D1645106

RLHQ

Kelso
26.6.95

BORDERS REGIONAL LIBRARY

Reference Only

NOT TO BE TAKEN AWAY

BORDERS REGIONAL LIBRARY

00219079

Class R 032-02

WHITAKER'S ALMANACK 1993

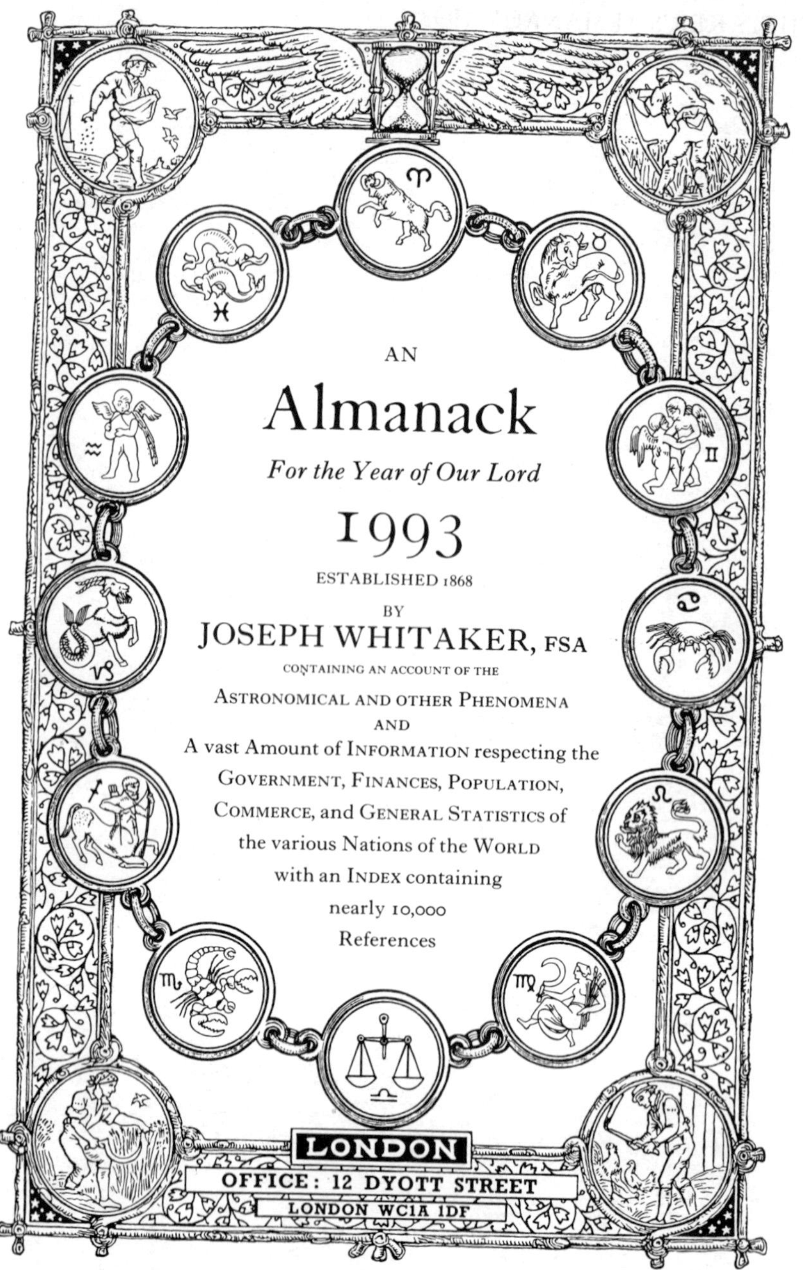
AN
Almanack
For the Year of Our Lord
1993
ESTABLISHED 1868
BY
JOSEPH WHITAKER, FSA
CONTAINING AN ACCOUNT OF THE
ASTRONOMICAL AND OTHER PHENOMENA
AND
A vast Amount of INFORMATION respecting the
GOVERNMENT, FINANCES, POPULATION,
COMMERCE, and GENERAL STATISTICS of
the various Nations of the WORLD
with an INDEX containing
nearly 10,000
References
LONDON
OFFICE: 12 DYOTT STREET
LONDON WC1A 1DF

The traditional design of the title page for Whitaker's Almanack which has appeared in each edition since 1868

Contents

CONTENTS CONTINUED

Preface

TO THE 125TH ANNUAL VOLUME 1993

This, the 125th edition of Whitaker's Almanack, is the first time in its 125 years that Whitaker has had a change of appearance. The decision to change size and layout was not taken lightly.

WHY CHANGE?

The principal intentions behind the changes are to make the text more legible through the use of larger print, and to enable readers to find their way around Whitaker's Almanack more easily through the use of stronger headings. The larger page size helps to accommodate the larger print without increasing the number of pages to an unwieldy and costly degree.

Although we have our regrets at the break with tradition, we feel that the new size and layout are great improvements in legibility and clarity. Testing of the initial designs on existing and potential readers evoked a very positive response and so we are confident that the majority will welcome the changes as an enhancement of a familiar and invaluable reference tool.

NEW IN THIS EDITION

Enhancements of the content of Whitaker are a more familiar feature of each edition for regular readers. New items include a section describing the framework of protection for investors and listing the main regulatory bodies. A summary of White Papers published during the past year has been compiled, and descriptions of some of the major non-Christian faiths in the United Kingdom have been added.

The major editorial change in this edition is the amalgamation of the Commonwealth and Foreign Countries sections to form one alphabetical listing of countries of the world. The information about the Commonwealth as an organization has been rewritten and is included in the International Organizations section.

In addition, the listing of newspapers and periodicals has been revised, and the information on the Royal family has been rewritten and rearranged. Following the general election of April 1992, the results of voting in each constituency have been compiled, and the list of Members of Parliament and other data revised.

In his preface to the first edition, Joseph Whitaker stated that 'It is not intended that the work shall take a stereotyped form, and thus become, as it were, fossilized', and he went on to solicit the criticism and suggestions of readers. (However, he entered the caveat that 'all suggestions will be adopted as far as they may be deemed judicious'!)

Our commitment to the continual improvement of Whitaker's Almanack remains as strong. The suggestions of readers are always welcome, indicating how the book may be even more useful to its readers.

125TH ANNIVERSARY

The usefulness of the information provided in Whitaker's Almanack was the spur to its publication 125 years ago. Joseph Whitaker was primarily a publisher but from 1856 to 1859 was also part-time editor of *The Gentleman's Magazine*, personally conducting the correspondence columns of the periodical, which were famous for their diversity. To help with this work, he compiled a commonplace book of newspaper cuttings, questions and answers which had appeared in his own or contemporary magazines, manuscript notes likely to be of future use, and extracts from such sources as government statistics.

From 1859 Joseph Whitaker's time was taken up by his publishing business and his work on *The Bookseller*, a journal for the book trade which he founded in 1858. However, after some years he started to look for further sources of income because of the financial demands of supporting a large and increasing family; he married twice and had thirteen children. He thought of his commonplace book and decided to publish for public use the accumulated facts which had proved so useful to himself.

Joseph Whitaker decided upon the title 'Almanack', meaning an annual book containing a calendar of months and days, astronomical data, ecclesiastical and other anniversaries, etc. To justify the title, he obtained the assistance of the Astronomer Royal of the day, who nominated a member of his staff to supply the astronomical data for the first edition. It is because of the inclusion of such data that each edition of Whitaker's Almanack is dated for the coming year.

Whitaker's Almanack for 1869 was published on 10 December 1868 and was a success from the first; 36,000 copies were subscribed before publication and the original printing order of 40,000 was increased several times.

By the tenth anniversary of the first edition, the standing of Whitaker's Almanack was such that a copy of the edition for 1878 was included in the foundations of Cleopatra's Needle when it was set up on the Embankment, along with a set of the current coins of the realm and a copy of *The Times* for the day.

However, Whitaker's Almanack's steady progress over 125 years has not been without its hitches; the destruction of Whitaker's premises in an incendiary raid on the City of London in December 1940 caused the loss of almost all the Almanack's records and led to delays in publication. On one occasion during the Second World War, the Prime Minister wrote to the Editor to express his concern at the non-appearance of the new edition. This was, however, merely delayed; in all its 125 years Whitaker's Almanack has never failed to publish.

Whitaker Today

The first edition of Whitaker's Almanack had 363 pages; the present edition contains 1,280 pages. Despite the considerable increase in size and in the variety of subjects which it covers, the basic concept and indeed the general organization of the book remain recognizably those of the first edition.

This Joseph Whitaker described in his preface as 'the knowledge ordinarily possessed of the Course of the Seasons, and other Astronomical phenomena, the nature of our Constitution, and the statistics of our Ecclesiastical, Legal, Naval, and Military systems. In addition to all such information, herein given in an unusually full and complete manner, the reader will discover other and important features not hitherto easily obtainable.'

The updating of each edition of Whitaker's Almanack now involves contacting several thousand organizations and individuals. The collation of their responses and the preparation of the text for printing is the work of four inhouse staff and over 25 specialist contributors.

We are, as ever, most grateful for the assistance of all those organizations and individuals who respond so readily to our requests for information. My personal thanks for their work also go to my staff and our contributors, and to everyone involved in ensuring a smooth introduction of the new design for our 125th anniversary.

12 Dyott Street
London WC1A 1DF
Tel 071-836 8911

Hilary Marsden
Editor

October 1992

BORDERS
REGIONAL
LIBRARY

The Year 1993

CHRONOLOGICAL CYCLES AND ERAS

Dominical Letter	C
Epact	6
Golden Number (Lunar Cycle)	XVIII
Julian Day, 1 January (from noon)	2,448,989
Julian Period	6706
Roman Indiction	1
Solar Cycle	14

	Beginning
Japanese year Heisei 5	1 January
Chinese year of the Chicken	23 January
Regnal year 42	6 February
Indian (Saka) year 1915	22 March
Hindu new year	24 March
Muslim year AH 1414	21 June
Jewish year AM 5754	16 September
Roman year 2746 AUC	

RELIGIOUS CALENDARS

Epiphany	6 January
Ramadan, first day	23 February
Ash Wednesday	24 February
Passover, first day	6 April
Good Friday	9 April
Easter Day (Western churches)	11 April
Easter Day (Greek Orthodox)	18 April
Rogation Sunday	16 May
Ascension Day	20 May
Feast of Weeks, first day	26 May
Pentecost (Whit Sunday)	30 May
Trinity Sunday	6 June
Corpus Christi	10 June
Yom Kippur (Day of Atonement)	25 September
Feast of Tabernacles, first day	30 September
First Sunday in Advent	28 November
Chanucah, first day	9 December
Christmas Day	25 December

CIVIL CALENDAR

Accession of Queen Elizabeth II	6 February
Duke of York's birthday	19 February
St David's Day	1 March
Commonwealth Day	8 March
Prince Edward's birthday	10 March
St Patrick's Day	17 March
Birthday of Queen Elizabeth II	21 April
St George's Day	23 April
Coronation of Queen Elizabeth II	2 June
Duke of Edinburgh's birthday	10 June
The Queen's Official Birthday	12 June
Princess of Wales' birthday	1 July
Queen Elizabeth the Queen Mother's birthday	4 August
Princess Royal's birthday	15 August
Princess Margaret's birthday	21 August
Lord Mayor's Day	13 November
Prince of Wales' birthday	14 November
Remembrance Sunday	14 November
Wedding Day of Queen Elizabeth II	20 November
St Andrew's Day	30 November

LEGAL CALENDAR

Law Terms

Hilary Term	11 January to 7 April
Easter Term	20 April to 28 May
Trinity Term	8 June to 31 July
Michaelmas Term	1 October to 21 December

Quarter Days

England, Wales and Northern Ireland

Lady	25 March
Midsummer	24 June
Michaelmas	29 September
Christmas	25 December

Term Days

Scotland

Candlemas	28 February
Whitsunday	28 May
Lammas	28 August
Martinmas	28 November
Removal Terms	28 May, 28 November

1993

JANUARY

Sunday		3	10	17	24	31
Monday		4	11	18	25	
Tuesday		5	12	19	26	
Wednesday		6	13	20	27	
Thursday		7	14	21	28	
Friday	1	8	15	22	29	
Saturday	2	9	16	23	30	

FEBRUARY

Sunday		7	14	21	28
Monday	1	8	15	22	
Tuesday	2	9	16	23	
Wednesday	3	10	17	24	
Thursday	4	11	18	25	
Friday	5	12	19	26	
Saturday	6	13	20	27	

MARCH

Sunday		7	14	21	28
Monday	1	8	15	22	29
Tuesday	2	9	16	23	30
Wednesday	3	10	17	24	31
Thursday	4	11	18	25	
Friday	5	12	19	26	
Saturday	6	13	20	27	

APRIL

Sunday		4	11	18	25
Monday		5	12	19	26
Tuesday		6	13	20	27
Wednesday		7	14	21	28
Thursday	1	8	15	22	29
Friday	2	9	16	23	30
Saturday	3	10	17	24	

MAY

Sunday		2	9	16	23	30
Monday		3	10	17	24	31
Tuesday		4	11	18	25	
Wednesday		5	12	19	26	
Thursday		6	13	20	27	
Friday		7	14	21	28	
Saturday	1	8	15	22	29	

JUNE

Sunday		6	13	20	27
Monday		7	14	21	28
Tuesday	1	8	15	22	29
Wednesday	2	9	16	23	30
Thursday	3	10	17	24	
Friday	4	11	18	25	
Saturday	5	12	19	26	

JULY

Sunday		4	11	18	25
Monday		5	12	19	26
Tuesday		6	13	20	27
Wednesday		7	14	21	28
Thursday	1	8	15	22	29
Friday	2	9	16	23	30
Saturday	3	10	17	24	31

AUGUST

Sunday	1	8	15	22	29
Monday	2	9	16	23	30
Tuesday	3	10	17	24	31
Wednesday	4	11	18	25	
Thursday	5	12	19	26	
Friday	6	13	20	27	
Saturday	7	14	21	28	

SEPTEMBER

Sunday		5	12	19	26
Monday		6	13	20	27
Tuesday		7	14	21	28
Wednesday	1	8	15	22	29
Thursday	2	9	16	23	30
Friday	3	10	17	24	
Saturday	4	11	18	25	

OCTOBER

Sunday		3	10	17	24	31
Monday		4	11	18	25	
Tuesday		5	12	19	26	
Wednesday		6	13	20	27	
Thursday		7	14	21	28	
Friday	1	8	15	22	29	
Saturday	2	9	16	23	30	

NOVEMBER

Sunday		7	14	21	28
Monday	1	8	15	22	29
Tuesday	2	9	16	23	30
Wednesday	3	10	17	24	
Thursday	4	11	18	25	
Friday	5	12	19	26	
Saturday	6	13	20	27	

DECEMBER

Sunday		5	12	19	26
Monday		6	13	20	27
Tuesday		7	14	21	28
Wednesday	1	8	15	22	29
Thursday	2	9	16	23	30
Friday	3	10	17	24	31
Saturday	4	11	18	25	

PUBLIC HOLIDAYS	*England and Wales*	*Scotland*	*Northern Ireland*
New Year	1 January	1, 4 January	1 January
St Patrick's Day	—	—	17 March
*Good Friday	9 April	9 April	9 April
Easter Monday	12 April	—	12 April
May Day	3 May	31 May	3 May
Spring	31 May	3 May	31 May
Battle of Boyne	—	—	12 July
Summer	30 August	2 August	30 August
*Christmas	27, 28 December	27, 28 December	27, 28 December

*In England, Wales, and Northern Ireland, Christmas Day and Good Friday are common law holidays.
In the Channel Islands, Liberation Day (9 May) is a bank and public holiday.

1994

JANUARY

Sunday		2	9	16	23	30
Monday		3	10	17	24	31
Tuesday		4	11	18	25	
Wednesday		5	12	19	26	
Thursday		6	13	20	27	
Friday		7	14	21	28	
Saturday	1	8	15	22	29	

FEBRUARY

Sunday		6	13	20	27
Monday		7	14	21	28
Tuesday	1	8	15	22	
Wednesday	2	9	16	23	
Thursday	3	10	17	24	
Friday	4	11	18	25	
Saturday	5	12	19	26	

MARCH

Sunday		6	13	20	27
Monday		7	14	21	28
Tuesday	1	8	15	22	29
Wednesday	2	9	16	23	30
Thursday	3	10	17	24	31
Friday	4	11	18	25	
Saturday	5	12	19	26	

APRIL

Sunday		3	10	17	24
Monday		4	11	18	25
Tuesday		5	12	19	26
Wednesday		6	13	20	27
Thursday		7	14	21	28
Friday	1	8	15	22	29
Saturday	2	9	16	23	30

MAY

Sunday	1	8	15	22	29
Monday	2	9	16	23	30
Tuesday	3	10	17	24	31
Wednesday	4	11	18	25	
Thursday	5	12	19	26	
Friday	6	13	20	27	
Saturday	7	14	21	28	

JUNE

Sunday		5	12	19	26
Monday		6	13	20	27
Tuesday		7	14	21	28
Wednesday	1	8	15	22	29
Thursday	2	9	16	23	30
Friday	3	10	17	24	
Saturday	4	11	18	25	

JULY

Sunday		3	10	17	24	31
Monday		4	11	18	25	
Tuesday		5	12	19	26	
Wednesday		6	13	20	27	
Thursday		7	14	21	28	
Friday	1	8	15	22	29	
Saturday	2	9	16	23	30	

AUGUST

Sunday		7	14	21	28
Monday	1	8	15	22	29
Tuesday	2	9	16	23	30
Wednesday	3	10	17	24	31
Thursday	4	11	18	25	
Friday	5	12	19	26	
Saturday	6	13	20	27	

SEPTEMBER

Sunday		4	11	18	25
Monday		5	12	19	26
Tuesday		6	13	20	27
Wednesday		7	14	21	28
Thursday	1	8	15	22	29
Friday	2	9	16	23	30
Saturday	3	10	17	24	

OCTOBER

Sunday		2	9	16	23	30
Monday		3	10	17	24	31
Tuesday		4	11	18	25	
Wednesday		5	12	19	26	
Thursday		6	13	20	27	
Friday		7	14	21	28	
Saturday	1	8	15	22	29	

NOVEMBER

Sunday		6	13	20	27
Monday		7	14	21	28
Tuesday	1	8	15	22	29
Wednesday	2	9	16	23	30
Thursday	3	10	17	24	
Friday	4	11	18	25	
Saturday	5	12	19	26	

DECEMBER

Sunday		4	11	18	25
Monday		5	12	19	26
Tuesday		6	13	20	27
Wednesday		7	14	21	28
Thursday	1	8	15	22	29
Friday	2	9	16	23	30
Saturday	3	10	17	24	31

PUBLIC HOLIDAYS	*England and Wales*	*Scotland*	*Northern Ireland*
New Year	3 January	3, 4 January	3 January
St Patrick's Day	—	—	17 March
*Good Friday	1 April	1 April	1 April
Easter Monday	4 April	—	4 April
May Day	2 May	30 May	2 May
Spring	30 May	2 May	30 May
Battle of Boyne	—	—	12 July
Summer	29 August	1 August	29 August
*Christmas	26, 27 December	26, 27 December	26, 27 December

*In England, Wales, and Northern Ireland, Christmas Day and Good Friday are common law holidays. In the Channel Islands, Liberation Day (9 May) is a bank and public holiday.

FORTHCOMING EVENTS 1993

This is the UN International Year for the World's Indigenous People, the EC Year of the Elderly and Solidarity amongst Generations, and the Arts Council Year for Dance

7–17 January	London International Boat Show Earls Court, London
14–17 January	Cruft's Dog Show National Exhibition Centre, Birmingham
18 March–12 April	Ideal Home Exhibition Earls Court, London
21–23 March	London International Book Fair Olympia, London
1–7 April	International Antiques Fair National Exhibition Centre, Birmingham
30 April–22 May	Mayfest 1993 Glasgow
30 April–9 October	Pitlochry Festival Theatre season Pitlochry, Tayside
May–September	Chichester Festival Theatre season, West Sussex
12–16 May	Royal Windsor Horse Show Home Park, Windsor
21 May–6 June	Bath International Festival, Bath
27–28 May	Chelsea Flower Show Royal Hospital, Chelsea
6 June–15 August	Royal Academy Summer Exhibition Piccadilly, London
11–27 June	Aldeburgh Festival of Music and Arts, Suffolk
12 June	Trooping the Colour Horse Guards Parade, London
14 July–1 August	Buxton Festival Derbyshire
5–8 July	The Royal Show Stoneleigh Park, Kenilworth, Warks
15–24 July	Welsh Proms 1993 St David's Hall, Cardiff
16 July–11 September	Promenade Concerts season Royal Albert Hall, London
20–31 July	Royal Tournament Earls Court, London
31 July–7 August	Royal National Eisteddfod of Wales Builth Wells, Powys
6–28 August	Edinburgh Military Tattoo Edinburgh Castle
12 August	Battle of Flowers, Jersey
15 August–4 September	Edinburgh International Festival
21–28 August	Three Choirs Festival, Worcester
3 September–7 November	Blackpool Illuminations
4 September	Braemar Royal Highland Gathering Braemar, Aberdeenshire
10–18 September	Southampton International Boat Show, Western Esplanade, Southampton
7 November	London to Brighton Veteran Car Run
8–23 November	London International Film Festival
13 November	Lord Mayor's Procession and Show, City of London
18–28 November	Huddersfield Contemporary Music Festival
28 November–2 December	Royal Smithfield Show and Agricultural Machinery Exhibition, Earls Court, London

SPORTS EVENTS

16 January	Rugby Union: England v. France Twickenham, London Scotland v. Ireland Murrayfield, Edinburgh
6 February	Rugby Union: Wales v. England Cardiff Arms Park France v. Scotland Parc des Princes, Paris
20 February	Rugby Union: Ireland v. France Lansdowne Road, Dublin Scotland v. Wales Murrayfield, Edinburgh
6 March	Rugby Union: Wales v. Ireland Cardiff Arms Park England v. Scotland Twickenham, London
20 March	Rugby Union: France v. Wales Parc des Princes, Paris Ireland v. England Lansdowne Road, Dublin
27 March	University Boat Race Putney–Mortlake, London
17 April–3 May	Snooker: World Professional Championships Crucible Theatre, Sheffield
18 April	Athletics: London Marathon
1 May	Rugby League: Challenge Cup Final Wembley Stadium, London
1 May	Rugby Union: Pilkington Cup Final Twickenham, London
6–9 May	Badminton Horse Trials Badminton, Avon
15 May	Football: FA Cup Final Wembley Stadium, London Welsh FA Cup Final Cardiff Arms Park
19 May	Cricket: One-Day International England v. Australia Old Trafford, Manchester
21 May	Cricket: One-Day International England v. Australia Edgbaston, Birmingham
23 May	Cricket: One-Day International England v. Australia Lord's, London
25–30 May	Golf: British Amateur Championship Royal Port Rush, Ireland
29 May	Football: Scottish FA Cup Final Hampden Park, Glasgow
30 May–12 June	Cycling: Milk Race
31 May–11 June	International TT Motorcycle Races Isle of Man
3–7 June	Cricket: 1st Test Match England v. Australia Old Trafford, Manchester
17–21 June	Cricket: 2nd Test Match Lord's, London
21 June–4 July	Lawn Tennis Championships Wimbledon, London
30 June–4 July	Henley Royal Regatta Henley-on-Thames

1–6 July	Cricket: 3rd Test Match Trent Bridge, Nottingham
10 July	Cricket: Benson & Hedges Cup Final Lord's, London
11 July	British Formula 1 Grand Prix Silverstone, Northants
12–26 July	Shooting: NRA Imperial Meetings Bisley Camp, Woking, Surrey
15–18 July	Golf: Open Championship Royal St George's, Sandwich, Kent
22–26 July	Cricket: 4th Test Match Headingley, Leeds
24 July–7 August	Yacht Racing: Admiral's Cup and Fastnet Race
31 July–7 August	Yachting: Cowes Week Isle of Wight
5–9 August	Cricket: 5th Test Match Edgbaston, Birmingham
19–23 August	Cricket: 6th Test Match The Oval, London
26–29 August	Showjumping: British Jumping Derby Hickstead, West Sussex
2–5 September	Eventing: Burghley Horse Trials Burghley, Lincs
4 September	Cricket: Nat West Trophy Final Lord's, London
6–10 October	Horse of the Year Show Wembley Arena, London

HORSE-RACING

18 March	Cheltenham Gold Cup Cheltenham
27 March	Lincoln Handicap Doncaster
3 April	Grand National Aintree
29 April	One Thousand Guineas Newmarket
1 May	Two Thousand Guineas Newmarket
2 June	The Derby Epsom
3 June	Coronation Cup Epsom
5 June	The Oaks Epsom
15–18 June	Royal Ascot
24 July	King George VI and Queen Elizabeth Diamond Stakes Ascot
11 September	St Leger Doncaster
2 October	Cambridgeshire Handicap Newmarket
16 October	Cesarewitch Newmarket

The horse-racing fixtures are the copyright of The Jockey Club.

CENTENARIES OF 1993

1593

30 May — Christopher Marlowe, poet and playwright, died
9 August — Izaak Walton, writer, born

1693

4 February — George Lillo, dramatist and jeweller, born

1793

21 January — Louis XVI, King of France, executed
3 March — William Macready, actor, born
17 July — Charlotte Corday, French assassin of Marat, executed
16 October — Marie Antoinette, wife of Louis XVI, executed
22 November — John Tillotson, Archbishop of Canterbury, died
28 December — Queen Mary II died

1893

12 January — Hermann Goering, German Nazi leader, born
14 January — Independent Labour Party founded
15 January — Fanny Kemble, actress, died
15 January — Ivor Novello, actor, playwright and composer, born
12 February — Gen. Omar Bradley, American commander in Second World War, born
18 March — Wilfred Owen, poet, born
8 April — Mary Pickford, American actress, born
20 April — Harold Lloyd, American actor, born
26 May — Sir Eugene Goossens, composer and conductor, born
13 June — Dorothy L. Sayers, writer, born
6 July — Guy de Maupassant, French author, died
6 October — Ford Madox Brown, artist, died
18 October — Charles Gounod, French composer, died
6 November NS — Piotr Tchaikovsky, Russian composer, died
12 December — Edward G. Robinson, American actor, born

CENTENARIES OF 1994

1494

20 April — Johannes Agricola, German Protestant reformer, born
4 May — Christopher Columbus landed in Jamaica

1594

2 February — Giovanni Palestrina, Italian composer, born
31 May — Jacopo Tintoretto, Venetian artist, died
22 November — Sir Martin Frobisher, navigator and explorer, died
5 December — Gerardus Mercator, Flemish mathematician and geographer, died

1694

27 July — Bank of England established by charter
21 November — François-Marie Voltaire, French philosopher, born

1794

16 January — Edward Gibbon, writer and historian, died
5 April — Georges Jacques Danton, French Revolutionary leader, executed
8 May — Antoine Lavoisier, French chemist, executed
1 June — Battle of the Glorious First of June
28 July — Maximilien Robespierre, French Revolutionary leader, executed

1894

1 January — Manchester Ship Canal opened to traffic
10 February — Harold Macmillan, 1st Earl of Stockton, Prime Minister 1957–63, born
21 February — Andres Segovia, Spanish classical guitarist, born
10 April — Ben Nicholson, artist, born
17 April NS — Nikita Krushchev, Soviet leader, born
23 June — King Edward VIII, later Duke of Windsor, born
30 June — Tower Bridge, London, opened
26 July — Aldous Huxley, author, born
1 August — Start of Sino-Japanese War
13 September — J. B. Priestley, author, born
14 October — e. e. cummings, American poet, born
24 November — Herbert Sutcliffe, cricketer, born
3 December — Robert Louis Stevenson, poet and author, died
7 December — Ferdinand de Lesseps, French diplomatist and maker of the Suez Canal, died
8 December — James Thurber, American humorist, born
20 December — Sir Robert Menzies, Australian Prime Minister 1939–41 and 1949–66, born
29 December — Christina Rossetti, poet and hymn writer, died
30 December — Amelia Bloomer, women's rights campaigner, died

Astronomy

The following pages give astronomical data for each month of the year 1993. There are four pages of data for each month. All data are given for 0h Greenwich Mean Time (GMT), i.e. at the midnight at the beginning of the day named. This applies also to data for the months when British Summer Time is in operation.

British Summer Time is in operation in 1993 from March 28d 01h GMT to October 24d 01h GMT.

The astronomical data are given in a form suitable for observation with the naked eye or with a small telescope. These data do not attempt to replace the *Astronomical Almanac* for professional astronomers.

A fuller explanation of how to use the astronomical data is given on pages 66–8.

Calendar for Each Month

The calendar for each month shows dates of religious, civil and legal significance for the year 1993.

The days in bold type are the principal holy days and the festivals and greater holy days of the Church of England as set out in the calendar of the *Alternative Service Book 1980*. Observance of certain festivals and greater holy days is transferred if the day falls on a principal holy day. The calendar shows the date on which holy days and festivals are to be observed in 1993.

The days in small capitals are dates of significance in the calendars of non-Anglican denominations and non-Christian religions.

The days in italic type are dates of civil and legal significance. The royal anniversaries shown in italic type are the days on which the Union flag is to be flown.

The rest of the calendar comprises days of general interest and the dates of birth or death of well-known people.

Fuller explanations of the various calendars can be found under Time Measurement and Calendars.

The Zodiacal signs through which the Sun is passing during each month are illustrated. The date of transition from one sign to the next, to the nearest hour, is also given.

SEASONS

The seasons are defined astronomically as follows:

Spring	from the vernal equinox to the summer solstice
Summer	from the summer solstice to the autumnal equinox
Autumn	from the autumnal equinox to the winter solstice
Winter	from the winter solstice to the vernal equinox

The seasons in 1993 are:

Northern hemisphere

Vernal equinox	March 20d 15h GMT
Summer solstice	June 21d 09h GMT
Autumnal equinox	September 23d 00h GMT
Winter solstice	December 21d 20h GMT

Southern hemisphere

Autumnal equinox	March 20d 15h GMT
Winter solstice	June 21d 09h GMT
Vernal equinox	September 23d 00h GMT
Summer solstice	December 21d 20h GMT

The longest day of the year, measured from sunrise to sunset, is at the summer solstice. For the remainder of this century the longest day in the United Kingdom will fall each year on 21 June. *See also* page 82.

The shortest day of the year is at the winter solstice. For the remainder of this century the shortest day in the United Kingdom will fall on 21 December in 1993, 1996, 1997, 2000, and on 22 December in 1994, 1995, 1998, 1999. *See also* page 82.

The equinox is the point at which day and night are of equal length all over the world. *See also* page 82.

In popular parlance, the seasons in the northern hemisphere comprise the following months:

Spring	March April May
Summer	June July August
Autumn	September October November
Winter	December January February

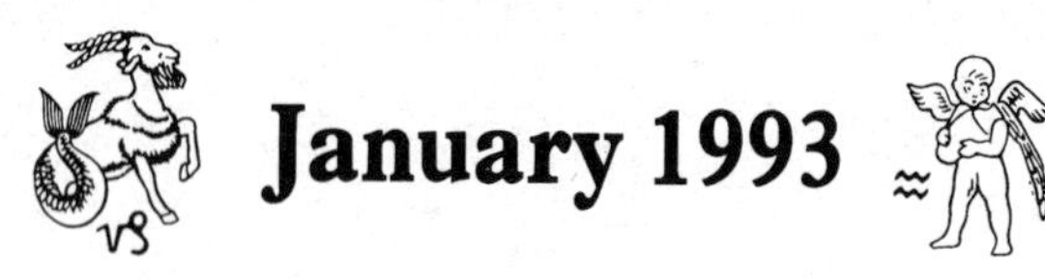

January 1993

FIRST MONTH, 31 DAYS. *Janus*, god of the portal, facing two ways, past and future

Sun's Longitude 300° ♒ $20^{d} 01^{h}$

1	*Friday*	**The Naming of Jesus.** *Bank Holiday in the UK.*	*week* 1 *day* 1
2	*Saturday*	Sir Michael Tippett *b.* 1905.	2
3	*Sunday*	**2nd S. after Christmas.** Josiah Wedgwood *d.* 1795.	*week* 2 *day* 3
4	*Monday*	*Bank Holiday in Scotland.* Augustus John *b.* 1878.	4
5	*Tuesday*	Catherine de Medici *d.* 1589.	5
6	*Wednesday*	**Epiphany.** Joan of Arc *b.* 1412.	6
7	*Thursday*	First manned balloon crossing of the English Channel 1785.	7
8	*Friday*	Sir Laurence Alma-Tadema *b.* 1836.	8
9	*Saturday*	Simone de Beauvoir *b.* 1908.	9
10	*Sunday*	**1st S. after Epiphany.** League of Nations founded 1920.	*week* 3 *day* 10
11	*Monday*	*Hilary Law Sittings begin.* Thomas Hardy *d.* 1928.	11
12	*Tuesday*	Edmund Burke *b.* 1729. John Singer Sargent *b.* 1856.	12
13	*Wednesday*	James Joyce *d.* 1941.	13
14	*Thursday*	Henri Fantin-Latour *b.* 1836. Sir Cecil Beaton *b.* 1904.	14
15	*Friday*	British Museum opened 1759. Ivor Novello *b.* 1893.	15
16	*Saturday*	Anton Chekhov *b.* 1860 os. Toscanini *d.* 1957.	16
17	*Sunday*	**2nd S. after Epiphany.** David Lloyd George *b.* 1863.	*week* 4 *day* 17
18	*Monday*	Captain Scott reached the South Pole 1912.	18
19	*Tuesday*	Edgar Allen Poe *b.* 1809. Paul Cézanne *b.* 1839.	19
20	*Wednesday*	David Garrick *d.* 1779. George V *d.* 1936.	20
21	*Thursday*	Louis XVI of France *exec.* 1793. Orwell *d.* 1950.	21
22	*Friday*	August Strindberg *b.* 1847. Walter Sickert *d.* 1942.	22
23	*Saturday*	*Chinese Year of the Chicken.*	23
24	*Sunday*	**3rd S. after Epiphany.** Sir Winston Churchill *d.* 1965.	*week* 5 *day* 24
25	*Monday*	**Conversion of St Paul.** Robert Burns *b.* 1759.	25
26	*Tuesday*	Jacqueline du Pré *b.* 1945.	26
27	*Wednesday*	Giuseppe Verdi *d.* 1901.	27
28	*Thursday*	Fyodor Dostoyevsky *d.* 1881.	28
29	*Friday*	The Victoria Cross instituted 1856.	29
30	*Saturday*	Edward Lear *d.* 1888. Mahatma Gandhi *assass.* 1948.	30
31	*Sunday*	**4th S. after Epiphany.** Franz Schubert *b.* 1797.	*week* 6 *day* 31

Astronomical Phenomena

d	h	
4	03	Earth at perihelion (147 million km)
7	23	Mars at opposition
8	09	Uranus in conjunction with Sun
8	11	Mars in conjunction with Moon. Mars 6° N.
8	22	Neptune in conjunction with Sun
14	10	Jupiter in conjunction with Moon. Jupiter 6° N.
19	16	Venus at greatest elongation E. 47°
22	17	Mercury in conjunction with Moon. Mercury 5° S.
23	16	Mercury in superior conjunction
24	03	Saturn in conjunction with Moon. Saturn 5° S.
27	01	Venus in conjunction with Moon. Venus 4° S.

Constellations

The following constellations are near the meridian at

December 1d, 24h	January 16d, 21h
December 16d, 23h	February 1d, 20h
January 1d, 22h	February 15d, 19h

Draco (below the Pole), Ursa Minor (below the Pole), Camelopardus, Perseus, Auriga, Taurus, Orion, Eridanus and Lepus

Minima of Algol

d	h	d	h	d	h
3	01.0	14	12.3	25	23.6
5	21.8	17	09.1	28	20.4
8	18.7	20	05.9	31	17.2
11	15.5	23	02.8		

The Moon

Phases, Apsides and Node	d	h	m
☽ First Quarter	1	03	38
○ Full Moon	8	12	37
☾ Last Quarter	15	04	01
● New Moon	22	18	27
☽ First Quarter	30	23	20
Perigee (362,264 km)	10	12	11
Apogee (406,028 km)	26	10	18

Mean longitude of ascending node on 1 Jan., 260°

THE SUN

s.d. 16′.3

Day	Right Ascension	Dec. −	Equation of time	Rise 52°	Rise 56°	Transit	Set 52°	Set 56°	Sidereal time	Transit of First Point of Aries
	h m s	° ′	m s	h m	h m	h m	h m	h m	h m s	h m s
1	18 46 03	23 01	− 3 25	8 08	8 31	12 04	15 59	15 36	6 42 38	17 14 32
2	18 50 28	22 56	− 3 54	8 08	8 31	12 04	16 00	15 38	6 46 34	17 10 36
3	18 54 52	22 50	− 4 21	8 08	8 31	12 05	16 02	15 39	6 50 31	17 06 40
4	18 59 16	22 44	− 4 49	8 08	8 30	12 05	16 03	15 40	6 54 27	17 02 45
5	19 03 40	22 38	− 5 16	8 07	8 30	12 05	16 04	15 42	6 58 24	16 58 49
6	19 08 03	22 31	− 5 43	8 07	8 29	12 06	16 05	15 43	7 02 21	16 54 53
7	19 12 26	22 24	− 6 09	8 06	8 29	12 06	16 07	15 45	7 06 17	16 50 57
8	19 16 48	22 16	− 6 34	8 06	8 28	12 07	16 08	15 46	7 10 14	16 47 01
9	19 21 10	22 08	− 6 59	8 05	8 27	12 07	16 09	15 48	7 14 10	16 43 05
10	19 25 31	21 59	− 7 24	8 05	8 26	12 08	16 11	15 49	7 18 07	16 39 09
11	19 29 51	21 50	− 7 48	8 04	8 25	12 08	16 12	15 51	7 22 03	16 35 13
12	19 34 11	21 41	− 8 12	8 04	8 24	12 08	16 14	15 53	7 26 00	16 31 17
13	19 38 31	21 31	− 8 34	8 03	8 23	12 09	16 15	15 55	7 29 56	16 27 21
14	19 42 50	21 20	− 8 57	8 02	8 22	12 09	16 17	15 56	7 33 53	16 23 25
15	19 47 08	21 10	− 9 18	8 01	8 21	12 09	16 18	15 58	7 37 50	16 19 30
16	19 51 25	20 58	− 9 39	8 00	8 20	12 10	16 20	16 00	7 41 46	16 15 34
17	19 55 42	20 47	−10 00	7 59	8 19	12 10	16 21	16 02	7 45 43	16 11 38
18	19 59 58	20 35	−10 19	7 58	8 18	12 10	16 23	16 04	7 49 39	16 07 42
19	20 04 14	20 23	−10 38	7 57	8 16	12 11	16 25	16 06	7 53 36	16 03 46
20	20 08 29	20 10	−10 56	7 56	8 15	12 11	16 26	16 08	7 57 32	15 59 50
21	20 12 43	19 57	−11 14	7 55	8 13	12 11	16 28	16 10	8 01 29	15 55 54
22	20 16 56	19 43	−11 31	7 54	8 12	12 12	16 30	16 12	8 05 25	15 51 58
23	20 21 09	19 29	−11 47	7 53	8 10	12 12	16 32	16 14	8 09 22	15 48 02
24	20 25 20	19 15	−12 02	7 51	8 09	12 12	16 33	16 16	8 13 19	15 44 06
25	20 29 31	19 01	−12 16	7 50	8 07	12 12	16 35	16 18	8 17 15	15 40 10
26	20 33 41	18 46	−12 30	7 49	8 06	12 13	16 37	16 20	8 21 12	15 36 14
27	20 37 51	18 30	−12 42	7 47	8 04	12 13	16 39	16 22	8 25 08	15 32 19
28	20 41 59	18 15	−12 54	7 46	8 02	12 13	16 41	16 24	8 29 05	15 28 23
29	20 46 07	17 59	−13 06	7 45	8 00	12 13	16 42	16 27	8 33 01	15 24 27
30	20 50 14	17 43	−13 16	7 43	7 59	12 13	16 44	16 29	8 36 58	15 20 31
31	20 54 20	17 26	−13 25	7 42	7 57	12 13	16 46	16 31	8 40 54	15 16 35

Duration of Twilight (in minutes)

Latitude	52°	56°	52°	56°
	1 January		11 January	
Civil	41	47	40	45
Nautical	84	96	82	93
Astronomical	125	141	123	138
	21 January		31 January	
Civil	38	43	37	41
Nautical	80	90	78	87
Astronomical	120	134	117	130

The Night Sky

Mercury is unsuitably placed for observation, superior conjunction occurring on the 23rd.

Venus is a brilliant evening object, magnitude −4.3, visible in the SW skies for several hours after sunset. The crescent Moon, four days old, passes 4° N. of the planet on the evening of the 26th.

Mars, magnitude −1.4, is at opposition on the 7th and is therefore visible throughout the hours of darkness. Mars is in Gemini moving slowly westwards south of Castor and Pollux. During the night of the 7th to 8th the Full Moon will be seen moving towards the planet, passing about 6° S. of it after dawn. The slightly reddish colour of Mars is a help in identification.

Jupiter, magnitude −2.1, is a brilliant morning object in Virgo. By the end of the month it is visible low in the ESE sky before midnight.

Saturn, magnitude +0.7, is an evening object at the beginning of the year, visible for a short while low above the SW horizon in the early evening. It gradually becomes more difficult to locate and well before the end of January it is lost to view.

THE MOON

Day	RA	Dec.	Hor. par.	Semi-diam.	Sun's co-long.	PA. of Bright Limb	Phase	Age	Rise 52°	Rise 56°	Transit	Set 52°	Set 56°
	h m	°	′	′	°	°	%	d	h m	h m	h m	h m	h m
1	0 25	+ 8.1	54.6	14.9	2	246	49	8.0	11 09	11 00	18 14	0 25	0 32
2	1 11	+12.4	55.1	15.0	15	248	58	9.0	11 29	11 16	18 59	1 33	1 45
3	1 59	+16.3	55.7	15.2	27	251	68	10.0	11 54	11 37	19 48	2 43	2 59
4	2 50	+19.5	56.5	15.4	39	255	77	11.0	12 26	12 05	20 40	3 54	4 15
5	3 45	+21.9	57.3	15.6	51	259	85	12.0	13 08	12 44	21 36	5 04	5 28
6	4 44	+23.1	58.2	15.9	63	264	92	13.0	14 03	13 37	22 35	6 08	6 33
7	5 44	+22.9	59.0	16.1	75	267	97	14.0	15 11	14 47	23 34	7 02	7 27
8	6 46	+21.3	59.7	16.3	87	261	100	15.0	16 29	16 10	—	7 47	8 07
9	7 46	+18.2	60.2	16.4	100	124	100	16.0	17 54	17 39	0 34	8 22	8 37
10	8 45	+14.0	60.5	16.5	112	116	97	17.0	19 20	19 11	1 31	8 50	9 00
11	9 42	+ 8.8	60.5	16.5	124	116	91	18.0	20 45	20 41	2 25	9 13	9 19
12	10 37	+ 3.2	60.3	16.4	136	117	83	19.0	22 09	22 10	3 18	9 35	9 35
13	11 31	− 2.5	59.8	16.3	148	116	74	20.0	23 31	23 38	4 09	9 55	9 51
14	12 24	− 8.0	59.3	16.2	160	115	63	21.0	—	—	5 00	10 17	10 08
15	13 17	−12.9	58.7	16.0	172	112	52	22.0	0 52	1 04	5 52	10 41	10 27
16	14 11	−17.1	58.0	15.8	184	109	41	23.0	2 10	2 27	6 44	11 09	10 51
17	15 06	−20.3	57.4	15.6	197	105	31	24.0	3 25	3 46	7 37	11 44	11 22
18	16 02	−22.3	56.8	15.5	209	100	21	25.0	4 32	4 57	8 31	12 28	12 03
19	16 58	−23.2	56.3	15.3	221	96	14	26.0	5 31	5 56	9 25	13 20	12 55
20	17 54	−22.8	55.8	15.2	233	92	7	27.0	6 18	6 42	10 18	14 21	13 57
21	18 47	−21.2	55.4	15.1	245	90	3	28.0	6 56	7 17	11 08	15 27	15 07
22	19 39	−18.7	55.0	15.0	258	98	1	29.0	7 25	7 42	11 56	16 35	16 19
23	20 28	−15.4	54.6	14.9	270	201	0	0.2	7 49	8 02	12 42	17 44	17 33
24	21 15	−11.4	54.3	14.8	282	235	2	1.2	8 09	8 17	13 25	18 52	18 45
25	22 00	− 7.1	54.1	14.7	294	239	5	2.2	8 26	8 31	14 06	19 58	19 56
26	22 44	− 2.6	54.0	14.7	306	241	9	3.2	8 42	8 43	14 47	21 05	21 06
27	23 27	+ 2.1	54.0	14.7	318	242	16	4.2	8 58	8 55	15 28	22 11	22 16
28	0 11	+ 6.6	54.2	14.8	331	243	23	5.2	9 15	9 08	16 10	23 18	23 27
29	0 56	+10.9	54.5	14.8	343	245	31	6.2	9 34	9 23	16 53	—	—
30	1 43	+14.9	54.9	15.0	355	248	41	7.2	9 56	9 41	17 39	0 26	0 40
31	2 32	+18.3	55.5	15.1	7	252	50	8.2	10 24	10 05	18 28	1 35	1 53

MERCURY

Day	RA	Dec.	Diam.	Phase	Transit	
	h m	°			h m	
1	17 49	−23.8	—	—	11 08	Mercury is
4	18 09	−24.2	—	—	11 16	too close to
7	18 30	−24.3	—	—	11 25	the Sun for
10	18 50	−24.3	—	—	11 34	observation
13	19 11	−24.0	—	—	11 43	
16	19 32	−23.6	—	—	11 52	
19	19 53	−22.9	—	—	12 01	
22	20 14	−21.9	—	—	12 10	
25	20 35	−20.8	—	—	12 20	
28	20 57	−19.4	—	—	12 29	
31	21 18	−17.8	—	—	12 38	

VENUS

Day	RA	Dec.	Diam.	Phase	Transit	5° high 52°	5° high 56°
	h m	°	″	%	h m	h m	h m
1	21 58	−14.1	20	60	15 15	19 26	19 09
6	22 19	−11.8	21	58	15 16	19 41	19 27
11	22 38	− 9.5	22	56	15 16	19 55	19 43
16	22 58	− 7.1	23	53	15 16	20 07	19 58
21	23 16	− 4.7	25	50	15 14	20 19	20 12
26	23 33	− 2.2	26	48	15 12	20 29	20 25
31	23 50	0.2	28	45	15 08	20 39	20 36

MARS

Day	RA	Dec.	Diam.	Phase	Transit	5° high 52°	5° high 56°
1	7 31	+25.7	15	100	0 48	8 36	8 57
6	7 22	+26.1	15	100	0 20	8 10	8 33
11	7 14	+26.5	15	100	23 46	7 44	8 07
16	7 05	+26.7	15	100	23 18	7 18	7 41
21	6 58	+26.9	14	99	22 51	6 52	7 16
26	6 51	+27.0	14	98	22 25	6 27	6 50
31	6 46	+27.0	13	98	22 00	6 02	6 26

SUNRISE AND SUNSET

	London		Bristol		Birmingham		Manchester		Newcastle		Glasgow		Belfast	
	0°05′	51°30′	2°35′	51°28′	1°55′	52°28′	2°15′	53°28′	1°37′	54°59′	4°14′	55°52′	5°56′	54°35′
	h m	h m	h m	h m	h m	h m	h m	h m	h m	h m	h m	h m	h m	h m
1	8 06	16 02	8 16	16 12	8 18	16 05	8 25	16 01	8 31	15 49	8 47	15 54	8 46	16 09
2	8 06	16 03	8 16	16 13	8 18	16 06	8 25	16 02	8 31	15 50	8 47	15 55	8 46	16 10
3	8 06	16 04	8 16	16 15	8 18	16 07	8 25	16 03	8 31	15 52	8 47	15 57	8 46	16 11
4	8 05	16 06	8 15	16 16	8 18	16 08	8 24	16 04	8 30	15 53	8 46	15 58	8 45	16 13
5	8 05	16 07	8 15	16 17	8 17	16 09	8 24	16 05	8 30	15 54	8 46	15 59	8 45	16 14
6	8 05	16 08	8 15	16 18	8 17	16 11	8 23	16 07	8 29	15 56	8 45	16 01	8 44	16 15
7	8 04	16 09	8 14	16 19	8 16	16 12	8 23	16 08	8 29	15 57	8 45	16 02	8 44	16 17
8	8 04	16 11	8 14	16 21	8 16	16 13	8 22	16 10	8 28	15 59	8 44	16 04	8 43	16 18
9	8 03	16 12	8 13	16 22	8 15	16 15	8 22	16 11	8 28	16 00	8 43	16 05	8 43	16 20
10	8 03	16 13	8 13	16 23	8 15	16 16	8 21	16 12	8 27	16 02	8 42	16 07	8 42	16 21
11	8 02	16 15	8 12	16 25	8 14	16 18	8 20	16 14	8 26	16 03	8 41	16 09	8 41	16 23
12	8 02	16 16	8 11	16 26	8 13	16 19	8 20	16 16	8 25	16 05	8 41	16 10	8 40	16 24
13	8 01	16 18	8 11	16 28	8 13	16 21	8 19	16 17	8 24	16 07	8 40	16 12	8 39	16 26
14	8 00	16 19	8 10	16 29	8 12	16 22	8 18	16 19	8 23	16 08	8 39	16 14	8 38	16 28
15	7 59	16 21	8 09	16 31	8 11	16 24	8 17	16 20	8 22	16 10	8 37	16 16	8 37	16 30
16	7 58	16 22	8 08	16 32	8 10	16 25	8 16	16 22	8 21	16 12	8 36	16 18	8 36	16 31
17	7 58	16 24	8 07	16 34	8 09	16 27	8 15	16 24	8 20	16 14	8 35	16 20	8 35	16 33
18	7 57	16 26	8 06	16 36	8 08	16 29	8 14	16 26	8 19	16 16	8 34	16 22	8 34	16 35
19	7 56	16 27	8 05	16 37	8 07	16 30	8 13	16 27	8 17	16 18	8 32	16 24	8 33	16 37
20	7 55	16 29	8 04	16 39	8 06	16 32	8 12	16 29	8 16	16 19	8 31	16 25	8 31	16 39
21	7 53	16 31	8 03	16 41	8 05	16 34	8 10	16 31	8 15	16 21	8 30	16 27	8 30	16 41
22	7 52	16 32	8 02	16 42	8 03	16 36	8 09	16 33	8 13	16 23	8 28	16 30	8 29	16 43
23	7 51	16 34	8 01	16 44	8 02	16 37	8 08	16 35	8 12	16 25	8 27	16 32	8 27	16 44
24	7 50	16 36	8 00	16 46	8 01	16 39	8 06	16 36	8 11	16 27	8 25	16 34	8 26	16 46
25	7 49	16 37	7 58	16 48	8 00	16 41	8 05	16 38	8 09	16 29	8 24	16 36	8 24	16 48
26	7 47	16 39	7 57	16 49	7 58	16 43	8 04	16 40	8 07	16 31	8 22	16 38	8 23	16 50
27	7 46	16 41	7 56	16 51	7 57	16 45	8 02	16 42	8 06	16 33	8 20	16 40	8 21	16 52
28	7 45	16 43	7 54	16 53	7 55	16 47	8 01	16 44	8 04	16 35	8 19	16 42	8 20	16 54
29	7 43	16 44	7 53	16 55	7 54	16 48	7 59	16 46	8 03	16 37	8 17	16 44	8 18	16 56
30	7 42	16 46	7 52	16 56	7 52	16 50	7 57	16 48	8 01	16 39	8 15	16 46	8 16	16 58
31	7 40	16 48	7 50	16 58	7 51	16 52	7 56	16 50	7 59	16 42	8 13	16 48	8 15	17 00

JUPITER

Day	*RA*	*Dec.*	*Transit*	*5° high*	
				52°	56°
	h m	° ′	h m	h m	h m
1	12 51.7	– 4 07	6 08	1 03	1 10
11	12 54.3	– 4 21	5 31	0 28	0 35
21	12 55.9	– 4 28	4 54	23 47	23 54
31	12 56.3	– 4 28	4 15	23 08	23 15

Diameters – equatorial 38″ polar 36″

SATURN

Day	*RA*	*Dec.*	*Transit*	*5° high*	
				52°	56°
	h m	° ′	h m	h m	h m
1	21 16.5	–16 54	14 32	18 21	18 00
11	21 20.8	–16 35	13 57	17 49	17 28
21	21 25.4	–16 14	13 22	17 16	16 56
31	21 30.1	–15 52	12 47	16 44	16 24

Diameters – equatorial 15″ polar 14″
Rings – major axis 35″ minor axis 9″

URANUS

Day	*RA*	*Dec.*	*Transit*	
	h m	° ′	h m	
1	19 16.8	–22 41	12 32	Uranus is
11	19 19.4	–22 36	11 56	too close to
21	19 21.9	–22 31	11 19	the Sun for
31	19 24.4	–22 27	10 42	observation

Diameter 4″

NEPTUNE

Day	*RA*	*Dec.*	*Transit*	
	h m	° ′	h m	
1	19 19.1	–21 31	12 35	Neptune is
11	19 20.8	–21 28	11 57	too close to
21	19 22.4	–21 25	11 19	the Sun for
31	19 23.9	–21 22	10 41	observation

Diameter 2″

February 1993

SECOND MONTH, 28 DAYS. *Februa*, Roman festival of Purification

Sun's Longitude 330° ♓ 18ᵈ 16ʰ

1	*Monday*	Mary Wollstonecraft Shelley *d.* 1851. Clark Gable *b.* 1901.	*week* 6 *day* 32
2	*Tuesday*	**Presentation of Christ.** Stan Getz *b.* 1927.	33
3	*Wednesday*	Beau Nash *d.* 1762. Felix Mendelssohn *b.* 1809.	34
4	*Thursday*	George Lillo *b.* 1693. Thomas Carlyle *d.* 1881.	35
5	*Friday*	Sir Robert Peel *b.* 1788.	36
6	*Saturday*	*Queen's Accession 1952.* François Truffaut *b.* 1932.	37
7	*Sunday*	**9th S. before Easter.** Charles Dickens *b.* 1812.	*week* 7 *day* 38
8	*Monday*	John Ruskin *b.* 1819. Sir Giles Gilbert Scott *d.* 1960.	39
9	*Tuesday*	Edward Carson *b.* 1854. Brendan Behan *b.* 1923.	40
10	*Wednesday*	Charles Montesquieu *d.* 1755. Charles Lamb *b.* 1775.	41
11	*Thursday*	René Descartes *d.* 1650. John Buchan *d.* 1940.	42
12	*Friday*	Lady Jane Grey *exec.* 1554. Escoffier *d.* 1935.	43
13	*Saturday*	Dame Christabel Pankhurst *d.* 1958.	44
14	*Sunday*	**8th S. before Easter.** Valentine's Day.	*week* 8 *day* 45
15	*Monday*	H. H. Asquith, 1st Earl of Oxford and Asquith *d.* 1928.	46
16	*Tuesday*	George Macaulay Trevelyan *b.* 1876.	47
17	*Wednesday*	Johann Pestalozzi *d.* 1827. Geronimo *d.* 1909.	48
18	*Thursday*	Martin Luther *d.* 1546. Dame Ngaio Marsh *d.* 1982.	49
19	*Friday*	*Duke of York b. 1960.* André Gide *d.* 1951.	50
20	*Saturday*	Benedict Spinoza *d.* 1677. Enzo Ferrari *b.* 1898.	51
21	*Sunday*	**7th S. before Easter.** Léo Delibes *b.* 1836.	*week* 9 *day* 52
22	*Monday*	Chopin *b.* 1810. Jean-Baptiste Corot *d.* 1875.	53
23	*Tuesday*	Shrove Tuesday. RAMADAN begins.	54
24	*Wednesday*	**Ash Wednesday.** Henry Cavendish *d.* 1810.	55
25	*Thursday*	Sir Christopher Wren *d.* 1723.	56
26	*Friday*	Maj.-Gen. Orde Wingate *b.* 1903.	57
27	*Saturday*	Dame Ellen Terry *b.* 1848. John Steinbeck *b.* 1902.	58
28	*Sunday*	**1st S. in Lent.** Sir John Tenniel *b.* 1820.	*week* 10 *day* 59

ASTRONOMICAL PHENOMENA

d	h	
2	02	Saturn in conjunction with Mercury. Saturn 0°.8 N.
4	09	Mars in conjunction with Moon. Mars 6° N.
9	16	Saturn in conjunction with Sun
10	17	Jupiter in conjunction with Moon. Jupiter 6° N.
20	16	Saturn in conjunction with Moon. Saturn 5° S.
21	09	Mercury at greatest elongation E. 18°
23	04	Mercury in conjunction with Moon. Mercury 3° S.
24	10	Venus at greatest brilliancy
25	05	Venus in conjunction with Moon. Venus 0°.4 N.

CONSTELLATIONS

The following constellations are near the meridian at

January 1d, 24h
January 16d, 23h
February 1d, 22h
February 15d, 21h
March 1d, 20h
March 16d, 19h

Draco (below the Pole), Camelopardus, Auriga, Taurus, Gemini, Orion, Canis Minor, Monoceros, Lepus, Canis Major and Puppis

MINIMA OF ALGOL

d	h	d	h	d	h
3	14.1	12	04.5	20	19.0
6	10.9	15	01.3	23	15.8
9	07.7	17	22.2	26	12.6

THE MOON

Phases, Apsides and Node	d	h	m
○ Full Moon	6	23	55
☾ Last Quarter	13	14	57
● New Moon	21	13	05
Perigee (357,905 km)	7	20	21
Apogee (406,627 km)	22	17	56

Mean longitude of ascending node on 1 Feb., 259°

THE SUN s.d. 16′.2

Day	Right Ascension	Dec. −	Equation of time	Rise 52°	Rise 56°	Transit	Set 52°	Set 56°	Sidereal time	Transit of First Point of Aries
	h m s	° ′	m s	h m	h m	h m	h m	h m	h m s	h m s
1	20 58 25	17 09	−13 34	7 40	7 55	12 14	16 48	16 33	8 44 51	15 12 39
2	21 02 29	16 52	−13 42	7 38	7 53	12 14	16 50	16 35	8 48 48	15 08 43
3	21 06 33	16 35	−13 49	7 37	7 51	12 14	16 52	16 37	8 52 44	15 04 47
4	21 10 36	16 17	−13 55	7 35	7 49	12 14	16 53	16 40	8 56 41	15 00 51
5	21 14 37	15 59	−14 00	7 33	7 47	12 14	16 55	16 42	9 00 37	14 56 55
6	21 18 38	15 41	−14 05	7 32	7 45	12 14	16 57	16 44	9 04 34	14 52 59
7	21 22 39	15 22	−14 08	7 30	7 43	12 14	16 59	16 46	9 08 30	14 49 04
8	21 26 38	15 03	−14 11	7 28	7 41	12 14	17 01	16 48	9 12 27	14 45 08
9	21 30 37	14 44	−14 13	7 26	7 39	12 14	17 03	16 51	9 16 23	14 41 12
10	21 34 35	14 25	−14 15	7 25	7 37	12 14	17 05	16 53	9 20 20	14 37 16
11	21 38 32	14 05	−14 15	7 23	7 34	12 14	17 06	16 55	9 24 17	14 33 20
12	21 42 28	13 45	−14 15	7 21	7 32	12 14	17 08	16 57	9 28 13	14 29 24
13	21 46 24	13 25	−14 14	7 19	7 30	12 14	17 10	16 59	9 32 10	14 25 28
14	21 50 19	13 05	−14 12	7 17	7 28	12 14	17 12	17 02	9 36 06	14 21 32
15	21 54 13	12 45	−14 10	7 15	7 25	12 14	17 14	17 04	9 40 03	14 17 36
16	21 58 06	12 24	−14 07	7 13	7 23	12 14	17 16	17 06	9 43 59	14 13 40
17	22 01 59	12 03	−14 03	7 11	7 21	12 14	17 18	17 08	9 47 56	14 09 44
18	22 05 51	11 42	−13 59	7 09	7 18	12 14	17 20	17 10	9 51 52	14 05 49
19	22 09 42	11 21	−13 53	7 07	7 16	12 14	17 21	17 13	9 55 49	14 01 53
20	22 13 33	10 59	−13 48	7 05	7 14	12 14	17 23	17 15	9 59 46	13 57 57
21	22 17 23	10 38	−13 41	7 03	7 11	12 14	17 25	17 17	10 03 42	13 54 01
22	22 21 13	10 16	−13 34	7 01	7 09	12 14	17 27	17 19	10 07 39	13 50 05
23	22 25 01	9 54	−13 26	6 59	7 06	12 13	17 29	17 21	10 11 35	13 46 09
24	22 28 50	9 32	−13 18	6 57	7 04	12 13	17 31	17 23	10 15 32	13 42 13
25	22 32 37	9 10	−13 09	6 55	7 02	12 13	17 32	17 26	10 19 28	13 38 17
26	22 36 24	8 48	−12 59	6 52	6 59	12 13	17 34	17 28	10 23 25	13 34 21
27	22 40 10	8 25	−12 49	6 50	6 57	12 13	17 36	17 30	10 27 21	13 30 25
28	22 43 56	8 02	−12 38	6 48	6 54	12 13	17 38	17 32	10 31 18	13 26 30

DURATION OF TWILIGHT (in minutes)

Latitude	52°	56°	52°	56°
	1 February		11 February	
Civil	37	41	35	39
Nautical	77	86	75	83
Astronomical	117	130	114	126
	21 February		28 February	
Civil	34	38	34	38
Nautical	74	81	73	81
Astronomical	113	125	112	124

THE NIGHT SKY

Mercury is visible in the evenings after the first ten days of the month, magnitude −1.1 to +1.0 low above the WSW horizon, around the end of evening civil twilight. This evening apparition is the most suitable one of the year for observers in the northern hemisphere.

Venus, magnitude −4.5, is a magnificent evening object, dominating the western sky for several hours after sunset. Keen-sighted observers may be able to detect the planet before sunset, especially if they know exactly where to look and can shield their eyes from direct sunlight. On the evening of the 22nd the thin sliver of the New Moon, only just over one day old, may be detected passing 3°N. of the planet.

Mars, not long past opposition, is visible for most of the night and is already high in the eastern sky when dusk falls. By the end of the month it is a whole magnitude fainter than when it was at opposition. Mars reaches a stationary point during the second half of the month, only 1° N. of ε Geminorum.

Jupiter is a brilliant morning object, magnitude −2.3, in Virgo.

Saturn passes through conjunction on the 9th and thus is too close to the Sun for observation.

Zodiacal Light. The evening cone may be observed in the western sky after the end of twilight, from the 8th to the 22nd. This faint phenomenon is only visible in good conditions, in the absence of both moonlight and artificial lighting.

THE MOON

Day	RA	Dec.	Hor. par.	Semi-diam.	Sun's co-long.	PA. of Bright Limb	Phase	Age	Rise 52°	Rise 56°	Transit	Set 52°	Set 56°
	h m	°	′	′	°	°	%	d	h m	h m	h m	h m	h m
1	3 24	+21.0	56.3	15.3	19	256	60	9.2	11 00	10 37	19 20	2 43	3 05
2	4 19	+22.6	57.2	15.6	31	261	70	10.2	11 47	11 22	20 16	3 48	4 13
3	5 18	+23.1	58.2	15.9	44	266	80	11.2	12 46	12 21	21 15	4 47	5 12
4	6 18	+22.1	59.1	16.1	56	270	88	12.2	13 58	13 36	22 14	5 36	5 58
5	7 18	+19.8	60.0	16.4	68	273	94	13.2	15 20	15 03	23 12	6 16	6 34
6	8 19	+16.1	60.7	16.5	80	269	98	14.2	16 46	16 35	—	6 47	7 01
7	9 17	+11.2	61.1	16.7	92	197	100	15.2	18 14	18 08	0 09	7 14	7 22
8	10 15	+ 5.7	61.3	16.7	104	129	98	16.2	19 42	19 41	1 05	7 37	7 40
9	11 11	− 0.2	61.1	16.6	116	122	94	17.2	21 08	21 13	1 58	7 59	7 57
10	12 06	− 6.0	60.6	16.5	129	119	87	18.2	22 33	22 43	2 52	8 21	8 15
11	13 01	−11.3	59.9	16.3	141	116	78	19.2	23 55	—	3 45	8 45	8 34
12	13 57	−15.9	59.1	16.1	153	112	68	20.2	—	0 10	4 39	9 13	8 57
13	14 53	−19.4	58.2	15.9	165	107	57	21.2	1 13	1 33	5 33	9 47	9 26
14	15 49	−21.8	57.4	15.6	177	102	46	22.2	2 24	2 48	6 28	10 28	10 04
15	16 46	−22.9	56.6	15.4	189	97	36	23.2	3 25	3 51	7 22	11 18	10 52
16	17 41	−22.8	55.9	15.2	202	92	26	24.2	4 16	4 41	8 14	12 15	11 51
17	18 35	−21.5	55.4	15.1	214	88	18	25.2	4 57	5 18	9 05	13 19	12 58
18	19 26	−19.3	54.9	15.0	226	85	11	26.2	5 28	5 46	9 54	14 26	14 09
19	20 16	−16.2	54.5	14.9	238	84	6	27.2	5 54	6 08	10 39	15 34	15 21
20	21 03	−12.5	54.2	14.8	250	87	2	28.2	6 15	6 25	11 23	16 41	16 33
21	21 48	− 8.3	54.1	14.7	262	108	0	29.2	6 33	6 39	12 05	17 48	17 44
22	22 32	− 3.9	53.9	14.7	275	203	0	0.5	6 50	6 52	12 46	18 54	18 54
23	23 16	+ 0.7	53.9	14.7	287	230	2	1.5	7 06	7 05	13 27	20 00	20 04
24	0 00	+ 5.3	54.0	14.7	299	237	6	2.5	7 23	7 17	14 08	21 07	21 15
25	0 44	+ 9.6	54.2	14.8	311	241	11	3.5	7 41	7 32	14 51	22 14	22 26
26	1 30	+13.7	54.5	14.8	323	245	17	4.5	8 02	7 49	15 35	23 22	23 38
27	2 18	+17.2	54.9	15.0	336	249	25	5.5	8 28	8 10	16 22	—	—
28	3 08	+20.0	55.5	15.1	348	253	34	6.5	8 59	8 38	17 12	0 29	0 49

MERCURY

Day	RA	Dec.	Diam.	Phase	Transit	5° high 52°	5° high 56°
	h m	°	″	%	h m	h m	h m
1	21 25	−17.3	5	98	12 41	16 33	16 11
4	21 45	−15.4	5	96	12 50	16 54	16 36
7	22 06	−13.3	5	93	12 59	17 16	17 00
10	22 26	−11.0	6	88	13 07	17 38	17 24
13	22 44	− 8.7	6	81	13 13	17 58	17 47
16	23 01	− 6.3	6	72	13 18	18 15	18 07
19	23 15	− 4.1	7	60	13 20	18 29	18 22
22	23 26	− 2.1	7	46	13 18	18 36	18 32
25	23 33	− 0.6	8	32	13 12	18 37	18 33
28	23 34	0.3	9	20	13 01	18 29	18 26
31	23 31	0.5	10	10	12 44	18 13	18 10

VENUS

Day	RA	Dec.	Diam.	Phase	Transit	5° high 52°	5° high 56°
	h m	°	″	%	h m	h m	h m
1	23 53	+ 0.7	28	44	15 08	20 40	20 38
6	0 08	+ 3.0	30	41	15 03	20 48	20 47
11	0 22	+ 5.3	32	38	14 57	20 53	20 54
16	0 34	+ 7.4	34	34	14 49	20 56	20 59
21	0 45	+ 9.4	37	30	14 40	20 57	21 02
26	0 54	+11.2	40	26	14 29	20 55	21 01
31	1 00	+12.7	43	22	14 15	20 48	20 56

MARS

Day	RA	Dec.	Diam.	Phase	Transit	5° high 52°	5° high 56°
1	6 45	+27.0	13	97	21 56	5 57	6 21
6	6 41	+27.0	13	96	21 33	5 34	5 57
11	6 39	+26.9	12	95	21 11	5 12	5 35
16	6 39	+26.8	12	95	20 51	4 51	5 14
21	6 40	+26.6	11	94	20 33	4 31	4 54
26	6 42	+26.5	10	93	20 16	4 12	4 35
31	6 45	+26.3	10	92	19 59	3 55	4 17

SUNRISE AND SUNSET

	London		Bristol		Birmingham		Manchester		Newcastle		Glasgow		Belfast	
	0°05′	51°30′	2°35′	51°28′	1°55′	52°28′	2°15′	53°28′	1°37′	54°59′	4°14′	55°52′	5°56′	54°35′
	h m	h m	h m	h m	h m	h m	h m	h m	h m	h m	h m	h m	h m	h m
1	7 39	16 50	7 49	17 00	7 49	16 54	7 54	16 52	7 57	16 44	8 11	16 51	8 13	17 02
2	7 37	16 52	7 47	17 02	7 48	16 56	7 52	16 54	7 55	16 46	8 09	16 53	8 11	17 05
3	7 36	16 54	7 45	17 04	7 46	16 58	7 51	16 56	7 54	16 48	8 07	16 55	8 09	17 07
4	7 34	16 55	7 44	17 05	7 44	17 00	7 49	16 58	7 52	16 50	8 05	16 57	8 07	17 09
5	7 32	16 57	7 42	17 07	7 43	17 02	7 47	17 00	7 50	16 52	8 03	16 59	8 06	17 11
6	7 31	16 59	7 40	17 09	7 41	17 03	7 45	17 02	7 48	16 54	8 01	17 01	8 04	17 13
7	7 29	17 01	7 39	17 11	7 39	17 05	7 43	17 04	7 46	16 56	7 59	17 04	8 02	17 15
8	7 27	17 03	7 37	17 13	7 37	17 07	7 42	17 06	7 44	16 58	7 57	17 06	8 00	17 17
9	7 25	17 04	7 35	17 15	7 35	17 09	7 40	17 08	7 42	17 00	7 55	17 08	7 58	17 19
10	7 24	17 06	7 34	17 16	7 34	17 11	7 38	17 10	7 40	17 03	7 53	17 10	7 56	17 21
11	7 22	17 08	7 32	17 18	7 32	17 13	7 36	17 12	7 38	17 05	7 51	17 12	7 54	17 23
12	7 20	17 10	7 30	17 20	7 30	17 15	7 34	17 14	7 36	17 07	7 49	17 15	7 52	17 25
13	7 18	17 12	7 28	17 22	7 28	17 17	7 32	17 16	7 33	17 09	7 46	17 17	7 49	17 27
14	7 16	17 14	7 26	17 24	7 26	17 19	7 30	17 18	7 31	17 11	7 44	17 19	7 47	17 29
15	7 14	17 15	7 24	17 26	7 24	17 21	7 28	17 19	7 29	17 13	7 42	17 21	7 45	17 31
16	7 12	17 17	7 22	17 27	7 22	17 22	7 26	17 21	7 27	17 15	7 40	17 23	7 43	17 33
17	7 10	17 19	7 20	17 29	7 20	17 24	7 23	17 23	7 25	17 17	7 37	17 25	7 41	17 36
18	7 08	17 21	7 18	17 31	7 18	17 26	7 21	17 25	7 22	17 19	7 35	17 28	7 39	17 38
19	7 06	17 23	7 16	17 33	7 16	17 28	7 19	17 27	7 20	17 21	7 33	17 30	7 36	17 40
20	7 04	17 25	7 14	17 35	7 14	17 30	7 17	17 29	7 18	17 24	7 30	17 32	7 34	17 42
21	7 02	17 26	7 12	17 36	7 12	17 32	7 15	17 31	7 15	17 26	7 28	17 34	7 32	17 44
22	7 00	17 28	7 10	17 38	7 09	17 34	7 13	17 33	7 13	17 28	7 26	17 36	7 30	17 46
23	6 58	17 30	7 08	17 40	7 07	17 36	7 10	17 35	7 11	17 30	7 23	17 38	7 27	17 48
24	6 56	17 32	7 06	17 42	7 05	17 37	7 08	17 37	7 08	17 32	7 21	17 41	7 25	17 50
25	6 54	17 34	7 04	17 44	7 03	17 39	7 06	17 39	7 06	17 34	7 18	17 43	7 23	17 52
26	6 52	17 35	7 02	17 45	7 01	17 41	7 04	17 41	7 04	17 36	7 16	17 45	7 20	17 54
27	6 50	17 37	7 00	17 47	6 59	17 43	7 01	17 43	7 01	17 38	7 13	17 47	7 18	17 56
28	6 48	17 39	6 58	17 49	6 56	17 45	6 59	17 45	6 59	17 40	7 11	17 49	7 16	17 58

JUPITER

Day	*RA*	*Dec.*	*Transit*	*5° high* 52°	56°
	h m	° ′	h m	h m	h m
1	12 56.3	− 4 28	4 11	23 04	23 11
11	12 55.4	− 4 19	3 31	22 22	22 29
21	12 53.4	− 4 04	2 49	21 40	21 46
31	12 50.4	− 3 43	2 07	20 55	21 02

Diameters – equatorial 42″ polar 39″

SATURN

Day	*RA*	*Dec.*	*Transit*	
	h m	° ′	h m	
1	21 30.5	−15 50	12 44	Saturn is
11	21 35.3	−15 27	12 09	too close to
21	21 40.0	−15 05	11 35	the Sun for
31	21 44.7	−14 42	11 00	observation

Diameters – equatorial 15″ polar 14″
Rings – major axis 35″ minor axis 8″

URANUS

Day	*RA*	*Dec.*	*Transit*	
	h m	° ′	h m	
1	19 24.6	−22 26	10 38	Uranus is
11	19 26.9	−22 22	10 01	too close to
21	19 29.1	−22 17	9 24	the Sun for
31	19 31.0	−22 13	8 47	observation

Diameter 4″

NEPTUNE

Day	*RA*	*Dec.*	*Transit*	
	h m	° ′	h m	
1	19 24.1	−21 21	10 38	Neptune is
11	19 25.5	−21 18	10 00	too close to
21	19 26.9	−21 16	9 22	the Sun for
31	19 28.1	−21 13	8 44	observation

Diameter 2″

March 1993

THIRD MONTH, 31 DAYS. *Mars*, Roman god of battle

Sun's Longitude 0° ♈ 20ᵈ 15ʰ

1	*Monday*	St David's Day. Paul Scott *d.* 1978.	*week* 10 *day* 60
2	*Tuesday*	John Wesley *d.* 1791. Horace Walpole *d.* 1797.	61
3	*Wednesday*	Alexander Graham Bell *b.* 1847.	62
4	*Thursday*	Opening of the Forth railway bridge 1890.	63
5	*Friday*	Geraldus Mercator *b.* 1512. Prokofiev *d.* 1953.	64
6	*Saturday*	Michelangelo *b.* 1474. Louisa M. Alcott *d.* 1888.	65
7	*Sunday*	**2nd S. in Lent.** Maurice Ravel *b.* 1875.	*week* 11 *day* 66
8	*Monday*	Commonwealth Day. William III *d.* 1702.	67
9	*Tuesday*	Comte de Mirabeau *b.* 1749. Ernest Bevin *b.* 1881.	68
10	*Wednesday*	*Prince Edward b. 1964.* Owen Brannigan *b.* 1908.	69
11	*Thursday*	Henry Walford Davies *d.* 1941.	70
12	*Friday*	Bishop George Berkeley *b.* 1685.	71
13	*Saturday*	Tsar Alexander II of Russia *assass.* 1881 NS.	72
14	*Sunday*	**3rd S. in Lent.** Strauss (the Elder) *b.* 1804.	*week* 12 *day* 73
15	*Monday*	Salvator Rosa *d.* 1673. Dame Rebecca West *d.* 1983.	74
16	*Tuesday*	Sir Austen Chamberlain *d.* 1937.	75
17	*Wednesday*	St Patrick's Day. *Bank Holiday in Northern Ireland.*	76
18	*Thursday*	Neville Chamberlain *b.* 1869. Wilfred Owen *b.* 1893.	77
19	*Friday*	**St Joseph of Nazareth.** Sir Richard Burton *b.* 1821.	78
20	*Saturday*	Henry IV *d.* 1413. Sir Isaac Newton *d.* 1727.	79
21	*Sunday*	**4th S. in Lent.** Mothering Sunday.	*week* 13 *day* 80
22	*Monday*	Goethe *d.* 1832. Stephen Sondheim *b.* 1930.	81
23	*Tuesday*	Princess Eugenie of York *b.* 1990.	82
24	*Wednesday*	HINDU NEW YEAR. William Morris *b.* 1834.	83
25	*Thursday*	**The Annunciation.** A. J. P. Taylor *b.* 1906.	84
26	*Friday*	Cecil Rhodes *d.* 1902. Sarah Bernhardt *d.* 1923.	85
27	*Saturday*	James I *d.* 1625. Arnold Bennett *d.* 1931.	86
28	*Sunday*	**5th S. in Lent.** Dame Flora Robson *b.* 1902.	*week* 14 *day* 87
29	*Monday*	Charles Wesley *d.* 1788. Vera Brittain *d.* 1970.	88
30	*Tuesday*	Vincent Van Gogh *b.* 1853. Sean O'Casey *b.* 1880.	89
31	*Wednesday*	John Donne *d.* 1631. Eiffel Tower completed 1889.	90

Astronomical Phenomena

d	h	
3	20	Mars in conjunction with Moon. Mars 5° N.
9	04	Mercury in inferior conjunction
10	00	Jupiter in conjunction with Moon. Jupiter 6° N.
20	04	Saturn in conjunction with Moon. Saturn 6° S.
20	15	Equinox
21	10	Mercury in conjunction with Moon. Mercury 4° S.
24	11	Venus in conjunction with Moon. Venus 4° N.
30	12	Jupiter at opposition
31	18	Mars in conjunction with Moon. Mars 5° N.

Constellations

The following are near the meridian at

February 1d, 24h
February 15d, 23h
March 1d, 22h
March 16d, 21h
April 1d, 20h
April 15d, 19h

Cepheus (below the Pole), Camelopardus, Lynx, Gemini, Cancer, Leo, Canis Minor, Hydra, Monoceros, Canis Major and Puppis

Minima of Algol

d	h	d	h	d	h
1	09.4	12	20.7	24	08.0
4	06.3	15	17.6	27	04.8
7	03.1	18	14.4	30	01.7
9	23.9	21	11.2		

The Moon

Phases, Apsides and Node	d	h	m
☽ First Quarter	1	15	47
○ Full Moon	8	09	46
☾ Last Quarter	15	04	17
● New Moon	23	07	14
☽ First Quarter	31	04	10
Perigee (356,528 km)	8	08	34
Apogee (406,632 km)	21	18	59

Mean longitude of ascending node on 1 March, 257°

THE SUN s.d. 16′.1

Day	Right Ascension	Dec.	Equation of time	Rise 52°	Rise 56°	Transit	Set 52°	Set 56°	Sidereal time	Transit of First Point of Aries
	h m s	° ′	m s	h m	h m	h m	h m	h m	h m s	h m s
1	22 47 42	−7 40	−12 27	6 46	6 52	12 12	17 40	17 34	10 35 15	13 22 34
2	22 51 26	−7 17	−12 15	6 44	6 49	12 12	17 41	17 36	10 39 11	13 18 38
3	22 55 11	−6 54	−12 03	6 42	6 47	12 12	17 43	17 38	10 43 08	13 14 42
4	22 58 54	−6 31	−11 50	6 39	6 44	12 12	17 45	17 40	10 47 04	13 10 46
5	23 02 38	−6 08	−11 37	6 37	6 41	12 12	17 47	17 43	10 51 01	13 06 50
6	23 06 21	−5 45	−11 23	6 35	6 39	12 11	17 49	17 45	10 54 57	13 02 54
7	23 10 03	−5 21	−11 09	6 33	6 36	12 11	17 50	17 47	10 58 54	12 58 58
8	23 13 45	−4 58	−10 55	6 30	6 34	12 11	17 52	17 49	11 02 50	12 55 02
9	23 17 27	−4 35	−10 40	6 28	6 31	12 11	17 54	17 51	11 06 47	12 51 06
10	23 21 08	−4 11	−10 24	6 26	6 29	12 10	17 56	17 53	11 10 44	12 47 10
11	23 24 49	−3 48	−10 09	6 24	6 26	12 10	17 57	17 55	11 14 40	12 43 15
12	23 28 29	−3 24	− 9 53	6 21	6 23	12 10	17 59	17 57	11 18 37	12 39 19
13	23 32 10	−3 00	− 9 37	6 19	6 21	12 09	18 01	17 59	11 22 33	12 35 23
14	23 35 50	−2 37	− 9 20	6 17	6 18	12 09	18 03	18 01	11 26 30	12 31 27
15	23 39 30	−2 13	− 9 03	6 14	6 16	12 09	18 04	18 03	11 30 26	12 27 31
16	23 43 09	−1 49	− 8 46	6 12	6 13	12 09	18 06	18 05	11 34 23	12 23 35
17	23 46 49	−1 26	− 8 29	6 10	6 10	12 08	18 08	18 08	11 38 19	12 19 39
18	23 50 28	−1 02	− 8 12	6 07	6 08	12 08	18 10	18 10	11 42 16	12 15 43
19	23 54 07	−0 38	− 7 55	6 05	6 05	12 08	18 11	18 12	11 46 13	12 11 47
20	23 57 46	−0 15	− 7 37	6 03	6 02	12 07	18 13	18 14	11 50 09	12 07 51
21	0 01 25	+0 09	− 7 19	6 01	6 00	12 07	18 15	18 16	11 54 06	12 03 55
22	0 05 04	+0 33	− 7 01	5 58	5 57	12 07	18 17	18 18	11 58 02	12 00 00
23	0 08 42	+0 57	− 6 43	5 56	5 55	12 07	18 18	18 20	12 01 59	11 56 04
24	0 12 21	+1 20	− 6 25	5 54	5 52	12 06	18 20	18 22	12 05 55	11 52 08
25	0 15 59	+1 44	− 6 07	5 51	5 49	12 06	18 22	18 24	12 09 52	11 48 12
26	0 19 38	+2 07	− 5 49	5 49	5 47	12 06	18 23	18 26	12 13 48	11 44 16
27	0 23 16	+2 31	− 5 31	5 47	5 44	12 05	18 25	18 28	12 17 45	11 40 20
28	0 26 54	+2 54	− 5 13	5 44	5 41	12 05	18 27	18 30	12 21 41	11 36 24
29	0 30 33	+3 18	− 4 55	5 42	5 39	12 05	18 29	18 32	12 25 38	11 32 28
30	0 34 11	+3 41	− 4 37	5 40	5 36	12 04	18 30	18 34	12 29 35	11 28 32
31	0 37 50	+4 04	− 4 19	5 37	5 33	12 04	18 32	18 36	12 33 31	11 24 36

DURATION OF TWILIGHT (in minutes)

Latitude	52°	56°	52°	56°
	1 March		11 March	
Civil	34	38	34	37
Nautical	73	81	73	80
Astronomical	112	124	113	125
	21 March		31 March	
Civil	34	37	34	38
Nautical	74	82	76	84
Astronomical	116	129	120	136

THE NIGHT SKY

Mercury may possibly be glimpsed low above the WSW horizon at the end of evening civil twilight on the first day of March. Thereafter it is unsuitably placed for observation, inferior conjunction occurring on the 9th.

Venus is a brilliant object in the west in the early evening skies. The period available for observation in the evening is shortening very noticeably and by the end of the month the planet is setting just before the Sun. However, Venus attains its greatest northern ecliptic latitude during the second half of March. As a result it will be possible to see it as a morning object for a few days before inferior conjunction on 1 April. It may be detected low above the ENE horizon shortly before sunrise.

Mars, magnitude +0.2, continues to fade as it moves away from opposition. It is now moving eastwards in Gemini. The Moon will be seen close to Mars on the evenings of the 3rd and 31st.

Jupiter, magnitude −2.4, reaches opposition on the 30th and is therefore visible throughout the hours of darkness. On the night of the 9th to 10th, the Moon just after Full passes 5° S. of Jupiter.

Saturn is too close to the Sun for observation.

Zodiacal Light. The evening cone may be observed in the western sky after the end of twilight, from the 9th to the 24th.

THE MOON

Day	RA	Dec.	Hor. par.	Semi-diam.	Sun's co-long.	P.A. of Bright Limb	Phase	Age	Rise 52°	Rise 56°	Transit	Set 52°	Set 56°
	h m	°	′	′	°	°	%	d	h m	h m	h m	h m	h m
1	4 01	+21.9	56.1	15.3	360	258	43	7.5	9 40	9 16	18 05	1 33	1 57
2	4 57	+22.8	57.0	15.5	12	264	54	8.5	10 32	10 07	19 00	2 33	2 58
3	5 54	+22.4	57.9	15.8	24	269	64	9.5	11 36	11 13	19 57	3 25	3 48
4	6 53	+20.7	58.9	16.0	36	274	74	10.5	12 50	12 31	20 54	4 07	4 28
5	7 52	+17.7	59.8	16.3	49	278	84	11.5	14 12	13 58	21 50	4 42	4 58
6	8 50	+13.5	60.6	16.5	61	280	91	12.5	15 38	15 29	22 46	5 11	5 22
7	9 48	+ 8.4	61.2	16.7	73	277	97	13.5	17 05	17 02	23 41	5 36	5 42
8	10 44	+ 2.6	61.5	16.8	85	252	100	14.5	18 34	18 35	—	5 59	6 00
9	11 41	− 3.3	61.4	16.7	97	143	99	15.5	20 01	20 08	0 36	6 22	6 18
10	12 38	− 9.0	61.0	16.6	109	124	96	16.5	21 28	21 40	1 30	6 46	6 37
11	13 35	−14.0	60.4	16.5	122	116	90	17.5	22 51	23 09	2 26	7 13	6 59
12	14 33	−18.0	59.5	16.2	134	111	82	18.5	—	—	3 22	7 46	7 27
13	15 32	−20.9	58.6	16.0	146	105	73	19.5	0 08	0 30	4 19	8 25	8 03
14	16 30	−22.4	57.6	15.7	158	99	62	20.5	1 15	1 40	5 15	9 13	8 49
15	17 27	−22.7	56.7	15.4	170	93	52	21.5	2 11	2 36	6 09	10 10	9 45
16	18 22	−21.7	55.9	15.2	182	88	42	22.5	2 55	3 18	7 02	11 12	10 50
17	19 14	−19.7	55.2	15.1	195	84	32	23.5	3 30	3 49	7 51	12 18	12 00
18	20 04	−16.9	54.7	14.9	207	80	24	24.5	3 58	4 13	8 38	13 26	13 12
19	20 51	−13.3	54.3	14.8	219	78	16	25.5	4 20	4 31	9 22	14 33	14 23
20	21 37	− 9.3	54.1	14.7	231	77	10	26.5	4 39	4 47	10 04	15 39	15 34
21	22 21	− 5.0	54.0	14.7	243	79	5	27.5	4 57	5 00	10 45	16 45	16 44
22	23 05	− 0.4	53.9	14.7	256	86	2	28.5	5 13	5 13	11 26	17 51	17 54
23	23 49	+ 4.1	54.0	14.7	268	122	0	29.5	5 30	5 26	12 07	18 57	19 04
24	0 33	+ 8.5	54.1	14.8	280	216	1	0.7	5 48	5 40	12 50	20 04	20 15
25	1 19	+12.6	54.4	14.8	292	236	3	1.7	6 09	5 57	13 34	21 12	21 27
26	2 07	+16.2	54.7	14.9	304	245	7	2.7	6 33	6 17	14 20	22 19	22 38
27	2 56	+19.2	55.1	15.0	317	251	12	3.7	7 03	6 43	15 09	23 24	23 47
28	3 48	+21.3	55.6	15.1	329	257	19	4.7	7 40	7 17	16 00	—	—
29	4 42	+22.4	56.2	15.3	341	262	28	5.7	8 27	8 03	16 53	0 25	0 49
30	5 38	+22.4	56.9	15.5	353	268	38	6.7	9 25	9 02	17 48	1 18	1 42
31	6 35	+21.1	57.7	15.7	5	274	48	7.7	10 33	10 13	18 43	2 02	2 24

MERCURY

Day	RA	Dec.	Diam.	Phase	Transit	
	h m	°			h m	
1	23 34	0.5	—	—	12 56	Mercury is
4	23 29	0.4	—	—	12 38	too close to
7	23 20	− 0.3	—	—	12 17	the Sun for
10	23 09	− 1.6	—	—	11 55	observation
13	22 59	− 3.1	—	—	11 34	
16	22 52	− 4.6	—	—	11 14	
19	22 47	− 5.8	—	—	10 59	
22	22 46	− 6.8	—	—	10 46	
25	22 48	− 7.3	—	—	10 37	
28	22 53	− 7.5	—	—	10 30	
31	23 00	− 7.4	—	—	10 26	

VENUS

Day	RA	Dec.	Diam.	Phase	Transit	5° high 52°	5° high 56°
	h m	°	″	%	h m	h m	h m
1	0 58	+12.1	42	23	14 21	20 51	20 58
6	1 02	+13.4	45	19	14 05	20 42	20 50
11	1 03	+14.3	49	14	13 46	20 27	20 36
16	1 00	+14.7	52	10	13 23	20 06	20 15
21	0 54	+14.6	55	6	12 57	19 38	19 47
26	0 45	+13.8	58	3	12 28	19 04	19 12
31	0 34	+12.4	59	1	11 58	18 26	18 33

MARS

Day	RA	Dec.	Diam.	Phase	Transit	5° high 52°	5° high 56°
1	6 44	+26.4	10	93	20 06	4 02	4 24
6	6 48	+26.2	10	92	19 50	3 44	4 07
11	6 52	+25.9	9	92	19 35	3 28	3 50
16	6 58	+25.7	9	91	19 22	3 12	3 34
21	7 05	+25.4	8	91	19 09	2 57	3 19
26	7 12	+25.1	8	90	18 56	2 43	3 04
31	7 20	+24.8	8	90	18 44	2 29	2 49

SUNRISE AND SUNSET

	London		Bristol		Birmingham		Manchester		Newcastle		Glasgow		Belfast	
	0°05′	51°30′	2°35′	51°28′	1°55′	52°28′	2°15′	53°28′	1°37′	54°59′	4°14′	55°52′	5°56′	54°35′
	h m	h m	h m	h m	h m	h m	h m	h m	h m	h m	h m	h m	h m	h m
1	6 46	17 41	6 56	17 51	6 54	17 47	6 57	17 47	6 57	17 42	7 08	17 51	7 13	18 00
2	6 43	17 42	6 53	17 52	6 52	17 49	6 55	17 49	6 54	17 44	7 06	17 53	7 11	18 02
3	6 41	17 44	6 51	17 54	6 50	17 50	6 52	17 51	6 52	17 46	7 03	17 55	7 08	18 04
4	6 39	17 46	6 49	17 56	6 48	17 52	6 50	17 52	6 49	17 48	7 01	17 58	7 06	18 06
5	6 37	17 48	6 47	17 58	6 45	17 54	6 48	17 54	6 47	17 50	6 58	18 00	7 04	18 08
6	6 35	17 49	6 45	17 59	6 43	17 56	6 45	17 56	6 44	17 52	6 56	18 02	7 01	18 10
7	6 33	17 51	6 43	18 01	6 41	17 58	6 43	17 58	6 42	17 54	6 53	18 04	6 59	18 12
8	6 30	17 53	6 40	18 03	6 38	17 59	6 41	18 00	6 39	17 56	6 51	18 06	6 56	18 14
9	6 28	17 55	6 38	18 05	6 36	18 01	6 38	18 02	6 37	17 58	6 48	18 08	6 54	18 16
10	6 26	17 56	6 36	18 06	6 34	18 03	6 36	18 04	6 34	18 00	6 45	18 10	6 51	18 18
11	6 24	17 58	6 34	18 08	6 31	18 05	6 33	18 06	6 32	18 02	6 43	18 12	6 49	18 20
12	6 21	18 00	6 31	18 10	6 29	18 07	6 31	18 08	6 29	18 04	6 40	18 14	6 46	18 22
13	6 19	18 01	6 29	18 11	6 27	18 08	6 29	18 09	6 27	18 06	6 38	18 16	6 44	18 24
14	6 17	18 03	6 27	18 13	6 25	18 10	6 26	18 11	6 24	18 08	6 35	18 18	6 41	18 26
15	6 15	18 05	6 25	18 15	6 22	18 12	6 24	18 13	6 22	18 10	6 32	18 20	6 39	18 28
16	6 12	18 07	6 22	18 17	6 20	18 14	6 21	18 15	6 19	18 12	6 30	18 22	6 36	18 29
17	6 10	18 08	6 20	18 18	6 17	18 16	6 19	18 17	6 17	18 14	6 27	18 24	6 34	18 31
18	6 08	18 10	6 18	18 20	6 15	18 17	6 17	18 19	6 14	18 16	6 25	18 27	6 31	18 33
19	6 06	18 12	6 15	18 22	6 13	18 19	6 14	18 20	6 12	18 18	6 22	18 29	6 29	18 35
20	6 03	18 13	6 13	18 23	6 10	18 21	6 12	18 22	6 09	18 20	6 19	18 31	6 26	18 37
21	6 01	18 15	6 11	18 25	6 08	18 23	6 09	18 24	6 06	18 22	6 17	18 33	6 24	18 39
22	5 59	18 17	6 09	18 27	6 06	18 24	6 07	18 26	6 04	18 24	6 14	18 35	6 21	18 41
23	5 56	18 18	6 06	18 28	6 03	18 26	6 04	18 28	6 01	18 26	6 11	18 37	6 19	18 43
24	5 54	18 20	6 04	18 30	6 01	18 28	6 02	18 30	5 59	18 28	6 09	18 39	6 16	18 45
25	5 52	18 22	6 02	18 32	5 59	18 30	6 00	18 31	5 56	18 30	6 06	18 41	6 14	18 47
26	5 50	18 23	6 00	18 33	5 56	18 31	5 57	18 33	5 54	18 32	6 04	18 43	6 11	18 49
27	5 47	18 25	5 57	18 35	5 54	18 33	5 55	18 35	5 51	18 34	6 01	18 45	6 09	18 51
28	5 45	18 27	5 55	18 37	5 52	18 35	5 52	18 37	5 49	18 36	5 58	18 47	6 06	18 53
29	5 43	18 29	5 53	18 39	5 49	18 37	5 50	18 39	5 46	18 38	5 56	18 49	6 04	18 55
30	5 40	18 30	5 50	18 40	5 47	18 38	5 47	18 41	5 44	18 40	5 53	18 51	6 01	18 56
31	5 38	18 32	5 48	18 42	5 45	18 40	5 45	18 42	5 41	18 41	5 50	18 53	5 59	18 58

JUPITER

Day	*RA*	*Dec.*	*Transit*	*5° high*	
				52°	56°
	h m	° ′	h m	h m	h m
1	12 51.1	− 3 48	2 15	21 04	21 11
11	12 47.3	− 3 22	1 32	20 19	20 25
21	12 43.0	− 2 54	0 49	19 33	19 38
31	12 38.3	− 2 23	0 05	18 46	18 51

Diameters – equatorial 44″ polar 41″

SATURN

Day	*RA*	*Dec.*	*Transit*	
	h m	° ′	h m	
1	21 43.7	−14 47	11 07	Saturn is
11	21 48.2	−14 25	10 32	too close to
21	21 52.5	−14 04	9 57	the Sun for
31	21 56.5	−13 44	9 22	observation

Diameters – equatorial 15″ polar 14″
Rings – major axis 35″ minor axis 8″

URANUS

Day	*RA*	*Dec.*	*Transit*	
	h m	° ′	h m	
1	19 30.7	−22 14	8 54	Uranus is
11	19 32.4	−22 11	8 16	too close to
21	19 33.8	−22 08	7 39	the Sun for
31	19 34.9	−22 06	7 00	observation

Diameter 4″

NEPTUNE

Day	*RA*	*Dec.*	*Transit*	
	h m	° ′	h m	
1	19 27.8	−21 14	8 51	Neptune is
11	19 28.9	−21 11	8 13	too close to
21	19 29.8	−21 09	7 34	the Sun for
31	19 30.4	−21 08	6 56	observation

Diameter 2″

April 1993

FOURTH MONTH, 30 DAYS. *Aperire*, to open; Earth opens to receive seed

Sun's Longitude 30° ♉ 20ᵈ 02ʰ

1	*Thursday*	End of the Spanish Civil War 1939. Max Ernst *d.* 1976.	*week* 14 *day* 91
2	*Friday*	Hans Christian Andersen *b.* 1805. C. S. Forester *d.* 1966.	92
3	*Saturday*	First run of the Pony Express 1860. Graham Greene *d.* 1991.	93
4	*Sunday*	**Palm Sunday.** Martin Luther King *assass.* 1968.	*week* 15 *day* 94
5	*Monday*	Thomas Hobbes *b.* 1588. A. C. Swinburne *b.* 1837.	95
6	*Tuesday*	PASSOVER begins. USA entered World War I 1917.	96
7	*Wednesday*	*Hilary Law Sittings end.* Phineas T. Barnum *d.* 1891.	97
8	*Thursday*	**Maundy Thursday.** Entente Cordiale signed 1904.	98
9	*Friday*	**Good Friday.** *Public Holiday in the UK.*	99
10	*Saturday*	**Easter Eve.** Ben Nicholson *b.* 1894.	100
11	*Sunday*	**Easter Day** (Western churches). Charles Hallé *b.* 1819.	*week* 16 *day* 101
12	*Monday*	*Bank Holiday in England, Wales and Northern Ireland.*	102
13	*Tuesday*	Edict of Nantes 1598. Samuel Beckett *b.* 1906.	103
14	*Wednesday*	Handel *b.* 1759. Arnold Toynbee *b.* 1889.	104
15	*Thursday*	Henry James *b.* 1843. Jean Genet *d.* 1986.	105
16	*Friday*	Ford Madox Brown *b.* 1821. Marie Tussaud *d.* 1850.	106
17	*Saturday*	Diet of Worms 1521. Nikita Krushchev *b.* 1894 NS.	107
18	*Sunday*	**1st S. after Easter.** EASTER DAY (Greek Orthodox).	*week* 17 *day* 108
19	*Monday*	Benjamin Disraeli, 1st Earl of Beaconsfield *d.* 1881.	109
20	*Tuesday*	*Easter Law Sittings begin.* Giovanni Canaletto *d.* 1768.	110
21	*Wednesday*	*Queen Elizabeth II b. 1926.* Mark Twain *d.* 1910.	111
22	*Thursday*	Kathleen Ferrier *b.* 1912. Yehudi Menuhin *b.* 1916.	112
23	*Friday*	St George's Day. William Shakespeare *b.* 1564, *d.* 1616.	113
24	*Saturday*	Trollope *b.* 1815. Easter Rising in Dublin began 1916.	114
25	*Sunday*	**St Mark. 2nd S. after Easter.**	*week* 18 *day* 115
26	*Monday*	Alfred Krupp *b.* 1812. Rudolf Hess *b.* 1894.	116
27	*Tuesday*	Edward Gibbon *b.* 1737. Ferdinand Magellan *killed.* 1521.	117
28	*Wednesday*	Anthony Ashley Cooper, 7th Earl of Shaftesbury *b.* 1801.	118
29	*Thursday*	Easter Rising in Dublin put down 1916.	119
30	*Friday*	Mary II *b.* 1662. Beatrice Webb *d.* 1943.	120

ASTRONOMICAL PHENOMENA

d	h	
1	13	Venus in inferior conjunction
5	18	Mercury at greatest elongation W. 28°
6	06	Jupiter in conjunction with Moon. Jupiter 6° N.
16	15	Saturn in conjunction with Moon. Saturn 6° S.
18	12	Venus in conjunction with Mercury. Venus 7° N.
19	16	Venus in conjunction with Moon. Venus 0°.4 S.
19	20	Mercury in conjunction with Moon. Mercury 7° S.
28	21	Mars in conjunction with Moon. Mars 6° N.

CONSTELLATIONS

The following constellations are near the meridian at

March 1d, 24h
March 16d, 23h
April 1d, 22h
April 15d, 21h
May 1d, 20h
May 16d, 19h

Cepheus (below the Pole), Cassiopeia (below the Pole), Ursa Major, Leo Minor, Leo, Sextans, Hydra and Crater

MINIMA OF ALGOL

d	h	d	h	d	h
1	22.5	13	09.8	24	21.0
4	19.3	16	06.6	27	17.9
7	16.1	19	03.4	30	14.7
10	12.9	22	00.2		

THE MOON

Phases, Apsides and Node	d	h	m
○ Full Moon	6	18	43
☾ Last Quarter	13	19	39
● New Moon	21	23	49
☽ First Quarter	29	12	41
Perigee (358,381 km)	5	19	29
Apogee (405,951 km)	18	05	06

Mean longitude of ascending node on 1 April, 256°

THE SUN

s.d. 16′.0

Day	Right Ascension	Dec. +	Equation of time	Rise 52°	Rise 56°	Transit	Set 52°	Set 56°	Sidereal time	Transit of First Point of Aries
	h m s	° ′	m s	h m	h m	h m	h m	h m	h m s	h m s
1	0 41 28	4 28	−4 01	5 35	5 31	12 04	18 34	18 38	12 37 28	11 20 40
2	0 45 07	4 51	−3 43	5 33	5 28	12 04	18 35	18 40	12 41 24	11 16 45
3	0 48 46	5 14	−3 25	5 30	5 26	12 03	18 37	18 42	12 45 21	11 12 49
4	0 52 25	5 37	−3 07	5 28	5 23	12 03	18 39	18 44	12 49 17	11 08 53
5	0 56 04	6 00	−2 50	5 26	5 20	12 03	18 41	18 46	12 53 14	11 04 57
6	0 59 43	6 22	−2 33	5 24	5 18	12 02	18 42	18 48	12 57 10	11 01 01
7	1 03 22	6 45	−2 15	5 21	5 15	12 02	18 44	18 50	13 01 07	10 57 05
8	1 07 02	7 08	−1 58	5 19	5 13	12 02	18 46	18 52	13 05 04	10 53 09
9	1 10 42	7 30	−1 42	5 17	5 10	12 02	18 47	18 54	13 09 00	10 49 13
10	1 14 22	7 52	−1 25	5 15	5 07	12 01	18 49	18 56	13 12 57	10 45 17
11	1 18 02	8 14	−1 09	5 12	5 05	12 01	18 51	18 59	13 16 53	10 41 21
12	1 21 43	8 36	−0 53	5 10	5 02	12 01	18 52	19 01	13 20 50	10 37 26
13	1 25 24	8 58	−0 38	5 08	5 00	12 01	18 54	19 03	13 24 46	10 33 30
14	1 29 05	9 20	−0 23	5 06	4 57	12 00	18 56	19 05	13 28 43	10 29 34
15	1 32 47	9 41	−0 08	5 04	4 55	12 00	18 58	19 07	13 32 39	10 25 38
16	1 36 29	10 03	+0 07	5 01	4 52	12 00	18 59	19 09	13 36 36	10 21 42
17	1 40 12	10 24	+0 21	4 59	4 50	12 00	19 01	19 11	13 40 33	10 17 46
18	1 43 55	10 45	+0 35	4 57	4 47	11 59	19 03	19 13	13 44 29	10 13 50
19	1 47 38	11 06	+0 48	4 55	4 45	11 59	19 04	19 15	13 48 26	10 09 54
20	1 51 21	11 27	+1 01	4 53	4 42	11 59	19 06	19 17	13 52 22	10 05 58
21	1 55 06	11 47	+1 13	4 51	4 40	11 59	19 08	19 19	13 56 19	10 02 02
22	1 58 50	12 08	+1 25	4 49	4 37	11 58	19 10	19 21	14 00 15	9 58 06
23	2 02 35	12 28	+1 37	4 46	4 35	11 58	19 11	19 23	14 04 12	9 54 11
24	2 06 20	12 48	+1 48	4 44	4 33	11 58	19 13	19 25	14 08 08	9 50 15
25	2 10 06	13 07	+1 59	4 42	4 30	11 58	19 15	19 27	14 12 05	9 46 19
26	2 13 53	13 27	+2 09	4 40	4 28	11 58	19 16	19 29	14 16 02	9 42 23
27	2 17 40	13 46	+2 18	4 38	4 25	11 58	19 18	19 31	14 19 58	9 38 27
28	2 21 27	14 05	+2 28	4 36	4 23	11 57	19 20	19 33	14 23 55	9 34 31
29	2 25 15	14 24	+2 36	4 34	4 21	11 57	19 21	19 35	14 27 51	9 30 35
30	2 29 03	14 43	+2 45	4 32	4 18	11 57	19 23	19 37	14 31 48	9 26 39

DURATION OF TWILIGHT (in minutes)

Latitude	52°	56°	52°	56°
	1 April		11 April	
Civil	34	38	35	40
Nautical	76	85	79	90
Astronomical	121	137	128	148
	21 April		30 April	
Civil	37	42	39	44
Nautical	84	96	89	105
Astronomical	138	167	152	200

THE NIGHT SKY

Mercury is unsuitably placed for observation.

Venus passes through inferior conjunction on the 1st and is a brilliant morning object, visible low above the ENE horizon just before sunrise. During April its magnitude brightens from −3.5 to −4.4. On the morning of the 19th the old crescent Moon, three days before New, will be seen close to the planet, an actual occultation being visible from North America later in the morning.

Mars, magnitude +0.8, continues to be visible as an evening object, moving eastwards from Gemini into Cancer. It is 5° S. of Pollux on the 14th.

Jupiter continues to be visible as an evening object, magnitude −2.4. Jupiter is moving very slowly westwards in Virgo. The four Galilean satellites are readily observable with a small telescope or a good pair of binoculars, provided that they are held rigidly. Times of eclipses and shadow transits of these satellites are given on pages 74–5.

Saturn, magnitude +0.9, is too close to the Sun to be detected at first but towards the end of the month it gradually becomes visible as a morning object low above the SE horizon between 03h and 04h.

THE MOON

Day	RA	Dec.	Hor. par.	Semi-diam.	Sun's co-long.	PA. of Bright Limb	Phase	Age	Rise 52°	Rise 56°	Transit	Set 52°	Set 56°
	h m	°	′	′	°	°	%	d	h m	h m	h m	h m	h m
1	7 32	+18.6	58.5	15.9	18	278	59	8.7	11 49	11 33	19 37	2 39	2 57
2	8 28	+15.0	59.3	16.2	30	282	70	9.7	13 10	12 59	20 31	3 09	3 22
3	9 24	+10.4	60.1	16.4	42	285	80	10.7	14 34	14 27	21 25	3 35	3 44
4	10 19	+ 5.1	60.7	16.5	54	285	89	11.7	15 59	15 58	22 18	3 59	4 02
5	11 15	− 0.6	61.1	16.6	66	283	95	12.7	17 26	17 30	23 12	4 21	4 20
6	12 11	− 6.4	61.2	16.7	78	271	99	13.7	18 53	19 03	—	4 45	4 38
7	13 09	−11.7	61.0	16.6	91	165	100	14.7	20 19	20 34	0 08	5 11	4 59
8	14 07	−16.2	60.4	16.5	103	120	98	15.7	21 41	22 01	1 05	5 41	5 25
9	15 07	−19.7	59.7	16.3	115	109	93	16.7	22 56	23 19	2 03	6 18	5 58
10	16 07	−21.8	58.8	16.0	127	102	86	17.7	23 59	—	3 01	7 04	6 40
11	17 06	−22.5	57.8	15.8	139	95	78	18.7	—	0 23	3 59	7 59	7 34
12	18 04	−21.9	56.9	15.5	151	89	68	19.7	0 49	1 12	4 53	9 01	8 38
13	18 58	−20.2	56.1	15.3	164	84	58	20.7	1 29	1 49	5 45	10 08	9 48
14	19 50	−17.5	55.3	15.1	176	80	48	21.7	1 59	2 16	6 34	11 15	11 00
15	20 38	−14.1	54.8	14.9	188	76	39	22.7	2 24	2 36	7 19	12 23	12 12
16	21 25	−10.2	54.4	14.8	200	74	30	23.7	2 44	2 53	8 02	13 30	13 23
17	22 09	− 6.0	54.1	14.7	212	73	21	24.7	3 03	3 07	8 44	14 36	14 33
18	22 53	− 1.5	54.0	14.7	225	73	14	25.7	3 20	3 20	9 24	15 41	15 43
19	23 37	+ 3.0	54.1	14.7	237	74	8	26.7	3 37	3 34	10 06	16 47	16 53
20	0 21	+ 7.4	54.2	14.8	249	78	4	27.7	3 54	3 48	10 48	17 54	18 04
21	1 07	+11.6	54.4	14.8	261	88	1	28.7	4 14	4 04	11 31	19 02	19 16
22	1 54	+15.3	54.8	14.9	274	161	0	0.0	4 37	4 23	12 17	20 10	20 28
23	2 44	+18.5	55.1	15.0	286	240	1	1.0	5 06	4 47	13 06	21 16	21 37
24	3 36	+20.8	55.6	15.1	298	253	4	2.0	5 41	5 20	13 57	22 18	22 42
25	4 30	+22.1	56.1	15.3	310	261	9	3.0	6 26	6 02	14 50	23 14	23 38
26	5 25	+22.3	56.6	15.4	322	267	15	4.0	7 21	6 57	15 44	—	—
27	6 22	+21.4	57.1	15.6	335	273	24	5.0	8 25	8 04	16 38	0 01	0 23
28	7 18	+19.2	57.7	15.7	347	279	34	6.0	9.37	9 20	17 31	0 39	0 58
29	8 13	+15.9	58.4	15.9	359	283	44	7.0	10 54	10 41	18 24	1 11	1 25
30	9 07	+11.7	59.0	16.1	11	286	55	8.0	12 14	12 06	19 16	1 37	1 47

MERCURY

Day	RA	Dec.	Diam.	Phase	Transit
	h m	°			h m
1	23 03	− 7.3	—	—	10 25
4	23 13	− 6.8	—	—	10 24
7	23 24	− 6.0	—	—	10 23
10	23 37	− 4.9	—	—	10 25
13	23 51	− 3.7	—	—	10 27
16	0 06	− 2.2	—	—	10 30
19	0 22	− 0.5	—	—	10 34
22	0 38	1.3	—	—	10 39
25	0 56	3.3	—	—	10 45
28	1 14	5.4	—	—	10 52
31	1 34	7.6	—	—	11 00

Mercury is too close to the Sun for observation

VENUS

Day	RA	Dec.	Diam.	Phase	Transit	5° high 52°	5° high 56°
	h m	°	″	%	h m	h m	h m
1	0 32	+12.1	59	1	11 52	5 24	5 17
6	0 22	+10.3	58	1	11 22	5 04	4 59
11	0 14	+ 8.4	56	4	10 54	4 46	4 42
16	0 09	+ 6.6	53	7	10 30	4 30	4 28
21	0 07	+ 5.2	50	12	10 10	4 17	4 16
26	0 10	+ 4.3	46	16	9 53	4 04	4 04
31	0 16	+ 3.7	42	21	9 39	3 53	3 53

MARS

Day	RA	Dec.	Diam.	Phase	Transit	5° high 52°	5° high 56°
1	7 21	+24.7	8	90	18 42	2 26	2 46
6	7 30	+24.3	7	90	18 31	2 12	2 32
11	7 38	+23.9	7	90	18 20	1 58	2 17
16	7 47	+23.4	7	90	18 09	1 45	2 03
21	7 57	+22.9	7	90	17 59	1 31	1 49
26	8 07	+22.3	6	90	17 49	1 18	1 35
31	8 17	+21.7	6	90	17 39	1 05	1 21

SUNRISE AND SUNSET

	London		Bristol		Birmingham		Manchester		Newcastle		Glasgow		Belfast	
	0°05′	51°30′	2°35′	51°28′	1°55′	52°28′	2°15′	53°28′	1°37′	54°59′	4°14′	55°52′	5°56′	54°35′
	h m	h m	h m	h m	h m	h m	h m	h m	h m	h m	h m	h m	h m	h m
1	5 36	18 34	5 46	18 44	5 42	18 42	5 43	18 44	5 38	18 43	5 48	18 55	5 56	19 00
2	5 34	18 35	5 44	18 45	5 40	18 44	5 40	18 46	5 36	18 45	5 45	18 57	5 54	19 02
3	5 31	18 37	5 41	18 47	5 38	18 45	5 38	18 48	5 33	18 47	5 43	18 59	5 51	19 04
4	5 29	18 39	5 39	18 49	5 35	18 47	5 35	18 50	5 31	18 49	5 40	19 01	5 49	19 06
5	5 27	18 40	5 37	18 50	5 33	18 49	5 33	18 52	5 28	18 51	5 37	19 03	5 46	19 08
6	5 25	18 42	5 35	18 52	5 31	18 51	5 31	18 53	5 26	18 53	5 35	19 05	5 44	19 10
7	5 22	18 44	5 32	18 54	5 28	18 52	5 28	18 55	5 23	18 55	5 32	19 07	5 41	19 12
8	5 20	18 45	5 30	18 55	5 26	18 54	5 26	18 57	5 21	18 57	5 30	19 09	5 39	19 14
9	5 18	18 47	5 28	18 57	5 24	18 56	5 23	18 59	5 18	18 59	5 27	19 11	5 36	19 16
10	5 16	18 49	5 26	18 59	5 21	18 58	5 21	19 01	5 16	19 01	5 25	19 13	5 34	19 17
11	5 14	18 50	5 24	19 00	5 19	18 59	5 19	19 02	5 13	19 03	5 22	19 15	5 31	19 19
12	5 11	18 52	5 21	19 02	5 17	19 01	5 16	19 04	5 11	19 05	5 19	19 17	5 29	19 21
13	5 09	18 54	5 19	19 04	5 15	19 03	5 14	19 06	5 08	19 07	5 17	19 19	5 27	19 23
14	5 07	18 55	5 17	19 05	5 12	19 05	5 12	19 08	5 06	19 09	5 14	19 21	5 24	19 25
15	5 05	18 57	5 15	19 07	5 10	19 06	5 09	19 10	5 04	19 11	5 12	19 23	5 22	19 27
16	5 03	18 59	5 13	19 09	5 08	19 08	5 07	19 12	5 01	19 13	5 09	19 25	5 19	19 29
17	5 01	19 00	5 11	19 10	5 06	19 10	5 05	19 13	4 59	19 15	5 07	19 27	5 17	19 31
18	4 58	19 02	5 08	19 12	5 04	19 11	5 03	19 15	4 56	19 17	5 04	19 29	5 15	19 33
19	4 56	19 04	5 06	19 14	5 01	19 13	5 00	19 17	4 54	19 18	5 02	19 31	5 12	19 35
20	4 54	19 05	5 04	19 15	4 59	19 15	4 58	19 19	4 52	19 20	5 00	19 33	5 10	19 37
21	4 52	19 07	5 02	19 17	4 57	19 17	4 56	19 21	4 49	19 22	4 57	19 35	5 08	19 39
22	4 50	19 09	5 00	19 19	4 55	19 18	4 54	19 22	4 47	19 24	4 55	19 38	5 05	19 40
23	4 48	19 10	4 58	19 20	4 53	19 20	4 51	19 24	4 45	19 26	4 52	19 40	5 03	19 42
24	4 46	19 12	4 56	19 22	4 51	19 22	4 49	19 26	4 42	19 28	4 50	19 42	5 01	19 44
25	4 44	19 14	4 54	19 24	4 49	19 24	4 47	19 28	4 40	19 30	4 47	19 44	4 58	19 46
26	4 42	19 15	4 52	19 25	4 47	19 25	4 45	19 30	4 38	19 32	4 45	19 46	4 56	19 48
27	4 40	19 17	4 50	19 27	4 45	19 27	4 43	19 32	4 35	19 34	4 43	19 48	4 54	19 50
28	4 38	19 19	4 48	19 28	4 43	19 29	4 41	19 33	4 33	19 36	4 40	19 50	4 52	19 52
29	4 36	19 20	4 46	19 30	4 41	19 31	4 39	19 35	4 31	19 38	4 38	19 52	4 50	19 54
30	4 34	19 22	4 44	19 32	4 39	19 32	4 37	19 37	4 29	19 40	4 36	19 54	4 47	19 56

JUPITER

Day	*RA*	*Dec.*	*Transit*	*5° high*	
				52°	56°
	h m	° ′	h m	h m	h m
1	12 37.8	− 2 20	0 00	5 15	5 09
11	12 33.1	− 1 51	23 12	4 33	4 29
21	12 28.8	− 1 24	22 28	3 52	3 48
31	12 25.1	− 1 02	21 46	3 11	3 07

Diameters – equatorial 44″ polar 41″

SATURN

Day	*RA*	*Dec.*	*Transit*	*5° high*	
				52°	56°
	h m	° ′	h m	h m	h m
1	21 56.9	−13 42	9 18	5 08	5 24
11	22 00.5	−13 25	8 42	4 30	4 47
21	22 03.7	−13 09	8 06	3 52	4 08
31	22 06.4	−12 56	7 30	3 14	3 30

Diameters – equatorial 16″ polar 14″
Rings – major axis 36″ minor axis 7″

URANUS

Day	*RA*	*Dec.*	*Transit*	*10° high*	
				52°	56°
	h m	° ′	h m	h m	h m
1	19 35.0	−22 05	6 56	4 39	5 35
11	19 35.8	−22 04	6 18	4 00	4 56
21	19 36.1	−22 03	5 39	3 21	4 17
31	19 36.2	−22 04	5 00	2 42	3 37

Diameter 4″

NEPTUNE

Day	*RA*	*Dec.*	*Transit*	*10° high*	
				52°	56°
	h m	° ′	h m	h m	h m
1	19 30.5	−21 08	6 52	4 24	5 12
11	19 30.8	−21 07	6 13	3 45	4 33
21	19 31.0	−21 06	5 34	3 05	3 53
31	19 30.9	−21 06	4 54	2 26	3 14

Diameter 2″

May 1993

FIFTH MONTH, 31 DAYS. *Maia*, goddess of growth and increase

Sun's Longitude 60° II 21ᵈ 01ʰ

1	*Saturday*	**SS Philip and James.** 1st Duke of Wellington *b.* 1769.	*week* 18 *day* 121
2	*Sunday*	**3rd S. after Easter.** Nancy Astor *d.* 1964.	*week* 19 *day* 122
3	*Monday*	*Bank Holiday in the UK.* Golda Meir *b.* 1898.	123
4	*Tuesday*	The Derby was first run 1780. Joseph Whitaker *b.* 1820.	124
5	*Wednesday*	Søren Kierkegaard *b.* 1813. Sir Gordon Richards *b.* 1904.	125
6	*Thursday*	Sigmund Freud *b.* 1856. First four-minute mile run 1954.	126
7	*Friday*	Antonio Salieri *d.* 1825. Johannes Brahms *b.* 1833.	127
8	*Saturday*	Antoine-Laurent Lavoisier *exec.* 1794.	128
9	*Sunday*	**4th S. after Easter.** Sir James Barrie *b.* 1860.	*week* 20 *day* 129
10	*Monday*	Indian Mutiny began with rising at Meerut 1857.	130
11	*Tuesday*	Spencer Perceval *assass.* 1812. Paul Nash *b.* 1889.	131
12	*Wednesday*	Dante Gabriele Rossetti *b.* 1828. Gabriel Fauré *b.* 1845.	132
13	*Thursday*	Sir Arthur Sullivan *b.* 1842. Daphne du Maurier *b.* 1907.	133
14	*Friday*	**St Matthias.** Otto Klemperer *b.* 1885.	134
15	*Saturday*	Pierre Curie *b.* 1859. Edwin Muir *b.* 1887.	135
16	*Sunday*	**5th S. after Easter.** H. E. Bates *b.* 1905.	*week* 21 *day* 136
17	*Monday*	Sandro Botticelli *d.* 1510. Paul Dukas *d.* 1935.	137
18	*Tuesday*	Pierre de Beaumarchais *d.* 1799. Gustav Mahler *d.* 1911.	138
19	*Wednesday*	T. E. Lawrence *d.* 1935. John Betjeman *d.* 1984.	139
20	*Thursday*	**Ascension Day.** Christopher Columbus *d.* 1506.	140
21	*Friday*	Elizabeth Fry *b.* 1780. Rajiv Gandhi *assass.* 1991.	141
22	*Saturday*	Victor Hugo *d.* 1885. Blackwall Tunnel opened 1897.	142
23	*Sunday*	**S. after Ascension Day.** Sir Hugh Casson *b.*1910.	*week* 22 *day* 143
24	*Monday*	Jan Smuts *b.* 1870. Duke Ellington *d.* 1974.	144
25	*Tuesday*	Ralph Waldo Emerson *b.* 1803. Lord Beaverbrook *b.* 1879.	145
26	*Wednesday*	FEAST OF WEEKS begins. Eugene Goossens *b.* 1893.	146
27	*Thursday*	Evacuation from Dunkirk began 1940. *Bismarck* sunk 1941.	147
28	*Friday*	*Easter Law Sittings end.* Patrick White *b.* 1912.	148
29	*Saturday*	Charles II *b.* 1630. G. K. Chesterton *b.* 1874.	149
30	*Sunday*	**Pentecost (Whit Sunday).** Boris Pasternak *d.* 1960.	*week* 23 *day* 150
31	*Monday*	*Bank Holiday in the UK.* Walt Whitman *b.* 1819.	151

ASTRONOMICAL PHENOMENA

d	h	
3	11	Jupiter in conjunction with Moon. Jupiter 6° N.
7	03	Venus at greatest brilliancy
14	02	Saturn in conjunction with Moon. Saturn 6° S.
14	23	Pluto at opposition
16	03	Mercury in superior conjunction
17	19	Venus in conjunction with Moon. Venus 5° S.
21		Partial eclipse of Sun (*see* page 71)
22	05	Mercury in conjunction with Moon. Mercury 0°.9 N.
27	04	Mars in conjunction with Moon. Mars 6° N.
30	16	Jupiter in conjunction with Moon. Jupiter 6° N.

CONSTELLATIONS

The following constellations are near the meridian at

April 1d, 24h	May 16d, 21h
April 15d, 23h	June 1d, 20h
May 1d, 22h	June 15d, 19h

Cepheus (below the Pole), Cassiopeia (below the Pole), Ursa Minor, Ursa Major, Canes Venatici, Coma Berenices, Bootes, Leo, Virgo, Crater, Corvus and Hydra

MINIMA OF ALGOL

Algol is inconveniently situated for observation during May.

THE MOON

Phases, Apsides and Node	d	h	m
○ Full Moon	6	03	34
☾ Last Quarter	13	12	20
● New Moon	21	14	07
☽ First Quarter	28	18	21
Perigee (362,698 km)	4	00	12
Apogee (404,908 km)	15	21	46
Perigee (367,759 km)	31	11	10

Mean longitude of ascending node on 1 May, 254°

THE SUN s.d. 15′.8

Day	Right Ascension	Dec. +	Equation of time	Rise 52°	Rise 56°	Transit	Set 52°	Set 56°	Sidereal time	Transit of First Point of Aries
	h m s	° ′	m s	h m	h m	h m	h m	h m	h m s	h m s
1	2 32 52	15 01	+2 52	4 30	4 16	11 57	19 25	19 39	14 35 44	9 22 43
2	2 36 41	15 19	+3 00	4 29	4 14	11 57	19 26	19 41	14 39 41	9 18 47
3	2 40 31	15 37	+3 06	4 27	4 12	11 57	19 28	19 43	14 43 37	9 14 51
4	2 44 22	15 54	+3 12	4 25	4 10	11 57	19 30	19 45	14 47 34	9 10 56
5	2 48 12	16 12	+3 18	4 23	4 07	11 57	19 31	19 47	14 51 31	9 07 00
6	2 52 04	16 29	+3 23	4 21	4 05	11 57	19 33	19 49	14 55 27	9 03 04
7	2 55 56	16 45	+3 28	4 19	4 03	11 57	19 35	19 51	14 59 24	8 59 08
8	2 59 49	17 02	+3 31	4 18	4 01	11 56	19 36	19 53	15 03 20	8 55 12
9	3 03 42	17 18	+3 35	4 16	3 59	11 56	19 38	19 55	15 07 17	8 51 16
10	3 07 36	17 34	+3 38	4 14	3 57	11 56	19 40	19 57	15 11 13	8 47 20
11	3 11 30	17 50	+3 40	4 13	3 55	11 56	19 41	19 59	15 15 10	8 43 24
12	3 15 25	18 05	+3 41	4 11	3 53	11 56	19 43	20 01	15 19 06	8 39 28
13	3 19 21	18 20	+3 42	4 09	3 51	11 56	19 44	20 03	15 23 03	8 35 32
14	3 23 17	18 35	+3 43	4 08	3 49	11 56	19 46	20 05	15 27 00	8 31 36
15	3 27 14	18 49	+3 43	4 06	3 47	11 56	19 47	20 07	15 30 56	8 27 41
16	3 31 11	19 03	+3 42	4 05	3 45	11 56	19 49	20 08	15 34 53	8 23 45
17	3 35 09	19 17	+3 40	4 03	3 44	11 56	19 50	20 10	15 38 49	8 19 49
18	3 39 07	19 30	+3 39	4 02	3 42	11 56	19 52	20 12	15 42 46	8 15 53
19	3 43 06	19 43	+3 36	4 00	3 40	11 56	19 53	20 14	15 46 42	8 11 57
20	3 47 06	19 56	+3 33	3 59	3 38	11 56	19 55	20 16	15 50 39	8 08 01
21	3 51 06	20 08	+3 29	3 58	3 37	11 57	19 56	20 17	15 54 35	8 04 05
22	3 55 07	20 21	+3 25	3 56	3 35	11 57	19 58	20 19	15 58 32	8 00 09
23	3 59 08	20 32	+3 21	3 55	3 34	11 57	19 59	20 21	16 02 29	7 56 13
24	4 03 10	20 44	+3 15	3 54	3 32	11 57	20 00	20 22	16 06 25	7 52 17
25	4 07 12	20 55	+3 10	3 53	3 31	11 57	20 02	20 24	16 10 22	7 48 21
26	4 11 15	21 05	+3 04	3 52	3 29	11 57	20 03	20 26	16 14 18	7 44 26
27	4 15 18	21 16	+2 57	3 51	3 28	11 57	20 04	20 27	16 18 15	7 40 30
28	4 19 21	21 26	+2 50	3 50	3 27	11 57	20 06	20 29	16 22 11	7 36 34
29	4 23 26	21 35	+2 42	3 49	3 25	11 57	20 07	20 30	16 26 08	7 32 38
30	4 27 30	21 44	+2 34	3 48	3 24	11 57	20 08	20 32	16 30 04	7 28 42
31	4 31 35	21 53	+2 26	3 47	3 23	11 58	20 09	20 33	16 34 01	7 24 46

DURATION OF TWILIGHT (in minutes)

Latitude	52°	56°	52°	56°
	1 May		11 May	
Civil	39	45	41	49
Nautical	90	106	97	121
Astronomical	154	209	179	TAN
	21 May		31 May	
Civil	44	53	46	57
Nautical	106	143	116	TAN
Astronomical	TAN	TAN	TAN	TAN

THE NIGHT SKY

Mercury is unsuitably placed for observation throughout the month, superior conjunction occurring on the 16th.

Venus continues to be visible as a magnificent morning object, attaining its greatest brilliancy, magnitude −4.4, on the 7th. However, it is never visible for more than an hour before sunrise. As seen through a telescope the apparent diameter shrinks from 42″ to 27″ during May as the distance from the Earth increases. At the same time, the phase increases from a 21 per cent to a 44 per cent illuminated disk. The old crescent Moon is near the planet on the mornings of the 21st and 22nd.

Mars is an evening object in Cancer and by the middle of the month is roughly halfway between Pollux and Regulus. Its magnitude is +1.2, so all three objects appear to be of equal brightness. By the end of the month it is no longer visible after midnight.

Jupiter, magnitude −2.3, is an evening object in Virgo.

Saturn is a morning object, magnitude +0.9. However, it is not an easy object to locate low above the SE horizon before the lengthening twilight inhibits observation.

THE MOON

Day	RA	Dec.	Hor. par.	Semi-diam.	Sun's co-long.	PA. of Bright Limb	Phase	Age	Rise 52°	Rise 56°	Transit	Set 52°	Set 56°
	h m	°	′	′	°	°	%	d	h m	h m	h m	h m	h m
1	10 01	+ 6.7	59.5	16.2	24	289	67	9.0	13 36	13 33	20 07	2 01	2 06
2	10 55	+ 1.3	60.0	16.4	36	289	77	10.0	14 59	15 00	20 59	2 23	2 23
3	11 49	− 4.2	60.3	16.4	48	288	86	11.0	16 23	16 30	21 52	2 45	2 41
4	12 44	− 9.6	60.5	16.5	60	285	93	12.0	17 48	18 00	22 48	3 09	3 00
5	13 42	−14.4	60.3	16.4	72	279	98	13.0	19 11	19 29	23 45	3 37	3 23
6	14 41	−18.3	60.0	16.3	84	236	100	14.0	20 30	20 52	—	4 10	3 52
7	15 41	−21.0	59.4	16.2	97	110	99	15.0	21 40	22 04	0 44	4 52	4 30
8	16 42	−22.3	58.6	16.0	109	98	96	16.0	22 38	23 02	1 42	5 44	5 19
9	17 41	−22.2	57.8	15.7	121	90	90	17.0	23 23	23 45	2 40	6 44	6 20
10	18 38	−20.8	56.9	15.5	133	84	83	18.0	23 58	—	3 34	7 51	7 30
11	19 32	−18.4	56.1	15.3	145	79	74	19.0	—	0 16	4 25	9 00	8 43
12	20 22	−15.2	55.4	15.1	158	75	65	20.0	0 26	0 39	5 13	10 09	9 56
13	21 10	−11.4	54.9	14.9	170	72	55	21.0	0 48	0 58	5 58	11 17	11 09
14	21 56	− 7.2	54.5	14.8	182	70	45	22.0	1 07	1 13	6 40	12 24	12 20
15	22 40	− 2.8	54.2	14.8	194	69	36	23.0	1 25	1 27	7 21	13 30	13 29
16	23 24	+ 1.7	54.2	14.8	206	69	27	24.0	1 42	1 40	8 02	14 35	14 39
17	0 08	+ 6.2	54.2	14.8	219	70	19	25.0	1 59	1 54	8 44	15 42	15 50
18	0 53	+10.4	54.5	14.8	231	72	12	26.0	2 18	2 09	9 27	16 49	17 01
19	1 40	+14.3	54.8	14.9	243	75	7	27.0	2 40	2 27	10 12	17 57	18 14
20	2 29	+17.6	55.2	15.1	255	80	3	28.0	3 07	2 50	11 00	19 05	19 25
21	3 21	+20.2	55.7	15.2	268	89	0	29.0	3 40	3 20	11 51	20 10	20 33
22	4 15	+21.8	56.2	15.3	280	253	0	0.4	4 22	3 59	12 44	21 09	21 32
23	5 11	+22.4	56.8	15.5	292	267	2	1.4	5 15	4 51	13 39	21 59	22 22
24	6 08	+21.6	57.3	15.6	304	274	6	2.4	6 17	5 55	14 34	22 41	23 00
25	7 05	+19.7	57.8	15.7	317	280	13	3.4	7 28	7 09	15 28	23 14	23 30
26	8 01	+16.6	58.2	15.9	329	284	21	4.4	8 44	8 30	16 21	23 42	23 53
27	8 55	+12.6	58.6	16.0	341	288	31	5.4	10 03	9 53	17 12	—	—
28	9 48	+ 7.9	59.0	16.1	353	290	41	6.4	11 22	11 18	18 03	0 06	0 12
29	10 41	+ 2.6	59.3	16.1	5	292	53	7.4	12 43	12 43	18 53	0 28	0 30
30	11 34	− 2.8	59.5	16.2	18	292	64	8.4	14 04	14 09	19 44	0 49	0 47
31	12 27	− 8.0	59.6	16.2	30	291	75	9.4	15 26	15 36	20 37	1 11	1 04

MERCURY

Day	RA	Dec.	Diam.	Phase	Transit	
	h m	°			h m	
1	1 34	+ 7.6	—	—	11 00	Mercury is
4	1 55	+ 9.9	—	—	11 09	too close to
7	2 17	+12.3	—	—	11 19	the Sun for
10	2 40	+14.7	—	—	11 31	observation
13	3 05	+17.0	—	—	11 44	
16	3 30	+19.2	—	—	11 58	
19	3 57	+21.2	—	—	12 13	
22	4 24	+22.8	—	—	12 29	
25	4 51	+24.1	—	—	12 44	
28	5 18	+25.0	—	—	12 58	
31	5 43	+25.5	—	—	13 11	

VENUS

Day	RA	Dec.	Diam.	Phase	Transit	5° high 52°	5° high 56°
	h m	°	″	%	h m	h m	h m
1	0 16	+ 3.7	42	21	9 39	3 53	3 53
6	0 24	+ 3.6	39	25	9 28	3 42	3 42
11	0 35	+ 3.9	36	29	9 19	3 32	3 32
16	0 47	+ 4.5	33	33	9 12	3 22	3 21
21	1 01	+ 5.3	31	37	9 06	3 12	3 11
26	1 16	+ 6.3	29	40	9 02	3 02	3 00
31	1 33	+ 7.5	27	44	8 59	2 52	2 50

MARS

Day	RA	Dec.	Diam.	Phase	Transit	5° high 52°	5° high 56°
1	8 17	+21.7	6	90	17 39	1 05	1 21
6	8 27	+21.1	6	90	17 30	0 51	1 07
11	8 37	+20.4	6	90	17 21	0 38	0 52
16	8 47	+19.7	6	91	17 11	0 24	0 38
21	8 58	+18.9	6	91	17 02	0 10	0 23
26	9 09	+18.0	5	91	16 53	23 54	0 09
31	9 19	+17.2	5	91	16 44	23 40	23 51

SUNRISE AND SUNSET

	London		Bristol		Birmingham		Manchester		Newcastle		Glasgow		Belfast	
	0°05′	51°30′	2°35′	51°28′	1°55′	52°28′	2°15′	53°28′	1°37′	54°59′	4°14′	55°52′	5°56′	54°35′
	h m	h m	h m	h m	h m	h m	h m	h m	h m	h m	h m	h m	h m	h m
1	4 32	19 24	4 42	19 33	4 37	19 34	4 35	19 39	4 27	19 42	4 34	19 56	4 45	19 58
2	4 30	19 25	4 41	19 35	4 35	19 36	4 33	19 41	4 24	19 44	4 31	19 58	4 43	19 59
3	4 29	19 27	4 39	19 37	4 33	19 37	4 31	19 42	4 22	19 46	4 29	20 00	4 41	20 01
4	4 27	19 28	4 37	19 38	4 31	19 39	4 29	19 44	4 20	19 47	4 27	20 02	4 39	20 03
5	4 25	19 30	4 35	19 40	4 29	19 41	4 27	19 46	4 18	19 49	4 25	20 04	4 37	20 05
6	4 23	19 32	4 33	19 42	4 27	19 42	4 25	19 48	4 16	19 51	4 23	20 06	4 35	20 07
7	4 22	19 33	4 32	19 43	4 25	19 44	4 23	19 49	4 14	19 53	4 21	20 08	4 33	20 09
8	4 20	19 35	4 30	19 45	4 24	19 46	4 21	19 51	4 12	19 55	4 19	20 10	4 31	20 11
9	4 18	19 36	4 28	19 46	4 22	19 47	4 19	19 53	4 10	19 57	4 17	20 11	4 29	20 12
10	4 16	19 38	4 27	19 48	4 20	19 49	4 17	19 55	4 08	19 59	4 14	20 13	4 27	20 14
11	4 15	19 40	4 25	19 49	4 18	19 51	4 16	19 56	4 06	20 01	4 13	20 15	4 25	20 16
12	4 13	19 41	4 23	19 51	4 17	19 52	4 14	19 58	4 04	20 02	4 11	20 17	4 24	20 18
13	4 12	19 43	4 22	19 52	4 15	19 54	4 12	20 00	4 03	20 04	4 09	20 19	4 22	20 20
14	4 10	19 44	4 20	19 54	4 13	19 55	4 10	20 01	4 01	20 06	4 07	20 21	4 20	20 21
15	4 09	19 46	4 19	19 55	4 12	19 57	4 09	20 03	3 59	20 08	4 05	20 23	4 18	20 23
16	4 07	19 47	4 17	19 57	4 10	19 59	4 07	20 05	3 57	20 09	4 03	20 25	4 16	20 25
17	4 06	19 49	4 16	19 58	4 09	20 00	4 06	20 06	3 56	20 11	4 01	20 26	4 15	20 26
18	4 04	19 50	4 14	20 00	4 07	20 02	4 04	20 08	3 54	20 13	4 00	20 28	4 13	20 28
19	4 03	19 51	4 13	20 01	4 06	20 03	4 03	20 09	3 52	20 15	3 58	20 30	4 12	20 30
20	4 02	19 53	4 12	20 03	4 05	20 05	4 01	20 11	3 51	20 16	3 56	20 32	4 10	20 31
21	4 00	19 54	4 10	20 04	4 03	20 06	4 00	20 12	3 49	20 18	3 55	20 34	4 09	20 33
22	3 59	19 56	4 09	20 06	4 02	20 08	3 58	20 14	3 48	20 20	3 53	20 35	4 07	20 35
23	3 58	19 57	4 08	20 07	4 01	20 09	3 57	20 15	3 46	20 21	3 51	20 37	4 06	20 36
24	3 57	19 58	4 07	20 08	3 59	20 10	3 56	20 17	3 45	20 23	3 50	20 39	4 04	20 38
25	3 56	20 00	4 06	20 10	3 58	20 12	3 54	20 18	3 43	20 24	3 49	20 40	4 03	20 39
26	3 54	20 01	4 05	20 11	3 57	20 13	3 53	20 20	3 42	20 26	3 47	20 42	4 02	20 41
27	3 53	20 02	4 04	20 12	3 56	20 14	3 52	20 21	3 41	20 27	3 46	20 43	4 00	20 42
28	3 52	20 03	4 03	20 13	3 55	20 16	3 51	20 22	3 40	20 29	3 44	20 45	3 59	20 44
29	3 51	20 05	4 02	20 14	3 54	20 17	3 50	20 24	3 38	20 30	3 43	20 46	3 58	20 45
30	3 51	20 06	4 01	20 16	3 53	20 18	3 49	20 25	3 37	20 31	3 42	20 48	3 57	20 46
31	3 50	20 07	4 00	20 17	3 52	20 19	3 48	20 26	3 36	20 33	3 41	20 49	3 56	20 48

JUPITER

Day	*RA*	*Dec.*	*Transit*	*5° high*	
				52°	56°
	h m	° ′	h m	h m	h m
1	12 25.1	− 1 02	21 46	3 11	3 07
11	12 22.3	− 0 46	21 04	2 30	2 26
21	12 20.5	− 0 36	20 22	1 50	1 46
31	12 19.8	− 0 34	19 43	1 10	1 06

Diameters – equatorial 41″ polar 39″

SATURN

Day	*RA*	*Dec.*	*Transit*	*5° high*	
				52°	56°
	h m	° ′	h m	h m	h m
1	22 06.4	−12 56	7 30	3 14	3 30
11	22 08.6	−12 46	6 52	2 36	2 52
21	22 10.2	−12 40	6 15	1 58	2 13
31	22 11.2	−12 36	5 36	1 19	1 35

Diameters – equatorial 17″ polar 15″
Rings – major axis 38″ minor axis 7″

URANUS

Day	*RA*	*Dec.*	*Transit*	*10° high*	
				52°	56°
	h m	° ′	h m	h m	h m
1	19 36.2	−22 04	5 00	2 42	3 37
11	19 35.8	−22 05	4 20	2 02	2 58
21	19 35.2	−22 07	3 40	1 22	2 19
31	19 34.2	−22 09	3 00	0 43	1 39

Diameter 4″

NEPTUNE

Day	*RA*	*Dec.*	*Transit*	*10° high*	
				52°	56°
	h m	° ′	h m	h m	h m
1	19 30.9	−21 06	4 54	2 26	3 14
11	19 30.6	−21 07	4 15	1 46	2 35
21	19 30.1	−21 08	3 35	1 07	1 55
31	19 29.4	−21 09	2 55	0 27	1 15

Diameter 2″

♊ June 1993 ♋

SIXTH MONTH, 30 DAYS. *Junius*, Roman *gens* (family)

Sun's Longitude 90° ♋ 21ᵈ 09ʰ

1	*Tuesday*	Sir David Wilkie *d.* 1841. Sir Frank Whittle *b.* 1907.	*week* 23 *day* 152
2	*Wednesday*	*Coronation Day 1953.* Vita Sackville-West *d.* 1962.	153
3	*Thursday*	Georges Bizet *d.* 1875. Johann Strauss (the Younger) *d.* 1899.	154
4	*Friday*	George III *b.* 1738. Magenta 1859.	155
5	*Saturday*	Igor Stravinsky *b.* 1882 OS. John Maynard Keynes *b.* 1883.	156
6	*Sunday*	**Trinity Sunday.** Alexander Pushkin *b.* 1799 NS.	*week* 24 *day* 157
7	*Monday*	Paul Gaugin *b.* 1848. Jean Harlow *d.* 1937.	158
8	*Tuesday*	*Trinity Law Sittings begin.* Robert Schumann *b.* 1810.	159
9	*Wednesday*	Charles Dickens *d.* 1870. Dame Sybil Thorndike *d.* 1976.	160
10	*Thursday*	**Corpus Christi.** *Duke of Edinburgh* *b.* 1921.	161
11	*Friday*	**St Barnabas.** Sir Frank Brangwyn *d.* 1956.	162
12	*Saturday*	*Queen's Official Birthday.* Anthony Eden *b.* 1897.	163
13	*Sunday*	**2nd S. after Pentecost.** Dorothy L. Sayers *b.* 1893.	*week* 25 *day* 164
14	*Monday*	Naseby 1645. Jerome K. Jerome *d.* 1927.	165
15	*Tuesday*	Wat Tyler *exec.* 1381. Edvard Grieg *b.* 1843.	166
16	*Wednesday*	Lady Diana Cooper *d.* 1986. Dame Eva Turner *d.* 1990.	167
17	*Thursday*	Joseph Addison *d.* 1719. Sir Edward Burne-Jones *d.* 1898.	168
18	*Friday*	William Cobbett *d.* 1835. Captain Matthew Webb *b.* 1848.	169
19	*Saturday*	1st Earl Haig *b.* 1861. Wallis Simpson *b.* 1896.	170
20	*Sunday*	**3rd S. after Pentecost.** Jacques Offenbach *b.* 1819.	*week* 26 *day* 171
21	*Monday*	MUSLIM NEW YEAR (1414). Prince William of Wales *b.* 1982.	172
22	*Tuesday*	Sir Peter Pears *b.* 1910. Germany invaded USSR 1941.	173
23	*Wednesday*	Plassey 1757. Sir Leonard Hutton *b.* 1916.	174
24	*Thursday*	**St John the Baptist.** Lucrezia Borgia *d.* 1519.	175
25	*Friday*	Lady Baden-Powell *d.* 1977. Korean War began 1950.	176
26	*Saturday*	UN Charter signed at San Francisco 1945.	177
27	*Sunday*	**4th S. after Pentecost.** Charles Stewart Parnell *b.* 1846.	*week* 27 *day* 178
28	*Monday*	Crash of first Zeppelin airliner 1910.	179
29	*Tuesday*	**St Peter.** *Daily Telegraph* first published 1855.	180
30	*Wednesday*	Margery Allingham *d.* 1966. Nancy Mitford *d.* 1973.	181

ASTRONOMICAL PHENOMENA

d	h	
4		Total eclipse of Moon (*see* page 71)
10	12	Saturn in conjunction with Moon. Saturn 6° S.
10	13	Venus at greatest elongation W. 46°
16	06	Venus in conjunction with Moon. Venus 5° S.
17	17	Mercury at greatest elongation E. 25°
21	09	Solstice
21	23	Mercury in conjunction with Moon. Mercury 4° N.
24	12	Mars in conjunction with Moon. Mars 6° N.
26	23	Jupiter in conjunction with Moon. Jupiter 6° N.

CONSTELLATIONS

The following constellations are near the meridian at

May 1d, 24h
May 16d, 23h
June 1d, 22h
June 15d, 21h
July 1d, 20h
July 16d, 19h

Cassiopeia (below the Pole), Ursa Minor, Draco, Ursa Major, Canes Venatici, Bootes, Corona, Serpens, Virgo and Libra

MINIMA OF ALGOL

Algol is inconveniently situated for observation during June.

THE MOON

Phases, Apsides and Node	d	h	m
○ Full Moon	4	13	02
☾ Last Quarter	12	05	36
● New Moon	20	01	52
☽ First Quarter	26	22	43
Apogee (404,242 km)	12	16	19
Perigee (369,357 km)	25	17	27

Mean longitude of ascending node on 1 June, 252°

THE SUN

s.d. 15′.8

Day	Right Ascension	Dec. +	Equation of time	Rise 52°	Rise 56°	Transit	Set 52°	Set 56°	Sidereal time	Transit of First Point of Aries
	h m s	° ′	m s	h m	h m	h m	h m	h m	h m s	h m s
1	4 35 40	22 01	+2 17	3 46	3 22	11 58	20 10	20 34	16 37 58	7 20 50
2	4 39 46	22 10	+2 08	3 45	3 21	11 58	20 11	20 36	16 41 54	7 16 54
3	4 43 52	22 17	+1 59	3 44	3 20	11 58	20 12	20 37	16 45 51	7 12 58
4	4 47 58	22 24	+1 49	3 44	3 19	11 58	20 13	20 38	16 49 47	7 09 02
5	4 52 05	22 31	+1 39	3 43	3 18	11 58	20 14	20 39	16 53 44	7 05 06
6	4 56 12	22 38	+1 28	3 42	3 17	11 59	20 15	20 41	16 57 40	7 01 10
7	5 00 20	22 44	+1 17	3 42	3 17	11 59	20 16	20 42	17 01 37	6 57 15
8	5 04 27	22 50	+1 06	3 41	3 16	11 59	20 17	20 43	17 05 33	6 53 19
9	5 08 36	22 55	+0 54	3 41	3 15	11 59	20 18	20 44	17 09 30	6 49 23
10	5 12 44	23 00	+0 43	3 41	3 15	11 59	20 19	20 44	17 13 27	6 45 27
11	5 16 52	23 04	+0 31	3 40	3 14	12 00	20 19	20 45	17 17 23	6 41 31
12	5 21 01	23 08	+0 19	3 40	3 14	12 00	20 20	20 46	17 21 20	6 37 35
13	5 25 10	23 12	+0 06	3 40	3 14	12 00	20 21	20 47	17 25 16	6 33 39
14	5 29 19	23 15	−0 06	3 40	3 13	12 00	20 21	20 48	17 29 13	6 29 43
15	5 33 28	23 18	−0 19	3 39	3 13	12 00	20 22	20 48	17 33 09	6 25 47
16	5 37 38	23 20	−0 32	3 39	3 13	12 01	20 22	20 49	17 37 06	6 21 51
17	5 41 47	23 22	−0 45	3 39	3 13	12 01	20 23	20 49	17 41 02	6 17 55
18	5 45 57	23 24	−0 58	3 39	3 13	12 01	20 23	20 50	17 44 59	6 14 00
19	5 50 07	23 25	−1 11	3 39	3 13	12 01	20 23	20 50	17 48 56	6 10 04
20	5 54 16	23 26	−1 24	3 39	3 13	12 02	20 24	20 50	17 52 52	6 06 08
21	5 58 26	23 26	−1 38	3 40	3 13	12 02	20 24	20 50	17 56 49	6 02 12
22	6 02 36	23 26	−1 51	3 40	3 13	12 02	20 24	20 51	18 00 45	5 58 16
23	6 06 46	23 26	−2 04	3 40	3 14	12 02	20 24	20 51	18 04 42	5 54 20
24	6 10 55	23 25	−2 17	3 41	3 14	12 02	20 24	20 51	18 08 38	5 50 24
25	6 15 05	23 24	−2 30	3 41	3 14	12 03	20 24	20 51	18 12 35	5 46 28
26	6 19 14	23 22	−2 42	3 41	3 15	12 03	20 24	20 51	18 16 31	5 42 32
27	6 23 23	23 20	−2 55	3 42	3 15	12 03	20 24	20 50	18 20 28	5 38 36
28	6 27 32	23 17	−3 07	3 42	3 16	12 03	20 24	20 50	18 24 25	5 34 40
29	6 31 41	23 14	−3 20	3 43	3 17	12 03	20 24	20 50	18 28 21	5 30 45
30	6 35 49	23 11	−3 32	3 44	3 17	12 04	20 23	20 49	18 32 18	5 26 49

Duration of Twilight (in minutes)

Latitude	52°	56°	52°	56°
	1 June		11 June	
Civil	47	58	48	61
Nautical	117	TAN	125	TAN
Astronomical	TAN	TAN	TAN	TAN
	21 June		30 June	
Civil	49	63	49	62
Nautical	128	TAN	125	TAN
Astronomical	TAN	TAN	TAN	TAN

The Night Sky

Mercury is a difficult evening object during the first half of the month, magnitude −0.7 to +0.4, visible low above the WNW horizon around the end of evening civil twilight. It attains its greatest eastern elongation on the 17th but afterwards the long duration of twilight renders it unobservable in the British Isles.

Venus is a brilliant morning object, magnitude −4.2, reaching greatest western elongation on the 10th. The old crescent Moon is near the planet on the mornings of the 15th and 16th.

Mars, magnitude +1.4, continues to be visible as an evening object in Leo passing north of Regulus on the 22nd (though closest approach occurs after the planet has set).

Jupiter continues to be visible as an evening object, magnitude −2.1. By the end of the month it is no longer visible after midnight.

Saturn, magnitude +0.8, is a morning object in Aquarius. By the end of the month it is visible low above the SE horizon before midnight.

Twilight. Reference to the section above shows that astronomical twilight lasts all night for a period around the summer solstice (i.e. in June and July), even in southern England. Under these conditions the sky never gets completely dark since the Sun is always less than 18° below the horizon.

THE MOON

Day	RA	Dec.	Hor. par.	Semi-diam.	Sun's co-long.	PA. of Bright Limb	Phase	Age	Rise 52°	Rise 56°	Transit	Set 52°	Set 56°
	h m	°	′	′	°	°	%	d	h m	h m	h m	h m	h m
1	13 22	−12.9	59.6	16.2	42	288	84	10.4	16 48	17 03	21 32	1 37	1 25
2	14 19	−17.0	59.4	16.2	54	285	92	11.4	18 07	18 27	22 28	2 07	1 50
3	15 18	−20.1	59.1	16.1	66	280	97	12.4	19 20	19 44	23 27	2 44	2 23
4	16 18	−21.9	58.7	16.0	79	276	100	13.4	20 24	20 48	—	3 30	3 06
5	17 17	−22.3	58.1	15.8	91	87	100	14.4	21 15	21 38	0 25	4 26	4 02
6	18 16	−21.5	57.4	15.6	103	83	97	15.4	21 55	22 14	1 21	5 31	5 09
7	19 11	−19.4	56.7	15.4	115	78	93	16.4	22 26	22 42	2 14	6 40	6 21
8	20 04	−16.4	56.0	15.3	127	74	87	17.4	22 51	23 02	3 04	7 51	7 36
9	20 53	−12.7	55.4	15.1	140	71	79	18.4	23 12	23 19	3 51	9 01	8 50
10	21 40	− 8.6	54.9	14.9	152	69	71	19.4	23 30	23 34	4 35	10 09	10 03
11	22 25	− 4.2	54.5	14.8	164	67	62	20.4	23 47	23 47	5 17	11 15	11 14
12	23 09	+ 0.3	54.3	14.8	176	67	52	21.4	—	—	5 58	12 21	12 24
13	23 53	+ 4.7	54.3	14.8	188	67	43	22.4	0.04	0 00	6 39	13 27	13 33
14	0 38	+ 9.1	54.4	14.8	201	68	34	23.4	0 23	0 15	7 21	14 34	14 44
15	1 24	+13.1	54.7	14.9	213	70	25	24.4	0 43	0 32	8 06	15 42	15 56
16	2 12	+16.6	55.1	15.0	225	73	17	25.4	1 08	0 52	8 52	16 49	17 08
17	3 03	+19.4	55.7	15.2	237	77	10	26.4	1 38	1 18	9 42	17 56	18 18
18	3 57	+21.4	56.3	15.3	250	80	5	27.4	2 16	1 54	10 34	18 58	19 22
19	4 53	+22.3	56.9	15.5	262	83	1	28.4	3 05	2 41	11 29	19 53	20 16
20	5 50	+22.0	57.6	15.7	274	34	0	29.4	4 04	3 41	12 25	20 38	20 59
21	6 48	+20.4	58.1	15.8	286	287	1	0.9	5 14	4 53	13 21	21 16	21 33
22	7 45	+17.6	58.6	16.0	299	288	5	1.9	6 30	6 14	14 16	21 46	21 59
23	8 41	+13.7	59.0	16.1	311	291	11	2.9	7 50	7 39	15 09	22 12	22 19
24	9 36	+ 9.1	59.2	16.1	323	293	19	3.9	9 10	9 04	16 00	22 34	22 38
25	10 29	+ 3.9	59.3	16.2	335	294	28	4.9	10 31	10 30	16 51	22 56	22 54
26	11 22	− 1.5	59.4	16.2	348	294	39	5.9	11 52	11 55	17 41	23 17	23 12
27	12 15	− 6.8	59.3	16.2	360	293	51	6.9	13 12	13 21	18 33	23 41	23 31
28	13 08	−11.7	59.1	16.1	12	291	62	7.9	14 33	14 46	19 25	—	23 54
29	14 04	−16.0	58.9	16.1	24	288	73	8.9	15 51	16 10	20 20	0 08	—
30	15 01	−19.3	58.6	16.0	37	285	82	9.9	17 06	17 28	21 16	0 42	0 23

MERCURY

Day	RA	Dec.	Diam.	Phase	Transit	5° high 52°	5° high 56°
	h m	°	″	%	h m	h m	h m
1	5 51	+25.5	6	74	13 15	21 05	21 26
4	6 14	+25.5	6	67	13 26	21 15	21 36
7	6 35	+25.3	7	60	13 35	21 21	21 42
10	6 54	+24.7	7	54	13 41	21 24	21 44
13	7 11	+24.0	7	47	13 46	21 23	21 42
16	7 25	+23.2	8	42	13 48	21 19	21 37
19	7 37	+22.2	—	—	13 48	Mercury is	
22	7 47	+21.2	—	—	13 45	too close to	
25	7 54	+20.2	—	—	13 40	the Sun for	
28	7 58	+19.3	—	—	13 32	observation	
31	8 00	+18.4	—	—	13 21		

VENUS

Day	RA	Dec.	Diam.	Phase	Transit	5° high 52°	5° high 56°
	h m	°	″	%	h m	h m	h m
1	1 36	+ 7.8	27	44	8 58	2 51	2 48
6	1 54	+ 9.1	25	47	8 56	2 41	2 37
11	2 12	+10.5	24	50	8 54	2 33	2 27
16	2 31	+12.0	22	52	8 54	2 24	2 18
21	2 51	+13.4	21	55	8 54	2 17	2 09
26	3 11	+14.8	20	57	8 55	2 10	2 01
31	3 32	+16.2	19	60	8 56	2 04	1 53

MARS

Day	RA	Dec.	Diam.	Phase	Transit	5° high 52°	5° high 56°
1	9 22	+17.0	5	91	16 42	23 37	23 48
6	9 32	+16.1	5	92	16 33	23 23	23 33
11	9 43	+15.1	5	92	16 25	23 09	23 18
16	9 54	+14.1	5	92	16 16	22 55	23 03
21	10 05	+13.1	5	93	16 07	22 40	22 48
26	10 16	+12.0	5	93	15 58	22 26	22 32
31	10 27	+10.9	5	93	15 50	22 11	22 17

SUNRISE AND SUNSET

	London		Bristol		Birmingham		Manchester		Newcastle		Glasgow		Belfast	
	0°05′	51°30′	2°35′	51°28′	1°55′	52°28′	2°15′	53°28′	1°37′	54°59′	4°14′	55°52′	5°56′	54°35′
	h m	h m	h m	h m	h m	h m	h m	h m	h m	h m	h m	h m	h m	h m
1	3 49	20 08	3 59	20 18	3 51	20 20	3 47	20 27	3 35	20 34	3 40	20 50	3 55	20 49
2	3 48	20 09	3 58	20 19	3 50	20 22	3 46	20 29	3 34	20 35	3 39	20 52	3 54	20 50
3	3 47	20 10	3 58	20 20	3 50	20 23	3 45	20 30	3 33	20 37	3 38	20 53	3 53	20 51
4	3 47	20 11	3 57	20 21	3 49	20 24	3 44	20 31	3 32	20 38	3 37	20 54	3 52	20 52
5	3 46	20 12	3 56	20 22	3 48	20 25	3 44	20 32	3 32	20 39	3 36	20 55	3 52	20 53
6	3 45	20 13	3 56	20 23	3 48	20 26	3 43	20 33	3 31	20 40	3 35	20 56	3 51	20 55
7	3 45	20 14	3 55	20 24	3 47	20 26	3 42	20 34	3 30	20 41	3 35	20 58	3 50	20 56
8	3 44	20 15	3 55	20 24	3 46	20 27	3 42	20 35	3 30	20 42	3 34	20 59	3 50	20 56
9	3 44	20 15	3 54	20 25	3 46	20 28	3 41	20 35	3 29	20 43	3 33	21 00	3 49	20 57
10	3 44	20 16	3 54	20 26	3 46	20 29	3 41	20 36	3 29	20 44	3 33	21 00	3 49	20 58
11	3 43	20 17	3 53	20 27	3 45	20 30	3 41	20 37	3 28	20 44	3 32	21 01	3 48	20 59
12	3 43	20 18	3 53	20 27	3 45	20 30	3 40	20 38	3 28	20 45	3 32	21 02	3 48	21 00
13	3 43	20 18	3 53	20 28	3 45	20 31	3 40	20 38	3 27	20 46	3 31	21 03	3 47	21 00
14	3 43	20 19	3 53	20 29	3 44	20 32	3 40	20 39	3 27	20 47	3 31	21 03	3 47	21 01
15	3 43	20 19	3 53	20 29	3 44	20 32	3 40	20 40	3 27	20 47	3 31	21 04	3 47	21 02
16	3 42	20 20	3 53	20 29	3 44	20 33	3 39	20 40	3 27	20 48	3 31	21 05	3 47	21 02
17	3 42	20 20	3 53	20 30	3 44	20 33	3 39	20 40	3 27	20 48	3 31	21 05	3 47	21 03
18	3 42	20 20	3 53	20 30	3 44	20 33	3 39	20 41	3 27	20 49	3 31	21 05	3 47	21 03
19	3 43	20 21	3 53	20 31	3 44	20 34	3 39	20 41	3 27	20 49	3 31	21 06	3 47	21 03
20	3 43	20 21	3 53	20 31	3 44	20 34	3 40	20 41	3 27	20 49	3 31	21 06	3 47	21 04
21	3 43	20 21	3 53	20 31	3 45	20 34	3 40	20 42	3 27	20 49	3 31	21 06	3 47	21 04
22	3 43	20 21	3 53	20 31	3 45	20 34	3 40	20 42	3 27	20 50	3 31	21 06	3 47	21 04
23	3 43	20 22	3 54	20 31	3 45	20 34	3 40	20 42	3 28	20 50	3 32	21 07	3 48	21 04
24	3 44	20 22	3 54	20 31	3 45	20 35	3 41	20 42	3 28	20 50	3 32	21 07	3 48	21 04
25	3 44	20 22	3 54	20 31	3 46	20 35	3 41	20 42	3 28	20 50	3 32	21 07	3 48	21 04
26	3 45	20 22	3 55	20 31	3 46	20 34	3 42	20 42	3 29	20 50	3 33	21 06	3 49	21 04
27	3 45	20 22	3 55	20 31	3 47	20 34	3 42	20 42	3 29	20 49	3 33	21 06	3 49	21 04
28	3 46	20 21	3 56	20 31	3 47	20 34	3 43	20 42	3 30	20 49	3 34	21 06	3 50	21 04
29	3 46	20 21	3 56	20 31	3 48	20 34	3 43	20 41	3 31	20 49	3 35	21 06	3 51	21 03
30	3 47	20 21	3 57	20 31	3 49	20 34	3 44	20 41	3 31	20 48	3 35	21 05	3 51	21 03

JUPITER

Day	*RA*	*Dec.*	*Transit*	*5° high*	
				52°	56°
	h m	° ′	h m	h m	h m
1	12 19.7	−0 35	19 39	1 06	1 02
11	12 20.2	−0 40	19 00	0 27	0 23
21	12 21.8	−0 53	18 22	23 44	23 40
31	12 24.3	−1 12	17 45	23 06	23 01

Diameters – equatorial 38″ polar 36″

SATURN

Day	*RA*	*Dec.*	*Transit*	*5° high*	
				52°	56°
	h m	° ′	h m	h m	h m
1	22 11.2	−12 36	5 32	1 15	1 31
11	22 11.5	−12 37	4 53	0 36	0 52
21	22 11.2	−12 41	4 14	23 53	0 13
31	22 10.3	−12 48	3 33	23 14	23 29

Diameters – equatorial 18″ polar 16″
Rings – major axis 40″ minor axis 7″

URANUS

Day	*RA*	*Dec.*	*Transit*	*10° high*	
				52°	56°
	h m	° ′	h m	h m	h m
1	19 34.1	−22 09	2 56	0 39	1 35
11	19 32.8	−22 12	2 15	23 55	0 56
21	19 31.3	−22 16	1 34	23 15	0 16
31	19 29.7	−22 19	0 53	22 34	23 33

Diameter 4″

NEPTUNE

Day	*RA*	*Dec.*	*Transit*	*10° high*	
				52°	56°
	h m	° ′	h m	h m	h m
1	19 29.4	−21 09	2 51	0 23	1 11
11	19 28.5	−21 11	2 11	23 39	0 32
21	19 27.5	−21 13	1 30	22 59	23 48
31	19 26.4	−21 16	0 50	22 19	23 08

Diameter 2″

July 1993

SEVENTH MONTH, 31 DAYS. *Julius* Caesar, formerly *Quintilis*, fifth month of Roman pre-Julian calendar

Sun's Longitude 120° ♌ 22ᵈ20ʰ

1	*Thursday*	*Princess of Wales b. 1961.* C. P. Snow *d.* 1980.	*week* 27 *day* 182
2	*Friday*	Hermann Hesse *b.* 1877. Joseph Chamberlain *d.* 1914.	183
3	*Saturday*	**St Thomas.** Leoš Janáček *b.* 1854. Tom Stoppard *b.* 1937.	184
4	*Sunday*	**5th S. after Pentecost.** Nathaniel Hawthorne *b.* 1804.	*week* 28 *day* 185
5	*Monday*	*Tynwald Day* (public holiday in the Isle of Man).	186
6	*Tuesday*	Sir Thomas More *exec.* 1535. Aneurin Bevan *d.* 1960.	187
7	*Wednesday*	Joseph Jacquard *b.* 1752. R. B. Sheridan *d.* 1816.	188
8	*Thursday*	Percy Bysshe Shelley *d.* 1822. Percy Grainger *b.* 1882.	189
9	*Friday*	Mrs Ann Radcliffe *b.* 1764. David Hockney *b.* 1937.	190
10	*Saturday*	Camille Pissarro *b.* 1830. Marcel Proust *b.* 1871.	191
11	*Sunday*	**6th S. after Pentecost.** George Gershwin *d.* 1937.	*week* 29 *day* 192
12	*Monday*	*Bank Holiday in Northern Ireland.* Alfred Dreyfus *d.* 1935.	193
13	*Tuesday*	Sidney Webb *b.* 1859. Arnold Schönberg *d.* 1951.	194
14	*Wednesday*	Isaac Bashevis Singer *b.* 1904. Ingmar Bergman *b.* 1918.	195
15	*Thursday*	St Swithin's Day. Rembrandt *b.* 1606.	196
16	*Friday*	Sir Joshua Reynolds *b.* 1723. Hilaire Belloc *d.* 1953.	197
17	*Saturday*	First issue of *Punch* 1841. James Whistler *d.* 1903.	198
18	*Sunday*	**7th S. after Pentecost. Jane Austen** *d.* 1817.	*week* 30 *day* 199
19	*Monday*	*Mary Rose* sank 1545. Edgar Degas *b.* 1834.	200
20	*Tuesday*	Francesco Petrarch *b.* 1304. Paul Valéry *d.* 1945.	201
21	*Wednesday*	Independence of Belgium 1831. Ernest Hemingway *b.* 1898.	202
22	*Thursday*	**St Mary Magdalen.** Falkirk 1298. Atlanta 1864.	203
23	*Friday*	Field Marshal (1st) Viscount Alanbrooke *b.* 1883.	204
24	*Saturday*	Alexandre Dumas (father) *b.* 1802. Treaty of Lausanne 1923.	205
25	*Sunday*	**St James. 8th S. after Pentecost.**	*week* 31 *day* 206
26	*Monday*	George Bernard Shaw *b.* 1856. Robert Graves *b.* 1895.	207
27	*Tuesday*	Alexandre Dumas (son) *b.* 1824. Gertrude Stein *d.* 1946.	208
28	*Wednesday*	Thomas Cromwell *exec.* 1540. Sir Garfield Sobers *b.* 1936.	209
29	*Thursday*	Frans Hals *d.* 1666. Benito Mussolini *b.* 1883.	210
30	*Friday*	Henry Ford *b.* 1863. Henry Moore *b.* 1898.	211
31	*Saturday*	*Trinity Law Sittings end.* Franz Lizst *d.* 1886.	212

Astronomical Phenomena

d	h	
4	22	Earth at aphelion (152 million km)
7	19	Saturn in conjunction with Moon. Saturn 6° S.
12	03	Neptune at opposition
12	14	Uranus at opposition
15	01	Mercury in inferior conjunction
16	03	Venus in conjunction with Moon. Venus 3° S.
19	00	Mercury in conjunction with Moon. Mercury 2° S.
22	23	Mars in conjunction with Moon. Mars 5° N.
24	10	Jupiter in conjunction with Moon. Jupiter 5° N.

Constellations

The following constellations are near the meridian at

June 1d, 24h
June 15d, 23h
July 1d, 22h
July 16d, 21h
August 1d, 20h
August 16d, 19h

Ursa Minor, Draco, Corona, Hercules, Lyra, Serpens, Ophiuchus, Libra, Scorpius and Sagittarius

Minima of Algol

d	h	d	h	d	h
2	16.6	14	03.8	25	15.1
5	13.4	17	00.6	28	11.9
8	10.2	19	21.4	31	08.7
11	07.0	22	18.3		

The Moon

Phases, Apsides and Node	d	h	m
○ Full Moon	3	23	45
☾ Last Quarter	11	22	49
● New Moon	19	11	24
☽ First Quarter	26	03	25
Apogee (404,412 km)	10	10	49
Perigee (365,146 km)	22	08	28

Mean longitude of ascending node on 1 July, 251°

THE SUN s.d. 15′.8

Day	Right Ascension	Dec. +	Equation of time	Rise 52°	Rise 56°	Transit	Set 52°	Set 56°	Sidereal time	Transit of First Point of Aries
	h m s	° ′	m s	h m	h m	h m	h m	h m	h m s	h m s
1	6 39 58	23 07	−3 43	3 44	3 18	12 04	20 23	20 49	18 36 14	5 22 53
2	6 44 06	23 03	−3 55	3 45	3 19	12 04	20 23	20 48	18 40 11	5 18 57
3	6 48 13	22 59	−4 06	3 46	3 20	12 04	20 22	20 48	18 44 07	5 15 01
4	6 52 21	22 54	−4 17	3 46	3 21	12 04	20 22	20 47	18 48 04	5 11 05
5	6 56 28	22 48	−4 27	3 47	3 22	12 05	20 21	20 46	18 52 00	5 07 09
6	7 00 35	22 43	−4 38	3 48	3 23	12 05	20 21	20 46	18 55 57	5 03 13
7	7 04 41	22 36	−4 48	3 49	3 24	12 05	20 20	20 45	18 59 54	4 59 17
8	7 08 47	22 30	−4 57	3 50	3 25	12 05	20 19	20 44	19 03 50	4 55 21
9	7 12 53	22 23	−5 06	3 51	3 27	12 05	20 19	20 43	19 07 47	4 51 25
10	7 16 58	22 16	−5 15	3 52	3 28	12 05	20 18	20 42	19 11 43	4 47 29
11	7 21 03	22 08	−5 23	3 53	3 29	12 05	20 17	20 41	19 15 40	4 43 34
12	7 25 08	22 00	−5 31	3 54	3 30	12 06	20 16	20 40	19 19 36	4 39 38
13	7 29 12	21 51	−5 39	3 55	3 32	12 06	20 15	20 39	19 23 33	4 35 42
14	7 33 15	21 43	−5 46	3 57	3 33	12 06	20 14	20 37	19 27 30	4 31 46
15	7 37 18	21 33	−5 52	3 58	3 35	12 06	20 13	20 36	19 31 26	4 27 50
16	7 41 21	21 24	−5 58	3 59	3 36	12 06	20 12	20 35	19 35 23	4 23 54
17	7 45 23	21 14	−6 04	4 00	3 38	12 06	20 11	20 33	19 39 19	4 19 58
18	7 49 25	21 04	−6 09	4 02	3 39	12 06	20 10	20 32	19 43 16	4 16 02
19	7 53 26	20 53	−6 14	4 03	3 41	12 06	20 09	20 31	19 47 12	4 12 06
20	7 57 26	20 42	−6 18	4 04	3 42	12 06	20 08	20 29	19 51 09	4 08 10
21	8 01 26	20 31	−6 21	4 06	3 44	12 06	20 06	20 27	19 55 05	4 04 14
22	8 05 26	20 19	−6 24	4 07	3 46	12 06	20 05	20 26	19 59 02	4 00 19
23	8 09 25	20 07	−6 26	4 08	3 48	12 06	20 04	20 24	20 02 59	3 56 23
24	8 13 23	19 55	−6 28	4 10	3 49	12 06	20 02	20 23	20 06 55	3 52 27
25	8 17 20	19 42	−6 29	4 11	3 51	12 06	20 01	20 21	20 10 52	3 48 31
26	8 21 17	19 29	−6 29	4 13	3 53	12 06	19 59	20 19	20 14 48	3 44 35
27	8 25 14	19 15	−6 29	4 14	3 55	12 06	19 58	20 17	20 18 45	3 40 39
28	8 29 10	19 02	−6 28	4 16	3 56	12 06	19 56	20 15	20 22 41	3 36 43
29	8 33 05	18 48	−6 27	4 17	3 58	12 06	19 55	20 13	20 26 38	3 32 47
30	8 36 59	18 34	−6 25	4 19	4 00	12 06	19 53	20 12	20 30 34	3 28 51
31	8 40 53	18 19	−6 22	4 20	4 02	12 06	19 52	20 10	20 34 31	3 24 55

DURATION OF TWILIGHT (in minutes)

Latitude	52°	56°	52°	56°
	1 July		11 July	
Civil	48	61	46	58
Nautical	124	TAN	116	TAN
Astronomical	TAN	TAN	TAN	TAN
	21 July		31 July	
Civil	44	53	41	49
Nautical	107	144	98	122
Astronomical	TAN	TAN	180	TAN

THE NIGHT SKY

Mercury is unsuitably placed for observation, inferior conjunction occurring on the 15th.

Venus continues to be observable as a brilliant morning object, magnitude −4.0. During the second half of the month, observers with a good ENE horizon should be able to see it shortly before 02h. The old crescent Moon will be seen near the planet on the mornings of the 15th and 16th. Venus is moving eastwards amongst the stars passing north of Aldebaran on the 14th.

Mars is a difficult evening object in Leo, magnitude +1.6. It is coming towards the end of its period of visibility and is only visible for a short while low in the WSW sky during evening nautical twilight.

Jupiter, magnitude −1.9, is an evening object visible in the SW sky, in the constellation of Virgo.

Saturn continues to be visible in the night sky, in Aquarius, magnitude +0.6. By the end of the month it is visible low above the SE horizon shortly after 21h.

Uranus is at opposition on the 12th, in Sagittarius. Uranus is barely visible to the naked eye since its magnitude is +5.6, but it is readily located with only small optical aid.

Neptune is at opposition on the 12th, in Sagittarius. It is not visible to the naked eye since its magnitude is +7.9. These two outer planets are now within a degree of each other in the sky, a situation which will not occur again until around the year 2164. The times of opposition (in longitude) are only half a day apart. However, the planets are so slow-moving that the times when the two planets have the same longitude do not occur during July. There are three such occasions: 2 February, 20 August and 24 October.

THE MOON

Day	RA	Dec.	Hor. par.	Semi-diam.	Sun's co-long.	PA. of Bright Limb	Phase	Age	Rise 52°	Rise 56°	Transit	Set 52°	Set 56°
	h m	°	′	′	°	°	%	d	h m	h m	h m	h m	h m
1	15 59	−21.5	58.2	15.9	49	280	90	10.9	18 12	18 36	22 13	1 23	1 01
2	16 58	−22.3	57.8	15.7	61	277	96	11.9	19 07	19 31	23 10	2 14	1 50
3	17 56	−21.9	57.3	15.6	73	278	99	12.9	19 51	20 12	—	3 15	2 51
4	18 52	−20.3	56.7	15.5	85	357	100	13.9	20 26	20 43	0 04	4 22	4 01
5	19 45	−17.6	56.1	15.3	97	64	99	14.9	20 53	21 07	0 55	5 32	5 16
6	20 36	−14.2	55.6	15.1	110	66	96	15.9	21 16	21 25	1 43	6 43	6 31
7	21 24	−10.2	55.1	15.0	122	65	91	16.9	21 35	21 41	2 29	7 52	7 44
8	22 10	− 5.8	54.7	14.9	134	64	84	17.9	21 53	21 54	3 12	9 00	8 56
9	22 55	− 1.3	54.4	14.8	146	64	77	18.9	22 10	22 08	3 54	10 06	10 07
10	23 39	+ 3.2	54.2	14.8	158	65	68	19.9	22 28	22 22	4 35	11 12	11 17
11	0 23	+ 7.6	54.2	14.8	171	66	59	20.9	22 47	22 37	5 16	12 18	12 27
12	1 08	+11.6	54.4	14.8	183	68	50	21.9	23 10	22 56	5 59	13 25	13 38
13	1 55	+15.3	54.8	14.9	195	70	40	22.9	23 37	23 19	6 44	14 32	14 49
14	2 45	+18.4	55.3	15.1	207	74	31	23.9	—	23 50	7 32	15 39	15 59
15	3 37	+20.7	55.9	15.2	220	77	22	24.9	0 11	—	8 23	16 42	17 05
16	4 31	+22.1	56.7	15.4	232	82	14	25.9	0 54	0 30	9 16	17 41	18 04
17	5 28	+22.2	57.4	15.7	244	85	8	26.9	1 48	1 24	10 12	18 31	18 53
18	6 26	+21.1	58.2	15.9	256	86	3	27.9	2 54	2 32	11 09	19 12	19 31
19	7 25	+18.8	58.9	16.1	269	71	0	28.9	4 08	3 50	12 05	19 46	20 01
20	8 22	+15.2	59.5	16.2	281	314	1	0.5	5 29	5 16	13 00	20 15	20 24
21	9 19	+10.7	59.9	16.3	293	300	3	1.5	6 51	6 43	13 54	20 39	20 44
22	10 14	+ 5.5	60.0	16.4	305	298	9	2.5	8 15	8 12	14 46	21 02	21 02
23	11 08	0.0	60.0	16.4	318	297	17	3.5	9 37	9 39	15 38	21 24	21 20
24	12 02	− 5.4	59.8	16.3	330	296	26	4.5	10 59	11 06	16 30	21 47	21 38
25	12 56	−10.5	59.5	16.2	342	294	37	5.5	12 21	12 33	17 22	22 14	22 00
26	13 51	−14.9	59.0	16.1	354	291	48	6.5	13 40	13 57	18 16	22 45	22 27
27	14 48	−18.5	58.6	16.0	7	287	60	7.5	14 55	15 16	19 12	23 23	23 01
28	15 45	−20.9	58.0	15.8	19	282	70	8.5	16 03	16 27	20 08	—	23 46
29	16 43	−22.1	57.5	15.7	31	278	80	9.5	17 01	17 25	21 03	0 10	—
30	17 40	−22.1	57.0	15.5	43	273	88	10.5	17 49	18 11	21 57	1 06	0 42
31	18 36	−20.8	56.5	15.4	55	271	94	11.5	18 26	18 45	22 49	2 10	1 48

MERCURY

Day	RA	Dec.	Diam.	Phase	Transit
	h m	°			h m
1	8 00	+18.4	—	—	13 21
4	7 58	+17.7	—	—	13 07
7	7 54	+17.1	—	—	12 51
10	7 48	+16.8	—	—	12 33
13	7 40	+16.7	—	—	12 13
16	7 32	+16.8	—	—	11 53
19	7 24	+17.1	—	—	11 34
22	7 19	+17.5	—	—	11 17
25	7 16	+18.1	—	—	11 04
28	7 18	+18.7	—	—	10 54
31	7 23	+19.3	—	—	10 47

Mercury is too close to the Sun for observation

VENUS

Day	RA	Dec.	Diam.	Phase	Transit	5° high 52°	5° high 56°
	h m	°	″	%	h m	h m	h m
1	3 32	+16.2	19	60	8 56	2 04	1 53
6	3 54	+17.5	18	62	8 58	1 59	1 47
11	4 16	+18.6	18	64	9 01	1 55	1 42
16	4 39	+19.7	17	66	9 04	1 52	1 38
21	5 02	+20.5	16	68	9 07	1 51	1 36
26	5 26	+21.2	16	70	9 12	1 51	1 35
31	5 50	+21.6	15	72	9 16	1 53	1 37

MARS

Day	RA	Dec.	Diam.	Phase	Transit	5° high 52°	5° high 56°
1	10 27	+10.9	5	93	15 50	22 11	22 17
6	10 38	+ 9.7	5	93	15 41	21 57	22 01
11	10 49	+ 8.6	5	94	15 32	21 42	21 45
16	11 00	+ 7.4	4	94	15 24	21 27	21 30
21	11 11	+ 6.1	4	94	15 15	21 12	21 14
26	11 22	+ 4.9	4	95	15 06	20 57	20 58
31	11 34	+ 3.6	4	95	14 58	20 43	20 42

SUNRISE AND SUNSET

	London		Bristol		Birmingham		Manchester		Newcastle		Glasgow		Belfast	
	0°05′	51°30′	2°35′	51°28′	1°55′	52°28′	2°15′	53°28′	1°37′	54°59′	4°14′	55°52′	5°56′	54°35′
	h m	h m	h m	h m	h m	h m	h m	h m	h m	h m	h m	h m	h m	h m
1	3 47	20 21	3 58	20 30	3 49	20 33	3 45	20 41	3 32	20 48	3 36	21 05	3 52	21 03
2	3 48	20 20	3 58	20 30	3 50	20 33	3 45	20 40	3 33	20 48	3 37	21 04	3 53	21 02
3	3 49	20 20	3 59	20 30	3 51	20 33	3 46	20 40	3 34	20 47	3 38	21 04	3 54	21 02
4	3 50	20 19	4 00	20 29	3 52	20 32	3 47	20 39	3 35	20 46	3 39	21 03	3 55	21 01
5	3 50	20 19	4 01	20 29	3 52	20 32	3 48	20 39	3 36	20 46	3 40	21 02	3 56	21 00
6	3 51	20 18	4 01	20 28	3 53	20 31	3 49	20 38	3 37	20 45	3 41	21 02	3 56	21 00
7	3 52	20 18	4 02	20 28	3 54	20 30	3 50	20 37	3 38	20 44	3 42	21 01	3 58	20 59
8	3 53	20 17	4 03	20 27	3 55	20 30	3 51	20 37	3 39	20 44	3 43	21 00	3 59	20 58
9	3 54	20 16	4 04	20 26	3 56	20 29	3 52	20 36	3 40	20 43	3 44	20 59	4 00	20 57
10	3 55	20 16	4 05	20 25	3 57	20 28	3 53	20 35	3 41	20 42	3 46	20 58	4 01	20 56
11	3 56	20 15	4 06	20 25	3 58	20 27	3 54	20 34	3 42	20 41	3 47	20 57	4 02	20 55
12	3 57	20 14	4 07	20 24	3 59	20 26	3 55	20 33	3 44	20 40	3 48	20 56	4 03	20 54
13	3 58	20 13	4 08	20 23	4 01	20 25	3 56	20 32	3 45	20 39	3 50	20 55	4 05	20 53
14	3 59	20 12	4 10	20 22	4 02	20 24	3 58	20 31	3 46	20 37	3 51	20 54	4 06	20 52
15	4 01	20 11	4 11	20 21	4 03	20 23	3 59	20 30	3 48	20 36	3 53	20 52	4 07	20 51
16	4 02	20 10	4 12	20 20	4 04	20 22	4 00	20 29	3 49	20 35	3 54	20 51	4 09	20 50
17	4 03	20 09	4 13	20 19	4 06	20 21	4 02	20 28	3 50	20 34	3 56	20 50	4 10	20 49
18	4 04	20 08	4 14	20 18	4 07	20 20	4 03	20 26	3 52	20 32	3 57	20 48	4 12	20 47
19	4 06	20 07	4 16	20 17	4 08	20 19	4 04	20 25	3 53	20 31	3 59	20 47	4 13	20 46
20	4 07	20 06	4 17	20 15	4 10	20 18	4 06	20 24	3 55	20 30	4 00	20 45	4 15	20 45
21	4 08	20 04	4 18	20 14	4 11	20 16	4 07	20 22	3 57	20 28	4 02	20 44	4 16	20 43
22	4 10	20 03	4 20	20 13	4 12	20 15	4 09	20 21	3 58	20 27	4 04	20 42	4 18	20 42
23	4 11	20 02	4 21	20 12	4 14	20 14	4 10	20 20	4 00	20 25	4 05	20 40	4 19	20 40
24	4 12	20 00	4 22	20 10	4 15	20 12	4 12	20 18	4 01	20 23	4 07	20 39	4 21	20 38
25	4 14	19 59	4 24	20 09	4 17	20 11	4 13	20 17	4 03	20 22	4 09	20 37	4 22	20 37
26	4 15	19 58	4 25	20 07	4 18	20 09	4 15	20 15	4 05	20 20	4 10	20 35	4 24	20 35
27	4 17	19 56	4 27	20 06	4 20	20 08	4 16	20 13	4 06	20 18	4 12	20 33	4 26	20 34
28	4 18	19 55	4 28	20 05	4 21	20 06	4 18	20 12	4 08	20 17	4 14	20 32	4 27	20 32
29	4 19	19 53	4 30	20 03	4 23	20 04	4 20	20 10	4 10	20 15	4 16	20 30	4 29	20 30
30	4 21	19 52	4 31	20 01	4 24	20 03	4 21	20 08	4 12	20 13	4 18	20 28	4 31	20 28
31	4 22	19 50	4 33	20 00	4 26	20 01	4 23	20 07	4 13	20 11	4 19	20 26	4 33	20 26

JUPITER

Day	*RA*	*Dec.*	*Transit*	*5° high*	
				52°	56°
	h m	° ′	h m	h m	h m
1	12 24.3	− 1 12	17 45	23 06	23 01
11	12 27.8	− 1 37	17 10	22 28	22 23
21	12 32.1	− 2 07	16 35	21 50	21 45
31	12 37.2	− 2 42	16 00	21 13	21 07

Diameters – equatorial 35″ polar 33″

SATURN

Day	*RA*	*Dec.*	*Transit*	*5° high*	
				52°	56°
	h m	° ′	h m	h m	h m
1	22 10.3	−12 48	3 33	23 14	23 29
11	22 08.8	−12 58	2 53	22 34	22 50
21	22 06.8	−13 11	2 11	21 54	22 10
31	22 04.4	−13 25	1 30	21 14	21 30

Diameters – equatorial 18″ polar 17″
Rings – major axis 42″ minor axis 8″

URANUS

Day	*RA*	*Dec.*	*Transit*	*10° high*	
				52°	56°
	h m	° ′	h m	h m	h m
1	19 29.7	−22 19	0 53	3 08	2 10
11	19 28.0	−22 23	0 12	2 27	1 27
21	19 26.3	−22 27	23 27	1 45	0 45
31	19 24.6	−22 30	22 46	1 03	0 03

Diameter 4″

NEPTUNE

Day	*RA*	*Dec.*	*Transit*	*10° high*	
				52°	56°
	h m	° ′	h m	h m	h m
1	19 26.4	−21 16	0 50	3 17	2 28
11	19 25.3	−21 18	0 10	2 36	1 47
21	19 24.1	−21 21	23 25	1 55	1 05
31	19 23.0	−21 23	22 45	1 14	0 24

Diameter 2″

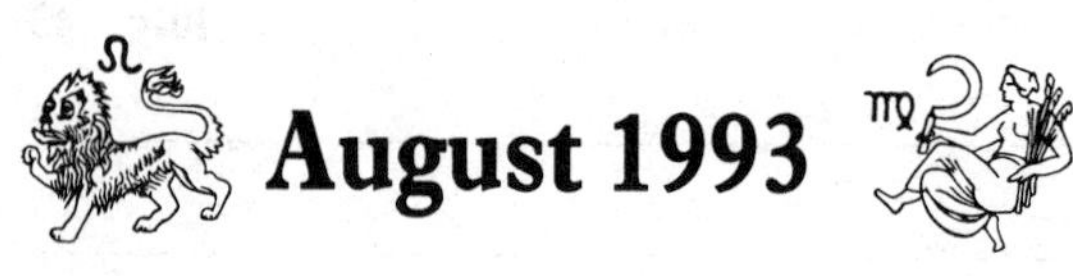

August 1993

EIGHTH MONTH, 31 DAYS. Julius Caesar *Augustus*, formerly *Sextilis*, sixth month of Roman pre-Julian calendar

Sun's Longitude 150° ♍ 23ᵈ 03ʰ

1	*Sunday*	**9th S. after Pentecost.** Queen Anne *d.* 1714.	*week* 32 *day* 213
2	*Monday*	*Bank Holiday in Scotland.* Thomas Gainsborough *d.* 1788.	214
3	*Tuesday*	Sir Joseph Paxton *b.* 1801. Rupert Brooke *b.* 1887.	215
4	*Wednesday*	*Queen Elizabeth the Queen Mother b. 1900.* Evesham 1265.	216
5	*Thursday*	Friedrich Engels *d.* 1895. Marilyn Monroe *d.* 1962.	217
6	*Friday*	**Transfiguration.** Anne Hathaway *d.* 1623.	218
7	*Saturday*	Oliver Hardy *d.* 1957.	219
8	*Sunday*	**10th S. after Pentecost.** Princess Beatrice of York *b.* 1988.	*week* 33 *day* 220
9	*Monday*	John Dryden *b.* 1631. Atomic bomb dropped on Nagasaki 1945.	221
10	*Tuesday*	Sir Charles Napier *b.* 1782. Charles Keene *b.* 1823.	222
11	*Wednesday*	Charlotte Yonge *b.* 1823. Edith Wharton *d.* 1937.	223
12	*Thursday*	George IV *b.* 1762. William Blake *d.* 1827.	224
13	*Friday*	Sir John Millais *d.* 1896. Sir Basil Spence *b.* 1907.	225
14	*Saturday*	William Randolph Hearst *d.* 1951. J. B. Priestley *d.* 1984.	226
15	*Sunday*	**11th S. after Pentecost.** *Princess Royal b. 1950.*	*week* 34 *day* 227
16	*Monday*	Andrew Marvell *d.* 1678. Peterloo Massacre 1819.	228
17	*Tuesday*	Davy Crockett *b.* 1786. Honoré de Balzac *d.* 1850.	229
18	*Wednesday*	1st Earl Russell *b.* 1792. Sir Frederick Ashton *d.* 1988.	230
19	*Thursday*	Blaise Pascal *d.* 1662. Ogden Nash *b.* 1902.	231
20	*Friday*	Gen. William Booth *d.* 1912. Invasion of Czechoslovakia 1968.	232
21	*Saturday*	*Princess Margaret b. 1930.* Constant Lambert *d.* 1951.	233
22	*Sunday*	**12th S. after Pentecost.** Jomo Kenyatta *d.* 1978.	*week* 35 *day* 234
23	*Monday*	William Wallace *exec.* 1305. Michel Fokine *d.* 1942.	235
24	*Tuesday*	**St Bartholomew.** William Wilberforce *b.* 1759.	236
25	*Wednesday*	First cross-channel swim by Captain Matthew Webb 1875.	237
26	*Thursday*	Sir Robert Walpole *b.* 1676. Charles Lindbergh *d.* 1974.	238
27	*Friday*	Dresden 1813. Emperor Haile Selassie *d.* 1975.	239
28	*Saturday*	Leigh Hunt *d.* 1859. Prince William of Gloucester *d.* 1972.	240
29	*Sunday*	**13th S. after Pentecost.** Ingrid Bergman *d.* 1982.	*week* 36 *day* 241
30	*Monday*	*Bank Holiday in England, Wales and Northern Ireland.*	242
31	*Tuesday*	Harley Granville Barker *d.* 1946. Rocky Marciano *d.* 1969.	243

Astronomical Phenomena

d	h	
3	23	Saturn in conjunction with Moon. Saturn 6° S.
4	02	Mercury at greatest elongation W. 19°
15	02	Venus in conjunction with Moon. Venus 2° N.
16	22	Mercury in conjunction with Moon. Mercury 5° N.
19	23	Saturn at opposition
20	12	Mars in conjunction with Moon. Mars 5° N.
21	01	Jupiter in conjunction with Moon. Jupiter 5° N.
29	08	Mercury in superior conjunction
31	02	Saturn in conjunction with Moon. Saturn 6° S.

Constellations

The following constellations are near the meridian at

July 1d, 24h	August 16d, 21h
July 16d, 23h	September 1d, 20h
August 1d, 22h	September 15d, 19h

Draco, Hercules, Lyra, Cygnus, Sagitta, Ophiuchus, Serpens, Aquila and Sagittarius

Minima of Algol

d	h	d	h	d	h
3	05.5	14	16.7	26	04.0
6	02.3	17	13.5	29	00.8
8	23.1	20	10.3	31	21.6
11	19.9	23	07.2		

The Moon

Phases, Apsides and Node	d	h	m
○ Full Moon	2	12	10
☾ Last Quarter	10	15	19
● New Moon	17	19	28
☽ First Quarter	24	09	57
Apogee (405,257 km)	7	03	57
Perigee (360,388 km)	19	06	52

Mean longitude of ascending node on 1 Aug., 249°

THE SUN

s.d. 15′.8

Day	Right Ascension	Dec. +	Equation of time	Rise 52°	Rise 56°	Transit	Set 52°	Set 56°	Sidereal time	Transit of First Point of Aries
	h m s	° ′	m s	h m	h m	h m	h m	h m	h m s	h m s
1	8 44 47	18 04	−6 19	4 22	4 04	12 06	19 50	20 08	20 38 28	3 20 59
2	8 48 39	17 49	−6 15	4 23	4 06	12 06	19 48	20 06	20 42 24	3 17 04
3	8 52 31	17 33	−6 11	4 25	4 07	12 06	19 47	20 03	20 46 21	3 13 08
4	8 56 23	17 18	−6 06	4 26	4 09	12 06	19 45	20 01	20 50 17	3 09 12
5	9 00 14	17 02	−6 00	4 28	4 11	12 06	19 43	19 59	20 54 14	3 05 16
6	9 04 04	16 45	−5 54	4 29	4 13	12 06	19 41	19 57	20 58 10	3 01 20
7	9 07 54	16 29	−5 47	4 31	4 15	12 06	19 39	19 55	21 02 07	2 57 24
8	9 11 43	16 12	−5 39	4 33	4 17	12 06	19 38	19 53	21 06 03	2 53 28
9	9 15 31	15 55	−5 31	4 34	4 19	12 05	19 36	19 51	21 10 00	2 49 32
10	9 19 19	15 37	−5 23	4 36	4 21	12 05	19 34	19 48	21 13 57	2 45 36
11	9 23 07	15 20	−5 14	4 37	4 23	12 05	19 32	19 46	21 17 53	2 41 40
12	9 26 54	15 02	−5 04	4 39	4 25	12 05	19 30	19 44	21 21 50	2 37 44
13	9 30 40	14 44	−4 54	4 41	4 27	12 05	19 28	19 41	21 25 46	2 33 49
14	9 34 26	14 26	−4 43	4 42	4 29	12 05	19 26	19 39	21 29 43	2 29 53
15	9 38 11	14 07	−4 32	4 44	4 31	12 04	19 24	19 37	21 33 39	2 25 57
16	9 41 56	13 48	−4 20	4 45	4 33	12 04	19 22	19 34	21 37 36	2 22 01
17	9 45 40	13 29	−4 08	4 47	4 35	12 04	19 20	19 32	21 41 32	2 18 05
18	9 49 24	13 10	−3 55	4 49	4 37	12 04	19 18	19 30	21 45 29	2 14 09
19	9 53 07	12 50	−3 42	4 50	4 39	12 04	19 16	19 27	21 49 25	2 10 13
20	9 56 50	12 31	−3 28	4 52	4 41	12 03	19 14	19 25	21 53 22	2 06 17
21	10 00 32	12 11	−3 14	4 54	4 42	12 03	19 11	19 22	21 57 19	2 02 21
22	10 04 14	11 51	−2 59	4 55	4 44	12 03	19 09	19 20	22 01 15	1 58 25
23	10 07 55	11 31	−2 43	4 57	4 46	12 03	19 07	19 17	22 05 12	1 54 29
24	10 11 36	11 10	−2 28	4 59	4 48	12 02	19 05	19 15	22 09 08	1 50 34
25	10 15 16	10 50	−2 12	5 00	4 50	12 02	19 03	19 12	22 13 05	1 46 38
26	10 18 56	10 29	−1 55	5 02	4 52	12 02	19 01	19 10	22 17 01	1 42 42
27	10 22 36	10 08	−1 38	5 03	4 54	12 01	18 58	19 07	22 20 58	1 38 46
28	10 26 15	9 47	−1 21	5 05	4 56	12 01	18 56	19 05	22 24 54	1 34 50
29	10 29 54	9 26	−1 03	5 07	4 58	12 01	18 54	19 02	22 28 51	1 30 54
30	10 33 32	9 04	−0 45	5 08	5 00	12 01	18 52	19 00	22 32 48	1 26 58
31	10 37 10	8 43	−0 26	5 10	5 02	12 00	18 50	18 57	22 36 44	1 23 02

Duration of Twilight (in minutes)

Latitude	52°	56°	52°	56°
	1 August		11 August	
Civil	41	48	39	45
Nautical	97	120	89	106
Astronomical	177	TAN	153	205
	21 August		31 August	
Civil	37	42	35	40
Nautical	83	96	79	89
Astronomical	138	166	127	147

The Night Sky

Mercury is a morning object during the first half of the month, magnitude +0.7 to −1.1, visible low above the ENE horizon around the time of beginning of morning civil twilight. On the morning of the 16th the old crescent Moon, only one and a half days before New, may be seen about 10° to the right of the planet.

Venus, magnitude −3.9, is a brilliant morning object, visible in the eastern sky for several hours before sunrise. The old crescent Moon is near the planet on the mornings of the 14th and 15th. Around the 22nd, Venus, continuing its eastward motion, passes south of the twins, Castor and Pollux.

Mars, magnitude +1.7, is moving towards the Sun and will not be visible again this year.

Jupiter is still a bright evening object, magnitude −1.7. It is moving towards the Sun and only visible for a short while in the SW sky before it sets. By the end of the month it is a difficult object to detect.

Saturn, magnitude +0.4, reaches opposition on the 20th, and thus is visible throughout the hours of darkness. The Moon, near Full, passes 6° S. of the planet on the night of 3–4 August and again on 30–31 August.

Meteors. The maximum of the famous Perseid meteor shower occurs on the the 12th. Even after midnight, when the old crescent Moon rises in the east, there will be little hindrance to observation.

THE MOON

Day	RA	Dec.	Hor. par.	Semi-diam.	Sun's co-long.	P.A. of Bright Limb	Phase	Age	Rise 52°	Rise 56°	Transit	Set 52°	Set 56°
	h m	°	′	′	°	°	%	d	h m	h m	h m	h m	h m
1	19 30	−18.5	56.0	15.3	68	272	98	12.5	18 56	19 11	23 38	3 18	3 00
2	20 21	−15.3	55.5	15.1	80	291	100	13.5	19 20	19 31	—	4 28	4 14
3	21 09	−11.5	55.1	15.0	92	34	100	14.5	19 41	19 48	0 24	5 37	5 28
4	21 56	− 7.3	54.7	14.9	104	54	98	15.5	19 59	20 02	1 08	6 46	6 40
5	22 41	− 2.9	54.4	14.8	116	59	94	16.5	20 17	20 16	1 50	7 53	7 51
6	23 25	+ 1.6	54.2	14.8	128	61	89	17.5	20 34	20 30	2 32	8 59	9 01
7	0 10	+ 6.0	54.1	14.7	141	63	82	18.5	20 53	20 45	3 13	10 04	10 11
8	0 54	+10.2	54.2	14.8	153	65	74	19.5	21 14	21 02	3 55	11 10	11 21
9	1 40	+14.0	54.4	14.8	165	68	66	20.5	21 39	21 23	4 39	12 16	12 31
10	2 28	+17.3	54.7	14.9	177	71	56	21.5	22 09	21 49	5 24	13 22	13 41
11	3 18	+19.8	55.3	15.1	190	75	47	22.5	22 47	22 25	6 13	14 26	14 48
12	4 11	+21.5	55.9	15.2	202	80	37	23.5	23 35	23 11	7 04	15 26	15 49
13	5 06	+22.2	56.8	15.5	214	84	27	24.5	—	—	7 58	16 19	16 42
14	6 03	+21.6	57.6	15.7	226	89	18	25.5	0 34	0 11	8 53	17 05	17 25
15	7 01	+19.8	58.6	16.0	238	92	11	26.5	1 44	1 24	9 49	17 42	17 59
16	7 59	+16.8	59.4	16.2	251	93	5	27.5	3 01	2 46	10 45	18 13	18 26
17	8 56	+12.6	60.1	16.4	263	85	1	28.5	4 24	4 13	11 40	18 40	18 48
18	9 53	+ 7.6	60.6	16.5	275	352	0	0.2	5 48	5 43	12 35	19 04	19 07
19	10 49	+ 2.2	60.8	16.6	287	309	2	1.2	7 13	7 13	13 28	19 28	19 26
20	11 44	− 3.5	60.8	16.6	300	301	7	2.2	8 39	8 43	14 22	19 51	19 45
21	12 40	− 8.8	60.5	16.5	312	297	15	3.2	10 03	10 13	15 16	20 18	20 06
22	13 36	−13.6	59.9	16.3	324	293	24	4.2	11 25	11 40	16 11	20 48	20 32
23	14 34	−17.5	59.3	16.2	336	289	34	5.2	12 44	13 03	17 07	21 25	21 04
24	15 32	−20.2	58.6	16.0	349	284	46	6.2	13 55	14 17	18 03	22 09	21 46
25	16 30	−21.8	57.8	15.8	1	279	57	7.2	14 56	15 20	18 59	23 02	22 39
26	17 27	−22.0	57.1	15.6	13	274	67	8.2	15 47	16 09	19 53	—	23 41
27	18 23	−21.0	56.5	15.4	25	269	76	9.2	16 27	16 47	20 45	0 03	—
28	19 17	−19.0	55.9	15.2	37	266	84	10.2	16 59	17 15	21 34	1 09	0 50
29	20 08	−16.1	55.4	15.1	50	263	91	11.2	17 25	17 37	22 21	2 18	2 03
30	20 57	−12.5	55.0	15.0	62	264	96	12.2	17 46	17 55	23 05	3 26	3 16
31	21 44	− 8.5	54.6	14.9	74	272	99	13.2	18 06	18 10	23 48	4 34	4 28

MERCURY

Day	RA	Dec.	Diam.	Phase	Transit	5° high 52°	5° high 56°
	h m	°	″	%	h m	h m	h m
1	7 25	+19.5	8	29	10 46	3 36	3 22
4	7 35	+19.9	8	39	10 45	3 32	3 18
7	7 50	+20.1	7	50	10 48	3 34	3 19
10	8 07	+20.0	6	61	10 54	3 40	3 26
13	8 27	+19.6	6	72	11 03	3 51	3 38
16	8 50	+18.7	6	82	11 14	4 07	3 54
19	9 13	+17.5	—	—	11 26	Mercury is	
22	9 37	+15.9	—	—	11 38	too close to	
25	10 01	+14.0	—	—	11 50	the Sun for	
28	10 24	+11.9	—	—	12 01	observation	
31	10 46	+ 9.7	—	—	12 11		

VENUS

Day	RA	Dec.	Diam.	Phase	Transit	5° high 52°	5° high 56°
	h m	°	″	%	h m	h m	h m
1	5 55	+21.7	15	72	9 17	1 53	1 37
6	6 20	+21.9	15	74	9 22	1 57	1 41
11	6 45	+21.8	14	75	9 28	2 03	1 47
16	7 10	+21.5	14	77	9 33	2 10	1 54
21	7 35	+21.0	14	79	9 38	2 19	2 03
26	8 00	+20.2	13	80	9 44	2 29	2 14
31	8 25	+19.1	13	82	9 49	2 40	2 27

MARS

Day	RA	Dec.	Diam.	Phase	Transit	5° high 52°	5° high 56°
1	11 36	3.4	4	95	14 56	20 40	20 39
6	11 47	2.1	4	95	14 48	20 25	20 23
11	11 59	0.8	4	95	14 40	20 10	20 07
16	12 10	− 0.5	4	96	14 31	19 55	19 51
21	12 22	− 1.8	4	96	14 23	19 40	19 35
26	12 33	− 3.1	4	96	14 15	19 25	19 19
31	12 45	− 4.5	4	97	14 07	19 10	19 03

SUNRISE AND SUNSET

	London		Bristol		Birmingham		Manchester		Newcastle		Glasgow		Belfast	
	0°05′	51°30′	2°35′	51°28′	1°55′	52°28′	2°15′	53°28′	1°37′	54°59′	4°14′	55°52′	5°56′	54°35′
	h m	h m	h m	h m	h m	h m	h m	h m	h m	h m	h m	h m	h m	h m
1	4 24	19 48	4 34	19 58	4 27	19 59	4 25	20 05	4 15	20 09	4 21	20 24	4 34	20 25
2	4 25	19 47	4 36	19 57	4 29	19 58	4 26	20 03	4 17	20 07	4 23	20 22	4 36	20 23
3	4 27	19 45	4 37	19 55	4 31	19 56	4 28	20 01	4 19	20 05	4 25	20 20	4 38	20 21
4	4 28	19 43	4 39	19 53	4 32	19 54	4 29	19 59	4 20	20 03	4 27	20 18	4 40	20 19
5	4 30	19 42	4 40	19 51	4 34	19 52	4 31	19 58	4 22	20 01	4 29	20 16	4 41	20 17
6	4 31	19 40	4 42	19 50	4 35	19 51	4 33	19 56	4 24	19 59	4 31	20 13	4 43	20 15
7	4 33	19 38	4 43	19 48	4 37	19 49	4 35	19 54	4 26	19 57	4 33	20 11	4 45	20 13
8	4 35	19 36	4 45	19 46	4 39	19 47	4 36	19 52	4 28	19 55	4 35	20 09	4 47	20 11
9	4 36	19 34	4 46	19 44	4 40	19 45	4 38	19 50	4 30	19 53	4 36	20 07	4 48	20 09
10	4 38	19 32	4 48	19 42	4 42	19 43	4 40	19 48	4 31	19 51	4 38	20 05	4 50	20 07
11	4 39	19 31	4 49	19 40	4 43	19 41	4 41	19 46	4 33	19 49	4 40	20 02	4 52	20 04
12	4 41	19 29	4 51	19 39	4 45	19 39	4 43	19 44	4 35	19 46	4 42	20 00	4 54	20 02
13	4 42	19 27	4 53	19 37	4 47	19 37	4 45	19 42	4 37	19 44	4 44	19 58	4 56	20 00
14	4 44	19 25	4 54	19 35	4 48	19 35	4 47	19 39	4 39	19 42	4 46	19 56	4 58	19 58
15	4 46	19 23	4 56	19 33	4 50	19 33	4 48	19 37	4 41	19 40	4 48	19 53	4 59	19 56
16	4 47	19 21	4 57	19 31	4 52	19 31	4 50	19 35	4 43	19 37	4 50	19 51	5 01	19 53
17	4 49	19 19	4 59	19 29	4 53	19 29	4 52	19 33	4 45	19 35	4 52	19 49	5 03	19 51
18	4 50	19 17	5 00	19 27	4 55	19 27	4 54	19 31	4 46	19 33	4 54	19 46	5 05	19 49
19	4 52	19 15	5 02	19 25	4 57	19 25	4 55	19 29	4 48	19 31	4 56	19 44	5 07	19 47
20	4 54	19 13	5 04	19 23	4 58	19 22	4 57	19 26	4 50	19 28	4 58	19 41	5 09	19 44
21	4 55	19 11	5 05	19 20	5 00	19 20	4 59	19 24	4 52	19 26	5 00	19 39	5 10	19 42
22	4 57	19 08	5 07	19 18	5 02	19 18	5 01	19 22	4 54	19 23	5 02	19 36	5 12	19 40
23	4 58	19 06	5 08	19 16	5 03	19 16	5 02	19 20	4 56	19 21	5 04	19 34	5 14	19 37
24	5 00	19 04	5 10	19 14	5 05	19 14	5 04	19 17	4 58	19 19	5 06	19 31	5 16	19 35
25	5 02	19 02	5 12	19 12	5 07	19 12	5 06	19 15	5 00	19 16	5 08	19 29	5 18	19 33
26	5 03	19 00	5 13	19 10	5 08	19 09	5 08	19 13	5 01	19 14	5 10	19 26	5 20	19 30
27	5 05	18 58	5 15	19 08	5 10	19 07	5 09	19 11	5 03	19 11	5 12	19 24	5 21	19 28
28	5 06	18 56	5 16	19 06	5 12	19 05	5 11	19 08	5 05	19 09	5 13	19 21	5 23	19 25
29	5 08	18 53	5 18	19 03	5 13	19 03	5 13	19 06	5 07	19 06	5 15	19 19	5 25	19 23
30	5 10	18 51	5 20	19 01	5 15	19 00	5 15	19 03	5 09	19 04	5 17	19 16	5 27	19 20
31	5 11	18 49	5 21	18 59	5 17	18 58	5 16	19 01	5 11	19 02	5 19	19 14	5 29	19 18

JUPITER

Day	*RA*	*Dec.*	*Transit*	*5° high*	
				52°	56°
	h m	° ′	h m	h m	h m
1	12 37.7	− 2 46	15 57	21 09	21 03
11	12 43.6	− 3 25	15 24	20 32	20 26
21	12 49.9	− 4 07	14 51	19 55	19 49
31	12 56.8	− 4 51	14 18	19 19	19 12

Diameters – equatorial 32″ polar 31″

SATURN

Day	*RA*	*Dec.*	*Transit*	*5° high*	
				52°	56°
	h m	° ′	h m	h m	h m
1	22 04.1	−13 27	1 25	21 10	21 26
11	22 01.4	−13 43	0 43	20 29	20 46
21	21 58.5	−13 59	0 01	19 49	20 06
31	21 55.6	−14 15	23 15	19 08	19 26

Diameters – equatorial 19″ polar 17″
Rings – major axis 43″ minor axis 9″

URANUS

Day	*RA*	*Dec.*	*Transit*	*10° high*	
				52°	56°
	h m	° ′	h m	h m	h m
1	19 24.5	−22 30	22 42	0 59	23 54
11	19 23.0	−22 33	22 01	0 18	23 12
21	19 21.7	−22 36	21 21	23 33	22 31
31	19 20.6	−22 38	20 40	22 52	21 50

Diameter 4″

NEPTUNE

Day	*RA*	*Dec.*	*Transit*	*10° high*	
				52°	56°
	h m	° ′	h m	h m	h m
1	19 22.9	−21 23	22 41	1 10	0 20
11	19 21.9	−21 25	22 00	0 29	23 35
21	19 21.0	−21 27	21 20	23 45	22 54
31	19 20.3	−21 29	20 40	23 05	22 14

Diameter 2″

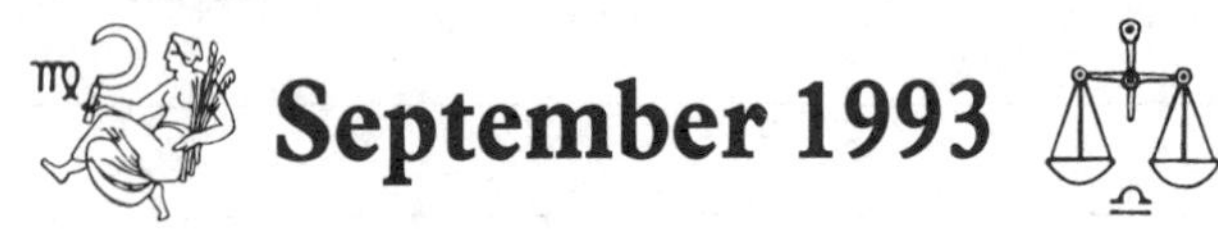

September 1993

NINTH MONTH, 30 DAYS. *Septem* (seven), seventh month of Roman pre-Julian calendar

Sun's Longitude 180° ♎ 23ᵈ 00ʰ

1	*Wednesday*	Pope Adrian IV *d.* 1159. Edgar Rice Burroughs *b.* 1875.	*week* 36 *day* 244
2	*Thursday*	Thomas Telford *d.* 1834. Omdurman 1898.	245
3	*Friday*	Dunbar 1650. Oliver Cromwell *d.* 1658.	246
4	*Saturday*	Darius Milhaud *b.* 1892. Georges Simenon *d.* 1989.	247
5	*Sunday*	**14th S. after Pentecost.** John Gilpin *d.* 1983.	*week* 37 *day* 248
6	*Monday*	*Mayflower* sailed from Plymouth 1620.	249
7	*Tuesday*	Borodino 1812. Sir Henry Campbell-Bannerman *b.* 1836.	250
8	*Wednesday*	**Blessed Virgin Mary.** Antonin Dvořák *b.* 1841.	251
9	*Thursday*	Captain William Bligh *b.* 1754. Mao Tse-tung *d.* 1976.	252
10	*Friday*	Wilfrid Scawen Blunt *d.* 1922. Arnold Palmer *b.* 1929.	253
11	*Saturday*	Malplaquet 1709. Nikita Krushchev *d.* 1971.	254
12	*Sunday*	**15th S. after Pentecost.** Marshal von Blücher *d.* 1819.	*week* 38 *day* 255
13	*Monday*	Roald Dahl *b.* 1916. Leopold Stokowski *d.* 1977.	256
14	*Tuesday*	Dante Alighieri *d.* 1321. Princess Grace of Monaco *d.* 1982.	257
15	*Wednesday*	Prince Henry of Wales *b.* 1984. Battle of Britain Day.	258
16	*Thursday*	JEWISH NEW YEAR (5754). John McCormack *d.* 1945.	259
17	*Friday*	Tobias Smollett *d.* 1771. Walter Savage Landor *d.* 1864.	260
18	*Saturday*	Greta Garbo *b.* 1905. Sean O'Casey *d.* 1964.	261
19	*Sunday*	**16th S. after Pentecost.** William Golding *b.* 1911.	*week* 39 *day* 262
20	*Monday*	Mungo Park *b.* 1771. Jean Sibelius *d.* 1957.	263
21	*Tuesday*	**St Matthew.** Girolamo Savonarola *b.* 1452.	264
22	*Wednesday*	Zutphen 1586. Irving Berlin *d.* 1989.	265
23	*Thursday*	Vincenzo Bellini *d.* 1835. Wilkie Collins *d.* 1889.	266
24	*Friday*	Scott Fitzgerald *b.* 1896. Dame Isobel Baillie *d.* 1983.	267
25	*Saturday*	YOM KIPPUR (Day of Atonement). Stamford Bridge 1066.	268
26	*Sunday*	**17th S. after Pentecost.** *Queen Mary* launched 1934.	*week* 40 *day* 269
27	*Monday*	Sir Martin Ryle *b.* 1918. *Queen Elizabeth* launched 1938.	270
28	*Tuesday*	Herman Melville *d.* 1891. Pres. Gamal Nasser *d.* 1970.	271
29	*Wednesday*	**St Michael and all Angels.** Horatio Nelson *b.* 1758.	272
30	*Thursday*	FEAST OF TABERNACLES begins. Pierre Corneille *d.* 1684.	273

ASTRONOMICAL PHENOMENA

d	h	
6	06	Jupiter in conjunction with Mars. Jupiter 0°.8 N.
13	23	Venus in conjunction with Moon. Venus 5° N.
17	05	Mercury in conjunction with Moon. Mercury 4° N.
17	19	Jupiter in conjunction with Moon. Jupiter 4° N.
18	04	Mars in conjunction with Moon. Mars 3° N.
23	00	Equinox
23	22	Jupiter in conjunction with Mercury. Jupiter 2° N.
27	04	Saturn in conjunction with Moon. Saturn 6° S.

CONSTELLATIONS

The following constellations are near the meridian at

August 1d, 24h
August 16d, 23h
September 1d, 22h
September 15d, 21h
October 1d, 20h
October 16d, 19h

Draco, Cepheus, Lyra, Cygnus, Vulpecula, Sagitta, Delphinus, Equuleus, Aquila, Aquarius and Capricornus

MINIMA OF ALGOL

d	h	d	h	d	h
3	18.4	15	05.6	23	20.1
6	15.2	18	02.4	26	16.9
9	12.0	20	23.3	29	13.7
12	08.8				

THE MOON

Phases, Apsides and Node	d	h	m
○ Full Moon	1	02	33
☾ Last Quarter	9	06	26
● New Moon	16	03	10
☽ First Quarter	22	19	32
○ Full Moon	30	18	54
Apogee (406,125 km)	3	17	01
Perigee (357,407 km)	16	14	40
Apogee (406,426 km)	30	21	23

Mean longitude of ascending node on 1 Sept., 248°

THE SUN

s.d. 15′.9

Day	Right Ascension	Dec.	Equation of time	Rise 52°	Rise 56°	Transit	Set 52°	Set 56°	Sidereal time	Transit of First Point of Aries
	h m s	° ′	m s	h m	h m	h m	h m	h m	h m s	h m s
1	10 40 48	+8 21	−0 07	5 12	5 04	12 00	18 47	18 55	22 40 41	1 19 06
2	10 44 25	+8 00	+0 12	5 13	5 06	12 00	18 45	18 52	22 44 37	1 15 10
3	10 48 03	+7 38	+0 31	5 15	5 08	11 59	18 43	18 49	22 48 34	1 11 14
4	10 51 40	+7 16	+0 51	5 16	5 10	11 59	18 40	18 47	22 52 30	1 07 19
5	10 55 16	+6 53	+1 11	5 18	5 12	11 59	18 38	18 44	22 56 27	1 03 23
6	10 58 53	+6 31	+1 31	5 20	5 14	11 58	18 36	18 42	23 00 23	0 59 27
7	11 02 29	+6 09	+1 51	5 21	5 16	11 58	18 34	18 39	23 04 20	0 55 31
8	11 06 05	+5 46	+2 12	5 23	5 18	11 58	18 31	18 36	23 08 17	0 51 35
9	11 09 41	+5 24	+2 32	5 25	5 20	11 57	18 29	18 34	23 12 13	0 47 39
10	11 13 17	+5 01	+2 53	5 26	5 22	11 57	18 27	18 31	23 16 10	0 43 43
11	11 16 52	+4 38	+3 14	5 28	5 24	11 57	18 24	18 28	23 20 06	0 39 47
12	11 20 28	+4 15	+3 35	5 29	5 25	11 56	18 22	18 26	23 24 03	0 35 51
13	11 24 03	+3 52	+3 56	5 31	5 27	11 56	18 20	18 23	23 27 59	0 31 55
14	11 27 39	+3 29	+4 17	5 33	5 29	11 56	18 17	18 20	23 31 56	0 28 00
15	11 31 14	+3 06	+4 39	5 34	5 31	11 55	18 15	18 18	23 35 52	0 24 04
16	11 34 49	+2 43	+5 00	5 36	5 33	11 55	18 13	18 15	23 39 49	0 20 08
17	11 38 24	+2 20	+5 21	5 38	5 35	11 54	18 10	18 12	23 43 46	0 16 12
18	11 42 00	+1 57	+5 42	5 39	5 37	11 54	18 08	18 10	23 47 42	0 12 16
19	11 45 35	+1 34	+6 04	5 41	5 39	11 54	18 06	18 07	23 51 39	0 08 20
20	11 49 10	+1 10	+6 25	5 43	5 41	11 53	18 03	18 04	23 55 35	0 04 24
21	11 52 46	+0 47	+6 46	5 44	5 43	11 53	18 01	18 02	23 59 32	{ 0 00 28 23 56 32
22	11 56 21	+0 24	+7 07	5 46	5 45	11 53	17 59	17 59	0 03 28	23 52 36
23	11 59 56	0 00	+7 28	5 47	5 47	11 52	17 56	17 57	0 07 25	23 48 40
24	12 03 32	−0 23	+7 49	5 49	5 49	11 52	17 54	17 54	0 11 21	23 44 45
25	12 07 08	−0 46	+8 10	5 51	5 51	11 52	17 52	17 51	0 15 18	23 40 49
26	12 10 44	−1 10	+8 31	5 52	5 53	11 51	17 49	17 49	0 19 15	23 36 53
27	12 14 20	−1 33	+8 51	5 54	5 55	11 51	17 47	17 46	0 23 11	23 32 57
28	12 17 56	−1 56	+9 12	5 56	5 57	11 51	17 45	17 43	0 27 08	23 29 01
29	12 21 32	−2 20	+9 32	5 57	5 59	11 50	17 42	17 41	0 31 04	23 25 05
30	12 25 09	−2 43	+9 52	5 59	6 01	11 50	17 40	17 38	0 35 01	23 21 09

DURATION OF TWILIGHT (in minutes)

Latitude	52°	56°	52°	56°
	1 September		11 September	
Civil	35	39	34	38
Nautical	79	89	76	84
Astronomical	127	146	120	135
	21 September		31 September	
Civil	34	37	34	37
Nautical	74	82	73	80
Astronomical	115	129	113	126

THE NIGHT SKY

Mercury is unsuitably placed for observation.

Venus is a brilliant morning object in the eastern sky, magnitude −3.8. By the end of September it is still visible for about two hours before sunrise. The old crescent Moon will be seen near the planet on the mornings of the 13th and 14th. Venus will be seen near Regulus on the mornings of the 20th and 21st.

Mars is unsuitably placed for observation.

Jupiter, although technically still an evening object, is lost in the gathering twilight and will not be seen again until November.

Saturn continues to be visible in the evening and through to the early morning skies. By the end of the month it is lost to view over the SW horizon by about 01h. Its retrograde motion has now taken it back along the ecliptic into Capricornus. Saturn's magnitude is +0.4.

Zodiacal Light. The morning cone may be seen stretching up from the eastern horizon before the beginning of morning twilight, from the 15th to the 28th.

THE MOON

Day	RA	Dec.	Hor. par.	Semi-diam.	Sun's co-long.	P.A. of Bright Limb	Phase	Age	Rise 52°	Rise 56°	Transit	Set 52°	Set 56°
	h m	°	′	′	°	°	%	d	h m	h m	h m	h m	h m
1	22 29	− 4.2	54.3	14.8	86	325	100	14.2	18 24	18 24	—	5 41	5 39
2	23 13	+ 0.3	54.1	14.8	98	41	99	15.2	18 41	18 38	0 30	6 47	6 49
3	23 58	+ 4.7	54.0	14.7	111	55	97	16.2	19 00	18 53	1 11	7 53	7 58
4	0 42	+ 8.9	54.0	14.7	123	60	92	17.2	19 20	19 10	1 53	8 59	9 08
5	1 28	+12.8	54.1	14.7	135	65	87	18.2	19 43	19 29	2 36	10 04	10 18
6	2 15	+16.2	54.3	14.8	147	69	80	19.2	20 11	19 53	3 20	11 10	11 26
7	3 03	+18.9	54.7	14.9	159	73	72	20.2	20 45	20 25	4 07	12 13	12 33
8	3 54	+20.8	55.2	15.0	171	78	63	21.2	21 28	21 05	4 56	13 13	13 36
9	4 48	+21.8	55.8	15.2	184	83	53	22.2	22 21	21 58	5 47	14 08	14 31
10	5 42	+21.7	56.6	15.4	196	88	43	23.2	23 24	23 03	6 41	14 56	15 17
11	6 38	+20.4	57.5	15.7	208	93	32	24.2	—	—	7 35	15 36	15 54
12	7 35	+18.0	58.5	15.9	220	97	23	25.2	0 35	0 18	8 29	16 09	16 24
13	8 31	+14.4	59.4	16.2	233	100	14	26.2	1 54	1 41	9 24	16 38	16 48
14	9 28	+ 9.9	60.3	16.4	245	100	7	27.2	3 16	3 08	10 18	17 04	17 09
15	10 24	+ 4.6	60.9	16.6	257	95	2	28.2	4 41	4 38	11 12	17 28	17 28
16	11 20	− 1.0	61.3	16.7	269	45	0	29.2	6 07	6 10	12 07	17 52	17 48
17	12 17	− 6.6	61.3	16.7	281	312	1	0.9	7 34	7 42	13 03	18 18	18 09
18	13 15	−11.7	61.0	16.6	294	299	5	1.9	9 00	9 13	13 59	18 48	18 34
19	14 14	−16.0	60.5	16.5	306	292	12	2.9	10 23	10 41	14 57	19 23	19 05
20	15 14	−19.3	59.7	16.3	318	286	21	3.9	11 40	12 01	15 55	20 06	19 44
21	16 13	−21.2	58.8	16.0	330	280	31	4.9	12 47	13 10	16 53	20 58	20 35
22	17 12	−21.8	57.9	15.8	343	274	41	5.9	13 42	14 05	17 49	21 57	21 35
23	18 10	−21.1	57.1	15.5	355	269	52	6.9	14 26	14 47	18 42	23 03	22 43
24	19 04	−19.4	56.3	15.3	7	264	62	7.9	15 01	15 18	19 32	—	23 54
25	19 56	−16.7	55.6	15.2	19	261	72	8.9	15 29	15 42	20 19	0 10	—
26	20 45	−13.3	55.1	15.0	31	258	80	9.9	15 52	16 01	21 04	1 18	1 06
27	21 32	− 9.4	54.6	14.9	44	257	87	10.9	16 12	16 17	21 47	2 26	2 18
28	22 18	− 5.2	54.3	14.8	56	257	93	11.9	16 30	16 32	22 29	3 33	3 29
29	23 02	− 0.8	54.1	14.7	68	261	97	12.9	16 48	16 46	23 10	4 38	4 38
30	23 46	+ 3.6	54.0	14.7	80	275	99	13.9	17 06	17 01	23 52	5 44	5 48

MERCURY

Day	RA	Dec.	Diam.	Phase	Transit	
	h m	°			h m	
1	10 53	8.9	—	—	12 14	Mercury is
4	11 14	6.6	—	—	12 22	too close to
7	11 33	4.2	—	—	12 30	the Sun for
10	11 52	1.9	—	—	12 37	observation
13	12 10	− 0.5	—	—	12 44	
16	12 28	− 2.7	—	—	12 49	
19	12 45	− 4.9	—	—	12 54	
22	13 02	− 7.1	—	—	12 59	
25	13 18	− 9.1	—	—	13 03	
28	13 34	−11.1	—	—	13 07	
31	13 49	−12.9	—	—	13 11	

VENUS

Day	RA	Dec.	Diam.	Phase	Transit	5° high 52°	5° high 56°
	h m	°	″	%	h m	h m	h m
1	8 30	+18.9	13	82	9 50	2 42	2 29
6	8 55	+17.6	13	83	9 55	2 55	2 43
11	9 19	+16.1	12	85	9 59	3 08	2 58
16	9 43	+14.4	12	86	10 04	3 22	3 13
21	10 07	+12.5	12	87	10 08	3 36	3 29
26	10 30	+10.5	12	88	10 11	3 50	3 45
31	10 54	+ 8.4	11	89	10 15	4 05	4 01

MARS

Day	RA	Dec.	Diam.	Phase	Transit	
1	12 47	− 4.7	—	—	14 06	Mars is
6	12 59	− 6.0	—	—	13 58	too close to
11	13 12	− 7.3	—	—	13 51	the Sun for
16	13 24	− 8.6	—	—	13 43	observation
21	13 36	− 9.9	—	—	13 36	
26	13 49	−11.1	—	—	13 29	
31	14 02	−12.4	—	—	13 22	

SUNRISE AND SUNSET

	London		Bristol		Birmingham		Manchester		Newcastle		Glasgow		Belfast	
	0°05′	51°30′	2°35′	51°28′	1°55′	52°28′	2°15′	53°28′	1°37′	54°59′	4°14′	55°52′	5°56′	54°35′
	h m	h m	h m	h m	h m	h m	h m	h m	h m	h m	h m	h m	h m	h m
1	5 13	18 47	5 23	18 57	5 18	18 56	5 18	18 59	5 13	18 59	5 21	19 11	5 31	19 16
2	5 14	18 45	5 24	18 54	5 20	18 53	5 20	18 56	5 14	18 57	5 23	19 09	5 32	19 13
3	5 16	18 42	5 26	18 52	5 22	18 51	5 21	18 54	5 16	18 54	5 25	19 06	5 34	19 11
4	5 17	18 40	5 28	18 50	5 23	18 49	5 23	18 52	5 18	18 52	5 27	19 03	5 36	19 08
5	5 19	18 38	5 29	18 48	5 25	18 46	5 25	18 49	5 20	18 49	5 29	19 01	5 38	19 06
6	5 21	18 36	5 31	18 45	5 27	18 44	5 27	18 47	5 22	18 46	5 31	18 58	5 40	19 03
7	5 22	18 33	5 32	18 43	5 28	18 42	5 28	18 44	5 24	18 44	5 33	18 56	5 42	19 01
8	5 24	18 31	5 34	18 41	5 30	18 39	5 30	18 42	5 26	18 41	5 35	18 53	5 43	18 58
9	5 25	18 29	5 36	18 39	5 32	18 37	5 32	18 40	5 27	18 39	5 37	18 50	5 45	18 56
10	5 27	18 26	5 37	18 36	5 33	18 35	5 34	18 37	5 29	18 36	5 39	18 48	5 47	18 53
11	5 29	18 24	5 39	18 34	5 35	18 32	5 35	18 35	5 31	18 34	5 41	18 45	5 49	18 51
12	5 30	18 22	5 40	18 32	5 37	18 30	5 37	18 32	5 33	18 31	5 43	18 42	5 51	18 48
13	5 32	18 20	5 42	18 30	5 38	18 28	5 39	18 30	5 35	18 29	5 45	18 40	5 53	18 45
14	5 33	18 17	5 43	18 27	5 40	18 25	5 41	18 27	5 37	18 26	5 46	18 37	5 54	18 43
15	5 35	18 15	5 45	18 25	5 42	18 23	5 42	18 25	5 39	18 23	5 48	18 35	5 56	18 40
16	5 37	18 13	5 47	18 23	5 43	18 21	5 44	18 22	5 40	18 21	5 50	18 32	5 58	18 38
17	5 38	18 10	5 48	18 20	5 45	18 18	5 46	18 20	5 42	18 18	5 52	18 29	6 00	18 35
18	5 40	18 08	5 50	18 18	5 47	18 16	5 48	18 18	5 44	18 16	5 54	18 27	6 02	18 33
19	5 41	18 06	5 51	18 16	5 48	18 13	5 49	18 15	5 46	18 13	5 56	18 24	6 04	18 30
20	5 43	18 03	5 53	18 13	5 50	18 11	5 51	18 13	5 48	18 11	5 58	18 21	6 05	18 28
21	5 45	18 01	5 55	18 11	5 52	18 09	5 53	18 10	5 50	18 08	6 00	18 19	6 07	18 25
22	5 46	17 59	5 56	18 09	5 53	18 06	5 55	18 08	5 52	18 05	6 02	18 16	6 09	18 23
23	5 48	17 57	5 58	18 07	5 55	18 04	5 56	18 05	5 54	18 03	6 04	18 13	6 11	18 20
24	5 49	17 54	5 59	18 04	5 57	18 02	5 58	18 03	5 55	18 00	6 06	18 11	6 13	18 18
25	5 51	17 52	6 01	18 02	5 58	17 59	6 00	18 00	5 57	17 58	6 08	18 08	6 15	18 15
26	5 53	17 50	6 03	18 00	6 00	17 57	6 02	17 58	5 59	17 55	6 10	18 06	6 16	18 13
27	5 54	17 47	6 04	17 57	6 02	17 54	6 03	17 56	6 01	17 53	6 12	18 03	6 18	18 10
28	5 56	17 45	6 06	17 55	6 04	17 52	6 05	17 53	6 03	17 50	6 14	18 00	6 20	18 07
29	5 58	17 43	6 08	17 53	6 05	17 50	6 07	17 51	6 05	17 48	6 16	17 58	6 22	18 05
30	5 59	17 40	6 09	17 50	6 07	17 47	6 09	17 48	6 07	17 45	6 18	17 55	6 24	18 02

JUPITER

Day	*RA*	*Dec.*	*Transit*	*5° high*	
				52°	56°
	h m	° ′	h m	h m	h m
1	12 57.5	− 4 56	14 15	19 15	19 08
11	13 04.8	− 5 42	13 43	18 39	18 31
21	13 12.4	− 6 30	13 11	18 03	17 54
31	13 20.3	− 7 18	12 40	17 27	17 18

Diameters – equatorial 31″ polar 29″

SATURN

Day	*RA*	*Dec.*	*Transit*	*5° high*	
				52°	56°
	h m	° ′	h m	h m	h m
1	21 55.4	−14 17	23 11	3 22	3 04
11	21 52.7	−14 31	22 29	2 38	2 20
21	21 50.3	−14 43	21 47	1 55	1 37
31	21 48.3	−14 53	21 06	1 13	0 54

Diameters – equatorial 19″ polar 17″
Rings – major axis 42″ minor axis 9″

URANUS

Day	*RA*	*Dec.*	*Transit*	*10° high*	
				52°	56°
	h m	° ′	h m	h m	h m
1	19 20.5	−22 38	20 36	22 48	21 45
11	19 19.7	−22 39	19 56	22 07	21 05
21	19 19.3	−22 40	19 17	21 28	20 25
31	19 19.3	−22 40	18 37	20 48	19 46

Diameter 4″

NEPTUNE

Day	*RA*	*Dec.*	*Transit*	*10° high*	
				52°	56°
	h m	° ′	h m	h m	h m
1	19 20.2	−21 29	20 36	23 00	22 10
11	19 19.7	−21 30	19 56	22 20	21 29
21	19 19.3	−21 31	19 17	21 41	20 50
31	19 19.2	−21 32	18 37	21 01	20 10

Diameter 2″

October 1993

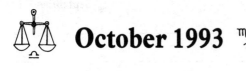

TENTH MONTH, 31 DAYS. *Octo* (eight), eighth month of Roman pre-Julian calendar

Sun's Longitude 210° ♏ 23^{d} 10^{h}

1	*Friday*	*Michaelmas Law Sittings begin.* Stanley Holloway *b.* 1890.	*week* 40 *day* 274
2	*Saturday*	Richard III *b.* 1452. Mahatma Gandhi *b.* 1869.	275
3	*Sunday*	**18th S. after Pentecost.** William Morris *d.* 1896.	*week* 41 *day* 276
4	*Monday*	First English Bible printed 1535. Damon Runyon *b.* 1884.	277
5	*Tuesday*	Denis Diderot *b.* 1713. Portugal declared a republic 1910.	278
6	*Wednesday*	Helen Wills-Moody *b.* 1905. Anwar Sadat *assass.* 1981.	279
7	*Thursday*	William Laud *b.* 1573. Marie Lloyd *d.* 1922.	280
8	*Friday*	Henry Fielding *d.* 1754. Great fire of Chicago 1871.	281
9	*Saturday*	Camille Saint-Saëns *b.* 1835. André Maurois *d.* 1967.	282
10	*Sunday*	**19th S. after Pentecost.** Sir Ralph Richardson *d.* 1983.	*week* 42 *day* 283
11	*Monday*	Second Boer War began 1899. Jean Cocteau *d.* 1963.	284
12	*Tuesday*	Elizabeth Fry *d.* 1845. Robert Stephenson *d.* 1859.	285
13	*Wednesday*	Joachim Murat *d.* 1815. Sir Henry Irving *d.* 1905.	286
14	*Thursday*	Harold II *d.* 1066. William Penn *b.* 1644.	287
15	*Friday*	Duchess of York *b.* 1959. P. G. Wodehouse *b.* 1881.	288
16	*Saturday*	Günter Grass *b.* 1927. Moshe Dayan *d.* 1981	289
17	*Sunday*	**20th S. after Pentecost.** Arthur Miller *b.* 1915.	*week* 43 *day* 290
18	*Monday*	**St Luke.** Leipzig 1813. Charles Babbage *b.* 1871.	291
19	*Tuesday*	King John *d.* 1216. Dean Jonathan Swift *d.* 1745.	292
20	*Wednesday*	Sir Christopher Wren *b.* 1632. Navarino 1827.	293
21	*Thursday*	Sir Georg Solti *b.* 1912. Geoffrey Boycott *b.* 1940.	294
22	*Friday*	Edict of Nantes revoked 1685. Pablo Casals *d.* 1973.	295
23	*Saturday*	First Parliament of Great Britain met 1707. Pelé *b.* 1940.	296
24	*Sunday*	**9th S. before Christmas.** Alessandro Scarlatti *d.* 1725.	*week* 44 *day* 297
25	*Monday*	King Stephen *d.* 1154. Pablo Picasso *b.* 1881.	298
26	*Tuesday*	Georges Danton *b.* 1759. Leon Trotsky *b.* 1879 os.	299
27	*Wednesday*	Dylan Thomas *b.* 1914.	300
28	*Thursday*	**SS Simon and Jude.** Evelyn Waugh *b.* 1903.	301
29	*Friday*	International Red Cross founded 1863.	302
30	*Saturday*	Ezra Pound *b.* 1885. Dame Rose Macaulay *d.* 1958.	303
31	*Sunday*	**8th S. before Christmas.** Hallowmass Eve.	*week* 45 *day* 304

Astronomical Phenomena

d	h	
5	08	Mars in conjunction with Mercury. Mars 2° N.
13	21	Venus in conjunction with Moon. Venus 6° N.
14	04	Mercury at greatest elongation E. 25°
15	15	Jupiter in conjunction with Moon. Jupiter 4° N.
16	22	Mars in conjunction with Moon. Mars 2° N.
17	06	Mercury in conjunction with Moon. Mercury 2° S.
18	10	Jupiter in conjunction with Sun
24	09	Saturn in conjunction with Moon. Saturn 6° S.
28	20	Mars in conjunction with Mercury. Mars 2° N.

Constellations

The following constellations are near the meridian at

September 1d, 24h	October 16d, 21h
September 15d, 23h	November 1d, 20h
October 1d, 22h	November 15d, 19h

Ursa Major (below the Pole), Cepheus, Cassiopeia, Cygnus, Lacerta, Andromeda, Pegasus, Capricornus, Aquarius and Piscis Austrinus

Minima of Algol

d	h	d	h	d	h
2	10.5	13	21.7	25	09.0
5	07.3	16	18.6	28	05.8
8	04.1	19	15.4	31	02.6
11	00.9	22	12.2		

The Moon

Phases, Apsides and Node	d	h	m
☾ Last Quarter	8	19	35
● New Moon	15	11	36
☽ First Quarter	22	08	52
○ Full Moon	30	12	38
Perigee (357,243 km)	15	01	47
Apogee (406,103 km)	27	23	56

Mean longitude of ascending node on 1 Oct., 246°

THE SUN

s.d. 16′.1

Day	Right Ascension	Dec. −	Equation of time	Rise 52°	Rise 56°	Transit	Set 52°	Set 56°	Sidereal time	Transit of First Point of Aries
	h m s	° ′	m s	h m	h m	h m	h m	h m	h m s	h m s
1	12 28 46	3 06	+10 11	6 01	6 03	11 50	17 38	17 35	0 38 57	23 17 13
2	12 32 23	3 30	+10 31	6 02	6 05	11 49	17 35	17 33	0 42 54	23 13 17
3	12 36 01	3 53	+10 50	6 04	6 07	11 49	17 33	17 30	0 46 50	23 09 21
4	12 39 38	4 16	+11 08	6 06	6 09	11 49	17 31	17 28	0 50 47	23 05 25
5	12 43 17	4 39	+11 27	6 07	6 11	11 48	17 28	17 25	0 54 43	23 01 30
6	12 46 55	5 02	+11 45	6 09	6 13	11 48	17 26	17 22	0 58 40	22 57 34
7	12 50 34	5 25	+12 02	6 11	6 15	11 48	17 24	17 20	1 02 37	22 53 38
8	12 54 14	5 48	+12 20	6 13	6 17	11 48	17 22	17 17	1 06 33	22 49 42
9	12 57 53	6 11	+12 36	6 14	6 19	11 47	17 19	17 15	1 10 30	22 45 46
10	13 01 34	6 34	+12 52	6 16	6 21	11 47	17 17	17 12	1 14 26	22 41 50
11	13 05 15	6 57	+13 08	6 18	6 23	11 47	17 15	17 10	1 18 23	22 37 54
12	13 08 56	7 19	+13 24	6 19	6 25	11 46	17 13	17 07	1 22 19	22 33 58
13	13 12 38	7 42	+13 38	6 21	6 27	11 46	17 10	17 04	1 26 16	22 30 02
14	13 16 20	8 04	+13 53	6 23	6 29	11 46	17 08	17 02	1 30 12	22 26 06
15	13 20 03	8 26	+14 06	6 25	6 31	11 46	17 06	16 59	1 34 09	22 22 11
16	13 23 46	8 49	+14 19	6 26	6 33	11 46	17 04	16 57	1 38 06	22 18 15
17	13 27 30	9 11	+14 32	6 28	6 35	11 45	17 02	16 54	1 42 02	22 14 19
18	13 31 15	9 32	+14 44	6 30	6 37	11 45	17 00	16 52	1 45 59	22 10 23
19	13 35 00	9 54	+14 55	6 32	6 39	11 45	16 58	16 50	1 49 55	22 06 27
20	13 38 46	10 16	+15 06	6 33	6 42	11 45	16 55	16 47	1 53 52	22 02 31
21	13 42 32	10 37	+15 16	6 35	6 44	11 45	16 53	16 45	1 57 48	21 58 35
22	13 46 19	10 59	+15 26	6 37	6 46	11 44	16 51	16 42	2 01 45	21 54 39
23	13 50 07	11 20	+15 34	6 39	6 48	11 44	16 49	16 40	2 05 41	21 50 43
24	13 53 55	11 41	+15 43	6 40	6 50	11 44	16 47	16 38	2 09 38	21 46 47
25	13 57 44	12 02	+15 50	6 42	6 52	11 44	16 45	16 35	2 13 35	21 42 51
26	14 01 34	12 22	+15 57	6 44	6 54	11 44	16 43	16 33	2 17 31	21 38 56
27	14 05 25	12 43	+16 03	6 46	6 56	11 44	16 41	16 31	2 21 28	21 35 00
28	14 09 16	13 03	+16 08	6 48	6 58	11 44	16 39	16 28	2 25 24	21 31 04
29	14 13 08	13 23	+16 13	6 49	7 00	11 44	16 37	16 26	2 29 21	21 27 08
30	14 17 00	13 43	+16 17	6 51	7 03	11 44	16 35	16 24	2 33 17	21 23 12
31	14 20 54	14 02	+16 20	6 53	7 05	11 44	16 34	16 22	2 37 14	21 19 16

DURATION OF TWILIGHT (in minutes)

Latitude	52°	56°	52°	56°
	1 October		11 October	
Civil	34	37	34	37
Nautical	73	80	73	80
Astronomical	113	125	112	124
	21 October		31 October	
Civil	34	38	36	40
Nautical	74	81	75	83
Astronomical	113	124	114	126

THE NIGHT SKY

Mercury is unsuitably placed for observation, even though it is at greatest eastern elongation on the 14th.

Venus is a brilliant morning object, magnitude −3.8, though gradually drawing closer to the Sun.

Mars is unsuitably placed for observation.

Jupiter is at conjunction on the 18th and thus remains too close to the Sun for observation throughout October.

Saturn, magnitude +0.5, continues to be visible as an evening object in the S. and SW sky, in Capricornus. The rings of Saturn present a beautiful spectacle to the observer, even with only a small telescope.

THE MOON

Day	RA	Dec.	Hor. par.	Semi-diam.	Sun's co-long.	PA. of Bright Limb	Phase	Age	Rise 52°	Rise 56°	Transit	Set 52°	Set 56°
	h m	°	′	′	°	°	%	d	h m	h m	h m	h m	h m
1	0 31	+ 7.8	54.0	14.7	92	6	100	14.9	17 26	17 17	—	6 49	6 57
2	1 16	+11.7	54.0	14.7	104	54	99	15.9	17 49	17 36	0 34	7 55	8 07
3	2 03	+15.2	54.1	14.8	117	64	96	16.9	18 15	17 59	1 18	9 00	9 16
4	2 51	+18.1	54.4	14.8	129	71	91	17.9	18 47	18 28	2 04	10 04	10 23
5	3 41	+20.2	54.7	14.9	141	76	85	18.9	19 27	19 05	2 52	11 05	11 27
6	4 33	+21.4	55.2	15.0	153	82	77	19.9	20 15	19 52	3 42	12 01	12 23
7	5 27	+21.6	55.8	15.2	165	87	68	20.9	21 13	20 51	4 34	12 50	13 12
8	6 21	+20.7	56.5	15.4	177	93	59	21.9	22 19	22 00	5 26	13 31	13 51
9	7 16	+18.7	57.3	15.6	190	97	48	22.9	23 32	23 17	6 19	14 06	14 22
10	8 10	+15.6	58.2	15.9	202	101	37	23.9	—	—	7 11	14 36	14 48
11	9 05	+11.6	59.1	16.1	214	104	27	24.9	0 49	0 39	8 04	15 02	15 10
12	10 00	+ 6.8	60.0	16.3	226	106	17	25.9	2 10	2 05	8 56	15 27	15 29
13	10 55	+ 1.5	60.7	16.5	238	105	9	26.9	3 34	3 33	9 50	15 50	15 48
14	11 51	− 4.1	61.2	16.7	251	102	4	27.9	4 59	5 04	10 44	16 15	16 09
15	12 48	− 9.4	61.4	16.7	263	84	0	28.9	6 26	6 36	11 41	16 44	16 32
16	13 47	−14.1	61.2	16.7	275	312	0	0.5	7 52	8 07	12 39	17 17	17 01
17	14 48	−17.9	60.8	16.6	287	291	3	1.5	9 15	9 34	13 39	17 58	17 37
18	15 50	−20.4	60.0	16.4	299	283	9	2.5	10 29	10 51	14 39	18 47	18 25
19	16 51	−21.5	59.2	16.1	312	276	17	3.5	11 31	11 54	15 38	19 46	19 23
20	17 51	−21.3	58.2	15.9	324	270	26	4.5	12 21	12 42	16 34	20 51	20 30
21	18 48	−19.8	57.2	15.6	336	264	36	5.5	13 00	13 18	17 27	22 00	21 42
22	19 42	−17.3	56.4	15.4	348	260	46	6.5	13 31	13 45	18 16	23 09	22 56
23	20 32	−14.0	55.6	15.2	0	256	56	7.5	13 56	14 06	19 02	—	—
24	21 20	−10.3	55.0	15.0	13	254	66	8.5	14 17	14 24	19 45	0 17	0 08
25	22 06	− 6.1	54.5	14.9	25	252	75	9.5	14 36	14 39	20 27	1 24	1 19
26	22 51	− 1.8	54.2	14.8	37	252	83	10.5	14 54	14 53	21 09	2 30	2 29
27	23 35	+ 2.5	54.0	14.7	49	253	89	11.5	15 12	15 08	21 50	3 35	3 38
28	0 19	+ 6.8	54.0	14.7	61	255	94	12.5	15 32	15 24	22 32	4 40	4 47
29	1 04	+10.8	54.0	14.7	73	259	98	13.5	15 53	15 42	23 16	5 46	5 56
30	1 51	+14.4	54.2	14.8	86	275	100	14.5	16 19	16 04	—	6 51	7 06
31	2 39	+17.4	54.4	14.8	98	53	100	15.5	16 49	16 31	0 02	7 56	8 14

MERCURY

Day	RA	Dec.	Diam.	Phase	Transit	
	h m	°			h m	
1	13 49	−12.9	—	—	13 11	Mercury is
4	14 04	−14.6	—	—	13 14	too close to
7	14 18	−16.2	—	—	13 16	the Sun for
10	14 32	−17.6	—	—	13 18	observation
13	14 45	−18.9	—	—	13 18	
16	14 56	−19.9	—	—	13 18	
19	15 06	−20.7	—	—	13 15	
22	15 13	−21.2	—	—	13 10	
25	15 17	−21.3	—	—	13 01	
28	15 16	−20.9	—	—	12 48	
31	15 10	−20.0	—	—	12 30	

VENUS

Day	RA	Dec.	Diam.	Phase	Transit	5° high 52°	5° high 56°
	h m	°	″	%	h m	h m	h m
1	10 54	8.4	11	89	10 15	4 05	4 01
6	11 17	6.1	11	90	10 18	4 20	4 18
11	11 40	3.8	11	91	10 21	4 35	4 35
16	12 02	1.4	11	92	10 25	4 50	4 53
21	12 25	− 1.0	11	93	10 28	5 06	5 10
26	12 48	− 3.5	11	94	10 31	5 22	5 28
31	13 11	− 5.9	11	95	10 34	5 38	5 47

MARS

Day	RA	Dec.	Diam.	Phase	Transit	
1	14 02	−12.4	—	—	13 22	Mars is
6	14 15	−13.6	—	—	13 16	too close to
11	14 28	−14.7	—	—	13 09	the Sun for
16	14 42	−15.8	—	—	13 03	observation
21	14 56	−16.9	—	—	12 57	
26	15 10	−17.9	—	—	12 51	
31	15 24	−18.9	—	—	12 46	

SUNRISE AND SUNSET

	London		Bristol		Birmingham		Manchester		Newcastle		Glasgow		Belfast	
	0°05′	51°30′	2°35′	51°28′	1°55′	52°28′	2°15′	53°28′	1°37′	54°59′	4°14′	55°52′	5°56′	54°35′
	h m	h m	h m	h m	h m	h m	h m	h m	h m	h m	h m	h m	h m	h m
1	6 01	17 38	6 11	17 48	6 09	17 45	6 10	17 46	6 09	17 42	6 20	17 52	6 26	18 00
2	6 02	17 36	6 12	17 46	6 10	17 43	6 12	17 43	6 11	17 40	6 22	17 50	6 28	17 57
3	6 04	17 34	6 14	17 44	6 12	17 40	6 14	17 41	6 13	17 37	6 24	17 47	6 30	17 55
4	6 06	17 31	6 16	17 41	6 14	17 38	6 16	17 39	6 14	17 35	6 26	17 45	6 31	17 52
5	6 07	17 29	6 17	17 39	6 15	17 36	6 18	17 36	6 16	17 32	6 28	17 42	6 33	17 50
6	6 09	17 27	6 19	17 37	6 17	17 33	6 19	17 34	6 18	17 30	6 30	17 39	6 35	17 47
7	6 11	17 25	6 21	17 35	6 19	17 31	6 21	17 31	6 20	17 27	6 32	17 37	6 37	17 45
8	6 12	17 22	6 22	17 32	6 21	17 29	6 23	17 29	6 22	17 25	6 34	17 34	6 39	17 43
9	6 14	17 20	6 24	17 30	6 22	17 27	6 25	17 27	6 24	17 22	6 36	17 32	6 41	17 40
10	6 16	17 18	6 26	17 28	6 24	17 24	6 27	17 24	6 26	17 20	6 38	17 29	6 43	17 38
11	6 17	17 16	6 27	17 26	6 26	17 22	6 28	17 22	6 28	17 17	6 40	17 27	6 45	17 35
12	6 19	17 14	6 29	17 24	6 28	17 20	6 30	17 20	6 30	17 15	6 42	17 24	6 47	17 33
13	6 21	17 11	6 31	17 22	6 29	17 17	6 32	17 17	6 32	17 13	6 44	17 22	6 49	17 30
14	6 22	17 09	6 32	17 19	6 31	17 15	6 34	17 15	6 34	17 10	6 46	17 19	6 50	17 28
15	6 24	17 07	6 34	17 17	6 33	17 13	6 36	17 13	6 36	17 08	6 48	17 17	6 52	17 26
16	6 26	17 05	6 36	17 15	6 35	17 11	6 38	17 11	6 38	17 05	6 50	17 14	6 54	17 23
17	6 28	17 03	6 38	17 13	6 37	17 09	6 40	17 08	6 40	17 03	6 52	17 12	6 56	17 21
18	6 29	17 01	6 39	17 11	6 38	17 07	6 41	17 06	6 42	17 01	6 54	17 09	6 58	17 19
19	6 31	16 59	6 41	17 09	6 40	17 04	6 43	17 04	6 44	16 58	6 56	17 07	7 00	17 16
20	6 33	16 57	6 43	17 07	6 42	17 02	6 45	17 02	6 46	16 56	6 58	17 04	7 02	17 14
21	6 35	16 55	6 44	17 05	6 44	17 00	6 47	16 59	6 48	16 54	7 00	17 02	7 04	17 12
22	6 36	16 53	6 46	17 03	6 45	16 58	6 49	16 57	6 50	16 51	7 02	17 00	7 06	17 09
23	6 38	16 51	6 48	17 01	6 47	16 56	6 51	16 55	6 52	16 49	7 04	16 57	7 08	17 07
24	6 40	16 49	6 50	16 59	6 49	16 54	6 53	16 53	6 54	16 47	7 07	16 55	7 10	17 05
25	6 41	16 47	6 51	16 57	6 51	16 52	6 55	16 51	6 56	16 44	7 09	16 53	7 12	17 03
26	6 43	16 45	6 53	16 55	6 53	16 50	6 57	16 49	6 58	16 42	7 11	16 50	7 14	17 01
27	6 45	16 43	6 55	16 53	6 55	16 48	6 58	16 47	7 00	16 40	7 13	16 48	7 16	16 58
28	6 47	16 41	6 57	16 51	6 56	16 46	7 00	16 45	7 02	16 38	7 15	16 46	7 18	16 56
29	6 48	16 39	6 58	16 49	6 58	16 44	7 02	16 42	7 04	16 36	7 17	16 43	7 20	16 54
30	6 50	16 37	7 00	16 47	7 00	16 42	7 04	16 40	7 06	16 34	7 19	16 41	7 22	16 52
31	6 52	16 35	7 02	16 45	7 02	16 40	7 06	16 38	7 08	16 31	7 21	16 39	7 24	16 50

JUPITER

Day	*RA*	*Dec.*	*Transit*	
	h m	° ′	h m	
1	13 20.3	−7 18	12 40	Jupiter is
11	13 28.4	−8 07	12 08	too close to
21	13 36.5	−8 54	11 37	the Sun for
31	13 44.7	−9 41	11 06	observation

Diameters – equatorial 31″ polar 29″

SATURN

Day	*RA*	*Dec.*	*Transit*	*5° high*	
				52°	56°
	h m	° ′	h m	h m	h m
1	21 48.3	−14 53	21 06	1 13	0 54
11	21 46.9	−15 00	20 25	0 31	0 13
21	21 46.1	−15 03	19 45	23 47	23 28
31	21 45.9	−15 03	19 06	23 07	22 49

Diameters – equatorial 18″ polar 16″
Rings – major axis 41″ minor axis 9″

URANUS

Day	*RA*	*Dec.*	*Transit*	*10° high*	
				52°	56°
	h m	° ′	h m	h m	h m
1	19 19.3	−22 40	18 37	20 48	19 46
11	19 19.6	−22 39	17 58	20 10	19 07
21	19 20.3	−22 38	17 20	19 31	18 29
31	19 21.3	−22 36	16 41	18 53	17 52

Diameter 4″

NEPTUNE

Day	*RA*	*Dec.*	*Transit*	*10° high*	
				52°	56°
	h m	° ′	h m	h m	h m
1	19 19.2	−21 32	18 37	21 01	20 10
11	19 19.4	−21 32	17 58	20 22	19 31
21	19 19.8	−21 32	17 19	19 43	18 52
31	19 20.4	−21 31	16 40	19 05	18 14

Diameter 2″

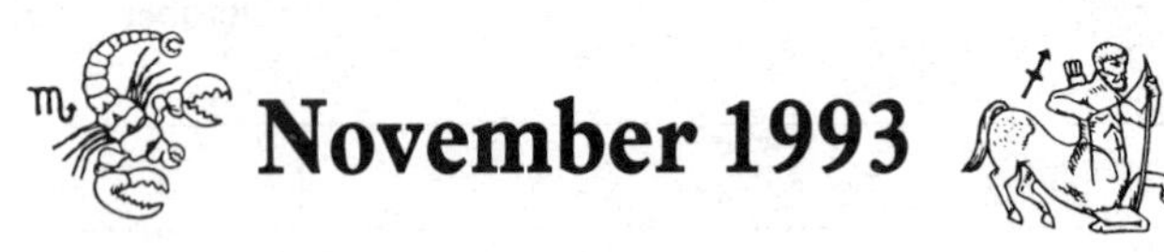

November 1993

ELEVENTH MONTH, 30 DAYS. *Novem* (nine), ninth month of Roman pre-Julian calendar

Sun's Longitude 240° ♐ 22d 07h

1	*Monday*	**All Saints.** Spencer Perceval *b.* 1762. L. S. Lowry *b.* 1887	*week* 45 *day* 305
2	*Tuesday*	Edward V *b.* 1470. *Daily Mirror* first issued 1903.	306
3	*Wednesday*	Vincenzo Bellini *b.* 1801. Henri Matisse *d.* 1954.	307
4	*Thursday*	William III *b.* 1650. Wilfred Owen *d.* 1918.	308
5	*Friday*	Angelica Kauffmann *d.* 1807. Vladimir Horowitz *d.* 1989.	309
6	*Saturday*	Colley Cibber *b.* 1671. John Philip Sousa *b.* 1854.	310
7	*Sunday*	**7th S. before Christmas.** Sir Godfrey Kneller *d.* 1723.	*week* 46 *day* 311
8	*Monday*	Thomas Bewick *d.* 1828. Sir Arnold Bax *b.* 1883.	312
9	*Tuesday*	Ramsay MacDonald *d.* 1937. Charles de Gaulle *d.* 1970.	313
10	*Wednesday*	William Hogarth *b.* 1697. Johann von Schiller *b.* 1759.	314
11	*Thursday*	Armistice Day. Sir Edward German *d.* 1936.	315
12	*Friday*	General Thomas Fairfax *d.* 1671. Sinking of the *Tirpitz* 1944.	316
13	*Saturday*	Lord Mayor's Day. Gioacchino Rossini *d.* 1868.	317
14	*Sunday*	**6th S. before Christmas.** *Prince of Wales b. 1948.*	*week* 47 *day* 318
15	*Monday*	George Romney *d.* 1802. Daniel Barenboim *b.* 1942.	319
16	*Tuesday*	Sir Oswald Mosley *b.* 1896. Arthur Askey *d.* 1982.	320
17	*Wednesday*	Viscount Montgomery of Alemein *b.* 1887.	321
18	*Thursday*	Louise Daguerre *b.* 1789. Niels Bohr *d.* 1962.	322
19	*Friday*	Gettysburg address by Abraham Lincoln 1863.	323
20	*Saturday*	*Queen's Wedding Day 1947.* General Franco *d.* 1975.	324
21	*Sunday*	**5th S. before Christmas.** Sir Arthur Quiller-Couch *b.* 1863.	*week* 48 *day* 325
22	*Monday*	Benjamin Britten *b.* 1913. Mae West *d.* 1981.	326
23	*Tuesday*	Perkin Warbeck *d.* 1499. Thomas Tallis *d.* 1585.	327
24	*Wednesday*	John Knox *d.* 1572. Grace Darling *b.* 1815.	328
25	*Thursday*	Leonard Woolf *b.* 1880. Lilian Baylis *d.* 1937.	329
26	*Friday*	William Cowper *b.* 1731. John McAdam *d.* 1836.	330
27	*Saturday*	Fanny Kemble *b.* 1809. Eugene O'Neill *d.* 1953.	331
28	*Sunday*	**1st S. in Advent.** Friedrich Engels *b.* 1820.	*week* 49 *day* 332
29	*Monday*	C. S. Lewis *b.* 1898. Cary Grant *d.* 1986.	333
30	*Tuesday*	**St Andrew.** Oscar Wilde *d.* 1900.	334

Astronomical Phenomena

d	h	
6	04	Mercury in inferior conjunction (transit)
8	20	Jupiter in conjunction with Venus. Jupiter 0°.3 S.
12	12	Jupiter in conjunction with Moon. Jupiter 4° N.
12	18	Venus in conjunction with Moon. Venus 4° N.
12	22	Mercury in conjunction with Moon. Mercury 4° N.
13		Partial eclipse of Sun (*see* page 71)
14	09	Venus in conjunction with Mercury. Venus 0°.6 S.
14	18	Mars in conjunction with Moon. Mars 0°.5 S.
17	18	Pluto in conjunction with Sun
20	17	Saturn in conjunction with Moon. Saturn 6° S.
22	16	Mercury at greatest elongation W. 20°
29		Total eclipse of Moon (*see* page 71)

Constellations

The following constellations are near the meridian at

October 1d, 24h	November 15d, 21h
October 16d, 23h	December 1d, 20h
November 1d, 22h	December 16d, 19h

Ursa Major (below the Pole), Cepheus, Cassiopeia, Andromeda, Pegasus, Pisces, Aquarius and Cetus

Minima of Algol

d	h	d	h	d	h
2	23.4	14	10.7	23	01.1
5	20.2	17	07.5	25	22.0
8	17.1	20	04.3	28	18.8
11	13.9				

The Moon

Phases, Apsides and Node	d	h	m
☾ Last Quarter	7	06	36
● New Moon	13	21	34
☽ First Quarter	21	02	03
○ Full Moon	29	06	31
Perigee (360,143 km)	12	12	01
Apogee (405,302 km)	24	12	33

Mean longitude of ascending node on 1 Nov., 244°

THE SUN

s.d. 16′.2

Day	Right Ascension	Dec. −	Equation of time	Rise 52°	Rise 56°	Transit	Set 52°	Set 56°	Sidereal time	Transit of First Point of Aries
	h m s	° ′	m s	h m	h m	h m	h m	h m	h m s	h m s
1	14 24 48	14 22	+16 22	6 55	7 07	11 44	16 32	16 20	2 41 10	21 15 20
2	14 28 43	14 41	+16 24	6 57	7 09	11 44	16 30	16 17	2 45 07	21 11 24
3	14 32 39	15 00	+16 24	6 58	7 11	11 44	16 28	16 15	2 49 04	21 07 28
4	14 36 36	15 18	+16 24	7 00	7 13	11 44	16 26	16 13	2 53 00	21 03 32
5	14 40 33	15 37	+16 23	7 02	7 15	11 44	16 25	16 11	2 56 57	20 59 36
6	14 44 32	15 55	+16 21	7 04	7 18	11 44	16 23	16 09	3 00 53	20 55 41
7	14 48 31	16 13	+16 19	7 06	7 20	11 44	16 21	16 07	3 04 50	20 51 45
8	14 52 31	16 31	+16 15	7 07	7 22	11 44	16 20	16 05	3 08 46	20 47 49
9	14 56 32	16 48	+16 11	7 09	7 24	11 44	16 18	16 03	3 12 43	20 43 53
10	15 00 34	17 05	+16 06	7 11	7 26	11 44	16 16	16 01	3 16 39	20 39 57
11	15 04 36	17 22	+16 00	7 13	7 28	11 44	16 15	15 59	3 20 36	20 36 01
12	15 08 40	17 38	+15 53	7 15	7 30	11 44	16 13	15 57	3 24 33	20 32 05
13	15 12 44	17 54	+15 45	7 16	7 32	11 44	16 12	15 56	3 28 29	20 28 09
14	15 16 50	18 10	+15 36	7 18	7 34	11 44	16 10	15 54	3 32 26	20 24 13
15	15 20 56	18 26	+15 26	7 20	7 36	11 45	16 09	15 52	3 36 22	20 20 17
16	15 25 03	18 41	+15 16	7 22	7 39	11 45	16 08	15 50	3 40 19	20 16 21
17	15 29 11	18 56	+15 05	7 23	7 41	11 45	16 06	15 49	3 44 15	20 12 26
18	15 33 19	19 10	+14 53	7 25	7 43	11 45	16 05	15 47	3 48 12	20 08 30
19	15 37 29	19 25	+14 40	7 27	7 45	11 45	16 04	15 46	3 52 08	20 04 34
20	15 41 39	19 39	+14 26	7 28	7 47	11 46	16 02	15 44	3 56 05	20 00 38
21	15 45 50	19 52	+14 12	7 30	7 49	11 46	16 01	15 43	4 00 02	19 56 42
22	15 50 02	20 05	+13 57	7 32	7 51	11 46	16 00	15 41	4 03 58	19 52 46
23	15 54 14	20 18	+13 40	7 33	7 52	11 46	15 59	15 40	4 07 55	19 48 50
24	15 58 27	20 30	+13 24	7 35	7 54	11 47	15 58	15 39	4 11 51	19 44 54
25	16 02 42	20 42	+13 06	7 37	7 56	11 47	15 57	15 37	4 15 48	19 40 58
26	16 06 56	20 54	+12 48	7 38	7 58	11 47	15 56	15 36	4 19 44	19 37 02
27	16 11 12	21 05	+12 29	7 40	8 00	11 48	15 55	15 35	4 23 41	19 33 06
28	16 15 28	21 16	+12 09	7 41	8 02	11 48	15 54	15 34	4 27 37	19 29 11
29	16 19 45	21 26	+11 49	7 43	8 03	11 48	15 54	15 33	4 31 34	19 25 15
30	16 24 03	21 37	+11 28	7 44	8 05	11 49	15 53	15 32	4 35 31	19 21 19

DURATION OF TWILIGHT (in minutes)

Latitude	52°	56°	52°	56°
	1 November		11 November	
Civil	36	40	37	41
Nautical	75	84	78	87
Astronomical	115	127	117	130
	21 November		30 November	
Civil	38	43	39	45
Nautical	80	90	82	93
Astronomical	120	134	123	137

THE NIGHT SKY

Mercury is visible in the mornings after the first twelve days of the month, magnitude +1.0 to −0.6, low above the SE horizon around the beginning of morning civil twilight. This is the most suitable morning apparition of the year for northern hemisphere observers. On the morning of the 12th the old crescent Moon, only one and a half days before New, may be seen about 10° to the right of, and a few degrees higher than, the planet, if conditions are good.

Venus, magnitude −3.8, is a brilliant morning object. It is drawing towards the Sun, the period available for observation shortening noticeably during the month. Venus passes Spica on the 2nd. On the morning of the 12th the thin crescent Moon will be seen approaching the planet. During the second half of the month Venus and Mercury are within a few degrees of each other.

Mars is unsuitably placed for observation.

Jupiter, magnitude −1.7, becomes visible as a bright morning object early in the month, low above the SE horizon for a short while before sunrise. Around 8–9 November Jupiter and Venus will be close together in the sky. Venus is two magnitudes brighter than Jupiter.

Saturn is an evening object, magnitude +0.7, in Capricornus.

THE MOON

Day	RA	Dec.	Hor. par.	Semi-diam.	Sun's co-long.	PA. of Bright Limb	Phase	Age	Rise 52°	Rise 56°	Transit	Set 52°	Set 56°
	h m	°	′	′	°	°	%	d	h m	h m	h m	h m	h m
1	3 29	+19.7	54.7	14.9	110	73	98	16.5	17 27	17 06	0 50	8 58	9 19
2	4 21	+21.1	55.1	15.0	122	81	94	17.5	18 13	17 50	1 39	9 56	10 18
3	5 14	+21.5	55.5	15.1	134	87	89	18.5	19 07	18 45	2 30	10 47	11 09
4	6 08	+20.9	56.0	15.3	146	93	82	19.5	20 10	19 51	3 22	11 30	11 51
5	7 02	+19.2	56.6	15.4	158	98	73	20.5	21 20	21 04	4 14	12 07	12 24
6	7 56	+16.4	57.2	15.6	171	102	64	21.5	22 33	22 22	5 05	12 38	12 51
7	8 49	+12.7	58.0	15.8	183	106	53	22.5	23 50	23 43	5 56	13 04	13 13
8	9 42	+ 8.3	58.7	16.0	195	108	42	23.5	—	—	6 47	13 28	13 32
9	10 34	+ 3.3	59.4	16.2	207	110	31	24.5	1 09	1 07	7 37	13 51	13 51
10	11 28	− 1.9	60.1	16.4	219	110	21	25.5	2 31	2 33	8 29	14 14	14 10
11	12 23	− 7.2	60.6	16.5	232	108	12	26.5	3 54	4 01	9 23	14 40	14 31
12	13 20	−12.1	60.8	16.6	244	105	5	27.5	5 19	5 31	10 20	15 10	14 56
13	14 20	−16.3	60.8	16.6	256	99	1	28.5	6 43	7 00	11 18	15 47	15 28
14	15 21	−19.4	60.6	16.5	268	318	0	0.1	8 02	8 23	12 19	16 32	16 10
15	16 24	−21.2	60.0	16.3	280	278	2	1.1	9 12	9 35	13 20	17 27	17 04
16	17 26	−21.5	59.2	16.1	293	270	6	2.1	10 10	10 32	14 19	18 32	18 10
17	18 26	−20.4	58.3	15.9	305	264	13	3.1	10 55	11 14	15 15	19 41	19 22
18	19 22	−18.2	57.4	15.6	317	259	21	4.1	11 30	11 46	16 07	20 52	20 38
19	20 15	−15.1	56.5	15.4	329	255	30	5.1	11 58	12 10	16 56	22 03	21 52
20	21 05	−11.4	55.7	15.2	341	252	39	6.1	12 21	12 29	17 41	23 12	23 05
21	21 52	− 7.3	55.1	15.0	353	250	49	7.1	12 41	12 45	18 24	—	—
22	22 38	− 3.0	54.6	14.9	6	249	59	8.1	12 59	13 00	19 06	0 19	0 16
23	23 22	+ 1.4	54.3	14.8	18	249	68	9.1	13 18	13 15	19 47	1 24	1 26
24	0 06	+ 5.6	54.1	14.7	30	249	76	10.1	13 37	13 30	20 29	2 29	2 35
25	0 51	+ 9.7	54.1	14.7	42	251	84	11.1	13 57	13 47	21 12	3 35	3 44
26	1 37	+13.4	54.2	14.8	54	253	90	12.1	14 21	14 07	21 57	4 40	4 53
27	2 25	+16.6	54.5	14.8	66	256	95	13.1	14 50	14 33	22 45	5 45	6 02
28	3 15	+19.2	54.8	14.9	79	259	98	14.1	15 25	15 05	23 34	6 49	7 09
29	4 07	+20.8	55.2	15.0	91	258	100	15.1	16 09	15 47	—	7 49	8 11
30	5 00	+21.5	55.6	15.2	103	92	99	16.1	17 01	16 39	0 26	8 43	9 06

MERCURY

Day	RA	Dec.	Diam.	Phase	Transit	5° high 52°	5° high 56°
	h m	°	″	%	h m	h m	h m
1	15 07	−19.5	10	9	12 22	8 50	9 16
4	14 55	−17.7	10	2	11 58	8 13	8 35
7	14 41	−15.6	10	0	11 32	7 33	7 52
10	14 28	−13.6	10	6	11 08	6 57	7 13
13	14 21	−12.2	9	18	10 50	6 30	6 45
16	14 20	−11.6	8	32	10 38	6 15	6 29
19	14 25	−11.8	7	46	10 32	6 10	6 25
22	14 34	−12.6	7	58	10 30	6 12	6 28
25	14 46	−13.7	6	68	10 31	6 20	6 37
28	15 01	−15.0	6	76	10 34	6 32	6 51
31	15 17	−16.4	6	82	10 38	6 45	7 06

VENUS

Day	RA	Dec.	Diam.	Phase	Transit	5° high 52°	5° high 56°
	h m	°	″	%	h m	h m	h m
1	13 16	− 6.4	11	95	10 35	5 42	5 51
6	13 39	− 8.7	10	95	10 39	5 58	6 10
11	14 03	−11.0	10	96	10 43	6 16	6 29
16	14 27	−13.2	10	97	10 47	6 33	6 50
21	14 51	−15.2	10	97	10 52	6 51	7 10
26	15 16	−17.1	10	98	10 57	7 09	7 31
31	15 42	−18.8	10	98	11 03	7 26	7 51

MARS

Day	RA	Dec.	Diam.	Phase	Transit	5° high
1	15 27	−19.1	—	—	12 45	Mars is
6	15 41	−20.0	—	—	12 40	too close to
11	15 56	−20.8	—	—	12 35	the Sun for
16	16 11	−21.5	—	—	12 31	observation
21	16 27	−22.2	—	—	12 26	
26	16 42	−22.8	—	—	12 22	
31	16 58	−23.3	—	—	12 18	

SUNRISE AND SUNSET

	London		Bristol		Birmingham		Manchester		Newcastle		Glasgow		Belfast	
	0°05′	51°30′	2°35′	51°28′	1°55′	52°28′	2°15′	53°28′	1°37′	54°59′	4°14′	55°52′	5°56′	54°35′
	h m	h m	h m	h m	h m	h m	h m	h m	h m	h m	h m	h m	h m	h m
1	6 54	16 33	7 04	16 43	7 04	16 38	7 08	16 37	7 10	16 29	7 23	16 37	7 26	16 48
2	6 56	16 32	7 05	16 42	7 06	16 36	7 10	16 35	7 12	16 27	7 26	16 35	7 28	16 46
3	6 57	16 30	7 07	16 40	7 07	16 34	7 12	16 33	7 14	16 25	7 28	16 33	7 30	16 44
4	6 59	16 28	7 09	16 38	7 09	16 33	7 14	16 31	7 16	16 23	7 30	16 31	7 32	16 42
5	7 01	16 26	7 11	16 36	7 11	16 31	7 16	16 29	7 18	16 21	7 32	16 28	7 34	16 40
6	7 03	16 25	7 12	16 35	7 13	16 29	7 17	16 27	7 20	16 19	7 34	16 26	7 36	16 38
7	7 04	16 23	7 14	16 33	7 15	16 27	7 19	16 25	7 22	16 17	7 36	16 24	7 38	16 36
8	7 06	16 21	7 16	16 32	7 17	16 26	7 21	16 24	7 24	16 15	7 38	16 22	7 40	16 34
9	7 08	16 20	7 18	16 30	7 18	16 24	7 23	16 22	7 26	16 14	7 40	16 21	7 42	16 32
10	7 10	16 18	7 20	16 28	7 20	16 22	7 25	16 20	7 28	16 12	7 42	16 19	7 44	16 31
11	7 11	16 17	7 21	16 27	7 22	16 21	7 27	16 18	7 30	16 10	7 44	16 17	7 46	16 29
12	7 13	16 15	7 23	16 25	7 24	16 19	7 29	16 17	7 32	16 08	7 47	16 15	7 48	16 27
13	7 15	16 14	7 25	16 24	7 26	16 18	7 31	16 15	7 34	16 07	7 49	16 13	7 50	16 25
14	7 17	16 12	7 26	16 23	7 27	16 16	7 33	16 14	7 36	16 05	7 51	16 11	7 52	16 24
15	7 18	16 11	7 28	16 21	7 29	16 15	7 35	16 12	7 38	16 03	7 53	16 10	7 54	16 22
16	7 20	16 10	7 30	16 20	7 31	16 13	7 36	16 11	7 40	16 02	7 55	16 08	7 56	16 21
17	7 22	16 08	7 32	16 19	7 33	16 12	7 38	16 09	7 42	16 00	7 57	16 06	7 58	16 19
18	7 23	16 07	7 33	16 17	7 35	16 11	7 40	16 08	7 44	15 59	7 59	16 05	8 00	16 18
19	7 25	16 06	7 35	16 16	7 36	16 09	7 42	16 07	7 46	15 57	8 01	16 03	8 02	16 16
20	7 27	16 05	7 37	16 15	7 38	16 08	7 44	16 05	7 48	15 56	8 03	16 02	8 03	16 15
21	7 28	16 04	7 38	16 14	7 40	16 07	7 45	16 04	7 50	15 54	8 05	16 00	8 05	16 14
22	7 30	16 03	7 40	16 13	7 41	16 06	7 47	16 03	7 52	15 53	8 07	15 59	8 07	16 12
23	7 32	16 02	7 41	16 12	7 43	16 05	7 49	16 02	7 54	15 52	8 09	15 58	8 09	16 11
24	7 33	16 01	7 43	16 11	7 45	16 04	7 51	16 00	7 55	15 50	8 11	15 56	8 11	16 10
25	7 35	16 00	7 45	16 10	7 46	16 03	7 52	15 59	7 57	15 49	8 12	15 55	8 12	16 09
26	7 36	15 59	7 46	16 09	7 48	16 02	7 54	15 58	7 59	15 48	8 14	15 54	8 14	16 08
27	7 38	15 58	7 48	16 08	7 49	16 01	7 56	15 57	8 01	15 47	8 16	15 53	8 16	16 06
28	7 39	15 57	7 49	16 07	7 51	16 00	7 57	15 56	8 02	15 46	8 18	15 52	8 18	16 05
29	7 41	15 56	7 51	16 06	7 53	15 59	7 59	15 56	8 04	15 45	8 20	15 51	8 19	16 05
30	7 42	15 56	7 52	16 06	7 54	15 58	8 00	15 55	8 06	15 44	8 21	15 50	8 21	16 04

JUPITER

Day	*RA*	*Dec.*	*Transit*	*5° high*	
				52°	56°
	h m	° ′	h m	h m	h m
1	13 45.6	−9 46	11 03	6 29	6 41
11	13 53.7	−10 31	10 32	6 02	6 15
21	14 01.7	−11 14	10 00	5 35	5 49
31	14 09.5	−11 55	9 29	5 07	5 22

Diameters – equatorial 31″ polar 29″

SATURN

Day	*RA*	*Dec.*	*Transit*	*5° high*	
				52°	56°
	h m	° ′	h m	h m	h m
1	21 45.9	−15 03	19 02	23 03	22 45
11	21 46.5	−14 59	18 23	22 25	22 07
21	21 47.7	−14 52	17 45	21 48	21 30
31	21 49.6	−14 41	17 08	21 12	20 54

Diameters – equatorial 17″ polar 15″
Rings – major axis 39″ minor axis 9″

URANUS

Day	*RA*	*Dec.*	*Transit*	
	h m	° ′	h m	
1	19 21.4	−22 35	16 38	Uranus is
11	19 22.8	−22 32	16 00	too close to
21	19 24.5	−22 29	15 22	the Sun for
31	19 26.4	−22 25	14 45	observation

Diameter 4″

NEPTUNE

Day	*RA*	*Dec.*	*Transit*	
	h m	° ′	h m	
1	19 20.4	−21 31	16 37	Neptune is
11	19 21.3	−21 29	15 58	too close to
21	19 22.3	−21 27	15 20	the Sun for
31	19 23.6	−21 25	14 42	observation

Diameter 2″

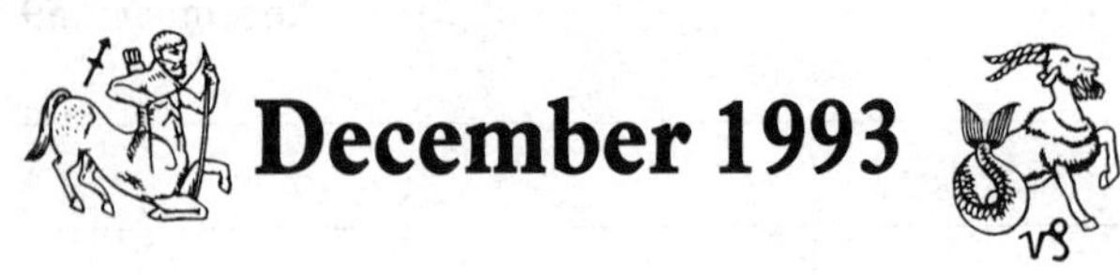

December 1993

TWELFTH MONTH, 31 DAYS. *Decem* (ten), tenth month of Roman pre-Julian calendar

Sun's Longitude 270° ♑ 21ᵈ 20ʰ

1	*Wednesday*	Edmund Campion *exec.* 1581. David Ben-Gurion *d.* 1973	*week* 49 *day* 335
2	*Thursday*	St Paul's Cathedral opened 1697. Maria Callas *b.* 1923.	336
3	*Friday*	Sir Rowland Hill *b.* 1795. Pierre Renoir *d.* 1919.	337
4	*Saturday*	Edith Cavell *b.* 1865. Edgar Wallace *b.* 1875.	338
5	*Sunday*	**2nd S. in Advent.** Wolfgang Amadeus Mozart *d.* 1791.	*week* 50 *day* 339
6	*Monday*	Henry VI *b.* 1421. Finland gained independence 1917.	340
7	*Tuesday*	Captain William Bligh *d.* 1817. Joyce Carey *b.* 1888.	341
8	*Wednesday*	Mary, Queen of Scots *b.* 1542. Golda Meir *d.* 1978.	342
9	*Thursday*	CHANUCAH begins. Dame Edith Sitwell *d.* 1964.	343
10	*Friday*	Royal Academy founded 1768. Emily Dickinson *b.* 1830.	344
11	*Saturday*	Hector Berlioz *b.* 1803. Alexander Solzhenitsyn *b.* 1918.	345
12	*Sunday*	**3rd S. in Advent.** Frank Sinatra *b.* 1915.	*week* 51 *day* 346
13	*Monday*	Dr Samuel Johnson *d.* 1784. Glen Byam Shaw *b.* 1904.	347
14	*Tuesday*	Prince Albert *d.* 1861. Amundsen reached South Pole 1911.	348
15	*Wednesday*	Jan Vermeer *d.* 1675. Walt Disney *d.* 1966.	349
16	*Thursday*	Ludwig von Beethoven *b.* 1770. Zoltan Kodaly *b.* 1882.	350
17	*Friday*	Simón Bolivar *d.* 1830. First flight by Wright brothers 1903.	351
18	*Saturday*	Christopher Fry *b.* 1907. Ben Travers *d.* 1980.	352
19	*Sunday*	**4th S. in Advent.** J. M. W. Turner *d.* 1851.	*week* 52 *day* 353
20	*Monday*	John Steinbeck *d.* 1968. Artur Rubinstein *d.* 1982.	354
21	*Tuesday*	*Michaelmas Law Sittings end.* Boccaccio *d.* 1375.	355
22	*Wednesday*	Dame Peggy Ashcroft *b.* 1907. Beatrix Potter *d.* 1943.	356
23	*Thursday*	Richard Arkwright *b.* 1732. Théophile Gautier *d.* 1872.	357
24	*Friday*	Christmas Eve. William Thackeray *d.* 1863.	358
25	*Saturday*	**Christmas Day.** Stone of Scone stolen 1950.	359
26	*Sunday*	**1st S. after Christmas.** Boxing Day.	*week* 53 *day* 360
27	*Monday*	**St John the Evangelist.** *Bank Holiday in the UK.*	361
28	*Tuesday*	**Holy Innocents.** *Bank Holiday in the UK.*	362
29	*Wednesday*	**St Stephen.** William Gladstone *b.* 1809.	363
30	*Thursday*	L. P. Hartley *b.* 1895. Josephine Butler *d.* 1906.	364
31	*Friday*	The farthing ceased to be legal tender 1960.	365

ASTRONOMICAL PHENOMENA

d	h	
10	06	Jupiter in conjunction with Moon. Jupiter 3° N.
12	11	Mercury in conjunction with Moon. Mercury 0°.1 S.
12	18	Venus in conjunction with Moon. Venus 0°.4 S.
13	16	Mars in conjunction with Moon. Mars 3° S.
18	05	Saturn in conjunction with Moon. Saturn 6° S.
21	20	Solstice
25	07	Venus in conjunction with Mercury. Venus 1° N.
27	02	Mars in conjunction with Sun

CONSTELLATIONS

The following constellations are near the meridian at

November 1d, 24h	December 16d, 21h
November 15d, 23h	January 1d, 20h
December 1d, 22h	January 16d, 19h

Ursa Major (below the Pole), Ursa Minor (below the Pole), Cassiopeia, Andromeda, Perseus, Triangulum, Aries, Taurus, Cetus and Eridanus

MINIMA OF ALGOL

d	h	d	h	d	h
1	15.6	13	02.9	24	14.1
4	12.4	15	23.7	27	11.0
7	09.2	18	20.5	30	07.8
10	06.0	21	17.3		

THE MOON

Phases, Apsides and Node	d	h	m
☾ Last Quarter	6	15	49
● New Moon	13	09	27
☽ First Quarter	20	22	26
○ Full Moon	28	23	05
Perigee (365,357 km)	10	14	07
Apogee (404,515 km)	22	07	49

Mean longitude of ascending node on 1 Dec., 243°

THE SUN s.d. 16′.3

Day	Right Ascension	Dec. −	Equation of time	Rise 52°	Rise 56°	Transit	Set 52°	Set 56°	Sidereal time	Transit of First Point of Aries
	h m s	° ′	m s	h m	h m	h m	h m	h m	h m s	h m s
1	16 28 21	21 46	+11 06	7 46	8 07	11 49	15 52	15 31	4 39 27	19 17 23
2	16 32 40	21 55	+10 43	7 47	8 08	11 49	15 52	15 30	4 43 24	19 13 27
3	16 37 00	22 04	+10 20	7 48	8 10	11 50	15 51	15 29	4 47 20	19 09 31
4	16 41 20	22 12	+ 9 57	7 50	8 12	11 50	15 51	15 29	4 51 17	19 05 35
5	16 45 41	22 20	+ 9 32	7 51	8 13	11 51	15 50	15 28	4 55 13	19 01 39
6	16 50 03	22 28	+ 9 07	7 52	8 15	11 51	15 50	15 27	4 59 10	18 57 43
7	16 54 25	22 35	+ 8 42	7 53	8 16	11 52	15 49	15 27	5 03 06	18 53 47
8	16 58 47	22 42	+ 8 16	7 55	8 17	11 52	15 49	15 26	5 07 03	18 49 51
9	17 03 10	22 48	+ 7 49	7 56	8 19	11 52	15 49	15 26	5 11 00	18 45 55
10	17 07 34	22 53	+ 7 23	7 57	8 20	11 53	15 49	15 26	5 14 56	18 42 00
11	17 11 58	22 59	+ 6 55	7 58	8 21	11 53	15 48	15 25	5 18 53	18 38 04
12	17 16 22	23 04	+ 6 27	7 59	8 22	11 54	15 48	15 25	5 22 49	18 34 08
13	17 20 47	23 08	+ 5 59	8 00	8 23	11 54	15 48	15 25	5 26 46	18 30 12
14	17 25 12	23 12	+ 5 31	8 01	8 24	11 55	15 48	15 25	5 30 42	18 26 16
15	17 29 37	23 15	+ 5 02	8 02	8 25	11 55	15 49	15 25	5 34 39	18 22 20
16	17 34 03	23 18	+ 4 33	8 03	8 26	11 56	15 49	15 25	5 38 35	18 18 24
17	17 38 28	23 21	+ 4 04	8 03	8 27	11 56	15 49	15 25	5 42 32	18 14 28
18	17 42 54	23 23	+ 3 34	8 04	8 28	11 57	15 49	15 25	5 46 29	18 10 32
19	17 47 20	23 24	+ 3 05	8 05	8 29	11 57	15 50	15 26	5 50 25	18 06 36
20	17 51 47	23 26	+ 2 35	8 05	8 29	11 58	15 50	15 26	5 54 22	18 02 40
21	17 56 13	23 26	+ 2 05	8 06	8 30	11 58	15 50	15 27	5 58 18	17 58 45
22	18 00 39	23 26	+ 1 35	8 06	8 30	11 59	15 51	15 27	6 02 15	17 54 49
23	18 05 06	23 26	+ 1 06	8 07	8 31	11 59	15 52	15 28	6 06 11	17 50 53
24	18 09 32	23 25	+ 0 36	8 07	8 31	12 00	15 52	15 28	6 10 08	17 46 57
25	18 13 58	23 24	+ 0 06	8 08	8 31	12 00	15 53	15 29	6 14 04	17 43 01
26	18 18 25	23 22	− 0 24	8 08	8 31	12 01	15 54	15 30	6 18 01	17 39 05
27	18 22 51	23 20	− 0 53	8 08	8 32	12 01	15 54	15 31	6 21 58	17 35 09
28	18 27 17	23 17	− 1 23	8 08	8 32	12 02	15 55	15 32	6 25 54	17 31 13
29	18 31 43	23 14	− 1 52	8 08	8 32	12 02	15 56	15 33	6 29 51	17 27 17
30	18 36 08	23 11	− 2 21	8 08	8 32	12 03	15 57	15 34	6 33 47	17 23 21
31	18 40 33	23 07	− 2 50	8 08	8 32	12 03	15 58	15 35	6 37 44	17 19 25

DURATION OF TWILIGHT (in minutes)

Latitude	52°	56°	52°	56°
	1 December		11 December	
Civil	40	45	41	47
Nautical	82	93	84	96
Astronomical	123	138	125	141
	21 December		31 December	
Civil	41	47	41	47
Nautical	85	97	84	96
Astronomical	126	142	125	141

THE NIGHT SKY

Mercury is visible as a difficult morning object, magnitude −0.6, low on the SE horizon around the beginning of morning civil twilight for the first week of the month. Thereafter it is unsuitably placed for observation.

Venus, magnitude −3.8, is a morning object for the first week of the month, but only visible low in the SE sky for a short while before dawn. Thereafter it is lost in the morning twilight.

Mars remains unsuitably placed for observation.

Jupiter is a bright morning object, magnitude −1.8, visible in the SE sky. By the end of the month it crosses the meridian at sunrise. During December Jupiter moves from Virgo into Libra. On the morning of the 10th the old crescent Moon passes 3° S. of the planet.

Saturn, magnitude +0.8, continues to be visible as an evening object in the SW sky. By the end of the year it is too low to be seen for long after 19h.

Meteors. The maximum of the well-known Geminid meteor shower occurs on the 13th. Conditions are favourable this year, in the absence of any moonlight.

THE MOON

Day	RA	Dec.	Hor. par.	Semi-diam.	Sun's co-long.	P.A. of Bright Limb	Phase	Age	Rise 52°	Rise 56°	Transit	Set 52°	Set 56°
	h m	°	′	′	°	°	%	d	h m	h m	h m	h m	h m
1	5 55	+21.1	56.1	15.3	115	96	97	17.1	18 03	17 42	1 18	9 30	9 51
2	6 49	+19.6	56.6	15.4	127	100	92	18.1	19 11	18 54	2 11	10 09	10 27
3	7 44	+17.1	57.1	15.5	139	104	86	19.1	20 23	20 10	3 02	10 41	10 56
4	8 37	+13.6	57.6	15.7	151	108	78	20.1	21 39	21 30	3 53	11 09	11 19
5	9 29	+ 9.4	58.1	15.8	163	110	68	21.1	22 56	22 51	4 43	11 33	11 39
6	10 21	+ 4.6	58.6	16.0	176	112	58	22.1	—	—	5 33	11 55	11 57
7	11 13	− 0.4	59.0	16.1	188	113	46	23.1	0 14	0 14	6 23	12 18	12 15
8	12 06	− 5.6	59.5	16.2	200	112	35	24.1	1 33	1 39	7 14	12 41	12 34
9	13 00	−10.5	59.8	16.3	212	110	24	25.1	2 54	3 04	8 07	13 08	12 57
10	13 57	−14.8	60.0	16.3	224	108	15	26.1	4 16	4 31	9 02	13 40	13 24
11	14 56	−18.3	60.0	16.3	237	104	8	27.1	5 36	5 55	10 01	14 20	14 00
12	15 57	−20.6	59.8	16.3	249	101	3	28.1	6 50	7 12	11 01	15 09	14 47
13	16 59	−21.5	59.4	16.2	261	109	0	29.1	7 53	8 16	12 01	16 09	15 46
14	18 00	−21.1	58.8	16.0	273	253	1	0.6	8 45	9 06	12 59	17 17	16 57
15	18 58	−19.3	58.1	15.8	285	255	3	1.6	9 26	9 44	13 54	18 29	18 12
16	19 54	−16.5	57.3	15.6	297	253	8	2.6	9 58	10 11	14 45	19 42	19 29
17	20 46	−12.9	56.5	15.4	310	250	15	3.6	10 23	10 33	15 33	20 53	20 45
18	21 35	− 8.9	55.8	15.2	322	248	23	4.6	10 45	10 51	16 18	22 02	21 58
19	22 22	− 4.6	55.2	15.0	334	247	32	5.6	11 04	11 07	17 01	23 09	23 09
20	23 07	− 0.1	54.7	14.9	346	246	41	6.6	11 23	11 21	17 43	—	—
21	23 52	+ 4.2	54.4	14.8	358	247	51	7.6	11 42	11 36	18 25	0 15	0 19
22	0 37	+ 8.4	54.2	14.8	10	248	60	8.6	12 01	11 53	19 07	1 21	1 28
23	1 22	+12.2	54.2	14.8	23	249	69	9.6	12 24	12 11	19 51	2 26	2 37
24	2 09	+15.6	54.4	14.8	35	252	77	10.6	12 50	12 34	20 38	3 31	3 46
25	2 58	+18.4	54.8	14.9	47	255	85	11.6	13 23	13 03	21 26	4 36	4 54
26	3 49	+20.4	55.2	15.0	59	258	91	12.6	14 03	13 41	22 17	5 38	5 59
27	4 43	+21.4	55.7	15.2	71	260	96	13.6	14 52	14 29	23 10	6 35	6 57
28	5 37	+21.4	56.3	15.3	83	258	99	14.6	15 50	15 29	—	7 25	7 47
29	6 33	+20.2	56.9	15.5	95	175	100	15.6	16 58	16 39	0 03	8 08	8 27
30	7 28	+18.0	57.4	15.6	108	115	99	16.6	18 10	17 56	0 57	8 44	8 59
31	8 23	+14.7	57.9	15.8	120	113	95	17.6	19 27	19 16	1 49	9 13	9 25

MERCURY

Day	RA	Dec.	Diam.	Phase	Transit	5° high 52°	5° high 56°
	h m	°	″	%	h m	h m	h m
1	15 17	−16.4	6	82	10 38	6 45	7 06
4	15 34	−17.8	5	86	10 44	7 00	7 24
7	15 52	−19.2	5	90	10 50	7 16	7 42
10	16 10	−20.4	5	92	10 57	7 33	8 01
13	16 29	−21.5	5	94	11 04	7 49	8 20
16	16 49	−22.5	5	96	11 12	8 05	8 39
19	17 09	−23.4	—	—	11 20	Mercury is	
22	17 29	−24.0	—	—	11 28	too close to	
25	17 49	−24.5	—	—	11 37	the Sun for	
28	18 10	−24.7	—	—	11 46	observation	
31	18 31	−24.8	—	—	11 55		

VENUS

Day	RA	Dec.	Diam.	Phase	Transit	5° high 52°	5° high 56°
	h m	°	″	%	h m	h m	h m
1	15 42	−18.8	10	98	11 03	7 26	7 51
6	16 08	−20.3	10	99	11 09	7 44	8 12
11	16 34	−21.5	10	99	11 16	8 00	8 31
16	17 01	−22.5	10	99	11 23	8 15	8 49
21	17 28	−23.2	10	99	11 30	8 29	9 05
26	17 55	−23.6	10	100	11 38	8 40	9 17
31	18 23	−23.7	10	100	11 46	8 48	9 26

MARS

Day	RA	Dec.	Diam.	Phase	Transit	5° high 52°	5° high 56°
1	16 58	−23.3	—	—	12 18	Mars is	
6	17 14	−23.6	—	—	12 15	too close to	
11	17 30	−23.9	—	—	12 11	the Sun for	
16	17 47	−24.1	—	—	12 08	observation	
21	18 03	−24.2	—	—	12 05		
26	18 20	−24.1	—	—	12 02		
31	18 36	−24.0	—	—	11 58		

SUNRISE AND SUNSET

	London		Bristol		Birmingham		Manchester		Newcastle		Glasgow		Belfast	
	0°05′	51°30′	2°35′	51°28′	1°55′	52°28′	2°15′	53°28′	1°37′	54°59′	4°14′	55°52′	5°56′	54°35′
	h m	h m	h m	h m	h m	h m	h m	h m	h m	h m	h m	h m	h m	h m
1	7 44	15 55	7 53	16 05	7 55	15 58	8 02	15 54	8 07	15 43	8 23	15 49	8 22	16 03
2	7 45	15 54	7 55	16 04	7 57	15 57	8 03	15 53	8 09	15 43	8 25	15 48	8 24	16 02
3	7 46	15 54	7 56	16 04	7 58	15 56	8 05	15 53	8 10	15 42	8 26	15 47	8 25	16 01
4	7 48	15 53	7 57	16 03	8 00	15 56	8 06	15 52	8 12	15 41	8 28	15 46	8 27	16 01
5	7 49	15 53	7 59	16 03	8 01	15 55	8 07	15 52	8 13	15 41	8 29	15 46	8 28	16 00
6	7 50	15 52	8 00	16 03	8 02	15 55	8 09	15 51	8 15	15 40	8 31	15 45	8 30	16 00
7	7 51	15 52	8 01	16 02	8 04	15 55	8 10	15 51	8 16	15 40	8 32	15 45	8 31	15 59
8	7 53	15 52	8 02	16 02	8 05	15 54	8 11	15 50	8 17	15 39	8 33	15 44	8 32	15 59
9	7 54	15 52	8 04	16 02	8 06	15 54	8 13	15 50	8 19	15 39	8 35	15 44	8 34	15 58
10	7 55	15 51	8 05	16 02	8 07	15 54	8 14	15 50	8 20	15 38	8 36	15 43	8 35	15 58
11	7 56	15 51	8 06	16 01	8 08	15 54	8 15	15 50	8 21	15 38	8 37	15 43	8 36	15 58
12	7 57	15 51	8 07	16 01	8 09	15 54	8 16	15 50	8 22	15 38	8 38	15 43	8 37	15 58
13	7 58	15 51	8 08	16 01	8 10	15 54	8 17	15 50	8 23	15 38	8 39	15 43	8 38	15 58
14	7 59	15 51	8 08	16 01	8 11	15 54	8 18	15 50	8 24	15 38	8 40	15 43	8 39	15 58
15	8 00	15 51	8 09	16 02	8 12	15 54	8 19	15 50	8 25	15 38	8 41	15 43	8 40	15 58
16	8 00	15 52	8 10	16 02	8 13	15 54	8 20	15 50	8 26	15 38	8 42	15 43	8 41	15 58
17	8 01	15 52	8 11	16 02	8 13	15 54	8 20	15 50	8 27	15 38	8 43	15 43	8 42	15 58
18	8 02	15 52	8 12	16 02	8 14	15 54	8 21	15 50	8 28	15 39	8 44	15 43	8 42	15 58
19	8 02	15 53	8 12	16 03	8 15	15 55	8 22	15 51	8 28	15 39	8 45	15 44	8 43	15 59
20	8 03	15 53	8 13	16 03	8 15	15 55	8 22	15 51	8 29	15 39	8 45	15 44	8 44	15 59
21	8 04	15 53	8 13	16 04	8 16	15 56	8 23	15 51	8 29	15 40	8 46	15 44	8 44	16 00
22	8 04	15 54	8 14	16 04	8 16	15 56	8 23	15 52	8 30	15 40	8 46	15 45	8 45	16 00
23	8 05	15 54	8 14	16 05	8 17	15 57	8 24	15 53	8 30	15 41	8 47	15 46	8 45	16 01
24	8 05	15 55	8 15	16 05	8 17	15 57	8 24	15 53	8 31	15 41	8 47	15 46	8 46	16 01
25	8 05	15 56	8 15	16 06	8 18	15 58	8 24	15 54	8 31	15 42	8 47	15 47	8 46	16 02
26	8 06	15 56	8 15	16 07	8 18	15 59	8 25	15 55	8 31	15 43	8 48	15 48	8 46	16 03
27	8 06	15 57	8 16	16 07	8 18	16 00	8 25	15 55	8 31	15 44	8 48	15 49	8 46	16 04
28	8 06	15 58	8 16	16 08	8 18	16 00	8 25	15 56	8 32	15 45	8 48	15 49	8 46	16 04
29	8 06	15 59	8 16	16 09	8 18	16 01	8 25	15 57	8 32	15 46	8 48	15 50	8 46	16 05
30	8 06	16 00	8 16	16 10	8 18	16 02	8 25	15 58	8 32	15 47	8 48	15 52	8 46	16 06
31	8 06	16 01	8 16	16 11	8 18	16 03	8 25	15 59	8 31	15 48	8 48	15 53	8 46	16 07

JUPITER

Day	*RA*	*Dec.*	*Transit*	*5° high*	
				52°	56°
	h m	° ′	h m	h m	h m
1	14 09.5	−11 55	9 29	5 07	5 22
11	14 16.9	−12 32	8 57	4 39	4 55
21	14 23.9	−13 06	8 24	4 10	4 26
31	14 30.3	−13 37	7 52	3 41	3 57

Diameters – equatorial 32″ polar 30″

SATURN

Day	*RA*	*Dec.*	*Transit*	*5° high*	
				52°	56°
	h m	° ′	h m	h m	h m
1	21 49.6	−14 41	17 08	21 12	20 54
11	21 52.1	−14 28	16 31	20 36	20 19
21	21 55.0	−14 12	15 54	20 02	19 44
31	21 58.5	−13 53	15 19	19 28	19 11

Diameters – equatorial 16″ polar 15″
Rings – major axis 37″ minor axis 8″

URANUS

Day	*RA*	*Dec.*	*Transit*	
	h m	° ′	h m	
1	19 26.4	−22 25	14 45	Uranus is
11	19 28.6	−22 20	14 08	too close to
21	19 30.9	−22 15	13 31	the Sun for
31	19 33.3	−22 10	12 54	observation

Diameter 4″

NEPTUNE

Day	*RA*	*Dec.*	*Transit*	
	h m	° ′	h m	
1	19 23.6	−21 25	14 42	Neptune is
11	19 24.9	−21 23	14 04	too close to
21	19 26.4	−21 20	13 26	the Sun for
31	19 28.0	−21 17	12 48	observation

Diameter 2″

RISING AND SETTING TIMES

TABLE 1. SEMI-DIURNAL ARCS (HOUR ANGLES AT RISING/SETTING)

Dec.	*Latitude* 0° h m	10° h m	20° h m	30° h m	40° h m	45° h m	50° h m	52° h m	54° h m	56° h m	58° h m	60° h m	*Dec.*
0°	6 00	6 00	6 00	6 00	6 00	6 00	6 00	6 00	6 00	6 00	6 00	6 00	0°
1°	6 00	6 01	6 01	6 02	6 03	6 04	6 05	6 05	6 06	6 06	6 06	6 07	1°
2°	6 00	6 01	6 03	6 05	6 07	6 08	6 10	6 10	6 11	6 12	6 13	6 14	2°
3°	6 00	6 02	6 04	6 07	6 10	6 12	6 14	6 15	6 17	6 18	6 19	6 21	3°
4°	6 00	6 03	6 06	6 09	6 13	6 16	6 19	6 21	6 22	6 24	6 26	6 28	4°
5°	6 00	6 04	6 07	6 12	6 17	6 20	6 24	6 26	6 28	6 30	6 32	6 35	5°
6°	6 00	6 04	6 09	6 14	6 20	6 24	6 29	6 31	6 33	6 36	6 39	6 42	6°
7°	6 00	6 05	6 10	6 16	6 24	6 28	6 34	6 36	6 39	6 42	6 45	6 49	7°
8°	6 00	6 06	6 12	6 19	6 27	6 32	6 39	6 41	6 45	6 48	6 52	6 56	8°
9°	6 00	6 06	6 13	6 21	6 31	6 36	6 44	6 47	6 50	6 54	6 59	7 04	9°
10°	6 00	6 07	6 15	6 23	6 34	6 41	6 49	6 52	6 56	7 01	7 06	7 11	10°
11°	6 00	6 08	6 16	6 26	6 38	6 45	6 54	6 58	7 02	7 07	7 12	7 19	11°
12°	6 00	6 09	6 18	6 28	6 41	6 49	6 59	7 03	7 08	7 13	7 20	7 26	12°
13°	6 00	6 09	6 19	6 31	6 45	6 53	7 04	7 09	7 14	7 20	7 27	7 34	13°
14°	6 00	6 10	6 21	6 33	6 48	6 58	7 09	7 14	7 20	7 27	7 34	7 42	14°
15°	6 00	6 11	6 22	6 36	6 52	7 02	7 14	7 20	7 27	7 34	7 42	7 51	15°
16°	6 00	6 12	6 24	6 38	6 56	7 07	7 20	7 26	7 33	7 41	7 49	7 59	16°
17°	6 00	6 12	6 26	6 41	6 59	7 11	7 25	7 32	7 40	7 48	7 57	8 08	17°
18°	6 00	6 13	6 27	6 43	7 03	7 16	7 31	7 38	7 46	7 55	8 05	8 17	18°
19°	6 00	6 14	6 29	6 46	7 07	7 21	7 37	7 45	7 53	8 03	8 14	8 26	19°
20°	6 00	6 15	6 30	6 49	7 11	7 25	7 43	7 51	8 00	8 11	8 22	8 36	20°
21°	6 00	6 16	6 32	6 51	7 15	7 30	7 49	7 58	8 08	8 19	8 32	8 47	21°
22°	6 00	6 16	6 34	6 54	7 19	7 35	7 55	8 05	8 15	8 27	8 41	8 58	22°
23°	6 00	6 17	6 36	6 57	7 23	7 40	8 02	8 12	8 23	8 36	8 51	9 09	23°
24°	6 00	6 18	6 37	7 00	7 28	7 46	8 08	8 19	8 31	8 45	9 02	9 22	24°
25°	6 00	6 19	6 39	7 02	7 32	7 51	8 15	8 27	8 40	8 55	9 13	9 35	25°
26°	6 00	6 20	6 41	7 05	7 37	7 57	8 22	8 35	8 49	9 05	9 25	9 51	26°
27°	6 00	6 21	6 43	7 08	7 41	8 03	8 30	8 43	8 58	9 16	9 39	10 08	27°
28°	6 00	6 22	6 45	7 12	7 46	8 08	8 37	8 52	9 08	9 28	9 53	10 28	28°
29°	6 00	6 22	6 47	7 15	7 51	8 15	8 45	9 01	9 19	9 41	10 10	10 55	29°
30°	6 00	6 23	6 49	7 18	7 56	8 21	8 54	9 11	9 30	9 55	10 30	12 00	30°

TABLE 2. CORRECTION FOR REFRACTION AND SEMI-DIAMETER

	m	m	m	m	m	m	m	m	m	m	m	m	
0°	3	3	4	4	4	5	5	5	6	6	6	7	0°
10°	3	3	4	4	4	5	5	6	6	6	7	7	10°
20°	4	4	4	4	5	5	6	7	7	8	8	9	20°
25°	4	4	4	4	5	6	7	8	8	9	11	13	25°
30°	4	4	4	5	6	7	8	9	11	14	21	—	30°

NB: Regarding Table 1. If latitude and declination are of the same sign, take out the respondent directly. If they are of opposite signs, subtract the respondent from 12h. *Examples*:

Lat.	Dec.	Semi-diurnal arc
+52°	+20°	7h 51m
+52°	−20°	4h 09m

SUNRISE AND SUNSET

The local mean time of sunrise or sunset may be found by obtaining the hour angle from Table 1 and applying it to the time of transit. The hour angle is negative for sunrise and positive for sunset. A small correction to the hour angle, which always has the effect of increasing it numerically, is necessary to allow for the Sun's semi-diameter (16′) and for refraction (34′); it is obtained from Table 2. The resulting local mean time may be converted into the standard time of the country by taking the difference between the longitude of the standard meridian of the country and that of the place, adding it to the local mean time if the place is west of the standard meridian, and subtracting it if the place is east.

Example – Required the New Zealand Mean Time (12h fast on GMT) of sunset on May 23 at Auckland, latitude 36° 50′ S. (or minus), longitude 11h 39m E. Taking the declination as +20°.7 (page 33), we find

		h m
Tabular entry for 30° Lat. and Dec. 20°, opposite signs	+	5 11
Proportional part for 6° 50′ of Lat.	−	15
Proportional part for 0°.7 of Dec.	−	2
Correction (Table 2)	+	4
Hour angle		4 58
Sun transits (page 33)		11 57
Longitudinal correction	+	21
New Zealand Mean Time		17 16

MOONRISE AND MOONSET

It is possible to calculate the times of moonrise and moonset using Table 1, though the method is more complicated because the apparent motion of the Moon is much more rapid and also more variable than that of the Sun.
The parallax of the Moon, about 57′, is near to the sum of the semi-diameter and refraction but has the opposite effect on these times. It is thus convenient to neglect all three quantities in the method outlined below.

TABLE 3. LONGITUDE CORRECTION

A \ X	40m	45m	50m	55m	60m	65m	70m
h	m	m	m	m	m	m	m
1	2	2	2	2	3	3	3
2	3	4	4	5	5	5	6
3	5	6	6	7	8	8	9
4	7	8	8	9	10	11	12
5	8	9	10	11	13	14	15
6	10	11	13	14	15	16	18
7	12	13	15	16	18	19	20
8	13	15	17	18	20	22	23
9	15	17	19	21	23	24	26
10	17	19	21	23	25	27	29
11	18	21	23	25	28	30	32
12	20	23	25	28	30	33	35
13	22	24	27	30	33	35	38
14	23	26	29	32	35	38	41
15	25	28	31	34	38	41	44
16	27	30	33	37	40	43	47
17	28	32	35	39	43	46	50
18	30	34	38	41	45	49	53
19	32	36	40	44	48	51	55
20	33	38	42	46	50	54	58
21	35	39	44	48	53	57	61
22	37	41	46	50	55	60	64
23	38	43	48	53	58	62	67
24	40	45	50	55	60	65	70

Notation

φ = latitude of observer
λ = longitude of observer (measured positively towards the west)
T_{-1} = time of transit of Moon on previous day
T_0 = time of transit of Moon on day in question
T_1 = time of transit of Moon on following day
δ_0 = approximate declination of Moon
δ_R = declination of Moon at moonrise
δ_S = declination of Moon at moonset
h_0 = approximate hour angle of Moon
h_R = hour angle of Moon at moonrise
h_S = hour angle of Moon at moonset
t_R = time of moonrise
t_S = time of moonset

Method

1. With arguments φ, δ_0 enter Table 1 on page 64 to determine h_0 where h_0 is negative for moonrise and positive for moonset.
2. Form approximate times from
   $t_R = T_0 + \lambda + h_0$
   $t_S = T_0 + \lambda + h_0$
3. Determine δ_R, δ_S for times t_R, t_S respectively.
4. Re-enter Table 1 on page 64 with—
   (*a*) arguments φ, δ_R to determine h_R
   (*b*) arguments φ, δ_S to determine h_S
5. Form $t_R = T_0 + \lambda + h_R + AX$
   $t_S = T_0 + \lambda + h_S + AX$

   where $A = (\lambda + h)$

   and $X = (T_0 - T_{-1})$ if $(\lambda + h)$ is negative
   $X = (T_1 - T_0)$ if $(\lambda + h)$ is positive

   AX is the respondent in Table 3.

Example – To find the times of moonrise and moonset at Vancouver ($\varphi = +49°$, $\lambda = +8h\ 12m$) on 1993 January 20. The starting data (page 18) are

T_{-1} = 9h 25m
T_0 = 10h 18m
T_1 = 11h 08m
δ = −23°

1. h_0 = 4h 02m
2. Approximate values
   t_R = 20d 10h 18m + 8h 12m + (−4h 02m)
   = 20d 14h 28m
   t_S = 20d 10h 18m + 8h 12m + (+4h 02m)
   = 20d 22h 32m
3. δ_R = −22°.0
   δ_S = −21°.3
4. h_R = −4h 09m
   h_S = +4h 14m
5. t_R = 20d 10h 18m + 8h 12m + (−4h 09m) + 8m
   = 20d 14h 29m
   t_S = 20d 10h 18m + 8h 12m + (+4h 14m) + 26m
   = 20d 23h 10m

To get the LMT of the phenomenon the longitude is subtracted from the GMT thus:
Moonrise = 20d 14h 29m − 8h 12m = 20d 06h 17m
Moonset = 20d 23h 10m − 8h 12m = 20d 14h 58m

ASTRONOMICAL CONSTANTS

Solar Parallax	8″.794
Astronomical unit	149597870 km
Precession for the year 1993	50″.289
Precession in Right Ascension	3s.075
Precession in Declination	20″.044
Constant of Nutation	9″.202
Constant of Aberration	20″.496
Mean Obliquity of Ecliptic (1993)	23° 26′ 24″
Moon's Equatorial Hor. Parallax	57′ 02″.70
Velocity of light in vacuo per second	299792.5 km
Solar motion per second	20.0 km
Equatorial radius of the Earth	6378.140 km
Polar radius of the Earth	6356.755 km

North Galactic Pole (IAU standard)
RA 12h 49m (1950.0). Dec. 27°.4 N.
Solar Apex RA 18h 06m Dec. +30°

Length of Year (in mean solar days)	
Tropical	365.24220
Sidereal	365.25636
Anomalistic (perihelion to perihelion)	365.25964
Eclipse	346.6200

Length of Month (mean values)	d	h	m	s
New Moon to New	29	12	44	02.9
Sidereal	27	07	43	11.5
Anomalistic (perigee to perigee)	27	13	18	33.2

EXPLANATION OF ASTRONOMICAL DATA

Positions of the heavenly bodies are given only to the degree of accuracy required by amateur astronomers for setting telescopes, or for plotting on celestial globes or star atlases. Where intermediate positions are required, linear interpolation may be employed.

Definitions of the terms used cannot be given here. They must be sought in astronomical literature and textbooks. Probably the best source for the amateur is Norton's *Star Atlas and Reference Handbook* (Longman, 18th edition, 1989; £17.50), which contains an introduction to observational astronomy, and a series of star maps for showing stars visible to the naked eye. Certain more extended ephemerides are available in the British Astronomical Association Handbook, an annual popular among amateur astronomers. (Secretary: Burlington House, Piccadilly, London, W1V 9AG)

A special feature has been made of the times when the various heavenly bodies are visible in the British Isles. Since two columns, calculated for latitudes 52° and 56°, are devoted to risings and settings, the range 50° to 58° can be covered by interpolation and extrapolation. The times given in these columns are GMTs for the meridian of Greenwich. An observer west of this meridian must add his/her longitude (in time) and vice versa.

In accordance with the usual convention in astronomy, + and − indicate respectively north and south latitudes or declinations.

All data are, unless otherwise stated, for 0h Greenwich Mean Time (GMT), i.e. at the midnight at the beginning of the day named.

PAGE ONE OF EACH MONTH

The calendar for each month is explained on page 15.

Under the heading Astronomical Phenomena will be found particulars of the more important conjunctions of the Sun, Moon and planets with each other, and also the dates of other astronomical phenomena of special interest.

The Constellations listed each month are those that are near the meridian at the beginning of the month at 22h local mean time. Allowance must be made for British Summer Time if necessary. The fact that any star crosses the meridian 4m earlier each night or 2h earlier each month may be used, in conjunction with the lists given each month, to find what constellations are favourably placed at any moment. The table preceding the list of constellations may be extended indefinitely at the rate just quoted.

Times of Minima of Algol are approximate times of the middle of the period of diminished light.

The principal phases of the Moon are the GMTs when the difference between the longitude of the Moon and that of the Sun is 0°, 90°, 180° or 270°. The times of perigee and apogee are those when the Moon is nearest to, and farthest from, the Earth, respectively. The nodes or points of intersection of the Moon's orbit and the ecliptic make a complete retrograde circuit of the ecliptic in about 19 years. From a knowledge of the longitude of the ascending node and the inclination, whose value does not vary much from 5°, the path of the Moon among the stars may be plotted on a celestial globe or star atlas.

PAGE TWO OF EACH MONTH

The Sun's semi-diameter, in arc, is given once a month.

The right ascension and declination (Dec.) is that of the true Sun. The right ascension of the mean Sun is obtained by applying the equation of time, with the sign given, to the right ascension of the true Sun, or, more easily, by applying 12h to the column Sidereal Time. The direction in which the equation of time has to be applied in different problems is a frequent source of confusion and error. Apparent Solar Time is equal to the Mean Solar Time plus the Equation of Time. For example at noon on August 8 the Equation of Time is − 5m 35s and thus at 12h Mean Time on that day the Apparent Time is 12h − 5m 35s = 11h 54m 25s.

The Greenwich Sidereal Time at 0h and the Transit of the First Point of Aries (which is really the mean time when the sidereal time is 0h) are used for converting mean time to sidereal time and vice versa.

The GMT of transit of the Sun at Greenwich may also be taken as the local mean time (LMT) of transit in any longitude. It is independent of latitude. The GMT of transit in any longitude is obtained by adding the longitude to the time given if west, and vice versa.

Lighting-up Time

The legal importance of Sunrise and Sunset is that the Road Vehicles Lighting Regulations 1989 (SI 1989 No. 1796) make the use of front and rear position lamps on vehicles compulsory during the period between sunset and sunrise. Headlamps on vehicles are required to be used during the hours of darkness on unlit roads or whenever visibility is seriously reduced. The hours of darkness are defined in these Regulations as the period between half an hour after sunset and half an hour before sunrise.

In all laws and regulations 'sunset' refers to the local sunset, i.e. the time at which the Sun sets at the place in question. This common-sense interpretation has been upheld by legal tribunals. Thus the necessity for providing for different latitudes and longitudes, as already described, is evident.

Sunrise and Sunset

The times of Sunrise and Sunset are those when the Sun's upper limb, as affected by refraction, is on the true horizon of an observer at sea-level. Assuming the mean refraction to be 34′, and the Sun's semi-diameter to be 16′, the time given is that when the true zenith distance of the Sun's centre is 90° + 34′ + 16′ or 90° 50′, or, in other words, when the depression of the Sun's centre below the true horizon is 50′. The upper limb is then 34′ below the true horizon, but is brought there by refraction. It is true, of course, that an observer on a ship might see the Sun for a minute or so longer, because of the dip of the horizon, while another viewing the sunset over hills or mountains would record an earlier time. Nevertheless, the moment when the true zenith distance of the Sun's centre is 90° 50′ is a precise time dependent only on the latitude and longitude of the place, and independent of its altitude above sea-level, the contour of its horizon, the vagaries of refraction or the small seasonal change in the Sun's semi-diameter; this moment is suitable in every way as a definition of sunset (or sunrise) for all statutory purposes. (For further information, *see* footnote.)

Sunrise, Sunset and Moonrise, Moonset

The tables have been constructed for the meridian of Greenwich, and for latitudes 52° and 56°. They give Greenwich Mean Time (GMT) throughout the year. To obtain the GMT of the phenomenon as seen from any other latitude and longitude in the British Isles, first interpolate or extrapolate for latitude by the usual rules of proportion. To the time thus found, the longitude (expressed in time) is to be added if west (as it usually is in Great Britain) or subtracted if east. If the longitude is expressed in degrees and minutes of arc, it must be converted to time at the rate of 1° = 4m and 15′ = 1m.

A method of calculating rise and set times for other places in the world is given on pages 64 and 65.

TWILIGHT

It is well known that light reaches us before sunrise and also continues to reach us for some time after sunset. The interval between darkness and sunrise or sunset and darkness is called twilight. Astronomically speaking, twilight is considered to begin or end when the Sun's centre is 18° below the horizon, as no light from the Sun can then reach the observer. As thus defined, twilight may last several hours; in high latitudes at the summer solstice the depression of 18° is not reached, and twilight lasts from sunset to sunrise.

The need for some sub-division of twilight is met by dividing the gathering darkness into four steps.

(1) *Sunrise or Sunset*, defined as above.
(2) *Civil twilight*, which begins or ends when the Sun's centre is 6° below the horizon. This marks the time when operations requiring daylight may commence or must cease. In England it varies from about 30 to 60 minutes after sunset and the same interval before sunrise.
(3) *Nautical twilight*, which begins or ends when the Sun's centre is 12° below the horizon. This marks the time when it is, to all intents and purposes, completely dark.
(4) *Astronomical twilight*, which begins or ends when the Sun's centre is 18° below the horizon. This marks theoretical perfect darkness. It is of little practical importance, especially if nautical twilight is tabulated.

To assist observers the durations of civil, nautical and astronomical twilights are given at intervals of ten days. The beginning of a particular twilight is found by subtracting the duration from the time of sunrise, while the end is found by adding the duration to the time of sunset. Thus the beginning of astronomical twilight in latitude 52°, on the Greenwich meridian, on March 11 is found as 06h 24m − 113m = 04h 31m and similarly the end of civil twilight as 17h 57m + 34m = 18h 31m.

The letters TAN (twilight all night) are printed when twilight lasts all night.

Under the heading The Night Sky will be found notes describing the position and visibility of all the planets and also of other phenomena.

PAGE THREE OF EACH MONTH

The Moon moves so rapidly among the stars that its position is given only to the degree of accuracy that permits linear interpolation. The right ascension (RA) and declination (Dec.) are geocentric, i.e. for an imaginary observer at the centre of the Earth. To an observer on the surface of the Earth the position is always different, as the altitude is always less on account of parallax, which may reach 1°.

The lunar terminator is the line separating the bright from the dark part of the Moon's disk. Apart from irregularities of the lunar surface, the terminator is elliptical, because it is a circle seen in projection. It becomes the full circle forming the limb, or edge, of the Moon at New and Full Moon. The selenographic longitude of the terminator is measured from the mean centre of the visible disk, which may differ from the visible centre by as much as 8°, because of libration.

Instead of the longitude of the terminator the Sun's selenographic co-longitude (Sun's co-long.) is tabulated. It is numerically equal to the selenographic longitude of the morning terminator, measured eastwards from the mean centre of the disk. Thus its value is approximately 270° at New Moon, 360° at First Quarter, 90° at Full Moon and 180° at Last Quarter.

The Position Angle (PA) of the Bright Limb is the position angle of the midpoint of the illuminated limb, measured eastward from the north point on the disk. The column Phase shows the percentage of the area of the Moon's disk illuminated; this is also the illuminated percentage of the diameter at right angles to the line of cusps. The terminator is a semi-ellipse whose major axis is the line of cusps, and whose semi-minor axis is determined by the tabulated percentage; from New Moon to Full Moon the east limb is dark, and vice versa.

The times given as moonrise and moonset are those when the upper limb of the Moon is on the horizon of an observer at sea-level. The Sun's horizontal parallax (Hor. par.) is about 9″, and is negligible when considering sunrise and sunset, but that of the Moon averages about 57′. Hence the computed time represents the moment when the true zenith distance of the Moon is 90° 50′ (as for the Sun) minus the horizontal parallax. The time required for the Sun or Moon to rise or set is about four minutes (except in high latitudes). *See also* page 65 and footnote on page 66.)

The GMT of transit of the Moon over the meridian of Greenwich is given; these times are independent of latitude, but must be corrected for longitude. For places in the British Isles it suffices to add the longitude if west, and vice versa. For more remote places a further correction is necessary because of the rapid movement of the Moon relative to the stars. The entire correction is conveniently determined by first finding the west longitude λ of the place. If the place is in west longitude, λ is the ordinary west longitude; if the place is in east longitude λ is the complement to 24h (or 360°) of the longitude and will be greater than 12h (or 180°). The correction then consists of two positive portions, namely λ and the fraction $\lambda/24$ (or $\lambda°/360$) multiplied by the difference between consecutive transits. Thus for Sydney, New South Wales, the longitude is 10h 05m east, so λ = 13h 55m and the fraction $\lambda/24$ is 0.58. The transit on the local date 1993 May 29 is found as follows:

		d	h	m
GMT of transit at Greenwich	May	28	18	03
λ			13	55
0.58 × (18h 53m − 18h 03m)				29
GMT of transit at Sydney		29	08	27
Corr. to NSW Standard Time			10	00
Local standard time of transit		29	18	27

As is evident, for any given place the quantities λ and the correction to local standard time may be combined permanently, being here 23h 55m.

Positions of Mercury are given for every third day, and those of Venus and Mars for every fifth day; they may be interpolated linearly. The diameter (Diam.) is given in seconds of arc. The phase is the illuminated percentage of the disk. In the case of the inner planets this approaches 100 at superior conjunction and 0 at inferior conjunction. When the phase is less than 50 the planet is crescent-shaped or horned; for greater phases it is gibbous. In the case of the exterior planet Mars, the phase approaches 100 at conjunction and opposition, and is a minimum at the quadratures.

Since the planets cannot be seen when on the horizon, the actual times of rising and setting are not given; instead, the time when the planet has an apparent altitude of 5° has been tabulated. If the time of transit is between 00h and 12h the time refers to an altitude of 5° above the eastern horizon; if between 12h and 24h, to the western horizon. The phenomenon tabulated is the one that occurs between sunset and sunrise; unimportant exceptions to these rules may occur because changes are not made during a month, except in the case of Mercury. The times given may be interpolated for latitude and corrected for longitude as in the case of the Sun and Moon.

The GMT at which the planet transits the Greenwich

meridian is also given. The times of transit are to be corrected to local meridians in the usual way, as already described.

PAGE FOUR OF EACH MONTH

The GMTs of sunrise and sunset for seven towns, whose adopted positions in longitude (W.) and latitude (N.) are given immediately below the name, may be used not only for these phenomena, but also for lighting-up times, which, under the Road Vehicles Lighting Regulations 1989, are from sunset to sunrise throughout the year. (*See* page 66 for a fuller explanation.)

The particulars for the four outer planets resemble those for the planets on Page Three of each month, except that, under Uranus and Neptune, times when the planet is 10° high instead of 5° high are given; this is because of the inferior brightness of these planets. The diameters given for the rings of Saturn are those of the major axis (in the plane of the planet's equator) and the minor axis respectively. The former has a small seasonal change due to the slightly varying distance of the Earth from Saturn, but the latter varies from zero when the Earth passes through the ring plane every 15 years to its maximum opening half-way between these periods. The rings were open at their widest extent in 1988.

TIME

From the earliest ages, the natural division of time into recurring periods of day and night has provided the practical time-scale for the everyday activities of the human race. Indeed, if any alternative means of time measurement is adopted, it must be capable of adjustment so as to remain in general agreement with the natural time-scale defined by the diurnal rotation of the Earth on its axis. Ideally the rotation should be measured against a fixed frame of reference; in practice it must be measured against the background provided by the celestial bodies. If the Sun is chosen as the reference point, we obtain Apparent Solar Time, which is the time indicated by a sundial. It is not a uniform time but is subject to variations which amount to as much as a quarter of an hour in each direction. Such wide variations cannot be tolerated in a practical time-scale, and this has led to the concept of Mean Solar Time in which all the days are exactly the same length and equal to the average length of the Apparent Solar Day.

The positions of the stars in the sky are specified in relation to a fictitious reference point in the sky known as the First Point of Aries (or the Vernal Equinox). It is therefore convenient to adopt this same reference point when considering the rotation of the Earth against the background of the stars. The time-scale so obtained is known as Apparent Sidereal Time.

Greenwich Mean Time

The daily rotation of the Earth on its axis causes the Sun and the other heavenly bodies to appear to cross the sky from east to west. It is convenient to represent this relative motion as if the Sun really performed a daily circuit around a fixed Earth. Noon in Apparent Solar Time may then be defined as the time at which the Sun transits across the observer's meridian. In Mean Solar Time, noon is similarly defined by the meridian transit of a fictitious Mean Sun moving uniformly in the sky with the same average speed as the true Sun. Mean Solar Time observed on the meridian of the transit circle telescope of the Old Royal Observatory at Greenwich is called Greenwich Mean Time (GMT). The mean solar day is divided into 24 hours and, for astronomical and other scientific purposes, these are numbered 0 to 23, commencing at midnight. Civil time is usually reckoned in two periods of 12 hours, designated a.m. (*ante meridiem*, i.e. before noon) and p.m. (*post meridiem*, i.e. after noon).

Universal Time

Before 1925 January 1, GMT was reckoned in 24 hours commencing at noon; since that date it has been reckoned from midnight. In view of the risk of confusion in the use of the designation GMT before and after 1925, the International Astronomical Union recommended in 1928 that astronomers should employ the term Universal Time (UT) or Weltzeit (WZ) to denote GMT measured from Greenwich Mean Midnight.

In precision work it is necessary to take account of small variations in Universal Time. These arise from small irregularities in the rotation of the Earth. Observed astronomical time is designated UT0. Observed time corrected for the effects of the motion of the poles (giving rise to a 'wandering' in longitude) is designated UT1. There is also a seasonal fluctuation in the rate of rotation of the Earth arising from meteorological causes, often called the annual fluctuation. UT1 corrected for this effect is designated UT2 and provides a time-scale free from short-period fluctuations. It is still subject to small secular and irregular changes.

Apparent Solar Time

As has been mentioned above, the time shown by a sundial is called Apparent Solar Time. It differs from Mean Solar Time by an amount known as the Equation of Time, which is the total effect of two causes which make the length of the apparent solar day non-uniform. One cause of variation is that the orbit of the Earth is not a circle, but an ellipse, having the Sun at one focus. As a consequence, the angular speed of the Earth in its orbit is not constant; it is greatest at the beginning of January when the Earth is nearest the Sun.

The other cause is due to the obliquity of the ecliptic; the plane of the equator (which is at right angles to the axis of rotation of the Earth) does not coincide with the ecliptic (the plane defined by the apparent annual motion of the Sun around the celestial sphere) but is inclined to it at an angle of 23° 26′. As a result, the apparent solar day is shorter than average at the equinoxes and longer at the solstices. From the combined effects of the components due to obliquity and eccentricity, the equation of time reaches its maximum values in February (−14 minutes) and early November (+16 minutes). It has a zero value on four dates during the year, and it is only on these dates (approx. April 15, June 14, September 1, and December 25) that a sundial shows Mean Solar Time.

Sidereal Time

A sidereal day is the duration of a complete rotation of the Earth with reference to the First Point of Aries. The term sidereal (or 'star') time is perhaps a little misleading since the time-scale so defined is not exactly the same as that which would be defined by successive transits of a selected star, as there is a small progressive motion between the stars and the First Point of Aries due to the precession of the Earth's axis. This makes the length of the sidereal day shorter than the true period of rotation by 0.008 seconds. Superimposed on this steady precessional motion are small oscillations called nutation, giving rise to fluctuations in apparent sidereal time amounting to as much as 1.2 seconds. It is therefore customary to employ Mean Sidereal Time, from which these fluctuations have been removed. The conversion of GMT to Greenwich sidereal time (GST) may be performed by adding the value of the GST at 0h on the day in question (Page Two of each month) to the GMT converted to sidereal time using the table on page 71.

Example – To find the GST at August 8d 02h 41m 11s GMT

	h	m	s
GST at 0h	21	06	03
GMT	2	41	11
Acceleration for 2h			20
Acceleration for 41m 11s			7
Sum = GST =	23	47	41

If the observer is not on the Greenwich meridian then his/her longitude, measured positively westwards from Greenwich, must be subtracted from the GST to obtain Local Sidereal Time (LST). Thus, in the above example, an observer 5h east of Greenwich, or 19h west, would find the LST as 4h 47m 41s.

Ephemeris Time

In the study of the motions of the Sun, Moon and planets, observations taken over an extended period are used in the preparation of tables giving the apparent position of the body each day. A table of this sort is known as an ephemeris, and may be used in the comparison of current observations with tabulated positions. A detailed examination of the observations made over the past 300 years shows that the Sun, Moon and planets appear to depart from their predicted positions by amounts proportional to their mean motions. The only satisfactory explanation is that the time-scale to which the observations were referred was not as uniform as had been supposed. Since the time-scale was based on the rotation of the Earth, it follows that this rotation is subject to irregularities. The fact that the discrepancies between the observed and ephemeris positions were proportional to the mean motions of the bodies made it possible to secure agreement by substituting a revised time-scale and recomputing the ephemeris positions. The time-scale which brings the ephemeris into agreement with the observations is known as Ephemeris Time (ET).

The new unit of time has been defined in terms of the apparent annual motion of the Sun. Thus the second is now defined in terms of the annual motion of the Earth in its orbit around the Sun (1/31556925.9747 of the Tropical Year for 1900 January 0d 12h ET) instead of in terms of the diurnal rotation of the Earth on its axis (1/86 400 of the Mean Solar Day). In many branches of scientific work other than astronomy there has been a demand for a unit of time that is invariable, and the second of Ephemeris time was adopted by the Comité International des Poids et Mesures in 1956. The length of the unit has been chosen to provide general agreement with UT throughout the 19th and 20th centuries. During 1993 the estimated difference ET – UT is 59 seconds. The precise determination of ET from astronomical observations is a lengthy process, as the accuracy with which a single observation of the Sun can be made is far less than that obtainable in, for instance, a comparison between clocks. It is therefore necessary to average the observations over an extended period. Largely on account of its faster motion, the position of the Moon may be observed with greater accuracy, and a close approximation to Ephemeris Time may be obtained by comparing observations of the Moon with its ephemeris position. Even in this case, however, the requisite standard of accuracy can only be achieved by averaging over a number of years.

Atomic Time

The fundamental standards of time and frequency must be defined in terms of a periodic motion adequately uniform, enduring and measurable. Progress has made it possible to use natural standards, such as atomic or molecular oscillations. Continuous oscillations are generated in an electrical circuit, the frequency of which is then compared or brought into coincidence with the frequency characteristic of the absorption or emission by the atoms or molecules when they change between two selected energy levels. The National Physical Laboratory routinely uses clocks of high stability produced by locking a quartz oscillator to the frequency defined by a caesium atomic beam.

International Atomic Time (TAI) is formed by combining the readings of many caesium clocks and was set close to the astronomically-based Universal Time (UT) near the beginning of 1958. It was formally recognized in 1971 and since 1988 January 1 has been maintained by the International Bureau of Weights and Measures (BIPM). The second markers are generated according to the SI definition of the second adopted in 1967 at the 13th General Conference of Weights and Measures: 'The second is the duration of 9 192 631 770 periods of the radiation corresponding to the transition between the two hyperfine levels of the ground state of the caesium-133 atom.'

Civil time in almost all countries is now based on Coordinated Universal Time (UTC), established through international collaboration and based on the readings of atomic clocks and the rotation of the Earth. It was designed to make both atomic time and UT accessible with accuracies appropriate for most users.

Radio Time-Signals

UTC is made generally available through time-signals and standard frequency broadcasts such as MSF in the UK, CHU in Canada and WWV and WWVH in the USA. These are based on national time-scales that are maintained in close agreement with UTC and provide traceability to the national time-scale and to UTC. The markers of seconds in the UTC scale coincide with those of TAI.

As the rate of rotation of the Earth is variable, the time-signals are adjusted by the introduction of a leap second when necessary in order that UTC shall not depart from UT by more than 0.9s. For convenience, leap seconds are introduced when necessary on the last second of the third, sixth, ninth or twelfth month, but preferably on December 31 and/or June 30. In the case of a positive leap second, 23h 59m 60s is followed one second later by 0h 0m 00s of the first day of the month. In the case of a negative leap second, 23h 59m 58s is followed one second later by 0h 0m 00s of the first day of the month. Notices concerning the insertion of leap seconds in UTC are issued by the International Earth Rotation Service at the Observatoire de Paris.

To disseminate the national time-scale in the UK, special signals are broadcast on behalf of the National Physical Laboratory from the BT (British Telecom) radio station at Rugby. The signals are controlled from a caesium beam atomic frequency standard and consist of a standard frequency carrier of 60 kHz (MSF) which switches off for half a second to denote the passing of one minute, and for a tenth of a second to denote the passing of one second. Also transmitted are two binary coded decimal (BCD) time codes giving time of day and calendar information. Summer and winter time changes are encoded on instruction from the British Government. Other broadcast signals in the UK include the BBC six pips signal, the BT Speaking Clock and a coded time-signal on the BBC 198 kHz Droitwich transmitter, which is used for timing in the electricity supply industry. From 1972 January 1 the six pips on the BBC have consisted of five short pips from second 55 to second 59 followed by one lengthened pip, the start of which indicates the exact minute. From 1990 February 5 these signals have been controlled by the BBC with respect to the broadcast MSF signal and are thus traceable to the National Physical Laboratory. Formerly they were generated by the Royal Greenwich Observatory. The BT Speaking Clock is connected to the National Physical Laboratory caesium beam atomic frequency standar at the Rugby radio station.

Accurate timing may also be obtained from the signals of international navigation systems, such as the ground-based Loran-C or Omega, or satellite-based Global Positioning System (GPS) of the USA or the Russian GLONASS system.

Standard Time

In the year 1880 it was enacted by statute that the word 'time', when it occurred in any legal document relating to Great Britain, was to be interpreted, unless otherwise specifically stated, as the mean time of the Greenwich meridian. Summer time is the 'legal' time during the period in which its use is ordained.

Since the year 1883 the system of standard time by zones ha been gradually accepted, and now almost throughout the world a standard time which differs from that of Greenwich by an integral number of hours, either fast or slow, is used. (For time zones of countries of the world, *see* Index.)

Variations from the standard time of some countries occur during part of the year; they are decided annually and are usually referred to as Summer Time or Daylight Saving Time.

The large territories of the United States and Canada are divided into zones approximately 7.5° on either side of central meridians.

At the 180th meridian the time can be either 12 hours fast on Greenwich Mean Time or 12 hours slow, and a change of date occurs. The internationally-recognized date or calendar line is a modification of the 180th meridian, drawn so as to include islands of any one group on the same side of the line, or for political reasons. The line is indicated by joining up the following co-ordinates:

Lat.	*Long.*	*Lat.*	*Long.*
60° S.	180°	48° N.	180°
51° S.	180°	53° N.	170° E.
45° S.	172.5° W.	65.5° N.	169° W.
15° S.	172.5° W.	75° N.	180°
5° S.	180°		

British Summer Time

In 1916 an Act ordained that during a defined period of that year the legal time for general purposes in Great Britain should be one hour in advance of Greenwich Mean Time. The Summer Time Acts 1922 to 1925 defined the period during which Summer Time was to be in force, stabilizing practice until the war.

During the Second World War the duration of Summer Time was extended and in the years 1941–5 and in 1947 Double Summer Time (two hours in advance of Greenwich Mean Time) was in force. After the war, Summer Time was extended in each year from 1948–52 and 1961–4 by Order in Council.

Between 1968 October 27 and 1971 October 31 clocks were kept one hour ahead of Greenwich Mean Time throughout the year. This was known as British Standard Time.

The most recent legislation is the Summer Time Act 1972, which enacted that 'the period of summer time for the purposes of this Act is the period beginning at two o'clock, Greenwich mean time, in the morning of the day after the third Saturday in March or, if that day is Easter Day, the day after the second Saturday in March, and ending at two o'clock, Greenwich mean time, in the morning of the day after the fourth Saturday in October.'

The duration of Summer Time can be varied by Order in Council and in recent years alterations have been made to bring the operation of Summer Time in Britain closer to similar provisions in other countries of the European Community. Subject to parliamentary approval of the Summer Time Order 1992, the duration of Summer Time in 1993 and 1994 will be as given below.* As in recent years, the hour of changeover will be 01h Greenwich Mean Time.

The duration of Summer Time in the following years was:

1990 March 25–October 28
1991 March 31–October 27
1992 March 29–October 25
1993 March 28–October 24*
1994 March 27–October 23*

MEAN AND SIDEREAL TIME

Acceleration

h	m s
1	0 10
2	0 20
3	0 30
4	0 39
5	0 49
6	0 59
7	1 09
8	1 19
9	1 29
10	1 39
11	1 48
12	1 58
13	2 08
14	2 18
15	2 28
16	2 38
17	2 48
18	2 57
19	3 07
20	3 17
21	3 27
22	3 37
23	3 47
24	3 57

m s	s
0 00	
	0
3 02	
	1
9 07	
	2
15 13	
	3
21 18	
	4
27 23	
	5
33 28	
	6
39 34	
	7
45 39	
	8
51 44	
	9
57 49	
	10
60 00	

Retardation

h	m s
1	0 10
2	0 20
3	0 29
4	0 39
5	0 49
6	0 59
7	1 09
8	1 19
9	1 28
10	1 38
11	1 48
12	1 58
13	2 08
14	2 18
15	2 27
16	2 37
17	2 47
18	2 57
19	3 07
20	3 17
21	3 26
22	3 36
23	3 46
24	3 56

m s	s
0 00	
	0
3 03	
	1
9 09	
	2
15 15	
	3
21 21	
	4
27 28	
	5
33 34	
	6
39 40	
	7
45 46	
	8
51 53	
	9
57 59	
	10
60 00	

The length of a sidereal day in mean time is 23h 56m 04s.09. Hence 1h MT = 1h + 9s.86 ST and 1h ST = 1h − 9s.83 MT.

To convert an interval of mean time to the corresponding interval of sidereal time, enter the acceleration table with the given mean time (taking the hours and the minutes and seconds separately) and add the acceleration obtained to the given mean time. To convert an interval of sidereal time to the corresponding interval of mean time, take out the retardation for the given sidereal time and subtract.

The columns for the minutes and seconds of the argument are in the form known as critical tables. To use these tables, find in the appropriate left-hand column the two entries between which the given number of minutes and seconds lies; the quantity in the right-hand column between these two entries is the required acceleration or retardation. Thus the acceleration for 11m 26s (which lies between the entries 9m 07s and 15m 13s) is 2s. If the given number of minutes and seconds is a tabular entry, the required acceleration or retardation is the entry in the right-hand column above the given tabular entry, e.g. the retardation for 45m 46s is 7s.

Example – Convert 14h 27m 35s from ST to MT

	h	m	s
Given ST	14	27	35
Retardation for 14h		2	18
Retardation for 27m 35s			5
Corresponding MT	14	25	12

For further explanation, *see* page 68–9.

The refraction table is also in the form of a critical table.

MEAN REFRACTION

Alt.	Ref.	Alt.	Ref.	Alt.	Ref.
° ′	′	° ′	′	° ′	′
1 20		3 12		7 54	
	21		13		6
1 30		3 34		9 27	
	20		12		5
1 41		4 00		11 39	
	19		11		4
1 52		4 30		15 00	
	18		10		3
2 05		5 06		20 42	
	17		9		2
2 19		5 50		32 20	
	16		8		1
2 35		6 44		62 17	
	15		7		0
2 52		7 54		90 00	
	14				
3 12					

ECLIPSES AND OCCULTATIONS 1993

Eclipses

There will be four eclipses during 1993, two of the Sun and two of the Moon. (Penumbral eclipses are not mentioned in this section as they are difficult to observe).

1. A partial eclipse of the Sun on May 21 is visible from North America (except the south-east and the eastern seaboard), arctic regions, Greenland, Iceland, northern Europe including Scotland, and the north-west part of the former USSR. The eclipse begins at 12h 19m and ends at 16h 20m. At the time of maximum eclipse 0.74 of the Sun's diameter is obscured. As seen from Edinburgh, the eclipse begins at 15h 06m and ends at 15h 29m, though even at maximum only 1% of the Sun's disk is obscured.
2. A total eclipse of the Moon on June 4 is visible from the extreme southern tip of South America, the western coast of North America, the Pacific Ocean, Antarctica, Australasia and south-east Asia. The eclipse begins at 11h 12m and ends at 14h 50m. Totality lasts from 12h 13m to 13h 49m.
3. A partial eclipse of the Sun on November 13 is visible from the southern tip of South America, Antarctica, most of New Zealand and the southern part of Australia. The eclipse begins at 19h 46m and ends at 23h 43m. At the time of maximum eclipse 93% of the Sun's diameter is obscured.
4. A total eclipse of the Moon on November 29 is visible from most of Europe including the British Isles, west Africa, Greenland, Iceland, the arctic regions, the Americas and north-east Asia. The eclipse begins at 04h 40m and ends at 08h 10m. Totality lasts from 06h 02m to 06h 48m.

Transit

There will be a near-grazing transit of Mercury across the disk of the Sun on November 6. Mercury (semi-diameter 5 arcseconds) will never be more than 0.7 arcminutes inside the SSW limb of the Sun. The phenomenon will be visible from the Pacific Ocean (Hawaii, not egress), part of Antarctica, Australasia, Asia, eastern and southern Africa, and eastern Europe (not ingress). The transit begins at 03h 06m and ends at 04h 47m.

Lunar Occultations

Observations of the times of occultations are made by both amateur and professional astronomers. Such observations are later analysed to yield accurate positions of the Moon; this is one method of determining the difference between ephemeris time and universal time.

Many of the observations made by amateurs are obtained with the use of a stop-watch which is compared with a time-signal immediately after the observation. Thus an accuracy of about one-fifth of a second is obtainable, though the observer's personal equation may amount to one-third or one-half of a second.

The list on page 72 includes most of the occultations visible under favourable conditions in the British Isles. No occultation is included unless the star is at least 10° above the horizon and the Sun sufficiently far below the horizon to permit the star to be seen with the naked eye or with a small telescope. The altitude limit is reduced from 10° to 2° for stars and planets brighter than magnitude 2.0 and such occultations are also predicted in daylight.

The column Phase shows (i) whether a disappearance (D) or reappearance (R) is to be observed; and (ii) whether it is at the dark limb (D) or bright limb (B). The column headed 'El. of Moon' gives the elongation of the Moon from the Sun, in degrees. The elongation increases from 0° at New Moon to 180° at Full Moon and on to 360° (or 0°) at New Moon again. Times and position angles (*P*), reckoned from the north point in the direction north, east, south, west, are given for Greenwich (lat. 51° 30′, long. 0°) and Edinburgh (lat. 56° 00′, long. 3° 12′ west).

The coefficients *a* and *b* are the variations in the GMT for each degree of longitude (positive to the west) and latitude (positive to the north) respectively; they enable approximate times (to within about 1m generally) to be found for any point in the British Isles. If the point of observation is $\Delta\lambda$ degrees west and $\Delta\phi$ degrees north, the approximate time is found by adding $a.\Delta\lambda + b.\Delta\phi$ to the given GMT.

Example: the disappearance of ZC465 on January 31 at Liverpool, found from both Greenwich and Edinburgh.

	Greenwich	Edinburgh
	°	°
Longitude	0.0	+3.2
Long. of Liverpool	+3.0	+3.0
$\Delta\lambda$	+3.0	−0.2
Latitude	+51.5	+56.0
Lat. of Liverpool	+53.4	+53.4
$\Delta\phi$	+1.9	−2.6
	h m	h m
GMT	17 33.9	17 26.2
$a.\Delta\lambda$	− 6.3	+ 0.3
$b.\Delta\phi$	− 2.5	− 0.5
	17 25.1	17 26.0

If the occultation is given for one station but not the other, the reason for the suppression is given by the following code.

N = star not occulted.

A = star's altitude less than 10° (2° for bright stars and planets).

S = Sun not sufficiently below the horizon.

G = occultation is of very short duration.

In some cases the coefficients *a* and *b* are not given; this is because the occultation is so short that prediction for other places by means of these coefficients would not be reliable.

LUNAR OCCULTATIONS 1993

Date		ZC No.	Mag.	Phase	El. of Moon	Greenwich UT	a	b	P	Edinburgh UT	a	b	P
					°	h m	m	m	°	h m	m	m	°
January	4	421	6.6	D.D.	123	0 33.7	−0.7	−0.5	56	0 29.9	−0.7	−0.1	43
	4	525	6.4	D.D.	133					20 44.8			142
	10	1341	4.3	R.D.	204	6 50.0	−0.2	−1.6	279	6 42.0	−0.3	−1.6	282
	29	244	6.9	D.D.	79	22 57.6	−0.3	0.0	39	22 57.5	−0.5	0.6	23
	30	371	6.4	D.D.	90	24 1.8	0.0	−1.2	78	23 56.2	−0.2	−1.1	68
	31	465	4.5	D.D.	99	17 33.9	−2.1	−1.3	124	17 26.2	−1.5	0.2	105
February	2	634	5.3	D.D.	114	0 49.0			163	0 33.2	0.2	−3.3	146
	2	657	5.4	D.D.	115	A				3 2.1			27
	2	784	6.2	D.D.	126	23 34.5			161	23 17.0	−0.5	−3.1	144
March	5	1198	6.2	D.D.	134	3 12.1	−0.1	−1.2	74	3 6.0	−0.2	−1.3	71
	6	1341	4.3	D.D.	148	3 56.3	0.0	−1.5	103	3 49.2	−0.1	−1.6	100
	26	415	6.0	D.D.	39	20 49.1	−0.1	−0.9	66	20 44.7	−0.2	−0.9	57
	29	817	4.8	D.D.	73	19 30.1	−1.0	−1.6	104	19 20.5	−1.1	−1.2	94
	30	989	6.6	D.D.	86	21 10.1	−0.9	−1.3	90	21 1.5	−1.0	−1.1	83
	30	991	6.1	D.D.	87	21 36.0	0.1	−3.2	157	21 22.3	−0.2	−2.8	147
	31	1114	6.8	D.D.	99	20 29.6	−0.4	−3.1	159	20 15.3	−0.7	−2.4	147
	31	1124	6.9	D.D.	99	21 47.7	−0.6	−2.1	131	21 36.7	−0.7	−1.9	125
April	2	1271	5.9	D.D.	114	0 38.3	−0.4	−1.4	81	0 30.4	−0.5	−1.4	78
	3	1397	5.5	D.D.	128	2 24.4	−0.1	−1.5	98	2 16.9	−0.2	−1.6	95
	24	631	5.6	D.D.	32	19 42.6			17				
	24	633	5.4	D.D.	32	19 59.4	0.4	−2.6	138	S			
	29	1341	4.3	D.D.	94	19 47.5	−1.7	−0.3	78	S			
	30	1359	5.1	D.D.	96	0 38.8	0.1	−1.6	108	0 31.4	0.0	−1.7	106
May	3	1713	5.8	D.D.	137	1 14.1	−0.7	−1.4	81	1 5.7	−0.7	−1.4	78
	12	2986	6.5	R.D.	254	2 35.4	−1.2	1.7	228	S			
	26	1318	5.7	D.D.	66	21 16.5			179	21 4.8			173
	28	1551	6.7	D.D.	92	21 40.9	−0.6	−1.9	129	S			
July	17	847	3.0	R.D.	330					3 0.0			203
	31	2704	5.8	D.D.	151	1 6.1	−0.6	−0.5	52	A			
August	13	847	3.0	D.B.	304	13 57.4	0.3	−2.1	130	13 48.6	0.1	−2.1	124
	13	847	3.0	R.D.	305	14 44.4	0.0	−1.0	247	14 39.3	0.0	−1.2	252
September	23	2757	5.1	D.D.	103	21 1.8			134	20 47.0	−1.6	−1.5	118
	23	2760	6.7	D.D.	103	21 20.3	−1.1	−1.1	86	A			
October	7	847	3.0	D.B.	251	4 2.9	−1.6	0.9	74	4 4.1	−1.4	1.7	58
	7	847	3.0	R.D.	251	5 19.5	−1.5	−1.3	294	5 8.3	−1.3	−1.7	308
	8	995	4.1	R.D.	262	2 53.4	−1.5	−1.7	328				
	20	2697	6.5	D.D.	71	18 46.5	−0.5	0.4	27	A			
	26	3455	6.4	D.D.	139	18 41.1	−0.8	2.2	35	18 48.8	−0.6	2.2	26
	27	3482	5.7	D.D.	142	1 13.0	−0.8	−1.7	90	1 4.4	−0.7	−1.1	74
November	1	628	4.8	R.D.	206	21 37.6	−1.0	0.8	295	21 37.2	−1.1	0.4	311
	3	915	4.7	R.D.	229	21 11.9	0.5	2.8	219	21 24.1	0.3	2.2	235
	26	326	6.0	D.D.	151	16 31.3	0.2	2.3	32	16 42.9	0.3	2.5	22
	29	628	4.8	D.D.	179	5 18.0	−0.4	−0.7	56	5 13.5	−0.6	−0.5	47
	29	628	4.8	R.D.	180	6 6.0	0.4	−2.1	306	5 56.9			315
December	1	915	4.7	R.D.	203	5 3.3			218	4 59.9	−1.2	−0.2	231
	15	2865	5.9	D.D.	30	16 35.8	−1.0	−0.8	73	16 29.9	−0.8	−0.6	62
	16	2995	6.2	D.D.	42	16 59.7			137	16 42.0	−1.7	−1.6	114
	19	3371	6.4	D.D.	78	19 32.9	−0.5	1.4	19	19 42.4			352
	24	326	6.0	D.D.	124	2 27.7	0.1	−1.3	82	2 22.1	−0.1	−1.2	72
	24	416	5.4	D.D.	132	18 37.9	−0.9	2.1	50	18 45.9	−0.6	2.5	35
	24	433	5.6	D.D.	134	23 35.1	−1.3	1.9	26				
	25	531	5.5	D.D.	143	19 40.8	−1.2	1.8	61	19 46.8	−0.8	2.3	46
	25	533	6.3	D.D.	144	20 31.7	−1.6	0.6	87	20 31.2	−1.2	1.2	73
	27	847	3.0	D.D.	168	23 55.9			29				
	28	847	3.0	R.B.	169	0 26.7			343				

MEAN PLACES OF STARS 1993.5

Name	Mag.	RA	Dec.	Spectrum
		h m	° ′	
α Andromedae *Alpheratz*	2.1	0 08.1	+29 03	A0*p*
β Cassiopeiae *Caph*	2.3	0 08.8	+59 07	F5
γ Pegasi *Algenib*	2.8	0 12.9	+15 09	B2
α Phoenicis	2.4	0 26.0	−42 21	K0
α Cassiopeiae *Schedar*	2.2	0 40.1	+56 30	K0
β Ceti *Diphda*	2.0	0 43.3	−18 01	K0
γ Cassiopeiae*	Var.	0 56.3	+60 41	B0*p*
β Andromedae *Mirach*	2.1	1 09.4	+35 35	M0
δ Cassiopeiae	2.7	1 25.4	+60 12	A5
α Eridani *Achernar*	0.5	1 37.5	−57 16	B5
β Arietis *Sheratan*	2.6	1 54.3	+20 47	A5
γ Andromedae *Almak*	2.3	2 03.5	+42 18	K0
α Arietis *Hamal*	2.0	2 06.8	+23 26	K2
α Ursae Minoris *Polaris*	2.0	2 24.8	+89 14	F8
β Persei *Algol**	Var.	3 07.7	+40 56	B8
α *Persei Mirfak*	1.8	3 23.9	+49 50	F5
η Tauri *Alcyone*	2.9	3 47.1	+24 05	B5*p*
α Tauri *Aldebaran*	0.9	4 35.5	+16 30	K5
β Orionis *Rigel*	0.1	5 14.2	− 8 13	B8*p*
α Aurigae *Capella*	0.1	5 16.2	+45 59	G0
γ Orionis *Bellatrix*	1.6	5 24.8	+ 6 21	B2
β Tauri *Elnath*	1.7	5 25.9	+28 36	B8
δ Orionis	2.2	5 31.7	− 0 18	B0
α Leporis	2.6	5 32.4	−17 50	F0
ε Orionis	1.7	5 35.9	− 1 12	B0
ζ Orionis	1.8	5 40.4	− 1 57	B0
κ Orionis	2.1	5 47.4	− 9 40	B0
α Orionis *Betelgeuse**	Var.	5 54.8	+ 7 24	M0
β Aurigae *Menkalinan*	1.9	5 59.1	+44 57	A0*p*
β Canis Majoris *Mirzam*	2.0	6 22.4	−17 57	B1
α Carinae *Canopus*	−0.7	6 23.8	−52 42	F0
γ Geminorum *Alhena*	1.9	6 37.3	+16 24	A0
α Canis Majoris *Sirius*	−1.5	6 44.9	−16 43	A0
ε Canis Majoris	1.5	6 58.4	−28 58	B1
δ Canis Majoris	1.9	7 08.1	−26 23	F8*p*
α Geminorum *Castor*	1.6	7 34.2	+31 54	A0
α Canis Minoris *Procyon*	0.4	7 39.0	+ 5 14	F5
β Geminorum *Pollux*	1.1	7 44.9	+28 03	K0
ζ Puppis	2.3	8 03.4	−39 59	Od
γ Velorum	1.8	8 09.3	−47 19	Oa*p*
ε Carinae	1.9	8 22.4	−59 29	K0
δ Velorum	2.0	8 44.5	−54 41	A0
λ Velorum *Suhail*	2.2	9 07.8	−43 24	K5
β Carinae	1.7	9 13.1	−69 41	A0
ι Carinae	2.2	9 16.9	−59 15	F0
α Hydrae *Alphard*	2.0	9 27.3	− 8 38	K2
α Leonis *Regulus*	1.3	10 08.0	+12 00	B8
γ Leonis *Algeiba*	1.9	10 19.6	+19 52	K0
β Ursae Majoris *Merak*	2.4	11 01.5	+56 25	A0
α Ursae Majoris *Dubhe*	1.8	11 03.3	+61 47	K0
δ Leonis	2.6	11 13.8	+20 34	A3
β Leonis *Denebola*	2.1	11 48.7	+14 36	A2
γ Ursae Majoris *Phecda*	2.4	11 53.5	+53 44	A0
γ Corvi	2.6	12 15.5	−17 30	B8
α Crucis	1.0	12 26.2	−63 04	B1
γ Crucis	1.6	12 30.8	−57 05	M3
γ Centauri	2.2	12 41.2	−48 55	A0
γ Virginis	2.7	12 41.3	− 1 25	F0
β Crucis	1.3	12 47.3	−59 39	B1
ε Ursae Majoris *Alioth*	1.8	12 53.7	+56 00	A0*p*
α Canum Venaticorum	2.9	12 55.7	+38 21	A0*p*
ζ Ursae Majoris *Mizar*	2.1	13 23.7	+54 58	A2*p*
α Virginis *Spica*	1.0	13 24.8	−11 08	B2
η Ursae Majoris *Alkaid*	1.9	13 47.3	+49 21	B3
β Centauri *Hadar*	0.6	14 03.4	−60 21	B1
θ Centauri	2.1	14 06.3	−36 20	K0
α Bootis *Arcturus*	0.0	14 15.4	+19 13	K0
α Centauri *Rigil Kent*	0.1	14 39.1	−60 48	G0
ε Bootis	2.4	14 44.7	+27 06	K0
β Ursae Minoris *Kochab*	2.1	14 50.7	+74 11	K5
α Coronae Borealis *Alphecca*	2.2	15 34.4	+26 44	A0
δ Scorpii	2.3	15 59.9	−22 36	B0
β Scorpii	2.6	16 05.1	−19 47	B1
α Scorpii *Antares*	1.0	16 29.0	−26 25	M0
α Trianguli Australis	1.9	16 48.0	−69 01	K2
ε Scorpii	2.3	16 49.7	−34 17	K0
α Herculis†	Var.	17 14.3	+14 24	M3
λ Scorpii	1.6	17 33.2	−37 06	B2
α Ophiuchi *Rasalhague*	2.1	17 34.6	+12 34	A5
θ Scorpii	1.9	17 36.8	−43 00	F0
κ Scorpii	2.4	17 42.0	−39 02	B2
γ Draconis	2.2	17 56.5	+51 29	K5
ε Sagittarii *Kaus Australis*	1.9	18 23.7	−34 23	A0
α Lyrae *Vega*	0.0	18 36.7	+38 47	A0
σ Sagittarii	2.0	18 54.9	−26 18	B3
β Cygni *Albireo*	3.1	19 30.5	+27 57	K0
α Aquilae *Altair*	0.8	19 50.5	+ 8 51	A5
α Capricorni	3.8	20 17.7	−12 34	G5
γ Cygni	2.2	20 22.0	+40 14	F8*p*
α Pavonis	1.9	20 25.1	−56 45	B3
α Cygni *Deneb*	1.3	20 41.2	+45 15	A2*p*
α Cephei *Alderamin*	2.4	21 18.4	+62 33	A5
ε Pegasi	2.4	21 43.9	+ 9 51	K0
δ Capricorni	2.9	21 46.7	−16 09	A5
α Gruis	1.7	22 07.8	−47 00	B5
δ Cephei†	3.7	22 28.9	+58 23	†
β Gruis	2.1	22 42.3	−46 55	M3
α Piscis Austrini *Fomalhaut*	1.2	22 57.3	−29 39	A3
β Pegasi *Scheat*	2.4	23 03.5	+28 03	M0
α Pegasi *Markab*	2.5	23 04.4	+15 10	A0

*γ Cassiopeiae, 1993 mag. 2.5. β Persei, mag. 2.1 to 3.4. α Orionis, mag. 0.1 to 1.2.

†α Herculis, mag. 3.1 to 3.9. δ Cephei, mag. 3.7 to 4.4, Spectrum F5 to G0.

The positions of heavenly bodies on the celestial sphere are defined by two co-ordinates, right ascension and declination, which are analogous to longitude and latitude on the surface of the Earth. If we imagine the plane of the terrestrial equator extended indefinitely, it will cut the celestial sphere in a great circle known as the celestial equator. Similarly the plane of the Earth's orbit, when extended, cuts in the great circle called the ecliptic. The two intersections of these circles are known as the First Point of Aries and the First Point of Libra. If from any star a perpendicular be drawn to the celestial equator, the length of this perpendicular is the star's declination. The arc, measured eastwards along the equator from the First Point of Aries to the foot of this perpendicular, is the right ascension. An alternative definition of right ascension is that it is the angle at the celestial pole (where the Earth's axis, if prolonged, would meet the sphere) between the great circles to the First Point of Aries and to the star.

The plane of the Earth's equator has a slow movement, so that our reference system for right ascension and declination is not fixed. The consequent alteration in these quantities from year to year is called precession. In right ascension it is an increase of about 3s a year for equatorial stars, and larger or smaller changes in either direction for stars near the poles, depending on the right ascension of the star. In declination it varies between +20″ and −20″ according to the right ascension of the star.

A star or other body crosses the meridian when the sidereal time is equal to its right ascension. The altitude is then a maximum, and may be deduced by remembering that the altitude of the elevated pole is numerically equal to the latitude, while that of the equator at its intersection with the meridian is equal to the co-latitude, or complement of the latitude.

Thus in London (lat. 51° 30′) the meridian altitude of *Sirius* is found as follows:

	° ′
Altitude of equator	38 30
Declination south	16 43
Difference	21 47

The altitude of *Capella* (Dec. +45° 59′) at lower transit is:

Altitude of pole	51 30
Polar distance of star	44 01
Difference	7 29

The brightness of a heavenly body is denoted by its magnitude. Omitting the exceptionally bright stars Sirius and Canopus, the twenty brightest stars are of the first magnitude, while the faintest stars visible to the naked eye are of the sixth magnitude. The magnitude scale is a precise one, as a difference of five magnitudes represents a ratio of 100 to 1 in brightness. Typical second magnitude stars are Polaris and the stars in the belt of Orion. The scale is most easily fixed in memory by comparing the stars with Norton's *Star Atlas* (*see* page 66). The stars Sirius and Canopus and the planets Venus and Jupiter are so bright that their magnitudes are expressed by negative numbers. A small telescope will show stars down to the ninth or tenth magnitude, while stars fainter than the twentieth magnitude may be photographed by long exposures with the largest telescopes.

ECLIPSES AND SHADOW TRANSITS OF JUPITER'S SATELLITES 1993

Jupiter's satellites transit across the disk from east to west, and pass behind the disk from west to east. The shadows that they cast also transit across the disk. With the exception at times of Satellite IV, the satellites also pass through the shadow of the planet, i.e. they are eclipsed. Just before opposition the satellite disappears in the shadow to the west of the planet and reappears from occultation on the east limb. Immediately after opposition the satellite is occulted at the west limb and reappears from eclipse to the east of the planet. At times approximately two to four months before and after opposition, both phases of eclipses of Satellite III may be seen. When Satellite IV is eclipsed, both phases may be seen.

The times given refer to the centre of the satellite. As the satellite is of considerable size, the immersion and emersion phases are not instantaneous. Even when the satellite enters or leaves the shadow along a radius of the shadow, the phase can last for several minutes. With satellite IV, grazing phenomena can occur so that the light from the satellite may fade and brighten again without a complete eclipse taking place.

The list of phenomena gives most of the eclipses and shadow transits visible in the British Isles under favourable conditions.

Ec. = Eclipse
Sh. = Shadow transit
D. = Disappearance
R. = Reappearance
I. = Ingress
E. = Egress

GMT	*Sat.*	*Phen.*
JANUARY		
d h m		
1 02 26	I	Sh.E.
2 02 31	II	Sh.I.
2 05 03	II	Sh.E.
6 03 26	III	Sh.I.
6 06 25	III	Sh.E.
6 07 38	I	Sh.I.
7 04 46	I	Ec.D.
8 02 07	I	Sh.I.
8 04 19	I	Sh.E.
9 05 05	II	Sh.I.
9 07 36	II	Sh.E.
13 07 25	III	Sh.I.
14 06 39	I	Ec.D.
15 04 00	I	Sh.I.
15 06 12	I	Sh.E.
16 01 07	I	Ec.D.
16 07 38	II	Sh.I.
17 00 26	III	Ec.R.
17 00 41	I	Sh.E.
22 05 53	I	Sh.I.
23 03 00	I	Ec.D.
24 00 21	I	Sh.I.
24 01 23	III	Ec.D.
24 02 34	I	Sh.E.
24 04 22	III	Ec.R.
25 05 15	II	Ec.D.
27 01 59	II	Sh.E.
30 04 53	I	Ec.D.
31 02 15	I	Sh.I.
31 04 27	I	Sh.E.
31 05 21	III	Ec.D.
FEBRUARY		
3 02 02	II	Sh.I.
3 04 32	II	Sh.E.
6 06 46	I	Ec.D.
7 04 08	I	Sh.I.
7 06 20	I	Sh.E.
8 01 15	I	Ec.D.
9 00 49	I	Sh.E.
10 04 36	II	Sh.I.
10 07 06	II	Sh.E.
10 23 15	III	Sh.I.
11 02 10	III	Sh.E.
11 23 43	II	Ec.D.
14 06 01	I	Sh.I.
15 03 08	I	Ec.D.
16 00 30	I	Sh.I.
16 02 42	I	Sh.E.
18 03 12	III	Sh.I.
18 06 06	III	Sh.E.
19 02 18	II	Ec.D.
20 22 57	II	Sh.E.
22 05 01	I	Ec.D.
23 02 23	I	Sh.I.
23 04 35	I	Sh.E.
23 23 29	I	Ec.D.
24 23 04	I	Sh.E.
26 04 52	II	Ec.D.
27 23 01	II	Sh.I.
28 01 32	II	Sh.E.
MARCH		
2 04 16	I	Sh.I.
3 01 23	I	Ec.D.
3 22 45	I	Sh.I.
4 00 57	I	Sh.E.
7 01 36	II	Sh.I.
7 04 06	II	Sh.E.
8 01 10	III	Ec.D.
10 03 17	I	Ec.D.
11 00 38	I	Sh.I.
11 02 51	I	Sh.E.
11 21 45	I	Ec.D.
12 21 19	I	Sh.E.
14 04 11	II	Sh.I.
15 05 08	III	Ec.D.
15 23 19	II	Ec.D.
17 05 10	I	Ec.D.
18 02 32	I	Sh.I.
18 04 44	I	Sh.E.
18 21 56	III	Sh.E.
18 23 39	I	Ec.D.
19 21 00	I	Sh.I.
19 23 13	I	Sh.E.
23 01 53	II	Ec.D.

GMT	*Sat.*	*Phen.*
MARCH		
d h m		
24 20 04	II	Sh.I.
24 22 34	II	Sh.E.
25 04 25	I	Sh.I.
25 23 02	III	Sh.I.
26 01 33	I	Ec.D.
26 01 53	III	Sh.E.
26 22 54	I	Sh.I.
27 01 06	I	Sh.E.
27 20 01	I	Ec.D.
30 04 28	II	Ec.D.
31 22 40	II	Sh.I.
APRIL		
1 01 10	II	Sh. E.
2 03 00	III	Sh. I.
2 20 15	II	Ec. R.
3 00 48	I	Sh. I.
3 03 00	I	Sh.E.
4 00 09	I	Ec.R.
4 19 16	I	Sh.I.
4 21 29	I	Sh.E.
5 19 54	III	Ec.R.
8 01 16	II	Sh.I.
8 03 46	II	Sh.E.
9 22 49	II	Ec.R.
10 02 42	I	Sh.I.
10 04 54	I	Sh.E.
11 02 03	I	Ec.R.
11 21 10	I	Sh.I.
11 23 22	I	Sh.E.
12 20 32	I	Ec.R.
12 23 52	III	Ec.R.
15 03 52	II	Sh.I.
17 01 23	II	Ec.R.
17 04 36	I	Sh.I.
18 03 57	I	Ec.R.
18 19 39	II	Sh.E.
18 23 04	I	Sh.I.
19 01 16	I	Sh.E.
19 22 26	I	Ec.R.
20 03 50	III	Ec.R.
20 19 45	I	Sh.E.
24 03 57	II	Ec.R.
25 22 16	II	Sh.E.
26 00 59	I	Sh.I.
26 03 10	I	Sh.E.
27 00 21	I	Ec.R.
27 21 39	I	Sh.E.
30 21 41	III	Sh.E.
MAY		
2 22 24	II	Sh.I.
3 00 52	II	Sh.E.
3 02 53	I	Sh.I.
4 02 16	I	Ec.R.
4 21 22	I	Sh.I.
4 23 33	I	Sh.E.
5 20 44	I	Ec.R.
7 22 54	III	Sh.I.
8 01 39	III	Sh.E.
10 01 01	II	Sh.I.
11 22 23	II	Ec.R.
11 23 16	I	Sh.I.
12 01 27	I	Sh.E.
12 22 39	I	Ec.R.
15 02 53	III	Sh.I.
19 00 57	II	Ec.R.
19 01 10	I	Sh.I.
19 03 21	I	Sh.E.
20 00 34	I	Ec.R.
20 21 50	I	Sh.E.
25 23 42	III	Ec.R.
27 21 34	I	Sh.I.
27 22 02	II	Sh.E.
27 23 44	I	Sh.E.
JUNE		
2 00 58	III	Ec.D.
3 22 12	II	Sh.I.
3 23 28	I	Sh.I.
4 00 39	II	Sh.E.
4 01 39	I	Sh.E.
4 22 53	I	Ec.R.
11 00 50	II	Sh.I.
11 01 23	I	Sh.I.
12 00 48	I	Ec.R.
12 21 29	III	Sh.E.
12 21 57	II	Ec.R.
12 22 02	I	Sh.E.
19 21 46	I	Sh.I.
19 22 05	II	Ec.D.
19 22 49	III	Sh.I.
19 23 56	I	Sh.E.
26 23 41	I	Sh.I.
27 23 08	I	Ec.R.
28 21 49	II	Sh.E.
JULY		
5 22 01	II	Sh.I.
5 22 14	I	Sh.E.
12 21 58	I	Sh.I.
14 21 32	II	Ec.R.
25 21 18	III	Sh.E.
30 21 37	II	Sh.E.
DECEMBER		
18 07 37	I	Ec.D.
19 04 48	I	Sh.I.
19 06 58	I	Sh.E.

ELEMENTS OF THE SOLAR SYSTEM

Orb	Mean distance from Sun (Earth = 1)	km 10^6	Sidereal period	Synodic period	Incl. of orbit to ecliptic	Diameter	Mass (Earth = 1)	Period of rotation on axis
			y d	days	° ′	km		d h m
Sun	—	—	—	—	—	1,392,000	332,948	25 09
Mercury	0.39	58	88	116	7 00	4,880	0.055	59
Venus	0.72	108	225	584	3 24	12,100	0.815	243
Earth	1.00	150	1 0	—	—	12,756*eq*	1.00	23 56
Mars	1.52	228	1 322	780	1 51	6,790	0.107	24 37
Jupiter	5.20	778	11 315	399	1 18	142,800*eq* 134,200*p*	318	9 50 9 56
Saturn	9.54	1427	29 167	378	2 29	120,000*eq* 108,000*p*	95	10 14 10 38
Uranus	19.19	2870	84 6	370	0 46	52,000	14.6	16–28
Neptune	30.07	4497	164 288	367	1 46	48,400	17.2	18–20
Pluto	39.46	5950	247 255	367	17 09	2,445	0.01	6 09

eq equatorial, *p* polar

THE SATELLITES

Name	Star mag.	Mean distance from primary	Sidereal period of revolution
		km	d
EARTH			
Moon	—	384,400	27.322
MARS			
Phobos	12	9,400	0.319
Deimos	13	23,500	1.262
JUPITER			
XVI Metis	17	128,000	0.295
XV Adrastea	19	129,000	0.298
V Amalthea	14	181,000	0.498
XIV Thebe	15	222,000	0.675
I Io	5	422,000	1.769
II Europa	5	671,000	3.551
III Ganymede	5	1,070,000	7.155
IV Callisto	6	1,880,000	16.689
XIII Leda	20	11,090,000	239
VI Himalia	15	11,480,000	251
X Lysithea	18	11,720,000	259
VII Elara	17	11,740,000	260
XII Ananke	19	21,200,000	631
XI Carme	18	22,600,000	692
VIII Pasiphae	18	23,500,000	735
IX Sinope	18	23,700,000	758
SATURN			
Pan	—	134,000	0.575
Atlas	18	138,000	0.602
Prometheus	16	139,000	0.613
Pandora	16	142,000	0.629
Epimetheus	15	151,000	0.694
Janus	14	151,000	0.695
Mimas	13	186,000	0.942
Enceladus	12	238,000	1.370
Tethys	10	295,000	1.888
Telesto	19	295,000	1.888
Calypso	18	295,000	1.888
Dione	10	377,000	2.737
Helene	18	377,000	2.737
Rhea	10	527,000	4.518
Titan	8	1,222,000	15.945
Hyperion	14	1,481,000	21.278
Iapetus	11	3,561,000	79.331
Phoebe	16	12,952,000	550.3
URANUS			
Cordelia	—	49,800	0.330
Ophelia	—	53,800	0.372
Bianca	—	59,200	0.433
Juliet	—	61,800	0.464
Desdemona	—	62,700	0.474
Rosalind	—	64,400	0.493
Portia	—	66,100	0.513
Cressida	—	69,900	0.558
Belinda	—	75,300	0.622
Puck	—	86,000	0.762
Miranda	17	129,000	1.414
Ariel	14	191,000	2.520
Umbriel	15	266,000	4.144
Titania	14	436,000	8.706
Oberon	14	583,000	13.463
NEPTUNE			
Naiad	—	48,000	0.30
Thalassa	—	50,000	0.31
Despina	—	52,000	0.33
Galatea	—	62,000	0.43
Larissa	—	74,000	0.55
Proteus	—	118,000	1.12
Triton	14	355,000	5.877
Nereid	19	5,510,000	360.21
PLUTO			
Charon	17	19,600	6.387

THE EARTH

The shape of the Earth is that of an oblate spheroid or solid of revolution whose meridian sections are ellipses not differing much from circles, whilst the sections at right angles are circles. The length of the equatorial axis is about 12,756 kilometres, and that of the polar axis is 12,714 kilometres. The mean density of the Earth is 5.5 times that of water, although that of the surface layer is less. The Earth and Moon revolve about their common centre of gravity in a lunar month; this centre in turn revolves round the Sun in a plane known as the ecliptic, that passes through the Sun's centre. The Earth's equator is inclined to this plane at an angle of 23.5°. This tilt is the cause of the seasons. In mid-latitudes, and when the Sun is high above the Equator, not only does the high noon altitude make the days longer, but the Sun's rays fall more directly on the Earth's surface; these effects combine to produce summer. In equatorial regions the noon altitude is large throughout the year, and there is little variation in the length of the day. In higher latitudes the noon altitude is lower, and the days in summer are appreciably longer than those in winter.

The average velocity of the Earth in its orbit is 30 kilometres a second. It makes a complete rotation on its axis in about 23h 56m of mean time, which is the sidereal day. Because of its annual revolution round the Sun, the rotation with respect to the Sun, or the solar day, is more than this by about four minutes (*see* page 68). The extremity of the axis of rotation, or the North Pole of the Earth, is not rigidly fixed, but wanders over an area roughly 20 metres in diameter.

TERRESTRIAL MAGNETISM

A magnetic compass points along the horizontal component of a magnetic line of force. These directions converge on the 'magnetic dip-poles', the places where a freely suspended magnetized needle would become vertical. Not only do the positions of these poles change with time, but their exact locations are ill-defined, particularly so in the case of the north dip-pole where the lines of force on the north side of it, instead of converging radially, tend to bunch into a channel. Although it is therefore unrealistic to attempt to specify the locations of the dip-poles exactly, the present adopted positions are 78°.2 N., 103°.7 W. and 64°.8 S., 138°.8 E. The two magnetic dip-poles are thus not antipodal, the line joining them passing the centre of the Earth at a distance of about 1,200 kilometres. The distances of the magnetic dip-poles from the north and south geographical poles are about 1,400 and 2,700 kilometres respectively.

There is also a 'magnetic equator', at all points of which the vertical component of the Earth's magnetic field is zero and a magnetized needle remains horizontal. This line runs between 2° and 10° north of the geographical equator in the eastern hemisphere, turns sharply south off the West African coast, and crosses South America through Brazil, Bolivia and Peru; it recrosses the geographical equator in mid-Pacific.

Reference has already been made to secular changes in the Earth's field. The following table indicates the changes in magnetic declination (or variation of the compass). Similar, though much smaller, changes have occurred in 'dip' or magnetic inclination. Secular changes differ throughout the world. Although the London observations strongly suggest a cycle with a period of several hundred years, an exact repetition is unlikely.

London		*Greenwich*	
1580	11° 15′ E.	1850	22° 24′ W.
1622	5° 56′ E.	1900	16° 29′ W.
1665	1° 22′ W.	1925	13° 10′ W.
1730	13° 00′ W.	1950	9° 07′ W.
1773	21° 09′ W.	1975	6° 39′ W.

In order that up-to-date information on the variation of the compass may be available, many governments publish magnetic charts on which there are lines (isogonic lines) passing through all places at which specified values of declination will be found at the date of the chart.

In the British Isles, isogonic lines now run approximately north-east to south-west. Though there are considerable local deviations due to geological causes, a rough value of magnetic declination may be obtained by assuming that at 50° N. on the meridian of Greenwich, the value in 1993 is 3° 50′ west and allowing an increase of 10′ for each degree of latitude northwards and one of 24′ for each degree of longitude westwards. For example, at 53° N., 5° W., declination will be about 3° 50′+30′+120′, i.e. 6° 20′ west. The average annual change at the present time is about 8′ decrease.

The number of magnetic observatories is about 200, widely scattered over the globe. There are three in Great Britain run by the British Geological Survey: at Hartland, North Devon; at Eskdalemuir, Dumfriesshire; and at Lerwick, Shetland Islands. The following are some recent annual mean values of the magnetic elements for Hartland.

Year	*Declination West*	*Dip or inclination*	*Horizontal force*	*Vertical force*
	° ′	° ′	oersted	oersted
1955	10 30	66 49	0.1859	0.4340
1960	9 59	66 44	0.1871	0.4350
1965	9 30	66 34	0.1887	0.4354
1970	9 06	66 26	0.1903	0.4364
1975	8 32	66 17	0.1921	0.4373
1980	7 44	66 10	0.1933	0.4377
1985	6 56	66 08	0.1938	0.4380
1990	6 15	66 10	0.1939	0.4388
1991	6 07	66 10	0.1940	0.4391

The normal world-wide terrestrial magnetic field corresponds approximately to that of a very strong small bar magnet near the centre of the Earth but with appreciable smooth spatial departures. The origin and slow secular change of the normal field are not yet fully understood but are generally ascribed to electric currents associated with fluid motions in the Earth's core. Superimposed on the normal field are local and regional anomalies whose magnitudes may in places exceed that of the normal field; these are due to the influence of mineral deposits in the Earth's crust. A small proportion of the field is of external origin, mostly associated with electric currents in the ionosphere. The configuration of the external field and the ionization of the atmosphere depend on the incident particle and radiation flux from the Sun. There are, therefore, short-term and non-periodic as well as diurnal, 27-day, seasonal and 11-year periodic changes in the magnetic field, dependent upon the position of the Sun and the degree of solar activity.

Magnetic Storms

Occasionally, sometimes with great suddenness, the Earth's magnetic field is subject for several hours to marked disturbance. In extreme cases, departures in field intensity of as much as one-tenth the normal value are experienced. In many instances, such disturbances are accompanied by widespread displays of aurorae, marked changes in the incidence of cosmic rays, an increase in the reception of 'noise' from the Sun at radio frequencies together with rapid changes in the ionosphere and induced electric currents within the Earth which adversely affect radio and telegraphic communications. The disturbances are generally ascribed to changes in the stream of neutral and ionized particles which emanates from the Sun and through which the Earth is continuously passing. Some of these changes are associated with visible eruptions on the Sun, usually in the region of sun-spots. There is a marked tendency for disturbances to recur after intervals of about 27 days, the apparent period of rotation of the Sun on its axis, which is consistent with the sources being located on particular areas of the Sun.

ARTIFICIAL SATELLITES

To consider the orbit of an artificial satellite, it is best to imagine that one is looking at the Earth from a distant point in space. The Earth would then be seen to be rotating about its axis inside the orbit described by the rapidly revolving satellite. The inclination of a satellite orbit to the Earth's equator (which generally remains almost constant throughout the satellite's lifetime) gives at once the maximum range of latitudes over which the satellite passes. Thus a satellite whose orbit has an inclination of 53° will pass overhead all latitudes between 53° S. and 53° N., but would never be seen in the zenith of any place nearer the poles than these latitudes. If we consider a particular place on the earth, whose latitude is less than the inclination of the satellite's orbit, then the Earth's rotation carries this place first under the northbound part of the orbit and then under the southbound portion of the orbit, these two occurrences being always less than 12 hours apart for satellites moving in direct orbits (i.e. to the east). (For satellites in retrograde orbits, the words 'northbound' and 'southbound' should be interchanged in the preceding statement.) As the value of the latitude of the observer increases and approaches the value of the inclination of the orbit, so this interval gets shorter until (when the latitude is equal to the inclination) only one overhead passage occurs each day.

Observation of Satellites

The regression of the orbit around the Earth causes alternate periods of visibility and invisibility, though this is of little concern to the radio or radar observer. To the visual observer the following cycle of events normally occurs (though the cycle may start in any position): invisibility, morning observations before dawn, invisibility, evening observations after dusk, invisibility, morning observations before dawn, and so on. With reasonably high satellites and for observers in high latitudes around the summer solstice, the evening observations follow the morning observations without interruption as sunlight passing over the polar regions can still illuminate satellites which are passing over temperate latitudes at local midnight. At the moment all satellites rely on sunlight to make them visible, though a satellite with a flashing light has been suggested for a future launching. The observer must be in darkness or twilight in order to make any useful observations and the durations of twilight and the sunrise, sunset times given on Page Two of each month will be a useful guide.

Some of the satellites are visible to the naked eye and much interest has been aroused by the spectacle of a bright satellite disappearing into the Earth's shadow. The event is even more fascinating telescopically as the disappearance occurs gradually as the satellite traverses the Earth's penumbral shadow, and during the last few seconds before the eclipse is complete the satellite may change colour (in suitable atmospheric conditions) from yellow to red. This is because the last rays of sunlight are refracted through the denser layers of our atmosphere before striking the satellite.

Some satellites rotate about one or more axes so that a periodic variation in brightness is observed. This was particularly noticeable in several of the Soviet satellites.

Satellite research has provided some interesting results. Among them may be mentioned a revised value of the Earth's oblateness, 1/298.2, and the discovery of the Van Allen radiation belts.

Launchings

Apart from their names, e.g. Cosmos 6 Rocket, the satellites are also classified according to their date of launch. Thus 1961 α refers to the first satellite launching of 1961. A number following the Greek letter indicated the relative brightness of the satellites put in orbit. From the beginning of 1963 the Greek letters were replaced by numbers and the numbers by roman letters e.g. 1963–01A. For all satellites successfully injected into orbit the table gives the designation and names of the main objects (in the order A, B, C . . . etc.), the launch date and some initial orbital data. These are the inclination to the equator (i), the nodal period of revolution (P), the eccentricity (e), and the perigee height.

Although most of the satellites launched are injected into orbits less than 1,000 km high there are an increasing number of satellites in geostationary orbits, i.e. where the orbital inclination is zero, the eccentricity close to zero, and the period of revolution is 1436.1 minutes. Thus the satellite is permanently situated over the equator at one selected longitude at a mean height of 35,786 km. Already this geostationary band is crowded; for example, the television satellite Astra 1A (1988–109B) has been placed only 0°.2 away from the communication satellite Arabsat 1A (1985–15A).

ARTIFICIAL SATELLITE LAUNCHES 1990–2

Designation	Satellite	Launch date	i	P	e	Perigee height
1990–			°	m		km
76	Cosmos 2097, launcher rocket, launcher, rocket	August 28	62.9	718.0	0.737	614
77	Yuri 3A	August 28	0.2	1436.1	0.000	35780
78	Cosmos 2098, rocket	August 28	83.0	109.2	0.104	396
79	Skynet 4C, Eutelsat 2 F-1	August 30	4.3	1436.0	0.000	35781
80	Cosmos 2099, rocket, engine	August 31	82.3	90.4	0.008	239
81	China 30-32, rocket	September 3	98.9	102.9	0.001	885
82	Resurs-F9, rocket, engine	September 7	82.6	89.9	0.001	261
83	Cosmos 2100, rocket	September 14	82.9	104.9	0.004	961
84	Molniya 3-39, launcher rocket, launcher, rocket	September 20	62.8	717.8	0.741	507
85	Progress-M5, rocket	September 27	51.6	90.5	0.002	284
86	Meteor 2-20, rocket	September 28	82.5	104.2	0.001	943
87	Cosmos 2101, rocket	October 1	64.7	89.5	0.006	212
88	Navstar 2-09	October 1	54.9	717.9	0.008	19972
89	China 33, rocket	October 5	57.0	89.7	0.008	208
90	STS 41	October 6	28.5	90.4	0.001	285
91	SBS 6, Galaxy 6	October 12	0.1	1436.1	0.002	35723
92	Cosmos 2102, rocket	October 16	62.8	90.0	0.012	191
93	Inmarsat 2F-1	October 30	2.5	1436.3	0.003	35660
94	Gorizont 21, launcher	November 3	1.4	1436.0	0.000	35780
95	USA 65	November 13				
96	Cosmos 2103, rocket	November 14	65.0	92.8	0.001	403
97	STS 38, USA 67	November 15	28.5	89.2	0.003	221
98	Cosmos 2104, rocket, engine	November 16	62.8	89.6	0.004	232
99	Cosmos 2105, launcher rocket, launcher, rocket	November 20	63.2	717.5	0.738	580
100	Satcom C1, G Star	November 20	0.0	1435.9	0.000	35776
101	Molniya 1-79, launcher rocket, launcher, rocket	November 23	62.8	717.5	0.737	607
102	Gorizont 22, launcher	November 23	1.4	1435.9	0.001	35760
103	Navstar 2A-01, rocket	November 26	54.9	718.0	0.004	20073
104	Cosmos 2106, rocket	November 28	82.5	95.2	0.001	518
105	DMSP 2-05	December 1	98.9	100.7	0.008	732

Designation	Satellite	Launch date	i	P	e	Perigee height
1990–			°	m		km
106	STS-35	December 2	28.5	91.4	0.001	347
107	Soyuz TM11, rocket	December 2	51.6	90.3	0.003	275
108	Cosmos 2107, rocket	December 4	65.0	92.8	0.001	404
109	Cosmos 2108, rocket	December 4	62.8	89.7	0.011	186
110	Cosmos 2109-2111	December 8	64.8	675.7	0.006	18970
111	Cosmos 2112, rocket	December 10	74.0	100.7	0.003	771
112	Raduga 26, launcher	December 20	1.4	1435.6	0.001	35756
113	Cosmos 2113, rocket	December 21	64.8	89.7	0.003	237
114	Cosmos 2113-2119, rocket	December 22	82.6	114.1	0.000	1410
115	Cosmos 2120, rocket	December 26	82.6	90.4	0.008	237
116	Raduga 1-02, launcher	December 27	1.5	1463.6	0.003	36189
1991–						
01	NATO, 4A, rocket	January 8	4.2	1409.4	0.008	34915
02	Progress-M6, rocket	January 14	51.6	90.3	0.007	248
03	Italsat 1, Eutelsat 2F-2	January 15	7.0	630.2	0.729	217
04	Cosmos 2121, rocket, engine	January 17	82.6	90.0	0.005	235
05	Cosmos 2122, rocket	January 18	65.0	92.8	0.001	404
06	Informator 1, rocket	January 29	82.9	104.8	0.003	959
07	Cosmos 2123, rocket	February 5	82.9	104.9	0.003	965
08	Cosmos 2124, rocket	February 7	62.8	89.2	0.008	182
09	Cosmos 2125-2132, rocket	February 12	74.0	115.3	0.001	1458
10	Cosmos 2133, launcher	February 14	2.3	1436.0	0.001	35760
11	Cosmos 2134, rocket	February 15	64.7	89.2	0.004	212
12	Molniya 1-80, launcher rocket, launcher, rocket	February 15	62.8	717.9	0.744	422
13	Cosmos 2135, rocket	February 26	82.8	104.6	0.007	925
14	Raduga 27, launcher	February 28	1.5	1436.1	0.000	35778
15	Astra 1B, Meteosat 5	March 2	0.2	1424.1	0.002	35470
16	Cosmos 2136, rocket, engine	March 6	62.8	89.1	0.004	206
17	USA 69	March 8	68.0	98.3	0.000	672
18	Inmarsat 2F-2	March 8	2.7	1436.2	0.001	35767
19	Nadezhda 3, rocket	March 12	82.9	104.9	0.004	958
20	Progress-M7, rocket	March 19	51.6	92.0	0.002	366
21	Cosmos 2137, rocket	March 19	65.8	94.0	0.003	449
22	Molniya 3-40, launcher rocket, launcher, rocket	March 22	62.9	700.9	0.740	429
23	Cosmos 2138, rocket	March 26	67.2	90.1	0.013	192
24	Almaz 1	March 31	72.7	90.0	0.001	268
25	Cosmos 2139-2141	April 4	64.8	675.7	0.001	19111
26	Anik E2	April 4	0.1	1432.8	0.001	35692
27	STS 37, Gama Ray Observatory	April 5	28.4	93.5	0.001	446
28	ASC-2	April 13	0.3	1428.3	0.002	35559
29	Cosmos 2142, rocket	April 16	83.0	105.0	0.004	962
30	Meteor 3-04, rocket	April 24	82.5	109.5	0.002	1187
31	STS 39, IBSS, MPEC	April 28	57.0	89.7	0.001	253
32	NOAA 12	May 14	98.7	101.4	0.001	812
33	Cosmos 2143-2148, rocket	May 16	82.6	114.0	0.001	1400
34	Soyuz TM12, rocket	May 18	51.6	90.2	0.004	259
35	Resurs-F10, rocket	May 21	82.3	89.2	0.000	230
36	Cosmos 2149, rocket	May 24	67.1	90.2	0.014	189
37	Aurora 2, rocket	May 29	0.1	1435.9	0.001	35731
38	Progress-M8, rocket	May 30	51.6	90.1	0.001	279
39	Okean 3, rocket	June 4	82.5	97.8	0.002	634
40	STS 40	June 5	39.0	90.1	0.001	279
41	Cosmos 2150, rocket	June 11	74.0	100.8	0.002	783
42	Cosmos 2151, rocket	June 13	82.5	97.8	0.002	636

Designation	Satellite	Launch date	*i*	*P*	*e*	Perigee height
1991–			°	m		km
43	Molniya 1-81, launcher rocket, launcher, rocket	June 18	62.9	717.7	0.743	446
44	Resurs-F11, rocket, engine	June 28	82.3	89.9	0.001	258
45	REX	June 29	89.6	101.4	0.007	773
46	Gorizont 23, launcher	July 1	1.5	1435.9	0.002	35687
47	Navstar 2A-02, Losat-X, rocket	July 4	55.3	717.9	0.004	20083
48	Cosmos 2152, rocket, engine	July 9	82.3	89.5	0.002	233
49	Cosmos 2153, rocket	July 10	64.9	89.7	0.003	242
50	ERS 1, UOSAT 5, Orbcomm-X, Tabsat, SARA	July 17	98.5	100.5	0.000	777
51	Microsat 1-7, rocket	July 17	82.0	92.7	0.007	358
52	Resurs-F12, rocket, engine	July 23	82.3	89.9	0.001	257
53	Molniya 1-82, launcher rocket, launcher, rocket	August 1	62.9	717.8	0.736	620
54	STS 43, TDRS 5	August 2	28.5	90.6	0.002	299
55	Intelsat 6F-5	August 14	0.0	1435.9	0.001	35751
56	Meteor 3-05, rocket	August 15	82.6	109.4	0.001	1188
57	Progress-M9, rocket	August 20	51.6	90.8	0.000	312
58	Resurs-F13, rocket	August 21	82.3	89.2	0.000	230
59	Cosmos 2154, rocket	August 22	82.9	105.0	0.002	973
60	Yuri 3B	August 25	28.5	659.5	0.738	197
61	IRS-1B, rocket	August 29	99.1	103.1	0.003	882
62	Yohkoh, rocket	August 30	31.3	97.7	0.019	523
63	STS 48, UARS	September 12	57.0	96.0	0.001	561
64	Cosmos 2155, launcher	September 13	1.3	1435.9	0.001	35761
65	Molniya 3-41, launcher rocket, launcher, rocket	September 17	62.8	717.9	0.743	453
66	Cosmos 2156, rocket	September 19	67.1	89.8	0.012	185
67	Anik E1	September 26	2.3	724.2	0.578	4903
68	Cosmos 2157-2162, rocket	September 28	82.6	114.1	0.001	1407
69	Soyuz TM13, rocket	October 2	51.6	90.1	0.002	271
70	Foton 4, rocket, engine	October 4	62.8	90.6	0.013	215
71	Cosmos 2163, rocket	October 9	64.8	90.3	0.011	214
72	Cosmos 2164, rocket	October 10	74.0	94.6	0.031	285
73	Progress-M10, rocket	October 17	51.6	91.1	0.004	304
74	Gorizont 24, launcher	October 23	1.5	1447.4	0.000	36008
75	Intelsat 6F-1	October 29	4.4	715.6	0.589	4531
76	USA 72, 74, 76, 77	November 8	n/a	n/a	n/a	n/a
77	Cosmos 2165-2170, rocket	November 12	82.6	113.9	0.001	1395
78	Cosmos 2171, rocket	November 20	62.8	89.6	0.010	189
79	Cosmos 2172, launcher	November 22	1.4	1463.2	0.000	36298
80	STS 44, USA 75	November 24	28.5	91.6	0.001	358
81	Cosmos 2173, rocket	November 27	82.9	104.8	0.005	947
82	DMSP 2-06	November 28	98.9	102.0	0.001	840
83	Eutelsat 2F-3	December 7	0.1	1434.0	0.003	35605
84	Telecom 2A, Inmarsat 2F-3	December 16	0.2	1433.3	0.001	35709
85	Cosmos 2174, rocket	December 17	64.9	89.3	0.004	209
86	Intercosmos 25, rocket, Magion 3	December 18	82.6	121.7	0.162	437
87	Raduga 28, launcher	December 19	1.4	1436.5	0.001	35761
88	China 34, rocket	December 28	31.0	112.2	0.145	213
1992–		1992				
01	Cosmos 2175, rocket	January 21	67.1	89.7	0.011	184
02	STS 42	January 22	57.0	90.5	0.001	294
03	Cosmos 2176, launcher rocket, launcher, rocket	January 24	62.8	717.7	0.737	604
04	Progress-M11, rocket	January 25	51.6	90.1	0.003	264
05	Cosmos 2177, 2178	January 29	64.8	676.1	0.000	19132
06	DSCS 3B-01, IABS-01	February 11	n/a	n/a	n/a	n/a
07	Fuyo 1	February 11	97.7	96.1	0.001	567

Designation	Satellite	Launch date	*i*	*P*	*e*	Perigee height
1992–			°	m		km
08	Cosmos 2180, rocket	February 17	82.9	104.9	0.004	962
09	Navstar 2A-03, rocket	February 23	55.0	715.0	0.008	19901
10	Superbird B1, Arabsat 1C	February 27	0.1	1355.1	0.040	32547
11	Molniya 1-83, launcher rocket, launcher, rocket	March 4	62.8	717.7	0.736	620
12	Cosmos 2181, rocket	March 9	82.9	105.0	0.003	973
13	Galaxy 5	March 14	0.1	1436.1	0.002	35695
14	Soyuz TM14, rocket	March 17	51.6	90.1	0.003	263
15	STS 45	March 24	57.0	90.4	0.001	292
16	Cosmos 2182, rocket	April 1	67.2	89.3	0.011	166
17	Gorizont 25, launcher	April 2	1.4	1435.8	0.000	35769
18	Cosmos 2183, rocket	April 8	64.9	89.8	0.004	240
19	Navstar 2A-04, rocket	April 10	55.1	717.9	0.008	19979
20	Cosmos 2184, rocket	April 15	82.9	105.0	0.003	967

The Royal Observatories

ROYAL GREENWICH OBSERVATORY

Madingley Road, Cambridge CB3 0EZ
Tel 0223-374000

The Royal Greenwich Observatory was founded at Greenwich by Charles II in 1675. Because of smog and light pollution the Observatory was moved to Herstmonceux after the Second World War. The development of first-class overseas sites for the country's telescopes obviated the need for telescopes in the UK and so the Observatory was relocated to Cambridge in 1990 and is now on a site next to the University's Institute of Astronomy.

The main task of the Observatory, which is an establishment of the Science and Engineering Research Council, is the provision of facilities for research in optical astronomy for astronomers in the universities. This involves running the Isaac Newton group of telescopes with their associated instrumentation at the Roque de los Muchachos Observatory on La Palma in the Canary Islands. This group comprises the 4.2 m William Herschel telescope, the 2.5 m Isaac Newton telescope and the 1 m Jacobus Kapteyn telescope. The running of these is shared with the Netherlands, and also, in the case of the Jacobus Kapteyn telescope, with the Republic of Ireland.

The Carlsberg Automatic Meridian Circle, also at the Roque de los Muchachos Observatory, is run as a collaborative project with Danish and Spanish astronomers and continues the Observatory's traditional work in positional astronomy, as does the reduction of data from the European Space Agency's HIPPARCOS astrometric satellite.

The Satellite Laser Ranger, used to monitor the Earth's rate of rotation and other geophysical parameters such as continental drift, remains at Herstmonceux.

At the UK headquarters in Cambridge, there are facilities for the design and manufacture of the complex instrumentation that is needed for modern optical astronomy. The Observatory runs the largest node of the Starlink computing network. This serves both the Observatory and the Institute of Astronomy and is used for the reduction of astronomical data from the Observatory's measuring machines, the La Palma telescopes and elsewhere. The observatory also houses HM Nautical Almanac Office, responsible for the production of almanacs and basic astronomical data.

Director, Prof. A. Boksenberg, FRS.

ROYAL OBSERVATORY

Blackford Hill, Edinburgh EH9 3HJ
Tel 031-668 8100

The Observatory was founded by the Astronomical Institution in 1818 and its Royal Charter dates from 1822. It is now responsible for some major national astronomical facilities funded by the Science and Engineering Research Council, including a 15.0 m millimetre-wave telescope and a 3.8 m infra-red telescope in Hawaii, and COSMOS, a fast automatic plate measuring machine, in Edinburgh. The Observatory is also part of the UK Starlink network for astronomical image and data processing. The Observatory specializes in the development of advanced technologies and the application of these to studies of the properties of matter in extreme environments in space.

Director, Dr P. G. Murdin, OBE.

Time Measurement and Calendars

MEASUREMENTS OF TIME

Measurements of time are based on the time taken by the earth to rotate on its axis (day); by the moon to revolve round the earth (month); and by the earth to revolve round the sun (year). From these, which are not commensurable, certain average or mean intervals have been adopted for ordinary use.

THE DAY

The day begins at midnight and is divided into 24 hours of 60 minutes, each of 60 seconds. The hours are counted from midnight up to 12 noon (when the sun crosses the meridian), and these hours are designated a.m. (*ante meridiem*); and again from noon up to 12 midnight, which hours are designated p.m. (*post meridiem*), except when the twenty-four hour reckoning is employed. The 24-hour reckoning ignores a.m. and p.m., and the hours are numbered 0 to 23 from midnight to midnight.

Colloquially the 24 hours are divided into day and night, day being the time while the sun is above the horizon (including the four stages of twilight defined on page 67). Day is subdivided further into morning, the early part of daytime, ending at noon; afternoon, from noon to 6 p.m.; and evening, which may be said to extend from 6 p.m. until midnight. Night, the dark period between day and day, begins at the close of astronomical twilight (*see* page 67) and extends beyond midnight to sunrise the next day.

The names of the days are derived from Old English translations or adaptations of the Roman titles.

Sunday	Sun	Sol
Monday	Moon	Luna
Tuesday	Tiw/Tyr (god of war)	Mars
Wednesday	Woden/Odin	Mercury
Thursday	Thor	Jupiter
Friday	Frigga/Freyja (goddess of love)	Venus
Saturday	Saeternes	Saturn

THE WEEK

The week is a period of seven days.

THE MONTH

The month in the ordinary calendar is approximately the twelfth part of a year, but the lengths of the different months vary from 28 (or 29) days to 31.

THE YEAR

The equinoctial or tropical year is the time that the earth takes to revolve round the sun from equinox to equinox, or 365.2422 mean solar days.

The calendar year consists of 365 days, but a year the date of which is divisible by four without remainder, is called bissextile (*see* Roman Calendar) or leap year and consists of 366 days, one day being added to the month February, so that a date 'leaps over' a day of the week. The last year of a century is not a leap year unless its number is divisible by 400 (e.g. the years 1800 and 1900 had only 365 days but the year 2000 will have 366 days).

THE SOLSTICE

A solstice is the point in the tropical year at which the sun attains its greatest distance, north or south, from the Equator. In the northern hemisphere the greatest distance north of the Equator is the summer solstice and the greatest distance south is the winter solstice.

The date of the solstice varies according to locality. If the summer solstice falls on 21 June late in the day by Greenwich time, that day will be the longest of the year at Greenwich even though it may be by only a second of time or a fraction thereof, but it will be on 22 June, local date, in Japan, and so 22 June will be the longest day there and at places in eastern longitudes.

The date of the solstice is also affected by the length of the tropical year, which is 365.24 days, less about 11 minutes. If a solstice happens late on 21 June in one year, it will be nearly six hours later in the next, i.e. early on 22 June, and that will be the longest day. This delay of the solstice is not permitted to continue because the extra day in leap year brings it back a day in the calendar.

However, because of the 11 minutes mentioned above, the additional day in leap year brings the solstice back too far by 44 minutes, and the time of the solstice in the calendar is earlier as the century progresses. (In the year 2000 the summer solstice reaches its earliest date for 100 years, i.e. 02 h on 21 June.) To remedy this the last year of a century is in most cases not a leap year, and the omission of the extra day puts the date of the solstice later by about six hours too much, compensation for which is made by making the fourth centennial year a leap year.

Similar considerations apply to the day of the winter solstice, the shortest day of the year. In the year 2000 the winter solstice reaches its earliest date, i.e. 13 h on 21 December. The difference due to locality also prevails in the same sense as for the longest day.

At Greenwich the sun sets at its earliest by the clock about ten days before the shortest day. The reason for this is twofold. First the daily change in the time of sunset is due in the first place to the sun's movement southwards at this time of the year, which diminishes the interval between the sun's transit and its setting. Second, the daily decrease of the Equation of Time causes the time of apparent noon to be continuously later day by day. This in a measure counteracts the first effect. The rates of the change of these two quantities are not equal, nor are they uniform, but are such that their combination causes the date of earliest sunset to be 12 or 13 December at Greenwich. In more southerly latitudes the effect of the movement of the sun is less, and the change in the time of sunset depends on that of the Equation of Time to a greater degree, and the date of earliest sunset is earlier than it is at Greenwich.

THE EQUINOX

The equinox is the point at which the sun crosses the Equator and day and night are of equal length all over the world. This occurs in March (vernal equinox) and September (autumnal equinox).

DOG DAYS

The days about the heliacal rising of the Dog Star, noted from ancient times as the hottest and most unwholesome period of the year in the northern hemisphere, are called the Dog Days. Their incidence has been variously calculated as depending on the Greater or Lesser Dog Star (Sirius or Procyon) and their duration has been reckoned as from 30 to 54 days. A generally accepted period is from 3 July to 15 August.

CHRISTIAN CALENDAR

In the Christian chronological system the years are distinguished by cardinal numbers before or after the Incarnation, the period being denoted by the letters BC (Before Christ) or, more rarely, AC (*Ante Christum*), and AD (*Anno Domini* – In the Year of Our Lord). The correlative dates of the epoch are the fourth year of the 194th Olympiad, the 753rd year from the foundation of Rome, AM 3761 (Jewish chronology), and the 4714th year of the Julian period.

The system was introduced into Italy in the sixth century. Though first used in France in the seventh century, it was not universally established there until about the eighth century. It has been said that the system was introduced into England by St Augustine (AD 596), but it was probably not generally used until some centuries later. It was ordered to be used by the Bishops at the Council of Chelsea (AD 816). The actual date of the birth of Christ is somewhat uncertain.

The Julian Calendar

In the Julian calendar all the centennial years were leap years, and for this reason towards the close of the sixteenth century there was a difference of ten days between the tropical and calendar years; the equinox fell on 11 March of the calendar, whereas at the time of the Council of Nicaea (AD 325), it had fallen on 21 March. In 1582 Pope Gregory ordained that 5 October should be called 15 October and that of the end-century years only the fourth should be a leap year (*see* page 82).

The Gregorian Calendar

The Gregorian Calendar was adopted by Italy, France, Spain, and Portugal in 1582, by Prussia, the Roman Catholic German states, Switzerland, Holland and Flanders on 1 January 1583, by Poland in 1586, Hungary in 1587, the Protestant German and Netherland states and Denmark in 1700, and by Great Britain and her Dominions (including the North American colonies) in 1752, by the omission of eleven days (3 September being reckoned as 14 September). Sweden omitted the leap day in 1700 but observed leap days in 1704 and 1708, and reverted to the Julian calendar by having two leap days in 1712; the Gregorian calendar was adopted in 1753 by the omission of eleven days (18 February being reckoned as 1 March). Japan adopted the calendar in 1872, China in 1912, Bulgaria in 1915, Turkey and Soviet Russia in 1918, Yugoslavia and Romania in 1919, and Greece in February 1923.

In the same year that the change was made in England from the Julian to the Gregorian calendar, the beginning of the new year was also changed from 25 March to 1 January (*see* page 87).

The Orthodox Churches

Some Orthodox Churches still use the Julian reckoning, but the majority of Greek Orthodox Churches and the Romanian Orthodox Church have adopted a modified 'New Calendar', observing the Gregorian calendar for fixed feasts and the Julian for movable feasts.

The Orthodox Church year begins on 1 September. There are four fast periods, and in addition to Pascha (Easter), twelve great feasts, as well as numerous commemorations of the saints of the Old and New Testaments throughout the year.

The Dominical Letter

The Dominical Letter is one of the letters A–G which are used to denote the Sundays in successive years. If the first day of the year is a Sunday the letter is A; if the second, B; the third, C; and so on. Leap year requires two letters, the first for 1 January to 29 February, the second for 1 March to 31 December (*see* page 85).

Epiphany

The feast of the Epiphany, commemorating the manifestation of Christ, later became associated with the offering of gifts by the Magi. The day was of exceptional importance from the time of the Council of Nicaea (AD 325), as the primate of Alexandria was charged at every Epiphany feast with the announcement in a letter to the churches of the date of the forthcoming Easter. The day was of considerable importance in Britain as it influenced dates, ecclesiastical and lay, e.g. Plough Monday, when work was resumed in the fields, falls upon the Monday in the first full week after Epiphany.

Lent

The Teutonic word *Lent*, which denotes the fast preceding Easter, originally meant no more than the spring season; but from Anglo-Saxon times at least it has been used as the equivalent of the more significant Latin term Quadragesima, meaning the 'forty days' or, more literally, the fortieth day. Ash Wednesday is the first day of Lent, which ends at midnight before Easter Day.

Palm Sunday

Palm Sunday, the Sunday before Easter and the beginning of Holy Week, commemorates the triumphal entry of Christ into Jerusalem and is celebrated in Britain (when palm is not available) by branches of willow gathered for use in the decoration of churches on that day.

Maundy Thursday

Maundy Thursday is the day before Good Friday, the name itself being a corruption of *dies mandati* (day of the mandate) when Christ washed the feet of the disciples and gave them the mandate to love one another.

Easter Day

Easter Day is the first Sunday after the full moon which happens upon, or next after, the 21st day of March; if the full moon happens upon a Sunday, Easter Day is the Sunday after.

This definition is contained in an Act of Parliament (24 Geo. II c. 23) and explanation is given in the preamble to the Act that the day of full moon depends on certain tables that have been prepared. These are the tables whose essential points are given in the early pages of the Book of Common Prayer. The moon referred to is not the real moon of the heavens, but a hypothetical moon on whose 'full' the date of Easter depends, and the lunations of this 'calendar' moon consist of twenty-nine and thirty days alternately, with certain necessary modifications to make the date of its full agree as nearly as possible with that of the real moon, which is known as the Paschal Full Moon. As at present ordained, Easter falls on one of 35 days (22 March–25 April).

A Fixed Easter

On 15 June 1928 the House of Commons agreed to a motion for the third reading of a bill proposing that Easter Day shall, in the calendar year next but one after the commencement of the Act and in all subsequent years, be the first Sunday after the second Saturday in April. Easter would thus fall between 9 and 15 April (inclusive), that is, on the second or third Sunday in April. A clause in the Bill provided that before it shall come into operation, regard shall be had to any opinion expressed officially by the various Christian churches. Efforts by the World Council of Churches to secure a unanimous choice of date for Easter by its member churches have so far been unsuccessful.

Rogation Days

Rogation Days are the Monday, Tuesday and Wednesday preceding Ascension Day and in the fifth century were ordered by the Church to be observed as public fasts with solemn processions and supplications. The processions were discontinued as religious observances at the Reformation, but survive in the ceremony known as 'Beating the Parish Bounds'. Rogation Sunday is the Sunday before Ascension Day.

Ember Days

The Ember Days at the four seasons are the Wednesday, Friday and Saturday (*a*) before the third Sunday in Advent, (*b*) before the second Sunday in Lent, and (*c*) before the Sundays nearest to the festivals of St Peter and of St Michael and All Angels.

Trinity Sunday

Trinity Sunday is eight weeks after Easter Day, on the Sunday following Whit Sunday. Subsequent Sundays are reckoned in the Book of Common Prayer calendar of the Church of England as 'after Trinity'.

Thomas Becket (1118–70) was consecrated Archbishop of Canterbury on the Sunday after Whit Sunday and his first act was to ordain that the day of his consecration should be held as a new festival in honour of the Holy Trinity. The observance thus originated spread from Canterbury throughout the whole of Christendom.

MOVABLE FEASTS TO THE YEAR 2025

Year	*Ash Wednesday*	*Easter*	*Ascension*	*Pentecost (Whit Sunday)*	*Sundays after Pentecost*	*Advent Sunday*
1993	24 February	11 April	20 May	30 May	20	28 November
1994	16 February	3 April	12 May	22 May	21	27 November
1995	1 March	16 April	25 May	4 June	20	3 December
1996	21 February	7 April	16 May	26 May	21	1 December
1997	12 February	30 March	8 May	18 May	22	30 November
1998	25 February	12 April	21 May	31 May	20	29 November
1999	17 February	4 April	13 May	23 May	21	28 November
2000	8 March	23 April	1 June	11 June	19	3 December
2001	28 February	15 April	24 May	3 June	20	2 December
2002	13 February	31 March	9 May	19 May	22	1 December
2003	5 March	20 April	29 May	8 June	19	30 November
2004	25 February	11 April	20 May	30 May	20	28 November
2005	9 February	27 March	5 May	15 May	22	27 November
2006	1 March	16 April	25 May	4 June	20	3 December
2007	21 February	8 April	17 May	27 May	21	2 December
2008	6 February	23 March	1 May	11 May	23	30 November
2009	25 February	12 April	21 May	31 May	20	29 November
2010	17 February	4 April	13 May	23 May	21	28 November
2011	9 March	24 April	2 June	12 June	18	27 November
2012	22 February	8 April	17 May	27 May	21	2 December
2013	13 February	31 March	9 May	19 May	22	1 December
2014	5 March	20 April	29 May	8 June	19	30 November
2015	18 February	5 April	14 May	24 May	21	29 November
2016	10 February	27 March	5 May	15 May	22	27 November
2017	1 March	16 April	25 May	4 June	20	3 December
2018	14 February	1 April	10 May	20 May	22	2 December
2019	6 March	21 April	30 May	9 June	19	1 December
2020	26 February	12 April	21 May	31 May	20	29 November
2021	17 February	4 April	13 May	23 May	21	28 November
2022	2 March	17 April	26 May	5 June	19	27 November
2023	22 February	9 April	18 May	28 May	21	3 December
2024	14 February	31 March	9 May	19 May	22	1 December
2025	5 March	20 April	29 May	8 June	19	30 November

Notes

Ash Wednesday (first day in Lent) can fall at earliest on 4 February and at latest on 10 March.

Mothering Sunday (fourth Sunday in Lent) can fall at earliest on 29 February and at latest on 4 April.

Easter Day can fall at earliest on 22 March and at latest on 25 April.

Ascension Day is forty days after Easter Day and can fall at earliest on 30 April and at latest on 3 June.

Pentecost (Whit Sunday) is seven weeks after Easter and can fall at earliest on 10 May and at latest on 13 June.

Trinity Sunday is the Sunday after Whit Sunday.

Corpus Christi falls on the Thursday after Trinity Sunday.

There are not less than 18 and not more than 23 Sundays after Pentecost.

Advent Sunday is the Sunday nearest to 30 November.

EASTER DAYS AND DOMINICAL LETTERS 1500 TO 2030

	1500–1599	1600–1699	1700–1799	1800–1899	1900–1999	2000–2025
March						
d 22	1573	1668	1761	1818		
e 23	1505/16	1600	1788	1845/56	1913	2008
f 24		1611/95	1706/99		1940	
g 25	1543/54	1627/38/49	1722/33/44	1883/94	1951	
A 26	1559/70/81/92	1654/65/76	1749/58/69/80	1815/26/37	1967/78/89	
b 27	1502/13/24/97	1608/87/92	1785/96	1842/53/64	1910/21/32	2005/16
c 28	1529/35/40	1619/24/30	1703/14/25	1869/75/80	1937/48	2027
d 29	1551/62	1635/46/57	1719/30/41/52	1807/12/91	1959/64/70	
e 30	1567/78/89	1651/62/73/84	1746/55/66/77	1823/34	1902/75/86/97	
f 31	1510/21/32/83/94	1605/16/78/89	1700/71/82/93	1839/50/61/72	1907/18/29/91	2002/13/24
April						
g 1	1526/37/48	1621/32	1711/16	1804/66/77/88	1923/34/45/56	2018/29
A 2	1553/64	1643/48	1727/38/52(NS)	1809/20/93/99	1961/72	
b 3	1575/80/86	1659/70/81	1743/63/68/74	1825/31/36	1904/83/88/94	
c 4	1507/18/91	1602/13/75/86/97	1708/79/90	1847/58	1915/20/26/99	2010/21
d 5	1523/34/45/56	1607/18/29/40	1702/13/24/95	1801/63/74/85/96	1931/42/53	2015/26
e 6	1539/50/61/72	1634/45/56	1729/35/40/60	1806/17/28/90	1947/58/69/80	
f 7	1504/77/88	1667/72	1751/65/76	1822/33/44	1901/12/85/96	
g 8	1509/15/20/99	1604/10/83/94	1705/87/92/98	1849/55/60	1917/28	2007/12
A 9	1531/42	1615/26/37/99	1710/21/32	1871/82	1939/44/50	2023
b 10	1547/58/69	1631/42/53/64	1726/37/48/57	1803/14/87/98	1955/66/77	
c 11	1501/12/63/74/85/96	1658/69/80	1762/73/84	1819/30/41/52	1909/71/82/93	2004
d 12	1506/17/28	1601/12/91/96	1789	1846/57/68	1903/14/25/36/98	2009/20
e 13	1533/44	1623/28	1707/18	1800/73/79/84	1941/52	
f 7	1504/77/88	1667/72	1751/65/76	1822/33/44	1901/12/85/96	
g 8	1509/15/20/99	1604/10/83/94	1705/87/92/98	1849/55/60	1917/28	2007/12
A 9	1531/42	1615/26/37/99	1710/21/32	1871/82	1939/44/50	2023
b 10	1547/58/69	1631/42/53/64	1726/37/48/57	1803/14/87/98	1955/66/77	
c 11	1501/12/63/74/85/96	1658/69/80	1762/73/84	1819/30/41/52	1909/71/82/93	2004
d 19	1500/79/84/90	1663/74/85	1747/67/72/78	1829/35/40	1908/81/87/92	
e 20	1511/22/95	1606/17/79/90	1701/12/83/94	1851/62	1919/24/30	2003/14/25
f 21	1527/38/49	1622/33/44	1717/28	1867/78/89	1935/46/57	2019/30
g 22	1565/76	1660	1739/53/64	1810/21/32	1962/73/84	
A 23	1508	1671		1848	1905/16	2000
b 24	1519	1603/14/98	1709/91	1859		2011
c 25	1546	1641	1736	1886	1943	

HINDU CALENDAR

The Hindu calendar is a lunar calendar of twelve months, each containing 29 days, 12 hours. Each month is divided into a light fortnight (Shukla or Shuddha) and a dark fortnight (Krishna or Vadya) based on the waxing and waning of the moon. In most parts of India the month starts with the light fortnight, i.e. the day after the new moon, although in some regions it begins with the dark fortnight, i.e. the day after the full moon.

The new year begins in the month of Chaitra (March/April) and ends in the month of Phalgun (March). The twelve months, Chaitra, Vaishakh, Jyeshtha, Ashadh, Shravan, Bhadrapad, Ashvin, Kartik, Margashirsh, Paush, Magh and Phalgun, have Sanskrit names derived from twelve asterisms (constellations). There are regional variations to the names of the months but the Sanskrit names are understood throughout India.

Whenever the difference between the Hindu year of 360 lunar days (354 days, 8 hours solar time) and the 365 days, 6 hours of the solar year reaches the length of one Hindu lunar month (29 days, 12 hours), a 'leap' month is added to the Hindu calendar.

The leap month may be added at any point in the Hindu year. The name given to the month varies according to when it occurs but is taken from the month immediately following it. Leap months will occur in 1993–4 (Bhadrapad), 1996–7 (Ashadh) and 1999–2000 (Jyeshtha).

The days of the week are called Raviwar (Sunday), Somawar (Monday), Mangalwar (Tuesday), Budhawar (Wednesday), Guruwar (Thursday), Shukrawar (Friday) and Shaniwar (Saturday). The names are derived from the Sanskrit names of the Sun, the Moon and five planets, Mars, Mercury, Jupiter, Venus and Saturn.

Most fasts and festivals are based on the lunar calendar but a few are determined by the apparent movement of the Sun, e.g. Sankranti, which is celebrated on 14/15 January to mark the start of the Sun's apparent journey northwards and a change of season.

Festivals celebrated throughout India are the New Year, Navaratri (a nine-night festival dedicated to the goddess Parvati), Dasara (the victory of Rama over the demon army), Diwali (a festival of lights), Shivaratri (dedicated to Shiva), and Holi (a spring festival).

Regional festivals are Durga-puja (dedicated to the goddess Durga (Parvati)), Sarasvati-puja (dedicated to the goddess Sarasvati), Raksha-bandhan (the renewal of the kinship bond between brothers and sisters), Ganesh Chaturthi (worship of

Ganesh on the fourth day (Chaturthi) of the light half of Bhadrapad), Ramanavami (the birth festival of the god Rama) and Janmashtami (the birth festival of the god Krishna).

The main festivals celebrated in Britain are Navaratri, Dasara, Durga-puja, Diwali, Holi, Sarasvati-puja, Ganesh Chaturthi, Raksha-bandhan, Ramanavami and Janmashtami.

JEWISH CALENDAR

The story of the Flood in the Book of Genesis relates that the Flood began on the seventeenth day of the second month, that after the end of 150 days the waters were abated, and that on the seventeenth day of the seventh month the Ark rested on Mount Ararat. This indicates the use of a calendar of some kind and that the writers recognized thirty days as the length of a lunation. However, after the diaspora, Jewish communities were left in considerable doubt as to the times of fasts and festivals. This led to the formation of the Jewish calendar as used today. It is said that this was done in AD 358 by Rabbi Hillel II, a descendant of Gamaliel, though some assert that it did not happen until much later.

The calendar is luni-solar, and is based on the lengths of the lunation and of the tropical year as found by Hipparchus (*c*.120 BC), which differ little from those adopted at the present day. The year AM 5753 (1992–3) is the 15th year of the 303rd Metonic (Minor or Lunar) cycle of 19 years and the 13th year of the 206th Solar (or Major) cycle of 28 years since the Era of the Creation. Jews hold that the Creation occurred at the time of the autumnal equinox in the year known in the Christian calendar as 3760 BC (954 of the Julian period). The epoch or starting point of Jewish chronology corresponds to 7 October 3761 BC. At the beginning of each solar cycle, the Tekufah of Nisan (the vernal equinox) returns to the same day and to the same hour.

The hour is divided into 1080 minims, and the month between one new moon and the next is reckoned as 29 days, 12 hours, 793 minims. The normal calendar year, called a Common Regular year, consists of 12 months of 30 days and 29 days alternately. Since twelve months such as these comprise only 354 days, in order that each of them shall not diverge greatly from an average place in the solar year, a thirteenth month is occasionally added after the fifth month of the civil year (which commences on the first day of the month Tishri), or as the penultimate month of the ecclesiastical year (which commences on the first day of month Nisan). The years when this happens are called Embolismic or leap years.

Of the 19 years that form a Metonic cycle, seven are leap years; they occur at places in the cycle indicated by the numbers 3, 6, 8, 11, 14, 17 and 19, these places being chosen so that the accumulated excesses of the solar years should be as small as possible.

A Jewish year is of one of the following six types:

Minimal Common	353 days
Regular Common	354 days
Full Common	355 days
Minimal Leap	383 days
Regular Leap	384 days
Full Leap	385 days.

The Regular year has alternate months of 30 and 29 days. In a Full year, whether common or leap, Marcheshvan, the second month of the civil year, has 30 days instead of 29; in Minimal years Kislev, the third month, has 29 instead of 30. The additional month in leap years is called Adar I and precedes the month called Adar in Common years. Adar II is called Ve-Adar, in leap years, and the usual Adar festivals are kept in Ve-Adar. Adar I and Adar II always have 30 days, but neither this, nor the other variations mentioned, is allowed to change the number of days in the other months which still follow the alternation of the normal twelve.

These are the main features of the Jewish calendar, which must be considered permanent because as a Jewish law it cannot be altered except by a great Sanhedrin.

The Jewish day begins between sunset and nightfall. The time used is that of the meridian of Jerusalem, which is 2h 21m in advance of Greenwich Mean Time. Rules for the beginning of sabbaths and festivals were laid down for the latitude of London in the eighteenth century and hours for nightfall are now fixed annually by the Chief Rabbi.

JEWISH CALENDAR 5753–4

AM 5753 (753) is a Minimal Common year of 12 months, 50 sabbaths and 353 days. AM 5754 (754) is a Full Common year of 12 months, 51 sabbaths and 355 days.

Jewish Month	AM 5753	AM 5754
Tishri 1	28 September 1992	16 September 1993
Marcheshvan 1	28 October	16 October
Kislev 1	26 November	15 November
Tebet 1	25 December	15 December
Shebat 1	23 January 1993	13 January 1994
**Adar* 1	22 February	12 February
Ve-Adar 1		
Nisan 1	23 March	13 March
Iyar 1	22 April	12 April
Sivan 1	21 May	11 May
Tammuz 1	20 June	10 June
Ab 1	19 July	9 July
Elul 1	18 August	8 August

*Known as Adar Rishon in leap years.

JEWISH FASTS AND FESTIVALS

(For dates of principal festivals in 1993, *see* page 9)

Tishri 1–2	Rosh Hashanah (New Year).
Tishri 3	*Fast of Gedaliah.
Tishri 10	Yom Kippur (Day of Atonement).
Tishri 15–21	Succoth (Feast of Tabernacles).
Tishri 21	Hoshana Rabba.
Tishri 22	Shemini Atseret (Solemn Assembly).
Tishri 23	Simchat Torah (Rejoicing of the Law).
Kislev 25	Chanukah (Dedication of the Temple) begins.
Tebet 10	Fast of Tebet.
†*Adar* 13	§Fast of Esther.
†*Adar* 14	Purim.
†*Adar* 15	Shushan Purim.
Nisan 15–22	Pesach (Passover).
Sivan 6–7	Shavuot (Feast of Weeks).
Tammuz 17	*Fast of Tammuz.
Ab 9	*Fast of Ab.

*If these dates fall on the sabbath the fast is kept on the following day.

†Ve-Adar in leap years.

§This fast is observed on Adar 11 (or Ve-Adar 11 in leap years) if Adar 13 falls on a sabbath.

THE MUSLIM CALENDAR

The basic date of the Muslim calendar is the *Hejira*, or flight of Muhammad from Mecca to Medina, the corresponding date of which is 16 July AD 622, in the Julian calendar. Hejira years are used principally in Iran, Turkey, Egypt, in various Arab states, in certain parts of India and in Malaysia. The system was adopted about AD 632, commencing from the first day of the month preceding the Hejira.

The years are purely lunar and consist of twelve months containing in alternate sequence 30 or 29 days, with the intercalation of one day at the end of the twelfth month at stated intervals in each cycle of thirty years. The object of the intercalation is to reconcile the date of the first of the month with the date of the actual new moon. Some adherents still take the date of the evening of the first visibility of the crescent as that of the first of the month.

The mean length of the Hejira year is 354 days, 8 hours, 48 minutes, and the period of mean lunation is 29 days, 12 hours, 44 minutes. In each cycle of thirty years, 19 are common and contain 354 days, and 11 are intercalary (355 days), the latter being called *kabishah*.

To ascertain if a Hejira year is common or *kabishah*, divide it by 30; the quotient gives the number of completed cycles and the remainder shows the place of the year in the current cycle. If the remainder is 2, 5, 7, 10, 13, 16, 18, 21, 24, 26 or 29, the year is *kabishah* and consists of 355 days.

Hejira year AH 1413 (remainder 1) is a common year and AH 1414 (remainder 1) is a common year.

HEJIRA YEARS 1413 AND 1414

Name and length of month	AH 1413	AH 1414
Muharram (30)	2 July 1992	21 June 1993
Safar (29)	1 August	21 July
Rabi' I (30)	30 August	19 August
Rabi' II (29)	29 September	18 September
Jumada I (30)	28 October	17 October
Jumada II (29)	27 November	16 November
Rajab (30)	26 December	15 December
Shaabân (29)	25 January 1993	14 January 1994
Ramadân (30)	23 February	12 February
Shawwâl (29)	25 March	14 March
Dhû'l-Qa'da (30)	23 April	12 April
Dhû'l-Hijjah (29 or 30)	23 May	12 May

CIVIL AND LEGAL CALENDAR

THE HISTORICAL YEAR

Before the year 1752, two calendar systems were in use in England. The civil or legal year began on 25 March, while the historical year began on 1 January. Thus the civil or legal date 24 March 1658, was the same day as the historical date 24 March 1659; and a date in that portion of the year is written as 24 March 165$\frac{8}{9}$, the lower figure showing the historical year.

THE NEW YEAR

In England in the seventh century, and as late as the thirteenth, the year was reckoned from Christmas Day, but in the twelfth century the Anglican Church began the year with the feast of the Annunciation of the Blessed Virgin (Lady Day) on 25 March and this practice was adopted generally in the fourteenth century. The civil or legal year in the British Dominions (exclusive of Scotland) began with 'Lady Day' until 1751. But in and since 1752 the civil year has begun with 1 January. Certain dividends are still paid by the Bank of England on dates based on Old Style. New Year's Day in Scotland was changed from 25 March to 1 January in 1600.

On the continent of Europe, 1 January was adopted as the first day of the year by Venice in 1522, Germany in 1544, Spain, Portugal, and the Roman Catholic Netherlands in 1556, Prussia, Denmark and Sweden in 1559, France in 1564, Lorraine in 1579, the Protestant Netherlands in 1583, Russia in 1725, and Tuscany in 1751.

REGNAL YEARS

The regnal years are the years of a sovereign's reign, and each begins on the anniversary of his or her accession, e.g. regnal year 42 of the present Queen begins on 6 February 1993.

The system was used for dating Acts of Parliament until 1962. The Summer Time Act 1925, for example, is quoted as 15 and 16 Geo. V c. 64, because it became law in the parliamentary session which extended over part of both of these regnal years. Acts of a parliamentary session during which a sovereign died were usually given two year numbers, the regnal year of the deceased sovereign and the regnal year of his or her successor. Acts passed in 1952 were dated 16 Geo. VI and 1 Elizabeth II. Since 1962, Acts of Parliament have been dated by the calendar year.

QUARTER AND TERM DAYS

Holy days and saints days were the normal factors in early times for setting the dates of future and recurrent appointments. The quarter days in England and Wales are the feast of the Nativity (25 December), the feast of the Annunciation (25 March), the feast of St John the Baptist (24 June) and the feast of St Michael and All Angels (29 September).

The term days in Scotland are Candlemas (the feast of the Purification), Whitsunday, Lammas (Loaf Mass), and Martinmas (St Martin's Day). These fell on 2 February, 15 May, 1 August and 11 November respectively. However, by the Term and Quarter Days (Scotland) Act 1990, the dates of the term days were changed to 28 February (Candlemas), 28 May (Whitsunday), 28 August (Lammas) and 28 November (Martinmas).

RED-LETTER DAYS

Red-letter days were originally the holy days and saints days indicated in early ecclesiastical calendars by letters printed in red ink. The days to be distinguished in this way were approved at the Council of Nicaea in AD 325.

These days still have a legal significance, as judges of the Queen's Bench Division wear scarlet robes on red-letter days falling during the law sittings. The days designated as red-letter days for this purpose are:

Holy and saints days
Conversion of St Paul, the Purification, Ash Wednesday, the Annunciation, the Ascension, the feasts of St Mark, SS Philip and James, St Matthias, St Barnabas, St Peter, St Thomas, St James, St Luke, SS Simon and Jude, All Saints, St Andrew.

Civil calendar
The anniversary of The Queen's accession, The Queen's birthday, The Queen's coronation, the birthday of the Duke of Edinburgh, the birthday of Queen Elizabeth the Queen Mother, the birthday of the Prince of Wales, and St David's Day and Lord Mayor's Day.

PUBLIC HOLIDAYS

Public holidays are divided into two categories, common law, and statutory. Common law holidays are holidays 'by habit and custom' – in England, Wales and Northern Ireland these are Good Friday and Christmas Day.

Statutory public holidays, known as bank holidays, were first established by the Bank Holidays Act 1871. They were, literally, days on which the banks (and other public institutions) were closed and financial obligations due on that day were payable the following day. The legislation currently governing public holidays in the United Kingdom is the Banking and Financial Dealings Act 1971. It stipulates which days are to be public holidays in England, Wales, Scotland and Northern Ireland.

Certain holidays are granted annually by royal proclamation, either throughout the United Kingdom, or in any place in the United Kingdom.

CHRONOLOGICAL CYCLES AND ERAS

Solar (or Major) Cycle

The solar cycle is a period of twenty-eight years, in any corresponding year of which the days of the week recur on the same day of the month.

Metonic (Lunar, or Minor) Cycle

In the year 432 BC, Meton, an Athenian astronomer, found that 235 lunations are very nearly, though not exactly, equal in duration to 19 solar years, and, hence, after 19 years the phases of the Moon recur on the same days of the month (nearly). The dates of full moon in a cycle of 19 years were inscribed in figures of gold on public monuments in Athens, and the number showing the position of a year in the cycle is called the golden number of that year.

Julian Period

The Julian period was proposed by Joseph Scaliger in 1582. The period is 7980 Julian years, and its first year coincides with the year 4713 BC. The figure of 7980 is the product of the number of years in the solar cycle, the Metonic cycle and the cycle of the Roman indiction (28 × 19 × 15).

Roman Indiction

The Roman indiction is a period of fifteen years, instituted for fiscal purposes about AD 300.

Epact

The epact is the age of the calendar Moon, diminished by one day, on 1 January, in the ecclesiastical lunar calendar.

Chinese Calendar

Until 1911 a lunar calendar was in force in China, but with the establishment of the Republic the government adopted the Gregorian calendar. The new and old systems were used simultaneously until 1930, when the publication and use of the old calendar were banned by the government, and an official Chinese calendar, corresponding with the European or Western system, compiled. The old Chinese calendar, with a cycle of 60 years, is still in use in Tibet, Hong Kong, Singapore, Malaysia and elsewhere in south-east Asia.

Coptic Calendar

In the Coptic calendar, which is used by part of the population of Egypt and Ethiopia, the year is made up of 12 months of 30 days each, followed, in general, by five complementary days. Every fourth year is an intercalary or leap year and in these years there are six complementary days. The intercalary year of the Coptic calendar immediately precedes the leap year of the Julian calendar. The era is that of Diocletian or the Martyrs, the origin of which is fixed at 29 August AD 284 (Julian date).

Indian Eras

In addition to the Muslim reckoning there are six eras used in India. The principal astronomical system was the Kaliyuga era, which appears to have been adopted in the fourth century AD. It began on 18 February 3102 BC. The chronological system of northern India, known as the Vikrama Samvat era, prevalent in western India, began on 23 February 57 BC. The year AD 1993 is, therefore, the year 2050 of the Vikrama era.

The Saka era of southern India dating from 3 March AD 78, was declared the uniform national calendar of the Republic of India with effect from 22 March 1957, to be used concurrently with the Gregorian calendar. As revised, the year of the new Saka era begins at the spring equinox, with five successive months of 31 days and seven of 30 days in ordinary years, and six months of each length in leap years. The year AD 1993 is 1915 of the revised Saka era.

The Saptarshi era dates from the moment when the Saptarshi, or saints, were translated and became the stars of the Great Bear in 3076 BC.

The Buddhists reckoned from the death of Buddha in 543 BC (the actual date being 487 BC); and the epoch of the Jains was the death of Vardhamana, the founder of their faith, in 527 BC.

Japanese Calendar

The Japanese calendar is essentially the same as the Gregorian calendar, the years, months and weeks being of the same length and beginning on the same days as those of the Gregorian calendar. The numeration of the years is different, for Japanese chronology is based on a system of epochs or periods, each of which begins at the accession of an Emperor or other important occurrence. The method is not unlike the former British system of regnal years, but differs from it in that each year of a period closes on 31 December. The Japanese chronology begins about AD 650 and the three latest epochs are defined by the reigns of Emperors, whose actual names are not necessarily used:

Epoch
Taishō 1 August 1912 to 25 December 1926
Shōwa 26 December 1926 to 7 January 1989
Heisei 8 January 1989

Hence the year Heisei 5 begins on 1 January 1993.

The months are not named. They are known as First Month, Second Month, etc., First Month being the equivalent to January. The days of the week are Nichiyōbi (Sun-day), Getsuyōbi (Moon-day), Kayōbi (Fire-day), Suiyōbi (Water-day), Mokuyōbi (Wood-day), Kinyōbi (Metal-day), Doyōbi (Earth-day).

The Masonic Year

Two dates are quoted in warrants, dispensations, etc., issued by the United Grand Lodge of England, those for the current year being expressed as *Anno Domini* 1993 – *Anno Lucis* 5993. This *Anno Lucis* (year of light) is based on the Book of Genesis 1:3, the 4000 year difference being derived, in modified form, from *Ussher's Notation*, published in 1654, which places the Creation of the World in 4004 BC.

Olympiads

Ancient Greek chronology was reckoned in Olympiads, cycles of four years corresponding with the periodic Olympic Games held on the plain of Olympia in Elis once every four years, the intervening years being the first, second, etc., of the Olympiad which received the name of the victor at the Games. The first recorded Olympiad is that of Choroebus, 776 BC.

Zoroastrian Calendar

Zoroastrians, followers of the Iranian prophet Zarathushtra (known to the Greeks as Zoroaster) are mostly to be found in Iran and in India, where they are known as Parsis.

The Zoroastrian era dates from the coronation of the last Zoroastrian Sasanian king in AD 631. The Zoroastrian calendar is divided into twelve months, each comprising 30 days.

In order to synchronize the calandar with the solar year of 365 days, an extra month was intercalated once every 120 years. However, this intercalation ceased in the twelfth century and the New Year, which had fallen in the spring, slipped back until it now falls in August. Because intercalation ceased at different times in Iran and India, there was one month's difference between the calendar followed in Iran (Kadmi calendar) and by the Parsis (Shenshai calendar).

In 1906 a group of Zoroastrians decided to bring the calendar back in line with the seasons again and restore the New Year to 21 March. This, the Fasli calendar, is now kept in line with the solar year by the addition of five days to the twelfth month to make the year consist of 365 days.

The Shenshai calendar (New Year, 23 August) is mainly used by Parsis. The Fasli calendar (New Year, 21 March) is mainly used by Zoroastrians living in Iran or away from Iran and the Indian subcontinent.

THE ROMAN CALENDAR

Roman historians adopted as an epoch the foundation of Rome, which is believed to have happened in the year 753 BC. The ordinal number of the years in Roman reckoning is followed by the letters AUC (*ab urbe condita*), so that the year 1993 is 2746 AUC (MMDCCXLVI). The calendar that we know has developed from one established by Romulus, who is said to have used a year of 304 days divided into ten months, beginning with March. To this Numa added January and February, making the year consist of 12 months of 30 and 29 days alternately, with an additional day so that the total was 355. It is also said that Numa ordered an intercalary month of 22 or 23 days in alternate years, making 90 days in eight years, to be inserted after 23 February. However, there is some doubt as to the origination and the details of the intercalation in the Roman calendar. It is certain that some scheme of this kind was inaugurated and not fully carried out, for in the year 46 BC Julius Caesar, who was then Pontifex Maximus, found that the calendar had been allowed to fall into some confusion. He therefore sought the help of the Egyptian astronomer Sosigenes, which led to the construction and adoption (45 BC) of the Julian calendar, and, by a slight alteration, to the Gregorian calendar now in use. The year 46 BC was made to consist of 445 days and is called the Year of Confusion.

In the Roman (Julian) calendar the days of the month were counted backwards from three fixed points, or days, and an intervening day was said to be so many days before the next coming point, the first and last being counted. These three points were the Kalends, the Nones, and the Ides. Their positions in the months and the method of counting from them will be seen in the table below. The year containing 366 days was called *bissextillis annus*, as it had a doubled sixth day (*bissextus dies*) before the March Kalends on 24 February – *ante diem sextum Kalendas Martias*, or a.d. VI Kal. Mart.

Present days of the month	*March, May, July, October have thirty-one days*	*January, August, December have thirty-one days*	*April, June, September, November have thirty days*	*February has twenty-eight days, and in leap year twenty-nine*
1	Kalendis.	Kalendis.	Kalendis.	Kalendis.
2	VI	IV ante	IV ante	IV ante
3	V ante	III Nonas.	III Nonas.	III Nonas.
4	IV Nonas.	pridie Nonas.	pridie Nonas.	pridie Nonas.
5	III	Nonis.	Nonis.	Nonis.
6	pridie Nonas.	VIII	VIII	VIII
7	Nonis.	VII	VII	VII
8	VIII	VI ante	VI ante.	VI ante
9	VII	V Idus.	V Idus.	V Idus.
10	VI ante	IV	IV	IV
11	V Idus.	III	III	III
12	IV	pridie Idus.	pridie Idus.	pridie Idus.
13	III	Idibus.	Idibus.	Idibus.
14	pridie Idus.	XIX	XVIII	XVI
15	Idibus.	XVIII	XVII	XV
16	XVII	XVII	XVI	XIV
17	XVI	XVI	XV	XIII
18	XV	XV	XIV	XII
19	XIV	XIV	XIII	XI
20	XIII	XIII	XII	X ante Kalendas
21	XII ante Kalendas	XII ante Kalendas	XI ante Kalendas	IX Martias.
22	XI (of the month	XI (of the month	X (of the month	VIII
23	X following).	X following).	IX following).	VII
24	IX	IX	VIII	*VI
25	VIII	VIII	VII	V
26	VII	VII	VI	IV
27	VI	VI	V	III
28	V	V	IV	pridie Kalendas
29	IV	IV	III	Martias.
30	III	III	pridie Kalendas	
31	pridie Kalendas (Aprilis, Iunias, Sextilis, Novembris).	pridie Kalendas (Februarias, Septembris, Ianuarias).	(Maias, Quinctilis, Octobris, Decembris).	* (repeated in leap year).

Calendar for Any Year 1770–2030

To select the correct calendar for any year between 1770 and 2030, consult the index below
* leap year

1770	C	1803	M	1836	L*	1869	K	1902	G	1935	E	1968	D*	2001	C
1771	E	1804	B*	1837	A	1870	M	1903	I	1936	H*	1969	G	2002	E
1772	H*	1805	E	1838	C	1871	A	1904	L*	1937	K	1970	I	2003	G
1773	K	1806	G	1839	E	1872	D*	1905	A	1938	M	1971	K	2004	J*
1774	M	1807	I	1840	H*	1873	G	1906	C	1939	A	1972	N*	2005	M
1775	A	1808	L*	1841	K	1874	I	1907	E	1940	D*	1973	C	2006	A
1776	D*	1809	A	1842	M	1875	K	1908	H*	1941	G	1974	E	2007	C
1777	G	1810	C	1843	A	1876	N*	1909	K	1942	I	1975	G	2008	F*
1778	I	1811	E	1844	D*	1877	C	1910	M	1943	K	1976	J*	2009	I
1779	K	1812	H*	1845	G	1878	E	1911	A	1944	N*	1977	M	2010	K
1780	N*	1813	K	1846	I	1879	G	1912	D*	1945	C	1978	A	2011	M
1781	C	1814	M	1847	K	1880	J*	1913	G	1946	E	1979	C	2012	B*
1782	E	1815	A	1848	N*	1881	M	1914	I	1947	G	1980	F*	2013	E
1783	G	1816	D*	1849	C	1882	A	1915	K	1948	J*	1981	I	2014	G
1784	J*	1817	G	1850	E	1883	C	1916	N*	1949	M	1982	K	2015	I
1785	M	1818	I	1851	G	1884	F*	1917	C	1950	A	1983	M	2016	L*
1786	A	1819	K	1852	J*	1885	I	1918	E	1951	C	1984	B*	2017	A
1787	C	1820	N*	1853	M	1886	K	1919	G	1952	F*	1985	E	2018	C
1788	F*	1821	C	1854	A	1887	M	1920	J*	1953	I	1986	G	2019	E
1789	I	1822	E	1855	C	1888	B*	1921	M	1954	K	1987	I	2020	H*
1790	K	1823	G	1856	F*	1889	E	1922	A	1955	M	1988	L*	2021	K
1791	M	1824	J*	1857	I	1890	G	1923	C	1956	B*	1989	A	2022	M
1792	B*	1825	M	1858	K	1891	I	1924	F*	1957	E	1990	C	2023	A
1793	E	1826	A	1859	M	1892	L*	1925	I	1958	G	1991	E	2024	D*
1794	G	1827	C	1860	B*	1893	A	1926	K	1959	I	1992	H*	2025	G
1795	I	1828	F*	1861	E	1894	C	1927	M	1960	L*	1993	K	2026	I
1796	L*	1829	I	1862	G	1895	E	1928	B*	1961	A	1994	M	2027	K
1797	A	1830	K	1863	I	1896	H*	1929	E	1962	C	1995	A	2028	N*
1798	C	1831	M	1864	L*	1897	K	1930	G	1963	E	1996	D*	2029	C
1799	E	1832	B*	1865	A	1898	M	1931	I	1964	H*	1997	G	2030	E
1800	G	1833	E	1866	C	1899	A	1932	L*	1965	K	1998	I		
1801	I	1834	G	1867	E	1900	C	1933	A	1966	M	1999	K		
1802	K	1835	I	1868	H*	1901	E	1934	C	1967	A	2000	N*		

A

	January	*February*	*March*
Sun.	1 8 15 22 29	5 12 19 26	5 12 19 26
Mon.	2 9 16 23 30	6 13 20 27	6 13 20 27
Tue.	3 10 17 24 31	7 14 21 28	7 14 21 28
Wed.	4 11 18 25	1 8 15 22	1 8 15 22 29
Thur.	5 12 19 26	2 9 16 23	2 9 16 23 30
Fri.	6 13 20 27	3 10 17 24	3 10 17 24 31
Sat.	7 14 21 28	4 11 18 25	4 11 18 25

	April	*May*	*June*
Sun.	2 9 16 23 30	7 14 21 28	4 11 18 25
Mon.	3 10 17 24	1 8 15 22 29	5 12 19 26
Tue.	4 11 18 25	2 9 16 23 30	6 13 20 27
Wed.	5 12 19 26	3 10 17 24 31	7 14 21 28
Thur.	6 13 20 27	4 11 18 25	1 8 15 22 29
Fri.	7 14 21 28	5 12 19 26	2 9 16 23 30
Sat.	1 8 15 22 29	6 13 20 27	3 10 17 24

	July	*August*	*September*
Sun.	2 9 16 23 30	6 13 20 27	3 10 17 24
Mon.	3 10 17 24 31	7 14 21 28	4 11 18 25
Tue.	4 11 18 25	1 8 15 22 29	5 12 19 26
Wed.	5 12 19 26	2 9 16 23 30	6 13 20 27
Thur.	6 13 20 27	3 10 17 24 31	7 14 21 28
Fri.	7 14 21 28	4 11 18 25	1 8 15 22 29
Sat.	1 8 15 22 29	5 12 19 26	2 9 16 23 30

	October	*November*	*December*
Sun.	1 8 15 22 29	5 12 19 26	3 10 17 24 31
Mon.	2 9 16 23 30	6 13 20 27	4 11 18 25
Tue.	3 10 17 24 31	7 14 21 28	5 12 19 26
Wed.	4 11 18 25	1 8 15 22 29	6 13 20 27
Thur.	5 12 19 26	2 9 16 23 30	7 14 21 28
Fri.	6 13 20 27	3 10 17 24	1 8 15 22 29
Sat.	7 14 21 28	4 11 18 25	2 9 16 23 30

Easter Days

March 26 1815, 1826, 1837, 1967, 1978, 1989
April 2 1809, 1893, 1899, 1961
April 9 1871, 1882, 1939, 1950, 2023
April 16 1775, 1786, 1797, 1843, 1854, 1865, 1911 1922, 1933, 1995, 2006, 2017
April 23 1905

B (leap year)

	January	*February*	*March*
Sun.	1 8 15 22 29	5 12 19 26	4 11 18 25
Mon.	2 9 16 23 30	6 13 20 27	5 12 19 26
Tue.	3 10 17 24 31	7 14 21 28	6 13 20 27
Wed.	4 11 18 25	1 8 15 22 29	7 14 21 28
Thur.	5 12 19 26	2 9 16 23	1 8 15 22 29
Fri.	6 13 20 27	3 10 17 24	2 9 16 23 30
Sat.	7 14 21 28	4 11 18 25	3 10 17 24 31

	April	*May*	*June*
Sun.	1 8 15 22 29	6 13 20 27	3 10 17 24
Mon.	2 9 16 23 30	7 14 21 28	4 11 18 25
Tue.	3 10 17 24	1 8 15 22 29	5 12 19 26
Wed.	4 11 18 25	2 9 16 23 30	6 13 20 27
Thur.	5 12 19 26	3 10 17 24 31	7 14 21 28
Fri.	6 13 20 27	4 11 18 25	1 8 15 22 29
Sat.	7 14 21 28	5 12 19 26	2 9 16 23 30

	July	*August*	*September*
Sun.	1 8 15 22 29	5 12 19 26	2 9 16 23 30
Mon.	2 9 16 23 30	6 13 20 27	3 10 17 24
Tue.	3 10 17 24 31	7 14 21 28	4 11 18 25
Wed.	4 11 18 25	1 8 15 22 29	5 12 19 26
Thur.	5 12 19 26	2 9 16 23 30	6 13 20 27
Fri.	6 13 20 27	3 10 17 24 31	7 14 21 28
Sat.	7 14 21 28	4 11 18 25	1 8 15 22 29

	October	*November*	*December*
Sun.	7 14 21 28	4 11 18 25	2 9 16 23 30
Mon.	1 8 15 22 29	5 12 19 26	3 10 17 24 31
Tue.	2 9 16 23 30	6 13 20 27	4 11 18 25
Wed.	3 10 17 24 31	7 14 21 28	5 12 19 26
Thur.	4 11 18 25	1 8 15 22 29	6 13 20 27
Fri.	5 12 19 26	2 9 16 23 30	7 14 21 28
Sat.	6 13 20 27	3 10 17 24	1 8 15 22 29

Easter Days

April 1 1804, 1888, 1956
April 8 1792, 1860, 1928, 2012
April 22 1832, 1984

C

	January	*February*	*March*
Sun.	7 14 21 28	4 11 18 25	4 11 18 25
Mon.	1 8 15 22 29	5 12 19 26	5 12 19 26
Tue.	2 9 16 23 30	6 13 20 27	6 13 20 27
Wed.	3 10 17 24 31	7 14 21 28	7 14 21 28
Thur.	4 11 18 25	1 8 15 22	1 8 15 22 29
Fri.	5 12 19 26	2 9 16 23	2 9 16 23 30
Sat.	6 13 20 27	3 10 17 24	3 10 17 24 31

	April	*May*	*June*
Sun.	1 8 15 22 29	6 13 20 27	3 10 17 24
Mon.	2 9 16 23 30	7 14 21 28	4 11 18 25
Tue.	3 10 17 24	1 8 15 22 29	5 12 19 26
Wed.	4 11 18 25	2 9 16 23 30	6 13 20 27
Thur.	5 12 19 26	3 10 17 24 31	7 14 21 28
Fri.	6 13 20 27	4 11 18 25	1 8 15 22 29
Sat.	7 14 21 28	5 12 19 26	2 9 16 23 30

	July	*August*	*September*
Sun.	1 8 15 22 29	5 12 19 26	2 9 16 23 30
Mon.	2 9 16 23 30	6 13 20 27	3 10 17 24
Tue.	3 10 17 24 31	7 14 21 28	4 11 18 25
Wed.	4 11 18 25	1 8 15 22 29	5 12 19 26
Thur.	5 12 19 26	2 9 16 23 30	6 13 20 27
Fri.	6 13 20 27	3 10 17 24 31	7 14 21 28
Sat.	7 14 21 28	4 11 18 25	1 8 15 22 29

	October	*November*	*December*
Sun.	7 14 21 28	4 11 18 25	2 9 16 23 30
Mon.	1 8 15 22 29	5 12 19 26	3 10 17 24 31
Tue.	2 9 16 23 30	6 13 20 27	4 11 18 25
Wed.	3 10 17 24 31	7 14 21 28	5 12 19 26
Thur.	4 11 18 25	1 8 15 22 29	6 13 20 27
Fri.	5 12 19 26	2 9 16 23 30	7 14 21 28
Sat.	6 13 20 27	3 10 17 24	1 8 15 22 29

EASTER DAYS

March 25	1883, 1894, 1951
April 1	1866, 1877, 1923, 1934, 1945, 2018, 2029
April 8	1787, 1798, 1849, 1855, 1917, 2007
April 15	1770, 1781, 1827, 1838, 1900, 1906, 1979, 1990, 2001
April 22	1810, 1821, 1962, 1973

D (LEAP YEAR)

	January	*February*	*March*
Sun.	7 14 21 28	4 11 18 25	3 10 17 24 31
Mon.	1 8 15 22 29	5 12 19 26	4 11 18 25
Tue.	2 9 16 23 30	6 13 20 27	5 12 19 26
Wed.	3 10 17 24 31	7 14 21 28	6 13 20 27
Thur.	4 11 18 25	1 8 15 22 29	7 14 21 28
Fri.	5 12 19 26	2 9 16 23	1 8 15 22 29
Sat.	6 13 20 27	3 10 17 24	2 9 16 23 30

	April	*May*	*June*
Sun.	7 14 21 28	5 12 19 26	2 9 16 23 30
Mon.	1 8 15 22 29	6 13 20 27	3 10 17 24
Tue.	2 9 16 23 30	7 14 21 28	4 11 18 25
Wed.	3 10 17 24	1 8 15 22 29	5 12 19 26
Thur.	4 11 18 25	2 9 16 23 30	6 13 20 27
Fri.	5 12 19 26	3 10 17 24 31	7 14 21 28
Sat.	6 13 20 27	4 11 18 25	1 8 15 22 29

	July	*August*	*September*
Sun.	7 14 21 28	4 11 18 25	1 8 15 22 29
Mon.	1 8 15 22 29	5 12 19 26	2 9 16 23 30
Tue.	2 9 16 23 30	6 13 20 27	3 10 17 24
Wed.	3 10 17 24 31	7 14 21 28	4 11 18 25
Thur.	4 11 18 25	1 8 15 22 29	5 12 19 26
Fri.	5 12 19 26	2 9 16 23 30	6 13 20 27
Sat.	6 13 20 27	3 10 17 24 31	7 14 21 28

	October	*November*	*December*
Sun.	6 13 20 27	3 10 17 24	1 8 15 22 29
Mon.	7 14 21 28	4 11 18 25	2 9 16 23 30
Tue.	1 8 15 22 29	5 12 19 26	3 10 17 24 31
Wed.	2 9 16 23 30	6 13 20 27	4 11 18 25
Thur.	3 10 17 24 31	7 14 21 28	5 12 19 26
Fri.	4 11 18 25	1 8 15 22 29	6 13 20 27
Sat.	5 12 19 26	2 9 16 23 30	7 14 21 28

EASTER DAYS

March 24	1940
March 31	1872, 2024
April 7	1776, 1844, 1912, 1996
April 14	1816, 1968

E

	January	*February*	*March*
Sun.	6 13 20 27	3 10 17 24	3 10 17 24 31
Mon.	7 14 21 28	4 11 18 25	4 11 18 25
Tue.	1 8 15 22 29	5 12 19 26	5 12 19 26
Wed.	2 9 16 23 30	6 13 20 27	6 13 20 27
Thur.	3 10 17 24 31	7 14 21 28	7 14 21 28
Fri.	4 11 18 25	1 8 15 22	1 8 15 22 29
Sat.	5 12 19 26	2 9 16 23	2 9 16 23 30

	April	*May*	*June*
Sun.	7 14 21 28	5 12 19 26	2 9 16 23 30
Mon.	1 8 15 22 29	6 13 20 27	3 10 17 24
Tue.	2 9 16 23 30	7 14 21 28	4 11 18 25
Wed.	3 10 17 24	1 8 15 22 29	5 12 19 26
Thur.	4 11 18 25	2 9 16 23 30	6 13 20 27
Fri.	5 12 19 26	3 10 17 24 31	7 14 21 28
Sat.	6 13 20 27	4 11 18 25	1 8 15 22 29

	July	*August*	*September*
Sun.	7 14 21 28	4 11 18 25	1 8 15 22 29
Mon.	1 8 15 22 29	5 12 19 26	2 9 16 23 30
Tue.	2 9 16 23 30	6 13 20 27	3 10 17 24
Wed.	3 10 17 24 31	7 14 21 28	4 11 18 25
Thur.	4 11 18 25	1 8 15 22 29	5 12 19 26
Fri.	5 12 19 26	2 9 16 23 30	6 13 20 27
Sat.	6 13 20 27	3 10 17 24 31	7 14 21 28

	October	*November*	*December*
Sun.	6 13 20 27	3 10 17 24	1 8 15 22 29
Mon.	7 14 21 28	4 11 18 25	2 9 16 23 30
Tue.	1 8 15 22 29	5 12 19 26	3 10 17 24 31
Wed.	2 9 16 23 30	6 13 20 27	4 11 18 25
Thur.	3 10 17 24 31	7 14 21 28	5 12 19 26
Fri.	4 11 18 25	1 8 15 22 29	6 13 20 27
Sat.	5 12 19 26	2 9 16 23 30	7 14 21 28

EASTER DAYS

March 24	1799
March 31	1771, 1782, 1793, 1839, 1850, 1861, 1907 1918, 1929, 1991, 2002, 2013
April 7	1822, 1833, 1901, 1985
April 14	1805, 1811, 1895, 1963, 1974
April 21	1867, 1878, 1889, 1935, 1946, 1957, 2019, 2030

F (LEAP YEAR)

	January	*February*	*March*
Sun.	6 13 20 27	3 10 17 24	2 9 16 23 30
Mon.	7 14 21 28	4 11 18 25	3 10 17 24 31
Tue.	1 8 15 22 29	5 12 19 26	4 11 18 25
Wed.	2 9 16 23 30	6 13 20 27	5 12 19 26
Thur.	3 10 17 24 31	7 14 21 28	6 13 20 27
Fri.	4 11 18 25	1 8 15 22 29	7 14 21 28
Sat.	5 12 19 26	2 9 16 23	1 8 15 22 29

	April	*May*	*June*
Sun.	6 13 20 27	4 11 18 25	1 8 15 22 29
Mon.	7 14 21 28	5 12 19 26	2 9 16 23 30
Tue.	1 8 15 22 29	6 13 20 27	3 10 17 24
Wed.	2 9 16 23 30	7 14 21 28	4 11 18 25
Thur.	3 10 17 24	1 8 15 22 29	5 12 19 26
Fri.	4 11 18 25	2 9 16 23 30	6 13 20 27
Sat.	5 12 19 26	3 10 17 24 31	7 14 21 28

	July	*August*	*September*
Sun.	6 13 20 27	3 10 17 24 31	7 14 21 28
Mon.	7 14 21 28	4 11 18 25	1 8 15 22 29
Tue.	1 8 15 22 29	5 12 19 26	2 9 16 23 30
Wed.	2 9 16 23 30	6 13 20 27	3 10 17 24
Thur.	3 10 17 24 31	7 14 21 28	4 11 18 25
Fri.	4 11 18 25	1 8 15 22 29	5 12 19 26
Sat.	5 12 19 26	2 9 16 23 30	6 13 20 27

	October	*November*	*December*
Sun.	5 12 19 26	2 9 16 23 30	7 14 21 28
Mon.	6 13 20 27	3 10 17 24	1 8 15 22 29
Tue.	7 14 21 28	4 11 18 25	2 9 16 23 30
Wed.	1 8 15 22 29	5 12 19 26	3 10 17 24 31
Thur.	2 9 16 23 30	6 13 20 27	4 11 18 25
Fri.	3 10 17 24 31	7 14 21 28	5 12 19 26
Sat.	4 11 18 25	1 8 15 22 29	6 13 20 27

EASTER DAYS

March 23	1788, 1856, 2008
April 6	1828, 1980
April 13	1884, 1952
April 20	1924

G

	January	*February*	*March*
Sun.	5 12 19 26	2 9 16 23	2 9 16 23 30
Mon.	6 13 20 27	3 10 17 24	3 10 17 24 31
Tue.	7 14 21 28	4 11 18 25	4 11 18 25
Wed.	1 8 15 22 29	5 12 19 26	5 12 19 26
Thur.	2 9 16 23 30	6 13 20 27	6 13 20 27
Fri.	3 10 17 24 31	7 14 21 28	7 14 21 28
Sat.	4 11 18 25	1 8 15 22	1 8 15 22 29

	April	*May*	*June*
Sun.	6 13 20 27	4 11 18 25	1 8 15 22 29
Mon.	7 14 21 28	5 12 19 26	2 9 16 23 30
Tue.	1 8 15 22 29	6 13 20 27	3 10 17 24
Wed.	2 9 16 23 30	7 14 21 28	4 11 18 25
Thur.	3 10 17 24	1 8 15 22 29	5 12 19 26
Fri.	4 11 18 25	2 9 16 23 30	6 13 20 27
Sat.	5 12 19 26	3 10 17 24 31	7 14 21 28

	July	*August*	*September*
Sun.	6 13 20 27	3 10 17 24 31	7 14 21 28
Mon.	7 14 21 28	4 11 18 25	1 8 15 22 29
Tue.	1 8 15 22 29	5 12 19 26	2 9 16 23 30
Wed.	2 9 16 23 30	6 13 20 27	3 10 17 24
Thur.	3 10 17 24 31	7 14 21 28	4 11 18 25
Fri.	4 11 18 25	1 8 15 22 29	5 12 19 26
Sat.	5 12 19 26	2 9 16 23 30	6 13 20 27

	October	*November*	*December*
Sun.	5 12 19 26	2 9 16 23 30	7 14 21 28
Mon.	6 13 20 27	3 10 17 24	1 8 15 22 29
Tue.	7 14 21 28	4 11 18 25	2 9 16 23 30
Wed.	1 8 15 22 29	5 12 19 26	3 10 17 24 31
Thur.	2 9 16 23 30	6 13 20 27	4 11 18 25
Fri.	3 10 17 24 31	7 14 21 28	5 12 19 26
Sat.	4 11 18 25	1 8 15 22 29	6 13 20 27

EASTER DAYS

March 23	1845, 1913
March 30	1777, 1823, 1834, 1902, 1975, 1986, 1997
April 6	1806, 1817, 1890, 1947, 1958, 1969
April 13	1800, 1873, 1879, 1941
April 20	1783, 1794, 1851, 1862, 1919, 1930, 2003 2014, 2025

H (LEAP YEAR)

	January	*February*	*March*
Sun.	5 12 19 26	2 9 16 23	1 8 15 22 29
Mon.	6 13 20 27	3 10 17 24	2 9 16 23 30
Tue.	7 14 21 28	4 11 18 25	3 10 17 24 31
Wed.	1 8 15 22 29	5 12 19 26	4 11 18 25
Thur.	2 9 16 23 30	6 13 20 27	5 12 19 26
Fri.	3 10 17 24 31	7 14 21 28	6 13 20 27
Sat.	4 11 18 25	1 8 15 22 29	7 14 21 28

	April	*May*	*June*
Sun.	5 12 19 26	3 10 17 24 31	7 14 21 28
Mon.	6 13 20 27	4 11 18 25	1 8 15 22 29
Tue.	7 14 21 28	5 12 19 26	2 9 16 23 30
Wed.	1 8 15 22 29	6 13 20 27	3 10 17 24
Thur.	2 9 16 23 30	7 14 21 28	4 11 18 25
Fri.	3 10 17 24	1 8 15 22 29	5 12 19 26
Sat.	4 11 18 25	2 9 16 23 30	6 13 20 27

	July	*August*	*September*
Sun.	5 12 19 26	2 9 16 23 30	6 13 20 27
Mon.	6 13 20 27	3 10 17 24 31	7 14 21 28
Tue.	7 14 21 28	4 11 18 25	1 8 15 22 29
Wed.	1 8 15 22 29	5 12 19 26	2 9 16 23 30
Thur.	2 9 16 23 30	6 13 20 27	3 10 17 24
Fri.	3 10 17 24 31	7 14 21 28	4 11 18 25
Sat.	4 11 18 25	1 8 15 22 29	5 12 19 26

	October	*November*	*December*
Sun.	4 11 18 25	1 8 15 22 29	6 13 20 27
Mon.	5 12 19 26	2 9 16 23 30	7 14 21 28
Tue.	6 13 20 27	3 10 17 24	1 8 15 22 29
Wed.	7 14 21 28	4 11 18 25	2 9 16 23 30
Thur.	1 8 15 22 29	5 12 19 26	3 10 17 24 31
Fri.	2 9 16 23 30	6 13 20 27	4 11 18 25
Sat.	3 10 17 24 31	7 14 21 28	5 12 19 26

EASTER DAYS

March 29	1812, 1964
April 5	1896
April 12	1868, 1936, 2020
April 19	1772, 1840, 1908, 1992

I

	January	*February*	*March*
Sun.	4 11 18 25	1 8 15 22	1 8 15 22 29
Mon.	5 12 19 26	2 9 16 23	2 9 16 23 30
Tue.	6 13 20 27	3 10 17 24	3 10 17 24 31
Wed.	7 14 21 28	4 11 18 25	4 11 18 25
Thur.	1 8 15 22 29	5 12 19 26	5 12 19 26
Fri.	2 9 16 23 30	6 13 20 27	6 13 20 27
Sat.	3 10 17 24 31	7 14 21 28	7 14 21 28

	April	*May*	*June*
Su.	5 12 19 26	3 10 17 24 31	7 14 21 28
Mon.	6 13 20 27	4 11 18 25	1 8 15 22 29
Tue.	7 14 21 28	5 12 19 26	2 9 16 23 30
Wed.	1 8 15 22 29	6 13 20 27	3 10 17 24
Thur.	2 9 16 23 30	7 14 21 28	4 11 18 25
Fri.	3 10 17 24	1 8 15 22 29	5 12 19 26
Sat.	4 11 18 25	2 9 16 23 30	6 13 20 27

	July	*August*	*September*
Sun.	5 12 19 26	2 9 16 23 30	6 13 20 27
Mon.	6 13 20 27	3 10 17 24 31	7 14 21 28
Tue.	7 14 21 28	4 11 18 25	1 8 15 22 29
Wed.	1 8 15 22 29	5 12 19 26	2 9 16 23 30
Thur.	2 9 16 23 30	6 13 20 27	3 10 17 24
Fri.	3 10 17 24 31	7 14 21 28	4 11 18 25
Sat.	4 11 18 25	1 8 15 22 29	5 12 19 26

	October	*November*	*December*
Sun.	4 11 18 25	1 8 15 22 29	6 13 20 27
Mon.	5 12 19 26	2 9 16 23 30	7 14 21 28
Tue.	6 13 20 27	3 10 17 24	1 8 15 22 29
Wed.	7 14 21 28	4 11 18 25	2 9 16 23 30
Thur.	1 8 15 22 29	5 12 19 26	3 10 17 24 31
Fri.	2 9 16 23 30	6 13 20 27	4 11 18 25
Sat.	3 10 17 24 31	7 14 21 28	5 12 19 26

EASTER DAYS

March 22	1818
March 29	1807, 1891, 1959, 1970
April 5	1795, 1801, 1863, 1874, 1885, 1931, 1942 1953, 2015, 2026
April 12	1789, 1846, 1857, 1903, 1914, 1925, 1998, 2009
April 19	1778, 1829, 1835, 1981, 1987

J (LEAP YEAR)

	January	*February*	*March*
Sun.	4 11 18 25	1 8 15 22 29	7 14 21 28
Mon.	5 12 19 26	2 9 16 23	1 8 15 22 29
Tue.	6 13 20 27	3 10 17 24	2 9 16 23 30
Wed.	7 14 21 28	4 11 18 25	3 10 17 24 31
Thur.	1 8 15 22 29	5 12 19 26	4 11 18 25
Fri.	2 9 16 23 30	6 13 20 27	5 12 19 26
Sat.	3 10 17 24 31	7 14 21 28	6 13 20 27

	April	*May*	*June*
Sun.	4 11 18 25	2 9 16 23 30	6 13 20 27
Mon.	5 12 19 26	3 10 17 24 31	7 14 21 28
Tue.	6 13 20 27	4 11 18 25	1 8 15 22 29
Wed.	7 14 21 28	5 12 19 26	2 9 16 23 30
Thur.	1 8 15 22 29	6 13 20 27	3 10 17 24
Fri.	2 9 16 23 30	7 14 21 28	4 11 18 25
Sat.	3 10 17 24	1 8 15 22 29	5 12 19 26

	July	*August*	*September*
Sun.	4 11 18 25	1 8 15 22 29	5 12 19 26
Mon.	5 12 19 26	2 9 16 23 30	6 13 20 27
Tue.	6 13 20 27	3 10 17 24 31	7 14 21 28
Wed.	7 14 21 28	4 11 18 25	1 8 15 22 29
Thur.	1 8 15 22 29	5 12 19 26	2 9 16 23 30
Fri.	2 9 16 23 30	6 13 20 27	3 10 17 24
Sat.	3 10 17 24 31	7 14 21 28	4 11 18 25

	October	*November*	*December*
Sun.	3 10 17 24 31	7 14 21 28	5 12 19 26
Mon.	4 11 18 25	1 8 15 22 29	6 13 20 27
Tue.	5 12 19 26	2 9 16 23 30	7 14 21 28
Wed.	6 13 20 27	3 10 17 24	1 8 15 22 29
Thur.	7 14 21 28	4 11 18 25	2 9 16 23 30
Fri.	1 8 15 22 29	5 12 19 26	3 10 17 24 31
Sat.	2 9 16 23 30	6 13 20 27	4 11 18 25

EASTER DAYS

March 28	1880, 1948
April 4	1920
April 11	1784, 1852, 2004
April 18	1824, 1976

K

	January	*February*	*March*
Sun.	3 10 17 24 31	7 14 21 28	7 14 21 28
Mon.	4 11 18 25	1 8 15 22	1 8 15 22 29
Tue.	5 12 19 26	2 9 16 23	2 9 16 23 30
Wed.	6 13 20 27	3 10 17 24	3 10 17 24 31
Thur.	7 14 21 28	4 11 18 25	4 11 18 25
Fri.	1 8 15 22 29	5 12 19 26	5 12 19 26
Sat.	2 9 16 23 30	6 13 20 27	6 13 20 27

	April	*May*	*June*
Sun.	4 11 18 25	2 9 16 23 30	6 13 20 27
Mon.	5 12 19 26	3 10 17 24 31	7 14 21 28
Tue.	6 13 20 27	4 11 18 25	1 8 15 22 29
Wed.	7 14 21 28	5 12 19 26	2 9 16 23 30
Thur.	1 8 15 22 29	6 13 20 27	3 10 17 24
Fri.	2 9 16 23 30	7 14 21 28	4 11 18 25
Sat.	3 10 17 24	1 8 15 22 29	5 12 19 26

	July	*August*	*September*
Sun.	4 11 18 25	1 8 15 22 29	5 12 19 26
Mon.	5 12 19 26	2 9 16 23 30	6 13 20 27
Tue.	6 13 20 27	3 10 17 24 31	7 14 21 28
Wed.	7 14 21 28	4 11 18 25	1 8 15 22 29
Thur.	1 8 15 22 29	5 12 19 26	2 9 16 23 30
Fri.	2 9 16 23 30	6 13 20 27	3 10 17 24
Sat.	3 10 17 24 31	7 14 21 28	4 11 18 25

	October	*November*	*December*
Sun.	3 10 17 24 31	7 14 21 28	5 12 19 26
Mon.	4 11 18 25	1 8 15 22 29	6 13 20 27
Tue.	5 12 19 26	2 9 16 23 30	7 14 21 28
Wed.	6 13 20 27	3 10 17 24	1 8 15 22 29
Thur.	7 14 21 28	4 11 18 25	2 9 16 23 30
Fri.	1 8 15 22 29	5 12 19 26	3 10 17 24 31
Sat.	2 9 16 23 30	6 13 20 27	4 11 18 25

EASTER DAYS

March 28	1869, 1875, 1937, 2027
April 4	1779, 1790, 1847, 1858, 1915, 1926, 1999 2010, 2021
April 11	1773, 1819, 1830, 1841, 1909, 1971, 1982, 1993
April 18	1802, 1813, 1897, 1954, 1965
April 25	1886, 1943

L (LEAP YEAR)

	January	*February*	*March*
Sun.	3 10 17 24 31	7 14 21 28	6 13 20 27
Mon.	4 11 18 25	1 8 15 22 29	7 14 21 28
Tue.	5 12 19 26	2 9 16 23	1 8 15 22 29
Wed.	6 13 20 27	3 10 17 24	2 9 16 23 30
Thur.	7 14 21 28	4 11 18 25	3 10 17 24 31
Fri.	1 8 15 22 29	5 12 19 26	4 11 18 25
Sat.	2 9 16 23 30	6 13 20 27	5 12 19 26

	April	*May*	*June*
Sun.	3 10 17 24	1 8 15 22 29	5 12 19 26
Mon.	4 11 18 25	2 9 16 23 30	6 13 20 27
Tue.	5 12 19 26	3 10 17 24 31	7 14 21 28
Wed.	6 13 20 27	4 11 18 25	1 8 15 22 29
Thur.	7 14 21 28	5 12 19 26	2 9 16 23 30
Fri.	1 8 15 22 29	6 13 20 27	3 10 17 24
Sat.	2 9 16 23 30	7 14 21 28	4 11 18 25

	July	*August*	*September*
Sun.	3 10 17 24 31	7 14 21 28	4 11 18 25
Mon.	4 11 18 25	1 8 15 22 29	5 12 19 26
Tue.	5 12 19 26	2 9 16 23 30	6 13 20 27
Wed.	6 13 20 27	3 10 17 24 31	7 14 21 28
Thur.	7 14 21 28	4 11 18 25	1 8 15 22 29
Fri.	1 8 15 22 29	5 12 19 26	2 9 16 23 30
Sat.	2 9 16 23 30	6 13 20 27	3 10 17 24

	October	*November*	*December*
Sun.	2 9 16 23 30	6 13 20 27	4 11 18 25
Mon.	3 10 17 24 31	7 14 21 28	5 12 19 26
Tue.	4 11 18 25	1 8 15 22 29	6 13 20 27
Wed.	5 12 19 26	2 9 16 23 30	7 14 21 28
Thur.	6 13 20 27	3 10 17 24	1 8 15 22 29
Fri.	7 14 21 28	4 11 18 25	2 9 16 23 30
Sat.	1 8 15 22 29	5 12 19 26	3 10 17 24 31

EASTER DAYS

March 27	1796, 1864, 1932, 2016
April 3	1836, 1904, 1988
April 17	1808, 1892, 1960

M

	January	*February*	*March*
Sun.	2 9 16 23 30	6 13 20 27	6 13 20 27
Mon.	3 10 17 24 31	7 14 21 28	7 14 21 28
Tue.	4 11 18 25	1 8 15 22	1 8 15 22 29
Wed.	5 12 19 26	2 9 16 23	2 9 16 23 30
Thur.	6 13 20 27	3 10 17 24	3 10 17 24 31
Fri.	7 14 21 28	4 11 18 25	4 11 18 25
Sat.	1 8 15 22 29	5 12 19 26	5 12 19 26

	April	*May*	*June*
Sun.	3 10 17 24	1 8 15 22 29	5 12 19 26
Mon.	4 11 18 25	2 9 16 23 30	6 13 20 27
Tue.	5 12 19 26	3 10 17 24 31	7 14 21 28
Wed.	6 13 20 27	4 11 18 25	1 8 15 22 29
Thur.	7 14 21 28	5 12 19 26	2 9 16 23 30
Fri.	1 8 15 22 29	6 13 20 27	3 10 17 24
Sat.	2 9 16 23 30	7 14 21 28	4 11 18 25

	July	*August*	*September*
Sun.	3 10 17 24 31	7 14 21 28	4 11 18 25
Mon.	4 11 18 25	1 8 15 22 29	5 12 19 26
Tue.	5 12 19 26	2 9 16 23 30	6 13 20 27
Wed.	6 13 20 27	3 10 17 24 31	7 14 21 28
Thur.	7 14 21 28	4 11 18 25	1 8 15 22 29
Fri.	1 8 15 22 29	5 12 19 26	2 9 16 23 30
Sat.	2 9 16 23 30	6 13 20 27	3 10 17 24

	October	*November*	*December*
Sun.	2 9 16 23 30	6 13 20 27	4 11 18 25
Mon.	3 10 17 24 31	7 14 21 28	5 12 19 26
Tue.	4 11 18 25	1 8 15 22 29	6 13 20 27
Wed.	5 12 19 26	2 9 16 23 30	7 14 21 28
Thur.	6 13 20 27	3 10 17 24	1 8 15 22 29
Fri.	7 14 21 28	4 11 18 25	2 9 16 23 30
Sat.	1 8 15 22 29	5 12 19 26	3 10 17 24 31

EASTER DAYS

March 27	1785, 1842, 1853, 1910, 1921, 2005
April 3	1774, 1825, 1831, 1983, 1994
April 10	1803, 1814, 1887, 1898, 1955, 1966, 1977
April 17	1870, 1881, 1927, 1938, 1949, 2022
April 24	1791, 1859, 2011

N (LEAP YEAR)

	January	*February*	*March*
Sun.	2 9 16 23 30	6 13 20 27	5 12 19 26
Mon.	3 10 17 24 31	7 14 21 28	6 13 20 27
Tue.	4 11 18 25	1 8 15 22 29	7 14 21 28
Wed.	5 12 19 26	2 9 16 23	1 8 15 22 29
Thur.	6 13 20 27	3 10 17 24	2 9 16 23 30
Fri.	7 14 21 28	4 11 18 25	3 10 17 24 31
Sat.	1 8 15 22 29	5 12 19 26	4 11 18 25

	April	*May*	*June*
Sun.	2 9 16 23 30	7 14 21 28	4 11 18 25
Mon.	3 10 17 24	1 8 15 22 29	5 12 19 26
Tue.	4 11 18 25	2 9 16 23 30	6 13 20 27
Wed.	5 12 19 26	3 10 17 24 31	7 14 21 28
Thur.	6 13 20 27	4 11 18 25	1 8 15 22 29
Fri.	7 14 21 28	5 12 19 26	2 9 16 23 30
Sat.	1 8 15 22 29	6 13 20 27	3 10 17 24

	July	*August*	*September*
Sun.	2 9 16 23 30	6 13 20 27	3 10 17 24
Mon.	3 10 17 24 31	7 14 21 28	4 11 18 25
Tue.	4 11 18 25	1 8 15 22 29	5 12 19 26
Wed.	5 12 19 26	2 9 16 23 30	6 13 20 27
Thur.	6 13 20 27	3 10 17 24 31	7 14 21 28
Fri.	7 14 21 28	4 11 18 25	1 8 15 22 29
Sat.	1 8 15 22 29	5 12 19 26	2 9 16 23 30

	October	*November*	*December*
Sun.	1 8 15 22 29	5 12 19 26	3 10 17 24 31
Mon.	2 9 16 23 30	6 13 20 27	4 11 18 25
Tue.	3 10 17 24 31	7 14 21 28	5 12 19 26
Wed.	4 11 18 25	1 8 15 22 29	6 13 20 27
Thur.	5 12 19 26	2 9 16 23 30	7 14 21 28
Fri.	6 13 20 27	3 10 17 24	1 8 15 22 29
Sat.	7 14 21 28	4 11 18 25	2 9 16 23 30

EASTER DAYS

March 26	1780
April 2	1820, 1972
April 9	1944
April 16	1876, 2028
April 23	1848, 1916, 2000

GEOLOGICAL TIME

The earth is thought to have come into existence approximately 4,600 million years ago, but for nearly half this time, the Archean era, it was uninhabited. Life is generally believed to have emerged in the succeeding Proterozoic era. The Archean and the Proterozoic eras are often together referred to as the Precambrian.

Although primitive forms of life, e.g. algae and bacteria, existed during the Proterozoic era, it is not until the strata of Palaeozoic rocks is reached that abundant fossilized remains appear, initially of small shellfish, followed by plants, primitive fishes and, in the Devonian period (*c*.400 million BC), land-living plants and amphibia.

Since the Precambrian, there have been three great geological eras:

PALAEOZOIC ('ancient life')
c.570–*c*.250 million BC

Cambrian - Mainly sandstones, slate and shales; limestones in Scotland. Shelled fossils and invertebrates, e.g. trilobites and brachiopods appear.
Ordovician - Mainly shales and mudstones, e.g. in north Wales; limestones in Scotland.
Silurian - Shales, mudstones and some limestones, found mostly in Wales and southern Scotland.
Devonian - Old red sandstone, shale, limestone and slate, e.g. in south Wales and the West Country. 'The age of fishes' - proliferation of fish fossils. First traces of land-living life.
Carboniferous - Coal-bearing rocks, millstone grit, limestone and shale.
Permian - Marls, sandstones and clays, named after the area of Russia where these strata are widespread. First large-scale appearance of reptile fossils.

There were two great phases of mountain building in the Palaeozoic era: the Caledonian, characterized in Britain by NE–SW lines of hills and valleys; and the later Hercyian, widespread in west Germany and adjacent areas, and in Britain exemplified in E–W lines of hills and valleys.

The end of the Palaeozoic era was marked by the extensive glaciations of the Permian period in the southern continents and the decline of amphibians. It was succeeded by an era of warm conditions.

MESOZOIC ('middle forms of life')
c.250–*c*.65 million BC

Triassic - Mostly sandstone, e.g. in the West Midlands.
Jurassic - Mainly limestones and clays, typically displayed in the Jura mountains, and in England in a NE–SW belt from Lincolnshire and the Wash to the Severn and the Dorset coast.
Cretaceous - Mainly chalk, clay and sands, e.g. in Kent and Sussex.

Giant reptiles were dominant during the Mesozoic era, but it was at this time that marsupial mammals first appeared, as well as *Archaeopteryx lithographica*, the earliest known species of bird. Coniferous trees and flowering plants also developed during the era and, with the birds and the mammals, were the main species to survive into the Caenozoic (or Cenozoic) era. The giant reptiles became extinct.

CAENOZOIC ('recent life')
from *c*.65 million BC

Eocene - The emergence of new forms of life, i.e. existing species.
Oligocene - Fossils of a few still existing species.
Miocene - Fossil remains show a balance of existing and extinct species.
Pliocene - Fossil remains show a majority of still existing species.
Pleistocene - The majority of remains are those of still existing species.
Holocene - The present, post-glacial period. Existing species only, except for a few exterminated by man.

In the last 25 million years, from the Miocene through the Pliocene periods, the Alpine-Himalayan and the circum-Pacific phases of mountain building reached their climax. During the Pleistocene period ice sheets repeatedly locked up masses of water as land ice; its weight depressed the land, but the locking-up of the water lowered the sea-level by 100–200 metres. The glaciations and interglacials of the Ice Age are extremely difficult to date and classify, but recent scientific opinion considers the Pleistocene period to have begun approximately 1.7 million years ago. The last glacial retreat, merging into the Holocene period, was 10,000 years ago.

HUMAN DEVELOPMENT

Any consideration of the history of man must start with the fact that all members of the human race belong to one species of animal, i.e. *Homo sapiens*, the definition of a species being in biological terms that all its members can interbreed. As a species of mammal it is possible to group man with other similar types, known as the primates. Amongst these is found a sub-group, the apes, which includes, in addition to man, the chimpanzees, gorillas, orang-utans and gibbons. All lack a tail, have shoulder blades at the back, and a Y-shaped chewing pattern on the surface of their molars, as well as showing the more general primate characteristics of four incisors, a thumb which is able to touch the fingers of the same hand, and finger and toe nails instead of claws. All the factors available to scientific study suggest that human beings have chimpanzees and gorillas as their nearest relatives in the animal world. However, there remains the possibility that there once lived creatures, now extinct, which were closer to modern man than the chimpanzees and gorillas, and which shared with modern man the characteristics of having flat faces (i.e. the absence of a pronounced muzzle), being bipedal, and possessing large brains.

There are two broad groups of extinct apes recognized by specialists. First the ramapithecines, the remains of which, mainly jaw fragments, have been found in east Africa, Asia, and Turkey. They lived about 14 to 8 million years ago, and from the evidence of their teeth it seems they chewed more in the manner of modern man than the other presently living apes. The second group, the australopithecines, have left much more numerous remains amongst which sub-groups may be detected, although the geographic spread is limited to south and east Africa. Living between 5 and 1.5 million years ago, they were closer relatives of modern man to the extent that they walked upright, did not have an extensive muzzle, and had similar types of pre-molars. The first australopithecine remains were recognized at Taung in South Africa in 1924, and subsequent discoveries include those at the famous site of Olduvai Gorge in Tanzania. Perhaps the most impressive discovery was made at Hadar in Ethiopia in 1974 when about half a skeleton, known as 'Lucy', was found.

Also in east Africa, between 2 million and 1.5 million years ago, lived a hominid group which not only walked upright, had a flat face, and a large brain case, but also made simple pebble and flake stone tools. On present evidence these habilines seem to have been the first people to make tools, however crude. This facility is related to the larger brain size and human beings are the only animals to make implements to be used in other processes. These early pebble tool users, because of their distinctive characteristics, have been grouped as a separate sub-species, now extinct, of the genus *Homo*, and are known as *Homo habilis*.

The use of fire, again a human characteristic, is associated with another group of extinct hominids whose remains, about a million years old, are found in south and east Africa, China, Indonesia, north Africa and Europe. No doubt the mastery of the techniques of making fire helped the colonization of the colder northern areas and in this respect the site of Vertesszollos in Hungary is of particular importance. *Homo erectus* is the name given to this group of fossils and it now includes a number of famous individual discoveries from earlier decades, for example, Solo Man, Heidelberg Man, and especially Peking Man who lived at the cave site at Choukoutien, which has yielded evidence of fire and burnt bone.

The well-known group, Neanderthal Man, or *Homo sapiens neandertalensis*, is an extinct form of modern man who lived between about 100,000 and 40,000 years ago, thus spanning the last Ice Age. Indeed, its ability to adapt to the cold climate on the edge of the ice sheets is one of its characteristic features, the remains being found only in Europe, Asia and the Middle East. Complete neanderthal skeletons were found during excavations at Tabun in Israel, together with evidence of tool-making and the use of fire. Distinguished by very large brains, it seems that neanderthal man was the first to develop recognizable social customs, especially deliberate burial rites. Why the neanderthalers became extinct is not clear, but it may be connected with the climatic changes at the end of the Ice Ages, which would have seriously affected their food supplies; possibly they became too specialized for their own good.

The Swanscombe skull is the only known human fossil remains found in England. Some specialists see Swanscombe Man (or, more probably, woman) as a neanderthaler. Others group these remains together with the Steinheim skull from Germany, seeing both as a separate sub-species, *Homo sapiens steinheimenses*. Unfortunately there is too little evidence as yet on which to form a final judgement.

Modern Man, *Homo sapiens sapiens*, the surviving sub-species of *Homo sapiens*, had evolved to our present physical condition and had colonized much of the world by about 30,000 years ago. There are many previously distinguished individual specimens, for example Cromagnon Man, which may now be grouped together as *Homo sapiens sapiens*. It was modern man who spread to the American continent by crossing the landbridge between Siberia and Alaska and thence moved south through North America and into South America. Equally it is modern man who over the last 30,000 years has been responsible for the major developments in technology, art and civilization generally.

One of the problems for those studying fossil man is the lack in many cases of sufficient quantities of fossil bone for analysis. It is important that theories should be tested against evidence, and not the evidence made to fit the theory. The celebrated Piltdown hoax is perhaps the best-known example of 'fossils' being forged to fit what was seen in some quarters as the correct theory of man's evolution.

CULTURAL DEVELOPMENT

The Eurocentric bias of early archaeologists meant that the search for a starting point for the development and transmission of cultural ideas, especially by migration, trade and warfare, concentrated unduly on Europe and the Near East. The Three Age system, whereby pre-history was divided into a Stone Age, a Bronze Age, and an Iron Age, was devised by Christian Thomsen, curator of the National Museum of Denmark in the early nineteenth century, to facilitate the classification of the museum's collections. The descriptive adjectives referred to the materials from which the implements and weapons were made, and came to be regarded as the dominant features of the societies to which they related. The refinement of the Three Age system once dominated archaeological thought and still remains a generally accepted concept in the popular mind. However, it is now seen by archaeologists as an inadequate model for human development.

Common sense alone suggests that there were no complete breaks between one so-called Age and another, any more than contemporaries would have regarded 1485 as a complete break between medieval and modern English history. Nor can the Three Age system be applied universally. In some areas it is necessary to insert a Copper Age, while in Africa south of the Sahara there would seem to be no Bronze Age at all; in Australia, Old Stone Age societies survived, while in South America, New Stone Age communities existed into modern times. The civilizations in other parts of the world clearly invalidate a Eurocentric theory of human development.

The concept of the 'Neolithic Revolution', associated with the domestication of plants and animals, was a development of particular importance in the human cultural pattern. It reflected change from the primitive hunter/gatherer economies to a more settled agricultural way of life and therefore, so the argument goes, made possible the development of urban civilization. However, it can no longer be argued that this 'revolution' took place only in one area from which all development stemmed. Though it appears that the cultivation of wheat and barley was first undertaken, together with the domestication of cattle and goats/sheep in the Fertile Crescent, there is evidence that rice was first deliberately planted and pigs domesticated in south-east Asia, maize first cultivated in Central America, and llamas first domesticated in South America. It has been recognized increasingly in recent years that cultural changes can take place independently of each other in different parts of the world at different rates and different times. There is no need for a general diffusionist theory.

Although scholars will continue to study the particular societies which interest them, it may be possible to obtain a reliable chronological framework, in absolute terms of years, against which the cultural development of any particular area may be set. The development and refinement of radiocarbon dating and other scientific methods of producing absolute chronologies is enabling the cross-referencing of societies to be undertaken. As the techniques of dating become more rigorous in application and the number of scientifically obtained dates increases, the attainment of an absolute chronology for prehistoric societies throughout the world comes closer to being achieved.

Tidal Tables

CONSTANTS

The constant tidal difference may be used in conjunction with the time of high water at a standard port shown in the Predictions data (pages 98–109) to find the time of high water at any of the ports or places listed below.

(pages 98–109)

EXAMPLE

Required times of high water at Stranraer at 1 *January* 1993
Appropriate time of high water at *Greenock*

Morning tide 1 *January*	0523 hrs
Tidal difference	−0020 hrs
High water at *Stranraer*	0503 hrs

The columns headed 'Springs' and 'Neaps' show the height, in metres, of the tide above datum for mean high water springs and mean high water neaps respectively.

† data very approximate * data for first high water springs only

Port		Diff. h m	Springs m	Neaps m
Aberdeen	*Leith*	−1 19	4.3	3.4
Aberdovey	*Liverpool*	−3 00	5.0	3.5
Aberystwyth	*Liverpool*	−3 30	5.0	3.5
Aldeburgh	*London*	−3 05	2.8	2.7
Alloa	*Leith*	+0 47	5.6	4.2
Amlwch	*Liverpool*	−0 33	7.2	5.7
Anstruther Easter	*Leith*	−0 22	5.5	4.4
Antwerp (Prosperpolder)	*London*	+0 50	5.8	4.8
Appledore	*Avonmouth*	−1 15	7.5	5.2
Arbroath	*Leith*	−0 33	5.0	4.1
Ardrossan	*Greenock*	−0 15	3.2	2.7
†Arundel	*London*	−2 03	3.2	2.1
Avonmouth	*A'mouth*	0 00	13.2	9.8
Ayr	*Greenock*	−0 25	3.0	2.6
Baie de Lampaul	*London*	+2 30	7.4	5.8
Ballycotton	*Avonmouth*	−1 47	4.2	3.2
Banff	*Leith*	−2 44	3.5	2.8
Bantry	*Liverpool*	+5 54	3.3	2.4
Bardsey Island	*Liverpool*	−3 18	4.4	3.2
Barmouth	*Liverpool*	−2 57	5.0	3.5
Barnstaple	*Avonmouth*	−1 00	4.1	1.4
Barrow (Docks)	*Liverpool*	+0 11	9.3	7.1
Barry	*Avonmouth*	−0 22	11.4	8.5
Belfast	*London*	−2 45	3.5	3.0
Berwick	*Leith*	−0 02	4.7	3.8
Bideford	*Avonmouth*	−1 15	5.9	3.6
Blackpool	*Liverpool*	−0 10	8.9	7.0
Blacktoft	*Hull*	+0 30	5.8	4.0
Blakeney	*Hull*	+0 44	3.4	2.0
Blyth	*Leith*	+0 50	5.0	3.9
Boscastle	*Avonmouth*	−1 20	7.3	5.6
Boulogne	*London*	−2 44	8.9	7.2
Bovisand Pier	*London*	+3 55	5.3	4.3
Bowling	*Greenock*	+0 15	4.0	3.4
Braye (Alderney)	*London*	+5 33	6.3	4.7
Brest	*London*	+2 28	7.5	5.9
Bridgwater	*Avonmouth*	−0 22	4.6	1.7
Bridlington	*Leith*	+2 03	6.1	4.7
Bridport (W. Bay)	*London*	+4 37	4.1	3.0
Brighton	*London*	−2 50	6.6	5.0
Buckie	*Leith*	−2 56	4.1	3.2
Bude Haven	*Avonmouth*	−1 33	7.7	5.8
Bull Sand Fort	*Hull*	−0 46	6.9	5.5
Burntisland	*Leith*	0 00	5.6	4.5
Calais	*London*	−2 04	7.1	5.9
Campbeltown	*Greenock*	+0 07	2.9	2.6
Cape Cornwall	*A'mouth*	−2 30	6.0	4.3
Cardiff (Penarth)	*Avonmouth*	−0 15	12.2	9.2
Cardigan Port	*Liverpool*	−3 37	4.7	3.4
Carmarthen	*Avonmouth*	−0 48	2.6	0.4
Cayeux	*London*	−2 55	10.2	7.9
Chatham	*London*	−1 10	6.0	4.9
Chepstow	*Avonmouth*	+0 20	No data	
Cherbourg	*London*	−6 00	6.4	5.0
Chester	*Liverpool*	+1 05	4.0	2.0
Chichester Hbr.	*London*	−2 25	4.9	4.0
*Christchurch Hbr.	*London*	−4 53	1.8	1.4
Cobh	*Liverpool*	−5 56	4.2	3.2
Coulport	*Greenock*	−0 05	3.4	2.9
Coverack	*Avonmouth*	−2 02	5.3	4.2
Cowes	*London*	−2 23	4.2	3.5
Cromarty	*Leith*	−2 56	4.3	3.4
Cromer	*Hull*	+0 15	5.2	4.1
Dartmouth	*London*	+4 25	4.9	3.8
Deal	*London*	−2 37	6.1	5.0
Dieppe	*London*	−3 03	9.3	7.2
Dingle Hbr.	*Liverpool*	+5 33	3.9	2.8
Donegal Hbr.	*Liverpool*	−5 24	3.9	3.0
Douglas (IOM)	*Liverpool*	−0 04	6.9	5.4
Dover	*London*	−2 52	6.7	5.3
Duclair	*London*	−1 48	7.5	6.3
Duddon Bar	*Liverpool*	+0 03	8.5	6.6
Dunbar	*Leith*	−0 07	5.2	4.2
Dundalk (Sldr's Pt)	*L'pool*	+0 22	5.1	4.2
Dundee	*Leith*	+0 11	5.4	4.3
Dungeness	*London*	−3 04	7.7	5.9
Dunkirk	*London*	−1 54	5.8	4.8
Eastbourne	*London*	−2 50	7.4	5.5
East Loch Tarbert	*G'nock*	+0 05	3.4	2.9
Exmouth Dock	*London*	+4 55	4.0	2.8
Eyemouth	*Leith*	−0 20	4.7	3.7
Falmouth	*London*	+3 35	5.3	4.2
Ferryside	*Avonmouth*	−0 58	6.7	4.5
Filey Bay	*Leith*	+1 50	5.8	4.9
Fishguard	*Liverpool*	−4 01	4.8	3.4
Folkestone	*London*	−3 04	7.1	5.7
Formby	*Liverpool*	−0 12	9.0	7.3
Fowey	*London*	+3 53	5.4	4.3
Fraserburgh	*Leith*	−2 29	3.7	2.9
*Freshwater Bay	*London*	−4 33	2.6	2.3
Galway	*Liverpool*	−6 08	5.1	3.9
Glasgow	*Greenock*	+0 28	4.7	4.1
Goole	*Hull*	+0 59	5.7	3.7
Gorleston	*London*	−5 00	2.4	2.0
Granton	*Leith*	0 00	5.6	4.5
Granville	*London*	+4 32	13.0	9.8
Grimsby	*Hull*	−0 28	7.0	5.6

Hartlepool	*Leith*	+0 58	5.4	4.2
Harwich	*London*	−2 02	4.0	3.4
Hastings	*London*	−2 57	7.5	5.8
Haverfordwest	*Liverpool*	−4 50	2.2	0.3
Hestan Islet	*Liverpool*	+0 25	8.3	6.3
Holyhead	*Liverpool*	−0 48	5.6	4.4
Hook of Holland	*London*	−0 01	2.1	1.7
*Hurst Point	*London*	−3 38	2.7	2.3
Ijmuiden	*London*	+1 04	2.0	1.6
Ilfracombe	*Avonmouth*	−1 10	9.2	6.9
Inveraray	*Greenock*	+0 11	3.3	3.0
Invergordon	*Leith*	−2 49	4.4	3.5
Ipswich	*London*	−1 42	4.2	3.4
Itchenor	*London*	−2 23	4.8	3.8
Kinsale	*Liverpool*	−6 08	4.0	3.2
Kirkcudbright	*Liverpool*	+0 15	7.5	5.9
Kirkwall	*Leith*	−4 15	2.9	2.2
Knights Town	*Liverpool*	+5 31	3.6	2.8
Lamlash	*Greenock*	−0 26	3.2	2.7
Le Havre	*London*	−3 55	7.9	6.6
Lerwick	*Leith*	−3 49	2.2	1.6
Limerick Dock	*Liverpool*	−4 27	6.1	4.6
Littlehampton	*London*	−2 38	5.9	4.5
Lizard Point	*Avonmouth*	−2 17	5.3	4.2
Llanddwyn Island	*Liverpool*	−1 53	4.9	3.9
Llanelli	*Avonmouth*	−0 56	7.8	5.8
Loch Moidart	*Greenock*	+6 00	4.8	3.5
Londonderry	*London*	−5 37	2.7	2.1
Looe	*London*	+3 55	5.4	4.2
Lossiemouth	*Leith*	−3 01	4.1	3.2
Lowestoft	*London*	−4 25	2.4	2.1
Lulworth Cove	*London*	+5 00	2.3	1.5
Lundy Island	*Avonmouth*	−1 23	8.0	5.9
Lyme Regis	*London*	+4 55	4.3	3.1
*Lymington	*London*	−3 33	3.0	2.6
Margate	*London*	−1 52	4.8	3.9
Maryport	*Liverpool*	+0 24	8.6	6.6
Menai Bridge	*Liverpool*	−0 28	7.3	5.8
Mevagissey	*London*	+3 53	5.4	4.3
Middlesbrough	*Leith*	+1 09	5.6	4.5
Milford Haven	*Liverpool*	−5 07	7.0	5.2
Minehead	*Avonmouth*	−0 40	10.6	7.9
Montrose	*Leith*	−0 19	4.8	3.9
Morecambe	*Liverpool*	+0 07	9.5	7.4
Mostyn Quay	*Liverpool*	−0 17	8.5	6.7
Newburgh	*Leith*	+0 48	4.1	3.0
Newcastle upon Tyne	*Leith*	+0 54	5.3	4.1
Newhaven	*London*	−2 48	6.7	5.1
Newlyn	*Avonmouth*	−2 24	5.6	4.4
Newport (Gwent)	*Avonmouth*	−0 15	12.1	8.8
Newquay	*Avonmouth*	−1 58	7.0	5.3
New Quay, Cardigan Bay	*Liverpool*	−3 30	4.9	3.4
North Shields	*Leith*	+0 51	5.0	3.9
North Sunderland	*Leith*	+0 05	4.8	3.7
N. Woolwich	*London*	−0 20	7.0	5.9
Oban	*Greenock*	+5 45	4.0	2.9
Old Lynn Road	*Hull*	+0 05	7.3	5.8
Orfordness	*London*	−2 50	2.8	2.7
Ostend	*London*	−1 32	5.1	4.2
Padstow	*Avonmouth*	−1 45	7.3	5.6
Peel (IOM)	*Liverpool*	−0 02	5.3	4.2
Peterhead	*Leith*	−1 59	3.8	3.1
Plymouth	*London*	+4 05	5.5	4.4
*Poole (Entrance)	*London*	−5 03	2.0	1.6
Porlock Bay	*Avonmouth*	−0 50	10.2	7.6
Porthcawl	*Avonmouth*	−0 53	9.9	7.5
Portmadoc	*Liverpool*	−2 45	5.1	3.4
Portland	*London*	+5 10	2.1	1.4

Portpatrick	*Liverpool*	+0 22	3.8	3.0
Portsmouth	*London*	−2 23	4.7	3.8
Port Talbot	*Avonmouth*	−0 53	9.6	7.3
Preston	*Liverpool*	+0 10	5.3	3.3
Pwllheli	*Liverpool*	−3 07	5.0	3.4
Ramsey (IOM)	*Liverpool*	+0 10	7.6	5.9
Ramsgate	*London*	−2 32	4.9	3.8
†Rosslare Hbr.	*Liverpool*	−5 23	1.9	1.4
Rosyth	*Leith*	+0 07	5.8	4.7
Ryde	*London*	−2 23	4.5	3.7
St Helier	*London*	+4 48	11.1	8.1
St Ives	*Avonmouth*	−1 55	6.6	4.9
St Malo	*London*	+4 27	12.2	9.2
St Peter Port	*London*	+4 54	9.3	7.0
Salcombe	*London*	+4 10	5.3	4.1
Saltash	*London*	+4 10	5.6	4.5
Scarborough	*Leith*	+1 33	5.7	4.6
Scheveningen	*London*	+1 02	2.1	1.7
Scrabster	*Leith*	−6 06	5.0	4.0
Seaham	*Leith*	+0 53	5.2	4.1
Selsey Bill	*London*	−2 28	5.3	4.4
Sennen Cove	*Avonmouth*	−2 30	6.1	4.8
Sharpness Dock	*A'mouth*	+0 42	9.3	5.6
Sheerness	*London*	−1 16	5.7	4.8
Shoreham	*London*	−2 43	6.3	4.9
Silloth	*Liverpool*	+0 35	9.2	7.1
Southampton (1st high water)	*London*	−2 52	4.5	3.7
Southend	*London*	−1 22	5.7	4.8
Southwold	*London*	−3 50	2.5	2.2
Stirling	*Leith*	+1 13	2.9	1.6
Stonehaven	*Leith*	−1 09	4.5	3.6
Stornoway	*Liverpool*	−4 15	4.8	3.7
Stranraer	*Greenock*	−0 20	3.0	2.5
Stromness	*Leith*	−5 26	3.6	2.7
Sunderland	*Leith*	+0 51	5.2	4.2
*Swanage	*London*	−5 13	2.0	1.6
Swansea	*Avonmouth*	−0 49	9.6	7.3
Tarn Point	*Liverpool*	+0 05	8.3	6.4
Tay River (Bar)	*Leith*	−0 19	5.2	4.2
Tees R. (Ent.)	*Leith*	+1 08	5.5	4.3
Teignmouth	*London*	+4 37	4.8	3.6
Tenby	*Avonmouth*	−1 05	8.4	6.3
Tilbury	*London*	−0 49	6.4	5.3
Tobermory	*Liverpool*	−5 12	4.4	3.3
Torquay	*London*	+4 40	4.9	3.7
*Totland Bay	*London*	−3 53	2.7	2.3
Troon	*Greenock*	−0 25	3.2	2.7
Truro	*London*	+3 43	3.5	2.4
Walton-on-Naze	*London*	−2 10	4.2	3.4
Waterford	*Liverpool*	−4 59	4.6	3.5
Weston S. Mare	*A'mouth*	−0 25	12.0	8.8
†Wexford Hbr	*Liverpool*	−5 03	1.7	1.4
Whitby	*Leith*	+1 22	5.6	4.3
Whitehaven	*Liverpool*	+0 10	8.0	6.3
Wick	*Leith*	−3 26	3.5	2.8
Wisbech Cut	*Hull*	+0 01	7.0	5.1
Workington	*Liverpool*	+0 21	8.2	6.4
Worthing	*London*	−2 38	6.2	4.7
*Yarmouth (IOW)	*London*	−3 28	3.1	2.5
Youghal	*Liverpool*	−5 51	4.0	3.1

The tidal predictions for London Bridge, Avonmouth, Liverpool, Hull, Leith and Dun Laoghaire have been computed by the Proudman Oceanographic Laboratory, copyright reserved. The tidal predictions for Greenock have been computed by the Hydrographer of the Navy, Crown copyright reserved.

JANUARY 1993 *High water* GMT

	London Bridge				Avonmouth				Liverpool				Hull (*Albert Dock*)			
	*Datum of predictions 3.20m below				*Datum of predictions 6.50m below				*Datum of predictions 4.93m below				*Datum of predictions 3.90m below			
	a.m. h m	ht. m	p.m. h m	ht. m	a.m. h m	ht. m	p.m. h m	ht. m	a.m. h m	ht. m	p.m. h m	ht. m	a.m. h m	ht. m	p.m. h m	ht. m
1 Friday	06 32	6.0	19 16	5.9	11 58	10.3	— —	—	04 00	7.5	16 26	7.7	11 22	5.9	23 39	6.2
2 Saturday	07 20	5.8	20 11	5.7	00 17	10.0	12 50	9.9	04 57	7.3	17 26	7.4	— —	—	12 22	5.7
3 Sunday	08 23	5.6	21 14	5.7	01 19	9.7	14 06	9.8	06 05	7.2	18 36	7.4	00 48	6.0	13 37	5.7
4 Monday	09 34	5.6	22 19	5.9	02 40	9.9	15 22	10.3	07 19	7.4	19 47	7.7	02 04	6.0	14 47	5.9
5 Tuesday	10 41	5.8	23 20	6.1	03 52	10.6	16 28	11.0	08 22	7.8	20 47	8.1	03 11	6.2	15 48	6.2
6 Wednesday	11 46	6.2	— —	—	04 55	11.5	17 27	11.8	09 15	8.4	21 39	8.5	04 12	6.4	16 41	6.6
7 Thursday	00 21	6.5	12 45	6.6	05 51	12.2	18 24	12.5	10 03	8.9	22 27	9.0	05 06	6.8	17 29	6.9
8 Friday	01 13	6.8	13 37	7.0	06 45	12.9	19 14	13.0	10 49	9.3	23 15	9.3	05 54	7.1	18 11	7.3
9 Saturday	02 01	7.1	14 25	7.3	07 34	13.4	20 02	13.4	11 34	9.6	— —	—	06 41	7.4	18 53	7.6
10 Sunday	02 46	7.3	15 11	7.6	08 19	13.8	20 47	13.6	00 00	9.6	12 19	9.8	07 23	7.6	19 33	7.8
11 Monday	03 29	7.4	15 56	7.6	09 04	13.9	21 31	13.6	00 46	9.7	13 04	9.9	08 06	7.7	20 13	8.0
12 Tuesday	04 12	7.4	16 41	7.5	09 48	13.8	22 14	13.3	01 31	9.6	13 49	9.8	08 49	7.6	20 56	7.9
13 Wednesday	04 54	7.2	17 26	7.2	10 31	13.3	22 58	12.7	02 16	9.3	14 36	9.5	09 32	7.4	21 41	7.7
14 Thursday	05 39	7.0	18 14	6.9	11 16	12.7	23 43	12.0	03 04	9.0	15 24	9.1	10 20	7.0	22 28	7.4
15 Friday	06 27	6.8	19 07	6.6	— —	—	12 04	11.9	03 55	8.5	16 19	8.6	11 12	6.7	23 26	6.9
16 Saturday	07 21	6.5	20 06	6.4	00 32	11.2	12 59	11.1	04 54	8.1	17 23	8.1	— —	—	12 17	6.3
17 Sunday	08 29	6.3	21 15	6.3	01 34	10.5	14 09	10.5	06 05	7.7	18 42	7.7	00 38	6.6	13 34	6.2
18 Monday	09 46	6.2	22 30	6.2	02 53	10.3	15 31	10.5	07 24	7.7	20 02	7.8	02 01	6.3	14 50	6.2
19 Tuesday	11 08	6.2	23 42	6.4	04 12	10.7	16 47	10.9	08 34	8.0	21 10	8.0	03 27	6.3	15 59	6.5
20 Wednesday	— —	—	12 15	6.4	05 19	11.4	17 49	11.5	09 34	8.4	22 03	8.4	04 35	6.4	16 54	6.7
21 Thursday	00 41	6.5	13 09	6.6	06 14	12.1	18 39	12.0	10 21	8.8	22 48	8.6	05 29	6.6	17 39	6.9
22 Friday	01 27	6.7	13 52	6.8	06 59	12.5	19 21	12.4	11 02	9.1	23 26	8.8	06 12	6.7	18 18	7.1
23 Saturday	02 08	6.8	14 32	6.9	07 40	12.8	19 59	12.6	11 39	9.2	— —	—	06 49	6.8	18 52	7.3
24 Sunday	02 43	6.9	15 07	7.0	08 15	12.9	20 33	12.7	00 00	8.9	12 14	9.3	07 23	6.9	19 23	7.4
25 Monday	03 15	7.0	15 41	7.1	08 47	12.9	21 01	12.6	00 32	8.9	12 46	9.3	07 52	7.0	19 54	7.5
26 Tuesday	03 46	7.0	16 12	7.0	09 15	12.8	21 29	12.5	01 03	8.8	13 17	9.1	08 22	7.0	20 25	7.5
27 Wednesday	04 17	6.9	16 44	6.9	09 45	12.5	21 57	12.1	01 33	8.7	13 48	9.0	08 51	6.9	20 57	7.4
28 Thursday	04 48	6.8	17 16	6.7	10 14	12.1	22 26	11.7	02 02	8.5	14 19	8.7	09 24	6.8	21 32	7.1
29 Friday	05 20	6.6	17 50	6.5	10 42	11.5	22 54	11.1	02 33	8.2	14 53	8.3	09 57	6.5	22 09	6.8
30 Saturday	05 56	6.3	18 27	6.2	11 12	10.9	23 25	10.6	03 10	7.9	15 32	8.0	10 34	6.2	22 51	6.4
31 Sunday	06 34	6.0	19 10	5.9	11 49	10.3	— —	—	03 55	7.6	16 24	7.6	11 19	5.9	23 46	6.0

FEBRUARY 1993 *High water* GMT

	London Bridge				Avonmouth				Liverpool				Hull (*Albert Dock*)			
1 Monday	07 24	5.7	20 08	5.7	00 10	10.0	12 49	9.8	04 57	7.3	17 37	7.3	— —	—	12 25	5.7
2 Tuesday	08 34	5.6	21 25	5.6	01 27	9.7	14 26	9.8	06 22	7.2	19 04	7.3	01 06	5.8	13 58	5.7
3 Wednesday	09 57	5.7	22 44	5.9	03 07	10.2	15 53	10.6	07 44	7.5	20 19	7.8	02 36	5.9	15 15	6.0
4 Thursday	11 18	6.0	23 56	6.3	04 24	11.1	17 04	11.5	08 50	8.1	21 21	8.4	03 49	6.3	16 17	6.4
5 Friday	— —	—	12 27	6.6	05 32	12.1	18 07	12.5	09 45	8.8	22 13	9.0	04 49	6.7	17 09	6.9
6 Saturday	00 55	6.8	13 21	7.1	06 29	13.0	19 00	13.2	10 34	9.4	23 01	9.5	05 40	7.1	17 53	7.4
7 Sunday	01 44	7.2	14 11	7.5	07 20	13.7	19 48	13.8	11 20	9.8	23 46	9.8	06 24	7.5	18 34	7.8
8 Monday	02 29	7.5	14 56	7.7	08 05	14.2	20 30	14.1	— —	—	12 05	10.1	07 06	7.8	19 13	8.2
9 Tuesday	03 11	7.6	15 39	7.8	08 47	14.4	21 12	14.1	00 29	10.0	12 49	10.2	07 47	7.9	19 55	8.4
10 Wednesday	03 53	7.7	16 23	7.6	09 29	14.2	21 53	13.7	01 13	9.9	13 31	10.1	08 27	7.9	20 37	8.3
11 Thursday	04 35	7.5	17 05	7.3	10 12	13.7	22 34	13.1	01 55	9.6	14 15	9.7	09 10	7.6	21 21	8.0
12 Friday	05 18	7.2	17 50	6.9	10 52	12.9	23 15	12.2	02 39	9.2	15 00	9.2	09 55	7.2	22 09	7.5
13 Saturday	06 04	6.9	18 36	6.6	11 34	11.9	23 58	11.2	03 25	8.6	15 49	8.5	10 42	6.8	23 04	6.9
14 Sunday	06 55	6.6	19 30	6.3	— —	—	12 22	10.8	04 20	8.0	16 52	7.8	11 40	6.3	— —	—
15 Monday	07 58	6.2	20 33	6.1	00 53	10.3	13 30	10.0	05 30	7.5	18 17	7.3	00 12	6.3	12 53	6.0
16 Tuesday	09 14	6.0	21 52	5.9	02 15	9.8	15 00	9.8	06 59	7.4	19 48	7.3	01 42	5.9	14 19	6.0
17 Wednesday	10 45	6.0	23 18	6.1	03 48	10.2	16 27	10.4	08 19	7.7	20 58	7.7	03 17	5.9	15 38	6.2
18 Thursday	11 57	6.4	— —	—	04 59	11.1	17 29	11.3	09 19	8.2	21 50	8.2	04 26	6.1	16 35	6.5
19 Friday	00 19	6.4	12 50	6.7	05 54	11.9	18 19	12.0	10 06	8.6	22 31	8.5	05 15	6.4	17 20	6.8
20 Saturday	01 07	6.7	13 34	6.9	06 39	12.5	19 02	12.4	10 44	9.0	23 06	8.8	05 54	6.6	17 57	7.1
21 Sunday	01 47	6.9	14 12	7.0	07 19	12.8	19 37	12.7	11 19	9.2	23 37	8.9	06 28	6.8	18 29	7.4
22 Monday	02 22	7.0	14 44	7.0	07 52	13.0	20 08	12.8	11 50	9.3	— —	—	06 57	7.0	18 59	7.5
23 Tuesday	02 53	7.0	15 14	7.0	08 22	13.0	20 34	12.9	00 07	9.0	12 21	9.3	07 26	7.1	19 30	7.6
24 Wednesday	03 21	7.0	15 43	7.0	08 49	13.0	21 00	12.8	00 35	9.0	12 50	9.2	07 52	7.2	19 59	7.6
25 Thursday	03 49	7.0	16 13	7.0	09 15	12.8	21 28	12.5	01 03	8.9	13 19	9.1	08 22	7.1	20 32	7.4
26 Friday	04 20	6.9	16 42	6.9	09 45	12.4	21 56	12.1	01 31	8.8	13 48	8.9	08 51	7.0	21 04	7.2
27 Saturday	04 51	6.8	17 15	6.7	10 13	11.8	22 21	11.5	02 01	8.6	14 19	8.6	09 22	6.7	21 38	6.8
28 Sunday	05 25	6.5	17 50	6.4	10 40	11.2	22 49	11.0	02 33	8.3	14 57	8.2	09 56	6.4	22 17	6.5

JANUARY 1993 *continued*

	Greenock				Leith				Dun Laoghaire			
	*Datum of predictions 1.62m below				*Datum of predictions 2.90m below				†Datum of predictions 0.20m above			
	a.m.	ht.	p.m.	ht.	a.m.	ht.	p.m.	ht.	a.m.	ht.	p.m.	ht.
	h m	m	h m	m	h m	m	h m	m	h m	m	h m	m
1 Friday	05 23	3.0	17 37	3.0	08 02	4.5	20 09	4.6	05 04	3.3	17 20	3.4
2 Saturday	06 12	2.9	18 30	2.9	08 58	4.4	21 10	4.5	06 09	3.2	18 23	3.4
3 Sunday	07 11	2.8	19 45	2.7	09 57	4.4	22 13	4.5	07 11	3.3	19 25	3.4
4 Monday	08 35	2.8	21 25	2.8	10 57	4.5	23 15	4.6	08 07	3.4	20 21	3.5
5 Tuesday	09 51	3.0	22 28	2.9	11 51	4.7	— —	—	08 55	3.5	21 11	3.6
6 Wednesday	10 44	3.2	23 19	3.0	00 14	4.8	12 42	4.9	09 39	3.7	21 58	3.8
7 Thursday	11 30	3.4	— —	—	01 09	5.0	13 31	5.2	10 21	3.9	22 43	3.9
8 Friday	00 07	3.2	12 14	3.5	02 01	5.3	14 18	5.4	11 02	4.1	23 27	4.1
9 Saturday	00 54	3.3	12 57	3.7	02 51	5.5	15 05	5.6	11 45	4.3	— —	—
10 Sunday	01 42	3.4	13 39	3.8	03 39	5.7	15 53	5.8	00 12	4.1	12 29	4.4
11 Monday	02 28	3.4	14 22	3.9	04 28	5.7	16 42	5.8	00 58	4.2	13 15	4.5
12 Tuesday	03 12	3.5	15 05	4.0	05 18	5.7	17 32	5.8	01 46	4.1	14 06	4.4
13 Wednesday	03 54	3.5	15 49	3.9	06 07	5.5	18 22	5.6	02 38	4.0	14 57	4.3
14 Thursday	04 37	3.4	16 34	3.8	06 57	5.3	19 16	5.4	03 33	3.8	15 56	4.1
15 Friday	05 23	3.3	17 24	3.6	07 49	5.0	20 12	5.2	04 35	3.7	17 03	4.0
16 Saturday	06 14	3.2	18 19	3.4	08 46	4.8	21 14	4.9	05 43	3.6	18 16	3.8
17 Sunday	07 17	3.1	19 25	3.1	09 48	4.7	22 23	4.8	06 54	3.6	19 27	3.7
18 Monday	08 37	3.0	20 48	3.0	10 55	4.6	23 36	4.8	08 00	3.7	20 34	3.8
19 Tuesday	09 57	3.1	22 16	2.9	— —	—	12 04	4.8	09 01	3.8	21 34	3.8
20 Wednesday	10 58	3.2	23 21	3.0	00 45	4.9	13 04	5.0	09 53	4.0	22 25	3.8
21 Thursday	11 46	3.3	— —	—	01 41	5.1	13 54	5.2	10 37	4.1	23 07	3.9
22 Friday	00 10	3.0	12 27	3.4	02 26	5.2	14 34	5.3	11 16	4.2	23 43	3.9
23 Saturday	00 51	3.1	13 04	3.5	03 05	5.3	15 10	5.4	11 51	4.2	— —	—
24 Sunday	01 27	3.1	13 38	3.5	03 39	5.3	15 39	5.4	00 15	3.8	12 25	4.2
25 Monday	02 00	3.2	14 11	3.6	04 10	5.2	16 07	5.4	00 47	3.8	12 58	4.1
26 Tuesday	02 31	3.2	14 43	3.5	04 41	5.2	16 35	5.3	01 18	3.8	13 32	4.0
27 Wednesday	03 02	3.2	15 14	3.5	05 13	5.1	17 08	5.2	01 52	3.7	14 07	3.9
28 Thursday	03 33	3.2	15 44	3.3	05 49	4.9	17 44	5.1	02 28	3.6	14 47	3.7
29 Friday	04 06	3.1	16 16	3.2	06 29	4.7	18 29	4.8	03 11	3.5	15 33	3.6
30 Saturday	04 43	3.1	16 51	3.0	07 16	4.5	19 23	4.6	04 01	3.4	16 26	3.4
31 Sunday	05 25	2.9	17 34	2.8	08 09	4.3	20 25	4.4	05 00	3.3	17 27	3.3

NOTES:

*Difference of height in metres from Ordnance datum (Newlyn)

†Difference of height in metres from Ordnance datum (Dublin)

FEBRUARY 1993 *continued*

	Greenock				Leith				Dun Laoghaire			
1 Monday	06 16	2.8	18 37	2.6	09 08	4.2	21 31	4.3	06 09	3.2	18 38	3.3
2 Tuesday	07 26	2.8	20 22	2.6	10 12	4.3	22 40	4.4	07 22	3.3	19 48	3.4
3 Wednesday	09 01	2.8	21 58	2.8	11 13	4.5	23 47	4.7	08 24	3.4	20 48	3.6
4 Thursday	10 12	3.1	22 56	3.0	— —	—	12 14	4.8	09 16	3.7	21 39	3.8
5 Friday	11 05	3.3	23 48	3.2	00 49	5.0	13 09	5.2	10 03	3.9	22 26	4.0
6 Saturday	11 53	3.5	— —	—	01 44	5.3	13 59	5.5	10 46	4.2	23 10	4.1
7 Sunday	00 38	3.3	12 39	3.7	02 34	5.6	14 49	5.8	11 28	4.4	23 54	4.2
8 Monday	01 26	3.4	13 24	3.8	03 22	5.8	15 36	6.0	— —	—	12 12	4.5
9 Tuesday	02 11	3.5	14 07	3.9	04 10	5.9	16 26	6.1	00 37	4.3	12 56	4.6
10 Wednesday	02 52	3.5	14 48	3.9	04 57	5.8	17 13	6.0	01 22	4.2	13 43	4.5
11 Thursday	03 31	3.5	15 29	3.9	05 43	5.6	18 03	5.8	02 08	4.1	14 33	4.4
12 Friday	04 09	3.4	16 12	3.8	06 31	5.3	18 53	5.5	02 59	3.9	15 29	4.1
13 Saturday	04 50	3.3	16 57	3.5	07 21	5.0	19 48	5.1	03 54	3.8	16 36	3.9
14 Sunday	05 35	3.2	17 46	3.2	08 15	4.7	20 49	4.8	05 03	3.6	17 52	3.7
15 Monday	06 30	3.0	18 46	2.9	09 17	4.5	22 00	4.5	06 20	3.5	19 08	3.6
16 Tuesday	07 53	2.8	20 24	2.7	10 27	4.4	23 20	4.5	07 34	3.6	20 21	3.6
17 Wednesday	09 37	2.9	22 16	2.7	11 43	4.5	— —	—	08 42	3.7	21 26	3.7
18 Thursday	10 43	3.1	23 14	2.8	00 35	4.7	12 49	4.8	09 39	3.9	22 16	3.7
19 Friday	11 30	3.2	23 57	2.9	01 27	4.9	13 37	5.0	10 25	4.0	22 55	3.8
20 Saturday	12 09	3.3	— —	—	02 08	5.1	14 13	5.2	11 00	4.1	23 26	3.8
21 Sunday	00 32	3.0	12 45	3.4	02 42	5.2	14 46	5.3	11 33	4.1	23 52	3.8
22 Monday	01 05	3.1	13 18	3.4	03 12	5.3	15 12	5.4	— —	—	12 04	4.1
23 Tuesday	01 35	3.1	13 49	3.4	03 42	5.3	15 41	5.4	00 21	3.8	12 33	4.0
24 Wednesday	02 04	3.2	14 19	3.4	04 12	5.2	16 09	5.3	00 47	3.8	13 03	4.0
25 Thursday	02 33	3.2	14 46	3.3	04 42	5.1	16 41	5.3	01 15	3.8	13 35	3.9
26 Friday	03 03	3.2	15 14	3.2	05 16	5.0	17 16	5.1	01 50	3.7	14 13	3.8
27 Saturday	03 34	3.2	15 44	3.1	05 53	4.8	17 58	4.9	02 32	3.6	14 57	3.6
28 Sunday	04 09	3.1	16 17	2.9	06 34	4.5	18 48	4.6	03 18	3.4	15 50	3.5

MARCH 1993 *High water* GMT

	London Bridge				Avonmouth				Liverpool				Hull (*Albert Dock*)			
	*Datum of predictions 3.20m below				*Datum of predictions 6.50m below				*Datum of predictions 4.93m below				*Datum of predictions 3.90m below			
	a.m.	ht.	p.m.	ht.	a.m.	ht.	p.m.	ht.	a.m.	ht.	p.m.	ht.	a.m.	ht.	p.m.	ht.
	h m	m	h m	m	h m	m	h m	m	h m	m	h m	m	h m	m	h m	m
1 Monday	06 04	6.3	18 29	6.1	11 12	10.6	23 30	10.4	03 15	7.9	15 46	7.7	10 37	6.1	23 08	6.1
2 Tuesday	06 50	6.0	19 21	5.8	— —	—	12 07	10.0	04 13	7.5	16 57	7.3	11 33	5.8	— —	—
3 Wednesday	07 57	5.7	20 39	5.6	00 43	9.9	13 44	9.7	05 37	7.2	18 31	7.2	00 22	5.8	13 06	5.6
4 Thursday	09 25	5.7	22 09	5.8	02 29	10.0	15 24	10.4	07 12	7.5	19 55	7.7	02 06	5.9	14 43	5.9
5 Friday	10 55	6.1	23 32	6.2	03 59	11.0	16 42	11.5	08 26	8.1	21 00	8.4	03 28	6.2	15 50	6.4
6 Saturday	— —	—	12 07	6.7	05 09	12.1	17 47	12.5	09 24	8.8	21 53	9.0	04 31	6.7	16 44	6.9
7 Sunday	00 32	6.8	13 03	7.2	06 10	13.1	18 41	13.3	10 14	9.4	22 41	9.6	05 20	7.2	17 29	7.5
8 Monday	01 23	7.2	13 51	7.6	07 00	13.8	19 28	14.0	11 01	9.9	23 25	9.9	06 04	7.6	18 10	8.0
9 Tuesday	02 08	7.5	14 36	7.7	07 45	14.3	20 11	14.3	11 44	10.2	— —	—	06 43	7.9	18 52	8.3
10 Wednesday	02 50	7.7	15 18	7.7	08 27	14.5	20 50	14.3	00 08	10.1	12 28	10.3	07 24	8.0	19 34	8.4
11 Thursday	03 32	7.7	16 00	7.6	09 07	14.3	21 31	13.9	00 50	10.0	13 10	10.1	08 04	8.0	20 18	8.3
12 Friday	04 14	7.6	16 42	7.3	09 48	13.7	22 10	13.1	01 31	9.7	13 52	9.7	08 46	7.7	21 03	7.9
13 Saturday	04 58	7.3	17 25	6.9	10 28	12.8	22 49	12.2	02 13	9.3	14 36	9.1	09 29	7.3	21 52	7.3
14 Sunday	05 43	7.0	18 07	6.6	11 09	11.7	23 30	11.1	02 57	8.7	15 25	8.3	10 16	6.8	22 47	6.6
15 Monday	06 32	6.5	18 55	6.2	11 54	10.5	— —	—	03 50	8.0	16 26	7.6	11 09	6.3	23 54	6.0
16 Tuesday	07 31	6.2	19 54	5.9	00 22	10.1	12 57	9.6	04 58	7.5	17 50	7.1	— —	—	12 15	5.9
17 Wednesday	08 42	5.9	21 08	5.7	01 41	9.5	14 26	9.4	06 28	7.3	19 24	7.1	01 23	5.6	13 38	5.8
18 Thursday	10 14	5.9	22 44	5.9	03 17	9.9	15 57	10.1	07 51	7.5	20 36	7.5	03 00	5.6	15 08	5.9
19 Friday	11 32	6.3	23 51	6.3	04 31	10.9	17 01	11.1	08 53	8.0	21 25	8.0	04 04	5.9	16 09	6.3
20 Saturday	— —	—	12 25	6.7	05 26	11.7	17 51	11.8	09 38	8.4	22 04	8.4	04 51	6.2	16 52	6.7
21 Sunday	00 41	6.6	13 09	6.9	06 11	12.3	18 34	12.3	10 17	8.8	22 38	8.7	05 29	6.5	17 30	7.0
22 Monday	01 21	6.8	13 45	7.0	06 50	12.6	19 09	12.5	10 51	9.0	23 09	8.9	06 01	6.8	18 03	7.3
23 Tuesday	01 55	6.9	14 16	7.0	07 24	12.8	19 38	12.7	11 22	9.2	23 39	9.0	06 29	7.1	18 32	7.5
24 Wednesday	02 25	7.0	14 44	7.0	07 52	12.9	20 05	12.9	11 53	9.2	— —	—	06 56	7.2	19 03	7.5
25 Thursday	02 53	7.0	15 12	7.0	08 19	12.9	20 32	12.9	00 07	9.1	12 22	9.2	07 24	7.3	19 35	7.5
26 Friday	03 21	7.0	15 42	7.0	08 49	12.8	21 00	12.7	00 35	9.0	12 52	9.1	07 54	7.2	20 08	7.3
27 Saturday	03 53	7.0	16 13	7.0	09 18	12.4	21 31	12.3	01 03	8.9	13 23	8.9	08 23	7.0	20 40	7.0
28 Sunday	04 26	6.9	16 47	6.8	09 49	11.9	22 00	11.8	01 34	8.8	13 57	8.6	08 54	6.8	21 15	6.7
29 Monday	05 02	6.7	17 22	6.6	10 20	11.4	22 33	11.3	02 09	8.5	14 36	8.3	09 28	6.5	21 56	6.5
30 Tuesday	05 43	6.5	18 03	6.3	10 58	10.8	23 16	10.7	02 53	8.1	15 27	7.8	10 09	6.2	22 49	6.2
31 Wednesday	06 34	6.2	18 55	5.9	11 56	10.2	— —	—	03 50	7.7	16 37	7.4	11 06	5.9	— —	—

APRIL 1993 *High water* GMT

	London Bridge				Avonmouth				Liverpool				Hull (*Albert Dock*)			
1 Thursday	07 38	5.9	20 09	5.7	00 28	10.1	13 23	9.9	05 12	7.4	18 05	7.4	00 01	5.9	12 29	5.7
2 Friday	09 04	5.9	21 41	5.8	02 05	10.2	15 00	10.5	06 42	7.6	19 30	7.8	01 42	5.9	14 08	5.9
3 Saturday	10 33	6.3	23 04	6.3	03 34	11.1	16 19	11.5	07 58	8.2	20 36	8.4	03 04	6.3	15 19	6.4
4 Sunday	11 44	6.8	— —	—	04 45	12.1	17 23	12.4	08 58	8.8	21 29	9.1	04 06	6.8	16 16	7.0
5 Monday	00 07	6.8	12 41	7.2	05 46	13.0	18 18	13.2	09 49	9.4	22 17	9.5	04 57	7.2	17 02	7.5
6 Tuesday	00 59	7.2	13 30	7.4	06 38	13.6	19 06	13.8	10 37	9.8	23 02	9.8	05 40	7.6	17 47	7.9
7 Wednesday	01 45	7.4	14 13	7.5	07 23	14.0	19 48	14.1	11 22	10.1	23 46	10.0	06 21	7.8	18 31	8.1
8 Thursday	02 27	7.5	14 56	7.5	08 05	14.1	20 27	14.1	— —	—	12 07	10.1	07 00	7.9	19 16	8.2
9 Friday	03 11	7.6	15 38	7.4	08 46	13.9	21 08	13.7	00 28	9.9	12 49	9.8	07 42	7.8	20 01	7.9
10 Saturday	03 55	7.5	16 19	7.3	09 28	13.3	21 48	13.0	01 09	9.6	13 33	9.4	08 25	7.6	20 49	7.5
11 Sunday	04 40	7.3	17 01	6.9	10 09	12.4	22 28	12.1	01 51	9.2	14 16	8.8	09 08	7.2	21 38	6.9
12 Monday	05 25	7.0	17 42	6.6	10 49	11.4	23 09	11.1	02 34	8.7	15 04	8.2	09 53	6.8	22 31	6.3
13 Tuesday	06 12	6.6	18 27	6.2	11 33	10.4	23 58	10.2	03 25	8.1	16 02	7.5	10 42	6.4	23 33	5.8
14 Wednesday	07 06	6.2	19 20	5.9	— —	—	12 29	9.6	04 27	7.6	17 16	7.1	11 40	6.0	— —	—
15 Thursday	08 11	5.9	20 26	5.7	01 09	9.6	13 47	9.4	05 46	7.3	18 43	7.1	00 49	5.5	12 50	5.8
16 Friday	09 28	5.8	21 50	5.7	02 32	9.8	15 10	9.8	07 06	7.4	19 55	7.4	02 22	5.4	14 15	5.8
17 Saturday	10 52	6.1	23 13	6.1	03 48	10.5	16 19	10.7	08 11	7.8	20 47	7.8	03 31	5.7	15 28	6.1
18 Sunday	11 50	6.5	— —	—	04 45	11.3	17 12	11.4	09 00	8.2	21 29	8.2	04 19	6.1	16 17	6.5
19 Monday	00 07	6.4	12 35	6.8	05 34	11.8	17 56	11.9	09 41	8.5	22 04	8.5	04 57	6.4	16 57	6.8
20 Tuesday	00 48	6.7	13 12	6.9	06 15	12.2	18 34	12.2	10 17	8.8	22 37	8.8	05 29	6.7	17 32	7.1
21 Wednesday	01 23	6.7	13 44	6.9	06 50	12.4	19 04	12.5	10 51	9.0	23 08	8.9	05 57	7.0	18 05	7.2
22 Thursday	01 54	6.8	14 13	6.9	07 21	12.6	19 34	12.7	11 23	9.1	23 37	9.0	06 27	7.1	18 38	7.3
23 Friday	02 23	6.9	14 43	7.0	07 52	12.7	20 05	12.8	11 56	9.1	— —	—	06 56	7.2	19 13	7.2
24 Saturday	02 56	6.9	15 15	7.0	08 25	12.6	20 37	12.7	00 10	9.1	12 28	9.0	07 28	7.1	19 48	7.1
25 Sunday	03 31	7.0	15 49	7.0	09 00	12.4	21 12	12.4	00 42	9.0	13 03	8.9	08 01	7.0	20 23	6.9
26 Monday	04 07	7.0	16 26	6.9	09 35	12.1	21 48	12.0	01 17	8.9	13 41	8.7	08 34	6.8	21 03	6.7
27 Tuesday	04 48	6.9	17 04	6.7	10 13	11.6	22 28	11.6	01 57	8.6	14 25	8.4	09 12	6.6	21 48	6.5
28 Wednesday	05 32	6.7	17 47	6.4	10 58	11.0	23 18	11.0	02 43	8.3	15 18	8.0	09 56	6.4	22 40	6.3
29 Thursday	06 24	6.4	18 41	6.1	11 56	10.5	— —	—	03 41	8.0	16 26	7.7	10 52	6.2	23 47	6.1
30 Friday	07 28	6.2	19 49	6.0	00 24	10.6	13 12	10.4	04 54	7.8	17 44	7.7	— —	—	12 05	6.0

MARCH 1993 *continued*

	Greenock				Leith				Dun Laoghaire			
	*Datum of predictions 1.62m below				*Datum of predictions 2.90m below				†Datum of predictions 0.20m above			
	a.m. h m	ht. m	p.m. h m	ht. m	a.m. h m	ht. m	p.m. h m	ht. m	a.m. h m	ht. m	p.m. h m	ht. m
1 Monday	04 48	3.0	16 58	2.8	07 24	4.3	19 49	4.4	04 14	3.3	16 52	3.4
2 Tuesday	05 37	2.9	17 57	2.6	08 25	4.2	20 58	4.3	05 23	3.2	18 06	3.3
3 Wednesday	06 42	2.8	19 39	2.6	09 32	4.2	22 12	4.3	06 44	3.3	19 22	3.4
4 Thursday	08 13	2.8	21 29	2.7	10 41	4.4	23 22	4.6	07 56	3.4	20 28	3.6
5 Friday	09 38	3.0	22 32	3.0	11 46	4.8	— —	—	08 54	3.7	21 22	3.8
6 Saturday	10 38	3.3	23 26	3.1	00 27	5.0	12 45	5.2	09 44	4.0	22 09	4.0
7 Sunday	11 30	3.5	— —	—	01 23	5.4	13 38	5.6	10 28	4.2	22 53	4.2
8 Monday	00 16	3.3	12 18	3.6	02 13	5.7	14 29	5.9	11 10	4.4	23 34	4.3
9 Tuesday	01 03	3.3	13 03	3.7	03 01	5.8	15 17	6.1	11 52	4.6	— —	—
10 Wednesday	01 47	3.4	13 46	3.8	03 48	5.9	16 04	6.1	00 15	4.3	12 36	4.6
11 Thursday	02 26	3.4	14 27	3.8	04 33	5.8	16 52	6.0	00 56	4.3	13 22	4.5
12 Friday	03 03	3.4	15 08	3.8	05 19	5.6	17 42	5.7	01 40	4.2	14 11	4.3
13 Saturday	03 40	3.4	15 49	3.6	06 04	5.3	18 31	5.4	02 27	4.0	15 06	4.1
14 Sunday	04 19	3.3	16 32	3.3	06 52	4.9	19 24	5.0	03 20	3.8	16 11	3.8
15 Monday	05 02	3.1	17 19	3.0	07 45	4.6	20 25	4.6	04 26	3.6	17 28	3.5
16 Tuesday	05 53	2.9	18 16	2.7	08 44	4.4	21 34	4.4	05 46	3.5	18 48	3.4
17 Wednesday	07 06	2.8	19 59	2.5	09 55	4.3	22 55	4.3	07 05	3.5	20 03	3.5
18 Thursday	09 04	2.8	21 55	2.6	11 12	4.4	— —	—	08 18	3.6	21 08	3.5
19 Friday	10 15	2.9	22 48	2.7	00 08	4.5	12 19	4.6	09 18	3.8	21 56	3.6
20 Saturday	11 03	3.1	23 27	2.9	01 00	4.8	13 07	4.9	10 03	3.9	22 33	3.7
21 Sunday	11 42	3.2	— —	—	01 38	5.0	13 42	5.1	10 39	3.9	23 02	3.7
22 Monday	00 02	3.0	12 19	3.2	02 12	5.1	14 13	5.2	11 09	4.0	23 27	3.8
23 Tuesday	00 34	3.0	12 52	3.3	02 42	5.2	14 43	5.3	11 38	3.9	23 52	3.8
24 Wednesday	01 05	3.1	13 24	3.2	03 12	5.2	15 12	5.3	— —	—	12 06	3.9
25 Thursday	01 35	3.1	13 53	3.2	03 42	5.2	15 45	5.3	00 18	3.8	12 35	3.9
26 Friday	02 04	3.2	14 20	3.1	04 14	5.1	16 19	5.2	00 47	3.8	13 07	3.8
27 Saturday	02 34	3.2	14 48	3.0	04 47	5.0	16 57	5.0	01 22	3.8	13 47	3.8
28 Sunday	03 06	3.2	15 19	3.0	05 22	4.8	17 39	4.8	02 01	3.7	14 32	3.7
29 Monday	03 41	3.2	15 56	2.9	06 01	4.6	18 29	4.6	02 50	3.5	15 25	3.5
30 Tuesday	04 22	3.1	16 41	2.8	06 50	4.5	19 28	4.4	03 46	3.4	16 29	3.4
31 Wednesday	05 10	3.0	17 45	2.6	07 52	4.3	20 36	4.3	04 55	3.3	17 43	3.4

Notes:

*Difference of height in metres from Ordnance datum (Newlyn)

†Difference of height in metres from Ordnance datum (Dublin)

APRIL 1993 *continued*

	Greenock				Leith				Dun Laoghaire			
1 Thursday	06 14	2.9	19 20	2.6	09 01	4.4	21 48	4.4	06 14	3.3	18 59	3.4
2 Friday	07 37	2.9	20 59	2.8	10 12	4.5	22 58	4.6	07 29	3.5	20 06	3.6
3 Saturday	09 02	3.0	22 05	3.0	11 19	4.9	— —	—	08 30	3.7	21 02	3.8
4 Sunday	10 07	3.2	23 00	3.1	00 03	5.0	12 19	5.2	09 22	4.0	21 51	4.0
5 Monday	11 02	3.4	23 50	3.2	00 59	5.3	13 14	5.6	10 08	4.2	22 33	4.1
6 Tuesday	11 52	3.5	— —	—	01 49	5.6	14 06	5.8	10 53	4.4	23 14	4.2
7 Wednesday	00 37	3.3	12 39	3.6	02 37	5.8	14 56	6.0	11 36	4.5	23 54	4.3
8 Thursday	01 20	3.3	13 23	3.6	03 24	5.8	15 45	6.0	— —	—	12 19	4.5
9 Friday	01 50	3.4	14 05	3.6	04 09	5.7	16 33	5.8	00 33	4.3	13 04	4.4
10 Saturday	02 36	3.4	14 46	3.5	04 54	5.5	17 22	5.6	01 15	4.2	13 53	4.2
11 Sunday	03 13	3.4	15 28	3.3	05 39	5.2	18 11	5.2	02 01	4.0	14 49	3.9
12 Monday	03 53	3.3	16 12	3.1	06 25	4.9	19 02	4.8	02 53	3.9	15 52	3.7
13 Tuesday	04 36	3.2	16 59	2.9	07 14	4.6	19 58	4.5	03 56	3.7	17 03	3.5
14 Wednesday	05 25	3.0	17 56	2.6	08 11	4.4	21 01	4.3	05 11	3.5	18 18	3.4
15 Thursday	06 29	2.8	19 22	2.5	09 14	4.2	22 12	4.3	06 30	3.5	19 32	3.4
16 Friday	08 09	2.7	21 08	2.6	10 24	4.3	23 22	4.4	07 41	3.5	20 34	3.4
17 Saturday	09 32	2.8	22 05	2.7	11 30	4.5	— —	—	08 44	3.6	21 22	3.5
18 Sunday	10 25	3.0	22 48	2.8	00 17	4.6	12 21	4.7	09 30	3.7	22 00	3.6
19 Monday	11 09	3.1	23 25	2.9	00 59	4.9	13 03	4.9	10 08	3.7	22 30	3.7
20 Tuesday	11 48	3.1	— —	—	01 34	5.0	13 38	5.0	10 40	3.8	22 58	3.7
21 Wednesday	00 01	3.0	12 24	3.1	02 08	5.1	14 12	5.1	11 10	3.8	23 24	3.8
22 Thursday	00 34	3.1	12 58	3.0	02 40	5.2	14 47	5.2	11 40	3.8	23 52	3.8
23 Friday	01 06	3.1	13 28	3.0	03 14	5.2	15 24	5.2	— —	—	12 12	3.8
24 Saturday	01 36	3.2	13 58	3.0	03 46	5.1	16 02	5.1	00 23	3.8	12 47	3.8
25 Sunday	02 09	3.2	14 30	2.9	04 21	5.0	16 44	5.0	01 00	3.8	13 29	3.8
26 Monday	02 43	3.3	15 06	2.9	04 58	4.9	17 29	4.9	01 43	3.8	14 15	3.7
27 Tuesday	03 21	3.3	15 48	2.9	05 40	4.8	18 19	4.7	02 32	3.7	15 10	3.6
28 Wednesday	04 04	3.2	16 39	2.8	06 32	4.7	19 17	4.6	03 28	3.6	16 11	3.5
29 Thursday	04 54	3.2	17 45	2.8	07 33	4.6	20 20	4.5	04 33	3.5	17 21	3.4
30 Friday	05 55	3.1	19 05	2.8	08 40	4.6	21 27	4.6	05 46	3.5	18 34	3.5

MAY 1993 *High water* GMT

	London Bridge				Avonmouth				Liverpool				Hull (*Albert Dock*)			
	*Datum of predictions 3.20m below				*Datum of predictions 6.50m below				*Datum of predictions 4.93m below				*Datum of predictions 3.90m below			
	a.m.	ht.	p.m.	ht.	a.m.	ht.	p.m.	ht.	a.m.	ht.	p.m.	ht.	a.m.	ht.	p.m.	ht.
	h m	m	h m	m	h m	m	h m	m	h m	m	h m	m	h m	m	h m	m
1 Saturday	08 47	6.2	21 12	6.1	01 45	10.7	14 34	10.7	06 14	7.9	19 00	8.0	01 16	6.1	13 30	6.2
2 Sunday	10 07	6.5	22 33	6.4	03 07	11.3	15 50	11.5	07 26	8.3	20 06	8.5	02 33	6.4	14 44	6.5
3 Monday	11 18	6.8	23 39	6.7	04 17	12.0	16 55	12.2	08 29	8.8	21 03	8.9	03 36	6.8	15 45	7.0
4 Tuesday	— —	—	12 17	7.1	05 19	12.6	17 51	12.8	09 24	9.2	21 53	9.3	04 30	7.1	16 38	7.4
5 Wednesday	00 35	7.0	13 07	7.2	06 14	13.0	18 41	13.2	10 14	9.5	22 40	9.6	05 16	7.4	17 27	7.6
6 Thursday	01 24	7.1	13 52	7.2	07 02	13.4	19 26	13.5	11 02	9.7	23 25	9.7	06 00	7.5	18 15	7.7
7 Friday	02 09	7.2	14 36	7.2	07 45	13.5	20 08	13.6	11 47	9.6	— —	—	06 41	7.6	19 03	7.7
8 Saturday	02 54	7.3	15 17	7.2	08 27	13.3	20 49	13.3	00 07	9.6	12 32	9.4	07 24	7.5	19 51	7.5
9 Sunday	03 38	7.4	15 59	7.1	09 10	12.9	21 31	12.8	00 50	9.5	13 16	9.1	08 06	7.4	20 37	7.1
10 Monday	04 23	7.3	16 40	6.9	09 52	12.2	22 12	12.0	01 33	9.1	13 59	8.6	08 49	7.1	21 25	6.7
11 Tuesday	05 08	7.0	17 19	6.6	10 33	11.4	22 52	11.2	02 15	8.7	14 44	8.2	09 31	6.9	22 13	6.3
12 Wednesday	05 53	6.7	18 00	6.3	11 13	10.6	23 36	10.5	03 03	8.3	15 34	7.7	10 16	6.6	23 04	5.9
13 Thursday	06 41	6.3	18 48	6.0	— —	—	12 00	10.0	03 55	7.9	16 34	7.3	11 05	6.2	— —	—
14 Friday	07 35	6.0	19 47	5.8	00 31	10.0	13 00	9.7	04 57	7.6	17 43	7.1	00 00	5.6	12 03	6.0
15 Saturday	08 39	5.9	20 56	5.7	01 38	9.9	14 09	9.8	06 07	7.4	18 56	7.2	01 10	5.5	13 12	5.9
16 Sunday	09 50	5.9	22 10	5.8	02 49	10.2	15 18	10.2	07 14	7.6	19 57	7.5	02 30	5.6	14 26	6.0
17 Monday	10 59	6.2	23 16	6.1	03 50	10.7	16 17	10.8	08 11	7.8	20 44	7.9	03 31	5.9	15 29	6.2
18 Tuesday	11 50	6.4	— —	—	04 45	11.2	17 08	11.3	08 58	8.2	21 25	8.3	04 14	6.2	16 17	6.5
19 Wednesday	00 04	6.3	12 31	6.6	05 32	11.6	17 51	11.8	09 41	8.5	22 02	8.6	04 51	6.5	16 59	6.8
20 Thursday	00 43	6.5	13 07	6.7	06 12	12.0	18 31	12.2	10 19	8.7	22 37	8.8	05 25	6.8	17 37	6.9
21 Friday	01 20	6.6	13 42	6.8	06 52	12.2	19 07	12.5	10 55	8.9	23 12	9.0	05 58	6.9	18 15	7.0
22 Saturday	01 57	6.7	14 19	6.9	07 28	12.4	19 44	12.7	11 32	9.0	23 49	9.1	06 32	7.0	18 53	7.0
23 Sunday	02 36	6.9	14 57	7.0	08 08	12.5	20 22	12.7	— —	—	12 10	9.0	07 09	7.0	19 33	7.0
24 Monday	03 15	7.0	15 35	7.0	08 47	12.5	21 03	12.6	00 27	9.1	12 50	9.0	07 45	7.0	20 13	7.0
25 Tuesday	03 56	7.1	16 13	7.0	09 29	12.3	21 43	12.4	01 06	9.1	13 33	8.8	08 23	6.9	20 56	6.9
26 Wednesday	04 40	7.1	16 54	6.8	10 13	12.0	22 28	12.1	01 49	8.9	14 19	8.6	09 04	6.8	21 41	6.7
27 Thursday	05 26	6.9	17 39	6.6	10 59	11.6	23 19	11.7	02 37	8.7	15 11	8.4	09 49	6.7	22 31	6.6
28 Friday	06 17	6.6	18 29	6.4	11 53	11.2	— —	—	03 32	8.5	16 12	8.1	10 41	6.5	23 32	6.4
29 Saturday	07 16	6.5	19 31	6.3	00 17	11.3	12 55	10.9	04 35	8.3	17 19	8.0	11 43	6.4	— —	—
30 Sunday	08 25	6.4	20 46	6.3	01 24	11.2	14 06	10.9	05 44	8.2	18 29	8.1	00 45	6.3	12 57	6.5
31 Monday	09 39	6.6	22 02	6.4	02 37	11.3	15 18	11.3	06 55	8.4	19 37	8.3	02 01	6.5	14 12	6.6

JUNE 1993 *High water* GMT

	London Bridge				Avonmouth				Liverpool				Hull (*Albert Dock*)			
1 Tuesday	10 49	6.7	23 12	6.6	03 48	11.6	16 26	11.7	08 02	8.6	20 37	8.7	03 05	6.7	15 18	6.9
2 Wednesday	11 53	6.8	— —	—	04 52	12.0	17 26	12.2	09 01	8.8	21 31	9.0	04 04	6.9	16 20	7.1
3 Thursday	00 14	6.7	12 48	6.8	05 51	12.3	18 19	12.6	09 56	9.1	22 21	9.2	04 57	7.1	17 16	7.2
4 Friday	01 07	6.8	13 35	6.8	06 43	12.6	19 07	12.9	10 47	9.2	23 08	9.4	05 43	7.2	18 07	7.3
5 Saturday	01 57	6.8	14 19	6.9	07 30	12.8	19 51	13.0	11 33	9.2	23 53	9.4	06 27	7.3	18 56	7.2
6 Sunday	02 42	7.0	15 01	6.9	08 13	12.8	20 34	13.0	— —	—	12 18	9.1	07 09	7.3	19 42	7.1
7 Monday	03 25	7.1	15 41	7.0	08 56	12.6	21 15	12.7	00 35	9.3	13 00	8.9	07 49	7.2	20 26	6.9
8 Tuesday	04 07	7.2	16 20	6.9	09 36	12.2	21 55	12.2	01 16	9.1	13 41	8.6	08 29	7.2	21 07	6.6
9 Wednesday	04 49	7.0	16 58	6.7	10 14	11.7	22 31	11.6	01 55	8.9	14 20	8.3	09 08	7.0	21 48	6.4
10 Thursday	05 29	6.8	17 34	6.5	10 49	11.1	23 09	11.1	02 36	8.6	15 03	8.0	09 48	6.8	22 27	6.2
11 Friday	06 11	6.5	18 15	6.2	11 27	10.7	23 50	10.6	03 21	8.2	15 49	7.7	10 30	6.6	23 11	5.9
12 Saturday	06 57	6.2	19 04	6.0	— —	—	12 10	10.2	04 10	7.9	16 42	7.4	11 18	6.3	— —	—
13 Sunday	07 51	6.0	20 04	5.8	00 41	10.2	13 04	9.9	05 06	7.6	17 44	7.2	00 04	5.7	12 17	6.0
14 Monday	08 51	5.9	21 08	5.7	01 42	10.0	14 09	9.9	06 10	7.5	18 50	7.3	01 07	5.6	13 26	5.9
15 Tuesday	09 52	5.9	22 10	5.8	02 49	10.1	15 15	10.2	07 14	7.5	19 52	7.6	02 16	5.7	14 33	6.0
16 Wednesday	10 49	6.0	23 08	5.9	03 50	10.5	16 16	10.7	08 12	7.8	20 43	7.9	03 17	6.0	15 34	6.2
17 Thursday	11 42	6.2	— —	—	04 47	11.1	17 09	11.3	09 04	8.1	21 29	8.3	04 09	6.3	16 26	6.4
18 Friday	00 00	6.1	12 31	6.4	05 37	11.6	17 58	11.9	09 49	8.4	22 10	8.7	04 52	6.6	17 12	6.6
19 Saturday	00 49	6.4	13 16	6.7	06 25	12.0	18 43	12.3	10 31	8.7	22 51	9.0	05 33	6.8	17 56	6.8
20 Sunday	01 35	6.7	13 59	6.8	07 10	12.4	19 28	12.7	11 13	9.0	23 32	9.2	06 14	6.9	18 39	7.0
21 Monday	02 20	6.9	14 43	7.0	07 55	12.6	20 12	12.9	11 56	9.1	— —	—	06 53	7.1	19 21	7.1
22 Tuesday	03 04	7.2	15 24	7.1	08 39	12.8	20 54	13.1	00 14	9.3	12 39	9.2	07 33	7.2	20 04	7.2
23 Wednesday	03 48	7.3	16 04	7.1	09 22	12.8	21 38	13.0	00 57	9.4	13 24	9.2	08 12	7.3	20 46	7.2
24 Thursday	04 31	7.3	16 45	7.0	10 06	12.7	22 23	12.8	01 41	9.3	14 09	9.0	08 53	7.3	21 29	7.1
25 Friday	05 16	7.1	17 29	6.8	10 51	12.3	23 09	12.4	02 27	9.2	14 58	8.8	09 36	7.2	22 17	6.9
26 Saturday	06 04	6.8	18 15	6.6	11 39	11.8	— —	—	03 18	8.9	15 50	8.5	10 24	7.0	23 09	6.7
27 Sunday	06 57	6.6	19 10	6.5	00 00	11.9	12 31	11.3	04 13	8.7	16 51	8.2	11 20	6.8	— —	—
28 Monday	07 59	6.5	20 18	6.4	00 56	11.4	13 34	11.0	05 15	8.4	17 58	8.1	00 14	6.5	12 28	6.6
29 Tuesday	09 08	6.5	21 32	6.4	02 05	11.1	14 46	10.9	06 27	8.2	19 09	8.1	01 27	6.4	13 44	6.6
30 Wednesday	10 20	6.5	22 48	6.4	03 18	11.1	15 57	11.1	07 40	8.2	20 16	8.3	02 37	6.5	15 00	6.6

MAY 1993 *continued*

NOTES:

*Difference of height in metres from Ordnance datum (Newlyn)

†Difference of height in metres from Ordnance datum (Dublin)

	Greenock				Leith				Dun Laoghaire			
	*Datum of predictions 1.62m below				*Datum of predictions 2.90m below				†Datum of predictions 0.20m above			
	a.m.	ht.	p.m.	ht.	a.m.	ht.	p.m.	ht.	a.m.	ht.	p.m.	ht.
	h m	m	h m	m	h m	m	h m	m	h m	m	h m	m
1 Saturday	07 08	3.1	20 27	2.9	09 46	4.7	22 33	4.7	06 59	3.6	19 40	3.6
2 Sunday	08 26	3.1	21 35	3.0	10 52	4.9	23 34	5.0	08 02	3.8	20 38	3.8
3 Monday	09 35	3.2	22 32	3.1	11 54	5.2	— —	—	08 58	4.0	21 28	3.9
4 Tuesday	10 33	3.3	23 23	3.2	00 32	5.3	12 52	5.5	09 49	4.2	22 14	4.1
5 Wednesday	11 26	3.4	— —	—	01 24	5.5	13 47	5.7	10 36	4.3	22 56	4.2
6 Thursday	00 10	3.3	12 16	3.4	02 13	5.6	14 39	5.8	11 21	4.3	23 37	4.2
7 Friday	00 54	3.3	13 02	3.4	03 01	5.6	15 28	5.7	— —	—	12 06	4.3
8 Saturday	01 34	3.4	13 46	3.4	03 46	5.5	16 17	5.6	00 16	4.2	12 51	4.2
9 Sunday	02 12	3.4	14 29	3.3	04 31	5.4	17 05	5.4	00 58	4.2	13 40	4.0
10 Monday	02 51	3.4	15 12	3.2	05 13	5.2	17 51	5.1	01 43	4.1	14 32	3.8
11 Tuesday	03 32	3.4	15 56	3.0	05 57	4.9	18 38	4.8	02 33	3.9	15 28	3.6
12 Wednesday	04 15	3.3	16 43	2.9	06 42	4.7	19 28	4.6	03 31	3.8	16 31	3.4
13 Thursday	05 02	3.1	17 34	2.7	07 33	4.5	20 22	4.4	04 35	3.6	17 36	3.3
14 Friday	05 56	2.9	18 37	2.6	08 29	4.3	21 19	4.3	05 46	3.5	18 42	3.3
15 Saturday	07 06	2.8	19 59	2.6	09 29	4.3	22 21	4.4	06 54	3.4	19 44	3.3
16 Sunday	08 34	2.8	21 11	2.7	10 31	4.4	23 19	4.5	07 56	3.5	20 35	3.4
17 Monday	09 41	2.8	22 04	2.8	11 27	4.5	— —	—	08 48	3.5	21 19	3.5
18 Tuesday	10 32	2.9	22 48	2.9	00 10	4.7	12 17	4.7	09 31	3.5	21 56	3.6
19 Wednesday	11 16	2.9	23 28	3.0	00 53	4.9	13 02	4.9	10 08	3.6	22 28	3.7
20 Thursday	11 56	2.9	— —	—	01 33	5.0	13 44	5.0	10 43	3.6	22 58	3.8
21 Friday	00 04	3.1	12 33	2.9	02 09	5.1	14 25	5.1	11 16	3.7	23 30	3.8
22 Saturday	00 39	3.2	13 09	2.9	02 46	5.1	15 05	5.1	11 52	3.8	— —	—
23 Sunday	01 14	3.3	13 45	2.9	03 22	5.1	15 49	5.1	00 05	3.9	12 32	3.8
24 Monday	01 50	3.3	14 23	3.0	04 00	5.1	16 34	5.1	00 44	3.9	13 14	3.8
25 Tuesday	02 28	3.4	15 04	3.0	04 42	5.1	17 20	5.0	01 29	3.9	14 03	3.8
26 Wednesday	03 08	3.4	15 50	3.0	05 29	5.0	18 11	4.9	02 17	3.9	14 56	3.7
27 Thursday	03 52	3.4	16 42	3.0	06 21	4.9	19 06	4.8	03 10	3.8	15 53	3.6
28 Friday	04 42	3.4	17 40	3.0	07 20	4.9	20 04	4.8	04 10	3.8	16 57	3.5
29 Saturday	05 39	3.3	18 44	3.0	08 20	4.8	21 04	4.7	05 17	3.7	18 06	3.5
30 Sunday	06 43	3.2	19 53	3.0	09 24	4.8	22 06	4.8	06 27	3.7	19 11	3.6
31 Monday	07 53	3.2	21 02	3.0	10 28	4.9	23 08	4.9	07 34	3.8	20 11	3.7

JUNE 1993 *continued*

	Greenock				Leith				Dun Laoghaire			
1 Tuesday	09 03	3.2	22 04	3.1	11 32	5.1	— —	—	08 35	3.9	21 07	3.8
2 Wednesday	10 07	3.2	22 59	3.2	00 07	5.1	12 34	5.3	09 31	4.0	21 56	4.0
3 Thursday	11 04	3.2	23 49	3.2	01 03	5.3	13 33	5.4	10 22	4.1	22 42	4.1
4 Friday	11 58	3.2	— —	—	01 55	5.4	14 26	5.5	11 10	4.1	23 24	4.2
5 Saturday	00 33	3.3	12 48	3.2	02 43	5.4	15 15	5.5	11 57	4.1	— —	—
6 Sunday	01 15	3.4	13 34	3.2	03 28	5.4	16 03	5.4	00 05	4.2	12 42	4.0
7 Monday	01 55	3.4	14 17	3.1	04 12	5.3	16 47	5.3	00 46	4.2	13 25	3.9
8 Tuesday	02 34	3.5	15 00	3.1	04 51	5.2	17 29	5.1	01 28	4.1	14 10	3.8
9 Wednesday	03 14	3.4	15 41	3.0	05 29	5.0	18 10	4.9	02 11	4.0	14 57	3.6
10 Thursday	03 55	3.4	16 23	3.0	06 08	4.8	18 52	4.7	03 00	3.9	15 49	3.5
11 Friday	04 37	3.2	17 05	2.9	06 52	4.7	19 38	4.5	03 53	3.7	16 45	3.4
12 Saturday	05 21	3.1	17 50	2.8	07 41	4.5	20 29	4.4	04 52	3.5	17 43	3.3
13 Sunday	06 10	2.9	18 42	2.7	08 37	4.4	21 25	4.4	05 56	3.4	18 44	3.3
14 Monday	07 12	2.7	19 50	2.7	09 36	4.4	22 23	4.4	06 59	3.3	19 41	3.3
15 Tuesday	08 40	2.7	21 11	2.7	10 37	4.4	23 19	4.5	08 00	3.3	20 34	3.4
16 Wednesday	09 51	2.7	22 09	2.8	11 33	4.5	— —	—	08 51	3.4	21 19	3.5
17 Thursday	10 43	2.8	22 56	3.0	00 10	4.7	12 28	4.7	09 35	3.4	21 58	3.6
18 Friday	11 29	2.8	23 37	3.1	00 56	4.8	13 17	4.8	10 16	3.5	22 33	3.7
19 Saturday	12 11	2.9	— —	—	01 38	5.0	14 04	5.0	10 55	3.7	23 09	3.9
20 Sunday	00 17	3.2	12 54	3.0	02 19	5.1	14 50	5.1	11 34	3.8	23 48	4.0
21 Monday	00 56	3.4	13 36	3.1	03 01	5.2	15 35	5.2	— —	—	12 16	3.8
22 Tuesday	01 36	3.5	14 20	3.1	03 45	5.3	16 21	5.3	00 29	4.1	13 00	3.9
23 Wednesday	02 17	3.6	15 04	3.2	04 30	5.4	17 09	5.3	01 13	4.1	13 46	3.9
24 Thursday	02 59	3.6	15 49	3.2	05 19	5.3	17 58	5.2	01 59	4.1	14 36	3.8
25 Friday	03 43	3.6	16 34	3.2	06 10	5.3	18 49	5.1	02 50	4.1	15 31	3.8
26 Saturday	04 30	3.6	17 23	3.2	07 04	5.2	19 42	5.0	03 45	4.0	16 29	3.7
27 Sunday	05 21	3.5	18 16	3.1	08 02	5.0	20 40	4.9	04 47	3.9	17 33	3.6
28 Monday	06 18	3.4	19 17	3.0	09 03	4.9	21 39	4.8	05 56	3.8	18 40	3.6
29 Tuesday	07 22	3.2	20 27	3.0	10 06	4.9	22 42	4.8	07 08	3.8	19 46	3.7
30 Wednesday	08 33	3.1	21 38	3.0	11 13	4.9	23 46	4.9	08 14	3.8	20 45	3.8

JULY 1993 *High water* GMT

	London Bridge				Avonmouth				Liverpool				Hull (*Albert Dock*)			
	*Datum of predictions 3.20m below				*Datum of predictions 6.50m below				*Datum of predictions 4.93m below				*Datum of predictions 3.90m below			
	a.m.	ht.	p.m.	ht.	a.m.	ht.	p.m.	ht.	a.m.	ht.	p.m.	ht.	a.m.	ht.	p.m.	ht.
	h m	m	h m	m	h m	m	h m	m	h m	m	h m	m	h m	m	h m	m
1 Thursday	11 29	6.6	23 58	6.5	04 28	11.3	17 04	11.6	08 47	8.4	21 17	8.6	03 43	6.7	16 12	6.7
2 Friday	— —	—	12 29	6.6	05 34	11.7	18 03	12.1	09 46	8.6	22 09	8.9	04 41	6.9	17 12	6.9
3 Saturday	00 56	6.6	13 21	6.6	06 29	12.1	18 53	12.5	10 37	8.8	22 57	9.2	05 32	7.0	18 04	6.9
4 Sunday	01 47	6.7	14 06	6.7	07 19	12.4	19 38	12.8	11 23	8.9	23 40	9.3	06 15	7.1	18 49	6.9
5 Monday	02 30	6.9	14 47	6.8	08 01	12.5	20 19	12.9	— —	—	12 04	8.9	06 55	7.2	19 30	6.9
6 Tuesday	03 11	7.0	15 24	6.9	08 40	12.6	20 57	12.8	00 19	9.3	12 42	8.9	07 33	7.3	20 08	6.9
7 Wednesday	03 50	7.1	16 00	6.9	09 17	12.4	21 32	12.5	00 56	9.2	13 19	8.7	08 08	7.3	20 43	6.8
8 Thursday	04 27	7.0	16 34	6.8	09 49	12.1	22 06	12.1	01 33	9.1	13 52	8.6	08 43	7.3	21 17	6.7
9 Friday	05 02	6.8	17 08	6.7	10 21	11.7	22 37	11.7	02 08	8.8	14 27	8.3	09 18	7.1	21 50	6.5
10 Saturday	05 39	6.6	17 43	6.5	10 51	11.3	23 11	11.2	02 44	8.5	15 05	8.0	09 55	6.9	22 27	6.3
11 Sunday	06 17	6.4	18 22	6.2	11 25	10.8	23 47	10.6	03 25	8.2	15 48	7.7	10 37	6.5	23 09	6.0
12 Monday	07 00	6.1	19 09	5.9	— —	—	12 03	10.2	04 10	7.8	16 38	7.4	11 26	6.2	— —	—
13 Tuesday	07 51	5.8	20 05	5.7	00 31	10.0	12 53	9.8	05 06	7.5	17 42	7.2	00 04	5.8	12 29	5.9
14 Wednesday	08 50	5.7	21 10	5.6	01 35	9.7	14 08	9.7	06 14	7.3	18 55	7.3	01 13	5.7	13 45	5.8
15 Thursday	09 52	5.7	22 16	5.7	02 56	9.9	15 27	10.2	07 26	7.4	20 02	7.6	02 25	5.8	14 54	5.9
16 Friday	10 54	5.9	23 20	5.9	04 04	10.5	16 31	11.0	08 30	7.8	20 58	8.1	03 29	6.1	15 57	6.2
17 Saturday	11 57	6.2	— —	—	05 06	11.3	17 30	11.8	09 24	8.2	21 48	8.6	04 24	6.4	16 52	6.5
18 Sunday	00 24	6.3	12 53	6.6	06 03	11.9	18 24	12.4	10 12	8.7	22 33	9.0	05 12	6.7	17 40	6.8
19 Monday	01 17	6.7	13 42	6.9	06 55	12.5	19 13	13.0	10 57	9.1	23 16	9.4	05 54	7.0	18 24	7.1
20 Tuesday	02 05	7.1	14 27	7.2	07 42	13.0	19 59	13.4	11 42	9.4	— —	—	06 35	7.3	19 06	7.4
21 Wednesday	02 50	7.4	15 10	7.3	08 26	13.3	20 42	13.6	00 00	9.7	12 25	9.5	07 14	7.6	19 47	7.6
22 Thursday	03 34	7.5	15 50	7.4	09 08	13.4	21 25	13.7	00 43	9.8	13 09	9.5	07 55	7.7	20 29	7.6
23 Friday	04 17	7.5	16 31	7.3	09 52	13.3	22 09	13.4	01 27	9.8	13 52	9.4	08 36	7.8	21 11	7.5
24 Saturday	05 01	7.2	17 12	7.1	10 34	12.9	22 52	12.9	02 11	9.6	14 37	9.1	09 18	7.6	21 55	7.2
25 Sunday	05 46	6.9	17 57	6.9	11 18	12.2	23 37	12.2	02 57	9.3	15 27	8.8	10 04	7.4	22 44	6.9
26 Monday	06 34	6.6	18 48	6.6	— —	—	12 04	11.5	03 48	8.8	16 21	8.3	10 58	7.0	23 43	6.5
27 Tuesday	07 30	6.4	19 51	6.4	00 28	11.4	13 00	10.8	04 48	8.3	17 27	8.0	— —	—	12 04	6.6
28 Wednesday	08 36	6.3	21 04	6.3	01 31	10.7	14 13	10.4	06 03	7.9	18 45	7.8	00 55	6.3	13 26	6.3
29 Thursday	09 49	6.2	22 27	6.2	02 50	10.4	15 34	10.6	07 24	7.8	20 02	8.0	02 13	6.3	14 54	6.3
30 Friday	11 06	6.3	23 43	6.4	04 12	10.8	16 48	11.3	08 39	8.0	21 07	8.4	03 28	6.4	16 10	6.4
31 Saturday	— —	—	12 12	6.5	05 22	11.4	17 50	12.0	09 39	8.3	22 00	8.8	04 30	6.7	17 09	6.6

AUGUST 1993 *High water* GMT

	London Bridge				Avonmouth				Liverpool				Hull (*Albert Dock*)			
1 Sunday	00 45	6.6	13 06	6.6	06 17	11.9	18 41	12.5	10 28	8.6	22 44	9.1	05 19	6.9	17 56	6.8
2 Monday	01 34	6.8	13 51	6.8	07 04	12.3	19 23	12.8	11 09	8.9	23 25	9.3	06 00	7.1	18 36	6.9
3 Tuesday	02 16	6.9	14 29	6.9	07 45	12.6	20 02	13.0	11 47	9.0	— —	—	06 36	7.3	19 12	6.9
4 Wednesday	02 54	7.0	15 04	7.0	08 20	12.7	20 36	13.0	00 00	9.4	12 21	9.0	07 12	7.4	19 44	7.0
5 Thursday	03 28	7.1	15 36	7.0	08 51	12.7	21 07	12.8	00 34	9.3	12 52	8.9	07 44	7.5	20 13	7.0
6 Friday	04 00	7.0	16 06	6.9	09 21	12.5	21 35	12.5	01 06	9.2	13 23	8.8	08 16	7.5	20 43	6.9
7 Saturday	04 31	6.9	16 37	6.8	09 49	12.2	22 04	12.1	01 37	9.0	13 52	8.6	08 49	7.3	21 14	6.8
8 Sunday	05 04	6.7	17 11	6.6	10 16	11.7	22 34	11.5	02 09	8.7	14 25	8.3	09 22	7.0	21 48	6.6
9 Monday	05 37	6.5	17 46	6.4	10 44	11.1	23 02	10.8	02 43	8.4	14 58	8.0	09 59	6.7	22 23	6.2
10 Tuesday	06 14	6.2	18 24	6.1	11 12	10.5	23 33	10.2	03 21	8.0	15 41	7.6	10 40	6.2	23 06	5.9
11 Wednesday	06 55	5.9	19 10	5.8	11 51	10.0	— —	—	04 09	7.5	16 40	7.3	11 32	5.9	— —	—
12 Thursday	07 45	5.7	20 12	5.5	00 24	9.6	12 56	9.6	05 18	7.2	18 00	7.1	00 07	5.7	12 52	5.6
13 Friday	08 54	5.5	21 29	5.5	01 54	9.5	14 36	9.8	06 42	7.2	19 24	7.4	01 38	5.6	14 20	5.7
14 Saturday	10 12	5.7	22 48	5.8	03 28	10.1	16 00	10.7	08 01	7.6	20 32	8.0	02 54	5.9	15 34	6.0
15 Sunday	11 29	6.0	— —	—	04 40	11.1	17 06	11.8	09 01	8.1	21 25	8.6	03 57	6.3	16 33	6.4
16 Monday	00 01	6.3	12 31	6.5	05 42	12.0	18 04	12.6	09 52	8.7	22 13	9.2	04 48	6.7	17 22	6.9
17 Tuesday	00 57	6.9	13 21	7.0	06 36	12.8	18 56	13.4	10 38	9.3	22 58	9.7	05 33	7.1	18 05	7.3
18 Wednesday	01 47	7.3	14 06	7.4	07 24	13.4	19 41	13.9	11 22	9.6	23 42	10.0	06 14	7.6	18 46	7.6
19 Thursday	02 32	7.6	14 49	7.6	08 08	13.8	20 25	14.2	— —	—	12 05	9.9	06 53	7.9	19 26	7.8
20 Friday	03 14	7.7	15 29	7.6	08 50	13.9	21 05	14.1	00 24	10.2	12 48	9.9	07 33	8.1	20 06	7.9
21 Saturday	03 56	7.6	16 10	7.5	09 31	13.7	21 48	13.7	01 07	10.1	13 31	9.7	08 15	8.1	20 47	7.7
22 Sunday	04 40	7.3	16 52	7.3	10 12	13.2	22 30	13.1	01 49	9.8	14 13	9.4	08 58	7.9	21 31	7.4
23 Monday	05 23	6.9	17 37	7.0	10 54	12.4	23 13	12.2	02 34	9.4	15 00	8.9	09 45	7.5	22 19	7.0
24 Tuesday	06 10	6.6	18 28	6.6	11 36	11.5	— —	—	03 24	8.8	15 53	8.3	10 40	6.9	23 13	6.5
25 Wednesday	07 00	6.3	19 28	6.3	00 00	11.1	12 29	10.6	04 23	8.1	17 01	7.8	11 46	6.3	— —	—
26 Thursday	08 02	6.1	20 40	6.1	01 03	10.2	13 44	10.0	05 43	7.5	18 25	7.6	00 25	6.2	13 16	6.0
27 Friday	09 15	6.0	22 04	6.1	02 26	9.9	15 14	10.3	07 14	7.5	19 48	7.8	01 49	6.1	14 51	6.0
28 Saturday	10 41	6.1	23 26	6.4	03 56	10.4	16 33	11.2	08 32	7.8	20 54	8.3	03 11	6.3	16 04	6.2
29 Sunday	11 53	6.4	— —	—	05 05	11.3	17 32	12.0	09 28	8.2	21 45	8.8	04 13	6.6	16 58	6.5
30 Monday	00 27	6.7	12 46	6.7	05 58	12.0	18 21	12.6	10 13	8.6	22 26	9.1	05 01	6.9	17 40	6.7
31 Tuesday	01 16	7.0	13 30	6.9	06 43	12.5	19 02	12.9	10 49	8.9	23 02	9.3	05 40	7.2	18 15	6.9

JULY 1993 *continued*

	Greenock				Leith				Dun Laoghaire			
	*Datum of predictions 1.62m below				*Datum of predictions 2.90m below				†Datum of predictions 0.20m above			
	a.m.	ht.	p.m.	ht.	a.m.	ht.	p.m.	ht.	a.m.	ht.	p.m.	ht.
	h m	m	h m	m	h m	m	h m	m	h m	m	h m	m
1 Thursday	09 46	3.1	22 41	3.1	— —	—	12 22	5.0	09 16	3.9	21 39	3.9
2 Friday	10 53	3.0	23 34	3.2	00 46	5.1	13 23	5.2	10 12	3.9	22 29	4.1
3 Saturday	11 53	3.0	— —	—	01 41	5.2	14 18	5.3	11 02	4.0	23 13	4.1
4 Sunday	00 21	3.3	12 44	3.1	02 29	5.3	15 04	5.4	11 48	3.9	23 54	4.2
5 Monday	01 03	3.4	13 28	3.1	03 12	5.4	15 48	5.3	— —	—	12 28	3.9
6 Tuesday	01 42	3.5	14 08	3.1	03 52	5.4	16 26	5.3	00 32	4.2	13 06	3.8
7 Wednesday	02 20	3.5	14 45	3.1	04 26	5.3	17 02	5.1	01 08	4.2	13 43	3.8
8 Thursday	02 57	3.5	15 21	3.1	04 59	5.2	17 37	5.0	01 47	4.1	14 21	3.7
9 Friday	03 33	3.4	15 55	3.1	05 32	5.0	18 14	4.8	02 27	3.9	15 04	3.6
10 Saturday	04 08	3.3	16 30	3.1	06 10	4.9	18 56	4.7	03 10	3.8	15 50	3.5
11 Sunday	04 44	3.2	17 06	3.0	06 56	4.7	19 42	4.5	03 57	3.6	16 40	3.4
12 Monday	05 22	3.0	17 48	2.9	07 49	4.5	20 36	4.4	04 50	3.4	17 38	3.3
13 Tuesday	06 07	2.8	18 38	2.8	08 49	4.4	21 34	4.3	05 53	3.3	18 41	3.3
14 Wednesday	07 06	2.6	19 46	2.7	09 50	4.3	22 33	4.4	07 03	3.2	19 44	3.3
15 Thursday	08 56	2.6	21 22	2.8	10 54	4.4	23 29	4.5	08 09	3.3	20 40	3.4
16 Friday	10 11	2.7	22 23	3.0	11 56	4.6	— —	—	09 04	3.4	21 27	3.5
17 Saturday	11 04	2.9	23 12	3.1	00 22	4.7	12 52	4.8	09 52	3.5	22 08	3.7
18 Sunday	11 51	3.0	23 56	3.3	01 10	5.0	13 42	5.0	10 35	3.7	22 49	3.9
19 Monday	12 37	3.1	— —	—	01 57	5.2	14 30	5.3	11 16	3.8	23 28	4.1
20 Tuesday	00 39	3.5	13 24	3.2	02 42	5.4	15 18	5.5	11 58	3.9	— —	—
21 Wednesday	01 23	3.6	14 10	3.3	03 28	5.6	16 04	5.6	00 09	4.3	12 40	4.0
22 Thursday	02 05	3.7	14 53	3.4	04 14	5.7	16 52	5.6	00 51	4.4	13 26	4.1
23 Friday	02 48	3.8	15 35	3.4	05 04	5.7	17 40	5.5	01 37	4.4	14 11	4.0
24 Saturday	03 30	3.8	16 15	3.4	05 54	5.6	18 29	5.3	02 25	4.3	15 01	3.9
25 Sunday	04 13	3.8	16 58	3.3	06 46	5.4	19 20	5.1	03 18	4.2	15 57	3.8
26 Monday	05 00	3.6	17 45	3.2	07 41	5.2	20 15	4.9	04 18	4.0	16 59	3.7
27 Tuesday	05 53	3.4	18 41	3.1	08 42	4.9	21 14	4.7	05 28	3.8	18 09	3.6
28 Wednesday	06 53	3.2	19 50	3.0	09 48	4.8	22 20	4.7	06 45	3.7	19 19	3.7
29 Thursday	08 07	3.0	21 15	3.0	10 59	4.7	23 29	4.8	08 00	3.7	20 27	3.8
30 Friday	09 38	2.9	22 29	3.1	— —	—	12 14	4.9	09 08	3.7	21 27	3.9
31 Saturday	10 56	2.9	23 25	3.3	00 34	5.0	13 16	5.1	10 07	3.8	22 19	4.0

NOTES:
*Difference of height in metres from Ordnance datum (Newlyn)
†Difference of height in metres from Ordnance datum (Dublin)

AUGUST 1993 *continued*

	Greenock				Leith				Dun Laoghaire			
1 Sunday	11 52	3.0	— —	—	01 30	5.2	14 06	5.2	10 56	3.8	23 02	4.1
2 Monday	00 10	3.4	12 38	3.1	02 15	5.3	14 49	5.3	11 37	3.8	23 38	4.2
3 Tuesday	00 51	3.5	13 16	3.1	02 54	5.4	15 27	5.3	— —	—	12 11	3.8
4 Wednesday	01 27	3.5	13 50	3.2	03 28	5.4	15 59	5.3	00 12	4.2	12 42	3.8
5 Thursday	02 02	3.5	14 22	3.2	03 57	5.4	16 31	5.2	00 46	4.2	13 13	3.8
6 Friday	02 35	3.5	14 53	3.2	04 24	5.3	17 02	5.1	01 18	4.1	13 44	3.8
7 Saturday	03 06	3.4	15 23	3.2	04 55	5.2	17 36	5.0	01 53	4.0	14 20	3.7
8 Sunday	03 37	3.3	15 54	3.2	05 30	5.0	18 14	4.8	02 29	3.8	15 01	3.6
9 Monday	04 07	3.2	16 28	3.1	06 14	4.8	18 59	4.6	03 13	3.7	15 47	3.5
10 Tuesday	04 41	3.0	17 06	3.0	07 06	4.6	19 51	4.4	04 01	3.5	16 40	3.4
11 Wednesday	05 20	2.8	17 52	2.9	08 05	4.4	20 49	4.3	04 59	3.3	17 43	3.3
12 Thursday	06 12	2.7	18 52	2.8	09 11	4.3	21 49	4.3	06 10	3.2	18 54	3.3
13 Friday	07 43	2.6	20 24	2.8	10 19	4.3	22 51	4.4	07 29	3.2	20 00	3.4
14 Saturday	09 40	2.7	21 50	3.0	11 25	4.5	23 50	4.7	08 35	3.4	20 57	3.5
15 Sunday	10 39	3.0	22 46	3.2	— —	—	12 27	4.8	09 28	3.5	21 44	3.8
16 Monday	11 29	3.1	23 34	3.4	00 43	5.1	13 20	5.1	10 15	3.7	22 25	4.0
17 Tuesday	12 18	3.3	— —	—	01 33	5.4	14 09	5.4	10 56	3.9	23 06	4.2
18 Wednesday	00 20	3.6	13 06	3.4	02 20	5.7	14 57	5.7	11 37	4.1	23 47	4.4
19 Thursday	01 05	3.7	13 51	3.5	03 07	5.9	15 43	5.8	— —	—	12 18	4.2
20 Friday	01 48	3.8	14 33	3.5	03 55	6.0	16 30	5.8	00 29	4.5	13 00	4.2
21 Saturday	02 30	3.9	15 12	3.5	04 44	6.0	17 16	5.7	01 14	4.5	13 46	4.2
22 Sunday	03 11	3.9	15 50	3.5	05 33	5.8	18 05	5.4	02 01	4.4	14 33	4.1
23 Monday	03 53	3.8	16 30	3.4	06 25	5.5	18 55	5.2	02 54	4.3	15 25	4.0
24 Tuesday	04 38	3.6	17 14	3.3	07 21	5.2	19 49	4.9	03 54	4.0	16 28	3.8
25 Wednesday	05 28	3.4	18 06	3.2	08 22	4.9	20 49	4.7	05 07	3.7	17 41	3.7
26 Thursday	06 26	3.1	19 13	3.0	09 29	4.6	21 56	4.6	06 30	3.6	18 55	3.7
27 Friday	07 46	2.9	20 54	3.0	10 47	4.6	23 11	4.7	07 50	3.5	20 07	3.7
28 Saturday	09 43	2.9	22 15	3.2	— —	—	12 04	4.8	09 04	3.6	21 14	3.9
29 Sunday	10 51	3.0	23 09	3.3	00 19	4.9	13 03	5.0	10 02	3.7	22 05	4.0
30 Monday	11 39	3.1	23 52	3.4	01 13	5.1	13 48	5.2	10 46	3.8	22 46	4.1
31 Tuesday	12 18	3.1	— —	—	01 55	5.3	14 26	5.3	11 21	3.8	23 19	4.1

SEPTEMBER 1993 *High water* GMT

	London Bridge				Avonmouth				Liverpool				Hull (*Albert Dock*)			
	*Datum of predictions 3.20m below				*Datum of predictions 6.50m below				*Datum of predictions 4.93m below				*Datum of predictions 3.90m below			
	a.m.	ht.	p.m.	ht.	a.m.	ht.	p.m.	ht.	a.m.	ht.	p.m.	ht.	a.m.	ht.	p.m.	ht.
	h m	m	h m	m	h m	m	h m	m	h m	m	h m	m	h m	m	h m	m
1 Wednesday	01 55	7.1	14 08	7.0	07 23	12.7	19 38	13.1	11 23	9.0	23 34	9.4	06 14	7.4	18 46	7.0
2 Thursday	02 30	7.1	14 40	7.0	07 55	12.9	20 09	13.1	11 54	9.1	— —	—	06 46	7.5	19 16	7.1
3 Friday	03 01	7.0	15 10	7.0	08 25	12.9	20 37	13.0	00 07	9.4	12 22	9.1	07 17	7.6	19 42	7.2
4 Saturday	03 31	7.0	15 36	7.0	08 50	12.7	21 04	12.7	00 36	9.3	12 52	9.0	07 48	7.5	20 11	7.1
5 Sunday	03 59	6.9	16 06	6.9	09 17	12.4	21 32	12.3	01 06	9.1	13 20	8.8	08 20	7.3	20 40	7.0
6 Monday	04 28	6.8	16 38	6.8	09 43	12.0	22 00	11.7	01 35	8.9	13 48	8.6	08 53	7.0	21 11	6.7
7 Tuesday	04 59	6.6	17 13	6.6	10 10	11.4	22 27	11.0	02 06	8.5	14 20	8.3	09 27	6.6	21 43	6.4
8 Wednesday	05 34	6.4	17 51	6.3	10 35	10.8	22 55	10.4	02 42	8.1	14 58	7.9	10 03	6.3	22 20	6.1
9 Thursday	06 12	6.1	18 35	6.0	11 11	10.2	23 42	9.8	03 28	7.7	15 52	7.5	10 51	5.9	23 12	5.8
10 Friday	07 00	5.8	19 33	5.7	— —	—	12 12	9.7	04 33	7.2	17 12	7.2	— —	—	12 00	5.6
11 Saturday	08 06	5.5	20 51	5.6	01 06	9.4	13 54	9.7	06 04	7.1	18 46	7.4	00 39	5.6	13 48	5.6
12 Sunday	09 34	5.6	22 21	5.9	02 54	9.9	15 31	10.6	07 30	7.5	20 01	8.0	02 19	5.8	15 07	6.0
13 Monday	10 59	6.0	23 37	6.4	04 14	11.1	16 41	11.8	08 36	8.2	21 00	8.7	03 27	6.2	16 09	6.5
14 Tuesday	— —	—	12 05	6.6	05 19	12.2	17 42	12.8	09 28	8.9	21 48	9.3	04 21	6.8	16 59	7.0
15 Wednesday	00 35	7.0	12 56	7.1	06 14	13.1	18 34	13.6	10 16	9.4	22 34	9.9	05 06	7.3	17 42	7.4
16 Thursday	01 24	7.4	13 42	7.5	07 03	13.7	19 20	14.2	10 59	9.8	23 18	10.2	05 49	7.7	18 22	7.8
17 Friday	02 09	7.6	14 25	7.7	07 47	14.1	20 02	14.4	11 42	10.1	— —	—	06 29	8.1	19 02	8.0
18 Saturday	02 51	7.7	15 07	7.8	08 27	14.2	20 44	14.3	00 01	10.3	12 25	10.1	07 10	8.3	19 41	8.0
19 Sunday	03 34	7.6	15 49	7.7	09 07	13.9	21 25	13.8	00 45	10.2	13 07	9.9	07 54	8.2	20 23	7.8
20 Monday	04 17	7.3	16 33	7.4	09 49	13.3	22 09	13.0	01 28	9.9	13 49	9.5	08 40	7.9	21 07	7.4
21 Tuesday	05 01	7.0	17 20	7.1	10 31	12.5	22 52	12.0	02 13	9.3	14 36	8.9	09 29	7.3	21 55	7.0
22 Wednesday	05 46	6.6	18 11	6.7	11 15	11.5	23 39	10.9	03 03	8.6	15 28	8.4	10 24	6.7	22 48	6.5
23 Thursday	06 35	6.2	19 07	6.3	— —	—	12 07	10.5	04 03	7.9	16 35	7.8	11 32	6.1	23 53	6.1
24 Friday	07 31	6.0	20 16	6.0	00 39	10.0	13 19	9.9	05 23	7.4	18 00	7.6	— —	—	13 03	5.7
25 Saturday	08 42	5.8	21 36	6.0	02 01	9.6	14 49	10.1	06 55	7.3	19 23	7.8	01 17	6.0	14 37	5.7
26 Sunday	10 09	5.9	23 01	6.3	03 32	10.2	16 09	11.0	08 11	7.7	20 29	8.2	02 44	6.1	15 46	6.0
27 Monday	11 26	6.3	— —	—	04 40	11.2	17 06	11.9	09 05	8.2	21 18	8.7	03 49	6.4	16 35	6.3
28 Tuesday	00 03	6.8	12 21	6.7	05 33	12.0	17 54	12.5	09 48	8.6	21 59	9.0	04 35	6.8	17 15	6.6
29 Wednesday	00 50	7.1	13 04	7.0	06 17	12.4	18 35	12.8	10 23	8.8	22 34	9.2	05 15	7.1	17 49	6.9
30 Thursday	01 30	7.1	13 41	7.1	06 55	12.7	19 12	12.9	10 55	9.0	23 06	9.3	05 49	7.3	18 18	7.1

OCTOBER 1993 *High water* GMT

	London Bridge				Avonmouth				Liverpool				Hull (*Albert Dock*)			
1 Friday	02 04	7.1	14 12	7.1	07 27	12.8	19 41	12.9	11 25	9.1	23 37	9.3	06 19	7.5	18 45	7.2
2 Saturday	02 33	7.0	14 40	7.0	07 54	12.8	20 08	12.9	11 53	9.1	— —	—	06 50	7.5	19 13	7.3
3 Sunday	02 58	7.0	15 08	7.0	08 19	12.8	20 34	12.7	00 07	9.3	12 21	9.1	07 23	7.4	19 41	7.2
4 Monday	03 27	6.9	15 38	7.0	08 46	12.6	21 04	12.3	00 38	9.1	12 50	9.0	07 54	7.2	20 09	7.0
5 Tuesday	03 56	6.9	16 12	6.9	09 15	12.2	21 34	11.8	01 07	8.9	13 20	8.8	08 26	7.0	20 40	6.8
6 Wednesday	04 30	6.8	16 48	6.7	09 45	11.7	22 04	11.2	01 40	8.6	13 52	8.5	09 01	6.6	21 11	6.5
7 Thursday	05 05	6.6	17 26	6.5	10 14	11.1	22 37	10.6	02 16	8.2	14 32	8.1	09 38	6.3	21 48	6.2
8 Friday	05 43	6.3	18 12	6.2	10 52	10.6	23 26	10.0	03 03	7.8	15 25	7.8	10 26	6.0	22 40	5.9
9 Saturday	06 31	6.0	19 09	5.9	11 54	10.0	— —	—	04 06	7.4	16 40	7.5	11 32	5.8	23 54	5.7
10 Sunday	07 34	5.7	20 26	5.8	00 45	9.6	13 26	9.9	05 32	7.3	18 10	7.6	— —	—	13 10	5.8
11 Monday	09 01	5.7	21 55	6.1	02 23	10.0	15 00	10.7	06 57	7.6	19 27	8.1	01 35	5.8	14 34	6.1
12 Tuesday	10 28	6.1	23 11	6.6	03 46	11.1	16 13	11.9	08 06	8.3	20 27	8.8	02 50	6.3	15 38	6.6
13 Wednesday	11 36	6.7	— —	—	04 51	12.2	17 15	12.8	09 01	8.9	21 21	9.4	03 48	6.8	16 31	7.1
14 Thursday	00 11	7.1	12 31	7.1	05 49	13.0	18 10	13.5	09 49	9.5	22 09	9.9	04 38	7.3	17 16	7.5
15 Friday	01 02	7.4	13 17	7.4	06 38	13.7	18 57	14.0	10 35	9.9	22 54	10.2	05 23	7.8	17 57	7.8
16 Saturday	01 47	7.5	14 02	7.6	07 23	14.1	19 41	14.2	11 19	10.1	23 39	10.2	06 07	8.1	18 38	7.9
17 Sunday	02 30	7.5	14 46	7.7	08 05	14.2	20 23	14.1	— —	—	12 03	10.1	06 52	8.2	19 20	7.9
18 Monday	03 12	7.5	15 31	7.7	08 46	13.9	21 07	13.7	00 24	10.1	12 46	9.9	07 38	8.0	20 02	7.7
19 Tuesday	03 56	7.3	16 17	7.5	09 28	13.4	21 50	12.9	01 09	9.7	13 30	9.5	08 26	7.7	20 46	7.4
20 Wednesday	04 40	7.0	17 05	7.2	10 12	12.5	22 34	11.9	01 55	9.1	14 15	9.0	09 17	7.1	21 32	7.0
21 Thursday	05 25	6.6	17 54	6.8	10 57	11.5	23 20	10.9	02 44	8.5	15 07	8.5	10 10	6.5	22 23	6.6
22 Friday	06 11	6.3	18 48	6.4	11 47	10.6	— —	—	03 42	7.8	16 07	8.0	11 12	6.0	23 20	6.2
23 Saturday	07 03	6.0	19 48	6.0	00 17	10.0	12 50	10.0	04 54	7.4	17 22	7.6	— —	—	12 29	5.6
24 Sunday	08 06	5.8	21 00	5.9	01 27	9.6	14 09	10.0	06 17	7.3	18 42	7.7	00 29	6.0	14 02	5.6
25 Monday	09 24	5.8	22 23	6.1	02 47	10.0	15 28	10.6	07 33	7.5	19 49	8.0	01 57	6.0	15 12	5.8
26 Tuesday	10 48	6.1	23 29	6.5	04 00	10.7	16 30	11.4	08 29	7.9	20 43	8.4	03 11	6.2	16 03	6.1
27 Wednesday	11 49	6.5	— —	—	04 57	11.5	17 19	12.0	09 14	8.3	21 25	8.7	04 02	6.5	16 44	6.5
28 Thursday	00 18	6.8	12 34	6.8	05 42	12.0	18 03	12.4	09 50	8.7	22 02	8.9	04 44	6.8	17 18	6.8
29 Friday	00 57	7.0	13 10	6.9	06 21	12.3	18 39	12.5	10 23	8.9	22 37	9.1	05 20	7.1	17 47	7.0
30 Saturday	01 31	7.0	13 42	7.0	06 55	12.5	19 12	12.6	10 54	9.0	23 09	9.2	05 53	7.2	18 15	7.2
31 Sunday	02 01	7.0	14 11	7.0	07 24	12.6	19 40	12.6	11 25	9.1	23 40	9.2	06 25	7.3	18 43	7.2

SEPTEMBER 1993 *continued*

	Greenock a.m.	ht.	p.m.	ht.	Leith a.m.	ht.	p.m.	ht.	Dun Laoghaire a.m.	ht.	p.m.	ht.
	*Datum of predictions 1.62m below				*Datum of predictions 2.90m below				†Datum of predictions 0.20m above			
	h m	m	h m	m	h m	m	h m	m	h m	m	h m	m
1 Wednesday	00 30	3.5	12 52	3.2	02 29	5.4	14 58	5.3	11 48	3.8	23 48	4.1
2 Thursday	01 05	3.5	13 23	3.3	02 58	5.5	15 29	5.3	— —	—	12 13	3.8
3 Friday	01 38	3.5	13 53	3.3	03 25	5.4	15 57	5.3	00 18	4.1	12 40	3.8
4 Saturday	02 09	3.4	14 22	3.3	03 52	5.4	16 27	5.2	00 47	4.0	13 10	3.8
5 Sunday	02 37	3.4	14 50	3.3	04 23	5.3	16 59	5.1	01 20	4.0	13 43	3.8
6 Monday	03 05	3.3	15 21	3.3	04 58	5.1	17 36	4.9	01 56	3.8	14 21	3.7
7 Tuesday	03 34	3.2	15 54	3.3	05 40	4.9	18 17	4.7	02 39	3.7	15 07	3.6
8 Wednesday	04 06	3.0	16 32	3.2	06 31	4.6	19 07	4.5	03 28	3.5	15 59	3.4
9 Thursday	04 45	2.9	17 16	3.1	07 30	4.4	20 05	4.3	04 25	3.4	17 00	3.3
10 Friday	05 38	2.7	18 15	2.9	08 37	4.3	21 10	4.3	05 35	3.2	18 11	3.3
11 Saturday	07 09	2.6	19 40	2.9	09 48	4.3	22 16	4.5	06 56	3.3	19 25	3.4
12 Sunday	09 10	2.8	21 13	3.1	10 57	4.5	23 19	4.8	08 07	3.4	20 25	3.6
13 Monday	10 12	3.1	22 15	3.3	— —	—	12 00	4.9	09 04	3.6	21 16	3.8
14 Tuesday	11 04	3.3	23 07	3.5	00 15	5.2	12 55	5.3	09 52	3.8	22 02	4.1
15 Wednesday	11 54	3.4	23 55	3.7	01 07	5.6	13 44	5.6	10 35	4.0	22 43	4.3
16 Thursday	12 41	3.5	— —	—	01 57	5.9	14 32	5.8	11 14	4.2	23 24	4.5
17 Friday	00 41	3.8	13 26	3.6	02 44	6.1	15 18	5.9	11 55	4.3	— —	—
18 Saturday	01 26	3.9	14 07	3.6	03 34	6.1	16 04	5.9	00 08	4.6	12 36	4.3
19 Sunday	02 08	3.9	14 45	3.6	04 23	6.1	16 52	5.7	00 53	4.6	13 20	4.3
20 Monday	02 50	3.9	15 23	3.6	05 13	5.8	17 40	5.5	01 42	4.4	14 07	4.2
21 Tuesday	03 32	3.7	16 02	3.6	06 05	5.5	18 29	5.2	02 35	4.2	14 59	4.1
22 Wednesday	04 17	3.5	16 46	3.5	07 02	5.2	19 23	4.9	03 38	3.9	16 00	3.9
23 Thursday	05 06	3.3	17 36	3.3	08 02	4.8	20 23	4.6	04 52	3.6	17 13	3.7
24 Friday	06 04	3.0	18 40	3.1	09 10	4.6	21 31	4.5	06 14	3.5	18 30	3.7
25 Saturday	07 30	2.8	20 22	3.1	10 26	4.5	22 45	4.6	07 37	3.5	19 44	3.7
26 Sunday	09 30	2.9	21 49	3.2	11 42	4.7	23 53	4.8	08 50	3.6	20 51	3.8
27 Monday	10 29	3.0	22 43	3.3	— —	—	12 38	4.9	09 44	3.7	21 42	3.9
28 Tuesday	11 12	3.2	23 25	3.4	00 45	5.0	13 20	5.1	10 25	3.7	22 21	4.0
29 Wednesday	11 48	3.2	— —	—	01 26	5.2	13 55	5.3	10 56	3.8	22 53	4.0
30 Thursday	00 03	3.5	12 21	3.3	01 58	5.4	14 27	5.4	11 20	3.8	23 20	4.0

NOTES:

* Difference of height in metres from Ordnance datum (Newlyn)

† Difference of height in metres from Ordnance datum (Dublin)

OCTOBER 1993 *continued*

	Greenock a.m.	ht.	p.m.	ht.	Leith a.m.	ht.	p.m.	ht.	Dun Laoghaire a.m.	ht.	p.m.	ht.
1 Friday	00 38	3.5	12 52	3.3	02 27	5.4	14 57	5.4	11 44	3.9	23 50	4.0
2 Saturday	01 11	3.4	13 22	3.4	02 56	5.4	15 25	5.3	— —	—	12 11	3.9
3 Sunday	01 41	3.3	13 51	3.4	03 25	5.4	15 56	5.3	00 19	4.0	12 39	3.9
4 Monday	02 08	3.2	14 20	3.4	03 59	5.3	16 27	5.1	00 51	3.9	13 13	3.9
5 Tuesday	02 36	3.2	14 51	3.4	04 35	5.1	17 02	5.0	01 29	3.8	13 52	3.8
6 Wednesday	03 06	3.1	15 26	3.4	05 18	4.9	17 40	4.8	02 13	3.7	14 38	3.7
7 Thursday	03 41	3.0	16 04	3.4	06 08	4.7	18 29	4.6	03 03	3.5	15 29	3.5
8 Friday	04 24	2.9	16 49	3.3	07 07	4.5	19 28	4.5	04 00	3.4	16 29	3.4
9 Saturday	05 23	2.8	17 47	3.2	08 12	4.4	20 36	4.5	05 10	3.3	17 38	3.4
10 Sunday	06 54	2.8	19 06	3.1	09 21	4.4	21 43	4.6	06 28	3.3	18 51	3.5
11 Monday	08 37	3.0	20 32	3.2	10 30	4.7	22 48	4.9	07 40	3.5	19 54	3.7
12 Tuesday	09 43	3.2	21 41	3.4	11 32	5.0	23 47	5.3	08 37	3.7	20 48	3.9
13 Wednesday	10 37	3.4	22 36	3.6	— —	—	12 28	5.3	09 26	3.9	21 37	4.2
14 Thursday	11 27	3.5	23 27	3.7	00 42	5.6	13 19	5.6	10 11	4.1	22 22	4.4
15 Friday	12 14	3.6	— —	—	01 33	5.9	14 06	5.8	10 53	4.3	23 06	4.5
16 Saturday	00 15	3.8	12 59	3.6	02 23	6.1	14 54	5.9	11 33	4.4	23 50	4.6
17 Sunday	01 01	3.8	13 40	3.7	03 14	6.1	15 41	5.9	— —	—	12 15	4.4
18 Monday	01 45	3.8	14 18	3.7	04 06	6.0	16 28	5.7	00 36	4.5	12 57	4.4
19 Tuesday	02 29	3.7	14 57	3.7	04 57	5.8	17 16	5.5	01 26	4.3	13 44	4.3
20 Wednesday	03 12	3.6	15 37	3.7	05 49	5.5	18 05	5.2	02 18	4.1	14 38	4.1
21 Thursday	03 58	3.4	16 21	3.6	06 42	5.1	18 57	4.9	03 21	3.8	15 36	4.0
22 Friday	04 48	3.2	17 11	3.4	07 40	4.8	19 54	4.7	04 33	3.6	16 45	3.8
23 Saturday	05 46	3.0	18 11	3.2	08 43	4.6	20 57	4.5	05 52	3.4	17 59	3.7
24 Sunday	07 03	2.9	19 35	3.1	09 52	4.5	22 04	4.5	07 11	3.4	19 11	3.7
25 Monday	08 48	2.9	21 06	3.2	10 59	4.6	23 11	4.7	08 18	3.5	20 16	3.7
26 Tuesday	09 51	3.1	22 06	3.3	11 57	4.8	— —	—	09 11	3.6	21 08	3.8
27 Wednesday	10 36	3.2	22 53	3.4	00 05	4.9	12 42	5.0	09 52	3.7	21 48	3.8
28 Thursday	11 14	3.3	23 33	3.4	00 48	5.1	13 20	5.2	10 23	3.8	22 22	3.9
29 Friday	11 49	3.3	— —	—	01 24	5.2	13 54	5.3	10 52	3.8	22 53	3.9
30 Saturday	00 09	3.3	12 22	3.4	01 58	5.3	14 25	5.4	11 17	3.9	23 23	3.9
31 Sunday	00 44	3.3	12 53	3.4	02 32	5.3	14 57	5.3	11 44	3.9	23 55	3.9

NOVEMBER 1993 *High water* GMT

	London Bridge				Avonmouth				Liverpool				Hull (*Albert Dock*)			
	*Datum of predictions 3.20m below				*Datum of predictions 6.50m below				*Datum of predictions 4.93m below				*Datum of predictions 3.90m below			
	a.m. h m	ht. m	p.m. h m	ht. m	a.m. h m	ht. m	p.m. h m	ht. m	a.m. h m	ht. m	p.m. h m	ht. m	a.m. h m	ht. m	p.m. h m	ht. m
1 Monday	02 29	7.0	14 42	7.0	07 52	12.7	20 11	12.6	11 56	9.1	— —	—	06 59	7.3	19 14	7.2
2 Tuesday	03 00	7.0	15 15	7.0	08 22	12.6	20 43	12.4	00 12	9.1	12 27	9.1	07 33	7.1	19 45	7.1
3 Wednesday	03 34	7.0	15 52	7.0	08 56	12.4	21 17	12.0	00 46	8.9	12 59	8.9	08 08	6.9	20 18	6.9
4 Thursday	04 07	6.9	16 30	6.9	09 29	12.0	21 53	11.6	01 21	8.7	13 35	8.7	08 44	6.7	20 51	6.7
5 Friday	04 44	6.7	17 11	6.7	10 06	11.6	22 34	11.1	02 02	8.4	14 18	8.4	09 25	6.5	21 32	6.4
6 Saturday	05 25	6.4	17 58	6.5	10 51	11.0	23 25	10.5	02 50	8.1	15 10	8.1	10 13	6.3	22 21	6.2
7 Sunday	06 11	6.2	18 55	6.2	11 49	10.6	— —	—	03 49	7.8	16 16	7.9	11 12	6.1	23 26	6.1
8 Monday	07 12	5.9	20 05	6.1	00 31	10.2	13 04	10.5	05 04	7.6	17 34	7.9	— —	—	12 31	6.0
9 Tuesday	08 30	5.9	21 28	6.2	01 54	10.4	14 29	10.9	06 22	7.8	18 49	8.2	00 49	6.1	13 57	6.2
10 Wednesday	09 55	6.2	22 42	6.6	03 14	11.1	15 42	11.7	07 33	8.3	19 55	8.7	02 09	6.4	15 04	6.6
11 Thursday	11 05	6.7	23 44	7.0	04 21	11.9	16 47	12.5	08 32	8.8	20 53	9.2	03 14	6.8	16 00	7.0
12 Friday	— —	—	12 04	7.0	05 20	12.7	17 44	13.1	09 24	9.3	21 45	9.6	04 10	7.3	16 51	7.4
13 Saturday	00 39	7.2	12 56	7.2	06 14	13.3	18 35	13.5	10 13	9.7	22 34	9.8	05 02	7.6	17 36	7.6
14 Sunday	01 27	7.2	13 44	7.3	07 02	13.7	19 23	13.7	10 59	9.9	23 22	9.9	05 51	7.8	18 19	7.7
15 Monday	02 11	7.2	14 30	7.4	07 45	13.9	20 08	13.7	11 44	9.9	— —	—	06 41	7.8	19 02	7.7
16 Tuesday	02 54	7.2	15 17	7.5	08 29	13.7	20 51	13.4	00 08	9.7	12 28	9.8	07 28	7.7	19 45	7.6
17 Wednesday	03 38	7.2	16 03	7.5	09 12	13.3	21 35	12.8	00 53	9.4	13 13	9.5	08 16	7.4	20 29	7.4
18 Thursday	04 21	7.1	16 49	7.2	09 56	12.6	22 19	12.0	01 40	9.0	13 58	9.1	09 04	7.0	21 12	7.2
19 Friday	05 05	6.8	17 36	6.9	10 40	11.8	23 02	11.2	02 26	8.5	14 44	8.7	09 52	6.5	21 56	6.9
20 Saturday	05 47	6.4	18 24	6.5	11 25	11.0	23 47	10.4	03 15	8.0	15 36	8.2	10 42	6.1	22 44	6.5
21 Sunday	06 34	6.1	19 16	6.1	— —	—	12 15	10.4	04 13	7.6	16 37	7.8	11 39	5.8	23 40	6.2
22 Monday	07 27	5.9	20 16	5.9	00 42	10.0	13 19	10.1	05 19	7.3	17 44	7.6	— —	—	12 48	5.6
23 Tuesday	08 33	5.7	21 27	5.9	01 48	9.8	14 27	10.2	06 34	7.3	18 53	7.7	00 48	6.0	14 12	5.6
24 Wednesday	09 49	5.8	22 40	6.1	02 58	10.1	15 35	10.6	07 38	7.5	19 55	7.9	02 05	6.0	15 15	5.9
25 Thursday	11 01	6.1	23 36	6.4	04 03	10.7	16 33	11.1	08 30	7.9	20 46	8.2	03 15	6.2	16 03	6.2
26 Friday	11 54	6.4	— —	—	04 57	11.2	17 22	11.6	09 14	8.3	21 28	8.5	04 06	6.5	16 41	6.5
27 Saturday	00 21	6.6	12 35	6.6	05 42	11.7	18 04	12.0	09 52	8.6	22 07	8.7	04 49	6.7	17 16	6.8
28 Sunday	00 57	6.7	13 10	6.7	06 21	12.1	18 41	12.2	10 27	8.8	22 42	8.9	05 27	6.9	17 47	7.0
29 Monday	01 30	6.8	13 45	6.8	06 56	12.4	19 17	12.4	11 01	9.0	23 18	9.0	06 03	7.0	18 19	7.1
30 Tuesday	02 05	6.9	14 22	6.9	07 30	12.6	19 52	12.5	11 34	9.1	23 54	9.1	06 39	7.1	18 53	7.2

DECEMBER 1993 *High water* GMT

	London Bridge				Avonmouth				Liverpool				Hull (*Albert Dock*)			
1 Wednesday	02 40	7.0	15 00	7.0	08 06	12.7	20 30	12.5	— —	—	12 10	9.2	07 16	7.1	19 27	7.2
2 Thursday	03 18	7.0	15 39	7.1	08 43	12.7	21 08	12.4	00 31	9.0	12 46	9.1	07 54	7.1	20 04	7.1
3 Friday	03 55	7.0	16 20	7.1	09 22	12.5	21 49	12.1	01 10	8.9	13 26	9.0	08 33	7.0	20 42	7.0
4 Saturday	04 33	6.9	17 02	6.9	10 04	12.2	22 31	11.8	01 52	8.7	14 09	8.8	09 15	6.8	21 22	6.9
5 Sunday	05 13	6.7	17 47	6.7	10 49	11.8	23 19	11.3	02 39	8.5	14 58	8.6	10 02	6.7	22 09	6.7
6 Monday	05 57	6.4	18 39	6.4	11 40	11.4	— —	—	03 32	8.2	15 55	8.4	10 54	6.5	23 04	6.5
7 Tuesday	06 52	6.2	19 42	6.3	00 14	10.9	12 42	11.1	04 35	8.0	17 01	8.3	11 57	6.3	— —	—
8 Wednesday	08 01	6.2	20 57	6.3	01 21	10.7	13 54	11.1	05 46	8.0	18 12	8.3	00 11	6.5	13 13	6.3
9 Thursday	09 21	6.3	22 12	6.6	02 37	10.9	15 10	11.4	06 57	8.2	19 24	8.5	01 28	6.5	14 27	6.5
10 Friday	10 35	6.5	23 19	6.8	03 49	11.5	16 19	11.9	08 04	8.5	20 29	8.8	02 42	6.8	15 32	6.8
11 Saturday	11 43	6.7	— —	—	04 54	12.1	17 22	12.4	09 03	8.9	21 28	9.1	03 49	7.0	16 30	7.1
12 Sunday	00 18	6.9	12 41	6.9	05 53	12.7	18 18	12.8	09 56	9.3	22 21	9.3	04 49	7.3	17 20	7.3
13 Monday	01 10	6.9	13 33	7.0	06 45	13.1	19 09	13.1	10 45	9.6	23 11	9.5	05 44	7.4	18 05	7.5
14 Tuesday	01 58	6.9	14 20	7.1	07 31	13.4	19 55	13.3	11 32	9.7	23 57	9.4	06 34	7.4	18 49	7.6
15 Wednesday	02 42	7.0	15 05	7.3	08 16	13.5	20 39	13.2	— —	—	12 15	9.7	07 20	7.4	19 31	7.6
16 Thursday	03 24	7.1	15 49	7.4	08 58	13.3	21 21	12.9	00 41	9.3	12 59	9.5	08 05	7.2	20 11	7.5
17 Friday	04 04	7.1	16 33	7.3	09 39	12.9	22 00	12.3	01 23	9.0	13 40	9.3	08 47	7.0	20 50	7.4
18 Saturday	04 44	7.0	17 13	7.0	10 19	12.3	22 38	11.7	02 04	8.7	14 20	8.9	09 28	6.7	21 29	7.2
19 Sunday	05 22	6.7	17 56	6.7	10 57	11.6	23 15	11.1	02 44	8.3	15 03	8.5	10 07	6.4	22 10	6.9
20 Monday	06 01	6.4	18 39	6.3	11 36	11.0	23 53	10.5	03 29	7.9	15 49	8.1	10 48	6.1	22 54	6.6
21 Tuesday	06 48	6.1	19 30	6.0	— —	—	12 21	10.4	04 19	7.5	16 42	7.7	11 37	5.8	23 49	6.2
22 Wednesday	07 42	5.8	20 29	5.8	00 42	10.0	13 19	10.0	05 19	7.3	17 46	7.5	— —	—	12 38	5.7
23 Thursday	08 49	5.7	21 32	5.8	01 44	9.7	14 27	9.9	06 28	7.2	18 55	7.4	00 56	6.0	13 51	5.7
24 Friday	09 55	5.7	22 35	5.9	02 56	9.9	15 35	10.2	07 37	7.4	19 59	7.6	02 09	6.0	15 03	5.9
25 Saturday	10 58	5.9	23 32	6.2	04 02	10.4	16 35	10.8	08 33	7.8	20 53	8.0	03 19	6.1	15 59	6.2
26 Sunday	11 53	6.1	— —	—	04 58	11.1	17 27	11.4	09 19	8.2	21 39	8.3	04 16	6.4	16 44	6.5
27 Monday	00 19	6.4	12 39	6.4	05 47	11.7	18 14	11.9	10 02	8.6	22 20	8.6	05 02	6.6	17 23	6.8
28 Tuesday	01 03	6.6	13 23	6.6	06 32	12.2	18 57	12.3	10 40	8.9	22 59	8.9	05 43	6.8	18 00	7.0
29 Wednesday	01 45	6.9	14 06	6.9	07 13	12.6	19 38	12.6	11 18	9.2	23 39	9.1	06 22	7.0	18 36	7.2
30 Thursday	02 26	7.1	14 47	7.2	07 54	13.0	20 19	12.9	11 57	9.4	— —	—	07 02	7.2	19 13	7.4
31 Friday	03 07	7.2	15 29	7.3	08 34	13.2	21 00	13.0	00 18	9.2	12 36	9.4	07 41	7.3	19 51	7.5

NOVEMBER 1993 *continued*

	Greenock a.m. h m	ht. m	p.m. h m	ht. m	Leith a.m. h m	ht. m	p.m. h m	ht. m	Dun Laoghaire a.m. h m	ht. m	p.m. h m	ht. m
	*Datum of predictions 1.62m below				*Datum of predictions 2.90m below				†Datum of predictions 0.20m above			
1 Monday	01 15	3.2	13 23	3.5	03 05	5.3	15 28	5.3	— —	—	12 15	4.0
2 Tuesday	01 45	3.2	13 54	3.5	03 42	5.2	16 02	5.2	00 29	3.9	12 49	4.0
3 Wednesday	02 15	3.1	14 27	3.6	04 23	5.1	16 37	5.1	01 07	3.8	13 29	3.9
4 Thursday	02 49	3.1	15 04	3.6	05 06	5.0	17 16	5.0	01 53	3.7	14 14	3.8
5 Friday	03 29	3.1	15 44	3.5	05 56	4.8	18 04	4.8	02 43	3.6	15 06	3.7
6 Saturday	04 17	3.0	16 30	3.5	06 50	4.7	19 03	4.7	03 40	3.5	16 03	3.6
7 Sunday	05 19	3.0	17 26	3.4	07 51	4.6	20 08	4.7	04 46	3.4	17 07	3.6
8 Monday	06 36	3.0	18 37	3.3	08 56	4.6	21 14	4.8	05 59	3.4	18 17	3.6
9 Tuesday	07 58	3.1	19 53	3.4	10 00	4.8	22 19	5.0	07 08	3.5	19 23	3.8
10 Wednesday	09 09	3.2	21 03	3.5	11 02	5.0	23 20	5.3	08 07	3.7	20 21	4.0
11 Thursday	10 07	3.4	22 04	3.6	— —	—	12 00	5.3	09 01	3.9	21 15	4.2
12 Friday	11 00	3.5	22 59	3.6	00 18	5.5	12 53	5.6	09 48	4.1	22 05	4.3
13 Saturday	11 48	3.6	23 50	3.7	01 14	5.8	13 44	5.7	10 33	4.3	22 52	4.4
14 Sunday	12 33	3.7	— —	—	02 08	5.9	14 33	5.8	11 16	4.4	23 38	4.4
15 Monday	00 39	3.7	13 15	3.7	03 01	5.9	15 21	5.8	11 58	4.4	— —	—
16 Tuesday	01 26	3.6	13 55	3.8	03 52	5.9	16 09	5.7	00 25	4.4	12 42	4.4
17 Wednesday	02 11	3.6	14 35	3.8	04 42	5.7	16 55	5.5	01 13	4.2	13 28	4.3
18 Thursday	02 57	3.5	15 17	3.8	05 32	5.4	17 42	5.3	02 04	4.0	14 15	4.2
19 Friday	03 43	3.3	16 00	3.7	06 21	5.1	18 29	5.0	03 01	3.8	15 10	4.0
20 Saturday	04 31	3.2	16 47	3.5	07 13	4.9	19 20	4.8	04 04	3.6	16 11	3.8
21 Sunday	05 22	3.1	17 40	3.4	08 06	4.6	20 15	4.6	05 11	3.4	17 17	3.7
22 Monday	06 22	3.0	18 43	3.2	09 04	4.5	21 14	4.5	06 23	3.4	18 26	3.6
23 Tuesday	07 39	2.9	20 07	3.1	10 03	4.5	22 14	4.6	07 27	3.4	19 29	3.6
24 Wednesday	08 58	3.0	21 22	3.1	11 02	4.6	23 12	4.7	08 24	3.5	20 24	3.6
25 Thursday	09 53	3.1	22 17	3.1	11 56	4.8	— —	—	09 09	3.6	21 11	3.7
26 Friday	10 38	3.2	23 02	3.2	00 04	4.8	12 39	5.0	09 48	3.7	21 51	3.7
27 Saturday	11 17	3.3	23 43	3.2	00 49	5.0	13 20	5.1	10 21	3.8	22 26	3.7
28 Sunday	11 53	3.4	— —	—	01 30	5.1	13 55	5.2	10 53	3.9	23 00	3.8
29 Monday	00 20	3.1	12 27	3.4	02 11	5.2	14 30	5.3	11 21	3.9	23 34	3.8
30 Tuesday	00 55	3.1	13 00	3.5	02 50	5.2	15 05	5.3	11 54	4.0	— —	—

NOTES:

*Difference of height in metres from Ordnance datum (Newlyn)

†Difference of height in metres from Ordnance datum (Dublin)

DECEMBER 1993 *continued*

	Greenock a.m.	ht.	p.m.	ht.	Leith a.m.	ht.	p.m.	ht.	Dun Laoghaire a.m.	ht.	p.m.	ht.
1 Wednesday	01 30	3.1	13 33	3.6	03 31	5.2	15 42	5.3	00 11	3.8	12 29	4.0
2 Thursday	02 05	3.2	14 09	3.7	04 13	5.2	16 20	5.3	00 50	3.8	13 08	4.0
3 Friday	02 44	3.2	14 48	3.7	04 57	5.1	17 02	5.2	01 35	3.8	13 53	4.0
4 Saturday	03 27	3.2	15 29	3.7	05 44	5.0	17 50	5.1	02 24	3.7	14 43	3.9
5 Sunday	04 15	3.2	16 15	3.6	06 35	4.9	18 46	5.0	03 17	3.6	15 38	3.8
6 Monday	05 09	3.1	17 07	3.6	07 31	4.8	19 45	5.0	04 17	3.6	16 38	3.8
7 Tuesday	06 10	3.1	18 08	3.5	08 30	4.8	20 49	4.9	05 24	3.5	17 45	3.8
8 Wednesday	07 18	3.1	19 16	3.4	09 31	4.8	21 52	5.0	06 34	3.6	18 54	3.9
9 Thursday	08 29	3.2	20 27	3.4	10 33	4.9	22 57	5.1	07 39	3.7	19 58	4.0
10 Friday	09 35	3.3	21 34	3.4	11 34	5.1	— —	—	08 37	3.9	20 57	4.1
11 Saturday	10 34	3.4	22 36	3.4	00 00	5.3	12 34	5.3	09 28	4.1	21 51	4.2
12 Sunday	11 26	3.5	23 32	3.5	01 02	5.5	13 27	5.5	10 16	4.2	22 42	4.3
13 Monday	12 13	3.6	— —	—	01 58	5.7	14 19	5.6	11 02	4.3	23 30	4.3
14 Tuesday	00 25	3.5	12 57	3.7	02 51	5.7	15 07	5.7	11 45	4.4	— —	—
15 Wednesday	01 14	3.4	13 38	3.8	03 41	5.7	15 53	5.7	00 16	4.2	12 28	4.4
16 Thursday	02 00	3.4	14 18	3.8	04 28	5.6	16 37	5.5	01 00	4.1	13 10	4.3
17 Friday	02 44	3.4	14 59	3.8	05 12	5.4	17 19	5.4	01 46	3.9	13 54	4.2
18 Saturday	03 26	3.3	15 40	3.7	05 56	5.2	17 58	5.2	02 33	3.8	14 42	4.1
19 Sunday	04 08	3.3	16 22	3.6	06 38	4.9	18 41	5.0	03 23	3.6	15 33	3.9
20 Monday	04 50	3.2	17 04	3.4	07 23	4.7	19 27	4.8	04 18	3.4	16 31	3.7
21 Tuesday	05 33	3.1	17 50	3.2	08 12	4.6	20 20	4.6	05 20	3.3	17 33	3.6
22 Wednesday	06 21	2.9	18 45	3.0	09 05	4.5	21 18	4.5	06 24	3.3	18 38	3.5
23 Thursday	07 26	2.9	20 14	2.8	10 04	4.5	22 19	4.5	07 26	3.4	19 40	3.5
24 Friday	08 57	2.9	21 37	2.8	11 02	4.6	23 19	4.6	08 23	3.5	20 34	3.5
25 Saturday	09 59	3.0	22 32	2.9	11 57	4.7	— —	—	09 11	3.6	21 22	3.6
26 Sunday	10 45	3.1	23 18	3.0	00 14	4.7	12 45	4.9	09 52	3.7	22 03	3.6
27 Monday	11 26	3.3	23 59	3.0	01 04	4.9	13 28	5.0	10 29	3.8	22 40	3.7
28 Tuesday	12 04	3.4	— —	—	01 49	5.1	14 08	5.2	11 02	3.9	23 16	3.8
29 Wednesday	00 39	3.1	12 41	3.5	02 33	5.2	14 47	5.3	11 36	4.0	23 52	3.9
30 Thursday	01 19	3.2	13 18	3.6	03 17	5.3	15 27	5.4	— —	—	12 11	4.1
31 Friday	02 00	3.2	13 56	3.7	04 00	5.4	16 07	5.5	00 32	3.9	12 50	4.1

World Geographical Statistics

THE EARTH

The shape of the Earth is that of an oblate spheroid or solid of revolution whose meridian sections are ellipses, whilst the sections at right angles are circles.

Dimensions

Equatorial diameter = 12,756.28 km (7,926.38 miles).
Polar diameter = 12,713.50 km (7,899.80 miles).
Equatorial circumference = 40,075.01 km (24,901.45 miles).
Polar circumference = 40,008.00 km (24,859.82 miles).

The equatorial circumference is divided into 360 degrees of longitude, which is measured in degrees, minutes and seconds east or west of the Greenwich meridian (0°) to 180° (the meridian 180° E. coinciding with 180° W.). This was internationally ratified in 1884.

Distance north and south of the Equator is measured in degrees, minutes and seconds of latitude. The Equator is 0°, the North Pole is 90° N. and the South Pole is 90° S. The Tropics lie at 23° 26′ N. (Tropic of Cancer) and 23° 26′ S. (Tropic of Capricorn). The Arctic Circle lies at 66° 34′ N. and the Antarctic Circle at 66° 34′ S. (NB The Tropics and the Arctic and Antarctic circles are of variable latitude due to the mean obliquity of the Ecliptic; the values given are for 1992.5.)

Area, etc.

The surface area of the Earth is 510,069,120 km^2 (196,938,800 miles^2), of which the water area is 70.92 per cent and the land area is 29.08 per cent.

The velocity of a given point of the Earth's surface at the Equator exceeds 1,000 miles an hour (24,901.8 miles in 24 hours, viz 1,037.56 mph); the Earth's velocity in its orbit round the Sun averages 66,620 mph (584,018,400 miles in 365.256366 days). The Earth is distant from the Sun 92,955,900 miles, on the average.

OCEAN AREAS

	Area km^2	miles^2
Pacific	166,240,000	64,186,300
Atlantic	86,550,000	33,420,000
Indian	73,427,000	28,350,500
Arctic	13,223,700	5,105,700

Greatest Ocean Depths

Greatest depth location	*Depth* metres	feet
Mariana Trench (Pacific)	10,916	35,839
Puerto Rico Trench (Atlantic)	8,605	28,232
Java Trench (Indian)	7,125	23,376
Eurasian Basin (Arctic)	5,450	17,880

SEA AREAS

	Area km^2	miles^2
South China	2,974,600	1,148,500
Caribbean	2,515,900	971,400
Mediterranean	2,509,900	969,100
Bering	2,226,100	873,000
Gulf of Mexico	1,507,600	582,100
Okhotsk	1,392,000	537,500
Japan	1,015,000	391,100
Hudson Bay	730,100	281,900
East China	664,600	256,600
Andaman	564,880	218,100
Black Sea	507,900	196,100
Red Sea	453,000	174,900
North Sea	427,100	164,900
Baltic Sea	382,000	147,500
Yellow Sea	294,000	113,500
Persian Gulf	230,000	88,800

THE CONTINENTS

There are six geographic continents, though America is often divided politically into North and Central America, and South America.

Africa is surrounded by sea except for the narrow isthmus of Suez in the north-east, through which is cut the Suez Canal. The Equator passes through the middle of the continent. Its extreme longitudes are 17° 20′ W. at Cape Verde, Senegal, and 51° 24′ E. at Ras Hafun, Somalia. The extreme latitudes are 37° 20′ N. at Cape Blanc, Tunisia, and 34° 50′ S. at Cape Agulhas, South Africa, about 4,400 miles apart.

North America, including Mexico, is surrounded by ocean except in the south, where the isthmian states of Central America link North America with South America. Its extreme longitudes are 168° 5′ W. at Cape Prince of Wales, Alaska, and 55° 40′ W. at Cape Charles, Newfoundland. The extreme continental latitudes are Point Barrow, Alaska (71°22′ N.) and 14°22′ N. at Ocós in the south of Mexico. The West Indies, about 65,000 square miles in area, extend from about 27° N. to 10° N. latitude.

South America lies mostly in the southern hemisphere; the Equator passes through the north of the continent. It is surrounded by ocean except where it is joined to Central America in the north by the narrow isthmus through which is cut the Panama Canal. Its extreme longitudes are 34° 47′ W. at Cape Branco in Brazil and 81° 20′ W. at Punta Pariña, Peru. The extreme latitudes are 12° 25′ N. at Punta Gallinas, Colombia, and 55° 59′ S. at Cape Horn, Chile.

Antarctica lies almost entirely within the Antarctic Circle (66° 34′ S.) and is the largest of the world's glaciated areas. The continent has an area of about 5.5 million square miles, 99 per cent of which is permanently ice-covered. The ice amounts to some 7.2 million cubic miles and represents more than 90 per cent of the world's fresh water. The environment is too hostile for unsupported human habitation. *See also* Countries of the World.

ASIA is the largest continent and occupies almost a third of the world's land surface. The extreme longitudes are about 26° E. on the west coast of Asia Minor and 169° 40′ W. at Mys Dežneva (East Cape), Russia, a distance of about 6,000 miles. Its extreme northern latitude is 77° 45′ N. at Cape Čeljuskin, Russia, and it extends over 5,000 miles south to about 1° 15′ N. of the Equator. The islands of Japan, the Philippines and Indonesia ring the continent to the east and south-east.

AUSTRALIA is the smallest of the continents and lies in the southern hemisphere. It is entirely surrounded by ocean. Its extreme longitudes are 113° 9′ E. at Steep Point and 153° 38′ E. at Cape Byron. The extreme latitudes are 10° 40′ S. at Cape York and 39° S. at South East Point.

EUROPE, including European Russia, is the smallest continent in the northern hemisphere. Its extreme latitudes are 71° 11′ N. at North Cape in Norway, and 36° 23′ N. at Cape Matapan in southern Greece, a distance of about 2,400 miles. Its breadth from Cape da Roca in Portugal (9° 30′ W.) in the west to the Urals in the east is about 3,300 miles. The division between Europe and Asia is generally regarded as being the Ural Mountains and, in the south, the valley of the Manych, which stretches from the Caspian Sea to the mouth of the Don.

	Area km²	miles²
Asia	43,998,000	16,988,000
America*	41,918,000	16,185,000
Africa	29,800,000	11,506,000
Antarctica	*c.*13,600,000	*c.*5,500,000
Europe†	9,699,000	3,745,000
Australia	7,618,493	2,941,526

*North and Central America has an area of 24,255,000 km² (9,365,000 miles²).

†Includes 5,571,000 km² (2,151,000 miles²) of CIS territory west of the Ural Mountains.

GLACIATED AREAS

It is estimated that 15,600,000 km² (6,020,000 miles²) or 10.51 per cent of the world's land surface is permanently covered with ice.

	Area km²	miles²
South Polar regions	13,597,000	5,250,000
North Polar regions (incl. Greenland or Kalaallit Nunaat)	1,965,000	758,500
Alaska-Canada	58,800	22,700
Asia	37,800	14,600
South America	11,900	4,600
Europe	10,700	4,128
New Zealand	984	380
Africa	238	92

PENINSULAS

	Area km²	miles²
Arabian	3,250,000	1,250,000
Southern Indian	2,072,000	800,000
Alaskan	1,500,000	580,000
Labradorian	1,300,000	500,000
Scandinavian	800,300	309,000
Iberian	584,000	225,500

LARGEST ISLANDS

Island (and Ocean)	*Area* km²	miles²
Greenland (Arctic)	2,175,500	840,000
New Guinea (Pacific)	792,500	306,000
Borneo (Pacific)	725,450	280,100
Madagascar (Indian)	587,040	226,658
Baffin Island (Arctic)	507,528	195,928
Sumatra (Indian)	427,350	165,000
Honshu (Pacific)	227,413	87,805
*Great Britain (Atlantic)	218,040	84,186
Victoria Island (Arctic)	217,290	83,895
Ellesmere Island (Arctic)	196,235	75,767
Sulawesi (Celebes) (Indian)	178,700	69,000
South Island, NZ (Pacific)	151,010	58,305
Java (Indian)	126,650	48,900
Cuba (Atlantic)	114,525	44,218
North Island, NZ (Pacific)	114,050	44,035
Newfoundland (Atlantic)	108,855	42,030
Luzon (Pacific)	105,880	40,880
Iceland (Atlantic)	103,000	39,770
Mindanao (Pacific)	95,247	36,775
Ireland (Atlantic)	82,462	31,839

*Mainland only

LARGEST DESERTS

	Area (approx.) km²	miles²
The Sahara (N. Africa)	8,400,000	3,250,000
Australian Desert	1,550,000	600,000
Arabian Desert	1,300,000	500,000
*The Gobi (Mongolia/China)	1,170,000	450,000
Kalahari Desert (Botswana/Namibia/S. Africa)	520,000	200,000
Sonoran Desert (USA/Mexico)	310,000	120,000
Namib Desert (Namibia)	310,000	120,000
†Kara Kum (Turkmenistan)	270,000	105,000
Thar Desert (India/Pakistan)	260,000	100,000
Somali Desert (Somalia)	260,000	100,000
Atacama Desert (Chile)	180,000	70,000
†Kyzyl Kum (Kazakhstan/Uzbekistan)	180,000	70,000
Dasht-e Lut (Iran)	52,000	20,000
Mojave Desert (USA)	35,000	13,500
Desierto de Sechura (Peru)	26,000	10,000

*Including the Takla Makan – 320,000 km² (125,000 miles²)

†Together known as the Turkestan Desert

DEEPEST DEPRESSIONS

	Maximum depth below sea level metres	feet
Dead Sea (Jordan/Israel)	395	1,296
Turfan Depression (Sinkiang, China)	153	505
Qattara Depression (Egypt)	132	436
Mangyshlak peninsula (Kazakhstan)	131	433
Danakil Depression (Ethiopia)	116	383
Death Valley (California, USA)	86	282
Salton Sink (California, USA)	71	235
W. of Ustyurt plateau (Kazakhstan)	70	230
Prikaspiyskaya Nizmennost' (Russia/ Kazakhstan)	67	220
Lake Sarykamysh (Uzbekistan/ Turkmenistan)	45	148
El Faiyûm (Egypt)	44	147
Valdies peninsula, Lago Enriquillo (Dominican Republic)	40	131

The world's largest exposed depression is the Prikaspiyskaya Nizmennost' covering the hinterland of the northern third of the Caspian Sea, which is itself 28 m (92 ft) below sea level.

Western Antarctica and Central Greenland largely comprise crypto-depressions under ice burdens. The Antarctic Wilkes subglacial basin has a bedrock 2,341 m (7,680 ft) below sea-level. In Greenland (lat. 73° N., long. 39° W.) the bedrock is 365 m (1,197 ft) below sea-level.

LONGEST MOUNTAIN RANGES

Range (location)	*Length* km	miles
Cordillera de Los Andes (W. South America)	7,200	4,500
Rocky Mountains (W. North America)	4,800	3,000
Himalaya-Karakoram-Hindu Kush (S. Central Asia)	3,800	2,400
Great Dividing Range (E. Australia)	3,600	2,250
Trans-Antarctic Mts (Antarctica)	3,500	2,200
Atlantic Coast Range (E. Brazil)	3,000	1,900
West Sumatran-Javan Range (Indonesia)	2,900	1,800
Aleutian Range (Alaska and NW Pacific)	2,650	1,650
Tien Shan (S. Central Asia)	2,250	1,400
Central New Guinea Range (Irian Jaya/ Papua New Guinea)	2,000	1,250

HIGHEST VOLCANOES

Volcano (last major eruption) and location	*Height* metres	feet
Guallatiri (1987), Andes, Chile	6,060	19,882
Lascar (1991), Andes, Chile	5,990	19,652
Cotopaxi (1975), Andes, Ecuador	5,897	19,347
Tupungatito (1986), Andes, Chile	5,640	18,504
Nevado del Ruiz, Colombia (1991)	5,400	17,716
Sangay (1988), Andes, Ecuador	5,230	17,159
Guagua Pichincha (1988), Andes, Ecuador	4,784	15,696
Purace (1977), Colombia	4,756	15,601
Klyuchevskaya Sopka (1990), Kamchatka peninsula, Russia	4,750	15,584
Nevado de Colima (1991), Mexico	4,268	14,003
Galeras, Colombia (1991)	4,266	13,996
Mauna Loa (1987), Hawaii Is.	4,170	13,680
Cameroon (1982), Cameroon	4,070	13,354
Acatenango (1972), Guatemala	3,960	12,992
Fuego (1991), Guatemala	3,835	12,582
Kerinci (1987), Sumatra, Indonesia	3,800	12,467
Erebus (1991), Ross Island, Antarctica	3,794	12,450
Tacana (1988), Guatemala	3,780	12,400
Santiaguito (1902, 1991), Guatemala	3,768	12,362
Rindjani (1966), Lombok, Indonesia	3,726	12,224
Semeru (1989), Java, Indonesia	3,675	12,060
Nyirgongo (1977), Zaïre	3,475	11,400
Koryakskaya (1957), Kamchatka, Russia	3,456	11,339
Irazú (1991), Costa Rica	3,432	11,260
Slamet (1988), Java, Indonesia	3,428	11,247
Spurr (1953), Alaska, USA	3,374	11,069
Mt. Etna (1169, 1669, 1992), Sicily, Italy	3,369	11,053
Raung, Java, Indonesia (1990)	3,322	10,932
Shiveluch (1964), Kamchatka, Russia	3,283	10,771
Agung (1964), Bali, Indonesia	3,142	10,308
Llaima (1990), Chile	3,128	10,239
Redoubt (1991), Alaska, USA	3,108	10,197
Tjareme (1938), Java, Indonesia	3,078	10,098
Iliamna (1978), Alaska, USA	3,076	10,092
On-Taka (1991), Japan	3,063	10,049
Nyamlagira (1988), Zaire	3,056	10,028

Other Notable Volcanoes

	Height metres	feet
Tambora (1815), Sumbawa, Indonesia	2,850	9,353
Mount St Helens (1986), Washington State, USA	2,530	8,300
Pinatubo (1991), Philippines	1,758	5,770
Hekla (1981), Iceland	1,491	4,892
Mount Pelée (1902), Martinique	1,397	4,583
Mt. Unzen (1991), Kyushu, Japan	1,360	4,462
Vesuvius (AD 79, 1944), Italy	1,280	4,198
Kilauea (1988), Hawaii, USA	1,242	4,077
Stromboli (1990), Lipari Is., Italy	926	3,038
Krakatau (1883), Sunda Strait, Indonesia	804	2,640
Santoriní (Thíra) (1628 BC), Aegean Sea, Greece	566	1,857
Vulcano (Monte Aria), Lipari Is., Italy	499	1,637
Tristan da Cunha (1961), South Atlantic	243	800
Surtsey (1963–7), off Iceland	173	568

HIGHEST MOUNTAINS

The world's 8,000-metre mountains (with six subsidiary peaks) are all in the 3,800 km (2,400 mile) long Himalaya-Karakoram-Hindu Kush range of south central Asia.

Mountain	*Height* metres	feet
Mount Everest*	8,863	29,078
K2	8,607	28,238
Kangchenjunga	8,597	28,208
Lhotse	8,511	27,923
Makalu I	8,481	27,824
Lhotse Shar	8,383	27,504
Dhaulagiri I	8,167	26,795
Manaslu I (Kutang I)	8,156	26,760
Cho Oyu	8,153	26,750
Nanga Parbat (Diamir)	8,125	26,660
Annapurna I	8,091	26,546
Gasherbrum I (Hidden Peak)	8,068	26,470
Broad Peak I	8,046	26,400
Shisha Pangma (Gosainthan)	8,046	26,398
Gasherbrum II	8,034	26,360
Annapurna East	8,010	26,280
Makalu South-East	8,010	26,280
Broad Peak Central	8,000	26,246

*Named after Sir George Everest (1790–1866), Surveyor-General of India 1830–43, in 1863. He pronounced his name Eve-rest.

The culminating summits in the other major mountain ranges are:

Mountain (range or country)	*Height* metres	feet
Pik Pobeda (Tien Shan)	7,439	24,406
Cerro Aconcagua (Cordillera de Los Andes)	6,960	22,834
Mt. McKinley, *S. Peak* (Alaska Range)	6,194	20,320
Kilimanjaro (Tanzania)	5,894	19,340
Hkakabo Razi (Myanmar)	5,881	19,296
Citlaltépetl (Orizaba) (Sierra Madre Oriental, Mexico)	5,699	18,700
El'brus, *W. Peak* (Caucasus)	5,663	18,481
Vinson Massif (E. Antarctica)	4,897	16,067
Puncak Jaya (Central New Guinea Range)	4,884	16,023
Mt. Blanc (Alps)	4,807	15,771
Klyuchevskaya Sopka (Kamchatka peninsula, Russia)	4,750	15,584
Ras Dashan (Ethiopian Highlands)	4,620	15,158
Zard Kūh (Zagros Mts, Iran)	4,547	14,921
Mt. Kirkpatrick (Trans Antarctic)	4,529	14,860
Mt. Belukha (Altai Mts, Russia/ Kazakhstan)	4,505	14,783
Mt. Elbert (Rocky Mountains)	4,400	14,433
Mt. Rainier (Cascade Range, N. America)	4,392	14,410
Nevado de Colima (Sierra Madre Occidental, Mexico	4,268	14,003
Jebel Toubkal (Atlas Mts, N. Africa)	4,165	13,665
Kinabalu (Crocker Range, Borneo)	4,101	13,455
Kerinci (West Sumatran-Javan Range, Indonesia)	3,800	12,467
Jabal an Nabī Shu'ayb (N. Tihāmat, Yemen)	3,760	12,336
Teotepec (Sierra Madre del Sur, Mexico)	3,703	12,149
Thaban Ntlenyana (Drakensberg, South Africa)	3,482	11,425
Pico de Bandeira (Atlantic Coast Range)	2,890	9,482
Shishaldin (Aleutian Range)	2,861	9,387
Kosciusko (Great Dividing Range)	2,228	7,310

LARGEST LAKES

The areas of some of these lakes are subject to seasonal variation.

	Area km²	miles²	*Length* km	miles
Caspian Sea – Iran/ Azerbaijan/Russia/ Turkmenistan/ Kazakhstan	371,000	143,000	1,171	728
Superior – Canada/USA	82,100	31,700	563	350
Victoria – Uganda/ Tanzania/Kenya	69,500	26,828	362	225
Huron – Canada/USA	59,570	23,000	331	206
Michigan – USA	57,750	22,300	494	307
Aral Sea – Kazakhstan/ Uzbekistan	40,400	15,600	331	235
Tanganyika – Zaïre/ Tanzania/Zambia/ Burundi	32,900	12,700	675	420
*Baykal (*Baikal*) – Russia	31,500	12,162	635	395
Great Bear – Canada	31,328	12,096	309	192
Malawi – Tanzania/ Malawi/Mozambique	28,880	11,150	580	360
Great Slave – Canada	28,570	11,031	480	298
Erie – Canada/USA	25,670	9,910	388	241
Winnipeg – Canada	24,390	9,417	428	266
Ontario – Canada/USA	19,550	7,550	310	193
Balkhash – Kazakhstan	18,427	7,115	605	376
Ladozhskoye (*Ladoga*) – Russia	17,700	6,835	200	124
UNITED KINGDOM (BY COUNTRY)				
Lough Neagh – Northern Ireland	381.73	147.39	28.90	18.00
Loch Lomond – Scotland	71.12	27.46	36.44	22.64
Windermere – England	14.74	5.69	16.90	10.50
Lake Vyrnwy – Wales (artificial)	4.53	1.75	7.56	4.70
Llyn Tegid (*Bala*) – Wales (natural)	4.38	1.69	5.80	3.65

*World's deepest lake (1,940 m/6,365 ft)

LONGEST RIVERS

River (source and outflow)	*Length* km	miles
Nile (*Bahr-el-Nil*) (R. Luvironza, Burundi – E. Mediterranean Sea)	6,670	4,145
Amazon (*Amazonas*) (Lago Villafro, Peru – S. Atlantic Ocean)	6,648	4,007
Mississippi-Missouri (R. Red Rock, Montana – Gulf of Mexico)	5,970	3,710
Yenisey-Angara (W. Mongolia – Kara Sea)	5,540	3,442
Yangtze-Kiang (*Chang Jiang*) (Kunlun Mts, W. China – Yellow Sea)	5,530	3,436
Ob'-Irtysh (W. Mongolia – Kara Sea)	5,410	3,362
Huang He (*Yellow River*) (Bayan Har Shan range, central China – Yellow Sea)	4,830	3,000
Zaire (*Congo*) (R. Lualaba, Zaire-Zambia – S. Atlantic Ocean)	4,700	2,920
Amur-Argun (R. Argun, Khingan Mts, N. China – Sea of Okhotsk)	4,670	2,903
Lena-Kirenga (R. Kirenga, W. of Lake Baykal – Arctic Ocean)	4,345	2,700
Mackenzie-Peace (Tatlatui Lake, British Columbia – Beaufort Sea)	4,240	2,635
Mekong (Lants'ang, Tibet – South China Sea)	4,184	2,600
Niger (Loma Mts, Guinea – Gulf of Guinea, E. Atlantic Ocean)	4,184	2,600
Rió de la Plata-Paraná (R. Paranáiba, central Brazil – S. Atlantic Ocean)	4,000	2,485
Murray-Darling (SE Queensland – Lake Alexandrina, S. Australia)	3,750	2,330
Volga (Valdai plateau – Caspian Sea)	3,690	2,293
Zambezi (NW Zambia – S. Indian Ocean)	3,540	2,200
Other Notable Rivers		
St Lawrence (Minnesota, USA – Gulf of St Lawrence)	3,130	1,945
Ganges-Brahmaputra (R. Matsang, SW Tibet – Bay of Bengal)	2,900	1,800
Indus (R. Sengge, SW Tibet – N. Arabian Sea)	2,880	1,790
Danube (*Donau*) (Black Forest, SW Germany – Black Sea)	2,850	1,770
Tigris-Euphrates (R. Murat, E. Turkey – Persian Gulf)	2,740	1,700
Irrawaddy (R. Mali Hka, N. Burma – Andaman Sea)	2,090	1,300
Don (SE of Novomoskovsk – Sea of Azov)	1,969	1,224
British Isles		
Shannon (Co. Cavan, Rep. of Ireland – Atlantic Ocean)	386	240
Severn (Powys, Wales – Bristol Channel)	354	220
Thames (Gloucestershire, England – North Sea)	346	215
Tay (Perthshire, Scotland – North Sea)	188	117
Clyde (Lanarkshire, Scotland – Firth of Clyde)	158	98½
Tweed (Peeblesshire, Scotland – North Sea)	155	96½
Bann (Upper and Lower) (Co. Down, N. Ireland – Atlantic Ocean)	122	76

GREATEST WATERFALLS – BY HEIGHT

Waterfall (river and location)	*Total drop* metres	feet	*Greatest single leap* metres	feet
Angel (Carrao, Venezuela)	979	3,212	807	2,648
Tugela (Tugela, S. Africa)	947	3,110	410	1,350
Utigård (Jostedal Glacier, Norway)	800	2,625	600	1,970
Mongefossen (Monge, Norway)	774	2,540	—	—
Yosemite (Yosemite Creek, USA)	739	2,425	435	1,430
Østre Mardøla Foss (Mardals, Norway)	656	2,154	296	974
Tyssestrengane (Tysso, Norway)	646	2,120	289	948
Cuquenán (Arabopó, Venezuela)	610	2,000	—	—
Sutherland (Arthur, NZ)	580	1,904	248	815
*Kjellfossen (Naeröfjord, Norway)	561	1,841	149	490
British Isles (by country)				
Eas a' Chuàl Aluinn (Glas Bheinn, Sutherland, Scotland)	200	658		
Powerscourt Falls (Dargle, Co. Wicklow, Rep. of Ireland)	106	350		
Pistyll-y-Llyn (Powys/ Dyfed border, Wales)	c.73	230–240	(cascades)	
Pistyll Rhyadr (Clwyd/ Powys border, Wales)	71.5	235	(single leap)	
Caldron Snout (R. Tees, Cumbria/Durham, England)	60	200	(cascades)	

*Volume often so low the fall atomizes into a 'bridal veil'.

GREATEST WATERFALLS – BY VOLUME

Waterfall (river and location)	*Mean annual flow* m³/sec	galls/sec
Boyoma (R. Lualaba, Zaïre)	c.17,000	c.3,750,000
*Guairá (Alto Parañá, Brazil/ Paraguay)	13,300	2,930,000
Khône (Mekong, Laos)	11,500	2,530,000
Niagara (Horseshoe) (R. Niagara/Lake Erie–Lake Ontario)	3,000	670,000
Paulo Afonso (R. São Francisco, Brazil)	2,750	605,000
Urubupunga (Alto Parañá, Brazil)	2,800	625,000
Cataratas del Iguazú (R. Iguaçu, Brazil/ Argentina)	1,725	380,000
Patos-Maribando (Rio Grande, Brazil)	1,500	330,000

Waterfall (river and location)	*Mean annual flow* m³/sec	galls/sec
Victoria (Mosi-oa-tunya) (R. Zambezi, Zambia/ Zimbabwe)	1,000	220,000
Churchill (R. Churchill, Canada)	975	215,000
Kaieteur (R. Potaro, Guyana)	660	145,000

*Peak flow 50,000 m³/sec, 11,000,000 galls/sec.

TALLEST INHABITED BUILDINGS

Building and city	*Height* metres	feet
Sears Tower, Chicago	443	[1]1,454
World Trade Center, New York	417	[2]1,368
Empire State Building, New York	381	[3]1,250
Bank of China, Hong Kong	368	1,209
Amoco Building, Chicago	346	1,136
John Hancock Center, Chicago	343	1,127
C. & S. Plaza, Atlanta	324	1,063
Chrysler Building, New York	319	1,046
First Interstate World Center, Los Angeles	310	1,017
Texas Commerce Tower, Houston	305	1,002
Allied Bank Plaza, Houston	302	992

[1] With TV antennae 475.18 m/1,559 ft
[2] With TV antennae, 521.2 m/1,710 ft
[3] With TV tower (added 1950–1), 430.9 m/1,414 ft

TALLEST STRUCTURES

Structure and location	*Height* metres	feet
*Warszawa Radio Mast, Konstantynow, Poland	646	2,120
KTHI-TV Mast, Fargo, North Dakota	629	2,063
CN Tower, Metro Centre, Toronto, Canada	555	1,822

*Collapsed during renovation, August 1991.

LONGEST BRIDGES – BY SPAN

Bridge and location	*Length* metres	feet
SUSPENSION SPANS		
Humber Estuary, Humberside, England	1,410	4,626
Verrazano Narrows, Brooklyn–Staten I, USA	1,298	4,260
Golden Gate, San Francisco Bay, USA	1,280	4,200
Mackinac Straits, Michigan, USA	1,158	3,800
Bosporus, Istanbul, Turkey	1,074	3,524
George Washington, Hudson River, New York City, USA	1,067	3,500
Ponte 25 Abril (Tagus), Lisbon, Portugal	1,013	3,323
Firth of Forth (road), nr. Edinburgh, Scotland	1,006	3,300
Severn River, Severn Estuary, England	988	3,240
CANTILEVER SPANS		
Pont de Québec (rail-road), St Lawrence, Canada	548.6	1,800
Ravenswood, W. Virginia, USA	525.1	1,723
Firth of Forth (rail), nr. Edinburgh, Scotland	521.2	1,710
Minato, Osaka, Japan	510.0	1,673
Commodore Barry, Chester, Pennsylvania, USA	494.3	1,622
Greater New Orleans, Algiers, Louisiana, USA	480.0	1,575
Howrah (rail-road), Calcutta, India	457.2	1,500
STEEL ARCH SPANS		
New River Gorge, Fayetteville, W. Virginia, USA	518.2	1,700
Bayonne (Kill van Kull), Bayonne, NJ–Staten I, USA	503.5	1,652
Sydney Harbour, Sydney, Australia	502.9	1,650

The 'floating' bridging at Evergreen, Seattle, Washington State, USA is 3,839 m/12,596 ft long.

The longest stretch of bridgings of any kind are those between Mandeville and Jefferson, Louisiana, USA; the Lake Pontchartrain Causeway II 38.422 km/23.87 miles and Causeway I 38.352 km/23.83 miles.

LONGEST VEHICULAR TUNNELS

Tunnel and location	*Length* km	miles
*Seikan (rail), Tsugaru Channel, Japan	53.90	33.49
Moscow metro, Belyaevo–Medved Kovo, Moscow, Russia	30.70	19.07
Northern line tube, East Finchley–Morden, London	27.84	17.30
Oshimizu, Honshū, Japan	22.17	13.78
Simplon II (rail), Brigue, Switzerland–Iselle, Italy	19.82	12.31
Simplon I (rail), Brigue, Switzerland–Iselle, Italy	19.80	12.30
Shin-Kanmon (rail), Kanmon Strait, Japan	18.68	11.61
Great Appennine (rail), Vernio, Italy	18.49	11.49
St Gotthard (road), Göschenen–Airolo, Switzerland	16.32	10.14
Rokko (rail), Ōsaka–Kōbe, Japan	16.09	10.00

*Sub-aqueous

The twin rail Eurotunnel under the English Channel between Cheriton, Kent and Sargette, near Calais, is due to be opened in November 1993. The tunnels are 49.94 km/31.03 miles in length.

The longest non-vehicular tunnelling in the world is the Delaware Aqueduct in New York State, USA, constructed in 1937–44 to a length of 168.9 km/105 miles.

British Rail

	miles	yards
Severn, Bristol – Newport	4	484
Totley, Manchester – Sheffield	3	950
Standedge, Manchester – Huddersfield	3	66
Sodbury, Swindon – Bristol	2	924
Disley, Stockport – Sheffield	2	346
Ffestiniog, Llandudno – Blaenau Ffestiniog	2	338
Bramhope, Leeds – Harrogate	2	241
Cowburn, Manchester – Sheffield	2	182

LONGEST SHIP CANALS

	Length km	miles	*Min. depth* metres	feet
White Sea-Baltic (formerly Stalin) Canalized river; canal 51.5 km/32 miles; opened 1933	227	141.00	5.0	16.5
*Suez Links Red and Mediterranean Seas; opened 1869	162	100.60	12.9	42.3
V. I. Lenin Volga-Don Links Black and Caspian Seas; opened 1952	100	62.20	n/a	n/a
Kiel (or North Sea) Links North and Baltic Seas; opened 1895	98	60.90	13.7	45.0
*Houston Links inland city with sea; opened 1940	91	56.70	10.4	34.0
Alphonse XIII Gives Seville access to sea; opened 1926	85	53.00	7.6	25.0
Panama Links Pacific Ocean and Caribbean Sea; lake chain, 78.9 km/49 miles dug; opened 1914	82	50.71	12.5	41.0
Manchester Ship Links city with Irish Channel; opened 1894	64	39.70	8.5	28.0
Welland Circumvents Niagara Falls and Rapids; opened 1931	45	28.00	8.8	29.0
Brussels (Rupel Sea) Renders Brussels an inland port; opened 1922	32	19.80	6.4	21.0

*Has no locks

The first section of China's Grand Canal, running 1,780 km/1,107 miles from Beijing to Hangchou, was opened AD 610 but in undredged parts is today only 1.8 m/6 ft deep.

The longest boat canal in the world is the Volga-Baltic canal from Astrakhan to St Petersburg with 2,300 route km/1,850 miles.

The Seven Wonders of the World

I. The Pyramids of Egypt

The pyramids are found from Gizeh, near Cairo, to a southern limit 60 miles distant. The oldest is that of Zoser, at Saqqara, built *c.*2650 BC. The Great Pyramid of Cheops covers more than 13.12 acres and was originally 481 ft. in height and 756 × 756 ft. at the base.

II. The Hanging Gardens of Babylon

These adjoined Nebuchadnezzar's palace, 60 miles south of Baghdad. The terraced gardens, ranging from 75 ft. to 300 ft. above ground level, were watered from storage tanks on the highest terrace.

III. The Tomb of Mausolus

Built at Halicarnassus, in Asia Minor, by the widowed Queen Artemisia about 350 BC. The memorial originated the term mausoleum.

IV. The Temple of Artemis at Ephesus

Ionic temple erected about 350 BC in honour of the goddess and burned by the Goths in AD 262.

V. The Colossus of Rhodes

A bronze statue of Apollo, set up about 280 BC. According to legend it stood at the harbour entrance of the seaport of Rhodes.

VI. The Statue of Zeus

Located at Olympia in the plain of Elis, and constructed of marble inlaid with ivory and gold by the sculptor Phidias, about 430 BC.

VII. The Pharos of Alexandria

A marble watch tower and lighthouse on the island of Pharos in the harbour of Alexandria, built *c.*270 BC.

Distances from London by Air

The list of the distances in statute miles from London, Heathrow, to various cities (airport) abroad has been supplied by the publishers of *IATA/IAL Air Distances Manual*, Sunbury-on-Thames, Middx.

To	*Miles*
Abidjan	3,197
Abu Dhabi	3,425
Addis Ababa	3,675
Aden	3,670
Algiers	1,035
Amman	2,287
Amsterdam	230
Ankara	1,770
Athens	1,500
Auckland	11,404
Baghdad	2,551
Bahrain	3,163
Bangkok	5,928
Barbados	4,193
Barcelona	712
Basle	447
Beijing/Peking	5,063
Beirut	2,161
Belfast	325
Belgrade	1,056
Berlin (Tegel)	588
Bermuda	3,428
Berne	476
Bombay	4,478
Brasilia	5,452
Brisbane	10,273
Brussels	217
Bucharest	1,307
Budapest	923
Buenos Aires	6,915
Cairo	2,194
Calcutta	4,958
Canberra	10,563
Cape Town	6,011
Caracas	4,639
Casablanca	1,300
Chicago (O'Hare)	3,941
Cologne	331
Colombo	5,411
Copenhagen	608
Dakar	2,706
Damascus	2,223
Dar-es-Salaam	4,662
Darwin	8,613
Delhi	4,180
Detroit	3,754
Dhaka	4,976
Doha	3,253
Dubai	3,414
Dublin	279
Durban	5,937
Düsseldorf	310
Entebbe	4,033
Frankfurt	406
Freetown	3,046
Geneva	468
Gibraltar	1,084
Gothenburg (Landvetter)	664
Hamburg	463
Harare	5,156
Havana	4,647
Helsinki (Vantaa)	1,147
Hong Kong	5,990
Honolulu	7,220
Istanbul	1,560
Jeddah	2,947
Johannesburg	5,634
Karachi	3,935
Khartoum	3,071
Kingston, Jamaica	4,668
Kuala Lumpur	6,557
Kuwait	2,903
Lagos	3,107
Larnaca, Cyprus	2,036
Lima	6,303
Lisbon	972
Lomé	3,129
Los Angeles	5,439
Madrid	773
Malta	1,305
Manila	6,685
Marseilles	614
Mauritius	6,075
Mexico City	5,529
Milan	609
Montego Bay	4,687
Montevideo	6,841
Montreal (Mirabel)	3,241
Moscow (Sheremetievo)	1,557
Munich	588
Nairobi	4,248
Naples	1,011
Nassau	4,333
New York (J. F. Kennedy)	3,440
Nice	645
Oporto	806
Oslo (Fornebu)	723
Ottawa	3,321
Palma, Majorca	836
Paris (Charles de Gaulle)	215
Paris (Le Bourget)	215
Paris (Orly)	227
Perth, Australia	9,008
Port of Spain, Trinidad	4,405
Prague	649
Reykjavik	1,167
Rhodes	1,743
Rio de Janeiro	5,745
Riyadh	3,067
Rome (Fiumicino)	895
St Petersburg	1,314
Salzburg	651
San Francisco	5,351
Seoul	5,507
Shannon	369
Singapore	6,756
Sofia	1,266
Stockholm (Arlanda)	908
Sydney, Australia	10,568
Tangier	1,120
Tehran	2,741
Tel Aviv	2,227
Tokyo (Narita)	5,956
Toronto	3,545
Tripoli	1,468
Tunis	1,137
Turin (Caselle)	570
Valencia	826
Vancouver	4,707
Venice (Tessera)	715
Vienna (Schwechat)	790
Warsaw	912
Washington	3,665
Wellington	11,692
Yangon/Rangoon	5,582
Zagreb	848
Zürich	490

The United Kingdom

The United Kingdom comprises Great Britain (England, Wales and Scotland) and Northern Ireland. The Isle of Man and the Channel Islands are Crown dependencies with their own legislative systems, and not a part of the United Kingdom.

AREA (as at 31 March 1981)

	Land miles²	Land km²	Inland water* miles²	Inland water* km²	Total miles²	Total km²
UK	93,027	240,939	1,242	3,218	94,269	244,157
England	50,085	129,720	293	758	50,377	130,478
Wales	7,968	20,636	50	130	8,018	20,766
Scotland	29,767	77,097	653	1,692	30,420	78,789
Northern Ireland†	5,206	13,483	246	638	5,452	14,121

The area of the Isle of Man is 221 sq. miles and of the Channel Islands is 75 sq. miles.

*Excluding tidal water.

†Excluding certain tidal waters that are parts of statutory areas in Northern Ireland.

POPULATION

The first official census of population in England, Wales and Scotland was taken in 1801 and a census has been taken every ten years since, except in 1941 when there was no census because of war. The last official census in the United Kingdom was taken on 21 April 1991 and the next is due in April 2001.

The first official census of population in Ireland was taken in 1841. However, all figures given below refer only to the area which is now Northern Ireland. Figures for Northern Ireland in 1921 and 1931 are estimates based on the censuses taken in 1926 and 1937 respectively.

Estimates of the population of England before 1801, calculated from the number of baptisms, burials and marriages, are:

1570	4,160,221	1670	5,773,646
1600	4,811,718	1700	6,045,008
1630	5,600,517	1750	6,517,035

Thousands	United Kingdom Total	Male	Female	England and Wales Total	Male	Female	Scotland Total	Male	Female	Northern Ireland Total	Male	Female
Census Results 1801–1991												
1801	—	—	—	8,893	4,255	4,638	1,608	739	869	—	—	—
1811	13,368	6,368	7,000	10,165	4,874	5,291	1,806	826	980	—	—	—
1821	15,472	7,498	7,974	12,000	5,850	6,150	2,092	983	1,109	—	—	—
1831	17,835	8,647	9,188	13,897	6,771	7,126	2,364	1,114	1,250	—	—	—
1841	20,183	9,819	10,364	15,914	7,778	8,137	2,620	1,242	1,378	1,649	800	849
1851	22,259	10,855	11,404	17,928	8,781	9,146	2,889	1,376	1,513	1,443	698	745
1861	24,525	11,894	12,631	20,066	9,776	10,290	3,062	1,450	1,612	1,396	668	728
1871	27,431	13,309	14,122	22,712	11,059	11,653	3,360	1,603	1,757	1,359	647	712
1881	31,015	15,060	15,955	25,974	12,640	13,335	3,736	1,799	1,936	1,305	621	684
1891	34,264	16,593	17,671	29,003	14,060	14,942	4,026	1,943	2,083	1,236	590	646
1901	38,237	18,492	19,745	32,528	15,729	16,799	4,472	2,174	2,298	1,237	590	647
1911	42,082	20,357	21,725	36,070	17,446	18,625	4,761	2,309	2,452	1,251	603	648
1921	44,027	21,033	22,994	37,887	18,075	19,811	4,882	2,348	2,535	1,258	610	648
1931	46,038	22,060	23,978	39,952	19,133	20,819	4,843	2,326	2,517	1,243	601	642
1951	50,225	24,118	26,107	43,758	21,016	22,742	5,096	2,434	2,662	1,371	668	703
1961	52,709	25,481	27,228	46,105	22,304	23,801	5,179	2,483	2,697	1,425	694	731
1971	55,515	26,952	28,562	48,750	23,683	25,067	5,229	2,515	2,714	1,536	755	781
1981	55,848	27,104	28,742	49,155	23,873	25,281	5,131	2,466	2,664	1,533*	750	783
1991p	55,500	—	—	48,960	—	—	4,957	—	—	1,583	—	—
Resident Population: Projections (mid-year)†												
1991	57,561	28,099	29,463	50,903	24,865	26,038	5,068	2,452	2,615	1,590	781	809
2001	59,174	29,069	30,105	52,526	25,819	26,708	5,026	2,449	2,577	1,622	802	820
2011	60,033	29,630	30,403	53,510	26,423	27,087	4,900	2,400	2,500	1,623	806	816
2021	60,743	30,049	30,694	54,411	26,927	27,484	4,727	2,322	2,405	1,605	800	805
2031	61,068	30,213	30,855	54,977	27,208	27,769	4,524	2,224	2,300	1,567	782	785

p preliminary. * figures include 44,500 non-enumerated persons. † projections are 1989 based.

Sources: HMSO–Annual Abstract 1992; OPCS–1991 Census (preliminary reports)

ISLANDS: Census Results 1901–91

	Isle of Man			Jersey			Guernsey*		
	Total	Male	Female	Total	Male	Female	Total	Male	Female
1901	54,752	25,496	29,256	52,576	23,940	28,636	40,446	19,652	20,794
1911	52,016	23,937	28,079	51,898	24,014	27,884	41,858	20,661	21,197
1921	60,284	27,329	32,955	49,701	22,438	27,263	38,315	18,246	20,069
1931	49,308	22,443	26,865	50,462	23,424	27,038	40,643	19,659	20,984
1951	55,123	25,749	29,464	57,296	27,282	30,014	43,652	21,221	22,431
1961	48,151	22,060	26,091	57,200	27,200	30,000	45,068	21,671	23,397
1971	56,289	26,461	29,828	72,532	35,423	37,109	51,458	24,792	26,666
1981	64,679	30,901	33,778	77,000	37,000	40,000	53,313	25,701	27,612
1991	69,788	33,693	36,095	84,082	40,862	43,220	58,867	28,297	30,570

* Population of Guernsey, Herm, Jethou and Lithou. Figures for 1901–71 record all persons present on census night; census figures for 1981 and 1991 record all persons resident in the islands on census night.

Sources: 1991 Census

RESIDENT POPULATION (mid-year estimate)

	1980	1990
United Kingdom	56,330,000	57,411,000
England	46,787,000	47,838,000
Wales	2,816,000	2,881,000
Scotland	5,194,000	5,102,000
Northern Ireland	1,533,000	1,589,000

Source: HMSO – Annual Abstract of Statistics 1992

RESIDENT POPULATION BY AGE AND SEX 1990

Males	*Under 16*	*Over 65**
United Kingdom	5,960,000	3,599,000
England	4,920,000	3,037,000
Wales	300,000	192,000
Scotland	524,000	294,000
Northern Ireland	215,000	76,000
Females		
United Kingdom	5,661,000	6,891,000
England	4,674,000	5,758,000
Wales	284,000	369,000
Scotland	498,000	609,000
Northern Ireland	205,000	155,000

*Females over 60

Source: HMSO – Population Trends 68

RESIDENT POPULATION BY ETHNIC GROUP

1988–90 Average (Great Britain)

Ethnic group	*Estimated population*	*Percentage*
West Indian/Guyanese	461,000	18
African	136,000	5
Indian	786,000	30
Pakistani	462,000	18
Bangladeshi	108,000	4
Chinese	135,000	5
Arab	64,000	2
Mixed	308,000	12
Other	163,000	6
Total ethnic minority groups	2,624,000	100
White	51,689,000	—
Not stated	509,000	—
All ethnic groups	54,823,000	—

Source: HMSO – Population Trends 67

IMMIGRATION 1990

Acceptances for settlement in the UK by nationality

Region	*Number of persons*
Europe: total	5,080
European Community	1,760
Other Western Europe	2,690
Eastern Europe	630
Americas: total	6,650
USA	3,660
Canada	850
Africa: total	8,250
Asia: total	23,270
Indian sub-continent	12,980
Middle East	2,980
Australasia: total	5,170
Other	2,570
Stateless	1,400
Total	52,400
Foreign	20,700
Commonwealth	31,690
Old Commonwealth	6,030
New Commonwealth	25,660

Source: HMSO – Annual Abstract of Statistics 1992

POPULATION DENSITY (Average)

Persons per hectare

	1981	1991
England	3.55	3.54
Wales	1.34	1.35
Scotland	0.66	0.64
Northern Ireland	1.12	n/a

Sources: Census 1981; Census 1991 (preliminary figures)

LIVE BIRTHS AND BIRTH RATES 1990

	Live births	*Birth rate**
United Kingdom	798,612	13.9
England and Wales	706,140	13.9
Scotland	65,973	12.9
Northern Ireland	26,499	16.7

*Live births per 1,000 population

Source: HMSO – Annual Abstract of Statistics 1992

LEGAL ABORTIONS 1990 (ENGLAND AND WALES)

Age Group	*Number*
Under 16	3,300
16–19	35,000
20–34	115,100
35–44	17,800
Over 45	390
Age not stated	10
Total	171,600

Source: HMSO – Population Trends 68

BIRTH RATE OUTSIDE MARRIAGE

Rate per 1,000 live births

	1981	1990
United Kingdom	125	279†
England	129	283
Wales	112	293
Scotland	122	271

†Provisional
Source: HMSO – Population Trends 68

MARRIAGE AND DIVORCE 1989

	Marriages	*Divorces**
United Kingdom	392,042	—
England and Wales	346,697	150,872
Scotland	35,326	11,659
Northern Ireland	10,019	2,385

*Decrees absolute granted (in Northern Ireland, divorce petitions filed)

Source: HMSO – Annual Abstract of Statistics 1992

DEATHS AND DEATH RATES 1990

Males	*Deaths*	*Death rate**
United Kingdom	314,601†	11.2†
England and Wales	277,336	—
Scotland	29,617	—
Northern Ireland	7,648†	—
Females		
United Kingdom	327,198	11.1†
England and Wales	287,510	—
Scotland	31,910	—
Northern Ireland	7,778†	—

*Deaths per 1,000 population
†Provisional
Source: HMSO – Annual Abstract of Statistics 1992

INFANT MORTALITY 1990

Deaths of infants under 1 year of age per 1,000 live births

	Number
United Kingdom	7.9†
England and Wales	7.9
Scotland	7.7
Northern Ireland	7.5†

†Provisional
Source: HMSO – Annual Abstract of Statistics 1992

EXPECTATION OF LIFE LIFE TABLES 1987–9 (INTERIM FIGURES)

	England and Wales		Scotland		Northern Ireland	
Age	Male	Female	Male	Female	Male	Female
0	72.7	78.2	70.5	76.4	71.1	77.1
5	68.5	74.0	66.4	72.1	66.9	72.8
10	63.6	69.0	61.4	67.1	62.0	67.8
15	58.7	64.1	56.5	62.2	57.0	62.9
20	53.9	59.2	51.7	57.3	52.3	58.0
25	49.1	54.2	47.0	52.4	47.6	53.1
30	44.3	49.3	42.2	47.5	42.9	48.2
35	39.5	44.5	37.5	42.6	38.2	43.3
40	34.7	39.6	32.8	37.8	33.5	38.5
45	30.1	34.9	28.2	33.1	28.8	33.8
50	25.6	30.3	23.8	28.6	24.4	29.2
55	21.3	25.8	19.7	24.2	20.1	24.8
60	17.4	21.6	16.1	20.2	16.3	20.6
65	13.9	17.7	12.8	16.5	13.0	16.8
70	10.9	14.1	10.1	13.1	10.1	13.3
75	8.3	10.9	7.7	10.4	7.7	10.1
80	6.3	8.1	5.8	7.6	5.7	7.3
85	4.8	5.8	4.3	5.4	4.1	5.1

Source: HMSO – Annual Abstract of Statistics 1992

DEATHS ANALYSED BY CAUSE, 1990

	England & Wales	*Scotland*	*N. Ireland*†
TOTAL DEATHS	564,846	61,527	15,426
DEATHS FROM NATURAL CAUSES	543,682	58,887	14,727
Infections and parasitic diseases	2,446	285	46
Intestinal infectious diseases	187	13	3
Tuberculosis of respiratory system	313	31	11
Other tuberculosis, including late effects	264	31	1
Whooping cough	7	1	—
Meningococcal infection	169	16	4
Measles	1	—	1
Malaria	3	—	—
Syphilis	18	1	—
Neoplasms	144,577	15,137	3,525
Malignant neoplasm of stomach	8,712	877	219
Malignant neoplasm of trachea, bronchus and lung	34,375	4,123	771
Malignant neoplasm of breast	13,741	1,257	295
Malignant neoplasm of uterus	3,235	298	68
Leukaemia	3,488	312	79
Benign and unspecified neoplasms	1,330	140	51
Endocrine, nutritional and metabolic diseases and immunity disorders	10,249	733	78
Diabetes mellitus	7,933	512	41
Nutritional deficiencies	125	18	1
Other metabolic and immunity disorders	1,512	156	27
Diseases of blood and blood-forming organs	2,427	169	35
Anaemias	1,217	73	19
Mental disorders	13,395	986	58
Diseases of nervous system and sense organs	11,644	890	177
Meningitis	203	26	15
Diseases of the circulatory system	259,247	29,437	7,110
Rheumatic heart disease	2,174	205	70
Hypertensive disease	3,269	260	81
Ischaemic heart disease	148,159	17,028	4,327
Diseases of pulmonary circulation and other forms of heart disease	19,847	2,305	625
Cerebrovascular disease	66,769	7,998	1,642
Diseases of the respiratory system	61,018	7,231	2,781
Influenza	791	126	48
Pneumonia	26,817	3,918	1,855
Bronchitis, emphysema	7,081	490	160
Asthma	1,858	148	49
Diseases of the digestive system	18,429	2,035	392
Ulcer of stomach and duodenum	4,355	370	90
Appendicitis	148	7	3
Hernia of abdominal cavity and other intestinal obstruction	1,988	174	41
Chronic liver disease and cirrhosis	3,063	490	70
Diseases of the genito-urinary system	7,317	817	251
Nephritis, nephrotic syndrome and nephrosis	3,919	538	159
Hyperplasia of prostate	450	11	4
Complications of pregnancy, childbirth, etc.	57	4	—
Abortion	10	1	—
Diseases of the skin and subcutaneous tissue	823	79	21
Diseases of the musculo-skeletal system	5,286	301	59
Congenital anomalies	1,621	206	85
Certain conditions originating in the perinatal period	249	206	68
Birth trauma, hypoxia, birth asphyxia and other respiratory conditions	68	104	37
Signs, symptoms and ill-defined conditions	4,897	371	41
Sudden infant death syndrome	1,079	132	14
DEATHS FROM ACCIDENTS AND VIOLENCE	17,943	2,640	699
All accidents	11,721	1,784	456
Motor vehicle accidents	4,968	547	186
Suicide and self-inflicted injury	3,950	535	158
All other external causes	2,272	321	85

† Provisional.
Source: HMSO – Annual Abstract of Statistics 1992

The National Flag

The national flag of the United Kingdom is the Union Flag, generally known as the Union Jack. (The name 'Union Jack' derives from the use of the Union Flag on the jack-staff of naval vessels.)

The Union Flag is a combination of the cross of St George, patron saint of England, the cross of St Andrew, patron saint of Scotland, and a cross similar to that of St Patrick, patron saint of Ireland.

Cross of St George: cross gules in a field argent (red cross on a white ground).
Cross of St Andrew: saltire argent in a field azure (white diagonal cross on a blue ground).
Cross of St Patrick: saltire gules in a field argent (red diagonal cross on a white ground).

The Union Flag was first introduced in 1606 after the union of England and Scotland. The cross of St Patrick was added in 1801 after the union of Great Britain and Ireland.

DAYS FOR FLYING FLAGS

The correct orientation of the Union Flag when flying is with the broader diagonal band of white uppermost in the hoist (i.e. near the pole) and the narrower diagonal band of white uppermost in the fly (i.e. farthest from the pole).

It is the practice to fly the Union Flag daily on some Customs Houses. In all other cases, flags are flown on government buildings by command of The Queen.

Days for hoisting the Union Flag are notified to the Department of the Environment by The Queen's command and communicated by the department to the other government departments. On the days appointed, the Union Flag is flown on all government buildings in London and elsewhere in the United Kingdom from 8 a.m. to sunset.

The Queen's Accession	6 February
Birthday of The Duke of York	19 February
St David's Day (in Wales only)	1 March
Commonwealth Day (1993)	8 March
Birthday of The Prince Edward	10 March
Birthday of The Queen	21 April
St George's Day (in England only) Where a building has two or more flagstaffs, the Cross of St George may be flown in addition to the Union Flag, but not in a superior position	23 April
Coronation Day	2 June
Birthday of The Duke of Edinburgh	10 June
The Queen's Official Birthday (1993)	12 June
Birthday of The Princess of Wales	1 July
Birthday of Queen Elizabeth the Queen Mother	4 August
Birthday of The Princess Royal	15 August
Birthday of The Princess Margaret	21 August
Remembrance Sunday (1993)	14 November
Birthday of The Prince of Wales	14 November
The Queen's Wedding Day	20 November
St Andrew's Day (in Scotland only)	30 November
The occasion of the opening and closing of Parliament by The Queen, whether or not Her Majesty performs the ceremony in person (on government buildings in the Greater London area only)	

Flags at Half-Mast

Flags are flown at half-mast on the following occasions:

(a) From the announcement of the death up to the funeral of the Sovereign, except on Proclamation Day, when flags are hoisted right up from 11 a.m. to sunset
(b) The funerals of members of the Royal Family, subject to special commands from The Queen in each case
(c) The funerals of foreign rulers, subject to special commands from The Queen in each case
(d) The funerals of Prime Ministers and ex-Prime Ministers of the United Kingdom
(e) Other occasions by special command of The Queen

On occasions when days for flying flags coincide with days for flying flags at half-mast, the following rules are observed. Flags are flown:

(a) although a member of the Royal Family, or a near relative of the Royal Family, may be lying dead, unless special commands be received from The Queen to the contrary
(b) although it may be the day of the funeral of a foreign ruler

If the body of a very distinguished subject is lying at a government office, the flag may fly at half-mast on that office until the body has left (provided it is a day on which the flag would fly) and then the flag is to be hoisted right up. On all other government buildings the flag will fly as usual.

The Royal Standard

The Royal Standard is hoisted only when The Queen is actually present in the building, and never when Her Majesty is passing in procession.

The Royal Family

THE SOVEREIGN

Elizabeth II, by the Grace of God, of the United Kingdom of Great Britain and Northern Ireland and of her other Realms and Territories Queen, Head of the Commonwealth, Defender of the Faith

Her Majesty Elizabeth Alexandra Mary of Windsor, elder daughter of King George VI and of HM Queen Elizabeth the Queen Mother
Born 21 April 1926, at 17 Bruton Street, London W1
Ascended the throne 6 February 1952
Crowned 2 June 1953, at Westminster Abbey
Married 20 November 1947, in Westminster Abbey, HRH The Duke of Edinburgh
Official residences: Buckingham Palace, London SW1; Windsor Castle, Berks; Palace of Holyroodhouse, Edinburgh
Private residences: Sandringham, Norfolk; Balmoral Castle, Aberdeenshire
Office: Buckingham Palace, London SW1A 1AA. Tel: 071-930 4832

HUSBAND OF HM THE QUEEN

HRH THE PRINCE PHILIP, DUKE OF EDINBURGH, KG, KT, OM, GBE, AC, QSO, PC, Ranger of Windsor Park
Born 10 June 1921, son of Prince and Princess Andrew of Greece and Denmark (*see* page 135), naturalized a British subject 1947, created Duke of Edinburgh, Earl of Merioneth and Baron Greenwich 1947

CHILDREN OF HM THE QUEEN

HRH THE PRINCE OF WALES (Prince Charles Philip Arthur George), KG, KT, GCB and Great Master of the Order of the Bath, AK, QSO, PC, ADC(P)
Born 14 November 1948, created Prince of Wales and Earl of Chester 1958, succeeded as Duke of Cornwall, Duke of Rothesay, Earl of Carrick and Baron Renfrew, Lord of the Isles and Prince and Great Steward of Scotland 1952
Married 29 July 1981 Lady Diana Frances Spencer, now HRH The Princess of Wales (*born* 1 July 1961, youngest daughter of the 8th Earl Spencer and the Hon. Mrs Shand Kydd)
Issue:
(1) HRH Prince William of Wales (Prince William Arthur Philip Louis), *born* 21 June 1982
(2) HRH Prince Henry of Wales (Prince Henry Charles Albert David), *born* 15 September 1984
Residences: Kensington Palace, London W8; Highgrove, Doughton, Tetbury, Glos.
Office: St James's Palace, London SW1A 1BS. Tel: 071-930 4832

HRH THE PRINCESS ROYAL (Princess Anne Elizabeth Alice Louise), GCVO
Born 15 August 1950, declared The Princess Royal 1987
Married 14 November 1973 Captain Mark Anthony Peter Phillips, CVO (*born* 22 September 1948); marriage dissolved 1992
Issue:
(1) Peter Mark Andrew Phillips, *born* 15 November 1977
(2) Zara Anne Elizabeth Phillips, *born* 15 May 1981
Residence: Gatcombe Park, Minchinhampton, Glos.
Office: Buckingham Palace, London SW1A 1AA. Tel: 071-930 4832

HRH THE DUKE OF YORK (Prince Andrew Albert Christian Edward), CVO, ADC(P)
Born 19 February 1960, created Duke of York, Earl of Inverness and Baron Killyleagh 1986
Married 23 July 1986 Sarah Margaret Ferguson, now HRH The Duchess of York (*born* 15 October 1959, younger daughter of Major Ronald Ferguson and Mrs Hector Barrantes), *separated* 1992
Issue:
(1) HRH Princess Beatrice of York (Princess Beatrice Elizabeth Mary), *born* 8 August 1988
(2) HRH Princess Eugenie of York (Princess Eugenie Victoria Helena), *born* 23 March 1990
Residences: Buckingham Palace, London SW1; Sunninghill Park, Ascot, Berks.
Office: Buckingham Palace, London SW1 1AA. Tel: 071-930 4832

HRH THE PRINCE EDWARD (Prince Edward Antony Richard Louis), CVO
Born 10 March 1964
Residence and Office: Buckingham Palace, London SW1A 1AA. Tel: 071-930 4832

SISTER OF HM THE QUEEN

HRH THE PRINCESS MARGARET, COUNTESS OF SNOWDON (Princess Margaret Rose), CI, GCVO, Royal Victorian Chain, Dame Grand Cross of the Order of St John of Jerusalem
Born 21 August 1930, younger daughter of King George VI and HM Queen Elizabeth the Queen Mother
Married 6 May 1960 Antony Charles Robert Armstrong-Jones, GCVO (*born* 7 March 1930, created Earl of Snowdon 1961, Constable of Caernarvon Castle); marriage dissolved 1978
Issue:
(1) David Albert Charles, Viscount Linley, *born* 3 November 1961
(2) Lady Sarah Armstrong-Jones (Sarah Frances Elizabeth), *born* 1 May 1964
Residence and Office: Kensington Palace, London W8 4PU. Tel: 071-930 3141

MOTHER OF HM THE QUEEN

HM QUEEN ELIZABETH THE QUEEN MOTHER (Elizabeth Angela Marguerite), Lady of the Garter, Lady of the Thistle, CI, GMVO, GBE, Dame Grand Cross of the Order of St John, Royal Victorian Chain, Lord Warden and

Admiral of the Cinque Ports and Constable of Dover Castle
Born 4 August 1900, youngest daughter of the 14th Earl of Strathmore and Kinghorne
Married 26 April 1923 (as Lady Elizabeth Bowes-Lyon) Prince Albert, Duke of York, afterwards King George VI (*see* page 134)
Residences: Clarence House, St James's Palace, London SW1; Royal Lodge, Windsor Great Park, Berks; Castle of Mey, Caithness
Office: Clarence House, St James's Palace, London SW1A 1BA. Tel: 071-930 3141

AUNT OF HM THE QUEEN

HRH PRINCESS ALICE, DUCHESS OF GLOUCESTER (Alice Christabel), GCB, CI, GCVO, GBE, Grand Cordon of Al Kamal
Born 25 December 1901, third daughter of the 7th Duke of Buccleuch and Queensberry
Married 6 November 1935 (as Lady Alice Montagu-Douglas-Scott) Prince Henry, Duke of Gloucester, third son of King George V (*see* page 134)

COUSINS OF HM THE QUEEN

HRH THE DUKE OF GLOUCESTER (Prince Richard Alexander Walter George), GCVO, Grand Prior of the Order of St John of Jerusalem
Born 26 August 1944
Married 8 July 1972 Birgitte Eva van Deurs, now HRH The Duchess of Gloucester, GCVO (*born* 20 June 1946, daughter of Asger Henriksen and Vivian van Deurs)
Issue:
(1) Alexander Patrick Gregers Richard, Earl of Ulster, *born* 24 October 1974
(2) Lady Davina Windsor (Davina Elizabeth Alice Benedikte), *born* 19 November 1977
(3) Lady Rose Windsor (Rose Victoria Birgitte Louise), *born* 1 March 1980
Residences: Kensington Palace, London W8; Barnwell Manor, Peterborough, Northants PE8 5PJ
Office: Kensington Palace, London W8 4PU. Tel: 071-937 6374

HRH THE DUKE OF KENT (Prince Edward George Nicholas Paul Patrick), KG, GCMG, GCVO, ADC(P)
Born 9 October 1935
Married 8 June 1961 Katharine Lucy Mary Worsley, now HRH The Duchess of Kent, GCVO (*born* 22 February 1933, daughter of Sir William Worsley, Bt.)
Issue:
(1) George Philip Nicholas, Earl of St Andrews, *born* 26 June 1962, *married* 9 January 1988 Sylvana Tomaselli, and has issue, Edward Edmund Maximilian George, Baron Downpatrick, *born* 2 December 1988
(2) Lady Helen Taylor (Helen Marina Lucy), *born* 28 April 1964, *married* 18 July 1992 Timothy Verner Taylor
(3) Lord Nicholas Windsor (Nicholas Charles Edward Jonathan), *born* 25 July 1970
Residences: York House, St James's Palace, London SW1; Crocker End House, Nettlebed, Oxon.
Office: York House, St James's Palace, London SW1A 1BQ. Tel: 071-930 4872

HRH PRINCESS ALEXANDRA, THE HON. LADY OGILVY (Princess Alexandra Helen Elizabeth Olga Christabel), GCVO
Born 25 December 1936
Married 24 April 1963 The Hon. Sir Angus Ogilvy, KCVO (*born* 14 September 1928, second son of 12th Earl of Airlie)
Issue:
(1) James Robert Bruce Ogilvy, *born* 29 February 1964, *married* 30 July 1988 Julia Rawlinson
(2) Marina Victoria Alexandra, Mrs Mowatt, *born* 31 July 1966, *married* 2 February 1990 Paul Mowatt, and has issue, Zenouska Mowatt, *born* 26 May 1990
Residence: Thatched House Lodge, Richmond Park, Surrey
Office: 22 Friary Court, St James's Palace, London SW1A 1BJ. Tel: 071-930 1860

HRH PRINCE MICHAEL OF KENT (Prince Michael George Charles Franklin), KCVO
Born 4 July 1942
Married 30 June 1978 Baroness Marie-Christine Agnes Hedwig Ida von Reibnitz, now HRH Princess Michael of Kent (*born* 15 January 1945, daughter of Baron Gunther von Reibnitz)
Issue:
(1) Lord Frederick Windsor (Frederick Michael George David Louis), *born* 6 April 1979
(2) Lady Gabriella Windsor (Gabriella Marina Alexandra Ophelia), *born* 23 April 1981
Residences: Kensington Palace, London W8; Nether Lypiatt Manor, Stroud, Glos.
Office: Kensington Palace, London W8 4PU. Tel: 071-938 3519

ORDER OF SUCCESSION

1 HRH The Prince of Wales
2 HRH Prince William of Wales
3 HRH Prince Henry of Wales
4 HRH The Duke of York
5 HRH Princess Beatrice of York
6 HRH Princess Eugenie of York
7 HRH The Prince Edward
8 HRH The Princess Royal
9 Peter Phillips
10 Zara Phillips
11 HRH The Princess Margaret, Countess of Snowdon
12 Viscount Linley
13 Lady Sarah Armstrong-Jones
14 HRH The Duke of Gloucester
15 Earl of Ulster
16 Lady Davina Windsor
17 Lady Rose Windsor
18 HRH The Duke of Kent
19 Baron Downpatrick
20 Lord Nicholas Windsor
21 Lady Helen Taylor
22 Lord Frederick Windsor
23 Lady Gabriella Windsor
24 HRH Princess Alexandra, the Hon. Lady Ogilvy
25 James Ogilvy
26 Marina, Mrs Paul Mowatt
27 Zenouska Mowatt

The Earl of St Andrews and HRH Prince Michael of Kent lost the right of succession to the throne under the Act of Settlement 1701, through marriage to a Roman Catholic. However, their children and descendants remain in succession, provided that they are in communion with the Church of England.

Royal Households

THE QUEEN'S HOUSEHOLD

Lord Chamberlain, The Earl of Airlie, KT, GCVO, PC.
Lord Steward, The Viscount Ridley, KG, TD.
Master of the Horse, The Lord Somerleyton.
Treasurer of the Household, D. Heathcoat-Amery, MP.
Comptroller of the Household, D. Lightbown, MP.
Vice-Chamberlain, S. Chapman, MP.

Gold Stick, Maj.-Gen. Lord Michael Fitzalan-Howard, GCVO, CB, CBE, MC; Gen. Sir Desmond Fitzpatrick, GCB, DSO, MBE, MC.
Vice-Adm. of the United Kingdom, Adm. Sir Anthony Morton, GBE, KCB.
Rear-Adm. of the United Kingdom, Adm. Sir James Eberle, GCB.
First and Principal Naval Aide-de-Camp, Adm. Sir Julian Oswald, GCB.
Flag Aide de Camp, Adm. Sir John Kerr, KCB.
Aides-de-Camp-General, Gen. Sir David Ramsbotham, KCB, CBE; Gen. Sir Peter Inge, GCB; Gen. Sir John Waters, KCB, CBE.
Air Aides-de-Camp, Air Chief Marshal Sir Peter Harding, GCB; Air Chief Marshal Sir Roger Palin, KCB, OBE.

Mistress of the Robes, The Duchess of Grafton, GCVO.
Ladies of the Bedchamber, The Countess of Airlie, CVO; The Lady Farnham.
Extra Ladies of the Bedchamber, The Marchioness of Abergavenny, DCVO; The Countess of Cromer, CVO..
Women of the Bedchamber, Hon. Mary Morrison, DCVO; Lady Susan Hussey, DCVO; Mrs John Dugdale, DCVO; The Lady Elton.
Extra Women of the Bedchamber, Mrs John Woodroffe, CVO; Lady Rose Baring, DCVO; Mrs Michael Wall, DCVO; Lady Abel Smith, DCVO; Mrs Robert de Pass.
Equerries, Lt.-Col. B. A. Stewart-Wilson, CVO; Capt. J. Patrick; Capt. P. Hopkins (temp.).
Extra Equerries, Vice-Adm. Sir Peter Ashmore, KCB, KCVO, DSC; Lt.-Col. The Lord Charteris of Amisfield, GCB, GCVO, OBE, QSO, PC; Air Cdre the Hon. T. Elworthy, CBE; The Rt Hon. Sir Robert Fellowes, KCB, KCVO; Sir Edward Ford, KCB, KCVO, ERD; Rear-Adm. Sir John Garnier, KCVO, CBE; Rear-Adm. Sir Paul Greening, KCVO, CBE; Brig. Sir Geoffrey Hardy-Roberts, KCVO, CB, CBE; The Rt. Hon. Sir William Heseltine, GCB, GCVO, AC, QSO; Rear-Adm. Sir Hugh Janion, KCVO; Lt.-Col. Sir John Johnston, GCVO, MC; Lt.-Col. A. Mather, OBE; Sir Peter Miles, KCVO; Lt.-Col. Sir John Miller, GCVO, DSO, MC; Air Cdre Sir Dennis Mitchell, KBE, CVO, DFC, AFC; The Lord Moore of Wolvercote, GCB, GCVO, CMG, QSO; Lt.-Col. Sir Eric Penn, GCVO, OBE, MC; Lt.-Gen. Sir John Richards, KCB; Lt.-Col. W. H. M. Ross, OBE; Air Vice-Marshal Sir John Severne, KCVO, OBE, AFC; Gp Capt P. Townsend, CVO, DSO, DFC; Rear-Adm. Sir Richard Trowbridge, KCVO; Lt.-Col. G. West, CVO; Air Cdre Sir Archie Winskill, KCVO, CBE, DFC, AE.

THE PRIVATE SECRETARY'S OFFICE
Buckingham Palace, London SW1A 1AA

Private Secretary to The Queen, The Rt Hon. Sir Robert Fellowes, KCB, KCVO.
Deputy Private Secretary, Sir Kenneth Scott, KCVO, CMG.
Assistant Private Secretary, R. B. Janvrin, LVO.
Press Secretary, C. V. Anson, LVO.
Deputy Press Secretary, J. Haslam, LVO.
Assistant Press Secretaries, G. Crawford; R. W. Arbiter.
Chief Clerk, Mrs G. S. Coulson, MVO.
Secretary to the Private Secretary, Mrs J. Bean, LVO.
Clerks, Miss A. Freeman; Mrs A. Hickson; Mrs G. Middleburgh; Miss E. Raikes; Miss H. Spiller; Miss H. Staveley; Mrs E. Walsh Waring.
Press Office, Miss K. McGrigor, MVO; Mrs R. Murdo-Smith, LVO; Miss C. Sillars; Miss L. Stewart.
Lady-in-Waiting's Office, Mrs D. Phillips; Mrs J. Vince.

THE QUEEN'S ARCHIVES
Round Tower, Windsor Castle, Berks.

Keeper of The Queen's Archives, The Rt Hon. Sir Robert Fellowes, KCB, KCVO.
Assistant Keeper, O. Everett, CVO.
Registrar, Lady de Bellaigue, MVO.
Assistant Registrar, Miss P. Clark.
Curator of the Photographic Collection, Miss F. Dimond, LVO.

THE PRIVY PURSE AND TREASURER'S OFFICE
Buckingham Palace, London SW1A 1AA

Keeper of the Privy Purse and Treasurer to The Queen, Maj. Sir Shane Blewitt, KCVO.
Deputy Keeper of the Privy Purse and Deputy Treasurer, J. Parsons.
Chief Accountant and Paymaster, D. Walker, LVO.
Personnel Officer, G. Franklin, CVO.
Pensions Manager, Miss P. Lloyd.
Assistant Chief Accountant and Paymaster, Miss R. Ward.
Assistant Personnel Officer, Mrs C. Jones.
Clerks, Mrs C. Auton, MVO; I. Biss; Mrs N. Broad; Miss L. Buggé; Mrs F. Burrows; J. Curr; Miss N. Mooney; Miss C. Robinson; Miss G. Wickham, MVO.
Clerk of Stationery, W. Cotton.
Land Agent, Sandringham, J. Major.
Resident Factor, Balmoral, M. Leslie, LVO.

FINANCE AND PROPERTY SERVICES

Director of Finance and Property Services, M. Peat.
Deputy Director, Property Services, J. H. Tiltman.
Superintending Architect, S. Dhargalkar.
Senior Architect, Miss H. Bell.
Property Administrator, Miss M. Green.
Deputy Property Administrator, M. Bourke.
Maintenance Manager, G. Griffiths, MVO.
Deputy Maintenance Manager, R. Mole.
Assistant Maintenance Managers, M. Harmer; A. Ryan.
Assistant Property Administrator, Mrs H. Dunlop.
Management Auditor, I. McGregor.
Assistant Management Auditor, Mrs D. Mowbray.
Information Systems Manager, I. Hardy.
Clerks, Mrs. J. Hillyer; Mrs C. Sharma; Mrs J. Thomas; Miss R. Wickenden.

WINDSOR CASTLE

Maintenance Manager, E. Norton.
Deputy Maintenance Manager, M. Thresher.
Administrative Assistant, Mrs C. Crook.

ROYAL ALMONRY

High Almoner, The Rt. Revd the Lord Bishop of St Albans.

Hereditary Grand Almoner, The Marquess of Exeter.
Sub-Almoner, Revd W. Booth.
Secretary, P. Wright, CVO.
Assistant Secretary, D. Waters, CVO.

THE LORD CHAMBERLAIN'S OFFICE

Buckingham Palace, London SW1A 1AA

Comptroller, Lt.-Col. M. Ross, OBE.
Assistant Comptroller, Lt.-Col. A. Mather, OBE.
Secretary, P. D. Hartley, MVO.
Assistant Secretary, J. Spencer.
State Invitations Assistant, J. Mordaunt, MVO.
Clerks, Miss L. Connor; Miss L. Dove; Mrs S. Scott; Miss A. Utting.
Permanent Lords-in-Waiting, Lt.-Col. The Lord Charteris of Amisfield, GCB, GCVO, OBE, QSO, PC; The Lord Moore of Wolvercote, GCB, GCVO, CMG, QSO; The Earl of Westmorland, GCVO.
Lords-in-Waiting, The Viscount Boyne; The Lord Camoys; The Viscount Long; The Viscount Astor; The Viscount St Davids; The Viscount Goschen.
Baroness-in-Waiting, Baroness Trumpington.
Gentlemen Ushers, C. Greig, CVO, CBE; Gp Capt J. Slessor; Maj. N. Chamberlayne-Macdonald, LVO, OBE; Air Marshal Sir Roy Austen-Smith, KBE, CB, DFC; Vice-Adm. Sir David Loram, KCB, LVO; Capt. M. Barrow, DSO, RN; Capt. M. Fulford-Dobson, RN; Lt.-Gen. Sir Richard Vickers, KCB, LVO, OBE; Air Vice-Marshal B. Newton, CB, OBE; Col. M. Havergal, OBE.
Extra Gentlemen Ushers, Maj. T. Harvey, CVO, DSO; Maj.-Gen. Sir Cyril Colquhoun, KCVO, CB, OBE; Lt.-Col. Sir John Hugo, KCVO, OBE; Vice-Adm. Sir Ronald Brockman, KCB, CSI, CIE, CVO, CBE; Air Marshal Sir Maurice Heath, KBE, CB, CVO; Sir James Scholtens, KCVO; Sir Patrick O'Dea, KCVO; Brig.-Gen. S. Cooper, CVO, OBE, CD; Adm. Sir David Williams, GCB; Capt. M. Tufnell, CVO, DSC, RN; H. Davis, CVO, CM; Maj.-Gen. R. Reid, CVO, MC, CD; Lt.-Cdr. J. Holdsworth, CVO, OBE, RN; Col. G. Leigh, CVO, CBE; Lt.-Cdr. Sir Russell Wood, KCVO, VRD; Air Chief Marshal Sir Neville Stack, KCB, CVO, CBE, AFC; Maj.-Gen. Sir Desmond Rice, KCVO, CBE; Lt.-Col. Sir Julian Paget, Bt., CVO.
Gentleman Usher to the Sword of State, Gen. Sir Edward Burgess, KCB, OBE.
Gentleman Usher of the Black Rod, Adm. Sir Richard Thomas, KCB, OBE.
Serjeants-at-Arms, M. Tims, CVO; G. Franklin, CVO; D. Walker, LVO.

Marshal of the Diplomatic Corps, Vice-Adm. Sir James Weatherall, KBE.
Vice-Marshal, A. St J. H. Figgis.

Constable and Governor of Windsor Castle, Gen. Sir Patrick Palmer, KBE.
Keeper of the Jewel House, Tower of London, Maj.-Gen. C. Tyler, CB.
Master of The Queen's Music, Malcolm Williamson, CBE, AO.
Poet Laureate, Ted Hughes, OBE.
Bargemaster, R. Crouch.
Keeper of the Swans, F. J. Turk, MVO.
Superintendent of the State Apartments, St James's Palace, T. Taylor, MVO, MBE.

ECCLESIASTICAL HOUSEHOLD

THE COLLEGE OF CHAPLAINS

Clerk of the Closet, Rt. Revd Bishop of Chelmsford.
Deputy Clerk of the Closet, Revd W. Booth.
Chaplains to The Queen, Revd A. H. H. Harbottle, LVO; Ven. D. N. Griffiths, RD; Revd Canon A. Glendining, LVO; Revd Canon J. V. Bean; Revd K. Huxley; Ven. P. Ashford; Revd Canon G. A. Elcoat; Revd Canon D. C. Gray, TD; Ven. D. Scott; Revd Canon E. James; Revd Canon J. Hester; Revd S. Pedley; Revd D. Tonge; Revd Canon C. Craston; Revd Canon N. M. Ramm; Revd Canon D. N. Hole; Revd Canon M. A. Moxon; Revd Canon R. T. W. McDermid; Revd Canon G. Murphy, LVO; Revd Canon R. H. C. Lewis; Revd D. J. Burgess; Revd E. R. Ayerst; Revd R. S. Clarke; Revd Canon C. J. Hill; Ven. K. Pound; Revd Canon J. Haslam; Revd Canon G. Hall; Revd Canon A. C. Hill; Revd J. C. Priestley; Revd Canon J. O. Colling; Revd Canon G. Jones; Revd D. G. Palmer; Revd Canon D. H. Wheaton; Revd Canon P. Boulton; Revd Canon R. A. Bowden; Revd Canon E. Buchanan.
Extra Chaplains, Revd Canon J. S. D. Mansel, KCVO, FSA; Preb. S. A. Williams, CVO; Ven. E. J. G. Ward, LVO; Revd J. R. W. Stott; Revd Canon A. D. Caesar, CVO.

CHAPELS ROYAL

Dean of the Chapels Royal, The Bishop of London.
Sub-Dean of Chapels Royal, Revd W. Booth.
Priests in Ordinary, Revd W. Booth; Revd G. Watkins; Revd H. Mead; Revd S. E. Young.
Organist, Choirmaster and Composer, R. J. Popplewell, FRCO, FRCM.
Domestic Chaplain, Buckingham Palace, Revd W. Booth.
Domestic Chaplain, Windsor Castle, The Dean of Windsor.
Domestic Chaplain, Sandringham, Revd Canon G. R. Hall.
Chaplain, Royal Chapel, Windsor Great Park, Revd Canon M. Moxon.
Chaplain, Hampton Court Palace, Revd Canon M. Moore.
Chaplain, Tower of London, Revd Canon J. G. M. W. Murphy, LVO.
Organist and Choirmaster, Hampton Court Palace, Gordon Reynolds, LVO.

MEDICAL HOUSEHOLD

Head of the Medical Household and Physician, A. Dawson, CVO, MD, FRCP.
Physician, R. W. Davey, MB, BS.
Serjeant Surgeon, B. T. Jackson, MS, FRCS.
Surgeon Oculist, P. Holmes Sellors, LVO, BM, B.Ch., FRCS.
Surgeon Gynaecologist, M. E. Setchell, FRCS, FRCOG.
Surgeon Dentist, N. A. Sturridge, CVO, LDS, BDS, DDS.
Orthopaedic Surgeon, R. H. Vickers, MA, BM, B.Ch., FRCS.
Physician to the Household, R. Thompson, DM, FRCP.
Surgeon to the Household, A. A. M. Lewis, MB, FRCS.
Surgeon Oculist to the Household, T. J. ffytche, FRCS.
Apothecary to The Queen and to the Household, N. R. Southward, LVO, MB, B.Chir.
Apothecary to the Household at Windsor, J. H. D. Briscoe, MB, B.Chir., D.Obst.
Apothecary to the Household at Sandringham, I. K. Campbell, MB, BS, FRCGP.
Coroner of The Queen's Household, J. Burton, CBE, MB, BS.

CENTRAL CHANCERY OF THE ORDERS OF KNIGHTHOOD

St James's Palace, London SW1

Secretary, Lt.-Col. A. Mather, OBE.
Assistant Secretary, Sqn. Ldr. B. Sowerby, MVO..
Clerks, J. Bagwell Purefoy; Miss F. Bean; Miss L. Hiney; Mrs T. Isaac; Miss S. Koller, MVO; J. McGurk, MVO; Miss R. Wells, MVO.

THE HONORABLE CORPS OF GENTLEMEN-AT-ARMS
St James's Palace, London SW1

Captain, The Lord Hesketh.
Lieutenant, Maj. T. St Aubyn.
Standard Bearer, Lt.-Col. Sir James Scott, Bt.
Clerk of the Cheque and Adjutant, Maj. Sir Torquil Matheson of Matheson, Bt.
Harbinger, Brig. A. N. Breitmeyer.

Gentlemen of the Corps

Colonels, T. Hall, OBE; Sir Piers Bengough, KCVO, OBE; Hon. N. Crossley, TD; T. Wilson; D. Fanshawe, OBE; J. Baker; R. ffrench Blake.
Lieutenant-Colonels, R. Mayfield, DSO; B. Lockhart; Hon. P. H. Lewis; R. Macfarlane; Hon. G. B. Norrie; J. H. Fisher, OBE; R. Ker, MC.
Majors, F. J. H. Matheson; J. A. J. Nunn; Sir Philip Duncombe, Bt.; I. B. Ramsden, MBE; M. J. Drummond-Brady; A. Arkwright; G. M. B. Colenso-Jones; T. Gooch, MBE; J. B. B. Cockcroft; C. J. H. Gurney; J. R. E. Nelson; P. D. Johnson.
Captain, The Lord Monteagle of Brandon.

THE QUEEN'S BODYGUARD OF THE YEOMEN OF THE GUARD
St James's Palace, London SW1

Captain, The Earl of Strathmore and Kinghorne.
Lieutenant, Col. A. B. Pemberton, CVO, MBE.
Clerk of the Cheque and Adjutant, Col. G. W. Tufnell.
Ensign, Lt.-Col. S. Longsdon.
Exons, Maj. C. Marriott; Maj. C. Enderby.

MASTER OF THE HOUSEHOLD'S DEPARTMENT

BOARD OF GREEN CLOTH
Buckingham Palace, London SW1A 1AA

Master of the Household, Maj.-Gen. Sir Simon Cooper, KCVO.
Deputy Master of the Household, Lt.-Col. B. A. Stewart-Wilson, CVO.
Assistant to the Master of the Household, M. T. Parker, MVO.
Chief Clerk, M. C. W. N. Jephson, MVO.
Chief Housekeeper, Miss H. Colebrook.
Deputy to Assistant, F. M. Bovaird.
Senior Clerk, G. S. Stacey.
Flower Arranger, Mrs P. Pentney.
Clerks, Miss S. Bell; Miss S. Derry, MVO; Miss S. Fergus, MVO; Miss S. Hargreaves; Miss L. Moran.
Palace Steward, A. Jarred, RVM.
Royal Chef, L. Mann, RVM.
Superintendent, Windsor Castle, Maj. B. Eastwood, MBE.
Assistant to Superintendent, Capt. R. McClosky, MVO.
Superintendent, The Palace of Holyroodhouse, Lt.-Col. D. Wickes, MVO.

ROYAL MEWS DEPARTMENT

Buckingham Palace, London SW1A 1AA

Crown Equerry, Lt.-Col. S. Gilbart-Denham.
Veterinary Surgeon, P. Scott Dunn, LVO, MRCVS.
Supt. Royal Mews, Buckingham Palace, Maj. A. Smith, MBE.
Comptroller of Stores, Maj. L. Marsham, MVO.
Chief Clerk, P. Almond, MVO.
Deputy Chief Clerk, A. Marshall.
Assistant Chief Clerk, Mrs J. Clark.

ROYAL COLLECTION DEPARTMENT

St James's Palace, London SW1

Director of Royal Collection and Surveyor of The Queen's Works of Art, Sir Geoffrey de Bellaigue, KCVO, FSA.
Deputy Director (Finance), J. Parsons, LVO.
Surveyor of The Queen's Pictures, C. Lloyd.
Surveyor Emeritus of The Queen's Pictures, Sir Oliver Millar, GCVO, FBA, FSA.
Librarian, The Royal Library, Windsor Castle, O. Everett, CVO.
Deputy Surveyor of The Queen's Works of Art, H. Roberts.
Adviser for The Queen's Works of Art, Sir Francis Watson, KCVO, FBA, FSA.
Librarian Emeritus, Sir Robin Mackworth-Young, GCVO, FSA.
Curator of the Print Room, The Hon. Mrs Roberts, MVO.
Registrar, M. Bishop, MVO.
Senior Picture Restorer, Miss V. Pemberton-Pigott, MVO.
Assistant to Surveyors (Military), D. Rankin-Hunt, TD.
Assistant to Surveyor of The Queen's Pictures, C. Noble, MVO.
Secretary to the Director, Miss C. Crichton-Stuart, MVO.
Clerks, J. Cowell; R. Cook; Miss H. Edwards; Miss A. Fairbank; Miss S. Goodbody; Mrs C. Gordon Lennox; Miss A. Leslie; Hon. C. Neville.
Computer Systems Manager, S. Patterson.
Superintendent, Public Enterprise, M. Hewlett.
Financial Controller, Mrs G. Johnson.
Clerks, Mrs C. Murphy; Miss M. O'Connell; Mrs W. Oates.

ASCOT OFFICE

St James's Palace, London SW1
Tel 071-930 9882

Her Majesty's Representative at Ascot, Col. Sir Piers Bengough, KCVO, OBE.
Secretary, Miss L. Thompson-Royd.

THE QUEEN'S HOUSEHOLD IN SCOTLAND

Hereditary Lord High Constable, The Earl of Erroll.
Hereditary Master of the Household, The Duke of Argyll.
Lord Lyon King of Arms, Sir Malcolm Innes of Edingight, KCVO, WS.
Hereditary Bearer of the Royal Banner of Scotland, The Earl of Dundee.
Hereditary Bearer of the Scottish National Flag, The Earl of Lauderdale.
Hereditary Keepers:
Palace of Holyroodhouse, The Duke of Hamilton and Brandon.
Falkland Castle, N. J. Crichton-Stuart.
Stirling Castle, The Earl of Mar and Kellie.
Dunstaffnage Castle, The Duke of Argyll.
Dunconnel Castle, Sir Fitzroy Maclean, Bt., CBE.
Hereditary Carver, Sir Ralph Anstruther, KCVO, MC.
Keeper of Dumbarton Castle, Brig. A. S. Pearson, CB, DSO, OBE, MC, TD.
Governor of Edinburgh Castle, Lt.-Gen. Sir Peter Graham, KCB, CBE.
Historiographer, Prof. G. Donaldson, CBE, FBA, FRSE.
Botanist, Prof. D. Henderson, CBE, FRSE.
Painter and Limner, D. A. Donaldson, RSA, RP.
Sculptor in Ordinary, Prof. Sir Eduardo Paolozzi.
Astronomer, Prof. M. S. Longair, Ph.D.
Heralds and Pursuivants, *see* page 289.

ECCLESIASTICAL HOUSEHOLD

Dean of the Order of the Thistle, The Very Revd G. I. Macmillan.
Dean of the Chapel Royal, Very Revd W. J. Morris, DD, LL.D.
Chaplains in Ordinary, Very Revd W. J. Morris, DD, LL.D.; Revd J. McLeod; Very Revd G. I. Macmillan; Rt Revd M. D. Craig; Revd W. B. R. Macmillan, LL.D.; Revd

J. L. Weatherhead; Revd M. I. Levison; Revd A. S. Todd, DD; Revd C. Robertson.
Extra Chaplains, Very Revd R. L. Small, CBE, DD; Very Revd W. R. Sanderson, DD; Very Revd R. W. V. Selby Wright, CVO, TD, DD, FRSE, FSAScot.; Revd T. J. T. Nicol, MVO, MBE, MC, TD; Very Revd Prof. J. McIntyre, CVO, DD, FRSE; Revd C. Forrester-Paton; Revd H. W. M. Cant; Very Revd R. A. S. Barbour, KCVO, MC, DD; Revd K. MacVicar, MBE, DFC, TD; Very Revd W. B. Johnston, DD; Revd A. J. C. Macfarlane.
Domestic Chaplain, Balmoral, Revd J. A. K. Angus, LVO, TD.

MEDICAL HOUSEHOLD
Physicians in Scotland, P. Brunt, MD, FRCP; A. L. Muir, MD, FRCP.
Surgeons in Scotland, I. B. Macleod, MB, ch.B., FRCS; J. Engeset, ch.M., FRCS.
Extra Surgeons in Scotland, Prof. Sir Charles Illingworth, CBE, MD, FRCSE; Prof. Sir Donald Douglas, MBE, ch.M., MS, D.SC., FRCS.
Apothecary to the Household at Balmoral, D. J. A. Glass, MB, ch.B.
Apothecary to the Household at the Palace of Holyroodhouse, Dr J. Cormack, MD, FRCGP.

THE QUEEN'S BODY GUARD FOR SCOTLAND

ROYAL COMPANY OF ARCHERS
Archers' Hall, Edinburgh

Captain-General and Gold Stick for Scotland, Col. the Lord Clydesmuir, KT, CB, MBE, TD.
Captains, Maj. the Lord Home of the Hirsel, KT; The Duke of Buccleuch and Queensberry, KT, VRD; Lt.-Col. Sir John Gilmour, Bt., DSO, TD; Maj. Sir Hew Hamilton-Dalrymple, Bt., KCVO.
Lieutenants, Maj. the Earl of Wemyss and March, KT; The Earl of Airlie, KT, GCVO; The Earl of Dalhousie, KT, GCVO, GBE, MC; Capt. Sir Iain Tennant, KT.
Ensigns, Capt. N. E. F. Dalrymple-Hamilton, CVO, MBE, DSC, RN; The Marquess of Lothian, KCVO; Cdre Sir John Clerk of Penicuik, Bt., CBE, VRD; The Earl of Elgin and Kincardine, KT.
Brigadiers, Col. G. R. Simpson, DSO, LVO, TD; Maj. Sir David Butter, KCVO, MC; The Earl of Minto, OBE; Maj.-Gen. Sir John Swinton, KCVO, OBE; Gen. Sir Michael Gow, GCB; The Hon. Lord Elliott, MC; Maj. the Hon. Sir Lachlan Maclean, Bt.; The Rt. Hon. Lord Younger of Prestwick, TD; Capt. G. Burnet, LVO; The Duke of Montrose; Lt.-Gen. Sir Norman Arthur, KCB; The Hon. Sir William Macpherson of Cluny, TD; Sir David Nickson, KBE.
Adjutant, Maj. the Hon. Sir Lachlan Maclean, Bt.
Surgeon, Dr P. A. P. Mackenzie, TD.
Chaplain, Very Revd R. Selby Wright, CVO, TD, DD, FRSE.
President of the Council and Silver Stick for Scotland, Maj. Sir Hew Hamilton-Dalrymple, Bt., KCVO.
Vice-President, The Earl of Dalhousie, KT, GCVO, GBE, MC.
Secretary, Col. H. F. O. Bewsher, OBE.
Treasurer, J. Martin Haldane.

HOUSEHOLD OF THE PRINCE PHILIP, DUKE OF EDINBURGH

Private Secretary and Treasurer, B. H. McGrath, CVO.
Assistant Private Secretary, Brig. M. G. Hunt-Davis, CBE.
Equerry, Wg Cdr. C. H. Moran.
Extra Equerries, J. B. V. Orr, CVO; Sir Richard Davies, KCVO, CBE; Lord Buxton of Alsa; Brig. C. Robertson, CVO.
Temporary Equerries, Capt. I. Grant, RM; Capt. G. Inglis-Jones.
Chief Clerk and Accountant, V. G. Jewell, MVO.

HOUSEHOLD OF QUEEN ELIZABETH THE QUEEN MOTHER

Lord Chamberlain, The Earl of Crawford and Balcarres, PC.
Comptroller and Extra Equerry, Capt. Sir Alastair Aird, KCVO.
Private Secretary and Equerry, Lt.-Col. Sir Martin Gilliat, GCVO, MBE.
Treasurer and Equerry, Maj. Sir Ralph Anstruther, Bt., GCVO, MC.
Equerries, Maj. R. Seymour, CVO; Capt. the Hon. E. Dawson-Damer (*temp.*).
Extra Equerries, Maj. Sir John Griffin, KCVO; The Lord Sinclair, CVO.
Apothecary to the Household, Dr N. Southward, LVO, MB, B.chir.
Surgeon-Apothecary to the Household (Royal Lodge, Windsor), Dr J. Briscoe, D.obst.
Mistress of the Robes, vacant.
Ladies of the Bedchamber, The Dowager Viscountess Hambleden, GCVO; The Lady Grimthorpe, CVO.
Women of the Bedchamber, Ruth, Lady Fermoy, DCVO, OBE; Dame Frances Campbell-Preston, DCVO; Lady Elizabeth Basset, DCVO; Lady Angela Oswald.
Extra Women of the Bedchamber, Lady Victoria Wemyss, CVO; Lady Jean Rankin, DCVO; Miss Jane Walker-Okeover; Lady Margaret Colville; The Hon. Mrs Rhodes.
Clerk Comptroller, M. Blanch, CVO.
Clerk Accountant, J. P. Kyle, LVO.
Information Officer, Mrs R. Murphy, LVO.
Clerks, Miss F. Fletcher, MVO; Mrs W. Stevens.

HOUSEHOLD OF THE PRINCE AND PRINCESS OF WALES

Private Secretary and Treasurer to The Prince of Wales, Cdr. R. J. Aylard, RN.
Private Secretary to the Princess of Wales, P. Jephson.
Deputy Private Secretary to The Prince of Wales, P. Westmacott.
Assistant Private Secretaries to The Prince of Wales, H. Merrill; Miss B. Harley.
Equerry to The Prince of Wales, Lt.-Cdr. R. Fraser.
Equerry to The Princess of Wales, Capt. E. Musto, RM.
Extra Equerries to The Prince of Wales, The Hon. Edward Adeane, CVO; Maj.-Gen. Sir Christopher Airy, KCVO, CBE; Sqn. Ldr. Sir David Checketts, KCVO; Sir John Riddle, Bt., CVO; G. J. Ward, CBE; Col. J. Q. Winter, LVO.
Ladies-in-Waiting, Miss Anne Beckwith-Smith, LVO; Viscountess Campden; Mrs Max Pike; Miss Alexandra Loyd; The Hon. Mrs Vivian Baring; Mrs James Lonsdale.
Extra Lady-in-Waiting, Lady Sarah McCorquodale.
Secretary to the Duchy of Cornwall and Keeper of the Records, D. W. N. Landale.

HOUSEHOLD OF THE DUKE AND DUCHESS OF YORK

Private Secretary and Treasurer to the Duke and Duchess of York, Capt. N. Blair, RN.
Comptroller and Assistant Private Secretary to the Duke and Duchess of York, Mrs Jonathan Mathias.
Equerry to The Duke of York, Capt. R. Maitland-Titterton.
Extra Equerry, Maj. G. W. McLean.
Ladies-in-Waiting, Mrs John Spooner; Mrs John Floyd.
Extra Ladies-in-Waiting (temp.), Miss Lucy Manners; Mrs Harry Cotterell.

HOUSEHOLD OF THE PRINCE EDWARD

Private Secretary and Equerry to The Prince Edward, Lt.-Col. S. G. O'Dwyer.
Assistant Private Secretary, Mrs R. Warburton, MVO.

HOUSEHOLD OF THE PRINCESS ROYAL

Private Secretary, Lt.-Col. P. Gibbs, LVO.
Assistant Private Secretary, The Hon. Mrs Louloudis.
Ladies-in-Waiting, Mrs Richard Carew Pole, LVO; Mrs Andrew Feilden, LVO; The Hon. Mrs Legge-Bourke, LVO; Mrs William Nunneley; Mrs Timothy Holderness-Roddam; Mrs Charles Ritchie; Mrs David Bowes Lyon.
Extra Ladies-in-Waiting, Miss Victoria Legge-Bourke, LVO; Mrs Malcolm Innes, LVO; The Countess of Lichfield.

HOUSEHOLD OF THE PRINCESS MARGARET, COUNTESS OF SNOWDON

Private Secretary and Comptroller, The Lord Napier and Ettrick, KCVO.
Lady-in-Waiting, The Hon. Mrs Whitehead, LVO.
Extra Ladies-in-Waiting, Lady Elizabeth Cavendish, LVO; Lady Aird, LVO; Mrs Robin Benson, LVO, OBE; Lady Juliet Townsend, LVO; Mrs Jane Stevens; The Hon. Mrs Wills, LVO; The Lady Glenconner, LVO; The Countess Alexander of Tunis, LVO; Mrs Charles Vyvyan.

HOUSEHOLD OF THE DUKE AND DUCHESS OF GLOUCESTER

Private Secretary, Comptroller and Equerry, Maj. N. M. L. Barne.
Assistant Private Secretary to The Duchess of Gloucester, Miss Suzanne Marland.
Extra Equerry, Lt.-Col. Sir Simon Bland, KCVO.
Ladies-in-Waiting, Mrs Michael Wigley, CVO; Mrs Euan McCorquodale, LVO; Mrs Howard Page.
Extra Lady-in-Waiting, Miss Jennifer Thomson.

HOUSEHOLD OF PRINCESS ALICE, DUCHESS OF GLOUCESTER

Private Secretary, Comptroller and Equerry, Maj. N. M. L. Barne.
Extra Equerry, Lt.-Col. Sir Simon Bland, KCVO.
Ladies-in-Waiting, Dame Jean Maxwell-Scott, DCVO; Mrs Michael Harvey.
Extra Ladies-in-Waiting, Miss Diana Harrison; The Hon. Jane Walsh, LVO; Miss Jane Egerton-Warburton, LVO.

HOUSEHOLD OF THE DUKE AND DUCHESS OF KENT

Private Secretary, Cdr. R. M. Walker.
Extra Equerry, Lt.-Cdr. Sir Richard Buckley, KCVO.
Equerry (temp.), Capt. the Hon. T. E. Coke.
Ladies-in-Waiting, Mrs Fiona Henderson, CVO; Mrs David Napier, LVO; Mrs Colin Marsh, LVO.
Extra Ladies-in-Waiting, Mrs Peter Wilmot-Sitwell, LVO; Mrs Julian Tomkins; Mrs Peter Troughton.

HOUSEHOLD OF PRINCE AND PRINCESS MICHAEL OF KENT

Private Secretary and Equerry, Lt.-Col. Sir Christopher Thompson, Bt.
Ladies-in-Waiting, The Hon. Mrs Sanders; Miss Anne Frost; Lady Thompson.
Extra Lady-in-Waiting, Mrs J. Fellowes.

HOUSEHOLD OF PRINCESS ALEXANDRA, THE HON. LADY OGILVY

Comptroller and Private Secretary, Rear-Adm. Sir John Garnier, KCVO, CBE.
Extra Equerry, Maj. Sir Peter Clarke, KCVO.
Lady-in-Waiting, Lady Mary Mumford, CVO.
Extra Ladies-in-Waiting, Mrs Peter Afia; Lady Mary Colman; Lady Nicholas Gordon Lennox; The Hon. Lady Rowley; Dame Mona Mitchell, DCVO.

THE CIVIL LIST

The land revenues of the Crown in England and Wales have been collected on the public account since 1760, when George III surrendered them and received a fixed annual payment or Civil List. (For details of income from the Crown Estate, *see* page 300).

The Civil List, the annuity payable to The Queen, is payable out of the Consolidated Fund under the authority of a Civil List Act following the recommendation of a Parliamentary select committee.

Until 1972, the amount of money allocated annually under the Civil List was set for the period of a reign. The system was then altered to a fixed annual payment for ten years but from 1975 high inflation made an annual review necessary. However, the system of payments reverted to the practice of a fixed annual payment for ten years from 1 January 1991. The annual payments for the years 1991–2000 are:

The Queen	£7,900,000
Queen Elizabeth The Queen Mother	640,000
The Duke of Edinburgh	360,000
The Duke of York	250,000
The Prince Edward	100,000
The Princess Royal	230,000
The Princess Margaret	220,000
Princess Alice, Duchess of Gloucester	90,000
*Duke of Gloucester *Duke of Kent *Princess Alexandra	630,000
	10,420,000
*Refunded to the Treasury by The Queen	630,000
Total	9,790,000

The Prince of Wales does not receive an allocation from the Civil List but derives his income from the revenues of the Duchy of Cornwall.

The Royal Arms

QUARTERS

1st and 4th quarters (representing England) – gules, three lions passant guardant in pale or.

2nd quarter (representing Scotland) – or, a lion rampant within a double tressure flory counterflory gules.

3rd quarter (representing Ireland) – azure, a harp or, stringed argent.

The whole shield is encircled with the Garter.

Scottish usage shows the Royal Arms with the Lion of Scotland in the 1st and 4th quarters, and the Lions of England in the 2nd quarter.

SUPPORTERS

Dexter (right) – a lion rampant guardant or, imperially crowned.

Sinister (left) – a unicorn argent, armed, crined, and unguled or, gorged with a coronet composed of crosses patées and fleurs-de-lis, a chain affixed, passing between the forelegs, and reflexed over the back.

Scottish usage shows the Royal Arms with the supporters transposed, the unicorn appearing on the right.

BADGES

England – the red and white rose united, slipped and leaved proper.

Scotland – a thistle, slipped and leaved proper.

Ireland – a shamrock leaf slipped vert; also a harp or, stringed argent.

United Kingdom – the rose of England, the thistle of Scotland, and the shamrock of Ireland engrafted on the same stem proper, and an escutcheon charged as the Union Flag (all ensigned with the Royal Crown).

Wales – upon a mount vert a dragon passant, wings elevated gules.

Royal Salutes

A salute of 62 guns is fired on the wharf at the Tower of London on the following occasions:

(a) the anniversaries of the birth, accession and coronation of the Sovereign

(b) the anniversary of the birth of HM Queen Elizabeth the Queen Mother

(c) the anniversary of the birth of HRH Prince Philip, Duke of Edinburgh

A salute of 41 guns only is fired on extraordinary and triumphal occasions, e.g. on the occasion of the Sovereign opening, proroguing or dissolving Parliament in person, or when passing through London in procession, except when otherwise ordered.

A salute of 41 guns is fired from the two saluting stations in London (the Tower of London and Hyde Park) on the occasion of the birth of a Royal infant.

Constable of the Royal Palace and Fortress of London, Field Marshal Sir John Stanier, GCB, MBE.

Lieutenant of the Tower of London, Lt.-Gen. Sir Robert Richardson, KCB, CVO, CBE.

Resident Governor and Keeper of the Jewel House, Maj.-Gen. C. Tyler, CB.

Master Gunner of St James's Park, Gen. Sir Martin Farndale, KCB.

Master Gunner within the Tower, Col. D. P. Spooner, TD.

Military Ranks and Titles

THE QUEEN

Lord High Admiral of the United Kingdom

Colonel-in-Chief
The Life Guards; The Blues and Royals (Royal Horse Guards and 1st Dragoons); The Royal Scots Dragoon Guards (Carabiniers and Greys); 16th/5th The Queen's Royal Lancers; Royal Tank Regiment; Corps of Royal Engineers; Grenadier Guards; Coldstream Guards; Scots Guards; Irish Guards; Welsh Guards; The Royal Welch Fusiliers; The Queen's Lancashire Regiment; The Argyll and Sutherland Highlanders (Princess Louise's); The Royal Green Jackets; Royal Army Ordnance Corps; Adjutant-General's Corps; The Queen's Own Mercian Yeomanry; The Duke of Lancaster's Own Yeomanry; The Governor-General's Horse Guards; The King's Own Calgary Regiment; Canadian Forces Military Engineers Branch; Royal 22e Regiment; Governor General's Foot Guards; The Canadian Grenadier Guards; Le Regiment de la Chaudiere; 2nd Bn Royal New Brunswick Regiment (North Shore); The 48th Highlanders of Canada; The Argyll and Sutherland Highlanders of Canada (Princess Louise's); The Calgary Highlanders; Royal Australian Engineers; Royal Australian Infantry Corps; Royal Australian Army Ordnance Corps; Royal Australian Army Nursing Corps; The Corps of Royal New Zealand Engineers; Royal New Zealand Infantry Regiment; Royal New Zealand Army Ordnance Corps; Royal Malta Artillery; The Malawi Rifles

Captain-General
Royal Regiment of Artillery; The Honourable Artillery Company; Combined Cadet Force; Royal Regiment of Canadian Artillery; Royal Regiment of Australian Artillery; Royal Regiment of New Zealand Artillery; Royal New Zealand Armoured Corps

Patron
Royal Army Chaplain's Department

Air Commodore-in-Chief
Royal Auxiliary Air Force; Royal Air Force Regiment; Royal Observer Corps; Air Reserve (of Canada); Royal Australian Air Force Reserve; Territorial Air Force (New Zealand)

Commandant-in-Chief
Royal Air Force College, Cranwell

Hon. Air Commodore
RAF Marham

HM QUEEN ELIZABETH THE QUEEN MOTHER

Colonel-in-Chief
1st The Queen's Dragoon Guards; The Queen's Own Hussars; 9th/12th Royal Lancers (Prince of Wales's); The King's Regiment; The Royal Anglian Regiment; The Light Infantry; The Black Watch (Royal Highland Regiment); Royal Army Medical Corps; The Black Watch (Royal Highland Regiment) of Canada; The Toronto Scottish Regiment; Canadian Forces Medical Services; Royal Australian Army Medical Corps; Royal New Zealand Army Medical Corps

Hon. Colonel
The Royal Yeomanry; The London Scottish; Inns of Court and City Yeomanry

Commandant-in-Chief
Women's Royal Naval Service; Women's Royal Air Force; RAF Central Flying School

HRH THE PRINCE PHILIP, DUKE OF EDINBURGH

Admiral of the Fleet
Field Marshal
Marshal of the Royal Air Force

Admiral of the Fleet, Royal Australian Navy
Field Marshal, Australian Military Forces
Marshal of the Royal Australian Air Force

Admiral of the Fleet, Royal New Zealand Navy
Field Marshal, New Zealand Army
Marshal of the Royal New Zealand Air Force

Captain-General, Royal Marines

Admiral
Royal Canadian Sea Cadets

Colonel-in-Chief
The Queen's Royal Irish Hussars; The Duke of Edinburgh's Royal Regiment (Berkshire and Wiltshire); The Queen's Own Highlanders (Seaforth and Camerons); Corps of Royal Electrical and Mechanical Engineers; Intelligence Corps; Army Cadet Force; The Royal Canadian Regiment; The Royal Hamilton Light Infantry (Wentworth Regiment); The Cameron Highlanders of Ottawa; The Queen's Own Cameron Highlanders of Canada; The Seaforth Highlanders of Canada; The Royal Canadian Army Cadets; The Royal Australian Corps of Electrical and Mechanical Engineers; The Australian Cadet Corps; The Royal New Zealand Corps of Electrical and Mechanical Engineers

Colonel
Grenadier Guards

Hon. Colonel
Edinburgh and Heriot-Watt Universities Officers' Training Corps; The Trinidad and Tobago Regiment

Air Commodore-in-Chief
Air Training Corps; Royal Canadian Air Cadets

Hon. Air Commodore
RAF Kinloss

HRH THE PRINCE OF WALES

Captain, Royal Navy
Group Captain, Royal Air Force

Colonel-in-Chief
The Royal Dragoon Guards; The Cheshire Regiment; The Royal Regiment of Wales (24th/41st Foot); The Gordon Highlanders; The Parachute Regiment; 2nd King Edward VII's Own Gurkha Rifles (The Sirmoor Rifles); Army Air Corps; The Royal Canadian Dragoons; Lord Strathcona's Horse (Royal Canadians); Royal Regiment of Canada; Royal Winnipeg Rifles; Royal Australian Armoured Corps; 2nd Bn The Royal Pacific Islands Regiment

Colonel
Welsh Guards

Air Commodore-in-Chief
Royal New Zealand Air Force

Hon. Air Commodore
RAF Brawdy

HRH THE PRINCESS OF WALES

Colonel-in-Chief
The Light Dragoons; The Princess of Wales's Royal Regiment; The Princess of Wales's Own Regiment (of Canada)

Hon. Air Commodore
RAF Wittering

HRH THE DUKE OF YORK

Lieutenant-Commander, Royal Navy

Admiral
Sea Cadet Corps

Colonel-in-Chief
The Staffordshire Regiment (The Prince of Wales's); The Royal Irish Regiment (27th (Inniskilling), 83rd, 87th and the Ulster Defence Regiment); Canadian Airborne Regiment

HRH THE PRINCESS ROYAL

Chief Commandant
Women's Royal Naval Service

Colonel-in-Chief
The King's Royal Hussars; Royal Corps of Signals; The Royal Scots (The Royal Regiment); The Worcestershire and Sherwood Foresters Regiment (29th/45th Foot); 8th Canadian Hussars (Princess Louise's); Canadian Forces Communications and Electronics Branch; The Grey and Simcoe Foresters; The Royal Regina Rifle Regiment; Royal Newfoundland Regiment; Royal Australian Corps of Signals; Royal New Zealand Corps of Signals; Royal New Zealand Nursing Corps

Hon. Colonel
London University Officers' Training Corps

Hon. Air Commodore
RAF Lyneham

Commandant-in-Chief
Women's Transport Service (FANY)

HRH THE PRINCESS MARGARET, COUNTESS OF SNOWDON

Colonel-in-Chief
The Royal Highland Fusiliers (Princess Margaret's Own Glasgow and Ayrshire Regiment); Queen Alexandra's Royal Army Nursing Corps; The Highland Fusiliers of Canada; The Princess Louise Fusiliers; The Bermuda Regiment

Deputy Colonel-in-Chief
The Royal Anglian Regiment

Hon. Air Commodore
RAF Coningsby

HRH PRINCESS ALICE, DUCHESS OF GLOUCESTER

Air Chief Marshal

Colonel-in-Chief
The King's Own Scottish Borderers; Royal Corps of Transport; Royal Australian Corps of Transport; Royal New Zealand Corps of Transport

Deputy Colonel-in-Chief
The King's Royal Hussars; The Royal Anglian Regiment

Air Chief Commandant
Women's Royal Air Force

HRH THE DUKE OF GLOUCESTER

Colonel-in-Chief
The Gloucestershire Regiment; Royal Pioneer Corps

Hon. Colonel
Royal Monmouthshire Royal Engineers (Militia)

HRH THE DUCHESS OF GLOUCESTER

Colonel-in-Chief
Royal Australian Army Educational Corps; Royal New Zealand Educational Corps

Deputy Colonel-in-Chief
Adjutant-General's Corps

HRH THE DUKE OF KENT

Major-General
Hon. Air Vice-Marshal

Colonel-in-Chief
The Royal Regiment of Fusiliers; The Devonshire and Dorset Regiment; The Lorne Scots Regiment (Peel, Dufferin and Hamilton Regiment)

Colonel
Scots Guards

HRH THE DUCHESS OF KENT

Hon. Major-General
Colonel-in-Chief
The Prince of Wales' Own Regiment of Yorkshire; Army Catering Corps

Deputy Colonel-in-Chief
The Royal Dragoon Guards; Adjutant-General's Corps

Hon. Colonel
The Yorkshire Volunteers

HRH PRINCE MICHAEL OF KENT

Major (retd), The Royal Hussars (Prince of Wales's Own)

Hon. Auxiliary Commodore
Royal Naval Auxiliary Service

HRH PRINCESS ALEXANDRA, THE HON. LADY OGILVY

Patron
Queen Alexandra's Royal Naval Nursing Service

Colonel-in-Chief
17th/21st Lancers; The King's Own Royal Border Regiment; The Queen's Own Rifles of Canada; The Canadian Scottish Regiment (Princess Mary's)

Deputy Colonel-in-Chief
The Light Infantry

Deputy Hon. Colonel
The Royal Yeomanry

Patron and Air Chief Commandant
Princess Mary's Royal Air Force Nursing Service

The House of Windsor

King George V assumed by royal proclamation (17 June 1917) for his House and family, as well as for all descendants in the male line of Queen Victoria who are subjects of these realms, the name of Windsor.

KING GEORGE V (George Frederick Ernest Albert), second son of King Edward VII, *born* 3 June 1865; *married* 6 July 1893 HSH Princess Victoria Mary Augusta Louise Olga Pauline Claudine Agnes of Teck (Queen Mary, *born* 26 May 1867; *died* 24 March 1953); *succeeded* to the throne 6 May 1910; *died* 20 January 1936. *Issue:*

1. HRH PRINCE EDWARD Albert Christian George Andrew Patrick David, *born* 23 June 1894, *succeeded* to the throne as King Edward VIII, 20 January 1936; *abdicated* 11 December 1936; created *Duke of Windsor*, 1936; *married* 3 June 1937, Mrs Wallis Warfield (Her Grace The Duchess of Windsor, *born* 19 June 1896; *died* 24 April 1986), *died* 28 May 1972.

2. HRH PRINCE ALBERT Frederick Arthur George, *born* 14 December 1895, *created* Duke of York 1920; *married* 26 April 1923, Lady Elizabeth Bowes-Lyon, youngest daughter of the 14th Earl of Strathmore and Kinghorne (HM Queen Elizabeth the Queen Mother, *see* page 123–4), *succeeded* to the throne as King George VI, 11 December 1936; *died* 6 Feburary 1952, having had issue (*see* page 123).

3. HRH PRINCESS (Victoria Alexandra Alice) MARY (*Princess Royal*), *born* 25 April 1897, *married* 28 February 1922, Viscount Lascelles, later the 6th Earl of Harewood (1882–1947), *died* 28 March 1965. *Issue:*

(1) George Henry Hubert Lascelles, 7th Earl of Harewood, KBE, *born* 7 February 1923; *married* (1) 29 September 1949, Maria (Marion) Stein (marriage dissolved 1967); *issue*, (*a*) David Henry George, Viscount Lascelles, *born* 21 October 1950; (*b*) James Edward, *born* 5 October 1953; (*c*) (Robert) Jeremy Hugh, *born* 14 February 1955; (2) 31 July 1967, Mrs Patricia Tuckwell; *issue*, (*d*) Mark Hubert, *born* 5 July 1964.
(2) Gerald David Lascelles, *born* 21 August 1924, *married* (1) 15 July 1952, Miss Angela Dowding (marriage dissolved 1978); *issue*, (*a*) Henry Ulick, *born* 19 May 1953; (2) 17 November 1978, Mrs Elizabeth Colvin; *issue*, (*b*) Martin David, *born* 9 February 1962.

4. HRH PRINCE HENRY William Frederick Albert, *born* 31 March 1900, *created* Duke of Gloucester, Earl of Ulster and Baron Culloden 1928, *married* 6 November 1935, Lady Alice Christabel Montagu-Douglas-Scott, daughter of the 7th Duke of Buccleuch (HRH Princess Alice, Duchess of Gloucester, *see* page 124); *died* 10 June 1974. *Issue:*

(1) HRH Prince William Henry Andrew Frederick, *born* 18 December 1941; *accidentally killed* 28 August 1972.
(2) HRH Prince Richard Alexander Walter George (HRH The Duke of Gloucester), *see* page 124.

5. HRH PRINCE GEORGE Edward Alexander Edmund, *born* 20 December 1902, *created* Duke of Kent, Earl of St Andrews and Baron Downpatrick 1934, *married* 29 November 1934, HRH Princess Marina of Greece and Denmark (*born* 30 November OS, 1906; *died* 27 August 1968); *killed on active service*, 25 August 1942. *Issue:*

(*1*) *HRH Prince Edward George Nicholas Paul Patrick (HRH The Duke of Kent), see* page 124.
(2) HRH Princess Alexandra Helen Elizabeth Olga Christabel (HRH Princess Alexandra, the Hon. Lady Ogilvy), *see* page 124.
(3) HRH Prince Michael George Charles Franklin (HRH Prince Michael of Kent), *see* page 124.

6. HRH PRINCE JOHN Charles Francis, *born* 12 July 1905; *died* 18 January 1919.

Descendants of Queen Victoria

QUEEN VICTORIA (Alexandrina Victoria), *born* 24 May 1819; *succeeded* to the throne 20 June 1837; *married* 10 February 1840 (Francis) Albert Augustus Charles Emmanuel, Duke of Saxony, Prince of Saxe-Coburg and Gotha (*HRH Albert, Prince Consort, born* 26 August 1819, *died* 14 December 1861); *died* 22 January 1901. *Issue:*

1. HRH PRINCESS VICTORIA Adelaide Mary Louisa (*Princess Royal*) (1840–1901), *m.* 1858, Frederic (1831–88), *Emperor of Germany* March–June 1888. *Issue:*

(1) HIM Wilhelm II (1859–1941), *Emperor of Germany* 1888–1918, *m.* (1) 1881 Princess Augusta Victoria of Schleswig-Holstein-Sonderburg-Augustenburg (1858–1921); (2) 1922 Princess Hermine of Reuss (1887–1947). *Issue:*
(*a*) Prince Wilhelm (1882–1951), *Crown Prince* 1888–1918, *m.* 1905 Duchess Cecilie of Mecklenburg-Schwerin; *issue:* Prince Wilhelm (1906–40); Prince Ludwig Ferdinand (*b.* 1907), *m.* 1938 Grand Duchess Kira (*see* page 135); Prince Hubertus (1909–50); Prince Friedrich Georg (1911–66); Princess Alexandrine Irene (1915–); Princess Cecilie (1917–75).
(*b*) Prince Eitel-Friedrich (1883–1942), *m.* 1906 Duchess Sophie of Oldenburg (marriage dissolved 1926).
(*c*) Prince Adalbert (1884–1948), *m.* 1914 Duchess Adelheid of Saxe-Meiningen; *issue:* Princess Victoria Marina (1917–81); Prince Wilhelm Victor (1919–89).
(*d*) Prince August Wilhelm (1887–1949), *m.* 1908 Princess Alexandra of Schleswig-Holstein-Sonderburg-Glücksburg (marriage dissolved 1920); *issue:* Prince Alexander (1912–85).
(*e*) Prince Oskar (1888–1958), *m.* 1914 Countess von Ruppin; *issue:* Prince Oskar (1915–39); Prince Burchard (1917–); Princess Herzeleide (1918–89); Prince Wilhelm (*b.* 1922).
(*f*) Prince Joachim (1890–1920), *m.* 1916 Princess Marie of Anhalt; *issue:* Prince Karl (1916–75).
(*g*) Princess Viktoria Luise (1892–1980), *m.* 1913 Ernst, Duke of Brunswick 1913–18 (1887–1953); *issue:* Prince Ernst (1914–87); Prince Georg (*b.* 1915), *m.* 1946 Princess Sophie of Greece (*see* page 135) and has issue (two sons, one daughter); Princess Frederika (1917–81), *m.* 1938 Paul I, King of the Hellenes (*see* page 135); Prince Christian (1919–81); Prince Welf Heinrich (*b.* 1923).
(2) Princess Charlotte (1860–1919), *m.* 1878 Bernhard, Duke of Saxe-Meiningen 1914 (1851–1914). *Issue:*
Princess Feodora (1879–1945), *m.* 1898 Prince Heinrich XXX of Reuss.
(3) Prince Heinrich (1862–1929), *m.* 1888 Princess Irene of Hesse (*see* page 135). *Issue:*
(*a*) Prince Waldemar (1889–1945), *m.* Princess Calixsta of Lippe.
(*b*) Prince Sigismund (1896–1978), *m.* Princess Charlotte of Saxe-Altenburg; *issue:* Princess Barbe (*b.* 1920); Prince Alfred (*b.* 1924).
(*c*) Prince Heinrich (1900–4).
(4) Prince Sigismund (1864–6).
(5) Princess Victoria (1866–1929), *m.* (1) 1890, Prince Adolf of Schaumburg-Lippe (1859–1916); (2) 1927 Alexander Zubkov.
(6) Prince Joachim Waldemar (1868–79).
(7) Princess Sophie (1870–1932), *m.* 1889 Constantine I (1868–1923), King of the Hellenes 1913–17, 1920–3. *Issue:*
(*a*) George II (1890–1947), King of the Hellenes 1923–4 and 1935–47, *m.* 1921 Princess Elisabeth of Roumania (marriage dissolved 1935), (*see* page 135).
(*b*) Alexander I (1893–1920), King of the Hellenes 1917–20, *m.*

1919 Aspasia Manos; *issue:* Princess Alexandra (*b.* 1921), *m.* 1944 King Petar II of Yugoslavia (*see* below).
(*c*) Princess Helena (1896–1982), *m.* 1921 King Carol of Roumania (*see* below), (marriage dissolved 1928).
(*d*) Paul I (1901–64), King of the Hellenes 1947–64, *m.* 1938 Princess Frederika of Brunswick (*see* page 134); *issue:* King Constantine II (*b.* 1940), *m.* 1964 Princess Anne-Marie of Denmark (*see* page 136), and has issue (three sons, two daughters); Princess Sophie (*b.* 1938), *m.* 1962 Juan Carlos I of Spain (*see* page 136); Princess Irene (*b.* 1942).
(*e*) Princess Irene (1904–74), *m.* 1939 4th Duke of Aosta; *issue:* Prince Amedeo (*b.* 1943).
(*f*) Princess Katherine (Lady Katherine Brandram) (*b.* 1913), *m.* 1947 Major R. C. A. Brandram, MC, TD; *issue:* R. Paul G. A. Brandram (*b.* 1948).
(8) Princess Margarethe (1872–1954), *m.* 1893 Prince Friedrich Karl of Hesse (1868–1940). *Issue:*
(*a*) Prince Friedrich Wilhelm (1893–1916).
(*b*) Prince Maximilian (1894–1914).
(*c*) Prince Philipp (1896–1980), *m.* 1925 Princess Mafalda of Italy; *issue:* Prince Moritz (*b.* 1926); Prince Heinrich (*b.* 1927); Prince Otto (*b.* 1937); Princess Elisabeth (*b.* 1940).
(*d*) Prince Wolfgang (*b.* 1896), *m.* (1) 1924 Princess Marie Alexandra of Baden; (2) 1948 Ottilie Möller.
(*e*) Prince Richard (1901–).
(*f*) Prince Christoph (1901–43), *m.* 1930 Princess Sophie of Greece (*see* below) and has issue (two sons, three daughters).

2. HRH PRINCE ALBERT EDWARD (HM KING EDWARD VII), *b.* 9 November 1841, *m.* 1863 HRH Princess Alexandra of Denmark (1844–1925), *succeeded* to the throne 22 January 1901, *d.* 6 May 1910. *Issue:*

(1) Albert Victor, Duke of Clarence and Avondale (1864–92).
(2) George (HM KING GEORGE V) (*see* page 134).
(3) Louise (1867–1931) Princess Royal 1905–31, *m.* 1889 1st Duke of Fife (1849–1912). *Issue:*
(*a*) Princess Alexandra, Duchess of Fife (1891–1959), *m.* 1913 Prince Arthur of Connaught (*see* page 136).
(*b*) Princess Maud (1893–1945), *m.* 1923 11th Earl of Southesk (1893–1992); *issue:* The Duke of Fife (*b.* 1929).
(4) Victoria (1868–1935).
(5) Maud (1869–1938), *m.* 1896 Prince Charles of Denmark (1872–1957), later King Haakon VII of Norway 1905–57. *Issue:*
(*a*) Olav V, King of Norway 1957–91 (1903–91), *m.* 1929 Princess Märtha of Sweden (1901–54); *issue:* Princess Ragnhild (*b.* 1930); Princess Astrid (*b.* 1932); Harald V, King of Norway (*b.* 1937).
(6) Alexander (6–7 April 1871).

3. HRH PRINCESS ALICE Maud Mary (1843–78), *m.* 1862 Prince Louis (1837–92), Grand Duke of Hesse 1877–92. *Issue:*

(1) Victoria (1863–1950), *m.* 1884 *Admiral of the Fleet* Prince Louis of Battenberg (1854–1921), *cr.* 1st Marquess of Milford Haven 1917. *Issue:*
(*a*) Alice (1885–1969), *m.* 1903 Prince Andrew of Greece (1882–1944); *issue:* Princess Margarita (1905–81) *m.* 1931 Prince Gottfried of Hohenlohe-Langenburg (*see* below); Princess Theodora (1906–69), *m.* Prince Berthold of Baden (1906–63) and has issue (2 sons, one daughter); Princess Cecilie (1911–37), *m.* George, Grand Duke of Hesse (*see* below); Princess Sophie (*b.* 1914), *m.* (1) 1930 Prince Christoph of Hesse (*see* above); (2) 1946 Prince Georg of Hanover (*see* page 134); Prince Philip, Duke of Edinburgh (*b.* 1921) (*see* page 123).
(*b*) Louise (1889–1965), *m.* 1923 Gustaf VI Adolf (1882–1973), King of Sweden 1950–73.
(*c*) George, 2nd Marquess of Milford Haven (1892–1938), *m.* 1916 Countess Nadejda, daughter of Grand Duke Michael of Russia; *issue:* Lady Tatiana (1917–88); David Michael, 3rd Marquess (1919–70).
(*d*) Louis, 1st Earl Mountbatten of Burma (1900–79), *m.* 1922 Edwina Ashley, daughter of Lord Mount Temple; *issue:* Patricia, Countess Mountbatten of Burma (*b.* 1924), Pamela (*b.* 1929).
(2) Elizabeth (1864–1918), *m.* 1884 Grand Duke Sergius of Russia (1857–1905).
(3) Irene (1866–1953), *m.* 1888 Prince Heinrich of Prussia (*see* page 134).
(4) Ernst Ludwig (1868–1937), Grand Duke of Hesse 1892–1918, *m.* (1) 1894 Princess Victoria Melita of Saxe-Coburg (*see* below), (marriage dissolved 1901); (2) 1905 Princess Eleonore of Solms-Hohensolmslich. *Issue:*
(*a*) Princess Elizabeth (1895–1903).
(*b*) George, Grand Duke of Hesse (1906–37), *m.* Princess Cecilie of Greece (*see* above), and had issue, 2 sons, accidentally killed with parents 1937.
(*c*) Ludwig, Grand Duke of Hesse (1908–68), *m.* 1937 Margaret, daughter of 1st Lord Geddes.
(5) Frederick William (1870–3).
(6) Alix (Tsaritsa of Russia) (1872–1918), *m.* 1894 Nicholas II (1868–1918) Tsar of All the Russias 1894–1917, assassinated 16 July 1918. *Issue:*
(*a*) Grand Duchess Olga (1895–1918).
(*b*) Grand Duchess Tatiana (1897–1918).
(*c*) Grand Duchess Marie (1899–1918).
(*d*) Grand Duchess Anastasia (1901–18).
(*e*) Alexis, Tsarevitch of Russia (1904–18).
(7) Marie (1874–8).

4. HRH PRINCE ALFRED Ernest Albert, Duke of Edinburgh, *Admiral of the Fleet* (1844–1900), *m.* 1874 Grand Duchess Marie Alexandrovna of Russia (1853–1920); succeeded as Duke of Saxe-Coburg and Gotha 22 August 1893. *Issue:*

(1) Alfred (Prince of Saxe-Coburg) (1874–99).
(2) Marie (1875–1938), *m.* 1893 Ferdinand (1865–1927), King of Roumania 1914–27. *Issue:*
(*a*) Carol II (1893–1953), King of Roumania 1930–40, *m.* (2) Princess Helena of Greece (*see* above), (marriage dissolved 1928); *issue:* Michael (*b.* 1921), King of Roumania 1927–30, 1940–7, *m.* 1948 Princess Anne of Bourbon-Palma, and has issue (five daughters).
(*b*) Elisabeth (1894–1956), *m.* 1921 George II (1890–1947) King of the Hellenes (*see* page 134).
(*c*) Marie (1900–61), *m.* 1922 Alexander (1888–1934), King of Yugoslavia 1921–34; *issue:* Petar II (1923–70), King of Yugoslavia 1934–45, *m.* 1944 Princess Alexandra of Greece (*see* page 134) and has issue (one son); Prince Tomislav (*b.* 1928), *m.* (1) 1957 Princess Margarita of Baden (daughter of Princess Theodora of Greece and Prince Berthold of Baden, *see* above); (2) 1982 Linda Bonney; and has issue (three sons, one daughter); Prince Andrej (1929–90), *m.* (1) Princess Christina of Hesse (daughter of Prince Christoph of Hesse and Princess Sophie of Greece, *see* above); (2) 1963 Princess Kira-Melita of Leiningen (*see* below); and has issue (three sons, one daughter).
(*d*) Prince Nicolas (1903–).
(*e*) Princess Ileana (1909–91), *m.* (1) 1931 Archduke Anton of Austria; (2) 1954 Dr Stefan Issarescu; *issue:* Archduke Stefan (*b.* 1932); Archduchess Maria Ileana (1933–59); Archduchess Alexandra (*b.* 1935); Archduke Dominic (*b.* 1937); Archduchess Maria Magdalena (*b.* 1939); Archduchess Elisabeth (*b.* 1942).
(*f*) Prince Mircea (1913–16).
(3) Victoria Melita (1876–1936), *m.* (1) 1894 Grand Duke Ernst of Hesse (*see* above) (marriage dissolved 1901); (2) 1905 the Grand Duke Kirill of Russia (1876–1938). *Issue:*
(*a*) Marie Kirillovna (1907–51), *m.* 1925 Prince Friedrich Karl of Leiningen; *issue:* Prince Emich (*b.* 1926); Prince Karl (*b.* 1928); Princess Kira-Melita (*b.* 1930), *m.* Prince Andrej of Yugoslavia (*see* above); Princess Margarita (*b.* 1932); Princess Mechtilde (*b.* 1936); Prince Friedrich (*b.* 1938).
(*b*) Kira Kirillovna (1909–67), *m.* 1938 Prince Ludwig of Prussia (*see* page 134); *issue:* Prince Friedrich Wilhelm (*b.* 1939); Prince Michael (*b.* 1940); Princess Marie (*b.* 1942); Princess Kira (*b.* 1943); Prince Louis Ferdinand (1944–77); Prince Christian (*b.* 1946); Princess Xenia (*b.* 1949).
(*c*) Vladimir Kirillovitch (1917–92), *m.* 1948 Princess Leonida Bagration-Mukhransky; *issue:* Grand Duchess Maria (*b.* 1953), *m.* and has issue.
(4) Alexandra (1878–1942), *m.* 1896 Ernst, Prince of Hohenlohe Langenburg. *Issue:*
(*a*) Gottfried (1897–1960), *m.* 1931 Princess Margarita of Greece (*see* above); *issue:* Prince Kraft (*b.* 1935), Princess Beatrix (*b.* 1936), Prince George (*b.* 1938), Prince Ruprecht and Prince Albrecht (*b.* 1944).
(*b*) Maria (1899–1967), *m.* 1916 Prince Frederick of Schleswig-Holstein-Sonderburg-Glücksburg; *issue:* Prince Peter (1922–80); Princess Marie (*b.* 1927).
(*c*) Princess Alexandra (1901–63).
(*d*) Princess Irma (1902–).
(5) Princess Beatrice (1884–1966), *m.* 1909 Alfonso of Orleans, Infante of Spain. *Issue:*

(*a*) Prince Alvaro (*b*. 1910), *m*. 1937 Carla Parodi-Delfino; *issue:* Princess Gerarda (*b*. 1939); Prince Alonso (1941–75); Princess Beatriz (*b*. 1943); Prince Alvaro (*b*. 1947).
(*b*) Prince Alonso (1912–36).
(*c*) Prince Ataulfo (1913–).

5. HRH Princess Helena Augusta Victoria (1846–1923), *m*. 1866 Prince Christian of Schleswig-Holstein-Sonderburg-Augustenburg (1831–1917). *Issue:*

(1) Prince Christian Victor (1867–1900).
(2) Prince Albert (1869–1931), Duke of Schleswig-Holstein 1921–31.
(3) Princess Helena (1870–1948).
(4) Princess Marie Louise (1872–1956), *m*. 1891 Prince Aribert of Anhalt (marriage dissolved 1900).
(5) Prince Harold (12–20 May 1876).

6. HRH Princess Louise Caroline Alberta (1848–1939), *m*. 1871 the Marquess of Lorne, afterwards 9th Duke of Argyll (1845–1914); without issue.

7. HRH Prince Arthur William Patrick Albert, Duke of Connaught, *Field Marshal* (1850–1942), *m*. 1879 Princess Louisa of Prussia (1860–1917). *Issue:*

(1) Margaret (1882–1920), *m*. 1905 Crown Prince Gustaf Adolf (1882–1973), afterwards King of Sweden 1950–73. *Issue:*
(*a*) Gustaf Adolf, Duke of Västerbotten (1906–47), *m*. 1932 Princess Sibylla of Saxe-Coburg-Gotha (*see* below); *issue:* Princess Margaretha (*b*. 1934); Princess Birgitta (*b*. 1937); Princess Désirée (*b*. 1938); Princess Christina (*b*. 1943); Carl XVI Gustaf, King of Sweden (*b*. 1946).
(*b*) Count Sigvard Bernadotte (*b*. 1907); *m*., *issue:* Count Michael (*b*. 1944).
(*c*) Princess Ingrid (Queen Mother of Denmark) (*b*. 1910), *m*. 1935 Frederick IX (1899–72), King of Denmark 1947–72; *issue:* Margrethe II, Queen of Denmark (*b*. 1940); Princess Benedikte (*b*. 1944); Princess Anne-Marie (*b*. 1946), *m*. 1964 Constantine II of Greece (*see* page 135).
(*d*) Prince Bertil, Duke of Halland (*b*. 1912), *m*. 1976 Mrs Lilian Craig.
(*e*) Count Carl Bernadotte (*b*. 1916), *m*. (1) 1946 Mrs Kerstin Johnson; (2) 1988 Countess Gunnila Busler.
(2) Arthur (1883–1938), *m*. 1913 HH the Duchess of Fife (*see* page 135). *Issue:*
Alastair Arthur, Duke of Connaught (1914–43).
(3) (Victoria) Patricia (1886–1974), *m*. 1919 Adm. Hon. Sir Alexander Ramsay. *Issue:*
Hon. Alexander Ramsay of Mar (*b*. 1919), *m*. 1956 Hon. Flora Fraser (Lady Saltoun).

8. HRH Prince Leopold George Duncan Albert, Duke of Albany (1853–84), *m*. 1882 Princess Helena of Waldeck (1861–1922). *Issue:*

(1) Alice (1883–1981), *m*. 1904 Prince Alexander of Teck (1874–1957), *cr*. 1st Earl of Athlone 1917. *Issue:*
(*a*) Lady May (*b*. 1906), *m*. 1931 Sir Henry Abel-Smith, KCMG, KCVO, DSO; *issue:* Anne (*b*. 1932); Richard (*b*. 1933); Elizabeth (*b*. 1936).
(*b*) Rupert, Viscount Trematon (1907–28).
(*c*) Prince Maurice (March–September 1910).
(2) Charles Edward (1884–1954), Duke of Albany 1884 until title suspended 1917, Duke of Saxe-Coburg-Gotha 1900–18, *m*. 1905 Princess Victoria Adelheid of Schleswig-Holstein-Sonderburg-Glücksburg. *Issue:*
(*a*) Prince Johann (1906–72), and has issue.
(*b*) Princess Sibylla (1908–72) *m*. 1932 Prince Gustav Adolf of Sweden (*see* above).
(*c*) Prince Dietmar (1909–).
(*d*) Princess Caroline (1912–83).
(*e*) Prince Friedrich (*b*. 1918).

9. HRH Princess Beatrice Mary Victoria Feodore (1857–1944), *m*. 1885 Prince Henry of Battenberg (1858–96). *Issue:*

(1) Alexander, 1st Marquess of Carisbrooke (1886–1960), *m*. 1917 Lady Irene Denison. *Issue:*
Lady Iris Mountbatten (1920–82).
(2) Victoria Eugénie (1887–1969), *m*. 1906 Alfonso XIII (1886–1941) King of Spain 1886–1931. *Issue:*
(*a*) Prince Alfonso (1907–38).
(*b*) Prince Jaime (1908–75).
(*c*) Princess Beatrice (*b*. 1909).
(*d*) Princess Maria (*b*. 1911).
(*e*) Prince Juan (*b*. 1913) Count of Barcelona, and has *issue:* Princess Maria (*b*. 1936); Juan Carlos I, King of Spain (*b*. 1938), *m*. 1962 Princess Sophie of Greece (*see* page 135) and has issue (1 son, 2 daughters); Princess Margarita (*b*. 1939).
(*f*) Prince Gonzale (1914–34).
(3) Major Lord Leopold Mountbatten (1889–1922).
(4) Maurice (1891–1914), died of wounds received in action.

Kings and Queens of England

Since 927

HOUSES OF CERDIC AND DENMARK

Reign

927–939 Æthelstan
Second son of Edward the Elder, by Ecgwynn, and grandson of Alfred
Acceded to Wessex and Mercia *c*.924, established direct rule over Northumbria 927, effectively creating the Kingdom of England
Reigned 15 years

939–946 Edmund I
Born 921, fourth son of Edward the Elder, by Eadgifu
Married (1) Ælfgifu (2) Æthelflæd
Killed aged 25, *reigned* 6 years

946–955 Eadred
Fifth son of Edward the Elder, by Eadgifu
Reigned 9 years

955–959 Eadwig
Born before 943, son of Edmund and Ælfgifu
Married Ælfgifu
Reigned 3 years

959–975 Edgar I
Born 943, son of Edmund and Ælfgifu
Married (1) Aethelflæd (2) Wulfthryth (3) Ælfthryth
Died aged 32, *reigned* 15 years

975–978 Edward I (the Martyr)
Born c.962, son of Edgar and Æthelflæd
Assassinated aged *c*.16, *reigned* 2 years

978–1016 Æthelred (the Unready)
Born c.968/969, son of Edgar and Ælfthryth
Married (1) Ælfgifu (2) Emma, daughter of Richard I, count of Normandy
1013–14 dispossessed of kingdom by Swegn Forkbeard (king of Denmark 987–1014)
Died aged *c*.47, *reigned* 38 years

1016 Edmund II (Ironside)
Born before 993, son of Æthelred and Ælfgifu
Married Ealdgyth
Died aged over 23, *reigned* 7 months (April–November)

1016–1035 Cnut (Canute)
*Born c.*995, son of Swegn Forkbeard, king of Denmark, and Gunhild
Married (1) Ælfgifu (2) Emma, widow of Æthelred the Unready
Gained submission of West Saxons 1015, Northumbrians 1016, Mercia 1016, king of all England after Edmund's death
King of Denmark 1019–35, king of Norway 1028–35
Died aged *c.*40, *reigned* 19 years

1035–1040 Harold I (Harefoot)
*Born c.*1016/17, son of Cnut and Ælfgifu
Married Ælfgifu
1035 recognized as regent for himself and his brother Harthacnut; 1037 recognized as king
Died aged *c.*23, *reigned* 4 years

1040–1042 Harthacnut
*Born c.*1018, son of Cnut and Emma
Titular king of Denmark from 1028
Acknowledged king of England 1035–7 with Harold I as regent; effective king after Harold's death
Died aged *c.*24, *reigned* 2 years

1042–1066 Edward II (the Confessor)
Born between 1002 and 1005, son of Æthelred the Unready and Emma
Married Eadgyth, daughter of Godwine, earl of Wessex
Died aged over 60, *reigned* 23 years

1066 Harold II (Godwinesson)
*Born c.*1020, son of Godwine, earl of Wessex, and Gytha
Married (1) Eadgyth (2) Ealdgyth
Killed in battle aged *c.*46, *reigned* 10 months (January–October)

THE HOUSE OF NORMANDY

1066–1087 William I (the Conqueror)
Born 1027/8, son of Robert I, duke of Normandy; obtained the Crown by conquest
Married Matilda, daughter of Baldwin, count of Flanders
Died aged *c.*60, *reigned* 20 years

1087–1100 William II (Rufus)
Born between 1056 and 1060, third son of William I; succeeded his father in England only
Killed aged *c.*40, *reigned* 12 years

1100–1135 Henry I (Beauclerk)
Born 1068, fourth son of William I
Married (1) Edith or Matilda, daughter of Malcolm III of Scotland (2) Adela, daughter of Godfrey, count of Louvain
Died aged 67, *reigned* 35 years

1135–1154 Stephen
Born not later than 1100, third son of Adela, daughter of William I, and Stephen, count of Blois
Married Matilda, daughter of Eustace, count of Boulogne
1141 (February–November) held captive by adherents of Matilda, daughter of Henry I, who contested the crown until 1153
Died aged over 53, *reigned* 18 years

THE HOUSE OF ANJOU (PLANTAGENETS)

1154–1189 Henry II (Curtmantle)
Born 1133, son of Matilda, daughter of Henry I, and Geoffrey, count of Anjou
Married Eleanor, daughter of William, duke of Aquitaine, and divorced queen of Louis VII of France
Died aged 56, *reigned* 34 years

1189–1199 Richard I (Coeur de Lion)
Born 1157, third son of Henry II
Married Berengaria, daughter of Sancho VI, king of Navarre
Died aged 42, *reigned* 9 years

1199–1216 John (Lackland)
Born 1167, fifth son of Henry II
Married (1) Isabella or Avisa, daughter of William, earl of Gloucester (divorced) (2) Isabella, daughter of Aymer, count of Angoulême
Died aged 48, *reigned* 17 years

1216–1272 Henry III
Born 1207, son of John and Isabella of Angoulême
Married Eleanor, daughter of Raymond, count of Provence
Died aged 65, *reigned* 56 years

1272–1307 Edward I (Longshanks)
Born 1239, eldest son of Henry III
Married (1) Eleanor, daughter of Ferdinand III, king of Castile (2) Margaret, daughter of Philip III of France
Died aged 68, *reigned* 34 years

1307–1327 Edward II
Born 1284, eldest surviving son of Edward I and Eleanor
Married Isabella, daughter of Philip IV of France
Deposed January 1327, *killed* September 1327 aged 43, *reigned* 19 years

1327–1377 Edward III
Born 1312, eldest son of Edward II
Married Philippa, daughter of William, count of Hainault
Died aged 64, *reigned* 50 years

1377–1399 Richard II
Born 1367, son of Edward (the Black Prince), eldest son of Edward III
Married (1) Anne, daughter of Emperor Charles IV (2) Isabelle, daughter of Charles VI of France
Deposed September 1399, *killed* February 1400 aged 33, *reigned* 22 years

THE HOUSE OF LANCASTER

1399–1413 Henry IV
Born 1366, son of John of Gaunt, fourth son of Edward III, and Blanche, daughter of Henry, duke of Lancaster
Married (1) Mary, daughter of Humphrey, earl of Hereford (2) Joan, daughter of Charles, king of Navarre, and widow of John, duke of Brittany
Died aged *c.*47, *reigned* 13 years

1413–1422 Henry V
Born 1387, eldest surviving son of Henry IV and Mary
Married Catherine, daughter of Charles VI of France
Died aged 34, *reigned* 9 years

1422–1471 Henry VI
Born 1421, son of Henry V
Married Margaret, daughter of René, duke of Anjou and count of Provence
Deposed March 1461, *restored* October 1470
Deposed April 1471, *killed* May 1471 aged 49, *reigned* 39 years

THE HOUSE OF YORK

1461–1483 Edward IV
Born 1442, eldest son of Richard of York, who was the grandson of Edmund, fifth son of Edward III, and the son of Anne, great-granddaughter of Lionel, third son of Edward III
Married Elizabeth Woodville, daughter of Richard, Lord Rivers, and widow of Sir John Grey
Acceded March 1461, *deposed* October 1470, *restored* April 1471
Died aged 40, *reigned* 21 years

1483 EDWARD V
Born 1470, eldest son of Edward IV
Deposed June 1483, *died* probably July–September 1483, aged 12, *reigned* 2 months (April–June)

1483–1485 RICHARD III
Born 1452, fourth son of Richard of York and brother of Edward IV
Married Anne Neville, daughter of Richard, earl of Warwick, and widow of Edward, Prince of Wales, son of Henry VI
Killed in battle aged 32, *reigned* 2 years

THE HOUSE OF TUDOR

1485–1509 HENRY VII
Born 1457, son of Margaret Beaufort, great-granddaughter of John of Gaunt, fourth son of Edward III, and Edmund Tudor, earl of Richmond
Married Elizabeth, daughter of Edward IV
Died aged 52, *reigned* 23 years

1509–1547 HENRY VIII
Born 1491, second son of Henry VII
Married (1) Catherine, daughter of Ferdinand II, king of Aragon, and widow of his elder brother Arthur (divorced) (2) Anne, daughter of Sir Thomas Boleyn (executed) (3) Jane, daughter of Sir John Seymour (died in childbirth) (4) Anne, daughter of John, duke of Cleves (divorced) (5) Catherine Howard, niece of the Duke of Norfolk (executed) (6) Catherine, daughter of Sir Thomas Parr and widow of Lord Latimer
Died aged 55, *reigned* 37 years

1547–1553 EDWARD VI
Born 1537, son of Henry VIII and Jane Seymour
Died aged 15, *reigned* 6 years

1553 JANE
Born 1537, daughter of Frances, daughter of Mary Tudor, the younger sister of Henry VIII, and Henry Grey, duke of Suffolk
Married Lord Guildford Dudley, son of the Duke of Northumberland
Deposed July 1553, *executed* February 1554 aged 16, *reigned* 14 days

1553–1558 MARY I
Born 1516, daughter of Henry VIII and Catherine of Aragon
Married Philip II of Spain
Died aged 42, *reigned* 5 years

1558–1603 ELIZABETH I
Born 1533, daughter of Henry VIII and Anne Boleyn
Died aged 69, *reigned* 44 years

THE HOUSE OF STUART

1603–1625 JAMES I (VI OF SCOTLAND)
Born 1566, son of Mary, queen of Scots and granddaughter of Margaret Tudor, eldest daughter of Henry VII, and Henry Stewart, Lord Darnley
Married Anne, daughter of Frederick II of Denmark
Died aged 58, *reigned* 22 years

1625–1649 CHARLES I
Born 1600, second son of James I
Married Henrietta Maria, daughter of Henry VI of France
Executed 1649 aged 48, *reigned* 23 years

COMMONWEALTH DECLARED 19 May 1649
1649–53 Government by a council of state
1653–8 Oliver Cromwell, *Lord Protector*
1658–9 Richard Cromwell, *Lord Protector*

1660–1685 CHARLES II
Born 1630, eldest son of Charles I
Married Catherine, daughter of John IV of Portugal
Died aged 54, *reigned* 24 years

1685–1688 JAMES II (VII of Scotland)
Born 1633, second son of Charles I
Married (1) Lady Anne Hyde, daughter of Edward, earl of Clarendon (2) Mary, daughter of Alphonso, duke of Modena
Reign ended with flight from kingdom December 1688
Died 1701 aged 67, *reigned* 3 years

INTERREGNUM 11 December 1688 to 12 February 1689

1689–1702 WILLIAM III
Born 1650, son of William II, prince of Orange, and Mary Stuart, daughter of Charles I
Married Mary, elder daughter of James II
Died aged 51, *reigned* 13 years

and

1689–1694 MARY II
Born 1662, elder daughter of James II and Anne
Died aged 32, *reigned* 5 years

1702–1714 ANNE
Born 1665, younger daughter of James II and Anne
Married Prince George of Denmark, son of Frederick III of Denmark
Died aged 49, *reigned* 12 years

THE HOUSE OF HANOVER

1714–1727 GEORGE I (Elector of Hanover)
Born 1660, son of Sophia (daughter of Frederick, elector palatine, and Elizabeth Stuart, daughter of James I) and Ernest Augustus, elector of Hanover
Married Sophia Dorothea, daughter of George William, duke of Lüneburg-Celle
Died aged 67, *reigned* 12 years

1727–1760 GEORGE II
Born 1683, son of George I
Married Caroline, daughter of John Frederick, margrave of Brandenburg-Anspach
Died aged 76, *reigned* 33 years

1760–1820 GEORGE III
Born 1738, son of Frederick, eldest son of George II
Married Charlotte, daughter of Charles Louis, duke of Mecklenburg-Strelitz
Died aged 81, *reigned* 59 years

REGENCY 1811–20
Prince of Wales regent owing to the insanity of George III

1820–1830 GEORGE IV
Born 1762, eldest son of George III
Married Caroline, daughter of Charles, duke of Brunswick-Wolfenbüttel
Died aged 67, *reigned* 10 years

1830–1837 WILLIAM IV
Born 1765, third son of George III
Married Adelaide, daughter of George, duke of Saxe-Meiningen
Died aged 71, *reigned* 7 years

1837–1901 VICTORIA
Born 1819, daughter of Edward, fourth son of George III
Married Prince Albert of Saxe-Coburg and Gotha
Died aged 81, *reigned* 63 years

THE HOUSE OF SAXE-COBURG AND GOTHA

1901–1910 EDWARD VII
Born 1841, eldest son of Victoria and Albert
Married Alexandra, daughter of Christian IX of Denmark
Died aged 68, *reigned* 9 years

THE HOUSE OF WINDSOR

1910–1936 GEORGE V
Born 1865, second son of Edward VII
Married Victoria Mary, daughter of Francis, duke of Teck
Died aged 70, *reigned* 25 years

1936 EDWARD VIII
Born 1894, eldest son of George V
Married (1937) Mrs Wallis Warfield
Abdicated 1936, *died* 1972 aged 77, *reigned* 10 months (20 January to 11 December)

1936–1952 GEORGE VI
Born 1895, second son of George V
Married Lady Elizabeth Bowes-Lyon, daughter of 14th Earl of Strathmore and Kinghorne (*see also* pages 123–4)
Died aged 56, *reigned* 15 years

1952– ELIZABETH II
Born 1926, elder daughter of George VI
Married Philip, son of Prince Andrew of Greece (*see also* page 123)
WHOM GOD PRESERVE

Kings and Queens of Scots

SINCE 1016

Reign

1016–1034 MALCOLM II
*Born c.*954, son of Kenneth II
Acceded to Alba 1005, secured Lothian *c.*1016, obtained Strathclyde for his grandson Duncan *c.*1016, thus forming the Kindom of Scotland
Died aged *c.*80, *reigned* 18 years

1034–1040 DUNCAN I
Son of Bethoc, daughter of Malcolm II, and Crinan
Married a cousin of Siward, earl of Northumbria
Reigned 5 years

1040–1057 MACBETH
*Born c.*1005, son of a daughter of Malcolm II and Finlaec, mormaer of Moray
Married Gruoch, granddaughter of Kenneth III
Died aged *c.*52, *reigned* 17 years

1057–1058 LULACH
*Born c.*1032, son of Gillacomgan, mormaer of Moray, and Gruoch (and stepson of Macbeth)
Died aged *c.*26, *reigned* 7 months (August–March)

1058–1093 MALCOLM III(Canmore)
*Born c.*1031, elder son of Duncan I
Married (1) Ingibiorg (2) Margaret (St Margaret), granddaughter of Edmund II of England
Killed in battle aged *c.*62, *reigned* 35 years

1093–1097 DONALD III BÁN
*Born c.*1033, second son of Duncan I
Deposed May 1094, *restored* November 1094, *deposed* October 1097, *reigned* 3 years

1094 DUNCAN II
*Born c.*1060, elder son of Malcolm III and Ingibiorg
Married Octreda of Dunbar
Killed aged *c.*34, *reigned* 6 months (May–November)

1097–1107 EDGAR
*Born c.*1074, second son of Malcolm III and Margaret
Died aged *c.*32, *reigned* 9 years

1107–1124 ALEXANDER I (The Fierce)
*Born c.*1077, fifth son of Malcolm III and Margaret
Married Sybilla, illegitimate daughter of Henry I of England
Died aged *c.*47, *reigned* 17 years

1124–1153 DAVID I (The Saint)
*Born c.*1085, sixth son of Malcolm III and Margaret
Married Matilda, daughter of Waltheof, earl of Huntingdon
Died aged *c.*68, *reigned* 29 years

1153–1165 MALCOLM IV (The Maiden)
*Born c.*1141, son of Henry, earl of Huntingdon, second son of David I
Died aged *c.*24, *reigned* 12 years

1165–1214 WILLIAM I (The Lion)
*Born c.*1142, brother of Malcolm IV
Married Ermengarde, daughter of Richard, viscount of Beaumont
Died aged *c.*72, *reigned* 49 years

1214–1249 ALEXANDER II
Born 1198, son of William I
Married (1) Joan, daughter of John, king of England (2) Marie, daughter of Ingelram de Coucy
Died aged 50, *reigned* 34 years

1249–1286 ALEXANDER III
Born 1241, son of Alexander II and Marie
Married (1) Margaret, daughter of Henry III of England (2) Yolande, daughter of the Count of Dreux
Killed accidentally aged 44, *reigned* 36 years

1286–1290 MARGARET (The Maid of Norway)
Born 1283, daughter of Margaret (daughter of Alexander III) and Eric II of Norway
Died aged 7, *reigned* 4 years

FIRST INTERREGNUM 1290–2
Throne disputed by 13 competitors. Crown awarded to John Balliol by adjudication of Edward I of England

THE HOUSE OF BALLIOL

1292–1296 JOHN (Balliol)
*Born c.*1250, son of Dervorguilla, great-great-granddaughter of David I, and John de Balliol
Married Isabella, daughter of John, earl of Surrey
Abdicated 1296, *died* 1313 aged *c.*63, *reigned* 3 years

SECOND INTERREGNUM 1296–1306
Edward I of England declared John Balliol to have forfeited the throne for contumacy in 1296 and took the government of Scotland into his own hands

THE HOUSE OF BRUCE

1306–1329 ROBERT I (Bruce)
Born 1274, son of Robert Bruce and Marjorie, countess of Carrick, and great-grandson of the second daughter of David, earl of Huntingdon, brother of William I
Married (1) Isabella, daughter of Donald, earl of Mar (2) Elizabeth, daughter of Richard, earl of Ulster
Died aged 54, *reigned* 23 years

1329–1371	DAVID II *Born* 1324, son of Robert I and Elizabeth *Married* (1) Joanna, daughter of Edward II of England (2) Margaret Drummond, widow of Sir John Logie (divorced) *Died* aged 46, *reigned* 41 years 1332 Edward Balliol, son of John Balliol, crowned King of Scots September, expelled December 1333–6 Edward Balliol restored as King of Scots

THE HOUSE OF STEWART

1371–1390	ROBERT II (Stewart) *Born* 1316, son of Marjorie, daughter of Robert I, and Walter, High Steward of Scotland *Married* (1) Elizabeth, daughter of Sir Robert Mure of Rowallan (2) Euphemia, daughter of Hugh, earl of Ross *Died* aged 74, *reigned* 19 years
1390–1406	ROBERT III *Born* c.1337, son of Robert II and Elizabeth *Married* Annabella, daughter of Sir John Drummond of Stobhall *Died* aged c.69, *reigned* 16 years
1406–1437	JAMES I *Born* 1394, son of Robert III *Married* Joan Beaufort, daughter of John, earl of Somerset *Assassinated* aged 42, *reigned* 30 years
1437–1460	JAMES II *Born* 1430, son of James I *Married* Mary, daughter of Arnold, duke of Gueldres *Killed* accidentally aged 29, *reigned* 23 years
1460–1488	JAMES III *Born* 1452, son of James II *Married* Margaret, daughter of Christian I of Denmark *Assassinated* aged 36, *reigned* 27 years
1488–1513	JAMES IV *Born* 1473, son of James III *Married* Margaret Tudor, daughter of Henry VII of England *Killed* in battle aged 40, *reigned* 25 years
1513–1542	JAMES V *Born* 1512, son of James IV *Married* (1) Madeleine, daughter of Francis I of France (2) Mary of Lorraine, daughter of the Duc de Guise *Died* aged 30, *reigned* 29 years
1542–1567	MARY *Born* 1542, daughter of James V and Mary *Married* (1) the Dauphin, afterwards Francis II of France (2) Henry Stewart, Lord Darnley (3) James Hepburn, earl of Bothwell *Abdicated* 1567, prisoner in England from 1568, *executed* 1587, *reigned* 24 years
1567–1625	JAMES VI (and I of England) *Born* 1566, son of Mary, queen of Scots, and Henry, Lord Darnley Acceded 1567 to the Scottish throne, *reigned* 58 years Succeeded 1603 to the English throne, so joining the English and Scottish crowns

Welsh Sovereigns and Princes

Wales was ruled by sovereign princes from the earliest times until the death of Llywelyn in 1282. The first English Prince of Wales was the son of Edward I, and was born in Caernarvon town on 25 April 1284. According to a discredited legend, he was presented to the Welsh chieftains as their prince, in fulfilment of a promise that they should have a prince who 'could not speak a word of English' and should be native born. This son, who afterwards became Edward II, was created 'Prince of Wales and Earl of Chester' at the Lincoln Parliament on 7 February 1301.

The title Prince of Wales is borne after individual conferment and is not inherited at birth, though some Princes have been declared and styled Prince of Wales but never formally so created (*s.*). The title was conferred on Prince Charles by The Queen on 26 July 1958. He was invested at Caernarvon on 1 July 1969.

INDEPENDENT PRINCES AD 844 to 1282

844–878	Rhodri the Great
878–916	Anarawd, son of Rhodri
916–950	Hywel Dda, the Good
950–979	Iago ab Idwal (or Ieuaf)
979–985	Hywel ab Ieuaf, the Bad
985–986	Cadwallon, his brother
986–999	Maredudd ab Owain ap Hywel Dda
999–1008	Cynan ap Hywel ab Ieuaf
1018–1023	Llywelyn ap Seisyll
1023–1039	Iago ab Idwal ap Meurig
1039–1063	Gruffydd ap Llywelyn ap Seisyll
1063–1075	Bleddyn ap Cynfyn
1075–1081	Trahaern ap Caradog
1081–1137	Gruffydd ap Cynan ab Iago
1137–1170	Owain Gwynedd
1170–1194	Dafydd ab Owain Gwynedd
1194–1240	Llywelyn Fawr, the Great
1240–1246	Dafydd ap Llywelyn
1246–1282	Llywelyn ap Gruffydd ap Llywelyn

ENGLISH PRINCES SINCE 1301

1301	Edward (Edward II)
1343	Edward the Black Prince, s. of Edward III
1376	Richard (Richard II), s. of the Black Prince
1399	Henry of Monmouth (Henry V)
1454	Edward of Westminster, son of Henry VI
1471	Edward of Westminster (Edward V)
1483	Edward, son of Richard III (d. 1484)
1489	Arthur Tudor, son of Henry VII
1504	Henry Tudor (Henry VIII)
1610	Henry Stuart, son of James I (d. 1612)
1616	Charles Stuart (Charles I)
c.1638 (*s.*)	Charles (Charles II)
1688 (*s.*)	James Francis Edward (The Old Pretender) (d. 1766)
1714	George Augustus (George II)
1729	Frederick Lewis, s. of George II (d. 1751)
1751	George William Frederick (George III)
1762	George Augustus Frederick (George IV)
1841	Albert Edward (Edward VII)
1901	George (George V)
1910	Edward (Edward VIII)
1958	Charles Philip Arthur George

The Peerage

and Members of the House of Lords

The rules which govern the creation and succession of peerages are extremely complicated. There are, technically, five separate peerages, the Peerage of England, of Scotland, of Ireland, of Great Britain, and of the United Kingdom. The Peerage of Great Britain dates from 1707 when an Act of Union combined the two Kingdoms of England and Scotland and separate peerages were discontinued. The Peerage of the United Kingdom dates from 1801 when Great Britain and Ireland were combined under an Act of Union. Some Scottish peers have received additional peerages of Great Britain or of the United Kingdom since 1707, and some Irish peers additional peerages of the United Kingdom since 1801.

The Peerage of Ireland was not entirely discontinued from 1801 but holders of Irish peerages, whether pre-dating or created subsequent to the Union of 1801, are not entitled to sit in the House of Lords if they have no additional English, Scottish, Great Britain or United Kingdom peerage. However, they are eligible for election to the House of Commons and to vote in Parliamentary elections, which other peers are not. An Irish peer holding a peerage of a lower grade which enables him to sit in the House of Lords is introduced there by the title which enables him to sit, though for all other purposes he is known by his higher title.

In the Peerage of Scotland there is no rank of Baron; the equivalent rank is Lord of Parliament, abbreviated to 'Lord' (the female equivalent is 'Lady'). All peers of England, Scotland, Great Britain or the United Kingdom who are of full age (21 years) and of British, Irish or Commonwealth nationality are entitled to sit in the House of Lords.

Women Peers in Their Own Right

Most hereditary peerages pass on death to the nearest male heir; but certain ancient peerages pass on death to the nearest heir, male or female, and several are held by women (*see* pages 149 and 161).

A woman peer in her own right retains her title after marriage, and if her husband's rank is the superior she is designated by the two titles jointly, the inferior one last. Her hereditary claim still holds good in spite of any marriage whether higher or lower. No rank held by a woman can confer any title or even precedence upon her husband but the rank of a woman peer in her own right is inherited by her eldest son (or perhaps daughter), to whomsoever she may have been married.

Since the Peerage Act 1963, women peers in their own right have been entitled to sit in the House of Lords, subject to the same qualifications as men.

Life Peers

Non-hereditary or life peerages, in the degree of Baron or Baroness, have been conferred by the Crown since 1876 on eminent judges, the Lords of Appeal or law lords, to enable them to carry out the judicial functions of the House of Lords, and since 1958 on men and women of distinction in public life, giving them seats in the House of Lords. Life peers are addressed identically as an hereditary peer, and their children have the same courtesy style as the children of an hereditary peer.

No fees for dignities have been payable since 1937. The House of Lords surrendered the ancient right of peers to be tried for treason or felony by their peers in 1948.

Peerages Extinct Since the Last Edition

Viscountcies: Muirshiel (*cr.* 1964).
Baronies: Lurgan (*cr.* 1839), Southborough (*cr.* 1917).
Life Peerages: Burton of Coventry (*cr.* 1962), Molson (*cr.* 1961), Salmon (*cr.* 1972), Hart of South Lanark (*cr.* 1988), Broxbourne (*cr.* 1983), Fieldhouse (*cr.* 1990), Evans of Claughton (*cr.* 1978), Briginshaw (*cr.* 1974), Havers (*cr.* 1987), Davies of Penrhys (*cr.* 1974), James of Rusholme (*cr.* 1959), McFadzean of Kelvinside (*cr.* 1980), Ferrier (*cr.* 1958), Kearton (*cr.* 1970), Winterbottom (*cr.* 1965), Cheshire (*cr.* 1991), Devlin (*cr.* 1961), Phillips (*cr.* 1964).

Disclaimer of Peerages

The Peerage Act 1963 enables peers to disclaim their peerages for life. Peers alive in 1963 could disclaim within twelve months after the passing of the Act (31 July 1963); a person subsequently succeeding to a peerage may disclaim within twelve months (one month if an MP) after the date of succession, or of attaining his or her majority, if later. The disclaimer is irrevocable but does not affect the descent of the peerage after the disclaimant's death, and children of a disclaimed peer may, if they wish, retain their precedence and any courtesy titles and styles borne as children of a peer.

Earls: Durham (1970); Home (1963); Sandwich (1964).
Viscounts: Hailsham (1963); Stansgate (1963).
Barons: Altrincham (1963); Archibald (1975); Merthyr (1977); Reith (1972); Sanderson of Ayot (1971); Silkin (1972).

Peers Who Are Minors (i.e. under 21 years of age)

Earls: Craven (*b.* 1989).
Barons: Gretton (*b.* 1975).

Contractions and Symbols

s. Scottish title
I. Irish title
* The peer holds also an Imperial title, specified after the name by Engl., Brit. or UK.
° there is no 'of' in the title.
b. born.
s. succeeded.
m. married.
w. widower or widow.
M. minor.
† *heir* not ascertained at time of going to press.

Hereditary Peers

ROYAL DUKES

Style, His Royal Highness The Duke of _.
Style of address (*formal*) May it please your Royal Highness; (*informal*) Sir.

Created	Title, order of succession, name, etc.	Heir
1947	*Edinburgh* (1st), The Prince Philip, Duke of Edinburgh, (*see* page 123)	The Prince of Wales
1337	*Cornwall*, Charles, Prince of Wales, *s.* 1952 (*see* page 123)	–
1398	*Rothesay*, Charles, Prince of Wales, *s.* 1952 (*see* page 123)	–
1986	*York* (1st), The Prince Andrew, Duke of York (*see* p. 123)	None
1928	*Gloucester* (2nd), Prince Richard, Duke of Gloucester, *s.* 1974 (*see* page 124)	Earl of Ulster (*see* page 124)
1934	*Kent* (2nd), Prince Edward, Duke of Kent, *s.* 1942 (*see* page 124)	Earl of St Andrews (*see* page 124)

DUKES

Coronet, Eight strawberry leaves.
Style, His Grace the Duke of _.
Wife's style, Her Grace the Duchess of _.
Eldest son's style, Takes his father's second title as a courtesy title.
Younger sons' style, 'Lord' before forename and family name.
Daughters' style, 'Lady' before forename and family name.
For forms of address, *see* page 218.

Created	Title, order of succession, name, etc.	Eldest son or heir
1868 I.*	*Abercorn* (5th), James Hamilton (6th *Brit. Marq.*, 1790, and 14th *Scott. Earl*, 1606, both *Abercorn*), *b.* 1934, *s.* 1979, *m.*	Marquess of Hamilton, *b.* 1969.
1701 S.*	*Argyll*, Ian Campbell (12th *Scottish* and 5th *UK Duke*, 1892, both *Argyll*), *b.* 1937, *s.* 1973, *m.*	Marquess of Lorne, *b.* 1968.
1703 S.	*Atholl* (10th), George Iain Murray, *b.* 1931, *s.* 1957.	John *M.*, *b.* 1929.
1682	*Beaufort* (11th), David Robert Somerset, *b.* 1928, *s.* 1984, *m.*	Marquess of Worcester, *b.* 1952.
1694	*Bedford* (13th), John Robert Russell, *b.* 1917, *s.* 1953, *m.*	Marquess of Tavistock, *b.* 1940.
1663 S.*	*Buccleuch* (9th) & *Queensberry* (11th) (1684), Walter Francis John Montagu Douglas Scott, KT, VRD (8th *Engl. Earl, Doncaster*, 1662), *b.* 1923, *s.* 1973, *m.*	Earl of Dalkeith, *b.* 1954.
1694	*Devonshire* (11th), Andrew Robert Buxton Cavendish, MC, PC, *b.* 1920, *s.* 1950, *m.*	Marquess of Hartington, *b.* 1944.
1900	*Fife* (3rd), James George Alexander Bannerman Carnegie (12th *Scott. Earl, Southesk*, 1633, *s.* 1992), *b.* 1929, *s.* 1959. (*see* page 135).	Earl of Southesk, *b.* 1961.
1675	*Grafton* (11th), Hugh Denis Charles FitzRoy, KG, *b.* 1919, *s.* 1970, *m.*	Earl of Euston, *b.* 1947.
1643 S.*	*Hamilton* (15th) & *Brandon* (12th) (*Brit.* 1711), Angus Alan Douglas Douglas-Hamilton (*Premier Peer of Scotland*), *b.* 1938, *s.* 1973, *m.*	Marquess of Douglas and Clydesdale, *b.* 1978.
1766 I.*	*Leinster* (8th), Gerald FitzGerald (*Premier Duke, Marquess and Earl of Ireland*; 8th *Brit. Visct., Leinster*, 1747), *b.* 1914, *s.* 1976, *m.*	Marquess of Kildare, *b.* 1948.
1719	*Manchester* (12th), Angus Charles Drogo Montagu, *b.* 1938, *s.* 1985, *m.*	Viscount Mandeville, *b.* 1962.
1702	*Marlborough* (11th), John George Vanderbilt Henry Spencer-Churchill, *b.* 1926, *s.* 1972, *m.*	Marquess of Blandford, *b.* 1955.
1707 S.*	*Montrose* (8th), James Graham (6th *Brit. Earl, Graham*, 1722), *b.* 1935, *s.* 1992, *m.*	Marquess of Graham, *b.* 1973.
1483	*Norfolk* (17th), Miles Francis Stapleton Fitzalan-Howard, KG, GCVO, CB, CBE, MC (*Premier Duke and Earl*; 12th *Eng. Baron Beaumont*, 1309, *s.* 1971; 4th *UK Baron Howard of Glossop*, 1869, *s.* 1972), *b.* 1915, *s.* 1975, *m. Earl Marshal*.	Earl of Arundel and Surrey, *b.* 1956.
1766	*Northumberland* (11th), Henry Alan Walter Richard Percy, *b.* 1953, *s.* 1988.	Lord Ralph G.A.*P.*, *b.* 1956.
1675	*Richmond* (10th) & *Gordon* (5th) (*UK* 1876), Charles Henry Gordon Lennox (10th *Scott. Duke, Lennox*, 1675), *b.* 1929, *s.* 1989, *m.*	Earl of March and Kinrara, *b.* 1955.

Created	Title, order of succession, name, etc.	Eldest son or heir
1707 s.*	*Roxburghe* (10th), Guy David Innes-Ker (5th *UK Earl, Innes*, 1837), *b.* 1954, *s.* 1974. (*Premier Baronet of Scotland*).	Marquess of Bowmont and Cessford, *b.* 1981.
1703	*Rutland* (10th), Charles John Robert Manners, CBE, *b.* 1919, *s.* 1940, *m.*	Marquess of Granby, *b.* 1959.
1684	*St Albans* (14th), Murray de Vere Beauclerk, *b.* 1939, *s.* 1988, *m.*	Earl of Burford, *b.* 1965.
1547	*Somerset* (19th), John Michael Edward Seymour, *b.* 1952, *s.* 1984, *m.*	Lord Seymour, *b.* 1982.
1833	*Sutherland* (6th), John Sutherland Egerton, TD (5th *UK Earl, Ellesmere*, 1846), *b.* 1915, *s.* 1963, *m.*	Cyril R. *E.*, *b.* 1905.
1814	*Wellington* (8th), Arthur Valerian Wellesley, KG, LVO, OBE, MC (9th *Irish Earl, Mornington*, 1760), *b.* 1915, *s.* 1972, *m.*	Marquess of Douro, *b.* 1945.
1874	*Westminster* (6th), Gerald Cavendish Grosvenor, *b.* 1951, *s.* 1979, *m.*	Earl Grosvenor, *b.* 1991.

MARQUESSES

Coronet, Four strawberry leaves alternating with four silver balls.
Style, The Most Hon. the Marquess of _. In Scotland the spelling 'Marquis' is preferred for pre-Union creations.
Wife's style, The Most Hon. the Marchioness of _.
Eldest son's style, Takes his father's second title as a courtesy title.
Younger sons' style, 'Lord' before forename and family name.
Daughters' style, 'Lady' before forename and family name.
For forms of address, *see* page 218.

Created	Title, order of succession, name, etc.	Eldest son or heir
1916	*Aberdeen and Temair* (6th), Alastair Ninian John Gordon (12th *Scott. Earl, Aberdeen*, 1682), *b.* 1920, *s.* 1984, *m.*	Earl of Haddo, *b.* 1955.
1876	*Abergavenny* (5th), John Henry Guy Nevill, KG, OBE, *b.* 1914, *s.* 1954, *m.*	Guy R. G. *N.*, *b.* 1945.
1821	*Ailesbury* (8th), Michael Sidney Cedric Brudenell-Bruce, *b.* 1926, *s.* 1974, *m.*	Earl of Cardigan, *b.* 1952.
1831	*Ailsa* (7th), Archibald David Kennedy, OBE, (19th *Scott. Earl, Cassillis*, 1509), *b.* 1925, *s.* 1957, *m.*	Earl of Cassillis, *b.* 1956.
1815	*Anglesey* (7th), George Charles Henry Victor Paget, *b.* 1922, *s.* 1947, *m.*	Earl of Uxbridge, *b.* 1950.
1789	*Bath* (7th), Alexander George Thynn, *b.* 1932, *s.* 1992, *m.*	Viscount Weymouth, *b.* 1974.
1826	*Bristol* (7th), (Frederick William) John Augustus Hervey, *b.* 1954, *s.* 1985.	Lord F. W. C. Nicholas W. *H.*, *b.* 1961.
1796	*Bute* (6th), John Crichton-Stuart (11th *Scott. Earl, Dumfries*, 1633), *b.* 1933, *s.* 1956, *m.*	Earl of Dumfries, *b.* 1958.
1812	°*Camden* (6th), David George Edward Henry Pratt, *b.* 1930, *s.* 1983.	Earl of Brecknock, *b.* 1965.
1815	*Cholmondeley* (7th), David George Philip Cholmondeley (11th *Irish Viscount, Cholmondeley*, 1661), *b.* 1960, *s.* 1990. *Lord Great Chamberlain.*	Charles G. *C.*, *b.* 1959.
1816 I.*	°*Conyngham* (7th), Frederick William Henry Francis Conyngham (7th *UK Baron, Minster, UK* 1821), *b.* 1924, *s.* 1974, *m.*	Earl of Mount Charles, *b.* 1951.
1791 I.*	*Donegall* (7th), Dermot Richard Claud Chichester, LVO (7th *Brit. Baron, Fisherwick*, 1790, 6th *Brit. Baron, Templemore*, 1831), *b.* 1916, *s.* to Marquessate, 1975: to Templemore Barony, 1953, *m.*	Earl of Belfast, *b.* 1952.
1789 I.*	*Downshire* (8th), (Arthur) Robin Ian Hill (8th *Brit. Earl, Hillsborough*, 1772), *b.* 1929, *s.* 1989, *m.*	Earl of Hillsborough, *b.* 1959.
1801 I.*	*Ely* (8th) Charles John Tottenham (8th *UK Baron, Loftus*, 1801), *b.* 1913, *s.* 1969, *m.*	Viscount Loftus, *b.* 1943.
1801	*Exeter* (8th), (William) Michael Anthony Cecil, *b.* 1935, *s.* 1988, *m.*	Lord Burghley, *b.* 1970.
1800 I.*	*Headfort* (6th), Thomas Geoffrey Charles Michael Taylour (4th *UK Baron, Kenlis*, 1831), *b.* 1932, *s.* 1960, *m.*	Earl of Bective, *b.* 1959.
1793	*Hertford* (8th), Hugh Edward Conway Seymour (9th *Irish Baron, Conway*, 1712), *b.* 1930, *s.* 1940, *m.*	Earl of Yarmouth, *b.* 1958.
1599 s.*	*Huntly* (13th), Granville Charles Gomer Gordon (*Premier Marquess of Scotland*) (5th *UK Baron, Meldrum*, 1815), *b.* 1944, *s.* 1987, *m.*	Earl of Aboyne, *b.* 1973.
1784	*Lansdowne* (8th), George John Charles Mercer Nairne Petty-Fitzmaurice, PC (8th *Irish Earl, Kerry*, 1723), *b.* 1912, *s.* 1944, *w.*	Earl of Shelburne, *b.* 1941.
1902	*Linlithgow* (4th), Adrian John Charles Hope (10th *Scott. Earl, Hopetoun* 1703), *b.* 1946, *s.* 1987, *m.*	Earl of Hopetoun, *b.* 1969.
1816 I.*	*Londonderry* (9th), Alexander Charles Robert Vane-Tempest-Stewart (6th *UK Earl, Vane*, 1823), *b.* 1937, *s.* 1955, *m.*	Viscount Castlereagh, *b.* 1972.

Created	*Title, order of succession, name, etc.*	*Eldest son or heir*
1701 S.*	*Lothian* (12th), Peter Francis Walter Kerr, KCVO (6th *UK Baron, Kerr,* 1821), *b.* 1922, *s.* 1940, *m.*	Earl of Ancram, MP, *b.* 1945.
1917	*Milford Haven* (4th), George Ivar Louis Mountbatten, *b.* 1961, *s.* 1970, *m.*	Lord Ivar A. M. *M.*, *b.* 1963.
1838	*Normanby* (4th), Oswald Constantine John Phipps, KG, CBE (8th *Irish Baron, Mulgrave,* 1767), *b.* 1912, *s.* 1932, *m.*	Earl of Mulgrave, *b.* 1954.
1812	*Northampton* (7th), Spencer Douglas David Compton, *b.* 1946, *s.* 1978, *m.*	Earl Compton, *b.* 1973.
1825 I.*	*Ormonde* (7th), James Hubert Theobald Charles Butler, MBE (7th *UK Baron, Ormonde,* 1821), *b.* 1899, *s.* 1971, *w.*	None to Marquessate. To Earldoms of Ormonde and Ossory, Viscount Mountgarret, *b.* 1936 (*see* p. 151).
1682 S.	*Queensberry* (12th), David Harrington Angus Douglas, *b.* 1929, *s.* 1954.	Viscount Drumlanrig, *b.* 1967.
1926	*Reading* (4th), Simon Charles Henry Rufus Isaacs, *b.* 1942, *s.* 1980, *m.*	Viscount Erleigh, *b.* 1986.
1789	*Salisbury* (6th), Robert Edward Peter Cecil, *b.* 1916, *s.* 1972, *m.*	Viscount Cranborne, *b.* 1946.
1800 I.*	*Sligo* (10th), Denis Edward Browne (10th *UK Baron, Monteagle,* 1806), *b.* 1908, *s.* 1952, *m.*	Earl of Altamont, *b.* 1939.
1787	°*Townshend* (7th), George John Patrick Dominic Townshend, *b.* 1916, *s.* 1921, *w.*	Viscount Raynham, *b.* 1945.
1694 S.*	*Tweeddale* (13th), Edward Douglas John Hay (4th *UK Baron, Tweeddale,* 1881), *b.* 1947, *s.* 1979.	Lord Charles D. M. *H.*, *b.* 1947.
1789 I.*	*Waterford* (8th), John Hubert de la Poer Beresford (8th *Brit. Baron, Tyrone,* 1786), *b.* 1933, *s.* 1934, *m.*	Earl of Tyrone, *b.* 1958.
1551	*Winchester* (18th), Nigel George Paulet (*Premier Marquess of England*), *b.* 1941, *s.* 1968, *m.*	Earl of Wiltshire, *b.* 1969.
1892	*Zetland* (4th), Lawrence Mark Dundas (6th *UK Earl of Zetland,* 1838, 7th *Brit. Baron Dundas,* 1794), *b.* 1937, *s.* 1989, *m.*	Earl of Ronaldshay, *b.* 1965.

EARLS

Coronet, Eight silver balls on stalks alternating with eight gold strawberry leaves.
Style, The Right Hon. the Earl of _
Wife's style, The Right Hon. the Countess of _
Eldest son's style, Takes his father's second title as a courtesy title.
Younger sons' style, 'The Hon.' before forename and family name.
Daughters' style, 'Lady' before forename and family name.
For forms of address, *see* page 218.

Created	*Title, order of succession, name, etc.*	*Eldest son or heir*
1639 S.	*Airlie* (13th), David George Coke Patrick Ogilvy, KT, GCVO, PC, *b.* 1926, *s.* 1968, *m. Lord Chamberlain.*	Lord Ogilvy, *b.* 1958.
1696	*Albemarle* (10th), Rufus Arnold Alexis Keppel, *b.* 1965, *s.* 1979.	Crispian W. J. *K.*, *b.* 1948.
1952	°*Alexander of Tunis* (2nd), Shane William Desmond Alexander, *b.* 1935, *s.* 1969, *m.*	Hon. Brian J. *A.*, *b.* 1939.
1826	°*Amherst* (5th), Jeffery John Archer Amherst, MC, *b.* 1896, *s.* 1927.	None.
1662 S.	*Annandale and Hartfell* (11th), Patrick Andrew Wentworth Hope Johnstone, *b.* 1941, *claim established* 1985, *m.*	Lord Johnstone, *b.* 1971.
1789 I.	°*Annesley* (10th), Patrick Annesley, *b.* 1924, *s.* 1979, *m.*	Hon. Philip H.*A.*, *b.* 1927.
1785 I.	*Antrim* (9th), Alexander Randal Mark McDonnell, *b.* 1935, *s.* 1977, *m.* (*Viscount Dunluce.*)	Hon. Randal A. St J. *M.*, *b.* 1967.
1762 I.*	*Arran* (9th), Arthur Desmond Colquhoun Gore (5th *UK Baron Sudley,* 1884), *b.* 1938, *s.* 1983, *m.*	Paul A. *G.*, CMG, CVO, *b.* 1921.
1955	°*Attlee* (3rd), John Richard Attlee, *b.* 1956, *s.* 1991.	None.
1714	*Aylesford* (11th), Charles Ian Finch-Knightley, *b.* 1918, *s.* 1958, *m.*	Lord Guernsey, *b.* 1947.
1937	°*Baldwin of Bewdley* (4th), Edward Alfred Alexander Baldwin, *b.* 1938, *s.* 1976, *m.*	Viscount Corvedale, *b.* 1973.
1922	*Balfour* (4th), Gerald Arthur James Balfour, *b.* 1925, *s.* 1968, *m.*	Eustace A. G. *B.*, *b.* 1921.
1772	°*Bathurst* (8th), Henry Allen John Bathurst, *b.* 1927, *s.* 1943, *m.*	Lord Apsley, *b.* 1961.
1919	°*Beatty* (3rd), David Beatty, *b.* 1946, *s.* 1972, *m.*	Viscount Borodale, *b.* 1973.
1797 I.	*Belmore* (8th), John Armar Lowry-Corry, *b.* 1951, *s.* 1960, *m.*	Viscount Corry, *b.* 1985.
1739 I.*	*Bessborough*, Frederick Edward Neuflize Ponsonby (10th *Irish* and 2nd *UK Earl*, 1937, both *Bessborough*), *b.* 1913, *s.* 1956, *m.*	To Irish Earldom and UK Barony only, Arthur M. L. *P.*, *b.* 1912.
1815	*Bradford* (7th), Richard Thomas Orlando Bridgeman, *b.* 1947, *s.* 1981, *m.*	Viscount Newport, *b.* 1980.
1677 S.	*Breadalbane and Holland* (10th), John Romer Boreland Campbell, *b.* 1919, *s.* 1959.	None.

Created	*Title, order of succession, name, etc.*	*Eldest son or heir*
1469 S.*	*Buchan* (17th), Malcolm Harry Erskine, (8th *UK Baron Erskine* 1806), *b.* 1930, *s.* 1984, *m.*	Lord Cardross, *b.* 1960.
1746	*Buckinghamshire* (10th), (George) Miles Hobart-Hampden, *b.* 1944, *s.* 1983, *m.*	Sir John Hobart, Bt., *b.* 1945.
1800	°*Cadogan* (7th), William Gerald Charles Cadogan, MC, *b.* 1914, *s.* 1933, *m.*	Viscount Chelsea, *b.* 1937.
1878	°*Cairns* (6th), Simon Dallas Cairns, CBE, *b.* y1939, *s.* 1989, *m.*	Viscount Garmoyle, *b.* 1965.
1455 S.	*Caithness* (20th), Malcolm Ian Sinclair, PC, *b.* 1948, *s.* 1965, *m.*	Lord Berriedale, *b.* 1981.
1800 I.	*Caledon* (7th), Nicholas James Alexander, *b.* 1955, *s.* 1980, *m.*	Viscount Alexander, *b.* 1990.
1661	*Carlisle* (12th), Charles James Ruthven Howard, MC (12th *Scott. Baron, Ruthven of Freeland*, 1651), *b.* 1923, *s.* 1963, *m.*	Viscount Morpeth, *b.* 1949.
1793	*Carnarvon* (7th), Henry George Reginald Molyneux Herbert, KCVO, KBE, *b.* 1924, *s.* 1987, *m.*	Lord Porchester, *b.* 1956.
1748 I.*	*Carrick* (9th), Brian Stuart Theobald Somerset Caher Butler (3rd *UK Baron, Butler,* 1912), *b.* 1931, *s.* 1957, *m.*	Viscount Ikerrin, *b.* 1953.
1800 I.	°*Castle Stewart* (8th), Arthur Patrick Avondale Stuart, *b.* 1928, *s.* 1961, *m.*	Viscount Stuart, *b.* 1953.
1814	°*Cathcart* (6th), Alan Cathcart, CB, DSO, MC (15th *Scott. Baron, Cathcart,* 1447), *b.* 1919, *s.* 1927, *m.*	Lord Greenock, *b.* 1952.
1647 I.	*Cavan* (13th), Roger Cavan Lambart, *b.* 1944, *s.* 1988.	Arthur O. R. *L.*, *b.* 1909.
1827	°*Cawdor* (6th), Hugh John Vaughan Campbell, *b.* 1932, *s.* 1970, *m.*	Viscount Emlyn, *b.* 1962.
1801	*Chichester* (9th), John Nicholas Pelham, *b.* 1944, *s.* 1944, *m.*	Richard A. H. *P.*, *b.* 1952.
1803 I.*	*Clancarty* (8th), William Francis Brinsley Le Poer Trench (7th *UK Visct. Clancarty,* 1823), *b.* 1911, *s.* 1975, *m.*	Nicholas P. R. *Le P. T.*, *b.* 1952.
1776 I.*	*Clanwilliam* (7th), John Herbert Meade (5th *UK Baron Clanwilliam,* 1828), *b.* 1919, *s.* 1989, *m.*	Lord Gillford, *b.* 1960.
1776	*Clarendon* (7th), George Frederick Laurence Hyde Villiers, *b.* 1933, *s.* 1955, *m.*	Lord Hyde, *b.* 1976.
1620 I.*	*Cork* (13th) & *Orrery* (13th)(I. 1660), Patrick Reginald Boyle (9th *Brit. Baron, Boyle of Marston,* 1711), *b.* 1910, *s.* 1967, *m.*	Hon. John W. *B.*, DSC, *b.* 1916.
1850	*Cottenham* (8th), Kenelm Charles Everard Digby Pepys, *b.* 1948, *s.* 1968, *m.*	Viscount Crowhurst, *b.* 1983.
1762 I.*	*Courtown* (9th), James Patrick Montagu Burgoyne Winthrop Stopford (8th *Brit. Baron, Saltersford,* 1796), *b.* 1954, *s.* 1975, *m.*	Viscount Stopford, *b.* 1988.
1697	*Coventry* (11th), George William Coventry, *b.* 1934, *s.* 1940, *m.*	Viscount Deerhurst, *b.* 1957.
1857	°*Cowley* (7th), Garret Graham Wellesley, *b.* 1934, *s.* 1975, *m.*	Viscount Dangan, *b.* 1965.
1892	*Cranbrook* (5th), Gathorne Gathorne-Hardy, *b.* 1933, *s.* 1978, *m.*	Lord Medway, *b.* 1968.
1801	*Craven* (9th), Benjamin Robert Joseph Craven, *b.* 1989, *s.* 1990, *M.*	Rupert J. E. *C.*, *b.* 1926.
1398 S.*	*Crawford* (29th) & *Balcarres* (12th) (S. 1651), Robert Alexander Lindsay, PC (*Premier Earl on Union Roll,* 5th *UK Baron, Wigan,* 1826, and *Baron Balniel* (Life Peer)), *b.* 1927, *s.* 1975, *m.*	Lord Balniel, *b.* 1958.
1861	*Cromartie* (5th), John Ruaridh Blunt Grant Mackenzie, *b.* 1948, *s.* 1989, *m.*	Viscount Tarbat, *b.* 1987.
1901	*Cromer* (4th), Evelyn Rowland Esmond Baring, *b.* 1946, *s.* 1991, *m.*	Hon. Vivian J. R. *B.*, *b.* 1950.
1633 S.*	*Dalhousie* (16th), Simon Ramsay, KT, GCVO, GBE, MC (4th *UK Baron, Ramsay,* 1875), *b.* 1914, *s.* 1950, *m.*	Lord Ramsay, *b.* 1948.
1725 I.*	*Darnley* (11th), Adam Ivo Stuart Bligh (20th *Engl. Baron, Clifton of Leighton Bromswold,* 1608), *b.* 1941, *s.* 1980, *m.*	Lord Clifton of Rathmore, *b.* 1968.
1711	*Dartmouth* (9th), Gerald Humphry Legge, *b.* 1924, *s.* 1962, *m.*	Viscount Lewisham, *b.* 1949.
1761	°*De La Warr* (11th), William Herbrand Sackville, *b.* 1948, *s.* 1988, *m.*	Lord Buckhurst, *b.* 1979.
1622	*Denbigh* (11th) & *Desmond* (10th) (I. 1622), William Rudolph Michael Feilding, *b.* 1943, *s.* 1966, *m.*	Viscount Feilding, *b.* 1970.
1485	*Derby* (18th), Edward John Stanley, MC, *b.* 1918, *s.* 1948, *w.*	Edward R. W. *S.*, *b.* 1962.
1553	*Devon* (17th), Charles Christopher Courtenay, *b.* 1916, *s.* 1935, *m.*	Lord Courtenay, *b.* 1942.
1800 I.*	*Donoughmore* (8th), Richard Michael John Hely-Hutchinson (8th *UK Visct., Hutchinson,* 1821), *b.* 1927, *s.* 1981, *m.*	Viscount Suirdale, *b.* 1952.
1661 I.*	*Drogheda* (12th), Henry Dermot Ponsonby Moore (3rd *UK Baron, Moore,* 1954), *b.* 1937, *s.* 1989, *m.*	Viscount Moore, *b.* 1983.
1837	*Ducie* (7th), David Leslie Moreton, *b.* 1951, *s.* 1991, *m.*	Lord Moreton, *b.* 1981.
1860	*Dudley* (4th), William Humble David Ward, *b.* 1920, *s.* 1969, *m.*	Viscount Ednam, *b.* 1947.
1660 S.*	*Dundee* (12th), Alexander Henry Scrymgeour (2nd *UK Baron, Glassary,* 1954), *b.* 1949, *s.* 1983, *m.*	Lord Scrymgeour, *b.* 1982.
1669 S.	*Dundonald* (15th), Iain Alexander Douglas Blair Cochrane, *b.* 1961, *s.* 1986, *m.*	Lord Cochrane, *b.* 1991.
1686 S.	*Dunmore* (11th), Kenneth Randolph Murray, *b.* 1913, *s.* 1981, *w.*	Viscount Fincastle, *b.* 1946.
1822 I.	*Dunraven and Mount-Earl* (7th), Thady Windham Thomas Wyndham-Quin, *b.* 1939, *s.* 1965, *m.*	None.
1833	*Durham.* Disclaimed for life 1970. (*Antony Claud Frederick Lambton, b.* 1922, *s.* 1970, *m.*)	Hon. Edward R. *L.*, *b.* 1961.

Created	*Title, order of succession, name, etc.*	*Eldest son or heir*
1837	*Effingham* (6th), Mowbray Henry Gordon Howard (16th *Engl. Baron, Howard of Effingham*, 1554), *b.* 1905, *s.* 1946, *m.*	Cdr. David P. M. A. *H.*, *b.* 1939.
1507 S.*	*Eglinton* (18th) & *Winton* (9th) (1600), Archibald George Montgomerie (6th *UK Earl, Winton*, 1859), *b.* 1939, *s.* 1966, *m.*	Lord Montgomerie, *b.* 1966.
1733 I.*	*Egmont* (11th), Frederick George Moore Perceval (9th *Brit. Baron, Lovel & Holland*, 1762), *b.* 1914, *s.* 1932, *m.*	Viscount Perceval, *b.* 1934.
1821	*Eldon* (5th), John Joseph Nicholas Scott, *b.* 1937, *s.* 1976, *m.*	Viscount Encombe, *b.* 1962.
1633 S.*	*Elgin* (11th), & *Kincardine* (15th) (S. 1647), Andrew Douglas Alexander Thomas Bruce (4th *UK Baron, Elgin*, 1849), KT, *b.* 1924, *s.* 1968, *m.*	Lord Bruce, *b.* 1961.
1789 I.*	*Enniskillen* (7th), Andrew John Galbraith Cole (5th *UK Baron, Grinstead*, 1815) *b.* 1942, *s.* 1989, *m.*	Arthur G. *C.*, *b.* 1920.
1789 I.*	*Erne* (6th), Henry George Victor John Crichton (3rd *UK Baron, Fermanagh*, 1876), *b.* 1937, *s.* 1940, *m.*	Viscount Crichton, *b.* 1971.
1452 S.	*Erroll* (24th), Merlin Sereld Victor Gilbert Hay, *b.* 1948, *s.* 1978, *m.* *Hereditary Lord High Constable and Knight Marischal of Scotland.*	Lord Hay, *b.* 1984.
1661	*Essex* (10th), Robert Edward de Vere Capell, *b.* 1920, *s.* 1981, *m.*	Viscount Malden, *b.* 1944.
1711	°*Ferrers* (13th), Robert Washington Shirley, PC, *b.* 1929, *s.* 1954, *m.*	Viscount Tamworth, *b.* 1952.
1789	°*Fortescue* (7th), Richard Archibald Fortescue, *b.* 1922, *s.* 1977, *m.*	Viscount Ebrington, *b.* 1951.
1841	*Gainsborough* (5th), Anthony Gerard Edward Noel, *b.* 1923, *s.* 1927, *m.*	Viscount Campden, *b.* 1950.
1623 S.*	*Galloway* (13th), Randolph Keith Reginald Stewart (6th *Brit. Baron, Stewart of Garlies*, 1796), *b.* 1928, *s.* 1978, *m.*	Andrew C. *S.*, *b.* 1949.
1703 S.*	*Glasgow* (10th), Patrick Robin Archibald Boyle (4th *UK Baron, Fairlie*, 1897), *b.* 1939, *s.* 1984, *m.*	Viscount of Kelburn, *b.* 1978.
1806 I.*	*Gosford* (7th), Charles David Nicholas Alexander John Sparrow Acheson (5th *UK Baron, Worlingham*, 1835), *b.* 1942, *s.* 1966, *m.*	Hon. Patrick B. V. M. *A.*, *b.* 1915.
1945	*Gowrie* (2nd), Alexander Patric Greysteil Hore-Ruthven, PC (3rd *UK Baron, Ruthven of Gowrie*, 1919), *b.* 1939, *s.* 1955, *m.*	Viscount Ruthven of Canberra, *b.* 1964.
1684 I.*	*Granard* (9th), Arthur Patrick Hastings Forbes, AFC (4th *UK Baron, Granard*, 1806), *b.* 1915, *s.* 1948, *m.*	Peter A. E. H. *F.*, *b.* 1957.
1833	°*Granville* (5th), Granville James Leveson-Gower, MC, *b.* 1918, *s.* 1953, *m.*	Lord Leveson, *b.* 1959.
1806	°*Grey* (6th), Richard Fleming George Charles Grey, *b.* 1939, *s.* 1963, *m.*	Philip K. *G.*, *b.* 1940.
1752	*Guilford* (9th), Edward Francis North, *b.* 1933, *s.* 1949, *w.*	Lord North, *b.* 1971.
1619 S.	*Haddington* (13th), John George Baillie-Hamilton, *b.* 1941, *s.* 1986, *m.*	Lord Binning, *b.* 1985.
1919	°*Haig* (2nd), George Alexander Eugene Douglas Haig, OBE, *b.* 1918, *s.* 1928, *m.*	Viscount Dawick, *b.* 1961.
1944	*Halifax* (3rd), Charles Edward Peter Neil Wood (5th *UK Viscount, Halifax*, 1866), *b.* 1944, *s.* 1980, *m.*	Lord Irwin, *b.* 1977.
1898	*Halsbury* (3rd), John Anthony Hardinge Giffard, FRS, FEng., *b.* 1908, *s.* 1943, *w.*	Adam E. *G.*, *b.* 1934.
1754	*Hardwicke* (10th), Joseph Philip Sebastian Yorke, *b.* 1971, *s.* 1974.	Richard C. J. *Y.*, *b.* 1916.
1812	*Harewood* (7th), George Henry Hubert Lascelles, KBE, *b.* 1923, *s.* 1947, *m.* (*See also* page 134).	Viscount Lascelles, *b.* 1950.
1742	*Harrington* (11th), William Henry Leicester Stanhope (8th *Brit. Viscount, Stanhope of Mahon*, 1717), *b.* 1922, *s.* 1929, *m.*	Viscount Petersham, *b.* 1945.
1809	*Harrowby* (7th), Dudley Danvers Granville Coutts Ryder, TD, *b.* 1922, *s.* 1987, *m.*	Viscount Sandon, *b.* 1951.
1605 S.	*Home.* Disclaimed for life 1963. (*See* Lord Home of the Hirsel, page 164.)	Hon. David A. C. *D.-H.*, *b.* 1943.
1821	°*Howe* (7th), Frederick Richard Penn Curzon, *b.* 1951, *s.* 1984, *m.*	Charles M. P. *C.*, *b.* 1967.
1529	*Huntingdon* (16th), William Edward Robin Hood Hastings Bass, *b.* 1948, *s.* 1990, *m.*	Simon A. R. H. *H. B.*, *b.* 1950.
1885	*Iddesleigh* (4th), Stafford Henry Northcote, *b.* 1932, *s.* 1970, *m.*	Viscount St Cyres, *b.* 1957.
1756	*Ilchester* (9th), Maurice Vivian de Touffreville Fox-Strangways, *b.* 1920, *s.* 1970, *m.*	Hon. Raymond G. *F.-S.*, *b.* 1921.
1929	*Inchcape* (3rd), Kenneth James William Mackay, *b.* 1917, *s.* 1939, *m.*	Viscount Glenapp, *b.* 1943.
1919	*Iveagh* (4th), Arthur Edward Rory Guinness, *b.* 1969, *s.* 1992.	Hon. Rory M. B. *G.*, *b.* 1974.
1925	°*Jellicoe* (2nd), George Patrick John Rushworth Jellicoe, KBE, DSO, MC, PC, *b.* 1918, *s.* 1935, *m.*	Viscount Brocas, *b.* 1950.
1697	*Jersey* (9th), George Francis Child-Villiers (12th *Irish Visct., Grandison*, 1620), *b.* 1910, *s.* 1923, *m.*	Viscount Villiers, *b.* 1948.
1822 I.	*Kilmorey* (6th), Richard Francis Needham, MP, *b.* 1942, *s.* 1977, *m.*	Viscount Newry and Morne, *b.* 1966.
1866	*Kimberley* (4th), John Wodehouse, *b.* 1924, *s.* 1941, *m.*	Lord Wodehouse, *b.* 1951.
1768 I.	*Kingston* (11th), Barclay Robert Edwin King-Tenison, *b.* 1943, *s.* 1948, *m.*	Viscount Kingsborough, *b.* 1969.
1633 S.*	*Kinnoull* (15th), Arthur William George Patrick Hay (9th *Brit. Baron, Hay of Pedwardine*, 1711), *b.* 1935, *s.* 1938, *m.*	Viscount Dupplin, *b.* 1962.
1677 S.*	*Kintore* (13th), Michael Canning William John Keith (3rd *UK Viscount Stonehaven*, 1938), *b.* 1939, *s.* 1989, *m.*	Lord Inverurie, *b.* 1976.

Created	Title, order of succession, name, etc.	Eldest son or heir
1914	°*Kitchener of Khartoum* (3rd), Henry Herbert Kitchener, TD, *b.* 1919, *s.* 1937.	None.
1756 I.	*Lanesborough* (9th), Denis Anthony Brian Butler, TD, *b.* 1918, *s.* 1950.	Henry A. B. C. *B.*, *b.* 1909.
1624 S.	*Lauderdale* (17th), Patrick Francis Maitland, *b.* 1911, *s.* 1968, *m.*	Viscount Maitland, *b.* 1937.
1837	*Leicester* (6th), Anthony Louis Lovel Coke, *b.* 1909, *s.* 1976, *m.*	Viscount Coke, *b.* 1936.
1641 S.	*Leven* (14th) & *Melville* (13th) (S. 1690), Alexander Robert Leslie Melville, *b.* 1924, *s.* 1947, *m.*	Lord Balgonie, *b.* 1954.
1831	*Lichfield* (5th), Thomas Patrick John Anson, *b.* 1939, *s.* 1960.	Viscount Anson, *b.* 1978.
1803 I.*	*Limerick* (6th), Patrick Edmund Pery, KBE (6th *UK Baron, Foxford*, 1815), *b.* 1930, *s.* 1967, *m.*	Viscount Glentworth, *b.* 1963.
1572	*Lincoln* (18th), Edward Horace Fiennes-Clinton, *b.* 1913, *s.* 1988, *m.*	Hon. Edward G. *F.-C.*, *b.* 1943.
1633 S.	*Lindsay* (16th), James Randolph Lindesay-Bethune, *b.* 1955, *s.* 1989, *m.*	Viscount Garnock, *b.* 1990.
1626	*Lindsey* (14th) *and Abingdon* (9th) (1682), Richard Henry Rupert Bertie, *b.* 1931, *s.* 1963, *m.*	Lord Norreys, *b.* 1958.
1776 I.	*Lisburne* (8th), John David Malet Vaughan, *b.* 1918, *s.* 1965, *m.*	Viscount Vaughan, *b.* 1945.
1822 I.*	*Listowel* (5th), William Francis Hare, GCMG, PC, (3rd *UK Baron, Hare*, 1869), *b.* 1906, *s.* 1931, *m.*	Viscount Ennismore, *b.* 1964.
1905	*Liverpool* (5th), Edward Peter Bertram Savile Foljambe, *b.* 1944, *s.* 1969, *m.*	Viscount Hawkesbury, *b.* 1972.
1945	°*Lloyd George of Dwyfor* (3rd), Owen Lloyd George, *b.* 1924, *s.* 1968, *m.*	Viscount Gwynedd, *b.* 1951.
1785 I.*	*Longford* (7th), Francis Aungier Pakenham, KG, PC (6th *UK Baron, Silchester*, 1821; 1st *UK Baron, Pakenham*, 1945), *b.* 1905, *s.* 1961, *m.*	Thomas F. D. *P.*, *b.* 1933.
1807	*Lonsdale* (7th), James Hugh William Lowther, *b.* 1922, *s.* 1953, *m.*	Viscount Lowther, *b.* 1949.
1838	*Lovelace* (5th), Peter Axel William Locke King (12th *Brit. Baron, King*, 1725), *b.* 1951, *s.* 1964, *m.*	None.
1795 I.*	*Lucan* (7th), Richard John Bingham (3rd *UK Baron, Bingham*, 1934), *b.* 1934, *s.* 1964, *m.*	Lord Bingham, *b.* 1967.
1880	*Lytton* (5th), John Peter Michael Scawen Lytton (18th *Engl. Baron, Wentworth*, 1529), *b.* 1950, *s.* 1985, *m.*	Viscount Knebworth, *b.* 1989.
1721	*Macclesfield* (8th), George Roger Alexander Thomas Parker, *b.* 1914, *s.* 1975, *m.*	Viscount Parker, *b.* 1943.
1800	*Malmesbury* (6th), William James Harris, TD, *b.* 1907, *s.* 1950, *m.*	Viscount FitzHarris, *b.* 1946.
1776 & 1792	*Mansfield and Mansfield* (8th), William David Mungo James Murray (14th *Scott. Visct., Stormont*, 1621), *b.* 1930, *s.* 1971, *m.*	Viscount Stormont, *b.* 1956.
1565 S.	*Mar* (13th) & *Kellie* (15th) (S. 1616), John Francis Hervey Erskine, *b.* 1921, *s.* 1955, *m.*	Lord Erskine, *b.* 1949.
1785 I.	*Mayo* (10th), Terence Patrick Bourke, *b.* 1929, *s.* 1962, *m.*	Lord Naas, *b.* 1953.
1627 I.*	*Meath* (14th), Anthony Windham Normand Brabazon (5th *UK Baron, Chaworth*, 1831), *b.* 1910, *s.* 1949, *m.*	Lord Ardee, *b.* 1941.
1766 I.	*Mexborough* (8th), John Christopher George Savile, *b.* 1931, *s.* 1980, *m.*	Viscount Pollington, *b.* 1959.
1813	*Minto* (6th), Gilbert Edward George Lariston Elliot-Murray-Kynynmound, OBE, *b.* 1928, *s.* 1975, *m.*	Viscount Melgund, *b.* 1953.
1562 S.*	*Moray* (20th) Douglas John Moray Stuart (12th *Brit. Baron, Stuart* of *Castle Stuart*, 1796), *b.* 1928, *s.* 1974, *m.*	Lord Doune, *b.* 1966.
1815	*Morley* (6th), John St Aubyn Parker, *b.* 1923, *s.* 1962, *m.*	Viscount Boringdon, *b.* 1956.
1458 S.	*Morton* (22nd), John Charles Sholto Douglas, *b.* 1927, *s.* 1976, *m.*	Lord Aberdour, *b.* 1952.
1789	*Mount Edgcumbe* (8th), Robert Charles Edgcumbe, *b.* 1939, *s.* 1982, *m.*	Piers V. *E.*, *b.* 1946.
1831	*Munster* (7th), Anthony Charles FitzClarence, *b.* 1926, *s.* 1983, *m.*	None.
1805	°*Nelson* (9th), Peter John Horatio Nelson, *b.* 1941, *s.* 1981, *m.*	Viscount Merton, *b.* 1971.
1660 S.	*Newburgh* (12th), Prince Filippo Giambattista Camillo Francesco Aldo Maria Rospigliosi, *b.* 1942, *s.* 1986, *m.*	Princess Benedetta F. M. *R.*, *b.* 1974.
1827 I.	*Norbury* (6th), Noel Terence Graham-Toler, *b.* 1939, *s.* 1955, *m.*	Viscount Glandine, *b.* 1967.
1806 I.*	*Normanton* (6th), Shaun James Christian Welbore Ellis Agar (9th *Brit. Baron, Mendip*, 1791, 4th *UK Baron, Somerton*, 1873), *b.* 1945, *s.* 1967, *m.*	Viscount Somerton, *b.* 1982.
1647 S.	*Northesk* (13th), Robert Andrew Carnegie, *b.* 1926, *s.* 1975, *m.*	Lord Rosehill, *b.* 1954.
1801	*Onslow* (7th), Michael William Coplestone Dillon Onslow, *b.* 1938, *s.* 1971, *m.*	Viscount Cranley, *b.* 1967.
1696 S.	*Orkney* (8th), Cecil O'Bryen Fitz-Maurice, *b.* 1919, *s.* 1951, *m.*	O. Peter *St John*, *b.* 1938.
1925	*Oxford and Asquith* (2nd), Julian Edward George Asquith, KCMG, *b.* 1916, *s.* 1928, *m.*	Viscount Asquith, OBE, *b.* 1952.
1929	°*Peel* (3rd), William James Robert Peel (4th *UK Viscount Peel*, 1895), *b.* 1947, *s.* 1969, *m.*	Viscount Clanfield, *b.* 1976.
1551	*Pembroke* (17th) & *Montgomery* (14th) (1605), Henry George Charles Alexander Herbert, *b.* 1939, *s.* 1969.	Lord Herbert, *b.* 1978.
1605 S.	*Perth* (17th), John David Drummond, PC, *b.* 1907, *s.* 1951, *m.*	Viscount Strathallan, *b.* 1935.
1905	*Plymouth* (3rd), Other Robert Ivor Windsor-Clive (15th *Engl. Baron, Windsor*, 1529), *b.* 1923, *s.* 1943, *m.*	Viscount Windsor, *b.* 1951.

Created	*Title, order of succession, name, etc.*	*Eldest son or heir*
1785 I.	*Portarlington* (7th), George Lionel Yuill Seymour Dawson-Damer, *b.* 1938, *s.* 1959, *m.*	Viscount Carlow, *b.* 1965.
1689	*Portland* (11th), Count Henry Noel Bentinck, *b.* 1919, *s.* 1990, *m.*	Viscount Woodstock, *b.* 1953.
1743	*Portsmouth* (10th), Quentin Gerard Carew Wallop, *b.* 1954, *s.* 1984, *m.*	Viscount Lymington, *b.* 1981.
1804	*Powis* (7th), George William Herbert (8th *Irish Baron, Clive*, 1762), *b.* 1925, *s.* 1988, *m.*	Viscount Clive, *b.* 1952.
1765	*Radnor* (8th), Jacob Pleydell-Bouverie, *b.* 1927, *s.* 1968, *m.*	Viscount Folkestone, *b.* 1955.
1831 I.*	*Ranfurly* (7th), Gerald Françoys Needham Knox (8th *UK Baron, Ranfurly*, 1826), *b.* 1929, *s.* 1988, *m.*	Viscount Northland, *b.* 1957.
1771 I.	*Roden* (9th), Robert William Jocelyn, *b.* 1909, *s.* 1956, *w.*	Viscount Jocelyn, *b.* 1938.
1801	*Romney* (7th), Michael Henry Marsham, *b.* 1910, *s.* 1975, *m.*	Julian C. *M.*, *b.* 1948.
1703 S.*	*Rosebery* (7th), Neil Archibald Primrose (3rd *UK Earl, Midlothian*, 1911), *b.* 1929, *s.* 1974, *m.*	Lord Dalmeny, *b.* 1967.
1806 I.	*Rosse* (7th), William Brendan Parsons, *b.* 1936, *s.* 1979, *m.*	Lord Oxmantown, *b.* 1969.
1801	*Rosslyn* (7th), Peter St Clair-Erskine, *b.* 1958, *s.* 1977, *m.*	Lord Loughborough, *b.* 1986.
1457 S.	*Rothes* (21st), Ian Lionel Malcolm Leslie, *b.* 1932, *s.* 1975, *m.*	Lord Leslie, *b.* 1958.
1861	°*Russell* (5th), Conrad Sebastian Robert Russell, *b.* 1937, *s.* 1987, *m.*	Viscount Amberley, *b.* 1968.
1915	°*St Aldwyn* (3rd), Michael Henry Hicks Beach, b. 1950, *s.* 1992, *m.*	Hon. David S. *H.B.*, *b.* 1955.
1815	*St Germans* (10th), Peregrine Nicholas Eliot, *b.* 1941, *s.* 1988.	Lord Eliot, *b.* 1966.
1660	*Sandwich.* Disclaimed for life 1964. ((*Alexander*) *Victor* (*Edward Paulet*) *Montagu*, *b.* 1906, *s.* 1962.)	John E. H. *M.*, *b.* 1943.
1690	*Scarbrough* (12th), Richard Aldred Lumley (13th *Irish Visct., Lumley*, 1628), *b.* 1932, *s.* 1969, *m.*	Viscount Lumley, *b.* 1973.
1701 S.	*Seafield* (13th), Ian Derek Francis Ogilvie-Grant, *b.* 1939, s. 1969, *m.*	Viscount Reidhaven, *b.* 1963.
1882	*Selborne* (4th), John Roundell Palmer, KBE, FRS, *b.* 1940, *s.* 1971, *m.*	Viscount Wolmer, *b.* 1971.
1646 S.	*Selkirk* (10th), (George) Nigel Douglas-Hamilton, KT, GCMG, GBE, AFC, AE, PC, QC, *b.* 1906, *s.* 1940, *m.*	The Master of Selkirk, *b.* 1939.
1672	*Shaftesbury* (10th), Anthony Ashley-Cooper, *b.* 1938, *s.* 1961, *m.*	Lord Ashley, *b.* 1977.
1756 I.*	*Shannon* (9th), Richard Bentinck Boyle (8th *Brit. Baron Carleton*, 1786), *b.* 1924, *s.* 1963.	Viscount Boyle, *b.* 1960.
1442	*Shrewsbury* & *Waterford* (22nd) (I. 1446), Charles Henry John Benedict Crofton Chetwynd Chetwynd-Talbot (*Premier Earl of England and Ireland; Earl Talbot*, 1784), *b.* 1952, *s.* 1980, *m.*	Viscount Ingestre, *b.* 1978.
1961	*Snowdon* (1st), Antony Charles Robert Armstrong-Jones, GCVO, *b.* 1930, *m.* (*See also* page 123).	Viscount Linley, *b.* 1961 (*see also* page 123).
1880	°*Sondes* (5th), Henry George Herbert Milles-Lade, *b.* 1940, *s.* 1970.	None.
1765	°*Spencer* (9th), Charles Edward Maurice Spencer, b. 1964, *s.* 1992, *m.*	G. C. Robert M. *S.*, *b.* 1932.
1703 S.*	*Stair* (13th), John Aymer Dalrymple, KCVO, MBE (6th *UK Baron, Oxenfoord*, 1841), *b.* 1906, *s.* 1961, *m.*	Viscount Dalrymple, *b.* 1961.
1984	*Stockton* (2nd), Alexander Daniel Alan Macmillan, *b.* 1943, *s.* 1986.	Viscount Macmillan of Ovenden, *b.* 1974.
1821	*Stradbroke* (6th), Robert Keith Rous, *b.* 1937, *s.* 1983, *m.*	Viscount Dunwich, *b.* 1961.
1847	*Strafford* (8th), Thomas Edmund Byng, *b.* 1936, *s.* 1984, *m.*	Viscount Enfield, *b.* 1964.
1606 S.*	*Strathmore* & *Kinghorne* (18th), Michael Fergus Bowes Lyon (16th *Scottish Earl, Strathmore*, 1677, & 18th *Kinghorne*, 1606; 5th *UK Earl, Strathmore* & *Kinghorne*, 1937), *b.* 1957, *s.* 1987, *m.*	Lord Glamis, *b.* 1986.
1603	*Suffolk* (21st) & *Berkshire* (14th) (1626), Michael John James George Robert Howard, *b.* 1935, *s.* 1941, *m.*	Viscount Andover, *b.* 1974.
1955	*Swinton* (2nd), David Yarburgh Cunliffe-Lister, *b.* 1937, *s.* 1972, *m.*	Hon. Nicholas J. *C.-L.*, *b.* 1939.
1714	*Tankerville* (10th), Peter Grey Bennet, *b.* 1956, *s.* 1980.	Revd the Hon. George A. G. *B.*, *b.* 1925.
1822	°*Temple of Stowe* (8th), (Walter) Grenville Algernon Temple-Gore-Langton, *b.* 1924, *s.* 1988, *m.*	Lord Langton, *b.* 1955.
1815	*Verulam* (7th), John Duncan Grimston (11th *Irish Visct., Grimston*, 1719; 16th *Scott. Baron, Forrester of Corstorphine*, 1633), *b.* 1951, *s.* 1973, *m.*	Viscount Grimston, *b.* 1978.
1729	°*Waldegrave* (12th), Geoffrey Noel Waldegrave, KG, GCVO, TD, *b.* 1905, *s.* 1936, *m.*	Viscount Chewton, *b.* 1940.
1759	*Warwick* & °*Brooke* (8th) (*Brit.* 1746), David Robin Francis Guy Greville (8th *Earl Brooke* and 8th *Earl of Warwick*), *b.* 1934, *s.* 1984.	Lord Brooke, *b.* 1957.
1633 S.*	*Wemyss* (12th) & *March* (8th) (S. 1697), Francis David Charteris, KT (5th *UK Baron, Wemyss*, 1821), *b.* 1912, *s.* 1937, *w.*	Lord Neidpath, *b.* 1948.
1621 I.	*Westmeath* (13th), William Anthony Nugent, *b.* 1928, *s.* 1971, *m.*	Hon. Sean C. W. *N.*, *b.* 1965.
1624	*Westmorland* (15th), David Anthony Thomas Fane, GCVO, *b.* 1924, *s.* 1948, *m.*	Lord Burghersh, *b.* 1951.
1876	*Wharncliffe* (5th), Richard Alan Montagu Stuart Wortley, *b.* 1953, *s.* 1987, *m.*	Viscount Carlton, *b.* 1980.
1801	*Wilton* (7th), Seymour William Arthur John Egerton, *b.* 1921, *s.* 1927, *m.*	Baron Ebury, *b.* 1934 (*see* page 155).

Created	Title, order of succession, name, etc.	Eldest son or heir
1628	*Winchilsea* (16th) & *Nottingham* (11th) (1675), Christopher Denys Stormont Finch Hatton, *b.* 1936, *s.* 1950, *m.*	Viscount Maidstone, *b.* 1967.
1766 I.	°*Winterton* (7th), Robert Chad Turnour, *b.* 1915, *s.* 1962, *m.*	D. David *T.*, *b.* 1943.
1956	*Woolton* (3rd), Simon Frederick Marquis, *b.* 1958, *s.* 1969, *m.*	None.
1837	*Yarborough* (8th), Charles John Pelham, *b.* 1963, *s.* 1991, *m.*	Lord Worsley, *b.* 1990.

COUNTESSES IN THEIR OWN RIGHT

Style, The Right Hon. the Countess (of) _.
Husband, Untitled.
Children's style, As for children of an Earl.
For forms of address, *see* page 218.

Created	Title, order of succession, name, etc.	Eldest son or heir
1643 S.	*Dysart* (11th in line), Rosamund Agnes Greaves, *b.* 1914, *s.* 1975.	Lady Katherine *Grant of Rothiemurchus*, *b.* 1918.
1633 S.	*Loudoun* (13th in line), Barbara Huddleston Abney-Hastings, *b.* 1919, *s.* 1960, *m.*	Lord Mauchline, *b.* 1942.
c.1115 S.	*Mar* (31st in line), Margaret of Mar (*Premier Earldom of Scotland*), *b.* 1940, *s.* 1975, *m.*	Mistress of Mar, *b.* 1963.
1947	°*Mountbatten of Burma* (2nd in line), Patricia Edwina Victoria Knatchbull, CBE, *b.* 1924, *s.* 1979, *m.*	Lord Romsey, *b.* 1947 (*see also* page 153).
c. 1235 S.	*Sutherland* (24th in line), Elizabeth Millicent Sutherland, *b.* 1921, *s.* 1963, *m.*	Lord Strathnaver, *b.* 1947.

VISCOUNTS

Coronet, Sixteen silver balls.
Style, The Right Hon. the Viscount _.
Wife's style, The Right Hon. the Viscountess _.
Children's style, 'The Hon.' before forename and family name.
In Scotland, the heir apparent to a Viscount may be styled 'The Master of _(title of peer)'.
For forms of address, *see* page 218.

Created	Title, order of succession, name, etc.	Eldest son or heir
1945	*Addison* (4th), William Matthew Wand Addison, *b.* 1945, *s.* 1992, *m.*	Hon. Paul W. *A.*, *b.* 1973.
1946	*Alanbrooke* (3rd), Alan Victor Harold Brooke, *b.* 1932, *s.* 1972.	None.
1919	*Allenby* (3rd), Lt.-Col. Michael Jaffray Hynman Allenby, *b.* 1931, *s.* 1984, *m.*	Hon. Henry J. H. *A.*, *b.* 1968.
1911	*Allendale* (3rd), Wentworth Hubert Charles Beaumont, *b.* 1922, *s.* 1956, *m.*	Hon. Wentworth P. I. *B.*, *b.* 1948.
1642 S.	*of Arbuthnott* (16th), John Campbell Arbuthnott, CBE, DSC, *b.* 1924, *s.* 1966, *m.*	Master of Arbuthnott, *b.* 1950.
1751 I.	*Ashbrook* (10th), Desmond Llowarch Edward Flower, KCVO, MBE, *b.* 1905. *s.* 1936, *m.*	Hon. Michael L. W. *F.*, *b.* 1935.
1917	*Astor* (4th), William Waldorf Astor, *b.* 1951, *s.* 1966, *m.*	Hon. William W. *A.*, *b.* 1979.
1781 I.	*Bangor* (7th), Edward Henry Harold Ward, *b.* 1905, *s.* 1950, *w.*	Hon. William M. D. *W.*, *b.* 1948.
1925	*Bearsted* (4th), Peter Montefiore Samuel, MC, TD, *b.* 1911, *s.* 1986, *m.*	Hon. Nicholas A. *S.*, *b.* 1950.
1963	*Blakenham* (2nd), Michael John Hare, *b.* 1938, *s.* 1982, *m.*	Hon. Caspar J. *H.*, *b.* 1972.
1935	*Bledisloe* (3rd), Christopher Hiley Ludlow Bathurst, QC, *b.* 1934, *s.* 1979.	Hon. Rupert E. L. *B.*, *b.* 1964.
1712	*Bolingbroke* (7th) & *St John* (8th) (1716), Kenneth Oliver Musgrave St John, *b.* 1927, *s.* 1974.	Hon. Henry F. *St J.*, *b.* 1957.
1960	*Boyd of Merton* (2nd), Simon Donald Rupert Neville Lennox-Boyd, *b.* 1939, *s.* 1983, *m.*	Hon. Benjamin A. *L.-B.*, *b.* 1964.
1717 I.*	*Boyne* (10th), Gustavus Michael George Hamilton-Russell (4th *UK Baron, Brancepeth*, 1866), *b.* 1931, *s.* 1942, *m.*	Hon. Gustavus M. S. *H.-R.*, *b.* 1965.

Created	Title, order of succession, name, etc.	Eldest son or heir
1929	*Brentford* (4th), Crispin William Joynson-Hicks, *b.* 1933, *s.* 1983, *m.*	Hon. Paul W. *J.-H.*, *b.* 1971.
1929	*Bridgeman* (3rd), Robin John Orlando Bridgeman, *b.* 1930, *s.* 1982, *m.*	Hon. William O. C. *B.*, *b.* 1968.
1868	*Bridport* (4th), Alexander Nelson Hood (7th *Duke of Brontë in Sicily*, 1799, *and* 6th *Irish Baron Bridport*, 1794), *b.* 1948, *s.* 1969, *m.*	Hon. Peregrine A. N. *H.*, *b.* 1974.
1952	*Brookeborough* (3rd), Alan Henry Brooke, *b.* 1952, *s.* 1987, *m.*	Hon. Christopher A. *B.*, *b.* 1954.
1933	*Buckmaster* (3rd), Martin Stanley Buckmaster, OBE, *b.* 1921, *s.* 1974.	Hon. Colin J. *B.*, *b.* 1923.
1939	*Caldecote* (2nd), Robert Andrew Inskip, KBE, DSC, FEng., *b.* 1917, *s.* 1947, *m.*	Hon. Piers J. H. *I.*, *b.* 1947.
1941	*Camrose* (2nd), (John) Seymour Berry, TD, *b.* 1909, *s.* 1954, *m.*	Baron Hartwell, MBE, TD, *b.* 1911 (*see* page 164).
1954	*Chandos* (3rd), Thomas Orlando Lyttelton, *b.* 1953, *s.* 1980, *m.*	Hon. Oliver A. *L.*, *b.* 1986.
1665 I.	*Charlemont* (14th), John Day Caulfeild (18th *Irish Baron, Caulfeild of Charlemont*, 1620), *b.* 1934, *s.* 1985, *m.*	Hon. John D. *C.*, *b.* 1966.
1921	*Chelmsford* (3rd), Frederic Jan Thesiger, *b.* 1931, *s.* 1970, *m.*	Hon. Frederic C. P. *T.*, *b.* 1962.
1717 I.	*Chetwynd* (10th), Adam Richard John Casson Chetwynd, *b.* 1935, *s.* 1965, *m.*	Hon. Adam D. *C.*, *b.* 1969.
1911	*Chilston* (4th), Alastair George Akers-Douglas, *b.* 1946, *s.* 1982, *m.*	Hon. Oliver I. *A.-D.*, *b.* 1973.
1902	*Churchill* (3rd), Victor George Spencer (5th *UK Baron Churchill*, 1815), *b.* 1934, *s.* 1973.	None to Viscountcy. To Barony, Richard H. R. *S.*, *b.* 1926.
1718	*Cobham* (11th), John William Leonard Lyttelton (8th *Irish Baron, Westcote*, 1776), *b.* 1943, *s.* 1977, *m.*	Hon. Christopher C. *L.*, *b.* 1947.
1902	*Colville of Culross* (4th), John Mark Alexander Colville, QC (13th *Scott. Baron, Colville of Culross*, 1604), *b.* 1933, *s.* 1945, *m.*	Master of Colville, *b.* 1959.
1826	*Combermere* (5th), Michael Wellington Stapleton-Cotton, *b.* 1929, *s.* 1969, *m.*	Hon. Thomas R. W. *S.-C.*, *b.* 1969.
1917	*Cowdray* (3rd), Weetman John Churchill Pearson, TD (3rd *UK Baron, Cowdray*, 1910), *b.* 1910, *s.* 1933, *m.*	Hon. Michael O. W. *P.*, *b.* 1944.
1927	*Craigavon* (3rd), Janric Fraser Craig, *b.* 1944, *s.* 1974.	None.
1886	*Cross* (3rd), Assheton Henry Cross, *b.* 1920, *s.* 1932.	None.
1943	*Daventry* (3rd), Francis Humphrey Maurice FitzRoy Newdegate, *b.* 1921, *s.* 1986, *m.*	Hon. James E. *F.N.*, *b.* 1960.
1937	*Davidson* (2nd), John Andrew Davidson, *b.* 1928, *s.* 1970, *m.*	Hon. Malcolm W. M. *D.*, *b.* 1934.
1956	*De L'Isle* (2nd), Philip John Algernon Sidney, MBE, (7th *Baron De L'Isle and Dudley*, 1835), *b.* 1945, *s.* 1991, *m.*	Hon. Philip W. E. *S.*, *b.* 1985.
1776 I.	*De Vesci* (7th), Thomas Eustace Vesey (8th *Irish Baron, Knapton*, 1750), *b.* 1955, *s.* 1983, *m.*	Hon. Damian B. J. *V.*, *b.* 1985.
1917	*Devonport* (3rd), Terence Kearley, *b.* 1944, *s.* 1973.	Chester D. H. *K.*, *b.* 1932.
1964	*Dilhorne* (2nd), John Mervyn Manningham-Buller, *b.* 1932, *s.* 1980, *m.*	Hon. James E.*M.-B.*, *b.* 1956.
1622 I.	*Dillon* (22nd), Henry Benedict Charles Dillon, *b.* 1973, *s.* 1982.	Hon. Richard A. L. *D.*, *b.* 1948.
1785 I.	*Doneraile* (10th), Richard Allen St Leger, *b.* 1946, *s.* 1983, *m.*	Hon. Nathaniel W. R. St J. *St L.*, *b.* 1971.
1680 I.*	*Downe* (11th), John Christian George Dawnay (4th *UK Baron, Dawnay*, 1897), *b.* 1935, *s.* 1965, *m.*	Hon. Richard H. *D.*, *b.* 1967.
1959	*Dunrossil* (2nd), John William Morrison, CMG, *b.* 1926, *s.* 1961, *m.*	Hon. Andrew W. R. *M.*, *b.* 1953.
1964	*Eccles* (1st), David McAdam Eccles, CH, KCVO, PC, *b.* 1904, *m.*	Hon. John D. *E.*, CBE, *b.* 1931.
1897	*Esher* (4th), Lionel Gordon Baliol Brett, CBE, *b.* 1913. *s.* 1963, *m.*	Hon. Christopher L. B. *B.*, *b.* 1936.
1816	*Exmouth* (10th), Paul Edward Pellew, *b.* 1940, *s.* 1970, *m.*	Hon. Edward F. *P.*, *b.* 1978.
1620 S.	*Falkland* (15th), Lucius Edward William Plantagenet Cary (*Premier Scottish Viscount on the Roll*), *b.* 1935, *s.* 1984, *m.*	Master of Falkland, *b.* 1963.
1720	*Falmouth* (9th), George Hugh Boscawen (26th *Eng. Baron, Le Despencer*, 1264), *b.* 1919, *s.* 1962, *m.*	Hon. Evelyn A. H. *B.*, *b.* 1955.
1918	*Furness* (2nd), William Anthony Furness, *b.* 1929, *s.* 1940.	None.
1720 I.*	*Gage* (7th), George John St Clere Gage, (6th *Brit. Baron, Gage*, 1790), *b.* 1932, *s.* 1982.	Hon. H. Nicholas *G.*, *b.* 1934.
1727 I.	*Galway* (12th), George Rupert Monckton-Arundell, *b.* 1922, *s.* 1980, *m.*	Hon. J. Philip *M.*, *b.* 1952.
1478 I.*	*Gormanston* (17th), Jenico Nicholas Dudley Preston (*Premier Viscount of Ireland*; 5th *UK Baron, Gormanston*, 1868), *b.* 1939, *s.* 1940, *w.*	Hon. Jenico F. T. *P.*, *b.* 1974.
1816 I.	*Gort* (8th), Colin Leopold Prendergast Vereker, *b.* 1916, *s.* 1975, *m.*	Hon. Foley R.S.P.*V.*, *b.* 1951.
1900	*Goschen* (4th), Giles John Harry Goschen, *b.* 1965, *s.* 1977.	None.
1849	*Gough* (5th), Shane Hugh Maryon Gough, *b.* 1941, *s.* 1951.	None.
1937	*Greenwood* (2nd), David Henry Hamar Greenwood, *b.* 1914, *s.* 1948.	Hon. Michael G. H. *G.*, *b.* 1923.
1929	*Hailsham.* Disclaimed for life 1963. (*See* Lord Hailsham of St Marylebone, page 164.)	Hon. Douglas M. *H.*, QC, MP, *b.* 1945.
1891	*Hambleden* (4th), William Herbert Smith, *b.* 1930, *s.* 1948, *m.*	Hon. William H. B. *S.*, *b.* 1955.
1884	*Hampden* (6th), Anthony David Brand, *b.* 1937, *s.* 1975.	Hon. Francis A. *B.*, *b.* 1970.
1936	*Hanworth* (2nd), David Bertram Pollock, *b.* 1916, *s.* 1936, *m.*	Hon. David S. G. *P.*, *b.* 1946.
1791 I.	*Harberton* (10th), Thomas de Vautort Pomeroy, *b.* 1910, *s.* 1980, *m.*	Hon. Robert W. *P.*, *b.* 1916.
1846	*Hardinge* (6th), Charles Henry Nicholas Hardinge, *b.* 1956, *s.* 1984, *m.*	Hon. Andrew H. *H.*, *b.* 1960.

Created	*Title, order of succession, name, etc.*	*Eldest son or heir*
1791 I.	*Hawarden* (9th), (Robert) Connan Wyndham Leslie Maude, *b.* 1961, *s.* 1991.	Hon. Thomas P. C. *M.*, *b.* 1964.
1960	*Head* (2nd), Richard Antony Head, *b.* 1937, *s.* 1983, *m.*	Hon. Henry J. *H.*, *b.* 1980.
1550	*Hereford* (18th), Robert Milo Leicester Devereux (*Premier Viscount of England*), *b.* 1932, *s.* 1952.	Hon. Charles R. de B. *D.*, *b.* 1975.
1842	*Hill* (8th), Antony Rowland Clegg-Hill, *b.* 1931, *s.* 1974.	Peter D. R. C. *C.-H.*, *b.* 1945.
1796	*Hood* (7th), Alexander Lambert Hood (7th *Irish Baron, Hood*, 1782), *b.* 1914, *s.* 1981, *m.*	Hon. Henry L. A. *H.*, *b.* 1958.
1956	*Ingleby* (2nd), Martin Raymond Peake, *b.* 1926, *s.* 1966, *m.*	None.
1945	*Kemsley* (2nd), (Geoffrey) Lionel Berry, *b.* 1909, *s.* 1968, *m.*	Richard G. *B.*, *b.* 1951.
1911	*Knollys* (3rd), David Francis Dudley Knollys, *b.* 1931, *s.* 1966, *m.*	Hon. Patrick N. M. *K.*, *b.* 1962.
1895	*Knutsford* (6th), Michael Holland-Hibbert, *b.* 1926, *s.* 1986, *m.*	Hon. Henry T. *H.-H.*, *b.* 1959.
1945	*Lambert* (3rd), Michael John Lambert, *b.* 1912, *s.* 1989, *m.*	None.
1954	*Leathers* (2nd), Frederick Alan Leathers, *b.* 1908, *s.* 1965, *m.*	Hon. Christopher G. *L.*, *b.* 1941.
1922	*Leverhulme* (3rd), Philip William Bryce Lever, KG, TD, *b.* 1915, *s.* 1949, *w.*	None.
1781 I.	*Lifford* (9th), (Edward) James Wingfield Hewitt, *b.* 1949, *s.* 1987, *m.*	Hon. James T. W. *H.*, *b.* 1979.
1921	*Long* (4th), Richard Gerard Long, *b.* 1929, *s.* 1967, *m.*	Hon. James R. *L.*, *b.* 1960.
1957	*Mackintosh of Halifax* (3rd), (John) Clive Mackintosh, *b.* 1958, *s.* 1980, *m.*	Hon. Thomas H. G. *M.*, *b.* 1985.
1955	*Malvern* (3rd), Ashley Kevin Godfrey Huggins, *b.* 1949, *s.* 1978.	Hon. M. James *H.*, *b.* 1928.
1945	*Marchwood* (3rd), David George Staveley Penny, *b.* 1936, *s.* 1979, *m.*	Hon. Peter G. W. *P.*, *b.* 1965.
1942	*Margesson* (2nd), Francis Vere Hampden Margesson, *b.* 1922, *s.* 1965, *m.*	Capt. Hon. Richard F. D. *M.*, *b.* 1960.
1660 I.*	*Massereene* (13th) & *Ferrard* (6th) (1797), John Clotworthy Talbot Foster Whyte-Melville Skeffington (6th *UK Baron, Oriel*, 1821), *b.* 1914, *s.* 1956, *m.*	Hon. John D. C. W.-M. F. *S.*, *b.* 1940.
1802	*Melville* (9th), Robert David Ross Dundas, *b.* 1937, *s.* 1971, *m.*	Hon. Robert H. K. *D.*, *b.* 1984.
1916	*Mersey* (4th), Richard Maurice Clive Bigham, *b.* 1934, *s.* 1979, *m.*	Hon. Edward J. H. *B.*, *b.* 1966.
1717 I.*	*Midleton* (12th), Alan Henry Brodrick (9th *Brit. Baron, Brodrick of Peper Harow*, 1796), *b.* 1949, *s.* 1988, *m.*	Hon. Ashley R. *B.*, *b.* 1980.
1962	*Mills* (3rd), Christopher Philip Roger Mills, *b.* 1956, *s.* 1988, *m.*	None.
1716 I.	*Molesworth* (11th), Richard Gosset Molesworth, *b.* 1907, *s.* 1961, *w.*	Hon. Robert B. K. *M.*, *b.* 1959.
1801 I.*	*Monck* (7th), Charles Stanley Monck (4th *UK Baron, Monck*, 1866), *b.* 1953, *s.* 1982.	Hon. George S. *M.*, *b.* 1957.
1957	*Monckton of Brenchley* (2nd), Gilbert Walter Riversdale Monckton, CB, OBE, MC, *b.* 1915, *s.* 1965, *m.*	Hon Christopher W. *M.*, *b.* 1952.
1935	*Monsell* (2nd), Henry Bolton Graham Eyres Monsell, *b.* 1905, *s.* 1969.	None.
1946	*Montgomery of Alamein* (2nd), David Bernard Montgomery, CBE, *b.* 1928, *s.* 1976, *m.*	Hon. Henry D. *M.*, *b.* 1954.
1550 I.*	*Mountgarret* (17th), Richard Henry Piers Butler (4th *UK Baron, Mountgarret*, 1911), *b.* 1936, *s.* 1966, *m.*	Hon. Piers J. R. *B.*, *b.* 1961.
1952	*Norwich* (2nd), John Julius Cooper, *b.* 1929, *s.* 1954, *m.*	Hon. Jason C. D. B. *C.*, *b.* 1959.
1651 S.	*of Oxfuird* (13th), George Hubbard Makgill, *b.* 1934, *s.* 1986, *m.*	Master of Oxfuird, *b.* 1969.
1873	*Portman*, (9th), Edward Henry Berkeley Portman, *b.* 1934, *s.* 1967, *m.*	Hon. Christopher E. B. *P.*, *b.* 1958.
1743 I.*	*Powerscourt* (10th), Mervyn Niall Wingfield (4th *UK Baron, Powerscourt*, 1885), *b.* 1935, *s.* 1973, *m.*	Hon. Mervyn A. *W.*, *b.* 1963.
1900	*Ridley* (4th), Matthew White Ridley, KG, TD, *b.* 1925, *s.* 1964, *m. Lord Steward.*	Hon. Matthew W. *R.*, *b.* 1958.
1960	*Rochdale* (1st), John Durival Kemp, OBE, TD (2nd *UK Baron, Rochdale*, 1913), *b.* 1906, *s.* to Barony 1945, *m.*	Hon. St John D. *K.*, *b.* 1938.
1919	*Rothermere* (3rd), Vere Harold Esmond Harmsworth, *b.* 1925, *s.* 1978, *w.*	Hon. H. Jonathan E. V. *H.*, *b.* 1967.
1937	*Runciman of Doxford* (3rd), Walter Garrison Runciman, CBE, FBA (4th *UK Baron, Runciman*, 1933), *b.* 1934, *s.* 1989, *m.*	Hon. David W. *R.*, *b.* 1967.
1918	*St Davids* (3rd), Colwyn Jestyn John Philipps (20th *Engl. Baron Strange of Knokin*, 1299, 8th *Engl. Baron Hungerford*, 1426, *and De Moleyns*, 1445), *b.* 1939, *s.* 1991, *m.*	Hon. Rhodri C. *P.*, *b.* 1966.
1801	*St Vincent* (7th), Ronald George James Jervis, *b.* 1905, *s.* 1940, *m.*	Hon. Edward R. J. *J.*, *b.* 1951.
1937	*Samuel* (3rd), David Herbert Samuel, Ph.D., *b.* 1922, *s.* 1978, *m.*	Hon. Dan J. *S.*, *b.* 1925.
1911	*Scarsdale* (3rd), Francis John Nathaniel Curzon (7th *Brit. Baron, Scarsdale*, 1761), *b.* 1924, *s.* 1977, *m.*	Hon. Peter G. N. *C.*, *b.* 1949.
1905	*Selby* (4th), Michael Guy John Gully, *b.* 1942, *s.* 1959, *m.*	Hon. Edward T. W. *G.*, *b.* 1967.
1805	*Sidmouth* (7th), John Tonge Anthony Pellew Addington, *b.* 1914, *s.* 1976, *w.*	Hon. Jeremy F. *A.*, *b.* 1947.
1940	*Simon* (2nd), John Gilbert Simon, CMG, *b.* 1902, *s.* 1954, *m.*	Hon. Jan D. *S.*, *b.* 1940.
1960	*Slim* (2nd), John Douglas Slim, OBE, *b.* 1927, *s.* 1970, *m.*	Hon. Mark W. R. *S.*, *b.* 1960.
1954	*Soulbury* (2nd), James Herwald Ramsbotham, *b.* 1915, *s.* 1971, *w.*	Hon. Sir Peter E. *R.*, GCMG, GCVO, *b.* 1919.
1776 I.	*Southwell* (7th), Pyers Anthony Joseph Southwell, *b.* 1930, *s.* 1960, *m.*	Hon. Richard A. P. *S.*, *b.* 1956.
1942	*Stansgate.* Disclaimed for life 1963. (*Rt. Hon. Anthony Neil Wedgwood Benn*, MP, *b.* 1925, *s.* 1960, *m.*)	Stephen M. W. *B.*, *b.* 1951.

Created	*Title, order of succession, name, etc.*	*Eldest son or heir*
1959	*Stuart of Findhorn* (2nd), David Randolph Moray Stuart, *b.* 1924, *s.* 1971, *m.*	Hon. J. Dominic *S.*, *b.* 1948.
1957	*Tenby* (3rd), William Lloyd George, *b.* 1927, *s.* 1983, *m.*	Hon. Timothy H. G. *L. G.*, *b.* 1962.
1952	*Thurso* (2nd), Robin Macdonald Sinclair, *b.* 1922, *s.* 1970, *m.*	Hon. John A. *S.*, *b.* 1953.
1983	*Tonypandy* (1st), (Thomas) George Thomas, PC, *b.* 1909.	None.
1721	*Torrington* (11th), Timothy Howard St George Byng, *b.* 1943, *s.* 1961, *m.*	John L. *B.*, MC, *b.* 1919.
1936	*Trenchard* (3rd), Hugh Trenchard, *b.* 1951, *s.* 1987, *m.*	Hon. Alexander T. *T.*, *b.* 1978.
1921	*Ullswater* (2nd), Nicholas James Christopher Lowther, *b.* 1942, *s.* 1949, *m.*	Hon. Benjamin J. *L.*, *b.* 1975.
1621 I.	*Valentia* (15th), Richard John Dighton Annesley, *b.* 1929, *s.* 1983, *m.*	Hon. Francis W. D. *A.*, *b.* 1959.
1964	*Watkinson* (1st), Harold Arthur Watkinson, CH, PC, *b.* 1910, *m.*	None.
1952	*Waverley* (3rd), John Desmond Forbes Anderson, *b.* 1949, *s.* 1990.	None.
1938	*Weir* (3rd), William Kenneth James Weir, *b.* 1933, *s.* 1975, *m.*	Hon. James W. H. *W.*, *b.* 1965.
1983	*Whitelaw* (1st), William Stephen Ian Whitelaw, KT, CH, MC, PC, *b.* 1918, *m.*	None.
1918	*Wimborne* (3rd), Ivor Fox-Strangways Guest (4th *UK Baron, Wimborne,* 1880), *b.* 1939, *s.* 1967, *m.*	Hon. Ivor M.V.*G.*, *b.* 1968.
1923	*Younger of Leckie* (3rd), Edward George Younger, OBE, TD, *b.* 1906, *s.* 1946, *w.*	Baron Younger of Prestwich, TD, PC, *b.* 1931 (*see* page 166).

BARONS

Coronet, Six silver balls.
Style, The Right Hon. the Lord _.
Wife's style, The Right Hon. the Lady _.
Children's style, 'The Hon.' before forename and family name.
In Scotland, the heir apparent to a Lord may be styled 'The Master of _ (title of peer)'.
For forms of address, *see* page 218.

Created	*Title, order of succession, name, etc.*	*Eldest son or heir*
1911	*Aberconway* (3rd), Charles Melville McLaren, *b.* 1913, *s.* 1953, *m.*	Hon. H. Charles *M.*, *b.* 1948.
1873	*Aberdare* (4th), Morys George Lyndhurst Bruce, KBE, PC, *b.* 1919, *s.* 1957, *m.*	Hon. Alastair J. L. *B.*, *b.* 1947.
1835	*Abinger* (8th), James Richard Scarlett, *b.* 1914, *s.* 1943, *m.*	Hon. James H. *S.*, *b.* 1959.
1869	*Acton* (4th), Richard Gerald Lyon-Dalberg-Acton, *b.* 1941, *s.* 1989, *m.*	Hon. John C. F. H. *L.-D.-A.*, *b.* 1966.
1887	*Addington* (6th), Dominic Bryce Hubbard, *b.* 1963, *s.* 1982.	Hon. Michael W. L. *H.*, *b.* 1965.
1955	*Adrian* (2nd), Richard Hume Adrian, FRS, *b.* 1927, *s.* 1977, *m.*	None.
1907	*Airedale* (4th), Oliver James Vandeleur Kitson, *b.* 1915, *s.* 1958.	None.
1896	*Aldenham* (6th), and *Hunsdon of Hunsdon* (4th) (1923), Vicary Tyser Gibbs, *b.* 1948, *s.* 1986, *m.*	Hon. Humphrey W. F. *G.*, *b.* 1989.
1962	*Aldington* (1st), Toby Austin Richard William Low, KCMG, CBE, DSO, TD, PC, *b.* 1914, *m.*	Hon Charles H. S. *L.*, *b.* 1948.
1945	*Altrincham.* Disclaimed for life 1963. (*John Edward Poynder Grigg, b.* 1924, *s.* 1955, *m.*)	Hon. Anthony U. D. D. *G.*, *b.* 1934.
1929	*Alvingham* (2nd), Maj.-Gen. Robert Guy Eardley Yerburgh, CBE, *b.* 1926, *s.* 1955, *m.*	Capt. Hon. Robert R. G. *Y.*, *b.* 1956.
1892	*Amherst of Hackney* (4th), William Hugh Amherst Cecil, *b.* 1940, *s.* 1980, *m.*	Hon. H. William A. *C.*, *b.* 1968.
1881	*Ampthill* (4th), Geoffrey Denis Erskine Russell, CBE, *b.* 1921, *s.* 1973.	Hon. David W. E. *R.*, *b.* 1947.
1947	*Amwell* (3rd), Keith Norman Montague, *b.* 1943, *s.* 1990, *m.*	Hon. Ian K. *M.*, *b.* 1973.
1863	*Annaly* (6th), Luke Richard White, *b.* 1954, *s.* 1990, *m.*	Hon. Luke H. *W.*, *b.* 1990.
1949	*Archibald.* Disclaimed for life 1975. (*George Christopher Archibald, b.* 1926, *s.* 1975, *m.*)	None.
1885	*Ashbourne* (4th), Edward Barry Greynville Gibson, *b.* 1933, *s.* 1983, *m.*	Hon. Edward C. d'O. *G.*, *b.* 1967.
1835	*Ashburton* (7th), John Francis Harcourt Baring, KCVO, *b.* 1928, *s.* 1991, *m.*	Hon. Mark F. R. *B.*, *b.* 1958.
1892	*Ashcombe* (4th), Henry Edward Cubitt, *b.* 1924, *s.* 1962, *m.*	M. Robin *C.*, *b.* 1936.
1911	*Ashton of Hyde* (3rd), Thomas John Ashton, TD, *b.* 1926, *s.* 1983, *m.*	Hon. Thomas H. *A.*, *b.* 1958.
1800 I.	*Ashtown* (7th), Nigel Clive Crosby Trench, KCMG, *b.* 1916, *s.* 1990, *m.*	Hon. Roderick N. G. *T.*, *b.* 1944.
1956	*Astor of Hever* (3rd), John Jacob Astor, *b.* 1946, *s.* 1984, *m.*	Hon. Charles G. J. *A.*, *b.* 1990.
1789 I.*	*Auckland* (9th), Ian George Eden (9th *Brit. Baron, Auckland,* 1793), *b.* 1926, *s.* 1957, *m.*	Hon. Robert I. B. *E.*, *b.* 1962.
1313	*Audley* (25th), Richard Michael Thomas Souter, *b.* 1914, *s.* 1973, *m.*	Three co-heiresses.

Created	*Title, order of succession, name, etc.*	*Eldest son or heir*
1900	*Avebury* (4th), Eric Reginald Lubbock, *b.* 1928, *s.* 1971, *m.*	Hon. Lyulph A. J. *L.*, *b.* 1954.
1718 I.	*Aylmer* (13th), Michael Anthony Aylmer, *b.* 1923, *s.* 1982, *m.*	Hon. A. Julian *A.*, *b.* 1951.
1929	*Baden-Powell* (3rd), Robert Crause Baden-Powell, *b.* 1936, *s.* 1962, *m.*	Hon. David M. *B.-P.*, *b.* 1940.
1780	*Bagot* (9th), Heneage Charles Bagot, *b.* 1914, *s.* 1979, *m.*	Hon. C. H. Shaun *B.*, *b.* 1944.
1953	*Baillieu* (3rd), James William Latham Baillieu, *b.* 1950, *s.* 1973, *m.*	Hon. Robert L. *B.*, *b.* 1979.
1607 S.	*Balfour of Burleigh* (8th), Robert Bruce, *b.* 1927, *s.* 1967, *m.*	Hon. Victoria B., *b.* 1973.
1945	*Balfour of Inchrye* (2nd), Ian Balfour, *b.* 1924, *s.* 1988, *m.*	None.
1924	*Banbury of Southam* (3rd), Charles William Banbury, *b.* 1953, *s.* 1981.	None.
1698	*Barnard* (11th), Harry John Neville Vane, TD, *b.* 1923, *s.* 1964, *m.*	Hon. Henry F. C. *V.*, *b.* 1959.
1887	*Basing* (5th), Neil Lutley Sclater-Booth, *b.* 1939, *s.* 1983, *m.*	Hon. Stuart W. *S.-B.*, *b.* 1969.
1917	*Beaverbrook* (3rd), Maxwell William Humphrey Aitken, *b.* 1951, *s.* 1985, *m.*	Hon. Maxwell F. *A*, *b.* 1977.
1647 S.	*Belhaven and Stenton* (13th), Robert Anthony Carmichael Hamilton, *b.* 1927, *s.* 1961, *m.*	Master of Belhaven, *b.* 1953.
1848 I.	*Bellew* (7th), James Bryan Bellew, *b.* 1920, *s.* 1981, *m.*	Hon. Bryan E. *B.*, *b.* 1943.
1856	*Belper* (4th), (Alexander) Ronald George Strutt, *b.* 1912, *s.* 1956.	Hon. Richard H. *S.*, *b.* 1941.
1938	*Belstead* (2nd), John Julian Ganzoni, PC, *b.* 1932, *s.* 1958.	None.
1922	*Bethell* (4th), Nicholas William Bethell, MEP, *b.* 1938, s. 1967, *m.*	Hon. James N. *B.*, *b.* 1967.
1938	*Bicester* (3rd), Angus Edward Vivian Smith, *b.* 1932, *s.* 1968.	Hugh C. V. *S.*, *b.* 1934.
1903	*Biddulph* (5th), (Anthony) Nicholas Colin Maitland Biddulph, *b.* 1959, *s.* 1988.	Hon. William I. R. *M.B.*, *b.* 1963.
1938	*Birdwood* (3rd), Mark William Ogilvie Birdwood, *b.* 1938, *s.* 1962, *m.*	None.
1958	*Birkett* (2nd), Michael Birkett, *b.* 1929, *s.* 1962, *m.*	Hon. Thomas *B.*, *b.* 1982.
1907	*Blyth* (4th), Anthony Audley Rupert Blyth, *b.* 1931, *s.* 1977, *m.*	Hon. Riley A. J. *B.*, *b.* 1955.
1797	*Bolton* (7th), Richard William Algar Orde-Powlett, *b.* 1929, *s.* 1963, *m.*	Hon. Harry A. N. *O.-P.*, *b.* 1954.
1452 S.	*Borthwick* (23rd), John Henry Stuart Borthwick, TD, *b.* 1905, *claim succeeded* 1986, *w.*	Master of Borthwick, *b.* 1940.
1922	*Borwick* (4th), James Hugh Myles Borwick, MC, *b.* 1917, *s.* 1961, *m.*	Hon. George S. *B.*, *b.* 1922.
1761	*Boston* (10th), Timothy George Frank Boteler Irby, *b.* 1939, *s.* 1978, *m.*	Hon. George W. E. B. *I.*, *b.* 1971.
1942	*Brabazon of Tara* (3rd), Ivon Anthony Moore-Brabazon, *b.* 1946, *s.* 1974, *m.*	Hon. Benjamin R. *M.-B.*, *b.* 1983.
1880	*Brabourne* (7th), John Ulick Knatchbull, *b.* 1924, *s.* 1943, *m.*	Lord Romsey, *b.* 1947 (*see* page 149).
1925	*Bradbury* (2nd), John Bradbury, *b.* 1914, *s.* 1950, *m.*	Hon. John *B.*, *b.* 1940.
1962	*Brain* (2nd), Christopher Langdon Brain, *b.* 1926, *s.* 1966, *m.*	Hon. Michael C. *B.*, DM, *b.* 1928.
1938	*Brassey of Apethorpe* (3rd), David Henry Brassey, *b.* 1932, *s.* 1967, *m.*	Hon. Edward *B.*, *b.* 1964.
1788	*Braybrooke* (10th), Robin Henry Charles Neville, *b.* 1932, *s.* 1990, *m.*	George *N.*, *b.* 1943.
1957	*Bridges* (2nd), Thomas Edward Bridges, GCMG, *b.* 1927, *s.* 1969, *m.*	Hon. Mark T. *B.*, *b.* 1954.
1945	*Broadbridge* (3rd), Peter Hewett Broadbridge, *b.* 1938, *s.* 1972, *m.*	Martin H. *B.*, *b.* 1929.
1933	*Brocket* (3rd), Charles Ronald George Nall-Cain, *b.* 1952, *s.* 1967, *m.*	Hon. Alexander C. C. *N.-C.*, *b.* 1984.
1860	*Brougham and Vaux* (5th), Michael John Brougham, *b.* 1938, *s.* 1967.	Hon. Charles W. *B.*, *b.* 1971.
1945	*Broughshane* (2nd), Patrick Owen Alexander Davison, *b.* 1903, *s.* 1953, *m.*	Hon. W. Kensington *D.*, DSO, DFC, *b.* 1914.
1776	*Brownlow* (7th), Edward John Peregrine Cust, *b.* 1936, *s.* 1978, *m.*	Hon. Peregrine E. Q. *C.*, *b.* 1974.
1942	*Bruntisfield* (1st), Victor Alexander George Anthony Warrender, MC, *b.* 1899, *m.*	Hon. John R. *W.*, OBE, MC, TD, *b.* 1921.
1950	*Burden* (2nd), Philip William Burden, *b.* 1916, *s.* 1970, *m.*	Hon. Andrew P. *B.*, *b.* 1959.
1529	*Burgh* (7th), Alexander Peter Willoughby Leith, *b.* 1935, *s.* 1959, *m.*	Hon. A. Gregory D. *L.*, *b.* 1958.
1903	*Burnham* (5th), William Edward Harry Lawson, *b.* 1920, *s.* 1963, *m.*	Hon. Hugh J. F. *L.*, *b.* 1931.
1897	*Burton* (3rd), Michael Evan Victor Baillie, *b.* 1924, *s.* 1962, *m.*	Hon. Evan M. R. *B.*, *b.* 1949.
1643	*Byron* (13th), Robert James Byron, *b.* 1950, *s.* 1989, *m.*	Hon. Charles R. G. *B.*, *b.* 1990.
1937	*Cadman* (3rd), John Anthony Cadman, *b.* 1938, *s.* 1966, *m.*	Hon. Nicholas A. J. *C.*, *b.* 1977.
1796	*Calthorpe* (10th), Peter Waldo Somerset Gough-Calthorpe, *b.* 1927, *s.* 1945, *m.*	None.
1945	*Calverley* (3rd), Charles Rodney Muff, *b.* 1946, *s.* 1971, *m.*	Hon. Jonathan E. *M.*, *b.* 1975.
1383	*Camoys* (7th), (Ralph) Thomas Campion George Sherman Stonor, *b.* 1940, *s.* 1976, *m.*	Hon. R. William R. T. *S.*, *b.* 1974.
1715 I.	*Carbery* (11th), Peter Ralfe Harrington Evans-Freke, *b.* 1920, *s.* 1970, *m.*	Hon. Michael P. *E.-F.*, *b.* 1942.
1834 I.*	*Carew* (6th), William Francis Conolly-Carew, CBE (6th *UK. Baron, Carew*, 1838), *b.* 1905, *s.* 1927, *w.*	Hon. Patrick T. *C.-C.*, *b.* 1938.
1916	*Carnock* (4th), David Henry Arthur Nicolson, *b.* 1920, *s.* 1982.	Nigel *N.*, MBE, *b.* 1917.
1796 I.*	*Carrington* (6th), Peter Alexander Rupert Carington, KG, GCMG, CH, MC, PC (6th *Brit. Baron, Carrington*, 1797), *b.* 1919, *s.* 1938, *m.*	Hon. Rupert F. J. *C.*, *b.* 1948.
1812 I.	*Castlemaine* (8th), Roland Thomas John Handcock, MBE, *b.* 1943, *s.* 1973, *m.*	Hon. Ronan M. E. *H.*, *b.* 1989.
1936	*Catto* (2nd), Stephen Gordon Catto, *b.* 1923, *s.* 1959, *m.*	Hon. Innes G. *C.*, *b.* 1950.
1918	*Cawley* (3rd), Frederick Lee Cawley, *b.* 1913, *s.* 1954, *m.*	Hon. John F. *C.*, *b.* 1946.
1937	*Chatfield* (2nd), Ernle David Lewis Chatfield, *b.* 1917, *s.* 1967, *m.*	None.
1858	*Chesham* (6th), Nicholas Charles Cavendish, *b.* 1941, *s.* 1989, *m.*	Hon. Charles G. C. *C.*, *b.* 1974.

Created	*Title, order of succession, name, etc.*	*Eldest son or heir*
1945	*Chetwode* (2nd), Philip Chetwode, *b.* 1937, *s.* 1950, *m.*	Hon. Roger *C.*, *b.* 1968.
1945	*Chorley* (2nd), Roger Richard Edward Chorley, *b.* 1930, *s.* 1978, *m.*	Hon. Nicholas R. D. *C.*, *b.* 1966.
1858	*Churston* (5th), John Francis Yarde-Buller, *b.* 1934, *s.* 1991, *m.*	Hon. Benjamin F. A. *Y.-B.*, *b.* 1974.
1946	*Citrine* (2nd), Norman Arthur Citrine, *b.* 1914, *s.* 1983, *m.*	Hon. Ronald E. *C.*, *b.* 1919.
1800 I.	*Clanmorris* (8th), Simon John Ward Bingham, *b.* 1937, *s.* 1988, *m.*	John T. *B.*, *b.* 1923.
1672	*Clifford of Chudleigh* (14th), Thomas Hugh Clifford, *b.* 1948, *s.* 1988, *m.*	Hon. Alexander T. H. *C.*, *b.* 1985.
1299	*Clinton* (22nd), Gerard Nevile Mark Fane Trefusis, *b.* 1934, *title called out of abeyance* 1965, *m.*	Hon. Charles P. R. F. *T.*, *b.* 1962.
1955	*Clitheroe* (2nd), Ralph John Assheton, *b.* 1929, *s.* 1984, *m.*	Hon. Ralph C. *A.*, *b.* 1962.
1919	*Clwyd* (3rd), (John) Anthony Roberts, *b.* 1935, *s.* 1987, *m.*	Hon. J. Murray *R.*, *b.* 1971.
1948	*Clydesmuir* (2nd), Ronald John Bilsland Colville, KT, CB, MBE, TD, *b.* 1917, *s.* 1954, *m.*	Hon. David R. *C.*, *b.* 1949.
1960	*Cobbold* (2nd), David Antony Fromanteel Lytton Cobbold, *b.* 1937, *s.* 1987, *m.*	Hon. Henry F. *L. C.*, *b.* 1962.
1919	*Cochrane of Cults* (4th), (Ralph Henry) Vere Cochrane, *b.* 1926, *s.* 1990, *m.*	Hon. Thomas H. V. *C.*, *b.* 1957.
1954	*Coleraine* (2nd), (James) Martin (Bonar) Law, *b.* 1931, *s.* 1980, *m.*	Hon. James P. B. *L.*, *b.* 1975.
1873	*Coleridge* (5th), William Duke Coleridge, *b.* 1937, *s.* 1984, *m.*	Hon. James D. *C.*, *b.* 1967.
1946	*Colgrain* (3rd), David Colin Campbell, *b.* 1920, *s.* 1973, *m.*	Hon. Alastair C. L. *C.*, *b.* 1951.
1917	*Colwyn* (3rd), (Ian) Anthony Hamilton-Smith, CBE, *b.* 1942, *s.* 1966, *m.*	Hon. Craig P. *H.-S.*, *b.* 1968.
1956	*Colyton* (1st), Henry Lennox d'Aubigné Hopkinson, CMG, PC, *b.* 1902, *m.*	Hon. Nicholas H. E. *H.*, *b.* 1932.
1841	*Congleton* (8th), Christopher Patrick Parnell, *b.* 1930, *s.* 1967, *m.*	Hon. John P. C. *P.*, *b.* 1959.
1927	*Cornwallis* (3rd), Fiennes Neil Wykeham Cornwallis, OBE, *b.* 1921, *s.* 1982, *m.*	Hon. F. W. Jeremy *C.*, *b.* 1946.
1874	*Cottesloe* (4th), John Walgrave Halford Fremantle, GBE, TD, *b.* 1900, *s.* 1956, *m.*	Cdr. Hon. John T. *F.*, *b.* 1927.
1929	*Craigmyle* (3rd), Thomas Donald Mackay Shaw, *b.* 1923, *s.* 1944, *m.*	Hon. Thomas C. *S.*, *b.* 1960.
1899	*Cranworth* (3rd), Philip Bertram Gurdon, *b.* 1940, *s.* 1964, *m.*	Hon. Sacha W. R. *G.*, *b.* 1970.
1959	*Crathorne* (2nd), Charles James Dugdale, *b.* 1939, *s.* 1977, *m.*	Hon. Thomas A. J. *D.*, *b.* 1977.
1892	*Crawshaw* (4th), William Michael Clifton Brooks, *b.* 1933, *s.* 1946.	Hon. David G. *B.*, *b.* 1934.
1940	*Croft* (2nd), Michael Henry Glendower Page Croft, *b.* 1916, *s.* 1947, *w.*	Hon. Bernard W. H. P. *C.*, *b.* 1949.
1797 I.	*Crofton* (7th), Guy Patrick Gilbert Crofton, *b.* 1951, *s.* 1989, *m.*	Hon. E. Harry P. *C.*, *b.* 1988.
1375	*Cromwell* (7th), Godfrey John Bewicke-Copley, *b.* 1960, *s.* 1982, *m.*	Hon. Thomas D. *B.-C.*, *b.* 1964.
1947	*Crook* (2nd), Douglas Edwin Crook, *b.* 1926, *s* 1989, *m.*	Hon. Robert D. E. *C.*, *b.* 1955.
1920	*Cullen of Ashbourne* (2nd), Charles Borlase Marsham Cokayne, MBE, *b.* 1912, *s.* 1932, *m.*	Hon. Edmund W. M. *C.*, *b.* 1916.
1914	*Cunliffe* (3rd), Roger Cunliffe, *b.* 1932, *s.* 1963, *m.*	Hon. Henry *C.*, *b.* 1962.
1927	*Daresbury* (3rd), Edward Gilbert Greenall, *b.* 1928, *s.* 1990, *m.*	Hon. Peter G. *G.*, *b.* 1953.
1924	*Darling* (2nd), Robert Charles Henry Darling, *b.* 1919, *s.* 1936, *m.*	Hon. R. Julian H. *D.*, *b.* 1944.
1946	*Darwen* (3rd), Roger Michael Davies, *b.* 1938, *s.* 1988, *m.*	Hon. Paul *D.*, *b.* 1962.
1923	*Daryngton* (2nd), Jocelyn Arthur Pike Pease, *b.* 1908, *s.* 1949.	None.
1932	*Davies* (3rd), David Davies, *b.* 1940, *s.* 1944, *m.*	Hon. David D. *D.*, *b.* 1975.
1812 I.	*Decies* (6th), Arthur George Marcus Douglas de la Poer Beresford, *b.* 1915, *s.* 1944, *m.*	Hon. Marcus H. T. *de la P. B.*, *b.* 1948.
1299	*de Clifford* (27th), John Edward Southwell Russell, *b.* 1928, *s.* 1982, *m.*	Hon. William S. *R.*, *b.* 1930.
1851	*De Freyne* (7th), Francis Arthur John French, *b.* 1927, *s.* 1935, *m.*	Hon. Fulke C. A. J. *F.*, *b.* 1957.
1821	*Delamere* (5th), Hugh George Cholmondeley, *b.* 1934, *s.* 1979, *m.*	Hon. Thomas P. G. *C.*, *b.* 1968.
1838	*de Mauley* (6th), Gerald John Ponsonby, *b.* 1921, *s.* 1962, *m.*	Col. Hon. Thomas M. *P.*, TD, *b.* 1930.
1937	*Denham* (2nd), Bertram Stanley Mitford Bowyer, KBE, PC, *b.* 1927, *s.* 1948, *m.*	Hon. Richard G. G. *B.*, *b.* 1959.
1834	*Denman* (5th), Charles Spencer Denman, CBE, MC, TD, *b.* 1916, *s.* 1971, *w.*	Hon. Richard T. S. *D.*, *b.* 1946.
1885	*Deramore* (6th), Richard Arthur de Yarburgh-Bateson, *b.* 1911, *s.* 1964, *m.*	None.
1887	*De Ramsey* (3rd), Ailwyn Edward Fellowes, KBE, TD, *b.* 1910, *s.* 1925, *w.*	Hon. John A. *F.*, *b.* 1942.
1264	*de Ros* (28th), Peter Trevor Maxwell, *b.* 1958, *s.* 1983, *m.* (*Premier Baron of England*).	Hon. Finbar J. *M.*, *b.* 1988.
1881	*Derwent* (5th), Robin Evelyn Leo Vanden-Bempde-Johnstone, LVO, *b.* 1930, *s.* 1986, *m.*	Hon. Francis P. H. *V.-B.-J.*, *b.* 1965.
1831	*de Saumarez* (7th), Eric Douglas Saumarez, *b.* 1956, *s.* 1991, *m.*	Hon. Victor T. *S.*, *b.* 1956.
1910	*de Villiers* (3rd), Arthur Percy de Villiers, *b.* 1911, *s.* 1934.	Hon. Alexander C. *de V.*, *b.* 1940.
1930	*Dickinson* (2nd), Richard Clavering Hyett Dickinson, *b.* 1926, *s.* 1943, *m.*	Hon. Martin H. *D.*, *b.* 1961.
1620 I. 1765*	*Digby* (12th), Edward Henry Kenelm Digby (6th *Brit. Baron, Digby*), *b.* 1924, *s.* 1964, *m.*	Hon. Henry N. K. *D.*, *b.* 1954.
1615	*Dormer* (16th), Joseph Spencer Philip Dormer, *b.* 1914, *s.* 1975.	Geoffrey H. *D.*, *b.* 1920.
1943	*Dowding* (2nd), Derek Hugh Tremenheere Dowding, *b.* 1919, *s.* 1970, *m.*	Hon. Piers H. T. *D.*, *b.* 1948.
1800 I.	*Dufferin and Clandeboye* (10th), Francis George Blackwood, *b.* 1916, *s.* 1988, *m.*	Hon. John F. *B.*, *b.* 1944.
1929	*Dulverton* (3rd), (Gilbert) Michael Hamilton Wills, *b.* 1944, *s.* 1992, *m.*	Hon. Robert A. H. *W.*, *b.* 1983.
1800 I.	*Dunalley* (7th), Henry Francis Cornelius Prittie, *b.* 1948, *s.* 1992, *m.*	Hon. Joel H. *P.*, *b.* 1981.

Created	*Title, order of succession, name, etc.*	*Eldest son or heir*
1324 I.	*Dunboyne* (28th), Patrick Theobald Tower Butler, VRD, *b.* 1917, *s.* 1945, *m.*	Hon. John F. *B.*, *b.* 1951.
1802	*Dunleath* (4th), Charles Edward Henry John Mulholland, TD, *b.* 1933, *s.* 1956, *m.*	Sir Michael H. *M.*, Bt., *b.* 1915.
1439 I.	*Dunsany* (19th), Randal Arthur Henry Plunkett (20th *Irish Baron Killeen*, 1449), *b.* 1906, *s.* 1957, *m.*	Hon. Edward J. C. *P.*, *b.* 1939.
1780	*Dynevor* (9th), Richard Charles Uryan Rhys, *b.* 1935, *s.* 1962.	Hon. Hugo G. U. *R.*, *b.* 1966.
1857	*Ebury* (6th), Francis Egerton Grosvenor, *b.* 1934, *s.* 1957, *m.*	Hon. Julian F. M. *G.*, *b.* 1959.
1963	*Egremont* (2nd), & *Leconfield* (7th) (1859), John Max Henry Scawen Wyndham, *b.* 1948, *s.* 1972, *m.*	Hon. George R. V. *W.*, *b.* 1983.
1643	*Elibank* (14th), Alan D'Ardis Erskine-Murray, *b.* 1923, *s.* 1973, *m.*	Master of Elibank, *b.* 1964.
1802	*Ellenborough* (8th), Richard Edward Cecil Law, *b.* 1926, *s.* 1945, *w.*	Maj. Hon. Rupert E. H. *L.*, *b.* 1955.
1509 S.*	*Elphinstone* (18th), James Alexander Elphinstone (4th *UK Baron Elphinstone*, 1885), *b.* 1953, *s.* 1975, *m.*	Master of Elphinstone, *b.* 1980.
1934	*Elton* (2nd), Rodney Elton, TD, *b.* 1930, *s.* 1973, *m.*	Hon. Edward P. *E.*, *b.* 1966.
1964	*Erroll of Hale* (1st), Frederick James Erroll, TD, PC, *b.* 1914, *m.*	None.
1964	*Erskine of Rerrick* (2nd), Iain Maxwell Erskine, *b.* 1926, *s.* 1980.	None.
1627 S.	*Fairfax of Cameron* (14th), Nicholas John Albert Fairfax, *b.* 1956, *s.* 1964, *m.*	Hon. Edward N. T. *F.*, *b.* 1984.
1961	*Fairhaven* (3rd), Ailwyn Henry George Broughton, *b.* 1936, *s.* 1973, *m.*	Hon. James H. A. *B.*, *b.* 1963.
1916	*Faringdon* (3rd), Charles Michael Henderson, *b.* 1937, *s.* 1977, *m.*	Hon. James H. *H.*, *b.* 1961.
1756 I.	*Farnham* (12th), Barry Owen Somerset Maxwell, *b.* 1931, *s.* 1957, *m.*	Hon. Simon K. *M.*, *b.* 1933.
1856 I.	*Fermoy* (6th), Patrick Maurice Burke Roche, *b.* 1967, *s.* 1984.	Hon. E. Hugh B. *R.*, *b.* 1972.
1826	*Feversham* (6th), Charles Antony Peter Duncombe, *b.* 1945, *s.* 1963, *m.*	Hon. Jasper O. S. *D.*, *b.* 1968.
1798 I.	*ffrench* (8th), Robuck John Peter Charles Mario ffrench, *b.* 1956, *s.* 1986, *m.*	Hon. John C. M. J. F. *ff.*, *b.* 1928.
1909	*Fisher* (3rd), John Vavasseur Fisher, DSC, *b.* 1921, *s.* 1955, *m.*	Hon. Patrick V. *F.*, *b.* 1953.
1295	*Fitzwalter* (21st), (Fitzwalter) Brook Plumptre, *b.* 1914, *title called out of abeyance*, 1953, *m.*	Hon. Julian B. *P.*, *b.* 1952.
1776	*Foley* (8th), Adrian Gerald Foley, *b.* 1923, *s.* 1927, *m.*	Hon. Thomas H. *F.*, *b.* 1961.
1445 S.	*Forbes* (22nd), Nigel Ivan Forbes, KBE (*Premier Baron of Scotland*), *b.* 1918, *s.* 1953, *m.*	Master of Forbes, *b.* 1946.
1821	*Forester* (8th), (George Cecil) Brooke Weld-Forester, *b.* 1938, *s.* 1977, *m.*	Hon. C. R. George *W.-F.*, *b.* 1975.
1922	*Forres* (4th), Alastair Stephen Grant Williamson, *b.* 1946, *s.* 1978, *m.*	Hon. George A. M. *W.*, *b.* 1972.
1917	*Forteviot* (3rd), Henry Evelyn Alexander Dewar, MBE, *b.* 1906, *s.* 1947, *w.*	Hon. John J. E. *D.*, *b.* 1938.
1951	*Freyberg* (2nd), Paul Richard Freyberg, OBE, MC, *b.* 1923, *s.* 1963, *m.*	Hon. Valerian B. *F.*, *b.* 1970.
1917	*Gainford* (3rd), Joseph Edward Pease, *b.* 1921, *s.* 1971, *m.*	Hon. George *P.*, *b.* 1926.
1818 I.	*Garvagh* (5th), (Alexander Leopold Ivor) George Canning, *b.* 1920, *s.* 1956, *m.*	Hon. Spencer G. S. de R. *C.*, *b.* 1953.
1942	*Geddes* (3rd), Euan Michael Ross Geddes, *b.* 1937, *s.* 1975, *m.*	Hon. James G. N. *G.*, *b.* 1969.
1876	*Gerard* (5th), Anthony Robert Hugo Gerard, *b.* 1949, *s.* 1992, *m.*	Hon. Rupert B. C. *G.*, *b.* 1981.
1824	*Gifford* (6th), Anthony Maurice Gifford, QC, *b.* 1940, *s.* 1961, *m.*	Hon. Thomas A. *G.*, *b.* 1967.
1917	*Gisborough* (3rd), Thomas Richard John Long Chaloner, *b.* 1927, *s.* 1951, *m.*	Hon. T. Peregrine L. *C.*, *b.* 1961.
1960	*Gladwyn* (1st), (Hubert Miles) Gladwyn Jebb, GCMG, GCVO, CB, *b.* 1900, *w.*	Hon. Miles A. G. *J.*, *b.* 1930.
1899	*Glanusk* (4th), David Russell Bailey, *b.* 1917, *s.* 1948, *m.*	Hon. Christopher R. *B.*, *b.* 1942.
1918	*Glenarthur* (4th), Simon Mark Arthur, *b.* 1944, *s.* 1976, *m.*	Hon. Edward A. *A.*, *b.* 1973.
1911	*Glenconner* (3rd), Colin Christopher Paget Tennant, *b.* 1926, *s.* 1983, *m.*	Hon. Charles E. P. *T.*, *b.* 1957.
1964	*Glendevon* (1st), John Adrian Hope, PC, *b.* 1912, *m.*	Hon. Julian J. S. *H.*, *b.* 1950.
1922	*Glendyne* (3rd), Robert Nivison, *b.* 1926, *s.* 1967, *m.*	Hon. John *N.*, *b.* 1960.
1939	*Glentoran* (2nd), Daniel Stewart Thomas Bingham Dixon, KBE, PC (NI), *b.* 1912, *s.* 1950, *w.*	Hon. Thomas R. V. *D.*, CBE, *b.* 1935.
1909	*Gorell* (4th), Timothy John Radcliffe Barnes, *b.* 1927, *s.* 1963, *m.*	Hon. Ronald A. H. *B.*, *b.* 1931.
1953	*Grantchester* (2nd), Kenneth Bent Suenson-Taylor, CBE, QC, *b.* 1921, *s.* 1976, *m.*	Hon. Christopher J. *S.-T.*, *b.* 1951.
1782	*Grantley* (7th), John Richard Brinsley Norton, MC, *b.* 1923, *s.* 1954, *m.*	Hon. Richard W. B. *N.*, *b.* 1956.
1794 I.	*Graves* (8th), Peter George Wellesley Graves, *b.* 1911, *s.* 1963, *w.*	Evelyn P. *G.*, *b.* 1926.
1445 S.	*Gray* (22nd), Angus Diarmid Ian Campbell-Gray, *b.* 1931, *s.* 1946, *w.*	Master of Gray, *b.* 1964.
1950	*Greenhill* (3rd), Malcolm Greenhill, *b.* 1924, *s.* 1989.	None.
1927	*Greenway* (4th), Ambrose Charles Drexel Greenway, *b.* 1941, *s.* 1975, *m.*	Hon. Mervyn S. K. *G.*, *b.* 1942.
1902	*Grenfell* (3rd), Julian Pascoe Francis St Leger Grenfell, *b.* 1935, *s.* 1976, *m.*	Francis P. J. *G.*, *b.* 1938.
1944	*Gretton* (4th), John Lysander Gretton, *b.* 1975, *s.* 1989, *M.*	None.
1397	*Grey of Codnor* (5th), Charles Legh Shuldham Cornwall-Legh, CBE, AE, *b.* 1903, *title called out of abeyance* 1989, *m.*	Hon. Richard H. *C.-L.*, *b.* 1936.
1955	*Gridley* (2nd), Arnold Hudson Gridley, *b.* 1906, *s.* 1965, *m.*	Hon. Richard D. A. *G.*, *b.* 1956.

Created	*Title, order of succession, name, etc.*	*Eldest son or heir*
1964	*Grimston of Westbury* (2nd), Robert Walter Sigismund Grimston, *b.* 1925, *s.* 1979, *m.*	Hon. Robert J. S. *G.*, *b.* 1951.
1886	*Grimthorpe* (4th), Christopher John Beckett, OBE, *b.* 1915, *s.* 1963, *m.*	Hon. Edward J. *B.*, *b.* 1954.
1945	*Hacking* (3rd), Douglas David Hacking, *b.* 1938, *s.* 1971, *m.*	Hon. Douglas F. *H.*, *b.* 1968.
1950	*Haden-Guest* (4th), Peter Haden Haden-Guest, *b.* 1913, *s.* 1987, *m.*	Hon. Christopher *H.-G.*, *b.* 1948.
1886	*Hamilton of Dalzell* (4th), James Leslie Hamilton, *b.* 1938, *s.* 1990, *m.*	Hon. Gavin G. *H.*, *b.* 1968.
1874	*Hampton* (6th), Richard Humphrey Russell Pakington, *b.* 1925, *s.* 1974, *m.*	Hon. John H. A. *P.*, *b.* 1964.
1939	*Hankey* (2nd), Robert Maurice Alers Hankey, KCMG, KCVO, *b.* 1905, *s.* 1963, *m.*	Hon. Donald R. A. *H.*, *b.* 1938.
1958	*Harding of Petherton* (2nd), John Charles Harding, *b.* 1928, *s.* 1989, *m.*	Hon. William A. J. *H.*, *b.* 1969.
1910	*Hardinge of Penshurst* (3rd), George Edward Charles Hardinge, *b.* 1921, *s.* 1960, *m.*	Hon. Julian A. *H.*, *b.* 1945.
1876	*Harlech* (6th), Francis David Ormsby-Gore, *b.* 1954, *s.* 1985, *m.*	Hon. Jasset D. C. *O.-G.*, *b.* 1986.
1939	*Harmsworth* (3rd), Thomas Harold Raymond Harmsworth, *b.* 1939, *s.* 1990, *m.*	Hon. Dominic M. E. *H.*, *b.* 1973.
1815	*Harris* (6th), George Robert John Harris, *b.* 1920, *s.* 1984.	Derek M. *H.*, *b.* 1916.
1954	*Harvey of Tasburgh* (2nd), Peter Charles Oliver Harvey, *b.* 1921, *s.* 1968, *m.*	Hon. John W. *H.*, *b.* 1923.
1295	*Hastings* (22nd), Edward Delaval Henry Astley, *b.* 1912, *s.* 1956, *m.*	Hon. Delaval T. H. *A.*, *b.* 1960.
1835	*Hatherton* (8th), Edward Charles Littleton, *b.* 1950, *s.* 1985, *m.*	Hon. Thomas E. *L.*, *b.* 1977.
1776	*Hawke* (11th), Edward George Hawke, *b.* 1950, *s.* 1992.	None.
1927	*Hayter* (3rd), George Charles Hayter Chubb, KCVO, CBE, b. 1911, *s.* 1967, *m.*	Hon. G. William M. *C.*, *b.* 1943.
1945	*Hazlerigg* (2nd), Arthur Grey Hazlerigg, MC, TD, *b.* 1910, *s.* 1949, *w.*	Hon. Arthur G. *H.*, *b.* 1951.
1797 I.	*Headley* (7th), Charles Rowland Allanson-Winn, *b.* 1902, *s.* 1969, *w.*	Hon. Owain G. *A.-W.*, *b.* 1906.
1943	*Hemingford* (3rd), (Dennis) Nicholas Herbert, *b.* 1934, *s.* 1982, *m.*	Hon. Christopher D. C. *H.*, *b.* 1973.
1906	*Hemphill* (5th), Peter Patrick Fitzroy Martyn Martyn-Hemphill, *b.* 1928, *s.* 1957, *m.*	Hon. Charles A. M. *M.-H.*, *b.* 1954.
1799 I.*	*Henley* (8th), Oliver Michael Robert Eden (6th *UK Baron, Northington*, 1885), *b.* 1953, *s.* 1977, *m.*	Hon. John W. O. *E.*, *b.* 1988.
1800 I.*	*Henniker* (8th), John Patrick Edward Chandos Henniker-Major, KCMG, CVO, MC (4th *UK Baron, Hartismere*, 1866), *b.* 1916, *s.* 1980, *m.*	Hon. Mark I. P. C. *H.-M.*, *b.* 1947.
1886	*Herschell* (3rd), Rognvald Richard Farrer Herschell, *b.* 1923, *s.* 1929, *m.*	None.
1935	*Hesketh* (3rd), Thomas Alexander Fermor-Hesketh, PC, *b.* 1950, *s.* 1955, *m.*	Hon. Frederick H. *F.-H.*, *b.*1988.
1828	*Heytesbury* (6th), Francis William Holmes à Court, *b.* 1931, *s.* 1971, *m.*	Hon. James W. *H. à C.*, *b.* 1967.
1886	*Hindlip* (5th), Henry Richard Allsopp, *b.* 1912, *s.* 1966, *m.*	Hon. Charles H. *A.*, *b.* 1940.
1950	*Hives* (2nd), John Warwick Hives, CBE, *b.* 1913, *s.* 1965, *m.*	Matthew P. *H.*, *b.* 1971.
1912	*Hollenden* (3rd), Gordon Hope Hope-Morley, *b.* 1914, *s.* 1977, *m.*	Hon. Ian H. *H.-M.*, *b.* 1946.
1897	*HolmPatrick* (4th), Hans James David Hamilton, *b.* 1955, *s.* 1991, *m.*	Hon. Ion H. J. *H.*, *b.* 1956.
1933	*Horder* (2nd), Thomas Mervyn Horder, *b.* 1910, *s.* 1955.	None.
1797 I.	*Hotham* (8th), Henry Durand Hotham, *b.* 1940, *s.* 1967, *m.*	Hon. William B. *H.*, *b.* 1972.
1881	*Hothfield* (6th), Anthony Charles Sackville Tufton, *b.* 1939, *s.* 1991, *m.*	Hon. William S. *T.*, *b.* 1977.
1597	*Howard de Walden* (9th), John Osmael Scott-Ellis, TD (5th *UK Baron, Seaford*, 1826), *b.* 1912, *s.* 1946, *m.*	To Barony of Howard de Walden, four co-heiresses. To Barony of Seaford, Colin H. F. *Ellis*, *b.* 1946.
1930	*Howard of Penrith* (2nd), Francis Philip Howard, *b.* 1905, *s.* 1939, *m.*	Hon. Philip E. *H.*, *b.* 1945.
1960	*Howick of Glendale* (2nd), Charles Evelyn Baring, *b.* 1937, *s.* 1973, *m.*	Hon. David E. C. *B.*, *b.* 1975.
1796 I.	*Huntingfield* (6th), Gerard Charles Arcedeckne Vanneck, *b.* 1915, *s.* 1969, *m.*	Hon. Joshua C. *V.*, *b.* 1954.
1866	*Hylton* (5th), Raymond Hervey Jolliffe, *b.* 1932, *s.* 1967, *m.*	Hon. William H. M. *J.*, *b.* 1967.
1933	*Iliffe* (2nd), Edward Langton Iliffe, *b.* 1908, *s.* 1960, *m.*	Robert P. R. *I.*, *b.* 1944.
1543 I.	*Inchiquin* (18th), Conor Myles John O'Brien, *b.* 1943, *s.* 1982.	Murrough R. *O'B.*, *b.* 1910.
1962	*Inchyra* (2nd), Robert Charles Reneke Hoyer Millar, *b.* 1935, *s.* 1989, *m.*	Hon. C. James C. H. *M.*, *b.* 1962.
1964	*Inglewood* (2nd), (William) Richard Fletcher-Vane, MEP, *b.* 1951, *s.* 1989, *m.*	Hon. Henry W. F. *F.-V.*, *b.* 1990.
1919	*Inverforth* (4th), Andrew Peter Weir, *b.* 1966, *s.* 1982.	Hon. John V. *W.*, *b.* 1935.
1941	*Ironside* (2nd), Edmund Oslac Ironside, *b.* 1924, *s.* 1959, *m.*	Hon. Charles E. G. *I.*, *b.* 1956.
1952	*Jeffreys* (3rd), Christopher Henry Mark Jeffreys, *b.* 1957, *s.* 1986, *m.*	Hon. Arthur M. H. *J.*, *b.* 1989.
1906	*Joicey* (4th), Michael Edward Joicey, *b.* 1925, *s.* 1966, *m.*	Hon. James M. *J.*, *b.* 1953.
1937	*Kenilworth* (4th), (John) Randle Siddeley, *b.* 1954, *s.* 1981, *m.*	None.
1935	*Kennet* (2nd), Wayland Hilton Young, *b.* 1923, *s.* 1960, *m.*	Hon. W. A. Thoby *Y.*, *b.* 1957.
1776 I.*	*Kensington* (8th), Hugh Ivor Edwardes (5th *UK Baron, Kensington*, 1886), *b.* 1933, *s.* 1981, *m.*	Hon. W. Owen A. *E.*, *b.* 1964.
1951	*Kenswood* (2nd), John Michael Howard Whitfield, *b.* 1930, *s.* 1963, *m.*	Hon. Michael C. *W.*, *b.* 1955.
1788	*Kenyon* (5th), Lloyd Tyrell-Kenyon, CBE, *b.* 1917, *s.* 1927, *m.*	Hon. Lloyd *T.-K.*, *b.* 1947.
1947	*Kershaw* (4th), Edward John Kershaw, *b.* 1936, *s.* 1962, *m.*	Hon. John C. E. *K.*, *b.* 1971.

Created	Title, order of succession, name, etc.	Eldest son or heir
1943	*Keyes* (2nd), Roger George Bowlby Keyes, *b.* 1919, *s.* 1945, *m.*	Hon. Charles W. P. *K.*, *b.* 1951.
1909	*Kilbracken* (3rd), John Raymond Godley, DSC, *b.* 1920, *s.* 1950.	Hon. Christopher J. *G.*, *b.* 1945.
1900	*Killanin* (3rd), Michael Morris, MBE, TD, *b.* 1914, *s.* 1927, *m.*	Hon. G. Redmond F. *M.*, *b.* 1947.
1943	*Killearn* (2nd), Graham Curtis Lampson, *b.* 1919, *s.* 1964, *m.*	Hon. Victor M. G. A. *L.*, *b.* 1941.
1789 I.	*Kilmaine* (7th), John David Henry Browne, *b.* 1948, *s.* 1978, *m.*	Hon. John F. S. *B.*, *b.* 1983.
1831	*Kilmarnock* (7th), Alastair Ivor Gilbert Boyd, *b.* 1927, *s.* 1975, *m.*	Hon. Robin J. *B.*, *b.* 1941.
1941	*Kindersley* (3rd), Robert Hugh Molesworth Kindersley, *b.* 1929, *s.* 1976, *m.*	Hon. Rupert J. M. *K.*, *b.* 1955.
1223 I.	*Kingsale* (35th), John de Courcy (*Premier Baron of Ireland*), *b.* 1941, *s.* 1969.	Nevinson R. *de C.*, *b.* 1920.
1682 S.*	*Kinnaird* (13th), Graham Charles Kinnaird (5th *UK Baron, Kinnaird*, 1860), *b.* 1912, *s.* 1972, *m.*	None.
1902	*Kinross* (5th), Christopher Patrick Balfour, *b.* 1949, *s.* 1985, *m.*	Hon. Alan I. *B.*, *b.* 1978.
1951	*Kirkwood* (3rd), David Harvie Kirkwood, PH.D., *b.* 1931, *s.* 1970, *m.*	Hon. James S. *K.*, *b.* 1937.
1800 I.	*Langford* (9th), Geoffrey Alexander Rowley-Conwy, OBE, *b.* 1912, *s.* 1953, *m.*	Hon. Owain G. *R.-C.*, *b.* 1958.
1942	*Latham* (2nd), Dominic Charles Latham, *b.* 1954, *s.* 1970.	Anthony M. *L.*, *b.* 1954.
1431	*Latymer* (8th), Hugo Nevill Money-Coutts, *b.* 1926, *s.* 1987, *m.*	Hon. Crispin J. A. N. *M.-C.*, *b.* 1955.
1869	*Lawrence* (5th), David John Downer Lawrence, *b.* 1937, *s.* 1968.	None.
1947	*Layton* (3rd), Geoffrey Michael Layton, *b.* 1947, *s.* 1989, *m.*	Hon. David *L.*, MBE, *b.* 1914.
1839	*Leigh* (5th), John Piers Leigh, *b.* 1935, *s.* 1979, *m.*	Hon. Christopher D. P. *L.*, *b.* 1960.
1962	*Leighton of St Mellons* (2nd), (John) Leighton Seager, *b.* 1922, *s.* 1963, *m.*	Hon. Robert W. H. L. *S.*, *b.* 1955.
1797	*Lilford* (7th), George Vernon Powys, *b.* 1931, *s.* 1949, *m.*	Hon. Mark V. *P.*, *b.* 1975.
1945	*Lindsay of Birker* (2nd), Michael Francis Morris Lindsay, *b.* 1909, *s.* 1952, *m.*	Hon. James F. *L.*, *b.* 1945.
1758 I.	*Lisle* (7th), John Nicholas Horace Lysaght, *b.* 1903, *s.* 1919, *m.*	Patrick J. *L.*, *b.* 1931.
1850	*Londesborough* (9th), Richard John Denison, *b.* 1959, *s.* 1968, *m.*	Hon. James F. *D.*, *b.* 1990.
1541 I.	*Louth* (16th), Otway Michael James Oliver Plunkett, *b.* 1929, *s.* 1950, *m.*	Hon. Jonathan O. *P.*, *b.* 1952.
1458 S.*	*Lovat* (15th), Simon Christopher Joseph Fraser, DSO, MC, TD (4th *UK Baron, Lovat*, 1837), *b.* 1911, *s.* 1933, *m.*	Master of Lovat *b.* 1939.
1946	*Lucas of Chilworth* (2nd), Michael William George Lucas, *b.* 1926, *s.* 1967, *m.*	Hon. Simon W. *L.*, *b.* 1957.
1663	*Lucas of Crudwell* (11th) & *Dingwall* (8th) (*Scottish Lordship* 1609), Ralph Matthew Palmer, *b.* 1951, *s.* 1992, *m.*	Hon. Lewis E. *P.*, *b.* 1987
1929	*Luke* (2nd), Ian St John Lawson-Johnston, KCVO, TD, *b.* 1905, *s.* 1943, *m.*	Hon. Arthur C. St J. *L.-J.*, *b.* 1933.
1914	*Lyell* (3rd), Charles Lyell, *b.* 1939, *s.* 1943.	None.
1859	*Lyveden* (6th), Ronald Cecil Vernon, *b.* 1915, *s.* 1973, *m.*	Hon. Jack L. *V.*, *b.* 1938.
1959	*MacAndrew* (3rd), Christopher Anthony Colin MacAndrew, *b.* 1945, *s.* 1989, *m.*	Hon. Oliver C. J. *M.*, *b.* 1983.
1776 I.	*Macdonald* (8th), Godfrey James Macdonald of Macdonald, *b.* 1947, *s.* 1970, *m.*	Hon. Godfrey E. H. T. *M.*, *b.* 1982.
1949	*Macdonald of Gwaenysgor* (2nd), Gordon Ramsay Macdonald, *b.* 1915, *s.* 1966, *m.*	None.
1937	*McGowan* (3rd), Harry Duncan Cory McGowan, *b.* 1938, *s.* 1966, *m.*	Hon. Harry J. C. *M.*, *b.* 1971.
1922	*Maclay* (3rd), Joseph Paton Maclay, *b.* 1942, *s.* 1969, *m.*	Hon. Joseph P. *M.*, *b.* 1977.
1955	*McNair* (3rd), Duncan James McNair, *b.* 1947, *s.* 1989, *m.*	Hon. Thomas J. *M.*, *b.* 1990.
1951	*Macpherson of Drumochter* (2nd), (James) Gordon Macpherson, *b.* 1924, *s.* 1965, *m.*	Hon. James A. *M.*, *b.* 1979.
1937	*Mancroft* (3rd), Benjamin Lloyd Stormont Mancroft, *b.* 1957, *s.* 1987, *m.*	None.
1807	*Manners* (5th), John Robert Cecil Manners, *b.* 1923, *s.* 1972, *m.*	Hon. John H. R. *M.*, *b.* 1956.
1922	*Manton* (3rd), Joseph Rupert Eric Robert Watson, *b.* 1924, *s.* 1968, *m.*	Capt. Hon. Miles R. M. *W.*, *b.* 1958.
1908	*Marchamley* (3rd), John William Tattersall Whiteley, *b.* 1922, *s.* 1949, *m.*	Hon. William F. *W.*, *b.* 1968.
1964	*Margadale* (1st), John Granville Morrison, TD, *b.* 1906, *w.*	Hon. James I. *M.*, TD, *b.* 1930.
1961	*Marks of Broughton* (2nd), Michael Marks, *b.* 1920, *s.* 1964.	Hon. Simon R. *M.*, *b.* 1950.
1964	*Martonmere* (2nd), John Stephen Robinson, *b.* 1963, *s.* 1989.	David A. *R.*, *b.* 1965.
1776 I.	*Massy* (9th), Hugh Hamon John Somerset Massy, *b.* 1921, *s.* 1958, *m.*	Hon. David H. S. *M.*, *b.* 1947.
1935	*May* (3rd), Michael St John May, *b.* 1931, *s.* 1950, *m.*	Hon. Jasper B. St J. *M.*, *b.* 1965.
1928	*Melchett* (4th), Peter Robert Henry Mond, *b.* 1948, *s.* 1973.	None.
1925	*Merrivale* (3rd), Jack Henry Edmond Duke, *b.* 1917, *s.* 1951, *m.*	Hon. Derek J. P. *D.*, *b.* 1948.
1911	*Merthyr.* Disclaimed for life 1977. (*Trevor Oswin Lewis, Bt.*, CBE, *b.* 1935, *s.* 1977, *m.*)	David T. *L.*, *b.* 1977.
1919	*Meston* (3rd), James Meston, *b.* 1950, *s.* 1984, *m.*	Hon. Thomas J. D. *M.*, *b.* 1977.
1838	*Methuen* (6th), Anthony John Methuen, *b.* 1925, *s.* 1975.	Hon. Robert A. H. *M.*, *b.* 1931.
1711	*Middleton* (12th), (Digby) Michael Godfrey John Willoughby, MC, *b.* 1921, *s.* 1970, *m.*	Hon. Michael C. J. *W.*, *b.* 1948.
1939	*Milford* (2nd), Wogan Philipps, *b.* 1902, *s.* 1962, *m.*	Hon. Hugo J. L. *P.*, *b.* 1929.
1933	*Milne* (2nd), George Douglass Milne, TD, *b.* 1909, *s.* 1948, *m.*	Hon. George A. *M.*, *b.* 1941.

Created	Title, order of succession, name, etc.	Eldest son or heir
1951	*Milner of Leeds* (2nd), Arthur James Michael Milner, AE, *b.* 1923, *s.* 1967, *m.*	Hon. Richard J. *M.*, *b.* 1959.
1947	*Milverton* (2nd), Revd Fraser Arthur Richard Richards, *b.* 1930, *s.* 1978, *m.*	Hon. Michael H. *R.*, *b.* 1936.
1873	*Moncreiff* (5th), Harry Robert Wellwood Moncreiff, *b.* 1915, *s.* 1942, *w.*	Hon. Rhoderick H. W. *M.*, *b.* 1954.
1884	*Monk Bretton* (3rd), John Charles Dodson, *b.* 1924, *s.* 1933, *m.*	Hon. Christopher M. *D.*, *b.* 1958.
1885	*Monkswell* (5th), Gerard Collier, *b.* 1947, *s.* 1984, *m.*	Hon. James A. *C.*, *b.* 1977.
1728	*Monson* (11th), John Monson, *b.* 1932, *s.* 1958, *m.*	Hon. Nicholas J. *M.*, *b.* 1955.
1885	*Montagu of Beaulieu* (3rd), Edward John Barrington Douglas-Scott-Montagu, *b.* 1926, *s.* 1929, *m.*	Hon. Ralph *D.-S.-M.*, *b.* 1961.
1839	*Monteagle of Brandon* (6th), Gerald Spring Rice, *b.* 1926, *s.* 1946, *m.*	Hon. Charles J. S. *R.*, *b.* 1953.
1943	*Moran* (2nd), (Richard) John (McMoran) Wilson, KCMG, *b.* 1924, *s.* 1977, *m.*	Hon. James M. *W.*, *b.* 1952.
1918	*Morris* (3rd), Michael David Morris, *b.* 1937, *s.* 1975, *m.*	Hon. Thomas A. S. *M.*, *b.* 1982.
1950	*Morris of Kenwood* (2nd), Philip Geoffrey Morris, *b.* 1928, *s.* 1954, *m.*	Hon. Jonathan D. *M.*, *b.* 1968.
1945	*Morrison* (2nd), Dennis Morrison, *b.* 1914, *s.* 1953.	None.
1831	*Mostyn* (5th), Roger Edward Lloyd Lloyd-Mostyn, MC, *b.* 1920, *s.* 1965, *m.*	Hon. Llewellyn R. L. *L.-M.*, *b.* 1948.
1933	*Mottistone* (4th), David Peter Seely, CBE, *b.* 1920, *s.* 1966, *m.*	Hon. Peter J. P. *S.*, *b.* 1949.
1945	*Mountevans* (3rd), Edward Patrick Broke Evans, *b.* 1943, *s.* 1974, *m.*	Hon. Jeffrey de C. R. *E.*, *b.* 1948.
1283	*Mowbray* (26th), *Segrave* (27th) (1283), & *Stourton* (23rd) (1448), Charles Edward Stourton, CBE, *b.* 1923, *s.* 1965, *m.*	Hon. Edward W. S. *S.*, *b.* 1953.
1932	*Moyne* (3rd), Jonathan Bryan Guinness, *b.* 1930, *s.* 1992, *m.*	Hon. Jasper J. R. *G.*, *b.* 1954.
1929	*Moynihan*, the 3rd Baron died November 1991. His trustees recognized Daniel Antony Patrick Berkeley Moynihan, (*b.* January 1991) as the financial heir of the 3rd Baron but the succession to the title is not settled.	
1781 I.	*Muskerry* (9th), Robert Fitzmaurice Deane, *b.* 1948, *s.* 1988, *m.*	Hon. Jonathan F. *D.*, *b.* 1986.
1627 S.	*Napier* (14th) & *Ettrick* (5th) (*UK* 1872), Francis Nigel Napier, KCVO, *b.* 1930, *s.* 1954, *m.*	Master of Napier, *b.* 1962.
1868	*Napier of Magdala* (6th), Robert Alan Napier, *b.* 1940, *s.* 1987, *m.*	Hon. James R. *N.*, *b.* 1966.
1940	*Nathan* (2nd), Roger Carol Michael Nathan, *b.* 1922, *s.* 1963, *m.*	Hon. Rupert H. B. *N.*, *b.* 1957.
1960	*Nelson of Stafford* (2nd), Henry George Nelson, FEng., *b.* 1917, *s.* 1962, *m.*	Hon. Henry R. G. *N.*, *b.* 1943.
1959	*Netherthorpe* (3rd), James Frederick Turner, *b.* 1964, *s.* 1982, *m.*	Hon. Patrick A. *T.*, *b.* 1971.
1946	*Newall* (2nd), Francis Storer Eaton Newall, *b.* 1930, *s.* 1963, *m.*	Hon. Richard H. E. *N.*, *b.* 1961.
1776 I.	*Newborough* (7th), Robert Charles Michael Vaughan Wynn, DSC, *b.* 1917, *s.* 1965, *m.*	Hon. Robert V. *W.*, *b.* 1949.
1892	*Newton* (5th), Richard Thomas Legh, *b.* 1950, *s.* 1992, *m.*	Hon. Piers R. *L.*, *b.* 1979.
1930	*Noel-Buxton* (3rd), Martin Connal Noel-Buxton, *b.* 1940, *s.* 1980, *m.*	Hon. Charles C. *N.-B.*, *b.* 1975.
1957	*Norrie* (2nd), (George) Willoughby Moke Norrie, *b.* 1936, *s.* 1977, *m.*	Hon. Mark W. J. *N.*, *b.* 1972.
1884	*Northbourne* (5th), Christopher George Walter James, *b.* 1926, *s.* 1982, *m.*	Hon. Charles W. H. *J.*, *b.* 1960.
1866	*Northbrook* (6th), Francis Thomas Baring, *b.* 1954, *s.* 1990, *m.*	None.
1878	*Norton* (7th), John Arden Adderley, OBE, *b.* 1915, *s.* 1961, *m.*	Hon. James N. A. *A.*, *b.* 1947.
1906	*Nunburnholme* (4th), Ben Charles Wilson, *b.* 1928, *s.* 1974.	Hon. Charles T. *W.*, *b.* 1935.
1950	*Ogmore* (2nd), Gwilym Rees Rees-Williams, *b.* 1931, *s.* 1976, *m.*	Hon. Morgan *R.-W.*, *b.* 1937.
1870	*O'Hagan* (4th), Charles Towneley Strachey, MEP, *b.* 1945, *s.* 1961, *m.*	Hon. Richard T. *S.*, *b.* 1950.
1868	*O'Neill* (4th), Raymond Arthur Clanaboy O'Neill, TD, *b.* 1933, *s.* 1944, *m.*	Hon. Shane S. C. *O'N.*, *b.* 1965.
1836 I.*	*Oranmore and Browne* (4th), Dominick Geoffrey Edward Browne (2nd *UK Baron Mereworth*, 1926), *b.* 1901, *s.* 1927, *m.*	Hon. Dominick G. T. *B.*, *b.* 1929.
1933	*Palmer* (4th), Adrian Bailie Nottage Palmer, *b.* 1951, *s.* 1990, *m.*	Hon. Hugo B. R. *P.*, *b.* 1980.
1914	*Parmoor* (4th), (Frederick Alfred) Milo Cripps, *b.* 1929, *s.* 1977.	M. Anthony L. *C.*, CBE, DSO, TD, QC, *b.* 1913.
1937	*Pender* (3rd), John Willoughby Denison-Pender, *b.* 1933, *s.* 1965, *m.*	Hon. Henry J. R. *D.-P.*, *b.* 1968.
1866	*Penrhyn* (6th), Malcolm Frank Douglas-Pennant, DSO, MBE, *b.* 1908, *s.* 1967, *m.*	Hon. Nigel *D.-P.*, *b.* 1909.
1603	*Petre* (18th), John Patrick Lionel Petre, *b.* 1942, *s.* 1989, *m.*	Hon. Dominic W. *P.*, *b.* 1966.
1918	*Phillimore* (4th), Claud Stephen Phillimore, *b.* 1911, *s.* 1990, *m.*	Hon. Francis S. *P.*, *b.* 1944.
1945	*Piercy* (3rd), James William Piercy, *b.* 1946, *s.* 1981.	Hon. Mark E. P. *P.*, *b.* 1953.
1827	*Plunket* (8th), Robin Rathmore Plunket, *b.* 1925, *s.* 1975, *m.*	Hon. Shaun A. F. S. *P.*, *b.* 1931.
1831	*Poltimore* (7th), Mark Coplestone Bampfylde, *b.* 1957, *s.* 1978, *m.*	Hon. Henry A. W. *B.*, *b.* 1985.
1690 S.	*Polwarth* (10th), Henry Alexander Hepburne-Scott, TD, *b.* 1916, *s.* 1944, *m.*	Master of Polwarth, *b.* 1947.
1930	*Ponsonby of Shulbrede* (4th), Frederick Matthew Thomas Ponsonby, *b.* 1958, *s.* 1990.	None.
1958	*Poole* (1st), Oliver Brian Sanderson Poole, CBE, TD, PC, *b.* 1911, *m.*	Hon. David C. *P.*, *b.* 1945.
1852	*Raglan* (5th), FitzRoy John Somerset, *b.* 1927, *s.* 1964.	Hon. Geoffrey *S.*, *b.* 1932.
1932	*Rankeillour* (4th), Peter St Thomas More Henry Hope, *b.* 1935, *s.* 1967.	Michael R. *H.*, *b.* 1940.

Created	*Title, order of succession, name, etc.*	*Eldest son or heir*
1953	*Rathcavan* (2nd), Phelim Robert Hugh O'Neill, PC (NI), *b.* 1909, *s.* 1982, *m.*	Hon. Hugh D. T. *O'N.*, *b.* 1939.
1916	*Rathcreedan* (3rd), Christopher John Norton, *b.* 1949, *s.* 1990, *m.*	Hon. Adam G. *N.*, *b.* 1952.
1868 I.	*Rathdonnell* (5th), Thomas Benjamin McClintock-Bunbury, *b.* 1938, *s.* 1959, *m.*	Hon. William L. *M.-B.*, *b.* 1966.
1911	*Ravensdale* (3rd), Nicholas Mosley, MC, *b.* 1923, *s.* 1966, *m.*	Hon. Shaun N. *M.*, *b.* 1949.
1821	*Ravensworth* (8th), Arthur Waller Liddell, *b.* 1924, *s.* 1950, *m.*	Hon. Thomas A. H. *L.*, *b.* 1954.
1821	*Rayleigh* (6th), John Gerald Strutt, *b.* 1960, *s.* 1988, *m.*	Hon. Hedley V. *S.*, *b.* 1915.
1937	*Rea* (3rd), John Nicolas Rea, MD, *b.* 1928, *s.* 1981, *m.*	Hon. Matthew J. *R.*, *b.* 1956.
1628 S.	*Reay* (14th), Hugh William Mackay, *b.* 1937, *s.* 1963, *m.*	Master of Reay, *b.* 1965.
1902	*Redesdale* (6th), Rupert Bertram Mitford, *b.* 1967, *s.* 1991.	None.
1940	*Reith.* Disclaimed for life 1972. (*Christopher John Reith*, *b.* 1928, *s.* 1971, *m.*)	Hon. James H. J. *R.*, *b.* 1971.
1928	*Remnant* (3rd), James Wogan Remnant, CVO, b. 1930, *s.* 1967, *m.*	Hon. Philip J. *R.*, *b.* 1954.
1806 I.	*Rendlesham* (8th), Charles Anthony Hugh Thellusson, *b.* 1915, *s.* 1943, *w.*	Hon. Charles W. B. *T.*, *b.* 1954.
1933	*Rennell* (3rd), (John Adrian) Tremayne Rodd, *b.* 1935, *s.* 1978, *m.*	Hon. James R. D. T. *R.*, *b.* 1978.
1964	*Renwick* (2nd), Harry Andrew Renwick, *b.* 1935, *s.* 1973, *m.*	Hon. Robert J. *R.*, *b.* 1966.
1885	*Revelstoke* (4th), Rupert Baring, *b.* 1911, *s.* 1934.	Hon. John *B.*, *b.* 1934.
1905	*Ritchie of Dundee* (5th), (Harold) Malcolm Ritchie, *b.* 1919, *s.* 1978, *m.*	Hon. C. Rupert R. *R.*, *b.* 1958.
1935	*Riverdale* (2nd), Robert Arthur Balfour, *b.* 1901, *s.* 1957, *m.*	Hon. Mark R. *B.*, *b.* 1927.
1961	*Robertson of Oakridge* (2nd), William Ronald Robertson, *b.* 1930, *s.* 1974, *m.*	Hon. William B. E. *R.*, *b.* 1975.
1938	*Roborough* (3rd), Henry Massey Lopes, *b.* 1940, *s.* 1992, *m.*	Hon. Massey J. H. *L.*, *b.* 1969.
1931	*Rochester* (2nd), Foster Charles Lowry Lamb, *b.* 1916, *s.* 1955, *m.*	Hon. David C. *L.*, *b.* 1944.
1934	*Rockley* (3rd), James Hugh Cecil, *b.* 1934, *s.* 1976, *m.*	Hon. Anthony R. *C.*, *b.* 1961.
1782	*Rodney* (9th), John Francis Rodney, *b.* 1920, *s.* 1973, *m.*	Hon. George B. *R.*, *b.* 1953.
1651 S.*	*Rollo* (13th), Eric John Stapylton Rollo (4th *UK Baron, Dunning*, 1869), *b.* 1915, *s.* 1947, *m.*	Master of Rollo, *b.* 1943.
1959	*Rootes* (3rd), Nicholas Geoffrey Rootes, *b.* 1951, *s.* 1992, *m.*	†
1796 I.*	*Rossmore* (7th), William Warner Westenra (6th *UK Baron, Rossmore*, 1838), *b.* 1931, *s.* 1958, *m.*	Hon. Benedict W. *W.*, *b.* 1983.
1939	*Rotherwick* (2nd), (Herbert) Robin Cayzer, *b.* 1912, *s.* 1958, *w.*	Hon. H. Robin *C.*, *b.* 1954.
1885	*Rothschild* (4th), (Nathaniel Charles) Jacob Rothschild, *b.* 1936, *s.* 1990, *m.*	Hon. Nathaniel P. V. J. *R.*, *b.* 1971.
1911	*Rowallan* (3rd), Arthur Cameron Corbett, *b.* 1919, *s.* 1977.	Hon. John P. C. *C.*, *b.* 1947.
1947	*Rugby* (3rd), Robert Charles Maffey, *b.* 1951, *s.* 1990, *m.*	Hon. Timothy J. H. *M.*, *b.* 1975.
1919	*Russell of Liverpool* (3rd), Simon Gordon Jared Russell, *b.* 1952, *s.* 1981, *m.*	Hon. Edward C. S. *R.*, *b.* 1985.
1876	*Sackville* (6th), Lionel Bertrand Sackville-West, *b.* 1913, *s.* 1965, *m.*	Hugh R. I. *S.-W.*, MC, *b.* 1919.
1964	*St Helens* (2nd), Richard Francis Hughes-Young, *b.* 1945, *s.* 1980, *m.*	Hon. Henry T. *H.-Y.*, *b.* 1986.
1559	*St John of Bletso* (21st), Anthony Tudor St John, *b.* 1957, *s.* 1978.	Edmund O. *St J.*, *b.* 1927.
1887	*St Levan* (4th), John Francis Arthur St Aubyn, DSC, *b.* 1919, *s.* 1978, *m.*	Hon. O. Piers *St A.*, MC, *b.* 1920.
1885	*St Oswald* (5th), Derek Edward Anthony Winn, *b.* 1919, *s.* 1984, *m.*	Hon. Charles R. A. *W.*, *b.* 1959.
1960	*Sanderson of Ayot.* Disclaimed for life 1971. (*Alan Lindsay Sanderson*, *b.* 1931, *s.* 1971, *m.*)	Hon. Michael *S.*, *b.* 1959.
1945	*Sandford* (2nd), Revd John Cyril Edmondson, DSC, *b.* 1920, *s.* 1959, *m.*	Hon. James J. M. *E.*, *b.* 1949.
1871	*Sandhurst* (5th), (John Edward) Terence Mansfield, DFC, *b.* 1920, *s.* 1964, *m.*	Hon. Guy R. J. *M.*, *b.* 1949.
1802	*Sandys* (7th), Richard Michael Oliver Hill, *b.* 1931, *s.* 1961, *m.*	Marcus T. *H.*, *b.* 1931.
1888	*Savile* (3rd), George Halifax Lumley-Savile, *b.* 1919, *s.* 1931.	Hon. Henry L. T. *L.-S.*, *b.* 1923.
1447	*Saye and Sele* (21st), Nathaniel Thomas Allen Fiennes, *b.* 1920, *s.* 1968, *m.*	Hon. Richard I. *F.*, *b.* 1959.
1932	*Selsdon* (3rd), Malcolm McEacharn Mitchell-Thomson, *b.* 1937, *s.* 1963, *m.*	Hon. Callum M. M. *M.-T.*, *b.* 1969.
1916	*Shaughnessy* (3rd), William Graham Shaughnessy, *b.* 1922, *s.* 1938, *m.*	Hon. Michael J. *S.*, *b.* 1946.
1946	*Shepherd* (2nd), Malcolm Newton Shepherd, PC, *b.* 1918, *s.* 1954, *m.*	Hon. Graeme G. *S.*, *b.* 1949.
1964	*Sherfield* (1st), Roger Mellor Makins, GCB, GCMG, FRS, *b.* 1904, *w.*	Hon. Christopher J. *M.*, *b.* 1942.
1902	*Shuttleworth* (5th), Charles Geoffrey Nicholas Kay-Shuttleworth, *b.* 1948, *s.* 1975, *m.*	Hon. Thomas E. *K.-S.*, *b.* 1976.
1950	*Silkin.* Disclaimed for life 1972. (*Arthur Silkin*, *b.* 1916, *s.* 1972, *m.*)	Hon. Christopher L. *S.*, *b.* 1947.
1963	*Silsoe* (2nd), David Malcolm Trustram Eve, QC, *b.* 1930, *s.* 1976, *m.*	Hon. Simon R. T. *E.*, *b.* 1966.
1947	*Simon of Wythenshawe* (2nd), Roger Simon, *b.* 1913, *s.* 1960, *m.*	Hon. Matthew *S.*, *b.* 1955.
1449 S.	*Sinclair* (17th), Charles Murray Kennedy St Clair, CVO, *b.* 1914, *s.* 1957, *m.*	Master of Sinclair, *b.* 1968.
1957	*Sinclair of Cleeve* (3rd), John Lawrence Robert Sinclair, *b.* 1953, *s.* 1985.	None.
1919	*Sinha* (3rd), Sudhindro Prosanno Sinha, *b.* 1920, *s.* 1967, *m.*	Hon. Susanta P. *S.*, *b.* 1953.
1828	*Skelmersdale* (7th), Roger Bootle-Wilbraham, *b.* 1945, *s.* 1973, *m.*	Hon. Andrew *B.-W.*, *b.* 1977.

Created	*Title, order of succession, name, etc.*	*Eldest son or heir*
1916	*Somerleyton* (3rd), Savile William Francis Crossley, *b.* 1928, *s.* 1959, *m.* *Master of the Horse.*	Hon. Hugh F. S. *C.*, *b.* 1971.
1784	*Somers* (8th), John Patrick Somers Cocks, *b.* 1907, *s.* 1953, *m.*	Philip S. *S. C.*, *b.* 1948.
1780	*Southampton* (6th), Charles James FitzRoy, *b.* 1928, *s.* 1989, *m.*	Hon. Edward C. *F.*, *b.* 1955.
1959	*Spens* (3rd), Patrick Michael Rex Spens, *b.* 1942, *s.* 1984, *m.*	Hon. Patrick N. G. *S.*, *b.* 1968.
1640	*Stafford* (15th), Francis Melfort William Fitzherbert, *b.* 1954, *s.* 1986, *m.*	Hon. Benjamin J. B. *F.*, *b.* 1983.
1938	*Stamp* (4th), Trevor Charles Bosworth Stamp, MD, FRCP, *b.* 1935, *s.* 1987, *m.*	Hon. Nicholas C. T. *S.*, *b.* 1978.
1839	*Stanley of Alderley* (8th) & *Sheffield* (8th) (1738 I.), Thomas Henry Oliver Stanley (7th *UK Baron Eddisbury*, 1848), *b.* 1927, *s.* 1971, *m.*	Hon. Richard O. *S.*, *b.* 1956.
1318	*Strabolgi* (11th), David Montague de Burgh Kenworthy, *b.* 1914, *s.* 1953, *m.*	Andrew D. W. *K.*, *b.* 1967.
1954	*Strang* (2nd), Colin Strang, *b.* 1922, *s.* 1978, *m.*	None.
1955	*Strathalmond* (3rd), William Roberton Fraser, *b.* 1947, *s.* 1976, *m.*	Hon. William G. *F.*, *b.* 1976.
1936	*Strathcarron* (2nd), David William Anthony Blyth Macpherson, *b.* 1924, *s.* 1937, *m.*	Hon. Ian D. P. *M.*, *b.* 1949.
1955	*Strathclyde* (2nd), Thomas Galloway Dunlop du Roy de Blicquy Galbraith, *b.* 1960, *s.* 1985, *m.*	Hon. Charles W. du R. de B. *G.*, *b.* 1962.
1900	*Strathcona and Mount Royal* (4th), Donald Euan Palmer Howard, *b.* 1923, *s.* 1959, *m.*	Hon. D. Alexander S. *H.*, *b.* 1961.
1836	*Stratheden & Campbell* (1841) (6th), Donald Campbell, *b.* 1934, *s.* 1987, *m.*	Hon. David A. *C.*, *b.* 1963.
1884	*Strathspey* (6th), James Patrick Trevor Grant of Grant, *b.* 1943, *s.* 1991, *m.*	Hon. Michael P. F. *G.*, *b.* 1953.
1838	*Sudeley* (7th), Merlin Charles Sainthill Hanbury-Tracy, *b.* 1939, *s.* 1941.	D. Andrew J. *H-T.*, *b.* 1928.
1786	*Suffield* (11th), Anthony Philip Harbord-Hamond, MC, *b.* 1922, *s.* 1951, *m.*	Hon. Charles A. A. *H.-H.*, *b.* 1953.
1893	*Swansea* (4th), John Hussey Hamilton Vivian, *b.* 1925, *s.* 1934, *m.*	Hon. Richard A. H. *V.*, *b.* 1957.
1907	*Swaythling* (4th), David Charles Samuel Montagu, *b.* 1928, *s.* 1990, *m.*	Hon. Charles E. S. *M.*, *b.* 1954.
1919	*Swinfen* (3rd), Roger Mynors Swinfen Eady, *b.* 1938, *s.* 1977, *m.*	Hon. Charles R. P. S. *E.*, *b.* 1971.
1935	*Sysonby* (3rd), John Frederick Ponsonby, *b.* 1945, *s.* 1956.	None.
1831 I.	*Talbot of Malahide* (10th), Reginald John Richard Arundell, *b.* 1931, *s.* 1987, *w.*	Hon. Richard J. T. *A.*, *b.* 1957.
1946	*Tedder* (2nd), John Michael Tedder, SC.D., Ph.D., D.SC., *b.* 1926, *s.* 1967, *m.*	Hon. Robin J. *T.*, *b.* 1955.
1884	*Tennyson* (5th), Mark Aubrey Tennyson, DSC, *b.* 1920, *s.* 1991, *m.*	James A. *T.*, *b.* 1913.
1918	*Terrington* (4th), (James Allen) David Woodhouse, *b.* 1915, *s.* 1961, *m.*	Hon. C. Montague *W.*, DSO, OBE, b. 1917.
1940	*Teviot* (2nd), Charles John Kerr, *b.* 1934, *s.* 1968, *m.*	Hon. Charles R. *K.*, *b.* 1971.
1616	*Teynham* (20th), John Christopher Ingham Roper-Curzon, *b.* 1928, *s.* 1972, *m.*	Hon. David J. H. I. *R.-C.*, *b.* 1965.
1964	*Thomson of Fleet* (2nd), Kenneth Roy Thomson, *b.* 1923, *s.* 1976, *m.*	Hon. David K. R. *T.*, *b.* 1957.
1792	*Thurlow* (8th), Francis Edward Hovell-Thurlow-Cumming-Bruce, KCMG, *b.* 1912, *s.* 1971, *w.*	Hon. Roualeyn R. *H.-T.-C.-B.*, *b.* 1952.
1876	*Tollemache* (5th), Timothy John Edward Tollemache, *b.* 1939, *s.* 1975, *m.*	Hon. Edward J. H. *T.*, *b.* 1976.
1564 S.	*Torphichen* (15th), James Andrew Douglas Sandilands, *b.* 1946, *s.* 1975, *m.*	Douglas R. A. *S.*, *b.* 1926.
1947	*Trefgarne* (2nd), David Garro Trefgarne, PC, *b.* 1941, *s.* 1960, *m.*	Hon. George G. *T.*, *b.* 1970.
1921	*Trevethin* (4th), *and Oaksey* (2nd), John Geoffrey Tristram Lawrence, OBE (2nd *UK Baron, Oaksey*, 1947), *b.* 1929, *s.* 1971, *m.*	Hon. Patrick J. T. *L.*, *b.* 1960.
1880	*Trevor* (4th), Charles Edwin Hill-Trevor, *b.* 1928, *s.* 1950, *m.*	Hon. Marke C. *H.-T.*, *b.* 1970.
1461 I.	*Trimlestown* (20th), Anthony Edward Barnewall, *b.* 1928, *s.* 1990, *m.*	Hon. Raymond C. *B.*, *b.* 1930.
1940	*Tryon* (3rd), Anthony George Merrik Tryon, *b.* 1940, *s.* 1976, *m.*	Hon. Charles G. B. *T.*, *b.* 1976.
1935	*Tweedsmuir* (2nd), John Norman Stuart Buchan, CBE, CD, *b.* 1911, *s.* 1940, *m.*	Hon. William *B.*, *b.* 1916.
1523	*Vaux of Harrowden* (10th), John Hugh Philip Gilbey, *b.* 1915, *s.* 1977, *m.*	Hon. Anthony W. *G.*, *b.* 1940.
1800 I.	*Ventry* (8th), Andrew Wesley Daubeny de Moleyns, *b.* 1943, *s.* 1987, *m.*	Hon. Francis W. *D. de M.*, *b.* 1965.
1762	*Vernon* (10th), John Lawrance Vernon, *b.* 1923, *s.* 1963, *m.*	Col. William R. D. *Vernon-Harcourt*, OBE, *b.* 1909.
1922	*Vestey* (3rd), Samuel George Armstrong Vestey, *b.* 1941, *s.* 1954, *m.*	Hon. William G. *V.*, *b.* 1983.
1841	*Vivian* (6th), Nicholas Crespigny Laurence Vivian, *b.* 1935, *s.* 1991, *m.*	Hon. Charles H. C. *V.*, *b.* 1966.
1934	*Wakehurst* (3rd), (John) Christopher Loder, *b.* 1925, *s.* 1970, *m.*	Hon. Timothy W. *L.*, *b.* 1958.
1723	*Walpole* (10th), Robert Horatio Walpole, *b.* 1938, *s.* 1989, *m.* (*8th Brit. Baron Walpole of Wolterton*, 1756).	Hon. Jonathan R. H. *W.*, *b.* 1967.
1780	*Walsingham* (9th), John de Grey, MC, *b.* 1925, *s.* 1965, *m.*	Hon. Robert *de G.*, *b.* 1969.
1936	*Wardington* (2nd), Christopher Henry Beaumont Pease, *b.* 1924, *s.* 1950, *m.*	Hon. William S. *P.*, *b.* 1925.
1792 I.	*Waterpark* (7th), Frederick Caryll Philip Cavendish, *b.* 1926, *s.* 1948, *m.*	Hon. Roderick A. *C.*, *b.* 1959.
1942	*Wedgwood* (4th), Piers Anthony Weymouth Wedgwood, *b.* 1954, *s.* 1970, *m.*	John *W.*, CBE, MD, *b.* 1919.

Created	Title, order of succession, name, etc.	Eldest son or heir
1861	*Westbury* (5th), David Alan Bethell, MC, *b.* 1922, *s.* 1961, *m.*	Hon. Richard N. *B.*, MBE, *b.* 1950.
1944	*Westwood* (3rd), (William) Gavin Westwood, *b.* 1944, *s.* 1991, *m.*	Hon. William F. *W.*, *b.* 1972.
1935	*Wigram* (2nd), (George) Neville (Clive) Wigram, MC, *b.* 1915, *s.* 1960, *w.*	Maj. Hon. Andrew F. C. *W.*, MVO, *b.* 1949.
1491	*Willoughby de Broke* (21st), Leopold David Verney, *b.* 1938, *s.* 1986, *m.*	Hon. Rupert G. *V.*, *b.* 1966.
1946	*Wilson* (2nd), Patrick Maitland Wilson, *b.* 1915, *s.* 1964, *w.*	None.
1937	*Windlesham* (3rd), David James George Hennessy, CVO, PC, *b.* 1932, *s.* 1962, *w.*	Hon. James R. *H.*, *b.* 1968.
1951	*Wise* (2nd), John Clayton Wise, *b.* 1923, *s.* 1968, *m.*	Hon. Christopher J. C. *W.*, Ph.D., *b.* 1949.
1869	*Wolverton* (7th), Christopher Richard Glyn, *b.* 1938, *s.* 1988, *m.*	Hon. Andrew J. *G.*, *b.* 1943.
1928	*Wraxall* (2nd), George Richard Lawley Gibbs, *b.* 1928, *s.* 1931.	Hon. Sir Eustace H. B. *G.*, KCVO, CMG, *b.* 1929.
1915	*Wrenbury* (3rd), John Burton Buckley, *b.* 1927, *s.* 1940, *m.*	Hon. William E. *B.*, *b.* 1966.
1838	*Wrottesley* (6th), Clifton Hugh Lancelot de Verdon Wrottesley, *b.* 1968, *s.* 1977.	Hon. Stephen J. *W.*, *b.* 1955.
1919	*Wyfold* (3rd), Hermon Robert Fleming Hermon-Hodge, *b.* 1915, *s.* 1942.	None.
1829	*Wynford* (8th), Robert Samuel Best, MBE, *b.* 1917, *s.* 1943, *m.*	Hon. John P. *B.*, *b.* 1950.
1308	*Zouche* (18th), James Assheton Frankland, *b.* 1943, *s.* 1965, *m.*	Hon. William T. A. *F.*, *b.* 1984.

BARONESSES IN THEIR OWN RIGHT

Style, The Right Hon. the Lady _, *or* The Right Hon. the Baroness _, according to her preference.
Husband, Untitled.
Children's style, As for children of a Baron.
For forms of address, *see* page 218.

Created	Title, order of succession, name, etc.	Eldest son or heir
1421	*Berkeley* (17th in line), Mary Lalle Foley Berkeley, *b.* 1905, *title called out of abeyance*, 1967.	Anthony F. Gueterbock, OBE, *b.* 1939.
1455	*Berners*, in abeyance between two co-heiresses, daughters of the late Baroness Berners.	
1529	*Braye* (8th in line), Mary Penelope Aubrey-Fletcher, *b.* 1941, *s.* 1985, *m.*	Two co-heiresses.
1321	*Dacre* (27th in line), Rachel Leila Douglas-Home, *b.* 1929, *title called out of abeyance*, 1970, *m.*	Hon. James T. A. *D.-H.*, *b.* 1952.
1332	*Darcy de Knayth* (18th in line), Davina Marcia Ingrams, *b.* 1938, *s.* 1943, *w.*	Hon. Caspar D. *I.*, *b.* 1962.
1439	*Dudley* (14th in line), Barbara Amy Felicity Hamilton, *b.* 1907, *s.* 1972, *m.*	Hon. Jim A. H. *Wallace*, *b.* 1930.
1490 S.	*Herries of Terregles* (14th in line), Anne Elizabeth Fitzalan-Howard, *b.* 1938, *s.* 1975, *m.*	Lady Mary *Mumford*, CVO, *b.* 1940.
1602 S.	*Kinloss* (12th in line), Beatrice Mary Grenville Freeman-Grenville, *b.* 1922, *s.* 1944, *m.*	Master of Kinloss, *b.* 1953.
1681 S.	*Nairne* (12th in line), Katherine Evelyn Constance Bigham (*Katherine, Viscountess Mersey*), *b.* 1912, *s.* 1944, *w.*	Viscount Mersey, *b.* 1934 (*see* page 151).
1445 S.	*Saltoun* (20th in line), Flora Marjory Fraser, *b.* 1930, *s.* 1979, *m.*	Hon. Katharine I. M. I. *F.*, *b.* 1957.
1489 S.	*Sempill* (20th in line), Ann Moira Sempill, *b.* 1920, *s.* 1965, *w.*	Master of Sempill, *b.* 1949.
1628	*Strange* (16th in line), (Jean) Cherry Drummond of Megginch, *b.* 1928, *title called out of abeyance*, 1986, *m.*	Hon. Adam H. *D. of M.*, *b.* 1953.
1544–5	*Wharton* (11th in line), Myrtle Olive Felix Robertson, *b.* 1934, *title called out of abeyance*, 1990, *m.*	Hon. Myles C. D. *R.*, *b.* 1964.
1313	*Willoughby de Eresby* (27th in line), (Nancy) Jane Marie Heathcote-Drummond-Willoughby, *b.* 1934, *s.* 1983.	Two co-heiresses.

Life Peers

Between 1 September 1991 and 31 August 1992, the conferment of 45 life peerages was announced, three under the Appellate Jurisdiction Act 1876 and 42 under the Life Peerages Act 1958:

NEW LORDS OF APPEAL IN ORDINARY (announced 23 September 1991): the Rt. Hon. Sir Nicolas Browne-Wilkinson; the Rt. Hon. Sir Michael Mustill; Sir Gordon Slynn

NEW YEAR HONOURS (31 December 1991): the Rt. Hon. Sir Reginald Prentice, Sir Brian Rix, CBE; Dame Shelagh Roberts, DBE (died 16 January 1992 before any title gazetted); the Rt. Hon. William Rodgers; Sir David Wilson, GCMG

NEW LORD CHIEF JUSTICE (25 February 1992): the Rt. Hon. Sir Peter Taylor

FOLLOW THE GENERAL ELECTION (13 April 1992): the Rt. Hon. Lynda Chalker; the Rt. Hon. Alan Rodger, QC; the Rt. Hon. John Wakeham

RESIGNATION HONOURS (6 June 1992): the Rt. Hon. Julian Amery; the Rt. Hon. Peter Archer, QC; the Rt. Hon. Jack Ashley, CH; Harry Ewing; the Rt. Hon. Sir Ian Gilmour, Bt.; the Rt. Hon. Denis Healey, CH, MBE; the Rt. Hon. Sir Geoffrey Howe, QC; the Rt. Hon. Denis Howell; Geraint Howells; the Rt. Hon. Nigel Lawson; the Rt. Hon. John Moore; the Rt. Hon. David Owen; the Rt. Hon. Cecil Parkinson; the Rt. Hon. Merlyn Rees; the Rt. Hon. Nicholas Ridley; the Rt. Hon. Norman Tebbit, CH; the Rt. Hon. Margaret Thatcher, OM; *Dafydd Elis Thomas; the Rt. Hon. Peter Walker, MBE; the Rt. Hon. Bernard Weatherill; the Rt. Hon. George Younger, TD

THE QUEEN'S BIRTHDAY HONOURS (13 June 1992): Jeffrey Archer; Sir Derek Barber; the Rt. Hon. Sir Bernard Braine; the Rt. Hon. Sir William Clark; Victor Cooke, OBE; John Eatwell; Sir Geoffrey Finsberg, MBE; the Rt. Hon. Sir Barney Hayhoe; Mrs Margaret Jay; Prof. Raymond Plant; the Rt. Hon. Sir Ian Stewart; Gareth Williams

*No title gazetted at time of going to press

CREATED UNDER THE APPELLATE JURISDICTION ACT 1876 (AS AMENDED)

BARONS

Created

1986 *Ackner*, Desmond James Conrad Ackner, PC, *b.* 1920, *m.* Lord of Appeal in Ordinary.

1981 *Brandon of Oakbrook*, Henry Vivian Brandon, MC, PC, *b.* 1920, *m.*

1980 *Bridge of Harwich*, Nigel Cyprian Bridge, PC, *b.* 1917, *m.*

1982 *Brightman*, John Anson Brightman, PC, *b.* 1911, *m.*

1991 *Browne-Wilkinson*, Nicolas Christopher Henry Browne-Wilkinson, PC, *b.* 1930, *m.* Lord of Appeal in Ordinary.

1957 *Denning*, Alfred Thompson Denning, PC, *b.* 1899, *m.*

1974 *Edmund-Davies*, (Herbert) Edmund Edmund-Davies, PC, *b.* 1906, *w.*

1986 *Goff of Chieveley*, Robert Lionel Archibald Goff, PC, *b.* 1926, *m.* Lord of Appeal in Ordinary.

1985 *Griffiths*, (William) Hugh Griffiths, MC, PC, *b.* 1923, *m.* Lord of Appeal in Ordinary.

1987 *Jauncey of Tullichettle*, Charles Eliot Jauncey, PC, *b.* 1925, *m.* Lord of Appeal in Ordinary.

1977 *Keith of Kinkel*, Henry Shanks Keith, PC, *b.* 1922, *m.* Lord of Appeal in Ordinary.

1979 *Lane*, Geoffrey Dawson Lane, AFC, PC, *b.* 1918, *m.*

1992 *Mustill*, Michael John Mustill, PC, *b.* 1931, *m.* Lord of Appeal in Ordinary.

1986 *Oliver of Aylmerton*, Peter Raymond Oliver, PC, *b.* 1921, *m.*

1980 *Roskill*, Eustace Wentworth Roskill, PC, *b.* 1911, *m.*

1977 *Scarman*, Leslie George Scarman, OBE, PC, *b.* 1911, *m.*

1992 *Slynn of Hadley*, Gordon Slynn, PC, *b.* 1930, *m.* Lord of Appeal in Ordinary.

1982 *Templeman*, Sydney William Templeman, MBE, PC, *b.* 1920, *w.* Lord of Appeal in Ordinary.

1964 *Wilberforce*, Richard Orme Wilberforce, CMG, OBE, PC, *b.* 1907, *m.*

CREATED UNDER THE LIFE PEERAGES ACT 1958

BARONS

Created

1974 *Alexander of Potterhill*, William Picken Alexander, Ph.D., *b.* 1905, *m.*

1988 *Alexander of Weedon*, Robert Scott Alexander, QC, *b.* 1936, *m.*

1976 *Allen of Abbeydale*, Philip Allen, GCB, *b.* 1912, *m.*

1961 *Alport*, Cuthbert James McCall Alport, TD, PC, *b.* 1912, *w.*

1992 *Amery of Lustleigh*, Julian Amery, PC, *b.* 1919, *w.*

1965 *Annan*, Noel Gilroy Annan, OBE, *b.* 1916, *m.*

1992 *Archer of Sandwell*, Peter Kingsley Archer, PC, QC, *b.* 1926, *m.*

1992 *Archer of Weston-super-Mare*, Jeffrey Howard Archer, *b.* 1940, *m.*

1970 *Ardwick*, John Cowburn Beavan, *b.* 1910, *m.*

1988 *Armstrong of Ilminster*, Robert Temple Armstrong, GCB, CVO, *b.* 1927, *m.*

1973 *Ashby*, Eric Ashby, D.SC., FRS, *b.* 1904, *m.*

1992 *Ashley of Stoke*, Jack Ashley, CH, PC, *b.* 1922, *m.*

1967 *Aylestone*, Herbert William Bowden, CH, CBE, PC, *b.* 1905, *m.*

1982 *Bancroft*, Ian Powell Bancroft, GCB, *b.* 1922, *m.*

1974 *Banks*, Desmond Anderson Harvie Banks, CBE, *b.* 1918, *m.*

1974 *Barber*, Anthony Perrinott Lysberg Barber, TD, PC, *b.* 1920, *m.*

1992 *Barber of Tewkesbury*, Derek Coates Barber, *b.* 19–, *m.*

1983 *Barnett*, Joel Barnett, PC, *b.* 1923, *m.*

1982 *Bauer*, Prof. Peter Thomas Bauer, D.SC., *b.* 1915.

1967 *Beaumont of Whitley*, Revd Timothy Wentworth Beaumont, *b.* 1928, *m.*

1979 *Bellwin*, Irwin Norman Bellow, *b.* 1923, *m.*

1981 *Beloff*, Max Beloff, *b.* 1913, *m.*

1981 *Benson*, Henry Alexander Benson, GBE, *b.* 1909, *m.*

1969 *Bernstein*, Sidney Lewis Bernstein, *b.* 1899, *w.*

Created

1971 *Blake*, Robert Norman William Blake, FBA, *b.* 1916, *m.*
1983 *Blanch*, Rt. Revd Stuart Yarworth Blanch, PC, *b.* 1918, *m.*
1978 *Blease*, William John Blease, *b.* 1914, *m.*
1980 *Boardman*, Thomas Gray Boardman, MC, TD, *b.* 1919, *m.*
1986 *Bonham-Carter*, Mark Raymond Bonham Carter, *b.* 1922, *m.*
1976 *Boston of Faversham*, Terence George Boston, QC, *b.* 1930, *m.*
1984 *Bottomley*, Arthur George Bottomley, OBE, PC, *b.* 1907, *m.*
1972 *Boyd-Carpenter*, John Archibald Boyd-Carpenter, PC, *b.* 1908, *m.*
1992 *Braine of Wheatley*, Bernard Richard Braine, PC, *b.* 1914, *w.*
1987 *Bramall*, Edwin Noel Westby Bramall, KG, GCB, OBE, MC, *Field Marshal*, *b.* 1923, *m.*
1976 *Briggs*, Asa Briggs, *b.* 1921, *m.*
1976 *Brimelow*, Thomas Brimelow, GCMG, OBE, *b.* 1915, *m.*
1975 *Brookes*, Raymond Percival Brookes, *b.* 1909, *m.*
1979 *Brooks of Tremorfa*, John Edward Brooks, *b.* 1927, *m.*
1974 *Bruce of Donington*, Donald William Trevor Bruce, *b.* 1912, *m.*
1976 *Bullock*, Alan Louis Charles Bullock, FBA, *b.* 1914, *m.*
1988 *Butterfield*, (William) John (Hughes) Butterfield, OBE, DM, *b.* 1920, *m.*
1985 *Butterworth*, John Blackstock Butterworth, CBE, *b.* 1918, *m.*
1978 *Buxton of Alsa*, Aubrey Leland Oakes Buxton, MC, *b.* 1918, *m.*
1987 *Callaghan of Cardiff*, (Leonard) James Callaghan, KG, PC, *b.* 1912, *m.*
1984 *Cameron of Lochbroom*, Kenneth John Cameron, PC, *b.* 1931, *m.*
1981 *Campbell of Alloway*, Alan Robertson Campbell, QC, *b.* 1917, *m.*
1974 *Campbell of Croy*, Gordon Thomas Calthrop Campbell, MC, PC, *b.* 1921, *m.*
1966 *Campbell of Eskan*, John (Jock) Middleton Campbell, *b.* 1912, *w.*
1987 *Carlisle of Bucklow*, Mark Carlisle, QC, PC, *b.* 1929, *m.*
1983 *Carmichael of Kelvingrove*, Neil George Carmichael, *b.* 1921.
1975 *Carr of Hadley*, (Leonard) Robert Carr, PC, *b.* 1916, *m.*
1987 *Carter*, Denis Victor Carter, *b.* 1932, *m.*
1977 *Carver*, (Richard) Michael (Power) Carver, GCB, CBE, DSO, MC, *Field Marshal*, *b.* 1915, *m.*
1990 *Cavendish of Furness*, (Richard) Hugh Cavendish, *b.* 1941, *m.*
1982 *Cayzer*, (William) Nicholas Cayzer, *b.* 1910, *m.*
1964 *Chalfont*, (Alun) Arthur Gwynne Jones, OBE, MC, PC, *b.* 1919, *m.*
1985 *Chapple*, Frank Joseph Chapple, *b.* 1921, *m.*
1978 *Charteris of Amisfield*, Martin Michael Charles Charteris, GCB, GCVO, OBE, PC, Royal Victorian Chain, *b.* 1913, *m.*
1963 *Chelmer*, Eric Cyril Boyd Edwards, MC, TD, *b.* 1914, *m.*
1987 *Chilver*, (Amos) Henry Chilver, FRS, FEng., *b.* 1926, *m.*
1977 *Chitnis*, Pratap Chidamber Chitnis, *b.* 1936, *m.*

Created

1992 *Clark of Kempston*, William Gibson Haig Clark, PC, *b.* 1917, *m.*
1979 *Cledwyn of Penrhos*, Cledwyn Hughes, CH, PC, *b.* 1916, *m.*
1990 *Clinton-Davis*, Stanley Clinton Davis, *b.* 1928, *m.*
1978 *Cockfield*, (Francis) Arthur Cockfield, PC, *b.* 1916, *m.*
1987 *Cocks of Hartcliffe*, Michael Francis Lovell Cocks, PC, *b.* 1929, *m.*
1980 *Coggan*, Rt. Revd (Frederick) Donald Coggan, PC, Royal Victorian Chain, *b.* 1909, *m.*
1964 *Collison*, Harold Francis Collison, CBE, *b.* 1909, *m.*
1987 *Colnbrook*, Humphrey Edward Gregory Atkins, KCMG, PC, *b.* 1922, *m.*
1981 *Constantine of Stanmore*, Theodore Constantine, CBE, AE, *b.* 1910, *w.*
1992 *Cooke of Islandreagh*, Victor Alexander Cooke, OBE, *b.* 1920, *m.*
1991 *Craig of Radley*, David Brownrigg Craig, GCB, OBE, *Marshal of the Royal Air Force*, *b.* 1929, *m.*
1959 *Craigton*, Jack Nixon Browne, CBE, PC, *b.* 1904, *m.*
1987 *Crickhowell*, (Roger) Nicholas Edwards, PC, *b.* 1934, *m.*
1978 *Croham*, Douglas Albert Vivian Allen, GCB, *b.* 1917, *m.*
1974 *Cudlipp*, Hugh Cudlipp, OBE, *b.* 1913, *m.*
1979 *Dacre of Glanton*, Hugh Redwald Trevor-Roper, *b.* 1914, *m.*
1986 *Dainton*, Frederick Sydney Dainton, Ph.D., Sc.D., FRS, *b.* 1914, *m.*
1983 *Dean of Beswick*, Joseph Jabez Dean, *b.* 1922.
1986 *Deedes*, William Francis Deedes, MC, PC, *b.* 1913, *m.*
1976 *Delfont*, Bernard Delfont, *b.* 1909, *m.*
1991 *Desai*, Prof. Meghnad Jagdishchandra Desai, Ph.D., *b.* 1940, *m.*
1970 *Diamond*, John Diamond, PC, *b.* 1907, *m.*
1967 *Donaldson of Kingsbridge*, John George Stuart Donaldson, OBE, *b.* 1907, *m.*
1988 *Donaldson of Lymington*, John Francis Donaldson, PC, *b.* 1920, *m.*
1985 *Donoughue*, Bernard Donoughue, D.Phil., *b.* 1934.
1987 *Dormand of Easington*, John Donkin Dormand, *b.* 1919, *m.*
1992 *Eatwell*, John Leonard Eatwell, *b.* 19_.
1983 *Eden of Winton*, John Benedict Eden, PC, *b.* 1925, *m.*
1985 *Elliott of Morpeth*, Robert William Elliott, *b.* 1920, *m.*
1972 *Elworthy*, (Samuel) Charles Elworthy, KG, GCB, CBE, DSO, LVO, DFC, AFC, *Marshal of the Royal Air Force*, *b.* 1911, *w.*
1981 *Elystan-Morgan*, Dafydd Elystan Elystan-Morgan, *b.* 1932, *m.*
1980 *Emslie*, George Carlyle Emslie, MBE, PC, *b.* 1919, *m.*
1983 *Ennals*, David Hedley Ennals, PC, *b.* 1922, *m.*
1992 *Ewing of Kirkford*, Harry Ewing, *b.* 1931, *m.*
1983 *Ezra*, Derek Ezra, MBE, *b.* 1919, *m.*
1983 *Fanshawe of Richmond*, Anthony Henry Fanshawe Royle, KCMG, *b.* 1927, *m.*
1992 *Finsberg*, Geoffrey Finsberg, MBE, *b.* 1926, *m.*
1983 *Fitt*, Gerard Fitt, *b.* 1926, *m.*
1979 *Flowers*, Brian Hilton Flowers, FRS, *b.* 1924, *m.*
1967 *Foot*, John Mackintosh Foot, *b.* 1909, *m.*
1982 *Forte*, Charles Forte, *b.* 1908, *m.*
1962 *Franks*, Oliver Shewell Franks, OM, GCMG, KCB, KCVO, CBE, PC, FBA, *b.* 1905, *w.*
1989 *Fraser of Carmyllie*, Peter Lovat Fraser, QC, PC, *b.* 1945, *m.*

Created

1974 *Fraser of Kilmorack*, (Richard) Michael Fraser, CBE, *b.* 1915, *m.*
1982 *Gallacher*, John Gallacher, *b.* 1920, *m.*
1979 *Galpern*, Myer Galpern, *b.* 1903.
1992 *Geraint*, Geraint Wyn Howells, *b.* 1925, *m.*
1975 *Gibson*, (Richard) Patrick (Tallentyre) Gibson, *b.* 1916, *m.*
1979 *Gibson-Watt*, (James) David Gibson-Watt, MC, PC, *b.* 1918, *m.*
1992 *Gilmour of Craigmillar*, Ian Hedworth John Little Gilmour, PC, *b.* 1926, *m.*
1977 *Glenamara*, Edward Watson Short, CH, PC, *b.* 1912, *m.*
1965 *Goodman*, Arnold Abraham Goodman, CH, *b.* 1913.
1987 *Goold*, James Duncan Goold, *b.* 1934, *m.*
1982 *Gormley*, Joseph Gormley, OBE, *b.* 1917, *m.*
1976 *Grade*, Lew Grade, *b.* 1906, *m.*
1983 *Graham of Edmonton*, (Thomas) Edward Graham, *b.* 1925, *m.*
1967 *Granville of Eye*, Edgar Louis Granville, *b.* 1899, *m.*
1983 *Gray of Contin*, James (Hamish) Hector Northey Gray, PC, *b.* 1927, *m.*
1974 *Greene of Harrow Weald*, Sidney Francis Greene, CBE, *b.* 1910, *m.*
1974 *Greenhill of Harrow*, Denis Arthur Greenhill, GCMG, OBE, *b.* 1913, *m.*
1975 *Gregson*, John Gregson, *b.* 1924.
1968 *Grey of Naunton*, Ralph Francis Alnwick Grey, GCMG, GCVO, OBE, *b.* 1910, *m.*
1991 *Griffiths of Fforestfach*, Brian Griffiths, *b.* 1941, *m.*
1983 *Grimond*, Joseph Grimond, TD, PC, *b.* 1913, *m.*
1970 *Hailsham of St Marylebone*, Quintin McGarel Hogg, KG, CH, PC, *b.* 1907, *m.*
1983 *Hanson*, James Edward Hanson, *b.* 1922, *m.*
1974 *Harmar-Nicholls*, Harmar Harmar-Nicholls, *b.* 1912, *m.*
1974 *Harris of Greenwich*, John Henry Harris, *b.* 1930, *m.*
1979 *Harris of High Cross*, Ralph Harris, *b.* 1924, *m.*
1968 *Hartwell*, (William) Michael Berry, MBE, TD, *b.* 1911, *w.*
1971 *Harvey of Prestbury*, Arthur Vere Harvey, CBE, *b.* 1906, *m.*
1974 *Harvington*, Robert Grant Grant-Ferris, AE, PC, *b.* 1907, *m.*
1990 *Haslam*, Robert Haslam, *b.* 1923, *m.*
1978 *Hatch of Lusby*, John Charles Hatch, *b.* 1917.
1992 *Hayhoe*, Bernard John (Barney) Hayhoe, PC, *b.* 1925, *m.*
1992 *Healey*, Denis Winston Healey, CH, MBE, PC, *b.* 1917, *m.*
1984 *Henderson of Brompton*, Peter Gordon Henderson, KCB, *b.* 1922, *m.*
1979 *Hill-Norton*, Peter John Hill-Norton, GCB, *Admiral of the Fleet*, *b.* 1915, *m.*
1967 *Hirshfield*, Desmond Barel Hirshfield, *b.* 1913, *m.*
1979 *Holderness*, Richard Frederick Wood, PC, *b.* 1920, *m.*
1991 *Hollick*, Clive Richard Hollick, *b.* 1945, *m.*
1990 *Holme of Cheltenham*, Richard Gordon Holme, CBE, *b.* 1936, *m.*
1974 *Home of the Hirsel*, Alexander Frederick Douglas-Home, KT, PC, *b.* 1903, *w.*
1979 *Hooson*, (Hugh) Emlyn Hooson, QC, *b.* 1925, *m.*
1974 *Houghton of Sowerby*, (Arthur Leslie Noel) Douglas Houghton, CH, PC, *b.* 1898, *m.*
1992 *Howe of Aberavon*, (Richard Edward) Geoffrey Howe, PC, QC, *b.* 1926, *m.*

Created

1992 *Howell*, Denis Herbert Howell, PC, *b.* 1923, *m.*
1978 *Howie of Troon*, William Howie, *b.* 1924, *m.*
1961 *Hughes*, William Hughes, CBE, PC, *b.* 1911, *m.*
1966 *Hunt*, (Henry Cecil) John Hunt, KG, CBE, DSO, *b.* 1910, *m.*
1980 *Hunt of Tanworth*, John Joseph Benedict Hunt, GCB, *b.* 1919, *m.*
1978 *Hunter of Newington*, Robert Brockie Hunter, MBE, FRCP, *b.* 1915, *m.*
1978 *Hutchinson of Lullington*, Jeremy Nicolas Hutchinson, QC, *b.* 1915, *m.*
1982 *Ingrow*, John Aked Taylor, OBE, TD, *b.* 1917, *m.*
1987 *Irvine of Lairg*, Alexander Andrew Mackay Irvine, QC, *b.* 1940, *m.*
1968 *Jacques*, John Henry Jacques, *b.* 1905, *m.*
1988 *Jakobovits*, Immanuel Jakobovits, *b.* 1921, *m.*
1987 *Jay*, Douglas Patrick Thomas Jay, PC, *b.* 1907, *m.*
1987 *Jenkin of Roding*, (Charles) Patrick (Fleeming) Jenkin, PC, *b.* 1926, *m.*
1987 *Jenkins of Hillhead*, Roy Harris Jenkins, PC, *b.* 1920, *m.*
1981 *Jenkins of Putney*, Hugh Gater Jenkins, *b.* 1908, *w.*
1981 *John-Mackie*, John John-Mackie, *b.* 1909, *m.*
1987 *Johnston of Rockport*, Charles Collier Johnston, TD, *b.* 1915, *m.*
1987 *Joseph*, Keith Sinjohn Joseph, CH, PC, *b.* 1918, *m.*
1991 *Judd*, Frank Ashcroft Judd, *b.* 1935, *m.*
1981 *Kadoorie*, Lawrence Kadoorie, CBE, *b.* 1899, *m.*
1976 *Kagan*, Joseph Kagan, *b.* 1915, *m.*
1980 *Keith of Castleacre*, Kenneth Alexander Keith, *b.* 1916, *m.*
1985 *Kimball*, Marcus Richard Kimball, *b.* 1928, *m.*
1983 *King of Wartnaby*, John Leonard King, *b.* 1918, *m.*
1965 *Kings Norton*, Harold Roxbee Cox, Ph.D., FEng., *b.* 1902, *m.*
1975 *Kirkhill*, John Farquharson Smith, *b.* 1930, *m.*
1974 *Kissin*, Harry Kissin, *b.* 1912, *m.*
1987 *Knights*, Philip Douglas Knights, CBE, QPM, *b.* 1920, *m.*
1991 *Laing of Dunphail*, Hector Laing, *b.* 1923, *m.*
1990 *Lane of Horsell*, Peter Stewart Lane, *b.* 1925, *w.*
1992 *Lawson of Blaby*, Nigel Lawson, PC, *b.* 1932, *m.*
1964 *Leatherland*, Charles Edward Leatherland, OBE, *b.* 1898, *w.*
1979 *Lever of Manchester*, Harold Lever, PC, *b.* 1914, *m.*
1982 *Lewin*, Terence Thornton Lewin, KG, GCB, LVO, DSC, *Admiral of the Fleet*, *b.* 1920, *m.*
1989 *Lewis of Newnham*, Jack Lewis, FRS, *b.* 1928, *m.*
1965 *Lloyd of Hampstead*, Dennis Lloyd, QC, Ll.D., *b.* 1915, *m.*
1974 *Lovell-Davis*, Peter Lovell Lovell-Davis, *b.* 1924, *m.*
1979 *Lowry*, Robert Lynd Erskine Lowry, PC, PC(NI), *b.* 1919, *w. Lord of Appeal in Ordinary.*
1984 *McAlpine of West Green*, (Robert) Alistair McAlpine, *b.* 1942, *m.*
1988 *Macaulay of Bragar*, Donald Macaulay, QC, *b.* 1933.
1975 *McCarthy*, William Edward John McCarthy, *b.* 1925, *m.*
1976 *McCluskey*, John Herbert McCluskey, *b.* 1929, *m.*
1989 *McColl of Dulwich*, Ian McColl, FRCS, FRCSE, *b.* 1933, *m.*
1966 *McFadzean*, William Hunter McFadzean, KT, *b.* 1903, *m.*
1991 *Macfarlane of Bearsden*, Norman Somerville Macfarlane, *b.* 1926, *m.*
1978 *McGregor of Durris*, Oliver Ross McGregor, *b.* 1921, *m.*

Created

1982 *McIntosh of Haringey*, Andrew Robert McIntosh, *b.* 1933, *m.*
1991 *Mackay of Ardbrecknish*, John Jackson Mackay, *b.* 1938, *m.*
1979 *Mackay of Clashfern*, James Peter Hymers Mackay, PC, *b.* 1927, *m. Lord High Chancellor.*
1988 *Mackenzie-Stuart*, Alexander John Mackenzie Stuart, , *b.* 1924, *m.*
1974 *Mackie of Benshie*, George Yull Mackie, CBE, DSO, DFC, *b.* 1919, *m.*
1982 *MacLehose of Beoch*, (Crawford) Murray MacLehose, KT, GBE, KCMG, KCVO, *b.* 1917, *m.*
1967 *Mais*, Alan Raymond Mais, GBE, TD, ERD, FEng., *b.* 1911, *m.*
1991 *Marlesford*, Mark Shuldham Schreiber, *b.* 1931, *m.*
1981 *Marsh*, Richard William Marsh, PC, *b.* 1928, *m.*
1985 *Marshall of Goring*, Walter Charles Marshall, CBE, FRS, *b.* 1932, *m.*
1987 *Mason of Barnsley*, Roy Mason, PC, *b.* 1924, *m.*
1980 *Matthews*, Victor Collin Matthews, *b.* 1919, *m.*
1983 *Maude of Stratford-upon-Avon*, Angus Edmund Upton Maude, TD, PC, *b.* 1912, *m.*
1981 *Mayhew*, Christopher Paget Mayhew, *b.* 1915, *m.*
1985 *Mellish*, Robert Joseph Mellish, PC, *b.* 1913, *m.*
1992 *Merlyn-Rees*, Merlyn Merlyn-Rees, PC, *b.* 1920, *m.*
1978 *Mishcon*, Victor Mishcon, *b.* 1915, *m.*
1981 *Molloy*, William John Molloy, *b.* 1918.
1992 *Moore of Lower Marsh*, John Edward Michael Moore, PC, *b.* 1937, *m.*
1986 *Moore of Wolvercote*, Philip Brian Cecil Moore, GCB, GCVO, CMG, PC, *b.* 1921, *m.*
1990 *Morris of Castle Morris*, Brian Robert Morris, D.Phil., *b.* 1930, *m.*
1985 *Morton of Shuna*, Hugh Drennan Baird Morton, *b.* 1930, *m.*
1971 *Moyola*, James Dawson Chichester-Clark, PC (NI), *b.* 1923, *m.*
1984 *Mulley*, Frederick William Mulley, PC, *b.* 1918, *m.*
1985 *Murray of Epping Forest*, Lionel Murray, OBE, PC, *b.* 1922, *m.*
1964 *Murray of Newhaven*, Keith Anderson Hope Murray, KCB, Ph.D., *b.* 1903.
1979 *Murton of Lindisfarne*, (Henry) Oscar Murton, OBE, TD, PC, *b.* 1914, *m.*
1975 *Northfield*, (William) Donald Chapman, *b.* 1923.
1966 *Nugent of Guildford*, (George) Richard (Hodges) Nugent, PC, *b.* 1907, *m.*
1973 *O'Brien of Lothbury*, Leslie Kenneth O'Brien, GBE, PC, *b.* 1908, *m.*
1976 *Oram*, Albert Edward Oram, *b.* 1913, *m.*
1971 *Orr-Ewing*, (Charles) Ian Orr-Ewing, OBE, *b.* 1912, *m.*
1992 *Owen*, David Anthony Llewellyn Owen, PC, *b.* 1938, *m.*
1991 *Palumbo*, Peter Garth Palumbo, *b.* 1935, *m.*
1992 *Parkinson*, Cecil Edward Parkinson, PC, *b.* 1931, *m.*
1975 *Parry*, Gordon Samuel David Parry, *b.* 1925, *m.*
1990 *Pearson of Rannoch*, Malcolm Everard MacLaren Pearson, *b.* 1942, *m.*
1982 *Pennock*, Raymond William Pennock, *b.* 1920, *m.*
1979 *Perry of Walton*, Walter Laing Macdonald Perry, OBE, FRS, FRSE, *b.* 1921, *m.*
1987 *Peston*, Maurice Harry Peston, *b.* 1931, *m.*
1983 *Peyton of Yeovil*, John Wynne William Peyton, PC, *b.* 1919, *m.*
1975 *Pitt of Hampstead*, David Thomas Pitt, *b.* 1913, *m.*
1992 *Plant of Highfield*, Prof. Raymond Plant, Ph.D., *b.* 1945, *m.*

Created

1959 *Plowden*, Edwin Noel Plowden, GBE, KCB, *b.* 1907, *m.*
1987 *Plumb*, (Charles) Henry Plumb, MEP, *b.* 1925, *m.*
1981 *Plummer of St Marylebone*, (Arthur) Desmond (Herne) Plummer, TD, *b.* 1914, *m.*
1973 *Porritt*, Arthur Espie Porritt, GCMG, GCVO, CBE, *b.* 1900, *m.*
1990 *Porter of Luddenham*, George Porter, OM, FRS, *b.* 1920, *m.*
1992 *Prentice*, Reginald Ernest Prentice, PC, *b.* 1923, *m.*
1987 *Prior*, James Michael Leathes Prior, PC, *b.* 1927, *m.*
1975 *Pritchard*, Derek Wilbraham Pritchard, *b.* 1910, *m.*
1982 *Prys-Davies*, Gwilym Prys Prys-Davies, *b.* 1923, *m.*
1987 *Pym*, Francis Leslie Pym, MC, PC, *b.* 1922, *m.*
1982 *Quinton*, Anthony Meredith Quinton, *b.* 1925, *m.*
1978 *Rawlinson of Ewell*, Peter Anthony Grayson Rawlinson, PC, QC, *b.* 1919, *m.*
1976 *Rayne*, Max Rayne, *b.* 1918, *m.*
1983 *Rayner*, Derek George Rayner, *b.* 1926.
1987 *Rees*, Peter Wynford Innes Rees, PC, QC, *b.* 1926, *m.*
1988 *Rees-Mogg*, William Rees-Mogg, *b.* 1928, *m.*
1970 *Reigate*, John Kenyon Vaughan-Morgan, PC, *b.* 1905, *m.*
1991 *Renfrew of Kaimsthorn*, (Andrew) Colin Renfrew, FBA, *b.* 1937, *m.*
1979 *Renton*, David Lockhart-Mure Renton, KBE, TD, PC, QC, *b.* 1908, *w.*
1990 *Richard*, Ivor Seward Richard, QC, *b.* 1932, *m.*
1979 *Richardson*, John Samuel Richardson, LVO, MD, FRCP, *b.* 1910, *w.*
1983 *Richardson of Duntisbourne*, Gordon William Humphreys Richardson, KG, MBE, TD, PC, *b.* 1915, *m.*
1992 *Ridley of Liddesdale*, Nicholas Ridley, PC, *b.* 1929, *m.*
1987 *Rippon of Hexham*, (Aubrey) Geoffrey (Frederick) Rippon, PC, QC, *b.* 1924, *m.*
1992 *Rix*, Brian Norman Roger Rix, CBE, *b.* 1924, *m.*
1961 *Robens of Woldingham*, Alfred Robens, PC, *b.* 1910, *m.*
1992 *Rodger of Earlsferry*, Alan Ferguson Rodger, PC, QC, FBA, *b.* 1944, *Lord Advocate.*
1992 *Rodgers of Quarry Bank*, William Thomas Rodgers, PC, *b.* 1928, *m.*
1977 *Roll of Ipsden*, Eric Roll, KCMG, CB, *b.* 1907, *m.*
1987 *Ross of Newport*, Stephen Sherlock Ross, *b.* 1926, *m.*
1991 *Runcie*, Rt Revd Robert Alexander Kennedy Runcie, MC, PC, Royal Victoria Chain, *b.* 1921, *m.*
1975 *Ryder of Eaton Hastings*, Sydney Thomas Franklin (Don) Ryder, *b.* 1916, *m.*
1962 *Sainsbury*, Alan John Sainsbury, *b.* 1902, *w.*
1989 *Sainsbury of Preston Candover*, John Davan Sainsbury, KG, *b.* 1927, *m.*
1987 *St John of Fawsley*, Norman Antony Francis St John-Stevas, PC, *b.* 1929.
1985 *Sanderson of Bowden*, Charles Russell Sanderson, *b.* 1933, *m.*
1979 *Scanlon*, Hugh Parr Scanlon, *b.* 1913, *m.*
1976 *Schon*, Frank Schon, *b.* 1912, *m.*
1978 *Sefton of Garston*, William Henry Sefton, *b.* 1915, *m.*
1958 *Shackleton*, Edward Arthur Alexander Shackleton, KG, OBE, PC, *b.* 1911, *m.*
1989 *Sharp of Grimsdyke*, Eric Sharp, CBE, *b.* 1916, *m.*
1959 *Shawcross*, Hartley William Shawcross, GBE, PC, QC, *b.* 1902, *w.*
1980 *Sieff of Brimpton*, Marcus Joseph Sieff, OBE, *b.* 1913, *m.*

Created

1971 *Simon of Glaisdale*, Jocelyn Edward Salis Simon, PC, *b.* 1911, *m.*

1991 *Skidelsky*, Robert Jacob Alexander Skidelsky, D.Phil., *b.* 1939, *m.*

1978 *Smith*, Rodney Smith, KBE, FRCS, *b.* 1914, *m.*

1965 *Soper*, Revd Donald Oliver Soper, Ph.D., *b.* 1903, *m.*

1990 *Soulsby of Swaffham Prior*, Ernest Jackson Lawson Soulsby, Ph.D., *b.* 1926, *m.*

1983 *Stallard*, Albert William Stallard, *b.* 1921, *m.*

1991 *Sterling of Plaistow*, Jeffrey Maurice Sterling, CBE, *b.* 1934, *m.*

1987 *Stevens of Ludgate*, David Robert Stevens, *b.* 1936, *m.*

1992 *Stewartby*, (Bernard Harold) Ian (Halley) Stewart, RD, PC, FBA, FRSE, *b.* 1935, *m.*

1981 *Stodart of Leaston*, James Anthony Stodart, PC, *b.* 1916, *m.*

1983 *Stoddart of Swindon*, David Leonard Stoddart, *b.* 1926, *m.*

1969 *Stokes*, Donald Gresham Stokes, TD, FEng., *b.* 1914, *m.*

1979 *Strauss*, George Russell Strauss, PC, *b.* 1901, *m.*

1971 *Tanlaw*, Simon Brooke Mackay, *b.* 1934, *m.*

1978 *Taylor of Blackburn*, Thomas Taylor, CBE, *b.* 1929, *m.*

1992 *Taylor of Gosforth*, Peter Murray Taylor, PC, *b.* 1930, *m.*, *Lord Chief Justice of England.*

1968 *Taylor of Gryfe*, Thomas Johnston Taylor, *b.* 1912, *m.*

1982 *Taylor of Hadfield*, Francis Taylor, *b.* 1905, *m.*

1992 *Tebbit*, Norman Beresford Tebbit, CH, PC, *b.* 1931, *m.*

1987 *Thomas of Gwydir*, Peter John Mitchell Thomas, PC, QC, *b.* 1920, *w.*

1981 *Thomas of Swynnerton*, Hugh Swynnerton Thomas, *b.* 1931, *m.*

1977 *Thomson of Monifieth*, George Morgan Thomson, KT, PC, *b.* 1921, *m.*

1967 *Thorneycroft*, (George Edward) Peter Thorneycroft, CH, PC, *b.* 1909, *m.*

1962 *Todd*, Alexander Robertus Todd, OM, D.SC., D.Phil., FRS, *b.* 1907, *w.*

1990 *Tombs*, Francis Leonard Tombs, FEng., *b.* 1924, *m.*

1981 *Tordoff*, Geoffrey Johnson Tordoff, *b.* 1928, *m.*

1974 *Tranmire*, Robert Hugh Turton, KBE, MC, PC, *b.* 1903, *m.*

1979 *Underhill*, (Henry) Reginall Underhill, CBE, *b.* 1914, *m.*

1990 *Varley*, Eric Graham Varley, PC, *b.* 1932, *m.*

1985 *Vinson*, Nigel Vinson, LVO, *b.* 1931, *m.*

1990 *Waddington*, David Charles Waddington, PC, QC, *b.* 1929, *m.*

1990 *Wade of Chorlton*, (William) Oulton Wade, *b.* 1932, *m.*

1992 *Wakeham*, John Wakeham, PC, *b.* 1932, *m.*

1992 *Walker of Worcester*, Peter Edward Walker, MBE, PC, *b.* 1932, *m.*

1974 *Wallace of Campsie*, George Wallace, *b.* 1915, *m.*

1974 *Wallace of Coslany*, George Douglas Wallace, *b.* 1906, *m.*

1989 *Walton of Detchant*, John Nicholas Walton, TD, FRCP, *b.* 1922, *m.*

1992 *Weatherill*, (Bruce) Bernard Weatherill, PC, *b.* 1920, *m.*

1977 *Wedderburn of Charlton*, Kenneth William Wedderburn, QC, *b.* 1927, *m.*

1976 *Weidenfeld*, (Arthur) George Weidenfeld, *b.* 1919, *m.*

1980 *Weinstock*, Arnold Weinstock, *b.* 1924, *m.*

1978 *Whaddon*, (John) Derek Page, *b.* 1927, *m.*

1991 *White of Hull*, (Vincent) Gordon (Lindsay) White, KBE, *b.* 1923, *m.*

1974 *Wigoder*, Basil Thomas Wigoder, QC, *b.* 1921, *m.*

1985 *Williams of Elvel*, Charles Cuthbert Powell Williams, CBE, *b.* 1933, *m.*

1992 *Williams of Mostyn*, Gareth Wyn Williams, QC, *b.* 1941, *m.*

1963 *Willis*, Edward Henry Willis, *b.* 1918, *m.*

1969 *Wilson of Langside*, Henry Stephen Wilson, PC, QC, *b.* 1916, *m.*

1983 *Wilson of Rievaulx*, (James) Harold Wilson, KG, OBE, PC, FRS, *b.* 1916, *m.*

1992 *Wilson of Tillyorn*, David Clive Wilson, GCMG, *b.* 1935, *m.*

1975 *Winstanley*, Michael Platt Winstanley, *b.* 1918, *m.*

1985 *Wolfson*, Leonard Gordon Wolfson, *b.* 1927, *m.*

1991 *Wolfson of Sunningdale*, David Wolfson, *b.* 1935, *m.*

1987 *Wyatt of Weeford*, Woodrow Lyle Wyatt, *b.* 1918, *m.*

1978 *Young of Dartington*, Michael Young, Ph.D., *b.* 1915, *m.*

1984 *Young of Graffham*, David Ivor Young, PC, *b.* 1932, *m.*

1992 *Younger of Prestwick*, George Kenneth Hotson Younger, TD, PC, *b.* 1931, *m.*

1971 *Zuckerman*, Solly Zuckerman, OM, KCB, FRS, MD, D.SC., *b.* 1904, *m.*

BARONESSES

The conferment of a life peerage on Dame Shelagh Marjorie Roberts, DBE, was announced in the New Year's Honours 1991 but Dame Shelagh died before a title was gazetted.

Created

1979 *Airey of Abingdon*, Diana Josceline Barbara Neave Airey, *b.* 1919, *w.*

1970 *Bacon*, Alice Martha Bacon, CBE, PC, *b.* 1911.

1967 *Birk*, Alma Birk, *b.* 1921, *m.*

1987 *Blackstone*, Tessa Ann Vosper Blackstone, Ph.D., *b.* 1942.

1987 *Blatch*, Emily May Blatch, CBE, *b.* 1937, *m.*

1990 *Brigstocke*, Heather Renwick Brigstocke, *b.* 1929, *w.*

1964 *Brooke of Ystradfellte*, Barbara Muriel Brooke, DBE, *b.* 1908, *w.*

1982 *Carnegy of Lour*, Elizabeth Patricia Carnegy of Lour, *b.* 1925.

1990 *Castle of Blackburn*, Barbara Anne Castle, PC, *b.* 1910, *w.*

1992 *Chalker of Wallasey*, Lynda Chalker, PC, *b.* 1942, *m.*

1982 *Cox*, Caroline Anne Cox, *b.* 1937, *m.*

1990 *Cumberlege*, Julia Frances Cumberlege, CBE, *b,* 1943, *m.*

1978 *David*, Nora Ratcliff David, *b.* 1913, *m.*

1974 *Delacourt-Smith of Alteryn*, Margaret Rosalind Delacourt-Smith, *b.* 1916, *m.*

1978 *Denington*, Evelyn Joyce Denington, DBE, *b.* 1907, *m.*

1991 *Denton of Wakefield*, Jean Denton, CBE, *b.* 1935.

1990 *Dunn*, Lydia Selina Dunn, DBE, MEC, *b.* 1940, *m.*

1990 *Eccles of Moulton*, Diana Catherine Eccles, *b.* 1933, *m.*

1972 *Elles*, Diana Louie Elles, *b.* 1921, *m.*

1958 *Elliot of Harwood*, Katharine Elliot, DBE, *b.* 1903, *w.*

Created

1981 *Ewart-Biggs*, (Felicity) Jane Ewart-Biggs, *b.* 1929, *w.*
1975 *Faithfull*, Lucy Faithfull, OBE, *b.* 1910.
1974 *Falkender*, Marcia Matilda Falkender, CBE, *b.* 1932.
1974 *Fisher of Rednal*, Doris Mary Gertrude Fisher, *b.* 1919, *w.*
1990 *Flather*, Shreela Flather, *b.* 19–, *m.*
1981 *Gardner of Parkes*, (Rachel) Trixie (Anne) Gardner, *b.* 1927, *m.*
1991 *Hamwee*, Sally Rachel Hamwee, *b.* 1947.
1991 *Hilton of Eggardon*, Jennifer Hilton, QPM, *b.* 1936.
1990 *Hollis of Heigham*, Patricia Lesley Hollis, D.Phil., *b.* 1941, *m.*
1985 *Hooper*, Gloria Dorothy Hooper, *b.* 1939.
1965 *Hylton-Foster*, Audrey Pellew Hylton-Foster, DBE, *b.* 1908, *w.*
1991 *James of Holland Park*, Phyllis Dorothy James (Mrs White), OBE, *b.* 1920, *w.*
1992 *Jay of Paddington*, Margaret Ann Jay, *b.* 19_.
1979 *Jeger*, Lena May Jeger, *b.* 1915, *w.*
1967 *Llewelyn-Davies of Hastoe*, (Annie) Patricia Llewelyn-Davies, PC, *b.* 1915, *w.*
1978 *Lockwood*, Betty Lockwood, *b.* 1924, *w.*
1979 *McFarlane of Llandaff*, Jean Kennedy McFarlane, *b.* 1926.
1971 *Macleod of Borve*, Evelyn Hester Macleod, *b.* 1915, *w.*
1991 *Mallalieu*, Ann Mallalieu, QC, *b.* 1945, *m.*
1970 *Masham of Ilton*, Susan Lilian Primrose Cunliffe-Lister, *b.* 1935, *m.* (*Countess of Swinton*).

Created

1982 *Nicol*, Olive Mary Wendy Nicol, *b.* 1923, *m.*
1991 *O'Cathain*, Detta O'Cathain, OBE, *b.* 1938, *m.*
1989 *Oppenheim-Barnes*, Sally Oppenheim-Barnes, PC, *b.* 1930, *m.*
1990 *Park of Monmouth*, Daphne Margaret Sybil Désirée Park, CMG, OBE, *b.* 1921.
1991 *Perry of Southwark*, Pauline Perry, *b.* 1931, *m.*
1974 *Pike*, (Irene) Mervyn (Parnicott) Pike, DBE, *b.* 1918.
1981 *Platt of Writtle*, Beryl Catherine Platt, CBE, FEng., *b.* 1923, *m.*
1974 *Robson of Kiddington*, Inga-Stina Robson, *b.* 1919, *w.*
1979 *Ryder of Warsaw*, (Margaret) Susan Cheshire, CMG, OBE, *b.* 1923, *w.*
1991 *Seccombe*, Joan Anna Dalziel Seccombe, DBE, *b.* 1930, *m.*
1971 *Seear*, (Beatrice) Nancy Seear, PC, *b.* 1913.
1967 *Serota*, Beatrice Serota, DBE, *b.* 1919, *m.*
1973 *Sharples*, Pamela Sharples, *b.* 1923, *m.*
1974 *Stedman*, Phyllis Stedman, OBE, *b.* 1916, *w.*
1992 *Thatcher*, Margaret Hilda Thatcher, OM, PC, *b.* 1925, *m.*
1980 *Trumpington*, Jean Alys Barker, *b.* 1922, *w.*
1985 *Turner of Camden*, Muriel Winifred Turner, *b.* 1927, *m.*
1974 *Vickers*, Joan Helen Vickers, DBE, *b.* 1907.
1985 *Warnock*, Helen Mary Warnock, DBE, *b.* 1924, *m.*
1970 *White*, Eirene Lloyd White, *b.* 1909, *w.*
1971 *Young*, Janet Mary Young, PC, *b.* 1926, *m.*

Lords Spiritual

The Lords Spiritual are the Archbishops of Canterbury and York and 24 diocesan bishops of the Church of England. The Bishops of London, Durham and Winchester always have seats in the House of Lords; the other 21 seats are filled by the remaining diocesan bishops in order of seniority. The Bishop of Sodor and Man and the Bishop of Gibraltar are not eligible to sit in the House of Lords.

ARCHBISHOPS

Style, The Most Revd and Right Hon. the Lord Archbishop of _.
Addressed as, Archbishop; *or*, Your Grace.

Introduced to House of Lords

1991 *Canterbury* (103rd), George Leonard Carey, PC, Ph.D., *b.* 1935, *m. Consecrated Bishop of Bath and Wells* 1988, *trans.* 1991.
1973 *York* (95th), John Stapylton Habgood, PC, Ph.D., *b.* 1927, *m. Consecrated Bishop of Durham* 1973, *trans.* 1983.

BISHOPS

Style, the Right Revd the Lord Bishop of _.
Addressed as, My Lord.
elected = date of election as Diocesan Bishop

Introduced to House of Lords

1990 *London* (131st), David Michael Hope, PC, *b.* 1940, *cons.* 1985, *elected* 1985, *trans.* 1991.
1984 *Durham* (92nd), David Edward Jenkins, *b.* 1925, *m.*, *cons.* 1984, *elected* 1984.
1982 *Winchester* (95th), Colin Clement Walter James, *b.* 1926, *m.*, *cons.* 1973, *elected* 1977, *trans.* 1985.
1979 *Chichester* (102nd), Eric Waldram Kemp, DD, *b.* 1915, *m.*, *cons.* 1974, *elected* 1974.
1980 *Liverpool* (6th), David Stuart Sheppard, *b.* 1929, *m.*, *cons.* 1969, *elected* 1975.
1984 *Ripon* (11th), David Nigel de Lorentz Young, *b.* 1931, *m.*, *cons.* 1977, *elected* 1977.
1985 *Chelmsford* (7th), John Waine, *b.* 1930, *m.*, *cons.* 1975, *elected* 1978, *trans.* 1986.
1985 *Manchester* (9th), Stanley Eric Francis Booth-Clibborn, *b.* 1924, *m.*, *cons.* 1979, *elected* 1979.
1985 *Sheffield* (5th), David Ramsay Lunn, *b.* 1930, *cons.* 1980, *elected* 1980.
1985 *St Albans* (8th), John Bernard Taylor, *b.* 1929, *m.*, *cons.* 1980, *elected* 1980.
1985 *Newcastle* (10th), Andrew Alexander Kenny Graham, *b.* 1929, *cons.* 1977, *elected* 1981.

1986 *Salisbury* (76th), John Austin Baker, *b.* 1928, *m.*, *cons.* 1982, *elected* 1982.
1987 *Worcester* (111th), Philip Harold Ernest Goodrich, *b.* 1929, *m.*, *cons.* 1973, *elected* 1982.
1987 *Chester* (39th), Michael Alfred Baughen, *b.* 1930, *m.*, *cons.* 1982, *elected* 1982.
1988 *Guildford* (7th), Michael Edgar Adie, *b.* 1929, *m.*, *cons.* 1983, *elected* 1983.
1988 *Southwark* (7th), Robert Kerr Williamson, *b.* 1932, *m.*, *cons.* 1984, *elected* 1984, *trans.* 1991.
1989 *Lichfield* (97th), Keith Norman Sutton, *b.* 1934, *m.*, *cons.* 1978, *elected* 1984.
1989 *Peterborough* (36th), William John Westwood, *b.* 1925, *m.*, *cons.* 1975, *elected* 1984.
1990 *Portsmouth* (7th), Timothy John Bavin, *b.* 1935, *cons.* 1974, *elected* 1985.
1990 *Exeter* (69th), (Geoffrey) Hewlett Thompson, *b.* 1929, *m.*, *cons.* 1974, *elected* 1985.
1990 *Bristol* (54th), Barry Rogerson, *b.* 1936, *m.*, *cons.* 1979, *elected* 1985.
1991 *Coventry* (7th), Simon Barrington-Ward, *b.* 1930, *m.*, *cons.* 1985, *elected* 1985.
1991 *Norwich* (70th), Peter John Nott, *b.* 1933, *m.*, *cons.* 1977, *elected* 1985.
1991 *St Edmundsbury and Ipswich* (8th), John Dennis, *b.* 1931, *m.*, *cons.* 1979, *elected* 1986.

Bishops awaiting seats, in order of seniority

Lincoln (70th), Robert Maynard Hardy, *b.* 1936, *m.*, *cons.* 1980, *elected* 1986.
Oxford (41st), Richard Douglas Harries, *b.* 1936, *m.*, *cons.* 1987, *elected* 1987.
Birmingham (7th), Mark Santer, *b.* 1936, *m.*, *cons.* 1981, *elected* 1987.
Derby (5th), Peter Spencer Dawes, *b.* 1928, *m.*, *cons.* 1988, *elected* 1988.
Southwell (9th), Patrick Burnet Harris, *b.* 1934, *m.*, *cons.* 1973, *elected* 1988.
Rochester (105th), (Anthony) Michael (Arnold) Turnbull, *b.* 1935, *m.*, *cons.* 1988, *elected* 1988.
Blackburn (7th), Alan David Chesters, *b.* 1937, *m.*, *cons.* 1989, *elected* 1989.
Carlisle (65th), Ian Harland, *b.* 1932, *m.*, *cons.* 1985, *elected* 1989.
Truro (13th), Michael Thomas Ball, *b.* 1932, *cons.* 1980, *elected* 1990.
Ely (67th), Stephen Whitefield Sykes, *b.* 1939, *m.*, *cons.* 1990, *elected* 1990.
Hereford (103rd), John Keith Oliver, *b.* 1935, *m.*, *cons.* 1990, *elected* 1990.
Leicester (5th), Thomas Frederick Butler, *b.* 1940, *m.*, *cons.* 1985, *elected* 1991.
Bath and Wells (77th), James Lawton Thompson, *b.* 1936, *m.*, *cons.* 1978, *elected* 1991.
Wakefield (11th), Nigel Simeon McCulloch, *b.* 1942, *m.*, *cons.* 1986, *elected* 1992.
Gloucester (38th), Peter John Ball, *b.* 1932, *cons.* 1977, *elected* 1992.
Bradford (8th), David James Smith, *b.* 1935, *m.*, *cons.* 1987, *elected* 1992.

The Order of St John

THE MOST VENERABLE ORDER OF THE HOSPITAL OF ST JOHN OF JERUSALEM
St John's Gate, Clerkenwell, London ECIM 4DA

Grand Prior, HRH The Duke of Gloucester, GCVO.
Lord Prior, The Lord Vestey.
Chancellor, Prof. A. R. Mellows, TD.

COURTESY TITLES

From this list it will be seen that, for example, the Marquess of Blandford is heir to the Dukedom of Marlborough, and Viscount Amberley to the Earldom of Russell. Titles of second heirs are also given, and the courtesy title of the father of a second heir is indicated by *; e.g., Earl of Burlington, eldest son of *Marquess of Hartington.
For forms of address, *see* page 218.

MARQUESSES

Blandford – *Marlborough, D.*
Bowmont and Cessford – *Roxburghe, D.*
Douglas and Clydesdale – *Hamilton, D.*
*Douro – *Wellington, D.*
*Graham – *Montrose, D.*
Granby – *Rutland, D.*
Hamilton – *Abercorn, D.*
*Hartington – *Devonshire, D.*
*Kildare – *Leinster, D.*
Lorne – *Argyll, D.*
*Tavistock – *Bedford, D.*
*Worcester – *Beaufort, D.*

EARLS

*Aboyne – *Huntly, M.*
Altamont – *Sligo, M.*
Ancram – *Lothian, M.*
Arundel and Surrey – *Norfolk, D.*
*Bective – *Headfort, M.*
*Belfast – *Donegall, M.*
*Brecknock – *Camden, M.*
Burford – *St Albans, D.*
Burlington – **Hartington, M.*
*Cardigan – *Ailesbury, M.*
Cassillis – *Ailsa, M.*
Compton – *Northampton, M.*
*Dalkeith – *Buccleuch, D.*
*Dumfries – *Bute, M.*
*Euston – *Grafton, D.*
Glamorgan – **Worcester, M.*
Grosvenor – *Westminster, D.*
*Haddo – *Aberdeen and Temair, M.*
Hillsborough – *Downshire, M.*
Hopetoun – *Linlithgow, M.*
March and Kinrara – *Richmond, D.*
*Mount Charles – *Conyngham, M.*
Mornington – **Douro, M.*
Mulgrave – *Normanby, M.*
Offaly – **Kildare, M.*
Ronaldshay – *Zetland, M.*
*St Andrews – *Kent, D.*
*Shelburne – *Lansdowne, M.*
*Southesk – *Fife, D.*
Sunderland – **Blandford, M.*
*Tyrone – *Waterford, M.*
Ulster – *Gloucester, D.*
*Uxbridge – *Anglesey, M.*
Wiltshire – *Winchester, M.*
Yarmouth – *Hertford, M.*

VISCOUNTS

Amberley – *Russell, E.*
Andover – *Suffolk and Berkshire, E.*
Anson – *Lichfield, E.*
Asquith – *Oxford & Asquith, E.*
Boringdon – *Morley, E.*
Borodale – *Beatty, E.*
Boyle – *Shannon, E.*
Brocas – *Jellicoe, E.*
Calne and Calstone – **Shelburne, E.*
Campden – *Gainsborough, E.*
Carlow – *Portarlington, E.*
Carlton – *Wharncliffe, E.*
Castlereagh – *Londonderry, M.*
Chelsea – *Cadogan, E.*
Chewton – *Waldegrave, E.*
Chichester – **Belfast, E.*
Clanfield – *Peel, E.*
Clive – *Powis, E.*
Coke – *Leicester, E.*
Corry – *Belmore, E.*
Corvedale – *Baldwin of Bewdley, E.*
Cranborne – *Salisbury, M.*
Cranley – *Onslow, E.*
Crichton – *Erne, E.*
Crowhurst – *Cottenham, E.*
Dalrymple – *Stair, E.*
Dangan – *Cowley, E.*
Dawick – *Haig, E.*
Deerhurst – *Coventry, E.*
Drumlanrig – *Queensberry, M.*
Dunwich – *Stradbroke, E.*
Dupplin – *Kinnoull, E.*
Ebrington – *Fortescue, E.*
Ednam – *Dudley, E.*
Emlyn – *Cawdor, E.*
Encombe – *Eldon, E.*
Ennismore – *Listowel, E.*
Enfield – *Strafford, E.*
Erleigh – *Reading, M.*
Feilding – *Denbigh, E.*
Fincastle – *Dunmore, E.*
FitzHarris – *Malmesbury, E.*
Folkestone – *Radnor, E.*
Garmoyle – *Cairns, E.*
Garnock – *Lindsay, E.*
Glandine – *Norbury, E.*
Glenapp – *Inchcape, E.*
Glentworth – *Limerick, E.*
Grimstone – *Verulam, E.*
Gwynedd – *Lloyd George of Dwyfor, E.*
Hawkesbury – *Liverpool, E.*
Ikerrin – *Carrick, E.*
Ingestre – *Shrewsbury, E.*
Ipswich – **Euston, E.*
Jocelyn – *Roden, E.*
Kelburn – *Glasgow, E.*
Kingsborough – *Kingston, E.*
Knebworth – *Lytton, E.*
Lascelles – *Harewood, E.*
Lewisham – *Dartmouth, E.*
Linley – *Snowdon, E.*
Loftus – *Ely, M.*
Lowther – *Lonsdale, E.*
Lumley – *Scarbrough, E.*
Lymington – *Portsmouth, E.*
Macmillan of Ovenden – *Stockton, E.*
Maidstone – *Winchilsea and Nottingham, E.*
Maitland – *Lauderdale, E.*
Malden – *Essex, E.*
Mandeville – *Manchester, D.*
Melgund – *Minto, E.*
Merton – *Nelson, E.*
Moore – *Drogheda, E.*
Morpeth – *Carlisle, E.*
Mount Stuart – **Dumfries, E.*
Newport – *Bradford, E.*
Newry and Mourne – *Kilmorey, E.*
Northland – *Ranfurly, E.*
Parker – *Macclesfield, E.*
Perceval – *Egmont, E.*
Petersham – *Harrington, E.*
Pollington – *Mexborough, E.*
Raynham – *Townshend, M.*
Reidhaven – *Seafield, E.*
Ruthven of Canberra – *Gowrie, E.*
St Cyres – *Iddesleigh, E.*
Sandon – *Harrowby, E.*
Savernake – **Cardigan, E.*
Slane – **Mount Charles, E.*
Somerton – *Normanton, E.*
Stopford – *Courtown, E.*
Stormont – *Mansfield, E.*
Strathallan – *Perth, E.*
Stuart – *Castle Stewart, E.*
Suirdale – *Donoughmore, E.*
Tamworth – *Ferrers, E.*
Tarbat – *Cromartie, E.*
Vaughan – *Lisburne, E.*
Villiers – *Jersey, E.*
Weymouth – *Bath, M.*
Windsor – *Plymouth, E.*
Wolmer – *Selborne, E.*
Woodstock – *Portland, E.*

BARONS (LORD –)

Aberdour – *Morton, E.*
Apsley – *Bathurst, E.*
Ardee – *Meath, E.*
Ashley – *Shaftesbury, E.*
Balgonie – *Leven & Melville, E.*
Balniel – *Crawford and Balcarres, E.*
Berriedale – *Caithness, E.*
Bingham – *Lucan, E.*
Binning – *Haddington, E.*
Brooke – *Warwick, E.*
Bruce – *Elgin, E.*
Buckhurst – *De La Warr, E.*
Burghersh – *Westmorland, E.*
Burghley – *Exeter, M.*
Cardross – *Buchan, E.*
Carnegie – **Southesk, E.*
Clifton of Rathmore – *Darnley, E.*
Cochrane – *Dundonald, E.*
Courtenay – *Devon, E.*
Dalmeny – *Rosebery, E.*
Doune – *Moray, E.*
Downpatrick – **St Andrews, E.*
Eliot – *St Germans, E.*
Erskine – *Mar & Kellie, E.*
Eskdail – **Dalkeith, E.*
Fintrie – **Graham, M.*
Formartine – **Haddo, E.*
Gillford – *Clanwilliam, E.*
Glamis – *Strathmore, E.*
Greenock – *Cathcart, E.*
Guernsey – *Aylesford, E.*
Hay – *Erroll, E.*
Herbert – *Pembroke, E.*
Howland – **Tavistock, M.*
Hyde – *Clarendon, E.*
Inverurie – *Kintore, E.*
Irwin – *Halifax, E.*
Johnstone – *Annandale and Hartfell, E.*

Kenlis – **Bective, E.*
Langton – *Temple of Stowe, E.*
La Poer – **Tyrone, E.*
Leslie – *Rothes, E.*
Leveson – *Granville, E.*
Loughborough – *Rosslyn, E.*
Maltravers – **Arundel and Surrey, E.*
Mauchline – *Loudoun, C.*
Medway – *Cranbrook, E.*
Montgomerie – *Eglinton and Winton, E.*
Moreton – *Ducie, E.*
Naas – *Mayo, E.*
Neidpath – *Wemyss & March, E.*
Norreys – *Lindsey & Abingdon, E.*
North – *Guilford, E.*
Ogilvy – *Airlie, E.*
Oxmantown – *Rosse, E.*
Paget de Beaudesert – **Uxbridge, E.*
Porchester – *Carnarvon, E.*
Ramsay – *Dalhousie, E.*
Romsey – *Mountbatten of Burma, C.*
Rosehill – *Northesk, E.*
Scrymgeour – *Dundee, E.*
Seymour – *Somerset, D.*
Strathnaver – *Sutherland, C.*
Wodehouse – *Kimberley, E.*
Worsley – *Yarborough, E.*

PEERS' SURNAMES WHICH DIFFER FROM THEIR TITLES

The following symbols indicate the rank of the peer holding each title:
C. Countess
D. Duke
E. Earl
M. Marquess
V. Viscount
* Life Peer
Where no designation is given, the title is that of an hereditary Baron or Baroness.

Abney-Hastings – *Loudoun, C.*
Acheson – *Gosford, E.*
Adderley – *Norton*
Addington – *Sidmouth, V.*
Agar – *Normanton, E.*
Airey – *A. of Abingdon**
Aitken – *Beaverbrook*
Akers-Douglas – *Chilston, V.*
Alexander – *A. of Potterhill**
Alexander – *A. of Tunis, E.*
Alexander – *A. of Weedon**
Alexander – *Caledon, E.*
Allen – *A. of Abbeydale**
Allen – *Croham**
Allanson-Winn – *Headley*
Allsopp – *Hindlip*
Amery – *A. of Lustleigh**
Anderson – *Waverley, V.*
Annesley – *Valentia, V.*
Anson – *Lichfield, E.*
Archer – *A. of Sandwell**
Archer – *A. of Weston-super-Mare**
Armstrong – *A. of Ilminster**
Armstrong-Jones – *Snowdon, E.*
Arthur – *Glenarthur*
Arundell – *Talbot of Malahide*
Ashley – *A. of Stoke**
Ashley-Cooper – *Shaftesbury, E.*
Ashton – *A. of Hyde*
Asquith – *Oxford & Asquith, E.*
Assheton – *Clitheroe*
Astley – *Hastings*
Astor – *A. of Hever*
Atkins – *Colnbrook**
Aubrey-Fletcher – *Braye*
Bailey – *Glanusk*
Baillie – *Burton*
Baillie Hamilton – *Haddington, E.*
Baldwin – *B. of Bewdley, E.*
Balfour – *B. of Inchrye*
Balfour – *Kinross*
Balfour – *Riverdale*
Bampfylde – *Poltimore*
Banbury – *B. of Southam*
Barber – *B. of Tewkesbury**
Baring – *Ashburton*
Baring – *Cromer, E.*
Baring – *Howick of Glendale*
Baring – *Northbrook*
Baring – *Revelstoke*
Barker – *Trumpington**
Barnes – *Gorell*
Barnewall – *Trimlestown*
Bathurst – *Bledisloe, V.*
Beauclerk – *St Albans, D.*
Beaumont – *Allendale, V.*
Beaumont – *B. of Whitley**
Beavan – *Ardwick**
Beckett – *Grimthorpe*
Bellow – *Bellwin**
Benn – *Stansgate, V.*
Bennet – *Tankerville, E.*
Bentinck – *Portland, E.*
Beresford – *Decies*
Beresford – *Waterford, M.*
Berry – *Camrose, V.*
Berry – *Hartwell**
Berry – *Kemsley, V.*
Bertie – *Lindsey, E.*
Best – *Wynford*
Bethell – *Westbury*
Bewicke-Copley – *Cromwell*
Bigham – *Mersey, V.*
Bigham – *Nairne*
Bingham – *Clanmorris*
Bingham – *Lucan, E.*
Blackwood – *Dufferin & Clandeboye*
Bligh – *Darnley, E.*
Bootle-Wilbraham – *Skelmersdale*
Boscawen – *Falmouth, V.*
Boston – *Boston of Faversham**
Bourke – *Mayo, E.*
Bowden – *Aylestone**
Bowes Lyon – *Strathmore, E.*
Bowyer – *Denham*
Boyd – *Kilmarnock*
Boyle – *Cork & Orrery, E.*
Boyle – *Glasgow, E.*
Boyle – *Shannon, E.*
Brabazon – *Meath, E.*
Braine – *B. of Wheatley**
Brand – *Hampden, V.*
Brandon – *B. of Oakbrook**
Brassey – *B. of Apethorpe*
Brett – *Esher, V.*
Bridge – *B. of Harwich**
Bridgeman – *Bradford, E.*
Brodrick – *Midleton, V.*
Brooke – *Alanbrooke, V.*
Brooke – *Brookeborough, V.*
Brooke – *B. of Ystradfellte**
Brooks – *B. of Tremorfa**
Brooks – *Crawshaw*
Brougham – *Brougham and Vaux*
Broughton – *Fairhaven*
Browne – *Craigton**
Browne – *Kilmaine*
Browne – *Oranmore and Browne*
Browne – *Sligo, M.*
Bruce – *Aberdare*
Bruce – *Balfour of Burleigh*
Bruce – *B. of Donington**
Bruce – *Elgin and Kincardine, E.*
Brudenell-Bruce – *Ailesbury, M.*
Buchan – *Tweedsmuir*
Buckley – *Wrenbury*
Butler – *Carrick, E.*
Butler – *Dunboyne*
Butler – *Lanesborough, E.*
Butler – *Mountgarret, V.*
Butler – *Ormonde, M.*
Buxton – *B. of Alsa**
Byng – *Strafford, E.*
Byng – *Torrington, V.*
Callaghan – *C. of Cardiff**
Cameron – *C. of Lochbroom**
Campbell – *Argyll, D.*
Campbell – *Breadalbane and Holland, E.*
Campbell – *C. of Alloway**
Campbell – *C. of Croy**
Campbell – *C. of Eskan**
Campbell – *Cawdor, E.*
Campbell – *Colgrain*
Campbell – *Stratheden and Campbell*
Campbell-Gray – *Gray*
Canning – *Garvagh*
Capell – *Essex, E.*
Carington – *Carrington*
Carlisle – *C. of Bucklow**
Carmichael – *C. of Kelvingrove**
Carnegie – *Fife, D.*
Carnegie – *Northesk, E.*
Carnegie – *Southesk, E.*
Carr – *C. of Hadley**
Cary – *Falkland, V.*
Castle – *C. of Blackburn**
Caulfeild – *Charlemont, V.*
Cavendish – *C. of Furness**
Cavendish – *Chesham*
Cavendish – *Devonshire, D.*
Cavendish – *Waterpark*
Cayzer – *Rotherwick*
Cecil – *Amherst of Hackney*
Cecil – *Exeter, M.*
Cecil – *Rockley*
Cecil – *Salisbury, M.*
Chalker – *C. of Wallasey**
Chaloner – *Gisborough*
Chapman – *Northfield**
Charteris – *C. of Amisfield**
Charteris – *Wemyss and March, E.*
Cheshire – *Ryder of Warsaw**
Chetwynd-Talbot – *Shrewsbury, E.*
Chichester – *Donegall, M.*
Chichester-Clark – *Moyola**
Child-Villiers – *Jersey, E.*
Cholmondeley – *Delamere*
Chubb – *Hayter*
Clark – *C. of Kempston**
Clegg-Hill – *Hill, V.*
Clifford – *Clifford of Chudleigh*
Cochrane – *C. of Cults*
Cochrane – *Dundonald, E.*
Cocks – *C. of Hartcliffe**

Cocks – *Somers*
Cokayne – *Cullen of Ashbourne*
Coke – *Leicester, E.*
Cole – *Enniskillen, E.*
Collier – *Monkswell*
Colville – *Clydesmuir*
Colville – *C. of Culross, V.*
Compton – *Northampton, M.*
Conolly-Carew – *Carew*
Constantine – *C. of Stanmore**
Cooke – *C. of Islandreagh**
Cooper – *Norwich, V.*
Corbett – *Rowallan*
Courtenay – *Devon, E.*
Cox – *Kings Norton**
Craig – *C. of Radley**
Craig – *Craigavon, V.*
Crichton – *Erne, E.*
Crichton-Stuart – *Bute, M.*
Cripps – *Parmoor*
Crossley – *Somerleyton*
Cubitt – *Ashcombe*
Cunliffe-Lister – *Masham of Ilton**
Cunliffe-Lister – *Swinton, E.*
Curzon – *Howe, E.*
Curzon – *Scarsdale, V.*
Cust – *Brownlow*
Dalrymple – *Stair, E.*
Daubeny de Moleyns – *Ventry*
Davies – *Darwen*
Davies – *D. of Penrhys**
Davis – *Clinton-Davis**
Davison – *Broughshane*
Dawnay – *Downe, V.*
Dawson-Damer – *Portarlington, E.*
Dean – *D. of Beswick**
Deane – *Muskerry*
de Courcy – *Kingsale*
de Grey – *Walsingham*
Delacourt-Smith – *Delacourt Smith of Alteryn**
Denison – *Londesborough*
Denison-Pender – *Pender*
Denton – *D. of Wakefield**
Devereux – *Hereford, V.*
Dewar – *Forteviot*
De Yarburgh-Bateson – *Deramore*
Dixon – *Glentoran*
Dodson – *Monk Bretton*
Donaldson – *D. of Kingsbridge**
Donaldson – *D. of Lymington**
Dormand – *D. of Easington**
Douglas – *Morton, E.*
Douglas – *Queensberry, M.*
Douglas-Hamilton – *Hamilton, D.*
Douglas-Hamilton – *Selkirk, E.*
Douglas-Home – *Dacre*
Douglas-Home – *Home of the Hirsel**
Douglas-Pennant – *Penrhyn*
Douglas-Scott-Montagu – *Montagu of Beaulieu*
Drummond – *Perth, E.*
Drummond of Megginch – *Strange*
Dugdale – *Crathorne*
Duke – *Merrivale*
Duncombe – *Feversham*
Dundas – *Melville, V.*
Dundas – *Zetland, M.*
Eady – *Swinfen*
Eccles – *E. of Moulton**
Eden – *Auckland*
Eden – *E. of Winton**
Eden – *Henley*
Edgcumbe – *Mount Edgcumbe, E.*
Edmondson – *Sandford*
Edwardes – *Kensington*
Edwards – *Chelmer**
Edwards – *Crickhowell**
Egerton – *Sutherland, D.*
Egerton – *Wilton, E.*
Eliot – *St Germans, E.*
Elliot – *E. of Harwood**
Elliot-Murray-Kynynmound – *Minto, E.*
Elliott – *E. of Morpeth**
Erroll – *E. of Hale*
Erskine – *Buchan, E.*
Erskine – *E. of Rerrick*
Erskine – *Mar & Kellie, E.*
Erskine-Murray – *Elibank*
Evans – *Mountevans*
Evans-Freke – *Carbery*
Eve – *Silsoe*
Ewing – *E. of Kirkford**
Eyres Monsell – *Monsell, V.*
Fairfax – *F. of Cameron*
Fane – *Westmorland, E.*
Feilding – *Denbigh, E.*
Fellowes – *De Ramsey*
Fermor-Hesketh – *Hesketh*
Fiennes – *Saye & Sele*
Fiennes-Clinton – *Lincoln, E.*
Finch Hatton – *Winchilsea, E.*
Finch-Knightley – *Aylesford, E.*
Fisher – *F. of Rednal**
Fitzalan-Howard – *Herries of Terregles*
Fitzalan-Howard – *Norfolk, D.*
FitzClarence – *Munster, E.*
FitzGerald – *Leinster, D.*
Fitzherbert – *Stafford*
Fitz-Maurice – *Orkney, E.*
FitzRoy – *Grafton, D.*
FitzRoy – *Southampton*
FitzRoy Newdegate – *Daventry, V.*
Fletcher-Vane – *Inglewood*
Flower – *Ashbrook, V.*
Foley Berkeley – *Berkeley*
Foljambe – *Liverpool, E.*
Forbes – *Granard, E.*
Fox-Strangways – *Ilchester, E.*
Frankland – *Zouche*
Fraser – *F. of Carmyllie**
Fraser – *F. of Kilmorack**
Fraser – *Lovat*
Fraser – *Saltoun*
Fraser – *Strathalmond*
Freeman-Grenville – *Kinloss*
Fremantle – *Cottesloe*
French – *De Freyne*
Galbraith – *Strathclyde*
Ganzoni – *Belstead*
Gardner – *G. of Parkes**
Gathorne-Hardy – *Cranbrook, E.*
Gibbs – *Aldenham*
Gibbs – *Wraxall*
Gibson – *Ashbourne*
Giffard – *Halsbury, E.*
Gilbey – *Vaux of Harrowden*
Gilmour – *G. of Craigmillar**
Glyn – *Wolverton*
Godley – *Kilbracken*
Goff – *G. of Chieveley**
Gordon – *Aberdeen, M.*
Gordon – *Huntly, M.*
Gordon Lennox – *Richmond, D.*
Gore – *Arran, E.*
Gough-Calthorpe – *Calthorpe*
Graham – *G. of Edmonton**
Graham – *Montrose, D.*
Graham-Toler – *Norbury, E.*
Grant of Grant – *Strathspey*
Grant-Ferris – *Harvington**
Granville – *G. of Eye**
Gray – *G. of Contin**
Greaves – *Dysart, C.*
Greenall – *Daresbury*
Greene – *G. of Harrow Weald**
Greenhill – *G. of Harrow**
Greville – *Warwick, E.*
Grey – *G. of Naunton**
Griffiths – *G. of Fforestfach**
Grigg – *Altrincham*
Grimston – *G. of Westbury*
Grimston – *Verulam, E.*
Grosvenor – *Ebury*
Grosvenor – *Westminster, D.*
Guest – *Wimborne, V.*
Guinness – *Iveagh, E.*
Guinness – *Moyne*
Gully – *Selby, V.*
Gurdon – *Cranworth*
Gwynne Jones – *Chalfont**
Hamilton – *Abercorn, D.*
Hamilton – *Belhaven and Stenton*
Hamilton – *Dudley*
Hamilton – *H. of Dalzell*
Hamilton – *Holm Patrick*
Hamilton-Russell – *Boyne, V.*
Hamilton-Smith – *Colwyn*
Hanbury-Tracy – *Sudeley*
Handcock – *Castlemaine*
Harbord-Hamond – *Suffield*
Harding – *H. of Petherton*
Hardinge – *H. of Penshurst*
Hare – *Blakenham, V.*
Hare – *Listowel, E.*
Harmsworth – *Rothermere, V.*
Harris – *H. of Greenwich**
Harris – *H. of High Cross**
Harris – *Malmesbury, E.*
Harvey – *H. of Prestbury**
Harvey – *H. of Tasburgh*
Hastings Bass – *Huntingdon, E.*
Hatch – *H. of Lusby**
Hay – *Erroll, E.*
Hay – *Kinnoull, E.*
Hay – *Tweeddale, M.*
Heathcote-Drummond-Willoughby – *Willoughby de Eresby*
Hely-Hutchinson – *Donoughmore, E.*
Henderson – *Faringdon*
Henderson – *H. of Brompton**
Hennessy – *Windlesham*
Henniker-Major – *Henniker*
Hepburne-Scott – *Polwarth*
Herbert – *Carnarvon, E.*
Herbert – *Hemingford*
Herbert – *Pembroke, E.*
Herbert – *Powis, E.*
Hermon-Hodge – *Wyfold*
Hervey – *Bristol, M.*
Hewitt – *Lifford, V.*
Hicks Beach – *St Aldwyn, E.*
Hill – *Downshire, M.*
Hill – *Sandys*
Hill-Trevor – *Trevor*
Hilton – *H. of Eggardon**
Hobart-Hampden – *Buckinghamshire, E.*
Hogg – *Hailsham of St Marylebone**
Holland-Hibbert – *Knutsford, V.*
Hollis – *H. of Heigham**
Holme – *H. of Cheltenham**
Holmes à Court – *Heytesbury*
Hood – *Bridport, V.*
Hope – *Glendevon*
Hope – *Linlithgow, M.*
Hope – *Rankeillour*
Hope Johnstone – *Annandale and Hartfell, E.*
Hope-Morley – *Hollenden*
Hopkinson – *Colyton*

Hore Ruthven – *Gowrie, E.*
Houghton – *H. of Sowerby**
Hovell-Thurlow-Cumming-Bruce – *Thurlow*
Howard – *Carlisle, E.*
Howard – *Effingham, E.*
Howard – *H. of Penrith*
Howard – *Strathcona*
Howard – *Suffolk and Berkshire, E.*
Howe – *H. of Aberavon**
Howells – *Geraint**
Howie – *H. of Troon**
Hubbard – *Addington*
Huggins – *Malvern, V.*
Hughes – *Cledwyn of Penrhos**
Hughes-Young – *St Helens*
Hunt – *H. of Tanworth**
Hunter – *H. of Newington**
Hutchinson – *H. of Lullington**
Ingrams – *Darcy de Knayth*
Innes-Ker – *Roxburghe, D.*
Inskip – *Caldecote, V.*
Irby – *Boston*
Irvine – *I. of Lairg**
Isaacs – *Reading, M.*
James – *J. of Holland Park**
James – *J. of Rusholme**
James – *Northbourne*
Jauncey – *J. of Tullichettle**
Jay – *J. of Paddington**
Jebb – *Gladwyn*
Jenkin – *J. of Roding**
Jenkins – *J. of Hillhead**
Jenkins – *J. of Putney**
Jervis – *St Vincent, V.*
Jocelyn – *Roden, E.*
Johnston – *J. of Rockport**
Jolliffe – *Hylton*
Joynson-Hicks – *Brentford, V.*
Kay-Shuttleworth – *Shuttleworth*
Kearley – *Devonport, V.*
Keith – *K. of Castleacre**
Keith – *K. of Kinkel**
Keith – *Kintore, E.*
Kemp – *Rochdale, V.*
Kennedy – *Ailsa, M.*
Kenworthy – *Strabolgi*
Keppel – *Albemarle, E.*
Kerr – *Lothian, M.*
Kerr – *Teviot*
King – *Lovelace, E.*
King – *K. of Wartnaby**
King-Tenison – *Kingston, E.*
Kitchener – *K. of Khartoum, E.*
Kitson – *Airedale*
Knatchbull – *Brabourne*
Knatchbull – *Mountbatten of Burma, C.*
Knox – *Ranfurly, E.*
Laing – *L. of Dunphail**
Lamb – *Rochester*
Lambart – *Cavan, E.*
Lambton – *Durham, E.*
Lampson – *Killearn*
Lane – *L. of Horsell**
Lascelles – *Harewood, E.*
Law – *Coleraine*
Law – *Ellenborough*
Lawrence – *Trevethin and Oaksey*
Lawson – *Burnham*
Lawson – *L. of Blaby**
Lawson-Johnston – *Luke*
Legge – *Dartmouth, E.*
Legh – *Grey of Codnor*
Legh – *Newton*
Leith – *Burgh*
Lennox-Boyd – *Boyd of Merton, V.*
Le Poer Trench – *Clancarty, E.*
Leslie – *Rothes, E.*
Leslie Melville – *Leven and Melville, E.*
Lever – *Leverhulme, V.*
Lever – *L. of Manchester**
Leveson-Gower – *Granville, E.*
Lewis – *L. of Newnham**
Lewis – *Merthyr*
Liddell – *Ravensworth*
Lindesay-Bethune – *Lindsay, E.*
Lindsay – *Crawford, E.*
Lindsay – *L. of Birker*
Littleton – *Hatherton*
Llewelyn-Davies – *Llewelyn-Davies of Hastoe**
Lloyd – *L. of Hampstead**
Lloyd George – *Lloyd George of Dwyfor, E.*
Lloyd George – *Tenby, V.*
Lloyd-Mostyn – *Mostyn*
Loder – *Wakehurst*
Lopes – *Roborough*
Low – *Aldington*
Lowry-Corry – *Belmore, E.*
Lowther – *Lonsdale, E.*
Lowther – *Ullswater, V.*
Lubbock – *Avebury*
Lucas – *L. of Chilworth*
Lumley – *Scarbrough, E.*
Lumley-Savile – *Savile*
Lyon-Dalberg-Acton – *Acton*
Lysaght – *Lisle*
Lyttelton – *Chandos, V.*
Lyttelton – *Cobham, V.*
Lytton Cobbold – *Cobbold*
McAlpine – *M. of West Green**
Macaulay – *M. of Bragar**
McClintock-Bunbury – *Rathdonnell*
McColl – *M. of Dulwich**
Macdonald – *M. of Gwaenysgor*
Macdonald of Macdonald – *Macdonald*
McDonnell – *Antrim, E.*
McFadzean – *M. of Kelvinside**
Macfarlane – *M. of Bearsden**
McFarlane – *M. of Llandaff**
McGregor – *M. of Durris**
McIntosh – *M. of Haringey**
Mackay – *Inchcape, E.*
Mackay – *M. of Ardbrecknish**
Mackay – *M. of Clashfern**
Mackay – *Reay*
Mackay – *Tanlaw**
Mackenzie – *Cromartie, E.*
Mackie – *John-Mackie**
Mackie – *M. of Benshie**
Mackintosh – *M. of Halifax, V.*
McLaren – *Aberconway*
MacLehose – *M. of Beoch**
Macleod – *M. of Borve**
Macmillan – *Stockton, E.*
Macpherson – *M. of Drumochter*
Macpherson – *Strathcarron*
Maffey – *Rugby*
Maitland – *Lauderdale, E.*
Makgill – *Oxfuird, V.*
Makins – *Sherfield*
Manners – *Rutland, D.*
Manningham-Buller – *Dilhorne, V.*
Mansfield – *Sandhurst*
Marks – *M. of Broughton*
Marquis – *Woolton, E.*
Marshall – *M. of Goring**
Marsham – *Romney, E.*
Martyn-Hemphill – *Hemphill*
Mason – *M. of Barnsley**
Maude – *Hawarden, V.*
Maude – *M. of Stratford-upon-Avon**
Maxwell – *de Ros*
Maxwell – *Farnham*
Meade – *Clanwilliam, E.*
Mercer Nairne Petty-Fitzmaurice – *Lansdowne, M.*
Millar – *Inchyra*
Milles-Lade – *Sondes, E.*
Milner – *M. of Leeds*
Mitchell-Thomson – *Selsdon*
Mitford – *Redesdale*
Monckton – *M. of Brenchley, V.*
Monckton-Arundell – *Galway, V.*
Mond – *Melchett*
Money-Coutts – *Latymer*
Montagu – *Manchester, D.*
Montagu – *Sandwich, E.*
Montagu – *Swaythling*
Montagu Douglas Scott – *Buccleuch, D.*
Montagu Stuart Wortley – *Wharncliffe, E.*
Montague – *Amwell*
Montgomerie – *Eglinton, E.*
Montgomery – *M. of Alamein, V.*
Moore – *Drogheda, E.*
Moore – *M. of Lower Marsh**
Moore – *M. of Wolvercote**
Moore-Brabazon – *Brabazon of Tara*
Moreton – *Ducie, E.*
Morris – *Killanin*
Morris – *M. of Castle Morris**
Morris – *M. of Kenwood*
Morrison – *Dunrossil, V.*
Morrison – *Margadale*
Morton – *M. of Shuna**
Mosley – *Ravensdale*
Mountbatten – *Milford Haven, M.*
Muff – *Calverley*
Mulholland – *Dunleath*
Murray – *Atholl, D.*
Murray – *Dunmore, E.*
Murray – *Mansfield and Mansfield, E.*
Murray – *M. of Epping Forest**
Murray – *M. of Newhaven**
Murton – *M. of Lindisfarne**
Nall-Cain – *Brocket*
Napier – *Napier and Ettrick*
Napier – *N. of Magdala*
Needham – *Kilmorey, E.*
Nelson – *N. of Stafford*
Nevill – *Abergavenny, M.*
Neville – *Braybrooke*
Nicolson – *Carnock*
Nivison – *Glendyne*
Noel – *Gainsborough, E.*
Noel-Paton – *Ferrier**
North – *Guilford, E.*
Northcote – *Iddesleigh, E.*
Norton – *Grantley*
Norton – *Rathcreedan*
Nugent – *N. of Guildford**
Nugent – *Westmeath, E.*
O'Brien – *Inchiquin*
O'Brien – *O'Brien of Lothbury**
Ogilvie-Grant – *Seafield, E.*
Ogilvy – *Airlie, E.*
Oliver – *O. of Aylmerton**
O'Neill – *Rathcavan*
Orde-Powlett – *Bolton*
Ormsby-Gore – *Harlech*
Page – *Whaddon**
Paget – *Anglesey, M.*
Pakenham – *Longford, E.*
Pakington – *Hampton*
Palmer – *Lucas of Crudwell*
Palmer – *Selborne, E.*
Park – *P. of Monmouth**
Parker – *Macclesfield, E.*
Parker – *Morley, E.*

Parnell – *Congleton*
Parsons – *Rosse, E.*
Paulet – *Winchester, M.*
Peake – *Ingleby, V.*
Pearson – *Cowdray, V.*
Pearson – *P. of Rannoch**
Pease – *Daryngton*
Pease – *Gainford*
Pease – *Wardington*
Pelham – *Chichester, E.*
Pelham – *Yarborough, E.*
Pellew – *Exmouth, V.*
Penny – *Marchwood, V.*
Pepys – *Cottenham, E.*
Perceval – *Egmont, E.*
Percy – *Northumberland, D.*
Perry – *P. of Southwark**
Perry – *P. of Walton**
Pery – *Limerick, E.*
Peyton – *P. of Yeovil**
Philipps – *Milford*
Philipps – *St Davids, V.*
Phipps – *Normanby, M.*
Pitt – *P. of Hampstead**
Plant – *P. of Highfield**
Platt – *P. of Writtle**
Pleydell-Bouverie – *Radnor, E.*
Plummer – *P. of St Marylebone**
Plumptre – *Fitzwalter*
Plunkett – *Dunsany*
Plunkett – *Louth*
Pollock – *Hanworth, V.*
Pomeroy – *Harberton, V.*
Ponsonby – *Bessborough, E.*
Ponsonby – *de Mauley*
Ponsonby – *P. of Shulbrede*
Ponsonby – *Sysonby*
Porter – *P. of Luddenham**
Powys – *Lilford*
Pratt – *Camden, M.*
Preston – *Gormanston, V.*
Primrose – *Rosebery, E.*
Prittie – *Dunalley*
Ramsay – *Dalhousie, E.*
Ramsbotham – *Soulbury, V.*
Rawlinson – *R. of Ewell**
Rees-Williams – *Ogmore*
Renfrew – *R. of Kaimsthorn**
Rhys – *Dynevor*
Richards – *Milverton*
Richardson – *R. of Duntisbourne**
Ridley – *R. of Liddesdale**
Rippon – *R. of Hexham**
Ritchie – *R. of Dundee*
Robens – *R. of Woldingham**
Roberts – *Clwyd*
Robertson – *R. of Oakridge*
Robertson – *Wharton*
Robinson – *Martonmere*
Robson – *R. of Kiddington**
Roche – *Fermoy*
Rodd – *Rennell*
Rodger – *R. of Earlsferry**
Rodgers – *R. of Quarry Bank**
Roll – *R. of Ipsden**
Roper-Curzon – *Teynham*
Rospigliosi – *Newburgh, E.*
Ross – *R. of Newport**
Rous – *Stradbroke, E.*
Rowley-Conwy – *Langford*
Royle – *Fanshawe of Richmond**
Runciman – *R. of Doxford, V.*
Russell – *Ampthill*
Russell – *Bedford, D.*
Russell – *de Clifford*
Russell – *R. of Liverpool*
Ryder – *Harrowby, E.*
Ryder – *R. of Eaton Hastings**
Ryder – *R. of Warsaw**
Sackville – *De La Warr, E.*
Sackville-West – *Sackville*
Sainsbury – *S. of Preston Candover**
St Aubyn – *St Levan*
St Clair – *Sinclair*
St Clair-Erskine – *Rosslyn, E.*
St John – *Bolingbroke and St John, V.*
St John – *St John of Blesto*
St John-Stevas – *St John of Fawsley**
St Leger – *Doneraile, V.*
Samuel – *Bearsted, V.*
Sanderson – *S. of Ayot*
Sanderson – *S. of Bowden**
Sandilands – *Torphichen*
Saumarez – *De Saumarez*
Savile – *Mexborough, E.*
Scarlett – *Abinger*
Schreiber – *Marlesford**
Sclater-Booth – *Basing*
Scott – *Eldon, E.*
Scott-Ellis – *Howard de Walden*
Scrymgeour – *Dundee, E.*
Seager – *Leighton of St Mellons*
Seely – *Mottistone*
Sefton – *S. of Garston**
Seymour – *Hertford, M.*
Seymour – *Somerset, D.*
Sharp – *S. of Grimsdyke**
Shaw – *Craigmyle*
Shirley – *Ferrers, E.*
Short – *Glenamara**
Siddeley – *Kenilworth*
Sidney – *De L'Isle, V.*
Sieff – *S. of Brimpton**
Simon – *S. of Glaisdale**
Simon – *S. of Wythenshawe*
Sinclair – *Caithness, E.*
Sinclair – *S. of Cleeve*
Sinclair – *Thurso, V.*
Skeffington – *Massereene, V.*
Slynn – *S. of Hadley**
Smith – *Bicester*
Smith – *Hambleden, V.*
Smith – *Kirkhill**
Somerset – *Beaufort, D.*
Somerset – *Raglan*
Souter – *Audley*
Spencer – *Churchill, V.*
Spencer-Churchill – *Marlborough, D.*
Spring Rice – *Monteagle of Brandon*
Stanhope – *Harrington, E.*
Stanley – *Derby, E.*
Stanley – *Stanley of Alderley & Sheffield*
Stapleton-Cotton – *Combermere, V.*
Sterling – *S. of Plaistow**
Stevens – *S. of Ludgate**
Stewart – *Galloway, E.*
Stewart – *Stewartby**
Stodart – *S. of Leaston**
Stoddart – *S. of Swindon**
Stonor – *Camoys*
Stopford – *Courtown, E.*
Stourton – *Mowbray*
Strachey – *O'Hagan*
Strutt – *Belper*
Strutt – *Rayleigh*
Stuart – *Castle Stewart, E.*
Stuart – *Moray, E.*
Stuart – *S. of Findhorn, V.*
Suenson-Taylor – *Grantchester*
Taylor – *Ingrow**
Taylor – *T. of Blackburn**
Taylor – *T. of Gosforth**
Taylor – *T. of Gryfe**
Taylor – *T. of Hadfield**
Taylour – *Headfort, M.*
Temple-Gore-Langton – *Temple of Stowe, E.*
Tennant – *Glenconner*
Thellusson – *Rendlesham*
Thesiger – *Chelmsford, V.*
Thomas – *T. of Gwydir**
Thomas – *T. of Swynnerton**
Thomas – *Tonypandy, V.*
Thomson – *T. of Fleet*
Thomson – *T. of Monifieth**
Thynn – *Bath, M.*
Thynne – *Bath, M.*
Tottenham – *Ely, M.*
Trefusis – *Clinton*
Trench – *Ashtown*
Trevor-Roper – *Dacre of Glanton**
Tufton – *Hothfield*
Turner – *Netherthorpe*
Turner – *T. of Camden**
Turnour – *Winterton, E.*
Turton – *Tranmire**
Tyrell-Kenyon – *Kenyon*
Vanden-Bempde-Johnstone – *Derwent*
Vane – *Barnard*
Vane – *Inglewood*
Vane-Tempest-Stewart – *Londonderry, M.*
Vanneck – *Huntingfield*
Vaughan – *Lisburne, E.*
Vaughan-Morgan – *Reigate**
Vereker – *Gort, V.*
Verney – *Willoughby de Broke*
Vernon – *Lyveden*
Vesey – *De Vesci, V.*
Villiers – *Clarendon, E.*
Vivian – *Swansea*
Wade – *W. of Chorlton**
Walker – *W. of Worcester**
Wallace – *W. of Campsie**
Wallace – *W. of Coslany**
Wallop – *Portsmouth, E.*
Walton – *W. of Detchant**
Ward – *Bangor, V.*
Ward – *Dudley, E.*
Warrender – *Bruntisfield*
Watson – *Manton*
Wedderburn – *W. of Charlton**
Weir – *Inverforth*
Weld-Forester – *Forester*
Wellesley – *Cowley, E.*
Wellesley – *Wellington, D.*
Westenra – *Rossmore*
White – *Annaly*
White – *W. of Hull**
Whiteley – *Marchamley*
Whitfield – *Kenswood*
Williams – *Berners*
Williams – *W. of Elvel**
Williams – *W. of Mostyn**
Williamson – *Forres*
Willoughby – *Middleton*
Wills – *Dulverton*
Wilson – *Moran*
Wilson – *Nunburnholme*
Wilson – *W. of Langside**
Wilson – *W. of Rievaulx**
Wilson – *W. of Tillyorn**
Windsor – *Gloucester, D.*
Windsor – *Kent, D.*
Windsor-Clive – *Plymouth, E.*
Wingfield – *Powerscourt, V.*
Winn – *St Oswald*
Wodehouse – *Kimberley, E.*
Wolfson – *W. of Sunningdale**
Wood – *Halifax, E.*
Wood – *Holderness**
Woodhouse – *Terrington*
Wyatt – *W. of Weeford**
Wyndham – *Egremont & Leconfield*
Wyndham-Quin – *Dunraven, E.*
Wynn – *Newborough*
Yarde-Buller – *Churston*
Yerburgh – *Alvingham*
Yorke – *Hardwicke, E.*
Young – *Kennet*
Young – *Y. of Dartington**
Young – *Y. of Graffham**
Younger – *Y. of Leckie, V.*
Younger – *Y. of Prestwick**

Orders of Chivalry

THE MOST NOBLE ORDER OF THE GARTER (1348)

KG

Ribbon, Garter Blue
Motto, Honi soit qui mal y pense (*Shame on him who thinks evil of it*)

The number of Knights Companions is limited to 24

SOVEREIGN OF THE ORDER
The Queen

LADY OF THE GARTER
HM Queen Elizabeth The Queen Mother, 1936

ROYAL KNIGHTS

HRH The Duke of Edinburgh, 1947.
HRH The Prince of Wales, 1958.
HRH The Duke of Kent, 1985.

EXTRA KNIGHTS COMPANIONS AND LADIES

HRH Princess Juliana of the Netherlands, 1958.
HM The King of The Belgians, 1963.
HRH The Grand Duke of Luxembourg, 1972.
HM The Queen of Denmark, 1979.
HM The King of Sweden, 1983
HM The King of Spain, 1988.
HM The Queen of the Netherlands, 1989.

KNIGHTS AND LADY COMPANIONS

Sir Cennydd Traherne, 1970.
The Earl Waldegrave, 1971.
The Earl of Longford, 1971.
The Lord Shackleton, 1974.
The Marquess of Abergavenny, 1974.
The Lord Wilson of Rievaulx, 1976.
The Duke of Grafton, 1976.
The Lord Elworthy, 1977.
The Lord Hunt, 1979.
Sir Paul Hasluck, 1979.
The Duke of Norfolk, 1983.
The Lord Lewin, 1983.
The Lord Richardson of Duntisbourne, 1983.
The Marquess of Normanby, 1985.
The Lord Carrington, 1985.
The Lord Callaghan of Cardiff, 1987.
The Viscount Leverhulme, 1988.
The Lord Hailsham of St Marylebone, 1988.
Lavinia, Duchess of Norfolk, 1990.
The Duke of Wellington, 1990.
Field Marshal Lord Bramall, 1990.
Sir Edward Heath, 1992.
The Viscount Ridley, 1992.
The Lord Sainsbury of Preston Candover, 1992.

Prelate, The Bishop of Winchester.
Chancellor, The Marquess of Abergavenny, KG, OBE.
Register, The Dean of Windsor.
Garter King of Arms, C. Swan, CVO, Ph.D., FSA.
Gentleman Usher of the Black Rod, Adm. Sir Richard Thomas, KCB, OBE.
Secretary, D. H. B. Chesshyre, LVO.

THE MOST ANCIENT AND MOST NOBLE ORDER OF THE THISTLE (REVIVED 1687)

KT

Ribbon, Green
Motto, Nemo me impune lacessit (*No one provokes me with impunity*)

The number of Knights is limited to 16

SOVEREIGN OF THE ORDER
The Queen

LADY OF THE THISTLE
HM Queen Elizabeth The Queen Mother, 1937

ROYAL KNIGHTS

HRH The Duke of Edinburgh, 1952.
HRH The Prince of Wales, Duke of Rothesay, 1977.

KNIGHTS

The Lord Home of the Hirsel, 1962.
The Earl of Wemyss and March, 1966.
The Earl of Dalhousie, 1971.
The Lord Clydesmuir, 1972.
Sir Donald Cameron of Lochiel, 1973.
The Earl of Selkirk, 1976.
The Lord McFadzean, 1976.
The Hon. Lord Cameron, 1978.
The Duke of Buccleuch and Queensberry, 1978.
The Earl of Elgin and Kincardine, 1981.
The Lord Thomson of Monifieth, 1981.
The Lord MacLehose of Beoch, 1983.
The Earl of Airlie, 1985.
Capt. Sir Iain Tennant, 1986.
The Viscount Whitelaw, 1990.

Chancellor, The Lord Home of the Hirsel.
Dean, The Very Revd G. I. Macmillan.
Secretary and Lord Lyon King of Arms, Sir Malcolm Innes of Edingight, KCVO, WS.
Usher of the Green Rod, Rear- Admiral D.A. Dunbar-Nasmith, CB, DSC.

THE MOST HONOURABLE ORDER OF THE BATH (1725)

GCB *Military*

GCB *Civil*

GCB, Knight (or Dame) Grand Cross
KCB, Knight Commander
DCB, Dame Commander
CB, Companion

Ribbon, Crimson
Motto, Tria juncta in uno (*Three joined in one*)

Remodelled 1815, and enlarged many times since. The Order is divided into civil and military divisions. Women became eligible for the Order from 1 January 1971.

THE SOVEREIGN

GREAT MASTER AND FIRST OR PRINCIPAL KNIGHT GRAND CROSS
HRH The Prince of Wales, KG, KT, GCB

Dean of the Order, The Dean of Westminster.
Bath King of Arms, Air Chief Marshal Sir David Evans, GCB, CBE.
Registrar and Secretary, Rear-Adm. D. E. Macey, CB.
Genealogist, C. Swan, CVO, Ph.D., FSA.
Gentleman Usher of the Scarlet Rod, Air Vice-Marshal Sir Richard Peirse, KCVO, CB.
Deputy Secretary, The Secretary of the Central Chancery of the Orders of Knighthood.
Chancery, Central Chancery of the Orders of Knighthood, St James's Palace, London SW1A 1BH.

THE ORDER OF MERIT (1902)

OM *Military* OM *Civil*

Ribbon, Blue and Crimson

This Order is designed as a special distinction for eminent men and women without conferring a knighthood upon them. The Order is limited in numbers to 24, with the addition of foreign honorary members. Membership is of two kinds, Military and Civil, the badge of the former having crossed swords, and the latter oak leaves.

THE SOVEREIGN

HRH THE DUKE OF EDINBURGH, 1968

Dorothy Hodgkin, 1965.
The Lord Zuckerman, 1968.
Dame Veronica Wedgwood, 1969.
Sir Isaiah Berlin, 1971.
Sir George Edwards, 1971.
Sir Alan Hodgkin, 1973.
The Lord Todd, 1977.
The Lord Franks, 1977.
Revd Prof. Owen Chadwick, KBE, 1983.
Sir Andrew Huxley, 1983.
Sir Sidney Nolan, 1983.
Sir Michael Tippett, 1983.
Frederick Sanger, 1986.
Air Commodore Sir Frank Whittle, 1986.
Sir Yehudi Menuhin, 1987.
Prof. Sir Ernst Gombrich, 1988.
Dr Max Perutz, 1988.
Dame Cicely Saunders, 1989.
The Lord Porter of Luddenham, 1990.
Rt. Hon. Baroness Thatcher, 1990.
Dame Joan Sutherland, 1991.
Prof. Francis Crick, 1991.
Honorary Member, Mother Teresa, 1983.

Secretary and Registrar, Sir Edward Ford, KCB, KCVO, ERD.
Chancery, Central Chancery of the Orders of Knighthood, St James's Palace, London SW1A 1BH.

THE MOST EXALTED ORDER OF THE STAR OF INDIA (1861)

GCSI, Knight Grand Commander
KCSI, Knight Commander
CSI, Companion

Ribbon, Light Blue, with White Edges
Motto, Heaven's Light our Guide

THE SOVEREIGN

Registrar, The Secretary of the Central Chancery of the Orders of Knighthood.
No conferments have been made since 1947.

THE MOST DISTINGUISHED ORDER OF ST MICHAEL AND ST GEORGE (1818)

GCMG KCMG

GCMG, Knight (or Dame) Grand Cross
KCMG, Knight Commander
DCMG, Dame Commander
CMG, Companion

Ribbon, Saxon Blue, with Scarlet centre
Motto, Auspicium melioris aevi (*Token of a better age*)

THE SOVEREIGN

Grand Master, HRH The Duke of Kent, KG, GCMG, GCVO, ADC.
Prelate, The Rt. Revd the Bishop of Coventry.
Chancellor, The Lord Carrington, KG, GCMG, CH, MC, PC.
Secretary, Sir David Gillmore, KCMG.
Registrar, Sir John Graham, Bt., GCMG.
King of Arms, Sir Oliver Wright, GCMG, GCVO, DSC.
Gentleman Usher of the Blue Rod, Sir John Margetson, KCMG.
Dean, The Dean of St Paul's.
Deputy Secretary, The Secretary of the Central Chancery of the Orders of Knighthood.
Chancery, Central Chancery of the Orders of Knighthood, St James's Palace, London SW1A 1BH.

THE MOST EMINENT ORDER OF THE INDIAN EMPIRE (1868)

GCIE, Knight Grand Commander
KCIE, Knight Commander
CIE, Companion

Ribbon, Imperial Purple
Motto, Imperatricis auspiciis (*Under the auspices of the Empress*)

THE SOVEREIGN

Registrar, The Secretary of the Central Chancery of the Orders of Knighthood.
No conferments have been made since 1947.

THE IMPERIAL ORDER OF THE CROWN OF INDIA (1877) FOR LADIES

CI

Badge, the royal cipher in jewels within an oval, surmounted by an Heraldic Crown and attached to a bow of light blue watered ribbon, edged white.
The honour does not confer any rank or title upon the recipient.
No conferments have been made since 1947.

HM The Queen, 1947.
HM Queen Elizabeth The Queen Mother, 1931.
HRH The Princess Margaret, Countess of Snowdon, 1947.
HRH The Princess Alice, Duchess of Gloucester, 1937.
HH Maharani of Travancore, 1929.

THE ROYAL VICTORIAN ORDER (1896)

GCVO KCVO

GCVO, Knight or Dame Grand Cross
KCVO, Knight Commander
DCVO, Dame Commander
CVO, Commander
LVO, Lieutenant
MVO, Member

Ribbon, Blue, with Red and White Edges
Motto, Victoria

THE SOVEREIGN

GRAND MASTER
HM Queen Elizabeth The Queen Mother.
Chancellor, The Lord Chamberlain.
Secretary, The Keeper of the Privy Purse.
Registrar, The Secretary of the Central Chancery of the Orders of Knighthood.
Chaplain, The Revd J. Robson.
Hon. Genealogist, D. H. B. Chesshyre, LVO.

THE MOST EXCELLENT ORDER OF THE BRITISH EMPIRE (1917)

GBE KBE

The Order was divided into Military and Civil divisions in December 1918

GBE, Knight or Dame Grand Cross
KBE, Knight Commander
DBE, Dame Commander
CBE, Commander
OBE, Officer
MBE, Member

Ribbon, Rose pink edged with pearl grey with vertical pearl stripe in centre (Military division); without vertical pearl stripe (Civil division)
Motto, For God and the Empire

THE SOVEREIGN

GRAND MASTER

HRH The Prince Philip, Duke of Edinburgh, KG, KT, OM, GBE, PC, FRS.
Prelate, The Bishop of London.
King of Arms, Admiral Sir Anthony Morton, GBE, KCB.
Registrar, The Secretary of the Central Chancery of the Orders of Knighthood.
Secretary, Sir Robin Butler, GCB, CVO.
Dean, The Dean of St Paul's.
Gentleman Usher of the Purple Rod, Sir Robin Gillett, Bt., GBE, RD.
Chancery, Central Chancery of the Orders of Knighthood, St James's Palace, London SW1A 1BH.

ORDER OF THE COMPANIONS OF HONOUR (1917)

CH

Ribbon, Carmine, with Gold Edges

This Order consists of one class only and carries with it no title. The number of awards is limited to 65 (excluding honorary members)

Anthony, Rt. Hon. John, 1981.
Ashley of Stoke, The Lord, 1975.
Aylestone, The Lord, 1975.
Baker, Rt. Hon. Kenneth, 1992.
Brenner, Sydney, 1986.
Brooke, Rt. Hon. Peter, 1992.
Carrington, The Lord, 1983.
Casson, Sir Hugh, 1984.
Cledwyn of Penrhos, The Lord, 1976.
de Valois, Dame Ninette, 1981.
Eccles, The Viscount, 1984.
Fraser, Rt. Hon. Malcolm, 1977.
Freud, Lucian, 1983.
Frink, Dame Elisabeth, 1992.
Gielgud, Sir John, 1977.
Glenamara, The Lord, 1976.
Goodman, The Lord, 1972.
Gorton, Rt. Hon. Sir John, 1971.
Hailsham of St Marylebone, The Lord, 1974.
Hawking, Prof. Stephen, 1989.
Healey, The Lord, 1979.
Houghton of Sowerby, The Lord, 1967.
Jones, James, 1977.
Joseph, The Lord, 1986.
King, Rt. Hon. Tom, 1992.
Lange, Rt. Hon. David, 1989.
Needham, Joseph, 1992.
Pasmore, Victor, 1980.
Perutz, Prof. Max, 1975.
Popper, Prof. Sir Karl, 1982.
Powell, Anthony, 1987.
Powell, Sir Philip, 1984.
Runciman, Hon. Sir Steven, 1984.
Rylands, George, 1987.
Sanger, Frederick, 1981.
Smith, Arnold Cantwell, 1975.
Somare, Rt. Hon. Sir Michael, 1978.
Summerson, Sir John, 1986.
Talboys, Rt. Hon. Sir Brian, 1981.
Tebbit, The Lord, 1987.
Thorneycroft, The Lord, 1979.
Tippett, Sir Michael, 1979.
Trudeau, Rt. Hon. Pierre, 1984.
Watkinson, The Viscount, 1962.
Whitelaw, The Viscount, 1974.
Honorary Members, Lee Kuan Yew, 1970; Dr Joseph Luns, 1971.

Secretary and Registrar, The Secretary of the Central Chancery of the Orders of Knighthood.

THE DISTINGUISHED SERVICE ORDER (1886)

DSO

Ribbon, Red, with Blue Edges

Bestowed in recognition of especial services in action of commissioned officers in the Navy, Army and Royal Air Force and (since 1942) Mercantile Marine. The members are Companions only. A Bar may be awarded for any additional act of service.

THE IMPERIAL SERVICE ORDER (1902)

ISO

Ribbon, Crimson, with Blue Centre

Appointment as Companion of this Order is open to members of the Civil Services whose eligibility is determined by the grade they hold. The Order consists of The Sovereign and Companions to a number not exceeding 1,900, of whom 1,300 may belong to the Home Civil Services and 600 to Overseas Civil Services.

Secretary, Sir Robin Butler, GCB, CVO.
Registrar, The Secretary of the Central Chancery of the Orders of Knighthood, St James's Palace, London SW1A 1BH.

THE ROYAL VICTORIAN CHAIN (1902)

It confers no precedence on its holders.

HM THE QUEEN

HM Queen Elizabeth The Queen Mother, 1937.
HRH Princess Juliana of the Netherlands, 1950.
HM The King of Thailand, 1960.
HIH The Crown Prince of Ethiopia, 1965.
HM The King of Jordan, 1966.
HM King Zahir Shah of Afghanistan, 1971.
HM The Queen of Denmark, 1974.
HM The King of Nepal, 1975.
HM The King of Sweden, 1975.
The Lord Coggan, 1980.
HM The Queen of the Netherlands, 1982.
General Antonio Eanes, 1985.
HM The King of Spain, 1986.
HM The King of Saudi Arabia, 1987.
HRH The Princess Margaret, Countess of Snowdon, 1990.
The Lord Runcie, 1991.
The Lord Charteris of Amisfield, 1992.
HE François Mitterand, 1992.

Baronetage and Knightage

BARONETS

Style, 'Sir' before forename and surname, followed by 'Bt.'
Wife's style, 'Lady' followed by surname.
For forms of address, *see* page 218.

There are five different creations of Baronetcies: Baronets of England (creations dating from 1611); Baronets of Ireland (creations dating from 1619); Baronets of Scotland or Nova Scotia (creations dating from 1625); Baronets of Great Britain (creations after the Act of Union 1707 which combined the Kingdoms of England and Scotland); and Baronets of the United Kingdom (creations after the union of Great Britain and Ireland in 1801).

Badge of Ulster

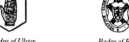

Badge of Baronets of Nova Scotia

Badge of Baronets of the United Kingdom

The patent of creation limits the destination of a baronetcy, usually to male descendants of the first baronet, although special remainders allow the baronetcy to pass, if the male issue of sons fail, to the male issue of daughters of the first baronet. In the case of baronetcies of Scotland or Nova Scotia, a special remainder of 'heirs male and of tailzie' allows the baronetcy to descend to heirs general, including women. There are four existing Scottish baronets with such a remainder, one of whom, the holder of the Dunbar of Hempriggs creation, is a Baronetess.

The Official Roll of Baronets is kept at the Home Office by the Registrar of the Baronetage. Anyone who considers that he is entitled to be entered on the Roll may petition the Crown through the Home Secretary. Every person succeeding to a Baronetcy must exhibit proofs of succession to the Home Secretary. A person whose name is not entered on the Official Roll will not be addressed or mentioned by the title of Baronet in any official document, nor will he be accorded precedence as a Baronet.

BARONETCIES EXTINCT SINCE THE LAST EDITION:
Hamilton (*cr.* 1937); Benn (*cr.* 1920); Fraser (*cr.* 1921); Younger

Registrar of the Baronetage, R. M. Morris.
Assistant Registrar, I. W. Jardine; *Office*, Home Office, Queen Anne's Gate, London SW1H 9AT. Tel: 071-273 3498.

KNIGHTS

Style, 'Sir' before forename and surname, followed by appropriate post-nominal initials if a Knight Grand Cross, Knight Grand Commander or Knight Commander.
Wife's style, 'Lady' followed by surname.
For forms of address, *see* page 218.

The prefix 'Sir' is not used by knights who are clerics of the Church of England, who do not receive the accolade. Their wives are entitled to precedence as the wife of a knight but not to the style of 'Lady'.

ORDERS OF KNIGHTHOOD

Knight Grand Cross, Knight Grand Commander, and Knight Commander are the higher classes of the Orders of Chivalry (*see* pages 174–6). Honorary knighthoods of these Orders may be conferred on men who are citizens of countries of which The Queen is not head of state. As a rule, the prefix 'Sir' is not used by honorary knights.

KNIGHTS BACHELOR

The Knights Bachelor do not constitute a Royal Order, but comprise the surviving representation of the ancient State Orders of Knighthood. The Register of Knights Bachelor, instituted by James I in the 17th century, lapsed, and in 1908 a voluntary association under the title of The Society of Knights (now The Imperial Society of Knights Bachelor by Royal command) was formed with the primary objects of continuing the various registers dating from 1257 and obtaining the uniform registration of every created Knight Bachelor. In 1926 a design for a badge to be worn by Knights Bachelor was approved and adopted, a miniature reproduction being shown above; in 1974 a neck badge and miniature were added.

Knight Principal, Sir Colin Cole, KCVO, TD
Chairman of Council, Sir David Napley
Prelate, Rt. Revd and Rt. Hon. The Bishop of London
Hon. Registrar, Sir Kenneth Newman, GBE, QPM
Hon. Treasurer, The Lord Lane of Horsell
Clerk to the Council, R. M. Esden
Office, 21 Old Buildings, Lincoln's Inn, London WC2A 3UJ.

LIST OF BARONETS AND KNIGHTS

Revised to 31 August 1992

Peers are not included in this list

† Not registered on the Official Roll of the Baronetage at the time of going to press.
() The date of creation of the baronetcy is given in parenthesis.
I Baronet of Ireland.
NS Baronet of Nova Scotia.
S Baronet of Scotland.

If a baronet or knight has a double barrelled or hyphenated surname, he is listed under the final element of the name.

A full entry in italic type indicates that the recipient of a knighthood died during the year in which the honour was conferred. The name is included for purposes of record.

Abal, Sir Tei, Kt., CBE.
Abbott, Sir Albert Francis, Kt., CBE.
Abdy, Sir Valentine Robert Duff, Bt. (1850).
Abel, Sir Seselo (Cecil) Charles Geoffrey, Kt., OBE.
Abeles, Sir (Emil Herbert) Peter, Kt.
Abell, Sir Anthony Foster, KCMG.
Abercromby, Sir Ian George, Bt. (S. 1636).
Abraham, Sir Edward Penley, Kt., CBE, FRS.
Acheson, *Prof.* Sir (Ernest) Donald, KBE.
Ackers, Sir James George, Kt.
Ackroyd, Sir John Robert Whyte, Bt. (1956).
Acland, Sir Antony Arthur, GCMG, GCVO.
Acland, *Maj.* Sir (Christopher) Guy (Dyke), Bt., MVO. (1890).
Acland, Sir John Dyke, Bt. (1644).
Acland, *Maj.-Gen.* Sir John Hugh Bevil, KCB, CBE.
Acton, Sir Harold Mario Mitchell, Kt., CBE.
Adam, Sir Christopher Eric Forbes, Bt. (1917).
Adams, Sir Philip George Doyne, KCMG.
Adams, Sir William James, KCMG.
Adams-Schneider, *Rt. Hon.* Sir Lancelot Raymond, KCMG.
Adamson, Sir (William Owen) Campbell, Kt.
Addison, Sir William Wilkinson, Kt.
Ademola, *Rt. Hon.* Sir Adetokunbo Adegboyega, KBE.
Adrien, *Hon.* Sir Maurice Latour-, Kt.
Agnew, Sir Crispin Hamlyn, Bt. (S. 1629).
Agnew, Sir (John) Anthony Stuart, Bt. (1895).
Agnew, Sir (William) Godfrey, KCVO, CB.
Ah-Chuen, Sir Moi Lin Jean Etienne, Kt.
Aiken, *Air Chief Marshal* Sir John Alexander Carlisle, KCB.
Ainsworth, Sir (Thomas) David, Bt. (1916).
Aird, *Capt.* Sir Alastair Sturgis, KCVO.
Aird, Sir (George) John, Bt. (1901).
Airey, Sir Lawrence, KCB.
Airy, *Maj.-Gen.* Sir Christopher John, KCVO, CBE.
Aisher, Sir Owen Arthur, Kt.
Aitchison, Sir Charles Walter de Lancey, Bt. (1938).
Aitken, Sir Robert Stevenson, Kt., MD, D.Phil.
Akehurst, *Gen.* Sir John Bryan, KCB, CBE.
Akers-Jones, Sir David, KBE, CMG.
Albert, Sir Alexis François, Kt., CMG, VRD.
Albu, Sir George, Bt. (1912).
Alcock, *Air Marshal* Sir (Robert James) Michael, KBE, CB.
Aldous, *Hon.* Sir William, Kt.
Alexander, Sir Alexander Sandor, Kt.
Alexander, Sir Charles Gundry, Bt. (1945).
Alexander, Sir Claud Hagart-, Bt. (1886).
Alexander, Sir Douglas, Bt. (1921).
Alexander, Sir (John) Lindsay, Kt.
Alexander, *Prof.* Sir Kenneth John Wilson, Kt.
Alexander, Sir Michael O'Donal Bjarne, GCMG.
Alexander, Sir Norman Stanley, Kt., CBE.
†Alexander, Sir Patrick Desmond William Cable-, Bt. (1809).
Allan, Sir Anthony James Allan Havelock-, Bt. (1858).
Allan, Sir Colin Hamilton, KCMG, OBE.
Allard, Sir Gordon Laidlaw, Kt.
Allen, *Rear-Adm.* Sir David, KCVO, CBE.
Allen, *Prof.* Sir Geoffrey, Kt., Ph.D., FRS.
Allen, *Hon.* Sir Peter Austin Philip Jermyn, Kt.
Allen, Sir Peter Christopher, Kt.
Allen, Sir Richard Hugh Sedley, KCMG.
Allen, Sir William Guilford, Kt.
Allen, Sir (William) Kenneth (Gwynne), Kt.
Alleyne, Sir George Allanmoore Ogarren, Kt.
Alleyne, *Revd* Sir John Olpherts Campbell, Bt. (1769).
Alliance, Sir David, Kt., CBE.
Allinson, Sir (Walter) Leonard, KCVO, CMG.
Alliott, *Hon.* Sir John Downes, Kt.
Alment, Sir (Edward) Anthony John, Kt.
Althaus, Sir Nigel Frederick, Kt.
Alun-Jones, Sir (John) Derek, Kt.
Ambo, *Rt. Revd* George, KBE.
Amies, Sir (Edwin) Hardy, KCVO.
Amis, Sir Kingsley William, Kt., CBE.
Amory, Sir Ian Heathcoat, Bt. (1874).
Anderson, *Prof.* Sir (James) Norman (Dalrymple), Kt., OBE, QC, FBA.
Anderson, *Maj.-Gen.* Sir John Evelyn, KBE.
Anderson, Sir John Muir, Kt., CMG.
Anderson, Sir Kenneth, KBE, CB.
Anderson, *Hon.* Sir Kevin Victor, Kt.
Anderson, *Vice-Adm.* Sir Neil Dudley, KBE, CB.
Anderson, *Prof.* Sir (William) Ferguson, Kt., OBE.
Anderton, Sir (Cyril) James, Kt., CBE, QPM.
Andrew, Sir Robert John, KCB.
Andrews, Sir Derek Henry, KCB, CBE.
Andrews, *Hon.* Sir Dormer George, Kt.
Angus, Sir Michael Richardson, Kt.
Annesley, Sir Hugh Norman, Kt., QPM.
Ansell, *Col.* Sir Michael Picton, Kt., CBE, DSO.
Anson, *Vice-Adm.* Sir Edward Rosebery, KCB.
Anson, Sir John, KCB.
Anson, *Rear-Adm.* Sir Peter, Bt., CB (1831).
Anstey, *Brig.* Sir John, Kt., CBE, TD.
Anstruther, *Maj.* Sir Ralph Hugo, Bt. GCVO, MC (S. 1694).
Antico, Sir Tristan Venus, Kt.
Antrobus, Sir Philip Coutts, Bt. (1815).
Appleyard, Sir Raymond Kenelm, KBE.
Arbuthnot, Sir Keith Robert Charles, Bt. (1823).
†Arbuthnot, Sir William Reierson, Bt. (1964).
Archdale, *Capt.* Sir Edward Folmer, Bt., DSC, RN (1928).
Archer, *Gen.* Sir (Arthur) John, KCB, OBE.
Archer, Sir Clyde Vernon Harcourt, Kt.
Arculus, Sir Ronald, KCMG, KCVO.
Armitage, *Air Chief Marshal* Sir Michael John, KCB, CBE.
Armstrong, Sir Andrew Clarence Francis, Bt., CMG (1841).
Armstrong, Sir Thomas Henry Wait, Kt., D.Mus..
Armytage, Sir John Martin, Bt. (1738).
Arnold, *Rt. Hon.* Sir John Lewis, Kt.
Arnold, Sir Thomas Richard, Kt., MP.
Arnott, Sir Alexander John Maxwell, Bt. (1896).
Arnott, *Prof.* Sir (William) Melville, Kt., TD, MD.
Arrindell, Sir Clement Athelston, GCMG, GCVO, QC.
Arthur, *Lt.-Gen.* Sir (John) Norman Stewart, KCB.
Arthur, Sir Stephen John, Bt. (1841).
Ash, *Prof.* Sir Eric Albert, Kt., CBE, FRS, FEng.
Ashburnham, Sir Denny Reginald, Bt. (1661).
Ashe, Sir Derick Rosslyn, KCMG.
Ashley, Sir Bernard Albert, Kt.
Ashmore, *Admiral of the Fleet* Sir Edward Beckwith, GCB, DSC.
Ashmore, *Vice-Adm.* Sir Peter William Beckwith, KCB, KCVO, DSC.
Ashworth, Sir Herbert, Kt.
Aske, *Revd* Sir Conan, Bt. (1922).
Askew, Sir Bryan, Kt.
Asscher, Prof. (Adolf) William, Kt., MD, FRCP
Astley, Sir Francis Jacob Dugdale, Bt. (1821).
Aston, Sir Harold George, Kt., CBE.
Aston, *Hon.* Sir William John, KCMG.
Astor, *Hon.* Sir John Jacob, Kt., MBE.
Astwood, *Hon.* Sir James Rufus, Kt.
Astwood, *Lt.-Col.* Sir Jeffrey Carlton, Kt., CBE, ED.
Atcherley, Sir Harold Winter, Kt.
Atiyah, Sir Michael Francis, Kt., Ph.D., FRS.

Atkinson, *Air Marshal* Sir David William, KBE.
Atkinson, Sir Frederick John, KCB.
Atkinson, Sir John Alexander, KCB, DFC.
Atkinson, Sir Robert, Kt., DSC, FEng.
Attenborough, Sir David Frederick, Kt., CVO, CBE, FRS.
Attenborough, Sir Richard Samuel, Kt., CBE.
Atwell, Sir John William, Kt., CBE, FRSE, FEng.
Atwill, Sir (Milton) John (Napier), Kt.
Audland, Sir Christopher John, KCMG.
Audley, Sir George Bernard, Kt.
Auld, *Hon.* Sir Robin Ernest, Kt.
Austin, Sir Michael Trescawen, Bt. (1894).
Austin, *Vice-Adm.* Sir Peter Murray, KCB.
Austin, *Air Marshal* Sir Roger Mark, KCB, AFC.
Aykroyd, Sir Cecil William, Bt. (1929).
Aykroyd, Sir William Miles, Bt., MC (1920).
Aylmer, Sir Richard John, Bt. (I. 1622).
Bacha, Sir Bhinod, Kt., CMG.
Backhouse, Sir Jonathan Roger, Bt. (1901).
Bacon, Sir Nicholas Hickman Ponsonby, Bt. *Premier Baronet of England* (1611 and 1627).
Bacon, Sir Sidney Charles, Kt., CB, FEng.
Baddeley, Sir John Wolsey Beresford, Bt. (1922).
Baddiley, *Prof.* Sir James, Kt., Ph.D., D.SC., FRS, FRSE.
Badenoch, Sir John, Kt., DM, FRCP.
Badger, Sir Geoffrey Malcolm, Kt.
Bagge, Sir (John) Jeremy Picton, Bt. (1867).
Bagnall, *Field Marshal* Sir Nigel Thomas, GCB, CVO, MC.
Bailey, Sir Alan Marshall, KCB.
Bailey, Sir Brian Harry, Kt., OBE.
Bailey, Sir Derrick Thomas Louis, Bt., DFC (1919).
Bailey, *Prof.* Sir Harold Walter, Kt., D.Phil., FBA.
Bailey, Sir John Bilsland, KCB.
Bailey, Sir Richard John, Kt., CBE.
Bailey, Sir Stanley Ernest, Kt., CBE, QPM.
Baillie, Sir Gawaine George Hope, Bt. (1823).
Baines, *Prof.* Sir George Grenfell-, Kt., OBE.
Baird, Sir David Charles, Bt. (1809).
Baird, *Lt.-Gen.* Sir James Parlane, KBE, MD.
Baird, Sir James Richard Gardiner, Bt., MC (S. 1695).
Baird, *Vice-Adm.* Sir Thomas Henry Eustace, KCB.
Bairsto, *Air Marshal* Sir Peter Edward, KBE, CB.
Baker, Sir (Allan) Ivor, Kt., CBE.
Baker, Sir Robert George Humphrey Sherston-, Bt. (1796).
Baker, *Hon.* Sir (Thomas) Scott (Gillespie), Kt.
Balcombe, *Rt. Hon.* Sir (Alfred) John, Kt.
Balderstone, Sir James Schofield, Kt.
Baldwin, Sir Peter Robert, KCB.
Balfour, *Gen.* Sir (Robert George) Victor FitzGeorge-, KCB, CBE, DSO, MC.
Ball, *Air Marshal* Sir Alfred Henry Wynne, KCB, DSO, DFC.
Ball, Sir Charles Irwin, Bt. (1911).
Ball, Sir Christopher John Elinger, Kt.
Ball, *Prof.* Sir Robert James, Kt., Ph.D.
Balmer, Sir Joseph Reginald, Kt.
Bamford, Sir Anthony Paul, Kt.
Banham, Sir John Michael Middlecott, Kt.
Bannerman, Sir David Gordon, Bt., OBE (S. 1682).
Bannister, Sir Roger Gilbert, Kt., CBE, DM, FRCP.
Barber, *Hon.* Sir (Edward Hamilton) Esler, Kt.
Barber, Sir William Francis, Bt., TD (1960).
Barbour, *Very Revd* Sir Robert Alexander Stewart, KCVO, MC.
Barclay, Sir Colville Herbert Sanford, Bt. (S. 1668).
Barclay, Sir Peter Maurice, Kt., CBE.
Barclay, Sir Roderick Edward, GCVO, KCMG.
Barder, Sir Brian Leon, KCMG.
Baring, *Hon.* Sir John Francis Harcourt, Kt., KCVO.
Barker, Sir Alwyn Bowman, Kt., CMG.
Barker, Sir Colin, Kt.
Barker, Sir Harry Heaton, Kt., KBE.
Barlow, Sir Christopher Hilaro, Bt. (1803).
Barlow, Sir (George) William, Kt., FEng.
Barlow, Sir John Kemp, Bt. (1907).
Barlow, Sir Thomas Erasmus, Bt., DSC (1902).
Barnard, Sir (Arthur) Thomas, Kt., CB, OBE.
Barnard, *Capt.* Sir George Edward, Kt.
Barnard, Sir Joseph Brian, Kt.
Barnes, Sir James George, Kt., MBE.
Barnes, Sir Kenneth, KCB.
Barnett, *Air Chief Marshal* Sir Denis Hensley Fulton, GCB, CBE, DFC.
Barnett, Sir Oliver Charles, Kt., CBE, QC.
Barnewall, Sir Reginald Robert, Bt. (I. 1623).
Baron, Sir Thomas, Kt., CBE.
Barraclough, *Air Chief Marshal* Sir John, KCB, CBE, DFC, AFC.
Barraclough, Sir Kenneth James Priestley, Kt., CBE, TD.
Barran, Sir David Haven, Kt.
Barran, Sir John Napoleon Ruthven, Bt. (1895).
Barratt, Sir Lawrence Arthur, Kt.
Barratt, Sir Richard Stanley, Kt., CBE, QPM.
Barrett, *Lt.-Gen.* Sir David William Scott-, KBE, MC.
Barrett, *Lt.-Col.* Sir Dennis Charles Titchener, Kt., TD.
Barrett, Sir Stephen Jeremy, KCMG.
Barrington, Sir Alexander (Fitzwilliam Croker), Bt. (1831).
Barrington, Sir Nicholas John, KCMG, CVO.
Barron, Sir Donald James, Kt.
Barrow, *Capt.* Sir Richard John Uniacke, Bt. (1835).
Barrowclough, Sir Anthony Richard, Kt., QC.
Barry, Sir (Lawrence) Edward (Anthony Tress), Bt. (1899).
Barry, Sir (Philip) Stuart Milner-, KCVO, CB, OBE.
Bartlett, Sir John Hardington, Bt. (1913).
Barton, *Prof.* Sir Derek Harold Richard, Kt., FRS, FRSE.
Barttelot, *Lt.-Col.* Sir Brian Walter de Stopham, Bt., OBE (1875).
Barwick, *Rt. Hon.* Sir Garfield Edward John, GCMG.
Basten, Sir Henry Bolton, Kt., CMG.
Batchelor, Sir Ivor Ralph Campbell, Kt., CBE.
Bate, Sir David Lindsay, KBE.
Bate, Sir (Walter) Edwin, Kt., OBE.
Bateman, Sir Cecil Joseph, KBE.
Bateman, Sir Geoffrey Hirst, Kt., FRCS.
Bateman, Sir Ralph Melton, KBE.
Bates, *Prof.* Sir David Robert, Kt., D.SC., FRS.
Bates, Sir Geoffrey Voltelin, Bt., MC (1880).
Bates, Sir John David, Kt., CBE, VRD.
Bates, Sir (John) Dawson, Bt., MC (1937).
Batho, Sir Peter Ghislain, Bt. (1928).
Bathurst, *Adm.* Sir (David) Benjamin, GCB.
Bathurst, Sir Frederick Peter Methuen Hervey-, Bt. (1818).
Bathurst, Sir Maurice Edward, Kt., CMG, CBE, QC.
Batten, Sir John Charles, KCVO.
Battersby, Prof. Sir Alan Rushton, Kt., FRS.
Battishill, Sir Anthony Michael William, KCB.
Batty, Sir William Bradshaw, Kt., TD.
Baxendell, Sir Peter Brian, Kt., CBE, FEng.
Bayliss, *Prof.* Sir Noel Stanley, Kt., CBE.
Bayliss, Sir Richard Ian Samuel, KCVO, MD, FRCP.
Bayly, *Vice-Adm.* Sir Patrick Uniacke, KBE, CB, DSC.
Bayne, Sir Nicholas Peter, KCMG.
Baynes, Sir John Christopher Malcolm, Bt. (1801).
Bazley, Sir Thomas Stafford, Bt. (1869).

Beach, *Gen.* Sir (William Gerald) Hugh, GBE, KCB, MC.
Beale, *Lt.-Gen.* Sir Peter John, KBE, FRCP.
Beament, Sir James William Longman, Kt., SC.D., FRS.
Beattie, *Hon.* Sir Alexander Craig, Kt.
Beattie, *Hon.* Sir David Stuart, GCMG, GCVO.
Beauchamp, Sir Christopher Radstock Proctor-, Bt. (1745).
Beaumont, Sir George (Howland Francis), Bt. (1661).
Beaumont, Sir Richard Ashton, KCMG, OBE.
Beavis, *Air Chief Marshal* Sir Michael Gordon, KCB, CBE, AFC.
Becher, Sir William Fane Wrixon, Bt., MC (1831).
Beck, Sir Edgar Charles, Kt., CBE, FEng.
Beck, Sir Edgar Philip, Kt.
Beckett, *Capt.* Sir (Martyn) Gervase, Bt., MC (1921).
Beckett, Sir Terence Norman, Kt., KBE, FEng.
Bedbrook, Sir George Montario, Kt., OBE.
Bedingfeld, *Capt.* Sir Edmund George Felix Paston-, Bt. (1661).
Beecham, Sir John Stratford Roland, Bt. (1914).
Beeley, Sir Harold, KCMG, CBE.
Beetham, *Marshal of the Royal Air Force* Sir Michael James, GCB, CBE, DFC, AFC.
Beevor, Sir Thomas Agnew, Bt. (1784).
Begg, Sir Neil Colquhoun, KBE.
Begg, *Admiral of the Fleet* Sir Varyl Cargill, GCB, DSO, DSC.
Beit, Sir Alfred Lane, Bt. (1924).
Beith, Sir John Greville Stanley, KCMG.
Belch, Sir Alexander Ross, Kt., CBE, FRSE.
Beldam, *Rt. Hon.* Sir (Alexander) Roy (Asplan), Kt.
Belich, Sir James, Kt.
Bell, Sir Gawain Westray, KCMG, CBE.
Bell, Sir (George) Raymond, KCMG, CB.
Bell, Sir John Lowthian, Bt. (1885).
Bell, Sir Timothy John Leigh, Kt.
Bell, Sir (William) Ewart, KCB.
Bell, Sir William Hollin Dayrell Morrison-, Bt. (1905).
Bellew, Hon. Sir George Rothe, KCB, KCVO, FSA.
Bellew, Sir Henry Charles Gratton-, Bt. (1838).
Bellinger, Sir Robert Ian, GBE.
Bellingham, Sir Noel Peter Roger, Bt. (1796).
Bengough, *Col.* Sir Piers, KCVO, OBE.
Benn, Sir (James) Jonathan, Bt. (1914).
Bennett, Sir Charles Moihi Te Arawaka, Kt., DSO.
Bennett, *Air Vice-Marshal* Sir Erik Peter, KBE, CB.
Bennett, *Rt. Hon.* Sir Frederic Mackarness, Kt.
Bennett, Sir Hubert, Kt.
Bennett, Sir John Mokonuiarangi, Kt.
Bennett, *Gen.* Sir Phillip Harvey, KBE, DSO.
Bennett, Sir Reginald Frederick Brittain, Kt., VRD.
Bennett, Sir Ronald Wilfrid Murdoch, Bt. (1929).
Benson, Sir Christopher John, Kt.
Benson, Sir (William) Jeffrey, Kt.
Bentley, Sir William, KCMG.
Beresford, Sir (Alexander) Paul, Kt., MP.
Berger, *Vice-Adm.* Sir Peter Egerton Capel, KCB, MVO, DSC.
Berghuser, *Hon.* Sir Eric, Kt., MBE.
Berlin, Sir Isaiah, Kt., OM, CBE.
Bernard, Sir Dallas Edmund, Bt. (1954).
Berney, Sir Julian Reedham Stuart, Bt. (1620).
Berrill, Sir Kenneth Ernest, GBE, KCB.
Berriman, Sir David, Kt.
Berthon, *Vice-Adm.* Sir Stephen Ferrier, KCB.
Berthoud, Sir Martin Seymour, KCVO, CMG.
Best, Sir Richard Radford, KCVO, CBE.
Bethune, Sir Alexander Maitland Sharp, Bt. (S. 1683).
Bethune, *Hon.* Sir (Walter) Angus, Kt.
Bevan, Sir Martyn Evan Evans, Bt. (1958).
Bevan, Sir Timothy Hugh, Kt.
Beverley, *Lt.-Gen.* Sir Henry York La Roche, KCB, OBE, RM.
Beynon, *Prof.* Sir (William John) Granville, Kt., CBE, Ph.D., D.SC., FRS.
Bibby, Sir Derek James, Bt., MC (1959).
Bickersteth, *Rt. Revd* John Monier, KCVO.
Biddulph, Sir Ian D'Olier, Bt. (1664).
Bide, Sir Austin Ernest, Kt.
Bidwell, Sir Hugh Charles Philip, GBE.
Biggs, Sir Norman Paris, Kt.
Billière, *Gen.* Sir Peter Edgar de la Cour de la, KCB, KBE, DSO, MC.
Bing, Sir Rudolf Franz Josef, KBE.
Bingham, *Hon.* Sir Eardley Max, Kt., QC.
Bingham, *Rt. Hon.* Sir Thomas Henry, Kt.
Birch, Sir Roger, Kt., CBE, QPM.
Bird, *Col.* Sir Richard Dawnay Martin-, Kt., CBE, TD.
Bird, Sir Richard Geoffrey Chapman, Bt. (1922).
Birkin, Sir John Christian William, Bt. (1905).
Birkin, Sir (John) Derek, Kt., TD.
Birkmyre, Sir Archibald, Bt. (1921).
Birley, Sir Derek Sydney, Kt.
Birtwistle, Sir Harrison, Kt.
Bishop, Sir Frederick Arthur, Kt., CB, CVO.
Bishop, Sir George Sidney, Kt., CB, OBE.
Bishop, Sir Michael David, Kt., CBE.
Bisson, *Rt Hon.* Sir Gordon Ellis, Kt.
Black, *Prof.* Sir Douglas Andrew Kilgour, Kt., MD, FRCP.
Black, Sir James Whyte, Kt., FRCP, FRS.
Black, *Adm.* Sir (John) Jeremy, GCB, DSO, MBE.
Black, Sir Robert Brown, GCMG, OBE.
Black, Sir Robert David, Bt. (1922).
Blacker, *Lt.-Gen.* Sir (Anthony Stephen) Jeremy, KCB, CBE.
Blacker, *Gen.* Sir Cecil Hugh, GCB, OBE, MC.
Blackett, Sir George William, Bt. (1673).
Blackman, Sir Frank Milton, KCVO, OBE.
Blackwell, Sir Basil Davenport, Kt, FEng.
Blair, Sir Alastair Campbell, KCVO, TD, WS.
Blair, *Lt.-Gen.* Sir Chandos, KCVO, OBE, MC.
Blair, Sir Edward Thomas Hunter, Bt. (1786).
Blake, Sir Alfred Lapthorn, KCVO, MC.
Blake, Sir Francis Michael, Bt. (1907).
Blake, Sir (Thomas) Richard (Valentine), Bt. (I. 1622).
Blaker, Sir John, Bt. (1919).
Blaker, *Rt. Hon.* Sir Peter Allan Renshaw, KCMG.
Blakiston, Sir Ferguson Arthur James, Bt. (1763).
Bland, Sir Henry Armand, Kt., CBE.
Bland, *Lt.-Col.* Sir Simon Claud Michael, KCVO.
Blelloch, Sir John Nial Henderson, KCB.
Blennerhassett, Sir (Marmaduke) Adrian Francis William, Bt. (1809).
Blewitt, *Maj.* Sir Shane Gabriel Basil, KCVO.
Blofield, *Hon.* Sir John Christopher Calthorpe, Kt.
Blois, Sir Charles Nicholas Gervase, Bt. (1686).
Blomefield, Sir Thomas Charles Peregrine, Bt. (1807).
Bloomfield, Sir Kenneth Percy, KCB.
Blosse, *Capt.* Sir Richard Hely Lynch-, Bt. (1622).
Blount, Sir Walter Edward Alpin, Bt., DSC (1642).
Blundell, Sir Michael, KBE.
Blunden, Sir George, Kt.
Blunden, Sir Philip Overington, Bt. (I. 1766).
Blunt, Sir David Richard Reginald Harvey, Bt. (1720).
Blyth, Sir James, Kt.
Boardman, *Prof.* Sir John, Kt., FSA, FBA.
Boardman, Sir Kenneth Ormrod, Kt.
Bodilly, *Hon.* Sir Jocelyn, Kt., VRD.
Bodmer, Sir Walter Fred, Kt., Ph.D., FRS.

Body, Sir Richard Bernard Frank Stewart, Kt., MP.
Boevey, Sir Thomas Michael Blake Crawley-, Bt. (1784).
Bogarde, Sir Dirk (Derek Niven van den Bogaerde), Kt.
Boileau, Sir Guy (Francis), Bt. (1838).
Boles, Sir Jeremy John Fortescue, Bt. (1922).
Boles, Sir John Dennis, Kt., MBE.
Bolland, Sir Edwin, KCMG.
Bollers, *Hon.* Sir Harold Brodie Smith, Kt.
Bolton, Sir Frederic Bernard, Kt., MC.
Bonallack, Sir Richard Frank, Kt., CBE.
Bonar, Sir Herbert Vernon, Kt., CBE.
Bond, Sir Kenneth Raymond Boyden, Kt.
Bondi, *Prof.* Sir Hermann, KCB, FRS.
Bonham, *Maj.* Sir Antony Lionel Thomas, Bt. (1852).
Bonsall, Sir Arthur Wilfred, KCMG, CBE.
Bonsor, Sir Nicholas Cosmo, Bt., MP (1925).
Boolell, Sir Satcam, Kt.
Boon, Sir Peter Coleman, Kt.
Boord, Sir Nicolas John Charles, Bt. (1896).
Boorman, *Lt.-Gen.* Sir Derek, KCB.
Booth, Sir Angus Josslyn Gore-, Bt. (I. 1760).
Booth, Sir Christopher Charles, Kt., MD, FRCP.
Booth, Sir Douglas Allen, Bt. (1916).
Booth, Sir Gordon, KCMG, CVO.
Booth, Sir Robert Camm, Kt., CBE, TD.
Boothby, Sir Brooke Charles, Bt. (1660).
Boreel, Sir Francis David, Bt. (1645).
Boreham, Sir (Arthur) John, KCB.
Boreham, *Hon.* Sir Leslie Kenneth Edward, Kt.
Bornu, The Waziri of, KCMG, CBE.
Borrie, Sir Gordon Johnson, Kt., QC.
Borthwick, Sir John Thomas, Bt. MBE (1908).
Bossom, *Hon.* Sir Clive, Bt. (1953).
Boswall, Sir (Thomas) Alford Houstoun-, Bt. (1836).
Boswell, *Lt.-Gen.* Sir Alexander Crawford Simpson, KCB, CBE.
Bosworth, Sir Neville Bruce Alfred, Kt., CBE.
Bottomley, Sir James Reginald Alfred, KCMG.
Boughey, Sir John George Fletcher, Bt. (1798).
Boulton, Sir Clifford John, KCB.
Boulton, Sir (Harold Hugh) Christian, Bt. (1905).
Boulton, Sir William Whytehead, Bt., CBE, TD (1944).
Bourn, Sir John Bryant, KCB.
Bourne, Sir (John) Wilfrid, KCB.
Bovell, *Hon.* Sir (William) Stewart, Kt.
Bowater, Sir Euan David Vansittart, Bt. (1939).
Bowater, Sir (John) Vansittart, Bt. (1914).
Bowden, Sir Frank, Bt. (1915).
Bowen, Sir Geoffrey Fraser, Kt.
Bowen, Sir Mark Edward Mortimer, Bt. (1921).
Bowen, *Hon.* Sir Nigel Hubert, KBE.
Bowlby, Sir Anthony Hugh Mostyn, Bt. (1923).
Bowman, Sir George, Bt. (1961).
Bowman, Sir Jeffery Haverstock, Kt.
Bowman, Sir John Paget, Bt. (1884).
Bowmar, Sir Charles Erskine, Kt.
Bowness, Sir Alan, Kt., CBE.
Bowness, Sir Peter Spencer, Kt., CBE.
Boxer, *Air Vice-Marshal* Sir Alan Hunter Cachemaille, KCVO, CB, DSO, DFC.
Boyce, Sir Robert Charles Leslie, Bt. (1952).
Boyd, Sir Alexander Walter, Bt. (1916).
Boyd, Sir John Dixon Iklé, KCMG.
Boyd, Sir (John) Francis, Kt.
Boyd, *Prof.* Sir Robert Lewis Fullarton, Kt., CBE, D.SC., FRS.
Boyes, Sir Brian Gerald Barratt-, KBE.
Boyle, *Marshal of the Royal Air Force* Sir Dermot Alexander, GCB, KCVO, KBE, AFC.
Boyle, Sir Stephen Gurney, Bt. (1904).
Boyne, Sir Henry Brian, Kt., CBE.
Boynton, Sir John Keyworth, Kt., MC.
Boyson, *Rt. Hon.* Sir Rhodes, Kt., MP.
Brabham, Sir John Arthur, Kt., OBE.
Bradbeer, Sir John Derek Richardson, Kt., OBE, TD.
Bradbury, *Surgeon Vice-Adm.* Sir Eric Blackburn, KBE, CB.
Bradford, Sir Edward Alexander Slade, Bt. (1902).
Bradley, Sir Burton Gyrth Burton-, Kt., OBE.
Bradman, Sir Donald George, Kt.
Bradshaw, Sir Kenneth Anthony, KCB.
Bradshaw, *Lt.-Gen.* Sir Richard Phillip, KBE.
Brain, Sir (Henry) Norman, KBE, CMG.
Braithwaite, Sir (Joseph) Franklin Madders, Kt.
Braithwaite, Sir Rodric Quentin, KCMG.
Bramall, Sir (Ernest) Ashley, Kt.
Bramley, *Prof.* Sir Paul Anthony, Kt.
Branch, Sir William Allan Patrick, Kt.
Brancker, Sir (John Eustace) Theodore, Kt., QC.
Branigan, Sir Patrick Francis, Kt., QC.
Bray, Sir Theodor Charles, Kt., CBE.
Braynen, Sir Alvin Rudolph, Kt.
Bremridge, Sir John Henry, KBE.
Brennan, *Hon.* Sir (Francis) Gerard, KBE.
Brett, Sir Charles Edward Bainbridge, Kt., CBE.
Brickwood, Sir Basil Greame, Bt. (1927).
Bridges, *Hon.* Sir Phillip Rodney, Kt., CMG.
Brierley, Sir Ronald Alfred, Kt.
Brierley, Sir Zachry, Kt., CBE.
Briggs, *Hon.* Sir Geoffrey Gould, Kt.
Bright, Sir Keith, Kt.
Brinckman, Sir Theodore George Roderick, Bt. (1831).
Brisco, Sir Donald Gilfrid, Bt. (1782).
Briscoe, Sir John Leigh Charlton, Bt., DFC (1910).
Brise, Sir John Archibald Ruggles-, Bt., CB, OBE, TD (1935).
Bristow, *Hon.* Sir Peter Henry Rowley, Kt.
Brittan, *Rt. Hon.* Sir Leon, Kt., QC.
Britton, Sir Edward Louis, Kt., CBE.
Broackes, Sir Nigel, Kt.
†Broadbent, Sir Andrew George, Bt. (1893).
Broadbent, Sir Ewen, KCB, CMG.
Broadhurst, *Air Chief Marshal* Sir Harry, GCB, KBE, DSO, DFC, AFC.
Brockhoff, Sir Jack Stuart, Kt.
Brocklebank, Sir Aubrey Thomas, Bt. (1885).
Brockman, *Vice-Adm.* Sir Ronald Vernon, KCB, CVO, CSI, CIE, CBE.
Brockman, *Hon.* Sir Thomas Charles Drake-, Kt., DFC.
Brodie, Sir Benjamin David Ross, Bt. (1834).
Brogan, *Lt.-Gen.* Sir Mervyn Francis, KBE, CB.
Bromhead, Sir John Desmond Gonville, Bt. (1806).
Bromley, Sir Rupert Charles, Bt. (1757).
Bromley, Sir Thomas Eardley, KCMG.
Brook, Sir Robin, Kt., CMG, OBE.
†Brooke, Sir Alistair Weston, Bt. (1919).
Brooke, Sir Francis George Windham, Bt. (1903).
Brooke, *Hon.* Sir Henry, Kt.
Brooke, Sir Richard Neville, Bt. (1662).
Brookes, Sir Wilfred Deakin, Kt., CBE, DSO.
Brooksbank, Sir (Edward) Nicholas, Bt. (1919).
Broom, *Air Marshal* Sir Ivor Gordon, KCB, CBE, DSO, DFC, AFC.
Broughton, *Air Marshal* Sir Charles, KBE, CB.
Broughton, Sir Evelyn Delves, Bt. (1661).
Broun, Sir Lionel John Law, Bt. (S. 1686).
Brown, Sir Allen Stanley, Kt., CBE.
Brown, Sir (Arthur James) Stephen, KBE.
Brown, *Adm.* Sir Brian Thomas, KCB, CBE.
Brown, *Lt.-Col.* Sir Charles Frederick Richmond, Bt. (1863).
Brown, Sir (Cyril) Maxwell Palmer, KCB, CMG.
Brown, Sir David, Kt.
Brown, *Vice-Adm.* Sir David Worthington, KCB.
Brown, Sir Derrick Holden-, Kt.
Brown, Sir Douglas Denison, Kt.

Brown, *Hon.* Sir Douglas Dunlop, Kt.
Brown, *Prof.* Sir (Ernest) Henry Phelps, Kt., MBE, FBA.
Brown, Sir (Frederick Herbert) Stanley, Kt., CBE, FEng.
Brown, *Prof.* Sir (George) Malcolm, Kt., FRS.
Brown, Sir George Noel, Kt.
Brown, Sir John Douglas Keith, Kt.
Brown, Sir John Gilbert Newton, Kt., CBE.
Brown, Sir Mervyn, KCMG, OBE.
Brown, *Hon.* Sir Ralph Kilner, Kt., OBE, TD.
Brown, Sir Robert Crichton-, KCMG, CBE, TD.
Brown, *Hon.* Sir Simon Denis, Kt.
Brown, *Rt. Hon.* Sir Stephen, Kt.
Brown, Sir Thomas, Kt.
Brown, Sir William Brian Piggott-, Bt. (1903).
Browne, *Rt. Hon.* Sir Patrick Reginald Evelyn, Kt., OBE, TD.
Brownrigg, Sir Nicholas (Gawen), Bt. (1816).
Bruce, Sir (Francis) Michael Ian, Bt. (S. 1628).
Bruce, Sir Hervey James Hugh, Bt. (1804).
Bruce, *Rt. Hon.* Sir (James) Roualeyn Hovell-Thurlow-Cumming-, Kt.
Brunner, Sir John Henry Kilian, Bt. (1895).
Brunton, Sir (Edward Francis) Lauder, Bt. (1908).
Brunton, Sir Gordon Charles, Kt.
Bryan, Sir Arthur, Kt.
Bryan, Sir Paul Elmore Oliver, Kt., DSO, MC.
Bryce, *Hon.* Sir (William) Gordon, Kt., CBE.
Bryson, *Adm.* Sir Lindsay Sutherland, KCB, FEng.
Buchan, Sir John, Kt., CMG.
Buchanan, Sir Andrew George, Bt. (1878).
Buchanan, Sir Charles Alexander James Leith-, Bt. (1775).
Buchanan, *Prof.* Sir Colin Douglas, Kt., CBE.
Buchanan, *Vice-Adm.* Sir Peter William, KBE.
Buchanan, Sir Robert Wilson (Robin), Kt.
Buchanan, Sir (Ranald) Dennis, Kt., MBE.
Buck, Sir (Philip) Antony (Fyson), Kt., QC.
Buckley, *Rt. Hon.* Sir Denys Burton, Kt., MBE.
Buckley, Sir John William, Kt.
Buckley, *Lt.-Cdr.* Sir (Peter) Richard, KCVO.
Buckley, *Hon.* Sir Roger John, Kt.
Bulkeley, Sir Richard Thomas Williams-, Bt. (1661).
Bull, Sir Simeon George, Bt. (1922).
Bull, Sir Walter Edward Avenon, KCVO.
Bullard, Sir Giles Lionel, KCVO, CMG.
Bullard, Sir Julian Leonard, GCMG.
Bullus, Sir Eric Edward, Kt.
Bulmer, Sir William Peter, Kt.
Bultin, Sir Bato, Kt., MBE.
Bunbury, Sir Michael William, Bt. (1681).
Bunbury, Sir (Richard David) Michael Richardson-, Bt. (I. 1787).
Bunch, Sir Austin Wyeth, Kt., CBE.
Bunting, Sir (Edward) John, KBE.
Bunyard, Sir Robert Sidney, Kt., CBE, QPM.
Burbidge, Sir Herbert Dudley, Bt. (1916).
Burbury, *Hon.* Sir Stanley Charles, KCMG, KCVO, KBE.
Burdett, Sir Savile Aylmer, Bt. (1665).
Burgen, Sir Arnold Stanley Vincent, Kt., FRS.
Burgess, *Gen.* Sir Edward Arthur, KCB, OBE.
Burgh, Sir John Charles, KCMG, CB.
Burke, Sir James Stanley Gilbert, Bt. (I. 1797).
Burke, Sir (Thomas) Kerry, Kt.
Burley, Sir Victor George, Kt., CBE.
Burman, Sir (John) Charles, Kt.
Burman, Sir Stephen France, Kt., CBE.
Burnet, Sir James William Alexander (Sir Alastair Burnet), Kt.
Burnett, *Air Chief Marshal* Sir Brian Kenyon, GCB, DFC, AFC.
Burnett, Sir David Humphery, Bt., MBE, TD (1913).
Burnett, Sir John Harrison, Kt.
Burnett, Sir Walter John, Kt.
Burney, Sir Cecil Denniston, Bt. (1921).
Burns, Sir Terence, Kt.
Burns, *Maj.-Gen.* Sir (Walter Arthur) George, GCVO, CB, DSO, OBE, MC.
Burrell, Sir John Raymond, Bt. (1774).
Burrenchobay, Sir Dayendranath, KBE, CMG, CVO.
Burrows, Sir Bernard Alexander Brocas, GCMG.
Burston, Sir Samuel Gerald Wood, Kt., OBE.
Burt, *Hon.* Sir Francis Theodore Page, KCMG.
Burton, Sir Carlisle Archibald, Kt., OBE.
Burton, Sir George Vernon Kennedy, Kt., CBE.
Burton, *Air Marshal* Sir Harry, KCB, CBE, DSO.
Busby, Sir Matthew, Kt., CBE.
Bush, *Adm.* Sir John Fitzroy Duyland, GCB, DSC.
Butler, *Rt. Hon.* Sir Adam Courtauld, Kt.
Butler, Sir Clifford Charles, Kt., Ph.D., FRS.
Butler, Sir (Frederick) (Edward) Robin, GCB, CVO.
Butler, Sir Michael Dacres, GCMG.
Butler, Sir (Reginald) Michael (Thomas), Bt. (1922).
Butler, *Hon.* Sir Richard Clive, Kt.
Butler, *Col.* Sir Thomas Pierce, Bt., CVO, DSO, OBE (1628).
Butt, Sir (Alfred) Kenneth Dudley, Bt. (1929).
Butter, *Maj.* Sir David Henry, KCVO, MC.
Butterworth, Sir (George) Neville, Kt.
Buxton, Sir Thomas Fowell Victor, Bt. (1840).
Buzzard, Sir Anthony Farquhar, Bt. (1929).
Byatt, Sir Hugh Campbell, KCVO, CMG.
Byers, Sir Maurice Hearne, Kt., CBE, QC.
Byford, Sir Lawrence, Kt., CBE, QPM.
Byrne, Sir Clarence Askew, Kt., OBE, DSC.
Cable, Sir James Eric, KCVO, CMG.
Cadbury, Sir (George) Adrian (Hayhurst), Kt.
Cadell, *Vice-Adm.* Sir John Frederick, KBE.
Cadogan, *Prof.* Sir John Ivan George, Kt., CBE, FRS, FRSE.
Cadwallader, Sir John, Kt.
Cahn, Sir Albert Jonas, Bt. (1934).
Cain, Sir Edward Thomas, Kt., CBE.
Cain, Sir Henry Edney Conrad, Kt.
Caine, Sir Michael Harris, Kt.
Caines, Sir John, KCB.
Cairncross, Sir Alexander Kirkland, KCMG.
Calcutt, Sir David Charles, Kt., QC.
Calderwood, Sir Robert, Kt.
Caldwell, *Surgeon Vice-Adm.* Sir (Eric) Dick, KBE, CB.
Callaghan, Sir Allan Robert, Kt., CMG.
Callaghan, Sir Bede Bertrand, Kt., CBE.
Callard, Sir Eric John, Kt., FEng.
Callaway, *Prof.* Sir Frank Adams, Kt., CMG, OBE.
Calley, Sir Henry Algernon, Kt., DSO, DFC.
Callinan, Sir Bernard James, Kt., CBE, DSO, MC.
Calne, *Prof.* Sir Roy Yorke, Kt., FRS.
Calthorpe, Sir Euan Hamilton Anstruther-Gough-, Bt. (1929).
Cameron of Lochiel, Sir Donald Hamish, KT, CVO, TD.
Cameron, Sir (Eustace) John, Kt., CBE.
Cameron, *Hon.* Sir John, KT, DSC, QC (Lord Cameron).
Cameron, Sir John Watson, Kt., OBE.
Campbell, Sir Alan Hugh, GCMG.
Campbell, Sir Colin Moffat, Bt., MC (S. 1668).
Campbell, *Col.* Sir Guy Theophilus Halswell, Bt., OBE, MC (1815).
Campbell, *Maj.-Gen.* Sir Hamish Manus, KBE, CB.
Campbell, Sir Ian Tofts, Kt., CBE, VRD.
Campbell, Sir Ilay Mark, Bt. (1808).
Campbell, Sir Matthew, KBE, CB, FRSE.
Campbell, Sir Niall Alexander Hamilton, Bt. (1831).
Campbell, Sir Robin Auchinbreck, Bt. (S. 1628).

Campbell, Sir Thomas Cockburn-, Bt. (1821).
Campbell, *Hon.* Sir Walter Benjamin, Kt.
Campbell, *Hon.* Sir William Anthony, Kt.
Campion, Sir Harry, Kt., CB, CBE.
Cantley, *Hon.* Sir Joseph Donaldson, Kt., OBE.
Carden, *Lt.-Col.* Sir Henry Christopher, Bt., OBE (1887).
Carden, Sir John Craven, Bt. (I. 1787).
Carew, Sir Rivers Verain, Bt. (1661).
Carey, Sir Peter Willoughby, GCB.
Carlill, *Vice-Adm.* Sir Stephen Hope, KBE, CB, DSO.
Carlisle, Sir John Michael, Kt.
Carmichael, Sir David Peter William Gibson-Craig-, Bt. (S. 1702 and 1831).
Carmichael, Sir John, KBE.
Carnac, *Revd Canon* Sir (Thomas) Nicholas Rivett-, Bt. (1836).
Carnegie, *Lt.-Gen.* Sir Robin Macdonald, KCB, OBE.
Carnegie, Sir Roderick Howard, Kt.
Carnwath, Sir Andrew Hunter, KCVO.
Caro, Sir Anthony Alfred, Kt., CBE.
Carpenter, *Very Revd* Edward Frederick, KCVO.
Carr, Sir (Albert) Raymond (Maillard), Kt.
Carr, *Air Marshal* Sir John Darcy Baker-, KBE, CB, AFC.
Carrick, *Hon.* Sir John Leslie, KCMG.
Carsberg, *Prof.* Sir Bryan Victor, Kt.
Carswell, *Hon.* Sir Robert Douglas, Kt.
Carter, Sir Charles Frederick, Kt., FBA.
Carter, Sir Derrick Hunton, Kt., TD.
Carter, Sir John, Kt., QC.
Carter, Sir John Alexander, Kt.
Carter, Sir Philip David, Kt., CBE.
Carter, Sir Richard Henry Alwyn, Kt.
Carter, Sir William Oscar, Kt.
Cartland, Sir George Barrington, Kt., CMG.
Cartledge, Sir Bryan George, KCMG.
Cary, Sir Roger Hugh, Bt. (1955).
Casey, *Rt. Hon.* Sir Maurice Eugene, Kt.
Cash, Sir Gerald Christopher, GCMG, GCVO, OBE.
Cass, Sir Geoffrey Arthur, Kt.
Cass, Sir John Patrick, Kt., OBE.
Cassel, Sir Harold Felix, Bt., TD, QC (1920).
Cassels, *Field Marshal* Sir (Archibald) James Halkett, GCB, KBE, DSO.
Cassels, Sir John Seton, Kt., CB.
Cassels, *Adm.* Sir Simon Alastair Cassillis, KCB, CBE.
Cassidi, *Adm.* Sir (Arthur) Desmond, GCB.
Casson, Sir Hugh Maxwell, CH, KCVO, PPRA, FRIBA.
Cater, Sir Jack, KBE.
Cater, Sir John Robert, Kt.
Catherwood, Sir (Henry) Frederick (Ross), Kt., MEP.
Catling, Sir Richard Charles, Kt., CMG, OBE.
Cato, *Hon.* Sir Arnott Samuel, KCMG.
Caughey, Sir Thomas Harcourt Clarke, KBE.
Caulfield, *Hon.* Sir Bernard, Kt.
Cave, Sir Charles Edward Coleridge, Bt. (1896).
Cave, Sir (Charles) Philip Haddon-, KBE, CMG.
Cave, Sir Robert Cave-Browne-, Bt. (1641).
Cawley, Sir Charles Mills, Kt., CBE, Ph.D.
Cayley, Sir Digby William David, Bt. (1661).
Cayzer, Sir James Arthur, Bt. (1904).
Cazalet, *Hon.* Sir Edward Stephen, Kt.
Cazalet, Sir Peter Grenville, Kt.
Cecil, *Rear-Adm.* Sir (Oswald) Nigel Amherst, KBE, CB.
Chacksfield, *Air Vice-Marshal* Sir Bernard Albert, KBE, CB.
Chadwick, *Revd Prof.* Henry, KBE.
Chadwick, *Hon.* Sir John Murray, Kt., ED.
Chadwick, Sir Joshua Kenneth Burton, Bt. (1935).
Chadwick, *Revd Prof.* (William) Owen, OM, KBE, FBA.
Chalk, *Hon.* Sir Gordon William Wesley, KBE.
Chamberlain, *Hon.* Sir Reginald Roderic St Clair, Kt.
Chan, *Rt. Hon.* Sir Julius, KBE.
Chance, Sir (George) Jeremy ffolliott, Bt. (1900).
Chandler, Sir Colin Michael, Kt.
Chandler, Sir Geoffrey, Kt., CBE.
Chaney, *Hon.* Sir Frederick Charles, KBE, AFC.
Chaplin, Sir Malcolm Hilbery, Kt., CBE.
Chapman, Sir David Robert Macgowan, Bt. (1958).
Chapman, Sir George Alan, Kt.
Chapple, *Field Marshal* Sir John Lyon, GCB, CBE.
Charles, Sir Joseph Quentin, Kt.
Charnley, Sir (William) John, Kt., CB, FEng.
Chaytor, Sir George Reginald, Bt. (1831).
Checketts, *Sqn. Ldr.* Sir David John, KCVO.
Checkland, Sir Michael, Kt.
Cheetham, Sir Nicolas John Alexander, KCMG.
Chesterman, Sir (Dudley) Ross, Kt., Ph.D.
Chesterton, Sir Oliver Sidney, Kt., MC.
Chetwood, Sir Clifford Jack, Kt.
Chetwynd, Sir Arthur Ralph Talbot, Bt. (1795).
Cheung, Sir Oswald Victor, Kt., CBE.
Cheyne, Sir Joseph Lister Watson, Bt., OBE (1908).
Chichester, Sir (Edward) John, Bt. (1641).
Child, Sir (Coles John) Jeremy, Bt. (1919).
Chilton, *Brig.* Sir Frederick Oliver, Kt., CBE, DSO.
Chilwell, *Hon.* Sir Muir Fitzherbert, Kt.
Chinn, Sir Trevor Edwin, Kt., CVO.
Chipperfield, Sir Geoffrey Howes, KCB.
Chitty, Sir Thomas Willes, Bt. (1924).
Cholmeley, Sir Montague John, Bt. (1806).
Christie, Sir George William Langham, Kt.
Christie, *Hon.* Sir Vernon Howard Colville, Kt.
Christie, Sir William, Kt., MBE.
Christison, *Gen.* Sir (Alexander Frank) Philip, Bt., GBE, CB, DSO, MC (1871).
Christofas, Sir Kenneth Cavendish, KCMG, MBE.
Christopherson, Sir Derman Guy, Kt., OBE, D.Phil., FRS, FEng.
Chung, Sir Sze-yuen, Kt., GBE, FEng.
Clapham, Sir Michael John Sinclair, KBE.
Clark, Sir Colin Douglas, Bt. (1917).
Clark, Sir Francis Drake, Bt. (1886).
Clark, Sir John Allen, Kt.
Clark, *Prof.* Sir John Grahame Douglas, Kt., CBE.
Clark, Sir John Stewart-, Bt., MEP (1918).
Clark, Sir Robert Anthony, Kt., DSC.
Clark, Sir Robin Chichester-, Kt.
Clark, Sir Terence Joseph, KBE, CMG, CVO.
Clark, Sir Thomas Edwin, Kt.
Clarke, Sir (Charles Mansfield) Tobias, Bt. (1831).
Clarke, *Prof.* Sir Cyril Astley, KBE, MD, SC.D., FRS, FRCP.
Clarke, Sir Ellis Emmanuel Innocent, GCMG.
Clarke, Sir (Henry) Ashley, GCMG, GCVO.
Clarke, Sir Jonathan Dennis, Kt.
Clarke, *Maj.* Sir Peter Cecil, KCVO.
Clarke, Sir Rupert William John, Bt., MBE (1882).
Clay, Sir Richard Henry, Bt. (1841).
Clayton, Sir David Robert, Bt., (1732).
Clayton, Sir Robert James, Kt., CBE, FEng.
Cleary, Sir Joseph Jackson, Kt.
Cleaver, Sir Anthony Brian, Kt.
Clegg, Sir Walter, Kt.
Cleminson, Sir James Arnold Stacey, KBE, MC.
Clerk, Sir John Dutton, Bt., CBE, VRD (S. 1679).
Clerke, Sir John Edward Longueville, Bt. (1660).
Clifford, Sir Roger Joseph, Bt. (1887).
Clothier, Sir Cecil Montacute, KCB, QC.
Clowes, *Col.* Sir Henry Nelson, KCVO, DSO, OBE.

Clucas, Sir Kenneth Henry, KCB.
Clutterbuck, *Vice-Adm.* Sir David Granville, KBE, CB.
Coates, Sir Ernest William, Kt., CMG.
Coates, Sir Frederick Gregory Lindsay, Bt. (1921).
Coats, Sir Alastair Francis Stuart, Bt. (1905).
Coats, Sir William David, Kt.
Cobban, Sir James Macdonald, Kt., CBE, TD.
Cochrane, Sir (Henry) Marc (Sursock), Bt. (1903).
Cockburn, Sir John Elliot, Bt. (s. 1671).
Cockburn, Sir Robert, KBE, CB, Ph.D., FEng.
Cockcroft, Sir Wilfred Halliday, Kt., D.Phil.
Cockerell, Sir Christopher Sydney, Kt., CBE, FRS.
Cockram, Sir John, Kt.
Cockshaw, Sir Alan, Kt., FEng.
Codrington, Sir Simon Francis Bethell, Bt. (1876).
Codrington, Sir William Alexander, Bt. (1721).
Coghill, Sir Egerton James Nevill Tobias, Bt. (1778).
Cohen, Sir Edward, Kt.
Cohen, Sir Ivor Harold, Kt., CBE, TD.
Cohen, Sir Stephen Harry Waley-, Bt. (1961).
Coldstream, Sir George Phillips, KCB, KCVO, QC.
Cole, Sir (Alexander) Colin, KCVO, TD.
Cole, Sir David Lee, KCMG, MC.
Cole, Sir (Robert) William, Kt.
Coles, Sir (Arthur) John, KCMG.
Colfox, Sir (William) John, Bt. (1939).
Collett, Sir Christopher, GBE.
Collett, Sir Ian Seymour, Bt. (1934).
Collins, Sir Arthur James Robert, KCVO.
Collyear, Sir John Gowen, Kt., FEng.
Colman, Sir Michael Jeremiah, Bt. (1907).
Colquhoun, *Maj.-Gen.* Sir Cyril Harry, KCVO, CB, OBE.
Colquhoun of Luss, Sir Ivar Iain, Bt. (1786).
Colt, Sir Edward William Dutton Bt. (1694).
Colthurst, Sir Richard La Touche, Bt. (1744).
Combs, Sir Willis Ide, KCVO, CMG.
Compston, *Vice-Adm.* Sir Peter Maxwell, KCB.
Compton, Sir Edmund Gerald, GCB, KBE.
Compton Miller, Sir John (Francis), Kt., MBE, TD.
Comyn, *Hon.* Sir James, Kt.
Conant, Sir John Ernest Michael, Bt. (1954).
Connell, *Hon.* Sir Michael Bryan, Kt.
Conran, Sir Terence Orby, Kt.
Cons, *Hon.* Sir Derek, Kt.
Constable, Sir Robert Frederick Strickland-, Bt. (1641).
Cook, *Prof.* Sir Alan Hugh, Kt.
Cook, Sir Christopher Wymondham Rayner Herbert, Bt. (1886).
Cooke, Sir Charles Fletcher-, Kt., QC.
Cooke, *Lt.-Col.* Sir David William Perceval, Bt. (1661).
Cooke, Sir Howard Felix Hanlan, GCMG, ON, CD.
Cooke, *Rt. Hon.* Sir Robin Brunskill, KBE.
Cooley, Sir Alan Sydenham, Kt., CBE.
Coop, Sir Maurice Fletcher, Kt.
Cooper, *Rt. Hon.* Sir Frank, GCB, CMG.
Cooper, Sir (Frederick Howard) Michael Craig-, Kt., CBE, TD.
Cooper, *Gen.* Sir George Leslie Conroy, GCB, MC.
Cooper, Sir Louis Jacques Blom-, Kt., QC.
Cooper, Sir Patrick Graham Astley, Bt. (1821).
Cooper, Sir Richard Powell, Bt. (1905).
Cooper, *Maj.-Gen.* Sir Simon Christie, KCVO.
Cooper, Sir William Daniel Charles, Bt. (1863).
Cooper, *Prof.* Sir (William) Mansfield, Kt.
Coote, Sir Christopher John, Bt., *Premier Baronet of Ireland* (I. 1621).
Copas, *Most Revd* Virgil, KBE, DD.
Cope, *Rt. Hon.* Sir John Ambrose, Kt., MP.
Copisarow, Sir Alcon Charles, Kt.
Corbet, Sir John Vincent, Bt., MBE (1808).
Corby, Sir (Frederick) Brian, Kt.
Corfield, *Rt. Hon.* Sir Frederick Vernon, Kt., QC.
Corfield, Sir Kenneth George, Kt.
Corley, Sir Kenneth Sholl Ferrand, Kt.
Cormack, Sir Magnus Cameron, KBE.
Corness, Sir Colin Ross, Kt.
Cornford, Sir (Edward) Clifford, KCB, FEng.
Cornforth, Sir John Warcup, Kt., CBE, D.Phil., FRS.
Corry, Sir William James, Bt. (1885).
Cortazzi, Sir (Henry Arthur) Hugh, GCMG.
Cory, Sir (Clinton Charles) Donald, Bt. (1919).
Costar, Sir Norman Edgar, KCMG.
Cotter, *Lt.-Col.* Sir Delaval James Alfred, Bt., DSO (I. 1763).
Cotterell, Sir John Henry Geers, Bt. (1805).
Cotton, Sir John Richard, KCMG, OBE.
Cotton, *Hon.* Sir Robert Carrington, KCMG.
Cottrell, Sir Alan Howard, Kt., Ph.D., FRS, FEng.
Cotts, Sir (Robert) Crichton Mitchell, Bt. (1921).
Coulson, Sir John Eltringham, KCMG.
Couper, Sir (Robert) Nicholas (Oliver), Bt. (1841).
Court, *Hon.* Sir Charles Walter Michael, KCMG, OBE.
Coutts, Sir David Burdett Money-, KCVO.
Couzens, Sir Kenneth Edward, KCB.
Covacevich, Sir (Anthony) Thomas, Kt., DFC.
Cowan, Sir Robert, Kt.
Coward, *Vice-Adm.* Sir John Francis, KCB, DSO.
Cowdrey, Sir (Michael) Colin, Kt., CBE.
Cowen, *Rt. Hon. Prof.* Sir Zelman, GCMG, GCVO, QC.
Cowie, Sir Thomas (Tom), Kt., OBE.
Cowley, *Lt.-Gen.* Sir John Guise, GC, KBE, CB.
Cowperthwaite, Sir John James, KBE, CMG.
Cox, Sir Anthony Wakefield, Kt., CBE, FRIBA.
Cox, *Prof.* Sir David Roxbee, Kt., FRS.
Cox, Sir (Ernest) Gordon, KBE, TD, D.Sc., FRS.
Cox, Sir Geoffrey Sandford, Kt., CBE.
Cox, Sir (George) Trenchard, Kt., CBE, FSA.
Cox, *Vice-Adm.* Sir John Michael Holland, KCB.
Cox, Sir Mencea Ethereal, Kt.,
Cradock, Sir Percy, GCMG.
Craig, Sir (Albert) James (Macqueen), GCMG.
Cramer, *Hon.* Sir John Oscar, Kt.
Crane, Sir James William Donald, Kt., CBE.
Craufurd, Sir Robert James, Bt. (1781).
Craven, *Air Marshal* Sir Robert Edward, KBE, CB, DFC.
Crawford, *Prof.* Sir Frederick William, Kt., FEng.
Crawford, *Hon.* Sir George Hunter, Kt.
Crawford, Sir (Robert) Stewart, GCMG, CVO.
Crawford, *Prof.* Sir Theodore, Kt.
Crawford, *Vice-Adm.* Sir William Godfrey, KBE, CB, DSC.
Crawshay, *Col.* Sir William Robert, Kt., DSO, ERD, TD.
Creagh, *Maj.-Gen.* Sir (Kilner) Rupert Brazier-, KBE, CB, DSO.

Cresswell, *Hon.* Sir Peter John, Kt.
Crichton, Sir Andrew James Maitland-Makgill-, Kt.
Crill, Sir Peter Leslie, Kt., CBE.
Cripps, Sir Cyril Humphrey, Kt.
Cripps, Sir John Stafford, Kt., CBE.
Crisp, Sir (John) Peter, Bt. (1913).
Critchett, Sir Ian (George Lorraine), Bt. (1908).
Croft, Sir Owen Glendower, Bt. (1671).
Croft, Sir Thomas Stephen Hutton, Bt. (1818).
†Crofton, Sir Hugh Denis, Bt. (1801).
Crofton, *Prof.* Sir John Wenman, Kt.
Crofton, Sir Malby Sturges, Bt. (1838).
Croker, Sir Walter Russell, KBE.
Crookenden, *Lt.-Gen.* Sir Napier, KCB, DSO, OBE.
Cross, Sir Barry Albert, Kt., CBE, FRS.
Cross, *Air Chief Marshal* Sir Kenneth Brian Boyd, KCB, CBE, DSO, DFC.
Crossland, *Prof.* Sir Bernard, Kt., CBE, FEng.
Crossland, Sir Leonard, Kt.
Crossley, Sir Nicholas John, Bt. (1909).
Crouch, Sir David Lance, Kt.
Cruthers, Sir James Winter, Kt.
Cubbon, Sir Brian Crossland, GCB.
Cubitt, Sir Hugh Guy, Kt., CBE.
Cuckney, Sir John Graham, Kt.
Cullen, Sir (Edward) John, Kt., F.Eng.
Cumming, Sir William Gordon Gordon-, Bt. (1804).
Cuninghame, Sir John Christopher Foggo Montgomery-, Bt. (NS 1672).
†Cuninghame, Sir William Henry Fairlie-, Bt. (S. 1630).
Cunliffe, Sir David Ellis, Bt. (1759)
Cunningham, Sir Charles Craik, GCB, KBE, CVO.
Cunningham, *Lt.-Gen.* Sir Hugh Patrick, KBE.
Cunynghame, Sir Andrew David Francis, Bt. (S. 1702).
Curle, Sir John Noel Ormiston, KCVO, CMG.
Curran, Sir Samuel Crowe, Kt., D.SC., Ph.D., FRS, FRSE, FEng.
Currie, *Prof.* Sir Alastair Robert, Kt., FRCP, FRCPE, FRSE.
†Currie, Sir Donald Scott, Bt. (1847).
Currie, Sir Neil Smith, Kt., CBE.
Curtis, Sir Barry John, Kt.
Curtis, Sir (Edward) Leo, Kt.
Curtis, Sir William Peter, Bt. (1802).
Curtiss, *Air Marshal* Sir John Bagot, KCB, KBE.
Curwen, Sir Christopher Keith, KCMG.
Cuthbertson, Sir Harold Alexander, Kt.
Cutler, Sir (Arthur) Roden, VC, KCMG, KCVO, CBE.
Cutler, Sir Charles Benjamin, KBE, ED.
Cutler, Sir Horace Walter, Kt., OBE.
Dacie, *Prof.* Sir John Vivian, Kt., MD, FRS.
Dalais, Sir Adrien Pierre, Kt.
Dale, Sir William Leonard, KCMG.
Dalrymple, *Maj.* Sir Hew Fleetwood Hamilton-, Bt., KCVO (S. 1697).
Dalton, Sir Alan Nugent Goring, Kt., CBE.
Dalton, *Vice-Adm.* Sir Geoffrey Thomas James Oliver, KCB.
Daly, *Lt.-Gen.* Sir Thomas Joseph, KBE, CB, DSO.
Dalyell, Sir Tam, Bt., MP (NS 1685).
Daniel, Sir Goronwy Hopkin, KCVO, CB, D.Phil.
Daniell, Sir Peter Averell, Kt., TD.
Danks, Sir Alan John, KBE.
Darby, Sir Peter Howard, Kt., CBE, QFSM.
Darell, Sir Jeffrey Lionel, Bt., MC (1795).
Dargie, Sir William Alexander, Kt., CBE.
Dark, Sir Anthony Michael Beaumont-, Kt.
Darling, Sir Clifford, Kt.
Darling, Sir James Ralph, Kt., CMG, OBE.
Darling, *Gen.* Sir Kenneth Thomas, GBE, KCB, DSO.
Darlington, *Rear-Adm.* Sir Charles Roy, KBE.
Darvall, Sir (Charles) Roger, Kt., CBE.
Dashwood, Sir Francis John Vernon Hereward, Bt., *Premier Baronet of Great Britain* (1707).
Dashwood, Sir Richard James, Bt. (1684).
Daunt, Sir Timothy Lewis Achilles, KCMG.
David, Sir Jean Marc, Kt., CBE, QC.
Davidson, Sir Robert James, Kt., FEng.
Davie, Sir Antony Francis Ferguson-, Bt. (1847).
Davies, *Air Marshal* Sir Alan Cyril, KCB, CBE.
Davies, *Hon.* Sir (Alfred William) Michael, Kt.
Davies, Sir Alun Talfan, Kt., QC.
Davies, Sir David Henry, Kt.
Davies, *Hon.* Sir (David Herbert) Mervyn, Kt., MC, TD.
Davies, *Vice-Adm.* Sir Lancelot Richard Bell, KBE.
Davies, Sir Oswald, Kt., CBE.
Davies, Sir Peter Maxwell, Kt., CBE.
Davies, Sir Richard Harries, KCVO, CBE.
Davies, Sir Victor Caddy, Kt., OBE.
Davis, Sir Charles Sigmund, Kt., CB.
Davis, Sir Colin Rex, Kt., CBE.
Davis, *Hon.* Sir (Dermot) Renn, Kt., OBE.
Davis, Sir (Ernest) Howard, Kt., CMG, OBE.
Davis, Sir John Gilbert, Bt. (1946).
Davis, Sir John Henry Harris, Kt.
Davis, Sir Maurice Herbert, Kt., OBE.
Davis, Sir Rupert Charles Hart-, Kt.
Davis, *Hon.* Sir Thomas Robert Alexander Harries, KBE.
Davis, Sir (William) Allan, GBE.
Davison, *Rt. Hon.* Sir Ronald Keith, GBE, CMG.
Dawbarn, Sir Simon Yelverton, KCVO, CMG.
Dawson, *Hon.* Sir Daryl Michael, KBE, CB.
Dawson, Sir Hugh Michael Trevor, Bt. (1920).
Dawson, *Air Chief Marshal* Sir Walter Lloyd, KCB, CBE, DSO.
Dawtry, Sir Alan (Graham), Kt., CBE, TD.
Day, Sir Derek Malcolm, KCMG.
Day, Sir (Judson) Graham, Kt.
Day, Sir Michael John, Kt., OBE.
Day, Sir Robin, Kt.
Deakin, Sir (Frederick) William (Dampier), Kt., DSO.
Dean, *Rt. Hon.* Sir (Arthur) Paul, Kt.
Dean, Sir Patrick Henry, GCMG.
Deane, *Hon.* Sir William Patrick, KBE.
Dearing, Sir Ronald Ernest, Kt., CB.
de Bellaigue, Sir Geoffrey, KCVO.
Debenham, Sir Gilbert Ridley, Bt. (1931).
de Deney, Sir Geoffrey Ivor, KCVO.
Deer, Sir (Arthur) Frederick, Kt., CMG.
de Hoghton, Sir (Richard) Bernard (Cuthbert), Bt. (1611).
De la Bère, Sir Cameron, Bt. (1953).
de la Mare, Sir Arthur James, KCMG, KCVO.
Delamere, Sir Monita Eru, KBE.
de la Rue, Sir Andrew George Ilay, Bt. (1898).
Dellow, Sir John Albert, Kt., CBE.
de Lotbinière, *Lt.-Col.* Sir Edmond Joly, Kt.
Delve, Sir Frederick William, Kt., CBE.
de Montmorency, Sir Arnold Geoffroy, Bt. (I. 1631).
Denholm, Sir John Ferguson (Ian), Kt., CBE.
Denman, Sir (George) Roy, KCB, CMG.
Denny, Sir Alistair Maurice Archibald, Bt. (1913).
Denny, Sir Anthony Coningham de Waltham, Bt. (I. 1782).
Dent, Sir John, Kt., CBE, FEng.
Dent, Sir Robin John, KCVO.

Denton, *Prof.* Sir Eric James, Kt., CBE, FRS.
Derbyshire, Sir Andrew George, Kt.
Derham, Sir Peter John, Kt..
de Trafford, Sir Dermot Humphrey, Bt. (1841).
Deverell, Sir Colville Montgomery, GBE, KCMG, CVO.
Devesi, Sir Baddeley, GCMG, GCVO.
De Ville, Sir Harold Godfrey Oscar, Kt., CBE.
Devitt, Sir Thomas Gordon, Bt. (1916).
de Waal, Sir (Constant Henrik) Henry, KCB, QC.
Dewey, Sir Anthony Hugh, Bt. (1917).
Dewhurst, *Prof.* Sir (Christopher) John, Kt.
d'Eyncourt, Sir Mark Gervais Tennyson-, Bt. (1930).
Dhenin, *Air Marshal* Sir Geoffrey Howard, KBE, AFC, GM, MD.
Dhrangadhra, HH the Maharaja Raj Saheb of, KCIE.
Dibela, *Hon.* Sir Kingsford, GCMG.
Dick, Sir John Alexander, Kt., MC, QC.
Dickenson, Sir Aubrey Fiennes Trotman-, Kt.
Dickinson, Sir Harold Herbert, Kt.
Dickinson, Sir Samuel Benson, Kt.
Dilbertson, Sir Geoffrey, Kt., CBE.
Dilke, Sir John Fisher Wentworth, Bt. (1862).
Dill, Sir Nicholas Bayard, Kt., CBE.
Dillon, *Rt. Hon.* Sir (George) Brian (Hugh), Kt.
Dillon, Sir John Vincent, Kt., CMG.
Dillon, Sir Max, Kt.
Diver, *Hon.* Sir Leslie Charles, Kt.
Dixon, Sir Jonathan Mark, Bt. (1919).
Dobbs, *Capt.* Sir Richard Arthur Frederick, KCVO.
Dobson, *Vice-Adm.* Sir David Stuart, KBE.
Dobson, Sir Denis William, KCB, OBE, QC.
Dobson, *Gen.* Sir Patrick John Howard-, GCB.
Dobson, Sir Richard Portway, Kt.
Dodds, Sir Ralph Jordan, Bt. (1964).
Dodson, Sir Derek Sherborne Lindsell, KCMG, MC.
Dodsworth, Sir John Christopher Smith-, Bt. (1784).
Doll, *Prof.* Sir (William) Richard (Shaboe), Kt., OBE, FRS, DM, MD, D.SC.
Dollery, Sir Colin Terence, Kt.
Donald, Sir Alan Ewen, KCMG.
Donald, *Air Marshal* Sir John George, KBE.
Donne, *Hon.* Sir Gaven John, KBE.
Donne, Sir John Christopher, Kt.
Dookun, Sir Dewoonarain, Kt.
Dorman, *Lt.-Col.* Sir Charles Geoffrey, Bt., MC (1923).
Dorman, Sir Maurice Henry, GCMG, GCVO.
Dos Santos, Sir Errol Lionel, Kt., CBE.
Dougherty, *Maj.-Gen.* Sir Ivan Noel, Kt., CBE, DSO, ED.
Doughty, Sir William Roland, Kt.
Douglas, *Prof.* Sir Donald Macleod, Kt., MBE.
Douglas, Sir (Edward) Sholto, Kt.
Douglas, Sir Robert McCallum, Kt., OBE.
Douglas, *Hon.* Sir Roger Owen, Kt.
Douglas, *Rt. Hon.* Sir William Randolph, KCMG.
Dover, *Prof.* Sir Kenneth James, Kt., D.Litt., FBA, FRSE.
Down, Sir Alastair Frederick, Kt., OBE, MC, TD.
Downes, Sir Edward Thomas, Kt., CBE.
Downey, Sir Gordon Stanley, KCB.
Downs, Sir Diarmuid, Kt., CBE, FEng.
Downward, Sir William Atkinson, Kt.
Dowson, Sir Philip Manning, Kt., CBE, ARA.
Doyle, Sir Reginald Derek Henry, Kt., CBE.
D'Oyly, Sir Nigel Hadley Miller, Bt. (1663).
Drake, Sir (Arthur) Eric (Courtney), Kt., CBE.
Drake, *Hon.* Sir (Frederick) Maurice, Kt., DFC.
Drew, Sir Arthur Charles Walter, KCB.
Dreyer, *Adm.* Sir Desmond Parry, GCB, CBE, DSC.
Drinkwater, Sir John Muir, Kt., QC.
Driver, Sir Antony Victor, Kt.
Driver, Sir Eric William, Kt.
Drury, Sir (Victor William) Michael, Kt., OBE.
Dryden, Sir John Stephen Gyles, Bt. (1733 and 1795).
du Cann, *Rt. Hon.* Sir Edward Dillon Lott, KBE.
Duckmanton, Sir Talbot Sydney, Kt., CBE.
Duckworth, *Maj.* Sir Richard Dyce, Bt. (1909).
du Cros, Sir Claude Philip Arthur Mallet, Bt. (1916).
Duff, *Rt. Hon.* Sir (Arthur) Antony, GCMG, CVO, DSO, DSC.
Duffell, *Lt.-Gen.* Sir Peter Royson, KCB, CBE, MC.
Duffus, *Hon.* Sir William Algernon Holwell, Kt.
Duffy, Sir (Albert) (Edward) Patrick, Kt., Ph.D.
Dugdale, Sir William Stratford, Bt., MC (1936).
Dunbar, Sir Archibald Ranulph, Bt. (S. 1700).
Dunbar, Sir David Hope-, Bt. (S. 1664).
Dunbar, Sir Drummond Cospatrick Ninian, Bt., MC (S. 1698).
Dunbar, Sir Jean Ivor, Bt. (S. 1694).
Dunbar of Hempriggs, Dame Maureen Daisy Helen (Lady Dunbar of Hempriggs), Btss. (S. 1706).
Duncan, Sir James Blair, Kt.
Duncombe, Sir Philip Digby Pauncefort-, Bt. (1859).
Dundas, Sir Hugh Spencer Lisle, Kt., CBE, DSO, DFC.
Dunham, Sir Kingsley Charles, Kt., Ph.D., FRS, FRSE, FEng.
Dunlop, Sir (Ernest) Edward, Kt., CMG, OBE.
Dunlop, Sir Thomas, Bt. (1916).
Dunlop, Sir William Norman Gough, Kt.
Dunn, *Air Marshal* Sir Eric Clive, KBE, CB, BEM.
Dunn, *Lt.-Col.* Sir (Francis) Vivian, KCVO, OBE.
Dunn, *Air Marshal* Sir Patrick Hunter, KBE, CB, DFC.
Dunn, *Rt. Hon.* Sir Robin Horace Walford, Kt., MC.
Dunnett, Sir (Ludovic) James, GCB, CMG.
Dunning, Sir Simon William Patrick, Bt. (1930).
Dunphie, *Maj.-Gen.* Sir Charles Anderson Lane, Kt., CB, CBE, DSO.
Dunstan, *Lt.-Gen.* Sir Donald Beaumont, KBE, CB.
†Duntze, Sir Daniel Evans, Bt. (1774).
Dupree, Sir Peter, Bt. (1921).
Durand, *Revd* Sir (Henry Mortimer) Dickon, Bt. (1892).
Durant, Sir (Robert) Anthony (Bevis), Kt., MP.
Durham, Sir Kenneth, Kt.
Durie, Sir Alexander Charles, Kt., CBE.
Durkin, *Air Marshal* Sir Herbert, KBE, CB.
Durrant, Sir William Henry Estridge, Bt. (1784).
Duthie, *Prof.* Sir Herbert Livingston, Kt.
Duthie, Sir Robert Grieve (Robin), Kt., CBE.
Duval, Sir (Charles) Gaetan, Kt.
Duxbury, *Air Marshal* Sir (John) Barry, KCB, CBE.
Dyer, *Prof.* Sir (Henry) Peter (Francis) Swinnerton-, Bt., KBE, FRS (1678).
Dyke, Sir David William Hart, Bt. (1677).
Earle, Sir (Hardman) George (Algernon), Bt. (1869).
East, Sir (Lewis) Ronald, Kt., CBE.
Eastham, *Hon.* Sir (Thomas) Michael, Kt.
Easton, Sir Robert William Simpson, Kt., CBE.
Eastwood, Sir John Bealby, Kt..
Eaton, *Vice-Adm.* Sir Kenneth John, KCB.
Eberle, *Adm.* Sir James Henry Fuller, GCB.
Ebrahim, Sir (Mahomed) Currimbhoy, Bt. (1910).
Eburne, Sir Sidney Alfred William, Kt., MC.

Eccles, Sir John Carew, Kt., D.Phil., FRS.
Echlin, Sir Norman David Fenton, Bt. (I. 1721).
Eckersley, Sir Donald Payze, Kt., OBE.
†Edge, Sir William, Bt. (1937).
Edmenson, Sir Walter Alexander, Kt., CBE.
Edmonstone, Sir Archibald Bruce Charles, Bt. (1774).
Edwardes, Sir Michael Owen, Kt.
Edwards, Sir Christopher John Churchill, Bt. (1866).
Edwards, Sir George Robert, Kt., OM, CBE, FRS, FEng.
Edwards, Sir (John) Clive (Leighton), Bt. (1921).
Edwards, Sir Llewellyn Roy, Kt.
Edwards, *Prof.* Sir Samuel Frederick, Kt., FRS.
Egan, Sir John Leopold, Kt.
Egerton, Sir John Alfred Roy, Kt.
Egerton, Sir (Philip) John (Caledon) Grey-, Bt. (1617).
Egerton, Sir Seymour John Louis, GCVO.
Egerton, Sir Stephen Loftus, KCMG.
Eggleston, *Hon.* Sir Richard Moulton, Kt.
Eichelbaum, *Rt. Hon.* Sir Thomas, GBE.
Eliott of Stobs, Sir Charles Joseph Alexander, Bt. (S. 1666).
Ellerton, Sir Geoffrey James, Kt., CMG, MBE.
Elliot, Sir Gerald Henry, Kt.
Elliott, Sir Clive Christopher Hugh, Bt. (1917).
Elliott, Sir Randal Forbes, KBE.
Elliott, *Prof.* Sir Roger James, Kt., FRS.
Elliott, Sir Ronald Stuart, Kt.
Ellis, Sir John Rogers, Kt., MBE, MD, FRCP.
Ellis, Sir Ronald, Kt., FEng.
Ellison, *Rt. Revd* and *Rt. Hon.* Gerald Alexander, KCVO.
Ellison, *Col.* Sir Ralph Harry Carr-, Kt., TD.
Ellwood, *Air Marshal* Sir Aubrey Beauclerk, KCB, DSC.
Elphinstone, Sir John, Bt. (S. 1701).
Elphinstone, Sir (Maurice) Douglas (Warburton), Bt., TD (1816).
Elton, Sir Arnold, Kt., CBE.
Elton, Sir Charles Abraham Grierson, Bt. (1717).
Elton, *Prof.* Sir Geoffrey Rudolph, Kt., FBA.
Elwood, Sir Brian George Conway, Kt., CBE.
Elworthy, Sir Peter Herbert, Kt.
Elyan, Sir (Isadore) Victor, Kt.
Emery, Sir Peter Frank Hannibal, Kt., MP.
Empson, *Adm.* Sir (Leslie) Derek, GBE, KCB.
Emson, *Air Marshal* Sir Reginald Herbert, KBE, CB, AFC.
Engineer, Sir Noshirwan Phirozshah, Kt.
Engle, Sir George Lawrence Jose, KCB, QC.
English, Sir Cyril Rupert, Kt.
English, Sir David, Kt.
English, Sir Terence Alexander Hawthorne, KBE, FRCS.
Entwistle, Sir (John Nuttall) Maxwell, Kt.
Epstein, *Prof.* Sir (Michael) Anthony, Kt., CBE, FRS.
Ereaut, Sir (Herbert) Frank Cobbold, Kt.
Eri, Sir Vincent Serei, GCMG.
Errington, *Col.* Sir Geoffrey Frederick, Bt. (1963).
Errington, Sir Lancelot, KCB.
Erskine, Sir (Thomas) David, Bt. (1821).
Esmonde, Sir Thomas Francis Grattan, Bt. (I. 1629).
Espie, Sir Frank Fletcher, Kt., OBE.
Esplen, Sir John Graham, Bt. (1921).
Eustace, Sir Joseph Lambert, GCMG, GCVO.
Evans, Sir Anthony Adney, Bt. (1920).
Evans, *Hon.* Sir Anthony Howell Meurig, Kt., RD.
Evans, *Air Chief Marshal* Sir David George, GCB, CBE.
Evans, *Air Chief Marshal* Sir David Parry-, GCB, CBE.
Evans, Sir Francis Loring Gwynne-, Bt. (1913).
Evans, Sir Geraint Llewellyn, Kt., CBE.
Evans, *Hon.* Sir Haydn Tudor, Kt.
Evans, Sir Richard Mark, KCMG, KCVO.
Evans, Sir (Robert) Charles, Kt.
Evans, Sir (William) Vincent (John), GCMG, MBE, QC.
Eveleigh, *Rt. Hon.* Sir Edward Walter, Kt., ERD.
Everard, *Maj.-Gen.* Sir Christopher Earle Welby-, KBE, CB.
Everard, Sir Robin Charles, Bt. (1911).
Everson, Sir Frederick Charles, KCMG.
Every, Sir Henry John Michael, Bt. (1641).
Ewans, Sir Martin Kenneth, KCMG.
Ewart, Sir (William) Ivan (Cecil), Bt., DSC (1887).
Ewbank, *Hon.* Sir Anthony Bruce, Kt..
Ewin, Sir (David) Ernest Thomas Floyd, Kt., OBE, MVO.
Ewing, *Vice-Adm.* Sir (Robert) Alastair, KBE, CB, DSC.
Ewing, Sir Ronald Archibald Orr-, Bt. (1886).
Eyre, Sir Graham Newman, Kt., QC.
Eyre, *Maj.-Gen.* Sir James Ainsworth Campden Gabriel, KCVO, CBE.
Eyre, Sir Reginald Edwin, Kt.
Faber, Sir Richard Stanley, KCVO, CMG.
Fadahunsi, Sir Joseph Odeleye, KCMG.
Fagge, Sir John William Frederick, Bt. (1660).
Fairbairn, *Hon.* Sir David Eric, KBE, DFC.
Fairbairn, Sir (James) Brooke, Bt. (1869).
Fairbairn, Sir Nicholas Hardwick, Kt., QC, MP.
Fairclough, Sir John Whitaker, Kt., FEng.
Fairfax, Sir Vincent Charles, Kt., CMG.
Fairgrieve, Sir (Thomas) Russell, Kt., CBE, TD.
Fairhall, *Hon.* Sir Allen, KBE.
Fairweather, Sir Patrick Stanislaus, KCMG.
Falconer, *Hon.* Sir Douglas William, Kt., MBE.
Falk, Sir Roger Salis, Kt., OBE.
Falkiner, Sir Edmond Charles, Bt. (I. 1778).
Falkner, Sir (Donald) Keith, Kt.
Fall, Sir Brian James Proetel, KCMG.
Falle, Sir Samuel, KCMG, KCVO, DSC.
Fareed, Sir Djamil Sheik, Kt.
Farmer, Sir (Lovedin) George Thomas, Kt.
Farndale, *Gen.* Sir Martin Baker, KCB.
Farquhar, Sir Michael Fitzroy Henry, Bt. (1796).
Farquharson, *Rt. Hon.* Sir Donald Henry, Kt.
Farquharson, Sir James Robbie, KBE.
Farr, Sir John Arnold, Kt.
Farrer, Sir Charles Matthew, KCVO.
Farrington, Sir Henry Francis Colden, Bt. (1818).
Fat, Sir (Maxime) Edouard (Lim Man) Lim, Kt.
Faulkner, Sir Eric Odin, Kt., MBE.
Faulkner, Sir (James) Dennis (Compton), Kt., CBE, VRD.
Fawcus, Sir (Robert) Peter, KBE, CMG.
Fawkes, Sir Randol Francis, Kt.
Fay, Sir (Humphrey) Michael Gerard, Kt.
Fayrer, Sir John Lang Macpherson, Bt. (1896).
Fearn, Sir (Patrick) Robin, KCMG.
Feilden, Sir Bernard Melchior, Kt., CBE.
Feilden, Sir Henry Wemyss, Bt., (1846).
Feldman, Sir Basil Samuel, Kt.
Fell, Sir Anthony, Kt.
Fellowes, *Rt. Hon.* Sir Robert, KCB, KCVO.
Fenn, Sir Nicholas Maxted, KCMG.
Fennell, *Hon.* Sir (John) Desmond Augustine, Kt., OBE.
Fennessy, Sir Edward, Kt., CBE.
†Ferguson, Sir Ian Edward Johnson-, Bt. (1906).
Fergusson of Kilkerran, Sir Charles, Bt. (S. 1703).
Fergusson, Sir Ewan Alastair John, GCVO, KCMG.
Fergusson, Sir James Herbert Hamilton Colyer-, Bt. (1866).
Feroze, Sir Rustam Moolan, Kt., FRCS.
Ferris, *Hon.* Sir Francis Mursell, Kt., TD.
ffolkes, Sir Robert Francis Alexander, Bt, OBE (1774).
Field, Sir Malcolm David, Kt.

Fielding, Sir Colin Cunningham, Kt., CB.
Fielding, Sir Leslie, KCMG.
Fiennes, Sir John Saye Wingfield Twisleton-Wykeham-, KCB, QC.
Fiennes, Sir Maurice Alberic Twisleton-Wykeham-, Kt.
Fiennes, Sir Ranulph Twisleton-Wykeham-, Bt. (1916).
Figg, Sir Leonard Clifford William, KCMG.
Figgess, Sir John George, KBE, CMG.
Figures, Sir Colin Frederick, KCMG, OBE.
Fingland, Sir Stanley James Gunn, KCMG.
Finlay, Sir David Ronald James Bell, Bt. (1964).
Finley, Sir Peter Hamilton, Kt., OBE, DFC.
Firth, *Prof.* Sir Raymond William, Kt., Ph.D., FBA.
Fish, Sir Hugh, Kt., CBE.
Fisher, Sir George Read, Kt., CMG.
Fisher, *Hon.* Sir Henry Arthur Pears, Kt.
Fisher, Sir Nigel Thomas Loveridge, Kt., MC.
Fison, Sir (Richard) Guy, Bt., DSC (1905).
Fitch, *Adm.* Sir Richard George Alison, KCB.
†Fitzgerald, *Revd* (Sir) Daniel Patrick, Bt. (1903).
FitzGerald, Sir George Peter Maurice, Bt., MC (*The Knight of Kerry*) (1880).
FitzHerbert, Sir Richard Ranulph, Bt. (1784).
Fitzpatrick, *Gen.* Sir (Geoffrey Richard) Desmond, GCB, DSO, MBE, MC.
Fitzpatrick, *Air Marshal* Sir John Bernard, KBE, CB.
Flanagan, Sir James Bernard, Kt., CBE.
Flavelle, Sir (Joseph) David Ellsworth, Bt. (1917).
Fleming, *Instructor Rear-Adm.* Sir John, KBE, DSC.
Fletcher, *Hon.* Sir Alan Roy, Kt.
†Fletcher, Sir Henry Egerton Aubrey-, Bt. (1782).
Fletcher, Sir James Muir Cameron, Kt.
Fletcher, Sir Leslie, Kt., DSC.
Fletcher, *Air Chief Marshal* Sir Peter Carteret, KCB, OBE, DFC, AFC.
Floissac, *Hon.* Sir Vincent Frederick, CMG, OBE, QC.
Floyd, Sir Giles Henry Charles, Bt. (1816).
Foley, Sir (Thomas John) Noel, Kt., CBE.
Follett, *Prof.* Sir Brian Keith, Kt., FRS.
Foot, Sir Geoffrey James, Kt.
Foots, Sir James William, Kt.
Forbes, *Hon.* Sir Alastair Granville, Kt.
Forbes, *Maj.* Sir Hamish Stewart, Bt., MBE, MC (1823).
†Forbes of Craigievar, Sir John Alexander Cumnock Forbes-Sempill, Bt. (S. 1630).
Forbes, *Vice-Adm.* Sir John Morrison, KCB.
†Forbes of Pitsligo, Sir William Daniel Stuart-, Bt. (S. 1626).
Ford, Sir Andrew Russell, Bt. (1929).
Ford, Sir David Robert, KBE, LVO, OBE.
Ford, *Maj.* Sir Edward William Spencer, KCB, KCVO.
Ford, *Air Marshal* Sir Geoffrey Harold, KBE, CB, FEng.
Ford, *Prof.* Sir Hugh, Kt., FRS, FEng.
†Ford, Sir James Anson St Clair-, Bt. (1793).
Ford, Sir John Archibald, KCMG, MC.
Ford, Sir Richard Brinsley, Kt., CBE.
Ford, *Gen.* Sir Robert Cyril, GCB, CBE.
Foreman, Sir Philip Frank, Kt., CBE, FEng.
Forman, Sir John Denis, Kt., OBE.
Forrest, *Prof.* Sir (Andrew) Patrick (McEwen), Kt.
Forrest, Sir James Alexander, Kt.
Forrest, *Rear-Adm.* Sir Ronald Stephen, KCVO.
Forster, Sir Archibald William, Kt., FEng.
Forster, Sir Oliver Grantham, KCMG, MVO.
Forwood, Sir Dudley Richard, Bt. (1895).
Foster, *Prof.* Sir Christopher David, Kt.
Foster, Sir John Gregory, Bt. (1930).
Foster, Sir Norman Robert, Kt.
Foster, Sir Robert Sidney, GCMG, KCVO.
Foulis, Sir Ian Primrose Liston-, Bt. (S. 1634).
Foulkes, Sir Nigel Gordon, Kt.
Fowden, Sir Leslie, Kt., FRS.
Fowke, Sir David Frederick Gustavus, Bt. (1814).
Fowler, Sir (Edward) Michael Coulson, Kt.
Fowler, *Rt. Hon.* Sir (Peter) Norman, Kt., MP.
Fox, Sir (Henry) Murray, GBE.
Fox, Sir (John) Marcus, Kt., MBE, MP.
Fox, *Rt. Hon.* Sir Michael John, Kt.
Fox, Sir Paul Leonard, Kt., CBE.
Frame, Sir Alistair Gilchrist, Kt., FEng.
France, Sir Arnold William, GCB.
France, Sir Christopher Walter, KCB.
Francis, Sir Horace William Alexander, Kt., CBE, FEng.
Frank, Sir Douglas George Horace, Kt., QC.
Frank, Sir (Frederick) Charles, Kt., OBE, FRS.
Frank, Sir Robert Andrew, Bt. (1920).
Frankel, Sir Otto Herzberg, Kt., D.SC., FRS.
Franklin, Sir Eric Alexander, Kt., CBE.
Franklin, Sir Michael David Milroy, KCB, CMG.
Franks, Sir Arthur Temple, KCMG.
Fraser, Sir Angus McKay, KCB, TD.
Fraser, Sir Bruce Donald, KCB.
Fraser, Sir Charles Annand, KCVO.
Fraser, *Gen.* Sir David William, GCB, OBE.
Fraser, *Air Marshal Revd* Sir (Henry) Paterson, KBE, CB, AFC.
Fraser, Sir Ian, Kt., DSO, OBE.
Fraser, Sir Ian James, Kt., CBE, MC.
Fraser, Sir (James) Campbell, Kt.
Fraser, *Prof.* Sir James David, Bt. (1943).
Fraser, Sir William Kerr, GCB.
Frederick, Sir Charles Boscawen, Bt. (1723).
Freeland, Sir John Redvers, KCMG.
Freeman, Sir James Robin, Bt. (1945).
Freeman, Sir Ralph, Kt., CVO, CBE, FEng.
Freer, *Air Chief Marshal* Sir Robert William George, GBE, KCB.
Freeth, *Hon.* Sir Gordon, KBE.
French, *Hon.* Sir Christopher James Saunders, Kt.
Fretwell, Sir (Major) John (Emsley), GCMG.
Freud, Sir Clement Raphael, Kt.
Froggatt, Sir Leslie Trevor, Kt.
Froggatt, Sir Peter, Kt.
Frossard, Sir Charles Keith, Kt., KBE.
Frost, *Hon.* Sir (Thomas) Sydney, Kt.
Fry, *Hon.* Sir William Gordon, Kt.
Fryberg, Sir Abraham, Kt., MBE.
Fuchs, Sir Vivian Ernest, Kt., Ph.D.
Fuller, *Hon.* Sir John Bryan Munro, Kt.
Fuller, Sir John William Fleetwood, Bt. (1910).
Fung, *Hon.* Sir Kenneth Ping-Fan, Kt., CBE.
Furness, Sir Stephen Roberts, Bt. (1913).
Gadsden, Sir Peter Drury Haggerston, GBE, FEng.
Gage, Sir Berkeley Everard Foley, KCMG.
Gairy, *Rt. Hon.* Sir Eric Matthew, Kt.
Gaius, *Rt. Revd* Saimon, KBE.
Gallwey, Sir Philip Frankland Payne-, Bt. (1812).
Gamble, Sir David Hugh Norman, Bt. (1897).
Ganilau, *Ratu* Sir Penaia Kanatabatu, GCMG, KCVO, KBE, DSO.
Gardiner, Sir George Arthur, Kt., MP.
Gardner, Sir Douglas Bruce Bruce-, Bt. (1945).
Gardner, Sir Edward Lucas, Kt., QC.
Garland, *Hon.* Sir Patrick Neville, Kt.
Garland, *Hon.* Sir Ransley Victor, KBE.
Garlick, Sir John, KCB.
Garner, Sir Anthony Stuart, Kt.
Garnier, *Rear-Adm.* Sir John, KCVO, CBE, LVO.
Garrett, *Hon.* Sir Raymond William, Kt., AFC.
Garrioch, Sir (William) Henry, Kt.

Garrod, *Lt.-Gen.* Sir (John) Martin Carruthers, KCB, OBE.
Garthwaite, Sir William Francis Cuthbert, Bt., DSC (1919).
Gaskell, Sir Richard Kennedy Harvey, Kt.
Gatehouse, *Hon.* Sir Robert Alexander, Kt.
Geddes, Sir (Anthony) Reay (Mackay), KBE.
Gentry, *Maj.-Gen.* Sir William George, KBE, CB, DSO.
George, Sir Arthur Thomas, Kt.
Gerken, *Vice-Adm.* Sir Robert William Frank, KCB, CBE.
Gery, Sir Robert Lucian Wade-, KCMG, KCVO.
Gethin, Sir Richard Joseph St Lawrence, Bt. (I. 1665).
Ghurburrun, Sir Rabindrah, Kt.
Gibb, Sir Francis Ross (Frank), Kt., CBE, FEng.
Gibbings, Sir Peter Walter, Kt.
Gibbon, *Gen.* Sir John Houghton, GCB, OBE.
Gibbons, Sir (John) David, KBE.
Gibbons, Sir William Edward Doran, Bt. (1752).
Gibbs, *Hon.* Sir Eustace Hubert Beilby, KCVO, CMG.
Gibbs, *Air Marshal* Sir Gerald Ernest, KBE, CIE, MC.
Gibbs, *Rt. Hon.* Sir Harry Talbot, GCMG, KBE.
Gibbs, *Field Marshal* Sir Roland Christopher, GCB, CBE, DSO, MC.
Gibson, Sir Alexander Drummond, Kt., CBE.
Gibson, Sir Christopher Herbert, Bt. (1931).
Gibson, *Revd* Sir David, Bt. (1926).
Gibson, *Vice-Adm.* Sir Donald Cameron Ernest Forbes, KCB, DSC.
Gibson, *Hon.* Sir Peter Leslie, Kt.
Gibson, *Rt. Hon.* Sir Ralph Brian, Kt.
Giddings, *Air Marshal* Sir (Kenneth Charles) Michael, KCB, OBE, DFC, AFC.
Gielgud, Sir (Arthur) John, Kt., CH.
Giffard, Sir (Charles) Sydney (Rycroft), KCMG.
Gilbert, *Air Chief Marshal* Sir Joseph Alfred, KCB, CBE.
†Gilbey, Sir Walter Gavin, Bt. (1893).
Gilchrist, Sir Andrew Graham, KCMG.
Giles, *Rear-Adm.* Sir Morgan Charles Morgan-, Kt., DSO, OBE, GM.
Gill, Sir Anthony Keith, Kt., F.Eng.
Gillett, Sir Robin Danvers Penrose, Bt., GBE, RD (1959).
Gilliat, *Lt.-Col.* Sir Martin John, GCVO, MBE.
Gillmore, Sir David Howe, KCMG.
Gilmour, *Col.* Sir Allan Macdonald, KCVO, OBE, MC.
Gilmour, Sir John Edward, Bt., DSO, TD (1897).
Gina, Sir Lloyd Maepeza, KBE.
Gingell, *Air Chief Marshal* Sir John, GBE, KCB, KCVO.
Girolami, Sir Paul, Kt.
Gladstone, Sir (Erskine) William, Bt. (1846).
Glasspole, Sir Florizel Augustus, GCMG, GCVO.
Glen, Sir Alexander Richard, KBE, DSC.
Glenn, Sir (Joseph Robert) Archibald, Kt., OBE.
Glidewell, *Rt. Hon.* Sir Iain Derek Laing, Kt.
Glock, Sir William Frederick, Kt., CBE.
Glover, *Gen.* Sir James Malcolm, KCB, MBE.
Glover, Sir Victor Joseph Patrick, Kt.
Glyn, Sir Alan, Kt., ERD.
Glyn, Sir Anthony Geoffrey Leo Simon, Bt. (1927).
Glyn, Sir Richard Lindsay, Bt. (1759 and 1800).
Goad, Sir (Edward) Colin (Viner), KCMG.
Godber, Sir George Edward, GCB, DM.
Goff, Sir Robert (William) Davis-, Bt. (1905).
Gohel, Sir Jayvantsinhji Kayaji, Kt., CBE.
Gold, Sir Arthur Abraham, Kt., CBE.
Gold, Sir Joseph, Kt.
Goldberg, *Prof.* Sir Abraham, Kt., MD, DSC, FRCP.
Golding, Sir John Simon Rawson, Kt., OBE.
Golding, Sir William Gerald, Kt., CBE.
Goldman, Sir Samuel, KCB.
Goldsmith, Sir James Michael, Kt.
Gombrich, *Prof.* Sir Ernst Hans Josef, Kt., OM, CBE, Ph.D., FBA, FSA.
Gooch, Sir (Richard) John Sherlock, Bt. (1746).
Gooch, Sir Trevor Sherlock (Sir Peter), Bt. (1866).
Goodall, Sir (Arthur) David Saunders, GCMG.
Goodenough, Sir Richard Edmund, Bt. (1943).
Goodhart, Sir Philip Carter, Kt.
Goodhart, Sir Robert Anthony Gordon, Bt. (1911).
Goodhart, Sir William Howard, Kt., QC.
Goodhew, Sir Victor Henry, Kt.
Goodison, Sir Alan Clowes, KCMG.
Goodison, Sir Nicholas Proctor, Kt.
Goodson, Sir Mark Weston Lassam, Bt. (1922).
Goodwin, Sir Matthew Dean, Kt., CBE.
Goody, *Most Revd* Launcelot John, KBE.
Goold, Sir George Leonard, Bt. (1801).
Gordon, Sir Alexander John, Kt., CBE.
Gordon, Sir Andrew Cosmo Lewis Duff-, Bt. (1813).
Gordon, Sir Charles Addison Somerville Snowden, KCB.
Gordon, Sir Keith Lyndell, Kt., CMG.
Gordon, Sir (Lionel) Eldred (Peter) Smith-, Bt. (1838).
Gordon, Sir Robert James, Bt. (S. 1706).
Gordon, Sir Sidney Samuel, Kt., CBE.
Gordon Lennox, Lord Nicholas Charles, KCMG, KCVO.
Gore, Sir Richard Ralph St George, Bt. (I. 1622).
Goring, Sir William Burton Nigel, Bt. (1627).
Gorton, *Rt. Hon.* Sir John Grey, GCMG, CH.
Goschen, Sir Edward Christian, Bt., DSO (1916).
Gosling, Sir (Frederick) Donald, Kt.
Goswell, Sir Brian Lawrence, Kt.
Goulding, Sir (Ernest) Irvine, Kt.
Goulding, Sir (William) Lingard Walter, Bt. (1904).
Gourlay, *Gen.* Sir (Basil) Ian (Spencer), KCB, OBE, MC, RM.
Gourlay, Sir Simon Alexander, Kt.
Govan, Sir Lawrence Herbert, Kt.
Gow, *Gen.* Sir (James) Michael, GCB.
Gow, Sir Leonard Maxwell Harper, Kt., MBE.
Gowans, Sir James Learmonth, Kt., CBE, FRCP, FRS.
Gowans, *Hon.* Sir (Urban) Gregory, Kt.
Graaff, Sir de Villiers, Bt., MBE (1911).
Grabham, Sir Anthony Henry, Kt.
Graesser, *Col.* Sir Alastair Stewart Durward, Kt., DSO, OBE, MC, TD.
Graham, Sir Alexander Michael, GBE.
Graham, Sir Charles Spencer Richard, Bt. (1783).
Graham, Sir James Bellingham, Bt. (1662).
Graham, Sir James Thompson, Kt., CMG.
Graham, Sir John Alexander Noble, Bt., GCMG (1906).
Graham, Sir John Moodie, Bt. (1964).
Graham, Sir (John) Patrick, Kt.
Graham, Sir Norman William, Kt., CB.
Graham, Sir Peter Alfred, Kt., OBE.
Graham, *Lt.-Gen.* Sir Peter Walter, KCB, CBE.
†Graham, Sir Ralph Stuart, Bt. (1629).
Graham, *Hon.* Sir Samuel Horatio, Kt., CMG, OBE.
Grandy, *Marshal of the Royal Air Force* Sir John, GCB, GCVO, KBE, DSO.
Grant, Sir Archibald, Bt. (S. 1705).
Grant, Sir Clifford, Kt.
Grant, Sir (John) Anthony, Kt., MP.
Grant, Sir (Matthew) Alistair, Kt.
Grant, Sir Patrick Alexander Benedict, Bt. (S. 1688).
Grantham, *Adm.* Sir Guy, GCB, CBE, DSO.
Gray, Sir John Archibald Browne, Kt., SC.D., FRS.
Gray, *Vice-Adm.* Sir John Michael Dudgeon, KBE, CB.
Gray, *Lt.-Gen.* Sir Michael Stuart, KCB, OBE.
Gray, Sir William Hume, Bt. (1917).

Gray, Sir William Stevenson, Kt.
Graydon, *Air Chief Marshal* Sir Michael James, KCB, CBE.
†Grayson, Sir Jeremy Brian Vincent Harrington, Bt. (1922).
Green, Sir Allan David, KCB, QC.
Green, Sir (Edward) Stephen (Lycett), Bt., CBE (1886).
Green, *Hon.* Sir Guy Stephen Montague, KBE.
Green, Sir Kenneth, Kt.
Green, Sir Owen Whitley, Kt.
Green, Sir Peter James Frederick, Kt.
Greenaway, Sir Derek Burdick, Bt., CBE (1933).
Greenborough, Sir John, KBE.
Greenbury, Sir Richard, Kt.
Greene, Sir (John) Brian Massy-, Kt.
Greengross, Sir Alan David, Kt.
Greening, *Rear-Adm.* Sir Paul Woollven, KCVO.
Greenwell, Sir Edward Bernard, Bt. (1906).
Gregson, Sir Peter Lewis, KCB.
Grenside, Sir John Peter, Kt., CBE.
Gretton, *Vice-Adm.* Sir Peter William, KCB, DSO, OBE, DSC.
Grey, Sir Anthony Dysart, Bt. (1814).
Grey, Sir Roger de, KCVO, PRA.
Grierson, Sir Michael John Bewes, Bt. (S. 1685).
Grierson, Sir Ronald Hugh, Kt.
Grieve, *Prof.* Sir Robert, Kt.
Griffin, *Adm.* Sir Anthony Templer Frederick Griffith, GCB.
Griffin, *Maj.* (Arthur) John (Stewart), KCVO.
Griffin, Sir (Charles) David, Kt., CBE.
Griffiths, Sir Eldon Wylie, Kt.
Griffiths, Sir (Ernest) Roy, Kt.
Griffiths, Sir John Norton-, Bt. (1922).
Grimwade, Sir Andrew Sheppard, Kt., CBE.
Grindrod, *Most Revd* John Basil Rowland, KBE.
Grinstead, Sir Stanley Gordon, Kt.
Grose, *Vice-Adm.* Sir Alan, KBE.
Grotrian, Sir Philip Christian Brent, Bt. (1934).
Grove, Sir Charles Gerald, Bt. (1874).
Grove, Sir Edmund Frank, KCVO.
Grugeon, Sir John Drury, Kt..
Grylls, Sir (William) Michael (John), Kt., MP.
Guinness, Sir Alec, Kt., CBE.
Guinness, Sir Howard Christian Sheldon, Kt., VRD.
Guinness, Sir Kenelm Ernest Lee, Bt. (1867).
Guise, Sir John Grant, Bt. (1783).
Gujadhur, Sir Radhamohun, Kt., CMG.
Gull, Sir Rupert William Cameron, Bt. (1872).
Gunn, *Prof.* Sir John Currie, Kt., CBE.
Gunn, Sir William Archer, KBE, CMG.
†Gunning, Sir Charles Theodore, Bt. (1778).
Gunston, Sir John Wellesley, Bt. (1938).
Guthrie, *Gen.* Sir Charles Ronald Llewelyn, KCB, LVO, OBE.
Guthrie, Sir Malcolm Connop, Bt., (1936)
Guy, *Gen.* Sir Roland Kelvin, GCB, CBE, DSO.
Habakkuk, Sir John Hrothgar, Kt., FBA.
Hackett, *Gen.* Sir John Winthrop, GCB, CBE, DSO, MC.
Hadlee, Sir Richard John, Kt., MBE.
Hadley, Sir Leonard Albert, Kt.
Hadow, Sir Gordon, Kt., CMG, OBE.
Hadow, Sir (Reginald) Michael, KCMG.
Hague, *Prof.* Sir Douglas Chalmers, Kt., CBE.
Halberg, Sir Murray Gordon, Kt., MBE.
Hale, *Prof.* Sir John Rigby, Kt.
Hall, Sir Arnold Alexander, Kt., FRS, FEng.
Hall, Sir Basil Brodribb, KCB, MC, TD.
Hall, *Air Marshal* Sir Donald Percy, KCB, CBE, AFC.
Hall, Sir Douglas Basil, Bt., KCMG (S. 1687).
Hall, Sir (Frederick) John (Frank), Bt. (1923).
Hall, Sir John, Kt.
Hall, Sir John Bernard, Bt. (1919).
Hall, Sir Peter Reginald Frederick, Kt., CBE.
Hall, Sir Robert de Zouche, KCMG.
Hall, *Brig.* Sir William Henry, KBE, DSO, ED.
Halliday, *Vice-Adm.* Sir Roy William, KBE, DSC.
Hallifax, Adm. Sir David John, KCB, KCVO, KBE.
Hallinan, Sir (Adrian) Lincoln, Kt.
Halpern, Sir Ralph Mark, Kt.
Halsey, *Revd* Sir John Walter Brooke, Bt. (1920).
Halstead, Sir Ronald, Kt., CBE.
Ham, Sir David Kenneth Rowe-, GBE.
Hambling, Sir (Herbert) Hugh, Bt. (1924).
Hamburger, Sir Sidney Cyril, Kt., CBE.
Hamer, *Hon.* Sir Rupert James, KCMG, ED.
Hamill, Sir Patrick, Kt., QPM.
Hamilton, Sir Edward Sydney, Bt. (1776 and 1819).
Hamilton, Sir James Arnot, KCB, MBE, FEng.
Hamilton, *Adm.* Sir John Graham, GBE, CB.
Hamilton, Sir Malcolm William Bruce Stirling-, Bt. (S. 1673).
Hamilton, Sir Michael Aubrey, Kt.
Hamilton, Sir (Robert Charles) Richard Caradoc, Bt. (S. 1646).
Hammett, *Hon.* Sir Clifford James, Kt.
Hammick, Sir Stephen George, Bt. (1834).
Hampshire, Sir Stuart Newton, Kt., FBA.
Hanbury, Sir John Capel, Kt., CBE.
Hancock, Sir David John Stowell, KCB.
Hancock, *Air Marshal* Sir Valston Eldridge, KBE, CB, DFC.
Hand, *Most Revd* Geoffrey David, KBE.
Handley, Sir David John Davenport-, Kt., OBE.
Hanham, Sir Michael William, Bt., DFC (1667).
Hanley, Sir Michael Bowen, KCB.
Hanmer, Sir John Wyndham Edward, Bt. (1774).
Hannam, Sir John Gordon, Kt., MP.
Hannay, Sir David Hugh Alexander, KCMG.
Hanson, Sir Anthony Leslie Oswald, Bt. (1887).
Hanson, Sir (Charles) John, Bt. (1918).
Hardcastle, Sir Alan John, Kt.
Harders, Sir Clarence Waldemar, Kt., OBE.
Hardie, Sir Charles Edgar Mathewes, Kt., CBE.
Hardie, Sir Douglas Fleming, Kt., CBE.
Harding, Sir Christopher George Francis, Kt.
Harding, Sir George William, KCMG, CVO.
Harding, *Marshal of the Royal Air Force* Sir Peter Robin, GCB.
Harding, Sir Roy Pollard, Kt., CBE.
Hardinge, Sir Robert Arnold, Bt. (1801).
Hardman, Sir Henry, KCB.
Hardy, Sir David William, Kt.
Hardy, Sir James Gilbert, Kt., OBE.
Hardy, Sir Rupert John, Bt. (1876).
Hare, Sir Thomas, Bt. (1818).
Harford, Sir James Dundas, KBE, CMG.
Harford, Sir (John) Timothy, Bt. (1934).
Hargroves, *Brig.* Sir Robert Louis, Kt., CBE.
Harington, *Gen.* Sir Charles Henry Pepys, GCB, CBE, DSO, MC.
Harington, Sir Nicholas John, Bt. (1611).
Harland, *Air Marshal* Sir Reginald Edward Wynyard, KBE, CB.
Harman, *Gen.* Sir Jack Wentworth, GCB, OBE, MC.
Harman, *Hon.* Sir Jeremiah LeRoy, Kt.
Harmer, Sir Frederic Evelyn, Kt., CMG.
Harmsworth, Sir Hildebrand Harold, Bt. (1922).
Harpham, Sir William, KBE, CMG.
Harris, *Prof.* Sir Alan James, Kt., CBE, FEng.
Harris, Sir Anthony Kyrle Travers, Bt. (1953).
Harris, *Prof.* Sir Charles Herbert Stuart-, Kt., CBE, MD.
Harris, *Lt.-Gen.* Sir Ian Cecil, KBE, CB, DSO.
Harris, Sir Jack Wolfred Ashford, Bt. (1932).

Harris, *Air Marshal* Sir John Hulme, KCB, CBE.
Harris, Sir Philip Charles, Kt.
Harris, Sir Ronald Montague Joseph, KCVO, CB.
Harris, Sir William Gordon, KBE, CB, FEng.
Harrison, Sir Donald Frederick Norris, Kt., FRCS.
Harrison, Sir Ernest Thomas, Kt., OBE..
Harrison, Sir Francis Alexander Lyle, Kt., MBE, QC.
Harrison, *Surgeon Vice-Adm.* Sir John Albert Bews, KBE.
Harrison, *Hon.* Sir (John) Richard, Kt., ED.
Harrison, Sir Michael James Harwood, Bt. (1961).
Harrison, *Prof.* Sir Richard John, Kt., FRS.
Harrison, Sir (Robert) Colin, Bt. (1922).
Harrop, Sir Peter John, KCB.
Hart, Sir Francis Edmund Turton-, KBE.
Hartley, *Air Marshal* Sir Christopher Harold, KCB, CBE, DFC, AFC.
Hartley, Sir Frank, Kt., CBE, Ph.D.
Hartopp, Sir John Edmund Cradock-, Bt. (1796).
Hartwell, Sir Brodrick William Charles Elwin, Bt. (1805).
Harvey, Sir Charles Richard Musgrave, Bt. (1933).
Haskard, Sir Cosmo Dugal Patrick Thomas, KCMG, MBE.
Haslam, *Hon.* Sir Alec Leslie, Kt.
Haslam, *Rear-Adm.* Sir David William, KBE, CB.
Hasluck, *Rt. Hon.* Sir Paul Meernaa Caedwalla, KG, GCMG, GCVO.
Hassan, Sir Joshua Abraham, GBE, KCMG, LVO, QC.
Hassett, *Gen.* Sir Francis George, KBE, CB, DSO, MVO.
Hastings, Sir Stephen Lewis Edmonstone, Kt., MC.
Hatty, *Hon.* Sir Cyril James, Kt.
Haughton, Sir James, Kt., CBE, QPM.
Havelock, Sir Wilfrid Bowen, Kt.
Hawkins, Sir Arthur Ernest, Kt.
Hawkins, Sir Humphry Villiers Caesar, Bt. (1778).
Hawkins, Sir Paul Lancelot, Kt., TD.
Hawley, Sir Donald Frederick, KCMG, MBE.
†Hawley, Sir Henry Nicholas, Bt. (1795).
Haworth, Sir Philip, Bt. (1911).
Hawthorne, *Prof.* Sir William Rede, Kt., CBE, SC.D., FRS, FEng.
Hay, Sir Arthur Thomas Erroll, Bt., ISO (S. 1663).
Hay, Sir David Osborne, Kt., CBE, DSO.
Hay, Sir David Russell, Kt., CBE, FRCP, MD.
Hay, Sir Hamish Grenfell, Kt.
Hay, Sir James Brian Dalrymple-, Bt. (1798).
†Hay, Sir Ronald Frederick Hamilton, Bt. (S. 1703).
Haydon, Sir Walter Robert, KCMG.
Hayes, Sir Brian David, GCB.
Hayes, Sir Claude James, KCMG.
Hayes, *Vice-Adm.* Sir John Osier Chattock, KCB, OBE.
Hayr, *Air Marshal* Sir Kenneth William, KCB, KBE, AFC.
Hayter, Sir William Goodenough, KCMG.
Hayward, Sir Anthony William Byrd, Kt.
Hayward, Sir Jack Arnold, Kt., OBE.
Hayward, Sir Richard Arthur, Kt., CBE.
Haywood, Sir Harold, KCVO, OBE.
Head, Sir Francis David Somerville, Bt. (1838).
Healey, Sir Charles Edward Chadwyck-, Bt. (1919).
Heap, Sir Desmond, Kt.
Heath, *Rt. Hon.* Sir Edward Richard George, KG, MBE, MP.
Heath, Sir Mark Evelyn, KCVO, CMG.
Heath, *Air Marshal* Sir Maurice Lionel, KBE, CB, CVO.
Heathcote, *Brig.* Sir Gilbert Simon, Bt., CBE (1733).
Heathcote, Sir Michael Perryman, Bt. (1733).
Heatley, Sir Peter, Kt., CBE.
Heaton, Sir Yvo Robert Henniker-, Bt. (1912).
Heiser, Sir Terence Michael, GCB.
Hele, Sir Ivor Thomas Henry, Kt., CBE.
Hellaby, Sir (Frederick Reed) Alan, Kt.
Henderson, Sir Denys Hartley, Kt.
Henderson, Sir James Thyne, KBE, CMG.
Henderson, Sir (John) Nicholas, GCMG, KCVO.
Henderson, *Adm.* Sir Nigel Stuart, GBE, KCB.
Henderson, Sir William MacGregor, Kt., D.SC., FRS.
Henley, Sir Douglas Owen, KCB.
Henley, *Rear-Adm.* Sir Joseph Charles Cameron, KCVO, CB.
Hennessy, Sir James Patrick Ivan, KBE, CMG.
Hennessy, Sir John Wyndham Pope-, Kt., CBE, FBA, FSA.
†Henniker, Sir Adrian Chandos, Bt. (1813).
Henry, Sir Denis Aynsley, Kt., OBE, QC.
Henry, *Hon.* Denis Robert Maurice, Kt.
Henry, *Hon.* Sir Geoffrey Arama, KBE.
Henry, Sir James Holmes, Bt., CMG, MC, TD, QC (1923).
Henry, *Hon.* Sir Trevor Ernest, Kt.
Hepburn, Sir John Alastair Trant Kidd Buchan-, Bt. (1815).
Herbecq, Sir John Edward, KCB.
Herbert, *Adm.* Sir Peter Geoffrey Marshall, KCB, OBE.
Hermon, Sir John Charles, Kt., OBE, QPM.
Heron, Sir Conrad Frederick, KCB, OBE.
Herries, Sir Michael Alexander Robert Young-, Kt., OBE, MC.
Hervey, Sir Roger Blaise Ramsay, KCVO, CMG.
Heseltine, *Rt. Hon.* Sir William Frederick Payne, GCB, GCVO.
Hetherington, Sir Arthur Ford, Kt., DSC, FEng.
Hetherington, Sir Thomas Chalmers, KCB, CBE, TD, QC.
Heward, *Air Chief Marshal* Sir Anthony Wilkinson, KCB, OBE, DFC, AFC.
Hewetson, Sir Christopher Raynor, Kt., TD.
Hewetson, *Gen.* Sir Reginald Hackett, GCB, CBE, DSO.
†Hewett, Sir Peter John Smithson, Bt., MM (1813).
Hewitt, Sir (Cyrus) Lenox (Simson), Kt., OBE.
Hewitt, Sir Nicholas Charles Joseph, Bt. (1921).
†Heygate, Sir Richard John Gage, Bt. (1831).
Heyman, Sir Horace William, Kt.
†Heywood, Sir Peter, Bt. (1838).
Hezlet, *Vice-Adm.* Sir Arthur Richard, KBE, CB, DSO, DSC.
Hibbert, Sir Jack, KCB.
Hibbert, Sir Reginald Alfred, GCMG.
Hickey, Sir Justin, Kt.
Hickman, Sir (Richard) Glenn, Bt. (1903).
Hidden, *Hon.* Sir Anthony Brian, Kt.
Hielscher, Sir Leo Arthur, Kt.
Higgins, Sir Christopher Thomas, Kt.
Higgins, *Hon.* John Patrick Basil, Kt.
Higginson, Sir Gordon Robert, Kt., Ph.D., FEng.
Higgs, Sir (John) Michael (Clifford), Kt.
Hildreth, *Maj.-Gen.* Sir (Harold) John (Crossley), KBE.
Hildyard, Sir David Henry Thoroton, KCMG, DFC.
Hiley, *Hon.* Sir Thomas Alfred, KBE.
Hill, Sir Alexander Rodger Erskine-, Bt. (1945).
Hill, Sir Arthur Alfred, Kt., CBE.
Hill, Sir Brian John, Kt.
Hill, Sir James Frederick, Bt. (1917).
Hill, Sir John McGregor, Kt., Ph.D., FEng.
Hill, Sir John Maxwell, Kt., CBE, DFC.
†Hill, Sir John Rowley, Bt. (I. 1779).
Hill, *Vice-Adm.* Sir Robert Charles Finch, KBE.
Hillary, Sir Edmund, KBE.
Hillhouse, Sir (Robert) Russell, KCB.
Hills, Sir Graham John, Kt.

Himsworth, Sir Harold Percival, KCB, MD, FRS.
Hine, *Air Chief Marshal* Sir Patrick Bardon, GCB, GBE.
Hines, Sir Colin Joseph, Kt., OBE.
Hinsley, *Prof.* Sir Francis Harry, Kt., OBE, FBA.
Hirsch, *Prof.* Sir Peter Bernhard, Kt., Ph.D., FRS.
Hirst, *Hon.* Sir David Cozens-Hardy, Kt.
Hirst, Sir Michael William, Kt.
Hoare, Sir Peter Richard David, Bt. (1786).
Hoare, Sir Timothy Edward Charles, Bt. (I. 1784).
Hobart, Sir John Vere, Bt. (1914).
Hobday, Sir Gordon Ivan, Kt.
Hobhouse, Sir Charles John Spinney, Bt. (1812).
Hobhouse, *Hon.* Sir John Stewart, Kt.
Hockaday, Sir Arthur Patrick, KCB, CMG.
Hockley, *Gen.* Sir Anthony Heritage Farrar-, GBE, KCB, DSO, MC.
Hodge, Sir John Rowland, Bt., MBE (1921).
Hodge, Sir Julian Stephen Alfred, Kt.
Hodges, *Air Chief Marshal* Sir Lewis MacDonald, KCB, CBE, DSO, DFC.
Hodgkin, *Prof.* Sir Alan Lloyd, OM, KBE, FRS, SC.D.
Hodgkin, Sir Gordon Howard Eliot, Kt., CBE.
Hodgkinson, *Air Chief Marshal* Sir (William) Derek, KCB, CBE, DFC, AFC.
Hodgson, Sir Maurice Arthur Eric, Kt., FEng.
Hodgson, *Hon.* Sir (Walter) Derek (Thornley), Kt.
Hodson, Sir Michael Robin Adderley, Bt. (I. 1789).
Hoffenberg, *Prof.* Sir Raymond, KBE.
Hoffman, *Hon.* Sir Leonard Hubert, Kt.
Hogg, *Maj.* Sir Arthur Ramsay, Bt., MBE (1846).
Hogg, Sir Christopher Anthony, Kt.
Hogg, Sir Edward William Lindsay-, Bt. (1905).
Hogg, *Vice-Adm.* Sir Ian Leslie Trower, KCB, DSC.
Hogg, Sir John Nicholson, Kt., TD.
Holcroft, Sir Peter George Culcheth, Bt. (1921).
Holden, Sir David Charles Beresford, KBE, CB, ERD.
Holden, Sir Edward, Bt. (1893).
Holden, Sir John David, Bt. (1919).
Holder, Sir John Henry, Bt. (1898).
Holder, *Air Marshal* Sir Paul Davie, KBE, CB, DSO, DFC, Ph.D.
Holderness, Sir Richard William, Bt. (1920).
Holdsworth, Sir (George) Trevor, Kt.
Holland, Sir Clifton Vaughan, Kt.
Holland, Sir Geoffrey, KCB.
Holland, Sir Guy (Hope), Bt. (1917).
Holland, Sir Kenneth Lawrence, Kt., CBE, QFSM.
Holland, Sir Philip Welsby, Kt.
Holliday, *Prof.* Sir Frederick George Thomas, Kt., CBE, FRSE.
Hollings, *Hon.* Sir (Alfred) Kenneth, Kt., MC.
Hollis, *Hon.* Sir Anthony Barnard, Kt.
Hollom, Sir Jasper Quintus, KBE.
Holloway, *Hon.* Sir Barry Blyth, KBE.
Holm, Sir Carl Henry, Kt., OBE.
Holmes, *Prof.* Sir Frank Wakefield, Kt.
Holmes, Sir Maurice Andrew, Kt.
Holmes, Sir Peter Fenwick, Kt., MC.
Holroyd, *Air Marshal* Sir Frank Martyn, KBE, CB.
Holt, *Prof.* Sir James Clarke, Kt.
Holt, Sir John Anthony Langford-, Kt.
†Home, Sir William Dundas, Bt. (s. 1671).
Hone, *Maj.-Gen.* Sir (Herbert) Ralph, KCMG, KBE, MC, TD, QC.
Honeycombe, *Prof.* Sir Robert William Kerr, Kt., FRS, FEng.
Honywood, Sir Filmer Courtenay William, Bt. (1660).
Hood, Sir Alexander William Fuller-Acland-, Bt. (1806).
Hood, Sir Harold Joseph, Bt., TD (1922).
Hookway, Sir Harry Thurston, Kt.
Hoole, Sir Arthur Hugh, Kt.
Hooper, Sir Leonard James, KCMG, CBE.
Hope, Sir (Charles) Peter, KCMG, TD.
Hope, Sir John Carl Alexander, Bt. (s. 1628).
Hope, Sir Robert Holms-Kerr, Bt. (1932).
Hopkin, Sir David Armand, Kt.
Hopkin, Sir (William Aylsham) Bryan, Kt., CBE.
Hopkins, Sir James Sidney Rawdon Scott-, Kt., MEP.
Hordern, Sir Michael Murray, Kt., CBE.
Hordern, Sir Peter Maudslay, Kt., MP.
Horlick, *Vice-Adm.* Sir Edwin John, KBE, FEng.
Horlick, Sir John James Macdonald, Bt. (1914).
Hornby, Sir Derek Peter, Kt.
Hornby, Sir Simon Michael, Kt.
Horne, Sir Alan Gray Antony, Bt. (1929).
Horsfall, Sir John Musgrave, Bt., MC, TD (1909).
Horsley, *Air Marshal* Sir (Beresford) Peter (Torrington), KCB, CBE, MVO, AFC.
Hort, Sir James Fenton, Bt. (1767).
Hoskyns, Sir Benedict Leigh, Bt. (1676).
Hoskyns, Sir John Austin Hungerford Leigh, Kt.
Houghton, Sir John Theodore, Kt., CBE, FRS.
†Houldsworth, Sir Richard Thomas Reginald, Bt. (1887).
Hounsfield, Sir Godfrey Newbold, Kt., CBE.
House, *Lt.-Gen.* Sir David George, GCB, KCVO, CBE, MC.
Houssemayne du Boulay, Sir Roger William, KCVO, CMG.
Howard, Sir (Hamilton) Edward de Coucey, Bt., GBE (1955).
Howard, *Prof.* Sir Michael Eliot, Kt., CBE, MC.
Howard, *Maj.-Gen.* Lord Michael Fitzalan-, GCVO, CB, CBE, MC.
Howard, Sir Walter Stewart, Kt., MBE.
Howie, Sir James William, Kt., MD.
Howlett, *Gen.* Sir Geoffrey Hugh Whitby, KBE, MC.
Hoyle, *Prof.* Sir Fred, Kt., FRS.
Hoyos, *Hon.* Sir Fabriciano Alexander, Kt.
Huckle, Sir (Henry) George, Kt., OBE.
Huddie, Sir David Patrick, Kt., FEng.
Hudleston, *Air Chief Marshal* Sir Edmund Cuthbert, GCB, CBE.
Hudson, Sir Havelock Henry Trevor, Kt.
Hudson, *Lt.-Gen.* Sir Peter, KCB, CBE.
Huggins, *Hon.* Sir Alan Armstrong, Kt.
Hugh-Jones, Sir Wynn Normington, Kt., MVO.
Hughes, Sir David Collingwood, Bt. (1773).
Hughes, *Prof.* Sir Edward Stuart Reginald, Kt., CBE.
Hughes, Sir Jack William, Kt.
Hughes, *Air Marshal* Sir (Sidney Weetman) Rochford, KCB, CBE, AFC.
Hughes, Sir Trevor Denby Lloyd-, Kt.
Hughes, Sir Trevor Poulton, KCB.
Hugo, *Lt.-Col.* Sir John Mandeville, KCVO, OBE.
Hulse, Sir (Hamilton) Westrow, Bt. (1739).
Hulton, Sir Geoffrey Alan, Bt. (1905).
Hume, Sir Alan Blyth, Kt., CB.
Humphreys, Sir Olliver William, Kt., CBE.
Humphreys, Sir (Raymond Evelyn) Myles, Kt.
Hunn, Sir Jack Kent, Kt., CMG.
Hunt, Sir David Wathen Stather, KCMG, OBE.
Hunt, Sir John Leonard, Kt., MP.
Hunt, *Adm.* Sir Nicholas John Streynsham, GCB, LVO.
Hunt, Sir Rex Masterman, Kt., CMG.
Hunt, Sir Robert Frederick, Kt., CBE, FEng.
Hunter, *Hon.* Sir Alexander Albert, KBE.
Hunter, Sir Ian Bruce Hope, Kt., MBE.
Hurrell, Sir Anthony Gerald, KCVO, CMG.
Hutchinson, *Hon.* Sir Ross, Kt., DFC.
Hutchison, *Lt.-Cdr.* Sir (George) Ian Clark, Kt., RN.
Hutchison, *Hon.* Sir Michael, Kt.

Hutchison, Sir Peter, Bt., CBE (1939).
Hutchison, Sir Peter Craft, Bt. (1956).
Hutson, Sir Francis Challenor, Kt., CBE.
Hutton, *Rt. Hon.* Sir (James) Brian Edward, Kt.
Huxley, *Prof.* Sir Andrew Fielding, Kt., OM, FRS.
Huxtable, *Gen.* Sir Charles Richard, KCB, CBE.
Hyatali, *Hon.* Sir Isaac Emanuel, Kt.
Hyslop, Sir Robert John (Robin) Maxwell-, Kt.
Ibbs, Sir (John) Robin, KBE.
Ihaka, *Ven.* Sir Kingi Matutaera, Kt., MBE.
Imbert, Sir Peter Michael, Kt., QPM.
Imray, Sir Colin Henry, KBE, CMG.
Inch, Sir John Ritchie, Kt., CVO, CBE.
Inge, *Gen.* Sir Peter Anthony, GCB.
Ingham, Sir Bernard, Kt.
Ingilby, Sir Thomas Colvin William, Bt. (1866).
Inglis, Sir Brian Scott, Kt.
Inglis of Glencorse, Sir Roderick John, Bt. (S. 1703).
Ingram, Sir James Herbert Charles, Bt. (1893).
†Innes, Sir David Charles Kenneth Gordon, Bt. (NS 1686).
Innes of Edingight, Sir Malcolm Rognvald, KCVO.
Innes, Sir Peter Alexander Berowald, Bt. (S. 1628).
Inniss, *Hon.* Sir Clifford de Lisle, Kt.
Irish, Sir Ronald Arthur, Kt., OBE.
Irvine, *Dr* Sir Robin Orlando Hamilton, Kt.
Irving, Sir Charles Graham, Kt.
Isham, Sir Ian Vere Gyles, Bt. (1627).
Jack, *Hon.* Sir Alieu Sulayman, Kt.
Jack, Sir David, GCMG, MBE.
Jackman, *Air Marshal* Sir (Harold) Douglas, KBE, CB.
Jackson, *Air Chief Marshal* Sir Brendan James, GCB.
Jackson, Sir (John) Edward, KCMG.
Jackson, *Hon.* Sir Lawrence Walter, KCMG.
Jackson, Sir Michael Roland, Bt. (1902).
Jackson, Sir Nicholas Fane St George, Bt. (1913).
Jackson, Sir Robert, Bt. (1815).
Jackson, *Gen.* Sir William Godfrey Fothergill, GBE, KCB, MC.
Jackson, Sir William Thomas, Bt. (1869)
Jacob, *Lt.-Gen.* Sir (Edward) Ian (Claud), GBE, CB.
Jacob, Sir Isaac Hai, Kt., QC.
Jacobi, *Dr* Sir James Edward, Kt., OBE.
Jacobs, Sir David Anthony, Kt.
Jacobs, *Hon.* Sir Kenneth Sydney, KBE.
Jacobs, Sir Piers, KBE.
Jacobs, Sir Wilfred Ebenezer, GCMG, GCVO, OBE, QC.
Jacomb, Sir Martin Wakefield, Kt.
Jaffray, Sir William Otho, Bt. (1892).
Jakeway, Sir (Francis) Derek, KCMG, OBE.
James, Sir Cynlais Morgan, KCMG.
James, Sir Gerard Bowes Kingston, Bt. (1823).
James, Sir Robert Vidal Rhodes, Kt.
Jamieson, *Air Marshal* Sir David Ewan, KBE, CB.
Janion, *Rear-Adm.* Sir Hugh Penderel, KCVO.
Jansen, Sir Ross Malcolm, KBE.
Janvrin, *Vice-Adm.* Sir (Hugh) Richard Benest, KCB, DSC.
Jardine, Sir Andrew Colin Douglas, Bt. (1916).
Jardine, *Maj.* Sir (Andrew) Rupert (John) Buchanan-, Bt., MC (1885).
Jardine of Applegirth, Sir Alexander Maule, Bt. (S. 1672).
Jarratt, Sir Alexander Anthony, Kt., CB.
Jarrett, Sir Clifford George, KBE, CB.
Jawara, *Hon.* Sir Dawda Kairaba, Kt.
Jay, Sir Antony Rupert, Kt.
Jeewoolall, Sir Ramesh, Kt.
Jeffcoate, Sir (Thomas) Norman (Arthur), Kt., MD, FRCS.
Jefferson, Sir George Rowland, Kt., CBE, FEng.
Jefferson, Sir Mervyn Stewart Dunnington-, Bt. (1958).
Jehangir, Sir Hirji, Bt. (1908).
Jejeebhoy, Sir Rustom, Bt. (1857).
Jellicoe, Sir Geoffrey Alan, Kt., CBE, FRIBA.
Jenkins, Sir Brian Garton, GBE.
Jenkins, Sir Michael Romilly Heald, KCMG.
Jenkins, Sir Owain Trevor, Kt.
Jenkinson, Sir John Banks, Bt. (1661).
Jenks, Sir Richard Atherley, Bt. (1932).
Jennings, Sir Albert Victor, Kt.
Jennings, Sir Raymond Winter, Kt., QC.
Jennings, *Prof.* Sir Robert Yewdall, Kt., QC.
Jenour, Sir (Arthur) Maynard (Chesterfield), Kt., TD.
Jephcott, Sir (John) Anthony, Bt. (1962).
Jessel, Sir Charles John, Bt. (1883).
Jewkes, Sir Gordon Wesley, KCMG.
Joel, *Hon.* Sir Asher Alexander, KBE.
John, Sir Rupert Godfrey, Kt.
Johnson, *Rt. Hon.* Sir David Powell Croom-, Kt., DSC, VRD.
Johnson, *Gen.* Sir Garry Dene, KCB, OBE, MC.
Johnson, Sir John Rodney, KCMG.
Johnson, Sir Peter Colpoys Paley, Bt. (1755).
Johnson, *Hon.* Sir Robert Lionel, Kt.
†Johnson, Sir Robin Eliot, Bt. (1818).
Johnson, Sir Ronald Ernest Charles, Kt., CB.
Johnston, Sir Alexander, GCB, KBE.
Johnston, Sir (David) Russell, Kt., MP.
Johnston, Sir John Baines, GCMG, KCVO.
Johnston, *Lt.-Col.* Sir John Frederick Dame, GCVO, MC.
Johnston, *Lt.-Gen.* Sir Maurice Robert, KCB, OBE.
Johnston, Sir Thomas Alexander, Bt. (S. 1626).
Johnstone, Sir Frederic Allan George, Bt. (S. 1700).
Jolliffe, Sir Anthony Stuart, GBE.
Jones, *Gen.* Sir (Charles) Edward Webb, KCB, CBE.
Jones, Sir Christopher Lawrence-, Bt. (1831).
Jones, *Air Marshal* Sir Edward Gordon, KCB, CBE, DSO, DFC.
Jones, Sir (Edward) Martin Furnival, Kt., CBE.
Jones, *Rt. Hon.* Sir Edward Warburton, Kt.
Jones, Sir Ewart Ray Herbert, Kt., D.SC., Ph.D., FRS.
Jones, Sir Francis Avery, Kt., CBE, FRCP.
Jones, Sir Gordon Pearce, Kt.
Jones, Sir Harry Ernest, Kt., CBE.
Jones, Sir James Duncan, KCB.
Jones, Sir John Henry Harvey-, Kt., MBE.
Jones, Sir (John) Kenneth (Trevor), Kt., CBE, QC.
Jones, Sir John Lewis, KCB, CMG.
Jones, Sir John Prichard-, Bt. (1910).
Jones, Sir Keith Stephen, Kt.
Jones, *Hon.* Sir Kenneth George Illtyd, Kt.
Jones, *Air Marshal* Sir Laurence Alfred, KCB, CB, AFC.
Jones, Sir (Owen) Trevor, Kt.
Jones, Sir (Peter) Hugh (Jefferd) Lloyd-, Kt.
Jones, Sir Richard Anthony Lloyd, KCB.
Jones, Sir Robert Edward, Kt.
Jones, Sir Simon Warley Frederick Benton, Bt. (1919).
Jones, Sir (Thomas) Philip, Kt., CB.
Jones, Sir (William) Emrys, Kt.
Jones, *Hon.* Sir William Lloyd Mars-, Kt., MBE.
Jordan, *Air Marshal* Sir Richard Bowen, KCB, DFC.
Joughin, Sir Michael, Kt., CBE.
Jowitt, *Hon.* Sir Edwin Frank, Kt.
Judge, *Hon.* Sir Igor, Kt.
Jugnauth, *Rt. Hon.* Sir Anerood, KCMG, QC.
Jungius, *Vice-Adm.* Sir James George, KBE.
Junor, Sir John Donald Brown, Kt.
Jupp, *Hon.* Sir Kenneth Graham, Kt., MC.
Kaberry, *Hon.* Sir Christopher Donald, Bt. (1960).
Kadoorie, Sir Horace, CBE.
Kalo, Sir Kwamala, Kt., MBE.
Kan Yuet-Keung, Sir, GBE.
Kapi, *Hon.* Sir Mari, Kt., CBE.

Katsina, The Emir of, KBE, CMG.
Katz, Sir Bernard, Kt., FRS.
Kavali, Sir Thomas, Kt., OBE.
Kawharu, *Prof.* Sir Ian Hugh, Kt.
Kay, *Prof.* Sir Andrew Watt, Kt.
Kaye, Sir David Alexander Gordon, Bt. (1923).
Kaye, Sir Emmanuel, Kt., CBE.
Kaye, Sir John Phillip Lister Lister-, Bt. (1812).
Keane, Sir Richard Michael, Bt. (1801).
Keatinge, Sir Edgar Mayne, Kt., CBE.
Keeble, Sir (Herbert Ben) Curtis, GCMG.
Keith, *Prof.* Sir James, KBE.
Kellett, Sir Brian Smith, Kt.
Kellett, Sir Stanley Charles, Bt. (1801).
Kelliher, Sir Henry Joseph, Kt.
Kelly, *Rt. Hon.* Sir (John William) Basil, Kt.
Kelly, Sir William Theodore, Kt., OBE.
Kemball, *Air Marshal* Sir (Richard) John, KCB, CBE.
Kemp, Sir (Edward) Peter, KCB.
Kendrew, Sir John Cowdery, Kt., CBE, SC.D., FRS.
Kenilorea, *Rt. Hon.* Sir Peter, KBE.
Kennard, *Lt.-Col.* Sir George Arnold Ford, Bt. (1891).
Kennaway, Sir John Lawrence, Bt. (1791).
Kennedy, Sir Clyde David Allen, Kt.
Kennedy, Sir Francis, KCMG, CBE.
Kennedy, *Hon.* Sir Ian Alexander, Kt.
Kennedy, Sir Michael Edward, Bt., (1836).
Kennedy, *Rt. Hon.* Sir Paul Joseph Morrow, Kt.
Kennedy, *Air Chief Marshal* Sir Thomas Lawrie, GCB, AFC.
Kennedy-Good, Sir John, KBE.
Kenny, Sir Anthony John Patrick, Kt., D.Phil., D.Litt., FBA.
Kenny, *Gen.* Sir Brian Leslie Graham, GCB, CBE.
Kent, Sir Harold Simcox, GCB, QC.
Kenyon, Sir George Henry, Kt.
Kermode, Sir (John) Frank, Kt., FBA.
Kermode, Sir Ronald Graham Quale, KBE.
Kerr, *Hon.* Sir Alastair Blair-, Kt.
Kerr, *Adm.* Sir John Beverley, KCB.
Kerr, Sir John Olav, KCMG.
Kerr, *Rt. Hon.* Sir Michael Robert Emanuel, Kt.
Kerruish, Sir (Henry) Charles, Kt., OBE.
Kerry, Sir Michael James, KCB, QC.
Kershaw, Sir (John) Anthony, Kt., MC.
Kidd, Sir Robert Hill, KBE, CB.
Kidu, *Hon.* Sir Buri (William), Kt.
Kikau, *Ratu* Sir Jone Latianara, KBE.
Kiki, *Hon.* Sir (Albert) Maori, KBE.
Kilfedder, Sir James Alexander, Kt., MP.
Killen, *Hon.* Denis James, KCMG.
Killick, Sir John Edward, GCMG.
Kilpatrick, *Prof.* Sir Robert, Kt., CBE.
Kimber, Sir Charles Dixon, Bt. (1904).
Kinahan, Sir Robert George Caldwell, Kt., ERD.
King, Sir Albert, Kt., OBE.
King, *Gen.* Sir Frank Douglas, GCB, MBE.
King, Sir John Christopher, Bt. (1888).
King, *Vice-Adm.* Sir Norman Ross Dutton, KBE.
King, Sir Richard Brian Meredith, KCB, MC.
King, Sir Sydney Percy, Kt., OBE.
King, Sir Wayne Alexander, Bt. (1815).
Kingman, *Prof.* Sir John Frank Charles, Kt., FRS.
Kingsland, Sir Richard, Kt., CBE, DFC.
Kingsley, Sir Patrick Graham Toler, KCVO.
Kinloch, Sir David, Bt. (S. 1686).
†Kinloch, Sir David Oliphant, Bt. (1873).
Kirby, *Hon.* Sir Richard Clarence, Kt.
Kirkpatrick, Sir Ivone Elliott, Bt. (S. 1685).
Kirwan, Sir (Archibald) Laurence Patrick, KCMG, TD.
Kitcatt, Sir Peter Julian, Kt., CB.
Kitson, *Gen.* Sir Frank Edward, GBE, KCB, MC.
Kitson, Sir Timothy Peter Geoffrey, Kt.
Kitto, *Rt. Hon.* Sir Frank Walters, KBE.
Kleinwort, Sir Kenneth Drake, Bt. (1909).
Klug, Sir Aaron, Kt.
Knight, Sir Allan Walton, Kt., CMG.
Knight, Sir Arthur William, Kt.
Knight, Sir Harold Murray, KBE, DSC.
Knight, *Air Chief Marshal* Sir Michael William Patrick, KCB, AFC.
Knill, Sir John Kenelm Stuart, Bt. (1893).
Knott, Sir John Laurence, Kt., CBE.
Knowles, Sir Charles Francis, Bt. (1765).
Knowles, Sir Leonard Joseph, Kt., CBE.
Knowles, Sir Richard Marchant, Kt.
Knox, Sir Bryce Muir, KCVO, MC, TD.
Knox, *Hon.* Sir John Leonard, Kt.
Knox, *Hon.* Sir William Edward, Kt.
Kornberg, *Prof.* Sir Hans Leo, Kt., D.SC., SC.D., Ph.D., FRS.
Korowi, Sir Wiwa, GCMG.
Krusin, Sir Stanley Marks, Kt., CB.
Kurongku, *Most. Revd* Peter, KBE.
Labouchere, Sir George Peter, GBE, KCMG.
Lacon, Sir Edmund Vere, Bt. (1818).
Lacy, Sir Hugh Maurice Pierce, Bt. (1921).
Lacy, Sir John Trend, Kt., CBE.
Lagesen, *Air Marshal* Sir Philip Jacobus, KCB, DFC, AFC.
Laidlaw, Sir Christophor Charles Fraser, Kt.
Laing, Sir (John) Maurice, Kt.
Laing, Sir (William) Kirby, Kt., FEng.
Lake, Sir (Atwell) Graham, Bt. (1711).
Laker, Sir Frederick Alfred, Kt.
Lakin, Sir Michael, Bt. (1909).
Laking, Sir George Robert, KCMG.
Lamb, Sir Albert (Larry), Kt.
Lamb, Sir Albert Thomas, KBE, CMG, DFC.
Lambert, Sir Anthony Edward, KCMG.
Lambert, Sir Edward Thomas, KBE, CVO.
Lambert, Sir John Henry, KCVO, CMG.
†Lambert, Sir Peter John Biddulph, Bt. (1711).
Lampl, Sir Frank William, Kt.
Landau, Sir Dennis Marcus, Kt.
Lane, Sir David William Stennis Stuart, Kt.
Lang, *Lt.-Gen.* Sir Derek Boileau, KCB, DSO, MC.
Langham, Sir James Michael, Bt. (1660).
Langley, *Maj.-Gen.* Sir Henry Desmond Allen, KCVO, MBE.
Langrishe, Sir Hercules Ralph Hume, Bt. (I. 1777).
Lapsley, *Air Marshal* Sir John Hugh, KBE, CB, DFC, AFC.
Lapun, *Hon.* Sir Paul, Kt.
Larcom, Sir (Charles) Christopher Royde, Bt. (1868).
Larmour, Sir Edward Noel, KCMG.
Lartigue, Sir Louis Cools-, Kt., OBE.
Lasdun, Sir Denys Louis, Kt., CBE, FRIBA.
Latey, *Rt. Hon.* Sir John Brinsmead, Kt., MBE.
Latham, *Hon.* Sir David Nicholas Ramsey, Kt.
Latham, Sir Richard Thomas Paul, Bt. (1919).
Latimer, Sir (Courtenay) Robert, Kt., CBE.
Latimer, Sir Graham Stanley, KBE.
Laucke, *Hon.* Sir Condor Louis, KCMG.
Lauder, Sir Piers Robert Dick-, Bt. (S. 1690).
Laughton, Sir Anthony Seymour, Kt.
Laurantus, Sir Nicholas, Kt., MBE.
Laurence, Sir Peter Harold, KCMG, MC.
Laurie, Sir Robert Bayley Emilius, Bt. (1834).
Lauti, *Rt. Hon.* Sir Toaripi, GCMG.
Lavan, *Hon.* Sir John Martin, Kt.
Law, *Adm.* Sir Horace Rochfort, GCB, OBE, DSC.
Lawes, Sir (John) Michael Bennet, Bt. (1882).
Lawler, Sir Peter James, Kt., OBE.
Lawrence, Sir David Roland Walter, Bt. (1906).
Lawrence, Sir Guy Kempton, Kt., DSO, OBE, DFC.
Lawrence, Sir Ivan John, Kt., QC, MP.
Lawrence, Sir John Patrick Grosvenor, Kt., CBE.
Lawrence, Sir John Waldemar, Bt., OBE (1858).

Lawrence, Sir William Fettiplace, Bt. (1867).
Laws, *Hon.* Sir John Grant McKenzie, Kt.
Lawson, Sir Christopher Donald, Kt.
Lawson, *Col.* Sir John Charles Arthur Digby, Bt., DSO, MC (1900).
Lawson, Sir John Philip Howard-, Bt. (1841).
Lawson, *Hon.* Sir Neil, Kt.
Lawson, *Gen.* Sir Richard George, KCB, DSO, OBE.
Lawton, *Prof.* Sir Frank Ewart, Kt.
Lawton, *Rt. Hon.* Sir Frederick Horace, Kt.
Layden, Sir John (Jack), Kt.
Layfield, Sir Frank Henry Burland Willoughby, Kt., QC.
Lazarus, Sir Peter Esmond, KCB.
Lea, *Vice-Adm.* Sir John Stuart Crosbie, KBE.
Lea, Sir Thomas William, Bt. (1892).
Leach, *Admiral of the Fleet* Sir Henry Conyers, GCB.
Leach, Sir Ronald George, GBE.
Leahy, Sir Daniel Joseph, Kt.
Leahy, Sir John Henry Gladstone, KCMG.
Learmont, *Gen.* Sir John Hartley, KCB, CBE.
Leask, *Lt.-Gen.* Sir Henry Lowther Ewart Clark, KCB, DSO, OBE.
Leather, Sir Edwin Hartley Cameron, KCMG, KCVO.
Leaver, Sir Christopher, GBE.
Le Bailly, *Vice-Adm.* Sir Louis Edward Stewart Holland, KBE, CB.
Le Cheminant, *Air Chief Marshal* Sir Peter de Lacey, GBE, KCB, DFC.
Lechmere, Sir Berwick Hungerford, Bt. (1818).
Ledger, Sir Frank, (Joseph Francis), Kt.
Ledwidge, Sir (William) Bernard (John), KCMG.
Lee, Sir Arthur James, KBE, MC.
Lee, *Air Chief Marshal* Sir David John Pryer, GBE, CB.
Lee, Sir (Henry) Desmond (Pritchard), Kt.
Lee, *Brig.* Sir Leonard Henry, Kt., CBE.
Lee, Sir Quo-wei, Kt., CBE.
Lee, *Col.* Sir William Allison, Kt., OBE, TD.
Leeds, Sir Christopher Anthony, Bt. (1812).
Lees, Sir David Bryan, Kt.
Lees, Sir Thomas Edward, Bt. (1897).
Lees, Sir Thomas Harcourt Ivor, Bt. (1804).
Lees, Sir (William) Antony Clare, Bt. (1937).
Leese, Sir John Henry Vernon, Bt. (1908).
Le Fanu, *Maj.* Sir (George) Victor (Sheridan), KCVO.
le Fleming, Sir Quintin John, Bt. (1705).
Legard, Sir Charles Thomas, Bt. (1660).
Leggatt, *Rt. Hon.* Sir Andrew Peter, Kt.
Leggatt, Sir Hugh Frank John, Kt.
Leggett, Sir Clarence Arthur Campbell, Kt., MBE.
Leigh, Sir Geoffrey Norman, Kt.
Leigh, Sir John, Bt. (1918).
Leigh, Sir Neville Egerton, KCVO.
Leighton, Sir Michael John Bryan, Bt. (1693).
Leitch, Sir George, KCB, OBE.
Leith, Sir Andrew George Forbes-, Bt. (1923).
Le Marchant, Sir Francis Arthur, Bt. (1841).
Le Masurier, Sir Robert Hugh, Kt., DSC.
Lemon, Sir (Richard) Dawnay, Kt., CBE.
Leng, *Gen.* Sir Peter John Hall, KCB, MBE, MC.
Lennard, *Revd* Sir Hugh Dacre Barrett-, Bt. (1801).
Leon, Sir John Ronald, Bt. (1911).
Leonard, *Rt. Revd* Graham Douglas, KCVO.
Leonard, *Hon.* Sir (Hamilton) John, Kt.
Lepping, Sir George Geria Dennis, GCMG, MBE.
Le Quesne, Sir (Charles) Martin, KCMG.
Le Quesne, Sir (John) Godfray, Kt., QC.
Leslie, Sir Colin Alan Bettridge, Kt.
Leslie, Sir John Norman Ide, Bt. (1876).
†Leslie, Sir (Percy) Theodore, Bt. (S. 1625).
Leslie, Sir Peter Evelyn, Kt.
Lethbridge, Sir Thomas Periam Hector Noel, Bt. (1804).
Leuchars, Sir William Douglas, KBE.
Leupena, Sir Tupua, GCMG, MBE.
Levene, Sir Peter Keith, KBE.
Lever, Sir (Tresham) Christopher Arthur Lindsay, Bt. (1911).
Levey, Sir Michael Vincent, Kt., MVO.
Levine, Sir Montague Bernard, Kt.
Levinge, Sir Richard George Robin, Bt. (I. 1704).
Levy, Sir Ewart Maurice, Bt. (1913).
Lewando, Sir Jan Alfred, Kt., CBE.
Lewis, Sir Allen Montgomery, GCMG, GCVO, QC.
Lewis, *Adm.* Sir Andrew Mackenzie, KCB.
Lewis, Sir Kenneth, Kt.
Lewis, Sir Terence Murray, Kt., OBE, QPM.
Lewthwaite, Sir William Anthony, Bt. (1927).
Ley, Sir Francis Douglas, Bt., MBE, TD (1905).
Leyland, Sir Philip Vyvyan Naylor-, Bt. (1895).
Lickley, Sir Robert Lang, Kt., CBE, FEng.
Lidbury, Sir John Towersey, Kt.
Lidderdale, Sir David William Shuckburgh, KCB.
Liggins, *Prof.* Sir Graham Collingwood, Kt., CBE, FRS.
Lighthill, Sir (Michael) James, Kt., FRS.
Lighton, Sir Christopher Robert, Bt., MBE (I. 1791).
Lim, Sir Han-Hoe, Kt., CBE.
Linacre, Sir (John) Gordon (Seymour), Kt., CBE, AFC, DFM.
Lincoln, Sir Anthony Handley, KCMG, CVO.
Lindley, Sir Arnold Lewis George, Kt., FEng.
Lindop, Sir Norman, Kt.
Lindsay, Sir James Harvey Kincaid Stewart, Kt.
Lindsay, Sir Ronald Alexander, Bt., (1962).
Lintott, Sir Henry John Bevis, KCMG.
Lipworth, Sir (Maurice) Sydney, Kt.
Lithgow, Sir William James, Bt. (1925).
Little, *Most Revd* Thomas Francis, KBE.
Littler, Sir (James) Geoffrey, KCB.
Livesay, *Adm.* Sir Michael Howard, KCB.
Llewellyn, Sir Henry Morton, Bt., CBE (1922).
Llewellyn, *Lt.-Col.* Sir Michael Rowland Godfrey, Bt. (1959).
Llewelyn, Sir John Michael Dillwyn-Venables-, Bt. (1890).
Lloyd, *Rt. Hon.* Sir Anthony John Leslie, Kt.
Lloyd, Sir Ian Stewart, Kt.
Lloyd, Sir (John) Peter (Daniel), Kt.
Lloyd, Sir Nicholas Markley, Kt.
Lloyd, Sir Richard Ernest Butler, Bt. (1960).
Loader, Sir Leslie Thomas, Kt., CBE.
Loane, *Most Revd* Marcus Lawrence, KBE.
Lobo, Sir Rogerio Hyndman, Kt., CBE.
Lock, *Cdr.* Sir (John) Duncan, Kt.
Lockhart, Sir Simon John Edward Francis Sinclair-, Bt. (S. 1636).
Loder, Sir Giles Rolls, Bt. (1887).
Lodge, Sir Thomas, Kt.
Logan, Sir Donald Arthur, KCMG.
Logan, Sir Raymond Douglas, Kt.
Lokoloko, Sir Tore, GCMG, GCVO, OBE.
Longden, Sir Gilbert James Morley, Kt., MBE.
Longland, Sir John Laurence, Kt.
Longley, Sir Norman, Kt., CBE.
Loram, *Vice-Adm.* Sir David Anning, KCB, MVO.
Lorimer, Sir (Thomas) Desmond, Kt.
Lousada, Sir Anthony Baruh, Kt.
Love, Sir Makere Rangiatea Ralph, Kt.
Lovell, Sir (Alfred Charles) Bernard, Kt., OBE, FRS.

Lovelock, Sir Douglas Arthur, KCB.
Loveridge, Sir John Henry, Kt., CBE.
Loveridge, Sir John Warren, Kt.
Lovill, Sir John Roger, Kt., CBE.
Low, Sir Alan Roberts, Kt.
Low, Sir James Richard Morrison-, Bt. (1908).
Lowe, *Air Chief Marshal* Sir Douglas Charles, GCB, DFC, AFC.
Lowe, Sir Thomas William Gordon, Bt. (1918).
Lowry, Sir John Patrick, Kt., CBE.
Lowson, Sir Ian Patrick, Bt. (1951).
Lowther, *Maj.* Sir Charles Douglas, Bt. (1824).
Loyd, Sir Francis Alfred, KCMG, OBE.
Loyd, Sir Julian St John, KCVO.
Lu, Sir Tseng Chi, Kt.
Lucas, Sir Cyril Edward, Kt., CMG, FRS.
Lucas, Sir Thomas Edward, Bt. (1887).
Luce, *Rt Hon.* Sir Richard Napier, Kt.
Luckhoo, *Hon.* Sir Joseph Alexander, Kt.
Luckhoo, Sir Lionel Alfred, KCMG, CBE, QC.
Lucy, Sir Edmund John William Hugh Cameron-Ramsay-Fairfax-, Bt. (1836).
Luddington, Sir Donald Collin Cumyn, KBE, CMG, CVO.
Lumsden, Sir David James, Kt.
Lus, *Hon.* Sir Pita, Kt., OBE.
Lush, *Hon.* Sir George Hermann, Kt.
Lushington, Sir John Richard Castleman, Bt. (1791).
Luyt, Sir Richard Edmonds, GCMG, KCVO, DCM.
Lyell, *Rt. Hon.* Sir Nicholas Walter, Kt., QC, MP.
Lygo, *Adm.* Sir Raymond Derek, KCB.
Lyle, Sir Gavin Archibald, Bt. (1929).
Lyons, Sir Edward Houghton, Kt.
Lyons, Sir James Reginald, Kt.
Lyons, Sir John, Kt.
McAdam, Sir Ian William James, Kt., OBE.
Macadam, Sir Peter, Kt.
McAlpine, Sir Robin, Kt., CBE.
McAlpine, Sir William Hepburn, Bt. (1918).
†Macara, Sir Hugh Kenneth, Bt. (1911).
Macartney, Sir John Barrington, Bt. (I. 1799).
McAvoy, Sir (Francis) Joseph, Kt., CBE.
McCaffrey, Sir Thomas Daniel, Kt.
McCall, Sir (Charles) Patrick Home, Kt., MBE, TD.
McCallum, Sir Donald Murdo, Kt., CBE, FEng.
McCamley, Sir Graham Edward, Kt., MBE.
McCarthy, *Rt. Hon.* Sir Thaddeus Pearcey, KBE.
McCaw, *Hon.* Sir Kenneth Malcolm, Kt., QC.
McClellan, *Col.* Sir Herbert Gerard Thomas, Kt., CBE, TD.
McClintock, Sir Eric Paul, Kt.
McColl, Sir Colin Hugh Verel, KCMG.
McCollum, *Hon.* Sir William, Kt.
McConnell, Sir Robert Shean, Bt. (1900).
McCowan, *Rt. Hon.* Sir Anthony James Denys, Kt..
McCowan, Sir Hew Cargill, Bt. (1934).
McCrea, *Prof.* Sir William Hunter, Kt., FRS.
McCrindle, Sir Robert Arthur, Kt.
McCullough, *Hon.* Sir (Iain) Charles (Robert), Kt.
McCusker, Sir James Alexander, Kt.
MacDermott, *Rt. Hon.* Sir John Clarke, Kt.
McDermott, Sir (Lawrence) Emmet, KBE.
MacDonald, *Gen.* Sir Arthur Leslie, KBE, CB.
McDonald, *Air Chief Marshal* Sir Arthur William Baynes, KCB, AFC.
McDonald, Sir Duncan, Kt., CBE, FEng.
Macdonald of Sleat, Sir Ian Godfrey Bosville, Bt. (S. 1625).
Macdonald, Sir Kenneth Carmichael, KCB.
Macdonald, *Vice-Adm.* Sir Roderick Douglas, KBE.
McDonald, Sir Tom, Kt., OBE.
McDonald, *Hon.* Sir William John Farquhar, Kt.
MacDougall, Sir (George) Donald (Alastair), Kt., CBE, FBA.
McDowell, Sir Eric Wallalce, Kt., CBE.
McDowell, Sir Henry McLorinan, KBE.
Mace, *Lt.-Gen.* Sir John Airth, KBE, CB.
McEwen, Sir John Roderick Hugh, Bt. (1953).
McFarland, Sir John Talbot, Bt. (1914).
Macfarlane, Sir (David) Neil, Kt.
Macfarlane, Sir George Gray, Kt., CB, FEng.
McFarlane, Sir Ian, Kt.
Macfarlane, Sir James Wright, Kt.
McGeoch, *Vice-Adm.* Sir Ian Lachlan Mackay, KCB, DSO, DSC.
Macgregor, Sir Edwin Robert, Bt. (1828).
MacGregor of MacGregor, Sir Gregor, Bt. (1795).
McGregor, Sir Ian Alexander, Kt., CBE, FRS.
MacGregor, Sir Ian Kinloch, Kt.
McGrigor, *Capt.* Sir Charles Edward, Bt. (1831).
McIntosh, *Vice-Adm.* Sir Ian Stewart, KBE, CB, DSO, DSC.
McIntosh, Sir Ronald Robert Duncan, KCB.
McIntyre, Sir Donald Conroy, Kt., CBE.
McIntyre, Sir Meredith Alister, Kt.
McKaig, *Adm.* Sir (John) Rae, KCB, CBE.
Mackay, Sir (George Patrick) Gordon, Kt., CBE.
McKay, Sir John Andrew, Kt., CBE.
McKee, *Maj.* Sir (William) Cecil, Kt., ERD.
McKellen, Sir Ian Murray, Kt., CBE.
McKenzie, Sir Alexander, KBE.
Mackenzie, Sir Alexander Alwyne Henry Charles Brinton Muir-, Bt. (1805).
Mackenzie, Sir (Alexander George Anthony) Allan, Bt. (1890).
Mackenzie, *Vice-Adm.* Sir Hugh Stirling, KCB, DSO, DSC.
Mackenzie, *Lt.-Gen.* Sir Jeremy John George, KCB, OBE.
†Mackenzie, Sir Peter Douglas, Bt. (S. 1673).
†Mackenzie, Sir Roderick McQuhae, Bt. (S. 1703).
McKenzie, Sir Roy Allan, KBE.
Mackeson, Sir Rupert Henry, Bt. (1954).
Mackie, Sir Maitland, Kt., CBE.
MacKinlay, Sir Bruce, Kt., CBE.
McKinnon, Sir James, Kt.
McKinnon, *Hon.* Sir Stuart Neil, Kt.
McKissock, Sir Wylie, Kt., OBE, FRCS.
Macklin, Sir Bruce Roy, Kt., OBE.
Mackworth, *Cdr.* Sir David Arthur Geoffrey, Bt. (1776).
McLaren, Sir Robin John Taylor, KCMG.
MacLaurin, Sir Ian Charter, Kt.
Maclean, Sir Donald Og Grant, Kt.
Maclean, Sir Fitzroy Hew, Bt., CBE (1957).
McLean, Sir Francis Charles, Kt., CBE.
MacLean, *Vice-Adm.* Sir Hector Charles Donald, KBE, CB, DSC.
Maclean, Sir Lachlan Hector Charles, Bt. (NS 1631).
Maclean, Sir Robert Alexander, KBE.
McLennan, Sir Ian Munro, KCMG, KBE.
McLeod, Sir Charles Henry, Bt. (1925).
MacLeod, Sir (Hugh) Roderick, Kt.
McLeod, Sir Ian George, Kt.
†MacLeod, *Hon.* Sir John Maxwell Norman, Bt. (1924).
McLintock, Sir Michael William, Bt. (1934).
Maclure, Sir John Robert Spencer, Bt. (1898).
McMahon, Sir Brian Patrick, Bt. (1817).
McMahon, Sir Christopher William, Kt.
McMichael, Sir John, Kt., MD, FRS, FRCP.
Macmillan, Sir (Alexander McGregor) Graham, Kt.
MacMillan, *Lt.-Gen.* Sir John Richard Alexander, KCB, CBE.
MacMillan, Sir Kenneth, Kt.
McMullin, *Rt. Hon.* Sir Duncan Wallace, Kt.
Macnab, *Brig.* Sir Geoffrey Alex Colin, KCMG, CB.

Macnaghten, Sir Patrick Alexander, Bt. (1836).
McNamara, *Air Chief Marshal* Sir Neville Patrick, KBE.
Macnaughton, *Prof.* Sir Malcolm Campbell, Kt.
McNee, Sir David Blackstock, Kt., QPM.
McNeice, Sir (Thomas) Percy (Fergus), Kt., CMG, OBE.
MacPhail, Sir Bruce Dugald, Kt.
MacPherson, Sir Keith Duncan, Kt.
Macpherson, Sir Ronald Thomas Steward (Tommy), CBE, MC, TD.
Macpherson of Cluny, *Hon.* Sir William Alan, Kt., TD.
McQuarrie, Sir Albert, Kt.
Macrae, *Col.* Sir Robert Andrew Scarth, KCVO, MBE.
Macready, Sir Nevil John Wilfrid, Bt. (1923).
Macrory, Sir Patrick Arthur, Kt.
McShine, *Hon.* Sir Arthur Hugh, Kt.
Mactaggart, Sir John Auld, Bt. (1938).
Macwhinnie, Sir Gordon Menzies, Kt., CBE.
Madden, *Adm.* Sir Charles Edward, Bt., GCB (1919).
Maddocks, Sir Kenneth Phipson, KCMG, KCVO.
Madigan, Sir Russel Tullie, Kt., OBE.
Magnus, Sir Laurence Henry Philip, Bt. (1917).
Maguire, *Air Marshal* Sir Harold John, KCB, DSO, OBE.
Mahon, Sir (John) Denis, Kt., CBE.
Mahon, Sir William Walter, Bt. (1819).
Maiden, Sir Colin James, Kt., D.Phil.
Main, Sir Peter Tester, Kt., ERD.
Maini, Sir Amar Nath, Kt., CBE.
Mais, *Hon.* Sir (Robert) Hugh, Kt.
Maitland, Sir Donald James Dundas, GCMG, OBE.
Maitland, Sir Richard John, Bt. (1818).
Makins, Sir Paul Vivian, Bt. (1903).
Malcolm, Sir David Peter Michael, Bt. (S. 1665).
Malet, Sir Harry Douglas St Lo, Bt.
Mallaby, Sir Christopher Leslie George, KCMG.
Mallinson, Sir William John, Bt. (1935).
Malone, *Hon.* Sir Denis Eustace Gilbert, Kt.
Mamo, Sir Anthony Joseph, Kt., OBE.
Manchester, Sir William Maxwell, KBE.
Mander, Sir Charles Marcus, Bt. (1911).
Manduell, Sir John, Kt., CBE.
Mann, *Rt. Hon.* Sir Michael, Kt.
Mann, *Rt. Revd* Michael Ashley, KCVO.
Mann, Sir Rupert Edward, Bt. (1905).
Mansel, *Revd Canon* James Seymour Denis, KCVO.
Mansel, Sir Philip, Bt. (1622).
Mansfield, *Vice-Adm.* Sir (Edward) Gerard (Napier), KBE, CVO.
Mansfield, Sir Philip (Robert Aked), KCMG.
Mantell, *Hon.* Sir Charles Barrie Knight, Kt.
Manzie, Sir (Andrew) Gordon, KCB.
Mara, *Rt. Hon. Ratu* Sir Kamisese Kapaiwai Tuimacilai, GCMG, KBE.
Margetson, Sir John William Denys, KCMG.
Marjoribanks, Sir James Alexander Milne, KCMG.
Mark, Sir Robert, GBE.
Markham, Sir Charles John, Bt. (1911).
Marking, Sir Henry Ernest, KCVO, CBE, MC.
Marling, Sir Charles William Somerset, Bt. (1882).
Marr, Sir Leslie Lynn, Bt. (1919).
Marriner, Sir Neville, Kt., CBE.
Marriott, Sir Hugh Cavendish Smith-, Bt. (1774).
Marsden, Sir Nigel John Denton, Bt. (1924).
Marshall, Sir Arthur Gregory George, Kt., OBE.
Marshall, Sir Colin Marsh, Kt.
Marshall, Sir Denis Alfred, Kt.
Marshall, *Prof.* Sir (Oshley) Roy, Kt., CBE.
Marshall, Sir Peter Harold Reginald, KCMG.
Marshall, Sir Robert Braithwaite, KCB, MBE.
Marshall, Sir (Robert) Michael, Kt., MP.
Martell, *Vice-Adm.* Sir Hugh Colenso, KBE, CB.
Martin, *Vice-Adm.* Sir John Edward Ludgate, KCB, DSC.
Martin, *Prof.* Sir (John) Leslie, Kt., Ph.D.
Martin, *Col.* Sir (Robert) Andrew (St George), KCVO, OBE.
Martin, Sir (Robert) Bruce, Kt., QC.
Martin, Sir Sidney Launcelot, Kt.
Marychurch, Sir Peter Harvey, KCMG.
Masefield, Sir Peter Gordon, Kt.
Mason, *Hon.* Sir Anthony Frank, KBE.
Mason, Sir (Basil) John, Kt., CB, D.Sc., FRS.
Mason, *Prof.* Sir David Kean, Kt., CBE.
Mason, Sir Frederick Cecil, KCVO, CMG.
Mason, Sir John Charles Moir, KCMG.
Mason, *Prof.* Sir Ronald, KCB, FRS.
Matane, Sir Paulias Nguna, Kt., CMG, OBE.
Mather, Sir (David) Carol (Macdonell), Kt., MC.
Mather, Sir William Loris, Kt., CVO, OBE, MC, TD.
Mathers, Sir Robert William, Kt.
Matheson, Sir (James Adam) Louis, KBE, CMG, FEng.
Matheson of Matheson, Sir Torquhil Alexander, Bt. (1882).
Matthews, Sir Peter Alec, Kt.
Matthews, Sir Peter Jack, Kt., CVO, OBE, QPM.
Matthews, Sir Stanley, Kt., CBE.
†Maxwell, Sir Michael Eustace George, Bt. (S. 1681).
Maxwell, Sir Nigel Mellor Heron-, Bt. (S. 1683).
Maxwell, Sir Robert Hugh, KBE.
May, *Hon.* Sir Anthony Tristram Kenneth, Kt.
May, *Rt. Hon.* Sir John Douglas, Kt.
May, Sir Kenneth Spencer, Kt., CBE.
Mayall, Sir (Alexander) Lees, KCVO, CMG.
Mayhew, *Rt. Hon.* Sir Patrick Barnabas Burke, Kt., QC, MP.
Maynard, *Hon.* Sir Clement Travelyan, Kt.
Maynard, *Air Chief Marshal* Sir Nigel Martin, KCB, CBE, DFC, AFC.
Meade, Sir (Richard) Geoffrey (Austin), KBE, CMG, CVO.
Medlycott, Sir Mervyn Tregonwell, Bt. (1808).
Megarry, *Rt. Hon.* Sir Robert Edgar, Kt., FBA.
Megaw, *Rt. Hon.* Sir John, Kt., CBE, TD.
Meinertzhagen, Sir Peter, Kt., CMG.
Mellon, Sir James, KCMG.
Melville, Sir Harry Work, KCB, Ph.D., D.Sc., FRS.
Melville, Sir Leslie Galfreid, KBE.
Melville, Sir Ronald Henry, KCB.
Mensforth, Sir Eric, Kt., CBE, F.Eng.
Menter, Sir James Woodham, Kt., Ph.D., Sc.D., FRS.
Menteth, Sir James Wallace Stuart-, Bt. (1838).
Menuhin, Sir Yehudi, OM, KBE.
Menzies, Sir Peter Thomson, Kt.
Messervy, Sir (Roney) Godfrey (Collumbell), Kt.
Meyer, Sir Anthony John Charles, Bt. (1910).
Meyjes, Sir Richard Anthony, Kt.
Meyrick, Sir David John Charlton, Bt. (1880).
Meyrick, Sir George Christopher Cadafael Tapps-Gervis-, Bt. (1791).
Miakwe, *Hon.* Sir Akepa, KBE.
Michael, Sir Peter Colin, Kt., CBE.
Micklethwait, Sir Robert Gore, Kt., QC.
Middleton, Sir George Humphrey, KCMG.
Middleton, Sir Peter Edward, GCB.
Middleton, Sir Stephen Hugh, Bt. (1662).
Miers, Sir (Henry) David Alastair Capel, KBE, CMG.
Milbank, Sir Anthony Frederick, Bt. (1882).
Milburn, Sir Anthony Rupert, Bt. (1905).
Miles, Sir Peter Tremayne, KCVO.
Miles, Sir William Napier Maurice, Bt. (1859).

Millais, Sir Geoffrey Richard Everett, Bt. (1885).
Millar, Sir Oliver Nicholas, GCVO, FBA.
Millar, Sir Ronald Graeme, Kt.
Millard, Sir Guy Elwin, KCMG, CVO.
Miller, Sir Donald John, Kt., FRSE, FEng.
Miller, Sir Douglas Sinclair, KCVO, CBE.
Miller, Sir Hilary Duppa (Hal), Kt.
Miller, Sir (Ian) Douglas, Kt.
Miller, Sir John Holmes, Bt. (1705).
Miller, *Lt.-Col.* Sir John Mansel, GCVO, DSO, MC.
Miller, Sir (Oswald) Bernard, Kt.
Miller, Sir Peter North, Kt.
Miller, Sir Stephen James Hamilton, KCVO, MD, FRCS.
Miller of Glenlee, Sir Stephen William Macdonald, Bt. (1788).
Millett, *Hon.* Sir Peter Julian, Kt.
Millichip, Sir Frederick Albert (Bert), Kt.
Milling, *Air Marshal* Sir Denis Crowley-, KCB, CBE, DSO, DFC.
Mills, *Vice-Adm.* Sir Charles Piercy, KCB, CBE, DSC.
Mills, Sir Frank, KCVO, CMG.
Mills, Sir John Lewis Ernest Watts, Kt., CBE.
Mills, Sir Peter Frederick Leighton, Bt. (1921).
Mills, Sir Peter McLay, Kt.
Milman, *Lt.-Col.* Sir Derek, Bt. (1800).
Milne, Sir John Drummond, Kt.
Milner, Sir (George Edward) Mordaunt, Bt. (1717).
Milnes Coates, Sir Anthony Robert, Bt. (1911).
Miskin, *Hon.* Sir James William, Kt., QC.
Mitchell, *Air Cdre* Sir (Arthur) Dennis, KBE, CVO, DFC, AFC.
Mitchell, Sir David Bower, Kt., MP.
Mitchell, Sir Derek Jack, KCB, CVO.
Mitchell, *Prof.* Sir (Edgar) William John, Kt., CBE, FRS.
Mobbs, Sir (Gerald) Nigel, Kt.
Moberly, Sir John Campbell, KBE, CMG.
Moberly, Sir Patrick Hamilton, KCMG.
Moffat, *Lt.-Gen.* Sir (William) Cameron, KBE.
Mogg, *Gen.* Sir (Herbert) John, GCB, CBE, DSO.
Moir, Sir Ernest Ian Royds, Bt. (1916).
Moller, *Hon.* Sir Lester Francis, Kt.
†Molony, Sir Thomas Desmond, Bt. (1925).
Monro, Sir Hector Seymour Peter, Kt., MP.
Monson, Sir (William Bonnar) Leslie, KCMG, CB.
Montgomery, Sir (Basil Henry) David, Bt. (1801).
Montgomery, Sir (William) Fergus, Kt., MP.
Mookerjee, Sir Birendra Nath, Kt.
Moollan, Sir Abdool Hamid Adam, Kt.
Moollan, *Hon.* Sir Cassam (Ismael), Kt.
Moon, Sir Peter Wilfred Giles Graham-, Bt. (1855).
†Moon, Sir Roger, Bt. (1887).
Moore, Sir Edward Stanton, Bt., OBE (1923).
Moore, Sir Francis Thomas, Kt.
Moore, Sir Henry Roderick, Kt., CBE.
Moore, *Hon.* Sir John Cochrane, Kt.
Moore, *Maj.-Gen.* Sir (John) Jeremy, KCB, OBE, MC.
Moore, Sir John Michael, KCVO, CB, DSC.
Moore, *Prof.* Sir Norman Winfrid, Bt. (1919).
Moore, Sir Patrick William Eisdell, Kt., OBE.
Moore, Sir William Roger Clotworthy, Bt., TD (1932).
Moores, Sir John, Kt., CBE.
Mootham, Sir Orby Howell, Kt.
Morauta, Sir Mekere, Kt.
Mordaunt, Sir Richard Nigel Charles, Bt. (1611).
Moreton, Sir John Oscar, KCMG, KCVO, MC.
Morgan, *Maj.-Gen.* Sir David John Hughes-, Bt., CB, CBE (1925).
Morgan, Sir Ernest Dunstan, KBE.
Morgan, Sir John Albert Leigh, KCMG.
Morland, *Hon.* Sir Michael, Kt.
Morland, Sir Robert Kenelm, Kt.
Morpeth, Sir Douglas Spottiswoode, Kt., TD.
Morris, *Air Marshal* Sir Arnold Alec, KBE, CB, FEng.
Morris, Sir (James) Richard (Samuel), Kt., CBE, FEng.
Morris, Sir Robert Byng, Bt. (1806).
Morrison, *Hon.* Sir Charles Andrew, Kt.
Morrison, Sir Howard Leslie, Kt., OBE.
Morrison, *Rt. Hon.* Sir Peter Hugh, Kt.
Morritt, *Hon.* Sir (Robert) Andrew, Kt., CVO.
Morrow, Sir Ian Thomas, Kt.
Morse, Sir Christopher Jeremy, KCMG.
Morton, *Adm.* Sir Anthony Storrs, GBE, KCB.
Morton, Sir (Robert) Alastair (Newton), Kt.
Morton, Sir William David, Kt., CBE.
Moseley, Sir George Walker, KCB.
Moser, *Prof.* Sir Claus Adolf, KCB, CBE, FBA.
†Moss, Sir David John Edwards-, Bt. (1868).
Mostyn, *Gen.* Sir (Joseph) David Frederick, KCB, CBE.
†Mostyn, Sir William Basil John, Bt. (1670).
Mott, Sir John Harmer, Bt. (1930).
Mott, Sir Nevill Francis, Kt., FRS.
Mount, Sir James William Spencer, Kt., CBE, BEM.
Mount, Sir William Malcolm, Bt. (1921).
Mountain, Sir Denis Mortimer, Bt. (1922).
Mowbray, Sir John, Kt.
Mowbray, Sir John Robert, Bt. (1880).
Moynihan, Sir Noel Henry, Kt.
Muir, Sir John Harling, Bt. (1892).
Muir, Sir Laurence Macdonald, Kt.
Muirhead, Sir David Francis, KCMG, CVO.
Mulholland, Sir Michael Henry, Bt. (1945).
Mullens, *Lt.-Gen.* Sir Anthony Richard Guy, KCB, OBE.
Mummery, *Hon.* Sir John Frank, Kt.
Munn, Sir James, Kt., OBE.
Munro, Sir Alan Gordon, KCMG.
Munro, Sir Alasdair Thomas Ian, Bt. (1825).
Munro, Sir Ian Talbot, Bt. (s. 1634).
Munro, *Hon.* Sir Robert Lindsay, Kt., CBE.
Munro, Sir Sydney Douglas Gun-, GCMG, MBE.
Murley, Sir Reginald Sydney, KBE, TD, FRCS.
Murphy, Sir Leslie Frederick, Kt.
Murray, *Rt. Hon.* Sir Donald Bruce, Kt.
Murray, Sir Donald Frederick, KCVO, CMG.
Murray, Sir James, KCMG.
Murray, Sir John Antony Jerningham, Kt., CBE.
Murray, Sir Nigel Andrew Digby, Bt. (s. 1628).
Murray, Sir Patrick Ian Keith, Bt. (s. 1673).
Murray, Sir Rowland William Patrick, Bt. (s. 1630).
Murrie, Sir William Stuart, GCB, KBE.
Mursell, Sir Peter, Kt., MBE.
Musgrave, Sir Christopher Patrick Charles, Bt. (1611).
Musgrave, Sir Richard James, Bt. (I. 1782).
Musson, *Gen.* Sir Geoffrey Randolph Dixon, GCB, CBE, DSO.
Myers, Sir Kenneth Ben, Kt., MBE.
Myers, Sir Philip Alan, Kt., OBE, QPM.
Myers, *Prof.* Sir Rupert Horace, KBE.
Mynors, Sir Richard Baskerville, Bt. (1964).
Nabarro, Sir John David Nunes, Kt., MD, FRCP.
Naipaul, Sir Vidiadhar Surajprasad, Kt.
Nairn, Sir Michael, Bt. (1904).
Nairn, Sir Robert Arnold Spencer-, Bt. (1933).
Nairne, *Rt. Hon.* Sir Patrick Dalmahoy, GCB, MC.
Nalder, *Hon.* Sir Crawford David, Kt.
Nall, Sir Michael Joseph, Bt., RN (1954).
Napier, Sir John Archibald Lennox, Bt. (s. 1627).
Napier, Sir Oliver John, Kt.

Napier, Sir Robin Surtees, Bt. (1867).
Napley, Sir David, Kt.
Narain, Sir Sathi, KBE.
Neal, Sir Eric James, Kt., CVO.
Neal, Sir Leonard Francis, Kt., CBE.
Neale, Sir Alan Derrett, KCB, MBE.
Neale, Sir Gerrard Anthony, Kt.
†Neave, Sir Paul Arundell, Bt. (1795).
Nedd, *Hon.* Sir Robert Archibald, Kt.
Neill, *Rt. Hon.* Sir Brian Thomas, Kt.
Neill, Sir Francis Patrick, Kt., QC.
Neill, *Rt. Hon.* Sir Ivan, Kt, PC(NI).
Nelson, *Maj.-Gen.* Sir (Eustace) John (Blois), KCVO, CB, DSO, OBE, MC.
†Nelson, Sir Jamie Charles Vernon Hope, Bt. (1912).
Nelson, *Air Marshal* Sir (Sidney) Richard (Carlyle), KCB, OBE, MD.
Nepean, *Lt.-Col.* Sir Evan Yorke, Bt. (1802).
Ness, *Air Marshal* Sir Charles Ernest, KCB, CBE.
Neubert, Sir Michael John, Kt., MP.
Nevile, *Capt.* Sir Henry Nicholas, KCVO.
Neville, Sir Richard Lionel John Baines, Bt. (1927).
New, *Maj.-Gen.* Sir Laurence Anthony Wallis, Kt., CB, CBE.
Newbold, Sir Charles Demorée, KBE, CMG, QC.
Newman, Sir Francis Hugh Cecil, Bt. (1912).
Newman, Sir Geoffrey Robert, Bt. (1836).
Newman, Sir Jack, Kt., CBE.
Newman, Sir Kenneth Leslie, GBE, QPM.
Newman, *Vice-Adm.* Sir Roy Thomas, KCB.
Newns, Sir (Alfred) Foley (Francis Polden), KCMG, CVO.
Newsam, Sir Peter Anthony, Kt.
Newton, Sir (Harry) Michael (Rex), Bt. (1900).
Newton, Sir Kenneth Garnar, Bt., OBE, TD (1924).
Newton, Sir (Leslie) Gordon, Kt.
Ngata, Sir Henare Kohere, KBE.
Niall, Sir Horace Lionel Richard, Kt., CBE.
Nicholas, Sir David, Kt., CBE.
Nicholas, Sir Herbert Richard, Kt., OBE.
Nicholas, Sir John William, KCVO, CMG.
Nicholls, *Rt. Hon.* Sir Donald James, Kt.
Nicholls, *Air Marshal* Sir John Moreton, KCB, CBE, DFC, AFC.
Nichols, Sir Edward Henry, Kt., TD.
Nicholson, Sir Bryan Hubert, Kt.
Nicholson, *Hon.* Sir David Eric, Kt.
Nicholson, Sir John Norris, Bt., KBE, CIE (1912).
Nicholson, *Hon.* Sir Michael, Kt.
Nicholson, Sir Robin Buchanan, Kt., Ph.D., FRS.
Nickson, Sir David Wigley, KBE.
Nicoll, Sir William, KCMG.
Nicolson, Sir David Lancaster, Kt, FEng.
Nield, Sir Basil Edward, Kt., CBE, QC.
Nield, Sir William Alan, GCMG, KCB.
Nightingale, Sir Charles Manners Gamaliel, Bt. (1628).
Nightingale, Sir John Cyprian, Kt., CBE, BEM, QPM.
Nimmo, *Hon.* Sir John Angus, Kt., CBE.
Niven, Sir (Cecil) Rex, Kt., CMG, MC.
Nixon, Sir Edwin Ronald, Kt., CBE.
Nixon, *Revd* Sir Kenneth Michael John Basil, Bt. (1906).
Noad, Sir Kenneth Beeson, Kt., MD.
Noble, Sir David Brunel, Bt. (1902).
Noble, Sir Iain Andrew, Bt., OBE (1923).
Noble, Sir (Thomas Alexander) Fraser, Kt., MBE.
Nolan, *Rt. Hon.* Sir Michael Patrick, Kt.
Nolan, Sir Sidney Robert, Kt., OM, CBE.
Nombri, Sir Joseph Karl, Kt., ISO, BEM.
Norman, Sir Arthur Gordon, KBE, DFC.
Norman, Sir Mark Annesley, Bt. (1915).
Norman, *Prof.* Sir Richard Oswald Chandler, KBE, FRS.
Norman, Sir Robert Henry, Kt., OBE.
Norman, Sir Robert Wentworth, Kt.
Normanton, Sir Tom, Kt., TD.
Norris, *Air Chief Marshal* Sir Christopher Neil Foxley-, GCB, DSO, OBE.
Norris, Sir Eric George, KCMG.
North, Sir Thomas Lindsay, Kt.
North, Sir (William) Jonathan (Frederick), Bt. (1920).
Norton, *Vice-Adm. Hon.* Sir Nicholas John Hill-, KCB.
Norwood, Sir Walter Neville, Kt.
Nossal, Sir Gustav Joseph Victor, Kt., CBE.
Nott, *Rt. Hon.* Sir John William Frederic, KCB.
Nourse, *Rt. Hon.* Sir Martin Charles, Kt.
Nugent, Sir John Edwin Lavallin, Bt. (I. 1795).
Nugent, *Maj.* Sir Peter Walter James, Bt. (1831).
Nugent, Sir Robin George Colborne, Bt. (1806).
Nursaw, Sir James, KCB, QC.
Nuttall, Sir Nicholas Keith Lillington, Bt. (1922).
Nutting, *Rt. Hon.* Sir (Harold) Anthony, Bt. (1903).
Oakeley, Sir John Digby Atholl, Bt. (1790).
Oakes, Sir Christopher, Bt. (1939).
Oakshott, Hon. Sir Anthony Hendrie, Bt. (1959).
Oates, Sir Thomas, Kt., CMG, OBE.
Oatley, Sir Charles William, Kt., OBE, FRS, FEng.
Obolensky, *Prof.* Sir Dimitri, Kt.
O'Brien, Sir Frederick William Fitzgerald, Kt.
O'Brien, Sir Richard, Kt., DSO, MC.
O'Brien, Sir Timothy John, Bt. (1849).
O'Brien, *Adm.* Sir William Donough, KCB, DSC.
O'Connell, Sir Maurice James Donagh MacCarthy, Bt. (1869).
O'Connor, *Rt. Hon.* Sir Patrick McCarthy, Kt.
O'Dea, Sir Patrick Jerad, KCVO.
Odell, Sir Stanley John, Kt.
Ogden, Sir (Edward) Michael, Kt., QC.
Ogilvie, Sir Alec Drummond, Kt.
Ogilvy, Hon. Sir Angus James Bruce, KCVO.
†Ogilvy, Sir Francis Gilbert Arthur, Bt. (S. 1626).
Ognall, *Hon.* Sir Harry Henry, Kt.
O'Halloran, Sir Charles Ernest, Kt.
Ohlson, Sir Brian Eric Christopher, Bt. (1920).
Okeover, *Capt.* Sir Peter Ralph Leopold Walker-, Bt. (1886).
Olewale, *Hon.* Sir Niwia Ebia, Kt.
Oliphant, Sir Mark (Marcus Laurence Elwin), KBE, FRS.
Oliver, Sir (Frederick) Ernest, Kt., CBE, TD.
O'Loghlen, Sir Colman Michael, Bt. (1838).
Olver, Sir Stephen John Linley, KBE, CMG.
O'Neil, *Hon.* Sir Desmond Henry, Kt.
Ongley, *Hon.* Sir Joseph Augustine, Kt.
Onslow, Sir John Roger Wilmot, Bt. (1797).
Oppenheim, Sir Alexander, Kt., OBE, D.SC., FRSE.
Oppenheim, Sir Duncan Morris, Kt.
Oppenheimer, Sir Michael Bernard Grenville, Bt. (1921).
Oppenheimer, Sir Philip Jack, Kt.
Opperman, *Hon.* Sir Hubert Ferdinand, Kt., OBE.
Orde, Sir John Alexander Campbell-, Bt. (1790).
O'Regan, *Hon.* Sir John Barry, Kt.
Orlebar, Sir Michael Keith Orlebar Simpson-, KCMG.
Ormond, Sir John Davies Wilder, Kt., BEM.
Orr, Sir David Alexander, Kt., MC.
Orr, Sir John Henry, Kt., OBE, QPM.
Osborn, Sir John Holbrook, Kt.
Osborn, Sir Richard Henry Danvers, Bt. (1662).
Osborne, Sir Peter George, Bt. (I. 1629).
Osifelo, Sir Frederick Aubarua, Kt., MBE.
Osman, Sir (Abdool) Raman Mahomed, GCMG, CBE.
Osmond, Sir Douglas, Kt., CBE.
Osmond, Sir (Stanley) Paul, Kt., CB.

Oswald, *Adm.* Sir (John) Julian Robertson, GCB.
Otton, Sir Geoffrey John, KCB.
Otton, *Hon.* Sir Philip Howard, Kt.
Oulton, Sir Antony Derek Maxwell, GCB, QC.
Outram, Sir Alan James, Bt. (1858).
Overall, Sir John Wallace, Kt., CBE, MC.
Owen, Sir Geoffrey, Kt.
Owen, Sir Hugh Bernard Pilkington, Bt. (1813).
†Owen, Sir Hugo Dudley Cunliffe-, Bt. (1920).
Owen, *Hon.* Sir John Arthur Dalziel, Kt.
Owo, The Olowo of, Kt.
Oxburgh, *Prof.* Sir Ernest Ronald, KBE, Ph.D., FRS.
Oxford, Sir Kenneth Gordon, Kt., CBE, QPM.
Packard, *Lt.-Gen.* Sir (Charles) Douglas, KBE, CB, DSO.
Padmore, Sir Thomas, GCB.
Page, Sir Alexander Warren, Kt., MBE.
Page, Sir (Arthur) John, Kt.
Page, Sir Frederick William, Kt., CBE, FEng.
Page, Sir John Joseph Joffre, Kt., OBE.
Paget, Sir Julian Tolver, Bt., CVO (1871).
Paget, Sir Richard Herbert, Bt. (1886).
Pain, *Lt.-Gen.* Sir (Horace) Rollo (Squarey), KCB, MC.
Pain, *Hon.* Sir Peter Richard, Kt.
Palin, *Air Chief Marshal* Sir Roger Hewlett, KCB, OBE.
Palliser, *Rt. Hon.* Sir (Arthur) Michael, GCMG.
Palmar, Sir Derek James, Kt.
Palmer, Sir (Charles) Mark, Bt. (1886).
Palmer, *Gen.* Sir (Charles) Patrick (Ralph), KBE.
Palmer, Sir Geoffrey Christopher John, Bt. (1660).
Palmer, *Rt. Hon.* Sir Geoffrey Winston Russell, KCMG.
Palmer, Sir John Chance, Kt.
Palmer, Sir John Edward Somerset, Bt. (1791).
Palmer, *Maj.-Gen.* Sir (Joseph) Michael, KCVO.
Paolozzi, Sir Eduardo Luigi, Kt., CBE, RA.
Pararajasingam, Sir Sangarapillai, Kt.
Parbo, Sir Arvi Hillar, Kt.
Parish, Sir David Elmer Woodbine, Kt., CBE.
Park, *Hon.* Sir Hugh Eames, Kt.
Parker, Sir (Arthur) Douglas Dodds-, Kt.
Parker, Sir Eric Wilson, Kt.
Parker, *Hon.* Sir Jonathan Frederic, Kt.
Parker, Sir Peter, Kt., LVO.
Parker, Sir Richard (William) Hyde, Bt. (1681).
Parker, *Rt. Hon.* Sir Roger Jocelyn, Kt.
Parker, *Vice-Adm.* Sir (Wilfred) John, KBE, CB, DSC.
Parker, Sir William Peter Brian, Bt. (1844).
Parkes, Sir Basil Arthur, Kt., OBE.
Parkes, Sir Edward Walter, Kt., FEng.
Parkinson, Sir Nicholas Fancourt, Kt.
Parry, Sir Ernest Jones-, Kt.
Parsons, Sir Anthony Derrick, GCMG, MVO, MC.
Parsons, Sir (John) Michael, Kt.
Parsons, Sir Richard Edmund (Clement Fownes), KCMG.
Partridge, Sir Michael John Anthony, KCB.
Pascoe, *Gen.* Sir Robert Alan, KCB, MBE.
Pasley, Sir John Malcolm Sabine, Bt. (1794).
Paterson, Sir Dennis Craig, Kt.
Paterson, Sir George Mutlow, Kt., OBE, QC.
Paterson, Sir John Valentine Jardine, Kt.
Paton, Sir (Thomas) Angus (Lyall), Kt., CMG, FRS, FEng.
Paton, *Prof.* Sir William Drummond Macdonald, Kt., CBE, DM, FRS, FRCP.
Pattie, *Rt. Hon.* Sir Geoffrey Edwin, Kt., MP.
Pattinson, *Hon.* Sir Baden, KBE.
Pattinson, Sir (William) Derek, Kt.
Paul, Sir John Warburton, GCMG, OBE, MC.
Paul, *Air Marshal* Sir Ronald Ian Stuart-, KBE.
Payne, Sir Norman John, Kt., CBE, FEng.
Peach, Sir Leonard Harry, Kt.
Peacock, *Prof.* Sir Alan Turner, Kt., DSC.
Pearce, Sir Austin William, Kt., CBE, Ph.D., FEng.
Pearce, Sir (Daniel Norton) Idris, Kt., CBE, TD.
Pearce, Sir Eric Herbert, Kt., OBE.
Peard, *Rear-Adm.* Sir Kenyon Harry Terrell, KBE.
Pearman, *Hon.* Sir James Eugene, Kt., CBE.
Pearson, Sir Francis Nicholas Fraser, Bt. (1964).
Pearson, *Gen.* Sir Thomas Cecil Hook, KCB, CBE, DSO.
Peart, *Prof.* Sir William Stanley, Kt., MD, FRS.
Pease, Sir (Alfred) Vincent, Bt. (1882).
Pease, Sir Richard Thorn, Bt. (1920).
Peat, Sir Gerrard Charles, KCVO.
Peat, Sir Henry, KCVO, DFC.
Peck, Sir Edward Heywood, GCMG.
Peck, Sir John Howard, KCMG.
Pedder, *Vice-Adm.* Sir Arthur Reid, KBE, CB.
Pedder, *Air Marshal* Sir Ian Maurice, KCB, OBE, DFC.
Peek, Sir Francis Henry Grenville, Bt. (1874).
Peek, *Vice-Adm.* Sir Richard Innes, KBE, CB, DSC.
Peel, Sir John Harold, KCVO.
Peel, Sir (William) John, Kt.
Peierls, Sir Rudolf Ernst, Kt., CBE, D.SC., D.Phil., FRS.
Peirse, Sir Henry Grant de la Poer Beresford-, Bt. (1814).
Peirse, *Air Vice-Marshal* Sir Richard Charles Fairfax, KCVO, CB.
Pelgen, Sir Harry Friedrich, Kt., MBE.
Pelly, Sir John Alwyne, Bt. (1840).
Pemberton, Sir Francis Wingate William, Kt., CBE.
Penn, *Lt.-Col.* Sir Eric Charles William Mackenzie, GCVO, OBE, MC.
Percival, Sir Anthony Edward, Kt., CB.
Percival, *Rt. Hon.* Sir (Walter) Ian, Kt., QC.
Pereira, Sir (Herbert) Charles, Kt., D.SC., FRS.
Perkins, *Surgeon Vice-Adm.* Sir Derek Duncombe Steele-, KCB, KCVO.
Perring, Sir Ralph Edgar, Bt. (1963).
Perris, Sir David (Arthur), Kt., MBE.
Perry, Sir David Howard, KCB.
Perry, Sir (David) Norman, Kt., MBE.
Pestell, Sir John Richard, KCVO.
Peterkin, Sir Neville, Kt.
Petersen, Sir Jeffrey Charles, KCMG.
Petersen, Sir Johannes Bjelke-, KCMG.
Petit, Sir Dinshaw Manockjee, Bt. (1890).
Peto, Sir Henry George Morton, Bt. (1855).
Peto, Sir Michael Henry Basil, Bt. (1927).
Petrie, Sir Peter Charles, Bt., CMG (1918).
Pettigrew, Sir Russell Hilton, Kt.
Pettit, Sir Daniel Eric Arthur, Kt.
Philips, *Prof.* Sir Cyril Henry, Kt.
Phillips, *Prof.* Sir David Chilton, KBE, Ph.D., FRS.
Phillips, Sir Fred Albert, Kt., CVO.
Phillips, Sir Henry Ellis Isidore, Kt., CMG, MBE.
Phillips, Sir Horace, KCMG.
Phillips, *Hon.* Sir Nicholas Addison, Kt.
Phillips, Sir Peter John, Kt., OBE.
Phillips, Sir Robin Francis, Bt. (1912).
Pickard, Sir Cyril Stanley, KCMG.
Pickering, Sir Edward Davies, Kt.
Pickthorn, Sir Charles William Richards, Bt. (1959).
Pidgeon, Sir John Allan Stewart, Kt.
Piers, Sir Charles Robert Fitzmaurice, Bt. (I. 1661).
Pigot, Sir George Hugh, Bt. (1764).
Pigott, Sir Berkeley Henry Sebastian, Bt. (1808).
Pike, Sir Michael Edmund, KCVO, CMG.
Pike, Sir Philip Ernest Housden, Kt., QC.

Pike, *Lt.-Gen.* Sir William Gregory Huddleston, KCB, CBE, DSO.
Pilcher, Sir (Charlie) Dennis, Kt., CBE.
Pilditch, Sir Richard Edward, Bt. (1929).
Pile, Sir Frederick Devereux, Bt. MC (1900).
Pile, Sir William Dennis, GCB, MBE.
Pilkington, Sir Antony Richard, Kt.
Pilkington, Sir Lionel Alexander Bethune, (Sir Alastair), Kt., FRS.
Pilkington, Sir Thomas Henry Milborne-Swinnerton-, Bt. (S. 1635).
Pill, *Hon.* Sir Malcolm Thomas, Kt.
Pillar, *Adm.* Sir William Thomas, GBE, KCB.
Pindling, *Rt. Hon.* Sir Lynden Oscar, KCMG.
Pinker, Sir George Douglas, KCVO.
Pinsent, Sir Christopher Roy, Bt. (1938).
Pippard, *Prof.* Sir (Alfred) Brian, Kt., FRS.
Pirie, *Gp Capt* Sir Gordon Hamish, Kt., CVO, CBE.
Pitblado, Sir David Bruce, KCB, CVO.
Pitcher, Sir Desmond Henry, Kt.
Pitoi, Sir Sere, Kt., CBE.
Pitt, Sir Harry Raymond, Kt., Ph.D., FRS.
Pitts, Sir Cyril Alfred, Kt.
Pixley, Sir Neville Drake, Kt., MBE, VRD.
Pizey, *Adm.* Sir (Charles Thomas) Mark, GBE, CB, DSO.
Plastow, Sir David Arnold Stuart, Kt.
†Platt, Sir (Frank) Lindsey, Bt. (1958).
Platt, *Prof.* Hon. Sir Peter, Bt. (1959).
Playfair, Sir Edward Wilder, KCB.
Pliatzky, Sir Leo, KCB.
Plowman, Sir (John) Anthony, Kt.
Plowman, *Hon.* Sir John Robin, Kt., CBE.
Plumb, *Prof.* Sir John Harold, Kt.
Pohai, Sir Timothy, Kt., MBE.
Pole, *Col.* Sir John Gawen Carew, Bt., DSO, TD (1628).
Pole, Sir Peter Van Notten, Bt. (1791).
Pollen, Sir John Michael Hungerford, Bt. (1795).
Pollock, Sir George Frederick, Bt. (1866).
Pollock, Sir Giles Hampden Montagu-, Bt. (1872).
Pollock, *Admiral of the Fleet* Sir Michael Patrick, GCB, MVO, DSC.
Pollock, Sir William Horace Montagu-, KCMG.
Ponsonby, Sir Ashley Charles Gibbs, Bt., MC (1956).
Pontin, Sir Frederick William, Kt.
Poore, Sir Herbert Edward, Bt. (1795).
Pope, *Vice-Adm.* Sir (John) Ernle, KCB.
Pope, Sir Joseph Albert, Kt., D.SC., Ph.D.
Popper, *Prof.* Sir Karl Raimund, Kt., CH, Ph.D., FRS.
Popplewell, *Hon.* Sir Oliver Bury, Kt.
Portal, Sir Jonathan Francis, Bt. (1901).
Porter, Sir John Simon Horsbrugh-, Bt. (1902).
Porter, Sir Leslie, Kt.
Porter, *Air Marshal* Sir (Melvin) Kenneth (Drowley), KCB, CBE.
Porter, *Hon.* Sir Murray Victor, Kt.
Porter, *Rt. Hon.* Sir Robert Wilson, Kt., PC(NI), QC.
Posnett, Sir Richard Neil, KBE, CMG.
Potter, Sir (Joseph) Raymond (Lynden), Kt.
Potter, *Hon.* Sir Mark Howard, Kt.
Potter, *Maj.-Gen.* Sir (Wilfrid) John, KBE, CB.
Potter, Sir (William) Ian, Kt.
Potts, *Hon.* Sir Francis Humphrey, Kt.
Pound, Sir John David, Bt. (1905).
Pountain, Sir Eric John, Kt.
Powell, Sir (Arnold Joseph) Philip, Kt., CH, OBE, RA, FRIBA.
Powell, Sir Charles David, KCMG.
Powell, Sir Nicholas Folliott Douglas, Bt. (1897).
Powell, Sir Richard Royle, GCB, KBE, CMG.
Power, Sir Alastair John Cecil, Bt. (1924).
Powles, Sir Guy Richardson, KBE, CMG, ED.
Poynton, Sir (Arthur) Hilton, GCMG.
Prendergast, Sir John Vincent, KBE, CMG, GM.
Prendergast, Sir (Walter) Kieran, KCVO, CMG.
Prentice, *Hon.* Sir William Thomas, Kt., MBE.
Prescott, Sir Mark, Bt. (1938).
Preston, Sir Kenneth Huson, Kt.
Preston, Sir Peter Sansome, KCB.
Preston, Sir Ronald Douglas Hildebrand, Bt. (1815).
Prevost, Sir Christopher Gerald, Bt. (1805).
Price, Sir Charles Keith Napier Rugge-, Bt. (1804).
Price, Sir David Ernest Campbell, Kt.
Price, Sir Francis Caradoc Rose, Bt. (1815).
Price, Sir Frank Leslie, Kt.
Price, Sir (James) Robert, KBE.
Price, Sir Leslie Victor, Kt., OBE.
Price, Sir Norman Charles, KCB.
Price, Sir Robert John Green-, Bt. (1874).
Prickett, *Air Chief Marshal* Sir Thomas Other, KCB, DSO, DFC.
Prideaux, Sir Humphrey Povah Treverbian, Kt., OBE.
Prideaux, Sir John Francis, Kt., OBE.
†Primrose, Sir John Ure, Bt. (1903).
Pringle, *Air Marshal* Sir Charles Norman Seton, KBE, FEng.
Pringle, *Lt.-Gen.* Sir Steuart (Robert), Bt., KCB, RM (S. 1683).
Pritchard, Sir Neil, KCMG.
Pritchett, Sir Victor Sawdon, Kt., CBE.
Proby, Sir Peter, Bt. (1952).
Proctor, Sir Roderick Consett, Kt., MBE.
Proud, Sir John Seymour, Kt.
Prout, Sir Christopher James, Kt., TD, QC, MEP.
Pryke, Sir David Dudley, Bt. (1926).
Pugh, Sir Idwal Vaughan, KCB.
Pugsley, *Prof.* Sir Alfred Grenvile, Kt., OBE, D.SC., FRS, FEng.
Pullen, Sir William Reginald James, KCVO.
Pullinger, Sir (Francis) Alan, Kt., CBE.
Pumphrey, Sir (John) Laurence, KCMG.
Purchas, *Rt. Hon.* Sir Francis Brooks, Kt.
Purvis, *Vice-Adm.* Sir Neville, KCB.
Quennell, Sir Peter, Kt., CBE.
Quicke, Sir John Godolphin, Kt., CBE.
Quilliam, *Hon.* Sir (James) Peter, Kt.
Quilter, Sir Anthony Raymond Leopold Cuthbert, Bt. (1897).
Quinlan, Sir Michael Edward, GCB.
Quinton, Sir James Grand, Kt.
Quirk, *Prof.* Sir (Charles)Randolph, Kt., CBE, FBA.
Rabukawaqa, Sir Josua Rasilau, KBE, MVO.
Radcliffe, Sir Sebastian Everard, Bt. (1813).
Radclyffe, Sir Charles Edward Mott-, Kt.
Radford, Sir Ronald Walter, KCB, MBE.
Radzinowicz, *Prof.* Sir Leon, Kt., LL D.
Rae, *Hon.* Sir Wallace Alexander Ramsay, Kt.
Raeburn, Sir Michael Edward Norman, Bt. (1923).
Raeburn, *Maj.-Gen.* Sir (William) Digby (Manifold), KCVO, CB, DSO, MBE.
Raffray, Sir Piat Joseph Raymond Andre, Kt.
Raikes, *Vice-Adm.* Sir Iwan Geoffrey, KCB, CBE, DSC.
Raison, *Rt. Hon.* Sir Timothy Hugh Francis, Kt.
Ralli, Sir Godfrey Victor, Bt., TD (1912).
Ramdanee, Sir Mookteswar Baboolall Kailash, Kt.
Ramphal, Sir Shridath Surendranath, Kt., GCMG.
Ramphul, Sir Baalkhristna, Kt.
Ramphul, Sir Indurduth, Kt.
Rampton, Sir Jack Leslie, KCB.
Ramsay, Sir Alexander William Burnett, Bt. (1806).
Ramsay, Sir Allan John (Hepple), KBE, CMG.
Ramsay, Sir Thomas Meek, Kt., CMG.
Ramsbotham, *Gen.* Sir David John, KCB, CBE.
Ramsbotham, *Hon.* Sir Peter Edward, GCMG, GCVO.
Ramsden, Sir John Charles Josslyn, Bt. (1689).
Ramsey, Sir Alfred Ernest, Kt.
Randle, *Prof.* Sir Philip John, Kt.
Ranger, Sir Douglas, Kt., FRCS.
Rank, Sir Benjamin Keith, Kt., CMG.

Rankin, Sir Alick Michael, Kt., CBE.
Rankin, Sir Ian Niall, Bt. (1898).
Rasch, *Maj.* Sir Richard Guy Carne, Bt. (1903).
Rashleigh, Sir Richard Harry, Bt. (1831).
Rattee, *Hon.* Sir Donald Keith, Kt.
Rault, Sir Louis Joseph Maurice, Kt.
Rawlins, *Surgeon Vice-Adm.* Sir John Stuart Pepys, KBE.
Rawlinson, Sir Anthony Henry John, Bt. (1891).
Read, *Air Marshal* Sir Charles Frederick, KBE, CB, DFC, AFC.
Read, *Gen.* Sir (John) Antony (Jervis), GCB, CBE, DSO, MC.
Read, Sir John Emms, Kt.
Reade, Sir Clyde Nixon, Bt. (1661).
Reay, *Lt.-Gen.* Sir (Hubert) Alan John, KBE.
Redgrave, *Maj.-Gen.* Sir Roy Michael Frederick, KBE, MC.
Redmayne, Sir Nicholas, Bt. (1964).
Redmond, Sir James, Kt., FEng.
Redwood, Sir Peter Boverton, Bt. (1911).
Reece, Sir Charles Hugh, Kt.
Reece, Sir James Gordon, Kt.
Reed, *Hon.* Sir Nigel Vernon, Kt., CBE.
Rees, Sir (Charles William) Stanley, Kt., TD.
Rees, *Prof.* Sir Martin John, Kt., FRS.
Reeve, Sir Anthony, KCMG.
Reeve, Sir (Charles) Trevor, Kt.
Reeves, *Most Revd* Paul Alfred, GCMG, GCVO.
Reffell, *Adm.* Sir Derek Roy, KCB.
Refshauge, *Maj-Gen.* Sir William Dudley, Kt., CBE.
Reid, Sir Alexander James, Bt. (1897).
Reid, *Hon.* Sir George Oswald, Kt., QC.
Reid, Sir (Harold) Martin (Smith), KBE, CMG.
Reid, Sir Hugh, Bt. (1922).
Reid, Sir John James Andrew, KCMG, CB, TD.
Reid, Sir Norman Robert, Kt.
Reid, Sir Robert Basil, Kt., CBE.
Reid, Sir Robert Paul, Kt.
Reiher, Sir Frederick Bernard Carl, KBE, CMG.
Reilly, Sir (D'Arcy) Patrick, GCMG, OBE.
Reilly, *Lt.-Gen.* Sir Jeremy Calcott, KCB, DSO.
Renals, Sir Stanley, Bt. (1895).
Rendell, Sir William, Kt.
Rennie, Sir John Shaw, GCMG, OBE.
Renouf, Sir Clement William Bailey, Kt.
Renouf, Sir Francis Henry, Kt.
Renshaw, Sir (Charles) Maurice Bine, Bt. (1903).
Renwick, Sir Richard Eustace, Bt. (1921).
Renwick, Sir Robin William, KCMG.
Reporter, Sir Shapoor Ardeshirji, KBE.
Rex, *Hon.* Sir Robert Richmond, KBE, CMG.
Reynolds, Sir David James, Bt. (1923).
Reynolds, Sir Peter William John, Kt., CBE.
Rhodes, Sir Basil Edward, Kt., CBE, TD.
Rhodes, Sir John Christopher Douglas, Bt. (1919).
Rhodes, Sir Peregrine Alexander, KCMG.
Rice, *Maj.-Gen.* Sir Desmond Hind Garrett, KCVO, CBE.
Richards, Sir (Francis) Brooks, KCMG, DSC.
Richards, *Lt.-Gen.* Sir John Charles Chisholm, KCB, KCVO, RM.
Richards, Sir Rex Edward, Kt., D.SC., FRS.
Richardson, Sir Anthony Lewis, Bt. (1924).
Richardson, *Gen.* Sir Charles Leslie, GCB, CBE, DSO.
Richardson, *Air Marshal* Sir (David) William, KBE.
Richardson, Sir Egerton Rudolf, Kt., CMG.
Richardson, *Rt. Hon.* Sir Ivor Lloyd Morgan, Kt.
Richardson, Sir (John) Eric, Kt., CBE.
Richardson, Sir Michael John de Rougemont, Kt.
Richardson, *Lt.-Gen.* Sir Robert Francis, KCB, CVO, CBE.
Richardson, Sir Simon Alaisdair Stewart-, Bt. (S. 1630).
Riches, Sir Derek Martin Hurry, KCMG.
Riches, *Gen.* Sir Ian Hurry, KCB, DSO.
Richmond, Sir Alan James, Kt.
Richmond, *Rt. Hon.* Sir Clifford Parris, KBE.
Richmond, Sir John Frederick, Bt. (1929).
Richmond, *Prof.* Sir Mark Henry, Kt., FRS.
Rickett, Sir Denis Hubert Fletcher, KCMG, CB.
Rickett, Sir Raymond Mildmay Wilson, Kt., CBE, Ph.D.
Ricketts, Sir Robert Cornwallis Gerald St Leger, Bt. (1828).
Riddell, Sir John Charles Buchanan, Bt., CVO (S. 1628).
Ridley, Sir Adam (Nicholas), Kt.
Ridley, Sir Sidney, Kt.
Ridsdale, Sir Julian Errington, Kt., CBE.
Rigby, *Lt.-Col.* Sir (Hugh) John (Macbeth), Bt. (1929).
Riley, Sir Ralph, Kt., FRS.
Ring, Sir Lindsay Roberts, GBE.
Ringadoo, *Hon.* Sir Veerasamy, GCMG.
Ripley, Sir Hugh, Bt. (1880).
Risk, Sir Thomas Neilson, Kt.
Risson, *Maj.-Gen.* Sir Robert Joseph Henry, Kt., CB, CBE, DSO, ED.
Rix, Sir John, Kt., MBE, FEng.
Roberts, Sir Bryan Clieve, KCMG, QC.
Roberts, *Hon.* Sir Denys Tudor Emil, KBE, QC.
Roberts, Sir (Edward Fergus) Sidney, Kt., CBE.
Roberts, Sir Frank Kenyon, GCMG, GCVO.
Roberts, Sir Geoffrey Newland, Kt., CBE, AFC.
Roberts, *Brig.* Sir Geoffrey Paul Hardy-, KCVO, CB, CBE.
Roberts, Sir Gilbert Howland Rookehurst, Bt. (1809).
Roberts, Sir Gordon James, Kt., CBE.
Roberts, *Rt. Hon.* Sir (Ieuan) Wyn Pritchard, Kt., MP.
Roberts, Sir Samuel, Bt. (1919).
Roberts, Sir Stephen James Leake, Kt.
Roberts, Sir William James Denby, Bt. (1909).
Robertson, Sir Lewis, Kt., CBE, FRSE.
Robertson, *Prof.* Sir Rutherford Ness, Kt., CMG.
Robins, Sir Ralph Harry, Kt., FEng.
Robinson, Sir Albert Edward Phineas, Kt.
†Robinson, Sir Christopher Philipse, Bt. (1854).
Robinson, *Prof.* Sir (Edward) Austin (Gossage), Kt., CMG, OBE, FBA.
Robinson, Sir John James Michael Laud, Bt. (1660).
Robinson, *Rt. Hon.* Sir Kenneth, Kt.
Robinson, Sir Niall Bryan Lynch-, Bt., DSC (1920).
Robinson, Sir Wilfred Henry Frederick, Bt. (1908).
Robotham, *Hon.* Sir Lascelles Lister, Kt.
Robson, *Prof.* Sir James Gordon, Kt., CBE.
Robson, Sir John Adam, KCMG.
Roch, *Hon.* Sir John Ormond, Kt.
Roche, Sir David O'Grady, Bt. (1838).
Rodgers, Sir John Charles, Bt. (1964).
Rodrigues, Sir Alberto Maria, Kt., CBE, ED.
Roe, *Air Chief Marshal* Sir Rex David, GCB, AFC.
Rogers, Sir Frank Jarvis, Kt.
Rogers, *Air Chief Marshal* Sir John Robson, KCB, CBE.
Rogers, Sir Philip James, Kt., CBE.
Rogers, Sir Richard George, Kt., RA.
Roll, *Revd* Sir James William Cecil, Bt. (1921).
Rooke, Sir Denis Eric, Kt., CBE, FRS, FEng.
Roper, *Hon.* Sir Clinton Marcus, Kt.
Ropner, Sir John Bruce Woollacott, Bt. (1952).
Ropner, Sir Robert Douglas, Bt. (1904).
Roscoe, Sir Robert Bell, KBE.
Rose, *Hon.* Sir Christopher Dudley Roger, Kt.
Rose, Sir Clive Martin, GCMG.
Rose, Sir David Lancaster, Bt. (1874).
Rose, Sir Julian Day, Bt. (1872 and 1909).

Rosier, *Air Chief Marshal* Sir Frederick Ernest, GCB, CBE, DSO.
Ross, Sir Alexander, Kt.
Ross, Sir Archibald David Manisty, KCMG.
Ross, Sir (James) Keith, Bt., RD, FRCS (1960).
Rosser, Sir Melvyn Wynne, Kt.
Rossi, Sir Hugh Alexis Louis, Kt.
Roth, *Prof.* Sir Martin, Kt., MD, FRCP.
Rothnie, Sir Alan Keir, KCVO, CMG.
Rothschild, Sir Evelyn Robert Adrian de, Kt.
Rougier, *Hon.* Sir Richard George, Kt.
Rous, Sir Anthony Gerald Roderick, KCMG, OBE.
Rous, *Lt.-Gen.* the Hon. Sir William Edward, KCB, OBE.
Row, *Hon.* Sir John Alfred, Kt.
Rowe, Sir Jeremy, Kt., CBE.
Rowell, Sir John Joseph, Kt., CBE.
Rowland, *Air Marshal* Sir James Anthony, KBE, DFC, AFC.
Rowlands, *Air Marshal* Sir John Samuel, GC, KBE.
Rowley, Sir Charles Robert, Bt. (1836).
Rowley, Sir Joshua Francis, Bt. (1786).
Rowling, *Rt. Hon.* Sir Wallace Edward, KCMG.
Roxburgh, *Vice-Adm.* Sir John Charles Young, KCB, CBE, DSO, DSC.
Royden, Sir Christopher John, Bt. (1905).
Rumbold, Sir Henry John Sebastian, Bt. (1779).
Rumbold, Sir (Horace) Algernon (Fraser), KCMG, CIE.
Rumbold, Sir Jack Seddon, Kt.
†Runchorelal, Sir Udayan Chinubhai, Bt. (1913).
Runciman, *Hon.* Sir James Cochran Stevenson (Sir Steven Runciman), Kt., CH.
Rusby, *Vice-Adm.* Sir Cameron, KCB, MVO.
Russell, Sir Archibald Edward, Kt., CBE, FRS, FEng.
Russell, Sir Charles Ian, Bt. (1916).
Russell, *Hon.* Sir David Sturrock West-, Kt.
Russell, Sir Evelyn Charles Sackville, Kt.
Russell, Sir George, Kt., CBE.
Russell, Sir George Michael, Bt. (1812).
Russell, Sir (Robert) Mark, KCMG.
Russell, Sir Spencer Thomas, Kt.
Russell, *Rt. Hon.* Sir (Thomas) Patrick, Kt.
Rutter, Sir Frank William Eden, KBE.
Rutter, *Prof.* Sir Michael Llewellyn, Kt., CBE, MD, FRS.
Ryan, Sir Derek Gerald, Bt. (1919).
Rycroft, Sir Richard Newton, Bt. (1784).
Ryrie, Sir William Sinclair, KCB.
Sainsbury, Sir Robert James, Kt.
St Aubyn, Sir (John) Arscott Molesworth-, Bt. (1689).
St George, Sir George Bligh, Bt. (I. 1766).
St Johnston, Sir Kerry, Kt.
Sainty, Sir John Christopher, KCB.
Sakzewski, Sir Albert, Kt.
Salt, Sir Patrick MacDonnell, Bt. (1869).
Salt, Sir (Thomas) Michael John, Bt. (1899).
Samuel, Sir Jon Michael Glen, Bt. (1898).
Samuelson, Sir (Bernard) Michael (Francis), Bt. (1884).
Sandberg, Sir Michael Graham Ruddock, Kt., CBE.
Sanders, Sir John Reynolds Mayhew-, Kt.
Sanders, Sir Robert Tait, KBE, CMG.
Sanderson, Sir (Frank Philip) Bryan, Bt. (1920).
Sandilands, Sir Francis Edwin Prescott, Kt., CBE.
Sarei, Sir Alexis Holyweek, Kt., CBE.
Sarell, Sir Roderick Francis Gisbert, KCMG, KCVO.
Sargant, Sir (Henry) Edmund, Kt.
Saunders, *Hon.* Sir John Anthony Holt, Kt., CBE, DSO, MC.
Saunders, Sir Owen Alfred, Kt., D.SC., FRS, FEng.
Saunders, Sir Peter, Kt.
Sauzier, Sir (André) Guy, Kt., CBE, ED.
Savage, Sir Ernest Walter, Kt.
Savile, Sir James Wilson Vincent, Kt., OBE.
Saville, *Hon.* Sir Mark Oliver, Kt.
Say, *Rt. Revd* Richard David, KCVO.
Schiemann, *Hon.* Sir Konrad Hermann Theodor, Kt.
Scholey, Sir David Gerald, Kt., CBE.
Scholey, Sir Robert, Kt., CBE, FEng.
Scholtens, Sir James Henry, KCVO.
Schubert, Sir Sydney, Kt.
Schuster, Sir (Felix) James Moncrieff, Bt., OBE (1906).
Scipio, Sir Hudson Rupert, Kt.
Scoon, Sir Paul, GCMG, GCVO, OBE.
Scopes, Sir Leonard Arthur, KCVO, CMG, OBE.
Scott, Sir Anthony Percy, Bt. (1913).
Scott, Sir (Charles) Peter, KBE, CMG.
Scott, Sir David Aubrey, GCMG.
†Scott, Sir Dominic James Maxwell, Bt. (1642).
Scott, Sir Ian Dixon, KCMG, KCVO, CIE.
Scott, Sir James Walter, Bt. (1962).
Scott, Sir Kenneth Bertram Adam, KCVO, CMG.
Scott, Sir Michael, KCVO, CMG.
Scott, Sir Oliver Christopher Anderson, Bt. (1909).
Scott, *Prof.* Sir Philip John, KBE.
Scott, *Rt. Hon.* Sir Richard Rashleigh Folliott, Kt.
Scott, Sir Walter, Bt. (1907).
Scott, *Rear-Adm.* Sir (William) David (Stewart), KBE, CB.
Scowen, Sir Eric Frank, Kt., MD, D.SC., LL D., FRCP, FRCS.
Scrivenor, Sir Thomas Vaisey, Kt., CMG.
Seale, Sir John Henry, Bt. (1838).
Seaman, Sir Keith Douglas, KCVO, OBE.
†Sebright, Sir Peter Giles Vivian, Bt. (1626).
Seccombe, Sir (William) Vernon Stephen, Kt.
Secombe, Sir Harry Donald, Kt., CBE.
Seconde, Sir Reginald Louis, KCMG, CVO.
Seely, Sir Nigel Edward, Bt. (1896).
Seeto, Sir Ling James, Kt., MBE.
Seeyave, Sir Rene Sow Choung, Kt., CBE.
Selby, Sir Kenneth, Kt.
Seligman, Sir Peter Wendel, Kt., CBE.
Sells, Sir David Perronet, Kt.
Senior, Sir Edward Walters, Kt., CMG.
Sergeant, Sir Patrick, Kt.
Series, Sir (Joseph Michel) Emile, Kt., CBE.
Serpell, Sir David Radford, KCB, CMG, OBE.
Seton, Sir Iain Bruce, Bt. (S. 1663).
Seton, Sir Robert James, Bt. (S. 1683).
Severne, *Air Vice-Marshal* Sir John de Milt, KCVO, OBE, AFC.
Sewell, Sir (John) Allan, Kt., ISO.
Seymour, *Cdr.* Sir Michael Culme-, Bt., RN (1809).
Shakerley, Sir Geoffrey Adam, Bt. (1838).
Shakespeare, Sir William Geoffrey, Bt. (1942).
Shapland, Sir William Arthur, Kt.
Sharp, Sir Adrian, Bt. (1922).
Sharp, Sir George, Kt., OBE.
Sharp, Sir Kenneth Johnston, Kt., TD.
Sharp, Sir Milton Reginald, Bt. (1920).
Sharp, Sir Richard Lyall, KCVO, CB.
Sharp, Sir (William Harold) Angus, KBE, QPM.
Sharpe, *Hon.* Sir John Henry, Kt., CBE.
Sharpe, Sir Reginald Taaffe, Kt., QC.
Shattock, Sir Gordon, Kt.
Shaw, Sir Brian Piers, Kt.
Shaw, Sir (Charles) Barry, Kt., CB, QC.
Shaw, Sir (George) Neville Bowan-, Kt.
Shaw, Sir (John) Giles (Dunkerley), Kt., MP.
Shaw, Sir John Michael Robert Best-, Bt. (1665).
Shaw, Sir Michael Norman, Kt.
Shaw, Sir Robert, Bt. (1821).
Shaw, Sir Roy, Kt.
Shaw, Sir Run Run, Kt., CBE.
Sheehy, Sir Patrick, Kt.
Sheen, *Hon.* Sir Barry Cross, Kt.
Sheffield, Sir Reginald Adrian Berkeley, Bt. (1755).
Shehadie, Sir Nicholas Michael, Kt., OBE.
Sheil, *Hon.* Sir John, Kt.
Shelbourne, Sir Philip, Kt.

Sheldon, *Hon.* Sir (John) Gervase (Kensington), Kt.
Shelley, Sir John Richard, Bt. (1611).
Shelton, Sir William Jeremy Masefield, Kt.
Shepheard, Sir Peter Faulkner, Kt., CBE.
Shepherd, Sir Peter Malcolm, Kt., CBE.
Sheppard, Sir Allen John George, Kt.
Shepperd, Sir Alfred Joseph, Kt.
Sherlock, Sir Philip Manderson, KBE.
Sherman, Sir Alfred, Kt.
Sherman, Sir Louis, Kt., OBE.
Shields, Sir Neil Stanley, Kt., MC.
Shields, *Prof.* Sir Robert, Kt., MD.
Shiffner, Sir Henry David, Bt. (1818).
Shillington, Sir (Robert Edward) Graham, Kt., CBE.
Shock, Sir Maurice, Kt.
Sholl, *Hon.* Sir Reginald Richard, Kt.
Shone, Sir Robert Minshull, Kt., CBE.
Short, *Brig.* Sir Noel Edward Vivian, Kt., MBE, MC.
Shuckburgh, Sir (Charles Arthur) Evelyn, GCMG, CB.
Shuckburgh, Sir Rupert Charles Gerald, Bt. (1660).
Siaguru, Sir Anthony Michael, KBE.
Sich, Sir Rupert Leigh, Kt., CB.
Siddall, Sir Norman, Kt., CBE, FEng.
Sidey, *Air Marshal* Sir Ernest Shaw, KBE, CB, MD.
Sie, Sir Banja Tejan-, GCMG.
Simeon, Sir John Edmund Barrington, Bt. (1815).
Simmons, *Air Marshal* Sir Michael George, KCB, AFC.
Simonet, Sir Louis Marcel Pierre, Kt., CBE.
Simpson, *Hon.* Sir Alfred Henry, Kt.
Simpson, Sir Joseph Trevor, KBE.
Simpson, Sir William James, Kt.
Sinclair, Sir Clive Marles, Kt.
Sinclair, Sir George Evelyn, Kt., CMG, OBE.
Sinclair, Sir Ian McTaggart, KCMG, QC.
Sinclair, *Prof.* Sir Keith, Kt., CBE.
Sinclair, *Air Vice-Marshal* Sir Laurence Frank, GC, KCB, CBE, DSO.
Sinclair, Sir Patrick Robert Richard, Bt. (S. 1704).
Sinclair, Sir Ronald Ormiston, KBE.
Singh, *Hon.* Sir Vijay Raghubir, Kt.
Singhania, Sir Padampat, Kt.
Singleton, Sir Edward Henry Sibbald, Kt.
Sinnamon, Sir Hercules, Kt., OBE.
Sisson, Sir Roy, Kt.
Sitwell, Sir (Sacheverell) Reresby, Bt. (1808).
Skeet, Sir Trevor Herbert Harry, Kt., MP.
Skeggs, Sir Clifford George, Kt.
Skingsley, *Air Chief Marshal* Sir Anthony Gerald, GBE, KCB.
Skinner, Sir Thomas Edward, KBE.
Skinner, Sir (Thomas) Keith (Hewitt), Bt. (1912).
Skipwith, Sir Patrick Alexander d'Estoteville, Bt. (1622).
Skyrme, Sir (William) Thomas (Charles), KCVO, CB, CBE, TD.
Slack, Sir William Willatt, KCVO, FRCS.
Slade, Sir Benjamin Julian Alfred, Bt. (1831).
Slade, *Rt. Hon.* Sir Christopher John, Kt.
Slaney, *Prof.* Sir Geoffrey, KBE.
Slater, *Adm.* Sir John (Jock) Cunningham Kirkwood, GCB, LVO.
Sleight, Sir Richard, Bt. (1920).
Slimmings, Sir William Kenneth MacLeod, Kt., CBE.
Sloan, Sir Andrew Kirkpatrick, Kt., QPM.
Sloman, Sir Albert Edward, Kt., CBE.
Smallwood, *Air Chief Marshal* Sir Denis Graham, GBE, KCB, DSO, DFC.
Smart, *Prof.* Sir George Algernon, Kt., MD, FRCP.
Smart, Sir Jack, Kt., CBE.
Smedley, Sir Harold, KCMG, MBE.
Smiley, *Lt.-Col.* Sir John Philip, Bt. (1903).
Smith, Sir Alan, Kt., CBE, DFC.
Smith, Sir Alexander Mair, Kt., Ph.D.
Smith, Sir Andrew Colin Hugh-, Kt.
Smith, Sir Charles Bracewell-, Bt. (1947).
Smith, Sir Christopher Sydney Winwood, Bt. (1809).
Smith, Sir Cyril, Kt., MBE.
Smith, *Prof.* Sir David Cecil, Kt., FRS.
Smith, *Air Chief Marshal* Sir David Harcourt-, GBE, KCB, DFC.
Smith, Sir David Iser, KCVO.
Smith, Sir Douglas Boucher, KCB.
Smith, Sir Dudley (Gordon), Kt., MP.
Smith, *Maj.-Gen.* Sir (Francis) Brian Wyldbore-, Kt., CB, DSO, OBE.
Smith, *Prof.* Sir (Francis) Graham, Kt., FRS.
Smith, Sir (Frank) Ewart, Kt., FEng.
Smith, Sir Geoffrey Johnson, Kt., MP.
Smith, *Col.* Sir Henry Abel, KCMG, KCVO, DSO.
Smith, Sir Howard Frank Trayton, GCMG.
Smith, *Hon.* Sir James Alfred, Kt., CBE, TD.
Smith, Sir John Hamilton-Spencer-, Bt. (1804).
Smith, Sir John Jonah Walker-, Bt. (1960).
Smith, Sir John Kenneth Newson-, Bt. (1944).
Smith, Sir John Lindsay Eric., Kt., CBE.
Smith, Sir John Wilson, Kt., CBE.
Smith, Sir Joseph William Grenville, Kt., MD, FRCP.
Smith, Sir Leslie Edward George, Kt.
Smith, *Rt. Hon.* Sir Murray Stuart-, Kt.
Smith, Sir Raymond Horace, KBE.
Smith, Sir Reginald Beaumont, Kt.
Smith, Sir Richard Rathbone Vassar-, Bt., TD (1917).
Smith, Sir (Richard) Robert Law-, Kt., CBE, AFC.
Smith, Sir Robert Courtney, Kt., CBE.
Smith, Sir Robert Hill, Bt. (1945).
Smith, *Prof.* Sir Roland, Kt.
Smith, *Air Marshal* Sir Roy David Austen-, KBE, CB, DFC.
Smith, Sir (Thomas) Gilbert, Bt. (1897).
Smith, *Adm.* Sir Victor Alfred Trumper, KBE, CB, DSC.
Smith, Sir William Reardon Reardon-, Bt. (1920).
Smith, Sir (William) Richard Prince-, Bt. (1911).
Smithers, *Prof.* Sir David Waldron, Kt., MD.
Smithers, Sir Peter Henry Berry Otway, Kt., VRD, D.Phil.
Smithers, *Hon.* Sir Reginald Allfree, Kt.
Smyth, Sir Thomas Weyland Bowyer-, Bt. (1661).
Smyth, Sir Timothy John, Bt. (1955).
Snelling, Sir Arthur Wendell, KCMG, KCVO.
Snelson, Sir Edward Alec Abbott, KBE.
Soame, Sir Charles John Buckworth-Herne-, Bt. (1697).
Sobell, Sir Michael, Kt.
Sobers, Sir Garfield St Auburn, Kt.
Solomon, Sir David Arnold, Kt., MBE.
Solomon, Sir Harry, Kt.
Solomons, *Hon.* Sir (Louis) Adrian, Kt.
Solti, Sir Georg, KBE.
Somare, *Rt. Hon.* Sir Michael Thomas, GCMG, CH.
Somers, *Rt. Hon.* Sir Edward Jonathan, Kt.
Somerset, Sir Henry Beaufort, Kt., CBE.
Somerville, *Brig.* Sir John Nicholas, Kt., CBE.
Somerville, Sir Quentin Charles Somerville Agnew-, Bt. (1957).
Sopwith, Sir Charles Ronald, Kt.
Soutar, *Air Marshal* Sir Charles John Williamson, KBE.
South, Sir Arthur, Kt.
Southby, Sir John Richard Bilbe, Bt. (1937).
Southern, Sir Richard William, Kt., FBA.
Southern, Sir Robert, Kt., CBE.
Southey, Sir Robert John, Kt., CMG.
Southgate, Sir Colin Grieve, Kt.
Southward, Sir Leonard Bingley, Kt., OBE.
Southward, Sir Ralph, KCVO, FRCP.
Southwood, *Prof.* Sir (Thomas) Richard (Edmund), Kt., FRS.
Southworth, Sir Frederick, Kt., QC.
Souyave, *Hon.* Sir (Louis) Georges, Kt.
Sowrey, *Air Marshal* Sir Frederick Beresford, KCB, CBE, AFC.

Soysa, Sir Warusahennedige Abraham Bastian, Kt., CBE.
Sparkes, Sir Robert Lyndley, Kt.
Sparrow, Sir John, Kt.
Spearman, Sir Alexander Young Richard Mainwaring, Bt. (1840).
Speed, Sir (Herbert) Keith, Kt., RD, MP.
Speed, Sir Robert William Arney, Kt., CB, QC.
Speelman, Sir Cornelis Jacob, Bt. (1686).
Speight, *Hon.* Sir Graham Davies, Kt.
Speir, Sir Rupert Malise, Kt.
Spencer, Sir Derek Harold, Kt., QC, MP.
Spencer, Sir Kelvin Tallent, Kt., CBE, MC.
Spender, *Prof.* Sir Stephen Harold, Kt., CBE.
Spicer, Sir James Wilton, Kt., MP.
Spicer, Sir Peter James, Bt. (1906).
Spooner, Sir James Douglas, Kt.
Spotswood, *Marshal of the Royal Air Force* Sir Denis Frank, GCB, CBE, DSO, DFC.
Spratt, *Col.* Sir Greville Douglas, GBE, TD.
Spreckley, Sir (John) Nicholas (Teague), KCVO, CMG.
Springer, Sir Hugh Worrell, GCMG, GCVO, CBE.
Spry, *Brig.* Sir Charles Chambers Fowell, Kt., CBE, DSO.
Spry, *Hon.* Sir John Farley, Kt.
Stabb, *Hon.* Sir William Walter, Kt., QC.
Stack, *Air Chief Marshal* Sir (Thomas) Neville, KCB, CVO, CBE, AFC.
Stainton, Sir (John) Ross, Kt., CBE.
Stakis, Sir Reo Argiros, Kt.
Stallard, Sir Peter Hyla Gawne, KCMG, CVO, MBE.
Stallworthy, Sir John Arthur, Kt., FRCS.
Stamer, Sir (Lovelace) Anthony, Bt. (1809).
Stanbridge, *Air Vice-Marshal* Sir Brian Gerald Tivy, KCVO, CBE, AFC.
Stanier, *Brig.* Sir Alexander Beville Gibbons, Bt., DSO, MC (1917).
Stanier, *Field Marshal* Sir John Wilfred, GCB, MBE.
Stanley, *Rt. Hon.* Sir John Paul, Kt., MP.
†Staples, Sir Thomas, Bt. (I. 1628).
Stapleton, Sir (Henry) Alfred, Bt. (1679).
Stark, Sir Andrew Alexander Steel, KCMG, CVO.
Starke, *Hon.* Sir John Erskine, Kt.
Starkey, Sir John Philip, Bt. (1935).
Starrit, Sir James, KCVO.
Statham, Sir Norman, KCMG, CVO.
Staughton, *Rt. Hon.* Sir Christopher Stephen Thomas Jonathan Thayer, Kt.
Staveley, Sir John Malfroy, KBE, MC.
Staveley, *Admiral of the Fleet* Sir William Doveton Minet, GCB.
Stear, *Air Chief Marshal* Sir Michael James Douglas, KCB, CBE.
Steel, Sir David Edward Charles, Kt., DSO, MC, TD.
Steel, *Rt. Hon.* Sir David Martin Scott, KBE, MP.
Steel, *Maj.* Sir (Fiennes) William Strang, Bt. (1938).
Steel, Sir James, Kt., CBE.
Steele, Sir (Philip John) Rupert, Kt.
Steere, Sir Ernest Henry Lee-, KBE.
Stenhouse, Sir Nicol, Kt.
Stening, *Col.* Sir George Grafton Lees, Kt., ED.
Stephen, *Rt. Hon.* Sir Ninian Martin, GCMG, GCVO, KBE.
Stephenson, Sir Henry Upton, Bt. (1936).
Stephenson, *Rt. Hon.* Sir John Frederick Eustace, Kt.
Sternberg, Sir Sigmund, Kt.
Stevens, Sir Laurence Houghton, Kt., CBE.
Stevenson, *Vice-Adm.* Sir (Hugh) David, KBE.
Stevenson, Sir Simpson, Kt.
Stewart, Sir Alan, KBE.
Stewart, Sir Alan d'Arcy, Bt. (I. 1623).
Stewart, Sir David Brodribb, Bt., TD (1960).
Stewart, Sir David James Henderson-, Bt. (1957).
Stewart, Sir Edward Jackson, Kt.
Stewart, *Prof.* Sir Frederick Henry, Kt., Ph.D., FRS, FRSE.
Stewart, Sir Houston Mark Shaw-, Bt., MC, TD (S. 1667).
Stewart, Sir Hugh Charlie Godfray, Bt. (1803).
Stewart, Sir James Douglas, Kt.
Stewart, Sir (John) Simon (Watson), Bt. (1920).
Stewart, Sir Michael Norman Francis, KCMG, OBE.
Stewart, Sir Robertson Huntly, Kt., CBE.
Stewart, Sir Ronald Compton, Bt. (1937).
Steyn, *Rt. Hon.* Sir Johan Van Zyl, Kt.
Stibbon, *Gen.* Sir John James, KCB, OBE.
Stirling, Sir Alexander John Dickson, KBE, CMG.
Stirling, Sir James Frazer, Kt., RA.
Stockdale, Sir Arthur Noel, Kt.
Stockdale, Sir Thomas Minshull, Bt. (1960).
Stocker, *Rt. Hon.* Sir John Dexter, Kt., MC, TD.
Stoddart, *Wg Cdr.* Sir Kenneth Maxwell, KCVO, AE.
Stoker, *Prof.* Sir Michael George Parke, Kt., CBE, FRCP, FRS, FRSE.
Stokes, Sir John Heydon Romaine, Kt.
Stones, Sir William Frederick, Kt., OBE.
Stonhouse, Sir Philip Allan, Bt. (1628).
Stonor, *Air Marshal* Sir Thomas Henry, KCB.
Storey, *Hon.* Sir Richard, Bt. (1960).
Stormonth Darling, Sir James Carlisle, Kt., CBE, MC, TD.
Stott, Sir Adrian George Ellingham, Bt. (1920).
Stow, Sir Christopher Philipson-, Bt., DFC (1907).
Stow, Sir John Montague, GCMG, KCVO.
Stowe, Sir Kenneth Ronald, GCB, CVO.
Stracey, Sir John Simon, Bt. (1818).
Strachey, Sir Charles, Bt. (1801).
Straker, Sir Michael Ian Bowstead, Kt., CBE.
Strawson, *Prof.* Sir Peter Frederick, Kt., FBA.
Street, *Hon.* Sir Laurence Whistler, KCMG.
Streeton, Sir Terence George, KBE, CMG.
Strong, Sir Roy Colin, Kt., Ph.D., FSA.
Stronge, Sir James Anselan Maxwell, Bt. (1803).
Stroud, *Prof.* Sir (Charles) Eric, Kt., FRCP.
Strutt, Sir Nigel Edward, Kt., TD.
Stuart, Sir James Keith, Kt.
Stuart, Sir Kenneth Lamonte, Kt.
†Stuart, Sir Phillip Luttrell, Bt. (1660).
Stubblefield, Sir (Cyril) James, Kt., D.SC., FRS.
Stubbs, Sir James Wilfrid, KCVO, TD.
Stucley, *Lt.* Sir Hugh George Coplestone Bampfylde, Bt. (1859).
Studd, Sir Edward Fairfax, Bt. (1929).
Studd, Sir Peter Malden, GBE, KCVO.
Studholme, Sir Henry William, Bt. (1956).
Style, *Lt.-Cdr.* Sir Godfrey William, Kt., CBE, DSC, RN.
†Style, Sir William Frederick, Bt. (1627).
Suffield, Sir (Henry John) Lester, Kt.
Sugden, Sir Arthur, Kt.
Sullivan, Sir Desmond John, Kt.
Sullivan, Sir Richard Arthur, Bt. (1804).
Summerfield, *Hon.* Sir John Crampton, Kt., CBE.
Summers, Sir Felix Roland Brattan, Bt. (1952).
Summerson, Sir John Newenham, Kt., CH, CBE, FBA, FSA.
Sunderland, *Prof.* Sir Sydney, Kt., CMG.
Sutherland, *Prof.* Sir James Runcieman, Kt., FBA.
Sutherland, Sir John Brewer, Bt. (1921).
Sutherland, Sir Maurice, Kt.
Sutherland, Sir William George MacKenzie, Kt.
Suttie, Sir (George) Philip Grant-, Bt. (S. 1702).
Sutton, Sir Frederick Walter, Kt., OBE.
Sutton, *Air Marshal* Sir John Matthias Dobson, KCB.
Sutton, Sir Richard Lexington, Bt. (1772).

Swaffield, Sir James Chesebrough, Kt., CBE, RD.
Swallow, Sir William, Kt.
Swan, Sir John William David, KBE.
Swann, Sir Michael Christopher, Bt., TD (1906).
Swanwick, Sir Graham Russell, Kt., MBE.
Swartz, *Hon.* Sir Reginald William Colin, KBE, ED.
Sweetnam, Sir (David) Rodney, KCVO, CBE, FRCS.
Swinburn, *Lt.-Gen.* Sir Richard Hull, KCB.
Swinson, Sir John Henry Alan, Kt., OBE.
Swinton, *Maj.-Gen.* Sir John, KCVO, OBE.
Swire, Sir Adrian Christopher, Kt.
Swire, Sir John Anthony, Kt., CBE.
Swiss, Sir Rodney Geoffrey, Kt., OBE.
Swynnerton, Sir Roger John Massy, Kt., CMG, OBE, MC.
Sykes, Sir Francis John Badcock, Bt. (1781).
Sykes, Sir John Charles Anthony le Gallais, Bt. (1921).
Sykes, *Prof.* Sir (Malcolm) Keith, Kt.
Sykes, Sir Tatton Christopher Mark, Bt. (1783).
Symington, *Prof.* Sir Thomas, Kt., MD, FRSE.
Symons, *Vice-Adm.* Sir Patrick Jeremy, KBE.
Synge, Sir Robert Carson, Bt. (1801).
Tait, *Adm.* Sir (Allan) Gordon, KCB, DSC.
Tait, Sir James Sharp, Kt., D.SC., LL D., Ph.D.
Tait, Sir Peter, KBE.
Talbot, *Vice-Adm.* Sir (Arthur Allison) FitzRoy, KBE, CB, DSO.
Talbot, *Hon.* Sir Hilary Gwynne, Kt.
Talboys, *Rt. Hon.* Sir Brian Edward, Kt., CH.
Tancred, Sir Henry Lawson-, Bt. (1662).
Tangaroa, *Hon.* Sir Tangoroa, Kt., MBE.
Tange, Sir Arthur Harold, Kt., CBE.
Tansley, Sir Eric Crawford, Kt., CMG.
Tapsell, Sir Peter Hannay Bailey, Kt., MP.
Tate, *Lt.-Col.* Sir Henry, Bt. (1898).
Taukala, Sir David Dawea, Kt., MBE.
Tavaiqia, *Ratu* Sir Josaia, KBE.
Tavare, Sir John, Kt., CBE.
Taylor, *Lt.-Gen.* Sir Allan Macnab, KBE, MC.
Taylor, Sir (Arthur) Godfrey, Kt.
Taylor, Sir Cyril Julian Hebden, Kt.
Taylor, Sir Edward Macmillan (Teddy), Kt., MP.
Taylor, Sir George, Kt., D.SC., FRS, FRSE.
Taylor, Sir Henry Milton, Kt.
Taylor, Sir James, Kt., MBE, D.SC.
Taylor, Sir John Lang, KCMG.
Taylor, Sir Nicholas Richard Stuart, Bt. (1917).
Taylor, *Prof.* Sir William, Kt., CBE.
Tebbit, Sir Donald Claude, GCMG.
Te Heuheu, Sir Hepi Hoani, KBE.
Telford, Sir Robert, Kt., CBE, FEng.
Temple, Sir Ernest Sanderson, Kt., MBE, QC.
Temple, Sir John Meredith, Kt.
Temple, Sir Rawden John Afamado, Kt., CBE, QC.
Temple, *Maj.* Sir Richard Anthony Purbeck, Bt., MC (1876).
Templeton, Sir John Marks, Kt.
Tennant, *Capt.* Sir Iain Mark, KT.
Tennant, Sir Anthony John, Kt.
Tennant, Sir Peter Frank Dalrymple, Kt., CMG, OBE.
Teo, Sir Fiatau Penitala, GCMG, GCVO, ISO, MBE.
Terry, Sir George Walter Roberts, Kt., CBE, QPM.
Terry, Sir John Elliott, Kt.
Terry, Sir Michael Edward Stanley Imbert-, Bt. (1917).
Terry, *Air Chief Marshal* Sir Peter David George, GCB, AFC.
Tetley, Sir Herbert, KBE, CB.
Tett, Sir Hugh Charles, Kt.
Thatcher, Sir Denis, Bt., MBE, TD (1990).
Thiess, Sir Leslie Charles, Kt., CBE.
Thomas, Sir Derek Morison David, KCMG.
Thomas, Sir Frederick William, Kt.
Thomas, Sir (Godfrey) Michael (David), Bt. (1694).
Thomas, Sir Jeremy Cashel, KCMG.
Thomas, Sir John Maldwyn, Kt.
Thomas, *Prof.* Sir John Meurig, Kt., FRS.
Thomas, Sir Keith Vivian, Kt.
Thomas, Sir Robert Evan, Kt.
Thomas, *Hon.* Sir Swinton Barclay, Kt.
Thomas, Sir William James Cooper, Bt., TD (1919).
Thomas, Sir (William) Michael (Marsh), Bt. (1918).
Thomas, *Adm.* Sir (William) Richard Scott, KCB, OBE.
Thompson, Sir Christopher Peile, Bt. (1890).
Thompson, Sir Donald, Kt., MP.
Thompson, Sir Edward Hugh Dudley, Kt., MBE, TD.
Thompson, *Surgeon Vice-Adm.* Sir Godfrey James Milton-, KBE.
Thompson, *Vice-Adm.* Sir Hugh Leslie Owen, KBE, FEng.
Thompson, Sir (Humphrey) Simon Meysey-, Bt. (1874).
Thompson, *Hon.* Sir John, Kt.
Thompson, *Prof.* Sir Michael Warwick, Kt., D.SC.
Thompson, Sir Paul Anthony, Bt. (1963).
Thompson, Sir Peter Anthony, Kt.
Thompson, Sir Ralph Patrick, Kt.
Thompson, Sir Richard Hilton Marler, Bt. (1963).
Thompson, Sir (Thomas) Lionel Tennyson, Bt. (1806).
Thomson, Sir Adam, Kt., CBE.
Thomson, *Air Chief Marshal* Sir (Charles) John, KCB, CBE, AFC.
Thomson, Sir Evan Rees Whitaker, Kt.
Thomson, Sir (Frederick Douglas) David, Bt. (1929).
Thomson, Sir John, KBE, TD.
Thomson, Sir John Adam, GCMG.
Thomson, Sir John (Ian) Sutherland, KBE, CMG.
Thomson, Sir Mark Wilfrid Home, Bt. (1925).
Thomson, Sir Thomas James, Kt., CBE, FRCP.
Thorn, Sir John Samuel, Kt., OBE.
Thorne, *Maj.-Gen.* Sir David Calthrop, KBE.
Thorne, Sir Neil Gordon, Kt., OBE, TD.
Thorne, Sir Peter Francis, KCVO, CBE.
Thornton, Sir (George) Malcolm, Kt., MP.
Thornton, *Lt.-Gen.* Sir Leonard Whitmore, KCB, CBE.
Thornton, Sir Peter Eustace, KCB.
Thorold, Sir Anthony Henry, Bt., OBE, DSC (1642).
Thorpe, *Hon.* Sir Mathew Alexander, Kt.
Thouron, Sir John Rupert Hunt, KBE.
†Throckmorton, Sir Anthony John Benedict, Bt. (1642).
Thwaites, Sir Bryan, Kt., Ph.D.
Thwin, Sir U, Kt.
Tibbits, *Capt.* Sir David Stanley, Kt., DSC.
Tickell, Sir Crispin Charles Cervantes, GCMG, KCVO.
Tidbury, Sir Charles Henderson, Kt.
Tikaram, Sir Moti, KBE.
Tilney, Sir John Dudley Robert Tarleton, Kt., TD.
Tippet, *Vice-Adm.* Sir Anthony Sanders, KCB.
Tippett, Sir Michael Kemp, Kt., OM, CH, CBE.
Tirvengadum, Sir Harry Krishnan, Kt.
Titman, Sir John Edward Powis, KCVO.
Tizard, Sir John Peter Mills, Kt.
Tod, *Air Marshal* Sir John Hunter Hunter-, KBE, CB.
Todd, Sir Ian Pelham, KBE, FRCS.
Todd, *Hon.* Sir (Reginald Stephen) Garfield, Kt.
Tollemache, Sir Lyonel Humphry John, Bt. (1793).
Tololo, Sir Alkan, KBE.
Tomkins, Sir Alfred George, Kt., CBE.
Tomkins, Sir Edward Emile, GCMG, CVO.
Tomkys, Sir (William) Roger, KCMG.
Tomlinson, *Prof.* Sir Bernard Evans, Kt., CBE.
Tomlinson, Sir (Frank) Stanley, KCMG.
Tooley, Sir John, Kt.
Tooth, Sir (Hugh) John Lucas-, Bt. (1920).

ToRobert, Sir Henry Thomas, KBE.
Tory, Sir Geofroy William, KCMG.
Touche, Sir Anthony George, Bt. (1920).
Touche, Sir Rodney Gordon, Bt. (1962).
Tovey, Sir Brian John Maynard, KCMG.
ToVue, Sir Ronald, Kt., OBE.
Townsend, *Rear-Adm.* Sir Leslie William, KCVO, CBE.
Townsing, Sir Kenneth Joseph, Kt., CMG.
Traherne, Sir Cennydd George, KG, TD.
Traill, Sir Alan Towers, GBE.
Trant, *Gen.* Sir Richard Brooking, KCB.
Travers, Sir Thomas à'Beckett, Kt.
Treacher, *Adm.* Sir John Devereux, KCB.
Trehane, Sir (Walter) Richard, Kt.
Trelawny, Sir John Barry Salusbury-, Bt. (1628).
Trench, Sir Nigel Clive Cosby, KCMG.
Trench, Sir Peter Edward, Kt., CBE, TD.
Trescowthick, Sir Donald Henry, KBE.
Trethowan, *Prof.* Sir William Henry, Kt., CBE, FRCP.
Trevelyan, Sir George Lowthian, Bt. (1874).
Trevelyan, Sir Norman Irving, Bt. (1662).
Trewby, *Vice-Adm.* Sir (George Francis) Allan, KCB, FEng.
Trippier, Sir David Austin, Kt., RD.
Tritton, Sir Anthony John Ernest, Bt. (1905).
†Trollope, Sir Anthony Simon, Bt. (1642).
Trotter, Sir Ronald Ramsay, Kt.
Troubridge, Sir Thomas Richard, Bt. (1799).
Troup, *Vice-Adm.* Sir (John) Anthony (Rose), KCB, DSC.
Trowbridge, *Rear-Adm.* Sir Richard John, KCVO.
Truscott, Sir George James Irving, Bt. (1909).
Tuck, Sir Bruce Adolph Reginald, Bt. (1910).
Tucker, *Hon.* Sir Richard Howard, Kt.
Tuckey, *Hon.* Sir Simon Lane, Kt.
Tudor, *Hon.* Sir James Cameron, KCMG.
Tugendhat, Sir Christopher Samuel, Kt.
Tuita, Sir Mariano Kelesimalefo, Kt., OBE.
Tuite, Sir Christopher Hugh, Bt., Ph.D. (1622).
Tuivaga, Sir Timoci Uluiburotu, Kt.
Tuke, Sir Anthony Favill, Kt.
Tupper, Sir Charles Hibbert, Bt. (1888).
Turbott, Sir Ian Graham, Kt., CMG, CVO.
Turing, Sir John Dermot, Bt. (s. 1638).
Turnbull, Sir George Henry, Kt.
Turnbull, Sir Richard Gordon, GCMG.
Turner, *Rt. Hon.* Sir Alexander Kingcome, KBE.
Turner, *Hon.* Sir Michael John, Kt.
Tuti, *Revd* Dudley, KBE.
Tuzo, *Gen.* Sir Harry Craufurd, GCB, OBE, MC.
Twiss, *Adm.* Sir Frank Roddam, KCB, KCVO, DSC.
Tyree, Sir (Alfred) William, Kt., OBE.
Tyrrell, Sir Murray Louis, KCVO, CBE.
Tyrwhitt, Sir Reginald Thomas Newman, Bt. (1919).
Udoma, *Hon.* Sir (Egbert) Udo, Kt.
Unsworth, *Hon.* Sir Edgar Ignatius Godfrey, Kt., CMG.
Unwin, Sir (James) Brian, KCB.
Ure, Sir John Burns, KCMG, LVO.
Urquhart, Sir Brian Edward, KCMG, MBE.
Urwick, Sir Alan Bedford, KCVO, CMG.
Usher, Sir Leonard Gray, KBE.
Usher, Sir Robert Edward, Bt. (1899).
Ustinov, Sir Peter Alexander, Kt., CBE.
Utting, Sir William Benjamin, Kt., CB.
Vallat, Sir Francis Aimé, GBE, KCMG, QC.
Vallings, *Vice-Adm.* Sir George Montague Francis, KCB.
Vanderfelt, Sir Robin Victor, KBE.
van der Post, Sir Laurens Jan, Kt., CBE.
Vane, Sir John Robert, Kt., D.Phil., D.SC., FRS.
Vanneck, *Air Cdre* Hon. Sir Peter Beckford Rutgers, GBE, CB, AFC.
van Straubenzee, Sir William Radcliffe, Kt., MBE.
Vasquez, Sir Alfred Joseph, Kt., CBE, QC.
Vaughan, Sir (George) Edgar, KBE.
Vaughan, Sir Gerard Folliott, Kt., MP, FRCP.
Vavasour, *Cdr.* Sir Geoffrey William, Bt., DSC, RN (1828).
Veale, Sir Alan John Ralph, Kt., FEng.
Veira, Sir Philip Henry, KBE.
Verco, Sir Walter John George, KCVO.
Verney, Sir John, Bt., MC, TD (1946).
Verney, Sir Ralph Bruce, Bt., KBE (1818).
Vernon, Sir James, Kt., CBE.
Vernon, Sir Nigel John Douglas, Bt. (1914).
Vesey, Sir (Nathaniel) Henry (Peniston), Kt., CBE.
Vestey, Sir (John) Derek, Bt. (1921).
Vial, Sir Kenneth Harold, Kt., CBE.
Vick, Sir (Francis) Arthur, Kt., OBE, Ph.D.
Vickers, *Lt.-Gen.* Sir Richard Maurice Hilton, KCB, MVO, OBE.
Victoria, Sir (Joseph Aloysius) Donatus, Kt., CBE.
Vincent, *Field Marshal* Sir Richard Frederick, GBE, KCB, DSO.
Vincent, Sir William Percy Maxwell, Bt. (1936).
Vinelott, *Hon.* Sir John Evelyn, Kt.
Vines, Sir William Joshua, Kt., CMG.
Vyse, *Lt.-Gen.* Sir Edward Dacre Howard-, KBE, CB, MC.
Vyvyan, Sir John Stanley, Bt. (1645).
Waddell, Sir Alexander Nicol Anton, KCMG, DSC.
Waddell, Sir James Henderson, Kt., CB.
Wade, *Prof.* Sir Henry William Rawson, Kt., QC, FBA.
Wade, *Air Chief Marshal* Sir Ruthven Lowry, KCB, DFC.
Wagner, Sir Anthony Richard, KCB, KCVO.
Waite, *Hon.* Sir John Douglas, Kt.
Wake, Sir Hereward, Bt. MC (1621).
Wakefield, Sir (Edward) Humphry (Tyrell), Bt. (1962).
Wakefield, Sir Norman Edward, Kt.
Wakefield, Sir Peter George Arthur, KBE, CMG.
Wakeford, *Air Marshal* Sir Richard Gordon, KCB, OBE, MVO, AFC.
Wakeley, Sir John Cecil Nicholson, Bt., FRCS (1952).
†Wakeman, Sir Edward Offley Bertram, Bt. (1828).
Walker, *Revd* Alan Edgar, Kt., OBE.
Walker, Sir Allan Grierson, Kt., QC.
Walker, *Gen.* Sir Antony Kenneth Frederick, KCB.
Walker, Sir Baldwin Patrick, Bt. (1856).
Walker, Sir (Charles) Michael, GCMG.
Walker, Sir Colin John Shedlock, Kt., OBE.
Walker, Sir David Alan, Kt.
Walker, Sir Gervas George, Kt.
Walker, *Rt. Hon.* Sir Harold, Kt., MP.
Walker, Sir Harold Berners, KCMG.
Walker, *Maj.* Sir Hugh Ronald, Bt. (1906).
Walker, Sir James Graham, Kt., MBE.
Walker, Sir James Heron, Bt. (1868).
Walker, *Air Marshal* Sir John Robert, KCB, CBE, AFC.
Walker, Sir Michael Leolin Forestier-, Bt. (1835).
Walker, Sir Patrick Jeremy, KCB.
Walker, *Gen.* Sir Walter Colyear, KCB, CBE, DSO.
Wall, *Dr Hon.* Sir Gerard Aloysius, Kt.
Wall, Sir Patrick Henry Bligh, Kt., MC, VRD.
Wall, Sir Robert William, Kt., OBE.
Wallace, Sir Ian James, Kt., CBE.
Waller, *Hon.* Sir (George) Mark, Kt.
Waller, *Rt. Hon.* Sir George Stanley, Kt., OBE.
Waller, Sir (John) Keith, Kt., CBE.
Waller, Sir John Stainer, Bt. (1815).
Waller, Sir Robert William, Bt. (I. 1780).
Walley, Sir John, KBE, CB.
Wallis, Sir Peter Gordon, KCVO.
Walsh, Sir Alan, Kt., D.SC., FRS.
Walsh, *Prof.* Sir John Patrick, KBE.

Walsham, *Rear-Adm.* Sir John Scarlett Warren, Bt., CB, OBE (1831).
Walter, Sir Harold Edward, Kt.
Walters, *Prof.* Sir Alan Arthur, Kt.
Walters, Sir Dennis Murray, Kt., MBE.
Walters, Sir Frederick Donald, Kt.
Walters, Sir Peter Ingram, Kt.
Walters, Sir Roger Talbot, KBE, FRIBA.
Walton, Sir John Robert, Kt.
Wan, Sir Wamp, Kt., MBE.
Wanstall, *Hon.* Sir Charles Gray, Kt.
Ward, *Hon.* Sir Alan Hylton, Kt.
Ward, Sir Arthur Hugh, KBE.
Ward, Sir Joseph James Laffey, Bt. (1911).
Ward, *Maj.-Gen.* Sir Philip John Newling, KCVO, CBE.
Wardale, Sir Geoffrey Charles, KCB.
Wardlaw, Sir Henry (John), Bt. (S. 1631).
Wardle, Sir Thomas Edward Jewell, Kt.
Waring, Sir (Alfred) Holburt, Bt. (1935).
Warmington, *Lt.-Cdr.* Sir Marshall George Clitheroe, Bt., RN (1908).
Warner, Sir (Edward Courtenay) Henry, Bt. (1910).
Warner, Sir Edward Redston, KCMG, OBE.
Warner, Sir Frederick Archibald, GCVO, KCMG.
Warner, *Prof.* Sir Frederick Edward, Kt., FRS, FEng.
Warner, *Hon.* Sir Jean-Pierre Frank Eugene, Kt.
Warnock, Sir Geoffrey James, Kt.
Warren, Sir Brian Charles Pennefather, Bt. (1784).
Warren, Sir Frederick Miles, KBE.
Warren, Sir (Harold) Brian (Seymour), Kt.
Wass, Sir Douglas William Gretton, GCB.
Waterhouse, *Hon.* Sir Ronald Gough, Kt.
Waterlow, Sir Christopher Rupert, Bt. (1873).
Waterlow, Sir (James) Gerard, Bt. (1930).
Waters, *Gen.* Sir (Charles) John, KCB, CBE.
Wates, Sir Christopher Stephen, Kt.
Watkins, *Rt. Hon.* Sir Tasker, VC, GBE.
Watson, Sir Bruce Dunstan, Kt.
Watson, Sir Francis John Bagott, KCVO, FBA, FSA.
Watson, Sir (James) Andrew, Bt. (1866).
Watson, Sir John Forbes Inglefield-, Bt. (1895).
Watson, Sir Michael Milne-, Bt., CBE (1937).
Watson, Sir (Noel) Duncan, KCMG.
Watson, *Vice-Adm.* Sir Philip Alexander, KBE, MVO.
Watt, *Surgeon Vice-Adm.* Sir James, KBE, FRCS.
Watt, Sir James Harvie-, Bt. (1945).
Watts, Sir Arthur Desmond, KCMG.
Watts, *Lt.-Gen.* Sir John Peter Barry Condliffe, KBE, CB, MC.
Watts, Sir Roy, Kt., CBE.
Wauchope, Sir Roger (Hamilton) Don-, Bt. (S. 1667).
Way, Sir Richard George Kitchener, KCB, CBE.
Weatherall, *Prof.* Sir David John, Kt., FRS.
Weatherall, *Vice-Adm.* Sir James Lamb, KBE.
Weatherstone, Sir Dennis, KBE.
Weaver, Sir Tobias Rushton, Kt., CB.
Webb, *Lt.-Gen.* Sir Richard James Holden, KBE, CB.
Webb, Sir Thomas Langley, Kt.
Webber, Sir Andrew Lloyd, Kt.
Webster, *Very Revd* Alan Brunskill, KCVO.
Webster, *Vice-Adm.* Sir John Morrison, KCB.
Webster, *Hon.* Sir Peter Edlin, Kt.
Wedderburn, Sir Andrew John Alexander Ogilvy-, Bt. (1803).
Wedgwood, Sir (Hugo) Martin, Bt. (1942).
Weinberg, Sir Mark Aubrey, Kt.
Weir, Sir Michael Scott, KCMG.
Weir, Sir Roderick Bignell, Kt.
Welby, Sir (Richard) Bruno Gregory, Bt. (1801).
Welch, Sir John Reader, Bt. (1957).
Weldon, Sir Anthony William, Bt. (I. 1723).
Wellings, Sir Jack Alfred, Kt., CBE.
Wells, Sir Charles Maltby, Bt., TD (1944).
Wells, Sir John Julius, Kt.
Westbrook, Sir Neil Gowanloch, Kt., CBE.
Westerman, Sir (Wilfred) Alan, Kt., CBE.
Weston, Sir Michael Charles Swift, KCMG, CVO.
Weston, Sir (Philip) John, KCMG.
Wheeler, Sir Frederick Henry, Kt., CBE.
Wheeler, Sir Harry Anthony, Kt., OBE.
Wheeler, *Air Chief Marshal* Sir (Henry) Neil (George), GCB, CBE, DSO, DFC, AFC.
Wheeler, Sir John Daniel, Kt., MP.
Wheeler, Sir John Hieron, Bt. (1920).
Wheeler, *Hon.* Sir Kenneth Henry, Kt.
Wheler, Sir Edward Woodford, Bt. (1660).
Whishaw, Sir Charles Percival Law, Kt.
Whitaker, *Maj.* Sir James Herbert Ingham, Bt. (1936).
White, Sir Christopher Robert Meadows, Bt. (1937).
White, Sir David Harry, Kt.
White, Sir Dick Goldsmith, KCMG, KBE.
White, Sir Frederick William George, KBE, Ph.D., FRS.
White, Sir George Stanley James, Bt. (1904).
White, Sir Harold Leslie, Kt., CBE.
White, *Wg Cdr.* Sir Henry Arthur Dalrymple-, Bt., DFC (1926).
White, *Vice-Adm.* Sir Hugo Moresby, KCB, CBE.
White, *Hon.* Sir John Charles, Kt., MBE.
White, Sir John Woolmer, Bt. (1922).
White, Sir Lynton Stuart, Kt., MBE. TD.
White, *Adm.* Sir Peter, GBE.
White, Sir Thomas Astley Woollaston, Bt. (1802).
Whitehead, Sir John Stainton, GCMG, CVO.
Whitehead, Sir Rowland John Rathbone, Bt. (1889).
Whiteley, Sir Hugo Baldwin Huntington-, Bt. (1918).
Whiteley, *Gen.* Sir Peter John Frederick, GCB, OBE, RM.
Whitford, *Hon.* Sir John Norman Keates, Kt.
Whitley, *Air Marshal* Sir John René, KBE, CB, DSO, AFC.
Whitmore, Sir Clive Anthony, GCB, CVO.
Whitmore, Sir John Henry Douglas, Bt. (1954).
Whitteridge, Sir Gordon Coligny, KCMG, OBE.
Whittle, *Air Cdre* Sir Frank, OM, KBE, CB, FRS, FEng.
Whittome, Sir Leslie Alan, Kt.
Wickerson, Sir John Michael, Kt.
Wicks, Sir James Albert, Kt.
Wicks, Sir Nigel Leonard, KCB, CVO, CBE.
Wigan, Sir Alan Lewis, Bt. (1898).
†Wiggin, Sir Charles Rupert John, Bt. (1892).
Wigglesworth, Sir Vincent Brian, Kt., CBE, MD, FRS.
Wigram, *Revd Canon* Sir Clifford Woolmore, Bt. (1805).
Wilbraham, Sir Richard Baker, Bt. (1776).
Wilford, Sir (Kenneth) Michael, GCMG.
Wilkes, *Lt.-Gen.* Sir Michael John, KCB, CBE.
Wilkins, Sir Graham John, Kt.
Wilkins, *Lt.-Gen.* Sir Michael Compton Lockwood, KCB, OBE.
Wilkinson, Sir (David) Graham (Brook) Bt. (1941).
Wilkinson, *Prof.* Sir Denys Haigh, Kt., FRS.
Wilkinson, *Prof.* Sir Geoffrey, Kt., FRS.
Wilkinson, Sir Peter Allix, KCMG, DSO, OBE.
Wilkinson, Sir Philip William, Kt.
Wilkinson, Sir William Henry Nairn, Kt.

Willatt, Sir (Robert) Hugh, Kt.
Willcocks, Sir David Valentine, Kt., CBE, MC.
Williams, Sir Alastair Edgcumbe James Dudley-, Bt. (1964).
Williams, Sir Alwyn, Kt., Ph.D., FRS.
Williams, Sir Arthur Dennis Pitt, Kt.
Williams, Sir (Arthur) Gareth Ludovic Emrys Rhys, Bt. (1918).
Williams, *Prof.* Sir Bruce Rodda, KBE.
Williams, *Adm.* Sir David, GCB.
Williams, *Prof.* Sir David Glyndwr Tudor, Kt.
Williams, Sir David Innes, Kt.
Williams, *Hon.* Sir Denys Ambrose, Kt.
Williams, Sir Donald Mark, Bt. (1866).
Williams, Sir Edgar Trevor, Kt., CB, CBE, DSO.
Williams, *Prof.* Sir (Edward) Dillwyn, Kt., FRCP.
Williams, *Hon.* Sir Edward Stratten, KCMG, KBE.
Williams, Sir Francis John Watkin, Bt., QC (1798).
Williams, Sir Henry Sydney, Kt., OBE.
Williams, Sir (John) Leslie, Kt., CBE.
Williams, Sir John Robert, KCMG.
Williams, Sir Leonard, KBE, CB.
Williams, Sir Osmond, Bt., MC (1909).
Williams, Sir Peter Watkin, Kt.
Williams, *Prof.* Sir Robert Evan Owen, Kt., MD, FRCP.
Williams, Sir (Robert) Philip Nathaniel, Bt. (1915).
Williams, Sir Robin Philip, Bt. (1953).
Williams, Sir (William) Maxwell (Harries), Kt.
Williamson, *Marshal of the Royal Air Force* Sir Keith Alec, GCB, AFC.
Williamson, Sir (Nicholas Frederick) Hedworth, Bt. (1642).
Willink, Sir Charles William, Bt. (1957).
Willis, *Hon.* Sir Eric Archibald, KBE, CMG.
Willis, *Vice-Adm.* Sir (Guido) James, KBE.
Willison, *Lt.-Gen.* Sir David John, KCB, OBE, MC.
Willison, Sir John Alexander, Kt., OBE.
Wills, Sir David Seton, Bt. (1904).
Wills, Sir (Hugh) David Hamilton, Kt., CBE, TD.
Wills, Sir John Vernon, Bt., TD (1923).
Wilmot, Sir Henry Robert, Bt. (1759).
Wilmot, *Cdr.* Sir John Assheton Eardley-, Bt., MVO, DSC, RN (1821).
Wilsey, *Lt.-Gen.* Sir John Finlay Willasey, KCB, CBE.
Wilson, Sir Alan Herries, Kt., FRS.
Wilson, *Lt.-Gen.* Sir (Alexander) James, KBE, MC.
Wilson, Sir Anthony, Kt.
Wilson, *Vice-Adm.* Sir Barry Nigel, KCB.
Wilson, Sir Charles Haynes, Kt.
Wilson, Sir David, Bt. (1920).
Wilson, Sir David Mackenzie, Kt.
Wilson, Sir Geoffrey Masterman, KCB, CMG.
Wilson, Sir James William Douglas, Bt. (1906).
Wilson, Sir John Foster, Kt., CBE.
Wilson, Sir John Gardiner, Kt., CBE.
Wilson, Sir John Martindale, KCB.
Wilson, *Brig.* Sir Mathew John Anthony, Bt., OBE, MC (1874).
Wilson, Sir Patrick Michael Ernest David McNair-, Kt., MP.
Wilson, Sir Reginald Holmes, Kt.
Wilson, Sir Robert, Kt., CBE.
Wilson, Sir Robert Donald, Kt.
Wilson, Sir (Robert) Michael Conal McNair-, Kt.
Wilson, *Rt. Revd* Roger Plumpton, KCVO, DD.
Wilson, Sir Roland, KBE.
Wilson, *Air Marshal* Sir (Ronald) Andrew (Fellowes), KCB, AFC.
Wilson, *Hon.* Sir Ronald Darling, KBE, CMG.
Wilton, Sir (Arthur) John, KCMG, KCVO, MC.
Wiltshire, Sir Frederick Munro, Kt., CBE.
Windeyer, Sir Brian Wellingham, Kt.
Wingate, *Capt.* Sir Miles Buckley, KCVO.
Winnifrith, Sir (Alfred) John (Digby), KCB.
Winnington, Sir Francis Salwey William, Bt. (1755).
Winskill, *Air Cdre* Sir Archibald Little, KCVO, CBE, DFC.
Winterbottom, Sir Walter, Kt., CBE.
Wiseman, Sir John William, Bt. (1628).
Wolfson, Sir Brian Gordon, Kt.
Wolseley, Sir Charles Garnet Richard Mark, Bt. (1628).
Wolseley, Sir Garnet, Bt. (I. 1745).
Wolstenholme, Sir Gordon Ethelbert Ward, Kt., OBE.
Wombwell, Sir George Philip Frederick, Bt. (1778).
Womersley, Sir Peter John Walter, Bt. (1945).
Wontner, Sir Hugh Walter Kingwell, GBE, CVO.
Wood, Sir Alan Marshall Muir, Kt., FRS, FEng.
Wood, Sir Anthony John Page, Bt. (1837).
Wood, Sir David Basil Hill-, Bt. (1921).
Wood, Sir Frederick Ambrose Stuart, Kt.
Wood, Sir Henry Peart, Kt., CBE.
Wood, *Prof.* Sir John Crossley, Kt., CBE.
Wood, *Hon.* Sir John Kember, Kt., MC.
Wood, Sir Martin Francis, Kt., OBE.
Wood, Sir Russell Dillon, KCVO, VRD.
Wood, Sir William Alan, KCVO, CB.
Woodcock, Sir John, Kt., CBE, QPM.
Woodfield, Sir Philip John, KCB, CBE.
Woodhead, *Vice-Adm.* Sir (Anthony) Peter, KCB.
Woodhouse, *Rt. Hon.* Sir (Arthur) Owen, KBE, DSC.
Wooding, Sir Norman Samuel, Kt., CBE.
Woodroffe, *Most Revd* George Cuthbert Manning, KBE.
Woodroofe, Sir Ernest George, Kt., Ph.D.
Woodruff, *Prof.* Sir Michael Francis Addison, Kt., D.Sc., FRS, FRCS.
Woods, Sir Colin Philip Joseph, KCVO, CBE.
Woods, *Most Revd* Frank, KBE, DD.
Woods, *Rt. Revd* Robert Wilmer, KCMG, KCVO.
Woodward, *Hon.* Sir (Albert) Edward, Kt., OBE.
Woodward, *Adm.* Sir John Forster, GBE, KCB.
Woolf, *Rt. Hon.* Sir Harry Kenneth, Kt.
Woolf, Sir John, Kt.
Woollaston, Sir (Mountford) Tosswill, Kt.
Wordie, Sir John Stewart, Kt., CBE, VRD.
Worsley, *Gen.* Sir Richard Edward, GCB, OBE.
Worsley, Sir (William) Marcus (John), Bt. (1838).
Worsthorne, Sir Peregrine Gerard, Kt.
Wraight, Sir John Richard, KBE, CMG.
Wratten, *Air Marshal* Sir William John, KBE, CB, AFC.
Wraxall, Sir Charles Frederick Lascelles, Bt. (1813).
†Wrey, Sir George Richard Bourchier, Bt. (1628).
Wrigglesworth, Sir Ian William, Kt.
Wright, Sir Allan Frederick, KBE.
Wright, Sir Denis Arthur Hepworth, GCMG.
Wright, Sir Edward Maitland, Kt., D.Phil., LL D., D.Sc., FRSE.
Wright, *Hon.* Sir (John) Michael, Kt.
Wright, Sir (John) Oliver, GCMG, GCVO, DSC.
Wright, Sir Patrick Richard Henry, GCMG.
Wright, Sir Paul Hervé Giraud, KCMG, OBE.
Wright, Sir Richard Michael Cory-, Bt. (1903).
Wrightson, Sir Charles Mark Garmondsway, Bt. (1900).
Wykeham, *Air Marshal* Sir Peter Guy, KCB, DSO, OBE, DFC, AFC.
Wylie, Sir Campbell, Kt., ED, QC.
Wynn, Sir David Watkin Williams-, Bt. (1688).
Yacoub, *Prof.* Sir Magdi Habib, Kt., FRCS.
Yang, *Hon.* Ti Liang, Kt.
Yapp, Sir Stanley Graham, Kt.
Yarranton, Sir Peter George, Kt.

Yarrow, Sir Eric Grant, Bt., MBE (1916).
Yeend, Sir Geoffrey John, Kt., CBE.
Yellowlees, Sir Henry, KCB.
Yocklunn, Sir John (Soong Chung), KCVO.
Yoo Foo, Sir (François) Henri, Kt.
Youens, Sir Peter William, Kt., CMG, OBE.
Young, Sir Brian Walter Mark, Kt.
Young, *Lt.-Gen.* Sir David Tod, KBE, CB, DFC.
Young, Sir George Samuel Knatchbull, Bt., MP (1813).
Young, *Hon.* Sir Harold William, KCMG.
Young, Sir John Kenyon Roe, Bt. (1821).
Young, *Hon.* Sir John McIntosh, KCMG.
Young, Sir Leslie Clarence, Kt., CBE.
Young, Sir Norman Smith, Kt.
Young, Sir Richard Dilworth, Kt.
Young, Sir Robert Christopher Mackworth-, GCVO.
Young, Sir Roger William, Kt.
Young, Sir Stephen Stewart Templeton, Bt. (1945).
Young, Sir William Neil, Bt. (1769).
Younger, *Maj.-Gen.* Sir John William, Bt., CBE (1911).
Zeeman, *Prof.* Sir (Erik) Christopher, Kt., FRS.
Zeidler, Sir David Ronald, Kt., CBE.
Zoleveke, Sir Gideon Pitabose, KBE.
Zunz, Sir Gerhard Jacob (Jack), Kt., FEng.
Zurenuo, *Rt. Revd* Zurewe Kamong, Kt., OBE.

The Military Knights of Windsor

The Military Knights of Windsor take part in all ceremonies of the Noble Order of the Garter and attend Sunday morning service in St George's Chapel, Windsor Castle, as representatives of the Knights of the Garter. The Knights receive a small stipend in addition to their army pensions and quarters in Windsor Castle.

The Knights of Windsor were originally founded in 1348 after the wars in France to assist English knights, who, having been prisoners in the hands of the French, had become impoverished by the payments of heavy ransoms. When Edward III founded the Order of the Garter later the same year, he incorporated the Knights of Windsor and the College of St George into its foundation and raised the number of Knights to 26 to correspond with the number of the Knights of the Garter. Known later as the Alms Knights or Poor Knights of Windsor, their establishment was reduced under the will of King Henry VIII to 13 and Statutes were drawn up by Queen Elizabeth I.

In 1833 King William IV changed their designation to The Military Knights and granted them their present uniform which consists of a scarlet tail-coat with white cross sword-belt, crimson sash and cocked hat with plume. The badges are the Shield of St George and the Star of the Order of the Garter.

Governor, Maj.-Gen. Peter Downward, CB, DSO, DFC.
Military Knights, Brig. A. L. Atkinson, OBE; Brig. J. F. Linder, OBE, MC; Maj. W. L. Thompson, MVO, MBE, DCM; Maj. L. W. Dickerson; Maj. J. C. Cowley, DCM; Lt.-Col. N. L. West; Maj. G. R. Mitchell; MBE, BEM; Lt.-Col. R. L. C. Tamplin; Maj. P. H. Bolton, MBE; Lt.-Col. H. R. Rogers, MBE; Brig. T. W. Hackworth, OBE.
Supernumerary, Brig. A. C. Tyler, CBE, MC.

Dames Grand Cross and Dames Commanders

Style, 'Dame' before forename and surname, followed by appropriate post-nominal initials. Where such an award is made to a lady already in enjoyment of a higher title, the appropriate initials follow her name.
Husband, Untitled.
For forms of address, *see* page 218.

Dame Grand Cross and Dames Commander are the higher classes for women of the Order of the Bath, the Order of St Michael and St George, the Royal Victorian Order, and the Order of the British Empire. Dames Grand Cross rank after the wives of Baronets and before the wives of Knights Grand Cross. Dames Commanders rank after the wives of Knights Grand Cross and before the wives of Knights Commanders.

Honorary Dame Commanders may be conferred on women who are citizens of countries of which The Queen is not head of state.

LIST OF DAMES *Revised to 31 August 1992*

Women peers in their own right and life peers are not included in this list.

HM Queen Elizabeth The Queen Mother, KG, KT, CI, GMVO.
HRH The Princess Royal, GCVO.
HRH The Princess Margaret, Countess of Snowdon, CI, GCVO.
HRH The Duchess of Gloucester, GCVO.
HRH The Princess Alice, Duchess of Gloucester, GCB, CI, GCVO, GBE.
HRH The Duchess of Kent, GCVO.
HRH The Princess Alexandra of Kent, GCVO.
Abaijah, Dame Josephine, DBE.
Abel Smith, Lady, DCVO.
Abergavenny, The Marchioness of, DCVO.
Albemarle, The Countess of, DBE.
Anderson, *Brig.* Hon. Dame Mary Mackenzie (Mrs Pihl), DBE.
Anglesey, The Marchioness of, DBE.
Baker, Dame Janet Abbott (Mrs Shelley), DBE.
Baring, Lady Rose Gwendolen Louisa, DCVO.
Barnes, Dame (Alice) Josephine (Mary Taylor), DBE, FRCP, FRCS.
Barrow, Dame Jocelyn Anita (Mrs Downer), DBE.
Barrow, Dame (Ruth) Nita, GCMG.
Basset, Lady Elizabeth, DCVO.
Beaurepaire, Dame Beryl Edith, DBE.
Berry, Dame Alice Miriam, DBE.
Bishop, Dame (Margaret) Joyce, DBE.
Blaize, Dame Venetia Ursula, DBE.
Blaxland, Dame Helen Frances, DBE.
Booth, *Hon.* Dame Margaret Myfanwy Wood, DBE.
Bottomley, Dame Bessie Ellen, DBE.
Bowman, Dame (Mary) Elaine Kellett-, DBE, MP.
Boyd, Dame Vivienne Myra, DBE.
Bracewell, *Hon.* Dame Joyanne Winifred (Mrs Copeland), DBE.
Brazill, Dame Josephine (Sister Mary Philippa), DBE.
Breen, Dame Marie Freda, DBE.
Bridges, Dame Mary Patricia, DBE.
Brown, Dame Beryl Paston, DBE.
Brown, Dame Gillian Gerda, DCVO, CMG.
Browne, Lady Moyra Blanche Madeleine, DBE.
Bryans, Dame Anne Margaret, DBE.
Bryce, Dame Isabel Graham, DBE.
Burnside, Dame Edith, DBE.
Buttfield, Dame Nancy Eileen, DBE.
Bynoe, Dame Hilda Louisa, DBE.
Cartland, Dame Barbara Hamilton, DBE.
Cartwright, Dame Mary Lucy, DBE, SC.D., D.Phil., FRS.
Cartwright, Dame Silvia Rose, DBE.
Casey, Dame Stella Katherine, DBE.
Cayford, Dame Florence Evelyn, DBE.
Charles, Dame (Mary) Eugenia, DBE.
Chesterton, Dame Elizabeth Ursula, DBE.
Clay, Dame Marie Mildred, DBE.
Clayton, Dame Barbara Evelyn (Mrs Klyne), DBE.
Cleland, Dame Rachel, DBE.
Clode, Dame (Emma) Frances (Heather), DBE.
Coles, Dame Mabel Irene, DBE.
Cooper, Dame Whina, DBE.
Coulshed, Dame (Mary) Frances, DBE, TD.
Cozens, *Brig.* Dame (Florence) Barbara, DBE, RRC.
Crowe, Dame Sylvia, DBE.
Daws, Dame Joyce Margaretta, DBE.
De La Warr, Sylvia, Countess, DBE.
Dell, Dame Miriam Patricia, DBE.
Dench, Dame Judith Olivia (Mrs Williams), DBE.
de Valois, Dame Ninette, CH, DBE.
Digby, Lady, DBE.
Donaldson, Dame (Dorothy) Mary (Lady Donaldson of Lymington), GBE.
Doyle, *Air Comdt.* Dame Jean Lena Annette Conan (Lady Bromet), DBE.
Drake, *Brig.* Dame Jean Elizabeth Rivett-, DBE.
Dugdale, Kathryn Edith Helen (Mrs John Dugdale), DCVO.
Durack, Dame Mary (Mrs H. C. Miller), DBE.
Ebsworth, *Hon.* Dame Ann Marian, DBE.
Emerton, Dame Audrey Caroline, DBE.
Fenner, Dame Peggy Edith, DBE, MP.
Fermoy, Ruth Sylvia, Lady, DCVO, OBE.
Fitton, Dame Doris Alice (Mrs Mason), DBE.
Fookes, Dame Janet Evelyn, DBE, MP.
Fraser, Dame Dorothy Rita, DBE.
Friend, Dame Phyllis Muriel, DBE.
Frink, Dame Elisabeth, CH, DBE, RA.
Frost, Dame Phyllis Irene, DBE.
Fry, Dame Margaret Louise, DBE.
Gallagher, Dame Monica Josephine, DBE.
Gardiner, Dame Helen Louisa, DBE, MVO.
Gibbs, Dame Molly Peel, DBE.
Giles, *Air Comdt.* Dame Pauline (Mrs Parsons), DBE, RRC.
Golding, Dame (Cecilie) Monica, DBE.
Goodman, Dame Barbara, DBE.
Gordon, Dame Minita Elmira, GCMG, GCVO.
Gow, Dame Jane Elizabeth, DBE.
Grafton, The Duchess of, GCVO.
Green, Dame Mary Georgina, DBE.
Grey, Dame Beryl Elizabeth (Mrs Svenson), DBE.
Guilfoyle, Dame Margaret Georgina Constance, DBE.
Hall, Dame Catherine Mary, DBE.
Hambleden, Patricia, Viscountess, GCVO.
Hammond, Dame Joan Hood, DBE.
Harris, Dame (Muriel) Diana Reader-, DBE.
Heilbron, *Hon.* Dame Rose, DBE.
Henrison, Dame Anne Elizabeth Rosina, DBE.
Herbison, Dame Jean Marjory, DBE, CMG.
Hercus, *Hon.* Dame (Margaret) Ann, DCMG.
Hetet, Dame Rangimarie, DBE.
Hill, Dame Elizabeth Mary, DBE.
Hill, *Air Cdre* Dame Felicity Barbara, DBE.
Hiller, Dame Wendy (Mrs Gow), DBE.
Horsman, Dame Dorothea Jean, DBE.

Howard, Dame Rosemary Christian, DBE.
Hunter, Dame Pamela, DBE.
Hurley, *Prof.* Dame Rosalinde (Mrs Gortvai), DBE.
Hussey, Lady Susan Katharine, DCVO.
Isaacs, Dame Albertha Madeline, DBE.
James, Dame Naomi Christine (Mrs Haythorne), DBE.
Jenkins, Dame (Mary) Jennifer (Lady Jenkins of Hillhead), DBE.
Jessel, Dame Penelope, DBE.
Jones, Dame Gwyneth (Mrs Haberfeld-Jones), DBE.
Kekedo, Dame Mary, DBE, BEM.
Kelleher, Dame Joan, DBE.
Kettlewell, *Comdt.* Dame Marion Mildred, DBE.
Kilroy, Dame Alix Hester Marie (Lady Meynell), DBE.
Kirk, Dame (Lucy) Ruth, DBE.
Knight, Dame (Joan Christabel) Jill, DBE, MP.
Kramer, *Prof.* Dame Leonie Judith, DBE.
Lancaster, Dame Jean, DBE.
Lewis, Dame Edna Leofrida (Lady Lewis), DBE.
Lister, Dame Unity Viola, DBE.
Litchfield, Dame Ruby Beatrice, DBE.
Lloyd, *Prof.* Dame June Kathleen, DBE, FRCP.
Lowrey, *Air Comdt.* Dame Alice, DBE, RRC.
Lympany, Dame Moura, DBE.
Lynn, Dame Vera (Mrs Lewis), DBE.
Mackinnon, Dame (Una) Patricia, DBE.
Macknight, Dame Ella Annie Noble, DBE, MD.
Macmillan of Ovenden, Katharine, Viscountess, DBE.
Maconchy, Dame Elizabeth Violet (Mrs Le Fanu), DBE.
Major, Dame Malvina Lorraine (Mrs Fleming), DBE.
Mann, Dame Ida Caroline, DBE, D.SC., FRCS.
Markova, Dame Alicia, DBE.
Martin, Rosamund Mary Holland-, Lady, DBE.
Menzies, Dame Pattie Maie, GBE.
Metge, *Dr* Dame (Alice) Joan, DBE.
Miles, Dame Margaret, DBE.
Miller, Dame Mabel Flora Hobart, DBE.
Miller, Dame Mary Elizabeth Hedley-, DCVO, CB.
Mitchell, Dame Mona, DCVO.
Mitchell, *Hon.* Dame Roma Flinders, DBE.
Mitchell, Dame Wendy, DBE.
Morrison, *Hon.* Dame Mary Anne, DCVO.
Mueller, Dame Anne Elisabeth, DCB.
Munro, Dame Alison, DBE.
Murdoch, Dame Elisabeth Joy, DBE.
Murdoch, Dame (Jean) Iris (Mrs Bayley), DBE.
Murray, Dame (Alice) Rosemary, DBE, D.Phil.
Niccol, Dame Kathleen Agnes, DBE.
Ollerenshaw, Dame Kathleen Mary, DBE, D.Phil.
Oxenbury, Dame Shirley Anne, DBE.
Park, Dame Merle Florence (Mrs Bloch), DBE.
Paterson, Dame Betty Fraser Ross, DBE.
Plowden, The Lady, DBE.
Poole, Dame Avril Anne Barker, DBE.
Porter, Dame Shirley (Lady Porter), DBE.
Prendergast, Dame Simone Ruth, DBE.
Prentice, Dame Winifred Eva, DBE.
Preston, Dame Frances Olivia Campbell-, DCVO.
Purves, Dame Daphne Helen, DBE.
Pyke, Lady, DBE.
Quinn, Dame Sheila Margaret Imelda, DBE.
Railton, *Brig.* Dame Mary, DBE.
Railton, Dame Ruth (Mrs King), DBE.
Rankin, Lady Jean Margaret Florence, DCVO.
Raven, Dame Kathleen Annie (Mrs Ingram), DBE.
Restieaux, *Dr* Dame Norma Jean, DBE.
Riddelsdell, Dame Mildred, DCB, CBE.
Ridley, Dame (Mildred) Betty, DBE.
Ridsdale, Dame Victoire Evelyn Patricia (Lady Ridsdale), DBE.
Rie, Dame Lucie, DBE.
Robertson, *Comdt.* Dame Nancy Margaret, DBE.
Roe, Dame Raigh Edith, DBE.
Rue, Dame (Elsie) Rosemary, DBE.
Rumbold, *Rt. Hon.* Dame Angela Claire Rosemary, DBE, MP.
Salas, Dame Margaret Laurence, DBE.
Saunders, Dame Cicely Mary Strode, OM, DBE, FRCP.
Schwarzkopf, Dame Elisabeth Friederike Marie Olga Legge-, DBE.
Scott, Dame Catherine Campbell, DBE.
Scott, Dame Jean Mary Monica Maxwell-, DCVO.
Scott, Dame Margaret, (Dame Catherine Margaret Mary Denton), DBE.
Shenfield, Dame Barbara Estelle, DBE.
Sherlock, *Prof.* Dame Sheila Patricia Violet, DBE, MD, FRCP.
Sloss, *Rt. Hon.* Dame (Ann) Elizabeth (Oldfield) Butler-, DBE.
Smieton, Dame Mary Guillan, DBE.
Smith, Dame Margaret Natalie (Maggie) (Mrs Cross), DBE.
Smith, Dame Margot, DBE.
Snagge, Dame Nancy Marion, DBE.
Soames, Mary, Lady, DBE.
Stark, Dame Freya (Mrs Perowne), DBE.
Stephens, *Air Comdt.* Dame Anne, DBE.
Stewart, Dame Muriel Acadia, DBE.
Sutherland, Dame Joan (Mrs Bonynge), OM, DBE.
Szaszy, Dame Miraka Petricevich, DBE.
Taylor, Dame Jean Elizabeth, DCVO.
Te Atairangikaahu, Te Arikinui, Dame, DBE.
Te Kanawa, Dame Kiri Janette (Mrs Park), DBE.
Tilney, Dame Guinevere (Lady Tilney), DBE.
Tinson, Dame Sue, DBE.
Tizard, Dame Catherine Anne, GCMG, DBE.
Tokiel, Dame Rosa, DBE.
Turner, *Brig.* Dame Margot, DBE, RRC.
Tyrwhitt, *Brig.* Dame Mary Joan Caroline, DBE, TD.
Uatioa, Dame Mere, DBE.
Uvarov, Dame Olga, DBE.
Varley, Dame Joan Fleetwood, DBE.
Vaughan, Dame Janet Maria (Mrs Gourlay), DBE, FRS.
Wakehurst, Margaret, Lady, DBE.
Walker, Dame Susan Armour, DBE.
Wall, (Alice) Anne, (Mrs Michael Wall), DCVO.
Warburton, Dame Anne Marion, DCVO, CMG.
Warwick, Dame Margaret Elizabeth Harvey Turner-, DBE, FRCP, FRCPEd.
Waterhouse, Dame Rachel Elizabeth, DBE, Ph.D.
Wedega, Dame Alice, DBE.
Wedgwood, Dame (Cicely) Veronica, OM, DBE.
Weston, Dame Margaret Kate, DBE.
Williamson, Dame (Elsie) Marjorie, DBE, Ph.D.
Winstone, Dame Dorothy Gertrude, DBE, CMG.
Wormald, Dame Ethel May, DBE.
Yonge, Dame (Ida) Felicity (Ann), DBE.

Chiefs of Clans and Names in Scotland

Only chiefs of whole Names or Clans are included, except certain special instances (marked *), who though not chiefs of a whole name, were, or are, for some reason (e.g. the Macdonald forfeiture), independent. Under decision (*Campbell-Gray*, 1950) that a bearer of a 'double or triple-barrelled' surname cannot be held chief of a part of such, several others cannot be included in the list at present.

THE ROYAL HOUSE: HM The Queen

AGNEW: Sir Crispin Agnew of Lochnaw, Bt., 6 Palmerston Road, Edinburgh.

ANSTRUTHER: Sir Ralph Anstruther of that Ilk, Bt., KCVO, MC, Balcaskie, Pittenweem, Fife.

ARBUTHNOTT: The Viscount of Arbuthnott, CBE, DSC, Arbuthnott House, Laurencekirk, Kincardineshire.

BARCLAY: Peter C. Barclay of that Ilk, Gatemans, Stratford St Mary, Colchester, Essex.

BORTHWICK: The Lord Borthwick, TD, Crookston, Heriot, Midlothian.

BOYD: The Lord Kilmarnock, Casa de Mondragon, Ronda (Malaga), Spain.

BOYLE: The Earl of Glasgow, Kelburn, Fairlie, Ayrshire.

BRODIE: Ninian Brodie of Brodie, Brodie Castle, Forres, Morayshire.

BRUCE: The Earl of Elgin and Kincardine, KT, Broomhall, Dunfermline, Fife.

BUCHAN: David S. Buchan of Auchmacoy, Auchmacoy, Ellon, Aberdeenshire.

BURNETT: J. C. A. Burnett of Leys, Crathes Castle, Kincardineshire.

CAMERON: Sir Donald Cameron of Lochiel, KT, CVO, TD, Achnacarry, Spean Bridge, Inverness-shire.

CAMPBELL: The Duke of Argyll, Inveraray, Argyll.

CARMICHAEL: Richard J. Carmichael of Carmichael, Carmichael, Thankerton, Biggar, Lanarkshire.

CARNEGIE: The Duke of Fife, Elsick House, Stonehaven, Kincardineshire.

CATHCART: Maj.-Gen. The Earl Cathcart, CB, DSO, MC, 2 Pembroke Gardens, London W8.

CHARTERIS: The Earl of Wemyss and March, KT, Gosford House, Longniddry, East Lothian.

CLAN CHATTAN: M. K. Mackintosh of Clan Chattan, Maxwell Park, Gwelo, Zimbabwe.

CHISHOLM: Alastair Chisholm of Chisholm (*The Chisholm*), Silver Willows, Bury St Edmunds.

COCHRANE: The Earl of Dundonald, Lochnell Castle, Ledaig, Argyllshire.

COLQUHOUN: Sir Ivar Colquhoun of Luss, Bt., Camstraddan, Luss, Dunbartonshire.

CRANSTOUN: David A. S. Cranstoun of that Ilk, Corehouse, Lanark.

CRICHTON: vacant.

DARROCH: Capt. Duncan Darroch of Gourock, The Red House, Branksome Park Road, Camberley, Surrey.

DEWAR: Kenneth M. J. Dewar of that Ilk and Vogrie, The Dower House, Grayshott, Nr. Hindhead, Surrey.

DRUMMOND: The Earl of Perth, PC, Stobhall, Perth.

DUNBAR: Sir Jean Dunbar of Mochrum, Bt., 45–55 39th Street, Long Island City, New York, USA.

DUNDAS: David D. Dundas of Dundas, 8 Derna Road, Kenwyn 7700, South Africa.

DURIE: Raymond V. D. Durie of Durie, Court House, Pewsey, Wilts.

ELIOTT: Mrs Margaret Eliott of Redheugh, Redheugh, Newcastleton, Roxburghshire.

ERSKINE: The Earl of Mar and Kellie, Claremont House, Alloa.

FARQUHARSON: Capt. A. A. C. Farquharson of Invercauld, MC, Invercauld, Braemar.

FERGUSSON: Sir Charles Fergusson of Kilkerran, Bt., Kilkerran, Maybole, Ayrshire.

FORBES: The Lord Forbes, KBE, Balforbes, Alford, Aberdeenshire.

FORSYTH: Alistair Forsyth of that Ilk, Ethie Castle, by Arbroath, Angus.

FRASER: The Lady Saltoun, Cairnbulg Castle, Fraserburgh, Aberdeenshire.

*FRASER (OF LOVAT): The Lord Lovat, DSO, MC, TD, Balblair House, Beauly, Inverness-shire.

GAYRE: Lt.-Col. Robert Gayre of Gayre and Nigg, 1–3 Gloucester Lane, Edinburgh.

GORDON: The Marquess of Huntly, Aboyne Castle, Aberdeenshire.

GRAHAM: The Duke of Montrose, Auchmar, Drymen, Stirlingshire.

GRANT: The Lord Strathspey, The House of Lords, London SW1A 0PW.

GRIERSON: Sir Michael Grierson of Lag, Bt., 40C Palace Road, London.

HAIG: The Earl Haig, OBE, Bemersyde, Melrose, Roxburghshire.

HALDANE: Alexander N. C. Haldane of Gleneagles, Auchterarder, Perthshire.

HANNAY: Ramsey W. R. Hannay of Kirkdale and of that Ilk, Cardoness House, Gatehouse-of-Fleet, Kirkcudbrightshire.

HAY: The Earl of Erroll, Wolverton Farm, Wolverton, Basingstoke, Hants.

HENDERSON: John W. P. Henderson of Fordell, 7 Owen Street, Toowoomba, Queensland, Australia.

HUNTER: Neil A. Hunter of Hunterston, Tour d'Escas, Carretera d'Escas, La Massana, Andorra.

IRVINE OF DRUM: C. F. Irvine of Drum, 29 Forest Road, Hoylake, Wirral, Merseyside.

JARDINE: Sir Alexander Jardine of Applegirth, Bt., Ash House, Thwaites, Millom, Cumbria.

JOHNSTONE: The Earl of Annandale and Hartfell, Raehills, Lockerbie, Dumfriesshire.

KEITH: The Earl of Kintore, Glenton House, Rickarton, Stonehaven, Kincardineshire.

KENNEDY: The Marquess of Ailsa, OBE, Blanefield, Kirkoswald, Ayrshire.

KERR: The Marquess of Lothian, KCVO, Monteviot, Ancrum, Roxburghshire.

KINCAID: Mrs Heather V. Kincaid of Kincaid, 4A Bristol Gardens, Brighton, E. Sussex.

LAMONT: Peter N. Lamont of that Ilk, St Patrick's College, Manly, NSW 2095, Australia.

LEASK: Madam Leask of Leask, 1 Vincent Road, Sheringham, Norfolk.

LENNOX: Edward J. H. Lennox of that Ilk, Pools Farm, Downton on the Rock, Ludlow, Shropshire.

LESLIE: The Earl of Rothes, Tanglewood, West Tytherley, Salisbury, Wilts.

LINDSAY: The Earl of Crawford and Balcarres, PC, Balcarres, Colinsburgh, Fife.

LOCKHART: Angus H. Lockhart of the Lee, Newholme, Dunsyre, Lanark.

LUMSDEN: Gillem Lumsden of that Ilk and Blanerne, Kinderslegh, Bois Avenue, Chesham Bois, Amersham, Bucks.

MCBAIN: J. H. McBain of McBain, 7025, North Finger Rock Place, Tucson, Arizona, USA.

MALCOLM (MACCALLUM): Robin N. L. Malcolm of Poltalloch, Duntrune Castle, Lochgilphead, Argyll.
MACDONALD: The Lord Macdonald (*The Macdonald of Macdonald*), Ostaig House, Skye.
*MACDONALD OF CLANRANALD: Ranald A. Macdonald of Clanranald, 55 Compton Road, London N1.
*MACDONALD OF SLEAT (CLAN HUSTEAIN): Sir Ian Bosville Macdonald of Sleat, Bt., Thorpe Hall, Rudston, Driffield, N. Humberside.
*MACDONELL OF GLENGARRY: Air Cdre Aeneas R. MacDonell of Glengarry, CB, DFC, Elonbank, Castle Street, Fortrose, Ross-shire.
MACDOUGALL: vacant.
MACDOWELL: Fergus D. H. Macdowell of Garthland, 16 Tower Road, Nepean, Ontario, Canada.
MACGREGOR: Sir Gregor MacGregor of MacGregor, Bt., Bannatyne, Newtyle, Angus.
MACINTYRE: James W. McIntyre of Glencoe, 15301 Pine Orchard Drive, Apartment 3H, Silver Spring, Maryland, USA.
MACKAY: The Lord Reay, House of Lords, London SW1.
MACKENZIE: The Earl of Cromartie, MC, TD, Castle Leod, Strathpeffer, Ross-shire.
MACKINNON: Madam Anne Mackinnon of Mackinnon, 16 Purleigh Road, Bridgwater, Somerset.
MACKINTOSH: The Mackintosh of Mackintosh, OBE, Moy Hall, Inverness.
MACLACHLAN: Madam Marjorie MacLachlan of MacLachlan, Castle Lachlan, Argyll.
MACLAREN: Donald MacLaren of MacLaren and Achleskine, c/o Foreign and Commonwealth Office, London SW1.
MACLEAN: The Hon. Sir Lachlan Maclean of Duart, Bt., Duart Castle, Mull.
MACLENNAN: vacant.
MACLEOD: J. MacLeod of MacLeod, Dunvegan Castle, Skye.
MACMILLAN: George MacMillan of MacMillan, Finlaystone, Langbank, Renfrewshire.
MACNAB: J. C. Macnab of Macnab (*The Macnab*), Finlarig, Killin, Perthshire.
MACNAGHTEN: Sir Patrick Macnaghten of Macnaghten and Dundarave, Bt., Dundarave, Bushmills, Co. Antrim.
MACNEACAIL: Iain Macneacail of Macneacail and Scorrybreac, 12 Fox Street, Ballina, NSW, Australia.
MACNEIL OF BARRA: Ian R. Macneil of Barra (*The Macneil of Barra*), Kisimul Castle, Barra.
MACPHERSON: The Hon. Sir William Macpherson of Cluny, TD, Newtown Castle, Blairgowrie, Perthshire.
MACTHOMAS: Andrew P. C. MacThomas of Finegand, c/o The Clan MacThomas Society, 19 Warriston Avenue, Edinburgh.
MAITLAND: The Earl of Lauderdale, 12 St Vincent Street, Edinburgh.
MAKGILL: The Viscount of Oxfuird, Hill House, St Mary Bourne, Andover, Hants.
MAR: The Countess of Mar, St Michael's Farm, Great Witley, Worcs.
MARJORIBANKS: Andrew Marjoribanks of that Ilk.
MATHESON: Sir Torquhil Matheson of Matheson, Bt., Sanderwick Court, Frome, Somerset.
MENZIES: David R. Menzies of Menzies, 20 Nardina Crescent, Dalkeith, Western Australia.
MOFFAT: Madam Moffat of that Ilk, St Jasual, Bullocks Farm Lane, Wheeler End Common, High Wycombe, Bucks.
MONCREIFFE: vacant.
MONTGOMERIE: The Earl of Eglinton and Winton, The Dutch House, West Green, Hartley Wintney, Hants.
MORRISON: Dr Iain M. Morrison of Ruchdi, Todhurst Farm, Lake Lane, Barnham, W. Sussex.
MUNRO: Patrick G. Munro of Foulis, TD, Foulis Castle, Ross.
MURRAY: The Duke of Atholl, Blair Castle, Blair Atholl, Perthshire.
NICOLSON: The Lord Carnock, 90 Whitehall Court, London SW1.
OGILVY: The Earl of Airlie, KT, GCVO, PC, Cortachy Castle, Kirriemuir, Angus.
RAMSAY: The Earl of Dalhousie, KT, GCVO, GBE, MC, Brechin Castle, Angus.
RATTRAY: James S. Rattray of Rattray, Craighall, Rattray, Perthshire.
ROBERTSON: Alexander G. H. Robertson of Struan (*Struan-Robertson*), The Breach Farm, Goudhurst Road, Cranbrook, Kent.
ROLLO: The Lord Rollo, Pitcairns, Dunning, Perthshire.
ROSE: Miss Elizabeth Rose of Kilravock, Kilravock Castle, Croy, Inverness.
ROSS: David C. Ross of that Ilk, The Old Schoolhouse, Fettercairn, Kincardineshire.
RUTHVEN: The Earl of Gowrie, PC, Castlemartin, Kilcullen, Co. Kildare, Republic of Ireland.
SCOTT: The Duke of Buccleuch and Queensberry, KT, VRD, Bowhill, Selkirk.
SCRYMGEOUR: The Earl of Dundee, Birkhill, Cupar, Fife.
SEMPILL: The Lady Sempill, Druminnor Castle, Rhynie, Aberdeenshire.
SHAW: John Shaw of Tordarroch, Newhall, Balblair, By Conon Bridge, Ross-shire.
SINCLAIR: The Earl of Caithness, Finstock Manor, Finstock, Oxon.
STIRLING: Fraser J. Stirling of Cader, 17 Park Row, Farnham, Surrey.
SUTHERLAND: The Countess of Sutherland, House of Tongue, Brora, Sutherland.
SWINTON: John Swinton of that Ilk, 123 Superior Avenue SW, Calgary, Alberta, Canada.
URQUHART: Kenneth T. Urquhart of that Ilk, 4713 Orleans Boulevard, Jefferson, Louisiana, USA.
WALLACE: Ian F. Wallace of that Ilk, 5 Lennox Street, Edinburgh EH4 1QB.
WEDDERBURN OF THAT ILK: The Master of Dundee, Birkhill, Cupar, Fife.
WEMYSS: David Wemyss of that Ilk, Invermay, Forteviot, Perthshire.

Decorations and Medals

PRINCIPAL DECORATIONS AND MEDALS
In order of precedence

VICTORIA CROSS (VC), 1856.
GEORGE CROSS (GC), 1940.

British Orders of Knighthood, etc.
(for order in which worn, *see* pages 174–6.

BARONET'S BADGE.
KNIGHT BACHELOR'S BADGE.

Decorations.

ROYAL RED CROSS Class I (RRC), 1883. For ladies.
DISTINGUISHED SERVICE CROSS (DSC), 1914. For officers of RN below the rank of Captain, and Warrant Officers.
MILITARY CROSS (MC), December 1914. Awarded to Captains, Lieutenants, and Warrant Officers (I and II) in the Army and Indian and Colonial forces.
DISTINGUISHED FLYING CROSS (DFC), 1918. For officers and Warrant Officers in the RAF (and Fleet Air Arm from 1941) for acts of gallantry when flying in active operations against the enemy.
AIR FORCE CROSS (AFC), 1918. Instituted as preceding, but for acts of courage or devotion to duty when flying, although not in active operations against the enemy (extended to Fleet Air Arm 1941).
ROYAL RED CROSS Class II (ARRC).
ORDER OF BRITISH INDIA.
KAISAR-I-HIND MEDAL.
ORDER OF ST JOHN.

Medals for Gallantry and Distinguished Conduct.

UNION OF SOUTH AFRICA QUEEN'S MEDAL FOR BRAVERY, in Gold.
DISTINGUISHED CONDUCT MEDAL (DCM), 1854. Awarded to warrant officers, non-commissioned officers and men of the Army and RAF.
CONSPICUOUS GALLANTRY MEDAL (CGM), 1874. Bestowed upon warrant officers and men of the RN and since 1942 of Mercantile Marine and RAF.
THE GEORGE MEDAL (GM), 1940.
QUEEN'S POLICE MEDAL FOR GALLANTRY.
QUEEN'S FIRE SERVICE MEDAL FOR GALLANTRY.
ROYAL WEST AFRICAN FRONTIER FORCE DISTINGUISHED CONDUCT MEDAL.
KING'S AFRICAN RIFLES DISTINGUISHED CONDUCT MEDAL.
INDIAN DISTINGUISHED SERVICE MEDAL.
UNION OF SOUTH AFRICA QUEEN'S MEDAL FOR BRAVERY, in Silver.
DISTINGUISHED SERVICE MEDAL (DSM), 1914. For chief petty officers, petty officers and men, of all branches of the Royal Navy, and since 1942 of Mercantile Marine; non-commissioned officers and men of the Royal Marines; all other persons holding corresponding positions in Her Majesty's service afloat.
MILITARY MEDAL (MM), 1916. For warrant and non-commissioned officers and men and serving women.
DISTINGUISHED FLYING MEDAL (DFM), 1918, and the AIR FORCE MEDAL (AFM). For warrant and non-commissioned officers and men for equivalent services as for DFC and AFC (extended to Fleet Air Arm 1941).
CONSTABULARY MEDAL (IRELAND).
MEDAL FOR SAVING LIFE AT SEA.
INDIAN ORDER OF MERIT (Civil).
INDIAN POLICE MEDAL FOR GALLANTRY.
CEYLON POLICE MEDAL FOR GALLANTRY.
SIERRA LEONE POLICE MEDAL FOR GALLANTRY.
SIERRA LEONE FIRE BRIGADES MEDAL FOR GALLANTRY.
COLONIAL POLICE MEDAL FOR GALLANTRY (CPM).
QUEEN'S GALLANTRY MEDAL, 1974.
ROYAL VICTORIAN MEDAL (RVM). (Gold, Silver and Bronze.)
BRITISH EMPIRE MEDAL (BEM), (formerly the Medal of the Order of the British Empire, for Meritorious Service; also includes the Medal of the Order awarded before 29 December 1922).
QUEEN'S POLICE (QPM) AND FIRE SERVICES MEDALS (QFSM) FOR DISTINGUISHED SERVICE.
QUEEN'S MEDAL FOR CHIEFS.

War Medals and Stars
(in order of date).

Polar Medals
(in order of date).

IMPERIAL SERVICE MEDAL.

Police Medals for Valuable Service.
BADGE OF HONOUR.

Jubilee, Coronation and Durbar Medals.
KING GEORGE V, KING GEORGE VI AND QUEEN ELIZABETH II LONG AND FAITHFUL SERVICE MEDALS.

Efficiency and Long Service Decorations and Medals.

MEDAL FOR MERITORIOUS SERVICE.
LONG SERVICE AND GOOD CONDUCT MEDAL (Military).
NAVAL LONG SERVICE AND GOOD CONDUCT MEDAL.
ROYAL MARINE MERITORIOUS SERVICE MEDAL.
ROYAL AIR FORCE MERITORIOUS SERVICE MEDAL.
ROYAL AIR FORCE LONG SERVICE AND GOOD CONDUCT MEDAL.
MEDAL FOR LONG SERVICE AND GOOD CONDUCT (ULSTER DEFENCE REGIMENT).
POLICE LONG SERVICE AND GOOD CONDUCT MEDAL.
FIRE BRIGADE LONG SERVICE AND GOOD CONDUCT MEDAL.
COLONIAL POLICE AND FIRE BRIGADES LONG SERVICE MEDAL.
COLONIAL PRISON SERVICE MEDAL.
ARMY EMERGENCY RESERVE DECORATION (ERD), 1952.
VOLUNTEER OFFICER'S DECORATION (VD).
VOLUNTEER LONG SERVICE MEDAL.
VOLUNTEER OFFICER'S DECORATION for India and the Colonies.
VOLUNTEER LONG SERVICE MEDAL for India and the Colonies.
COLONIAL AUXILIARY FORCES OFFICER'S DECORATION.
COLONIAL AUXILIARY FORCES LONG SERVICE MEDAL.
MEDAL FOR GOOD SHOOTING (Naval).
MILITIA LONG SERVICE MEDAL.
IMPERIAL YEOMANRY LONG SERVICE MEDAL.
TERRITORIAL DECORATION (TD), 1908.
EFFICIENCY DECORATION (ED).

TERRITORIAL EFFICIENCY MEDAL.
EFFICIENCY MEDAL.
SPECIAL RESERVE LONG SERVICE AND GOOD CONDUCT MEDAL.
DECORATION FOR OFFICERS, ROYAL NAVY RESERVE (RD), 1910.
DECORATION FOR OFFICERS, RNVR (VRD).
ROYAL NAVAL RESERVE LONG SERVICE AND GOOD CONDUCT MEDAL.
RNVR LONG SERVICE AND GOOD CONDUCT MEDAL.
ROYAL NAVAL AUXILIARY SICK BERTH RESERVE LONG SERVICE AND GOOD CONDUCT MEDAL.
ROYAL FLEET RESERVE LONG SERVICE AND GOOD CONDUCT MEDAL.
ROYAL NAVAL WIRELESS AUXILIARY RESERVE LONG SERVICE AND GOOD CONDUCT MEDAL.
AIR EFFICIENCY AWARD (AE), 1942.
ULSTER DEFENCE REGIMENT MEDAL.
The QUEEN'S MEDAL. For champion shots in the RN, RM, RNZN, Army, RAF.
CADET FORCES MEDAL, 1950.
COAST LIFE SAVING CORPS LONG SERVICE MEDAL, 1911.
SPECIAL CONSTABULARY LONG SERVICE MEDAL.
ROYAL OBSERVER CORPS MEDAL.
CIVIL DEFENCE LONG SERVICE MEDAL.
ROYAL ULSTER CONSTABULARY SERVICE MEDAL.
SERVICE MEDAL OF THE ORDER OF ST JOHN.
BADGE OF THE ORDER OF THE LEAGUE OF MERCY.
VOLUNTARY MEDICAL SERVICE MEDAL, 1932.
WOMEN'S ROYAL VOLUNTARY SERVICE MEDAL.
COLONIAL SPECIAL CONSTABULARY MEDAL.

Foreign Orders, Decorations and Medals (in order of date).

THE VICTORIA CROSS (1856)
FOR CONSPICUOUS BRAVERY

VC

Ribbon, Crimson, for all Services (until 1918 it was blue for Royal Navy).

Instituted on 29 January 1856, the Victoria Cross was awarded retrospectively to 1854, the first being held by Lt. C. D. Lucas, RN, for bravery in the Baltic Sea on 21 June 1854 (gazetted 24 February 1857). The first 62 Crosses were presented by Queen Victoria in Hyde Park, London, on 26 June 1857.

The Victoria Cross is worn before all other decorations, on the left breast, and consists of a cross-pattée of bronze, one and a half inches in diameter, with the Royal Crown surmounted by a lion in the centre, and beneath there is the inscription *For Valour*. Holders of the VC receive a tax-free annuity of £100, irrespective of need or other conditions. In 1911, the right to receive the Cross was extended to Indian soldiers, and in 1920 to Matrons, Sisters and Nurses, and the staff of the Nursing Services and other services pertaining to hospitals and nursing, and to civilians of either sex regularly or temporarily under the orders, direction or supervision of the Naval, Military, or Air Forces of the Crown.

SURVIVING RECIPIENTS OF THE VICTORIA CROSS *as at 31 August 1992*

Agansing Rai, *Havildar*, MM (Gurkha Rifles) 1944 *World War*
Ali Haidar, *Jemadar* (Frontier Force Rifles) 1945 *World War*
Annand, *Capt.* R. W. (Durham Light Infantry) 1940 *World War*
Bhan Bhagta Gurung, *Capt.* (2nd Gurkha Rifles) 1945 *World War*
Bhandari Ram, *Capt.* (Baluch R.) 1944 *World War*
Burton, *Cpl.* R. H. (Duke of Wellington's R.) 1944 *World War*
Chapman, *Sgt.* E. T., BEM (Monmouthshire R.) 1945 *World War*
Cruickshank, *Flt. Lt.* J. A. (RAFVR) 1944 *World War*
Cutler, Sir Roden, AK, KCMG, KCVO, CBE (Australia) 1941 *World War*
Ervine-Andrews, *Lt.-Col.* H. M. (E. Lancs. R.) 1940 *World War*
Foote, *Maj.-Gen.* H. R. B., CB, DSO (R. Tank R.) 1942 *World War*
Fraser, *Lt. Cdr.* I. E., DSC (RNR) 1945 *World War*
Gaje Ghale, *Subedar* (Gurkha Rifles) 1943 *World War*
Ganju Lama, *Jemadar*, MM (Gurkha Rifles) 1944 *World War*
Gardner, *Capt.* P. J., MC (RTR) 1941 *World War*
Gian Singh, *Jemadar* (Punjab R.) 1945 *World War*
Gould, *Lt.* T. W. (RN) 1942 *World War*
Hinton, *Sgt.* J. D. (NZMF) 1941 *World War*
Jackson, *WO* N. C. (RAFVR) 1944 *World War*
Jamieson, *Maj.* D. A., CVO (R. Norfolk R.) 1944 *World War*
Kenna, *Pte.* E. (Australian M. F.) 1945 *World War*
Kenneally, *C-Q-M-S* J. P. (Irish Guards) 1943 *World War*
Lachiman Gurung, *Rifleman* (Gurkha Rifles) 1945 *World War*
Learoyd, *Wg Cdr.* R. A. B. (RAF) 1940 *World War*
Merritt, *Lt.-Col.* C. C. I., CD (S. Saskatchewan R.) 1942 *World War*
Norton, *Capt.* G. R., MM (SAMF) 1944 *World War*
Payne, *WO* K. (Australian Army) 1969 *Vietnam*
Place, *Rear-Adm.* B. C. G., CB, CVO, DSC (RN) 1943 *World War*
Porteous, *Col.* P. A. (RA) 1942 *World War*
Rambahadur Limbu, *Lt.*, MVO (Gurkha Rifles) 1965 *Sarawak*
Reid, *Flt. Lt.* W. (RAFVR) 1943 *World War*
Smith, *Sgt.* E. A., CD (Seaforth Highlanders of Canada) 1944 *World War*
Smythe, *Capt.* Q. G. M. (SAMF) 1942 *World War*

Speakman-Pitt, *Sgt.* W. (Black Watch)
1951 *Korea*
Tilston, *Maj.* F. A., CD (Essex Scottish, Canada)
1945 *World War*
Tulbahadur Pun, *WOI* (Gurkha Rifles)
1944 *World War*
Umrao Singh, *Sub-Major* (IA)
1944 *World War*
Upham, *Capt.* C. H. (and Bar, 1942), (NZMF)
1941 *World War*
Watkins, *Maj. Rt. Hon.* Sir Tasker, GBE (Welch R.)
1944 *World War*
Wilson, *Lt.-Col.* E. C. T. (E. Surrey R.)
1940 *World War*

THE GEORGE CROSS (1940)
FOR GALLANTRY

GC

Ribbon, Dark Blue, threaded through a bar adorned with laurel leaves.

Instituted 24 September 1940 (with amendments, 3 November 1942).

The George Cross is worn before all other decorations (except the VC) on the left breast (when worn by a woman it may be worn on the left shoulder from a ribbon of the same width and colour fashioned into a bow). It consists of a plain silver cross with four equal limbs, the cross having in the centre a circular medallion bearing a design showing St George and the Dragon. The inscription *For Gallantry* appears round the medallion and in the angle of each limb of the cross is the Royal cypher 'G VI' forming a circle concentric with the medallion. The reverse is plain and bears the name of the recipient and the date of the award. The cross is suspended by a ring from a bar adorned with laurel leaves on dark blue ribbon one and a half inches wide.

The cross is intended primarily for civilians; awards to the fighting services are confined to actions for which purely military honours are not normally granted. It is awarded only for acts of the greatest heroism or of the most conspicuous courage in circumstances of extreme danger. From 1 April 1965, holders of the Cross have received a tax-free annuity of £100.

The Royal Warrant which ordained that the grant of the Empire Gallantry Medal should cease authorized holders of that medal to return it to the Central Chancery of the Orders of Knighthood and to receive in exchange the George Cross. A similar provision applied to posthumous awards of the Empire Gallantry Medal made after the outbreak of war in 1939. In October 1971 all surviving holders of the Albert Medal and the Edward Medal exchanged those decorations for the George Cross.

SURVIVING RECIPIENTS OF THE GEORGE CROSS
as at 31 August 1992

If the recipient originally received the Empire Gallantry Medal, the Albert Medal or the Edward Medal, this is indicated by the initials in parenthesis.

Archer, *Col.* B. S. T., GC, OBE, ERD, 1941
Atkinson, T., GC (EGM), 1939
Baker, J. T., GC (EM), 1929
Baldwin, W. C. G., GC, Ph.D. (EM), 1943
Bamford, J., GC, 1952
Baxter, W. F., GC (EM), 1942
Beaton, J., GC, CVO, 1974
Biggs, *Maj.* K. A., GC, 1946
Bridge, *Cdr.* J., GC, GM, 1944
Butson, *Col.* A. R. C., GC, CD, MD (AM), 1948
Bywater, R. A. S., GC, GM, 1944
Cobham, *Cdr.* A. J., GC, MBE (EGM), 1930
Copperwheat, *Lt. Cdr.* D. A., GC, 1942
Cowley, *Lt.-Gen.* Sir John, GC, KCB, CBE (AM), 1935
Durrani, *Lt.-Col.* M. K., GC, 1946
Easton, J. M. C., GC, 1941
Errington, H., GC, 1941
Fairfax, F. W., GC, 1953
Farrow, K., GC (AM), 1948
Flintoff, H. H., GC (EM), 1944
Gledhill, A. J., GC, 1967
Goad, W., GC (AM), 1943
Goldsworthy, *Lt. Cdr.* L. V., GC, DSC, GM, 1944
Gregson, J. S., GC (AM), 1943
Hallowes, Mrs O. M. C., GC, MBE, Légion d'Honneur, 1946
Hawkins, E., GC (AM), 1943
Hodge, *Capt.* A. M., GC, VRD (EGM), 1940
Idris, Shawish Taha, GC (EGM), 1934
Johnson, *WO1 (SSM)* B., GC, 1990
Kinne, D. G., GC, 1954
Lowe, A. R., GC (AM), 1949
Lynch, J., GC, BEM (AM), 1948
McAloney, *Gp. Capt.* W. S., GC, OBE (AM), 1938
McClymont, J. M., GC (EGM), 1940
Malta, GC, 1942
Manwaring, T. G., GC (EM), 1949
May, P. R. S., GC (AM), 1947
Miller, *Lt. Cdr.* J. B. P., GC, 1941
Moore, R. V., GC, 1940
Moss, B., GC, 1940
Naughton, F., GC (EGM), 1937
Nix, F. E., GC (EM), 1944
Patton, The Hon. John, GC, CBE, 1940
Pearson, Miss J. D. M., GC (EGM), 1940
Pratt, M. K., GC, 1978
Purves, Mrs M., GC (AM), 1949
Raweng, Awang anak, GC, 1951
Riley, G., GC (AM), 1944
Rimmer, R., GC (EGM), 1931
Rogerson, S., GC, 1946
Rowlands, *Air Marshal* Sir John, GC, KBE, 1943
Sinclair, *Air Vice-Marshal* Sir Laurence, GC, KCB, CBE, DSO, 1941
Stevens, H. W., GC, 1958
Stronach, *Capt.* G. P., GC, 1943
Styles, *Lt.-Col.* S. G., GC, 1972
Sylvester, W. G., GC (EGM), 1940
Taylor, *Lt. Cdr.* W. H., GC, MBE, 1941
Walker, C., GC, 1972
Walker, C. H., GC (AM), 1942
Walton, E. W. K., GC (AM), 1948
Western, D., GC (AM), 1948
Wilcox, C., GC (EM), 1949
Wiltshire, S. N., GC (EGM), 1930
Yates, P. W., GC (EM), 1932
Younger, W., GC (EM), 1948

Forms of address

It is only possible to cover here the forms of address for peers, their wife and children. Greater detail should be sought in one of the publications devoted to the subject.

Both formal and social forms of address are given where usage differs; increasingly, the social form is preferred to the formal, though this is used for official documents and on very formal occasions.

F _ represents forename.
S _ represents surname.

BARON – *Envelope (formal)*, The Right Hon. Lord _; *(social)*, The Lord _. *Letter (formal)*, My Lord; *(social)*, Dear Lord _. *Spoken*, Lord _.

BARON'S WIFE – *Envelope (formal)*, The Right Hon. Lady _; *(social)*, The Lady _. *Letter (formal)*, My Lady; *(social)*, Dear Lady _. *Spoken*, Lady _.

BARON'S CHILDREN – *Envelope*, The Hon. F _ S _. *Letter*, Dear Mr/Miss/Mrs S _. *Spoken*, Mr/Miss/Mrs [F _] S _.

BARONESS IN OWN RIGHT – *Envelope*, may be addressed in same way as a Baron's wife or, if she prefers *(formal)*, The Right Hon. the Baroness _; *(social)*, The Baroness _. Otherwise as for a Baron's wife.

BARONET – *Envelope*, Sir F _ S _, Bt. *Letter (formal)*, Dear Sir; *(social)*, Dear Sir F _. *Spoken*, Sir F _.

BARONET'S WIFE – *Envelope*, Lady S _. *Letter (formal)*, Dear Madam; *(social)*, Dear Lady S _. *Spoken*, Lady S _.

COUNTESS IN OWN RIGHT – As for an Earl's wife.

COURTESY TITLES – The heir apparent to a Duke, Marquess or Earl uses the highest of his father's other titles as a courtesy title. (For list, *see* pages 169–70.) The holder of a courtesy title is not styled The Most Hon. or The Right Hon., and in correspondence 'The' is omitted before the title. The heir apparent to a Scottish title may use the title 'Master' (*see* below).

DAME – *Envelope*, Dame F _ S _, followed by appropriate post-nominal letters. *Letter (formal)*, Dear Madam; *(social)*, Dear Dame F _. *Spoken*, Dame F _.

DUKE – *Envelope (formal)*, His Grace the Duke of _; *(social)*, The Duke of _. *Letter (formal)*, My Lord Duke; *(social)*, Dear Duke. *Spoken (formal)*, Your Grace; *(social)*, Duke.

DUKE'S WIFE – *Envelope (formal)*, Her Grace the Duchess of _; *(social)*, The Duchess of _. *Letter (formal)*, Dear Madam; *(social)*, Dear Duchess. *Spoken*, Duchess.

DUKE'S ELDEST SON – See Courtesy titles.

DUKE'S YOUNGER SONS – *Envelope*, Lord F _ S _. *Letter (formal)*, My Lord; *(social)*, Dear Lord F _. *Spoken (formal)*, My Lord; *(social)*, Lord F _.

DUKE'S DAUGHTER – *Envelope*, Lady F _ S _. *Letter (formal)*, Dear Madam; *(social)*, Dear Lady F _. *Spoken*, Lady F _.

EARL – *Envelope (formal)*, The Right Hon. the Earl of _; *(social)*, The Earl of _. *Letter (formal)*, My Lord; *(social)*, Dear Lord _. *Spoken (formal)*, My Lord; *(social)*, Lord _.

EARL'S WIFE – *Envelope (formal)*, The Right Hon. the Countess (of) _; *(social)*, The Countess (of) _. *Letter (formal)*, Madam; *(social)*, Lady _. *Spoken (formal)*, Madam; *(social)*, Lady _.

EARL'S CHILDREN – *Eldest son*, see Courtesy titles. *Younger sons*, The Hon. F _ S _ (for forms of address, see Baron's children). *Daughters*, Lady F _ S _ (for forms of address, see Duke's daughter).

KNIGHT (BACHELOR) – *Envelope*, Sir F _ S _. *Letter (formal)*, Dear Sir; *(social)*, Dear Sir F _. *Spoken*, Sir F _.

KNIGHT (ORDERS OF CHIVALRY) – *Envelope*, Sir F _ S _, followed by appropriate post-nominal letters. Otherwise as for Knight Bachelor.

KNIGHT'S WIFE – As for Baronet's wife.

MARQUESS – *Envelope (formal)*, The Most Hon. the Marquess of _; *(social)*, The Marquess of _. *Letter (formal)*, My Lord; *(social)*, Dear Lord _. *Spoken (formal)*, My Lord; *(social)*, Lord _.

MARQUESS'S WIFE – *Envelope (formal)*, The Most Hon. the Marchioness of _; *(social)*, The Marchioness of _. *Letter (formal)*, Madam; *(social)*, Dear Lady _. *Spoken*, Lady _.

MARQUESS'S CHILDREN – *Eldest son*, see Courtesy titles. *Younger sons*, Lord F _ S _ (for forms of address, see Duke's younger sons). *Daughters*, Lady F _ S _ (for forms of address, see Duke's daughter).

MASTER – The title is used by the heir apparent to a Scottish peerage, though usually the heir apparent to a Duke, Marquess or Earl uses his courtesy title rather than 'Master'. *Envelope*, The Master of _. *Letter (formal)*, Dear Sir; *(social)*, Dear Master of _. *Spoken (formal)*, Master, or Sir; *(social)*, Master, or Mr S _.

MASTER'S WIFE – Addressed as for the wife of the appropriate peerage style, otherwise as Mrs S _.

PRIVY COUNSELLOR – *Envelope*, The Right (or Rt.) Hon. F _ S _. *Letter*, Dear Mr/Miss/Mrs S _. *Spoken*, Mr/Miss/Mrs S _. It is incorrect to use the letters PC after the name, unless the Privy Counsellor is a peer below the rank of Marquess and so is styled The Right Hon. In this case the post-nominal letters may be used in conjunction with the prefix The Right Hon.

VISCOUNT – *Envelope (formal)*, The Right Hon. the Viscount _; *(social)*, The Viscount _. *Letter (formal)*, My Lord; *(social)*, Dear Lord _. *Spoken*, Lord _.

VISCOUNT'S WIFE – *Envelope (formal)*, The Right Hon. the Viscountess of _; *(social)*, The Viscountess _. *Letter (formal)*, Madam; *(social)*, Dear Lady _. *Spoken*, Lady _.

VISCOUNT'S CHILDREN – As for Baron's children.

The Privy Council

The Sovereign in Council, or Privy Council, was the chief source of executive power until the system of Cabinet government developed in the 18th century. Now the Privy Council's main functions are to advise the Sovereign and to exercise its own statutory responsibilities independent of the Sovereign in Council (*see also* page 222).

Membership of the Privy Council is automatic upon appointment to certain government and judicial positions in the United Kingdom, e.g. Cabinet ministers must be Privy Counsellors and are sworn in on first assuming office. Membership is also accorded by The Queen to eminent people in the United Kingdom and independent countries of the Commonwealth of which Her Majesty is Queen, on the recommendation of the British Prime Minister. Membership of the Council is retained for life, except for very occasional removals.

The administrative functions of the Privy Council are carried out by the Privy Council Office (*see* page 348) under the direction of the Lord President of the Council, who is always a member of the Cabinet.

Lord President of the Council, The Rt. Hon. Anthony Newton, OBE, MP.
Clerk of the Council, Sir Geoffrey de Deney, KCVO.

MEMBERS *as at 31 August 1992*

HRH The Duke of Edinburgh, 1951
HRH The Prince of Wales, 1977

Aberdare, Lord, 1974
Ackner, Lord, 1980
Adams-Schneider, Sir Lancelot, 1980
Ademola, Sir Adetokunbo, 1963
Airlie, Earl of, 1984
Aldington, Lord, 1954
Alebua, Ezekiel, 1988
Alison, Michael, 1981
Alport, Lord, 1960
Amery of Lustleigh, Lord, 1960
Anthony, Douglas, 1971
Archer of Sandwell, Lord, 1977
Armstrong, Ernest, 1979
Arnold, Sir John, 1979
Ashdown, Paddy, 1989
Ashley of Stoke, Lord, 1979
Avonside, Lord, 1962
Aylestone, Lord, 1962
Azikiwe, Nnamdi, 1960
Bacon, Baroness, 1966
Baker, Kenneth, 1984
Balcombe, Sir John, 1985
Barber, Lord, 1963
Barnett, Lord, 1975
Barwick, Sir Garfield, 1964
Beith, Alan, 1992
Beldam, Sir Roy, 1989
Belstead, Lord, 1983
Benn, Anthony, 1964
Bennett, Sir Frederic, 1985
Bevins, John, 1959
Biffen, John, 1979
Bingham, Sir Thomas, 1986
Birch, William, 1992
Bird, Vere, 1982
Bisson, Sir Gordon, 1987
Blaker, Sir Peter, 1983
Blanch, Lord, 1975
Bolger, James, 1991
Booth, Albert, 1976
Boothroyd, Betty, 1992
Boscawen, Hon. Robert, 1992
Bottomley, Lord, 1952
Bottomley, Virginia, 1992
Boyd-Carpenter, Lord, 1954
Boys, Michael, 1989
Boyson, Sir Rhodes, 1987
Braine, Lord, 1985
Braithwaite, Nicholas, 1991
Brandon of Oakbrook, Lord, 1978
Bridge of Harwich, Lord, 1975
Brightman, Lord, 1979
Brittan, Sir Leon, 1981
Brooke, Peter, 1988
Brown, Sir Stephen, 1983
Browne, Sir Patrick, 1974
Browne-Wilkinson, Lord, 1983
Buckley, Sir Denys, 1970
Butler, Sir Adam, 1984
Butler-Sloss, Dame Elizabeth, 1988
Caithness, Earl of, 1990
Callaghan of Cardiff, Lord, 1964
Cameron of Lochbroom, Lord, 1984
Campbell of Croy, Lord, 1970
Canterbury, The Archbishop of, 1991
Carlisle of Bucklow, Lord, 1979
Carr of Hadley, Lord, 1963
Carrington, Lord, 1959
Casey, Sir Maurice, 1986
Castle of Blackburn, Baroness, 1964
Cato, Robert, 1981
Chalfont, Lord, 1964
Chalker of Wallasey, Baroness, 1987
Chan, Sir Julius, 1981
Channon, Paul, 1980
Charteris of Amisfield, Lord, 1972
Chataway, Christopher, 1970
Clark, Alan, 1991
Clark, Helen, 1990
Clark of Kempston, Lord, 1990
Clarke, Kenneth, 1984
Cledwyn of Penrhos, Lord, 1966
Cockfield, Lord, 1982
Cocks of Hartcliffe, Lord, 1976
Coggan, Lord, 1961
Colman, Fraser, 1986
Colnbrook, Lord, 1973
Colyton, Lord, 1952
Compton, John, 1983
Concannon, John, 1978
Cooke, Sir Robin, 1977
Cooper, Sir Frank, 1983
Cope, Sir John, 1988
Corfield, Sir Frederick, 1970
Cowen, Sir Zelman, 1981
Craigton, Lord, 1961
Crawford and Balcarres, Earl of, 1972
Crickhowell, Lord, 1979
Croom-Johnson, Sir David, 1984
Cumming-Bruce, Sir Roualeyn, 1977
Davies, Denzil, 1978
Davison, Sir Ronald, 1978
Dean, Sir Paul, 1991
Deedes, Lord, 1962
Dell, Edmund, 1970
Denham, Lord, 1981
Denning, Lord, 1948
Devonshire, Duke of, 1964
Diamond, Lord, 1965
Dillon, Sir Brian, 1982
Donaldson of Lymington, Lord, 1979
Douglas, Sir William, 1977
du Cann, Sir Edward, 1964
Duff, Sir Antony, 1980
Dunn, Sir Robin, 1980
Eccles, Viscount, 1951
Eden of Winton, Lord, 1972
Edmund-Davies, Lord, 1966
Eichelbaum, Sir Thomas, 1989
Ellison, Rt. Revd Gerald, 1973
Emslie, Lord, 1972
Ennals, Lord, 1970
Erroll of Hale, Lord, 1960
Esquivel, Manuel, 1986
Eveleigh, Sir Edward, 1977
Farquharson, Sir Donald, 1989
Fellowes, Sir Robert, 1990
Ferguson, Alan, 1992
Fernyhough, Ernest, 1970
Ferrers, Earl, 1982
Foot, Michael, 1974
Fowler, Sir Norman, 1979
Fox, Sir Michael, 1981
Franks, Lord, 1949
Fraser, Malcolm, 1976
Fraser of Carmyllie, Lord, 1989
Freeman, John, 1966
Freeson, Reginald, 1976
Gairy, Sir Eric, 1977
Garel-Jones, Tristan, 1992
Gault, Thomas, 1992
Georges, Telford, 1986
Gibbs, Sir Harry, 1972
Gibson, Sir Ralph, 1985
Gibson-Watt, Lord, 1974
Gilbert, John, 1978

Gilmour of Craigmillar, Lord, 1973
Glenamara, Lord, 1964
Glendevon, Lord, 1959
Glidewell, Sir Iain, 1985
Goff of Chieveley, Lord, 1982
Goodlad, Alastair, 1992
Gorton, Sir John, 1968
Gowrie, Earl of, 1984
Gray of Contin, Lord, 1982
Griffiths, Lord, 1980
Grimond, Lord, 1961
Gummer, John, 1985
Hailsham of St Marylebone, Lord, 1956
Hamilton, Archie, 1991
Harrison, Walter, 1977
Harvington, Lord, 1971
Hasluck, Sir Paul, 1966
Hattersley, Roy, 1975
Hayhoe, Lord, 1985
Healey, Lord, 1964
Heath, Sir Edward, 1955
Herbison, Margaret, 1964
Heseltine, Michael, 1979
Heseltine, Sir William, 1986
Hesketh, Lord, 1991
Higgins, Terence, 1979
Hogg, Hon. Douglas, 1992
Holderness, Lord, 1959
Home of the Hirsel, Lord, 1951
Hope, Lord, 1989
Houghton of Sowerby, Lord, 1964
Howard, Michael, 1990
Howe of Aberavon, Lord, 1972
Howell, David, 1979
Howell, Lord, 1976
Hughes, Lord, 1970
Hunt, David, 1990
Hunt, Jonathan, 1989
Hurd, Douglas, 1982
Hutton, Sir Brian, 1988
Jauncey of Tullichettle, Lord, 1988
Jay, Lord, 1952
Jellicoe, Earl, 1963
Jenkin of Roding, Lord, 1973
Jenkins of Hillhead, Lord, 1964
Jones, Aubrey, 1955
Jones, Sir Edward, 1979
Jopling, Michael, 1979
Joseph, Lord, 1962
Jugnauth, Sir Anerood, 1987
Kaufman, Gerald, 1978
Keith of Kinkel, Lord, 1976
Kelly, Sir Basil, 1984
Kenilorea, Sir Peter, 1979
Kennedy, Sir Paul, 1992
Kerr, Sir Michael, 1981
King, Thomas, 1979
Kinnock, Neil, 1983
Kitto, Sir Frank, 1963
Lamont, Norman, 1986
Lane, Lord, 1975
Lang, Ian, 1990
Lange, David, 1984
Lansdowne, Marquess of, 1964
Latey, Sir John, 1986
Lauti, Sir Toaripi, 1979
Lawson of Blaby, Lord, 1981
Lawton, Sir Frederick, 1972
Leggatt, Sir Andrew, 1990
Leigh-Pemberton, Robin, 1987
Leonard, Graham, 1981
Lever of Manchester, Lord, 1969
Lilley, Peter, 1990
Listowel, Earl of, 1946
Llewelyn-Davies of Hastoe, Baroness, 1975
Lloyd, Sir Anthony, 1984
London, The Bishop of, 1991
Longford, Earl of, 1948
Louisy, Allan, 1981
Lowry, Lord, 1974
Luce, Sir Richard, 1986
Lyell, Sir Nicholas, 1990
Mabon, Dickson, 1977
McCarthy, Sir Thaddeus, 1968
McCowan, Sir Anthony, 1989
MacDermott, Sir John, 1987
MacGregor, John, 1985
MacIntyre, Duncan, 1980
Mackay of Clashfern, Lord, 1979
McKay, Ian, 1992
McKinnon, Donald, 1992
McMullin, Sir Duncan, 1980
Major, John, 1987
Manley, Michael, 1989
Mann, Sir Michael, 1988
Mara, Sir Kamisese, 1973
Marsh, Lord, 1966
Mason of Barnsley, Lord, 1968
Maude of Stratford-upon-Avon, Lord, 1979
Maude, Hon. Francis, 1992
May, Sir John, 1982
Mayhew, Sir Patrick, 1986
Megarry, Sir Robert, 1978
Megaw, Sir John, 1969
Mellish, Lord, 1967
Mellor, David, 1990
Merlyn-Rees, Lord, 1974
Millan, Bruce, 1975
Mitchell, James, 1985
Molyneaux, James, 1983
Moore of Lower Marsh, Lord, 1986
Moore, Michael, 1990
Moore of Wolvercote, Lord, 1977
Morris, Alfred, 1979
Morris, Charles, 1978
Morris, John, 1970
Morrison, Sir Peter, 1988
Moyle, Roland, 1978
Mulley, Lord, 1964
Murray, *Hon.* Lord, 1974
Murray, Sir Donald, 1989
Murray of Epping Forest, Lord, 1976
Murton of Lindisfarne, Lord, 1976
Mustill, Lord, 1985
Nairne, Sir Patrick, 1982
Namaliu, Robbie, 1989
Neill, Sir Brian, 1985
Newton, Antony, 1988
Nicholls, Sir Donald, 1986
Nolan, Sir Michael, 1991
Nott, Sir John, 1979
Nourse, Sir Martin, 1985
Nugent of Guildford, Lord, 1962
Nutting, Sir Anthony, 1954
Oakes, Gordon, 1979
O'Brien of Lothbury, Lord, 1970
O'Connor, Sir Patrick, 1980
O'Donnell, Turlough, 1979
O'Flynn, Francis, 1987
Oliver of Aylmerton, Lord, 1980
Onslow, Cranley, 1988
Oppenheim-Barnes, Baroness, 1979
Orme, Stanley, 1974
Owen, Lord, 1976
Palliser, Sir Michael, 1983
Palmer, Sir Geoffrey, 1986
Parker, Sir Roger, 1983
Parkinson, Lord, 1981
Patten, Christopher, 1989
Patten, John, 1990
Pattie, Sir Geoffrey, 1987
Percival, Sir Ian, 1983
Perth, Earl of, 1957
Peyton of Yeovil, Lord, 1970
Pindling, Sir Lynden, 1976
Poole, Lord, 1963
Portillo, Michael, 1992
Powell, Enoch, 1960
Prentice, Lord, 1966
Price, George, 1982
Prior, Lord, 1970
Puapua, Tomasi, 1982
Purchas, Sir Francis, 1982
Pym, Lord, 1970
Raison, Sir Timothy, 1982
Ramsden, James, 1963
Rawlinson of Ewell, Lord, 1964
Rees, Lord, 1983
Reigate, Lord, 1961
Renton, Lord, 1962
Renton, Timothy, 1989
Richardson, Sir Ivor, 1978
Richardson of Duntisbourne, Lord, 1976
Richmond, Sir Clifford, 1973
Ridley of Liddesdale, Lord, 1983
Rifkind, Malcolm, 1986
Rippon of Hexham, Lord, 1962
Robens of Woldingham, Lord, 1951
Roberts, Sir Wyn, 1991
Robinson, Sir Kenneth, 1964
Rodger of Earlsferry, Lord, 1992
Rodgers of Quarry Bank, Lord, 1975
Roskill, Lord, 1971
Ross, *Hon.* Lord, 1985
Rowling, Sir Wallace, 1974
Rumbold, Dame Angela, 1991
Runcie, Lord, 1980
Russell, Sir Patrick, 1987
Ryder, Richard, 1990
Sainsbury, Hon. Timothy, 1992
St John of Fawsley, Lord, 1979
Sandiford, Erskine, 1989
Scarman, Lord, 1973
Scott, Nicholas, 1989
Scott, Sir Richard, 1992
Seaga, Edward, 1981
Seear, Baroness, 1985
Selkirk, Earl of, 1955
Shackleton, Lord, 1966
Shawcross, Lord, 1946
Shearer, Hugh, 1969
Sheldon, Robert, 1977
Shephard, Gillian, 1992

Shepherd, Lord, 1965
Shore, Peter, 1967
Simmonds, Kennedy, 1984
Simon of Glaisdale, Lord, 1961
Sinclair, Ian, 1977
Slade, Sir Christopher, 1982
Slynn of Hadley, Lord, 1992
Smith, John, 1978
Somare, Sir Michael, 1977
Somers, Sir Edward, 1981
Stanley, Sir John, 1984
Staughton, Sir Christopher, 1988
Steel, Sir David, 1977
Stephen, Sir Ninian, 1979
Stephenson, Sir John, 1971
Stewartby, Lord, 1989
Steyn, Sir Johan, 1992
Stocker, Sir John, 1986
Stodart of Leaston, Lord, 1974
Stott, Lord, 1964
Strauss, Lord, 1947
Stuart-Smith, Sir Murray, 1988
Talboys, Sir Brian, 1977
Taylor of Gosforth, Lord, 1988
Tebbit, Lord, 1981
Templeman, Lord, 1978
Thatcher, Baroness, 1970
Thomas of Gwydir, Lord, 1964
Thomson, David, 1981
Thomson of Monifieth, Lord, 1966
Thorneycroft, Lord, 1951
Thorpe, Jeremy, 1967
Tizard, Robert, 1986
Tonypandy, Viscount, 1968
Tranmire, Lord, 1955
Trefgarne, Lord, 1989
Trumpington, Baroness, 1992
Turner, Sir Alexander, 1968
Varley, Lord, 1974
Waddington, Lord, 1987
Wakeham, Lord, 1983
Waldegrave, William, 1990
Walker, Sir Harold, 1979
Walker of Worcester, Lord, 1970
Waller, Sir George, 1976
Watkins, Sir Tasker, 1980
Watkinson, Viscount, 1955
Weatherill, Lord, 1980
Whitelaw, Viscount, 1967
Wilberforce, Lord, 1964
Williams, Alan, 1977
Williams, Shirley, 1974
Wilson of Langside, Lord, 1967
Wilson of Rievaulx, Lord, 1947
Windlesham, Lord, 1973
Wingti, Paias, 1987
Withers, Reginald, 1977
Woodhouse, Sir Owen, 1974
Woolf, Sir Harry, 1986
Wylie, *Hon.* Lord, 1970
York, The Archbishop of, 1983
Young, Baroness, 1981
Young of Graffham, Lord, 1984
Younger of Prestwick, Lord, 1979

The Privy Council of Northern Ireland

The Privy Council of Northern Ireland had responsibilities in Northern Ireland similar to those of the Privy Council in Great Britain until the Northern Ireland Act 1974 instituted direct rule and a United Kingdom Cabinet minister became responsible for the functions previously exercised by the Northern Ireland government.

Membership of the Privy Council of Northern Ireland is retained for life. The postnominal initials PC(NI) are used to differentiate its members from those of the Privy Council.

MEMBERS *as at 31 August 1992*

Bailie, Robin, 1971
Bleakley, David, 1971
Bradford, Roy, 1969
Craig, William, 1963
Dobson, John, 1969
Glentoran, The Lord, 1953
Jones, Sir Edward, 1965
Kelly, Sir Basil, 1969
Kirk, Herbert, 1962
Long, William, 1966
Lowry, The Lord, 1971
McConnell, Robert, 1964
McIvor, Basil, 1971
Morgan, William, 1961
Moyola, The Lord, 1966
Neill, Sir Ivan, 1950
Porter, Sir Robert, 1969
Rathcavan, The Lord, 1969
Simpson, Robert, 1969
Taylor, John, MP, 1970
West, Henry, 1960

Parliament

The United Kingdom constitution is not contained in any single document but has evolved in the course of time, formed partly by statute, partly by common law and partly by convention. A constitutional monarchy, the United Kingdom is governed by Ministers of the Crown in the name of the Sovereign, who is head both of the state and of the government.

The organs of government are the legislature (Parliament), the executive and the judiciary. The executive consists of Her Majesty's Government (Cabinet and other Ministers) (*see* pages 282–3), government departments (*see* pages 284–372), local authorities (*see* Local Government), and public corporations operating nationalized industries or social or cultural services (*see* pages 284–372). The judiciary (*see* Law Courts and Offices) pronounces on the law, both written and unwritten, interprets statutes and is responsible for the enforcement of the law; the judiciary is independent of both the legislature and the executive.

THE MONARCHY

The Sovereign personifies the state and is, in law, an integral part of the legislature, head of the executive, head of the judiciary, the commander-in-chief of all armed forces of the Crown and the 'Supreme Governor' of the Church of England. The seat of the monarchy is in the United Kingdom. In the Channel Islands and the Isle of Man, which are Crown dependencies, the Sovereign is represented by a Lieutenant-Governor. In the member states of the Commonwealth of which the Sovereign is head of state, her representative is a Governor-General, in United Kingdom dependencies the Sovereign is usually represented by a Governor, who is responsible to the British Government.

Although the powers of the monarchy are now very limited, restricted mainly to the advisory and ceremonial, there are important acts of government which require the participation of the Sovereign. These include summoning, proroguing and dissolving Parliament, giving royal assent to Bills passed by Parliament, appointing important office-holders, e.g. government ministers, judges, bishops, and governors, conferring peerages, knighthoods and other honours, and granting pardon to a person wrongly convicted of a crime. An important function is appointing a Prime Minister, by convention the leader of the political party which enjoys, or can secure, a majority of votes in the House of Commons. In international affairs the Sovereign as head of state has the power to declare war and make peace, to recognize foreign states and governments, to conclude treaties and to annex or cede territory. However, as the Sovereign entrusts executive power to Ministers of the Crown and acts on the advice of her Ministers, which she cannot ignore, in practice royal prerogative powers are exercised by Ministers, who are responsible to Parliament.

Ministerial responsibility does not diminish the Sovereign's importance to the smooth working of government. She holds meetings of the Privy Council, gives audiences to her Ministers and other officials at home and overseas, receives accounts of Cabinet decisions, reads dispatches and signs state papers; she must be informed and consulted on every aspect of national life; and she must show complete impartiality.

COUNSELLORS OF STATE

In the event of the Sovereign's absence abroad, it is necessary to appoint Counsellors of State under Letters Patent to carry out the chief functions of the Monarch, including the holding of Privy Councils and giving royal assent to Acts passed by Parliament. The normal procedure is to appoint as Counsellors three or four members of the Royal family among those remaining in the United Kingdom. In the event of the Sovereign on accession being under the age of eighteen years, or at any time unavailable or incapacitated by infirmity of mind or body for the performance of the royal functions, provision is made for a regency.

THE PRIVY COUNCIL

The Sovereign in Council, or Privy Council, was the chief source of executive power until the system of Cabinet government developed. Now its main function is to advise the Sovereign to approve Orders in Council and to advise on the issue of royal proclamations. The Council's own statutory responsibilities (independent of the powers of the Sovereign in Council) include powers of supervision over the registering bodies for the medical and allied professions. A full Council is summoned only on the death of the Sovereign or when the Sovereign announces his or her intention to marry. (For full list of Counsellors, *see* pages 219–21)

There are a number of advisory Privy Council committees, whose meetings the Sovereign does not attend. Some are prerogative committees, such as those dealing with legislative matters submitted by the legislatures of the Channel Islands and the Isle of Man or with applications for charters of incorporation; and some are provided for by statute, e.g. those for the universities of Oxford and Cambridge and the Scottish universities.

The Judicial Committee of the Privy Council is the final court of appeal from courts of the United Kingdom dependencies, courts of independent Commonwealth countries which have retained the right of appeal, courts of the Channel Islands and the Isle of Man, some professional and disciplinary committees, and church sources. The Committee is composed of all Privy Counsellors who hold, or have held, high judicial office, although usually only three or five hear each case.

Administrative work is carried out by the Privy Council Office under the direction of the Lord President of the Council, a Cabinet Minister.

PARLIAMENT

Parliament is the supreme law-making authority and can legislate for the United Kingdom as a whole or for any parts of it separately (the Channel Islands and the Isle of Man are Crown dependencies and not part of the United Kingdom). The main functions of Parliament are to pass laws, to provide (by voting taxation) the means of carrying on the work of government and to scrutinize government policy and administration, particularly proposals for expenditure. International treaties and agreements are by custom presented to Parliament before ratification.

Parliament emerged during the late thirteenth and early fourteenth centuries. The officers of the King's household and the King's judges were the nucleus of early Parliaments, joined by such ecclesiastical and lay magnates as the King might summon to form a prototype 'House of Lords', and occasionally by the knights of the shires, burgesses and proctors of the lower clergy. By the end of Edward III's reign a 'House of Commons' was beginning to appear; the first known Speaker was elected in 1377.

Parliamentary procedure is based on custom and precedent, partly formulated in the Standing Orders of both Houses (*see* Standing Orders, page 228), and each House has the right to control its own internal proceedings and to commit for contempt. The system of debate in the two Houses is similar; when a motion has been moved, the Speaker proposes the question as the subject of a debate. Members speak from wherever they have been sitting. Questions are decided by a vote on a simple majority. Draft legislation is introduced, in either House, as a Bill. Bills can be introduced by a Government Minister or a private Member, but in practice the majority of Bills which become law are introduced by the Government. To become law, a Bill must be passed by each House (for parliamentary stages, *see* Bill, page 226) and then sent to the Sovereign for the royal assent, after which it becomes an Act of Parliament.

Proceedings of both Houses are public, except on extremely rare occasions. The minutes (called Votes and Proceedings in the Commons, and Minutes of Proceedings in the Lords) and the speeches (The Official Report of Parliamentary Debates, *Hansard*) are published daily. Proceedings are also recorded for transmission on radio and television and stored in the Parliamentary Recording Unit before transfer to the National Sound Archive. Television cameras have been allowed into the House of Lords since January 1985, and into the House of Commons since November 1989; committee meetings may also be televised.

By the Parliament Act of 1911, the maximum duration of a Parliament is five years (if not previously dissolved), the term being reckoned from the date given on the writs for the new Parliament. The maximum life has been prolonged by legislation in such rare circumstances as the two world wars (31 January 1911 to 25 November 1918; 26 November 1935 to 15 June 1945). Dissolution and writs for a general election are ordered by The Queen on the advice of the Prime Minister. The life of a Parliament is divided into sessions, usually of one year in length, beginning and ending most often in October or November.

THE HOUSE OF LORDS

London SW1A 0PW
Tel 071-219 3000

The House of Lords consists of the Lords Spiritual and Temporal. The Lords Spiritual are the Archbishops of Canterbury and York, the Bishops of London, Durham and Winchester, and the 21 senior diocesan bishops of the Church of England. The Lords Temporal consist of all hereditary peers of England, Scotland, Great Britain and the United Kingdom who have not disclaimed their peerages, life peers created under the Life Peerages Act 1958, and those Lords of Appeal in Ordinary created life peers under the Appellate Jurisdiction Act 1876, as amended (law lords). Disclaimants of an hereditary peerage lose their right to sit in the House of Lords but gain the right to vote at Parliamentary elections and to offer themselves for election to the House of Commons (*see also* page 141). Those peers disqualified from sitting in the House include:

- aliens, i.e. any peer who is not a British citizen, a Commonwealth citizen (under the British Nationality Act 1981) or a citizen of the Republic of Ireland
- peers under the age of 21
- undischarged bankrupts or, in Scotland, those whose estate is sequestered
- peers convicted of treason

Peers who do not wish to attend sittings of the House of Lords may apply for leave of absence for the duration of a Parliament.

Until the beginning of this century the House of Lords had considerable power, being able to veto any Bill submitted to it by the House of Commons, but those powers were greatly reduced by the Parliament Act of 1911 and subsequently by the Parliament Act of 1949 (*see* Parliament Acts 1911 and 1949, page 227).

Combined with its legislative role, the House of Lords has judicial powers as the ultimate Court of Appeal for courts in Great Britain and Northern Ireland, except for criminal cases in Scotland. These powers are exercised by the Lord Chancellor and the law lords.

Members of the House of Lords are unpaid. However, they are entitled to reimbursement of travelling expenses on parliamentary business within the UK and certain other expenses incurred for the purpose of attendance at sittings of the House, within a maximum for each day of £68.00 for overnight subsistence, £29.00 for day subsistence and incidental travel, and £29.00 for secretarial costs, postage and certain additional expenses.

Composition *as at 9 July 1992*

Archbishops and Bishops, 26
Peers by succession, 758 (18 women)
Hereditary Peers of first creation (including the Prince of Wales), 19
Life Peers under the Appellate Jurisdiction Act 1876, 20
Life Peers under the Life Peerages Act 1958, 382 (61 women)
Total 1,205
Of whom:
Peers without Writs of Summons, 84
Peers on leave of absence from the House, 97

State of Parties *as at 9 July 1992*

About half of the members of the House of Lords take the whip of one of the political parties. The other members sit on the cross-benches or as independents.

Conservative, 473
Labour, 117
Liberal Democrats, 59
Cross-bench, 264
Other (including Bishops), 292

OFFICERS

The House is presided over by the Lord Chancellor, who is *ex officio* Speaker of the House. A panel of deputy Speakers is appointed by Royal Commission. The first deputy Speaker is the Chairman of Committees, appointed at the beginning of each session, a salaried officer of the House who takes the chair in committee of the whole House and in some select committees. He is assisted by a panel of deputy chairmen, headed by the salaried Principal Deputy Chairman of Committees, who is also chairman of the European Communities Committee of the House.

The permanent officers include the Clerk of the Parliaments, who is in charge of the administrative staff collectively known as the Parliament Office; the Gentleman Usher of the Black Rod, who is also Serjeant-at-Arms in attendance upon the Lord Chancellor and is responsible for security and for accommodation and services in the House of Lords; and the Yeoman Usher who is Deputy Serjeant-at-Arms and assists Black Rod in his duties.

Speaker (£110,940), The Rt. Hon. the Lord Mackay of Clashfern.
Private Secretary, Ms J. Rowe.
Chairman of Committees (£46,167), The Lord Ampthill, CBE.
Principal Deputy Chairman of Committees (£42,188), The Lord Boston of Faversham, QC.
Clerk of the Parliaments (£84,250), M. A. J. Wheeler-Booth.
Clerk Assistant and Clerk of the Journals (£60,100–£70,400), J. M. Davies.
Reading Clerk (£51,300–£59,000), P. D. G. Hayter, LVO.
Counsel to Chairman of Committees (£60,100–£70,400), D. Rippengal, CB, QC.
Second Counsel (£51,300–£59,000), Mrs E. Denza, CMG.
Assistant Counsel (£41,152–£55,490), N. J. Adamson, CB, QC.
Principal Clerks (£46,140–£51,540), J. A. Vallance White (*Judicial Office and Fourth Clerk at the Table*); M. G. Pownall (*Committees*); B. P. Keith (*Private Bills*).
Chief Clerks (£37,928–£49,671), C. A. J. Mitchell; R. H. Walters, D.Phil.; D. R. Beamish; D. F. Slater.
Senior Clerks (£26,129–£36,417), Dr F. P. Tudor; E. C. Ollard (*seconded as Secretary to the Leader of the House and Chief Whip*); Miss M. E. De Groose; A. Makower; E. J. J. Wells; T. V. Mohan; W. G. Sleath; S. P. Burton.
Clerk (£13,869–£24,097), Mrs. M. B. Bloor.
Clerk of the Records (£37,928–£49,671), D. J. Johnson, FSA.
Deputy Clerk of the Records (£29,569–£44,474), S. K. Ellison.
Accountant (£26,129–£44,474), C. Preece.
Assistant Accountant (£19,117–£26,296), Miss J. M. Lansdown.
Judicial Taxing Clerk (£19,117–£26,296), C. G. Osborne.
Librarian (£37,928–£49,671), D. L. Jones.
Deputy Librarian (£29,569–£44,474), P. G. Davis, Ph.D.
Library Clerk (£26,129–£36,417), Miss I. L. Victory, Ph.D.
Examiners of Petitions for Private Bills, B. P. Keith; R. J. Willoughby.
Gentleman Usher of the Black Rod and Serjeant-at-Arms (£51,300–£59,000), Adm. Sir Richard Thomas, KCB, OBE.
Yeoman Usher of the Black Rod and Deputy Serjeant-at-Arms (£26,129–£36,417), Air Cdre A. C. Curry, OBE.
Staff Superintendent, Maj. F. P. Horsfall, MBE.
Shorthand Writer (fees), Mrs E. M. C. Holland.
Editor, Official Report (*Hansard*), (£35,757–£46,796), Mrs M. E. Villiers.
Deputy Editor, Official Report (£26,787–£40,202), G. R. Goodbarne.

THE HOUSE OF COMMONS

London SW1A 0AA
Tel 071-219 3000

The members of the House of Commons are elected by universal adult suffrage. For electoral purposes, the United Kingdom is divided into constituencies, each of which returns one member to the House of Commons, the member being the candidate who obtains the largest number of votes cast in the constituency. To ensure equitable representation the four Boundary Commissions keep constituency boundaries under review and recommend any redistribution of seats which may seem necessary because of population movements, etc. The number of seats was raised to 640 in 1945, then reduced to 625 in 1948, and subsequently rose to 630 in 1955, 635 in 1970, 650 in 1983 and 651 in 1992. Of the present 651 seats, there are 524 for England, 38 for Wales, 72 for Scotland and 17 for Northern Ireland.

Elections

Elections are by secret ballot, each elector casting one vote; voting is not compulsory. When a seat becomes vacant between general elections, a by-election is held.

British subjects and citizens of the Irish Republic can stand for election as Members of Parliament (MPs) provided they are 21 or over and not subject to disqualification. Those disqualified from sitting in the House include:
- undischarged bankrupts
- people sentenced to more than one year's imprisonment
- clergy of the Church of England, Church of Scotland, Church of Ireland and Roman Catholic Church
- members of the House of Lords
- holders of certain offices listed in the House of Commons Disqualification Act 1975, e.g. members of the judiciary, Civil Service, regular armed forces, police forces, some local government officers and some members of public corporations and government commissions

For entitlement to vote in parliamentary elections, *see* Legal Notes section.

A candidate does not require any party backing but his or her nomination for election must be supported by the signatures of ten people registered in the constituency. A candidate must also deposit with the returning officer £500, which is forfeit if the candidate does not receive more than 5 per cent of the votes cast. All election expenses, except the candidate's personal expenses, are subject to a statutory limit of £4,330, plus 3.7 pence for each elector in a borough constituency or 4.9 pence for each elector in a county constituency.

See pages 232–9 for an alphabetical list of MPs, pages 241–75 for the results of the last General Election, and page 275 for the results of recent by-elections.

State of Parties *as at 31 July 1992*

Conservative, 336 (20 women)
Labour, 270 (36 women)
Liberal Democrats, 20 (2 women)
Plaid Cymru, 4
Scottish Nationalist, 3 (1 woman)
Democratic Unionist, 3
Social Democratic and Labour, 4
Ulster Popular Unionist, 1
Ulster Unionist, 9
The Speaker, 1
Total, 651 (60 women)

Business

The week's business of the House is outlined each Thursday by the Leader of the House, after consultation between the Chief Government Whip and the Chief Opposition Whip. A quarter to a third of the time will be taken up by the Government's legislative programme, and the rest by other business, e.g. question time. As a rule, Bills likely to raise political controversy are introduced in the Commons before going on to the Lords, and the Commons claims exclusive control in respect of national taxation and expenditure. Bills such as the Finance Bill, which imposes taxation, and the Consolidated Fund Bills, which authorize expenditure, must begin in the Commons. A Bill of which the financial provisions are subsidiary may begin in the Lords; and the Commons may waive its rights in regard to Lords' amendments affecting finance.

The Commons has a public register of MPs' financial, and certain other, interests. Members must also disclose any relevant financial interest or benefit in a matter before the House when taking part in a debate, in certain other proceedings of the House, or in consultations with other MPs, with Ministers or civil servants.

MEMBERS' PAY AND ALLOWANCES

Since 1911 members of the House of Commons have received salary payments; facilities for free travel were introduced in 1924. Members are entitled to claim income tax relief on expenses incurred in the course of their Parliamentary duties. Salary rates since 1911 are as follows:

1911	£400 p.a.	1979 June	£9,450 p.a.
1931	360	1980 June	11,750
1934	380	1981 June	13,950
1935	400	1982 June	14,510
1937	600	1983 June	15,308
1946	1,000	1984 Jan	16,106
1954	1,250	1985 Jan	16,904
1957	1,750	1986 Jan	17,702
1964	3,250	1987 Jan	18,500
1972 Jan	4,500	1988 Jan	22,548
1975 June	5,750	1989 Jan	24,107
1976 June	6,062	1990 Jan	26,701
1977 July	6,270	1991 Jan	28,970
1978 June	6,897	1992 Jan	30,854

In October 1969 MPs were granted an allowance for secretarial and research expenses. In 1987 this became known as the Office Costs Allowance. For the year 1992 the allowance is £39,960.

Since January 1972 MPs can claim reimbursement for the additional cost of staying overnight away from their main residence while on Parliamentary business. This was set at £10,786 for the 1991–2 financial year. Since 1984 this has been non-taxable.

From April 1980 provision was made enabling each MP in receipt of Office Costs Allowance to contribute sums to an approved pension scheme for the provision of a pension, or other benefits, for or in respect of persons whose salary is met by him/her from the Office Costs Allowance.

The cost of travel allowances for 1991–2 was stated in June 1992 to be £7,272,075.

MEMBERS' PENSIONS

A contributory pension fund exists to provide pensions for former Members of Parliament and for dependants of deceased former MPs. The arrangements currently provide a pension of one-fiftieth of salary for each year of pensionable service with a maximum of two-thirds of salary at age 65. Pension is payable normally at age 65, for men and women, or on later retirement. Pensions may be paid earlier, e.g. on ill-health retirement. The widow/widower of a former MP receives a pension of one-half of the late MP's pension. Pensions are index-linked. Members currently contribute 6 per cent of salary to the pension fund; there is an Exchequer contribution, currently slightly less than half the amount contributed by MPs.

The House of Commons Members' Fund provides for annual or lump sum grants to ex-MPs, their widows or widowers, and children whose incomes are below certain limits. Alternatively, payments of £1,884 per annum to ex-MPs with at least ten years' service and who left the House of Commons before October 1964, and £942 per annum to their widows or widowers are made as of right. Members contribute £24 per annum and the Exchequer £115,000 per annum to the fund. The net assets of the fund as at 30 September 1990 amounted to £1,692,676.

OFFICERS AND OFFICIALS

The House of Commons is presided over by the Speaker, who has considerable powers to maintain order in the House. A deputy, the Chairman of Ways and Means, and two Deputy Chairmen may preside over sittings of the House of Commons; they are elected by the House, and, like the Speaker, neither speak nor vote other than in their official capacity.

The staff of the House are employed by a Commission chaired by the Speaker. The heads of House of Commons departments (*see* below) are permanent officers of the House, not MPs. The Clerk of the House is the principal adviser to the Speaker on the privileges and procedures of the House, the conduct of the business of the House, and Committees. The Serjeant-at-Arms is responsible for security, ceremonial, and for accommodation in the Commons part of the Palace of Westminster.

Speaker (£63,047), The Rt. Hon. Betty Boothroyd, MP for West Bromwich West.
Chairman of Ways and Means (£51,402), Michael Morris, MP for Northampton South.
First Deputy Chairman of Ways and Means (£47,989), Geoffrey Lofthouse, MP for Pontefract and Castleford.
Second Deputy Chairman of Ways and Means (£47,989), Dame Janet Fookes, DBE, MP for Plymouth Drake.

OFFICES OF THE SPEAKER AND CHAIRMAN OF WAYS AND MEANS

Speaker's Secretary (£37,928–£42,870), Sir Peter Kitcatt, CB.
Speaker's Counsel (£51,300–£59,000), H. Knorpel, CB, QC; G. E. Gammie, CB, QC.
Assistant to Speaker's Counsel (£28,372–£33,497), P. Harvey, CB.
Chaplain to the Speaker, The Revd Canon D. Gray, TD.
Secretary to the Chairman of Ways and Means, Ms P. A. Helme.

DEPARTMENT OF THE CLERK OF THE HOUSE

Clerk of the House of Commons (£84,250), Sir Clifford Boulton, KCB.
Clerk Assistant (£60,100–£70,400), D. W. Limon.
Clerk of Committees (£60,100–£70,400), J. F. Sweetman, CB, TD.
Principal Clerks (£51,300–£59,000)
Public Bills, W. R. McKay.
Table Office, C. B. Winnifrith.
Select Committees, R. B. Sands.
Overseas Office, G. Cubie.
Journals, A. J. Hastings.
Private Bills, R. J. Willoughby.
Second Clerk of Select Committees, D. G. Millar.
Standing Committees, M. R. Jack, Ph.D.
Domestic Committees, R. W. G. Wilson.
Financial Committees, W. A. Proctor.
Deputy Principal Clerks (£37,928–£42,870), S. A. L. Panton; Mrs J. Sharpe; Ms A. Milner-Barry; F. A. Cranmer; R. J. Rogers; C. R. M. Ward, Ph.D.; Ms H. E. Irwin; D. W. N. Doig; A. Sandall; D. L. Natzler; A. R. Kennon; D. W. Robson; L. C. Laurence Smyth; S. J. Patrick; D. J. Gerhold; C. J. Poyser; D. F. Harrison; S. J. Priestley; A. H. Doherty; P. A. Evans; R. I. S. Phillips; R. G. James.
Senior Clerks (£26,129–£30,823), Ms P. A. Helme; D. R Lloyd; R. A. Lambert; B. M. Hutton; J. S. Benger; Ms E. C. Samson; N. P. Walker; M. D. Hamlyn; P. C. Seaward; C. G. Lee; C. D. Stanton; J. M. Hope (*acting*); H. R. Neilson (*acting*); M. J. Reeves (*acting*); D. Steel (*acting*).
Clerks of Domestic Committees (£26,129–£30,813), K. J. Brown; P. G. Moon.
Examiners of Petitions for Private Bills, R. J. Willoughby; B. P. Keith.

Registrar of Members' Interests, R. B. Sands.
Taxing Officer, R. J. Willoughby.

DEPARTMENT OF THE SERJEANT-AT-ARMS

Serjeant-at-Arms (£51,300–£59,000) Sir Alan Urwick, KCVO, CMG.
Deputy Serjeant-at-Arms (£37,928–£42,870), P. N. W. Jennings.
Assistant Serjeant-at-Arms (£29,569–£37,928), M. J. A. Cummins.
Deputy Assistant Serjeants-at-Arms (£26,129–£30,823), P. A. J. Wright; J. F. Collins.

PARLIAMENTARY WORKS DIRECTORATE

Director of Works (£48,501), H. P. Webber.
Deputy Director of Works (£37,928), B. C. Sewell.
Principal Works Officers (£26,129–£30,823), A. Makepeace; B. R. Hall; J. Whyte; R. Bentley; M. Moone; G. Goode; J. F. Moore.
Senior Planning Technical Officers (£20,976–£26,296), J. Stone; S. Howard; B. O'Boyle; W. Knowles.

DEPARTMENT OF THE LIBRARY

Librarian (£51,300–£59,000), D. J. T. Englefield.
Deputy Librarian, (£46,140–47,872), Miss J. B. Tanfield.

Library and Information Service

Assistant Librarians (£37,928–£42,870), S. Z. Young; Miss P. J. Baines.
Deputy Assistant Librarians (£29,569–£37,928), K. G. Cunninghame; Mrs J. M. Wainwright; C. C. Pond, Ph.D.; Mrs C. B. Andrews; R. C. Clements; Mrs J. M. Laurie; R. J. Ware, D.Phil.; C. R. Barclay; Mrs J. M. Fiddick.
Senior Library Clerks (£26,129–£30,823), Ms F. Poole; Mrs C. M. Gillie; Miss C. E. Nield; R. J. Twigger; T. N. Edmonds; R. J. Cracknell; Miss O. M. Gay; Miss E. M. McInnes; Miss M. Baber; Ms A. Muir; Mrs H. V. Holden; Mrs G. L. Allen; Miss J. Seaton; Mrs P. L. Carling; A. J. L. Crompton; Mrs K. Greener; Miss P. J. Strickland.

Vote Office

Deliverer of the Vote (£37,928–£42,870), G. R. Russell.
Deputy Deliverer of the Vote (£26,129–£30,823), H. C. Foster.

DEPARTMENT OF FINANCE AND ADMINISTRATION

Director of Finance and Administration (£51,300–£59,000), J. Rodda.
Accountant (£46,140–£47,872), A. J. Lewis.
Deputy Accountant (£37,928–£42,870), A. R. Marskell.
Assistant Accountants (£26,129–£30,823), M. Fletcher; Mrs G. Crowther.
Head of Establishments Office (£37,928–£42,870), B. A. Wilson.
Head of Finance Office (£29,589–£37,928), M. J. Barram.
Financial Accountant (£26,129–£30,823), Miss M. McColl.
Management Accountant (£26,129–£30,823), R. H. A. Russell.
Deputy Head of Establishments Office (£29,569–£37,928), J. A. Robb.
Computer Officer (£37,928–£42,870), R. S. Morgan.
Internal Auditor (£26,129–£30,823), A. A. Cameron.
Staff Inspector (£26,129–£30,823), R. C. Collins.

DEPARTMENT OF THE OFFICIAL REPORT

Editor (£46,140–£47,872), I. D. Church.
Deputy Editor (£37,928–£42,870), P. Walker.
Principal Assistant Editors (£27,799–£35,671), J. Gourley; W. G. Garland; Miss H. Hales.
Assistant Editors (£25,079–£32,130), Miss V. Grainger; Miss V. A. A. Clarke; Miss G. L. Sutherland; S. Hutchinson; Miss C. Fogarty.

REFRESHMENT DEPARTMENT

Director of Catering Services (£37,928–£42,870), Mrs S. J. Harrison.
Catering Accountant (£26,129–£30,823), vacant.

PARLIAMENTARY INFORMATION

The following is a short glossary of aspects of the work of Parliament. Unless otherwise stated, references are to House of Commons procedures.

ADJOURNMENT DEBATE – Usually a half-hour debate introduced by a backbencher at the end of business for the day. The subjects raised are often local or personal issues.

BILL – Proposed legislation is termed a Bill. The stages of a Public Bill (for Private Bills, *see* page 227) in the House of Commons are as follows:
First Reading: There is no debate at this stage, which nowadays merely constitutes an order to have the Bill printed.
Second Reading: The debate on the principles of the Bill.
Committee Stage: The detailed examination of a Bill, clause by clause. In most cases this takes place in a Standing Committee, or the whole House may act as a Committee. A Special Standing Committee may take evidence before embarking on detailed scrutiny of the Bill. Very rarely, a Bill may be examined by a Select Committee (*see* below).
Report Stage: Detailed review of a Bill as amended in Committee.
Third Reading: Final debate on a Bill.
Public Bills go through the same stages in the House of Lords, except that in almost all cases the Committee stage is taken in Committee of the Whole House.

A Bill may start in either House, and has to pass through both Houses to become law.

Both Houses have to agree the same text of a Bill, so that the amendments made by the second House are then considered in the originating House, and if not agreed, sent back or themselves amended, until agreement is reached.

CHILTERN HUNDREDS – A legal fiction, a nominal office of profit under the Crown, the acceptance of which requires an MP to vacate his seat. The Manor of Northstead is similar. These are the only means by which an MP may resign.

CLOSURE AND GUILLOTINE – To prevent deliberate waste of time of either House, a motion may be made that the question be now put. In the House of Commons, if the Speaker decides that the rights of a minority are not being prejudiced and 100 members support the closure motion in a division, if carried, the original motion is put to the House without further debate.

The guillotine represents a more rigorous and systematic application of the closure. Under this system, a Bill proceeds in accordance with a rigid timetable and discussion is limited to the time allotted to each group of clauses. The closure is hardly ever used in the Lords, and there is no procedure for a guillotine. The completion of business in the Lords is ensured by agreement from all sides of the House.

CONSOLIDATED FUND BILL – A Bill to authorize issue of money to maintain Government services. The Bill is dealt with without debate, but afterwards members may raise topics of public or local importance.

DELEGATED LEGISLATION – Many statutes empower Ministers to make delegated legislation, with little or no reference back to Parliament, usually by means of Statutory Instruments. These fall into four broad categories:
(i) Affirmative Instruments, which are subject to approval by resolutions of both Houses before they can come into or remain in force
(ii) Negative Instruments, which are subject to annulment by resolution of either House
(iii) General Instruments, which include those not required to be laid before Parliament and those which are required to be so laid but are not subject to approval or annulment
(iv) Special Procedure Orders, against which parties outside Parliament may lodge petitions

DISSOLUTION – Parliament comes to an end either by dissolution by the Sovereign, on the advice of the Prime Minister, or on the expiration of the term of five years for which the House of Commons was elected. Dissolution is normally effected by a Royal Proclamation.

EARLY DAY MOTION – A motion put on the Notice Paper by an MP without in general the real prospect of its being debated. Such motions are expressions of back-bench opinion.

EMERGENCY DEBATE – In the Commons a method of obtaining prompt discussion of a matter of urgency is by moving the adjournment under Standing Order No. 20 for the purpose of discussing a specific and important matter that should have urgent consideration. A member may ask leave to make this motion by giving written notice to the Speaker, usually before 12 noon, and if the Speaker considers the matter of sufficient importance and the House agrees, it is discussed usually at 7 p.m. on the following day.

FATHER OF THE HOUSE – The Member whose continuous service in the House of Commons is the longest. The present Father of the House is the Rt. Hon. Sir Edward Heath, KG, MBE, elected first in 1950.

GENERAL SYNOD MEASURE – A measure passed by the national assembly of the Church of England under the Church of England Assembly (Powers) Act 1919. These measures are considered by the Joint Ecclesiastical Committee, who make a report. They are then considered by both Houses and, if approved, sent for the royal assent.

HANSARD – The official report of debates in both Houses (and in Standing Committees) published by HMSO, normally on the day after the sitting concerned.

HOURS OF MEETING – The House of Commons meets on Monday, Tuesday, Wednesday and Thursday at 2.30 p.m., and on Friday at 9.30 a.m. Changes to these hours are under consideration. The House of Lords normally meets at 2.30 p.m. on Monday, Tuesday and Wednesday and at 3 p.m. on Thursday. In the latter part of the session, the House of Lords sometimes sits on Fridays at 11 a.m.

HYBRIDITY – Public Bill which is considered to affect specific private or local interests, as distinct from all such interests of a single category, is called a Hybrid Bill and is subject to a special form of scrutiny to enable people affected to object. In the House of Lords, affirmative instruments (*see* Delegated Legislation above) may also be treated as hybrid.

LEADER OF THE OPPOSITION – In 1937 the office of Leader of the Opposition was recognized and a salary of £2,000 per annum was assigned to the post. From January 1992 the salary was £59,736 (including Parliamentary salary of £23,227). The present Leader of the Opposition is the Rt. Hon. John Smith, QC, MP.

THE LORD CHANCELLOR – The Lord High Chancellor of Great Britain is (*ex officio*) the Speaker of the House of Lords. Unlike the Speaker of the House of Commons, he is a member of the Government, takes part in debates and votes in divisions. He has none of the powers to maintain order that the Speaker in the Commons has, these powers being exercised in the Lords by the House as a whole. The Lord Chancellor sits in the Lords on one of the Woolsacks, couches covered with red cloth and stuffed with wool. If he wishes to address the House in any way except formally as Speaker, he leaves the Woolsack.

NAMING – When a member has been named by the Speaker for a breach of order, i.e. contrary to the practice of the House, called by surname and not addressed as the 'Hon. Member for . . . (her/his constituency)', the Leader of the House moves that the offender 'be suspended from the service of the House' for (in the case of a first offence) a period of five sitting days. Should the member offend again, the period of suspension is increased.

OPPOSITION DAY – A day on which the topic for debate is chosen by the Opposition. There are twenty such days in a normal session. On seventeen days, subjects are chosen by the Leader of the Opposition; on the remaining three days by the leader of the next largest opposition party.

PARLIAMENT ACTS 1911 AND 1949 – Under these Acts, Bills may become law without the consent of the Lords.

Since at least the eighteenth century the Commons have had the privilege of having Bills concerned with supply (i.e. taxation and money matters) passed without amendment by the Lords, though until 1911 the Lords retained the right to reject such Bills outright.

By the Parliament Act 1911, a Bill which has been endorsed by the Speaker of the House of Commons as a Money Bill, and has been passed by the Commons and sent up to the Lords at least one month before the end of a session, can become law without the consent of the Lords if it is not passed by them without amendment within a month.

Under the Parliament Acts 1911 and 1949, if the Lords reject any other Public Bill (except one to prolong the life of a Parliament) which has been passed by the Commons in two successive sessions, then that Bill shall (unless the Commons direct to the contrary) become law without the consent of the Lords. The Lords have power, therefore, to delay a Public Bill for thirteen months from its first Second Reading in the House of Commons.

PRIME MINISTER'S QUESTIONS – The Prime Minister answers questions from 3.15 to 3.30 p.m. on Tuesdays and Thursdays. Nowadays the 'open question' predominates. Members tend to ask the Prime Minister what are her or his official engagements for the day; a supplementary question on virtually any topic can then be put.

PRIVATE BILL – A Bill promoted by a body or an individual to give powers additional to, or in conflict with, the general law, and to which a special procedure applies to enable people affected to object.

PRIVATE MEMBERS' BILL – A Public Bill promoted by a Member who is not a member of the Government.

PRIVATE NOTICE QUESTION – A question adjudged of urgent importance on submission to the Speaker (in the Lords, the Leader of the House), answered at the end of oral questions – usually at 3.30 p.m.

PRIVILEGE – The following are covered by the privilege of Parliament:
(i) freedom from interference in going to, attending at, and going from, Parliament
(ii) freedom of speech in Parliamentary proceedings
(iii) the printing and publishing of anything relating to the proceedings of the two Houses is subject to privilege
(iv) each House is the guardian of its dignity and may punish any insult to the House as a whole

PROROGATION – The bringing to an end, by the Sovereign on the advice of the Government, of a session of Parliament. Public Bills which have not completed all their stages lapse on prorogation.

QUEEN'S SPEECH – The Speech delivered by The Queen at the State Opening of Parliament, in which the Government's programme for the session is set forth. The Speech is, in fact, drafted by civil servants and approved by the Cabinet.

QUESTION TIME – Oral questions are answered by Ministers in the Commons from 2.30 to 3.30 p.m. every day except Friday. They are also taken at the start of the Lords sittings, with a daily limit of four oral questions.

ROYAL ASSENT – The royal assent is signified by Letters Patent to such Bills and Measures as have passed both Houses of Parliament (or Bills which have been passed under the Parliament Acts 1911 and 1949). The Sovereign has not given royal assent in person since 1854. On occasion, for instance in the prorogation of Parliament, royal assent may be pronounced to the two Houses by Lords Commissioners. More usually royal assent is notified to each House sitting separately in accordance with the Royal Assent Act 1967. The old French formulae for royal assent are then endorsed on the Acts by the Clerk of the Parliaments.

The power to withhold assent resides with the Sovereign but has not been exercised in the United Kingdom since 1707, in the reign of Queen Anne.

SELECT COMMITTEES – Consisting usually of 10–15 members of all parties are a means used by both Houses in order to investigate certain matters.

Most select committees in the House of Commons are now tied to departments; each committee investigates subjects within a government department's remit.

There are other House of Commons select committees dealing with Public Accounts (i.e. the spending by the Government of money voted by Parliament) and European legislation, and also domestic committees dealing, for example, with privilege and procedure. Major select committees usually take evidence in public; their evidence and reports are published by HMSO.

The principal select committee in the House of Lords is that on the European Communities, which has, at present, six sub-committees dealing with all areas of Community policy. The House of Lords also has a select committee on science and technology, which appoints sub-committees to deal with specific subjects. In addition, *ad hoc* select committees have been set up from time to time to investigate specific subjects, e.g. overseas trade, murder and life imprisonment. There are also some joint committees of the two Houses, e.g. the Joint Committee on Statutory Instruments.

DEPARTMENTAL COMMITTEES

Agriculture - *Chair*, Jerry Wiggin, MP;
Clerk, D. W. Robson.

Defence - *Chair*, Sir Nicholas Bonsor, MP;
Clerk, D. L. Natzler.

Education - *Chair*, Sir Malcolm Thornton, MP;
Clerk, A. Sandall.

Employment - *Chair*, Ron Leighton, MP;
Clerk, R. I. S. Phillips.

Environment - *Chair*, Robert Jones, MP;
Clerk, S. J. Priestley.

Foreign Affairs - *Chair*, Rt. Hon. David Howell, MP;
Clerks, Ms H. E. Irwin, M. Hamlyn.

Health - *Chair*, Marion Roe, MP;
Clerks, P. A. Evans, F. Reid.

Home Affairs - *Chair*, Sir Ivan Lawrence, MP;
Clerk, E. P. Silk.

National Heritage - *Chair*, Gerald Kaufman, MP;
Clerk, J. Sharpe.

Science and Technology - *Chair*, Sir Giles Shaw, MP;
Clerk, E. C. Samson.

Scottish Affairs - *Chair*, William McKelvey, MP;
Clerk, A. H. Doherty.

Social Security - *Chair*, Frank Field, MP;
Clerk, D. Lloyd.

Trade and Industry - *Chair*, Richard Caborn, MP;
Clerks, D. J. Gerhold, Ms L. Gardner.

Transport - *Chair*, Robert Adley, MP;
Clerks, D. W. Doig, C. Stanton.

Treasury and Civil Service - *Chair*, John Watts, MP;
Clerks, W. A. Proctor, C. G. Lee.

Welsh Affairs - *Chair*, Gareth Wardell, MP;
Clerk, B. M. Hutton.

NON-DEPARTMENTAL COMMITTEES

European Legislation - *Chair*, James Hood, MP;
Clerk, C. R. M. Ward.

Public Accounts - *Chair*, Rt. Hon. Robert Sheldon, MP;
Clerk, Dr J. Benger.

The Members' Interests, Parliamentary Commissioner, Privileges, and Procedure committees had still to be reconstituted at the time of going to press.

THE SPEAKER – The Speaker of the House of Commons is the spokesman and president of the Chamber. He or she is elected by the House at the beginning of each Parliament or when the previous Speaker retires or dies. The Speaker neither speaks in debates nor votes in divisions except when the voting is equal.

STANDING ORDERS – Rules which have from time to time been agreed by each House of Parliament to regulate the conduct of its business. These orders may be amended or repealed, and are from time to time suspended or dispensed with.

STATE OPENING – This marks the start of each new session of Parliament. Parliament is normally opened, in the presence of both Houses, by The Queen in person, who makes the Speech from the Throne which outlines the Government's policies for the coming session (*see* Queen's Speech). In the absence of The Queen, Parliament is opened by Royal Commission, and The Queen's Speech is read by one of the Lords Commissioners specially appointed by Letters Patent for the occasion.

STRANGERS – Anyone who is not a Member or Officer of the House is a stranger. Visitors are generally admitted to debates of both Houses but may be excluded if the House so decides. In practice this happens only in time of war.

TEN MINUTE RULE – A colloquial term for Standing Order No. 19, under which back-benchers have an opportunity on Tuesdays and Wednesdays to state for about ten minutes why a Bill on a certain subject should be introduced. Time is also available for a short opposing speech.

VACANT SEATS – When a vacancy occurs in the House of Commons during a session of Parliament, the writ for the by-election is moved by a Whip of the party to which the member whose seat has been vacated belonged. If the House is in recess, the Speaker can issue a warrant for a writ, should two members certify to him that a seat is vacant.

WHIPS – In order to secure the attendance of Members of a particular party in Parliament on all occasions, and particularly on the occasion of an important vote, Whips (originally known as 'Whippers-in') are appointed. The written appeal or circular letter issued by them is also known as a 'whip', its urgency being denoted by the number of times it is underlined. Failure to respond to a three-line whip, headed 'Most important', is tantamount in the Commons to secession (at any rate temporarily) from the party. Whips are officially recognized by Parliament and are provided with office accommodation in both Houses. In both Houses, Government and some Opposition Whips receive salaries from public funds.

PUBLIC INFORMATION SERVICES

HOUSE OF COMMONS – Public Information Office, House of Commons, London SW1A 0AA. Tel: 071-219 4272.
HOUSE OF LORDS – The Journal and Information Office, House of Lords, London SW1A 0PW. Tel: 071–219 3107.

GOVERNMENT OFFICE

The Government is the body of Ministers responsible for the administration of national affairs, determining policy and introducing into Parliament any legislation necessary to give effect to government policy. The majority of Ministers are members of the House of Commons but members of the House of Lords or of neither House may also hold Ministerial responsibility. The Lord Chancellor is always a member of the House of Lords. The Prime Minister is, by current convention, always a member of the House of Commons.

THE PRIME MINISTER

The office of Prime Minister, which had been in existence for nearly 200 years, was officially recognized in 1905 and its holder was granted a place in the table of precedence. The Prime Minister, by tradition also First Lord of the Treasury and Minister for the Civil Service, is appointed by the Sovereign and is usually the leader of the party which enjoys, or can secure, a majority in the House of Commons. Other Ministers are appointed by the Sovereign on the recommendation of the Prime Minister, who also allocates functions amongst Ministers and has the power to obtain their resignation or dismissal individually.

The Prime Minister informs the Sovereign of state and political matters, advises on the dissolution of Parliament, and makes recommendations for important Crown appointments, the award of honours, etc.

As the chairman of Cabinet meetings and leader of a political party, the Prime Minister is responsible for translating party policy into government activity. As leader of the Government, the Prime Minister is responsible to Parliament and to the electorate for the policies and their implementation.

The Prime Minister also represents the nation in international affairs, e.g. summit conferences.

THE CABINET

The Cabinet developed during the eighteenth century as an inner committee of the Privy Council, which was the chief source of executive power until that time. The Cabinet is composed of about twenty Ministers chosen by the Prime Minister, usually the heads of government departments (generally known as Secretaries of State unless they have a special title, e.g. Chancellor of the Exchequer), the leaders of the two Houses of Parliament, and the holders of various traditional offices.

The Cabinet's functions are the final determination of policy, control of government and coordination of government departments. The exercise of its functions is dependent upon enjoying majority support in the House of Commons. Cabinet meetings are held in private, taking place once or twice a week during parliamentary sittings and less often during a recess. Proceedings are confidential, the members being bound by their oath as Privy Counsellors not to disclose information about the proceedings.

The convention of collective responsibility means that the Cabinet acts unanimously even when Cabinet Ministers do not all agree on a subject. The policies of departmental Ministers must be consistent with the policies of the Government as a whole, and once the Government's policy has been decided, each Minister is expected to support it or resign.

The convention of Ministerial responsibility holds a Minister, as the political head of his or her department, accountable to Parliament for the department's work. Departmental Ministers usually decide all matters within their responsibility, although on matters of political importance they normally consult their colleagues collectively. A decision by a departmental Minister is binding on the Government as a whole.

POLITICAL PARTIES

Before the reign of William and Mary the principal officers of state were chosen by and were responsible to the Sovereign alone and not to Parliament or the nation at large. Such officers acted sometimes in concert with one another but more often independently, and the fall of one did not, of necessity, involve that of others, although all were liable to be dismissed at any moment.

In 1693 the Earl of Sunderland recommended to William III the advisability of selecting a Ministry from the political party which enjoyed a majority in the House of Commons and the first united Ministry was drawn in 1696 from the Whigs, to which party the King owed his throne. This group became known as the Junto and was regarded with suspicion as a novelty in the political life of the nation, being a small section meeting in secret apart from the main body of Ministers. It may be regarded as the forerunner of the Cabinet and in course of time it led to the establishment of the principle of joint responsibility of Ministers, so that internal disagreement caused a change of personnel or resignation of the whole body of Ministers.

The accession of George I, who was unfamiliar with the English language, led to a disinclination on the part of the Sovereign to preside at meetings of his Ministers and caused the appearance of a Prime Minister, a position first acquired by Robert Walpole in 1721 and retained without interruption for 20 years and 326 days.

Development of Parties

In 1828 the old party of the Whigs became known as Liberals, a name originally given to it by its opponents to imply laxity of principles, but gradually accepted by the party to indicate its claim to be pioneers and champions of political reform and progressive legislation. In 1861 a Liberal Registration Association was founded and Liberal Associations became widespread. In 1877 a National Liberal Federation was formed, with headquarters in London. The Liberal Party was in power for long periods during the second half of the nineteenth century and for several years during the first quarter of the twentieth century, but after a split in the party the numbers elected were small from 1931. In March 1988, the Liberals and the Social Democratic Party merged under the title Social and Liberal Democrats. Since October 1989 they have been known as the Liberal Democrats.

Soon after the change from Whig to Liberal the Tory Party became known as Conservative, a name traditionally believed to have been invented by John Wilson Croker in 1830 and to have been generally adopted about the time of the passing of the Reform Act of 1832 to indicate that the preservation of national institutions was the leading principle of the party. After the Home Rule crisis of 1886 the dissentient Liberals entered into a compact with the Conservatives, under which the latter undertook not to contest their seats, but a separate Liberal Unionist organization was maintained until 1912, when it was united with the Conservatives.

Labour candidates for Parliament made their first appearance at the general election of 1892, when there were 27 standing as Labour or Liberal-Labour. In 1900 the Labour Representation Committee was set up in order to establish a distinct Labour group in Parliament, with its own whips, its own policy, and a readiness to co-operate with any party which might be engaged in promoting legislation in the direct interest of labour. In 1906 the LRC became known as The Labour Party.

The Council for Social Democracy was announced by four former Labour Cabinet Ministers on 25 January 1981. Subsequently a number of sitting Labour Members of Parliament, together with one Conservative, joined the new group, and on 26 March 1981 the Social Democratic Party was launched. Later that year the SDP and the Liberal Party formed an electoral alliance. In 1988 a majority of the SDP agreed on a merger with the Liberal Party (*see* above) but a minority continued as a separate party under the SDP title. In June 1990 it was decided to wind up the party organization and its three sitting MPs were known as independent social democrats. None were returned at the 1992 general election.

Government and Opposition

The government of the day is formed by the party which wins the largest number of seats in the House of Commons at a general election, or which has the support of a majority of members in the House of Commons. By tradition, the leader of the majority party is asked by the Sovereign to form a government, while the largest minority party becomes the official Opposition with its own leader and 'Shadow Cabinet'. Leaders of the Government and Opposition sit on the front benches of the Commons with their supporters (the backbenchers) sitting behind them.

When a party is in opposition and its leadership becomes vacant, it makes its free choice among the various personalities available; but if the party is in office, the Sovereign's choice may anticipate, and in a certain sense forestall, the decision of the party.

PARTIES

The parties included here are those with MPs sitting in the House of Commons in the present Parliament. Addresses of other political parties may be found in the Societies and Institutions section.

Conservative and Unionist Party, Central Office, 32 Smith Square, London SW1P 3HH. Tel: 071-222 9000.
Chairman, The Rt. Hon. Sir Norman Fowler, MP
Deputy Chairman, The Rt. Hon. Dame Angela Rumbold, DBE, MP; Gerald Malone, MP
Hon. Treasurers, The Lord Laing of Dunphail; T. J. Smith, MP.

Scottish Conservative and Unionist Central Office, Suite 1/1, 14 Links Place, Leith, Edinburgh EH6 7EX. Tel: 031-555 2900.
Chairman, The Lord Sanderson of Bowden
Deputy Chairmen, W. Y. Hughes, CBE; Sir Matthew Goodwin, CBE; Mrs N. Milne
Hon. Treasurers, D. Mitchell, CBE; M. Tennant
Director of the Party in Scotland, J. Goodsman

Labour Party, 150 Walworth Road, London SE17 1JT. Tel: 071-701 1234.
Parliamentary Party Leader, The Rt. Hon. John Smith, QC, MP
Deputy Party Leader, Margaret Beckett, MP
Leader in the Lords, The Lord Cledwyn of Penrhos, CH (standing down in autumn 1992)
Chair, John Evans, MP
Vice-Chair, A. Clarke
Treasurer, S. McCluskie
General Secretary, L. Whitty

Shadow Cabinet *since July 1992*
Leader of the Opposition, The Rt. Hon. John Smith, QC, MP
Leader of the House, Margaret Beckett, MP
Treasury and Economic Affairs, Gordon Brown, MP
Home Affairs, Tony Blair, MP
Trade and Industry, Robin Cook, MP
Employment, Frank Dobson, MP
Transport, John Prescott, MP
National Heritage, vacant.
Chief Secretary to the Treasury, Harriet Harman, MP
Citizen's Charter and Women, Marjorie Mowlam, MP
Environmental Protection, Chris Smith, MP
Wales, Ann Clwyd, MP
Education, Ann Taylor, MP
Foreign and Commonwealth Affairs, Jack Cunningham, MP
Development and Co-operation, Michael Meacher, MP
Social Security, Donald Dewar, MP
Health, David Blunkett, MP
Environment (Local Government), Jack Straw, MP
Scotland, Tom Clarke, MP
Defence, Disarmament and Arms Control, David Clark, MP
Food, Agriculture and Rural Affairs, Ron Davies, MP
Northern Ireland, Kevin McNamara, MP
Chief Whip, Derek Foster, MP
Chair of the Parliamentary Labour Party, Douglas Hoyle, MP

Labour Whips
House of Lords, The Lord Graham of Edmonton
House of Commons, Derek Foster, MP

Liberal Democrats, 4 Cowley Street, London SW1P 3NB. Tel: 071-222 7999.
President, Charles Kennedy, MP
Deputy Chair, Sir Ian Wrigglesworth
Hon. Treasurer, T. Razzall
General Secretary, G. Elson

Parliamentary Party Leader, The Rt. Hon. Paddy Ashdown, MP
Leader in the Lords, The Rt. Hon. the Lord Jenkins of Hillhead

LIBERAL DEMOCRAT SPOKESMEN
Treasury and Civil Service, Alan Beith, MP
Trade, Industry and Employment, Malcolm Bruce, MP
Agriculture and Rural Affairs, Paul Tyler, MP
Environment and Natural Resources, Simon Hughes, MP
Transport, Nicholas Harvey, MP
Home Affairs and National Heritage, Robert Maclennan, MP
England, Local Government and Housing, Nigel Jones, MP
Citizen's Charter and Youth Issues, Matthew Taylor, MP
Women's Issues, Ray Michie, MP
Sport, Menzies Campbell, MP
Scotland, Jim Wallace, MP (also fisheries policy); Ray Michie, MP
Northern Ireland, Lord Holme of Cheltenham
Wales, Alex Carlile, MP
Social Security, Older People and Disabled People, Archy Kirkwood, MP
Health and Community Care, Liz Lynne, MP
Education and Training, Don Foster, MP
Foreign Affairs, The Rt. Hon. Sir David Steel, MP
Defence and Disarmament, Menzies Campbell, MP
Europe and East-West Relations, Sir Russell Johnston, MP; Charles Kennedy, MP
Overseas Development, The Lord Bonham Carter

LIBERAL DEMOCRAT WHIPS
House of Lords, The Lord Tordoff
House of Commons, Archy Kirkwood, MP (*Chief Whip*); Simon Hughes, MP (*Deputy Whip*)

WELSH LIBERAL DEMOCRATS, 57 St Mary Street, Cardiff CF1 1FE. Tel: 0222-382210.
Party President, Revd R. Roberts
Party Leader, Alex Carlile, MP
Chairman, G. Williams
Treasurer, B. Lopez
Secretary, Ms K. Lloyd

SCOTTISH LIBERAL DEMOCRATS, 4 Clifton Terrace, Edinburgh EH12 5DR. Tel: 031-337 2314.
Party President, Sir Russell Johnston, MP
Party Leader, Jim Wallace, MP
Chair, Ray Michie, MP
Vice-Chairs, M. Ford; Ms S. Grieve
Hon. Treasurer, N. Stephen
Secretary, Ms R. Grant

PLAID CYMRU, 51 Cathedral Road, Cardiff CF1 9HD. Tel: 0222-231944.
Party President, Dafydd Wigley, MP
Vice-President, D. Iwan
Chairman, I. Wyn Jones, MP
Deputy Chairman, J. Dixon
Hon. Treasurer, S. R. Morgan
Secretary, D. Williams

SCOTTISH NATIONAL PARTY, 6 North Charlotte Street, Edinburgh EH2 4JH. Tel: 031-226 3661.
Parliamentary Party Leader, Margaret Ewing, MP
Chief Whip, Andrew Welsh, MP
National Convener, Alex Salmond, MP
Deputy Vice-Conveners, A. Morgan; J. Sillars
National Treasurer, T. Chalmers
National Secretary, J. Swinney

NORTHERN IRELAND

SOCIAL DEMOCRATIC AND LABOUR PARTY, 24 Mount Charles, Belfast BT7 1NZ. Tel: 0232-323428.
Parliamentary Party Leader, John Hume, MP, MEP
Deputy Leader, Seamus Mallon, MP
Chief Whip, Eddie McGrady, MP
Chairman, M. Durkan
Vice-Chairmen, Ms A. Hegarty; G. Murphy
Hon. Treasurer, Ms D. Field
Party Administrator, Mrs G. Cosgrove

ULSTER DEMOCRATIC UNIONIST PARTY, 296 Albertbridge Road, Belfast BT5 4GX. Tel: 0232-458597.
Parliamentary Party Leader, I. Paisley, MP, MEP
Deputy Leader, Peter Robinson, MP
Chairman, W. J. McClure
Deputy Chairman, S. Gibson
Hon. Treasurer, D. F. Herron
General Secretary, vacant

ULSTER UNIONIST COUNCIL, 3 Glengall Street, Belfast BT12 5AE. Tel: 0232-324601.
President, J. Cunningham
Party Leader, The Rt. Hon. James Molyneaux, MP
Chief Whip, William Ross, MP
Chairman, J. Nicholson, MEP
Vice-Chairman, A. J. Wilson
Treasurer, J. Allen
Party Secretary, J. Wilson

MEMBERS OF PARLIAMENT AS AT 31 JULY 1992

For abbreviations, *see* page 241
* Denotes membership of the last Parliament

*Abbott, Ms Diane J. (*b.* 1953) *Lab., Hackney North and Stoke Newington*, maj. 10,727
*Adams, Mrs Irene (*b.* 1948) *Lab., Paisley North*, maj. 9,329
*Adley, Robert J. (*b.* 1935) *C., Christchurch*, maj. 23,015
Ainger, Nicholas R. (*b.* 1949) *Lab., Pembroke*, maj. 755
Ainsworth, Peter M. (*b.* 1956) *C., Surrey East*, maj. 17,656
Ainsworth, Robert W. (*b.* 1952) *Lab., Coventry North East*, maj. 11,676
*Aitken, Jonathan W. P. (*b.* 1942) *C., Thanet South*, maj. 11,513
*Alexander, Richard T. (*b.* 1934) *C., Newark*, maj. 8,229
*Alison, Rt. Hon. Michael J. H. (*b.* 1926) *C., Selby*, maj. 9,508
*Allason, Rupert W. S. (*b.* 1951) *C., Torbay*, maj. 5,787
*Allen, Graham W. (*b.* 1953) *Lab., Nottingham North*, maj. 10,743
*Alton, David P. (*b.* 1951) *LD, Liverpool, Mossley Hill*, maj. 2,606
*Amess, David A. A. (*b.* 1952) *C., Basildon*, maj. 1,480
Ancram, Michael A. F. J. K. (Earl of Ancram) (*b.* 1945) *C., Devizes*, maj. 19,712
*Anderson, Donald (*b.* 1939) *Lab., Swansea East*, maj. 23,482
Anderson, Mrs Janet (*b.* 1949) *Lab., Rossendale and Darwen*, maj. 120
*Arbuthnot, James N. (*b.* 1952) *C., Wanstead and Woodford*, maj. 16,885
*Armstrong, Miss Hilary J. (*b.* 1945) *Lab., Durham North West*, maj. 13,987
*Arnold, Jacques A. (*b.* 1947) *C., Gravesham*, maj. 5,493
*Arnold, Sir Thomas (*b.* 1947) *C., Hazel Grove*, maj. 929
*Ashby, David G. (*b.* 1940) *C., Leicestershire North West*, maj. 979
*Ashdown, Rt. Hon. J. J. D. (Paddy) (*b.* 1941) *LD, Yeovil*, maj. 8,833
*Ashton, Joseph W. (*b.* 1933) *Lab., Bassetlaw*, maj. 9,997
*Aspinwall, Jack H. (*b.* 1933) *C., Wansdyke*, maj. 13,341
*Atkins, Robert J. (*b.* 1946) *C., South Ribble*, maj. 5,973
*Atkinson, David A. (*b.* 1940) *C., Bournemouth East*, maj. 14,823
Atkinson, Peter (*b.* 1943) *C., Hexham*, maj. 13,438
Austin-Walker, John E. (*b.* 1944) *Lab., Woolwich*, maj. 2,225
*Baker, Rt. Hon. Kenneth W., CH (*b.* 1934) *C., Mole Valley*, maj. 15,950
*Baker, Nicholas B. (*b.* 1938) *C., Dorset North*, maj. 10,080
*Baldry, Antony B. (*b.* 1950) *C., Banbury*, maj. 16,720
Banks, Matthew (*b.* 1961) *C., Southport*, maj. 3,063
*Banks, Robert G., MBE (*b.* 1937) *C., Harrogate*, maj. 12,589
*Banks, Tony L. (*b.* 1943) *Lab., Newham North West*, maj. 9,171
*Barnes, Harold (*b.* 1936) *Lab., Derbyshire North East*, maj. 6,270
*Barron, Kevin J. (*b.* 1946) *Lab., Rother Valley*, maj. 17,222
Bates, Michael W. (*b.* 1961) *C., Langbaurgh*, maj. 1,564
*Batiste, Spencer L. (*b.* 1945) *C., Elmet*, maj. 3,261
*Battle, John D. (*b.* 1951) *Lab., Leeds West*, maj. 13,828
Bayley, Hugh (*b.* 1952) *Lab., York*, maj. 6,342
*Beckett, Mrs Margaret M. (*b.* 1953) *Lab., Derby South*, maj. 6,936
*Beggs, Roy (*b.* 1936) *UUP, Antrim East*, maj. 7,422
*Beith, Rt. Hon. Alan J. (*b.* 1943) *LD, Berwick-upon-Tweed*, maj. 5,043
*Bell, Stuart (*b.* 1938) *Lab., Middlesbrough*, maj. 15,784
*Bellingham, Henry C. (*b.* 1955) *C., Norfolk North West*, maj. 11,564
*Bendall, Vivian W. H. (*b.* 1938) *C., Ilford North*, maj. 9,071
*Benn, Rt. Hon. Anthony N. W. (*b.* 1925) *Lab., Chesterfield*, maj. 6,414
*Bennett, Andrew F. (*b.* 1939) *Lab., Denton and Reddish*, maj. 12,084
*Benton, Joseph E. (*b.* 1933) *Lab., Bootle*, maj. 29,442
Beresford, Sir Paul (*b.* 1946) *C., Croydon Central*, maj. 9,650
*Bermingham, Gerald E. (*b.* 1940) *Lab., St Helens South*, maj. 18,209
Berry, Roger L., D.Phil (*b.* 1948) *Lab., Kingswood*, maj. 2,370
Betts, Clive J. C. (*b.* 1950) *Lab., Sheffield, Attercliffe*, maj. 15,480
*Biffen, Rt. Hon. John W. (*b.* 1930) *C., Shropshire North*, maj. 16,211
*Blackburn, John G., Ph.D. (*b.* 1933) *C., Dudley West*, maj. 5,789
*Blair, Anthony C. L. (*b.* 1953) *Lab., Sedgefield*, maj. 14,859
*Blunkett, David (*b.* 1947) *Lab., Sheffield, Brightside*, maj. 22,681
*Boateng, Paul Y. (*b.* 1951) *Lab., Brent South*, maj. 9,705
*Body, Sir Richard (*b.* 1927) *C., Holland with Boston*, maj. 13,831
*Bonsor, Sir Nicholas, Bt. (*b.* 1942) *C., Upminster*, maj. 13,821
Booth, Hartley, Ph.D. (*b.* 1946) *C., Finchley*, maj. 6,388
*Boothroyd, Rt. Hon. Betty (*b.* 1929) *The Speaker, West Bromwich West*, maj. 7,830
*Boswell, Timothy E. (*b.* 1942) *C., Daventry*, maj. 20,274
*Bottomley, Peter J. (*b.* 1944) *C., Eltham*, maj. 1,666
*Bottomley, Rt. Hon. Virginia H. B. M. (*b.* 1948) *C., Surrey South West*, maj. 14,975
*Bowden, Andrew, MBE (*b.* 1930) *C., Brighton, Kemptown*, maj. 3,056
*Bowis, John C., OBE (*b.* 1945) *C., Battersea*, maj. 4,840
Boyce, James (*b.* 1947) *Lab., Rotherham*, maj. 17,561
*Boyes, Roland (*b.* 1937) *Lab., Houghton and Washington*, maj. 20,808
*Boyson, Rt. Hon. Sir Rhodes (*b.* 1925) *C., Brent North*, maj. 10,131
*Bradley, Keith J. C. (*b.* 1950) *Lab., Manchester, Withington*, maj. 9,735
Brandreth, Gyles D. (*b.* 1948) *C., City of Chester*, maj. 1,101
*Bray, Jeremy W., Ph.D. (*b.* 1930) *Lab., Motherwell South*, maj. 14,013
*Brazier, Julian W. H. (*b.* 1953) *C., Canterbury*, maj. 10,805
*Bright, Graham F. J. (*b.* 1942) *C., Luton South*, maj. 799
*Brooke, Rt. Hon. Peter L., CH (*b.* 1934) *C., City of London and Westminster South*, maj. 13,369
*Brown, J. Gordon, Ph.D. (*b.* 1951) *Lab., Dunfermline East*, maj. 17,444
*Brown, Michael R. (*b.* 1951) *C., Brigg and Cleethorpes*, maj. 9,269
*Brown, Nicholas H. (*b.* 1950) *Lab., Newcastle upon Tyne East*, maj. 13,877
Browning, Mrs Angela F. (*b.* 1946) *C., Tiverton*, maj. 11,089
*Bruce, Ian C. (*b.* 1947) *C., Dorset South*, maj. 13,508
*Bruce, Malcolm G. (*b.* 1944) *LD, Gordon*, maj. 274
*Budgen, Nicholas W. (*b.* 1937) *C., Wolverhampton South West*, maj. 4,966

Burden, Richard (*b.* 1954) *Lab., Birmingham, Northfield*, maj. 630
*Burns, Simon H. M. (*b.* 1952) *C., Chelmsford*, maj. 18,260
*Burt, Alistair J. H. (*b.* 1955) *C., Bury North*, maj. 4,764
*Butcher, John P. (*b.* 1946) *C., Coventry South West*, maj. 1,436
Butler, Peter (*b.* 1951) *C., Milton Keynes North East*, maj. 14,176
*Butterfill, John V. (*b.* 1941) *C., Bournemouth West*, maj. 12,703
Byers, Stephen J. (*b.* 1953) *Lab., Wallsend*, maj. 19,470
*Caborn, Richard G. (*b.* 1943) *Lab., Sheffield Central*, maj. 17,294
*Callaghan, James (*b.* 1927) *Lab., Heywood and Middleton*, maj. 8,074
Campbell, Mrs Anne (*b.* 1940) *Lab., Cambridge*, maj. 580
*Campbell, Ronald (*b.* 1943) *Lab., Blyth Valley*, maj. 8,044
*Campbell, W. Menzies, CBE, QC (*b.* 1941) *LD, Fife North East*, maj. 3,308
*Campbell-Savours, Dale N. (*b.* 1943) *Lab., Workington*, maj. 10,449
*Canavan, Dennis A. (*b.* 1942) *Lab., Falkirk West*, maj. 9,812
Cann, James (*b.* 1946) *Lab., Ipswich*, maj. 265
*Carlile, Alexander C., QC (*b.* 1948) *LD, Montgomery*, maj. 5,209
*Carlisle, John R. (*b.* 1942) *C., Luton North*, maj. 13,094
*Carlisle, Kenneth M. (*b.* 1941) *C., Lincoln*, maj. 2,049
*Carrington, Matthew H. M. (*b.* 1947) *C., Fulham*, maj. 6,579
*Carttiss, Michael R. H. (*b.* 1938) *C., Great Yarmouth*, maj. 5,309
*Cash, William N. P. (*b.* 1940) *C., Stafford*, maj. 10,900
*Channon, Rt. Hon. H. Paul G. (*b.* 1935) *C., Southend West*, maj. 11,902
Chaplin, Mrs Judith (*b.* 1939) *C., Newbury*, maj. 12,357
*Chapman, Sydney B. (*b.* 1935) *C., Chipping Barnet*, maj. 13,951
Chisholm, Malcolm (*b.* 1949) *Lab., Edinburgh, Leith*, maj. 4,985
*Churchill, Winston S. (*b.* 1940) *C., Davyhulme*, maj. 4,426
Clapham, Michael (*b.* 1943) *Lab., Barnsley West and Penistone*, maj. 14,504
Clappison, W. James (*b.* 1956) *C., Hertsmere*, maj. 18,735
*Clark, David G., PH.D. (*b.* 1939) *Lab., South Shields*, maj. 13,477
*Clark, Dr Michael (*b.* 1935) *C., Rochford*, maj. 26,036
Clarke, Eric L. (*b.* 1933) *Lab., Midlothian*, maj. 10,334
*Clarke, Rt. Hon. Kenneth H., QC (*b.* 1940) *C., Rushcliffe*, maj. 19,766
*Clarke, Thomas, CBE (*b.* 1941) *Lab., Monklands West*, maj. 17,065
*Clelland, David G. (*b.* 1943) *Lab., Tyne Bridge*, maj. 15,210
Clifton-Brown, Geoffrey R. (*b.* 1953) *C., Cirencester and Tewkesbury*, maj. 16,058
*Clwyd, Ms Ann (*b.* 1937) *Lab., Cynon Valley*, maj. 21,364
Coe, Sebastian N., OBE (*b.* 1956) *C., Falmouth and Camborne*, maj. 3,267
Coffey, Ms M. Ann (*b.* 1946) *Lab., Stockport*, maj. 1,422
*Cohen, Harry (*b.* 1949) *Lab., Leyton*, maj. 11,484
*Colvin, Michael K. B. (*b.* 1932) *C., Romsey and Waterside*, maj. 15,304
Congdon, David L. (*b.* 1949) *C., Croydon North East*, maj. 7,473
Connarty, Michael (*b.* 1949) *Lab., Falkirk East*, maj. 7,969
*Conway, Derek L. (*b.* 1953) *C., Shrewsbury and Atcham*, maj. 10,965
*Cook, Francis (*b.* 1935) *Lab., Stockton North*, maj. 10,474
*Cook, R. F. (Robin) (*b.* 1946) *Lab., Livingston*, maj. 8,105
*Coombs, Anthony M. V. (*b.* 1952) *C., Wyre Forest*, maj. 10,341
*Coombs, Simon C. (*b.* 1947) *C., Swindon*, maj. 2,826
*Cope, Rt. Hon. Sir John (*b.* 1937) *C., Northavon*, maj. 11,861
*Corbett, Robin (*b.* 1933) *Lab., Birmingham, Erdington*, maj. 4,735
*Corbyn, Jeremy B. (*b.* 1949) *Lab., Islington North*, maj. 12,784
*Cormack, Patrick T. (*b.* 1939) *C., Staffordshire South*, maj. 22,633
Corston, Ms Jean (*b.* 1942) *Lab., Bristol East*, maj. 2,692
*Couchman, James R. (*b.* 1942) *C., Gillingham*, maj. 16,638
*Cousins, James M. (*b.* 1944) *Lab., Newcastle upon Tyne Central*, maj. 5,288
*Cox, Thomas M. (*b.* 1930) *Lab., Tooting*, maj. 4,107
*Cran, James D. (*b.* 1944) *C., Beverley*, maj. 16,517
*Critchley, Julian M. G. (*b.* 1930) *C., Aldershot*, maj. 19,188
*Cryer, G. Robert (*b.* 1934) *Lab., Bradford South*, maj. 4,902
*Cummings, John S. (*b.* 1943) *Lab., Easington*, maj. 26,390
*Cunliffe, Lawrence F. (*b.* 1929) *Lab., Leigh*, maj. 18,827
Cunningham, James (*b.* 1941) *Lab., Coventry South East*, maj. 1,311
*Cunningham, Dr John A. (*b.* 1939) *Lab., Copeland*, maj. 2,439
*Currie, Mrs Edwina (*b.* 1946) *C., Derbyshire South*, maj. 4,658
*Curry, David M. (*b.* 1944) *C., Skipton and Ripon*, maj. 19,330
Dafis, Cynog G. (*b.* 1938) *PC, Ceredigion and Pembroke North*, maj. 3,193
*Dalyell, Tam (Sir Thomas Dalyell of the Binns, Bt.) (*b.* 1932) *Lab., Linlithgow*, maj. 7,026
*Darling, Alistair M. (*b.* 1953) *Lab., Edinburgh Central*, maj. 2,126
Davidson, Ian (*b.* 1950) *Lab., Glasgow, Govan*, maj. 4,125
Davies, Bryan (*b.* 1939) *Lab., Oldham Central and Royton*, maj. 8,606
*Davies, Rt. Hon. D. J. Denzil (*b.* 1938) *Lab., Llanelli*, maj. 19,270
*Davies, J. Quentin (*b.* 1944) *C., Stamford and Spalding*, maj. 22,869
*Davies, Ronald (*b.* 1946) *Lab., Caerphilly*, maj. 22,672
*Davis, David M. (*b.* 1948) *C., Boothferry*, maj. 17,535
*Davis, Terence A. G. (*b.* 1938) *Lab., Birmingham, Hodge Hill*, maj. 7,068
*Day, Stephen R. (*b.* 1948) *C., Cheadle*, maj. 15,778
Denham, John V. (*b.* 1953) *Lab., Southampton, Itchen*, maj. 551
Deva, Niranjan J. A. (*b.* 1948) *C., Brentford and Isleworth*, maj. 2,086
*Devlin, Timothy R. (*b.* 1959) *C., Stockton South*, maj. 3,369
*Dewar, Donald C. (*b.* 1937) *Lab., Glasgow, Garscadden*, maj. 13,340
*Dickens, Geoffrey K. (*b.* 1931) *C., Littleborough and Saddleworth*, maj. 4,494
*Dicks, Terence P. (*b.* 1937) *C., Hayes and Harlington*, maj. 53
*Dixon, Donald (*b.* 1929) *Lab., Jarrow*, maj. 17,907
*Dobson, Frank G. (*b.* 1940) *Lab., Holborn and St Pancras*, maj. 10,824
Donohoe, Brian H. (*b.* 1948) *Lab., Cunninghame South*, maj. 10,680
*Dorrell, Stephen J. (*b.* 1952) *C., Loughborough*, maj. 10,883
*Douglas-Hamilton, Lord James (*b.* 1942) *C., Edinburgh West*, maj. 879
*Dover, Densmore (*b.* 1938) *C., Chorley*, maj. 4,246
Dowd, James P. (*b.* 1951) *Lab., Lewisham West*, maj. 1,809
Duncan, Alan J. C. (*b.* 1957) *C., Rutland and Melton*, maj. 25,535
Duncan-Smith, G. Iain (*b.* 1954) *C., Chingford*, maj. 14,938
*Dunn, Robert J. (*b.* 1946) *C., Dartford*, maj. 10,314

*Dunnachie, James F. (*b.* 1930) *Lab., Glasgow, Pollok*, maj. 7,883
*Dunwoody, Hon. Mrs Gwyneth P. (*b.* 1930) *Lab., Crewe and Nantwich*, maj. 2,695
*Durant, Sir Anthony (*b.* 1928) *C., Reading West*, maj. 13,298
*Dykes, Hugh J. (*b.* 1939) *C., Harrow East*, maj. 11,098
Eagle, Ms Angela (*b.* 1961) *Lab., Wallasey*, maj. 3,809
*Eastham, Kenneth (*b.* 1927) *Lab., Manchester, Blackley*, maj. 12,389
*Eggar, Timothy J. C. (*b.* 1951) *C., Enfield North*, maj. 9,430
Elletson, Harold D. H. (*b.* 1960) *C., Blackpool North*, maj. 3,040
*Emery, Sir Peter (*b.* 1926) *C., Honiton*, maj. 16,511
*Enright, Derek A. (*b.* 1935) *Lab., Hemsworth*, maj. 22,075
Etherington, William (*b.* 1941) *Lab., Sunderland North*, maj. 17,004
*Evans, David J. (*b.* 1935) *C., Welwyn Hatfield*, maj. 8,465
*Evans, John (*b.* 1930) *Lab., St Helens North*, maj. 16,244
Evans, Jonathan P. (*b.* 1950) *C., Brecon and Radnor*, maj. 130
Evans, Nigel M. (*b.* 1957) *C., Ribble Valley*, maj. 6,542
Evans, Roger (*b.* 1947) *C., Monmouth*, maj. 3,204
*Evennett, David A. (*b.* 1939) *C., Erith and Crayford*, maj. 2,339
*Ewing, Mrs Margaret A. (*b.* 1945) *SNP, Moray*, maj. 2,844
Faber, David J. C. (*b.* 1961) *C., Westbury*, maj. 12,606
Fabricant, Michael L. D. (*b.* 1950) *C., Staffordshire Mid*, maj. 6,236
*Fairbairn, Sir Nicholas, QC (*b.* 1933) *C., Perth and Kinross*, maj. 2,094
*Fatchett, Derek J. (*b.* 1945) *Lab., Leeds Central*, maj. 15,020
*Faulds, Andrew M. W. (*b.* 1923) *Lab., Warley East*, maj. 7,794
*Fenner, Dame Peggy, DBE (*b.* 1922) *C., Medway*, maj. 8,786
*Field, Barry J. A., TD (*b.* 1946) *C., Isle of Wight*, maj. 1,827
*Field, Frank (*b.* 1942) *Lab., Birkenhead*, maj. 17,613
*Fishburn, J. Dudley (*b.* 1946) *C., Kensington*, maj. 3,548
*Fisher, Mark (*b.* 1944) *Lab., Stoke-on-Trent Central*, maj. 13,420
*Flynn, Paul P. (*b.* 1935) *Lab., Newport West*, maj. 7,779
*Fookes, Dame Janet, DBE (*b.* 1936) *C., Plymouth, Drake*, maj. 2,013
*Forman, F. Nigel (*b.* 1943) *C., Carshalton and Wallington*, maj. 9,943
*Forsyth, Michael B. (*b.* 1954) *C., Stirling*, maj. 703
*Forsythe, Clifford (*b.* 1929) *UUP, Antrim South*, maj. 24,559
*Forth, Eric (*b.* 1944) *C., Worcestershire Mid*, maj. 9,870
*Foster, Derek (*b.* 1937) *Lab., Bishop Auckland*, maj. 10,087
Foster, Donald M. E. (*b.* 1937) *LD, Bath*, maj. 3,768
*Foulkes, George (*b.* 1942) *Lab., Carrick, Cumnock and Doon Valley*, maj. 16,626
*Fowler, Rt. Hon. Sir Norman (*b.* 1938) *C., Sutton Coldfield*, maj. 26,036
Fox, Dr Liam (*b.* 1961) *C., Woodspring*, maj. 17,509
*Fox, Sir Marcus, MBE (*b.* 1927) *C., Shipley*, maj. 12,382
*Fraser, John D. (*b.* 1934) *Lab., Norwood*, maj. 7,216
*Freeman, Roger N. (*b.* 1942) *C., Kettering*, maj. 11,154
*French, Douglas C. (*b.* 1944) *C., Gloucester*, maj. 6,058
*Fry, Peter D. (*b.* 1931) *C., Wellingborough*, maj. 11,816
*Fyfe, Mrs Maria (*b.* 1938) *Lab., Glasgow, Maryhill*, maj. 13,419
*Galbraith, Samuel L. (*b.* 1945) *Lab., Strathkelvin and Bearsden*, maj. 3,162
*Gale, Roger J. (*b.* 1943) *C., Thanet North*, maj. 18,210
Gallie, Philip (*b.* 1939) *C., Ayr*, maj. 85
*Galloway, George (*b.* 1954) *Lab., Glasgow, Hillhead*, maj. 4,826
Gapes, Michael J. (*b.* 1952) *Lab., Ilford South*, maj. 402
*Gardiner, Sir George (*b.* 1935) *C., Reigate*, maj. 17,664
*Garel-Jones, W. A. T. Tristan (*b.* 1941) *C., Watford*, maj. 9,590
Garnier, Edward (*b.* 1952) *C., Harborough*, maj. 13,543
*Garrett, John L. (*b.* 1931) *Lab., Norwich South*, maj. 6,181
*George, Bruce T. (*b.* 1942) *Lab., Walsall South*, maj. 3,178
Gerrard, Neil F. (*b.* 1942) *Lab., Walthamstow*, maj. 3,022
*Gilbert, Rt. Hon. Dr John W. (*b.* 1927) *Lab., Dudley East*, maj. 9,200
*Gill, Christopher J. F., RD (*b.* 1936) *C., Ludlow*, maj. 14,152
Gillan, Ms Cheryl E. K. (*b.* 1952) *C., Chesham and Amersham*, maj. 22,220
*Godman, Norman A., Ph.D. (*b.* 1938) *Lab., Greenock and Port Glasgow*, maj. 14,979
Godsiff, Roger D. (*b.* 1946) *Lab., Birmingham, Small Heath*, maj. 13,989
*Golding, Mrs Llinos (*b.* 1933) *Lab., Newcastle under Lyme*, maj. 9,839
*Goodlad, Alistair R. (*b.* 1943) *C., Eddisbury*, maj. 12,697
*Goodson-Wickes, Dr Charles (*b.* 1945) *C., Wimbledon*, maj. 14,761
*Gordon, Mrs Mildred (*b.* 1923) *Lab., Bow and Poplar*, maj. 8,404
*Gorman, Mrs Teresa E. (*b.* 1931) *C., Billericay*, maj. 22,494
*Gorst, John M. (*b.* 1928) *C., Hendon North*, maj. 7,122
*Gould, Bryan C. (*b.* 1939) *Lab., Dagenham*, maj. 6,733
*Graham, Thomas (*b.* 1944) *Lab., Renfrew West and Inverclyde*, maj. 1,744
*Grant, Sir Anthony (*b.* 1925) *C., Cambridgeshire South West*, maj. 19,637
*Grant, Bernard A. M. (*b.* 1944) *Lab., Tottenham*, maj. 11,968
*Greenway, Harry (*b.* 1934) *C., Ealing North*, maj. 5,966
*Greenway, John R. (*b.* 1946) *C., Ryedale*, maj. 18,439
*Griffiths, Nigel (*b.* 1955) *Lab., Edinburgh South*, maj. 4,176
*Griffiths, Peter H. S. (*b.* 1928) *C., Portsmouth North*, maj. 13,881
*Griffiths, Winston J. (*b.* 1943) *Lab., Bridgend*, maj. 7,326
*Grocott, Bruce J. (*b.* 1940) *Lab., The Wrekin*, maj. 6,648
*Grylls, Sir Michael (*b.* 1934) *C., Surrey North West*, maj. 28,394
*Gummer, Rt. Hon. John S. (*b.* 1939) *C., Suffolk Coastal*, maj. 19,285
Gunnell, W. John (*b.* 1933) *Lab., Leeds South and Morley*, maj. 7,372
*Hague, William J. (*b.* 1961) *C., Richmond (Yorks)* maj. 23,504
*Hain, Peter G. (*b.* 1950) *Lab., Neath*, maj. 23,975
Hall, Michael T. (*b.* 1952) *Lab., Warrington South*, maj. 191
*Hamilton, Rt. Hon. Archibald G. (*b.* 1941) *C., Epsom and Ewell*, maj. 20,021
*Hamilton, M. Neil (*b.* 1949) *C., Tatton*, maj. 15,860
*Hampson, Dr Keith (*b.* 1943) *C., Leeds North West*, maj. 7,671
*Hanley, Jeremy J. (*b.* 1945) *C., Richmond and Barnes*, maj. 3,869
*Hannam, Sir John (*b.* 1929) *C., Exeter*, maj. 4,045
Hanson, David G. (*b.* 1957) *Lab., Delyn*, maj. 2,039
*Hardy, Peter (*b.* 1931) *Lab., Wentworth*, maj. 22,449
*Hargreaves, Andrew R. (*b.* 1955) *C., Birmingham, Hall Green*, maj. 3,665
*Harman, Ms Harriet (*b.* 1950) *Lab., Peckham*, maj. 12,005
*Harris, David A. (*b.* 1937) *C., St Ives*, maj. 1,645
Harvey, Nicholas B. (*b.* 1961) *LD, Devon North*, maj. 794
*Haselhurst, Alan G. B. (*b.* 1937) *C., Saffron Walden*, maj. 17,424
*Hattersley, Rt. Hon. Roy S. G. (*b.* 1932) *Lab., Birmingham, Sparkbrook*, maj. 13,572
Hawkins, Nicholas J. (*b.* 1957) *C., Blackpool South*, maj. 1,667
Hawksley, P. Warren (*b.* 1943) *C., Halesowen and Stourbridge*, maj. 9,582

*Hayes, Jeremy J. J. (*b.* 1953) *C., Harlow*, maj. 2,940
Heald, Oliver (*b.* 1954) *C., Hertfordshire North*, maj. 16,531
*Heath, Rt. Hon. Sir Edward, KG, MBE (*b.* 1916) *C., Old Bexley and Sidcup*, maj. 15,699
*Heathcoat-Amory, David P. (*b.* 1949) *C., Wells*, maj. 6,649
*Henderson, Douglas J. (*b.* 1949) *Lab., Newcastle upon Tyne North*, maj. 8,946
Hendron, Dr Joseph G. (*b.* 1932) *SDLP, Belfast West*, maj. 589
Hendry, Charles (*b.* 1959) *C., High Peak*, maj. 4,819
Heppell, John B. (*b.* 1948) *Lab., Nottingham East*, maj. 7,680
*Heseltine, Rt. Hon. Michael R. D. (*b.* 1933) *C., Henley*, maj. 18,392
*Hicks, Robert (*b.* 1938) *C., Cornwall South East*, maj. 7,704
*Higgins, Rt. Hon. Terence L. (*b.* 1928) *C., Worthing*, maj. 16,533
*Hill, S. James A. (*b.* 1926) *C., Southampton, Test*, maj. 585
Hill, T. Keith (*b.* 1943) *Lab., Streatham*, maj. 2,317
*Hinchliffe, David M. (*b.* 1948) *Lab., Wakefield*, maj. 6,590
*Hoey, Ms Catharine (Kate) L. (*b.* 1946) *Lab., Vauxhall*, maj. 10,488
*Hogg, Rt. Hon. Douglas M., QC (*b.* 1945) *C., Grantham*, maj. 19,588
*Hogg, Norman (*b.* 1938) *Lab., Cumbernauld and Kilsyth*, maj. 9,215
*Home Robertson, John D. (*b.* 1948) *Lab., East Lothian*, maj. 10,036
*Hood, James (*b.* 1948) *Lab., Clydesdale*, maj. 10,187
Hoon, Geoffrey W. (*b.* 1953) *Lab., Ashfield*, maj. 12,987
Horam, John R. (*b.* 1939) *C., Orpington*, maj. 12,935
*Hordern, Sir Peter (*b.* 1929) *C., Horsham*, maj. 25,072
*Howard, Rt. Hon. Michael, QC (*b.* 1941) *C., Folkestone and Hythe*, maj. 8,910
*Howarth, Alan T., CBE (*b.* 1944) *C., Stratford-upon-Avon*, maj. 22,892
*Howarth, George E. (*b.* 1949) *Lab., Knowsley North*, maj. 22,403
*Howell, Rt. Hon. David A. R. (*b.* 1936) *C., Guildford*, maj. 13,404
*Howell, Ralph F. (*b.* 1923) *C., Norfolk North*, maj. 12,545
*Howells, Kim S., Ph.D. (*b.* 1946) *Lab., Pontypridd*, maj. 19,797
*Hoyle, E. Douglas H. (*b.* 1930) *Lab., Warrington North*, maj. 12,622
Hughes, Kevin M. (*b.* 1952) *Lab., Doncaster North*, maj. 19,813
*Hughes, Robert (*b.* 1932) *Lab., Aberdeen North*, maj. 9,237
*Hughes, Robert G. (*b.* 1951) *C., Harrow West*, maj. 17,897
*Hughes, Royston J. (*b.* 1925) *Lab., Newport East*, maj. 9,899
*Hughes, Simon H. W. (*b.* 1951) *LD, Southwark and Bermondsey*, maj. 9,845
*Hume, John (*b.* 1937) *SDLP, Foyle*, maj. 13,005
*Hunt, Rt. Hon. David J. F., MBE (*b.* 1942) *C., Wirral West*, maj. 11,064
*Hunt, Sir John (*b.* 1929) *C., Ravensbourne*, maj. 19,714
*Hunter, Andrew R. F. (*b.* 1943) *C., Basingstoke*, maj. 21,198
*Hurd, Rt. Hon. Douglas R., CBE (*b.* 1930) *C., Witney*, maj. 22,568
Hutton, John M. P. (*b.* 1955) *Lab., Barrow and Furness*, maj. 3,578
*Illsley, Eric E. (*b.* 1955) *Lab., Barnsley Central*, maj. 19,361
*Ingram, Adam P. (*b.* 1947) *Lab., East Kilbride*, maj. 11,992
*Jack, J. Michael (*b.* 1946) *C., Fylde*, maj. 20,991
Jackson, Ms Glenda, CBE (*b.* 1936) *Lab., Hampstead and Highgate*, maj. 1,440
Jackson, Mrs Helen (*b.* 1939) *Lab., Sheffield, Hillsborough*, maj. 7,068
*Jackson, Robert V. (*b.* 1946) *C., Wantage*, maj. 16,473
Jamieson, David C. (*b.* 1947) *Lab., Plymouth, Devonport*, maj. 7,412
*Janner, Hon. Greville E., QC (*b.* 1928) *Lab., Leicester West*, maj. 3,978
Jenkin, Hon. Bernard (*b.* 1959) *C., Colchester North*, maj. 16,492
*Jessel, Toby F. H. (*b.* 1934) *C., Twickenham*, maj. 5,711
*Johnson Smith, Sir Geoffrey (*b.* 1924) *C., Wealden*, maj. 20,931
*Johnston, Sir Russell (*b.* 1932) *LD, Inverness, Nairn and Lochaber*, maj. 458
*Jones, Gwilym H. (*b.* 1947) *C., Cardiff North*, maj. 2,969
*Jones, Ieuan W. (*b.* 1949) *PC, Ynys Môn*, maj. 1,106
Jones, Jon O. (*b.* 1954) *Lab., Cardiff Central*, maj. 3,465
Jones, Ms Lynne M., Ph.D. (*b.* 1951) *Lab., Birmingham, Selly Oak*, maj. 2,060
*Jones, Martyn D. (*b.* 1947) *Lab., Clwyd South West*, maj. 4,941
Jones, Nigel D. (*b.* 1948) *LD, Cheltenham*, maj. 1,668
*Jones, Robert B. (*b.* 1950) *C., Hertfordshire West*, maj. 13,940
*Jones, S. Barry (*b.* 1938) *Lab., Alyn and Deeside*, maj. 7,851
*Jopling, Rt. Hon. T. Michael (*b.* 1930) *C., Westmorland and Lonsdale*, maj. 16,436
Jowell, Ms Tessa (*b.* 1947) *Lab., Dulwich*, maj. 2,056
*Kaufman, Rt. Hon. Gerald B. (*b.* 1930) *Lab., Manchester, Gorton*, maj. 16,279
Keen, Alan (*b.* 1937) *Lab., Feltham and Heston*, maj. 1,995
*Kellett-Bowman, Dame Elaine, DBE (*b.* 1924) *C., Lancaster*, maj. 2,953
*Kennedy, Charles P. (*b.* 1959) *LD, Ross, Cromarty and Skye*, maj. 7,630
Kennedy, Mrs Jane (*b.* 1958) *Lab., Liverpool, Broadgreen*, maj. 7,027
*Key, S. Robert (*b.* 1945) *C., Salisbury*, maj. 8,973
Khabra, Piara C. (*b.* 1924) *Lab., Ealing, Southall*, maj. 6,866
*Kilfedder, Sir James (*b.* 1928) *UPUP, Down North*, maj. 4,934
*Kilfoyle, Peter (*b.* 1946) *Lab., Liverpool, Walton*, maj. 28,299
*King, Rt. Hon. Thomas J., CH (*b.* 1933) *C., Bridgwater*, maj. 9,716
*Kinnock, Rt. Hon. Neil G. (*b.* 1942) *Lab., Islwyn*, maj. 24,728
*Kirkhope, Timothy J. R. (*b.* 1945) *C., Leeds North East*, maj. 4,244
*Kirkwood, Archibald J. (*b.* 1946) *LD, Roxburgh and Berwickshire*, maj. 4,257
*Knapman, Roger M. (*b.* 1944) *C., Stroud*, maj. 13,405
Knight, Mrs Angela A. (*b.* 1950) *C., Erewash*, maj. 5,703
*Knight, Gregory (*b.* 1949) *C., Derby North*, maj. 4,453
*Knight, Dame Jill, DBE (*b.* 1923) *C., Birmingham, Edgbaston*, maj. 4,307
*Knox, David L. (*b.* 1933) *C., Staffordshire Moorlands*, maj. 7,410
Kynoch, George A. B. (*b.* 1946) *C., Kincardine and Deeside*, maj. 4,495
Lait, Ms Jacqui (*b.* 1947) *C., Hastings and Rye*, maj. 6,634
*Lamont, Rt. Hon. Norman S. H. (*b.* 1942) *C., Kingston upon Thames*, maj. 10,153
*Lang, Rt. Hon. Ian B. (*b.* 1940) *C., Galloway and Upper Nithsdale*, maj. 2,468
*Lawrence, Sir Ivan, QC (*b.* 1936) *C., Burton*, maj. 5,996
Legg, Barry (*b.* 1949) *C., Milton Keynes South West*, maj. 4,687
*Leigh, Edward J. E. (*b.* 1950) *C., Gainsborough and Horncastle*, maj. 16,245
*Leighton, Ronald (*b.* 1930) *Lab., Newham North East*, maj. 9,986

*Lennox-Boyd, Hon. Mark A. (*b.* 1943) *C., Morecambe and Lunesdale*, maj. 11,509
*Lester, James T. (*b.* 1932) *C., Broxtowe*, maj. 9,891
*Lestor, Miss Joan (*b.* 1931) *Lab., Eccles*, maj. 13,226
*Lewis, Terence (*b.* 1935) *Lab., Worsley*, maj. 10,012
Lidington, David R., Ph.D. (*b.* 1956) *C., Aylesbury*, maj. 18,860
*Lightbown, David L. (*b.* 1932) *C., Staffordshire South East*, maj. 7,192
*Lilley, Rt. Hon. Peter B. (*b.* 1943) *C., St Albans*, maj. 16,404
*Litherland, Robert K. (*b.* 1930) *Lab., Manchester Central*, maj. 18,037
*Livingstone, Ken (*b.* 1945) *Lab., Brent East*, maj. 5,971
*Lloyd, Anthony J. (*b.* 1950) *Lab., Stretford*, maj. 11,137
*Lloyd, Peter R. C. (*b.* 1937) *C., Fareham*, maj. 24,141
Llwyd, Elfyn (*b.* 1951) *PC, Meirionnydd Nant Conwy*, maj. 4,613
*Lofthouse, Geoffrey (*b.* 1925) *Lab., Pontefract and Castleford*, maj. 23,495
*Lord, Michael N. (*b.* 1938) *C., Suffolk Central*, maj. 16,031
*Loyden, Edward (*b.* 1923) *Lab., Liverpool, Garston*, maj. 12,279
Luff, Peter J. (*b.* 1955) *C., Worcester*, maj. 6,152
*Lyell, Rt. Hon. Sir Nicholas, QC (*b.* 1938) *C., Bedfordshire Mid*, maj. 25,138
Lynne, Ms Elizabeth (*b.* 1948) *LD, Rochdale*, maj. 1,839
*McAllion, John (*b.* 1948) *Lab., Dundee East*, maj. 4,564
*McAvoy, Thomas M. (*b.* 1943) *Lab., Glasgow, Rutherglen*, maj. 15,270
*McCartney, Ian (*b.* 1951) *Lab., Makerfield*, maj. 18,118
*McCrea, Revd Dr R. T. William (*b.* 1948) *DUP, Ulster Mid*, maj. 6,187
*MacDonald, Calum A. (*b.* 1956) *Lab., Western Isles*, maj. 1,703
*McFall, John (*b.* 1944) *Lab., Dumbarton*, maj. 6,129
*McGrady, Edward K. (*b.* 1935) *SDLP, Down South*, maj. 6,342
*MacGregor, Rt. Hon. John R. R., OBE (*b.* 1937) *C., Norfolk South*, maj. 17,565
*Mackay, Andrew J. (*b.* 1949) *C., Berkshire East*, maj. 28,680
*McKelvey, William (*b.* 1934) *Lab., Kilmarnock and Loudoun*, maj. 6,979
MacKinlay, Andrew S. (*b.* 1949) *Lab., Thurrock*, maj. 1,172
*Maclean, David J. (*b.* 1953) *C., Penrith and the Border*, maj. 18,449
*McLeish, Henry B. (*b.* 1948) *Lab., Fife Central*, maj. 10,578
*Maclennan, Robert A. R. (*b.* 1936) *LD, Caithness and Sutherland*, maj. 5,365
*McLoughlin, Patrick A. (*b.* 1957) *C., Derbyshire West*, maj. 18,769
*McMaster, Gordon J. (*b.* 1960) *Lab., Paisley South*, maj. 9,549
*McNair-Wilson, Sir Patrick (*b.* 1929) *C., New Forest*, maj. 20,405
*McNamara, J. Kevin (*b.* 1934) *Lab., Hull North*, maj. 15,384
*McWilliam, John D. (*b.* 1941) *Lab., Blaydon*, maj. 13,343
*Madden, Maxwell F. (*b.* 1941) *Lab., Bradford West*, maj. 9,502
*Madel, W. David (*b.* 1938) *C., Bedfordshire South West*, maj. 21,273
*Maginnis, Kenneth (*b.* 1938) *UUP, Fermanagh and South Tyrone*, maj. 14,113
*Mahon, Ms Alice (*b.* 1937) *Lab., Halifax*, maj. 478
Maitland, Lady Olga (*b.* 1944) *C., Sutton and Cheam*, maj. 10,756
*Major, Rt. Hon. John (*b.* 1943) *C., Huntingdon*, maj. 36,230
*Mallon, Seamus (*b.* 1936) *SDLP, Newry and Armagh*, maj. 7,091
Malone, P. Gerald (*b.* 1950) *C., Winchester*, maj. 8,121
Mandelson, Peter B. (*b.* 1953) *Lab., Hartlepool*, maj. 8,782
*Mans, Keith D. R. (*b.* 1946) *C., Wyre*, maj. 11,664
*Marek, John, Ph.D. (*b.* 1940) *Lab., Wrexham*, maj. 6,716
*Marland, Paul (*b.* 1940) *C., Gloucestershire West*, maj. 4,958
*Marlow, Antony R. (*b.* 1940) *C., Northampton North*, maj. 3,908
*Marshall, David (*b.* 1941) *Lab., Glasgow, Shettleston*, maj. 14,834
*Marshall, James (*b.* 1941) *Lab., Leicester South*, maj. 9,440
*Marshall, John L. (*b.* 1940) *C., Hendon South*, maj. 12,047
*Marshall, Sir Michael (*b.* 1930) *C., Arundel*, maj. 19,863
*Martin, David J. P. (*b.* 1945) *C., Portsmouth South*, maj. 242
*Martin, Michael J. (*b.* 1945) *Lab., Glasgow, Springburn*, maj. 14,506
*Martlew, Eric A. (*b.* 1949) *Lab., Carlisle*, maj. 3,108
*Mates, Michael J. (*b.* 1934) *C., Hampshire East*, maj. 29,165
*Mawhinney, Brian S., Ph.D. (*b.* 1940) *C., Peterborough*, maj. 5,376
*Maxton, John A. (*b.* 1936) *Lab., Glasgow, Cathcart*, maj. 8,001
*Mayhew, Rt. Hon. Sir Patrick, QC (*b.* 1929) *C., Tunbridge Wells*, maj. 17,132
*Meacher, Michael H. (*b.* 1939) *Lab., Oldham West*, maj. 8,333
*Meale, J. Alan (*b.* 1949) *Lab., Mansfield*, maj. 11,724
*Mellor, Rt. Hon. David J., QC (*b.* 1949) *C., Putney*, maj. 7,526
Merchant, Piers R. G. (*b.* 1951) *C., Beckenham*, maj. 15,285
*Michael, Alun E. (*b.* 1943) *Lab., Cardiff South and Penarth*, maj. 10,425
*Michie, Mrs J. Ray (*b.* 1934) *LD, Argyll and Bute*, maj. 2,622
*Michie, William (*b.* 1935) *Lab., Sheffield, Heeley*, maj. 14,954
Milburn, Alan (*b.* 1958) *Lab., Darlington*, maj. 2,798
Miller, Andrew (*b.* 1949) *Lab., Ellesmere Port and Neston*, maj. 1,989
Milligan, Stephen (*b.* 1948) *C., Eastleigh*, maj. 17,702
*Mills, Iain C. (*b.* 1940) *C., Meriden*, maj. 14,699
*Mitchell, Andrew J. B. (*b.* 1956) *C., Gedling*, maj. 10,637
*Mitchell, Austin V. (*b.* 1934) *Lab., Great Grimsby*, maj. 7,504
*Mitchell, Sir David (*b.* 1928) *C., Hampshire North West*, maj. 17,848
*Moate, Roger D. (*b.* 1938) *C., Faversham*, maj. 16,351
*Molyneaux, Rt. Hon. James H. (*b.* 1920) *UUP, Lagan Valley*, maj. 23,565
*Monro, Sir Hector, AE (*b.* 1922) *C., Dumfries*, maj. 6,415
*Montgomery, Sir Fergus (*b.* 1927) *C., Altrincham and Sale*, maj. 16,791
*Moonie, Dr Lewis G. (*b.* 1947) *Lab., Kirkcaldy*, maj. 9,126
*Morgan, H. Rhodri (*b.* 1939) *Lab., Cardiff West*, maj. 9,291
*Morley, Elliot A. (*b.* 1952) *Lab., Glanford and Scunthorpe*, maj. 8,412
*Morris, Rt. Hon. Alfred (*b.* 1928) *Lab., Manchester, Wythenshawe*, maj. 11,996
Morris, Ms Estelle (*b.* 1952) *Lab., Birmingham, Yardley*, maj. 162
*Morris, Rt. Hon. John, QC (*b.* 1931) *Lab., Aberavon*, maj. 21,310
*Morris, Michael W. L. (*b.* 1936) *C., Northampton South*, maj. 16,973
*Moss, Malcolm D. (*b.* 1943) *C., Cambridgeshire North East*, maj. 15,093
*Mowlam, Dr Marjorie (*b.* 1949) *Lab., Redcar*, maj. 11,577
Mudie, George (*b.* 1945) *Lab., Leeds East*, maj. 12,697
*Mullin, Christopher J. (*b.* 1947) *Lab., Sunderland South*, maj. 14,501
*Murphy, Paul P. (*b.* 1948) *Lab., Torfaen*, maj. 20,754
*Needham, Richard F. (The Earl of Kilmorey) (*b.* 1942) *C., Wiltshire North*, maj. 16,388
*Nelson, R. Anthony (*b.* 1948) *C., Chichester*, maj. 20,887

*Neubert, Sir Michael (*b.* 1933) *C.*, *Romford*, maj. 11,420
*Newton, Rt. Hon. Antony H., OBE (*b.* 1937) *C.*, *Braintree*, maj. 17,494
*Nicholls, Patrick C. M. (*b.* 1948) *C.*, *Teignbridge*, maj. 8,856
*Nicholson, David J. (*b.* 1944) *C.*, *Taunton*, maj. 3,336
*Nicholson, Miss Emma H. (*b.* 1941) *C.*, *Devon West and Torridge*, maj. 3,614
*Norris, Steven J. (*b.* 1945) *C.*, *Epping Forest*, maj. 20,188
*Oakes, Rt. Hon. Gordon J. (*b.* 1931) *Lab.*, *Halton*, maj. 18,204
O'Brien, Michael (*b.* 1954) *Lab.*, *Warwickshire North*, maj. 1,454
*O'Brien, William (*b.* 1929) *Lab.*, *Normanton*, maj. 8,950
*O'Hara, Edward (*b.* 1937) *Lab.*, *Knowsley South*, maj. 22,011
Olner, William J. (*b.* 1942) *Lab.*, *Nuneaton*, maj. 1,631
*O'Neill, Martin J. (*b.* 1945) *Lab.*, *Clackmannan*, maj. 8,503
*Onslow, Rt. Hon. Cranley G. D. (*b.* 1926) *C.*, *Woking*, maj. 19,842
*Oppenheim, Hon. Phillip A. C. L. (*b.* 1956) *C.*, *Amber Valley*, maj. 712
*Orme, Rt. Hon. Stanley (*b.* 1923) *Lab.*, *Salford East*, maj. 11,235
Ottaway, Richard G. J. (*b.* 1945) *C.*, *Croydon South*, maj. 20,425
*Page, Richard L. (*b.* 1941) *C.*, *Hertfordshire South West*, maj. 20,107
*Paice, James E. T. (*b.* 1949) *C.*, *Cambridgeshire South East*, maj. 23,810
*Paisley, Revd Ian R. K. (*b.* 1926) *DUP*, *Antrim North*, maj. 14,936
*Parry, Robert (*b.* 1933) *Lab.*, *Liverpool, Riverside*, maj. 17,437
*Patchett, Terry (*b.* 1940) *Lab.*, *Barnsley East*, maj. 24,777
*Patnick, C. Irvine, OBE (*b.* 1929) *C.*, *Sheffield, Hallam*, maj. 6,741
*Patten, Rt. Hon. John H. C. (*b.* 1945) *C.*, *Oxford West and Abingdon*, maj. 3,539
*Pattie, Rt. Hon. Sir Geoffrey (*b.* 1936) *C.*, *Chertsey and Walton*, maj. 22,819
*Pawsey, James F. (*b.* 1933) *C.*, *Rugby and Kenilworth*, maj. 13,247
*Peacock, Mrs Elizabeth J. (*b.* 1937) *C.*, *Batley and Spen*, maj. 1,408
*Pendry, Thomas (*b.* 1934) *Lab.*, *Stalybridge and Hyde*, maj. 8,831
Pickles, Eric J. (*b.* 1952) *C.*, *Brentwood and Ongar*, maj. 15,145
Pickthall, Colin (*b.* 1944) *Lab.*, *Lancashire West*, maj. 2,077
*Pike, Peter L. (*b.* 1937) *Lab.*, *Burnley*, maj. 11,491
Pope, Gregory J. (*b.* 1960) *Lab.*, *Hyndburn*, maj. 1,960
*Porter, David J. (*b.* 1948) *C.*, *Waveney*, maj. 6,702
*Porter, G. B. (Barry) (*b.* 1939) *C.*, *Wirral South*, maj. 8,183
*Portillo, Rt. Hon. Michael D. X. (*b.* 1953) *C.*, *Enfield, Southgate*, maj. 15,563
*Powell, Raymond (*b.* 1928) *Lab.*, *Ogmore*, maj. 23,827
*Powell, William R. (*b.* 1948) *C.*, *Corby*, maj. 342
Prentice, Mrs Bridget (*b.* 1952) *Lab.*, *Lewisham East*, maj. 1,095
Prentice, Gordon (*b.* 1951) *Lab.*, *Pendle*, maj. 2,113
*Prescott, John L. (*b.* 1938) *Lab.*, *Hull East*, maj. 18,719
*Primarolo, Ms Dawn (*b.* 1954) *Lab.*, *Bristol South*, maj. 8,919
Purchase, Kenneth (*b.* 1939) *Lab.*, *Wolverhampton North East*, maj. 3,939
*Quin, Miss Joyce G. (*b.* 1944) *Lab.*, *Gateshead East*, maj. 18,530
*Radice, Giles H. (*b.* 1936) *Lab.*, *Durham North*, maj. 19,637
*Randall, Stuart J. (*b.* 1938) *Lab.*, *Hull West*, maj. 10,585
*Rathbone, J. R. (Tim) (*b.* 1933) *C.*, *Lewes*, maj. 12,175
Raynsford, W. R. N. (Nick) (*b.* 1945) *Lab.*, *Greenwich*, maj. 1,357
*Redmond, Martin (*b.* 1937) *Lab.*, *Don Valley*, maj. 13,534
*Redwood, John A. (*b.* 1951) *C.*, *Wokingham*, maj. 25,709
*Reid, Dr John (*b.* 1947) *Lab.*, *Motherwell North*, maj. 18,910
*Renton, Rt. Hon. R. Timothy (*b.* 1932) *C.*, *Sussex Mid*, maj. 20,528
Richards, Roderick (*b.* 1947) *C.*, *Clwyd North West*, maj. 6,050
*Richardson, Ms Josephine (*b.* 1923) *Lab.*, *Barking*, maj. 6,268
*Riddick, Graham E. G. (*b.* 1955) *C.*, *Colne Valley*, maj. 7,225
*Rifkind, Rt. Hon. Malcolm L., QC (*b.* 1946) *C.*, *Edinburgh, Pentlands*, maj. 4,290
Robathan, Andrew R. G. (*b.* 1951) *C.*, *Blaby*, maj. 25,347
*Roberts, Rt. Hon. Sir Wyn (*b.* 1930) *C.*, *Conwy*, maj. 995
*Robertson, George I. M. (*b.* 1946) *Lab.*, *Hamilton*, maj. 16,603
Robertson, Raymond S. (*b.* 1959) *C.*, *Aberdeen South*, maj. 1,517
*Robinson, Geoffrey (*b.* 1938) *Lab.*, *Coventry North West*, maj. 6,432
Robinson, Mark N. F. (*b.* 1946) *C.*, *Somerton and Frome*, maj. 4,341
*Robinson, Peter D. (*b.* 1948) *DUP*, *Belfast East*, maj. 7,787
Roche, Mrs Barbara M. R. (*b.* 1954) *Lab.*, *Hornsey and Wood Green*, maj. 5,177
*Roe, Mrs Marion A. (*b.* 1936) *C.*, *Broxbourne*, maj. 23,970
*Rogers, Allan R. (*b.* 1932) *Lab.*, *Rhondda*, maj. 28,816
*Rooker, Jeffrey W. (*b.* 1941) *Lab.*, *Birmingham, Perry Barr*, maj. 8,590
*Rooney, Terence H. (*b.* 1950) *Lab.*, *Bradford North*, maj. 7,664
*Ross, Ernest (*b.* 1942) *Lab.*, *Dundee West*, maj. 10,604
*Ross, William (*b.* 1936) *UUP*, *Londonderry East*, maj. 18,527
*Rowe, Andrew (*b.* 1935) *C.*, *Kent Mid*, maj. 19,649
*Rowlands, Edward (*b.* 1940) *Lab.*, *Merthyr Tydfil and Rhymney*, maj. 26,713
*Ruddock, Mrs Joan M. (*b.* 1943) *Lab.*, *Lewisham, Deptford*, maj. 12,238
*Rumbold, Rt. Hon. Dame Angela, DBE (*b.* 1932) *C.*, *Mitcham and Morden*, maj. 1,734
*Ryder, Rt. Hon. Richard A., OBE (*b.* 1949) *C.*, *Norfolk Mid*, maj. 18,948
*Sackville, Hon. Thomas G. (*b.* 1950) *C.*, *Bolton West*, maj. 1,079
*Sainsbury, Hon. Timothy A. D. (*b.* 1932) *C.*, *Hove*, maj. 12,268
*Salmond, Alexander E. A. (*b.* 1954) *SNP*, *Banff and Buchan*, maj. 4,108
*Scott, Rt. Hon. Nicholas P., MBE (*b.* 1933) *C.*, *Chelsea*, maj. 12,789
*Sedgemore, Brian C. J. (*b.* 1937) *Lab.*, *Hackney South and Shoreditch*, maj. 9,016
*Shaw, David L. (*b.* 1950) *C.*, *Dover*, maj. 833
*Shaw, Sir Giles (*b.* 1931) *C.*, *Pudsey*, maj. 8,972
*Sheerman, Barry J. (*b.* 1940) *Lab.*, *Huddersfield*, maj. 7,258
*Sheldon, Rt. Hon. Robert E. (*b.* 1923) *Lab.*, *Ashton-under-Lyne*, maj. 10,935
*Shephard, Rt. Hon. Mrs Gillian P. (*b.* 1940) *C.*, *Norfolk South West*, maj. 16,931
*Shepherd, Colin (*b.* 1938) *C.*, *Hereford*, maj. 3,413
*Shepherd, Richard C. S. (*b.* 1942) *C.*, *Aldridge-Brownhills*, maj. 11,024
*Shersby, J. Michael (*b.* 1933) *C.*, *Uxbridge*, maj. 13,179
*Shore, Rt. Hon. Peter D. (*b.* 1924) *Lab.*, *Bethnal Green and Stepney*, maj. 12,230
*Short, Ms Clare (*b.* 1946) *Lab.*, *Birmingham, Ladywood*, maj. 15,283

Simpson, Alan (*b.* 1948) *Lab., Nottingham South*, maj. 3,181
*Sims, Roger E. (*b.* 1930) *C., Chislehurst*, maj. 15,276
*Skeet, Sir Trevor (*b.* 1918) *C., Bedfordshire North*, maj. 11,618
*Skinner, Dennis E. (*b.* 1932) *Lab., Bolsover*, maj. 20,660
*Smith, Andrew D. (*b.* 1951) *Lab., Oxford East*, maj. 7,538
*Smith, Christopher R., Ph.D. (*b.* 1951) *Lab., Islington South and Finsbury*, maj. 10,652
*Smith, Sir Dudley (*b.* 1926) *C., Warwick and Leamington*, maj. 8,935
*Smith, Rt. Hon. John, QC (*b.* 1938) *Lab., Monklands East*, maj. 15,712
Smith, Llewellyn T. (*b.* 1944) *Lab., Blaenau Gwent*, maj. 30,067
*Smith, Timothy J. (*b.* 1947) *C., Beaconsfield*, maj. 23,597
*Smyth, Revd W. Martin (*b.* 1931) *UUP, Belfast South*, maj. 10,070
*Snape, Peter C. (*b.* 1942) *Lab., West Bromwich East*, maj. 2,813
*Soames, Hon. A. Nicholas W. (*b.* 1948) *C., Crawley*, maj. 7,765
*Soley, Clive S. (*b.* 1939) *Lab., Hammersmith*, maj. 4,754
*Spearing, Nigel J. (*b.* 1930) *Lab., Newham South*, maj. 2,502
*Speed, Sir Keith, RD (*b.* 1934) *C., Ashford*, maj. 17,359
Spellar, John F. (*b.* 1947) *Lab., Warley West*, maj. 5,472
Spencer, Sir Derek, QC (*b.* 1936) *C., Brighton, Pavilion*, maj. 3,675
*Spicer, Sir James (*b.* 1925) *C., Dorset West*, maj. 8,010
*Spicer, W. Michael H. (*b.* 1943) *C., Worcestershire South*, maj. 16,151
Spink, Dr Robert M. (*b.* 1948) *C., Castle Point*, maj. 16,830
Spring, Richard J. G. (*b.* 1946) *C., Bury St Edmunds*, maj. 18,787
Sproat, Iain M. (*b.* 1938) *C., Harwich*, maj. 17,159
Squire, Ms Rachel (*b.* 1954) *Lab., Dunfermline West*, maj. 7,484
*Squire, Robin C. (*b.* 1944) *C., Hornchurch*, maj. 9,165
*Stanley, Rt. Hon. Sir John (*b.* 1942) *C., Tonbridge and Malling*, maj. 21,558
*Steel, Rt. Hon. Sir David, KBE (*b.* 1938) *LD, Tweeddale, Ettrick and Lauderdale*, maj. 2,520
*Steen, Anthony D. (*b.* 1939) *C., South Hams*, maj. 13,711
*Steinberg, Gerald N. (*b.* 1945) *Lab., City of Durham*, maj. 15,058
Stephen, B. Michael L. (*b.* 1942) *C., Shoreham*, maj. 14,286
*Stern, Michael C. (*b.* 1942) *C., Bristol North West*, maj. 45
Stevenson, George W. (*b.* 1938) *Lab., Stoke-on-Trent South*, maj. 6,909
*Stewart, J. Allan (*b.* 1942) *C., Eastwood*, maj. 11,688
*Stott, Roger, CBE (*b.* 1943) *Lab., Wigan*, maj. 21,842
*Strang, Gavin S., Ph.D. (*b.* 1943) *Lab., Edinburgh East*, maj. 7,211
*Straw, J. W. (Jack) (*b.* 1946) *Lab., Blackburn*, maj. 6,027
Streeter, Gary (*b.* 1955) *C., Plymouth, Sutton*, maj. 11,950
*Sumberg, David A. G. (*b.* 1941) *C., Bury South*, maj. 788
Sweeney, Walter E. (*b.* 1949) *C., Vale of Glamorgan*, maj. 19
Sykes, John D. (*b.* 1956) *C., Scarborough*, maj. 11,734
*Tapsell, Sir Peter (*b.* 1930) *C., Lindsey East*, maj. 11,846
*Taylor, Sir Edward (Teddy) (*b.* 1937) *C., Southend East*, maj. 13,111
*Taylor, Ian C., MBE (*b.* 1945) *C., Esher*, maj. 20,371
*Taylor, Rt. Hon. John D. (*b.* 1937) *UUP, Strangford*, maj. 8,911
*Taylor, John M. (*b.* 1941) *C., Solihull*, maj. 25,146
*Taylor, Matthew O. J. (*b.* 1963) *LD, Truro*, maj. 7,570
*Taylor, Mrs W. Ann (*b.* 1947) *Lab., Dewsbury*, maj. 634
*Temple-Morris, Peter (*b.* 1938) *C., Leominster*, maj. 16,680
Thomason, K. Roy, OBE (*b.* 1944) *C., Bromsgrove*, maj. 13,702
*Thompson, Sir Donald (*b.* 1931) *C., Calder Valley*, maj. 4,878
*Thompson, H. Patrick (*b.* 1935) *C., Norwich North*, maj. 266
*Thompson, John (*b.* 1928) *Lab., Wansbeck*, maj. 18,174
*Thornton, Sir Malcolm (*b.* 1939) *C., Crosby*, maj. 14,806
*Thurnham, Peter G. (*b.* 1938) *C., Bolton North East*, maj. 185
Tipping, S. Paddy (*b.* 1949) *Lab., Sherwood*, maj. 2,910
*Townend, John E. (*b.* 1934) *C., Bridlington*, maj. 16,358
*Townsend, Cyril D. (*b.* 1937) *C., Bexleyheath*, maj. 14,086
*Tracey, Richard P. (*b.* 1943) *C., Surbiton*, maj. 9,639
*Tredinnick, David A. S. (*b.* 1950) *C., Bosworth*, maj. 19,094
Trend, Hon. Michael St J. (*b.* 1952) *C., Windsor and Maidenhead*, maj. 12,928
*Trimble, W. David (*b.* 1944) *UUP, Upper Bann*, maj. 16,163
*Trotter, Neville G. (*b.* 1932) *C., Tynemouth*, maj. 597
*Turner, Dennis (*b.* 1942) *Lab., Wolverhampton South East*, maj. 10,240
*Twinn, Dr Ian D. (*b.* 1950) *C., Edmonton*, maj. 593
Tyler, Paul A., CBE (*b.* 1941) *LD, Cornwall North*, maj. 1,921
*Vaughan, Sir Gerard (*b.* 1923) *C., Reading East*, maj. 14,555
*Vaz, N. Keith A. S. (*b.* 1956) *Lab., Leicester East*, maj. 11,316
*Viggers, Peter J. (*b.* 1938) *C., Gosport*, maj. 16,318
*Waldegrave, Rt. Hon. William A. (*b.* 1946) *C., Bristol West*, maj. 6,071
*Walden, George G. H., CMG (*b.* 1939) *C., Buckingham*, maj. 19,791
*Walker, A. Cecil (*b.* 1924) *UUP, Belfast North*, maj. 9,625
*Walker, Rt. Hon. Sir Harold (*b.* 1927) *Lab., Doncaster Central*, maj. 10,682
*Walker, William C. (*b.* 1929) *C., Tayside North*, maj. 3,995
*Wallace, James R. (*b.* 1954) *LD, Orkney and Shetland*, maj. 5,033
*Waller, Gary P. A. (*b.* 1945) *C., Keighley*, maj. 3,596
*Walley, Ms Joan L. (*b.* 1949) *Lab., Stoke-on-Trent North*, maj. 14,777
*Ward, John D., CBE (*b.* 1925) *C., Poole*, maj. 12,831
*Wardell, Gareth L. (*b.* 1944) *Lab., Gower*, maj. 7,018
*Wardle, Charles F. (*b.* 1939) *C., Bexhill and Battle*, maj. 16,307
*Wareing, Robert N. (*b.* 1930) *Lab., Liverpool, West Derby*, maj. 20,425
Waterson, Nigel C. (*b.* 1950) *C., Eastbourne*, maj. 5,481
*Watson, Michael G. (*b.* 1949) *Lab., Glasgow Central*, maj. 11,019
*Watts, John A. (*b.* 1947) *C., Slough*, maj. 514
*Wells, Bowen (*b.* 1935) *C., Hertford and Stortford*, maj. 20,210
*Welsh, Andrew P. (*b.* 1944) *SNP, Angus East*, maj. 954
*Wheeler, Sir John (*b.* 1940) *C., Westminster North*, maj. 3,733
*Whitney, Raymond W., OBE (*b.* 1930) *C., Wycombe*, maj. 17,076
Whittingdale, John F. L., OBE (*b.* 1959) *C., Colchester South and Maldon*, maj. 21,821
Wicks, Malcolm H. (*b.* 1947) *Lab., Croydon North West*, maj. 1,526
*Widdecombe, Miss Ann N. (*b.* 1947) *C., Maidstone*, maj. 16,286
*Wiggin, A. W. (Jerry), TD (*b.* 1937) *C., Weston-super-Mare*, maj. 5,342
*Wigley, Dafydd (*b.* 1943) *PC, Caernarfon*, maj. 14,476
*Wilkinson, John A. D. (*b.* 1940) *C., Ruislip-Northwood*, maj. 19,791
Willetts, David L. (*b.* 1956) *C., Havant*, maj. 17,584
*Williams, Rt. Hon. Alan J. (*b.* 1930) *Lab., Swansea West*, maj. 9,478
*Williams, Dr Alan W. (*b.* 1945) *Lab., Carmarthen*, maj. 2,922

*Wilshire, David (*b.* 1943) *C., Spelthorne*, maj. 19,843
*Wilson, Brian D. H. (*b.* 1948) *Lab., Cunninghame North*, maj. 2,939
*Winnick, David J. (*b.* 1933) *Lab., Walsall North*, maj. 3,824
*Winterton, Mrs J. Ann (*b.* 1941) *C., Congleton*, maj. 11,120
*Winterton, Nicholas R. (*b.* 1938) *C., Macclesfield*, maj. 22,767
*Wise, Mrs Audrey (*b.* 1935) *Lab., Preston*, maj. 12,175
*Wolfson, G. Mark (*b.* 1934) *C., Sevenoaks*, maj. 19,154
*Wood, Timothy J. R. (*b.* 1940) *C., Stevenage*, maj. 4,888
*Worthington, Anthony (*b.* 1941) *Lab., Clydebank and Milngavie*, maj. 12,430
*Wray, James (*b.* 1938) *Lab., Glasgow, Provan*, maj. 10,703
Wright, Anthony W., D.Phil. (*b.* 1948) *Lab., Cannock and Burntwood*, maj. 1,506
*Yeo, Timothy S. K. (*b.* 1945) *C., Suffolk South*, maj. 17,289
*Young, David W. (*b.* 1930) *Lab., Bolton South East*, maj. 12,691
*Young, Sir George, Bt. (*b.* 1941) *C., Ealing, Acton*, maj. 7,007

MEMBERS WITH SMALL MAJORITIES

The following MPs were returned in April 1992 with majorities of fewer than 1,000 votes
*denotes membership of last Parliament

	Maj.
Walter Sweeney, *C., Vale of Glamorgan*	19
*Michael Stern, *C., Bristol North West*	45
*Terry Dicks, *C., Hayes and Harlington*	53
Phil Gallie, *C., Ayr*	85
Janet Anderson, *Lab., Rossendale and Darwen*	120
Jonathan Evans, *C., Brecon and Radnor*	130
Estelle Morris, *Lab., Birmingham Yardley*	162
*Peter Thurnham, *C., Bolton North East*	185
Mike Hall, *Lab., Warrington South*	191
*David Martin, *C., Portsmouth South*	242
Jamie Cann, *Lab., Ipswich*	265
*Patrick Thompson, *C., Norwich North*	266
*Malcolm Bruce, *LD, Gordon*	274
*William Powell, *C., Corby*	342
Mike Gapes, *Lab., Ilford South*	402
*Sir Russell Johnston, *LD, Inverness, Nairn and Lochaber*	458
*Alice Mahon, *Lab., Halifax*	478
*John Watts, *C., Slough*	514
John Denham, *Lab., Southampton Itchen*	551
Anne Campbell, *Lab., Cambridge*	580
*James Hill, *C., Southampton Test*	585
Dr Joe Hendron, *SDLP, Belfast West*	589
*Dr Ian Twinn, *C., Edmonton*	593
Neville Trotter, *C., Tynemouth*	597
Richard Burden, *Lab., Birmingham Northfield*	630
*Ann Taylor, *Lab., Dewsbury*	634
*Michael Forsyth, *C., Stirling*	703
*Phillip Oppenheim, *C., Amber Valley*	712
Nick Ainger, *Lab., Pembroke*	755
*David Sumberg, *C., Bury South*	788
Nick Harvey, *LD, Devon North*	794
*Graham Bright, *C., Luton South*	799
*David Shaw, *C., Dover*	833
*Lord James Douglas-Hamilton, *C., Edinburgh West*	879
*Sir Tom Arnold, *C., Hazel Grove*	929
*Andrew Welsh, *SNP, Angus East*	954
*David Ashby, *C., Leicestershire North West*	979
*Sir Wyn Roberts, *C., Conwy*	995

MEMBERS WHO LEFT THE HOUSE AT THE GENERAL ELECTION 1992

RETIRED

Rt. Hon. Julian Amery (*C., Brighton Pavilion*)
Alan Amos (*C., Hexham*)
Rt. Hon. Peter Archer (*Lab., Warley West*)
Rt. Hon. Jack Ashley (*Lab., Stoke-on-Trent South*)
William Benyon (*C., Milton Keynes*)
Rt. Hon. Sir Peter Blaker (*C., Blackpool South*)
Hon. Robert Boscawen (*C., Somerton and Frome*)
Rt. Hon. Sir Bernard Braine (*C., Castle Point*)
Sir Antony Buck (*C., Colchester North*)
Rt. Hon. Alan Clark (*C., Plymouth Sutton*)
Rt. Hon. Sir William Clark (*C., Croydon South*)
Robert Clay (*Lab., Sunderland North*)
Stanley Crowther (*Lab., Rotherham*)
Rt. Hon. Sir Paul Dean (*C., Woodspring*)
†Richard Douglas (*Ind.* (formerly *Lab.*), *Dunfermline West*)
Sir Patrick Duffy (*Lab., Sheffield Attercliffe*)
Alexander Eadie (*Lab., Midlothian*)
Harry Ewing (*Lab., Falkirk East*)
Sir John Farr (*C., Harborough*)
Sir Geoffrey Finsberg (*C., Hampstead and Highgate*)
Martin Flannery (*Lab., Sheffield Hillsborough*)
Rt. Hon. Michael Foot (*Lab., Blaenau Gwent*)
William Garrett (*Lab., Wallsend*)
Rt. Hon. Sir Ian Gilmour (*C., Chesham and Amersham*)
Sir Alan Glyn (*C., Windsor and Maidenhead*)
Sir Philip Goodhart (*C., Beckenham*)
Sir Eldon Griffiths (*C., Bury St Edmunds*)
Christopher Hawkins (*C., High Peak*)
Rt. Hon. Sir Barney Hayhoe (*C., Brentford and Isleworth*)
Frank Haynes (*Lab., Ashfield*)
Rt. Hon. Denis Healey (*Lab., Leeds East*)
Rt. Hon. Sir Geoffrey Howe (*C., Surrey East*)
Rt. Hon. Denis Howell (*Lab., Birmingham Small Heath*)
Sir Charles Irving (*C., Cheltenham*)
David Lambie (*Lab., Cunninghame South*)
James Lamond (*Lab., Oldham Central and Royton*)
Michael Latham (*C., Rutland and Melton*)
Rt. Hon. Nigel Lawson (*C., Blaby*)
Edward Leadbitter (*Lab., Hartlepool*)
Sir Ian Lloyd (*C., Havant*)
Rt. Hon. Sir Richard Luce (*C., Shoreham*)
Sir Robert McCrindle (*C., Brentwood and Ongar*)
Sir Neil Macfarlane (*C., Sutton and Cheam*)
Allen McKay (*Lab., Barnsley West and Penistone*)
Sir Michael McNair-Wilson (*C., Newbury*)
Sir Robin Maxwell-Hyslop (*C., Tiverton*)

*Sir Anthony Meyer, Bt. (*C. Clywd, North West*)
Sir Hal Miller (*C., Bromsgrove*)
Norman Miscampbell (*C., Blackpool North*)
Rt. Hon. John Moore (*C., Croydon Central*)
Hon. Sir Charles Morrison (*C., Devizes*)
Rt. Hon. Sir Peter Morrison (*C., City of Chester*)
David Mudd (*C., Falmouth and Camborne*)
Rt. Hon. David Owen (*SD, Plymouth Devonport*)
Rt. Hon. Cecil Parkinson (*C., Hertsmere*)
Sir David Price (*C., Eastleigh*)
Keith Raffan (*C., Delyn*)
Rt. Hon. Sir Timothy Raison (*C., Aylesbury*)
Rt. Hon. Merlyn Rees (*Lab., Leeds South and Morley*)
Sir Robert Rhodes James (*C., Cambridge*)
Rt. Hon. Nicholas Ridley (*C., Cirencester and Tewkesbury*)
Sir Julian Ridsdale (*C., Harwich*)
Sir Hugh Rossi (C., Hornsey and Wood Green)
Peter Rost (*C., Erewash*)
Sir Michael Shaw (*C., Scarborough*)
Sir Cyril Smith (*LD, Rochdale*)
Ivor Stanbrook (*C., Orpington*)
Rt. Hon. Sir Ian Stewart (*C., Hertfordshire North*)
Sir John Stokes (*C., Halesowen and Stourbridge*)
Rt. Hon. Norman Tebbit (*C., Chingford*)
Rt. Hon. Margaret Thatcher (*C., Finchley*)
Dafydd Thomas (*PC, Meirionnydd Nant Conwy*)
Rt. Hon. John Wakeham (*C., Colchester South and Maldon*)
Rt. Hon. Peter Walker (*C., Worcester*)
Sir Dennis Walters (*C., Westbury*)
Kenneth Warren (*C., Hastings and Rye*)
Rt. Hon. Bernard Weatherill (*The Speaker, Croydon North East*)
Michael Welsh (*Lab., Doncaster North*)
Michael Woodcock (*C., Ellesmore Port and Neston*)
Rt. Hon. George Younger (*C., Ayr*)

LOST SEAT

Gerry Adams (*SF, Belfast West*)
Mrs Rosemary Barnes (*SD, Greenwich*)
Anthony Beaumont-Dark (*C., Birmingham Selly Oak*)
David Bellotti (*LD, Eastbourne*)
Nicholas Bennett (*C., Pembroke*)
David Bevan (*C., Birmingham Yardley*)
*Sydney Bidwell (formerly *Lab., Ealing Southall*, standing as *True Labour* candidate)
Gerald Bowden (*C., Dulwich*)
Martin Brandon-Bravo (*C., Nottingham South*)
*Ronald Brown (formerly *Lab., Edinburgh Leith*, standing as *Independent Labour* candidate)
*John Browne (formerly *C., Winchester*, standing as *Independent Conservative* candidate)
Christopher Butler (*C., Warrington South*)
Michael Carr (*LD, Ribble Valley*)
John Cartwright (*SD, Woolwich*)
Rt. Hon. Lynda Chalker (*C., Wallasey*)
Christopher Chope (*C., Southampton Itchen*)
Frank Doran (*Lab., Aberdeen South*)
†Richard Douglas (fought Glasgow Garscadden for *SNP*)
Huw Edwards (*Lab., Monmouth*)
Michael Fallon (*C., Darlington*)
Anthony Favell (*C., Stockport*)
Ronald Fearn (*LD, Southport*)
‡Terry Fields (formerly *Lab., Liverpool Broadgreen*, standing as *Socialist Labour* candidate)
Cecil Franks (*C., Barrow and Furness*)
Conal Gregory (*C., York*)
Ian Grist (*C., Cardiff Central*)
Patrick Ground (*C., Feltham and Heston*)
Kenneth Hargreaves (*C., Hyndburn*)
Robert Hayward (*C., Kingswood*)
Mrs Sylvia Heal (*Lab., Staffordshire Mid*)
Mrs Maureen Hicks (*C., Wolverhampton North East*)
Kenneth Hind (*C., Lancashire West*)
Gerald Howarth (*C., Cannock and Burntwood*)
Geraint Howells (*LD, Ceredigion and Pembroke North*)
*John Hughes (formerly *Lab., Coventry North East*, standing as *Independent Labour* candidate)
Michael Irvine (*C., Ipswich*)
Timothy Janman (*C., Thurrock*)
Roger King (*C., Birmingham Northfield*)
Michael Knowles (*C., Nottingham East*)
Ashok Kumar (*Lab., Langbaurgh*)
John Lee (*C., Pendle*)
Richard Livsey (*LD, Brecon and Radnor*)
Humfrey Malins (*C., Croydon North West*)
John Maples (*C., Lewisham West*)
Hon. Francis Maude (*C., Warwickshire North*)
Hon. Colin Moynihan (*C., Lewisham East*)
Sir Gerrard Neale (*C., Cornwall North*)
‡David Nellist (formerly *Lab., Coventry South East*, standing as *Independent Labour* candidate)
Rt. Hon. Christopher Patten (*C., Bath*)
Jonathan Sayeed (*C., Bristol East*)
Sir William Shelton (*C., Streatham*)
James Sillars (*SNP, Glasgow Govan*)
John Smith (*Lab., Vale of Glamorgan*)
Antony Speller (*C., Devon North*)
Nicol Stephen (*LD, Kincardine and Deeside*)
Lewis Stevens (*C., Nuneaton*)
Andrew Stewart (*C., Sherwood*)
Hugo Summerson (*C., Walthamstow*)
Neil Thorne (*C., Ilford South*)
David Trippier (*C., Rossendale and Darwen*)

*Not selected as candidate by constituency party
†Retired as MP for Dunfermline West; stood and lost in Glasgow Garscadden
‡Expelled from Labour Party in December 1991

PARLIAMENTARY CONSTITUENCIES 9 April 1992

The results of voting in each parliamentary division at the General Election of 9 April 1992 are given below. The majority in the 1987 General Election, and any subsequent by-elections, is given below the 1992 result.

Symbols

E.	Total number of electors in the constituency at the 1992 General Election
T.	Turnout of electors at the 1992 General Election
*	Member of the last Parliament

Abbreviations

All.	Alliance Party (NI)
C.	Conservative
DUP	Democratic Unionist Party
Green	Green Party
Ind.	Independent
Lab.	Labour
L./All.	Liberal Alliance
LD	Liberal Democrat
Lib.	Liberal
PC	Plaid Cymru
SD	Social Democrat
SDLP	Social Democratic and Labour Party
SDP	Social Democrat Party
SF	Sinn Fein
SNP	Scottish National Party
UPUP	Ulster Popular Unionist Party
UUP	Ulster Unionist Party
ADS	After Dinner Speaker
AFE	Anti-Federal Europe
Alt.	Alternative
Anti Fed.	Anti Federalist League
Anti H.	Anti-Heseltine Independent
APAKBI	Anti-Paddy Ashdown Keep Britain Independent
AS	Anglo Saxon
Bastion	Bastion Party
BNP	British National Party
Brewer	Jolly Small Brewers Party
Brit. Ind.	British Independence Party
CD	Christian Democrat
Century	21st Century Party
Choice	People's Choice
CL	Communist League
Comm. GB	Communist Party of Great Britain
CRA	Chauvinist Raving Alliance
CSP	Common Sense Party
C. Thatch.	Conservative Thatcherite
DLC	Democrat Liberal Conservative
DOS	Doctor of Stockwell
EFRA	Epping Forest Residents Association
ERIP	Equal Representation in Parliament
EUVJJ	End Unemployment Vote Justice for the Jobless
FDP	Fancy Dress Party
Fellowship	Fellowship Party
FP	Feudal Party
FTA	Fair Trials Abroad
FTM	Forward to Mars Party
Fun	Funstermentalist
Gremloids	Gremloids
Hardcore	The Altern-8-ive (Hardcore) Party
Homeland	Independent British Homeland Defence
Hove C.	Official Conservative Hove Party
IFM	Irish Freedom Movement
ILP	Independent Labour Party
Ind. U.	Independent Unionist
Int. Comm.	International Communist Party
Islamic	Islamic Party
ISS	Illegal Sunday Shopping
JBR	Justice from British Rail
Loony	Official Monster Raving Loony Party
Loony G.	Loony Green
LP	Lodestar Party
LTU	Labour and Trade Union
MBI	Morecambe Bay Independent
NA	Noise Abatement
Nat.	Nationalist
NF	National Front
NLP	Natural Law Party
Pensioners	Pensioners' Party
PP	People's Party
PPP	Peoples' Peace Party
PR	Proportional Representation
Prog. Soc.	Independent Progressive Socialist
Prot. Ref.	Protestant Reformation
QFL	Quality for Life Party
RAVA	Rainbow Ark Voters Association
RCC	Revolutionary Christian Communist
Real Bean	Real Bean
Rev. Comm.	Revolutionary Communist
Rizz	Rizz Party - Rainbow
Scallywagg	Scallywagg
SML	Scottish Militant Labour
SOADDA	Struck Off and Die Doctor's Alliance
Soc.	Socialist
Soc. Lab.	Socialist Labour
True Lab.	True Labour
UTCHAP	Up The Creek Have A Party
WAR	Workers Against Racism
Wessex	Save Wessex
Whiplash	Whiplash Corrective
WP	Workers' Party
WRP	Workers' Revolutionary Party
WUWC	Wake Up Wokingham Campaign
YSOR	Young Socialist - Occupy Ravenscraig

ENGLAND

ALDERSHOT (Hants)
*E.*81,754 *T.*78.71%

*J. Critchley, *C.*	36,974
A. Collett, *LD*	17,786
J. Anthony Smith, *Lab.*	8,552
D. Robinson, Lib.	1,038
C. majority	19,188

(June 1987, C. maj. 17,784)

ALDRIDGE-BROWNHILLS (W. Midlands)
*E.*63,404 *T.*82.55%

*R. Shepherd, *C.*	28,431
N. Fawcett, *Lab.*	17,407
S. Reynolds, *LD*	6,503
C. majority	11,024

(June 1987, C. maj. 12,396)

ALTRINCHAM AND SALE (Greater Manchester)
*E.*65,897 *T.*80.66%

*Sir Fergus Montgomery, *C.*	29,066
Ms M. Atherton, *Lab.*	12,275
J. Mulholland, *LD*	11,601
J. Renwick, *NLP*	212
C. majority	16,791

(June 1987, C. maj. 14,228)

AMBER VALLEY (Derbys)
*E.*70,155 *T.*84.69%

*Hon. P. Oppenheim, *C.*	27,418
J. Cooper, *Lab.*	26,706
G. Brocklebank, *LD*	5,294
C. majority	712

(June 1987, C. maj. 9,500)

ARUNDEL (W. Sussex)
*E.*79,241 *T.*77.06%

*Sir Michael Marshall, *C.*	35,405
Dr J. Walsh, *LD*	15,542
R. Nash, *Lab.*	8,321
Mrs D. Renson, *Lib.*	1,103
R. Corbin, *Green*	693
C. majority	19,863

(June 1987, C. maj. 18,880)

ASHFIELD (Notts)
*E.*75,075 *T.*77.70%

G. Hoon, *Lab.*	32,018
L. Robertson, *C.*	19,031
J. Turton, *LD*	7,291
Lab. majority	12,987

(June 1987, Lab. maj. 4,400)

ASHFORD (Kent)
*E.*71,767 *T.*79.20%

*K. Speed, *C.*	31,031
Ms C. Headley, *LD*	13,672
Ms D. Cameron, *Lab.*	11,365
Dr A. Porter, *Green*	773
C. majority	17,359

(June 1987, C. maj. 15,488)

ASHTON-UNDER-LYNE (Greater Manchester)
*E.*58,701 *T.*73.87%

*Rt. Hon. R. Sheldon, *Lab.*	24,550
J. Pinniger, *C.*	13,615
C. Turner, *LD*	4,005

C. Hall, *Lib.* 907
J. Brannigan, *NLP* 289
Lab. majority 10,935
(June 1987, Lab. maj. 9,286)

AYLESBURY (Bucks)
*E.*79,208 *T.*80.29%
D. Lidington, *C.* 36,500
Ms S. Bowles, *LD* 17,640
R. Priest, *Lab.* 8,517
N. Foster, *Green* 702
B. D'Arcy, *NLP* 239
C. majority 18,860
(June 1987, C. maj. 16,558)

BANBURY (Oxon)
*E.*71,840 *T.*81.51%
*A. Baldry, *C.* 32,215
Ms A. Billingham, *Lab.* 15,495
G. Fisher, *LD* 10,602
Dr R. Ticiiati, *NLP* 250
C. majority 16,720
(June 1987, C. maj. 17,330)

BARKING (Greater London)
*E.*50,454 *T.*69.99%
*Ms J. Richardson, *Lab.* 18,224
J. Kennedy, *C.* 11,956
S. Churchman, *LD* 5,133
Lab. majority 6,268
(June 1987, Lab. maj. 3,409)

BARNSLEY CENTRAL (S. Yorks)
*E.*55,373 *T.*70.53%
*E. Illsley, *Lab.* 27,048
D. Senior, *C.* 7,687
S. Cowton, *LD* 4,321
Lab. majority 19,361
(June 1987, Lab. maj. 19,051)

BARNSLEY EAST (S. Yorks)
*E.*54,051 *T.*72.73%
*T. Patchett, *Lab.* 30,346
J. Procter, *C.* 5,569
Ms S. Anginotti, *LD* 3,399
Lab. majority 24,777
(June 1987, Lab. maj. 23,511)

BARNSLEY WEST AND PENISTONE (S. Yorks)
*E.*63,374 *T.*75.75%
M. Clapham, *Lab.* 27,965
G. Sawyer, *C.* 13,461
I. Nicolson, *LD* 5,610
D. Jones, *Green* 970
Lab. majority 14,504
(June 1987, Lab. maj. 14,191)

BARROW AND FURNESS (Cumbria)
*E.*67,764 *T.*82.11%
J. Hutton, *Lab.* 26,568
*C. Franks, *C.* 22,990
C. Crane, *LD* 6,089
Lab. majority 3,578
(June 1987, C. maj. 3,928)

BASILDON (Essex)
*E.*67,585 *T.*79.61%
*D. Amess, *C.* 24,159
J. Potter, *Lab.* 22,679
G. Williams, *LD* 6,967
C. majority 1,480
(June 1987, C. maj. 2,649)

BASINGSTOKE (Hants)
*E.*82,952 *T.*82.79%
*A. Hunter, *C.* 37,521
D. Bull, *Lab.* 16,323
C. Curtis, *LD* 14,119
Ms V. Oldaker, *Green* 714
C. majority 21,198
(June 1987, C. maj. 17,893)

BASSETLAW (Notts)
*E.*58,583 *T.*92.97%
*J. Ashton, *Lab.* 29,061
Mrs C. Spelman, *C.* 19,064
M. Reynolds, *LD* 6,340
Lab. majority 9,997
(June 1987, Lab. maj. 5,613)

BATH (Avon)
*E.*63,689 *T.*82.54%
D. Foster, *LD* 25,718
*Rt. Hon. C. Patten, *C.* 21,950
Ms P. Richards, *Lab.* 4,102
D. McCanlis, *Green* 433
Ms M. Barker, *Lib.* 172
Dr A. Sked, *Anti Fed.* 117
J. Rumming, *Ind.* 79
LD majority 3,768
(June 1987, C. maj. 1,412)

BATLEY AND SPEN (W. Yorks)
*E.*76,417 *T.*79.63%
*Mrs E. Peacock, *C.* 27,629
Mrs E. Durkin, *Lab.* 26,221
G. Beever, *LD* 6,380
C. Lord, *Green* 628
C. majority 1,408
(June 1987, C. maj. 1,362)

BATTERSEA (Greater London)
*E.*68,218 *T.*76.63%
*J. Bowis, *C.* 26,390
A. Dubs, *Lab.* 21,550
R. O'Brien, *LD* 3,659
I. Wingrove, *Green* 584
W. Stevens, *NLP* 98
C. majority 4,840
(June 1987, C. maj. 857)

BEACONSFIELD (Bucks)
*E.*64,268 *T.*82.27%
*T. Smith, *C.* 33,817
Ms A. Purse, *LD* 10,220
G. Smith, *Lab.* 7,163
W. Foulds, *Ind. C.* 1,317
A. Foss, *NLP* 196
Ms J. Martin, *ERIP* 166
C. majority 23,597
(June 1987, C. maj. 21,339)

BECKENHAM (Greater London)
*E.*59,440 *T.*77.86%
P. Merchant, *C.* 26,323
K. Ritchie, *Lab.* 11,038
Ms M. Williams, *LD* 8,038
G. Williams, *Lib.* 643
P. Shaw, *NLP* 243
C. majority 15,285
(June 1987, C. maj. 13,464)

BEDFORDSHIRE MID
*E.*81,864 *T.*84.45%
*Rt. Hon. Sir N. Lyell, *C.* 40,230
R. Clayton, *Lab.* 15,092
N. Hills, *LD* 11,957
P. Cottier, *Lib.* 1,582
M. Lorys, *NLP* 279
C. majority 25,138
(June 1987, C. maj. 22,851)

BEDFORDSHIRE NORTH
*E.*73,789 *T.*80.03%
*Sir T. Skeet, *C.* 29,920
P. Hall, *Lab.* 18,302
M. Smithson, *LD* 10,014
Ms L. Smith, *Green* 643
B. Bench, *NLP* 178
C. majority 11,618
(June 1987, C. maj. 16,505)

BEDFORDSHIRE SOUTH WEST
*E.*79,662 *T.*82.39%
*W. D. Madel, *C.* 37,498
B. Elliott, *Lab.* 16,225
M. Freeman, *LD* 10,988
P. Rollings, *Green* 689
D. Gilmour, *NLP* 239
C. majority 21,273
(June 1987, C. maj. 22,305)

BERKSHIRE EAST
*E.*90,365 *T.*81.41%
*A. Mackay, *C.* 43,898
Ms L. Murray, *LD* 15,218
K. Dibble, *Lab.* 14,458
C. majority 28,680
(June 1987, C. maj. 22,626)

BERWICK-UPON-TWEED (Northumberland)
*E.*54,919 *T.*79.12%
*A. Beith, *LD* 19,283
Dr A. Henfrey, *C.* 14,240
Dr G. Adam, *Lab.* 9,933
LD majority 5,043
(June 1987, L./All. maj. 13,945)

BETHNAL GREEN AND STEPNEY (Greater London)
*E.*55,675 *T.*65.45%

*Rt. Hon. P. Shore, *Lab.*	20,350
J. Shaw, *LD*	8,120
Miss J. Emmerson, *C.*	6,507
R. Edmonds, *BNP*	1,310
S. Kelsey, *Comm. GB*	156
Lab. majority	12,230

(June 1987, Lab. maj. 5,284)

BEVERLEY (Humberside)
*E.*81,198 *T.*79.69%

*J. Cran, *C.*	34,503
A. Collinge, *LD*	17,986
C. Challen, *Lab.*	12,026
D. Hetherington, *NLP*	199
C. majority	16,517

(June 1987, C. maj. 12,595)

BEXHILL AND BATTLE (E. Sussex)
*E.*65,850 *T.*78.99%

*C. Wardle, *C.*	31,330
Ms S. Prochak, *LD*	15,023
F. Taylor, *Lab.*	4,883
J. Prus, *Green*	594
Mrs M. Smith, *CSP*	190
C. majority	16,307

(June 1987, C. maj. 20,519)

BEXLEYHEATH (Greater London)
*E.*57,684 *T.*82.17%

*C. Townsend, *C.*	25,606
J. Browning, *Lab.*	11,520
Ms W. Chaplin, *LD*	10,107
R. Cundy, *Ind.*	170
C. majority	14,086

(June 1987, C. maj. 11,687)

BILLERICAY (Essex)
*E.*80,388 *T.*82.34%

*Mrs T. Gorman, *C.*	37,406
F. Bellard, *LD*	14,912
Ms A. Miller, *Lab.*	13,880
C. majority	22,494

(June 1987, C. maj. 18,016)

BIRKENHEAD (Merseyside)
*E.*62,682 *T.*72.96%

*F. Field, *Lab.*	29,098
R. Hughes, *C.*	11,485
P. Williams, *LD*	4,417
Ms T. Fox, *Green*	543
Ms B. Griffiths, *NLP*	190
Lab. majority	17,613

(June 1987, Lab. maj. 15,372)

BIRMINGHAM EDGBASTON (W. Midlands)
*E.*53,041 *T.*71.29%

*Dame J. Knight, *C.*	18,529
J. Wilton, *Lab.*	14,222
I. Robertson-Steel, *LD*	4,419
P. Simpson, *Green*	643
C. majority	4,307

(June 1987, C. maj. 8,581)

BIRMINGHAM ERDINGTON (W. Midlands)
*E.*52,398 *T.*70.15%

*R. Corbett, *Lab.*	18,549
S. Hope, *C.*	13,814
Dr J. Campbell, *LD*	4,398
Lab. majority	4,735

(June 1987, Lab. maj. 2,467)

BIRMINGHAM HALL GREEN (W. Midlands)
*E.*60,091 *T.*78.17%

*A. Hargreaves, *C.*	21,649
Ms J. Slowey, *Lab.*	17,984
D. McGrath, *LD*	7,342
C. majority	3,665

(June 1987, C. maj. 7,621)

BIRMINGHAM HODGE HILL (W. Midlands)
*E.*57,651 *T.*70.82%

*T. Davis, *Lab.*	21,895
Miss E. Gibson, *C.*	14,827
S. Hagan, *LD*	3,740
E. Whicker, *NF*	370
Lab. majority	7,068

(June 1987, Lab. maj. 4,789)

BIRMINGHAM LADYWOOD (W. Midlands)
*E.*56,970 *T.*65.92%

*Ms C. Short, *Lab.*	24,887
Mrs B. Ashford, *C.*	9,604
B. Worth, *LD*	3,068
Lab. majority	15,283

(June 1987, Lab. maj. 10,028)

BIRMINGHAM NORTHFIELD (W. Midlands)
*E.*70,533 *T.*76.08%

R. Burden, *Lab.*	24,433
*R. King, *C.*	23,803
D. Cropp, *LD*	5,431
Lab. majority	630

(June 1987, C. maj. 3,135)

BIRMINGHAM PERRY BARR (W. Midlands)
*E.*72,161 *T.*71.62%

*J. Rooker, *Lab.*	27,507
G. Green, *C.*	18,917
T. Philpott, *LD*	5,261
Lab. majority	8,590

(June 1987, Lab. maj. 6,933)

BIRMINGHAM SELLY OAK (W. Midlands)
*E.*72,150 *T.*76.61%

Ms L. Jones, *Lab.*	25,430
*A. Beaumont-Dark, *C.*	23,370
D. Osborne, *LD*	5,679
P. Slatter, *Green*	535
C. Barwood, *NLP*	178
K. Malik, *Rev Comm*	84
Lab. majority	2,060

(June 1987, C. maj. 2,584)

BIRMINGHAM SMALL HEATH (W. Midlands)
*E.*55,213 *T.*62.95%

R. Godsiff, *Lab.*	22,675
A. Qayyum Chaudhary, *C.*	8,686
H. Thomas, *LD*	2,575
Ms H. Clawley, *Green*	824
Lab. majority	13,989

(June 1987, Lab. maj. 15,521)

BIRMINGHAM SPARKBROOK (W. Midlands)
*E.*51,677 *T.*66.80%

*Rt. Hon. R. Hattersley, *Lab.*	22,116
M. Khamisa, *C.*	8,544
D. Parry, *LD*	3,028
C. Alldrick, *Green*	833
Lab. majority	13,572

(June 1987, Lab. maj. 11,859)

BIRMINGHAM YARDLEY (W. Midlands)
*E.*54,749 *T.*77.98%

Ms E. Morris, *Lab.*	14,884
*A. D. G. Bevan, *C.*	14,722
J. Hemming, *LD*	12,899
Miss P. Read, *NF*	192
Lab. majority	162

(June 1987, C. maj. 2,522)

BISHOP AUCKLAND (Durham)
*E.*72,572 *T.*76.52%

*D. Foster, *Lab.*	27,763
D. Williamson, *C.*	17,676
W. Wade, *LD*	10,099
Lab. majority	10,087

(June 1987, Lab. maj. 7,035)

BLABY (Leics)
*E.*81,790 *T.*83.39%

A. Robathan, *C.*	39,498
Ms E. Ranson, *Lab.*	14,151
Ms M. Lewin, *LD*	13,780
J. Peacock, *BNP*	521
Ms S. Lincoln, *NLP*	260
C. majority	25,347

(June 1987, C. maj. 22,176)

BLACKBURN (Lancs)
*E.*73,251 *T.*75.05%

*J. Straw, *Lab.*	26,633
R. Coates, *C.*	20,606
D. Mann, *LD*	6,332
R. Field, *Green*	878
Mrs M. Carmichael-Grimshaw, *LP*	334
W. Ayliffe, *NLP*	195
Lab. majority	6,027

(June 1987, Lab. maj. 5,497)

BLACKPOOL NORTH (Lancs)
*E.*58,087 *T.*77.55%
H. Elletson, *C.* 21,501
E. Kirton, *Lab.* 18,461
A. Lahiff, *LD* 4,786
Sir G. Francis, *Loony* 178
H. Walker, *NLP* 125
C. majority 3,040
(June 1987, C. maj. 7,321)

BLACKPOOL SOUTH (Lancs)
*E.*56,801 *T.*77.35%
N. Hawkins, *C.* 19,880
G. Marsden, *Lab.* 18,213
R. Wynne, *LD* 5,675
D. Henning, *NLP* 173
C. majority 1,667
(June 1987, C. maj. 6,744)

BLAYDON (Tyne & Wear)
*E.*66,044 *T.*77.69%
*J. McWilliam, *Lab.* 27,028
P. Pescod, *C.* 13,685
P. Nunn, *LD* 10,602
Lab. majority 13,343
(June 1987, Lab. maj. 12,488)

BLYTH VALLEY (Northumberland)
*E.*60,913 *T.*80.77%
*R. Campbell, *Lab.* 24,542
P. Tracey, *LD* 16,498
M. Revell, *C.* 7,691
S. Tyley, *Green* 470
Lab. majority 8,044
(June 1987, Lab. maj. 853)

BOLSOVER (Derbys)
*E.*66,693 *T.*78.94%
*D. Skinner, *Lab.* 33,973
T. James, *C.* 13,313
Ms S. Barber, *LD* 5,363
Lab. majority 20,660
(June 1987, Lab. maj. 14,120)

BOLTON NORTH EAST (Greater Manchester)
*E.*58,659 *T.*82.26%
*P. Thurnham, *C.* 21,644
D. Crausby, *Lab.* 21,459
B. Dunning, *LD* 4,971
P. Tong, *NLP* 181
C. majority 185
(June 1987, C. maj. 813)

BOLTON SOUTH EAST (Greater Manchester)
*E.*65,600 *T.*75.53%
*D. Young, *Lab.* 26,906
N. Wood-Dow, *C.* 14,215
D. Lee, *LD* 5,243
W. Hardman, *Ind. Lab.* 2,894
L. Walch, *NLP* 290
Lab. majority 12,691
(June 1987, Lab. maj. 11,381)

BOLTON WEST (Greater Manchester)
*E.*71,344 *T.*83.53%
*Hon. T. Sackville, *C.* 26,452
C. Morris, *Lab.* 25,373
Ms B. Ronson, *LD* 7,529
Ms J. Phillips, *NLP* 240
C. majority 1,079
(June 1987, C. maj. 4,593)

BOOTHFERRY (Humberside)
*E.*80,747 *T.*79.73%
*D. Davis, *C.* 35,266
Ms L. Coubrough, *Lab.* 17,731
J. Goss, *LD* 11,388
C. majority 17,535
(June 1987, C. maj. 18,970)

BOOTLE (Merseyside)
*E.*69,308 *T.*72.46%
*J. Benton, *Lab.* 37,464
C. Varley, *C.* 8,022
J. Cunningham, *LD* 3,301
Ms M. Hall, *Lib.* 1,174
T. Haynes, *NLP* 264
Lab. majority 29,442
(June 1987, Lab. maj. 24,477)
(May 1990, Lab. maj. 23,517)
(November 1990, Lab. maj. 19,465)

BOSWORTH (Leics)
*E.*80,234 *T.*84.13%
*D. Tredinnick, *C.* 36,618
D. Everitt, *Lab.* 17,524
G. Drozdz, *LD* 12,643
B. Fewster, *Green* 716
C. majority 19,094
(June 1987, C. maj. 17,016)

BOURNEMOUTH EAST (Dorset)
*E.*75,089 *T.*72.82%
*D. Atkinson, *C.* 30,820
N. Russell, *LD* 15,997
P. Brushett, *Lab.* 7,541
Ms S. Holmes, *NLP* 329
C. majority 14,823
(June 1987, C. maj. 14,683)

BOURNEMOUTH WEST (Dorset)
*E.*74,738 *T.*75.72%
*J. Butterfill, *C.* 29,820
Ms J. Dover, *LD* 17,117
B. Grower, *Lab.* 9,423
A. Springham, *NLP* 232
C. majority 12,703
(June 1987, C. maj. 12,651)

BOW AND POPLAR (Greater London)
*E.*56,685 *T.*65.84%
*Mrs M. Gordon, *Lab.* 18,487
P. Hughes, *LD* 10,083
S. Pearce, *C.* 6,876
J. Tyndall, *BNP* 1,107
S. Petter, *Green* 612
W. Hite, *NLP* 158
Lab. majority 8,404
(June 1987, Lab. maj. 4,631)

BRADFORD NORTH (W. Yorks)
*E.*66,719 *T.*73.38%
*T. Rooney, *Lab.* 23,420
M. Riaz, *C.* 15,756
D. Ward, *LD* 9,133
W. Beckett, *Loony* 350
M. Nasr, *Islamic* 304
Lab. majority 7,664
(June 1987, Lab. maj. 1,663)
(November 1990, Lab. maj. 9,514)

BRADFORD SOUTH (W. Yorks)
*E.*69,914 *T.*75.61%
*G. R. Cryer, *Lab.* 25,185
A. Popat, *C.* 20,283
B. Boulton, *LD* 7,243
M. Naseem, *Islamic* 156
Lab. majority 4,902
(June 1987, Lab. maj. 309)

BRADFORD WEST (W. Yorks)
*E.*70,016 *T.*69.90%
*M. Madden, *Lab.* 26,046
Dr A. Ashworth, *C.* 16,544
A. Griffiths, *LD* 5,150
P. Braham, *Green* 735
D. Pidcock, *Islamic* 471
Lab. majority 9,502
(June 1987, Lab. maj. 7,551)

BRAINTREE (Essex)
*E.*78,880 *T.*83.41%
*Rt. Hon. A. Newton, *C.* 34,415
I. Willmore, *Lab.* 16,921
Ms D. Wallis, *LD* 13,603
J. Abbott, *Green* 855
C. majority 17,494
(June 1987, C. maj. 16,857)

BRENT EAST (Greater London)
*E.*53,319 *T.*68.82%
*K. Livingstone, *Lab.* 19,387
D. Green, *C.* 13,416
M. Cummins, *LD* 3,249
Ms T. Dean, *Green* 548
Ms A. Murphy, *Comm. GB* 96
Lab. majority 5,971
(June 1987, Lab. maj. 1,653)

BRENT NORTH (Greater London)
*E.*58,917 *T.*70.57%
*Rt. Hon. Sir R. Boyson, *C.* 23,445
J. Moher, *Lab.* 13,314
P. Lorber, *LD* 4,149
T. Vipul, *Ind.* 356
T. Davids, *NLP* 318
C. majority 10,131
(June 1987, C. maj. 15,720)

BRENT SOUTH (Greater London)
*E.*56,034 *T.*64.10%

*P. Boateng, *Lab.*	20,662
R. Blackman, *C.*	10,957
M. Harskin, *LD*	3,658
D. Johnson, *Green*	479
C. Jani, *NLP*	166
Lab. majority	9,705

(June 1987, Lab. maj. 7,931)

BRENTFORD AND ISLEWORTH (Greater London)
*E.*70,880 *T.*76.22%

N. Deva, *C.*	24,752
Ms A. Keen, *Lab.*	22,666
Ms J. Salmon, *LD*	5,683
J. Bradley, *Green*	927
C. majority	2,086

(June 1987, C. maj. 7,953)

BRENTWOOD AND ONGAR (Greater London)
*E.*65,830 *T.*84.70%

E. Pickles, *C.*	32,145
Ms E. Bottomley, *LD*	17,000
F. Keohane, *Lab.*	6,080
Ms C. Bartley, *Green*	535
C. majority	15,145

(June 1987, C. maj. 18,921)

BRIDGWATER (Somerset)
*E.*71,567 *T.*79.51%

*Rt. Hon. T. King, *C.*	26,610
W. Revans, *LD*	16,894
P. James, *Lab.*	12,365
G. Dummett, *Green*	746
A. Body, *Ind.*	183
Ms G. Sanson, *NLP*	112
C. majority	9,716

(June 1987, C. maj. 11,195)

BRIDLINGTON (Humberside)
*E.*84,829 *T.*77.93%

*J. Townend, *C.*	33,604
J. Leeman, *LD*	17,246
S. Hatfield, *Lab.*	15,263
C. majority	16,358

(June 1987, C. maj. 17,321)

BRIGG AND CLEETHORPES (Humberside)
*E.*82,377 *T.*77.98%

*M. Brown, *C.*	31,673
I. Cawsey, *Lab.*	22,404
Ms M. Cockbill, *LD*	9,374
N. Jacques, *Green*	790
C. majority	9,269

(June 1987, C. maj. 12,250)

BRIGHTON KEMPTOWN (E. Sussex)
*E.*57,646 *T.*76.14%

*A. Bowden, *C.*	21,129
Ms G. Haynes, *Lab.*	18,073
P. Scott, *LD*	4,461
Ms E. Overall, *NLP*	230
C. majority	3,056

(June 1987, C. maj. 9,260)

BRIGHTON PAVILION (E. Sussex)
*E.*57,616 *T.*76.81%

D. Spencer, *C.*	20,630
D. Lepper, *Lab.*	16,955
T. Pearce, *LD*	5,606
I. Brodie, *Green*	963
Ms E. Turner, *NLP*	103
C. majority	3,675

(June 1987, C. maj. 9,142)

BRISTOL EAST (Avon)
*E.*62,577 *T.*80.40%

Ms J. Corston, *Lab.*	22,418
*J. Sayeed, *C.*	19,726
J. Kiely, *LD*	7,903
I. Anderson, *NF*	270
Lab. majority	2,692

(June 1987, C. maj. 4,123)

BRISTOL NORTH WEST (Avon)
*E.*72,726 *T.*82.35%

*M. Stern, *C.*	25,354
D. Naysmith, *Lab.*	25,309
J. Taylor, *LD*	8,498
H. Long, *SD*	729
C. majority	45

(June 1987, C. maj. 6,952)

BRISTOL SOUTH (Avon)
*E.*64,309 *T.*78.04%

*Ms D. Primarolo, *Lab.*	25,164
J. Bercow, *C.*	16,245
P. Crossley, *LD*	7,892
J. Boxall, *Green*	756
N. Phillips, *NLP*	136
Lab. majority	8,919

(June 1987, Lab. maj. 1,404)

BRISTOL WEST (Avon)
*E.*70,579 *T.*74.37%

*Rt. Hon. W. Waldegrave, *C.*	22,169
C. Boney, *LD*	16,098
H. Bashforth, *Lab.*	12,992
A. Sawday, *Green*	906
D. Cross, *NLP*	104
B. Brent, *Rev. Comm.*	92
P. Hammond, *SOADDA*	87
T. Hedges, *Anti Fed.*	42
C. majority	6,071

(June 1987, C. maj. 7,703)

BROMSGROVE (H & W)
*E.*71,111 *T.*82.49%

K. R. Thomason, *C.*	31,709
Ms C. Mole, *Lab.*	18,007
Ms A. Cassin, *LD*	8,090
J. Churchman, *Green*	856
C. majority	13,702

(June 1987, C. maj. 16,685)

BROXBOURNE (Herts)
*E.*72,116 *T.*79.95%

*Mrs M. Roe, *C.*	36,094
M. Hudson, *Lab.*	12,124
Mrs J. Davies, *LD*	9,244
G. Woolhouse, *NLP*	198
C. majority	23,970

(June 1987, C. maj. 22,995)

BROXTOWE (Notts)
*E.*73,123 *T.*83.40%

*J. Lester, *C.*	31,096
J. Walker, *Lab.*	21,205
J. Ross, *LD*	8,395
D. Lukehurst, *NLP*	293
C. majority	9,891

(June 1987, C. maj. 16,651)

BUCKINGHAM
*E.*56,063 *T.*84.21%

*G. Walden, *C.*	29,496
T. Jones, *LD*	9,705
K. White, *Lab.*	7,662
L. Sheaff, *NLP*	353
C. majority	19,791

(June 1987, C. maj. 18,526)

BURNLEY (Lancs)
*E.*68,952 *T.*74.38%

*P. Pike, *Lab.*	27,184
Mrs B. Binge, *C.*	15,693
G. Birtwistle, *LD*	8,414
Lab. majority	11,491

(June 1987, Lab. maj. 7,557)

BURTON (Staffs)
*E.*75,292 *T.*82.43%

*I. Lawrence, *C.*	30,845
Ms P. Muddyman, *Lab.*	24,849
R. Renold, *LD*	6,375
C. majority	5,996

(June 1987, C. maj. 9,830)

BURY NORTH (Greater Manchester)
*E.*69,529 *T.*84.77%

*A. Burt, *C.*	29,266
J. Dobbin, *Lab.*	24,502
C. McGrath, *LD*	5,010
M. Sullivan, *NLP*	163
C. majority	4,764

(June 1987, C. maj. 6,929)

BURY SOUTH (Greater Manchester)
*E.*65,793 *T.*82.10%

*D. Sumberg, *C.*	24,873
Ms H. Blears, *Lab.*	24,085
A. Cruden, *LD*	4,832
Mrs N. Sullivan, *NLP*	228
C. majority	788

(June 1987, C. maj. 2,679)

BURY ST EDMUNDS (Suffolk)
*E.*79,967 *T.*78.38%

R. Spring, *C.* 33,554
T. Sheppard, *Lab.* 14,767
J. Williams, *LD* 13,814
Ms J. Lillis, *NLP* 550
C. majority 18,787
(June 1987, C. maj. 21,458)

CALDER VALLEY (W. Yorks)
*E.*74,417 *T.*82.09%

*Sir D. Thompson, *C.* 27,753
D. Chaytor, *Lab.* 22,875
S. Pearson, *LD* 9,842
Ms V. Smith, *Green* 622
C. majority 4,878
(June 1987, C. maj. 6,045)

CAMBRIDGE
*E.*69,022 *T.*73.18%

Mrs A. Campbell, *Lab.* 20,039
M. Bishop, *C.* 19,459
D. Howarth, *LD* 10,037
T. Cooper, *Green* 720
D. Brettell-Winnington, *Loony* 175
R. Chalmers, *NLP* 83
Lab. majority 580
(June 1987, C. maj. 5,060)

CAMBRIDGESHIRE NORTH EAST
*E.*79,935 *T.*79.38%

*M. Moss, *C.* 34,288
M. Leeke, *LD* 19,195
R. Harris, *Lab.* 8,746
C. Ash, *Lib.* 998
Mrs M. Chalmers, *NLP* 227
C. majority 15,093
(June 1987, C. maj. 1,428)

CAMBRIDGESHIRE SOUTH EAST
*E.*78,600 *T.*80.57%

*J. Paice, *C.* 36,693
R. Wotherspoon, *LD* 12,883
M. Jones, *Lab.* 12,688
J. Marsh, *Green* 836
Ms B. Langridge, *NLP* 231
C. majority 23,810
(June 1987, C. maj. 17,502)

CAMBRIDGESHIRE SOUTH WEST
*E.*84,418 *T.*81.10%

*Sir A. Grant, *C.* 38,902
Ms S. Sutton, *LD* 19,265
K. Price, *Lab.* 9,378
Ms L. Whitebread, *Green* 699
F. Chalmers, *NLP* 225
C. majority 19,637
(June 1987, C. maj. 18,251)

CANNOCK AND BURNTWOOD (Staffs)
*E.*72,600 *T.*84.21%

A. Wright, *Lab.* 28,139
*G. Howarth, *C.* 26,633
P. Treasaden, *LD* 5,899
M. Hartshorne, *Loony* 469
Lab. majority 1,506
(June 1987, C. maj. 2,689)

CANTERBURY (Kent)
*E.*75,181 *T.*78.12%

*J. Brazier, *C.* 29,827
M. Vye, *LD* 19,022
M. Whitemore, *Lab.* 8,936
Ms W. Arnall, *Green* 747
Ms S. Curphey, *NLP* 203
C. majority 10,805
(June 1987, C. maj. 14,891)

CARLISLE (Cumbria)
*E.*55,140 *T.*79.39%

*E. Martlew, *Lab.* 20,479
C. Condie, *C.* 17,371
R. Aldersey, *LD* 5,740
Ms N. Robinson, *NLP* 190
Lab. majority 3,108
(June 1987, Lab. maj. 916)

CARSHALTON AND WALLINGTON (Surrey)
*E.*65,179 *T.*80.94%

*F. N. Forman, *C.* 26,243
T. Brake, *LD* 16,300
Ms M. Moran, *Lab.* 9,333
R. Steel, *Green* 614
D. Bamford, *Loony G.* 266
C. majority 9,943
(June 1987, C. maj. 14,409)

CASTLE POINT (Essex)
*E.*66,229 *T.*80.50%

Dr R. Spink, *C.* 29,629
D. Flack, *Lab.* 12,799
A. Petchey, *LD* 10,208
Ms I. Willis, *Green* 683
C. majority 16,830
(June 1987, C. maj. 19,248)

CHEADLE (Greater Manchester)
*E.*66,131 *T.*84.43%

*S. Day, *C.* 32,504
Ms P. Calton, *LD* 16,726
Ms S. Broadhurst, *Lab.* 6,442
Ms P. Whittle, *NLP* 168
C. majority 15,778
(June 1987, C. maj. 10,631)

CHELMSFORD (Essex)
*E.*83,441 *T.*84.61%

*S. Burns, *C.* 39,043
H. Nicholson, *LD* 20,783
Dr R. Chad, *Lab.* 10,010
Ms E. Burgess, *Green* 769
C. majority 18,260
(June 1987, C. maj. 7,761)

CHELSEA (Greater London)
*E.*42,371 *T.*63.31%

*Rt. Hon. N. Scott, *C.* 17,471
Ms R. Horton, *Lab.* 4,682
Ms S. Broidy, *LD* 4,101
Ms N. Kortvelyessy, *Green* 485
D. Armstrong, *Anti Fed.* 88
C. majority 12,789
(June 1987, C. maj. 13,319)

CHELTENHAM (Glos)
*E.*79,808 *T.*80.32%

N. Jones, *LD* 30,351
J. Taylor, *C.* 28,683
Ms P. Tatlow, *Lab.* 4,077
M. Rendall, *AFE* 665
H. Brighouse, *NLP* 169
M. Bruce-Smith, *Ind.* 162
LD majority 1,668
(June 1987, C. maj. 4,896)

CHERTSEY AND WALTON (Surrey)
*E.*70,465 *T.*80.52%

*Rt. Hon. Sir G. Pattie, *C.* 34,163
A. Kremer, *LD* 11,344
Ms I. Hamilton, *Lab.* 10,791
Ms S. Bennell, *NLP* 444
C. majority 22,819
(June 1987, C. maj. 17,469)

CHESHAM AND AMERSHAM (Bucks)
*E.*69,895 *T.*81.93%

Ms C. Gillan, *C.* 36,273
A. Ketteringham, *LD* 14,053
Ms C. Atherton, *Lab.* 5,931
Ms C. Strickland, *Green* 753
T. Griffith-Jones, *NLP* 255
C. majority 22,220
(June 1987, C. maj. 19,440)

CHESTER, CITY OF
*E.*63,370 *T.*83.84%

G. Brandreth, *C.* 23,411
D. Robinson, *Lab.* 22,310
G. Smith, *LD* 6,867
T. Barker, *Green* 448
S. Cross, *NLP* 98
C. majority 1,101
(June 1987, C. maj. 4,855)

CHESTERFIELD (Derbys)
*E.*71,783 *T.*77.98%

*A. Benn, *Lab.* 26,461
A. Rogers, *LD* 20,047
P. Lewis, *C.* 9,473
Lab. majority 6,414
(June 1987, Lab. maj. 8,577)

CHICHESTER (W. Sussex)
*E.*82,124 *T.*77.77%

*R. A. Nelson, *C.* 37,906
P. Gardiner, *LD* 17,019
Ms D. Andrewes, *Lab.* 7,192

E. Paine, *Green* 876
Ms J. Weights, *Lib.* 643
Ms J. Jackson, *NLP* 238
C. majority 20,887
(June 1987, C. maj. 20,177)

CHINGFORD (Greater London)
*E.*55,401 *T.*78.41%

G. I. Duncan-Smith, *C.* 25,730
P. Dawe, *Lab.* 10,792
S. Banks, *LD* 5,705
D. Green, *Lib.* 602
J. Baguley, *Green* 575
Revd C. John, *Ind.* 41
C. majority 14,938
(June 1987, C. maj. 17,955)

CHIPPING BARNET (Greater London)
*E.*57,153 *T.*78.57%

*S. Chapman, *C.* 25,589
A. Williams, *Lab.* 11,638
D. Smith, *LD* 7,247
Ms D. Derksen, *NLP* 222
C. Johnson, *Fun.* 213
C. majority 13,951
(June 1987, C. maj. 14,871)

CHISLEHURST (Greater London)
*E.*53,782 *T.*78.89%

*R. Sims, *C.* 24,761
I. Wingfield, *Lab.* 9,485
W. Hawthorne, *LD* 6,683
I. Richmond, *Lib.* 849
Dr F. Speed, *Green* 652
C. majority 15,276
(June 1987, C. maj. 14,507)

CHORLEY (Lancs)
*E.*78,531 *T.*82.81%

*D. Dover, *C.* 30,715
R. McManus, *Lab.* 26,469
Ms J. Ross-Mills, *LD* 7,452
P. Leadbetter, *NLP* 402
C. majority 4,246
(June 1987, C. maj. 8,057)

CHRISTCHURCH (Dorset)
*E.*71,438 *T.*80.70%

*R. Adley, *C.* 36,627
Revd D. Bussey, *LD* 13,612
A. Lloyd, *Lab.* 6,997
J. Barratt, *NLP* 243
A. Wareham, *CRA* 175
C. majority 23,015
(June 1987, C. maj. 22,374)

CIRENCESTER AND TEWKESBURY (Glos)
*E.*88,299 *T.*82.05%

G. Clifton-Brown, *C.* 40,258
E. Weston, *LD* 24,200
T. Page, *Lab.* 7,262
R. Clayton, *NLP* 449
P. Trice-Rolph, *Ind.* 287
C. majority 16,058
(June 1987, C. maj. 12,662)

CITY OF LONDON AND WESTMINSTER SOUTH
*E.*55,021 *T.*63.08%

*Rt. Hon. P. Brooke, *C.* 20,938
C. Smith, *Lab.* 7,569
Ms J. Smithard, *LD* 5,392
G. Herbert, *Green* 458
P. Stockton, *Loony* 147
A. Farrell, *IFM* 107
R. Johnson, *NLP* 101
C. majority 13,369
(June 1987, C. maj. 12,034)

COLCHESTER NORTH (Essex)
*E.*86,479 *T.*79.11%

Hon. B. Jenkin, *C.* 35,213
Dr J. Raven, *LD* 18,721
D. Lee, *Lab.* 13,870
M. Tariq Shabbeer, *Green* 372
M. Mears, *NLP* 238
C. majority 16,492
(June 1987, C. maj. 13,623)

COLCHESTER SOUTH AND MALDON (Essex)
*E.*86,410 *T.*79.22%

J. Whittingdale, *C.* 37,548
I. Thorn, *LD* 15,727
C. Pearson, *Lab.* 14,158
M. Patterson, *Green* 1,028
C. majority 21,821
(June 1987, C. maj. 15,483)

COLNE VALLEY (W. Yorks)
*E.*72,043 *T.*81.97%

*G. Riddick, *C.* 24,804
J. Harman, *Lab.* 17,579
N. Priestley, *LD* 15,953
R. Stewart, *Green* 443
Mrs M. Staniforth, *Loony* 160
J. Hasty, *Ind.* 73
J. Tattersall, *NLP* 44
C. majority 7,225
(June 1987, C. maj. 1,677)

CONGLETON (Cheshire)
*E.*70,477 *T.*84.47%

*Mrs J. A. Winterton, *C.* 29,163
I. Brodie-Browne, *LD* 18,043
M. Finnegan, *Lab.* 11,927
P. Brown, *NLP* 399
C. majority 11,120
(June 1987, C. maj. 7,969)

COPELAND (Cumbria)
*E.*54,911 *T.*83.54%

*Dr J. Cunningham, *Lab.* 22,328
P. Davies, *C.* 19,889
R. Putnam, *LD* 3,508
J. Sinton, *NLP* 148
Lab. majority 2,439
(June 1987, Lab. maj. 1,894)

CORBY (Northants)
*E.*68,333 *T.*82.88%

*W. Powell, *C.* 25,203
S. Feather, *Lab.* 24,861
M. Roffe, *LD* 5,792
Ms J. Wood, *Lib.* 784
C. majority 342
(June 1987, C. maj. 1,805)

CORNWALL NORTH
*E.*76,844 *T.*81.51%

P. Tyler, *LD* 29,696
*Sir G. Neale, *C.* 27,775
F. Jordan, *Lab.* 4,103
P. Andrews, *Lib.* 678
G. Rowe, *Ind.* 276
Mrs H. Treadwell, *NLP* 112
LD majority 1,921
(June 1987, C. maj. 5,682)

CORNWALL SOUTH EAST
*E.*73,027 *T.*82.14%

*R. Hicks, *C.* 30,565
R. Teverson, *LD* 22,861
Mrs L. Gilroy, *Lab.* 5,536
Miss M. Cook, *Lib.* 644
A. Quick, *Anti Fed.* 227
Miss R. Allen, *NLP* 155
C. majority 7,704
(June 1987, C. maj. 6,607)

COVENTRY NORTH EAST (W. Midlands)
*E.*64,787 *T.*73.20%

R. Ainsworth, *Lab.* 24,896
K. Perrin, *C.* 13,220
V. McKee, *LD* 5,306
*J. Hughes, *Ind. Lab.* 4,008
Lab. majority 11,676
(June 1987, Lab. maj. 11,867)

COVENTRY NORTH WEST (W. Midlands)
*E.*50,670 *T.*77.63%

*G. Robinson, *Lab.* 20,349
Mrs A. Hill, *C.* 13,917
Ms A. Simpson, *LD* 5,070
Lab. majority 6,432
(June 1987, Lab. maj. 5,663)

COVENTRY SOUTH EAST (W. Midlands)
*E.*48,796 *T.*74.87%

J. Cunningham, *Lab.* 11,902
Mrs M. Hyams, *C.* 10,591
*D. Nellist, *Ind. Lab.* 10,551
A. Armstrong, *LD* 3,318
N. Tompkinson, *NF* 173
Lab. majority 1,311
(June 1987, Lab. maj. 6,653)

COVENTRY SOUTH WEST (W. Midlands)
*E.*63,474 *T.*80.14%

*J. Butcher, *C.* 23,225
R. Slater, *Lab.* 21,789
G. Sewards, *LD* 4,666
R. Wheway, *Lib.* 989
D. Morris, *NLP* 204
C. majority 1,436
(June 1987, C. maj. 3,210)

CRAWLEY (W. Sussex)
*E.*78,277 *T.*79.16%

*Hon. A. N. Soames, *C.* 30,204
Ms L. Moffatt, *Lab.* 22,439
G. Seekings, *LD* 8,558
M. Wilson, *Green* 766
C. majority 7,765
(June 1987, C. maj. 12,138)

CREWE AND NANTWICH (Cheshire)
*E.*74,993 *T.*81.87%

*Hon. Mrs G. Dunwoody, *Lab.* 28,065
B. Silvester, *C.* 25,370
G. Griffiths, *LD* 7,315
Ms N. Wilkinson, *Green* 651
Lab. majority 2,695
(June 1987, Lab. maj. 1,092)

CROSBY (Merseyside)
*E.*82,537 *T.*82.45%

*M. Thornton, *C.* 32,267
Ms M. Eagle, *Lab.* 17,461
Ms F. Clucas, *LD* 16,562
J. Marks, *Lib.* 1,052
S. Brady, *Green* 559
N. Paterson, *NLP* 152
C. majority 14,806
(June 1987, C. maj. 6,853)

CROYDON CENTRAL (Greater London)
*E.*55,798 *T.*71.73%

Sir P. Beresford, *C.* 22,168
G. Davies, *Lab.* 12,518
Ms D. Richardson, *LD* 5,342
C. majority 9,650
(June 1987, C. maj. 12,617)

CROYDON NORTH EAST (Greater London)
*E.*64,405 *T.*72.01%

D. Congdon, *C.* 23,835
Ms M. Walker, *Lab.* 16,362
J. Fraser, *LD* 6,186
C. majority 7,473
(June 1987, C. maj. 12,519)

CROYDON NORTH WEST (Greater London)
*E.*57,241 *T.*70.76%

M. Wicks, *Lab.* 19,152
*H. Malins, *C.* 17,626
Ms L. Hawkins, *LD* 3,728
Lab. majority 1,526
(June 1987, C. maj. 3,988)

CROYDON SOUTH (Greater London)
*E.*64,768 *T.*77.57%

R. Ottaway, *C.* 31,993
P. Billenness, *LD* 11,568
Miss H. Salmon, *Lab.* 6,444
M. Samuel, *Choice* 239
C. majority 20,425
(June 1987, C. maj. 19,063)

DAGENHAM (Greater London)
*E.*59,645 *T.*70.65%

*B. Gould, *Lab.* 22,027
D. Rossiter, *C.* 15,294
C. Marquand, *LD* 4,824
Lab. majority 6,733
(June 1987, Lab. maj. 2,469)

DARLINGTON (Durham)
*E.*66,094 *T.*83.60%

A. Milburn, *Lab.* 26,556
*M. Fallon, *C.* 23,758
P. Bergg, *LD* 4,586
Dr D. Clarke, *BNP* 355
Lab. majority 2,798
(June 1987, C. maj. 2,661)

DARTFORD (Kent)
*E.*72,366 *T.*83.14%

*B. Dunn, *C.* 31,194
Dr H. Stoate, *Lab.* 20,880
P. Bryden, *LD* 7,584
A. Munro, *FDP* 262
Ms A. Holland, *NLP* 247
C. majority 10,314
(June 1987, C. maj. 14,929)

DAVENTRY (Northants)
*E.*71,824 *T.*82.75%

*T. Boswell, *C.* 34,734
Ms L. Koumi, *Lab.* 14,460
A. Rounthwaite, *LD* 9,820
R. France, *NLP* 422
C. majority 20,274
(June 1987, C. maj. 19,690)

DAVYHULME (Greater Manchester)
*E.*61,679 *T.*81.82%

*W. Churchill, *C.* 24,216
B. Brotherton, *Lab.* 19,790
Ms J. Pearcey, *LD* 5,797
T. Brotheridge, *NLP* 665
C. majority 4,426
(June 1987, C. maj. 8,199)

DENTON AND REDDISH (Greater Manchester)
*E.*68,463 *T.*76.77%

*A. Bennett, *Lab.* 29,021
J. Horswell, *C.* 16,937
Dr F. Ridley, *LD* 4,953
M. Powell, *Lib.* 1,296
J. Fuller, *NLP* 354
Lab. majority 12,084
(June 1987, Lab. maj. 8,250)

DERBY NORTH
*E.*73,176 *T.*80.65%

*G. Knight, *C.* 28,574
R. Laxton, *Lab.* 24,121
R. Charlesworth, *LD* 5,638
E. Wall, *Green* 383
P. Hart, *NF* 245
N. Onley, *NLP* 58
C. majority 4,453
(June 1987, C. maj. 6,280)

DERBY SOUTH
*E.*66,328 *T.*75.52%

*Mrs M. Beckett, *Lab.* 25,917
N. Brown, *C.* 18,981
S. Hartropp, *LD* 5,198
Lab. majority 6,936
(June 1987, Lab. maj. 1,516)

DERBYSHIRE NORTH EAST
*E.*70,707 *T.*83.61%

*H. Barnes, *Lab.* 28,860
J. Hayes, *C.* 22,590
D. Stone, *LD* 7,675
Lab. majority 6,270
(June 1987, Lab. maj. 3,720)

DERBYSHIRE SOUTH
*E.*82,342 *T.*85.49%

*Mrs E. Currie, *C.* 34,266
M. Todd, *Lab.* 29,608
Ms D. Brass, *LD* 6,236
T. Mercer, *NLP* 291
C. majority 4,658
(June 1987, C. maj. 10,311)

DERBYSHIRE WEST
*E.*71,201 *T.*84.99%

*P. McLoughlin, *C.* 32,879
R. Fearn, *LD* 14,110
S. Clamp, *Lab.* 13,528
C. majority 18,769
(June 1987, C. maj. 10,527)

DEVIZES (Wilts)
*E.*89,745 *T.*81.67%

M. Ancram, *C.* 39,090
Ms J. Mactaggart, *LD* 19,378
Ms R. Berry, *Lab.* 13,060
S. Coles, *Lib.* 962
D. Ripley, *Green* 808
C. majority 19,712
(June 1987, C. maj. 17,830)

DEVON NORTH
*E.*68,998 *T.*84.36%

N. Harvey, *LD* 27,414
*A. Speller, *C.* 26,620
P. Donner, *Lab.* 3,410

Ms C. Simmons, *Green* 658
G. Treadwell, *NLP* 107
LD majority 794
(June 1987, C. maj. 4,469)

DEVON WEST AND TORRIDGE
*E.*76,933 *T.*81.46%
*Miss E. Nicholson, *C.* 29,627
D. McBride, *LD* 26,013
D. Brenton, *Lab.* 5,997
Dr F. Williamson, *Green* 898
D. Collins, *NLP* 141
C. majority 3,614
(June 1987, C. maj. 6,468)

DEWSBURY (W. Yorks)
*E.*72,839 *T.*80.18%
*Mrs W. A. Taylor, *Lab.* 25,596
J. Whitfield, *C.* 24,962
R. Meadowcroft, *LD* 6,570
Lady J. Birdwood, *BNP* 660
N. Denby, *Green* 471
Mrs J. Marsden, *NLP* 146
Lab. majority 634
(June 1987, Lab. maj. 445)

DONCASTER CENTRAL (S. Yorks)
*E.*68,890 *T.*74.24%
*Rt. Hon. H. Walker, *Lab.* 27,795
W. Glossop, *C.* 17,113
C. Hampson, *LD* 6,057
M. Driver, *WRP* 184
Lab. majority 10,682
(June 1987, Lab. maj. 8,196)

DONCASTER NORTH (S. Yorks)
*E.*74,732 *T.*73.92%
K. Hughes, *Lab.* 34,135
R. Light, *C.* 14,322
S. Whiting, *LD* 6,787
Lab. majority 19,813
(June 1987, Lab. maj. 19,938)

DON VALLEY (S. Yorks)
*E.*76,327 *T.*76.25%
*M. Redmond, *Lab.* 32,008
N. Paget-Brown, *C.* 18,474
M. Jevons, *LD* 6,920
S. Platt, *Green* 803
Lab. majority 13,534
(June 1987, Lab. maj. 11,467)

DORSET NORTH
*E.*76,718 *T.*81.79%
*N. Baker, *C.* 34,234
Ms L. Siegle, *LD* 24,154
J. Fitzmaurice, *Lab.* 4,360
C. majority 10,080
(June 1987, C. maj. 11,907)

DORSET SOUTH
*E.*75,788 *T.*76.91%
*I. Bruce, *C.* 29,319
B. Ellis, *LD* 15,811
Dr A. Chedzoy, *Lab.* 12,298
Mrs J. Nager, *Ind.* 673
M. Griffiths, *NLP* 191
C. majority 13,508
(June 1987, C. maj. 15,067)

DORSET WEST
*E.*67,256 *T.*81.18%
*Sir J. Spicer, *C.* 27,766
R. Legg, *LD* 19,756
J. Mann, *Lab.* 7,082
C. majority 8,010
(June 1987, C. maj. 12,364)

DOVER (Kent)
*E.*68,962 *T.*83.50%
*D. Shaw, *C.* 25,395
G. Prosser, *Lab.* 24,562
M. Sole, *LD* 6,212
A. Sullivan, *Green* 637
P. Sherred, *Ind.* 407
B. Philp, *Ind. C.* 250
C. Percy, *NLP* 127
C. majority 833
(June 1987, C. maj. 6,541)

DUDLEY EAST (W. Midlands)
*E.*75,355 *T.*74.96%
*Dr J. Gilbert, *Lab.* 29,806
J. Holland, *C.* 20,606
I. Jenkins, *LD* 5,400
G. Cartwright, *NF* 675
Lab. majority 9,200
(June 1987, Lab. maj. 3,473)

DUDLEY WEST (W. Midlands)
*E.*86,632 *T.*82.08%
*J. Blackburn, *C.* 34,729
K. Lomax, *Lab.* 28,940
G. Lewis, *LD* 7,446
C. majority 5,789
(June 1987, C. maj. 10,244)

DULWICH (Greater London)
*E.*55,141 *T.*67.91%
Ms T. Jowell, *Lab.* 17,714
*G. Bowden, *C.* 15,658
Dr A. Goldie, *LD* 4,078
Lab. majority 2,056
(June 1987, C. maj. 180)

DURHAM, CITY OF
*E.*68,165 *T.*74.61%
*G. Steinberg, *Lab.* 27,095
M. Woodroofe, *C.* 12,037
N. Martin, *LD* 10,915
Ms S. J. Banks, *Green* 812
Lab. majority 15,058
(June 1987, Lab. maj. 6,125)

DURHAM NORTH
*E.*73,694 *T.*76.08%
*G. Radice, *Lab.* 33,567
Ms E. Sibley, *C.* 13,930
P. Appleby, *LD* 8,572
Lab. majority 19,637
(June 1987, Lab. maj. 18,433)

DURHAM NORTH WEST
*E.*61,139 *T.* 75.58%
*Miss H. Armstrong, Lab. 26,734
Mrs T. May, C. 12,747
T. Farron, LD 6,728
Lab. majority 13,987
(June 1987, Lab. maj. 10,162)

EALING ACTON (Greater London)
*E.*58,687 *T.*76.03%
*Sir G. Young, *C.* 22,579
Ms Y. Johnson, *Lab.* 15,572
L. Rowe, *LD* 5,487
Ms A. Seibe, *Green* 554
T. Pitt-Aikens, *Ind. C.* 432
C. majority 7,007
(June 1987, C. maj. 12,233)

EALING NORTH (Greater London)
*E.*63,528 *T.*78.84%
*H. Greenway, *C.* 24,898
M. Stears, *Lab.* 18,932
P. Hankinson, *LD* 5,247
D. Earl, *Green* 554
C. Hill, *NF* 277
R. Davis, *CD* 180
C. majority 5,966
(June 1987, C. maj. 15,153)

EALING SOUTHALL (Greater London)
*E.*65,574 *T.*75.49%
P. Khabra, *Lab.* 23,476
P. Treleaven, *C.* 16,610
*S. Bidwell, *True Lab.* 4,665
Ms P. Nandhra, *LD* 3,790
N. Goodwin, *Green* 964
Lab. majority 6,866
(June 1987, Lab. maj. 7,977)

EASINGTON (Durham)
*E.*65,061 *T.*72.46%
*J. Cummings, *Lab.* 34,269
W. Perry, *C.* 7,879
P. Freitag, *LD* 5,001
Lab. majority 26,390
(June 1987, Lab. maj. 24,639)

EASTBOURNE (E. Sussex)
*E.*76,103 *T.*80.97%
N. Waterson, *C.* 31,792
*D. Bellotti, *LD* 26,311
I. Gibbons, *Lab.* 2,834
D. Aherne, *Green* 391
Ms T. Williamson, *Lib.* 296
C. majority 5,481
(June 1987, C. maj 16,923)
(October 1990, LD maj. 4,550)

EASTLEIGH (Hants)
*E.*91,736 *T.*82.91%

S. Milligan, *C.*	38,998
D. Chidgey, *LD*	21,296
Ms J. Sugrue, *Lab.*	15,768
C. majority	17,702

(June 1987, C. maj. 13,355)

ECCLES (Greater Manchester)
*E.*64,910 *T.*74.12%

*Miss J. Lestor, *Lab.*	27,357
G. Ling, *C.*	14,131
G. Reid, *LD*	5,835
R. Duriez, *Green*	521
Miss J. Garner, *NLP*	270
Lab. majority	13,226

(June 1987, Lab. maj. 9,699)

EDDISBURY (Cheshire)
*E.*75,089 *T.*82.55%

*A. Goodlad, *C.*	31,625
Ms N. Edwards, *Lab.*	18,928
D. Lyon, *LD*	10,543
A. Basden, *Green*	783
N. Pollard, *NLP*	107
C. majority	12,697

(June 1987, C. maj. 15,835)

EDMONTON (Greater London)
*E.*63,052 *T.*75.66%

*Dr I. Twinn, *C.*	22,076
A. Love, *Lab.*	21,483
E. Jones, *LD*	3,940
Ms E. Solley, *NLP*	207
C. majority	593

(June 1987, C. maj. 7,286)

ELLESMERE PORT AND NESTON (Cheshire)
*E.*71,572 *T.*84.12%

A. Miller, *Lab.*	27,782
A. Pearce, *C.*	25,793
Ms E. Jewkes, *LD*	5,944
Dr M. Money, *Green*	589
Dr A. Rae, *NLP*	105
Lab. majority	1,989

(June 1987, C. maj. 1,853)

ELMET (W. Yorks)
*E.*70,558 *T.*82.53%

*S. Batiste, *C.*	27,677
C. Burgon, *Lab.*	24,416
Mrs A. Beck, *LD*	6,144
C. majority	3,261

(June 1987, C. maj. 5,356)

ELTHAM (Greater London)
*E.*51,989 *T.*78.72%

*P. Bottomley, *C.*	18,813
C. Efford, *Lab.*	17,147
C. McGinty, *LD*	4,804
A. Graham, *Ind. C.*	165
C. majority	1,666

(June 1987, C. maj. 6,460)

ENFIELD NORTH (Greater London)
*E.*67,421 *T.*77.91%

*T. Eggar, *C.*	27,789
M. Upham, *Lab.*	18,359
Ms S. Tustin, *LD*	5,817
J. Markham, *NLP*	565
C. majority	9,430

(June 1987, C. maj. 14,015)

ENFIELD SOUTHGATE (Greater London)
*E.*64,311 *T.*76.28%

*M. Portillo, *C.*	28,422
Ms K. Livney, *Lab.*	12,859
K. Keane, *LD*	7,080
Ms M. Hollands, *Green*	696
C. majority	15,563

(June 1987, C. maj. 18,345)

EPPING FOREST (Essex)
*E.*67,585 *T.*80.55%

*S. Norris, *C.*	32,407
S. Murray, *Lab.*	12,219
Mrs B. Austen, *LD*	9,265
A. O'Brien, *EFRA*	552
C. majority	20,188

(June 1987, C. maj. 21,513)
(December 1988, C. maj. 4,504)

EPSOM AND EWELL (Surrey)
*E.*68,138 *T.*80.14%

*Rt. Hon. A. Hamilton, *C.*	32,861
M. Emerson, *LD*	12,840
R. Warren, *Lab.*	8,577
G. Hatchard, *NLP*	334
C. majority	20,021

(June 1987, C. maj. 20,761)

EREWASH (Derbys)
*E.*75,627 *T.*83.78%

Mrs A. Knight, *C.*	29,907
S. Stafford, *Lab.*	24,204
P. Tuck, *LD*	8,606
L. Johnson, *BNP*	645
C. majority	5,703

(June 1987, C. maj. 9,754)

ERITH AND CRAYFORD (Kent)
*E.*59,213 *T.*79.66%

*D. Evennett, *C.*	21,926
N. Beard, *Lab.*	19,587
Ms F. Jamieson, *LD*	5,657
C. majority	2,339

(June 1987, C. maj. 6,994)

ESHER (Surrey)
*E.*58,840 *T.*80.80%

*I. Taylor, *C.*	31,115
J. Richling, *LD*	10,744
Ms J. Reay, *Lab.*	5,685
C. majority	20,371

(June 1987, C. maj. 19,068)

EXETER (Devon)
*E.*76,723 *T.*82.21%

*Sir J. Hannam, *C.*	26,543
J. Lloyd, *Lab.*	22,498
G. Oakes, *LD*	12,059
Ms A. Micklem, *Lib.*	1,119
T. Brenan, *Green*	764
M. Turnbull, *NLP*	98
C. majority	4,045

(June 1987, C. maj. 7,656)

FALMOUTH AND CAMBORNE (Cornwall)
*E.*70,702 *T.*81.10%

S. Coe, *C.*	21,150
Ms T. Jones, *LD*	17,883
J. Cosgrove, *Lab.*	16,732
P. Holmes, *Lib.*	730
K. Saunders, *Green*	466
F. Zapp, *Loony*	327
A. Pringle, *NLP*	56
C. majority	3,267

(June 1987, C. maj. 5,039)

FAREHAM (Hants)
*E.*81,124 *T.*81.85%

*P. Lloyd, *C.*	40,482
J. Thompson, *LD*	16,341
Ms E. Weston, *Lab.*	8,766
M. Brimecome, *Green*	818
C. majority	24,141

(June 1987, C. maj. 18,795)

FAVERSHAM (Kent)
*E.*81,977 *T.*79.71%

*R. Moate, *C.*	32,755
Ms H. Brinton, *Lab.*	16,404
R. Truelove, *LD*	15,896
R. Bradshaw, *NLP*	294
C. majority	16,351

(June 1987, C. maj. 13,978)

FELTHAM AND HESTON (Greater London)
*E.*81,221 *T.*73.90%

A. Keen, *Lab.*	27,660
*P. Ground, *C.*	25,665
M. Hoban, *LD*	6,700
Lab. majority	1,995

(June 1987, C. maj. 5,430)

FINCHLEY (Greater London)
*E.*52,907 *T.*77.64%

H. Booth, *C.*	21,039
Ms A. Marjoram, *Lab.*	14,651
Ms H. Leighter, *LD*	4,568
A. Gunstock, *Green*	564
Ms S. Johnson, *Loony*	130
J. Macrae, *NLP*	129
C. majority	6,388

(June 1987, C. maj. 8,913)

FOLKESTONE AND HYTHE (Kent)
*E.*65,856 *T.*79.61%

*Rt. Hon. M. Howard, *C.*	27,437
Mrs L. Cufley, *LD*	18,527
P. Doherty, *Lab.*	6,347
A. Hobbs, *NLP*	123
C. majority	8,910

(June 1987, C. maj. 9,126)

FULHAM (Greater London)
*E.*52,740 *T.*76.16%

*M. Carrington, *C.*	21,438
N. Moore, *Lab.*	14,859
P. Crystal, *LD*	3,339
Ms E. Streeter, *Green*	443
J. Darby, *NLP*	91
C. majority	6,579

(June 1987, C. maj. 6,322)

FYLDE (Lancs)
*E.*63,573 *T.*78.50%

*M. Jack, *C.*	30,639
N. Cryer, *LD*	9,648
Ms C. Hughes, *Lab.*	9,382
P. Leadbetter, *NLP*	239
C. majority	20,991

(June 1987, C. maj. 17,772)

GAINSBOROUGH AND HORNCASTLE (Lincs)
*E.*72,038 *T.*80.87%

*E. Leigh, *C.*	31,444
N. Taylor, *LD*	15,199
Ms F. Jones, *Lab.*	11,619
C. majority	16,245

(June 1987, C. maj. 9,723)

GATESHEAD EAST (Tyne & Wear)
*E.*64,355 *T.*73.63%

*Miss J. Quin, *Lab.*	30,100
M. Callanan, *C.*	11,570
R. Beadle, *LD*	5,720
Lab. majority	18,530

(June 1987, Lab. maj. 17,228)

GEDLING (Notts)
*E.*68,953 *T.*82.34%

*A. J. B. Mitchell, *C.*	30,191
V. Coaker, *Lab.*	19,554
D. George, *LD*	6,863
Ms A. Miszeweka, *NLP*	168
C. majority	10,637

(June 1987, C. maj. 16,539)

GILLINGHAM (Kent)
*E.*71,851 *T.*80.32%

*J. Couchman, *C.*	30,201
P. Clark, *Lab.*	13,563
M. Wallbank, *LD*	13,509
C. MacKinlay, *Ind.*	248
D. Jolicoeur, *NLP*	190
C. majority	16,638

(June 1987, C. maj. 12,549)

GLANFORD AND SCUNTHORPE (Humberside)
*E.*73,479 *T.*78.91%

*E. Morley, *Lab.*	30,623
Dr A. Saywood, *C.*	22,211
W. Paxton, *LD*	4,172
C. Nottingham, *SD*	982
Lab. majority	8,412

(June 1987, Lab. maj. 512)

GLOUCESTER
*E.*80,578 *T.*80.24%

*D. French, *C.*	29,870
K. Stephens, *Lab.*	23,812
J. Sewell, *LD*	10,978
C. majority	6,058

(June 1987, C. maj. 12,035)

GLOUCESTERSHIRE WEST
*E.*80,007 *T.*83.89%

*P. Marland, *C.*	29,232
Ms D. Organ, *Lab.*	24,274
L. Boait, *LD*	13,366
A. Reeve, *Brit. Ind.*	172
C. Palmer, *Century*	75
C. majority	4,958

(June 1987, C. maj. 11,679)

GOSPORT (Hants)
*E.*69,638 *T.*76.79%

*P. Viggers, *C.*	31,094
M. Russell, *LD*	14,776
Ms M. Angus, *Lab.*	7,275
P. Ettie, *Pensioners*	332
C. majority	16,318

(June 1987, C. maj. 13,723)

GRANTHAM (Lincs)
*E.*83,463 *T.*79.29%

*Hon. D. Hogg, *C.*	37,194
S. Taggart, *Lab.*	17,606
J. Heppell, *LD*	9,882
J. Hiley, *Lib.*	1,500
C. majority	19,588

(June 1987, C. maj. 21,303)

GRAVESHAM (Kent)
*E.*70,740 *T.*83.48%

*J. Arnold, *C.*	29,322
G. Green, *Lab.*	23,829
D. Deedman, *LD*	5,269
A. Bunstone, *Ind.*	273
R. Khilkoff-Boulding, *ILP*	187
B. Buxton, *Soc.*	174
C. majority	5,493

(June 1987, C. maj. 8,792)

GREAT GRIMSBY (Humberside)
*E.*67,427 *T.*75.28%

*A. V. Mitchell, *Lab.*	25,895
P. Jackson, *C.*	18,391
Ms P. Frankish, *LD*	6,475
Lab. majority	7,504

(June 1987, Lab. maj. 8,784)

GREAT YARMOUTH (Norfolk)
*E.*68,263 *T.*77.94%

*M. Carttiss, *C.*	25,505
Ms B. Baughan, *Lab.*	20,196
M. Scott, *LD*	7,225
Ms P. Larkin, *NLP*	284
C. majority	5,309

(June 1987, C. maj. 10,083)

GREENWICH (Greater London)
*E.*47,789 *T.*74.63%

W. R. N. Raynsford, *Lab.*	14,630
*Mrs R. Barnes, *SD*	13,273
Mrs A. McNair, *C.*	6,960
R. McCracken, *Green*	483
R. Mallone, *Fellowship*	147
M. Hardee, *UTCHAP*	103
J. Small, *NLP*	70
Lab. majority	1,357

(June 1987, SDP/All. maj. 2,141)

GUILDFORD (Surrey)
*E.*77,265 *T.*78.48%

*Rt. Hon. D. Howell, *C.*	33,516
Mrs M. Sharp, *LD*	20,112
H. Mann, *Lab.*	6,781
A. Law, *NLP*	234
C. majority	13,404

(June 1987, C. maj. 12,607)

HACKNEY NORTH AND STOKE NEWINGTON (Greater London)
*E.*54,655 *T.*63.53%

*Ms D. Abbott, *Lab.*	20,083
C. Manson, *C.*	9,356
K. Fitchett, *LD*	3,996
Ms H. Hunt, *Green*	1,111
J. Windsor, *NLP*	178
Lab. majority	10,727

(June 1987, Lab. maj. 7,678)

HACKNEY SOUTH AND SHOREDITCH (Greater London)
*E.*57,935 *T.*63.82%

*B. Sedgemore, *Lab.*	19,730
A. Turner, *C.*	10,714
G. Wintle, *LD*	5,533
L. Lucas, *Green*	772
Ms G. Norman, *NLP*	226
Lab. majority	9,016

(June 1987, Lab. maj. 7,522)

HALESOWEN AND STOURBRIDGE (W. Midlands)
*E.*77,644 *T.*82.28%

P. W. Hawksley, *C.*	32,312
A. Hankon, *Lab.*	22,730
V. Sharma, *LD*	7,941
T. Weller, *Green*	908
C. majority	9,582

(June 1987, C. maj. 13,808)

HALIFAX (W. Yorks)
*E.*73,401 *T.*78.69%

*Ms A. Mahon, *Lab.*	25,115
T. Martin, *C.*	24,637
I. Howell, *LD*	7,364
R. Pearson, *Nat.*	649
Lab. majority	478

(June 1987, Lab. maj. 1,212)

HALTON (Cheshire)
*E.*74,906 *T.*78.34%

*Rt. Hon. G. Oakes, *Lab.*	35,025
G. Mercer, *C.*	16,821
D. Reaper, *LD*	6,104
S. Herley, *Loony*	398
N. Collins, *NLP*	338
Lab. majority	18,204

(June 1987, Lab. maj. 14,578)

HAMMERSMITH (Greater London)
*E.*47,229 *T.*71.90%

*C. Soley, *Lab.*	17,329
A. Hennessy, *C.*	12,575
J. Bates, *LD*	3,380
R. Crosskey, *Green*	546
K. Turner, *NLP*	89
Ms H. Szamuely, *Anti Fed.*	41
Lab. majority	4,754

(June 1987, Lab. maj. 2,415)

HAMPSHIRE EAST
*E.*92,139 *T.*80.35%

*M. Mates, *C.*	47,541
Ms S. Baring, *LD*	18,376
J. Phillips, *Lab.*	6,840
I. Foster, *Green*	1,113
S. Hale, *RCC*	165
C. majority	29,165

(June 1987, C. maj. 23,786)

HAMPSHIRE NORTH WEST
*E.*73,101 *T.*80.75%

*Sir D. Mitchell, *C.*	34,310
M. Simpson, *LD*	16,462
M. Stockwell, *Lab.*	7,433
Ms D. Ashley, *Green*	825
C. majority	17,848

(June 1987, C. maj. 13,437)

HAMPSTEAD AND HIGHGATE (Greater London)
*E.*58,203 *T.*73.04%

Ms G. Jackson, *Lab.*	19,193
O. Letwin, *C.*	17,753
D. Wrede, *LD*	4,765
S. Games, *Green*	594
Dr R. Prosser, *NLP*	86
Ms A. Hall, *RAVA*	44
C. Scallywag Wilson, *Scallywag*	44
Captain Rizz, *Rizz*	33
Lab. majority	1,440

(June 1987, C. maj. 2,221)

HARBOROUGH (Leics)
*E.*76,514 *T.*82.11%

E. Garnier, *C.*	34,280
M. Cox, *LD*	20,737
Ms C. Mackay, *Lab.*	7,483
A. Irwin, *NLP*	328
C. majority	13,543

(June 1987, C. maj. 18,810)

HARLOW (Essex)
*E.*68,615 *T.*82.56%

*J. Hayes, *C.*	26,608
W. Rammell, *Lab.*	23,668
Ms L. Spenceley, *LD*	6,375
C. majority	2,940

(June 1987, C. maj. 5,877)

HARROGATE (N. Yorks)
*E.*76,250 *T.*77.98%

*R. Banks, *C.*	32,023
T. Hurren, *LD*	19,434
A. Wright, *Lab.*	7,230
A. Warneken, *Green*	780
C. majority	12,589

(June 1987, C. maj. 11,902)

HARROW EAST (Greater London)
*E.*74,733 *T.*77.83%

*H. Dykes, *C.*	30,752
A. McNulty, *Lab.*	19,654
Ms V. Chamberlain, *LD*	6,360
P. Burrows, *Lib.*	1,142
Mrs S. Hamza, *NLP*	212
J. Lester, *Anti Fed.*	49
C. majority	11,098

(June 1987, C. maj. 18,273)

HARROW WEST (Greater London)
*E.*69,616 *T.*78.69%

*R. G. Hughes, *C.*	30,240
C. Moraes, *Lab.*	12,343
C. Noyce, *LD*	11,050
G. Aitman, *Lib.*	845
Mrs J. Argyle, *NLP*	306
C. majority	17,897

(June 1987, C. maj. 15,444)

HARTLEPOOL (Cleveland)
*E.*67,968 *T.*76.07%

P. Mandelson, *Lab.*	26,816
G. Robb, *C.*	18,034
I. Cameron, *LD*	6,860
Lab. majority	8,782

(June 1987, Lab. maj. 7,289)

HARWICH (Essex)
*E.*80,260 *T.*77.70%

I. Sproat, *C.*	32,369
Mrs P. Bevan, *LD*	15,210
R. Knight, *Lab.*	14,511
Mrs E. McGrath, *NLP*	279
C. majority	17,159

(June 1987, C. maj. 12,082)

HASTINGS AND RYE (E. Sussex)
*E.*71,838 *T.*74.86%

Ms J. Lait, *C.*	25,573
M. Palmer, *LD*	18,939
R. Stevens, *Lab.*	8,458
Ms S. Phillips, *Green*	640
T. Howell, *Loony*	168
C. majority	6,634

(June 1987, C. maj. 7,347)

HAVANT (Hants)
*E.*74,217 *T.*79.01%

D. Willetts, *C.*	32,233
S. van Hagen, *LD*	14,649
G. Morris, *Lab.*	10,968
T. Mitchell, *Green*	793
C. majority	17,584

(June 1987, C. maj. 16,510)

HAYES AND HARLINGTON (Greater London)
*E.*54,449 *T.*79.70%

*T. Dicks, *C.*	19,489
J. McDonnell, *Lab.*	19,436
T. Little, *LD*	4,472
C. majority	53

(June 1987, C. maj. 5,965)

HAZEL GROVE (Greater Manchester)
*E.*64,302 *T.*84.94%

*Sir T. Arnold, *C.*	24,479
A. Stunell, *LD*	23,550
C. McAllister, *Lab.*	6,390
M. Penn, *NLP*	204
C. majority	929

(June 1987, C. maj. 1,840)

HEMSWORTH (W. Yorks)
*E.*55,679 *T.*75.91%

*D. Enright, *Lab.*	29,942
G. Harrison, *C.*	7,867
Ms V. Megson, *LD*	4,459
Lab. majority	22,075

(June 1987, Lab. maj. 20,700)
(November 1991, Lab. maj. 11,087)

HENDON NORTH (Greater London)
*E.*51,513 *T.*75.08%

*J. Gorst, *C.*	20,569
D. Hill, *Lab.*	13,447
P. Kemp, *LD*	4,136
Ms P. Duncan, *Green*	430
Ms P. Orr, *NLP*	95
C. majority	7,122

(June 1987, C. maj. 10,932)

HENDON SOUTH (Greater London)
*E.*48,401 *T.*72.38%

*J. Marshall, *C.*	20,593
Ms L. Lloyd, *Lab.*	8,546
J. Cohen, *LD*	5,609
J. Leslie, *NLP*	289

C. majority	12,047
(June 1987, C. maj. 11,124)	

HENLEY (Oxon)
*E.*64,702 *T.*79.84%

*Rt. Hon. M. Heseltine, *C.*	30,835
D. Turner, *LD*	12,443
I. Russell-Swinnerton, *Lab.*	7,676
A. Plane, *Anti H.*	431
Ms S. Banerji, *NLP*	274
C. majority	18,392
(June 1987, C. maj. 17,082)	

HEREFORD
*E.*69,676 *T.*81.29%

*C. Shepherd, *C.*	26,727
G. Jones, *LD*	23,314
Ms J. Kelly, *Lab.*	6,005
C. Mattingly, *Green*	596
C. majority	3,413
(June 1987, C. maj. 1,413)	

HERTFORD AND STORTFORD
*E.*76,654 *T.*81.05%

*B. Wells, *C.*	35,716
C. White, *LD*	15,506
A. Bovaird, *Lab.*	10,125
J. Goth, *Green*	780
C. majority	20,210
(June 1987, C. maj. 17,140)	

HERTFORDSHIRE NORTH
*E.*80,066 *T.*84.44%

O. Heald, *C.*	33,679
R. Liddle, *LD*	17,148
Ms S. Bissett Johnson, *Lab.*	16,449
B. Irving, *NLP*	339
C. majority	16,531
(June 1987, C. maj. 11,442)	

HERTFORDSHIRE SOUTH WEST
*E.*70,836 *T.*83.76%

*R. Page, *C.*	33,825
Ms A. Shaw, *LD*	13,718
A. Gale, *Lab.*	11,512
C. Adamson, *NLP*	281
C. majority	20,107
(June 1987, C. maj. 15,784)	

HERTFORDSHIRE WEST
*E.*78,573 *T.*82.36%

*R. Jones, *C.*	33,340
Mrs E. McNally, *Lab.*	19,400
M. Trevett, *LD*	10,464
J. Hannaway, *Green*	674
J. McAuley, *NF*	665
G. Harvey, *NLP*	175
C. majority	13,940
(June 1987, C. maj. 14,924)	

HERTSMERE (Herts)
*E.*69,951 *T.*80.89%

W. J. Clappison, *C.*	32,133
Dr D. Souter, *Lab.*	13,398
Mrs Z. Gifford, *LD*	10,681
Ms D. Harding, *NLP*	373
C. majority	18,735
(June 1987, C. maj. 18,106)	

HEXHAM (Northumberland)
*E.*57,812 *T.*82.37%

P. Atkinson, *C.*	24,967
I. Swithenbank, *Lab.*	11,529
J. Wallace, *LD*	10,344
J. Hartshorne, *Green*	781
C. majority	13,438
(June 1987, C. maj. 8,066)	

HEYWOOD AND MIDDLETON (Greater Manchester)
*E.*57,176 *T.*74.92%

*J. Callaghan, *Lab.*	22,380
E. Ollerenshaw, *C.*	14,306
Dr M. Taylor, *LD*	5,262
P. Burke, *Lib.*	757
Ms A. M. Scott, *NLP*	134
Lab. majority	8,074
(June 1987, Lab. maj. 6,848)	

HIGH PEAK (Derbys)
*E.*70,793 *T.*84.62%

C. Hendry, *C.*	27,538
T. Levitt, *Lab.*	22,719
S. Molloy, *LD*	8,861
R. Floyd, *Green*	794
C. majority	4,819
(June 1987, C. maj. 9,516)	

HOLBORN AND ST PANCRAS (Greater London)
*E.*64,480 *T.*62.99%

*F. Dobson, *Lab.*	22,243
A. McHallam, *C.*	11,419
Ms J. Horne-Roberts, *LD*	5,476
P. Wolf-Light, *Green*	959
M. Hersey, *NLP*	212
R. Headicar, *Soc.*	175
N. Lewis, *WAR*	133
Lab. majority	10,824
(June 1987, Lab. maj. 8,853)	

HOLLAND WITH BOSTON (Lincs)
*E.*67,900 *T.*77.93%

*Sir R. Body, *C.*	29,159
J. Hough, *Lab.*	15,328
N. Ley, *LD*	8,434
C. majority	13,831
(June 1987, C. maj. 17,595)	

HONITON (Devon)
*E.*79,223 *T.*80.74%

*Sir P. Emery, *C.*	33,533
Ms J. Sharratt, *LD*	17,022
R. Davison, *Lab.*	8,142
D. Owen, *Ind. C.*	2,175
S. Hughes, *Loony G.*	1,442
G. Halliwell, *Lib.*	1,005
A. Tootill, *Green*	650
C. majority	16,511
(June 1987, C. maj. 16,562)	

HORNCHURCH (Greater London)
*E.*60,522 *T.*79.78%

*R. Squire, *C.*	25,817
Ms L. Cooper, *Lab.*	16,652
B. Oddy, *LD*	5,366
T. Matthews, *SD*	453
C. majority	9,165
(June 1987, C. maj. 10,694)	

HORNSEY AND WOOD GREEN (Greater London)
*E.*73,491 *T.*75.85%

Mrs B. Roche, *Lab.*	27,020
A. Boff, *C.*	21,843
P. Dunphy, *LD*	5,547
Ms L. Crosbie, *Green*	1,051
P. Davies, *NLP*	197
W. Massey, *Rev. Comm.*	89
Lab. majority	5,177
(June 1987, C. maj. 1,779)	

HORSHAM (W. Sussex)
*E.*84,158 *T.*81.27%

*Sir P. Hordern, *C.*	42,210
Ms J. Stainton, *LD*	17,138
S. Uwins, *Lab.*	6,745
Ms J. Elliott, *Lib.*	1,281
T. King, *Green*	692
J. Duggan, *PPP*	332
C. majority	25,072
(June 1987, C. maj. 23,907)	

HOUGHTON AND WASHINGTON (Tyne & Wear)
*E.*79,325 *T.*70.60%

*R. Boyes, *Lab.*	34,733
A. Tyrie, *C.*	13,925
O. Dumpleton, *LD*	7,346
Lab. majority	20,808
(June 1987, Lab. maj. 20,193)	

HOVE (E. Sussex)
*E.*67,450 *T.*74.26%

*Hon. T. Sainsbury, *C.*	24,525
D. Turner, *Lab.*	12,257
A. Jones, *LD*	9,709
N. Furness, *Hove C.*	2,658
G. Sinclair, *Green*	814
J. Morilly, *NLP*	126
C. majority	12,268
(June 1987, C. maj. 18,218)	

HUDDERSFIELD (W. Yorks)
*E.*67,604 *T.*72.32%

*B. Sheerman, *Lab.*	23,832
Ms J. Kenyon, *C.*	16,574
Ms A. Denham, *LD*	7,777
N. Harvey, *Green*	576
M. Cran, *NLP*	135
Lab. majority	7,258
(June 1987, Lab. maj. 7,278)	

HULL EAST
*E.*69,036 *T.*69.29%

*J. Prescott, *Lab.* 30,092
J. Fareham, *C.* 11,373
J. Wastling, *LD* 6,050
C. Kinzell, *NLP* 323
Lab. majority 18,719
(June 1987, Lab. maj. 14,689)

HULL NORTH
*E.*71,363 *T.*66.71%

*J. K. McNamara, *Lab.* 26,619
B. Coleman, *C.* 11,235
A. Meadowcroft, *LD* 9,504
G. Richardson, *NLP* 253
Lab. majority 15,384
(June 1987, Lab. maj. 12,169)

HULL WEST
*E.*56,111 *T.*65.70%

*S. Randall, *Lab.* 21,139
D. Stewart, *C.* 10,554
R. Tress, *LD* 4,867
B. Franklin, *NLP* 308
Lab. majority 10,585
(June 1987, Lab. maj. 8,130)

HUNTINGDON (Cambs)
*E.*92,913 *T.*79.16%

*Rt. Hon. J. Major, *C.* 48,662
H. Seckleman, *Lab.* 12,432
A. Duff, *LD* 9,386
P. Wiggin, *Lib.* 1,045
Miss D. Birkhead, *Green* 846
Lord D. Sutch, *Loony* 728
M. Flanagan, *C. Thatch.* 231
Lord Buckethead, *Gremloids* 107
C. Cockell, *FTM* 91
D. Shepheard, *NLP* 26
C. majority 36,230
(June 1987, C. maj. 27,044)

HYNDBURN (Lancs)
*E.*58,539 *T.*83.97%

G. Pope, *Lab.* 23,042
*K. Hargreaves, *C.* 21,082
Ms Y. Stars, *LD* 4,886
S. Whittle, *NLP* 150
Lab. majority 1,960
(June 1987, C. maj. 2,220)

ILFORD NORTH (Greater London)
*E.*58,670 *T.*77.98%

*V. Bendall, *C.* 24,698
Ms L. Hilton, *Lab.* 15,627
R. Scott, *LD* 5,430
C. majority 9,071
(June 1987, C. maj. 12,090)

ILFORD SOUTH (Greater London)
*E.*55,741 *T.*76.83%

M. Gapes, *Lab.* 19,418
*N. Thorne, *C.* 19,016
G. Hogarth, *LD* 4,126
N. Bramachari, *NLP* 269
Lab. majority 402
(June 1987, C. maj. 4,572)

IPSWICH (Suffolk)
*E.*67,261 *T.*80.32%

J. Cann, *Lab.* 23,680
*M. Irvine, *C.* 23,415
J. White, *LD* 6,159
Ms J. Scott, *Green* 591
E. Kaplan, *NLP* 181
Lab. majority 265
(June 1987, C. maj. 874)

ISLE OF WIGHT
*E.*99,838 *T.*79.76%

*B. Field, *C.* 38,163
Dr P. Brand, *LD* 36,336
K. Pearson, *Lab.* 4,784
C. Daly, *NLP* 350
C. majority 1,827
(June 1987, C. maj. 6,442)

ISLINGTON NORTH (Greater London)
*E.*56,270 *T.*67.26%

*J. Corbyn, *Lab.* 21,742
Mrs L. Champagnie, *C.* 8,958
Ms S. Ludford, *LD* 5,732
C. Ashby, *Green* 1,420
Lab. majority 12,784
(June 1987, Lab. maj. 9,657)

ISLINGTON SOUTH AND FINSBURY (Greater London)
*E.*55,541 *T.*72.52%

*C. Smith, *Lab.* 20,586
M. Jones, *C.* 9,934
C. Pryce, *LD* 9,387
Ms R. Hersey, *JBR* 149
Ms M. Avino, *Loony* 142
M. Spinks, *NLP* 83
Lab. majority 10,652
(June 1987, Lab. maj. 805)

JARROW (Tyne & Wear)
*E.*62,611 *T.*74.44%

*D. Dixon, *Lab.* 28,956
T. Ward, *C.* 11,049
K. Orrell, *LD* 6,608
Lab. majority 17,907
(June 1987, Lab. maj. 18,795)

KEIGHLEY (W. Yorks)
*E.*66,358 *T.*82.58%

*G. Waller, *C.* 25,983
T. Flanagan, *Lab.* 22,387
I. Simpson, *LD* 5,793
M. Crowson, *Green* 642
C. majority 3,596
(June 1987, C. maj. 5,606)

KENSINGTON (Greater London)
*E.*42,129 *T.*73.29%

*J. D. Fishburn, *C.* 15,540
Ms A. Holmes, *Lab.* 11,992
C. Shirley, *LD* 2,770
Ms A. Burlingham-Johnson, *Green* 415
A. Hardy, *NLP* 90
Ms A. Bulloch, *Anti Fed.* 71
C. majority 3,548
(June 1987, C. maj. 4,447)
(July 1988, C. maj. 815)

KENT MID
*E.*74,459 *T.*79.66%

*A. Rowe, *C.* 33,633
T. Robson, *Lab.* 13,984
G. Colley, *LD* 11,476
G. Valente, *NLP* 224
C. majority 19,649
(June 1987, C. maj. 14,768)

KETTERING (Northants)
*E.*67,853 *T.*82.58%

*R. Freeman, *C.* 29,115
P. Hope, *Lab.* 17,961
R. Denton-White, *LD* 8,962
C. majority 11,154
(June 1987, C. maj. 11,327)

KINGSTON UPON THAMES (Greater London)
*E.*51,077 *T.*78.41%

*Rt. Hon. N. Lamont, *C.* 20,675
D. Osbourne, *LD* 10,522
R. Markless, *Lab.* 7,748
A. Amer, *Lib.* 771
D. Beaupre, *Loony* 212
G. Woollcoombe, *NLP* 81
A. Scholefield, *Anti Fed.* 42
C. majority 10,153
(June 1987, C. maj. 11,186)

KINGSWOOD (Avon)
*E.*71,727 *T.*83.85%

R. Berry, *Lab.* 26,774
*R. Hayward, *C.* 24,404
Ms J. Pinkerton, *LD* 8,960
Lab. majority 2,370
(June 1987, C. maj. 4,393)

KNOWSLEY NORTH (Merseyside)
*E.*48,761 *T.*72.81%

*G. Howarth, *Lab.* 27,517
S. Mabey, *C.* 5,114
J. Murray, *LD* 1,515
Mrs K. Lappin, *Lib.* 1,180
V. Ruben, *NLP* 179
Lab. majority 22,403
(June 1987, Lab. maj. 21,098)

KNOWSLEY SOUTH (Merseyside)
*E.*62,260 *T.*74.77%

*E. O'Hara, *Lab.* 31,933
L. Byrom, *C.* 9,922
I. Smith, *LD* 4,480
M. Raiano, *NLP* 217
Lab. majority 22,011
(June 1987, Lab. maj. 20,846)
(September 1990, Lab. maj. 11,367)

LANCASHIRE WEST
*E.*77,462 *T.*82.55%

C. Pickthall, *Lab.*	30,128
*K. Hind, *C.*	28,051
P. Reilly, *LD*	4,884
P. Pawley, *Green*	546
B. Morris, *NLP*	336
Lab. majority	2,077

(June 1987, C. maj. 1,353)

LANCASTER (Lancs)
*E.*58,714 *T.*78.78%

*Dame E. Kellett-Bowman, *C.*	21,084
Ms R. Henig, *Lab.*	18,131
J. Humberstone, *LD*	6,524
Ms G. Dowding, *Green*	433
R. Barcis, *NLP*	83
C. majority	2,953

(June 1987, C. maj. 6,453)

LANGBAURGH (Cleveland)
*E.*79,566 *T.*83.05%

M. Bates, *C.*	30,018
*A. Kumar, *Lab.*	28,454
P. Allen, *LD*	7,615
C. majority	1,564

(June 1987, C. maj. 2,088)
(November 1991, C. maj. 1,975)

LEEDS CENTRAL (W. Yorks)
*E.*62,058 *T.*61.29%

*D. Fatchett, *Lab.*	23,673
Mrs T. Holdroyd, *C.*	8,653
D. Pratt, *LD*	5,713
Lab. majority	15,020

(June 1987, Lab. maj. 11,505)

LEEDS EAST (W. Yorks)
*E.*61,695 *T.*70.02%

G. Mudie, *Lab.*	24,929
N. Carmichael, *C.*	12,232
P. Wrigley, *LD*	6,040
Lab. majority	12,697

(June 1987, Lab. maj. 9,526)

LEEDS NORTH EAST (W. Yorks)
*E.*64,372 *T.*76.89%

*T. Kirkhope, *C.*	22,462
F. Hamilton, *Lab.*	18,218
C. Walmsley, *LD*	8,274
J. Noble, *Green*	546
C. majority	4,244

(June 1987, C. maj. 8,419)

LEEDS NORTH WEST (W. Yorks)
*E.*69,406 *T.*72.84%

*Dr K. Hampson, *C.*	21,750
Ms B. Pearce, *LD*	14,079
Ms S. Egan, *Lab.*	13,782
D. Webb, *Green*	519
N. Nowosielski, *Lib.*	427
C. majority	7,671

(June 1987, C. maj. 5,201)

LEEDS SOUTH AND MORLEY
(W. Yorks)
*E.*63,107 *T.*72.58%

W. J. Gunnell, *Lab.*	23,896
R. Booth, *C.*	16,524
Ms J. Walmsley, *LD*	5,062
R. Thurston, *NLP*	327
Lab. majority	7,372

(June 1987, Lab. maj. 6,711)

LEEDS WEST (W. Yorks)
*E.*67,084 *T.*71.14%

*J. Battle, *Lab.*	26,310
P. Bartlett, *C.*	12,482
G. Howard, *LD*	4,252
M. Meadowcroft, *Lib.*	3,980
Ms A. Mander, *Green*	569
R. Tenny, *NF*	132
Lab. majority	13,828

(June 1987, Lab. maj. 4,692)

LEICESTER EAST
*E.*63,434 *T.*78.40%

*N. K. A. S. Vaz, *Lab.*	28,123
J. Stevens, *C.*	16,807
Ms S. Mitchell, *LD*	4,043
M. Frankland, *Green*	453
D. Taylor, *Homeland*	308
Lab. majority	11,316

(June 1987, Lab. maj. 1,924)

LEICESTER SOUTH
*E.*71,120 *T.*75.09%

*J. Marshall, *Lab.*	27,934
Dr M. Dutt, *C.*	18,494
Ms A. Crumbie, *LD*	6,271
J. McWhirter, *Green*	554
Ms P. Saunders, *NLP*	154
Lab. majority	9,440

(June 1987, Lab. maj. 1,877)

LEICESTER WEST
*E.*65,510 *T.*73.66%

*Hon. G. Janner, *Lab.*	22,574
J. Guthrie, *C.*	18,596
G. Walker, *LD*	6,402
Ms C. Wintram, *Green*	517
Ms J. Rosta, *NLP*	171
Lab. majority	3,978

(June 1987, Lab. maj. 1,201)

LEICESTERSHIRE NORTH WEST
*E.*72,414 *T.*86.11%

*D. Ashby, *C.*	28,379
D. Taylor, *Lab.*	27,400
J. Beckett, *LD*	6,353
J. Fawcett, *NLP*	229
C. majority	979

(June 1987, C. maj. 7,828)

LEIGH (Greater Manchester)
*E.*70,064 *T.*75.02%

*L. Cunliffe, *Lab.*	32,225
J. Egerton, *C.*	13,398
R. Bleakley, *LD*	6,621
A. Tayler, *NLP*	320
Lab. majority	18,827

(June 1987, Lab. maj. 16,606)

LEOMINSTER (H & W)
*E.*70,873 *T.*81.69%

*P. Temple-Morris, *C.*	32,783
D. Short, *LD*	16,103
C. Chappell, *Lab.*	6,874
Ms F. Norman, *Green*	1,503
Capt. E. Carlise, *Anti Fed.*	640
C. majority	16,680

(June 1987, C. maj. 14,075)

LEWES (E. Sussex)
*E.*73,918 *T.*81.81%

*J. R. Rathbone, *C.*	33,042
N. Baker, *LD*	20,867
Ms A. Chapman, *Lab.*	5,758
A. Beaumont, *Green*	719
N. Clinch, *NLP*	87
C. majority	12,175

(June 1987, C. maj. 13,620)

LEWISHAM DEPTFORD (Greater London)
*E.*57,014 *T.*65.05%

*Mrs J. Ruddock, *Lab.*	22,574
Miss T. O'Neill, *C.*	10,336
Ms J. Brightwell, *LD*	4,181
Lab. majority	12,238

(June 1987, Lab. maj. 6,771)

LEWISHAM EAST (Greater London)
*E.*57,674 *T.*74.78%

Mrs B. Prentice, *Lab.*	19,576
*Hon. C. Moynihan, *C.*	18,481
J. Hawkins, *LD*	4,877
Ms G. Mansour, *NLP*	196
Lab. majority	1,095

(June 1987, C. maj. 4,814)

LEWISHAM WEST (Greater London)
*E.*59,317 *T.*73.11%

J. Dowd, *Lab.*	20,378
*J. Maples, *C.*	18,569
Ms E. Neale, *LD*	4,295
P. Coulam, *Anti Fed.*	125
Lab. majority	1,809

(June 1987, C. maj. 3,772)

LEYTON (Greater London)
*E.*57,271 *T.*67.38%

*H. Cohen, *Lab.*	20,334
Miss C. Smith, *C.*	8,850
J. Fryer, *LD*	8,180
L. de Pinna, *Lib.*	561
K. Pervez, *Green*	412
R. Archer, *NLP*	256
Lab. majority	11,484

(June 1987, Lab. maj. 4,641)

LINCOLN
*E.*78,905 *T.*79.15%

*K. Carlisle, *C.*	28,792
N. Butler, *Lab.*	26,743
D. Harding-Price, *LD*	6,316
Ms S. Wiggin, *Lib.*	603
C. majority	2,049

(June 1987, C. maj. 7,483)

LINDSEY EAST (Lincs)
*E.*80,026 *T.*78.07%

*Sir P. Tapsell, *C.*	31,916
J. Dodsworth, *LD*	20,070
D. Shepherd, *Lab.*	9,477
Ms R. Robinson, *Green*	1,018
C. majority	11,846

(June 1987, C. maj. 8,616)

LITTLEBOROUGH AND SADDLEWORTH (Greater Manchester)
*E.*65,576 *T.*81.61%

*G. Dickens, *C.*	23,682
C. Davies, *LD*	19,188
A. Brett, *Lab.*	10,649
C. majority	4,494

(June 1987, C. maj. 6,202)

LIVERPOOL BROADGREEN
*E.*60,080 *T.*69.59%

Mrs J. Kennedy, *Lab.*	18,062
Ms R. Cooper, *LD*	11,035
*T. Fields, *Soc. Lab.*	5,952
Mrs H. Roche, *C.*	5,405
S. Radford, *Lib.*	1,211
Mrs A. Brennan, *NLP*	149
Lab. majority	7,027

(June 1987, Lab. maj. 6,047)

LIVERPOOL GARSTON
*E.*57,538 *T.*70.60%

*E. Loyden, *Lab.*	23,212
J. Backhouse, *C.*	10,933
W. Roberts, *LD*	5,398
A. Conrad, *Lib.*	894
P. Chandler, *NLP*	187
Lab. majority	12,279

(June 1987, Lab. maj. 13,777)

LIVERPOOL MOSSLEY HILL
*E.*60,409 *T.*68.52%

*D. Alton, *LD*	19,809
N. Bann, *Lab.*	17,203
S. Syder, *C.*	4,269
B. Rigby, *NLP*	114
LD majority	2,606

(June 1987, L./All. maj. 2,226)

LIVERPOOL RIVERSIDE
*E.*49,595 *T.*54.57%

*R. Parry, *Lab.*	20,550
Dr A. Zsigmond, *C.*	3,113
M. Akbar Ali, *LD*	2,498
L. Brown, *Green*	738
J. Collins, *NLP*	169
Lab. majority	17,437

(June 1987, Lab. maj. 20,689)

LIVERPOOL WALTON
*E.*70,102 *T.*67.40%

*P. Kilfoyle, *Lab.*	34,214
B. Greenwood, *C.*	5,915
J. Lang, *LD*	5,672
T. Newall, *Lib.*	963
D. Carson, *Prot. Ref.*	393
Ms D. Raiano, *NLP*	98
Lab. majority	28,299

(June 1987, Lab. maj. 23,253)
(July 1991, Lab. maj. 6,860)

LIVERPOOL WEST DERBY
*E.*56,718 *T.*69.84%

*R. Wareing, *Lab.*	27,014
S. Fitzsimmons, *C.*	6,589
Ms G. Bundred, *LD*	4,838
D. Curtis, *Lib.*	1,021
C. Higgins, *NLP*	154
Lab. majority	20,425

(June 1987, Lab. maj. 20,496)

LOUGHBOROUGH (Leics)
*E.*75,450 *T.*78.52%

*S. Dorrell, *C.*	30,064
A. Reed, *Lab.*	19,181
A. Stott, *LD*	8,953
I. Sinclair, *Green*	817
P. Reynolds, *NLP*	233
C. majority	10,883

(June 1987, C. maj. 17,648)

LUDLOW (Salop)
*E.*68,935 *T.*80.87%

*C. Gill, *C.*	28,719
D. Phillips, *LD*	14,567
Ms B. Mason, *Lab.*	11,709
N. Appleton-Fox, *Green*	758
C. majority	14,152

(June 1987, C. maj. 11,699)

LUTON NORTH (Beds)
*E.*76,857 *T.*81.91%

*J. Carlisle, *C.*	33,777
A. McWalter, *Lab.*	20,683
Ms J. Jackson, *LD*	7,570
R. Jones, *Green*	633
K. Buscombe, *NLP*	292
C. majority	13,094

(June 1987, C. maj. 15,573)

LUTON SOUTH (Beds)
*E.*73,016 *T.*79.10%

*G. Bright, *C.*	25,900
W. McKenzie, *Lab.*	25,101
D. Rogers, *LD*	6,020
Ms L. Bliss, *Green*	550
D. Cooke, *NLP*	191
C. majority	799

(June 1987, C. maj. 5,115)

MACCLESFIELD (Cheshire)
*E.*76,548 *T.*82.29%

*N. Winterton, *C.*	36,447
Mrs M. Longworth, *Lab.*	13,680
Dr P. Beatty, *LD*	12,600
Mrs C. Penn, *NLP*	268
C. majority	22,767

(June 1987, C. maj. 19,092)

MAIDSTONE (Kent)
*E.*72,834 *T.*80.08%

*Miss A. Widdecombe, *C.*	31,611
Ms P. Yates, *LD*	15,325
Ms A. Logan, *Lab.*	10,517
Ms P. Kemp, *Green*	707
F. Ingram, *NLP*	172
C. majority	16,286

(June 1987, C. maj. 10,364)

MAKERFIELD (Greater Manchester)
*E.*71,425 *T.*76.09%

*I. McCartney, *Lab.*	32,832
Mrs D. Dickson, *C.*	14,714
S. Jeffers, *LD*	5,097
Ms S. Cairns, *Lib.*	1,309
C. Davies, *NLP*	397
Lab. majority	18,118

(June 1987, Lab. maj. 15,558)

MANCHESTER BLACKLEY
*E.*55,234 *T.*69.31%

*K. Eastham, *Lab.*	23,031
W. Hobhouse, *C.*	10,642
S. Wheale, *LD*	4,324
M. Kennedy, *NLP*	288
Lab. majority	12,389

(June 1987, Lab. maj. 10,122)

MANCHESTER CENTRAL
*E.*56,446 *T.*56.90%

*R. Litherland, *Lab.*	23,336
P. Davies, *C.*	5,299
M. Clayton, *LD*	3,151
A. Buchanan, *CL*	167
Ms V. Mitchell, *NLP*	167
Lab. majority	18,037

(June 1987, Lab. maj. 19,867)

MANCHESTER GORTON
*E.*62,410 *T.*60.84%

*Rt. Hon. G. Kaufman, *Lab.*	23,671
J. Bullock, *C.*	7,392
P. Harris, *LD*	5,327
T. Henderson, *Lib.*	767
M. Daw, *Green*	595
Ms P. Lawrence, *Rev. Comm.*	108
P. Mitchell, *NLP*	84
Ms C. Smith, *Int. Comm.*	30
Lab. majority	16,279

(June 1987, Lab. maj. 14,065)

MANCHESTER WITHINGTON
*E.*63,838 *T.*71.27%

*K. Bradley, *Lab.*	23,962
E. Farthing, *C.*	14,227
G. Hennell, *LD*	6,457
B. Candeland, *Green*	725
C. Menhinick, *NLP*	128
Lab. majority	9,735

(June 1987, Lab. maj. 3,391)

MANCHESTER WYTHENSHAWE
*E.*53,548 *T.*69.68%

*Rt. Hon. A. Morris, *Lab.*	22,591
K. McKenna, *C.*	10,595
S. Fenn, *LD*	3,633
G. Otten, *Green*	362
Ms E. Martin, *NLP*	133
Lab. majority	11,996

(June 1987, Lab. maj. 11,855)

MANSFIELD (Notts)
*E.*66,964 *T.*82.23%

*J. A. Meale, *Lab.*	29,932
G. Mond, *C.*	18,208
S. Thompstone, *LD*	6,925
Lab. majority	11,724

(June 1987, Lab. maj. 56)

MEDWAY (Kent)
*E.*61,736 *T.*80.22%

*Dame P. Fenner, *C.*	25,924
R. Marshall-Andrews, *Lab.*	17,138
C. Trice, *LD*	4,751
M. Austin, *Lib.*	1,480
P. Kember, *NLP*	234
C. majority	8,786

(June 1987, C. maj. 9,929)

MERIDEN (W. Midlands)
*E.*76,994 *T.*78.85%

*I. Mills, *C.*	33,462
N. Stephens, *Lab.*	18,763
Ms J. Morris, *LD*	8,489
C. majority	14,699

(June 1987, C. maj. 16,820)

MIDDLESBROUGH (Cleveland)
*E.*58,844 *T.*69.85%

*S. Bell, *Lab.*	26,343
P. Rayner, *C.*	10,559
Ms R. Jordan, *LD*	4,201
Lab. majority	15,784

(June 1987, Lab. maj. 14,958)

MILTON KEYNES NORTH EAST (Bucks)
*E.*62,748 *T.*80.95%

P. Butler, *C.*	26,212
Ms M. Cosin, *Lab.*	12,036
P. Gaskell, *LD*	11,693
A. Francis, *Green*	529
Mrs M. Kavanagh-Dowsett, *Ind. C.*	249
M. Simson, *NLP*	79
C. majority	14,176

(New constituency)

MILTON KEYNES SOUTH WEST (Bucks)
*E.*66,422 *T.*77%

B. Legg, *C.*	23,840
K. Wilson, *Lab.*	19,153
C. Pym, *LD*	7,429
Dr C. Field, *Green*	525
H. Kelly, *NLP*	202
C. majority	4,687

(New constituency)

MITCHAM AND MORDEN (Greater London)
*E.*63,723 *T.*80.32%

*Rt. Hon. A. Rumbold, *C.*	23,789
Ms S. McDonagh, *Lab.*	22,055
J. Field, *LD*	4,687
T. Walsh, *Green*	655
C. majority	1,734

(June 1987, C. maj. 6,183)

MOLE VALLEY (Surrey)
*E.*66,949 *T.*81.97%

*Rt. Hon. K. Baker, *C.*	32,549
M. Watson, *LD*	16,599
Dr T. Walsh, *Lab.*	5,291
Ms J. Thomas, *NLP*	442
C. majority	15,950

(June 1987, C. maj. 16,076)

MORECAMBE AND LUNESDALE (Lancs)
*E.*56,426 *T.*78.35%

*Hon. M. Lennox-Boyd, *C.*	22,507
Ms J. Yates, *Lab.*	10,998
A. Saville, *LD*	9,584
M. Turner, *MBI*	916
R. Marriott, *NLP*	205
C. majority	11,509

(June 1987, C. maj. 11,785)

NEWARK (Notts)
*E.*68,801 *T.*82.17%

*R. Alexander, *C.*	28,494
D. Barton, *Lab.*	20,265
P. Harris, *LD*	7,342
Ms P. Wood, *Green*	435
C. majority	8,229

(June 1987, C. maj. 13,543)

NEWBURY (Berks)
*E.*80,252 *T.*82.75%

Mrs J. Chaplin, *C.*	37,135
D. Rendel, *LD*	24,778
R. Hall, *Lab.*	3,962
J. Wallis, *Green*	539
C. majority	12,357

(June 1987, C. maj. 16,658)

NEWCASTLE UNDER LYME (Staffs)
*E.*66,595 *T.*80.34%

*Mrs L. Golding, *Lab.*	25,652
A. Brierley, *C.*	15,813
A. Thomas, *LD*	11,727
R. Lines, *NLP*	314
Lab. majority	9,839

(June 1987, Lab. maj. 5,132)

NEWCASTLE UPON TYNE CENTRAL
*E.*59,973 *T.*71.32%

*J. Cousins, *Lab.*	21,123
M. Summersby, *C.*	15,835
L. Opik, *LD*	5,816
Lab. majority	5,288

(June 1987, Lab. maj. 2,483)

NEWCASTLE UPON TYNE EAST
*E.*57,165 *T.*70.73%

*N. Brown, *Lab.*	24,342
J. Lucas, *C.*	10,465
A. Thompson, *LD*	4,883
G. Edwards, *Green*	744
Lab. majority	13,877

(June 1987, Lab. maj. 12,500)

NEWCASTLE UPON TYNE NORTH
*E.*66,187 *T.*76.80%

*D. Henderson, *Lab.*	25,121
I. Gordon, *C.*	16,175
P. Maughan, *LD*	9,542
Lab. majority	8,946

(June 1987, Lab. maj. 5,243)

NEW FOREST (Hants)
*E.*75,413 *T.*80.76%

*Sir P. McNair-Wilson, *C.*	37,986
Ms J. Vernon-Jackson, *LD*	17,581
M. Shutler, *Lab.*	4,989
Ms F. Carter, *NLP*	350
C. majority	20,405

(June 1987, C. maj. 21,732)

NEWHAM NORTH EAST (Greater London)
*E.*59,555 *T.*60.34%

*R. Leighton, *Lab.*	20,952
J. Galbraith, *C.*	10,966
J. Aves, *LD*	4,020
Lab. majority	9,986

(June 1987, Lab. maj. 8,236)

NEWHAM NORTH WEST (Greater London)
*E.*46,471 *T.*56.02%

*T. Banks, *Lab.*	15,911
M. Prisk, *C.*	6,740
A. Sawdon, *LD*	2,445
Ms A. Standford, *Green*	587
T. Jug, *Loony G.*	252
D. O'Sullivan, *Int. Comm.*	100

Lab. majority 9,171
(June 1987, Lab. maj. 8,496)

NEWHAM SOUTH (Greater London)
*E.*51,143 *T.*60.19%
*N. Spearing, *Lab.* 14,358
Ms J. Foster, *C.* 11,856
A. Kellaway, *LD* 4,572
Lab. majority 2,502
(June 1987, Lab. maj. 2,766)

NORFOLK MID
*E.*80,336 *T.*81.64%
*Rt. Hon. R. Ryder, *C.* 35,620
M. Castle, *Lab.* 16,672
J. Gleed, *LD* 13,072
Ms C. Waite, *NLP* 226
C. majority 18,948
(June 1987, C. maj. 18,008)

NORFOLK NORTH
*E.*73,780 *T.*80.84%
*R. Howell, *C.* 28,810
N. Lamb, *LD* 16,265
M. Cullingham, *Lab.* 13,850
Ms A. Zelter, *Green* 559
Ms S. Jackson, *NLP* 167
C. majority 12,545
(June 1987, C. maj. 15,310)

NORFOLK NORTH WEST
*E.*77,438 *T.*80.67%
*H. Bellingham, *C.* 32,554
Dr G. Turner, *Lab.* 20,990
A. Waterman, *LD* 8,599
S. Pink, *NLP* 330
C. majority 11,564
(June 1987, C. maj. 10,825)

NORFOLK SOUTH
*E.*81,647 *T.*83.99%
*Rt. Hon. J. MacGregor, *C.* 36,081
C. Brocklebank-Fowler, *LD* 18,516
C. Needle, *Lab.* 12,422
Ms S. Ross-Wagenknecht, *Green* 702
N. Clark, *NLP* 320
R. Peacock, *Ind.* 304
R. Watkins, *Ind. C.* 232
C. majority 17,565
(June 1987, C. maj. 12,418)

NORFOLK SOUTH WEST
*E.*77,652 *T.*79.30%
*Mrs G. Shephard, *C.* 33,637
Ms M. Page, *Lab.* 16,706
J. Marsh, *LD* 11,237
C. majority 16,931
(June 1987, C. maj. 20,436)

NORMANTON (W. Yorks)
*E.*65,562 *T.*76.35%
*W. O'Brien, *Lab.* 25,936
R. Sturdy, *C.* 16,986
M. Galdas, *LD* 7,137
Lab. majority 8,950
(June 1987, Lab. maj. 7,287)

NORTHAMPTON NORTH
*E.*69,139 *T.*78.52%
*A. Marlow, *C.* 24,865
Ms J. Thomas, *Lab.* 20,957
R. Church, *LD* 8,236
B. Spivack, *NLP* 232
C. majority 3,908
(June 1987, C. maj. 9,256)

NORTHAMPTON SOUTH
*E.*83,477 *T.*79.90%
*M. Morris, *C.* 36,882
J. Dickie, *Lab.* 19,909
G. Mabbutt, *LD* 9,912
C. majority 16,973
(June 1987, C. maj. 17,803)

NORTHAVON (Avon)
*E.*83,496 *T.*84.16%
*Rt. Hon. Sir J. Cope, *C.* 35,338
Ms H. Larkins, *LD* 23,477
Ms J. Norris, *Lab.* 10,290
Ms J. Greene, *Green* 789
P. Marx, *Lib.* 380
C. majority 11,861
(June 1987, C. maj. 14,270)

NORWICH NORTH (Norfolk)
*E.*63,308 *T.*81.82%
*H. P. Thompson, *C.* 22,419
I. Gibson, *Lab.* 22,153
D. Harrison, *LD* 6,706
L. Betts, *Green* 433
R. Arnold, *NLP* 93
C. majority 266
(June 1987, C. maj. 7,776)

NORWICH SOUTH (Norfolk)
*E.*63,603 *T.*80.60%
*J. Garrett, *Lab.* 24,965
D. Baxter, *C.* 18,784
C. Thomas, *LD* 6,609
A. Holmes, *Green* 803
B. Parsons, *NLP* 104
Lab. majority 6,181
(June 1987, Lab. maj. 336)

NORWOOD (Greater London)
*E.*52,496 *T.*65.87%
*J. Fraser, *Lab.* 18,391
J. Samways, *C.* 11,175
Ms S. Lawman, *LD* 4,087
S. Collins, *Green* 790
M. Leighton, *NLP* 138
Lab. majority 7,216
(June 1987, Lab. maj. 4,723)

NOTTINGHAM EAST
*E.*67,939 *T.*70.08%
J. Heppell, *Lab.* 25,026
*M. Knowles, *C.* 17,346
T. Ball, *LD* 3,695
A. Jones, *Green* 667
C. Roylance, *Lib.* 598
J. Ashforth, *NLP* 283
Lab. majority 7,680
(June 1987, C. maj. 456)

NOTTINGHAM NORTH
*E.*69,494 *T.*74.98%
*G. Allen, *Lab.* 29,052
I. Bridge, *C.* 18,309
A. Skelton, *LD* 4,477
A. Cadman, *NLP* 274
Lab. majority 10,743
(June 1987, Lab. maj. 1,665)

NOTTINGHAM SOUTH
*E.*72,796 *T.*74.22%
A. Simpson, *Lab.* 25,771
*M. Brandon-Bravo, *C.* 22,590
G. D. Long, *LD* 5,408
Ms J. Christou, *NLP* 263
Lab. majority 3,181
(June 1987, C. maj. 2,234)

NUNEATON (Warwicks)
*E.*70,906 *T.*83.70%
W. Olner, *Lab.* 27,157
*L. Stevens, *C.* 25,526
Ms R. Merritt, *LD* 6,671
Lab. majority 1,631
(June 1987, C. maj. 5,655)

OLD BEXLEY AND SIDCUP (Greater London)
*E.*49,449 *T.*81.94%
*Rt. Hon. E. Heath, *C.* 24,450
Ms D. Brierly, *Lab.* 8,751
D. Nicolle, *LD* 6,438
B. Rose, *Alt. C.* 733
R. Stephens, *NLP* 148
C. majority 15,699
(June 1987, C. maj. 16,274)

OLDHAM CENTRAL AND ROYTON (Greater Manchester)
*E.*61,333 *T.*74.20%
B. Davies, *Lab.* 23,246
Mrs T. Morris, *C.* 14,640
Ms A. Dunn, *LD* 7,224
I. Dalling, *NLP* 403
Lab. majority 8,606
(June 1987, Lab. maj. 6,279)

OLDHAM WEST (Greater Manchester)
*E.*54,063 *T.*75.65%
*M. Meacher, *Lab.* 21,580
J. Gillen, *C.* 13,247
J. Smith, *LD* 5,525
Ms S. Dalling, *NLP* 551
Lab. majority 8,333
(June 1987, Lab. maj. 5,967)

ORPINGTON (Greater London)
*E.*57,318 *T.*83.67%

J. Horam, *C.*	27,421
C. Maines, *LD*	14,486
S. Cowan, *Lab.*	5,512
R. Almond, *Lib.*	539
C. majority	12,935

(June 1987, C. maj. 12,732)

OXFORD EAST
*E.*63,075 *T.*74.59%

*A. Smith, *Lab.*	23,702
Dr M. Mayall, *C.*	16,164
M. Horwood, *LD*	6,105
Mrs C. Lucas, *Green*	933
Miss A. Wilson, *NLP*	101
K. Thompson, *Rev. Comm.*	48
Lab. majority	7,538

(June 1987, Lab. maj. 1,288)

OXFORD WEST AND ABINGDON
*E.*72,328 *T.*76.68%

*Rt. Hon. J. Patten, *C.*	25,163
Sir W. Goodhart, *LD*	21,624
B. Kent, *Lab.*	7,652
M. Woodin, *Green*	660
R. Jenking, *Lib.*	194
Miss S. Nelson, *Anti Fed.*	98
G. Wells, *NLP*	75
C. majority	3,539

(June 1987, C. maj. 4,878)

PECKHAM (Greater London)
*E.*58,269 *T.*53.87%

*Ms H. Harman, *Lab.*	19,391
C. Frazer, *C.*	7,386
Mrs R. Colley, *LD*	4,331
G. Dacres, *WRP*	146
V. Emmanuel, *Whiplash*	140
Lab. majority	12,005

(June 1987, Lab. maj. 9,489)

PENDLE (Lancs)
*E.*64,063 *T.*82.91%

G. Prentice, *Lab.*	23,497
*J. Lee, *C.*	21,384
A. Davies, *LD*	7,976
Mrs V. Thome, *Anti Fed.*	263
Lab. majority	2,113

(June 1987, C. maj. 2,639)

PENRITH AND THE BORDER (Cumbria)
*E.*73,769 *T.*79.67%

*D. Maclean, *C.*	33,808
G. Walker, *LD*	15,359
J. Metcalfe, *Lab.*	8,871
R. Gibson, *Green*	610
I. Docker, *NLP*	129
C. majority	18,449

(June 1987, C. maj. 17,366)

PETERBOROUGH (Cambs)
*E.*87,638 *T.*75.12%

*B. Mawhinney, *C.*	31,827
Ms J. Owens, *Lab.*	26,451
Ms A. Taylor, *LD*	5,208
E. Murat, *Lib.*	1,557
R. Heaton, *BNP*	311
P. Beasley, *PP*	271
C. Brettell, *NLP*	215
C. majority	5,376

(June 1987, C. maj. 9,784)

PLYMOUTH DEVONPORT (Devon)
*E.*65,799 *T.*77.83%

D. Jamieson, *Lab.*	24,953
K. Simpson, *C.*	17,541
M. Mactaggart, *LD*	6,315
H. Luscombe, *SD*	2,152
F. Lyons, *NLP*	255
Lab. majority	7,412

(June 1987, SDP/All. maj. 6,470)

PLYMOUTH DRAKE (Devon)
*E.*51,667 *T.*75.56%

*Dame J. Fookes, *C.*	17,075
P. Telford, *Lab.*	15,062
Ms V. Cox, *LD*	5,893
D. Stanbury, *SD*	476
Ms A. Harrison, *Green*	441
T. Pringle, *NLP*	95
C. majority	2,013

(June 1987, C. maj. 3,125)

PLYMOUTH SUTTON (Devon)
*E.*67,430 *T.*81.17%

G. Streeter, *C.*	27,070
A. Pawley, *Lab.*	15,120
J. Brett-Freeman, *LD*	12,291
J. Bowler, *NLP*	256
C. majority	11,950

(June 1987, C. maj. 4,013)

PONTEFRACT AND CASTLEFORD (W. Yorks)
*E.*64,648 *T.*74.25%

*G. Lofthouse, *Lab.*	33,546
A. Rockall, *C.*	10,051
D. Ryan, *LD*	4,410
Lab. majority	23,495

(June 1987, Lab. maj. 21,626)

POOLE (Dorset)
*E.*79,221 *T.*79.39%

*J. Ward, *C.*	33,445
B. Clements, *LD*	20,614
H. White, *Lab.*	6,912
M. Steen, *Ind. C.*	1,620
A. Bailey, *NLP*	303
C. majority	12,831

(June 1987, C. maj. 14,808)

PORTSMOUTH NORTH (Hants)
*E.*79,592 *T.*77.05%

*P. Griffiths, *C.*	32,240
A. Burnett, *Lab.*	18,359
A. Bentley, *LD*	10,101
Ms H. Palmer, *Green*	628
C. majority	13,881

(June 1987, C. maj. 18,401)

PORTSMOUTH SOUTH (Hants)
*E.*77,645 *T.*69.09%

*D. Martin, *C.*	22,798
M. Hancock, *LD*	22,556
S. Rapson, *Lab.*	7,857
A. Zivkovic, *Green*	349
W. Trend, *NLP*	91
C. majority	242

(June 1987, C. maj. 205)

PRESTON (Lancs)
*E.*64,158 *T.*71.74%

*Mrs A. Wise, *Lab.*	24,983
S. O'Toole, *C.*	12,808
W. Chadwick, *LD*	7,897
Ms J. Ayliffe, *NLP*	341
Lab. majority	12,175

(June 1987, Lab. maj. 10,645)

PUDSEY (W. Yorks)
*E.*70,847 *T.*80.14%

*Sir G. Shaw, *C.*	25,067
A. Giles, *Lab.*	16,095
D. Shutt, *LD*	15,153
Ms J. Wynne, *Green*	466
C. majority	8,972

(June 1987, C. maj. 6,436)

PUTNEY (Greater London)
*E.*61,914 *T.*77.91%

*Rt. Hon. D. Mellor, *C.*	25,188
Ms J. Chegwidden, *Lab.*	17,662
J. Martyn, *LD*	4,636
K. Hagenbach, *Green*	618
P. Levy, *NLP*	139
C. majority	7,526

(June 1987, C. maj. 6,907)

RAVENSBOURNE (Greater London)
*E.*57,259 *T.*81.24%

*Sir J. Hunt, *C.*	29,506
P. Booth, *LD*	9,792
E. Dyer, *Lab.*	6,182
I. Mouland, *Green*	617
P. White, *Lib.*	318
J. Shepheard, *NLP*	105
C. majority	19,714

(June 1987, C. maj. 16,919)

READING EAST (Berks)
*E.*72,151 *T.*75.02%

*Sir G. Vaughan, *C.*	29,148
Ms G. Parker, *Lab.*	14,593

D. Thair, *LD* 9,528
Ms A. McCubbin, *Green* 861
C. majority 14,555
(June 1987, C. maj. 16,217)

READING WEST (Berks)
*E.*67,937 *T.*77.98%

*Sir A. Durant, *C.* 28,048
P. Ruhemann, *Lab.* 14,750
K. Lock, *LD* 9,572
P. Unsworth, *Green* 613
C. majority 13,298
(June 1987, C. maj. 16,753)

REDCAR (Cleveland)
*E.*62,494 *T.*77.73%

*Dr M. Mowlam, *Lab.* 27,184
R. Goodwill, *C.* 15,607
C. Abbott, *LD* 5,789
Lab. majority 11,577
(June 1987, Lab. maj. 7,735)

REIGATE (Surrey)
*E.*71,853 *T.*78.54%

*Sir G. Gardiner, *C.* 32,220
B. Newsome, *LD* 14,556
Ms H. Young, *Lab.* 9,150
M. Dilcliff, *SD* 513
C. majority 17,664
(June 1987, C. maj. 18,173)

RIBBLE VALLEY (Lancs)
*E.*64,996 *T.*85.73%

N. Evans, *C.* 29,178
*M. Carr, *LD* 22,636
R. Pickup, *Lab.* 3,649
D. Beesley, *Loony G.* 152
Ms N. Holmes, *NLP* 112
C. majority 6,542
(June 1987, C. maj. 19,528)
(March 1991, LD maj. 4,641)

RICHMOND AND BARNES
(Greater London)
*E.*53,081 *T.*85.01%

*J. Hanley, *C.* 22,894
Dr J. Tonge, *LD* 19,025
D. Touhig, *Lab.* 2,632
Ms J. Maciejowska, *Green* 376
C. Cunningham, *NLP* 89
R. Meacock, *QFL* 62
Ms A. Ellis-Jones, *Anti Fed.* 47
C. majority 3,869
(June 1987, C. maj. 1,766)

RICHMOND (N. Yorks)
*E.*82,879 *T.*78.41%

*W. Hague, *C.* 40,202
G. Irwin, *LD* 16,698
R. Cranston, *Lab.* 7,523
M. Barr, *Ind.* 570
C. majority 23,504
(June 1987, C. maj. 19,576)
(Feb 1989, C. maj. 2,634)

ROCHDALE (Greater Manchester)
*E.*69,522 *T.*76.47%

Ms E. Lynne, *LD* 22,776
D. Williams, *Lab.* 20,937
D. Goldie-Scott, *C.* 8,626
K. Henderson, *BNP* 620
V. Lucker, *NLP* 211
LD majority 1,839
(June 1987, L./All. maj. 2,779)

ROCHFORD (Essex)
*E.*76,869 *T.*82.99%

*Dr M. Clark, *C.* 38,967
N. Harris, *LD* 12,931
D. Quinn, *Lab.* 10,537
Ms L. Farmer, *Lib.* 1,362
C. majority 26,036
(June 1987, C. maj. 19,694)

ROMFORD (Greater London)
*E.*54,001 *T.*78%

*Sir M. Neubert, *C.* 23,834
Ms E. Gordon, *Lab.* 12,414
Ms P. Atherton, *LD* 5,329
F. Gibson, *Green* 546
C. majority 11,420
(June 1987, C. maj. 13,471)

ROMSEY AND WATERSIDE
(Hants)
*E.*82,628 *T.*83.15%

*M. Colvin, *C.* 37,375
G. Dawson, *LD* 22,071
Mrs A. Mawle, *Lab.* 8,688
J. Spottiswood, *Green* 577
C. majority 15,304
(June 1987, C. maj. 15,272)

ROSSENDALE AND DARWEN
(Lancs)
*E.*76,909 *T.*83.06%

Mrs J. Anderson, *Lab.* 28,028
*D. Trippier, *C.* 27,908
K. Connor, *LD* 7,226
J. Gaffney, *Green* 596
P. Gorrod, *NLP* 125
Lab. majority 120
(June 1987, C. maj. 4,982)

ROTHERHAM (S. Yorks)
*E.*60,937 *T.*71.68%

J. Boyce, *Lab.* 27,933
S. Yorke, *C.* 10,372
D. Wildgoose, *LD* 5,375
Lab. majority 17,561
(June 1987, Lab. maj. 16,012)

ROTHER VALLEY (S. Yorks)
*E.*68,303 *T.*74.98%

*K. Barron, *Lab.* 30,977
T. Horton, *C.* 13,755
K. Smith, *LD* 6,483
Lab. majority 17,222
(June 1987, Lab. maj. 15,790)

RUGBY AND KENILWORTH
(Warwicks)
*E.*77,766 *T.*83.72%

*J. Pawsey, *C.* 34,110
J. Airey, *Lab.* 20,863
J. Roodhouse, *LD* 9,934
S. Withers, *NLP* 202
C. majority 13,247
(June 1987, C. maj. 16,264)

RUISLIP-NORTHWOOD (Greater
London)
*E.*54,151 *T.*81.91%

*J. Wilkinson, *C.* 28,097
Ms R. Brooks, *Lab.* 8,306
H. Davies, *LD* 7,739
M. Sheehan, *NLP* 214
C. majority 19,791
(June 1987, C. maj. 16,971)

RUSHCLIFFE (Notts)
*E.*76,253 *T.*83.04%

*Rt. Hon. K. Clarke, *C.* 34,448
A. Chewings, *Lab.* 14,682
Dr A. Wood, *LD* 12,660
S. Anthony, *Green* 775
M. Maelor-Jones, *Ind. C.* 611
D. Richards, *NLP* 150
C. majority 19,766
(June 1987, C. maj. 20,839)

RUTLAND AND MELTON (Leics)
*E.*80,976 *T.*80.82%

A. Duncan, *C.* 38,603
Ms J. Taylor, *Lab.* 13,068
R. Lustig, *LD* 12,682
J. Berreen, *Green* 861
R. Grey, *NLP* 237
C. majority 25,535
(June 1987, C. maj. 23,022)

RYEDALE (N. Yorks)
*E.*87,048 *T.*81.73%

*J. Greenway, *C.* 39,888
Mrs E. Shields, *LD* 21,449
J. Healey, *Lab.* 9,812
C. majority 18,439
(June 1987, C. maj. 9,740)

SAFFRON WALDEN (Essex)
*E.*74,878 *T.*83.21%

*A. Haselhurst, *C.* 35,272
M. Hayes, *LD* 17,848
J. Kotz, *Lab.* 8,933
M. Miller, *NLP* 260
C. majority 17,424
(June 1987, C. maj. 16,602)

ST ALBANS (Herts)
*E.*74,188 *T.*83.47%

*Rt. Hon. P. Lilley, *C.* 32,709
Ms M. Howes, *LD* 16,305
K. Pollard, *Lab.* 12,016
C. Simmons, *Green* 734
D. Lucas, *NLP* 161

C. majority 16,404
(June 1987, C. maj. 10,881)

ST HELENS NORTH (Merseyside)
*E.*71,261 *T.*77.35%

*J. Evans, *Lab.* 31,930
B. Anderson, *C.* 15,686
J. Beirne, *LD* 7,224
Ms A. Lynch, *NLP* 287
Lab. majority 16,244
(June 1987, Lab. maj. 14,260)

ST HELENS SOUTH (Merseyside)
*E.*67,507 *T.*73.77%

*G. Bermingham, *Lab.* 30,391
Mrs P. Buzzard, *C.* 12,182
B. Spencer, *LD* 6,933
Dr H. Jump, *NLP* 295
Lab. majority 18,209
(June 1987, Lab. maj. 13,801)

ST IVES (Cornwall)
*E.*71,152 *T.*80.29%

*D. Harris, *C.* 24,528
A. George, *LD* 22,883
S. Warran, *Lab.* 9,144
Dr G. Stephens, *Lib.* 577
C. majority 1,645
(June 1987, C. maj. 7,555)

SALFORD EAST (Greater Manchester)
*E.*52,616 *T.*64.36%

*Rt. Hon. S. Orme, *Lab.* 20,327
D. Berens, *C.* 9,092
N. Owen, *LD* 3,836
M. Stanley, *Green* 463
C. Craig, *NLP* 150
Lab. majority 11,235
(June 1987, Lab. maj. 12,056)

SALISBURY (Wilts)
*E.*75,916 *T.*79.89%

*S. R. Key, *C.* 31,546
P. Sample, *LD* 22,573
S. Fear, *Lab.* 5,483
Dr S. Elcock, *Green* 609
S. Fletcher, *Ind.* 233
T. Abbott, *Wessex* 117
Ms A. Martell, *NLP* 93
C. majority 8,973
(June 1987, C. maj. 11,443)

SCARBOROUGH (N. Yorks)
*E.*76,364 *T.*77.18%

J. Sykes, *C.* 29,334
D. Billing, *Lab.* 17,600
B. Davenport, *LD* 11,133
Dr D. Richardson, *Green* 876
C. majority 11,734
(June 1987, C. maj. 13,626)

SEDGEFIELD (Durham)
*E.*61,024 *T.*77.06%

*A. Blair, *Lab.* 28,453
N. Jopling, *C.* 13,594
G. Huntington, *LD* 4,982
Lab. majority 14,859
(June 1987, Lab. maj. 13,058)

SELBY (N. Yorks)
*E.*77,178 *T.*80.16%

*Rt. Hon. M. Alison, *C.* 31,067
J. Grogan, *Lab.* 21,559
E. Batty, *LD* 9,244
C. majority 9,508
(June 1987, C. maj. 13,779)

SEVENOAKS (Kent)
*E.*71,050 *T.*81.35%

*G. M. Wolfson, *C.* 33,245
R. Walshe, *LD* 14,091
Ms J. Evans, *Lab.* 9,470
Ms M. Lawrence, *Green* 786
P. Wakeling, *NLP* 210
C. majority 19,154
(June 1987, C. maj. 17,345)

SHEFFIELD ATTERCLIFFE (S. Yorks)
*E.*69,177 *T.*71.81%

C. Betts, *Lab.* 28,563
G. Millward, *C.* 13,083
Ms H. Woolley, *LD* 7,283
G. Ferguson, *Green* 751
Lab. majority 15,480
(June 1987, Lab. maj. 17,191)

SHEFFIELD BRIGHTSIDE (S. Yorks)
*E.*63,810 *T.*66.26%

*D. Blunkett, *Lab.* 29,771
T. Loughton, *C.* 7,090
R. Franklin, *LD* 5,273
D. Hyland, *Int. Comm.* 150
Lab. majority 22,681
(June 1987, Lab. maj. 24,191)

SHEFFIELD CENTRAL (S. Yorks)
*E.*59,059 *T.*56.12%

*R. Caborn, *Lab.* 22,764
V. Davies, *C.* 5,470
A. Sangar, *LD* 3,856
G. Wroe, *Green* 750
M. Clarke, *EUVJJ* 212
Ms J. O'Brien, *CL* 92
Lab. majority 17,294
(June 1987, Lab. maj. 19,342)

SHEFFIELD HALLAM (S. Yorks)
*E.*76,584 *T.*70.83%

*C. I. Patnick, *C.* 24,693
Dr P. Gold, *LD* 17,952
Ms V. Hardstaff, *Lab.* 10,930
M. Baker, *Green* 473
R. Hurford, *NLP* 101
Ms T. Clifford, *Rev. Comm.* 99
C. majority 6,741
(June 1987, C. maj. 7,637)

SHEFFIELD HEELEY (S. Yorks)
*E.*70,953 *T.*70.89%

*W. Michie, *Lab.* 28,005
D. Beck, *C.* 13,051
P. Moore, *LD* 9,247
Lab. majority 14,954
(June 1987, Lab. maj. 14,440)

SHEFFIELD HILLSBOROUGH (S. Yorks)
*E.*77,343 *T.*77.19%

Mrs H. Jackson, *Lab.* 27,568
D. Chadwick, *LD* 20,500
S. Cordle, *C.* 11,640
Lab. majority 7,068
(June 1987, Lab. maj. 3,286)

SHERWOOD (Notts)
*E.*73,354 *T.*85.48%

S. P. Tipping, *Lab.* 29,788
*A. Stewart, *C.* 26,878
J. Howard, *LD* 6,039
Lab. majority 2,910
(June 1987, C. maj. 4,495)

SHIPLEY (W. Yorks)
*E.*68,816 *T.*82.12%

*Sir M. Fox, *C.* 28,463
Ms A. Lockwood, *Lab.* 16,081
J. Cole, *LD* 11,288
C. Harris, *Green* 680
C. majority 12,382
(June 1987, C. maj. 12,630)

SHOREHAM (W. Sussex)
*E.*71,252 *T.*81.17%

B. M. L. Stephen, *C.* 32,670
M. King, *LD* 18,384
P. Godwin, *Lab.* 6,123
W. Weights, *Lib.* 459
J. Dreben, *NLP* 200
C. majority 14,286
(June 1987, C. maj. 17,070)

SHREWSBURY AND ATCHAM (Salop)
*E.*70,620 *T.*82.45%

*D. Conway, *C.* 26,681
K. Hemsley, *LD* 15,716
Ms E. Owen, *Lab.* 15,157
G. Hardy, *Green* 677
C. majority 10,965
(June 1987, C. maj. 9,064)

SHROPSHIRE NORTH
*E.*82,675 *T.*77.68%

*Rt. Hon. J. Biffen, *C.* 32,443
J. Stevens, *LD* 16,232
R. Hawkins, *Lab.* 15,550

C. majority 16,211
(June 1987, C. maj. 14,415)

SKIPTON AND RIPON (N. Yorks)
*E.*75,628 *T.*81.34%
*D. Curry, *C.* 35,937
R. Hall, *LD* 16,607
Ms K. Allott, *Lab.* 8,978
C. majority 19,330
(June 1987, C. maj. 17,174)

SLOUGH (Berks)
*E.*73,889 *T.*78.24%
*J. Watts, *C.* 25,793
E. Lopez, *Lab.* 25,279
P. Mapp, *LD* 4,041
J. Clark, *Lib.* 1,426
D. Alford, *Ind. Lab.* 699
A. Carmichael, *NF* 290
M. Creese, *NLP* 153
Ms E. Smith, *ERIP* 134
C. majority 514
(June 1987, C. maj. 4,090)

SOLIHULL (W. Midlands)
*E.*77,303 *T.*81.61%
*J. Taylor, *C.* 38,385
M. Southcombe, *LD* 13,239
Ms N. Kutapan, *Lab.* 10,544
C. Hards, *Green* 925
C. majority 25,146
(June 1987, C. maj. 21,786)

SOMERTON AND FROME (Somerset)
*E.*71,354 *T.*82.75%
M. Robinson, *C.* 28,052
D. Heath, *LD* 23,711
R. Ashford, *Lab.* 6,154
Ms L. Graham, *Green* 742
Ms J. Pollock, *Lib.* 388
C. majority 4,341
(June 1987, C. maj. 9,538)

SOUTHAMPTON ITCHEN (Hants)
*E.*72,104 *T.*76.93%
J. Denham, *Lab.* 24,402
*C. Chope, *C.* 23,851
J. Hodgson, *LD* 7,221
Lab. majority 551
(June 1987, C. maj. 6,716)

SOUTHAMPTON TEST (Hants)
*E.*72,932 *T.*77.40%
*S. J. A. Hill, *C.* 24,504
A. Whitehead, *Lab.* 23,919
Ms D. Maddock, *LD* 7,391
J. Michaelis, *Green* 535
D. Plummer, *NLP* 101
C. majority 585
(June 1987, C. maj. 6,954)

SOUTHEND EAST (Essex)
*E.*56,708 *T.*73.80%
*Sir E. Taylor, *C.* 24,591
G. Bramley, *Lab.* 11,480
Ms J. Horne, *LD* 5,107
B. Lynch, *Lib.* 673
C. majority 13,111
(June 1987, C. maj. 13,847)

SOUTHEND WEST (Essex)
*E.*64,198 *T.*77.80%
*Rt. Hon. P. Channon, *C.* 27,319
Ms N. Stimson, *LD* 15,417
G. Viney, *Lab.* 6,139
A. Farmer, *Lib.* 495
C. Keene, *Green* 451
P. Warburton, *NLP* 127
C. majority 11,902
(June 1987, C. maj. 8,400)

SOUTH HAMS (Devon)
*E.*83,061 *T.*81.09%
*A. Steen, *C.* 35,951
V. Evans, *LD* 22,240
Ms E. Cohen, *Lab.* 8,091
C. Titmuss, *Green* 846
Mrs L. Summerville, *NLP* 227
C. majority 13,711
(June 1987, C. maj. 13,146)

SOUTHPORT (Merseyside)
*E.*71,443 *T.*77.60%
M. Banks, *C.* 26,081
*R. Fearn, *LD* 23,018
J. King, *Lab.* 5,637
J. Walker, *Green* 545
G. Clements, *NLP* 159
C. majority 3,063
(June 1987, L./All. maj. 1,849)

SOUTH RIBBLE (Lancs)
*E.*78,173 *T.*82.99%
*R. Atkins, *C.* 30,828
Dr G. Smith, *Lab.* 24,855
S. Jones, *LD* 8,928
Dr R. Decter, *NLP* 269
C. majority 5,973
(June 1987, C. maj. 8,430)

SOUTH SHIELDS (Tyne & Wear)
*E.*59,392 *T.*70.07%
*D. Clark, *Lab.* 24,876
J. Howard, *C.* 11,399
A. Preece, *LD* 5,344
Lab. majority 13,477
(June 1987, Lab. maj. 13,851)

SOUTHWARK AND BERMONDSEY (Greater London)
*E.*60,251 *T.*62.62%
*S. Hughes, *LD* 21,459
R. Balfe, *Lab.* 11,614
A. Raca, *C.* 3,794
S. Tyler, *BNP* 530
T. Blackham, *NF* 168
Dr G. Barnett, *NLP* 113
J. Grogan, *CL* 56
LD majority 9,845
June 1987, L./All. maj. 2,779

SPELTHORNE (Surrey)
E.69,343 *T.*80.36%
*D. Wilshire, C. 32,627
Ms A. Leedham, Lab. 12,784
R. Roberts, LD 9,202
Ms J. Wassell, Green 580
D. Rea, Loony 338
D. Ellis, NLP 195
C. majority 19,843
(June 1987, C. maj. 20,050)

STAFFORD
*E.*74,663 *T.*82.91%
*W. Cash, *C.* 30,876
D. Kidney, *Lab.* 19,976
Mrs J. Calder, *LD* 10,702
C. Peat, *Hardcore* 178
P. Lines, *NLP* 176
C. majority 10,900
(June 1987, C. maj. 13,707)

STAFFORDSHIRE MID
*E.*73,414 *T.*85.66%
M. Fabricant, *C.* 31,227
*Mrs S. Heal, *Lab.* 24,991
B. Stamp, *LD* 6,432
Ms D. Grice, *NLP* 239
C. majority 6,236
(June 1987, C. maj. 14,654)
(March 1990, Lab. maj. 9,449)

STAFFORDSHIRE MOORLANDS
*E.*75,036 *T.*83.66%
*D. Knox, *C.* 29,240
J. Siddelley, *Lab.* 21,830
Ms C. Jebb, *LD* 9,326
M. Howson, *Anti Fed.* 2,121
P. Davies, *NLP* 261
C. majority 7,410
(June 1987, C. maj. 14,427)

STAFFORDSHIRE SOUTH
*E.*82,758 *T.*81.54%
*P. Cormack, *C.* 40,266
B. Wylie, *Lab.* 17,633
I. Sadler, *LD* 9,584
C. majority 22,633
(June 1987, C. maj. 25,268)

STAFFORDSHIRE SOUTH EAST
*E.*70,199 *T.*82.05%
*D. Lightbown, *C.* 29,180
B. Jenkins, *Lab.* 21,988
G. Penlington, *LD* 5,540
Miss J. Taylor, *SD* 895
C. majority 7,192
(June 1987, C. maj. 10,885)

STALYBRIDGE AND HYDE (Greater Manchester)
*E.*68,189 *T.*73.46%

*T. Pendry, *Lab.*	26,207
S. Mort, *C.*	17,376
I. Kirk, *LD*	4,740
R. Powell, *Lib.*	1,199
D. Poyzer, *Loony*	337
E. Blomfield, *NLP*	238
Lab. majority	8,831

(June 1987, Lab. maj. 5,663)

STAMFORD AND SPALDING (Lincs)
*E.*75,153 *T.*81.16%

*J. Q. Davies, *C.*	35,965
C. Burke, *Lab.*	13,096
B. Lee, *LD*	11,939
C. majority	22,869

(June 1987, C. maj. 14,007)

STEVENAGE (Herts)
*E.*70,233 *T.*83.03%

*T. Wood, *C.*	26,652
Ms J. Church, *Lab.*	21,764
A. Reilly, *LD*	9,668
A. Calcraft, *NLP*	233
C. majority	4,888

(June 1987, C. maj. 5,340)

STOCKPORT (Greater Manchester)
*E.*58,095 *T.*82.27%

Ms M. A. Coffey, *Lab.*	21,096
*A. Favell, *C.*	19,674
Ms A. Corris, *LD*	6,539
Ms J. Filmore, *Green*	436
D. Saunders, *NLP*	50
Lab. majority	1,422

(June 1987, C. maj. 2,853)

STOCKTON NORTH (Cleveland)
*E.*69,451 *T.*76.83%

*F. Cook, *Lab.*	27,918
S. Brocklebank-Fowler, *C.*	17,444
Ms S. Fletcher, *LD*	7,454
K. McGarvey, *Ind. Lab.*	550
Lab. majority	10,474

(June 1987, Lab. maj. 8,801)

STOCKTON SOUTH (Cleveland)
*E.*75,959 *T.*82.77%

*T. Devlin, *C.*	28,418
J. Scott, *Lab.*	25,049
Ms K. Kirkham, *LD*	9,410
C. majority	3,369

(June 1987, C. maj. 774)

STOKE-ON-TRENT CENTRAL (Staffs)
*E.*65,527 *T.*68.12%

*M. Fisher, *Lab.*	25,897
N. Gibb, *C.*	12,477
M. Dent, *LD*	6,073
N. Pullen, *NLP*	196
Lab. majority	13,420

(June 1987, Lab. maj. 9,770)

STOKE-ON-TRENT NORTH (Staffs)
*E.*73,141 *T.*73.42%

*Ms J. Walley, *Lab.*	30,464
L. Harris, *C.*	15,687
J. Redfern, *LD*	7,167
A. Morrison, *NLP*	387
Lab. majority	14,777

(June 1987, Lab. maj. 8,513)

STOKE-ON-TRENT SOUTH (Staffs)
*E.*71,316 *T.*74.33%

G. Stevenson, *Lab.*	26,380
R. Ibbs, *C.*	19,471
F. Jones, *LD*	6,870
Mrs E. Lines, *NLP*	291
Lab. majority	6,909

(June 1987, Lab. maj. 5,053)

STRATFORD-UPON-AVON (Warwicks)
*E.*82,824 *T.*82.07%

*A. Howarth, *C.*	40,251
N. Fogg, *LD*	17,359
Ms S. Brookes, *Lab.*	8,932
R. Roughan, *Green*	729
A. Saunders, *Ind. C.*	573
M. Twite, *NLP*	130
C. majority	22,892

(June 1987, C. maj. 21,165)

STREATHAM (Greater London)
*E.*56,825 *T.*69.03%

K. Hill, *Lab.*	18,925
*Sir W. Shelton, *C.*	16,608
J. Pindar, *LD*	2,858
R. Baker, *Green*	443
A. Hankin, *Islamic*	154
Mrs C. Payne, *ADS*	145
J. Parsons, *NLP*	97
Lab. majority	2,317

(June 1987, C. maj. 2,407)

STRETFORD (Greater Manchester)
*E.*54,467 *T.*68.76%

*A. Lloyd, *Lab.*	22,300
C. Rae, *C.*	11,163
F. Beswick, *LD*	3,722
A. Boyton, *NLP*	268
Lab. majority	11,137

(June 1987, Lab. maj. 9,402)

STROUD (Glos)
*E.*82,553 *T.*84.49%

*R. Knapman, *C.*	32,201
D. Drew, *Lab.*	18,796
M. Robinson, *LD*	16,751
Ms S. Atkinson, *Green*	2,005
C. majority	13,405

(June 1987, C. maj. 12,375)

SUFFOLK CENTRAL
*E.*82,735 *T.*80.26%

*M. Lord, *C.*	32,917
Ms L. Henniker-Major, *LD*	16,886
J. Harris, *Lab.*	15,615
J. Matthissen, *Green*	800
Ms J. Wilmot, *NLP*	190
C. majority	16,031

(June 1987, C. maj. 16,290)

SUFFOLK COASTAL
*E.*79,333 *T.*81.62%

*Rt. Hon. J. Gummer, *C.*	34,680
P. Monk, *LD*	15,395
T. Hodgson, *Lab.*	13,508
A. Slade, *Green*	943
Ms F. Kaplan, *NLP*	232
C. majority	19,285

(June 1987, C. maj. 15,280)

SUFFOLK SOUTH
*E.*84,833 *T.*81.73%

*T. Yeo, *C.*	34,793
Ms K. Pollard, *LD*	17,504
S. Hesford, *Lab.*	16,623
T. Aisbitt, *NLP*	420
C. majority	17,289

(June 1987, C. maj. 16,243)

SUNDERLAND NORTH (Tyne & Wear)
*E.*72,874 *T.*68.86%

W. Etherington, *Lab.*	30,481
Miss J. Barnes, *C.*	13,477
V. Halom, *LD*	5,389
Ms W. Lundgren, *Lib.*	841
Lab. majority	17,004

(June 1987, Lab. maj. 14,672)

SUNDERLAND SOUTH (Tyne & Wear)
*E.*72,607 *T.*69.87%

*C. Mullin, *Lab.*	29,399
G. Howe, *C.*	14,898
J. Lennox, *LD*	5,844
T. Scouler, *Green*	596
Lab. majority	14,501

(June 1987, Lab. maj. 12,613)

SURBITON (Greater London)
*E.*42,421 *T.*82.44%

*R. Tracey, *C.*	19,033
Ms B. Janke, *LD*	9,394
R. Hutchinson, *Lab.*	6,384
W. Parker, *NLP*	161
C. majority	9,639

(June 1987, C. maj. 9,741)

SURREY EAST
*E.*57,878 *T.*82.53%

P. Ainsworth, *C.*	29,767
R. Tomlin, *LD*	12,111
Mrs G. Roles, *Lab.*	5,075
I. Kilpatrick, *Green*	819

C. majority 17,656
(June 1987, C. maj. 18,126)

SURREY NORTH WEST
*E.*83,648 *T.*78.27%

*Sir M. Grylls, *C.* 41,772
Mrs C. Clark, *LD* 13,378
M. Hayhurst, *Lab.* 8,886
Ms Y. Hockey, *Green* 1,441
C. majority 28,394
(June 1987, C. maj. 23,575)

SURREY SOUTH WEST
*E.*72,288 *T.*82.77%

*Mrs V. Bottomley, *C.* 35,008
N. Sherlock, *LD* 20,033
P. Kelly, *Lab.* 3,840
N. Bedrock, *Green* 710
K. Campbell, *NLP* 147
D. Newman, *AS* 98
C. majority 14,975
(June 1987, C. maj. 14,343)

SUSSEX MID
*E.*80,827 *T.*82.85%

*Rt. Hon. T. Renton, *C.* 39,524
Ms M. Collins, *LD* 18,996
Ms L. Gregory, *Lab.* 6,951
H. Stevens, *Green* 772
P. Berry, *Loony* 392
P. Hodkin, *PR* 246
Dr A. Hankey, *NLP* 89
C. majority 20,528
(June 1987, C. maj. 18,292)

SUTTON AND CHEAM (Greater London)
*E.*60,949 *T.*82.39%

Lady O. Maitland, *C.* 27,710
P. Burstow, *LD* 16,954
G. Martin, *Lab.* 4,980
J. Duffy, *Green* 444
Ms A. Hatchard, *NLP* 133
C. majority 10,756
(June 1987, C. maj. 15,718)

SUTTON COLDFIELD (W. Midlands)
*E.*71,410 *T.*79.51%

*Rt. Hon. Sir N. Fowler, *C.* 37,001
J. Whorwood, *LD* 10,965
Ms J. Bott-Obi, *Lab.* 8,490
H. Meads, *NLP* 324
C. majority 26,036
(June 1987, C. maj. 21,183)

SWINDON (Wilts)
*E.*90,067 *T.*81.46%

*S. Coombs, *C.* 31,749
J. D'Avila, *Lab.* 28,923
S. Cordon, *LD* 11,737
W. Hughes, *Green* 647
R. Gillard, *Loony G.* 236
V. Farrar, *Ind.* 78
C. majority 2,826
(June 1987, C. maj. 4,857)

TATTON (Cheshire)
*E.*71,085 *T.*80.83%

*M. N. Hamilton, *C.* 31,658
J. Kelly, *Lab.* 15,798
Ms C. Hancox, *LD* 9,597
M. Gibson, *FP* 410
C. majority 15,860
(June 1987, C. maj. 17,094)

TAUNTON (Somerset)
*E.*78,036 *T.*82.32%

*D. Nicholson, *C.* 29,576
Ms J. Ballard, *LD* 26,240
Ms J. Hole, *Lab.* 8,151
P. Leavey, *NLP* 279
C. majority 3,336
(June 1987, C. maj. 10,380)

TEIGNBRIDGE (Devon)
*E.*74,892 *T.*83.43%

*P. Nicholls, *C.* 31,272
R. Younger-Ross, *LD* 22,416
R. Kennedy, *Lab.* 8,128
A. Hope, *Loony* 437
N. Hayes, *NLP* 234
C. majority 8,856
(June 1987, C. maj. 10,425)

THANET NORTH (Kent)
*E.*70,978 *T.*76.02%

*R. Gale, *C.* 30,867
A. Bretman, *Lab.* 12,657
Ms J. Phillips, *LD* 9,563
Ms H. Dawe, *Green* 873
C. majority 18,210
(June 1987, C. maj. 17,480)

THANET SOUTH (Kent)
*E.*62,441 *T.*78.17%

*J. Aitken, *C.* 25,253
M. James, *Lab.* 13,740
W. Pitt, *LD* 8,948
Ms S. Peckham, *Green* 871
C. majority 11,513
(June 1987, C. maj. 13,683)

THURROCK (Essex)
*E.*69,171 *T.*78.15%

A. MacKinlay, *Lab.* 24,791
*T. Janman, *C.* 23,619
A. Banton, *LD* 5,145
C. Rogers, *Pensioners* 391
P. Compobassi, *Anti Fed.* 117
Lab. majority 1,172
(June 1987, C. maj. 690)

TIVERTON (Devon)
*E.*71,024 *T.*82.98%

Mrs A. Browning, *C.* 30,376
D. Cox, *LD* 19,287
Ms S. Gibb, *Lab.* 5,950
D. Morrish, *Lib.* 2,225
P. Foggitt, *Green* 1,007
B. Rhodes, *NLP* 96
C. majority 11,089
(June 1987, C. maj. 9,212)

TONBRIDGE AND MALLING (Kent)
*E.*77,292 *T.*82.66%

*Rt. Hon. Sir J. Stanley, *C.* 36,542
P. Roberts, *LD* 14,984
Ms M. O'Neill, *Lab.* 11,533
J. Tidy, *Green* 612
Mrs J. Hovarth, *NLP* 221
C. majority 21,558
(June 1987, C. maj. 16,429)

TOOTING (Greater London)
*E.*68,306 *T.*74.79%

*T. Cox, *Lab.* 24,601
M. Winters, *C.* 20,494
B. Bunce, *LD* 3,776
Ms C. Martin, *Lib.* 1,340
P. Owens, *Green* 694
F. Anklesalria, *NLP* 119
M. Whitelaw, *CD* 64
Lab. majority 4,107
(June 1987, Lab. maj. 1,441)

TORBAY (Devon)
*E.*71,171 *T.*80.63%

*R. Allason, *C.* 28,624
A. Sanders, *LD* 22,837
P. Truscott, *Lab.* 5,503
R. Jones, *NF* 268
Ms A. Thomas, *NLP* 157
C. majority 5,787
(June 1987, C. maj. 8,820)

TOTTENHAM (Greater London)
*E.*68,319 *T.*65.60%

*B. Grant, *Lab.* 25,309
A. Charalambous, *C.* 13,341
A. L'Estrange, *LD* 5,120
P. Budge, *Green* 903
Ms M. Obomanu, *NLP* 150
Lab. majority 11,968
(June 1987, Lab. maj. 4,141)

TRURO (Cornwall)
*E.*75,101 *T.*82.35%

*M. Taylor, *LD* 31,230
N. St Aubyn, *C.* 23,660
J. Geach, *Lab.* 6,078
L. Keating, *Green* 569
C. Tankard, *Lib.* 208
Ms M. Hartley, *NLP* 108
LD majority 7,570
(June 1987, L./All. maj. 4,753)

TUNBRIDGE WELLS (Kent)
*E.*76,808 *T.*78.11%

*Rt. Hon. Sir P. Mayhew, *C.* 34,162
A. Clayton, *LD* 17,030
E. Goodman, *Lab.* 8,300

E. Fenna, *NLP* 267
R. Edey, *ISS* 236
C. majority 17,132
(June 1987, C. maj. 16,122)

TWICKENHAM (Greater London)
*E.*63,072 *T.*84.27%

*T. Jessel, *C.* 26,804
Dr V. Cable, *LD* 21,093
M. Gold, *Lab.* 4,919
G. Gill, *NLP* 152
D. Griffith, *DLC* 103
A. Miners, *Lib.* 85
C. majority 5,711
(June 1987, C. maj. 7,127)

TYNE BRIDGE (Tyne & Wear)
*E.*53,079 *T.*62.64%

*D. Clelland, *Lab.* 22,328
C. Liddell-Grainger, *C.* 7,118
J. Burt, *LD* 3,804
Lab. majority 15,210
(June 1987, Lab. maj. 15,573)

TYNEMOUTH (Tyne & Wear)
*E.*74,955 *T.*80.39%

*N. Trotter, *C.* 27,731
P. Cosgrove, *Lab.* 27,134
P. Selby, *LD* 4,855
A. Buchanan-Smith, *Green* 543
C. majority 597
(June 1987, C. maj. 2,583)

UPMINSTER (Greater London)
*E.*64,138 *T.*80.46%

*Sir N. Bonsor, *C.* 28,791
T. Ward, *Lab.* 14,970
T. Hurlstone, *LD* 7,848
C. majority 13,821
(June 1987, C. maj. 16,857)

UXBRIDGE (Greater London)
*E.*61,744 *T.*78.87%

*J. M. Shersby, *C.* 27,487
R. Evans, *Lab.* 14,308
S. Carey, *LD* 5,900
I. Flindall, *Green* 538
M. O'Rourke, *BNP* 350
A. Deans, *NLP* 120
C. majority 13,179
(June 1987, C. maj. 15,970)

VAUXHALL (Greater London)
*E.*62,473 *T.*62.35%

*Ms C. Hoey, *Lab.* 21,328
B. Gentry, *C.* 10,840
M. Tuffrey, *LD* 5,678
Ms P. Shepherd, *Green* 803
A. Khan, *DOS* 156
Ms S. Hill, *Rev. Comm.* 152
Lab. majority 10,488
(June 1987, Lab. maj. 9,019)
(June 1989, Lab. maj. 9,766)

WAKEFIELD (W. Yorks)
*E.*69,794 *T.*76.27%

*D. Hinchliffe, *Lab.* 26,964
D. Fanthorpe, *C.* 20,374
T. Wright, *LD* 5,900
Lab. majority 6,590
(June 1987, Lab. maj. 2,789)

WALLASEY (Merseyside)
*E.*65,676 *T.*82.50%

Ms A. Eagle, *Lab.* 26,531
*Rt. Hon. L. Chalker, *C.* 22,722
N. Thomas, *LD* 4,177
Ms S. Davis, *Green* 650
G. Gay, *NLP* 105
Lab. majority 3,809
(June 1987, C. maj. 279)

WALLSEND (Tyne & Wear)
*E.*77,941 *T.*74.12%

S. Byers, *Lab.* 33,439
Miss M. Gibbon, *C.* 13,969
M. Huscroft, *LD* 10,369
Lab. majority 19,470
(June 1987, Lab. maj. 19,384)

WALSALL NORTH (W. Midlands)
*E.*69,604 *T.*74.98%

*D. Winnick, *Lab.* 24,387
R. Syms, *C.* 20,563
A. Powis, *LD* 6,629
K. Reynolds, *NF* 614
Lab. majority 3,824
(June 1987, Lab. maj. 1,790)

WALSALL SOUTH (W. Midlands)
*E.*65,642 *T.*76.26%

*B. George, *Lab.* 24,133
L. Jones, *C.* 20,955
G. Williams, *LD* 4,132
R. Clarke, *Green* 673
J. Oldbury, *NLP* 167
Lab. majority 3,178
(June 1987, Lab. maj. 1,116)

WALTHAMSTOW (Greater London)
*E.*49,140 *T.*72.35%

N. Gerrard, *Lab.* 16,251
*H. Summerson, *C.* 13,229
P. Leighton, *LD* 5,142
Ms J. Lambert, *Green* 594
V. Wilkinson, *Lib.* 241
A. Planton, *NLP* 94
Lab. majority 3,022
(June 1987, C. maj. 1,512)

WANSBECK (Northumberland)
*E.*63,457 *T.*79.29%

*J. Thompson, *Lab.* 30,046
G. Sanderson, *C.* 11,872
B. Priestley, *LD* 7,691
N. Best, *Green* 710
Lab. majority 18,174
(June 1987, Lab. maj. 16,789)

WANSDYKE (Avon)
*E.*77,156 *T.*84.33%

*J. Aspinwall, *C.* 31,389
D. Norris, *Lab.* 18,048
Ms D. Darby, *LD* 14,834
F. Hayden, *Green* 800
C. majority 13,341
(June 1987, C. maj. 16,144)

WANSTEAD AND WOODFORD (Greater London)
*E.*55,821 *T.*78.28%

*J. Arbuthnot, *C.* 26,204
Ms L. Brown, *Lab.* 9,319
G. Staight, *LD* 7,362
F. Roads, *Green* 637
A. Brickell, *NLP* 178
C. majority 16,885
(June 1987, C. maj. 16,412)

WANTAGE (Oxon)
*E.*68,328 *T.*82.68%

*R. Jackson, *C.* 30,575
R. Morgan, *LD* 14,102
V. Woodell, *Lab.* 10,955
R. Ely, *Green* 867
C. majority 16,473
(June 1987, C. maj. 12,156)

WARLEY EAST (W. Midlands)
*E.*51,717 *T.*71.72%

*A. Faulds, *Lab.* 19,891
G. Marshall, *C.* 12,097
A. Harrod, *LD* 4,547
A. Groucott, *NLP* 561
Lab. majority 7,794
(June 1987, Lab. maj. 5,585)

WARLEY WEST (W. Midlands)
*E.*57,164 *T.*73.90%

J. Spellar, *Lab.* 21,386
Mrs S. Whitehouse, *C.* 15,914
Ms E. Todd, *LD* 4,945
Lab. majority 5,472
(June 1987, Lab. maj. 5,393)

WARRINGTON NORTH (Cheshire)
*E.*78,548 *T.*77.38%

*E. D. H. Hoyle, *Lab.* 33,019
C. Daniels, *C.* 20,397
I. Greenhalgh, *LD* 6,965
B. Davies, *NLP* 400
Lab. majority 12,622
(June 1987, Lab. maj. 8,013)

WARRINGTON SOUTH (Cheshire)
*E.*77,694 *T.*82.04%

M. Hall, *Lab.* 27,819
*C. Butler, *C.* 27,628
P. Walker, *LD* 7,978
S. Benson, *NLP* 321
Lab. majority 191
(June 1987, C. maj. 3,609)

WARWICK AND LEAMINGTON
E.71,259 T.81.54%

*Sir D. Smith, *C.*	28,093
M. Taylor, *Lab.*	19,158
Ms S. Boad, *LD*	9,645
Ms J. Alty, *Green*	803
R. Newby, *Ind.*	251
J. Brewster, *NLP*	156
C. majority	8,935

(June 1987, C. maj. 13,982)

WARWICKSHIRE NORTH
E.71,473 T.83.82%

M. O'Brien, *Lab.*	27,599
*Hon. F. Maude, *C.*	26,145
N. Mitchell, *LD*	6,167
Lab. majority	1,454

(June 1987, C. maj. 2,829)

WATFORD (Herts)
E.72,291 T.82.34%

*W. A. T. T. Garel-Jones, *C.*	29,072
M. Jackson, *Lab.*	19,482
M. Oaten, *LD*	10,231
J. Hywel-Davies, *Green*	566
L. Davis, *NLP*	176
C. majority	9,590

(June 1987, C. maj. 11,736)

WAVENEY (Suffolk)
E.84,181 T.81.81%

*D. Porter, *C.*	33,174
E. Leverett, *Lab.*	26,472
A. Rogers, *LD*	8,925
D. Hook, *NLP*	302
C. majority	6,702

(June 1987, C. maj. 11,783)

WEALDEN (E. Sussex)
E.74,665 T.80.83%

*Sir G. Johnson Smith, *C.*	37,263
M. Skinner, *LD*	16,332
S. Billcliffe, *Lab.*	5,579
I. Guy-Moore, *Green*	1,002
Dr R. Graham, *NLP*	182
C. majority	20,931

(June 1987, C. maj. 20,110)

WELLINGBOROUGH (Northants)
E.73,875 T.81.89%

*P. Fry, *C.*	32,302
P. Sawford, *Lab.*	20,486
Ms J. Trevor, *LD*	7,714
C. majority	11,816

(June 1987, C. maj. 14,070)

WELLS (Somerset)
E.69,833 T.82.71%

*D. Heathcoat-Amory, *C.*	28,620
H. Temperley, *LD*	21,971
J. Pilgrim, *Lab.*	6,126
M. Fenner, *Green*	1,042
C. majority	6,649

(June 1987, C. maj. 8,541)

WELWYN HATFIELD (Herts)
E.72,146 T.84.39%

*D. Evans, *C.*	29,447
R. Little, *Lab.*	20,982
R. Parker, *LD*	10,196
Ms E. Lucas, *NLP*	264
C. majority	8,465

(June 1987, C. maj. 10,903)

WENTWORTH (S. Yorks)
E.64,914 T.74.03%

*P. Hardy, *Lab.*	32,939
M. Brennan, *C.*	10,490
Ms C. Roderick, *LD*	4,629
Lab. majority	22,449

(June 1987, Lab. maj. 20,092)

WEST BROMWICH EAST (W. Midlands)
E.56,940 T.75.25%

*P. Snape, *Lab.*	19,913
C. Blunt, *C.*	17,100
M. Smith, *LD*	5,360
J. Lord, *NF*	477
Lab. majority	2,813

(June 1987, Lab. maj. 983)

WEST BROMWICH WEST (W. Midlands)
E.57,655 T.70.41%

*Miss B. Boothroyd, *Lab.*	22,251
D. Swayne, *C.*	14,421
Miss S. Broadbent, *LD*	3,925
Lab. majority	7,830

(June 1987, Lab. maj. 5,253)

WESTBURY (Wilts)
E.87,356 T.82.99%

D. Faber, *C.*	36,568
Ms V. Rayner, *LD*	23,962
W. Stallard, *Lab.*	9,642
P. Macdonald, *Lib.*	1,440
P. French, *Green*	888
C. majority	12,606

(June 1987, C. maj. 10,097)

WESTMINSTER NORTH (Greater London)
E.58,847 T.75.75%

*Sir J. Wheeler, *C.*	21,828
Ms J. Edwards, *Lab.*	18,095
J. Wigoder, *LD*	3,341
Ms A. Burke, *Green*	1,017
J. Hinde, *NLP*	159
M. Kelly, *Anti Fed.*	137
C. majority	3,733

(June 1987, C. maj. 3,310)

WESTMORLAND AND LONSDALE (Cumbria)
E.71,865 T.77.76%

*Rt. Hon. M. Jopling, *C.*	31,798
S. Collins, *LD*	15,362
D. Abbott, *Lab.*	8,436
R. Johnstone, *NLP*	287
C. majority	16,436

(June 1987, C. maj. 14,920)

WESTON-SUPER-MARE (Avon)
E.78,839 T.79.75%

*A. W. Wiggin, *C.*	30,022
B. Cotter, *LD*	24,680
D. Murray, *Lab.*	6,913
Dr R. Lawson, *Green*	1,262
C. majority	5,342

(June 1987, C. maj. 7,998)

WIGAN (Greater Manchester)
E.72,739 T.76.16%

*R. Stott, *Lab.*	34,910
E. Hess, *C.*	13,068
G. Davies, *LD*	6,111
K. White, *Lib.*	1,116
Ms A. Taylor, *NLP*	197
Lab. majority	21,842

(June 1987, Lab. maj. 20,462)

WILTSHIRE NORTH
E.85,851 T.81.71%

*R. Needham, *C.*	39,028
Ms C. Napier, *LD*	22,640
Ms C. Reid, *Lab.*	6,945
Ms L. Howitt, *Green*	850
G. Hawkins, *Lib.*	622
S. Martienssen, *Bastion*	66
C. majority	16,388

(June 1987, C. maj. 10,939)

WIMBLEDON (Greater London)
E.61,917 T.80.23%

*Dr C. Goodson-Wickes, *C.*	26,331
K. Abrams, *Lab.*	11,570
Ms A. Willott, *LD*	10,569
V. Flood, *Green*	860
H. Godfrey, *NLP*	181
G. Hadley, *Ind.*	170
C. majority	14,761

(June 1987, C. maj. 11,301)

WINCHESTER (Hants)
E.79,218 T.83.46%

P. G. Malone, *C.*	33,113
A. Barron, *LD*	24,992
P. Jenks, *Lab.*	4,917
*J. Browne, *Ind. C.*	3,095
C. majority	8,121

(June 1987, C. maj. 7,479)

WINDSOR AND MAIDENHEAD (Berks)
E.77,327 T.81.68%

Hon. M. Trend, *C.*	35,075
J. Hyde, *LD*	22,147
Ms C. Attlee, *Lab.*	4,975
R. Williams, *Green*	510
D. Askwith, *Loony*	236

Miss E. Bigg, *Ind.* 110
M. Grenville, *NLP* 108
C. majority 12,928
(June 1987, C. maj. 17,836)

WIRRAL SOUTH (Merseyside)
*E.*61,116 *T.*82.37%

*G. B. Porter, *C.* 25,590
Ms H. Southworth, *Lab.* 17,407
E. Cunniffe, *LD* 6,581
N. Birchenough, *Green* 584
G. Griffiths, *NLP* 182
C. majority 8,183
(June 1987, C. maj. 10,963)

WIRRAL WEST (Merseyside)
*E.*62,453 *T.*81.57%

*Rt. Hon. D. Hunt, *C.* 26,852
Ms H. Stephenson, *Lab.* 15,788
J. Thornton, *LD* 7,420
Ms G. Bowler, *Green* 700
N. Broome, *NLP* 188
C. majority 11,064
(June 1987, C. maj. 12,723)

WITNEY (Oxon)
*E.*78,521 *T.*81.89%

*Rt. Hon. D. Hurd, *C.* 36,256
J. Plaskitt, *Lab.* 13,688
I. Blair, *LD* 13,393
Ms C. Beckford, *Green* 716
Ms S. Catling, *NLP* 134
Miss M. Brown, *FTA* 119
C. majority 22,568
(June 1987, C. maj. 18,464)

WOKING (Surrey)
*E.*80,842 *T.*79.20%

*Rt. Hon. C. Onslow, *C.* 37,744
Mrs D. Buckrell, *LD* 17,902
J. Dalgleish, *Lab.* 8,080
Mrs T. Macintyre, *NLP* 302
C. majority 19,842
(June 1987, C. maj. 16,544)

WOKINGHAM (Berks)
*E.*85,914 *T.*82.41%

*J. Redwood, *C.* 43,497
P. Simon, *LD* 17,788
N. Bland, *Lab.* 8,846
P. Owen, *Loony* 531
P. Harriss, *WUWC* 148
C. majority 25,709
(June 1987, C. maj. 20,387)

WOLVERHAMPTON NORTH EAST (W. Midlands)
*E.*62,695 *T.*78%

K. Purchase, *Lab.* 24,106
*Mrs M. Hicks, *C.* 20,167
M. Gwinnett, *LD* 3,546
K. Bullman, *Lib.* 1,087
Lab. majority 3,939
(June 1987, C. maj. 204)

WOLVERHAMPTON SOUTH EAST (W. Midlands)
*E.*56,158 *T.*72.86%

*D. Turner, *Lab.* 23,215
P. Bradbourn, *C.* 12,975
R. Whitehouse, *LD* 3,881
Ms C. Twelvetrees, *Lib.* 850
Lab. majority 10,240
(June 1987, Lab. maj. 6,398)

WOLVERHAMPTON SOUTH WEST (W. Midlands)
*E.*67,288 *T.*78.28%

*N. Budgen, *C.* 25,969
S. Murphy, *Lab.* 21,003
M. Wiggin, *LD* 4,470
C. Hallmark, *Lib.* 1,237
C. majority 4,966
(June 1987, C. maj. 10,318)

WOODSPRING (Avon)
*E.*77,534 *T.*83.21%

Dr L. Fox, *C.* 35,175
Ms N. Kirsen, *LD* 17,666
R. Stone, *Lab.* 9,942
N. Brown, *Lib.* 836
Ms R. Knifton, *Green* 801
B. Lee, *NLP* 100
C. majority 17,509
(June 1987, C. maj. 17,852)

WOOLWICH (Greater London)
*E.*55,977 *T.*70.91%

J. Austin-Walker, *Lab.* 17,551
*J. Cartwright, *SD* 15,326
K. Walmsley, *C.* 6,598
Ms S. Hayward, *NLP* 220
Lab. majority 2,225
(June 1987, SDP/All. maj. 1,937)

WORCESTER
*E.*74,211 *T.*80.99%

P. Luff, *C.* 27,883
R. Berry, *Lab.* 21,731
J. Caiger, *LD* 9,561
M. Foster, *Green* 592
M. Soden, *Brewer* 343
C. majority 6,152
(June 1987, C. maj. 10,453)

WORCESTERSHIRE MID
*E.*84,269 *T.*81.07%

*E. Forth, *C.* 33,964
Ms J. Smith, *Lab.* 24,094
D. Barwick, *LD* 9,745
P. Davis, *NLP* 520
C. majority 9,870
(June 1987, C. maj. 14,911)

WORCESTERSHIRE SOUTH
*E.*80,423 *T.*79.99%

*W. M. H. Spicer, *C.* 34,792
P. Chandler, *LD* 18,641
N. Knowles, *Lab.* 9,727
G. Woodford, *Green* 1,178
C. majority 16,151
(June 1987, C. maj. 13,645)

WORKINGTON (Cumbria)
*E.*57,597 *T.*81.52%

*D. Campbell-Savours, *Lab.* 26,719
S. Sexton, *C.* 16,270
Ms C. Neale, *LD* 3,028
D. Langstaff, *Loony* 755
Ms N. Escott, *NLP* 183
Lab. majority 10,449
(June 1987, Lab. maj. 7,019)

WORSLEY (Greater Manchester)
*E.*72,244 *T.*77.74%

*T. Lewis, *Lab.* 29,418
N. Cameron, *C.* 19,406
R. Boyd, *LD* 6,490
P. Connolly, *Green* 677
G. Phillips, *NLP* 176
Lab. majority 10,012
(June 1987, Lab. maj. 7,337)

WORTHING (W. Sussex)
*E.*77,540 *T.*77.41%

*Rt. Hon. T. Higgins, *C.* 34,198
Mrs S. Bucknall, *LD* 17,665
J. Deen, *Lab.* 6,679
Mrs P. Beever, *Green* 806
N. Goble, *Lib.* 679
C. majority 16,533
(June 1987, C. maj. 18,501)

THE WREKIN (Salop)
*E.*90,892 *T.*77.14%

*B. Grocott, *Lab.* 33,865
Mrs E. Holt, *C.* 27,217
A. West, *LD* 8,032
R. Saunders, *Green* 1,008
Lab. majority 6,648
(June 1987, Lab. maj. 1,456)

WYCOMBE (Bucks)
*E.*72,564 *T.*78.01%

*R. Whitney, *C.* 30,081
T. Andrews, *LD* 13,005
J. Huddart, *Lab.* 12,222
J. Laker, *Green* 686
A. Page, *SD* 449
T. Anton, *NLP* 168
C. majority 17,076
(June 1987, C. maj. 13,819)

WYRE (Lancs)
*E.*67,778 *T.*79.54%

*K. Mans, *C.* 29,449
D. Borrow, *Lab.* 17,785
J. Ault, *LD* 6,420
R. Perry, *NLP* 260
C. majority 11,664
(June 1987, C. maj. 14,661)

WYRE FOREST (H & W)
*E.*73,550 *T.*82.36%

*A. Coombs, *C.*	28,983
R. Maden, *Lab.*	18,642
M. Jones, *LD*	12,958
C. majority	10,341

(June 1987, C. maj. 7,224)

YEOVIL (Somerset)
*E.*73,057 *T.*81.98%

*Rt. Hon. J. J. D. Ashdown, *LD*	30,958
J. Davidson, *C.*	22,125
Ms V. Nelson, *Lab.*	5,765
J. Risbridger, *Green*	639
D. Sutch, *Loony*	338
R. Simmerson, *APAKBI*	70
LD majority	8,833

(June 1987, L./All. maj. 5,700)

YORK (N. Yorks)
*E.*79,242 *T.*80.97%

H. Bayley, *Lab.*	31,525
*C. Gregory, *C.*	25,183
Ms K. Anderson, *LD*	6,811
S. Kenwright, *Green*	594
Ms P. Orr, *NLP*	54
Lab. majority	6,342

(June 1987, C. maj. 147)

WALES

ABERAVON (W. Glamorgan)
*E.*51,650 *T.*77.57%

*Rt. Hon. J. Morris, *Lab.*	26,877
H. Williams, *C.*	5,567
Mrs M. Harris, *LD*	4,999
D. Saunders, *PC*	1,919
Capt. Beany, *Real Bean*	707
Lab. majority	21,310

(June 1987, Lab. maj. 20,609)

ALYN AND DEESIDE (Clwyd)
*E.*60,477 *T.*80.08%

*S. B. Jones, *Lab.*	25,206
J. Riley, *C.*	17,355
R. Britton, *LD*	4,687
J. Rogers, *PC*	551
V. Button, *Green*	433
J. Cooksey, *Ind.*	200
Lab. majority	7,851

(June 1987, Lab. maj. 6,383)

BLAENAU GWENT
*E.*55,638 *T.*78.13%

L. Smith, *Lab.*	34,333
D. Melding, *C.*	4,266
A. Burns, *LD*	2,774
A. Davies, *PC*	2,099
Lab. majority	30,067

(June 1987, Lab. maj. 27,861)

BRECON AND RADNOR (Powys)
*E.*51,509 *T.*85.94%

J. P. Evans, *C.*	15,977
*R. Livsey, *LD*	15,847
C. Mann, *Lab.*	11,634
Ms S. Meredudd, *PC*	418
H. Richards, *Green*	393
C. majority	130

(June 1987, L./All. maj. 56)

BRIDGEND (Mid Glamorgan)
*E.*58,531 *T.*80.44%

*W. Griffiths, *Lab.*	24,143
D. Unwin, *C.*	16,817
D. Mills, *LD*	4,827
A. Lloyd Jones, *PC*	1,301
Lab. majority	7,326

(June 1987, Lab. maj. 4,380)

CAERNARFON (Gwynedd)
*E.*46,468 *T.*78.15%

*D. Wigley, *PC*	21,439
P. Fowler, *C.*	6,963
Ms S. Mainwaring, *Lab.*	5,641
R. Arwel Williams, *LD*	2,101
G. Evans, *NLP*	173
PC majority	14,476

(June 1987, *PC maj. 12,812)*

CAERPHILLY (Mid Glamorgan)
*E.*64,529 *T.*77.20%

*R. Davies, *Lab.*	31,713
H. Philpott, *C.*	9,041
L. Whittle, *PC*	4,821
S. Wilson, *LD*	4,247
Lab. majority	22,672

(June 1987, Lab. maj. 19,167)

CARDIFF CENTRAL
(S. Glamorgan)
*E.*57,716 *T.*74.35%

J. O. Jones, *Lab.*	18,014
*I. Grist, *C.*	14,549
Ms J. Randerson, *LD*	9,170
H. Marshall, *PC*	748
C. von Ruhland, *Green*	330
B. Francis, *NLP*	105
Lab. majority	3,465

(June 1987, C. maj. 1,986)

CARDIFF NORTH (S. Glamorgan)
*E.*56,721 *T.*84.15%

*G. H. Jones, *C.*	21,547
Ms J. Morgan, *Lab.*	18,578
Ms E. Warlow, *LD*	6,487
Ms E. Bush, *PC*	916
J. Morse, *BNP*	121
D. Palmer, *NLP*	86
C. majority	2,969

(June 1987, C. maj. 8,234)

CARDIFF SOUTH AND PENARTH (S. Glamorgan)
*E.*61,484 *T.*77.25%

*A. Michael, *Lab.*	26,383
T. Hunter Jarvie, *C.*	15,958
P. Verma, *LD*	3,707
Ms B. Anglezarke, *PC*	776
L. Davey, *Green*	676
Lab. majority	10,425

(June 1987, Lab. maj. 4,574)

CARDIFF WEST (S. Glamorgan)
*E.*58,898 *T.*77.56%

*H. R. Morgan, *Lab.*	24,306
M. Prior, *C.*	15,015
Ms J. Gasson, *LD*	5,002
Ms P. Bestic, *PC*	1,177
A. Harding, *NLP*	184
Lab. majority	9,291

(June 1987, Lab. maj. 4,045)

CARMARTHEN (Dyfed)
*E.*68,887 T. 82.70%

*Dr A. W. Williams, *Lab.*	20,879
R. Thomas, *PC*	17,957
S. Cavenagh, *C.*	12,782
Mrs J. Hughes, *LD*	5,353
Lab. majority	2,922

(June 1987, Lab. maj. 4,317)

CEREDIGION AND PEMBROKE NORTH (Dyfed)
*E.*66,180 *T.*77.36%

C. Dafis, *PC*	16,020
*G. Howells, *LD*	12,827
J. Williams, *C.*	12,718
J. Davies, *Lab.*	9,637
PC majority	3,193

(June 1987, *L./All. maj. 4,700)*

CLWYD NORTH WEST
*E.*67,351 *T.*78.64%

R. Richards, *C.*	24,488
C. Ruane, *Lab.*	18,438
R. Ingham, *LD*	7,999
T. Neil, *PC*	1,888
Ms M. Swift, *NLP*	158
C. majority	6,050

(June 1987, C. maj. 11,781)

CLWYD SOUTH WEST
*E.*60,607 *T.*81.52%

*M. Jones, *Lab.*	21,490
G. Owen, *C.*	16,549
G. Williams, *LD*	6,027
E. Lloyd Jones, *PC*	4,835
N. Worth, *Green*	351
Mrs J. Leadbetter, *NLP*	155

Lab. majority	4,941
(June 1987, Lab. maj. 1,028)	

CONWY (Gwynedd)
*E.*53,576 *T.*78.85%

*Rt. Hon. Sir W. Roberts, *C.*	14,250
Revd R. Roberts, *LD*	13,255
Ms E. Williams, *Lab.*	10,883
R. Davies, *PC*	3,108
O. Wainwright, *Ind. C.*	637
Ms D. Hughes, *NLP*	114
C. majority	995
(June 1987, C. maj. 3,024)	

CYNON VALLEY (Mid Glamorgan)
*E.*49,695 *T.*76.46%

*Ms A. Clwyd, *Lab.*	26,254
A. Smith, *C.*	4,890
T. Benney, *PC*	4,186
M. Verma, *LD*	2,667
Lab. majority	21,364
(June 1987, Lab. maj. 21,571)	

DELYN (Clwyd)
*E.*66,591 *T.*83.40%

D. Hanson, *Lab.*	24,979
M. Whitby, *C.*	22,940
R. Dodd, *LD*	6,208
A. Drake, *PC*	1,414
Lab. majority	2,039
(June 1987, C. maj. 1,224)	

GOWER (W. Glamorgan)
*E.*57,231 *T.*81.84%

*G. Wardell, *Lab.*	23,455
A. Donnelly, *C.*	16,437
C. Davies, *LD*	4,655
A. Price, *PC*	1,658
B. Kingzett, *Green*	448
G. Egan, *Loony G.*	114
M. Beresford, *NLP*	74
Lab. majority	7,018
(June 1987, Lab. maj. 5,764)	

ISLWYN (Gwent)
*E.*51,079 *T.*81.48%

*Rt. Hon. N. Kinnock, *Lab.*	30,908
P. Bone, *C.*	6,180
M. Symonds, *LD*	2,352
Ms H. Jones, *PC*	1,636
Lord Sutch, *Loony*	547
Lab. majority	24,728
(June 1987, Lab. maj. 22,947)	

LLANELLI (Dyfed)
*E.*65,058 *T.*77.80%

*Rt. Hon. D. Davies, *Lab.*	27,802
G. Down, *C.*	8,532
M. Phillips, *PC*	7,878
K. Evans, *LD*	6,404
Lab. majority	19,270
(June 1987, Lab. maj. 20,935)	

MEIRIONNYDD NANT CONWY (Gwynedd)
*E.*32,413 *T.*81.47%

E. Llwyd, *PC*	11,608
G. Lewis, *C.*	6,995
R. Williams, *Lab.*	4,978
Mrs R. Parry, *LD*	2,358
W. Pritchard, *Green*	471
PC majority	4,613
(June 1987, PC maj. 3,026)	

MERTHYR TYDFIL AND RHYMNEY (Mid Glamorgan)
*E.*58,430 *T.*75.84%

*E. Rowlands, *Lab.*	31,710
R. Rowland, *LD*	4,997
M. Hughes, *C.*	4,904
A. Cox, *PC*	2,704
Lab. majority	26,713
(June 1987, Lab. maj. 28,207)	

MONMOUTH (Powys)
*E.*59,147 *T.*86.06%

R. Evans, *C.*	24,059
*H. Edwards, *Lab.*	20,855
Mrs F. David, *LD*	5,562
M. Witherden, *Green/PC*	431
C. majority	3,204
(June 1987, C. maj. 9,350)	
(May 1991, Lab. maj. 2,406)	

MONTGOMERY (W. Glamorgan)
*E.*41,386 *T.*79.87%

*A. Carlile, *LD*	16,031
Mrs J. France-Hayhurst, *C.*	10,822
S. Wood, *Lab.*	4,115
H. Parsons, *PC*	1,581
P. Adams, *Green*	508
LD majority	5,209
(June 1987, L./All. maj. 2,558)	

NEATH (W. Glamorgan)
*E.*56,392 *T.*80.58%

*P. Hain, *Lab.*	30,903
D. Adams, *C.*	6,928
Dr D. Evans, *PC*	5,145
M. Phillips, *LD*	2,467
Lab. majority	23,975
(June 1987, Lab. maj. 20,578)	
(April 1991, Lab. maj. 9,830)	

NEWPORT EAST (Gwent)
*E.*51,603 *T.*81.21%

*R. J. Hughes, *Lab.*	23,050
Mrs A. Emmett, *C.*	13,151
W. Oliver, *LD*	4,991
S. Ainley, *Green/PC*	716
Lab. majority	9,899
(June 1987, Lab. maj. 7,064)	

NEWPORT WEST (Gwent)
*E.*54,871 *T.*82.82%

*P. Flynn, *Lab.*	24,139
A. Taylor, *C.*	16,360
A. Toye, *LD*	4,296
P. Keelan, *PC*	653
Lab. majority	7,779
(June 1987, Lab. maj. 2,708)	

OGMORE (Mid Glamorgan)
*E.*52,195 *T.*80.62%

*R. Powell, *Lab.*	30,186
D. Edwards, *C.*	6,359
J. Warman, *LD*	2,868
Ms L. McAllister, *PC*	2,667
Lab. majority	23,827
(June 1987, Lab. maj. 22,292)	

PEMBROKE (Dyfed)
*E.*73,187 *T.*82.86%

N. Ainger, *Lab.*	26,253
*N. Bennett, *C.*	25,498
P. Berry, *LD*	6,625
C. Bryant, *PC*	1,627
R. Coghill, *Green*	484
M. Stoddart, *Anti Fed.*	158
Lab. majority	755
(June 1987, C. maj. 5,700)	

PONTYPRIDD (Mid Glamorgan)
*E.*61,685 *T.*79.25%

*K. Howells, *Lab.*	29,722
Dr P. Donnelly, *C.*	9,925
Dr D. Bowen, *PC*	4,448
S. Belzak, *LD*	4,180
Ms E. Jackson, *Green*	615
Lab. majority	19,797
(June 1987, Lab. maj. 17,277)	
(Feb. 1989, Lab. maj. 10,794)	

RHONDDA (Mid Glamorgan)
*E.*59,955 *T.*76.61%

*A. Rogers, *Lab.*	34,243
G. Davies, *PC*	5,427
J. Richards, *C.*	3,588
P. Nicholls-Jones, *LD*	2,431
M. Fisher, *Comm. GB*	245
Lab. majority	28,816
(June 1987, Lab. maj. 30,596)	

SWANSEA EAST (W. Glamorgan)
*E.*59,196 *T.*75.56%

*D. Anderson, *Lab.*	31,179
H. Davies, *C.*	7,697
R. Barton, *LD*	4,248
Ms E. Bonner-Evans, *PC*	1,607
Lab. majority	23,482
(June 1987, Lab. maj. 19,338)	

SWANSEA WEST (W. Glamorgan)
*E.*59,785 *T.*73.34%

*Rt. Hon. A. Williams, *Lab.*	23,238
R. Perry, *C.*	13,760
M. Shrewsbury, *LD*	4,620
Dr D. Lloyd, *PC*	1,668
B. Oubridge, *Green*	564
Lab. majority	9,478
(June 1987, Lab. maj. 7,062)	

TORFAEN (Gwent)
*E.*61,104 *T.*77.47%

*P. Murphy, *Lab.* 30,352
M. Watkins, *C.* 9,598
M. Hewson, *LD* 6,178
Dr J. Cox, *Green/PC* 1,210
Lab. majority 20,754
(June 1987, Lab. maj. 17,550)

VALE OF GLAMORGAN (S. Glamorgan)
*E.*66,672 *T.*81.93%

W. Sweeney, *C.* 24,220
*J. Smith, *Lab.* 24,201
K. Davies, *LD* 5,045
D. Haswell, *PC* 1,160
C. majority 19
(June 1987, C. maj 6,251)
(May 1989, Lab. maj. 6,028)

WREXHAM (Clwyd)
*E.*63,720 *T.*80.71%

*J. Marek, *Lab.* 24,830
O. Paterson, *C.* 18,114
A. Thomas, *LD* 7,074
G. Wheatley, *PC* 1,415
Lab. majority 6,716
(June 1987, Lab. maj. 4,152)

YNYS MÔN (Gwynedd)
*E.*53,412 *T.*80.62%

*I. W. Jones, *PC* 15,984
G. Price Rowlands, *C.* 14,878
Dr R. Jones, *Lab.* 10,126
Ms P. Badger, *LD* 1,891
Mrs S. Parry, *NLP* 182
PC majority 1,106
(June 1987, PC maj. 4,298)

SCOTLAND

ABERDEEN NORTH (Grampian)
*E.*60,217 *T.*66.52%

*R. Hughes, *Lab.* 18,845
J. McGugan, *SNP* 9,608
P. Cook, *C.* 6,836
Dr M. Ford, *LD* 4,772
Lab. majority 9,237
(June 1987, Lab. maj. 16,278)

ABERDEEN SOUTH (Grampian)
*E.*58,881 *T.*69.78%

R. Robertson, *C.* 15,808
*F. Doran, *Lab.* 14,291
J. Davidson, *SNP* 6,223
Ms I. Keith, *LD* 4,767
C. majority 1,517
(June 1987, Lab. maj. 1,198)

ANGUS EAST (Tayside)
*E.*63,170 *T.*75.03%

*A. Welsh, *SNP* 19,006
Dr R. Harris, *C.* 18,052
G. Taylor, *Lab.* 5,994
C. McLeod, *LD* 3,897
D. McCabe, *Green* 449
SNP majority 954
(June 1987, SNP maj. 1,544)

ARGYLL AND BUTE (Strathclyde)
*E.*47,894 *T.*76.19%

*Mrs J. R. Michie, *LD* 12,739
J. Corrie, *C.* 10,117
Prof. N. MacCormick, *SNP* 8,689
D. Browne, *Lab.* 4,946
LD majority 2,622
(June 1987, L./All. maj. 1,394)

AYR (Strathclyde)
*E.*65,481 *T.*83.08%

P. Gallie, *C.* 22,172
A. Osborne, *Lab.* 22,087
Mrs B. Mullin, *SNP* 5,949
J. Boss, *LD* 4,067
R. Scott, *NLP* 132
C. majority 85
(June 1987, C. maj. 182)

BANFF AND BUCHAN (Grampian)
*E.*64,873 *T.*71.20%

*A. Salmond, *SNP* 21,954
S. Manson, *C.* 17,846
B. Balcombe, *Lab.* 3,803
Mrs R. Kemp, *LD* 2,588
SNP majority 4,108
(June 1987, SNP maj. 2,441)

CAITHNESS AND SUTHERLAND (Highland)
*E.*30,905 *T.*71.93%

*R. Maclennan, *LD* 10,032
G. Bruce, *C.* 4,667
K. MacGregor, *SNP* 4,049
M. Coyne, *Lab.* 3,483
LD majority 5,365
(June 1987, SDP/All. maj. 8,494)

CARRICK, CUMNOCK AND DOON VALLEY (Strathclyde)
*E.*55,330 *T.*76.94%

*G. Foulkes, *Lab.* 25,142
J. Boswell, *C.* 8,516
C. Douglas, *SNP* 6,910
Ms M. Paris, *LD* 2,005
Lab. majority 16,626
(June 1987, Lab. maj. 16,802)

CLACKMANNAN (Central)
*E.*48,963 *T.*78.34%

*M. O'Neill, *Lab.* 18,829
A. Brophy, *SNP* 10,326
J. Mackie, *C.* 6,638
Ms A. Watters, *LD* 2,567
Lab. majority 8,503
(June 1987, Lab. maj. 12,401)

CLYDEBANK AND MILNGAVIE (Strathclyde)
*E.*47,337 *T.*77.79%

*A. Worthington, *Lab.* 19,637
G. Hughes, *SNP* 7,207
W. Harvey, *C.* 6,654
A. Tough, *LD* 3,216
Ms J. Barrie, *NLP* 112
Lab. majority 12,430
(June 1987, Lab. maj. 16,304)

CLYDESDALE (Strathclyde)
*E.*61,878 *T.*77.62%

*J. Hood, *Lab.* 21,418
Ms C. Goodwin, *C.* 11,231
I. Gray, *SNP* 11,084
Ms E. Buchanan, *LD* 3,957
S. Cartwright, *BNP* 342
Lab. majority 10,187
(June 1987, Lab. maj. 10,502)

CUMBERNAULD AND KILSYTH (Strathclyde)
*E.*46,489 *T.*79.06%

*N. Hogg, *Lab.* 19,855
T. Johnston, *SNP* 10,640
I. Mitchell, *C.* 4,143
Ms J. Haddow, *LD* 2,118
Lab. majority 9,215
(June 1987, Lab. maj. 14,403)

CUNNINGHAME NORTH (Strathclyde)
*E.*54,803 *T.*78.21%

*B. Wilson, *Lab.* 17,564
Ms E. Clarkson, *C.* 14,625
D. Crossan, *SNP* 7,813
D. Herbison, *LD* 2,864
Lab. majority 2,939
(June 1987, Lab. maj. 4,422)

CUNNINGHAME SOUTH (Strathclyde)
*E.*49,010 *T.*75.88%

B. Donohoe, *Lab.* 19,687
R. Bell, *SNP* 9,007
S. Leslie, *C.* 6,070
B. Ashley, *LD* 2,299
W. Jackson, *NLP* 128
Lab. majority 10,680
(June 1987, Lab. maj. 16,633)

DUMBARTON (Strathclyde)
*E.*57,222 *T.*77.11%

*J. McFall, *Lab.*	19,255
T. Begg, *C.*	13,126
W. McKechnie, *SNP*	8,127
J. Morrison, *LD*	3,425
Ms D. Krass, *NLP*	192
Lab. majority	6,129

(June 1987, Lab. maj. 5,222)

DUMFRIES (D & G)
*E.*61,145 *T.*79.97%

*Sir H. Monro, *C.*	21,089
P. Rennie, *Lab.*	14,674
A. Morgan, *SNP*	6,971
N. Wallace, *LD*	5,749
G. McLeod, *Ind. Green*	312
T. Barlow, *NLP*	107
C. majority	6,415

(June 1987, C. maj. 7,493)

DUNDEE EAST (Tayside)
*E.*58,959 *T.*72.10%

*J. McAllion, *Lab.*	18,761
D. Coutts, *SNP*	14,197
S. Blackwood, *C.*	7,549
I. Yuill, *LD*	1,725
Ms S. Baird, *Green*	205
R. Baxter, *NLP*	77
Lab. majority	4,564

(June 1987, Lab. maj. 1,015)

DUNDEE WEST (Tayside)
*E.*59,953 *T.*69.82%

*E. Ross, *Lab.*	20,498
K. Brown, *SNP*	9,894
A. Spearman, *C.*	7,746
Ms E. Dick, *LD*	3,132
Ms E. Hood, *Green*	432
D. Arnold, *NLP*	159
Lab. majority	10,604

(June 1987, Lab. maj. 16,526)

DUNFERMLINE EAST (Fife)
*E.*50,179 *T.*75.62%

*J. G. Brown, *Lab.*	23,692
M. Tennant, *C.*	6,248
J. Lloyd, *SNP*	5,746
Ms T. Little, *LD*	2,262
Lab. majority	17,444

(June 1987, Lab. maj. 19,589)

DUNFERMLINE WEST (Fife)
*E.*50,948 *T.*76.44%

Ms R. Squire, *Lab.*	16,374
M. Scott-Hayward, *C.*	8,890
J. Smith, *SNP*	7,563
Ms E. Harris, *LD*	6,122
Lab. majority	7,484

(June 1987, Lab. maj. 9,402)

EAST KILBRIDE (Strathclyde)
*E.*64,080 *T.*80.01%

*A. Ingram, *Lab.*	24,055
Ms K. McAlorum, *SNP*	12,063
G. Lind, *C.*	9,781
Ms S. Grieve, *LD*	5,377
Lab. majority	11,992

(June 1987, Lab. maj. 12,624)

EAST LOTHIAN
*E.*66,699 *T.*82.37%

*J. Home Robertson, *Lab.*	25,537
J. Hepburne Scott, *C.*	15,501
G. Thomson, *SNP*	7,776
T. McKay, *LD*	6,126
Lab. majority	10,036

(June 1987, Lab. maj. 10,105)

EASTWOOD (Strathclyde)
*E.*63,685 *T.*80.97%

*J. A. Stewart, *C.*	24,124
P. Grant-Hutchison, *Lab.*	12,436
Miss M. Craig, *LD*	8,493
P. Scott, *SNP*	6,372
Dr L. Fergusson, *NLP*	146
C. majority	11,688

(June 1987, C. maj. 6,014)

EDINBURGH CENTRAL (Lothian)
*E.*56,527 *T.*69.26%

*A. Darling, *Lab.*	15,189
P. Martin, *C.*	13,063
Ms L. Devine, *SNP*	5,539
A. Myles, *LD*	4,500
R. Harper, *Green*	630
D. Wilson, *Lib.*	235
Lab. majority	2,126

(June 1987, Lab. maj. 2,262)

EDINBURGH EAST (Lothian)
*E.*45,687 *T.*73.89%

*G. Strang, *Lab.*	15,446
K. Ward, *C.*	8,235
D. McKinney, *SNP*	6,225
D. Scobie, *LD*	3,432
G. Farmer, *Green*	424
Lab. majority	7,211

(June 1987, Lab. maj. 9,295)

EDINBURGH LEITH (Lothian)
*E.*56,520 *T.*71.30%

M. Chisholm, *Lab.*	13,790
Ms F. Hyslop, *SNP*	8,805
M. Bin Ashiq Rizvi, *C.*	8,496
Mrs H. Campbell, *LD*	4,975
*R. Brown, *Ind. Lab.*	4,142
A. Swan, *NLP*	96
Lab. majority	4,985

(June 1987, Lab. maj. 11,327)

EDINBURGH PENTLANDS (Lothian)
*E.*55,567 *T.*80.18%

*Rt. Hon. M. Rifkind, *C.*	18,128
M. Lazarowicz, *Lab.*	13,838
Ms K. Caskie, *SNP*	6,882
K. Smith, *LD*	5,597
D. Rae, *NLP*	111
C. majority	4,290

(June 1987, C. maj. 3,745)

EDINBURGH SOUTH (Lothian)
*E.*61,355 *T.*72.67%

*N. Griffiths, *Lab.*	18,485
S. Stevenson, *C.*	14,309
B. McCreadie, *LD*	5,961
R. Knox, *SNP*	5,727
G. Manclark, *NLP*	108
Lab. majority	4,176

(June 1987, Lab. maj. 1,859)

EDINBURGH WEST (Lothian)
*E.*58,998 *T.*82.67%

*Lord J. Douglas-Hamilton, *C.*	18,071
D. Gorrie, *LD*	17,192
Ms I. Kitson, *Lab.*	8,759
G. Sutherland, *SNP*	4,117
A. Fleming, *Lib.*	272
Ms L. Hendry, *Green*	234
D. Bruce, *BNP*	133
C. majority	879

(June 1987, C. maj. 1,234)

FALKIRK EAST (Central)
*E.*51,918 *T.*76.91%

M. Connarty, *Lab.*	18,423
R. Halliday, *SNP*	10,454
K. Harding, *C.*	8,279
Miss D. Storr, *LD*	2,775
Lab. majority	7,969

(June 1987, Lab. maj. 14,023)

FALKIRK WEST (Central)
*E.*50,126 *T.*76.77%

*D. Canavan, *Lab.*	19,162
W. Houston, *SNP*	9,350
M. Macdonald, *C.*	7,558
M. Reilly, *LD*	2,414
Lab. majority	9,812

(June 1987, Lab. maj. 13,552)

FIFE CENTRAL
*E.*56,152 *T.*74.33%

*H. McLeish, *Lab.*	21,036
Mrs T. Marwick, *SNP*	10,458
Ms C. Cender, *C.*	7,353
C. Harrow, *LD*	2,892
Lab. majority	10,578

(June 1987, Lab. maj. 15,709)

FIFE NORTH EAST
*E.*53,747 *T.*77.84%

*W. M. Campbell, *LD*	19,430
Mrs M. Scanlon, *C.*	16,122
D. Roche, *SNP*	3,589
Miss L. Clark, *Lab.*	2,319
T. Flynn, *Green*	294
D. Senior, *Lib.*	85
LD majority	3,308

(June 1987, L./All. maj. 1,447)

GALLOWAY AND UPPER NITHSDALE (D & G)
*E.*54,474 *T.*81.66%

*Rt. Hon. I. Lang, *C.*	18,681
M. Brown, *SNP*	16,213
J. Dowson, *Lab.*	5,766
J. McKerchar, *LD*	3,826
C. majority	2,468

(June 1987, C. maj. 3,673)

GLASGOW CATHCART (Strathclyde)
*E.*44,689 *T.*75.38%

*J. Maxton, *Lab.*	16,265
J. Young, *C.*	8,264
W. Steven, *SNP*	6,107
G. Dick, *LD*	2,614
Ms K. Allan, *Green*	441
Lab. majority	8,001

(June 1987, Lab. maj. 11,203)

GLASGOW CENTRAL (Strathclyde)
*E.*48,107 *T.*63.05%

*M. Watson, *Lab.*	17,341
B. O'Hara, *SNP*	6,322
E. Stewart, *C.*	4,208
A. Rennie, *LD*	1,921
Ms I. Brandt, *Green*	435
T. Burn, *Comm. GB*	106
Lab. majority	11,019

(June 1987, Lab. maj. 17,253)
(June 1989, Lab. maj. 6,462)

GLASGOW GARSCADDEN (Strathclyde)
*E.*41,289 *T.*71.13%

*D. Dewar, *Lab.*	18,920
R. Douglas, *SNP*	5,580
J. Scott, *C.*	3,385
C. Brodie, *LD*	1,425
W. Orr, *NLP*	61
Lab. majority	13,340

(June 1987, Lab. maj. 18,977)

GLASGOW GOVAN (Strathclyde)
*E.*45,822 *T.*76.03%

I. Davidson, *Lab.*	17,051
*J. Sillars, *SNP*	12,926
J. Donnelly, *C.*	3,458
R. Stewart, *LD*	1,227
D. Spaven, *Green*	181
Lab. majority	4,125

(June 1987, Lab. maj. 19,509)
(Nov. 1988, SNP maj. 3,554)

GLASGOW HILLHEAD (Strathclyde)
*E.*57,223 *T.*68.80%

*G. Galloway, *Lab.*	15,148
C. Mason, *LD*	10,322
Ms A. Bates, *C.*	6,728
Miss S. White, *SNP*	6,484
Ms L. Collie, *Green*	558
Ms H. Gold, *Rev. Comm.*	73
D. Patterson, *NLP*	60
Lab. majority	4,826

(June 1987, Lab. maj. 3,251)

GLASGOW MARYHILL (Strathclyde)
*E.*48,426 *T.*65.16%

*Mrs M. Fyfe, *Lab.*	19,452
C. Williamson, *SNP*	6,033
J. Godfrey, *C.*	3,248
J. Alexander, *LD*	2,215
P. O'Brien, *Green*	530
M. Henderson, *NLP*	78
Lab. majority	13,419

(June 1987, Lab. maj. 19,364)

GLASGOW POLLOK (Strathclyde)
*E.*46,139 *T.*70.74%

*J. Dunnachie, *Lab.*	14,170
T. Sheridan, *SML*	6,287
R. Gray, *C.*	5,147
G. Leslie, *SNP*	5,107
D. Jago, *LD*	1,932
Lab. majority	7,883

(June 1987, Lab. maj. 17,983)

GLASGOW PROVAN (Strathclyde)
*E.*36,560 *T.*65.31%

*J. Wray, *Lab.*	15,885
Ms A. MacRae, *SNP*	5,182
A. Rosindell, *C.*	1,865
C. Bell, *LD*	948
Lab. majority	10,703

(June 1987, Lab. maj. 18,372)

GLASGOW RUTHERGLEN (Strathclyde)
*E.*52,709 *T.*75.23%

*T. McAvoy, *Lab.*	21,962
B. Cooklin, *C.*	6,692
J. Higgins, *SNP*	6,470
D. Baillie, *LD*	4,470
Ms B. Slaughter, *Int. Comm.*	62
Lab. majority	15,270

(June 1987, Lab. maj. 13,995)

GLASGOW SHETTLESTON (Strathclyde)
*E.*51,910 *T.*68.91%

*D. Marshall, *Lab.*	21,665
Ms N. Sturgeon, *SNP*	6,831
N. Mortimer, *C.*	5,396
Ms J. Orskov, *LD*	1,881
Lab. majority	14,834

(June 1987, Lab. maj. 18,981)

GLASGOW SPRINGBURN (Strathclyde)
*E.*45,842 *T.*65.65%

*M. Martin, *Lab.*	20,369
S. Miller, *SNP*	5,863
A. Barnett, *C.*	2,625
R. Ackland, *LD*	1,242
Lab. majority	14,506

(June 1987, Lab. maj. 22,063)

GORDON (Grampian)
*E.*80,103 *T.*73.86%

*M. Bruce, *LD*	22,158
J. Porter, *C.*	21,884
B. Adam, *SNP*	8,445
P. Morrell, *Lab.*	6,682
LD majority	274

(June 1987, L./All. maj. 9,519)

GREENOCK AND PORT GLASGOW (Strathclyde)
*E.*52,053 *T.*73.72%

*N. Godman, *Lab.*	22,258
I. Black, *SNP*	7,279
Dr J. McCullough, *C.*	4,479
C. Lambert, *LD*	4,359
Lab. majority	14,979

(June 1987, Lab. maj. 20,055)

HAMILTON (Strathclyde)
*E.*61,531 *T.*76.15%

*G. Robertson, *Lab.*	25,849
W. Morrison, *SNP*	9,246
Ms M. Mitchell, *C.*	8,250
J. Oswald, *LD*	3,515
Lab. majority	16,603

(June 1987, Lab. maj. 21,662)

INVERNESS, NAIRN AND LOCHABER (Highland)
*E.*69,468 *T.*73.27%

*Sir R. Johnston, *LD*	13,258
D. Stewart, *Lab.*	12,800
F. Ewing, *SNP*	12,562
J. Scott, *C.*	11,517
J. Martin, *Green*	766
LD majority	458

(June 1987, L./All maj. 5,431)

KILMARNOCK AND LOUDOUN (Strathclyde)
*E.*62,002 *T.*79.99%

*W. McKelvey, *Lab.*	22,210
A. Neil, *SNP*	15,231
R. Wilkinson, *C.*	9,438
Mrs K. Philbrick, *LD*	2,722
Lab. majority	6,979

(June 1987, Lab. maj. 14,127)

KINCARDINE AND DEESIDE (Grampian)
*E.*66,617 *T.*78.74%

G. Kynoch, *C.*	22,924
*N. Stephen, *LD*	18,429
Dr A. Macartney, *SNP*	5,927
M. Savidge, *Lab.*	4,795
S. Campbell, *Green*	381
C. majority	4,495

(June 1987, C. maj. 2,063)
(Nov. 1991, LD maj. 7,824)

KIRKCALDY (Fife)
*E.*51,762 *T.*75.06%

*Dr L. Moonie, *Lab.*	17,887
S. Hosie, *SNP*	8,761

S. Wosley, *C.* 8,476
Ms S. Leslie, *LD* 3,729
Lab. majority 9,126
(June 1987, Lab. maj. 11,570)

LINLITHGOW (Lothian)
*E.*61,082 *T.*78.66%

*T. Dalyell, *Lab.* 21,603
K. MacAskill, *SNP* 14,577
Ms E. Forbes, *C.* 8,424
M. Falchikov, *LD* 3,446
Lab. majority 7,026
(June 1987, Lab. maj. 10,373)

LIVINGSTON (Lothian)
*E.*61,092 *T.*74.62%

*R. Cook, *Lab.* 20,245
P. Johnston, *SNP* 12,140
H. Gordon, *C.* 8,824
F. Mackintosh, *LD* 3,911
A. Ross-Smith, *Green* 469
Lab. majority 8,105
(June 1987, Lab. maj. 11,105)

MIDLOTHIAN
*E.*60,255 *T.*77.87%

E. Clarke, *Lab.* 20,588
A. Lumsden, *SNP* 10,254
J. Stoddart, *C.* 9,443
P. Sewell, *LD* 6,164
I. Morrice, *Green* 476
Lab. majority 10,334
(June 1987, Lab. maj. 12,253)

MONKLANDS EAST (Strathclyde)
*E.*48,391 *T.*75.07%

*Rt. Hon. J. Smith, *Lab.* 22,266
J. Wright, *SNP* 6,554
S. Walters, *C.* 5,830
P. Ross, *LD* 1,679
Lab. majority 15,712
(June 1987, Lab. maj. 16,389)

MONKLANDS WEST (Strathclyde)
*E.*49,269 *T.*77.45%

*T. Clarke, *Lab.* 23,384
K. Bovey, *SNP* 6,319
A. Lownie, *C.* 6,074
Ms S. Hamilton, *LD* 2,382
Lab. majority 17,065
(June 1987, Lab. maj. 18,333)

MORAY (Grampian)
*E.*63,255 *T.*72.46%

*Mrs M. Ewing, *SNP* 20,299
Ms R. Hossack, *C.* 17,455
C. Smith, *Lab.* 5,448
B. Sheridan, *LD* 2,634
SNP majority 2,844
(June 1987, *SNP maj. 3,685)*

MOTHERWELL NORTH
(Strathclyde)
*E.*57,290 *T.*76.71%

*Dr J. Reid, *Lab.* 27,852
D. Clark, *SNP* 8,942
R. Hargrave, *C.* 5,011
Miss H. Smith, *LD* 2,145
Lab. majority 18,910
(June 1987, Lab. maj. 23,595)

MOTHERWELL SOUTH
(Strathclyde)
*E.*50,042 *T.*76.17%

*J. Bray, *Lab.* 21,771
Mrs K. Ullrich, *SNP* 7,758
G. McIntosh, *C.* 6,097
A. Mackie, *LD* 2,349
D. Lettice, *YSOR* 146
Lab. majority 14,013
(June 1987, Lab. maj. 16,930)

ORKNEY AND SHETLAND
*E.*31,472 *T.*65.53%

*J. Wallace, *LD* 9,575
Dr P. McCormick, *C.* 4,542
J. Aberdein, *Lab.* 4,093
Mrs F. McKie, *SNP* 2,301
Ms C. Wharton, *NLP* 115
LD majority 5,033
(June 1987, L./All maj. 3,922)

PAISLEY NORTH (Strathclyde)
*E.*46,403 *T.*73.39%

*Mrs I. Adams, *Lab.* 17,269
R. Mullin, *SNP* 7,940
D. Sharpe, *C.* 5,576
Miss E. McCartin, *LD* 2,779
D. Mellor, *Green* 412
N. Brennan, *NLP* 81
Lab. majority 9,329
(June 1987, Lab. maj. 14,442)
(Nov. 1990, Lab. maj. 3,770)

PAISLEY SOUTH (Strathclyde)
*E.*47,889 *T.*75.01%

*G. McMaster, *Lab.* 18,202
I. Lawson, *SNP* 8,653
Ms S. Laidlaw, *C.* 5,703
A. Reid, *LD* 3,271
S. Porter, *NLP* 93
Lab. majority 9,549
(June 1987, Lab. maj. 15,785)
(Nov. 1990, Lab. maj. 5,030)

PERTH AND KINROSS (Tayside)
*E.*65,410 *T.*76.86%

*Sir N. Fairbairn, *C.* 20,195
Ms R. Cunningham, *SNP* 18,101
M. Rolfe, *Lab.* 6,267
M. Black, *LD* 5,714
C. majority 2,094
(June 1987, C. maj. 5,676)

RENFREW WEST AND
INVERCLYDE (Strathclyde)
*E.*58,122 *T.*80.32%

*T. Graham, *Lab.* 17,085
Ms A. Goldie, *C.* 15,341
C. Campbell, *SNP* 9,444
S. Nimmo, *LD* 4,668
D. Maltman, *NLP* 149
Lab. majority 1,744
(June 1987, Lab. maj. 4,063)

ROSS, CROMARTY AND SKYE
(Highland)
*E.*55,524 *T.*73.90%

*C. Kennedy, *LD* 17,066
J. Gray, *C.* 9,436
R. Gibson, *SNP* 7,618
J. MacDonald, *Lab.* 6,275
D. Jardine, *Green* 642
LD majority 7,630
(June 1987, SDP/All. maj. 11,319)

ROXBURGH AND
BERWICKSHIRE (Borders)
*E.*43,485 *T.*77.71%

*A. Kirkwood, *LD* 15,852
S. Finlay-Maxwell, *C.* 11,595
M. Douglas, *SNP* 3,437
S. Lambert, *Lab.* 2,909
LD majority 4,257
(June 1987, L./All maj. 4,008)

STIRLING (Central)
*E.*58,266 *T.*82.29%

*M. Forsyth, *C.* 19,174
Ms K. Phillips, *Lab.* 18,471
G. Fisher, *SNP* 6,558
W. Robertson, *LD* 3,337
W. Thomson, *Green* 342
R. Sharp, *Loony* 68
C. majority 703
(June 1987, C. maj. 548)

STRATHKELVIN AND
BEARSDEN (Strathclyde)
*E.*61,116 *T.*82.33%

*S. Galbraith, *Lab.* 21,267
M. Hirst, *C.* 18,105
T. Chalmers, *SNP* 6,275
Ms B. Waterfield, *LD* 4,585
D. Whitley, *NLP* 90
Lab. majority 3,162
(June 1987, Lab. maj. 2,452)

TAYSIDE NORTH
*E.*55,969 *T.*77.64%

*W. Walker, *C.* 20,283
J. Swinney, *SNP* 16,288
S. Horner, *LD* 3,791
S. Maclennan, *Lab.* 3,094
C. majority 3,995
(June 1987, C. maj. 5,016)

TWEEDDALE, ETTRICK AND LAUDERDALE (Borders)
*E.*39,493 *T.*78.04%

*Rt. Hon. Sir D. Steel, *LD*	12,296
L. Beat, *C.*	9,776
Mrs C. Creech, *SNP*	5,244
A. Dunton, *Lab.*	3,328
J. Hein, *Lib.*	177
LD majority	2,520

(June 1987, L./All. maj. 5,942)

WESTERN ISLES
*E.*22,784 *T.*70.35%

*C. MacDonald, *Lab.*	7,664
Ms F. MacFarlane, *SNP*	5,961
R. Heany, *C.*	1,362
N. Mitchison, *LD*	552
A. Price, *Ind*	491
Lab. majority	1,703

(June 1987, Lab. maj. 2,340)

NORTHERN IRELAND

ANTRIM EAST
*E.*62,839 *T.*62.46%

*R. Beggs, *UUP*	16,966
N. Dodds, *DUP*	9,544
S. Neeson, *All.*	9,132
Miss M. Boal, *C.*	3,359
Ms A. Palmer, *NLP*	250
UUP majority	7,422

(June 1987, UUP maj. 15,360)

ANTRIM NORTH
*E.*69,124 *T.*65.82%

*Revd I. Paisley, *DUP*	23,152
J. Gaston, *UUP*	8,216
S. Farren, *SDLP*	6,512
G. Williams, *All.*	3,442
R. Sowler, *C.*	2,263
J. McGarry, *SF*	1,916
DUP majority	14,936

(June 1987, DUP maj. 23,234)

ANTRIM SOUTH
*E.*68,013 *T.*62.10%

*C. Forsythe, *UUP*	29,956
D. McClelland, *SDLP*	5,397
J. Blair, *All.*	5,224
H. Cushinan, *SF*	1,220
D. Martin, *Loony G.*	442
UUP majority	24,559

(June 1987, UUP maj. 19,587)

BELFAST EAST
*E.*52,833 *T.*67.74%

*P. Robinson, *DUP*	18,437
Dr J. Alderdice, *All.*	10,650
D. Greene, *C.*	3,314
Ms D. Dunlop, *Ind. U.*	2,256
J. O'Donnell, *SF*	679
J. Bell, *WP*	327
G. Redden, *NLP*	128
DUP majority	7,787

(June 1987, DUP maj. 9,798)

BELFAST NORTH
*E.*55,062 *T.*65.22%

*A. C. Walker, *UUP*	17,240
A. Maginness, *SDLP*	7,615
P. McManus, *SF*	4,693
T. Campbell, *All.*	2,246
Ms M. Redpath, *C.*	2,107
S. Lynch, *NA*	1,386
Ms M. Smith, *WP*	419
D. O'Leary, *NLP*	208
UUP majority	9,625

(June 1987, UUP maj. 8,560)

BELFAST SOUTH
*E.*52,032 *T.*64.54%

*Revd W. M. Smyth, *UUP*	16,336
Dr A. McDonnell, *SDLP*	6,266
J. Montgomery, *All.*	5,054
L. Fee, *C.*	3,356
S. Hayes, *SF*	1,123
P. Hadden, *LTU*	875
P. Lynn, *WP*	362
Ms T. Mullan, *NLP*	212
UUP majority	10,070

(June 1987, UUP maj. 11,954)

BELFAST WEST
*E.*54,609 *T.*73.19%

Dr J. Hendron, *SDLP*	17,415
*G. Adams, *SF*	16,826
F. Cobain, *UUP*	4,766
J. Lowry, *WP*	750
M. Kennedy, *NLP*	213
SDLP majority	589

(June 1987, SF maj. 2,221)

DOWN NORTH
*E.*68,662 *T.*65.47%

*J. Kilfedder, *UPUP*	19,305
Dr L. Kennedy, *C.*	14,371
Ms A. Morrow, *All.*	6,611
D. Vitty, *DUP*	4,414
A. Wilmot, *NLP*	255
UPUP majority	4,934

(June 1987, UPUP maj. 3,953)

DOWN SOUTH
*E.*76,093 *T.*80.92%

*E. McGrady, *SDLP*	31,523
D. Nelson, *UUP*	25,181
S. Fitzpatrick, *SF*	1,843
M. Healey, *All.*	1,542
Mrs S. McKenzie-Hill, *C.*	1,488
SDLP majority	6,342

(June 1987, SDLP maj. 731)

FERMANAGH AND SOUTH TYRONE
*E.*70,192 *T.*78.53%

*K. Maginnis, *UUP*	26,923
T. Gallagher, *SDLP*	12,810
F. Molloy, *SF*	12,604
D. Kettyles, *Prog. Soc.*	1,094
E. Bullick, *All.*	950
G. Cullen, *NA*	747
UUP majority	14,113

(June 1987, UUP maj. 12,823)

FOYLE
*E.*74,585 *T.*69.57%

*J. Hume, *SDLP*	26,710
G. Campbell, *DUP*	13,705
M. McGuinness, *SF*	9,149
Ms L. McIlroy, *All.*	1,390
G. McKenzie, *WP*	514
J. Burns, *NLP*	422
SDLP majority	13,005

(June 1987, SDLP maj. 9,860)

LAGAN VALLEY
*E.*72,645 *T.*67.39%

*Rt. Hon. J. H. Molyneaux, *UUP*	29,772
S. Close, *All.*	6,207
H. Lewsley, *SDLP*	4,626
T. Coleridge, *C.*	4,423
P. Rice, *SF*	3,346
Ms A.-M. Lowry, *WP*	582
UUP majority	23,565

(June 1987, UUP maj. 23,373)

LONDONDERRY EAST
*E.*75,559 *T.*69.79%

*W. Ross, *UUP*	30,370
A. Doherty, *SDLP*	11,843
Ms P. Davey-Kennedy, *SF*	5,320
P. McGowan, *All.*	3,613
A. Elder, *C.*	1,589
UUP majority	18,527

(June 1987, UUP maj. 20,157)

NEWRY AND ARMAGH
*E.*67,508 *T.*77.87%

*S. Mallon, *SDLP*	26,073
J. Speers, *UUP*	18,982
B. Curran, *SF*	6,547
Mrs E. Bell, *All.*	972
SDLP majority	7,091

(June 1987, SDLP maj. 5,325)

STRANGFORD
*E.*68,870 *T.*65.02%

*Rt. Hon. J. Taylor, *UUP*	19,517
S. Wilson, *DUP*	10,606

K. McCarthy, *All.* 7,585
S. Eyre, *C.* 6,782
D. Shaw, *NLP* 295
UUP majority 8,911
(June 1987, UUP maj. 20,646)

ULSTER MID
*E.*69,071 *T.*79.28%
*Revd Dr R. T. W. McCrea, *DUP* 23,181
D. Haughey, *SDLP* 16,994
B. McElduff, *SF* 10,248
J. McLoughlin, *Ind.* 1,996
Ms A. Gormley, *All.* 1,506
H. Hutchinson, *LTU* 389
T. Owens, *WP* 285
J. Anderson, *NLP* 164
DUP majority 6,187
(June 1987, DUP maj. 9,360)

UPPER BANN
*E.*67,446 *T.*67.43%
*W. D. Trimble, *UUP* 26,824
Mrs B. Rodgers, *SDLP* 10,661
B. Curran, *SF* 2,777
Dr W. Ramsey, *All.* 2,541
Mrs C. Jones, *C.* 1,556
T. French, *WP* 1,120
UUP majority 16,163
(June 1987, OUP maj. 17,361)
(May 1990, OUP maj. 13,849)

BY-ELECTIONS Since the Last Edition

KINCARDINE AND DEESIDE
(7 November 1991)
N. Stephen, *LD* 20,779
M. Humphrey, *C.* 12,955
A. Macartney, *SNP* 4,705
M. Savidge, *Lab.* 3,271
S. Campbell, *Green* 683
LD majority 7,824

HEMSWORTH
(7 November 1991)
D. Enright, *Lab.* 15,895
V. Megson, *LD* 4,808
G. Harrison, *C.* 2,512
P. Ablett, *Ind. Lab.* 648
T. Smith, *Corrective* 108
Lab. majority 11,087

LANGBAURGH
(7 November 1991)
A. Kumar, *Lab.* 22,442
M. Bates, *C.* 20,467
P. Allen, *LD* 8,421
G. Parr, *Green* 456
R. Holt, *Yorkshire* 216
Ms L. St Clair, *Corrective* 198
N. Downing, *Football Supporters* 163
Lab. majority 1,975

European Parliament

UK MEMBERS (as at end July 1991)

* Denotes membership of the last Parliament

*Adam, Gordon J. (*b.* 1934), *Lab., Northumbria*, maj. 60,040
*Balfe, Richard A. (*b.* 1944), *Lab. Co-op, London South Inner*, maj. 45,018
Barton, Roger (*b.* 1945), *Lab., Sheffield*, maj. 69,276
*Beazley, Christopher J. P. (*b.* 1952), *C., Cornwall and Plymouth*, maj. 19,817
*Beazley, Peter G. (*b.* 1922), *C., Bedfordshire South*, maj. 2,977
*Bethell, The Lord (*b.* 1938), *C., London North West*, maj. 7,400
*Bird, John A. W. (*b.* 1926), *Lab. Co-op, Midlands West*, maj. 42,364
Bowe, David (*b.* 1955), *Lab., Cleveland and Yorkshire North*, maj. 24,092
*Buchan, Mrs Janey O. (*b.* 1926), *Lab., Glasgow*, maj. 59,232
*Cassidy, Bryan M. D. (*b.* 1934), *C., Dorset East and Hampshire West*, maj. 61,774
*Catherwood, Sir Frederick (*b.* 1925), *C., Cambridge and Bedfordshire North*, maj. 32,321
Coates, Kenneth (*b.* 1939), *Lab., Nottingham*, maj. 14,513
*Collins, Kenneth D. (*b.* 1939), *Lab., Strathclyde East*, maj. 60,317
Crampton, Peter D. (*b.* 1932), *Lab., Humberside*, maj. 16,328
*Crawley, Mrs Christine M. (*b.* 1950), *Lab., Birmingham East*, maj. 46,948
*Daly, Mrs Margaret E. (*b.* 1938), *C., Somerset and Dorset West*, maj. 52,220
David, Wayne (*b.* 1957), *Lab., Wales South*, maj. 62,557
Donnelly, Alan J. (*b.* 1957), *Lab., Tyne and Wear*, maj. 95,780
*Elles, James E. M. (*b.* 1949), *C., Oxford and Buckinghamshire*, maj. 47,518
*Elliott, Michael N. (*b.* 1932), *Lab., London West*, maj. 14,808
*Ewing, Mrs Winifred M. (*b.* 1929), *SNP, Highlands and Islands*, maj. 44,695
*Falconer, Alec (*b.* 1940), *Lab., Scotland Mid and Fife*, maj. 52,157
Fletcher-Vane, *see* Inglewood
*Ford, J. Glyn (*b.* 1950), *Lab., Greater Manchester East*, maj. 34,501
Green, Ms Pauline (*b.* 1948), *Lab. Co-op, London North*, maj. 5,837
Harrison, Lyndon (*b.* 1947), *Lab., Cheshire West*, maj. 23,201
*Hindley, Michael J. (*b.* 1947), *Lab., Lancashire East*, maj. 39,148
*Hoon, Geoffrey W. (*b.* 1953), *Lab., Derbyshire*, maj. 33,388
*Howell, Paul F. (*b.* 1951), *C., Norfolk*, maj. 20,907
*Hughes, Stephen S. (*b.* 1952), *Lab., Durham*, maj. 86,848
*Hume, John, MP (*b.* 1937), *SDLP, Northern Ireland*, polled 136,335 votes
Inglewood, The Lord (Richard Fletcher-Vane) (*b.* 1951), *C., Cumbria and Lancashire North*, maj. 2,391
*Jackson, Mrs Caroline F. (*b.* 1946), *C., Wiltshire*, maj. 46,313
*Jackson, Christopher M. (*b.* 1935), *C., Kent East*, maj. 28,961

*Kellett-Bowman, Edward T. (*b.* 1931), *C.*, *Hampshire Central*, maj. 27,674
*Lomas, Alfred (*b.* 1928), *Lab.*, *London North East*, maj. 47,767
*McGowan, Michael (*b.* 1940), *Lab.*, *Leeds*, maj. 42,518
McCubbin, Henry (*b.* 1942), *Lab.*, *Scotland North East*, maj. 2,613
McIntosh, Miss Anne C. B. (*b.* 1954), *C.*, *Essex North East*, maj. 39,398
*McMahon, Hugh R. (*b.* 1938), *Lab.*, *Strathclyde West*, maj. 39,591
*McMillan-Scott, Edward H. C. (*b.* 1949), *C.*, *York*, maj. 15,102
*Martin, David W. (*b.* 1954), *Lab.*, *Lothians*, maj. 38,826
*Megahy, Thomas (*b.* 1929), *Lab.*, *Yorkshire South West*, maj. 65,901
*Moorhouse, C. James O. (*b.* 1924), *C.*, *London South and Surrey East*, maj. 30,816
*Morris, Revd David R. (*b.* 1930), *Lab.*, *Wales Mid and West*, maj. 51,912
*Newens, A. Stanley (*b.* 1930), *Lab. Co-op*, *London Central*, maj. 11,542
*Newman, Edward (*b.* 1953), *Lab.*, *Greater Manchester Central*, maj. 38,867
*Newton Dunn, William F. (*b.* 1941), *C.*, *Lincolnshire*, maj. 20,650
Nicholson, James F. (*b.* 1945), *UUP*, *Northern Ireland*, polled 118,785 votes
Oddy, Ms Christine M. (*b.* 1955), *Lab.*, *Midlands Central*, maj. 5,093
*O'Hagan, The Lord (*b.* 1945), *C.*, *Devon*, maj. 57,298
*Paisley, Revd Ian R. K., MP (*b.* 1926), *DUP*, *Northern Ireland*, polled 160,110 votes
*Patterson, G. Benjamin (Ben) (*b.* 1939), *C.*, *Kent West*, maj. 24,050
*Plumb, The Lord (*b.* 1925), *C.*, *The Cotswolds*, maj. 45,678
Pollack, Ms Anita J. (*b.* 1946), *Lab.*, *London South West*, maj. 518
*Prag, Derek (*b.* 1923), *C.*, *Hertfordshire*, maj. 43,342
*Price, Peter N. (*b.* 1942), *C.*, *London South East*, maj. 7,590
*Prout, Sir Christopher, TD, QC (*b.* 1942), *C.*, *Shropshire and Stafford*, maj. 2,544
Rawlings, Miss Patricia (*b.* 1939), *C.*, *Essex South West*, maj. 9,403
Read, Ms Mel (*b.* 1939), *Lab.*, *Leicester*, maj. 15,322
*Scott-Hopkins, Sir James (*b.* 1921), *C.*, *Hereford and Worcester*, maj. 25,665
*Seal, Barry H. (*b.* 1937), *Lab.*, *Yorkshire West*, maj. 37,927
*Seligman, R. Madron (*b.* 1918), *C.*, *Sussex West*, maj. 46,233
*Simmonds, Richard J. (*b.* 1944), *C.*, *Wight and Hampshire East*, maj. 39,430
*Simpson, Anthony M. H., TD (*b.* 1935), *C.*, *Northamptonshire*, maj. 20,447
Simpson, Brian (*b.* 1953), *Lab.*, *Cheshire East*, maj. 1,864
Smith, Alexander (*b.* 1943), *Lab.*, *Scotland South*, maj. 15,693
*Smith, Llewellyn T. (*b.* 1944), *Lab.*, *Wales South East*, maj. 108,488
Spencer, Thomas N. B. (*b.* 1948), *C.*, *Surrey West*, maj. 49,342
Stevens, John C. C. (*b.* 1955), *C.*, *Thames Valley*, maj. 26,491
*Stevenson, George W. (*b.* 1938), *Lab.*, *Staffordshire East*, maj. 31,769
*Stewart, Kenneth A. (*b.* 1925), *Lab.*, *Merseyside West*, maj. 49,817
*Stewart-Clark, Sir John, Bt. (*b.* 1929), *C.*, *Sussex East*, maj. 53,294
Titley, Gary (*b.* 1950), *Lab.*, *Greater Manchester West*, maj. 50,135
*Tomlinson, John E. (*b.* 1939), *Lab.*, *Birmingham West*, maj. 30,860
*Tongue, Miss Carole (*b.* 1955), *Lab.*, *London East*, maj. 27,385
*Turner, Amédée E., QC (*b.* 1929), *C.*, *Suffolk*, maj. 25,693
*Welsh, Michael J. (*b.* 1942), *C.*, *Lancashire Central*, maj. 5,688
*West, Norman (*b.* 1935), *Lab.*, *Yorkshire South*, maj. 91,784
White, Ian (*b.* 1947), *Lab.*, *Bristol*, maj. 9,982
Wilson, Joseph (*b.* 1937), *Lab.*, *Wales North*, maj. 4,460
Wynn, Terence (*b.* 1946), *Lab.*, *Merseyside East*, maj. 76,867

UK CONSTITUENCIES 15 June 1989

Corr. Corrective Party
Grn. Green
Hum. Humanist Party
ICP International Communist Party
Lab. RG Labour for Regional Government
MK Mebyon Kernow
W. Reg. Wessex Regionalists
For other abbreviations, *see* page 241)

BEDFORDSHIRE SOUTH
E. 569,506

*P. G. Beazley, *C.*	73,406
T. McWalter, *Lab.*	70,429
D. Everett, *Grn*	34,508
W. M. Johnston, *SLD*	8,748
R. Muller, *SDP*	3,067
C. majority	2,977

(June 1984, C. maj. 14,982)

BIRMINGHAM EAST
E. 531,081

*Mrs C. M. Crawley, *Lab.*	96,588
M. J. C. Harbour, *C.*	49,640
P. M. Simpson, *Grn.*	22,589
J. C. Binns, *SDP*	5,424
J. M. E. C. Roodhouse, *SLD*	4,010
M. Wingfield, *NF*	1,471
Lab. majority	46,948

(June 1984, Lab. maj. 21,383)

BIRMINGHAM WEST
E. 515,817

*J. E. Tomlinson, *Lab.*	86,545
C. F. Robinson, *C.*	55,685
J. D. Bentley, *Grn.*	21,384
S. Reynolds, *SLD*	7,673
Lab. majority	30,860

(June 1984, Lab. maj. 6,244)

BRISTOL
E. 562,277

I. White, *Lab.*	87,753
*R. J. Cottrell, *C.*	77,771
D. N. Wall, *Grn.*	39,436
C. Boney, *SLD*	16,309
G. McEwen *W. Reg.*	1,017
Lab. majority	9,982

(June 1984, C. maj. 17,644)

CAMBRIDGE AND BEDFORDSHIRE NORTH
E. 562,539

*Sir F. Catherwood, *C.*	84,044
M. Strube, *Lab.*	51,723
Ms M. E. Wright, *Grn.*	37,956
A. N. Duff, *SLD*	15,052
C. majority	32,321

(June 1984, C. maj. 47,216)

CHESHIRE EAST
E. 518,311

B. Simpson, *Lab.*	74,721
*Sir T. Normanton, *C.*	72,857
C. C. White, *Grn.*	21,456
Mrs B. Fraenkel, *SLD*	12,344
Lab. majority	1,864

(June 1984, C. maj. 18,376)

CHESHIRE WEST
E. 543,256

L. Harrison, *Lab.*	102,962
*A. Pearce, *C.*	79,761

G. L. Nicholls, *Grn.* 25,933
J. Rankin, *SLD* 9,333
Lab. majority 23,201
(June 1984, C. maj. 9,692)

CLEVELAND AND YORKSHIRE NORTH
E. 571,254
D. Bowe, *Lab.* 94,953
*Sir P. Vanneck, *C.* 70,861
O. Dumpleton, *Grn.* 17,225
T. M. Mawston, *SLD* 8,470
R. I. Andrew *SDP* 7,970
Lab. majority 24,092
(June 1984, C. maj. 2,625)

CORNWALL AND PLYMOUTH
E. 542,527
*C. J. P. Beazley, *C.* 88,376
P. A. Tyler, *SLD* 68,559
Ms D. Kirk, *Lab.* 41,466
H. Hoptrough, *Grn.* 24,581
C. Lawry, *MK* 4,224
C. majority 19,817
(June 1984, C. maj. 17,751)

THE COTSWOLDS
E. 558,115
*The Lord Plumb, *C.* 94,852
Mrs S. Limb, *Grn.* 49,174
T. Levitt, *Lab.* 48,180
L. A. Rowe, *SLD* 18,196
C. majority 45,678
(June 1984, C. maj. 48,942)

CUMBRIA AND LANCASHIRE NORTH
E. 561,263
W. R. Fletcher-Vane, *C.* 84,035
J. M. P. Hutton, *Lab.* 81,644
Mrs C. E. Smith, *Grn.* 21,262
E. E. Hill, *SLD* 12,590
J. Bates, *SDP* 4,206
C. majority 2,391
(June 1984, C. maj. 23,795)

DERBYSHIRE
E. 564,429
*G. W. Hoon, *Lab.* 105,018
P. Jenkinson, *C.* 72,630
E. Wall, *Grn.* 20,781
S. Molloy, *SLD* 4,613
Mrs A. M. Ayres, *SDP* 3,858
Lab. majority 33,388
(June 1984, Lab maj. 6,853)

DEVON
E. 596,671
*The Lord O'Hagan, *C.* 110,518
P. S. Christie, *Grn.* 53,220
W. J. Cairns, *Lab.* 40,675
M. Edmunds, *SLD* 23,306
R. Edwards, *SDP* 7,806
S. B. F. Hughes, *LM* 2,241
Lady Rous, *W. Reg.* 385
C. majority 57,298
(June 1984, C. maj. 56,610)

DORSET EAST AND HAMPSHIRE WEST
E. 608,895
*B. M. D. Cassidy, *C.* 111,469
Ms K. I. Bradbury, *Grn.* 49,695
H. R. White, *Lab.* 38,011
H. R. Legg, *SLD* 21,809
C. majority 61,774
(June 1984, C. maj. 59,891)

DURHAM
E. 530,137
*S. S. Hughes, *Lab.* 124,448
R. Hull, *C.* 37,600
Ms H. I. Lennox, *Grn.* 18,770
P. Freitag, *SLD* 8,369
Lab. majority 86,848
(June 1984, Lab. maj. 61,227)

ESSEX NORTH EAST
E. 598,542
Miss A. C. B. McIntosh, *C.* 92,758
Ms H. J. Bryan, *Lab.* 53,360
C. R. Keene, *Grn.* 45,163
Miss D. P. Wallis, *SLD* 16,939
C. majority 39,398
(June 1984, C. maj. 54,302)

ESSEX SOUTH WEST
E. 569,011
Miss P. E. Rawlings, *C.* 77,408
J. W. Orpe, *Lab.* 68,005
Mrs M. E. Willis, *Grn.* 32,242
T. P. Allen, *SLD* 10,618
C. majority 9,403
(June 1984, C. maj. 16,021)

GLASGOW
E. 487,199
*Mrs J. O. Buchan, *Lab.* 107,818
A. Brophy, *SNP* 48,586
Mrs A. K. Bates, *C.* 20,761
D. L. Spaven, *Grn.* 12,229
J. Morrison, *SLD* 3,887
D. Chalmers, *Comm.* 1,164
J. Simons, *ICP* 193
Lab. majority 59,232
(June 1984, Lab. maj. 65,733)

GREATER MANCHESTER CENTRAL
E. 481,023
*E. Newman, *Lab.* 86,914
Miss C. E. Gillan, *C.* 48,047
B. Candeland, *Grn.* 19,742
J. H. Mulholland, *SLD* 9,437
S. M. Millson, *SDP* 2,769
S. Knight, *Hum.* 1,045
Lab. majority 38,867
(June 1984, Lab. maj. 28,077)

GREATER MANCHESTER EAST
E. 506,930
*J. G. Ford, *Lab.* 93,294
R. N. Greenwood, *C.* 58,793
M. J. Shipley, *Grn.* 19,090
A. B. Leah, *SLD* 16,645
Lab. majority 34,501
(June 1984, Lab. maj. 8,651)

GREATER MANCHESTER WEST
E. 522,476
G. Titley, *Lab.* 109,228
P. H. Twyman, *C.* 59,093
D. W. Milne, *Grn.* 22,778
A. H. Cruden, *SLD* 6,940
Mrs B. Archer, *SDP* 4,526
Lab. majority 50,135
(June 1984, Lab. maj. 37,698)

HAMPSHIRE CENTRAL
E. 546,630
*E. T. Kellett-Bowman, *C.* 78,651
Ms A. Mawle, *Lab.* 50,977
Mrs S. J. Penton, *Grn.* 33,186
D. W. G. Chidgey, *SLD* 18,418
C. majority 27,674
(June 1984, C. maj. 44,821)
(Dec. 1988, C. maj. 21,442)

HEREFORD AND WORCESTER
E. 595,504
*Sir James Scott-Hopkins, *C.* 87,898
C. A. Short, *Lab.* 62,233
Ms F. M. Norman, *Grn.* 49,296
Mrs J. D. Davies, *SLD* 13,569
C. majority 25,665
(June 1984, C. maj. 39,934)

HERTFORDSHIRE
E. 517,137
*D. N. Prag, *C.* 86,898
V. S. Anand, *Lab.* 43,556
M. F. Ames, *Grn.* 37,277
M. D. Phelan, *SLD* 13,456
Mrs C. Treves Brown, *SDP* 5,048
C. majority 43,342
(June 1984, C. maj. 45,932)

HIGHLANDS AND ISLANDS
E. 313,877
*Mrs W. M. Ewing, *SNP* 66,297
Sir A. McQuarrie, *C.* 21,602
N. MacAskill, *Lab.* 17,848
M. Gregson, *Grn.* 12,199
N. Michison, *SLD* 10,644
SNP majority 44,695
(June 1984, SNP maj. 16,277)

HUMBERSIDE
E. 504,219
P. D. Crampton, *Lab.* 74,163
*R. C. Battersby, *C.* 57,835
Mrs J. C. Clark, *Grn.* 23,835
F. L. Parker, *SLD* 3,989
S. W. Unwin, *SDP* 3,419

Lab. majority 16,328
(June 1984, C. maj. 8,015)

KENT EAST
E. 575,789
*C. M. Jackson, *C.* 85,667
G. N. J. Perry, *Lab.* 56,706
Ms P. A. Kemp, *Grn.* 36,931
A. F. C. Morris, *SLD* 15,470
C. majority 28,961
(June 1984, C. maj. 48,867)

KENT WEST
E. 569,725
*G. B. Patterson, *C.* 82,519
P. L. Sloman, *Lab.* 58,469
J. Tidy, *Grn.* 33,202
J. B. Doherty, *SLD* 16,087
C. majority 24,050
(June 1984, C. maj. 34,630)

LANCASHIRE CENTRAL
E. 537,610
*M. J. Welsh, *C.* 81,125
G. W. T. Smith, *Lab.* 75,437
Mrs H. Ingham, *Grn.* 28,777
Ms J. Ross-Mills, *SLD* 7,378
C. majority 5,688
(June 1984, C. maj. 26,195)

LANCASHIRE EAST
E. 529,740
*M. J. Hindley, *Lab.* 96,926
R. W. Sturdy, *C.* 57,778
S. Barker, *Grn.* 20,728
M. Hambley, *SLD* 12,661
Lab. majority 39,148
(June 1984, Lab. maj. 7,905)

LEEDS
E. 519,631
*M. McGowan, *Lab.* 97,385
J. W. Tweddle, *C.* 54,867
C. R. Lord, *Grn.* 22,558
Mrs J. Ewens, *SLD* 11,720
Lab. majority 42,518
(June 1984, Lab. maj. 10,357)

LEICESTER
E. 579,050
Ms I. M. Read, *Lab.* 90,798
*F. A. Tuckman, *C.* 75,476
C. J. Davis, *Grn.* 33,081
A. G. Barrett, *Ind. C.* 6,996
G. W. Childs, *SLD* 6,791
Lab. majority 15,322
(June 1984, C. maj. 2,892)

LINCOLNSHIRE
E. 586,156
*W. F. Newton Dunn, *C.* 92,043
S. Taggart, *Lab.* 71,393
Ms J. Steranka, *Grn.* 24,908
J. P. Heppell, *SLD* 14,341
C. majority 20,650
(June 1984, C. maj. 45,445)

LONDON CENTRAL
E. 486,558
*A. S. Newens, *Lab. Co-op.* 78,561
Ms H. S. Crawley, *C.* 67,019
Ms N. Kortvelyessy, *Grn.* 28,087
Miss S. A. Ludford, *SLD* 7,864
W. D. E. Mallinson, *SDP* 2,957
'Lord' D. E. Sutch, *LM* 841
Ms L. St-Claire, *Corr.* 707
J. S. Swinden, *Hum.* 304
Lab. Co-op majority 11,542
(June 1984, Lab. maj. 13,297)

LONDON EAST
E. 530,548
*Miss C. Tongue, *Lab.* 92,803
A. R. Tyrrell, *C.* 65,418
Ms E. L. Crosbie, *Grn.* 21,388
J. K. Gibb, *SLD* 7,341
D. A. O'Sullivan, *ICP* 717
Lab. majority 27,385
(June 1984, Lab. maj. 12,159)

LONDON NORTH
E. 573,043
Ms P. Green, *Lab. Co-op.* 85,536
R. M. Lacey, *C.* 79,699
S. Clark, *Grn.* 30,807
Ms H. F. Leighter, *SLD* 8,917
P. Burns, *Ind.* 2,016
Ms L. Reith, *Comm.* 850
Lab. Co-op. majority 5,837
(June 1984, C. maj. 4,853)

LONDON NORTH EAST
E. 510,138
*A. Lomas, *Lab.* 76,085
M. Trend, *C.* 28,318
Mrs J. D. Lambert, *Grn.* 25,949
S. Banks, *SLD* 9,575
Ms N. C. Temple, *Comm.* 1,129
Lab. majority 47,767
(June 1984, Lab. maj. 52,665)

LONDON NORTH WEST
E. 506,707
*The Lord Bethell, *C.* 74,900
A. K. Toms, *Lab.* 67,500
I. E. Flindall, *Grn.* 28,275
C. D. Noyce, *SLD* 10,553
C. majority 7,400
(June 1984, C. maj. 7,422)

LONDON SOUTH AND SURREY EAST
E. 495,942
*C. J. O. Moorhouse, *C.* 78,256
R. J. E. Evans, *Lab.* 47,440
G. F. Brand, *Grn.* 31,854
P. H. Billenness, *SLD* 14,967
C. majority 30,816
(June 1984, C. maj. 44,657)

LONDON, SOUTH EAST
E. 558,815
*P. N. Price, *C.* 80,619
D. J. Earnshaw, *Lab.* 73,029
Dr E. C. McPhee, *Grn.* 37,576
A. A. Kinch, *SDP* 10,196
Mrs M. C. Williams, *SLD* 9,052
W. E. Turner, *Ind.* 456
C. majority 7,590
(June 1984, C. maj. 20,015)

LONDON, SOUTH INNER
E. 528,188
*R. A. Balfe, *Lab Co-op* 90,378
R. J. Wheatley, *C.* 45,360
Ms P. A. Shepherd, *Grn.* 26,230
M. J. Pindar, *SLD* 10,277
P. N. Power, *Comm.* 1,277
Ms D. Weppler, *Comm. League* 323
Lab. Co-op majority 45,018
(June 1984, Lab. maj. 31,481)

LONDON SOUTH WEST
E. 486,412
Ms A. J. Pollack, *Lab.* 74,298
*Dame S. M. Roberts, *C.* 73,780
Ms M. A. Elson, *Grn.* 35,476
J. C. Field, *SLD* 10,400
Lab. majority 518
(June 1984, C. maj. 6,867)

LONDON WEST
E. 515,581
*M. N. Elliott, *Lab.* 92,959
B. Donnelly, *C.* 78,151
J. R. Hywell-Davies, *Grn.* 32,686
J. G. Parry, *SLD* 9,309
J. Rogers-Davies, *SDP* 2,877
Lab. majority 14,808
(June 1984, Lab. maj. 5,229)

LOTHIANS
E. 523,506
*D. W. Martin, *Lab.* 90,840
Mrs C. M. Blight, *C.* 52,014
J. Smith, *SNP* 44,935
R. C. M. Harper, *Grn.* 22,983
K. Leadbetter, *SLD* 9,222
Lab. majority 38,826
(June 1984, Lab. maj. 25,924)

MERSEYSIDE EAST
E. 519,514
T. Wynn, *Lab.* 107,288
E. N. Farthing, *C.* 30,421
R. L. Georgeson, *Grn.* 20,018
R. M. Clayton, *SLD* 5,658
Lab. majority 76,867
(June 1984, Lab. maj. 49,039)

MERSEYSIDE WEST
E. 508,722
*K. A. Stewart, *Lab.* 93,717
M. D. Byrne, *C.* 43,900
L. Brown, *Grn.* 23,052
Mrs H. F. Clucas, *SLD* 16,327
D. J. E. Carson, *PRP* 1,747
Lab. majority 49,817
(June 1984, Lab. maj. 13,197)

MIDLANDS CENTRAL
E. 539,211
Ms C. M. Oddy, *Lab.* 76,736
*J. de Courcy Ling, *C.* 71,643
Ms J. A. Alty, *Grn.* 42,622
I. Cundy, *SLD* 8,450
Lab. majority 5,093
(June 1984, C. maj. 12,729)

MIDLANDS WEST
E. 529,505
*J. A. W. Bird, *Lab. Co-op.* 105,529
M. J. Whitby, *C.* 63,165
J. Raven, *Grn.* 21,787
Mrs F. M. Oborski, *SLD* 6,974
Lab. Co-op majority 42,364
(June 1984, Lab. maj. 19,685)

NORFOLK
E. 577,576
*P. F. Howell, *C.* 92,385
Ms M. Page, *Lab.* 71,478
M. Macartney-Filgate, *Grn.* 40,575
R. A. Lawes, *SLD* 8,902
S. D. Maxwell, *SDP* 4,934
C. majority 20,907
(June 1984, C. maj. 36,857)

NORTHAMPTONSHIRE
E. 587,733
*A. M. H. Simpson, *C.* 86,695
M. Coyne, *Lab.* 66,248
Ms A. T. Bryant, *Grn.* 43,071
R. Church, *SLD* 11,619
C. majority 20,447
(June 1984, C. maj. 39,859)

NORTHUMBRIA
E. 514,083
*G. J. Adam, *Lab.* 110,688
P. Yeoman, *C.* 50,648
Ms A. Lipman, *Grn.* 24,882
Viscount Morpeth, *SLD* 10,983
Lab. majority 60,040
(June 1984, Lab. maj. 15,700)

NOTTINGHAM
E. 565,354
K. Coates, *Lab.* 92,261
*M. L. Kilby, *C.* 77,748
Mrs S. E. Blount, *Grn.* 34,097
A. Swift, *SLD* 6,693
Lab. majority 14,513
(June 1984, C. maj. 16,126)

OXFORD AND BUCKINGHAMSHIRE
E. 560,730
*J. E. M. Elles, *C.* 92,483
R. Gifford, *Lab.* 44,965
T. H. Andrewes, *Grn.* 42,058
R. Johnston, *SLD* 14,405
R. C. Turner, *Ind.* 3,696
C. majority 47,518
(June 1984, C. maj. 49,081)

SCOTLAND MID AND FIFE
E. 534,638
*A. Falconer, *Lab.* 102,246
K. W. MacAskill, *SNP* 50,089
A. Christie, *C.* 46,505
G. Moreton, *Grn.* 14,165
M. Black, *SLD* 8,857
Lab. majority 52,157
(June 1984, Lab. maj. 27,166)

SCOTLAND NORTH EAST
E. 554,408
H. McGubbin, Lab. 65,348
Dr A. Macartney, *SNP* 62,735
*J. L. C. Provan, *C.* 56,835
M. Hill, *Grn.* 15,584
S. Horner, *SLD* 12,704
Lab. majority 2,613
(June 1984, C. maj. 9,171)

SCOTLAND SOUTH
E. 491,865
A. Smith, *Lab.* 81,366
*A. H. Hutton, *C.* 65,673
M. Brown, *SNP* 35,155
J. Button, *Grn.* 11,658
J. E. McKercher, *SLD* 10,368
Lab. majority 15,693
(June 1984, C. maj. 3,137)

SHEFFIELD
E. 564,409
R. Barton, *Lab.* 109,677
T. S. R. Mort, *C.* 40,401
P. L. Scott, *Grn.* 26,844
A. H. Rogers, *SLD* 10,910
D. E. Hyland, *ICP* 657
Lab. majority 69,276
(June 1984, Lab. maj. 46,283)

SHROPSHIRE AND STAFFORD
E. 597,554
*C. J. Prout, *C.* 85,896
D. J. A. Hallam, *Lab.* 83,352
R. T. C. Saunders, *Grn.* 29,637
C. Hards, *SLD* 10,568
C. majority 2,544
(June 1984, C. maj. 24,932)

SOMERSET AND DORSET WEST
E. 582,098
*Mrs M. E. Daly, *C.* 106,716
Dr R. H. Lawson, *Grn.* 54,496
Ms D. M. Organ, *Lab.* 46,210
M. Mactaggart, *SLD* 28,662
A. P. B. Mockler *W. Reg.* 930
C. majority 52,220
(June 1984, C. maj. 40,251)

STAFFORDSHIRE EAST
E. 581,127
*G. W. Stevenson, *Lab.* 94,873
M. F. Spungin, *C.* 63,104
S. Parker, *Grn.* 23,415
R. C. Dodson, *SLD* 7,046
Lab. majority 31,769
(June 1984, Lab. maj. 7,867)

STRATHCLYDE EAST
E. 494,274
*K. D. Collins, *Lab.* 109,170
G. A. Leslie, *SNP* 48,853
M. Dutt, *C.* 22,233
A. Whitelaw, *Grn.* 9,749
G. Lait, *SLD* 4,276
Lab. majority 60,317
(June 1984, Lab. maj. 63,462)

STRATHCLYDE WEST
E. 493,067
*H. R. McMahon, *Lab.* 89,627
C. M. Campbell, *SNP* 50,036
S. J. Robin, *C.* 45,872
G. Campbell, *Grn.* 16,461
D. J. Herbison, *SLD* 8,098
Lab. majority 39,591
(June 1984, Lab. maj. 23,038)

SUFFOLK
E. 550,131
*A. E. Turner, *C.* 82,481
M. D. Cornish, *Lab.* 56,788
A. C. Slade, *Grn.* 37,305
P. R. Odell, *SLD* 12,660
C. majority 25,693
(June 1984, C. maj. 47,098)

SURREY WEST
E. 515,881
T. N. B. Spencer, *C.* 89,674
E. Haywood, *Grn.* 40,332
H. G. Trace, *Lab.* 28,313
A. Davies, *SLD* 18,042
B. M. Collignon, *SDP* 3,676
C. majority 49,342
(June 1984, C. maj. 52,588)

SUSSEX EAST
E. 553,536
*Sir John Stewart-Clark, Bt., *C.* 96,388
Ms G. Roles, *Lab.* 43,094
Ms R. Addison, *Grn* 42,316
Mrs D. Venables, *SLD* 16,810
D. Howells, *LM* 1,181
C. majority 53,294
(June 1984, C. maj. 65,621)

SUSSEX WEST
E. 554,664
*R. M. Seligman, *C.* 95,821
I. F. N. Bagnall, *Grn.* 49,588
M. Shrimpton, *Lab.* 32,006
Dr J. M. M. Walsh, *SLD* 24,855
C. majority 46,233
(June 1984, C. maj. 57,502)

THAMES VALLEY
E. 542,855
J. C. C. Stevens, *C.* 73,070
Ms H. B. de Lyon, *Lab.* 46,579

P. Gordon, *Grn.* 36,865
D. B. Griffiths, *SLD* 14,603
C. majority 26,491
(June 1984, C. maj. 38,805)

TYNE AND WEAR
E. 530,953
A. J. Donnelly, *Lab.* 126,682
N. C. Gibbon, *C.* 30,902
R. Stather, *Grn.* 18,107
P. J. Arnold, *SLD* 6,101
T. P. Kilgallon, *SPGB* 919
Lab. majority 95,780
(June 1984, Lab. maj. 49,414)

WALES MID AND WEST
E. 547,740
*Revd D. R. Morris, *Lab.* 105,670
O. J. Williams, *C.* 53,758
Ms B. I. McPake, *Grn.* 29,852
Dr P. J. S. Williams, *PC* 26,063
G. A. Sinclair, *SLD* 10,031
Lab. majority 51,912
(June 1984, Lab. maj. 36,452)

WALES NORTH
E. 540,230
J. Wilson, *Lab.* 83,638
*Miss B. A. Brookes, *C.* 79,178
Dr D. E. Thomas, *PC* 64,120
P. H. W. Adams, *Grn.* 15,832
R. K. Marshall, *SLD* 10,056
Lab. majority 4,460
(June 1984, C. maj. 12,278)

WALES SOUTH
E. 520,911
W. David, *Lab.* 108,550
A. R. Taylor, *C.* 45,993
G. P. Jones, *Grn.* 25,993
P. J. Keelan, *PC* 10,727
P. K. Verma, *SLD* 4,037
D. A. T. Thomas, *SDP* 3,513
Lab. majority 62,557
(June 1984, Lab. maj. 44,258)

WALES SOUTH EAST
E. 561,068
*L. T. Smith, *Lab.* 138,872
R. J. Young, *C.* 30,384
M. J. Witherden, *Grn.* 27,869
Ms J. Evans, *PC* 14,152
P. Nicholls-Jones, *SLD* 4,661
Lab. majority 108,488
(June 1984, Lab. maj. 95,557)

WIGHT AND HAMPSHIRE EAST
E. 574,332
*R. J. Simmonds, *C.* 90,658
Dr A. D. Burnett, *Lab.* 51,228
S. L. Rackett, *Grn.* 40,664
Ms V. A. Rayner, *SLD* 19,569
C. majority 39,430
(June 1984, C. maj. 42,928)

WILTSHIRE
E. 568,875
*Mrs C. F. Jackson, *C.* 93,200
G. A. Harris, *Lab.* 46,887
J. V. Hughes, *Grn.* 46,735
P. N. Crossley, *SLD* 18,302
J. A. Cade, *Ind.* 4,809
C. majority 46,313
(June 1984, C. maj. 26,469)

YORK
E. 542,998
*E. H. C. McMillan-Scott, *C.* 81,453
J. T. Grogan, *Lab.* 66,351
R. Bell, *Grn.* 27,525
A. Collinge, *SLD* 12,542
C. majority 15,102
(June 1984, C. maj. 36,402)

YORKSHIRE SOUTH
E. 518,995
*N. West, *Lab.* 121,060
W. J. Clappison, *C.* 29,276
A. Grace, *Grn.* 19,063
B. Boulton, *SLD* 5,039
Lab. majority 91,784
(June 1984, Lab. maj. 67,749)

YORKSHIRE SOUTH WEST
E. 523,322
*T. Megahy, *Lab.* 108,444
G. T. Horton, *C.* 42,543
Mrs S. Leyland, *Grn.* 25,677
J. A. D. Ridgway, *SLD* 10,352
Lab. majority 65,901
(June 1984, Lab. maj. 44,173)

YORKSHIRE WEST
E. 564,001
*B. H. Seal, *Lab.* 108,644
G. T. Hall, *C.* 70,717
N. Parrott, *Grn.* 28,308
P. Wrigley, *SLD* 9,765
Lab. majority 37,927
(June 1984, Lab. maj. 20,854)

NORTHERN IRELAND
E. 1,105,551
*Revd I. R. K. Paisley, MP, *DUP* 160,110
*J. Hume, MP, *SDLP* 136,335
J. F. Nicholson, UUP 118,785
D. Morrison *SF* 48,914
J. T. Alderdice, *All.* 27,905
A. Kennedy, *C.* 25,789
M. H. Samuel, *Ecol.* 6,569
S. Lynch, *WP* 5,590
M. Langhammer, *Lab. RG* 3,540
B. Caul, *Lab. 87* 1,274

Revd I. R. K. Paisley, J. Hume and J. F. Nicholson were elected by the single transferable voting system.

COMMONWEALTH PARLIAMENTARY ASSOCIATION (1911)

The Commonwealth Parliamentary Association consists of 119 branches in the national, state, provincial or territorial parliaments in the countries of the Commonwealth. Conferences and general assemblies are held every year in different countries of the Commonwealth.

President (1991–2), Hon. Darrell Rolle, MP, Minister of National Security and Leader of the House (*The Bahamas*).
Vice-President (1991–2), His Excellency Alexis Galanos, MP, President of the House of Representatives (*Cyprus*).
Chairman of the Executive Committee (1990–3), Hon. Clive Griffiths, MLC, President of the Legislative Council (*Western Australia*).
Secretary-General, D. Tonkin, 7 Old Palace Yard, London SW1P 3JY.

UNITED KINGDOM BRANCH

Hon. Presidents, The Lord Chancellor; Madam Speaker.
Chairman of Branch, The Rt. Hon. John Major, MP.
Chairman of Executive Committee, C. Shepherd, MP.
Secretary, P. Cobb, OBE, Westminster Hall, Palace of Westminster, London, SW1.

THE INTER-PARLIAMENTARY UNION (1889)

To facilitate personal contact between members of all Parliaments in the promotion of representative institutions, peace and international co-operation.
Secretary-General, P. Cornillon, Place du Petit-Saconnex, BP 99, 1211 Geneva 19, Switzerland.

BRITISH GROUP

Palace of Westminster, London SW1A 0AA

Hon. Presidents, The Lord Chancellor; Madam Speaker.
President, The Rt. Hon. John Major, MP.
Chairman, Dr M. Clark, MP.
Secretary, D. Ramsay.

Parliamentary statistics

PRINCIPAL PARTIES IN PARLIAMENT SINCE 1970

	1970	1974 *Feb.*	1974 *Oct.*	1979	1983	1987	1992
Conservative	330*a*	296	276	339	397	375	336
Labour	287	301	319	268	209	229	270
Liberal/LD	6	14	13	11	17	17	20
Social Democrat	—	1	—	—	6	5	—
Independent	5*b*	1	1	2	—	—	—
Plaid Cymru	—	2	3	2	2	3	4
Scottish Nationalist	1	7	11	2	2	3	3
Democratic Unionist	—	—	—	3	3	3	3
SDLP	—	1	1	1	1	3	4
Sinn Fein	—	—	—	—	1	1	—
Ulster Popular Unionist	—	—	—	—	1	1	1
Ulster Unionist *c*	*a*	11	10	6	10	9	9
The Speaker	1	1	1	1	1	1	1
Total	630	635	635	635	650	650	651

a Including 8 Ulster Unionists
b Comprising: Independent Labour 1, Independent Unity 1, Protestant Unity 1, Republican Labour 1, Unity 1
c Comprises:
1974 (February) United Ulster Unionist Council 11
1974 (October) United Ulster Unionist 10
1979 Ulster Unionist 5, United Ulster Unionist 1
1983 Official Unionist 10

PARLIAMENTS SINCE 1970

Assembled	*Dissolved*	*Duration* *yr*	*m.*	*d.*
29 June 1970	8 February 1974	3	7	10
6 March 1974	20 September 1974	0	6	14
22 October 1974	7 April 1979	4	5	16
9 May 1979	13 May 1983	4	0	4
15 June 1983	18 May 1987	3	11	3
17 June 1987	16 March 1992	4	8	28
27 April 1992				

MAJORITIES IN THE HOUSE OF COMMONS SINCE 1970

Year	*Party*	*Maj.*
1970	Conservative	31
1974 Feb.	No majority	
1974 Oct.	Labour	5
1979	Conservative	43
1983	Conservative	144
1987	Conservative	102
1992	Conservative	21

VOTES CAST AT 1987 AND 1992 GENERAL ELECTIONS

General Election, 1987*

Conservative	13,760,525
Labour	10,029,944
Liberal/SDP Alliance	7,341,152
Scottish Nationalist	416,873
Plaid Cymru	123,589
†Green	89,753
Others	37,576

General Election, 1992*

Conservative	14,048,283
Labour	11,559,735
Liberal Democrats	5,999,384
Scottish Nationalist	629,552
Plaid Cymru	154,439
Others	436,207

*Excluding Northern Ireland seats
†Excluding Ecology candidate in Northern Ireland

The Government

THE CABINET AS AT 31 JULY 1992

Prime Minister, First Lord of the Treasury and Minister for the Civil Service
The Rt. Hon. John Major, MP, since November 1990
Lord High Chancellor
The Lord Mackay of Clashfern, PC, since October 1987
Secretary of State for Foreign and Commonwealth Affairs
The Rt. Hon. Douglas Hurd, CBE, MP, since October 1989
Chancellor of the Exchequer
The Rt. Hon. Norman Lamont, MP, since November 1990
Secretary of State for the Home Department
The Rt. Hon. Kenneth Clarke, QC, MP, since April 1992
President of the Board of Trade and Secretary of State for Trade and Industry
The Rt. Hon. Michael Heseltine, MP, since April 1992
Secretary of State for Transport
The Rt. Hon. John MacGregor, MP, since April 1992
Secretary of State for Defence
The Rt. Hon. Malcolm Rifkind, QC, MP, since April 1992
Lord Privy Seal and Leader of the House of Lords
The Lord Wakeham, PC, since April 1992
Lord President of the Council and Leader of the House of Commons
The Rt. Hon. Antony Newton, OBE, MP, since April 1992
Secretary of State for National Heritage
The Rt. Hon. Peter Brooke, MP, since September 1992
Minister of Agriculture, Fisheries and Food
The Rt. Hon. John Gummer, MP, since July 1989
Secretary of State for the Environment
The Rt. Hon. Michael Howard, QC, MP, since April 1992
Secretary of State for Wales
The Rt. Hon. David Hunt, MBE, MP, since May 1990
Secretary of State for Social Security
The Rt. Hon. Peter Lilley, MP, since April 1992
Chancellor of the Duchy of Lancaster (and Minister of Public Service and Science)
The Rt. Hon. William Waldegrave, MP, since April 1992
Secretary of State for Scotland
The Rt. Hon. Ian Lang, MP, since November 1990
Secretary of State for Northern Ireland
The Rt. Hon. Sir Patrick Mayhew, QC, MP, since April 1992
Secretary of State for Education
The Rt. Hon. John Patten, MP, since April 1992
Secretary of State for Health
The Rt. Hon. Virginia Bottomley, MP, since April 1992
Secretary of State for Employment
The Rt. Hon. Gillian Shephard, MP, since April 1992
Chief Secretary to the Treasury
The Rt. Hon. Michael Portillo, MP, since April 1992

LAW OFFICERS

Attorney-General
The Rt. Hon. Sir Nicholas Lyell, QC, MP, since April 1992
Lord Advocate
The Lord Rodger of Earlsferry, PC, QC, since April 1992
Solicitor-General
Sir Derek Spencer, QC, MP, since April 1992
Solicitor-General for Scotland
Thomas Dawson, QC, since April 1992

MINISTERS OF STATE

Agriculture, Fisheries and Food
David Curry, MP
Defence
The Rt. Hon. Archibald Hamilton, MP (*Armed Forces*)
Jonathan Aitken, MP (*Defence Procurement*)
Education
The Baroness Blatch, CBE
Employment
Michael Forsyth, MP
Environment
Sir George Young, MP (*Minister for Housing and Planning*)
John Redwood, MP (*Minister for Local Government and Inner Cities*)
David Maclean, MP (*Minister for Environment and Countryside*)
Foreign and Commonwealth Affairs
The Baroness Chalker of Wallasey, PC (*Minister for Overseas Development*)
The Rt. Hon. Douglas Hogg, QC, MP; The Rt. Hon. Tristan Garel-Jones, MP; The Rt. Hon. Alastair Goodlad, MP
Health
Brian Mawhinney, MP (*Minister for Health*)
Home Office
The Earl Ferrers, PC; Peter Lloyd, MP; Michael Jack, MP
Northern Ireland Office
Robert Atkins, MP; Michael Mates, MP
Scottish Office
The Lord Fraser of Carmyllie, PC, QC
Social Security
The Rt. Hon. Nicholas Scott, MBE, MP (*Minister for Social Security and Disabled People*)
Trade and Industry
The Rt. Hon. Timothy Sainsbury, MP (*Minister for Industry*)
Richard Needham, MP (*Minister for Trade*)
Timothy Eggar, MP (*Minister for Energy*)
Transport
The Earl of Caithness, PC (*Minister for Aviation and Shipping*)
Roger Freeman, MP (*Minister for Public Transport*)
Treasury
Stephen Dorrell, MP (*Financial Secretary*)
The Rt. Hon. Sir John Cope, MP (*Paymaster-General*)
Anthony Nelson, MP (*Economic Secretary*)
Welsh Office
The Rt. Hon. Sir Wyn Roberts, MP

UNDER SECRETARIES OF STATE

Agriculture, Fisheries and Food
The Earl Howe; the Hon. Nicholas Soames, MP
Office of the Minister for the Civil Service
Robert Jackson, MP

Defence
Viscount Cranborne
Education
Eric Forth, MP; Nigel Forman, MP
Employment
Patrick McLoughlin, MP; The Viscount Ullswater
Environment
The Lord Strathclyde; Anthony Baldry, MP; Robin Squire, MP
Foreign and Commonwealth Affairs
The Hon. Mark Lennox-Boyd, MP
Health
The Hon. Thomas Sackville, MP; Timothy Yeo, MP; The Baroness Cumberlege, CBE
Home Office
Charles Wardle, MP
Lord Chancellor's Department
John Taylor, MP
National Heritage
Robert Key, MP
Northern Ireland
The Earl of Arran; Jeremy Hanley, MP
Scottish Office
Lord James Douglas-Hamilton, MP; Allan Stewart, MP; Sir Hector Monro, MP
Social Security
The Lord Henley; Ann Widdecombe, MP; Alistair Burt, MP
Trade and Industry
Neil Hamilton, MP (*Corporate Affairs*)
Edward Leigh, MP (*Technology*)
The Baroness Denton of Wakefield, CBE (*Consumer Affairs and Small Firms*)
Transport
Kenneth Carlisle, MP (*Minister for Roads and Traffic*)
Steven Norris, MP (*Minister for Transport in London*)
Treasury
The Lords Commissioners, *see* Government Whips
Welsh Office
Gwilym Jones, MP

GOVERNMENT WHIPS

HOUSE OF LORDS

Captain of the Honourable Corps of Gentlemen-at-Arms (Chief Whip)
The Lord Hesketh, PC
Captain of The Queen's Bodyguard of the Yeomen of the Guard (Deputy Chief Whip)
The Earl of Strathmore and Kinghorne
Lords-in-Waiting
The Viscount Long; The Viscount Astor; The Viscount St Davids; The Viscount Goschen
Baroness-in-Waiting
The Baroness Trumpington, PC

HOUSE OF COMMONS

Parliamentary Secretary to the Treasury (Chief Whip)
The Rt. Hon. Richard Ryder, OBE, MP
Treasurer of HM Household (Deputy Chief Whip)
David Heathcoat-Amory, MP
Comptroller of HM Household
David Lightbown, MP
Vice-Chamberlain of HM Household
Sydney Chapman, MP
Lord Commissioners
Gregory Knight, MP; Irvine Patnick, MP; Nicholas Baker, MP; Timothy Wood, MP; Timothy Boswell, MP
Assistant Whips
Timothy Kirkhope, MP; David Davis, MP; Andrew MacKay, MP; Robert Hughes, MP; James Arbuthnot, MP

Government Departments and Public Offices

SALARIES 1992–3

MINISTERIAL SALARIES
as at 1 January 1992

Prime Minister	£53,007
Secretary of State	£39,820
Minister of State (Lords)	£44,945
Minister of State (Commons)	£28,175
Parliamentary Under Secretary (Lords)	£37,689
Parliamentary Under Secretary (Commons)	£21,384

Ministers who are Members of the House of Commons receive a reduced Parliamentary salary (£23,227 in 1992) in addition to this ministerial salary.

CIVIL SERVICE (BASIC) SALARIES
as at 1 April 1992

+Secretary to the Cabinet and Head of the Home Civil Service	£108,940
+Permanent Secretary to the Treasury	£101,920
+Head of the Diplomatic Service	£101,920
+Grade 1	£87,620
+Grade 1A	£80,600
+Grade 2	£62,504–£73,216
*Grade 3	£49,920–£57,928
Grade 4	£44,390–£49,790
Grade 5	£36,019–£47,921
Grade 6	£27,660–£42,724
Grade 7	£24,239–£34,469
Senior Executive Officer	£18,082–£22,618
Higher Executive Officer (D)	£15,869–£19,963
Higher Executive Officer	£14,456–£18,454
Executive Officer	£8,517–£14,753
Administration Trainee	£12,640–£14,701

*£51,272–£59,280 if in London
+These grades do not attract London weighting. London weighting, since 1 July 1989, is:

Inner zone	£1,750 a year
Intermediate zone	£1,000 a year
Outer zone	£725 a year

The Home Civil Service's unified pay and grading structure for senior personnel represents the following:

Grade	*Title*
1	Permanent Secretary
1A	Second Permanent Secretary
2	Deputy Secretary
3	Under Secretary
4	Chief Scientific Officer B, Professional and Technology Directing A
5	Assistant Secretary, Deputy Chief Scientific Officer, Professional and Technology Directing B
6	Senior Principal, Senior Principal Scientific Officer, Professional and Technology Superintending Grade
7	Principal

ADVISORY, CONCILIATION AND ARBITRATION SERVICE

27 Wilton Street, London SW1X 7AX
Tel 071-210 3000

The Advisory, Conciliation and Arbitration Service (ACAS) is an independent organization set up under the Employment Protection Act 1975. ACAS is directed by a Council consisting of a chairman and employer, trade union and independent members, all appointed by the Secretary of State for Employment. The functions of the Service are to provide facilities for conciliation, mediation and arbitration as means of avoiding and resolving industrial disputes, and to provide advisory services to industry on industrial relations and matters affecting the quality of working life.

ACAS also has offices in Accrington, Birmingham, Bristol, Cardiff, Fleet, Glasgow, Leeds, Liverpool, Manchester, Newcastle upon Tyne and Nottingham.

Chairman, Sir Douglas Smith, KCB
Chief Conciliation Officer (*G4*), D. Evans
Director of Resources and General Policy Branch (*G5*), E. Norcross

MINISTRY OF AGRICULTURE, FISHERIES AND FOOD

Whitehall Place, London SW1A 2HH†
Tel 071-270 3000

The Ministry of Agriculture, Fisheries and Food is responsible for administering government policy for agriculture, horticulture and fisheries in England and for policies relating to the safety and quality of food in the United Kingdom as a whole. In association with the other Agricultural Departments in the UK and the Intervention Board for Agricultural Produce, the Ministry is responsible for the negotiation and administration of the EC common agricultural and fisheries policies and for matters relating to the single European market.

The Ministry administers policies for the control and eradication of animal, plant and fish diseases and for assistance to capital investment in farm and horticultural businesses; it exercises responsibilities relating to the protection and enhancement of the countryside and the marine environment as well as to flood defence and other rural issues and appropriate research and development.

The Ministry has responsibility for ensuring public health standards in the manufacture, preparation and distribution of basic foods, and planning to safeguard essential food supplies in times of emergency. The Ministry is responsible for government relations with the UK food and drink

†Unless otherwise stated, this is the main address of divisions of the Ministry

manufacturing industries, and the food and drink importing, distributive and catering trades.

The Food Safety Directorate is responsible for many aspects of food safety and quality. These include analytical and research work, pesticide safety approval, biotechnology, meat hygiene, animal health and welfare, and related public health issues.

Minister, The Rt. Hon. John Gummer, MP
Principal Private Secretary (G7), T. D. Rossington
Private Secretary, F. M. Marlow
Parliamentary Private Secretary, J. Paice, MP
Special Adviser, K. Adams
Minister of State, David Curry, MP (*Farming and Fisheries*)
Private Secretary, Ms A. M. Gartland
Parliamentary Secretary (Lords), The Earl Howe (*Countryside*)
Private Secretary, C. L. Young
Parliamentary Secretary, The Hon. Nicholas Soames, MP (*Food*)
Private Secretary, S. C. Tanner
Parliamentary Clerk, Miss A. Evans
Permanent Secretary (G1), Sir Derek Andrews, KCB, CBE
Private Secretary, Miss S. E. Hendry

ESTABLISHMENT DEPARTMENT

Director of Establishments (G3), D. H. Griffiths

Establishments (General) Division

Victory House, 30–34 Kingsway, London WC2B 6TU
Tel 071-405 4310
Head of Division (G6), vacant

Staff Training Branch*

Principal (G7), Miss E. M. Berthoud

Welfare Branch

Victory House, 30–34 Kingsway, London WC2B 6TU
Tel 071-405 4310
Chief Welfare Officer (SEO), D. J. Jones

Personnel Division

Victory House, 30–34 Kingsway, London WC2B 6TU
Tel 071-405 4310
Head of Division (G5), G. P. McLachlan

Office Services Division*

Head of Division (G6), P. A. Cocking

Departmental Health and Safety Unit

Head of Unit (G7), P. A. Greatorex

Building and Estate Management

Eastbury House, 30–34 Albert Embankment, London SE1 7TL
Tel 071-238 3000
Head of Division (G5), J. S. Buchanan

Information

Chief Information Officer (G5), S. Dugdale
Chief Press Officer, M. Smith
Principal Librarian (G7), P. McShane

FINANCE DEPARTMENT

19–29 Woburn Place, London WC1H 0LU
Tel 071-917 1000

Principal Finance Officer (G3), A. R. Cruickshank

Financial Planning Division

Head of Division (G5), Miss V. A. Smith

Financial Management Division

Head of Division (G5), A. G. Kuyk
Deputy Head of Financial Management (G6), J. M. Lowi

Audit Consultancy and Management Services Division

Director of Audit (G5), D. V. Fisher
Deputy Director of Audit (G6), D. J. Littler

Purchasing and Supply Unit*

Director (G5), G. Lander

LEGAL DEPARTMENT

55 Whitehall, London SW1A 2EY
Tel 071-270 3000

Legal Adviser and Solicitor (G2), G. J. Jenkins, QC
Principal Assistant Solicitors (G3), A. E. Munir; B. T. Atwood

Legal Division A1

Assistant Solicitor (G5), P. D. Davis

Legal Division A2

Assistant Solicitor (G5), Mrs C. Davis

Legal Division A3

Assistant Solicitor (G5), M. C. P. Thomas

Legal Division A4

Assistant Solicitor (G5), Miss E. A. Stephens

Legal Division A5

Assistant Solicitor (G5), L. Gunatilleke

Legal Division B1

Assistant Solicitor (G5), Ms C. A. Crisham

Legal Division B2

Assistant Solicitor (G4), D. J. Pearson

Legal Division B3

Assistant Solicitor (G5), A. I. Corbett

Legal Division B4

Assistant Solicitor (G5), Dr M. R. Parke

Investigation Unit

Chief Investigation Officer (SEO), L. R. Blake

AGRICULTURAL COMMODITIES

Deputy Secretary (G2), R. J. Packer

EUROPEAN COMMUNITY

Under Secretary (G3), S. Wentworth

European Community Division I

Head of Division (G5), C. I. Llewelyn

European Community Division II

Head of Division (G6), L. G. Mitchell

---

*At Nobel/Ergon House, 17 Smith Square, London SW1P 3JR. Tel: 071-238 3000

HORTICULTURE, PLANT PROTECTION AND AGRICULTURAL RESOURCES

Under Secretary (G3), Mrs E. A. J. Attridge

HORTICULTURE AND POTATOES DIVISION
Head of Division (G5), R. A. Saunderson

PLANT HEALTH DIVISION*
Head of Division (G4), G. M. Trevelyan

PLANT VARIETY, RIGHTS OFFICE AND SEEDS
White House Lane, Huntingdon Road, Cambridge CB3 OLF
Tel 0223-277151
Head of Division (G5), J. Harvey

AGRICULTURAL RESOURCES POLICY DIVISION
Head of Division (G5), R. C. McIvor

ARABLE CROPS

Under Secretary (G3), C. J. Barnes

CEREALS AND SET-ASIDE DIVISION
Head of Division (G5), Ms J. Allfrey

SUGAR, TOBACCO, OILSEEDS AND PROTEINS DIVISION
Head of Division (G5), R. S. Thomas

ALCOHOLIC DRINKS DIVISION
Head of Division (G5), P. M. Boyling

MEAT GROUP

Under Secretary (G3), G. A. Hollis

BEEF DIVISION
Head of Division (G5), J. R. Cowan

SHEEP AND LIVESTOCK SUBSIDIES DIVISION
Head of Division (G5), A. J. Lebrecht

PIGS, EGGS AND POULTRY DIVISION
Head of Division (G5), G. W. Noble

FOOD, MILK AND MARKETING POLICY

Under Secretary (G3), J. W. Hepburn

MILK MARKETING AND LEGISLATION DIVISION
Head of Division (G5), P. Elliott

MILK AND MILK PRODUCTS
Head of Division (G5), B. J. Harding

FOOD INDUSTRY, MARKETING AND COMPETITION POLICY DIVISION
Head of Division (G5), R. E. Melville

EXTERNAL RELATIONS AND TRADE PROMOTION DIVISION
Head of Division (G5), D. V. Orchard

TRADE POLICY AND TROPICAL FOODS
Head of Division (G5), D. P. Hunter

MARKET TASK FORCE
Head of Division (G5), H. B. Brown

*At Nobel/Ergon House, 17 Smith Square, London SWIP 3JR. Tel: 071-238 3000

FOOD SAFETY

Deputy Secretary (G2), C. W. Capstick, CB, CMG

FOOD SAFETY GROUP

Under Secretary (G3), B. H. B. Dickinson
Chief Scientist (Fisheries and Food) (G3), Dr W. H. B. Denner

CHEMICAL SAFETY OF FOOD DIVISION*
Head of Division (G5), R. C. McKinley

CONSUMER PROTECTION DIVISION*
Head of Division (G5), C. A. Cockbill

MICROBIOLOGICAL SAFETY OF FOOD DIVISION*
Head of Division (G5), Mrs A. M. Pickering

FOOD SCIENCE DIVISION I*
Head of Division (G5), vacant

FOOD SCIENCE DIVISION II*
Head of Division (G5), Dr J. R. Bell.

FOOD SCIENCE LABORATORY
Colney Lane, Norwich NR4 7UQ
Tel 0603-501102
Head of Laboratory (G5), Dr J. Gilbert

TORRY RESEARCH STATION
PO Box 31, 135 Abbey Road, Aberdeen AB9 8DG
Tel 0224-877071
Director (G5), G. Hobbs, Ph.D

CHIEF SCIENTIST'S GROUP*

Head of Division (G6), Dr D. G. Lindsay

PESTICIDES, VETERINARY MEDICINES AND EMERGENCIES

Under Secretary (G3), P. W. Murphy

EMERGENCIES AND FOOD PROTECTION DIVISION
Head of Division (G5), Dr J. R. Park

PESTICIDES SAFETY DIRECTORATE
Chief Executive (G4), G. K. Bruce

BIOTECHNOLOGY UNIT
Head of Unit (G7), J. A. Bainton

STATE VETERINARY SERVICE
Government Buildings, Hook Rise South, Tolworth, Surbiton, Surrey KT15 3NB
Tel 081-330 4411
Director of Veterinary Field Services (G3), I. Crawford

LASSWADE VETERINARY LABORATORY
East of Scotland College of Agriculture, The Bush Estate, Penicuik, Midlothian EH26 0QN
Tel 031-445 4811

ANIMAL HEALTH AND VETERINARY GROUP

Under Secretary (G3), M. T. Haddon
Chief Veterinary Officer (G3), K. C. Meldrum

ANIMAL HEALTH (ZOONOSES) DIVISION
Government Buildings, Hook Rise South, Tolworth, Surbiton, Surrey KT6 7NF
Tel 081-330 4411

Head of Division (*G5*), R. J. G. Cawthorne

ANIMAL HEALTH (DISEASE CONTROL) DIVISION
Government Buildings, Hook Rise South, Tolworth, Surbiton, Surrey KT6 7NF
Tel 081-330 4411

Head of Division (*G5*), R. C. Lowson

ANIMAL HEALTH (INTERNATIONAL TRADE) DIVISION
Government Buildings, Hook Rise South, Tolworth, Surbiton, Surrey KT6 7NF
Tel 081-330 4411

Head of Division (*G5*), R. A. Bell

ANIMAL WELFARE DIVISION
Government Buildings, Hook Rise South, Tolworth, Surbiton, Surrey KT6 7NF
Tel 081-330 4411

Head of Division (*G5*), A. J. Perrins

MEAT HYGIENE DIVISION
Tolworth Tower, Surbiton, Surrey KT6 7DX
Tel 081-330 4411

Head of Division (*G5*), Mrs K. J. A. Brown

RESOURCE MANAGEMENT DIVISION
Government Buildings, Hook Rise South, Tolworth, Surbiton, Surrey KT6 7NF
Tel 081-330 4411

Head of Division (*G5*), M. J. Atkinson

COUNTRYSIDE, MARINE ENVIRONMENT AND FISHERIES

Deputy Secretary (*G2*), C. R. Cann

LAND USE, CONSERVATION AND RURAL ECONOMY

Under Secretary (*G3*), G. R. Waters*

RURAL STRUCTURES AND GRANTS DIVISION*
Head of Division (*G5*), T. E. D. Eddy

LAND USE AND TENURE DIVISION*
Head of Division (*G5*), T. J. Osmond

CONSERVATION POLICY DIVISION*
Head of Division (*G5*), C. R. Bodrell

ENVIRONMENT TASK FORCE*
Head of Division (*G5*), J. Robbs

FISHERIES DEPARTMENT*

Fisheries Secretary (*G3*), R. J. D. Carden

MARINE ENVIRONMENTAL PROTECTION DIVISION
Head of Division (*G5*), G. F. Meekings

FISHERIES DIVISION I
Head of Division (*G5*), I. C. Redfern

FISHERIES DIVISION II
Head of Division (*G5*), C. J. Ryder

FISHERIES DIVISION III
Head of Division (*G5*), Mrs A. M. Blackburn

SEA FISHERIES INSPECTORATE
Chief Inspector (*G6*), M. G. Jennings

FISHERIES RESEARCH
Director of Fisheries Research and Development for Great Britain (*G4*), D. J. Garrod, Ph.D.
Deputy Directors of Fisheries Research (*G5*), Dr J. G. Shepherd; Dr C. E. Purdom

FISHERIES LABORATORY
Pakefield Road, Lowestoft, Suffolk NR33 OHT
Tel 0502-62244

FISHERIES LABORATORY
Remembrance Avenue, Burnham-on-Crouch, Essex CMO 8HA
Tel 0621-782658

FISHERIES EXPERIMENT STATION
Benarth Road, Conwy, Gwynedd LL32 8UB
Tel 049-263 3883

FISH DISEASES LABORATORY
The Nothe, Weymouth, Dorset DT4 8UB
Tel 03057-72137
Officer-in-Charge (*Principal Scientific Officer*) (*G6*), B. J. Hill, Ph.D

ENVIRONMENT POLICY

Under Secretary (*G3*), M. Madden

ENVIRONMENTAL PROTECTION DIVISION*
Head of Division (*G5*), P. P. Nash

FLOOD DEFENCE DIVISION
Eastbury House, 30–34 Albert Embankment, London SE1 7TL
Tel 071-238 3000

Head of Division (*G5*), R. A. Hathaway

ECONOMICS AND STATISTICS

Under Secretary (*G3*), R. E. Mordue

ECONOMICS (FARM BUSINESS) DIVISION
Senior Economic Adviser (*G5*), J. P. Muriel

ECONOMICS (INTERNATIONAL) DIVISION
Senior Economic Adviser (*G5*), R. W. Irving

ECONOMICS (RESOURCE USE) DIVISION
Senior Economic Adviser (*G5*), A. P. Power, Ph.D

STATISTICS (AGRICULTURAL COMMODITIES) DIVISION*
Chief Statistician (*G5*), P. J. Lund, Ph.D

STATISTICS (CENSUS AND PRICES) DIVISION
Government Buildings, Epsom Road, Guildford GU1 2LD
Tel 0483-68121

Chief Statistician (*G5*), D. E. Bradbury

ECONOMICS AND STATISTICS (FOOD)
Senior Economic Adviser (*G5*), J. M. Slater, Ph.D

---

*At Nobel/Ergon House, 17 Smith Square, London SW1P 3JR. Tel: 071-238 3000

CHIEF SCIENTIFIC ADVISER

Chief Scientific Adviser (*G2*), P. J. Bunyan, DSC, Ph.D
Chief Scientist (*Agriculture and Horticulture*) (*G3*), D. W. F. Shannon, Ph.D*
Assistant Chief Scientist (*Agriculture and Horticulture*) (*G5*), Dr M. Parker
Scientific Liaison Officer (*Fisheries*) (*G6*), Dr D. G. Smith*

POLICY COORDINATION DIVISION*

Head of Division (*G5*), J. Suich

REGIONAL ORGANIZATION

Director of Regional Administration (*G3*), D. J. Coates*

REGIONAL SERVICES AND AGENCIES SUPPORT DIVISION

Head of Division (*G5*), G. Belchamber

RESOURCE MANAGEMENT STRATEGY UNIT

Head of Division (*G5*), J. D. Garnett

REGIONAL SERVICE CENTRES

WESSEX REGION, Block 3, Government Buildings, Burghill Road, Westbury-on-Trym, Bristol BS10 6NJ. Tel: 0272-591000. *Regional Director* (*G6*), Mrs A. J. L. Ould
ANGLIA REGION, Block C, Government Buildings, Brooklands Avenue, Cambridge CB2 2DR. Tel: 0223-462727. *Regional Director* (*G5*), D. A. Boreham
NORTHERN REGION, Eden Bridge House, Lowther Street, Carlisle CA3 8DX. Tel: 0228-23400. *Regional Director* (*G5*), D. E. Jones
NORTH MERCIA REGION, Berkeley Towers, Crewe, Cheshire CW2 6PT. Tel: 0270-69211. *Regional Director* (*G6*), R. Bettley-Smith
EAST MIDLANDS REGION, Block 7, Chalfont Drive, Nottingham NG8 3SN. Tel: 0602-291191. *Regional Director* (*G5*), M. J. Finnigan
NORTH-EAST REGION, Government Buildings, Crosby Road, Northallerton DL6 1AD. Tel: 0609-773751. *Regional Director* (*G6*), P. Watson
SOUTH-EAST REGION, Block A, Government Buildings, Coley Park, Reading, Berks. RG1 6DT. Tel: 0734-581222. *Regional Director* (*G5*), R. Anderson
SOUTH MERCIA REGION, Block C, Government Buildings, Whittington Road, Worcester WR5 2LQ. Tel: 0905-763355. *Regional Director* (*G6*), P. G. Gething
SOUTH-WEST REGION, Government Buildings, Alphington Road, Exeter EX2 8NQ. Tel: 0392-77951. *Regional Director* (*G6*), M. R. W. Highman

INFORMATION TECHNOLOGY DIRECTORATE

Government Buildings, Epsom Road, Guildford, Surrey GU1 2LD
Tel 0483-68121

Director (*G4*), D. Selwood
Assistant Directors (*G5*), A. G. Matthews; D. J. Dunthorne; (*G6*), D. D. Brown; R. F. Syrett

EXECUTIVE AGENCIES

CENTRAL VETERINARY LABORATORY

New Haw, Weybridge, Surrey KT15 3NB
Tel 0932-341111

The Central Veterinary Laboratory provides scientific and technical expertise in animal and public health.

Director and Chief Executive (*G3*), Dr T. W. A. Little
Director of Research (*G4*), Dr B. J. Shreeve
Director of Operations (*G5*), R. W. Saunders
Director of Business (*G5*), Dr J. A. Morris

VETERINARY MEDICINES DIRECTORATE

Woodham Lane, New Haw, Weybridge, Surrey KT15 3NB
Tel 0932-336911

The Veterinary Medicines Directorate is responsible for all aspects of licensing and control of animal medicines, including the protection of the consumer from hazardous or unacceptable residues.

Chief Executive and Director of Veterinary Medicines (*G4*), Dr J. M. Rutter
Director (*Policy and Finance*) (*G5*), C. J. Lawson
Director (*Licensing*) (*G5*), Dr K. N. Woodward
Professional Head, Pharmaceuticals Team (*G6*), vacant
Professional Head, Feed Additives Team (*G6*), J. P. O'Brien
Professional Head, Biological and Recombinant Products Team (*G6*), Dr A. M. T. Lee

CENTRAL SCIENCE LABORATORY

Chief Executive (*G3*), Dr P. I. Stanley
Research Director (*G5*), Dr A. R. Hardy

Comprising:

CENTRAL SCIENCE LABORATORY SLOUGH, London Road, Slough, Berks. SL3 7HJ. Tel 0753-534626
CENTRAL SCIENCE LABORATORY HARPENDEN, Hatching Green, Harpenden, Herts. AL5 2BD. Tel 0582-75241

AGRICULTURAL DEVELOPMENT AND ADVISORY SERVICE (ADAS)

Tel 071-238 5619/5631

The Agricultural Development and Advisory Service (ADAS) provides a comprehensive range of consultancy services to the land-based industries. It also carries out research; performs certain statutory functions; and provides advice on policy for MAFF and the Welsh Office. ADAS became an executive agency on 1 April 1992.

Chief Executive (*G2*), Dr J. Walsh*
Director of Farm and Countryside Service (*G3*), P. Needham*
Research Director (*G4*), Dr A. D. Hughes*
Finance Director (*G5*), Dr C. Herring*
Personnel Director (*G5*), Ms S. Nason*
Director for Wales (*G5*), W. I. C. Davies
Non-Executive Directors, C. Bystram (*Chairman*); P. Christensen, CBE; K. Fraser

---

AGRICULTURAL AND FOOD RESEARCH COUNCIL

Polaris House, North Star Avenue, Swindon SN2 1UH
Tel 0793-413200

The Agricultural and Food Research Council (AFRC) is an independent body established by Royal Charter. It is funded by the Office of Science and Technology, receives commissions from the Ministry of Agriculture, Fisheries and Food, and does research for industry and other bodies.

The Council is responsible for research done in its institutes and in UK university departments funded through its research grants scheme. It advises the Scottish Office

*At Nobel/Ergon House, 17 Smith Square, London SW1P 3JR. Tel: 071-238 3000

Agriculture and Fisheries Department (SOAFD) on research in the Scottish Agricultural Research Institutes.

The institutes funded through AFRC and SOAFD, and the university groups supported, form the Agricultural and Food Research Service.

Chairman, Sir Alistair Grant
Deputy Chairman and Director-General, Prof. T. L. Blundell, FRS
Members, Dr P. J. Bunyan; C. R. Cann; Prof. E. C. D. Cocking, FRS; Prof. J. R. Coggins, FRSE; Prof. J. M. M. Cunningham, CBE; Sir Sam Edwards, FRS; Dr D. A. Evans; D. F. R. George, OBE; A. B. N. Gill; Prof. R. M. Hicks, OBE; Prof. G. Horn, FRS; R. M. Knapman, MP; Prof. J. R. Krebs, FRS; Prof. C. J. Leaver, FRS; Dr T. Little; K. J. MacKenzie; Prof. T. Mansfield, FRS; J. L. C. Provan; G. T. Pryce; Dr D. W. F. Shannon; Prof. W. V. Shaw
Assessors, K. Meldrum; Dr C. McMurray; Prof. H. Smith, FRS; O. Rees, CB; Dr G. W. Robinson; D. Wilkinson; Dr E. Buttle; Prof. H. J. Newby; Dr D. A. Rees, FRS; Sir Mark Richmond, FRS
Deputy Secretary (G2), vacant
Director of Administration, Central Office (G3), B. G. Jamieson, Ph.D.
Heads of Divisions (G5), S. H. Visscher (*Finance*); R. J. Price (*Personnel*); Dr J. N. Wingfield (*Science*); Dr A. V. Harrison (*Policy*)
Commercial Policy Section (G7), S. M. Lawrie
Principal Information Officer (G7), M. A. Winstanley

For institutes and units of the Agricultural and Food Research Service, *see* page 693.

COLLEGE OF ARMS OR HERALDS COLLEGE

Queen Victoria Street, London EC4V 4BT
Tel 071-248 2762

The College is the official repository of the Arms and pedigrees of English, Northern Irish, and Commonwealth families and their descendants, and its records include official copies of the records of Ulster King of Arms, the originals of which remain in Dublin. The 13 officers of the College specialize in genealogical and heraldic work for their respective clients.

Arms have been and still are granted by Letters Patent from the Kings of Arms under authority delegated to them by the Sovereign, such authority having been expressly conferred on them since at least the fifteenth century. A right to Arms can only be established by the registration in the official records of the College of Arms of a pedigree showing direct male line descent from an ancestor already appearing therein as being entitled to Arms, or by making application through the College of Arms for a Grant of Arms.

The College of Arms is open Mon.–Fri. 10–4, when an Officer of Arms is in attendance to deal with enquiries by the public, though such enquiries may also be directed to any of the Officers of Arms, either personally or by letter.

Earl Marshal, His Grace the Duke of Norfolk, KG, GCVO, CB, CBE, MC

KINGS OF ARMS

Garter, C. M. J. F. Swan, CVO, Ph.D., FSA
Clarenceux, Sir Anthony Wagner, KCB, KCVO, FSA
Norroy and Ulster, J. P. B. Brooke-Little, CVO, FSA

HERALDS

York (and Registrar), D. H. B. Chesshyre, LVO, FSA
Chester, vacant
Windsor, T. D. Mathew
Lancaster, P. L. Gwynn-Jones
Somerset, T. Woodcock, FSA
Richmond, P. L. Dickinson

Earl Marshal's Secretary, Sir Walter Verco, KCVO, Surrey Herald Extraordinary

PURSUIVANTS

Portcullis, P. B. Spurrier
Rouge Croix, H. E. Paston-Bedingfeld
Rouge Dragon, T. H. S. Duke
Bluemantle, vacant

COURT OF THE LORD LYON

HM New Register House, Edinburgh EH1 3YT
Tel 031-556 7255

The Court of the Lord Lyon is the Scottish Court of Chivalry (including the genealogical jurisdiction of the *Ri-Sennachie* of Scotland's Celtic Kings), and adjudicates rights to arms and administers the Scottish Public Register of All Arms and Bearings and the Public Register of All Genealogies. The Lord Lyon presides and judicially establishes rights to existing arms or succession to Chiefship, or for cadets with scientific 'differences' showing position in clan or family. Pedigrees are also established by decrees of Lyon Court and by Letters Patent. As Royal Commissioner in Armory, he grants Patents of Arms (which constitute the grantee and heirs noble in the Noblesse of Scotland) to 'virtuous and well-deserving' Scotsmen, and petitioners (personal or corporate) in Her Majesty's overseas realms of Scottish connection, and issues birthbrieves.

Lord Lyon King of Arms, Sir Malcolm Innes of Edingight, KCVO, WS, FSA scot

HERALDS

Albany, J. A. Spens, RD, WS
Rothesay, Sir Crispin Agnew of Lochnaw, Bt
Ross, C. J. Burnett, FSA scot

PURSUIVANTS

Kintyre, J. C. G. George, FSA scot
Unicorn, Alastair Campbell of Airds, FSA scot
Carrick, Mrs C. G. W. Roads, MVO, FSA scot

Lyon Clerk and Keeper of Records, Mrs C. G. W. Roads, MVO, FSA scot
Procurator-Fiscal, I. R. Guild, CBE, FRSE, WS
Herald Painter, Mrs J. Phillips
Macer, A. M. Clark

ARTS COUNCIL OF GREAT BRITAIN

14 Great Peter Street, London SW1P 3NQ
Tel 071-333 0100

The Arts Council, an independent body established in 1946, is the principal channel for the Government's support of the arts. It funds the major arts organizations in England, the Regional Arts Boards (which replaced the Regional Arts Associations in October 1991) and the Scottish and Welsh

Arts Councils. It also provides a service of advice, information and help to artists, arts organizations and the general public.

Its objectives are to develop and improve the understanding and practice of the arts and to increase their accessibility to the public.

The Council distributes an annual grant from the Office of Arts and Libraries, and for the year 1992–3 the amount is £221.2 million.

Chairman, Lord Palumbo
Secretary-General, A. Everitt

REGIONAL ARTS BOARDS

NORTH-WEST ARTS BOARD, 12 Harter Street, Manchester M1 6HY. Tel: 061-228 3062. *Chair*, M. Unger
EAST MIDLANDS ARTS BOARD, Mountfields House, Forest Road, Loughborough, Leics. LE11 3HU. Tel: 0509-218292. *Chair*, M. Hutchinson
EASTERN ARTS BOARD, Cherry Hinton Hall, Cherry Hinton Road, Cambridge CB1 4DW. Tel: 0223-215355. *Chair*, Prof. D. Hargreaves
LONDON ARTS BOARD, Elme House, 133 Long Acre, London WC2E 9AF. Tel: 071-240 1313. *Chair*, C. Priestley
NORTHERN ARTS BOARD, 9–10 Osborne Terrace, Newcastle upon Tyne NE2 1NZ. Tel: 091-281 6334. *Chair*, Mrs S. Robinson
SOUTH-EAST ARTS BOARD, 10 Mount Ephraim, Tunbridge Wells, Kent TN4 8AS. Tel: 0892-515210. *Chair*, B. Nicholson
SOUTH-WEST ARTS BOARD, Bradninch Place, Gandy Street, Exeter EX4 3LS. Tel: 0392-218188. *Chair*, Ms M. Guillebaud
SOUTHERN ARTS BOARD, 13 St Clement Street, Winchester SO23 9DQ. Tel: 0962-855099. *Chair*, D. Reid
WEST MIDLANDS ARTS BOARD, 82 Granville Street, Birmingham B1 2LH. Tel: 021-631 3121. *Chair*, R. Southgate
YORKSHIRE AND HUMBERSIDE ARTS BOARD, 21 Bond Street, Dewsbury, W. Yorks. WF13 1AX. Tel: 0924-455555. *Chair*, E. Hall

SCOTTISH ARTS COUNCIL
12 Manor Place, Edinburgh EH3 7DD
Tel 031-226 6051

Chairman, W. Brown

WELSH ARTS COUNCIL
Holst House, 9 Museum Place, Cardiff CF1 3NX
Tel 0222-394 711

Chairman, M. Prichard, CBE

ART GALLERIES, ETC

ROYAL FINE ART COMMISSION
7 St James's Square, London SW1Y 4JU
Tel 071-839 6537

Established in 1924, the Commission is an autonomous authority on the aesthetic implications of any project or development, primarily but not exclusively architectural, which affects the visual environment.

Chairman, The Lord St John of Fawsley, PC
Commissioners, R. D. Carter, CBE; Dame Elizabeth Chesterton, DBE; Sir Philip Dowson, CBE, RA; M. Girouard, Ph.D.; The Duke of Grafton, KG, FSA; D. Hamilton Fraser, RA; M. J. Hopkins, CBE; S. A. Lipton; R. MacCormac; H. T. Moggridge, OBE; Mrs J. Nutting; Sir Philip Powell, CH, OBE, RA; J. Sutherland; Miss W. Taylor, CBE; W. Whitfield, CBE; J. Winter, MBE
Secretary (G6), S. Cantacuzino, CBE

ROYAL FINE ART COMMISSION FOR SCOTLAND
9 Atholl Crescent, Edinburgh EH3 8HA
Tel 031-229 1109

The Commission was established in 1927 and advises ministers and local authorities on the visual impact and quality of design of construction projects. It is an independent body and gives its opinions impartially.

Chairman, The Hon. Lord Prosser
Commissioners, Miss K. Borland; W. D. Cadell; W. D. Campbell; Mrs K. Dalyell; Dr Deborah Howard, Ph.D., FSA; A. S. Matheson, FRIBA; G. Ogilvie-Laing; Prof. T. Ridley; R. R. Steedman, RSA; Prof. R. Webster; R. Wedgwood
Secretary, C. Prosser

NATIONAL GALLERY
Trafalgar Square, London WC2N 5DN
Tel 071-839 3321

Open weekdays 10–6, Sun. 2–6. Closed on Good Friday, 24–26 December, New Year's Day and May Day Bank Holiday. Admission free.

The National Gallery was founded in 1824, following a Parliamentary grant of £60,000 for the purchase and exhibition of the Angerstein collection of pictures. The present site was first occupied in 1838 and enlarged and improved at various times throughout the years. A substantial extension to the north of the building with a public entrance in Orange Street was opened in 1975, and a new wing, the Sainsbury wing, was opened by The Queen on 9 July 1991. Government grants-in-aid for 1992–3 total £17.9 million.

BOARD OF TRUSTEES

Chairman, N. H. Baring
Trustees, Sir Rex Richards, FRS D.Phil.; HRH The Prince of Wales, KG, KT, GCB, PC; Lord Alexander of Weedon, QC; F. St J. Gore, CBE; B. Gascoigne; P. Troughton; The Countess of Airlie, CVO; Sir Derek Oulton, KCB, QC; E. Uglow; Sir Keith Thomas; Hon. Simon Sainsbury

OFFICERS

Director (£56,550), R. N. MacGregor
Chief Curator (G5), Dr C. P. H. Brown
Senior Curators (G6), Dr N. Penny; *(G7)*, Dr S. Foister; Dr D. Gordon; J. Leighton
Chief Restorer (G5), M. H. Wyld
Head of Exhibitions (G6), M. J. Wilson
Scientific Adviser (G6), Dr A. Roy
Director of Administration (G5), M. A. Cowdy
Head of Finance and Personnel (G6), T. Tarkowski
Head of Building, Mrs J. Evans
Head of Press and Public Relations, Miss J. Liddiard

NATIONAL PORTRAIT GALLERY
St Martin's Place, London WC2H 0HE
Tel 071-306 0055

Open Mon.–Fri. 10–5, Sat. 10–6, Sun. 2–6. Closed on Good Friday, May Day Bank Holiday, 24–26 December and New Year's Day. Admission free.

A grant was made in 1856 to form a gallery of the portraits of the most eminent persons in British history. The present building was opened in 1896, £80,000 being contributed to its cost by W. H. Alexander; an extension erected at the expense of Lord Duveen was opened in 1933. There are four outstations displaying portraits in appropriate settings: Montacute House, Gawthorpe Hall, Beningbrough Hall and Bodelwyddan Castle.

Chairman, The Revd Prof. W. O. Chadwick, OM, KBE, FBA
Trustees, The Lord President of the Council (ex officio); The President of the Royal Academy of Arts (ex officio); Sir Oliver Millar, GCVO, FBA, FSA; J. Roberts, D.Phil.; The Lord Morris of Castle Morris, D.Phil.; H. Keswick; Prof. N. Lynton; The Lord Weidenfeld; Sir Eduardo Paolozzi; J. Tusa; Sir Antony Acland, GCMG, GCVO; Mrs J. E. Benson, LVO, OBE; Mrs W. Tumim

Director (£49,671), J. T. Hayes, CBE, Ph.D., FSA
Keeper and Deputy Director (£44,474), M. Rogers, D.Phil

TATE GALLERY
Millbank, London SW1P 4RG
Tel 071-821 1313

Open weekdays 10–5.50, Sun. 2–5.50. Closed on New Year's Day, Good Friday, May Day Bank Holiday and 24–26 December. Admission free.

The Tate Gallery comprises the National Collections of British painting and 20th century painting and sculpture. The Gallery was opened in 1897, the cost of erection (£80,000) being defrayed by Sir Henry Tate, who also contributed the nucleus of the present collection. The Turner Wing, built at the expense of Sir Joseph Duveen, was opened in 1920. Lord Duveen defrayed the cost of galleries to contain the collection of modern foreign painting, completed in 1926, and a new sculpture hall, completed in 1937. In 1979 a further extension was built with a contribution from the Calouste Gulbenkian Foundation. The latest extension to the Tate Gallery, the Clore Gallery for the Turner Collection, was opened by The Queen on 1 April 1987. The Tate Gallery Liverpool, sited in the Albert Dock, opened in May 1988. The Tate Gallery St Ives is due to open in 1993. Total government funding for 1992–3 is £16,596,000.

BOARD OF TRUSTEES

Chairman, D. Stevenson
Trustees, The Countess of Airlie, CVO; The Hon. Mrs J. de Botton; R. Deacon; C. LeBrun; D. Puttnam, CBE; W. Govett; Mrs P. Ridley; M. Craig-Martin; Sir Rex Richards; D. Verey

OFFICERS

Salaries 1992

Director	£56,500
Grade 5	£34,667–£49,671
Grade 6	£26,622–£44,474

Director, N. Serota
Deputy Director, F. Carnwath
Keeper of the British Collection (G5), A. Wilton
Keeper of the Modern Collection (G5), R. Morphet
Deputy Keepers (G6), L. A. Parris; J. Lewison

TATE GALLERY LIVERPOOL
Albert Dock, Liverpool L3 4BB
Tel 051-709 3223
Open Wed.–Sun., 10–6, Tues. 11–6. Closed Mondays.
Curator (G6), L. Biggs

WALLACE COLLECTION
Hertford House, Manchester Square, London W1M 6BN
Tel 071-935 0687

Open weekdays 10–5, Sun. 2–5. Closed on Good Friday, 24–26 December, 1 January and May Day. Admission free.

The Wallace Collection was bequeathed to the nation by the widow of Sir Richard Wallace, Bt., on her death in 1897, and Hertford House was subsequently acquired by the Government. The collection includes pictures, drawings and miniatures, French furniture, sculpture, bronzes, porcelain, armour and miscellaneous *objets d'art*. The total net expenses for 1992–3 were estimated at £2,230,000.

Director, Miss R. J. Savill
Assistant to Director, P. Hughes
Head of Administration, A. W. Houldershaw

NATIONAL GALLERIES OF SCOTLAND
The Mound, Edinburgh EH2 2EL
Tel 031-556 8921

TRUSTEES

Chairman of the Trustees, A. M. Grossart, CBE
Trustees, J. Packer, OBE; A. R. Cole-Hamilton; Mrs L. W. Gibbs; Lord Macfarlane of Bearsden; Dr T. Johnston; Prof. A. A. Tait; E. Hagman; Prof. E. Fernie; M. Shea

OFFICERS

Salaries 1992

Director	£42,724–£44,390
Keeper	£26,622–£34,667
Assistant Keeper/Curator	£23,329–£27,819

Director, T. Clifford
Keeper of Conservation, J. P. Dick
Keeper of Information (Asst. Keeper), Miss L. S. Callander
Keeper of Education (Asst. Keeper), M. Cassin
Registrar (Asst. Keeper), J. Patterson, Ph.D
Secretary (Keeper), Ms S. Edwards
Buildings (Asst. Keeper), C. P. Fotheringham

NATIONAL GALLERY OF SCOTLAND
The Mound, Edinburgh
Tel 031-556 8921

Open Mon.–Sat. 10–5, Sun. 2–5. Closed 25, 26, 31 December, 1, 2, 4 January. Admission free.
Keeper, M. Clarke
Assistant Keepers, Miss L. M. Errington, Ph.D.; Ms J. Lloyd Williams
Assistant Keeper, R. M. M. Campbell

SCOTTISH NATIONAL PORTRAIT GALLERY
1 Queen Street, Edinburgh
Tel 031-556 8921

Hours: as for National Gallery of Scotland
Keeper, D. Thomson, Ph.D
Assistant Keepers, Miss R. K. Marshall, Ph.D.; J. E. Holloway
Curator of Photography, Miss S. F. Stevenson

SCOTTISH NATIONAL GALLERY OF MODERN ART
Belford Road, Edinburgh EH4 3DR
Tel 031-556 8921

Hours: as for National Gallery of Scotland
Keeper, R. Calvocoressi
Assistant Keepers, K. S. Hartley; P. Elliott, Ph.D

For other British Art Galleries, *see* Index

UNITED KINGDOM ATOMIC ENERGY AUTHORITY (AEA TECHNOLOGY)

Harwell, Oxfordshire OX11 ORA
Tel 0235-821111

The UKAEA was established by the Atomic Energy Authority Act 1954. Since April 1986 the UKAEA has been required by the Government to operate on a commercial footing and in 1990 it adopted the trading name AEA Technology. It provides scientific and technical services, products and consultancy in nuclear and non-nuclear fields to governments, utilities and industries worldwide. The UKAEA has seven research and engineering centres.

Chairman (part-time), J. N. Maltby, CBE
Deputy Chairman and Chief Executive, Dr B. L. Eyre
Members (part-time), Prof. Sir Peter Hirsch, FRS; J. Bullock; R. Sanderson, OBE; Prof. Sir Roger Elliott, FRS; J. A. Gardiner
Secretary, J. R. Bretherton
Executive Director, Finance, P. G. Daffern
Managing Director, Sites and Personnel, A. W. Hills
Managing Director, Industrial Business Group, Dr R. S. Nelson
Managing Director, Nuclear Business Group, Dr D. Pooley

THE AUDIT COMMISSION FOR LOCAL AUTHORITIES AND THE NATIONAL HEALTH SERVICE IN ENGLAND AND WALES

1 Vincent Square, London SW1P 2PN
Tel 071-828 1212

The Audit Commission was set up in 1983 with responsibility for the external audit of local authorities. This remit was extended from October 1990 to include the audit of the National Health Service bodies in England and Wales. The Commission appoints the auditors, who may be from the District Audit Service or from a private firm of accountants. The Commission also has responsibility for promoting value for money in the services provided by local authorities and health bodies.

The Commission has 15–17 members appointed by the Secretary of State for the Environment in consultation with the Secretaries of State for Wales and for Health. Though appointed by the Secretary of State, the Commissioners are responsible to Parliament.

Chairman, D. J. S. Cooksey
Deputy Chairman, C. M. Stuart
Controller of Audit, A. Foster
Deputy Controller, J. C. Nicholson, CBE

THE COMMISSION FOR LOCAL AUTHORITY ACCOUNTS IN SCOTLAND

18 George Street, Edinburgh EH2 2QU
Tel 031-226 7346

The Commission was set up in 1975. It is responsible for securing the audit of the accounts of Scottish local authorities and certain joint boards and joint committees. Amongst its duties the Commission is required to deal with reports made by the Controller of Audit on items of account contrary to law; incorrect accounting; and losses due to misconduct, negligence and failure to carry out statutory duties. Since 1988 the Commission has had responsibility for value-for-money audits of authorities.

Members are appointed by the Secretary of State for Scotland.

Chairman, Prof. J. R. Small, CBE
Controller of Audit, J. Broadfoot
Secretary, J. Ritchie

THE BANK OF ENGLAND

Threadneedle Street, London EC2R 8AH
Tel 071-601 4444

The Bank of England was incorporated in 1694 under Royal Charter. It is the banker of the Government on whose behalf it executes monetary policy and manages the Note Issue and the National Debt. It is also responsible for promoting the efficiency and competitiveness of financial services. As the central reserve bank of the country, the Bank keeps the accounts of British banks, who maintain with it a proportion of their cash resources, and of most overseas central banks.

Governor, Rt. Hon. Robin Leigh-Pemberton (until June 1993)
Deputy Governor, E. A. J. George
Directors, Sir Adrian Cadbury; A. L. Coleby; Sir Frederick Corby; Sir Colin Corness; A. D. Crockett; The Lord Haslam; Sir Christopher Hogg; Sir Martin Jacomb; Prof. M. A. King; G. H. Laird, CBE; Sir David Lees; B. Quinn; Sir David Scholey, CBE; Prof. Sir Roland Smith; C. G. Southgate; Sir David Walker
Associate Directors, P. H. Kent; H. C. E. Harris; I. Plenderleith
Advisers to the Governor, J. P. Charkham; Sir Peter Petrie
Assistant Director, R. A. Barnes
Chief of Banking Department (Chief Cashier), G. E. A. Kentfield
Chief Registrar, D. A. Bridger
General Manager, Printing Works, A. W. Jarvis
Secretary, G. A. Croughton
Head of Information Division, J. R. E. Footman
The Auditor, M. J. W. Phillips

BOUNDARY COMMISSIONS

The Commissions are constituted under the Parliamentary Constituencies Act 1986. The Speaker of the House of Commons is ex-officio chairman of all four Commissions in the United Kingdom. Each of the four Commissions is required by law to keep the parliamentary constituencies in their part of the United Kingdom under review. Each of the three Commissions in Great Britain is required by law to keep the European Parliamentary constituencies in their part of Great Britain under review.

ENGLAND

St Catherine's House, 10 Kingsway, London WC2B 6JP
Tel 071-242 0262

Deputy Chairman, The Hon. Mr Justice Knox
Joint Secretaries, R. McLeod; Mrs J. S. Morris

WALES
St Catherine's House, 10 Kingsway, London WC2B 6JP
Tel 071-242 0262

Deputy Chairman, The Hon. Mr Justice Anthony Evans
Joint Secretaries, R. McLeod; Mrs J. S. Morris

SCOTLAND
St Andrew's House, Edinburgh EH1 3DG
Tel 031-244 2196/2027

Deputy Chairman, The Hon. Lord Davidson
Secretary, D. K. C. Jeffrey

NORTHERN IRELAND
c/o Northern Ireland Office, Whitehall, London SW1A 2AZ
Tel 071-210 6569

Deputy Chairman, The Hon. Mr Justice Higgins
Secretary, J. R. Fisher

BRITISH BROADCASTING CORPORATION

Broadcasting House, London W1A 1AA
Tel 071-580 4468

The BBC was incorporated under Royal Charter as successor to the British Broadcasting Company Ltd, whose licence expired on 31 December 1926. Its present Charter came into force on 1 August 1981, for 15 years. The Chairman, Vice-Chairman and other Governors are appointed by The Queen-in-Council. The BBC is financed by revenue from receiving licences for the home services and by grant-in-aid from Parliament for the external services. The total number of receiving licences in the UK at 31 March 1992 was 19,630,848, of which 1,205,115 were for monochrome receivers and 18,425,733 for colour receivers. Annual television licence fees are: monochrome £26.50; colour £80.

BOARD OF GOVERNORS
as at 1 August 1992

Chairman (£55,155), M. Hussey
Vice-Chairman (£14,150), The Lord Barnett, PC
Governors (*each* £14,150), Sir Kenneth Bloomfield, KCB (*N. Ireland*); Dr G. Jones (*Wales*); Sir Graham Hills, FRSE (*Scotland*); (*each* £7,075), Dr J. Roberts; W. B. Jordan; J. K. Oates, OBE; The Baroness James of Holland Park; Miss J. Glover, D.Phil; Mrs S. Sadeque; Lord Nicholas Gordon Lennox, KCMG, KCVO

BOARD OF MANAGEMENT

Director-General, Sir Michael Checkland (*from March 1993*, J. Birt)
Deputy Director-General, J. Birt
Managing Directors, W. Wyatt (*Network Television*); D. Hatch (*Network Radio*); J. Tusa (*World Service*) (until end 1992); R. Neil (*Regional Broadcasting*)
Directors, W. Dennay (*Engineering*); H. James (*Corporate Affairs*); I. Phillips (*Finance*); J. Arnold-Baker (BBC Enterprises); Ms M. Salmon (*Personnel*)

OTHER SENIOR STAFF

Director, News and Current Affairs, T. Hall
Director, Resources, Radio, D. Thomas
Director, Resources, Television, C. Taylor
Deputy Managing Director, World Service, D. Witherow
Head of Policy and Planning Unit, Ms P. Hodgson
Controller, BBC1, J. Powell
Controller, BBC2, A. Yentob
Assistant Managing Director, Network Television, Ms J. Drabble
Controller, Radio 1, J. Beerling
Controller, Radio 2, Ms F. Line
Controller, Radio 3, N. Kenyon
Controller, Radio 4, M. Green
Controller, Radio 5, Ms P. Ewing
Controller, Scotland, J. McCormick
Controller, Wales, G. Talfan Davies
Controller, N. Ireland, R. Walsh
Chief Political Adviser, Ms M. Douglas
Controller, Editorial Policy, J. Wilson
Controller, Information Services and International Relations, D. Barlow
The Secretary, M. Stevenson
Legal Adviser, G. Roscoe

BRITISH COAL CORPORATION

Hobart House, Grosvenor Place, London SW1X 7AE
Tel 071-235 2020

The British Coal Corporation (formerly the National Coal Board) was constituted in 1946 and took over the mines on 1 January 1947.

Chairman, J. N. Clarke
Deputy Chairmen, Dr K. Moses, CBE; A. Wheeler, CBE
Executive Members, M. H. Butler (*Finance Director*); K. Hunt (*Employee Relations*)
Non-Executive Members, Dr D. V. Atterton, CBE; Dr T. J. Parker; D. B. Walker; J. P. Erbé; A. P. Hichens
Secretary, M. S. Shelton

THE BRITISH COUNCIL

10 Spring Gardens, London SW1A 2BN
Tel 071-930 8466
Medlock Street, Manchester M15
Tel 061-957 7000

The British Council was established in 1934 and incorporated by Royal Charter in 1940.

It is an independent, non-political organization which promotes Britain abroad. It provides access to British ideas, talents and experience in education and training, books and periodicals, the English language, the arts, the sciences and technology.

The Council is represented in 95 countries and runs 162 offices, 116 libraries and 68 English language schools around the world.

The Council's annual turnover in 1992–3 is estimated at £408 million, including grants from the Foreign and Commonwealth Office and the Overseas Development Administration. The Council's own revenue now exceeds £120 million.

Chairman, Sir Martin Jacomb
Director-General (£77,500) (*acting*), J. Hanson

BRITISH FILM COMMISSION

70 Baker Street, London WIM IDJ
Tel 071-224 5000

The British Film Commission was established in January 1992 to promote the use of British locations, production services, technicians and facilities. It is funded by the Department of National Heritage. It offers a free service to international producers and directs enquiries to local film commissions throughout the UK. It also encourages the development of local commissions where they do not already exist.

Commissioner and Chairman of the Board, S. W. Samuelson, CBE
Chief Executive, A. Patrick

BRITISH FILM INSTITUTE

21 Stephen Street, London WIP IPL
Tel 071-255 1444

The British Film Institute was established in 1933 under Royal Charter. Its aims are to encourage the development of the art of film and its use as a record of contemporary life in Great Britain, and to foster the study, appreciation and use of films for television. It includes the National Film Archive, the National Film Theatre and the Museum of the Moving Image, and it supports a network of 40 regional film theatres. The BFI Library contains the world's largest collection of material relating to film and television. Total government funding for 1992–3 is £14.97 million.

Chairman, Sir Richard Attenborough, CBE
Director, W. Stevenson

BRITISH PHARMACOPOEIA COMMISSION

Market Towers, 1 Nine Elms Lane, London SW8 5NQ
Tel 071-273 0561

The British Pharmacopoeia Commission sets standards for medicinal products used in human and veterinary medicine. It is responsible for the British Pharmacopoeia (a publicly-available statement of the standard that a product must meet throughout its shelf-life), the British Pharmacopoeia (Veterinary) and the selection of British Approved Names. It also participates in the work of the European Pharmacopoeia on behalf of the United Kingdom. It has 18 members who are appointed by the Secretary of State for Health and the Minister for Agriculture, Fisheries and Food.

Chairman, Prof. D. Ganderton
Vice-Chairman, Prof. P. Turner, CBE
Secretary (*G6*), Dr R. C. Hutton

BRITISH RAILWAYS BOARD

Euston House, 24 Eversholt Street, PO Box 100, London NWI IDZ
Tel 071-928 5151

The British Railways Board came into being in 1963 under the terms of the Transport Act 1962. The Board is responsible for the provision of railway services in Great Britain and for catering and other related services.

Chairman (£221,000), Sir Robert Reid
Chief Executive, Railways, J. K. Welsby
Members, P. Allen, CBE*; Ms A. Biss*; Miss K. T. Kantor*; J. B. Cameron, CBE*; D. E. Rayner, CBE; J. C. P. Edmonds; K. H. M. Dixon*; Sir Fred Holliday, CBE*; J. J. Jerram; E. Sanderson*; Dr P. Watson
* part-time members

BRITISH STANDARDS INSTITUTION (BSI)

2 Park Street, London WIA 2BS
Enquiry Section: BSI, Linford Wood, Milton Keynes MK14 6LE
Tel 0908-221166

The British Standards Institution is the recognized authority in the UK for the preparation and publication of national standards for industrial and consumer products. In consultation with the interests concerned, BSI prepares standards relating to nearly every sector of the nation's industry and trade. It also represents the UK at European and international standards meetings. About 80 per cent of its standards work is now internationally linked.

British Standards are issued for voluntary adoption, though in a number of cases compliance with a British Standard is required by legislation. BSI operates certification schemes under which industrial and consumer products are certified as complying with the relevant British Standard and may carry the Institution's certification trade marks, known as the 'Kitemark' and the 'Safety Mark'. It assesses and registers companies which meet the requirements of the quality management standard, BS5750. BSI runs one of the largest testing laboratories in Europe and has an advisory service for exporters called Technical Help to Exporters.

BSI is financed by voluntary subscriptions, an annual government grant, the sale of its publications, and fees for testing and certification. There are more than 27,000 subscribing members of BSI.

Chief Executive, Dr M. Sanderson.

BRITISH TOURIST AUTHORITY

Thames Tower, Black's Road, London W6 9EL
Tel 081-846 9000

Established under the Development of Tourism Act 1969, the British Tourist Authority has specific responsibility for promoting tourism to Great Britain from overseas. It also has a general responsibility for the promotion and development of tourism and tourist facilities within Great Britain as a whole, and for advising the Government on tourism matters.

Chairman (*part-time*), W. Davis
Chief Executive, M. G. Medlicott

BRITISH WATERWAYS

Willow Grange, Church Road, Watford, Herts. WDI 3QA
Tel 0923-226422

British Waterways is the navigational authority for over 2,000 miles of canals and river navigations in England,

Scotland and Wales. Some 380 miles are maintained and are being developed as commercial waterways for use by freight-carrying vessels, and another 1,200 miles, the cruising waterways, are being developed for boating, fishing and other leisure activities. The remaining 500 miles, the remainder waterways, are maintained with due regard to safety, public health and the preservation of amenities. Of this remaining mileage, nearly two-thirds is navigable or has been restored to navigation over the last twenty years.

Chairman (part-time), D. C. Ingman
Vice-Chairman (part-time), Sir Peter Hutchison, Bt.
Members (all part-time), J. Gordon; D. H. R. Yorke; M. Cairns; D. Porter
Chief Executive, B. C. Dice
Secretary and Solicitor, R. J. Duffy

BROADCASTING STANDARDS COUNCIL

5–8 The Sanctuary, London SW1P 3JS
Tel 071-233 0544

The Council was set up in 1988 but received its statutory powers under the Broadcasting Act 1990. It monitors the portrayal of violence, sex and matters of taste and decency in any television or radio programme or broadcast advertisement. The Council publishes a code of practice, considers complaints and undertakes relevant research. Members of the Council are appointed by the Secretary of State for National Heritage. The appointments are part-time.

Chairman (£36,925), The Lord Rees-Mogg
Deputy Chairman (£27,885), Dame Jocelyn Barrow, DBE
Members (*each* £11,105), R. Baker, OBE, RD; The Bishop of Peterborough; A. Dubs; Ms R. Bevan; Dr Jean Curtis-Raleigh; Revd C. Robertson
Director, C. Shaw
Deputy Director, T. Cobley

THE BROADS AUTHORITY

Thomas Harvey House, 18 Colegate, Norwich NR3 1BQ
Tel 0603-610734

The Broads Authority is a special statutory authority set up under the Norfolk and Suffolk Broads Act 1988, with powers and responsibilities similar to those of National Park Authorities. The functions of the Authority are to conserve and enhance the natural beauty of the Broads; to promote the enjoyment of the Broads by the public; and to protect the interests of navigation.

The Authority comprises 35 members, appointed by Norfolk County Council (4); Suffolk County Council (2); Broadland District Council (2); Great Yarmouth Borough Council (2); North Norfolk District Council (2); Norwich City Council (2); South Norfolk District Council (2); Waveney District Council (2); the Countryside Commission (2); English Nature (1); the Great Yarmouth Port Authority (2); National Rivers Authority (Anglian Region) (1); the Secretary of State for the Environment (9); and two from amongst members of the Authority's statutory Navigation Committee who are not already members of the Authority.

Chairman, J. S. Peel, MC
Chief Executive, M. A. Clark

CABINET OFFICE

The Cabinet Office comprises the Secretariat, who support Ministers collectively in the conduct of Cabinet business; and the Office of Public Service and Science (OPSS) which is responsible for the Citizen's Charter initiative, the Next Steps programme, policy on open government, senior Civil Service and public appointments, and the management and organization of the Civil Service and recruitment into it. It is also responsible for the Civil Service College, the Recruitment and Assessment Services Agency, the Occupational Health Service, HMSO, CCTA (the Government Centre for Information Systems), the Central Office of Information, and the Chessington Computer Centre. The Office of Science and Technology also forms part of the OPSS.

The OPSS supports the Prime Minister in his capacity as Minister for the Civil Service, with responsibility for day-to-day supervision delegated to the Chancellor of the Duchy of Lancaster.

PRIME MINISTER'S OFFICE

Prime Minister and Minister for the Civil Service, The Rt. Hon. John Major, MP
Principal Private Secretary to the Prime Minister (*G2*), A. Allan
Private Secretaries to the Prime Minister, J. S. Wall (*Overseas Affairs*); Mrs M. Francis (*Economic Affairs*); W. Chapman (*Parliamentary Affairs*); M. Adams (*Home Affairs*)
Diary Secretary to the Prime Minister, Miss S. Phillips
Secretary for Appointments (*G5*), J. R. Catford, CBE
Foreign Affairs Adviser, Sir Rodric Braithwaite, KCMG
Efficiency and Competition Adviser, Sir Peter Levene, KBE
Political Secretary, J. Hill
Policy Unit, The Hon. Mrs S. Hogg; N. True; A. Rosling; the Hon. D. Poole; Mrs K. Ramsey; Miss L. Neville-Rolfe; Ms J. Rutter; D. Green
Chief Press Secretary, A. T. O'Donnell
Deputy Chief Press Secretary, J. Haslam
Assistant Private Secretaries to Prime Minister, Miss A. Hordern; Miss J. L. Wilkinson
Parliamentary Private Secretary, G. Bright, MP

Secretary to the Cabinet and Head of Home Civil Service, Sir Robin Butler, GCB, CVO
Private Secretary, Miss S. C. Phippard

SECRETARIAT

70 Whitehall, London SW1A 2AS
Tel 071-270 3000

Deputy Secretaries (*G2*), Miss L. Neville-Jones, CMG; P. F. Owen, CB; D. Hadley, CB
Under Secretaries (*G3*), M. Russell; N. Bevan, CB; T. J. Burr; B. G. Bender
Grade 5, J. Dilling; J. Sibson; Brig. J. A. J. Budd; S. G. Eldon
Grade 6, R. Hope

ESTABLISHMENT OFFICER'S GROUP

Government Offices, Great George Street, London SW1P 3AL
Tel 071-270 3000

Principal Establishment and Finance Officer (*G3*), S. R. Davie
Deputy Establishment Officer (*G5*), G. S. Royston
Senior Finance Officer (*G6*), Miss J. M. E. Buchan

HISTORICAL AND RECORDS SECTION
Hepburn House, Marsham Street, London SW1P 4HW
Tel 071-217 6032

Grade 6, Miss P. M. Andrews

CEREMONIAL OFFICER
53 Parliament Street, London SW1A 2NG
Tel 071-210 5056

Grade 6, J. H. Thompson, CB

OFFICE OF PUBLIC SERVICE AND SCIENCE (OPSS)

Horse Guards Road, London SW1P 3AL
70 Whitehall, London SW1A 2AS
Tel 071-270 5811

Chancellor of the Duchy of Lancaster and Minister of Public Service and Science, The Rt. Hon. William Waldegrave, MP
Principal Private Secretary, A. T. Cahn
Special Advisers, Sir Peter Levene, KBE; I. Wilton
Parliamentary Private Secretary, I. Taylor, MBE, MP
Parliamentary Under Secretary of State, Robert Jackson, MP
Private Secretary, W. E. Jones
Second Permanent Secretary (G1A), R. C. Mottram
Parliamentary Clerk, Miss T. N. Terry

CITIZEN'S CHARTER UNIT
Government Offices, Great George Street, London SW1P 3AL
Tel 071-270 6343

Director (G2), B. Hilton, CB
Deputy Director (G6), Mrs D. A. Goldsworthy

NEXT STEPS PROJECT TEAM
Government Offices, Great George Street, London SW1P 3AL
Tel 071-270 6454

Director (G5), Miss S. C. Phippard

EFFICIENCY UNIT
70 Whitehall, London SW1A 2AS
Tel 071-260 0273

Prime Minister's Adviser on Efficiency and Effectiveness, Sir Peter Levene, KBE
Head of Unit (G3), D. Brereton
Deputy Head of Unit (G5), G. D. Coley

MANAGEMENT DEVELOPMENT GROUP

Under Secretary (G3), J. K. Moore
Grade 5, R. D. J. White; Miss S. Haird; C. J. Parry

TOP MANAGEMENT PROGRAMME

Director of Programme (G3), Miss M. T. Neville-Rolfe
Course Directors (G5), Mrs P. Clarkson; Mrs M. Chapman

SENIOR AND PUBLIC APPOINTMENTS GROUP AND EUROPEAN STAFFING

Under Secretary (G3), A. J. Merifield
Grade 5, D. Laughrin; Mrs K. B. Elliott

INFORMATION DIVISION

Press Secretary and Head of Information (G5), P. Rose

MACHINERY OF GOVERNMENT

Grade 5, A. D. Whetnall

SECURITY DIVISION

Grade 5, R. D. J. Wright

OFFICE OF THE CIVIL SERVICE COMMISSIONERS (OCSC)
Alencon Link, Basingstoke, Hants. RG21 1JB
Tel 0256-29222

First Commissioner (G2), J. H. Holroyd (*London*)
Commissioner (G3), M. D. Geddes (*Chief Executive, RAS*)
Commissioners (part-time), Ms U. Prashar; Mrs J. Rubin; A. Maddrell; K. E. C. Sorensen

MANAGEMENT UNIT

Information Officer (G5), T. J. Perks

CHESSINGTON COMPUTER CENTRE
Government Buildings, Leatherhead Road, Chessington, Surrey KT9 2LT
Tel 081-391 3800

Director (G6), R. N. Edwards

CCTA (THE GOVERNMENT CENTRE FOR INFORMATION SYSTEMS)
Riverwalk House, 157–161 Millbank, London SW1P 4RT
Tel 071-217 3000
Gildengate House, Upper Green Lane, Norwich NR3 1DW
Tel 0603-694620

Director (G3), I. P. Wilson
Deputy Director (G4), W. Houldsworth

OFFICE OF SCIENCE AND TECHNOLOGY

70 Whitehall, London SW1A 2AS
Tel 071-270 3000
Grove House, 16 Orange Street, London WC2H 7ED
Tel 071-270 6944
Sanctuary Buildings, Great Smith Street, London SW1P 3BT
Tel 071-925 5000

Chief Scientific Adviser and Head of Office, Prof. W. D. P. Stewart, FRS, FRSE

BRANCH A

Grade 3, R. Foster
Grade 5, Dr D. P. Walker (*Domestic S. & T. issues*); D. A. Warren (*International S. & T. issues*); Dr J. McGuinness (*ACOST Secretariat*)

BRANCH B

Grade 3, D. A. Wilkinson
Grade 5, Dr J. Partington (*General Science Policy*); R. P. Ritzema (*International Science*)
Grade 6, Dr K. Root (*Science Budget*)

ADVISORY BOARD FOR THE RESEARCH COUNCILS

Chairman, Sir David Phillips, KBE, FRS
Secretary (G3), Dr D. G. Libby

EXECUTIVE AGENCIES

OCCUPATIONAL HEALTH SERVICE
18–20 Hill Street, Edinburgh EH2 3NB
Tel 031-220 4177

Medical Adviser and Director, Dr G. S. Sorrie
Deputy Medical Adviser, Dr P. Brown

CIVIL SERVICE COLLEGE
Sunningdale Park, Ascot, Berks. SL5 0QE
Tel 0344-634000
11 Belgrave Road, London SW1V 1RB
Tel 071-834 6644

Chief Executive (G3), Miss M. T. Neville-Rolfe
Director of Studies (G5), D. R. Smith

Director of Services and Resources (*G5*), I. Cameron
Business Group Directors (*G5/G6*), Ms C. M. Bentley; Ms E. Chennells; P. A. Daffern; J. G. Fuller; P. J. C. O'Connell; P. G. Tebby; Miss J. A. Topham
College Secretary (*G6*), Miss M. A. Wood

RECRUITMENT AND ASSESSMENT SERVICES (RAS)
Alencon Link, Basingstoke, Hants. RG21 1JB
Tel 0256-29222
24 Whitehall, London SW1A 2ED
Tel 071-210 3000

Chief Executive, M. D. Geddes
Grade 5, A. A. Carter (*London*); Miss E. Goodison
Grade 6, F. D. Bedford (*London*); P. Cook; K. N. Bastin

CENTRAL STATISTICAL OFFICE

Great George Street, London SW1P 3AQ
Tel 071-270 6363/6364

The work of the Central Statistical Office encompasses data collection from businesses; the preparation and publication of macro-economic statistics and social statistics abstracts; statistics relating to institutional sectors and financial statistics; the retail prices index and the family expenditure survey; liaison with international statistical bodies; and central management of the Government Statistical Service (GSS). The Central Statistical Office became an executive agency in November 1991.

Director and Head of the Government Statistical Service (*G1A*), W. McLennan
Private Secretary, Miss H. Shanks
Deputy Director and Director of National Accounts (*G3*), D. C. L. Wroe
Head of Division 1 (*G3*), R. G. Ward
Head of Division 2 (*G3*), N. Harvey
Head of Division 3 (*G3*), J. E. Kidgell
Head of Division 4 and Principal Establishment and Finance Officer (*G4*), F. Martin
Head of Information (*G5*), J. B. Wright

DIVISION 1

Heads of Branches (*G5*):
Branch 1, D. C. K. Stirling (*GSS policy and management*)
Branch 2, T. J. Griffin (*Social, regional and international*)
Branch 3, D. J. Sellwood (*Consumer prices; family expenditure survey; distribution and redistribution of income*)
Branch 4, R. J. Scott (*Registers; energy and materials inquiries; classifications; survey control*)

DEPUTY DIRECTOR'S OFFICE

Heads of Branches (*G5*):
Branch 5, Miss S. P. Carter (*Central national accounts coordination; national accounts training; economic assessment*)
Branch 6, P. B. Kenny (*Research, development and evaluation*)

DIVISION 2

Heads of Branches (*G5*):
Branch 7, K. Francombe (*Index of production and manufacturing output*)
Branch 8, C. J. Spiller (*Annual censuses of production and construction; stocks and capital expenditure inquiries*)
Branch 9, R. M. Norton (*Distribution and services*)
Branch 10, R. G. Lynch (*Producer prices; annual and quarterly sales inquiries*)
Branch 11, K. Mansell (*Consumers' expenditure; capital formation; output other than production industries*)

DIVISION 3

Heads of Branches (*G5*):
Branch 12, G. Jenkinson (*External trade*)
Branch 13, B. J. Buckingham (*Balance of payments*)
Branch 14, Mrs P. Walker (*Company and personal sector accounts*)
Branch 15, P. Turnbull (*Financial statistics; public sector accounts; R&D statistics*)

DIVISION 4

Heads of Branches (*G5*):
Branch 16, Dr J. Ludley (*Information systems*)
Branch 17, J. B. Wright (*Press, publications and publicity*)
Branch 18, D. R. Lewis (*Establishment and finance*)
Branch 19, S. Clark (*Financial Institutions*)

CERTIFICATION OFFICE FOR TRADE UNIONS AND EMPLOYERS' ASSOCIATIONS

27 Wilton Street, London SW1X 7AZ
Tel 071-210 3734/5

The Certification Office is an independent statutory authority. The Certification Officer is appointed by the Secretary of State for Employment and is responsible for receiving and scrutinizing annual returns from trade unions and employers' associations; for reimbursing certain costs of trade unions' postal ballots; for dealing with complaints concerning trade union elections; for ensuring observance of statutory requirements governing political funds and trade union mergers; and for certifying the independence of trade unions.

Certification Officer, M. Wake
Assistant Certification Officer, G. S. Osborne

SCOTLAND
58 Frederick Street, Edinburgh EH2 1LN
Tel 031-226 3224
Assistant Certification Officer for Scotland, J. L. J. Craig

CHARITY COMMISSION

St Alban's House, 57–60 Haymarket, London SW1Y 4QX
Tel 071-210 3000
Graeme House, Derby Square, Liverpool L2 7SB
Tel 051-227 3191
Woodfield House, Tangier, Taunton, Somerset TA1 4BL
Tel 0823-345000

The Charity Commissioners are appointed under the Charities Act 1960, principally to further the work of charities in England and Wales by giving advice and information, and information, and by investigating and checking abuses. The Commissioners maintain a register of charities; give consent to land transactions; help to modernize the purposes and administrative machinery of charities; and, in the name of one of their staff, the Official Custodian for Charities, hold investments for charities.

At the end of 1991 the total number of registered charities was 166,503.

Chief Commissioner (G3), R. Fries
Commissioners (G3), J. Farquharson; R. M. C. Venables
Commissioners (part-time) (G4), M. Webber; Mrs D. H. Yeo
Deputy Commissioners (G5), J. A. Dutton; J. F. Claricoat; G. S. Goodchild; K. M. Dibble; S. Slack
Secretary and Executive Director (G4), Mrs E. A. Shaw
Director of Operations (G5), V. F. Mitchell
Grade 6, Mrs H. M. Phillips; Miss D. F. Taylor; S. K. Sen; P. P. White; N. M. Mackenzie; M. J. Harbottle; J. Tipping; R. E. Edwards; Miss V. A. Nuttall
Senior Legal Assistants, A. H. Bilbrough; I. M. Davies
Grade 7, R. E. Hatton; A. O. Polak; M. C. T. Seymour; K. M. Dickin; M. J. McManus; G. B. Ward; Mrs M. E. Whittaker; J. S. Holdsworth; M. Pearson; P. W. Somerfield; R. G. Dawes; Miss G. Fletcher; A. J. George; J. Thorne; I. Spencer; A. P. Kelly; Mrs P. D. W. Holt; J. Kilby; R. Jones; Miss B. Lythgoe
Official Custodian for Charities (G6), Mrs S. E. Gillingham
Deputy Official Custodian (G7), M. Fry
Establishment Officer (G5), D. Truman

The departments responsible for charities in Scotland and Northern Ireland are:

SCOTLAND – Scottish Home and Health Department, Charities Division, New St Andrews House, Edinburgh EH1 3DE. Tel: 031-244 2206

NORTHERN IRELAND – Department of Finance and Personnel, Charities Branch, Rosepark House, Upper Newtownards Road, Belfast BT4 3NR. Tel: 0232-484567

CHIEF ADJUDICATION SERVICES

Quarry House, Leeds LS2 7UB
Tel 0532-324000

The Chief Adjudication Officer and Chief Child Support Officer are independent statutory authorities under the Social Security Act 1975 (as amended) and the Child Support Act 1991. They are appointed by the Secretary of State for Social Security to give advice to adjudication officers and child support officers, to keep under review the operation of the systems of adjudication, and to report annually to the Secretary of State on adjudication standards.

Adjudication officers make decisions of first instance on all claims for social security cash benefits, and child support officers will make decisions of first instance on applications for child maintenance made to the Child Support Agency from April 1993. Officers of the Chief Adjudication Officer also enter written observations on all appeals made to the Social Security Commissioners, and from April 1993 officers of the Chief Child Support Officer will make observations on appeals to the Child Support Commissioners.

Chief Adjudication Officer and Chief Child Support Officer, K. Bellamy

CHURCH COMMISSIONERS

1 Millbank, London SW1P 3JZ
Tel 071-222 7010

The Church Commissioners were established in 1948 by the amalgamation of Queen Anne's Bounty (established 1704) and the Ecclesiastical Commissioners (established 1836).

The Commissioners are responsible for the management of the greater part of the Church of England's assets, the income from which is predominantly used to pay, house and pension the clergy. The Commissioners own over 150,000 acres of agricultural land, a number of residential estates in central London, and commercial property in Great Britain and the USA. They also carry out administrative duties in connection with pastoral reorganization and redundant churches, and have been designated by the General Synod as the central stipends authority of the Church of England.

INCOME AND EXPENDITURE

for year ended 31 December 1991

INCOME	*£ million*
Stock exchange investments	66.0
Property	54.8
Interest from loans, etc.	45.7
Diocesan/parish contributions for stipends	76.9
Total	£243.4
EXPENDITURE	
Clergy stipends	141.0
Clergy and widows' pensions	58.3
Clergy houses	12.5
Episcopal administration and payments to Chapters	10.3
Church buildings	2.9
Administrative expenses of the Commissioners and related bodies	12.7
Carried forward	5.7
Total	£243.4

CONSTITUTION

The Archbishops of Canterbury and of York; the 41 diocesan Bishops; five deans or provosts, ten other clergy and ten laymen appointed by the General Synod; four laymen nominated by The Queen; four persons nominated by the Archbishop of Canterbury; The Lord Chancellor; The Lord President of the Council; the First Lord of the Treasury; The Chancellor of the Exchequer; The Secretary of State for the Home Department; The Speaker of the House of Commons; The Lord Chief Justice; The Master of the Rolls; The Attorney-General; The Solicitor-General; The Lord Mayor and two Aldermen of the City of London; The Lord Mayor of York and one representative from each of the Universities of Oxford and Cambridge.

CHURCH ESTATES COMMISSIONERS

First, Sir Douglas Lovelock, KCB
Second, Rt. Hon. Michael Alison, MP
Third, Mrs M. H. Laird

OFFICERS

Secretary, P. Locke
Assistant Secretaries:
Chief Accountant, D. I. Archer
Deputy Accountant, G. C. Baines
Commercial Property, M. G. S. Farrell
Computer Manager, J. W. Ferguson
Establishment Officer, W. R. Herbert
Estates, P. H. P. Shaw, LVO
General Purposes, M. D. Elengorn
Houses, D. J. B. Long
Investments Manager, A. S. Hardy
Pastoral, D. N. Goodwin
Redundant Churches, J. M. Davies
Stipends and Allocations, R. S. Hopgood
Senior Architect, J. A. Taylor
Senior Principal, B. J. Hardy
Principals, A. W. Atkins; Miss A. M. Mackie; G. Wills; J. A. W. Elloy; C. R. Bullen; D. W. H. Lewis; N. J. Neil-Smith; J. W. Wallace; R. A. Scott

Legal Department

Official Solicitor, E. W. Wills
Deputy Solicitor, J. P. Guy
Solicitors, Miss J. M. Bland; J. D. Carter; Miss J. A. Egar; Miss S. M. S. Jones; R. D. C. Murray; T. Tayleur; Ms A. R. Usher

CIVIL AVIATION AUTHORITY

CAA House, 45–59 Kingsway, London WC2B 6TE
Tel 071-379 7311

The CAA is responsible for the economic regulation of UK airlines by licensing air routes, air travel organizers and approving fares; for the safety regulation of UK civil aviation by the certification of airlines and aircraft, and by licensing aerodromes, flight crew and aircraft engineers; and, through the National Air Traffic Services, for the provision of air traffic control and telecommunications services.

Chairman (part-time) (£57,750), The Rt. Hon. C. Chataway
Managing Director, T. Murphy, CBE
Secretary, Miss G. M. E. White

COMMONWEALTH DEVELOPMENT CORPORATION

1 Bessborough Gardens, London SW1V 2JQ
Tel 071-828 4488

The Commonwealth Development Corporation is charged with the task of assisting overseas countries in the development of their economies. Its main activity is providing long-term finance, as loans and risk capital, for projects. The Corporation's area of operations covers British dependent territories and, with ministerial approval, any Commonwealth or other developing country. At present, the Corporation is authorized to operate in about 50 countries in addition to the British dependent territories. The Corporation is authorized to borrow up to £850,000,000.

Chairman (part-time), Sir Peter Leslie
Deputy Chairman (part-time), Sir Michael Caine
Members (part-time), Mrs A. Wright; M. D. Nightingale, OBE; Prof. M. Faber; E. B. Waide, OBE; M. D. McWilliam
Chief Executive, J. D. Eccles, CBE

Commonwealth Secretariat – *see* Index

COMMONWEALTH WAR GRAVES COMMISSION

2 Marlow Road, Maidenhead, Berkshire SL6 7DX
Tel 0628-34221

The Commonwealth War Graves Commission (formerly Imperial War Graves Commission) was founded by Royal Charter in 1917. It is responsible for the commemoration of 1,695,000 members of the forces of the Commonwealth who fell in the two world wars. More than one million graves are maintained in 23,071 burial grounds throughout the world. Over three-quarters of a million men and women who have no known grave or who were cremated are commemorated by name on memorials built by the Commission.

The funds of the Commission are derived from the six governments participating in its work, the UK, Australia, Canada, India, New Zealand and South Africa.

President, HRH The Duke of Kent, KG, GCMG, GCVO, ADC
Chairman, The Secretary of State for Defence in the UK
Vice-Chairman, Gen. Sir Robert Ford, GCB, CBE
Members, The Secretary of State for the Environment in the UK; The High Commissioners in London for Australia, Canada, India and New Zealand; the Ambassador in London for the Republic of South Africa; The Rt. Hon. J. D. Concannon; Dame Janet Fookes, DBE, MP; Sir Derek Day, KCMG; Sir Nigel Mobbs; Adm. Sir Nicholas Hunt, GCB, LVO; Air Chief Marshal Sir Joseph Gilbert, KCB, CBE; The Viscount Ridley, KG, TD; Prof. R. J. O'Neill, AO
Director-General, J. Saynor, CMG
Deputy Director-Generals, T. F. Penfold (*Administration*); R. J. Dalley (*Operations*)
Directors, T. V. Reeves (*Finance*); A. Coombe (*Works*); D. C. Parker (*Horticulture*); H. Mackay (*Management Services*); D. R. Parker (*Personnel*); J. P. D. Gee (*Information and Secretariat*)
Legal Adviser and Solicitor, G. C. Reddie
Hon. Artistic Adviser, Prof. Sir Peter Shepheard, CBE
Hon. Botanical Adviser, Prof. G. T. Prance, D.Phil., FLS

Imperial War Graves Endowment Fund

Trustees, H. U. A. Lambert (*chairman*); Gen. Sir Robert Ford, GCB, CBE; The Lord Remnant, CVO
Secretary to the Trustees, T. V. Reeves

COUNTRYSIDE COMMISSION

John Dower House, Crescent Place, Cheltenham, Glos. GL50 3RA
Tel 0242-521381

The Countryside Commission is an independent agency set up in 1968 to promote the conservation and enhancement of landscape beauty in England and Wales, to encourage the provision and improvement of facilities in the countryside for enjoyment, including the need to secure access for open air recreation. Since April 1982 the Commission has been funded by annual grant from the Department of the Environment. Members of the Commission are appointed by the Secretary of State for the Environment.

Since 1 April 1991, the Countryside Commission's responsibilities in Wales have been discharged by the new Countryside Council for Wales.

Chairman, Sir John Johnson, KCMG
Director-General (G3), M. Dower
Directors (G5), R. Clarke (*Policy*); M. J. Kirby (*Operations*); M. Taylor (*Resources*)
Deputy Director (Operations) (G6), D. E. Coleman
National Heritage Adviser, P. Walshe
Head of Corporate Planning (G7), T. Robinson
Head of Land Use Branch (G7), R. Roberts
Head of Recreation and Access Branch (G7), J. W. B. Worth
Head of Communications Branch (G7), C. Pugsley
Head of Finance and Establishments (G7), V. Ellis
Head of National Parks and Planning Branch (G7), R. Lloyd
Head of Environmental Protection Branch (G7), I. Mitchell
Regional Officers (G7), K. Buchanan, (*Newcastle*); Dr M. Carroll (*Cambridge*); Dr S. A. Bucknall (*Leeds*); E. Holdaway (*Bristol*); R. T. Thomas (*Manchester*); L. Leeson (*London*); F. S. Walmsley (*Birmingham*)
Special Initiatives, Dr M. Rawson (*Community Forests*); S. Bell (*National Forest*); T. Allen (*Countryside Stewardship*)

COUNTRYSIDE COUNCIL FOR WALES

(CYNGOR CEFN GWLAD CYMRU)
Plas Penrhos, Fford Penrhos, Bangor, Gwynedd LL57 2LQ
Tel 0248-370444

The Countryside Council for Wales took over the functions of the Nature Conservancy Council in Wales and the Countryside Commission in Wales on 1 April 1991. It is accountable to the Secretary of State for Wales and exists to promote the conservation and enhancement of the quality of the Welsh landscape and wildlife and to encourage opportunities for public access and enjoyment of the counryside.

Chairman, E. M. W. Griffith, CBE
Chief Executive, I. Mercer

COVENT GARDEN MARKET AUTHORITY

Covent House, New Covent Garden Market, London SW8 5NX
Tel 071-720 2211

The Covent Garden Market Authority is constituted under the Covent Garden Market Acts 1961 to 1977, the members being appointed by the Minister of Agriculture, Fisheries and Food. The Authority owns and operates the 56-acre New Covent Garden Markets (fruit, vegetable, flowers) which have been trading since 1974.

Chairman (part-time), W. P. Bowman, OBE
Members (part-time), P. J. Hunt; J. A. Harvey, CBE; R. Smith, OBE; Sir Peter Reynolds, CBE
General Manager, Dr P. M. Liggins
Secretary, C. Farey

CRIMINAL INJURIES COMPENSATION BOARD

Blythswood House, 200 West Regent Street, Glasgow G2 4SW
Tel 041-221 0945
Whittington House, 19 Alfred Place, London WC1E 7LG
Tel 071-636 9501 and 071-636 2812

The Board was constituted in 1964 to administer the government scheme for *ex gratia* payments of compensation to victims of crimes of violence.

Chairman (part-time) (£24,050), The Lord Carlisle of Bucklow, PC, QC
Members, J. F. A. Archer, QC; D. Barker, QC, Sir Derek Bradbeer, OBE; D. Brennan, QC; Sir David Calcutt, QC; H. Carlisle, QC; B. W. Chedlow, QC; J. Cherry, QC; M. Churchouse; Miss B. Cooper, QC; Miss D. Cotton, QC; J. D. Crowley, QC; His Hon. Judge da Cunha; T. A. K. Drummond, QC; C. Fawcett, QC; W. Gage, QC; E. Gee; B. Green, QC; G. M. Hamilton, QC; C. Holland, QC; Sir Arthur Hoole; His Hon. Judge Kellock, QC; His Hon. Judge Kingham; J. Law, QC; M. E. Lewer, QC; J. Leighton Williams, QC; C. Lindsay, QC; Lord Macaulay of Bragar, QC; J. M. McGhie, QC, D. MacKay, QC; I. M. S. Park, CBE; T. Preston, QC; Miss S. Ritchie, QC; D. B. Robertson, QC; C. Seagroatt, QC; Mrs J. Smith, QC; E. Stone, QC; D. M. Thomas, OBE, QC; D. O. Thomas, QC; P. Weitzman, QC; Sir David West-Russell; C. H. Whitby, QC
Director, Mrs L. Palletti

CROFTERS COMMISSION

4–6 Castle Wynd, Inverness IV2 3EQ
Tel 0463-237231

The Crofters Commission was established by Act of Parliament in 1955 and is responsible for reorganizing, developing and regulating crofting in the seven crofting (and former county) areas of Argyll, Caithness, Inverness, Orkney, Ross and Cromarty, Shetland and Sutherland. The Commission keeps under review all matters relating to crofting, advises the Secretary of State for Scotland on crofting matters and liaises with other relevant bodies. The Commission also administers the Crofting Counties Agricultural Grants (Scotland) Scheme 1988.

Chairman, H. A. M. Maclean
Members (part-time), B. T. Hunter; D. A. Morrison; P. Morrison; A. Cameron; W. Ritchie
Secretary (G6), A. Johnston

CROWN AGENTS FOR OVERSEA GOVERNMENTS AND ADMINISTRATIONS

St Nicholas House, St Nicholas Road, Sutton, Surrey SM1 1EL
Tel 081-643 3311

Incorporated by Act of Parliament, the Crown Agents are commercial, financial and professional agents for over 100 governments and over 300 public authorities, international bodies and other organizations, primarily in the public sector.

Chairman, D. H. Probert
Managing Director, P. F. Berry

CROWN ESTATE

16 Carlton House Terrace, London SW1Y 5AH
Tel 071-210 4377

The land revenues of the Crown in England and Wales have been collected on the public account since 1760, when George III surrendered them and received a fixed annual payment or Civil List. At the time of the surrender the gross revenues amounted to about £89,000 and the net return to about £11,000.

In the year ended 31 March 1992, the gross income from the Crown Estate totalled £113,693,000. The sum of £70,000,000 was paid to the Exchequer in 1991–2 as surplus revenue.

The land revenues in Ireland have been carried to the Consolidated Fund since 1820; from 1 April 1923, as regards the Republic of Ireland, they have been collected and administered by the Irish Government.

The land revenues in Scotland were transferred to the Crown Estate Commissioners in 1833.

First Commissioner and Chairman (part-time), The Earl of Mansfield and Mansfield
Second Commissioner and Chief Executive, C. K. Howes

Commissioners (part-time), R. B. Caws, CBE; P. Sober; G. D. I. Lillingston, CBE; J. N. C. James, CBE; A. S. Macdonald, CBE; J. H. M. Norris, CBE
Deputy Chief Executive, H. B. Clarke
Crown Estate Surveyor, C. F. Hynes
Asset Managers (Urban Estates), M. W. Dillon; J. S. Ellingford; B. T. O'Connoll; M. Tree
Housing Manager, R. Wyatt
Business Manager, Agricultural Estates, R. J. Mulholland
Asset Managers, Agricultural Estates, J. Stumbke; I. Gorwyn
Business Manager, Marine Estates, F. G. Parrish
Asset Managers, Marine Estates, P. Davies; A. Murray
Accountant and Receiver-General, D. E. G. Griffiths
Information Systems Manager, D. Kingston-Smith
Property Services and Technical Manager, P. Shearmur
Head of Valuation and Investment Analysis, R. Spence
Head of Building Services, R. Turner
Internal Audit Manager, J. E. Ford
Finance Manager, J. G. Lelliott
Corporate Services Manager, M. E. Beckwith
Legal Adviser, M. L. Davies
Deputy Legal Adviser, H. Turnsek
Solicitors, J. B. Postgate; R. T. Hayward; M. Drayton; P. Horner; D. R. Apthorpe
Senior Legal Assistant, M. A. J. Cordingley
Personnel Manager, R. J. Blake
Public Relations and Press Officer, Mrs G. Coates

SCOTLAND
10 Charlotte Square, Edinburgh EH2 4BR
Tel 031-226 2741

Crown Estate Receiver for Scotland, M. J. Gravestock
Asset Managers (Scottish Estates), N. Ruck Keene; I. Pritchard; Ms S. Harvey
Glenlivet Estate Ranger, A. Wells

WINDSOR ESTATE
The Great Park, Windsor, Berks. SL4 2HT
Tel 0753-860222

Surveyor and Deputy Ranger, A. R. Wiseman, MVO
Keeper of Gardens, J. Bond

CROWN PROSECUTION SERVICE – *see* pages 381–2

BOARD OF CUSTOMS AND EXCISE

New King's Beam House, 22 Upper Ground, London SE1 9PJ
Tel 071-620 1313

Commissioners of Customs were first appointed in 1671 and housed by the King in London. The present 'Long Room' in the Custom House, Lower Thames Street, London EC3, replaced that built by Charles II and was rebuilt after destruction by fire in 1718 and 1814. The Excise Department was formerly under the Inland Revenue Department and was amalgamated with the Customs Department in 1909.

HM Customs and Excise is responsible for collecting and administering customs and excise duties and value added tax, and advises the Chancellor of the Exchequer on any matters connected with them. The Department is also responsible for preventing and detecting the evasion of revenue laws and for enforcing a range of prohibitions and restrictions on the importation of certain classes of goods. In addition, the Department undertakes certain agency work on behalf of other departments, including the compilation of UK overseas trade statistics from customs import and export documents.

THE BOARD

Chairman (G1), Sir Brian Unwin, KCB
Private Secretaries, S. Harlen; Miss J. C. Huneburg
Deputy Chairmen (G2), Mrs V. P. M. Strachan, CB; P. Jefferson Smith, CB
Commissioners (G3), A. W. Russell; P. R. H. Allen; D. F. O. Battle; A. C. Sawyer; L. J. Harris; Ms E. Woods; M. J. Eland

HEADQUARTERS OFFICE

Head of Information Technology (G4), A. G. H. Paynter
Assistant Secretaries (G5), P. Kent; D. A. Walton; J. W. Tracey; M. R. Brown; I. Walton; A. Killikelly; M. Peach; K. M. Romanski; Ms D. Barrett; B. E. G. Banks; J. P. Bone; D. C. Hewett; A. Ferguson; A. F. Cross-Rudkin; C. J. Holloway; P. Trevett; B. G. Dawbarn; Mrs M. Smith; J. Campbell; V. C. Whittington; P. A. Blomfield; C. Arnott; D. P. Child; J. Strachan; R. Kellaway; M. F. Knox; M. W. Summers; F. A. D. Rush; W. L. Parker; L. I. Stark; A. P. Allen; J. Meyler
Head of Information (G7), Ms L. J. Sinclair

VAT CENTRAL UNIT

Controller (G5), M. J. Wardle
Deputy Controller (G6), B. Smith

SOLICITOR'S OFFICE

Solicitor (G2), vacant
Principal Assistant Solicitors (G3), G. F. Butt; R. D. S. Wylie
Assistant Solicitors (G5), M. Michael; M. A. Cooper; D. E. T. S. Keefe; M. C. K. Gasper; Miss A. E. Bolt; D. Pratt; Miss S. G. Linton; J. A. Quin; I. D. Napper; G. Fotherby; G. W. H. McFarlane; D. J. C. McIntyre; D. M. North

ACCOUNTANT AND COMPTROLLER-GENERAL'S OFFICE

Accountant and Comptroller-General (G5), P. A. Blomfield
Deputy Accountants-General (G6), M. Deedman; G. B. Fox

STATISTICAL OFFICE

Controller (G5), A. H. Cowley

INVESTIGATION DIVISION

Chief Investigation Officer (G5), F. D. Tweddle

COLLECTORS OF CUSTOMS AND EXCISE (*G5*)

England and Wales

Birmingham, R. A. Flavill
Dover, R. Crossley
East Anglia, R. C. Shephard
East Midlands, M. D. Patten
Leeds, W. J. G. Prollins
Liverpool, C. Roberts
London Airports, J. Bugge
London Central, Mrs F. Boardman
London North and West, C. A. Bray
London Port, R. L. H. Lawrence
London South, T. S. Archer
Manchester, J. C. Barnard
Northampton, P. E. St Quinton
Northern England, J. McKenzie
Reading, A. Bowen
Southampton, C. J. Packman
South Wales and the Borders, W. I. Stuttle
South West England, P. B. Grange

Scotland

Edinburgh, W. F. Coghill
Glasgow and Clyde, T. F. Jessop

Northern Ireland

Belfast, R. N. McAfee

OFFICE OF THE DATA PROTECTION REGISTRAR

Wycliffe House, Water Lane, Wilmslow, Cheshire SK9 5AX
Tel 0625-535711 (*administration*); 0625-535777 (*enquiries*)

The Office of the Data Protection Registrar was created by the Data Protection Act 1984. It is the Registrar's duty to compile and maintain the Register of Data Users and Computer Bureaux and provide facilities for members of the public to examine the Register; to promote observance of the data protection principles; to consider complaints made by data subjects; to disseminate information about the Act; to encourage the production of codes of practice by trade associations and other bodies; to guide data users in complying with the data protection principles; to co-operate with other parties to the Council of Europe Convention and act as UK authority for the purposes of Article 13 of the Convention; and to report annually to Parliament on the performance of his functions.

Registrar, E. J. Howe, CBE

MINISTRY OF DEFENCE, *see* pages 395–8

DESIGN COUNCIL

28 Haymarket, London SW1Y 4SU
Tel 071-839 8000

The Design Council's aim is to improve the design of British products and hence their competitiveness by advising companies on up-to-date practice in engineering and industrial design; presenting the annual British Design Awards; publishing information to help manufacturers, designers, and others professionally involved in design; and promoting improvements in design education and training at all levels. The headquarters and main exhibition area are in London and there are offices in Glasgow, Leeds, Newcastle upon Tyne, Belfast, Wolverhampton, Manchester, and Treforest in Wales. The Design Council is funded partly by a government grant-in-aid and partly by earned revenues.

Chairman, Sir Simon Hornby
Director, I. Owen, CBE

THE DUCHY OF CORNWALL

10 Buckingham Gate, London SW1E 6LA
Tel 071-834 7346

The Duchy of Cornwall was instituted by Edward III in 1337 for the support of his eldest son, Edward, the Black Prince, and since 1503 the eldest surviving son of the Sovereign has, as heir apparent, succeeded to the dukedom by inheritance. It is the oldest of the English duchies. Before elevation to a dukedom, it was an earldom from 1227, when Richard, King of the Romans and younger brother of Henry III, was created Earl of Cornwall.

THE PRINCE'S COUNCIL

HRH The Prince of Wales, KG, KT, GCB; The Lord Ashburton, KCVO (*Lord Warden of the Stannaries*); The Earl Cairns (*Receiver-General*); R. J. A. Carnwath, QC (*Attorney-General to the Prince of Wales*); D. W. N. Landale (*Secretary and Keeper of the Records*); Earl of Shelburne; Cdr. R. J. Aylard, RN; J. E. Pugsley; J. N. C. James, CBE; A. M. J. Galsworthy; C. Howes

OTHER OFFICERS OF THE DUCHY OF CORNWALL

Auditors, Sir Jeffery Bowman; P. L. Ainger; H. Hughes
Sheriff (1992–3), E. M. L. Latham

THE DUCHY OF LANCASTER

Lancaster Place, Strand, London WC2E 7ED
Tel 071-836 8277

The estates and jurisdiction known as the Duchy and County Palatine of Lancaster have been attached to the Crown since 1399, when John of Gaunt's son came to the throne as Henry IV. As the Lancaster inheritance it goes back to 1265. Edward III erected Lancashire into a County Palatine in 1351.

Chancellor of the Duchy of Lancaster, The Rt. Hon. William Waldegrave, MP
Private Secretary, I. Dougal
Attorney-General and Attorney and Serjeant within the County Palatine of Lancaster, Miss M. Arden, QC
Receiver-General, Maj. Sir Shane Blewitt, KCVO
Vice-Chancellor, The Hon. Mr Justice Morritt, CVO
Clerk of the Council and Keeper of Records, M. K. Ridley, CVO
Solicitor, I. J. Dicker
Chief Clerk, Col. F. N. J. Davies

ECONOMIC AND SOCIAL RESEARCH COUNCIL

Polaris House, North Star Avenue, Swindon SN2 1UJ
Tel 0793-413000

The ESRC is an independent, government-funded body established by Royal Charter in 1965. It supports research carried out in universities, polytechnics and research centres in Britain into economic life and social behaviour. The Council carries out its role by awarding research grants, by initiating research and research contracts, by funding designated research centres, and by awarding postgraduate studentships and bursaries. In addition, the Council provides advice and disseminates knowledge on the social sciences.

Chairman, Prof. H. Newby
Secretary, W. Solesbury

For research centres of the Economic and Social Science Research Council, *see* page 694.

DEPARTMENT FOR EDUCATION

Sanctuary Buildings, Great Smith Street, London SW1P 3BT
Tel 071-925 5000

The Government Department of Education was, until the establishment of a separate office, a Committee of the Privy Council appointed in 1839 to supervise the distribution of certain grants which had been made by Parliament since 1834. The Act of 1899 established the Board of Education, with a President and Parliamentary Secretary, and created a Consultative Committee. The Education Act of 1944 established the Ministry of Education. In April 1964 the office of the Minister of Science was combined with the Ministry to form the Department of Education and Science. In July 1992, responsibility for science was transferred to the Office of Public Service and Science, which was formed following the 1992 General Election, and the department was re-named the Department for Education.

Secretary of State for Education and Science, The Rt. Hon. John Patten, MP
Private Secretary, C. Bienkowska
Parliamentary Private Secretary, M. Carrington, MP
Special Adviser, C. Grantham
Minister of State, The Baroness Blatch, CBE
Private Secretary, A. Pokorny
Parliamentary Private Secretary, D. Evennett, MP
Parliamentary Under Secretaries of State, Nigel Forman, MP; Erich Forth, MP
Permanent Secretary (G1), Sir Geoffrey Holland, KCB
Private Secretary, Miss J. L. Spatcher
Deputy Secretaries (G2), R. J. Dawe, CB, OBE; J. M. M. Vereker, CB; J. C. Hedger
Under Secretaries (G3), M. M. Capey (*Director of Establishments*); C. A. Clark; D. M. Forrester; R. D. Horne; S. R. C. Jones; D. G. Libby; E. R. Morgan; B. M. Norbury; M. J. Richardson; R. N. Ricks (*Legal Adviser*); N. J. Sanders (*Accountant-General*); C. H. Saville; N. Summers; (G4), D. Allnutt
Chief Architect (G4), P. Benwell

SCHOOLS BRANCH 1

Assistant Secretaries (G5), Miss S. L. Scales; A. Clarke; A. J. Shaw
Principals (G7), B. C. Willett; M. E. Malt; C. P. Barnham; A. G. Short; T. C. Tarrant; Miss L. M. Clarke; N. R. Flint; Mrs A. C. Jeffery; C. Dee; R. S. Daruwalla; Mrs S. G. Evans; Mrs R. M. King; Ms M. Pedersen; Mrs C. K. Saville

SCHOOLS BRANCH 2

Assistant Secretaries (G5), Miss D. C. Fordham; Ms J. F. Cramphorn; Mrs P. A. Masters; P. S. Lewis
Principals (G7), C. Dowe; I. C. Loveless; D. Noble; G. A. Holley; I. M. Hughes; M. Spearing; Miss S. A. Clarke; S. Burt; S. Dance; J. Ratcliff; A. B. Thompson; Mrs M. Farthing; M. Rabarts

SCHOOLS BRANCH 3

Assistant Secretaries (G5), M. B. Baker; H. W. B. Davies; Mrs C. M. Chattaway; M. F. Neale
Principals (G7), Mrs S. Jetha; Mrs J. Baker; M. Wardle; Mrs C. Hadijimatheou; Ms G. Beauchamp; Ms A. Rushton; Ms N. Bartman; J. Lawrence; Ms E. Casbon; R. Troedson; S. James

SCHOOLS BRANCH 4

Assistant Secretaries (G5), M. C. Stark; R. L. Smith; A. D. Adamson
Senior Principal (G6), L. Webb
Principals (G7), Mrs P. Bailey; Mrs L. J. Chapman; S. M. Hillier; R. A. V. Jacobs; Mrs M. Moon; J. Moore; G. D. S. Sandeman; Ms E. Slater; J. Sutzbacher; Mrs S. Todd

ARCHITECTS AND BUILDING BRANCH

Chief Architect (G4), P. Benwell
Deputy Chief Architect (G5), A. J. Branton
Chief Quantity Surveyor (G5), B. G. Whitehouse
Superintending Architects (G5), G. J. Parker; J. J. Wilson; D. H. Griffin
Principals (G7), K. L. R. English; A. G. Myatt
Principal Research Officer, Dr G. B. Kenny
Principal Architects, E. C. Bissell; Mrs D. Holt; Miss E. J. Lloyd-Jones, OBE; P. Lenssen; D. S. Nightingale; Miss B. M. T. Sanders; D. F. Wicks; A. J. Benson-Wilson; J. R. C. Brooke; A. C. Thompson; Miss S. A. Legg
Principal Quantity Surveyors, A. A. Jones; W. Horsnell; M. E. H. Sturt
Principal Engineer, M. J. Patel
Principal Furniture Designer, N. J. Carter
SPTO Architects, G. E. Hughes; Miss L. Watson; T. J. Williamson; W. Beadling; R. H. Bishop; A. V. Brock; F. G. Cassidy
SPTO Quantity Surveyor, G. Wonnacott
SPTO Engineer, R. L. Daniels

FURTHER AND HIGHER EDUCATION BRANCH 1

Assistant Secretaries (G5), A. Woollard; R. D. Hull
Principals (G7), A. Sevier; A. Smyth; M. P. Markus; P. Cohen; K. Davey; A. Callaghan

FURTHER AND HIGHER EDUCATION BRANCH 2

Assistant Secretaries (G5), S. T. Crowne; Mrs I. Wilde
Principals (G7), A. J. Coles; P. W. Fulford-Jones; Miss C. E. Treen; Ms S. P. Gane; G. Carters; S. E. Kershaw; Mrs C. West

FURTHER AND HIGHER EDUCATION BRANCH 3

Assistant Secretaries (G5), T. B. Jeffery; M. D. Phipps; A. J. Wye; J. S. Street; S. R. Williams
Principals (G7), Miss A. Barlow; D. D. Cook; P. S. Sharples; J. K. Bushnell; D. M. Carter; C. T. Moorcroft; Ms S. A. Gray; R. H. Campbell; J. Abbott; P. V. Chorley; Ms V. Berkeley; E. D. Foster; O. A. Pereira; Mrs M. Pegg; R. M. Johnston; Mrs P. Tansley; I. Mounteney; Mrs J. Brown

INFORMATION BRANCH

Assistant Secretary (G5), J. W. Coe
Senior Principal Information Officer (G6), K. B. Kerslake
Chief Information Officer (G7), M. Paterson
Marketing Manager (G7), J. M. Brown

INTERNATIONAL RELATIONS, YOUTH AND GENERAL BRANCH

Assistant Secretaries (G5), R. W. Chattaway; Miss C. E. Hodkinson; Miss M. D'Armenia
Principals (G7), Miss L. Hanmer; J. C. Sheridan; R. J. Wood; D. Barwick; Ms C. Dale; D. A. Robins; N. Cornwell

TEACHERS BRANCH

Assistant Secretaries (G5), J. W. Whitaker; A. J. Sargent; J. Wilde
Principals (G7), Mrs G. W. Dishart; S. A. Mellor; M. Barker; E. G. Hartman; P. B. Long; R. H. Mace; D. F. Miller; N. Cornwell; T. Dracup

INFORMATION SYSTEMS BRANCH

Assistant Secretary (G5), A. F. Cowan
Senior Principals (G6), P. D. Gott; A. K. C. Gibson; N. Rudd
Principals (G7), B. Lillburn; Mrs N. A. T. Malt; M. Midwood; A. P. Thompson; D. Craggs; J. Winkle; K. Miles; K. Doherty

ANALYTICAL SERVICES BRANCH

Chief Statisticians (G5), J. W. Gardner; H. M. Dale
Head of Economics (G5), D. J. Thompson
Head of Operations Research Unit (G5), R. B. Ladley
Statisticians (G7), A. J. Barnett; R. K. Jain; S. N. Kew; J. Pascoe; T. C. Knight; M. J. Davidson; N. Rudoe; Mrs H. E. Evans; S. K. Cook; Miss A. C. Kennedy; Mrs J. Airs
Economics Advisers (G7), J. Tarsh; M. Thompson

LEGAL BRANCH

Legal Adviser (G3), R. Ricks
Assistant Legal Advisers (G5), D. J. Aries; A. D. Preston; M. Harris
Assistant Solicitor (G6), Ms J. L. C. Brooks
Senior Legal Assistants (G6), N. P. Beach; S. T. Harker

LIBRARY

Chief Librarian, Miss M. Wilson

FINANCE BRANCH

Assistant Secretaries (G5), Mrs H. M. Williams; P. F. Slade; R. J. Green; N. J. Thirtle
Senior Principal (G6), P. J. Edwards (*Assistant Accountant-General*)
Principals (G7), P. L. Jones; D. R. Pollard; B. G. Townsend; R. J. Gardner; S. N. Jardine; K. Fleay; J. Browning; P. G. Dalgleish; P. V. D. Swift; J. J. Watson; C. Walker; Miss P. Slight

OFFICE FOR STANDARDS IN EDUCATION (OFSTED)

HM Chief Inspector (G2), Prof. S. Sutherland
Director of Administration (G3), T. Flescher
Director of Inspection (G3), Miss A. C. Millett

ESTABLISHMENTS AND ORGANIZATION BRANCH

Assistant Secretaries (G5), Miss J. Gilbey; M. F. Hipkins; A. F. Cowan
Senior Principals (G6), H. H. Barrick; G. H. N. Evans
Principals (G7), C. Bramley; K. R. Fitzgerald; Mrs M. J. Lawrence; S. J. Bishop; Mrs J. M. Craggs; D. Greensmith; M. L. Lyons; Miss B. M. Smart; A. W. Wilshaw

TEACHERS PENSION AGENCY
Staindrop Road, Darlington, Co. Durham DL2 9EE
Tel 0325-392929

An executive agency of the Department for Education.

Chief Executive, Mrs D. Metcalfe
Directors, D. G. Halladay; P. M. Bleasdale; A. Allison; D. G. Sanders

OFFICE OF ELECTRICITY REGULATION

Hagley House, Hagley Road, Birmingham B16 8QG
Tel 021-456 2100

The Office of Electricity Regulation (OFFER) is a regulatory body headed by the Director-General of Electricity Supply, which was set up under the Electricity Act 1989 but is independent of ministerial control.

Director-General of Electricity Supply, Prof. S. C. Littlechild
Deputy Director-General, Miss P. A. Boys
Deputy Director-General for Scotland, R. N. Irvine

DEPARTMENT OF EMPLOYMENT

Caxton House, Tothill Street, London SW1H 9NF
Tel 071-273 3000

The Department of Employment is responsible for government policies aimed at producing a competitive and efficient labour market conducive to the growth of employment and the reduction of unemployment. Its main tasks are to help people acquire and improve their skills and competence for work, to help unemployed people, and to encourage industries to train their workforce. It is also responsible for policies aimed at countering sex discrimination. The Secretary of State for Employment is responsible for setting the strategic policy framework in consultation with the Secretaries of State for Scotland and Wales.

Many of the executive functions carried out in the Department's area of policy interest are exercised by separate public agencies reporting to the Secretary of State for Employment. These include the Health and Safety Commission and ACAS and, within the Department, the Employment Service. The training, enterprise and education functions of the Department are carried out by the Training, Enterprise and Education Directorate; the responsibility for planning and delivering many government-funded training and enterprise programmes rests with the network of 82 independent Training and Enterprise Councils in England and Wales and 22 local enterprise companies in Scotland (for addresses, see local telephone directories).

Secretary of State for Employment, The Rt. Hon. Gillian Shephard, MP
Principal Private Secretary (G5), D. Russell
Special Adviser, Dr Elizabeth Cottrell
Parliamentary Private Secretary, J. Brazier, MP
Minister of State, Michael Forsyth, MP
Parliamentary Private Secretary, D. Conway, MP
Under Secretaries of State, Patrick McLoughlin, MP; The Viscount Ullswater
Private Secretaries, A. Loy; M. Daly; Ms C. Pride
Parliamentary Clerk, Ms M. East
Permanent Secretary (G1), N. Monck
Private Secretary, A. Virgo
Deputy Secretaries (G2), N. W. Stuart, CB; G. Reid, CB; I. Johnston
Legal Adviser (G3), H. R. L. Purse
Special Advisers, I. Wilton; Ms C. Stratton

THE EMPLOYMENT SERVICE

An executive agency within the Department of Employment.

Chief Executive (G3+), M. E. G. Fogden
Deputy Chief Executive (G3), J. Turner
Director of Field Operations (G4), J. W. Cooper, CBE
Director of Personnel and Business Services (G4), D. B. Price
Director of Programmes (G4), M. Emmott

TRAINING, ENTERPRISE AND EDUCATION DIRECTORATE
Moorfoot, Sheffield S1 4PQ
Tel 0742-753275

Director-General (G2), I. Johnston
Director of Operations (G3), S. Loveman
Head of Financial Control Unit (G5), N. Gregory
Regional Directors (G5), Ms C. Johnson (*Eastern*); P. Lauener (*East Midlands*); W. Harris (*London*); K. Heslop (*Northern*); Ms B. Thomas (*Greater Manchester*); Ms F. Everiss (*North West*); D. Main (*South East*); Ms J. Henderson (*South West*); P. Thomas (*West Midlands*); J. Walker (*Yorkshire and Humberside*)

Youth and Education

Director (G3), Mrs V. Bayliss
Heads of Branches (G5); J. West (*Schools and Partnerships Policy*); A. Davies (*Careers Service*); G. Dyche (*Young People and Work*); K. Franklin (*Further and Higher Education*)

Training Strategy and Infrastructure

Director (G3), D. Grover
Heads of Branches (G5), B. Shaw (*Training Strategy and Secretariat*); P. Keen (*Employer Investment*); R. Wye (*Learning Methods*); C. Capella (*European Training Policy, Programmes and Funding*); J. Fuller (*Qualifications and Standards*); J. Wiltshire (*Industry Training Organizations*)

Planning

Director (G4), K. White
Heads of Branches (G5), M. Nicholas (*Operational Policy*); B. Heatley (*Resource Planning*); N. Atkinson (*Operational Monitoring*); M. Christie (*The Field Systems*)

Adult Learning

Director (G3), J. Lambert
Head of Branches (G5/G6), D. Tansley (*Adult Training*); G. Macnair (*Special Needs and Equal Opportunities*); J. Smith (*Individual Commitment*)

Quality Assurance

Director (G3), N. Schofield
Heads of Branches (G5), C. Williams (*Financial Analysis and Review*); J. Blizard (*Quality Assurance*); T. Fellows (*Quality Policy and Networking*)

National Training Task Force Unit

Director (Special Adviser), Ms C. Stratton

INDUSTRIAL RELATIONS AND INTERNATIONAL DIRECTORATE

Director (G2), G. Reid
International Division (G3), L. Lewis
Industrial Relations Division I (G3), C. Tucker
Industrial Relations Division II (G3), R. Hillier
Statistical Services Division (G3), P. Stibbard
Chief Wages Inspector (G6), C. Beach
Secretary of Wages Councils, G. Knorpel

RESOURCES AND STRATEGY DIRECTORATE

Director (G2), N. W. Stuart, CB
Finance and Resource Management Division (G3), M. Addison
Economics, Research and Evaluation Division (G3), Ms P. Meadows
Strategy and Employment Policy Division (G3), P. Makeham
Personnel and Development Division (G3), D. Norrington
Business Services Division (G4), K. Jordan
Information Branch (G5), B. Sutlieff

ENGLISH NATURE

Northminster House, Peterborough PE1 1UA
Tel 0733-340345

English Nature (the Nature Conservancy Council for England) was established by Act of Parliament in 1991 as a result of the dissolution of the Nature Conservancy Council and the creation of three new independent bodies responsible for promoting nature conservation in the three component countries of Great Britain. English Nature is responsible for advising the Government on nature conservation in England. It promotes, directly and through others, the conservation of England's wildlife and natural features. It selects, establishes and manages National Nature Reserves and identifies and notifies Sites of Special Scientific Interest. It provides advice and information about nature conservation, and supports and conducts research relevant to these functions. Through the Joint Nature Conservation Committee, it works with its sister organizations in Scotland and Wales on UK and international nature conservation issues.

Chairman, The Earl of Cranbrook
Chief Executive, Dr D. R. Langslow
Chief Scientist, Dr K. L. Duff
Director, Operations, E. T. Idle
Director, Corporate Services, Miss C. E. M. Wood
Director, Policy and Development, Mrs S. Collins
Director, Communications and Corporate Affairs, I. Dair
Environmental Audit Manager, M. R. Felton
Head of Lands, W. J. Hopkin
Director, East Region, J. M. Schofield

DEPARTMENT OF THE ENVIRONMENT

2 Marsham Street, London SW1P 3EB
Tel 071-276 3000

The Department of the Environment is responsible for planning and land use; local government; housing and construction; inner city areas; new towns; environmental protection; conservation areas and countryside affairs; energy efficiency; and property holdings.
PSA SERVICES – *see* page 348

Secretary of State for the Environment, The Rt. Hon. Michael Howard, QC, MP
Private Secretary, A. G. Riddell
Special Advisers, T. Burke; P. Rock
Private Secretaries, J. Cressy; Miss P. Thompson
Parliamentary Private Secretary, P. Thurnham, MP
Minister for Local Government and Inner Cities, John Redwood, MP
Private Secretary, Ms K. Jennings
Parliamentary Private Secretary, D. Evans, MP
Minister for Environment and Countryside, David Maclean, MP
Private Secretary, C. R. Bates
Parliamentary Private Secretary, J. Arnold, MP
Minister for Housing and Planning, Sir George Young, Bt., MP

Private Secretary, A. Allberry
Parliamentary Private Secretary, Dr C. Goodson-Wickes, MP
Special Adviser to Ministers of State, J. Gray
Private Secretary, Miss C. Martyres
Parliamentary Under Secretaries of State, Tony Baldry, MP; The Lord Strathclyde; Robin Squire, MP
Private Secretaries, S. E. S. Stringer; N. Ratcliffe; G. Cory
Lord in Waiting, The Viscount Goschen
Private Secretary, Miss A. Moore
Parliamentary Clerk, D. S. Demorais
Permanent Secretary (G1), R. Wilson, CB
Private Secretary, Mrs B. Houlden
Chief Executive, PSA (G1A), Sir Geoffrey Chipperfield, KCB
Private Secretary, Mrs N. Baxter

ORGANIZATION AND ESTABLISHMENTS

Lambeth Bridge House, London SE1 7SB
Tel 071-238 3000

Principal Establishments and Finance Officer (G2), D. J. Burr

PERSONNEL

Director (G3), J. A. Owen
Grade 5, C. P. Evans; K. G. Arnold; L. B. Hicks
Grade 6, M. A. L. Ross; R. E. Vidler; Miss J. A. Clark; J. Kingdom
Chief Librarian (G6), P. Kirwan
Chief Welfare Officer (G7), R. J. Lintern

FINANCE CENTRAL

Under Secretary (G3), R. S. Dudding
Heads of Divisions (G5), B. Redfern; D. A. C. Heigham; J. F. Stoker, B. L. Glicksman; *(G6)*, G. Knowles
Head of Internal Audit (G6), M. R. Haselip

ADMINISTRATION RESOURCES

Director (G3), D. A. R. Peel
Grade 4, B. G. Rosser
Grade 5, I. C. McBrayne; M. J. Bailey; D. L. H. Roberts
Grade 6, R. H. Cheeseman; D. Tridgell; R. Bendall; M. J. Burt

RELOCATION DIVISION

Director (G3), D. A. McDonald
Grade 5, J. Whaley

PLANNING INSPECTORATE

Tollgate House, Houlton Street, Bristol BS2 9DJ
Tel 0272-218950
An executive agency within the Department of the Environment.

Chief Executive and Chief Inspector of Planning (G3), H. S. Crow
Deputy Chief Inspector of Planning (G4), J. R. Mossop
Director of Planning Appeals (G4), A. J. M. Morgan
Assistant Chief Planning Inspectors (G5), Miss G. M. Pain; J. T. Graham; M. I. Montague-Smith; J. Acton; J. T. Dunlop; D. F. Harris; R. E. Wilson; M. C. Hurley; I. H. Nicol
Head of Administration (G5), D. A. C. Marshall
Head of Finance and Management Services (G5), M. Brasher

REGIONAL OFFICES

WEST MIDLANDS, Birmingham – *Regional Director (G3)*, D. R. Ritchie; *Regional Controllers (G5)*, J. E. Northover; D. L. Saunders; Mrs P. M. Holland
YORKSHIRE AND HUMBERSIDE, Leeds – *Regional Director (G3)*, J. P. Henry; *Regional Controllers (G5)*, I. H. Crowther; Mrs E. A. Kerry
NORTH-WEST, Manchester – *Regional Director (G3)*, D. C. Renshaw; *Regional Controllers (G5)*, B. C. Isherwood; P. Styche
NORTHERN, Newcastle upon Tyne – *Regional Director (G3)*, P. A. Shaw; *Regional Controllers (G5)*, Ms D. Caudle; R. G. Bell
SOUTH-WEST, Bristol – *Regional Director (G3)*, Ms E. A. Hopkins; *Regional Controller (G5)*, S. McQuillin
EAST MIDLANDS, Nottingham – *Regional Director (G4)*, D. J. Morrison; *Regional Controller (G6)*, G. Meynell, MBE; R. J. Smith
SOUTH-EAST, London W14 – *Regional Director (G3)*, J. W. Fellows; *Regional Controllers (G5)*, Mrs J. A. Bridges; T. E. Radice; *(G6)*, E. G. Everett
EASTERN, Bedford – *Regional Director (G3)*, P. F. Emms; *Regional Controllers (G5)*, A. Z. Levy; R. A. Bird

LONDON REGIONAL OFFICE

Under Secretary (G3), Mrs L. A. Heath
Grade 5, A. Buchanan; B. Strong; A. M. Wells; I. J. Scotter

INFORMATION

Director (G4), M. S. D. Granatt
Grade 5, J. Gee

PLANNING, RURAL AFFAIRS AND WATER

Deputy Secretary (G2), P. C. McQuail

PLANNING AND DEVELOPMENT CONTROL

Director (G3), P. J. Fletcher
Grade 5, D. N. Donaldson; R. Jones; R. G. Wakeford; C. L. L. Braun; J. M. Leigh-Pollitt; M. R. Ash

PLANNING SERVICES

Director (G4), J. B. Wilson
Grade 5, R. C. Mabey; J. A. Zetter; A. F. Richardson; A. M. Oliver
Grade 6, D. C. Stroud

DIRECTORATE OF RURAL AFFAIRS

Under Secretary (G3), R. J. A. Sharp
Grade 4, P. L. Leonard
Grade 5, R. Bunce; R. M. Pritchard; Ms S. Carter
Grade 6, J. C. Peters

WATER DIRECTORATE

Director (G3), N. W. Summerton
Heads of Divisions (G5), N. Dorling; A. J. C. Simcock; J. Vaughan

Drinking Water Inspectorate

Grade 5, M. G. Healey

MERSEYSIDE TASK FORCE

Director (G3), vacant
Controllers (G5), S. P. Sage; I. Urquhart

CHIEF ARCHITECTURAL ADVISER ON THE BUILT ENVIRONMENT

Grade 2, J. B. Jefferson, CB
Grade 5, J. E. Turner

HOUSING AND URBAN GROUP

Deputy Secretary (G2), Miss E. C. Turton

INNER CITIES

Director (G3), M. B. Gahagan
Heads of Divisions (G5), G. L. Laufer; P. F. Unwin; Mrs R. Le Guen; J. P. Channing; R. A. Beattie

HOUSING POLICY AND PRIVATE SECTOR

Director (G4), N. A. J. Kinghan
Heads of Divisions (G5), R. J. Dorrington; Ms P. E. Alexander; P. D. Walton; J. E. Roberts; Mrs H. Ghosh
Grade 6, J. S. Gill

HOUSING MONITORING AND ANALYSIS

Under Secretary (G3), N. J. Glass
Grade 5, J. E. Turner; A. E. Holmans, CBE; Mrs J. Littlewood; M. Hughes; D. A. C. Heigham

HOUSING RESOURCES AND MANAGEMENT

Under Secretary (G3), Mrs M. McDonald
Heads of Divisions (G5), R. A. Mills; B. H. Leonard; R. S. Horsman
Grade 6, P. J. Radley

PROPERTY HOLDINGS CONSTRUCTION AND CENTRAL SUPPORT SERVICES

Deputy Secretary (G2), Miss D. A. Nichols
Under Secretary (G3), Mrs D. S. Phillips
Director, Property Holdings (G3), N. E. Borrett

DIRECTORATE OF ESTATE PLANNING

Grade 4, D. O. McCreadie
Grade 5, R. J. Dinwiddy
Grade 6, N. Lee; J. H. Bilsby; R. M. D. Smith; M. S. Jennett

DIRECTORATE OF ESTATE OPERATIONS

Grade 4, vacant
Head of Operations Division (G5), R. W. P. Brice
Heads of Outstations (G6), *Scotland*, P. R. Stewart; *North-East*, J. C. Lewis; *North-West*, A. R. Jones; *Midlands*, M. J. Hathaway; *South-West/Wales*, R. M. Barry
Head of Central London Division (G5), A. R. Edwards
Deputy Head of Central London Division (G6), J. Glen
Heads of Outstations (G6), *Thames North*, A. J. Partridge; *Thames South*, C. G. H. Young

FINANCE

Grade 5, M. Nelson

ADMINISTRATION DIVISION

Head of Division (G6), D. M. Gillen

CENTRAL POLICY DIVISION

Grade 5, M. H. Bowles

TRANSPORT AND SECURITY SERVICES

Grade 5, J. C. King

CONSTRUCTION POLICY DIRECTORATE

Under Secretary (G3), A. A. Pelling
Heads of Divisions (G5), A. D. Fagin; I. C. Macpherson; J. N. Lithgow; P. F. Everall
Grade 6, W. J. Marsh; R. F. Window

QUEEN ELIZABETH II CONFERENCE CENTRE

Broad Sanctuary, London SW1P 3EE
Tel 071-798 4010

An executive agency within the Department of the Environment.

Chief Executive (G5), M. C. Buck

BUILDING RESEARCH ESTABLISHMENT

Garston, Watford WD2 7JR
Tel 0923-894040

An executive agency within the Department of the Environment.

Chief Executive (G3), R. G. Courtney
Deputy Chief Executive (G4), N. O. Milbank
Directors of Groups and Stations (G5), B. O. Hall; Dr W. D. Woolley; Dr N. J. Cook, Dr V. H. C. Crisp; C. R. Durham
Heads of Services/Research (G6), Dr A. B. Birties; R. E. Baldwin; B. B. Pigott; J. R. Britten; R. M. C. Driscoll; Dr P. J. Nixon; Dr J. R. F. Burdett; Dr J. P. Cornish; A. J. Butler; Dr P. R. Warren; H. Gulvanessian; Dr A. J. Bravery; Dr J. W. Llewellyn; M. R. Shaw; R. Hood-Leader; Dr M. McCall; R. J. Currie, OBE
Heads of Laboratories and Services (G7), P. W. Staff; Dr D. J. T. Webb, OBE; C. J. Judge; R. H. Welsh

THE BUYING AGENCY

Royal Liver Building, Pier Head, Liverpool L3 1PE
Tel 051-227 4262

An executive agency within the Department of the Environment.

Chief Executive (G5), R. M. Powell

LOCAL GOVERNMENT

Deputy Secretary (G2), C. J. S. Brearley

LOCAL GOVERNMENT FINANCE POLICY

Director, Local Government Finance Policy (G3), P. J. J. Britton
Heads of Divisions (G5), P. Rowsell; Mrs C. Wells; M. H. Coulshed; Mrs H. J. Chipping; R. J. Gibson; A. C. B. Ramsay

LOCAL GOVERNMENT REVIEW TEAM

Under Secretary (G3), R. U. Young
Grade 5, Ms L. F. Bell; J. Adams

LOCAL GOVERNMENT

Under Secretary (G3), R. J. Green
Heads of Divisions (G5), A. J. C. Simcock; H. C. T. Fawcett; Ms D. S. Kahn
Grade 6, P. G. Iredale; T. B. J. Crossley

LEGAL

Solicitor and Legal Adviser (G2), Mrs M. A. Morgan
Deputy Solicitors (G3), J. A. Catlin; Ms D. Unerman
Assistant Solicitors (G5), J. L. Comber; P. J. Szell; I. D. Day; Mrs S. Headley; Miss R. A. Lester; Mrs P. J. Conlon; Mrs G. Hedley-Dent; D. W. Jordan; Miss D. C. S. Phillips; N. S. Lefton

CHIEF SCIENTIST

Chief Scientist (G3), Dr D. J. Fisk
Head of Division (G5), C. L. Robson

ENVIRONMENT PROTECTION

Deputy Secretary (G2), F. A. Osborn, CB

HM INSPECTORATE OF POLLUTION

Director and Chief Inspector (G3), Dr D. H. Slater
Deputy Chief Inspector (G4), Dr A. Duncan
Heads of Division (G5), M. F. Tunnicliffe; Dr K. Speakman; L. N. Stuffins; L. Packer; Dr D. J. Bryce; I. Handyside

DIRECTORATE OF AIR, CLIMATE AND TOXIC SUBSTANCES

Under Secretary (G3), Dr D. J. Fisk
Heads of Division (G5), A. Davis; Dr N. J. King; M. J. C. Faulkner
Grade 6, Dr A. J. Apling; D. L. Pounder; Dr P. J. Corcoran; R. Derwent; Dr L. M. Smith

DIRECTORATE OF POLLUTION CONTROL AND WASTES

Under Secretary (G3), J. Hobson
Heads of Division (G5), J. Grevatt; Mrs L. A. C. Simcock; Dr M. W. Jones; N. Sanders; J. Jacobs; Dr P. Hinchcliffe; J. J. Rendell

ENVIRONMENTAL POLICY AND ANALYSIS

Director (G3), A. G. Watson
Heads of Division (G5), J. Stoker; N. J. Hartley; J. P. Plowman; Mrs H. Hillier; G. Handley; J. S. Stevens

ENERGY EFFICIENCY UNIT

Director-General (G3), W. F. S. Rickett
Grade 5, Dr N. Williams; Dr C. J. Myerscough; Dr J. Miles
Grade 6, Mrs A. J. Wandsworth

ROYAL COMMISSION ON ENVIRONMENTAL POLLUTION

Church House, Great Smith Street, London SW1P 3BZ
Tel 071-276 2080

The Commission was set up in 1970 to advise on matters, both national and international, concerning the pollution of the environment; on the adequacy of research in this field; and the future possibilities of danger to the environment.

Chairman, Sir John Houghton, CBE, FRS
Members, Sir Geoffrey Allen, FRS; Prof. H. Charnock, CBE, FRS; Prof. Dame Barbara Clayton, DBE; H. R. Fell; P. R. A. Jacques, CBE; Prof. J. H. Lawton, FRS; Prof. R. Macrory, FRSA; Prof. J. G. Morris; D. A. D. Reeve, CBE; W. N. Scott, OBE; Prof. E. M. Rothschild; Prof. Z. A. Silberston, OBE
Secretary, D. R. Lewis

EQUAL OPPORTUNITIES COMMISSION

Overseas House, Quay Street, Manchester M3 3HN
Tel 061-833 9244

Press Office, Swan House, 53 Poland Street, London W1V 3DF. Tel: 071-287 3953
Regional Offices, St Andrew House, 141 West Nile Street, Glasgow G1 2RN. Tel: 041-332 8018; Caerwys House, Windsor Place, Cardiff. Tel: 0222-43552

The Commission was set up by Parliament in 1975 as a result of the passing of the Sex Discrimination Act. It works towards the elimination of discrimination on the grounds of sex or marital status and to promote equality of opportunity between men and women generally.

Chair (£48,990), Mrs J. Foster
Deputy Chair (£26,280), Mrs J. Bridgeman
Members, Miss M. Monk; Mrs M. Prosser; Lady Brittan; Mrs A. Hasan; Ms B. Hillon; Ms A. Watts; Ms N. Bray; Ms A. Gibson; Mrs B. Kelly; Miss J. Trotter; Ms C. Wells; C. Mather
Chief Executive, Ms V. Amos

EQUAL OPPORTUNITIES COMMISSION FOR NORTHERN IRELAND
Chamber of Commerce House, 22 Great Victoria Street, Belfast BT2 7BA
Tel 0232-242752

Chair and Chief Executive, Mrs J. Smyth

EXCHEQUER AND AUDIT DEPARTMENT – *see* National Audit Office

ECGD (EXPORT CREDITS GUARANTEE DEPARTMENT)

PO Box 2200, 2 Exchange Tower, Harbour Exchange Square, London E14 9GS
Tel 071-512 7000

ECGD (Export Credits Guarantee Department), the official export credit insurer, is a separate government department responsible to the President of the Board of Trade and functions under the Export and Investment Guarantees Act 1991. This enables ECGD to facilitate UK exports by making available export credit insurance to British firms engaged in selling overseas and to guarantee repayment to banks in Britain providing finance for export credit for goods sold on credit terms of two years or more.

The Act also empowers ECGD to insure British private investment overseas against polical risks, such as war, expropriation and restrictions on remittances.

Chief Executive, W. B. Willott
Group Directors (G3), M. T. Hawtin; J. R. Weiss; T. M. Jaffray
Grade 5, G. Bromley; R. P. Burnett; P. J. Callaghan; D. C. Cooper; A. P. Fowell; R. F. Lethbridge; K. G. Lockwood; V. P. Lunn Rockliffe; R. W. MacGregor; M. E. Maddox; M. D. Pentecost; R. A. Ranson; J. W. Roberts; B. M. Sidwell, TD; J. S. Snowden; Miss J. West
Grade 6, J. M. Foster; R. P. D. Crick; Ms S. Rice; E. Walsby; J. D. Cameron; F. O. H. Coulson; J. C. W. Croall; R. O. L. Drummond; I. M. N. Ejiegbu; N. Harington; G. G. Jones; D. I. Robbins; A. V. Thomas
Grade 7, J. S. Astruc; D. I. Calvert; Mrs A. C. Cowie; G. P. Cox; A. B. Coyne; M. J. Crane; S. R. Dodgson; R. X. Fear; G. C. Fisher; P. C. Gaudoin; N. F. George; R. Gotts; R. Hardy; P. Jackson; K. Jones; R. Jones; N. A. Lambert; D. J. M. Lucas; I. Mackay; S. Merchack; A. J. E. Muckersie; P. L. Neal; G. A. Newhouse; S. C. Pond; P. J. Radford; A. B. Redmayne; S. Rosenthal; R. Scott; K. R. Smith; Miss V. M. Taylor; R. N. Tolliday;

J. A. Tyler; T. West; J. M. Willis; D. L. Wyatt; J. A. Youd; G. A. Young; M. R. Hodson; C. J. Leeds; P. J. Rossington; A. C. Faulkner; I. Wilson; D. M. Cox; M. Cranwell; D. L. Dyke; R. T. Griffiths; R. Holloway; B. S. Hooper; S. J. Johnson; C. King; E. Lynch; J. Maguire; R. C. Parry; J. K. Peacock; V. G. M. Robertson; R. S. Summers; J. Sweeney; C. M. Thorogood; J. W. H. Watts; C. J. Welch; D. Wood

EXPORT GUARANTEES ADVISORY COUNCIL

Chairman, R. T. Fox
Deputy Chairman, A. G. Gormly, CBE
Other Members, Sir Robert Davidson; The Hon. D. Douglas-Home, CBE; J. Melbourne; C. Smallwood; Sir Derek Thomas, KCMG; The Viscount Weir

OFFICE OF FAIR TRADING

Field House, Bream's Buildings, London EC4A 1PR
Tel 071-242 2858

The Office of Fair Trading is a non-ministerial government department, headed by the Director-General of Fair Trading. It keeps commercial activities in the UK under review and seeks to protect consumers against unfair trading practices. The Director-General's consumer protection duties under the Fair Trading Act 1973, together with his responsibilities under the Consumer Credit Act 1974, the Estate Agents Act 1979, and Control of Misleading Advertisements Regulations 1988, are administered by the Office's Consumer Affairs Division. The Competition Policy Division is concerned with monopolies and mergers (under the Fair Trading Act 1973), and the Director-General's other responsibilities for competition matters, including those under the Restrictive Trade Practices Act 1976, the Resale Prices Act 1976, the Competition Act 1980, the Financial Services Act 1986 and the Broadcasting Act 1990. The Office is the UK competent authority on the application of the European Commission's competition rules, and also liaises with the Commission on consumer protection initiatives.

Director-General, Sir Bryan Carsberg
Deputy Director-General (*G2*), J. W. Preston, CB

CONSUMER AFFAIRS DIVISION

Director (*G3*), J. F. Mills
Assistant Directors (*G5*), M. Lanyon; D. W. Lightfoot; J. Chapman

COMPETITION POLICY DIVISION

Director (*G3*), Dr M. Howe
Assistant Directors (*G5*), A. G. Atkinson; A. J. White; D. Roots-Parsons
Head of International Section (*G6*), H. L. Emden

LEGAL DIVISION

Director (*G3*), A. M. Inglese
Assistant Directors (*G5*), M. A. Khan; P. T. Rostron

Senior Economic Adviser (*G5*), D. Elliott
Establishment and Finance Officer (*G5*), Miss C. Banks
Chief Information Officer (*G6*), J. Stubbs

FOREIGN AND COMMONWEALTH OFFICE

Downing Street, London SW1A 2AL
Tel 071-270 3000

The Foreign and Commonwealth Office provides, mainly through diplomatic missions, the means of communication between the British Government and other governments and international governmental organizations for the discussion and negotiation of all matters falling within the field of international relations. It is responsible for alerting the British Government to the implications of developments overseas; for protecting British interests overseas; for protecting British citizens abroad; for explaining British policies to, and cultivating friendly relations with, governments overseas; and for the discharge of British responsibilities to the dependent territories.

DIPLOMATIC SERVICE SALARIES
since 1 April 1992

Permanent Under Secretary and Head of the Diplomatic Service	£98,000
Senior Grade Salary Point 1 (*SP1*)	£84,250
Senior Grade Salary Point 2 (*SP2*)	£70,400
Senior Grade Salary Point 3 (*SP3*)	£60,100
Senior Grade Salary Point 4 (*SP4*)	£56,530
Senior Grade Salary Point 5 (*SP5*)	£51,300
Diplomatic Service Grade 4 (*DS4*)	£37,928–£42,870
Diplomatic Service Grade 5 (*DS5*)	£26,129–£30,823

Secretary of State, The Rt. Hon. Douglas Hurd, CBE, MP
Private Secretary, R. H. T. Gozney
Assistant Private Secretaries, S. L. Gass; C. N. R. Prentice; Miss H. Drysdale
Social Secretary, Miss C. A. Smyth
Special Advisers, E. Bickham; M. Fraser
Parliamentary Private Secretary, D. Martin, MP
Minister of State for Foreign and Commonwealth Affairs (*Minister for Overseas Development*), The Baroness Chalker, PC
Private Secretary, S. Chakrabarti
Parliamentary Private Secretary, M. Robinson, MP
Ministers of State for Foreign and Commonwealth Affairs, The Rt. Hon. Douglas Hogg, QC, MP; The Rt. Hon. Alastair Goodlad, MP; The Rt. Hon. Tristan Garel-Jones, MP
Private Secretaries, N. S. Archer; P. H. Tibber; T. M. Hitchens
Parliamentary Private Secretary to Mr Garel-Jones, M. Moss, MP
Parliamentary Under Secretary of State, The Hon. Mark Lennox-Boyd, MP
Private Secretary, P. A. Speller
Parliamentary Private Secretary, M. Robinson, MP
Parliamentary Relations Unit, R. Calder (*Head*); J. P. Rodgers (*Deputy Head and Parliamentary Clerk*)
Permanent Under Secretary of State and Head of the Diplomatic Service, Sir David Gillmore, KCMG
Private Secretary, T. M. J. Simmons
Deputy Under Secretaries (*SP2*), A. M. Wood, CMG (*Chief Clerk*); M. Elliott; B. L. Crowe, CMG; L. V. Appleyard, CMG (*Political Director*); N. H. R. A. Broomfield, CMG; Sir John Coles, KCMG.
HM Vice-Marshal of the Diplomatic Corps, A. St J. H. Figgis
Assistant Under Secretaries (*SP5*), A. J. Beamish, CMG; P. J. Goulden, CMG; Mrs V. E. Sutherland, CMG (*Deputy Chief Clerk*); R. J. S. Muir (*Principal Finance Officer and Chief Inspector*); The Hon. D. Gore-Booth, CMG; R. D. Bone; A. M. Goodenough, CMG; J. Ling, CMG

(*Director of Communications and Technical Services*); Miss R. J. Spencer, CMG; D. B. C. Logan, CMG; J. Q. Greenstock, CMG; R. O. Miles, CMG; M. H. Jay, CMG; J. T. Masefield, CMG; C. O. Hum
Legal Adviser, F. D. Berman, CMG
Second Legal Adviser, D. H. Anderson, CMG
Deputy Legal Advisers, M. R. Eaton, CMG; K. J. Chamberlain, CMG
Legal Counsellors, A. Aust; Mrs A. Glover; Miss S. Brooks; Ms E. Wilmshurst; C. Whomersley
International Labour Adviser, A. E. Smith
Overseas Police Adviser (*DS4*), J. W. Kelland, LVO, QPM

HEADS OF DEPARTMENTS (DS4) AND ASSISTANT HEADS OF DEPARTMENT (DS5)

**Aid Policy Dept.*, D. L. Stanton; *Asst.*, G. Hand
Arms Control and Disarmament Dept., P. W. M. Vereker; *Asst.*, J. Nichols
Aviation and Maritime Dept., E. J. Hughes
Central and Southern African Dept., R. Christopher; *Asst.*, C. Robbins
Central European Dept., N. J. Thorpe
Commonwealth Co-ordination Dept., D. Broad; *Asst.*, M. W. Powles
Commonwealth Foreign and Security Policy Unit, N. J. Westcott
Conference on Security and Co-operation in Europe Unit, R. Dalton
Consular Dept., C. J. A. Denne; *Asst.*, B. Midgley, OBE
Cultural Relations Dept., J. N. Elam; *Assts.*, Ms A. Lewis; P. Holmes
East African Dept., T. J. Harris; *Asst.*, A. Maclean
Eastern European Dept., R. Lyne, CMG; *Assts.*, C. Crawford; Mrs R. Aron
**Economic Advisers*, S. H. Broadbent; *Asst.*, N. R. Chrimes
**Economic Relations Dept.*, K. Tebbit; *Asst.*, P. J. Millett
Environment Science and Energy Dept., A. R. Brenton; *Asst.*, M. Bourke
European Community Dept. (*External*), E. Jones Parry, CMG; *Asst.*, Q. M. Quayle
European Community Dept. (*Internal*), M. Arthur, CMG; *Asst.*, N. Sheinwald
Far Eastern Dept., H. L. Davies; *Asst.*, W. Morris
Finance Dept., G. F. Griffiths; *Asst.*, A. R. Ingle
Home Estate and Services Dept., D. Brown; *Asst.*, M. Hannant
Hong Kong Dept., P. Ricketts; *Asst.*, Miss N. J. Cox
Information Dept. A. D. Harris, LVO; *Assts.*, G. Davies; D. Wyatt
Information Systems Division (*Operations*), S. I. Soutar; *Assts.*, L. Walters; P. Jones
Information Systems Division (*Projects*), K. Willis
Information Systems Division (*Resources*), D. Wright, OBE; *Assts.*, C. Compton; J. Monk
Information Systems Division (*Services*), D. Briggs; *Assts.*, N. Paget; A. Taylor
Latin America Dept., A. R. Murray; *Asst.*, W. B. Sinton
Library and Records Dept., R. Bone; *Assts.*, R. L. E. Foreman; I. S. Lockhart, MBE; B. Barrett
**Management Review Staff*, A. C. Hunt, CMG; *Deputy Head*, N. Hoult
Medical and Staff Welfare Unit, F. J. Savage, OBE, LVO; *Deputy Head*, J. Gibb
Middle East Dept., P. M. Nixon, CMG, OBE
Migration and Visa Dept., vacant; *Assts.*, M. J. Peart, LVO; D. Cockaham
Narcotics Control and Aids Dept., P. Thomson; *Asst.*, D. Snoxell
Nationality, Treaty and Claims Dept., M. F. Sullivan, MBE; *Asst.*, C. Hayward
Near East and North Africa Dept., S. W. J. Fuller; *Asst.*, D. Richmond
News Dept., R. F. Cornish, LVO
Non-Proliferation and Defence Dept., J. B. Donnelly; *Assts.*, T. Dowse; E. Callway
North America Dept., M. E. Pellew, LVO; *Asst.*, R. French
Overseas Estate Dept., M. H. R. Bertram; *Deputy Head*, D. L. Brown
Overseas Inspectorate, R. J. S. Muir (*Chief Inspector and Principal Finance Officer*); *Inspectors*, D. I. Lewty; S. D. M. Jack; D. Carter; I. J. Rawlinson, OBE
**Overseas Trade Services Directorate, Dir.-Gen.*, R. O. Miles, CMG; *Dir.*, M. G. Dougal
Permanent Under Secretary's Dept., I. R. Callan, CMG; *Deputy Head*, S. Howarth
Personnel Management Dept., E. Clay; *Deputy Head*, S. M. J. Lamport
Personnel Policy Dept., D. Walker
Personnel Services Dept., R. G. Short, MVO; *Assts.*, J. Long; W. Stump
Policy Planning Staff, R. Cooper, MVO; *Asst.*, R. Clarke
Protocol Dept., D. C. B. Beaumont; *Assts.*, T. C. Almond, OBE; S. W. F. Martin, LVO (*First Assistant Marshal of the Diplomatic Corps*)
Republic of Ireland Dept., G. R. Archer; *Asst.*, D. F. G. Farr
Research and Analysis Dept., *Director*, B. S. Eastwood; *Regional Directors*, C. J. S. Rundle, OBE (*Africa and Middle East*); K. C. Walker (*Asia*); Miss S. Morphet (*Atlantic*); J. R. Banks, OBE (*Eastern Europe*)
Resource Management Dept., R. J. Chase; *Asst.*, J. A. Dew
Security Dept., J. W. Hodge; *Asst.*, R. Anderson
Security Policy Dept., S. J. Gomersall; *Asst.*, S. Cowper-Coles
South Asian Dept., M. J. Williams, CVO, OBE; *Asst.*, R. Codrington
South Atlantic and Antarctic Dept., P. M. Newton; *Asst.*, P. L. Hunt
South-East Asian Dept., G. Hewitt; *Asst.*, B. Stewart
Southern European Dept., D. C. A. Madden; *Asst.*, D. D. Pearey
South Pacific Dept., R. Thomas; *Asst.*, A. C. Walder
Technical Security Dept., M. J. B. Smith; *Assts.*, R. Read; J. Gould
Training Dept., T. D. Curran; *Director of Language Centre*, J. Moore
United Nations Dept., Miss M. G. D. Evans, CMG; *Asst.*, J. Watt
West African Dept., M. E. Cook
West Indian and Atlantic Dept., G. M. Baker; *Asst.*, J. Wilde
Western European Dept., Miss M. MacGlashen; *Asst.*, Ms A. Grant

CORPS OF QUEEN'S MESSENGERS
Foreign and Commonwealth Office, London SW1A 2AH
Tel 071-270 2779

Superintendent of the Corps of Queen's Messengers, Maj. I. G. M. Bamber
Queen's Messengers, Maj. J. E. A. Andre; Cdr. R. D. D. Bamford; Cdr. D. H. Barraclough; Maj. A. N. D. Bols; Lt.-Cdr. K. E. Brown; Lt.-Col. W. P. A. Bush; Lt.-Col. M. B. de S. Clayton; Capt. G. Courtauld; Maj. F. C. W. Courtenay-Thompson; Maj. P. C. H. Dening-Smitherman; Maj. P. T. Dunn; Sqn. Ldr. J. S. Frizzell; Capt. N. C. E. Gardner; Cdr. P. G. Gregson; Maj. D. A. Griffiths; Wg Cdr. J. O. Jewiss;

---

*Joint Foreign and Commonwealth Office/Overseas Development Administration Department

Lt.-Col. P. S. Kerr-Smiley; Lt.-Col. J. M. C. Kimmins;
Lt.-Col. R. C. Letchworth; G. F. Miller;
Lt.-Col. A. R. Murray; Maj. D. R. Nevile;
Maj. K. J. Rowbottom; Maj. M. R. Senior;
Cdr. K. M. C. Simmons, AFC; Maj. P. M. O. Springfield;
Maj. J. S. Steele; Col. D. W. F. Taylor

MI6

Director-General, Sir Colin McColl

GOVERNMENT COMMUNICATIONS HEADQUARTERS (GCHQ)
Priors Road, Cheltenham, Glos. GL52 5AJ
Tel 0242-221491

GCHQ is an autonomous government department under the Secretary of State for Foreign and Commonwealth Affairs.

FOREIGN COMPENSATION COMMISSION

Old Admiralty Building, London SW1A 2AF
Tel 071-210 6158

The Commission was set up by the Foreign Compensation Act 1950 primarily to distribute, under Orders in Council, funds received from other governments in accordance with agreements to pay compensation for expropriated British property and other losses sustained by British nationals.

The Commission has the further duty of registering claims for British-owned property in contemplation of agreements with other countries, and it has done so in seven instances since 1950.

Chairman, A. W. E. Wheeler, CBE
Commissioner, J. A. S. Hall, DFC, QC
Secretary and Chief Examiner, D. H. Wright

FORESTRY COMMISSION

231 Corstorphine Road, Edinburgh EH12 7AT
Tel 031-334 0303

The Forestry Commission is the government department responsible for forestry policy in Great Britain. It reports directly to Forestry Ministers (i.e. the Minister of Agriculture, Fisheries and Food, the Secretary of State for Scotland, and the Secretary of State for Wales), to whom it is responsible for advice on forestry policy and for the implementation of that policy in Great Britain. There is a statutorily-appointed Chairman and Board of Commissioners (four full-time and seven part-time) with prescribed duties and powers. The full-time Commissioners form the Executive Board.

On 1 April 1992 the Commission implemented a reorganization to distinguish between its departmental, regulatory and management functions. A Policy and Resources Group is responsible for the Parliamentary and policy aspects of the Commission's duties as a government department. As the Forestry Authority, the Commission provides advice and sets the standards for the forestry industry, administers the grant-aid schemes for private woodlands, carries out regulatory functions for plant health and felling control and undertakes forest research. As the Forest Enterprise, the Commission manages its forestry estate on a multi-use basis. In discharging their functions, the Forestry Commissioners have a statutory duty to endeavour to achieve a reasonable balance between the needs of forestry and the environment.

Chairman (part-time) (£31,830), J. R. Johnstone, CBE
Director-General and Deputy Chairman (G2), T. R. Cutler
Commissioner, Policy and Resources (G3), D. S. Grundy
Head of the Forestry Authority (G3), R. T. Bradley
Chief Executive, Forest Enterprise (G3), D. L. Foot
Secretary to the Commissioners (G4). P. J. Clarke

REGISTRY OF FRIENDLY SOCIETIES

15 Great Marlborough Street, London W1V 2AX
Tel 071-437 9992

The Registry of Friendly Societies is a government department serving two statutory bodies, the Building Societies Commission and the Central Office of the Registry of Friendly Societies (together with the Assistant Registrar of Friendly Societies for Scotland).

The Building Societies Commission was established by the Building Societies Act 1986. The Commission is responsible for the supervision of building societies, and administers the system of regulation. It also advises the Treasury and other government departments on matters relating to building societies.

The Central Office of the Registry of Friendly Societies provides a public registry for mutual organizations registered under the Building Societies Act 1986, Friendly Societies Act 1974, and the Industrial and Provident Societies Act 1965. It is responsible for the supervision of friendly societies and credit unions, and advises the Government on issues affecting those societies. The Chief Registrar has certain powers to arbitrate in disputes between members and registered societies. He also acts as the Industrial Assurance Commissioner.

BUILDING SOCIETIES COMMISSION

Chairman, Mrs R. E. J. Gilmore
Deputy Chairman, H. G. Walsh
Commissioners, T. F. Mathews; S. Proctor, CBE; H. R. C. Walden, CBE; F. E. Worsley

CENTRAL OFFICE

Chief Registrar, Mrs R. E. J. Gilmore
Assistant Registrars, A. Wilson; D. W. Lee; A. J. Perrett; R. N. Williams

THE REGISTRY

First Commissioner and Chief Registrar (G2), Mrs R. E. J. Gilmore

BUILDING SOCIETIES COMMISSION STAFF

Grade 3, H. G. Walsh
Grade 4, T. F. Matthews
Grade 5, D. A. W. Stevens; J. M. Palmer; A. T. Gosling
Grade 6, N. F. Digance
Grade 7, A. G. Tebbutt; Mrs S. A. Russell; E. Engstrom; M. E. Duff; N. J. Lock; B. Champion; B. Morbin; M. Turner; Mrs S. de Mont; R. Trew; A. Smith; Ms J. Page.

CENTRAL OFFICE STAFF

Assistant Registrar (G4), A. Wilson
Assistant Registrar (G5), D. W. Lee
Grade 7, F. da Rocha; N. J. F. Fawcett; C. T. Martyn; Ms S. Eden; D. Cobbett

CENTRAL SERVICES STAFF
Assistant Registrar (G5), A. J. Perrett
Establishment and Finance Officer (G5), K. Blackburn
Legal Staff (G6), Mrs V. Edwards; P. G. Ashcroft; Miss E. Long; R. Caune

REGISTRY OF FRIENDLY SOCIETIES, SCOTLAND
58 Frederick Street, Edinburgh, EH2 1NB
Tel 031-226 3224
Assistant Registrar (G5), J. L. J. Craig, WS

GAMING BOARD FOR GREAT BRITAIN
Berkshire House, 168–173 High Holborn, London WC1V 7AA
Tel 071-240 0821

The Board was established in 1968 to keep under review the extent and character of gaming in Great Britain; to approve prospective gaming licensees' management and staff; to inspect gaming establishments; and to advise the Home Secretary on changes in the law which may be needed for the further control of gaming.

Chairman (part-time) (£29,400), Lady Littler
Members (part-time) (each £11,790), Sir Richard Barratt, CBE, VRD; Lady Trethowan; W. B. Kirkpatrick; M. H. Hogan
Secretary, T. Kavanagh

OFFICE OF GAS SUPPLY
Stockley House, 130 Wilton Road, London SW1
Tel 071-828 0898

The Office of Gas Supply (Ofgas) is a regulatory body set up under the Gas Act 1986. It is headed by the Director-General of Gas Supply, who is independent of ministerial control.

The principal function of Ofgas is to monitor British Gas's activities as a public gas supplier and, where necessary, enforce the conditions of that company's authorization to act as a public gas supplier. Other functions are to grant authorizations to other suppliers of gas through pipes; to investigate complaints on matters where enforcement powers may be exercisable; to fix and publish maximum charges for reselling gas; to publish information and advice for the benefit of tariff customers; to keep under review developments concerning the gas supply industry, including competition; and to settle the terms on which other suppliers have access to British Gas pipelines in the event of disagreement.

Director-General, Sir James McKinnon
Deputy Director-General, J. Dorken
Legal Adviser, D. R. M. Long
Director, Competition and Tariffs, G. McGregor
Director, Public Affairs, I. Cooke
Director, Consumer Affairs, W. Macleod

THE GOVERNMENT ACTUARY
22 Kingsway, London WC2B 6LE
Tel 071-242 6828

The Government Actuary provides a consulting service to government departments, the public sector, and overseas governments. The actuaries advise on social security schemes and superannuation arrangements within the public sector at home and abroad, on population and other statistical studies, and on government supervision of insurance companies and friendly societies.

Government Actuary, C. D. Daykin
Directing Actuaries, D. G. Ballantine; D. H. Loades; M. A. Pickford
Chief Actuaries, P. L. Burt; J. L. Field; R. T. Foster; T. W. Hewitson; P. H. Hinton; A. I. Johnston; A. G. Young
Actuaries, E. I. Battersby; A. B. Chughtai; W. H. P. Davies; A. P. Gallop; C. A. Harris; V. P. Knowles; Mrs I. W. Lane; P. Merricks; S. M. O'Ceallaigh; A. P. Pavelin; J. W. Peers; H. J. Prescott; J. C. Rathbone; A. H. Silverman; J. G. Spain; D. I. Tomlinson; D. M. Webber

GOVERNMENT HOSPITALITY FUND
8 Cleveland Row, London SW1A 1DH
Tel 071-210 3000

The Government Hospitality Fund was instituted in 1908 for the purpose of organizing official hospitality on a regular basis, with a view to the promotion of international goodwill.

Minister in Charge, The Rt. Hon. Alastair Goodlad, MP
Secretary, Brig. A. Cowan, CBE

DEPARTMENT OF HEALTH
Richmond House, 79 Whitehall, London SW1A 2NS
Tel 071-210 3000

The Department of Health is responsible for the administration of the National Health Service in England and for the personal social services run by local authorities in England for children, the elderly, the infirm, the handicapped and other persons in need. It has functions relating to public and environmental health, food safety and nutrition. The Department is also responsible for the ambulance and emergency first aid services, under the Civil Defence Act 1948. The Department represents the UK at the World Health Organization.

Secretary of State for Health, The Rt. Hon. Virginia Bottomley, MP
Principal Private Secretary, C. Phillips
Special Adviser, R. Marsh
Parliamentary Private Secretary, K. Mans, MP
Minister of State, Dr Brian Mawhinney, MP
Private Secretary, Ms T. Ing
Parlimentary Private Secretary, P. Thompson, MP
Parliamentary Under Secretaries of State, The Baroness Cumberlege, CBE; The Hon. Thomas Sackville, MP; Timothy Yeo, MP
Permanent Secretary (G1), G. A. Hart, CB
Private Secretary, Ms K. Wright
Chief Medical Officer (G1A), Dr K. Calman
Director of Research and Development, Prof. M. Peckham

NATIONAL HEALTH SERVICE POLICY BOARD
Chairman, The Secretary of State
Deputy Chairman, Sir Roy Griffiths
Members, Dr K. Calman (*Chief Medical Officer*); Sir James Ackers; Dr B. Mawhinney, MP (*Minister of State*); Prof. C. Chantler; The Baroness Cumberledge, CBE; The

Hon. T. Sackville, MP; T. Yeo, MP (*Parliamentary Under Secretaries*); Sir Kenneth Durham; G. A. Hart, CB (*Permanent Secretary*); D. Nichol, CBE; Sir Robert Scholey, CBE; P. Gummer; Ms Y. Moores; Miss K. Jenkins

NATIONAL HEALTH SERVICE MANAGEMENT EXECUTIVE

Chief Executive, D. Nichol, CBE
Deputy Chief Executive and Director of Performance Management, vacant
Director of Corporate Affairs, M. Malone-Lee
Director of Personnel, E. Caines
Director of Finance and Corporate Information, G. Greenshields
Medical Director, Dr D. Walford
Chief Nursing Officer, Mrs Y. Moores
Director of Research and Development, Prof. M. Peckham

HEALTH AND PERSONAL SOCIAL SERVICES GROUP

Deputy Secretary (G2), T. S. Heppell, CB

HEALTH ASPECTS OF THE ENVIRONMENT AND FOOD

Under Secretary (G3), Miss R. O. B. Pease
Assistant Secretaries (G5), C. P. Kendall; R. Cunningham; Ms L. Lockyer
Senior Principal (G6), Mrs M. Fry

HEALTH CARE (ADMINISTRATIVE) DIVISION

Under Secretary (G3), C. H. Wilson
Assistant Secretaries (G5), J. H. Garlick; A. W. McCulloch; R. M. T. Scofield; K. Jacobsen; I. Jewesbury

COMMUNITY SERVICES DIVISION

Under Secretary (G3), T. Luce
Assistant Secretaries (G5), Mrs A. De Peyer; J. A. Parker; R. P. S. Hughes, CBE; A. McKeon

HEALTH PROMOTION (ADMINISTRATIVE) DIVISION

Under Secretary (G3), N. M. Hale, CB
Assistant Secretaries (G5), J. E. Knight; C. A. Muir; J. F. Sharpe; J. C. Middleton

HEALTH CARE DIRECTORATE

Deputy Secretary (G2), Dr D. Walford

DIVISION HCD-SD

Under Secretary (G3), J. H. Barnes
Assistant Secretaries (G5), Miss H. Gwynn; Ms M. Purvis; P. Garland

DIVISION P

Under Secretary (G3), B. Bridges
Assistant Secretaries (G5), S. J. Furniss; J. Tross; J. Thompson; M. Siswick; S. Alcock

MEDICINES CONTROL AGENCY

An executive agency within the Department of Health.
Chief Executive (G3), Dr K. H. Jones
Grade 4, D. O. Hagger; R. K. Alder; D. H. Hartley; Dr J. B. Jefferys; Dr S. M. Wood

NHS SUPPLIES AUTHORITY

Chairman, Sir Robin Buchanan
National Director of Supplies, T. Hunt
Directors, E. Sutherland (*Purchasing*); R. Chantler (*Finance and Information*); C. Uden (*Human Resources*); Mrs R. Sutton (*Communications*)

MEDICAL DEVICES DIRECTORATE

Director (G4), A. B. Barton

EC DIRECTIVES AND STANDARDS

Head of Business (G5), Dr D. C. Potter

PROFESSIONAL AND TECHNOLOGICAL ADVICE

Head of Business (G5), Miss M. N. Duncan

COMMUNITY HEALTH, NON-ACUTE AND DIAGNOSTIC IMAGING SERVICES GROUP

Group Manager (G6), A. D. C. Shipley

ACUTE CARE SERVICES GROUP

Group Manager (G6), C. S. Bray

EVALUATION OF MEDICAL DEVICES (INCLUDING PUBLICATIONS)

Head of Business (G6), Dr N. A. Slark

MANUFACTURERS' REGISTRATION SCHEME

Head of Business (G6), R. W. B. Allen

CORPORATE MANAGEMENT

Head of Business (G6), T. F. Crawley

MEDICAL AND NURSING

Senior Medical Officers (G5), Dr S. M. Ludgate; Dr S. P. Vahl
Nursing Officer (G6), Mrs P. A. Collinson

NHS MANAGEMENT EXECUTIVE PERSONNEL GROUP

Director of Operations (Personnel) (G2), E. Caines

DIVISION HAP

Under Secretary (G3), R. W. D. Venning
Executive Director (G4), R. M. Drury
Assistant Secretaries (G5), M. G. Sturges; Miss S. Norman; M. Staniforth; J. Ashe
Senior Principal (G6), B. A. J. Bennett

INFORMATION SYSTEMS DIRECTORATE

Director of Information Systems (G4), Dr A. A. Holt
Deputy Director (G5), R. Grimshaw
Grade 5, Mrs L. Masterman
Grade 6, Miss S. Blackburn; J. Wormald; P. Cobb

RESEARCH AND DEVELOPMENT DIVISION

Director of Research and Development, Prof. M. Peckham
Director of Research Management (G4), Dr W. J. Burroughs
Deputy Director of Research Management (G4), Dr H. Pickles
Assistant Secretaries (G5), Miss M. Edwards; Mrs J. Griffin; Mrs B. Soper; M. Woolley; Dr P. Woodford
Senior Medical Officers (G5), Dr R. Singh; Dr G. Lewis
Senior Principal Research Officers (G6), Ms A. Kauder; Dr C. Davies; J. Ennis; Dr C. Henshall

SOCIAL SERVICES INSPECTORATE

Chief Inspector (G2), H. Laming, CBE
Deputy Chief Inspectors (G4), D. C. Brand; Miss C. M. Hey
Assistant Chief Inspectors (HQ), Miss J. Baraclough; J. Kennedy; S. Mitchell; J. G. Smith; Mrs W. Rose
Assistant Chief Inspectors (Regions), S. Allard; J. K. Corcoran; J. Cypher; D. Gilroy; B. D. Harrison; A. Jones; D. G. Lambert; Miss A. Taylor; Mrs P. K. Hall; C. P. Brearley

MEDICAL DIVISIONS (HEALTH AND PERSONAL SOCIAL SERVICES)

Chief Medical Officer (G1A), Dr K. Calman
Deputy Chief Medical Officers (G2), Dr M. E. Abrams, CB; Dr J. S. Metters; Dr D. Walford

MEDICAL DIVISIONS UNDER DR ABRAMS

Divisions HP(M)1–4, CHMU, Medical Editorial Unit

Senior Principal Medical Officer (G3), Dr E. Rubery
Principal Medical Officers (G4), Dr G. Lewis; Dr D. McInnes; Dr J. D. F. Bellamy
Senior Medical Officers (G5), Dr P. E. Exon; Dr D. Salisbury; Dr S. Lader; Dr J. Hilton; Dr J. Leese; Dr E. Tebbs; Dr M. McGovern; Dr H. Williams; Dr M. Powlson; Dr H. Markowe; Dr F. Harvey; Dr K. Binysh; Dr V. Press; Dr M. Farrell

Division HEF(M)

Senior Principal Medical Officer (G3), Dr J. H. S. Steadman
Principal Medical Officers (G4), Dr E. Smales; Dr G. E. Diggle; Dr R. Skinner
Senior Medical Officers (G5), Dr M. Waring; Dr N. Lazarus; Dr T. Meredith; Dr R. L. Maynard; Dr T. Marrs; Dr A. Bulman; Dr P. Clarke; Dr A. Dawson; Dr L. Robinson; Dr C. Swinson; Dr A. Wight; Dr M. Wiseman

Division E

Principal Medical Officer (G4), Dr J. D. F. Bellamy

MEDICAL DIVISIONS UNDER DR METTERS

Divisions HP(M) 5 and 6

Senior Principal Medical Officer (G3), Dr E. Rubery
Principal Medical Officer (G4), J. D. F. Bellamy
Senior Medical Officers (G5), Dr D. Ernaelsteen; Dr W. J. Modle; Dr I. A. Lister-Cheese; Dr S. Shepherd; Dr D. Milner; Dr R. Stanwell-Smith

Health Care (Medical) Division

Senior Principal Medical Officer (G3), Dr J. L. Reed
Principal Medical Officers (G4), Dr J. R. W. Hangartner; Dr J. E. Shanks; Dr R. Jenkins
Senior Medical Officers (G5), Dr J. Ashwell; Dr D. Rothman; Dr N. Halliday; Dr N. Melia; Dr E. Hills; Dr H. Sutton; Dr P. Furnell; Dr A. Rejman; Dr E. Clissold; Dr A. Rawson; Dr S. Munday; Dr D. Brooksbank; Dr D. Kingdon, Dr D. Jones; Prof. S. Ebrahim; Dr E. Miller

MEDICAL DIVISIONS UNDER DR WALFORD

Division HCD–PH

Principal Medical Officer (G4), Dr A. Lakhani
Senior Medical Officers (G5), Dr G. N. Brown; Dr G. Bickler; Dr A. Stevens; Dr J. Linnane; Dr P. Old; Dr G. Pollock; Dr J. Rees; Dr M. Campbell-Stern; Dr G. Thorn

Division MME

Senior Principal Medical Officer (G3), Dr P. J. Bourdillon
Senior Medical Officers (G5), Dr H. S. Bloom; Dr M. Smith; Dr P. I. M. Allen; Dr D. Ewing
Assistant Secretary (G5), S. D. Catling
Principals (G7), H. Tolland; T. G. Bennett

Dental Division

Chief Dental Officer, R. B. Mouatt
Senior Dental Officers, C. Howard; J. M. G. Hunt; K. A. Eaton

Nursing Division

Chief Nursing Officer/Director of Nursing, Mrs Y. Moores
Deputy Director of Nursing, M. Clark
Deputy Chief Nursing Officer, J. Tait, OBE
Principal Nursing Officer/Business Manager, M. Hill
Principal Nursing Officer, Miss S. Norman

Pharmaceutical Division

Chief Pharmaceutical Officer (G3), B. H. Hartley
Deputy Chief Pharmaceutical Officer (G5), Dr J. R. V. Merrills
Senior Principal Pharmaceutical Officer (G6), P. E. Green

Information Division

Director of Information (G4), Miss R. Christopherson
Deputy Directors (G6), C. P. Wilson (*news*); Mrs A. Rea (*publicity*)

NATIONAL HEALTH SERVICE

Regional Health Authorities

The chairmen and members of Regional Health Authorities are appointed by the Secretary of State for Health.

Northern, Benfield Road, Walker Gate, Newcastle upon Tyne. *Chairman*, P. Carr, CBE; *Regional General Manager*, Prof. L. Donaldson
Yorkshire, Park Parade, Harrogate. *Chairman*, Sir Bryan Askew; *Regional General Manager*, C. McLean
Trent, Fulwood House, Old Fulwood Road, Sheffield. *Chairman*, Sir Michael Carlisle; *Regional General Manager*, B. Edwards, CBE
East Anglia, Union Lane, Chesterton, Cambridge. *Chairman*, Sir Colin Walker, OBE; *Regional General Manager*, A. Liddell
North-East Thames, 40 Eastbourne Terrace, London W2 3QR. *Chairman*, T. Chessells; *Regional General Manager*, B. Harrison
North-West Thames, 40 Eastbourne Terrace, London W2 3QR. *Chairman*, Sir William Doughty; *Regional General Manager*, A. Langlands
South-East Thames, Thrift House, Collington Avenue, Bexhill-on-Sea, E. Sussex. *Chairman*, P. Barker; *Regional General Manager*, Ms P. Saunders
South-West Thames, 40 Eastbourne Terrace, London W2 3QR. *Chairman*, vacant; *Regional General Manager*, Ms J. Turner
Wessex, Highcroft, Romsey Road, Winchester, Hants. *Chairman*, Sir Robin Buchanan; *Regional General Manager*, K. Jarrold
Oxford, Old Road, Headington, Oxford. *Chairman*, Dr S. Burgess; *Regional General Manager*, R. M. Nicholls
South-Western, King Square House, 26–27 King Square, Bristol. *Chairman*, C. Stuart; *Regional General Manager*, Miss C. E. Hawkins, CBE
West Midlands, Arthur Thompson House, 146–150 Hagley Road, Birmingham. *Chairman*, Sir James Ackers; *Regional General Manager*, S. Fletcher
Mersey, Hamilton House, 24 Pall Mall, Liverpool L3 6AL. *Chairman*, Sir Donald Wilson; *Regional General Manager*, G. Scaife

NORTH-WESTERN, Gateway House, Piccadilly South, Manchester M60 7LP. *Chairman*, Sir Bruce Martin, QC; *Regional General Manager*, D. Allison, CB

SPECIAL HEALTH AUTHORITIES

HEALTH EDUCATION AUTHORITY, Hamilton House, Mabledon Place, London WC1H 9TX. *Chairman*, Sir Donald Maitland, GCMG, OBE; *Chief Executive*, Dr Spencer Hagard

NHS SUPPLIES AUTHORITY, Apex Plaza, Forbury Road, Reading, Berks. RG1 1AX. *Chairman*, Sir Robin Buchanan

SPECIAL HOSPITALS SERVICE AUTHORITY, Charles House, Kensington High Street, London W14

The Special Hospitals Service is provided by four hospitals: Rampton; Broadmoor; Moss Side; and Park Lane. *Chairman*, Dr D. E. Edmond; *Chief Executive*, C. Kaye

NATIONAL HEALTH SERVICE, SCOTLAND – *see* page 357

DEPARTMENTAL RESOURCES AND SERVICES GROUP

Deputy Secretary (G2), Mrs A. E. Bowtell, CB

FINANCE AND CORPORATE INFORMATION DIRECTORATE

FINANCIAL MANAGEMENT DIRECTORATE

Director of Finance NHSHE (G2), G. Greenshields

FINANCE BRANCH

Under Secretary (Health) (G3), Ms M. E. Stuart
Assistant Secretaries (G5), J. M. Brownlee; K. J. Guinness; Miss A. Mithani; Ms G. Fletcher-Cook
Senior Principals (G6), R. J. Tredgett; R. Churchill; A. C. Symes

FINANCE AND CORPORATE INFORMATION DIVISION A

Deputy Director (G3), Mrs J. Firth
Heads of Branch (G5), A. Simkins; C. Dobson; M. A. Harris; A. Angilley

FINANCE AND CORPORATE INFORMATION DIVISION B

Deputy Director (G3), B. Marsden
Heads of Branch (G5), J. Rushfirth; B. J. Derry; J. Tomlinson; E. Hunter Johnston; M. Ruane; *(G6)*, R. Douglas; M. Gayton; *(G7)*, G. Smith

FINANCE DIVISION D

Under Secretary (Social Security) (G3), J. Tross
Assistant Secretaries (G5), S. Lord; Dr L. Mayhew; G. Foster

NHS SUPERANNUATION BRANCH

Executive Director (Personnel) (G4), R. M. Drury
Senior Principal (G6), D. Napier

STATISTICS AND MANAGEMENT INFORMATION DIVISION (S7)

Director of Statistics and Management Information (G3), Mrs R. J. Butler
Chief Statisticians (G5), Miss P. W. Annesley; R. K. Willmer; G. J. O. Phillpotts

ECONOMICS AND OPERATIONAL RESEARCH DIVISION (HEALTH)

Chief Economic Adviser (G3), C. H. Smee
Senior Economic Advisers (G5), M. A. Parsonage; J. W. Hurst

CENTRAL RESOURCE MANAGEMENT

Assistant Secretary (G5), M. Brown
Senior Principal (G6), T. Thorne

DEPARTMENTAL MANAGEMENT

Principal Establishment Officer (G3), M. G. Lillywhite
Assistant Secretaries (G5), Ms R. J. Darbyshire; M. Brown; Mrs S. Hughes; Ms P. A. Stewart

SOLICITOR'S OFFICE

Solicitor (G2), P. K. J. Thompson
Principal Assistant Solicitors (G3), Mrs G. S. Kerrigan; A. D. Roberts
Proceedings Operational Director (G4), P. C. Nilsson

NHS ESTATES

An executive agency within the Department of Health.

Chief Executive (G3), J. C. Locke
Estate Policy Director (G5), G. G. Mayers
Director of Business Development (G5), A. R. Tanner
Director of Resources (G5), L. J. Wardle
Head of Consultancy Services (G5), C. Davies
Chief Engineer (G5), L. W. M. Arrowsmith
Chief Surveyor (G6), D. A. Eastwood
Principal Nursing Adviser (G6), Miss S. B. R. Scott

NHS TRUSTS UNIT

Head of Unit (G4), N. Beverly
Operations Manager (G5), D. W. F. Lye

COMMITTEE ON THE SAFETY OF MEDICINES
Market Towers, 1 Nine Elms Lane, London SW8 5NQ
Tel 071-273 0451
Chairman, Prof. M. D. Rawlins

COMMITTEE ON DENTAL AND SURGICAL MATERIALS
Market Towers, 1 Nine Elms Lane, London SW8 5NQ
Tel 071-273 0502
Chairman, Prof. D. E. Poswillo, CBE

ADVISORY COMMITTEE ON THE MICROBIOLOGICAL SAFETY OF FOOD
Room 627, Eileen House, 80–94 Newington Causeway, London SE1 6EF
Tel 071-972 2924
Chairman, Prof. H. M. Dick

CLINICAL STANDARDS ADVISORY GROUP
Room 318, Eileen House, 80–94 Newington Causeway, London SE1 6EF
Tel 071-972 2768
Chairman, Sir Gordon Higginson

HEALTH AND SAFETY COMMISSION

Baynards House, 1 Chepstow Place, Westbourne Grove, London W2 4TF
Tel 071-243 6000

The Health and Safety Commission was created under the Health and Safety at Work etc. Act 1974, with duties to reform health and safety law, to propose new regulations, and generally to promote the protection of people at work and of the public from hazards arising from industrial (including commercial) activity, including major industrial accidents and the transportation of hazardous materials.

The Commission members are appointed by the Secretary of State for Employment, although the Commission assists a number of Secretaries of State concerned with aspects of its functions. It is made up of representatives of employers, trades unions and local authorities, and a full-time chairman.

The Commission can appoint agents, and it works in conjunction with local authorities who enforce the Act in such premises as offices and warehouses.

Chairman, Sir John Cullen
Members, Dr M. C. Shannon, CBE; P. Jacques, CBE; A. Tuffin; R. Symons; P. Gallagher; J. Marvin; E. Carrick, Dame Rachel Waterhouse, DBE, Ph.D; N. J. Pitcher
Secretary, J. L. Grubb

HEALTH AND SAFETY EXECUTIVE

Baynards House, 1 Chepstow Place, Westbourne Grove, London W2 4TF
Tel 071-243 6000

The Health and Safety Executive is the Health and Safety Commission's major instrument. Through its inspectorates it enforces health and safety law in the majority of industrial premises, to protect both people at work and the public. The Executive advises the Commission in its major task of laying down safety standards through regulations and practical guidance for many industrial processes, liaising as necessary with government departments and other institutions. The Executive is also the licensing authority for nuclear installations. In carrying out its functions the Executive acts independently of the Government, guided only by the Commission as to general health and safety policy.

Director-General (G2), J. D. Rimington, CB
Deputy Directors-General (G2), D. C. T. Eves; Miss J. H. Bacon

HM FACTORY INSPECTORATE
HM Chief Inspector of Factories (G3), Dr J. T. Carter

HM AGRICULTURAL INSPECTORATE
HM Chief Agricultural Inspector (G3), C. Boswell

HM MINES INSPECTORATE
HM Chief Inspector of Mines (G3), K. Twist

NUCLEAR SAFETY DIVISION
HM Chief Inspector of Nuclear Installations (G3), Dr S. A. Harbison

HM RAILWAY INSPECTORATE
HM Chief Inspector of Railways (G3), R. Seymour

STRATEGY AND GENERAL DIVISION
Director (G3), Dr J. M. McQuaid

TECHNOLOGY AND HEALTH SCIENCES DIVISION
Includes HM Explosives Inspectorate
Director (G3), Dr A. Ellis

SAFETY POLICY DIVISION
Director (G3), R. S. Allison

RESEARCH AND LABORATORY SERVICES DIVISION
Director (G4), Dr A. Roberts

HEALTH POLICY DIVISION
Director of Medical Services (G3), A. W. Brown, CB

SOLICITOR'S OFFICE
Solicitor (G4), B. J. Ecclestone

RESOURCES AND PLANNING DIVISION
Including the Accident Prevention Advisory Unit
Director (G3), D. J. Hodgkins

OFFSHORE SAFETY DIVISION
Chief Executive (G3), A. C. Barrell

HIGHER EDUCATION FUNDING COUNCIL FOR ENGLAND

Northavon House, Coldharbour Lane, Bristol BS16 1QD
Tel 0272-317317

The Higher Education Funding Council for England was established on 6 May 1992 under the provision of the Further and Higher Education Act 1992 to administer funds made available by the Secretary of State for Education for the provision of teaching and research in higher education institutions in England. It will take over this responsibility from the Universities Funding Council and the Polytechnics and Colleges Funding Council on 1 April 1993.

Chairman, Sir Ron Dearing, CB
Chief Executive, Prof. G. Davies, FEng
Members, Prof. C. Campbell; Prof. Sir Brian Follet, FRS; R. Gunn; Prof. K.-T. Khaw; Sir Idris Pearce, CBE, TD; Sir David Phillips, KBE, FRS; Sir Robert Scholey, CBE, FEng; Prof. J. Shaw, CBE; Dr R. Telfer, CBE; Miss J. Trotter, OBE; Prof. D. Watson
Secretary, F. Scott

HIGHER EDUCATION FUNDING COUNCIL FOR SCOTLAND

PO Box 1037, Edinburgh EH1 1DJ
Tel 031-244 5345

The Higher Education Funding Council for Scotland will assume its responsibilities in April 1993.

Chief Executive, Prof. J. Sizer

HIGHER EDUCATION FUNDING COUNCIL FOR WALES

Lambourne House, Lambourne Crescent, Cardiff Business Park, Llansihen, Cardiff CF4 5GL
Tel 0222-641 841

The Higher Education Funding Council for Wales will assume its responsibilities in April 1993.

Chief Executive, Prof. J. A. Andrews

HIGHLANDS AND ISLANDS ENTERPRISE

Bridge House, 20 Bridge Street, Inverness IV1 1QR
Tel 0463-234171

Highlands and Islands Enterprise is the core body of a network of ten local enterprise companies, which encourage and deliver economic and social development plans and training and environmental renewal schemes at local level. It brings together the powers of the former Highlands and Islands Development Board (HIDB), the Training Agency in the former HIDB area, and the land renewal functions of the Scottish Development Agency in the former HIDB area.

Chairman, F. Morrison
Chief Executive, I. A. Robertson

HISTORIC BUILDINGS AND MONUMENTS COMMISSION FOR ENGLAND (ENGLISH HERITAGE)

Fortress House, 23 Savile Row, London W1X 1AB
Tel 071-973 3000

Under the National Heritage Act 1983, the duties of the Commission are to secure the preservation of ancient monuments and historic buildings; to promote the preservation and enhancement of conservation areas; and to promote the public's enjoyment of, and advance their knowledge of, ancient monuments and historic buildings and their preservation. The Commission has advisory committees on historic buildings, ancient monuments, historic areas, and London.

Chairman, J. Stevens
Commissioners, HRH The Duke of Gloucester; Miss J. A. Page (*Chief Executive*); Dr R. W. Brunskill; A. Chancellor; M. B. Caroe; Dr N. Cossons; Sir Hugh Cubitt; Prof. B. Cunliffe; T. Farrell; Sir David Wilson; Mrs R. Lycett-Green; R. Suddards; G. Wilson

HISTORIC BUILDINGS COUNCIL FOR WALES

Brunel House, 2 Fitzalan Road, Cardiff CF2 1UY
Tel 0222-465511

The Council's function is to advise the Secretary of State for Wales through Cadw: Welsh Historic Monuments (*see* page 370), which is an executive agency within the Welsh Office.

Chairman, T. Lloyd, FSA
Members, W. Lindsay Evans; Prof. J. Eynon, OBE, FRIBA, FSA; The Earl Lloyd George of Dwyfor; R. Haslam; Dr P. Morgan
Secretary, R. W. Hughes

HISTORIC BUILDINGS COUNCIL FOR SCOTLAND

20 Brandon Street, Edinburgh EH3 5RA
Tel 031-244 2966

Chairman, Sir Nicholas Fairbairn, QC, MP
Members, Sir Ilay Campbell, Bt.; Mrs P. Chalmers; Prof. J. D. Dunbar-Nasmith, CBE, FRSA, FRSE; M. Ellington; J. Hunter Blair; I. Hutchison, OBE; The Lord Jauncey of Tullichettle, PC; K. Martin; J. A. M. Mitchell, CB, CVO, MC; Miss G. Nayler; Revd C. Robertson; Prof. A. J. Rowan
Secretary, I. G. Dewar

ROYAL COMMISSION ON THE HISTORICAL MONUMENTS OF ENGLAND

Fortress House, 23 Savile Row, London W1X 2JQ
Tel 071-973 3500

The Royal Commission on the Historical Monuments of England was established in 1908. It is the national body charged with the recording and analysing of ancient and historical monuments and buildings. It compiles, preserves and makes publicly available the national archive of such material, which is housed in the National Monuments Record.

Chairman, The Baroness Park of Monmouth, CMG, OBE
Commissioners, Prof. R. Bradley, FSA; R. A. Buchanan, Ph.D.; D. J. Keene, Ph.D.; Prof. G. H. Martin, CBE, D.Phil., FSA; Prof. G. I. Meirion-Jones, Ph.D., FSA; Prof. J. K. Downes, Ph.D., FSA; Prof. A. C. Thomas, CBE, D.Litt., FSA; Prof. M. Biddle, FBA, FSA; Prof. M. Todd, FSA; Mrs B. K. Cherry, FSA; R. D. H. Gem, Ph.D., FSA; T. R. M. Longman; R. A. Yorke; Miss A. Riches, FSA
Secretary, T. G. Hassall, FSA

ROYAL COMMISSION ON ANCIENT AND HISTORICAL MONUMENTS IN WALES

The Crown Building, Plas Crug, Aberystwyth SY23 2HP
Tel 0970-624381

The Commission was established in 1908 to make an inventory of the ancient and historical monuments in Wales and Monmouthshire. It currently has a Royal Warrant of 1992 empowering it to survey, record, publish and maintain a database of ancient and historical sites, structures and landscapes in Wales. The Commission is also responsible for the National Monuments Record for Wales.

Chairman, Prof. J. B. Smith
Commissioners, R. W. Brunskill, OBE, Ph.D., FSA; Prof. D. Ellis Evans, D.Phil., FBA; Prof. R. A. Griffiths, Ph.D.; D. Gruffyd Jones; R. M. Haslam, FSA; Prof. G. B. D. Jones, D.Phil., FSA; S. B. Smith; G. J. Wainwright, MBE, Ph.D., FSA
Secretary, P. R. White, FSA

ROYAL COMMISSION ON THE ANCIENT AND HISTORICAL MONUMENTS OF SCOTLAND

John Sinclair House, 16 Bernard Terrace, Edinburgh EH8 9NX
Tel 031-662 1446

The Commission was established in 1908 and is appointed to provide for the survey and recording of ancient and historical monuments connected with the culture, civilization and conditions of life of the people in Scotland from the earliest times. It compiles and maintains the National Monuments Record of Scotland as the national record of the archaeological and historical environment. The National Monuments Record is open for reference Mon.–Thurs. 9.30–4.30, Fri. 9.30–4.

Chairman, The Earl of Crawford and Balcarres, PC
Commissioners, Prof. J. M. Coles, PH.D., FBA; Prof. J. D. Dunbar-Nasmith, CBE, FRIBA; Prof. Rosemary Cramp, CBE, FSA; Prof. L. Alcock, OBE, FSA, FRHists; Mrs P. E. Durham; Prof. T. C. Smout, Ph.D.; The Hon. Lord Cullen; Dr D. J. Howard, FSA; The Hon. P. D. E. M. Moncreiffe
Secretary, R. J. Mercer, FSA

ANCIENT MONUMENTS BOARD FOR WALES

Brunel House, 2 Fitzalan Road, Cardiff CF2 1UY
Tel 0222-465511

The Ancient Monuments Board for Wales advises the Secretary of State for Wales on his statutory functions in respect of ancient monuments.

Chairman, Prof. G. Williams, CBE, FBA, FSA
Members, R. B. Heaton, OBE, FRIBA; Prof. R. R. Davies, FBA, D.Phil.; Dr S. H. R. Aldhouse-Green, FSA; R. G. Keen; Miss F. Lynch, FSA; Prof. W. H. Manning, Ph.D., FSA; D. Moore, RD, FSA; Dr P. Smith, FSA; Prof. J. B. Smith
Secretary, S. Morris

ANCIENT MONUMENTS BOARD FOR SCOTLAND

20 Brandon Street, Edinburgh EH3 5RA
Tel 031-244 3076

The Ancient Monuments Board for Scotland advises the Secretary of State for Scotland on his statutory functions of providing protection for monuments of national importance.

Chairman, Prof. E. C. Fernie, FSA, FSA scot.
Members, Prof. A. Fenton, CBE, FRSE, FSA scot.; J. Simpson, FSA scot.; Sir Jamie Stormonth Darling, CBE, MC, TD, WS; Mrs E. V. W. Proudfoot, FSA, FSA scot.; Mrs K. Dalyell; J. H. A. Gerrard, FRSA; T. R. H. Godden, CB; L. J. Masters, FSA; Dr A. Richie; R. D. Kernohan, OBE; Dr J. Morgan, FSA scot.; Prof. C. D. Morris, FSA, FSA scot.; The Duchess of Roxburghe; R. J. Mercer, FSA; W. D. H. Sellar, FSA scot.
Secretary, Ms J. Hutchison, FSA, scot.
Assessor, D. J. Breeze, Ph.D., FSA

HOME-GROWN CEREALS AUTHORITY

Hamlyn House, Highgate Hill, London N19 5PR
Tel 071-263 3391

Constituted under the Cereals Marketing Act 1965, the Authority consists of nine members representing UK cereal growers, nine representing dealers in, or processors of, grain and three independent members. The purpose of the Authority is to improve the production and marketing of UK-grown cereals through a research and development programme, the provision of a market information service, and the promotion of UK cereals in export markets. The Authority also undertakes agency work for the Intervention Board for Agricultural Produce in connection with the application in the UK of the Common Agricultural Policy for cereals.

Chairman, G. B. Nelson
General Manager, C. J. Ames

BRITISH CEREAL EXPORTS
Chairman, R. J. Cherrington
Manager, J. B. Rose

HOME OFFICE

50 Queen Anne's Gate, London SW1H 9AT
Tel 071-273 3000

The Home Office deals with those internal affairs in England and Wales which have not been assigned to other government departments. The Home Secretary is particularly concerned with the administration of justice; criminal law; the treatment of offenders, including probation and the prison service; the police; immigration and nationality; passport policy matters; community relations; certain public safety matters; and fire and civil emergencies services. The Home Secretary personally is the link between The Queen and the public, and exercises certain powers on her behalf, including that of the Royal Pardon.

Other subjects dealt with include electoral arrangements; addresses and petitions to The Queen; ceremonial and formal business connected with honours; requests for extradition of criminals; scrutiny of local authority byelaws; granting of licences for scientific procedures involving animals; cremations, burials and exhumations; firearms; dangerous drugs and poisons; general policy on laws relating to shops, liquor licensing, gaming and lotteries, charitable collections and marriage; theatre and cinema licensing; co-ordination of government action in relation to the voluntary social services; and race relations policy.

The Home Secretary is also the link between the UK government and the governments of the Channel Islands and the Isle of Man.

Secretary of State for the Home Department, The Rt. Hon. Kenneth Clarke, QC, MP
Principal Private Secretary (G5), C. J. Walters
Private Secretaries, Miss L. M. Hellmuth; Mrs S. J. McCarthy
Special Adviser, Mrs T. Keswick
Parliamentary Private Secretary, P. Oppenheim, MP
Ministers of State, The Earl Ferrers, PC; Peter Lloyd, MP; Michael Jack, MP
Special Adviser, D. Ruffley

Parliamentary Under Secretary of State, Charles Wardle, MP
Parliamentary Private Secretaries:
To Mr Lloyd, D. Wilshire, MP
To Mr Jack, Miss E. Nicholson, MP
Parliamentary Clerk, B. E. R. Kinney
Permanent Under Secretary of State (G1), Sir Clive Whitmore, GCB, CVO
Private Secretary, C. Dolphin
Chief Medical Officer (at Department of Health), Dr K. Calman

LEGAL ADVISER'S BRANCH

Legal Adviser (G2), M. L. Saunders, CB
Principal Assistant Legal Advisers (G3), D. J. Bentley; Miss P. A. Edwards
Assistant Legal Advisers, R. J. Clayton; Mrs S. A. Evans; J. R. O'Meara; C. M. L. Osborne; D. Seymour
Senior Principal Legal Assistants, S. M. S. Bramley; Miss R. P. Davies; Mrs J. M. Jones; Mrs C. Price

CRIMINAL RESEARCH AND STATISTICS DEPARTMENTS

Deputy Under Secretary (G2), J. F. Halliday

CRIMINAL POLICY DEPARTMENT

Assistant Under Secretary of State (G3), A. P. Wilson
Heads of Divisions (G5), R. J. Baxter; Miss J. MacNaughton; Miss C. Macready; Miss S. Marshall; Miss C. J. Stewart; P. R. C. Storr
Senior Principals (G6), A. Norbury; T. C. Morris; P. Rose
Principals (G7), Dr S. R. E. Atkins; Miss D. Collings; R. G. W. Dyce; M. H. S. de Pulford; R. Eagle; D. H. Evans; J. Glaze; L. D. Hay; L. T. Hughes; N. Jordon; Ms K. Lidbetter; K. MacKenzie; Miss H. L. McKinnon; Mrs R. M. Mitev; M. J. Narey; Ms S. A. Rex; D. Rigby; Ms L. Rogerson; Mrs E. A. Sandars; G. H. H. Sonnenberg; G. Sutton; Ms F. Taylor; J. R. Thew; G. Underwood; P. F. Vallance
Chief Inspector, Drugs Branch (G6), A. McFarlane

RESEARCH AND STATISTICS DEPARTMENT

Assistant Under Secretary of State (G3), C. P. Nuttall

RESEARCH AND PLANNING UNIT

Head of Unit (G5), R. Tarling
Grade 6, J. M. Hough; P. J. Jordan; Mrs P. Mayhew; G. R. Walmsley
Principals (G7), A. C. Barton; D. C. Brown; J. A. Ditchfield; Dr P. J. Ekblom; Dr S. Field; Ms M. Fitzgerald; J. H. Graham; Dr P. Grove; Mrs K. E. Howard; Mrs M. B. Manolias; T. Marshall; Ms P. M. Morgan; Miss J. W. Mott; Dr G. I. U. Mair; J. F. Mcleod; A. D. Moxon; Dr L. J. F. Smith; F. P. E. Southgate; Dr I. P. Williamson

STATISTICS DEPARTMENT

Chief Statisticians (G5), K. Childs; C. G. Lewis; J. L. Walker
Grade 6, L. Davidoff; N. Frater; Mrs C. L. Lehmann; R. Pape; D. A. Povey; P. Sheriff; P. White
Statisticians (G7), Ms A. Barber; G. G. Barclay; Mrs P. Dowdeswell; P. F. Collier; Miss G. Goddard; Mrs S. Keith; M. Lock; Z. J. Frosztega; K. M. Jackson; Miss A. Maxwell; Mrs P. A. Penneck; P. E. Ramell; R. M. Taylor; M. Uglow

CRIMINAL JUSTICE AND CONSTITUTIONAL DEPARTMENT

Assistant Under Secretary of State (G3), R. M. Morris
Heads of Divisions (G5), Miss P. C. Drew; P. J. Honour
Grade 6, A. F. C. Crook; G. H. Marriage
Principals (G7), Ms J. Cooke; S. L. Cox; Miss R. M. Fletton; Ms M. Gorman; Mrs G. Hetherington; H. D. Hillier; Mrs C. J. Jenkins; D. Ross; F. Smith; Ms F. Spencer; J. Wake; S. M. K. Willmington; R. W. Wootton
Chief Inspector of Probation (G4), G. W. Smith
Deputy Chief Inspector of Probation (G5), J. C. Haines
Grade 7, Dr C. Kershaw

ANIMALS (SCIENTIFIC PROCEDURE) INSPECTORATE

Chief Inspector, Dr R. M. Watt

POLICE DEPARTMENT

Deputy Under Secretary (G2), I. M. Burns, CB

POLICE DEPARTMENT

Assistant Under Secretaries of State (G3), Miss M. A. Clayton; Miss C. Sinclair; G. J. Wasserman
Heads of Divisions (G5), Mrs P. G. W. Catto; J. W. Cane; M. Cunliffe; J. B. Duke-Evans; Miss A. M. Edwards; J. L. Goddard; R. A. Harrington; K. H. Heal; R. R. Tilt
Senior Principals (G6), D. R. Birleson; R. Crick; G. J. Daly; R. A. Ginman
Principals (G7), R. C. Barron; J. W. Bradley; R. Brett; G. Brown; P. R. Curwen; P. Dawson; D. Faulks; A. Ford; N. Hancock; Mrs C. Heald; M. J. I. Hill; K. Hopley; A. Maclean; E. Maclean; Mrs S. G. Mann; D. Massey; Mrs S. J. McCarthy; N. F. Montgomery-Pott; Mrs G. I. Moody; D. D. O'Brien; M. Phillips; Mrs I. Posen; P. W. Pugh; C. Roden; S. J. Rimmer; Miss J. B. Rumble; K. W. Smalldon; P. T. Smith; D. Theobald; A. G. Thomson; P. Tomlinson; P. D. White; Mrs C. Wilson; D. Wright; Miss M. S. Wooldridge

POLICE SCIENTIFIC DEVELOPMENT BRANCH
Sandridge Laboratories, Woodcock Hill, Sandridge, St Albans, Herts. AL4 9HQ
Tel 0727-865051
Head of Laboratory (G6), Dr P. A. Young

Langhurst House, Langhurstwood Road, Nr. Horsham, Sussex RH12 4WX
Tel 0403-55451

HEADQUARTERS FORENSIC SCIENCE SERVICE
Horseferry House, Dean Ryle Street, London SW1
Tel 071-217 3000
An executive agency within the Home Office.

Director General (G3), Dr J. Thompson
Grade 5, P. W. Ward
Head of Personnel and Administration (G6), J. P. Emery
Grade 6, Dr T. Rothwell
Grade 7, Mrs E. Sadler (*policy*); Mrs D. Grice

POLICE NATIONAL COMPUTER ORGANIZATION
Horseferry House, Dean Ryle Street, London SW1
Tel 071-217 3000

Head of Organization (G6), J. Ladley
Senior Principals (G6), Dr G. Turnbull; R. Creedon
Principals (G7), B. J. Blain; E. L. Brannan; Mrs P. Cocks; G. T. Coulthard; B. G. Cox; Mrs J. D. Erwteman; D. H. Faulks; J. A. Henderson; P. D. Hill-Jones; A. F. G. Hitchman; D. C. Moulton; Dr F. Preston; P. T. Price; R. J. Reason; D. G. Skene; G. H. Thomas; R. H. Watt

DTELS (Directorate of Telecommunications)
Horseferry House, Dean Ryle Street, London SW1
Tel 071-217 3000

Head of Directorate (*G5*), N. F. K. Finlayson
Assistant Director (*G6*), J. F. Nicholson
Head of Operations (*G6*), I. Aitken
Head of Marketing (*G6*), vacant
Head of Engineering Consultancy (*G6*), J. L. Mumford
Principals (*G7*), F. W. Catterall; S. R. Cole; W. Hogg; A. Hulme; A. N. Kent; T. J. Logan; K. O'Sullivan; R. J. Sanders; K. Staves; L. T. Whiteside

HM Inspectorate of Constabulary

HM Chief Inspector of Constabulary (£78,820), Sir John Woodcock, CBE, QPM
HM Inspectors (£64,640–£71,266), C. J. Dear, QPM; D. Elliott, CBE, QPM; B. Hayes, CBE, QPM; T. A. Morris, CBE, QPM; Sir Philip Myers, OBE, QPM; C. Smith, CVO, QPM

Police Staff College
Bramshill House, Basingstoke, Hampshire RG27 0JW
Tel 025 126-2931
Commandant, Sir Robert Bunyard, KBE, QPM
Deputy Commandant and Director of Courses, P. J. Lewis
Secretary (*G7*), K. J. Sheehan

MI5

Director-General, Mrs S. Rimington

EQUAL OPPORTUNITIES, IMMIGRATION AND NATIONALITY DEPARTMENTS

Deputy Under Secretary (*G2*), A. J. Langdon

Equal Opportunities and General Department

Assistant Under Secretary of State (*G3*), M. E. Head, CVO
Heads of Divisions (*G5*), N. M. Johnson; R. Kornicki; A. Harding
Principals (*G7*), Mrs M. K. Bramwell; P. R. Edmundson; P. J. Goulder; Miss G. F. Harrison; C. C. R. Hudson; Mrs J. S. Morris; S. Pike; C. P. Stevens; R. A. Wright

Voluntary Services Unit

Assistant Secretary (*G5*), D. J. Hardwick
Principals (*G7*), Miss C. Byrne; Miss V. R. Hatcher; A. V. H. Stainer; Ms N. Williams

Immigration and Nationality Department
Lunar House, 40 Wellesley Road, Croydon, Surrey, CR9 2BY
Tel 081-760 plus ext

Assistant Under Secretaries of State (*G3*), W. A. Jeffrey; A. R. Rawsthorne
Heads of Divisions (*G5*), Miss V. M. Dews; E. B. Nicholls; N. C. Sanderson; K. D. Sutton; N. R. Varney; P. N. Wrench; R. G. Yates
Senior Principals (*G6*), T. Farrage; C. J. Saunders; A. Walmsley
Principals (*G7*), C. A. Allison; G. Brindle; W. F. Bryant; D. Burgess; J. Casey; J. Couch; A. Cunningham; W. M. Dawnie; J. Gilbert; Mrs C. Kellas; T. L. Neale; Ms C. Pelham; D. A. Peters; Miss G. M. Romney; G. Stadlen; P. A. Stanton; D. Truscott; J. Sweet; Mrs F. Webster

Immigration Service

Director (*Ports*) (*G5*), Miss K. J. Collins
Director (*Immigration Service Enforcement*) (*G5*), C. B. Manchip
Deputy Directors (*G6*), J. M. de Llanos; D. J. McDonough
Assistant Directors (*G7*), B. R. Barrett; J. M. Durose; Miss G. M. Griffith; V. Hogg; D. I. Ingham; G. Maguire; C. Passey; K. Richardson

Passport Agency
Clive House, Petty France, London SW1H 9HD
Tel 071-271 3000

An executive agency within the Home Office
Chief Executive (*G5*), J. E. Hayzelden
Deputy Chief Executive and Director of Operations (*G6*), Miss A. Smith
Director of Planning and Resources (*G6*), N. S. Benger
Director of Systems (*G6*), T. Lonsdale
Principals (*G7*), J. Burgess; M. Copley; E. Downham; R. G. Le Marechal; R. I. Henderson; J. McColl

PRISON SERVICE

Cleland House, Page Street, London SW1P 4LN
Tel 071-217 3000

Non-Civil Service grade salaries

HM Chief Inspector of Prisons	£61,600
Prison Service Governor 1	£44,710
Prison Service Governor 2	£40,372
Prison Service Governor 3	£34,866
Prison Service Governor 4	£27,626-£29,986

The Prisons Board

Chairman, and Director-General of the Prison Service (*G2*), J. G. Pilling
Director of Personnel and Finance (*G3*), A. J. Butler
Director of Inmate Administration (*G3*), I. Dunbar
Director of Inmate Programmes (*G3*), B. Emes
Director of Custody (*G3*), Miss P. C. Drew
Director of Services and Parole (*G3*), Ms J. Reisz
Director of Prison Health Care (*G3*), Dr R. Wool
Non-Executive Members, Mrs U. Banerjee; F. W. Bentley

Prisons Department

Heads of Divisions (*G5*), P. E. Bolton; B. M. Caffarey; J. I. Chisholm; Miss L. F. Gill; Mrs E. J. Grimsey; G. E. Guy; Mrs V. V. R. Harris; S. B. Hickson; R. C. Masefield; H. H. Taylor; T. Wilson
Assistant Director of Prison Medical Services (*G4*), Dr J. Sinclair
Principal Medical Officers (*G4*), Dr P. Arrowsmith; Dr R. Gooch; Dr M. Longfield; Dr P. B. Pattison; Dr G. Penton; Dr R. Ralli; Dr D. Speed; Dr A. Todd
Senior Principals (*G6*), J. F. Acton; Mrs H. M. Bayne; P. Cook; R. E. Corrigan; C. F. Drewitt; M. Ireson; B. Johnson; R. W. Lockett; B. S. Luetchford; Dr C. McDougall; P. Sleightholme
Governors (1), J. W. Dring; R. Jacques; G. Gregory-Smith; I. Ward; I. Boon
Principals (*G7*), D. M. Ackland; A. J. Adams; D. Aldridge; Mrs J. Anderson; J. H. Attridge; A. J. Beasley; R. M. Bradley; A. D. Burgess; N. Burton; H. M. C. Crudge; L. Curran; P. Done; H. D. R. Ferris; J. A. Greenland; N. F. M. Home; S. S. Horlock; Ms L. M. Jackson; M. W. Jarvis; R. S. H. Kettle; Ms P. Lowe; N. Maclean; Mrs S. McDougall; K. Marshall; Mrs E. Moody; B. Moore; N. Newcomen; J. S. Nottingham; J. Page; S. J. Rimmer; T. E. Russell; R. Rhodes; J. S. Sarjantson; S. Sirikanda; R. E. Smith; C. L. Spencer; R. M. Sutcliffe; D. J. Tallock; M. Todd; J. M. G. Toon; G. Utteridge; M. Walsh; T. A. Ward; Miss S. Weinel; S. C. Wells; W. F. Whiteing; Ms A. Wickington; A. T. Williams; A. Woolfenden; R. J. Wood; P. Wright

Governors (2), C. T. Erickson; C. Lambert; Miss S. F. McCormick; M. Morrison; S. R. Robinson; D. Shaw; C. D. Sherwood; A. G. Smith
Chaplain-General and Archdeacon of the Prison Service, Ven. K. Pound
Chief Education Officer (*G6*), I. G. Benson
Chief Physical Education Officer (*G6*), M. W. Denton
Governors (3), H. Bagshaw; J. R. Dovell; W. S. Duff; R. Fielder; P. L. Hanaway; Ms U. McCollom; D. Myers; S. O'Neill; P. Quinn; I. Truffet; J. Uzzell; R. W. Walker; D. Waplington; I. G. Windebank

DIRECTORATE OF WORKS
Abell House, John Islip Street, London SWIP 4LH
Tel 071-217 3000

Director of Works (*G4*), W. L. Sparks
Group Managers:
Superintending Architect (*G6*), S. Mahraj
Chief Civil Structural Engineer (*G6*), R. W. T. Haines
Chief Mechanical and Electrical Engineer (*G6*), R. Putland
Chief Quantity Surveyor (*G6*), A. W. Gillman
Grade 6, B. Stickley
Principals (G7), O. Astaniotis; P. J. Attwater; B. J. Bleet; J. K. Chamberlain; M. J. Davies; J. B. Dawson; A. Dick; J. A. Doohan; P. Enticknap; J. V. Gleed; M. C. Hayes; G. E. Hickey; J. J. Hurley; C. J. Lawton; R. T. Lewis; D. Newton; J. W. Plumb; S. Richards; M. Ryland; M. Sweeny; R. J. Tricker; A. Weeks; N. L. Wilson

DSP3 (PRISON SERVICE INDUSTRIES AND FARMS)
Lunar House, Wellesley Road, Croydon, Surrey CR9 2BY
Tel 081-760 plus ext.

Director (*G5*), P. R. A. Fulton
Group Managers (*G6*), M. Codd; R. K. Fisher; A. Sweeney; J. Weller
Governor (*1*), K. M. Brewer
Principals (*G7*), C. Allars; J. Cairns; R. Daw; J. W. Fallows; B. D. Feist; Mrs J. M. Flaschner; J. A. Gillcrist; C. Handley; D. E. Neville; T. Senior; A. S. Wilson

SUPPLY AND TRANSPORT BRANCH
Crown House, 52 Elizabeth Street, Corby, Northants
Tel 0536-202101

Director (*G5*), vacant
Principals (*G7*), R. C. Brett; D. J. Brown; B. David; M. Fitzgerald; D. J. Miller

AREA MANAGERS (GOVERNORS I)
Directorate of Custody (*DOC*)

East Anglia, J. Simmons
Kent, J. Hunter
London North, A. J. Pearson
London South, P. J. Kitteridge
South Coast, A. Rayfield

Directorate of Inmate Administration (*DIA*)

Central, M. D. Jenkins
Mercia, D. Curtis
Chilterns, A. de Frisching
Wales and the West, J. Wilkinson
Wessex, R. J. May

Directorate of Inmate Programmes (*DIP*)

East Midland, P. Wheatley
North-East, A. H. Papps
North-West, D. I. Lockwood
Trans-Pennine, T. Bone
Yorkshire, J. Blakey

PRISONS
ACKLINGTON (DIP), Morpeth, Northumberland NE65 9XF. *Governor*, F. P. Masserick
ALBANY (DOC), Newport, Isle of Wight PO30 5RS. *Governor*, R. Mitchell
ALDINGTON (DOC), Ashford, Kent TN25 7BQ. *Governor*, D. A. Bratton
ASHWELL (DIA), Oakham, Leics. LE15 7LS. *Governor*, H. Reid
*ASKHAM GRANGE (DIP), Askham Richard, York YO2 3PT. *Governor*, H. E. Crew
BEDFORD (DOC), St Loyes Street, Bedford MK40 1HG. *Governor*, S. P. Moore
BELMARSH (DOC), Western Way, Thamesmead, London SE28 0EB. *Governor*, H. D. Jones
BIRMINGHAM (DIA), Winson Green Road, Birmingham B18 4AS. *Governor*, C. B. Scott
BLAKENHURST (PRIVATE PRISON), Hewell Lane, Redditch, Worcs. B97 6QS. *Governor*, C. Williams
BLANTYRE HOUSE (DOC), Goudhurst, Cranbrook, Kent TN17 2NH. *Governor*, J. Semple
BLUNDESTON (DOC), Lowestoft, Suffolk NR32 5BG. *Governor*, Miss J. M. Fowler
BRISTOL (DIA), Cambridge Road, Bristol BS7 8PS. *Governor*, R. Smith
BRIXTON (DOC), PO Box 369, Jebb Avenue, London SW2 5XF. *Governor*, Dr A. Coyle
BROCKHILL (DIA), Redditch, Worcs. B97 6RD. *Governor*, P. J. Hanglin
BULLINGDON (DIA), Padrick Haugh Road, Arncott, Bicester, Oxon. OX6 0PZ. *Governor*, J. Thomas-Ferrand
*BULLWOOD HALL (DOC), High Road, Hockley, Essex SS5 4TE. *Governor*, Miss S. Ryan
CAMP HILL (DOC), Newport, Isle of Wight PO30 5PB. *Governor*, vacant
CANTERBURY (DOC), Longport, Canterbury, Kent CT1 1PJ. *Governor*, J. L. Harrison
CARDIFF (DIA), Knox Road, Cardiff CF2 1UG. *Governor*, R. S. Brandon
CASTINGTON (DIP), Morpeth, Northumberland NE65 9XF. *Governor*, J. W. Mullen
CHANNINGS WOOD (DIA), Denbury, Newton Abbott, Devon TQ12 6DW. *Governor*, J. C. Mullens
CHELMSFORD (DOC), Springfield Road, Chelmsford, Essex CM2 6LQ. *Governor*, D. B. Sinclair
COLDINGLEY (DIA), Bisley, Woking, Surrey GU24 9EX. *Governor*, J. Capel
*COOKHAM WOOD (DOC), Cookham Wood, Rochester, Kent ME1 3LU. *Governor*, R. Chapman
DARTMOOR (DIA), Princetown, Yelverton, Devon PL20 6RR. *Governor*, J. Powls
DORCHESTER (DIA), North Square, Dorchester, Dorset DT1 1JD. *Governor*, B. Coatsworth
DOWNVIEW (DOC), Sutton Lane, Sutton, Surrey SM2 5PD. *Governor*, D. Aram
*DRAKE HALL (DIA), Eccleshall, Staffs. ST21 6LQ. *Governor*, R. J. Crouch
*DURHAM (DIP), Old Elvet, Durham DH1 3HU. *Governor*, M. Mogg
*EAST SUTTON PARK (DOC), Sutton Valence, Maidstone, Kent ME17 3DF. *Governor*, W. S. Duff
*ELMLEY (DOC), Church Road, Eastchurch, Sheerness, Kent ME12 4DZ. *Governor*, W. J. Cooper
ERLESTOKE HOUSE (DIA), Devizes, Wilts. SN10 5TU. *Governor*, N. D. Clifford

---

*Women's establishments/establishments with units for women

EVERTHORPE (DIP), Brough, North Humberside HU15 1RB. *Governor*, T. Davies
EXETER (DIA), New North Road, Exeter, Devon EX4 4EX. *Governor*, D. Alderson
FEATHERSTONE (DIA), New Road, Featherstone, Wolverhampton WV10 7PU. *Governor*, L. M. Wiltshire
FORD (DOC), Arundel, W. Sussex BN18 0BX. *Governor*, Maj. B. Smith
FRANKLAND (DIP), Frankland, Brasside, Durham, DH1 5YD. *Governor*, P. Buxton
FULL SUTTON (DIP), Full Sutton, York YO4 1PS. *Governor*, J. W. Staples
GARTH (DIP), Ulnes Walton Lane, Leyland, Preston, Lancs. PR5 3NE. *Governor*, A. J. Fitzpatrick
GARTREE (DIA), Leicester Road, Market Harborough, Leics. LE16 7RP. *Governor*, R. J. Perry
GLOUCESTER (DIA), Barrack Square, Gloucester GL1 2JN. *Governor*, P. W. Winkley
GRENDON (DOC), Grendon Underwood, Aylesbury, Bucks. HP18 0TL. *Governor*, T. C. Newell
HASLAR (DOC), Dolphin Way, Gosport, Hants. PO12 2AW. *Governor*, T. Hinchcliffe
HAVERIGG (DIP), Haverigg Camp, Millom, Cumbria LA18 4NA. *Governor*, B. Wilson
HIGH DOWN (DOC), Sutton Lane, Sutton, Surrey SM2 5PJ. *Governor*, S. Pryor
HIGHPOINT (DOC), Stradishall, Newmarket, Suffolk CB8 9YG. *Governor*, R. Curtis
HINDLEY (DIP), Gibson Street, Bickershaw, Hindley, Wigan, Lancs. WN2 5TH. *Governor*, D. Roberts
*HOLLOWAY (DOC), Parkhurst Road, London N7 0NU. *Governor*, T. M. O'Sullivan
HOLME HOUSE (DIP), Holme House Road, Stockton-on-Tees, Cleveland TS18 2QU. *Governor*, A. K. Rawson
HULL (DIP), Hedon Road, Hull, N. Humberside HU9 5LS. *Governor*, R. Daly
KINGSTON (DOC), Milton Road, Portsmouth PO3 6AS. *Governor*, R. Merricks
KIRKHAM (DIP), Preston, Lancs. PR4 2RA. *Governor*, A. F. Jennings
LANCASTER (DIP), The Castle, Lancaster LA1 1YL. *Governor*, D. G. McNaughton
LATCHMERE HOUSE (DOC), Church Road, Ham Common, Richmond, Surrey TW10 5HH. *Governor*, S. O'Neill
LEEDS (DIP), Armley, Leeds LS12 2TJ. *Governor*, vacant
LEICESTER (DIA), Welford Road, Leicester LE2 7AJ. *Governor*, G. Ross
LEWES (DOC), Brighton Road, Lewes, E. Sussex BN7 1EA. *Governor*, T. M. Turner
LEYHILL (DIA), Wotton-under-Edge, Glos. GL12 8HL. *Governor*, N. W. A. Wall
LINCOLN (DIP), Greetwell Road, Lincoln LN2 4BD. *Governor*, W. J. MacGowan
LINDHOLME (DIP), Bawtry Road, Hatfield, Woodhouse, Doncaster DN7 6EE. *Governor*, P. Leonard
LITTLEHEY (DOC), Perry, Huntingdon, Cambs. PE18 0SR. *Governor*, M. L. Knight
LIVERPOOL (DIP), 68 Hornby Road, Liverpool L9 3DF. *Governor*, R. D. Dixon
LONG LARTIN (DIA), South Littleton, Evesham, Worcs. WR11 5TZ. *Governor*, P. Atherton
MAIDSTONE (DOC), County Road, Maidstone ME14 1UZ. *Governor*, P. J. Meakings
MANCHESTER (DIP), Southall Street, Manchester M60 9AH. *Governor*, R. P. Halward

*Women's establishments/establishments with units for women

MOORLAND (DIP), Hatfield Woodhouse, Doncaster DN7 6BW. *Governor*, M. Sheldrick
MORTON HALL (DIP), Swinderby, Lincoln LN6 9PS. *Governor*, M. F. Clarke
THE MOUNT (DIA), Molyneaux Avenue, Bovingdon, Hemel Hempstead HP3 0NZ. *Governor*, Mrs M. Donnelly
*NEW HALL (DIP), Dial Wood, Flockton, Wakefield, W. Yorks. WF4 4AX. *Governor*, D. England
NORTHEYE (DOC), Barnhorn Road, Bexhill-on-Sea, E. Sussex TN39 4QW. *Governor*, D. A. Godfrey
NORTH SEA CAMP (DIP), Freiston, Boston, Lincs. PE22 0QX. *Governor*, R. Reveley
NORWICH (DIP), Mousehold, Norwich NR1 4LU. *Governor*, M. R. J. Gander
NOTTINGHAM (DIP), Perry Road, Sherwood, Nottingham NG5 3AG. *Governor*, L. Lavender
OXFORD (DIA), New Road, Oxford OX1 1LZ. *Governor*, R. J. Talbot
PARKHURST (DOC), Newport, Isle of Wight PO30 5NX. *Governor*, J. R. Marriott
PENTONVILLE (DOC), Caledonian Road, London N7 8TT. *Governor*, W. J. Abbott
PRESTON (DIP), 2 Ribbleton Lane, Preston, Lancs. OR1 5AB. *Governor*, R. Doughty
RANBY (DIP), Ranby, Retford, Notts. DN22 8EU. *Governor*, F. Abbott
READING (DIA), Forbury Road, Reading RG1 3HY. *Governor*, P. Dixon
*RISLEY (DIP), Warrington Road, Risley, Warrington WA3 6BP. *Governor*, F. B. O'Friel.
ROCHESTER (DOC), Rochester, Kent ME1 3QS. *Governor*, D. Wilson
RUDGATE (DIP), Wetherby, W. Yorks. LS23 7AZ. *Governor*, H. Jones
SEND (DOC), Ripley Road, Send, Woking, Surrey GU23 7LJ. *Governor*, J. F. Dixon
SHEPTON MALLET (DIA), Cornhill, Shepton Mallet, Somerset BA4 5LU. *Governor*, C. P. Gibbard
SHREWSBURY (DIA), The Dana, Shrewsbury, Salop SY1 2HR. *Governor*, D. J. Bradley
SPRING HILL (DOC), Grendon Underwood, Aylesbury, Bucks. HP18 0TH. *Governor*, T. C. Newell
STAFFORD (DIA), 54 Gaol Road, Stafford ST16 3AW. *Governor*, C. Harder
STANDFORD HILL (DOC), Church Road, Eastchurch, Sheerness, Kent ME12 4AA. *Governor*, D. M. Twiner
STOCKEN (DIP), Stocken Hall Road, Stretton, Nr Oakham, Leics. LE15 7RD. *Governor*, R. P. Feeney
STOCKE HEATH (DIA), Market Drayton, Shropshire TF9 2JL. *Governor*, J. Alldridge
*STYAL (DIP), Wilmslow, Cheshire SK9 4HR. *Governor*, G. Walker
SUDBURY (DIA), Sudbury, Derbyshire DE6 5HW. *Governor*, Miss C. A. Carden
SWALESIDE (DOC), Eastchurch, Isle of Sheppey, Kent ME12 4AX. *Governor*, B. W. Sutton
SWANSEA (DIA), Oystermouth Road, Swansea SA1 2SR. *Governor*, J. Heyes
THORP ARCH (DIP), Wetherby, W. Yorks. LS23 7AY. *Governor*, G. Barnard
USK (DIA), 29 Maryport Street, Usk, Gwent NP5 1XP. *Governor*, B. T. Williams
THE VERNE (DIA), Portland, Dorset DT5 1EQ. *Governor*, D. G. Longley
WAKEFIELD (DIP), Love Lane, Wakefield WF2 9AG. *Governor*, R. S. Duncan
WANDSWORTH (DOC), PO Box 757, Heathfield Road, London SW18 3HS. *Governor*, C. G. Clarke

Wayland (doc), Wayland, Griston, Thetford, Norfolk IP25 6RL. *Governor*, T. C. H. Newth
Wellingborough (doc), Millers Park, Doddington Road, Wellingborough, Northants. NN8 2NH. *Governor*, J. Whetton
Whatton (dip), Whatton, Notts. NG13 9FQ. *Governor*, M. A. Lewis
Whitemoor (doc), Longhill Road, March, Cambs. PE15 0PR. *Governor*, A. J. Barclay
Winchester (doc), Romsey Road, Winchester, Hants. SO22 5DF. *Governor*, M. K. Pascoe
Woodhill (doc), Tattenhoe Street, Milton Keynes MK4 4DA. *Governor*, R. B. Clark
Wormwood Scrubbs (doc), PO Box 757, Du Cane Road, London W12 0AE. *Governor*, J. F. Perriss
Wymott (dip), Moss Lane, Ulnes Walton, Leyland, Preston, Lancs. PR5 3LW. *Governor*, W. J. Mansfield

Young Offender Institutions

Aylesbury (dia), Bierton Road, Aylesbury, Bucks. HP20 1EH. *Governor*, C. Welsh
Brinsford (dia), New Road, Featherstone, Wolverhampton WV10 7PY. *Governor*, P. J. Earnshaw
*Bullwood Hall (doc), High Road, Hockley, Essex SS5 4TE. *Governor*, Miss S. Ryan
Castington (dip), Morpeth, Northumberland NE65 9XF. *Governor*, J. W. Mullen
Deerbolt (dip), Bowes Road Barnard Castle, Co. Durham DL12 9BG. *Governor*, P. A. Whitehouse, OBE
Dover (doc), The Citadel, Western Heights, Dover, Kent CT17 9DR. *Governor*, T. G. Murtagh, OBE
*Drake Hall (dia), Eccleshall, Staffs. ST21 6LQ. *Governor*, R. J. Crouch
*East Sutton Park (doc), Sutton Valence, Maidstone, Kent ME17 3DF. *Governor*, W. S. Duff
Eastwood Park (dia), Falfield, Wotton-under-Edge, Glos. GL12 8DB. *Governor*, R. J. Monksummers
Feltham (doc), Bedfont Road, Feltham, Middx. TW13 4ND. *Governor*, J. Whitty
Finnamore Wood (dia), Finnamore Wood, Frieth Road, Medmenham, Marlow, Bucks. SL7 2HX. *Governor*, Miss A. W. Hair.
Glen Parva (dia), Tigers Road, Wigston, Leics. LE8 2TN. *Governor*, J. H. Rumball
Guys Marsh (dia), Shaftesbury, Dorset SP7 0AH. *Governor*, P. B. Tucker
Hatfield (dip), Hatfield, Doncaster DN7 6EL. *Governor*, W. J. Clark
Hewell Grange (dia), Redditch, Worcs. B97 6QQ. *Governor*, D. W. Bamber
Hollesley Bay Colony (doc), Hollesley, Woodbridge, Suffolk IP12 3JS. *Governor*, Miss J. M. King
Huntercombe (dia), Huntercombe Place, Nuffield, Henley-on-Thames RG9 5SB. *Governor*, Miss A. W. Hair
Kirklevington Grange (dip), Yarm, Cleveland TS15 9PA. *Governor*, M. K. Lees
Lancaster Farms (dip), Stone Row Head, off Quernmore Road, Lancaster LA1 3QZ. *Governor*, D. J. Waplington
*New Hall (dip), Dial Wood, Flockton, Wakefield WF4 4AX. *Governor*, D. England
Northallerton (dip), East Road, Northallerton, N. Yorks. DL6 1NW. *Governor*, J. N. Brooke.
Onley (dia), Willoughby, Rugby, Warks. CV23 8AP. *Governor*, J. O'Neill
Portland (dia), Easton, Portland, Dorset DT5 1DL. *Governor*, B. McLuckie
Prescoed (dia), 29 Maryport Street, Usk, Gwent NP4 0TD. *Governor*, D. T. Williams
Stoke Heath (dia), Market Drayton, Salop TF9 2JL. *Governor*, J. Alldridge
*Styal (dip), Wilmslow, Cheshire, SK9 4HR. *Governor*, G. Walker
Swinfen Hall (dia), Lichfield, Staffs. WS14 9QS. *Governor*, C. Scott
Thorn Cross (dip), Arley Road, Appleton Thorn, Warrington WA4 4RL. *Governor*, C. R. Griffiths
Werrington (dia), Stoke-on-Trent ST9 0DX. *Governor*, P. E. Salter
Wetherby (dip), York Road, Wetherby, W. Yorks. LS22 5ED. *Governor*, P. J. Atkinson

Remand Centres

Brinsford (dia), New Road, Featherstone, Wolverhampton WV10 7PY. *Governor*, P. J. Earnshaw
Cardiff (dia), Knox Road, Cardiff CF2 1UG. *Governor*, R. S. Brandon
Feltham (doc), Bedfont Road, Feltham, Middx. TW13 4ND. *Governor*, J. Whitty
Glen Parva (dia), Tigers Road, Wigston, Leics. LE8 2TN. *Governor*, J. H. Rumball
Low Newton (dip), Brasside, Durham DH1 5SD. *Governor*, A. Holman
Pucklechurch (dia), Bristol BS17 3QJ. *Governor*, P. Mortimore
Stoke Heath (dia), Market Drayton, Salop TF9 2JL. *Governor*, J. Alldridge
Winchester (doc), Romsey Road, Winchester, Hants. SO22 5DF. *Governor*, M. K. Pascoe
The Wolds (private remand prison), Everthorpe, Brough, N. Humberside HU15 2JZ. *Governor*, S. Twinn

Inspectorate of Prisons

HM Chief Inspector of Prisons, His Hon. Judge Tumim
HM Deputy Chief Inspector of Prisons (G5), B. V. Smith
HM Inspectors (Gov. 1), C. Allen; D. M. Brooke; *(Gov. 4)*, J. Gallagher; D. A. Strong; *(G7)*, J. J. Courtney; B. J. Wells
Principal (G7), S. E. Bass

ESTABLISHMENT, FINANCE AND MANPOWER, FIRE AND EMERGENCY PLANNING DEPARTMENTS

Deputy Under Secretary (G2), T. C. Platt

Establishment Department

Assistant Under Secretary of State (G3), C. L. Scoble *(Personnel, Organization and Management Services)*
Heads of Divisions (G5), B. W. Buck; P. Canovan; Mrs C. Crawford; Mrs E. I. France; R. M. Whalley
Senior Principals (G6), R. C. Case; F. R. Hayhurst; D. C. Houghton
Principals (G7), Miss M. A. Allibone; K. Aylen; F. Bannister; J. A. Black; W. Black; P. Buley; M. Carr; A. Fishwick; J. Fleming; I. C. Gaskell; R. A. Hemmings; W. Heppolette; M. C. Jennings; D. G. Jones; B. J. Jordan; Mrs J. Morgan; D. Mould; Mrs B. Moxon; H. O'Connor; R. Ritchie; K. E. R. Rogers; Mrs M. Rolfe; G. R. Sampher; T. Sargent; N. Shackleford; A. Silver; S. E. Wharton; A. T. Williams; Mrs V. M. Wilsdon; Mrs L. Wishart

ASSESSMENT CONSULTANCY UNIT

Director (*G5*), Miss S. E. Paul
Deputy Director (*G6*), vacant
Principal Psychologist (*G7*), D. J. Murray

PUBLIC RELATIONS BRANCH

Director of Information Services (*G4*), A. E. Moorey
Deputy Director of Information Services (*G6*), Miss A. Maclean
Head Publicity Officer (*G6*), C. Skinner
Chief Press Officer (*Prisons*) (*G7*), I. R. Scott

FINANCE AND MANPOWER DEPARTMENT

Assistant Under Secretary of State (*Principal Finance Officer*) (*G3*), S. G. Norris
Heads of Divisions (*G5*), B. O. Bubbear; J. L. Haugh; J. A. Ingman; G. C. Robertson
Senior Principals (*G6*), P. G. Davies; T. A. S. Devon; A. K. Holman
Principals (*G7*), B. D. Bishop; Ms J. Bonelle; D. Burge; Mrs C. Burrows; G. Cassell; K. I. Cole; Mrs M. Cooper; T. A. S. Daniels; C. I. Dickinson; G. F. Edwards; F. H. Eggleston; B. Elliott; C. Harnett; P. W. Jones; D. J. Kent; M. Lee; Miss D. Loudon; R. P. Ritchie; I. F. Smith

FIRE AND EMERGENCY PLANNING DEPARTMENT

Assistant Under Secretary of State (*G3*), W. J. A. Innes
Civil Emergencies Adviser, D. C. G. Brook, CB, CBE
Heads of Divisions (*G5*), R. J. Miles; Dr D. M. S. Peace; J. R. K. de Quidt; E. Soden; P. G. Spurgeon
Grade 6, D. R. Dewick; Dr J. R. Stealey; D. Meakin
Principals (*G7*), D. Boyle; Dr G. A. Carr-Hill; J. A. Chalmers; F. T. Chambers; R. Chick; E. Cook; J. A. Foster; Dr J. A. Harwood; A. J. Lewis; A. E. Mantle; D. A. Peters; A. N. Pickersgill; P. Regan; Dr G. E. Scott; R. C. Stephen; Dr M. D. Thomas; P. Topping; K. Wallace

HM FIRE SERVICE INSPECTORATE

HM Chief Inspector, Sir Reginald Doyle, CBE
HM Inspectors, B. H. A. Buswell; S. D. Christian; B. T. A. Collins, OBE; T. Greenwood, OBE; A. F. Kilford; P. A. Kilshaw; W. Lumb; D. N. McCallum, OBE; N. Musselwhite, QFSM; W. C. Perry, MBE; K. T. Phillips; R. W. Rawlinson; H. V. Reed; D. F. Robins, CBE; R. M. Simpson, OBE; G. J. Tinley
Senior Engineering Inspector, vacant
Principal (*G7*), R. G. W. Cooke

FIRE SERVICE COLLEGE

Moreton-in-Marsh, Glos. GL56 0RH
Tel 0608-50831

An executive agency within the Home Office.
Chief Executive, B. Fuller, CBE
Deputy Chief Executive, A. Salisbury
Director of Studies, Dr R. Willis-Lee
Secretary (*G7*), J. A. Gundersen

EMERGENCY PLANNING COLLEGE

The Hawkhills, Easingwold, Yorks. YO6 3EG
Tel 0347-21406

Head of College (*G5*), J. B. Bettridge, CBE
Vice-Principal, Col. H. H. Evans

HOME OFFICE HQ UK WARNING AND MONITORING ORGANIZATION

James Wolfe Road, Cowley, Oxford OX4 2PT
Tel 0865-776005

Group 7, W. P. Lawrie

HORSERACE TOTALISATOR BOARD

74 Upper Richmond Road, London SW15 2SU
Tel 081-874 6411

The Horserace Totalisator Board was established by the Betting, Gaming and Lotteries Act 1963, as successor to the Racecourse Betting Control Board. Its function is to operate totalisators on approved racecourses in Great Britain, and it also provides on- and off-course cash and credit offices. Under the Horserace Totalisator and Betting Levy Board Act 1972, it is further empowered to offer bets at starting price (or other bets at fixed odds) on any sporting event.

Chairman (£88,935), The Lord Wyatt of Weeford
Members, B. McDonnell (*Chief Executive*); P. S. Winfield; T. J. Phillips (*Finance*); J. F. Sanderson; The Hon. D. Sieff; The Lord Swaythling

HOUSING CORPORATION

149 Tottenham Court Road, London W1P 0BN
Tel 071-387 9466

Established by Parliament in 1964, the Housing Corporation registers, promotes, funds and supervises housing associations. There are over 2,300 registered associations in England providing more than 600,000 homes for people in need of housing. Housing associations are non-profit making bodies run by voluntary committees.

The Corporation's duties were extended under the provisions of the Housing Act 1988 to cover the payment of capital and revenue grants to housing associations, advice for tenants interested in Tenants' Choice, and the approval and revocation of potential new landlords under this policy.

Chairman, Sir Christopher Benson
Chief Executive, A. Mayer

HUMAN FERTILIZATION AND EMBRYOLOGY AUTHORITY

Paxton House, 30 Artillery Lane, London E1 7LS
Tel 071-377 5077

The Authority was established under the Human Fertilization and Embryology Act 1990. Its function is to license persons carrying out any of the following activities: the creation or use of embryos outside the body in the provision of infertility treatment services; the use of donated gametes in infertility treatment; the storage of gametes or embryos; and research on human embryos. The Authority also keeps under review information about embryos and, when requested to do so, gives advice to the Secretary of State for Health.

Chairman, Prof. C. Campbell
Deputy Chairman, Lady Brittan
Members, Ms M. Auld; Prof. R. J. Berry; Prof. I. Cooke; Prof. A. Cox; Ms E. Forgan; Ms J. Harbison; S. Hillier; Ph.D; Prof. B. Hoggett, QC; The Rt. Revd R. Holloway; Ms P. Keith; Ms A. Mays; Dr A. McLaren; Dr J. Naish; Rabbi Julia Neuberger; Prof. R. W. Shaw; D. Shilson; Prof. R. Snowden; Ms C. Walby; Prof. D. Whittingham
Chief Executive, Mrs F. Goldhill

INDEPENDENT TELEVISION COMMISSION

70 Brompton Road, London SW3 1EY
Tel 071-584 7011

The Independent Television Commission replaced the Independent Broadcasting Authority at the beginning of 1991 under the terms of the Broadcasting Act 1990. The Commission is responsible for licensing and regulating all commercially funded UK television services.

Chairman, Sir George Russell, CBE
Deputy Chairman, J. Stevens
Members, Earl of Dalkeith; Prof. J. F. Fulton; Ms P. Mathias; Lady Popplewell; Prof. J. Ring; P. Sheth; R. Goddard; Mrs E. Wynne Jones
Chief Executive, D. Glencross

INDUSTRIAL INJURIES ADVISORY COUNCIL

The Adelphi, 1–11 John Adam Street, London WC2N 6HT
Tel 071-962 8066

The Industrial Injuries Advisory Council is a statutory body under the Social Security Act 1975 which considers and advises the Secretary of State for Social Services on regulations and other questions relating to industrial injuries benefits or their administration.

Chairman, Prof. J. M. Harrington, CBE
Members, G. Appleby; P. Arscott; Dr J. Asherson; Miss J. C. Brown; Prof. M. J. Cinnamond; Dr D. Coggon; Prof. A. Dayan; P. R. A. Jacques; Dr C. P. Juniper; Prof. A. J. Newman Taylor; R. Pickering; Dr E. Roman; Dr A. Sinclair; O. Tudor; Ms M. Twomey
Secretary, R. Heigh

CENTRAL OFFICE OF INFORMATION

Hercules Road, London SE1 7DU
Tel 071-928 2345

The Central Office of Information (COI) is the government executive agency which provides publicity and information services to government departments, other executive agencies and public sector bodies. It provides consultancy, design, production, procurement and project management services for a wide range of publicity services in all media. Though the majority of COI's work is for government departments in the UK, it also produces a range of publicity materials for overseas consumption.

Administrative responsibility for the COI rests with the Minister of Public Service and Science, while the ministers whose departments it serves are responsible for the policy expressed in its work.

Chief Executive and Head of the Government Information Service (G3), G. M. Devereau
Private Secretary, Mrs J. Shinn
Deputy Chief Executive (G5), J. Bolitho

MARKETING AND CLIENT SERVICES GROUP

Group Director (G5), R. N. Hooper
Head, Business Development and Communications Services (G7), W. Roberts

CAMPAIGNS GROUP

Group Director (G5), R. Windsor
Director, Advertising (G6), M. Brodie
Director, Research (G6), M. Warren
Director, Direct Marketing (G7), C. Noble

PUBLICATIONS, PRESS AND EXHIBITIONS

Group Director (G5), D. A. Low
Director, Press and PR (G6), vacant
Director, Publications (G6), J. Murray
Director, Reference and Translations (G6), D. Beynon
Director, Exhibitions and Pictures (G6), D. Beynon
Director, Films Television and Radio Division (G6), M. Nisbet
Principal Finance Officer (G5), K. Williamson
Principal Establishment Officer (G6), M. Langhorne

NETWORK AND EMERGENCY PLANNING SERVICES GROUP

Group Director (G5), P. Brazier

NETWORK OFFICES

NORTH-EASTERN

Wellbar House, Gallowgate, Newcastle upon Tyne NE1 4TB
Network Director (G7), H. Cozens

YORKSHIRE AND HUMBERSIDE

City House, New Station Street, Leeds LS1 4JG
Network Director (G6), R. P. Haslam

EASTERN

Three Crowns House, 72–80 Hills Road, Cambridge CB2 1LL
Network Director (G7), Mrs V. Burdon

LONDON AND SOUTH-EASTERN

Lincoln House, Westminster Bridge Road, London SE1 7DU
Network Director (G6), D. Smith

SOUTH-WESTERN

The Pithay, Bristol BS1 2NF
Network Director (G7), B. Garner

MIDLANDS

Five Ways Tower, Frederick Road, Edgbaston, Birmingham B15 1SH
Network Director (G6), O. J. B. Prince-White

NORTH-WESTERN

Sunley Tower, Piccadilly Plaza, Manchester M1 4BD
Network Director (G7), Mrs E. Jones

BOARD OF INLAND REVENUE

Somerset House, London WC2R 1LB
Tel 071-438 6622

The Board of Inland Revenue was constituted under the Inland Revenue Board Act 1849, by the consolidation of the Board of Excise and the Board of Stamps and Taxes. In 1909 the administration of excise duties was transferred to the Board of Customs. The Board of Inland Revenue administers and collects direct taxes – mainly income tax, stamp duty, development land tax and petroleum revenue tax – and advises the Chancellor of the Exchequer on policy questions involving them.

The Department is organized into a series of accountable management units under the Next Steps programme. The day-to-day operations in assessing and collecting tax and in providing internal support services are carried out by 34 Executive Offices. The Department's Valuation Office is an executive agency responsible for valuing property for tax purposes, for compensation, for compulsory purchase, and (in England and Wales) for local rating purposes. In 1990–1 the Inland Revenue collected over £82,500 million in tax.

THE BOARD

Chairman (G1), Sir Anthony Battishill, KCB
Private Secretary, G. Lloyd
Deputy Chairmen (G2), T. J. Painter, CB; L. J. H. Beighton, CB
Private Secretary, Miss F. Huskisson
Directors-General (G2), S. C. T. Matheson; C. W. Corlett

SUBJECT DIVISIONS

Directors (G3), E. McGivern; M. F. Cayley; B. Mace; M. Templeman; P. Lewis; I. R. Spence; E. F. Gribbon
Senior Principal Inspectors of Taxes (G4), R. H. Allen; R. E. Creed; M. D. E. Newstead; R. N. Page, CBE; M. A. Keith; R. M. Elliss; R. E. Haigh; I. N. Hunter; P. R. P. Stokes; A. J. O'Brien; B. Sadler
Grade 5, A. W. Kuczys; R. B. Willis; L. E. Jaundoo; I. Stewart; C. Stewart; Miss R. A. Dyall; J. D. Farmer; M. T. Evans; M. D. R. Haigh; R. Warden; C. D. Sullivan; J. P. B. Bryce; P. W. Fawcett; J. B. Shepherd; M. Hay; M. J. G. Elliott
Principal Inspectors of Taxes (G5), B. Jones; J. H. Keelty; A. P. Beauchamp; Mrs M. E. Williams; R. S. Hurcombe; J. E. Morris; M. D. Phelps; J. P. Crisp; M. Waters; A. H. Williams; P. H. Linford

STATISTICS AND ECONOMICS OFFICE

Director (G3), J. W. Calder
Grade 5, Dr G. A. Keenay; J. B. Dearman; R. J. Eason; E. Ko
Information Technology (G6), Dr R. James
Senior Economics Adviser (G5), W. M. McNie

INFORMATION TECHNOLOGY OFFICE

Director (G3), G. H. Bush
Grade 4, C. J. Thompson
Grade 5, R. A. Assirati; Dr W. Woodard

PERSONNEL DIRECTORATE

Director of Personnel (G3), P. B. G. Jones, CB
Deputy Directors (G4), R. Neilson; N. C. Munro
Assistant Directors (G5), A. Pardoe; J. Eastman; Mrs C. B. Hubbard; S. Mitha; *(G6)*, M. Jarrett; R. Cartwright; M. K. Robins

MANPOWER AND SUPPORT SERVICES

Director (G3), J. M. Crawley
Assistant Directors (G5), R. F. Moore; J. Gray; Miss M. A. Hill; R. P. R. Tilley; A. W. Bryant

TRAINING OFFICE

Royal Exchange House, Boar Lane, Leeds LS1 5PG
Controller (G5), D. J. Timmons

CENTRAL DIVISION

Director (G3), M. A. Johns
Grade 5, R. Golding; B. Glassberg

CHANGE MANAGEMENT GROUP

Head (G4), J. Yard

CORPORATE COMMUNICATIONS OFFICE

Controller (G5), Mrs S. Cullum
Press Secretary (G7), Mrs S. J. Bradley

FINANCE DIVISION

Principal Finance Officer (G3), J. M. Crawley, CB
Grade 5, J. H. Reed; R. R. Martin; J. R. Cavell

INTERNAL AUDIT OFFICE

22 Kingsway, London WC2B 6NR
Chief Internal Auditor (G5), N. R. Buckley

FINANCIAL SERVICES OFFICE

Barrington Road, Worthing, W. Sussex BN12 4XH
Controller (G6), D. Easey

FINANCIAL AND MANAGEMENT ACCOUNTING SYSTEMS OFFICE

Barrington Road, Worthing, W. Sussex BN12 4XH
Controller (G6), C. R. F. Jury

SOLICITOR FOR INLAND REVENUE

Solicitor (G2), B. E. Cleave
Principal Assistant Solicitors (G3), J. D. H. Johnston; P. L. Ridd; J. G. H. Bates
Assistant Solicitors (G5), Miss M. P. E. Boland; A. J. Gunz; A. K. S. Shaw; A. P. Douglas; W. J. Durrans; S. Bousher; R. S. Waterson; R. F. Walters; Miss A. Hawkings; K. Brown; C. J. C. Baron; R. W. Thornhill; Miss A. E. Wyman
Board's Advisory Accountant (G5), T. C. Carne

SOLICITOR OF INLAND REVENUE (SCOTLAND)

80 Lauriston Place, Edinburgh EH3 9SL
Solicitor, T. H. Scott

DIRECTORATE, OPERATIONS 1

Director (G3), K. V. Deacon
Deputy Director (G4), D. W. Muir
Assistant Directors (G5), T. R. Evans; J. M. Thomas; S. H. Banyard; J. Calder; E. C. Jones; A. McClure; S. J. McManus; J. P. Gilbody; Dr E. A. Harrison; M. G. Oakley

REGIONAL OFFICES

INLAND REVENUE EAST LONDON, New Court, Carey Street, London WC2A 2JE
INLAND REVENUE SOUTH LONDON, New Court, Carey Street, London WC2A 2JE
INLAND REVENUE NORTH AND WEST LONDON, New Court, Carey Street, London WC2A 2JE
INLAND REVENUE NORTH, Corporation House, 73 Albert Road, Middlesbrough, Cleveland TS1 2RZ
INLAND REVENUE SOUTH YORKSHIRE, Sovereign House, 40 Silver Street, Sheffield S1 2EN
INLAND REVENUE EAST, Midgate House, Peterborough PE1 1TD
INLAND REVENUE SOUTH-EAST, Albion House, Chertsey Road, Woking GU21 1BT
INLAND REVENUE SOUTH-WEST, Finance House, Barnfield Road, Exeter EX1 1QX
INLAND REVENUE MIDLANDS, Chadwick House, Blenheim Court, Solihull, W. Midlands B91 2AA
INLAND REVENUE GREATER MANCHESTER, Apsley House, Wellington Road North, Stockport SK4 1EY
INLAND REVENUE NORTH-WEST, The Triad, Stanley Road, Bootle, Merseyside L20 3PD
INLAND REVENUE WALES, Brunel House, 2 Fitzalan Road, Cardiff CF2 1SE
INLAND REVENUE SCOTLAND, 80 Lauriston Place, Edinburgh EH3 9SL

INLAND REVENUE NORTHERN IRELAND, Windsor House, 9–15 Bedford Street, Belfast BT2 7EL

DIRECTORATE, OPERATIONS 2

Director (*G3*), J. H. Roberts
Deputy Director (*G4*), J. M. L. Davenport

SPECIAL COMPLIANCE OFFICE
Angel Court, 199 Borough High Street, London SE1 1HZ
Controller (*G4*), F. J. Brannigan
Grade 5, J. T. Cawdron; J. Mawson, D. F. Parrett; Miss K. C. S. H. Linnell
Board's Investigating Officer (*G6*), F. B. Dunbar

CLAIMS BRANCH
St John's House, Merton Road, Bootle L69 9BB
Controller (*G5*), D. A. Hartnett

CLAIMS BRANCH (SCOTLAND)
Trinity Park House, South Trinity Road, Edinburgh EH5 3SD
Officer in Charge (*G7*), J. Duguid

PENSION SCHEMES OFFICE
Lynwood Road, Thames Ditton, Surrey KT7 0DP
Controller (*G5*), R. G. Lusk

THE STAMP OFFICE

Controller (*G6*), K. S. Hodgson

THE STAMP OFFICE (SCOTLAND)
16 Picardy Place, Edinburgh EH1 3NF
Controller, D. G. Hunter

CAPITAL TAXES OFFICE
Minford House, Rockley Road, London W14 0DF
Controller (*G4*), B. D. Kent
Deputy Controllers (*G5*), H. V. Capon; A. G. Nield; R. J. Draper
Assistant Controllers (*G6*), D. J. Ferley; B. K. Lakhanpaul; T. J. Plumb; P. R. Twiddy; C. A. Oldridge; F. A. Cook; R. J. Shanks; N. S. Tant; M. J. Francis; A. D. Tytherleigh

CAPITAL TAXES OFFICE (SCOTLAND)
Mulberry House, 16 Picardy Place, Edinburgh, EH1 3NB
Registrar (*G5*), I. Fraser
Deputy Registrar (*G7*), W. Young
Chief Examiners (*G7*), Mrs J. A. Templeton; Miss K. M. Patrick; D. McL. Paterson; T. E. Naysmith; J. Telford; C. G. Hogg; Miss A. Forbes

OFFICE OF THE INSPECTOR OF FOREIGN DIVIDENDS
Lynwood Road, Thames Ditton, Surrey KT7 0DP
Inspector of Foreign Dividends (*G6*), T. R. Diggins

OIL TAXATION OFFICE
Melbourne House, Aldwych, London WC2B 4LL
Controller (*G4*), R. C. Mountain
Grade 5, K. Cartwright; I. M. Griffin; D. C. Howard; D. Newlyn; D. J. Slattery

THE VALUATION OFFICE EXECUTIVE AGENCY
New Court, 48 Carey Street, London WC2A 2JE
Tel 071-324 1183/1057
Meldrum House, 15 Drumsheugh Gardens, Edinburgh EH3 7UN
Tel 031-225 8511

Chief Executive (*G2*), R. R. B. Shutler, CB
Deputy Chief Executives (*G3*), A. J. Langford (*Management*); R. J. Pawley (*Technical*)
Chief Valuer, Scotland (*G4*), J. A. Sutherland

THE INTERCEPTION COMMISSIONER
c/o The Home Office, 50 Queen Anne's Gate, London SW1H 9AT

The Commissioner is appointed by the Prime Minister. He keeps under review the issue by the Secretary of State of warrants under the Interception of Communications Act 1985 and safeguards made in respect of intercepted material obtained through the use of such warrants. He is also required to give all such assistance as the Interception of Communications Tribunal may require to enable it to carry out its functions, and to submit an annual report to the Prime Minister with respect to the carrying out of his functions.

Commissioner, The Rt. Hon. Lord Justice Bingham

INTERCEPTION OF COMMUNICATIONS TRIBUNAL
PO Box 44, London SE1 0TX

The Tribunal comprises senior members of the legal profession, who are appointed by The Queen. Under the Interception of Communications Act 1985, the Tribunal is required to investigate applications from any person who believes that communications sent to or by them have been intercepted in the course of their transmission by post or by means of a public telecommunications system.

President, The Hon. Mr Justice Macpherson of Cluny
Vice-President, Sir Cecil Clothier, KCB, QC
Members, Sir David Calcutt, QC; I. Guild, CBE; P. Scott, QC

INTERVENTION BOARD
Fountain House, Queen's Walk, Reading RG1 7QW
Tel 0734-583626

The Intervention Board was established as a government department in 1972 and became operational in February 1973. It became an executive agency in April 1990. The Board is responsible for the implementation of European Community regulations covering the market support arrangements of the Common Agricultural Policy. Members of the Board are appointed by and are responsible to the Minister of Agriculture and the Secretaries of State for Scotland, Wales and Northern Ireland.

Chairman, A. J. Ellis, CBE
Chief Executive (*G3*), G. Stapleton

HEADS OF DIVISIONS

Finance Division (*G5*), J. N. Diserens
External Trade Division (*G5*), G. N. Dixon
Crops Division (*G5*), H. MacKinnon
Livestock Products Division (*G5*), M. J. Griffiths
Corporate Services Division (*G5*), J. W. M. Peffers
Legal Division (*G5*), T. Middleton
Chief Accountant (*G6*), R. Bryant
External Operations (*G6*), J. P. Bradbury
Procurement and Supply (*G6*), P. J. Offer
Establishments (*G6*), R. J. Lovell
Information Technology (*G6*), T. T. Simpson

LAND AUTHORITY FOR WALES

The Custom House, Customhouse Street, Cardiff CF1 5AP
Tel 0222-223444

The Authority is responsible for acquiring and disposing of land needed for private development in Wales.

Chairman (part-time) (£29,015), G. D. Inkin, OBE
Chief Executive, B. Ryan

LAND REGISTRIES

HM LAND REGISTRY

Lincoln's Inn Fields, London WC2A 3PH
Tel 071-405 3488

The registration of title to land was first introduced in England and Wales by the Land Registry Act 1862; HM Land Registry operates today under the Land Registration Acts 1925 to 1988. The object of registering title to land is to create and maintain a register of land owners whose title is guaranteed by the state and so to simplify the transfer, mortgage and other dealings with real property. Compulsory registration on sale was introduced in stages affecting only certain areas but it is now compulsory throughout England and Wales. The register, which used to be private and could only be inspected with the consent of the registered proprietor, became open to inspection by the public on 3 December 1990.

HM Land Registry is an executive agency administered under the Lord Chancellor by the Chief Land Registrar. The work is decentralized to a number of regional offices. The Chief Land Registrar is also responsible for the Land Charges Department and the Agricultural Credits Department.

HEADQUARTERS OFFICE

Chief Land Registrar and Chief Executive (G2), J. J. Manthorpe
Solicitor to Land Registry (G3), C. J. West
Senior Land Registrar (G5), Mrs J. G. Totty
Principal Establishment Officer (G5), E. G. Beardsall
Director of Operations (G5), G. N. French
Director of Information Technology (G5), R. J. Fenn
Director of Management Services (G6), P. J. Smith
Land Registrar (G5), M. L. Wood
Deputy Establishment Officer (G6), J. Hodder
Controller of Operations Development (G6), P. R. Laker

BIRKENHEAD DISTRICT LAND REGISTRY
Old Market House, Hamilton Street, Birkenhead L41 5JW
Tel 051-647 2377
District Land Registrar (G5), M. G. Garwood
Area Manager (G6), J. Eccles

COVENTRY DISTRICT LAND REGISTRY
Greyfriars Business Centre, 2 Eaton Road, Coventry CV1 2SD
Tel 0203-632442
District Land Registrar (G5), S. P. Kelway
Area Manager (G6), J. C. Lillistone

CROYDON DISTRICT LAND REGISTRY
Sunley House, Bedford Park, Croydon CR9 3LE
Tel 081-686 8833
District Land Registrar (G5), D. M. J. Moss
Area Manager (G6), V. J. C. Shorney

DURHAM DISTRICT LAND REGISTRY
Southfield House, Southfield Way, Durham DH1 5TR
Tel 091-3866151
District Land Registrar (G5), C. W. Martin
Area Manager (G6), B. Warriner

GLOUCESTER DISTRICT LAND REGISTRY
Twyver House, Bruton Way, Gloucester GL1 1DQ
Tel 0452-511111
District Land Registrar (G5), W. W. Budden
Area Manager (G6), D. J. Thomas

HARROW DISTRICT LAND REGISTRY
Lyon House, Lyon Road, Harrow, Middx. HA1 2EU
Tel 081-427 8811
District Land Registrar (G5), J. V. Timothy
Area Manager (G6), M. J. Wyatt

KINGSTON UPON HULL DISTRICT LAND REGISTRY
Earle House, Portland Street, Hull HU2 8JN
Tel 0482-223244
District Land Registrar (G5), S. R. Coveney
Area Manager (G6), E. Howard

LAND CHARGES AND AGRICULTURAL CREDITS DEPARTMENT
Burrington Way, Plymouth PL5 3LP
Tel 0752-779831
Superintendent of Land Charges (G7), H. Myers

LEICESTER DISTRICT LAND REGISTRY
Thames Tower, 99 Burleys Way, Leicester LE1 3UB
Tel 0533-510010
District Land Registrar (G6), L. M. Pope
Area Manager (G7), G. M. Johns

LYTHAM DISTRICT LAND REGISTRY
Birkenhead House, Lytham St Annes, Lancs. FY8 5AB
Tel 0253-736999
District Land Registrar (G5), J. G. Cooper
Area Manager (G6), E. J. Stringer

NOTTINGHAM DISTRICT LAND REGISTRY
Chalfont Drive, Nottingham NG8 3RN
Tel 0602-291166
District Land Registrar (G5), P. J. Timothy
Area Manager, (G6), W. Whitaker

PETERBOROUGH DISTRICT LAND REGISTRY
Touthill Close, City Road, Peterborough PE1 1XN
Tel 0733-555666
District Land Registrar (G5), M. Avens
Area Manager (G6), B. J. Andrews

PLYMOUTH DISTRICT LAND REGISTRY
Plumer House, Tailyour Road, Crownhill, Plymouth PL6 5HY
Tel 0752-701234
District Land Registrar (G5), A. J. Pain
Area Manager(G6), K. Robinson

PORTSMOUTH DISTRICT LAND REGISTRY
St Andrews Court, St Michael's Road, Portsmouth PO1 2JH
Tel 0705-865022
District Land Registrar (G6), S. R. Sehrawat
Area Manager (G7), A. W. Howarth

STEVENAGE DISTRICT LAND REGISTRY
Brickdale House, Swingate, Stevenage, Herts. SG1 1XG
Tel 0438-313003
District Land Registrar (G5), D. M. T. Mullett
Area Manager (G6), A. D. Gould

SWANSEA DISTRICT LAND REGISTRY
Tybryn Glas, High Street, Swansea SA1 1PW
Tel 0792-458877
District Land Registrar (G5), G. A. Hughes
Area Manager (G6), R. T. Davis

TELFORD DISTRICT LAND REGISTRY
Stafford Park 15, Telford, Shropshire TF3 3AL
Tel 0952-290355
District Land Registrar (G5), M. A. Roche
Area Manager (G6), R. D. Moseley

TUNBRIDGE WELLS DISTRICT LAND REGISTRY
Curtis House, Hawkenbury, Tunbridge Wells, Kent TN2 5AQ
Tel 0892-510015
District Land Registrar (G5), G. R. Tooke
Area Manager (G6), B. S. Crozier

WEYMOUTH DISTRICT LAND REGISTRY
1 Cumberland Drive, Weymouth, Dorset DT4 9TT
Tel 0305-776161
District Land Registrar (G5), Mrs P. M. Reeson
Area Manager (G6), J. Dodd

YORK DISTRICT LAND REGISTRY
James House, James Street, York YO1 3YZ
Tel 0904-450000
Area Manager (G7), P. Wright

COMPUTER SERVICES DIVISION
Burrington Way, Plymouth PL5 3LP
Tel 0752-779831
Head of Services Division (G6), P. A. Maycock
Head of Development Division (G6), R. J. Smith

REGISTERS OF SCOTLAND (EXECUTIVE AGENCY)

Meadowbank House, 153 London Road, Edinburgh EH8 7AU
Tel 031-659 6111

The Registers of Scotland consist of: General Register of Sasines and Land Register of Scotland; Register of Deeds in the Books of Council and Session; Register of Protests; Register of English and Irish Judgments; Register of Service of Heirs; Register of the Great Seal; Register of the Quarter Seal; Register of the Prince's Seal; Register of Crown Grants; Register of Sheriffs' Commissions; Register of the Cachet Seal; Register of Inhibitions and Adjudications; Register of Entails; Register of Hornings.

The General Register of Sasines and the Land Register of Scotland form the chief security in Scotland of the rights of land and other heritable (or real) property.

Keeper of the Registers of Scotland (G4), J. W. Barron
Senior Directors (G5), A. W. Ramage; A. G. Rennie
Senior Assistant Directors (G6), B. J. Corr; A. M. Falconer
Assistant Directors (G7), D. G. Cant (*computers*); R. Glen (*personnel*); J. Knox (*Land Register*); D. McCallum (*Land Register*); L. J. Mitchell (*management services*); A. G. T. New (*Land Register*); I. M. Nicol (*finance*); Mrs P. M. Stewart (*training*)
Assistant Keeper (G7), I. A. Davis
Grade 7, J. Anderson; J. F. Campbell; R. C. Clark; J. Cogle; A. B. Farmer; H. Hosken; J. S. McKinlay; D. Manson; J. B. Marshall; W. F. Rankin; J. Rynn; M. J. Wilczynski

LAW COMMISSION (England and Wales)

Conquest House, 37–38 John Street, Theobalds Road, London WC1N 2BQ
Tel 071-411 1220

The Law Commission was set up in 1965, under the Law Commissions Act 1965, to make proposals to the Government for the examination of the law and for its revision where it is unsuited for modern requirements, obscure, or otherwise unsatisfactory. It recommends to the Lord Chancellor programmes for the examination of different branches of the law and suggests whether the examination should be carried out by the Commission itself or by some other body. The Commission is also responsible for the preparation of Consolidation and Statute Law (Repeals) Bills.

Chairman, The Hon. Mr Justice Peter Gibson
Members, T. M. Aldridge QC; J. Beatson; R. Buxton, QC; Prof. B. M. Hoggett, QC
Secretary, M. H. Collon

SCOTTISH LAW COMMISSION

140 Causewayside, Edinburgh EH9 1PR
Tel 031-668 2131

Chairman, The Hon. Lord Davidson
Commissioners (full-time), Dr E. M. Clive; I. D. MacPhail, QC; (*part-time*) Prof. P. N. Love, CBE; W. Nimmo Smith, QC
Secretary, K. F. Barclay

LAW OFFICERS' DEPARTMENTS

Attorney-General's Chambers, 9 Buckingham Gate, London SW1E 6JP
Tel 071-828 7155
Attorney-General's Chambers, Royal Courts of Justice, Belfast BT1 3JY
Tel 0232-235111

The Law Officers of the Crown for England and Wales are the Attorney-General and the Solicitor-General. The Attorney-General is the Minister responsible for the work of the Law Officers' Departments: the Treasury Solicitor's Department, the Crown Prosecution Service, the Serious Fraud Office, and the Legal Secretariat to the Law Officers. The Director of Public Prosecutions (who is head of the Crown Prosecution Service), the Director of Public Prosecutions for Northern Ireland, and the Director of the Serious Fraud Office are responsible to the Attorney-General for the performance of their duties.

The Attorney-General is the Government's principal legal adviser, dealing with questions of law arising on Bills, issues of legal policy, and major international and domestic litigation involving the Government. The Solicitor-General is responsible for such matters as the Attorney-General delegates to him.

Attorney-General (£42,314†), The Rt. Hon. Sir Nicholas Lyell, QC, MP
Parliamentary Private Secretary, T. Devlin, MP
Solicitor-General (£34,695†), Sir Derek Spencer, QC, MP
Legal Secretary (G3), Miss J. L. Wheldon
Assistant Legal Secretary (G4), M. L. Carpenter

† Excluding reduced Parliamentary salary of £23,227

LEGAL AID BOARD

5th and 6th Floors, 29–37 Red Lion Street, London WC1R 4PP
Tel 071-831 4209

The Legal Aid Board has the general function of ensuring that advice, assistance and representation are available, in accordance with the Legal Aid Act 1988. In 1989 it took over from the Law Society responsibility for administering legal aid. The Board is a non-departmental government body whose members are appointed by the Lord Chancellor.

Chairman, J. Pitts
Members, S. Orchard (*Chief Executive*); M. Acland; Ms D. Beale; A. Blake; L. Devonald; K. Farrow; P. Jones; D. Sinker; J. Smith; P. Soar; Ms V. Boakes; F. Collins

SCOTTISH LEGAL AID BOARD

44 Drumsheugh Gardens, Edinburgh EH3 7SW
Tel 031-226 7061

The Scottish Legal Aid Board was set up under the Legal Aid (Scotland) Act 1986. It is responsible for ensuring that advice, assistance and representation are available in accordance with the Act. The Board is a non-departmental government body whose members are appointed by the Secretary of State for Scotland.

Chairman, Mrs C. A. M. Davis
Members, G. Barrie; Mrs P. A. M. Bolton; Miss L. Clark, QC; A. Gilchrist; Prof. P. H. Grinyer; G. D. Holmes, CB; D. A. Leitch; R. J. Livingstone; Mrs I. McColl; C. N. McEachran, QC; R. G. McEwan, QC; Mrs G. M. Peebles; Mrs M. Tait; Miss P. R. Wright
Chief Executive, A. E. M. Douglas

OFFICE OF THE LEGAL SERVICES OMBUDSMAN

22 Oxford Court, Oxford Street, Manchester M2 3WQ
Tel 061-236 9532

The Legal Services Ombudsman is appointed by the Lord Chancellor under the Courts and Legal Services Act 1990 to oversee the handling of complaints against solicitors, barristers and licensed conveyancers by their professional bodies. The Ombudsman replaced the Lay Observer on 1 January 1991. He is independent of the legal profession and his services are free of charge.

Legal Services Ombudsman, M. Barnes
Secretary, K. Fox

LIBRARIES

THE BRITISH LIBRARY

2 Sheraton Street, London W1V 4BH
Tel 071-636 1544

The British Library is the UK's national library and occupies the central position in the library and information network. The Library aims to serve scholarship, research, industry, commerce and all other major users of information. Its services are based on collections which include over 18 million volumes, 1 million discs, and 55,000 hours of tape recordings, at 18 buildings in London and one complex in West Yorkshire.

The British Library was established on 1 July 1973 and brought together the library departments of the British Museum, the National Central Library, the National Lending Library for Science and Technology, the British National Bibliography Ltd and, in 1974, the Office for Scientific and Technical Information. Subsequently the Library took responsibility for the India Office Library and Records, the HMSO Binderies, and the National Sound Archive.

Access to the Humanities and Social Sciences reading rooms in Great Russell Street is limited to holders of a British Library Reader's Pass, and information about eligibility is available from the Reader Admissions Office. The Aldwych and Holborn reading rooms of the Science Reference and Information Service are open to the general public without charge or formality.

The Library's exhibition galleries are housed in the British Museum building in Great Russell Street.

The British Library is in the process of moving to purpose-built accommodation at St Pancras, London NW1 (open to the public in 1994).

British Library Board
96 Euston Road, London NW1 2DB
Tel 071-323 7262

Chairman, Cdr. L. M. M. Saunders Watson
Chief Executive and Deputy Chairman, B. Lang
Directors-General, J. M. Smethurst; D. Russon
Part-time Members, The Lord Adrian, MD, FRS; The Lord Windlesham, CVO, PC; Prof. A. S. Forty, Ph.D., D.Sc.; Sir Robin Mackworth-Young, KCVO, FSA; R. E. Utiger, CBE; T. J. Rix; Dame Anne Warburton, DCVO, CMG; H. Heaney; D. Peake; The Rt. Revd M. A. Mann, KCVO; Dr A. Kenny; E. M. W. Griffith, CBE

BRITISH LIBRARY, BOSTON SPA

Boston Spa, Wetherby, W. Yorks. LS23 7BQ
Tel 0937-546000

Director-General, D. Russon

Document Supply Centre
Tel 0937-546000

Director, D. Bradbury

National Bibliographic Service
Tel 0937-546585

Director, S. J. Ede

London Unit
2 Sheraton Street, London W1V 4BH
Tel 071-323 7077

Acquisitions Processing and Cataloguing
Tel 0937-546000

Director, Mrs J. E. Butcher

Computing and Telecommunications*
2 Sheraton Street, London W1V 4BH
Tel 071-323 7210

Director, J. R. Mahoney

BRITISH LIBRARY, LONDON

Great Russell Street, London WC1B 3DG
Tel 071-636 1544

Director-General, J. M. Smethurst

*Scheduled to relocate to Yorkshire by the mid-1990s.

HUMANITIES AND SOCIAL SCIENCES
Tel 071-323 7676

Director, A. Phillips

WEST EUROPEAN COLLECTIONS, SLAVONIC AND EAST EUROPEAN COLLECTIONS, ENGLISH LANGUAGE COLLECTIONS
Tel 071-323 7676

INFORMATION BRANCH, OFFICIAL PUBLICATIONS AND SOCIAL SCIENCE SERVICE
Tel 071-323 7676

EXHIBITIONS AND EDUCATION SERVICE
Tel 071-323 7595

READER ADMISSIONS
Tel 071-323 7677

COLLECTIONS AND PRESERVATION
Tel 071-323 7676

Director, Dr M. Foot

PRESERVATION SERVICE (NATIONAL PRESERVATION OFFICE)
Tel 071-323 7612

SPECIAL COLLECTIONS
Tel 071-323 7513

Director, Dr A. Prochaska

Western Manuscripts, Map Library, Music Library, Philatelic Collections
Tel 071-323 7513

INFORMATION SCIENCES SERVICE (BLISS)
Ridgmount Street, London WC1E 7AE
Tel 071-323 7688

NEWSPAPER LIBRARY
Colindale Avenue, London NW9 5HE
Tel 071-323 7353

NATIONAL SOUND ARCHIVE
29 Exhibition Road, London SW7 2AS
Tel 071-589 6603

Director (acting), C. Jewitt

ORIENTAL AND INDIA OFFICE COLLECTIONS
197 Blackfriars Road, London SE1 8NG
Tel 071-412 7873

SCIENCE REFERENCE AND INFORMATION SERVICE
25 Southampton Buildings, London WC2A 1AW
Tel 071-323 7494
9 Kean Street, London WC2B 4AT
Tel 071-323 7288

Director, A. Gomersall

RESEARCH AND DEVELOPMENT DEPARTMENT
2 Sheraton Street, London W1V 4BH
TEL 071-323 7060

Director, B. J. Perry

ADMINISTRATION
2 Sheraton Street, London W1V 4BH
Tel 071-323 7132

Director, R. Ball

PRESS AND PUBLIC RELATIONS
96 Euston Road, London NW1 2DB
Tel 071-323 7111

Head, M. Jackson

NATIONAL LIBRARY OF SCOTLAND

George IV Bridge, Edinburgh EH1 1EW
Tel 031-226 4531

Opening hours: Reading Room, weekdays, 9.30–8.30 (Wed., 10–8.30); Sat. 9.30–1. Map Library, weekdays, 9.30–5; Sat. 9.30–1. Exhibition, weekdays, 9.30–5; Sat. 9.30–1; Sun. 2–5. Scottish Science Library, weekdays, 9.30–5 (Wed., 10–8.30).

The Library, which was founded as the Advocates' Library in 1682, became the National Library of Scotland by Act of Parliament in 1925. Its collections of printed books and MSS, augmented by purchase and gift, are very large and it has an unrivalled Scottish collection.

The Reading Room is for reference and research which cannot conveniently be pursued elsewhere. Admission is by ticket issued to an approved applicant.

SALARIES

Librarian	£44,390–£49,790
Keeper	£27,819–£42,724
Curator Grade C	£24,379–£34,667

Chairman of the Trustees, The Earl of Crawford and Balcarres, PC
Librarian and Secretary to the Trustees, I. D. McGowan
Secretary of the Library, M. C. Graham
Curators Grade C, A. Cameron; W. Jackson; J. E. McIntyre
Keepers of Printed Books, A. M. Marchbank, Ph.D.; Ms A. Matheson, Ph.D
Curators Grade C, T. A. Cherry; Ms A. E. Harvey Wood; B. P. Hillyard, D.Phil.; S. Holland; Ms R. I. Hope; W. A. Kelly; J. M. Morris
Keeper of Manuscripts, I. C. Cunningham
Curators Grade C, I. G. Brown, Ph.D., FSA; R. Duce; I. F. Maciver; S. M. Simpson; Ms J. M. Wilkes; Ms E. D. Yeo
Director of Computer Services and Research (Keeper), B. Gallivan
Curator Grade C, R. F. Guy
Director of Scottish Science Library (Keeper), Ms A. J. Bunch

THE NATIONAL LIBRARY OF WALES

(LLYFRGELL GENEDLAETHOL CYMRU)
Aberystwyth, Dyfed SY23 3BU
Tel 0970-623816

Readers' room open on weekdays, 9.30–6 (Sat. 9.30–5); closed first week of October. Admission by Reader's Ticket.

The National Library of Wales was founded by Royal Charter in 1907, and is maintained by annual grant from the Treasury. It contains about 4,000,000 printed books, 40,000 manuscripts, 4,000,000 deeds and documents, numerous maps, prints and drawings, and an audio-visual collection. It specializes in manuscripts and books relating to Wales and the Celtic peoples. It is the repository for pre-1858 Welsh probate records. It is approved by the Master of the Rolls as a repository for manorial records and tithe documents, and by the Lord Chancellor for certain legal records. It is the Bureau of the Regional Libraries Scheme for Wales.

Librarian, B. F. Roberts, Ph.D., FSA
Heads of Departments, M. W. Mainwaring (*Head of Administration and Technical Services*); G. Jenkins (*Manuscripts and Records*); J. L. Madden (*Printed Books*); D. H. Owen (*Pictures and Maps*)

LIGHTHOUSE AUTHORITIES

CORPORATION OF TRINITY HOUSE
Trinity House, Tower Hill, London EC3N 4DH
Tel 071-480 6601

Trinity House, the first general lighthouse and pilotage authority in the Kingdom, was a body of importance when Henry VIII granted the institution its first charter in 1514. The Corporation is the general lighthouse authority for England, Wales and the Channel Islands, with certain statutory jurisdiction over aids to navigation maintained by local harbour authorities. It is also responsible for dealing with wrecks dangerous to navigation, except those occurring within port limits or wrecks of HM ships.

The Trinity House Lighthouse Service is maintained out of the General Lighthouse Fund which is provided from light dues levied on ships at ports of the UK and Republic of Ireland. The Corporation is also a deep-sea pilotage authority and a charitable organization.

The affairs of the Corporation are controlled by a board of Elder Brethren, who are master mariners with long experience of command in the Royal or Merchant Navy, together with figures from the world of commerce, and the Secretary. A separate board, which comprises Elder Brethren, senior staff and outside representatives currently controls the Lighthouse Service. The Board is assisted by administrative and technical staff. The Elder Brethren also act as nautical assessors in marine cases in the Admiralty Division of the High Court of Justice.

ELDER BRETHREN

Master, HRH The Duke of Edinburgh, KG, KT
Deputy Master, Capt. P. M. Edge
Elder Brethren, Capt. I. R. C. Saunders; Capt. P. F. Mason, CBE; HRH The Prince of Wales, KG, KT; Capt. Sir George Barnard, FRSA; Capt. R. N. Mayo, CBE; Capt. Sir David Tibbits, DSC, RN; Capt. D. A. G. Dickens; Capt. J. E. Bury; Capt. J. A. N. Bezant, DSC, RD, RNR (retd.); Capt. D. J. Cloke; The Lord Wilson of Rievaulx, KG, OBE, PC, FRS; Capt. Sir Miles Wingate, KCVO; Rt. Hon. Sir Edward Heath, KG, MBE, MP; Capt. T. Woodfield, OBE; Sir Eric Drake, CBE; The Lord Simon of Glaisdale, PC; Admiral of the Fleet the Lord Lewin, KG, GCB, LVO, DSC; Capt. D. T. Smith, RN; Commander Sir Robin Gillett, GBE, RD, RNR; The Lord Shackleton, KG, OBE, PC, FRS; Sir John Cuckney; Capt. D. J. Orr; The Lord Carrington, KG, GCMG, CH, MC, PC; Sir Brian Shaw; The Lord Mackay of Clashfern, PC; Sir Adrian Swire; Capt. N. M. Turner, RD; HRH The Duke of York, CVO, ADC; Capt. P. H. King; Capt. The Lord Sterling of Plaistow, CBE, RNR; Cdr. M. J. Rivett-Carnac, RN

OFFICERS

Secretary and Director of Administration, M. J. Faulkner
Director of Finance, K. W. Clark
Director of Engineering, D. A. S. Vennings
Personnel and General Services Manager, Mrs B. C. Heesom
Navigation Manager, N. J. Cutmore
Legal and Information Manager, D. I. Brewer
General Manager Operations, Capt. J. M. Barnes
Operations Administration Manager, S. J. W. Dunning
Deputy Director of Engineering, F. E. J. Holden
Senior Inspector of Shipping, J. R. Dunnett
Manager, Corporate Department, R. Dobb
Information Officer, H. L. Cooper

COMMISSIONERS OF NORTHERN LIGHTHOUSES
84 George Street, Edinburgh EH2 3DA
Tel 031-226 7051

The Commissioners of Northern Lighthouses are the general lighthouse authority for Scotland and the Isle of Man. The present board owes its origin to an Act of Parliament passed in 1786. At present the Commissioners operate under the Merchant Shipping Act 1894 and are 19 in number.

The Commissioners control 18 major manned lighthouses, 66 major automatic lighthouses, 112 minor lights and many lighted and unlighted buoys. They have a fleet of two motor vessels.

COMMISSIONERS

The Lord Advocate; the Solicitor-General for Scotland; the Lord Provosts of Edinburgh, Glasgow and Aberdeen; the Provost of Inverness; the Chairman of Argyll and Bute District Council; the Sheriffs-Principal of North Strathclyde, Tayside, Central, Fife, Grampian, Highlands and Islands, South Strathclyde, Dumfries and Galloway, Lothians and Borders, and Glasgow and Strathkelvin; T. Macgill; Capt. A. F. Dickson, OBE; Capt. D. M. Cowell; A. J. Struthers; W. F. Hay, CBE; J. Hann, CBE

OFFICERS

General Manager, Cdr. J. M. Mackay, MBE
Secretary, I. A. Dickson
Engineer-in-Chief, W. Paterson

LOCAL COMMISSIONERS

COMMISSION FOR LOCAL ADMINISTRATION IN ENGLAND
21 Queen Anne's Gate, London SW1H 9BU
Tel 071-222 5622

Local Commissioners (local government ombudsmen) are responsible for investigating complaints from members of the public against local authorities (but not town and parish councils); police authorities; the Commission for New Towns and new town development corporations (housing functions); urban development corporations (town and country planning functions) and certain other authorities. The Commissioners are appointed by the Crown on the recommendation of the Secretary of State for the Environment.

Certain types of action are excluded from investigation, including personnel matters and commercial transactions unless they relate to the purchase or sale of land. Complaints can be sent direct to the Local Government Ombudsman or through a councillor, although the Local Government Ombudsman will not consider a complaint unless the council has had an opportunity to investigate and reply to a complainant.

A free booklet *Complaint about the Council? How to Complain to the Local Government Ombudsman* is available from the Commission's office.

Chairman of the Commission and Local Commissioner (£84,250), D. C. M. Yardley, D.Phil.
Vice-Chairman and Local Commissioner (£61,100), F. G. Laws
Local Commissioner (£60,100), Mrs P. A. Thomas
Member (ex officio), The Parliamentary Commissioner for Administration
Secretary (£43,698), G. D. Adams

COMMISSION FOR LOCAL ADMINISTRATION IN WALES
Derwen House, Court Road, Bridgend CF31 1BN
Tel 0656-661325

The Local Commissioner for Wales has similar powers to the Local Commissioners in England. The Commissioner is appointed by the Crown on the recommendation of the Secretary of State for Wales. A free booklet *Your Local Ombudsman in Wales* is available from the Commission's office.

Local Commissioner, E. R. Moseley
Secretary, D. Bowen
Member (ex officio), The Parliamentary Commissioner for Administration

COMMISSIONER FOR LOCAL ADMINISTRATION IN SCOTLAND
23 Walker Street, Edinburgh EH3 7HX
Tel 031-225 5300

The Local Commissioner for Scotland has similar powers to the Local Commissioners in England, and is appointed by the Crown on the recommendation of the Secretary of State for Scotland.

Local Commissioner, R. G. E. Peggie, CBE
Deputy and Secretary, Ms J. H. Renton

LONDON REGIONAL TRANSPORT
55 Broadway, London SW1H 0BD
Tel 071-222 5600

Subject to the financial objectives and principles approved by the Secretary of State for Transport, London Regional Transport has a general duty to provide or secure the provision of public transport services for Greater London.

Chairman (£106,500), C. W. Newton
Member (£76,150), A. J. Sheppeck

LORD ADVOCATE'S DEPARTMENT
Fielden House, 10 Great College Street, London SW1P 3SL
Tel 071-276 3000

The Law Officers for Scotland are the Lord Advocate and the Solicitor-General for Scotland. The Lord Advocate's Department is responsible for drafting Scottish legislation, for providing legal advice to other departments on Scottish questions and for assistance to the Law Officers for Scotland in certain of their legal duties.

Lord Advocate (£50,638), The Lord Rodger of Earlsferry, PC, QC
Solicitor-General for Scotland (£44,342), Thomas C. Dawson, QC
Legal Secretary and First Scottish Parliamentary Counsel (£61,100), J. C. McCluskie, QC
Assistant Legal Secretaries and Scottish Parliamentary Counsel (£50,800–£52,293), G. M. Clark; G. Kowalski; P. J. Layden, TD
Assistant Legal Secretaries and Depute Scottish Parliamentary Counsel (£46,122–£47,921), J. D. Harkness; D. C. Macrae; C. A. M. Wilson
Assistant Legal Secretary and Assistant Scottish Parliamentary Counsel (£29,070), Miss M. Mackenzie

LORD CHANCELLOR'S DEPARTMENT
House of Lords, London SW1A 0PW
Tel 071-219 3000

The Lord Chancellor is responsible for promoting general reforms in the civil law, for the procedure of the civil courts and for the administration of the Supreme Court (Court of Appeal, High Court and Crown Court) and county courts in England and Wales, and for legal aid schemes. He also now has Ministerial responsibility for magistrates' courts, which are administered locally. The Lord Chancellor is responsible for advising the Crown on the appointment of judges and certain other officers and is himself responsible for the appointment of Masters and Registrars of the High Court, Judges of the Principal Registry of the Family Division, District Judges and magistrates. He is responsible for ensuring that letters patent and other formal documents are passed in the proper form under the Great Seal of the Realm, of which he is the custodian. The work in connection with this is carried out under his direction in the Office of the Clerk of the Crown in Chancery.

Lord Chancellor (£110,940), The Lord Mackay of Clashfern, PC
Private Secretary, Miss J. Rowe
Parliamentary Under Secretary, John Taylor, MP
Private Secretary, Ms J. L. Morgan
Permanent Secretary (G1), T. S. Legg, CB, QC
Private Secretary, N. P. Chibnall

CROWN OFFICE
Clerk of the Crown in Chancery (G1), T. S. Legg, CB, QC
Deputy Clerk of the Crown in Chancery (G2), R. Potter, CB
Clerk of the Chamber, Miss J. L. Waine

JUDICIAL APPOINTMENTS GROUP
House of Lords, London SW1A 0PW
Tel 071-219 4311

Head of Group (G3), R. E. E. Holmes
Grade 5, D. E. Staff; R. J. Clark; R. V. Grobler; G. Norman; P. G. Taylor

LAW AND POLICY GROUPS
Trevelyan House, Great Peter Street, London SW1P 2BY
Tel 071-210 8734

Head of Group (G2), M. Huebner
Grade 5, P. L. Jacob

LEGAL GROUP
26 Old Queen Street, London SW1H 9HF
Tel 071-210 3508

Grade 3, R. H. H. White
Grade 5, R. Venne; J. Watherston; M. Kron; J. Gibson

POLICY AND LEGAL SERVICES GROUP
Trevelyan House, Great Peter Street, London SW1P 2BY
Tel 071-210 8769

Grade 3, C. Everett
Grade 5, Mrs N. A. Oppenheimer; S. Smith; M. Sayers

COURT SERVICE GROUP
Trevelyan House, Great Peter Street, London SW1P 2BY
Tel 071-210 8719

Head of Group (G2), R. Potter, CB

COURT SERVICE MANAGEMENT GROUP

Grade 4, J. F. Brindley
Grade 5, R. Stoate; D. Nooney; E. Grant; P. White

ESTABLISHMENT AND FINANCE GROUP
Trevelyan House, Great Peter Street, London SWIP 2BY
Tel 071-210 8803

Head of Group (G3), B. Cousins, CBE
Grade 5, R. A. Vincent; A. Cogbill; P. Matthews
Grade 6, R. Sams; J. Isaacs; K. Gregeen

LORD CHANCELLOR'S ADVISORY COMMITTEE ON STATUTE LAW
House of Lords, London SWIA OPW

The Advisory Committee advises the Lord Chancellor on all matters relating to the revision, modernization and publication of the statute book.

Chairman, T. S. Legg, CB
Members, M. A. J. Wheeler-Booth; Sir Clifford Boulton, KCB; The Hon. Mr Justice (Peter) Gibson; The Hon. Lord Davidson; P. Graham, CB, QC; J. C. McCluskie, QC; T. R. Erskine, CB; G. Hosker; R. Brodie, CB; R. H. H White; J. Gibson; Dr P. Freeman
Secretary, J. D. Saunders

ECCLESIASTICAL PATRONAGE
10 Downing Street, London SWI
Tel 071-930 4433

Secretary for Ecclesiastical Patronage, J. R. Catford, CBE
Assistant Secretary for Ecclesiastical Patronage, N. C. Wheeler

See also Law Courts and Offices section

LORD GREAT CHAMBERLAIN'S OFFICE

House of Lords, London SWIA OPW
Tel 071-219 3100

The Lord Great Chamberlain is a Great Officer of State, the office being hereditary since the grant of Henry I to the family of De Vere, Earls of Oxford.

Lord Great Chamberlain, The Marquess of Cholmondeley
Secretary to the Lord Great Chamberlain, Admiral Sir Richard Thomas, KCB, OBE
Clerk to the Lord Great Chamberlain, Mrs S. E. Douglas

LORD PRIVY SEAL'S OFFICE

Privy Council Office, 68 Whitehall, London SWIA 2AT
Tel 071-270 3000

As leader of the House of Lords, the Lord Privy Seal is responsible to the Prime Minister for the arrangement of government business in the House. He also has a responsibility to the House itself to advise it on procedural matters and other difficulties which arise.

Lord Privy Seal, and Leader of the House of Lords, Lord Wakeham, PC
Private Secretary, Miss G. M. Kirton
Assistant Private Secretary, R. A'Court

OFFICE OF MANPOWER ECONOMICS

22 Kingsway, London WC2B 6JY
Tel 071-405 5944

The Office of Manpower Economics was set up in 1971. It is an independent non-statutory organization which is responsible for servicing independent review bodies which advise on the pay of various public service groups (*see* Review Bodies, page 352), the Pharmacists Review Panel, the Police Negotiating Board and the Civil Service Arbitration Tribunal. The Office is also responsible for servicing *ad hoc* bodies of inquiry and for undertaking research into pay and associated matters as requested by the Government.

Director, M. J. Horsman
Assistant Secretaries (G5), H. E. Miller; P. J. H. Edwards; Dr M. E. McDowall; P. J. Thorpe

MEDICAL RESEARCH COUNCIL

20 Park Crescent, London WIN 4AL
Tel 071-636 5422

The Medical Research Council is the main government agency for the promotion of medical and related biological research. The council employs its own research staff and also provides grants for other institutions and for individuals who are not members of its own staff, thus complementing the research resources of the universities and hospitals.

Chairman, Sir David Plastow
Deputy Chairman and Secretary, D. A. Rees, Ph.D., D.SC., FRS
Members, Prof. I. V. Allen, D.SC., MD; Dr D. T. Baird, D.SC., MD, FRCPath.; R. P. Bauman; Prof. M. Bobrow, D.SC.; Prof. M. R. Bond, Ph.D., FRCSEd., FRCPsych., FRCP(Glas.); Prof. I. A. D. Bouchier, CBE; Prof. A. M. Breckenridge, MD, FRCP, FRCPEd., FRSEd.; K. C. Calman, MD, Ph.D., FRCS(Glas.), FRCP; Sir Michael Carlisle; J. T. Carter, FRCP; P. Doyle, Ph.D.; Prof. C. R. W. Edwards, MD, FRCP, FRCPEd.; Prof. J. Grimley Evans, MD, FRCP, FRCM; R. E. Kendell, CBE, MD, FRCP, FRCPsych., FRCPEd.; A. McLaren, D.Phil., FRCOG, FRS; Prof. Sir Aaron Klug, SC.D., FRS; Prof. M. J. Peckham, FRCP, FRCP(Glas.), FRCR; Miss E. Nicholson, MP; Prof. J. R. Pattison; Prof. Sir Michael Rutter, CBE, MD, FRCP, FRCPsych., FRS; Prof. Sir David Weatherall, MD, FRCP, FRCPath., FRS; D. Wilkinson.
Administrative Secretary, Ms N. Morris

NEUROSCIENCES AND MENTAL HEALTH BOARD
Chairman, Prof. Sir Michael Rutter, CBE

MOLECULAR AND CELLULAR MEDICINE BOARD
Chairman, Prof. M. Bobrow

PHYSIOLOGICAL MEDICINE AND INFECTIONS BOARD
Chairman, Prof. C. L. Berry, Ph.D., MD, FRCPath

HEALTH SERVICES AND PUBLIC HEALTH RESEARCH BOARD
Chairman, Prof. J. Grimley Evans, MD, FRCP, FRCM

HEADQUARTERS OFFICE
Second Secretary, D. Evered, D.SC., MD, FRCP
Director of Finance, B. C. Dodd
Headquarters Office Management, J. E. A. Hay

Director of Personnel, D. Smith, PH.D.
Director of Corporate Affairs Group, N. H. Winterton
Director of Research Management Group, Dr D. Dunstan
Director of Research Planning, Dr M. B. Davies
Research Policy Development Manager, Dr M. B. Kemp
Research Business Manager, J. M. Lee
Executive Board Secretaries, Dr P. Dukes; Dr A. B. Stone; Dr D. J. McLaren; Dr R. D. Lang; Dr A. C. Peatfield

For units of Medical Research Council, *see* pages 694–5

MENTAL HEALTH ACT COMMISSION

Maid Marian House, 56 Hounds Gate, Nottingham NGI 6BG
Tel 0602-504040

The Mental Health Act Commission was established in 1983. Its functions are to keep under review the operation of the Mental Health Act 1983; to visit and interview patients detained under the Act; to investigate complaints falling within the Commission's remit; to monitor the implementation of the Code of Practice; and to advise ministers. Commissioners are appointed by the Secretary of State for Health in the following categories: lay; legal; medical; nursing; psychology; social worker; and specialist.

Chairman, Sir Louis Blom-Cooper, QC
Vice-Chairman, Prof. E. Murphy
Chief Executive (G6), W. Bingley

MONOPOLIES AND MERGERS COMMISSION

New Court, 48 Carey Street, London WC2A 2JT
Tel 071-324 1467

The Commission was established in 1948 as the Monopolies and Restrictive Practices Commission and became the Monopolies and Mergers Commission in 1973. The Commission has the duty of investigating and reporting on questions referred to it with respect to the existence or possible existence of monopolies not registrable under the Restrictive Trade Practices Act 1976 and relating to the supply of goods or services in the UK or part of the UK or to the supply of goods for export; the transfer of a newspaper or newspaper's assets; and the creation or possible creation of a merger qualifying for investigation within the meaning of the Fair Trading Act 1973. References may be made to the Commission on the general effect on the public interest of specified monopoly or other uncompetitive practices and of restrictive labour practices.

The Competition Act 1980 provides for the reference to the Commission of particular anti-competitive practices and of questions of efficiency, costs, service provided and possible abuse of monopolies in the public sector. In respect of recently-privatized industries, references to the Commission may be made in certain circumstances, with regard to their respective industries, by the Director-General of Telecommunications, the Civil Aviation Authority, the Director-General of Gas Supply, the Director-General of Water Services and the Director-General of Electricity Supply.

Under the Broadcasting Act 1990 the Commission can investigate and report on the competition aspects of networking arrangements between holders of regional Channel 3 licences.

Chairman (£84,250), Sir Sydney Lipworth
Deputy Chairmen (£29,555), H. H. Liesner, CB; P. H. Dean; D. G. Goyder
Members (£11,900/*£7,933 each), A. G. Armstrong; C. C. Baillieu; I. Barter; Prof. M. E. Beesley, CBE; Mrs C. Blight; F. E. Bonner, CBE; *P. Brenan; J. S. Bridgeman; K. S. Carmichael, CBE; R. Davies; Prof. S. Eilon; J. Evans; A. Ferry, MBE; M. R. Hoffman; *A. L. Kingshott; Miss P. K. R. Mann; G. C. S. Mather; *N. F. Matthews; Prof. J. S. Metcalfe; Mrs D. Miller, MBE; Prof. P. Minford; J. D. Montgomery; Dr D. J. Morris; B. C. Owens; *Prof. J. Pickering; *L. Priestley; D. P. Thomson; C. A. Unwin, MBE; Prof. G. Whittington
Secretary, S. N. Burbridge, CB

MUSEUMS

MUSEUMS AND GALLERIES COMMISSION

16 Queen Anne's Gate, London SW1H 9AA
Tel 071-233 4200

Established in 1931 as the Standing Commission on Museums and Galleries, the Commission was re-named and took up new functions in September 1981. Its sponsor department is the Department of National Heritage. The Commission advises the Government, including the Department of Education for Northern Ireland, the Scottish Education Department and the Welsh Office, on museum affairs. There are 15 Commissioners, appointed by the Prime Minister.

The Commission's executive functions include the services of the National Museums Security Adviser; allocation of grants to the seven Area Museum Councils in England; funding and monitoring of the work of the Museum Documentation Association; directly administering a capital grant scheme for non-national museums, and various other grant schemes. The Commission administers the arrangements for government indemnities and the acceptance of works of art in lieu of Inheritance Tax, and it has responsibility for the two purchase grant funds for local museums managed on its behalf by the Victoria and Albert Museum and the Science Museum. The Commission's Conservation Unit advises on conservation and operates grants schemes for conservators. The Travelling Exhibitions Unit promotes and encourages travelling exhibitions. A Disability Adviser promotes better provision for disabled people in museums, and an Environmental Adviser is drawing up guidelines on environmental standards in museums. A registration scheme for museums in the UK is being implemented with the assistance of the Commission.

Chairman, G. Greene, CBE
Members, The Marchioness of Anglesey, DBE; F. Atkinson, OBE; The Baroness Brigstocke; F. Dunning, OBE; Prof. Sir John Hale, FBA; J. Last, CBE; Sir Hugh Leggatt; Prof. D. Michie; The Lord O'Neill, TD; The Lord Rees, PC, QC; R. H. Smith; Dame Margaret Weston, DBE; Adm. Sir David Williams, GCB
Director and Secretary, P. Longman

THE BRITISH MUSEUM

Great Russell Street, London WC1B 3DG
Tel 071-636 1555

The British Museum houses antiquities collections, coins and medals, prints and drawings. Open daily (including Bank Holidays) 10–5; Sun. 2.30–6. Closed on Good Friday, 24–26 December, New Year's Day and the first Monday in May. Admission free. The ethnographical collections are displayed in the Museum of Mankind, 6 Burlington Gardens, London W1. Opening times as above.

The British Museum may be said to date from 1753, when Parliament granted funds for the purchase of the collections of Sir Hans Sloane and the Harleian manuscripts, and for their proper housing and maintenance. The building (Montagu House) was opened in 1759. The present buildings were erected between 1823 and the present day, and the original collection has increased to its present dimensions by gifts and purchases. Government grants for running costs and works and building projects were estimated at £30,992,000 in 1992–3.

BOARD OF TRUSTEES

Appointed by the Sovereign, HRH The Duke of Gloucester, GCVO.
Appointed by the Prime Minister, The Lord Windlesham, CVO, PC (*Chairman*); Sir Matthew Farrer, KCVO; G. C. Greene, CBE; Prof. E. T. Hall, D.Phil., FSA, FBA; C. E. A. Hambro; Sir Peter Harrop, KCB; S. Keswick; Hon. Mrs Marten, OBE; Mrs M. Moore; Sir John Morgan, KCMG; The Rt. Hon. Sir Timothy Raison; S. Towneley, D.Phil.; Prof. G. H. Treitel, DCL., FBA, QC; The Lord Weinstock; Prof. W. Whitfield, CBE
Nominated by the Learned Societies, The Lord Adrian, MD, FRS (*Royal Society*); A. Jones, RA (*Royal Academy*); Sir Claus Moser, KCB, CBE, FBA (*British Academy*); The Lord Renfrew of Kaimsthorn, FBA, FSA (*Society of Antiquaries*)
Appointed by the Trustees of the British Museum, Sir David Attenborough, CVO, CBE, FRS; Prof. Rosemary Cramp, CBE, FSA; Prof. Sir John Hale, FSA, FBA, FRHists, FRSA; Prof. P. Lasko, CBE, FSA, FBA; The Lord Egremont

SALARIES

Grade 2	£62,504
Grade 4	£44,390–£46,122
Grade 5	£36,178–£41,120
Grade 6	£27,819–£36,178
Grade 7	£24,379–£29,073
Senior Information Officer	£17,227–£21,797

OFFICERS

Director (*G2*), Dr R. G. W. Anderson
Deputy Director (*G4*), Miss J. M. Rankine
Secretary (*G6*), G. B. Morris
Assistant to the Director (*G7*), Ms M. L. Caygill
Head of Public Services (*G6*), G. A. L. House
Head of Design (*G6*), Margaret Hall, OBE
Head of Education (*G7*), J. F. Reeve
Head of Press and Public Relations (*SIO*), A. E. Hamilton
Head of Administration (*G5*), C. E. I. Jones
Head of Building and Security Services (*G6*), K. T. Stannard
Head of Architectural and Building Services (*G7*), C. J. Walker
Head of Finance (*G7*), D. E. Williams
Head of Personnel and Office Services (*G7*), Miss B. A. Hughes
Keeper of Prints and Drawings (*G5*), A. V. Griffiths
Keeper of Coins and Medals (*G5*), A. M. Burnett
Keeper of Egyptian Antiquities (*G5*), W. V. Davies
Keeper of Western Asiatic Antiquities (*G5*), J. E. Curtis
Keeper of Greek and Roman Antiquities (*G5*), B. F. Cook
Keeper of Medieval and Later Antiquities (*G5*), N. M. Stratford
Keeper of Prehistoric and Romano-British Antiquities (*G5*), I. H. Longworth
Keeper of Japanese Antiquities (*G5*), L. R. H. Smith
Keeper of Oriental Antiquities (*G5*), Ms J. M. Rawson
Keeper of Ethnography (*G5*), J. B. Mack
Keeper of Scientific Research (*G5*), Ms S. G. E. Bowman
Keeper of Conservation (*G5*), W. A. Oddy

THE NATURAL HISTORY MUSEUM
Cromwell Road and Exhibition Road, London SW7 5BD
Tel 071-938 9123

Open Mon.–Sat. 10–6 (closed New Year's Day and 24–26 December). Sun. 11–6. Admission, £4.00.

The Natural History Museum originates from the natural history departments of the British Museum. During the 19th century the natural history collections grew extensively and in 1881 they were moved to South Kensington. In 1963 the Natural History Museum became completely independent with its own body of trustees. The Zoological Museum, Tring, bequeathed by the second Lord Rothschild, has formed part of the Museum since 1938. The Geological Museum merged with the Natural History Museum in 1985 (opening times are as given above). Research workers are admitted to the libraries and study collections by Student's Ticket, applications for which should be made in writing to the Director.

The administrative expenses were estimated at £21,734,000 in 1991–2.

BOARD OF TRUSTEES

Appointed by the Prime Minister: Sir Walter Bodmer, FRS (*Chairman*); Sir Owen Green; The Baroness Blackstone, Ph.D; E. N. K. Clarkson, FRS; Mrs J. M. d'Abo; Sir Denys Henderson; Prof. R. May, FRS; Sir Crispin Tickell, GCMG, KCVO
Nominated by the Royal Society, Prof. J. L. Harper, FRS
Appointed by the Trustees of the Natural History Museum, R. J. Carter; Prof. B. K. Follett, FRS; Sir Anthony Laughton, FRS

OFFICERS

Director (*G3*), N. R. Chalmers, Ph.D
Associate Directors (*Scientific Development*) (*G5*), Dr S. Blackmore; Dr P. Henderson
Secretary (*G5*), C. J. E. Legg
Assistant to the Director (*G7*), Miss R. P. Baillon
Head of Marketing and Commerce Department (*G6*), Mrs R. Laughton-Scott.
Marketing Manager (*G6*), Ms J. Batchelor
Science Marketing (*G6*), Mrs A. Wendelaar
Public Relations Manager (*G6*), Miss J. Bevan
Keeper of Zoology (*G5*), C. R. Curds, D.Sc
Deputy Keepers (*G6*), R. J. Lincoln, Ph.D.; I. R. Bishop, OBE (*acting*)
Grade 6, J. D. Taylor, Ph.D
Bird Section, Park Street, Tring, Herts. Tel: 044 282-4181.
Grade 6, I. R. Bishop, OBE
Keeper of Entomology (*G5*), Dr R. P. Lane
Keeper of Botany (*G5*), S. Blackmore, Ph.D
Keeper of Palaeontology (*G5*), L. R. M. Cocks, D.Sc
Keeper of Mineralogy (*G5*), P. Henderson, D.Phil
Head of Finance and Establishment Officer (*G5*), C. J. E. Legg
Personnel Officer (*G7*), Mrs P. H. I. Orchard
Head of Library Services (*G6*), R. E. R. Banks
Head of Public Services (*G5*), R. S. Miles, D.Sc
Head of Exhibition and Design (*G7*), R. M. Bloomfield, Ph.D

MUSEUM OF LONDON
London Wall, London EC2Y 5HN
Tel 071-600 3699

Open Tues.–Sat. 10–6, Sun. 12–6. Closed Mondays, Christmas Day and Boxing Day. Admission, £3 (three months), £6 (one year); concessions, £1.50/£3.00.

The Museum of London opened in 1976. It is based on the amalgamation of the former Guildhall Museum and London Museum. The Museum is controlled by a Board of Governors, appointed (nine each) by the Government and the Corporation of London. The exhibition illustrates the history of London from prehistoric times to the present day.

Chairman of Board of Governors, P. Revell-Smith, CBE
Director, M. G. Hebditch, FSA

THE SCIENCE MUSEUM

South Kensington, London SW7 2DD
Tel 071-938 8000

Open Mon.–Sat. 10–6, Sun. 11–6. Closed on New Year's Day, Christmas Day and Boxing Day. Admission charge. Library open Mon.–Sat. 10–5.30. Closed on Sundays and Bank Holiday weekends.

The Science Museum, part of the National Museum of Science and Industry, houses the national collections of science, technology, industry and medicine. The Museum began as the science collection of the South Kensington Museum and first opened in 1857. In 1883 it acquired the collections of the Patent Museum and in 1909 the science collections were transferred to the new Science Museum, leaving the art collections with the Victoria and Albert Museum.

Some of the Museum's commercial aircraft, agricultural machinery, and road and rail transport collections are at Wroughton, near Swindon, Wilts., and are open for public viewing on selected weekends during the summer.

The Museum is responsible for the Concorde Exhibition at the Fleet Air Arm Museum, Yeovilton.

The total running expenses, including building costs, of the Museum, the Science Museum Library, the National Railway Museum and the National Museum of Photography, Film and Television are estimated at £26,507,000 for 1992–3. This includes £1.6 million for building a new storage site at Wroughton.

BOARD OF TRUSTEES

Chairman, Sir Austin Pearce, CBE
Members, HRH The Duke of Kent, KG, GCMG, GCVO, ADC; Dr Mary Archer; Prof. Sir Eric Ash, CBE, FRS; The Lord Brabourne; Adm. Sir Desmond Cassidi, GCB; Sir Kenneth Corfield; The Viscount Downe; Miss M. S. Goldring, OBE; Prof. E. T. Hall, CBE, FBA, FSA; Mrs A. Higham; Dr Bridget Ogilvie; Sir Robert Reid; Sir Denis Rooke, CBE, FRS; L. de Rothschild, CBE; Prof. Sir John Thomas, FRS; Sir Christopher Wates
Director, Dr N. Cossons, OBE
Assistant Director and Head of Resource Management Division (*G5*), J. J. Defries
Head of Personnel and Training (*G7*), C. Gosling
Assistant Director and Head of Collections Division (*G5*), Dr T. Wright
Head of Physical Sciences Group (*G5*), Dr D. A. Robinson
Head of Life and Environmental Sciences Group (*G5*), Dr R. F. Bud
Head of Technology Group (*G5*), Dr E. J. S. Becklake
Head of Collections Group (*G6*), Ms S. Keene
Assistant Director and Head of Public Affairs Division (*G5*), C. M. Pemberton
Assistant Director and Head of Science Communication Division (*G5*), Prof. J. R. Durant
Head of Library and Information Services (*G6*), Dr L. D. Will
Head of Interpretation and Education (*G6*), Dr G. Farmelo
Assistant Director and Head of Project Development Division (*G5*), vacant

NATIONAL RAILWAY MUSEUM

Leeman Road, York YO2 4XJ
Tel 0904-621261

The Museum, opened in 1975, houses the national rail transport collection. Locomotives, rolling stock and carriages are displayed to illustrate the technical, social and economic story of the development of railways in Britain. Open Mon.–Sat. 10–6, Sun. 11–6.

Head of Museum (*G5*), A. R. G. Dow

NATIONAL MUSEUM OF PHOTOGRAPHY, FILM AND TELEVISION

Prince's View, Bradford BD5 0TR
Tel 0274-727488

The Museum, opened in 1983, collects, conserves and displays photography, film and television materials and equipment. It has the only IMAX cinema in the UK. Open Tues.–Sun. 11–6, with special exhibition galleries open to 7.30.

Head of Museum (*G5*), C. J. Ford

THE VICTORIA AND ALBERT MUSEUM

South Kensington, London SW7 2RL
Tel 071-938 8500

Open Mon.–Sat. 10–5.50, Sun. 2.30–5.50. Closed 24–26 December, New Year's Day, Good Friday and May Day Bank Holiday. The National Art Library is open Tues.–Sat. 10–5 and the Print Room Tues.–Fri. 10–4.30, Sat. 10–1, 2–4.30. (The National Art Slide Library is now housed at De Montfort University, Leicester.) Donations are invited.

A museum of all branches of fine and applied art, the Victoria and Albert Museum descends directly from the Museum of Manufactures, which opened in Marlborough House in 1852 after the Great Exhibition of 1851. The Museum was moved in 1857 to become part of the collective South Kensington Museum. It was renamed the Victoria and Albert Museum in 1899. The branch museum at Bethnal Green was opened in 1872 and the building is the most important surviving example of the type of glass and iron construction used by Paxton for the Great Exhibition. The Victoria and Albert Museum also administers the Wellington Museum (Apsley House), and the Theatre Museum.

BOARD OF TRUSTEES

Chairman, The Lord Armstrong of Ilminster, GCB, CVO
Deputy Chairman, Sir Michael Butler, GCMG
Members, The Lord Barnett, PC; Miss N. Campbell; Sir Clifford Chetwood; I. H. Davison; E. Dawe; R. Fitch, CBE; Prof. C. Frayling, Ph.D.; Pamela, Lady Harlech; R. Gorlin; Sir Nevil Macready, Bt., CBE; Miss J. Muir, CBE; Miss A. Plowden; Prof. M. Podro, Ph.D.; M. Saatchi; Prof. J. Steer, FSA
Secretary to the Board of Trustees (*G7*), P. A. Wilson

OFFICERS

Director (*G3*), Mrs E. A. L. Esteve-Coll
Assistant Directors (*G5*), J. D. W. Murdoch (*Collections*); J. W. Close (*Administration*)
Head of Buildings and Estate (*G5*), J. G. Charlesworth
Curator, Ceramics Collection (*G6*), Dr O. Watson
Surveyor of Collections (*G5*), Mrs G. F. Miles
Head of Conservation Department (*G5*), Dr J. Ashley-Smith
Development Director, Miss S. Mason
Curator, Far Eastern Collection (*G6*), Miss R. Kerr
Head of Finance and Central Services (*G5*), Miss R. M. Sykes
Curator, Furniture and Woodwork Collection (*G6*), C. Wilk
Curator, Indian and South-East Asian Collection (*G6*), Dr D. Swallow

Curator, Metalwork Collection (G6), Mrs P. Glanville
Head of Personnel (G6), Mrs G. Henchley
Curator, Prints, Drawings and Paintings Collection (G6), Miss S. B. Lambert
Head of Public Affairs (G5), R. Cole-Hamilton
Head of Marketing and Public Relations (G7), Miss R. Griffith-Jones
Head of Research (G5), Dr C. R. Saumarez Smith
Curator, Sculpture Collection (G6), P. E. D. Williamson
Curator, Textiles and Dress Collection (G6), Mrs V. D. Mendes
Managing Director, V. & A. Enterprises Ltd, M. Cass

NATIONAL ART LIBRARY

Curator and Chief Librarian (G5), J. F. van den Wateren

BETHNAL GREEN MUSEUM OF CHILDHOOD
Cambridge Heath Road, Bethnal Green, London E2 9PA
Tel 081-980 3204
Open Mon.–Thurs. and Sat. 10–6, Sun. 2.30–6. Closed every Friday, May Day Bank Holiday, 24–26 December and New Year's Day.

Head of the Museum (G6), A. P. Burton

THEATRE MUSEUM
1E Tavistock Street, London WC2E 7PA
Tel 071-836 7891
Open Tues.–Sun. 11–7. Closed Mondays, 24–26 December, New Year's Day, Good Friday and May Day Bank Holiday. Admission £2.25, concessions £1.25.

Head of the Museum (G6), Ms M. Benton

WELLINGTON MUSEUM (APSLEY HOUSE)
149 Piccadilly, Hyde Park Corner, London W1V 9RA
Tel 071-499 5676
Open Tues.–Sun. 11–5. Closed Mondays. Apsley House is closed for essential works until spring 1994.
Curator (E), J. R. S. Voak

THE COMMONWEALTH INSTITUTE

Kensington High Street, London W8 6NQ
Tel 071-603 4535

Open Mon.–Sat. 10–5, Sun. 2–5. Closed Good Friday, May Day Bank Holiday, 24–26 December and New Year's Day. Admission free.

The Commonwealth Institute is a centre for information about the Commonwealth. It is funded by the British government with contributions from other Commonwealth governments. The Institute is controlled by a Board of Governors which includes the High Commissioners of all Commonwealth countries represented in London. There are also centres in Bradford and Edinburgh. The Institute has permanent exhibitions on all Commonwealth nations, plus educational resource, information and conference centres.

Director General, S. Cox
Director of Education, G. Brandt
Chief Administrative Officer, P. Kennedy
Senior Exhibitions Officer, S. Brownlow

IMPERIAL WAR MUSEUM

Lambeth Road, London SE1 6HZ
Tel 071-416 5000

Open daily 10–6. Closed 24–26 December and New Year's Day. Admission £3.50; concessions £2.50/£1.75. Free admission after 4 p.m. daily. The Reference departments are open Mon.–Sat. 10–5, Sat. by appointment only.

The Museum, founded in 1917, illustrates and records all aspects of the two world wars and other military operations involving Britain and the Commonwealth since 1914. It was opened in its present home, formerly Bethlem Hospital or Bedlam, in 1936. The Museum also administers HMS *Belfast* in the Pool of London, Duxford Airfield near Cambridge and the Cabinet War Rooms in Westminster.

Expenses for 1992–3 are estimated at £19,811,000.

Director-General (G4), A. C. N. Borg, CBE, Ph.D., FSA
Deputy Director-General (G5), R. W. K. Crawford
Secretary (G6), J. J. Chadwick
Personnel Officer (G7), P. L. Cracknell
Finance Officer (G7), Mrs P. A. Whitfield
Museum Superintendent (G7), D. A. Needham
Information Systems Officer (G7), J. C. Barrett
Director of Duxford Airfield (G5), E. O. Inman
Director of HMS Belfast (G6), Capt. F. A. Collins, RN

KEEPERS

Department of Museum Services (G6), C. Dowling, D.Phil
Department of Documents (G6), R. W. A. Suddaby
Department of Exhibits and Firearms (G6), D. J. Penn
Department of Printed Books (G6), G. M. Bayliss, Ph.D
Department of Art (G6), Miss A. H. Weight
Department of Film (G6), R. B. N. Smither
Department of Photographs (G6), Miss K. J. Carmichael
Department of Sound Records (G6), Mrs M. A. Brooks
Department of Marketing and Training (G6), Miss A. Godwin
Curator of the Cabinet War Rooms (G7), E. J. Wenzel

NATIONAL MARITIME MUSEUM

Greenwich, London SE10 9NF
Tel 081-858 4422

Open Mon.–Sat., 10–6 (10–5 in winter); Sun. 12–6 (2–5 in winter). Closed 24–26 December. Admission charge. Reference Library open Mon.–Fri., 10–5; Sats. by appointment only; readers' tickets available on written application to the Librarian.

Established by Act of Parliament in 1934, the National Maritime Museum illustrates the maritime history of Great Britain in the widest sense, underlining the importance of the sea and its influence on the nation's power, wealth, culture, technology and institutions. The Museum is in three groups of buildings in Greenwich Park – the main building, the Queen's House (built by Inigo Jones, 1616–35) and the Old Royal Observatory (including Wren's Flamsteed House) – and also includes the *Cutty Sark* and a Special Exhibitions Centre. The collections include paintings, actual craft and ship models, ships' lines, prints and drawings, atlases and charts, navigational and astronomical instruments, clocks, uniforms and relics, books and MSS.

Director, R. L. Ormond

NATIONAL ARMY MUSEUM

Royal Hospital Road, London SW3 4HT
Tel 071-730 0717

Open daily, 10–5.30. Closed 24–26 December, New Year's Day, Good Friday and May Day Bank Holiday. Admission free.

The National Army Museum was established by Royal Charter in 1960. It covers the history of five centuries of the British Army, including the story of the Indian Army up to independence in 1947. The Indian Army room at the Royal Military Academy Sandhurst, Camberley, Surrey may be viewed by appointment.

Director, I. G. Robertson
Personal Assistant to the Director, Mrs C. Marrable
Assistant Directors, D. K. Smurthwaite; A. J. Guy; Maj. P. R. Bateman

ROYAL AIR FORCE MUSEUM
Grahame Park Way, London NW9 5LL
Tel 081-205 2266

Open daily, 10–6. Closed 24–26 December and New Year's Day. Admission charge.
Situated on the former airfield at Hendon, the Museum illustrates the development of aviation from before the Wright brothers to the present-day RAF. About 65 historic aircraft are on display from the Museum's collection. The complex includes Battle of Britain and Bomber Command halls and the 'Battle of Britain Experience'.

Director, Dr M. A. Fopp
Deputy Director, J. D. Freeborn
Keepers, D. C. R. Elliott; P. G. Murton; P. Elliott; D. F. Lawrence

THE NATIONAL MUSEUMS AND GALLERIES ON MERSEYSIDE
William Brown Street, Liverpool L3 8EN
Tel 051-207 0001

All museums and galleries are open all year except 24–26 December, New Year's Day and Good Friday. Opening times (except for the Maritime Museum) are Mon.–Sat. 10–5, Sun. 12–5. Opening times for the Maritime Museum are 10.30–5.30. Admission charge.

The Board of Trustees of the National Museums and Galleries on Merseyside was established in 1986 to take over responsibility for the museums and galleries previously administered by Merseyside County Council. Various stores ancillary to the collections are also the responsibility of the body. It is grant-aided by the Department of National Heritage.

Chairman of the Board of Trustees, Sir Leslie Young, CBE
Director, R. Foster
Head of Central Services, P. Sudbury, Ph.D
Keeper of Art Galleries, J. Treuherz
Keeper of Conservation, J. France

LIVERPOOL MUSEUM
William Brown Street, Liverpool
Keeper, E. Greenwood

MERSEYSIDE MARITIME MUSEUM
Albert Dock, Liverpool
Keeper, M. Stammers

WALKER ART GALLERY
William Brown Street, Liverpool

LADY LEVER ART GALLERY
Port Sunlight Village, Bebington, Wirral

SUDLEY (ART GALLERY)
Mossley Hill Road, Liverpool

THE NATIONAL MUSEUM OF WALES
(AMGUEDDFA GENEDLAETHOL CYMRU)
Main Building, Cathays Park, Cardiff CF1 3NP
Tel 0222-397951

Open Tues.–Sat., 10–5. Sun. 2.30–5. Closed on Mondays (except Bank Holidays), 24–26 December, New Year's Day and Good Friday. Admission charge.

President, Hon. J. Davies
Vice-President, C. R. T. Edwards
Director, A. Wilson
Head of Administration, T. Arnold
Keepers, M. G. Bassett, Ph.D. (*Geology*); B. A. Thomas, Ph.D. (*Botany*); P. M. Morgan (*Zoology*); H. S. Green, Ph.D. (*Archaeology*); T. J. Stevens, Ph.D. (*Art*)

WELSH FOLK MUSEUM (AMGUEDDFA WERIN CYMRU)
St Fagans, Nr. Cardiff
Open April–Oct., daily 10–5; Nov.–March, Mon.–Sat. 10–5. Closed 24–26 December, New Year's Day and Good Friday. Admission charge.
Curator, Dr E. Williams
Keepers, E. Scourfield, Ph.D; J. W. Davies.

ROMAN LEGIONARY MUSEUM, CAERLEON
Caerleon, Gwent
Contains material found on the site of the Roman fortress of Isca and its suburbs. Open Mon.–Sat. 10–6, Sun. 2–6 (closes 4.30 p.m. mid-Oct. to mid-March). Closed 24–26 December, New Year's Day and Good Friday. Admission charge.
Officer in Charge, D. Zienkiewicz

TURNER HOUSE ART GALLERY
Plymouth Road, Penarth, Nr. Cardiff
Open Tues.–Fri. 11–12.45 and 2–5, Sun. 2–5. Closed Mondays except Bank Holidays, Saturdays, 24–26 December, New Year's Day and Good Friday.
Keeper in Charge, T. Stevens, Ph.D

MUSEUM OF THE NORTH
Llanberis, Gwynedd
A multi-media presentation of the history of Wales, and about the electricity supply industry. Open June to mid-Sept. 9.30–6; mid-Sept.–Oct. and May, 10–5; Nov.–April, pre-booked parties only. Closed 24–26 December, New Year's Day and Good Friday. Admission charge.
Keeper, D. Roberts, Ph.D

WELSH SLATE MUSEUM
Llanberis, Gwynedd
Open Easter–30 Sept daily 9.30–5.30. Admission charge.
Keeper in Charge, D. Roberts, Ph.D

SEGONTIUM ROMAN FORT MUSEUM
Beddgelert Road, Caernarfon, Gwynedd
Open weekdays at 9.30, Sundays at 2. Closes at 6 from May to September, at 5.30 in March, April and October (5 on Suns.), and at 4 from November to February. Closed 24–26 December, New Year's Day and Good Friday.
Officer in Charge, R. J. Brewer

MUSEUM OF THE WELSH WOOLLEN INDUSTRY
Dre-fach Felindre, nr. Llandysul, Dyfed
The museum occupies part of a working mill. Open April–Sept., Mon.–Sat. 10–5; Oct.–March, Mon.–Fri. 10–5. Admission charge.
Keeper in Charge, E. Scourfield, Ph.D

WELSH INDUSTRIAL AND MARITIME MUSEUM
Bute Street, Cardiff
Open Tues.–Sat. 10–5; Sun. 2.30–5. Closed Mondays, 24–26 December, New Year's Day and Good Friday. Admission charge.
Keeper, S. Owen-Jones, Ph.D

THE GRAHAM SUTHERLAND GALLERY AND PICTON CASTLE GROUNDS
The Rhos, Haverfordwest
Open Easter–end Oct., Tues.–Sun. 10.30–12.30, 1.30–5.00. Closed Mondays (except Bank Holidays). Admission charge.
Officer in Charge, S. Moss

NATIONAL MUSEUMS OF SCOTLAND
Chambers Street, Edinburgh EH1 1JF
Tel 031-225 7534

BOARD OF TRUSTEES
Members, The Marquess of Bute; Prof. L. Bown, OBE; W. Brown, CBE; R. D. Cramond, CBE; Sir Nicholas

Fairbairn, QC, MP; Dr H. A. P. Ingram; Prof. P. H. Jones; D. H. Pringle, CBE; R. Smith; Prof. T. C. Smout

OFFICERS

Director, M. Jones
Museums Administrator, I. Hooper
Keeper, Department of History and Applied Art (G5), Miss D. Idiens
Keeper, Department of Archaeology, D. V. Clarke, D.Phil
Keeper, Department of Geology (G5), W. D. I. Rolfe, Ph.D
Keeper, Department of Natural History (G5), M. Shaw, D.Phil
Keeper, Department of Science, Technology and Working Life (G5), D. J. Bryden
Head, Department of Public Affairs (G6), S. Brock, Ph.D
Head, Department of Museum Services (G6), S. R. Elson

ROYAL MUSEUM OF SCOTLAND
Chambers Street, Edinburgh and Queen Street, Edinburgh
Open Mon.–Sat. 10–5, Sun. 2–5. Closed 25–26 December and 1–2 January. Admission free.

SCOTTISH UNITED SERVICES MUSEUM
Edinburgh Castle
Open 1 April–30 Sept., Mon.–Sat. 9.30–5.50, Sun. 11–5.50; 1 Oct.–31 March, Mon.–Sat. 9.30–5.05, Sun. 12.30–4.20. Closed 25–26 December and 1–2 January. Admission free.
Keeper, S. C. Wood

SCOTTISH AGRICULTURAL MUSEUM
Ingliston, Edinburgh
Open May and Sept. Mon.–Fri. 10–4.30; June–Aug. Mon.–Sat. 10–4.30. Admission free.
Curator, G. Sprott

MUSEUM OF FLIGHT
East Fortune Airfield, East Lothian
Open Easter–end Sept. daily 10.30–4.30. Admission free.
Curator, Sqn. Ldr. R. Major

BIGGAR GASWORKS MUSEUM
Biggar, Lanarkshire
Open June–Sept. daily 2–5. Admission free.
Curator, J. Wood

SHAMBELLIE HOUSE MUSEUM OF COSTUME
New Abbey, nr Dumfries
Reopens July 1993 after refurbishment. Admission free.
Keeper, Miss D. Idiens

NATIONAL AUDIT OFFICE

157–197 Buckingham Palace Road, London SW1W 9SP
Tel 071–798 7000

The National Audit Office came into existence under the National Audit Act 1983, to replace and continue the work of the former Exchequer and Audit Department. The Act reinforced the Office's total financial and operational independence from the Government and brought its head, the Comptroller and Auditor-General, into a closer relationship with Parliament as an officer of the House of Commons.

The National Audit Office provides independent information, advice and assurance to Parliament and the public about all aspects of the financial operations of government departments and many other bodies receiving public funds. This it does by examining and certifying the accounts of these organizations and by regularly publishing reports to Parliament on the results of its value for money investigations of the economy, efficiency and effectiveness with which public resources have been used. The National Audit Office is also the auditor by agreement of the accounts of certain international and other organizations. In addition, the Office authorizes the issue of public funds to government departments.

Comptroller and Auditor-General, Sir John Bourn, KCB
Private Secretary, J. Rickleton
Deputy Comptroller and Auditor-General, R. N. Le Marechal
Assistant Auditor-Generals, D. A. Dewar; M. J. Goodson; J. A. Higgins; P. J. C. Keemer; L. H. Hughes
Directors, A. G. Brown; T. J. Lovett; C. L. Press; B. D. Baker; C. K. Beauchamp; M. C. Pfleger; R. M. Bennett; B. Hogg; G. G. Jones; R. J. McCourt; J. Marshall; A. R. Murray; J. Parsons; J. M. Pearce; A. G. Roberts; R. A. Skeen; R. E. Spurgeon; M. Easteal; A. Fiander; Ms M. Bibby; M. Daynes
Deputy Directors, C. J. Day; D. R. Corsby; J. J. Jones; D. J. Woodward; A. Burchell; J. B. Cavanagh; J. Darling; P. R. Duncombe; R. J. Eales; D. A. Ferguson; N. Gale; T. Griffiths; K. Hawkswell; Miss J. Lawler; J. S. McEwen; Miss C. Mawhood; R. Parker; R. A. Pocock; M. J. Reeves; N. Sloan; P. G. Woodward; R. Goacher; M. Whitehouse; P. Cannon; R. Swan; M. Sinclair; M. Reeves.

NATIONAL CONSUMER COUNCIL

20 Grosvenor Gardens, London SW1W 0DH
Tel 071-730 3469

The National Consumer Council was set up by the Government in 1975 to give an independent voice to consumers in the UK. Its job is to advocate the consumer interest to decision-makers in business, industry, the public utilities, the professions, and central and local government. It does this through a combination of research and campaigning. It is funded by a grant-in-aid from the Department of Trade and Industry.

Chairman, Lady Wilcox
Vice-Chairman, Mrs A. Scully
Members, Miss B. Brookes; Prof. K. Bhattacharyya; A. Burton, OBE; P. Circus; Prof. P. Fairest; Miss J. Francis; J. Hughes; L. N. Hunter; Mrs D. Hutton; Prof. G. Jones; J. Mitchell; Ms M. McAnally; Lady McCollum; Mrs J. Moore, OBE; Mrs J. Varnam; A. White; M. Wolf
Director, R. Evans

NATIONAL DEBT OFFICE – *see* National Investment and Loans Office

NATIONAL GALLERIES – *see* Art Galleries

DEPARTMENT OF NATIONAL HERITAGE

Horse Guards Road, London SW1P 3AL
Tel 071-270 3000
(*temporary address*)

The Department of National Heritage was established in 1992. It is responsible for aspects of government policy previously covered by six other government departments. It has taken over all the functions of the former Office of Arts and Libraries, heritage policy from the Department of the Environment, tourism policy from the Department of Employment, sports policy from the Department for Education, broadcasting and media policy and the safety of sports grounds from the Home Office, and films policy and the export licensing of antiques from the Department of Trade and Industry. The Department is also responsible for policy and legislation surrounding the introduction of the proposed National Lottery.

Secretary of State for National Heritage, The Rt. Hon. Peter Brooke, MP
Principal Private Secretary, N. Holgate
Parliamentary Under Secretary of State, Robert Key, MP
Private Secretary, K. Parker
Permanent Secretary (*G1*), G. H. Phillips, CB
Private Secretary, Miss H. Wilkinson

ARTS GROUP

Director (*G3*), Ms M. O'Mara
Head of Arts Group (*G5*), Miss S. Brown
Head of Libraries Group (*G5*), P. Bolt
Head of Galleries and Museums Group (*G5*), P. Gregory
Director, British Library Project St Pancras (*G5*), J. Pardey
Director, Government Art Collection (*G6*), Dr Wendy Baron, OBE
Head of Works of Art Unit (*G7*), Miss C. Morrison

BROADCASTING, FILMS AND SPORT GROUP

Director (*G3*), P. Wright
Head of Broadcasting Group (*G5*), Miss J. Goose
Head of Media Group (*G5*), P. Edwards
Head of Sport Group (*G5*), Miss A. Stewart
Head of Film Group (*G7*), J. Melville

HERITAGE AND TOURISM GROUP

Director (*G3*), J. Gunn
Head of Royal Parks Executive Agency (*G5*), D. Welch
Head of Heritage Group (*G5*), A. Corner
Head of Royal Estate Group (*G5*), C. Douglas
Head of Tourism Group (*G5*), C. Leamy

FINANCE AND RESOURCES

Director (*G4*), N. Pittman
Grade 5, Ms S. Booth

INFORMATION

Head of Press and Publicity (*G5*), Miss A. MacLean

HISTORIC ROYAL PALACES AGENCY
The Birdwood Annexe, Hampton Court Palace, East Molesey, Surrey KT8 9AU

An executive agency within the Department of the Environment, the Historic Royal Palaces Agency manages the Tower of London, Hampton Court Palace, Kensington Palace, Kew Palace with Queen Charlotte's Cottage, and the Banqueting House, Whitehall.

Chief Executive (*G3*), D. C. Beeton.
Director of Finance and Resources (*G5*), Ms B. Darbyshire
Surveyor of the Fabric (*G5*), S. Bond.
Director of Marketing (*G6*), P. D. Hammond
Administrator, Hampton Court Palace (*G6*), D. J. C. MacDonald
Resident Governor, HM Tower of London (*G5*), Maj.-Gen. C. Tyler, CB (retd)
Administrator, Kensington Palace (*G7*), N. J. Arch

NATIONAL HERITAGE MEMORIAL FUND

10 St James's Street, London SW1A 1EF
Tel 071-930 0963

The National Heritage Memorial Fund was established in 1980 as an independent body, and is intended as a memorial to those who have died for the UK. The Fund is empowered, by the National Heritage Act 1980, to give financial assistance towards the cost of acquiring, maintaining or preserving land, buildings, works of art and other objects of outstanding interest which are also of importance to the national heritage. The Fund is administered by up to eleven trustees, appointed by the Prime Minister.

The Fund's major source of money is the Department of National Heritage, which gives an annual grant. In its first 12 years, the Fund has spent over £140 million in carrying out its responsibilities.

TRUSTEES

Chairman, The Lord Rothschild
Members, R. Carew Pole; The Lord Crathorne; W. L. Evans; Sir Nicholas Goodison; Sir Martin Jacomb; The Lord Macfarlane of Bearsden; Prof. P. J. Newbould; Mrs J. Nutting; Mrs C. Porteous; Cdr. L. M. M. Saunders Watson
Director, Miss G. Nayler

NATIONAL INSURANCE JOINT AUTHORITY

The Adelphi, 1–11 John Adam Street, London WC2N 6HT
Tel 071-962 8000

The Authority's function is to co-ordinate the operation of social security legislation in Great Britain and Northern Ireland, including the necessary financial adjustments between the two National Insurance Funds.

Members, The Secretary of State for Social Security; the Head of the Department of Health and Social Services for Northern Ireland.
Secretary, Mrs D. M. Joannou

NATIONAL INVESTMENT AND LOANS OFFICE

1 King Charles Street, London SW1A 2AP
Tel 071-270 3863

The National Investment and Loans Office was set up in 1980 by the merger of the National Debt Office and the Public Works Loan Board. The Department provides staff and services for the National Debt Commissioners and the Public Works Loan Commissioners.

Director, I. H. Peattie
Establishment Officer, A. G. Ladd

NATIONAL DEBT OFFICE

Comptroller-General, I. H. Peattie

PUBLIC WORKS LOAN BOARD

Chairman, Sir Robin Dent, KCVO
Deputy Chairman, Miss F. M. Cook

Other Commissioners, Miss V. J. Di Palma, OBE; G. Ross Russell; P. Brackfield; D. H. Adams; R. A. Chapman; A. Morton; I. C. Wilson, OBE; G. G. Williams; R. G. Tettenborn; J. E. Scotford
Secretary, I. H. Peattie
Assistant Secretary, Miss L. M. Ashcroft

NATIONAL RADIOLOGICAL PROTECTION BOARD

Chilton, Didcot, Oxon. OX11 0RG
Tel 0235-831600

The National Radiological Protection Board is an independent statutory body created by the Radiological Protection Act 1970. It is the national point of authoritative reference on radiological protection for both ionizing and non-ionizing radiations.

Chairman, Sir Richard Southwood, FRS.
Director, Dr R. H. Clarke

NATIONAL RIVERS AUTHORITY

Rivers House, Waterside Drive, Aztec West, Almondsbury, Bristol BS12 4UD
Tel 0454-624400

The National Rivers Authority (NRA) is an independent body set up under the Water Act 1989. Its responsibilities include monitoring the quality of water, controlling pollution, and the management of water resources, flood defence and fisheries. The NRA has a board of 15 members, two of whom are appointed by the Minister of Agriculture, Fisheries and Food, one by the Secretary of State for Wales, and the rest by the Secretary of State for the Environment.

Chairman, The Lord Crickhowell, PC.
Chief Executive, E. Gallagher
Chief Scientist, Dr J. Pentreath
Technical Director, Dr C. Swinnerton
Finance Director, N. Reader
Personnel Director, P. Humphreys
Director, Chief Executive's Office, Ms M. Evans

DEPARTMENT FOR NATIONAL SAVINGS

Charles House, 375 Kensington High Street, London W14 8SD
Tel 071-605 9300

The Department for National Savings was established as a government department in 1969. The Department is responsible for the administration of a wide range of schemes for personal savers.
For details of schemes, *see* National Savings section.

Director of Savings (G2), C. D. Butler
Deputy Director (G3), D. Howard
Establishment Officer (G5), D. S. Speedie
Finance Officer (G5), C. Ward
Controllers (G5), Miss A. Nash (*Marketing and Information*); A. S. McGill; D. H. Monaghan; E. B. Senior; P. N. S. Hickman Robertson
Senior Principals (G6), D. W. Kellaway; W. J. Herd; I. Forsyth; M. A. Nicholls; D. Newton; T. Threlfall
Principals (G7), D. K. Paterson; A. J. V. Cummings; Dr A. Fort; W. J. Ferrier; H. Johnson; J. W. Davison; A. B. Wood; P. Finnie; C. E. Funk; I. Jordinson; A. Brown; B. Paley; H. Webster; J. Wheatley; T. J. F. McMahon; C. McVey; R. A. Nichol; J. B. Dunphy; J. C. Foreman; D. Wilson; P. B. Robinson; G. V. Wise; A. S. Lamond; D. Jeffrey; J. Bolam; R. W. Day; I. S. Campbell; C. Dodsworth; R. R. Hesketh; R. J. McLelland; M. J. Tan; M. McDade; I. Rich; Miss J. S. Clark; M. C. Richards; M. Taylor; J. M. Anderson; W. Carroll

NATIONAL TRAINING TASK FORCE

214 Gray's Inn Road, London WC1X 8HL
Tel 071-278 0363

The National Training Task Force was established by the Government in 1989 to advise the Secretary of State for Employment on strategic policy objectives for training, vocational education and enterprise development.

Chairman, Sir Brian Wolfson
Members, Sir Peter Bowness, CBE; L. Spencer; Sir Peter Thompson; Sir Antony Cleaver; M. Rowarth, OBE; S. Elliott; W. Jordan, CBE; Sir Allen Sheppard; A. Collier; Sir Bob Reid; I. Wood, CBE; T. Farmer, CBE; C. Darby, CBE; C. Hadley; T. Booth, CBE; Sir Anthony Gill, FEng.; The Baroness O'Cathain, OBE
Secretary, R. Dawe, CB, OBE

NATURAL ENVIRONMENT RESEARCH COUNCIL

Polaris House, North Star Avenue, Swindon SN2 1EU
Tel 0793-411500

The Natural Environment Research Council was established in 1965 to encourage, plan and conduct research in the physical and biological sciences which relate to the natural environment and its resources. The Council carries out research and training through its own institutes and by grants, fellowships and post-graduate awards to universities and other institutions of higher education.

Chairman, Prof. J. Knill, Ph.D., D.Sc
Secretary, Dr Eileen Buttle
Director of Earth Sciences, Prof. J. C. Briden, Ph.D
Director of Terrestrial and Fresh Water Sciences, P. B. Tinker, D.Sc., Ph.D
Director of Marine and Atmospheric Sciences, J. D. Woods, CBE, Ph.D

CENTRAL SERVICES

NERC SCIENTIFIC SERVICES, Polaris House, North Star Avenue, Swindon, Wilts. SN2 1EU. Tel: 0793-411500. *Director*, B. J. Hinde

RESEARCH VESSEL SERVICES, No. 1 Dock, Barry, S. Glamorgan. Tel: 0446-737451. *Head*, Dr C. Fay

NERC COMPUTER SERVICE, Holbrook House, Station Road, Swindon, Wilts. SN1 1DE. Tel: 0793-411500. *Director*, H. J. Down

For research institutes and units of the Natural Environment Research Council, *see* page 695–6.

JOINT NATURE CONSERVATION COMMITTEE

Monkstone House, City Road, Peterborough PE1 1JY
Tel 0733-62626

The Committee was established under the Environmental Protection Act 1990 and began work on 1 April 1991. It advises the Government and others on UK and international nature conservation issues and disseminates knowledge on these subjects. It establishes common standards for the monitoring of nature conservation and research, and analyses the resulting information. It commissions research relevant to these roles, and provides guidance to English Nature, Scottish Natural Heritage, the Countryside Council for Wales and the Department of the Environment for Northern Ireland.

Chairman, The Earl of Selborne, KBE, FRS
Chief Officer, Dr F. B. O'Connor
Director, Life Sciences and Resources, Dr M. W. Pienkowski

NORTHERN IRELAND OFFICE

Whitehall, London SW1A 2AZ
Tel 071-210 3000

The Northern Ireland Office is the office of the Secretary of State for Northern Ireland. It was established in 1972, when the Northern Ireland (Temporary Provisions) Act transferred the legislative and executive powers of the Northern Ireland Government and Parliament to the UK Parliament and a Secretary of State. The Northern Ireland Constitution Act 1973 provided for devolution in Northern Ireland through an assembly and executive, but agreement has not been reached on arrangements for involving locally-elected representatives in the government of Northern Ireland, and so responsibility still rests with the United Kingdom Government.

In 1985 the Governments of the United Kingdom and the Republic of Ireland signed the Anglo-Irish Agreement, establishing an intergovernmental conference in which the Irish Government may put forward views and proposals on certain aspects of Northern Ireland affairs.

Secretary of State for Northern Ireland, The Rt. Hon. Sir Patrick Mayhew, QC, MP
Parliamentary Private Secretary, M. Brown, MP
Ministers of State, Michael Mates, MP; Robert Atkins, MP
Parliamentary Private Secretary to Mr Atkins, J. Hayes, MP
Parliamentary Under Secretaries of State, Jeremy Hanley, MP; The Earl of Arran
Permanent Under Secretary of State(G1), J. A. Chilcot, CB
Second Permanent Under Secretary of State, Head of the NICS, (G1A); D. Fell, CB

NORTHERN IRELAND CIVIL SERVICE (NICS), Stormont Castle, Belfast BT4 3TT. Tel: 0232-763011
DEPARTMENT OF AGRICULTURE FOR NORTHERN IRELAND, Dundonald House, Upper Newtownards Road, Belfast BT4 3SB. Tel: 0232-650111
DEPARTMENT OF ECONOMIC DEVELOPMENT NORTHERN IRELAND, Netherleigh, Massey Avenue, Belfast BT4 2JP. Tel: 0232-763244
DEPARTMENT OF EDUCATION FOR NORTHERN IRELAND, Rathgael House, Balloo Road, Bangor, Co. Down BT19 2PR. Tel: 0247-270077
DEPARTMENT OF THE ENVIRONMENT FOR NORTHERN IRELAND, Parliament Buildings, Stormont, Belfast BT4 3SS. Tel: 0232-763210
DEPARTMENT OF FINANCE AND PERSONNEL, Parliament Buildings, Stormont, Belfast BT4 3SW. Tel: 0232-763210
DEPARTMENT OF HEALTH AND SOCIAL SERVICES NORTHERN IRELAND, Dundonald House, Upper Newtownards Road, Belfast BT4 3SF. Tel: 0232-650111

OCCUPATIONAL PENSIONS BOARD

PO Box 2EE, Newcastle upon Tyne NE99 2EE
Tel 091-225 6414

The Occupational Pensions Board (OPB) is an independent statutory body set up under the Social Security Act 1973 to administer the contracting-out of occupational pensions from the State Earnings Related Pension Scheme (SERPS), and to advise the Secretary of State. Its functions have been extended by subsequent legislation and it is now also responsible for administering equal access, preservation and modification requirements and appropriate personal pension schemes. Following the Social Security Act 1990, the OPB was appointed as Registrar of Occupational and Personal Pension Schemes and granted powers to make grants to approved bodies in the field. The OPB now funds the operation of the Occupational Pensions Advisory Service (OPAS).

Chairman, Sir Jeremy Rowe, CBE
Deputy Chairman, Miss C. H. Dawes
Members, R. J. Amy; Mrs R. Brown; R. Ellison; R. J. Hebblethwaite, TD; A. U. Lyburn; R. Neale; A. Pickering; W. M. R. Ramsey, D.Phil.; K. R. Thomas; The Baroness Turner of Camden; Miss H. Wiesner
Secretary to the Board and General Manager of Executive Office (G6), A. Scaife

OMBUDSMAN – *see* Local Commissioners *and* Parliamentary Commissioner. For non-statutory Ombudsmen, *see* Index

ORDNANCE SURVEY

Romsey Road, Maybush, Southampton SO9 4DH
Tel 0703-792000

The Ordnance Survey is the national mapping agency for Britain. It became an executive agency in May 1990 and reports to the Secretary of State for the Environment.

The Ordnance Survey has military origins. It produces over 220,000 large scale maps of the country at three basic scales. These are 1:1,250 (50 inches to 1 mile) for urban areas; 1:2,500 (25 inches to 1 mile) for rural areas; and 1:10,000 (6 inches to 1 mile) for mountain and moorland. In addition, Ordnance Survey produces a range of small scale maps and other products for general use.

Director-General, Prof. D. Rhind
Directors:
Surveys and Production, A. S. Macdonald
Marketing, Planning and Development, J. Leonard
Establishments and Finance, I. Lock
Heads of Functions:
Production, D. Davies
Topographic Surveys, D. Toft

Marketing, P. Wesley
Research and Development, I. T. Logan
Finance, D. James
Establishments, D. R. Evans
Information and Computer Service, B. W. Nanson
OS International, E. Gilbert

OVERSEAS DEVELOPMENT ADMINISTRATION

94 Victoria Street, London SWIE 5JL
Tel 071-917 7000
Abercrombie House, Eaglesham Road, East Kilbride, Glasgow G75 8EA
Tel 0355-844000

The Overseas Development Administration deals with British development assistance to overseas countries. This includes both capital aid on concessional terms and technical assistance (mainly in the form of specialist staff abroad and training facilities in the United Kingdom), whether provided directly to developing countries or through the various multilateral aid organizations, including the United Nations and its specialized agencies.

Minister for Overseas Development, The Baroness Chalker of Wallasey, PC
Private Secretary (G7), S. Chakrabarti
Permanent Secretary (G1A), T. P. Lankester
Private Secretary, Ms G. J. Lyons
Deputy Secretary (G2), R. M. Ainscow, CB
Under Secretaries (G3), N. B. Hudson; B. R. Ireton; J. V. Kerby; R. G. Manning; A. J. Bennett; J. B. Wilmshurst; J. L. Faint; P. D. M. Freeman

Economic and Social Division

Head of the Economic Service (G3), J. B. Wilmshurst
Senior Economic Advisers (G5), J. C. H. Morris; A. G. Coverdale; B. P. Thomas; J. Roberts; M. Foster; P. Sandersley
Economic Advisers (G6), P. J. Ackroyd; P. L. Owen; *(G7)*, P. D. Balacs; B. Carstairs; Dr F. C. Clift; J. G. Clarke; D. B. Crapper; P. J. Dearden; D. Donaldson; P. D. Grant; N. F. Gregory; Dr G. Haley; A. B. D. Hall; E. Hawthorn; N. Highton
Economists (G7), J. L. Hoy; W. Kingsmill; M. Lewis; A. Moon; R. Teuten; Ms R. Turner; Mrs J. White; A. Whitworth; Ms C. Laing; E. Cassidy; Ms R. Phillipson; J. Burton; M. Surr; R. Moberly; Ms J. Alston; P. G. Hill
Senior Small Enterprise Development Adviser (G6), D. L. Wright
Small Enterprise Development Adviser (G7) vacant
Chief Statistician (G5), R. M. Allen
Statisticians (G6), A. B. Williams; *(G7)*, J. R. B. King; P. J. Crook; Ms J. J. Church; M. Dyble
Principal Finance Management and Administration Adviser (G5), K. L. Sparkhall
Senior Finance Management and Administration Advisers (G6), Dr R. Thomas; Dr G. Glentworth
Finance Management and Administration Adviser (G7), Dr M. Greaves
Senior Finance and Management Advisers (G6), D. W. Heffer; D. J. Wood
Overseas Policy Adviser (G6), L. Grundy
Chief Social Development Adviser (G5), Dr R. J. Eyben
Senior Social Development Adviser (G6), Dr S. Conlin
Social Development Advisers (G7), Ms P. Holden; M. Schultz

Information Department

Head of Information (G5), A. Bearpark
Principal Information Officer (G7), R. W. Fosker

Administrative Staff

Grade 5, Miss A. M. Archbold; J. H. S. Chard; Ms M. Cund; A. D. Davis; J. R. Drummond; M. J. Dinham; R. Elias; D. S. Fish; R. M. Graham-Harrison; B. W. Hammond; W. Hobman; J. Hodges; Mrs S. Jay; Mrs B. M. Kelly; M. C. McCulloch; J. C. Machin; V. J. McClean; C. Myhill; M. A. Power; C. P. Raleigh; S. Ray; D. Sands-Smith; D. L. Stanton; G. M. Stegmann; D. P. Turner; Ms S. E. Unsworth; M. Wickstead; Mrs P. M. Wilkinson; R. J. Wilson
Grade 6, J. A. Anning; D. R. Curran; K. D. Grimshaw; Ms P. J. Hilton; D. Richards; D. Trotter; G. A. Williams
Grade 7, G. F. H. Aicken; J. D. Aitken; R. Allen; G. A. Armstrong; C. B. Austin; N. Bailey; D. W. Baker; D. G. Bell; F. Black; H. Britton; W. A. Brownlie; P. J. Burton; R. T. Calvert; P. H. Charters; D. J. Church; T. F. G. Connor; R. G. Cousins; G. Crabtree; A. O. Davies; P. Dean; M. J. Ellis; J. R. Gilbert; M. A. Hammond; Ms V. M. Harris; B. Hefferon; M. I. Holland; N. Hoult; G. I. James; W. Jardine; Mrs J. Laurence; D. Lawless; G. G. Leader; J. Lingham; M. A. B. Lowcock; I. M. McKendry; M. Mallalieu; G. H. Malley; P. S. Mason; J. Maund; C. A. Metcalf; J. C. H. Millett; D. J. Moran; M. L. S. Mosselmans; J. D. Moye; G. A. Mustard; P. T. Perris; R. J. Plumb; G. M. Porter; Mrs J. Radice; C. N. Raynor; S. R. J. Robbins; P. T. Rose; C. R. Roth; Dr P. W. K. Rundell; Ms P. Schofield; Mrs P. A. Scutt; S. J. Sharpe; R. J. Smith; Miss R. B. Stevenson; M. J. Sexton; I. D. Stuart; A. J. Sutherland; D. J. C. Taylor; E. C. N. Taylor; N. Thomas; B. A. Thorpe; R. G. Toulmin; N. A. Tranter; R. Vernon; Ms S. T. Wardell; C. W. Warren; R. S. White; J. M. Winter; A. K. C. Wood; M. C. Wood; Mrs G. B. Wright; M. S. S. Wyatt

Advisory and Specialist Staff

Chief Education Adviser (G5), Dr R. O. Iredale
Senior Education Advisers (G6), M. D. Francis; Ms M. Harrison; M. E. Seath; Dr D. G. Swift
Chief Engineering Adviser (G5), T. D. Pike
Senior Engineering Advisers (G6), A. G. Colley; C. I. Ellis; D. Gillett; B. Dolton; H. B. Jackson; P. W. D. H. Roberts; M. F. Sergeant
Engineering Advisers (G7), R. J. Cadwallader; A. Barker; A. Smallwood; M. McCarthy; D. Robson; C. Hunt
Senior Renewable Energy and Research Adviser (G6), Dr J. L. D. Harrison
Senior Electrical and Mechanical Engineering Adviser (G6), R. P. Jones
Senior Architectural and Physical Planning Advisers (G6), M. W. Parkes; W. M. Housego-Woolgar
Chief Health and Population Advisers (G6), Dr P. Key, OBE; Miss J. Isard; Dr M. Kapila; Ms S. Simmonds; J. Lambert
Chief Natural Resources Adviser (G3), A. J. Bennett
Deputy Chief Natural Resources and Principal Agricultural Adviser (G5), J. M. Scott
Deputy Chief Natural Resources Adviser (G5), Dr J. C. Davies, OBE *(Research)*
Senior Natural Resources Advisers (G6), Ms L. C. Brown; B. E. Grimwood; Dr I. Haines; J. R. F. Hansell; D. J. Salmon; A. J. Tainsh; D. Trotman; M. J. Wilson; *(G7)*, G. A. Gilman; J. A. Harvey; Dr H. Potter; Dr P. Dobie; T. Barrett

Animal Health Advisers (*G6*), G. G. Freeland; Dr A. D. Irvin; Ms L. Bell
Senior Fisheries Advisers (*G6*), Dr J. Tarbit; R. W. Beales
Senior Forestry Advisers (*G6*), W. J. Howard; R. Jenkin; P. Wood
Senior Procurement Adviser (*G6*), vacant
Contract Adviser (*G7*), R. Davidson
Senior Technical Education Advisers (*G6*), C. Lewis; Dr G. R. H. Jones
Industrial Training Advisers (*G7*), W. Wray; D. G. Marr
Population Adviser (*G7*), C. Allison
Agricultural Education and Training Adviser (*G7*), A. Hall

NATURAL RESOURCES INSTITUTE
Central Avenue, Chatham Maritime, Chatham, Kent ME4 4TB
Tel 0634-880088

An executive agency within the ODA, the NRI provides scientific and technical expertise in renewable natural resources for the overseas aid programme.

Director and Chief Executive (*G3*), G. A. Beattie

OFFICE OF THE PARLIAMENTARY COMMISSIONER AND HEALTH SERVICE COMMISSIONER

Church House, Great Smith Street, London SW1P 3BW
Tel 071-276 3000

The Parliamentary Commissioner for Administration (the Ombudsman) is responsible for investigating complaints referred to him by Members of the House of Commons from members of the public who claim to have sustained injustice in consequence of maladministration by or on behalf of government departments and certain non-departmental public bodies. Certain types of action by government departments or bodies are excluded from investigation. Actions taken by other public bodies (such as local authorities, the police, the Post Office and nationalized industries) are outside the Commissioner's scope.

The Health Service Commissioners for England, for Scotland and for Wales are responsible for investigating complaints against National Health Service authorities that are not dealt with by those authorities to the satisfaction of the complainant. Complaints can be referred direct by the member of the public who claims to have sustained injustice or hardship in consequence of the failure in a service provided by a relevant body, failure of that body to provide a service or in consequence of any other action by that body. Certain types of action are excluded, in particular, action taken solely in consequence of the exercise of clinical judgment. The three offices are presently held by the Parliamentary Commissioner.

Parliamentary Commissioner and Health Service Commissioner (*G1*), W. K. Reid, CB
Deputy Parliamentary Commissioner (*G3*), J. E. Avery
Deputy Health Service Commissioner (*G3*), R. A. Oswald
Directors (*G5*), Mrs J. M. Fowler; M. D. Randall; J. C. Bateman; M. P. Cornwell-Kelly; P. J. Belsham; Miss D. Fordham
Principals (*G7*), G. M. Keil; Mrs C. Bentley; T. J. Corkett; T. J. Hull; (*Establishment Officer*); S. J. Drummond; B. P. Jones; K. O'Brien; D. Bates; Miss C. Corrigan; D. S. Coleman; E. J. Drake; S. Lillington; Miss S. Pearson; Mrs S. Skingley

PARLIAMENTARY COUNSEL

36 Whitehall, London SW1A 2AY
Tel 071-210 6633

Parliamentary Counsel draft all government Bills (i.e. primary legislation) except those relating exclusively to Scotland, the latter being drafted by the Lord Advocate's Department. They also advise on all aspects of parliamentary procedure in connection with such Bills and draft government amendments to them as well as any motions (including financial resolutions) necessary to secure their introduction into, and passage through, Parliament.

First Counsel (£82,780), P. Graham, CB, QC
Second Counsel (£73,900), J. C. Jenkins, CB
Counsel (£59,020), J. S. Mason, CB; D. W. Saunders, CB; E. G. Caldwell, CB; E. G. Bowman, CB; G. B. Sellers, CB; E. R. Sutherland; P. F. A. Knowles; S. C. Laws; R. S. Parker

PAROLE BOARD FOR ENGLAND AND WALES

Abell House, John Islip Street, London SW1P 4LH
Tel 071-217 5705

The Board was constituted under section 59 of the Criminal Justice Act 1967 and continued under section 32 of the Criminal Justice Act 1991. Its duty is to advise the Secretary of State for the Home Department with respect to matters referred to it by him which are connected with the early release or recall of prisoners. Its functions include giving directions concerning the release on licence of prisoners serving discretionary life sentences and of certain prisoners serving long-term determinate sentences; and making recommendations to the Secretary of State concerning the early release on licence of other prisoners, the conditions of parole and licences and the variation and cancellation of such conditions, and the recall of long-term and life prisoners while on licence.

Chairman, The Viscount Colville of Culross, QC
Vice-Chairman, The Hon. Mr Justice Ian Kennedy
Secretary, T. E. Russell

PAROLE BOARD FOR SCOTLAND

Calton House, 5 Redheughs Rigg, Edinburgh EH12 9HW
Tel 031-244 8530

The Board advises the Secretary of State for Scotland on the release of prisoners on licence, and related matters.

Chairman, Mrs J. D. O. Morris, CBE
Vice-Chairman, J. M. Scott
Secretary, Miss W. M. Doonan

PATENT OFFICE

Cardiff Road, Newport, Gwent NP9 1RH
Tel 0633-814000

The Patent Office is an executive agency of the Department of Trade and Industry. The duties of the Patent Office consist in the administration of the Patent Acts, the Registered Designs Act and the Trade Marks Act, and in dealing with questions relating to the Copyright Designs and Patents Act 1988. The Search and Advisory Service carries out commercial searches through patent information. In 1991 the Office granted 9,346 patents and registered 6,271 designs and 30,421 trade and service marks.

Comptroller-General (G3), P. R. S. Hartnack
Assistant Comptroller, Industrial Property and Copyright Department (G4), A. Sugden
Assistant Comptroller, Patents and Designs (G4), T. W. Sage
Assistant Registrar, Trade Marks (G4), J. M. Myall
Head of Marketing and Information Services (Supt. Examiner), E. F. Blake
Head of Administration and Resources (G5), T. Cassidy
Head of ADP Unit (G6), G. Bennett

PAYMASTER-GENERAL'S OFFICE

HM Treasury, Parliament Street, London SW1P 3AG
Tel 071-270 4349
Sutherland House, Russell Way, Crawley, West Sussex RH10 1UH
Tel 0293-560999

The Paymaster-General's Office was formed by the consolidation in 1835 of various separate pay departments then existing, some of which dated back at least to 1660. Its function is that of paying agent for government departments, other than the revenue departments. Most of its payments are made through banks, to whose accounts the necessary transfers are made at the Bank of England. The payment of over one million public service pensions is an important feature of its work.

Paymaster-General, The Rt. Hon. Sir John Cope, MP
Assistant Paymaster-General, (G5), K. Sullens
Grade 6, G. Harbottle; G. Thomas; M. D. West
Grade 7, D. R. Alexander; Mrs D. F. Ambrose; M. L. Card; T. R. George; R. G. Hollands; A. Edwards; D. Nunn; C. A. Ulph

OFFICE OF THE PENSIONS OMBUDSMAN

11 Belgrave Road, London SW1V 1RB
Tel 071-834 9144

The Pensions Ombudsman is appointed by the Secretary of State for Social Security under the Social Security Act 1990 to deal with complaints against, and disputes with, occupational and personal pension schemes. He is completely independent.

Pensions Ombudsman, M. Platt

POLICE COMPLAINTS AUTHORITY

10 Great George Street, London SW1P 3AE
Tel 071-273 6450

The Police Complaints Authority was established under the Police and Criminal Evidence Act 1984 to introduce a further independent element into the procedure for dealing with complaints by members of the public against police officers in England and Wales. (In Scotland, complaints are investigated by independent public prosecutors.) The Authority has powers to supervise the investigation of certain categories of serious complaints and certain statutory functions in relation to the disciplinary aspects of complaints. It does not as a rule deal with complaints about police operations; these are usually dealt with by the Chief Constable of the relevant force.

Chairman, Sir Leonard Peach
Deputy Chairman (Investigations), Brig. J. Pownall
Deputy Chairman (Discipline), P. W. Moorhouse
Members, Mrs L. Cawsey; M. Chapman; J. Crawford; G. V. Marsh; W. McCall; K. Singh; Capt. N. Taylor; Brig. A. Vivian; Miss B. Wallis; E. Wignall; Mrs R. Wolff

POLITICAL HONOURS SCRUTINY COMMITTEE

Cabinet Office, 53 Parliament Street, London SW1A 2NG
Tel 071-210 5058

The function of the Political Honours Scrutiny Committee is set out in an Order in Council dated 31 May 1979. The Prime Minister submits certain particulars to the Committee about persons proposed to be recommended for honour for their political services. The Committee, after such enquiry as they think fit, report to the Prime Minister whether, so far as they believe, the persons whose names are submitted to them are fit and proper persons to be recommended.

Chairman, The Lord Shackleton, KG, OBE, PC, FRS
Members, The Lord Grimond, TD, PC; The Lord Pym, MC, PC
Secretary, J. H. Thompson, CB

THE POLYTECHNICS AND COLLEGES FUNDING COUNCIL

Northavon House, Coldharbour Lane, Bristol BS16 1QD
Tel 0272-317317

The Polytechnics and Colleges Funding Council (PCFC) was established as a result of the Education Act 1988 to oversee the sector of higher education formerly controlled by local authorities. It will be replaced by the Higher Education Funding Council for England (*see* page 316) in April 1993.

OFFICE OF POPULATION CENSUSES AND SURVEYS

St Catherine's House, 10 Kingsway, London WC2B 6JP
Tel 071-242 0262

The Office of Population Censuses and Surveys was created by the merger in May 1970 of the General Register Office and the Government Social Survey Department. The Registrar General controls the local registration service in England and Wales in the exercise of its registration and marriage duties. Copies of the original registrations of births, still births, marriages and deaths are kept at Southport. A register of adopted children is held at Titchfield, Hants. Central indexes are compiled annually and certified copies of entries may be obtained, on payment of certain fees, either by personal application from St Catherine's House or by post from Smedley Hydro, Southport PR8 2HH.

Since 1841 the Registrar General has been responsible for taking the census of population. He also prepares and publishes a wide range of statistics and appropriate commentary relating to population, fertility, births, still births, marriages, deaths and cause of death and infectious diseases. The Registrar General is also responsible for conducting surveys on a range of subjects for other government departments. He maintains, at Southport, the National Health Service Central Register.

Hours of access to Public Search Room, St Catherine's House, Mon.–Fri., 8.30–4.30.

Director and Registrar General for England and Wales (G2), P. J. Wormald, CB
Deputy Director and Director of Statistics (G3), E. J. Thompson
Deputy Director and Chief Medical Statistician (G3), A. J. Fox, Ph.D
Deputy Registrar General (G5), J. V. Ribbins
Principal Finance Officer (G5), B. S. Smith
Principal Establishment Officer (G6), N. E. Auckland
Principal Information Officer (G7), Miss S. Wallace
Heads of Division (G5), I. K. G. Arnold (*Information Technology*); J. F. A. Ashley (*Medical Support and Disease Classification*); R. Barnes (*Social Survey Division*); J. Craig (*Population Statistics*); Ms K. Dunnell (*Health Statistics*); B. H. Mahon (*Census*)
Heads of Division (G6), E. Barton (*NHS Central Register*); B. W. Meakings (*Data Services*)
Grade 6, B. S. T. Alcock; Mrs M. Bone; R. J. Butcher; A. M. Clark; J. Denton; Mrs W. Jenkins; I. B. Knight; D. L. Pearce; R. K. Thomas; R. McLeod; T. D. Proudfoot; Mrs J. Martin
Grade 7, R. I. Armitage; F. L. Ashwood; R. A. P. Bailey; N. Bateson; R. J. Beacham; D. E. Birch; Mrs B. J. Botting; A. F. Bradbury; M. J. Bradley; J. A. Brown; T. B. Bryson; L. Bulusu; D. Capron; R. J. Carpenter; J. R. H. Charlton; J. Cloyne; B. C. Collett; Mrs J. Cooper; C. J. Denham; T. L. F. Devis; J. M. Dixie; Mrs J. C. Dobbs; Ms P. A. Dodd; D. Elliot; Miss C. M. Ellis; Ms E. M. Goddard; I. Golds; Mrs J. R. Gregory; P. C. Gregory; J. Haskey; A. J. H. Hayes (*Chief Inspector of Registration*); P. J. Heady; G. Hughes; Mrs J. Humby; J. Jackson; S. P. King; I. B. Knight; B. G. Little; Miss C. S. J. Lloyd; D. Lockyer; W. F. Loomes; Mrs S. M. McCartney; Miss E. M. McCrossan; Mrs I. MacDonald-Davies; Mrs M. Machin; A. J. Manners; V. A. Mason; Ms J. Matheson; H. I. Meltzer; I. D. Mills; M. F. G. Murphy; Miss D. Pace; A. Parr; M. Quinn; Mrs I. Rauta; A. P. Read; S. Robinson-Grindey; C. I. Rooney; Miss J. M. R. Rosenbaum; J. A. Salvetti; C. Savage; Ms J. M. Sharp; D. Stewart; Mrs L. M. Street; A. D. Teague; A. W. Tester; Miss J. Todd; Mrs M. J. Wagget; I. S. G. White; A. J. White; E. W. Williams

---

PORT OF LONDON AUTHORITY

Devon House, 58–60 St Katharine's Way, London E1 9LB
Tel 071-481 8484

The Port of London Authority is a public trust constituted under the Port of London Act 1968 (as amended) and a Harbour Revision Order of 1975. The Board comprises a chairman and up to ten non-executive members appointed by the Secretary of State for Transport, and up to six executive members appointed by the Board.

The Port of London Authority is the governing body for the Port of London, covering the tidal portion of the River Thames from Teddington to the seaward limit.

Chairman, Sir Brian Kellett.
Vice-Chairman, R.Crawford, CBE
Chief Executive, River, D. Jeffery
Secretary, G. E. Ennals

THE POST OFFICE

30 St James's Square, London SW1Y 4PY
Tel 071-490 2888

Crown services for the carriage of government despatches were set up in about 1516. The conveyance of public correspondence began in 1635 and the mail service was made a parliamentary responsibility with the setting up of a Post Office in 1657. Telegraphs came under the Post Office control in 1870 and the Post Office Telephone Service began in 1880. The National Girobank service of the Post Office began in 1968. The Post Office ceased to be a government department on 1 October 1969 and responsibility for the running of the postal, telecommunications, giro and remittance services was transferred to a public authority called the Post Office. The 1981 British Telecommunications Act separated the functions of the Post Office, making it solely responsible for postal services and Girobank, which was privatized in 1990.

The chairman and members of the Post Office Board are appointed by the Secretary of State for Trade and Industry but responsibility for the running of the Post Office as a whole rests with the Board in its corporate capacity.

FINANCIAL RESULTS

	1990–1 £m	1991–2 £m
Post Office Group		
Turnover	4,719.0	5,149.0
Trading profit before tax	153.0*	247.0
Royal Mail and Parcel force		
Turnover	3,979.0	4,419.0
Trading profit before tax and interest on long-term loans	96.0*	190.0
Post Office Counters		
Turnover	959.0	1,028.0
Trading profit before tax and interest on long-term loans	28.0	26.0

* Before exceptional items

POST OFFICE BOARD

Chairman, W. Cockburn, CBE, TD
Deputy Chairman, K. M. Young, CBE
Members, P. Howarth (*Managing Director, Royal Mail*); M. Kitchener (*Acting Managing Director, Parcelforce*); A. J. Roberts, CBE (*Managing Director, Counters Ltd*); R. Close (*Corporate Finance and Planning*)
Secretary, Miss M. MacDonald

PRIVY COUNCIL OFFICE

Whitehall, London SW1A 2AT
Tel 071-270 3000

The Office is responsible for the arrangements leading to the making of all Royal Proclamations and Orders in Council; for certain formalities connected with ministerial changes; for considering applications for the granting (or amendment) of Royal Charters; for the scrutiny and approval of by-laws and statutes of chartered bodies; and for the appointment of High Sheriffs and many Crown and Privy Council appointments to governing bodies.

Lord President of the Council (and Leader of the House of Commons), The Rt. Hon. Anthony Newton, OBE, MP
Private Secretary, T. Sutton
Clerk of the Council (£51,300), Sir Geoffrey de Deney, KCVO
Deputy Clerk of the Council (£41,152), R. P. Bulling
Senior Clerk (£19,473), J. Laverick

PROCURATOR FISCAL SERVICE – *see* pages 385

PSA SERVICES

2 Marsham Street, London SW1P 3EB
Tel 071-276 3000

PSA Services (formerly the Property Services Agency) is an executive agency within the Department of the Environment. It provides and maintains government property, operating commercially in competition with the private sector. Government departments are free to go elsewhere for services and PSA Services is free to seek work in other markets. PSA Services is split into three businesses. PSA Projects is to be offered for sale in 1992–3. PSA Building Management is to be reorganized and managed by the private sector before being offered for sale. PSA International will be closed down in late 1993.

Permanent Secretary and Chief Executive (*G1A*), Sir Geoffrey Chipperfield, KCB
Private Secretary, Mrs N. Baxter

PRIVATIZATION AND STRATEGY DIRECTORATE

Grade 3, Mrs J. Williams
Grade 5, J. Clayton; J. Rogers

GROUP PERSONNEL DIRECTORATE

Director (G3), P. D. Draper
Grade 5, J. Bird; A. Hazeldine

GROUP FINANCE DIRECTORATE

Director (*G3*), A. Marson
Grade 5, M. Taylor; Mrs H. Parker-Brown
Head of Internal Audit (*G5*), M. Reece
Group Management Accountant (*G5*), J. Tomlinson

PSA PROJECTS

Chairman (*G2*), J. B. Jefferson, CBE
Managing Director (*G2*), J. P. G. Rowcliffe

OPERATIONS I

Director and Chairman (*G3*), S. G. D. Duguid
Managing Directors, Projects Offices:
Project Management (*G4*), M. R. Sutton
London A (G4), K. Jeavons
Edinburgh (*G4*), J. T. Wilson
Leeds (*G5*), G. Sowden
Birmingham (*G5*), A. Towers
Cardiff (*G4*), J. Clemits

OPERATIONS 2

Director and Chairman (*G3*), A. S. Kennedy
Managing Director, London B (*G4*), F. Rymill
Director, Building and Quantity Surveying (*G4*), M. Barnes
Director, Mechanical and Electrical Engineering Services (*G5*), J. Fisher

MARKETING AND PLANNING

Director (*G3*), R. Gray
Sales Director (*G3*), A. G. Gosling
Personnel Director (*G5*), R. G. Jones
Finance Director (*G5*), B. Law

PSA INTERNATIONAL

Chairman (*G2*), J. P. G. Rowcliffe
Managing Director (*G3*), R. G. S. Johnston

OPERATIONS

Director (*G5*), J. Reynolds
Director, Central Services and Personnel (*G5*), Miss R. Doidge
Director, Finance (*G5*), T. Sannia

GERMANY

Director (*G4*), R. B. Perry

PSA BUILDING MANAGEMENT

Managing Director (*G2*), J. Anderson
Director of Operations (*G3*), P. Butter, CB
Finance Director (*G5*), D. Cheal
Personnel Director (*G5*), Dr M. Barrett

MANAGING DIRECTORS/DIRECTORS OF REGIONAL OFFICES

South-East (*G4*), P. Livesey
Scotland (*G4*), B. Taylor
South-West (*G4*), S. Todd
North-East (*G4*), A. Staveley
North-West and Midland (*G4*), M. Harrison

PUBLIC HEALTH LABORATORY SERVICE

61 Colindale Avenue, London NW9 5DF
Tel 081-200 1295

The Public Health Laboratory Service comprises 52 regional or area laboratories in England and Wales, the Central Public Health Laboratory, the Communicable Disease Surveillance Centre, and the Centre for Applied Microbiology and Research. The PHLS provides diagnostic microbiological services to hospitals, and has reference facilities that are available nationally. It collates information on the incidence of infection, and when necessary it institutes special inquiries into outbreaks and the epidemiology of infectious disease. It also undertakes bacteriological surveillance of the quality of food and water for local authorities and others. The PHLS is often called upon to advise central and local government and the hospital service on many aspects of infectious disease. It maintains close contact with veterinary organizations in areas of mutual interest, and collaborates with the World Health Organization and with national laboratory and epidemiological services overseas.

THE BOARD

Chairman, Dr M. P. W. Godfrey, CBE, FRCP
Members, Prof. J. P. Arbuthnott, Ph.D.; Dr W. Bogie; D. F. R. Crofton; Prof. G. Crompton; A. E. Eames; Prof. C. S. F. Easmon; Dr J. M. Forsythe; J. Godfrey; A. Graham-Dixon, QC; Dr H. H. John; Prof. M. D. Lilly; D. Noble, CBE; Dr M. J. Painter; Prof. J. R. Pattison; Prof. C. S. Peckham; Prof. I. Phillips; J. J. Skehel, Ph.D., FRS; Prof. L. Southgate

HEAD OFFICE

Director, Sir Joseph Smith, MD, FRCP
Deputy Directors, Dr E. M. Cooke; Dr C. Roberts
Deputy Director (Administration) and Board Secretary, K. M. Saunders
Deputy Secretary, J. M. Harker

CENTRAL PUBLIC HEALTH LABORATORY
Colindale Avenue, London NW9 5HT
Director, Dr M. C. Timbury

COMMUNICABLE DISEASES SURVEILLANCE CENTRE
Colindale Avenue, NW9 5EQ
Director, Dr C. L. R. Bartlett

CENTRE FOR APPLIED MICROBIOLOGY AND RESEARCH
Porton Down, Salisbury, Wilts. SP4 0JG
Director (acting), Prof. J. Melling, Ph.D

OTHER SPECIAL LABORATORIES AND UNITS

ANAEROBE REFERENCE UNIT, Public Health Laboratory, Cardiff. *Director*, Prof. B. I. Duerden
CRYPTOSPROIDIUM REFERENCE UNIT, Public Health Laboratory, Rhyl. *Director*, D. P. Casemore, Ph.D
GONOCOCCUS REFERENCE UNIT, Public Health Laboratory, Bristol. *Director*, A. E. Jephcott, MD
LEPTOSPIRA REFERENCE LABORATORY, Public Health Laboratory, Hereford. *Director*, I. R. Fergusson, TD
MALARIA REFERENCE LABORATORY, London School of Hygiene and Tropical Medicine, London WC1. *Directors*, Prof. D. J. Bradley, DM; Prof. W. Peters, MD, D.Sc
MENINGOCOCCAL REFERENCE LABORATORY, Public Health Laboratory, Manchester. *Director*, D. M. Jones, MD
MYCOBACTERIUM REFERENCE UNIT, Public Health Laboratory, Cardiff. *Director*, P. A. Jenkins, Ph.D
TOXOPLASMA REFERENCE LABORATORIES, Public Health Laboratory, Leeds. *Director*, R. N. Peel; Public Health Laboratory, Swansea. *Director*, D. H. M. Joynson; Public Health Laboratory, Tooting, London. *Director*, R. E. Holliman
WATER AND ENVIRONMENTAL LABORATORY, Public Health Laboratory, Nottingham. *Director*, J. V. Lee, Ph.D

REGIONAL LABORATORIES

Birmingham, I. D. Farrell, Ph.D.; *Bristol*, A. E. Jephcott; *Cambridge*, vacant; *Cardiff*, Prof. B. I. Duerden; *Leeds*, R. N. Peel; *Liverpool*, J. H. Pennington, MD; *Manchester*, D. M. Jones, MD; *Newcastle*, N. F. Lightfoot; *Oxford*, J. B. Selkon, TD; *Portsmouth*, O. A. Okubadejo, MD; *Sheffield*, P. Norman

AREA LABORATORIES

Ashford, C. Dulake, TD; *Bath*, D. G. White; *Brighton*, B. T. Thom; *Carlisle*, M. A. Knowles; *Carmarthen*, M. D. Simmons; *Chelmsford*, R. E. Tettmar, D.Path.; *Chester*, P. Hunter, MD; *Coventry*, P. R. Mortimer, MD; *Dorchester*, A. Rampling, Ph.D.; *Epsom*, S. A. Chambers; *Exeter*, J. G. Cruickshank, MD; *Gloucester*, K. A. V. Cartwright; *Guildford*, Prof. R. Y. Cartwright; *Hereford*, I. R. Ferguson, TD; *Hull*, S. L. Mawer; *Ipswich*, P. H. Jones; *Leicester*, C. J. Mitchell; *Lincoln*, E. R. Youngs; LONDON: *Central Middlesex Hospital*, M. S. Shafi (*acting*); *Dulwich*, A. H. C. Uttley, Ph.D.; *Tooting*, Prof. A. R. M. Coates; *Whipps Cross*, B. Chattopadhyay, MD; *Luton*, Dr S. A. Rousseau (*acting*); *Middlesbrough*, E. McKay-Ferguson, MD; *Norwich*, P. M. B. White; *Nottingham*, M. J. Lewis, MD; Peterborough, R. S. Jobanputra, MD; *Plymouth*, P. J. Wilkinson; *Poole*, W. L. Hooper; *Preston*, D. N. Hutchinson, MD; *Reading*, J. V. Dadswell; *Rhyl*, D. N. Looker; *Salisbury*, S. Patrick; *Shrewsbury*, C. A. Morris, MD; *Southampton*, J. A. Lowes; *Stoke-on-Trent*, J. Gray; *Swansea*, D. H. M. Joynson; *Taunton*, J. V. S. Pether; *Truro*, W. A. Telfer Brunton; *Watford*, M. T. Moulsdale; *Wolverhampton*, R. G. Thompson

---

REGISTRAR OF PUBLIC LENDING RIGHT

Bayheath House, Prince Regent Street,
Stockton-on-Tees, TS18 1DF
Tel 0642-604699

Under the Public Lending Right system, in operation since 1983, payment is made from public funds to authors whose books are lent out from public libraries. Payment is made once a year (in February) and the amount each author receives is proportionate to the number of times (established from a sample) that each registered book has been lent out during the previous year.

The Registrar of PLR, who is appointed by the Secretary of State for National Heritage, compiles the register of authors and books. Only living authors resident in the UK or Germany are eligible to apply. (The term 'author' covers writers, illustrators, translators, and some editors/compilers.)

A payment of 1.81 pence was made in 1991–2 for each estimated loan of a registered book, up to a top limit of £6,000 for the books of any one registered author; the money for loans above this level is used to augment the remaining PLR payments.

In February 1992, the sum of £3,757,000 was made available for distribution to 16,884 registered authors and assignees as the annual payment of PLR.

The PLR Advisory Committee advises the Secretary of State for National Heritage and the Registrar of Public Lending Right. Its members are appointed by the Secretary of State.

Chairman of Advisory Committee, D. H. Whitaker, OBE
Registrar, Dr J. Parker

PUBLIC RECORD OFFICE – *see* pages 350–1

PUBLIC TRUST OFFICE

Stewart House, 24 Kingsway, London WC2B 6JX
Tel 071-269 7000

The Public Trustee is a trust Corporation created to undertake the business of executorship and trusteeship; he can act as executor or administrator of the estate of a deceased person, or as trustee of a will or settlement. The Public Trustee is also responsible for the performance of all the administrative, but not the judicial, tasks required of the Court of Protection under Part VII of the Mental Health Act 1983, relating to the management and administration of the property and affairs of persons suffering from mental disorder. The Public Trustee also acts as Receiver when so directed by the Court, usually where there is no other person willing or able so to act.

The Accountant-General of the Supreme Court, through the Court Funds Office, is responsible for the investment and accounting of funds in Court for persons under a disability, monies in Court subject to litigation and statutory deposits.

The Court Funds Office is at 22 Kingsway, London WC2B 6LE. Tel: 071-936 6000

Public Trustee and Accountant-General, P. J. Farmer
Assistant Public Trustee, H. N. Mather
Investment Manager, H. Stevenson
Chief Property Adviser, A. Nightingale

CLIENT SERVICES SECTOR

Head, E. J. Dober
Receivership Division, Mrs H. Bratton
Protection Division, I. S. Price

INTERNAL SERVICES SECTOR

Head, I. J. MacBean
Court Funds Office, F. J. Eddy

PUBLIC WORKS LOAN BOARD – *see* National Investment and Loans Office

COMMISSION FOR RACIAL EQUALITY

Elliot House, 10–12 Allington Street, London SW1E 5EH
Tel 071-828 7022

The Commission was established in 1977, under the Race Relations Act 1976, to work towards the elimination of discrimination and promote equality of opportunity and good relations between different racial groups.

Chairman, Sir Michael Day, OBE
Deputy Chairs, J. Abrams, OBE; R. Singh
Members, Mrs S. Sadeque; M. Skillicorn; D. A. C. Lambert; Dr D. Ray; R. Kent; Revd E. A. Brown; Dr M. C. K. Chan, MBE; T. A. Khan; A. Rose, OBE; R. Sondhi; A. Ward; Miss P. Scotland, QC
Chief Executive, Dr P. Sanders

THE RADIO AUTHORITY

Holbrook House, 14 Great Queen Street, London WC2B 5DG
Tel 071-430 2724

The Radio Authority was established in January 1991 under the Broadcasting Act 1990 as one of the two successor bodies to the Independent Broadcasting Authority. Its function is to plan frequencies, to grant licences for the provision of independent radio services, and to regulate the output of the services in accordance with published codes dealing with standards for programming, advertising and sponsorship.

Members of the Authority are appointed by the Secretary of State for National Heritage. Senior executive staff are appointed by the Authority.

Chairman, The Lord Chalfont OBE, MC, PC
Deputy Chairman, Mrs J. McIvor
Members, Mrs M. Corrigan; J. Grant; R. Hooper; R. Sondhi; M. Moriarty, CB
Chief Executive, P. Baldwin
Deputy Chief Executive and Head of Regulation, P. Brown
Head of Development, D. Vick
Head of Finance, N. Romain
Head of Engineering, M. Thomas
Secretary to the Authority, J. Norrington

RECORD OFFICES, ETC.

ADVISORY COUNCIL ON PUBLIC RECORDS

Trevelyan House, Great Peter Street, London SW1P 2BY
Tel 071-210 8500

Council members are appointed by the Lord Chancellor, under the Public Records Act 1958, to advise him on matters concerning public records in general and, in particular, on those aspects of the work of the Public Record Office which affect members of the public who make use of it. The Council meets quarterly and produces an annual report which is published alongside the Report of the Keeper of Public Records as a House of Commons sessional paper.

Chairman, The Master of the Rolls
Members, Prof. B. W. E. Alford; Miss S. Beesley; A. C. Carlile, QC, MP; Miss V. Cromwell; T. A. G. Davis, MP; Prof. R. B. Dobson; J. S. W. Gibson; Prof. Shula Marks; Prof. R. Skidelsky; D. G. Vaisey
Assessor, Mrs S. Tyacke
Secretary, P. Kennedy

THE PUBLIC RECORD OFFICE

Chancery Lane, London WC2A 1LR
Tel 081-876 3444
Ruskin Avenue, Kew, Richmond, Surrey TW9 4DU
Tel 081-876 3444

The Office, originally established in 1838 under the Master of the Rolls, was placed by the Public Records Act 1958 under the direction of the Lord Chancellor. He appoints a Keeper of Public Records, whose duties are to co-ordinate and supervise the selection of records of government departments and the English law courts for permanent preservation, to safeguard the records and to make them available to the public.

The Office holds records of central government dating from the *Domesday Book* (1086) to the present. Under the Public Records Act 1967 they are normally open to inspection when 30 years old, and are then available, without charge, in the reading rooms, Mon.–Fri., 9.30–5. The museum at Chancery Lane is open Mon.–Fri., 10–5.

The Public Records Office became an executive agency on 1 April 1992.

Keeper of Public Records (G3), Mrs S. Tyacke

PUBLIC SERVICES DIVISION

Director (G5), C. D. Chalmers
Reader Services Department (G6), Miss G. L. Beech
Editorial Services Department (G6), Dr D. L. Thomas
Publishing and Public Relations Department (G6), vacant
Preservation Department (G7), Dr H. Forde

GOVERNMENT SERVICES DIVISION

Director (G5), Dr N. G. Cox
Appraisal and Accessions Department (G6), Mrs A. N. Nicol
Team leaders (G7), A. H. W. Medlicott; E. J. Higgs; K. J. Smith; Ms J. Rose

CORPORATE SERVICES DIVISION

Director (G5), W. Arnold
Management Support Department (G6), J. L. Walford
IT Department (G7), Miss J. K. Lawlor
Finance Department (G7), Ms P. Ewens
Personnel Department (SEO), Mrs M. Bull
Purchasing and Contracts Department (SEO), Mrs S. Flatman

HOUSE OF LORDS RECORD OFFICE

House of Lords, London SW1A 0PW
Tel 071-219 3074

Since 1497, the records of Parliament have been kept within the Palace of Westminster. They are in the custody of the Clerk of the Parliaments. In 1946 a record department was established to supervise their preservation and their availability to the public. The search room of the office is open to the public Mon.–Fri., 9.30–5.

Some 3,000,000 documents are preserved, including Acts of Parliament from 1497, journals of the House of Lords from 1510, minutes and committee proceedings from 1610, and papers laid before Parliament from 1531. Amongst the records are the Petition of Right, the Death Warrant of Charles I, the Declaration of Breda, and the Bill of Rights. The House of Lords Record Office also has charge of the journals of the House of Commons (from 1547), and other surviving records of the Commons (from 1572), which include plans and annexed documents relating to Private Bill legislation from 1818. Among other documents are the records of the Lord Great Chamberlain, the political papers of certain members of the two Houses, and documents relating to Parliament acquired on behalf of the nation. All the manuscripts and other records are preserved in the Victoria Tower of the Houses of Parliament. A permanent exhibition was established in the Royal Gallery in 1979.

Clerk of the Records (£36,178–£41,120), D. J. Johnson, FSA
Deputy Clerk of the Records (£27,819–£42,724), S. K. Ellison
Assistant Clerks of the Records (£13,530–£34,667), J. C. Morgan; D. L. Prior

ROYAL COMMISSION ON HISTORICAL MANUSCRIPTS

Quality House, Quality Court, Chancery Lane, London WC2A 1HP
Tel 071-242 1198

The Commission was set up by Royal Warrant in 1869 to enquire and report on collections of papers of value for the study of history which were in private hands. In 1959 a new warrant enlarged these terms of reference to include all historical records, wherever situated, outside the Public Records and gave it added responsibilities as a central co-ordinating body to promote, assist and advise on their proper preservation and storage. The Commission has published over 200 volumes of reports. It holds a further 35,000 unpublished reports and computerized indices in the National Register of Archives, which is available for consultation in its search room. It also administers the Manorial and Tithe Documents Rules on behalf of the Master of the Rolls.

Chairman, G. E. Aylmer, FBA
Commissioners, The Lord Blake, FBA; J. P. W. Ehrman, FBA, FSA; Prof. S. F. C. Milsom, FBA; P. T. Cormack, FSA, MP; D. G. Vaisey, FSA; The Viscount of Arbuthnott, CBE, DSC; The Lord Camoys; The Lord Egremont and Leconfield; Mrs J. Thirsk, FBA; Sir Matthew Farrer, KCVO; Miss B. Harvey, FBA, FSA; Sir John Sainty, KCB, FSA; Prof. R. H. Campbell, Ph.D.; Very Revd H. E. C. Stapleton, FSA; Sir Keith Thomas
Secretary, C. J. Kitching, Ph.D., FSA

SCOTTISH RECORD OFFICE

HM General Register House, Edinburgh EH1 3YY
Tel 031-556 6585

The history of the national archives of Scotland can be traced back to the 13th century. The present headquarters of the Scottish Record Office, the General Register House, was founded in 1774. Here are preserved the administrative records of pre-Union Scotland, the registers of central and local courts of law, the public registers of property rights and legal documents, and many collections of local and church records and private archives. Certain groups of records, mainly the modern records of government departments in Scotland, the Scottish railway records, the plans collection, and private archives of an industrial or commercial nature are preserved in the branch repository at the West Register House in Charlotte Square. The search rooms in both buildings open Mon.–Fri., 9–4.45. A permanent exhibition at the West Register House and changing exhibitions at the General Register House are open to the public on weekdays, 10–4. The National Register of Archives (Scotland), which is a branch of the Scottish Record Office, is based in the West Register House.

Keeper of the Records of Scotland, P. M. Cadell

CORPORATION OF LONDON RECORDS OFFICE

Guildhall, London EC2P 2EJ
Tel 071-260 1251

The Corporation of London Records Office contains the municipal archives of the City of London which are regarded as the most complete collection of ancient municipal records in existence. The collection includes charters of William the Conqueror, Henry II, and later kings and queens to 1957; ancient custumals: Liber Horn, Dunthorne, Custumarum, Ordinacionum, Memorandorum and Albus, Liber de Antiquis Legibus, and collections of Statutes; continuous series of judicial rolls and books from 1252 and Council minutes from 1275; records of the Old Bailey and Guildhall Sessions from 1603; financial records from the 16th century; the records of London Bridge from the 12th century; and numerous subsidiary series and miscellanea of historical interest. Readers' Room open Mon.–Fri., 9.30–4.45.

Keeper of the City Records, The Town Clerk
City Archivist, J. R. Sewell
Deputy City Archivist, Mrs J. M. Bankes

RED DEER COMMISSION

Knowsley, 82 Fairfield Road, Inverness IV3 5LH
Tel 0463-231751

The Red Deer Commission has the general functions of furthering the conservation and control of red and sika deer in Scotland and of keeping under review all matters relating to roe deer. It has the statutory duty, with powers, to prevent damage to agriculture and forestry by red and sika deer. The Commission also has the power to advise in the interest of conservation any owner of land on questions relating to the carrying of stocks of red deer, sika deer and roe deer on that land, and to carry out research into matters of scientific importance relating to deer.

Chairman (part-time), (£17,500), I. K. Mackenzie, OBE
Secretary (£21,000), A. Rinning
Senior Field Officer, L. A. H. K. Stewart, MBE

REVIEW BODIES

The secretariat for these bodies is provided by the Office of Manpower Economics (*see* page 334)

ARMED FORCES PAY

The Review Body on Armed Forces Pay was appointed in 1971 to advise the Prime Minister on the pay and allowances of members of Naval, Military and Air Forces of the Crown and of any women's service administered by the Defence Council.

Chairman, Sir Peter Cazalet
Members, P. Ball, OBE; C. M. Bolton; G. M. Hourston; R. Sanderson, OBE; Sir Richard Trant, KCB; Mrs D. Venables; Prof. J. White, CBE

DOCTORS' AND DENTISTS' REMUNERATION

The Review Body on Doctors' and Dentists' Remuneration was set up in 1971 to advise the Prime Minister on the remuneration of doctors and dentists taking any part in the National Health Service.

Chairman, Sir Trevor Holdsworth
Members, D. G. Boyd; D. Fredjohn, MBE; J. W. Hougham; Sir Geoffrey Leigh; Prof. G. F. Thomason, CBE; A. J. P. Vineall

NURSING STAFF, MIDWIVES, HEALTH VISITORS AND PROFESSIONS ALLIED TO MEDICINE

The Review Body for nursing staff, midwives, health visitors and professions allied to medicine was set up in 1983 to advise the Prime Minister on the remuneration of nursing staff, midwives and health visitors employed in the National Health Service; and also of physiotherapists, radiographers, remedial gymnasts, occupational therapists, orthoptists, chiropodists, dietitians and related grades employed in the National Health Service.

Chairman, M. Bett, CBE
Members, Mrs M. Cameron; J. Hildreth; Miss A. Mackie, OBE; Dame Anne Mueller, DCB; Mrs R. Pickavance; Prof. G. F. Thomason, CBE; Miss D. Whittingham

SCHOOL TEACHERS

The School Teachers' Review Body (STRB) was established in 1991. It replaced an Interim Advisory Committee which made recommendations on school teachers' pay and conditions from 1988–92, following the breakdown of longstanding collective bargaining arrangements (the Burnham Committee). Unlike the other review bodies, the STRB is a statutory body, set up under the School Teachers' Pay and Conditions Act 1991. It is required to examine and report on such matters relating to the statutory conditions of employment of school teachers in England and Wales as may from time to time be referred to it by the Secretary of State for Education. The STRB's reports are submitted to the Prime Minister and the Secretary of State and the latter is required to publish them.

Chairman, Sir Graham Day
Members, Mrs B. Amey; Miss F. Cairncross; R. Carter, CBE; A. G. Cox, CBE; P. Halsey, CB, LVO

TOP SALARIES

The Review Body on Top Salaries was set up in 1971 to advise the Prime Minister on the remuneration of the higher judiciary and other judicial appointments, senior civil servants, and senior officers of the armed forces. The Review Body has also been asked on a number of occasions to advise on the remuneration of Members of Parliament and of Ministers and on the level of parliamentary allowances.

Chairman, Sir David Nickson, KBE
Members, Ms L. Botting; Ms A. Burdus; Sir Peter Cazalet; Sir Cecil Clothier, KCB, QC; A. G. Gormly; H. S. Pigott; J. J. R. Pope, OBE; Sir Anthony Wilson.

ROYAL BOTANIC GARDEN EDINBURGH

Inverleith Row, Edinburgh EH3 5LR
Tel 031-552 7171

The Royal Botanic Garden (RBG) Edinburgh originated as the Physic Garden, established in 1670 beside the Palace of Holyroodhouse. Since 1986, RBG Edinburgh has been administered by a Board of Trustees established under the National Heritage (Scotland) Act 1985.

RBG Edinburgh is an international centre for scientific research on plant diversity, maintaining collections of living plants and reference resources, including a herbarium of some two million specimens of preserved plants. Other statutory functions of RBG Edinburgh include the provision of education and information on botany and horticulture, and the provision of public access to the living plant collections.

The Garden moved to its present site at Inverleith, Edinburgh in 1821. There are also three specialist gardens: Younger Botanic Garden, Benmore, near Dunoon, Argyllshire; Logan Botanic Garden, near Stranraer, Wigtownshire; and Dawyck Botanic Garden, near Stobo, Peeblesshire. Public opening hours: RBG Edinburgh – daily (except Christmas Day and New Year's Day) Nov.–Feb. 10–4; March–April and Sept.–Oct. 10–6; May–Aug. 10–8; specialist gardens – March–Oct. 10–6.

Chairman of the Board of Trustees, Sir Peter Hutchison, Bt., CBE
Regius Keeper, Prof. D. S. Ingram
Assistant Keeper, Dr D. J. Mann

ROYAL BOTANIC GARDENS KEW

Richmond, Surrey TW9 3AB
Tel 081-940 1171
Wakehurst Place, Ardingly, nr. Haywards Heath, W. Sussex RH17 6TN
Tel 0444-892701

The Royal Botanic Gardens (RBG) Kew were founded in 1759 by HRH Princess Augusta. In 1965 the garden at Wakehurst Place was acquired; it is owned by the National Trust and managed by RBG Kew. Under the National Heritage Act 1983 a Board of Trustees was set up to administer the Gardens which in 1984 became an independent body supported by a grant-in-aid.

The functions of RBG Kew are to carry out research into plant sciences, to disseminate knowledge about plants and to provide the public with the opportunity to gain knowledge and enjoyment from the Gardens' collections. There are extensive national reference collections of living and preserved plants and a comprehensive library and archive. The main emphasis is on tropical and subtropical plants.

Open daily (except Christmas Day and New Year's Day) from 9.30. The closing hour varies from 4 in mid-winter to 6.30 on week-days, and 8 on Sundays and Bank Holidays, in mid-summer. Admission (1992), £3.30. Concessionary schemes available. Museums open 9.30; Glasshouses, 9.30–4.30 (weekdays); 9.30–5.30 (Sundays). No dogs except guide-dogs for the blind.

BOARD OF TRUSTEES

Chairman, R. A. E. Herbert
Members, Sir David Attenborough, CBE, FRS; R. P. Bauman; The Viscount Blakenham; Prof. W. G. Chaloner, FRS; Prof. E. C. D. Cocking, FRS; Sir Philip M. Dowson, CBE; Sir Leslie Fowden, FRS; Mrs A. Lennox-Boyd; Prof. R. May, Ph.D.; Dr Jane Renfrew; Mrs V. R. Wakefield
Director, Dr G. T. Prance

ROYAL COMMISSION FOR THE EXHIBITION OF 1851

Sherfield Building, Imperial College of Science and Technology, London SW7 2AZ
Tel 071-225 6110

The Royal Commission was incorporated by supplemental charter as a permanent Commission after winding up the affairs of the Great Exhibition of 1851. Its object is to promote scientific and artistic education by means of funds derived from its Kensington estate, purchased with the surplus left over from the Great Exhibition.

President, HRH The Duke of Edinburgh, KG, KT, PC
Chairman, Board of Management, Sir Denis Rooke, CBE, FRS
Secretary to Commissioners, M. C. Neale, CB

ROYAL COMMISSION ON CRIMINAL JUSTICE

Whittington House, 19 Alfred Place, London WC1E 7LU
Tel 071-436 5022

The setting up of a Royal Commission on Criminal Justice was announced on the day of the release of the Birmingham Six in March 1991, and its members were announced in May 1991. Members were appointed by The Queen upon advice from the Home Secretary. The Commission is undertaking a major review of the criminal justice system in England and Wales and expects to complete its work in June 1993. Neither the chairman nor the Commission members receive a salary.

Chairman, The Viscount Runciman of Doxford, CB, FBA
Members, Sir Robert Bunyard, CBE, QPM; Prof. Sir John Cadogan, CBE, FRS; Prof. J. Gunn; The Rt. Hon. Sir John May; Mrs Y. Newbold; Ms U. Prashar; Miss A. Rafferty, QC; Sir John Wickerson; Sir Philip Woodfield, KCB, CBE; Prof. M. Zander
Secretary (*G5*), M. J. A. Addison

THE ROYAL MINT

Llantrisant, nr Pontyclun, Mid Glamorgan CF7 8YT
Tel 0443-222111

The Royal Mint became an executive agency responsible to the Chancellor of the Exchequer in April 1990.

The prime responsibility of the Royal Mint is the provision of United Kingdom coinage, but it actively competes in world markets for a share of the available circulating coin business and, on average, two-thirds of the 15,000 tonnes of coins produced annually is exported to more than 100 countries. The Mint also manufactures special proof and uncirculated quality coins in gold, silver and other metals; military and civil decorations and medals; commemorative and prize medals; and royal and official seals.

Master of the Mint, The Chancellor of the Exchequer (ex officio)
Deputy Master and Comptroller, A. D. Garrett

ROYAL NATIONAL THEATRE BOARD

South Bank, London, SE1 9PX
Tel 071-928 2033

Chairman, The Lady Soames, DBE
Members, The Hon. P. Benson; The Hon. Lady Cazalet; R. Clutton; M. Codron, CBE; Dame Judi Dench, DBE; Sir John Hannam, MP; S. Lipton; Sonia Melchett; Sir Derek Mitchell, KCB, CVO; D. Nandy; The Rt. Hon. Sir Michael Palliser, GCMG; L. Sieff, OBE; B. Simons; T. Stoppard, CBE; J. Whitney; S. Yassukovich, CBE
Company Secretary and Head of Finance, A. Blackstock
Board and Committee Secretary, Ms Y. Bird, MBE

RURAL DEVELOPMENT COMMISSION

141 Castle Street, Salisbury, Wilts. SP1 3TP
Tel 0722-336255

The Rural Development Commission was formed in 1988 by the merger of the Development Commission for Rural England and the Council for Small Industries in Rural Areas. It is a statutory body funded by government grant-in-aid. It advises the Government on economic and social matters affecting rural areas, and its prime aim is to stimulate job creation and the provision of essential services in the countryside.

Chairman, The Lord Shuttleworth
Deputy Chairman, G. Gray
Chief Executive, R. Butt
Deputy Chief Executive, J. Taylor

SCIENCE AND ENGINEERING RESEARCH COUNCIL

Polaris House, North Star Avenue, Swindon, Wilts. SN2 1ET
Tel 0793-411000

The Science and Engineering Research Council (SERC) is one of five research councils funded through the Office of Science and Technology. Its purposes are to develop the natural and social sciences, including engineering; to maintain a fundamental capacity of research and scholarship; and to support relevant postgraduate education. SERC's role is to encourage and support research and advanced training in UK higher education institutions in all the basic areas of science and engineering.

Chairman, Sir Mark Richmond, FRS
Members, Prof. P. G. Burke; D. A. Davis; Prof. A. Donnachie; G. H. Fairtlough; Dr K. W. Gray; Prof. R. E. Hester; Sir Gordon Higginson, FEng.; Prof. C. J. Humphreys; Dr S. D. Iversen; Dr A. Ledwith; Dr J. S. Mason; D. P. Nash; Prof. E. R. Oxburgh, FRS; Prof. J. T. Stuart, FRS; Prof. J. O. Thomas, FRS; Prof. D. J. Wallace, FRS; Prof. A. W. Wolfendale
For research establishments, *see* page 696.

SCOTTISH COURTS ADMINISTRATION – *see* page 383.

SCOTTISH ENTERPRISE

120 Bothwell Street, Glasgow G2 7JP
Tel 041-248 2700

On 1 April 1991 Scottish Enterprise took over the economic development and environmental improvement functions of the Scottish Development Agency and the training functions of the Training Agency in lowland Scotland. Its remit is to further the development of Scotland's economy, to enhance the skills of the Scottish workforce, to promote Scotland's international competitiveness and to improve the environment. Many of its functions are contracted-out to a network of local enterprise companies. Through Locate in Scotland, Scottish Enterprise is also concerned with attracting firms to Scotland.

Chairman, Sir David Nickson
Chief Executive, C. Beveridge
Managing Director, Strategy and Local Enterprise Company Operations, J. Condliffe
Managing Director, Corporate Services, L. Gold

SCOTTISH NATURAL HERITAGE

Battleby, Redgorton, Perth PH1 3EW
Tel 0738-27921
12 Hope Terrace, Edinburgh EH9 2AS
Tel 031-447 4784

Scottish Natural Heritage came into existence on 1 April 1992 under the Natural Heritage (Scotland) Act 1991. It was created by the merger of the Countryside Commission for Scotland and the Nature Conservancy Council for Scotland and combines the functions of those bodies. It provides advice on nature conservation to all those whose activities affect wildlife, landforms and features of geological interest in Scotland, and seeks to develop and improve facilities for the enjoyment of the Scottish countryside.

Chairman, M. Magnusson, KBE
Chief Executive, R. Crofts
Chief Scientific Adviser, M. B. Usher

SCOTTISH OFFICE

The Secretary of State for Scotland is responsible in Scotland for a wide range of statutory functions which in England and Wales are the responsibility of a number of departmental ministers. He also works closely with ministers in charge of Great Britain departments on topics of special significance to Scotland within their fields of responsibility. His statutory functions are administered by five main departments: the Scottish Office Agriculture and Fisheries Department, the Scottish Office Education Department, the Scottish Office Environment Department, the Scottish Office Home and Health Department, and the Scottish Office Industry Department. These departments (plus Central Services embracing the Solicitor's Office, the Scottish Office Information Directorate, Establishment, Liaison and Finance Divisions) are collectively known as The Scottish Office. In addition there are a number of other Scottish departments for which the Secretary of State has some degree of responsibility; these include the Scottish Courts Administration, the Department of the Registrar-General for Scotland (the General Register Office), the Scottish Record Office and the Department of the Registers of Scotland. The Secretary of State also bears ministerial responsibility for the activities in Scotland of several statutory bodies whose functions extend throughout Great Britain, such as the Training Commission and the Forestry Commission.

Dover House, Whitehall, London, SW1A 2AU
Tel 071-270 3000

Secretary of State for Scotland, The Rt. Hon. Ian Lang, MP
Private Secretary (G5), A. W. Fraser
Assistant Private Secretaries, J. S. Hynd; Mrs L. J. Stirling
Special Advisers, A. Young; G. Mackay
Parliamentary Private Secretary, S. Coombs, MP
Minister of State, The Lord Fraser of Carmyllie, PC, QC (*Education, Health and Home Affairs*)
Private Secretary, I. D. Kernohan
Parliamentary Under Secretaries of State, Lord James Douglas-Hamilton, MP; J. Allan Stewart, MP; Sir Hector Monro, MP
Private Secretaries, O. D. Kelly (*Lord James Douglas-Hamilton*); B. K. Pedie (*J. Allan Stewart*); A. E. Sim (*Sir Hector Monro*)
Parliamentary Clerk, I. Campbell
Permanent Under Secretary of State (G1), Sir Russell Hillhouse, KCB
Private Secretary, J. Taylor
Liaison Staff:
Assistant Secretary (G5), E. W. Ferguson

St Andrew's House, Edinburgh EH1 3DG
Tel 031-556 8400

MANAGEMENT GROUP SUPPORT STAFF
Principal (G7), vacant

CENTRAL SERVICES

Grade 2, G. R. Wilson, CB

PERSONNEL GROUP
16 Waterloo Place Edinburgh, EHI 3DN
Tel 031-556 8400

Principal Establishment Officer (G3), C. C. MacDonald
Assistant Secretaries (G5), G. D. Calder; Mrs V. Macniven; J. A. Rennie
Senior Principals (G6), C. D. Henderson; I. C. Henderson; W. E. Bennet

ADMINISTRATIVE SERVICES
James Craig Walk, Edinburgh EHI 3BA
Tel 031-556 8400

Director of Administrative Services (G4), R. S. B. Gordon
Assistant Secretary (G5), D. Stevenson
Director of Information Technology (G5), J. Duffy
Deputy Director (G6), I. W. Goodwin
Director of Telecommunications (G6), K. Henderson
Director of Office Management (G6), B. V. Surridge, ISO
Chief Estates Officer (G6), R. I. K. White

FINANCE DIVISION
New St Andrew's House, Edinburgh EHI 3TB
Tel 031-556 8400

Finance Group

Principal Finance Officer (G3), Miss E. A MacKay
Assistant Secretaries (G5), S. F. Hampson; J. W. H. Irvine; L. Mosco; B. Naylor; D. G. N. Reid; W. T. Tait
Director of Financial Systems Unit (G6), R. Smith

SOLICITOR'S OFFICE
For the Scottish departments and certain UK services, including HM Treasury, in Scotland

Solicitor (G2), R. Brodie, CB
Deputy Solicitor (G3), N. W. Boe
Divisional Solicitors (G5), J. B. Allan; †K. F. Barclay; R. Bland; G. C. Duke; I. H. Harvie; R. M. Henderson; G. Jackson; J. L. Jamieson; H. F. Macdiarmid; Mrs L. A. Wallace
†Seconded to Scottish Law Commission

SCOTTISH OFFICE INFORMATION DIRECTORATE
For the Scottish departments and certain UK services

Director (G5), Ms E. S. B. Drummond
Deputy Director (G6), D. C. M. Beveridge, OBE

SCOTTISH OFFICE AGRICULTURE AND FISHERIES DEPARTMENT

Pentland House, 47 Robb's Loan, Edinburgh EH14 1TW
Tel 031-556 8400
Dover House, Whitehall, London, SWIA 2AU
Tel 071-270 3000

Secretary (G2), K. J. MacKenzie
Under Secretary (G3), T. A. Cameron
Fisheries Secretary (G3), G. Robson
Assistant Secretaries (G5), P. S. Collings; E. C. Davison; I. W. Gordon; R. A. Grant; T. J. Kelly; A. K. MacLeod; K. W. Moore; A. J. Rushworth; I. M. Whitelaw
Chief Agricultural Officer (G4), J. F. Hutcheson
Deputy Chief Agricultural Officer (G5), W. A. Macgregor
Assistant Chief Agricultural Officers (G6), D. R. J. Craven; J. A. Hardie; J. G. Muir; A. Robb; J. I. Woodrow
Chief Agricultural Economist (G6), J. R. Wildgoose, D.Phil
Chief Meat and Livestock Inspector (G7), J. Miller
Chief Food and Dairy Officer (G7), D. J. MacDonald
Chief Surveyor (G6), N. Taylor
Scientific Adviser (G5), T. W. Hegarty, Ph.D
Senior Principal Scientific Officers (G6), R. J. Dowdell, Ph.D.; D. Thornton

AGRICULTURAL SCIENCE AGENCY
East Craigs, Edinburgh EH12 8NJ
Tel 031-556 8400

An executive agency within the Scottish Office.
Director (G5), Dr R. K. M. Hay
Deputy Director (G6), R. S. Cooper
Senior Principal Scientific Officer (G6), M. J. Richardson

FISHERIES RESEARCH SERVICES
Marine Laboratory, PO Box 101,
Victoria Road, Torry, Aberdeen AB9 8DB
Tel 0224-876544

Director of Fisheries Research for Scotland (G4), Prof. A. D. Hawkins, Ph.D., FRSE
Deputy Director (G5), D. N. MacLennan
Senior Principal Scientific Officers (G6), R. M. Cook, Ph.D.; J. M. Davies, Ph.D.; A. L. S. Munro, Ph.D.; P. A. M. Stewart, Ph.D.; C. S. Wardle, Ph.D

Freshwater Fisheries Laboratory
Faskally, Pitlochry, Perthshire PH16 5LB
Tel 0796-2060

Senior Principal Scientific Officers (G6), R. G. J. Shelton, Ph.D.; J. E. Thorpe, Ph.D
Inspector of Salmon and Freshwater Fisheries for Scotland (G7), R. B. Williamson

Scottish Fisheries Protection Agency
Pentland House, 47 Robb's Loan, Edinburgh EH14 1TW
Tel 031-556 8400

An executive agency within the Scottish Office.
Chief Executive (G5), A. K. MacLeod
Director of Policy and Resources (G6), J. B. Roddin
Chief Inspector of Sea Fisheries (G6), J. F. Fenton
Marine Superintendent, Capt. R. M. Mill-Irving

SCOTTISH OFFICE ENVIRONMENT DEPARTMENT

St Andrew's House, Edinburgh EHI 3DD
Tel 031-556 8400
Dover House, Whitehall, London SWI 2AU
Tel 071-270 3000

Secretary (G2), H. H. Mills
Under Secretaries (G3), J. S. Graham; J. F. Laing
Assistant Secretaries (G5), C. M. Baxter; J. T. Birley; D. J. Chalmers; Ms L. Clare; Dr J. L. Cuthbert; W. J. Fearnley; I. C. Freeman; K. W. McKay; D. F. Middleton; J. N. Randall; E. C. Reavley; R. E. S. Robinson

PROFESSIONAL STAFF

Chief Engineer (G3), A. C. Paton
Deputy Chief Engineer (G5), T. D. Macdonald
Assistant Chief Engineers (G6), T. Bolton; D. MacFarlane; P. Wright
Director of Building and Chief Architect (G3), J. E. Gibbons, Ph.D
Deputy Director of Building and Deputy Chief Architect (G5), M. R. Miller
Deputy Director (G5), A. F. Affolter
Assistant Directors (G6), G. Gray; H. R. McCallum
Chief Planner (G4), A. Mackenzie
Deputy Chief Planner (G5), D. R. Dare
Assistant Chief Planners (G6), T. Williamson; A. W. Denham; I. R. Duncan; S. G. Fulton

HM Chief Industrial Pollution Inspector (G5), I. W. W. Wright

HISTORIC SCOTLAND
20 Brandon Street, Edinburgh EH3 5RA
Tel 031-244 3144

An executive agency within the Scottish Office.
Chief Executive (G3), G. N. Munro
Directors (G5), F. J. Lawrie; D. Macniven, TD; I. Maxwell; S. Rosie

LOCAL GOVERNMENT FINANCE GROUP
New St Andrew's House, Edinburgh EH1 3TB
Tel 031-556 8400

Assistant Secretaries (G5), C. M. Baxter; K. W. McKay

INQUIRY REPORTERS
16 Waterloo Place, Edinburgh EH1 3DN
Tel 031-556 8400

Chief Reporter (G3), A. G. Bell, CB
Deputy Chief Reporter (G5), R. M. Hickman

SCOTTISH OFFICE INDUSTRY DEPARTMENT

New St Andrew's House, Edinburgh EH1 3TA
Tel 031-556 8400
Dover House, Whitehall, London, SW1A 2AU
Tel 071-270 3000

Secretary (G2), P. MacKay
Under Secretaries (G3), A. D. F. Findlay; E. J. Weeple
Assistant Secretaries (G5), D. A. Brew; D. A. Campbell; M. J. P. Cunliffe; J. W. Elvidge; I. F. Gray; P. Heatherington; R. MacEwan; Mrs N. S. Munro
Senior Economic Advisers (G5), A. Goudie; J. A. Peat

PROFESSIONAL STAFF
Director of Roads and Chief Engineer (G4), J. A. L. Dawson
Deputy Chief Engineer (Roads) (G5), G. S. Marshall, CBE
Deputy Chief Engineer (Bridges) (G5), J. Innes
Assistant Chief Engineers (G6), N. B. MacKenzie; R. D. Udall; J. A. Howison

INDUSTRIAL EXPANSION
Alhambra House, 45 Waterloo Street, Glasgow G2 6AT
Tel 041-248 2855

Under Secretary (G3), H. Morison
Industrial Adviser, Dr C. K. Benington
Scientific Adviser, I. McGhee
Assistant Secretaries (G5), J. Meldrum; J. Thornton
Senior Principal (G6), J. McGhee

LOCATE IN SCOTLAND
120 Bothwell Street, Glasgow G2 7JP
Tel 041-248 2700

Director (G4), R. Crawford
Senior Principal (G6), W. Malone
Principal (G7), A. McCabe; J. Wilson
Director (North America), R. Crawford

SCOTTISH OFFICE EDUCATION DEPARTMENT

New St Andrew's House, Edinburgh EH1 3SY
Tel 031-556 8400
Dover House, Whitehall, London, SW1A 2AU
Tel 071-270 3000

Secretary (G2), G. R. Wilson, CB
Under Secretaries (G3), W. A. P. Weatherston; J. S. B. Martin
Assistant Secretaries (G5), P. Brady; D. S. Henderson; R. D. Jackson; J. W. L. Lonie; G. McHugh; Miss M. MacLean; K. Macrae; Mrs R. Menlowe; D. Salmond (*Chief Statistician*)
Senior Principal (G6), D. Wann

HM INSPECTORS OF SCHOOLS
Senior Chief Inspector (G3), T. N. Gallacher
Deputy Senior Chief Inspectors (G4), W. T. Beveridge; D. A. Osler
Chief Inspectors (G5), W. F. L. Bigwood; G. H. C. Donaldson; G. P. D. Donaldson; J. T. Donaldson; J. P. D. Gordon; J. Howgego; J. J. McDonald; A. S. McGlynn; A. M. Rankin; M. Roebuck; H. M. Stocker; R. M. S. Tuck.
There are 96 Grade 6 Inspectors.

SCOTTISH OFFICE HOME AND HEALTH DEPARTMENT

St Andrew's House, Edinburgh EH1 3DE
Tel 031-556 8400
Dover House, Whitehall, London, SW1A 2AU
Tel 071-270 3000

Secretary (G2), J. Hamill
Under Secretaries (G3), D. Belfall; N. G. Campbell; D. J. Essery; Mrs G. M. Stewart
Assistant Secretaries (G5), Mrs M. H. Brannan; J. T. Brown; A. M. Burnside; C. M. A. Lugton; C. K. McIntosh; P. M. Russell; R. H. Scott
Senior Principal (G6), N. MacLeod

NATIONAL HEALTH SERVICE IN SCOTLAND MANAGEMENT EXECUTIVE
Chief Executive, D. Cruickshank
Private Secretary, Ms J. A. Stirton
Director of Strategic Management, G. A. Anderson
Director of Finance, M. Collier
Director of Administration, D. Steel
Director of Information Services, C. B. Knox
Director of Manpower, A. J. Matheson
Assistant Secretaries (G5), W. J. Farquhar; Ms I. M. Low; W. Moyes; Mrs A. Robson; G. M. D. Thomson; G. W. Tucker
Assistant Director (G6), H. R. McCallum
Senior Principal (G6), Miss J. McGregor

MEDICAL SERVICES
Chief Medical Officer (G2), Prof. R. E. Kendell
Deputy Chief Medical Officer (G3), Dr A. B. Young
Principal Medical Officers, J. V. Basson; C. F. Fleming; G. Gilray; Margaret Hennigan; A. D. McIntyre; Dr Elizabeth Sowler
Senior Medical Officers, R. E. G. Aitken, TD; I. R. Bashford; P. W. Brooks; S. Capewell; W. Dodd; Dr A. Findlay; Dr Margaret Hally; Ms E. Keel; A. MacLeod; P. Massen; B. T. Potter; D. U. Sinclair; Dr R. D. Skinner; Dr M. A. R. Thomson; O. A. Thores; M. I. Ullah
Chief Scientist, I. A. D. Bouchier, CBE
Chief Dental Officer, N. K. Colquhoun
Deputy Chief Dental Officer, J. R. Wild
Regional Dental Officers, K. J. McKenzie; M. G. Platt; Miss A. J. Power; G. A. Reid
Chief Nursing Officer, Miss A. Jarvie
Chief Pharmacist (G6), G. Calder
Chief Research Officer, Dr C. P. A. Levein
Senior Principal Research Officers (G6), Mrs B. Doig; Dr Jacqueline Tombs

Social Work Services Group
43 Jeffrey Street, Edinburgh EH1 1DN
Tel 031-556 8400

The Social Work Services Group administers the provisions of the Social Work (Scotland) Act 1968.

Assistant Secretaries (G5), M. J. P. Cunliffe; J. W. Sinclair; D. Wishart
Chief Inspector of Social Work Services, A. Skinner
Assistant Chief Inspectors, Mrs H. Dempster; Ms M. L. Hunt; F. A. O'Leary; D. Pia; I. C. Robertson; J. I. Smith

Miscellaneous Appointments
HM Chief Inspector of Constabulary, C. Sampson, CBE, QPM
HM Chief Inspector of Prisons, A. H. Bishop, CB
Commandant, Scottish Police College, T. J. Whitson, OBE
HM Chief Inspector of Fire Services, A. Winton, QFSM
Commandant, Scottish Fire Service Training School, C. F. McManus, QFSM
Secretary, Scottish Health Service Advisory Council, W. J. Farquhar

Scottish Prison Service
Calton House, 5 Redheughs Rigg, Edinburgh EH12 9HW
Tel 031-556 8400

Chief Executive of Scottish Prison Service (G3), E. W. Frizzell
Deputy Chief Executive and Director of Prisons (G5), A. R. Walker
Director, Human Resources (G5), J. D. Gallagher
Director, Strategy and Planning (G5), D. A. Stewart
Deputy Director, Regime Services and Supplies (G6), N. Harvey
Deputy Director, Estates and Buildings (G6), D. D. Sutherland
Area Director, South and West (G5), J. Milne
Area Director, North and East (G5), J. Pearce

Prison Governors

Aberdeen, W. A. R. Rattray
Barlinnie, P. Withers
Barlinnie Special Unit, I. A. Bannatyne
Castle Huntly Young Offenders Institution, Miss M. Wood
Cornton Vale, P. L. Abernethy
Dumfries Young Offenders Institution, G. Taylor
Dungavel, A. P. Spencer
Edinburgh, R. McCowan (*acting*)
Friarton, J. A. Harker
Glenochil Prison and Young Offenders Institution, R. Kendrick
Greenock, D. E. Gunn
Inverness, P. Smeaton
Longriggend Remand Institution, A. F. King
Low Moss, W. Davidson
Noranside, J. C. Stuart
Penninghame, D. Croft (*acting*)
Perth, R. Kite
Peterhead, A. Ogilvie
Polmont Young Offenders Institution, G. R. Bond
Shotts, E. J. Campbell
Shotts Alternative Unit, A. MacDonald
Scottish Prison Service College, R. L. Houchin

Mental Welfare Commission for Scotland
25 Drumsheugh Gardens, Edinburgh EH3 7NS
Tel 031-225 7034

Chairman, Sheriff H. J. Aronson
Commissioners, Mrs A. Baxter; Dr D. Blaney; P. H. Brodie; R. G. Davis; Mrs A. M. Glen; Ms A. M. Green; Mrs H. L. Grieve; Mrs J. I. D. Isbister; D. A. Macdonald, OBE; Mrs H. S. Mein; Sir David Montgomery, Bt.; M. O'Reilly; J. G. Sutherland
Medical Commissioners, J. A. T. Dyer; A. A. McKechnie
Social Work Commissioner, J. H. L. Richards
Secretary, D. Wishart

Counsel to the Secretary of State for Scotland under the Private Legislation Procedure (Scotland) Act 1936
50 Frederick Street, Edinburgh
Tel 031-226 6499

Senior Counsel, G. S. Douglas, QC
Junior Counsel, N. M. P. Morrison

NATIONAL HEALTH SERVICE, SCOTLAND

Health Boards

Argyll and Clyde, Gilmour House, Paisley. *Chairman*, R. R. Reid; *General Manager*, I. C. Smith
Ayrshire and Arran, PO Box 13, Hunters Avenue, Ayr. *Chairman*, W. S. Fyfe, CBE; *General Manager*, J. M. Eckford, OBE
Borders, Huntlyburn, Melrose, Roxburghshire. *Chairman*, Dr D. H. Pringle,CBE; *General Manager*, D. A. Peters
Dumfries and Galloway, Nithbank, Dumfries. *Chairman*, J. A. M. McIntyre, OBE; *General Manager*, M. D. Cook
Fife, Glenrothes House, North Street, Glenrothes. *Chairman*, Mrs P. A. H. Ferguson; *General Manager*, vacant
Forth Valley, 33 Spittal Street, Stirling. *Chairman*, Mrs J. D. Isbister; *General Manager*, Miss L. Barrie
Grampian, 1–7 Albyn Place, Aberdeen. *Chairman*, J. Kyle, CBE; *General Manager*, F. E. L. Hartnett
Greater Glasgow, 112 Ingram Street, Glasgow. *Chairman*, Sir Thomas Thomson, CBE; *General Manager*, L. Peterken, CBE
Highland, Reay House, 17 Old Edinburgh Road, Inverness. *Chairman*, J. D. M. Robertson, OBE; *General Manager*, R. R. W. Stewart
Lanarkshire, 14 Beckford Street, Hamilton, Lanarkshire. *Chairman*, Mrs B. M. Gunn, OBE; *General Manager*, F. Clark, CBE
Lothian, 148 The Pleasance, Edinburgh. *Chairman*, Dr J. W. Baynham; *General Manager*, J. Lusby
Orkney, Balfour Hospital, New Scapa Road, Kirkwall, Orkney. *Chairman*, J. Leslie; *General Manager*, Dr J. I. Cromarty
Shetland, 28 Burgh Road, Lerwick. *Chairman*, Mrs F. Grains; *General Manager*, B. J. Atherton
Tayside, PO Box 75, Vernonholme, Riverside Drive, Dundee. *Chairman*, J. C. MacFarlane; *General Manager*, Dr R. C. Graham, CBE
Western Isles, 37 South Beach Street, Stornoway, Isle of Lewis. *Chairman*, Mrs M. A. Macmillan, OBE; *General Manager*, J. J. Glover

Health Education Board for Scotland
Woodburn House, Canaan Lane, Edinburgh EH10 4SG

Chairman, E. Walker
General Manager, Dr A. Tannahill

State Hospital
Carstairs Junction, Lanark ML11 8RP

Chairman, P. Hamilton-Grierson
General Manager, R. Manson

COMMON SERVICES AGENCY
Trinity Park House, South Trinity Road, Edinburgh EH5 3SE

Chairman, D. G. Cruickshank
General Manager, J. T. Donald

GENERAL REGISTER OFFICE
New Register House, Edinburgh EH1 3YT
Tel 031-334 0380

The General Register Office for Scotland is the Scottish equivalent of the Office of Population Censuses and Surveys. The main records in the custody of the Registrar General for Scotland are the statutory registers of births, deaths, marriages, still births, adoptions and divorces; the old parish registers (recording births, marriages, deaths, etc. before civil registration began in 1855); and records of censuses of the population in Scotland.

Hours of public access: Mon.–Thurs. 9–4.30; Fri. 9–4.

Registrar-General (G4), Dr C. M. Glennie
Deputy Registrar-General (G5), B. V. Philp
Senior Principal (G6), D. A. Orr
Principals (G7), D. B. L. Brownlee; R. C. Lawson; F. D. Garvie
Statisticians (G7), J. Arrundale; G. W. L. Jackson; F. G. Thomas

SEA FISH INDUSTRY AUTHORITY
Unit 9, 18 Logie Mill, Beaverbank Office Park, Logie Green Road, Edinburgh EH7 4HG
Tel 031-558 3331

Chairman, Lord Mackay of Ardbrecknish
Chief Executive, P. D. Chaplin
Assistant Secretary, D. Robertson
Technical Director, A. G. Hopper
Marketing Director, R. M. Kennedy
Training Director, K. Waind

THE SECURITY SERVICE COMMISSIONER
c/o The Home Office, 50 Queen Anne's Gate, London SW1H 9AT

The Commissioner is appointed by the Prime Minister. He keeps under review the issue of warrants by the Secretary of State under the Security Service Act 1989 and is required to give the Security Service Tribunal help by investigating complaints which allege interference with property and by offering all such assistance in discharging its functions as it may require. He is also required to submit an annual report on the discharge of his functions to the Prime Minister.

Commissioner, The Rt. Hon. Lord Justice Stuart-Smith

SECURITY SERVICE TRIBUNAL
PO Box 18, London SE1 0TZ

The Security Service Act 1989 established a tribunal of three to five senior members of the legal profession, independent of the Government and appointed by The Queen, to investigate complaints from any person about anything which they believe the Security Service has done to them or to their property.

President, The Hon. Mr Justice Simon Brown
Vice President, Sheriff J. McInnes, QC
Member, Sir Richard Gaskell

SERIOUS FRAUD OFFICE
Elm House, 10–16 Elm Street, London, WC1X 0BJ
Tel 071-239 7272

The Serious Fraud Office is an autonomous department under the superintendence of the Attorney-General. Its remit is to investigate and prosecute serious and complex fraud. The scope of its powers covers England, Wales and Northern Ireland. The staff includes lawyers, accountants and other support staff; investigating teams work closely with the police.

Director, G. Staple
Deputy Director, J. Knox

OFFICE OF THE SOCIAL FUND COMMISSIONER
Millbank Towers, 21–24 Millbank, London, SW1P 4QU
Tel 071-217 4799
4th Floor, Centre City Podium, 5 Hill Street, Birmingham B5 4UB
Tel 021-631 4000

The Social Fund Commissioner is appointed by the Secretary of State for Social Security. The Commissioner appoints Social Fund Inspectors, who provide an independent review of decisions made by Social Fund Officers in the Benefits Agency of the Department of Social Security.

Social Fund Commissioner, Mrs R. Mackworth

DEPARTMENT OF SOCIAL SECURITY
Richmond House, 79 Whitehall, London, SW1A 2NS
Tel 071-210 3000

The Department of Social Security is responsible for the provision of social security services in England, Wales and Scotland.

Secretary of State for Social Security, The Rt. Hon. Peter Lilley, MP
Private Secretary, A. Woods
Special Adviser, J. Mayhew
Parliamentary Private Secretary, P. Merchant, MP
Minister of State, Rt. Hon. Nicholas Scott, MBE, MP (*Social Security and Disabled People*)
Private Secretary, Ms C. Mitchell
Parliamentary Private Secretary, Mrs E. Peacock, MP
Parliamentary Under Secretary of State (*Lords*), The Lord Henley
Private Secretary, T. Lowe
Parliamentary Under Secretaries of State (*Commons*), Ann Widdecombe, MP; Alistair Burt, MP
Private Secretaries, D. Higlett; Mrs C. Sweetenham
Permanent Secretary (G1), Sir Michael Partridge, KCB
Private Secretary, Mrs V. Andrews

RESOURCE MANAGEMENT AND PLANNING GROUP

Deputy Secretary (*G2*), B. Gilmore

BENEFITS AGENCY
Quarry House, Quarry Hill, Leeds LS2 7UA
Tel 0532-324000

An executive agency within the Department of Social Security.

Chief Executive (*G2*), M. Bichard
Private Secretary, S. G. Appleton
Directors (*G3*), Mrs M. A. Robinson (*policy and planning*); D. Riggs (*finance*); G. Bardwell (*personnel*)

BENEFITS AGENCY TERRITORIES

SCOTLAND/NORTHERN ENGLAND, Sandyford House, Archbold Terrace, Newcastle upon Tyne NE2 1AA. *Director* (*G3*), A. J. Laurance
SOUTHERN ENGLAND, Olympic House, Olympic Way, Wembley, Middx. HA9 0DL. *Director* (*G3*), I. Magee
WALES/CENTRAL ENGLAND, Five Ways Tower, Frederick Road, Edgbaston, Birmingham B15 1ST. *Director* (*G3*), J. T. Green

BENEFITS AGENCY MEDICAL SERVICES

Director (*G3*), Dr P. Castaldi
Principal Medical Officers, Dr M. Aylward; Dr P. Dewis; Dr D. R. Findlay; Dr C. Hudson

INFORMATION TECHNOLOGY SERVICES AGENCY

An executive agency within the Department of Social Security.

Chief Executive, F. J. Kenworthy
Deputy Chief Executive, P. T. F. Dunn
Directors, Ms A. Cleveland; K. Caldwell; G. McCorkell; S. Williams; J. Y. Marshall; V. Seeney; N. Haighton
Non-Executive Directors, J. M. Bankier, CBE; G. Beavan

CONTRIBUTIONS AGENCY

An executive agency within the Department of Social Security.

Chief Executive (*G4*), Miss A. Chant
Deputy Chief Executive (*G5*), G. Bertram
Directors, K. Wilson; S. Heminsley; R. Roberts; D. Gatenby; A. Cass; I. Hutton
Non-Executive Director, M. Brimblecombe

SOCIAL SECURITY DIVISION A

Under Secretary (*G3*), B. Walmsley
Assistant Secretaries (*G5*), Mrs U. Brennan; Miss S. Fraenkel; R. H. Layton; Mrs A. Lingwood

SOCIAL SECURITY DIVISION B

Under Secretary (*G3*), Miss M. Pierson
Assistant Secretaries (*G5*), I. Knight-Smith; J. Moor; Miss L. Richards; A. Stott

SOCIAL SECURITY DIVISION C

Under Secretary (*G3*), D. J. Clarke
Assistant Secretaries (*G5*), Mrs C. Souter; Miss J. Liebling; A. Thompson

SOCIAL SECURITY DIVISION D

Under Secretary (*G3*), B. J. Ellis
Assistant Secretaries (*G5*), M. Street; P. Tansley; Miss N. Bastin; I. Williams

INFORMATION DIVISION

Head of Information (*G5*), S. Reardon
Deputy Head of Information (*G6*), T. Grace
Principal Information Officer (*G7*), J. Bretherton
Chief Publicity Officer (*G7*), Mrs H. Midlane

RESETTLEMENT AGENCY
Euston Tower, 286 Euston Road, London, NW1 3DN
Tel 071-388 1188

An executive agency within the Department of Social Security.

Chief Executive (*G6*), A. J. Ward

CHILD SUPPORT UNIT

Unit set up in advance of Child Support Agency. From April 1993 the Child Support Agency will be an executive agency within the Department of Social Security.
Chief Executive (*G4*), Mrs R. Hepplewhite

CENTRAL ADVISORY COMMITTEE ON WAR PENSIONS
Room 1138, The Adelphi, 1–11 John Adam Street, London WC2N 6HT
Tel 071-962 8028

Secretary, S. Adams

SOCIAL SECURITY ADVISORY COMMITTEE
New Court, Carey Street, London, WC2A 2LS
Tel 071-412 1507

The Social Security Advisory Committee (SSAC) was established by the Social Security Act 1980 to advise the Secretary of State for Social Security and the Department of Health and Social Services for Northern Ireland on all social security matters except those relating to benefits for industrial injuries and diseases and occupational pensions. The Social Security Housing Benefit Act 1982 added housing benefit to the Committee's responsibilities.

Chairman, Sir Peter Barclay, CBE
Members, Mrs J. Anelay, OBE; Revd G. H. Good, OBE; D. Guereca; H. Hodge; P. F. Naish; Hon. Mrs R. H. P. Price; Lady Scott, CBE; A. M. Sealey; Dr A. V. Stokes, OBE; Prof. Olive Stevenson; O. Tudor; R. G. Wendt
Secretary, L. C. Smith

SPORTS COUNCIL
16 Upper Woburn Place, London WC1H 0QP
Tel 071-388 1277

The Sports Council, created under Royal Charter, promotes the development of sport and fosters the provision of facilities for sport and recreation in Great Britain.

Chairman, Sir Peter Yarranton

HMSO (HER MAJESTY'S STATIONERY OFFICE)
St Crispins, Duke Street, Norwich NR3 1PD
Tel 0603-622211

HMSO (Her Majesty's Stationery Office) was established in 1786 and is the government executive agency that provides printing, binding and business supplies to government departments and publicly funded organizations. HMSO is also the Government's publisher and has bookshops for the sale of government publications in six major cities, as well as appointed agents in other cities. HMSO obtains most of its supplies and printing from commercial sources by competitive tender, apart from about 20 per cent of its printing requirement, such as Hansard and Bills and Acts of Parliament, which are produced in its own printing works. HMSO is a self-financing government trading fund and competes for its business with other commercial suppliers.

Controller and Chief Executive, P. I. Freeman, CB
Executive Assistant, Mrs J. B. Ward
Deputy Chief Executive, M. D. Lynn
Director-General of Corporate Services, P. J. Macdonald

HEADS OF DIVISIONS
Publications, C. N. Southgate
Business Supplies, A. J. Davies
Print Procurement, B. Ekers
Finance and Planning, V. G. Bell
Information Technology, D. C. Kerry
Technological Innovation, J. R. Eveson
Engineering and Estates, W. E. Scott
Human Resources, J. McDonald
Organization Development, C. J. Penn
Quality and Consultancy, A. M. Cole

BIRMINGHAM – *Bookshop*, 258 Broad Street, Birmingham B1 2HE.
BRISTOL, Ashton Vale Road, Bristol BS3 2HN – *Bookshop*, 33 Wine Street, Bristol BS1 2BQ.
LONDON – *Publications Centre*, 51 Nine Elms Lane, London SW8 5DR. *Bookshop*, 49 High Holborn, London WC1V 6HB.
MANCHESTER, Broadway, Chadderton, Oldham, Lancs. OL9 9QH – *Bookshop*, 9–21 Princess Street, Manchester M60 8AS.
SCOTLAND, South Gyle Crescent, Edinburgh EH12 9EB. *Director, Edinburgh*, G. W. Bedford – *Bookshop*, 71 Lothian Road, Edinburgh EH3 9AZ.
NORTHERN IRELAND, IDB House, Chichester Street, Belfast BT1 4PS. *Director, Belfast*, M. McNeill – *Retail and Trade Bookshop*, 16 Arthur Street, Belfast BT1 4GD.

STUDENT LOANS COMPANY LTD
100 Bothwell Street, Glasgow G2 7JD
Tel 041-306 2000

The Company was established in November 1989. It administers the student loans scheme on behalf of the Government.

Chief Executive, R. J. Harrison

OFFICE OF TELECOMMUNICATIONS
Export House, 50 Ludgate Hill, London EC4M 7JJ
Tel 071-822 1600

The Office of Telecommunications (Oftel) is a non-ministerial government department which is responsible for supervising telecommunications activities in the UK. Its principal functions are to ensure that holders of telecommunications licences comply with their licence conditions; to maintain and promote effective competition in telecommunications; and to promote, in respect of prices, quality and variety the interests of consumers, purchasers and other users of telecommunication services and apparatus.

The Director-General has powers to deal with anti-competitive practices and monopoly situations. He also has a duty to consider all reasonable complaints and representations about telecommunication apparatus and services.

Director-General (acting), W. R. B. Wigglesworth
Director of PTO Licensing, G. P. Knight
Director of Consumer and International Affairs, D. G. Hyde
Head of Information, D. C. Redding

TOURIST BOARDS

The English Tourist Board, the Scottish Tourist Board, the Wales Tourist Board and the Northern Ireland Tourist Board are responsible for developing and marketing the tourist industry in their respective countries. The Boards' main objectives are to promote holidays and to encourage the provision and improvement of tourist amenities.

ENGLISH TOURIST BOARD, Thames Tower, Black's Road, London W6 9EL. Tel: 081-846 9000. *Chief Executive*, J. East
SCOTTISH TOURIST BOARD, 23 Ravelston Terrace, Edinburgh EH4 3EU. Tel: 031-332 2433. *Chief Executive*, T. M. Band
WALES TOURIST BOARD, Brunel House, 2 Fitzalan Road, Cardiff CF2 1UY. Tel: 0222-499909. *Chief Executive*, P. Loveluck
NORTHERN IRELAND TOURIST BOARD, St Anne's Court, 59 North Street, Belfast BT1 1NB. Tel: 0232-231221. *Chief Executive*, I. Henderson

DEPARTMENT OF TRADE AND INDUSTRY
Ashdown House, 123 Victoria Street, London SW1E 6RB
Tel 071-215 5000

Enterprise Initiative, Tel 0800-500200
Single European Market, Tel 081-200 1992
Environmental Enquiries, Tel 0800-585794

The Department is responsible for:
(a) international trade policy, including the promotion of UK trade interests in the European Community, GATT, OECD, UNCTAD and other international organizations
(b) the promotion of UK exports and assistance to exporters
(c) policy in relation to industry and commerce, including policy towards small firms, regional policy and regional industrial assistance (some of this applying only to England), and policy in relation to British Shipbuilders and the Post Office
(d) competition policy and consumer protection, including relations with the Office of Fair Trading, the Office of Telecommunications and the Monopolies and Mergers Commission; co-ordination of policy on deregulation
(e) the development of national policies in relation to all forms of energy and the development of new sources of energy; international aspects of energy policy. Links with British Coal, the Atomic Energy Authority, the electricity supply industry, the nuclear power construction industry, and the oil and gas industries
(f) policy on science and technology research and development; space; standards, quality and design; the following

executive agencies: the Laboratory of the Government Chemist, the National Engineering Laboratory, the National Physical Laboratory, the National Weights and Measures Laboratory, and Warren Spring Laboratory
(g) company legislation and Companies House executive agency; the Insolvency Service executive agency; the regulation of insurance industries; the Radiocommunications Agency (executive agency); and the Patent Office and Accounts Services executive agencies

President of the Board of Trade and Secretary of State for Trade and Industry, The Rt. Hon. Michael Heseltine, MP
Principal Private Secretary, P. Smith
Private Secretaries, Ms E. Jones; K. Loader
Special Advisers, Lady Strathnever; Dr A. Kemp
Parliamentary Private Secretary, R. Ottaway, MP
Minister for Industry, The Rt. Hon. Timothy Sainsbury, MP
Private Secretary, Ms J. Knight
Minister for Energy, Timothy Eggar, MP
Private Secretary, J. Neilson
Parliamentary Private Secretary, S. Burns, MP
Minister for Trade, Richard Needham, MP
Private Secretary, J. Warren
Parliamentary Private Secretary, A. Rowe, MP
Parliamentary Under Secretary of State for Technology, Edward Leigh, MP.
Principal Private Secretary, C. Thresh
Parliamentary Under Secretary of State for Corporate Affairs, Neil Hamilton, MP
Private Secretary, Ms K. Spall
Parliamentary Under Secretary of State for Consumer Affairs and Small Firms, The Baroness Denton of Wakefield, CBE
Private Secretary, S. Speed
British Overseas Trade Board Chairman, Sir Derek Hornby
Permanent Secretary (G1), Sir Peter Gregson, KCB
Private Secretary, J. Foggo
Deputy Secretaries (G2), Dr G. Robinson (*Chief Adviser on Science and Technology*); C. W. Roberts, CB; R. Williams, CB; A. Lane, CB; A. Hammond, CB (*The Solicitor*); C. Henderson, CB; R. J. Priddle; A. C. Hutton; A. Macdonald, CB
Parliamentary Clerk, T. Williams

DIVISIONAL ORGANIZATION

Accounts Services Executive Agency
Government Buildings, Cardiff Road, Newport, Gwent NP9 1ZA
Tel 0633-812271
Director and Chief Executive (G5), D. M. Hoddinott

Aerospace Division
Tel 071-215 5000
Under Secretary (G3), A. Nieduszynski

Atomic Energy
1 Palace Street, London SW1E 5HE
Tel 071-215 5000
Under Secretary (G3), Dr T. E. Walker
Heads of Branch (G5), Dr D. Hauser; P. H. Aggrell; Dr J. M. Bird; Mrs H. Haddon; Dr D. Lumley

British National Space Centre
Dean Bradley House, Horseferry Road, London SW1P 2AG
Tel 071-276 3000
Director-General (G3), A. J. Pryor
Deputy Director-General (G4), J. S. Shrimplin
Heads of Branch (G5), Prof. J. E. Harries; Dr R. Jude; K. Inglis; *(G6)*, Dr G. W. D. Findlay; Dr D. Williams; J. Thomas

Business Task Forces Division 1
151 Buckingham Palace Road, London SW1W 9SS
Tel 071-215 5000
Under Secretary (G3), R. W. Simpson
Heads of Branch (G5), C. J. Brewer; M. R. Cohen; Miss S. E. Harding

Business Task Forces Division 2
151 Buckingham Palace Road, London SW1W 9SS
Tel 071-215 5000
Under Secretary (G3), A. J. Nieduszynski
Heads of Branch (G5), C. E. Blundell; T. M. H. Shearer; H. J. Charman; Dr G. T. Coleman; *(G6)*, M. O. Ralph

Central Unit
Ashdown House, 123 Victoria Street, London SW1E 6RB
Tel 071-215 5000
Head of Unit (G3), J. A. Cooke
Grade 5, J. Green

Chemicals and Biotechnology Division
Tel 071-215 5000
Under Secretary (G3), Dr E. Finer

Coal Division
1 Palace Street, London SW1E 5HE
Tel 071-215 5000
Under Secretary (G3), W. I. MacIntyre, CB
Heads of Branch (G5), J. A. V. Collett, N. Hirst

Companies Division
10–18 Victoria Street, London SW1H 0NN
Tel 071-215 5000
Under Secretary (G3), A. C. Russell
Heads of Branch (G5), M. J. C. Butcher; C. W. Johnston; J. Healey; F. C. Jenkins

Companies House
Companies House, Crown Way, Cardiff CF4 3UZ
Tel 0222-388588
An executive agency of the Department of Trade and Industry.
Registrar of Companies for England and Wales (G4), D. Durham
London Search Room, 55–71 City Road, London EC1Y 1BB
Tel 071-253 9393
102 George Street, Edinburgh EH2 3DJ
Tel 031-225 5774
Registrar for Scotland, J. Henderson

Competition Policy Division
Ashdown House, 123 Victoria Street, London SW1E 6RB
Tel 071-215 5000
Under Secretary (G3), Dr C. E. D. Bell
Heads of Branch (G5), G. C. Riggs; J. Alty; Mrs M. Bloom; C. C. Bridge

Consumer Affairs Division
10–18 Victoria Street, London SW1H 0NN
Tel 071-215 5000
Under Secretary (G3), C. Kerse
Heads of Branch (G5), D. Jones; M. A. R. Lunn; M. Oldham; D. W. Hellings

Deregulation Unit
Ashdown House, 123 Victoria Street, London SW1E 6RB
Tel 071-215 5000
Director (G3), Dr C. E. Bell
Heads of Branch (G5), R. M. Watson; Mrs G. V. Alliston

Economics and Statistics Division
Ashdown House, 123 Victoria Street, London SW1E 6RB
Tel 071-215 5000

Chief Economic Adviser (G3), D. R. Coates
Departmental reorganization in progress.

Electricity Division
1 Palace Street, London SW1E 5HE
Tel 071-215 5000

Under Secretary (G3), C. C. Wilcock
Heads of Branch (G5), M. A. Higson; S. F. D. Powell; C. J. C. Wright; J. G. Lindsay

Electronics and Electrical Engineering Division
Tel 071-215 5000
Under Secretary (G3), J. Cammell

Energy Technology
1 Palace Street, London SW1E 5HE
Tel 071-215 5000

Under Secretary (G3), Dr W. D. Evans
Heads of Branch (G5), Dr D. Fairmaner, G. G. Bevan; Dr. M. A. Eggington

Enterprise Initiative Division
Kingsgate House, 66–74 Victoria Street, London SW1E 6SW
Tel 071-215 5000

Under Secretary (G3), Mrs S. Brown
Heads of Branches (G5), H. P. Brown; M. Garrod; T. Roberts; Mrs E. Ryle

Environment Division
Tel 071-215 5000

Under Secretary (G3), D. Evans

Europe Division
Ashdown House, 123 Victoria Street, London SW1E 6RB
Tel 071-215 5000

Under Secretary (G3), N. R. Thornton
Grade 4, K. W. N. George
Heads of Branch (G5), J. Rhodes; D. I. Richardson; Dr H. M. Sutton; E. W. Beston

Finance and Resource Management Division
Ashdown House, 123 Victoria Street, London SW1E 6RB
Tel 071-215 5000

Under Secretary (G3), M. K. O'Shea
Heads of Branch (G5), W. Stow; D. T. Smith

Gas and Oil Measurement Branch
3 Tigers Road, South Wigston, Leicester LE8 2US
Tel 0533-785354

Director (G5), J. Plant

Industrial Competitiveness Division
151 Buckingham Palace Road, London SW1W 9SS
Tel 071-215 5000

Under Secretary (G3), Dr R. Dobbie
Heads of Branch (G5), M. Gibson; G. Dart

Information Division
Ashdown House, 123 Victoria Street, London SW1E 6RB
Tel 071-215 5000

Head of Information (G4), Ms J. M. Caines
Head of News (G6), A. Marre

Publicity
Bridge Place, 88–89 Eccleston Square, London SW1V 1PT
Tel 071-215 5000

Grade 5, S. Lyle-Smythe

Information and Manufacturing Technology Division
151 Buckingham Palace Road, London SW1W 9SS
Tel 071-215 5000

Director (G3), Dr K. C. Shotton
Departmental reorganization in progress.

The Insolvency Service
Bridge Place, 88–89 Eccleston Square, London SW1V 1PT
Tel 071-215 5000

An executive agency of the Department of Trade and Industry.
Inspector-General of the Insolvency Service and Chief Executive, P. R. Joyce
Deputy Inspectors-General, D. J. Flynn; J. R. Donnison; Ms R. J. R. Anderson

Insurance Division
10–18 Victoria Street, London SW1H 0NN
Tel 071-215 5000

Under Secretary (G3), J. Spencer
Heads of Branch (G5), M. G. Roberts; Ms S. Seymour; Miss A. Lambert; Miss V. Evans

Internal Audit
151 Buckingham Palace Road, London SW1W 9SS
Tel 071-215 5000

Head of Internal Audit (G5), A. C. Elkington

International Trade Policy Division
Ashdown House, 123 Victoria Street, London SW1E 6RB
Tel 071-215 5000

Under Secretary (G3), J. Cooke
Heads of Branch (G5), M. D. C. Johnson; R. E. Allen; S. J. Bowen

International Energy Unit
1 Palace Street, London SW1E 5EH
Tel 071-215 5000
Grade 4, S. W. Freemantle

Investigations Division
Ashdown House, 123 Victoria Street, London SW1E 6RB
Tel 071-215 5000

Head of Branch (G3), H. V. B. Brown
Head of Legal Services (G4), Mrs T. J. Dunstan
Inspector of Companies, G. Harp
Heads of Branch (G5), B. J. Welch; A. Mier; R. Burton; H. Bradshaw; Mrs B. Chase; A. Robertshaw

Joint Directorate (FCO/DTI)
Kingsgate House, 66–74 Victoria Street, London SW1E 6SW
Tel 071-215 5000

Under Secretary (G3), R. O. Miles, CMG
Directors (G5), D. Saunders; *(DS4)* M. Dougal

Laboratory of the Government Chemist
Queens Road, Teddington, Middx. TW11 0LY
Tel 081-943 7000

An executive agency of the Department of Trade and Industry.
Government Chemist (G3), Dr R. Worswick

Mechanical Engineering Division
Tel 071-215 5000

Under Secretary (G3), J. Cammell

NATIONAL ENGINEERING LABORATORY
East Kilbride, Glasgow G75 0QU
Tel 03552-20222

An executive agency of the Department of Trade and Industry.

Chief Executive (G3), W. Edgar

NATIONAL PHYSICAL LABORATORY
Teddington, Middx. TW11 0LW
Tel 081-977 3222

An executive agency of the Department of Trade and Industry.

Director (G3), Dr P. B. Clapham

NATIONAL WEIGHTS AND MEASURES LABORATORY
Stanton Avenue, Teddington, Middx. TW11 0JZ
Tel 081-943 7272

An executive agency of the Department of Trade and Industry.

Chief Executive (G5), S. Bennett

OFFSHORE SUPPLIES OFFICE
Alhambra House, 45 Waterloo Street, Glasgow G2 6AS
Tel 041-221 8777

1 Palace Street, London SW1E 5HE
Tel 071-215 5000

Director-General (G3), J. E. d'Ancona
Heads of Branch (G5), A. E. Maule; C. P. Carter; *(G6)*, J. Roddie

OIL AND GAS DIVISION
1 Palace Street, London SW1E 5HE
Tel 071-215 5000

Under Secretary (G3), D. R. Davis
Heads of Branch (G5), M. H. Atkinson; J. R. Wakely; W. C. F. Butler; H. W. Joiner
Director of Petroleum Engineering (RES1), I. W. G. Hughes

OVERSEAS TRADE DIVISIONS
Ashdown House, 123 Victoria Street, London SW1E 6RB
Tel 071-215 5000

DIVISION 1

Projects and Export Policy
Under Secretary (G3), D. J. Hall
Heads of Branch (G5), R. I. Rogers; P. Casey; N. Worman

DIVISION 2

North America, NE and SE Asia, China, Hong Kong and Export Licensing Operation
Under Secretary (G3), R. J. Meadway
Heads of Branch (G5), J. V. Hagestadt; D. E. Love; M. V. Coolican

DIVISION 3

Under Secretary (G3), P. Bryant
Head of Exports to Europe Branch (G5), K. D. Levinson
Head of Overseas Promotions Support (G6), L. D. Rabstaff
Head of Export Data Branch (G6), A. Reynolds
Head of Overseas Trade Fairs (G5), K. R. Timmins

DIVISION 4

Under Secretary (G3), M. M. Baker
Head of Middle East and North Africa Branch (G5), M. G. Petter
Head of Mexico, Central America, Caribbean, South America and Australasia Branch (G5), J. M. Bowder
Head of Sub-Saharan Africa and South Asia Branch (G5), G. Berg

PATENT OFFICE – *see* pages 345–6

PERSONNEL DIVISION
Allington Towers, 19 Allington Street, London SW1E 5EB
Tel 071-215 5000

Under Secretary (G3), A. Titchener
Heads of Branch (G5), J. Thompson; J. Phillips; A. Mantle
Director of Training (G5), T. Bryan

RADIOCOMMUNICATIONS AGENCY
Waterloo Bridge House, Waterloo Road, London SE1 8UA
Tel 071-215 5000

An executive agency of the Department of Trade and Industry.
Chief Executive (G3), M. J. Michell
Heads of Branch (G5), M. Goddard; S. Spivey; R. A. Bedford; D. Reed; R. M. Skiffins; *(G6)*, B. A. Maxwell

REGIONAL DEVELOPMENT AND INWARD INVESTMENT DIVISION
Kingsgate House, 66–74 Victoria Street, London SW1E 6SW
Tel 071-215 5000

Director (G3), P. M. S. Corley
Directors, IDU (G3), C. R. Jenkins; Mrs D. A. King
Heads of Branch (G5), R. H. S. Wells; J. C. S. Priston; K. Holt; Mrs A. Taylor; Dr H. N. M. Stewart; M. A. Wilks; *(G6)*, M. P. Briggs

RESEARCH AND TECHNOLOGY POLICY DIVISION
151 Buckingham Palace Road, London SW1W 9SS
Tel 071-215 5000

Under Secretary (G3), Dr C. Hicks
Heads of Branch (G5), R. J. Allpress; J. Hobday; A. Keddie; I. C. Downing; P. L. Bunn

SERVICES MANAGEMENT DIVISION
Kingsgate House, 66–74 Victoria Street, London SW1E 6SW
Tel 071-215 5000

Under Secretaries (G3), R. M. Rumbelow; Dr R. Heathcote
Director of Administrative Information Technology Services (G4), R. J. Wheeler
Heads of Branch (G5), Miss D. Gane; K. M. Long

SMALL FIRMS DIVISION
c/o Employment Department, Moorfoot, Sheffield S1 4PQ
Tel 0742-753275
Kingsgate House, 66–74 Victoria Street, London SW1E 6SW
Tel 071-215 5000

Under Secretary (G3), Mrs S. Brown
Heads of Branch (G5), Miss S. C. Newton; J. R. Reid

SOLICITOR'S OFFICE
10–18 Victoria Street, London SW1H 0NN
Tel 071-215 5000

The Solicitor (G2), A. Hammond, CB
Grade 3, P. H. Bovey; R. Woolman; D. E. J. Nissen; J. M. Stanley
Assistant Solicitors (G5), H. D. M. Bailey; Mrs N. M. P. Chappell; Mrs J. Darvell; R. D. Fayers; Miss P. A. E. Granados; R. D. B. Green; D. H. M. Ingham; D. S. Mangat; I. K. Mathers; S. G. Milligan; S. Morgan; Miss K. Morton; R. Nicklen; Miss E. N. O'Flynn; S. A. Parker; R. C. Perkins; Miss J. Richardson; J. W. Roberts; Miss J. V. Stokes; A. M. Susman

STEEL, METALS AND MINERALS DIVISION
Tel 071-215 5000

Under Secretary (G3), R. Simpson

TELECOMMUNICATIONS AND POSTS DIVISION
151 Buckingham Palace Road, London SW1W 9SS
Tel 071-215 5000

Under Secretary (G3), P. Salvidge
Grade 4, S. R. Temple
Heads of Branch (G5), D. D. Sibbick; P. Smith; S. Pride; Mrs L. Brown; P. Waller; N. McMillan

TEXTILES AND RETAILING DIVISION
Tel 071-215 5000

Under Secretary (G3), T. Muir

VEHICLES DIVISION
Tel 071-215 5000

Under Secretary (G3), M. Stanley

WARREN SPRING LABORATORY
Gunnels Wood Road, Stevenage, Herts. SG1 2BX
Tel 0438-741122

An executive agency of the Department of Trade and Industry.

Director (G3), Dr D. Cormack

BRITISH OVERSEAS TRADE BOARD

Kingsgate House, 66–74 Victoria Street, London SW1E 6SW
Tel 071-215 5000

President, The President of the Board of Trade
Chairman, Sir Derek Hornby
Vice-Chairman, HRH The Duke of Kent, KG, GCMG, GCVO
Members, J. M. Banham; Sir Hugh Bidwell; C. J. Bull; R. Burman; Sir Alan Cockshaw; B. L. Crowe, CMG; I. L. Dale, OBE; T. P. Frost; Dr A. Hayes, CBE; D. Lanigan; R. O. Miles, CMG; H. B. G. Montgomery; J. W. Parsons, CBE; M. S. Perry, CBE; C. W. Roberts, CB; B. D. Taylor; B. W. Willott
Secretary (G5), D. Saunders

REGIONAL OFFICES

DTI NORTH-EAST, Stanegate House, 2 Groat Market, Newcastle upon Tyne NE1 1YN. Tel: 091-232 4722. *Regional Director (G3)*, P. A. Denham; *Regional Industrial Adviser (G3)*, J. W. Armstrong
DTI NORTH-WEST, Sunley Tower, Piccadilly Plaza, Manchester M1 4BA. Tel: 061-236 2171. *Regional Director (G3)*, J. H. Pownall
DTI YORKSHIRE AND HUMBERSIDE, 25 Queen Street, Leeds LS1 2TW. Tel: 0532 443171. *Regional Director (G3)*, E. Wright
DTI EAST MIDLANDS, Severns House, 20 Middle Pavement, Nottingham NG1 7DW. Tel: 0602 506181. *Regional Director (G5)*, R. M. Anderson
DTI WEST MIDLANDS, 77 Paradise Circus, Queensway, Birmingham B1 2DT. Tel: 021-212 5000. *Regional Director (G3)*, S. G. Linstead
DTI EAST, Westbrook Centre, Milton Road, Cambridge CB4 1YG. Tel: 0223-461939. *Regional Director (G5)*, W. J. Hall; *Deputy Regional Director (G6)*, R. D. Dennis
DTI SOUTH-EAST, Bridge Place, 88–89 Eccleston Square, London SW1V 1PT. Tel: 071-215 5000. *Regional Director (G5)*, I. Jones; *Deputy Regional Director (G6)*, Dr A. Thorpe
DTI SOUTH-WEST, The Pithay, Bristol BS1 2PB. Tel: 0272-272666. *Regional Director (G5)*, D. B. Lodge; *Deputy Regional Director (G6)*, vacant

---

DEPARTMENT OF TRANSPORT

2 Marsham Street, London SW1P 3EB
Tel 071-276 3000

The Department of Transport is responsible for land, sea and air transport, including sponsorship of the rail and bus industries; airports; domestic and international civil aviation; shipping and the ports industry; navigational lights, pilotage, HM Coastguard and marine pollution; motorways and other trunk roads; oversight of road transport including vehicle standards, registration and licensing, driver testing and licensing, bus and road freight licensing, regulation of taxis and private hire cars and road safety; and oversight of local authorities transport planning, including payment of Transport Supplementary Grant.

Secretary of State for Transport, The Rt. Hon. John MacGregor, OBE, MP
Private Secretary, P. J. Coby
Special Advisers, Mrs E. Laing; Sir Christopher Foster
Parliamentary Private Secretary, G. Riddick, MP
Minister of State for Public Transport, Roger Freeman, MP
Private Secretary, Ms S. M. Watkins
Parliamentary Private Secretary, B. Wells, MP
Minister of State for Aviation and Shipping, The Earl of Caithness, PC
Private Secretary, A. N. Bowmer
Parliamentary Private Secretary, B. Wells, MP
Parliamentary Under Secretaries, Kenneth Carlisle, MP (*Roads and Traffic*); Steven Norris, MP (*Transport in London*)
Private Secretaries, P. Downie; Mrs C. L. Spink
Parliamentary Private Secretary to Parliamentary Under Secretaries, B. Wells, MP
Parliamentary Clerk, N. Duncan
Permanent Under Secretary of State (G1), A. P. Brown
Private Secretary, Ms J. Osborne

INFORMATION

Head of Information (G5), M. J. Helm

PUBLIC TRANSPORT

Deputy Secretary (G2), N. L. J. Montagu

RAILWAYS 1

Under Secretary (G3), D. J. Rowlands, CB
Heads of Division (G5), A. Burchell; Mrs J. C. Cotton; N. K. McDonald

RAILWAYS 2

Under Secretary (G3), P. Wood
Heads of Division (G5), A. T. Baker; P. H. McCarthy; B. Wadsworth; R. S. Peal

PUBLIC TRANSPORT

Under Secretary (G3), H. M. G. Stevens
Heads of Division (G5), M. N. Lambirth; G. J. Skinner

URBAN AND GENERAL

Under Secretary (G3), J. R. Coates, CB
Heads of Division (G5), P. E. Pickering; D. R. Instone; P. R. Smith

CENTRAL SERVICES

2 Marsham Street, London SW1 3EB

Principal Establishment and Finance Officer (G2), E. B. C. Osmotherley, CB

PERSONNEL
Lambeth Bridge House, London SE1 7SB
Tel 071-238 3000
Director of Personnel (G3), R. A. Allan
Grade 5, Mrs M. Clare; R. T. Bishop; Mrs C. M. Dixon; Mrs E. A. Baker
Chief Welfare Officer (G7), Miss E. T. Haines
Grade 6, K. A. Wyatt; K. Wight; C. Payne; B. Donaldson
Chief Librarian (G6), P. Kirwan

FINANCE
Under Secretary (G3), C. R. Grimsey
Heads of Division (G5), M. J. Fuhr; J. S. Parker; J. L. Gansler; H. C. S. Derwent
Accounting Adviser (G4), A. R. Allum

INTERNAL AUDIT
Head of Branch (G6), P. Houston

CENTRAL SERVICES UNIT
Grade 4, M. R. Newey
Heads of Division (G5), D. E. Bridge; S. C. Whiteley
Grade 6, I. Harris

ECONOMICS
Chief Economic Adviser (G3), M. J. Spackman
Grade 5, T. E. Worsley; M. C. Mann

STATISTICS
Under Secretary (G3), D. W. Flaxen
Grade 5, Miss B. J. Wood; H. Collings; G. R. Emes; R. P. Donachie

CHIEF SCIENTIST
Chief Scientist (G4), Dr D. H. Metz

VEHICLE INSPECTORATE EXECUTIVE AGENCY
Chief Executive (G4), R. J. Oliver
Deputy Chief Executive (G5), J. A. T. David
Director of Administration (G6), K. Walton

DRIVING STANDARDS EXECUTIVE AGENCY
Chief Executive (G5), Dr C. M. Woodman

TRANSPORT RESEARCH LABORATORY EXECUTIVE AGENCY
Chief Executive (G3), H. J. Wootton
Deputy Chief Executive (G4), Dr R. S. Hinsley
Grade 5, Dr P. H. Bly; G. Maycock; J. Porter; Dr G. P. Tilly

DRIVER AND VEHICLE LICENSING EXECUTIVE AGENCY
Chief Executive (G3), S. R. Curtis
Heads of Division (G5), R. J. Verge; T. J. Horton; Dr R. J. M. Irvine; I. R. Heawood
Grade 6, P. G. Desborough

DRIVERS, VEHICLES AND OPERATORS INFORMATION TECHNOLOGY EXECUTIVE AGENCY
Chief Executive (G4), D. Evans
Grade 5, J. K. Griffiths

HIGHWAYS, SAFETY AND TRAFFIC

Director-General, Highways (G2), J. W. S. Dempster

ROAD PROGRAMME
Director (G3), A. Whitfield

HIGHWAYS PROGRAMME SUPPORT SERVICES
Director (G4), D. A. Holland
Heads of Division (G5), Ms A. Munro; Miss P. M. Williams; M. R. Nevard
Grade 7, G. Hoy

MOTORWAY WIDENING UNIT
Director (G4), Dr J. H. Denning
Grade 5, N. E. Firkins
Grade 6, D. E. Oddy

CONSTRUCTION PROGRAMME DIVISION
EASTERN – *Director (G4)*, A. J. Homer; *G5*, J. P. Boud
NORTH-WEST – *Director (G4)*, vacant; *G5*, E. A. Sherwin
SOUTH-EAST – *Director (G4)*, B. A. Sperring; *G5*, M. G. Quinn
SOUTH-WEST – *Director (G4)*, P. E. Nutt; *G5*, G. D. Rowe
WEST MIDLANDS – *Director (G4)*, P. E. Nutt; *G5*, J. M. Bradley
YORKSHIRE AND HUMBERSIDE – *Director (G5)*, D. York

NETWORK MANAGEMENT AND CONSTRUCTION
EAST MIDLANDS – *Director (G5)*, S. Rose
NORTHERN – *Director (G5)*, D. W. Ward

NETWORK MANAGEMENT AND MAINTENANCE
Under Secretary (G3), B. J. Billington
Heads of Division (G5), A. S. D. Whybrow; R. S. Wilson; Dr R. M. Kimber; M. R. Fawcett

HIGHWAYS POLICY AND RESOURCES
Grade 3, D. J. Lyness
Grade 5, D. J. Kershaw; J. B. W. Robins; R. W. Linnard; P. G. Collis

ENGINEERING POLICY
Director and Chief Highway Engineer (G3), T. A. Rochester
Grade 5, P. H. Dawe; J. A. Kerman; N. S. Organ

ROAD AND VEHICLE SAFETY
Under Secretary (G3), Miss S. J. Lambert
Heads of Division (G5), I. R. Jordan; Dr P. H. Martin
Grade 6, J. Winder

TRAFFIC AREA OFFICES
Traffic Commissioners and Licensing Authorities
EASTERN (*Nottingham and Cambridge*), Brig. C. M. Boyd
NORTH-EASTERN (*Newcastle upon Tyne and Leeds*), F. Whalley
NORTH-WESTERN (*Manchester*), M. S. Albu
SCOTTISH (*Edinburgh*), K. R. Waterworth
SOUTH-EASTERN AND METROPOLITAN (*Eastbourne*), Brig. M. H. Turner
WEST MIDLANDS (*Birmingham*), J. M. C. Pugh
WESTERN (*Bristol*), Air Vice-Marshal R. G. Ashford, CBE
SOUTH WALES (*Cardiff*), J. M. C. Pugh

CHIEF MECHANICAL ENGINEER'S OFFICE
Director and Chief Mechanical Engineer (G4), E. Dunn

VEHICLE CERTIFICATION EXECUTIVE AGENCY
Chief Executive (G5), D. W. Harvey

Departmental Medical Adviser (G4), vacant
Head of Medical Advisory Board (G5), Dr R. J. M. Irvine

London Region

Under Secretary (G3), I. Yass
Grade 4, P. R. Smethurst; W. E. Gallagher
Heads of Division (G5), R. J. Mance; P. E. Butler; Dr S. Chatterjee; Dr J. C. Miles; D. M. Smith

REGIONAL OFFICES

West Midlands, Birmingham – *Regional Director (G3)*, D. R. Ritchie; *Director, Network Management (G5)*, W. S. C. Wadrup
Yorkshire and Humberside, Leeds – *Regional Director (G3)*, J. P. Henry; *Director, Network Management (G5)*, J. R. Wilkins
North-West, Manchester – *Regional Director (G3)*, D. C. Renshaw; *Director, Network Management (G5)*, M. M. Niven
Northern, Newcastle upon Tyne – *Regional Director (G3)*, P. A. Shaw; *Director, Network Management and Construction (G5)*, D. W. Ward
South-West, Bristol – *Regional Director (G3)*, Ms E. A. Hopkins; *Director, Network Management (G5)*, A. P. Moss
East Midlands, Nottingham – *Regional Director (G4)*, D. J. Morrison; *Director Network Management and Construction (G5)*, S. Rose
South-East, London – *Regional Director (G3)*, J. W. Fellows; *Director, Network Management (G5)*, A. D. Rowland
Eastern, Bedford – *Regional Director (G3)*, P. F. Emms; *Director, Network Management (G5)*, R. T. Thorndike

AVIATION, SHIPPING AND INTERNATIONAL

Deputy Secretary (G2), G. R. Sunderland, CB

Civil Aviation Policy Directorate

Under Secretary (G3), A. J. Goldman
Grade 5, E. C. Neve; A. G. Thorning
Grade 6, C. C. Thame

International Aviation Directorate

Under Secretary (G3), D. C. Moss
Heads of Division (G5), D. B. Cooke; M. L. Fielder; R. S. Balme; D. S. Evans

Air Accidents Investigation Branch

Chief Inspector of Air Accidents (G4), K. P. R. Smart
Grade 5, R. C. McKinlay

International and Freight Directorate

Under Secretary (G3), J. D. Henes
Grade 5, P. D. Burgess; A. J. Hunt; J. R. Fells
Grade 6, D. J. Blackman

Channel Tunnel Safety Unit

Grade 3, E. Ryder, CB
Deputy Chief Inspector of Mines and Quarries, A. Hall

Shipping Policy, Emergencies and Security Directorate

Under Secretary (G3), R. E. Clarke
Heads of Division (G5), A. Fortnam; H. Ditmas; J. Jack, MBE; L. S. Moyle
Grade 7, A. Crosswell

Marine Directorate

Under Secretary (G3), H. B. Wenban-Smith
Heads of Division (G5), Mrs A. M. Moss; M. W. Jackson

Marine Emergency Operations and Marine Pollution Control Unit

Director (G4), C. J. Harris
Chief Coastguard (G5), Cdr. D. T. Ascona, RN (retd)
Surveyor General (G4), G. Thompson
Grade 5, P. J. Hambling; W. A. Graham; Capt. D. Bell

Marine Accidents Investigation Branch

Chief Inspector of Marine Accidents (G5), Capt. P. B. Marriott

---

THE TREASURY

Parliament Street, London SW1P 3AG
Tel 071-270 3000

The Office of the Lord High Treasurer has been continuously in commission for well over 200 years. The Lord High Commissioners of HM Treasury consist of the First Lord of the Treasury (who is also the Prime Minister), the Chancellor of the Exchequer and five junior Lords. This Board of Commissioners is assisted at present by the Chief Secretary, a Parliamentary Secretary who is also the government Chief Whip, a Financial Secretary, an Economic Secretary, the Paymaster-General, and the Permanent Secretary.

The Prime Minister and First Lord is not primarily concerned in the day-to-day aspects of Treasury business. The junior lords are government whips in the House of Commons. The management of the Treasury devolves upon the Chancellor of the Exchequer and, under him, the Chief Secretary, the Financial Secretary, the Economic Secretary and the Paymaster-General.

The Chief Secretary is responsible for the control of public expenditure; pay in the public sector, including nationalized industries but excluding the Civil Service; parliamentary pay; export credit; and efficiency in the public sector.

The Financial Secretary discharges the traditional responsibility of the Treasury for the largely formal procedure for the voting of funds by Parliament. He also has responsibility for other parliamentary financial business; the legislative programme; Inland Revenue duties and taxes; privatization policy; competition and deregulation policy; and Civil Service pay, management and industrial relations.

The Paymaster-General is responsible for Customs and Excise duties and taxes; procurement policy; environment; women's issues; charities; the environment (including energy efficiency); the EC budget; general accounting issues; the Paymaster-General's Office; and ministerial correspondence.

The Economic Secretary has responsibility for monetary policy; the Royal Mint; the financial system (including banks, building societies and other financial institutions); the Central Office of Information; the Government Actuary's Department; Forward (the Civil Service catering organization); the Central Statistical Office; international financial business; Economic and Monetary Union; stamp duties; the Valuation Office; the Department for National Savings; the Registry of Friendly Societies; the National Investment and Loans Office; public expenditure casework; and the Treasury Bulletin and Economic Briefing.

The Paymaster-General's Office (*see* page 346) acts as a clearing bank and provides financial information for all government departments; it has particular responsibility for public sector pensions. All Treasury Ministers are concerned in tax matters.

Prime Minister and First Lord of the Treasury, The Rt. Hon. John Major, MP
Chancellor of the Exchequer (£39,820), The Rt. Hon. Norman Lamont, MP

Principal Private Secretary, J. Heywood
Private Secretary, Miss S. M. A. James
Special Adviser, Dr W. Robinson
Parliamentary Private Secretary, W. Hague, MP
Parliamentary Clerk, B. O. Dyer
Chief Secretary to the Treasury (£39,820), The Rt. Hon. Michael Portillo, MP
Private Secretary, P. T. Wanless
Assistant Private Secretary, J. G. Wray
Parliamentary Private Secretary, D. Amess, MP
Financial Secretary to the Treasury (£28,175), Stephen Dorrell, MP
Private Secretary, A. W. Bridges
Special Adviser, D. Cameron
Paymaster-General (£28,175), The Rt. Hon. Sir John Cope, MP
Private Secretary, P. Child
Parliamentary Private Secretary, Dr I. Twinn, MP
Economic Secretary (£21,384), Anthony Nelson, MP
Private Secretary, M. R. Buckler
Parliamentary Secretary to the Treasury and Government Chief Whip (£33,142), The Rt. Hon. Richard Ryder, OBE, MP
Private Secretary, M. Maclean
Treasurer of HM Household and Deputy Chief Whip (£28,175), David Heathcoat-Amory, MP
Lord Commissioners of the Treasury (£18,130), G. Knight, MP; I. Patnick, OBE, MP; N. Baker, MP; T. Wood, MP; T. Boswell, MP
Assistant Whips(£18,130), T. Kirkhope, MP; D. Davis, MP; A. MacKay, MP; R. Hughes, MP; J. Arbuthnot, MP
NOTE: All salaries shown above do not include Parliamentary salary

Permanent Secretary to the Treasury (*G1*), Sir Terence Burns
Private Secretary, P. W. Owen
Second Permanent Secretaries (*G1A*), Sir Nigel Wicks, KCB, CVO, CBE (*Overseas Finance*); A. Turnbull, CB, CVO (*Public Expenditure*)
Head of Government Economics Service and Chief Economic Adviser to the Treasury, Prof. A. Budd
Head of Government Accountancy Service, Sir Alan Hardcastle
Deputy Secretaries (*G2*), vacant (*Public Finance*); H. P. Evans (*Overseas Finance*); A. J. C. Edwards (*Public Services, and General Expenditure*); R. Mountfield, CB (*Industry*); M. C. Scholar, CB (*Civil Service Management and Pay*); Mrs J. R. Lomax (*Financial Services*)

INDUSTRY

INDUSTRY, AGRICULTURE AND EMPLOYMENT GROUP

Under Secretary (*G3*), G. Monger
Assistant Secretaries (*G5*), Miss J. Barber; M. C. Mercer; D. Revolta

PUBLIC ENTERPRISES GROUP

Under Secretary (*G3*), S. A. Robson
Assistant Secretaries (*G5*), S. Sargent; T. R. Fellgett

HOME TRANSPORT AND EDUCATION GROUP

Under Secretary (*G3*), M. Whippman
Assistant Secretaries (*G5*), Miss G. M. Noble; D. J. Batt

PUBLIC SERVICES AND GENERAL EXPENDITURE

SOCIAL SERVICES AND TERRITORIAL GROUP

Under Secretary (*G3*), vacant
Assistant Secretaries (*G5*), Mrs P. Diggle; J. W. Grice; S. Kelly

LOCAL GOVERNMENT GROUP

Under Secretary (*G3*), R. I. G. Allen
Assistant Secretaries (*G5*), N. J. Ilett; R. Bent

CENTRAL UNIT ON PURCHASING

Director, P. Forshaw
Deputy Director, M. J. Hoare

TREASURY OFFICER OF ACCOUNTS GROUP

Under Secretary (*G3*), J. S. Beastall
Assistant Secretary (*G5*), I. S. Thomson

GENERAL EXPENDITURE

GENERAL EXPENDITURE POLICY GROUP

Under Secretary (*G3*), C. W. Kelly
Assistant Secretaries (*G5*), J. Hibberd; F. K. Jones; I. W. V. Taylor

DEFENCE POLICY, MANPOWER AND MATERIAL GROUP

Under Secretary (*G3*), D. J. L. Moore
Assistant Secretaries (*G5*), H. J. Bush; M. L. Williams

OVERSEAS FINANCE

INTERNATIONAL FINANCE GROUP

Under Secretary (*G3*), P. N. Sedgwick
Assistant Secretaries (*G5*), D. Owen; Ms E. Young; C. R. Pickering

AID AND EXPORT FINANCE GROUP

Under Secretary (*G3*), J. E. Mortimer
Assistant Secretaries (*G5*), S. N. Wood; Mrs S. D. Brown

EUROPEAN COMMUNITY GROUP

Under Secretary (*G3*), D. J. Bostock
Assistant Secretaries (*G5*), R. C. Pratt; N. J. Kroll; M. E. Corcoran

ACCOUNTANCY ADVICE GROUP

Grade 4, D. Cooke
Assistant Secretary (*G5*), D. Jamieson
Senior Principals (*G6*), K. E. Bradley; J. L. Constantine

CHIEF ECONOMIC ADVISER'S SECTOR

FORECASTS AND ANALYSIS GROUP

Under Secretary (*G3*), C. J. Mowl
Senior Economic Advisers (*G5*), C. M. Kelly; S. Brooks

MEDIUM TERM AND POLICY ANALYSIS GROUP

Under Secretary (*G3*), C. Riley
Assistant Secretaries (*G5*), D. Savage; S. W. Matthews

PUBLIC EXPENDITURE ECONOMICS DIVISION

Under Secretary (*G3*), Dr J. H. Rickard
Assistant Secretaries (*G5*), R. Weeden; R. B. Stannard

PUBLIC FINANCE

FISCAL POLICY GROUP

Under Secretary (*G3*), R. P. Culpin
Assistant Secretary (*G5*), A. Sharples; R. P. Short

MONETARY GROUP

Under Secretary (*G3*), P. R. C. Gray
Assistant Secretaries (*G5*), S. J. Davies; J. P. McIntyre

FINANCIAL INSTITUTIONS AND MARKETS GROUP

BANKING GROUP

Under Secretary (G3), E. J. W. Gieve
Assistant Secretaries (G5), L. Watts (*Accounts*); Miss C. Farthing; J. M. G. Taylor

SECURITIES AND INVESTMENT GROUP

Under Secretary (G3), A. Whiting
Grade 5, Dr J. P. Compton; Miss R. Thompson; A. Loughead

PUBLIC SECTOR FINANCE

Assistant Secretary (G5), A. W. Ritchie
Statistician (G7), Mrs H. F. Patterson

CIVIL SERVICE MANAGEMENT AND PAY

CIVIL SERVICE PAY

Under Secretary (G3), Mrs A. F. Case
Assistant Secretaries (G5), J. S. Cunliffe; J. Strachan; R. J. Evans
Grade 6, F. S. G. Easton

PERSONNEL POLICY GROUP

Under Secretary (G3), B. A. E. Taylor
Assistant Secretaries (G5), D. G. Pain; D. W. Rayson; S. Kingaby; N. M. Hansford; J. Dixon

MANAGEMENT POLICY AND RUNNING COSTS

Under Secretary (G3), S. Boys-Smith
Assistant Secretaries (G5), P. M. Rayner; M. Perfect

SPECIALIST SUPPORT GROUP

Grade 4, C. J. A. Chivers
Grade 5, J. B. Jones
Grade 6, J. A. Barker

CENTRAL DIVISIONS

ESTABLISHMENT AND ORGANIZATION DIVISION

Under Secretary (G3), B. M. Fox
Assistant Secretaries (G5), E. I. Cooper; A. J. T. MacAuslan; D. Todd; J. Gilhooly
Senior Principals (G6), J. W. Stevens; B. J. Porteus; D. Rampton; D. N. Walters; P. Tickner

ECONOMIC BRIEFING DIVISION

Assistant Secretary (G5), M. C. Mercer

INFORMATION DIVISION

Assistant Secretary (G5), A. Hudson
Deputy Head of Division (G6), P. L. Patterson

TREASURY REPRESENTATIVES IN USA

Economic Minister and UK Representative IMF/IBRD, D. L. C. Peretz

FORWARD (CIVIL SERVICE CATERING)

Executive Director (G4), R. V. Wheeler

THE TREASURY SOLICITOR

DEPARTMENT OF HM PROCURATOR-GENERAL AND TREASURY SOLICITOR
Queen Anne's Chambers, 28 Broadway, London SW1H 9JS
Tel 071-210 3000

The Treasury Solicitor's Department provides legal services for many government departments. Those that do not have their own lawyers are given legal advice, and both they and other departments are provided with litigation and conveyancing services. The Department also deals with Bona Vacantia. The Treasury Solicitor is also the Queen's Proctor.

Procurator-General and Treasury Solicitor (G1), G. A. Hosker, CB, QC
Deputy Treasury Solicitor (G2), T. J. G. Pratt

CENTRAL ADVISORY DIVISION

Principal Assistant Solicitor (G3), M. A. Blythe
Assistant Solicitors (G5), Mrs P. A. Dayer; M. J. Hemming
Grade 6, C. J. Gregory; Miss P. F. Henderson; C. A. R. Bird; A. K. Fraser; Mrs I. G. Letwin

LITIGATION DIVISIONS

Principal Assistant Solicitor (G3), D. A. Hogg
Grade 4, F. L. Croft; D. Brummell
Assistant Solicitors (G5), R. A. D. Jackson; A. D. Lawton; A. Leithead; C. P. J. Muttukumaru; A. J. Sandal; S. Sargant; P. F. O. Whitehurst; R. J. Phillips
Grade 6, A. P. M. Aylett; Mrs D. Babar; Miss R. M. Caudwell; M. R. M. Davis; J. N. Desai; P. D. F. Grant; J. D. Howes; B. E. McHenry; P. Messer; D. Palmer; Miss A. J. Rees; H. O. J. R. Shepheard; D. A. Stalker; A. Turek; R. J. Walter
Principals (G7), T. C. Adcock; L. Blake; Miss S. Brzezina; A. P. Chapman; J. M. Crane; M. S. Esdale; M. P. Gold; L. John-Charles; Mrs K. Lester; N. Magyar; Miss C. R. Manuel; J. B. Matthews; P. J. Moran; Miss J. A. Murnane; Miss C. R. Musaala-Mukasa; A. C. Nwanodi; F. G. O'Connell; R. C. J. Opie; R. M. Pierce; C. Stephens; M. J. Stubbs; D. Trinchero; G. Tuttle; J. C. Youdell; J. Ziegel

QUEEN'S PROCTOR DIVISION

Queen's Proctor, G. A. Hosker, CB, QC
Assistant Queen's Proctor, vacant

PROPERTY DIVISION

Principal Assistant Solicitor (G3), A. D. Osborne
Assistant Solicitors (G5), M. Benmayor; Miss G. Gilder; P. L. Noble; P. F. Nockles; M. F. Rawlins; A. M. Scarfe
Grade 6, D. G. Ager; M. V. Cooper; R. L. Coward; R. F. Good; R. D. Harris; P. K. Hicks; J. B. Howe; R. S. Lugg; R. C. Paddock; P. Page; I. Parker; A. W. Prior; P. A. Redgrove; R. J. B. Stenhouse; T. Sylvester Jones; B. D. Thurley
Senior Legal Assistants, T. Forrester; A. R. Lilleystone
Grade 7, T. P. Baker; S. R. Bould; Miss G. Bowles; A. M. Cross; Ms J. K. Dabbs; H. S. Davis; Miss M. F. Davitt; D. I. Deuchar; Mrs A. M. Foxhuntley; Q. J. Hawkes; T. J. Howe; C. R. Irving; P. S. Jaskolski; J. H. Leggatt; J. L. Leonard; Miss S. Lomas; P. J. Lowe; D. Roberts; M. D. Savage; Miss J. C. Shotter; R. C. Stewart; J. P. Trent

Establishments, Finance and Departmental Services Division

Principal Establishment and Finance and Security Officer (G5), A. J. E. Hollis
Departmental Services Manager and Deputy Establishment and Security Officer (G7), P. Pegler
Chief Accountant (G7), R. B. Smith
Head of Information Systems Development (G7), G. N. Younger
Business Support Manager (G7), P. Francis

Bona Vacantia Division

Assistant Solicitor (G5), Miss S. L. Sargant
Senior Legal Assistant, M. R. M. Davies
Grade 7, Miss H. Donnelly; Mrs P. L. Woods

Ministry of Defence Branch
Neville House, Page Street, London SW1P 4LS
Tel 071-218 4691

Principal Assistant Solicitor (G3), D. F. W. Pickup
Grade 5, J. R. J. Braggins; R. Batstone; P. Visagie
Grade 6, A. L. Norris; M. B. Sturdy; Miss V. F. Dewhurst
Grade 7, Miss E. Polledri

Department for Education Branch
Sanctuary Buildings, Great Smith Street, London SW1P 3BT
Tel 071-925 5000

Principal Assistant Solicitor (G3), R. N. Ricks
Assistant Solicitors (G5), D. J. Aries; M. Harris; A. D. Preston
Grade 6, Miss J. L. C. Brooks; S. T. Harker; N. P. Beach; C. J. Reay; C. J. Hales

Department of Employment Branch
Caxton House, Tothill Street, London SW1H 9NF
Tel 071-273 3000

Principal Assistant Solicitor (G3), H. R. L. Purse
Assistant Solicitors (G5), R. J. Baker; Mrs V. Collett; C. House; Mrs A. Leale
Grade 6, R. H. Britten; J. Hall; P. H. Kilgarriff; N. A. D. Lambert; J. K. Winayak
Grade 7, Mrs K. Booth; S. J. Gibbon; Miss C. Smith

Department of Transport Branch
2 Marsham Street, London SW1P 3EB
Tel 071-276 3000

Principal Assistant Solicitor (G3), G. H. Beetham, CB
Assistant Solicitors (G5), R. G. Bellis; G. B. Claydon; P. D. Coopman; C. W. M. Ingram; A. G. Jones; R. Lines; D. F. Pascho
Grade 6, G. W. M. Galliford; A. Lancaster; A. L. Norris; A. M. H. Prosser; S. W. Rock; N. C. Thomas,
Senior Legal Assistants, B. J. Hammersley; A. K. Johnston
Grade 7, R. C. Drabble; B. Golds; Mrs A. Heilpern; R. J. R. Jones; N. Magyar; A. W. Stewart

COUNCIL ON TRIBUNALS

7th Floor, 22 Kingsway, London WC2B 6LE
Tel 071-936 7045

The Council on Tribunals is an independent statutory body. It keeps under review the constitution and working of the various tribunals which have been placed under its general supervision, and considers and reports on administrative procedures relating to statutory inquiries. It is consulted by government departments on proposals for legislation affecting tribunals and inquiries, and on proposals where the need for an appeals procedure may arise. It also offers advice on draft primary legislation.

Some 60 tribunals are currently under the Council's supervision. The matters with which they deal range from agriculture to immigration, pensions, road traffic, taxation, and the allocation of school places.

The Scottish Committee of the Council generally considers Scottish tribunals and matters relating only to Scotland.

Members of the Council are appointed by the Lord Chancellor and the Lord Advocate. The Scottish Committee is composed partly of members of the Council designated by the Lord Advocate and partly of others appointed by him. The Parliamentary Commissioner for Administration is *ex officio* a member of both the Council and the Scottish Committee.

Chairman, Sir Cecil Clothier, KCB, QC
Members, The Parliamentary Commissioner for Administration; Mrs A. Anderson; G. A. Anderson; T. N. Biggart, CBE, WS (Chairman of the Scottish Committee); M. B. Dempsey; Prof. D. L. Foulkes; Mrs S. Friend; T. R. H. Godden, CB; C. Heaps; B. Hill, CBE; Prof. M. J. Hill; W. N. Hyde; Mrs J. U. Kellock; L. F. Read, QC
Secretary, C. W. Dyment

Scottish Committee
20 Walker Street, Edinburgh EH3 7HR
Tel 031-220 1236

Chairman, T. N. Biggart, CBE, WS
Members, The Parliamentary Commissioner for Administration; G. A. Anderson; W. J. Campbell; Mrs C. A. M. Davis; T. R. H. Godden, CB; J. Langan; Lady Scott, CBE, WS
Secretary, Ms L. Wilkie

Tribunals – *see* pages 387–90

UNIVERSITIES FUNDING COUNCIL

Northavon House, Coldharbour Lane, Bristol BS16 1QD
Tel 0272-317317

The Universities Funding Council was established under the provisions of the Education Reform Act 1988, and came into existence formally on 1 April 1989. It will be replaced by the Higher Education Funding Council for England (*see* page 316) in April 1993.

UNRELATED LIVE TRANSPLANT REGULATORY AUTHORITY

Department of Health, Room 518, Eileen House, 80–94 Newington Causeway, London SE1 6EF
Tel 071-972 2736

The Unrelated Live Transplant Regulatory Authority (ULTRA) is a statutory body established on 1 January 1990. In every case where the transplant of an organ within the definition of the Human Organ Transplants Act 1989 is proposed between a living donor and a recipient who are not genetically related, the proposal must be referred to ULTRA. Applications must be made by registered medical practitioners.

The Authority comprises a chairman and 11 members appointed by the Secretary of State for Health. The secretariat is provided by Department of Health Officials.

Chairman, Prof. M. Bobrow

Members, Revd Prof. G. R. Dunstan; Dr P. A. Dyer; Mrs D. Eccles; Prof. M. G. McGeown; Sir Michael McNair-Wilson; S. G. Macpherson; Dr N. P. Mallick; Prof. J. R. Salaman; Miss F. Smithers; Miss S. M. Taber; J. Wellbeloved
Administrative Secretary, P. Pudlo
Medical Secretary, Dr R. Hangartner

URBAN REGENERATION AGENCY

The agency will start work in early 1993 under legislation planned for autumn 1992, its primary aim being to bring 150,000 acres of vacant and derelict land in towns and cities back into use and ease the pressure for development in the countryside.

Chairman, The Lord Walker of Worcester, MBE, PC

WALES YOUTH AGENCY

Leslie Court, Lon-y-Llyn, Caerphilly, Mid Glamorgan CF8 1BQ
Tel 0222-880088

The Wales Youth Agency is a non-departmental public body funded by the Welsh Office. Its functions include the encouragement and development of the partnership between statutory and voluntary agencies relating to young people; the promotion of staff development and training; and the extension of marketing and information services in the relevant fields. The board of directors is appointed by the Secretary of State for Wales; directors do not receive a salary.

Chairman of the Board of Directors, G. Davies
Vice-Chairman of the Board of Directors, Dr H. Williamson
Executive Director, B. Williams

OFFICE OF WATER SERVICES

Centre City Tower, 7 Hill Street, Birmingham B5 4UA
Tel 021-625 1300

The Office of Water Services (Ofwat) was set up under the Water Act 1989 and came into being on 1 September 1989. Its role is to support the Director-General of Water Services, who regulates the economic framework of the water industry in England and Wales. His main duties are to ensure that water companies (*see* page 514) comply with the terms of their appointments (or licences) and to protect the interests of water consumers. The Director-General has established ten regional customer service committees which investigate complaints and identify customer concerns. The Director-General is independent of ministerial control and directly accountable to Parliament.

Director-General of Water Services, I. C. R. Byatt

WELSH OFFICE

The Welsh Office has responsibility in Wales for ministerial functions relating to health and personal social services; education, except for terms and conditions of service and student awards; training; the Welsh language and culture; local government; housing; water and sewerage; environmental protection; sport; agriculture and fisheries; forestry; land use, including town and country planning and countryside and nature conservation; new towns; ancient monuments and historic buildings; roads; tourism; financial assistance to industry; the urban programme in Wales; the operation of the European Regional Development Fund in Wales and other European Community matters; civil emergencies; and all financial aspects of these matters, including Welsh rate support grant. It has oversight responsibilities for economic affairs and regional planning in Wales.

Gwydyr House, Whitehall, London SW1A 2ER
Tel 071-270 3000

Secretary of State for Wales, The Rt. Hon. David Hunt, MBE, MP
Private Secretary, Miss J. C. Simpson
Special Adviser, M. McManus
Parliamentary Private Secretary, J. Bowis, MP
Minister of State, The Rt. Hon. Sir Wyn Roberts, MP
Private Secretary, H. O. Jones
Parliamentary Private Secretary, D. Tredinnick, MP
Parliamentary Under-Secretary, Gwilym Jones, MP
Private Secretary, Ms J. Allen
Parliamentary Clerk, V. R. Watkin
Permanent Secretary (G1), Sir Richard Lloyd Jones, KCB
Private Secretary, P. J. Higgins

Cathays Park, Cardiff CF1 3NQ
Tel 0222-825111

Deputy Secretaries (G2), J. W. Lloyd, CB; J. F. Craig

ESTABLISHMENT GROUP

Principal Establishment Officer (G3), G. C. G. Craig
Heads of Divisions (G5), R. M. Abel; G. A. Thomas; Ms H. Angus
Senior Economic Adviser (G5), O. T. Hooker
Chief Statistician (G5), Dr M. P. G. Pepper
Head of Health Intelligence Unit (G6), G. J. Cockell
Principals (G7), R. J. Callen; J. F. Bowley; Mrs J. Leitch; P. Lunn; Mrs B. Hollick; M. Stevenson; P. H. Skellon; Miss C. M. Owen; C. Tudor
Economic Adviser (G7), V. W. F. McPherson
Principal Research Officers (G7), E. Darwin; Mrs M. A. J. Gronow
Statisticians (G7), D. D. Baird; M. R. Brand; G. P. Davies; J. T. Fletcher; K. Francombe; Ms C. Fullerton; P. J. Fullerton; E. Swires Hennessy; J. D. James; H. M. Jones; R. Jones; J. D. Kinder; Mrs S. Stansfield

CADW: WELSH HISTORIC MONUMENTS

Brunel House, Fitzalan Road, Cardiff CF2 1UY
Tel 0222-465511

An executive agency of the Welsh Office.

Chief Executive, E. A. J. Carr
Director of Properties in Care, J. H. Pavitt
Director of Policy and Administration, R. W. Hughes
Conservation Architect (G6), J. D. Hogg
Principal Inspector of Ancient Monuments and Historic Buildings, J. R. Avent
Inspectors of Ancient Monuments and Historic Buildings, J. K. Knight; A. D. McLees; Dr S. E. Rees; R. C. Turner; M. J. Yates

FINANCE GROUP

Principal Finance Officer (G3), R. A. Wallace
Heads of Divisions (G4), C. L. Jones; *(G5)*, D. H. Jones; L. A. Pavelin; J. Shortridge; Mrs E. A. Taylor; B. Wilcox
Grade 6, M. G. Horlock

Principals (*G7*), Mrs J. Blamire; B. R. Davies; M. H. Harper; Mrs H. Usher; I. R. Miller; D. A. Powell; H. F. Rawlings
Head of Internal Audit (*G7*), D. Howarth

HOUSING, HEALTH AND SOCIAL SERVICES POLICY GROUP

Head of Group (*G3*), R. W. Jarman
Heads of Divisions (*G5*), D. Adams; R. J. Davies; Mrs B. J. M. Wilson; A. Thornton
Chief Inspector, Social Services Inspectorate (*Wales*) (*G5*), D. G. Evans
Deputy Chief Inspectors, J. K. Fletcher; R. C. Woodward
Grade 6, A. C. Elmer
Principals (*G7*), J. A. Atkins; Mrs K. Cassidy; C. Coombs; P. Godden-Kent; D. B. Hilbourne; Miss E. M. Jones; R. Patterson; I. Price Jones; D. M. Rolph; M. Shannahan; I. I. Thomas; A. C. Wood
Social Services Inspectors (*G7*), D, Barker; D. A. Brushett; G. H. Davies; Miss R. E. Evans; I. Forster; Mrs J. Jenkins; J. F. Mooney; C. D. Vyvyan; Mrs P. White
Principal Professional and Technology Officers (*G7*), G. N. Harding; W. Ross

HEALTH PROFESSIONAL GROUP

Chief Medical Officer (*G3*), Dr D. J. Hine

Environmental Health Sub Group (*HPG M1*)

Deputy Chief Medical Officer (*G4*), Dr A. M. George
Senior Medical Officers (*G5*), Dr R. Jacobs; Dr J. Ludlow
Environmental (*Non Medical*) *Health Adviser* (G6), R. Alexander

Hospital Services Sub Group (*HPG M2*)

Principal Medical Officer (*acting*) (*G4*), Dr D. W. Owen
Senior Medical Officers (*G5*), Dr B. Davies; Dr D. Salter; (*part-time*) Dr J. N. P. Hughes

Community and Primary Care Services Sub Group (*HPG M3*)

Principal Medical Officer (*G4*), Dr J. K. Richmond
Senior Medical Officers (*G5*), Dr A. K. Thomas; Dr B. Fuge; Dr R. Owen

Divisional Medical Officer (*G5*), Dr D. E. Davies
Medical Officers (*G6*), Dr J. W. Crossley; Dr J. D. Andrews; Dr H. Williams; Dr T. Lyons; Dr T. I. Evans; Dr N. E. Thomas
Chief Dental Officer (*G5*), D. M. Heap
Senior Dental Officer (*G5*), B. A. C. Turner
Dental Officers (*G6*), J. D. O. Parkholm; Ms J. Bullen; T. M. Davies; T. A. Williams
Chief Scientific Adviser (*G5*), Dr J. A. V. Pritchard
Deputy Scientific Adviser (*G6*), Dr E. O. Crawley
Chief Pharmaceutical Adviser (*G5*), Dr G. B. A. Veitch
Deputy Pharmaceutical Adviser (*G6*), Mrs D. Kay Roberts

NURSING DIVISION

Chief Nursing Officer (*G3*), Miss M. Bull
Deputy Chief Nursing Officer (*G4*), Mrs B. Melvin
Nursing Officers (*G6*), Mrs R. Cohen; Mrs S. M. Drayton; Miss G. Harris; Dr D. Keyzer; M. F. Tonkin

NATIONAL HEALTH SERVICE DIRECTORATE

Director of the NHS in Wales, J. W. Owen
Heads of Divisions (*G5*), D. H. Jones; D. A. Pritchard; N. E. Thomas; B. Wilcox; R. C. Williams
Senior Principals (*G6*), D. M. Timlin; Mrs D. Vass
Principals (*G7*), Mrs J. D. Annand; M. A. C. Brooke; M. D. Chown; P. Davenport; J. Duggan; R. J. Dodd; J. H. Grainger; R. J. Keveren; E. J. McDonald; R. A. Jones; Ms J. Plastow; E. Roberts; P. Williams; Mrs J. E. Wood; K. Orchard; R. O'Sullivan; K. S. Sleight

LEGAL DIVISION

Legal Adviser (*G3*), D. G. Lambert
Assistant Solicitors (*G5*), P. J. Murrin; J. H. Turnbull
Grade 6, H. D. Evans; J. D. H. Evans; Miss A. L. Ferguson; C. P. Jones; C. G. Longville; A. J. Park; Mrs A. T. Parkes; A. J. Watkins; A. Widdrington
Senior Legal Assistants (*G7*), Mrs K. R. Davies; T. R. E. Heywood; Ms T. L. Jones; Miss K. Nicholas; M. Partridge; Mrs P. Turnbull; Miss E. Stallard; Mrs R. J. Wiles; D. H. J. Williams

INFORMATION DIVISION

Director of Information (*G5*), H. G. Roberts
Chief Press Officer (*G7*), E. M. Bowen, MVO
Principal Publicity Officer (*G7*), W. J. Edwards

ECONOMIC AND REGIONAL POLICY GROUP

Head of Group (*G3*), M. J. Cochlin
Heads of Divisions (*G5*), M. E. Bevan; M. J. Clancy; Miss E. N. M. Davies; M. L. Evans; D. T. Richards
Senior Principals (*G6*), H. D. Brodie; G. W. George
Principals (*G7*), D. Beames; M. H. Bendon; C. J. Burdett; M. C. Dunn; Ms J. M. Gordon; Mrs A. M. Jackson; A. D. Lansdown; Miss J. E. Paulett; J. N. Roberts; M. A. J. Roberts; A. J. Davies; Dr J. Milligan

INDUSTRY DEPARTMENT

Director (*G3*), C. D. Stevens
Industrial Director (*G4*), J. Cameron
Heads of Divisions (*G5*), D. Jones; G. T. Evans
Business Services Division Director (*G6*), Dr R. J. Loveland
Principals (*G7*), N. Barry; C. F. Francis; J. A. Grimes; G. Jones; J. H. Roberts; K. Smith; R. Waller; J. W. Wallington; J. Neal; G. Madden; I. Shuttleworth

EDUCATION DEPARTMENT

Head of Department (*G3*), S. H. Martin
Heads of Divisions (*G5*)°, W. G. Davies; H. Evans; B. J. Mitchell
Head of Division (*G6*)°, R. C. Simpson
Principals (*G7*)°, Mrs J. Booker; P. F. Brown; D. A. Bullen; Mrs L. L. Changkee; C. E. J. Daniels; R. O. Evans; B. Hayward-Blake; Mrs J. Hopkins; J. R. Howells; G. W. Jones; Mrs C. Peat; M. G. Richards; A. Whittaker

OFFICE OF HM CHIEF INSPECTOR FOR SCHOOLS IN WALES

Chief Inspector (*G4*), R. L. James
Staff Inspectors (*G5*)°, S. J. Adams; W. R. Jenkins; T. E. Parry; G. Thomas; P. Thomas; R. Thomas; M. J. F. Wynn
There are 50 Grade 6 Inspectors.

TRANSPORT, PLANNING AND ENVIRONMENT GROUP

Head of Group (*G3*), P. R. Gregory
Director of Highways (*G4*), K. J. Thomas°
Deputy Director of Highways (*G5*), J. G. Evans*
Heads of Divisions (*G5*), A. H. H. Jones; D. I. Westlake°; H. R. Bollington°; (*G6*), D. M. Timlin

---

Based at:
°Ty Glan Road, Llanishen, Cardiff CF4 5WE. Tel: 0222-761456
*Government Buildings, Pinerth Road, Rhos on Sea, Colwyn Bay LL28 4UL. Tel: 0492-44261

Superintending Engineers (G6), J. R. Rees; B. H. Hawker, OBE*
Superintending Estates Officer (G6), G. K. Hoad
Senior Principal (G6), P. R. Marsden
Scientific Adviser (G6), Dr H. Prosser
Chief Planning Adviser (G6), W. P. Roderick
Principals (G7), P. M. Bishop; W. M. P. Cooper; M. D. Evans; T. W. Hunter; H. R. Payne; D. Powell°; G. R. Jones; D. Hadfield°; G. Quarrell; D. C. Quinlan
Principal Planning Officers (G7), D. B. Courtier; L. Owen; J. V. Spear
Principal Research Officers (G7), A. S. Dredge; Ms L. J. Roberts
Principal Estates Officer (G7), R. W. Wilson
Principal Professional and Technology Officers, Highways Directorate (G7), P. Dunstan°; M. J. Gilbert; I. A. Grindulais; A. P. Howcroft; A. L. Perry; R. H. Powell°; S. C. Shouler; C. W. W. Smart°; J. Collins°; K. J. Alexander°; R. H. Hooper*

PLANNING INSPECTORATE

Principal Planning Inspectors (G5), F. Cosgrove; R. Pierce; D. Sheers
Senior Housing and Planning Inspectors (G6), T. W. B. Barnes; J. H. Chadwick; R. Davies; P. V. Farrow; M. Griffin; G. Rees; G. Sloan; S. B. Wild; D. N. Wilks

HM INSPECTORATE OF POLLUTION FOR WALES

Inspector, Hazardous Wastes (G7), G. Taylor
Inspector, Radiation and Chemicals (G7), Dr C. Hardman
Inspector, Water (G7), A. A. Houlden

AGRICULTURE DEPARTMENT

Head of Department (G3), O. Rees, CB
Heads of Divisions (G5), G. Podmore; D. R. Thomas; L. K. Walford
Principals (G7), Mrs B. Harding; A. G. Huws; R. A. Norris; R. F. Patterson; C. E. Taylor°; B. E. Price°; P. N. S. Wolfenden
Divisional Executive Officers (G7), W. K. Griffiths (*Carmarthen*); E. Hughes (*Caernarfon*); J. C. Alexander (*Llandrindod Wells*)

WOMEN'S NATIONAL COMMISSION

Level 2, Caxton House, Tothill Street, London SW1H 9NF
Tel 071-273 5486

The Women's National Commission is an advisory committee to the Government whose remit is to ensure by all possible means that the informed opinions of women are given their due weight in the deliberations of the Government. The Commission's fifty members are all women who are elected or appointed by national organizations with a large and active membership of women. The organizations include the women's sections of the major political parties, trades unions, religious groups, professional women's organizations and other bodies broadly representative of women.

Based at:
°Ty Glan Road, Llanishen, Cardiff CF4 5WE. Tel: 0222-761456
*Government Buildings, Pinerth Road, Rhos on Sea, Colwyn Bay LL28 4UL. Tel: 0492-44261

Government Co-Chairman, The Baroness Denton of Wakefield, CBE (*nominated by the Prime Minister* 1992)
Elected Co-Chairman, Mrs E. Martin (*elected* 1991)
Secretary, Ms M. Jones

WOMEN'S ROYAL VOLUNTARY SERVICE

234–244 Stockwell Road, London SW9 9SP
Tel 071-416 0146

The Women's Royal Voluntary Service (WRVS) assists government departments, local authorities and voluntary bodies in organizing and carrying out welfare and emergency work for the community on a nationwide network operated through area, county, district and London borough organizers. Activities include work for the elderly and handicapped, for young families, and for offenders and their families; non-medical work in hospitals; welfare work for HM Forces and for Service families; and trained teams to assist in national and local emergencies.

National Chairman, The Hon. Mrs M. Corsar

Law Courts and Offices

THE JUDICIAL COMMITTEE OF THE PRIVY COUNCIL

The Judicial Committee of the Privy Council is the final court of appeal from courts of the United Kingdom dependencies and courts of independent Commonwealth countries which have retained the right of appeal (Antigua and Barbuda, the Bahamas, Barbados, Belize, Brunei, Dominica, The Gambia, Jamaica, Kiribati, Mauritius, New Zealand, Singapore, St Christopher and Nevis, St Lucia, St Vincent and the Grenadines, Trinidad and Tobago, and Tuvalu). The Committee also hears appeals from courts of the Channel Islands and the Isle of Man, the disciplinary and health committees of the medical and allied professions, and some ecclesiastical appeals under the Pastoral Measure 1983.

The Judicial Committee includes the Lord Chancellor, the Lords of Appeal in Ordinary (*see* below) and other members of the Privy Council who hold or have held high judicial office, and certain judges from the Commonwealth. Commonwealth appeals are usually heard by a board of five judges.

PRIVY COUNCIL OFFICE (JUDICIAL DEPARTMENT), Downing Street, London SW1A 2AJ. Tel: 071-270 0483
Registrar of the Privy Council, D. H. O. Owen
Chief Clerk, K. N. Stringer

The Judicature of England and Wales

The legal system of England and Wales is separate from those of Scotland and Northern Ireland and differs from them in law, judicial procedure and court structure, although there is a common distinction between civil law (disputes between individuals) and criminal law (acts harmful to the community).

The supreme judicial authority for England and Wales is the House of Lords, which is the ultimate Court of Appeal from all courts in Great Britain and Northern Ireland (except criminal courts in Scotland). As a Court of Appeal it consists of the Lord Chancellor and the Lords of Appeal in Ordinary (Law Lords).

The Supreme Court of Judicature comprises the Court of Appeal, the Crown Court and the High Court of Justice. The High Court of Justice is the superior civil court and is divided into three divisions. The Chancery Division is concerned mainly with equity, bankruptcy and contentious probate business; the Queen's Bench Division deals with commercial and maritime law, with civil cases not assigned to other courts, and hears appeals from lower courts; and the Family Division deals with matters relating to family law. Sittings are held at the Royal Courts of Justice in London or at 26 Crown Court centres outside the capital. High Court judges sit alone to hear cases at first instance. Appeals from lower courts are heard by two or three judges, or by single judges of the appropriate division.

The decision to prosecute in the majority of cases rests with the Crown Prosecution Service, an independent prosecuting body established in 1986 to serve all of England and Wales (*see* pages 381–2). At the head of the service is the Director of Public Prosecutions, who discharges her duties under the superintendence of the Attorney-General. Certain categories of offence continue to require the Attorney-General's consent for prosecution.

Minor criminal offences (summary offences) are dealt with in magistrates' courts, which usually consist of three unpaid lay magistrates (Justices of the Peace) sitting without a jury, who are advised on points of law and procedure by a legally-qualified clerk to the justices. There were approximately 30,000 Justices of the Peace at 1 June 1992. In busier courts a full-time, salaried and legally-qualified stipendiary magistrate presides alone. Cases involving people under 16 are heard in youth courts, specially constituted magistrates' courts which sit apart from other courts. Preliminary proceedings in a serious case to decide whether there is evidence to justify committal for trial in the Crown Court are also held in the magistrates' courts. Appeals from magistrates' courts against sentence or conviction are made to the Crown Court. Appeals upon a point of law are made to the High Court, and may go on to the House of Lords.

The Crown Court sits in about 90 centres, divided into six circuits, and is presided over by High Court judges, full-time circuit judges, and part-time recorders, sitting with a jury in all trials which are contested. It deals with trials of the more serious criminal offences, the sentencing of offenders committed for sentence by magistrates' courts (when the magistrates consider their own power of sentence inadequate), and appeals from lower courts. Magistrates usually sit with a circuit judge or recorder to deal with appeals and committals for sentence. Appeals from the Crown Court, either against sentence or conviction, are made to the Court of Appeal (Criminal Division), presided over by the Lord Chief Justice. A further appeal from the Court of Appeal to the House of Lords can be brought if a point of law of general public importance is considered to be involved.

Most minor civil cases are dealt with by the county courts, of which there are about 300 (details may be found in the local telephone directory). For cases involving small claims there are special arbitration facilities and simplified procedures. Where there are financial limits on county court jurisdiction, claims which exceed those limits may be tried in the county courts with the consent of the parties, or in certain circumstances on transfer from the High Court. Outside London, bankruptcy proceedings can be heard in designated county courts. Magistrates' courts can deal with certain classes of civil case and committees of magistrates licence public houses, clubs and betting shops. For the implementation of the Children Act 1989 on 14 October 1991, a new structure of hearing centres was set up for family proceedings cases, involving magistrates' courts (family proceedings courts), divorce county courts, family hearing centres and care centres.

Appeals in family matters heard in the family proceedings courts go to the Family Division of the High Court; affiliation appeals and appeals from decisions of the licensing committees of magistrates go to the Crown Court. Appeals from the High Court and county courts are heard in the Court of Appeal (Civil Division), presided over by the Master of the Rolls, and may go on to the House of Lords.

Coroners' courts investigate violent and unnatural deaths or sudden deaths where the cause is unknown. Cases may be brought before a local coroner (a senior lawyer or doctor) by doctors, the police, various public authorities or members of the public. Where a death is sudden and the cause is unknown, the coroner may order a post-mortem examination to determine the cause of death rather than hold an inquest in court.

RECENT CHANGES

Responsibility for the finance, organization and management of magistrates' courts was transferred from the Home Secretary to the Lord Chancellor from 1 April 1992. Responsibility for the criminal and procedural law remains with the Home Secretary. A Lord Chancellor's Department junior minister in the House of Commons (*see* page 333) was appointed to improve further Parliament's access to the work of the Department.

Most of the provisions of the Criminal Justice Act 1991 came into effect in October 1992. The Act changed sentencing procedures and practice; set out criteria for custodial sentences; increased the range of community penalties; made changes to the ways in which young people are dealt with in the criminal justice system; and provided more effective and efficient administration of criminal justice services, in particular the magistrates' courts, the probation service and the accommodation of remand prisoners. Probation was established as a sentence in its own right; partly-suspended prison sentences were abolished; and the system of parole and remission of sentence was completely revised, with remission being abolished, prisoners being required to serve at least half their sentence in custody, a system of discretionary early release being introduced for those serving terms of more than four years, and all prisoners becoming eligible for recall throughout the whole of the original sentence on conviction of an imprisonable offence. The power to decide on the release of discretionary life sentence prisoners was transferred from the Home Secretary to the Parole Board; the use as evidence of a video recording of an early interview with a child victim of crime was allowed; a framework for abolishing remand to prison custody for 15- and 16-year-old boys was established; and 17-year-olds were brought within the jurisdiction of the juvenile courts, which were renamed the youth courts. Some provisions of the Act were implemented in October 1991, at which time HM Inspectorate of Probation was placed on a statutory footing and the Home Secretary was authorized to provide for the operation and management of prisons by the private sector.

THE HOUSE OF LORDS
AS FINAL COURT OF APPEAL

The Lord High Chancellor
The Rt. Hon. the Lord Mackay of Clashfern, *born* 1927, *apptd* 1987

Lords of Appeal in Ordinary (each £100,880)

Rt. Hon. Lord Keith of Kinkel, *born* 1922, *apptd* 1977
Rt. Hon. Lord Templeman, MBE, *born* 1920, *apptd* 1982
Rt. Hon. Lord Griffiths, MC, *born* 1923, *apptd* 1985
Rt. Hon. Lord Ackner, *born* 1920, *apptd* 1986
Rt. Hon. Lord Goff of Chieveley, *born* 1926, *apptd* 1986
Rt. Hon. Lord Jauncey of Tullichettle, *born* 1925, *apptd* 1988
Rt. Hon. Lord Lowry, *born* 1919, *apptd* 1988
Rt. Hon. Lord Browne-Wilkinson, *born* 1930, *apptd* 1991
Rt. Hon. Lord Mustill, *born* 1931, *apptd* 1992
Rt. Hon. Lord Slynn of Hadley, *born* 1930, *apptd* 1992
Registrar, The Clerk of the Parliaments (*see* page 224)

SUPREME COURT OF JUDICATURE

COURT OF APPEAL

The Master of the Rolls (£100,880), The Rt. Hon. Sir Thomas Bingham, *born* 1933, *apptd* 1992
Secretary, Miss V. Seymour
Clerk, D. G. Grimmett

Lords Justices of Appeal (each £96,720)

Rt. Hon. Sir Tasker Watkins, VC, GBE, *born* 1918, *apptd* 1980
Rt. Hon. Sir Michael Fox, *born* 1921, *apptd* 1981
Rt. Hon. Sir Francis Purchas, *born* 1919, *apptd* 1982
Rt. Hon. Sir Brian Dillon, *born* 1923, *apptd* 1982
Rt. Hon. Sir Roger Parker, *born* 1923, *apptd* 1983
Rt. Hon. Sir Anthony Lloyd, *born* 1929, *apptd* 1984
Rt. Hon. Sir Brian Neill, *born* 1923, *apptd* 1985
Rt. Hon. Sir Martin Nourse, *born* 1932, *apptd* 1985
Rt. Hon. Sir Iain Glidewell, *born* 1924, *apptd* 1985
Rt. Hon. Sir John Balcombe, *born* 1925, *apptd* 1985
Rt. Hon. Sir Ralph Gibson, *born* 1922, *apptd* 1985
Rt. Hon. Sir John Stocker, MC, TD, *born* 1918, *apptd* 1986
Rt. Hon. Sir Harry Woolf, *born* 1933, *apptd* 1986
Rt. Hon. Sir Patrick Russell, *born* 1926, *apptd* 1987
Rt. Hon. Dame Elizabeth Butler-Sloss, DBE, *born* 1933, *apptd* 1988
Rt. Hon. Sir Murray Stuart-Smith, *born* 1927, *apptd* 1988
Rt. Hon. Sir Christopher Staughton, *born* 1933, *apptd* 1988
Rt. Hon. Sir Michael Mann, *born* 1930, *apptd* 1988
Rt. Hon. Sir Donald Farquharson, *born* 1928, *apptd* 1989
Rt. Hon. Sir Anthony McCowan, *born* 1928, *apptd* 1989
Rt. Hon. Sir Roy Beldam, *born* 1925, *apptd* 1989
Rt. Hon. Sir Andrew Leggatt, *born* 1930, *apptd* 1990
Rt. Hon. Sir Michael Nolan, *born* 1928, *apptd* 1991
Rt. Hon. Sir Richard Scott, *born* 1934, *apptd* 1991
Rt. Hon. Sir Johan Steyn, *born* 1932, *apptd* 1992
Rt. Hon. Sir Paul Kennedy, *born* 1935, *apptd* 1992

Ex officio Judges, The Lord High Chancellor; the Lord Chief Justice of England; the Master of the Rolls; the President of the Family Division; and the Vice-Chancellor

COURT OF APPEAL (CRIMINAL DIVISION)

Judges, The Lord Chief Justice of England; the Master of the Rolls; Lords Justices of Appeal; and Judges of the High Court of Justice

COURTS-MARTIAL APPEAL COURT

Judges, The Lord Chief Justice of England; the Master of the Rolls; Lords Justices of Appeal; and Judges of the High Court of Justice

HIGH COURT OF JUSTICE
CHANCERY DIVISION

President, The Lord High Chancellor
The Vice-Chancellor (£96,720), The Rt. Hon. Sir Donald Nicholls, *born* 1933, *apptd* 1991
Clerk, W. Northfield, BEM

Judges (each £87,620)

Hon. Sir John Vinelott, *born* 1923, *apptd* 1978
Hon. Sir Jean-Pierre Warner, *born* 1924, *apptd* 1981
Hon. Sir Peter Gibson, *born* 1934, *apptd* 1981

Hon. Sir Mervyn Davies, MC, TD, *born* 1918, *apptd* 1982
Hon. Sir Jeremiah Harman, *born* 1930, *apptd* 1982
Hon. Sir Leonard Hoffman, *born* 1934, *apptd* 1985
Hon. Sir John Knox, *born* 1925, *apptd* 1985
Hon. Sir Peter Millett, *born* 1932, *apptd* 1986
Hon. Sir Andrew Morritt, CVO, *born* 1938, *apptd* 1988
Hon. Sir William Aldous, *born* 1936, *apptd* 1988
Hon. Sir John Mummery, *born* 1938, *apptd* 1989
Hon. Sir Francis Ferris, TD, *born* 1932, *apptd* 1990
Hon. Sir John Chadwick, ED, *born* 1941, *apptd* 1991
Hon. Sir Jonathan Parker, *born* 1937, *apptd* 1991

HIGH COURT OF JUSTICE IN BANKRUPTCY

Judges, The Vice-Chancellor and judges of the Chancery Division of the High Court

COMPANIES COURT

Judges, The Vice Chancellor and judges of the Chancery Division of the High Court

PATENT COURT (APPELLATE SECTION)
Tel 071-936 6000

Judges, The Hon. Mr Justice Aldous; The Hon. Mr Justice Mummery; The Hon. Mr Justice Morritt; The Hon. Mr Justice Hoffman

QUEEN'S BENCH DIVISION

The Lord Chief Justice of England (£108,940) The Rt. Hon. the Lord Taylor of Gosforth, *born* 1930, *apptd* 1992
Secretary, Mrs J. Simpson
Clerk, J. Bond

Judges (each £87,620)

Hon. Sir Leslie Boreham, *born* 1918, *apptd* 1972
Hon. Sir Haydn Tudor Evans, *born* 1920, *apptd* 1974
Hon. Sir Ronald Waterhouse, *born* 1926, *apptd* 1978
Hon. Sir Maurice Drake, DFC, *born* 1923, *apptd* 1978
Hon. Sir Barry Sheen, *born* 1918, *apptd* 1978
Hon. Sir Christopher French, *born* 1925, *apptd* 1979
Hon. Sir Charles McCullough, *born* 1931, *apptd* 1981
Hon. Sir John Leonard, *born* 1926, *apptd* 1981
Hon. Sir David Hirst, *born* 1925, *apptd* 1982
Hon. Sir John Stewart Hobhouse, *born* 1932, *apptd* 1982
Hon. Sir Oliver Popplewell, *born* 1927, *apptd* 1983
Hon. Sir William Macpherson, TD, *born* 1926, *apptd* 1983
Hon. Sir Philip Otton, *born* 1933, *apptd* 1983
Hon. Sir Michael Hutchison, *born* 1933, *apptd* 1983
Hon. Sir Simon Brown, *born* 1937, *apptd* 1984
Hon. Sir Anthony Evans, *born* 1934, *apptd* 1984
Hon. Sir Mark Saville, *born* 1936, *apptd* 1985
Hon. Sir Christopher Rose, *born* 1937, *apptd* 1985
Hon. Sir Swinton Thomas, *born* 1931, *apptd* 1985
Hon. Sir Richard Tucker, *born* 1931, *apptd* 1985
Hon. Sir Robert Gatehouse, *born* 1924, *apptd* 1985
Hon. Sir Patrick Garland, *born* 1929, *apptd* 1985
Hon. Sir John Roch, *born* 1934, *apptd* 1985
Hon. Sir Michael Turner, *born* 1931, *apptd* 1985
Hon. Sir John Alliott, *born* 1932, *apptd* 1986
Hon. Sir Harry Ognall, *born* 1934, *apptd* 1986
Hon. Sir Konrad Schiemann, *born* 1937, *apptd* 1986
Hon. Sir John Owen, *born* 1925, *apptd* 1986
Hon. Sir Denis Henry, *born* 1931, *apptd* 1986
Hon. Sir Humphrey Potts, *born* 1931, *apptd* 1986
Hon. Sir Richard Rougier, *born* 1932, *apptd* 1986
Hon. Sir Ian Kennedy, *born* 1930, *apptd* 1986
Hon. Sir Nicholas Phillips, *born* 1938, *apptd* 1987
Hon. Sir Robin Auld, *born* 1937, *apptd* 1988
Hon. Sir Malcolm Pill, *born* 1938, *apptd* 1988
Hon. Sir Stuart McKinnon, *born* 1938, *apptd* 1988
Hon. Sir Mark Potter, *born* 1937, *apptd* 1988
Hon. Sir Henry Brooke, *born* 1936, *apptd* 1988
Hon. Sir Igor Judge, *born* 1941, *apptd* 1988
Hon. Sir Edwin Jowitt, *born* 1929, *apptd* 1988
Hon. Sir Michael Morland, *born* 1929, *apptd* 1989
Hon. Sir Mark Waller, *born* 1940, *apptd* 1989
Hon. Sir Roger Buckley, *born* 1939, *apptd* 1989
Hon. Sir Anthony Hidden, *born* 1936, *apptd* 1989
Hon. Sir Michael Wright, *born* 1932, *apptd* 1990
Hon. Sir Charles Mantell, *born* 1937, *apptd* 1990
Hon. Sir John Blofeld, *born* 1932, *apptd* 1990
Hon. Sir Peter Cresswell, *born* 1944, *apptd* 1991
Hon. Sir Anthony May, *born* 1940, *apptd* 1991
Hon. Sir John Laws, *born* 1945, *apptd* 1992
Hon. Dame Ann Ebsworth, DBE, *born* 1937, *apptd* 1992
Hon. Sir Simon Tuckey, *born* 1941, *apptd* 1992
Hon. Sir David Latham, *born* 1942, *apptd* 1992

FAMILY DIVISION

President (£96,720) Rt. Hon. Sir Stephen Brown, *born* 1929, *apptd* 1988
Secretary, Mrs S. Leung
Clerk, Mrs S. Bell

Judges (each £87,620)

Hon. Sir Kenneth Hollings, MC, *born* 1918, *apptd* 1971
Hon. Sir John Wood, MC, *born* 1922, *apptd* 1977
Hon. Sir Michael Eastham, *born* 1920, *apptd* 1978
Hon. Dame Margaret Booth, DBE, *born* 1933, *apptd* 1979
Hon. Sir Anthony Ewbank, *born* 1925, *apptd* 1980
Hon. Sir John Waite, *born* 1932, *apptd* 1982
Hon. Sir Anthony Hollis, *born* 1927, *apptd* 1982
Hon. Sir Mathew Thorpe, *born* 1938, *apptd* 1988
Hon. Sir Edward Cazalet, *born* 1936, *apptd* 1988
Hon. Sir Alan Ward, *born* 1938, *apptd* 1988
Hon. Sir Scott Baker, *born* 1937, *apptd* 1988
Hon. Sir Robert Johnson, *born* 1933, *apptd* 1989
Hon. Sir Douglas Brown, *born* 1931, *apptd* 1989
Hon. Sir Donald Rattee, *born* 1937, *apptd* 1989
Hon. Dame Joyanne Bracewell, DBE, *born* 1934, *apptd* 1990
Hon. Sir Michael Connell, *born* 1939, *apptd* 1991

RESTRICTIVE PRACTICES COURT

President, (*acting*), The Hon. Mr Justice Warner
Lay Members, N. L. Salmond; I. G. Stewart; B. M. Currie; L. Robertson; R. Garrick; Z. A. Silberstone

OFFICIAL REFEREES' COURTS

St Dunstan's House, 133–137 Fetter Lane, London EC4A 1HD
Tel 071–936 7429

Judges (each £76,180)

His Hon. Judge Newey, QC
His Hon. Judge Lewis, QC
His Hon. Judge John Davies, QC
His Hon. Judge Fox-Andrews, QC
His Hon. Judge Bowsher, QC
His Hon. Judge Loyd, QC
His Hon. Judge Forbes, QC

LORD CHANCELLOR'S DEPARTMENT – *see* Government Departments and Public Offices

SUPREME COURT DEPARTMENTS AND OFFICES

Royal Courts of Justice, London WC2A 2LL
Tel 071–936 6000

Administrator (£36,178–£41,120), G. A. Calvett

CENTRAL OFFICE OF THE SUPREME COURT

Senior Master of the Supreme Court (QBD), and Queen's Remembrancer (£64,064), W. K. Topley
Masters of the Supreme Court (QBD) (£52,520), P. B. Creightmore; D. L. Prebble; G. H. Hodgson; R. L. Turner; J. Trench; M. Tennant; P. Miller; N. O. G. Murray; I. H. Foster; G. H. Rose
Chief Clerk (Central Office) (£24,379–£29,073), C. F. Jones

COURT OF APPEAL (CIVIL DIVISION) OFFICE

Registrar (£64,064), J. D. R. Adams
Chief Clerk (£17,367–£21,724), Miss H. M. Goddard

CRIMINAL APPEAL OFFICE

Registrar (£64,064), M. McKenzie, QC
Deputy Registrar (£36,178–£41,120), J. P. Stockton
Chief Clerk (£24,379–£29,073), K. M. Dickerson

COURTS-MARTIAL APPEALS OFFICE

Registrar, M. McKenzie, QC
Chief Clerk, K. M. Dickerson

CROWN OFFICE OF THE SUPREME COURT

Master of the Crown Office, and Queen's Coroner and Attorney (£64,064), M. McKenzie, QC
Head of Crown Office (£39,402–£44,390), Mrs L. Knapman

SUPREME COURT TAXING OFFICE

Chief Master (£64,064), P. T. Hurst
Masters of the Supreme Court (£52,520), C. R. N. Martyn; C. A. Prince; M. Ellis; T. H. Seager Berry (*Taxing Master*); C. C. Wright
Chief Clerk, vacant
Principal Taxing Officer (£24,379–£29,073), T. J. Ryan

EXAMINERS OF THE COURT

(Empowered to take examination of witnesses in all Divisions of the High Court)

M. F. Meredith-Hardy; B. Rathbone; N. W. Briggs; R. Jacobs

CHANCERY CHAMBERS

Chief Master of the Supreme Court (£64,064), J. M. Dyson
Masters of the Supreme Court (£52,520), J. S. Gowers; G. A. Barratt; J. I. Winegarten
Chief Clerk (£17,367–£21,724), G. Robinson
Conveyancing Counsel of the Supreme Court, J. Monckton; S. G. Maurice; M. J. Roth

BANKRUPTCY DEPARTMENT

Thomas More Building, Royal Courts of Justice, Strand, London WC2A 2LL
Tel 071–936 6000

Chief Registrar (£64,064), T. L. Dewhurst
Chief Clerk (£17,367–£21,724), M. Brown

OFFICIAL RECEIVERS' DEPARTMENT

21 Bloomsbury Street, London WC1B 3SS
Tel 071–323 3090

Senior Official Receiver, J. R. Donnison
Official Receivers, M. J. Pugh; L. T. Cramp; M. W. A. Sanderson; G. J. A. Harp

COMPANIES COURT

Thomas More Building, Royal Courts of Justice, London WC2A 2LL
Tel 071–936 6000

Registrar, M. Buckley
Chief Clerk, A. Roberts
Senior Official Receiver, Companies Department, J. R. Donnison

RESTRICTIVE PRACTICES COURT

Thomas More Building, Royal Courts of Justice, London WC2A 2LL
Tel 071–936 6000

Clerk of the Court, M. Buckley
Chief Clerk, A. Roberts

PRINCIPAL REGISTRY (FAMILY DIVISION)

Somerset House, London WC2R 1LP
Tel 071–936 6000

Senior District Judge (£64,064), G. B. N. A. Angel
District Judges (£52,520), T. G. Guest; J. E. Artro-Morris; R. B. Rowe; B. P. F. Kenworthy-Browne; Mrs K. T. Moorhouse; D. T. A. Davies; Mrs N. Pearce; M. J. Segal; R. Conn; Miss I. M. Plumstead; G. J. Maple; Miss H. C. Bradley; K. J. White; A. R. S. Bassett-Cross
Secretary (£24,379–£29,073), R. P. Knight

DISTRICT PROBATE REGISTRARS

Birmingham and Stoke-on-Trent, C. Marsh
Brighton and Maidstone, M. N. Emery
Bristol, Exeter and Bodmin, P. L. Speyer
Ipswich, Norwich and Peterborough, E. R. Alexander
Leeds, Lincoln and Sheffield, A. P. Dawson
Liverpool, Lancaster and Chester, B. J. Thomas
Llandaff, Bangor, Carmarthen and Gloucester, R. F. Yeldham
Manchester and Nottingham, M. A. Moran
Newcastle, Carlisle, York and Middlesbrough, P. Sanderson
Oxford, R. R. Da Costa
Winchester, A. K. Biggs

ADMIRALTY AND COMMERCIAL REGISTRY AND MARSHAL'S OFFICE

Royal Courts of Justice, London WC2A 2LL
Tel 071–936 6000

Registrar (£64,064), P. Miller
Marshal and Chief Clerk (£24,379–£29,073), A. Ferrigno

COURT OF PROTECTION

Stewart House, 24 Kingsway, London WC2B 6HD
Tel 071-269 7000

Master (£64,064), Mrs A. B. Macfarlane

OFFICIAL SOLICITOR'S DEPARTMENT

81 Chancery Lane, London WC2A 1DD

Official Solicitor to the Supreme Court (£48,000–£55,700), H. D. S. Venables
Deputy Official Solicitor (£39,402–£44,390), H. J. Baker
Chief Clerk (£24,379–£29,078), Mrs V. J. Carter

ELECTION PETITIONS OFFICE

Room E218, Royal Courts of Justice, Strand, London WC2A 2LL
Tel 071-936 6131

The office accepts petitions and deals with all matters relating to the questioning of Parliamentary, European Parliament and local government elections, and with applications for relief under the Representation of the People legislation.

Prescribed Officer, W. K. Topley
Chief Clerk, C. I. P. Denyer

OFFICE OF THE LORD CHANCELLOR'S VISITORS

Trevelyan House, 30 Great Peter Street, London SW1
Tel 071-210 8563

Legal Visitor, A. R. Tyrrell
Medical Visitors, A. G. Fullerton; F. E. Kenyon; K. Kahn; P. A. Morris; D. Parr; J. Roberts

---

OFFICE OF THE JUDGE ADVOCATE OF THE FLEET

The Law Courts, Barker Road, Maidstone ME16 8EQ
Tel 0622-754966

Judge Advocate of the Fleet, His Hon. Judge Waley, VRD, QC

OFFICE OF THE JUDGE ADVOCATE-GENERAL OF THE FORCES

(*Joint Service for the Army and the Royal Air Force*)
22 Kingsway, London WC2B 6LE
Tel 071-430 5335

Judge Advocate-General (£68,400), His Hon. Judge J. W. Rant, QC
Vice-Judge Advocate-General (£61,600), G. L. Chapman
Assistant Judge Advocates-General (£40,050–£46,200), E. G. Moelwyn-Hughes; A. P. Pitts; D. M. Berkson; M. A. Hunter; T. R. King; T. G. Pontius; J. P. Camp
Deputy Judge Advocates (£28,050–£39,250), Miss S. E. Woollam; R. C. C. Seymour

---

HIGH COURT AND CROWN COURT CENTRES

First-tier centres deal with both civil and criminal cases and are served by High Court and circuit judges. Second-tier centres deal with criminal cases only and are served by High Court and circuit judges. Third-tier centres deal with criminal cases only and are served only by circuit judges.

MIDLAND AND OXFORD CIRCUIT

First-tier - Birmingham, Lincoln, Nottingham, Oxford, Stafford, Warwick
Second-tier - Leicester, Northampton, Shrewsbury, Worcester
Third-tier - Coventry, Derby, Grimsby, Hereford, Peterborough, Stoke-on-Trent, Wolverhampton
Circuit Administrator, L. Oates, 2 Newton Street, Birmingham B4 7LU. Tel: 021-627 1700
Courts Administrators, Birmingham Group, V. C. Grove; *Nottingham Group*, Mrs E. A. Folman; *Stafford Group*, A. F. Parker

NORTH-EASTERN CIRCUIT

First-tier - Leeds, Newcastle upon Tyne, Sheffield, Teesside
Second-tier - York
Third-tier - Beverley, Doncaster, Durham, Huddersfield, Wakefield
Circuit Administrator, S. W. L. James, 17th Floor, West Riding House, Albion Street, Leeds LS1 5AA. Tel: 0532-441841
Courts Administrators, Leeds Group, P. Delany; *Newcastle upon Tyne Group*, K. Budgen; *Sheffield Group*, G. Bingham

NORTHERN CIRCUIT

First-tier - Carlisle, Liverpool, Manchester, Preston
Third-tier - Barrow-in-Furness, Bolton, Burnley, Lancaster
Circuit Administrator, P. M. Harris, Aldine House, West Riverside, New Bailey Street, Salford M3 5EU. Tel: 061-832 9571
Courts Administrators, Manchester Group, A. H. Howard; *Liverpool Group*, D. A. Beaumont; *Preston Group*, Mrs A. Prior

SOUTH-EASTERN CIRCUIT

First-tier - Chelmsford, Lewes, Norwich
Second-tier - Ipswich, London (Central Criminal Court), Luton, Maidstone, Reading, St Albans
Third-tier - Aylesbury, Bury St Edmunds, Cambridge, Canterbury, Chichester, Guildford, King's Lynn, London (Croydon, Harrow, Inner London Session House, Isleworth, Kingston upon Thames, Knightsbridge, Middlesex Guildhall, Snaresbrook, Southwark and Wood Green), Southend
The High Court in Greater London sits at the Royal Courts of Justice.
Circuit Administrator, B. Cooke, New Cavendish House, 18 Maltravers Street, London WC2R 3EU. Tel: 071-936 7235
Deputy Circuit Administrator, Miss B. J. Kenny
Courts Administrators, Chelmsford Group, P. Handcock; *Maidstone Group*, Mrs H. Hartwell; *Kingston Group*, P. M. Thomas; *London (Civil)*, P. Risk; *London (Crime)*, G. F. Addicott

WALES AND CHESTER CIRCUIT

First-tier - Caernarfon, Cardiff, Chester, Mold, Swansea
Second-tier - Carmarthen, Merthyr Tydfil, Newport, Welshpool
Third-tier - Dolgellau, Haverfordwest, Knutsford, Warrington
Circuit Administrator, D. Howe, Churchill House, Churchill Way, Cardiff CF1 4HH. Tel: 0222-396925
Courts Administrators, Cardiff Group, G. Jones; *Chester Group*, T. D. Beckett

WESTERN CIRCUIT

First-tier - Bristol, Exeter, Truro, Winchester
Second-tier - Dorchester, Gloucester, Plymouth
Third-tier - Barnstaple, Bournemouth, Devizes, Newport (IOW), Portsmouth, Salisbury, Southampton, Swindon, Taunton
Circuit Administrator, G. Jones, CBE, Bridge House, Sion Place, Clifton, Bristol BS8 4BN. Tel: 0272-743763
Courts Administrators, Bristol Group, A. C. Butler; *Exeter Group*, J. Ardern; *Winchester Group*, P. Matthews

CIRCUIT JUDGES

**Senior Circuit Judges*, each £76,180
Circuit Judges, each £64,064

MIDLAND AND OXFORD CIRCUIT

W. A. L. Allardice; F. A. Allen; B. J. Appleby, QC; M. J. Astill; I. J. Black, QC; D. W. Brunning;

F. A. Chapman; F. L. Clark, QC; P. N. R. Clark; R. R. B. Cole; P. F. Crane; P. J. Crawford, QC; R. H. Curtis, QC; I. T. R. Davidson, QC; P. N. de Mille; T. M. Dillon, QC; C. H. Durman; J. F. Evans, QC; B. A. Farrer, QC; Miss E. N. Fisher; J. E. Fletcher; R. J. H. Gibbs, QC; H. G. A. Gosling; J. Hall; M. K. Harrison-Hall; T. R. Heald; J. R. Hopkin; R. H. Hutchinson; J. E. M. Irvine; R. P. V. Jenkins; J. G. Jones; J. T. C. Lee; M. H. Mander; K. Matthewman, QC; R. G. May; H. R. Mayor, QC; P. W. Medd, OBE, QC; K. S. W. Mellor, QC; N. Micklem; P. R. Morrell; A. J. H. Morrison; M. D. Mott; A. J. D. Nicholl; J. F. F. Orrell; D. S. Perrett, QC; C. J. Pitchers; R. F. D. Pollard; F. M. Potter; D. P. Pugsley; J. R. Pyke; D. E. Roberts; J. A. O. Shand; J. R. S. Smyth; P. J. Stretton; C. S. Stuart-White; G. C. Styler; H. C. Tayler, QC; A. B. Taylor; K. J. Taylor; M. B. Ward; R. L. Ward, QC; D. J. R. Wilcox; D. H. Wild; H. Wilson; J. W. Wilson; B. Woods; C. G. Young

NORTH-EASTERN CIRCUIT

J. Altman; T. G. F. Atkinson; G. Baker, QC; P. M. Baker, QC; T. W. Barber; J. M. A. Barker; G. N. Barr Young; D. R. Bentley, QC; A. N. J. Briggs; D. M. A. Bryant; J. W. M. Bullimore; B. Bush; M. C. Carr; M. L. Cartlidge; P. J. Charlesworth; G. J. K. Coles, QC; J. A. Cotton; J. Crabtree; M. T. Cracknell; W. H. R. Crawford, QC; P. J. Fox, QC; A. N. Fricker, QC; M. S. Garner; W. Hannah; G. F. R. Harkins; J. A. Henham; D. Herrod, QC; P. M. L. Hoffman; R. Hunt; A. E. Hutchinson, QC; J. R. Johnson; N. H. Jones, QC; T. D. Kent-Jones, TD; C. F. Kolbert; G. M. Lightfoot; A. C. Macdonald; Miss M. B. M. MacMurray, QC; M. K. Mettyear; A. L. Myerson, QC; D. A. Orde; Miss H. E. Paling; R. A. Percy; *D. M. Savill, QC; A. Simpson; J. Stephenson; R. A. R. Stroyan, QC; R. C. Taylor; G. M. Vos; M. Walker; P. H. C. Walker

NORTHERN CIRCUIT

H. H. Andrew, QC; J. F. Appleton; J. R. Arthur, DFC; A. W. Bell; R. C. W. Bennett; Miss I. Bernstein; M. S. Blackburn; R. Brown; I. B. Campbell; F. B. Carter, QC; B. I. Caulfield; D. Clark; G. P. Crowe, QC; *R. E. Davies, QC (*Recorder of Manchester*); M. Dean, QC; Miss A. E. Downey; B. R. Duckworth; S. B. Duncan; D. M. Evans, QC; S. J. D. Fawcus; D. G. F. Franks; J. A. D. Gilliland, QC; R. G. Hamilton; J. A. Hammond; R. J. Hardy; F. D. Hart, QC; M. Hedley; T. D. T. Hodson; F. R. B. Holloway; Miss M. Holt; G. W. Humphries; A. C. Jolly; H. A. Kershaw; P. M. Kershaw, QC (*Commercial Circuit Judge*); H. L. Lachs; C. N. Lees; J. M. Lever, QC; R. J. D. Livesey, QC; R. Lockett; J. H. Lord; D. Lynch; D. I. Mackay; B. C. Maddocks; C. J. Mahon; J. A. Morgan; M. O'Donoghue; F. D. Owen, TD; F. D. Paterson; R. E. I. Pickering; D. A. Pirie; A. J. Proctor; M. A. G. Sachs; H. S. Singer; Miss A. H. Steel; Miss E. M. Steel; I. R. Taylor, QC; J. P. Townend; P. W. Urquhart; I. S. Webster; W. R. Wickham (*Recorder of Liverpool*); B. Woodward

SOUTH-EASTERN CIRCUIT

J. R. S. Adams; F. J. Aglionby; M. J. Anwyl-Davies, QC; J. A. Baker; J. B. Baker, QC; M. J. D. Baker; P. V. Baker, QC; A. F. Balston; C. J. A. Barnett, QC; K. Bassingthwaighte; G. A. Bathurst Norman; P. T. S. Batterbury, TD; P. J. L. Beaumont, QC; N. E. Beddard; F. E. Beezley; G. J. Binns; M. Birks; P. C. Bowsher, QC; A. V. Bradbury; P. N. Brandt; L. J. Bromley, QC; A. E. Brooks; R. G. Brown; J. M. Bull, QC; G. N. Butler, QC; *N. M. Butter, QC; H. J. Byrt, QC; C. V. Callman; B. E. Capstick, QC; B. L. Charles, QC; A. W. Clark; D. J. Clarkson, QC; P. C. Clegg; M. Cohen, QC; S. H. Colgan; P. H. Collins; C. C. Colston, QC; S. S. Coltart; J. S. Colyer, QC; C. D. Compston; T. A. C. Coningsby, QC; R. D. Connor; M. J. Cook; R. A. Cooke; G. H. Coombe; M. R. Coombe; A. Cooray; Margaret D. Cosgrave; Dr E. Cotran; R. C. Cox; D. L. Croft, QC; G. L. Davies; I. H. Davies, TD; L. J. Davies, QC; W. L. M. Davies, QC; W. N. Denison, QC; K. M. Devlin; M. N. Devonshire, TD; A. E. J. Diamond, QC; A. H. Durrant; C. M. Edwards; Q. T. Edwards, QC; F. P. L. Evans; J. K. Q. Evans; S. J. Evans; J. D. Farnworth; J. J. Finney; T. J. Forbes, QC; P. Ford; J. J. Fordham; G. C. F. Forrester; J. Fox-Andrews, QC; Ms D. A. Freedman A. Garfitt; R. Gee; L. Gerber; S. A. Goldstein; P. W. Goldstone; M. B. Goodman; C. G. M. Gordon; J. B. Gosschalk; J. H. Gower, QC; M. Graham, QC; P. B. Greenwood; D. J. Griffiths; G. D. Grigson; R. B. Groves, TD, VRD; N. T. Hague, QC; P. J. Halnan; J. Hamilton; R. E. Hammerton; C. R. H. Hardy; B. Hargrove, OBE, QC; J. P. Harris, DSC, QC; M. F. Harris; R. G. Hawkins, QC; A. H. Head; M. R. Hickman; J. C. Hicks, QC; A. N. Hitching; D. Holden; A. C. W. Hordern, QC; R. W. Howe; Sir David Hughes-Morgan, Bt., CB, CBE; J. G. Hull, QC; J. Hunter; M. J. Hyam; Dr P. J. E. Jackson; C. P. James; M. Kennedy, QC; A. M. Kenny; L. G. Krikler; L. H. C. Lait; P. St J. H. Langan, QC; Capt. J. B. R. L. Langdon, RN; G. F. B. Laughland, QC; R. Laurie; T. Lawrence; D. M. Levy, QC; E. Lewis, QC; D. T. Lloyd; F. R. Lockhart; D. B. D. Lowe; R. H. Lownie; Mrs N. M. Lowry; R. J. Lowry, QC; J. A. T. Loyd, QC; R. D. Lymbery, QC (*Common Serjeant*); K. M. McHale; K. A. Machin, QC; M. B. McMullan; K. C. Macrae; J. R. Main, QC; B. A. Marder, QC; F. J. M. Marr-Johnson; L. A. Marshall; O. S. Martin, QC; N. A. Medawar, QC; D. J. Mellor; J. H. E. Mendl; G. D. Mercer; A. L. Mildon, QC; D. Q. Miller; S. G. Mitchell, QC; E. F. Monier-Williams; D. Morton Jack; J. I. Murchie Mrs N. F. Negus; M. H. D. Neligan; J. H. R. Newey, QC; C. W. F. Newman, QC; Mrs M. F. Norrie; Suzanne F. Norwood; P. W. O'Brien; C. R. Oddie; M. A. Oppenheimer; A. Owen; D. A. Paiba; R. H. S. Palmer; M. C. Parker, QC; Miss V. A. Pearlman; J. R. Peppitt, QC; F. H. L. Petre; A. J. Phelan; N. A. J. Philpot; D. C. Pitman; J. R. Platt; P. B. Pollock; H. C. Pownall, QC; R. J. C. V. Prendergast; J. E. Previté, QC; B. H. Pryor, QC; J. E. Pullinger; J. W. Rant, QC; E. V. P. Reece; G. K. Rice; M. S. Rich, QC; K. A. Richardson, QC; G. Rivlin, QC; J. H. P. Roberts; D. A. H. Rodwell, QC; J. W. Rogers, QC; G. H. Rooke, TD, QC; P. C. R. Rountree; K. W. R. Rubin; J. H. Rucker; T. R. G. Ryland; R. B. Sanders; Maj.-Gen. D. H. D. Selwood; J. L. Sessions; J. D. Sheerin; *G. J. Shindler, QC; D. R. A. Sich; A. G. Simmons; K. T. Simpson; P. R. Simpson; M. Singh, QC; J. K. E. Slack, TD; P. M. J. Slot; F. B. Smedley, QC; C. M. Smith, QC; R. J. Southan; S. B. Spence; *R. O. C. Stable, QC; E. Stockdale; C. J. Sumner; W. F. C. Thomas; A. A. R. Thompson, QC; A. G. Y. Thorpe; A. H. Tibber; C. H. Tilling; A. M. Troup; S. Tumim; J. T. Turner; C. J. M. Tyrer; Mrs A. P. Uziell-Hamilton; J. E. van der Werff; L. J. Verney, TD (*Recorder of London*); A. O. R. Vick, QC; Miss M. S. Viner, QC; A. F. Waley, VRD, QC; R. Walker; D. B. Watling, QC; V. B. Watts; F. J. White; S. M. Willis; C. G. P. Woodford; G. N. Worthington; E. G. Wrintmore; K. H. Zucker, QC

WALES AND CHESTER CIRCUIT

T. R. Crowther, QC; G. H. M. Daniel; R. D. G. David, QC; J. B. S. Diehl, QC; D. E. H. Edwards; G. O. Edwards, QC; Lord Elystan-Morgan; T. M. Evans, QC; W. N. Francis; M. Gibbon, QC; D. M. Hughes; G. J. Jones; H. D. H. Jones; G. E. Kilfoil; T. E. I. Lewis-Bowen; D. G. Morgan; D. C. Morton; T. H. Moseley, QC; D. A. Phillips; D. W. Powell; E. J. Prosser, QC; H. W. J. ap Robert; H. E. P. Roberts, QC; *J. C. Rutter; S. M. Stephens, QC; D. B. Williams, TD, QC; H. V. Williams, QC; R. G. Woolley

WESTERN CIRCUIT

M. F. Addison; S. T. Bates, QC; C. L. Boothman; M. J. L. Brodrick; R. D. H. Bursell, QC; J. R. Chalkley; Sir Jonathan Clarke; M. G. Cotterill; Hazel Counsell; J. A. Cox; Mrs S. P. Darwall Smith; Mrs L. H. Davies; M. Dyer; *P. Fallon, QC; P. D. Fanner; B. J. F. Galpin; D. L. Griffiths; I. S. Hill, QC; G. B. Hutton; R. E. Jack, QC; A. C. Lauriston, QC; D. McCarraher, VRD; Miss S. M. D. McKinney; I. S. McKintosh; I. G. McLean; J. G. McNaught; T. J. Milligan; E. G. Neville; S. K. O'Malley; S. K. Overend; R. C. Pryor, QC; J. N. P. Rudd; D. A. Smith, QC; W. E. M. Taylor; H. J. M. Tucker, QC; D. M. Webster, QC; J. H. Weeks, QC; J. R. Whitley; J. A. J. Wigmore; K. M. Willcock, QC; J. C. Willis; J. H. Wroath

RECORDERS

J. D. R. Adams; I. D. G. Alexander, QC; M. P. Allweis; Miss C. Alton; W. P. Andreae-Jones, QC; P. J. Andrews, QC; R. A. Anelay; A. R. L. Ansell; Ms L. E. Appleby, QC; J. F. A. Archer, QC; Rt. Hon. P. K. Archer, QC, MP; A. J. Arlidge, QC; E. K. Armitage; R. Ashton; P. Ashworth, QC; J. M. Aspinall; B. Atchley; N. J. Atkinson, QC; M. G. Austin-Smith, QC; W. S. Aylen, QC; J. F. Badenoch, QC; P. G. N. Badge; A. B. Baillie; M. F. Baker, QC; N. R. J. Baker, QC; G. S. Barham; A. Barker, QC; B. J. Barker, QC; D. Barker, QC; R. O. Barlow; D. M. W. Barnes, QC; T. P. Barnes, QC; W. E. Barnett, QC; J. E. Barry; G. R. Bartlett, QC; J. C. T. Barton, QC; D. C. Bate; S. D. Batten, QC; J. J. Baughan, QC; R. A. Bayliss; J. F. Beashel; C. H. Beaumont; C. O. M. Bedingfield, TD, QC; C. O. J. Behrens; R. W. Belben; R. Bell, QC; The Hon. M. J. Beloff, QC; D. P. Bennett; H. P. D. Bennett, QC; J. M. Bennett; P. Bennett, QC; R. S. A. Benson; K. C. Bentall; H. L. Bentham; D. M. Berkson; M. Bethel, QC; J. P. V. Bevan; J. C. Beveridge, QC; P. V. Birkett, QC; P. W. Birts, QC; J. E. Bishop; B. M. Black; J. A. Blair-Gould; A. N. H. Blake; C. Bloom, QC; D. J. Blunt, QC; J. G. Boal; G. T. K. Boney, QC; D. J. Boulton; P. H. Bowers; J. J. Boyle; R. W. A. Bray; D. J. Brennan, QC; M. L. Brent, QC; G. J. B. G. Brice, QC; J. N. W. Bridges-Adams; A. J. Brigden; P. J. Briggs; R. P. Brittain; D. K. Brown; S. C. Brown, QC; A. J. N. Brunner; A. Bueno, QC; D. L. Bulmer; J. M. J. Burford, QC; J. P. Burgess; J. K. Burke, QC; J. P. Burke, QC; M. A. B. Burke-Gaffney, QC; H. W. Burnett, QC; M. R. Burr; M. J. Burton, QC; A. J. Butcher, QC; A. N. L. Butterfield, QC; R. J. Buxton, QC; M. D. Byrne

Mrs B. A. Calvert, QC; D. Calvert-Smith; Miss S. M. C. Cameron, QC; A. N. B. Campbell; J. Q. Campbell; G. M. C. Carey, QC; A. C. Carlile, QC, MP; The Lord Carlisle of Bucklow, PC, QC; H. B. H. Carlisle, QC; R. Carus, QC; B. E. F. Catlin; J. J. Cavell; J. A. Chadwin, QC; N. M. Chambers, QC; B. W. Chedlow, QC; J. M. Cherry, QC; J. R. Cherryman, QC; C. F. Chruszcz; C. H. Clark, QC; A. P. Clarke, QC; C. S. C. S. Clarke, QC; D. C. Clarke, QC; P. W. Clarke; S. P. Clarke; R. N. B. Clegg, QC; W. Clegg, QC; G. M. Clifton; P. J. Cockcroft; D. J. Cocks, QC; J. J. Coffey; T. A. Coghlan; W. J. Coker; J. R. Cole; N. J. Coleman; N. B. C. Coles, QC; P. N. Collier; A. D. Collins, QC; J. M. Collins; A. D. Colman, QC; Ms M. Colton; Viscount Colville of Culross, QC; Mrs J. R. Comyns; P. R. C. Coni, QC; G. D. Conlin; J. G. Connor; C. S. Cook; Miss B. P. Cooper, QC; S. M. Corkhill; T. G. E. Corrie; P. J. Cosgrove; G. W. A. Cottle; Miss D. R. Cotton, QC; J. S. Coward, QC; P. R. Cowell; B. R. E. Cox, QC; P. J. Cox, DSC, QC; D. I. Crigman, QC; M. L. S. Cripps; C. A. Critchlow; J. F. Crocker; I. W. Crompton; J. D. Crowley, QC; E. J. R. Crowther, OBE; W. R. H. Crowther, QC; H. M. Crush; Miss E. A. M. Curnow, QC; P. D. Curran; J. W. O. Curtis; M. J. Curwen; Ms J. M. P. Daley; A. J. G. Dalziel; S. C. Darwall-Smith; G. W. Davey; C. P. M. Davidson; D. T. A. Davies; Mrs J. Davies; A. W. Dawson; D. H. Day, QC; J. J. Deave; J. B. Deby, QC; P. G. Dedman; C. F. Dehn, QC; P. A. de la Piquerie; M. A. de Navarro, QC; W. E. Denny, CBE, QC; R. L. Denyer, QC; S. C. Desch, QC; H. A. D. de Silva; J. E. Devaux; A. D. Dinkin, QC; I. J. Dobkin; R. A. M. Doggett; Ms B. Dohmann, QC; A. M. Donne, QC; S. M. Duffield; P. R. Dunkels; W. H. Dunn, QC; R. T. Dutton; J. A. Dyson, QC

D. Eady, QC; Ms D. B. Eaglestone; T. K. Earnshaw; J. S. Eastwood; H. W. P. Eccles, QC; D. F. Elfer, QC; G. Elias, QC; B. J. Elliott; D. R. Ellis; R. M. Englehart, QC; G. A. Ensor; D. A. Evans, QC; D. H. Evans, QC; D. R. Evans, QC; E. C. Evans-Lombe, QC; Sir Graham Eyre, QC; W. D. Fairclough; D. J. Farrer, QC; K. J. Farrow; E. J. Faulks; M. H. Fauvelle; R. Fernyhough, QC; P. Fingret; P. S. Fish; D. P. Fisher; G. D. Flather, QC; P. E. J. Focke, QC; J. D. Foley; R. A. Fordham; A. J. Forrest; J. R. Foster, QC; R. M. Foster; R. H. K. Frisby, QC; J. H. Fryer-Spedding, OBE; M. T. Fugard, CB

W. M. Gage, QC; M. Gale, QC; J. R. B. Geake; A. C. Geddes; A. H. Gee, QC; D. S. Gee; D. S. Geey; C. A. H. Gibson; N. B. D. Gilmour, QC; L. Giovene; A. T. Glass, QC; H. B. Globe; Miss A. F. Goddard, QC; H. K. Goddard, QC; H. A. Godfrey, QC; Ms L. S. Godfrey, QC; J. B. Goldring, QC; A. R. Goldsack, QC; P. H. Goldsmith, QC; L. C. Goldstone; I. F. Goldsworthy; A. J. J. Gompertz, QC; A. A. Gordon; J. P. Gorman, QC; T. J. C. Goudie, QC; C. O. G. Gould; A. A. Goymer; G. Gozem; A. S. Grabiner, QC; C. A. St J. Gray, QC; G. Gray, QC; J. M. Gray; R. I. Gray, QC; R. M. K. Gray, QC; B. S. Green, QC; H. Green, QC; J. C. Greenwood; J. G. Grenfell; S. P. Grenfell; R. D. Grey, QC; J. C. Griffiths, CMG, QC; J. P. G. Griffiths; L. Griffiths; J. D. Griggs; M. G. Grills; M. S. E. Grime, QC; Mrs H. M. Grindrod, QC; P. Grobel; M. A. W. Grundy; S. J. Gullick

A. S. Hacking, QC; Mrs C. M. A. Hagen; M. F. Haigh; J. W. Haines; D. R. Halbert; D. J. Hale; V. E. Hall; D. T. Hallchurch; Ms H. C. Hallett, QC; A. B. R. Hallgarten, QC; G. Hallon; A. W. Hamilton, QC; D. R. D. Hamilton; G. M. Hamilton, TD, QC; S. T. Hammond; J. Hampton; J. L. Hand, QC; Miss R. S. A. Hare, QC; R. D. Harman, QC; P. J. Harrington; D. M. Harris, QC; G. C. W. Harris, QC; M. G. V. Harrison, QC; R. M. Harrison, QC; C. P. Hart-Leverton, QC; B. Harvey; C. S. Harvey, MBE, TD; M. L. T. Harvey, QC; R. O. Havery, QC; T. S. A. Hawkesworth, QC; R. J. Haworth; R. W. P. Hay;

Prof. D. J. Hayton; R. Hayward-Smith, QC; A. J. Healey; T. B. Hegarty; G. E. Heggs; R. A. Henderson, QC; R. H. Q. Henriques, QC; P. J. M. Heppel; R. B. Hickman; B. J. Higgs, QC; E. M. Hill, QC; J. W. Hillyer; A. J. H. Hilton, QC; Ms E. J. Hindley; W. T. J. Hirst; J. D. Hitchen; S. A. Hockman, QC; C. R. Hodson; The Hon. Mary Hogg, QC; A. J. C. Hoggett, QC; Ms B. M. Hoggett, QC; C. J. Holland, QC; D. A. Hollis, VRD, QC; R. C. Holman; C. J. Holmes; J. F. Holt; R. M. Hone; A. T. Hoolahan, QC; A. Hooper, QC; The Lord Hooson, QC; K. A. D. Hornby; M. Horowitz, QC; C. P. Hotten; B. F. Houlder; R. Houlker, QC; M. Howard, QC, MP; N. J. G. Howarth; C. I. Howells; M. J. Hubbard, QC; M. Hucker; A. P. G. Hughes, QC; P. T. Hughes; T. M. Hughes; J. Hugill, QC; D. R. N. Hunt, QC; P. J. Hunt, QC; I. G. A. Hunter, QC; M. Hussain; B. A. Hytner, QC

N. J. Inglis-Jones, QC; D. A. Inman; A. B. Issard-Davies; D. G. A. Jackson; M. R. Jackson; R. M. Jackson, QC; I. E. Jacob; P. J. Jacobs; C. E. F. James; N. F. B. Jarman, QC; J. M. Jarvis, QC; D. A. Jeffreys, QC; J. Jeffs, QC; J. D. Jenkins, QC; D. B. Johnson, QC; M. H. Johnson; A. G. H. Jones; G. R. Jones; R. A. Jones, QC; S. E. Jones; T. G. Jones; T. J. C. Joseph; W. H. Joss; P. S. L. Joyce, QC; M. D. L. Kalisher, QC; M. L. Kallipetis, QC; G. H. Kamil; J. W. Kay, QC; M. R. Kay, QC; M. L. Keane; K. R. Keen, QC; D. W. Keene, QC; C. L. Kelly; C. J. B. Kemp; D. A. M. Kemp, QC; L. D. Kershen; G. M. Khayat; R. I. Kidwell, QC; A. W. P. King; T. R. A. King, QC; W. M. Kingston; A. T. H. Kirkwood, QC; R. C. Klevan, QC; B. J. Knight, QC; S. E. Kramer

L. P. Laity; C. A. Lamb; D. G. Lane, QC; G. J. H. Langley, QC; R. B. Latham, QC; S. W. Lawler; I. J. Lawrence, QC, MP; M. H. Lawson, QC; G. S. Lawson Rogers; L. D. Lawton, QC; D. Lederman, QC; M. K. Lee, QC; R. T. L. Lee; B. W. T. Leech; I. Leeming, QC; C. H. de V. Leigh, QC; Sir Godfrey Le Quesne, QC; A. P. Lester, QC; B. H. Leveson, QC; S. Levine; M. E. Lewer, QC; A. K. Lewis, QC; M. ap G. Lewis, QC; R. S. Lewis; C. C. D. Lindsay, QC; S. J. Linehan; J. S. Lipton; B. J. E. Livesey, QC; C. G. Llewellyn-Jones, QC; H. J. Lloyd, QC; J. Lloyd-Eley, QC; A. J. C. Lodge, Q.C.; A. G. Longden; A. C. Longmore, QC; D. C. Lovell-Pank; R. P. Lowden; G. W. Lowe; G. W. Lowther; F. D. L. Loy; G. Lumley; Sir Nicholas Lyell, QC, MP; E. Lyons, QC; Capt. S. Lyons, RN

A. G. McCallum; A. W. McCreath; A. G. MacDuff; D. D. McEvoy, QC; R. D. Machell, QC; C. C. Mackay, QC; T. N. MacKean; D. L. Mackie; N. R. B. Macleod, QC; N. J. C. McLusky; J. B. MacMillan; D. G. Maddison; T. Maher; A. R. Malcolm; The Baroness Mallalieu, QC; J. H. Mance, QC; M. E. Mann, QC; A. C. B. Markham-David; A. S. Marron; R. G. Marshall-Andrews, QC; D. N. N. Martineau; H. R. A. Martineau; C. G. Masterman; D. Matheson, QC; W. D. Matthews; P. B. Mauleverer, QC; R. B. Mawrey, QC; M. Meggeson; D. B. Meier; N. F. Merriman, QC; J. T. Milford, QC; R. A. Miller; Mrs B. J. L. Mills, QC; J. B. M. Milmo, QC; N. A. Miscampbell, QC, MP; C. R. Mitchell; J. E. Mitting, QC; E. G. Moelwyn-Hughes; H. J. Montlake; M. J. Moore-Bick, QC; H. M. Morgan; W. G. O. Morgan, QC; G. E. Moriarty, QC; T. R. A. Morison, QC; A. P. Morris, QC; D. G. Morris; The Rt. Hon. J. Morris, QC, MP; J. I. Morris; W. P. Morris; C. Morris-Coole; T. J. Mort; A. G. Moses, QC; R. T. Moss; P. C. Mott, QC; R. W. Moxon-Browne, QC; J. H. Muir; J. Mulcahy, QC; F. J. Muller, QC; I. P. Murphy; M. J. A. Murphy; N. J. Mylne, QC

T. M. E. Nash; R. F. Nelson, QC; D. E. Neuberger, QC; R. E. Newbold; A. R. H. Newman, QC; G. M. Newman, QC; J. D. Newton; G. Nice, QC; C. A. A. Nicholls, QC; C. V. Nicholls, QC; M. C. Nicholson; A. S. T. E. Nicol; B. Nolan; Col. A. P. Norris, OBE; P. H. Norris; J. G. Nutting; D. P. O'Brien, QC; E. M. Ogden, QC; B. R. Oliver; C. P. L. Openshaw, QC; R. T. N. Orme; R. C. C. O'Rorke; G. V. Owen, QC; R. M. Owen, QC; S. R. Page; D. C. J. Paget; A. O. Palmer, QC; A. W. Palmer, QC; A. D. W. Pardoe, QC; S. A. B. Parish; A. E. W. Park, QC; G. C. Parkins, QC; G. E. Parkinson; M. P. Parroy, QC; D. J. Parry; D. J. T. Parry; E. O. Parry; M. A. Parry Evans; N. S. K. Pascoe, QC; A. Patience, QC; J. G. Paulusz; Mrs N. Pearce; Prof. D. S. Pearl; R. J. Pearse Wheatley; D. H. Penry-Davey, QC; Sir Ian Percival, QC; J. Perry, QC; M. Pert, QC; B. J. Phelvin; W. B. Phillips; M. A. Pickering, QC; C. J. Pitchford, QC; A. P. Pitts; Miss E. F. Platt, QC; J. R. Playford, QC; A. G. S. Pollock, QC; D. A. Poole, QC; L. R. Portnoy; W. D. C. Poulton; M. J. Pratt, QC; S. Pratt; T. W. Preston, QC; G. A. L. Price; J. A. Price, QC; N. P. L. Price; P. J. Price, QC; R. N. M. Price; A. C. Pugh, QC; G. V. Pugh, QC; C. P. B. Purchas, QC; R. M. Purchas, QC; N. R. Purnell, QC; P. O. Purnell, QC

D. A. Radcliffe; Ms A. J. Rafferty, QC; A. Rankin, QC; A. D. Rawley, QC; L. F. Read, QC; A. R. F. Redgrave; J. Reeder, QC; P. Rees; J. R. Reid, QC; R. E. Rhodes, QC; D. G. Rice; D. W. Richards; H. A. Richardson; N. P. Riddell; S. V. Riordan; Miss S. A. Ritchie, QC; B. A. Rix, QC; S. D. Robbins; J. A. Roberts, QC; J. D. Roberts; J. H. Roberts; J. M. G. Roberts, QC; P. B. Roberts; P. E. Robertshaw; V. Robinson, QC; D. E. H. Robson, QC; G. W. Roddick, QC; J. M. T. Rogers, QC; K. S. Rokison, QC; P. C. Rouch; J. J. Rowe, QC; R. J. Royce, QC; Ms G. D. Ruaux; R. J. Rubery; A. A. Rumbelow, QC; R. R. Russell; G. C. Ryan, QC

J. E. A. Samuels, QC; A. T. Sander; G. R. Sankey, QC; J. H. B. Saunders, QC; M. P. Sayers, QC; R. J. Scholes, QC; R. M. Scott; R. J. Seabrook, QC; C. Seagroatt, QC; H. M. Self, QC; M. R. Selfe; O. M. Sells; J. S. Sennitt; D. Serota, QC; A. J. Seys-Llewellyn; A. R. F. Sharp; R. M. Shawcross; P. P. Shears; S. J. Sher, QC; M. D. Sherrard, QC; J. M. Shorrock, QC; S. R. Silber, QC; J. P. Singer, QC; P. F. Singer; J. C. N. Slater, QC; S. P. Sleeman; E. Slinger; A. T. Smith, QC; J. H. Smith, QC; R. S. Smith, QC; S. A. R. Smith; W. P. Smith; Ms Z. P. Smith; S. M. Solley, QC; R. F. Solman; E. Somerset Jones, QC; R. C. E. Southwell; Miss J. M. Southworth, QC; M. H. Spence, QC; Sir Derek Spencer, QC, MP; J. Spencer, QC; M. G. Spencer, QC; S. M. Spencer, QC; L. Spittle; J. A. C. Spokes, QC; R. W. Spon-Smith; D. P. Stanley; D. W. Steel, QC; D. Steer; M. T. Steiger; D. H. Stembridge, QC; Mrs L. J. Stern, QC; A. W. Stevenson, TD; J. S. H. Stewart, QC; R. M. Stewart, QC; G. J. C. Still; D. M. A. Stokes, QC; M. G. T. Stokes; E. D. R. Stone, QC; P. L. Storr; T. M. F. Stow, QC; D. M. A. Strachan, QC; M. Stuart-Moore, QC; F. R. C. Such; A. B. Suckling, QC; J. M. Sullivan, QC; Ms L. E. Sullivan; D. M. Sumner; Mrs L. Sutcliffe; L. Swift, QC; M. R. Swift, QC

J. A. Tackaberry, QC; G. F. Tattersall, QC; E. Taylor; N. Taylor, QC; J. J. Teare; A. D. Temple, QC; V. B. A. Temple; M. I. Tennant; K. J. Tetley; C. B. Tetlow; Lord Thomas of Gwydir, PC, QC; D. M. Thomas, OBE, QC; D. O. Thomas, QC; P. M. Thomas; R. J. L. Thomas, QC; R. L. Thomas; R. U. Thomas, QC; J. Tiley; M. B. Tillett; R. N. Titheridge, QC; J. K. Toulmin, QC; R. G. Toulson, QC;

J. B. S. Townend, QC; C. M. Treacy, QC; H. B. Trethowan; I. J. C. Trigger; A. D. H. Trollope, QC; H. W. Turcan; D. A. Turner, QC; P. A. Twigg, QC; A. R. Tyrrell, QC; J. G. G. Ungley; N. P. Valios, QC; A. R. Vandermeer, QC; M. J. D. Vere-Hodge; T. L. Viljoen; C. D. Voelcker; Rt. Hon. Lord Waddington, QC, MP; J. P. Wadsworth, QC; D. St J. Wagstaff; R. M. Wakerley, QC; W. H. Waldron, QC; J. D. G. Walford; R. J. Walker, QC; T. E. Walker, QC; J. J. Walker-Smith; N. P. R. Wall, QC; B. Walsh, QC; D. E. B. Waters; Sir James Watson, Bt.; C. D. G. Waud; B. J. Waylen; P. A. Webster; M. Weisman; P. Weitzman, QC; C. P. C. Whelon; G. Whitburn, QC; C. H. Whitby, QC; W. J. M. White; D. R. B. Whitehouse, QC; P. G. Whiteman, QC; P. J. M. Whiteman, TD; A. Whitfield, QC; D. G. Widdicombe, QC; R. Wigglesworth; J. S. Wiggs; A. D. F. Wilcken; S. R. Wilkinson; D. B. Williams; G. H. G. Williams, QC; Lord Williams of Mostyn, QC; J. G. Williams, QC; J. L. Williams, QC; The Hon. J. M. Williams, QC; M. J. Williams; W. L. Williams, QC; S. W. Williamson, QC; A. M. Wilson, QC; N. A. R. Wilson, QC; C. Wilson-Smith, QC; G. W. Wingate-Saul, QC; M. E. Wolff; J. S. Wolstenholme; H. Wolton, QC; D. A. Wood, QC; D. R. Wood; W. R. Wood; L. G. Woodley, QC; S. Woodley; J. T. Woods; W. C. Woodward, QC; Ms A. F. W. Woolley; D. R. Woolley, QC; N. G. Wootton; A. M. Worrall, QC; N. J. Worsley; P. F. Worsley, QC; D. E. M. Young, QC

STIPENDIARY MAGISTRATES

PROVINCIAL (each £52,520)

Cheshire, P. K. Dodd, OBE, *apptd* 1991
Greater Manchester, W. D. Fairclough, *apptd* 1982; C. T. Latham, OBE, *apptd* 1976; Miss J. E. Hayward, *apptd* 1991
Hampshire, T. G. Cowling, *apptd* 1989
Humberside, N. H. White, *apptd* 1985
Lancashire/Merseyside, J. Finestein, *apptd* 1992
Merseyside, N. G. Wootton, *apptd* 1976; D. R. G. Tapp, *apptd* 1992
Middlesex, N. A. McKittrick, *apptd* 1989; S. Somjee, *apptd* 1991; S. N. Day, *apptd* 1991
Mid Glamorgan, B. R. Oliver, *apptd* 1983; J. T. Curran, *apptd* 1990
Nottinghamshire, P. F. Nuttall, *apptd* 1991; M. L. R. Harris, *apptd* 1991
South Glamorgan, Sir Lincoln Hallinan, *apptd* 1976
South Yorkshire, I. W. Crompton, *apptd* 1983; J. E. Barry, *apptd* 1985; W. D. Thomas, *apptd* 1989
Staffordshire, P. G. G. Richards, *apptd* 1991
West Midlands, W. M. Probert, *apptd* 1983; B. Morgan, *apptd* 1989; I. Gillespie, *apptd* 1991; M. F. James, *apptd* 1991
West Yorkshire, F. D. L. Loy, *apptd* 1972; Mrs P. A. Hewitt, *apptd* 1990; G. H. Kamil, *apptd* 1990

METROPOLITAN

Chief Metropolitan Stipendiary Magistrate and Chairman of Committee of Magistrates for Inner London Area (£57,500), P. G. N. Badge (*Bow Street*)

Magistrates (each £52,520)

Bow Street, The Chief Magistrate; R. D. Bartle; J. G. Connor; D. A. Cooper
Camberwell Green, C. P. M. Davidson; P. Fingret; Mrs H. Mitcham; J. R. D. Phillips; T. H. Workman
Clerkenwell, M. L. R. Romer; C. J. Bourke; M. A. Johnstone
Greenwich and Woolwich, Mrs K. R. Keating; B. Loosley; W. A. Kennedy
Highbury Corner, D. Barr; Miss D. Quick; G. Wicks; N. Crichton
Horseferry Road, Miss P. A. Long; A. R. Davies; R. T. Moss; T. Maher
Marlborough Street, K. J. H. Nichols; J. Q. Campbell
Marylebone, G. L. J. Noel; Sir Bryan Roberts, KCMG, QC; B. Black; A. C. Baldwin
Old Street, D. B. Meier; Miss G. B. Babington-Browne
South Western, S. G. Clixby; C. D. Voelcker; A. Ormerod
Thames, D. M. Fingleton; Miss D. Wickham; G. E. Parkinson
Tower Bridge, Mrs J. R. Comyns; T. M. English; A. T. Evans
Wells Street, Miss A. M. Jennings; K. L. Maitland-Davies; I. M. Baker; C. L. Pratt
West London, H. J. Cook; D. Kennett Brown
Unattached Magistrates, G. B. Breen; D. L. Thomas; M. Kelly; I. Bing

COMMITTEE OF MAGISTRATES FOR INNER LONDON AREA
3rd Floor, North West Wing, Bush House, Aldwych, London WC2B 4PJ. Tel: 071-836 9331

Principal Chief Clerk and Clerk to the Committee (£45,174), I. Fowler
Chief Clerk (Training) (£40,563), J. W. Greenhill

CROWN PROSECUTION SERVICE

4–12 Queen Anne's Gate, London SW1H 9AZ
Tel 071-273 8152
Casework: 10 Furnival Street, London EC4A 1PE
Tel 071-417 7000

The Crown Prosecution Service (CPS) is responsible for the independent review and conduct of criminal proceedings instituted by police forces in England and Wales (with the exception of cases conducted by the Serious Fraud Office and certain minor cases).

The Director of Public Prosecutions is the head of the CPS and discharges her statutory functions under the superintendence of the Attorney-General.

The CPS comprises a headquarters office and 31 areas covering England and Wales. Each of the 31 CPS Areas is supervised by a Chief Crown Prosecutor.

For salaries, *see* page 284

Director of Public Prosecutions (G1), Mrs B. Mills, QC
Deputy Director and Chief Executive (G2), D. S. Gandy, CB, OBE
Principal Establishment and Finance Officer (G3), D. J. Wiblin, CB
Director, Headquarters Casework (G3), C. Newell
Field Director, Operations (G3), G. Duff
Field Director, Resources (G3), G. D. Etherington
Director, Policy and Communications Group (G3), K. Ashken

CPS AREAS

AVON/SOMERSET, 1st Floor, Block A, Froomsgate House, Rupert Street, Bristol BS1 2QJ. Tel: 0272-273093. *Chief Crown Prosecutor (G5)*, C. T. Jones

CAMBRIDGESHIRE/LINCOLNSHIRE, Justinian House, Spitfire Close, Ermine Business Park, Huntingdon, Cambs. PE18 6XY. Tel: 0480–432333. *Chief Crown Prosecutor (G5)*, D. G. Lewis

CHESHIRE, 2nd Floor, Windsor House, Pepper Street, Chester CH1 1TD. Tel: 0244–348043. *Chief Crown Prosecutor (G5)*, Mrs N. E. Hollingsworth

CLEVELAND/NORTH YORKSHIRE, 6th Floor, Ryedale Building, 60 Piccadilly, York YO1 1NS. Tel: 0904–610726. *Chief Crown Prosecutor (G5)*, D. M. Sharp

DERBYSHIRE, Celtic House, Heritage Gate, Friary Street, Derby DE1 1QX. Tel: 0332–42956. *Chief Crown Prosecutor (G5)*, D. R. K. Seddon

DEVON/CORNWALL, Hawkins House, Pynes Hill, Rydon Lane, Exeter EX2 5SS. Tel: 0392–422555. *Chief Crown Prosecutor (G5)*, R. J. Green

DORSET/HAMPSHIRE, 1st Floor, Eastleigh House, Upper Market Street, Eastleigh, Hants. SO5 4FD. Tel: 0703–651128. *Chief Crown Prosecutor (G5)*, P. Boeuf

ESSEX, Gemini Centre, 88 New London Road, Chelmsford, Essex CM2 0PD. Tel: 0245–252939. *Chief Crown Prosecutor (G5)*, J. J. Goodwin

GLOUCESTERSHIRE/WILTSHIRE, 7 Avon Reach, Monkton Hill, Chippenham, Wilts. SN15 1EE. Tel: 0249–655149. *Chief Crown Prosecutor (G5)*, R. A. Prickett

GREATER MANCHESTER, PO Box 377, Sunlight House, Quay Street, Manchester M60 3LU. Tel: 061–837 7402. *Chief Crown Prosecutor (G4)*, A. R. Taylor

HERTFORDSHIRE/BEDFORDSHIRE, Queens House, 58 Victoria Street, St Albans AL1 3HZ. Tel: 0727–44753. *Chief Crown Prosecutor (G5)*, C. Ingham

HUMBERSIDE, 3rd Floor, Queens House, Paragon Street, Hull HU1 3DA. Tel: 0482–586611. *Chief Crown Prosecutor (G5)*, L. M. Bell

KENT, Priory Gate, 29 Union Street, Maidstone, Kent ME14 1PT. Tel: 0622–686425. *Chief Crown Prosecutor (G5)*, R. A. Crabb

LANCASHIRE/CUMBRIA, 3rd Floor, Robert House, 2 Starkie Street, Preston, Lancs. PR1 3NY. Tel: 0772–555030. *Chief Crown Prosecutor (G5)*, J. V. Bates

LEICESTERSHIRE/NORTHAMPTONSHIRE, Princes Court, 34 York Road, Leicester LE1 5TU. Tel: 0533–549333. *Chief Crown Prosecutor (G5)*, P. J. M. Hollingworth

LONDON (INNER), Portland House, Stag Place, London SW1E 5BH. Tel: 071–828 9050. *Chief Crown Prosecutor (G4)*, B. McArdle

LONDON (NORTH), Solar House, 1–9 Romford Road, Stratford, London E15 4LJ. Tel: 081–534 6601. *Chief Crown Prosecutor (G4)*, R. J. Chronnell

LONDON (SOUTH)/SURREY, Tolworth Tower, Surbiton KT6 7DS. Tel: 081–399 5171. *Chief Crown Prosecutor (G4)*, D. E. Dracup

MERSEYSIDE, 7th Floor (South), Royal Liver Building, Liverpool L3 1HN. Tel: 051–236 7575. *Chief Crown Prosecutor (G4)*, E. C. Woodcock

NORFOLK/SUFFOLK, Saxon House, 1 Cromwell Square, Ipswich, Suffolk IP1 1TS. Tel: 0473–230332. *Chief Crown Prosecutor (G5)*, M. F. C. Harvey

NORTHUMBRIA/DURHAM, 3rd Floor, Benton House, 136 Sandyford Road, Newcastle upon Tyne NE2 1QE. Tel: 091–230 0800. *Chief Crown Prosecutor (G5)*, D. A. Farmer

NORTH WALES/DYFED/POWYS, 491 Abergele Road, Old Colwyn, Colwyn Bay, Clwyd LL29 9AE. Tel: 0492–512353. *Chief Crown Prosecutor (G5)*, A. S. R. Clarke

NOTTINGHAMSHIRE, 2 King Edward Court, King Edward Street, Nottingham NG1 1EL. Tel: 0602–480480. *Chief Crown Prosecutor (G5)*, D. C. Beal

SOUTH WALES/GWENT, Pearl Assurance House, Greyfriars Road, Cardiff CF1 3PL. Tel: 0222–382777. *Chief Crown Prosecutor (G4)*, H. G. Wallace

SOUTH YORKSHIRE, Belgrave House, 47 Bank Street, Sheffield S1 2EH. Tel: 0742–761601. *Chief Crown Prosecutor (G4)*, M. J. Rose

STAFFORDSHIRE/WARWICKSHIRE, Government Buildings, 11A Princes Street, Stafford ST16 2EU. Tel: 0785–223511. *Chief Crown Prosecutor (G5)*, D. V. Dickenson

SUSSEX, Unit 3, Clifton Mews, Clifton Hill, Brighton, E. Sussex BN1 3HR. Tel: 0273–207562. *Chief Crown Prosecutor (G5)*, D. Thompson

THAMES VALLEY, The Courtyard, Lombard Street, Abingdon, Oxon. OX14 5SE. Tel: 0235–555678. *Chief Crown Prosecutor (G5)*, J. Wilcox

WEST MERCIA, Orchard House, Victoria Square, Droitwich, Worcester WR9 8QT. Tel: 0905–779502. *Chief Crown Prosecutor (G5)*, D. R. Stott

WEST MIDLANDS, Dale House, 31 Dale End, Birmingham B4 7NR. Tel: 021–233 3133. *Chief Crown Prosecutor (G4)*, T. M. McGowan

WEST YORKSHIRE, 4–5 South Parade, Wakefield WF1 1LR. Tel: 0924–290620. *Chief Crown Prosecutor (G4)*, R. Otley

The Scottish Judicature

Scotland has a legal system separate from and differing greatly from the English legal system in enacted law, judicial procedure and the structure of courts.

There is in Scotland a system of public prosecution headed by the Lord Advocate which is independent of the police, who have no say in the decision to prosecute. The Lord Advocate, discharging his functions through the Crown Office in Edinburgh, is responsible for prosecutions in the High Court, sheriff courts and district courts. Prosecutions in the High Court are prepared by the Crown Office and conducted in court by one of the law officers or an advocate-depute. In the inferior courts the decision to prosecute is made and prosecution is preferred by procurators fiscal, who are lawyers and full-time civil servants, subject to the directions of the Crown Office. A permanent legally-qualified civil servant known as the Crown Agent is responsible for the running of the Crown Office and the organization of the Procurator Fiscal Service, of which he is the head.

Scotland is divided into six Sheriffdoms, each with a full-time Sheriff Principal. The Sheriffdoms are further divided into sheriff court districts, each of which has a legally-qualified, resident sheriff or sheriffs, who are the judges of the court.

In criminal cases sheriffs principal and sheriffs have the same powers; sitting with a jury of 15 members, they may try more serious cases on indictment, or, sitting alone, may try lesser cases under summary procedure. Minor summary offences are dealt with in district courts which are administered by the district and the islands local government authorities and presided over by lay justices of the peace (of whom there are about 4,400) and, in Glasgow only, by stipendiary magistrates. Juvenile offenders (children under 16) may be brought before an informal children's hearing comprising three local lay people. The superior criminal court is the High Court of Justiciary which is both a trial and an appeal court. Cases on indictment are tried by a High Court judge, sitting with a jury of 15, in Edinburgh and on circuit in other towns. Appeals from the lower courts against conviction or sentence are heard also by the High Court, which sits as an appeal court only in Edinburgh. There is no further appeal to the House of Lords in criminal cases.

In civil cases the jurisdiction of the sheriff court extends to most kinds of action. Appeal against decisions of the sheriff may be made to the Sheriff Principal and thence to the Court of Session, or direct to the Court of Session, which sits only in Edinburgh. The Court of Session is divided into the Inner and the Outer House. The Outer House is a court of first instance in which cases are heard by judges sitting singly, sometimes with a jury of 12. The Inner House, itself subdivided into two divisions of equal status, is mainly an appeal court. Appeals may be made to the Inner House from the Outer House as well as from the sheriff court. An appeal may be made from the Inner House to the House of Lords.

The judges of the Court of Session are the same as those of the High Court of Justiciary, the Lord President of the Court of Session also holding the office of Lord Justice General in the High Court. Senators of the College of Justice are Lords Commissioners of Justiciary as well as judges of the Court of Session.

The office of coroner does not exist in Scotland. The local procurator fiscal inquires privately into sudden and suspicious deaths and may report findings to the Crown Agent. In some cases a fatal accident inquiry may be held before the sheriff.

COURT OF SESSION AND HIGH COURT OF JUSTICIARY

The Lord President and Lord Justice General (£97,000)
The Rt. Hon. Lord Hope, *born* 1938, *apptd* 1989

INNER HOUSE

Lords of Session (each £93,000)

FIRST DIVISION

The Lord President
Hon. Lord Allanbridge (William Ian Stewart), *born* 1925, *apptd* 1977
Hon. Lord Cowie (William Lorn Kerr Cowie), *born* 1926, *apptd* 1977
Hon. Lord Mayfield (Ian MacDonald, MC), *born* 1921, *apptd* 1981

SECOND DIVISION

Lord Justice Clerk (£94,000), The Rt. Hon. Lord Ross, (Donald MacArthur Ross), *born* 1927, *apptd* 1985
Rt. Hon. Lord Murray (Ronald King Murray), *born* 1922, *apptd* 1979
Hon. The Lord McCluskey, *born* 1929, *apptd* 1984
Hon. Lord Morison (Alastair Malcolm Morison), *born* 1931, *apptd* 1985

OUTER HOUSE

Lords of Session (each £84,230)

Hon. Lord Davidson (Charles Kemp Davidson) (*seconded to Scottish Law Commission*), *born* 1929, *apptd* 1983
Hon. Lord Sutherland (Ranald Iain Sutherland), *born* 1932, *apptd* 1985
Hon. Lord Weir (David Bruce Weir), *born* 1931, *apptd* 1985
Hon. Lord Clyde (James John Clyde), *born* 1932, *apptd* 1985
Hon. Lord Cullen (William Douglas Cullen), *born* 1935, *apptd* 1986
Hon. Lord Prosser (William David Prosser), *born* 1934, *apptd* 1986
Hon. Lord Kirkwood (Ian Candlish Kirkwood), *born* 1932, *apptd* 1987
Hon. Lord Coulsfield (John Taylor Cameron), *born* 1934, *apptd* 1987
Hon. Lord Milligan (James George Milligan), *born* 1934, *apptd* 1988
Hon. The Lord Morton of Shuna, *born* 1930, *apptd* 1988
Hon. Lord Caplan (Philip Isaac Caplan), *born* 1929, *apptd* 1989
Rt. Hon. The Lord Cameron of Lochbroom, *born* 1931, *apptd* 1989
Hon. Lord Marnoch (Michael Stewart Rae Bruce), *born* 1938, *apptd* 1990
Hon. Lord MacLean (Ranald Norman Munro MacLean), *born* 1938, *apptd* 1990
Hon. Lord Penrose (George William Penrose), *born* 1938, *apptd* 1990
Hon. Lord Osborne (Kenneth Hilton Osborne), *born* 1937, *apptd* 1990
Hon. Lord Abernethy (John Alastair Cameron), *born* 1938, *apptd* 1992

COURT OF SESSION AND HIGH COURT OF JUSTICIARY

Parliament House, Parliament Square, Edinburgh EH1 1RQ
Tel 031-225 2595

Principal Clerk of Session and Justiciary (£34,667–£46,122), H. S. Foley
Deputy Principal Clerk of Justiciary and Administration (£23,329–£33,175), E. Cumming
Deputy Principal Clerk of Session and Principal Extractor (£23,329–£33,175), M. Weir
Deputy Principal Clerk (Keeper of the Rolls) (£23,329–£33,175), M. G. Bonar
Depute Clerks of Session and Justiciary (£16,675–£23,567), T. D. McIntosh; A. Hogg; N. J. Dowie; J. M. Clark; I. Smith; J. A. R. Cowie; T. Higgins; T. B. Cruickshank; Q. Oliver; F. Shannly; R. D. Sinclair; Mrs A. Leighton; T. M. Thomson; D. D. Mackay; A. S. Moffat; J. Atkinson; D. J. Shand; G. Ellis; Mrs G. McKeand; D. G. Lynn; R. Cockburn; W. Dunn; A. Finlayson

SCOTTISH COURTS ADMINISTRATION

26–27 Royal Terrace, Edinburgh EH7 5AH
Tel 031-556 0755

Director, G. Murray

SHERIFF COURT OF CHANCERY

16 North Bank Street, Edinburgh EH1 2NH
Tel 031-226 7181

Sheriff of Chancery, C. G. B. Nicholson, QC

HM COMMISSARY OFFICE
16 North Bank Street, Edinburgh EH1 2NJ
Tel 031-226 7181

Commissary Clerk, I. E. Scott

SCOTTISH LAND COURT
1 Grosvenor Crescent, Edinburgh EH12 5ER
Tel 031-225 3595

Chairman (£68,400), The Hon. Lord Elliott, MC
Members, A. B. Campbell, OBE; D. D. McDiarmid; D. M. MacDonald; J. Kinloch (*part-time*)

SHERIFFDOMS

SALARIES

Sheriff Principal	£68,400
Sheriff	£61,600
Regional Sheriff Clerk	£26,622–£46,122
Sheriff Clerk	£17,017–£46,122

*Floating Sheriff

GRAMPIAN, HIGHLAND AND ISLANDS

Sheriff Principal, R. D. Ireland, QC
Regional Sheriff Clerk, J. Robertson

SHERIFFS AND SHERIFF CLERKS

Aberdeen and Stonehaven, D. J. Risk; D. W. Bogie; G. C. Warner; D. Kelbie; L. A. S. Jessop; *Sheriff Clerks*, J. Rodden; W. A. Mouser
Peterhead and Banff, K. A. McLernan; *Sheriff Clerk*, H. Hempseed; *Sheriff Clerk Depute*, W. H. Connon
Elgin, N. McPartlin; *Sheriff Clerk*, A. Lynch
Inverness, Lochmaddy, Portree, Stornoway, Dingwall, Tain, Wick and Dornoch, W. J. Fulton; D. Booker-Milburn; J. O. A. Fraser; E. Stewart; *Sheriff Clerk*, J. Robertson
Kirkwall and Lerwick, G. S. MacKenzie; *Sheriff Clerks Depute*, Miss H. M. Phillips; A. C. Norris
Fort William, D. Noble (also *Oban and Campbeltown*); *Sheriff Clerk Depute*, C. Morrison

TAYSIDE, CENTRAL AND FIFE

Sheriff Principal, J. J. Maguire, QC
Regional Sheriff Clerk, J. S. Doig

SHERIFFS AND SHERIFF CLERKS

Arbroath and Forfar, S. O. Kermack; G. N. R. Stein; *Sheriff Clerks*, M. Herbertson; P. Dougan
Dundee, G. L. Cox; A. L. Stewart; *Sheriff Clerk*, J. S. Doig
Perth, J. F. Wheatley; J. C. McInnes, QC; *Sheriff Clerk*, W. Jones
Falkirk, A. V. Sheehan; A. J. Murphy; *Sheriff Clerk*, D. Nicoll
Stirling, A. Pollock; R. E. G. Younger; *Sheriff Clerk*, P. Crow
Alloa, R. E. G. Younger; *Sheriff Clerk*, J. M. Murphy
Cupar, C. Smith (also *Dundee*); *Sheriff Clerk*, B. Sullivan
Dunfermline, J. S. Forbes; W. M. Reid; *Sheriff Clerk*, J. Ross
Kirkcaldy, W. J. Christie; Mrs L. G. Patrick; *Sheriff Clerk*, I. Hay

LOTHIAN AND BORDERS

Sheriff Principal, C. G. B. Nicholson, QC
Regional Sheriff Clerk, I. E. Scott

SHERIFFS AND SHERIFF CLERKS

Edinburgh, N. E. D. Thomson; J. L. M. Mitchell; P. G. B. McNeill, PH.D.; Miss H. J. Aronson, QC; R. G. Craik, QC; G. I. W. Shiach; Miss I. A. Poole; R. J. D. Scott; A. M. Bell; J. M. S. Horsburgh; G. W. S. Presslie; J. A. Farrell*; I. A. Cameron; *Sheriff Clerk*, I. E. Scott
Peebles, N. E. D. Thomson (also *Edinburgh*); *Sheriff Clerk*, I. E. Scott
Linlithgow, M. Stone; H. R. MacLean; *Sheriff Clerk*, R. Sinclair
Haddington, G. W. S. Presslie (also *Edinburgh*); *Sheriff Clerk*, B. W. S. Manthorpe
Jedburgh and Duns, J. V. Paterson; *Sheriff Clerk*, J. W. Williamson
Selkirk, J. V. Paterson; *Sheriff Clerk*, L. McFarlane

NORTH STRATHCLYDE

Sheriff Principal, R. C. Hay, CBE
Regional Sheriff Clerk, A. A. Brown

SHERIFFS AND SHERIFF CLERKS

Oban and Campbeltown, D. Noble (also *Fort William*); *Sheriff Clerk Deputes*, W. M. Cochrane; K. L. Graham
Dumbarton, J. T. Fitzsimons; T. Scott; S. W. H. Fraser; *Sheriff Clerk*, N. R. Weir
Paisley, R. G. Smith; C. N. Stoddart; J. Spy; C. K. Higgins; C. W. Palmer; C. G. McKay*; *Sheriff Clerk*, A. A. Brown
Greenock, J. Herald (also *Rothesay*); Sir Stephen Young; *Sheriff Clerk*, P. G. Corcoran
Kilmarnock, T. M. Croan; D. B. Smith; T. F. Russell; *Sheriff Clerk*, J. Shaw
Dunoon, C. W. Palmer (also *Dumbarton*); *Sheriff Clerk Depute*, Mrs C. Carson

GLASGOW AND STRATHKELVIN

Sheriff Principal, N. D. MacLeod, QC
Regional Sheriff Clerk, C. McLay

SHERIFFS AND SHERIFF CLERKS

Glasgow, A. C. Horsfall (*seconded to Scottish Lands Tribunal*); A. A. Bell, QC; B. Kearney; G. H. Gordon, QC; A. C. McKay; A. Lothian; J. C. M. Jardine; Mrs D. J. B. Robertson; B. A. Lockhart; I. G. Pirie; Mrs A. L. A. Duncan; W. G. Stevenson, QC; G. J. Evans; E. H. Galt; F. J. Keane; A. C. Henry; J. K. Mitchell; A. G. Johnston; J. P. Murphy; M. Sischy; A. B. Wilkinson; *Sheriff Clerk*, C. McLay

SOUTH STRATHCLYDE, DUMFRIES AND GALLOWAY

Sheriff Principal, J. S. Mowat, QC
Regional Sheriff Clerk, H. Findlay

SHERIFFS AND SHERIFF CLERKS

Hamilton, L. S. Lovat; A. C. MacPherson; W. F. Lunny; D. G. Russell; V. J. Canavan (also *Airdrie*); W. E. Gibson; *Sheriff Clerk*, J. Cumming
Lanark, J. D. Allan; *Sheriff Clerk*, D. M. Cameron
Ayr, N. Gow, QC; R. G. McEwan, QC; *Sheriff Clerk*, G. W. Waddell
Stranraer and Kirkcudbright, J. R. Smith; *Sheriff Clerk*, N. L. Hodgson; *Sheriff Clerk Depute*, B. Lindsay
Dumfries, K. G. Barr; L. Cameron; *Sheriff Clerk*, P. McGonigle
Airdrie, J. H. Stewart; V. J. Canavan (also *Hamilton*); R. H. Dickson; I. C. Simpson; *Sheriff Clerk*, H. Findlay

STIPENDIARY MAGISTRATES

GLASGOW

R. Hamilton, *apptd* 1984; J. B. C. Nisbet, *apptd* 1984; R. B. Christie, *apptd* 1985; Mrs J. A. M. MacLean, *apptd* 1990

PROCURATOR FISCAL SERVICE

CROWN OFFICE

Regent Road, Edinburgh EH7 5BL
Tel 031-557 3800

Crown Agent (£60,100), J. D. Lowe
Deputy Crown Agent (£46,122), A. D. Vannet

PROCURATORS FISCAL

SALARIES

Regional Procurator Fiscal-grade 3	£48,000
Regional Procurator Fiscal-grade 4	£46,122
Procurator Fiscal-upper level	£34,667–£39,402
Procurator Fiscal-lower level	£24,928–£33,921

GRAMPIAN, HIGHLANDS AND ISLANDS REGION

Regional Procurator Fiscal, S. W. Lockhart, CBE (*Aberdeen*)
Procurators Fiscal, J. D. McNaughton (*Stonehaven*); A. J. M. Colley (*Banff*); I. S. McNaughtan (*Peterhead*); A. Wither (*Elgin*); A. N. MacDonald (*Wick*); C. B. McClory (*Portree and Lochmaddy*); Mrs D. Wilson (*Stornoway*); H. T. Westwater (*Dornoch* and *Tain*); W. W. Orr (*Inverness*); D. K. Adam (*Kirkwall* and *Lerwick*); Mrs A. Neizer (*Fort William*); D. R. Hingston (*Dingwall*)

TAYSIDE, CENTRAL AND FIFE REGION

Regional Procurator Fiscal, B. K. Heywood (*Dundee*)
Procurators Fiscal, C. D. G. Hillary (*Arbroath*); A. L. Ingram (*Forfar*); I. A. McLeod (*Perth*); G. E. Scott (*Falkirk*); K. Valentine (*Stirling*); I. D. Douglas (*Alloa*); E. B. Russell (*Cupar*); R. T. Hamilton (*Dunfermline*); F. R. Crowe (*Kirkcaldy*)

LOTHIAN AND BORDERS REGION

Regional Procurator Fiscal, R. F. Lees (*Edinburgh*)
Procurators Fiscal, F. J. M. Brown (*Peebles*); H. R. Annan (*Linlithgow*); A. J. P. Reith (*Haddington*); J. C. Whitelaw (*Duns* and *Jedburgh*); D. McNeill (*Selkirk*)

NORTH STRATHCLYDE REGION

Regional Procurator Fiscal, J. D. Friel (*Paisley*)
Procurators Fiscal, I. Henderson (*Campbeltown*); J. Cardle (*Dumbarton*); C. C. Donnelly (*Greenock* and *Rothesay*); D. L. Webster (*Dunoon*); J. G. MacGlennan (*Kilmarnock*); B. R. Maguire (*Oban*)

GLASGOW AND STRATHKELVIN REGION

Regional Procurator Fiscal, A. C. Normand (*Glasgow*)

SOUTH STRATHCLYDE, DUMFRIES AND GALLOWAY REGION

Regional Procurator Fiscal, W. G. Carmichael (*Hamilton*)
Procurators Fiscal, S. R. Houston (*Lanark*); N. G. O'Brien (*Ayr*); F. Walkingshaw (*Stranraer*); J. T. MacDougall, CBE (*Dumfries* and *Kirkcudbright*); A. T. Wilson (*Airdrie*)

Northern Ireland Judicature

In Northern Ireland the legal system and the structure of courts closely resemble those of England and Wales; there are, however, often differences in enacted law.

The Supreme Court of Judicature of Northern Ireland comprises the Court of Appeal, the High Court of Justice and the Crown Court. The practice and procedure of these Courts is similar to that in England. The superior civil court is the High Court of Justice, from which an appeal lies to the Northern Ireland Court of Appeal; the House of Lords is the final civil appeal court.

The Crown Court, served by High Court and county court judges, deals with criminal trials on indictment. Cases are heard before a judge and, except those involving offences specified under emergency legislation, a jury. Appeals from the Crown Court against conviction or sentence are heard by the Northern Ireland Court of Appeal; the House of Lords is the final court of appeal.

The decision to prosecute in cases tried on indictment and in summary cases of a serious nature rests in Northern Ireland with the Director of Public Prosecutions, who is responsible to the Attorney-General. Minor summary offences are prosecuted by the police.

Minor criminal offences are dealt with in magistrates' courts by a full-time, legally qualified resident magistrate and, where an offender is under 17, by juvenile courts each consisting of a resident magistrate and two lay members specially qualified to deal with juveniles (at least one of whom must be a woman). There are 977 Justices of the Peace in Northern Ireland. Appeals from magistrates' courts are heard by the county court, or by the Court of Appeal on a point of law or an issue as to jurisdiction.

Magistrates' courts in Northern Ireland can deal with certain classes of civil case but most minor civil cases are dealt with in county courts. Judgments of all civil courts are enforceable through a centralized procedure administered by the Enforcement of Judgments Office.

SUPREME COURT OF JUDICATURE

The Royal Courts of Justice, Belfast BT1 3JF
Tel 0232-235111

Lord Chief Justice of Northern Ireland (£100,880), The Rt. Hon. Sir Brian Hutton, *born* 1931, *apptd* 1988

Lords Justices of Appeal (each £96,720)
Rt. Hon. Sir Donald Murray, *born* 1923, *apptd* 1975
Rt. Hon. Sir Basil Kelly, *born* 1920, *apptd* 1984
Rt. Hon. Sir John MacDermott, *born* 1927, *apptd* 1987

Puisne Judges (each £87,620)
Hon. Sir John Higgins, *born* 1927, *apptd* 1984
Hon. Sir Robert Carswell, *born* 1934, *apptd* 1984
Hon. Sir Michael Nicholson, *born* 1933, *apptd* 1986
Hon. Sir William McCollum, *born* 1933, *apptd* 1987
Hon. Sir Anthony Campbell, *born* 1936, *apptd* 1988
Hon. Sir John Sheil, *born* 1938, *apptd* 1989

LORD CHIEF JUSTICE'S OFFICE

Principal Secretary to the Lord Chief Justice and Clerk of the Crown for Northern Ireland, J. A. L. McLean, QC
Legal Secretary to the Lord Chief Justice, Mrs. D. M. Kennedy

MASTERS OF SUPREME COURT (each £50,500)

Master, Central Office, V. A. Care, QC
Master, High Court, J. W. Wilson, QC
Master, Office of Care and Protection, F. B. Hall
Master, Chancery Office, V. G. Bridges
Master, Bankruptcy and Companies Office, J. B. C. Glass
Master, Probate and Matrimonial Office, R. T. Millar
Master, Taxing Office, J. C. Napier

COUNTY COURTS

JUDGES (each £68,400)

Judge Babington, DSC, QC; Rt. Hon. Judge Sir Robert Porter, QC; Judge Russell, QC; Judge Curran, QC; Judge McKee, QC; Judge Gibson, QC; Judge Hart, QC; Judge Petrie, QC; Judge Smyth, QC; Judge Martin, QC

RECORDERS (each £68,400)

Belfast, Judge Pringle, QC
Londonderry, Judge Higgins, QC

MAGISTRATES COURTS

Resident Magistrates (each £50,500)

There are 17 resident magistrates in Northern Ireland.

CROWN SOLICITOR'S OFFICE
Royal Courts of Justice, Belfast BT1 3JF
Tel 0232-235111

Crown Solicitor, H. A. Nelson

DEPARTMENT OF THE DIRECTOR OF PUBLIC PROSECUTIONS
Royal Courts of Justice, Belfast BT1 3JF
Tel 0232-235111

Director of Public Prosecutions, A. Fraser, CB, QC
Deputy Director of Public Prosecutions, D. Magill

Ecclesiastical Courts

Original jurisdiction is exercised by the Consistory Court of each diocese in England, presided over by the Chancellor of that diocese. Appellate jurisdiction is exercised by the Provincial Courts detailed below, and by the Court for Ecclesiastical Causes Reserved, and by Commissions of Review (the membership of these being newly constituted for each case).

COURT OF ARCHES (PROVINCE OF CANTERBURY)
Registry, 16 Beaumont Street, Oxford OX1 2LZ
Tel 0865-241974

Dean of the Arches, The Rt. Worshipful Sir John Owen

COURT OF THE VICAR-GENERAL OF THE PROVINCE OF CANTERBURY

Registry, 16 Beaumont Street, Oxford OX1 2LZ
Tel 0865-241974

Vicar-General, The Rt. Worshipful Miss S. Cameron, QC

CHANCERY COURT OF YORK
Registry, 1 Peckitt Street, York YO1 1SG
Tel 0904-623487

Auditor, The Rt. Worshipful Sir John Owen

THE VICAR-GENERAL OF THE PROVINCE OF YORK
Registry, 1 Peckitt Street, York YO1 1SG
Tel 0904-623487

Vicar-General, His Honour the Worshipful Judge T. A. C. Coningsby, QC

COURT OF FACULTIES
Registry, 1 The Sanctuary, London SW1P 3JT
Tel 071-222 5381

Office for the use of special and ordinary marriage licences, appointment of notaries public, etc. Office hours, Monday–Friday, 10–4.
Master of the Faculties, The Rt. Worshipful Sir John Owen

Tribunals

AGRICULTURAL LAND TRIBUNALS

c/o Land Use and Tenure Division, Ministry of Agriculture, Fisheries and Food, Nobel House, 17 Smith Square, London SW1P 3JR
Tel 071-238 3000

Agricultural Land Tribunals were set up under the Agriculture Act 1947 and settle disputes and other issues between agricultural landlords and tenants. They also settle drainage disputes between neighbours.

There are seven tribunals covering England and one covering the whole of Wales. For each tribunal the Lord Chancellor appoints a chairman and one or more deputies, who must be barristers or solicitors of at least seven years standing. The Lord Chancellor also appoints lay members to three statutory panels of members: the 'landowners' panel, the 'farmers' panel and the 'drainage' panel.

Each of the eight tribunals is an independent statutory body with jurisdiction only within its own area. A separate tribunal is constituted for each case, and consists of a chairman (who may be the chairman or one of the deputy chairmen) and two lay members nominated by the chairman. The chairmen and deputy chairmen are entitled to claim a fee of £207 per day.

Chairmen (England), W. D. Greenwood; K. J. Fisher; E. C. Evans-Lombe, QC; C. H. Beaumont; N. J. Worsley; G. L. Newsom; His Hon. Judge Robert Taylor
Chairman (Wales), vacant

COMMONS COMMISSIONERS

Golden Cross House, Duncannon Street, London WC2N 4JF
Tel 071-210 4584

The Commons Commissioners are responsible for deciding disputes arising under the Commons Registration Act 1965 and the Common Land (Rectification of Registers) Act 1989. They also enquire into the ownership of unclaimed common land. Commissioners are appointed by the Lord Chancellor.

Chief Commons Commissioner, P. G. Langdon-Davies
Commissioners, M. Roth; I. L. R. Romer; D. M. Burton
Clerk, Miss F. A. A. Buchan

COPYRIGHT TRIBUNAL

Room 4/6, Hazlitt House, 45 Southampton Buildings, London WC2A 1AR
Tel 071-438 4776

The Copyright Tribunal is the successor to the Performing Right Tribunal which was established by the Copyright Act 1956 to resolve various classes of copyright dispute, principally in the field of collective licensing. Its jurisdiction was extended by the Copyright, Designs and Patents Act 1988 and the Broadcasting Act 1990.

The chairman and two deputy chairmen are appointed by the Lord Chancellor. Up to eight ordinary members are appointed by the President of the Board of Trade.

Chairman, J. M. Bowers
Secretary (acting), G. Belsham

THE DATA PROTECTION TRIBUNAL

c/o The Home Office, Queen Anne's Gate, London SW1H 9AT
Tel 071-273 3755

The Data Protection Tribunal was established under the Data Protection Act 1984 to determine appeals against decisions of the Data Protection Registrar. The chairman and two deputy chairmen are appointed by the Lord Chancellor and must be legally qualified. Lay members are appointed by the Home Secretary to represent the interests of data users or data subjects.

A tribunal consists of a legally-qualified chairman sitting with equal numbers of the lay members appointed to represent the interests of data users and data subjects. The chairman and members receive an *ad hoc* daily fee when the tribunal is sitting.

Chairman, J. A. C. Spokes, QC
Secretary, J. M. Priestley

EMPLOYMENT APPEAL TRIBUNAL

Central Office, Audit House, 58 Victoria Embankment, London EC4Y 0DS
Tel 071-273 1041
Divisional Office, 11 Melville Crescent, Edinburgh EH3 7LU
Tel 031-225 3963

The Employment Appeal Tribunal was established as a superior court of record under the provisions of the Employment Protection Act 1975, hearing appeals on a question of law arising from any decision of an industrial tribunal.

A tribunal consists of a legally-qualified chairman and two lay members, one from each side of industry. They are appointed by The Queen on the recommendation of the Lord Chancellor and the Secretary of State for Employment.

President, The Hon. Mr Justice Wood
Scottish Chairman, The Hon. Lord Coulsfield
Registrar, Miss V. J. Selio

IMMIGRATION APPELLATE AUTHORITIES

Thanet House, 231 Strand, London WC2R 1DA
Tel 071-353 8060

The Immigration Appeal Adjudicators hear appeals from immigration decisions concerning the need for, and refusal of, leave to enter or remain in the UK, decisions to make deportation orders and directions to remove persons subject to immigration control from the UK. The Immigration Appeal Tribunal hears appeals direct from decisions to make deportation orders in matters concerning conduct contrary to the public good. Its principal jurisdiction is, however, the hearing of appeals from adjudicators by the party (Home Office or individual) who is aggrieved by the decision. Most such appeals are subject to leave being granted by the tribunal.

An adjudicator sits alone. The tribunal sits in divisions of three – normally a legally qualified member and two lay members. Members of the tribunal and adjudicators are appointed by the Lord Chancellor.

IMMIGRATION APPEAL TRIBUNAL

President, G. W. Farmer
Vice-Presidents, Prof. D. C. Jackson; Mrs J. Chatwani

IMMIGRATION APPEAL ADJUDICATORS

Chief Adjudicator, M. Patey, MBE
Deputy Chief Adjudicator, R. G. Care

INDEPENDENT TRIBUNAL SERVICE

City Gate House, Finsbury Square, London EC2A 1UU

The service is an independent statutory authority which exercises judicial and administrative control over social security appeal tribunals, medical appeal tribunals, vaccine damage tribunals and disability appeal tribunals.

President (£68,400), His Hon. Judge Thorpe
Chief Administrator, J. Read

THE INDUSTRIAL TRIBUNALS

CENTRAL OFFICE (ENGLAND AND WALES)
93 Ebury Bridge Road, London SW1W 8RE
Tel 071-730 9161

Industrial Tribunals for England and Wales sit in 11 regions. The tribunals deal with matters of employment law, redundancy, dismissal, sexual and racial discrimination and related areas of dispute which may arise in the workplace. The tribunals are funded by the Department of Employment.

Chairmen, who may be full-time or part-time, are legally qualified. They are appointed by the Lord Chancellor. Tribunal members are nominated by the CBI and TUC, and appointed by the Secretary of State for Employment.

President, His Hon. Judge T. Lawrence

CENTRAL OFFICE (SCOTLAND)
St Andrew House, 141 West Nile Street, Glasgow G1 2RU
Tel 041-331 1601

Tribunals in Scotland have the same remit as those in England and Wales. Chairmen are appointed by the Lord President of the Court of Session and lay members by the Secretary of State for Employment.

President (£65,250), Mrs D. Littlejohn

INDUSTRIAL TRIBUNALS AND THE FAIR EMPLOYMENT TRIBUNAL (NORTHERN IRELAND)

Long Bridge House, 20–24 Waring Street, Belfast BT1 2EB
Tel 0232-327666

The industrial tribunal system in Northern Ireland was set up in 1965 and is similar to the system operating in the rest of the UK. The main legislation in Northern Ireland giving jurisdiction to industrial tribunals to hear complaints relating to employment matters corresponds to legislation enacted in Great Britain, except that there is no equivalent legislation to the Race Relations Act.

Since 1 January 1990 there has been a separate Fair Employment Tribunal in Northern Ireland. The Fair Employment Tribunal hears and determines individual cases of alleged religious or political discrimination in employment. Employers can also appeal to the Fair Employment Tribunal if they consider the directions of the Fair Employment Commission to be unreasonable, inappropriate or unnecessary, and the Fair Employment Commission can make application to the Tribunal for the enforcement of undertakings or directions with which an employer has not complied.

The president, vice-president and part-time chairmen of the Fair Employment Tribunal are appointed by the Lord Chancellor. The full-time chairman and the part-time chairmen of the industrial tribunals and the panel members to both the industrial tribunals and the Fair Employment Tribunal are appointed by the Department of Economic Development Northern Ireland.

President of the Industrial Tribunals and the Fair Employment Tribunal (£66,500), J. Maguire
Vice-President of the Industrial Tribunals and the Fair Employment Tribunal (£59,900), Mrs M. Perceval-Price
Secretary, J. Murphy

LANDS TRIBUNAL

48–49 Chancery Lane, London WC2A 1JR
Tel 071–936 7200

The Lands Tribunal is an independent judicial body constituted by the Lands Tribunal Act 1949 for the purpose of determining a wide range of questions relating to the valuation of land, rating appeals from local Valuation Courts and the discharge or modification of restrictive covenants. The Act also empowers the tribunal to accept the function of arbitration under references by consent. The tribunal consists of a president and a number of other members, who are appointed by the Lord Chancellor.

President (£76,180), V. G. Wellings, QC
Members (£64,064), Dr T. Hoyes; His Hon. Judge B. Marder, QC; His Hon. Judge M. O'Donoghue; M. S. J. Hopper, FRICS
Member (part-time) (£280 per day), J. C. Hill, TD
Registrar, C. A. McMullan

LANDS TRIBUNAL FOR SCOTLAND

1 Grosvenor Crescent, Edinburgh EH12 5ER
Tel 031-225 7996

The Lands Tribunal for Scotland was constituted by the Lands Tribunal Act 1949. Its remit is the same as the tribunal for England and Wales but also covers questions relating to tenants rights. The president is appointed by the Lord President of the Court of Session.

President (£66,500), The Hon. Lord Elliott, MC
Members (£59,900), Sheriff A. C. Horsfall, QC; A. R. MacLeary; J. Devine (*full-time*); R. A. Edwards, CBE, WS (*part-time*)
Clerk, D. Pentland

NATIONAL HEALTH SERVICE TRIBUNAL

The NHS Tribunal inquires into representations that the continued inclusion of a family practitioner (doctor, dentist, pharmacist or optician) on a Family Practitioner Committee's list would be prejudicial to the efficiency of the services concerned. The tribunal sits when required, about eight times a year, and usually in London.

Chairman, R. Bell, QC
Clerk, I. D. Keith, 1-2 Judges Terrace, East Grinstead, W. Sussex RH19 3AA. Tel: 0342-321111

NATIONAL HEALTH SERVICE TRIBUNAL (SCOTLAND)

33 Queen Street, Edinburgh EH2 1LE
Tel 031-226 6541

The tribunal was set up under the National Health Service (Scotland) Act 1978, and exists to consider representations that the continued inclusion of a registered medical practitioner, dental practitioner, optometrist or pharmacist on a health board's list would be prejudicial to the continuing efficiency of the service in question.

The tribunal meets when required and is composed of a chairman, one lay member, and one practitioner member drawn from a representative professional panel. The chairman is appointed by the Lord President of the Court of Session and the lay member and the members of the professional panel are appointed by the Secretary of State for Scotland. The chairman and members receive an *ad hoc* daily fee when the tribunal is sitting.

Chairman, W. C. Galbraith
Lay member, J. D. M. Robertson
Clerk to the Tribunal, D. G. Brash, WS

PENSIONS APPEAL TRIBUNALS

CENTRAL OFFICE (ENGLAND AND WALES)
48-49 Chancery Lane, London WC2A 1JR
Tel 071-936 7034

The Pensions Appeal Tribunals are responsible for hearing appeals from ex-servicemen or women and widows who have had their claims for a war pension rejected by the Secretary of State for Social Security. The Entitlement Appeal Tribunals hear appeals in cases where the Secretary of State has refused to grant a war pension. The Assessment Appeal Tribunals hear appeals against the Secretary of State's assessment of the degree of disablement caused by an accepted condition.

The tribunal members are appointed by the Lord Chancellor.

President (£52,520), M. H. Fauvelle
Secretary, S. J. Pye

PENSIONS APPEAL TRIBUNALS FOR SCOTLAND
20 Walker Street, Edinburgh EH3 7HS
Tel 031-220 1404

President, A. C. Hamilton, QC

OFFICE OF THE SOCIAL SECURITY COMMISSIONERS

London: Harp House, 83-86 Farringdon Street, EC4A 4DH
Tel 071-353 5145
Edinburgh: 23 Melville Street, EH3 7PW
Tel 031-225 2201

The Social Security Commissioners are the final statutory authority to decide appeals relating to entitlement to social security benefits. Appeals may be made only on a point of law. The Commissioners' jurisdiction covers England, Wales and Scotland. The commissioners are all qualified lawyers.

Chief Social Security Commissioner, His Hon. Judge K. Machin, QC
Secretary, Mrs M. White (*London*); R. Lindsay (*Edinburgh*)

OFFICE OF THE SOCIAL SECURITY COMMISSIONERS FOR NORTHERN IRELAND

Lancashire House, 5 Linenhall Street, Belfast BT2 8AA
Tel 0232-332344

The role of Northern Ireland Social Security Commissioners is similar to that of the Commissioners in Great Britain.

Chief Commissioner (£68,400), His Hon. Judge Chambers, QC
Registrar of Appeals, J. E. P. Millar

THE SOLICITORS' DISCIPLINARY TRIBUNAL

16 Bell Yard, London WC2A 1PL
Tel 071-242 0219

The Solicitors' Disciplinary Tribunal was constituted under the provisions of the Solicitors Act 1974. It is an independent statutory body whose members are appointed by the Master of the Rolls. The tribunal considers applications made to it alleging either professional misconduct and/or a breach of the statutory rules by which solicitors are bound against an individually named solicitor, or former solicitor. The tribunal's jurisdiction extends to solicitor's clerks, in respect of whom they may make an order restricting that clerk's employment by solicitors.

President, G. B. Marsh
Clerk, Mrs S. C. Elson

SPECIAL COMMISSIONERS OF INCOME TAX

15–19 Bedford Avenue, London WC1B 3AS
Tel 071–631 4242

The Special Commissioners are an independent body appointed by the Lord Chancellor to hear appeals concerning income taxes, etc.

Presiding Special Commissioner (£65,250), His Hon. Judge Stephen Oliver, QC
Special Commissioners (£49,100), T. H. K. Everett; D. A. Shirley
Deputy Special Commissioners, D. C. Potter, QC; R. H. Widdows, CB
Clerk (£21,724), R. P. Lester

TRANSPORT TRIBUNAL

48–49 Chancery Lane, London, WC2A 1JR
Tel 071–936 7494

The Transport Tribunal was set up in 1947 and hears appeals against decisions made by Traffic Commissioners at public inquiries. The tribunal consists of a legally-qualified president, two legal members who may sit as chairmen, and four lay members. The president and legal members are appointed by the Lord Chancellor and the lay members are appointed by the Secretary of State for Transport.

President (part-time), His Hon. Judge Harold Wilson
Legal members (£201 per day), His Hon. Judge Michael Brodrick (*part-time*); R. Owen, QC
Lay members (£161 per day), T. W. Hall; J. W. Whitworth; G. Simms; Miss E. B. Haran
Secretary, P. Harris

VAT TRIBUNALS

15–19 Bedford Avenue, London WC1B 3AS
Tel 071–631 4242

VAT Tribunals are administered by the Lord Chancellor's Department in England and Wales, and by the Secretary of State in Scotland. They are independent and decide disputes between taxpayers and the Commissioners of Customs and Excise, who manage VAT. In England and Wales, the president and chairmen are appointed by the Lord Chancellor, and members are appointed by the Treasury. Chairmen in Scotland are appointed by the Lord President of the Court of Session.

President (£65,250), His Hon. Judge Stephen Oliver, QC
Vice-President, Scotland (£48,200), R. A. Bennett, CBE, QC
Registrar, R. P. Lester

TRIBUNAL CENTRES

LONDON (including Belfast), 15–19 Bedford Avenue, London WC1B 3AS. Tel: 071–631 4242
EDINBURGH, 44 Palmerston Place, Edinburgh EH12 5BJ. Tel: 031–226 3551
MANCHESTER, Warwickgate House, Warwick Road, Old Trafford, Manchester M16 0GP. Tel: 061–872 6471

The Police Service

There are 52 police forces in the United Kingdom, each responsible for law enforcement in its area. Most forces' area is conterminous with an English or Welsh county or Scottish region, though there are several combined forces. Law enforcement in London is carried out by the Metropolitan Police and the City of London Police; in Northern Ireland by the Royal Ulster Constabulary; and by the Isle of Man, States of Jersey, and Guernsey forces in their respective islands and bailiwicks.

Each police force is maintained by a police authority. The authorities of English and Welsh forces comprise committees of local councillors and magistrates; in Scotland, the regional and islands councils are the authorities. The authority for the Metropolitan Police is the Home Secretary. In Northern Ireland the Secretary of State appoints the police authority.

Police authorities are financed by central and local government. Subject to the approval of the Home Secretary and to regulations, they appoint the chief constable, decide the maximum size of the force and provide buildings and equipment.

The National Criminal Intelligence Service was set up in April 1992 to gather and collate information on serious crime. It is independent of any other police organization.

The Home Secretary and the Secretaries of State for Scotland and Northern Ireland are responsible for the organization, administration and operation of the police service. They make regulations covering matters such as police ranks, discipline, hours of duty, and pay and allowances.

All police forces (including the Metropolitan Police at the request of the Commissioner) are subject to inspection by HM Inspectors of Constabulary, who report to the respective Secretary of State.

The investigation of a serious complaint against a police officer is supervised by the Police Complaints Authority (*see* page 346) in England and Wales. An officer may appeal against the finding of an investigation, or against the resulting punishment, to the Home Secretary; appeals are heard by private Police Appeal tribunals, whose members are appointed on an *ad hoc* basis. In Scotland, complaints are investigated by independent public prosecutors.

BASIC RATES OF POLICE PAY

as at 1 September 1992

Chief Constable	£55,482–£70,521
Deputy Chief Constable	£48,870–£56,418
Assistant Chief Constable	£46,542
Chief Superintendent	£39,480–£41,919
Superintendent	£35,508–£38,556
Chief Inspector	£26,103–£29,037
Inspector	£22,992–£26,103
Sergeant	£20,043–£22,992
Constable	£12,555–£20,952

**Metropolitan Police*

(including London weighting and London allowance for ranks from Inspector to Commissioner)

Metropolitan Commissioner	£82,780
Deputy Commissioner	£70,551
Assistant Commissioner	£62,241
Deputy Assistant Commissioner	£49,794
Commander	£43,701
Chief Superintendent	£37,071–£39,360
Superintendent	£34,191–£36,204
Chief Inspector	£25,686–£28,431
Inspector	£22,749–£25,686
Sergeant	£18,819–£21,588
Constable	£11,790–£19,674

*1991 figures

THE SPECIAL CONSTABULARY

The Special Constabulary is the part-time volunteer branch of the police force. Special Constables have full police powers within their force area and undertake regular officers' routine policing duties when required, thus freeing regulars at times of emergency for those tasks which only they can perform. There were 18,072 Special Constables in England and Wales at the end of 1991.

POLICE AUTHORITIES

Strength = actual strength of force as at mid June 1992
Chair = Chairman/Convener of the Police Authority/Police Committee

ENGLAND

AVON AND SOMERSET CONSTABULARY, *HQ*, PO Box 37, Valley Road, Portishead, Bristol BS20 8QJ. Tel: 0272-277777. *Strength*, 3,130; *Chief Constable*, D. J. Shattock, QPM; *Chair*, R. Mullett

BEDFORDSHIRE POLICE, *HQ*, Woburn Road, Kempston, Bedford MK43 9AX. Tel: 0234-841212. *Strength*, 1,097; *Chief Constable*, A. Dyer, QPM; *Chair*, elected at each meeting

CAMBRIDGESHIRE CONSTABULARY, *HQ*, Hinchingbrooke Park, Huntingdon, Cambs. PE18 8NP. Tel: 0480-56111. *Strength*, 1,220; *Chief Constable*, I. H. Kane, QPM; *Chair*, K. Spink, OBE

CHESHIRE CONSTABULARY, *HQ*, Castle Esplanade, Chester, CH1 2PP. Tel: 0244-350000. *Strength*, 1,905; *Chief Constable*, D. J. Graham, QPM; *Chair*, J. H. Collins, OBE

CLEVELAND CONSTABULARY, *HQ*, PO Box 70, Ladgate Lane, Middlesbrough, Cleveland TS8 9EH. Tel: 0642-326326. *Strength*, 1,483; *Chief Constable*, K. Hellawell, QPM; *Chair*, I. Jeffrey

CUMBRIA CONSTABULARY, *HQ*, Carleton Hall, Penrith, Cumbria CA10 2AU. Tel: 0768-64411. *Strength*, 1,180; *Chief Constable*, A. G. Elliott; *Chair*, R. Watson

DERBYSHIRE CONSTABULARY, *HQ*, Butterley Hall, Ripley, Derbyshire DE5 3RS. Tel: 0773-570100. *Strength*, 1,788; *Chief Constable*, J. F. Newing, QPM; *Chair*, E. H. Swain

DEVON AND CORNWALL CONSTABULARY, *HQ*, Middlemoor, Exeter EX2 7HQ. Tel: 0392-52101. *Strength*, 2,928; *Chief Constable*, J. S. Evans, QPM; *Chair*, S. J. Day

DORSET POLICE FORCE, *HQ*, Winfrith, Dorchester, Dorset DT2 8DZ. Tel: 0929-462727. *Strength*, 1,306; *Chief Constable*, B. H. Weight, QPM; *Chair*, Sir Stephen Hammick, Bt.

DURHAM CONSTABULARY, *HQ*, Aykley Heads, Durham DH1 5TT. Tel: 091-386 4929. *Strength*, 1,384; *Chief Constable*, F. W. Taylor, QPM; *Chair*, Mrs J. Parkin

ESSEX POLICE, *HQ*, PO Box 2, Springfield, Chelmsford CM2 6DA. Tel: 0245-491491. *Strength*, 2,904; *Chief Constable*, J. H. Burrow, OBE; *Chair*, G. C. Waterer, MBE

GLOUCESTERSHIRE CONSTABULARY, *HQ*, Holland House, Lansdown Road, Cheltenham, Glos. GL51 6QH. Tel: 0242-521321. *Strength*, 1,170; *Chief Constable*, A. H. Pacey, QPM; *Chairs*, Dr W. A. Whitehouse; Lt.-Col. W. McLelland

GREATER MANCHESTER POLICE, *HQ*, PO Box 22 (S. West PDO), Chester House, Boyer Street, Manchester M16 ORE. Tel: 061-872 5050. *Strength*, 7,075; *Chief Constable*, D. Wilmot, QPM; *Chair*, S. Murphy

HAMPSHIRE CONSTABULARY, *HQ*, West Hill, Winchester, Hants. SO22 5DB. Tel: 0962-68133. *Strength*, 3,219; *Chief Constable*, J. C. Hoddinott, QPM; *Chair*, B. L. P. Blacker

HERTFORDSHIRE CONSTABULARY, *HQ*, Stanborough Road, Welwyn Garden City, Herts. AL8 6XF. Tel: 0707-331177. *Strength*, 1,690; *Chief Constable*, B. H. Skitt, BEM, QPM; *Chair*, F. J. Cogan, CBE

HUMBERSIDE POLICE, *HQ*, Queens Gardens, Kingston upon Hull, N. Humberside HU1 3DJ. Tel: 0482-26111. *Strength*, 1,997; *Chief Constable*, D. A. Leonard, QPM; *Chair*, G. T. Berry

KENT CONSTABULARY, *HQ*, Sutton Road, Maidstone, Kent ME15 9BZ. Tel: 0622-65432. *Strength*, 3,091; *Chief Constable*, P. Condon, QPM; *Chair*, C. R. Carr

LANCASHIRE CONSTABULARY, *HQ*, PO Box 77, Hutton, Preston PR4 5SB. Tel: 0772-614444. *Strength*, 3,201; *Chief Constable*, R. B. Johnson, CBE, QPM; *Chair*, Mrs R. B. Henig

LEICESTERSHIRE CONSTABULARY, *HQ*, PO Box 999, Leicester LE99 1AZ. Tel: 0533-530066. *Strength*, 1,853; *Chief Constable*, M. J. Hirst, QPM; *Chair*, R. R. Angrave, CBE

LINCOLNSHIRE POLICE, *HQ*, PO Box 999, Lincoln LN5 7PH. Tel: 0522-532222. *Strength*, 1,198; *Chief Constable*, N. G. Ovens, QPM; *Chair*, M. D. Kennedy

MERSEYSIDE POLICE, *HQ*, PO Box 59, Canning Place, Liverpool L69 1JD. Tel: 051-709 6010. *Strength*, 4,737; *Chief Constable*, J. Sharples, QPM; *Chair*, G. Bundred, CBE

NORFOLK CONSTABULARY, *HQ*, Martineau Lane, Norwich NR1 2DJ. Tel: 0603-615111. *Strength*, 1,410; *Chief Constable*, P. J. Ryan, QPM; *Chair*, R. T. Chase

NORTHAMPTONSHIRE POLICE, *HQ*, Wootton Hall, Northampton NN4 0JQ. Tel: 0604-700700. *Strength*, 1,190; *Chief Constable*, D. O'Dowd, QPM; *Chair*, A. Morby

NORTHUMBRIA POLICE, *HQ*, Ponteland, Newcastle upon Tyne NE20 0BL. Tel: 0661-72555. *Strength*, 3,551; *Chief Constable*, J. A. Stevens, QPM; *Chair*, G. Gill

NORTH YORKSHIRE POLICE, *HQ*, Newby Wiske Hall, Newby Wiske, Northallerton, N. Yorks. DL7 9HA. Tel: 0609-783131. *Strength*, 1,397; *Chief Constable*, D. M. Burke, QPM; *Chair*, J. H. G. Parfect, MBE

NOTTINGHAMSHIRE CONSTABULARY, *HQ*, Sherwood Lodge, Arnold, Nottingham NG5 8PP. Tel: 0602-670999. *Strength*, 2,341; *Chief Constable*, D. Crompton, QPM; *Chair*, C. P. Winterton

SOUTH YORKSHIRE POLICE, *HQ*, Snig Hill, Sheffield S3 8LY. Tel: 0742-768522. *Strength*, 3,031; *Chief Constable*, R. Wells, QPM; *Chair*, Sir John Layden

STAFFORDSHIRE POLICE, *HQ*, Cannock Road, Stafford ST17 0QG. Tel: 0785-57717. *Strength*, 2,184; *Chief Constable*, C. H. Kelly, CBE, QPM; *Chair*, Miss I. H. Moseley

SUFFOLK CONSTABULARY, *HQ*, Martlesham Heath, Ipswich IP5 7QS. Tel: 0473-611611. *Strength*, 1,234; *Chief Constable*, A. T. Coe, QPM; *Chair*, Capt. R. J. Sheepshanks, CBE

SURREY CONSTABULARY, *HQ*, Mount Browne, Sandy Lane, Guildford, Surrey GU3 1HG. Tel: 0483-571212. *Strength*, 1,673; *Chief Constable*, D. J. Williams, QPM; *Chair*, Mrs D. James

SUSSEX POLICE, *HQ*, Malling House, Church Lane, Lewes, E. Sussex BN7 2DZ. Tel: 0273-475432. *Strength*, 2,981; *Chief Constable*, Sir Roger Birch, KBE, QPM; *Chair*, J. P. Sheridan

THAMES VALLEY POLICE, *HQ*, Oxford Road, Kidlington, Oxford OX5 2NX. Tel: 0865-846000. *Strength*, 3,877; *Chief Constable*, C. Pollard, QPM; *Chair*, C. F. Robinson, OBE

WARWICKSHIRE CONSTABULARY, *HQ*, PO Box 4, Leek Wootton, Warwick CV35 7QB. Tel: 0926-410111. *Strength*, 994; *Chief Constable*, P. D. Joslin, QPM; *Chair*, J. L. Findon

WEST MERCIA CONSTABULARY, *HQ*, PO Box 55, Hindlip Hall, Hindlip, Worcester WR3 8SP. Tel: 0905-723000. *Strength*, 2,043; *Chief Constable*, D. C. Blakey; *Chair*, R. A. H. Lloyd, TD

WEST MIDLANDS POLICE, *HQ*, PO Box 52, Lloyd House, Colmore Circus, Queensway, Birmingham B4 6NQ. Tel: 021-236 5000. *Strength*, 6,897; *Chief Constable*, R. Hadfield, QPM; *Chair*, L. V. Jones

WEST YORKSHIRE POLICE, *HQ*, PO Box 9, Laburnum Road, Wakefield, W. Yorks. WF1 3QP. Tel: 0924-292208. *Strength*, 5,052; *Chief Constable*, P. J. Nobes, QPM; *Chair*, T. Brennan

WILTSHIRE CONSTABULARY, *HQ*, London Road, Devizes, Wilts. SN10 2DN. Tel: 0380-722141. *Strength*, 1,123; *Chief Constable*, W. R. Girvan, QPM; *Chair*, Lt.-Col. D. B. W. Jarvis, DFC

WALES

DYFED–POWYS POLICE, *HQ*, PO Box 99, Llangunnor, Carmarthen, Dyfed SA31 2PF. Tel: 0267-236444. *Strength*, 969; *Chief Constable*, R. White, QPM; *Chair*, A. L. Pritchard

GWENT CONSTABULARY, *HQ*, Croesyceiliog, Cwmbran, Gwent NP44 2XJ. Tel: 0633-838111. *Strength*, 1,002; *Chief Constable*, J. E. Over, QPM, CPM; *Chair*, B. Sutton

NORTH WALES POLICE, *HQ*, Glan-y-Don, Colwyn Bay, Clwyd LL29 8AW. Tel: 0492-517171. *Strength*, 1,369; *Chief Constable*, D. Owen, CBE, QPM; *Chair*, W. E. Conway

SOUTH WALES CONSTABULARY, *HQ*, Cowbridge Road, Bridgend, Mid Glamorgan CF31 3SU. Tel: 0656-655555. *Strength*, 3,167; *Chief Constable*, W. R. Lawrence, QPM; *Chair*, D. McDonald

SCOTLAND

CENTRAL SCOTLAND POLICE, *HQ*, Randolphfield, Stirling FK8 2HD. Tel: 0786-560000. *Strength*, 647; *Chief Constable*, W. J. M. Wilson, QPM; *Convener*, Mrs A. Wallace

DUMFRIES AND GALLOWAY CONSTABULARY, *HQ*, Loreburn Street, Dumfries DG1 1HP. Tel: 0387-52112. *Strength*, 382; *Chief Constable*, G. A. Esson, QPM; *Chair*, R. Brown

FIFE CONSTABULARY, *HQ*, Wemyss Road, Dysart, Kirkcaldy, Fife KY1 2YA. Tel: 0592-52611. *Strength*, 775; *Chief Constable*, W. M. Moodie, CBE, QPM; *Chair*, C. J. Groom

GRAMPIAN POLICE, *HQ*, Queen Street, Aberdeen AB9 1BA. Tel: 0224-639111. *Strength*, 1,168; *Chief Constable*, I. T. Oliver, QPM, Ph.D.; *Chair*, Dr J. K. A. Thomaneck

LOTHIAN AND BORDERS POLICE, *HQ*, Fettes Avenue, Edinburgh EH4 1RB. Tel: 031-311 3131. *Strength*, 2,489; *Chief Constable*, Sir William Sutherland, QPM; *Chair*, R. B. Martin

NORTHERN CONSTABULARY, *HQ*, Perth Road, Inverness IV2 3SY. Tel: 0463-239191. *Strength*, 654; *Chief Constable*, H. C. MacMillan, QPM; *Chair*, Mrs I. C. Rhind

STRATHCLYDE POLICE, *HQ*, 173 Pitt Street, Glasgow G2 4JS. Tel: 041-204 2626. *Strength*, 6,954; *Chief Constable*, L. Sharp, QPM; *Chair*, J. Jennings

TAYSIDE POLICE, *HQ*, PO Box 59, West Bell Street, Dundee DD1 9JU. Tel: 0382-23200. *Strength*, 1,053; *Chief Constable*, J. W. Bowman, CBE, QPM; *Chair*, W. Smith

NORTHERN IRELAND

ROYAL ULSTER CONSTABULARY, *HQ*, Brooklyn, Knock Road, Belfast BT5 6LE. Tel: 0232-650222. *Strength*, 8,353; *Chief Constable*, Sir Hugh Annesley, QPM; *Chair*, T. Rainey

ISLANDS

ISLAND POLICE FORCE, *HQ*, St Peter Port, Guernsey, Channel Islands. Tel: 0481-725111. *Strength*, 149; *Chief Officer*, M. Le Moignan, QPM; *Chair*, M. Torode

STATES OF JERSEY POLICE, *HQ*, Rouge Bouillon, St Helier, Jersey, Channel Islands. Tel: 0534-69996. *Strength*, 232; *Chief Officer*, D. Parkinson, QPM; *Chair*, M. Wavell

ISLE OF MAN CONSTABULARY, *HQ*, Glencrutchery Road, Douglas, Isle of Man. Tel: 0624-26222. *Strength*, 213; *Chief Constable*, R. E. N. Oake; *Minister for Home Affairs*, The Hon. A. A. Callin

---

METROPOLITAN POLICE FORCE

New Scotland Yard, Broadway, London SW1H 0BG
Tel 071-230 1212

Establishment, 28,472

Commissioner, Sir Peter Imbert, QPM
Deputy Commissioner, J. A. Smith, QPM
Receiver, G. M. Angel

TERRITORIAL OPERATIONS DEPARTMENT

Assistant Commissioner, R. A. Hunt, OBE, QPM
Deputy Assistant Commissioner, T. J. Siggs, OBE
Commanders, J. J. Allinson; C. R. Pearman; D. N. Stevens

AREA HEADQUARTERS

Deputy Assistant Commissioners, W. E. E. Boreham, OBE; M. B. Taylor, QPM; D. J. Osland, QPM; A. G. Fry, QPM; L. T. Roach, QPM; A. J. Speed, QPM; D. Flanders
Commanders, T. O. Jones, MBE; J. A. Coo, QPM; M. G. Farbrother; L. J. Poole; D. M. T. Kendrick; J. F. Purnell, CGM; B. J. Luckhurst; T. D. Laidlow; A. V. Comben; B. S. Plaxton; J. D. Gibson; J. P. O'Connor; B. F. Aitchison; I. Quinn; M. R. Campbell, QPM; J. Townshend

SPECIALIST OPERATIONS DEPARTMENT

Assistant Commissioner, W. Taylor, QPM
Deputy Assistant Commissioners, D. M. Meynell, OBE; J. A. Howley, QPM; D. C. Veness
Commanders, K. G. Churchill-Coleman, QPM; G. M. Ness, QPM; P. R. Nove; R. A. Penrose; D. C. Stockley; D. Buchanan; R. C. Marsh, QPM; D. M. Tucker; B. G. Moss

Metropolitan Police Laboratory

Director, Dr B. Sheard
Deputy Directors, G. J. O. Lee; M. R. Loveland; P. D. Martin; Dr W. D. C. Wilson

PERSONNEL DEPARTMENT

Director of Personnel, E. Mitchell, QPM
Director of Civil Staff Personnel Management, R. M. Gregory
Director of Police Personnel Management, M. J. Sullivan, QPM
Director of Manpower Planning and Personnel Policy, J. S. Steele
Director of Catering, A. Thompson
Director of Occupational Health, Dr A. Johnson

MEDICAL AND DENTAL BRANCH

Chief Medical Officer, Dr E. C. A. Bott, CBE

INSPECTION AND REVIEW

Assistant Commissioner, P. J. J. Winship, QPM

COMPLAINTS INVESTIGATION BUREAU

Commander, E. Humphrey, QPM

CENTRAL STAFF

Commander, M. Briggs

DIRECTORATE OF PUBLIC AFFAIRS

Director of Public Affairs, vacant

DIRECTORATE OF PERFORMANCE REVIEW AND MANAGEMENT SERVICES

Director, Mrs S. M. Merchant

SOLICITOR'S DEPARTMENT

Solicitor, C. S. Porteous

'F' DEPARTMENT

Director of Finance, J. A. Crutchlow

PROPERTY SERVICES DEPARTMENT

Director of Property Services, T. G. Lawrence

DEPARTMENT OF TECHNOLOGY

Director of Technology, N. Boothman

CITY OF LONDON POLICE

26 Old Jewry, London EC2R 8DJ
Tel 071-601 2222

Strength of force (June 1992), 829

Commissioner (£70,182), O. Kelly, QPM
Assistant Commissioner (£53,373), C. Coxall
Commander (£44,796), H. J. Moore, QPM
Chief Superintendents (£37,071–£39,360):
'B' Division, G. Marshall
'C' Division, T. Dickinson
CID, P. Gwynn
Company Fraud, R. Knevett
Management Support, R. Friend
Operational Support, T. Hillier

BRITISH TRANSPORT POLICE

15 Tavistock Place, London WC1H 9SJ
Tel 071-388 7541

Strength of force (April 1992), 2,041

The Force provides a policing service to the British Railways Board and London Underground Ltd. Police stations are located throughout England, Wales and Scotland.

The Chief Constable reports to the British Transport Police Committee, a statutory body set up under the Transport Act 1962. The members of the Committee are appointed by the British Railways Board and London Underground Ltd.

Chief Constable, D. O'Brien, OBE
Deputy Chief Constable, A. Parker
Assistant Chief Constables:
Support Services, vacant
Operations, W. I. McGregor, QPM
Scottish Area, S. Mannion
Communications and Technology, A. Horn

MINISTRY OF DEFENCE POLICE

Ministry of Defence, Empress State Building, Lillie Road, London SW6 1TR
Tel 071-385 1244

Strength of force (May 1992), 5,192

The Ministry of Defence Police is a statutory police force directly responsible to the Secretary of State for Defence for the policing of all military land, stations and establishments in the United Kingdom.

Chief Constable, J. Reddington, QPM
Deputy Chief Constable, N. L. Chapple, QPM
Head of Secretariat, W. A. T. Aves
Assistant Chief Constables:
Inspectorate and Firearms, S. G. Edwards, QPM
Operations, R. E. Murray
Personnel and Training, B. J. Smith
Scotland, A. F. Grant
Support, P. A. Bedwell

ROYAL PARKS CONSTABULARY

2 Marsham Street, London SW1P 3EB
Tel 071-276 3761/3

Strength of force (June 1992), 158

The Royal Parks Constabulary is maintained by the Department of National Heritage and is responsible for the policing of twenty Royal Parks in and around London. These comprise an area in excess of 6,000 acres. Officers of the Force are appointed under the Parks Regulations Act 1872, as amended by the Parks Regulations (Amendment) Act 1974.

Chief Officer, W. Ross
Deputy Chief Officer, M. J. Loader

UNITED KINGDOM ATOMIC ENERGY AUTHORITY CONSTABULARY

Building E6, Culham Laboratory, Abingdon, Oxon. OX14 3DB
Tel 0235-463760

Strength of force (June 1992), 541

The Constabulary is responsible for policing United Kingdom Atomic Energy Authority and British Nuclear Fuels PLC establishments and for escorting nuclear material between establishments.

The Chief Constable is responsible, through the Atomic Energy Authority Police Committee, to the President of the Board of Trade.

Chief Constable, H. J. McMorris, QPM
Deputy Chief Constable, E. H. Miller

STAFF ASSOCIATIONS

ASSOCIATION OF CHIEF POLICE OFFICERS OF ENGLAND, WALES AND NORTHERN IRELAND, Room 311, Wellington House, 67–73 Buckingham Gate, London SW1E 5BE. Represents the Chief Constables, Deputy Chief Constables and Assistant Chief Constables of England, Wales and Northern Ireland, and officers of the rank of Commander and above in the Metropolitan and City of London Police. *General Secretary*, Miss M. C. E. Barton

THE POLICE SUPERINTENDENTS' ASSOCIATION OF ENGLAND AND WALES, 67A Reading Road, Pangbourne, Reading RG8 7JD. Represents officers of the rank of Superintendent and Chief Superintendent. *Secretary*, Chief Supt. P. G. Wall

THE POLICE FEDERATION OF ENGLAND AND WALES, 15–17 Langley Road, Surbiton, Surrey KT6 6LP. Represents officers up to and including the rank of Chief Inspector. *General Secretary*, Insp. V. Neild (Miss)

ASSOCIATION OF CHIEF POLICE OFFICERS IN SCOTLAND, Police Headquarters, Fettes Avenue, Edinburgh EH4 1RB. Represents the Chief Constables, Deputy Chief Constables and Assistant Chief Constables of the Scottish police forces. *Hon. Secretary*, Sir William Sutherland, QPM

THE ASSOCIATION OF SCOTTISH POLICE SUPERINTENDENTS, Hon. Secretary's Office, Strathclyde Police, 'P' Division, Divisional Headquarters, 217 Windmillhill Street, Motherwell ML1 1RZ. Represents officers of the rank of Superintendent and Chief Superintendent. *Hon. Secretary*, Chief Supt. J. Urquhart

THE SCOTTISH POLICE FEDERATION, 5 Woodside Place, Glasgow G3 7PD. Represents officers up to and including the rank of Chief Inspector. *General Secretary*, A. W. A. Wallace

THE SUPERINTENDENT ASSOCIATION OF NORTHERN IRELAND, Ormiston House, Hawthornden Road, Belfast BT4 3JW. Represents Superintendents and Chief Superintendents in the RUC. *Hon. Secretary*, W/Chief Supt. A. Donald

THE POLICE FEDERATION FOR NORTHERN IRELAND, Royal Ulster Constabulary, Garnerville, Garnerville Road, Belfast BT4 2NX. Represents officers up to and including the rank of Chief Inspector. *Secretary*, D. A. McClurg

Defence

MINISTRY OF DEFENCE

Main Building, Whitehall, London SW1A 2HB
Tel 071-218 9000

The Ministry of Defence is concerned with the control, administration, equipment and support of the Armed Forces of the Crown. The research, development, production and purchase of weapons systems and equipment for the Armed Forces is the concern of the Procurement Executive of the Ministry of Defence.

SALARIES

Secretary of State	£39,820
Minister of State	£28,175
Parliamentary Under Secretary	£37,689
Grade 1	£87,620
Grade 1A	£80,600
Grade 2	£62,504–£73,216
Grade 3	£49,920–£57,928*
Grade 4	£44,390–£49,790*
Grade 5	£36,178–£47,921*

*Plus London weighting (*see* page 284)
For Services salaries, *see* pages 405–6

Secretary of State for Defence, The Rt. Hon. Malcolm Rifkind, QC, MP
Private Secretary (*G5*), S. Webb, CBE
Parliamentary Private Secretary, H. Bellingham, MP
Minister of State for the Armed Forces, The Rt. Hon. Archibald Hamilton, MP
Private Secretary, J. A. Miller
Parliamentary Private Secretary, R. Gale, MP
Minister of State for Defence Procurement, The Rt. Hon. Jonathan Aitken, MP
Private Secretary, P. Watkins
Parliamentary Under Secretary of State, Viscount Cranborne
Private Secretary, P. A. Wilson
Permanent Under Secretary of State (*G1*), Sir Christopher France, KCB
Private Secretary, T. C. McKane
Chief of the Defence Staff, Field Marshal Sir Richard Vincent, GBE, KCB, DSO (Marshal of the RAF Sir Peter Harding, GCB, ADC, *w.e.f. Jan. 1993*)

THE DEFENCE COUNCIL

The Defence Council is responsible for running the Armed Forces. It is chaired by the Secretary of State for Defence and consists of: the Ministers of State; the Permanent Under Secretary of State; the Chief of the Defence Staff and the Vice-Chief of the Defence Staff; the Parliamentary Under Secretary of State; the Chief Scientific Adviser; the Chief of Defence Procurement; the Second Permanent Under Secretary of State; the Chief of the Naval Staff; the Chief of the General Staff; and the Chief of the Air Staff.

DEFENCE STAFF

Vice-Chief of the Defence Staff, Adm. Sir Benjamin Bathurst, KCB (Adm. Sir Jock Slater, GCB, LVO, *w.e.f. Feb. 1993*)
Deputy Under Secretary (*Policy*) (*G2*), vacant
Defence Services Secretary, Maj.-Gen. B. T. Pennicott
Deputy CDS (*Commitments*), Adm. the Hon. Sir Nicholas Hill-Horton, KCB
Asst Under Secretary (*Commitments*) (*G3*), W. D. Reeves
Asst CDS (*Overseas*), Maj.-Gen. A. G. H. Harley, CB, OBE
Asst CDS (*Logistics*), Air Vice-Marshal D. J. Saunders, CBE
Deputy CDS (*Systems*), Air Marshal Sir Roger Austin, KCB, AFC
Head of Manpower Structure Study Team, Air Vice-Marshal A. L. Roberts, CBE, AFC
Asst CDS, Operational Requirements (*Sea*), Rear-Adm. R. F. Cobbold
Asst CDS, Operational Requirements (*Land*), Maj.-Gen. S. Cowan, CBE
Asst CDS, Operational Requirements (*Air*), Air Vice-Marshal I. D. Macfadyen, CB, OBE
Asst CDS (*CIS*), Rear-Adm. R. Walmsley
Asst CDS (*Policy and Nuclear*), Rear-Adm. J. J. R. Tod, CBE
Asst Under Secretary (*Policy*) (*G3*), I. D. Dawson
Deputy CDS (*Programmes and Personnel*), Lt.-Gen. the Hon. T. P. J. Boyd-Carpenter, MBE
Asst CDS (*Programmes*), Air Vice-Marshal D. O. Crwys-Williams, CB
Deputy Surgeon-General (*Health Services*) *and Director-General Medical Services* (*RAF*), Air Vice-Marshal J. M. Brook, QHS
Deputy Surgeon-General (*Ops. and Plans*) *and Medical Director-General* (*Naval*), Surgeon Rear-Adm. D. A. Lammiman, LVO, QHS
Surgeon-General and Director-General Army Medical Services, Lt.-Gen. Sir Peter Beale, KBE, QHP
Director, Defence Nursing Services, Commandant Nursing Officer Miss J. Titley
Director Army Nursing Services, Brig. H. S. Dixon-Nuttal, QHNS
Director, Defence Dental Services, Air Vice-Marshal J. Mackey, QHDS
Head of Medical Services (*Fin. and Sect. Div.*) (*G5*), P. G. Schulte
Director, Army Medicine and Consultant Physician, Brig. G. O. Cowan, OBE, QHP
Director, Army Surgeon and Consultant Surgeon, Maj.-Gen. R. P. Craig, QHS
Director, Army Psychiatry and Consultant Psychiatrist, Col. R. M. L. Anderson

DEFENCE INTELLIGENCE STAFF

Director, Defence Intelligence (*Secretariat*) (*G5*), J. N. L. Morrison

NAVAL DEPARTMENT

Chief of the Naval Staff and First Sea Lord, Adm. Sir Julian Oswald, GCB, ADC (Adm. Sir Benjamin Bathurst, KCB, *w.e.f. Feb. 1993*)
Asst Chief of Naval Staff, Rear-Adm. P. C. Abbott
Commandant-General Royal Marines, Lt.-Gen. Sir Henry Beverley, KCB, OBE
Chief of Naval Personnel and Second Sea Lord, Adm. Sir Michael Livesay, KCB
Naval Secretary, Rear-Adm. M. C. Rutherford, CBE
Director-General, Naval Manpower and Training, Rear-Adm. N. J. Wilkinson
Asst Under Secretary (*Naval Personnel*) (*G3*), J. M. Moss
Chief of Fleet Support, Vice-Adm. Sir Neville Purvis, KCB
Hydrographer of the Royal Navy, Rear-Adm. J. A. L. Myres
Asst Under Secretary (*Fleet Support*) (*G3*), D. C. R. Heyhoe

Director-General, Ship Refitting (G3), G. A. Allin
Director-General, Supplies and Transport (N) (G3), J. T. Baugh
Principal Director, Supplies and Transport (Ops.) (G4), W. N. Cooke
Principal Director, Supplies and Transport (Stores and Victualling) (G4), G. E. Miller
Principal Director, Supplies and Transport (Armaments) (G4), M. A. Holder
Director-General, Fleet Support (Policy and Services), Rear-Adm. G. N. Davis
Director, Naval Shore Telecommunications (G5), M. Frowde
Director-General, Aircraft (Navy), Rear-Adm. R. C. Moylan-Jones
Director, Women's Royal Naval Services, Cmdt. A. C. Spencer, ADC
Chaplain of The Fleet, Ven. M. H. G. Henley, QHC

HYDROGRAPHIC OFFICE
Taunton, Somerset TA1 2DN
Tel 0823-337900

The Hydrographic Office was established as a defence support agency in April 1990 and provides charts and publications for the Royal Navy and other customers in the UK and overseas.

Chief Executive, Rear-Adm. J. A. L. Myres

ARMY DEPARTMENT

Chief of the General Staff, Gen. Sir Peter Inge, KCB, ADC (Gen.)
Asst Chief of the General Staff, Maj.-Gen. R. N. Wheeler, CBE
Director-General, TA, Maj.-Gen. A. I. J. Kennedy, CBE
Director-General, Army Training, Maj.-Gen. S. C. Grant
Inspector-General, Doctrine and Training, Lt.-Gen. P. R. Duffell, CBE, MC
Director, Royal Armoured Corps, Maj.-Gen. R. J. Hayman-Joyce, CBE
Director, Royal Artillery, Maj.-Gen. M. T. Tennant
Director, Infantry, Maj.-Gen. B. H. Dutton, CBE
Director, Army Air Corps, Maj.-Gen. S. W. St J. Lytle
Engineer in Chief (Army), Maj.-Gen. J. A. J. P. Barr, CBE
Director-General, Communications and Info. Systems (Army) and Signals Officer in Chief (Army), Maj.-Gen. A. H. Boyle
Military Secretary, Lt.-Gen. the Hon. Sir William Rous, KCB, OBE
Adjutant-General, Gen. Sir David Ramsbotham, KCB, CBE, ADC (Gen.)
Asst Under Secretary (Army) (G3), M. L. Scicluna
Asst Under Secretary (Command Secretary, HQ UK Land Forces) (G3), D. Dreher
Director-General, Army Manning and Recruiting, Maj.-Gen. J. F. J. Johnston, CBE
Paymaster in Chief, Maj.-Gen. P. S. Bray
Director-General, Personal Services (Army), Maj.-Gen. M. D. Jackson, MBE
Provost Marshal (Army), Brig. I. Cameron
Director, Army Legal Services, Maj.-Gen. M. H. F. Clarke
Director, Educational and Training Services (Army), Maj.-Gen. C. A. Kinvig
Quartermaster-General, Gen. Sir John Learmont, KCB, CBE
Asst Under Secretary (Quartermaster) (G3), N. J. Beaumont
Director-General, Logistics Policy (Army), Maj.-Gen. G. W. Field, OBE
Director-General, Transport and Movements, Maj.-Gen. J. D. Macdonald, CBE
Director, Royal Army Veterinary Corps, Brig. A. H. Parker-Bowles, OBE
Director-General, Management and Support of Intelligence, Maj.-Gen. A. L. Meier, OBE
Director-General, Ordnance Services, Maj.-Gen. D. F. E. Botting, CB, CBE
Director-General, Equipment Support (Army), Maj.-Gen. M. S. Heath
Director, Women, Brig. J. M. Roulstone
Chaplain General, Rev. J. Harkness, OBE, QHC

MILITARY SURVEY
Elmwood Avenue, Feltham, Middx. TW13 7AH
Tel 081-890 3622

Military Survey was established as a defence support agency in April 1991. Its role is to give the armed forces the geographic support required to enable them to plan, train and fight effectively.

Chief Executive and Director-General, Maj.-Gen. R. Wood

AIR FORCE DEPARTMENT

Chief of the Air Staff, Air Chief Marshal Sir Michael Graydon, KCB, CBE
Asst Chief of Air Staff, Air Vice-Marshal T. Garden, CB
Commandant-General and Director-General of Security (RAF), Air Vice-Marshal D. R. Hawkins, MBE
Chief Executive, National Air Traffic Services (G3), D. J. McLauchlan
Director-General, Policy and Planning, National Air Traffic Services, Air Vice-Marshal M. J. Gibson, OBE
Air Member for Personnel, Air Chief Marshal Sir Roger Palin, KCB, OBE, ADC
Air Secretary, Air Vice-Marshal R. J. Honey, CB, CBE
Director-General, Training and Personnel (RAF), Air Vice-Marshal P. G. Beer, CBE, LVO
Director, Legal Services (RAF) Air Vice-Marshal G. W. Carleton
Chief of Logistic Support (RAF), Air Marshal Sir Michael Alcock, KBE, CB
Asst Under Secretary (Personnel (Air)) (G3), M. D. Tidy
Air Member for Supply and Organization, Air Chief Marshal Sir Brendan Jackson, GCB.
Director-General, Support Services (RAF), Air Vice-Marshal R. H. Kyle, MBE
Director-General, Support Management (RAF), Air Vice-Marshal C. P. Baker, CB
Asst Under Secretary (Supply and Organization (Air)) (G3), D. J. Gould
Chaplain Services (RAF), Ven. B. H. Lucas, CB, QHC

RAF SUPPORT COMMAND MAINTENANCE GROUP
RAF Brampton, Huntingdon, Cambs. PE18 8QL
Tel 0480-52151

The Group became a defence support agency in April 1991. It supplies engineering, warehousing, transportation and communications services to the RAF and some other UK and NATO services.

Chief Executive, Air Marshal D. R. French

DEFENCE SCIENTIFIC STAFF

Chief Scientific Adviser (G1A), Prof. Sir Ernest Oxburgh, KBE, Ph.D
Deputy Chief Scientific Adviser (G2), Dr G. G. Pope, CB
Asst Chief Scientific Advisers (G3), J. W. Britton (*Projects and Research*); G. H. B. Jordan (*Capabilities*); Dr T. Buckley (*Research*); (*G4*) Dr G. Pocock (*Nuclear*)
Chief Executive, Defence Operational Analysis Centre (G3), Dr D. Leadbeater
Director-General, Strategic Defence Initiative Participation Office (G5), A. L. C. Quigley

OFFICE OF MANAGEMENT AND BUDGET

Second Permanent Under Secretary of State (G1A), J. M. Stewart, CB
Deputy Under Secretaries (G2), M. J. V. Bell (*Finance*); J. F. Howe, OBE (*Civilian Management*); R. L. L. Facer, CB (*Personnel and Logistics*); R. T. Jackling, CBE (*Resources and Programmes*)
Asst Under Secretaries (G3), T. J. Brack (*General Finance*); M. J. Culham, CB (*Civilian Management (Administration)*); Dr M. J. Harte (*Resources*); M. J. Dymond (*Director-General Defence Accounts*); A. G. Rucker (*Security and Common Services*); A. J. Cragg (*Director-General of Management Audit*); M. Gainsborough (*Personnel*); D. B. Omand (*Programmes*); N. H. Nicholls, CBE (*Systems*); I. D. Fauset (*Civilian Management (Specialists)*); B. F. Rule (*Director-General, Information Technology Services*); B. W. Stanley (*Director, Works Services*); T. F. W. B. Knapp (*Infrastructure and Logistics*)
Chief Statistical Adviser and Chief Executive of Defence Analytical Services Agency, P. Altobell
Chief of Ministry of Defence Police, J. Reddington, QPM

DIRECTORATE-GENERAL OF DEFENCE ACCOUNTS
Warminster Road, Bath BA1 5AA
Tel 0225-828106

This defence support agency was established in April 1991 and is responsible for providing accounting services to the MOD.

Chief Executive (G4), M. J. Dymond

PUBLIC RELATIONS

Chief of Public Relations (G4), Ms G. Samuel
Deputy Chief of Public Relations (G5), C. Verey
Director, Public Relations (Navy), Capt. C. Esplin-Jones
Director, Public Relations (Army), Brig. T. A. L. Glass, CBE
Director, Public Relations (RAF), Air Cdre B. E. A. Pegnall

PROCUREMENT EXECUTIVE

Chief of Defence Procurement (G1), Dr M. K. McIntosh
Private Secretary, S. H. Lowe

PROCUREMENT EXECUTIVE POLICY AND ADMINISTRATION

Deputy Under Secretary (Defence Procurement) (G2), A. J. P. Macdonald, CB
Asst Under Secretary (International and Domestic Procurement) (G3), J. A. Gulvin
President of the Ordnance Board, Maj.-Gen. C. R. S. Notley, CBE
Director-General, Test and Evaluation (G3), B. Miller
Director-General, Defence Contracts (G3), G. E. Roe
Principal Director, Accountancy, Estimating and Pricing Services (G4), J. V. A. Crawford
Director, Intellectual Property Rights (G4), D. J. Isaaks
Commandant, Aeroplane and Armament Experimental Establishment, Air Cdre J. E. Houghton, AFC

DEFENCE RESEARCH AGENCY
Farnborough, Hants. GU14 6TD
Tel 0252-373434

The Defence Research Agency (DRA) was set up on 1 April 1991. It incorporated the Royal Aerospace Establishment (now Aerospace Division), the Admiralty Research Establishment (now Maritime Division), the Royal Armament Research and Development Establishment (now Military Division), and the Royal Signals and Radar Establishment (now Electronics Division).

Chief Executive (G2), J. A. R. Chisholm
Directors (G3), Dr A. L. Mears (*technical and quality*); Dr D. C. Tyte (*rationalization*); M. Goodfellow (*commercial*); Dr D. J. L. Smith (*group services*); G. Love (*finance*); (*G5*), R. Hack (*personnel*); J. Holmes (*marketing*)
Managing Director, Maritime Division (G3), P. D. Ewins
Directors (G3), P. M. Sutcliffe; (*G4*), B. P. Blaydes
Managing Director, Military and Aerospace Division (G3), Dr R. H. Warren
Managing Director, Electronics Division (G3), P. D. Ewins
Company Secretary (G5), Mrs E. Peace

CHEMICAL AND BIOLOGICAL DEFENCE ESTABLISHMENT
Porton Down, Salisbury, Wilts. SP4 0JQ
Tel 0980-610211

This defence support agency was established in April 1991 and is the United Kingdom's scientific and technical authority on chemical and biological defence matters. It carries out research, provides advice and support to the MOD and other government departments, and assists the development and production in industry of appropriate equipment for the armed forces.

Chief Executive (G3), Dr G. S. Pearson, CB

NUCLEAR PROGRAMMES

Deputy Controller (Nuclear) (G3), G. N. Beavan
Director, Atomic Weapons Establishment (G2), B. H. Richards

SEA SYSTEMS CONTROLLERATE

Controller of the Navy, Vice-Adm. Sir Kenneth Eaton, KCB
Asst Under Secretary (Material Naval) (G3), B. R. Hawtin
Principal Director, Navy and Nuclear Contracts (G4), A. T. Phipps
Director-General, Submarines and Deputy Controller, Vice-Adm. Sir Robert Hill, KBE
Director-General, Surface Ships (G3), H. Perkins
Director-General, Surface Weapons (G4), Cdre F. P. Scourse, MBE
Director-General, Marine Engineering, Cdre R. F. James, ADC
Naval Ships Acceptance, Cdre S. Taylor
Director (Finance and Sect.), Underwater Systems (G3), J. A. Kenny
Director-General, Underwater Weapons (G4), D. McArthur
Director, Naval Architect/Submarines (G5), P. Davies
Chief, Strategic Systems Executive, Rear-Adm. R. D. Irwin
Deputy Chief, Strategic Systems Executive, Cdre P. L. Bryan
Director-General, Strategic Weapons Systems, Dr J. P. Catchpole
Director (Fin. and Sect.), Strategic Systems (G5), J. P. Colston
Director-General, Procurement and Support Organization (Navy), vacant
Director, Abovewater Systems (Finance and Sect.) (G5), P. A. Rotheram
Director, Future Projects (G5), P. C. Bryan

LAND SYSTEMS CONTROLLERATE

Master-General of the Ordnance, Lt.-Gen. Sir Jeremy Blacker, KCB, CBE
Director-General, Policy and Special Projects, J. G. H. Walker
Asst Under Secretary (Ordnance) (G3), Dr A. Fox
Principal Director, Contracts (Ordnance) (G4), R. C. Harford
Director-General, Guided Weapons and Electronic Systems (G3), J. D. Maines

Director-General, Land Fighting Systems, Maj.-Gen. A. C. P. Stone

AIR SYSTEMS CONTROLLERATE

Controller, Aircraft, D. M. Spiers, CB, TD
Deputy Controller, Aircraft, Air Marshal Sir Michael Simmons, KCB, AFC
Asst Under Secretary (Air (Procurement Executive)) (G3), Ms D. J. Seammen
Principal Director, Contracts (Air) (G4), D. A. Oakley
Director-General, Aircraft 1, (G3), J. A. Gordon
Director-General, Aircraft 2, Air Vice-Marshal P. C. Norriss, AFC
Director-General, Avionics Weapons and Information Systems (G3), J. C. Mabberley

DEFENCE EXPORT SERVICES ORGANIZATION

Head of Defence Export Services (G2), J. A. Thomas
Military Deputy to Head of DES, vacant
Director-General Saudi Armed Forces Project, Air Marshal Sir William Wratten, KBE, CB, AFC
Director-General, Marketing (G3), N. Paren
Asst Under Secretary (Export Policy and Finance) (G3), C. T. Sandars
Malaysian Project Office (G5), J. B. Taylor

METEOROLOGICAL OFFICE
London Road, Bracknell, Berks. RG12 2SZ
Tel 0344-420242

The Meteorological Office is the national meteorological service. It became an executive support agency within the Ministry of Defence in April 1990. It provides meteorological services for the Services departments and civilian aviation, shipping, public services, the press, industry and the general public. It collects, distributes and publishes meteorological information from all parts of the world and undertakes research related to meteorology and climate.

Chief Executive (G2), Prof. J. Hunt, FRS
Director of Operations (G3), Dr P. Ryder
Director of Research (G4), Dr P. Mason

The Royal Navy

LORD HIGH ADMIRAL OF THE UNITED KINGDOM, HM THE QUEEN

ADMIRALS OF THE FLEET

HRH The Prince Philip, Duke of Edinburgh, KG, KT, OM, GBE, AC, QSO, PC, *apptd* 1953
Sir Varyl Begg, GCB, DSO, DSC, *apptd* 1968
The Lord Hill-Norton, GCB, *apptd* 1971
Sir Michael Pollock, GCB, LVO, DSC, *apptd* 1974
Sir Edward Ashmore, GCB, DSC, *apptd* 1977
The Lord Lewin, KG, GCB, LVO, DSC, *apptd* 1979
Sir Henry Leach, GCB, *apptd* 1982
Sir William Staveley, GCB, *apptd* 1989

ADMIRALS

Oswald, Sir Julian, GCB, ADC (*Chief of the Naval Staff and First Sea Lord, until Feb. 1993*)
Bathurst, Sir Benjamin, GCB (*Chief of the Naval Staff and First Sea Lord, w.e.f. Feb. 1993*)
Slater, Sir Jock, GCB, LVO, (*Vice-Chief of the Defence Staff, w.e.f. Feb. 1993*)
Livesay, Sir Michael, KCB (*Chief of Personnel and Second Sea Lord*)
Kerr, Sir John, KCB, ADC (*C.-in-C. Naval Home Command*)

VICE-ADMIRALS

Coward, Sir John, KCB, DSO (*Commandant, Royal College of Defence Studies*)
Eaton, Sir Kenneth, KCB (*Controller of the Navy*)
Hill, Sir Robert, KBE (*Director-General, Submarines and Deputy Controller*)
Hill-Norton, The Hon. Sir Nicholas, KCB (*Deputy CDS (Commitments)*)
Purvis, Sir Neville, KCB (*Chief of Fleet Support*)
Dobson, Sir David, KBE (*Chief of Staff to Commander, Allied Naval Forces Southern Europe*)
White, Sir Hugo, KCB, CBE (*C.-in-C. Fleet*)
Newman, Sir Roy, KCB (*Flag Officer Plymouth and Naval Base Comd. Devonport*)
Woodhead, Sir Peter, KCB (*Deputy Supreme Allied Commander Atlantic*)
Layard, M. H. G. (*Head, Officers Study Group*)
Biggs, G. W. R. (*Deputy Comd. Fleet*)
Morgan, C. C. (*Flag Officer Scotland and N. Ireland*)

REAR-ADMIRALS

Frere, R. T. (*Flag Officer Submarines and Comd. Sub. Area East Atlantic*)
Cooke-Priest, C. H. D. (*Flag Officer Naval Aviation until Feb. 1993*)
Tod, J. J. R., CBE (*Asst CDS (Policy and Nuclear)*)
Abbott, P. C. (*Asst Chief of the Naval Staff*)
Walmsley, R. (*Asst CDS (CIS)*)
Myres, J. A. L. (*Chief Executive, Hydrographic Office Defence Support Agency*)
Hoddinott, A. P., OBE (*Commander British Naval Staff Washington, Naval Attaché Washington and UK National Liaison Representative to SACLANT*)
Musson, J. G. R. (*Senior Directing Staff (Naval) RCDS*)
Bawtree, D. K. (*Flag Officer Portsmouth and Naval Base Commander Portsmouth*)
Woodard, R. N. (*Flag Officer Royal Yachts*)
Moore, M. A. C., LVO (*Deputy Asst Chief of Staff (Operations) on the Staff of the Supreme Allied Commander Europe*)
Wilkinson, N. J. (*Director-General, Naval Manpower and Training*)
Brigstocke, J. R. (*COMUKTG*)
Cobbold, R. F. (*Asst CDS Operational Requirements (Sea Systems) and Asst CDS (Joint Systems)*)
Boyce, M. C., OBE (*Flag Officer Surface Flotilla*)
Davis, G. N. (*Director-General, Fleet Support (Policy and Services)*)
Shiffner, J. R. (*Chief of Staff to C.-in-C. Naval Home Command*)
Lang, J. S. (*Director-General, Intelligence (Assessments)*)
Saunders, J. T., OBE (*Comd. British Forces Gibraltar*)
Moylan-Jones, R. C. (*Director-General, Aircraft (Navy)*)
Rankin, N. E., CBE (*Comd. British Forces Falkland Islands*)
Tolhurst, J. G. (*Flag Officer Sea Training*)
Garnett, I. D. G. (*Flag Officer Naval Aviation, w.e.f. Feb. 1993*)
Rutherford, M. C., CBE (*Naval Secretary*)
Irwin, R. D. (*Chief Strategic Systems Executive*)

The strength of the Navy at 1 April 1992 was 62,119.

HER MAJESTY'S FLEET
(as at 1 April 1992)

SUBMARINES

Polaris
Operational: Repulse, Resolution
Refitting/standby: Renown

Fleet
Operational: Sceptre, Sovereign, Spartan, Superb, Talent, Tireless, Torbay, Trafalgar, Trenchant, Triumph, Turbulent, Valiant
Refitting/standby: Splendid

Type 2400
Operational: Unseen†, Ursula
Refitting/standby: Upholder

Oberon Class
Operational: Opossum, Opportune, Oracle

ASW CARRIERS

Operational: Ark Royal, Invincible
Refitting/standby: Illustrious

ASSAULT SHIPS

Operational: Fearless
Refitting/standby: Intrepid

DESTROYERS

Type 42
Operational: Birmingham, Cardiff, Edinburgh, Exeter, Glasgow, Gloucester, Liverpool, Newcastle, Nottingham, Southampton, York
Refitting/standby: Manchester

FRIGATES

Type 23
Operational: Argyll†, Iron Duke*, Lancaster†, Marlborough†, Monmouth†, Norfolk

Type 22
Operational: Battleaxe, Beaver, Boxer, Brave, Brazen, Brilliant, Broadsword, Campbelltown, Chatham, Cornwall, Coventry, Cumberland, London, Sheffield

Type 21
Operational: Active, Alacrity, Amazon, Ambuscade, Arrow, Avenger

Leander Class
Operational: Andromeda, Argonaut, Cleopatra, Sirius, Scylla

Navigation Training Ship
Operational: Juno

OFFSHORE PATROL

Castle Class
Operational: Dumbarton Castle, Leeds Castle

Island Class
Operational: Alderney, Anglesey, Guernsey, Jersey, Lindisfarne, Orkney, Shetland

MINESWEEPERS

River Class
Operational: Arun, Blackwater, Carron, Dovey, Helford, Humber, Itchen, Orwell, Spey, Waveney
Refitting/standby: Helmsdale, Ribble

Minehunters Ton Class
Operational: Brinton, Iveston, Kellington, Nurton, Sheraton, Wilton (Dartmouth Navigation Training Ship)

Hunt Class
Operational: Atherstone, Berkeley, Brecon, Brocklesby, Cattistock, Chiddingford, Cottesmore, Dulverton, Hurworth, Ledbury, Middleton, Quorn
Refitting/standby: Bicester

Single Role Minehunter
Operational: Cromer†, Inverness, Sandown, Walney*

PATROL CRAFT

Bird Class
Operational: Cygnet, Kingfisher, Redpole

Coastal Training Craft
Operational: Archer, Biter, Blazer, Charger, Dasher, Puncher, Pursuer, Smiter

Peacock Class
Operational: Peacock, Plover, Starling

Gibraltar Search and Rescue Craft
Operational: Ranger, Trumpeter

ROYAL YACHT/HOSPITAL SHIP

Operational: Britannia

TRAINING SHIPS

Fleet Tenders
Operational: Messina

ICE PATROL SHIP

Operational: Endurance

SURVEY SHIPS

Operational: Beagle, Gleaner, Herald, Roebuck
Refitting/standby: Bulldog, Hecla

DISPOSAL/SALE APPROVED 1991–2

Attacker, Brereton, Bristol, Charybdis, Chaser, Cleopatra, Courageous, Danae, Endurance, Fawn, Fencer, Hunter, Kedleston, Manly, Mentor, Millbrook, Ocelet, Otter, Otus, Soberton, Striker, Swiftsure

† Engaged in trials or training at 1 April 1992
* Under construction at 1 April 1992 and planned to enter service 1992–3
1 Ships solely engaged in harbour training duties are not included
2 River Class vessels, apart from HMS *Blackwater*, are operated by the RNR
3 Coastal training craft are operated by the RNR and University Royal Naval Units

ROYAL FLEET AUXILIARY (RFA)

The Royal Fleet Auxiliary supplies ships of the fleet with fuel, food, water, spares and ammunition while at sea. Its ships are manned by merchant seamen.

FLEET AIR ARM

The Fleet Air Arm was established in 1937 and operates aircraft and helicopters for the Royal Navy.

ROYAL NAVAL RESERVE (RNR)

The Royal Naval Reserve is a totally integrated part of the Royal Navy. It comprises about 6,000 men and women nationwide who volunteer to train in their spare time for a variety of sea and shore tasks which they would carry out in time of tension or war.

Chief Staff Officer, Capt. C. W. Pile

ROYAL NAVAL AUXILIARY SERVICE (RNXS)

The RNXS is a uniformed, unarmed and, in peacetime, volunteer civilian service of some 2,700 men and women, under the direction of the Commander-in-Chief Naval Home Command. Members train in their spare time in units around the coasts of the United Kingdom for duties in times of tension and war. Their role includes manning port headquarters in support of the Naval Control of Shipping Organization, and providing crews for vessels engaged in the defence of ports and anchorages.

Patron and Hon. Auxiliary Commodore, HRH Prince Michael of Kent
Captain, Capt. J. M. Neville-Rolfe, RN

ROYAL MARINES

The Corps of Royal Marines was formed in 1664 and is part of the Naval Service. The Royal Marines provide Britain's sea soldiers and in particular 3 Commando Brigade Royal Marines, two-thirds of which is trained and equipped for arctic warfare. Royal Marines also serve in HM Ships, provide landing craft crews, special boat sections and other detachments for naval and amphibious operations. They also provide the Naval Band Service. The Corps is about 7,000 strong.

Commandant-General, Royal Marines, Lt.-Gen. Sir Henry Beverley, KCB, OBE
Major-Generals, A. M. Keeling (*Chief of Staff*); R. J. Ross, OBE (*Commando Forces*); P. T. Stevenson; M. P. J. Hunt, OBE (*Royal College Defence Studies*)

ROYAL MARINES RESERVE (RMR)

The Royal Marines Reserve is a force of commando-trained volunteers who train to combat-readiness in order to support the regular Royal Marines should the need arise. About 50 per cent are trained and equipped for arctic warfare and most regular Royal Marine specializations are open to the reservist. There are RMR centres in London, Glasgow, Bristol, Liverpool and Newcastle, each with a number of outlying detachments. The present strength of the RMR is about 1,200.

Director, Brig. J. S. Chester, OBE

QUEEN ALEXANDRA'S ROYAL NAVAL NURSING SERVICE

The first nursing sisters were appointed to naval hospitals in 1884 and the Queen Alexandra's Royal Naval Nursing Service (QARNNS) gained its current title under the patronage of Queen Alexandra in 1902. Nursing ratings were introduced in 1960 and men were integrated into the Service in 1982; both men and women serve as officers and ratings. Female medical assistants were introduced in 1987. Qualified staff and learners are mainly based at the UK Royal Naval Hospitals, and continue their responsibility for the health and fitness of naval personnel. The strength is about 600.

Patron, HRH Princess Alexandra, the Hon. Lady Ogilvy
Matron-in-Chief, Commandant Nursing Officer Miss J. Titley

WOMEN'S ROYAL NAVAL SERVICE

Originally founded in 1917, the Women's Royal Naval Service (WRNS) was temporarily disbanded between the First and Second World Wars. The contribution of the Service is now established as a professional and integral part of the Royal Navy with personnel serving in the United Kingdom and abroad in a wide range of specialist roles. From 6 February 1990, the role of the WRNS was expanded to include sea service , and from 1 January 1991 to include aircrew. WRNS officers adopted Royal Navy rank titles from 1 December 1990. The strength of the WRNS is about 4,500.

Chief Commandant, HRH The Princess Royal
Director, Commandant A. C. Spencer, ADC

The Army

THE QUEEN

FIELD MARSHALS

HRH The Prince Philip, Duke of Edinburgh, KG, KT, OM, GBE, AC, QSO, PC, *apptd* 1953
Sir James Cassels, GCB, KBE, DSO, *apptd* 1968
The Lord Carver, GCB, CBE, DSO, MC, *apptd* 1973
Sir Roland Gibbs, GCB, CBE, DSO, MC, *apptd* 1979
The Lord Bramall, KG, GCB, OBE, MC, *apptd* 1982
Sir John Stanier, GCB, MBE, *apptd* 1985
Sir Nigel Bagnall, GCB, CVO, MC, *apptd* 1988
Sir Richard Vincent, GBE, KCB, DSO (*Chairman of NATO's Military Committee, w.e.f. Jan. 1993*), *apptd* 1991
Sir John Chapple, GCB, CBE, *apptd* 1992

GENERALS

Kenny, Sir Brian, GCB, CBE, Col. Cmdt. RAVC, Col. QRIH, Col. Cmdt. RAC (*D. SACEUR*)
Inge, Sir Peter, GCB, ADC (*Gen.*), Col. Green Howards, Col. Cmdt. APTC (*Chief of the General Staff*)
Waters, Sir John, KCB, CBE, (*C.-in-C. UK Land Forces*)
Ramsbotham, Sir David, KCB, CBE, ADC (*Gen.*), (*Adjutant-General*)
Guthrie, Sir Charles, KCB, LVO, OBE, Col. Cmdt. Int. Corps (*C.-in-C. BAOR and Comdt, Northern Army Group*)
Jones, Sir Edward, KCB, CBE, Col. Cmdt. 2 RGJ (*UK Military Rep. to NATO*)
Learmont, Sir John, KCB, CBE, Col. Cmdt. AAC, Col. Cmdt. RA (*Quartermaster-General*)
Johnson, Sir Garry, KCB, OBE, MC, Col. 10 GR, Col. Cmdt. The Light Division (*C.-in-C. AFNORTH*)

LIEUTENANT-GENERALS

Swinburn, Sir Richard, KCB (*GOC S District*)

Wilsey, Sir John, KCB, CBE, Col. D and D, Col. Cmdt ACC, Col. Cmdt. POW Division (*GOC Northern Ireland*)

Wilkes, Sir Michael, KCB, CBE, Col. Cmdt. Hon. Artillery Company (TA) (*Cmdt. UK Fd. Army and Inspector-General TA*)

Graham, Sir Peter, KCB, CBE, Col. Gordons, Col. Cmdt. The Scottish Division (*GOC Scotland*)

Blacker, Sir Jeremy, KCB, CBE, Col. Cmdt. REME, Col. Cmdt. RTR (*Master-General of the Ordnance*)

Rous, The Hon. Sir William, KCB, OBE (*Military Secretary*)

Mackenzie, Sir Jeremy, KCB, OBE, Col. Cmdt. AG Corps (*Cmdt. NATO Rapid Reaction Corps*)

Duffell, Sir Peter, KCB, CBE, MC (*Inspector-General Doctrine and Training*)

Beale, Sir Peter, KBE, QHP (*Surgeon-General*)

Boyd-Carpenter, the Hon. T. P. J., MBE (*Deputy CDS (Programmes and Personnel)*)

MAJOR-GENERALS

Corbett, R. J. S., CB (*GOC London District*)

Hayman-Joyce, R. J., CBE (*Director, Royal Armoured Corps*)

Cowan, S., CBE, Col. QGS, (*Asst Chief of the Defence Staff OR (Land)*)

Pennicott, B. T. (*Defence Services Secretary*)

Barr, J. A. J. P., CBE (*Engineer-in-Chief (Army)*)

Cook, R. F. L.

Wheeler, R. N., CBE, (*Asst Chief of General Staff*)

Crawford, I. P., GM, QHP, (*Cmdt. Royal Army Medical College*)

Rose, H. M., OBE, QGM (*Comdt. Staff College*)

Barron, R. E.

Grist, R. D., OBE, Col. Gloucesters (*Director-General AG Corps*)

Thomson, D. P., CBE, MC (*Senior Army Member, Royal College of Defence Studies*)

Denison-Smith, A. A., MBE (*GOC 4 Armd Division*)

Johnston, J. F. J., CBE (*Director-General Army Manning and Recruiting*)

Field, G. W., OBE (*Director-General Logistics Policy (Army)*)

Ashenhurst, F. E., QHDS (*Director of Army Dental Services*)

Botting, D. F. E., CB, CBE (*Director-General Ordnance Services LE (A)*)

Stone, A. C. P., CB (*Director-General Land Fighting Systems*)

Wallace, C. B. Q., OBE, Col. Cmdt. RMP (*Cmdt. 3 Armed Division*)

Harley, A. G. H., CB, OBE (*Asst Chief of the Defence Staff (Overseas)*)

Kinvig, C. A. (*Director Educational and Training Services (Army)*)

Baskervyle-Glegg, J., MBE (*SBLSO RAO*)

Smith, R. A., DSO, OBE, QGM, (*Cmdt. 1 Armed Division*)

Ticehurst, A. C., QHS (*Cmdt. MED. UK Land Forces*)

Wood, R. (*Director-General Military Survey*)

Courage, W. J., MBE (*Chief Joint Services Liaison Organization Bonn*)

Mayes, F. B., QHS (*Cmdt. Med. BAOR*)

Toyne Sewell, T. P. (*Cmdt. RMAS*)

Tennant, M. T. (*Director Royal Artillery*)

Macdonald, J. D., CBE (*Director-General Transport and Movements*)

Heath, M. S., CBE (*Director-General Equipment Support (Army)*)

Burton, E. F. G., OBE (*Cmdt. RMCS*)

Grove, D. A., OBE (*Team Leader, AG Study Group*)

Meier, A. L., OBE (*Director-General Management and Support of Intelligence, MOD*))

Pett, R. A., MBE (*Deputy Chief of Staff (Support) AFNORTH*)

Grant, S. C. (*Director-General Army Training*)

Gordon, J., CBE (*Chief of Staff HQ UK Land Forces*)

Sheppard, P. J., CBE (*Chief of Staff HQ BAOR*)

Walker, M. J. D., CBE, Col. Cmdt. The Queen's Division (*GOC E District*)

Regan, M. D., OBE (*GOC Wales and W District*)

Freer, I. L., CBE, Col. Staffords (*CLF and DD Ops. N. Ireland*)

Foley, J. P., CB, OBE, MC (*Comd. BFHK and Maj.-Gen. Brigade of Gurkhas*)

Hollands, G. S. (*Cmdt. Artillery 1 (Br) Corps*)

Lytle, S. W. St J. (*Director Army Air Corps*)

Notley, C. R. S., CBE (*President, Ordnance Board*)

Dutton, B. H., CBE (*Director Infantry*)

Pike, H. W. R., DSO, MBE, Col. SASC (*GOC UK Division*)

Carr-Smith, S. R. (*Chief C3 NACISA*)

Clarke, M. F. H. (*Director, Army Legal Services*)

Jackson, M. D., MBE (*Director-General, Personal Services (Army)*)

Kennedy, A. I. G., CBE (*Director-General, TA*)

Burden, D. L., CBE (*Director-General, Logistic Support (Army)*)

Craig, R. P., QHS (*Director, Army Surgery and Consultant Surgeon*)

Boyle, A. H. (*Director-General, CCCIS (Army) and Signal Officer in Chief (Army)*)

CONSTITUTION OF THE BRITISH ARMY

The strength of the Army at 1 April 1992 was 145,363; this will be reduced to about 116,000 by mid-1995. A programme of cuts and regiment mergers is under way to achieve this reduction.

The Regular Forces include the following Arms, Branches and Corps. Soldiers' record offices are shown at the end of each group; records of officers are maintained at the Ministry of Defence.

THE ARMS

HOUSEHOLD CAVALRY – The Life Guards; The Blues and Royals (Royal Horse Guards and 1st Dragoons). *Records*, Horse Guards, London SW1.

ROYAL ARMOURED CORPS – Cavalry Regiments: 1st The Queen's Dragoon Guards; The Royal Scots Dragoon Guards (Carabiniers and Greys); The Royal Dragoon Guards; The Queen's Own Hussars; The Queen's Royal Irish Hussars; 9th/12th Royal Lancers (Prince of Wales's); The King's Royal Hussars; The Light Dragoons; 16th/5th The Queen's Royal Lancers; 17th/21st Lancers; Royal Tank Regiment comprising two regular regiments. *Records*, Queen's Park, Chester.

ARTILLERY – Royal Regiment of Artillery. *Records*, Imphal Barracks, Fulford Road, York.

ENGINEERS – Corps of Royal Engineers. *Records*, Kentigern House, Brown Street, Glasgow.

SIGNALS – Royal Corps of Signals. *Records*, Kentigern House, Brown Street, Glasgow.

THE INFANTRY

The Foot Guards and Regiments of Infantry of the Line are grouped in Divisions as follows:

GUARDS DIVISION – Grenadier, Coldstream, Scots, Irish and Welsh Guards. *Divisional HQ*, HQ Household Division, Horse Guards, London SW1. *Depot*, Pirbright

Camp, Brookwood, Surrey. *Records*, Imphal Barracks, Fulford Road, York.

SCOTTISH DIVISION – The Royal Scots (The Royal Regiment); The Royal Highland Fusiliers (Princess Margaret's Own Glasgow and Ayrshire Regiment); The King's Own Scottish Borderers; The Black Watch (Royal Highland Regiment); Queen's Own Highlanders (Seaforth and Camerons); The Gordon Highlanders; The Argyll and Sutherland Highlanders (Princess Louise's). *Divisional HQ*, The Castle, Edinburgh. *Depots*, Scottish Divisional Depots, Glencorse, Milton Bridge, Midlothian; Albemarle Barracks, Ouston, Newcastle. *Records*, Imphal Barracks, Fulford Road, York.

QUEEN'S DIVISION – The Princess of Wales's Royal Regiment (Queen's and Royal Hampshire's); The Royal Regiment of Fusiliers; The Royal Anglian Regiment. *Divisional HQ* and *Depot*, Bassingbourn Barracks, Royston, Herts. *Records*, Higher Barracks, Exeter, Devon.

KING'S DIVISION – The King's Own Royal Border Regiment; The King's Regiment; The Prince of Wales's Own Regiment of Yorkshire; The Green Howards (Alexandra, Princess of Wales's Own Yorkshire Regiment); The Queen's Lancashire Regiment; The Duke of Wellington's Regiment (West Riding). *Divisional HQ*, Imphal Barracks, York. *Depots*, The King's Division Depot (Yorkshire), Queen Elizabeth Barracks, Strensall, Yorks.; Albemarle Barracks, Ouston, Newcastle. *Records*, Imphal Barracks, Fulford Road, York.

PRINCE OF WALES'S DIVISION – The Devonshire and Dorset Regiment; The Cheshire Regiment; The Royal Welch Fusiliers; The Royal Regiment of Wales (24th/41st Foot); The Gloucestershire Regiment; The Worcestershire and Sherwood Foresters Regiment (29th/45th Foot); The Staffordshire Regiment (The Prince of Wales's); The Duke of Edinburgh's Royal Regiment (Berkshire and Wiltshire). *Divisional HQ* and *Depot*, Whittington Barracks, Lichfield, Staffs. *Records*, Imphal Barracks, Fulford, York.

LIGHT DIVISION – The Light Infantry; The Royal Green Jackets. *Divisional HQ* and *Depot*, Sir John Moore Barracks, Winchester, Hants. *Records*, Higher Barracks, Exeter.

BRIGADE OF GURKHAS – 2nd King Edward VII's Own Gurkha Rifles (The Sirmoor Rifles); 6th Queen Elizabeth's Own Gurkha Rifles; 7th Duke of Edinburgh's Own Gurkha Rifles; 10th Princess Mary's Own Gurkha Rifles; The Queen's Gurkha Engineers; Queen's Gurkha Signals; Gurkha Transport Regiment. *Brigade HQ*, HMS *Tamar*, Hong Kong, BFPO 1. *Depot*, Training Depot, Brigade of Gurkhas, Malaya Lines, Sek Kong, BFPO 1. *Records*, Record Office, Brigade of Gurkhas, Hong Kong, BFPO 1.

THE ROYAL IRISH REGIMENT (two general service and seven home service battalions) – 27th (Inniskilling), 83rd, 87th and the Ulster Defence Regiment. *Depot*, St Patrick's Barracks, Ballymena, N. Ireland. *Records*, Imphal Barracks, Fulford Road, York.

THE PARACHUTE REGIMENT (three regular battalions) – *Depot*, Browning Barracks, Aldershot, Hants. *Records*, Higher Barracks, Exeter.

SPECIAL AIR SERVICE REGIMENT – *Regimental HQ*, Duke of York's Headquarters, Sloane Square, London SW3. *Depot*, Stirling Lines, Hereford. *Records*, Higher Barracks, Exeter, Devon.

ARMY AIR CORPS – Regimental HQ and *Depot*, Middle Wallop, Hants. *Records*, Higher Barracks, Exeter.

THE SERVICES

Royal Army Chaplain's Department – *Regimental HQ* and *Depot*, Bagshot Park, Surrey.

Royal Corps of Transport – *Records*, Kentigern House, Brown Street, Glasgow.

Royal Army Medical Corps, Royal Army Dental Corps and Queen Alexandra's Royal Army Nursing Corps. – *Records*, Queen's Park, Chester.

Adjutant-General's Corps – *Depot*, Worthy Down, Winchester, Hants. *Records*, Queen's Park, Chester.

Royal Army Ordnance Corps, Corps of Royal Electrical and Mechanical Engineers – *Records*, Glen Parva Barracks, Saffron Road, Wigston, Leicester.

Small Arms School Corps – *Records*, Higher Barracks, Exeter.

General Service Corps – *Records*, Imphal Barracks, Fulford Road, York.

Corps of Royal Military Police, Royal Army Pay Corps, Royal Army Veterinary Corps, Royal Pioneer Corps, Intelligence Corps, Army Catering Corps, Army Physical Training Corps, Sandhurst, Officers Training Corps – *Records*, Higher Barracks, Exeter, Devon.

THE TERRITORIAL ARMY (TA)

The Territorial Army is designed to provide a highly-trained and well-equipped force which will complete the Regular Army order of battle in a time of national emergency. Its establishment is approximately 91,000, reducing to 65,000, due to TA restructuring, by 1995.

QUEEN ALEXANDRA'S ROYAL ARMY NURSING CORPS

The Queen Alexandra's Royal Army Nursing Corps (QARANC) was founded in 1902 as Queen Alexandra's Imperial Military Nursing Service (QAIMNS) and gained its present title in 1949. The QARANC has trained nurses for the register and roll since 1950 and has eight other employment categories. A non-nursing officer element was introduced in 1959 for personnel work. Since 1 April 1992 men have been eligible to join the QARANC. The Corps provides service in military hospitals in the United Kingdom (including Northern Ireland), BAOR, Hong Kong, Cyprus, Falkland Islands and Belize.

Colonel-in-Chief, HRH The Princess Margaret, Countess of Snowdon, GCVO, CI

Matron-in-Chief (Army), Col. H. Dixon-Nuttall

WOMEN'S ROYAL ARMY CORPS

Formed 1 February 1949; disbanded April 1992.

The Royal Air Force

THE QUEEN

MARSHALS OF THE ROYAL AIR FORCE

HRH The Prince Philip, Duke of Edinburgh, KG, KT, OM, GBE, AC, QSO, PC, *apptd* 1953

Sir Dermot Boyle, GCB, KCVO, KBE, AFC, *apptd* 1958

The Lord Elworthy, KG, GCB, CBE, DSO, MVO, DFC, AFC, *apptd* 1967

Sir John Grandy, GCB, GCVO, KBE, DSO, *apptd* 1971

Sir Denis Spotswood, GCB, CBE, DSO, DFC, *apptd* 1974
Sir Michael Beetham, GCB, CBE, DFC, AFC, *apptd* 1982
Sir Keith Williamson, GCB, AFC, *apptd* 1985
Sir Peter Harding, GCB, ADC (*Chief of the Defence Staff, w.e.f. Jan. 1993*), *apptd* 1993

AIR CHIEF MARSHALS

Jackson, Sir Brendan, GCB (*Air Member for Supply and Organization*)
Graydon, Sir Michael, KCB, CBE (*Chief of the Air Staff*)
Palin, Sir Roger, KCB, OBE, ADC (*Air Member for Personnel*)
Stear, Sir Michael, KCB, CBE (*Deputy C.-in-C. Allied Forces Central Europe*)
Thomson, Sir John, KCB, CBE, AFC (*AOC.-in-C. Strike Command and C.-in-C. UK Air Forces*)

AIR MARSHALS

Hayr, Sir Kenneth, KCB, CBE, AFC (*until Dec. 1992*)
Simmons, Sir Michael, KCB, AFC (*Deputy Controller Aircraft*)
Kemball, Sir John, KCB, CBE (*Chief of Staff and Deputy C.-in-C. Strike Command*)
Wilson, Sir Andrew, KCB, AFC (*C.-in-C. RAF Germany*)
Alcock, Sir Michael, KBE, CB (*Chief of Logistic Support*)
Walker, Sir John, KCB, CBE, AFC (*Chief of Defence Intelligence*)
Austin, Sir Roger, KCB, AFC (*Deputy CDS (Systems)*)
Harris, Sir John, KCB, CBE (*AOC No. 18 Group*)
Wratten, Sir William, KBE, CB, AFC (*DG Saudi Armed Forces Project*)

AIR VICE-MARSHALS

Pilkington, M. J., CB, CBE
Roberts, A. L., CB, CBE, AFC (*Head of Manpower Structure Study Team*)
Honey, R. J., CB, CBE (*Air Secretary and AOC RAF Personnel Management Centre*)
Crwys-Williams, D. O., CB (*Asst CDS (Programmes)*)
Blackley, A. B., CBE, AFC (*Air Officer Scotland and N. Ireland*)
Johns, R. E., CB, CBE, LVO (*AOC No. 1 Group*)
Willis, J. F., CB, CBE (*AOC.-in-C. RAF Support Command*)
Harding, P. J., CBE, AFC (*Deputy Chief of Staff (Operations) Allied Air Forces Central Europe*)
Hunter, A. F. C., CBE, AFC (*Comd. British Forces Cyprus*)
Cousins, D., CB, AFC (*Cmdt. RAF College, Cranwell*)
Dawson, R. T., CBE
Allison, J. S., CBE (*AOC No. 11 Group*)
Baker, C. P., CB (*Director-General of Support Management (RAF)*)
Peters, R. G., CB (*Cmdt. RAF Staff College, Bracknell*)
Ernsting, J., CB, OBE, QHS, Ph.D (*Senior Consultant*)
Dodworth, P., OBE, AFC (*Defence Attaché and Head of British Defence Staff, Washington*)
Garden, T., CB (*Asst Chief of the Air Staff*)
Baird, J. A., QHP (*Principal Medical Officer Strike Command*)
Beer, P. G., CBE, LVO (*Director-General Training and Personnel (RAF)*)
Clark, P. D. (*Air Officer Engineering Strike Command*)
Ferguson, G. M., CBE (*Air Officer Admin. Strike Command*)
French, D. R., MBE (*Air Officer Maintenance RAF Support Command*)
Gibson, M. J., OBE (*Director-General Policy and Planning, National Air Traffic Services*)
Hawkins, D. R., CB, MBE (*Director-General of Security (RAF)*)
Macfadyen, I. D., CB, OBE (*Asst CDS Operational Requirements (Air Systems)*)
Saunders, D. J., CBE (*Asst CDS (Logistics)*)
Squire, P. T., DFC, AFC (*Senior Air Staff Officer Strike Command*)
Robertson, G. A., CBE (*Deputy Commander, RAF Germany*)
Lucas, Ven. B. H., QHC (*Chaplain Services (RAF)*)
Davison, D. J., QHS (*Dean of Air Force Medicine*)
Brook, J. M., QHS (*Director-General Medical Services (RAF)*)
Chapple, R., QHP (*Principal Medical Officer, RAF Support Command*)
Cheshire, J. A., CBE (Asst COS (*Policy*), *SHAPE*)
Kyle, R. H., MBE (*Director-General Support Services (RAF)*)
Mackey, J., QHDS (*Director, Defence Dental Services*)
Norriss, P. C., AFC (*Director-General Aircraft 2*)
Rae, W. M. (*Senior Director Staff, Royal College of Defence Studies*)
Sherrington, T. B., OBE (*Air Officer Admin., RAF Support Command*)
Carleton, G. W. (*Director of Legal Services (RAF)*)
Coville, C. C. C. (*Air Officer Training RAF Support Command*)
O'Brien, R. P., OBE (*Cmdt. Joint Service Defence College*)

CONSTITUTION OF THE ROYAL AIR FORCE

The strength of the Royal Air Force at 1 April 1992 was 85,962.

The RAF consists of three Commands: Strike Command and Support Command in the United Kingdom, and RAF Germany. Strike Command is responsible for providing the air defence of the United Kingdom and reinforcement forces for NATO; its roles include strike/attack, air defence, control and reporting, maritime surveillance, air reconnaissance, air-to-air refuelling, offensive support, air transport, aero-medical facilities, and search and rescue. Support Command is responsible for air and ground training, communications, engineering support, logistics, hospitals and for providing a range of administrative support. RAF Germany provides tactical air support in NATO's Central Region; its roles include strike/attack, interdiction, counter air operations, air defence, close air support of land forces, tactical reconnaissance and helicopter support.

To carry out its tasks, the Royal Air Force is equipped (as at 1 April 1992) with 8 Victor, 280 Tornado, 27 Buccaneer, 26 Phantom, 67 Harrier, 53 Jaguar, 23 Canberra, 33 Nimrod, 19 VC10, 8 Tristar, 54 Hercules, 145 Hawk, 85 Jet Provost, 68 Tucano, 64 Chipmunk and 118 Bulldog aircraft; 42 Puma, 62 Wessex, 17 Sea King and 29 Chinook helicopters; miscellaneous communications aircraft, etc.; Bloodhound and Rapier missiles; and the Skyguard system.

ROYAL AUXILIARY AIR FORCE (RAUXAF)

Formed in 1924, the Auxiliary Air Force served with great distinction in the Second World War and in recognition of its war record King George VI conferred the prefix 'Royal' in 1947. Following a major reduction of units in the late 1950s, the benefits to be gained by using auxiliary forces in certain roles has resulted in a subsequent expansion. Today, the Royal Auxiliary Air Force supports the RAF in maritime air operations, air and ground defence of major airfields, air movements and aero-medical evacuation.

Air Commodore-in-Chief, HM The Queen
Director of Reserve Forces (*RAF*), Air Cdre R. P. Skelley

ROYAL AIR FORCE VOLUNTEER RESERVE (RAFVR)

The Royal Air Force Volunteer Reserve was created in 1936 with the object of providing training for the increased number of aircrew who were seen as necessary for the forthcoming conflict. The RAFVR was reconstituted in 1947 following war service and today is a small but important part of the Air Force Reserve. There are RAFVR aircrew with the Harrier, Nimrod and Tornado Forces, and RAFVR units specializing in intelligence-orientated duties and public relations.

Director of Reserve Forces (RAF), Air Cdre R. P. Skelley

PRINCESS MARY'S ROYAL AIR FORCE NURSING SERVICE

The Princess Mary's Royal Air Force Nursing Service (PMRAFNS) is open to both male and female candidates. Commissions are offered to those who are Registered General Nurses (RGN) with a minimum of two years experience after obtaining RGN and normally with a second qualification. RGNs with no additional experience or qualification are also recruited as non-commissioned officers in the grade of Staff Nurse.

Air Chief Commandant, HRH Princess Alexandra, the Hon. Lady Ogilvy, GCVO
Matron-in-Chief, Group Captain E. M. Hancock, QHNS

WOMEN'S ROYAL AIR FORCE

Formed on 1 April 1918, the Women's Royal Air Force (WRAF) was disbanded on 1 April 1920 and re-formed on 1 February 1949 from the Women's Auxiliary Air Force, the Second World War service which had been formed on 28 June 1939, and from the RAF companies of the Auxiliary Territorial Service.

WRAF officers and airwomen serve in most of the RAF branches and trades including as aircrew and as pilots of combat jets. WRAF personnel are employed at RAF stations and higher formations at home and abroad, and they compete on equal terms with their RAF counterparts for appointments, promotion and places on training courses.

Commandant-in-Chief, HM Queen Elizabeth The Queen Mother
Air Chief Commandant, HRH Princess Alice, Duchess of Gloucester
Director, Air Commodore, R. M. B. Montague, ADC

ROYAL OBSERVER CORPS

Established in 1925; stood down 31 March 1992.

SERVICE SALARIES AND PENSIONS

The following rates of pay have been introduced as part of the 1992 pay award for service personnel.

The increasing integration of women in the armed services is reflected in equal pay for equal work and the X factor addition is now the same for men and women (11.5 per cent).

Annual salaries are derived from daily rates in whole pence and rounded to the nearest £.

OFFICERS' SALARIES

Army ranks are shown in these tables; the pay rates apply equally to equivalent ranks in the other services.

Normal Rates

Rank	*Daily*	*Annual*
Second Lieutenant	£34.04	£12,425
Lieutenant		
On appointment	45.01	16,429
After 1 year in the rank	46.19	16,860
After 2 years in the rank	47.37	17,290
After 3 years in the rank	48.55	17,721
After 4 years in the rank	49.73	18,151
Captain		
On appointment	57.28	20,901
After 1 year in the rank	58.83	21,473
After 2 years in the rank	60.38	22,039
After 3 years in the rank	61.93	22,604
After 4 years in the rank	63.48	23,170
After 5 years in the rank	65.03	23,736
After 6 years in the rank	66.58	24,302
Major		
On appointment	72.19	26,350
After 1 year in the rank	73.98	27,003
After 2 years in the rank	75.77	27,656
After 3 years in the rank	77.56	28,309
After 4 years in the rank	79.35	28,963
After 5 years in the rank	81.14	29,616
After 6 years in the rank	82.93	30,270
After 7 years in the rank	84.72	30,923
After 8 years in the rank	86.51	31,576
Special List Lieutenant-Colonel	£99.54	£36,332
Lieutenant-Colonel		
On appointment with less than 19 years service	101.27	36,964
After 2 years in the rank or with 19 years service	103.94	37,938
After 4 years in the rank or with 21 years service	106.61	38,913
After 6 years in the rank or with 23 years service	109.28	38,792
After 8 years in the rank or with 25 years service	111.95	40,861
Colonel		
On appointment	117.95	43,052
After 2 years in the rank	121.05	44,183
After 4 years in the rank	124.15	45,315
After 6 years in the rank	127.25	46,446
After 8 years in the rank	130.35	47,578
Brigadier	144.68	52,808
Major-General	151.01	55,120
Lieutenant-General	172.66	63,024
General	240.05	87,620
Field Marshal	298.48	108,940

SALARIES OF OFFICERS COMMISSIONED FROM THE RANKS

Years of Commissioned Service	Years of Non-commissioned Service from Age 18					
	Less than 12 years		*12 years but less than 15 years*		*15 years or more*	
	Daily	*Annual*	*Daily*	*Annual*	*Daily*	*Annual*
On appointment	£62.95	£22,976	£66.15	£24,144	£69.35	£25,313
After 1 year service	64.55	23,561	67.75	24,729	70.39	25,681
After 2 years service	66.15	24,145	69.35	25,313	71.43	26,072
After 3 years service	67.75	24,729	70.39	25,692	72.47	26,452
After 4 years service	69.35	25,313	71.43	26,072	73.51	26,831
After 5 years service	70.39	25,692	72.47	26,452	74.55	27,211
After 6 years service	71.43	26,025	73.51	26,831	75.59	27,590
After 8 years service	62.47	27,452	74.55	27,211	76.63	27,970
After 10 years service	73.51	26,831	75.59	27,590	76.63	27,970
After 12 years service	74.55	27,211	76.63	27,970	76.63	27,970
After 14 years service	75.59	27,590	76.63	27,970	76.63	27,970
After 16 years service	76.63	27,970	76.63	27,970	76.63	27,970

SALARIES OF WARRANT OFFICERS AND SENIOR NCOs

Rates shown are for army personnel. The rates apply also to personnel of equivalent rank and pay band in the other services.

The pay structure below officer level is divided into pay bands. Jobs at each rank are allocated to bands according to their score in the job evaluation system.

Scale A: committed to serve/have completed less than 6 years
Scale B: committed to serve/have completed 6 years but less than 9 years
Scale C: committed to serve/have completed more than 9 years

RANK	SCALE A				SCALE B				SCALE C			
	Band 1	*Band 2*	*Band 3*	*Band 4*	*Band 1*	*Band 2*	*Band 3*	*Band 4*	*Band 1*	*Band 2*	*Band 3*	*Band 4*
Sergeant	£41.84	£46.00	£50.55	£—	£42.14	£46.30	£50.85	£—	£42.59	£46.75	£51.30	£—
Staff Sergeant	44.24	48.40	52.96	58.46	44.54	48.70	53.26	58.76	44.99	49.15	53.71	59.21
Warrant Officer												
Class 2	47.31	51.47	57.09	62.70	47.61	51.77	57.39	63.00	48.06	52.22	57.84	63.45
Class 1	50.45	54.61	60.29	65.90	50.75	54.91	60.59	66.20	51.20	55.36	61.04	66.64

SALARIES OF ADULT PERSONNEL OF THE RANK OF CORPORAL AND BELOW

RANK	SCALE A			SCALE B			SCALE C		
	Band 1	*Band 2*	*Band 3*	*Band 1*	*Band 2*	*Band 3*	*Band 1*	*Band 2*	*Band 3*
Private									
Class 4	£21.30	£—	£—	£21.60	£—	£—	£22.05	£—	£—
Class 3	23.86	27.71	31.98	24.16	28.01	32.28	24.61	28.46	32.73
Class 2	26.69	30.55	34.82	26.99	30.85	35.12	27.44	31.30	35.57
Class 1	28.96	32.81	37.08	29.26	33.11	37.38	29.71	33.56	37.83
Lance-Corporal									
Class 3	28.96	32.81	37.08	29.26	33.11	37.38	29.71	33.56	37.83
Class 2	30.94	34.80	39.41	31.24	35.10	39.71	31.69	35.55	40.16
Class 1	33.29	37.15	41.76	33.59	37.45	42.06	34.04	37.90	42.51
Corporal									
Class 2	35.75	39.60	44.22	36.05	39.90	44.52	36.50	40.35	44.97
Class 1	38.37	42.23	46.85	38.67	42.53	47.15	39.12	42.98	47.60

SERVICE RETIREMENT BENEFITS, ETC.

Those who leave the services having served at least five years, but not long enough to qualify for the appropriate immediate pension, now qualify for a preserved pension and terminal grant both of which are payable at age 60. The tax-free resettlement grants shown below are payable on release to those who qualify for a preserved pension and who have completed nine years service from age 21 (officers) or 12 years from age 18 (other ranks). The annual rates for the army are given (as at mid-July 1992). These figures apply to equivalent ranks in all services, including the nursing services.

OFFICERS

No. of years reckonable service over age 21	*Capt. (incl. QM) and below*	*Major (incl. QM)*	*Lt.-Col.*	*Col. (incl. Deputy Chaplain General)*	*Brigadier*	*Major-General*	*Lieutenant-General*	*General*
16	£ 6,926	£ 8,254	£10,812	£—	£—	£—	£—	£—
17	7,245	8,646	11,312	—	—	—	—	—
18	7,565	9,038	11,813	13,757	—	—	—	—
19	7,884	9,431	12,313	14,339	—	—	—	—
20	8,204	9,823	12,813	14,922	—	—	—	—
21	8,523	10,215	13,314	15,504	—	—	—	—
22	8,843	10,607	13,814	16,086	18,571	—	—	—
23	9,162	11,000	14,314	16,669	19,157	—	—	—
24	9,482	11,392	14,815	17,251	19,744	19,480	—	—
25	9,801	11,784	15,315	17,834	20,331	20,059	—	—
26	10,120	12,176	15,815	18,416	20,918	20,638	—	—
27	10,440	12,568	16,316	18,998	21,505	21,217	22,519	—
28	10,759	12,961	16,816	19,581	22,091	21,796	24,870	—
29	11,079	13,353	17,316	20,163	22,678	22,375	25,530	—
30	11,398	13,745	17,817	20,745	23,265	22,953	26,191	36,478
31	11,718	14,137	18,317	21,328	23,852	23,532	26,851	37,398
32	12,037	14,530	18,817	21,910	24,438	24,111	27,512	38,318
33	12,357	14,922	19,318	22,493	25,025	24,690	28,172	39,238
34	12,667	15,314	19,818	23,075	25,612	25,269	28,833	40,158

WARRANT OFFICERS, NCOS AND PRIVATES

Number of years reckonable service	*Below Corporal*	*Corporal*	*Sergeant*	*Staff Sergeant*	*Warrant Officer Class II*	*Warrant Officer Class I*
22	£4,021	£5,139	£5,647	£6,428	£ 6,644	£ 7,342
23	4,161	5,318	5,844	6,652	6,879	7,606
24	4,302	5,498	6,041	6,877	7,715	7,870
25	4,442	5,677	6,238	7,101	7,350	8,134
26	4,583	5,857	6,435	7,325	7,586	8,398
27	4,723	6,036	6,632	7,550	7,821	8,662
28	4,863	6,215	6,829	7,774	8,056	8,926
29	5,004	6,395	7,026	7,998	8,292	9,190
30	5,144	6,574	7,224	8,223	8,527	9,453
31	5,285	6,754	7,421	8,447	8,763	9,717
32	5,425	6,933	7,618	8,871	8,998	9,981
33	5,565	7,112	7,815	8,896	9,223	10,245
34	5,706	7,292	8,012	9,120	9,469	10,509
35	5,846	7,471	8,209	9,344	9,704	10,773
36	5,987	7,651	8,406	9,569	9,940	11,037
37	6,127	7,830	8,603	9,793	10,175	11,301

TERMINAL GRANTS AND GRATUITIES

Terminal grants are in each case three times the rate of retired pay or pension. There are special rates of retired pay for Chaplains and certain other ranks not shown above. Lower rates are payable in cases of voluntary retirement.

A gratuity of £2,230 for each year completed is payable for officers with short service commissions. Resettlement grants are: officers £8,101; non-commissioned ranks £5,357.

Relative Rank – Armed Forces

Royal Navy

1 Admiral of the Fleet
2 Admiral (Adm.)
3 Vice-Admiral (Vice-Adm.)
4 Rear-Admiral (Rear-Adm.)
5 Commodore (1st & 2nd Class) (Cdre)
6 Captain (Capt.)
7 Commander (Cdr.)
8 Lieutenant-Commander (Lt.-Cdr.)
9 Lieutenant (Lt.)
10 Sub-Lieutenant (Sub-Lt.)
11 Acting Sub-Lieutenant (Acting Sub-Lt.)

Army

1 Field Marshal
2 General (Gen.)
3 Lieutenant-General (Lt.-Gen.)
4 Major-General (Maj.-Gen.)
5 Brigadier (Brig.)
6 Colonel (Col.)
7 Lieutenant-Colonel (Lt.-Col.)
8 Major (Maj.)
9 Captain (Capt.)
10 Lieutenant (Lt.)
11 Second Lieutenant (2nd Lt.)

Royal Air Force

1 Marshal of the RAF
2 Air Chief Marshal
3 Air Marshal
4 Air Vice-Marshal
5 Air Commodore (Air Cdre)
6 Group Captain (Gp Capt)
7 Wing Commander (Wg Cdr.)
8 Squadron Leader (Sqn. Ldr.)
9 Flight Lieutenant (Flt. Lt.)
10 Flying Officer (FO)
11 Pilot Officer (PO)

The Christian Churches

The Church of England

The Church of England is the established (i.e. state) church in England and the mother church of the Anglican Communion. It originated in the conflicts between church and state throughout the Middle Ages, culminating in the Act of Supremacy issued by Henry VIII in 1534. This broke with Rome and declared the King to be the supreme head of the Church in England. Since 1534 the English monarch has been termed the Supreme Governor of the Church of England. The Thirty-Nine Articles, a set of doctrinal statements defining the position of the Church of England, were adopted in their final form in 1571 and include the emphasis on personal faith and the authority of the scriptures common to the Protestant Reformation throughout Europe.

The Church of England is divided into the two provinces of Canterbury and York, each under an archbishop. The two provinces are subdivided into 44 dioceses. Decisions on matters concerning the Church of England are made by the General Synod, established in 1970. It also discusses and expresses opinion on any other matter of religious or public interest. The General Synod has 574 members in total, divided between three houses: the House of Bishops, the House of Clergy and the House of Laity. It is presided over jointly by the Archbishops of Canterbury and York and normally meets three times a year. The Synod has the power, delegated by Parliament, to frame statute law (known as a Measure) on any matter concerning the Church of England. A Measure must be laid before both Houses of Parliament, who may accept or reject it but cannot amend it. Once accepted the Measure is submitted for Royal Assent and then has the full force of law. The Synod appoints a number of committees, boards and councils which deal with, or advise the synod on, a wide range of matters. In addition to the General Synod, there are synods of clergy and laity at diocesan level.

The Church of England has an estimated 1.6 million members, of whom about 1.2 million regularly attend Sunday services. There are two archbishops, 109 diocesan and suffragan bishops, 10,375 male and 674 female full-time stipendiary clergy, and over 16,000 churches and places of worship.

General Synod of the Church of England, Church House, Dean's Yard, London SW1P 3NZ. Tel: 071-222 9011. *Secretary-General*, P. Mawer.
House of Bishops: *Chairman*, The Archbishop of Canterbury; *Vice-Chairman*, The Archbishop of York.
House of Clergy: *Joint Chairmen*, The Archdeacon of Leicester; Canon J. Stanley.
House of Laity: *Chairman*, Prof. J. D. McClean; *Vice-Chairman*, Dr Christina Baxter.

Stipends 1992–3

Archbishop of Canterbury	£43,550
Archbishop of York	£38,150
Bishop of London	£35,560
Bishop of Durham	£31,380
Bishop of Winchester	£26,160
Other Diocesan Bishops	£23,610
Suffragan Bishops	£19,410
Deans and Provosts	£19,410
Residentiary Canons	£15,870

Province of Canterbury

CANTERBURY

103rd Archbishop and Primate of All England
Most Revd and Rt. Hon. George L. Carey, Ph.D. *cons.* 1987, *trans.* 1991, *apptd* 1991; Lambeth Palace, London SE1 7JU. *Signs* George Cantuar:

Bishops Suffragan
Dover, Rt. Revd John R. A. Llewellin, *cons.* 1985, *apptd* 1992; Upway, St Martin's Hill, Canterbury, CT1 1PR.
Maidstone, Rt. Revd Gavin H. Reid, *cons.* 1992, *apptd* 1992; Bishop's House, Pett Lane, Charing, Ashford TN27 0DL

Assistant Bishops
Rt. Revd Ross Hook, MC, *cons.* 1965, *apptd* 1986; Rt. Revd William Franklin, OBE, *cons.* 1972, *apptd* 1987; Rt. Revd Richard Say, KCVO, *cons.* 1961, *apptd* 1988.

Dean
Very Revd John Arthur Simpson, *apptd* 1986.

Canons Residentiary
J. H. R. De Sausmarez, *apptd* 1981; P. Brett, *apptd* 1983; Ven. M. Till, *apptd* 1986; C. A. Lewis, *apptd* 1987.

Archdeacons
Canterbury, Ven. M. Till, *apptd* 1986.
Maidstone, Ven. P. Evans, *apptd* 1989.

Stipendiary Male Clergy, 189.
Stipendiary Women Deacons, 11.

Vicar-General of Province and Diocese, Chancellor S. Cameron, QC.
Commissary-General, J. H. R. Newey, QC, *apptd* 1971.
Joint Registrars of the Province, F. E. Robson, OBE, 16 Beaumont Street, Oxford; B. J. T. Hanson, Church House, Dean's Yard, London SW1P 3NZ.
Registrar of the Diocese of Canterbury, A. O. E. Davies, 9 The Precincts, Canterbury CT1 2EE.

LONDON

131st Bishop
Rt. Revd and Rt. Hon. David M. Hope, D.Phil., *cons.* 1985, *trans.* 1991, *apptd* 1991; 8 Barton Street, London SW1P 3NE. *Signs* David Londin:

Area Bishops
Edmonton, Rt. Revd Brian J. Masters, *cons.* 1982, *apptd* 1984; 1 Regent's Park Terrace, London NW1 7EE.
Kensington, Rt. Revd John Hughes, Ph.D., *cons.* 1987, *apptd* 1987; 19 Campden Hill Square, London W8 7JY.
Stepney, Rt. Revd Richard C. Chartres; 63 Coborn Road, London E3 2DB.
Willesden, Rt. Revd Graham G. Dow; 173 Willesden Lane, London NW6 7YN.

BISHOP SUFFRAGAN
Fulham, Rt. Revd C. John Klyberg, *cons.* 1985, *apptd* 1985; 4 Cambridge Place, London W8 5PB.

ASSISTANT BISHOPS
Rt. Revd Maurice Wood, DSC, *cons.* 1971, *apptd* 1985; Rt. Revd Michael Marshall, *cons.* 1975, *apptd* 1984.

DEAN OF ST PAUL'S
Very Revd T. Eric Evans, *apptd* 1988.

CANONS RESIDENTIARY
Ven. G. Cassidy, *apptd* 1987; C. J. Hill, *apptd* 1989;
R. J. Halliburton, *apptd* 1990; M. J. Saward, *apptd* 1991.
Receiver of St Paul's, Brig. R. Ackworth.

ARCHDEACONS
Charing Cross, Rt. Revd C. J. Klyberg, *apptd* 1989.
Hackney, vacant.
Hampstead, Ven. R. A. W. Coogan, *apptd* 1985.
London, Ven. G. Cassidy, *apptd* 1987.
Middlesex, Ven. T. J. Raphael, *apptd* 1983.
Northolt, vacant.

Stipendiary Male Clergy, 568.
Stipendiary Women Deacons, 49.

Chancellor and Commissary of the Dean and Chapter, Miss S. Cameron, QC, *apptd* 1992.
Registrar, D. W. Faull, 35 Great Peter Street, London SW1P 3LR.

WESTMINSTER

The Collegiate Church of St Peter (A Royal Peculiar)

DEAN
Michael Clement Otway Mayne, *apptd* 1986.

SUB DEAN AND ARCHDEACON
A. E. Harvey, *apptd* 1987.

CANONS OF WESTMINSTER
A. E. Harvey, *apptd* 1982; D. C. Gray, *apptd* 1987;
C. D. Semper, *apptd* 1987; P. S. Bates, *apptd* 1990.

Chapter Clerk and Receiver-General, Rear-Adm. K. A. Snow, CB, *apptd* 1987.
Legal Secretary, C. L. Hodgetts, *apptd* 1973.
Registrar, S. J. Holmes, MVO, *apptd* 1984, 20 Dean's Yard, London SW1P 3PA.

WINCHESTER

95TH BISHOP
Rt. Revd Colin C. W. James, *cons.* 1973, *trans.* 1977 and 1985, *apptd* 1985; Wolvesey, Winchester SO23 9ND. *Signs* Colin Winton:

BISHOPS SUFFRAGAN
Basingstoke, Rt. Revd Michael R. J. Manktelow, *cons.* 1977, *apptd* 1977; Bishop's Lodge, Skippetts Lane West, Basingstoke RG21 3HP.
Southampton, Rt. Revd John F. Perry, *cons.* 1989, *apptd* 1989; Ham House, The Crescent, Romsey SO51 7NG.

ASSISTANT BISHOPS
Rt. Revd Hassan Dehqani-Tafti, *cons.* 1961, *apptd* 1982; Rt. Revd Leslie Rees, *cons.* 1980, *apptd* 1986.

DEAN
Very Revd Trevor R. Beeson, *apptd* 1987.

Dean of Jersey (A Peculiar), Very Revd Basil A. O'Ferrall, CB, *apptd* 1985.
Dean of Guernsey (A Peculiar), Very Revd Jeffery Fenwick, *apptd* 1989.

CANONS RESIDENTIARY
E. G. Job, *apptd* 1979; P. A. Britton, *apptd* 1980;
A. K. Walker, *apptd* 1987; Ven. A. F. Knight, *apptd* 1991.

ARCHDEACONS
Basingstoke, Ven. A. F. Knight, *apptd* 1990.
Winchester, Ven. A. G. Clarkson, *apptd* 1984.

Stipendiary Male Clergy, 274.
Stipendiary Women Deacons, 10.

Chancellor, J. Spokes, QC, *apptd* 1985.
Registrar and Legal Secretary, P. M. White, 19 St Peter Street, Winchester SO23 8BU.

BATH AND WELLS

76TH BISHOP
Rt. Revd James L. Thompson, *cons.* 1978, *apptd* 1991; The Palace, Wells BA5 2PD. *Signs* James Bath & Wells.

BISHOP SUFFRAGAN
Taunton, Rt. Revd J. H. Richard Lewis, *cons.* 1992, *apptd* 1992; Sherford Farm House, Sherford, Taunton TA1 3RF.

DEAN
Very Revd Richard Lewis, *apptd* 1990.

CANONS RESIDENTIARY
S. R. Cutt, *apptd* 1979; C. E. Thomas, *apptd* 1983;
P. de N. Lucas, *apptd* 1988; G. O. Farran, *apptd* 1985.

ARCHDEACONS
Bath, Ven. J. E. Burgess, *apptd* 1975.
Taunton, Ven. R. M. C. Frith, *apptd* 1992.
Wells, Ven. C. E. Thomas, *apptd* 1983.

Stipendiary Male Clergy, 253.
Stipendiary Women Deacons, 8.

Chancellor, R. Bursell, QC, *apptd* 1992.
Registrar, Secretary and Chapter Clerk, T. Berry, Diocesan Registry, Market Place, Wells BA5 2RE.

BIRMINGHAM

7TH BISHOP
Rt. Revd Mark Santer, *cons.* 1981, *apptd* 1987; Bishop's Croft, Harborne, Birmingham B17 0BG. *Signs* Mark Birmingham.

BISHOP SUFFRAGAN
Aston, Rt. Revd John Austin, *cons.* 1992, *apptd* 1992; Strensham House, 8 Strensham Hill, Moseley, Birmingham B13 8AG.

STIPENDIARY ASSISTANT BISHOP
Rt. Revd Michael Whinney, *cons.* 1982, *apptd* 1989.

PROVOST
Very Revd Peter A. Berry, *apptd* 1986.

Canons Residentiary
Ven. C. J. G. Barton, *apptd* 1990; A. H. F. Luff, *apptd* 1992.

Archdeacons
Aston, Ven. C. J. G. Barton, *apptd* 1990.
Birmingham, Ven. J. F. Duncan, *apptd* 1985.
Coleshill, Ven. J. L. Cooper, *apptd* 1990.

Stipendiary Male Clergy, 210.
Stipendiary Women Deacons, 15.

Chancellor, His Honour Judge Aglionby, *apptd* 1970.
Registrar and Legal Secretary, M. B. Shaw, St Philip's House, St Philip's Place, Birmingham B3 2PP.

BRISTOL

54th Bishop
Rt. Revd Barry Rogerson, *cons.* 1979, *apptd* 1985; Bishop's House, Clifton Hill, Bristol BS8 1BW. *Signs* Barry Bristol.

Bishop Suffragan
Malmesbury, Rt. Revd Peter J. Firth, *cons.* 1983, *apptd* 1983; 7 Ivywell Road, Bristol BS9 1NX.

Dean
Very Revd Arthur W. Carr, *apptd* 1987.

Canons Residentiary
J. Rogan, *apptd* 1983; A. L. J. Redfern, *apptd* 1987; J. L. Simpson, *apptd* 1989; P. F. Johnson, *apptd* 1990.

Archdeacons
Bristol, Ven. D. J. Banfield, *apptd* 1990.
Swindon, Ven. M. Middleton, *apptd* 1992.

Stipendiary Male Clergy, 162.
Stipendiary Women Deacons, 19.

Chancellor, Sir David Calcutt, QC, *apptd* 1971.
Registrar and Secretary, T. R. Urquhart, 30 Queen Charlotte Street, Bristol BS13 8HE.

CHELMSFORD

7th Bishop
Rt. Revd John Waine, *cons.* 1975, *apptd* 1986; Bishopscourt, Margaretting, Ingatestone CM4 0HD. *Signs* John Chelmsford.

Bishops Suffragan
Barking, Rt. Revd Roger F. Sainsbury, *cons.* 1991, *apptd* 1991; 110 Capel Road, Forest Gate, London E7 0JS.
Bradwell, vacant; 21 Elmhurst Avenue, Benfleet SS7 5RY.
Colchester, Rt. Revd Michael E. Vickers, *cons.* 1988, *apptd* 1988; 1 Fitzwalter Road, Lexden, Colchester CO3 3SS.

Provost
Very Revd John H. Moses, Ph.D., *apptd* 1982.

Canons Residentiary
P. G. Brett, *apptd* 1985; P. G. Southwell-Sander, *apptd* 1985; T. Thompson, *apptd* 1988; B. P. Thompson, *apptd* 1988.

Archdeacons
Colchester, Ven. E. C. F. Stroud, *apptd* 1983.
Southend, Ven. D. Jennings, *apptd* 1992.
West Ham, Ven. T. J. Stevens, *apptd* 1991.

Stipendiary Male Clergy, 502.
Stipendiary Women Deacons, 25.

Chancellor, Miss S. M. Cameron, QC, *apptd* 1970.
Diocesan Registrar, B. Hood, 53 New Street, Chelmsford CM1 1NG.

CHICHESTER

102nd Bishop
Rt. Revd Eric W. Kemp, DD, *cons.* 1974, *apptd* 1974; The Palace, Chichester PO19 1PY. *Signs* Eric Cicestr:

Bishops Suffragan
Horsham, Rt. Revd John W. Hind, *cons.* 1991, *apptd* 1991; Bishop's Lodge, Worth, nr. Crawley RH10 4RT.
Lewes, Rt. Revd Ian P. M. Cundy, *cons.* 1992, *apptd* 1992; Beacon House, Berwick, Polegate BN26 6ST.

Assistant Bishops
Rt. Revd William Hunt, *cons.* 1955, *apptd* 1980; Rt. Revd Mark Green, *cons.* 1972, *apptd* 1982; Rt. Revd Simon Phipps, *cons.* 1968, *apptd* 1987; Rt. Revd Edward Knapp-Fisher, *cons.* 1960, *apptd* 1987; Rt. Revd Morris Maddocks, *cons.* 1972, *apptd* 1987.

Dean
Very Revd John D. Treadgold, LVO, *apptd* 1989.

Canons Residentiary
R. T. Greenacre, *apptd* 1975; J. F. Hester, *apptd* 1985.

Archdeacons
Chichester, Ven. M. Brotherton, *apptd* 1991.
Horsham, Ven. W. C. L. Filby, *apptd* 1983.
Lewes and Hastings, Ven. H. Glaisyer, *apptd* 1991.

Stipendiary Male Clergy, 362.
Stipendiary Women Deacons, 5.

Chancellor, His Honour Judge Q. T. Edwards, QC, *apptd* 1978.
Legal Secretary to the Bishop, and Diocesan Registrar, C. L. Hodgetts, 5 East Pallant, Chichester PO19 1TS.

COVENTRY

7th Bishop
Rt. Revd Simon Barrington-Ward, *cons.* 1985, *apptd* 1985; The Bishop's House, 23 Davenport Road, Coventry CV5 6PW. *Signs* Simon Coventry.

Bishop Suffragan
Warwick, Rt. Revd George C. Handford, *cons.* 1990, *apptd* 1990; 139 Kenilworth Road, Coventry CV4 7AF.

Assistant Bishops
Rt. Revd John Daly, *cons.* 1935, *apptd* 1968; Rt. Revd Vernon Nicholls, *cons.* 1974, *apptd* 1984.

Provost
Very Revd John F. Petty, *apptd* 1987.

Canons Residentiary
P. Oestreicher, *apptd* 1986; M. Sadgrove, *apptd* 1987; G. T. Hughes, *apptd* 1989.

ARCHDEACONS
Coventry, Ven. H. I. L. Russell, *apptd* 1989.
Warwick, Ven. M. J. J. Paget-Wilkes, *apptd* 1990.

Stipendiary Male Clergy, 186.
Stipendiary Women Deacons, 12.

Chancellor, W. M. Gage, *apptd* 1980.
Registrar, D. J. Dumbleton, 8 The Quadrant, Coventry CVI 2EL.

DERBY

5TH BISHOP
Rt. Revd Peter S. Dawes, *cons.* 1988, *apptd* 1988; The Bishop's House, 6 King Street, Duffield, Derby DE56 4EU. *Signs* Peter Derby.

BISHOP SUFFRAGAN
Repton, Rt. Revd Francis H. A. Richmond, *cons.* 1986, *apptd* 1986; Repton House, Lea, Matlock DE4 5JP.

PROVOST
Very Revd Benjamin H. Lewers, *apptd* 1981.

CANONS RESIDENTIARY
Ven. R. S. Dell, *apptd* 1981; I. Gatford, *apptd* 1984; G. A. Chesterman, *apptd* 1989.

ARCHDEACONS
Chesterfield, Ven. G. R. Phizackerley, *apptd* 1978.
Derby, Ven. R. S. Dell, *apptd* 1973.

Stipendiary Male Clergy, 202.
Stipendiary Women Deacons, 15.

Chancellor, J. W. M. Bullimore, *apptd* 1981.
Registrar, J. S. Battie, Derby Church House, Full Street, Derby DEI 3DR.

ELY

67TH BISHOP
Rt. Revd Stephen W. Sykes, *cons.* 1990, *apptd* 1990; The Bishop's House, Ely CB7 4DW. *Signs* Stephen Ely.

BISHOP SUFFRAGAN
Huntingdon, Rt. Revd William G. Roe, D.Phil., *cons.* 1980, *apptd* 1980; 14 Lynn Road, Ely, Cambs. CB6 IDA.

DEAN
Very Revd Michael Higgins, *apptd* 1991.

CANONS RESIDENTIARY
D. J. Green, *apptd* 1980; J. Rone, *apptd* 1989.

ARCHDEACONS
Ely, Ven. D. Walser, *apptd* 1981.
Huntingdon, Ven. R. K. Sledge, *apptd* 1978.
Wisbech, Ven. D. Fleming, *apptd* 1984.

Stipendiary Male Clergy, 170.
Stipendiary Women Deacons, 7.

Chancellor, W. Gage, QC.
Registrar, W. H. Godfrey, 18 The Broadway, St Ives, Huntingdon PE17 4BS.
Joint Registrar, P. F. B. Beesley, 1 The Sanctuary, London SWIP 3JT.

EXETER

69TH BISHOP
Rt. Revd G. Hewlett Thompson, *cons.* 1974, *apptd* 1985; The Palace, Exeter EXI IHY. *Signs* Hewlett Exon:

BISHOPS SUFFRAGAN
Crediton, Rt. Revd Peter E. Coleman, *cons.* 1984, *apptd* 1984; 10 The Close, Exeter EXI IEZ.
Plymouth, Rt. Revd Richard S. Hawkins, *cons.* 1988, *apptd* 1988; 31 Riverside Walk, Tamerton Foliot, Plymouth PL5 4AQ.

ASSISTANT BISHOPS
Rt. Revd Ronald Goodchild, *cons.* 1964, *apptd* 1983; Rt. Revd Philip Pasterfield, *cons.* 1974, *apptd* 1984; Rt. Revd Richard Cartwright, *cons.* 1972, *apptd* 1988; Rt. Revd Colin Docker, *cons.* 1975, *apptd* 1991.

DEAN
Very Revd Richard Montague Stephens Eyre, *apptd* 1981.

CANONS RESIDENTIARY
A. C. Mawson, *apptd* 1979; Ven. J. Richards, *apptd* 1981; K. C. Parry, *apptd* 1991.

ARCHDEACONS
Barnstaple, Ven. T. Lloyd, *apptd* 1989.
Exeter, Ven. J. Richards, *apptd* 1981.
Plymouth, Ven. R. G. Ellis, *apptd* 1982.
Totnes, Ven. A. F. Tremlett, *apptd* 1988.

Stipendiary Male Clergy, 280.
Stipendiary Women Deacons, 11.

Chancellor, Sir David Calcutt, QC, *apptd* 1971.
Registrar, R. K. Wheeler, 18 Cathedral Yard, Exeter EXI IHE.
Diocesan Secretary, Revd R. R. Huddleson, Diocesan House, Palace Gate, Exeter EXI IHX.

GIBRALTAR IN EUROPE

1ST BISHOP
Rt. Revd John R. Satterthwaite, CMG, *cons.* 1970, *apptd* 1970; 5A Gregory Place, London W8 4NG. *Signs* John Gibraltar.

BISHOP SUFFRAGAN
In Europe, Rt. Revd Edward Holland, *apptd* 1986.

AUXILIARY BISHOPS
Rt. Revd E. M. H. Capper, OBE, *cons.* 1967, *apptd* 1973; Rt. Revd D. de Pina Cabral, *cons.* 1967, *apptd* 1976; Rt. Revd A. W. M. Weeks, CB, *cons.* 1977, *apptd* 1988.

Vicar-General, Revd W. G. Reid.
Bishop's Commissaries, Canon L. Tyzack; Canon J. D. Beckwith; Canon D. H. Palmer; A. M. Apostol.
Dean, Cathedral Church of the Holy Trinity, Gibraltar, Very Revd B. W. Horlock, OBE.
Chancellor, Pro-Cathedral of St Paul, Valletta, Malta, Canon P. Cousins.
Chancellor, Pro-Cathedral of the Holy Trinity, Brussels, Belgium, Ven. J. Lewis.

ARCHDEACONS
Aegean, Ven. G. B. Evans.
North-west Europe, Ven. J. Lewis.
North France, Ven. M. B. Lea.
Gibraltar, Rt. Revd D. de Pina Cabral.
Italy, Rt. Revd E. Devenport.
Riviera, Ven. J. Livingstone.
Scandinavia, Ven. G. A. C. Brown.
Switzerland, Ven. P. J. Hawker.

Chancellor, Sir David Calcutt, QC.
Diocesan Registrar and Legal Secretary, J. G. Underwood, 37A Walbrook, London EC4 8BS.

GLOUCESTER

38TH BISHOP
Rt. Revd Peter J. Ball, *cons.* 1977, *apptd* 1992; Bishopscourt, Gloucester GL1 2BQ. *Signs* Peter Gloucester.

BISHOP SUFFRAGAN
Tewkesbury, Rt. Revd Geoffrey D. J. Walsh, *cons.* 1986, *apptd* 1986; Green Acre, Hempsted, Gloucester GL2 6LS.

DEAN
Very Revd Kenneth N. Jennings, *apptd* 1982.

CANONS RESIDENTIARY
A. L. Dunstan, *apptd* 1978; R. D. M. Grey, *apptd* 1982; P. R. Greenwood, *apptd* 1986.

ARCHDEACONS
Cheltenham, Ven. J. A. Lewis, *apptd* 1988.
Gloucester, Ven. C. J. H. Wagstaff, *apptd* 1982.

Stipendiary Male Clergy, 185.
Stipendiary Women Deacons, 12.

Chancellor and Vicar-General, Ms D. J. Rogers, *apptd* 1990.
Registrar, C. G. Peak, 34 Brunswick Road, Gloucester GL1 1JJ.
Diocesan Secretary, R. Anderton, Church House, College Green, Gloucester GL1 2LY.

GUILDFORD

7TH BISHOP
Rt. Revd Michael E. Adie, *cons.* 1983, *apptd* 1983; Willow Grange, Woking Road, Guildford GU4 7QS. *Signs* Michael Guildford.

BISHOP SUFFRAGAN
Dorking, Rt. Revd David P. Wilcox, *cons.* 1986, *apptd* 1986; 13 Pilgrims Way, Guildford GU4 8AD.

DEAN
Very Revd Alexander G. Wedderspoon, *apptd* 1987.

CANONS RESIDENTIARY
F. S. Telfer, *apptd* 1973; P. G. Croft, *apptd* 1983; R. D. Fenwick, *apptd* 1990.

ARCHDEACONS
Dorking, Ven. C.W. Herbert, *apptd* 1990.
Surrey, Ven. J. S. Went, *apptd* 1989.

Stipendiary Male Clergy, 194.
Stipendiary Women Deacons, 15.

Chancellor, M. B. Goodman.
Legal Secretary and Registrar, P. F. B. Beesley, 1 The Sanctuary, London SW1P 3JT.

HEREFORD

103RD BISHOP
Rt. Revd John Oliver, *cons.* 1990, *apptd* 1990; The Palace, Hereford HR4 9BN. *Signs* John Hereford.

BISHOP SUFFRAGAN
Ludlow, Rt. Revd Ian M. Griggs, *cons.* 1987, *apptd* 1987; Halford Vicarage, Craven Arms, Shropshire SY7 9BT.

DEAN
Very Revd Robert A. Willis, *apptd* 1992.

CANONS RESIDENTIARY
P. Iles, *apptd* 1983; J. Tiller, *apptd* 1984.

ARCHDEACONS
Hereford, Ven. L. G. Moss, *apptd* 1992.
Ludlow, Ven. J. C. Saxbee, *apptd* 1992.

Stipendiary Male Clergy, 129.
Stipendiary Women Deacons, 9.

Chancellor, J. M. Henty.
Joint Registrars, V. T. Jordan, 44 Bridge Street, Hereford; P. Beesley, 1 The Sanctuary, London SW1P 3JT.

LEICESTER

5TH BISHOP
Rt. Revd Thomas F. Butler, Ph.D., *cons.* 1985, *apptd* 1991; Bishop's Lodge, 10 Springfield Road, Leicester LE2 3BD. *Signs* Thomas Leicester.

ASSISTANT BISHOPS
Rt. Revd John Mort, CBE, *cons.* 1952, *apptd* 1972; Rt. Revd Godfrey Ashby, *cons.* 1980, *apptd* 1988.

PROVOST
Very Revd Derek Hole, *apptd* 1992.

CANONS RESIDENTIARY
M. T. H. Banks, *apptd* 1988; M. Wilson, *apptd* 1988.

ARCHDEACONS
Leicester, Ven. R. D. Silk, *apptd* 1980.
Loughborough, Ven. I. Stanes, *apptd* 1992.

Stipendiary Male Clergy, 180.
Stipendiary Women Deacons, 12.

Chancellor, N. Seed, *apptd* 1989.
Registrars, P. C. E. Morris, 35 Great Peter Street, London SW1P 3LR; R. H. Bloor, 23 Friar Lane, Leicester LE1 5QQ.

LICHFIELD

97TH BISHOP
Rt. Revd Keith N. Sutton, *cons.* 1978, *apptd* 1984; Bishop's House, The Close, Lichfield WS13 7LG. *Signs* Keith Lichfield.

Bishops Suffragan

Shrewsbury, Rt. Revd John D. Davies, *cons.* 1987, *apptd* 1987; Athlone House, 68 London Road, Shrewsbury SY2 6PG.

Stafford, Rt. Revd Michael C. Scott-Joynt, *cons.* 1987, *apptd* 1987; Ash Garth, Broughton Crescent, Barlaston ST12 9DD.

Wolverhampton, Rt. Revd Christopher J. Mayfield, *cons.* 1985, *apptd* 1985; 61 Richmond Road, Wolverhampton WV3 9JH.

Assistant Bishop

Rt. Revd Ronald O. Bowlby, *cons.* 1973, *apptd* 1991.

Dean

Very Revd John H. Lang, *apptd* 1980.

Canons Residentiary

Ven. R. B. Ninis, *apptd* 1974; A. N. Barnard, *apptd* 1977; W. J. Turner, *apptd* 1983; J. Howe, *apptd* 1988.

Archdeacons

Lichfield, Ven. R. B. Ninis, *apptd* 1974.
Salop, Ven. G. Frost, *apptd* 1987.
Stoke-on-Trent, Ven. D. Ede, *apptd* 1989.

Stipendiary Male Clergy, 403.
Stipendiary Women Deacons, 28.

Chancellor, His Honour Judge Shand.
Diocesan Registrar, J. P. Thorneycroft, St Mary's House, The Close, Lichfield WS13 7LD.

LINCOLN

70th Bishop

Rt. Revd Robert M. Hardy, *cons.* 1980, *apptd* 1987; Bishop's House, Eastgate, Lincoln LN2 1QQ. *Signs* Robert Lincoln.

Bishops Suffragan

Grantham, Rt. Revd William Ind, *cons.* 1987, *apptd* 1987; Fairacre, Barrowby High Road, Grantham NG31 8NP.

Grimsby, Rt. Revd David Tustin, *cons.* 1979, *apptd* 1979; Bishop's House, Church Lane, Irby-upon-Humber, Grimsby DN37 7JR.

Assistant Bishops

Rt. Revd Gerald Colin, *cons.* 1966, *apptd* 1979; Rt. Revd Harold Darby, *cons.* 1975, *apptd* 1989.

Dean

Very Revd Brandon D. Jackson, *apptd* 1989.

Canon Residentiary

B. R. Davis, *apptd* 1977.

Archdeacons

Lincoln, Ven. M. P. Brackenbury, *apptd* 1988.
Lindsey, Ven. J. H. C. Laurence, *apptd* 1985.
Stow, Ven. R. J. Wells, *apptd* 1989.

Stipendiary Male Clergy, 244.
Stipendiary Women Deacons, 21.

Chancellor, His Honour Judge Goodman, *apptd* 1971.
Registrar and Legal Secretary, D. M. Wellman, 28 West Parade, Lincoln LN1 1JT.

NORWICH

70th Bishop

Rt. Revd Peter J. Nott, *cons.* 1977, *apptd* 1985; Bishop's House, Norwich, NR3 1SB. *Signs* Peter Norvic:

Bishops Suffragan

Lynn, Rt. Revd David E. Bentley, *cons.* 1986, *apptd* 1986; The Old Vic, Castle Acre, King's Lynn PE32 2AA.

Thetford, Rt. Revd Hugo F. de Waal, *cons.* 1992, *apptd* 1992; Rectory Meadow, Bramerton, Norwich NR14 7DW.

Dean

Very Revd John P. Burbridge, *apptd* 1983.

Canons Residentiary

C. Beswick, *apptd* 1984; M. S. McLean, *apptd* 1986; M. F. Perham, *apptd* 1992.

Archdeacons

Lynn, Ven. A. C. Foottit, *apptd* 1987.
Norfolk, Ven. P. Dawson, *apptd* 1977.
Norwich, Ven. A. M. Handley, *apptd* 1981.

Stipendiary Male Clergy, 237.
Stipendiary Women Deacons, 10.

Chancellor, His Honour J. H. Ellison, VRD, *apptd* 1955.
Registrar and Secretary, J. W. F. Herring, Francis House, 3–7 Redwell Street, Norwich NR2 4TJ.

OXFORD

41st Bishop

Rt. Revd Richard D. Harries, *cons.* 1987, *apptd* 1987; Diocesan Church House, North Hinksey, Oxford OX2 0NB. *Signs* Richard Oxon:

Area Bishops

Buckingham, Rt. Revd Simon H. Burrows, *cons.* 1974, *apptd* 1974; Sheridan, Grimms Hill, Great Missenden HP16 9BD.

Dorchester, Rt. Revd Anthony J. Russell, *cons.* 1988, *apptd* 1988; Holmby House, Sibford Ferris, Banbury, Oxon. OX15 5RG.

Reading, Rt. Revd John F. E. Bone, *cons.* 1989, *apptd* 1989; Greenbanks, Old Bath Road, Sonning, Reading RG4 0SY.

Assistant Bishops

Rt. Revd Albert Cragg, DD, *cons.* 1970, *apptd* 1982; Rt. Revd Leonard Ashton, CB, *cons.* 1974, *apptd* 1984; Rt. Revd Richard Watson, *cons.* 1970, *apptd* 1988; Rt. Revd Peter Walker, *cons.* 1972, *apptd* 1990; Rt. Revd Maurice Wood, *cons.* 1971, *apptd* 1991; Rt. Revd Stephen Verney, *cons.* 1977, *apptd* 1991.

Dean of Christ Church

Very Revd John H. Drury, *apptd* 1991.

Canons Residentiary

Ven. F. V. Weston, *apptd* 1982; O. M. T. O'Donovan, D.Phil., *apptd* 1982; J. M. Pierce, *apptd* 1987; J. S. K. Ward, *apptd* 1991; Rt. Revd A. R. M. Gordon, *apptd* 1991.

Archdeacons

Berkshire, vacant.
Buckingham, Ven. J. A. Morrison, *apptd* 1989.
Oxford, Ven. F. V. Weston, *apptd* 1982.

Stipendiary Male Clergy, 449.
Stipendiary Women Deacons, 29.

Chancellor, P. T. S. Boydell, QC, *apptd* 1958.
Registrar and Legal Secretary, Dr F. E. Robson, OBE, 16 Beaumont Street, Oxford OX1 2LZ.

WINDSOR

The Queen's Free Chapel of St George within Her Castle of Windsor (A Royal Peculiar)

DEAN
Very Revd Patrick Reynolds Mitchell, FSA, *apptd* 1989.

CANONS RESIDENTIARY
J. A. White, *apptd* 1982; D. M. Stanesby, Ph.D., *apptd* 1985; A. A. Coldwells, *apptd* 1987; M. A. Moxon, *apptd* 1990.

Chapter Clerk, Lt.-Col. N. J. Newman, *apptd* 1990.

PETERBOROUGH

36TH BISHOP
Rt. Revd William J. Westwood, *cons.* 1975, *apptd* 1984; The Palace, Peterborough PE1 1YA. *Signs* William Petriburg:

BISHOP SUFFRAGAN
Brixworth, Rt. Revd Paul E. Barber, *cons.* 1989, *apptd* 1989; 4 The Avenue, Dallington, Northampton NN1 4RZ.

DEAN
Very Revd Michael Bunker, *apptd* 1992.

CANONS RESIDENTIARY
T. R. Christie, *apptd* 1980; J. Higham, *apptd* 1983; T. Willmott, *apptd* 1989.

ARCHDEACONS
Northampton, Ven. M. R. Chapman, *apptd* 1991.
Oakham, Ven. B. Fernyhough, *apptd* 1977.

Stipendiary Male Clergy, 175.
Stipendiary Women Deacons, 9.

Chancellor, T. A. C. Coningsby, QC, *apptd* 1989.
Registrar and Legal Secretary, R. Hemingray, 4 Holywell Way, Longthorpe, Peterborough PE3 6SS.

PORTSMOUTH

7TH BISHOP
Rt. Revd Timothy J. Bavin, *cons.* 1974, *apptd* 1985; Bishopswood, Fareham, Hants. PO14 1NT. *Signs* Timothy Portsmouth.

PROVOST
Very Revd David S. Stancliffe, *apptd* 1982.

CANONS RESIDENTIARY
M. D. Doe, *apptd* 1989; C. J. Bradley, *apptd* 1990; D. T. Isaac, *apptd* 1990.

ARCHDEACONS
Isle of Wight, Ven. A. H. M. Turner, *apptd* 1986.
Portsmouth, Ven. N. H. Crowder, *apptd* 1985.

Stipendiary Male Clergy, 145.
Stipendiary Women Deacons, 13.

Chancellor, His Honour Judge Aglionby, *apptd* 1978.
Registrar, Miss H. A. G. Tyler, 132 High Street, Portsmouth PO1 2HR.

ROCHESTER

105TH BISHOP
Rt. Revd A. Michael Arnold Turnbull, *cons.* 1988, *apptd* 1988; Bishopscourt, Rochester ME1 1TS. *Signs* Michael Roffen:

BISHOP SUFFRAGAN
Tonbridge, Rt. Revd David H. Bartleet, *cons.* 1982, *apptd* 1982; Bishop's Lodge, St Botolph's Road, Sevenoaks TN13 3AG.

ASSISTANT BISHOPS
Rt. Revd Colin Buchanan, *cons.* 1985, *apptd* 1989; Rt. Revd William Flagg, *cons.* 1969, *apptd* 1987.

DEAN
Very Revd Edward F. Shotter, *apptd* 1990.

CANONS RESIDENTIARY
E. R. Turner, *apptd* 1981; R. J. R. Lea, *apptd* 1988; J. Armson, *apptd* 1989; N. Warren, *apptd* 1989.

ARCHDEACONS
Bromley, Ven. E. R. Francis, *apptd* 1979.
Rochester, Ven. N. L. Warren, *apptd* 1989.
Tonbridge, Ven. R. J. Mason, *apptd* 1977.

Stipendiary Male Clergy, 231.
Stipendiary Women Deacons, 21.

Chancellor, His Honour Judge M. B. Goodman, *apptd* 1971.
Registrar, O. R. Woodfield, The Precinct, Rochester ME1 1SZ.

ST ALBANS

8TH BISHOP
Rt. Revd John B. Taylor, *cons.* 1980, *apptd* 1980; Abbey Gate House, St Albans AL3 4HD. *Signs* John St Albans.

BISHOPS SUFFRAGAN
Bedford, Rt. Revd David J. Farmbrough, *cons.* 1981, *apptd* 1981; 168 Kimbolton Road, Bedford MK41 8DN.
Hertford, Rt. Revd Robin J. N. Smith, *cons.* 1990, *apptd* 1990; Hertford House, Abbey Mill Lane, St Albans AL3 4HE.

ASSISTANT BISHOP
Rt. Revd The Lord Runcie, *cons.* 1970, *apptd* 1991.

DEAN
Very Revd Peter C. Moore, D.Phil., *apptd* 1973.

CANONS RESIDENTIARY
C. B. Slee, *apptd* 1982; C. Garner, *apptd* 1984; G. R. S. Ritson, *apptd* 1987; M. Sansom, *apptd* 1988.

ARCHDEACONS
Bedford, Ven. M. G. Bourke, *apptd* 1986.
St Albans, Ven. P. B. Davies, *apptd* 1987.

Stipendiary Male Clergy, 323.
Stipendiary Women Deacons, 26.

Chancellor, His Honour Judge Bursell, QC, *apptd* 1992.
Registrar and Legal Secretary, D. N. Cheetham, Holywell Lodge, 41 Holywell Hill, St Albans AL1 1HE.

ST EDMUNDSBURY AND IPSWICH

8TH BISHOP
Rt. Revd John Dennis, *cons.* 1979, *apptd* 1986; Bishop's House, Ipswich IP1 3ST. *Signs* John St Edmunds and Ipswich.

BISHOP SUFFRAGAN
Dunwich, Rt. Revd Jonathan S. Bailey, *cons.* 1992, *apptd* 1992; The Old Vicarage, Stowupland, Stowmarket IP14 4BQ.

PROVOST
Very Revd Raymond Furnell, *apptd* 1981.

CANONS RESIDENTIARY
G. J. Tarris, *apptd* 1982; R. Garrard, *apptd* 1987; A. M. Shaw, *apptd* 1989.

ARCHDEACONS
Ipswich, Ven. T. A. Gibson, *apptd* 1987.
Sudbury, Ven. R. Garrard, *apptd* 1992.
Suffolk, Ven. N. Robinson, *apptd* 1987.

Stipendiary Male Clergy, 192.
Stipendiary Women Deacons, 11.

Chancellor, His Honour Judge Blofeld, QC, *apptd* 1974.
Registrar, J. D. Mitson, 22–28 Museum Street, Ipswich IP1 1JA.

SALISBURY

76TH BISHOP
Rt. Revd John A. Baker, *cons.* 1982, *apptd* 1982; South Canonry, The Close, Salisbury SP1 2ER. *Signs* John Sarum.

BISHOPS SUFFRAGAN
Ramsbury, Rt. Revd Peter St G. Vaughan, *cons.* 1989, *apptd* 1989; Bishop's House, Urchfont, Devizes, Wilts. SN10 4QH.
Sherborne, Rt. Revd John D. G. Kirkham, *cons.* 1976, *apptd* 1976; Little Bailie, Sturminster Marshall, Wimborne BH21 4AD.

ASSISTANT BISHOP
Rt. Revd John Cavell, *cons.* 1972, *apptd* 1988.

DEAN
Very Revd the Hon. Hugh G. Dickinson, *apptd* 1986.

CANONS RESIDENTIARY
D. J. C. Davies, *apptd* 1985; J. R. Stewart, *apptd* 1990; D. M. K. Durston, *apptd* 1992.

ARCHDEACONS
Dorset, Ven. G. E. Walton, *apptd* 1982.
Sarum, Ven. B. J. Hopkinson, *apptd* 1986.
Sherborne, Ven. P. C. Wheatley, *apptd* 1991.
Wilts, Ven. B. J. Smith, *apptd* 1980.

Stipendiary Male Clergy, 260.
Stipendiary Women Deacons, 11

Chancellor of the Diocese, His Honour J. H. Ellison, VRD, *apptd* 1955.
Registrar and Legal Secretary, F. M. Broadbent, 42 Castle Street, Salisbury SP1 3TX.

SOUTHWARK

8TH BISHOP
Rt. Revd Robert K. Williamson, *cons.* 1984, *trans.* 1991, *apptd* 1991; Bishop's House, 38 Tooting Bec Gardens, London SW16 1QZ. *Signs* Robert Southwark.

BISHOPS SUFFRAGAN
Croydon, Rt. Revd Wilfred D. Wood, DD, *cons.* 1985, *apptd* 1985; St Matthew's House, George Street, Croydon CR0 1PE.
Kingston upon Thames, vacant; *Office*, Whitelands College, West Hill, London SW15 3SN.
Woolwich, Rt. Revd Albert P. Hall, *cons.* 1984, *apptd* 1984; 8B Hilly Fields Crescent, London SE4 1QA.

ASSISTANT BISHOPS
Rt. Revd Edmund Capper, OBE, *cons.* 1967, *apptd* 1981; Rt. Revd John Hughes, *cons.* 1956, *apptd* 1986; Rt. Revd Hugh Montefiore, *cons.* 1970, *apptd* 1987; Rt. Revd Simon Phipps, *cons.* 1976, *apptd* 1987; Rt. Revd Michael Nazir-Ali, *cons.* 1984, *apptd* 1990.

PROVOST
Very Revd David L. Edwards, *apptd* 1983.

CANON RESIDENTIARY
D. Painter, *apptd* 1991.

ARCHDEACONS
Croydon, Ven. F. R. Hazell, *apptd* 1984.
Lambeth, Ven. C. R. B. Bird, *apptd* 1988.
Lewisham, Ven. G. Kuhrt, *apptd* 1989.
Reigate, Ven. P. B. Coombs, *apptd* 1988.
Southwark, Ven. D. L. Bartles-Smith, *apptd* 1985.
Wandsworth, Ven. D. Gerrard, *apptd* 1989.

Stipendiary Male Clergy, 404.
Stipendiary Women Deacons, 34.

Chancellor, R. M. K. Gray, QC, *apptd* 1990.
Joint Registrars, D. W. Faull and P. Morris, 35 Great Peter Street, London SW1P 3LR.

TRURO

13TH BISHOP
Rt. Revd Michael T. Ball, *cons.* 1980, *apptd* 1990; Lis Escop, Truro TR3 6QQ. *Signs* Michael Truro.

BISHOP SUFFRAGAN
St Germans, vacant; 32 Falmouth Road, Truro TR1 2HX.

ASSISTANT BISHOP
Rt. Revd Conrad Meyer, *cons.* 1979, *apptd* 1991.

DEAN
Very Revd David J. Shearlock, *apptd* 1982.

CANONS RESIDENTIARY
W. J. P. Boyd, Ph.D., *apptd* 1985; Ven. R. L. Ravenscroft, *apptd* 1988; R. O. Osborne, *apptd* 1988.

ARCHDEACONS
Cornwall, Ven. R. L. Ravenscroft, *apptd* 1988.
Bodmin, Ven. R. D. C. Whiteman, *apptd* 1989.

Stipendiary Male Clergy, 149.
Stipendiary Women Deacons, 2.

Chancellor, P. T. S. Boydell, QC, *apptd* 1957.
Registrar and Secretary, M. J. Follett, Messrs Follett Blair, Riverside Business Centre, Malpas Road, Truro TR1 1QH.

WORCESTER

111TH BISHOP
Rt. Revd Philip H. E. Goodrich, *cons.* 1973, *apptd* 1982; The Bishop's House, Hartlebury Castle, Kidderminster DY11 7XX. *Signs* Philip Worcester.

BISHOP SUFFRAGAN
Dudley, Rt. Revd Anthony C. Dumper, *cons.* 1977, *apptd* 1977; The Bishop's House, Brooklands, Halesowen Road, Cradley Heath B64 7JF.

ASSISTANT BISHOPS
Rt. Revd John Maund, CBE, MC, *cons.* 1950, *apptd* 1984; Rt. Revd Kenneth Woollcombe, *cons.* 1971, *apptd* 1989; Rt. Revd George Briggs, *cons.* 1973, *apptd* 1990; Rt. Revd Derek Bond, *cons.* 1976, *apptd* 1992.

DEAN
Very Revd Robert M. C. Jeffery, *apptd* 1987.

CANONS RESIDENTIARY
Ven. F. Bentley, *apptd* 1984; D. G. Thomas, *apptd* 1987; I. M. MacKenzie, *apptd* 1989.

ARCHDEACONS
Dudley, Ven. J. Gathercole, *apptd* 1987.
Worcester, Ven. F. Bentley, *apptd* 1984.

Stipendiary Male Clergy, 150.
Stipendiary Women Deacons, 14.

Chancellor, P. T. S. Boydell, QC, *apptd* 1959.
Registrar, M. Huskinson, Diocesan Registry, 8 Sansome Walk, Worcester WR1 1LW.

Province of York

YORK

95TH ARCHBISHOP AND PRIMATE OF ENGLAND
Most Revd and Rt. Hon. John S. Habgood, Ph.D., *cons.* 1973, *trans.* 1983, *apptd* 1983; Bishopthorpe, York YO2 1QE. *Signs* John Ebor:

BISHOPS SUFFRAGAN
Hull, Rt. Revd Donald G. Snelgrove, TD, *cons.* 1981, *apptd* 1981; Hullen House, Woodfield Lane, Hessle, Hull HU13 0ES.
Selby, Rt. Revd Humphrey V. Taylor, *cons.* 1991, *apptd* 1991; 8 Bankside Close, Upper Poppleton, York YO2 6LH.
Whitby, Rt. Revd Gordon Bates, *cons.* 1983, *apptd* 1983; 60 West Green, Stokesley, Middlesbrough TS9 5BD.

ASSISTANT BISHOPS
Rt. Revd George Cockin, *cons.* 1959, *apptd* 1969; Rt. Revd Richard Wimbush, *cons.* 1963, *apptd* 1977; Rt. Revd Richard Wood, *cons.* 1973, *apptd* 1985; Rt. Revd Ronald Foley, *cons.* 1982, *apptd* 1989; Rt. Revd David Galliford, *cons.* 1975, *apptd* 1991; Rt. Revd Clifford Barker, *cons.* 1976, *apptd* 1991.

DEAN
Very Revd John E. Southgate, *apptd* 1984.

CANONS RESIDENTIARY
R. A. Hockley, *apptd* 1976; R. Mayland, *apptd* 1982; J. Toy, Ph.D., *apptd* 1983; R. Metcalfe, *apptd* 1988.

ARCHDEACONS
Cleveland, Ven. C. J. Hawthorn, *apptd* 1991.
East Riding, Ven. H. F. Buckingham, *apptd* 1988.
York, Ven. G. B. Austin, *apptd* 1988.

Stipendiary Male Clergy, 329.
Stipendiary Women Deacons, 23.

Official Principal and Auditor of the Chancery Court, J. A. D. Owen, QC.
Chancellor of the Diocese, His Honour Judge Coningsby, QC, *apptd* 1977.
Vicar-General of the Province and Official Principal of the Consistory Court, His Honour Judge Coningsby, QC.
Registrar and Legal Secretary, L. P. M. Lennox, 1 Peckitt Street, York YO1 1SG.

DURHAM

92ND BISHOP
Rt. Revd David E. Jenkins, *cons.* 1984, *apptd* 1984; Auckland Castle, Bishop Auckland DL14 7NR. *Signs* David Dunelm.

BISHOP SUFFRAGAN
Jarrow, Rt. Revd Alan Smithson, *cons.* 1990, *apptd* 1990; The Old Vicarage, Hallgarth, Pittington, Durham DH6 1AB.

DEAN
Very Revd John R. Arnold, *apptd* 1989.

CANONS RESIDENTIARY
Ven. M. C. Perry, *apptd* 1970; R. L. Coppin, *apptd* 1974; Ven. J. D. Hodgson, *apptd* 1983; D. W. Brown, *apptd* 1990.

ARCHDEACONS
Auckland, Ven. J. D. Hodgson, *apptd* 1983.
Durham, Ven. M. C. Perry, *apptd* 1970.

Stipendiary Male Clergy, 272.
Stipendiary Women Deacons, 22.

Chancellor, His Honour Judge Bursell, QC, *apptd* 1989.
Registrar and Legal Secretary, D. M. Robertson, Diocesan Registry, Auckland Castle, Bishop Auckland DL14 7QJ.

BLACKBURN

7TH BISHOP
Rt. Revd Alan D. Chesters, *cons.* 1989, *apptd* 1989; Bishop's House, Ribchester Road, Blackburn BB1 9EF. *Signs* Alan Blackburn.

BISHOPS SUFFRAGAN
Burnley, Rt. Revd Ronald J. Milner, *cons.* 1988, *apptd* 1988; Dean House, 449 Padiham Road, Burnley BB12 6TE.
Lancaster, Rt. Revd John Nicholls, *cons.* 1990, *apptd* 1990; Wheatfields, 7 Dallas Road, Lancaster LA1 1TN.

PROVOST
vacant.

CANONS RESIDENTIARY
J. M. Taylor, *apptd* 1976; G. I. Hirst, *apptd* 1987; M. A. Kitchener, *apptd* 1990.

ARCHDEACONS
Blackburn, Ven. W. D. Robinson, *apptd* 1986.
Lancaster, Ven. K. H. Gibbons, *apptd* 1989.

Stipendiary Male Clergy, 267.
Stipendiary Women Deacons, 8.

Chancellor, J. W. M. Bullimore, *apptd* 1990.
Registrar, T. A. Hoyle, Diocesan Registry, Cathedral Close, Blackburn BBI 5AB.

BRADFORD

8TH BISHOP
Rt. Revd David J. Smith, *cons.* 1987, *apptd* 1992; Bishopscroft, Ashwell Road, Heaton, Bradford BD9 4AU. *Signs* David Bradford.

PROVOST
Very Revd John S. Richardson, *apptd* 1990.

CANONS RESIDENTIARY
K. H. Cook, *apptd* 1977; J. M. Wharton, *apptd* 1992.

ARCHDEACONS
Bradford, Ven. D. H. Shreeve, *apptd* 1984.
Craven, Ven. B. A. Smith, *apptd* 1987.

Stipendiary Male Clergy, 134.
Stipendiary Women Deacons, 11.

Chancellor, D. M. Savill, QC, *apptd* 1976.
Registrar and Secretary, J. G. H. Mackrell, 6–14 Devonshire Street, Keighley BD21 2AY.

CARLISLE

65TH BISHOP
Rt. Revd Ian Harland, *cons.* 1985, *apptd* 1989; Rose Castle, Dalston, Carlisle CA5 7BZ. *Signs* Ian Carliol:

BISHOP SUFFRAGAN
Penrith, Rt. Revd George L. Hacker, *cons.* 1979, *apptd* 1979; The Rectory, Great Salkeld, Penrith CA11 9NA.

DEAN
Very Revd Henry E. C. Stapleton, *apptd* 1988.

CANONS RESIDENTIARY
R. A. Chapman, *apptd* 1978; Ven. C. P. Stannard, *apptd* 1984; R. C. Johns, *apptd* 1989; D. T. I. Jenkins, *apptd* 1991.

ARCHDEACONS
Carlisle, Ven. C. P. Stannard, *apptd* 1984.
West Cumberland, J. R. Packer, *apptd* 1991.
Westmorland and Furness, Ven. L. J. Peat, *apptd* 1989.

Stipendiary Male Clergy, 194.
Stipendiary Women Deacons, 5.

Chancellor, His Honour Judge Aglionby, *apptd* 1991.
Registrar and Secretary, Mrs S. Holmes, Woodside, Great Corby, Carlisle CA4 8LL.

CHESTER

39TH BISHOP
Rt. Revd Michael A. Baughen, *cons.* 1982, *apptd* 1982; Bishop's House, Chester CH1 2JD. *Signs* Michael Cestr:

BISHOPS SUFFRAGAN
Birkenhead, vacant; Trafford House, Queen's Park, Chester CH4 7AX.
Stockport, Rt. Revd Frank P. Sargeant, *cons.* 1984, *apptd* 1984; 32 Park Gate Drive, Cheadle Hulme, Cheshire SK8 7DF.

DEAN
Very Revd Stephen S. Smalley, *apptd* 1986.

CANONS RESIDENTIARY
C. D. Biddell, *apptd* 1986; R. M. Rees, *apptd* 1990; C. J. Bennetts, *apptd* 1990; O. A. Conway, *apptd* 1991.

ARCHDEACONS
Chester, vacant.
Macclesfield, Ven. J. S. Gaisford, *apptd* 1986.

Stipendiary Male Clergy, 322.
Stipendiary Women Deacons, 7.

Chancellor, H. H. Lomas, *apptd* 1977.
Registrar and Legal Secretary, A. K. McAllester, Friars, 20 White Friars, Chester CH1 1XS.

LIVERPOOL

6TH BISHOP
Rt. Revd David S. Sheppard, *cons.* 1969, *apptd* 1975; Bishop's Lodge, Woolton Park, Liverpool L25 6DT. *Signs* David Liverpool.

BISHOP SUFFRAGAN
Warrington, Rt. Revd Michael Henshall, *cons.* 1976, *apptd* 1976; Martinsfield, Elm Avenue, Great Crosby, Liverpool L23 2SX.

ASSISTANT BISHOPS
Rt. Revd Graham Chadwick, *cons.* 1976, *apptd* 1990; Rt. Revd James Roxburgh, *cons.* 1983, *apptd* 1991.

DEAN
Very Revd Rhys D. C. Walters, *apptd* 1983.

CANONS RESIDENTIARY
M. M. Wolfe, *apptd* 1982; D. J. Hutton, *apptd* 1983; K. J. Riley, *apptd* 1983; H. Thomas, *apptd* 1988.

ARCHDEACONS
Liverpool, Ven. S. Durant, *apptd* 1991.
Warrington, Ven. C. D. S. Woodhouse, *apptd* 1981.

Stipendiary Male Clergy, 274.
Stipendiary Women Deacons, 23.

Chancellor, R. G. Hamilton.
Registrar and Cathedral Chapter Clerk, R. H. Arden, 1 Hanover Street, Liverpool L1 3DW.

MANCHESTER

BISHOP
vacant; Bishopscourt, Bury New Road, Manchester M7 OLE. *Signs* – Manchester.

BISHOPS SUFFRAGAN
Bolton, Rt. Revd David Bonser, *cons.* 1991, *apptd* 1991; 4 Sandfield Drive, Lostock, Bolton BL6 4DU.
Hulme, Rt. Revd Colin J. F. Scott, *cons.* 1984, *apptd* 1984; 1 Raynham Avenue, Didsbury, Manchester M20 OBW.
Middleton, Rt. Revd Donald A. Tytler, *cons.* 1982, *apptd* 1982; The Hollies, Manchester Road, Rochdale OL11 3QY.

ASSISTANT BISHOP
Rt. Revd Edward Wickham, *cons.* 1959, *apptd* 1982.

DEAN
Very Revd Robert M. Waddington, *apptd* 1984.

CANONS RESIDENTIARY
Ven. R. B. Harris, *apptd* 1980; J. R. Atherton, PH.D., *apptd* 1984; B. Duncan, *apptd* 1986; A. E. Radcliffe, *apptd* 1991.

ARCHDEACONS
Bolton, Ven. L. M. Davies, *apptd* 1992.
Manchester, Ven. R. B. Harris, *apptd* 1980.
Rochdale, Ven. J. M. M. Dalby, *apptd* 1991.

Stipendiary Male Clergy, 377.
Stipendiary Women Deacons, 16.

Chancellor, G. C. H. Spafford, *apptd* 1976.
Registrar and Bishop's Secretary, M. Darlington, 90 Deansgate, Manchester M3 2GH.

NEWCASTLE

10TH BISHOP
Rt. Revd Andrew A. K. Graham, *cons.* 1977, *apptd* 1981; Bishop's House, 29 Moor Road South, Gosforth, Newcastle upon Tyne NE3 1PA. *Signs* A. Newcastle.

ASSISTANT BISHOP
Rt. Revd Kenneth Gill, *cons.* 1972, *apptd* 1980.

PROVOST
Very Revd Nicholas G. Coulton, *apptd* 1990.

CANONS RESIDENTIARY
W. J. Thomas, *apptd* 1983; R. Langley, *apptd* 1985; P. R. Strange, *apptd* 1986; I. F. Bennett, *apptd* 1988.

ARCHDEACONS
Lindisfarne, Ven. M. E. Bowering, *apptd* 1987.
Northumberland, Ven. W. J. Thomas, *apptd* 1983.

Stipendiary Male Clergy, 176.
Stipendiary Women Deacons, 6.

Chancellor, His Honour A. J. Blackett-Ord, CVO, *apptd* 1971.
Registrar and Secretary, R. R. V. Nicholson, 46 Grainger Street, Newcastle upon Tyne NE1 5LB.

RIPON

11TH BISHOP
Rt. Revd David N. de L. Young, *cons.* 1977, *apptd* 1977; Bishop Mount, Ripon HG4 5DP. *Signs* David Ripon.

BISHOP SUFFRAGAN
Knaresborough, Rt. Revd Malcolm J. Menin, *cons.* 1986, *apptd* 1986; 16 Shaftesbury Avenue, Roundhay, Leeds LS8 1DT.

ASSISTANT BISHOPS
Rt. Revd Ralph Emmerson, *cons.* 1972, *apptd* 1986; Rt. Revd Derek Rawcliffe, *cons.* 1974, *apptd* 1991.

DEAN
Very Revd Christopher R. Campling, *apptd* 1984.

CANONS RESIDENTIARY
D. G. Ford, *apptd* 1980; P. J. Marshall, *apptd* 1985; M. R. Glanville Smith, *apptd* 1990.

ARCHDEACONS
Leeds, Ven. J. M. Oliver, *apptd* 1992.
Richmond, Ven. N. G. L. R. McDermid, *apptd* 1983.

Stipendiary Male Clergy, 174.
Stipendiary Women Deacons, 17.

Chancellor, S. P. Grenfell, *apptd* 1992.
Registrar and Legal Secretary, J. R. Balmforth, York House, York Place, Knaresborough HG5 0AD.
Diocesan Secretary, G. M. Royal, Diocesan Office, St Mary's Street, Leeds LS9 7DP.

SHEFFIELD

5TH BISHOP
Rt. Revd David R. Lunn, *cons.* 1980, *apptd* 1980; Bishopscroft, Snaithing Lane, Sheffield S10 3LG. *Signs* David Sheffield.

BISHOP SUFFRAGAN
Doncaster, Rt. Revd. Michael F. Gear (from Dec. 1992), *cons.* 1992, *apptd* 1992; Bishops Lodge, Rotherham S65 4PF.

ASSISTANT BISHOPS
Rt. Revd Kenneth Skelton, CBE, *cons.* 1962, *apptd* 1984; Rt. Revd Kenneth Pillar, *cons.* 1982, *apptd* 1989.

PROVOST
Very Revd John W. Gladwin, *apptd* 1988.

CANONS RESIDENTIARY
T. M. Page, *apptd* 1982; Ven. S. R. Lowe, *apptd* 1988; C. M. Smith, *apptd* 1991.

ARCHDEACONS
Doncaster, Ven. D. Carnelley, *apptd* 1985.
Sheffield, Ven. S. R. Lowe, *apptd* 1988.

Stipendiary Male Clergy, 216.
Stipendiary Women Deacons, 16.

Chancellor, vacant.
Registrar and Legal Secretary, C. P. Rothwell, 30 Bank Street, Sheffield S1 2DS.

SODOR AND MAN

79TH BISHOP
Rt. Revd Noel D. Jones, CB, *cons.* 1989, *apptd* 1989; The Bishop's House, Quarterbridge Road, Douglas, IOM. *Signs* Noel Sodor and Man.

CANONS
B. H. Kelly, *apptd* 1980; J. D. Gelling, *apptd* 1980;
B. H. Partington, *apptd* 1985; J. Sheen, *apptd* 1991.

ARCHDEACON
Isle of Man, Ven. D. A. Willoughby, *apptd* 1982.

Stipendiary Male Clergy, 21.

Vicar-General and Registrar, P. W. S. Farrant, 24 Athol Street, Douglas.

SOUTHWELL

9TH BISHOP
Rt. Revd Patrick B. Harris, *cons.* 1973, *apptd* 1988; Bishop's Manor, Southwell NG25 OJR. *Signs* Patrick Southwell.

BISHOP SUFFRAGAN
Sherwood, Rt. Revd Alan W. Morgan, *cons.* 1989, *apptd* 1989; Sherwood House, High Oakham Road, Mansfield NG18 5AJ.

PROVOST
Very Revd David Leaning, *apptd* 1991.

CANONS RESIDENTIARY
D. P. Keene, *apptd* 1981; I. G. Collins, *apptd* 1985;
M. Austin, *apptd* 1992; P. Boulton, *apptd* 1992.

ARCHDEACONS
Newark, Ven. D. C. Hawtin, *apptd* 1992.
Nottingham, Ven. T. O. Walker, *apptd* 1991.

Stipendiary Male Clergy, 212.
Stipendiary Women Deacons, 9.

Chancellor, J. Shand, *apptd* 1981.
Registrar, C. C. Hodson, Diocesan Office, Westgate, Southwell NG25 OJL.

WAKEFIELD

11TH BISHOP
Rt. Revd Nigel S. McCulloch, *cons.* 1986, *apptd* 1992; Bishop's Lodge, Woodthorpe Lane, Wakefield WF2 6JL. *Signs* Nigel Wakefield.

BISHOP SUFFRAGAN
Pontefract, Rt. Revd Thomas R. Hare, *cons.* 1971, *apptd* 1971; 306 Barnsley Road, Wakefield WF2 6AX.

PROVOST
Very Revd John E. Allen, *apptd* 1982.

CANONS RESIDENTIARY
C. Dawson, *apptd* 1982; R. D. Baxter, *apptd* 1986;
I. C. Knox, *apptd* 1989.

ARCHDEACONS
Halifax, Ven. D. Hallett, *apptd* 1989.
Pontefract, Ven. K. Unwin, *apptd* 1981.

Stipendiary Male Clergy, 211.
Stipendiary Women Deacons, 11.

Chancellor, G. B. Graham, QC, *apptd* 1959.
Registrar and Secretary, E. Chapman, Burton Street, Wakefield WF1 2DA.

The Anglican Communion

The Anglican Communion consists of 33 independent provincial or national Christian Churches or extra-provincial dioceses throughout the world, many of which are in Commonwealth countries and originated from missionary activity by the Church of England. There is no single world authority linking the Communion, but all recognize the leadership of the Archbishop of Canterbury and have strong ecclesiastical and historical links with the Church of England. Every ten years all the bishops in the Communion meet at the Lambeth Conference, convened by the Archbishop of Canterbury. The Conference has no policy-making authority but is an important forum for the discussion of issues of common concern. The Anglican Consultative Council was set up in 1968 to function between conferences and the meeting of the Primates every two years.

There are about 70 million Anglicans and 700 archbishops and bishops world-wide.

THE CHURCH IN WALES

The Anglican Church was the established church in Wales from the 16th century until 1920, when the estrangement of the majority of Welsh people from Anglicanism, in particular in favour of Presbyterianism, resulted in disestablishment. Since then the Church in Wales has been an autonomous province consisting of six sees, with one of the diocesan bishops being elected Archbishop of Wales by an electoral college comprising elected lay and clerical members.

The legislative body of the Church in Wales is the Governing Body, which has 346 members in total, divided between the three orders of bishops, clergy and laity. It is presided over by the Archbishop of Wales and meets twice annually. Its decisions are binding upon all members of the Church. There are 120,892 members of the Church in Wales, with six bishops, about 600 clergy and 1,178 parishes.

THE GOVERNING BODY OF THE CHURCH IN WALES, 39 Cathedral Road, Cardiff CF1 9XF. Tel: 0222-231638. *Secretary-General*, J. W. D. McIntyre.

10TH ARCHBISHOP OF WALES, Most Revd Alwyn R. Jones (Bishop of St Asaph), *elected* 1991.

THE RT. REVD BISHOPS
Bangor (*79th*), Rt. Revd J. Cledan Mears, *b.* 1922, *cons.* 1982, *apptd* 1982; Tŷ'r Esgob, Bangor LL57 2SS. *Signs* Cledan Bangor. *Stipendiary clergy*, 66.
Llandaff (*101st*), Rt. Revd Roy T. Davies, *b.* 1934, *cons.* 1985, *apptd* 1985; Llys Esgob, The Cathedral Green, Llandaff, Cardiff CF5 2YE. *Signs* Roy Landav. *Stipendiary clergy*, 154.
Monmouth (*8th*), Rt. Revd Rowan D. Williams, *b* 1950, *cons.* 1992, *apptd* 1992; Bishopstow, Stow Hill, Newport NP9 4EA. *Signs* Rowan Monmouth. *Stipendiary clergy*, 110.
St Asaph (*74th*), Most Revd Alwyn R. Jones, *b.* 1934, *cons.* 1982, *apptd* 1982; Esgobty, St Asaph, Clwyd LL17 OTW. *Signs* Alwyn Cambrensis. *Stipendiary clergy*, 112.
St David's (*125th*), Rt. Revd J. Ivor Rees, *b.* 1926, *cons.* 1988, *apptd* 1991; Llys Esgob, Abergwili, Dyfed SA31 2JG. *Signs* Ivor St Davids. *Stipendiary clergy*, 132.

Swansea and Brecon (7th), Rt. Revd Dewi M. Bridges, *b.* 1933, *cons.* 1988, *apptd* 1988; Ely Tower, Brecon, Powys LD3 9DE. *Signs* Dewi Swansea & Brecon. *Stipendiary clergy*, 100.

(Stipend of diocesan bishop of the Church in Wales was £22,570 a year in 1992.)

THE EPISCOPAL CHURCH IN SCOTLAND

The Episcopal Church in Scotland was founded after the Act of Settlement (1690) established the presbyterian nature of the Church of Scotland. The Episcopal Church is in full communion with the Church of England but is autonomous. The governing authority is the General Synod, an elected body of 160 members which meets once a year. The diocesan bishop who convenes and presides at meetings of the General Synod is called the Primus and is elected by his fellow bishops.

There are 57,194 members of the Episcopal Church in Scotland, of whom 34,794 are communicants. There are seven bishops, 209 clergy, and 341 churches and places of worship.

THE GENERAL SYNOD OF THE EPISCOPAL CHURCH IN SCOTLAND, 21 Grosvenor Crescent, Edinburgh EH12 5EE. Tel: 031-225 6357. *Secretary-General*, J. G. Davies.

PRIMUS OF THE EPISCOPAL CHURCH IN SCOTLAND, Most Revd George Henderson (Bishop of Argyll and the Isles), *elected* 1990.

THE RT. REVD BISHOPS

Aberdeen and Orkney, A. Bruce Cameron, *b.* 1941, *cons.* 1992, *apptd* 1992. *Clergy* 14.

Argyll and the Isles, George K. B. Henderson, *b.* 1921, *cons.* 1977, *apptd* 1977. *Clergy* 10.

Brechin, Robert T. Halliday, *b.* 1932, *cons.* 1990, *apptd* 1990. *Clergy* 16.

Edinburgh, Richard F. Holloway, *b.* 1933, *cons.* 1986, *apptd* 1986. *Clergy* 63.

Glasgow and Galloway, John M. Taylor, *b.* 1932, *cons.* 1991, *apptd* 1991. *Clergy* 44.

Moray, Ross and Caithness, George M. Sessford, *b.* 1928, *cons.* 1970, *apptd* 1970. *Clergy* 16.

St Andrews, Dunkeld and Dunblane, Michael G. Hare-Duke, *b.* 1925, *cons.* 1969, *apptd* 1969. *Clergy* 31.

(Stipend of diocesan bishop of the Episcopal Church in Scotland was £16,110 in 1992.)

THE CHURCH OF IRELAND

The Anglican Church was the established church in Ireland from the 16th century but never secured the allegiance of a majority of the Irish, and was disestablished in 1871. The Church in Ireland is divided into the provinces of Armagh and Dublin, each under an archbishop. The provinces are subdivided into 12 dioceses.

The legislative body is the General Synod, which has 660 members in total, divided between the House of Bishops and the House of Representatives. The Archbishop of Armagh is elected by the House of Bishops; other episcopal elections are made by an electoral college.

There are about 375,000 members of the Church of Ireland, with two archbishops, ten bishops, about 600 clergy and about 1,000 churches and places of worship.

CENTRAL OFFICE, Church of Ireland House, Church Avenue, Rathmines, Dublin 6. Tel: 0001-978422. *Assistant Secretary of the General Synod*, J. F. Buttimore.

PROVINCE OF ARMAGH

Archbishop of Armagh and Primate of All Ireland, Most Revd Robert H. A. Eames, PH.D., *b.* 1937, *cons.* 1975, *trans.* 1986. *Clergy* 55.

THE RT. REVD BISHOPS

Clogher, Brian D. A. Hannon, *b.* 1936, *cons.* 1986, *apptd* 1986. *Clergy* 31.

Connor, Samuel G. Poyntz, PH.D., *b.* 1926, *cons.* 1978, *trs.* 1987. *Clergy* 115.

Derry and Raphoe, James Mehaffey, PH.D., *b.* 1931, *cons.* 1980, *apptd* 1980. *Clergy* 53.

Down and Dromore, Gordon McMullan, PH.D., *b.* 1934, *cons.* 1980, *trs.* 1986. *Clergy* 114.

Kilmore, Elphin and Ardagh, William G. Wilson, PH.D., *b.* 1918, *cons.* 1981, *apptd* 1981. *Clergy* 26.

Tuam, Killala and Achonry, John R. W. Neill, *b.* 1945, *cons.* 1986, *apptd* 1986. *Clergy* 9.

PROVINCE OF DUBLIN

Archbishop of Dublin, Bishop of Glendalough, and Primate of Ireland, Most Revd Donald A. Caird, DD, *b.* 1925, *cons.* 1970, *trans.* 1976, 1985. *Clergy* 86.

THE RT. REVD BISHOPS

Cashel and Ossory, Noel V. Willoughby, *b.* 1926, *cons.* 1980, *apptd* 1980. *Clergy* 36.

Cork, Cloyne and Ross, Robert A. Warke, *b.* 1930, *cons.* 1988, *apptd* 1988. *Clergy* 27.

Limerick and Killaloe, Edward F. Darling, *b.* 1933, *cons.* 1985, *apptd* 1985. *Clergy* 24.

Meath and Kildare, Most Revd Walton N. F. Empey, *b.* 1934, *cons.* 1981, *trans.* 1985. *Clergy* 20.

Anglican Communion Overseas

ANGLICAN CHURCH OF AOTEAROA, NEW ZEALAND AND POLYNESIA

PRIMATE AND ARCHBISHOP OF NEW ZEALAND, The Most Revd Brian N. Davis (Bishop of Wellington), *cons.* 1980, *apptd* 1986.

THE RT. REVD BISHOPS

Aotearoa, Whakahuhui Vercoe, *cons.* 1981, *apptd* 1981.

Auckland, Bruce Gilberd, *cons.* 1985, *apptd* 1985.

Christchurch, David Coles, *cons.* 1990, *apptd* 1990.

Dunedin, Penelope Jamieson, *cons.* 1990, *apptd* 1990.

Nelson, Derek Eaton, *cons.* 1990, *apptd* 1990.

Polynesia, Jabez Bryce, *cons.* 1975, *apptd* 1975.

Waiapu, Murray Mills, *cons.* 1991, *apptd* 1991.

Waikato, Roger Herft, *cons.* 1986, *apptd* 1986.

Wellington (*see* above).

ANGLICAN CHURCH OF AUSTRALIA

PRIMATE OF AUSTRALIA, The Most Revd Keith Rayner (Archbishop of Melbourne), *cons.* 1969, *trans.* 1991.

PROVINCE OF NEW SOUTH WALES

METROPOLITAN
Archbishop of Sydney, The Most Revd Donald W. B. Robinson, *cons.* 1973, *trans.* 1982 (until Jan. 1993).

THE RT. REVD BISHOPS
Armidale, P. Chiswell, *cons.* 1976, *apptd* 1976.
Bathurst, B. W. Wilson, *cons.* 1984, *trans.* 1989.
Canberra and Goulburn, vacant.
Grafton, B. A. Schultz, *cons.* 1985, *apptd* 1985.
Newcastle, vacant.
Riverina, vacant.

PROVINCE OF QUEENSLAND

METROPOLITAN
Archbishop of Brisbane, The Most Revd Peter Hollingworth, *cons.* 1985, *trans.* 1990.

THE RT. REVD BISHOPS
Carpentaria, A. F. B. Hall-Matthews, *cons.* 1984.
North Queensland, H. J. Lewis, *cons.* 1971.
Northern Territory, R. F. Appleby, *cons.* 1992.
Rockhampton, G. A. Hearn, *cons.* 1981.

PROVINCE OF SOUTH AUSTRALIA

METROPOLITAN
Archbishop of Adelaide, The Most Revd Ian G. George, *cons.* 1989, *trans.* 1991.

THE RT. REVD BISHOPS
The Murray, G. H. Walden, *cons.* 1981, *trans.* 1989.
Willochra, W. D. H. McCall, *cons.* 1987, *apptd* 1987.

PROVINCE OF VICTORIA

METROPOLITAN
Archbishop of Melbourne, The Most Revd Keith Rayner, *cons.* 1969, *trans.* 1975, 1990 (*see* above).

THE RT. REVD BISHOPS
Ballarat, J. Hazlewood, *cons.* 1975, *apptd* 1975.
Bendigo, B. Wright, *cons.* 1988, *apptd* 1992.
Gippsland, C. D. Sheumack, *cons.* 1987, *apptd* 1987.
Wangaratta, R. G. Beal, *cons.* 1985, *apptd* 1985.

PROVINCE OF WESTERN AUSTRALIA

METROPOLITAN
Archbishop of Perth, The Most Revd Peter F. Carnley, Ph.D., *cons.* 1981, *apptd* 1981.

THE RT. REVD BISHOPS
Bunbury, H. J. U. Jamieson, *cons.* 1974, *trans.* 1984.
North-West Australia, A. Nicholls, *cons.* 1992.

EXTRA-PROVINCIAL DIOCESE

Tasmania, P. K. Newell, *cons.* 1982, *apptd* 1982.

EPISCOPAL CHURCH OF BRAZIL
(Igreja Episcopal Do Brasil)

Primate, The Most Revd Olavo V. Luiz (Bishop of South-Western Brazil), *cons.* 1976, *elected* 1986.

THE RT. REVD BISHOPS
Brasilia, A. Santos, *cons.* 1989, *apptd* 1989.
Central Brazil, S. A. Ruiz, *cons.* 1985, *apptd* 1985.
Northern Brazil, C. E. Rodrigues, *cons.* 1985, *apptd* 1986.
Pelotas, L. O. P. Prado, *cons.* 1987, *apptd* 1989.
South Central Brazil, G. Soares de Lima, *cons.* 1989, *apptd* 1989.
Southern Brazil, C. V. S. Gastal, *cons.* 1984, *apptd* 1984.
South-Western Brazil, (*see* above), *apptd* 1976.

CHURCH OF THE PROVINCE OF BURUNDI, RWANDA AND ZAIRE

ARCHBISHOP OF PROVINCE, The Most Revd Samuel Sindamuka (Bishop of Matana), *cons.* 1975, *apptd* 1989.

THE RT. REVD BISHOPS
Boga Zaire, Byanka Njojo, *apptd* 1980.
Bujumbura, Pie Ntukamazina, *cons.* 1990, *apptd* 1990.
Bukavu, Balufuga Dirokpa, *apptd* 1982.
Butare, Augustin Nshamihigo, *apptd* 1991.
Buye, Samuel Ndayisenga, *apptd* 1979.
Gitega, Jean Nduwayo, *apptd* 1985.
Kigali, Adonia Sebununguri, *cons.* 1965.
Kisangani, Sylvestre Mugera, *apptd* 1980.
Matana (*see* above).
Shaba, Mbona Kolini.
Shyira, Augustin Nshamihigo, *cons.* 1984, *apptd* 1984.

ANGLICAN CHURCH OF CANADA

ARCHBISHOP AND PRIMATE, The Most Revd Michael G. Peers, *cons.* 1977, *trans.* 1986.

PROVINCE OF BRITISH COLUMBIA

METROPOLITAN
Archbishop of New Westminster, The Most Revd Douglas W. Hambidge, *cons.* 1969, *elected* 1981.

THE RT. REVD BISHOPS
British Columbia, Barry Jenks, *cons.* 1992, *elected* 1992.
Caledonia, John Hannen, *cons.* 1981, *elected* 1981.
Cariboo, James Cruickshank, *cons.* 1992, *elected* 1992.
Kootenay, David Crawley, *cons.* 1990, *elected* 1990.
New Westminster (*see* above).
Yukon, Ronald Ferris, *cons.* 1981, *elected* 1981.

PROVINCE OF CANADA

METROPOLITAN
Archbishop of West Newfoundland, Most Revd Stewart S. Payne, *cons.* 1978, *elected* 1990.

THE RT. REVD BISHOPS
Central Newfoundland, Edward Marsh, *cons.* 1990, *elected* 1990.
Eastern Newfoundland and Labrador, Martin Mate, *cons.* 1980, *elected* 1980.
Fredericton, George Lemon, *cons.* 1989, *elected* 1989.
Montreal, Andrew Hutchison, *cons.* 1990, *elected* 1990.
Nova Scotia, Arthur Peters, *cons.* 1982, *elected* 1982.
Quebec, Bruce Stavert, *cons.* 1991, *elected* 1991.
Western Newfoundland (*see* above).

PROVINCE OF ONTARIO

METROPOLITAN
Archbishop of Ottawa, The Most Revd Edwin Lackey, *cons.* 1981, *elected* 1991.

THE RT. REVD BISHOPS
Algoma, Leslie Peterson, *cons.* 1983, *elected* 1983.
Huron, Percival O'Driscoll, *cons.* 1987, *elected* 1990.
Moosonee, Caleb Lawrence, *cons.* 1980, *elected* 1980.
Niagara, Walter Asbil, *cons.* 1990, *elected* 1990.
Ontario, Peter Mason, *cons.* 1992, *elected* 1992.
Ottawa (*see* above).
Toronto, Terence Finlay, *cons.* 1986, *elected* 1990.

PROVINCE OF RUPERT'S LAND

METROPOLITAN
Archbishop of Rupert's Land, The Most Revd Walter H. Jones, *cons.* 1970, *elected* 1988.

THE RT. REVD BISHOPS
Arctic, J. C. R. Williams, *cons.* 1987, *elected* 1991.
Athabasca , John Clarke, *cons.* 1992, *elected* 1992.
Brandon, Malcolm Harding, *cons.* 1992, *elected* 1992.
Calgary, Barry Curtis, *cons.* 1983, *elected* 1983.
Edmonton, Kenneth Genge, *cons.* 1988, *elected* 1988.
Keewatin, Thomas Collings, *cons.* 1991, *elected* 1991.
Qu' Appelle, Eric Bays, *cons.* 1986, *elected* 1986.
Rupert's Land (*see* above).
Saskatchewan, Thomas Morgan, *cons.* 1985, *elected* 1985.
Saskatoon, Roland Wood, *cons.* 1981, *elected* 1981.

CHURCH OF THE PROVINCE OF CENTRAL AFRICA

ARCHBISHOP OF PROVINCE, The Most Revd Walter P. K. Makhulu (Bishop of Botswana), *cons.* 1979, *apptd* 1980.

THE RT. REVD BISHOPS
Botswana (*see* above).
Central Zambia, Clement Shaba, *cons.* 1984, *apptd* 1984.
Harare, Ralph Hatendi, *cons.* 1979, *apptd* 1981.
Lake Malawi, Peter Nyanja, *cons.* 1978, *apptd* 1978.
The Lundi, Jonathan Siyachitema, *cons.* 1981, *apptd* 1981.
Lusaka, Stephen Mumba, *cons.* 1981, *apptd* 1981.
Manicaland, Elijah Masuko, *cons.* 1981, *apptd* 1981.
Matabeleland, Theophilus Naledi, *cons.* 1987, *apptd* 1987.
Northern Zambia, Bernard Malango, *cons.* 1988, *apptd* 1988.
Southern Malawi, Nathaniel Aipa, *cons.* 1987, *apptd* 1987.

CHURCH OF THE PROVINCE OF THE INDIAN OCEAN

ARCHBISHOP OF PROVINCE, The Most Revd French Chang-Him (Bishop of Seychelles), *cons.* 1979, *apptd* 1984.

THE RT. REVD BISHOPS
Antananarivo, Remi Rabenirina, *cons.* 1984, *apptd* 1984.
Antsiranana, Keith Benzies, *cons.* 1982, *apptd* 1982.
Mauritius, Rex Donat, *cons.* 1984, *apptd* 1984.
Seychelles, (*see* above).
Toamasina, Donald Smith, *cons.* 1990, *apptd* 1990.

THE HOLY CATHOLIC CHURCH IN JAPAN *(Nippon Sei Ko Kai)*

PRIMATE, The Most Revd Christopher Ichiro Kikawada (Bishop of Osaka), *cons.* 1975, *apptd* 1986.

THE RT. REVD BISHOPS
Chubu, Samuel W. Hoyo, *cons.* 1987, *apptd* 1987.
Hokkaido, Augustine H. Amagi, *cons.* 1987, *apptd* 1987.
Kita Kanto, James T. Yashiro, *cons.* 1985, *apptd* 1985.
Kobe, John J. Furumoto, *cons.* 1992, *apptd* 1992.
Kyoto, John T. Okano, *cons.* 1991, *apptd* 1991.
Kyushu, Joseph N. Iida, *cons.* 1982, *apptd* 1982.
Okinawa, Paul S. Nakamura, *cons.* 1972, *apptd* 1972.
Osaka, (*see* above).
Tohoku, Cornelius Y. Tazaki, *cons.* 1979, *apptd* 1979.
Tokyo, John M. Takeda, *cons.* 1988, *apptd* 1988.
Yokohama, Raphael S. Kajiwara, *cons.* 1984, *apptd* 1984.

THE EPISCOPAL CHURCH IN JERUSALEM AND THE MIDDLE EAST

PRESIDENT-BISHOP, Rt. Revd Samir Kafity, *apptd* 1986.

Jerusalem, Samir Kafity, *cons.* 1984.
Iran, Iraj Mottahedeh, *cons.* 1990.
Egypt, Ghais A. Malik, *cons.* 1984.
Cyprus and the Gulf, John Brown, *cons.* 1986.

CHURCH OF THE PROVINCE OF KENYA

ARCHBISHOP OF PROVINCE, The Most Revd Manasses Kuria (Bishop of Nairobi), *cons.* 1970, *apptd* 1980.

THE RT. REVD BISHOPS
Eldoret, vacant.
Embu, Moses Njue.
Kirinyaga, David Gitari, *cons.* 1975, *apptd* 1975.
Machakos, Benjamin Nzimbi, *cons.* 1985, *apptd* 1985.
Maseno North, James Mundia, *cons.* 1970, *apptd* 1970.
Maseno South, Henry Okullu, *cons.* 1974, *apptd* 1974.
Maseno West, Joseph Wesonga, *apptd* 1991.
Mombasa, Crispus Nzano, *cons.* 1975, *apptd* 1981.
Mount Kenya Central, John Mahiaini, *cons.* 1984, *apptd* 1984.
Mount Kenya South, George Njuguna, *cons.* 1984, *apptd* 1985.
Nairobi, (*see* above).
Nakuru, Laadan Mbiu, *apptd* 1991.
Nambale, Isaac Namango, *cons.* 1984, *apptd* 1987.

CHURCH OF THE PROVINCE OF MELANESIA

ARCHBISHOP OF PROVINCE, The Most Revd Amos S. Waiaru (Bishop of Central Melanesia), *cons.* 1981, *apptd* 1988.

THE RT. REVD BISHOPS
Central Melanesia, (*see* above).
Hanuato'o, James Mason, *cons.* 1991, *apptd* 1991.
Malaita, Raymond Aumae, *cons.* 1990, *apptd* 1990.
Temotu, Lazarus Munamua, *cons.* 1987, *apptd* 1987.
Vanuatu, Michael Tavoa, *cons.* 1990, *apptd* 1990.
Ysabel, Ellison Pogo, *cons.* 1981, *apptd* 1981.

CHURCH OF THE PROVINCE OF MYANMAR

ARCHBISHOP OF PROVINCE, The Most Revd Andrew Mya Han (Bishop of Yangon), *cons.* 1988, *apptd* 1988.

THE RT. REVD BISHOPS
Hpa'an, D. Hoi Kyin, *cons.* 1992, *apptd* 1992.
Mandalay, T. Mya Wah, *cons.* 1984, *apptd* 1984.
Myitkyina, A. Hla Aung, *cons.* 1988, *apptd* 1988.
Sittwe, B. Theaung Hawi, *cons.* 1978, *apptd* 1980.
Yangon (*Rangoon*), (*see* above).

CHURCH OF THE PROVINCE OF NIGERIA

ARCHBISHOP OF THE PROVINCE, The Most Revd Joseph Adetiloye, *apptd* 1991.

THE RT. REVD BISHOPS
Aba, A. O. Iwuagwu, *apptd* 1985.
Abuja, Peter Akinole, *apptd* 1989.
Akoko, J. O. K. Olowokure, *apptd* 1986.
Akure, Emmanuel Gbonigi, *apptd* 1983.
Asaba, Roland Nwosu, *apptd* 1977.
Awka, Maxwell Anikwenwa, *apptd* 1987.
Bauchi, E. O. Chukwuma, *apptd* 1990.
Benin, John George, *apptd* 1985.
Calabar, W. G. Ekprikpo.
Egbado, Timothy Bolaji.
Egba-Egbado, T. I. Akintayo, *apptd* 1977.
Ekiti, C. A. Akinbola, *apptd* 1986.
Enugu, Gideon Otubelu, *apptd* 1969.
Ibadan, Gideon Olajide, *apptd* 1988.
Ife, Gabriel Oloniyo.
Ijebu, Abraham Olowoyo, *apptd* 1990.
Ijebu Remo, E. O. I. Ogundana, *apptd* 1984.
Ilesha, E. A. Ademowo, *apptd* 1989.
Jos, Timothy Adesola, *apptd* 1985.
Kaduna, Titus Ogbonyomi, *apptd* 1975.
Kafanchan, W. Diya, *apptd* 1990.
Kano, B. O. Omoseibi, *apptd* 1990.
Katsina, J. S. Kwasu, *apptd* 1990.
Kwara, Herbert Haruna, *apptd* 1974.
Lagos, Jospeh Adetiloye, *apptd* 1985.
Maiduguri, E. K. Mani, *apptd* 1990.
Makurdi, J. T. Iyangemar, *apptd* 1990.
Minna, J. A. Yisa, *apptd* 1990.
The Niger, Jonathan Onyemelukwe, *apptd* 1975.
Niger Delta, Samuel Elenwo, *apptd* 1981.
Okigwe/Orlu, Samuel Ebo, *apptd* 1984.
Ondo, Samuel Aderin, *apptd* 1981.
Osun, Seth Fagbemi, *apptd* 1987.
Owerri, Benjamin Nwankiti, *apptd* 1968.
Owo, Abraham Awosan, *apptd* 1983.
Sokoto, J. A. Idowu-Fearon, *apptd* 1990.
Warri, John Dafiewhare, *apptd* 1980.
Yola, C. O. Efobi, *apptd* 1990.

ANGLICAN CHURCH OF PAPUA NEW GUINEA

ARCHBISHOP OF PROVINCE, The Most Revd Bevan Meredith (Bishop of New Guinea Islands), *cons.* 1967, *apptd* 1990.

THE RT. REVD BISHOPS
Aipo Rongo, Paul Richardson, *cons.* 1987, *apptd* 1987.
Dogura, vacant.
New Guinea Islands (*see* above).
Popondota, Walter Siba, *cons.* 1990, *apptd* 1990.
Port Moresby, Isaac Gadebo, *cons.* 1983, *apptd* 1983.

PHILIPPINE EPISCOPAL CHURCH

PRIME BISHOP, The Most Revd Richard Abellon, *cons.* 1975, *apptd* 1990.

THE RT. REVD BISHOPS
Central Philippines, Manuel C. Lumpias, *cons.* 1977, *apptd* 1978.
North Central Philippines, Artemio M. Zabala, *cons.* 1989, *apptd* 1989.
Northern Luzon, Ignacio C. Soliba, *cons.* 1990, *apptd* 1990.
Northern Philippines, Robert L. Longid, *cons.* 1983, *apptd* 1986.
Southern Philippines, Narisco Ticobay, *cons.* 1986, *apptd* 1986.

CHURCH OF THE PROVINCE OF SOUTHERN AFRICA

METROPOLITAN
Archbishop of Cape Town, The Most Revd Desmond M. B. Tutu, *cons.* 1976, *trans.* 1986.

THE RT. REVD BISHOPS
Bloemfontein, Thomas Stanage, *cons.* 1978, *apptd* 1982.
Christ the King, Peter Lee, *cons.* 1990, *apptd* 1990.
George, Derek Damant, *cons.* 1985, *apptd* 1985.
Grahamstown, David Russell, *cons.* 1986, *apptd* 1987.
Johannesburg, Duncan Buchanan, *cons.* 1986, *apptd* 1986.
Kimberley and Kuruman, W. N. Ndungane, *cons.* 1991, *apptd* 1991.
Klerksdorp, David Nkwe, *cons.* 1990, *apptd* 1990.
Lebombo, Dinis Sengulane, *cons.* 1976, *apptd* 1976.
Lesotho, Philip Mokuku, *cons.* 1978, *apptd* 1978.
Namibia, James Kauluma, *cons.* 1978, *apptd* 1981.
Natal, Michael Nuttall, *cons.* 1975, *apptd* 1982.
Niassa, Paulino Manhique, *cons.* 1986, *apptd* 1986.
Port Elizabeth, Bruce Evans, *cons.* 1975, *apptd* 1975.
Pretoria, Richard Kraft, *cons.* 1982, *apptd* 1982.
St Helena, John Ruston, *cons.* 1985, *apptd* 1991.
St John's, Jacob Dlamini, *cons.* 1980, *apptd* 1985.
St Mark the Evangelist, Rollo Le Feuvre, *cons.* 1987, *apptd* 1987.
South-Eastern Transvaal, David Beetge, *cons.* 1990, *apptd* 1990.
Swaziland, Bernard Mkhabela, *cons.* 1975, *apptd* 1975.
Umzimvubu, Geoffrey Davies, *cons.* 1987, *apptd* 1991.
Zululand, Lawrence Zulu, *cons.* 1975, *apptd* 1975.

Order of Ethiopia, Sigqibo Dwane, *cons.* 1983, *apptd* 1983.

ANGLICAN CHURCH OF THE SOUTHERN CONE OF AMERICA

PRESIDING BISHOP, Rt. Revd Colin Bazley.

THE RT. REVD BISHOPS
Argentina, David Leake, *cons.* 1969, *apptd* 1990.
Chile, Colin Bazley, *cons.* 1969, *apptd* 1977.

Northern Argentina, Maurice Sinclair, *cons.* 1990, *apptd* 1990.
Paraguay, John Ellison, *cons.* 1988, *apptd* 1988.
Peru, Alan Winstanley, *cons.* 1988, *apptd* 1988.
Uruguay, Harold Godfrey, *cons.* 1986, *apptd* 1986.

CHURCH OF THE PROVINCE OF THE SUDAN

ARCHBISHOP OF PROVINCE, The Most Revd Benjamina W. Yugusuk (Bishop of Juba).

THE RT. REVD BISHOPS
Bor, Nathaniel Garang.
Juba (*see* above).
Kadugli, Mubarek Khamis.
Kajo-Kaji, Manasse Dawidi.
Khartoum, Bulus Tia.
Maridi, Joseph Marona.
Mundri, Eluzai Munda.
Rumbek, Gabriel Jur.
Wau, Gabriel Jur (*acting*).
Yambio, Daniel Zindo, *cons.* 1984, *apptd* 1984.
Yei, Seme Solomona.

CHURCH OF THE PROVINCE OF TANZANIA

ARCHBISHOP OF PROVINCE, The Most Revd John A. Ramadhani (Bishop of Zanzibar and Tanga), *cons.* 1980, *apptd* 1984.

THE RT. REVD BISHOPS
Central Tanganyika, Godfrey Mhogolo, *cons.* 1989, *apptd* 1989.
Dar es Salaam, Basil Sambano, *cons.* 1992, *apptd* 1992.
Kagera, Christopher Ruhuza, *cons.* 1985, *apptd* 1985.
Mara, Gershom Nyaronga, *cons.* 1985, *apptd* 1985.
Masasi, Christopher Sadiki, *cons.* 1992, *apptd* 1992.
Morogoro, Dudley Mageni, *cons.* 1987, *apptd* 1987.
Mount Kilimanjaro, S. Makundi, *cons.* 1991, *apptd* 1991.
Mpwapwa, S. Chiwanga, *cons.* 1991, *apptd* 1991.
Rift Valley, A. Mohamed, *cons.* 1982, *apptd* 1991.
Ruaha, D. Mtetemela, *cons.* 1982, *apptd* 1990.
Ruvuma, Stanford Shauri, *cons.* 1989, *apptd* 1989.
South-West Tanganyika, Charles Mwaigoga, *cons.* 1983, *apptd* 1983.
Tabora, Francis Ntiruka, *cons.* 1989, *apptd* 1989.
Victoria Nyanza, vacant.
Western Tanganyika, George Mpango, *cons.* 1983, *apptd* 1983.
Zanzibar and Tanga (*see* above).

CHURCH OF THE PROVINCE OF UGANDA

ARCHBISHOP OF THE PROVINCE, The Most Revd Dr Yona Okoth (Bishop of Kampala), *cons.* 1972, *apptd* 1984.

THE RT. REVD BISHOPS
Bukedi, Nicodemus Okille, *apptd* 1984.
Bunyoro-Kitara, Wilson Turumanya, *apptd* 1981.
Busoga, Cyprian Bamwoze, *apptd* 1972.
East Ankole, Elisha Kyamugambi, *cons.* 1992, *apptd* 1992.
Kampala (*see* above).
Karamoja, Peter Lomongin, *apptd* 1987.
Kigezi, William Rukirande.
Lango, Melchizedek Otim, *apptd* 1976.
Luwero, M. Bugimbi, *cons.* 1990, *apptd* 1990.
Madi and West Nile, Caleb Nguma, *apptd* 1991.
Mbale, Israel Koboyi, *cons.* 1992, *apptd* 1992.
Mityana, Wilson Mutebi, *apptd* 1977.
Muhabura, E. M. Shalita, *cons.* 1990, *apptd* 1990.
Mukono, Livingstone Mpalanyi-Nkoyoyo, *apptd* 1985.
Namirembe, Misaeri Kauma, *apptd* 1985.
North Mbale, Peter Mudonyi, *cons.* 1992, *apptd* 1992.
North Kigezi, Yustasi Ruhindi, *apptd* 1981.
Northern Uganda, Allan Oboma.
Ruwenzori, Eustace Kamanyire, *apptd* 1981.
Soroti, Geresom Ilukor, *apptd* 1976.
South Ruwenzori, Zebidee Masereka.
West Ankole, Yorumu Bamunoba, *apptd* 1977.
West Buganda, Christopher Senyonjo, *apptd* 1974.

EPISCOPAL CHURCH IN THE USA

PRESIDING BISHOP AND PRIMATE, Most Revd Edmond Lee Browning, DD, *cons.* 1968, *apptd* 1986.

RT. REVD BISHOPS
(*missionary diocese)

PROVINCE I

Connecticut, Arthur E. Walmsley, *cons.* 1979, *apptd* 1981.
Maine, Edward C. Chalfant, *cons.* 1984, *apptd* 1986.
Massachusetts, David E. Johnson, *cons.* 1985, *apptd* 1986.
New Hampshire, Douglas E. Theuner, *cons.* 1986, *apptd* 1986.
Rhode Island, George N. Hunt, *cons.* 1980, *apptd* 1980.
Vermont, Daniel L. Swensen, *cons.* 1986, *apptd* 1987.
Western Massachusetts, Andrew F. Wissemann, *cons.* 1984, *apptd* 1984.

PROVINCE II

Albany, David S. Ball, *cons.* 1984, *apptd* 1984.
Central New York, O'Kelley Whitaker, *cons.* 1981, *apptd* 1983.
Europe, Convocation of American Churches in, Matthew P. Bigliardi, *cons.* 1974, *apptd* 1988.
**Haiti*, Luc A. J. Garnier, *cons.* 1971, *apptd* 1971.
Long Island, Orris Walker, *apptd* 1991.
New Jersey, G. P. Mellick Belshaw, *cons.* 1975, *apptd* 1983.
New York, Richard Grein, *cons.* 1981, *apptd* 1989.
Newark, John S. Spong, *cons.* 1976, *apptd* 1979.
Rochester, William G. Burrill, *cons.* 1984, *apptd* 1984.
**Virgin Islands*, Don. E. Taylor, *cons.* 1987, *apptd* 1987.
Western New York, David C. Bowman, *cons.* 1986, *apptd* 1987.

PROVINCE III

Bethlehem, J. Mark Dyer, *cons.* 1982, *apptd* 1983.
Central Pennsylvania, Charles F. McNutt, *cons.* 1980, *apptd* 1982.
Delaware, C. Cabell Tennis, *cons.* 1986, *apptd* 1986.
Easton, Elliott L. Sorge, *cons.* 1971, *apptd* 1983.
Maryland, A. Theodore Eastman, *cons.* 1982, *apptd* 1986.
North-Western Pennsylvania, Robert D. Rowley jun., *cons.* 1989, *apptd* 1991.
Pennsylvania, Allen L. Bartlett, *cons.* 1986, *apptd* 1987.
Pittsburgh, Alden M. Hathaway, *cons.* 1981, *apptd* 1983.
Southern Virginia, Frank Vest, *apptd* 1991.

South-Western Virginia, Arthur H. Light, *cons.* 1979, *apptd* 1979.
Virginia, Peter J. Lee, *cons.* 1984, *apptd* 1985.
Washington, Ronald Haines, *cons.* 1986, *apptd* 1990.
West Virginia, John H. Smith, *cons.* 1989, *apptd* 1989.

PROVINCE IV

Alabama, Robert O. Miller, *cons.* 1988, *apptd* 1988.
Atlanta, Frank K. Allen, *cons.* 1988, *apptd* 1989.
Central Florida, John Howe, *cons.* 1989, *apptd* 1990.
Central Gulf Coast, Charles F. Duvall, *cons.* 1981, *apptd* 1981.
East Carolina, B. Sidney Sanders, *cons.* 1979, *apptd* 1983.
East Tennessee, William E. Saunders, *cons.* 1979, *apptd* 1985.
Florida, Frank S. Cerveny, *cons.* 1974, *apptd* 1975.
Georgia, Harry W. Shipps, *cons.* 1984, *apptd* 1985.
Kentucky, David B. Reed, *cons.* 1964, *apptd* 1974.
Lexington, Don A. Wimberley, *cons.* 1984, *apptd* 1985.
Louisiana, James B. Brown, *cons.* 1976, *apptd* 1976.
Mississippi, Duncan M. Gray jun., *cons.* 1974, *apptd* 1974.
North Carolina, Robert W. Estill, *cons.* 1980, *apptd* 1983.
South Carolina, Edward Salmon jun., *cons.* 1990, *apptd* 1990.
South-East Florida, Calvin O. Schofield jun., *cons.* 1979, *apptd* 1980.
South-West Florida, Roger Harris, *cons.* 1989, *apptd* 1989.
Tennessee, George L. Reynolds, *cons.* 1985, *apptd* 1985.
Upper South Carolina, William A. Beckham, *cons.* 1979, *apptd* 1979.
West Tennessee, Alex D. Dickson jun., *cons.* 1983, *apptd* 1983.
Western Louisiana, Robert Hargrove jun., *cons.* 1989, *apptd* 1990.
Western North Carolina, Robert Johnson., *cons* 1989, *apptd* 1990.

PROVINCE V

Chicago, Frank T. Griswold III, *cons.* 1985, *apptd* 1987.
Eau Claire, William C. Wantland, *cons.* 1980, *apptd* 1980.
Fond Du Lac, William L. Stevens, *cons.* 1980, *apptd* 1980.
Indianapolis, Edward W. Jones, *cons.* 1977, *apptd* 1977.
Michigan, R. Stewart Wood, *cons.* 1990, *apptd* 1990.
Milwaukee, Roger J. White, *cons.* 1984, *apptd* 1985.
Missouri, William A. Jones jun., *cons.* 1975, *apptd* 1975 (*from 1993*, Hayes Rockwell).
Northern Indiana, Francis C. Gray, *cons.* 1986, *apptd* 1987.
Northern Michigan, Thomas K. Ray, *cons.* 1982, *apptd* 1982.
Ohio, James R. Moodey, *cons.* 1983, *apptd* 1984.
Quincy, Edward Macburney, *cons.* 1988, *apptd* 1988.
Southern Ohio, William G. Black, *cons.* 1979, *apptd* 1980.
Springfield, Donald M. Hultstrand, *cons.* 1982, *apptd* 1982.
Western Michigan, Edward L. Lee jun., *cons.* 1989, *apptd* 1989.

PROVINCE VI

Colorado, William Winterrowd, *cons.* 1991, *apptd* 1991.
Iowa, C. Christopher Epting, *cons.* 1988, *apptd* 1988.
Minnesota, Robert M. Anderson, *cons.* 1978, *apptd* 1978.
Montana, Charles I. Jones, *cons.* 1986, *apptd* 1986.
Nebraska, James E. Krotz, *cons.* 1989, *apptd* 1989.
**North Dakota*, Andrew H. Fairfield, *cons.* 1990, *apptd* 1990.
South Dakota, Craig B. Anderson, *cons.* 1984, *apptd* 1984.
Wyoming, Bob G. Jones, *cons.* 1977, *apptd* 1977.

PROVINCE VII

Arkansas, Herbert A. Donovan jun., *cons.* 1980, *apptd* 1981.
Dallas, Donis D. Patterson, *cons.* 1983, *apptd* 1983.
Fort Worth, Clarence C. Pope jun., *cons.* 1985, *apptd* 1986.
Kansas, William E. Smalley, *cons.* 1989, *apptd* 1989.
North-West Texas, Sam B. Hulsey, *cons.* 1980, *apptd* 1980.
Oklahoma, Robert M. Moodey, *cons.* 1988, *apptd* 1989.
Rio Grande, Terence Kelshaw, *cons.* 1989, *apptd* 1989.
Texas, Maurice M. Benitez, *cons.* 1980, *apptd* 1980.
West Missouri, John C. Buchanan, *cons.* 1989, *apptd* 1989.
West Texas, John H. MacNaughton, *cons.* 1986, *apptd* 1987.
Western Kansas, John F. Ashby, *cons.* 1981, *apptd* 1981.

PROVINCE VIII

Alaska, Stephen Charleston, *cons.* 1991, *apptd* 1991.
Arizona, Joseph T. Heistand, *cons.* 1976, *apptd* 1979.
California, William E. Swing, *cons.* 1979, *apptd* 1980.
El Camino Real, Richard L. Skimpfky, *cons.* 1990, *apptd* 1990.
Eastern Oregon, Rustin R. Kimsey, *cons.* 1980, *apptd* 1980.
Hawaii, Donald P. Hart, *cons.* 1986, *apptd* 1986.
Idaho, John Thornton, *cons.* 1990, *apptd* 1990.
Los Angeles, Frederick L. Borsch, *cons.* 1988, *apptd* 1988.
**Navajoland Area Mission*, Steven T. Plummer, *cons.* 1989, *apptd* 1989.
Nevada, Stewart C. Zabriskie, *cons.* 1986, *apptd* 1986.
Northern California, John L. Thompson III, *cons.* 1978, *apptd* 1978.
Olympia, Vincent W. Warner, *cons.* 1989, *apptd* 1990.
Oregon, Robert L. Ladehoff, *cons.* 1985, *apptd* 1986.
San Diego, vacant.
San Joaquin, John-David Schofield, *cons.* 1988, *apptd* 1989.
Spokane, Frank Terry, *cons.* 1990, *apptd* 1991.
**Taiwan*, John C. T. Chien, *cons.* 1988, *apptd* 1988.
Utah, George E. Bates, *cons.* 1986, *apptd* 1986.

PROVINCE IX

**Central Ecuador*, Neptali L. Moreno, *cons.* 1990, *apptd* 1990.
**Colombia*, Bernardo Merino-Botero, *cons.* 1979, *apptd* 1979.
Cuernavaca, Jose G. Saucedo, *cons.* 1958, *apptd* 1989.
**Dominican Republic*, Julio C. Holguin, *apptd* 1991.
**Guatemala*, Armando Guerra-Soria, *cons.* 1982, *apptd* 1982.
**Honduras*, Leopold Frade, *cons.* 1984, *apptd* 1984.
**Mexico*, Sergio Cananga-Gomez, *cons.* 1989, *apptd* 1989.
**Nicaragua*, Sturdie W. Downs, *cons.* 1985, *apptd* 1985.
**Northern Mexico*, German Martinez, *cons.* 1987, *apptd* 1987.
**Panama*, James H. Ottley, *cons.* 1984, *apptd* 1984.
**El Salvador*, James H. Ottley, *cons.* 1984, *apptd* 1989.
**South-East Mexico*, Claro H. Rames, *cons.* 1980, *apptd* 1989.
**Western Mexico*, Samuel Espinoza-Venegas, *cons.* 1981, *apptd* 1983.

EXTRA-PROVINCIAL

Costa Rica, Cornelius J. Wilson, *cons.* 1978, *apptd* 1978.
Puerto Rico, David Alvarez, *cons.* 1987, *apptd* 1987.
Venezuela, Onell A. Soto, *cons.* 1987, *apptd* 1987.

CHURCH OF THE (ON-GOING) PROVINCE OF WEST AFRICA

ARCHBISHOP OF PROVINCE, The Most Revd George D. Browne, DD (Bishop of Liberia), *cons.* 1970, *apptd* 1982.

THE RT. REVD BISHOPS
Accra, Francis Thompson, *cons.* 1983, *apptd* 1983.
Bo, Michael Keili, OBE, *cons.* 1981, *apptd* 1981.
Cape Coast, vacant.

Freetown, Prince Thompson, *cons.* 1981, *apptd* 1981.
Gambia, Solomon Johnson, *cons.* 1990, *apptd* 1990.
Guinea, vacant.
Koforidua, Robert Okine, *cons.* 1981, *apptd* 1981.
Kumasi, Edmund Yeboah, *cons.* 1985, *apptd* 1985.
Liberia (*see* above).
Sekondi, Theophilus Annobil, *cons.* 1981, *apptd* 1981.
Sunyani/Tamale, Joseph Dadson, *cons.* 1981, *apptd* 1981.

The Anglican Church of Cameroon is a missionary area of the Province.

CHURCH IN THE PROVINCE OF THE WEST INDIES

ARCHBISHOP OF PROVINCE, The Most Revd Orland Lindsay (Bishop of North-Eastern Caribbean and Aruba), *cons.* 1970, *apptd* 1986.

THE RT. REVD BISHOPS
Barbados, Drexel Gomez, *cons.* 1972, *apptd* 1972.
Belize, Desmond Smith, *cons.* 1989, *apptd* 1989.
Guyana, Randolph George, *cons.* 1976, *apptd* 1980.
Jamaica, Neville de Souza, *cons.* 1973, *apptd* 1979.
Nassau and the Bahamas, Michael Eldon, CMG, *cons.* 1971, *apptd* 1972.
North-Eastern Caribbean and Aruba (*see* above).
Trinidad and Tobago, Clive Abdulah, *cons.* 1970, *apptd* 1970.
Windward Islands, Philip Elder, *cons.* 1966.

OTHER CHURCHES AND EXTRA-PROVINCIAL DIOCESES

ANGLICAN CHURCH OF BERMUDA, Rt. Revd William Down, *apptd* 1990.
EPISCOPAL CHURCH OF CUBA, Rt. Revd Emilio H. Albalate.
ANGLICAN CHURCH IN KOREA:
Pusan, Rt. Revd Bundo Kim, *apptd* 1988.
Seoul, Rt. Revd Simon Kim.
Taejon, Rt. Revd Paul Hwan Yoon, *apptd* 1988.
HONG KONG AND MACAO, Rt. Revd Peter Kwong.
KUCHING, Rt. Revd Datuk John Leong Chee Yun.
SABAH, Rt. Revd Yong Ping Chung.
SINGAPORE, Rt. Revd Moses Leng Kong Tay, *apptd* 1982.
WEST MALAYSIA, Rt. Revd Tan Sri John Savarimuthu, *apptd* 1973.
LUSITANIAN CHURCH (*Portuguese Episcopal Church*), Rt. Revd Fernando Soares, *apptd* 1971.
SPANISH REFORMED CHURCH, Rt. Revd Arturo Sánchez Galan, *apptd* 1982.

The Church of Scotland

The Church of Scotland is the established (i.e. state) church of Scotland. The Church is Calvinistic and evangelical in doctrine, and presbyterian in constitution. In 1560 the jurisdiction of the Roman Catholic Church was abolished and the first assembly of the Church of Scotland ratified the Confession of Faith, drawn up by a committee including John Knox. In 1592 Parliament passed an Act guaranteeing the liberties of the Church and its presbyterian government. James VI (James I of England) and later Stuart monarchs attempted to restore episcopacy, but a presbyterian church was finally restored in 1690 and secured by the Act of Settlement (1690) and the Act of Union (1707). The Free Church of Scotland was formed in 1843 in a dispute over patronage and state interference; in 1900 most of its ministers joined with the United Presbyterian Church (formed in 1847) to form the United Free Church of Scotland. In 1929 most of this body rejoined the Church of Scotland to form the united Church of Scotland.

The Church of Scotland is presbyterian in its organization, i.e. based on a hierarchy of councils of ministers and elders. At local level the kirk session consists of the parish minister and ruling elders, and at district level the presbyteries, of which there are 46, consist of all the ministers in the district and one ruling elder from each congregation. The 12 provincial synods comprise three or more presbyteries. The General Assembly is the supreme authority, and is presided over by a Moderator chosen annually by the Assembly. The Sovereign, if not present in person, is represented by a Lord High Commissioner who is appointed each year by the Crown.

The Church of Scotland has about 770,000 members, 1,250 ministers and 1,700 churches. There are about 100 ministers and other personnel working overseas.

Lord High Commissioner (1992), The Lord Macfarlane of Bearsden.
Moderator of the General Assembly (1992), Rt. Revd H. R. Wyllie.
Principal Clerk, Revd J. L. Weatherhead.
Deputy Clerk, Revd A. G. McGillivray.
Procurator, A. Dunlop, QC.
Law Agent and Solicitor of the Church, R. A. Paterson.
Parliamentary Agent, I. McCulloch (*London*).
General Treasurer, W. G. P. Colledge.
CHURCH OFFICE, 121 George Street, Edinburgh EH2 4YN. Tel: 031-225 5722.

SYNODS AND PRESBYTERIES (WITH NAMES OF CLERKS)

SYNOD I – LOTHIAN, Revd A. B. Forrest
Edinburgh, Revd A. G. McGillivray
West Lothian, Revd D. Shaw
Lothian, Revd J. Ritchie

SYNOD II – THE BORDERS, Revd H. Mackay
Melrose and Peebles, Revd C. A. Duncan
Duns, Revd W. P. Graham
Jedburgh, Revd N. R. Combe

SYNOD III – DUMFRIES AND GALLOWAY, Revd A. B. Elder
Annandale and Eskdale, Revd C. B. Haston
Dumfries and Kirkcudbright, Revd G. M. A. Savage
Wigtown and Stranraer, Revd D. Dutton

SYNOD IV – AYR, Revd C. L. Johnston
Ayr, Revd J. Crichton
Irvine and Kilmarnock, Revd C. G. F. Brochie
Ardrossan, Revd D. Broster

SYNOD V – CLYDESDALE, Revd W. W. M. Bell
Lanark, Revd J. Hardie
Paisley, Revd J. P. Lubie
Greenock, Revd D. Mill
Glasgow, Revd A. Cunningham
Hamilton, Revd J. H. Wilson
Dumbarton, Revd D. P. Munro

SYNOD VI – ARGYLL, Revd W. T. Hogg
South Argyll, Revd R. H. McMidder

Dunoon, Revd R. Samuel
Lorn and Mull, Revd W. M. Ritchie

Synod VII – Forth, Revd T. Kinloch
Falkirk, Revd D. E. McClements
Stirling, Revd G. A. McCutcheon

Synod VIII – Fife, Revd P. McPhail
Dunfermline, Revd W. E. Farquhar
Kirkcaldy, Revd B. L. Tomlinson
St Andrews, Revd J. W. Patterson

Synod IX – Perth and Angus, Revd J. Macdonald
Dunkeld and Meigle, Revd F. M. C. Stewart
Perth, Revd G. G. Stewart
Dundee, Revd J. A. Roy
Angus, Revd A. F. M. Downie

Synod X – Grampian, Revd E. C. P. Hood
Aberdeen, Revd A. M. Douglas
Kincardine and Deeside, Revd J. W. S. Brown
Gordon, Revd I. U. Thomson
Buchan, Revd R. Neilson
Moray, Revd J. T. Stuart

Synod XI – Southern Highlands, Revd R. J. V. Logan
Abernethy, Revd J. A. I. MacEwan
Inverness, Revd R. J. V. Logan
Lochaber, Revd A. Ramsay

Synod XII – Ross, Sutherland and Caithness, Revd R. M. MacKinnon
Ross, Revd R. M. MacKinnon
Sutherland, Revd J. L. Goskirk
Caithness, Revd M. G. Mappin
Locharron/Skye, Revd A. I. Macarthur
Uist, Revd A. P. J. Varwell
Lewis, Revd T. S. Sinclair

Orkney (*Finstown*), Revd D. A. Williams
Shetland (*Lerwick*), Revd M. Cheyne
England (*London*), Revd W. A. Cairns
Europe (*Portugal*), Revd R. Hill

The Roman Catholic Church

The Roman Catholic Church is one world-wide Christian Church acknowledging as its head the Bishop of Rome, known as the Pope (Father). The Pope is held to be the successor of St Peter and thus invested with the power which was entrusted to St Peter by Jesus Christ. A direct line of succession is therefore claimed from the earliest Christian communities. Papal authority over the doctrine and jurisdiction of the Church in western Europe developed early and was unrivalled after the split with the Eastern Orthodox Church until the Protestant Reformation in the 16th century. With the fall of the Roman Empire the Pope also became an important political leader. His temporal power is now limited to the 107 acres of the Vatican City State.

The Pope exercises spiritual authority over the Church with the advice and assistance of the Sacred College of Cardinals, the supreme council of the Church. He is also advised about the concerns of the Church locally by his ambassadors, who liaise with the Bishops' Conference in each country.

In addition to advising the Pope, those members of the Sacred College of Cardinals who are under the age of 80 also elect a successor following the death of a Pope. The assembly of the Cardinals at the Vatican for the election of a new Pope is known as the Conclave in which, in complete seclusion, the Cardinals elect by a secret ballot; a two-thirds majority is necessary before the vote can be accepted as final. When a Cardinal receives the necessary votes, the Dean of the Sacred College formally asks him if he will accept election and the name by which he wishes to be known. On his acceptance of the office the Conclave is dissolved and the First Cardinal Deacon announces the election to the assembled crowd in St Peter's Square. On the first Sunday or Holyday following the election, the new Pope assumes the pontificate at High Mass in St Peter's Square. A new pontificate is dated from the assumption of the pontificate.

The number of cardinals was fixed at 70 by Pope Sixtus V in 1586, but has been steadily increased since the pontificate of John XXIII and now stands at 163 (as at end June 1992). The governing body of the Church is the Curia, which is made up of the Secretariat of State, the Sacred Council for the Public Affairs of the Church, and various congregations, secretariats and tribunals assisted by commissions and offices. All are headed by cardinals.

The Vatican State has its own diplomatic service, with representatives known as nuncios. Papal nuncios with full diplomatic recognition are given precedence over all other ambassadors to the country to which they are appointed; where precedence is not recognized, as in Britain, the Papal representative is known as a pro-nuncio. Where the representation is only to the local churches and not to the government of a country, the Papal representative is known as an apostolic delegate. The Roman Catholic Church has an estimated 890,907,000 adherents world-wide.

Sovereign Pontiff

His Holiness Pope John Paul II (Karol Wojtyla), *born* Wadowice, Poland, 18 May 1920; *ordained priest* 1946; *appointed Archbishop* of Krakow 1964; *created Cardinal* 1967; *assumed Pontificate* 16 October 1978.

GREAT BRITAIN AND IRELAND

The Roman Catholic Church in England and Wales is governed by the Bishops' Conference, membership of which includes the Diocesan Bishops, the Apostolic Exarch of the Ukrainians, the Bishop of the Forces and the Auxiliary Bishops. The Conference is headed by the President (Cardinal Basil Hume, Archbishop of Westminster) and Vice-President (Archbishop Worlock, Archbishop of Liverpool). There are five departments, each with an episcopal chairman: the Department for Christian Life and Worship (the Archbishop of Southwark), the Department for Mission and Unity (the Bishop of East Anglia), the Department for Catholic Education and Formation (the Bishop of Leeds), the Department for Christian Responsibility and Citizenship (the Bishop of Middlesbrough), and the Department for International Affairs (the Bishop of Salford).

The Bishops' Standing Committee, made up of all the Archbishops and the chairman of each of the above departments, has general responsibility for continuity and policy between the plenary sessions of the Conference. It prepares the Conference agenda and implements its decisions. It is serviced by a General Secretariat. There are also agencies and consultative bodies affiliated to the Conference.

The Bishops' Conference of Scotland has as its president Archbishop Winning of Glasgow and is the permanently constituted assembly of the Bishops of Scotland. To promote its work, the Conference establishes various agencies which have an advisory function in relation to the Conference. The more important of these agencies are called Commissions and each one has a Bishop President who, with the other members of the Commissions, are appointed by the Conference.

The Irish Episcopal Conference has as its Acting President Archbishop Connell of Dublin. Its membership comprises all the Archbishops and Bishops of Ireland and it appoints various Commissions to assist it in its work. There are three types of Commissions: (a) those made up of lay and clerical members chosen for their skills and experience, and staffed by full-time expert secretariats; (b) Commissions whose members are selected from existing institutions and whose services are supplied on a part-time basis; and (c) Commissions of Bishops only.

The Roman Catholic Church in Britain and Ireland has an estimated 8,992,092 members, 11 archbishops, 67 bishops, 12,698 priests, and 8,588 churches and chapels open to the public.

Catholic Bishops' Conferences secretariats:

ENGLAND AND WALES, 39 Eccleston Square, London SW1V 1PD. Tel: 071-630 8220. *General Secretary*, Revd Philip Carroll.

SCOTLAND, Candida Casa, 8 Corsehill Road, Ayr, Scotland KA7 2ST. Tel: 0292-256750. *General Secretary*, Rt. Revd Maurice Taylor, Bishop of Galloway.

IRELAND, Iona, 67 Newry Road, Dundalk, Co. Louth. *Executive Secretary*, Revd Gerard Clifford.

GREAT BRITAIN

APOSTOLIC PRO-NUNCIO TO THE UNITED KINGDOM OF GREAT BRITAIN AND NORTHERN IRELAND
The Most Revd Luigi Barbarito.

ENGLAND AND WALES

THE MOST REVD ARCHBISHOPS
Westminster, HE Cardinal Basil Hume, *cons.* 1976.
Auxiliary, John Crowley, *cons.* 1986.
Auxiliary, Victor Guazzelli, *cons.* 1970.
Auxiliary, Vincent Nichols, *cons.* 1992.
Auxiliary, James J. O'Brien, *cons.* 1977.
Clergy, 839.
Birmingham, Maurice Couve de Murville, *cons.* 1982, *apptd* 1982.
Auxiliary, Terence Brain, *cons.* 1991.
Auxiliary, Philip Pargeter, *cons.* 1989.
Clergy, 426.
Cardiff, John A. Ward, *cons.* 1981, *apptd* 1983.
Clergy, 163.
Liverpool, Derek Worlock, *cons.* 1965, *apptd* 1976.
Auxiliary, Kevin O'Connor, *cons.* 1979.
Auxiliary, John Rawsthorne, *cons.* 1981.
Auxiliary, Vincent Malone, *cons.* 1989.
Clergy, 515.
Southwark, Michael Bowen, *cons.* 1970, *apptd* 1977.
Auxiliary, Charles Henderson, *cons.* 1972.
Auxiliary, Howard Tripp, *cons.* 1980.
Auxiliary, John Jukes, *cons.* 1980.
Clergy, 518.

THE RT. REVD BISHOPS
Arundel and Brighton, Cormac Murphy-O'Connor, *cons.* 1977. *Clergy*, 255.
Brentwood, Thomas McMahon, *cons.* 1980, *apptd* 1980.
Clergy, 188.
Clifton, Mervyn Alexander, *cons.* 1972, *apptd* 1975.
Clergy, 242.
East Anglia, Alan Clark, *cons.* 1969, *apptd* 1976. *Clergy*, 112.
Hallam, Gerald Moverley, *cons.* 1968, *apptd* 1980.
Clergy, 100.
Hexham and Newcastle, Michael Ambrose Griffiths, *cons.* 1992. *Clergy*, 309.
Auxiliary, Owen Swindelhurst, *cons.* 1977.
Lancaster, John Brewer, *cons.* 1971, *apptd* 1985. *Clergy*, 228.
Leeds, David Konstant, *cons.* 1977, *apptd* 1985. *Clergy*, 225.
Menevia (Wales, Daniel Mullins, *cons.* 1970, *apptd* 1987.
Clergy, 59.
Middlesbrough, Augustine Harris, *cons.* 1966, *apptd* 1978.
Clergy, 201.
Auxiliary, Thomas O'Brien, *cons.* 1981.
Northampton, Patrick Leo McCartie, *cons.* 1977. *Clergy*, 123.
Nottingham, James McGuinness, *cons.* 1972, *apptd* 1975.
Clergy, 224.
Plymouth, Christopher Budd, *cons.* 1986. *Clergy*, 168.
Portsmouth, F. Crispian Hollis, *cons.* 1987, *apptd* 1989.
Clergy, 282.
Salford, Patrick Kelly, *cons.* 1984. *Clergy*, 455.
Shrewsbury, Joseph Gray, *cons.* 1969, *apptd* 1980.
Clergy, 226.
Wrexham (Wales), James Hannigan, *cons.* 1983, *apptd* 1987.
Clergy, 94.

SCOTLAND

THE MOST REVD ARCHBISHOPS
St Andrews and Edinburgh, Keith Patrick O'Brian, *cons.* 1985.
Auxiliary, Kevin Rafferty, *cons.* 1990.
Clergy, 213.
Glasgow, Thomas Winning, *cons.* 1971, *apptd* 1974.
Clergy, 338.

THE RT. REVD BISHOPS
Aberdeen, Mario Conti, *cons.* 1977. *Clergy*, 59.
Argyll and the Isles, Roderick Wright, *cons.* 1990. *Clergy*, 35.
Dunkeld, Vincent Logan, *cons.* 1981. *Clergy*, 67.
Galloway, Maurice Taylor, *cons.* 1981. *Clergy*, 75.
Motherwell, Joseph Devine, *cons.* 1977, *apptd* 1983.
Clergy, 190.
Paisley, John A. Mone, *cons.* 1984, *apptd* 1988. *Clergy*, 98.

IRELAND

There is one hierarchy for the whole of Ireland. Several of the dioceses have territory partly in the Republic of Ireland and partly in Northern Ireland.

NUNCIO TO IRELAND
Most Revd Emanuele Gerada (titular Archbishop of Nomenta).

THE MOST REVD ARCHBISHOPS
Armagh, HE Cardinal Cahal B. Daly, *cons.* 1990.
Auxiliary, Gerard Clifford, *cons.* 1991.
Clergy, 271.
Cashel, Dermot Clifford, *cons.* 1986.
Clergy, 122.
Dublin, Desmond Connell, *cons.* 1988, *apptd* 1988.
Auxiliary, Donal Murray, *cons.* 1982.
Auxiliary, Dermot O'Mahony, *cons.* 1975.
Auxiliary, James Moriarty, *cons.* 1992.
Auxiliary, Eamonn Walsh, *cons.* 1990.
Auxiliary, Desmond Williams, *cons.* 1985.
Clergy, 994.
Tuam, Joseph Cassidy, *cons.* 1979, *apptd* 1987.
Auxiliary, Michael Neary, *cons.* 1992.
Clergy, 165.

THE MOST REVD BISHOPS
Achonry, Thomas Flynn, *cons.* 1975. *Clergy*, 55.
Ardagh and Clonmacnois, Colm O'Reilly, *cons.* 1983. *Clergy*, 108.
Clogher, Joseph Duffy, *cons.* 1979. *Clergy*, 124.
Clonfert, Joseph Kirby, *cons.* 1988. *Clergy*, 76.
Cloyne, John Magee, *cons.* 1987. *Clergy*, 155.
Cork and Ross, Michael Murphy, *cons.* 1976. *Clergy*, 360.
Auxiliary, John Buckley, *cons.* 1984.
Derry, Edward Daly, *cons.* 1974. *Clergy*, 149.
Auxiliary, Francis Lagan, *cons.* 1988.
Down and Connor, Patrick J. Walsh, *cons.* 1991. *Clergy*, 324.
Auxiliary, Anthony Farquhar, *cons.* 1983.
Auxiliary, William Philbin, *cons.* 1991.
Dromore, Francis Brooks, *cons.* 1976. *Clergy*, 71.
Elphin, Dominic Conway, *cons.* 1970. *Clergy*, 104.
Ferns, Brendon Comiskey, *cons.* 1980. *Clergy*, 148.
Galway and Kilmacduagh, vacant.
Kerry, Dermot O'Sullivan, *cons.* 1985. *Clergy*, 143.
Kildare and Leighlin, Laurence Ryan, *cons.* 1984. *Clergy*, 225.
Killala, Thomas Finnegan, *cons.* 1970. *Clergy*, 51.
Killaloe, Michael Harty, *cons.* 1967. *Clergy*, 186.
Kilmore, Francis McKiernan, *cons.* 1972. *Clergy*, 103.
Limerick, Jeremiah Newman, *cons.* 1974. *Clergy*, 234.
Meath, Michael Smith, *cons.* 1984, *apptd* 1990. *Clergy*, 270.
Ossory, Laurence Forristal, *cons.* 1980. *Clergy*, 125.
Raphoe, Seamus Hegarty, *cons.* 1984. *Clergy*, 102.
Waterford and Lismore, Michael Russell, *cons.* 1965. *Clergy*, 206.

RESIDENTIAL ARCHBISHOPRICS THROUGHOUT THE WORLD

This list is set out with the name of the relevant country first; then the name of the diocese; and finally the Archbishop's name. It does not include England and Wales, Scotland or Ireland which are above.

ALBANIA
Durrës, vacant (Apostolic Administrator, Mgr Nicola Troshani).
Shkodër, vacant (Apostolic Administrator, Mgr Ernesto Coba).

ALGERIA
Algiers, Henri Teissier.

ANGOLA
Huambo, Francisco Viti.
Luanda, HE Cardinal Alexandre do Nascimento.
Lubango, Manuel Franklin da Costa.

ARGENTINA
Bahia Blanca, Romulo Garcia.
Buenos Aires, HE Cardinal Antonio Quarracino.
Córdoba, HE Cardinal Raúl Francisco Primatesta.
Corrientes, Fortunato A. Rossi.
La Plata, Carlos Galán.
Mendoza, Candido Genaro Rubiolo.
Paraná, Estanislao Esteban Karlic.
Resistencia, vacant.
Rosario, Jorge Manuel López.
Salta, Moises J. Blanchoud.
San Juan de Cuyo, Italo Severino Di Stefano.
Santa Fe, Edgardo Gabriel Storni.
Tucumán, Horatio A. Bozzoli.

AUSTRALIA
Adelaide, Leonard Anthony Faulkner.
Brisbane, John A. Bathersby.
Canberra, Francis P. Carroll.
Hobart, Joseph E. D'Arcy.
Melbourne, Thomas Francis Little.
Perth, Barry J. Hickey.
Sydney, HE Cardinal Edward B. Clancy.

AUSTRIA
Salzburg, Georg Eder.
Vienna, HE Cardinal Hans Hermann Groer.

BANGLADESH
Dhaka, Michael Rozario.

BELGIUM
Malines-Bruxelles, HE Cardinal Godfried Danneels.

BENIN
Cotonou, Isidore de Souzá.

BOLIVIA
Cochabamba, Rene Fernandez Apaza.
La Paz, Luis Sainz Hinojosa.
Santa Cruz de la Sierra, Julio T. Sandoval.
Sucre, Jesus G. Pérez Rodriguez.

BRAZIL
Aparacida, Geraldo Maria de Morais Penido.
Aracaju, Luciano José Cabral Duarte.
Bélem do Pará, Vicente Joaquim Zico.
Belo Horizonte, Serafim Fernandes de Araújo.
Botucatu, Antonio M. Mucciolo.
Brasilia, HE Cardinal Jose Freire Falcao.
Campinas, Gilberto Pereira Lopes.
Campo Grande, Vitorio Pavanello.
Cascavel, Armando Cirio.
Cuiaba, Bonifacio Piccinini.
Curitiba, Pedro Antonio Fedalto.
Diamantina, Geraldo Majelo Reis.
Florianópolis, Eusebio Oscar Scheid.
Fortaleza, HE Cardinal Aloisio Lorscheider.
Goiania, Antonio Ribeiro de Oliveira.
Juiz de Fora, Clovis Frainer.
Londrina, Albano Bortoletto.
Maceió, Edvaldo G. Amaral.
Manaus, Luiz S. Vieira.
Mariana, Luciano Mendes de Almeida.
Maringá, Jaime Luis Coelho.
Natal, Alair V. Fernandes de Melo.
Niteroi, Carlos A. Navarro.
Olinda and Recife, José Cardoso Sobrinho.
Paraiba, José M. Pires.
Porto Alegre, Altamiro Rossato.
Porto Velho, José Martins da Silva.
Pouso Alegre, João Bergese.
Ribeirão Preto, Arnaldo Ribeiro.
São Luis do Maranhão, Paulo Eduardo Andrade Ponte.
São Paulo, HE Cardinal Paulo Evaristo Arns.
São Salvador da Bahia, HE Cardinal Lucas Moreira Neves.
São Sebastião do Rio de Janeiro, HE Cardinal Eugenio de Araújo Sales.
Sorocaba, José Lambert.
Teresina, Miguel F. Camara Filho.
Uberaba, Benedito de Ulhôa Vieira.
Vitória, Silvestre L. Scandian.

BURKINA
Ouagadougou, HE Cardinal Paul Zoungrana.

BURUNDI
Gitega, Joachim Ruhuna.

Cameroon
Bamenda, Paul Verdzekov.
Douala, HE Cardinal Christian W. Tumi.
Garoua, Antoine Ntalou.
Yaoundé, Jean Zoa.

Canada
Edmonton, Joseph N. MacNeil.
Gatineau-Hull, Roger Ebacher.
Grouard-McLennon, Henri Légaré.
Halifax, Austin-Emile Burke.
Keewatin-Le Pas, Peter Alfred Sutton.
Kingston, Francis John Spence.
Moncton, Donat Chiasson.
Montreal, Jean-Claude Turcotte.
Ottawa, Marcel A. Gervais.
Quebec, Maurice Couture.
Regina, Charles Halpin.
Rimouski, Gilles Ouellet.
St Boniface, Antoine Hacault.
St Johns, Newfoundland, James H. MacDonald.
Sherbrooke, Jean Marie Fortier.
Toronto, Aloysius Matthew Ambrosic.
Vancouver, Adam J. Exner.
Winnipeg, Leonard J. Wall; (Ukrainian Rite), Maxim Hermaniuk.

Central African Republic
Bangui, Joachim N'Dayen.

Chad
Ndjamena, Charles Vandame.

Chile
Antofagasta, Patricio Infante Alfonso.
Concepción, Antonio M. Casamitjana.
La Serena, Francisco J. C. Huneeus.
Puerto Montt, Savino B. C. Bertollo.
Santiago de Chile, Carlos Oviedo Cavada.

China
Anking, Huai-Ning, vacant.
Canton, Dominic Tang Yee-Ming.
Changsha, vacant.
Chungking, vacant.
Foochow, Min-Hou, vacant.
Hangchow, vacant.
Hankow, vacant.
Kaifeng, vacant.
Kunming, vacant.
Kweiyang, vacant.
Lanchow, vacant.
Mukden, vacant.
Nanchang, vacant.
Nanking, vacant.
Nanning, vacant.
Peking (Beijing), vacant.
Sian, vacant.
Suiyüan, Francis Wang Hsueh-Ming.
Taiyuan, vacant.
Tsinan, vacant.

Colombia
Barranquilla, Felix Maria Torres Parra.
Bogotá, HE Cardinal Mario Revollo Bravo.
Bucaramanga, vacant.
Cali, Pedro Rubiano Sáenz.
Cartagena, Carlos José Ruiseco Vieira.
Ibague, José Joaquin Flórez Hernández.
Manizales, José de Jesús Pimiento Rodriguez.
Medellin, Hector Rueda Hernández.
Nueva Pamplona, Rafael Sarmiento Peralta.
Popayán, Alberto G. Jaramillo.
Sante Fe de Antioquia, Eladio Acosta Arteaga.
Tunja, Augusto Trujillo Arango.

Congo
Brazzaville, Barthélémy Batantu.

Costa Rica
San José, Román Arrieta Villalobos.

Côte d'Ivoire
Abidjan, HE Cardinal Bernard Yago.

Cuba
San Cristóbal de la Habana, Jaime Lucas Ortega y Alamino.
Santiago de Cuba, Pedro Meurice Estiu.

Cyprus
Cyprus (Maronite Seat at Nicosia), Boutros Gemayel.

Czechoslovakia
Olomouc, vacant.
Praha, Miloslav Vlk.
Trnava, Jan Sokol.

Dominican Republic
Santo Domingo, HE Cardinal Nicolás de Jesús López Rodriguez.

Ecuador
Cuenca, Alberto Luna Tobar.
Guayaquil, Ignacio Larrea Holguin.
Quito, Antonio J. González Zumárraga.

Equatorial Guinea
Malabo, Idlefonso Obama Obono.

Ethiopia
Addis Ababa, HE Cardinal Paul Tzadua.

France
Aix, Bernard Panafieu.
Albi, Roger Meindre.
Auch, Gabriel Vanel.
Avignon, Raymond Bouchex.
Besançon, Lucien Daloz.
Bordeaux, Pierre Eyt.
Bourges, Pierre Plateau.
Cambrai, Jacques Delaporte.
Chambéry, Claude Feidt.
Lyon, HE Cardinal Albert Decourtray.
Marseilles, HE Cardinal Robert Coffy.
Paris, HE Cardinal J. M. Lustiger.
Reims, Jean Balland.
Rennes, Jacques Jullien.
Rouen, Joseph Duval.
Sens, Gérard Defois.
Strasbourg, Charles Amarin Brand.
Toulouse, André Collini.
Tours, Jean Honoré.

French Polynesia
Papeete, Michel Coppenrath.

Gabon
Libreville, André Fernand Anguilé.

Germany
Bamberg, Elmar Maria Kredel.
Cologne, HE Cardinal Joachim Meisner.
Freiburg im Breisgau, Oskar Saier.
Munich and Freising, HE Cardinal Friedrich Wetter.
Paderborn, Johannes Joachim Degenhardt.

GHANA
Cape Coast, vacant.
Tamale, Peter Poreiku Dery.

GREECE
Athens, Nicholaos Foscolos.
Corfu, Antonio Varthalitis.
Naxos, Jean Perris.
Rhodes, vacant (Apostolic Administrator, Michel Pierre Franzidis).

GUATEMALA
Guatemala, Prospero Penandos del Barrio.

GUINEA
Conakry, Robert Sarah.

HAITI
Cap-Haitien, François Gayot.
Port au Prince, François-Wolff Ligondé.

HONDURAS
Tegucigalpa, Hector Enrique Santos Hernández.

HONG KONG
Hong Kong, HE Cardinal J. B. Wu Cheng Chung.

HUNGARY
Eger, Istvan Seregely.
Esztergom, HE Cardinal Laslo Paskai.
Kalocsa, Laszlo Danko.

INDIA
Agra, Cecil de Sa.
Bangalore, Alphonsus Mathias.
Bhopal, Eugene D' Souza.
Bombay, HE Cardinal I. Pimenta.
Calcutta, Henry Sebastian D'Souza.
Changanacherry, Joseph Powathil.
Cuttack-Bhubaneswar, Raphael Cheenath.
Delhi, Alan de Lastic.
Ernakulam, HE Cardinal Anthony Padiyara.
Goa and Daman, Raul Nicolau Gonsalves.
Hyderabad, Saminini Arulappa.
Madras and Mylapore, Casimir Gnanadickam.
Madurai, Marianus Arokiasamy.
Nagpur, Leobard D'Souza.
Pondicherry and Cuddalore, Michael Augustine.
Ranchi, Telesphore P. Toppo.
Shillong-Gauhati, Hubert D'Rosario.
Trivandrum (Syrian Melekite Rite), Benedict Varghese Mar Gregorios Thangalathil.
Verapoly, Cornelius Elanjikal.

INDONESIA
Ende, Donatus Djagom.
Jakarta, Leo Soekoto.
Kupang, Gregorius Manteiro.
Medan, Alfred Gonti Pius Datubara.
Merauke, Jacobus Duivenvoorde.
Pontianak, Hieronymus Herculanus Bumbun.
Semarang, Julius R. Darmaatmadja.
Ujung Pandang, R. P. Francis van Roessel.

IRAN
Ahváz, Hanna Zora.
Tehran, Youhannan Semaan Issayi.
Urmyā, Thomas Meram.

IRAQ
Arbil, Stephane Babaca.
Baghdad (Latin Rite), Paul Dahdah; (Syrian Rite), Athanase M. S. Matoka; (Armenian Rite), Paul Coussa.
Basra, Yousif Thomas.
Kirkuk, André Sana.
Mosul, Georges Garmo.

ISRAEL
Akka (Greek Melekite Catholic Rite), Maximos Salloum.

ITALY
Acerenza, Michele Scandiffio.
Amalfi, Beniamino De Palma.
Ancona, Franco Festorazzi.
Bari, Mariano Magrassi.
Benevento, Serafino Sprovieri.
Bologna, HE Cardinal Giacomo Biffi.
Brindisi, Settimio Todisco.
Cagliari, Otterino Pietro Alberti.
Camerino, Francesco Gioia.
Campobasso-Boiano, Ettore Di Filippo.
Capua, Luigi Diligenza.
Catania, Luigi Bommarito.
Catanzaro, Antonio Cantisani.
Chieti, Antonio Valentini.
Conza, Mario Milano.
Cosenza, Dino Trabalzini.
Crotone-Santa Severina, Giuseppe Agostino.
Fermo, Cleto Bellucci.
Ferrara, Luigi Maverna.
Florence, HE Cardinal Silvano Piovanelli.
Foggia, Giuseppe Casale.
Gaeta, Vincenzo Farano.
Genoa, HE Cardinal Giovanni Canestri.
Gorizia and Gradisca, Antonio Vitale Bommarco.
Lanciano, Enzio d'Antonio.
L'Aquila, Mario Peressin.
Lecce, Cosmo F. Ruppi.
Lucca, Bruno Tommasi.
Manfredonia, Vincenzo D'Addario.
Matera, Ennio Appignanesi.
Messina, Ignazio Cannavó.
Milan, HE Cardinal Carlo Maria Martini.
Modena, Santo B. Quadri.
Monreale, Salvatore Cassisa.
Naples, HE Cardinal Michele Giordano.
Oristano, Pier Luigi Tiddia.
Otranto, Vincenzo Franco.
Palermo, HE Cardinal Salvatore Pappalardo.
Perugia, Ennio Antonelli.
Pescara-Penne, Francesco Cuccarese.
Pisa, Alessandro Plotti.
Potenza, Giuseppe Vairo.
Ravenna, Luigi Amaducci.
Reggio Calabria, Vittorio L. Mondello.
Rossano-Cariati, Andrea Cassone.
Salerno, Gerardo Pierro.
Sassari, Salvatore Isgrò.
Siena, Gaetano Bonicelli.
Siracusa, Giuseppe Costanzo.
Sorrento, Felice Cece.
Spoleto, Antonio Ambrosanio.
Taranto, Luigi Papa.
Turin, HE Cardinal Giovanni Saldarini.
Trani and Barletta, Carmelo Cassati.
Trento, Giovanni Sartori.
Udine, Alfredo Battisti.
Urbino, Donato U. Bianchi.
Vercelli, Tarcisio Bertone.

JAMAICA
Kingston, Samuel Emmanuel Carter.

JAPAN
Nagasaki, Francis Xavier Shimamoto.
Osaka, Paul Hisao Yasuda.
Tokyo, Peter Seiichi Shirayanagi.

JORDAN
Petra and Filadelfia (Greek Melekite Catholic Rite), Saba Youakim.

KENYA
Kisumu, Zaccharus Okoth.
Mombasa, John Njenga.
Nairobi, HE Cardinal Maurice Otunga.
Nyeri, Nicodemus Kirima.

KOREA
Kwangju, Victorinus Kong-Hi Youn.
Seoul, HE Cardinal Stephen Sou Hwan Kim.
Taegu, Paul Moun-Hi Ri.

LATVIA
Riga, Jānis Pujats.

LEBANON
Antelias (Maronite Rite), Joseph Mohsen Bechara.
Baalbek, Eliopoli (Greek Melekite Catholic Rite), Salim Bustros.
Baniyas (Greek Melekite Catholic Rite), Antoine Hayek.
Beirut (Greek Melekite Catholic Rite), Habib Bacha; (Maronite Rite), Khalil Abinader.
Saïda (Greek Melekite Catholic Rite), Georges Kwaiter.
Tripoli (Maronite Rite), Antoine Joubeir; (Greek Melekite Catholic Rite), Elias Nijmé.
Tyre (Greek Melekite Catholic Rite), Jean A. Haddad; (Maronite Rite), Joseph Khoury.
Zahle and Furzol (Greek Melekite Catholic Rite), Andre Haddad.

LESOTHO
Maseru, Bernard Mohlalisi.

LIBERIA
Monrovia, Michael Kpakala Francis.

LITHUANIA
Kaunas, HE Cardinal Vincentas Sladkevicius.
Vilnius, Audris J. Bačkis.

LUXEMBOURG
Luxembourg, Fernand Franck.

MADAGASCAR
Antananarive, HE Cardinal Victor Razafimahatratra.
Antsiranana, Albert Joseph Tsiahoana.
Fianarantsoa, vacant.

MALAYSIA
Kuala Lumpur, Anthony S. Fernandez.
Kuching, Peter Chung Hoan Ting.

MALI
Bamako, Luc Auguste Sangaré.

MALTA
Malta, Joseph Mercieca.

MARTINIQUE
Fort de France, Maurice Marie-Sainte.

MAURITIUS
Port Louis, HE Cardinal Jean Margeot.

MEXICO
Acapulco, Rafael Bello Ruiz.
Antequera, Bartolomé Carrasco Briseno.
Chihuahua, José Fernández Arteaga.
Durango, Antonio L. Avina.
Guadalajara, HE Cardinal Juan J. P. Ocampo.
Hermosillo, Carlos Quintero Arce.
Jalapa, Sergio Obeso Rivero.
Mexico City, HE Cardinal Ernesto Corripio Ahumada.
Monterrey, Adolfo Suarez Rivera.
Morelia, Estanislao Alcarez Figueroa.
Puebla de los Angeles, Rosendo Huesca Pacheco.
San Luis Potosi, Arturo A. Szymanski Ramirez.
Tlalnepantla, Manuel P. Gil Gonzalez.
Yucatán, Manuel Castro Ruiz.

MONACO
Monaco, Joseph-Marie Sardou.

MOROCCO
Rabat, Hubert Michon.
Tangier, Antonio J. Peteiro Freire.

MOZAMBIQUE
Beira, Jaime P. Goncalves.
Maputo, HE Cardinal Alexandre José Maria dos Santos.
Nampula, Manuel Vieira Pinto.

MYANMAR (BURMA)
Mandalay, Alphonse U. Than Aung.
Yangon (Rangoon), Gabriel Thohey Mahn Gaby.

NETHERLANDS
Utrecht, HE Cardinal Adrianus J. Simonis.

NEW ZEALAND
Wellington, HE Cardinal Thomas Stafford Williams.

NICARAGUA
Managua, HE Cardinal Miguel Obando Bravo.

NIGERIA
Kaduna, Peter Yariyok Jatau.
Lagos, Anthony Okogie.
Onitsha, Stephen Nweke Ezeanya.

OCEANIA
Agaña, Anthony Sablan Apuron.
Honiara, Adrian Thomas Smith.
Nouméa, Michel-Marie-Bernard Calvet.
Samoa, Apia and Tokelau, HE Cardinal Pio Taofino'u.
Suva, Petero Mataca.

PAKISTAN
Karachi, HE Cardinal Joseph Cordeiro.

PANAMA
Panama, Marcos Gregorio McGrath.

PAPUA NEW GUINEA
Madang, Benedict To Varpin.
Mount Hagen, Michael Meier.
Port Moresby, Peter Kurongku.
Rabaul, Karl Hesse.

PARAGUAY
Asuncion, Felipe Santiago B. Avalos.

PERU
Arequipa, Fernando Vargas Ruiz de Somocurcio.
Ayacucho o Huamanga, vacant.
Cuzco, Alcides Mendoza Castro.
Huancayo, vacant.
Lima, Augusto Vargas Alzamora.
Piura, Oscar Rolando Cantuarias Pastor.
Trujillo, Manuel Prado Pérez-Rosas.

PHILIPPINES
Caceres, Leonardo Legazpi.
Cagayan de Oro, Jesus B. Tuquib.
Capiz, Onesimo C. Gordoncillo.
Cebu, HE Cardinal Ricardo Vidal.

Cotabato, Philip Frances Smith.
Davao, Antonio Mabutas.
Jaro, Alberto J. Piamonte.
Lingayen-Dagupan, Oscar V. Cruz.
Lipa, Mariano Gaviola.
Manila, HE Cardinal Jaime L. Sin.
Nueva Segovia, Orlando Quevedo.
Ozamiz, Jesus Dosado.
Palo, Pedro R. Dean.
San Fernando, Paciano Aniceto.
Tuguegarao, Diosdado A. Talamayan.
Zamboanga, Francisco Raval Cruces.

POLAND
Bialystok, Edward Kisiel.
Czestochowa, Stanislaw Nowak.
Gdańsk, Tadeusz Goclowski.
Gniezno, Henryk Muszyński.
Katowice, Damian Zimoń.
Kraków, HE Cardinal Franciszek Macharski.
Lodz, Wladyslaw Ziolek.
Lublin, Boleslaw Pylak.
Poznań, Jerzy Stroba.
Przemyśl of the Latins, Ignacy Tokarczuk.
Szczecin-Kamień, Marian Przykucki.
Warmia, Edmund Piszcz.
Warsaw, HE Cardinal Józef Glemp.
Wroclaw, HE Cardinal Henryk Roman Gulbinowicz.

PORTUGAL
Braga, Eurico Dias Nogueira.
Evora, Maurilio Jorge Quintal de Gouveia.

PUERTO RICO
San Juan, HE Cardinal Luis Aponte Martinez.

ROMANIA
Alba Julia (Latin Rite), Lajos Balint.
Bucarest, Ioan Robu.
Fagaras and Alba Julia (Romanian Byzantine Rite), HE Cardinal Alexandru Todea.

RWANDA
Kigali, Vincent Nsengiyumva.

EL SALVADOR
San Salvador, Arturo Rivera Damas.

SENEGAL
Dakar, HE Cardinal Hyacinthe Thiandoum.

SIERRA LEONE
Freetown and Bo, Joseph Ganda.

SINGAPORE
Singapore, Gregory Yong Sooi Nghean.

SOUTH AFRICA
Bloemfontein, Peter John Butelezi.
Cape Town, Lawrence Patrick Henry.
Durban, Denis Eugene Hurley.
Pretoria, George Francis Daniel.

FORMER SOVIET UNION
Latin Rite
Karaganda Apostolic Administration (covering Kazakhstan), Apostolic Administrator, Mgr Jan Lenga (titular Bishop of Arba).
Lvov, Marian Jaworski (Archbishop of Lvov of the Latins).
Minsk-Mohilev Archdiocese (covering Belorussia), Kazimierz Swiatek.
Moscow Apostolic Administration (covering European Russia), Apostolic Administrator, Archbishop Tadeusz Kondrusiewicz.
Novosibirsk Apostolic Administration (covering Siberia), Apostolic Administrator, Mgr Joseph Werth, SJ (titular Bishop of Bulna).

Ukrainian Rite
Lvov, HE Cardinal Myroslav I. Lubachivsky (Major Archbishop of Lvov of the Ukrainians).

SPAIN
Barcelona, Ricardo Maria Carles Gordó.
Burgos, Theodoro C. Fernandez.
Granada, José Méndez Asensio.
Madrid, HE Cardinal Angel Suquia Goicoechea.
Oviedo, Gabino Diaz Merchán.
Pamplona, José Mariá Cirardo Lachiondo.
Santiago de Compostela, Antonio Rouco Varela.
Sevilla, Carlos Amigo Vallejo.
Tarragona, Ramon Torrella Cascante.
Toledo, HE Cardinal Marcelo González Martin.
Valencia, Miguel Roca Cabanellas.
Valladolid, José Delicado Baeza.
Zaragoza, Elíaz Yanez Alvarez.

SRI LANKA
Colombo, Nicholas Marcus Fernando.

SUDAN
Khartoum, Gabriel Zubeir Wako.

SYRIA
Alep, Beroea, Halab (Greek Melekite Catholic Rite), Néophytes Edelby; (Syrian Rite), Raboula A. Beylouni; (Maronite Rite), Pierre Callaos; (Armenian Rite), Boutros Marayati.
Baniyas (Greek Melekite Catholic Rite), Antoine Hayek.
Bosra, Bostra, Boulos Nassif Borkhoche.
Damascus (Greek Melekite Catholic Rite), vacant; (Syrian Rite), Eustache J. Mounayer; (Maronite Rite), Hamid A. Mourany.
Hassaké-Nisibi, Georges Habib Hafouri.
Homs, Emesa (Greek Melekite Catholic Rite), Abraham Nehmé; (Syrian Catholic Rite), Jean Dahi.
Laodicea (Greek Melekite Catholic Rite), Michel Yatim.

TAIWAN
Taipei, Joseph Ti-Kang.

TANZANIA
Dar es Salaam, HE Cardinal Laurean Rugambwa.
Mwanza, Antony Mayala.
Tabora, Mario E. A. Mgulunde.

THAILAND
Bangkok, HE Cardinal Michael Michai Kitbunchu.
Tharé and Nonseng, Lawrence Khai Saen-Phon-On.

TOGO
Lomé, vacant (Apostolic Administrator Jean Gbikpi-Benissan).

TRINIDAD
Port of Spain, Gordon Anthony Pantin.

TURKEY
Diarbekir, Paul Karatas.
Istanbul (*Constantinople*), Jean Tcholakian.
Izmir, Giuseppe G. Bernardini.

UGANDA
Kampala, Emmanuel Wamala.

URUGUAY
Montevideo, José Gottardi Cristelli.

USA
Anchorage, Francis Thomas Hurley.
Atlanta, James P. Lyke.
Baltimore, William Henry Keeler.
Boston, HE Cardinal Bernard F. Law.
Chicago, HE Cardinal Joseph L. Bernardin.
Cincinnati, Daniel E. Pilarczyk.
Denver, James Francis Stafford.
Detroit, Adam J. Maida.
Dubuque, Daniel W. Kucera.
Hartford, Daniel A. Cronin.
Indianapolis, Edward T. O'Meara.
Kansas City, Ignatius J. Strecker.
Los Angeles, HE Cardinal Roger M. Mahony.
Louisville, Thomas C. Kelly.
Miami, Edward A. McCarthy.
Milwaukee, Rembert G. Weakland.
Mobile, Oscar H. Lipscomb.
Newark, Theodore E. McCarrick.
New Orleans, Francis B. Schulte.
New York, HE Cardinal John J. O'Connor.
Oklahoma City, Charles A. Salatka.
Omaha, Daniel E. Sheehan.
Philadelphia, HE Cardinal Anthony J. Bevilacqua; (Ukrainian Rite), Stephen Sulyk.
Pittsburgh (Byzantine Rite), Thomas V. Dolinay.
Portland (*Oregon*), William J. Levada.
St Louis (*Missouri*), John L. May.
St Paul and Minneapolis, John Robert Roach.
San Antonio, Patrick F. Flores.
San Francisco, John R. Quinn.
Santa Fe, Robert F. Sanchez.
Seattle, Thomas J. Murphy.
Washington, HE Cardinal James A. Hickey.

Venezuela
Barquisimeto, Julio Manuel Chirivella Varela.
Caracas, HE Cardinal José Ali Lebrún Moratinos; (Greek Melekite Catholic Rite), Pierre Rai.
Ciudad Bolivar, Medardo Luzardo Romero.
Cumana, Alfredo J. R. Figueroa.
Maracaibo, Domingo Roa Pérez.
Mérida, Baltazar P. Cardozo.
Valencia, Jorge Liberato Urosa Savino.

Vietnam
Hanoi, vacant.
Hue, vacant.
Thanh-Phô Hôchiminh, Paul Nguyên Van Binh.

West Indies
Castries, Kelvin Edward Felix, OBE.

Former Yugoslavia
Bar, Petar Perkolić.
Belgrade, Franc Perko.
Ljubljana, Alojzij Šuštar.
Rijeka-Senj, Anton Tamarut.
Split-Makarska, Ante Juric.
Vrhbosna and Sarajevo, Vinko Puljic.
Zadar, Marijan Oblak.
Zagreb, HE Cardinal Franjo Kuharić.

Zaire
Bukavu, Mulindwa Mutabesha Mweru.
Kananga, Bakole wa Ilunga.
Kinshasa, HE Cardinal Frederick Etsou-Nzabi-Bamungwabi.
Kisangani, Laurent Monsengwo Pasinya.
Lubumbashi, Kabanga Songasonga.
Mbandaka-Bikoro, Joseph Kumuondala Mbimba.

Zambia
Kasama, James Spaita.
Lusaka, Adrian Mungandu.

Zimbabwe
Harare, Patrick Chakaipa.

ARCHBISHOPS OF TITULAR SEES

Abari, Carlo Furno.
Abbirmaius, Bernard Jacqueline.
Adana (Greek Melekite Catholic Rite), Gregoire Haddad.
Aeclanum, Antonio M. Vegliò
Amantia, Edward Idris Cassidy.
Amasya, James Patrick Carroll.
Amiterno, Agostino Cacciavillan.
Aquileia, Marcello Costalunga.
Augusta, Justo M. Garcia.
Balneoregium, Mario Rizzi.
Beroe, Victor Sartre.
Cadi, Stefan M. Marusyn.
Caesarea in Numidia, Alberto Bouone.
Celene, Gabriel Montaluo.
Cesarea in Palaestina (Greek Melekite Catholic Rite), Hilarion Capucci.
Cesariana, Giovanni Lajolo.
Claudiopolis in Honoriade, Alfredo Bruniera.
Corinthus, Gennaro Verolino.
Dara, Nicholas T. Elko.
Diocletiana, Lorenzo Baldisseri.
Doclea, Pier Luigi Celata.
Drivastum, Bruno Bertagna.
Edessa in Osrhoëne (Syrian Catholic Rite), Gregoire Ephrem Jarjour.
Ephesus, John Henry Boccella.
Fidene, Giacinto Berloco.
Fiorentino, Luigi Barbarito.
Formiae, Mario Tagliaferri.
Forum Novum, Giovanni Battista Re.
Gabala, Gérard de Milleville.
Germania in Numidia, Erwin J. Ender.
Gradum, José López Ortiz.
Hadrianopolis in Haemimonto, Lino Zanini.
Heraclea, Jozef Kowalczyk.
Hippo Diarrhytus, Tadeusz Kondrusiewicz.
Horta, Paul Marcinkus.
Idicra, Georg Weinhold.
Kaškar, Emmanuel-Karim Delly.
Litterae, Luigi Travaglino.
Macra, John Dooley.
Macri, Pablo Puente.
Madaurus, Janusz Bolonek.
Marcianopolis, Volodymyr Sterniuk.
Medeli, Carlo Curis.
Mesembria, Loris Francesco Capovilla.
Meta, Audrys J. Backis.
Midila, Beniamino Stella.
Narona, Giovanni Bulaitis.
Neapoli, HE Cardinal Jacques Martin.
Nicaea Parva, Paolino Limongi.
Novaliciana, Faustino Sainz Munoz.
Novi, Ernesto M. Fiore.
Nubia, Paul Antaki.
Octava, Blasco Francisco Collaco.
Otriculum, Pietro Biggio.
Pia, Osvaldo Padilla.
Razia Ria, Marian Oles.

Rebellum, Giovanni Marray.
Rusellae, Lorenzo Antonetti.
Rusubisir, Ivan Dias.
Salamis, Joseph Kuo Joshih.
Satrianum, Patrick Coveney.
Scytopolis, Joseph Raya.
Segermes, Renato R. Martino.
Serta, Giovanni Coppa.
Severiana, Luigi Bressan.
Silli, Jan Schotte.
Sinna, Paul F. Tabet.
Soteropolis, Ettore Cunial.
Tagase, Giovanni Ceirano.
Tagora, Cipriano Calderon Polo.
Tarsus (Greek Melekite Catholic Rite), Loutfi Laham.
Tharros, Giuseppe Uhač.
Thibica, Lajos Kada.
Tiburnia, Donato Squicciarini.
Tiddi, Eugenio Sbarbaro.
Tongeren, Henri Lemaître.
Truentum, Francesco Colasuonno.
Turris, Vincenzo Moreni.
Tyndaris, Paolo Giglio.
Vannida, Felix del Blanco Prieto.
Vartena, Giovanni Moretti.
Villamagna, Giulio Einaudi.
Viminacium, Franco Brambilla.
Volsinium, Justin Francis Rigali.
Zella, Angelo Acerbi.

PATRIARCHS IN COMMUNION WITH THE ROMAN CATHOLIC CHURCH

Alexandria, HB Stephanos II Ghattas (Patriarch for Catholic Copts).
Antioch, HB Ignace Antoine II Hayek (Patriarch for Syrian Rite Catholics); HB Maximos V. Hakim (Patriarch for Greek Melekite Rite Catholics); HB Nasrallah Pierre Sfeir (Patriarch for Maronite Rite Catholics).
Jerusalem, HB Michel Sabbah (Patriarch for Latin Rite Catholics).
Babilonia of the Chaldeans, HB Raphael I Bidawid.
Cilicia of the Armenians, HB Jean Pierre XVIII Kasparian (Patriarch for Armenian Rite Catholics).
Oriental India, Archbishop Raul Nicolau Gonsalves.
Lisbon, HE Cardinal Antonio Ribeiro.
Venice, HE Cardinal Marco Ce.

Other Churches in the UK

AFRICAN AND AFRO-CARIBBEAN CHURCHES

There are more than 160 Christian churches or groups of African or Afro-Caribbean origin in the United Kingdom. These include the Apostolic Faith Church, the Cherubim and Seraphim Church, the New Testament Church Assembly, the New Testament Church of God and the Wesleyan Holiness Church.

The Council of African and Allied Churches was initiated by the Most Revd Father Olu Abiola in 1979 to give one voice to the various Christian churches of African origin in the UK. Membership increased in the early 1980s and some churches of Caribbean origin also joined, resulting in 1986 in the change of name to the Council of African and Afro-Caribbean Churches UK. The Council is the medium through which the member churches can work jointly to provide services they cannot easily provide individually.

There are about 68,500 adherents of African and Afro-Caribbean churches in the United Kingdom, and about 950 churches. The Council has 25 member churches, with 70 congregations, 12,000 members and 150 ministers.

Council Chairman, His Grace The Most Revd Father Olu A. Abiola, 31 Norton House, Sidney Road, London SW9 0UJ. Tel: 071-274 5589

ASSOCIATED PRESBYTERIAN CHURCHES OF SCOTLAND

The Associated Presbyterian Churches came into being in 1989 as a result of a division within the Free Presbyterian Church of Scotland. Following two controversial disciplinary cases, the culmination of deepening differences within the Church, a Deed of Separation was drawn up by several members of the Church's synod. This held that the Church, in contravention of its constitution, had denied its members freedom of judgement in matters relating to the application of the Christian faith to daily living. A presbytery was formed calling itself the Associated Presbyterian Churches (APC). The APC claims that it represents the Free Presbyterian Church of Scotland as constituted in 1893. The Associated Presbyterian Churches has about 20 churches, 1,000 members and 13 ministers.

Clerk of the Scottish Presbytery, Revd H. I. MacKinnon, Fernhill, Polvinster Road, Oban, Argyll PA34 5TN. Tel: 0631-64789

THE BAPTIST CHURCH

Baptists trace their origins to John Smyth, who in 1609 in Amsterdam reinstituted the baptism of conscious believers as the basis of the fellowship of a gathered church. Members of Smyth's church established the first Baptist church in England in 1612. They came to be known as 'General' Baptists and their theology was Arminian, whereas a later group of Calvinists who adopted the baptism of believers came to be known as 'Particular' Baptists. The two sections of the Baptists were united into one body, the Baptist Union of Great Britain and Ireland, in 1891. In 1988 the title was changed to the Baptist Union of Great Britain.

Baptists emphasize the complete independence of the local church, although individual churches are linked in various kinds of associations. There are international bodies (such as the Baptist World Alliance) and national bodies, but many Baptist churches belong to neither. However, in Great Britain the majority of churches and associations belong to the Baptist Union of Great Britain. There are also Baptist Unions in Wales, Scotland and Ireland which are much smaller than the Baptist Union of Great Britain, and there is some overlap of membership.

There are over 38 million Baptist church members worldwide; in the Baptist Union of Great Britain there are 160,800 members, 1,585 pastors and 2,000 churches. In the Baptist

Union of Scotland there are 16,212 members, 130 pastors and 166 churches. In the Baptist Union of Wales there are 27,700 members, 117 pastors and 560 churches. In the Baptist Union of Ireland there are 8,505 members, 72 pastors and 103 churches.

President of the Baptist Union of Great Britain (1992–3), Revd E. J. Westwood

General Secretary, Revd D. R. Coffey, Baptist House, PO Box 44, 129 Broadway, Didcot, Oxon. OX11 8RT. Tel: 0235-512077

THE CHURCH OF CHRIST, SCIENTIST

The Church of Christ, Scientist, was founded by Mary Baker Eddy in the United States of America in 1879 to 'reinstate primitive Christianity and its lost element of healing'. Christian Science is concerned with spiritual regeneration and salvation from sin, but is best known for its reliance on prayer alone in the healing of sickness. Adherents believe that such healing is in direct line with that practised by Jesus Christ (revered, not as God, but as the Son of God) and by the early Christian Church.

The denomination consists of the First Church of Christ, Scientist, in Boston, Massachusetts, USA (the Mother Church) and its branch churches in over 60 countries world-wide. Branch churches are democratically governed by their members. There is also a five-member Board of Directors which oversees Church matters. There are no clergy. Those engaged in full-time healing ministry are called practitioners, of whom there are 3,500 world-wide.

No membership figures are available, since Mary Baker Eddy felt that numbers are no measure of spiritual vitality and ruled that such statistics should not be published. There are over 2,500 branch churches world-wide, including 210 in the United Kingdom.

CHRISTIAN SCIENCE COMMITTEE ON PUBLICATION, 108 Palace Gardens Terrace, London W8 4RT. Tel: 071-221 5650. *District Manager for Great Britain and Ireland*, G. Phaup

THE CONGREGATIONAL FEDERATION

The Congregational Federation was founded by members of Congregational churches in England and Wales who did not join the United Reformed Church (q.v.) in 1972. There are also churches in Scotland and Australia. The Federation exists to encourage congregations of believers to worship in free assembly, but has no authority over them and emphasizes their right to independence and self-government.

The Federation has 9,515 members, 116 ministers, 38 pastors, about 270 lay preachers and 282 churches.

President of the Federation (1992–3), Revd A. Avent

General Secretary, G. M. Adams, The Congregational Centre, 4 Castle Gate, Nottingham NG1 7AS. Tel: 0602-413801

FREE CHURCH OF ENGLAND

The Free Church of England, also known as the Reformed Episcopal Church, traces its beginnings to a dispute over the influence of the Oxford Movement in the established church between the Bishop of Exeter and one of his clergy, James Shore, in 1843. The Church defined its beliefs in 1863, accepting the Church of England's Thirty-Nine Articles and recognizing the legitimacy of the principle of episcopacy. Although its government was at first presbyterian, the Church later became affiliated to the Reformed Episcopal Church in the USA (a connection which has not been maintained) and adopted episcopal organization.

The Free Church of England has 1,700 members, 35 ministers and 30 churches in England. It also has three churches and three ministers in New Zealand, and one church and one minister in St Petersburg, Russia.

General Secretary, Rt. Revd A. Ward, 28 Sedgebrook, Liden, Swindon, Wilts. SN3 6EY. Tel: 0793-695838

THE FREE CHURCH OF SCOTLAND

The Free Church of Scotland was formed in 1843 when over 400 ministers withdrew from the Church of Scotland as a result of interference in the internal affairs of the church by the civil authorities. In 1900, all but 26 ministers joined with others to form the United Free Church (most of which rejoined the Church of Scotland in 1929). In 1904 the remaining 26 ministers were recognized by the House of Lords as continuing the Free Church of Scotland.

The Church maintains strict adherence to the Westminster Confession of Faith (1648) and accepts the Bible as the sole rule of faith and conduct. Its General Assembly meets annually. It also has links with Reformed Churches overseas. The Free Church of Scotland has about 18,000 members, 100 ministers and 120 churches.

General Treasurer, I. D. Gill, The Mound, Edinburgh EH1 2LS. Tel: 031-226 5286

THE FREE PRESBYTERIAN CHURCH OF SCOTLAND

The Free Presbyterian Church of Scotland was formed in 1893 by two ministers of the Free Church of Scotland who refused to accept a Declaratory Act passed by the Free Church General Assembly in 1892. The Free Presbyterian Church of Scotland is Calvinistic in doctrine and emphasizes observance of the Sabbath. It adheres strictly to the Westminster Confession of Faith of 1648.

The Church has 5,000 members, 23 ministers and 34 churches.

Moderator, Revd D. MacLean, 104 Barronald Drive, Glasgow G12 0HE. Tel: 041-357 2315

Clerk of Synod, Revd D. B. MacLeod, 8 Colinton Road, Edinburgh EH10 5DS. Tel: 031-447 1920

THE INDEPENDENT METHODIST CHURCHES

The Independent Methodist Churches seceded from the Wesleyan Methodist Church in 1805 and remained independent when the Methodist Church in Great Britain was formed in 1932. They are mainly concentrated in the industrial areas of the north of England.

The churches are Methodist in doctrine but their organization is congregational. All the churches are members of the Independent Methodist Connexion of Churches. The controlling body of the Connexion is the Annual Meeting, to which churches send delegates. The Connexional President is elected annually. Between annual meetings the affairs of the Connexion are handled by departmental committees. Ministers are appointed by the churches and trained through the Connexion, but are not titled 'Reverend'. The ministry is open to both men and women and is unpaid.

There are 3,600 members, 132 ministers and 106 churches in Great Britain.

Connexional President (1992–3), W. K. Sewell
General Secretary, Revd J. M. Day, The Old Police House, Croxton, Stafford ST21 6PE. Tel: 063-082 671

THE LUTHERAN CHURCH

Lutheranism is based on the teachings of Martin Luther, the German leader of the Protestant Reformation. The authority of the scriptures is held to be supreme over Church tradition and creeds, and the key doctrine is that of justification by faith alone.

Lutheranism is one of the largest Protestant denominations and it is particularly strong in northern Europe and the USA. Some Lutheran churches are episcopal, while others have a synodal form of organization; unity is based on doctrine rather than structure. Most Lutheran churches are members of the Lutheran World Federation, based in Geneva.

Lutheran services in Great Britain are held in many languages to serve members of different nationalities. English-language congregations are members either of the Lutheran Church in Great Britain–United Synod, or of the Evangelical Lutheran Church of England. The United Synod and most of the various national congregations are members of the Lutheran Council of Great Britain.

There are over 70 million Lutherans world-wide; in Great Britain there are 27,000 members, 45 ministers and 100 churches.

Chairman of the Lutheran Council of Great Britain, Very Revd R. J. Patkai, 8 Collingham Gardens, London SW5 0HW. Tel: 071-373 1141

THE METHODIST CHURCH

The Methodist movement started in England in 1729 when the Revd John Wesley, an Anglican priest, and his brother Charles met with others in Oxford and resolved to conduct their lives and study by 'rule and method'. In 1739 the Wesleys began evangelistic preaching and the first Methodist chapel was founded in Bristol in the same year. In 1744 the first annual conference was held, at which the Articles of Religion were drawn up. Doctrinal emphases included repentance, faith, the assurance of salvation, social concern and the priesthood of all believers. After John Wesley's death in 1791 the Methodists withdrew from the established Church to form the Methodist Church. Methodists gradually drifted into many groups, but in 1932 the Wesleyan Methodist Church, the United Methodist Church and the Primitive Methodist Church united to form the Methodist Church in Great Britain as it now exists.

The governing body and supreme authority of the Methodist Church is the Conference, but there are also 33 district synods, consisting of all the ministers and selected lay people in each district, and circuit meetings of the ministers and lay people of each circuit.

There are over 54 million Methodists world-wide; in Great Britain (1989 figures) there are 431,549 members, 3,514 ministers, 10,359 lay preachers and 7,207 churches.

President of the Conference in Great Britain (1992–3), Revd K. M. Richardson
Vice-President of the Conference (1992–3), E. I. Marshall
Secretary of the Conference, Revd B. E. Beck, Methodist Church, Conference Office, 1 Central Buildings, Storeys Gate, London SW1H 9NH. Tel: 071-222 8010

THE METHODIST CHURCH IN IRELAND

The Methodist Church in Ireland is closely linked to British Methodism but is autonomous. It has 19,217 members, 196 ministers, 296 lay preachers and 234 churches.

President of the Conference in Ireland (1992–3), Revd J. D. H. Ritchie
Secretary of the Conference in Ireland, Revd E. T. I. Mawhinney, 1 Fountainville Avenue, Belfast BT9 6AN. Tel: 0232-324554

THE ORTHODOX CHURCH

The Orthodox Church (or Eastern Orthodox Church) is a communion of self-governing Christian churches recognizing the honorary primacy of the Oecumenical Patriarch of Constantinople.

In the first millennium of the Christian era the faith was slowly formulated. Between AD 325 and 787 there were seven Oecumenical Councils at which bishops from the entire Christian world assembled to resolve various doctrinal disputes which had arisen. The estrangement between East and West began after Constantine moved the centre of the Roman Empire from Rome to Constantinople, and it gained momentum after the temporal administration was divided. Linguistic and cultural differences between Greek East and Latin West served to encourage separate ecclesiastical developments which became pronounced in the tenth and early eleventh centuries.

The administration of the church was divided between five ancient patriarchates: Rome and all the West, Constantinople (the imperial city – the 'New Rome'), Jerusalem and all Palestine, Antioch and all the East, and Alexandria and all Africa. Of these, only Rome was in the Latin West and after the Great Schism in 1054, Rome developed a structure of authority centralized on one source, the Papacy, while the Orthodox East maintained the style of localized administration.

To the older patriarchates were later added the Patriarchates of Russia, Georgia, Serbia, Bulgaria and Romania. The Orthodox Church also includes autocephalous (self-governing) national churches in Greece, Cyprus, Poland, Albania, Czechoslovakia and Sinai, and autonomous national churches in Finland and Japan. The Estonian and Latvian Orthodox Churches are in practice part of the Moscow Patriarchate. The Belorussians and Ukrainians have recently been given greater autonomy by Moscow, but some Ukrainians have broken away to establish an independent Ukrainian Patriarchate. In Macedonia the local hierarchy has declared itself independent of the Serbian Patriarchate. The Russian dioceses in the diaspora fall into four groups: those under the direct control of the Moscow Patriarchate; the Russian Orthodox Church Outside Russia, sometimes known as the Synod in Exile; the Russian Archdiocese centred at the cathedral in rue Daru, Paris, which is part of the Patriarchate in Constantinople; and the Orthodox Church in America, which was granted autocephalous status in 1970.

The position of Orthodox Christians is that the faith was

fully defined during the period of the Oecumenical Councils. In doctrine it is strongly trinitarian, and stresses the mystery and importance of the sacraments. It is episcopal in government. The structure of the Orthodox Christian year differs from that of Western Churches (*see* page 83).

Orthodox Christians throughout the world are estimated to number about 150 million.

PATRIARCHS

Archbishop of Constantinople, New Rome and Oecumenical Patriarch, Bartholomew, *elected* 1991

Pope and Patriarch of Alexandria and All Africa, Parthenios III, *elected* 1987

Patriarch of Antioch and All the East, Ignatios IV, *elected* 1979

Patriarch of Jerusalem and All Palestine, Diodoros, *elected* 1981

Patriarch of Moscow and All Russia, Alexei II, *elected* 1990

Archbishop of Tbilisi and Mtskheta, Catholicos-Patriarch of All Georgia, Ilia II, *elected* 1977

Archbishop of Pec, Metropolitan of Belgrade and Karlovci, Patriarch of Serbia, Paul, *elected* 1990

Archbishop of Bucharest and Patriarch of Romania, Teoctist, *elected* 1986

Metropolitan of Sofia and Patriarch of Bulgaria, Maxim, *elected* 1971

Patriarch of Kiev and All Ukraine, Mstyslav, *elected* 1990 (not officially recognized by other national Orthodox churches)

ORTHODOX CHURCHES IN THE UK

THE GREEK ORTHODOX CHURCH (PATRIARCHATE OF CONSTANTINOPLE)

The presence of Greek Orthodox Christians in Britain dates back to 1677 when Archbishop Joseph Geogirenes of Samos fled from Turkish persecution and came to London, where a church was built for him in Soho. The present Greek cathedral in Moscow Road, Bayswater, was opened for public worship in 1879 and the Diocese of Thyateira and Great Britain was established in 1922. There are now 87 parishes in Great Britain, served by eight bishops and 87 churches.

In Great Britain the Patriarchate of Constantinople is represented by Archbishop Gregorios of Thyateira and Great Britain, 5 Craven Hill, London W2 3EN. Tel: 071–723 4787.

THE RUSSIAN ORTHODOX CHURCH (PATRIARCHATE OF MOSCOW) AND THE RUSSIAN ORTHODOX CHURCH OUTSIDE RUSSIA

The earliest records of Russian Orthodox Church activities in Britain date from the visit to England of Tsar Peter I at the beginning of the 18th century. Clergy were sent from Russia to serve the chapel established to minister to the staff of the Imperial Russian Embassy in London.

After 1917 the Church of Russia was persecuted. The Patriarch of Moscow, St Tikhon the New Martyr, anathematized both the atheistic persecutors of the Church and all who collaborated with them. Because of the civil war normal administrative contact with Russian Orthodox Christians outside the country was impossible, and he therefore authorized the establishment of a higher church administration, i.e. a synod in exile, by Russian bishops who were then outside Russia. This is the origin of the Russian Orthodox Church Outside Russia. The attitude of the Church of Russia to the former Soviet regime was always a source of contention between the two hierarchies; tensions are now lessening but remain unresolved.

In Britain the Patriarchate of Moscow is represented by Metropolitan Anthony of Sourozh, 67 Ennismore Gardens, London SW7 1NH. Tel: 071-584 0096. There are 15 parishes, with two bishops and 13 priests.

The Russian Orthodox Church Outside Russia is represented by Archbishop Mark of Richmond and Great Britain (who is also Archbishop of Berlin and Germany), 14 St Dunstan's Road, London W6 8RB. Tel: 081-748 4232. There are eight parishes and two monasteries, served by six priests.

THE SERBIAN ORTHODOX CHURCH (PATRIARCHATE OF SERBIA)

There was a small congregation of Orthodox Christian Serbs in London before the Second World War, but most Serbian parishes in Britain have been established since 1945. There is no resident bishop as the parishes are part of the Serbian Orthodox Diocese of Western Europe, which has its centre in Germany. There are five main parishes in Britain and several smaller communities served by seven priests.

In Britain the Patriarchate of Serbia is represented by the Episcopal Vicar, the Very Revd Milun Kostic, 89 Lancaster Road, London W11 1QQ. Tel: 071-727 8367.

OTHER NATIONALITIES

Latvian, Polish and some Belorussian Orthodox parishes in Britain are under the care of the Patriarchate of Constantinople. The Patriarchates of Antioch, Bulgaria and Romania are represented by one priest each. Both the Ukrainian Autocephalous Orthodox Church and the Belorussian Autocephalic Orthodox Church have a few parishes in Britain.

ORTHODOX CHURCH PUBLIC RELATIONS OFFICE, St George Orthodox Information Service, 64 Prebend Gardens, London W6 0XU. Tel: 081-741 9624. *Secretary*, A. Bond.

PENTECOSTAL CHURCHES

Pentecostalism is inspired by the descent of the Holy Spirit upon the apostles at Pentecost. The movement began in Los Angeles, USA, in 1906 and is characterized by baptism with the Holy Spirit, faith healing, speaking in tongues (glossolalia), and a literal interpretation of the scriptures. The Pentecostal movement in Britain dates from 1907. Initially, groups of Pentecostalists were led by laymen and did not organize formally. However, in 1915 the Elim Foursquare Gospel Alliance (more usually called the Elim Pentecostal Church) was founded in Ireland by George Jeffreys and in 1924 about 70 independent assemblies formed a fellowship, the Assemblies of God in Great Britain and Ireland. The Apostolic Church grew out of the 1904–5 revivals in south Wales and was established in 1916, and the New Testament Church of God was established in England in 1953. In recent years many aspects of Pentecostalism have been adopted by the growing charismatic movement within the Roman Catholic Church and Protestant and Eastern Orthodox churches.

There are about 22 million Pentecostalists world-wide, with about 115,000 adult adherents in Great Britain and Ireland.

THE APOSTOLIC CHURCH, International Administration Offices, PO Box 389, 24–27 St Helens Road, Swansea, West Glamorgan SA1 1ZH. Tel: 0792-473992. *President*, Pastor P. Cawthorne; *Administrator*, Pastor W. W. Morris. The Apostolic Church has about 130 churches, 5,500 adherents and 83 ministers.

THE ASSEMBLIES OF GOD IN GREAT BRITAIN AND IRELAND, General Offices, 106–114 Talbot Street, Nottingham NG1 5GH. Tel: 0602-474525. *General*

Superintendent, W. Shenton; *General Administrator*, B. D. Varnam. The Assemblies of God has about 608 churches, 70,000 adherents (including children) and 560 accredited ministers.

THE ELIM PENTECOSTAL CHURCH, PO Box 38, Cheltenham, Glos. GL50 3HN. Tel: 0242-519904. *General Superintendent*, Pastor I. W. Lewis; *Administrator*, Pastor B. Hunter. The Elim Pentecostal Church has about 430 churches, 35,000 adherents and 475 accredited ministers.

THE NEW TESTAMENT CHURCH OF GOD, Main House, Overstone Park, Overstone, Northampton NN6 0AD. Tel: 0604-645944. *National Overseer*, Revd Dr S. E. Arnold. The New Testament Church of God has 106 organized congregations, 7,042 baptized members, about 20,000 adherents and 216 accredited ministers.

THE PRESBYTERIAN CHURCH IN IRELAND

The Presbyterian Church in Ireland is Calvinistic in doctrine and presbyterian in constitution. Presbyterianism was established in Ireland as a result of the Ulster plantation in the early 17th century, when English and Scottish Protestants settled in the north of Ireland.

There are 21 presbyteries and five regional synods under the chief court known as the General Assembly. The General Assembly meets annually and is presided over by a Moderator who is elected for one year. The ongoing work of the Church is undertaken by 18 boards under which there are a number of specialist committees.

There are about 330,000 Presbyterians in Ireland, mainly in the north, in 562 congregations and with 400 ministers.

Moderator (1992–3), Rt. Revd Dr J. Dunlop

Clerk of Assembly and General Secretary, Revd S. Hutchinson, Church House, Belfast BT1 6DW. Tel: 0232-322284

THE PRESBYTERIAN CHURCH OF WALES

The Presbyterian Church of Wales or Calvinistic Methodist Church of Wales is Calvinistic in doctrine and presbyterian in constitution. It was formed in 1811 when Welsh Calvinists severed the relationship with the established church by ordaining their own ministers. It secured its own confession of faith in 1823 and a Constitutional Deed in 1826, and since 1864 the General Assembly has met annually, presided over by a Moderator elected for a year. The doctrine and constitutional structure of the Presbyterian Church of Wales was confirmed by Act of Parliament in 1931–2.

The Church has 59,815 members, 127 ministers and 1,012 churches.

Moderator (1992–3), Dr A. Hughes, OBE

General Secretary, Revd D. H. Owen, 53 Richmond Road, Cardiff CF2 3UP. Tel: 0222-494913

THE RELIGIOUS SOCIETY OF FRIENDS (QUAKERS)

Quakerism is a movement, not a church, which was founded in the 17th century by George Fox and others in an attempt to revive what they saw as 'primitive Christianity'. The movement was based originally in the Midlands, Yorkshire and north-west England, but there are now Quakers in 36 countries around the world. The colony of Pennsylvania, founded by William Penn, was originally Quaker.

Emphasis is placed on the experience of God in daily life rather than on sacraments or religious occasions. There is no church calendar. Worship is largely silent and there are no appointed ministers; the responsibility for conducting a meeting is shared equally among those present. Social reform and religious tolerance have always been important to Quakers, together with a commitment to non-violence in resolving disputes.

There are 213,800 Quakers world-wide, with 18,070 in Great Britain and Ireland. There are 464 meeting houses in Great Britain.

CENTRAL OFFICES: (GREAT BRITAIN) Friends House, Euston Road, London NW1 2BJ. Tel: 071-387 3601; (IRELAND) Swanbrook House, Morehampton Road, Dublin 4. Tel: 0001-683684

THE SALVATION ARMY

The Salvation Army was founded by a Methodist minister, William Booth, in the east end of London in 1865, and has since become established in 94 countries world-wide. It was first known as the Christian Mission, and took its present name in 1878 when it adopted a quasi-military command structure intended to inspire and regulate its endeavours and to reflect its view that the Church was engaged in spiritual warfare. Salvationists emphasize evangelism, social work and the relief of poverty.

The world leader, known as the General, is elected by a High Council composed of the Chief of Staff and senior ranking officers known as commissioners.

There are about 1.5 million soldiers, 16,907 active officers (full-time ordained ministers) and 14,248 corps (churches) world-wide. In Great Britain and Ireland there are 55,000 soldiers, 1,792 active officers and 837 corps.

International Leader, Eva Burrows.

UK Territorial Commander, Commissioner John Larsson.

INTERNATIONAL AND TERRITORIAL HEADQUARTERS, PO Box 249, 101 Queen Victoria Street, London EC4P 4EP. Tel: 071-236 5222

THE SEVENTH-DAY ADVENTIST CHURCH

The Seventh-day Adventist Church was founded in 1863 in the USA. Its members look forward to the second coming of Christ and observe the Sabbath as a day of rest, worship and ministry. The Church bases its faith and practice wholly on the Bible and has developed 27 fundamental beliefs.

The World Church is divided into 12 divisions, each made up of unions of churches. The Seventh-day Adventist Church in the British Isles is known as the British Union of Seventh-day Adventists and is a member of the Trans-European

Division. In the British Isles the administrative organization of the church is arranged in three tiers: the local churches; the regional conferences for south England, north England, Wales, Scotland and Ireland, which are held every three years; and the national 'union' conference which is held every five years.

There are over 6 million Adventists and 25,000 churches in 190 countries world-wide. In the United Kingdom and Ireland there are 17,873 members, 153 ministers and 241 churches.

President of the British Union Conference (1991–6), Pastor C. Perry.

BRITISH ISLES HEADQUARTERS, Stanborough Park, Watford WD2 6JP. Tel: 0923-672251

UNDEB YR ANNIBYNWYR CYMRAEG

The Union of Welsh Independents

The Union of Welsh Independents was formed in 1872 and is a voluntary association of Welsh Congregational Churches and personal members. It is entirely Welsh-speaking. Congregationalism in Wales dates back to 1639 when the first Welsh Congregational Church was opened in Gwent. Member Churches are Calvinistic in doctrine and congregationalist in organization. Each church has complete independence in the government and administration of its affairs.

The Union has 49,915 members, 120 ministers and 625 chapels.

President of the Union (1992–3), Revd Dr E. S. John

General Secretary, Revd D. Morris Jones, Tŷ John Penry, 11 Heol Sant Helen, Swansea SA1 4AL. Tel: 0792-467040

UNITARIAN AND FREE CHRISTIAN CHURCHES

Unitarianism has its historical roots in the Judaeo-Christian tradition but denies the divinity of Christ and the doctrine of the trinity. It allows the individual to embrace insights from all the world's faiths and philosophies, as there is no formal creed. It is accepted that beliefs may evolve in the light of personal experience.

Unitarian communities first became established in Poland and Transylvania in the 16th century. The first avowedly Unitarian place of worship in the British Isles opened in London in 1774. The General Assembly of Unitarian and Free Christian Churches came into existence in 1928 as the result of the amalgamation of two earlier organizations.

There are about 10,000 Unitarians in Great Britain and Ireland, and 150 Unitarian ministers. About 250 self-governing congregations and fellowship groups, including a small number overseas, are members of the General Assembly.

GENERAL ASSEMBLY OF UNITARIAN AND FREE CHRISTIAN CHURCHES, Essex Hall, 1–6 Essex Street, Strand, London WC2R 3HY. Tel: 071-240 2384. *General Secretary*, Dr R. W. Smith

THE UNITED REFORMED CHURCH

The United Reformed Church was formed by the union of most of the Congregational churches in England and Wales with the Presbyterian Church of England in 1972.

Congregationalism dates from the mid 16th century. It is Calvinistic in doctrine, and its followers form independent self-governing congregations bound under God by covenant, a principle laid down in the writings of Robert Browne (1550–1633). From the late 16th century the movement was driven underground by persecution, but the cause was defended at the Westminster Assembly in 1643 and the Savoy Declaration of 1658 laid down its principles. Congregational churches formed county associations for mutual support and in 1832 these associations merged to form the Congregational Union of England and Wales.

The Presbyterian Church in England also dates from the mid 16th century, and was Calvinistic and evangelical in its doctrine. It was governed by a hierarchy of courts.

In the 1960s there was close co-operation locally and nationally between Congregational and Presbyterian Churches. This led to union negotiations and a Scheme of Union, supported by Act of Parliament in 1972. In 1981 a further unification took place, with the Reformed Association of Churches of Christ becoming part of the URC. In its basis the United Reformed Church reflects local church initiative and responsibility with a conciliar pattern of oversight. The General Assembly is the central body, and is made up of equal numbers of ministers and lay members.

The United Reformed Church is divided into 12 Provinces, each with a Provincial Moderator who chairs the Synod, and 70 Districts. There are 126,000 members, 730 full-time ministers and 1,800 local churches.

General Secretary of the United Reformed Church, Revd A. G. Burnham, 86 Tavistock Place, London WC1H 9RT. Tel: 071-916 2020

THE WESLEYAN REFORM UNION

The Wesleyan Reform Union was founded by Methodists who left or were expelled from Wesleyan Methodism in 1849 following a period of internal conflict. Its doctrine is Methodist but its organization is congregational, each church having complete independence in the government and administration of its affairs. The main concentration of churches is in Yorkshire.

The Union has 2,804 members, 20 ministers, 142 lay preachers and 124 churches.

President (1992–3), The Revd A. J. Williams.

General Secretary, Revd E. W. Downing, Wesleyan Reform Church House, 123 Queen Street, Sheffield S1 2DU. Tel: 0742-721928

Non-Christian Faiths

Buddhism

Buddhism originated in northern India, in the teachings of Siddharta Gautama, who was born near Kapilavastu about 560 BC. After a long spiritual quest he experienced enlightenment beneath a tree at the place now known as Bodhgaya, and began missionary work.

Fundamental to Buddhism is the concept that there is no such thing as a permanent soul or self; when someone dies, consciousness is the only one of the elements of which they were composed which is lost. All the other elements regroup in a new body and carry with them the consequences of the conduct of the earlier life (known as the law of *karma*). This cycle of death and rebirth is broken only when the state of *nirvana* has been reached. Buddhism steers a middle path between belief in personal immortality and belief in death as the final end.

The Four Noble Truths of Buddhism (*dukkha*, suffering; *tanha*, a thirst or desire for continued existence which causes dukkha; *nirvana*, the final liberation from desire and ignorance; and *ariya*, the path to nirvana) are all held to be universal and to sum up the *dhamma* or true nature of life. Necessary qualities to promote spiritual development are *sila* (morality), *samadhi* (meditation) and *panna* (wisdom).

There are two main schools of Buddhism: *Theravada* Buddhism, the earliest extant school, which is more traditional, and *Mahayana* Buddhism, which began to develop about 100 years after the Buddha's death and is more liberal; it teaches that all people may attain Buddahood. Important schools which have developed within Mahayana Buddhism are *Zen* Buddhism, *Nichiren* Buddhism and Pure Land Buddhism or *Amidism*. There are also distinctive Tibetan forms of Buddhism. Buddhism began to establish itself in the West at the beginning of the 20th century.

The scripture of Theravada Buddhism is the *Pali Canon*, which dates from the first century BC. Mahayana Buddhism uses a Sanskrit version of the Pali Canon but also has many other works of scripture.

There is no set time for Buddhist worship, which may take place in a temple or in the home. Worship centres around *paritta* (chanting), acts of devotion centring on the image of the Buddha, and, where possible, offerings to a relic of the Buddha. Buddhist festivals vary according to local traditions and within Theravada and Mahayana Buddhism. For religious purposes Buddhists use solar and lunar calendars, the New Year being celebrated in April. Other festivals mark events in the life of the Buddha.

There is no supreme governing authority in Buddhism. In the United Kingdom communities representing all schools of Buddhism have developed and operate independently. The Buddhist Society was established in 1924; it runs courses and lectures, and publishes books about Buddhism. It represents no one school of Buddhism.

There are estimated to be at least 300 million Buddhists world-wide, with about 200 groups, an estimated 25,000 adherents and 15 temples or monasteries in the United Kingdom.

THE BUDDHIST SOCIETY, 58 Eccleston Square, London SW1V 1PH. Tel: 071-834 5858. *General Secretary*, R. C. Maddox

Hinduism

Hinduism has no historical founder but is known to have been highly developed in India by about 1200 BC. Its adherents originally called themselves Aryans; Muslim invaders first called the Aryans 'Hindus' (derived from the word 'Sindhu', the name of the river Indus) in the eighth century.

Hinduism's evolution has been complex and it embraces many different religious beliefs, mythologies and practices. Most Hindus hold that *satya* (truthfulness), *ahimsa* (non-violence), honesty, physical labour and tolerance of other faiths are essential for good living. They believe in one supreme spirit (*Brahman*), and in the transmigration of *atman* (the soul). Most Hindus accept the doctrine of *karma* (consequences of actions), the concept of *samsara* (successive lives) and the possibility of all atmans achieving *moksha* (liberation from samsara) through *jnana* (knowledge), *yoga* (meditation), *karma* (work or action) and *bhakti* (devotion).

Most Hindus offer worship to *murtis* (images or statues) representing different aspects of Brahman, and follow their *dharma* (religious and social duty) according to the traditions of their *varna* (social class), *ashrama* (stage in life), *jati* (caste) and *kula* (family).

Hinduism's sacred texts are divided into *shruti* ('heard' or divinely inspired), including the *Vedas*; or *smriti* ('remembered' tradition), including the *Ramayana*, the *Mahabharata*, the *Puranas* (ancient myths), and the sacred law books. Most Hindus recognize the authority of the *Vedas*, the oldest holy books, and accept the philosophical teachings of the *Upanishads*, the *Vedanta Sutras* and the *Bhagavad-Gita*.

Brahman is formless, limitless and all-pervading, and is represented in worship by murtis which may be male or female and in the form of a human, animal or bird. Brahma, Vishnu and Shiva are the most important gods worshipped by Hindus; their respective consorts are Saraswati, Lakshmi and Durga or Parvati, also known as Shakti. There are held to have been ten *avatars* (incarnations) of Vishnu, of whom the most important are Rama and Krishna. Other popular gods are Ganesha, Hanuman and Subrahmanyam. All gods are seen as aspects of the supreme God, not as competing deities.

Orthodox Hindus revere all gods and goddesses equally, but there are many sects, including the Hare-Krishna movement (ISKCon), the Arya Samaj, the Swami Narayan Hindu mission and the Satya Sai-Baba movement. Worship in the sects is concentrated on one deity to the exclusion of others. In some sects a human *guru* (spiritual teacher), usually the head of the organization, is revered more than the deity, while in other sects the guru is seen as the source of spiritual guidance.

Hinduism does not have a centrally-trained and ordained priesthood. The pronouncements of the *shankaracharyas* (heads of monasteries) of Shringeri, Puri, Dwarka and Badrinath are heeded by the orthodox but may be ignored by the various sects.

The commonest form of worship is a *puja*, in which offerings of red and yellow powders, rice grains, water, flowers, food, fruit, incense and light are made to the image of a deity. Puja may be done either in a home shrine or a *mandir* (temple). For details of the Hindu calendar, main festivals etc, *see* pages 85–6.

The largest communities of Hindus in Britain are in Leicester, London, Birmingham and Bradford, and developed as a result of immigration from India, east Africa and Sri Lanka. Many Hindus now are British by birth, with English as their first language; the main ethnic languages are Gujarati, Hindi, Punjabi, Tamil, Bengali and Marathi.

There are an estimated 650 million Hindus world-wide; there are about 350,000 adherents and over 150 temples in the UK.

ARYA PRATINIDHI SABHA (UK), 69A Argyle Road, London W13 0LY

BHARATIYA VIDYA BHAVAN, Old Church Building, 4 Castletown Road, London W14 9HE. Tel: 071-381 3036

INTERNATIONAL SOCIETY FOR KRISHNA CONSCIOUSNESS (ISKCon), Bhakti Vedanta Manor, Radlett, Herts. Tel: 0923-857244

NATIONAL COUNCIL OF HINDU TEMPLES, 559 St Alban's Road, Watford, Herts. WD2 6JH

SWAMI NARAYAN HINDU MISSION, 54 Meadow Garth, London NW10 8HD. Tel: 081-965 2651

VISHVA HINDU PARISHAD (UK), 5 Rosemary Drive Redbridge, Ilford, Essex IG4 5JD

Islam

Islam (which means 'peace arising from submission to the wisdom of Allah' in Arabic) is a monotheistic religion which originated in Arabia through the prophet Muhammad, who was born in Mecca in AD 570. Islam spread to Egypt, North Africa, Spain and the borders of China in the century following the prophet's death, and is now the predominant religion in Indonesia, the Near and Middle East, North Africa, Pakistan, Bangladesh and Malaysia. There are also large Muslim communities in many other countries.

For Muslims (adherents of Islam), God (*Allah*) is one and holds absolute power. His commands were revealed to mankind through the prophets, who include Abraham, Moses and Jesus, but his message was gradually corrupted until revealed finally and in perfect form to Muhammad by the angel *Jibril* (Gabriel) over a period of 23 years. This last, incorruptible message has been recorded in the *Qur'an* (Koran), which contains 114 divisions called *surahs*, each made up of *ayahs*, and is held to be the essence of all previous scriptures. The *Hadith* is the record of the prophet Muhammad's deeds and sayings (the *Sunnah*) as recounted by his immediate followers. A culture and a system of law and theology based on the Hadith and the Qur'an gradually developed to form a distinctive Islamic civilization. Islam makes no distinction between sacred and worldly affairs and provides rules for every aspect of human life.

The 'five pillars of Islam' are *shahada* (a declaration of faith in the oneness and supremacy of Allah); *salat* (formal prayer, to be performed five times a day facing the holy city of Mecca); *zakat* (alms-giving); *saum* (fasting during the month of Ramadan); and *hajj* (pilgrimage to Mecca); some Muslims would add *jihad* (striving for the cause of good and resistance to evil). Together with other prescriptions, the five pillars make up the *Shari'a* (sacred law) of Islam.

Two main groups, with distinct legal and theological characteristics, developed among Muslims. *Sunni* Muslims accept the legitimacy of Muhammad's first three *caliphs* (successors) and of the authority of the community of Muslims as a whole. About 90 per cent of Muslims are *Sunni* Muslims. *Shi'ites* recognize Muhammad's son-in-law Ali as his rightful successor and the *Imams* (descendants of Ali, not to be confused with *imams* (prayer leaders or religious teachers)) as the principal legitimate religious authority. The largest group within *Shi'ism* is *Twelver Shi'ism*, which has been the official religion of Iran since the 16th century, and other subsects include the *Ismailis* and the *Druze* (the latter being an offshoot of the Ismailis and differing considerably from the main body of Muslims).

There is no organized priesthood, but holy men such as *ulama*, *imams* and *ayatollahs* are accorded great respect. The *Sufis* are the mystics of Islam. Mosques are centres for worship and teaching and also for social and welfare activities. For details of the Muslim calendar, *see* page 87.

Islam was first known in western Europe in the eighth century AD when 800 years of Muslim rule began in Spain. Later, Islam spread to eastern Europe. More recently, Muslims came to Europe from Africa, the Middle East and Asia in the late 19th century. Both the Sunni and Shi'a traditions are represented in Britain, but the majority of Muslims belong to the *Barelvi* movement, a branch of Sunni Islam.

The largest communities are in London, Liverpool, Manchester, Birmingham, Bradford, Cardiff, Edinburgh and Glasgow. There is no central organization, but the Islamic Cultural Centre, which is the London Central Mosque, and the Imams and Mosques Council are influential bodies; there are many other Muslim organizations in Britain.

There are at least 700 million Muslims world-wide. The estimated number of adherents in Britain is between one and two million, with over 300 mosques.

ISLAMIC CULTURAL CENTRE, 146 Park Road, London NW8 7RG. Tel: 071-724 3363. *Director*, Dr M. A. al-Ghamdi

IMAMS AND MOSQUES COUNCIL, 20–22 Creffield Road, London W5 3RP. Tel: 081-992 6636. *Director of the Council and Principal of the Muslim College*, Dr M. A. Z. Badawi

Judaism

Judaism is the oldest monotheistic faith. The Hebrew Bible, which records how the descendants of Abraham were led by Moses out of their slavery in Egypt to Mount Sinai where God's law (*Torah*) was revealed to them as the chosen people, is the primary authority of Judaism. The *Talmud*, which consists of commentaries on the *Mishnah* (the first text of rabbinical Judaism), is also held to be authoritative, and may be divided into two main categories: the *halakah* (dealing with legal and ritual matters) and the *Aggadah* (dealing with theological and ethical matters not directly concerned with the regulation of conduct). The *halakah* has become a source of division; Orthodox Jews regard Jewish law as derived from God and therefore unalterable; Reform and Liberal Jews seek to interpret it in the light of contemporary considerations; and Conservative Jews aim to maintain most of the traditional rituals but to allow changes in accordance with that tradition. Reconstructionist Judaism, a 20th century movement, regards Judaism as a culture rather than a theological system and therefore accepts all forms of Jewish practice.

The family is the basic unit of Jewish ritual, with the synagogue playing an important role as the centre for public worship and religious study. A synagogue is led by a group of laymen who are elected to office; there are no priestly roles. The Rabbi is primarily a teacher and spiritual guide. The Sabbath is the central religious observance. For details of the Jewish calendar, fasts and festivals, *see* page 86. Most British Jews are descendants of either the *Ashkenazim* of central and eastern Europe or the *Sephardim* of Spain and Portugal.

The Chief Rabbi of the United Hebrew Congregation and the Commonwealth is appointed by a Chief Rabbinate Conference, and is the rabbinical authority only to the Orthodox sector of the Ashkenazi Jewish community, whose main organization is the United Hebrew Congregation. His authority is not recognized by the Reform Synagogues of Great Britain (the largest progressive group), the Union of Liberal and Progressive Synagogues, the Union of Orthodox Hebrew Congregations, the Federation of Synagogues, the Sephardi community, or the Assembly of Masorti Synagogues. He is, however, generally recognized both outside the Jewish community and within it as the public religious representative of the totality of British Jewry.

The *Beth Din* (Court of Judgment) is the rabbinic court. The *Dayanim* (Assessors) adjudicate in disputes or on matters of Jewish law and tradition; they also oversee dietary law administration. The Chief Rabbi is President of the *Beth Din* of the United Synagogue.

The Board of Deputies of British Jews was established in 1760 and is the representative body of British Jewry. The basis of representation is mainly synagogal, but communal organizations are also represented. It watches over the interests of British Jewry and seeks to counter anti-Jewish discrimination.

There are over 12.5 million Jews world-wide; in Great Britain and Ireland there are an estimated 300,000 adherents and 356 synagogues. Of these, 207 congregations and about 150 rabbis and ministers are under the jurisdiction of the Chief Rabbi. A further 82 orthodox congregations have a more independent status, and 67 congregations do not recognize the authority of the Chief Rabbi.

Chief Rabbi, Dr Jonathan Sacks

BETH DIN (COURT OF THE CHIEF RABBI), Adler House, Tavistock Square, London WC1H 0EP. Tel: 071-387 5772. *Executive Director*, J. Kestenbaum; *Registrar*, J. Phillips; *Dayanim*, Rabbi C. Ehrentreu; Rabbi I. Binstock; Rabbi C. D. Kaplin; Rabbi I. D. Berger

UNITED SYNAGOGUE HEAD OFFICE, Woburn House, Upper Woburn Place, London WC1H 0EZ. Tel: 071-387 4300. *Chief Executive*, J. M. Lew

REFORM SYNAGOGUES OF GREAT BRITAIN, The Sternberg Centre, Manor House, 80 East End Road, London N3 2SY. Tel: 081-349 4731. *Executive Director*, R. M. Goldman

UNION OF LIBERAL AND PROGRESSIVE SYNAGOGUES (JEWISH RELIGIOUS UNION), 109 Whitfield Street, London W1P 5RP. Tel: 071-580 1663. *Director*, Mrs R. Rosenberg

UNION OF ORTHODOX HEBREW CONGREGATIONS, 40 Queen Elizabeth's Walk, London N16 0HH. Tel: 081-802 6226

FEDERATION OF SYNAGOGUES, 65 Watford Way, London NW4 3AQ. Tel: 081-202 2263. *Administrator*, G. Kushner

SEPHARDI COMMUNAL CENTRE, Montefiore Hall, 2 Ashworth Road, London W9 1JY. Tel: 071-289 2573

ASSEMBLY OF MASORTI SYNAGOGUES, 33 Abbey Road, London NW8 0AT. Tel: 071-624 0539

BOARD OF DEPUTIES OF BRITISH JEWS, Woburn House, Tavistock Square, London WC1H 0EZ. Tel: 071-387 3952). *President*, His Hon. I. Finestein, QC; *Chief Executive*, N. A. Nagler

Sikhism

The Sikh religion dates from the birth of Guru Nanak in the Punjab in 1469. The word 'guru' means 'teacher', but in Sikh tradition it has come to represent the divine presence of God giving inner spiritual guidance. Nanak's role as the human vessel of the divine guru was passed on to nine successors, the last of whom (Guru Gobind Singh) died in 1708. The immortal guru is now held to reside in the sacred scripture, *Guru Granth Sahib*, and so to be present in all Sikh gatherings.

Guru Nanak taught that there is one God and that different religions are like different roads leading to the same destination. He condemned religious conflict, ritualism and caste prejudices. The fifth Guru, Guru Arjan, compiled the Sikh Holy Book, a collection of hymns (*gurbani*) known as the *Adi Granth*. It contains the writings of the first five Gurus and selected writings of Hindu and Muslim saints whose views are in accord with the Guru's teachings. Guru Arjan also built the Golden Temple at Amritsar, the centre of Sikhism. The tenth Guru, Guru Gobind Singh, passed on the guruship to the sacred scripture, Guru Granth Sahib. He also founded the *Khalsa*, an order intended to fight against tyranny and injustice. Male initiates to the order added 'Singh' to their given names and women added 'Kaur'. Guru Gobind Singh also made five symbols obligatory: *kaccha* (a special undergarment), *kara* (a steel bangle), *kirpan* (a small sword), *kesh* (long unshorn hair, and consequently the wearing of a turban), and *kangha* (a comb). These practices are still compulsory for those Sikhs who are initiated into the *Khalsa* (the *Amritdharis*). Those who do not seek initiation are known as *Sahajdharis*.

There are no professional priests in Sikhism; anyone with a reasonable proficiency in the Punjabi language can conduct a service. Worship can be offered individually or communally, and in a private house or a *gurdwara* (temple). Sikhs are forbidden to eat meat prepared by ritual slaughter; they are also asked to abstain from smoking, alcohol and other intoxicants. There are no prescribed feast days and fasting is forbidden as a means of seeking salvation. The main celebrations are *Amrit* or *Baisakhi Mela* (the new year and the anniversary of the founding of the *Khalsa*), *Diwali Mela* (a festival of light), *Hola Mohalla Mela* (a spring festival held in the Punjab), and the *Gurpurbs* (anniversaries associated with the ten Gurus).

Sikhs first came to Britain in the 1950s, mainly for economic and political reasons. The largest Sikh communities are in London, Bradford, Leeds, Huddersfield, Birmingham, Nottingham, Coventry and Wolverhampton. Every gurdwara manages its own affairs and there is no central body. The Sikh Missionary Society UK works for the advancement of Sikhism and provides an information service.

There are about 12.5 million Sikhs world-wide and an estimated 400,000 adherents and 170 gurdwaras in Great Britain.

SIKH MISSIONARY SOCIETY UK, 10 Featherstone Road, Southall, Middx. UB2 5AA. Tel: 081-574 1902. *Hon. General Secretary*, H. S. Kular

Archbishops of Canterbury since 1414

Henry Chichele (1362–1443), translated 1414
John Stafford (?–1452), translated 1443
John Kemp (*c.*1380–1454), translated 1452
Thomas Bourchier (*c.*1410–86), translated 1454
John Morton (*c.*1420–1500), translated 1486
Henry Deane (?–1503), translated 1501
William Warham (1450–1532), translated 1503
Thomas Cranmer (1489–1556), translated 1533
Reginald Pole (1500–58), translated 1556
Matthew Parker (1504–75), translated 1559
Edmund Grindal (*c.* 1519–83), translated 1576
John Whitgift (*c.*1530–1604), translated 1583
Richard Bancroft (1544–1610), translated 1604
George Abbot (1562–1633), translated 1611
William Laud (1573–1645), translated 1633
William Juxon (1582–1663), translated 1660
Gilbert Sheldon (1598–1677), translated 1663
William Sancroft (1617–93), translated 1678
John Tillotson (1630–94), translated 1691
Thomas Tenison (1636–1715), translated 1695
William Wake (1657–1737), translated 1716
John Potter (*c.* 1674–1747), translated 1737
Thomas Herring (1693–1757), translated 1747
Matthew Hutton (1693–1758), translated 1757
Thomas Secker (1693–1768), translated 1758
Hon. Frederick Cornwallis (1713–83), translated 1768
John Moore (1730–1805), translated 1783
Charles Manners-Sutton (1755–1828), translated 1805
William Howley (1766–1848), translated 1828
John Bird Sumner (1780–1862), translated 1848
Charles Longley (1794–1868), translated 1862
Archibald Campbell Tait (1811–82), translated 1868
Edward White Benson (1829–96), translated 1883
Frederick Temple (1821–1902), translated 1896
Randall Thomas Davidson (1848–1930), translated 1903
Cosmo Gordon Lang (1864–1945), translated 1928
William Temple (1881–1944), translated 1942
Geoffrey Fisher (1887–1972), translated 1945
Arthur Ramsey (1904–88), translated 1961
Donald Coggan (1909–), translated 1974
Robert Runcie (1921–), translated 1980
George Carey (1935–), translated 1991

Archbishops of York since 1606

Tobias Matthew (1546–1628), translated 1606
George Montaigne (1569–1628), translated 1628
Samuel Harsnett (1561–1631), translated 1629
Richard Neile (1562–1640), translated 1632
John Williams (1582–1650), translated 1641
Accepted Frewen (1588–1664), translated 1660
Richard Sterne (1596–1683), translated 1664
John Dolben (1625–86), translated 1683
Thomas Lamplugh (1615–91), translated 1688
John Sharp (1645–1714), translated 1691
William Dawes (1671–1724), translated 1714
Launcelot Blackburn (1658–1743), translated 1724
Thomas Herring (1693–1757), translated 1743
Matthew Hutton (1693–1758), translated 1747
John Gilbert (1693–1761), translated 1757
Robert Hay Drummond (1711–76), translated 1761
William Markham (1719–1807), translated 1777
Edward Venables Vernon Harcourt (1757–1847), translated 1808
Thomas Musgrave (1788–1860), translated 1847
Charles Longley (1794–1868), translated 1860
William Thomson (1819–90), translated 1862
William Connor Magee (1821–91), translated 1891
William Dalrymple Maclagan (1826–1910), translated 1891
Cosmo Gordon Lang (1864–1945), translated 1909
William Temple (1881–1944), translated 1929
Cyril Garbett (1875–1955), translated 1942
Arthur Ramsey (1904–88), translated 1956
Donald Coggan (1909–), translated 1961
Stuart Blanch (1918–), translated 1975
John Habgood (1927–), translated 1983

Popes since 1800

The family name is in italics

Pius VII, *Chiaramonti*, elected 1800
Leo XII, *della Genga*, elected 1823
Pius VIII, *Castiglioni*, elected 1829
Gregory XVI, *Cappellari*, elected 1831
Pius IX, *Mastai-Ferretti*, elected 1846
Leo XIII, *Pecci*, elected 1878
Pius X, *Sarto*, elected 1903
Benedict XV, *della Chiesa*, elected 1914
Pius XI, *Ratti*, elected 1922
Pius XII, *Pacelli*, elected 1939
John XXIII, *Roncalli*, elected 1958
Paul VI, *Montini*, elected 1963
John Paul I, *Luciani*, elected 1978
John Paul II, *Wojyla*, elected 1978

Adrian IV is the only Englishman to be elected pope. He was born Nicholas Breakspear at Langley, near St Albans, and was elected Pope in 1154 on the death of Anastasius IV. He died in 1159.

Education

For addresses of national education departments, *see* Government Departments and Public Offices. For other addresses, *see* Education Directory

Responsibility for education in the United Kingdom is largely decentralized. The Secretary of State for Education has overall responsibility for all aspects of education in England, and for government policy for higher education throughout Britain in consultation with the Secretaries of State for Wales and Scotland. Responsibility in Wales for nursery, primary, secondary and further education, the youth and community services, and adult education lies with the Secretary of State for Wales. The general supervision of the national system of education in Scotland, except for higher education, is the responsibility of the Secretary of State for Scotland acting through the Scottish Office Education Department. All aspects of education in Northern Ireland, schools, and further and higher education are the responsibility of the Secretary of State for Northern Ireland.

The main concerns of the education departments (the Department for Education (DFE), the Welsh Office, the Scottish Office Education Department (SOED), and the Department of Education for Northern Ireland (DENI)) are the formulation of national policies for education, and the maintenance of consistency in educational standards. They are responsible for the broad allocation of resources for education, for the rate and distribution of educational building and for the supply, training and superannuation of teachers. Hitherto, none of the education departments have run any schools or colleges directly, nor employed any teachers. However, under the provisions of the Education Reform Act 1988 and the Self-Governing Schools etc. (Scotland) Act 1989, the Department for Education in England and Wales and the Scottish Office Education Department fund individual schools which have opted out of local education authority control and applied for direct funding from the Secretaries of State. In addition, the Department for Education, in association with sponsors from industry, funds the new City Technology Colleges (CTCs) and the City College for the Technology of the Arts. Technology Academies are to be instituted on a similar basis in Scotland.

Schools in Northern Ireland providing integrated education are able to apply for grant-maintained status from the Department of Education for Northern Ireland.

Expenditure

The Department for Education, the Welsh Office, the Scottish Office and the Northern Ireland Office act within a framework of estimates approved by Parliament.

In real terms expenditure on education by central government departments was as follows (£ million):

	1991–2 estimated outturn	1992–3 planned
DFE	7,345	7,947
Welsh Office	99	144
SOED	557	641
DENI	1,122	1,211

In the United Kingdom in 1989–90, central government provisional expenditure on education was apportioned as follows (£million):

Schools	13,915
Further and higher education	6,283
Other education and related expenditure	1,236

Most of this expenditure is incurred by local authorities, which make their own expenditure decisions according to their local situations and needs and which, until April 1993, are also responsible for funding most further education courses. The bulk of direct expenditure by central government is by the DFE, which supports the universities in England, Wales and Scotland through the Universities Funding Council (UFC). It also supports higher education courses in those universities which were formerly polytechnics, and in colleges of higher education, and prescribed higher education courses in local education authority colleges in England through the Polytechnics and Colleges Funding Council (PCFC). From 1 April 1993, both the UFC and the PCFC will be replaced by Higher Education Funding Councils for England, Wales and Scotland, funded by the DFE, Welsh Office and Scottish Office respectively. In the schools sector, the DFE funds grant-maintained schools and CTCs.

The Welsh Office funds grants for adult, higher and further education and supports bilingual education and the Welsh language.

In Scotland, as in England and Wales, the bulk of expenditure on education is at a local level by the regional and islands councils. The main elements of central government expenditure are grant-aided special schools, self-governing schools, student awards, capital and recurrent grants to central institutions and colleges of education, and, from April 1993, further education.

The Department of Education for Northern Ireland finances higher education, teacher education, teacher salaries and superannuation, student awards, grant-maintained integrated schools, and voluntary grammar schools. Remaining expenditure is by education and library boards at local level.

Current net expenditure on education by local education authorities in England and Wales, regional and islands councils in Scotland, and education and library boards in Northern Ireland is as follows (£million):

	1991–2 estimated outturn	1992–3 planned
England	19,100	20,500
Wales	1,166	1,175
Scotland	2,265	2,403
Northern Ireland	643	691

Local Education Administration

The education service at present is a national service in which the provision of school education and post-school further education is (until 1 April 1993) locally administered; its administration is still largely decentralized.

England and Wales – In England and Wales the education service is administered by local education authorities (LEAs), which carry the day-to-day responsibility for providing most state primary and secondary education and adult education to meet the needs of their areas.

Each local education authority is required by statute to appoint an education committee, or committees, authorized to exercise on its behalf any of the authority's functions with respect to education, except the power to borrow money. Members of the council make up a majority of these committees, but a number of people with experience in education and knowledge of the local education situation are also included.

The LEAs own and maintain schools and colleges, build new ones and provide equipment. Most of the public money spent on education is disbursed by the local authorities. LEAs are financed largely from the community charge and Aggregate External Finance (AEF) from the Department of the Environment in England and the Welsh Office in Wales.

The powers of local education authorities as regards the control of their schools have been modified in recent years. The Education (No. 2) Act 1986 legislated for equal numbers of parents and local authority representatives as governors in most maintained schools. This modification was continued by the Education Reform Act 1988, which delegated control of their budgets directly to secondary and larger primary schools, although LEAs can exercise their discretion to delegate to primary schools. It also provided for schools to opt out of local authority control and to be funded directly by central government.

SCOTLAND – The duty of providing education locally in Scotland rests with the nine regional and three islands councils. They are responsible for the construction of buildings, the employment of teachers and other staff, and the provision of equipment and materials. Their responsibility for the curricula taught in schools is shared with headteachers under the guidance of the Secretary of State for Scotland and the Scottish Consultative Council on the Curriculum.

The powers of local authorities over educational institutions under their control have been reduced also in Scotland. Under the School Boards (Scotland) Act 1988, education authorities are required to establish school boards consisting of parents and teachers as well as co-opted members, responsible among other things for the appointment of staff. The Self-Governing Schools etc. (Scotland) Act 1989 provides for schools to withdraw from local authority control and become self-governing; for the institution of Technology Academies directly funded by central government; and for the composition of further education college councils on which at least half the members are employers, and for the delegation of substantial functions to these new councils.

NORTHERN IRELAND – Education is administered locally in Northern Ireland by five education and library boards. All grant-aided schools include elected parents and teachers on their boards of governors. Provision has been made for schools wishing to provide integrated education to have grant-maintained integrated status from the outset. All secondary schools and colleges of further education have had full responsibility for their own budgets, including staffing costs, since April 1991. Full delegation is being phased in for primary and nursery schools from April 1992.

The Council for Catholic Maintained Schools forms an upper tier of management for Catholic schools and provides advice on matters relating to management and administration.

THE INSPECTORATE

Under the Education (Schools) Act 1992, the office of HM Chief Inspector of Schools (HMCI) has been created separately from the DFE, to supervise inspection of schools, teacher training, adult education and the youth service in England, Wales and Scotland. HMCI will advise the Secretaries of State on quality, standards and efficiency, and will be responsible for regulating a new system of inspection by independent inspectors approved by HMCI. Governors of schools will be free to select their own inspectors, who must be approved, and are obliged to send a copy of the inspection report to each parent, followed by a copy of the governors' action plan thereon. The inspection of further and higher education will be the responsibility of inspectors appointed to the Further and Higher Education Funding Councils when they are set up in April 1993. Inspection visits are the main way in which the Inspectors perform their functions. Inspection is carried out in Northern Ireland by the Education and Training Inspectorate of the Department of Education which performs a similar advisory function to the Secretary of State for Northern Ireland.

There were, in 1991–2, 475 HMIs in England, 58 in Wales, 107 in Scotland, and 62 members of the Inspectorate in Northern Ireland.

Schools and Pupils

Schooling is compulsory in the United Kingdom for all children between five and 16 years. Some provision is made for children under five and many pupils remain at school after the minimum leaving age. No fees are charged in any publicly maintained school in England, Wales and Scotland. In Northern Ireland, fees are paid by pupils in preparatory departments of grammar schools, but pupils admitted to the secondary departments of grammar schools do not pay fees.

In the United Kingdom, parents have a right to express a preference for a particular school and have a right to appeal if dissatisfied. Parental choice has been increased by the introduction of a policy known as more open enrolment whereby schools are required to admit children up to the limit of their capacity if there is a demand for places, and to publish their criteria for selection if they are over-subscribed, in which case parents have a right of appeal.

Schools are now required to make available information about themselves, their public examination and national curriculum test results, truancy rates, and destination of leavers. Corporal punishment is no longer legal in publicly maintained schools in the United Kingdom.

FALL AND RISE IN NUMBERS

In primary education, and increasingly in secondary education, pupil numbers in the United Kingdom have declined. In primary schools pupil numbers reached their lowest figure of 4.6 million in 1990. Numbers are expected to increase gradually year by year until by 1999 they reach about 5 million. In secondary schools pupil numbers rose to 4.6 million in 1981. They stood at 3.3 million in 1990 and are projected to decrease slightly in 1991, before rising to 3.6 million in 1999.

ENGLAND AND WALES

There are two main categories of school in England and Wales: those maintained by local education authorities (26,915), which charge no fees; and independent schools (2,347), which charge fees (*see* page 449). To these categories may be added two more as a result of the Education Reform Act 1988, consisting of institutions funded directly by the Secretary of State. These comprise primary and secondary schools which, although still providing free education, have applied to opt out of local education authority control in favour of grant-maintained status; and City Technology Colleges (*see* below).

Maintained schools are of two types: (i) county schools (17,210 in 1991) which are owned by LEAs and wholly funded by them. They are non-denominational and provide primary and secondary education; (ii) voluntary schools (7,675 in 1991) which also provide primary and secondary education. Although the buildings are in many cases provided by the voluntary bodies (mainly religious denominations) they are financially maintained by an LEA.

Voluntary schools are of three kinds: controlled (3,163), aided (4,440) and special agreement (72). In controlled schools the LEA bears all costs. In aided schools the building is usually provided by the voluntary body. The managers or governors are responsible for repairs to the outside of the school building and for improvements and alterations to it, though the Department for Education may reimburse part of approved capital expenditure. The LEA pays for internal maintenance and other running costs. Special agreement schools are those where the LEA may, by special agreement, pay between one-half and three-quarters of the cost of building a new, or extending an existing, voluntary school, almost always a secondary school. There are no special agreement schools in Wales. In voluntary schools the majority of the managers or governors are appointed by the voluntary body and at least one by the LEA. The managers or governors control the appointment of teachers. Expenditure is normally apportioned between the authority and the voluntary body.

All publicly maintained schools have a governing body usually made up of an equal number of parent representatives and governors appointed by the LEA, the headteacher (unless he or she chooses otherwise), and serving teachers. Parental involvement in the running of schools has increased considerably in recent years, and parents have also been given the power to decide by ballot whether their child's school should opt out of local authority control. Governors are responsible for the overall policies of schools and their academic aims and objectives; they also now control matters of school discipline and the appointment and dismissal of staff. Under the Education (Schools) Act 1992, governing bodies will select inspectors for their schools, be responsible for action as a result of inspection reports and make these reports and their action plans thereon available to parents. The Education Reform Act 1988 delegated control of the administration of the major part of school budgets, including staffing costs, from LEAs directly to schools under an initiative known as Local Management of Schools (LMS).

Technology schools – The technology schools initiative, launched in December 1991, provides capital and project funding for a network of schools committed to offering innovative technology teaching of a vocational nature. In 1992–3 £25 million of capital funding has been made available to 100 schools which submitted successful bids, with additional support of about £250,000 for individual schools for the up-grading of technology facilities.

Grant-maintained (GM) schools – All secondary schools and larger primary schools are eligible to apply for grant-maintained status, subject to a ballot of parents. GM schools are maintained directly by the Secretary of State, not the LEA, and are wholly run by their own governing body. The Funding Agency for Schools (FAS) will be set up to take over the payment of grants to grant maintained schools. By September 1992 there were at least 266 GM schools. Of these, 214 were secondary schools, 35.5 per cent of them comprehensive.

City Technology Colleges (CTCs) and *City Colleges for the Technology of the Arts (CCTAs)* are state-aided but independent of LEAs. Their aim is to widen the choice of secondary education in disadvantaged urban areas and to teach a broad curriculum with an emphasis on science, technology, business understanding and arts technologies. Capital costs are shared by government and sponsors from industry and commerce, and running costs are covered by a per capita grant from the DFE in line with comparable costs in an LEA maintained school.

The first city technology college opened in September 1988 in Solihull. By September 1993 there will be fifteen. The first CCTA, known as Britschool, opened in Croydon in September 1991.

Scotland

Schools in Scotland fall into three main categories: education authority schools (3,792) (known as public schools), which are managed by the regional and islands councils and financed jointly by the councils and central government; grant aided schools (8), conducted by voluntary managers who receive grants direct from the Scottish Office Education Department; and independent schools (122), which receive no direct grant and charge fees, but are subject to inspection and registration. An additional category is created under the provisions of the Self-Governing Schools etc. (Scotland) Act 1989, of schools opting to be managed entirely by a board of management consisting of the headmaster, parent and staff representatives and co-opted members. The change of status will require a ballot of parents and the publication of proposals by the board, and the achievement of self-government is subject to a final decision by the Secretary of State. These schools will remain in the public sector and will be funded by direct government grant set to match the resources the school would have received under education authority management. None have as yet been established.

Under the School Boards (Scotland) Act 1988, education authorities are required to establish school boards to participate in the administration and management of schools. These boards consist of elected parents and staff members as well as co-opted members.

Technology Academies (TAs) – The Self-Governing Schools etc. (Scotland) Act 1989 provides for setting up technology academies in areas of urban deprivation. These secondary schools are intended to be so placed as to draw on a wide catchment, and will offer a broad curriculum with an emphasis on science and technology. They are to be founded and managed in partnership with industrial sponsors, with central government meeting the running costs by grant-aid thereafter. None have as yet been set up.

Northern Ireland

There are three main categories of grant-aided school in Northern Ireland: controlled schools (710), which are controlled by the education and library boards with all costs paid from public funds; voluntary maintained schools (580), mainly under Roman Catholic management, which receive grants towards capital costs and running costs in whole or in part; and voluntary grammar schools (52), which may be under Roman Catholic or non-denominational management and receive grants from the Department of Education for Northern Ireland. All grant-aided schools include elected parents and teachers on their boards of governors, whose responsibilities also include financial management under the Local Management of Schools (LMS) initiative. There are also 19 independent schools in Northern Ireland.

The majority of children in Northern Ireland are educated in schools which in practice are segregated on religious lines. The Education Reform (Northern Ireland) Order 1989, however, makes provision for parents to opt for integrated education more easily. These provisions include arrangements to fund new integrated schools from the outset and procedures for balloting parents in existing segregated schools to determine whether they want instead to have integrated schools. By September 1992, 16 integrated schools had been established.

THE STATE SYSTEM

Nursery Education – Nursery education is for children from two to five years and is not compulsory. In the United Kingdom it takes place in nursery schools or nursery classes in primary schools. In 1989–90, 769,500 pupils under five years of age were receiving education in maintained nursery and primary schools, an increase of 47,000 on the previous year. Of the total, 84,000 were in nursery schools, 633,100 in primary schools, and 46,100 in non-maintained nursery schools. Expressed as a percentage of the population aged three and four years, the 769,500 represented 51 per cent, compared to 49 per cent in the previous year.

Many children also attend pre-school playgroups organized by parents and voluntary bodies such as the Pre-School Playgroups Association.

PRIMARY EDUCATION – Primary education begins at five years and is almost always co-educational. In England, Wales and Northern Ireland the transfer to secondary school is generally made at 11 years. In Scotland, the primary school course lasts for seven years and pupils transfer to secondary courses at about the age of 12.

Primary schools consist mainly of infants' schools for children aged five to seven, junior schools for those aged seven to 11, and combined junior and infant schools for both age groups. In addition, first schools in some parts of England cater for ages five to ten. (They are the first stage of a three-tier system: first, middle and secondary). Many primary schools provide nursery classes for children under five (*see* above).

The number of primary schools in the United Kingdom in 1989–90 was 24,268, which was 76 fewer than in 1988–9, with 4,564,000 full- and part-time pupils, of which 814,000 were under five. Between 1989 and 1999 primary school pupil numbers are projected to rise by about 2.8 per cent.

Pupil-teacher ratios in maintained primary schools in the United Kingdom are:

	1988–9	1989–90
England	22.0	21.8
Wales	22.3	22.3
Scotland	20.3	19.7
Northern Ireland	23.2	23.2
UK	21.9	21.7

The average size of classes 'as taught' has fallen from 25.5 in 1981 to 23.8 in 1991.

MIDDLE SCHOOLS – Middle schools (which take children from first schools), mostly in England, cover varying age ranges between eight and 14 and usually lead on to comprehensive upper schools.

SECONDARY EDUCATION – Secondary schools are for children aged 11 to 16 and for those who choose to stay on to 18. At 16, many students prefer to move on to tertiary or sixth form colleges (*see* page 453). Most secondary schools in England, Wales and Scotland are co-educational. The largest secondary schools have over 2,000 pupils but only 2.7 per cent of the schools take over 1,000 pupils.

In England and Wales the main types of secondary schools are: comprehensive schools (85.9 per cent of pupils in England, 99.2 in Wales), whose admission arrangements are without reference to ability or aptitude; middle deemed secondary schools for children aged variously between eight and 14 years who then move on to senior comprehensive schools at 12, 13 or 14 (6.5 per cent of pupils in England only); secondary modern schools (3.8 per cent of pupils in England, 0.2 per cent in Wales) providing a general education with a practical bias; secondary grammar schools (3.4 per cent of pupils in England, 0.2 per cent in Wales) with selective intake providing an academic course from 11 to 16–18 years; and technical schools (0.1 per cent) in England only, providing an integrated academic and technical education.

In January 1991 there were in England and Wales 3,038,493 pupils in maintained secondary schools, including 11.4 per cent in England and 11.6 per cent in Wales who were 16 or over. After falling by 16 per cent between 1987 and 1991, numbers are projected to rise by 9.3 per cent by 1999.

Pupil-teacher ratios improved steadily from 15.7 in 1987 to 15.3 in 1990 in England and Wales, then rose to 15.4 in 1991. The average class size in England was 20.3 in 1991. In Wales the average class size in 1991 was 19.2.

In Scotland all pupils in education authority secondary schools attend schools with a comprehensive intake. Most of these schools provide a full range of courses appropriate to all levels of ability from first to sixth year. In 1990–1 there were 293,702 pupils in education authority schools, of whom 22 per cent were 16 or over. Numbers are projected to increase to 300,000 in 1995. Pupil-teacher ratios worsened from 12.2 in 1990 to 12.4 in 1991. The average class size in 1991 was 18.9.

In most areas of Northern Ireland there is a selective system of secondary education with pupils transferring either to grammar schools or secondary schools at 11–12 years of age. Parents can choose the school they would like their children to attend and all those who apply must be admitted if they meet the criteria. If a school is over-subscribed beyond its statutory admissions number, selection is on the basis of published criteria, which, for most grammar schools, place emphasis on performance in the transfer procedure tests which are centrally administered by the Department for Education. When parents consider that a school has not applied its criteria fairly they have access to independent appeals tribunals. Grammar schools provide an academic type of secondary education with A-levels at the end of the seventh year, while secondary non-grammar schools follow a curriculum suited to a wider range of aptitudes and abilities.

In 1991 there were 141,146 pupils in public sector secondary schools, of whom 86,667 (62.9 per cent) attended non-grammar secondary and 54,479 (37.1 per cent) attended grammar schools. Of these 18.9 per cent were 16 or over. Pupil-teacher ratios in Northern Ireland were 18.7 in 1991.

SPECIAL EDUCATION – Special education is provided for children with special educational needs, usually because they have a disability which either prevents or hinders them from making use of educational facilities of a kind generally provided for children of their age in schools within the area of the local authority concerned. However, wherever possible, such children are now educated in ordinary schools, taking the parents' wishes into account. Maintained special schools are run by education authorities which pay all the costs of maintenance, and by April 1994 Local Management of Schools (LMS) will be extended to those that are able and wish to manage their own budgets. Non-maintained special schools are run by voluntary bodies; they may receive some grant from central government for capital expenditure and for equipment, but their current expenditure is met primarily from the fees charged to the education authorities for pupils placed in the schools. Some independent schools provide education wholly or mainly for children with special educational needs and are required to meet similar standards to those for maintained and non-maintained special schools. The national curriculum also applies to children with a statement of special needs, but there is provision for them to be exempt from it, or for it to be modified to suit the individual child's capabilities. Legislation is being planned to give parents greater choice of schools and to extend their right of appeal by establishing the Special Educational Needs (SEN) Tribunal.

In January 1990 in the United Kingdom there was a total of 113,700 full-time pupils in special schools (of whom 1,600 were in hospital schools in England, Wales and Northern Ireland). Of the total, 95,800 were in England, 3,600 in Wales, 8,800 in Scotland and 3,900 in Northern Ireland.

Numbers have decreased since 1975–6 as education authorities in England, Wales and Northern Ireland must now ensure that children with special needs are educated as far as possible in ordinary schools with support teaching.

In Scotland, school placing is a matter of agreement between education authorities and parents. Parents have the right to say which school they want their child to attend, and a right of appeal where their wishes are not being met. Whenever possible, children with special needs are integrated into ordinary schools. However, for those who require a different environment or specialized facilities, there are special schools, both grant-aided by central government and independent, and special classes within ordinary schools. The Self-Governing Schools etc. (Scotland) Act 1989 obliges education authorities to respond to reasonable requests for independent special schools, and provides for them to send children with special needs to schools outside Scotland if appropriate provision is not available within the country. A new centre has been opened which practices conductive education methods for children with motor impairments.

Alternative Provision

There is no legal obligation on parents in the United Kingdom to educate their children at school provided that the local education authority is satisfied that the child is receiving full-time education suited to its age, abilities and aptitudes. The education authority need not be informed that a child is being educated at home unless the child is already registered at a state school. In this case the parents must arrange for the child's name to be removed from the school's register (by writing to the headteacher) before education at home can begin. Failure to de-register a child leaves the parents liable to prosecution for condoning non-attendance.

In most cases an initial visit is made by an education adviser or education welfare officer, and sometimes subsequent inspections are made, but practice varies according to the individual education authority. There is no requirement for parents educating their children at home to be in possession of a teaching qualification.

Further advice on educating children other than at school can be obtained from Education Otherwise (*see* page 462).

INDEPENDENT SCHOOLS

Independent schools receive no grants from public funds. They charge fees, and are owned and managed under special trusts, with profits being used for the benefit of the schools concerned. There is a wide variety of provision, from kindergartens to large day and boarding schools, and from experimental schools to traditional institutions. A number of independent schools have been instituted by religious and ethnic minorities.

All independent schools in the United Kingdom are open to inspection by inspectors approved by HMCI (*see* page 446) and must register with the appropriate government education department. The education departments lay down certain minimum standards and can make schools remedy any unacceptable features of their building or instruction and exclude any unsuitable teacher or proprietor. Most independent schools offer a similar range of courses to state schools and enter pupils for the same public examinations. Introduction of the national curriculum and the associated education targets and assessment procedures is not obligatory in the independent sector.

The term public schools is often applied to those independent schools in membership of the Headmasters' Conference, the Governing Bodies Association or the Governing Bodies of Girls' Schools Association. Most public schools are single-sex (about half of them for girls) but there are some mixed schools and an increasing number of schools have mixed sixth forms.

Preparatory schools are so-called because they prepare children for the Common Entrance Examination to senior independent schools. Most cater for boys from about seven to 13 years, some are for girls, and an increasing number are co-educational. The Common Entrance Examination is set by the Common Entrance Examination Board, but marked by the independent school to which the pupil intends to go. It is taken at 13 by boys, and from 11 to 13 by girls.

In 1991 there were in England 2,280 independent schools with 565,900 full-time pupils and a pupil-teacher ratio of 10.75.

In Wales in 1990–1 there were 71 independent schools, with 12,074 pupils and a pupil-teacher ratio of 9.8.

In Scotland in 1990–1 there were 122 registered independent schools with 33,300 pupils. Most independent schools in Scotland follow the English examination system, i.e. GCSE followed by A-levels, although some take the Scottish Education Certificate at Ordinary/Standard grade followed by Highers.

There are 19 independent schools in Northern Ireland with 1,138 pupils and a pupil-teacher ratio of 13.2.

Assisted Places Scheme

The Assisted Places Scheme enables children to attend independent secondary schools which their parents could not otherwise afford. The scheme provides help with tuition fees and other expenses, except boarding costs, on a sliding scale depending on the family's income. The take-up rate for places available at age 11 to 13 at the 303 participating schools in England and Wales is around 98 per cent, and the proportion of pupils receiving full fee remission is 34.8 per cent. Over 34,500 places were offered in England and Wales in the academic year 1991–2. The 58 participating schools in Scotland will admit about 3,000 pupils on the scheme in 1991–2, which, unlike that in England and Wales, is cash-limited. The proportion of pupils receiving full fee remission will be 50 per cent.

The scheme is administered and funded in England by the Department for Education, in Wales by the Welsh Office, and in Scotland by the Scottish Office Education Department.

The scheme does not operate in Northern Ireland as the independent sector admits non-fee paying pupils. There is, however, a similar scheme known as the Talented Children's Scheme to help pupils gifted in music and dance.

Further information can be obtained from the Independent Schools Information Service (*see* page 462).

THE CURRICULUM

England and Wales

The Education Reform Act 1988 legislated for the progressive introduction of a national curriculum in primary and secondary schools from autumn 1989. During the period of compulsory schooling for children aged five to 16 the curriculum includes mathematics, English and science as core subjects and history, geography, technology, music, art, physical education and (for pupils in secondary schools) a modern foreign language as foundation subjects. For the core and foundation subjects attainment targets and assessment procedures have been instituted for seven year-olds, and are being phased in for 11 and 14 year-olds; at 16 the

GCSE will be the main form of assessment. It is intended that pupils with special educational needs should have access to as much of the national curriculum as possible. Religious education is required to be available in schools, with the curriculum devised locally, but parents have the right to remove their children if they wish.

In Wales in 1990–1 the Welsh language was in use as the main or secondary medium of instruction in 35.1 per cent of primary and 24.7 per cent of secondary schools. Following the introduction of the national curriculum it will constitute a core subject in Welsh-speaking schools and a foundation subject in the others, although there is provision for exemptions to be made.

In England the National Curriculum Council, funded by the Department for Education, is responsible for the promotion and support of curriculum development, in addition to advising the Secretary of State on the national curriculum. It is to combine with the School Examinations and Assessment Council to form the School Curriculum and Assessment Authority. In Wales its functions are performed by the Curriculum Council for Wales, funded by the Welsh Office.

Scotland

The content and management of the curriculum in Scotland is the responsibility of education authorities and individual headteachers. Advice and guidance is provided by the Scottish Office Education Department and the Scottish Consultative Council on the Curriculum. Scotland effectively has a national curriculum for 14–16 year-olds, who are required to study English, mathematics and a science subject plus five other subjects. These form the core area, supplemented by other activities forming the elective area. There is a recommended percentage of class time to be devoted to each area over the two years. Provision is made for teaching in Gaelic in Gaelic-speaking areas.

The Scottish Consultative Council on the Curriculum, which is responsible for development and advisory work on the curriculum in Scotland, has undertaken a major review of the balance of the primary curriculum, and produced new guidelines for each of the subject areas for the age group five to 14. There are new guidelines on assessment across the whole curriculum, and standardized tests have been introduced in English language and mathematics at five stages for this age group. For 16–18 year-olds, there is available a modular system of vocational courses in addition to academic courses.

Northern Ireland

Major programmes of curriculum review and development are in progress in primary and secondary schools. A curriculum common to all schools is being introduced over a three-year period to 1992–3, with six broad areas of study within which ten subjects will be compulsory; religious education will also be a compulsory part of the curriculum. The Irish language will be a compulsory subject in Irish-medium primary schools and can be chosen as the compulsory foreign language in secondary schools. Arrangements for the assessment of pupils, broadly in line with those in England and Wales, are proposed at the ages of eight, 11, 14 and 16. Pilot assessments are to be carried out in February 1993 and May 1993 for 11 and 14 year-olds respectively.

The Northern Ireland Curriculum Council advises the Government on all matters concerning the curriculum for grant-aided schools in Northern Ireland.

Records of Achievement

National records of achievement are documents which set down the range of school-leavers' achievements and activities both inside and outside the classroom, including those not tested by examination. They are issued to all those leaving school in England and Wales and will be introduced in Scotland. Under the Education (Schools) Act 1992, parents in England and Wales must receive a written yearly progress report on all aspects of their children's achievements. There is a similar commitment for Northern Ireland. In Scotland the school report card is being reformed to give parents more information on their children's progress.

Technical and Vocational Education Initiative

The Technical and Vocational Education Initiative (TVEI), funded by the Department of Employment, operates across the curriculum within a framework of general education in England, Wales and Scotland. It aims to make the secondary curriculum more relevant to adult life and work. Following pilot projects, it is now a national scheme with newly established criteria which complement and are compatible with the requirements of the new national curriculum in England and Wales. Participation is voluntary, and is open to all maintained schools and colleges providing for young people of all abilities aged 14–18. TVEI is not an examination or a qualification.

THE PUBLIC EXAMINATION SYSTEM

England, Wales and Northern Ireland

Until the end of 1987, secondary school pupils at the end of compulsory schooling around the age of 16, and others, took the General Certificate of Education (GCE) Ordinary-level or the Certificate of Secondary Education (CSE). From 1988 these were replaced by a single system of examinations, the General Certificate of Secondary Education (GCSE), which is usually taken after five years of secondary education. The first examinations took place in summer 1988.

The GCSE differs from its predecessors in that there are syllabuses based on national criteria covering course objectives, content and assessment methods; differentiated assessment (i.e. different papers or questions for different ranges of ability); and grade-related criteria (i.e. grades awarded on absolute rather than relative performance).

The GCSE certificates are awarded on a seven-point scale, A to G. Grades A to C are the equivalent of the corresponding O-level grades A to C, or CSE grade 1. Grades D, E, F and G record achievement at least as high as that represented by CSE grades 2 to 5. There is no restriction on entry to any examination. All GCSE syllabuses, assessments and grading procedures are monitored by the School Examinations and Assessment Council (*see* below) to ensure that they conform to the national criteria.

Of school leavers in the United Kingdom who left school without A-levels or SCE H-grades in 1989–90, 37.5 per cent had achieved one or more graded GCE O-level, CSE, GCSE or SCE O-grade results.

From September 1991, many maintained schools have offered BTEC Firsts (*see* below) and it is hoped that more schools will offer BTEC Nationals than do so at present. National Vocational Qualifications in the form of General NVQs have been available to students in schools from September 1992 (*see* page 451).

Certificate of Extended Education – The Certificate of Extended Education (CEE) comprises a number of single-subject examinations set and awarded by certain GCSE examining boards and taken a year after GCSE. Apart from English and mathematics, subjects are non-traditional and include social, environmental, technological, business and health studies.

Advanced levels – Advanced (A-level) examinations, taken by those who choose to continue their education after GCSE, continue as before although changes have been made to the grading system.

A-level courses last two years and have traditionally provided the foundation for entry to higher education. A-levels are marked on a seven-point scale, from A to E, N (narrow failure) and U (unclassified), which latter grade will not be certificated.

Advanced Supplementary levels – As an alternative to, and to complement, A-level examinations, Advanced Supplementary level (AS-level) examinations were introduced in September 1987, with the first examinations taking place in summer 1989. AS-levels are for full-time A-level students but are also open to other students. An AS-level syllabus covers not less than half the amount of ground covered by the corresponding A-level syllabus and, where possible, is related to it. An AS-level course lasts two years and requires not less than half the teaching time of the corresponding A-level course, and two AS-levels are equivalent to one A-level. AS-level courses are intended to supplement and broaden A-level studies, and examinations are held at the same time as A-levels. AS-level passes are graded A to E, with grade standards related to the A-level grades.

A mixture of A-level courses in the subjects to be specialized in and AS-levels will form the standard for admission to higher education.

In the United Kingdom in 1989–90, 26 per cent of all 17 year-olds (25 per cent of boys, 28 per cent of girls) achieved one or more A-level or SCE H-grade result. This figure includes those continuing their education in maintained further education establishments including tertiary colleges, as well as school leavers.

Of school leavers alone (706,000), 21.8 per cent achieved at least one A-level or SCE H-grade (20.9 per cent of boys, 22 per cent of girls). Of those in Great Britain obtaining two or more A-levels, or three or more SCE H-grades, 14 per cent studied sciences (19 per cent of boys, 9 per cent of girls), 42 per cent studied arts/social studies (33 per cent of boys, 51 per cent of girls), and 44 per cent (48 per cent of boys, 39 per cent of girls) studied a combination of science and arts/social studies.

S-levels – Most examining boards allow the option of an additional paper of greater difficulty to be taken by A-level candidates to obtain what is known as a Special-level or Scholarship-level qualification. S-level papers are available in most of the traditional academic subjects and are marked on a three-point scale, grade A or 1, grade B or 2, and unclassified.

The Diploma of Vocational Education – The Diploma of Vocational Education superseded the Certificate of Pre-Vocational Education (CPVE) in schools and colleges in England, Wales and Northern Ireland from September 1992. It is intended for a wide ability range, including pupils who might not go on to A-levels but would like to continue their education on completion of their secondary schooling. The qualification is offered by the City and Guilds of London Institute.

The Diploma of Vocational Education provides recognition of achievement at three levels: foundation, intermediate and national; the two latter broadly corresponding to the one- and two-year CPVE programmes, and linked with the GNVQ (*see* below) at levels 2 and 3. Within guidelines schools and colleges design their own courses, which stress activity-based learning, basic numeracy and work experience. The Diploma of Vocational Education is mainly for those who want to find out what aptitudes they may have and to prepare themselves for work, but who are not yet committed to a particular occupation. It can be taken alongside other courses such as GCSEs, A- or AS-levels.

Advanced Diploma – Introduced in September 1992 in schools and colleges in England, Wales and Northern Ireland, the Advanced Diploma is not an examination but a record of the achievement of three advanced GCE passes (of which two may be at AS-level) or a NVQ at level 3. It also denotes evidence of a certain level of attainment in English, mathematics and a modern foreign language. The first awards are expected to be made in summer 1994. The introduction of an Ordinary Diploma is under consideration.

Co-ordination and Advisory Bodies

The School Examinations and Assessment Council (SEAC), which was set up to advise the Government on all school examination and assessment matters in England and Wales, is to be combined with the National Curriculum Council to form a single new body, the School Curriculum and Assessment Authority. The Council is funded wholly by the Department for Education.

The Northern Ireland Schools Examinations and Assessment Council performs the same function in Northern Ireland, funded by the Department of Education for Northern Ireland.

Scotland

The system of public examinations in Scotland is different from that elsewhere in the United Kingdom. At the end of the fourth year of secondary education (equivalent to the fifth year in the rest of the United Kingdom), at about the age of 16, pupils take either the Ordinary grade of the Scottish Certificate of Education Examination (corresponding to the old GCE Ordinary level) or the Standard grade. By 1994–5, the Ordinary grade will have been replaced by Standard grade courses and examinations, which have been designed to suit every level of ability, with assessment against nationally determined standards of performance.

For most courses there are three separate examination papers at the end of the two-year Standard grade course. They are set at Credit (leading to awards at grade 1 or 2), General (leading to awards at grade 3 or 4) and Foundation (leading to awards at grade 5 or 6) levels. Grade 7 is available to those who, although they have completed the course, have shown no significant level of attainment. Normally pupils will take examinations covering two pairs of grades, either grades 1–4 or grades 3–6.

Pupils may attempt as many of a wide range of subjects as they are capable of, on either the Ordinary/Standard grades, or on the Higher grade which is normally taken one year after Ordinary/Standard grades, at the age of 17 or thereabouts. The shorter course means that Higher grades are normally studied to a lesser depth than A-levels; on the other hand it is common for pupils to be presented for four or more Higher grades at a single diet of the examination.

The Certificate of Sixth Year Studies (CSYS) is designed to give direction and purpose to sixth-year work by encouraging pupils who have completed their main subjects at Higher grade to study a maximum of three of these subjects in depth. Pupils may also use the sixth year to gain improved or additional Higher grades or Ordinary/Standard grades. The Scottish Office Education Department is proposing a number of changes in the system of Highers and CSYS as a result of recommendations made in the report of the Howie Committee in 1992.

The Scottish Certificate of Education Examination and the Certificate of Sixth Year Studies are conducted by the Scottish Examination Board.

National Certificates – National Certificates were introduced in 1984–5 as an alternative to, and to complement, Highers and CSYS. They are awarded to pupils normally over the age of 16 who have successfully completed a programme of vocational courses based on modular study units, and the assessment system is based on national criteria. National Certificates are validated by the Scottish Vocational Education Council (*see also* pages 453–4).

The International Baccalaureate

The International Baccalaureate is an internationally recognized two-year pre-university course and examination designed to facilitate the mobility of students and to promote international understanding. Candidates must offer one subject from each of six subject groups, at least three at higher level and the remainder at subsidiary level. Single subjects can be offered, for which a certificate is received. There are 26 schools and colleges in the United Kingdom which offer the International Baccalaureate diploma.

TEACHERS

England and Wales

Teachers are appointed by local education authorities, school governing bodies, or school managers. Those in publicly maintained schools must be approved as qualified by the Department for Education. To become a qualified teacher it is necessary to have successfully completed a course of initial teacher training, usually either a Bachelor of Education (B.Ed.) degree or the Postgraduate Certificate of Education (PGCE). Teacher training has hitherto been largely integrated with the rest of higher education, with training places concentrated in universities and institutes or colleges of education, but recent proposals will result in teacher training being largely school-based, with student teachers on secondary PGCE courses spending two-thirds of their training in the classroom by September 1994. Primary phase teacher training is also being reviewed. Under the articled teacher scheme, graduates are paid a bursary in addition to a salary to complete a school-based PGCE course over two years involving a progressively increasing teaching load. From September 1993, this scheme will be restricted to primary phase teacher training only.

With certain exceptions the profession now has an all-graduate entry. Teachers in further education are not required to have qualified teacher status, though roughly half have a teaching qualification and most have industrial, commercial or professional experience.

The licensed teacher scheme is designed to attract into the teaching profession entrants over 24 years of age without formal teaching qualifications but with relevant training and experience. All licensees are required to have the equivalent of two years' higher education in the United Kingdom and the equivalent of grade C in GCSE maths and English. Local education authorities will be involved in devising a suitable two-year training programme for any licensed teachers they may appoint to their schools; for grant-maintained schools and City Technology Colleges this will be a matter for the schools themselves. LEAs have discretion to recommend qualified teacher status after one year for a licensee with at least two years' experience as an instructor prior to becoming a licensed teacher.

Scotland

All teachers in maintained schools must be registered with the General Teaching Council for Scotland. They are registered provisionally for a two-year probationary period which can be extended if necessary. Only graduates are accepted as entrants to the teaching profession in Scotland. A review of initial teacher training was instituted in 1992 which has recommended that a greater proportion of training be classroom-based.

Northern Ireland

Teacher training in Northern Ireland is provided by the two universities and two colleges of education. The colleges are concerned with teacher education mainly for the primary school sector. They also provide B.Ed. courses for intending secondary school teachers of religious education, commercial studies, and craft, design and technology. With these exceptions, the training of teachers for secondary schools is provided in the education departments of the universities.

Accreditation of Training Institutions

The role of the Council for the Accreditation of Teacher Education (CATE) has hitherto been to advise on course accreditation in England, Wales and Northern Ireland, and monitor and disseminate good practice. In future, its function will be the accreditation of the higher education institutions themselves rather than the courses; its advisory role with regard to central government will be maintained.

In Scotland all training courses in colleges of education must be approved by the Scottish Office Education Department and a validating body.

Newly-Trained Teachers

Of teachers who in 1989 had successfully completed initial training courses in the United Kingdom, 10,400 had completed a postgraduate course and 7,000 a course for non-graduates.

In the year to January 1991, 14,400 teachers took up first full-time appointments, either permanently or for at least one term's duration, in maintained nursery, primary and secondary schools in England and Wales. In Scotland and Northern Ireland, figures for 1991 were 1,302 and 550 respectively.

Because of a shortage of teachers in a number of secondary subjects, a tax-free bursary scheme for trainee teachers on one- or two-year courses has been introduced. The subjects are mathematics, chemistry, biology, modern languages (including Welsh in Wales), and technology CDT, which attract a bursary of £1,500, and physics, which attracts a bursary of £2,000.

Serving Teachers

In 1989–90 there were 559,000 teachers (full-time and full-time equivalent) in public sector schools and establishments of further education in the United Kingdom. Of these, 469,000 were in maintained schools and 90,000 in further education. There were 210,000 full-time teachers in public sector primary schools, 239,000 in public sector secondary schools and 20,000 in special schools.

Salaries

All qualified teachers in England, Wales and Northern Ireland, other than heads and deputy heads, are paid on a ten-point scale ranging from £11,184 to £18,837 (April 1992 figures). Entry points vary depending on qualification and according to the discretion of the appointing authority. In addition, incentive allowances are payable on a range of five rates. Headteachers' salaries range from £22,911 to £50,181 (principals from £23,271 to £45,239 in Northern Ireland); deputy headteachers' salaries range from £22,182 to £36,489 (vice-principals from £22,182 to £33,453 in Northern Ireland). There is a statutory superannuation scheme in maintained schools.

Teachers in Scotland are paid (April 1992 figures) on a ten-point scale from £11,283 to £18,756 (£11,391 to £18,933 from October 1992). As in the rest of the United Kingdom, the entry point depends on type of qualification, and additional allowances are payable under certain circumstances. Headteachers are paid on a scale from £23,790 to £44,604 (£24,015 to £44,484 from October 1992) and depute headteachers from £23,790 to £32,970 (£24,015 to £33,285 from October 1992), depending on whether the school is primary or secondary and the size of school roll.

Further Education

The Education Reform Act 1988 defines further education as all provision outside schools to people aged over 16 of education up to and including A-level and its equivalent. All education authorities have a duty to secure provision of adequate facilities for further education in their area.

England and Wales

Responsibility for co-ordinating further education provision rested formerly with ten Regional Advisory Councils set up by the local education authorities (LEAs) in each region. The councils operated in accordance with terms of reference agreed between the participating LEAs, which met staffing and other expenses.

The Further and Higher Education Act 1992 has now removed all further education and sixth form colleges from local authority control as of April 1993, and provided for them to be funded directly by central government through the Further Education Council for England (FEFC) and the Further Education Funding Council for Wales (FEFCW). These councils will also be responsible for the assessment of quality. The colleges will become independent corporations, owning their own assets and employing their own staff. Their funding will be determined in part by the number of students recruited.

In England and Wales further education courses are taught at a variety of institutions. These range from universities which were formerly polytechnics and colleges of further and higher education (most of which also offer higher education courses) to tertiary colleges and sixth form colleges, which concentrate on the provision of normal sixth form school courses as well as a range of vocational courses. A number of institutions specific to a particular form of training, e.g. the Royal College of Music, are also involved. Until April 1993, all such courses are funded by local education authorities, including further education courses in universities and colleges of higher education. Thereafter, funding will be provided by the Further Education Funding Councils.

Every institution providing full-time further education under a further education scheme is required to appoint a board of governors. At least half the governors must represent employment interests or be independent of local authority or college interests. Since 1989, local authorities have been required to delegate to these bodies extensive powers over the appointment of staff and the management of college budgets under the local management of further and higher education colleges initiative. From April 1993, governing boards and principals will have total responsibility and accountability for their institutions.

The position of teaching staff in further education establishments is similar to that in schools with respect to qualifications and regular appraisal of teachers' performance.

Much of the post-school provision outside the higher education sector is broadly vocational in purpose. It ranges from lower-level technical and commercial courses through courses for those aiming at higher-level posts in industry, commerce and administration, to professional courses. Facilities for GCSE courses, CEE (Certificate of Extended Education), Diploma of Vocational Education, AS-levels and A-level courses are also provided (*see* pages 450–1). These courses can form the foundation for progress to higher education qualifications (*see* below).

The main courses and examinations in the vocational field, all of which link in with the NVQ framework, are offered by the following bodies, but there are also many others:

Business and Technology Education Council (BTEC) provides courses across a wide range of subject areas and four main qualifications: the BTEC First Certificate (one year part-time), the BTEC First Diploma (one year full-time or two years part-time), the BTEC National Certificate (two years part-time), and the BTEC National Diploma (two years full-time or three years part-time or as a sandwich course).

City and Guilds of London Institute (C&G) offers a wide range of technical and vocational qualifications and has sole responsibility for administering the Diploma of Vocational Education (*see* page 451). Most courses are part-time for students already in employment, but some full-time courses are available.

RSA (Royal Society of Arts) Examinations Board schemes cover a wide range of vocational qualifications, including business and administration, language schemes and teaching qualifications. Many schemes are offered at levels matching those established by the NCVQ (*see* below), and a policy operates of credit accumulation, so that candidates can take a single unit or complete qualifications.

There are 418 further education establishments in England and Wales and 2,669 adult education centres. In 1990–1 there were 428,273 full-time and sandwich students and 793,625 part-time students on further education courses.

Scotland

Education authorities have hitherto provided further education comprising non-advanced courses up to SCE Highers grade, GCE A-level and SCOTVEC vocational courses in Scotland, but under the Further and Higher Education (Scotland) Act 1992 funding of further education colleges is to be transferred to central government by April 1993; a further education funding council is proposed at a later stage. Courses are taught mainly at colleges of further education, including technical colleges, and in some schools.

The Self-Governing Schools etc. (Scotland) Act 1989 legislated for Further Education College Councils to be set up with extensive powers to run their colleges. The Act specifies that at least half the members of college councils must be private or public sector employers and not more than one-fifth local authority representatives; that education authorities must delegate substantial functions to the new councils; and that colleges must be allowed to earn income from commercial activities.

The Scottish Vocational Education Council (SCOTVEC) provides qualifications for most occupations (paralleling the work of the Business and Technology Education Council, City and Guilds of London Institute, the Royal Society of Arts and other bodies in England, Wales and Northern Ireland. It provides at non-advanced level the National Certificate which is completely comprehensive and covers the whole range of non-advanced further education provision in Scotland. Students may study for the National Certificate on a full-time, part-time, open learning or work-based learning basis. The system is based on modules and National Certificate modules and modular programmes can be taken in further education colleges, secondary schools and other centres, normally from the age of 16 onwards. SCOTVEC also offers modular advanced level HNC/HND qualifications and a few post-graduate or post-experience qualifications which are available in further education colleges and higher education institutions. Scottish Vocational Qualifications (SVQs) combine programmes of SCOTVEC's National Certificate modules or Higher National Units. They correspond to the system of NVQs which pertains in the rest of the UK. They were introduced in schools, further education colleges and other centres from August 1992.

The Record of Education and Training (RET) has been introduced to provide a single certificate recording SCOTVEC achievements; an updated version is provided as and when necessary.

In 1989–90 there were 35,971 full-time and sandwich students and 92,165 part-time students on non-advanced vocational courses of further education in the 49 further education colleges, eight central institutions and five colleges of education (*see also* page 457).

NORTHERN IRELAND

Education and library boards are obliged to prepare and submit for approval to the Department of Education for Northern Ireland, schemes setting out the principles to be applied by the boards in planning the further education provision to be made by colleges under their management.

The colleges of further education are maintained by the education and library boards, but financial powers and responsibilities are delegated to the boards of governors of the colleges. A review of further education provision is taking place during 1992–3, with a view to re-examining its administration and funding and rationalizing college and course provision. The boards of governors must include at least 50 per cent membership from the professions, local business or industry, or other fields of employment relevant to the activities of the college.

On reaching school-leaving age, pupils may attend colleges of further education to pursue the same type of vocational courses as are provided in colleges in England and Wales, administered by the same examining bodies.

Northern Ireland has 24 institutions of further education with 308 out-centres. In 1989–90 there were 16,208 full-time students and 33,112 part-time students on non-advanced vocational courses of further education.

COURSE INFORMATION

Applications for further education courses are generally made directly to the colleges concerned. Information on further education courses in the United Kingdom and addresses of colleges can be found in the *Directory of Further Education* published annually by the Careers Research and Advisory Centre.

NATIONAL COUNCIL FOR VOCATIONAL QUALIFICATIONS

The National Council for Vocational Qualifications (NCVQ) was set up by the Government in October 1986 to achieve a coherent national framework for vocational qualifications in England, Wales and Northern Ireland. The Council does not award qualifications but works with and through the established examining and awarding bodies to reform the existing vocational qualifications system and introduce simplified arrangements. SCOTVEC (*see* above) performs similar functions in Scotland, but its role includes the awarding of qualifications.

The name and style National Vocational Qualification is accorded to qualifications accredited by NCVQ. The NVQ framework is currently based on five levels incorporating qualifications up to and including the Higher National standard. From September 1992 General National Vocational Qualifications are to be introduced into colleges and schools. They cover broad categories in the NVQ framework and are aimed at those wishing to familiarize themselves with a range of opportunities. GNVQ level 3 is designed to be equivalent to two A-levels; at level 2 it provides a one year post-GCSE course. GNVQs at level 1 and level 4 are under consideration.

The National Record of Vocational Achievement (NRVA) is to be replaced by the National Record of Achievement (NRA) by autumn 1993. The NRA is intended to be a record of achievement, both formal and informal, in education, training and employment, in a single format.

Higher Education

The term higher education is used to describe education above A-level and Higher grade or their equivalent, which is provided in universities and colleges of higher education.

The Further and Higher Education Act 1992 marked the end of the so-called 'binary' system in higher education in Great Britain; a unitary system already exists in Northern Ireland. It removed the distinction between higher education provided by the universities, which were funded by the Universities Funding Council, and that provided by the polytechnics and colleges of higher education, funded by the Polytechnics and Colleges Funding Council. They are now brought under a single funding structure, the Higher Education Funding Councils for England, Wales and Scotland. The HEFCs will take over from the UFC and PCFC from April 1993. The Act also provides for other changes to bring the non-university sector in line with the universities, including the right for all polytechnics and other higher education institutions which satisfy the necessary criteria to award their own taught course and research degrees and to adopt the title of university, subject to Privy Council approval of the new name.

STUDENTS

In 1989–90, there were 689,100 full-time and sandwich students in higher education in the United Kingdom, of whom 72,800 were from overseas. The number of part-time students in the United Kingdom, including the Open University, was 396,000. The proportion of 16 to 20 year-olds entering full-time higher education in Great Britain rose from 16.1 per cent in 1985–6 to 18.9 per cent in 1989–90. The number of mature entrants (those aged 21 and over when starting an undergraduate course and 25 and over when starting a postgraduate course) to higher education in 1989 (excluding those at the Open University) was 216,000, up by 55 per cent on 1981. The number of full-time students on science courses in 1989–90 was 130,800, of whom 38,100 were female.

ACADEMIC STAFF

Each university appoints its own academic staff on its own conditions, though there is a common salary structure and, except for Oxford and Cambridge, a common career structure. The University Commissioners were appointed under the Education Reform Act 1988 to secure changes in university statutes to abolish the granting of tenure, thus enabling staff to be dismissed for good cause and for redundancy.

The Education Reform Act 1988 took polytechnics and higher education colleges in England and Wales out of local education authority control, turning them into employers on their own account. The Universities and Colleges Employers'

Forum, originally the Polytechnics and Colleges Employers' Forum, was set up to look after terms and conditions of employment and has negotiated the introduction of an academic contract similar to that obtaining in the universities which pre-dated the Higher and Further Education Act 1992.

Teaching staff in higher education require no formal teaching qualification, but teacher trainers are required to spend a certain amount of time in schools to ensure that they have sufficient recent practical experience.

In 1990–1 there were 55,852 full-time and part-time academic staff in universities in the United Kingdom and 114,257 in public sector further and higher education.

The 1992–3 salary scales for non-clinical academic staff in universities are as follows: lecturer grade A £14,428–£18,897; lecturer grade B £19,686–£25,183; senior lecturer £26,417–£29,855; professor £30,467 (minimum). Salary scales for lecturers in polytechnics, now universities, and colleges of higher education can be obtained from the Universities and Colleges Employers' Forum. The salaries of clinical academic staff are kept broadly comparable to those of doctors and dentists in the National Health Service.

UNIVERSITIES

The universities which pre-date the Higher and Further Education Act 1992 are self-governing institutions, usually established by Royal Charter. They have academic freedom and are responsible for their own academic appointments, curricula and student admissions.

Overall responsibility for universities in Great Britain rests with the Secretary of State for Education, who consults with the Secretaries of State for Scotland and Wales as necessary. Universities in Northern Ireland are the responsibility of the Secretary of State for Northern Ireland.

Advice to the Government on university matters is provided by the Universities Funding Council (UFC) until March 1993, when all its functions will be taken over by the Higher Education Funding Councils, which will also advise the Secretary of State for Northern Ireland. The UFC acts as a buffer between the Government, from which it receives a block grant of money, and the universities, to which it allocates its grant. Its brief is to secure more effective use of public funds allocated to higher education and to be instrumental in promoting government policy with regard to universities.

Before June 1992, when 28 former polytechnics adopted the title, there were 46 universities in the United Kingdom. Of these 46, 35 were in England, one (a federal institution) in Wales, eight in Scotland and two in Northern Ireland. In 1990–1 there was a total of 370,254 full-time students at universities in the United Kingdom (15,968 from EC countries; 42,771 from other overseas countries) and 58,604 part-time students. Women form 43.7 per cent of the full-time total and 44.6 per cent of the part-time total.

The non-residential Open University provides courses leading to degrees nationally. Teaching is through a combination of television and radio programmes, correspondence, tutorials, short residential courses and local audio-visual centres. No qualifications are needed for entry. The Open University offers undergraduate, post-experience and post-graduate courses. The University also has a programme of higher degrees: B.Phil., M.Phil. and Ph.D. through research, and MA, MBA and M.Sc. through taught courses.

The Open University will continue to be grant-aided directly by the Department for Education until April 1993, when the Higher Education Funding Council for England will take over. For Open University purposes, Northern Ireland is administered as a separate section of the United Kingdom and the cost is met by the Department of Education for Northern Ireland.

In 1992, 79,500 undergraduates were registered at the Open University, of whom 38,160 were women and 41,340 were men. Estimated cost (1992) of a BA general degree was around £2,400 and of a BA Hons. degree over £3,200.

The independent University of Buckingham provides a two-year course leading to a bachelor's degree and its tuition fees were £8,052 for 1992. It receives no capital or recurrent income from the Government but its students are eligible for mandatory awards from local education authorities. Its academic year consists of four terms of ten weeks each.

COURSES

All universities, including the Open University, award their own degrees and sometimes act as awarding and validating bodies for neighbouring colleges of higher education which are not yet accredited. This latter function will probably increase when the Council for National Academic Awards (*see* below), the major validating body, ceases to operate in October 1992. With the exception of certain Scottish universities where Master is sometimes used for a first degree in arts subjects, undergraduate courses lead to the title of Bachelor – Bachelor of Arts (BA) and Bachelor of Science (B.Sc.) being the most common – and for a higher degree, Master of Arts (MA), Master of Science (M.Sc.) (usually taught courses) and the research degrees of Master of Philosophy (M.Phil.) and Doctor of Philosophy (Ph.D. or, at a few universities, D.Phil.).

Most undergraduate programmes at British universities run for three years, except in Scotland and at the University of Keele where they may take four years. Professional courses in subjects such as medicine, dentistry and veterinary science take longer. Details of courses on offer and of entry requirements to first degree courses can be found in the annual handbook produced co-operatively by the universities, *University Entrance: The Official Guide*, published by the Association of Commonwealth Universities (for address, *see* page 464).

Postgraduate programmes vary in length. Taught courses which lead to certificates, diplomas or master's degrees usually take one year full-time or two years part-time. Research degrees take from two to three years full-time and much longer if completed on a part-time basis. Details of taught courses and research degree opportunities can be found in *Graduate Studies* published annually for the Careers Research and Advisory Council by Hobsons Publishing PLC (for address, *see* page 464).

Post-experience short courses are forming an increasing part of university provision, reflecting the need to update professional and technical training. Most of these courses finance themselves.

ADMISSIONS

Apart from quotas for medical, dental and veterinary students, there are no limits set for student intakes and the individual university decides which students to accept and which to reject. Students applying for admission to a first degree course at most universities do not apply direct but through a clearing-house, the Universities' Central Council on Admissions (UCCA) on a joint UCCA/PCAS (*see* below) form. A single admissions system is to be established for 1994 entry. All universities in the United Kingdom participate in the UCCA scheme except the Open University, which conducts its own admissions direct. The *UCCA handbook* is issued free for use in completing UCCA application forms, and is available from schools, colleges, or direct from the Universities' Central Council on Admissions (for address, *see* page 464).

For admission as a postgraduate student, universities normally require a good first degree in a subject related to the proposed course of study or research, but each candidate is considered on his or her merits. Application is normally to the institution direct.

Finance

Although universities are being expected to look to a much wider range of funding sources than before, and to generate additional revenue in collaboration with industry, they are still largely financed, directly or indirectly, from government resources.

In the academic year 1990–1 the total recurrent income of universities in the United Kingdom was £4,422 million (£4,040 million in 1989–90). The exchequer grant was £1,590 million (£1,795 million in 1989–90), forming 36.6 per cent of total income (44.4 per cent in 1989–90), compared to 1976–7 when it formed 75 per cent. Income from research grants and contracts was £877 million, an increase of 14.8 per cent on the previous year.

NON-UNIVERSITY SECTOR

England and Wales

Polytechnics, most of which changed their names to include the title 'university' from October 1992, colleges of higher education, and other major establishments provide both further and higher education courses in England and Wales. These public sector higher education establishments were under local education authority control until April 1989, when the Education Reform Act 1988 legislated for the polytechnics and higher education colleges in England to be incorporated as independent institutions, each run by a Higher Education Corporation (HEC), responsible for providing higher education and carrying out research in these institutions. HECs are controlled by boards of governors appointed by the Secretary of State. At least half the members of each board must be drawn from industry, business, commerce and the professions.

Until March 1993 the HECs will continue to be funded by the Polytechnics and Colleges Funding Council (PCFC), which allocates funds between individual institutions for the provision of higher education, both in its own sector, and in colleges under local education authority control. The PCFC also advises the Secretary of State for Education on matters relevant to its sector. In April 1993, however, all its functions, together with those of the UFC, will be taken over by the Higher Education Funding Council for England (HEFC). Institutions of higher education in Wales became independent of the Wales Advisory Body for Local Authority Higher Education (WAB) in April 1992 and received their funding directly from the Welsh Office. WAB was concurrently dissolved, but advises the Secretary of State on funding for the sector for 1992–3. From April 1993 the Higher Education Funding Council for Wales (HEFCW) will take over. All higher education institutions are expected to supplement their income by undertaking consultancy work and exploiting commercial possibilities.

In 1989–90, there was a total of 301,019 students enrolled at polytechnics: 285,519 (44 per cent of them women) were on higher education courses, and of this number, 194,874 (45 per cent of them women) were full-time or sandwich course students. In those colleges of higher education now in the PCFC sector, there were (1989–90) 148,600 students, 112,442 on higher education courses, of whom 71,000 were full-time or sandwich course students.

There are 377 major establishments of higher education (maintained, assisted by LEAs, in receipt of direct grant from the DFE, or voluntary) in addition to the polytechnics. In England and Wales in 1989–90 they catered for 134,779 students on higher education courses including 32,957 on full-time or sandwich courses.

Courses

Higher education courses comprise courses for the further training of teachers, and other courses which last full-time for at least four weeks or, if part-time, involve more than 60 hours of instruction. They include first degree and postgraduate courses (including research), courses for Diploma of Higher Education, Higher National Diploma and Higher National Certificate, courses in preparation for professional examinations, and other courses above GCE A-level or Ordinary National Certificate standard. Facilities are available for full-time and part-time study, and day release, sandwich or block release courses are more commonly available than in the traditional universities.

The Diploma of Higher Education (Dip.HE) is a two-year diploma usually intended to serve as a stepping-stone to a degree course or other further study. The Dip.HE was formerly awarded by the Council for National Academic Awards (*see* below), but from September 1992 will be awarded by the colleges if they are accredited; by an accredited institution of their choice if they are not.

The BTEC Higher National Certificate (HNC) is awarded after two years part-time study. The BTEC Higher National Diploma (HND) is awarded after two years full-time, or three years sandwich or part-time study.

The Council for National Academic Awards (CNAA) was established by Royal Charter in 1964 as a self-governing body to award degrees to students taking courses approved by it in non-university institutions. Since then academic responsibility has increasingly been devolved to accredited institutions which control the academic standards of their own taught courses and research as well as having the authority to validate new courses and to modify existing ones. All the former polytechnics, together with five colleges of higher education, have so far been accredited. Under the Further and Higher Education Act 1992, the CNAA is to cease its functions by October 1992 and to be dissolved by March 1993.

CNAA degrees comprised: BA, B.Ed., B.Sc., and higher degrees including MA and M.Sc. (for postgraduate course work) and M.Phil. and Ph.D. (for research). Some colleges of higher education retained their traditional links with a university which validates and awards their degrees. All institutions which are accredited will be able to undertake validation and awarding for colleges which are not. The newly-instituted Higher Education Quality Council (HEQC) will be responsible for advising the Secretary of State on applications for degree awarding powers from September 1992.

Admissions

Information on all higher education courses in polytechnics including postgraduate courses up to the 1993 intake, can be found in the *Polytechnic Courses Handbook* available from the Committee of Directors of Polytechnics (for address, *see* page 464). Postgraduate courses in all higher education institutions are included in *Graduate Studies* (*see* page 455).

The entry requirements are two or three GCSEs at grades A to C, or equivalent, and two or three A-levels/AS levels for first degrees, and a good first degree in a related subject for postgraduate study, although each candidate is considered on his or her merits. Alternative entry qualifications, particularly technician-level awards, are often favourably considered.

The Polytechnics Central Admissions System (PCAS) acts as a clearing-house for all full-time and sandwich first degree, HND and Dip.HE courses listed in the *Polytechnic Courses Handbook*. Applications for art and design courses are made elsewhere (*see* below). Applicants can obtain a copy of the *Guide for Applicants* and the joint UCCA/PCAS application form either from their school or college or from PCAS. A joint admissions system for higher education is to operate from the 1994 entry.

For first degree and postgraduate courses in art and design and BTEC HND courses in design and associated studies, applications should be made through the Art and Design Admissions Registry.

For courses other than the above, applications are made to the institution direct, using the Institution Standard Application Form, available in schools or colleges or from Pennine Packaging Co. Ltd. Applications for courses at colleges of higher education outside the clearing-house schemes are also made direct to the institutions.

Scotland

In Scotland advanced full-time courses are provided by the universities and the Scottish centrally-funded colleges which include the eight central institutions, five colleges of education and the agricultural college. They are funded by central government through the Scottish Office Education Department (Agricultural College through the Department of Agriculture and Fisheries for Scotland). Each is managed by an independent governing body which includes representatives of industrial, commercial, professional and educational interests. Most of the courses have a vocational orientation and a substantial number are sandwich courses. They are intended to complement provision in the universities. The degree courses are validated either by individual institutions which have degree awarding powers, or by a university or by CNAA (until October 1992).

Major changes are taking place arising from the implementation of the Further and Higher Education (Scotland) Act 1992. Four of the central institutions become universities, while funding arrangements are transferred to the Scottish Higher Education Funding Council. Advanced courses are also provided through the 49 local education authority colleges. Major changes are also taking place here arising from the Act.

In 1989–90, 73,701 students were enrolled on advanced courses of higher education (50 per cent of them women): 34,708 at central institutions, 5,934 at colleges of education, and 33,059 at education authority colleges. Of the total number, 39,350 were on full-time or sandwich courses (50 per cent of them women).

Application arrangements vary from one institution to another; four have joined PCAS and for others some applications are made through UCCA. A joint system will operate for the 1994 intake. The remainder ask candidates to apply direct to the institution concerned. Application for teacher training courses is made to TEACH (*see* page 464). Further information can be obtained from the institutions themselves or from the secretariat of the Scottish Centrally-Funded Colleges (*see* page 464).

Northern Ireland

In Northern Ireland advanced courses are provided by 24 institutions of further education and by the University of Ulster. As well as offering first and postgraduate degrees, the University runs courses leading to the BTEC Higher National Diploma and professional qualifications. Applications to undertake courses other than degree courses are made to the institutions direct.

In 1989–90, 3,444 students were enrolled on advanced courses of higher education in the institutions of further education (44.8 per cent of them women). There were 854 students on full-time or sandwich courses, including 513 women.

FEES

The tuition fees for students with mandatory awards (*see* p. 458) are paid by the grant-awarding body. Students from member states of the European Community pay fees at home student rates. Since 1980–1 students from outside the EC have paid fees that are meant to cover the cost of their education, but financial help is available under a number of schemes. Information about these schemes is available from British Council offices world-wide.

Although universities are free to set their own charges, the Committee of Vice-Chancellors and Principals recommend minimum fees for students from non-EC countries. Those for 1992–3 are £5,320 for arts students, £7,055 for science students, and £12,990 for students following clinical courses in medicine, dentistry and veterinary science. These compare with undergraduate fees for home and EC students of £1,855 for arts courses, £2,770 for laboratory or workshop based courses, mainly science and £4,985 for clinical courses in the academic year 1992–3.

All institutions of higher education charge the same fees for home students and EC nationals, but no recommended minimum fees have been set for non-EC overseas students for 1992–3 at the former polytechnics and colleges of higher education.

For postgraduate students, the maximum tuition fee that will be reimbursed through the awards system is £2,200 in 1992–3.

GRANTS FOR STUDENTS

Students in the United Kingdom who plan to take a full-time or sandwich course of further study after leaving school may be eligible for a grant. A parental contribution is deductible on a sliding scale dependent on income. For married students this may be deducted from their spouse's income instead. However, parental contribution is not deducted from the grant to students over 25 years of age who have been self-supporting for at least three years. The main rates of mandatory grant have been frozen from 1991–2, as it is envisaged that students will increasingly support themselves by loans (*see* below). Tuition fees are paid in full for all students in receipt of a grant, regardless of parental income, and they are usually paid direct to the university or college by the education authority.

Grants are paid by local education authorities in England, Wales and Northern Ireland, which are reimbursed for 100 per cent of the cost by central government, and by the Scottish Office Education Department in Scotland. Applications are made to the authority in the area in which the student normally lives. Applications should not, however, be made earlier than the January preceding the start of the course.

Types of Grant

Grants are of two kinds: mandatory and discretionary. Mandatory grants are those which awarding authorities must pay to students who are attending designated courses (*see* below) and who can satisfy certain other conditions. Such a grant is awarded normally to enable the student to attend only one designated course and there is no general entitlement to an award for any particular number of years. Discretionary grants are those for which each awarding authority has discretion to decide its own policy.

Designated courses are those full-time or sandwich courses leading to: a degree; the Diploma of Higher Education (Dip.HE); the Higher National Diploma (HND) of the Business and Technology Education Council; initial teacher-training courses, including those for the postgraduate certificate of education and the art teachers' certificate or diploma; a university certificate or diploma course lasting at least three years; other qualifications which are specifically designated as being comparable to first degree courses; and the SCOTVEC Higher National Diploma.

To be eligible for a mandatory grant, students admitted to a designated course must usually have been ordinarily resident in the United Kingdom for the three years immediately preceding the academic year in which the course begins; have not previously attended a course of advanced further education of more than two years' duration; and apply for the grant before the end of the first term of the course. The local education authority should be consulted for advice about eligibility.

Students taking designated courses who do not satisfy the residency condition may be eligible for a mandatory grant if they come from other member states of the EC and can establish migrant worker status, or their parents are migrant workers; or if they, or their spouse and children, are asylees or refugees.

A means-tested maintenance grant, usually paid once a term, covers periods of attendance during term as well as the Christmas and Easter vacations, but not the summer vacation. It is subject to deduction on account of the student's own income and her/his parents' or spouse's income. The basic grant rates are: £2,845 if living in a hall of residence or lodgings and studying within the London area; £2,265 as above but outside the London area; £1,795 if living at the parental home. Additional allowances are available if, for example, the course requires a period of study abroad.

Education authority and Scottish Office Education Department expenditure on student maintenance in 1990–1 was £1,454.8 million; 578.6 thousand mandatory awards were made.

Student Loans

The Education (Student Loans) Act 1990 legislated for interest-free but indexed top-up loans of up to £830 in 1992–3 to be made available to eligible students in the United Kingdom. This will increase the resources available to students by 20 per cent. The government expects that at least £176.3 million will be taken up in loans in 1992–3.

Students apply direct to the Student Loans Company Ltd, which will require a certificate of eligibility from their place of study. Loans are available to students on designated courses within the scope of mandatory awards and the same residency conditions apply. Repayment is normally over five to seven years, although it can be deferred if income is low.

Postgraduate Awards

Unlike funding for undergraduates, which is mandatory for most degree and equivalent level courses, grants for postgraduate study are usually discretionary. Grants are also often dependent on the class of first degree, especially for research degrees.

A number of schemes of postgraduate bursaries or studentships for residents in England and Wales are funded by the Department for Education, the five government research councils, the Ministry of Agriculture, Fisheries and Food, and the British Academy, which awards grants for study in the humanities.

In Scotland postgraduate funding is provided by the Scottish Office Education Department, the Scottish Office Agriculture and Fisheries Department, and the research councils as in England and Wales.

Awards in Northern Ireland are made by the Department of Education for Northern Ireland, the Department of Agriculture for Northern Ireland, and the Medical Research Council.

In 1989–90 in the United Kingdom 26,800 awards were made.

The national rates for twelve-month studentships in 1992–3 were: £5,195 in college or lodgings in London; £4,130 in college or lodgings outside London; £3,045 for those living with parents or spouse's parents. The rates for 30-week bursaries for 1992–3 were: £3,085 in college or lodgings in London; £2,435 in college or lodgings outside London; £1,840 if living with parents or spouse's parents.

Adult and Continuing Education

The term adult education covers a broad spectrum of educational activities ranging from non-vocational courses of general interest, through the acquiring of special vocational skills needed in industry or commerce, to study for a degree at the Open University.

Providers

Courses specifically for adults are funded and/or provided by many bodies. They include, in the statutory sector: local education authorities in England and Wales; the regional and islands education authorities in Scotland and the Scottish Office Education Department; education and library boards in Northern Ireland; the Open University; the extra-mural departments of other universities and Birkbeck College of the University of London; residential colleges; the Open College; the BBC, independent television and local radio stations. There are, in addition, a number of voluntary bodies.

The local education authorities in England and Wales operate through 'area' adult education centres (2,669 in 1990), institutes or colleges, and the adult studies departments of colleges of further education. The regional and islands education authorities in Scotland fund adult education, including that provided by the universities and the Workers' Educational Association, at vocational further education colleges (49 in 1990). In addition, the Scottish Office Education Department provides grants to a number of voluntary organizations. Provision in the statutory sector in Northern Ireland is the responsibility of the universities and the education and library boards, which operate 24 further education colleges and a number of community schools.

Over 40 universities have extra-mural, adult education or continuing education departments which serve their local areas or regions, and Birkbeck College in the University of London caters solely for part-time students. Institutions of higher education formerly in the PCFC sector in England and Wales, because of their range of courses and flexible patterns of student attendance, provide substantial opportunities in the field of adult and continuing education. The Polytechnic Association for Continuing Education (PACE) exists to promote collaboration between the former polytechnics and the colleges of higher education active in this area. The Open University, in partnership with the BBC, provides distance teaching leading to ordinary or honours first degrees, and also offers post-experience and higher degree courses (*see* page 474).

Of the voluntary bodies, the biggest is the Workers' Educational Association (WEA) which operates throughout the United Kingdom and comprises about 900 branches, organized into 19 districts, and nearly 1,500 affiliated educational and workers' organizations, reaching about 180,000 adult students annually. The Department for Education (DFE), Welsh Office, Scottish Office Education Department, Department of Education for Northern Ireland and local education authorities make grants towards provision.

The National Institute of Adult Continuing Education (England and Wales) (NIACE) provides information and advice to organizations and individuals on all aspects of adult continuing education. NIACE conducts research, project and development work, and is funded by the DFE, the Welsh Office, the LEAs and other funding bodies. The Welsh committee, NIACE Cymru, receives financial support from the Welsh Office Education Department, support in kind from the Welsh Joint Education Committee, and advises government, voluntary bodies and education providers on adult continuing education and training matters in Wales.

The voluntary organization which formerly advised on adult education in Scotland, the Scottish Institute of Adult and Continuing Education (SIACE) , has gone into sequestration.

The Northern Ireland Council for Continuing Education has an advisory role. Its membership includes representatives of most organizations involved in the field, together with appointees of the Northern Ireland Minister responsible for education.

The Universities Council for Adult and Continuing Education consists of one or two representatives from each university in the United Kingdom. It was established in 1947 for the interchange of ideas and the formulation of common policies on adult and continuing education.

Courses

Although lengths vary, most courses are part-time. Long-term residential colleges, which are grant-aided by the DFE, the Welsh Office or the Scottish Office, provide full-time courses lasting one or two years.

Some colleges and centres offer short-term residential courses, lasting from a few days to a few weeks, in a wide range of subjects. Local education authorities directly sponsor many of the colleges, while others are sponsored by universities or voluntary organizations. A booklet listing courses, *Residential Short Courses*, is published by NIACE.

Grants

Although full-time courses at degree level attract mandatory awards regardless of the age of the student, for courses below that level all students over the age of 19 must pay a fee. However, discretionary grants may be available. Adult education bursaries for students at the long-term residential colleges of adult education are the responsibility of the colleges themselves. Until March 1993 the awards are administered for the colleges by the Awards Officer of the Residential Colleges Committee for students resident in England; by the Welsh Office Education Department for those resident in Wales; by the Scottish Office Education Department for those resident in Scotland; and by the Department of Education for Northern Ireland for students resident there. The bursaries are paid in accordance with the rates and conditions set from time to time by the DFE. From April 1993 the bursary scheme will be funded by the Further Education Funding Council, and further changes may be made to the scheme after this date. *Adult Education Bursaries* can be obtained from the Awards Officer, Adult Education Bursaries, c/o Ruskin College (*see* page 477), who will also provide further details of the changes in funding to prospective applicants.

Numbers

There are no comprehensive statistics covering all aspects of adult education. However, it is known that enrolments on evening courses in further education establishments in the United Kingdom numbered 2,870,000 in 1989–90 (53.4 per cent women). This number included 1,586,000 students at adult education centres. In 1990–1, 339,927 students attended courses of liberal adult education provided by university extra-mural departments, including joint courses with the WEA, in the United Kingdom.

Education Directory

Local Education Authorities

ENGLAND

COUNTY COUNCILS

AVON, PO Box 57, Avon House North, St James Barton, Bristol BS99 7EB. Tel: 0272-290777. *Director*, G. Badman.

BEDFORDSHIRE, County Hall, Cauldwell Street, Bedford MK42 9AP. Tel: 0234-363222. *Director*, D. G. Wadsworth.

BERKSHIRE, Shire Hall, Shinfield Park, Reading RG2 9XE. Tel: 0734-233400. *Chief Education Officer*, S. R. Goodchild.

BUCKINGHAMSHIRE, County Hall, Aylesbury HP20 1UZ. Tel: 0296-395000. *Chief Education Officer*, S. Sharp.

CAMBRIDGESHIRE, Castle Court, Castle Hall, Cambridge CB3 0AP. Tel: 0223-317667. *Director*, J. Ferguson.

CHESHIRE, County Hall, Chester CH1 1SF. Tel: 0244-602424. *Director*, D. Cracknell.

CLEVELAND, Woodlands Road, Middlesbrough TS1 3BN. Tel: 0642-248155. *County Education Officer*, B. Worthy.

CORNWALL, County Hall, Truro TR1 3AY. Tel: 0872-74282. *Secretary of Education*, D. W. Fryer.

CUMBRIA, 5 Portland Square, Carlisle CA1 1PU. Tel: 0228-23456. *Director*, Ms P. Black.

DERBYSHIRE, County Offices, Matlock DE4 3AG. Tel: 0629-580000. *Chief Education Officer*, G. Lennox.

DEVON, County Hall, Exeter EX2 4QG. Tel: 0392-382000. *Chief Education Officer*, S. W. Jenkin.

DORSET, County Hall, Dorchester DT1 1XJ. Tel: 0305-251000. *Director*, P. L. Gedling.

DURHAM, County Hall, Durham DH1 5UJ. Tel: 091-386 4411. *Director*, K. Mitchell.

EAST SUSSEX, PO Box 4, County Hall, St Anne's Crescent, Lewes BN7 1SG. Tel: 0273-481000. *County Education Officer*, D. Mallen.

ESSEX, PO Box 47, Threadneedle House, Market Road, Chelmsford CM1 1LD. Tel: 0245-492211. *County Education Officer*, R. M. Sharp.

GLOUCESTERSHIRE, Shire Hall, Gloucester GL1 2TP. Tel: 0452-425300. *Director*, K. D. Anderson.

HAMPSHIRE, The Castle, Winchester SO23 8UJ. Tel: 0962-841841. *County Education Officer*, P. J. Coles.

HEREFORD AND WORCESTER, Castle Street, Worcester WR1 3AG. Tel: 0905-763763. *County Education Officer*, J. W. Turnball.

HERTFORDSHIRE, County Hall, Hertford SG13 8DF. Tel: 0992-555700. *County Education Officer*, Mrs H. du Quesnay.

HUMBERSIDE, County Hall, Beverley HU17 9BA. Tel: 0482-867131. *Director*, Dr M. W. Garnett.

ISLE OF WIGHT, County Hall, Newport PO30 1UD. Tel: 0983-821000. *Director*, J. A. Williams.

KENT, Springfield, Maidstone ME14 2LJ. Tel: 0622-671411. *Director*, R. Pryke.

LANCASHIRE, PO Box 61, County Hall, Preston PR1 8RJ. Tel: 0772-54868. *Chief Education Officer*, A. J. Collier.

LEICESTERSHIRE, County Hall, Glenfield, Leicester LE3 8RA. Tel: 0533-323232. *Director*, K. H. Wood-Allum.

LINCOLNSHIRE, County Offices, Newland, Lincoln LN1 1YL. Tel: 0522-552222. *Director*, A. M. Ridings.

NORFOLK, County Hall, Martineau Lane, Norwich NR1 2DH. Tel: 0603-222146. *Director*, M. H. Edwards.

NORTHAMPTONSHIRE, Northampton House, Northampton NN1 2HX. Tel: 0604-236250. *Director*, J. R. Atkinson.

NORTHUMBERLAND, County Hall, Morpeth NE61 2EF. Tel: 0670-514343. *Director*, C. C. Tipple.

NORTH YORKSHIRE, County Hall, Racecourse Lane, Northallerton DL7 8AE. Tel: 0609-780780. *Director*, F. F. Evans.

NOTTINGHAMSHIRE, County Hall, West Bridgford, Nottingham NG2 7QP. Tel: 0602-823823. *Director*, P. J. Housden.

OXFORDSHIRE, Macclesfield House, New Road, Oxford OX1 1NA. Tel: 0865-815449. *Chief Education Officer*, Mrs J. Stephens.

SHROPSHIRE, The Shirehall, Abbey Foregate, Shrewsbury SY2 6ND. Tel: 0743-254301. *County Education Officer*, P. B. Cates.

SOMERSET, County Hall, Taunton TA1 4DY. Tel: 0823-333451. *Chief Education Officer*, Mrs J. Wisker.

STAFFORDSHIRE, Tipping Street, Stafford ST16 2DH. Tel: 0785-223121. *Chief Education Officer*, Dr P. J. Hunter.

SUFFOLK, St Andrew House, County Hall, Ipswich IP4 1LJ. Tel: 0473-230000. *County Education Officer*, T. R. Cornthwaite.

SURREY, County Hall, Penrhyn Road, Kingston upon Thames KT1 2DJ. Tel: 081-541 9501. *County Education Officer*, M. C. Pinchin.

WARWICKSHIRE, PO Box 24, 22 Northgate Street, Warwick CV34 4SR. Tel: 0926-410410. *Director*, Ms M. Maden.

WEST SUSSEX, County Hall, Chichester PO19 1RF. Tel: 0243-777100. *Director*, R. D. C. Bunker.

WILTSHIRE, County Hall, Bythesea Road, Trowbridge BA14 8JE. Tel: 0225-753641. *Director*, I. M. Slocombe.

METROPOLITAN DISTRICT COUNCILS

BARNSLEY, Berneslai Close, Barnsley. Tel: 0226-733252. *Director (acting)*, M. Warrington.

BIRMINGHAM, Council House, Margaret Street, B3 3BU. Tel: 021-235 2550. *Chief Education Officer*, D. Hammond.

BOLTON, Paderborn House, Civic Centre, BL1 1JW. Tel: 0204-22311. *Education Officer*, B. Hughes.

BRADFORD, Flockton House, Flockton Road, BD4 7RY. Tel: 0274-752111. *Education Officer*, Mrs S. Conway.

BURY, Athenaeum House, Market Street, BL9 0BN. Tel: 061-705 5000. *Chief Education Officer (acting)*, J. Beech.

CALDERDALE, Northgate House, Halifax HX1 1UN. Tel: 0422-357257. *Director*, Miss J. Tonge.

COVENTRY, New Council Offices, Earl Street, CV1 5RS. Tel: 0203-831501. *Director*, C. Farmer.

DONCASTER, Princegate, DN1 3EP. Tel: 0302-734102. *Director*, A. M. Taylor.

DUDLEY, Westox House, 1 Trinity Road, DY1 1JB. Tel: 0384-452201. *Chief Education Officer*, R. K. Westerby.

GATESHEAD, Civic Centre, Regent Street, NE8 1HH. Tel: 091-477 1011. *Director*, D. Arbon.

KIRKLEES, Oldgate House, 2 Oldgate, Huddersfield HD1 6QW. Tel: 0484-422133. *Chief Education Officer*, Ms J. Devlin.

KNOWSLEY, Huyton Hey Road, Huyton, Merseyside L36 5YH. Tel: 051-489 6000. *Education Officer*, A. Culley.

LEEDS, Merrion House, Woodhouse Lane, LS2 8DT. Tel: 0532-348080. *Chief Education Officer*, R. S. Johnson, CBE.

LIVERPOOL, 14 Sir Thomas Street, L1 6BJ. Tel: 051-227 3911. *Director*, M. F. Cogley.

MANCHESTER, Cumberland House, Crown Square, M60 3BB. Tel: 061-234 5000. *Education Officer*, R. Jobson.

NEWCASTLE UPON TYNE, Civic Centre, NE1 8BU. Tel: 091-232 8520. *Education Officer*, N. Purser.

NORTH TYNESIDE, Stevenson House, Stevenson Street, North Shields NE30 1QA. Tel: 091-257 6621. *Education Officer*, P. Bainbridge.

OLDHAM, Old Town Hall, Middleton Road, Chadderton, OL9 6PP. Tel: 061-624 0505. *Education Officer*, W. R. Kneen, Ph.D.

ROCHDALE, PO Box 70, Municipal Offices, Smith Street, OL16 1YD. Tel: 0706-47474. *Director*, Mrs D. Cavanagh.

ROTHERHAM, Norfolk House, Walker Place, Rotherham. Tel: 0709-382121. *Education Officer*, B. H. Yemm.

ST HELENS, Century House, Hardshaw Street, St Helens WA10 1RN. Tel: 0744-24061. *Director (acting)*, B. M. Mainwaring.

SALFORD, Chapel Street, M3 5LT. Tel: 061-832 9751. *Chief Education Officer*, A. Lockhart.

SANDWELL, PO Box 41, Shaftesbury House, 402 High Street, West Bromwich B70 9LT. Tel: 021-525 7366. *Director*, S. Gallacher.

SEFTON, Town Hall, Bootle, Merseyside L20 7AE. Tel: 051-922 4040. *Education Officer*, J. A. Marsden.

SHEFFIELD, PO Box 67, Leopold Street, S1 1RJ. Tel: 0742-726341. *Director*, Ms A. Muller.

SOLIHULL, PO Box 20, Council House, B91 3QU. Tel: 021-704 6000. *Director*, C. J. Trinick.

SOUTH TYNESIDE, Town Hall and Civic Offices, South Shields NE33 2RL. Tel: 091-427 1717. *Education Officer*, I. L. Reid.

STOCKPORT, Stopford House, SK1 3XE. Tel: 061-480 4949. *Director*, J. E. Hendy.

SUNDERLAND, PO Box 101, Town Hall and Civic Centre, SR2 7DN. Tel: 091-567 6161. *Education Officer*, D. A. Bowers.

TAMESIDE, Council Offices, Wellington Road, Ashton-under-Lyne OL6 6DL. Tel: 061-330 8355. *Director*, A. M. Webster.

TRAFFORD, Town Hall, School Road, Sale M33 1YR. Tel: 061-872 2101. *Director*, vacant.

WAKEFIELD, County Hall, WF1 2QW. Tel: 0924-290900. *Education Officer*, A. Lenney.

WALSALL, Civic Centre, Darwall Street, WS1 1DQ. Tel: 0922-650000. *Education Officer*, M. J. Quinn.

WIGAN, Gateway House, Standishgate, WN1 1AE. Tel: 0942-44991. *Education Officer*, J. K. Hampson.

WIRRAL, Hamilton Building, Conway Street, Birkenhead L41 4FD. Tel: 051-666 2121. *Director*, D. Rigby.

WOLVERHAMPTON, Civic Centre, St Peter's Square, WV1 1RR. Tel: 0902-27811. *Director*, Ms C. Adams.

LONDON

The ILEA was abolished on 1 April 1990 and from that date the inner London boroughs(*) and the Corporation of the City of London assumed responsibility for the provision of education within their own areas.

BARKING AND DAGENHAM, Town Hall, Barking, Essex IG11 7LU. Tel: 081-592 4500. *Education Officer*, A. Larbalastier.

BARNET, Town Hall, Friern Barnet, N11 3DL. Tel: 081-368 1255. *Education Officer*, N. M. Gill.

BEXLEY, Hill View, Hill View Drive, Welling, Kent DA16 3RS. Tel: 081-303 7777. *Director*, J. Hall.

BRENT, PO Box 1, 9 Park Lane, Wembley, Middx. HA9 7RW. Tel: 081-904 1244. *Director*, G. Benham.

BROMLEY, Town Hall, Tweedy Road, Bromley, Kent BR1 1SB. Tel: 081-464 3333. *Director*, G. Grainge.

*CAMDEN, Crowndale Centre, 216–220 Eversholt Street, NW1 1BD. Tel: 071-860 1525. *Education Officer*, P. Mitchell.

*CITY OF LONDON, Education Department, Corporation of London, PO Box 270, Guildhall, EC2P 2EJ. Tel: 071-260 1750. *City Education Officer*, D. Smith.

*CITY OF WESTMINSTER, City Hall, PO Box 240, Victoria Street, SW1E 6QP. Tel: 071-828 8070. *Education Officer*, Mrs D. Tuck.

CROYDON, Taberner House, Park Lane, CR9 1TP. Tel: 081-686 4433. *Director*, P. Benians.

EALING, Perceval House, 14–16 Uxbridge Road, W5 2HL. Tel: 081-579 2424. *Director*, M. Herman.

ENFIELD, PO Box 56, Civic Centre, Silver Street, EN1 3XQ. Tel: 081-366 6565. *Director*, G. Hutchinson.

*GREENWICH, Riverside House, Woolwich High Street, Woolwich, SE18 6DN. Tel: 081-854 8888. *Director*, N. McClelland.

*HACKNEY, 77–83 East Road, N1 6AH. Tel: 071-490 8838. *Director*, G. John.

*HAMMERSMITH AND FULHAM, Cambridge House, Cambridge Grove, W6 9JU. Tel: 081-748 3020. *Director*, Ms C. Whatford.

HARINGEY, 48 Station Road, N22 4TY. Tel: 081-975 9700. *Director*, R. L. Jones.

HARROW, Civic Centre, Station Road, Harrow HA1 2UW. Tel: 081-863 5611. *Director*, Mrs C. Gilbert.

HAVERING, Mercury House, Mercury Gardens, Romford RM1 3DR. Tel: 0708-766999. *Director*, C. Hardy.

HILLINGDON, Civic Centre, Uxbridge, Middx. UB8 1UW. Tel: 0895-250111. *Education Officer*, Ms K. Higgins.

HOUNSLOW, Civic Centre, Lampton Road, Hounslow, Middx. TW3 4DN. Tel: 081-570 7728. *Director*, J. D. Trickett.

*ISLINGTON, Laycock Street, N1 1TH. Tel: 071-226 1234. *Education Officer*, C. Webb.

*KENSINGTON AND CHELSEA, Town Hall, Hornton Street, W8 7NX. Tel: 071-937 5464. *Education Officer*, M. Stoten.

KINGSTON UPON THAMES, Guildhall, KT1 1EU. Tel: 081-546 2121. *Director*, W. Dickinson.

*LAMBETH, Blue Star House, 234–244 Stockwell Road, SW9 9SP. Tel: 071-926 1000. *Chief Education Officer*, R. Burchell.

*LEWISHAM, Laurence House, Catford, SE6 4SW. Tel: 081-695 6000. *Director*, L. Fullick.

MERTON, Crown House, London Road, Morden, Surrey SM4 5DX. Tel: 081-543 2222. *Director*, R. Davies.

NEWHAM, Broadway House, 322 High Street, E15 1AJ. Tel: 081-555 5552. *Director (acting)*, Ms D. Green.

REDBRIDGE, Lynton House, 255–259 High Road, Ilford, IG1 1NN. Tel: 081-478 3020. *Director*, K. G. M. Ratcliffe.

RICHMOND UPON THAMES, Regal House, London Road, Twickenham, TW1 3QB. Tel: 081-891 1411. *Director*, G. Alexander.

*SOUTHWARK, 1 Bradenham Close, SE5. Tel: 071-525 5000. *Education Officer*, G. Mott.

SUTTON, The Grove, Carshalton, Surrey SM5 3AL. Tel: 081-770 6500. *Director*, C. Blurton.

*TOWER HAMLETS, Birkbeck Street Complex, 27 Birkbeck Street, E2 6LA. Tel: 071-739 4344. *Education Officer*, Mrs A. Sofer.

Waltham Forest, Municipal Offices, High Road, Leyton E10 5QJ. Tel: 081-527 5544. *Director (acting)*, M. Meredith.
*Wandsworth, Town Hall, Wandsworth High Street, SW18 2PU. Tel: 081-871 7890. *Director*, D. Naismith.

WALES

County Councils

Clwyd, Shire Hall, Mold CH7 6NB. Tel: 0352-752121. *Director*, K. McDonogh.
Dyfed, Pibwrlwyd, Carmarthen SA31 2NH. Tel: 0267-233333. *Director*, J. G. Ellis.
Gwent, County Hall, Cwmbran NP44 2XG. Tel: 0633-838838. *Director*, G. V. Drought.
Gwynedd, County Offices, Caernarfon LL55 1SH. Tel: 0286-672255. *Director*, G. E. Humphreys.
Mid Glamorgan, County Hall, Cathays Park, Cardiff CF1 3NE. Tel: 0222-820820. *Director*, E. Roberts.
Powys, County Hall, Llandrindod Wells LD1 5LG. Tel: 0597-826422. *Director*, R. W. Bevan.
South Glamorgan, County Hall, Atlantic Wharf, Cardiff CF1 5UW. Tel: 0222-872000. *Director*, D. Orrell.
West Glamorgan, County Hall, Swansea SA1 3SN. Tel: 0792-471111. *Director*, J. Beale.

SCOTLAND

Regional and Islands Councils

Borders, Regional Headquarters, Newtown St Boswells, Melrose TD6 0SA. Tel: 0835-23301. *Director*, I. Dutton.
Central, Regional Council Offices, Viewforth, Stirling FK8 2ET. Tel: 0786-442000. *Director*, I. Collie.
Dumfries and Galloway, 30 Edinburgh Road, Dumfries DG1 1JQ. Tel: 0387-61234. *Director*, W. C. Fordyce.
Fife, Fife House, North Street, Glenrothes KY7 5LT. Tel: 0592-754411. *Director*, P. B. Welsh.
Grampian, Woodhill House, Westburn Road, Aberdeen AB9 2LU. Tel: 0224-682222. *Director*, J. Graham.
Highland, Regional Buildings, Glenurquhart Road, Inverness IV3 5NX. Tel: 0463-702000. *Director*, Dr C. E. Stewart.
Lothian, 40 Torphichen Street, Edinburgh EH3 8JB. Tel: 031-229 9166. *Director*, W. D. C. Semple, CBE.
Orkney, Council Offices, Kirkwall KW15 1NY. Tel: 0856-873535. *Director*, J. Anderson.
Shetland, 1 Harbour Street, Lerwick ZE1 0LS. Tel: 0595-3535. *Director*, J. Halcrow.
Strathclyde, 20 India Street, Glasgow G2 4PF. Tel: 041-204 2900. *Director*, F. Pignatelli.
Tayside, Tayside House, 28 Crichton Street, Dundee DD1 3RJ. Tel: 0382-23281. *Director*, A. B. Watson.
Western Isles, Council Offices, Sandwick Road, Stornoway, Isle of Lewis PA87 2BW. Tel: 0851-703773. *Director*, N. R. Galbraith.

NORTHERN IRELAND

Education and Library Boards

Belfast, Board Headquarters, 40 Academy Street, Belfast BT1 2NQ. Tel: 0232-329211. *Chief Executive*, T. G. J. Moag.
North Eastern, County Hall, 182 Galgorm Road, Ballymena, Co. Antrim BT42 1HN. Tel: 0266-653333. *Chief Executive*, G. Topping.
South Eastern, 18 Windsor Avenue, Belfast BT9 6EF. Tel: 0232-381188. *Chief Executive*, T. Nolan, OBE.
Southern, 3 Charlemont Place, The Mall, Armagh BT61 9AX. Tel: 0861-523811. *Chief Executive*, J. G. Kelly.
Western, 1 Hospital Road, Omagh, Co. Tyrone BT79 0AW. Tel: 0662-240240. *Chief Executive*, M. H. F. Murphy, OBE.

ISLANDS, ETC.

Guernsey, PO Box 32, Grange Road, St Peter Port. Tel: 0481-710821. *Director*, J. D. Stephenson.
Jersey, PO Box 142, St Saviour JE4 8QJ. Tel: 0534-509500. *Director*, B. Grady.
Isle of Man, Department of Education, Murray House, Mount Havelock, Douglas. Tel: 0624-626262. *Director*, G. Baker.
Isles of Scilly, Town Hall, St Mary's TR21 0LW. Tel: 0720-22537. *Secretary for Education*, P. S. Hygate.

Advisory Bodies

Schools

Education Otherwise, 36 Kinross Road, Leamington Spa, Warks. CV32 7EF. *Helpline*, Tel: 0926-886828.
International Baccalaureate, Examinations Office, Pascal Close, Cardiff CF3 0YP. Tel: 0222-770770. *Director of Examinations*, C. Carthew.
Schools Examination and Assessment Council, Newcombe House, 45 Notting Hill Gate, London W11 3JB. Tel: 071-243 9238. *Chairman*, The Lord Griffiths of Fforestfach; *Chief Executive*, Dr H. A. Nicolle.

Independent Schools

Assisted Places Committee, 26 Queen Anne's Gate, London SW1H 9AN. Tel: 071-222 9595. *Secretary*, Mrs M. L. Shaw.
Common Entrance Board, Drax House, Tilshead, Salisbury, Wilts. SP3 4SJ. Tel: 0980-620473. *Secretary*, Mrs E. J. Twiston-Davies.
Governing Bodies Association, Windleshaw Lodge, Withyham, Nr. Hartfield, E. Sussex TN7 4DB. Tel: 0892-770879. *Secretary*, D. G. Banwell.
Governing Bodies of Girls' Schools Association, Windleshaw Lodge, Withyham, Nr. Hartfield, E. Sussex TN7 4DB. Tel: 0892-770879. *Secretary*, D. G. Banwell.
Independent Schools Information Service, 56 Buckingham Gate, London SW1E 6AG. Tel: 071-630 8793. *National Director*, D. J. Woodhead.

Further Education

Further Education Unit, Citadel Place, Tinworth Street, London SE11 5EH. Tel: 071-962 1280. *Chief Officer*, G. Stanton.
National Council for Vocational Qualifications, 222 Euston Road, London NW1 2BZ. Tel: 071-387 9898. *Chief Executive*, J. Hillier.

Regional Advisory Councils

Centra (North Western Regional Advisory Council for Further Education) ,Walkden

Road, Worsley, Manchester M28 4QE. Tel: 061-702 8700. *Manager*, R. S. Welsh.

EAST ANGLIAN REGIONAL ADVISORY COUNCIL FOR FURTHER EDUCATION, 2 Looms Lane, Bury St Edmunds, Suffolk IP33 1HE. Tel: 0284-764977. *Director*, Mrs H. Herrington.

EMFEC (EAST MIDLAND FURTHER EDUCATION COUNCIL), Robins Wood House, Robins Wood Road, Aspley, Nottingham NG8 3NH. Tel: 0602-293291. *Chief Executive*, R. Ainscough.

LONDON AND SOUTH EAST REGION ADVISORY COUNCIL FOR EDUCATION AND TRAINING (LASER), 232 Vauxhall Bridge Road, London SW1V 1AU. Tel: 071-233 6199. *Director*, L. South.

NORTHERN COUNCIL FOR FURTHER EDUCATION, 5 Grosvenor Villas, Grosvenor Road, Newcastle upon Tyne NE2 2RU. Tel: 091-281 3242. *Secretary*, J. F. Pearce.

SOUTHERN REGIONAL COUNCIL FOR EDUCATION AND TRAINING, The Mezzanine Suite, Civic Centre, Reading RG1 7TD. Tel: 0734-390592. *Secretary*, B. J. Knowles.

SOUTH WEST ASSOCIATION FOR FURTHER EDUCATION AND TRAINING, Bishops Hull House, Bishops Hull, Taunton, Somerset TA1 5RA. Tel: 0823-335491. *Secretary*, F. S. Fisher.

WELSH JOINT EDUCATION COMMITTEE, 245 Western Avenue, Cardiff CF5 2YX. Tel: 0222-561231. *Secretary*, C. Heycock.

WEST MIDLANDS ADVISORY COUNCIL FOR FURTHER EDUCATION AND TRAINING, Norfolk House, Smallbrook Queensway, Birmingham B5 4NB. Tel: 021-643 8924. *Chief Officer*, C. H. Smith.

YORKSHIRE AND HUMBERSIDE ASSOCIATION FOR FURTHER AND HIGHER EDUCATION, 13 Wellington Road, Dewsbury, W. Yorks. WF13 1XG. Tel: 0924-450900. *Secretary (acting)*, Ms P. Cole.

HIGHER EDUCATION

COMMITTEE OF VICE-CHANCELLORS AND PRINCIPALS OF THE UNIVERSITIES OF THE UNITED KINGDOM, 29 Tavistock Square, London WC1H 9EZ. Tel: 071-387 9231. *Chairman*, Dr D. Harrison.

HIGHER EDUCATION QUALITY COUNCIL, 344–354 Gray's Inn Road, London WC1X 8BP. Tel: 071-278 4411.

CURRICULUM COUNCILS, ETC.

NATIONAL CURRICULUM COUNCIL, Albion Wharf, 25 Skeldergate, York YO1 2XL. Tel: 0904-622533. *Chief Executive*, C. Woodhead.

NORTHERN IRELAND CURRICULUM COUNCIL, Stranmillis College, Stranmillis Road, Belfast BT9 5DY. Tel: 0232-381414. *Chief Executive*, Mrs C. Coxhead.

SCOTTISH CONSULTATIVE COUNCIL ON THE CURRICULUM, Gardyne Road, Broughty Ferry, Dundee DD5 1NY. Tel: 0382-455053. *Chief Executive*, C. E. Harrison.

CURRICULUM COUNCIL FOR WALES, Castle Buildings, Womanby Street, Cardiff CF1 9SX. Tel: 0222-344946. *Chief Executive*, B. Jones.

TVEI UNIT, Training Agency, Moorfoot, Sheffield S1 4PQ.

Examining Bodies

GCSE

NORTHERN EXAMINATIONS AND ASSESSMENT BOARD, Devas Street, Manchester M15 6EX. Tel: 061-953 1180. *Chief Executive*, Ms K. Tattersall.

NORTH WEST REGIONAL EXAMINATIONS BOARD, Orbit House, Albert Street, Eccles, Manchester M30 0WL. Tel: 061-953 1185. *Secretary (acting)*, Ms M. E. Hutchinson.

SOUTHERN EXAMINING GROUP, Stag Hill House, Guildford, Surrey GU2 5XJ. Tel. 0483-506506. *Joint Secretaries*, J. A. Day; J. Pailing.

UNIVERSITY OF LONDON EXAMINATIONS AND ASSESSMENT COUNCIL, The Lindens, 139 Lexden Road, Colchester CO3 3RL. Tel: 0206-549595; Stewart House, 32 Russell Square, London WC1B 5DN. Tel: 071-753 0053. *Chief Executive*, A. Smith.

WEST MIDLANDS EXAMINATIONS BOARD, Norfolk House, Smallbrook Queensway, Birmingham B5 4NJ. Tel: 021-631 2151. *Secretary*, B. Swift.

NORTHERN IRELAND SCHOOLS EXAMINATIONS AND ASSESSMENT COUNCIL, Beechill House, 42 Beechill Road, Belfast BT8 4RS. Tel. 0232-704666. *Chief Officer*, W. J. Caves.

WELSH JOINT EDUCATION COMMITTEE, 245 Western Avenue, Cardiff CF5 2YX. Tel. 0222-561231. *Secretary*, C. Heycock.

A-LEVEL

ASSOCIATED EXAMINING BOARD, Stag Hill House, Guildford, Surrey GU2 5XJ. Tel: 0483-506506. *Secretary-General*, J. A. Day.

NORTHERN EXAMINATIONS AND ASSESSMENT BOARD, Devas Street, Manchester M15 6EX. Tel: 061-953 1180. *Chief Executive*, Ms K. Tattersall.

OXFORD AND CAMBRIDGE SCHOOLS EXAMINATION BOARD, Purbeck House, Purbeck Road, Cambridge CB2 2PU. Tel: 0223-411211. *Secretary-General*, H. F. King.

OXFORD AND CAMBRIDGE SCHOOLS EXAMINATION BOARD, Elsfield Way, Oxford OX2 8EP. Tel: 0865-54421. *Secretary (acting)*, J. G. Lloyd.

UNIVERSITY OF CAMBRIDGE LOCAL EXAMINATIONS SYNDICATE, Syndicate Buildings, 1 Hills Road, Cambridge CB1 2EU. Tel: 0223-61111. *Secretary*, J. L. Reddaway.

UNIVERSITY OF LONDON EXAMINATIONS AND ASSESSMENT COUNCIL, Stewart House, 32 Russell Square, London WC1B 5DN. Tel: 071-331 4000. *Chief Executive*, A. Smith.

UNIVERSITY OF OXFORD DELEGACY OF LOCAL EXAMINATIONS, Ewert House, Ewert Place, Summertown, Oxford OX2 7BZ. Tel: 0865-54291. *Secretary*, J. Pailing.

SCOTLAND

SCOTTISH EXAMINATION BOARD, Ironmills Road, Dalkeith, Midlothian EH22 1LE. Tel: 031-663 6601. *Director*, H. A. Long, Ph.D.

SCOTTISH VOCATIONAL EDUCATION COUNCIL, Hanover House, 24 Douglas Street, Glasgow G2 7NQ. Tel: 041-248 7900. *Chief Executive*, T. J. McCool.

FURTHER EDUCATION

BUSINESS AND TECHNOLOGY EDUCATION COUNCIL, Central House, Upper Woburn Place, London WC1H 0HH. Tel: 071-413 8400. *Chief Executive*, J. E. Sellars.

CITY AND GUILDS OF LONDON INSTITUTE, 76 Portland Place, London W1N 4AA. Tel: 071-278 2468. *Director-General*, J. Barnes.

JOINT UNIT FOR DIP.VE AND FOUNDATION PROGRAMMES, 46 Britannia Street, London WC1X 9RG. Tel: 071-278 3344. *Chairman*, A. Ainsworth; *Head of Unit*, Ms S. Fifer.

RSA EXAMINATIONS BOARD, Westwood Way, Coventry CV4 8HS. Tel: 0203-470033. *Chief Executive*, M. F. Cross.

Funding Councils

FURTHER EDUCATION

From April 1993

FURTHER EDUCATION FUNDING COUNCIL UNIT, 22 Percy Street, London WIP 9FF. Tel: 071-637 1132. *Chief Executive*, W. H. Stubbs.

SCOTTISH FURTHER EDUCATION FUNDING UNIT, Scottish Office Education Department, 43 Jeffrey Street, Edinburgh EHI IDN. *Director*, J. G. Henderson.

WELSH FUNDING COUNCIL, FURTHER EDUCATION DIVISION, Lambourne House, Lambourne Crescent, Cardiff Business Park, Llanishen, Cardiff CF4 5GL. Tel: 0222-641841. *Chief Executive*, Prof. J. A. Andrews.

HIGHER EDUCATION

See also Government Departments and Public Offices section

Until April 1993

POLYTECHNICS AND COLLEGES FUNDING COUNCIL, Northavon House, Coldharbour Lane, Bristol BS16 IQD.

UNIVERSITIES' FUNDING COUNCIL, Northavon House, Coldharbour Lane, Bristol BS16 IQD.

From April 1993

HIGHER EDUCATION FUNDING COUNCIL FOR ENGLAND, Northavon House, Coldharbour Lane, Bristol BS16 IQD. Tel: 0272-317317. *Chief Executive*, Prof. G. Davies, FEng.

SCOTTISH HIGHER EDUCATION FUNDING COUNCIL, PO Box 1037, Edinburgh EHI IDJ. Tel: 031-244 5345. *Chief Executive*, Prof. J. Sizer.

WELSH FUNDING COUNCIL, HIGHER EDUCATION DIVISION, Lambourne House, Lambourne Crescent, Cardiff Business Park, Llanishen, Cardiff CF4 5GL. Tel: 0222-641841. *Chief Executive*, Prof. J. A. Andrews.

Admissions and Course Information

ART AND DESIGN ADMISSIONS REGISTRY, Penn House, 9 Broad Street, Hereford HR4 9AP. Tel: 0432-266653. *Registrar*, T. W. M. Gourdie.

THE ASSOCIATION OF COMMONWEALTH UNIVERSITIES, John Foster House, 36 Gordon Square, London WCIH OPF. Tel: 071-387 8572. *Secretary-General*, Dr A. Christodoulou, CBE.

CAREERS RESEARCH AND ADVISORY COUNCIL (CRAC), Sheraton House, Castle Park, Cambridge CB3 OAX. Tel: 0223-460277. *Director*, D. Blandford. *Publishers*, Hobsons Publishing PLC, Bateman Street, Cambridge CB2 ILZ.

COMMITTEE OF DIRECTORS OF POLYTECHNICS, Kirkman House, 12–14 Whitfield Street, London WIP 6AX. Tel: 071-637 9939. *Chief Executive*, Dr R. Brown.

GRADUATE TEACHER TRAINING REGISTRY, PO Box 239, Cheltenham, Glos. GL50 3SL.

PENNINE PACKAGING CO. LTD, Gale Street, Rochdale, Lancs. OL12 ODB. Tel: 0706-55787.

POLYTECHNICS CENTRAL ADMISSIONS SYSTEM, Fulton House, Jessop Avenue, Cheltenham, Glos. GL50 3SH. Tel: 0242-227788. *Chief Executive*, M. A. Higgins.

SCOTTISH CENTRALLY FUNDED COLLEGES, PO Box 142, Holyrood Road, Edinburgh EH8 8AH. Tel: 031-557 6309. *Secretary*, J. W. Robinson.

TEACHER EDUCATION ADMISSIONS CLEARING HOUSE (TEACH) (Scotland only), PO Box 165, Holyrood Road, Edinburgh EH8 8AT. *Registrar*, Miss R. C. Williamson.

UNIVERSITIES' CENTRAL COUNCIL ON ADMISSIONS, PO Box 28, Cheltenham, Glos. GL50 3SA. Tel: 0242-222444. *General Secretary*, P. A. Oakley.

Universities

Under the provisions of the Higher and Further Education Act 1992, polytechnics were permitted to apply to change their status to that of universities. Twenty-four polytechnics and Scottish central institutions will become universities from the beginning of the 1992–3 academic year. However, at the time of going to press, a few had not proposed or received approval of a proposed new name.

THE UNIVERSITY OF ABERDEEN (1495)
Regent Walk, Aberdeen AB9 IFX
Tel 0224-272000

Full-time Students (1990–1), 7,200.
Chancellor, Sir Kenneth Alexander, FRSE (1987).
Principal, Prof. J. Maxwell Irvine, Ph.D.
Secretary, N. R. D. Begg.
Rector, C. Bell (1991–3).

ANGLIA POLYTECHNIC UNIVERSITY (1992)
Victoria Road South, Chelmsford, Essex CMI ILL
Tel 0245-493131

Full-time Students (1990–1), 6,361.
Director, M. J. Salmon.
Head of Student Administration, D. Davies.

ASTON UNIVERSITY (1966)
Aston Triangle, Birmingham B4 7ET
Tel 021-359 3611

Full-time Students (1991–2), 4,570.
Chancellor, Sir Adrian Cadbury (1979).
Vice-Chancellor, Prof. Sir Frederick Crawford, Ph.D., D.Eng., D.Sc, FEng.
Registrar and Secretary, R. D. A. Packham.

THE UNIVERSITY OF BATH (1966)
Claverton Down, Bath BA2 7AY
Tel 0225-826826

Full-time Students (1991–2), 4,600.
Chancellor, vacant.
Vice-Chancellor, Dr V. D. VanderLinde.
Secretary and Registrar, R. M. Mawditt, OBE, FRSA.

THE UNIVERSITY OF BIRMINGHAM (1900)
Edgbaston, Birmingham B15 2TT
Tel 021-414 3344

Full-time Students (1990–1), 9,742.
Chancellor, Sir Alexander Jarratt, CB (1983).
Vice-Chancellor, Prof. Sir Michael Thompson, D.SC.
Registrar and Secretary, D. R. Holmes.

BOURNEMOUTH UNIVERSITY (1992)
(formerly Bournemouth Polytechnic)
Poole House, Talbot Campus, Fern Barrow, Dorset BH12 5BB
Tel 0202-524111

Full-time Students (1991-2), 6,800.
Chancellor, The Baroness Cox.
Vice-Chancellor, Dr B. R. MacManus.
Secretary and Registrar, D. Gibson.

THE UNIVERSITY OF BRADFORD (1966)
Bradford BD7 1DP
Tel 0274-733466

Full-time Students (1991–2), 5,647.
Chancellor, Sir Trevor Holdsworth (1992).
Vice-Chancellor, Prof. D. J. Johns, Ph.D., D.SC. (1989).
Registrar and Secretary, D. W. Granger, MBE.

THE UNIVERSITY OF BRIGHTON (1992)
(formerly Brighton Polytechnic)
Mithras House, Lewes Road, Brighton BN2 4AT
Tel 0273-600900

Full-time Students (1991–2), 8,500.
Chairman of the Board, M. J. Aldrich.
Director, Prof. D. J. Watson.
Deputy Director, D. E. House.

THE UNIVERSITY OF BRISTOL (1909)
Bristol BS8 1TH
Tel 0272-303030

Full-time Students (1991–2), 9,265.
Chancellor, Sir Jeremy Morse, KCMG (1989).
Vice-Chancellor, Sir John Kingman, FRS.
Registrar, Mrs C. M. Cunningham.
Secretary, J. H. M. Parry.

BRUNEL UNIVERSITY (1966)
Uxbridge, Middx. UB8 3PH
Tel 0895-274000

Full-time Students (1991–2), 4,900.
Chancellor, The Earl of Halsbury, FRS (1966).
Vice-Chancellor, Prof. M. J. H. Sterling.
Registrar, D. Neave.
Secretary, J. Alexander.

THE UNIVERSITY OF BUCKINGHAM (1983)
Founded 1976 as University College at Buckingham
Buckingham MK18 1EG
Tel 0280-814080

Full-time Students (1991–2), 901.
Chancellor, The Baroness Thatcher, OM, PC, FRS (1992).
Vice-Chancellor, The Rt. Hon. Sir Richard Luce (1992).
Registrar and Secretary, M. Lavis, Ph.D.

THE UNIVERSITY OF CAMBRIDGE

Number of undergraduates in residence 1992–3: *Men*, 6,116; *Women*, 4,331

UNIVERSITY OFFICERS, ETC.*

Chancellor, HRH The Duke of Edinburgh, KG, KT, OM, GBE, PC, *elected* 1977.
Vice-Chancellor, Prof. Sir David Williams (*Wolfson*), *elected* 1989.
High Steward, The Lord Runcie, PC, DD, *elected* 1991.
Deputy High Steward, The Lord Richardson of Duntisbourne, PC, MBE, TD, *elected* 1983.
Commissary, The Lord Oliver of Aylmerton, PC (*Trinity Hall*), *elected* 1989.
Proctors, W. C. Nixon, SC.D. (*Peterhouse*); P. Searby (*Fitzwilliam*), *elected* 1992.
Orator, J. Diggle, Litt.D. (*Queens'*), *elected* 1982.
Registrary, S. G. Fleet, Ph.D. (*Downing*), *elected* 1983.
Deputy Registrary, R. F. Holmes (*Darwin*), *elected* 1972.
Librarian, F. W. Ratcliffe, Ph.D. (*Corpus Christi*), *elected* 1980.
Treasurer, M. P. Halstead, Ph.D. (*Gonville & Caius*), *elected* 1985.
Secretary-General of the Faculties, D. A. Livesey, Ph.D. (*Emmanuel*), *elected* 1992.
Director of the Fitzwilliam Museum, S. S. Jervis (*Corpus Christi*), *elected* 1990.

COLLEGES AND HALLS, ETC.
with dates of foundation

CHRIST'S (1505), *Master*, Prof. Sir Hans Kornberg, Ph.D., D.SC., SC.D., FRS (1983).
CHURCHILL (1960), *Master*, Prof. A. N. Broers, Ph.D., FRS (1990).
CLARE (1326), *Master*, Prof. R. C. O. Matthews, CBE, FBA (1975).
CLARE HALL (1966), *President*, Prof. D. A. Low, Ph.D. (1987).
CORPUS CHRISTI (1352), *Master*, M. W. McCrum (1980).
DARWIN (1964), *Master*, Prof. G. E. R. Lloyd, Ph.D., FBA (1989).
DOWNING (1800), *Master*, P. Mathias, CBE, Litt.D., FBA (1987).
EMMANUEL (1584), *Master*, The Lord St John of Fawsley, PC, Ph.D. (1991).
FITZWILLIAM (1966), *Master*, Prof. A. W. Cuthbert, Ph.D., FRS (1991).

*Correspondence for the Vice-Chancellor and other administrative officers should be sent to the University Offices, The Old Schools, Cambridge CB2 1TN. Tel: 0223-337733.

GIRTON (1869), *Mistress*, Mrs J. J. d'A. Campbell, CMG (1992).
GONVILLE AND CAIUS (1348), *Master*, Prof. P. Gray, SC.D., FRS (1988).
HOMERTON (1824) (for B. Ed. Students), *Principal*, Mrs K. B. Pretty, Ph.D. (1991).
HUGHES HALL (1885), (for post-graduate students), *President*, T. D. Hawkins (1989).
JESUS (1496), *Master*, Prof. the Lord Renfrew of Kaimsthorn, SC.D. (1986).
KING'S (1441), *Provost*, Prof. P. P. G. Bateson, SC.D., FRS (1987).
*LUCY CAVENDISH COLLEGE (1965) (for women research students and mature and affiliated undergraduates), *President*, Dame Anne Warburton, DCVO, CMG (1985).
MAGDALENE (1542), *Master*, Sir David Calcutt, QC (1985).
*NEW HALL (1954), *President*, Mrs V. L. Pearl, Ph.D. (1981).
*NEWNHAM (1871), *Principal*, Ms O. S. O'Neill (1992).
PEMBROKE (1347), *Master*, Sir Roger Tomkys, KCMG (1992).
PETERHOUSE (1284), *Master*, Prof. H. Chadwick, KBE, DD, FBA (1987).
QUEENS' (1448), *President*, Revd J. C. Polkinghorne, SC.D., FRS (1989).
ROBINSON (1977), *Warden*, Prof. the Lord Lewis of Newnham, SC.D., FRS (1977).
ST CATHARINE'S (1473), *Master*, Prof. B. E. Supple, Ph.D. (1984).
ST EDMUND'S (1896), *Master*, R. M. Laws, CBE, Ph.D. (1986).
ST JOHN'S (1511), *Master*, Prof. R. A. Hinde, SC.D., FRS (1989).
SELWYN (1882), *Master*, Prof. Sir Alan Cook, SC.D., FRS (1983).
SIDNEY SUSSEX (1596), *Master*, Prof. G. Horn, SC.D., FRS (1992).
TRINITY (1546), *Master*, Sir Michael Atiyah, Ph.D., FRS, FRSE (1990).
TRINITY HALL (1350), *Master*, Sir John Lyons, Ph.D. (1984).
WOLFSON (1965), *President*, vacant.

*Colleges for women only.

THE UNIVERSITY OF CENTRAL ENGLAND IN BIRMINGHAM (1992)
(formerly Birmingham Polytechnic)
Perry Barr, Birmingham B42 5SU
Tel 021-331 5000

Full-time Students (1991–2), 11,316.
Vice-Chancellor, Dr P. C. Knight.
Secretary and Registrar, Ms M. Penlington.

THE UNIVERSITY OF CENTRAL LANCASHIRE (1992)
(formerly Lancashire Polytechnic)
Preston PR1 2TQ
Tel 0772-201201

Full-time Students (1991–2), 9,300.
Rector and Chief Executive, B. Booth.
Secretary, D. Sharrocks.

CITY OF LONDON POLYTECHNIC
31 Jewry Street, London EC3N 2EY
Tel 071-320 1000

Full-time Students (1990–1), 6,986.
Provost, Prof. R. Floud, D.Phil.
Registrar, B. High.

THE CITY UNIVERSITY (1966)
Northampton Square, London EC1V 0HB
Tel 071-477 8000

Full-time Students (1990–1), 4,468.
Chancellor, The Rt. Hon. the Lord Mayor of London.
Vice-Chancellor and Principal, Prof. R. N. Franklin, D.Phil., D.SC.
Registrar, A. H. Seville, Ph.D.
Secretary, M. M. O'Hara.

COVENTRY UNIVERSITY (1992)
(formerly Coventry Polytechnic)
Priory Street, Coventry CV1 5FB
Tel 0203-631313

Full-time Students (1990–1), 8,300.
Director, M. Goldstein, Ph.D., D.SC.
Registrar, Ms S. Haselgrove.

DE MONTFORT UNIVERSITY (1992)
(formerly Leicester Polytechnic)
PO Box 143, Leicester LE1 9BH
Tel 0533-551551

Full-time Students (1991–2), 14,500.
Chancellor, Dame Anne Mueller.
Vice-Chancellor and Chief Executive, Prof. K. Barker.
Secretary and Registrar, J. Wools.

THE UNIVERSITY OF DUNDEE (1967)
Dundee DD1 4HN
Tel 0382-23181

Full-time Students (1991–2), 4,550.
Chancellor, Sir James Black, FRCP, FRS (1992).
Vice-Chancellor, Prof. M. J. Hamlin, FRSE, FEng.
Secretary, R. Seaton.
Rector, S. Fry (1992–5).

THE UNIVERSITY OF DURHAM
Founded 1832; re-organized 1908, 1937 and 1963
Old Shire Hall, Durham DH1 3HP
Tel 091-374 2000

Full-time Students (1991–2), 6,061.
Chancellor, Sir Peter Ustinov, CBE, FRSL.
Vice-Chancellor and Warden, Prof. E. A. V. Ebsworth, Ph.D., D.SC., FRSE.
Registrar and Secretary, J. C. F. Hayward.

COLLEGES

Collingwood, *Principal*, G. H. Blake, ph.D.
Graduate Society, *Principal*, M. Richardson, ph.D.
Grey, *Master*, V. E. Watts.
Hatfield, *Master*, J. P. Barber, ph.D.
St Aidan's, *Principal*, R. J. Williams.
St Chad's, *Principal*, E. Halladay.
St Cuthbert's Society, *Principal*, S. G. C. Stoker.
St Hild and St Bede, *Principal*, J. V. Armitage, ph.D.
St John's, *Principal*, vacant.
St Mary's, *Principal*, Miss J. M. Kenworthy.
Trevelyan, *Principal*, Miss D. Lavin.
University, *Master*, E. C. Salthouse, ph.D.
Ushaw, *President*, Rt. Revd Mgr R. Atherton, OBE.
Van Mildert, *Principal*, Ms J. Turner, ph.D.

THE UNIVERSITY OF EAST ANGLIA (1963)
Norwich NR4 7TJ
Tel 0603-56161

Full-time Students (1991–2), *c.*5,500.
Chancellor, Revd Prof. W. O. Chadwick, OM, KBE, DD, FBA (1985).
Vice-Chancellor, Prof. D. C. Burke, ph.D.
Registrar and Secretary, M. G. E. Paulson-Ellis, OBE.

THE UNIVERSITY OF EAST LONDON (1992)
(formerly Polytechnic of East London)
Romford Road, London E15 4LZ
Tel 081-590 7722

Full-time Students (1991–2), 7,400.
Rector, Prof. F. Gould.
Secretary and Registrar, G. D. Miller.

THE UNIVERSITY OF EDINBURGH (1583)
Old College, South Bridge, Edinburgh EH8 9YL
Tel 031-667 1011

Full-time Students (1991–2), 13,080.
Chancellor, HRH The Prince Philip, Duke of Edinburgh, KG, KT, OM, GBE, PC, FRS (1952).
Vice-Chancellor and Principal, Sir David Smith, D.Phil., FRS, FRSE.
Secretary, M. J. B. Lowe, ph.D.
Rector, D. Munro (1991–4).

THE UNIVERSITY OF ESSEX (1964)
Wivenhoe Park, Colchester CO4 3SQ
Tel 0206-873333

Full-time Students (1991–2), 4,369.
Chancellor, The Rt. Hon. Sir Patrick Nairne, GCB, MC (1983).
Vice-Chancellor, Prof. R. J. Johnston, ph.D.
Registrar and Secretary, A. F. Woodburn.

THE UNIVERSITY OF EXETER (1955)
Exeter EX4 4QJ
Tel 0392-263263

Full-time Students (1991–2), 6,838.
Chancellor, Sir Rex Richards, D.SC., FRS (1981).
Vice-Chancellor, D. Harrison, CBE, ph.D., SC.D., FEng.
Academic Registrar and Secretary, I. H. C. Powell.

GLAMORGAN UNIVERSITY (1992)
(formerly Polytechnic of Wales)
Pontypridd, Mid Glamorgan CF37 1DL
Tel 0443-480480

Full-time Students (1990–1), 5,500.
Vice-Chancellor, vacant.
Registrar, J. O'Shea.

GLASGOW POLYTECHNIC
(proposed name: The Queen's University, Glasgow)
Cowcaddens Road, Glasgow G4 0BA
Tel 041-331 3000

Principal, Prof. J. S. Mason.

THE UNIVERSITY OF GLASGOW (1451)
Glasgow G12 8QQ
Tel 041-339 8855

Full-time Students (1991–2), 13,054.
Chancellor, Sir Alexander Cairncross, KCMG, FBA (1972).
Vice-Chancellor, Sir William Fraser, GCB, LL D, FRSE.
Registrar, J. M. Black.
Secretary, R. Ewen, OBE, TD.
Rector, P. Kane (1990–3).

THE UNIVERSITY OF GREENWICH (1992)
(formerly Thames Polytechnic)
Wellington Street, Woolwich, London SE18 6PF
Tel 081-316 8000

Full-time Students (1991–2), 9,700.
Vice-Chancellor, N. Singer, CBE, ph.D.
Academic Registrar, A. I. Mayfield.

HERIOT-WATT UNIVERSITY (1966)
Riccarton, Edinburgh EH14 4AS
Tel 031-449 5111

Full-time Students (1991–2), *c.*8,000.
Chancellor, The Lord Mackay of Clashfern, PC, QC, FRSE (1979).
Principal and Vice-Chancellor, Prof. A. G. J. MacFarlane, CBE, ph.D., FRS, FRSE, FEng. (1989).
Secretary, P. L. Wilson.
Registrar, D. Sturgeon.

THE UNIVERSITY OF HERTFORDSHIRE (1992)
(formerly Hatfield Polytechnic)
College Lane, Hatfield, Herts. AL10 9AB
Tel 0707-279000

Full-time Students (1990–1), 6,750.
Director, Prof. N. K. Buxton.
Registrar, P. G. Jeffreys.

THE UNIVERSITY OF HUDDERSFIELD (1992)
(formerly Polytechnic of Huddersfield)
Queensgate, Huddersfield HD1 3DH
Tel 0484-422288

Full-time Students (1991–2), 7,993.
Vice-Chancellor, Prof. K. J. Durrands, CBE.
Registrar, M. E. Bond.
Secretary, D. J. Lock.

THE UNIVERSITY OF HULL (1954)
Cottingham Road, Hull HU6 7RX
Tel 0482-46311

Full-time Students (1990–1), 6,819.
Chancellor, The Lord Wilberforce, CMG, OBE, PC (1978).
Vice-Chancellor, Prof. D. Dilks.
Registrar and Secretary, F. T. Mattison.

THE UNIVERSITY OF HUMBERSIDE (1992)
(formerly Humberside Polytechnic)
Cottingham Road, Hull HU6 7RT
Tel 0482-440552

Full-time Students (1991–2), 8,380.
Pro-Chancellor, Dr Harry Hooper.
Vice-Chancellor, Prof. R. King.
Registrar, Mrs P. Jackson.
Secretary, Miss M. Harries-Jenkins.

THE UNIVERSITY OF KEELE (1962)
Keele, Newcastle under Lyme, Staffs. ST5 5BG
Tel 0782-621111

Full-time Students (1991–2), 4,247.
Chancellor, Sir Claus Moser, KCB, CBE, FBA (1986).
Vice-Chancellor, Prof. B. E. Fender, CMG, Ph.D.
Registrar, D. Cohen, Ph.D.

THE UNIVERSITY OF KENT AT CANTERBURY (1965)
Canterbury CT2 7LX
Tel 0227-764000

Full-time Students (1991–2), 5,538.
Chancellor, R. Horton (1990).
Vice-Chancellor, D. J. E. Ingram, CBE, D.Phil., D.Sc.
Registrar, T. Mead, Ph.D.

KINGSTON UNIVERSITY (1992)
(formerly Kingston Polytechnic)
Penrhyn Road, Kingston upon Thames, Surrey KT1 2EE
Tel 081-547 2000

Full-time Students (1991-2), 11,019.
Vice-Chancellor, R. C. Smith, CBE, Ph.D.
Academic Registrar, Miss A. Hynes.
Secretary, E. Lang.

THE UNIVERSITY OF LANCASTER (1964)
Lancaster LA1 4YW
Tel 0524-65201

Full-time Students (1991–2), 6,040.
Chancellor, HRH Princess Alexandra, the Hon. Lady Ogilvy, GCVO (1964).
Vice-Chancellor, Prof. H. J. Hanham, Ph.D.
Secretary, G. M. Cockburn.

LEEDS METROPOLITAN UNIVERSITY
(formerly Leeds Polytechnic)
Calverley Street, Leeds LS1 3HE
Tel 0532-832600

Full-time Students (1990–1), 8,187.
Director, C. Price.

THE UNIVERSITY OF LEEDS (1904)
Leeds LS2 9JT
Tel 0532-431751

Full-time Students (1991–2), 13,553.
Chancellor, HRH The Duchess of Kent, GCVO (1966).
Vice-Chancellor, Prof. A. G. Wilson.
Registrar, E. Newcomb.

THE UNIVERSITY OF LEICESTER (1957)
Leicester LE1 7RH
Tel 0533-522522

Full-time Students (1991–2), 6,893.
Chancellor, The Lord Porter of Luddenham, OM, FRS, Ph.D., Sc.D. (1985).
Vice-Chancellor, K. J. R. Edwards, Ph.D.
Registrar, Prof. G. Bernbaum.

THE UNIVERSITY OF LIVERPOOL (1903)
PO Box 147, Liverpool L69 3BX
Tel 051-794 2000

Full-time Students (1991–2), 11,150.
Chancellor, The Viscount Leverhulme, KG, TD (1980).
Vice-Chancellor, Prof. P. N. Love, CBE.
Registrar and Secretary, M. D. Carr.

LIVERPOOL JOHN MOORES UNIVERSITY (1992)
(formerly Liverpool Polytechnic)
Rodney House, 70 Mount Pleasant, Liverpool L3 5UX
Tel 051-231 2121

Full-time Students (1990–1), c.8,500.
Chancellor, H. Cotton.
Vice-Chancellor, Prof. P. Toyne.
Registrar, Miss A. Richardson.

THE UNIVERSITY OF LONDON (1836)
Senate House, London WC1E 7HU
Tel 071-636 8000

Internal Students (1991–2), 51,392, External Students, 24,856.
Visitor, HM The Queen in Council.
Chancellor, HRH The Princess Royal, GCVO, FRS (1981).
Vice-Chancellor, Prof. S. R. Sutherland.
Chairman of the Court, The Lord Rippon of Hexham, PC, QC.
Chairman of Convocation, Prof. C. D. Cowan, CBE, Ph.D.
Principal, P. Holwell.

PRINCIPAL OFFICERS

Director of Resources and Planning, P. J. Griffiths.
Director of Finance, H. M. Green.
Director of Administration, J. R. Davidson.
Chief Executive to School Examinations Council, A. Smith.

SCHOOLS OF THE UNIVERSITY

BIRKBECK COLLEGE, Malet Street, London WC1E 7HX. *Master*, The Baroness Blackstone, Ph.D.
GOLDSMITHS' COLLEGE, Lewisham Way, New Cross, London SE14 6NW. *Warden*, Prof. K. J. Gregory, Ph.D.
IMPERIAL COLLEGE OF SCIENCE, TECHNOLOGY AND MEDICINE (includes St Mary's Hospital Medical School), Prince Consort Road, London SW7 2AZ. *Rector*, Prof. Sir Eric Ash, CBE, Ph.D., FRS.
INSTITUTE OF EDUCATION, 20 Bedford Way, London WC1H 0AL. *Director*, Sir Peter Newsam.
KING'S COLLEGE LONDON (includes former Chelsea College and Queen Elizabeth College), Strand, London WC2R 2LS. *Principal*, vacant.
LONDON SCHOOL OF ECONOMICS AND POLITICAL SCIENCE, Houghton Street, London WC2A 2AE. *Director*, J. M. Ashworth, Ph.D., D.Sc.
QUEEN MARY AND WESTFIELD COLLEGE, Mile End Road, London E1 4NS. *Principal*, Prof. G. Zellick.
ROYAL HOLLOWAY AND BEDFORD NEW COLLEGE, Egham Hill, Egham, Surrey TW20 0EX. *Principal*, Prof. N. Gowar.
ROYAL VETERINARY COLLEGE, Royal College Street, London NW1 0TU. *Principal and Dean*, Prof. L. E. Lanyon, Ph.D.
SCHOOL OF ORIENTAL AND AFRICAN STUDIES, Thornhaugh Street, London WC1H 0XG. *Director*, M. D. McWilliam.
SCHOOL OF PHARMACY, 29–39 Brunswick Square, London WC1N 1AX. *Dean*, Prof. A. T. Florence, Ph.D., FRSE.
UNIVERSITY COLLEGE, Gower Street, London WC1E 6BT. *Provost*, Dr D. H. Roberts, CBE, FRS.
WYE COLLEGE, Wye, Ashford, Kent TN25 5AH. *Principal*, Prof. J. H. D. Prescott, Ph.D.
*HEYTHROP COLLEGE, 11–13 Cavendish Square, London W1M 0AN. *Principal*, Revd B. A. Callaghan, SJ.

*Not in receipt of UFC/HEFCE grants.

MEDICAL SCHOOLS

CHARING CROSS AND WESTMINSTER MEDICAL SCHOOL, The Reynolds Building, St Dunstan's Road, London W6 8RP. *Dean*, J. E. H. Pendower.
ROYAL FREE HOSPITAL SCHOOL OF MEDICINE, Rowland Hill Street, London NW3 2PF. *Dean*, Prof. A. J. Zuckerman, MD, FRCP.
THE LONDON HOSPITAL MEDICAL COLLEGE, Turner Street, London E1 2AD. *Dean*, Prof. R. Duckworth, CBE, MD, FRCS, FRCPath.
ST BARTHOLOMEW'S HOSPITAL MEDICAL COLLEGE, West Smithfield, London EC1A 7BE. *Dean*, L. H. Rees, MD, FRCP.
ST GEORGE'S HOSPITAL MEDICAL SCHOOL, Cranmer Terrace, London SW17 0RE. *Dean*, Prof. A. W. Asscher, MD, FRCP.
UNITED MEDICAL AND DENTAL SCHOOLS OF GUY'S AND ST THOMAS' HOSPITALS, Guy's: London Bridge, London SE1 9RT; St Thomas': Lambeth Palace Road, London SE1 7EH. *Dean*, vacant.

POSTGRADUATE MEDICAL INSTITUTIONS

LONDON SCHOOL OF HYGIENE AND TROPICAL MEDICINE, Keppel Street, London WC1E 7HT. *Dean*, Prof. R. G. Feachem, Ph.D.
ROYAL POSTGRADUATE MEDICAL SCHOOL, Du Cane Road, London W12 0SH. *Dean*, Prof. Sir Colin Dollery.
BRITISH POSTGRADUATE MEDICAL FEDERATION (University of London), 33 Millman Street, London WC1N 3EJ. *Director*, Dr M. Green, DM, FRCP.
Comprises:
INSTITUTE OF CANCER RESEARCH, Royal Cancer Hospital, 17A Onslow Gardens, London SW7 3AL. *Director*, Prof. R. A. Weiss, Ph.D.
INSTITUTE OF CHILD HEALTH, 30 Guilford Street, London WC1N 1EH. *Dean*, Prof. R. J. Levinsky, MD, FRCP.
INSTITUTE OF DENTAL SURGERY, Eastman Dental Hospital, Gray's Inn Road, London WC1X 8LD. *Dean*, Prof. G. B. Winter, D.Ch., FDS.
NATIONAL HEART AND LUNG INSTITUTE, Dovehouse Street, London SW3 6LY. *Dean*, Prof. T. Clark, MD, FRCP.
HUNTERIAN INSTITUTE, Royal College of Surgeons of England, Lincoln's Inn Fields, London WC2A 3PN. *Master*, Prof. Sir Stanley Peart, FRS, FRCP; *Academic Dean*, Prof. G. P. Lewis, Ph.D.
INSTITUTE OF NEUROLOGY, National Hospital, Queen Square, London WC1N 3BG. *Dean*, Prof. D. N. Landon.
INSTITUTE OF OPHTHALMOLOGY, Judd Street, London WC1H 9QS. *Dean*, R. K. Blatch, MD, FRCS.
INSTITUTE OF PSYCHIATRY, De Crespigny Park, Denmark Hill, London SE5 8AF. *Dean*, D. S. Checkley, MD.

SENATE INSTITUTES

BRITISH INSTITUTE IN PARIS, 9–11 Rue de Constantine, 75007, Paris. *Director*, Prof. C. L. Campos, L-ès-L., Ph.D. *London office:* Senate House, Malet Street, London WC1E 7HU.
CENTRE FOR DEFENCE STUDIES, King's College London, Strand, London WC2R 2LS. *Director*, Prof. L. Freedman.

COURTAULD INSTITUTE OF ART, North Block, Somerset House, Strand, London WC2R 2LS. *Director*, Prof. C. M. Kauffman, Ph.D.
INSTITUTE OF ADVANCED LEGAL STUDIES, Charles Clore House, 17 Russell Square, London WC1B 5DR. *Director*, Prof. T. C. Daintith.
INSTITUTE OF CLASSICAL STUDIES, 31–34 Gordon Square, London WC1H 0PY. *Director*, Prof. R. R. K. Sorabji.
INSTITUTE OF COMMONWEALTH STUDIES, 27–28 Russell Square, London WC1B 5DS. *Director*, Prof. Shula E. Marks, Ph.D.
INSTITUTE OF GERMANIC STUDIES, 29 Russell Square, London WC1B 5DP. *Hon. Director*, Prof. M. W. Swales, Ph.D.
INSTITUTE OF HISTORICAL RESEARCH (including the Institute of United States Studies), Senate House, Malet Street, London WC1E 7HU. *Director*, Prof. P. K. O'Brien, D.Phil.
INSTITUTE OF LATIN AMERICAN STUDIES, 31 Tavistock Square, London WC1H 9HA. *Director*, Prof. L. M. Bethell, Ph.D.
INSTITUTE OF ROMANCE STUDIES, Senate House, Malet Street, London WC1E 7HU. *Director*, Prof. M. M. Bowie, D.Phil.
SCHOOL OF SLAVONIC AND EAST EUROPEAN STUDIES, Senate House, Malet Street, London WC1E 7HU. *Director*, Prof. M. A. Branch, Ph.D.
WARBURG INSTITUTE, Woburn Square, London WC1H 0AB. *Director*, Dr N. Mann.
INSTITUTE OF ZOOLOGY, Royal Zoological Society, Regent's Park, London NW1 4RY. *Director*, Prof. A. P. F. Flint, Ph.D., D.Sc.

INSTITUTIONS HAVING RECOGNIZED TEACHERS

JEWS' COLLEGE, 44A Albert Road, London NW4 2SJ. *Principal*, Rabbi I. Jacobs.
LONDON BUSINESS SCHOOL, Sussex Place, London NW1 4SA. *Principal*, Prof. G. Bain, D.Phil.
ROYAL ACADEMY OF MUSIC, Marylebone Road, London NW1 5HT. *Principal*, Sir David Lumsden, D.Phil., FRCM.
ROYAL COLLEGE OF MUSIC, Prince Consort Road, London SW7 2BS. *Director*, M. G. Matthews, FRSA, FRCM.
TRINITY COLLEGE OF MUSIC, Mandeville Place, London W1M 6AQ. *Principal*, P. Jones, CBE, FRCM.

LOUGHBOROUGH UNIVERSITY OF TECHNOLOGY (1966)

Loughborough LE11 3TU
Tel 0509-263171

Full-time Students (1991–2), 6,888.
Chancellor, Sir Denis Rooke, CBE, FRS, FEng (1989).
Vice-Chancellor, Prof. D. E. N. Davies, CBE, Ph.D., D.Sc., FRS, FEng.
Registrar, D. E. Fletcher, Ph.D.
Academic Secretary, N. A. McHard.

MANCHESTER METROPOLITAN UNIVERSITY

(formerly Manchester Polytechnic)
All Saints, Manchester M15 6BH
Tel 061-247 2000

Full-time Students (1990–1), c.12,500.
Director, Sir Kenneth Green.
Registrar, J. Karczewski-Slowikowski.

THE UNIVERSITY OF MANCHESTER

(Founded 1851; re-organized 1880 and 1903)
Oxford Road, Manchester M13 9PL

Full-time Students (1991–2), 14,150.
Chancellor, Prof. J. A. G. Griffiths, FBA (1986).
Vice-Chancellor, Prof. M. B. Harris, Ph.D.
Registrar and Secretary, K. E. Kitchen.

UNIVERSITY OF MANCHESTER INSTITUTE OF SCIENCE AND TECHNOLOGY (1824)

PO Box 88, Manchester M60 1QD
Tel 061-236 3311

Full-time Students (1991–2), 5,347.
President, Sir John Mason, CB, D.Sc., FRS (1986).
Principal, Prof. H. C. A. Hankins, Ph.D.
Secretary and Registrar, P. C. C. Stephenson.

MIDDLESEX UNIVERSITY (1992)

(formerly Middlesex Polytechnic)
White Hart Lane, London N17 8HR
Tel 081-362 5000

Full-time Students (1991–2), 9,599.
Vice-Chancellor, Prof. D. Melville, Ph.D.
Registrar, G. Jones.

NAPIER UNIVERSITY (1992)

(formerly Napier Polytechnic)
219 Colinton Road, Edinburgh EH14 1DJ
Tel 031-444 2266

Vice-Chancellor and Principal, Prof. W. Turmeau, CBE, FRSE.
Secretary and Registrar, I. J. Miller.

THE UNIVERSITY OF NEWCASTLE UPON TYNE

Founded 1852; re-organized 1908, 1937 and 1963
6 Kensington Terrace, Newcastle upon Tyne NE1 7RU
Tel 091-222 6000

Full-time Students (1990–1), 9,090.
Chancellor, The Viscount Ridley, KG, TD (1989).
Vice-Chancellor, J. R. G. Wright.
Registrar, D. E. T. Nicholson.

UNIVERSITY OF NORTH LONDON (1992)

(formerly Polytechnic of North London)
Holloway Road, London N7 8DB
Tel 071-607 2789

Full-time Students (1992–3), 7,300.
Vice-Chancellor, L. Wagner.
Academic Registrar, Dr M. Storey.

UNIVERSITY OF NORTHUMBRIA AT NEWCASTLE
(formerly Newcastle upon Tyne Polytechnic)
Newcastle upon Tyne NE1 8ST
Tel 091-232 6002

Full-time Students (1990–1), 10,043.
Vice-Chancellor, Prof. L. Barden, CBE, Ph.D., D.Sc.
Registrar, R. A. Bott.

NOTTINGHAM POLYTECHNIC
(proposed name: Nottingham Trent University)
Burton Street, Nottingham NG1 4BU
Tel 0602-418418

Full-time Students (1991–2), 12,260.
Director, Prof. R. Cowell, Ph.D.
Registrar, Ms A. E. Foster.

THE UNIVERSITY OF NOTTINGHAM (1948)
University Park, Nottingham NG7 2RD
Tel 0602-484848

Full-time Students (1991–2), 10,500.
Chancellor, Sir Gordon Hobday, Ph.D. (1979).
Vice-Chancellor, Prof. C. M. Campbell.
Registrar, G. E. Chandler.

OXFORD POLYTECHNIC
Headington, Oxford OX3 0BP
Tel 0865-741111

Full-time Students (1991–2), 8,000.
Director, Dr C. Booth.
Registrar, R. M. Tulloch.

THE UNIVERSITY OF OXFORD

Number of students in residence 1991–2:
Men, 8,693; *Women*, 5,595

UNIVERSITY OFFICERS, ETC.†

Chancellor, The Lord Jenkins of Hillhead, PC (*Balliol*), *elected* 1987
High Steward, The Lord Goff of Chieveley (*Lincoln* and *New College*), *elected* 1990
Vice-Chancellor, Sir Richard Southwood, D.Sc., FRS (*Merton*), *elected* 1989
Proctors, J. F. Iles, D.Phil. (*St Hugh's*); M. H. Matthews (*University*), *elected* 1992.
Assessor, D. S. Fairweather (*Corpus Christi*), *elected* 1992.
Public Orator, J. Griffin (*Balliol*), *elected* 1992
Bodley's Librarian, D. G. Vaisey (*Exeter*), *elected* 1986
Keeper of Archives, J. Hackney (*Wadham*), *elected* 1988
Director of the Ashmolean Museum, C. J. White (*Worcester*), *elected* 1985
Registrar of the University, A. J. Dorey, D.Phil. (*Linacre*), *elected* 1979
Surveyor to the University, D. W. Bending, *elected* 1985
Secretary of Faculties, A. P. Weale (*Worcester*), *elected* 1984
Secretary of the Chest, I. G. Thompson (*Merton*), *elected* 1986
Deputy Registrar (Administration), P. W. Jones (*Green*), *elected* 1991

OXFORD COLLEGES AND HALLS
with dates of foundation

ALL SOULS (1438), *Warden*, Sir Patrick Neill, QC (1977).
BALLIOL (1263), *Master*, B. S. Blumberg (1989).
BRASENOSE (1509), *Principal*, The Lord Windlesham, CVO, PC (1989).
CHRIST CHURCH (1546), *Dean*, Very Revd J. H. Drury (1991).
CORPUS CHRISTI (1517), *President*, Prof. Sir Keith Thomas, FBA (1986).
EXETER (1314), *Rector*, Sir Richard Norman, KBE, D.Sc., FRS (1987).
GREEN (1979), *Warden*, Sir Crispin Tickell, GCMG, KCVO (1990).
HERTFORD (1874), *Principal*, Prof. Sir Erik Zeeman, KBE, FRS (1988).
JESUS (1571), *Principal*, Dr P. M. North, CBE, DCL (1984).
KEBLE (1868), *Warden*, G. B. Richardson, CBE (1989).
LADY MARGARET HALL (1878), *Principal*, D. M. Stewart (1979).
LINACRE (1962), *Principal*, Sir Bryan Cartledge, KCMG (1988).
LINCOLN (1427), *Rector*, Sir Maurice Shock (1987).
MAGDALEN (1458), *President*, A. D. Smith, CBE (1988).
MERTON (1264), *Warden*, J. M. Roberts, D.Phil. (1985).
NEW COLLEGE (1379), *Warden*, H. McGregor, QC, DCL (1985).
NUFFIELD (1937), *Warden*, Sir David Cox, FRS (1988).
ORIEL (1326), *Provost*, E. W. Nicholson, DD, FBA (1990).
PEMBROKE (1624), *Master*, Sir Roger Bannister, CBE, DM, FRCP (1985).
QUEEN'S (1340), *Provost*, J. Moffatt, D.Phil. (1987).
REWLEY HOUSE (1990), *President*, G. P. Thomas, Ph.D. (1990).
ST ANNE'S (1952) (Originally Society of Oxford Home-Students (1879)), *Principal*, Mrs R. L. Deech (1991).
ST ANTONY'S (1950), *Warden*, R. Dahrendorf, Hon. KBE, Ph.D., FBA (1987).
ST CATHERINE'S (1962), *Master*, E. B. Smith, D.Sc. (1988).
ST CROSS (1965), *Master*, R. C. Repp, D.Phil. (1987).
ST EDMUND HALL (*c.* 1278), *Principal*, J. C. B. Gosling (1983).
*ST HILDA'S (1893), *Principal*, Miss E. Llewellyn-Smith, CB (1990).
ST HUGH'S (1886), *Principal*, D. Wood, QC (1991).
ST JOHN'S (1555), *President*, W. Hayes, D.Phil. (1987).
ST PETER'S (1929), *Master*, J. P. Barron, D.Phil. (1991).
*SOMERVILLE (1879), *Principal*, Mrs C. E. Hughes, CMG (1989).
TRINITY (1554), *President*, Sir John Burgh, KCMG, CB (1987).
UNIVERSITY (1249), *Master*, W. J. Albery, D.Phil., FRS (1989).
WADHAM (1612), *Warden*, Sir Claus Moser, KCB, CBE, FBA (1984).

* Colleges for women only.

---

† Correspondence for the Vice-Chancellor and other administrative officers should be sent to the University Offices, Wellington Square, Oxford OX1 2JD. Tel: 0865-270001.

WOLFSON (1966), *President*, Sir Raymond Hoffenberg, KBE, FRCP (1985).
WORCESTER (1714), *Provost*, R. G. Smethurst (1991).
CAMPION HALL (1896), *Master*, Revd J. A. Munitiz (1989).
GREYFRIARS (1910), *Warden*, Revd M. W. Sheehan, D.Phil. (1990).
MANCHESTER (1990), *Principal*, Revd R. Waller, Ph.D. (1990).
MANSFIELD (1886), *Principal*, D. J. Trevelyan, CB (1989).
REGENT'S PARK (1810), *Principal*, Revd P. S. Fiddes, D.Phil. (1989).
ST BENET'S HALL (1897), *Master*, Revd P. F. Cowper, OSB (1989).

UNIVERSITY OF PAISLEY (1992)
(formerly Paisley College of Technology)
High Street, Paisley PA1 2BE
Tel 041-848 3000

Full-time Students (1991–2), 5,000.
Vice-Chancellor and Principal, Prof. R. W. Shaw.
Registrar, D. Rigg.
Secretary, J. Fraser.

UNIVERSITY OF PLYMOUTH (1992)
(formerly Polytechnic South West)
Drake Circus, Plymouth PL4 8AA
Tel 0752-600600

Full-time Students (1991–2), 10,299.
Vice-Chancellor, R. J. Bull.
Registrar, Dr C. J. Sparrow.
Secretary, Dr R. M. Thorpe.

PORTSMOUTH UNIVERSITY (1992)
(formerly Portsmouth Polytechnic)
University House, Winston Churchill Avenue, Portsmouth PO1 1UP
Tel 0705-827681

Full-time Students (1991–2), 9,222.
Chancellor, The Lord Palumbo.
Vice-Chancellor, N. Merritt.
Academic Registrar, R. Moore.

THE QUEEN'S UNIVERSITY OF BELFAST (1908)
Belfast BT7 1NN
Tel 0232-245133

Full-time Students (1991–2), 9,259.
Chancellor, Sir David Orr.
President and Vice-Chancellor, G. Beveridge, Ph.D., FRSE.
Secretary, D. Wilson.

THE UNIVERSITY OF READING (1926)
Whiteknights, PO Box 217, Reading RG6 2AHA
Tel 0734-875123

Full-time Students (1991–2), 8,244.
Chancellor, The Lord Carrington, KG, GCMG, CH, MC, PC (1992).
Vice-Chancellor, E. S. Page, Ph.D.
Registrar, D. C. R. Frampton.

THE ROBERT GORDON UNIVERSITY (1992)
(formerly Robert Gordon Institute of Technology)
Schoolhill, Aberdeen AB9 1FR
Tel 0224-633611

Full-time Students (1991–2), *c*.4,500.
Principal, Dr D. A. Kennedy.
Academic Registrar, Mrs H. Douglas.
Secretary, D. Caldwell.

THE UNIVERSITY OF ST ANDREWS (1411)
College Gate, St Andrews KY16 9AJ
Tel 0334-76161

Full-time Students (1991–2), 4,484.
Chancellor, Sir Kenneth Dover, D.Litt., FRSE, FBA (1981).
Vice-Chancellor, Prof. S. Arnott, Ph.D., FRS, FRSE.
Secretary of Court, D. J. Corner.
Rector, N. Campbell (1992–4).

THE UNIVERSITY OF SALFORD (1967)
Salford M5 4WT
Tel 061-745 5000

Full-time Students (1991–2), 5,185.
Chancellor, HRH The Duchess of York (1990).
Vice-Chancellor, Prof. T. M. Husband, Ph.D, FEng.
Registrar (acting), M. D. Winton, Ph.D.

THE UNIVERSITY OF SHEFFIELD (1905)
Western Bank, Sheffield S10 2TN
Tel 0742-768555

Full-time Students (1991–2), 10,723.
Chancellor, The Lord Dainton, Ph.D., Sc.D., FRS (1979).
Vice-Chancellor, Prof. G. G. Roberts.
Registrar and Secretary, Dr J. S. Padley.

SHEFFIELD HALLAM UNIVERSITY
(formerly Sheffield Polytechnic)
Pond Street, Sheffield S1 1WB
Tel 0742-720911

Full-time Students (1991–2), 14,367.
Principal, J. Stoddart.
Registrar, Ms J. Tory.

THE UNIVERSITY OF SOUTHAMPTON (1952)
Highfield, Southampton SO9 5NH
Tel 0703-595000

Full-time Students (1991–2), 8,528.
Chancellor, The Earl Jellicoe, KBE, DSO, MC, PC, FRS (1984).
Vice-Chancellor, Sir Gordon Higginson, Ph.D, FEng.
Secretary and Registrar, J. F. D. Lauwerys.
Academic Registrar, Miss A. E. Clarke.

SOUTH BANK UNIVERSITY (1992)
(formerly South Bank Polytechnic)
103 Borough Road, London SE1 0AA
Tel 071-928 8989

Full-time Students (1991–2), 10,627.
Chancellor and Chairman of the Board of Governors, C. McLaren.
Vice-Chancellor, Baroness Perry of Southwark.
Registrar, N. Andrew.
Secretary, Ms L. Gander.

STAFFORDSHIRE UNIVERSITY (1992)
(formerly Staffordshire Polytechnic)
College Road, Stoke-on-Trent ST4 2DE
Tel 0782-744531

Full-time Students (1991–2), 8,121.
Director, K. Thompson.
Registrar, Miss F. Francis.
Secretary, K. Sproston.

THE UNIVERSITY OF STIRLING (1967)
Stirling FK9 4LA
Tel 0786-73171

Full-time Students (1992–3), 4,200.
Chancellor, The Lord Balfour of Burleigh, FRSE (1988).
Principal and Vice-Chancellor, Prof. A. J. Forty, CBE, Ph.D., D.Sc., FRSE.
Registrar, D. J. Farrington, D.Phil.
Secretary, R. G. Bomont.

THE UNIVERSITY OF STRATHCLYDE (1964)
16 Richmond Street, Glasgow G1 1XQ
Tel 041-552 4400

Full-time Students (1991–2), 9,980.
Chancellor, The Lord Tombs, LL D, D.Sc., FEng. (1990).
Principal and Vice-Chancellor, Prof. J. P. Arbuthnott.
Secretary, P. W. A. West.

UNIVERSITY OF SUNDERLAND (1992)
(formerly Sunderland Polytechnic)
Langham Tower, Ryhope Road, Sunderland SR2 7EE
Tel 091-515 2000

Full-time Students (1991–2), 8,200.
Vice-Chancellor, A. Wright, Ph.D.
Registrar, S. Porteous.
Secretary, J. D. Pacey.

THE UNIVERSITY OF SURREY (1966)
Guildford, Surrey GU2 5XH
Tel 0483-300800

Full-time Students (1991–2), 5,300.
Chancellor, HRH The Duke of Kent, KG, GCMG, GCVO (1977).
Vice-Chancellor, Prof. A. Kelly, CBE, Sc.D., FRS, FEng.
Secretary, H. W. B. Davies.

THE UNIVERSITY OF SUSSEX (1961)
Falmer, Brighton BN1 9RH
Tel 0273-678416

Full-time Students (1991–2), 6,659.
Chancellor, The Duke of Richmond and Gordon (1985).
Vice-Chancellor, Prof. G. Conway.
Registrar and Secretary, G. Lockwood, D.Phil.

UNIVERSITY OF TEESSIDE (1992)
(formerly Teesside Polytechnic)
Middlesbrough, Cleveland TS1 3BA
Tel 0642-218121

Full-time Students (1990–1), 7,239.
Vice-Chancellor, Dr D. Fraser.
University Secretary, M. McClintock.
Head of Academic Operations, M. White.

THAMES VALLEY UNIVERSITY (1992)
(formerly Polytechnic of West London)
St Mary's Road, Ealing, London W5 5RF
Tel 081-579 5000

Full-time Students (1991–2), 11,000.
Director, Dr M. Fitzgerald.
Registrar, Ms A. Denton.

THE UNIVERSITY OF ULSTER (1984)
(Amalgamation of New University of Ulster and Ulster Polytechnic)
Cromore Road, Coleraine BT52 1SA
Tel 0232-852926

Full-time Students (1991–2), 12,123.
Chancellor, The Lord Grey of Naunton, GCMG, GCVO, OBE (1985).
Vice-Chancellor, Prof. T. A. Smith.
Academic Registrar, K. Millar, Ph.D.
Secretary, J. A. Hunter.

THE UNIVERSITY OF WALES (1893)
King Edward VII Avenue, Cathays Park, Cardiff CF1 3NS
Tel 0222-382656

Chancellor, HRH The Prince of Wales, KG, KT, GCB, PC (1976).
Vice-Chancellor, Sir Aubrey Trotman-Dickenson.
Registrar, D. P. L. Davies.

COLLEGES

UNIVERSITY COLLEGE OF WALES, Aberystwyth. *Principal*, Prof. K. O. Morgan, D.Phil. (1979).
UNIVERSITY COLLEGE OF NORTH WALES, Bangor. *Principal*, Prof. E. Sunderland, Ph.D. (1984).
UNIVERSITY OF WALES COLLEGE OF CARDIFF, Cardiff. *Principal*, Sir Aubrey Trotman-Dickenson, Ph.D., D.Sc. (1968).
ST DAVID'S COLLEGE, Lampeter. *Principal*, Prof. K. Robbins, D.Litt, D.Phil., FRSE (1992).
UNIVERSITY COLLEGE, Swansea. *Principal*, Prof. B. L. Clarkson, Ph.D. (1982).
UNIVERSITY OF WALES COLLEGE OF MEDICINE, Cardiff. *Provost*, Prof. Sir Herbert Duthie, MD, Ch.M., FRCS (1979).

THE UNIVERSITY OF WARWICK (1965)

Coventry CV4 7AL
Tel 0203-523523

Full-time Students (1991–2), 7,896.
Chancellor, Sir Shridath Surendranath Ramphal, GCMG, QC (1989).
Vice-Chancellor, vacant.
Registrar, M. L. Shattock, OBE.

UNIVERSITY OF THE WEST OF ENGLAND, BRISTOL (1992)

(formerly Bristol Polytechnic)
Coldharbour Lane, Frenchay, Bristol BS16 1QY
Tel 0272-656261

Full-time Students (1991–2), 9,803.
Vice-Chancellor/Director, A. C. Morris.
Registrar, Mrs H. C. Croft.

THE UNIVERSITY OF WESTMINSTER (1992)

(formerly Polytechnic of Central London)
309 Regent Street, London W1R 8AL
Tel 071-911 5000.

Full-time Students (1991–2), 5,000.
Rector, T. E. Burlin.
Deputy-Rector, G. M. Copland.
Registrar, Ms J. Hopkinson.

UNIVERSITY OF WOLVERHAMPTON (1992)

(formerly Wolverhampton Polytechnic)
Molineux Street, Wolverhampton WV1 1SB
Tel 0902-321000

Full-time Students (1991–2), 12,059.
Director, Prof. M. J. Harrison.
Assistant Director, G. R. Brooks.

THE UNIVERSITY OF YORK (1963)

Heslington, York YO1 5DD
Tel 0904-430000

Full-time Students (1991–2), 4,626.
Chancellor, Dame Janet Baker, DBE.
Vice-Chancellor, Prof. S. B. Saul, Ph.D.
Registrar, D. J. Foster.

CRANFIELD INSTITUTE OF TECHNOLOGY (1969)

Cranfield, Bedford MK43 0AL
Tel 0908-672974

Under Royal Charter (1969) the Cranfield Institute of Technology grants degrees in applied science, engineering, technology and management.
Full-time Students (1991–2), 2,213.
Chancellor, The Lord Kings Norton, Ph.D., FEng. (1969).
Vice-Chancellor, Prof. F. R. Hartley, D.Sc.
Secretary and Registrar, J. K. Pettifer.

THE OPEN UNIVERSITY (1969)

Walton Hall, Milton Keynes MK7 6AA
Tel 0908-274066

Students and clients (1992), 195,000.
Tuition by correspondence linked with special radio and television programmes, video and audio cassettes, residential schools and a locally-based tutorial and counselling service. Under Royal Charter the University awards degrees of BA, B.Phil., MA, MBA, M.Sc., M.Phil., Ph.D., D.Sc. and D.Litt. There are eight faculties: arts; education; health, welfare and community education; management; mathematics; science; social sciences; technology; and a wide range of qualification courses and study packs.
Chancellor, The Lord Briggs, FBA (1978).
Vice-Chancellor, Dr J. S. Daniel.
Secretary, D. J. Clinch.

THE ROYAL COLLEGE OF ART (1837)

Kensington Gore, London SW7 2EU
Tel 071-584 5020

Under Royal Charter (1967) the Royal College of Art grants the degrees of Doctor, Doctor of Philosophy, Master of Arts, Master of Design and Master of Design (Engineering) (RCA).
Students (1991–2), 700 (all postgraduate).
Provost, The Earl of Gowrie, PC (1986).
Registrar, A. Selby.

Non-University Sector

SCOTTISH CENTRAL INSTITUTIONS

DUNCAN OF JORDANSTONE COLLEGE OF ART, Perth Road, Dundee DD1 4HT. Tel: 0382-23261. *Principal*, R. Miller-Smith.
DUNDEE INSTITUTE OF TECHNOLOGY, Bell Street, Dundee DD1 1HG. Tel: 0382-308000. *Principal*, Prof. B. King.
EDINBURGH COLLEGE OF ART, Lauriston Place, Edinburgh EH3 9DF. Tel: 031-229 9311. *Principal*, Prof. A. J. Rowan, Ph.D.
GLASGOW SCHOOL OF ART, 167 Renfrew Street, Glasgow G3 6RQ. Tel: 041-332 9797. *Director*, D. Cameron.
QUEEN MARGARET COLLEGE, Clerwood Terrace, Edinburgh EH12 8TS. Tel: 031-317 3000. *Principal*, D. F. Leach.
THE QUEEN'S COLLEGE, GLASGOW, 1 Park Drive, Glasgow G3 6LP. Tel: 041-337 4000. *Principal*, Prof. J. C. Phillips.
ROYAL SCOTTISH ACADEMY OF MUSIC AND DRAMA, 100 Renfrew Street, Glasgow G2 3DB. Tel: 041-332 4101. *Principal*, Dr P. Ledger, CBE, FRSE.
SAC: THE NATIONAL COLLEGE FOR FOOD, LAND AND ENVIRONMENTAL STUDIES, Central Office, West Mains Road, Edinburgh EH9 3JG. Tel: 031-662 1303. Campuses at Aberdeen, Auchincruive, and Edinburgh. *Principal and Chief Executive*, Prof. P. C. Thomas.
SCOTTISH COLLEGE OF TEXTILES, Netherdale, Galashiels, Selkirkshire TD1 3HF. Tel: 0896-3351. *Principal*, C. E. R. Maddox, Ph.D.

COLLEGES

It is not possible to name here all the colleges offering courses of higher or further education. The list of English colleges that follows is confined to those in the PCFC sector; there are many more colleges in England providing higher education courses, some with PCFC funding. (The PCFC will be replaced by the Higher Education Funding Council for England in April 1993.)

The list of colleges in Wales, Scotland and Northern Ireland includes institutions providing at least one full-time course leading to a first degree granted by an accredited validating body. It does not include colleges forming part of a polytechnic or a university, nor does it include Scottish central institutions.

ENGLAND

PCFC SECTOR

BATH COLLEGE OF HIGHER EDUCATION, Newton Park, Newton St Loe, Bath BA2 9BN. Tel: 0225-873701. *Director*, B. L. Gomes da Costa.
BISHOP GROSSETESTE COLLEGE, Lincoln LN1 3DY. Tel: 0522-527347. *Principal*, Prof. L. Marsh, OBE, D.Phil.
BOLTON INSTITUTE OF HIGHER EDUCATION, Deane Road, Bolton BL3 5AB. Tel: 0204-28851. *Principal*, R. Oxtoby, Ph.D.
BRETTON HALL, COLLEGE OF THE UNIVERSITY OF LEEDS, West Bretton, Wakefield, W. Yorks. WF4 4LG. Tel: 0924-830261. *Principal*, Prof. J. L. Taylor, OBE, Ph.D.
BUCKINGHAMSHIRE COLLEGE OF HIGHER EDUCATION, Queen Alexandra Road, High Wycombe, Bucks. HP11 2JZ. Tel: 0494-522141. *Director*, P. B. Mogford.
CAMBORNE SCHOOL OF MINES, Pool, Redruth, Cornwall TR15 3SE. Tel: 0209-714866. *Principal*, P. Hackett, OBE, Ph.D., FEng.
CANTERBURY CHRIST CHURCH COLLEGE, North Holmes Road, Canterbury, Kent CT1 1QU. Tel: 0227-767700. *Principal*, M. H. A. Berry, TD.
THE CENTRAL SCHOOL OF SPEECH AND DRAMA, Embassy Theatre, Eton Avenue, London NW3 3HY. Tel: 071-722 8183. *Principal*, R. S. Fowler.
CHELTENHAM AND GLOUCESTER COLLEGE OF HIGHER EDUCATION, PO Box 220, The Park, Cheltenham GL50 2QF. Tel: 0242-532701. *Director*, Miss J. O. Trotter, OBE.
CHESTER COLLEGE, Cheyney Road, Chester CH1 4BJ. Tel: 0244-375444. *Principal*, Revd E. V. Binks.
COLLEGE OF ST MARK AND ST JOHN, Derriford Road, Plymouth PL6 8BH. Tel: 0752-777188. *Principal*, J. E. Anderson.
CREWE AND ALSAGER COLLEGE OF HIGHER EDUCATION, Crewe Green Road, Crewe CW1 1DU. Tel: 0270-500661. *Director*, Miss B. P. R. Ward, CBE.
DARTINGTON COLLEGE OF ARTS, Totnes, Devon TQ9 6EJ. Tel: 0803-862224. *Principal*, Dr J. Ritterman.
DERBYSHIRE COLLEGE OF HIGHER EDUCATION, Kedleston Road, Derby DE3 1GB. Tel: 0332-47181. *Director*, R. Waterhouse.
EDGE HILL COLLEGE OF HIGHER EDUCATION, St Helens Road, Ormskirk, Lancs. L39 4QP. Tel: 0695-575171. *Director*, Prof. R. Gee.
FALMOUTH SCHOOL OF ART AND DESIGN, Woodlane, Falmouth, Cornwall TR11 4RA. Tel: 0326-211077. *Principal*, Prof. A. G. Livingston.
HARPER ADAMS AGRICULTURAL COLLEGE, Newport, Shropshire TF10 8NB. Tel: 0952-820280. *Principal*, A. G. Harris, OBE.
HOMERTON COLLEGE, Cambridge CB2 2PH. Tel: 0223-411141. *Principal*, Mrs K. Pretty, Ph.D.
INSTITUTE OF ADVANCED NURSING, Royal College of Nursing, 20 Cavendish Square, London W1M 0AB. Tel: 071-355 1396. *Principal*, J. C. A. Wells.
KENT INSTITUTE OF ART AND DESIGN, Oakwood Park, Oakwood Road, Maidstone ME16 8AG (*also* New Dover Road, Canterbury CT1 3AN; and Fort Pitt, Rochester ME1 1DZ. Tel: 0622-757286. *Director*, P. I. Williams.
KING ALFRED'S COLLEGE, Sparkford Road, Winchester SO22 4NR. Tel: 0962-841515. *Principal*, J. P. Dickinson.
LIVERPOOL INSTITUTE OF HIGHER EDUCATION, PO Box 6, Stand Park Road, Liverpool L16 9JD. Tel: 051-737 3000. *Rector*, J. Burke, OBE, Ph.D.
THE LONDON INSTITUTE, 388–396 Oxford Street, London W1R 1FE. *Rector*, Prof. J. C. McKenzie. Comprising:
Camberwell College of Arts, Peckham Road, London SE5 8UF.
Central St Martin's College of Art and Design, Southampton Row, London WC1B 4AP.
Chelsea College of Art and Design, Manresa Road, London SW3 6LS.
London College of Fashion, 20 John Prince's Street, London W1M 9HE.
London College of Printing and Distributive Trades, Elephant and Castle, London SE1 6SB.
LOUGHBOROUGH COLLEGE OF ART AND DESIGN, Radmoor, Loughborough, Leics. LE11 3BT. Tel: 0509-261515. *Principal*, I. Pugh.

LSU COLLEGE OF HIGHER EDUCATION, The Avenue, Southampton SO9 5HB. Tel: 0703-228761. *Principal*, Dr A. C. Chitnis.

LUTON COLLEGE OF HIGHER EDUCATION, Park Square, Luton LU1 3JU. Tel: 0582-34111. *Director*, A. J. Wood, Ph.D.

NENE COLLEGE, Moulton Park, Northampton NN2 7AL. Tel: 0604-735500. *Director*, S. M. Gaskell, Ph.D.

NEWMAN COLLEGE, Genners Lane, Bartley Green, Birmingham B32 3NT. Tel: 021-476 1181. *Principal*, Joan S. Cuming, Ph.D.

RAVENSBOURNE COLLEGE OF DESIGN AND COMMUNICATION, Walden Road, Chislehurst, Kent BR7 5SN. Tel: 081-468 7071. *Director*, N. J. Frewing.

ROEHAMPTON INSTITUTE, Senate House, Roehampton Lane, SW15 5PU. Comprises Digby Stuart College, Froebel Institute College, Southlands College and Whitelands College. Tel: 081-392 3000. *Rector*, Prof. S. C. Holt, Ph.D.

ROSE BRUFORD COLLEGE OF SPEECH AND DRAMA, Lamorbey Park, Burnt Oak Lane, Sidcup, Kent DA15 9DF. Tel: 081-300 3024. *Principal*, P. Robins.

ROYAL ACADEMY OF MUSIC, Marylebone Road, London NW1 5HT. Tel: 071-935 5461. *Principal*, Sir David Lumsden, D.Phil.

ROYAL COLLEGE OF MUSIC, Prince Consort Road, London SW7 2BS. Tel: 071-589 3643. *Director*, M. G. Matthews.

ROYAL NORTHERN COLLEGE OF MUSIC, 124 Oxford Road, Manchester M13 9RD. Tel: 061-273 6283. *Principal*, Sir John Manduell, CBE.

S. MARTIN'S COLLEGE LANCASTER, Lancaster LA1 3JD. Tel: 0524-63446. *Principal*, D. Edynbry, Ph.D.

ST MARY'S COLLEGE, Strawberry Hill, Twickenham TW1 4SX. Tel: 081-892 0051. *Principal*, Dr A. Naylor.

SALFORD COLLEGE OF TECHNOLOGY, Frederick Road, Salford M6 6PU. Tel: 061-736 6541. *Principal (acting)*, J. Squires.

SOUTHAMPTON INSTITUTE OF HIGHER EDUCATION, East Park Terrace, Southampton SO9 4WW. Tel: 0703-229381. *Director*, D. G. Leyland.

TRINITY AND ALL SAINTS' COLLEGE, Brownberrie Lane, Horsforth, Leeds LS18 5HD. Tel: 0532-584341. *Principal*, Dr G. L. Turnbull.

TRINITY COLLEGE OF MUSIC, 11–13 Mandeville Place, London W1M 6AQ. Tel: 071-935 5773. *Principal*, P. Jones, CBE.

UNIVERSITY COLLEGE OF RIPON AND YORK ST JOHN, Lord Mayor's Walk, York YO3 7EX. Tel: 0904-656771. *Principal*, Prof. G. P. McGregor.

UNIVERSITY COLLEGE SCARBOROUGH, THE NORTH RIDING COLLEGE, Filey Road, Scarborough, N. Yorks. YO11 3AZ. Tel: 0723-362392. *Principal*, R. A. Withers, Ph.D.

WESTHILL COLLEGE, Hamilton Building, Weoley Park Road, Selly Oak, Birmingham B29 6LL. Tel: 021-472 7245. *Principal*, Dr J. G. Priestley.

WEST LONDON INSTITUTE OF HIGHER EDUCATION, Lancaster House, Borough Road, Isleworth, Middx. TW7 5DU. Tel: 081-568 8741. *Principal*, J. E. Kane, OBE, Ph.D.

WESTMINSTER COLLEGE, Oxford OX2 9AT. Tel: 0865-247644. *Principal*, Revd Dr K. B. Wilson, CBE.

WEST SURREY COLLEGE OF ART AND DESIGN, Falkner Road, The Hart, Farnham, Surrey GU9 7DS. Tel: 0252-722441. *Director*, N. J. Taylor.

WEST SUSSEX INSTITUTE OF HIGHER EDUCATION, The Dome, Upper Bognor Road, Bognor Regis, West Sussex PO21 1HR. Tel: 0243-787911. *Director*, Dr J. F. Wyatt.

WINCHESTER SCHOOL OF ART, Park Avenue, Winchester, Hants. SO23 8DL. Tel: 0962-842500. *Principal*, M. Sadler-Forster.

WORCESTER COLLEGE OF HIGHER EDUCATION, Henwick Grove, Worcester WR2 6AJ. Tel: 0905-748080. *Principal*, Ms D. Urwin.

WALES

BANGOR NORMAL COLLEGE, Bangor, Gwynedd LL57 2PX. Tel: 0248-370171. *Principal*, R. Williams.

GWENT COLLEGE OF HIGHER EDUCATION, College Crescent, Caerleon, Newport, Gwent NP6 1XJ. Tel: 0633-430088. *Principal*, Dr K. J. Overshott.

THE NORTH EAST WALES INSTITUTE (NEWI Plas Coch), Mold Road, Wrexham, Clwyd LL11 2AW. Tel: 0978-290666. Also NEWI Cartrefle at Cefn Road, Wrexham, NEWI College at Art and Design Technology at Grove Park Road, Wrexham and NEWI Deeside at Kelsterton Road, Deeside. *Principal*, Prof. J. O. Williams, Ph.D, D.Sc.

SOUTH GLAMORGAN INSTITUTE OF HIGHER EDUCATION, Western Avenue, Llandaff, Cardiff CF5 2YB. *Principal*, E. J. Brent, Ph.D.

TRINITY COLLEGE, Carmarthen, Dyfed, SA31 3EP. Tel: 0267-237971. *Principal*, D. C. Jones-Davies, OBE.

WELSH AGRICULTURAL COLLEGE, Llanbadarn Fawr, Aberystwyth, Dyfed SY23 3AL. Tel: 0970-624471. *Principal*, J. R. Gill.

WELSH COLLEGE OF MUSIC AND DRAMA, Castle Grounds, Cathays Park, Cardiff CF1 3ER. Tel: 0222-342854. *Principal*, E. Fivet.

WEST GLAMORGAN INSTITUTE OF HIGHER EDUCATION, Townhill Road, Swansea SA2 0UT. Tel: 0792-203482. *Principal*, G. Stockdale, Ph.D.

SCOTLAND

BELL COLLEGE OF TECHNOLOGY, Almada Street, Hamilton ML3 0JB. Tel: 0698-283100. *Principal*, J. Reid.

CRAIGIE COLLEGE OF EDUCATION, Beech Grove, Ayr KA8 0SR. Tel: 0292-260321. *Principal*, G. M. Wilson, Ph.D.

JORDANHILL COLLEGE OF EDUCATION, 73 Southbrae Drive, Jordanhill, Glasgow G13 1PP. Tel: 041-950 3000. *Principal*, T. R. Bone, CBE, Ph.D.

MORAY HOUSE INSTITUTE OF EDUCATION, Heriot Watt University, Holyrood Campus, Edinburgh EH8 8AQ. Tel: 031-556 8455. *Principal*, Prof. G. Kirk.

NORTHERN COLLEGE OF EDUCATION, Hilton Place, Aberdeen AB9 1FA. Tel: 0224-283500; Gardyne Road, Dundee DD5 1NY. Tel: 0382-453433. *Principal*, D. A. Adams.

ST ANDREW'S COLLEGE, Duntocher Road, Bearsden, Glasgow G61 4QA. Tel: 041-943 1424. *Principal*, B. J. McGettrick.

NORTHERN IRELAND

ST MARY'S COLLEGE, 191 Falls Road, Belfast BT12 6FE. Tel: 0232-327678. *Principal*, Revd M. O'Callaghan.

STRANMILLIS COLLEGE, Stranmillis Road, Belfast BT9 5DY. Tel: 0232-381271. *Principal*, R. J. Rodgers, Ph.D.

Adult and Continuing Education

NATIONAL INSTITUTE OF ADULT CONTINUING EDUCATION, 19B De Montfort Street, Leicester LE1 7GE. Tel: 0533-551451. *Director*, A. Tuckett.

NIACE CYMRU, 245 Western Avenue, Cardiff CF5 2YX. Tel: 0222-571201. *National Officer for Wales*, Ms A. Poole.

NORTHERN IRELAND COUNCIL FOR CONTINUING EDUCATION, Department of Education for Northern Ireland, Rathgael House, Balloo Road, Bangor BT19 2PR. Tel: 0247-270077. *Secretary*, Miss S. Pidduck.

THE POLYTECHNIC ASSOCIATION FOR CONTINUING EDUCATION, Educational Development Officer, Polytechnic of Wales, Pontypridd, Mid Glam. CF37 1DL. Tel: 0443-480480. *Secretary*, P. Race.

THE RESIDENTIAL COLLEGES COMMITTEE, c/o Ruskin College, Oxford OX1 2HE. Tel: 0865-56360. *Awards Officer*, Mrs F. A. Bagchi.

THE UNIVERSITIES COUNCIL FOR ADULT AND CONTINUING EDUCATION, Department of Continuing Education, The University of Warwick, Coventry CV4 7AL. Tel: 0203-523835. *Hon. Secretary*, Prof. C. Duke, Ph.D.

THE WORKER'S EDUCATIONAL ASSOCIATION, 17 Victoria Park Square, London E2 9PB. Tel: 081-983 1515. *General Secretary*, R. Lochrie.

LONG-TERM RESIDENTIAL COLLEGES FOR ADULT EDUCATION

COLEG HARLECH, Harlech, Gwynedd LL46 2PU. Tel: 0766-780363. *Warden*, J. W. England.

CO-OPERATIVE COLLEGE, Stanford Hall, Loughborough, Leics. LE12 5QR. Tel: 0509-852333. *Principal*, Dr R. Houlton.

FIRCROFT COLLEGE, 1018 Bristol Road, Selly Oak, Birmingham B29 6LH. Tel: 021-472 0116. *Principal*, K. Jackson.

HILLCROFT COLLEGE, South Bank, Surbiton, Surrey KT6 6DF. Tel: 081-399 2688. (For women only). *Principal*, Ms E. Aird.

NEWBATTLE ABBEY COLLEGE, Dalkeith, Midlothian EH22 3LL. Tel: 031-662 1921. *Principal (acting)*, W. M. Conboy.

NORTHERN COLLEGE, Wentworth Castle, Stainborough, Barnsley, S. Yorks. S75 3ET. Tel: 0226-285426. *Principal*, R. H. Fryer.

PLATER COLLEGE, Pullens Lane, Oxford OX3 0DT. Tel: 0865-741676. *Principal*, M. Blades.

RUSKIN COLLEGE, Walton Street, Oxford OX1 2HE. Tel: 0865-54331. *Principal*, S. Yeo, D.Phil.

Professional Education

Excluding postgraduate study

The organizations listed below are those which, by providing specialist training or conducting examinations, control entry into a profession, or organizations responsible for maintaining a register of those with professional qualifications in their sector.

Many professions now have a largely graduate entry, and possession of a first degree can exempt entrants from certain of the professional examinations. Enquiries about obtaining professional qualifications should be made to the relevant professional organization(s). Details of higher education providers of first degrees may be found in *University Entrance: The Official Guide* and in the *Polytechnic Courses Handbook*.

ACCOUNTANCY

The main bodies granting membership on examination after a period of practical work are:

INSTITUTE OF CHARTERED ACCOUNTANTS IN ENGLAND AND WALES, Chartered Accountants' Hall, PO Box 433, Moorgate Place, London EC2P 2BJ. Tel: 071-628 7060. *Chief Executive*, A. J. Colquhoun.

INSTITUTE OF CHARTERED ACCOUNTANTS OF SCOTLAND, 27 Queen Street, Edinburgh EH2 1LA. Tel: 031-225 5673. *Chief Executive*, P. W. Johnston.

CHARTERED ASSOCIATION OF CERTIFIED ACCOUNTANTS, 29 Lincoln's Inn Fields, London WC2A 3EE. Tel: 071-242 6855. *Secretary*, A. W. Sansom.

CHARTERED INSTITUTE OF MANAGEMENT ACCOUNTANTS, 63 Portland Place, London W1N 4AB. Tel: 071-637 2311. *Secretary*, Sir George Vallings, KCB.

CHARTERED INSTITUTE OF PUBLIC FINANCE AND ACCOUNTANCY, 3 Robert Street, London WC2N 6BH. Tel: 071-895 8823. *Secretary*, N. P. Hepworth, OBE.

ACTUARIAL SCIENCE

Two professional organizations grant qualifications after examination:

INSTITUTE OF ACTUARIES, Staple Inn Hall, High Holborn, London WC1V 7QJ. Tel: 071-242 0106. *Secretary-General*, A. G. Tait.

FACULTY OF ACTUARIES IN SCOTLAND, 23 St Andrew Square, Edinburgh EH2 1AQ. Tel: 031-557 1575. *Secretary*, W. W. Mair.

ARCHITECTURE

The Education and Professional Development Committee of the Royal Institute of British Architects sets standards and guides the whole system of architectural education throughout the United Kingdom. Courses at Schools recognized by the RIBA exempt students from the RIBA's own examinations.

THE ROYAL INSTITUTE OF BRITISH ARCHITECTS, 66 Portland Place, London W1N 4AD. Tel: 071-580 5533. *President*, R. MacCormac; *Director-General*, The Lord Rodgers of Quarry Bank, PC.

Schools of architecture outside the universities include:

THE ARCHITECTURAL ASSOCIATION, 34–36 Bedford Square, London WC1B 2ES. *Secretary*, E. A. Le Maistre.

BANKING

Professional organizations granting qualifications after examination are:

CHARTERED INSTITUTE OF BANKERS, 10 Lombard Street, London EC3V 9AS. Tel: 071-623 3531. *Secretary-General*, E. Glover.

CHARTERED INSTITUTE OF BANKERS IN SCOTLAND, 19 Rutland Square, Edinburgh EH1 2DE. Tel: 031-229 9869. *Chief Executive*, Dr C. W. Munn.

BIOLOGY, CHEMISTRY, PHYSICS

Professional qualifications are awarded by:

INSTITUTE OF BIOLOGY, 20–22 Queensberry Place, London SW7 2DZ. Tel: 071-581 8333. *President*, Prof. P. M. Biggs, CBE, FRS; *General Secretary*, Dr R. H. Priestley.

ROYAL SOCIETY OF CHEMISTRY, Burlington House, Piccadilly, London W1V 0BN. Tel: 071-437 8656. *President*, Prof. C. W. Rees, FRS; *Secretary*, J. S. Gow, Ph.D., FRSC, FRSE.

INSTITUTE OF PHYSICS, 47 Belgrave Square, London SW1X 8QX. Tel: 071-235 6111. *Chief Executive*, Dr A. Jones.

BUILDING

Examinations are conducted by:

CHARTERED INSTITUTE OF BUILDING, Englemere, King's Ride, Ascot, Berks. SL5 8BJ. Tel: 0344-23355. *Chief Executive*, K. Banbury.

INSTITUTE OF BUILDING CONTROL, 21 High Street, Ewell, Epsom, Surrey KT17 1SB. Tel: 081-393 6860. *Director*, Ms R. Raywood.

INSTITUTE OF CLERKS OF WORKS OF GREAT BRITAIN, 41 The Mall, London W5 3TJ. Tel: 081-579 2917-8. *Secretary*, A. P. Macnamara.

BUSINESS, MANAGEMENT AND ADMINISTRATION

Professional bodies conducting training and/or examinations in business, administration, management or commerce include:

ROYAL INSTITUTE OF PUBLIC ADMINISTRATION, 3 Birdcage Walk, London SW1H 9JH. Tel: 071-222 2248. *Director-General*, D. Falcon.

AMETS (ASSOCIATION FOR MANAGEMENT EDUCATION AND TRAINING IN SCOTLAND), c/o University of Stirling, Stirling FK9 4LA. Tel: 0786-50906. *Vice-Chairman*, M. Makower.

CAM FOUNDATION, Abford House, 15 Wilton Road, London SW1V 1NJ. Tel: 071-828 7506. *Registrar*, Ms K. Hutchinson.

CHARTERED INSTITUTE OF MARKETING, Moor Hall, Cookham, Maidenhead, Berks. SL6 9QH. Tel: 0628-524922. *Director-General*, J. McAinsh.

CHARTERED INSTITUTE OF TRANSPORT, 80 Portland Place, London W1N 4DP. *Director-General*, R. P. Botwood.

FACULTY OF SECRETARIES AND ADMINISTRATORS, 15 Church Street, Godalming, Surrey GU7 1EL. Tel: 0483-425144. *Secretary*, Mrs D. M. Rummery.

INSTITUTE OF ADMINISTRATIVE MANAGEMENT, 40 Chatsworth Parade, Petts Wood, Orpington, Kent BR5 1RW. Tel: 0689-875555. *Chief Executive*, Ms C. Hayhurst.

INSTITUTE OF CHARTERED SECRETARIES AND ADMINISTRATORS, 16 Park Crescent, London W1N 4AH. Tel: 071-580 4741. *Secretary*, M. J. Ainsworth.

INSTITUTE OF CHARTERED SHIPBROKERS, 24 St Mary Axe, London EC3A 8DE. Tel: 071-928 6810. *Secretary*, J. H. Parker.

INSTITUTE OF EXPORT, Export House, 64 Clifton Street, London EC2A 4HB. Tel: 071-247 9812. *Secretary*, I. J. Campbell.

INSTITUTE OF HEALTH SERVICES MANAGEMENT, 75 Portland Place, London W1N 4AN. Tel: 071-580 5041. *Director*, Ms M. P. Charlwood.

INSTITUTE OF HOUSING, Octavia House, Westwood Way, Coventry CV4 8JP. Tel: 0203-694433. *Director*, P. McGurk.

INSTITUTION OF INDUSTRIAL MANAGERS, Management House, Cottingham Road, Corby, Northants. NN17 1TT. Tel: 0536-407600. *Chief Executive*, J. Dixon.

INSTITUTE OF PERSONNEL MANAGEMENT, IPM House, Camp Road, London SW19 4UX. Tel: 081-946 9100. *Director-General*, G. Armstrong.

INSTITUTE OF PRACTITIONERS IN ADVERTISING, 44 Belgrave Square, London SW1X 8QS. Tel: 071-235 7020. *Secretary*, J. Raad.

INSTITUTE OF PURCHASING AND SUPPLY, Easton House, Easton on the Hill, Stamford, Lincs. PE9 3NZ. Tel: 0780-56777. *Director-General*, P. Thomson.

HENLEY MANAGEMENT COLLEGE, Greenlands, Henley-on-Thames, Oxon. RG9 3AU. Tel: 0491-571454. *Principal*, Prof. R. Wild.

LONDON BUSINESS SCHOOL, Sussex Place, Regent's Park, London NW1 4SA. Tel: 071-262 5050. *Principal*, Prof. G. Bain, Ph.D.

MANCHESTER BUSINESS SCHOOL, Booth Street West, Manchester M15 6PB. Tel: 061-275 6333. *Director*, Prof. T. Cannon.

LONDON CHAMBER OF COMMERCE AND INDUSTRY EXAMINATIONS BOARD, Marlowe House, Station Road, Sidcup, Kent DA15 7BJ. Tel: 081-302 0261. *Director*, Prof. C. Bateson.

DANCE

ROYAL ACADEMY OF DANCING, 36 Battersea Square, London SW11 3RA. Tel: 071-223 0091. *Chief Executive*, D. Watchman; *Artistic Director*, J. Byrne.

ROYAL BALLET SCHOOL, 155 Talgarth Road, London W14 9DE. Tel: 081-748 6335. Also at White Lodge, Richmond Park, Surrey TW10 5HR. Tel: 081-876 5547. *Director*, Dame Merle Park, DBE.

IMPERIAL SOCIETY OF TEACHERS OF DANCING, Euston Hall, Birkenhead Street, London WC1H 8BE. Tel: 071-837 9967. *General Secretary*, M. J. Browne.

DEFENCE

ROYAL NAVAL COLLEGES

ROYAL NAVAL COLLEGE, Greenwich, London SE10 9NN. Tel: 081-858 2154. *Admiral President*, Adm. Sir Michael Livesay, KCB; *Dean of the College*, Prof. G. Till.

BRITANNIA ROYAL NAVAL COLLEGE, Dartmouth, Devon TQ6 0HJ. Tel: 0803-832141. Provides initial officer training. *Captain*, Capt. R. G. Hastilow.

ROYAL NAVAL ENGINEERING COLLEGE, Manadon, Plymouth PL5 3AQ. Provides BA, B.Eng., M.Sc. and specialist training in naval engineering. Students are selected uniformed officers of the Royal Navy, Commonwealth and foreign navies, and civilians. *Captain*, Capt. T. J. England; *Dean*, Capt. J. N. McGrath; *Executive Officer*, Cdr. B. V. C. Reeves, LVO.

MILITARY COLLEGES

STAFF COLLEGE, Camberley, Surrey GU15 4NP. Tel: 0276-412614. *Commandant*, Maj.-Gen. H. M. Rose, CBE.

ROYAL MILITARY ACADEMY, Sandhurst, Camberley, Surrey GU15 4PQ. Tel: 0276-63344. *Commandant*, Maj.-Gen. T. P. Toyne Sewell.

ROYAL MILITARY COLLEGE OF SCIENCE, Shrivenham, Swindon, Wilts. SN6 8LA. Tel: 0793-785434. Students from UK and overseas study from degree to postgraduate levels in management, science and technology. There is an increasing range of research and consultancy activity as the College is now a Faculty of the Cranfield Institute of Technology. *Commandant*, Maj.-Gen. E. F. B. Burton, OBE; *Principal*, Prof. A. C. Baynham, Ph.D.

INSTITUTE OF ARMY EDUCATION, Court Road, Eltham, London SE9 5NR. Tel: 081-854 2242. *Director*, Maj.-Gen. C. A. Kinvig.

ROYAL AIR FORCE COLLEGES

ROYAL AIR FORCE STAFF COLLEGE, Bracknell, Berks. RG12 3DD. Prepares selected senior officers for high-grade command and staff appointments. Two-thirds of the students are RAF officers; the others are officers from the other UK Services and overseas air forces. *Air Officer Commanding and Commandant*, Air Vice-Marshal R. G. Peters.

ROYAL AIR FORCE COLLEGE, Cranwell, Sleaford, Lincs. NG34 8HB. Provides initial officer training for officers of the RAF, WRAF and PMRAFNS, and initial specialist training for officers of the Engineer and Supply Branches. Advanced specialist training is provided for officers of the General Duties, Engineer and Supply Branches and basic flying training for pilots of the General Duties Branch. *Air Officer Commanding and Commandant*, Air Vice-Marshal D. Cousins, CB, AFC.

ROYAL AIR FORCE SCHOOL OF EDUCATION AND TRAINING SUPPORT, RAF Newton, Nottingham NG13 8HL. Tel: 0949-20771. *Commanding Officer*, Gp. Capt. J. Rennie.

DENTISTRY

To be entitled to be registered in the Dentists Register, a person must hold the degree or diploma in dental surgery of a university in the United Kingdom or Republic of Ireland or the diploma of any of the licensing authorities (The Royal College of Surgeons of England, of Edinburgh and in Ireland, and the Royal College of Physicians and Surgeons of Glasgow). Nationals of an EC member state holding an appropriate European diploma, and holders of certain overseas diplomas, may also be registered. The Dentists Register is maintained by:

THE GENERAL DENTAL COUNCIL, 37 Wimpole Street, London W1M 8DQ. Tel: 071-486 2171. *Registrar*, N. T. Davies, MBE.

DIETETICS

See also FOOD AND NUTRITION SCIENCE

The professional association is The British Dietetic Association. Full membership is open to dietitians holding a recognized qualification, who may also become State Registered Dietitians through the Council for Professions Supplementary to Medicine (*see* Medicine).

THE BRITISH DIETETIC ASSOCIATION, 7th Floor, Elizabeth House, 22 Suffolk Street, Queensway, Birmingham B1 1LS. Tel: 021-643 5483.

DRAMA

The national validating body for courses providing training in drama is The National Council for Drama Training. It currently has accredited courses at the following: Academy of Live and Recorded Arts; Arts Educational Schools; Birmingham School of Speech Training & Dramatic Art; Bristol Old Vic Theatre School; Central School of Speech and Drama; Drama Centre, London; Drama Studio; Guildford School of Acting; Guildhall School of Music and Drama; London Academy of Music and Dramatic Art; Manchester Polytechnic School of Theatre; Mountview Theatre School; Rose Bruford College of Speech and Drama; Royal Academy of Dramatic Art; Royal Scottish Academy of Music and Drama; Webber Douglas Academy of Dramatic Art; Welsh College of Music and Drama.

The accreditation of a course in a school does not necessarily imply that other courses of different type or duration in the same school are also accredited.

THE NATIONAL COUNCIL FOR DRAMA TRAINING, 5 Tavistock Place, London WC1H 9SS. *Secretary*, Miss E. M. McKay.

ENGINEERING

The Engineering Council supervises the engineering profession through the 46 nominated engineering institutions who are represented on its Board for Engineers' Registration. Working with and through the institutions, the Council sets the standards for the registration of individuals, and also the accreditation for academic courses in universities, polytechnics and technical colleges and the practical training in industry.

THE ENGINEERING COUNCIL, 10 Maltravers Street, London WC2R 3ER. *Secretary*, L. Chelton.

The principal qualifying bodies are:

BRITISH COMPUTER SOCIETY, PO Box 1454, Station Road, Swindon SN1 1TG. Tel: 0793 480269. *Chief Executive*, G. Kirkpatrick.

CHARTERED INSTITUTION OF BUILDING SERVICES ENGINEERS, Delta House, 222 Balham High Road, London SW12 9BS. Tel: 071-675 5211. *Secretary*, A. V. Ramsay.

INSTITUTION OF CHEMICAL ENGINEERS, The Davis Building, 165–171 Railway Terrace, Rugby, Warks. CV21 3HQ. Tel: 0788-578214. *General Secretary*, Dr T. J. Evans.

INSTITUTION OF CIVIL ENGINEERS, Great George Street, London SW1P 3AA. *Secretary*, R. Dobson.

INSTITUTION OF ELECTRICAL ENGINEERS, Savoy Place, London WC2R 0BL. Tel: 071-240 1871. *Secretary*, Dr J. C. Williams, FEng.
INSTITUTE OF ENERGY, 18 Devonshire Street, London W1N 2AU. Tel: 071-580 7124. *Secretary* C. Rigg, TD.
INSTITUTION OF GAS ENGINEERS, 17 Grosvenor Crescent, London SW1X 7ES. Tel: 071-245 9811. *Secretary*, D. J. Chapman.
INSTITUTE OF MARINE ENGINEERS, The Memorial Building, 76 Mark Lane, London EC3R 7JN. Tel: 071-481 8493. *Secretary*, J. E. Sloggett.
INSTITUTE OF MEASUREMENT AND CONTROL, 87 Gower Street, London WC1E 6AA. Tel: 071-387 4949. *Secretary*, M. J. Yates.
INSTITUTION OF MECHANICAL ENGINEERS, 1 Birdcage Walk, London SW1H 9JJ. Tel: 071-222 7899. *Secretary*, R. Mellor, CBE, FEng.
INSTITUTE OF METALS, 1 Carlton House Terrace, London SW1Y 5DB. Tel: 071-839 4071. *Secretary*, Dr J. A. Catterall.
INSTITUTION OF MINING ENGINEERS, Danum House, 6A South Parade, Doncaster DN1 2DY. Tel: 0302-320486. *Secretary*, W. J. W. Bourne, OBE.
INSTITUTION OF MINING AND METALLURGY, 44 Portland Place, London W1N 4BR. Tel: 071-580 3802. *Secretary*, M. J. Jones.
INSTITUTION OF STRUCTURAL ENGINEERS, 11 Upper Belgrave Street, London SW1X 8BH. Tel: 071-235 4535. *Secretary*, D. J. Clark.
ROYAL AERONAUTICAL SOCIETY, 4 Hamilton Place, London W1V 0BQ. Tel: 071-499 3515. *Director*, R. J. Kennett.
ROYAL INSTITUTION OF NAVAL ARCHITECTS, 10 Upper Belgrave Street, London SW1X 8BQ. Tel: 071-235 4622. *Secretary*, J. Rosewarn.

FOOD AND NUTRITION SCIENCE

See also DIETETICS and HOME ECONOMICS
Scientific and professional bodies include:
INSTITUTE OF FOOD SCIENCE & TECHNOLOGY, 5 Cambridge Court, 210 Shepherd's Bush Road, London W6 7NL. Tel: 071-603 6316. *Executive Secretary*, Ms H. G. Wild.
NUTRITION SOCIETY, Grosvenor Gardens House, 35–37 Grosvenor Gardens, London SW1W 0BS. *Hon. Secretary*, Dr R. F. Grimble.

FORESTRY AND TIMBER STUDIES

Professional organizations include:
ROYAL FORESTRY SOCIETY OF ENGLAND, WALES AND NORTHERN IRELAND, 102 High Street, Tring, Herts., HP23 4AF. Tel: 0442-822028. *Director*, J. E. Jackson, Ph.D.
ROYAL SCOTTISH FORESTRY SOCIETY, Camsie House, Charlestown, Dunfermline, Fife KY11 3EE. Tel: 0383-873014. *Director*, M. Osborne.
INSTITUTE OF CHARTERED FORESTERS, 22 Walker Street, Edinburgh EH3 7HR. *Secretary*, Mrs M. W. Dick.
COMMONWEALTH FORESTRY ASSOCIATION, c/o Oxford Forestry Institute, South Parks Road, Oxford OX1 3RB. Tel: 0865-275072. *Secretary (acting)*, P. J. Wood.

FUEL AND ENERGY SCIENCE

The principal professional bodies are:
INSTITUTE OF ENERGY, 18 Devonshire Street, London W1N 2AU. Tel: 071-580 7124. *Secretary*, C. Rigg, TD.
INSTITUTION OF GAS ENGINEERS, 17 Grosvenor Crescent, London SW1X 7ES. Tel: 071-245 9811. *Secretary*, D. J. Chapman.
INSTITUTE OF PETROLEUM, 61 New Cavendish Street, London W1M 8AR. Tel: 071-636 1004. *Director-General*, I. Ward.

HOTELKEEPING, CATERING AND INSTITUTIONAL MANAGEMENT

See also DIETETICS, and FOOD
The qualifying professional body in the subjects is:
HOTEL CATERING AND INSTITUTIONAL MANAGEMENT ASSOCIATION, 191 Trinity Road, London SW17 7HN. *Director*, Ms E. Gadsby.

INDUSTRIAL AND VOCATIONAL TRAINING

There are 120 Industry Training Organizations, employer-led independent organizations whose role includes setting the standards of National and Scottish Vocational Qualifications.
NATIONAL COUNCIL OF INDUSTRY TRAINING ORGANIZATIONS, 5 George Lane, Royston, Herts. SG8 9AR. Tel: 0763-247285. *Chairman*, P. Morley.

INSURANCE

Organizations conducting examinations and awarding diplomas are:
ASSOCIATION OF AVERAGE ADJUSTERS, HQS *Wellington*, Temple Stairs, Victoria Embankment, London WC2R 2PN. Tel: 071-240 5516. *Secretary*, Mrs P. J. Albano.
CHARTERED INSURANCE INSTITUTE, 20 Aldermanbury, London EC2V 7HY. Tel: 071-606 3835. *Director-General*, Dr D. E. Bland.
CHARTERED INSTITUTE OF LOSS ADJUSTERS, Manfield House, 376 The Strand, London WC2R 0LR. Tel: 071-240 1496. *Director*, A. F. Clack.

JOURNALISM

Courses for trainee newspaper journalists are available at 11 centres. One-year full-time courses are available for selected students. Particulars of all these courses are available from the National Council for Training of Journalists. Short courses for experienced journalists are also arranged by the National Council.

For periodical journalists, there are four centres running courses approved by The Periodicals Training Council.

THE NATIONAL COUNCIL FOR TRAINING OF JOURNALISTS, Latton Bush Centre, Southern Way, Harlow, Essex CM18 7BL. Tel: 0279-430009. *Chief Executive*, D. K. Hall.

THE PERIODICALS TRAINING COUNCIL, Imperial House, 15–19 Kingsway, London WC2B 6UN. Tel: 071-836 8798. *Director*, D. Longbottom, MBE.

LAW

THE BAR

Admission to the Bar of England and Wales is controlled by the Inns of Court, and admission to the Bar of Northern Ireland by the Honorable Society of the Inn of Court of Northern Ireland. Admission as an Advocate of the Scottish Bar is controlled by the Faculty of Advocates.

THE GENERAL COUNCIL OF THE BAR, 11 South Square, Gray's Inn, London WC1R 5EL.Tel: 071-242 0082. The governing body of the barristers' branch of the legal profession in England and Wales. *Chairman*, The Lord Williams of Mostyn, QC; *Chief Executive*, J. Mottram, CB, LVO, OBE.

The Inns of Court

THE INNER TEMPLE, London EC4Y 7HL. Tel: 071-353 8462. *Treasurer*, The Rt. Hon. Sir John May; *Sub-Treasurer*, Capt. P. T. Sheehan, CBE, RN.

THE MIDDLE TEMPLE, London EC4Y 9AT. *Treasurer*, A. Heyman, QC; *Deputy Treasurer*, Rear-Adm. J. R. Hill.

GRAY'S INN, 8 South Square, London WC1R 5EU. *Treasurer*, R. Stone, QC; *Under-Treasurer*, D. Machin.

LINCOLN'S INN, London WC2A 3TL. Tel: 071-405 1393. *Treasurer*, The Lord Oliver of Aylmerton, PC; *Under-Treasurer*, Capt. P. M. Carver, RN.

The education and examination of students for the Bar of England and Wales is superintended by the COUNCIL OF LEGAL EDUCATION, Inns of Court School of Law, 39 Eagle Street, London WC1R 4AJ. Tel: 071-404 5787. *Chairman*, The Hon. Mr Justice Phillips; *Dean, Inns of Court School of Law*, Mrs M. A. Phillips.

FACULTY OF ADVOCATES, Advocates Library, Parliament House, Edinburgh EH1 1RF. *Dean*, A. C. M. Johnston, QC; *Clerk*, J. R. Doherty.

THE HONORABLE SOCIETY OF THE INN OF COURT OF NORTHERN IRELAND, Royal Courts of Justice, Belfast BT1 3JF. *Treasurer* (1992), His Honour Judge Babington, DSC, QC; *Under-Treasurer*, J. A. L. McLean, QC.

SOLICITORS

Qualifications for Solicitor are obtainable only from one of the Law Societies, which control the education and examination of articled clerks, and the admission of solicitors.

LAW SOCIETY OF ENGLAND AND WALES, 113 Chancery Lane, London WC2A 1PL. *President* (1992–3), M. H. Sheldon; *Vice-President* (1992–3), R. J. Pannone. *Secretary-General*, J. W. Hayes.

THE COLLEGE OF LAW provides courses for the Law Society examinations at Braboeuf Manor, St Catherine's, Guildford, Surrey GU3 1HA; 33–35 Lancaster Gate, London W2 3LU; 14 Store Street, London WC1E 7DE; Christleton Hall, Chester CH3 7AB; Bishopthorpe Road, York YO2 1QA.

THE SOLICITORS COMPLAINTS BUREAU, Portland House, Stag Place, London SW1E 5BL. Tel: 071-834 2288, is an independent arm of the Law Society set up to handle complaints about solicitors.

LAW SOCIETY OF SCOTLAND, Law Society's Hall, 26 Drumsheugh Gardens, Edinburgh EH3 7YR. Tel: 031-226 7411. *President* (1992–3), B. C. Adair; *Secretary*, K. W. Pritchard, OBE.

LAW SOCIETY OF NORTHERN IRELAND, Law Society House, 90–106 Victoria Street, Belfast BT1 3JZ. Tel: 0232-231614. *Secretary*, M. C. Davey.

LIBRARIANSHIP AND INFORMATION MANAGEMENT

Two-thirds of entrants into library and information management take a one- or two-year postgraduate course accredited by the Library Association, in order to qualify. The Library Association maintains a professional register of Chartered Members. A full list of accredited degree and postgraduate courses is available from the Education Department.

THE LIBRARY ASSOCIATION, 7 Ridgmount Street, London WC1E 7AE. Tel: 071-636 7543. *Chief Executive*, R. Shimmon.

MATERIALS STUDIES

The qualifying body is:

INSTITUTE OF METALS, 1 Carlton House Terrace, London SW1Y 5DB. *Secretary*, Dr J. A. Catterall.

MEDICINE

LICENSING CORPORATIONS GRANTING DIPLOMAS

ROYAL COLLEGE OF PHYSICIANS OF LONDON AND THE ROYAL COLLEGE OF SURGEONS OF ENGLAND, Examining Board in England, 35–43 Lincoln's Inn Fields, London WC2A 3PN. Tel: 071-405 3474.

SOCIETY OF APOTHECARIES OF LONDON, Black Friars Lane, London EC4V 6EJ. Tel: 071-236 1189. *Clerk*, Maj. J. C. O'Leary; *Registrar*, D. H. C. Barrie.

SCOTTISH TRIPLE QUALIFICATION BOARD, Nicolson Street, Edinburgh EH8 9DW and 242 St Vincent Street, Glasgow.

COLLEGES HOLDING POSTGRADUATE MEMBERSHIP AND DIPLOMA EXAMINATIONS

ROYAL COLLEGE OF GENERAL PRACTITIONERS, 14 Princes Gate, London SW7 1PU. Tel: 071-581 3232. *President*, HRH The Prince of Wales; *Secretary*, Dr M. McBride.

ROYAL COLLEGE OF OBSTETRICIANS AND GYNAECOLOGISTS, 27 Sussex Place, London NW1 4RG. Tel: 071-262 5425. *President*, S. Simmons; *Secretary*, P. A. Barnett.

ROYAL COLLEGE OF PATHOLOGISTS, 2 Carlton House Terrace, London SW1Y 5AF. Tel: 071-930 5863. *President*, Prof. P. J. Lachmann, FRS, FRCP; *Secretary*, K. Lockyer.

ROYAL COLLEGE OF PHYSICIANS, 11 St Andrews Place, London NW1 4LE. Tel: 071-935 1174. *President*, L. A. Turnberg; *Secretary*, D. B. Lloyd.

ROYAL COLLEGE OF PHYSICIANS OF EDINBURGH, 9 Queen Street, Edinburgh EH2 1JQ. Tel: 031-225 7324. *President*, Dr A. D. Toft; *Secretary*, Dr J. L. Anderton.

ROYAL COLLEGE OF PHYSICIANS AND SURGEONS OF GLASGOW, 234–242 St Vincent Street, Glasgow G2 5RJ. Tel: 041-221 6072. *President*, Dr R. Hume; *Hon. Secretary*, Dr B. Williams.

ROYAL COLLEGE OF PSYCHIATRISTS, 17 Belgrave Square, London SW1X 8PG. Tel: 071-235 2351. *President*, Prof. A. Sims; *Secretary*, Mrs V. Cameron.

ROYAL COLLEGE OF RADIOLOGISTS, 38 Portland Place, London W1N 3DG. Tel: 071-636 4432. *President*, Dr C. H. Paine; *Secretary*, A. J. Cowles.

ROYAL COLLEGE OF SURGEONS OF ENGLAND, 35 Lincoln's Inn Fields, London WC2A 3PN. Tel: 071-405 3474. *President*, Prof. N. L. Browse, PRCS; *Secretary*, R. H. E. Duffett.

ROYAL COLLEGE OF SURGEONS OF EDINBURGH, Nicolson Street, Edinburgh EH8 9DW. Tel: 031-556 6206. *President*, Prof. P. S. Boulter; *Secretary*, A. C. B. Dean.

PROFESSIONS SUPPLEMENTARY TO MEDICINE

The standard of professional education in chiropody, dietetics, medical laboratory sciences, occupational therapy, orthoptics, physiotherapy and radiography is the responsibility of seven professional boards, which also publish an annual register of qualified practitioners. The work of the Boards is co-ordinated by THE COUNCIL FOR PROFESSIONS SUPPLEMENTARY TO MEDICINE, Park House, 184 Kennington Park Road, London SE11 4BU. Tel: 071-582 0866. *Registrar*, R. Pickis.

CHIROPODY

Professional recognition is granted by The Society of Chiropodists to students who are awarded BSc. degrees in Podiatry or Podiatric medicine after attending a course of full-time training for three or four years at one of the 14 recognized schools in the UK (11 in England and Wales, two in Scotland and one in Northern Ireland). Qualifications granted and degrees recognized by the Society are approved by the Chiropodists Board for the purpose of State Registration, which is a condition of employment within the National Health Service.

THE SOCIETY OF CHIROPODISTS, 53 Welbeck Street, London W1M 7HE. Tel: 071-486 3381. *General Secretary*, J. G. C. Trouncer.

See also DIETETICS

MEDICAL LABORATORY SCIENCES

Qualifications from higher or further education establishments and training in medical laboratories are required for progress to the professional examinations and qualifications of the INSTITUTE OF MEDICAL LABORATORY SCIENCES, 12 Queen Anne Street, London W1M 0AU. *Chief Executive*, A. Potter.

OCCUPATIONAL THERAPY

Professional qualifications are awarded by the College of Occupational Therapists upon completion of one of the 27 training courses approved by the College.

THE COLLEGE OF OCCUPATIONAL THERAPISTS, 6–8 Marshalsea Road, London SE1 1HL. Tel: 071-357 8480. *Secretary*, M. D. Hall, OBE.

ORTHOPTICS

See also OPHTHALMIC OPTICS

Orthoptists undertake the diagnosis and treatment of all types of squint and other anomalies of binocular vision, working in close collaboration with ophthalmologists. The training and maintenance of professional standards are the responsibility of the Orthoptists Board of the Council for the Professions Supplementary to Medicine. The professional body is the British Orthoptic Society. Training is at degree level.

THE BRITISH ORTHOPTIC SOCIETY, Tavistock House North, Tavistock Square, London WC1H 9HX. *Secretary*, Mrs A. Charnock.

PHYSIOTHERAPY

Full-time three- or four-year degree courses are available at 32 recognized Schools in the UK. Information about courses leading to eligibility for Membership of the Chartered Society of Physiotherapy and to State Registration is available from THE CHARTERED SOCIETY OF PHYSIOTHERAPY, 14 Bedford Row, London WC1R 4ED. Tel: 071-242 1941. *Secretary*, T. Simon.

RADIOGRAPHY AND RADIOTHERAPY

In order to practise both diagnostic and therapeutic radiography in the United Kingdom, it is necessary to have successfully completed a course of education and training recognized by the Privy Council. Such courses are offered by universities, polytechnics and colleges throughout the United Kingdom and lead to the award of either a degree in radiography or the Diploma of the College of Radiographers. Further information is available from THE COLLEGE OF RADIOGRAPHERS, 14 Upper Wimpole Street, London W1M 8BN. Tel: 071-935 5726. *Chief Executive*, R. M. Jordan.

MERCHANT NAVY TRAINING SCHOOLS

TRAINING SCHOOLS FOR OFFICERS

THE COLLEGE OF MARITIME STUDIES, Southampton Institute of Higher Education, Warsash Campus, Warsash, Southampton SO3 6ZL. Tel: 0489-576161.

TRAINING SCHOOLS FOR SEAMEN

INDEFATIGABLE AND NATIONAL SEA TRAINING SCHOOL FOR BOYS, Plas Llanfair, Llanfairpwllgwyngyll, Gwynedd LL61 6NT. Tel: 0248-714338. *Headmaster*, Capt. P. White.

NATIONAL SEA TRAINING COLLEGE, Denton, Gravesend, Kent DA12 2HR. Tel: 0474-363656. *Principal*, M. Bolton.

MUSIC

ASSOCIATED BOARD OF THE ROYAL SCHOOLS OF MUSIC, 14 Bedford Square, London WC1B 3JG. Conducts the local examinations in centres throughout the world in music and speech for the Royal Academy of Music and the Royal College of Music in London, the Royal Northern College of Music, Manchester and the Royal Scottish Academy of Music and Drama, Glasgow. *Chief Executive*, R. Smith.

ROYAL ACADEMY OF MUSIC, Marylebone Road, London NW1 5HT. Tel: 071-935 5461. *Principal*, Sir David Lumsden, D.Phil.

ROYAL COLLEGE OF MUSIC, Prince Consort Road, London SW7 2BS. Tel: 071-589 3643. *Director*, M. G. Matthews.

ROYAL NORTHERN COLLEGE OF MUSIC, 124 Oxford Road, Manchester M13 9RD. Tel: 061-273 6283. *Principal*, Sir John Manduell, CBE.

ROYAL SCOTTISH ACADEMY OF MUSIC AND DRAMA, 100 Renfrew Street, Glasgow G2 3DB. *Principal*, Dr P. Ledger, CBE.
ROYAL COLLEGE OF ORGANISTS, 7 St Andrew Street, London EC4A 3LQ. Tel: 071-936 3606. *Clerk*, V. Waterhouse.
GUILDHALL SCHOOL OF MUSIC AND DRAMA, Silk Street, London EC2Y 8DT. Tel: 071-628 2571. *Principal*, I. Horsbrugh.
LONDON COLLEGE OF MUSIC AT EALING, Thames Valley University, St Mary's Road, London W5 5RF. Tel: 081-579 5000. *Director*, W. Webb.
TRINITY COLLEGE OF MUSIC, 11–13 Mandeville Place, London W1M 6AQ. Tel: 071-935 5773. *Principal*, P. Jones, CBE.

NURSING

Three-year courses are undertaken for State Registration in general, sick children's, mental and mental deficiency nursing. Two-year courses lead to State enrolment.

The Royal College of Nursing, within its Institute of Advanced Nursing Education, provides education at post-basic level in hospital, occupational health and community health fields. Advanced courses are held in preparation for senior posts in management and teaching; and other short and special courses.

THE ROYAL COLLEGE OF NURSING OF THE UNITED KINGDOM, 20 Cavendish Square, London W1M 0AB. Tel: 071-409 3333. *General Secretary*, Miss C. Hancock; *Principal of the Institute of Advanced Nursing Education*, J. C. A. Wells.
ENGLISH NATIONAL BOARD FOR NURSING, MIDWIFERY AND HEALTH VISITING, Victory House, 170 Tottenham Court Road, London W1P 0HA. Tel: 071-388 3131. *Chief Executive Officer*, A. P. Smith.
WELSH NATIONAL BOARD FOR NURSING, MIDWIFERY AND HEALTH VISITING, Floor 13, Pearl Assurance House, Greyfriars Road, Cardiff CF1 3AG. Tel: 0222-395535. *Chief Executive Officer*, D. A. Ravey.
NATIONAL BOARD FOR NURSING, MIDWIFERY AND HEALTH VISITING FOR SCOTLAND, 22 Queen Street, Edinburgh EH2 1JX. Tel: 031-226 7371. *Chief Executive Officer*, Mrs E. C. Mitchell.
NATIONAL BOARD FOR NURSING, MIDWIFERY AND HEALTH VISITING FOR NORTHERN IRELAND, RAC House, 79 Chichester Street, Belfast BT1 4JE. Tel: 0232-238152. *Chief Executive Officer*, J. J. Walsh.

OPHTHALMIC OPTICS

Professional bodies are:
THE BRITISH COLLEGE OF OPTOMETRISTS, 10 Knaresborough Place, London SW5 0TG. Tel: 071-373 7765. Grants qualifications as an optometrist. *General Secretary*, P. D. Leigh.
THE ASSOCIATION OF BRITISH DISPENSING OPTICIANS, 6 Hurlingham Business Park, Sulivan Road, London SW6 3DU. Tel: 071-736 0088. Grants qualifications as a dispensing optician. *Registrar*, D. G. Baker.

PHARMACY

Information may be obtained from The Secretary and Registrar, ROYAL PHARMACEUTICAL SOCIETY OF GREAT BRITAIN, 1 Lambeth High Street, London SE1 7JN. *Secretary and Registrar*, J. Ferguson.

PHOTOGRAPHY

The professional body is:
BRITISH INSTITUTE OF PROFESSIONAL PHOTOGRAPHY, Amwell End, Ware, Herts. SG12 9HN. Tel: 0920-464011. *Chief Executive*, A. M. Berkeley.

PRINTING

Details of courses in general and technical design can be obtained from the Institute of Printing and the British Printing Industries Federation. In addition to these examining and organizing bodies, examinations are held by various independent regional examining boards in further education.
BRITISH PRINTING INDUSTRIES FEDERATION, 11 Bedford Row, London WC1R 4DX. Tel: 071-242 6904. *Director-General*, C. Stanley.
INSTITUTE OF PRINTING, 8 Lonsdale Gardens, Tunbridge Wells, Kent TN1 1NU. Tel: 0892-538118. *Secretary*, C. F. Partridge.

SOCIAL WORK

The Council for Education and Training in Social Work promotes education and training for social work and social care throughout the UK. It approves training programmes, including those leading to one of two social work qualifying awards: the Diploma in Social Work and the Certificate of Qualification in Social Work.
THE CENTRAL COUNCIL FOR EDUCATION AND TRAINING IN SOCIAL WORK, Derbyshire House, St Chad's Street, London WC1H 8AD. Tel: 071-278 2455. *Director*, A. Hall.

SPEECH THERAPY

The College of Speech and Language Therapists provides details of courses leading to qualification as a speech therapist. The College also sponsors advanced clinical courses. Associate Membership is available for professionals in other disciplines. A directory of registered members is published annually.
THE COLLEGE OF SPEECH AND LANGUAGE THERAPISTS, 7 Bath Place, Rivington Street, London EC2A 3DR. Tel: 071-613 3855. *Director*, Ms S. Davis.

SURVEYING

The qualifying professional bodies include:

ROYAL INSTITUTION OF CHARTERED SURVEYORS (incorporating The Institute of Quantity Surveyors), 12 Great George Street, London SW1P 3AD. Tel: 071-222 7000. *Secretary-General*, M. Pattison.

ARCHITECTS AND SURVEYORS INSTITUTE, 15 St Mary Street, Chippenham, Wilts. SN15 3JN. Tel: 0249-444505. *Chief Executive.*, B. A. Hunt.

INCORPORATED ASSOCIATION OF ARCHITECTS AND SURVEYORS, Jubilee House, Billing Brook Road, Weston Favell, Northampton NN3 4NW. Tel: 0604-404121. *Administrator*, B. D. Hughes.

INSTITUTE OF REVENUES, RATING AND VALUATION, 41 Doughty Street, London WC1N 2LF. Tel: 071-831 3505. *Director*, C. Farrington.

INCORPORATED SOCIETY OF VALUERS AND AUCTIONEERS (1968), 3 CADOGAN GATE, LONDON SW1X 0AS. Tel: 071-235 2282. *Chief Executive*, H. Whitty.

TEACHING

To become a qualified teacher it is necessary to have successfully completed a course of initial teacher training. Non-graduates usually qualify by way of a three- or four-year course leading to a Bachelor of Education (B.Ed.) honours degree, but some universities offer first degree courses (BA, B.Sc.) taken concurrently with a certificate of education. Graduates take a one-year postgraduate certificate of education (PGCE).

Details of courses in England and Wales are contained in the *Handbook of Degree and Advanced Courses* published annually by the National Association of Teachers in Further and Higher Education.

Applications for B.Ed. courses in England and Wales at institutions other than universities are made through the Central Register and Clearing House Ltd, from which application forms can be obtained. For all PGCE courses in England and Wales, applications are handled by the Graduate Teacher Training Registry at the same address. (For address, *see* page 464).

Details of courses in Scotland can be obtained from the colleges of education and from TEACH (*see* page 464). Details of courses in Northern Ireland can be obtained from the Department of Education for Northern Ireland. Applications for teacher training courses in Scotland and Northern Ireland are made to the institutions direct.

TEXTILES

THE TEXTILE INSTITUTE, 10 Blackfriars Street, Manchester M3 5DR. Tel: 061-834 8457. *General Secretary*, R. G. Denyer.

THEOLOGICAL COLLEGES

The number of students for the academic year 1991–2 is shown in parenthesis.

ANGLICAN

CHICHESTER THEOLOGICAL COLLEGE, Chichester, W. Sussex PO19 1SG. (42). *Principal*, Revd Canon P. Atkinson.

COATES HALL, College of the Scottish Episcopalian Church, Rosebery Crescent, Edinburgh EH12 5JT. (22). *Principal*, Revd Canon K. Mason.

CRANMER HALL, St John's College, Durham DH1 3RJ. (59). *Warden*, vacant.

LINCOLN THEOLOGICAL COLLEGE, Drury Lane, Lincoln LN1 3BP. (65). *Warden*, Revd Canon W. M. Jacob, Ph.D.

OAK HILL COLLEGE, Chase Side, London N14 4PS. (58). *Principal*, Revd Canon G. Bridger.

COLLEGE OF THE RESURRECTION, Mirfield, W. Yorks. WF14 0BW. (36). *Principal*, Revd Dr D. J. Lane.

RIDLEY HALL, Cambridge CB3 9HG. (51). *Principal*, Revd G. A. Cray.

RIPON COLLEGE, Cuddesdon, Oxford OX9 9EX. (70). *Principal*, Revd Canon J. H. Garton.

ST DEINIOL'S LIBRARY, Hawarden, Deeside, Clwyd CH5 3DF. (3). *Principal*, Revd Dr P. J. Jagger.

ST JOHN'S COLLEGE, Bramcote, Nottingham NG9 3DS. (122). *Principal*, Revd Dr J. Goldingay.

ST MICHAEL'S THEOLOGICAL COLLEGE, Llandaff, Cardiff CF5 2YJ. (35). *Warden*, Revd Canon J. H. L. Rowlands.

ST STEPHEN'S HOUSE, 16 Marston Street, Oxford OX4 1JX. (55). *Principal*, Revd E. R. Barnes.

SALISBURY AND WELLS THEOLOGICAL COLLEGE, 19 The Close, Salisbury SP1 2EE. (145). *Principal*, Revd P. A. Crowe.

TRINITY COLLEGE, Stoke Hill, Bristol BS9 1JP. (79). *Principal*, Revd Canon D. Gillett.

WESTCOTT HOUSE, Jesus Lane, Cambridge CB5 8BP. (50). *Principal*, Revd Dr R. W. N. Hoare.

WYCLIFFE HALL, 54 Banbury Road, Oxford OX2 6PW. (80). *Principal*, Revd Dr R. T. France.

CHURCH OF SCOTLAND

CHRIST'S COLLEGE, Aberdeen AB1 1YD. (42). *Master*, Revd Prof. A. Main, TD, Ph.D.

NEW COLLEGE, Mound Place, Edinburgh EH1 2LU. (438). *Principal*, Revd Prof. D. B. Forrester.

TRINITY COLLEGE, 4 The Square, University of Glasgow, Glasgow G12 8QQ. (70). *Principal*, Revd Prof. D. M. Newlands.

PRESBYTERIAN CHURCH OF WALES

UNITED THEOLOGICAL COLLEGE, Aberystwyth SY23 2LT. (42). *Principal*, Revd Prof. E. ap Nefydd Roberts.

PRESBYTERIAN

UNION THEOLOGICAL COLLEGE, Belfast BT7 1JT. (76). *Principal*, Revd Prof. R. F. G. Holmes.

METHODIST

EDGHILL THEOLOGICAL COLLEGE, 9 Lennoxvale, Belfast BT9 5BY. (13). *Principal*, Revd W. D. D. Cooke, Ph.D.

HARTLEY VICTORIA COLLEGE, Luther King House, Brighton Grove, Manchester M14 5JP. (27). *Principal*, Revd G. Slater.

LINCOLN THEOLOGICAL COLLEGE, Drury Lane, Lincoln LN1 3BP. (65). *Warden*, Revd Canon W. M. Jacob, Ph.D.

WESLEY COLLEGE, College Park Drive, Henbury Road, Bristol BS10 7QD. (70). *Principal*, Dr H. McKeating.

WESLEY HOUSE, Cambridge CB5 8BJ. (39). *Principal*, Revd Dr I. H. Jones.

WESLEY STUDY CENTRE, 55 The Avenue, Durham DH1 4EB. (20). *Principal*, Revd P. Luscombe, Ph.D.

BAPTIST

BRISTOL BAPTIST COLLEGE, Woodland Road, Bristol BS8 1UN. (18). *Principal*, Revd Dr J. E. Morgan-Wynne.
NORTHERN BAPTIST COLLEGE, Luther King House, Brighton Grove, Rusholme, Manchester M14 5JP. (40). *Principal*, Revd Dr B. Haymes.
NORTH WALES BAPTIST COLLEGE, Ffordd Ffriddoedd, Bangor, Gwynedd LL57 2EH. (3). *Principal*, Revd J. R. Rowlands.
REGENT'S PARK COLLEGE, Oxford OX1 2LB. (29). *Principal*, Revd Dr P. S. Fiddes.
THE SCOTTISH BAPTIST COLLEGE, 12 Aytoun Road, Glasgow G41 5RT. (28). *Principal*, Revd I. J. W. Oakley.
SOUTH WALES BAPTIST COLLEGE, 54 Richmond Road, Cardiff CF2 3UR. (21). *Principal*, Revd D. H. Matthews.
SPURGEON'S COLLEGE, South Norwood Hill, London SE25 6DJ. (115). *Principal*, vacant.

UNITED REFORMED

BALA-BANGOR INDEPENDENT COLLEGE, Bangor LL57 2EH. (15). *Principal*, R. T. Jones, D.Phil., DD.
MANSFIELD COLLEGE, Mansfield Road, Oxford OX1 3TF. (21). *Principal*, D. J. Trevelyan, CB.
NORTHERN COLLEGE, Luther King House, Brighton Grove, Rusholme, Manchester M14 5JP. (35). *Principal*, Revd R. J. McKelvey, Ph.D.
WESTMINSTER COLLEGE, Madingley Road, Cambridge CB3 0AA. (35). *Principal*, Revd M. H. Cressey.

CONGREGATIONAL

COLLEGE OF THE WELSH INDEPENDENTS, 38 Pier Street, Aberystwyth, Dyfed. *Principal*, Revd Dr E. S. John.
SCOTTISH CONGREGATIONAL COLLEGE, Rosebery Crescent, Edinburgh EH12 5YN. (8). *Principal*, Revd Dr J. W. S. Clark.

UNITARIAN

UNITARIAN COLLEGE, Luther King House, Brighton Grove, Rusholme, Manchester M14 5JP. (4). *Principal*, Revd L. Smith, Ph.D.

ECUMENICAL

QUEEN'S COLLEGE, Somerset Road, Edgbaston, Birmingham B15 2QH. (75). *Principal*, Revd Dr J. B. Walker.

NON-DENOMINATIONAL

ST MARY'S COLLEGE, The University, St Andrews, Fife KY16 9JU. (190). *Principal*, Very Revd D. W. D. Shaw.

ROMAN CATHOLIC

ALLEN HALL COLLEGE, 28 Beaufort Street, London SW3 5AA. (49). *Principal*, Revd K. Barltrop.
CAMPION HOUSE COLLEGE, 112 Thornbury Road, Isleworth, Middx. TW7 4NN. (35). *Principal*, Revd M. Barrow, SJ.
CHESTERS COLLEGE, 2 Chesters Road, Bearsden, Glasgow G61 4AG. (40). *Rector*, Very Revd P. Tartaglia.
OSCOTT COLLEGE, Chester Road, Sutton Coldfield, W. Midlands B73 5AA. (67). *Rector*, Rt. Revd Mgr P. McKinney.
ST JOHN'S SEMINARY, Wonersh, Guildford, Surrey GU5 0QX. (39). *Rector*, Rt. Revd Mgr P. Smith.
USHAW COLLEGE, Durham DH7 9RH. (92). *Principal*, Rt. Revd Mgr R. Atherton, OBE.

JEWISH

JEWS' COLLEGE, Albert Road, London NW4 2SJ. (13). *Principal*, Rabbi Dr I. Jacobs.
LEO BAECK COLLEGE, Sternberg Centre for Judaism, 80 East End Road, London N3 2SY. (16). *Principal*, Rabbi Dr J. Magonet.

TOWN AND COUNTRY PLANNING

Degree and diploma courses in town planning are accredited by the Royal Town Planning Institute.
THE ROYAL TOWN PLANNING INSTITUTE, 26 Portland Place, London W1N 4BE. Tel: 071-636 9107. *Secretary-General*, D. Fryer.

TRANSPORT

Qualifying examinations in transport management leading to chartered professional status are conducted by the Chartered Institute of Transport.
THE CHARTERED INSTITUTE OF TRANSPORT, 80 Portland Place, London W1N 4DP. Tel: 071-636 9952. *Director-General*, R. P. Botwood.

Independent Schools

The following pages list those independent schools whose Head is a member of the Headmasters' Conference, the Society of Headmasters and Headmistresses of Independent Schools or the Girls' Schools Association.

THE HEADMASTERS' CONFERENCE

Chairman (1993), R. J. Wilson (Trinity School, Surrey).
Secretary, V. S. Anthony, 130 Regent Road, Leicester LEI 7PG. Tel: 0533-854810.
Membership Secretary, R. N. P. Griffiths, 1 Russell House, Bepton Road, Midhurst, W. Sussex GU29 9NB. Tel: 0730-815635. The annual meeting is, as a rule, held at the end of September.

* Woodard Corporation School, 1 The Sanctuary, London SWIP 3JT. Tel: 071-222 5381
† Girls in VI form
‡ Co-educational

Name of School	*Founded*	*No. of pupils*	*Annual fees* Boarding	Day	*Head (with date of appointment)*
ENGLAND AND WALES					
Abbotsholme School, Staffs.	1889	245‡	£9,756	£6,504	D. J. Farrant (1984)
Abingdon School, Oxon.	1256	760	8,649	4,590	M. St J. Parker (1975)
Ackworth School, W. Yorks.	1779	422‡	8,031	4,575	D. S. Harris (1989)
Aldenham School, Herts.	1597	330†	10,476	8,301	M. Higginbottom (1983)
Alleyn's School, SE22	1619	922‡	—	5,205	C. H. R. Niven (1992)
Allhallows School, Dorset	1515	250‡	10,224	5,112	P. S. Larkman, LVO (1983)
Ampleforth College (*RC*), Yorks.	1802	643	10,350	8,550	Revd G. F. L. Chamberlain, OSB (1993)
*Ardingly College, W. Sussex	1858	500‡	10,350	8,220	J. W. Flecker (1980)
Arnold School, Blackpool	1896	820‡	3,321	3,258	J. A. B. Kelsall (1987)
Ashville College, Harrogate	1877	490‡	8,000	4,300	M. H. Crosby (1987)
Bablake School, Coventry	1560	800†	—	3,168	Dr S. Nuttall (1991)
Bancroft's School, Essex	1727	715‡	—	4,920	Dr P. C. D. Southern (1985)
Barnard Castle School, Co. Durham	1883	500†	7,355	4,352	F. S. McNamara (1980)
Batley Grammar School, W. Yorks.	1612	600	—	3,102	C. S. Parker (1986)
Bedales School, Hants.	1893	400‡	11,334	8,124	R. E. I. Newton (1992)
Bedford School	1552	706	9,435	5,985	Dr I. P. Evans (1990)
Bedford Modern School	1566	950	7,119	3,804	P. J. Squire (1977)
Berkhamsted School, Herts.	1541	480	9,552	5,454	Revd K. H. Wilkinson (1989)
Birkenhead School, Merseyside	1860	760	—	3,081	S. J. Haggett (1988)
Bishop's Stortford College, Herts.	1868	360†	9,520	6,880	S. G. G. Benson (1984)
*Bloxham School, Oxon.	1860	360†	10,500	7,850	D. K. Exham (1991)
Blundell's School, Devon	1604	430†	10,000	6,480	J. Leigh (1992)
Bolton School	1524	850	—	3,996	A. W. Wright (1983)
Bootham School, York	1823	350‡	9,040	5,847	I. M. Small (1988)
Bradfield College, Berks.	1850	580†	11,100	8,325	P. B. Smith (1985)
Bradford Grammar School	1662	1,023†	—	3,411	D. A. G. Smith (1974)
Brentwood School, Essex	1557	940†	8,712	4,974	J. A. E. Evans (1981)
Brighton College, E. Sussex	1845	477‡	10,395	6,831	J. D. Leach (1987)
Bristol Cathedral School	1542	460†	—	3,678	R. A. Collard (1990)
Bristol Grammar School	1532	1,000‡	—	3,537	C. E. Martin (1986)
Bromsgrove School, Worcs.	1553	575‡	9,060	5,670	T. M. Taylor (1986)
Bryanston School, Dorset	1928	660‡	11,670	7,782	T. D. Wheare (1983)
Bury Grammar School, Lancs.	1634	590	—	3,300	K. Richards (1990)
Canford School, Dorset	1923	510†	11,050	7,180	J. D. Lever (1992)
Caterham School, Surrey	1811	440†	9,060	4,935	S. R. Smith (1974)
Charterhouse, Surrey	1611	700†	11,565	9,540	P. J. Attenborough (1982)
Cheadle Hulme School, Cheshire	1855	904‡	7,905	3,660	D. J. Wilkinson (1990)
Cheltenham College, Glos.	1841	563†	10,935	8,265	P. D. V. Wilkes (1990)
Chetham's School of Music, Manchester	1653	270‡	14,307	11,079	Revd P. F. Hullah (1992)
Chigwell School, Essex	1629	340†	8,544	5,619	A. R. M. Little (1989)
Christ College, Brecon	1541	369†	8,136	5,607	S. W. Hockey (1982)
Christ's Hospital, W. Sussex	1553	804‡	varies	—	R. C. Poulton (1987)

Name of School	*Founded*	*No. of pupils*	*Annual fees* Boarding	Day	*Head (with date of appointment)*
Churcher's College, Hants.	1722	515‡	£8,220	£4,440	G. W. Buttle (1988)
City of London, EC4	1442	600	—	5,202	B. G. Bass (1990)
City of London Freemen's School, Surrey	1854	370‡	8,001	5,139	D. C. Haywood (1987)
Clifton College, Bristol	1862	680‡	11,085	7,770	H. Monro (1990)
Colfe's School, SE12	1652	698†	—	4,245	Dr D. Richardson (1990)
Colston's Collegiate School, Bristol	1710	330†	8,130	4,905	S. B. Howarth (1988)
Cranleigh School, Surrey	1863	550†	11,280	8,460	A. Hart (1984)
Culford School, Suffolk	1881	420‡	8,742	5,682	J. Richardson (1992)
Dame Allan's School, Newcastle upon Tyne	1705	436†	—	3,141	T. A. Willcocks (*Principal*) (1988)
Dauntsey's School, Wiltshire	1543	610‡	9,345	5,784	C. R. Evans (1985)
Dean Close School, Cheltenham	1884	450‡	10,500	7,350	C. J. Bacon (1979)
*Denstone College, Staffs.	1873	304‡	9,591	6,837	H. C. K. Carson (1990)
Douai School (*RC*), Berks.	1903	260	9,360	6,030	Revd G. Scott, Ph.D. (1987)
Dover College, Kent	1871	300‡	9,600	5,970	M. P. G. Wright (1991)
Downside School (*RC*), Somerset	1607	444	9,918	6,360	Dom. A. Bellenger (1991)
Dulwich College, SE21	1619	1,386	11,370	5,685	A. C. F. Verity (*Master*) (1986)
Durham School	1414	374†	10,500	6,999	M. A. Lang (1982)
Eastbourne College, E. Sussex	1867	542†	10,539	7,794	C. J. Saunders (1981)
*Ellesmere College, Shropshire	1884	380†	9,300	6,600	D. R. du Croz (1988)
Eltham College, SE9	1842	560†	10,155	4,315	D. M. Green (1990)
Emanuel School, SW11	1594	515	—	4,110	P. F. Thomson (1984)
Epsom College, Surrey	1855	660†	9,990	7,500	A. H. Beadles (1993)
Eton College, Berks.	1440	1,266	11,610	—	Dr W. E. K. Anderson (1980)
Exeter School	1633	722†	6,696	3,546	N. W. Gamble (1992)
Felsted School, Essex	1564	430†	10,980	8,670	E. J. H. Gould (1983)
Forest School, E17	1834	1,200‡	6,717	4,851	A. Boggis (*Warden*) (1992)
Framlingham College, Suffolk	1864	435‡	8,613	5,526	J. F. X. Miller (1989)
Frensham Heights, Surrey	1925	285‡	10,650	6,795	P. de Voile (1993)
Giggleswick School, N. Yorks.	1512	304‡	10,461	6,936	P. Hobson (1986)
Gresham's School, Norfolk	1555	470‡	9,696	6,786	J. H. Arkell (1991)
Haberdashers' Aske's School, Herts.	1690	1,100	—	5,028	K. Dawson (1987)
Haileybury, Herts.	1862	613†	11,340	8,055	D. J. Jewell (1987)
Hampton School, Middx.	1557	900	—	4,050	G. G. Able (1988)
Harrow School, Middx.	1571	775	11,925	—	N. R. Bomford (1991)
Hereford Cathedral School	1384	595‡	6,870	3,990	Dr H. C. Tomlinson (1987)
Highgate School, N6	1565	576	10,206	6,205	R. P. Kennedy (1989)
Hulme Grammar School, Oldham	1611	740	—	3,100	G. F. Dunkin (1987)
*Hurstpierpoint College, W. Sussex	1849	370	10,200	8,160	S. A. Watson (1986)
Hymers College, Hull	1889	720	—	4,640	J. C. Morris (1990)
Ipswich School, Suffolk	1390	616†	7,464	4,362	Dr J. M. Blatchly (1972)
John Lyon School, Middx.	1876	505	—	4,725	Revd T. J. Wright (1986)
Kelly College, Devon	1877	309‡	10,110	6,750	C. H. Hirst (1985)
Kent College, Canterbury	1885	570‡	8,622	4,830	R. J. Wicks (1980)
Kimbolton School, Cambs.	1600	555‡	7,860	4,560	R. V. Peel (1987)
King Edward VI School, Southampton	1553	945†	—	4,119	T. R. Cookson (1990)
King Edward VII School, Lytham	1908	550	—	3,069	D. Heap (1982)
King Edward's School, Bath	1552	675†	—	3,600	J. P. Wroughton (1982)
King Edward's School, Birmingham	1552	830	—	5,934	H. R. Wright (*Chief Master*) (1991)
King Edward's School, Witley, Surrey	1553	525‡	8,055	5,955	R. J. Fox (1988)
King Henry VIII School, Coventry	1545	826‡	—	3,168	G. R. James (1991)
*King's College, Taunton	1880	475‡	10,111	7,160	R. S. Funnell (1988)
King's College School, SW19	1829	670	—	5,070	R. M. Reeve (1980)
King's School, Bruton, Somerset	1519	347†	9,945	7,050	R. I. Smyth (1993)
King's School, Canterbury	600	710‡	11,250	7,875	Revd Canon A. C. J. Phillips (1986)
King's School, Chester	1541	490	—	3,645	A. R. D. Wickson (1981)
King's School, Ely, Cambs.	970	400‡	10,413	6,639	R. H. Youdale (1992)
King's School, Macclesfield	1502	910†	—	3,895	A. G. Silcock (1987)
King's School, Rochester, Kent	604	336†	9,753	5,742	Dr I. R. Walker (1986)
King's School, Tynemouth	1860	680‡	—	3,138	W. T. Gillen (1987)
King's School, Worcester	1541	775‡	7,953	4,752	Dr J. M. Moore (1983)
Kingston Grammar School, Surrey	1561	585‡	—	4,710	C. D. Baxter (1991)

Name of School	Founded	No. of pupils	Annual fees Boarding	Annual fees Day	Head (with date of appointment)
Kingswood School, Bath	1748	476‡	£9,798	£6,372	G. M. Best (1987)
*Lancing College, W. Sussex	1848	542†	10,770	8,085	J. S. Woodhouse (1981)
Latymer Upper School, London W6	1642	963	—	4,860	C. Diggory (1991)
Leeds Grammar School	1552	1,002	—	3,681	B. W. Collins (1986)
Leighton Park School, Reading	1890	350†	9,720	7,290	J. A. Chapman (1986)
The Leys School, Cambridge	1875	400†	10,740	7,950	Revd J. C. A. Barrett (1990)
Liverpool College	1840	339†	—	3,444	B. R. Martin (1992)
Llandovery College, Dyfed	1848	230‡	8,061	5,259	Dr C. E. Evans (*Warden*) (1988)
Lord Wandsworth College, Hants.	1912	444†	8,460	6,600	G. A. G. Dodd (1982)
Loughborough Grammar School	1495	920	7,290	3,906	D. N. Ireland (1984)
Magdalen College School, Oxford	1480	500‡	—	4,200	P. M. Tinniswood (*Master*) (1991)
Malvern College, Worcs.	1865	700‡	10,980	7,995	R. de C. Chapman (1983)
Manchester Grammar School	1515	1,447	—	3,642	J. G. Parker (*High Master*) (1985)
Marlborough College, Wilts.	1843	875‡	11,265	8,448	D. R. Cope (*Master*) (1986)
Merchant Taylors' School, Liverpool	1620	732	—	3,330	S. J. R. Dawkins (1986)
Merchant Taylors' School, Middx.	1561	705	9,715	5,965	J. R. Gabitass (1991)
Mill Hill School, NW7	1807	560†	10,185	6,750	E. A. M. MacAlpine (1992)
Monkton Combe School, Bath	1868	335‡	10,455	7,695	M. J. Cuthbertson (1990)
Monmouth School, Gwent	1614	542	7,374	4,428	R. D. Lane (1982)
Mount St Mary's College (*RC*), Derbys.	1842	323‡	8,025	5,421	P. Fisher (1991)
Newcastle under Lyme School	1874	1,200‡	—	3,150	Dr R. M. Reynolds (*Principal*) (1990)
Norwich School	1250	600	7,218	3,918	C. D. Brown (1984)
Nottingham High School	1513	850	—	3,960	D. T. Witcombe, PH.D. (1970)
Oakham School, Rutland	1584	750‡	10,065	5,565	G. Smallbone (1985)
The Oratory School (*RC*), Berks.	1859	360	10,557	7,377	S. W. Barrow (1992)
Oundle School, Northants	1556	805‡	11,670	—	D. B. McMurray (1984)
Pangbourne College, Berks.	1917	400†	10,050	7,050	A. B. E. Hudson (1988)
Perse School, Cambridge	1615	486	7,839	3,939	Dr G. M. Stephen (1987)
Plymouth College	1877	640	7,395	3,825	A. J. Morsley (1992)
Pocklington School, York	1514	597‡	7,563	4,122	J. N. D. Gray (1992)
Portsmouth Grammar School	1732	770‡	—	3,705	A. C. V. Evans (1983)
Prior Park College (*RC*), Bath	1830	440‡	9,105	5,034	J. W. R. Goulding (1989)
Queen Elizabeth GS, Wakefield	1591	746†	—	3,663	R. P. Mardling (1985)
Queen Elizabeth's GS, Blackburn	1567	1,100†	—	3,465	P. F. Johnston (1978)
Queen Elizabeth's Hospital, Bristol	1590	480	6,177	3,519	Dr R. Gliddon (1985)
Queen's College, Taunton	1843	470‡	8,755	5,400	C. T. Bradnock (1991)
Radley College, Oxon.	1847	604	11,025	—	R. M. Morgan (*Warden*) (1991)
Ratcliffe College (*RC*), Leicester	1844	470‡	8,007	5,340	Revd L. G. Hurdidge (1986)
Reading Blue Coat School	1646	560†	8,088	4,434	Revd A. Sanders (1974)
Reed's School, Surrey	1813	340†	9,075	6,855	D. E. Prince (1983)
Reigate Grammar School, Surrey	1675	850†	—	4,260	J. G. Hamlin (1982)
Rendcomb College, Glos.	1920	250‡	9,576	2,526	J. Tolputt (1987)
Repton School, Derby	1557	570‡	10,440	7,830	G. E. Jones (1987)
RNIB New College, Worcester	1987	120‡	19,629	13,086	Revd B. R. Manthorp (1980)
Rossall School, Lancs.	1844	485‡	10,500	7,095	R. D. W. Rhodes (1987)
Royal Grammar School, Guildford	1552	806	—	5,410	T. M. S. Young (1992)
Royal Grammar School, Newcastle upon Tyne	1545	955	—	3,180	A. S. Cox (1972)
Royal Grammar School, Worcester	1291	768	6,669	3,942	T. E. Savage, TD (1978)
Rugby School, Warwicks.	1567	650‡	11,520	6,825	M. B. Mavor, CVO (1990)
Rydal School, Clwyd	1885	340‡	8,433	6,411	N. W. Thorne (1991)
Ryde School, Isle of Wight	1921	425‡	7,176	3,594	M. D. Featherstone (1990)
St Albans School, Herts.	1570	665†	—	4,710	S. C. Wilkinson (1984)
St Ambrose College, Cheshire	1946	650	—	2,817	G. E. Hester (1991)
St Anselm's College (*RC*), Birkenhead	1933	655	—	2,826	Revd Br. C. J. Sreenan, OBE (1987)
St Bede's College (*RC*), Manchester	1876	950‡	—	3,486	J. Byrne (1983)
St Bees School, Cumbria	1583	331‡	9,327	6,480	P. A. Chamberlain (1988)
St Benedict's School (*RC*), W5	1902	600†	—	4,260	Dr A. J. Dachs (1987)
St Dunstan's College, SE6	1888	620	—	4,437	B. D. Dance (1973)

Name of School	*Foun-ded*	*No. of pupils*	*Annual fees* Boarding	Day	*Head (with date of appointment)*
St Edmund's College (*RC*), Herts.	1568	454‡	£8,178	£5,232	D. J. J. McEwen (1984)
St Edmund's School, Canterbury	1749	314‡	10,452	6,825	J. V. Tyson (1978)
St Edward's College (*RC*), Liverpool	1853	676‡	—	3,150	J. E. Waszek (1992)
St Edward's School, Oxford	1863	581†	11,025	8,280	D. Christie (*Warden*) (1988)
St George's College (*RC*), Surrey	1869	550†	—	5,550	P. A. Johnson, D.Phil. (1992)
St John's School, Surrey	1851	400†	8,850	6,300	C. H. Tongue (1993)
St Lawrence College, Kent	1879	385‡	9,750	6,540	J. H. Binfield (1983)
St Mary's College (*RC*), Merseyside	1919	565‡	—	3,165	W. Hammond (1991)
St Paul's School, SW13	1509	753	11,400	7,200	R. S. Baldock (*High Master*) (1992)
St Peter's School, York	627	480‡	9,402	5,595	R. N. Pittman (1985)
Sedbergh School, Cumbria	1525	460	10,560	7,410	Dr R. G. Baxter (1982)
Sevenoaks School, Kent	1418	915‡	10,305	6,264	R. P. Barker (1981)
Sherborne School, Dorset	1550	650	11,325	8,625	P. H. Lapping (1988)
Shrewsbury School	1552	670	10,950	7,725	F. E. Maidment (1988)
Silcoates School, W. Yorks.	1820	560‡	8,490	4,740	A. P. Spillane (1991)
Solihull School, Warwicks	1560	839†	—	3,468	A. Lee (1983)
Stamford School, Lincs.	1532	580	7,092	3,546	G. J. Timm (1978)
Stockport Grammar School	1487	1,005‡	—	3,537	D. R. J. Bird (1985)
Stonyhurst College (*RC*), Lancs.	1593	430†	10,188	5,862	Dr R. G. G. Mercer (1985)
Stowe School, Bucks.	1923	590†	11,730	8,205	J. G. L. Nichols (1989)
Sutton Valence School, Kent	1576	380‡	10,400	6,600	M. R. Haywood (1980)
Taunton School	1847	550‡	10,290	6,600	B. B. Sutton (1987)
Tettenhall College, Staffs.	1863	300‡	7,905	4,860	W. J. Dale (1968)
Tonbridge School, Kent	1553	643	11,310	7,974	J. M. Hammond (1990)
Trent College, Derbys.	1868	650‡	9,349	5,699	J. S. Lee (1988)
Trinity School, Surrey	1596	830	—	4,548	R. J. Wilson (1972)
Truro School	1879	885‡	7,650	4,110	B. K. Hobbs (1986)
University College School, NW3	1830	520	—	5,925	G. D. Slaughter (1983)
Uppingham School, Leics.	1584	620†	11,400	6,840	S. C. Winkley (1991)
Warwick School	914	982	8,688	4,038	P. J. Cheshire (1989)
Wellingborough School, Northants.	1595	430‡	7,965	4,785	G. Garrett (1973)
Wellington College, Berks.	1856	799†	11,175	8,160	C. J. Driver (1989)
Wells Cathedral School, Somerset	1180	610‡	7,887	4,635	J. S. Baxter (1986)
West Buckland School, Devon	1858	482‡	7,701	4,176	M. Downward (1979)
Westminster School, SW1	1560	651†	11,325	7,575	D. M. Summersale (1986)
Whitgift School, Surrey	1596	945	—	4,794	C. A. Barnett, D.Phil. (1991)
William Hulme's GS, Manchester	1887	790‡	—	3,705	P. D. Briggs (1987)
Winchester College, Hants.	1382	650	11,700	8,775	J. P. Sabben-Clare (1985)
Wisbech Grammar School, Cambs.	1379	621‡	—	1,340	R. S. Repper (1988)
Wolverhampton Grammar School	1512	654‡	—	4,086	B. St J. Trafford (1990)
Woodbridge School, Suffolk	1662	550‡	8,208	4,998	Dr D. Younger (1985)
Woodhouse Grove School, Bradford	1812	570‡	7,650	4,575	D. W. Welsh (1991)
*Worksop College, Notts.	1895	370‡	9,504	6,558	R. D. V. Knight (1990)
Worth School (*RC*), W. Sussex	1959	308	10,350	7,770	Revd R. S. Ortiger (1983)
Wrekin College, Shropshire	1880	350‡	10,050	7,065	P. Johnson (1991)
Wycliffe College, Glos.	1882	310‡	10,665	7,455	A. P. Millard (1987)
SCOTLAND					
Daniel Stewart's and Melville College, Edinburgh320	1832	785	7,116	3,666	P. J. F. Tobin (*Warden*) (1989)
Dollar Academy, Clackmannanshire	1818	750‡	7,869	3,549	L. Harrison (*Rector*) (1984)
Dundee High School, Tayside	1239	1,000‡	—	3,381	R. Nimmo, OBE (*Rector*) (1977)
The Edinburgh Academy	1824	579‡	9,801	4,635	A. J. D. Rees (*Rector*) (1992)
Fettes College, Edinburgh	1870	350‡	11,055	7,425	M. T. Thyne (1988)
George Heriot's School, Edinburgh	1659	960‡	—	3,420	K. P. Pearson (1983)
George Watson's College, Edinburgh	1741	1,267	7,230	3,630	F. E. Gerstenberg (*Principal*) (1985)
Glasgow Academy	1845	1,000‡	—	3,795	C. W. Turner (*Rector*) (1983)
Glenalmond College, Perth	1841	300†	10,650	7,095	I. G. Templeton (*Warden*) (1992)
Gordonstoun School, Moray	1934	470‡	10,650	6,870	M. C. S.-R. Pyper (1990)
The High School of Glasgow	1124	599‡	—	3,681	R. G. Easton (1983)
Hutchesons' Grammar School, Glasgow	1641	1,087‡	—	3,177	D. R. Ward (*Rector*) (1987)

Name of School	Founded	No. of pupils	Annual fees Boarding	Day	Head (with date of appointment)
Kelvinside Academy, Glasgow	1878	475	—	£3,600	J. H. Duff (*Rector*) (1980)
Loretto School, E. Lothian	1827	306†	10,170	6,780	Revd N. W. Drummond (1984)
Merchiston Castle School, Edinburgh	1833	380	10,200	6,600	D. M. Spawforth (1981)
Morrison's Academy, Perthshire	1860	560‡	8,754	3,162	H. A. Ashmall (*Rector*) (1979)
Robert Gordon's College, Aberdeen	1729	925‡	7,225	3,325	G. A. Allan (1978)
Strathallan School, Perth	1913	400‡	9,750	6,500	C. D. Pighills (1975)
NORTHERN IRELAND					
Bangor Grammar School, Co. Down	1856	900	—	504	T. W. Patton (1979)
Belfast Royal Academy	1785	1,300‡	—	185	W. M. Sillery (1980)
Campbell College, Belfast	1894	600	4,860	860	Dr R. J. I. Pollock (1987)
Coleraine Academical Institution	1856	860	3,000	nil	R. S. Forsythe (1984)
Methodist College, Belfast	1868	1,710	2,700	95	T. W. Mulryne (1988)
Portora Royal School, Enniskillen	1618	400	2,601	nil	R. L. Bennett (1983)
Royal Belfast Academical Institution	1810	950	—	230	R. M. Ridley (1990)
CHANNEL ISLANDS AND ISLE OF MAN					
Elizabeth College, Guernsey	1563	570	5,475	2,100	J. H. F. Doulton (1988)
King William's College, Isle of Man	1668	355‡	9,450	6,750	S. A. Westley (1989)
EUROPE					
Aiglon College, Switzerland	1949	280‡	*Fr.*46,635	*Fr.*31,815	P. Parsons (1976)
British School in the Netherlands	1935	540‡	—	*Fl.*17,820	M. J. Cooper (*Principal*) (1990)
British School of Brussels	1970	575‡	—	*Fr.*527,000	Dr J. Jackson (1983)
British School of Paris, France	1954	280‡	—	*Fr.*68,825	A. Slesser (1992)
The English School, Nicosia, Cyprus	1900	830‡	—	*C£*1,450	A. M. Hudspeth (1988)
The International School of Paris	1964	250‡	—	*Fr.*74,000	N. M. Prentki (1988)
St Columba's College, Dublin	1843	299‡	*IR£*5,310	*IR£*2,970	T. E. Macey (*Warden*) (1988)
St Edward's College, Malta	1929	450†	—	*M£*495	G. Briscoe (1989)
St George's English School, Rome	1958	450‡	—	*L*16,200,000	F. Ruggiero (1991)
Sir James Henderson School, Milan	1969	170†	—	*L*12,400,000	C. T. G. Leech (1986)

OTHER OVERSEAS MEMBERS

AFRICA

FALCON COLLEGE, PO Esigodini, Zimbabwe. *Head*, P. N. Todd

HILTON COLLEGE, Natal 3245, SA. *Head*, P. Marsh

MICHAELHOUSE, Balgowan, Natal 3275, SA. *Head*, J. H. Pluke

PETERHOUSE, Marondera, Zimbabwe. *Head*, Revd Dr A. J. Megahey

ST GEORGE'S COLLEGE, Harare, Zimbabwe. *Head*, M. F. Hackett

DIOCESAN COLLEGE, Rondebosch, SA. *Head*, J. B. Gardener

ST JOHN'S COLLEGE, Johannesburg, SA. *Head*, W. Macfarlane

ST STITHIAN'S COLLEGE, Randburg, SA. *Head*, D. B. Wylde

AUSTRALIA

ANGLICAN CHURCH GRAMMAR SCHOOL, Brisbane. *Head*, C. V. Ellis

BRIGHTON GRAMMAR SCHOOL, Brighton, Victoria. *Head*, R. L. Rofe

CAMBERWELL GRAMMAR SCHOOL, Balwyn, Victoria 3101. *Head*, C. F. Black

CANBERRA GS, Red Hill, ACT 2603. *Head*, T. C. Murray

CAULFIELD GRAMMAR SCHOOL, East St Kilda, Victoria. *Head*, Revd A. S. Holmes

CHRIST CHURCH GRAMMAR SCHOOL, Claremont 6010, W. Australia. *Head*, J. J. S. Madin

CHURCH OF ENGLAND GRAMMAR SCHOOL, Melbourne. *Head*, A. J. de V. Hill

CHURCH OF ENGLAND GRAMMAR SCHOOL, Sydney, NSW. *Head*, R. A. I. Grant

CRANBROOK SCHOOL, Sydney, NSW. *Head*, Dr B. N. Carter

GEELONG CHURCH OF ENGLAND GRAMMAR SCHOOL, Corio. *Head*, J. E. Lewis

THE GEELONG COLLEGE, Geelong, Victoria. *Head*, A. P. Sheahan

GUILDFORD GRAMMAR SCHOOL, W. Australia. *Head*, J. M. Moody

HAILEYBURY COLLEGE, Keysborough, Victoria 3175. *Head*, A. H. M. Aikman

HALE SCHOOL, Wembley Downs, W. Australia. *Head*, K. G. Tregonning

KING'S SCHOOL, Parramatta, NSW. *Head*, J. A. Wickham

KINROSS WOLAROI SCHOOL, NSW. *Head*, A. E. S. Anderson

KNOX GS, Wahroonga 2076 NSW. *Head*, Dr I. Paterson

NEWINGTON COLLEGE, Stanmore, NSW. *Head*, A. J. Rae

THE PENINSULA SCHOOL, Mt Eliza, Victoria. *Head*, H. A. Macdonald

ST PETER'S COLLEGE, St Peter's, S. Australia. *Head*, Dr A. J. Shinkfield

SCOTCH COLLEGE, Adelaide, S. Australia. *Head*, W. M. Miles
SCOTCH COLLEGE, Hawthorn, Melbourne, Victoria. *Head*, Dr F. G. Donaldson
SCOTCH COLLEGE, Swanbourne, W. Australia. *Head*, W. R. Dickinson
SCOTS COLLEGE, Sydney, NSW. *Head*, G. A. W. Renney
THE SOUTHPORT SCHOOL, Southport, Queensland. *Head*, B. A. Cook
SYDNEY GRAMMAR SCHOOL, NSW. *Head*, Dr R. D. Townsend
WESLEY COLLEGE, Melbourne. *Head*, D. H. Prest

CANADA

BRENTWOOD COLLEGE SCHOOL, Vancouver, BC. *Head*, W. T. Ross
GLENLYON-NORFOLK SCHOOL, Victoria, BC. *Head*, D. Brooks
HILLFIELD-STRATHALLAN COLLEGE, Hamilton, Ontario. *Head*, M. B. Wansbrough
PICKERING COLLEGE, Newmarket, Ontario. *Head*, S. H. Clark
ST ANDREW'S COLLEGE, Aurora, Ontario. *Head*, R. P. Bedard
TORONTO FRENCH SCHOOL. *Head*, A. S. Troubetzkoy
TRINITY COLLEGE SCHOOL, Port Hope, Ontario. *Head*, R. C. N.Wright
UPPER CANADA COLLEGE, Toronto. *Head*, J. D. Blakey

HONG KONG

ISLAND SCHOOL, Borrett Road. *Head*, D. J. James
KING GEORGE V SCHOOL, Kowloon. *Head*, M. J. Behennah

INDIA

BIRLA PUBLIC SCHOOL, Pilani 333 031, Rajasthan. *Head*, B. K. Sood
LAWRENCE SCHOOL, Lovedale, Nilgiris. *Head*, B. S. Bhatnagar
LAWRENCE SCHOOL, Sanawar. *Head*, Sumer Singh
THE SCINDIA SCHOOL, GWALIOR. *Head*, Dr S. D. Singh

NEW ZEALAND

CHRIST'S COLLEGE, Christchurch, Canterbury. *Head*, Dr M. J. Rosser
KING'S COLLEGE, Auckland. *Head*, J. S. Taylor
ST ANDREW'S COLLEGE, Christchurch, Canterbury. *Head*, Dr A. J. Rentoul
RATHKEALE COLLEGE, Masterton. *Head*, B. R. Levick
THE COLLEGIATE SCHOOL, Wanganui. *Head*, T. S. McKinlay
WAITAKI BOYS' HIGH SCHOOL, Oamaru. *Head*, B. R. Gollop

SOUTH AMERICA

ACADEMIA BRITANICA CUSCATLECA, El Salvador. *Head*, A. J. McGuiggan
MARKHAM COLLEGE, Lima, Peru. *Head*, W. J. Baker
ST ANDREW'S SCOTS SCHOOL, Argentina. *Head*, K. Prior
ST GEORGE'S COLLEGE, Quilmes, Argentina. *Head*, N. P. O. Green
ST PAULS' SCHOOL, São Paulo, Brazil. *Head*, M. T. M. C. McCann
THE BRITISH SCHOOLS, Montevideo, Uruguay. *Head*, J. H. Sidwell

ADDITIONAL MEMBERS

The headteachers of some maintained schools are by invitation Additional Members of the HMC. They include the following:

AYLESBURY GRAMMAR SCHOOL, Bucks. *Head*, K. D. Smith
EASINGWOLD SCHOOL, York. *Head*, R. F. Kirk
HABERDASHERS' ASKE'S HATCHAM BOYS' SCHOOL, Pepys Road, London SE14 5SF. *Head*, G. J. Walker
HAYWARDS HEATH SIXTH FORM COLLEGE, W. Sussex. *Head*, B. W. Derbyshire
THE JOHN FISHER SCHOOL, Purley, Surrey. *Head*, T. J. King
THE JUDD SCHOOL, Tonbridge, Kent. *Head*, K. A. Starling
LISKEARD SCHOOL, Cornwall. *Head*, A. D. Wood
THE LONDON ORATORY SCHOOL, London SW6. *Head*, J. C. McIntosh
PRESCOT SCHOOL, Merseyside. *Head*, P. A. Barlow
PRINCE WILLIAM SCHOOL, Oundle, Cambs. *Head*, C. J. Lowe
THE ROYAL GRAMMAR SCHOOL, High Wycombe, Bucks. *Head*, R. P. Brown
THE ROYAL GRAMMAR SCHOOL, Lancaster. *Head*, P. J. Mawby
ST BARTHOLOMEW'S SCHOOL, Newbury, Bucks. *Head*, R. P. H. Mermagen
SETTLE HIGH SCHOOL, N. Yorks. *Head*, R. Haslam
STOWMARKET HIGH SCHOOL, Suffolk. *Head*, Dr R. J. Montgomery

SOCIETY OF HEADMASTERS AND HEADMISTRESSES OF INDEPENDENT SCHOOLS

Hon. Secretary, A. E. R. Dodds, Mantons, Park Road, Winchester, Hants. SO23 7BE. Tel: 0962-862579.

The Society was founded in 1961 and, in general, represents smaller boarding schools.

Headmasters of the following schools are members of both HMC and SHMIS; details of these schools appear in the HMC list: Abbotsholme School, Ackworth School, Bedales School, Churcher's College, City of London Freemen's School, Colston's Collegiate School, King's School, Tynemouth, Lord Wandsworth College, Pangbourne College, Reading Blue Coat School, Reed's School, Rendcomb College, Ryde School, St George's College, Silcoates School, Tettenhall College, Wells Cathedral School, West Buckland School, Wisbech Grammar School, Woodbridge School.

* Woodard Corporation School
† Girls in VI form
‡ Co-educational

Name of School	*Founded*	*No. of pupils*	*Annual fees* Boarding	Day	*Head (with date of appointment)*
Abbey Gate College, Chester	1977	300‡	—	£3,294	E. W. Mitchell (1991)
Austin Friars School (*RC*), Carlisle	1951	310‡	6,585	3,927	Revd T. Lyons, OSA (1981)
Bearwood College, Berks.	1827	300	8,850	5,025	The Hon. M. C. Penney (1980)
Bedstone College, Shropshire	1948	170‡	7,995	4,932	M. S. Symonds (1990)
Belmont Abbey (*RC*), Hereford	1926	200	7,800	4,500	Revd D. C. Jenkins, OSB (1988)
Bembridge School, Isle of Wight	1919	200‡	8,085	6,945	J. High (1986)
Bentham School, N. Yorks	1726	250‡	7,215	3,570	N. K. D. Ward (1992)
Bethany School, Kent	1866	270‡	8,394	5,370	W. M. Harvey (1988)
Box Hill School, Surrey	1959	300‡	9,105	5,655	Dr R. A. S. Atwood (1987)
Carmel College (*Jewish*), Oxon.	1948	242‡	15,636	7,200	P. D. Skelker (1984)
Claremont Fan Court School, Surrey	1932	550‡	8,175	5,145	J. H. Scott (1987)
Clayesmore School, Dorset	1896	311‡	10,140	7,098	D. J. Beeby (1986)
Cokethorpe School, Oxon.	1957	200‡	10,500	6,900	D. G. Crawford (1989)
Duke of York's Military School, Dover	1803	475	n/a	—	Lt.-Col. G. H. Wilson (1992)
Embley Park School, Romsey, Hants.	1946	225†	8,985	5,490	D. F. Chapman (1987)
Ewell Castle School, Surrey	1926	330†	—	3,880	R. A. Fewtrell (1983)
Friends' School, Essex	1702	280‡	8,490	5,370	Miss S. H. Evans (1989)
Fulneck Boys' School, W. Yorks.	1753	335†	7,773	4,011	I. D. Cleland (1980)
*Grenville College, Devon	1954	330	8,601	4,218	N. C. V. Cane, Ph.D. (1992)
Halliford School, Middx.	1956	320†	—	3,900	J. R. Crook (1984)
Hipperholme Grammar School, Halifax	1648	380‡	—	2,880	C. C. Robinson (1988)
Keil School, Dumbarton	1915	224‡	8,082	7,941	vacant
Kingham Hill School, Oxon.	1886	180‡	7,725	4,635	M. Payne (*Warden*) (1990)
King's School, Gloucester	1541	320‡	7,851	4,647	P. Lacey (1993)
Kirkham Grammar School, Lancs.	1549	510‡	5,778	3,078	B. Stacey (1991)
Licensed Victuallers' School, Ascot, Berks.	1803	508‡	7,884	4,455	W. J. Powell (1989)
Lord Mayor Treloar College, Hants.	1908	274‡	17,976	13,482	H. Heard (1990)
Milton Abbey School, Dorset	1954	270	10,110	7,077	R. H. Hardy (1987)
Oswestry School, Shropshire	1407	300‡	8,091	4,821	J. V. Light (1992)
Pierrepont School, Surrey	1947	200‡	9,144	5,502	N. Taylor (1993)
The Purcell School (music), Middx.	1962	150‡	12,033	7,110	K. J. Bain (1983)
Rannoch School, Perthshire	1959	250‡	9,210	5,385	M. Barratt (1982)
Rishworth School, W. Yorks.	1724	482‡	8,295	4,290	M. J. Elford (1992)
Rougemont School, Gwent	1919	255‡	—	3,840	G. R. Sims (1991)
Royal Hospital School, Ipswich	1712	620‡	6,255	—	M. A. B. Kirk (1983)
Royal Russell School, Surrey	1853	450‡	8,970	4,725	R. D. Balaam (1981)
Royal School, Dungannon, N. Ireland	1614	597‡	5,145	85	P. D. Hewitt (1984)
Royal Wolverhampton School	1850	320‡	7,920	4,530	P. Gorring (1985)
Ruthin School, Clwyd	1574	175‡	8,475	5,340	F. R. Ullmann (1986)
St Bede's School, E. Sussex	—	350‡	9,900	6,150	R. A. Perrin (1978)
St David's College, Gwynedd	1965	230	8,130	5,250	W. Seymour (1991)
Scarborough College, N. Yorks.	1898	428‡	8,520	4,620	D. S. Hempsall, Ph.D. (1985)
Seaford College, W. Sussex	1884	350†	9,030	6,285	R. C. Hannaford (1990)
Shebbear College, Devon	1841	260‡	8,040	4,410	R. J. Buley (1983)
Shiplake College, Oxon.	1959	320	10,170	6,810	N. V. Bevan (1988)
Sidcot School, Avon	1808	325‡	8,580	5,145	C. J. Greenfield (1986)
Stafford Grammar School, Staffs.	1982	290‡	—	3,399	M. James (1992)
Stanbridge Earls School, Hants.	1952	187‡	10,470	7,860	H. Moxon (1984)
Warminster School, Wilts.	1707	486‡	7,995	4,725	T. D. Holgate (1990)
Yarm School, Cleveland	1978	450†	—	4,168	R. Neville Tate (1978)

GIRLS' SCHOOLS ASSOCIATION

THE GIRLS' SCHOOLS ASSOCIATION, 130 Regent Road, Leicester LEI 7PG. Tel: 0533-541619.
President (1992–3), Miss J. Jefferson.
Secretary, Miss A. C. Parkin.

CSC Church Schools Company, IA Doughty Street, London WCIN 2PH. Tel: 071-404 3134.
§ Girls Public Day School Trust, 26 Queen Anne's Gate, London SWIH 9AN. Tel: 071-222 9595.
* Woodard Corporation School
† Boys in VI form
‡ Co-educational

Name of School	*Founded*	*No. of pupils*	*Annual fees* Boarding	Day	*Head (with date of appointment)*
ENGLAND AND WALES					
Abbey School, Reading	1887	760	—	£3,630	Miss B. C. L. Sheldon (1991)
Abbot's Hill, Herts.	1912	170	£9,075	5,355	Mrs J. Kingsley (1979)
Adcote School, Shropshire	1907	80	7,665	4,545	Mrs S. B. Cecchet (1979)
Alice Ottley School, Worcester	1883	596	—	4,074	Miss C. Sibbit (1986)
Amberfield School, Ipswich	1952	180	—	3,525	Mrs P. F. Webb (1979)
Ashford School, Kent	1910	450	8,178	4,716	Mrs P. Metham (1992)
Assumption School, N. Yorks.	1852	125	7,398	4,473	Mrs V. Fisher (1990)
Atherley School, Southampton (*CSC*)	1926	320	—	3,744	Mrs M. Williams (1988)
Badminton School, Bristol	1858	300	9,900	5,550	C. J. T. Gould (1981)
§Bath High School	1875	388	—	3,444	Miss M. A. Winfield (1985)
Battle Abbey School, E. Sussex	1912	112	8,310	5,130	D. J. A. Teall (1982)
Bedford High School	1882	804	7,750	4,147	Mrs D. M. Willis (1987)
Bedgebury School, Kent	1860	340	9,498	5,880	Mrs M. E. A. Kaye (1987)
§Belvedere School, Liverpool	1880	435	—	3,444	Mrs C. H. Evans (1992)
Benenden School, Kent	1923	423	11,280	—	Mrs G. D. duCharme (1985)
Berkhamsted School, Herts.	1888	460	8,061	4,443	Miss V. E. M. Shepherd (1980)
§Birkenhead High School	1901	718	—	3,444	Mrs K. R. Irving (1986)
§Blackheath High School, SE3	1880	322	—	4,020	Miss R. K. Musgrave (1989)
Bolton School, Lancs.	1877	945	—	3,996	Mrs M. A. Spurr (1979)
Bradford Girls' Grammar School	1875	670	—	3,600	Mrs L. J. Warrington (1987)
§Brighton and Hove High School	1876	484	—	3,444	Miss R. A. Woodbridge (1989)
Brigidine Convent, Windsor	1948	278	—	3,819	Mrs M. B. Cairns (1986)
§Bromley High School, Kent	1883	524	—	4,020	Mrs E. J. Hancock (1989)
Bruton School, Somerset	1900	500	5,967	3,231	Mrs J. M. Wade (1987)
Burgess Hill School, W. Sussex	1906	281	7,875	4,740	Mrs R. F. Lewis (1992)
Bury Grammar School, Lancs.	1884	830	—	3,300	Miss J. M. Lawley (1987)
Casterton School, Cumbria	1823	315	7,920	4,878	A. F. Thomas (1990)
§Central Newcastle High School	1895	569	—	3,444	Mrs A. M. Chapman (1985)
Channing School, N6	1885	306	—	5,010	Mrs I. R. Raphael (1984)
§Charters-Ancaster School, E. Sussex	1906	246	7,539	3,744	Mrs K. Lewis (1990)
Cheltenham Ladies' College, Glos.	1853	849	10,725	6,810	Miss E. Castle (*Principal*) (1987)
City of London School for Girls, EC2	1894	542	—	4,734	Lady France (1986)
Clifton High School, Bristol	1877	498	7,410	3,885	Mrs J. D. Walters (1985)
Cobham Hall, Kent	1962	250	10,719	7,191	Mrs R. J. McCarthy (1989)
Colston's Girls' School, Bristol	1891	580	—	3,159	Mrs J. P. Franklin (1989)
Combe Bank School, Kent	1868	240	—	4,800	Mrs A. J. K. Austin (1982)
Commonweal Lodge School, Surrey	1916	150	—	3,510	Miss J. M. Brown (1982)
Cranford House School, Oxon.	1931	260	—	4,050	Mrs A. B. Gray (1992)
Croft House School, Dorset	1941	160	8,610	6,075	Mrs S. Rawlinson (1985)
Croham Hurst School, Surrey	1899	560	—	3,780	Miss J. M. Shelmerdine (1986)
§Croydon High School, Surrey	1874	697	—	4,020	Mrs P. E. Davies (1990)
Dame Alice Harpur School, Bedford	1882	797	—	3,555	Mrs R. Randle (1990)
Dame Allan's Girls' School, Newcastle upon Tyne	1705	418†	—	3,141	T. A. Willcocks (*Principal*) (1988)
Derby High School	1892	309	—	3,810	Dr G. H. Goddard (1983)
Downe House, Berks.	1907	432	10,890	7,890	Miss S. Cameron (1989)
Dunottar School, Surrey	1926	285	—	3,675	Miss J. Burnell (1985)

Name of School	Founded	No. of pupils	Annual fees Boarding	Annual fees Day	Head (with date of appointment)
Durham High School	1884	282	—	£3,015	M. L. Walters (1992)
Edgbaston Church of England College	1886	300	—	4,149	Mrs A. Varley-Tipton (1992)
Edgbaston High School	1876	559	—	3,825	Mrs S. J. Horsman (1987)
Edgehill College, Devon	1884	370	£8,190	4,470	Mrs E. M. Burton (1987)
Elmslie Girls' School, Lancs.	1918	350	—	3,255	Miss E. M. Smithies (1978)
Eothen School, Surrey (*CSC*)	1892	180	—	4,000	Mrs A. Coutts (1992)
Farlington School, W. Sussex	1896	245	7,800	4,800	Mrs P. Mawer (1992)
Farnborough Hill, Hants.	1889	500	—	3,768	Sr E. McCormack (1988)
Farringtons, Kent	1911	350	7,980	4,368	Mrs B. J. Stock (1987)
Felixstowe College, Suffolk	1929	240	9,780	6,090	Mrs A. F. Woodings (1988)
Fernhill Manor School, Hants.	1890	170	7,275	4,635	Revd A. J. Folks (1985)
Francis Holland School, NW1	1878	360	—	4,530	Mrs P. H. Parsonson (1988)
Francis Holland School, SW1	1881	168	—	4,995	Mrs J. A. Anderson (1982)
Gateways School, Leeds	1941	200	—	3,090	Miss L. M. Brown (1984)
Godolphin School, Wilts.	1726	360	9,525	5,655	Mrs H. Fender (1990)
Godolphin and Latymer School, W6	1905	700	—	4,830	Miss M. Rudland (1986)
Greenacre School, Surrey	1933	376	—	4,272	Mrs P. M. Wood (1990)
The Grove School, Hindhead, Surrey	1877	200	7,920	5,022	C. Brooks (1984)
Guildford High School (*CSC*)	1888	450	—	4,392	Mrs S. H. Singer (1991)
Haberdashers' Aske's School for Girls, Herts.	1873	840	—	3,330	Mrs P. Penney (1991)
Haberdashers' Monmouth School, Gwent	1891	550	6,651	3,519	vacant
Harrogate Ladies' College	1893	400	8,085	5,430	Mrs J. C. Lawrance (1974)
Headington School, Oxford	1915	560	7,719	3,939	Miss E. M. Tucker (1982)
Heathfield School, Ascot, Berks.	1900	210	10,770	—	Mrs J. Ben Ammar (1992)
§Heathfield School, Pinner, Middx.	1900	348	—	4,020	Mrs J. Merritt (1988)
Hethersett Old Hall School, Norwich	1928	196	7,080	3,690	Mrs V. M. Redington (1982)
Highclare School, W. Midlands	1932	340†	—	3,255	Mrs C. A. Hanson (1973)
Hollygirt School, Nottingham	1877	316	—	3,195	Mrs M. R. Banks (1985)
Holy Child School, Birmingham	1933	215	7,530	3,870	Miss J. M. Johnson (1987)
Holy Trinity College Bromley Trust, Bromley	1886	290	—	3,771	Sr B. Wetz (1986)
Holy Trinity School, Kidderminster	1903	220	—	2,940	Mrs S. M. Bell (1990)
Howell's School, Denbigh, Clwyd	1859	250	8,970	5,805	Mrs M. Steel (1991)
§Howell's School, Llandaff, Cardiff	1860	564	7,239	3,444	Mrs C. J. Fitz (1991)
Hull High School (*CSC*)	1890	180	5,520	3,480	Miss C. M. B. Radcliffe (1976)
Hulme Grammar School, Oldham	1895	520	—	3,210	Miss M. S. Smolenski (1992)
Huyton College, Liverpool	1894	209	7,775	3,585	Mrs C. Bradley (1991)
§Ipswich High School	1878	395	—	3,444	Miss V. MacCuish (*from April* 1993)
James Allen's Girls' School, SE22	1741	750	—	5,100	Mrs B. Davies (1984)
School of Jesus and Mary, Suffolk	1860	180	—	3,510	Mrs E. A. McKay (1982)
Kent College	1885	262	9,060	5,400	Miss B. Crompton (1990)
King Edward VI High School for Girls, Birmingham	1883	545	—	3,669	Miss E. W. Evans (1977)
King's HS for Girls, Warwick	1879	550	—	3,390	Mrs J. M. Anderson (1987)
Kingsley School, Warwicks.	1884	430	—	3,675	Mrs M. A. Webster (1988)
Lady Eleanor Holles School, Middx.	1711	620	—	4,335	Miss E. M. Candy (1981)
La Retraite School, Wilts.	1953	180	—	3,840	Mrs M. Paisey (1986)
La Sagesse Convent High School, Newcastle upon Tyne	1906	350	—	3,210	Mrs D. C. Parker (1988)
La Sagesse Convent School, Hants.	1896	125	—	2,600	Sr Thomas Cox (1977)
Lavant House School, W. Sussex	1952	92	8,835	5,385	Mrs Y. Graham (1990)
Lawnside, Worcs.	1818	100	9,120	5,370	Miss J. Harvey (1991)
Leeds Girls' High School	1876	588	—	3,822	Miss P. A. Randall (1976)
Leicester High School	1906	379	—	3,510	Mrs P. A. Watson (1992)
Loughborough High School	1850	528	5,559	3,510	Miss J. E. L. Harvatt (1978)
Luckley-Oakfield School, Berks.	1895	300	7,185	4,470	R. C. Blake (1984)
Malvern Girls' College, Worcs.	1893	500	10,188	6,792	Dr V. B. Payne (1986)
Manchester High School	1874	728	—	3,480	Miss M. M. Moon (1983)
Manor House School, Little Bookham, Surrey	1927	206	8,997	4,812	Mrs L. Mendes (1989)
Maynard School, Exeter	1877	487	—	3,504	Miss F. Murdin (1980)
Merchant Taylors' School, Liverpool	1888	640	—	3,384	Miss E. J. Panton (1988)
Micklefield School, E. Sussex	1910	170	8,865	5,085	E. Reynolds (1987)

Name of School	*Founded*	*No. of pupils*	*Annual fees*		*Head (with date of appointment)*
			Boarding	Day	
Moira House School, E. Sussex	1875	300	£9,429	£6,216	A. R. Underwood (1975)
More House School, SW1	1953	230	—	4,635	Miss M. Connell (1991)
Moreton Hall, Shropshire	1913	300	9,750	6,750	J. Forster (1992)
Mount School, York	1831	280	9,060	6,030	Miss B. J. Windle (1986)
Newcastle upon Tyne Church HS	1885	387	—	3,300	Miss P. E. Davies (1974)
New Hall, Essex	1642	510	9,621	6,162	Sr. Margaret Mary (1986)
Northampton High School	1878	517	—	3,390	Mrs L. A. Mayne (1988)
North Foreland Lodge, Hants.	1909	185	9,600	—	Miss D. L. Matthews (1983)
North London Collegiate School	1850	707	—	4,251	Mrs J. L. Clanchy (1986)
Northwood College, Middx.	1878	320	—	4,257	Mrs J. A. Mayou (1991)
§Norwich High School	1875	617	—	3,444	Mrs V. C. Bidwell (1985)
§Nottingham High School	1875	798	—	3,444	Mrs C. Bowering (1984)
§Notting Hill and Ealing High School	1873	563	—	4,020	Mrs S. M. Whitfield
Ockbrook School, Derby	1799	230	5,034	3,156	Ms M. Rennie, Ph.D. (1987)
Old Palace School, Surrey	1887	600	—	3,465	Miss K. L. Hilton (1974)
§Oxford High School	1875	550	—	3,444	Mrs J. Townsend (1981)
Palmers Green High School, N21	1905	130	—	3,450	Mrs S. Grant (1989)
Park School, Somerset	1851	93	7,620	4,380	Mrs M. J. Hannon (1987)
Parsons Mead, Surrey	1897	290	8,265	4,305	Miss E. B. Plant (1990)
Penrhos College, Clwyd	1880	255	8,415	5,760	N. C. Peacock (1974)
Perse School for Girls, Cambridge	1881	540	—	3,873	Miss H. S. Smith (1989)
*Peterborough High School	1939	225	6,540	3,255	Mrs A. Storey (1977)
Pipers Corner School, Bucks.	1930	390	8,130	4,635	Dr M. M. Wilson (1986)
Polam Hall, Co. Durham	1848	350	7,830	3,831	Mrs H. C. Hamilton (1987)
§Portsmouth High School	1882	509	—	3,444	Mrs J. M. Dawtrey (1984)
Princess Helena College, Herts.	1820	150	8,970	6,270	Miss H. Davidson-Wall (1990)
Prior's Field, Surrey	1902	245	8,685	5,490	Mrs J. M. McCallum (1987)
§Putney High School, SW15	1893	591	—	4,020	Mrs E. Merchant (1991)
Queen Anne's School, Berks.	1698	388	9,870	6,174	Miss A. M. Scott (1977)
Queen Ethelburga's College, York	1912	200	7,425	4,785	Mrs J. M. Town (1988)
Queen Margaret's School, York	1901	364	8,940	5,670	C. S. McGarrigle (1983)
Queen Mary School, Lytham, Lancs.	1930	600	—	3,069	Miss M. C. Ritchie (1981)
Queen's College, W1	1848	408	8,775	5,175	Lady Goodhart (1991)
Queen's Gate School, SW7	1891	198	—	4,560	Mrs A. M. Holyoak (*Principal*) (1987)
Queen's School, Chester	1878	416	—	3,828	Miss D. M. Skilbeck (1989)
Queenswood, Herts.	1894	410	10,272	6,065	Mrs A. M. B. Butler (1981)
Redland High School, Bristol	1882	485	—	3,465	Mrs C. Lear (1989)
Red Maids' School, Bristol	1634	500	6,780	3,420	Miss S. Hampton (1987)
Rickmansworth Masonic School, Herts.	1788	530	7,029	4,029	Mrs I. M. Andrews (1992)
Roedean School, Brighton	1885	475	11,655	—	Mrs A. R. Longley (1984)
Rosemead, W. Sussex	1919	133	8,085	4,680	Mrs H. Kingham (*Principal*) (1991)
Royal Naval School, Surrey	1840	260	8,280	5,520	Dr J. L. Clough (1987)
Royal School, Bath	1864	310	9,972	6,360	Dr J. McClure (1987)
Rye St Antony School (*RC*), Oxford	1930	400	7,185	4,305	Miss A. M. Jones (1990)
Sacred Heart School (*RC*), Kent	1915	190	9,810	5,775	J. A. Fallon, Ph.D. (1979)
St Albans High School, Herts.	1889	520	—	4,098	Miss E. M. Diggory (1983)
St Andrew's School, Bedford	1897	171	—	2,880	Mrs J. E. Stephen (1991)
St Anne's School, Cumbria	1863	280	8,685	5,760	M. P. Hawkins (1986)
St Antony's-Leweston School (*RC*), Dorset	1891	380	9,090	5,925	Mrs P. Cartwright (1983)
St Catherine's School, Surrey	1885	435	7,980	4,875	J. R. Palmer (1982)
*School of St Clare, Penzance	1889	120	7,305	3,864	I. Halford (1986)
St David's School, Middx.	1716	254†	7,980	4,605	Mrs J. G. Osborne (1985)
St Dunstan's Abbey, Devon	1850	230	6,060	3,750	R. A. Bye (1991)
St Elphin's School, Derbys.	1844	228	8,847	5,151	A. P. C. Pollard (1979)
St Felix School, Suffolk	1897	265	9,168	5,895	Mrs S. R. Campion (1991)
St Francis' College (*RC*), Herts.	1933	215	8,430	4,350	Mrs J. Frith (1987)
S. Gabriel's School, Berks.	1929	162	—	4,350	D. Cobb (1990)
St George's School, Ascot, Berks.	1923	288	9,900	5,550	Mrs A. M. Griggs (1989)
School of S. Helen and S. Katharine, Oxon.	1903	501	6,900	3,600	Miss Y. Paterson (1973)
St Helen's School, Middx.	1899	560	7,908	4,194	Mrs Y.A. Burne, Ph.D. (1987)
*S. Hilary's School, Cheshire	1880	188	—	3,630	Mrs J. Tracey (1985)

Name of School	Founded	No. of pupils	Annual fees Boarding	Annual fees Day	Head (with date of appointment)
St James's and the Abbey, Worcs.	1896	210	£9,300	£6,240	Miss E. M. Mullenger (1986)
St Joseph's Convent School (*RC*), Berks.	1909	500	—	3,465	Mrs V. Brookes (1990)
St Joseph's School, Lincoln	1905	210	6,600	3,300	Mrs A. Scott (1983)
St Leonards-Mayfield School, E. Sussex	1850	525	8,860	5,905	Sr J. Sinclair (1980)
St Margaret's School, Bushey, Herts.	1749	460	7,725	4,890	Miss M. de Villiers (1992)
*St Margaret's School, Exeter	1904	380	5,490	3,348	Mrs J. M. Giddings (1984)
St Martin's School, Solihull, W. Midlands	1941	270	—	4,000	Mrs S. J. Williams (1988)
*School of St Mary and St Anne, Abbots Bromley, Staffs.	1874	250	9,519	6,342	A. Grigg (1989)
St Mary's Convent School, Worcester	1934	280	—	2,925	Mrs M. Kilbride (1986)
St Mary's Hall, Brighton	1836	219	8,199	5,430	Mrs M. T. Broadbent (1988)
St Mary's School (*RC*), Ascot, Berks.	1885	330	10,818	5,901	Sr M. M. Orchard (1982)
St Mary's School, Calne, Wilts.	1872	315	10,050	5,970	Miss D. H. Burns (1985)
St Mary's School, Cambridge	1898	600	5,910	3,300	Miss M. Conway (1989)
St Mary's School, Colchester	1908	300	—	3,225	Mrs G. M. G. Mouser (1981)
St Mary's School, Gerrards Cross	1872	200	—	4,390	Mrs J. P. G. Smith (1984)
St Mary's School (*RC*), Shaftesbury	1945	310	8,355	5,250	Sr M. Campion Livesey (1985)
St Mary's School, Wantage, Oxon.	1873	292	9,600	—	Revd Mrs P. H. Johns (1980)
St Maur's Convent School, Weybridge	1898	450	—	3,690	Mrs M. E. Dodds (1991)
*S. Michaels Burton Park, W. Sussex	1844	140	8,850	5,940	Mrs L. J. Griffin (1991)
St Michael's, Limpsfield, Surrey	1850	122	8,655	5,025	Ms M. J. Hustler, PH.D. (1989)
St Paul's Girls' School, W6	1904	618	—	5,652	Miss J. Gough (*High Mistress*) (*acting*)
St Swithun's School, Winchester	1884	454	9,930	6,000	Miss J. E. Jefferson (1986)
St Teresa's School, Dorking	1928	370	9,030	4,440	L. Allan (1987)
Selwyn School, Glos.	—	200	5,385	4,050	A. Beatson (1990)
§Sheffield High School	1878	524	—	3,444	Mrs M. A. Houston (1989)
Sherborne School for Girls, Dorset	1899	458	9,960	6,630	Miss J. M. Taylor (1985)
§Shrewsbury High School	1885	391	—	3,444	Miss S. Gardner (1990)
Sir William Perkins's School, Surrey	1725	516	—	3,315	Mrs A. F. Darlow (1982)
§South Hampstead High School, NW3	1876	573	—	4,020	Mrs D. A. Burgess (1975)
Stamford High School, Lincs.	1876	736	7,164	3,582	Miss G. K. Bland (1978)
Stonar School, Wilts.	1921	450	8,610	4,770	Mrs S. Hopkinson (1986)
Stover School, Devon	1932	265	7,290	3,825	Mrs W. E. Lunel (1984)
Stratford House School, Kent	1912	250	—	4,260	Mrs A. A. Williamson (1974)
§Streatham Hill and Clapham High School, SW2	1887	392	—	4,020	Miss G. M. Ellis (1979)
Sunderland Church High School (*CSC*)	1884	529‡	—	3,549	Mrs M. Thrush (1980)
Surbiton High School (*CSC*), Surrey	1884	473	—	4,218	Mrs R. A. Thynne (1979)
§Sutton High School, Surrey	1884	547	—	4,020	Miss A. E. Cavendish (1980)
§Sydenham High School, SE26	1887	478	—	4,020	Mrs G. Baker (1988)
Talbot Heath, Dorset	1886	466	7,425	4,215	Mrs C. Dipple (1991)
Teesside High School, Cleveland	1970	385	—	3,270	Mrs H. Coles (1982)
Tormead School, Surrey	1905	400	—	4,800	Mrs H. E. M. Alleyne (1992)
Truro High School	1880	330	7,023	3,849	J. Graham-Brown (1992)
Tudor Hall School, Oxon.	1850	248	9,150	5,700	Miss N. Godfrey (1984)
Upper Chine, Isle of Wight	1799	150	8,085	4,305	Dr H. Harvey (1990)
Ursuline Convent School, Kent	1904	300	8,724	4,419	Sr M. Murphy (1977)
Ursuline High School, Ilford	1903	400	—	3,879	Miss J. Reddington (1990)
Wadhurst College, E. Sussex	1930	180	9,210	5,865	Miss A. M. Phillips (1991)
Wakefield Girls' High School	1878	950	—	3,663	Mrs P. A. Langham (1987)
Walthamstow Hall, Kent	1838	415	9,360	5,040	Mrs J. S. Lang (1984)
Wentworth Milton Mount, Dorset	1962	310	7,755	4,845	Miss S. Coe (1991)
Westfield School, Newcastle upon Tyne	1962	220	—	£3,591	Mrs M. Farndale (1990)
West Heath, Kent	1867	170	10,026	7,032	Mrs L. Cohn-Sherbok (*Principal*) (1988)
Westholme School, Lancs.	1923	650	—	3,126	Mrs L. Croston (*Principal*) (1988)
Westonbirt, Glos.	1928	280	9,546	6,144	Mrs G. Hylson-Smith (1986)
§Wimbledon High School, SW19	1880	503	—	4,020	Mrs E. M. Baker (1992)
Wispers School, Surrey	1946	180	8,040	5,181	L. H. Beltran (1978)
Withington Girls' School, Manchester	1890	475	—	3,360	Mrs M. Kenyon (1986)
Woldingham School, Surrey	1842	450	9,723	5,883	Ms P. Dineen, PH.D. (1985)
Wroxall Abbey School, Warwick	1872	100	9,000	5,250	Mrs I. D. M. Iles (1980)

Name of School	*Foun-ded*	*No. of pupils*	*Annual fees*		*Head (with date of appointment)*
			Boarding	Day	
Wychwood School, Oxford	1897	160	£6,270	£3,840	Mrs M. L. Duffill (1981)
Wycombe Abbey School, Bucks.	1896	500	11,088	—	Mrs J. M. Goodland (1989)
Wykeham House School, Fareham, Hants.	1913	233	—	3,393	Mrs E. M. Moore (1983)
York College for Girls (*CSC*)	1908	210	—	4,600	Mrs J. L. Clare (1982)
SCOTLAND					
Kilgraston School, Perthshire	1930	245	8,160	4,305	Sr B. Farquharson (1987)
Laurel Bank School, Glasgow	1903	410	—	3,726	Miss L. G. Egginton (1984)
Mary Erskine School, Edinburgh	1694	560	7,116	3,936	P. F. J. Tobin (*Principal*) (1989)
Oxenfoord Castle School, Midlothian	1931	72	10,170	5,295	Miss M. Carmichael (1979)
Park School, Glasgow	1880	300	—	3,483	Mrs M. E. Myatt (1986)
St Denis and Cranley School, Edinburgh	1858	140	7,995	3,975	Mrs J. M. Munro (1984)
St George's School, Edinburgh	1888	563	7,530	3,840	Mrs J. G. Scott (1986)
St Leonards School, St Andrews	1877	360	10,650	5,625	Mrs L. E. James (1988)
St Margaret's School, Aberdeen	1846	423	—	3,201	Miss L. M. Ogilvie (1989)
St Margaret's School, Edinburgh	1890	350	7,550	3,680	Mrs M. J. Cameron (1984)
Wellington School for Girls, Ayr	1849	300	8,160	4,095	Mrs D. A. Gardner (1988)
CHANNEL ISLANDS					
The Ladies' College, Guernsey	1872	345	—	1,890	Miss M. Macdonald (1992)

Social Welfare

National Health Service

and Local Authority Personal Social Services

The National Health Service came into being on 5 July 1948, as a result of the National Health Service Act 1946. The Act placed a duty on the Secretary of State for Social Services to promote the establishment in England and Wales of a comprehensive health service designed to secure improvement in the mental and physical health of the people and the prevention, diagnosis and treatment of illness. The Secretary of State for Wales administers the National Health Service in Wales. There are separate Acts for Scotland and Northern Ireland, where the health services are run on very similar lines and the respective Secretaries of State are responsible to Parliament.

The National Health Service covers a comprehensive range of hospital, specialist, family practitioner (medical, dental, ophthalmic and pharmaceutical), artificial limb and appliance, ambulance, and community health services. Everyone normally resident in this country is entitled to use any of these services, there are no contribution conditions and the charges made (except those for amenity beds) are reduced or waived in cases of hardship. In addition, the Secretary of State for Social Services is responsible under the Local Authority Social Services Act 1970 for the provision by local authorities of social services for the elderly, the disabled, those with mental disorders and for families and children.

Structure

The 1980 Health Services Act led to major changes in the structure of the Health Service. Since April 1982, District Health Authorities (DHAs) have been responsible for the operational management of health services and for planning within regional and national strategic guidelines. There are 179 DHAs in England and nine in Wales. Each DHA is required to arrange its services into units of management at hospital and community services level, and as many decisions as possible are delegated to unit level. Four of the London postgraduate teaching hospitals are now managed by DHAs (and eight are managed by special health authorities). Arrangements for the Family Doctor Service are administered by Family Health Services Authorities, 90 in England and eight in Wales. FHSAs also contribute to the planning of health services.

The 14 Regional Health Authorities (RHAs) in England are responsible for regional planning, the allocation of resources to District Authorities, FHSAs and GP fundholders, and the promotion of national policies and priorities. They also monitor the performance of DHAs and FHSAs, and assess manpower needs. Each DHA and FHSA is accountable to an RHA. The RHA is the link between them and the NHS Management Executive at the Department of Health. Professional advisory machinery incorporated within the structure ensures that health authorities and their staffs make decisions in the full knowledge of expert opinion.

The NHS is financed mainly from taxation and the cost met from moneys voted by Parliament. In the United Kingdom this will amount to £35.8 billion in 1992–3. The Department of Health makes capital and revenue allocations to the RHAs and from these the RHAs meet the cost of their own services and make allocations to DHAs as well as funding Community Health Councils.

Recent Changes

The National Health Service and Community Care Act 1990 provides for wide-ranging reforms in management and patient care. The reforms are intended to offer better health care and a greater choice of services to patients, and to encourage those working in the NHS to respond to local needs in a more specific and cost-conscious way. Reforms in the NHS have been implemented between April 1990 and April 1991, and those in community care are being implemented between April 1991 and April 1993.

THE HEALTH SERVICES

Family Doctor Service

In England and Wales the Family Doctor Service (or General Medical Services) is managed by 98 Family Health Services Authorities (FHSAs) which also organize the general dental, pharmaceutical and ophthalmic services for their areas. There is a Family Health Services Authority for one or more District Health Authorities. In Wales the chairman and non-executive members are appointed by the Secretary of State. In England the chairman is appointed by the Secretary of State and the non-executive members by the Regional Health Authority. There are nine non-executive members: a general medical practitioner, a general dental practitioner, a community pharmacist, a nurse, and five lay members.

Any doctor may take part in the Family Doctor Service (provided the area in which he/she wishes to practise has not already an adequate number of doctors) and about 28,000 general practitioners in England and Wales do so. They may at the same time have private fee-paying patients. Family doctors are paid for their Health Service work in accordance with a scheme of remuneration which includes *inter alia* a basic practice allowance, capitation fees, reimbursement of certain practice expenses and payments for out of hours work.

The National Health Service and Community Care Act 1990 enables general practitioner practices with at least 9,000 patients (7,000 from 1993) to apply for fund-holding status. This makes the practice responsible for its own NHS budget for a specified range of goods and services. There are currently 586 fund-holding practices, with as many more preparing to become fundholders from April 1993.

Everyone aged 16 or over can choose their doctor (parents or guardians choose for children under 16) and the doctor is also free to accept a person or not as he or she chooses. A person may change their doctor if they wish, by going to the surgery of a general practioner of their choice who is willing to accept them, and either handing in their medical card to register or filling in a form. When people are away from home they can still use the Family Doctor Service if they ask to be treated as temporary residents, and in an emergency, if a person's own doctor is not available, any doctor in the service will give treatment and advice.

Patients are treated either in the doctor's surgery or, when necessary, at home. Doctors may prescribe for their patients all drugs and medicines which are medically necessary for their treatment and also a certain number of surgical appliances (the more elaborate being provided through hospitals).

Dental Service

Dentists, like doctors, may take part in the National Health Service and may also have private patients. About 16,000 of the dentists available for general practice in England provide NHS general dental services. They are responsible to the Family Health Services Authorities in whose areas they provide services.

Patients are free to go to any dentist taking part in the Service and willing to accept them. Dentists are paid a capitation fee for patients registered with them who are under 18 years of age. They receive payment for items of treatment for individual adult patients and, in addition, a continuing care payment for those registered with them.

Patients are asked to pay three-quarters of the cost of NHS dental treatment. The maximum charge for a course of treatment is £200. There is no charge for arrest of bleeding, repairs to dentures, home visits by the dentist or re-opening a surgery in an emergency (in these two cases, payment will be for treatment given in the normal way). The following are exempt from dental charges:

(i) young people under 18
(ii) full time students under 19
(iii) expectant mothers who were pregnant when accepted for treatment
(iv) women who have had a child in the previous 12 months

People receiving Income Support or Family Credit, and members of the same family as someone receiving Income Support or Family Credit, are automatically entitled to full remission of charges.

Leaflet AB11 available from post offices and leaflet D11 available from local social security offices explain how other people on a low income can, depending on their financial circumstances, get free treatment or help with charges.

Pharmaceutical Service

Patients may obtain medicines, appliances and oral contraceptives prescribed under the NHS from any pharmacy whose owner has entered into arrangements with the Family Health Services Authority to provide this service. Almost all pharmacy owners have done so and display notices that they dispense under the NHS; the number of these pharmacies in England and Wales at the end of 1990 was about 10,400. There are also some appliance suppliers who only provide special appliances. In country areas where access to a pharmacy may be difficult, patients may be able to obtain medicines, etc., from their doctor.

Except for contraceptives (for which there is no charge), a charge of £3.75 is payable for each item supplied unless the patient is exempt and the declaration on the back of the prescription form is completed. Exemptions cover:

(i) children under 16
(ii) young people under 19 and still in full-time education
(iii) men aged 65 and over
(iv) women aged 60 and over
(v) pregnant women
(vi) mothers who have had a baby within the last 12 months
(vii) people suffering from certain medical conditions
(viii) people who receive Income Support or Family Credit and their dependants
(ix) people who hold an AG2 certificate issued by the Health Benefits Unit, and their dependants
(x) war pensioners (for their accepted disablements)

Prepayment certificates (£19.40 valid for four months, £53.50 valid for a year) may be purchased by those patients not entitled to exemption who require frequent prescriptions. Further information about the exemption and prepayment arrangements is given in leaflet P11.

General Ophthalmic Services

General Ophthalmic Services, which are administered by Family Practitioner Committees, form part of the ophthalmic services available under the National Health Service. The NHS sight test is available free to:

(i) children under 16
(ii) full-time students under the age of 19
(iii) those people and their partners in receipt of Income Support and Family Credit
(iv) people prescribed complex lenses
(v) the registered blind and partially sighted
(vi) diagnosed diabetic and glaucoma patients
(vii) close relatives aged 40 or over of diagnosed glaucoma patients

Those on a low income may qualify for help with the cost.

Certain groups are automatically entitled to help with the purchase of glasses under an NHS voucher scheme:

(i) children under 16
(ii) full-time students under 19
(iii) people who are themselves or whose partners are in receipt of Income Support or Family Credit
(iv) people wearing certain complex lenses
(v) people whose spectacles are lost or damaged as a result of their disability, injury or illness

The value of the voucher depends on the lenses required. Vouchers may be used to help pay for the glasses or contact lenses of the patient's choice. People with a low income may claim help on form AG1. Glasses or contact lenses should not be purchased until the result of a claim is known as no refunds can be given. Booklet G11 gives further details.

Diagnosis and specialist treatment of eye conditions is available through the Hospital Eye Service as well as the provision of glasses of a special type. Testing of sight may be carried out by any ophthalmic medical practitioner or ophthalmic optician and can cost between £10 and £15. The optician must hand the prescription, and a voucher if eligible, to the patient who can take this to any supplier of glasses of his/her choice to have dispensed. However, only registered opticians can supply glasses to children and to people registered as blind or partially sighted.

Primary Health Care Services

Primary health care services include the general medical, dental, ophthalmic and pharmaceutical services and the family doctor service. They also include community services run by district health authorities, health centres and clinics, family planning outside the hospital service, and preventive activities in the community including vaccination, immunization and fluoridation.

The district nursing and health visiting services include community psychiatric nursing for mentally ill people living outside hospital, and school nursing for the health surveillance of schoolchildren of all ages. Ante- and post-natal care and chiropody are also an integral part of the primary health care service.

Community Child Health Services

Pre-school services, usually at child health clinics, provide regular surveillance of children's physical, mental and emotional health and development, and advice to parents on their children's health and welfare.

The School Health Service provides for the medical and dental examination of schoolchildren, and advises the local education authority, the school, the parents and the pupil of any health factors which may require special consideration during the pupil's school life. GPs are increasingly undertaking child health surveillance to aid identification of curable disorders.

Hospitals and Other Services

The Secretary of State for Health has a duty to provide, to such extent as he/she considers necessary to meet all reasonable requirements, hospital and other accommodation; medical, dental, nursing and ambulance services; other facilities for the care of expectant and nursing mothers and young children; facilities for the prevention of illness and the care and after-care of persons suffering from illness; and such other services as are required for the diagnosis and treatment of illness. Rehabilitation services (occupational therapy, physiotherapy and speech therapy) may also be provided for those who need it and surgical and medical appliances are supplied in appropriate cases.

Specialists and consultants who take part in the Health Service can engage in private practice, including the treatment of their private patients in NHS hospitals.

Charges

In a number of hospitals, accommodation is available for the treatment of private in-patients who undertake to pay the full costs of hospital accommodation and services and (usually) separate medical fees to a specialist as well. The amount of the medical fees is a matter for agreement between doctor and patient. Hospital charges for private resident patients are determined by District Health Authorities either on a local basis or in line with a central 'model' list.

Certain hospitals have accommodation in single rooms or small wards which, if not required for patients who need privacy for medical reasons, may be made available to patients who desire it as an amenity. In such cases the patients are treated in every other respect as National Health patients.

There is no charge for drugs supplied to National Health hospital in-patients but out-patients pay £3.75 per item unless they are exempt.

With certain exceptions, hospital out-patients have to pay fixed charges for dentures, contact lenses and certain appliances. Glasses may be obtained either from the hospital or an optician and the charge will be related to the type of lens prescribed and the choice of frame.

Trusts

The National Health Service and Community Care Act 1990 enables hospitals and other providers of health care, to become independent of health authority control as self-governing NHS Trusts run by boards of directors. The Trusts derive their income principally from contracts to provide health services to health authorities and fund-holding general practitioners. In April 1992 there were 99 NHS Trusts, and applications from hospitals wishing to become Trusts in April 1993 are currently under consideration.

LOCAL AUTHORITY PERSONAL SOCIAL SERVICES

Local authorities are responsible for the organization, management and administration of the personal social services and each authority has a Director of Social Services and a Social Services Committee responsible for the social services functions placed upon them by the Local Authority Social Services Act 1970.

National Insurance and Related Cash Benefits

The State insurance and assistance schemes, comprising schemes of national insurance and industrial injuries insurance, national assistance, and non-contributory old age pensions came into force from 5 July 1948. The Ministry of Social Security Act 1966 replaced national assistance and non-contributory old age pensions with a scheme of non-contributory benefits, termed supplementary allowances and pensions. These, and subsequent measures relating to social security provision in Great Britain, were consolidated by the Social Security Act 1975; the Social Security (Consequential Provisions) Act 1975; and the Industrial Injuries and Diseases (Old Cases) Act 1975. Corresponding measures were passed for Northern Ireland. The Social Security Pensions Act 1975 introduced a new State pensions scheme, which came into force on 6 April 1978, and the graduated pension scheme 1961 to 1975 has been wound up, existing rights being preserved. The Pensioners' Payments and Social Security Act 1979 provided for a £10 bonus for pensioners in 1979 and for the payment of a bonus in succeeding years at levels then to be determined. The Child Benefit Act 1975 replaced family allowances (introduced 1946) with child benefit and one parent benefit.

Some of the above legislation has been superseded by the provisions of the Social Security Acts 1968 to 1991.

NATIONAL INSURANCE SCHEME

The National Insurance scheme operates under the Social Security Contributions and Benefits Act 1992 and the Social Security Administration Act 1992, and orders and regulations made thereunder. The scheme is financed by contributions payable by earners, employers and others (such as non-employed persons, paying voluntary contributions). It provides the funds required for paying benefits payable under the Social Security Acts out of the National Insurance Fund and not out of other public money and for the making of payments towards the cost of the National Health Service. In 1991 the Redundancy Fund was absorbed into the National Insurance Fund. The yearly Treasury supplement to the National Insurance Fund was abolished in April 1989.

CONTRIBUTIONS

Contributions are of four classes:

Class 1 contributions

These are earnings-related, based on a percentage of the employee's earnings.

(a) primary Class 1 contributions are payable by employed earners and office-holders over age 16 with gross earnings at or above the lower earnings limit of £54.00 per week. For those with gross earnings at or above this level, contributions are payable on all earnings up to an upper limit of £405.00 per week. 'Gross earnings' include overtime pay, commission, bonus, etc., without deduction of any superannuation contributions.

(b) secondary Class 1 contributions are payable by employers of employed earners, and by the appropriate authorities in the case of office-holders. On 6 October 1985 the upper earnings limit for employers' contributions was abolished and secondary contributions are payable on all the employee's earnings if they reach or exceed £54.00 per week.

Women who marry for the first time no longer have a right to elect not to pay the full contribution rate. Married women and widows who before 12 May 1977 elected not to pay contributions at the full rate retain the right to pay a reduced rate over the same earnings range, which includes a contribution to the National Health Service. They lose this right if, after 5 April 1978, there are two consecutive tax years in which they receive no earnings on which primary Class 1 contributions are payable and in which they have not been at any time self-employed earners. No primary contributions are due on earnings paid for a period on or after the employee's pension age, even when retirement is deferred.

Primary contributions are deducted from earnings by the employer and are paid, together with the employer's contributions, to the Inland Revenue along with income tax collected under the PAYE system. On 6 October 1985 several lower percentage rates of contribution for lower paid employees and their employers were introduced.

Class 2 contributions

These are flat-rate, paid weekly by self-employed earners over age 16. Those with earnings below £3,030 a year for the tax year 1992–3 can apply for exemption from liability to pay Class 2 contributions. People who while self-employed are exempted from liability to pay contributions on the grounds of small earnings may pay either Class 2 or Class 3 contributions voluntarily. Self-employed earners (whether or not they pay Class 2 contributions) may also be liable to pay Class 4 contributions based on profits or gains within certain limits. There are special rules for those who are concurrently employed and self-employed.

Married women and widows can no longer choose not to pay Class 2 contributions. Those who elected not to pay Class 2 contributions before 12 May 1977 retain the right until there is a period of two consecutive tax years after 5 April 1978 in which they were not at any time either self-employed earners or had earnings on which primary Class 1 contributions were payable.

Class 2 contributions may be paid by direct debit through a bank or National Giro account or by stamping a contribution card.

Class 3 contributions

These are voluntary flat-rate contributions payable by persons over school-leaving age who would otherwise be unable to qualify for retirement pension and certain other benefits because they have an insufficient record of Class 1 or Class 2 contributions. Married women and widows who on or before 11 May 1977 elected not to pay Class 1 (full rate) or Class 2 contributions cannot pay Class 3 contributions while they retain this right.

Payment may be made by stamping a contribution card or by direct debit through a bank or National Giro account.

Class 4 contributions

These are payable by self-employed earners, whether or not they pay Class 2 contributions, on annual profits or gains from a trade, profession or vocation chargeable to income tax under Schedule D, where these fall between £6,120 and £21,060 a year. The maximum Class 4 contribution, payable on profits or gains of £21,060 or more, is £941.22.

Class 4 contributions are generally assessed and collected by the Inland Revenue along with Schedule D income tax. Self-employed persons under 16, or who at the beginning of a tax year are over pension age even where retirement is deferred, are not liable to pay Class 4 contributions. There are special rules for people who have more than one job, or who pay Class I contributions on earnings which are chargeable to income tax under Schedule D.

Regulations state the cases in which earners may be exempted from liability to pay contributions, and the conditions upon which contributions are credited to persons who are exempted. Leaflet NI 208 is obtainable from local social security offices.

The Secretary of State for Social Services is empowered by the Social Security Acts to alter certain rates of contributions by order approved by both Houses of Parliament, and is required by the same enactments to make annual reviews of the general level of earnings in order to determine whether such an order should be made.

For the period 6 April 1992 to 4 April 1993 the earnings brackets determining Class I contributions are:

	Weekly earnings
1	£54.00– 89.99
2	90.00–134.99
3	135.00–189.99
4	190.00–405.00
5	over 405.00

Contribution rates for the period 6 April 1992 to 5 April 1992 are:

CLASS I CONTRIBUTIONS – NOT CONTRACTED OUT

Employee's rates

Earnings bracket	Percentage of reckonable income On first £54.00		On earnings from £54.00–£405.00	
	standard	reduced	standard	reduced
1	2	3.85	9	3.85
2	2	3.85	9	3.85
3	2	3.85	9	3.85
4	2	3.85	9	3.85
5	*2	*3.85	*9	*3.85

*to a maximum of £405.00 per week.

CLASS I CONTRIBUTIONS – CONTRACTED OUT

(*see also* page 503)

Employee's rates

Earnings bracket	On first £54.00		On earnings from £54.00–£405.00	
	standard	reduced	standard	reduced
1	2	3.85	7	3.85
2	2	3.85	7	3.85
3, 4, 5	2	3.85	7	3.85

Employer's rates

Earnings bracket	On first £54.00	On earnings from £54.00–£405.00	On any earnings over £405.00
1	4.6	0.8	0
2	6.6	2.8	0
3	8.6	4.8	0
4	10.4	6.6	0
5	10.4	6.6	10.4

	Weekly flat rate
CLASS 2 CONTRIBUTIONS	£5.35
CLASS 3 CONTRIBUTIONS	£5.25
CLASS 4 CONTRIBUTIONS	6.3% of profits or gains

From 5 October 1989 there was a change in the assessment of National Insurance contributions for employees. Where earnings were paid or were due to be paid on or after 5 October 1989, employees' contributions were paid at 2 per cent of earnings at the lower earnings limit (£54.00 a week or equivalent) plus 9 per cent (not contracted out) or 7 per cent (contracted out) of earnings between the lower earnings limit up to and including the employees' upper earnings limit (£405.00 a week or equivalent). Employees contributing at the reduced rate continue to pay contributions at 3.85 per cent on all earnings up to and including the employees' upper earnings limit.

The Social Security (Contributions) Act 1991 added a new class of contributions: IA, payable in respect of car fuel by persons liable to pay secondary Class I contributions. It has effect with regard to the 1991–2 tax year and thereafter.

Employees earning less than the lower earnings limit continue not to pay any contributions.

There was no change in the assessment of employers' contributions.

THE STATE EARNINGS RELATED PENSION SCHEME (SERPS)

The Social Security Pensions Act 1975, which came into force in April 1978, aims to reduce reliance upon means-tested benefit in old age, in widowhood and in chronic ill-health by providing better pensions; to ensure that occupational pension schemes which are contracted out of part of the State scheme fulfil the conditions of a good scheme; that pensions are adequately protected against inflation; and that in both the State and occupational schemes men and women are treated equally. Retirement, widow's and invalidity pensions under the new scheme started to be paid in April 1979. Since 6 April 1979 flat-rate retirement and other State pensions have been augmented for employed earners by additional pensions related to earnings, but it will be twenty years before these additional pensions become payable at the full rate.

Under the scheme, retirement, invalidity and widow's pensions for employees are related to the earnings on which national insurance contributions have been paid. For employees of either sex with a complete insurance record, the scheme provides a category A retirement pension in two parts, a basic and an additional pension. The basic pension corresponds to the old personal flat-rate national insurance pension. The additional pension is 1.25 per cent of average earnings between the lower weekly earnings limit for Class I contribution liability and the upper earnings limit for each year of such earnings under the scheme, and will thus build up to 25 per cent in twenty years.

The additional pension will be calculated in a different way for individuals who reach pension age after 6 April 1999. The changes are to be phased in over ten years. From 2010 a lifetime's earnings will be included in the calculation and for years from 1988–9 onwards the accrual rate on these surplus earnings will be 20 per cent. The accrual rate on surplus earnings for the years from 1978–9 to 1987–8 will remain at 25 per cent.

Actual earnings are to be revalued in terms of the earnings level current in the last complete tax year before pension age (or death or incapacity). Both components of pensions in payment will be uprated annually in line with the movement of prices. Graduated retirement pensions in payment, and rights to such pensions earned by people who are still working, will be brought into the annual review of benefits.

Self-employed persons pay contributions towards the basic pension. The non-employed and employees with earnings below the lower limit may contribute voluntarily for basic pension. Although no primary Class 1 contributions or Class 2 or Class 4 contributions are payable by persons who work beyond pension age (65 for men, 60 for women), the employer's liability for secondary Class 1 contributions continues if earnings are at or above the lower earnings limit. Class 4 contributions are still payable up to the end of the tax year during which pension age is reached.

Widows will get the whole of any additional pensions earned by their husbands with their widowed mother's allowances or widow's pensions; and can add to the retirement pensions earned by their own contributions any additional pensions earned by their husbands up to the maximum payable on one person's contributions. Men whose wives die when they are both over pension age can add together their own and their wives' pension rights in the same way as widows.

Among the steps taken to give women equal treatment in benefit provision, the State scheme permits years of home responsibilities to reduce the number of qualifying years (since 1978) needed for retirement pension, widowed mother's allowance and widow's pension; and the 'half-test', by which a married woman who married before age 55 could not qualify for a Category A retirement pension unless she had contributed on earnings at the basic level in at least half the years between marriage and pension age, has been abolished with effect from 22 December 1984. The range of short-term social security benefits and industrial injury benefits under the Social Security Act 1975 continues with only minor changes.

Contracted-Out and Personal Pension Schemes

Members of occupational pension schemes which meet the standards laid down in the Social Security Pensions Act 1975 can be contracted-out of the earnings related part of the state scheme relating to retirement and widows' benefits. Regulations made under the Act require employers to consult employees and their organizations and inform them of their intention to contract out. (Leaflets relating to pensions and guidance for employers about contracting-out are available from local social security offices.) The Act also contains provisions ensuring equal access to membership of schemes for men and women.

Until 6 April 1988 occupational pension schemes could only contract out if they promised a pension that was related to earnings. These are known as contracted-out salary related schemes. They must provide a pension that is not less than the guaranteed minimum pension (GMP), which is broadly equivalent to the state earnings related pension. However, new options have been introduced by the Social Security Act 1986. Since 6 April 1988 occupational pension schemes which promise a minimum level of contributions have also been able to contract out. These are known as contracted-out money purchase schemes. They provide a pension based on the fund built up in the scheme over the years plus the results of the way they have been invested.

In addition, since July 1988 employees whose employers do not provide a pension scheme have been able to start their own personal pension instead of staying in the state earnings related pension scheme. Since 6 April 1988, this choice has been open to all employees even if their employer does have a pension scheme. A personal pension, like a contracted-out money purchase scheme, provides a pension based on the fund built up in the scheme over the years plus the results of the way they have been invested.

The decision on whether or not an occupational pension scheme may become contracted-out lies with the Occupational Pension Board, an independent statutory body who have a general responsibility for supervising contracting-out. They also consider and approve personal pension schemes which can be used instead of state additional pension.

The State earnings related pension payable to a member of a contracted-out salary related scheme, or his widow, will be reduced by the amount of GMP payable (which in the case of a widow must be at least half of the late husband's GMP entitlement). Members of contracted-out money purchase schemes and personal pension schemes, or their widows, have no GMP entitlement as such. But the state earnings related pension payable will be reduced by an amount equivalent to a GMP (or widow's GMP).

Since 6 April 1988 contracted-out salary related schemes must also provide a widower's GMP which must be at least half of the late wife's GMP entitlement built up from 6 April 1988. (A scheme need not provide entitlement to a GMP for widowers of earners dying before April 1989.) Contracted-out money purchase schemes and personal pension schemes must provide half-rate widower's benefit.

In contracted-out schemes, both the employee and the employer pay the full ordinary rate of contribution on the first £54.00 (1992–3 figure) of earnings but earnings above that amount attract a lower rate of contribution from the employee, and from the employer where the employee's earnings are under £405.00; where the employee's earnings exceed this amount, the full ordinary rate of contribution is payable only by the employer and the employee has no liability for contributions on these earnings (*see also* page 502).

An employee who chooses a personal pension in place of SERPS or their employer's pension scheme must pay National Insurance contributions at the full ordinary rate (the employer's share must also be paid at the same rate). The DSS pays the difference between the lower contracted-out rate and the full ordinary rate directly into the personal pension scheme.

NATIONAL INSURANCE FUND

The National Insurance Fund receives all social security contributions (less only the National Health Service and Redundancy Fund and Maternity Pay Fund allocations and the National Insurance surcharge for taxation purposes) and it bears the cost of all contributory benefits provided by the Social Security Acts and the cost of administration.

Approximate receipts and payments of the National Insurance Fund for the year ended 31 March, 1990, were as follows:

Receipts		£'000
Balance, 1 April 1989		10,368,808
Contributions under the Social Security Acts (net of SSP)		29,405,362
Consolidated Fund Supplement		—
Income from investments		1,040,377
Other receipts		1,018
		40,815,565
Payments	£'000	£'000
Unemployment benefit	733,411	
Sickness benefit	203,692	
Invalidity benefit	3,836,636	
Maternity allowance	30,309	
Widow's benefit	852,303	
Guardian's allowance and child's special allowance	1,355	
Retirement pension	20,697,363	

Payments	£'000	£'000
Disablement benefits	469,261	
Death benefit	59,339	
Other industrial injury benefits	4,278	
Pensioners' lump sum payments	112,000	27,000,207
Personal pensions		2,434,461
Transfers to Northern Ireland		210,000
Administration		856,536
Other payments		7,222
Write offs		—
Balance, 31 March 1990		10,307,139
		40,815,565

NB: There have been changes to the National Insurance Fund. Payments will no longer be paid into surcharges or the Maternity Pay Fund. However, residual payments are still being paid in respect of late paid contributions for premium years.

BENEFITS

The benefits payable under the Social Security Acts are as follows:

Contributory Benefits

Unemployment benefit
Sickness benefit
Invalidity pension and allowance
Maternity allowance
Widow's benefit, comprising widow's payment, widowed mother's allowance and widow's pension
Retirement pensions, categories A and B

Non-contributory Benefits

Child benefit
One parent benefit
Guardian's allowance
Invalid care allowance
Mobility allowance
Severe disablement allowance
Attendance allowance
Disability Living Allowance
Disability Working Allowance
Retirement pensions, categories C and D
Income Support
Family Credit
Social Fund

Benefits for Industrial Injuries, Disablement and Death

Other

Statutory sick pay
Statutory maternity pay

Leaflets relating to the various benefits and payments are obtainable from local social security offices.

The Social Security Acts empower the Secretary of State to increase certain rates of benefit by order approved by both Houses of Parliament, and require him to increase certain rates by such an order if an annual review shows that they have not retained their value in relation to the general level of prices obtaining in Great Britain as measured by the Retail Price Index.

The latest order providing for increases in benefit rates took effect from the week commencing 6 April 1992. It did not apply to all benefits.

CONTRIBUTORY BENEFITS

Entitlement to contributory benefits depends on contribution conditions being satisfied either by the client or by some other person (depending on the kind of benefit). The class or classes of contribution which for this purpose are relevant to each benefit are as follows:

Short-term benefits	
Unemployment benefit	Class 1
Sickness benefit	Class 1 or 2
Maternity allowance	Class 1 or 2
Widow's payment	Class 1, 2 or 3
Other benefits	
Widowed mother's allowance	Class 1, 2 or 3
Widow's pension	Class 1, 2 or 3
Category A retirement pension	Class 1, 2 or 3
Category B retirement pension	Class 1, 2 or 3
Invalidity benefit	Class 1 or 2

The system of contribution conditions relates to yearly levels of earnings on which contributions have been paid. The contribution conditions for different benefits are set out in summary form in leaflets available at local social security offices.

Unemployment Benefit

Benefit is payable in a period of interruption of employment for up to 312 days (a year, excluding Sundays). Spells of unemployment and sickness not separated by more than eight weeks count as one period of interruption of employment. A person who has exhausted benefit requalifies when he has again worked as an employed earner for at least 16 hours a week for 13 weeks. These weeks need not be consecutive but must generally fall within 26 weeks prior to the date of the claim.

There are disqualifications from receiving benefit, e.g. for a period not exceeding 26 weeks if a person has lost his employment through his misconduct, or has voluntarily left his employment without just cause, or has, without good cause, refused an offer of employment or training.

Sickness Benefit

Sickness benefit is payable for up to 28 weeks of sickness in a period of interruption of employment and is then replaced by invalidity benefit (*see* below).

There are disqualifications from receiving sickness or invalidity benefit for a period not exceeding six weeks if a person has become incapable of work through his own misconduct or if he fails without good cause to attend for or submit himself to prescribed medical or other examination or treatment, or observe prescribed rules of behaviour.

Statutory sick pay (SSP) was introduced from 6 April 1983 and was payable for up to eight weeks. Since 6 April 1986 employers are responsible for paying SSP to their employees for up to 28 weeks of sickness in any period of incapacity for work. SSP replaces the employee's entitlement to State Sickness Benefit, which is not payable as long as any SSP liability remains. SSP is subject to PAYE and to NI deductions. From 6 April 1991 employers can recover 80 per cent (previously 100 per cent) of the SSP they have paid out. Employees who cannot get SSP can claim State Sickness Benefit instead.

Invalidity Benefit

Normally, after 28 weeks of sickness, sickness benefit, or SSP where the underlying conditions for sickness benefit are satisfied, is replaced by an invalidity pension. In addition, an invalidity allowance is payable if incapacity for work begins more than five years before pension age. The allowance varies according to the age on falling sick, and if still in payment at pension age will continue as an addition to retirement pension. From 16 September 1985 invalidity allowance has been reduced or withdrawn completely if there is entitlement to an additional earnings-related pension and/or a guaranteed minimum pension.

Maternity Benefit

Statutory maternity pay (SMP) is administered by employers but there is still a state maternity allowance scheme for women who are self-employed or otherwise do not qualify for SMP.

In general, employers pay SMP to pregnant women who have been employed by them for at least 26 weeks and earned at least the lower earnings limit for the payment of NI contributions. For those who have been employed for at least two years, payment of SMP for the first six weeks is related to earnings, followed by up to twelve weeks at a standard rate of £46.30. Those who have been employed for at least 26 weeks but less than two years receive payment at standard rate only for the 18 weeks. Part-time working women also qualify for the earnings-related element if employed for at least five years. Women have some choice in deciding when to begin maternity leave but SMP is not payable for any week in which work is done.

A woman may qualify for maternity allowance (MA) if she has been working and paying contributions at the full rate for at least 26 weeks in the 52-week period which ends 15 weeks before the baby is due. She also has an element of choice in deciding when to stop work and receive MA, which is not payable for any period she works.

Widow's Benefits

Only the late husband's contributions of any class count for widow's benefit in any of its three forms.

Widow's Payment – may be received by a woman who at her husband's death is under 60, or whose husband was not entitled to a Category A retirement pension when he died.

Widowed Mother's Allowance – payable to a widow if she is receiving child benefit for one of her children; if her husband was receiving child benefit; or if she is expecting her husband's baby.

Widow's Pension – a widow may receive this pension if aged 45 or over at the time of her husband's death or when her widowed mother's allowance ends. If aged 55 or over she will receive the full widow's pension rate.

Widow's benefit of any form ceases upon re-marriage.

Retirement Pension – Categories A and B

A Category A pension is payable for life to men or women on their own contributions if they are over pension age (65 for a man and 60 for a woman).

Where a person defers making a claim at 65 (60 for a woman) or later opts to be treated as if he/she had not made a claim, and does not draw a Category A pension, the weekly rate of pension is increased, when he or she finally makes a claim or reaches the age of 70 (65 for a woman), in respect of weeks when pension is forgone during the five years after reaching minimum pension age. Details of the increase in the rate of pension due to deferred retirement are given in leaflet NP46, available at social security offices. If a married man defers his own Category A pension, his wife has to defer receiving her Category B pension based on his contribution record. During this time she earns increments to the Category B pension, which is payable to her (and not her husband) when they both claim their pensions.

A Category B pension is normally payable for life to a woman on her husband's contributions when he has claimed, or is over 70, and has qualified for his own Category A pension, and she has reached 60. It is also payable on widowhood after 60 whether or not the late husband had retired and qualified for his own pension. The weekly pension is payable at the rate of the increase for a wife while the husband is alive, and at the single person's rate on widowhood after 60. Where a woman is widowed before she reaches 60, a Category B pension is paid to her on reaching 60 at the same weekly rate as her widow's pension if she claims. If a woman qualifies for a pension of each category she receives whichever pension is the larger. Details of the increase in the rate of pension due to deferred retirement are given in leaflet NP46, available at social security offices.

The earnings rule which stated that a man aged 65 to 70, or a woman aged 60 to 65, who has qualified for pension would have it reduced if he or she earned more than a certain amount was abolished on 1 October 1989. Where an adult dependant is living with the client, an Adult Dependants Allowance will only be payable if the dependant's earnings do not exceed the standard rate of unemployment benefit for a single person under pensionable age (*see* below). For the purpose of the dependency rule only, earnings will include payments by way of occupational pension. The earnings of a separated spouse affect the increase of retirement pension if they exceed £31.25 a week.

Unemployment, sickness or invalidity benefit is payable to men between 65 and 70, and women between 60 and 65 who have not claimed their retirement pension and who would have been entitled to a retirement pension if they had claimed at pension age. This applies in the case of sickness and invalidity benefit if incapacity for work is the result of an industrial accident or prescribed disease. These rates of benefit for people over pension age are shown in leaflet NI 196. A retirement pension will be increased by the amount of any invalidity allowance the pensioner was getting within the period of eight weeks and one day before reaching minimum pension age but this will be offset against any Additional Pension or Guaranteed Minimum Pension. An age addition of 25p per week is payable if a retirement pensioner is aged 80 or over.

Graduated Pension

The graduated pension scheme under which national insurance contributions and retirement pensions were graduated within specified limits, according to earnings, was discontinued in April 1975 under the Social Security Act 1975. Any graduated pension which an employed person over 18 and under 70 (65 for a woman) had earned by paying graduated contributions between 6 April 1961, when the scheme started, and 5 April 1975, will be paid when the contributor claims retirement pension or at 70 (65 for a woman), in addition to any retirement pension for which he or she qualifies.

Graduated pension is at the rate of 6.81p a week for each 'unit' of graduated contributions paid by the employee (half a unit or more counts as a whole unit). A unit of contributions is £7.50 for men, and £9.00 for women, of graduated contributions paid.

A wife can get a graduated pension in return for her own graduated contributions, but not for her husband's. A widow gets a graduated addition to her retirement pension equal to half of any graduated additions earned by her late husband, plus any additions earned by her own graduated contributions. If a person defers making a claim beyond 65 (60 for a woman), entitlement may be increased by one seventh of a penny per £1 of its weekly rate for each complete week of deferred retirement, as long as the retirement is deferred for a minimum of seven weeks.

RATES OF BENEFITS
from week commencing 6 April 1992

	Weekly rate
Unemployment Benefit: standard rate	
Person under pension age	£43.10
Increase for wife/other adult dependant	26.60
*Person over pension age	54.15
Increase for wife/other adult dependant	32.55
Sickness Benefit: standard rate	
Person under pension age	41.20
Increase for wife/other adult dependant	25.50
*Person over pension age	51.95
Increase for wife/other adult dependant	31.20
*Invalidity Pension	
Person (under or over pension age)	54.15
Increase for wife or adult dependant	32.55
Invalidity Allowance: maximum amount payable	
Higher rate	11.55
Middle rate	7.20
Lower rate	3.60
Maternity Allowance	42.25
Widow's Benefits	
Widow's Payment (lump sum)	1,000.00
*Widowed Mother's Allowance	54.15
*Widow's Pension	54.15
**Retirement pension: categories A and B*	
Single person	54.15
Increase for wife or adult dependant	32.55

*These benefits attract an increase for each dependent child (in addition to child benefit) of £10.85. (£9.75 for only, elder or eldest child for whom higher rate of Child Benefit payable.)

NON-CONTRIBUTORY BENEFITS

CHILD BENEFIT

Child benefit is payable for virtually all children aged under 16, and for those aged 16–18 who are studying full-time up to and including A-level or equivalent standard. It is also payable for a short period if the child has left school recently and is registered for work or youth training at a careers office.

ONE PARENT BENEFIT

This benefit may be paid to a person in receipt of Child Benefit who is responsible for bringing up one or more children on his/her own. It is a flat rate non-means tested, non-contributory benefit payable for the eldest child.

GUARDIAN'S ALLOWANCE

Where the parents of a child are dead, the person who has the child in his/her family may claim a guardian's allowance in addition to child benefit. The allowance, in exceptional circumstances, is payable on the death of only one parent.

INVALID CARE ALLOWANCE

Invalid care allowance is payable to persons of working age, who are not gainfully employed because they are regularly and substantially engaged in caring for a severely disabled person who is receiving attendance allowance, the middle or highest rate of disability living allowance or constant attendance allowance with either a war or services pension, industrial disablement workman's compensation, or an allowance under the Pneumoconiosis, Byssinosis and Miscellaneous Diseases Benefit Scheme.

SEVERE DISABLEMENT ALLOWANCE

Persons under pensionable age who have been continuously incapable of work for a period of at least 28 weeks but who do not qualify for a contributory invalidity pension may be entitled to severe disablement allowance. People who first become incapable of work after their twentieth birthday must be at least 80 per cent disabled.

ATTENDANCE ALLOWANCE

This is payable to disabled people over 65 who need a lot of care or supervision because of physical or mental disability for a period of at least six months. People not expected to live for six months because of an illness do not have to wait six months. The allowance has two rates: the lower rate is for day or night care, and the higher rate is for day and night care.

DISABILITY LIVING ALLOWANCE

This is payable to disabled people under 65 who have personal care and mobility needs because of an illness or disability for a period of at least three months. People not expected to live for six months because of an illness do not have to wait three months. The allowance has two components: the care component, which has three rates of help, and the mobility component, which has two rates. The amount payable depends on the care and mobility needs of the claimant. The mobility component is payable only to those aged five or over.

DISABILITY WORKING ALLOWANCE

This is a tax-free, income-related benefit for people who are working 16 hours a week or more but have an illness or disability which puts them at a disadvantage in getting a job. To qualify a person must be aged 16 or over and must, at the date of the claim, have one of the 'qualifying benefits', such as Disability Living Allowance. The amount payable depends on the size of the family and weekly income. DWA is not payable if any savings exceed £16,000.

NON-CONTRIBUTORY RETIREMENT PENSION – CATEGORIES C AND D

A Category C pension is provided, subject to a residence test, for persons who were over pensionable age on 5 July 1948, and for women whose husbands are so entitled if they are over pension age, with increases for adult and child dependants. A Category D pension is provided for others when they reach 80 if they are not already getting a retirement pension of any category or if they are getting that pension at less than these rates. An age addition of 25p per week is payable if persons entitled to retirement pension are aged 80 or over.

RATES OF BENEFITS
from week commencing 6 April, 1992

	Weekly rate
Child Benefit (first child)	£9.65
Each subsequent child	7.80
One Parent Benefit	
First or only child of certain lone parents	5.85
Guardian's Allowance (eldest child)	9.75
Each subsequent child	10.85
**Severe Disablement Allowance*	
†Basic rate	32.55
Under 40	11.55
40–49	7.20
50–59	3.60
Increase for wife/other adult dependant	19.45
**Invalid Care Allowance*	32.55
Increase for wife/other adult dependant	19.45

	Weekly rate
Attendance Allowance	
Higher rate	£43.35
Lower rate	28.95
Disability Living Allowance	
Care component	
Higher rate	43.45
Middle rate	28.95
Lower rate	11.55
Mobility component	
Higher rate	30.30
Lower rate	11.55
Disability Working Allowance	
Single person	42.40
Couple or single parent	58.80
Child aged under 11	10.40
aged 11–15	17.25
aged 16–17	21.45
aged 18	29.90
‡*Applicable amount* (income threshold)	
Single person	39.95
Couple or single parent	66.60
*Retirement Pension: Categories *C and D*	
Single person	32.55
Increase for wife/other adult dependant (not payable with Category D pension)	19.45

*These benefits attract an increase for each dependent child (in addition to child benefit) of £9.75 for the first child and £10.85 for each subsequent child.

†The age addition applies to the age when incapacity began.

‡70 pence is deducted from the maximum DWA payable (this is obtained by adding up the appropriate allowance for each person in the family) for every pound coming in each week over the appropriate applicable amount. Where weekly income is below the applicable amount, maximum DWA is payable.

INCOME SUPPORT

Income Support is a benefit for those aged 18 and over (although certain vulnerable 16- and 17-year-olds may be eligible) whose income is inadequate and who are unemployed. Others who may be eligible include people: over 60; bringing up children alone; unable to work through sickness; caring for a disabled person; or working part-time. Except in special cases Income Support is not available to those who work for more than 16 hours per week or who have a partner who works for more than 16 hours per week.

Income Support is not payable if the client, or client and partner, have capital or savings in excess of £8,000. The rate of benefits is affected by possession of capital or savings in excess of £3,000 and may be affected by a client's earnings.

Sums payable depend on fixed allowances laid down by law for people in different circumstances. Special rates apply for people living in board and lodging, hostels, residential care or nursing homes. Details are available from local social security offices. Income Support is payable via post offices, either by order book or, for the unemployed, by girocheque.

Applications for Income Support are made on form IS1, available from post offices; Income Support claim forms, available from social security offices; or on form B1 (for the unemployed), available from unemployment benefit offices. If both partners are entitled to Income Support, either may claim it for the couple. People receiving Income Support will be able to receive Housing Benefit, help with mortgage or home loan interest and help with health care. They may also be eligible for help with exceptional expenses, from the Social Fund. Leaflet IS20 gives a detailed explanation of Income Support.

Income Support Premiums

Income Support Premiums are additional weekly payments for those with special needs. They are payable as part of the Income Support scheme. People qualifying for more than one premium will normally only receive the highest single premium for which they qualify. However Family Premium, Disabled Child's Premium, Severe Disability Premium and Carer Premium are payable in addition to other premiums.

People with children qualify for a Family Premium if they have at least one child; a Disabled Child's Premium if they have a child who receives Attendance Allowance or certain components of Disability Living Allowance or is registered blind; or a Lone Parent Premium if they are bringing up one or more children alone. If someone receives Invalid Care Allowance, they qualify for the Carer Premium.

Long-term sick or disabled people qualify for a Disability Premium if they or their partner are receiving certain benefits because they are disabled or cannot work; are registered blind; or have been sending in doctor's statements for at least 28 weeks stating inability to work through sickness. If someone is living alone and they are in receipt of Attendance Allowance or Disability Living Allowance, without anyone receiving Invalid Care Allowance for looking after them, they will qualify for a Severe Disability Premium in addition to a Disability Premium.

People qualify for a Pensioner Premium if they or their partner are aged between 60 and 79, and for a Higher Pensioner Premium if they or their partner are aged 80 or over. A Higher Pensioner Premium is also payable to people aged between 60 and 79 who receive Attendance Allowance, Mobility Allowance, Invalidity Benefit or Severe Disablement Allowance, or who are registered blind. A Higher Pensioner Premium may be paid as well as a Severe Disability Premium. Enhanced Pensioner Premium is payable to pensioners aged between 75 and 79 in addition to Pensioner Premium.

Rates of Benefit

from week commencing 6 April 1992

	Weekly rate
Income Support	
Single people	
aged 16–17	£25.55
aged 18 – 24	33.60
aged 25 and over	42.45
aged 18 and over and a single parent	42.45
Couples	
both under 18	50.60
one or both aged 18 or over	66.60
For each child in a family	
under 11	14.55
aged 11–15	21.40
*aged 16–17	25.55
*aged 18 and over	33.60

*if in full-time education up to A level or equivalent standard.

Premiums	
Family Premium	9.30
Disabled Child's Premium	17.80
Lone Parent Premium	4.75
Disability Premium	
Single	17.80
Couple	25.55
Severe Disability Premium	
Single	32.55
Couple (one person qualified)	32.55
Couple (both qualified)	65.10
Pensioner Premium	
Single	14.70
Couple	22.35
Higher Pensioner Premium	
Single	20.75
Couple	29.55
Enhanced Pensioner Premium	
Single	16.65
Couple	25.00

FAMILY CREDIT

Family Credit is a tax-free benefit for working families with children. It is not a loan and does not have to be paid back. To qualify, a family must include at least one child under 16 (under 19 if in full-time education up to A-level or equivalent standard), and the client, or partner (if there is one), must be working for at least 16 hours per week. It does not matter which partner is working and they may be employed or self-employed. The right to Family Credit does not depend on NI contributions and the same rates of benefit are paid to one- and two-parent families. Family Credit is not payable if the client, or client and partner, have capital or savings in excess of £8,000. The rate of benefit is affected if capital or savings in excess of £3,000 are held. The rate of benefit payable depends upon the client's (and partner's) net income (excluding Child Benefit), number of children, and children's ages. Family Credit is paid for 26 weeks and the amount payable will usually remain the same throughout this period, regardless of change of circumstances. Payment is made weekly via post offices or every four-weeks directly into a bank or building society account. Family Credit is claimed by post. A claim pack FC1 which includes a claim form can be obtained at a post office or social security office. In two-parent families the woman should claim.

RATES OF BENEFIT

from week commencing 6 April 1992

	Weekly rate
The maximum amount will be payable where net income is no more than £66.60 per week. Where net income exceeds that amount, the maximum credit is reduced by 70 per cent of the excess and the result is the Family Credit payable. The maximum rate consists of:	
Adult credit (for one or two parents)	£41.00
plus for each child	
aged under 11	10.40
aged 11–15	17.25
aged 16–17	21.45
aged 18	29.90

CLAIMS AND QUESTIONS

With a few exceptions, claims and questions relating to Social Security benefits are decided by statutory authorities who act independently of the Department of Social Security and Department of Employment.

The first of the statutory authorities, the Adjudication Officer, determines entitlement to benefit. A client who is dissatisfied with that decision has the right of appeal to a Social Security Appeal Tribunal. There is a further right of appeal to a Social Security Commissioner against the Tribunal's decision but leave to appeal must first be obtained. Appeals to the Commissioner must be on a point of law. Provision is also made for the determination of certain questions by the Secretary of State for Social Services.

Disablement questions are decided by adjudicating medical authorities or Medical Appeal Tribunals. Appeal to the Commissioner against a tribunal's decision is with leave and on a point of law only.

Leaflet NI 246, which is available from social security offices, explains how to appeal, and leaflet NI260 is a guide to reviews and appeals.

THE SOCIAL FUND

The Social Fund helps people with expenses which are difficult to meet from regular income. Regulated Maternity, Funeral and Cold Weather payments are decided by Adjudication Officers and are not cash-limited. Discretionary Community Care Grants, and Budgeting and Crisis Loans are decided by Social Fund Officers and come out of a yearly budget which is allocated to each district (1992–3, grants £79.6 million; loans £197.8 million).

REGULATED PAYMENTS

Maternity Payments

A flat-rate payment of £100 for each baby expected, born or adopted. It is payable to people on Income Support and Family Credit and is non-repayable.

Funeral Payments

Payable for reasonable funeral expenses incurred by people receiving Income Support, Family Credit, Housing Benefit or Community Charge Rebate. It is recoverable from the estate of the deceased.

Cold Weather Payments

£6 for any consecutive seven days when the average temperature is 0°C or below. Paid to people on Income Support who are pensioners, disabled or parents with a child under the age of five. It is non-repayable.

DISCRETIONARY PAYMENTS

Community Care Grants

They are intended to help people on Income Support to move into the community or avoid institutional care; ease exceptional pressures on families; and/or meet certain essential travelling expenses. They are usually non-repayable.

Budgeting Loans

These are interest-free loans to people who have been receiving Income Support for at least six months, for intermittent expenses that may be difficult to budget for.

Crisis Loans

These are interest-free loans to anyone, whether receiving benefit or not, who is without resources in an emergency, where there is no other means of preventing serious risk or damage to health or safety.

Loans are normally repaid over a period of up to 78 weeks at 15, 10 or 5 per cent of Income Support (less housing costs), depending on other commitments.

SAVINGS

Savings over £500 (£1,000 for people aged 60 or over) are taken into account for Maternity and Funeral Payments, Community Care Grants and Budgeting Loans. All savings are taken into account for crisis loans.

APPEALS AND REVIEWS

For regulated payment there is a right of appeal to an independent Social Security Appeal and thereafter to a Social Security Commissioner. For discretionary payments there is a review system where persons can ask for a review at the local office with a further right of review to an independent Social Fund Inspector.

INDUSTRIAL INJURIES, DISABLEMENT AND DEATH BENEFITS

The Industrial Injuries scheme, administered under the Social Security Contributions and Benefits Act 1992, provides a range of benefits designed to compensate for disablement resulting from an industrial accident (i.e. an accident arising out of and in the course of an employed earner's employment) or from a prescribed disease due to the nature of a person's employment. Rates of benefit are increased periodically.

CLAIMS AND QUESTIONS

Provision is made for the determination of certain questions by the Secretary of State for Social Security, and of 'disablement questions' by a medical board (or a single doctor) or, on appeal, by a medical appeal tribunal. An appeal on a point of law against a medical appeal tribunal decision is determined by the Social Security Commissioner.

Claims for benefit and certain questions arising in connection with a claim for or award of benefit (e.g. whether the accident arose out of and in the course of the employment) are determined by an adjudication officer appointed by the Secretary of State, or a Social Security Appeal Tribunal, or in certain circumstances, on further appeal, by the Commissioners.

BENEFITS

Disablement Benefit is normally payable 15 weeks (90 days) after the date of accident or onset of disease if the employed earner suffers from loss of physical or mental faculty such that the resulting disablement is assessed at not less than 14 per cent. The amount of disablement benefit payable varies according to the degree of disablement (in the form of a percentage) assessed by an adjudicating medical authority or medical appeal tribunal.

Disablement assessed at less than 14 per cent does not normally attract basic benefit except for certain chest diseases. A weekly pension is payable where the assessment of disablement is between 14 and 100 per cent (assessments of 14 to 19 per cent are payable at the 20 per cent rate). Payment can be made for a limited period or for life.

The basic rates are applicable to adults and to juveniles entitled to an increase for a child or adult dependant; other juveniles receive lower rates.

Basic rates of pension are not related to the pensioner's loss of earning power, and are payable whether he/she is in work or not. If disablement is assessed at 1 per cent or more, loss of earnings may be compensated by a reduced earnings allowance. This may be paid even if basic disablement pension is not paid because disablement is assessed at less than 14 per cent, providing there is a current disablement assessment of at least 1 per cent. However, reduced earnings allowance cannot be paid where the date of the accident or the onset of a prescribed disease was on or after 1 October 1990. There is provision also for increases of pension if the pensioner requires constant attendance or if his disablement is exceptionally severe. A pensioner may draw SSP, sickness or invalidity benefit as appropriate, in addition to disablement pension, during spells of incapacity for work.

Death Benefit, in the form of a pension, is available for women widowed before 11 April 1988. The amount of pension depends on the widow's circumstances at the date of the death and not upon the deceased's earnings.

Regulations impose certain obligations on clients and beneficiaries and on employers, including, in the case of clients for disablement benefit, that of submitting themselves for medical examination.

SUPPLEMENTARY ALLOWANCES

Special schemes under the Industrial Injuries and Diseases (Old Cases) Act 1975 provide supplementary allowances to those entitled to receive weekly payments of workmen's compensation for loss of earnings due to injury at work, or disease contracted during employment before 5 July 1948 when the Industrial Injuries scheme was introduced. Other schemes under the Act provide allowances to those who contracted slowly-developing diseases during employment before July 1948 where neither workmen's compensation nor Industrial Injuries Benefits are payable. A lump sum death benefit of up to £300 may also be payable to a dependant of such a person.

RATES OF BENEFITS

from April 1992

	Weekly Rate
Disablement Benefit/Pension	
Degree of disablement	
100 per cent	£88.40
90	79.56
80	70.72
70	61.88
60	53.04
50	44.20
40	35.36
30	26.52
20	17.68
*Unemployability supplement	54.15
Addition for adult dependant (subject to earnings rule)	32.55
Reduced earnings allowance (maximum)	35.36
Constant Attendance allowance (normal maximum rate)	35.40
Exceptionally severe disablement allowance	35.40
*Industrial death benefit widow's pension	
Higher permanent rate	54.15
Lower permanent rate	16.25

*These benefits attract an increase for each dependent child (in addition to child benefit) of £9.75 for the first child and £10.85 for each subsequent child.

War Pensions

War pensions are awarded under The Naval, Military and Air Forces, Etc. (Disablement and Death) Service Pensions Order 1983, which was a consolidation of the previous Royal Warrants, Orders in Council and Orders by Her Majesty.

The Department of Social Security awards war pensions to members of the armed forces in respect of the periods 4 August 1914 to 30 September 1921 and subsequent to 3 September 1939 (including present members of the armed forces). The DSS also has special schemes for the Merchant Navy, Naval Auxiliary personnel, former members of the Ulster Defence Regiment, civil defence volunteers, civilians, coastguards, Home Guard, Polish armed forces under British command and Polish resettlement forces.

War pensions for the period 1 October 1921 to 2 September 1939 are dealt with by the Ministry of Defence, which is also responsible for the Armed Forces Pension Scheme.

Pensions

War disablement pension is awarded for the disabling effects of any injury, wound or disease which is attributable to, or has been aggravated by, conditions of service in the armed forces. It cannot be paid until the serviceman or woman has left the armed forces.

Disablement is assessed by comparison of the disabled person's health with that of a normal, healthy person of the same age and sex, without taking into account the disabled person's earning capacity or occupation, and is expressed on a percentage scale up to 100 per cent. Disablement of 20 per cent and above, for which a pension is awarded, is assessed in steps of 10 per cent. Maximum assessment does not necessarily imply total incapacity. For assessment of less than 20 per cent a lump sum is payable.

The Dependency Allowance, formerly payable in respect of a wife or child, was abolished in April 1992 and an equivalent amount incorporated into the basic War Disablement Pension.

War widow's pension is awarded where death occurs as a result of service or where a war disablement pensioner was receiving constant attendance allowance at the time of his death, or would have been receiving it if he were not in hospital, in which case his widow has automatic entitlement to a war widow's pension, regardless of the cause of death.

Additional allowances are payable for dependent children, in addition to child benefit.

A reduced weekly rate is payable to war widows of men below the rank of Lieutenant-Colonel who are under the age of 40, without children and capable of maintaining themselves. This is increased to the standard rate at age 40.

Rank additions to disablement and widows pensions may be paid where the rank held was above that of private (or equivalent).

Claims

Where a claim is made no later than seven years after the termination of service, the client does not have to prove that the disablement or death on which the claim is based is related to service and receives the benefit of any reasonable doubt. Where a claim is made more than seven years after the termination of service the claimant has to show that disablement or death is related to service. However, the claim succeeds if reliable evidence is produced which raises a reasonable doubt whether or not disablement or death is related to service. There is no time limit for making a claim for war pension.

Supplementary Allowances

A number of supplementary allowances may be awarded to a war pensioner which are intended to meet the various needs such as mobility, unemployability, constant nursing care, which may result from disablement or death and take account of its particular effect on the pensioner.

The principal supplementary allowances are:

Unemployability supplement – with additional allowances for dependants, this may be paid to a war pensioner whose pensioned disablement is so serious as to make him unemployable. In addition, an invalidity allowance may be payable if the incapacity for work began more than five years before normal retirement age.

Allowance for lowered standard of occupation – this may be awarded to a partially disabled pensioner whose pensioned disablement permanently prevents him from following his pre-service occupation and from doing another job of equivalent financial standard. The allowance, together with the basic war disablement pension, must not exceed pension at the 100 per cent rate.

Widow's age allowance – this is paid at three different rates according to age (65–69, 70–79 and over 80).

Widow's child's allowance – this may be paid in addition to child benefit.

Other supplementary allowances include constant attendance allowance, exceptionally severe disablement allowance, severe disablement occupational allowance, mobility supplement, treatment allowance, age allowance and education allowance.

Decisions on supplementary allowances are made on a discretionary basis on behalf of the Secretary of State and there is no provision for a statutory right of appeal against them. However, war pensioners may discuss any aspect of their pension position with their local War Pensions Committee, which may be able to arrange help or make representations to the war pensions branch of the DSS.

War Pensioners Abroad

The DSS is responsible for the payment of war pensions, and provision of necessary treatment for accepted disablement, to pensioners who reside overseas. They receive the same pension rates as war pensioners in this country and benefit from the same annual upratings.

Social Security Benefits

When a war disablement pensioner is sick, unemployed or retired, the appropriate social security benefits are paid in addition to the war pension, unless he is entitled to war pensioner's unemployability supplement or severe disablement occupational allowance instead.

Any sickness, invalidity, unemployment benefit or retirement pension for which a war widow qualifies on her own contributions, and any graduated retirement benefit, or additional earnings related pension inherited from her husband, can be paid in addition to her war widow's pension or temporary allowance.

A war pensioner or war widow who claims Income Support, Family Credit or Disability Working Allowance has the first £10 of pension disregarded. A similar provision operates for housing benefit and community charge relief; but the local authority may, at its discretion, disregard any or all of the balance.

A special tax-free Christmas bonus of £10.00 is payable to war disablement pensioners who are in receipt of unemployability supplement, constant attendance allowance, have retired, or are aged over 70 (65 for women); and to all war widows who do not otherwise receive this payment.

Pensions Appeal Tribunals

There are independent Pensions Appeal Tribunals which hear appeals against the decisions of the DSS on entitlement, and assessment of disablement, in respect of the 1939–45 War and subsequent service cases. There are no time limits within which an entitlement appeal must be made but there are time limits within which an assessment appeal should be made. However, there are now no rights of appeal in the 1914–21 War disablement cases, the great majority of which were given final assessment in the 1920s with a 12 months' right of appeal at the time. An appeal by a 1914 war widow must be made within twelve months of the date on which the rejection of the claim is notified.

War Pensioners Welfare Service

The DSS operates a war pensioners welfare service to advise and assist war pensioners and their widows on any matters affecting their welfare. Welfare officers are attached to War Pensioners' Welfare Offices located in the major towns, and work closely with central and local government agencies as well as the various ex-service organizations. The service is available on call to any war pensioner or widow who needs it. In addition the service takes the initiative in arranging regular visits in certain cases.

Rates of Pensions and Allowances

from week commencing 6 April 1992

	Weekly rates
War Disablement pension	
(for Private or equivalent rank)	
Degree of disablement:	
100 per cent	£89.00
90 per cent	80.10
80 per cent	71.20
70 per cent	62.30
60 per cent	53.40
50 per cent	44.50
40 per cent	35.60
30 per cent	26.70
20 per cent	17.80
Unemployability supplement	
Personal allowance	70.35
Increase for wife/other adult dependant	13.75
Increase for first child	14.85
Increase for other children	16.25
Allowance for lowered standard of occupation (maximum)	35.36
Widow's pension	
(widow of Private or equivalent rank)	
Standard rate	70.35
Increase for first child	13.75
Increase for other children	14.85
Childless widow under 40	23.10
Widow's age allowance	
aged 65–69	8.05
aged 70–79	15.55
aged 80 and over	23.10

The current rates of all war pensions and allowances are listed in leaflet MPL154 *Rates of War Pensions and Allowances* which is obtainable from War Pensioners Welfare Offices or from The Leaflets Unit, PO Box 21, Stanmore, Middx. HA7 1AY.

British Passport Regulations

Applications for United Kingdom passports must be made on the forms obtainable at any of the Passport Offices (addresses given below) or at any main post office (except in Northern Ireland).

LONDON, Clive House, 70–78 Petty France, London SW1H 9HD. Tel: 071-279 3434
LIVERPOOL, India Buildings, Water Street, Liverpool L2 0QZ. Tel: 051-237 3010
NEWPORT, Olympia House, Upper Dock Street, Newport, Gwent NP9 1XA. Tel: 0633-244500
PETERBOROUGH, Passport Office, Aragon Court, Northminster Road, Peterborough PE1 1QG. Tel: 0733-895555
GLASGOW, 3 Northgate, 96 Milton Street, Cowcaddens, Glasgow G4 0BT. Tel: 041-332 0271
BELFAST, Passport Office, Hampton House, 47–53 High Street, Belfast BT1 2QS. Tel: 0232-232371

The above offices are open Monday–Friday 9 a.m. to 4.30 p.m. (9 a.m. to 4 p.m. in London). The Passport Office in London is also open for cases of special emergency (e.g. death or serious illness) arising outside normal office hours between 4 p.m. and 6 p.m. and on Saturdays between 10 a.m. and noon.

The busy season for the issue of passports is January to July, when applications can take up to 20 days to process. At other times applications are likely to take 10–15 days to process. Applying in person does not guarantee that an application will be given priority.

Completed application forms should be posted to one of the six passport offices, with photographs, supporting documents and the fee of £15, in the form of a cheque or postal order which should be crossed and made payable to the passport office.

A passport cannot be issued or extended on behalf of a person already abroad; such person should apply to the nearest British High Commission or Consulate.

United Kingdom passports are granted to:

(i) British Citizens
(ii) British Dependent Territories Citizens
(iii) British Nationals (Overseas)
(iv) British Overseas Citizens
(v) British Subjects
(vi) British Protected Persons

A passport granted to a child under 16 will normally be valid for an initial period of five years, after which it may be extended for a further five years with no extra charge. Children who have reached the age of 16 require separate passports. Their application must be signed by one of their parents.

A passport granted to a person over 16 will normally be valid for ten years and will not be renewable. Thereafter, or if at any time the passport contains no further space for visas, a new passport must be obtained.

The issue of passports including details of the holder's spouse has been discontinued, but existing family passports may be used until expiry. A spouse who is included in a family passport cannot travel on the passport without the holder.

Completed passport applications should be countersigned by a Member of Parliament, Justice of the Peace, minister of religion, a professionally qualified person (e.g. doctor, engineer, lawyer, teacher), bank officer, established Civil Servant, police officer or a person of similar standing who has personally known the applicant for at least two years, and who is either a British Citizen, a British Dependent Territories Citizen, a British National (Overseas), a British Overseas Citizen, a British subject or a citizen of a Commonwealth country. A relative must not countersign the application. The applicant's birth certificate or previous British passport, and other evidence in support of the statements made in the application must be produced.

In the case of children under the age of 16 requiring a separate passport, an application should be made by one of the parents on Form B.

If the applicant for a passport is a British national by naturalization or registration, the certificate of naturalization or registration must be produced with the application, unless the applicant holds a previous United Kingdom passport issued after registration or naturalization.

United Kingdom passports are generally available for travel to all countries. The possession of a passport does not, however, exempt the holder from compliance with any immigration regulations in force in British or foreign countries, or from the necessity of obtaining a visa where required.

PHOTOGRAPHS

Duplicate unmounted photographs of the applicant must be sent. These photographs should be printed on normal thin photographic paper. They should measure 45 mm by 35 mm (1.77 in by 1.38 in) and should be taken full face without a hat. One photograph should be certified as a true likeness of the applicant by the person who countersigns the application form.

EXTENSION OF PASSPORTS

Applications for the extension of United Kingdom passports which have been valid for less than ten years must be made on Form D.

48-PAGE PASSPORTS

The 48-page passport is intended to meet the needs of frequent travellers who fill standard passports well before the validity has expired. It is valid for ten years and costs £22.50.

BRITISH VISITOR'S PASSPORTS

A simplified form of travel document is available for British Citizens, British Dependent Territories Citizens or British Overseas Citizens wishing to pay short visits (not exceeding three months) to the following countries:

Andorra; Austria; Belgium; Bermuda; Denmark; Finland; France (including Corsica); Greece (and the Greek islands); Germany; Gibraltar; Iceland; Italy (including Elba, Sardinia and Sicily); Liechtenstein; Luxembourg; Malta; Monaco; Netherlands; Norway; Portugal (including Madeira and the Azores); San Marino; Spain (including the Balearic Islands and the Canary Islands); Sweden; Switzerland; Tunisia; Turkey; the former Yugoslavia.

A fee of £7.50 (£11.25 if particulars of spouse included) is charged for the issue of a British Visitor's Passport, which is valid for 12 months, cannot be amended and is not renewable. On expiry, application should be made for a new passport if required. Particulars of an applicant's spouse and/or children under 16 years can be included at the time of issue only. A child of 8 years of age and over is eligible to hold a British Visitor's Passport. Applications for, or including, a person under 18 years of age (unless married or serving in HM Forces) must be countersigned by the legal guardian.

British Visitor's Passports are obtainable from main post offices in England, Scotland and Wales, and from Passport Offices in Northern Ireland, Jersey, Guernsey and the Isle of Man.

Two recent passport photographs will be required of the applicant and the spouse if included. Photographs of children included on the British Visitor's Passport are not required. Size of photographs must be 45 mm by 35 mm (1.77 in × 1.38 in). They should be unmounted and must be printed on normal thin photographic paper. No visas are required on British Visitor's Passports. Applicants must also produce for the purpose of identification the documents listed on the application form.

Visas

The visa requirements of a country may vary depending upon the purpose or the length of the visit. Visa regulations are also liable to change, sometimes at short notice, and enquiries should always be made at the Consulate or Embassy concerned (addresses and telephone numbers are given in the Countries of the World section).

For entry for tourist purposes into the following countries a visa or permit may be required: Afghanistan; Albania; Algeria; Angola; Australia; Bangladesh; Benin; Bhutan; Bulgaria; Burkina; Burundi; Cameroon Republic; Cape Verde; Central African Republic; Chad; China; Congo; Cuba; Djibouti; Egypt; Equatorial Guinea; Estonia; Ethiopia; Gabon; Ghana; Guatemala; Guinea; Guinea Bissau; Guyana; Haiti; Hong Kong; India; Indonesia; Iran; Iraq; Jordan; Kuwait; Laos; Latvia; Lebanon; Liberia; Libya; Madagascar; Mali; Mauritania; Mongolia; Mozambique; Myanmar; Nepal; Nigeria; Oman; Pakistan; Papua New Guinea; Romania; Rwanda; Saudi Arabia; Sierra Leone; Somalia; former Soviet republics; Sudan; Syria; Turkey; Uganda; Venezuela; Vietnam; Yemen; Zaire.

Immunization

In very general terms immunization against typhoid and polio, and protection against hepatitis A by immunoglobulin or vaccine are recommended for all countries outside Europe, except North America, Australia and New Zealand. Protection against malaria, in the form of tablets, is advised for visits to malarious areas.

Immunization against yellow fever is compulsory for entry into some countries, either for all travellers or for those arriving from a yellow fever infected area.

Fuller details are set out in Department of Health leaflet *Health Advice for Travellers*. Health care professionals can obtain up-to-date information about immunization requirements from:

ENGLAND – Communicable Disease Surveillance Centre, 61 Colindale Avenue, London NW9 5EQ. Tel: 081-200 6868

WALES – Welsh Office, Cathays Park, Cardiff CF1 3NQ. Tel: 0222-825111

SCOTLAND – Scottish Home and Health Department, St Andrew's House, Edinburgh EH1 3DE. Tel: 031-556 8501. Or the Communicable Diseases (Scotland) Unit, Ruchill Hospital, Bilsland Drive, Glasgow G20 9NB. Tel: 041-946 7120

NORTHERN IRELAND – DHSS, Dundonald House, Upper Newtownards Road, Belfast BT4 3SF. Tel: 0232-63939

Your doctor should be consulted at least eight weeks before departure, and will advise you and arrange vaccinations. If children will be travelling outside Europe, North America, Australia and New Zealand, the doctor should be informed, especially if they have not completed their full course of childhood immunization.

Details of free or reduced cost emergency medical treatment when visiting other European countries, and those countries with which the UK has concluded reciprocal health arrangements are set out in leaflet T4, available from some travel agents, local post offices or the Health Publications Unit, No. 2 Site, Manchester Road, Heywood, Lancs. OL10 2PZ.

Work and Business Overseas

A passport issued after 31 December 1982 showing the holder's national status as British citizen will secure for the holder the right to take employment or to establish himself/herself in business or other self-employed activity in another member state of the European Community. A passport bearing the endorsement 'holder has the right of abode in the United Kingdom' where the holder so qualifies will also secure the same right. Employment permits are required in most other countries, even for casual labour. The nearest representative of the country concerned should be consulted. Local employment offices have a booklet entitled *Working Abroad*.

Those planning to travel abroad on export business are advised to contact the Department of Trade and Industry–British Overseas Trade Board, Kingsgate House, 66–74 Victoria Street, London SW1E 6SW or its regional offices in London, Birmingham, Bristol, Cambridge, Leeds, Manchester, Newcastle upon Tyne and Nottingham. In Wales, contact the Welsh Office Industry Division, Cathays Park, Cardiff CF1 3NQ; in Scotland, Scottish Trade International, 120 Bothwell Street, Glasgow G2 7PJ; in Northern Ireland, the Industrial Development Board for Northern Ireland, Department of Economic Development, Netherleigh, Massey Avenue, Belfast BT4 2JP. These offices will send advance notification of visits to the Commercial Section of the relevant Consulate or Embassy, and can offer advice and information about the markets to be visited.

The Water Industry

ENGLAND AND WALES

In England and Wales the Secretaries of State for the Environment and for Wales, and the Director-General of Water Services, are responsible for the general oversight of the industry and for ensuring that the private water companies fulfil their statutory obligation to provide water supply and sewerage services.

The Minister of Agriculture, Fisheries and Food and the Secretary of State for Wales are responsible for policy relating to land drainage, flood protection, sea defences and the protection and development of fisheries.

The National Rivers Authority is responsible for water quality and the control of pollution, the management of water resources and nature conservation.

THE WATER COMPANIES

Until the end of 1989, nine regional water authorities in England and the Welsh Water Authority in Wales were responsible for water supply and the development of water resources, sewerage and sewage disposal, pollution control, freshwater fisheries, flood protection, water recreation, and environmental conservation. The Water Act 1989 provided for the creation of a privatized water industry under public regulation.

Of the 99 per cent of the population of England and Wales who are connected to a public water supply, 75 per cent are supplied by the new water companies (through their principal operating subsidiaries, the water service companies), which have replaced the regional water authorities. The remaining 25 per cent are supplied by statutory water companies which were already in the private sector. Many of these have now converted to public limited company (PLC) status. The ten water service companies are also responsible for sewerage and sewage disposal throughout England and Wales.

The water service companies are:

ANGLIAN WATER SERVICES LTD, Compass House, Chivers Way, Histon, Cambs. CB4 4ZY

DWR CYMRU (WELSH WATER), Cambrian Way, Brecon, Powys LD3 7HP

NORTHUMBRIAN WATER LTD, Abbey Road, Pity Me, Durham DH1 5FS

NORTH WEST WATER LTD, Dawson House, Liverpool Road, Great Sankey, Warrington WA5 3LW

SEVERN TRENT WATER LTD, 2297 Coventry Road, Sheldon, Birmingham B26 3PU

SOUTHERN WATER SERVICES LTD, Southern House, Yeoman Road, Worthing, W. Sussex BN13 3NX

SOUTH WEST WATER SERVICES LTD, Peninsula House, Rydon Lane, Exeter EX2 7HR

THAMES WATER UTILITIES LTD, Nugent House, Vastern Road, Reading RG1 8DB

WESSEX WATER SERVICES PLC, Wessex House, Passage Street, Bristol BS2 0JQ

YORKSHIRE WATER SERVICES LTD, West Riding House, 67 Albion Street, Leeds LS1 5AA

REGULATORY BODIES

The Director-General of Water Services is appointed by the Secretaries of State for the Environment and for Wales. Independent of ministers and directly accountable to Parliament, his main duties are to ensure that the water companies comply with the terms of their appointments (or licences) and to protect the interests of the consumer. All the water companies are subject to a system of price control which sets a limit on the average increase in their prices each year. The Office of Water Services (*see* page 370) was set up to support the director general's activities.

An independent national body, the National Rivers Authority (*see* page 342) was established under the Water Act 1989 to take over the regulatory and river management functions of the regional water authorities. It has statutory duties and powers in relation to water resources, pollution control, flood defence, fisheries, recreation, conservation and navigation in England and Wales.

The Drinking Water Inspectorate (*see* page 306) was established under the Water Act 1989, and is responsible for assessing the quality of the drinking water supplied by all the water companies in England and Wales and for inspecting the companies themselves. The inspectors look at records, check operational manuals, visit laboratories and water treatment works, and question company officials. They also investigate any accidents affecting drinking water quality. The Chief Inspector presents an annual report to the Secretaries of State for the Environment and for Wales.

METHODS OF CHARGING

In England and Wales, householders have up to now paid for domestic water supply and sewerage services through charges based on the assessed value of their property under the old domestic rating system. Industrial and most commercial users are charged according to consumption, which is recorded by meter.

The abolition of domestic rates necessitated new methods of charging the private consumer for water and sewerage services. The Water Act 1989 gave the water companies until the end of the century to decide on and introduce a suitable method of charging. Three options under consideration are a flat-rate licence fee, property banding, and metering. Trials of domestic metering are currently taking place.

SCOTLAND

Overall responsibility for national water policy in Scotland rests with the Secretary of State for Scotland. Most aspects of water policy are administered through the Scottish Office Environment Department, but fisheries and certain aspects of land drainage are the responsibility of the Scottish Office Agriculture and Fisheries Department. The supply of water and sewerage services and the development of water resources are administered by separate authorities from those responsible for the control of water pollution.

Water supply and sewerage services are local authority responsibilities and are provided by the nine Regional Councils and the three Islands Councils.

Seven river purification boards and the Islands Councils of Orkney, Shetland and the Western Isles have the specific duty of promoting the cleanliness of Scotland's rivers, lochs and coastal waters and conserving water resources. They are responsible for the prevention and control of pollution within their own areas.

The Central Scotland Water Development Board was established in 1967 with the main statutory function of developing new sources of water supply for the purpose of providing water in bulk to water authorities whose limits of supply are within the board's area, i.e. Central, Fife, Lothian, Strathclyde and Tayside Regional Councils.

The community charge, which was introduced in Scotland in April 1989, includes a community water charge set by each Regional and Islands Council.

CENTRAL SCOTLAND WATER DEVELOPMENT BOARD, Balmore, Torrance, Glasgow G64 4AJ. *Director*, W. G. Mitchell

NORTHERN IRELAND

In Northern Ireland ministerial responsibility for water services lies with the Secretary of State for Northern Ireland. The Department of the Environment for Northern Ireland, operating through the Water Service, is responsible for policy and co-ordination with regard to supply and distribution of water, and provision and maintenance of sewerage services.

The Water Service is divided into four regions, the Eastern, Northern, Western and Southern Divisions. These are based in Belfast, Ballymena, Londonderry and Craigavon respectively.

On all major policy issues the Department of the Environment for Northern Ireland seeks the views of the Northern Ireland Water Council, a body appointed to advise the Department on the exercise of its water and sewerage functions. The Council includes representatives from agriculture, angling, industry, commerce, tourism, trade unions and local government.

Usually householders do not pay directly for water and sewerage services; the costs of these services are allowed for in the Northern Ireland regional rate. Water consumed by industry, commerce and agriculture in excess of 100 cubic metres (22,000 gallons) per half year is charged through meters. Traders operating from industrially derated premises are required to pay for the treatment and disposal of the trade effluent which they discharge into the public sewerage system.

HM Coastguard

Founded in 1822, originally to guard the coasts against smuggling, HM Coastguard's role today is the very different one of guarding and saving life at sea. The Service is responsible for co-ordinating all civil marine search and rescue operations around the 2,500 mile coastline of Great Britain and Northern Ireland and 1,200 miles into the Atlantic. In addition, it co-operates with search and rescue organizations of neighbouring countries both in western Europe and around the Atlantic seaboard. The Service maintains a 24-hour radar watch on the Dover Strait, providing a Channel navigation information service for all shipping in one of the busiest sea lanes in the world. The Service is administered by the Department of Transport.

Since 1978 HM Coastguard has been organized into six regions, each with a Regional Controller, operating from a Maritime Rescue Co-ordination Centre. Each region is subdivided into districts under District Controllers, operating from Maritime Rescue Sub-Centres. In all there are 21 of these centres. They are on 24-hour watch and are fitted with a comprehensive range of communications and rescue equipment. They are supported by some 350 smaller stations manned by Auxiliary Coastguards under the direction of Regulars, each of which keeps its parent centre fully informed of day-to-day casualty risk, particularly on the more remote danger spots around the coast.

Between 1 January and 31 December 1991, the 500 Regular and 4,500 Auxiliary Coastguards co-ordinated 7,212 incidents incidents requiring search and rescue facilities, resulting in assistance being given to 13,048 persons. All distress telephone and radio calls are centralized on the 21 centres, which are on the alert for people or vessels in distress, shipping hazards and oil slicks. Using modern telecommunications equipment and the facilities provided by British Telecom's coast radio stations, they can alert and co-ordinate the most appropriate rescue facilities; RNLI lifeboats, Royal Navy, RAF or Coastguard helicopters, fixed-wing aircraft, naval vessels, ships in the vicinity, or Coastguard shore and cliff rescue teams.

For those who regularly sail in local waters or make longer passages, the Coastguard Yacht and Boat Safety Scheme provides a valuable free service. Its aim is to give the Coastguard a record of the details of craft, their normal operating areas and their passage plans. Yacht and Boat Safety Scheme cards are available from all Coastguard stations, harbourmasters' offices, and most yacht clubs and marinas.

Members of the public who see an accident or a potentially dangerous incident on or around the coast should dial 999 and ask for the Coastguard.

Energy

COAL: SUPPLY AND DEMAND *million tonnes*

	1985	1986	1987	1988	1989	1990
Supply						
Production of deep-mined coal	75.3	90.4	86.0	83.8	79.6	71.5
Production of opencast coal	15.6	14.3	15.8	17.9	18.7	17.8
Recovered slurry, fines, etc.	3.3	3.5	2.8	2.4	2.8	3.6
Imports	12.7	10.6	9.8	11.7	12.1	14.8
Change in colliery stocks	−5.3	+0.3	−1.1	+0.7	+1.3	−0.9
Change in stocks at opencast sites	−6.3	−0.8	−1.5	+0.5	+1.5	−0.1
Total supply	118.3	119.2	116.9	114.6	110.6	108.8
Home Consumption						
Electricity supply industry	73.9	82.7	86.2	82.5	80.6	82.6
Coke ovens	11.1	11.1	10.9	10.9	10.8	10.8
Low temperature carbonization plants	1.4	1.0	1.0	0.8	0.8	0.8
Manufactured fuel plants	0.8	1.0	1.0	1.2	0.9	0.8
Railways	—	—	—	—	—	—
Collieries	0.3	0.3	0.2	0.2	0.1	0.1
Industry (disposals to users)	7.4	8.2	8.0	8.1	7.5	7.2
Domestic (disposals to users)	8.6	8.4	7.2	6.6	5.7	4.5
Public services	1.3	1.3	1.2	1.0	0.9	0.9
Miscellaneous	0.4	0.2	0.2	0.2	0.2	0.3
Total home consumption	105.4	114.2	115.9	111.5	107.6	108.0
Overseas shipments and bunkers	2.4	2.7	2.4	1.8	2.0	2.5
Total consumption and shipments	107.8	116.9	118.2	113.3	109.6	110.5
*Change in distributed stocks	+10.0	+4.0	−2.8	+1.7	+0.4	−0.5
†Balance	+0.5	−1.8	+1.3	−0.4	+0.6	−1.3

*Stock change excludes industrial and domestic stocks

†This is the balance between supply and consumption, shipments and changes in known distributed stocks

Source: HMSO – Annual Abstract of Statistics 1992

FUEL INPUT AND GAS OUTPUT: GAS SALES *million therms*

	1985	1986	1987	1988	1989	1990
Fuel Input to Gas Industry						
Petroleum (*million tonnes*)	0.1	0.1	—	—	—	—
*Petroleum gases	28	36	6	1	3	1
Natural gas	—	—	—	—	—	—
Coke oven gas	—	—	—	—	—	—
Total to gas works	57	55	20	6	3	1
Natural gas for direct supply	18,988	19,747	20,198	19,083	18,826	19,242
Total fuel input	19,046	19,802	20,218	19,089	18,829	19,243
Gas Output and Sales						
Gas output:						
Town gas	20	18	13	4	1	1
Natural gas supplied direct	19,017	19,775	20,205	19,083	18,826	19,242
Gross total available	19,038	19,793	20,218	19,087	18,827	19,243
Own use	−140	−152	−137	−120	−101	−81
†Statistical difference	−531	−613	−708	−328	−377	−357
Total sales	18,367	18,496	19,373	18,639	18,349	18,832
Analysis of gas sales						
Power stations	197	75	79	83	82	86
Final users:						
Iron and steel industry	449	419	468	449	471	465
Other industries	5,310	4,804	5,275	4,811	4,915	5,066
Domestic	9,684	10,242	10,500	10,255	9,914	10,189
Public administration	1,184	1,286	1,326	1,242	1,188	1,204
Miscellaneous	1,463	1,597	1,636	1,725	1,699	1,745

Source: HMSO – Annual Abstract of Statistics 1992

*Butane, propane, ethane and refinery tail gases

†Supply greater than recorded demand (−). Includes losses in distribution

THE ELECTRICITY SUPPLY INDUSTRY

Under the Electricity Act 1989 twelve new public electricity supply companies were formed from the twelve Area Electricity Boards in England and Wales. These companies were floated on the stock market in November 1990. Four new companies were formed from the Central Electricity Generating Board: three new generating companies (National Power PLC, Nuclear Electric PLC and PowerGen PLC) and the National Grid Company PLC. National Power PLC and PowerGen PLC were floated on the stock market in February 1991, the Government retaining a 40 per cent holding in both companies.

In Scotland, there are three new companies: Scottish Power PLC, Scottish Hydro-Electric PLC and Scottish Nuclear Ltd. Flotation of Scottish Power PLC and Scottish Hydro-Electric PLC on the stock market took place in May 1991.

A new trade and representational organization, the Electricity Association, was created by the newly formed British electricity companies; its principal subsidiaries are Electricity Association Services Ltd (for representational and professional services) and Electricity Association Technology Ltd (for distribution and utilization research, development and technology transfer).

ELECTRICITY ASSOCIATION SERVICES LTD, 30 Millbank, London SW1P 4RD. Tel: 071–834 2333. *Chief Executive*, R. Farrance

ELECTRICITY ASSOCIATION TECHNOLOGY LTD, Capenhurst, Chester CH1 6ES. Tel: 051-339 4181. *Managing Director*, Dr S. F. Exell

CEGB SUCCESSOR COMPANIES

THE NATIONAL GRID COMPANY PLC, National Grid House, Sumner Street, London SE1 9JU. Tel: 071–620 8000. *Chief Executive*, B. Kerss

NATIONAL POWER PLC, Senator House, 85 Queen Victoria Street, London EC4V 4DP. Tel: 071–454 9494. *Chief Executive*, J. Baker

NUCLEAR ELECTRIC PLC, Barnett Way, Barnwood, Glos GL4 7RS. Tel: 0452–652222. *Chairman*, J. Collier

POWERGEN PLC, 53 New Broad Street, London EC2M 1JJ. Tel: 071–638 5742. *Chief Executive*, E. Walliss

REGIONAL ELECTRICITY COMPANIES

EAST MIDLANDS ELECTRICITY PLC, PO Box 4 North PDO, 398 Coppice Road, Arnold, Nottingham NG5 7HX

EASTERN ELECTRICITY PLC, PO Box 40, Wherstead, Ipswich IP2 9AQ

LONDON ELECTRICITY PLC, Templar House, 81–87 High Holborn, London WC1V 6NU

MANWEB PLC, Sealand Road, Chester CH1 4LR

MIDLANDS ELECTRICITY PLC, Mucklow Hill, Halesowen, W. Midlands B62 8BP

NORTHERN ELECTRIC PLC, Carliol House, Newcastle upon Tyne NE99 1SE

NORWEB PLC, Talbot Road, Manchester M16 0MQ

SEEBOARD PLC, Grand Avenue, Hove, E. Sussex BN3 2LS

SOUTH WALES ELECTRICITY PLC, St Mellons, Cardiff CF3 9XW

SOUTH WESTERN ELECTRICITY PLC, 800 Park Avenue, Aztec West, Almondsbury, Avon BS12 4SE

SOUTHERN ELECTRIC PLC, Littlewick Green, Maidenhead, Berks SL6 3QB

YORKSHIRE ELECTRICITY GROUP PLC, Scarcroft, Leeds LS14 3HS

SCOTTISH COMPANIES

SCOTTISH HYDRO-ELECTRIC PLC, 16 Rothesay Terrace, Edinburgh EH3 7SE. Tel: 031–225 1361. *Chief Executive*, R. Young

SCOTTISH NUCLEAR LTD, Minto Building, 6 Inverlair Avenue, Glasgow G44 4AD. Tel: 041–633 1166. *Chief Executive*, Dr R. C. Jeffrey

SCOTTISH POWER PLC, Cathcart House, Spean Street, Glasgow G44 4BE. Tel: 041–637 7177. *Chief Executive*, Dr I. Preston

GENERATION, SUPPLY AND CONSUMPTION

	gigawatt-hours 1989	1990
Electricity generated		
All generating companies: total	313,825	318,979
Conventional steam stations	234,991	245,732
Nuclear stations	71,734	65,747
Gas turbines	529	437
Hydro-electric stations:		
Natural flow	4,659	5,080
Pumped storage	1,910	1,982
Other (mainly wind)	2	n/a
Electricity used on works: total	20,234	19,558
Major generating companies	18,610	17,891
Other generators	1,624	1,666
Electricity supplied (gross)		
All generating companies: total	293,592	299,421
Conventional steam stations	223,037	233,391
Nuclear stations	63,602	58,664
Gas turbines and oil engines	494	407
Hydro-electric stations:		
Natural flow	4,645	5,067
Pumped storage	1,812	1,892
Other (mainly wind)	2	n/a
Electricity used in pumping		
Major generating companies	2,572	2,626
Electricity supplied (net): total	291,019	296,795
Major generating companies	271,714	277,978
Other generators	19,305	18,817
Net imports	12,631	11,943
Electricity available	303,650	308,738
Losses in transmission, etc	24,251	23,930
Electricity consumption: total	279,399	284,808
Fuel industries	9,001	9,974
Final users: total	270,398	274,834
Industrial sector	99,417	100,358
Domestic sector	92,270	93,793
Other sectors	78,711	80,683

Source: HMSO - Annual Abstract of Statistics 1992

THE GAS INDUSTRY

The gas industry in the United Kingdom was nationalized in 1949 under the Gas Act 1948, and operated as the Gas Council. The Gas Act 1972 replaced the Gas Council with the British Gas Corporation and led to greater centralization of the industry. The British Gas Corporation was privatized in 1986 as British Gas PLC and remains the main supplier of gas in Great Britain.

The principal business of British Gas is the purchase, transmission and sale of natural gas to domestic, industrial and commercial customers in Great Britain. British Gas has hydrocarbon exploration and production operations offshore and onshore, both in Great Britain and overseas, and it has an interest in gas-related activities world-wide.

BRITISH GAS PLC, Rivermill House, 152 Grosvenor Road, London SW1V 3JL. Tel: 071-821 1444. *Chairman and Chief Executive*, R. Evans, CBE

REGIONS

The Regions are largely concerned with the management of the gas business locally, including distribution and sale of gas, installation and servicing of appliances, meter reading, and the maintenance of emergency services.

EAST MIDLANDS, PO Box 145, De Montfort Street, Leicester LE1 9DB
EASTERN, Star House, Potters Bar, Herts. EN6 2PD
NORTH EASTERN, New York Road, Leeds LS2 7PE
NORTH THAMES, North Thames House, London Road, Staines, Middx. TW18 4AE
NORTH WESTERN, Welman House, Altrincham, Cheshire WA15 8AE
NORTHERN, PO Box 1GB, Killingworth, Newcastle upon Tyne NE99 1GB
SCOTLAND, Granton House, 4 Marine Drive, Edinburgh EH5 1YB
SOUTH EASTERN, Katherine Street, Croydon CR9 1JU
SOUTH WESTERN, Riverside, Temple Street, Keynsham, Bristol BS19 1EQ
SOUTHERN, 80 St Mary's Road, Southampton SO9 7GL
WALES, Helmont House, Churchill Way, Cardiff CF1 4NB
WEST MIDLANDS, Wharf Lane, Solihull, W. Midlands B91 2JP

SUPPLY AND TRANSMISSION

British Gas obtains natural gas from fields on mainland Britain, in coastal waters and in the North Sea. It also imports gas from other countries. In 1991 total gas production from UK continental shelf and Norwegian fields with gas contracted to British Gas was 62,037 million cubic metres, of which 61,839 million cubic metres was offshore production and 198 million cubic metres was onshore production.

The mainland national transmission system is operated by British Gas, with other gas suppliers entering contracts with British Gas to use the system. British Gas operates six reception terminals and 3,400 miles of pipeline. The length of mains in use in 1991 was 159,500 miles: 148,300 miles of distribution mains and 11,200 miles of transmission mains.

SALES

Total gas sold and used (1991) was (*million therms*):

Domestic	11,262
Commercial	3,414
Industrial	5,184
Used for own purposes	103
Total	20,096

Charges for domestic use are (from 4 July 1992):

Standing Charge per day (pence)	10.30
Unit charges (pence per kilowatt hour):	
Annual consumption	
1–5,000 therms	1.507
5,001–10,000 therms	1.439
10,001–15,000 therms	1.405
15,001–25,000 therms	1.371

BRITISH GAS FINANCE

	1990–1*	*£ million* 1991†
Turnover		
UK gas supply	7,930	8,423
Overseas gas supply	378	879
Exploration and production	978	980
UK marketing activities	745	774
Other activities	87	105
Less: intra-group sales	(627)	(676)
Total	9,491	10,485
Operating costs include:		
UK gas supply (includes levy)	3,674	3,834
Overseas gas supply	266	581
Payroll costs	1,390	1,647
Current cost depreciation less replacement expenditure	726	786
Current cost working capital adjustments	79	88
Total	7,836	8,812
Current cost operating profit	1,655	1,673
Gearing adjustment	41	39
Net interest payable	(140)	(243)
Current cost profit before tax	1,556	1,469
Current cost profit after tax	916	913
Minority shareholders' interest	2	8
Current cost profit attributable to British Gas shareholders	918	921
Dividends	(533)	(571)
Current cost profit retained	385	350

*Year ended 31 March
†Calendar year

New Towns in Great Britain

COMMISSION FOR THE NEW TOWNS

Glen House, Stag Place, London SWIE 5AJ

The Commission was established under the New Towns Act 1959. Its remit is to:

(a) take over and, with a view to its eventual disposal, to hold, manage and turn to account the property of development corporations transferred to the Commission

(b) dispose of property so transferred and any other property held by it, as soon as it considers it expedient to do so

In carrying out its remit the Commission must have due regard to the convenience and welfare of persons residing, working or carrying on business there and, until disposal, the maintenance and enhancement of the value of the land held and return obtained from it.

The Commission has such responsibilities in Basildon, Bracknell, Central Lancashire, Corby, Crawley, Harlow, Hatfield, Hemel Hempstead, Milton Keynes, Northampton, Peterborough, Redditch, Skelmersdale, Stevenage, Warrington and Runcorn, Washington and Welwyn Garden City.

The Commission has minimal responsibilities (principally financial and litigation) in Aycliffe and Peterlee, and Cwmbran following the wind-up of their development corporations in 1988.

Chairman, Sir Neil Shields, MC.
Members, R. B. Caws, CBE; W. J. Mackenzie, OBE; Sir Gordon Roberts, CBE; The Lord Bellwin; Sir Brian Jenkins, CBE; M. H. Mallinson; R. W. P. Luff; F. C. Graves, OBE; J. Trustram Eve; Ms W. Luscombe.
General Manager, N. J. Walker.

PROPERTIES

BASILDON, Essex. *Executive Officer*, H. Bacon. *Offices*, Gifford House, London Road, Bowers Gifford, Basildon SS13 2EX.
BRACKNELL, Berks. Glen House, London SWIE 5AJ.
CENTRAL LANCASHIRE, Lancs. *Executive Officer*, B. Birtwistle. *Offices*, Cuerden Pavilion, Shady Lane, Bamber Bridge, Preston PR5 6AZ.
CORBY, Northants. *Executive Officer*, J. G. Lloyd. *Offices*, Chisholm House, 9 Queen's Square, Corby NN17 IPA.
CRAWLEY, Sussex. Glen House, London SWIE 5AJ.
HARLOW, Essex. Glen House, London SWIE 5AJ.
HATFIELD, Herts. Glen House, London SWIE 5AJ.
HEMEL HEMPSTEAD, Herts. Glen House, London SWIE 5AJ.
MILTON KEYNES, Bucks. *Executive Officer*, J. Napleton. *Offices*, Saxon Court, 502 Avebury Boulevard, Central Milton Keynes MK9 3HS.
NORTHAMPTON. *Executive Officer*, I. McKay. *Offices*, Highfield House, Headless Cross Drive, Redditch B97 5EU.
PETERBOROUGH, Cambs. Glen House, London SWIE 5AJ.
REDDITCH, Worcs. *Executive Officer*, I. McKay. *Offices*, Highfield House, Headless Cross Drive, Reddich B97 5EU.
SKELMERSDALE, Lancs. *Executive Officer*, M. V. Anderson. *Offices*, Pennylands, Skelmersdale WN8 8AR.
STEVENAGE, Herts. Glen House, London SWIE 5AJ.
WARRINGTON AND RUNCORN, Cheshire. *Executive Officer*, J. Leigh. *Offices*, PO Box 49, New Town House, Buttermarket Street, Warrington WAI 2LF.
WASHINGTON, Tyne and Wear. *Executive Officer*, J. Edwards. *Offices*, 19 Parsons Road, District 2, Washington NE37 IEZ.
WELWYN GARDEN CITY, Herts. Glen House, London SWIE 5AJ.

DEVELOPMENT CORPORATIONS

ENGLAND

TELFORD, Shropshire. Formed 1963. *Chairman*, F. J. Jones. *General Manager*, M. D. Morgan. *Offices*, New Town House, Telford Square, Town Centre, Telford, Shropshire TF3 4JS. Area, 19,311 acres. Population, 117,500. Estimated eventual population, 130,000.

WALES

DEVELOPMENT BOARD FOR RURAL WALES. Formed 1977. *Chairman*, G. Davies. *Offices*, Ladywell House, Newtown, Powys SY16 IJB. TEL: 0686-626965.

SCOTLAND

CUMBERNAULD, Strathclyde. Formed 1956. *Chairman*, D. W. Mitchell, CBE. *Chief Executive*, D. Millan. *Headquarters*, Cumbernauld House, Cumbernauld G67 3JH. Area, 7,788 acres. Population, 50,100. Estimated eventual population, 55,000.
EAST KILBRIDE, Strathclyde. Formed 1947. *Chairman*, J. A. Denholm, CBE. *Managing Director*, J. C. Shaw. *Offices*, Atholl House, East Kilbride, Glasgow G74 ILU. Area, 10,250 acres. Population, 70,100. Estimated eventual population, 70,250.
GLENROTHES, Fife. Formed 1948. *Chairman*, Prof. C. Blake, CBE. *Chief Executive*, W. M. Cracknell. *Offices*, Unicorn House, Falkland Place, Glenrothes KY7 5PD. Area, 5,760 acres. Population, 38,900. Estimated eventual population, 48,000.
IRVINE, Ayrshire. Formed, 1966. *Chairman*, M. Crichton. *Managing Director*, Brig. R. A. Rickets. *Offices*, Perceton House, Irvine, Ayrshire KAII.2AL. Area, 12,800 acres. Population, 57,850. Estimated eventual population, 70,000.
LIVINGSTON, West Lothian. Formed 1962. *Chairman*, R. S. Watt, CBE. *Chief Executive*, J. A. Pollock. *Offices*, Sidlaw House, Almondvale, Livingston, West Lothian EH54 6QA. Area, 6,868 acres. Population, 42,480. Estimated eventual population, 55,000.

Local Government

ENGLAND AND WALES

The London Government Act 1963 and the Local Government Acts of 1972 and 1985 have brought about the present system of local government in England and Wales. The system is based on two tiers of local authorities, county and district councils, in the non-metropolitan areas; and a single tier, of metropolitan district and London borough councils, in the six metropolitan areas of England and in London respectively. Under the terms of the Local Government Act 1992, the two-tier structure of local government in England is to be reviewed.

Structure in England

England outside Greater London is divided into counties. Each county is divided into districts. Six metropolitan counties cover the main conurbations outside Greater London; Tyne and Wear, West Midlands, Merseyside, Greater Manchester, West Yorkshire and South Yorkshire. They are divided into 36 metropolitan districts, most of which have a population of over 200,000. There are 39 non-metropolitan counties; each of these is divided into non-metropolitan districts, of which there are 296. These districts have populations broadly in the range of 60,000 to 100,000; some however, have larger populations, because of the need to avoid dividing large towns, and some in mainly rural areas have smaller populations.

Greater London is divided into 32 London boroughs, with populations between 130,000 and 300,000, and the City, with a daytime population of 340,000 but only 4,000 by night.

There are also about 10,000 parishes, in 219 of the non-metropolitan and 18 of the metropolitan districts.

A permanent Local Government Boundary Commission keeps the areas and electoral arrangements under review, and makes proposals to the Secretary of State for changes found necessary.

Constitution and Elections

For districts, non-metropolitan counties, London boroughs, the City, and for about 8,000 parishes, there are elected councils, consisting of directly elected councillors. Broadly, county councils range from 60 to 100 members; metropolitan district councils 50–80 members; non-metropolitan district councils 30–60 members. The councillors elect annually one of their number as chairman.

The general pattern in England is that councillors serve four years and there are no elections of district and parish councillors in county election years. In metropolitan districts one-third of the councillors for each ward are elected each year except in the year of county elections. Non-metropolitan districts can choose whether to have elections by thirds or whole council elections. In the former case, one-third of the council, as nearly as may be, is elected in each year of metropolitan district elections. If whole council elections are chosen, these are held in the year midway between county elections. The London boroughs have whole council elections, in the year immediately following the county council election years. Local elections are normally held on the first Thursday in May.

Generally speaking, all British subjects or citizens of the Republic of Ireland of 18 years or over, resident on the qualifying date in the area for which the election is being held, are entitled to vote at local government elections. A register of electors is prepared and published annually by local electoral registration officers.

A returning officer has the overall responsibility for an election. Voting takes place at polling stations, arranged by the local authority and under the supervision of a presiding officer specially appointed for the purpose. Candidates, who are subject to various statutory qualifications and disqualifications designed to ensure that they are suitable persons to hold office, must be nominated by electors for the electoral area concerned.

Internal Organization

The council as a whole is the final decision-making body within any authority. Councils are free to a great extent to make their own internal organizational arrangements. Normally, questions of major policy are settled by the full council, while the administration of the various services is the responsibility of committees of members. Day-to-day decisions are delegated to the council's officers, who act within the policies laid down by the members.

Functions

Local authorities are empowered or required by various Acts of Parliament to carry out functions in their areas. The legislation concerned comprises public general Acts and 'local' Acts which local authorities have promoted as private bills. In non-metropolitan areas, functions are divided between the districts and counties, those requiring the larger area or population for their efficient performance going to the county. The metropolitan district councils, with the larger population in their areas, already had wider functions than non-metropolitan councils, and following abolition of the metropolitan county councils have now been given most of their functions also. A few functions continue to be exercised over the larger area by joint bodies, made up of councillors from each district.

The allocation of functions is as follows:

County councils: education; strategic planning; traffic, transport and highways; police; fire service; consumer protection; refuse disposal; smallholdings; social services; libraries.

Non-metropolitan district councils: local planning; housing; highways (maintenance of certain urban roads and off-street car parks); building regulations; environmental health; refuse collection; cemeteries and crematoria.

Metropolitan district and London borough councils: their functions are all those listed above, except that fire, civil defence (and in some cases, refuse disposal) in all areas and police and passenger transport in the metropolitan counties only are exercised by joint bodies.

Concurrently by county and district councils and London boroughs: recreation (parks, playing fields, swimming pools); museums; encouragement of the arts, tourism and industry.

The sewerage and sewage disposal functions of local authorities were transferred initially to water authorities and subsequently to the National Rivers Authority (NRA) and privatized public water companies.

The personal health functions of local authorities were transferred in 1977 to area health authorities, which were replaced in April 1982 by district health authorities. They work in close collaboration with local education, social services and environmental health authorities.

Parish Councils

Parishes with 200 or more electors must generally have parish councils, and about three-quarters of the parishes have councils. A parish council comprises at least five members, the number being fixed by the district council. Elections are held every four years, in the year in which the local district council is elected. All parishes have parish meetings, comprising the electors of the parish. Where there is no council, the meeting must be held at least twice a year.

Parish council functions include: allotments; encouragement of arts and crafts; community halls, recreational facilities (e.g. open spaces, swimming pools), cemeteries and crematoria; and many minor functions. They must also be given an opportunity to comment on planning applications. They may, like county and district councils, spend limited sums for the general benefit of the parish. They levy a precept on the district councils for their funds.

Civic Dignities

District councils may petition for a Royal Charter granting borough status to the district. In boroughs the chairman of the council is the mayor. The status 'City' and the right to call the mayor 'Lord Mayor' may also be granted by letters patent. Parish councils may call themselves 'town councils', in which case their chairman is the 'town mayor'.

Charter trustees were established for those former boroughs which were too large to have parish councils when local government was reorganized in 1974 and they became part of districts without city or borough status. The charter trustees are the district councillors representing the area of the former borough and they elect a town mayor, continue civic tradition, and look after the charters, insignia and civic plate of the former borough.

Local Commissioners

Commissioners for Local Administration in England and in Wales (*see* pages 332–3) have been appointed with the duty of investigating complaints of maladministration in aspects of local government; they report to the local council concerned.

WALES

Since 1974 Wales, including the former Monmouthshire, has been divided into eight counties. These are divided into 37 districts, many of those in the less populated parts reflecting the areas of former Welsh counties.

The arrangements for Welsh counties and districts are generally similar to those for English non-metropolitan counties and districts. There are some differences in functions; Welsh district councils have refuse disposal as well as refuse collection functions, and they may provide on-street as well as off-street car parks with the consent of the county council. A few districts have also been designated as library authorities.

Community Councils

In Wales parishes have been replaced by communities. Unlike England, where many areas are not in any parish, communities have been established for the whole of Wales, approximately 865 communities in all. Community meetings may be convened as and when desired.

Community councils exist in about 735 communities and further councils may be established at the request of a community meeting. Community councils have broadly the same range of powers as English parish councils. Community councillors are elected en bloc on the same basis as parish councillors in England, i.e. at the same time as a district council election and for a term of four years.

LOCAL GOVERNMENT FINANCE

Local government is financed mainly from three sources: community charges, non-domestic rates and government grants.

Community Charges

Community charges replaced domestic rates on 1 April 1990 under the provisions of the Local Government Finance Act 1988. They are raised by the charging authorities (district councils and, in London, borough councils and the City Corporation). Liability to pay a community charge arises from an entry in the community charges register which is compiled by the community charges registration officer of each charging authority. Sums required by county and parish councils and joint boards for police, fire and transport are included by the charging authority when calculating its community charge.

There are three types of charge: the personal community charge, payable by people aged 18 or over (unless exempt); the collective community charge paid in respect of certain designated buildings whose occupants move frequently and are difficult to register, and who will therefore pay their community charge contributions to the landlord; and the standard community charge which is payable in respect of domestic property which is not occupied.

The Personal Community Charge (Reductions) (England) Regulations provide for a scheme to limit household increases over rates. In general, reductions are awarded to individuals and households where the total community charge liability would otherwise have exceeded the rates payable in 1989–90 by more than £52 for the first two adults plus £52 for each successive chargepayer. There is additional help for the elderly or disabled who were not ratepayers.

The Local Government Finance Act 1992 provides for the community charge to be replaced from 1 April 1993 by the council tax. The tax will be payable by the occupiers of domestic property and will be related to the value of the dwelling. For this purpose, all dwellings will be placed in one of eight bands of value. There will be discounts in the case of dwellings occupied by fewer than two adults.

Non-domestic Rates

Non-domestic (business) rates have been collected since 1 April 1990 by charging authorities, i.e. by district councils, the Council of the Isles of Scilly, and in London by the borough councils and the Common Council of the City of London. The Local Government Finance Act 1988 provides for liability for rates to be assessed on the basis of a poundage (multiplier) tax on the rateable value of property (hereditaments). The multiplier is set by central government and rates collected by the charging authority for the area where a property is located. Rate income collected by charging authorities is paid into a central national non-domestic rating (NNDR) pool and redistributed to individual authorities on the basis of adult resident population. For the years 1990–1 to 1994–5 actual payment of rates in certain cases will be subjected to transitional arrangements, to phase in the larger increases and reductions in rates resulting from the combined effects of the 1990 revaluation and the introduction of a uniform national business rate (UBR).

Rateable values for the rating lists came into force on 1 April 1990. They are derived from the rental value of property as at 1 April 1988 and determined on certain statutory assumptions by valuation officers of the Board of Inland Revenue. New property is added to the list, and significant changes to existing property, necessitate amendments to the rateable value on the same basis. Rating lists remain in force until the next general revaluation, which is scheduled for 1 April 1995.

Certain types of property are exempt from rates, e.g. agricultural land and buildings, and places of public religious worship. Charities and other non-profit-making organizations may receive full or partial relief. Specified classes of empty property are liable to pay rates at 50 per cent.

Government Grants

In addition to specific grants in support of revenue expenditure on particular services, central government pays revenue support grant to local authorities. This grant is paid to each charging authority so that if all authorities in its area spend at a level sufficient to provide a standard level of service, it can set the same community charge before taking account of any transitional arrangements. In 1992–3 there are a number of transitional arrangements in operation to ease the transition from the old system of local authority finance.

Expenditure 1992–3

Local authority budgeted net revenue expenditure for 1992–3 in England was as follows. The amounts given are at 1992–3 cash prices.

Service	£m
Education	20,480
School catering	408
Libraries, museums and art galleries	704
Personal social services	5,015
Police	5,231
Fire	1,127
Other Home Office services	755
Local transport	2,479
Local environmental services	4,869
Agricultural services	31
Consumer protection and trading standards	130
Employment	182
Non-housing revenue account housing	339
Housing benefits	2,525
New Net Current Expenditure	44,274
Capital charges	3,526
Capital charged to revenue	655
Other non-current expenditure	2,477
Interest receipts	−1,062
Gross Revenue Expenditure	49,871
Specific grants	−10,842
Additional grant for teachers' pay	−51
Other income	−46
Net Revenue Expenditure	38,932

Aggregate external finance for 1992–3 was originally determined at £33,106 million. Of this, specific grants were estimated at £3,818 million and transitional grants at £359 million. £16,623 million was in respect of revenue support grant and £12,306 million was support from the national non-domestic rate pool. Following the teachers' pay award, an additional grant of £57 million was added to aggregate external finance, bringing the total to £33,163 million. Total standard spending by local authorities considered for grant purposes was £41,868 million.

Average Community Charges

The average charges levied in England for 1992–3 were: London boroughs, £264; metropolitan districts, £303; shire districts, £278. The average charge levied in England was £282.

Non-domestic Rates

National non-domestic rate (or uniform business rate) in England for 1992–3 is 40.2p. The amount estimated to be raised is £12.8 billion. Total rateable value held on local authority lists at 31 December 1991 was £31.0 billion.

SCOTLAND

Since 1975, mainland Scotland has been divided for local government purposes into nine regions within which there are 53 districts. Regional and district councils have separate responsibility for specific functions. In the three islands areas, Orkney, Shetland and the Western Isles, there are single tier Islands Councils responsible for most local authority functions.

Elections

In 1992 the register showed 3,927,427 electors in Scotland. Elections took place in 1990 for regional and island councils, and in 1992 for district councils.

Functions

Regional Councils: education; social work; strategic planning; the provision of infrastructure such as roads, water and sewerage; consumer protection; flood prevention; coast protection; valuation and rating; the police and fire services; civil defence; electoral registration; public transport; registration of births, deaths and marriages.

District Councils: housing; leisure and recreation, including tourism, parks, libraries, museums and galleries; development control and building control; environmental health, including cleansing, refuse collection and disposal, food hygiene, inspection of shops, offices and factories, clean air, markets and slaughterhouses, burial and cremation; licensing, including liquor, cinemas and theatres, taxis, street traders, betting and gaming, and charitable collections; allotments; public conveniences; the administration of district courts.

Community Councils

Unlike the parish councils of England or community councils of Wales, Scottish community councils are not local authorities. Their purpose as defined in statute is to ascertain and express the views of the communities which they represent, and to take in the interests of their communities such action as appears to be expedient or practicable. Over 1,000 community councils have been established under schemes drawn up by district and islands councils in Scotland.

Finance

In 1990–1 a total of £1,149,826,000 was received from non-domestic rates of local government in Scotland. The average non-domestic rate level was 57.3p. Total non-domestic water rate income was £17,611,000 and the average non-domestic water rate levied was 4.8p. Non-domestic sewerage rate income was £93,115,000 and the average non-domestic sewerage rate levied was 4.7p. Total metered water income was £77,961,000 and the average metered water rate levied was 32.5p.

A total of £1,007,723,000 was received from the community charge of local government in Scotland and the average personal community charge levied was £306.37. The community water charge receipts were £88,828,000 and the average community water charge levied was £22.99.

Provisional figures for 1991–2 show total receipts from non-domestic rates of £1,271,481,000 and £1,062,856,000 from the community charge. The average non-domestic rate per £ levied for 1991–2 was 48.1p and the average personal community charge payable in Scotland was £247.36.

LOCAL COMMISSIONER

The Commissioner for Local Administration in Scotland is responsible for investigating complaints from members of the public who claim to have suffered injustice as a consequence of maladministration in local government (*see* page 333).

NORTHERN IRELAND

For the purpose of local government Northern Ireland has a system of 26 single-tier district councils. There are 566 members of the councils, elected for periods of four years at a time on the principle of proportional representation.

The district councils all have the same three main roles. These are:

an executive role: responsibility for a wide range of local services including the provision of recreational, social, community, and cultural facilities; environmental health; consumer protection; the enforcement of building regulations; the promotion of tourist development schemes; street cleansing; refuse collection and disposal; litter prevention; and miscellaneous licensing and registration provisions, including dog control

a representative role: nominating representatives to sit as members of the various statutory bodies responsible for the administration of regional services such as education and libraries, health and personal social services, drainage, fire and electricity

a consultative role: acting as the media through which the views of local people are expressed on the operation in their area of other regional services, notably planning, roads, and conservation (including water supply and sewerage services) provided by those departments of central government which have an obligation, either statutorily or otherwise, to consult the district councils about proposals affecting their areas.

Political Composition of Local Councils

AS AT END MAY 1992

Abbreviations:

C.	Conservative
Com.	Communist
Dem.	Democrat
Green	Green
Ind.	Independent
Lab.	Labour
Lib.	Liberal
LD	Liberal Democrat
MK	Mebyon Kernow
NP	Non-political/Non-party
PC	Plaid Cymru
RA	Ratepayers'/Residents' Associations
SD	Social Democrat
SNP	Scottish National Party

ENGLAND

COUNTY COUNCILS

Avon	*Lab.* 36, *C.* 33, *LD* 7
Bedfordshire	*C.* 35, *Lab.* 25, *Official LD* 7, *LD* 3, *Others* 3
Berkshire	*C.* 37, *Lab.* 18, *LD* 15, *Ind.* 4, *Ind.C.* 1, *Lib.* 1
Buckinghamshire	*C.* 49, *Lab.* 12, *LD* 6, *Ind.* 2, *Lib.* 1, *SD* 1
Cambridgeshire	*C.* 45, *Lab.* 21, *LD* 8, *Ind.* 1, *Lib.* 1, *vacant* 1
Cheshire	*Lab.* 32, *C.* 29, *LD* 10
Cleveland	*Lab.* 48, *C.* 19, *LD* 10
Cornwall	*LD* 29, *Ind.* 24, *C.* 14, *Lab.* 8, *Lib.* 3, *MK* 1
Cumbria	*Lab.* 38, *C.* 35, *LD* 7, *Ind.* 3
Derbyshire	*Lab.* 52, *C.* 26, *LD* 4, *Ind.* 2
Devon	*C.* 56, *Lab.* 13, *LD* 11, *Ind.* 2, *SD* 2, *Lib.* 1
Dorset	*C.* 41, *LD* 23, *Ind.* 6, *Lab.* 6, *vacant* 1
Durham	*Lab.* 57, *C.* 7, *Ind.* 4, *LD* 4
East Sussex	*C.* 37, *Lab.* 17, *LD* 16
Essex	*C.* 57, *Lab.* 25, *LD* 15, *Ind.* 1
Gloucestershire	*C.* 23, *LD* 22, *Lab.* 17, *Others* 1
Hampshire	*C.* 55, *LD* 26, *Lab.* 20, *Ind.* 1
Hereford and Worcester	*C.* 38, *Lab.* 22, *LD* 12, *Ind.* 4
Hertfordshire	*C.* 45, *Lab.* 27, *LD* 5
Humberside	*Lab.* 42, *C.* 30, *LD* 3
Isle of Wight	*LD* 26, *C.* 15, *Ind.* 2
Kent	*C.* 54, *Lab.* 25, *LD* 20
Lancashire	*Lab.* 50, *C.* 42, *LD* 7
Leicestershire	*C.* 41, *Lab.* 32, *LD* 11, *vacant* 1
Lincolnshire	*C.* 42, *Lab.* 19, *LD* 12, *Ind.* 3
Norfolk	*C.* 46, *Lab.* 28, *LD* 10
Northamptonshire	*C.* 34, *Lab.* 31, *LD* 2, *Ind.* 1
Northumberland	*Lab.* 40, *C.* 17, *LD* 8, *Ind.* 1
North Yorkshire	*C.* 46, *Lab.* 21, *LD* 20, *Ind.* 6, *SD* 3
Nottinghamshire	*Lab.* 50, *C.* 35, *LD* 3
Oxfordshire	*C.* 33, *Lab.* 23, *LD* 13, *Ind.* 1

Shropshire	C. 29, Lab. 25, LD 9, NP 3
Somerset	C. 31, LD 17, Lab. 5, Ind. 2, vacant 2
Staffordshire	Lab. 48, C. 30, LD 2, RA 2
Suffolk	C. 46, Lab. 27, LD 4, Ind. 3
Surrey	C. 56, LD 10, Lab. 7, RA 2, Ind. 1
Warwickshire	C. 31, Lab. 24, LD 4, Ind. 3
West Sussex	C. 45, LD 17, Lab. 9
Wiltshire	C.&Ind. 38, LD 19, Lab. 15, Ind.&Lib. 3

METROPOLITAN DISTRICT COUNCILS

Greater Manchester

Bolton	Lab. 39, C. 16, LD 4, Ind.Lab. 1
Bury	Lab. 24, C. 22, LD 2
Manchester	Lab. 80, LD 12, C. 5, Others 2
Oldham	Lab. 33, LD 19, C. 7, Ind.Lab. 1
Rochdale	Lab. 23, LD 20, C. 16, Ind. Lab. 1
Salford	Lab. 54, C. 6
Stockport	LD 26, C. 17, Lab. 17, Ind. 3
Tameside	Lab. 48, C. 7, Others 1, vacant 1
Trafford	C. 37, Lab. 22, LD 4
Wigan	Lab. 61, LD 8, C. 2, Ind. Lab. 1

Merseyside

Knowsley	Lab. 60, C. 2, Ind. 2, Ind.Lab. 1, vacant 1
Liverpool	Lab. 40, LD 37, C. 2, Lib. 1, SD 1, Others 18
St Helens	Lab. 32, LD 15, C. 6, Others 1
Sefton	Lab. 27, C. 25, LD 17
Wirral	Lab. 31, C. 29, LD 6

South Yorkshire

Barnsley	Lab. 63, C. 2, Ind. 1
Doncaster	Lab. 54, C. 9
Rotherham	Lab. 64, C. 2
Sheffield	Lab. 67, C. 10, LD 9, vacant 1

Tyne and Wear

Gateshead	Lab. 55, LD 8, C. 1, Lib. 1, Others 1
Newcastle upon Tyne	Lab. 61, LD 11, C. 6
North Tyneside	Lab. 37, C. 16, LD 7
South Tyneside	Lab. 55, LD 4, Others 1
Sunderland	Lab. 64, C. 8, LD 3

West Midlands

Birmingham	Lab. 61, C. 43, LD 13
Coventry	Lab. 41, C. 13
Dudley	C. 36, Lab. 35, vacant 1
Sandwell	Lab. 42, C. 24, LD 6
Solihull	C. 24, Lab. 15, LD 6, RA 6
Walsall	Lab. 24, C. 23, LD 9, Ind. 4
Wolverhampton	Lab. 29, C. 28, LD 3

West Yorkshire

Bradford	Lab. 50, C. 38, LD 2
Calderdale	C. 25, Lab. 22, LD 7
Kirklees	Lab. 41, C. 19, LD 10, Ind. 2
Leeds	Lab. 67, C. 22, LD 8, Ind. 1, vacant 1
Wakefield	Lab. 55, C. 6, Others 2

NON-METROPOLITAN DISTRICT COUNCILS

* denotes councils where one third of councillors retire each year except the year of county council elections

*Adur	LD 22, C. 14, RA 2, Lab. 1
Allerdale	Lab. 31, C. 11, Ind. 11, LD 2
Alnwick	LD 15, C. 7, Ind. 5, Lab. 2
*Amber Valley	Lab. 22, C. 16, Ind. 3, Others 2
Arun	C. 36, LD 12, Lab. 7, Ind. 1
Ashfield	Lab. 32, C. 1
Ashford	C. 29, LD 12, Lab. 6, Ind. 2
Aylesbury Vale	C. 29, LD 22, Ind. 6, Lab. 1
Babergh	C. 15, Ind. 10, Lab. 6, LD 5, Others 6
*Barrow-in-Furness	C. 18, Lab. 18, Ind. 2
*Basildon	C. 26, Lab. 13, LD 3
*Basingstoke and Deane	C. 35, Lab. 11, LD 9, Ind. 2
*Bassetlaw	Lab. 30, Ind. 1, Ind.Lab. 1, LD 1
*Bath	C. 24, LD 17, Lab. 7
Berwick-upon-Tweed	LD 11, C. 7, Ind. 6, Lab. 1, Others 3
Beverley	C. 31, Lib. 19, Lab. 2, Ind. 1
Blaby	C. 30, Ind. 4, LD 4, Lab. 1
*Blackburn	Lab. 37, C. 19, LD 4
Blackpool	Lab. 27, C. 12, LD 5
Blyth Valley	Lab. 28, LD 19
Bolsover	Lab. 35, RA 2
Boothferry	C. 18, Lab. 12, Ind. 5
Boston	C. 11, Lab. 8, LD 8, Ind. 7
Bournemouth	LD 26, C. 21, Lab. 6, Ind. 4
Bracknell Forest	C. 32, Lab. 7, LD 1
Braintree	C. 24, Lab. 21, Ind. 9, LD 6
Breckland	C. 33, Ind. 11, Lab. 8, LD 1
*Brentwood	LD 24, C. 14, Lab. 1
Bridgnorth	C. 11, Ind. 8, LD 4, Ind.Lab. 2, NP 2, Lab. 1, Others 5
*Brighton	Lab. 24, C. 23, Ind. Lab. 1
*Bristol	Lab. 40, C. 22, LD 6
*Broadland	C. 27, Ind. 8, LD 8, Lab. 6
Bromsgrove	C. 26, Lab. 14, LD 1
*Broxbourne	C. 36, Lab. 4, LD 2
Broxtowe	C. 27, Lab. 15, LD 5, Ind. 2
*Burnley	Lab. 34, C. 8, LD 6
*Cambridge	Lab. 21, LD 12, C. 9
*Cannock Chase	Lab. 29, C. 9, LD 3, Ind. 1
Canterbury	LD 22, C. 19, Lab. 7, Ind. C. 1
Caradon	Ind. 21, LD 10, C. 6, RA 2, Lab. 1, vacant 1
*Carlisle	Lab. 30, C. 18, LD 2, Ind. 1
Carrick	LD 23, Ind. 9, C. 8, Lab. 4, vacant 1
Castle Morpeth	Ind. 9, Lab. 9, C. 8, LD 8
Castle Point	C. 37, Lab. 2
Charnwood	C. 34, Lab. 15, LD 2, Ind. 1
Chelmsford	C. 29, LD 21, Ind. 4, Lab. 2
*Cheltenham	LD 22, C. 12, Ind. 4, Lab. 3
*Cherwell	C. 33, Lab. 15, Ind. 1, Others 3
*Chester	C. 23, Lab. 19, LD 16, Ind. 2
Chesterfield	Lab. 31, LD 11, C. 5
Chester-le-Street	Lab. 27, Ind. 4, C. 1, Lib. 1
Chichester	C. 34, LD 14, Ind. 2
Chiltern	C. 39, LD 9, RA 2
*Chorley	Lab. 22, C. 20, LD 3, Ind.C. 2, Ind. 1
Christchurch	C. 13, Ind. 12
Cleethorpes	Lab. 16, C. 14, LD 11
*Colchester	LD 30, C. 21, Lab. 7
*Congleton	LD 19, C. 16, Lab. 10

Council	Composition
Copeland	Lab. 28, C. 20, Ind. 3
Corby	Lab. 23, LD 2, C. 1, Ind. 1
Cotswold	Ind. 16, C. 9, LD 3, Lab. 1, Others 16
*Craven	C. 13, LD 11, Ind. 5, Lab. 3, Ind.C. 1, Lib. 1
*Crawley	Lab. 22, C. 9, LD 1
*Crewe and Nantwich	Lab. 31, C. 24, LD 2
Dacorum	C. 38, Lab. 16, LD 4
Darlington	Lab. 30, C. 18, Ind. 2, LD 2
Dartford	C. 25, Lab. 20, RA 2
*Daventry	C. 19, Lab. 11, LD 3, Ind. 2
*Derby	C. 22, Lab. 22
Derbyshire Dales	C. 26, LD 9, Lab. 4
Derwentside	Lab. 38, Ind. 15, C. 2
Dover	C. 28, Lab. 20, LD 6, Ind. 2
Durham	Lab. 28, LD 15, Ind. 6
Easington	Lab. 39, Ind. 5, Lib. 4, Ind. Lab. 3
*Eastbourne	LD 17, C. 13
East Cambridgeshire	Ind. 10, C. 6, LD 4, Ind. C. 1, Lab. 1, Others 15
East Devon	C. 41, LD 10, Ind. 3, Green 2, Lib. 1, Ind.C. 1, Others 2
East Dorset	C. 20, LD 14, RA 2
East Hampshire	LD 20, C. 16, Ind. 6
East Hertfordshire	C. 32, LD 12, Ind. 3, Lab. 2, RA 1
*Eastleigh	C. 20, LD 18, Lab. 6
East Lindsey	Ind. 45, C. 6, LD 5, Lab. 4
East Northamptonshire	C. 23, Lab. 9, LD 3, vacant 1
East Staffordshire	Lab. 23, C. 19, LD 4
East Yorkshire	Ind. 20, C. 16, Lab. 4, SD 3
Eden	Ind. 24, RA 8, LD 4, Ind.C. 1
*Ellesmere Port and Neston	Lab. 30, C. 11
*Elmbridge	C. 21, RA 19, LD 10, Lab. 8, Ind. 1, vacant 1
*Epping Forest	C. 31, Lab. 13, RA 10, SD 3, LD 2
Epsom and Ewell	NP 30, LD 6, Lab. 3
Erewash	Lab. 27, C. 22, Ind. 2, LD 1
*Exeter	Lab. 16, C. 14, LD 5, Lib. 1
*Fareham	C. 30, LD 8, Lab. 4
Fenland	C. 27, Lab. 6, Ind. 4, LD 2, vacant 1
Forest Heath	C. 12, Ind. 9, LD 3, Lab. 1
Forest of Dean	Lab. 25, Ind. 9, SD 6, C. 4, Others 5
Fylde	C. 23, Ind. 11, RA 9, LD 4, Green 1, Lab. 1
Gedling	C. 38, Lab. 15, LD 3, Ind. 1
*Gillingham	LD 17, C. 16, Lab. 9
Glanford	C. 21, Ind. 10, Lab. 7, Green 3
*Gloucester	Lab. 16, C. 13, LD 5, Ind. 1
*Gosport	LD 17, C. 8, Lab. 3, Ind. 2
Gravesham	C. 22, Lab. 22
*Great Grimsby	Lab. 29, C. 13, LD 2, Ind. 1
*Great Yarmouth	Lab. 29, C. 18, LD 1
Guildford	C. 19, LD 19, Lab. 6, Ind. 1
*Halton	Lab. 44, LD 7, C. 2
Hambleton	C. 24, Ind. 13, LD 5, SD 3, Lab. 2
Harborough	C. 18, LD 12, Ind. 4, Lab. 3
*Harlow	Lab. 31, C. 8, LD 3
*Harrogate	LD 29, C. 20, Lab. 4, Ind. 2, Ind.C. 2, Green 1, Lib. 1, SD 1
*Hart	C. 16, LD 12, Ind. 7
*Hartlepool	Lab. 28, C. 12, LD 6, Ind. 1
*Hastings	C. 14, Lab. 9, LD 9
*Havant	C. 20, Lab. 12, Ind. 5, LD 5
*Hereford	LD 22, Lab. 4, C. 1
*Hertsmere	C. 23, Lab. 12, LD 3, Ind. 1
High Peak	Lab. 16, C. 15, LD 10, Ind. 3
Hinckley and Bosworth	C. 21, LD 9, Lab. 3, Ind. 1
Holderness	Ind. 24, LD 7
Horsham	C. 27, LD 13, Ind.C. 2, vacant 1
Hove	C. 21, Lab. 6, LD 3
*Huntingdonshire	C. 42, LD 7, Lab. 3, Ind. 1
*Hyndburn	Lab. 32, C. 12, LD 3
*Ipswich	Lab. 33, C. 15
Kennet	C. 17, Ind. 14, LD 8, Lab. 1
Kerrier	LD 16, Lab. 11, NP 11, C. 5, vacant 1
Kettering	Lab. 20, C. 11, LD 8, Ind. 6
King's Lynn and West Norfolk	C. 38, Lab. 16, LD 5, Ind. 1
*Kingston upon Hull	Lab. 57, LD 2, C. 1
Kingswood	Lab. 26, C. 18, LD 5, Ind. 1
Lancaster	Lab. 24, C. 15, Ind. 14, LD 7
Langbaurgh on Tees	Lab. 29, C. 22, LD 7, Ind.Lab. 1
Leicester	Lab. 37, C. 13, LD 6
*Leominster	Ind. 15, LD 7, C. 6, Ind.C. 3, Lab. 2, Green 1, Lib. 1, vacant 1
Lewes	LD 27, C. 17, Ind. 3, vacant 1
Lichfield	C. 37, Lab. 15, Ind.Lab. 3, Ind. 1
*Lincoln	Lab. 30, C. 3
Luton	Lab. 28, C. 11, LD 9
*Macclesfield	C. 34, LD 13, Lab. 10, RA 3
*Maidstone	C. 26, LD 15, Lab. 8, Ind. 6
Maldon	C. 13, Ind. 9, Lib. 6, Ind.C. 1, Lab. 1
Malvern Hills	Ind. 18, LD 16, C. 14, Lab. 2, Green 1
Mansfield	Lab. 39, C. 5, LD 2
Medina	C. 18, LD 13, Lab. 3, Ind. 2
Melton	C. 18, LD 8
Mendip	LD 20, C. 13, Ind. 7, Lab. 3
Mid Bedfordshire	C. 43, LD 4, Ind. 3, Lab. 3
Mid Devon	Ind. 27, LD 9, Lib. 2, Lab. 1, Ind.SD 1
Middlesbrough	Lab. 38, C. 9, LD 5, Ind. 1
Mid Suffolk	C. 17, LD 10, Lab. 8, Ind.C. 5
*Mid Sussex	C. 34, LD 13, Ind. 5, Lab. 2
*Milton Keynes	Lab. 21, C. 15, LD 9, Ind. 1
*Mole Valley	LD 18, C. 13, Ind. 9, Lab. 1
Newark and Sherwood	Lab. 28, C. 19, LD 4, Ind. 3
Newbury	LD 23, C. 20, Ind. 1, vacant 1
*Newcastle under Lyme	Lab. 36, C. 10, LD 10
New Forest	LD 30, C. 22, Ind. 6
Northampton	Lab. 21, C. 18, LD 4
Northavon	LD 25, C. 20, Lab. 11, Ind. 1
*North Bedfordshire	C. 25, Lab. 15, LD 10, Ind. 3
North Cornwall	Ind. 30, LD 5, Lab. 2, C. 1
North Devon	LD 25, Ind. 15, C. 2, vacant 2
North Dorset	Ind. 21, LD 12
North East Derbyshire	Lab. 33, C. 12, Ind. 4, LD 3, vacant 1
*North Hertfordshire	C. 27, Lab. 16, LD 3, RA 3, Ind. 1
North Kesteven	C. 10, Lab. 6, LD 5, Ind. 2, Ind.C. 1, Others 15
North Norfolk	C. 24, Lab. 6, LD 5, Ind. 4, Others 7
North Shropshire	Ind. 29, C. 7, Lab. 4
North Warwickshire	Lab. 20, C. 12, Ind. 1, NP 1
North West Leicestershire	Lab. 25, C. 10, Ind. 4, vacant 1

North Wiltshire	*LD* 29, *C.* 16, *Ind.* 3, *Lab.* 3, *Others* 1
*Norwich	*Lab.* 35, *LD* 10, *C.* 3
Nottingham	*Lab.* 37, *C.* 17, *Green* 1
*Nuneaton and Bedworth	*Lab.* 36, *C.* 9
*Oadby and Wigston	*LD* 19, *C.* 7
Oswestry	*Ind.* 11, *C.* 8, *Lab.* 6, *LD* 3, *vacant* 1
*Oxford	*Lab.* 35, *C.* 10, *LD* 5, *Ind. LD* 1
*Pendle	*Lab.* 27, *LD* 16, *C.* 7, *vacant* 1
*Penwith	*C.* 11, *Lab.* 10, *Ind.* 7, *LD* 4, *Ind.Lab.* 1, *MK* 1
*Peterborough	*C.* 22, *Lab.* 19, *Lib.* 6, *vacant* 1
Plymouth	*Lab.* 41, *C.* 17, *LD* 1, *vacant* 1
Poole	*LD* 20, *C.* 16
*Portsmouth	*C.* 17, *Lab.* 14, *LD* 7, *Ind.* 1
*Preston	*Lab.* 32, *C.* 20, *LD* 5
*Purbeck	*C.* 11, *Ind.* 6, *LD* 5
*Reading	*Lab.* 29, *C.* 11, *LD* 4, *Others* 1
*Redditch	*Lab.* 20, *C.* 9
*Reigate and Banstead	*C.* 24, *Lab.* 11, *LD* 10, *RA* 3, *Ind.* 1
Restormel	*LD* 28, *Ind.* 13, *C.* 2, *Lab.* 1
Ribble Valley	*C.* 24, *LD* 13, *Ind.* 1, *Lab.* 1
Richmondshire	*Ind.* 28, *LD* 4, *C.* 1, *Ind.C.* 1
Rochester upon Medway	*C.* 21, *Lab.* 21, *LD* 7, *vacant* 1
*Rochford	*LD* 19, *C.* 12, *Lab.* 7, *Ind.* 2
*Rossendale	*Lab.* 21, *C.* 15
Rother	*C.* 19, *LD* 16, *Ind.* 7, *Lab.* 3
*Rugby	*C.* 20, *Lab.* 15, *RA* 6, *Ind.* 3, *LD* 3, *vacant* 1
*Runnymede	*C.* 28, *Lab.* 7, *Ind.* 6, *Green* 1
Rushcliffe	*C.* 43, *LD* 6, *Lab.* 5
*Rushmoor	*C.* 30, *LD* 9, *Lab.* 6
Rutland	*Ind.* 9, *C.* 7, *LD* 4
Ryedale	*LD* 20, *Ind.* 14, *C.* 6, *Lab.* 2
*St Albans	*LD* 24, *C.* 23, *Lab.* 9, *Ind.* 1
St Edmundsbury	*C.* 25, *Lab.* 11, *LD* 5, *Ind.* 2, *vacant* 1
Salisbury	*C.* 32, *Ind.* 11, *LD* 9, *Lab.* 6
Scarborough	*Lab.* 16, *C.* 15, *Ind.* 10, *LD* 8
*Scunthorpe	*Lab.* 33, *C.* 6, *SD* 1
Sedgefield	*Lab.* 33, *LD* 8, *Ind.* 4, *C.* 2, *Others* 2
Sedgemoor	*C.* 26, *Lab.* 12, *LD* 7, *Ind.* 4
Selby	*C.* 22, *Lab.* 13, *Ind.* 10, *LD* 3, *Ind.Lab.* 2
Sevenoaks	*C.* 31, *Ind.* 11, *LD* 11
Shepway	*LD* 32, *C.* 18, *Lab.* 3, *Ind.* 2, *vacant* 1
*Shrewsbury and Atcham	*C.* 21, *Lab.* 18, *LD* 5, *Ind.* 4
*Slough	*Lab.* 29, *C.* 5, *LD* 5
*Southampton	*Lab.* 30, *C.* 9, *LD* 6
*South Bedfordshire	*C.* 37, *Lab.* 8, *LD* 6, *Ind.* 1, *vacant* 1
South Bucks	*C.* 30, *Ind.* 10, *LD* 1
*South Cambridgeshire	*C.* 26, *Ind.* 20, *Lab.* 5, *LD* 4
South Derbyshire	*Lab.* 20, *C.* 11, *Ind. C.* 2, *Ind.* 1
*Southend-on-Sea	*C.* 25, *LD* 8, *Lab.* 6
South Hams	*C.* 23, *Ind.* 8, *NP* 7, *LD* 4, *Ind.C.* 1, *Lab.* 1
*South Herefordshire	*Ind.* 30, *C.* 4, *LD* 4, *RA* 1
South Holland	*Lab.* 9, *C.* 6, *Ind.* 2, *Others* 20, *vacant* 1
South Kesteven	*C.* 24, *Lab.* 13, *Ind.* 10, *LD* 9, *Lib.* 1
*South Lakeland	*C.* 17, *LD* 15, *Ind.* 14, *Lab.* 6
South Norfolk	*C.* 22, *LD.* 22, *Ind.* 3
South Northamptonshire	*C.* 28, *Ind.C.* 9, *Lab.* 2, *Lib.* 1
South Oxfordshire	*C.* 29, *LD* 8, *Ind.* 5, *Lab.* 5, *RA* 3
South Ribble	*C.* 33, *Lab.* 15, *LD* 6
South Shropshire	*C.* 7, *Ind.* 6, *LD* 3, *Lab.* 2, *Others* 22
South Somerset	*LD* 41, *C.* 14, *Ind.* 5
South Staffordshire	*C.* 37, *Lab.* 9, *LD* 3, *Ind.* 1
South Wight	*LD* 12, *C.* 7, *Ind.* 4, *Others* 1
Spelthorne	*C.* 33, *Lab.* 4, *LD* 3
Stafford	*C.* 28, *Lab.* 18, *LD* 13, *vacant* 1
Staffordshire Moorlands	*RA* 23, *C.* 14, *Lab.* 9, *Ind.* 6, *LD* 4
*Stevenage	*Lab.* 32, *C.* 4, *LD* 3
Stockton-on-Tees	*Lab.* 26, *C.* 17, *LD* 11, *Ind. Lab.* 1
*Stoke-on-Trent	*Lab.* 48, *C.* 12
*Stratford-upon-Avon	*C.* 28, *LD* 19, *Ind.* 7, *Lab.* 1
*Stroud	*C.* 23, *Lab.* 14, *LD* 10, *Green* 5, *Ind.* 3
Suffolk Coastal	*C.* 37, *Ind.* 7, *Lab.* 7, *LD* 4
Surrey Heath	*C.* 31, *LD* 4, *Lab.* 1
*Swale	*C.* 20, *Lab.* 14, *LD* 14, *Ind.* 1
*Tamworth	*Lab.* 21, *C.* 8, *Ind.* 1
*Tandridge	*C.* 20, *LD* 18, *Lab.* 4
Taunton Deane	*LD* 29, *C.* 13, *Lab.* 7, *Ind.* 4
Teesdale	*Ind.* 21, *Lab.* 8, *C.* 2
Teignbridge	*Ind.* 23, *C.* 18, *LD* 13, *Lab.* 4
Tendring	*LD* 20, *C.* 17, *Lab.* 12, *RA* 4, *Ind.* 3, *Ind.C.* 2, *Others* 2
Test Valley	*C.* 26, *LD* 15, *Ind.* 2, *NP* 1
Tewkesbury	*Ind.* 20, *C.* 7, *LD* 6, *Lab.* 3
*Thamesdown	*Lab.* 33, *C.* 14, *LD* 6, *Ind.* 1
Thanet	*C.* 29, *Lab.* 14, *Ind.* 8, *LD* 2, *vacant* 1
*Three Rivers	*C.* 21, *LD* 18, *Lab.* 9
*Thurrock	*Lab.* 29, *C.* 9, *Ind.* 1
*Tonbridge and Malling	*C.* 32, *LD* 17, *Lab.* 6
*Torbay	*LD* 20, *C.* 13, *Lab.* 2, *SD* 1
Torridge	*C.* 6, *Ind.* 4, *Lab.* 4, *LD* 4, *Green* 1, *Others* 17
*Tunbridge Wells	*C.* 30, *LD* 14, *Lab.* 3, *Ind.* 1
Tynedale	*C.* 17, *Lab.* 14, *LD* 9, *Ind.* 6, *Others* 1
Uttlesford	*C.* 24, *LD* 11, *Ind.* 6, *Lab.* 1
Vale of White Horse	*C.* 29, *LD* 18, *Ind.* 2, *Lab.* 2
Vale Royal	*Lab.* 32, *C.* 24, *LD* 3, *Ind.* 1
Wansbeck	*Lab.* 44, *LD* 2
Wansdyke	*C.* 23, *Lab.* 20, *Ind.Lab.* 3, *LD* 1
Warrington	*Lab.* 42, *LD* 9, *C.* 8, *Ind.Lab.* 1
Warwick	*C.* 24, *Lab.* 10, *LD* 8, *RA* 3
*Watford	*Lab.* 22, *C.* 10, *LD* 4
*Waveney	*Lab.* 25, *C.* 17, *LD* 5, *vacant* 1
Waverley	*C.* 28, *LD* 27, *Lab.* 2
Wealden	*C.* 44, *LD* 11, *Ind.* 3
Wear Valley	*LD*, 28, *Lab.* 8, *Ind.* 4
Wellingborough	*C.* 19, *Lab.* 11, *Ind.* 4
*Welwyn Hatfield	*C.* 24, *Lab.* 23
West Devon	*Ind.* 17, *LD* 6, *C.* 5, *Green* 1, *Lab.* 1
West Dorset	*C.* 18, *LD* 12, *NP* 11, *Ind.* 7, *Lab.* 4, *Ind.C.* 1, *SD* 1, *vacant* 1
*West Lancashire	*C.* 27, *Lab.* 27, *LD* 1
*West Lindsey	*Ind.* 11, *C.* 10, *LD* 9, *Lab.* 7
*West Oxfordshire	*Ind.* 20, *C.* 15, *LD* 8, *Lab.* 6
West Somerset	*Ind.* 23, *C.* 5, *Lab.* 3, *LD* 1
West Wiltshire	*LD* 21, *C.* 9, *Lib.* 6, *Lab.* 3, *Ind.* 2, *Ind.Lib.* 1, *Others* 1
*Weymouth and Portland	*C.* 10, *Lab.* 10, *LD* 10, *Ind.* 5

*Winchester	*C.* 23, *LD* 23, *Lab.* 6, *Ind.* 3
Windsor and Maidenhead	*C.* 26, *LD* 25, *RA* 7
*Woking	*C.* 19, *LD* 11, *Lab.* 5
*Wokingham	*C.* 34, *LD* 19, *Lab.* 1
Woodspring	*C.* 36, *LD* 14, *Ind.* 4, *Lab.* 4, *Green* 1
*Worcester	*Lab.* 22, *C.* 11, *Ind.* 1, *LD* 1, *vacant* 1
*Worthing	*C.* 22, *LD* 14
Wrekin	*Lab.* 33, *C.* 10, *LD* 2, *Ind.* 1
Wychavon	*C.* 32, *LD* 10, *Lab.* 6, *Ind.* 1
Wycombe	*C.* 38, *LD* 10, *Lab.* 9, *Ind.* 3
Wyre	*C.* 32, *Lab.* 17, *LD* 5, *Ind.* 1, *RA* 1
*Wyre Forest	*Lab.* 21, *LD* 11, *C.* 9, *Ind.* 1
*York	*Lab.* 33, *C.* 7, *LD* 4, *vacant* 1

GREATER LONDON BOROUGHS

Barking and Dagenham	*Lab.* 44, *RA* 3, *LD* 1
Barnet	*C.* 39, *Lab.* 18, *LD* 3
Bexley	*C.* 35, *Lab.* 17, *LD* 9, *Ind.* 1
Brent	*C.* 31, *Lab.* 24, *LD* 7, *Ind.* 2, *Ind.C.* 2
Bromley	*C.* 43, *Lab.* 11, *LD* 6
Camden	*Lab.* 41, *C.* 15, *LD* 2, *Ind.* 1
City of Westminster	*C.* 45, *Lab.* 15
Croydon	*C.* 39, *Lab.* 29, *vacant* 2
Ealing	*C.* 40, *Lab.* 30
Enfield	*C.* 35, *Lab.* 31
Greenwich	*Lab.* 44, *C.* 11, *SD* 4, *LD* 2, *vacant* 1
Hackney	*Lab.* 44, *C.* 8, *LD* 6, *Ind.* 2
Hammersmith and Fulham	*Lab.* 28, *C.* 21, *vacant* 1
Haringey	*Lab.* 44, *C.* 15
Harrow	*C.* 28, *Lab.* 13, *LD* 12, *Ind.C.* 7, *Ind.* 3
Havering	*Lab.* 25, *C.* 19, *RA* 13, *LD* 6
Hillingdon	*C.* 35, *Lab.* 34
Hounslow	*Lab.* 44, *C.* 15, *LD* 1
Islington	*Lab.* 47, *LD* 4, *C.* 1
Kensington and Chelsea	*C.* 39, *Lab.* 14, *vacant* 1
Kingston upon Thames	*C.* 25, *LD* 18, *Lab.* 7
Lambeth	*Lab.* 39, *C.* 20, *LD* 5
Lewisham	*Lab.* 58, *C.* 6, *LD* 3
Merton	*Lab.* 29, *C.* 22, *RA* 5, *Ind. Lab.* 1
Newham	*Lab.* 52, *C.* 3, *LD* 2, *vacant* 3
Redbridge	*C.* 42, *Lab.* 18, *LD* 3
Richmond upon Thames	*LD* 48, *C.* 4
Southwark	*Lab.* 36, *LD* 22, *C.* 6
Sutton	*LD* 32, *C.* 18, *Lab.* 6
Tower Hamlets	*LD* 29, *Lab.* 21
Waltham Forest	*Lab.* 30, *C.* 15, *LD* 11, *Ind.* 1
Wandsworth	*C.* 48, *Lab.* 13

WALES

COUNTY COUNCILS

Clwyd	*Lab.* 33, *Ind.* 14, *C.* 10, *Others* 7, *vacant* 2
Dyfed	*Ind.* 32, *Lab.* 27, *PC* 4, *LD* 3, *Ind.Lab.* 1, *Lib.* 1, *RA* 1, *vacant* 1
Gwent	*Lab.* 53, *C.* 7, *Ind.* 1, *vacant* 2
Gwynedd	*Ind.* 27, *Lab.* 12, *PC* 12, *LD* 6, *NP* 5
Mid Glamorgan	*Lab.* 63, *PC* 6, *Ind.* 2, *LD* 1, *RA* 1, *vacant* 1
Powys	*Ind.* 40, *Lab.* 5, *vacant* 1
South Glamorgan	*Lab.* 42, *C.* 14, *LD* 5, *PC* 1
West Glamorgan	*Lab.* 45, *C.* 5, *Ind.* 5, *LD* 2, *PC* 1, *RA* 1, *vacant* 2

DISTRICT COUNCILS

Aberconwy	*Lab.* 11, *LD* 10, *C.* 9, *Ind.* 6, *PC* 1, *Others* 4
Alyn and Deeside	*Lab.* 27, *C.* 8, *Ind.C.* 4, *LD* 2, *Ind.Lab.* 1, *vacant* 1
Arfon	*Ind.* 14, *PC* 14, *Lab.* 8, *LD* 2, *Others* 1
Blaenau Gwent	*Lab.* 32, *RA* 5, *Ind.* 3, *PC* 2, *C.* 1, *Lib.* 1
Brecknock	*Ind.* 29, *Lab.* 13, *LD* 2
Cardiff	*Lab.* 39, *C.* 16, *LD* 9, *Ind.* 1
Carmarthen	*Ind.* 27, *Lab.* 6, *PC* 2, *LD* 1, *RA* 1
Ceredigion	*Ind.* 31, *LD* 9, *PC* 3, *Lab.* 1
Colwyn	*Ind.* 12, *LD* 12, *C.* 7, *Lab.* 3
Cynon Valley	*Lab.* 25, *PC* 10, *Ind.* 2, *Others* 1
Delyn	*Ind.* 19, *Lab.* 12, *LD* 3, *C.* 2, *PC* 2, *Others* 4
Dinefwr	*Lab.* 15, *Ind.C.* 9, *PC* 4, *Ind.* 3, *vacant* 1
Dwyfor	*PC* 7, *Others* 22
Glyndŵr	*Ind.* 25, *Lab.* 6, *LD* 2, *PC* 1, *vacant* 1
Islwyn	*Lab.* 30, *PC* 5
Llanelli	*Lab.* 20, *LD* 3, *Green* 2, *Ind.* 1, *PC* 1, *Others* 8
Lliw Valley	*Lab.* 22, *Ind.* 6, *PC* 4, *C.* 1
Meirionnydd	*Ind.* 24, *PC* 13, *Lab.* 4
Merthyr Tydfil	*Lab.* 20, *RA* 7, *Ind.Lab.* 3, *PC* 1, *Others* 2
Monmouth	*C.* 22, *Lab.* 14, *Ind.* 3, *LD* 1
Montgomeryshire	*NP* 36, *Lab.* 4, *LD* 3, *C.* 1, *PC* 1, *vacant* 1
Neath	*Lab.* 25, *PC* 5, *LD* 2, *Ind.* 1, *Others* 1
Newport	*Lab.* 40, *C.* 7
Ogwr	*Lab.* 38, *C.* 8, *Ind.Lab.* 1, *LD* 1, *vacant* 1
Port Talbot	*Lab.* 21, *RA* 6, *SD* 2, *Ind.* 1, *LD* 1
Preseli Pembrokeshire	*Ind.* 36, *Lab.* 2, *C.* 1, *LD* 1
Radnorshire	*Ind.* 29, *Lab.* 4
Rhondda	*Lab.* 26, *PC* 4, *RA* 3
Rhuddlan	*Lab.* 11, *Others* 21
Rhymney Valley	*Lab.* 27, *PC* 13, *Ind.* 4, *Ind.Lab.* 1, *RA* 1
South Pembrokeshire	*Ind.* 26, *Lab.* 2, *PC* 2
Swansea	*Lab.* 30, *C.* 11, *LD* 6, *Ind.* 5
Taff-Ely	*Lab.* 19, *PC* 14, *Ind.* 4, *C.* 2, *LD* 2, *RA* 1, *SD* 1
Torfaen	*Lab.* 36, *Ind.* 3, *LD* 3, *C.* 1, *Com.* 1
Vale of Glamorgan	*Lab.* 20, *C.* 18, *PC* 3, *Others* 5
Wrexham Maelor	*Lab.* 29, *Ind.* 6, *LD&Lib.* 6, *C.* 4, *PC* 1
Ynys Môn	*Ind.* 25, *PC* 8, *Lab.* 5, *C.* 1

SCOTLAND

REGIONAL AND ISLANDS COUNCILS

Borders	*Ind.* 13, *LD* 6, *C.* 2, *SNP* 2
Central	*Lab.* 22, *SNP* 6, *C.* 5, *Ind.* 1
Dumfries and Galloway	*Lab.* 11, *Ind.* 9, *SNP* 3, *Lib.* 2, *C.* 1, *Ind.Lab.* 1, *Others* 8
Fife	*Lab.* 30, *LD* 10, *C.* 2, *SNP* 2, *Com.* 1, *Ind.* 1
Grampian	*Lab.* 17, *SNP* 14, *C.* 13, *LD* 9, *Ind.* 3, *Ind.Lab.* 1
Highland	*Ind.* 34, *Lab.* 10, *LD* 3, *SNP* 2, *C.* 1, *Green* 1, *Ind.LD* 1
Lothian	*Lab.* 34, *C.* 12, *LD* 2, *SNP* 1
Orkney	*Ind.* 23, *SNP* 1
Shetland	*Ind.* 25
Strathclyde	*Lab.* 89, *C.* 5, *LD* 4, *Ind.* 3, *SNP* 1, *vacant* 1
Tayside	*Lab.* 18, *C.* 14, *SNP* 10, *LD* 2, *Ind.* 1, *Ind.Lab.* 1
Western Isles	*Ind.* 30

DISTRICT COUNCILS

Aberdeen	*Lab.* 27, *LD* 13, *C.* 10, *SNP* 2
Angus	*SNP* 11, *C.* 7, *Ind.* 2, *Others* 1
Annandale and Eskdale	*LD* 10, *NP* 5, *Lab.* 1
Argyll and Bute	*Ind.* 10, *C.* 4, *LD* 3, *SNP* 2, *Lab.* 1, *Others* 6
Badenoch and Strathspey	*Ind.* 11
Banff and Buchan	*Ind.* 10, *SNP* 7, *LD* 1
Bearsden and Milngavie	*C.* 5, *LD* 4, Lab. 1
Berwickshire	*C.* 8, *Ind.* 3, *LD* 1
Caithness	*Ind.* 15, *LD* 1
Clackmannan	*Lab.* 8, *SNP* 3, *C.* 1
Clydebank	*Lab.* 8, *SNP* 2, *C.* 1, *Ind.* 1
Clydesdale	*Lab.* 7, *SNP* 4, *C.* 3, *Ind.* 2
Cumbernauld and Kilsyth	*Lab.* 7, *SNP* 5
Cumnock and Doon Valley	*Lab.* 10
Cunninghame	*Lab.* 20, *C.* 6, *SNP* 3, *Ind.* 1
Dumbarton	*Lab.* 8, *C.* 5, *SNP* 2, *NP* 1
Dundee	*Lab.* 26, *C.* 12, *SNP* 6
Dunfermline	*Lab.* 22, *LD* 5, *SNP* 4, *C.* 2, *Others* 1
East Kilbride	*Lab.* 12, *C.* 2, *SNP* 2
East Lothian	*Lab.* 9, *C.* 7, *SNP* 1
Eastwood	*C.* 8, *RA* 2, *Lab.* 1, *LD* 1
Edinburgh	*Lab.* 30, *C.* 23, *LD* 7, *SNP* 2
Ettrick and Lauderdale	*Ind.* 15, SNP 1
Falkirk	*Lab.* 16, *SNP* 14, *C.* 3, *Ind.* 3
Glasgow	*Lab.* 54, *C.* 5, *Ind. Lab.* 2, *SNP* 2, *LD* 1, *Others* 2
Gordon	*Ind.* 9, *LD* 5, *C.* 2
Hamilton	*Lab.* 15, *C.* 2, *LD* 2, *Ind.Lab.* 1
Inverclyde	*Lab.* 11, *LD* 8, *C.* 1
Inverness	*Ind.* 13, *Lab.* 8, *LD* 5, *Lib.* 1, *SNP* 1
Kilmarnock and Loudoun	*Lab.* 8, *SNP* 7, *C.* 3
Kincardine and Deeside	*C.* 5, *Ind.* 5, *LD* 1, *SNP* 1
Kirkcaldy	*Lab.* 26, *SNP* 7, *Ind.* 3, *C.* 2, *LD* 2
Kyle and Carrick	*C.* 16, *Lab.* 9
Lochaber	*Ind.* 8, *Lab.* 3, *SNP* 3, *Ind.Lab.* 1
Midlothian	*Lab.* 12, *C.* 2, *SNP* 1
Monklands	*Lab.* 17, *SNP* 3
Moray	*Ind.* 9, *SNP* 7, *C.*1, *Lab.* 1
Motherwell	*Lab.* 22, *SNP* 4, *C.* 2, *Ind.* 2
Nairn	*Ind.* 8, *C.* 1, *SNP* 1
Nithsdale	*Lab.* 9, *Ind.* 8, *C.* 5, *SNP* 5, *LD* 1
North East Fife	*LD* 13, *C.* 4, *Ind.* 1
Perth and Kinross	*C.* 16, *SNP* 5, *Ind.* 3, *Lab.* 3, *LD* 2
Renfrew	*Lab.* 23, *SNP* 12, *C.* 8, *LD* 2
Ross and Cromarty	*Ind.* 16, *SNP* 4, *C.* 1, *Lab.* 1
Roxburgh	*Ind.* 7, *LD* 5, *C.* 1, *NP* 1, *SNP* 1, *Others* 1
Skye and Lochalsh	*Ind.* 10, *SNP* 1
Stewartry	*Ind.* 4, *C.* 1, *Others* 7
Stirling	*C.* 10, *Lab.* 10
Strathkelvin	*Lab.* 9, *C.* 6
Sutherland	*Ind.* 14
Tweeddale	*Ind.* 6, *LD* 2, *Lab.* 1, *SNP* 1
West Lothian	*SNP* 11, *Lab.* 10, *C.* 2, *Ind.* 1
Wigtown	*Ind.* 6, *NP* 4, *SNP* 2, *C.* 1, *Lab.* 1

England

Position and Extent

The Kingdom of England lies between 55° 46′ and 49° 57′ 30″ N. latitude (from a few miles north of the mouth of the Tweed to the Lizard), and between 1° 46′ E. and 5° 43′ W. (from Lowestoft to Land's End). England is bounded on the north by the Cheviot Hills; on the south by the English Channel; on the east by the Straits of Dover (Pas de Calais) and the North Sea; and on the west by the Atlantic Ocean, Wales and the Irish Sea. It has a total area of 50,377 sq. miles (130,478 sq. km): land 50,085 sq. miles (129,720 sq. km); inland water 293 sq. miles (758 sq. km).

Population

The population at the 1981 Census was 46,362,836 (males 22,520,723; females 23,842,113). The preliminary report on the 1991 Census put the population at 46,161,000. The average density of the population in 1981 was 915 per square mile.

Flag

The cross of St George, the patron saint of England (cross gules in a field argent), has been used since the 13th century.

Relief

There is a marked division between the upland and lowland areas of England. In the extreme north the Cheviot Hills (highest point, The Cheviot, 2,674 ft) form a natural boundary with Scotland. Running south from the Cheviots, though divided from them by the Tyne Gap, is the Pennine range (highest point, Cross Fell, 2,930 ft), the main orological feature of the country. The Pennines culminate in the Peak District of Derbyshire (Kinder Scout, 2,088 ft). West of the Pennines are the Cumbrian mountains, which include Scafell Pike (3,210 ft), the highest peak in England, and to the east are the Yorkshire Moors, their highest point being Urra Moor (1,490 ft).

In the west, the foothills of the Welsh mountains extend into the bordering English counties of Shropshire (the Wrekin, 1,334 ft; Long Mynd, 1,694 ft) and Hereford and Worcester (the Malvern Hills – Worcestershire Beacon, 1,394 ft). Extensive areas of high land and moorland are also to be found in the south-western peninsula formed by Somerset, Devon and Cornwall: principally Exmoor (Dunkery Beacon, 1,704 ft), Dartmoor (High Willhays, 2,038 ft) and Bodmin Moor (Brown Willy, 1,377 ft). Ranges of low, undulating hills run across the south of the country, including the Cotswolds in the Midlands and south-west, the Chilterns to the north of London, and the North (Kent) and South (Sussex) Downs of the south-east coastal areas.

The lowlands of England lie in the Vale of York, East Anglia and the area around the Wash. The lowest-lying are the Cambridgeshire Fens in the valleys of the Great Ouse and the River Nene, which are below sea-level in places. Since the 17th century extensive drainage has brought much of the Fens under cultivation. The North Sea coast between the Thames and the Humber, low-lying and formed of sand and shingle for the most part, is subject to erosion and defences against further incursion have been built along many stretches.

Hydrography

The Severn is the longest river in Great Britain, rising in the north-eastern slopes of Plinlimmon (Wales) and entering England in Shropshire with a total length of 220 miles (354 km) from its source to its outflow into the Bristol Channel, where it receives on the east the Bristol Avon, and on the west the Wye, its other tributaries being the Vyrnwy, Tern, Stour, Teme and Upper (or Warwickshire) Avon. The Severn is tidal below Gloucester, and a high bore or tidal wave sometimes reverses the flow as high as Tewkesbury (13½ miles above Gloucester). The scenery of the greater part of the river is very picturesque and beautiful, and the Severn is a noted salmon river, some of its tributaries being famous for trout. Navigation is assisted by the Gloucester and Berkeley Ship Canal (16¾ miles), which admits vessels of 350 tons to Gloucester. The Severn Tunnel was begun in 1873 and completed in 1886 at a cost of £2,000,000 and after many difficulties from flooding. It is 4 miles 628 yards in length (of which 2¼ miles are under the river). The Severn road bridge between Haysgate, Gwent, and Almondsbury, Glos., with a centre span of 3,240 ft, was opened in 1966.

The longest river wholly in England is the Thames, with a total length of 215 miles (346 km) from its source in the Cotswold hills to the Nore, and is navigable by ocean-going ships to London Bridge. The Thames is tidal to Teddington (69 miles from its mouth) and forms county boundaries almost throughout its course; on its banks are situated London, Windsor Castle, the home of the Sovereign, Eton College, the first of the public schools, and Oxford, the oldest university in the kingdom.

Of the remaining English rivers those flowing into the North Sea are the Tyne, Wear, Tees, Ouse and Trent from the Pennine Range, the Great Ouse (160 miles), which rises in Northamptonshire, and the Orwell and Stour from the hills of East Anglia. Flowing into the English Channel are the Sussex Ouse from the Weald, the Itchen from the Hampshire Hills, and the Axe, Teign, Dart, Tamar and Exe from the Devonian hills. Flowing into the Irish Sea are the Mersey, Ribble and Eden from the western slopes of the Pennines and the Derwent from the Cumbrian mountains.

The English Lakes, noteworthy for their picturesque scenery and poetic associations, lie in Cumbria, the largest being Windermere (10 miles long), Ullswater and Derwentwater.

Islands

The Isle of Wight is separated from Hampshire by the Solent. The capital, Newport, stands at the head of the estuary of the Medina, Cowes (at the mouth) being the chief port. Other centres are Ryde, Sandown, Shanklin, Ventnor, Freshwater, Yarmouth, Totland Bay, Seaview and Bembridge.

Lundy (= Puffin Island), 11 miles north-west of Hartland Point, Devon, is about two miles long and about half a mile broad (average), with a total area of about 1,116 acres, and a population of about 20. It became the property of the National Trust in 1969 and is now principally a bird sanctuary.

The Isles of Scilly consist of about 140 islands and skerries (total area, 6 square miles/10 square km) situated 28 miles south-west of Land's End. Only five are inhabited: St Mary's, St Agnes, Bryher, Tresco and St Martin's. The population is 1,978. The entire group has been designated a Conservation Area, a Heritage Coast, and an Area of Outstanding Natural Beauty, and has been given National Nature Reserve status by the Nature Conservancy Council because of its unique flora and fauna. Tourism and the winter/spring flower trade for the home market form the basis of the economy of the Isles. The island group is a recognized rural development area.

Climate

England has a generally mild and temperate climate. Because of the prevailing south-westerly winds, the weather day to day is variable, being affected mainly by depressions moving eastwards across the Atlantic Ocean. This maritime influence means that the west of the country tends to experience wetter but also milder weather than the east. Rainfall also increases with altitude, the mountainous areas of the north and west having more rain than the lowlands of the south and east. Rain is fairly well distributed throughout the year in all areas but, on average, the driest months are March to June, and the wettest September to January.

The mean annual temperature reduced to sea-level varies from 11°C in the south-west to 9°C near Berwick-upon-Tweed. In winter, temperatures tend to be higher in the south and west than in the east, while the warmest in summer are the south and inland areas. Latitude for latitude the mean annual temperature is lower in the east; the decrease of mean temperature with height is about 0.6°C per 100 metres.

EARLY HISTORY

Prehistoric Inhabitants

Archaeological evidence suggests that England has been inhabited since at least the Palaeolithic period, though the extent of the various Palaeolithic cultures was dependent upon the degree of glaciation. The succeeding Neolithic and Bronze Age cultures have left abundant remains throughout the country, the best-known of these being the henges and stone circles of Stonehenge (ten miles north of Salisbury, Wilts.) and Avebury (Wilts.), both of which are believed to have been of religious significance. In the latter part of the Bronze Age the Goidels, a people of Celtic race, and in the Iron Age other Celtic races of Brythons and Belgae, invaded the country and brought with them Celtic civilization and dialects, place names in England bearing witness to the spread of the invasion over the whole kingdom.

The Roman Conquest

The Roman conquest of Gaul (57–50 BC) brought Britain into close contact with Roman civilization, but although Julius Caesar raided the south of Britain in 55 BC and 54 BC, conquest was not undertaken until nearly 100 years later. In AD 43 the Emperor Claudius dispatched Aulus Plautius, with a well-equipped force of 40,000, and himself followed with reinforcements in the same year. Success was delayed by the resistance of Caratacus (Caractacus), the British leader from AD 48–51, who was finally captured and sent to Rome, and by a great revolt in AD 61 led by Boudicca (Boadicea), Queen of the Iceni; but the south of Britain was secured by AD 70, and Wales and the area north to the Tyne by about AD 80.

In AD 122, the Emperor Hadrian visited Britain and built a continuous rampart, since known as Hadrian's Wall, from Wallsend to Bowness (Tyne to Solway). The work was entrusted by the Emperor Hadrian to Aulus Platorius Nepos, legate of Britain from AD 122 to 126, and it was intended to form the northern frontier of the Roman Empire.

The Romans administered Britain as a province under a Governor, with a well-defined system of local government, each Roman municipality ruling itself and surrounding territory, while London was the centre of the road system and the seat of the financial officials of the Province of Britain. Colchester, Lincoln, York, Gloucester and St Albans stand on the sites of five Roman municipalities, and Wroxeter, Caerleon, Chester, Lincoln and York were at various times the sites of legionary fortresses. Well-preserved Roman towns have been uncovered at (or near) Silchester (*Calleva Atrebatum*), ten miles south of Reading, Wroxeter (*Viroconium Cornoviorum*), near Shrewsbury, and St Albans (*Verulamium*) in Hertfordshire.

Four main groups of roads radiated from London, and a fifth (the Fosse) ran obliquely from Lincoln through Leicester, Cirencester and Bath to Exeter. Of the four groups radiating from London, one ran south-east to Canterbury and the coast of Kent, a second to Silchester and thence to parts of western Britain and south Wales, a third (later known as Watling Street) ran through Verulamium to Chester, with various branches, and the fourth reached Colchester, Lincoln, York and the eastern counties.

In the fourth century Britain was subject to raids along the east coast by Saxon pirates, which led to the establishment of a system of coast defence from the Wash to Southampton Water, with forts at Brancaster, Burgh Castle (Yarmouth), Walton (Felixstowe), Bradwell, Reculver, Richborough, Dover, Lympne, Pevensey and Porchester (Portsmouth). The Irish (Scoti) and Picts in the north were also becoming more aggressive; from about AD 350 incursions became more frequent and more formidable. As the Roman Empire came under attack increasingly towards the end of the fourth century, many troops were removed from Britain for service in other parts of the empire. The island was eventually cut off from Rome by the Teutonic conquest of Gaul, and with the withdrawal of the last Roman garrison early in the fifth century, the Romano-British were left to themselves.

Saxon Settlement

According to legend, the British King Vortigern called in the Saxons to defend him against the Picts, the Saxon chieftains being Hengist and Horsa, who landed at Ebbsfleet, Kent, and established themselves in the Isle of Thanet; but the events during the one and a half centuries between the final break with Rome and the re-establishment of Christianity are unclear. However, it would appear that in the course of this period the raids turned into large-scale settlement by invaders traditionally known as Angles (England north of the Wash and East Anglia), Saxons (Essex and southern England) and Jutes (Kent and the Weald), which pushed the Romano-British into the mountainous areas of the north and west, Celtic culture outside Wales and Cornwall surviving only in topographical names. Various kingdoms were established at this time which attempted to claim overlordship of the whole country, hegemony finally being achieved by Wessex (capital, Winchester) in the ninth century. This century also saw the beginning of raids by the Vikings (Danes), which were resisted by Alfred the Great (871–899), who fixed a limit to the advance of Danish settlement by the Treaty of Wedmore (878), giving them the area north and east of Watling Street, on condition that they adopt Christianity.

In the tenth century the kings of Wessex recovered the whole of England from the Danes, but subsequent rulers were unable to resist a second wave of invaders. England paid tribute (*Danegeld*) for many years, and was invaded in 1013 by the Danes and ruled by Danish kings from 1016 until 1042, when Edward the Confessor was recalled from exile in Normandy. In 1066 Harold Godwinson (brother-in-law of Edward and son of Earl Godwin of Wessex) was chosen King of England. After defeating (at Stamford Bridge, Yorkshire, 25 September) an invading army under Harald Hadraada, King of Norway (aided by the outlawed Earl Tostig of Northumbria, Harold's brother), Harold was himself defeated at the Battle of Hastings on 14 October 1066, and the Norman conquest secured the throne of England for Duke William of Normandy, a cousin of Edward the Confessor.

CHRISTIANITY

Christianity reached the Roman province of Britain from Gaul in the third century (or possibly earlier); Alban, traditionally Britain's first martyr, was put to death as a Christian during the persecution of Diocletian (22 June 303), at his native town Verulamium; and the Bishops of Londinium, Eboracum (York), and Lindum (Lincoln) attended the Council of Arles in 314. However, the Anglo-Saxon invasions submerged the Christian religion in England until the sixth century when conversion was undertaken in the north from 563 by Celtic missionaries from Ireland led by St Columba, and in the south by a mission sent from Rome in 597 which was led by St Augustine, who became the first archbishop of Canterbury. England appears to have been converted again by the end of the seventh century and followed, after the Council of Whitby in 663, the practices of the Roman Church, which brought the kingdom into the mainstream of European thought and culture.

PRINCIPAL CITIES

BIRMINGHAM

Birmingham (West Midlands) is Britain's second city and the largest metropolitan district in the country. It is a focal point in national communications networks with a rapidly expanding International Airport. The generally accepted derivation of 'Birmingham' is the *ham* or dwelling-place of the *ing* or family of *Beorma*, presumed to have been a Saxon. During the Industrial Revolution the town grew into a major manufacturing centre. In 1889 Birmingham was granted City status.

Despite the decline in manufacturing, Birmingham is still a major hardware trade and motor component industry centre. Recent development includes the National Exhibition Centre and the Aston Science Park. An Urban Development Agency has been set up.

The principal buildings are the Town Hall, built in 1832–4; the Council House (1879); Victoria Law Courts (1891); the University (1909); the 13th century Church of St Martin (rebuilt 1873); the Cathedral (formerly St Philip's Church) (1711) and the Roman Catholic Cathedral of St Chad (1839–41).

BRADFORD

Bradford (West Yorkshire), 192 miles north-north-west of London, is the administrative centre of the Metropolitan District of Bradford. The District covers an area of 91,444 acres and lies on the southern edge of the Yorkshire Dales National Park, including within its boundaries the village of Haworth, home of the Brontë sisters, and Ilkley Moor.

Originally a Saxon township, Bradford received a market charter in 1251 but developed only slowly until the industrialization of the textile industry brought rapid growth during the 19th century. The prosperity of that period is reflected in much of the city's architecture, particularly the public buildings: City Hall (1873), Wool Exchange (1867), St George's Hall (Concert Hall, 1853), Cartwright Hall (Art Gallery, 1904) and Technical College (1882). Other chief buildings are the Cathedral (15th century) and Bolling Hall (14th century).

Textiles still play an important part in the city's economy but industry is now more broadly based, including engineering and micro-electronics. The city has a strong banking, insurance and building society sector, and a growing tourism industry.

BRISTOL

Bristol (Avon) is the largest non-metropolitan district in population in the country, and lies 119 miles west of London. The present municipal area is 10,954 hectares.

Bristol was a Royal Borough before the Norman Conquest. The earliest form of the name is *Bricgstow*. In 1373 it received from Edward III a charter granting it county status.

The chief buildings include the 12th century Cathedral (with later additions), with Norman chapter house and gateway, the 14th century Church of St Mary Redcliffe, Wesley's Chapel, Broadmead, the Merchant Venturers' Almshouses, the Council House (1956), Guildhall, Exchange (erected from the designs of John Wood in 1743), Cabot Tower, the University and Clifton College. The Roman Catholic Cathedral at Clifton was opened in 1973.

The Clifton Suspension Bridge, with a span of 702 feet over the Avon, was projected by Brunel in 1836 but was not completed until 1864. Brunel's SS *Great Britain*, the first ocean-going propeller-driven ship, is now being restored in the City Docks from where she was launched in 1843. The docks themselves have been extensively restored and redeveloped.

CAMBRIDGE

Cambridge, a settlement far older than its ancient University, lies on the River Cam or Granta, 51 miles north of London. It has an area of 10,060 acres.

The city is a county town and regional headquarters. Its industries include electronics, flour milling, cement making and the manufacture of scientific instruments. Among its open spaces are Jesus Green, Sheep's Green, Coe Fen, Parker's Piece, Christ's Pieces, the University Botanic Garden, and the Backs, or lawns and gardens through which the Cam winds behind the principal line of college buildings. East of the Cam, King's Parade, upon which stand Great St Mary's Church, Gibbs' Senate House and King's College Chapel with Wilkins' screen, joins Trumpington Street to form one of the most beautiful throughfares in Europe.

University and college buildings provide the outstanding features of Cambridge architecture but several churches (especially St Benet's, the oldest building in the City, and St Sepulchre's, the Round Church) also are notable. The modern Guildhall (1939) stands on a site of which at least part has held municipal buildings since 1224.

CANTERBURY

Canterbury, the Metropolitan City of the Anglican Communion, has a history going back to prehistoric times. It was the Roman *Durovernum Cantiacorum* and the Saxon *Cant-wara-byrig* (stronghold of the men of Kent). Here in 597 St Augustine began the conversion of the English to Christianity, when Ethelbert, King of Kent, was baptized.

Of the Benedictine St Augustine's Abbey, burial place of the Jutish Kings of Kent (whose capital Canterbury was) only extensive ruins remain. St Martin's Church, on the eastern outskirts of the city, is stated by Bede to have been the place of worship of Queen Bertha, the Christian wife of King Ethelbert, before the advent of St Augustine.

In 1170 the rivalry of Church and State culminated in the murder in Canterbury Cathedral, by Henry II's knights, of Archbishop Thomas Becket, whose shrine became a great centre of pilgrimage, as described by Chaucer in his *Canterbury Tales*. After the Reformation pilgrimages ceased, but the prosperity of the city was strengthened by an influx of Huguenot refugees, who introduced weaving. The Elizabethan poet and playwright Christopher Marlowe was born and reared in Canterbury, and there are literary associations also with Defoe, Dickens, Joseph Conrad and Somerset Maugham.

The Cathedral, with architecture ranging from the 11th to 15th centuries, is world famous. Modern pilgrims are attracted particularly to the Martyrdom, the Black Prince's Tomb, the Warriors' Chapel and the many examples of medieval stained glass.

The medieval city walls are built on Roman foundations and the 14th century West Gate is one of the finest buildings of its kind in the country.

The 1,000 seat Marlowe Theatre is the base for the Canterbury International Festival of the Arts each autumn.

CARLISLE

Carlisle is situated at the confluence of the River Eden and River Caldew, 309 miles north-west of London and about ten miles from the Scottish border. It has an area of 254,955 acres, and was granted a charter in 1158.

The city stands at the western end of Hadrian's Wall and dates from the original Roman settlement of ***Luguvalium***. Granted to Scotland in the tenth century, Carlisle is not included in the Domesday Book. William Rufus reclaimed the area in 1092 and the castle and city walls were built to guard Carlisle and the western border; the citadel is a Tudor addition to protect the south of the city. Until the Union of the Crowns in 1603, Carlisle changed hands several times and was frequently besieged. During the Civil War the city remained Royalist; in 1745 it supported the Young Pretender.

The Cathedral, originally a 12th century Augustinian priory, was enlarged in the 13th and 14th centuries after the diocese was created in 1133. To the south is a restored Tithe Barn and nearby the 18th century church of St Cuthbert, the third to stand on a site dating from the seventh century.

Carlisle is the major shopping, commercial and agricultural centre for the area, and industries include the manufacture of metal goods, biscuits and textiles. However, the largest employer is the services sector, notably in retailing and transport. The city has an important communications position at the centre of a network of major roads, as an important stage on the main west coast rail services, and with its own airport at Crosby.

CHESTER

Chester is situated on the River Dee, 189 miles north-west of London. The city administers an area of 173 square miles and was granted Borough and City status in 1974.

Chester's recorded history dates from the first century when the Romans founded the fortress of *Deva*. The city's name is derived from the Latin *castra* (a camp or encampment). During the Middle Ages, Chester was the principal port of north-west England but declined with the silting of the Dee estuary and competition from Liverpool. The city was also an important military centre, notably during Edward I's Welsh campaigns and the Elizabethan Irish campaigns. During the Civil War, Chester supported the King and was besieged from 1643–6. Chester's first charter was granted *c.*1175 and the city was incorporated in 1506. The office of Sheriff is the earliest created in the country (*c.*1120s), and in 1992 the Mayor was granted the title of Lord Mayor. He also enjoys the title 'Admiral of the Dee'.

The city's architectural features include the city walls (an almost complete two-mile circuit), the unique Rows (covered galleries above the street level shops), the Victorian Gothic Town Hall (1869), the Castle (rebuilt 1788 and 1822) and numerous half-timbered buildings. The Cathedral was a Benedictine abbey until the Dissolution. Remaining monastic buildings include the chapter house, refectory and cloisters and there is a modern free-standing bell tower. The Norman church of St John the Baptist was a cathedral church in the early Middle Ages.

Chester is primarily a regional service centre and has considerable tourist appeal. In 1984 the city was awarded Development Area status, which has attracted a range of nationally-known companies to expand or locate in Chester.

COVENTRY

Coventry (West Midlands) is 92 miles north-west of London, and has an important industrial centre, producing vehicles, machine tools, agricultural machinery, man-made fibres, aerospace components and telecommunications equipment. New investment has come from the financial services, power transmission, professional services and educational sectors.

The city owes its beginning to Leofric, Earl of Mercia, and his wife Godiva who, in 1043, founded a Benedictine monastery. The guildhall of St Mary dates from the 14th century, three of the city's churches date from the 14th and 15th centuries and 16th century almshouses may still be seen. Coventry's first cathedral was destroyed at the Reformation, its second in the 1940 blitz (its walls and spire remain) and the new cathedral designed by Sir Basil Spence, consecrated in 1962, now draws innumerable visitors.

Coventry is the home of the University of Warwick and its Science Park, Coventry University, the rapidly-expanding Westwood Business Park and the Museum of British Road Transport.

DERBY

Derby stands on the banks of the River Derwent, 127 miles north-north-west of London, and covers an area of 30 square miles. The name Derby dates back to 880 when the Danes settled in the locality and changed the original Saxon name of *Northworthy* to *Deoraby*.

Derby has a wide range of industries: its products include aero engines, lawn mowers, pipework, specialized mechanical engineering equipment, textiles, chemicals, plastics and the Royal Crown Derby porcelain. The city is an established railway centre, the site of British Rail's Technical Centre with its research laboratories.

Buildings of interest include St Peter's Church and the Old Abbey Building (14th century), the Cathedral (1525), St Mary's Roman Catholic Church (1839) and the Industrial Museum, formerly the Old Silk Mill (1721). The traditional city centre is complemented by the new Eagle Centre and 'out-of-centre' retail developments. In addition to the Derby Playhouse, the Assembly Rooms are a multi-purpose venue.

The first charter granting a Mayor and Aldermen was that of Charles I in 1637. Previous charters date back to 1154. It was granted City status in 1977.

DURHAM

The city of Durham is a district in the county of Durham and covers an area of 73 square miles. The city is a major tourist attraction in the county because of its prominent Norman Cathedral and Castle set high on a wooded peninsula overlooking the River Wear. The Cathedral was founded as a shrine for the body of St Cuthbert in 995. The present building dates from 1093 and among its many treasures is the tomb of the Venerable Bede (673–735). Durham's Prince Bishops had unique powers up to 1836, being lay rulers as well as religious leaders. As a palatinate Durham could have its own army, nobility, coinage and courts. The Castle was the main seat of the Prince Bishops for nearly 800 years; it is now used as a college by the University.

The University, founded on the initiative of Bishop William Van Mildert, is England's third oldest. Its students live in 14 colleges spread across the city.

Among other buildings of interest is the Guildhall in the Market Place which dates originally from the 14th century. Much work has been carried out to conserve this area, forming part of the city's major contribution to the Council of Europe's Urban Renaissance Campaign. Annual events include Durham's Regatta in June (claimed to be the oldest rowing event in Britain) and the Annual Gala (formerly Durham Miners' Gala) in July.

In the past 20 years the economy of Durham has undergone a significant change with the replacement of mining as the dominant feature by 'white collar' employment. Although still a predominantly rural area, the industrial and commercial sector is growing and a wide range of manufacturing and service industries are based on industrial estates in and around the City area.

EXETER

Exeter lies on the River Exe 170 miles south-west of London and ten miles from the sea. It covers an area of 11,661 acres and was granted a Royal Charter by Henry II.

The Romans founded *Isca Dumnoniorum* in the first century AD, and in the third century a stone wall (most of which remains) was built, providing protection against Saxon, and then Danish invasions. After the Conquest, the city led resistance to William in the west, until reduced by siege. The Normans built the motte and bailey castle of Rougemont, the gatehouse and one tower of which remain, although the rest was pulled down in 1784. The first bridge across the Exe was built in the 13th century. The city's role as a port declined due to the silting of the river, but was somewhat restored by the construction in the 1560s of the first ship canal in England. Exeter was the Royalist headquarters in the west during the Civil War.

The diocese of Exeter was established by Edward the Confessor in 1050, although a church existed on the Cathedral site in the early tenth century. A new cathedral was built in the 12th century but the present building was begun *c.*1275 in the Gothic style, although incorporating the Norman towers, and completed about a century later with the west front. The Guildhall dates from the 12th century and there are many other medieval buildings in the city, as well as architecture in the Georgian and Regency styles (Custom House, The Quay). Damage suffered by bombing in 1942 led to the redevelopment of the city centre.

Exeter's prosperity from medieval times was based on trade in wool and woollen cloth (commemorated by Tuckers Hall), which remained at its height until the late 18th century when export trade was hit by the French Wars. Subsequently Exeter has developed as an administrative and commercial centre, notably in the distributive trades, light manufacturing industries and tourism.

KINGSTON UPON HULL

Hull (officially Kingston upon Hull) lies in the mostly rural county of Humberside, at the junction of the River Hull with the Humber, 22 miles from the North Sea and 205 miles north of London. The municipal area is 17,535 acres.

Hull is one of the great seaports of the United Kingdom. It has docks covering a water area of 172 acres, equipped to handle cargoes by unit-load techniques, and is a departure point for car ferry services to continental Europe. There is a great variety of industry and service industries, as well as increasing tourism and conference business.

The city, restored after very heavy air raid damage during the Second World War, has good office and administrative buildings, its municipal centre being the Guildhall, its educational centre the University of Hull and its religious centre the Parish Church of the Holy Trinity. The old town area is being renovated and includes a new marina and shopping complex. Just west of the city is the Humber Bridge, the world's longest single span suspension bridge, which was officially opened by The Queen in July 1981.

Kingston upon Hull was so named by Edward I. City status was accorded in 1897 and the office of Mayor raised to the dignity of Lord Mayor in 1914.

LEEDS

Leeds (West Yorkshire), a Metropolitan District from 1 April 1974, is a junction for road, rail, canal and air services and an important commercial centre, situated in the lower Aire Valley, 195 miles by road north-north-west of London. The metropolitan area is 138,915 acres.

Seventy per cent of employment is in services, notably the distributive trades, public administration, medical services and business services. The main manufacturing industries are mechanical engineering, printing and publishing, metal goods and clothing.

The principal buildings are the Civic Hall (1933), the Town Hall (1858), the Municipal Buildings and Art Gallery (1884) with the Henry Moore Gallery (1982), the Corn Exchange (1863) and the University. The Parish Church (St Peter's) was rebuilt in 1841; the 17th century St John's Church has a fine interior with a famous English Renaissance screen; the last remaining 18th century church is Holy Trinity, Boar Lane (1727). Kirkstall Abbey (about three miles from the centre of the city), founded by Henry de Lacy in 1152, is one of the most complete examples of Cistercian houses now remaining. Temple Newsam, birthplace of Lord Darnley, was acquired by the Council in 1922. The present house was largely rebuilt by Sir Arthur Ingram in about 1620. Adel Church, about five miles from the centre of the city, is a fine Norman structure.

Leeds was first incorporated by Charles I in 1626. The earliest forms of the name are *Loidis* or *Ledes*, the origins of which are obscure.

LEICESTER

Leicester is situated geographically in the centre of England, 100 miles north of London. The city dates back to pre-Roman times and was one of the five Danish *Burghs*. In 1589 Queen Elizabeth I granted a Charter to the City and the ancient title was confirmed by Letters Patent in 1919. Under local government reorganization Leicester's area remained unchanged at 18,141 acres, and it retains its designation as a City.

The principal industries of the city are hosiery, knitwear, footwear manufacturing and engineering. The growth of Leicester as a hosiery centre increased rapidly from the introduction there of the first stocking frame in 1670 and today it has some of the largest hosiery factories in the world, with much of the output being exported.

The principal buildings in the city are the Town Hall, the New Walk Centre, the University of Leicester, De Montfort University, De Montfort Hall, one of the finest concert halls in the provinces seating over 2,750 people, and the Granby Halls, a major indoor sports facility. The ancient Churches of St Martin (now Leicester Cathedral), St Nicholas, St Margaret, All Saints, St Mary de Castro, and buildings such as the Guildhall, the 14th century Newarke Gate, the Castle and the Jewry Wall Roman site still exist. The Haymarket Theatre, an integral part of a large shopping and car-parking complex, was opened in 1973 and The Shires, a new shopping centre, was opened in 1992.

LINCOLN

Situated 143 miles north of London and 40 miles inland on the River Witham, Lincoln derives its name from a contraction of *Lindum Colonia*, the settlement founded in AD 48 by the Romans to command the crossing of Ermine Street and Fosse Way. Sections of the third century Roman city wall can be seen, including an extant gateway (Newport Arch), and excavations have discovered traces of a sewerage system unique in Britain. The Romans also drained the surrounding fenland and created a canal system, laying the foundations of Lincoln's agricultural prosperity, and also of the city's importance in the medieval wool trade as a port and Staple town.

As one of the Five Boroughs of the Danelaw, Lincoln was an important trading centre in the ninth and tenth centuries and medieval prosperity from the wool trade lasted until the 14th century, enabling local merchants to build parish churches (of which three survive), and attracting in the 12th century a Jewish community (Jew's House and Court, Aaron's House). However, the removal of the Staple to Boston in 1369 heralded a decline from which the city only recovered fully in the 19th century when improved fen drainage made Lincoln agriculturally important, and improved canal and rail links led to industrial development, mainly in the manufacture of machinery, components and engineering products.

The castle was built shortly after the Conquest and is unusual in having two mounds; on one motte stands a Keep (Lucy's Tower) added in the 12th century. The Cathedral was begun *c.*1073 when the first Norman bishop moved the see of Lindsey to Lincoln, but was mostly destroyed by fire and earthquake in the 12th century. Rebuilding was begun by St Hugh and completed over a century later. The Wren library contains manuscripts including one of the four surviving originals of the Magna Carta. Other notable architectural features of the city are the 12th century High Bridge, the oldest in Britain still to carry buildings, and the Guildhall situated above the 15th–16th century Stonebow gateway.

LIVERPOOL

Liverpool (Merseyside) on the right bank of the River Mersey, three miles from the Irish Sea and 210 miles north-west of London, is the UK's fourth most important port and the foremost for the Atlantic trade. The municipal area of 27,864 acres includes 2,840 acres in the bed of the river Mersey. Tunnels link Liverpool with Birkenhead and Wallasey.

There are 2,100 acres of dockland on both sides of the river and the Gladstone and Royal Seaforth Docks can accommodate the largest vessels afloat. Annual tonnage of cargo handled is approximately 23,000,000 tonnes. The main imports are crude oil, grain, ores, edible oils, timber, containers and break-bulk cargo. Liverpool Free Port, Britain's largest, was opened in 1984.

Liverpool was created a free borough in 1207 and a city in 1880. From the early 18th century it expanded rapidly with the growth of industrialization and Atlantic trade. Surviving buildings from this date include the Bluecoat Chambers (1717, formerly the Bluecoat School), the Town Hall (1754, rebuilt to the original design 1795), and buildings in Rodney Street, Canning Street and the suburbs. Notable from the 19th and 20th centuries are the Anglican Cathedral, built from the designs of Sir Giles Gilbert Scott (the foundation stone was laid in 1904, and the building was completed only in 1980), the Catholic Metropolitan Cathedral (designed by Sir Frederick Gibberd, consecrated 1967) and St George's Hall (1838–54), regarded as one of the finest modern examples of classical architecture. The recently refurbished Albert Dock (designed by Jesse Hartley) contains the Merseyside Maritime Museum and Tate Gallery, Liverpool.

In 1852 an Act was obtained for establishing a public library, museum and art gallery: as a result Liverpool had one of the first public libraries in the country. The Brown, Picton and Hornby libraries now form one of the country's major libraries. The Victoria Building of Liverpool University, the Royal Liver, Cunard and Mersey Docks & Harbour Company buildings at the Pier Head, the Municipal Buildings and the Philharmonic Hall are other examples of the City's fine buildings. Britain's first International Garden Festival was held in Liverpool in 1984.

MANCHESTER

Manchester (the *Mamucium* of the Romans, who occupied it in AD 79) is 204 miles north-west of London and covers about 43 square miles.

Manchester is a commercial and industrial centre with a population engaged in the engineering, chemical, clothing, food processing and textile industries and in education. Banking, insurance and a growing leisure industry are among the prime commercial activities. The city is connected with the sea by the Manchester Ship Canal, opened in 1894, 35½ miles long, and accommodating ships up to 15,000 tons. Manchester Airport handles more than 11 million passengers yearly.

The principal buildings are the Town Hall, erected in 1877 from the designs of Alfred Waterhouse, RA, together with a large extension of 1938; the Royal Exchange (1869, enlarged 1921); the Central Library (1934); Heaton Hall; the 17th century Chetham Library; the Rylands Library (1900), which includes the Althorp collection; the University precinct; the 15th century Cathedral (formerly the parish church); G-MEX and the Free Trade Hall. Manchester is the home of the Hallé Orchestra, the Royal Northern College of Music, the Royal Exchange Theatre and seven public art galleries. Metrolink, the new light rail system, opened in 1992.

The town received its first charter of incorporation in 1838 and was created a city in 1853. The title of City was retained under local government reorganization.

NEWCASTLE UPON TYNE

Newcastle upon Tyne (Tyne and Wear), a Metropolitan District on the north bank of the River Tyne, is eight miles from the North Sea, 272 miles north of London and has an area of 27,640 acres. A Cathedral and University City, it is the administrative, commercial and cultural centre for north-east England and the principal port. It is an important manufacturing centre with a wide variety of industries.

The principal buildings include the Castle Keep (12th century), Black Gate (13th century), Blackfriars (13th century), West Walls (13th century), St Nicholas's Cathedral (15th century, fine lantern tower), St Andrew's Church (12th–14th century), St John's (14th–15th century), All Saints (1786 by Stephenson), St Mary's Roman Catholic Cathedral (1844), Trinity House (17th century), Sandhill (16th century houses), Guildhall (Georgian), Grey Street (1834–9), Central Station (1846–50), Laing Art Gallery (1904), University of Newcastle Physics Building (1962) and Medical Building (1985), Civic Centre (1963), Central Library (1969) and Eldon Square Shopping Development (1976). Open spaces include the Town Moor (927 acres) and Jesmond Dene. Eight bridges span the Tyne at Newcastle.

The City derives its name from the 'new castle' (1080) erected as a defence against the Scots. In 1400 it was made a County, and in 1882 a City.

NORWICH

Norwich (Norfolk) is an ancient city 110 miles north-east of London. It grew from an early Anglo-Saxon settlement near the confluence of the Rivers Yare and Wensum, and now serves as provincial capital for the predominantly agricultural region of East Anglia. The name is thought to relate to the most northerly of a group of Anglo-Saxon villages or *wics*. The present city has an area of 9,655 acres. The city's first known Charter was granted in 1158 by Henry II.

Norwich serves its surrounding area as a market town and commercial centre, banking and insurance being prominent among the city's businesses. From the 14th century until the Industrial Revolution, Norwich was the regional centre of the woollen industry, but now the biggest single industry is financial services and principal trades are engineering, printing, shoemaking, double glazing, and the production of chemicals, clothing, confectionery and other foodstuffs. Norwich is accessible to seagoing vessels by means of the River Yare, entered at Great Yarmouth, 20 miles to the east.

Among many historic buildings are the Cathedral (completed in the 12th century and surmounted by a 15th century spire 315 feet in height), the Keep of the Norman Castle (now a museum and art gallery), the 15th century flint-walled Guildhall (now a tourist information centre), some thirty medieval parish churches, St Andrew's and Blackfriars' Halls, the Tudor houses preserved in Elm Hill and the Georgian Assembly House. The University of East Anglia has been established in Norwich on a site at Earlham on the city's western boundary and received its first students in 1963.

NOTTINGHAM

Nottingham stands on the River Trent, 124 miles north-north-west of London, in one of the most valuable coalfields of the country and connected by canal with the Atlantic and the North Sea. The municipal area is 18,364 acres.

The principal industries include textiles, pharmaceuticals, food manufacturing, engineering and telecommunications. There are two universities within the city boundaries.

Nottingham is a major sporting centre, home to Nottingham Forest FC, Notts County FC (the world's oldest Football league side), Nottingham Racecourse and the National Watersports Centre.

Architecturally, Nottingham has a wealth of notable buildings, particularly those designed in the Victorian era by T. C. Hine and Watson Fothergill. The City Council owns the Castle, of Norman origin but restored in 1878, Wollaton Hall (1580–8), Newstead Abbey (home of Lord Byron), the Guildhall (1888) and Council House (1929). St Mary's, St Peter's and St Nicholas's Churches are of interest, as is the Roman Catholic Cathedral (Pugin, 1842–4).

Snotingaham or *Notingeham*, literally the homestead of the people of Snot, is the Anglo-Saxon name for the Celtic settlement of *Tigguocobauc*, or the house of caves. In 878, Nottingham became one of the Five Boroughs of the Danelaw following a treaty signed by Alfred the Great and the Danish King Guthrum. William the Conqueror ordered the construction of Nottingham Castle, while the town itself developed rapidly under Norman rule. Its laws and rights were later formally recognized by Henry II's Charter in 1155. The Castle became a favoured residence of King John. In 1642 King Charles I raised his personal standard at Nottingham Castle at the start of the Civil War.

Nottingham was granted City status in 1897.

OXFORD

Oxford is a University City, an important industrial centre, and a market town, with an area of 10,798 acres. Industry played a minor part in Oxford until the motor industry was established in 1912.

It is for its architecture that Oxford is of most interest to the visitor, its oldest specimens being the reputed Saxon tower of St Michael's church, the remains of the Norman castle and city walls and the Norman church at Iffley. It is chiefly famous, however, for its Gothic buildings, such as the Divinity Schools, the Old Library at Merton College, William of Wykeham's New College, Magdalen College and Christ Church and many other college buildings. Later centuries are represented by the Laudian quadrangle at St John's College, the Renaissance Sheldonian Theatre by Wren, Trinity College Chapel, and All Saints Church; Hawksmoor's mock-Gothic at All Souls College, and the 18th century Queen's College. In addition to individual buildings, High Street and Radcliffe Square, just off it, both form architectural compositions of great beauty. Most of the Colleges have gardens, those of Magdalen, New College, St John's (designed by 'Capability' Brown) and Worcester being the largest.

PLYMOUTH

Plymouth is situated on the borders of Devon and Cornwall at the confluence of the Rivers Tamar and Plym, 210 miles from London, with an area of 19,572 acres.

The city has a long maritime history; it was the home port of Sir Francis Drake and the starting point for his circumnavigation of the world, as well as the last port of call for the *Mayflower* when the Pilgrim Fathers sailed for the New World in 1620. Today Plymouth is host to many international yacht races. The Barbican harbour area has many Elizabethan buildings, and on Plymouth Hoe stands the first lighthouse to be built on the Eddystone Rocks, 13 miles offshore.

Following extensive war damage, the city centre, comprising a large shopping centre, municipal offices, law courts and public buildings, has been rebuilt. The main employment is provided at the naval base, though many new industrial firms and service industries have become established in the post-war period and the city is a growing tourism centre. In 1982 the Theatre Royal was opened. In conjunction with the Cornwall County Council, the Tamar Bridge was constructed linking the city by road with Cornwall.

PORTSMOUTH

Portsmouth occupies Portsea Island, Hampshire, with boundaries extending to the mainland. It has an area of 15½ sq. miles and is 70 miles south-west of London.

Portsmouth is a centre of industry and commerce, including many high technology and manufacturing industries. It is the UK headquarters of several major international companies. The Royal Navy base still has a substantial work force, although this has decreased in recent years. The commercial port and continental ferry port is owned and run by the City Council, and carries passengers and vehicles to France.

A major port since the 16th century, Portsmouth is also a thriving seaside resort catering for thousands of visitors and day-trippers annually. Among many historic attractions are Lord Nelson's flagship, HMS *Victory*, the Tudor warship *Mary Rose*, Britain's first 'ironclad', HMS *Warrior*, the D-Day Museum, Charles Dickens' birthplace at 393 Old Commercial Road, the Royal Naval and Royal Marine museums, Southsea Castle (built by Henry VIII), the Round Tower and Point Battery, which for hundreds of years have guarded the entrance to Portsmouth Harbour, Fort Nelson on Portsdown Hill and the Sealife Centre.

ST ALBANS

Twenty-five miles north-west of London and situated on the River Ver, St Albans' origins stem from the major Roman town of *Verulamium*. Named after the first Christian martyr in Britain, who was executed here, St Albans has developed around the Norman Abbey and Cathedral Church (consecrated 1115), built partly of materials from the old Roman city. The museums house Iron Age and Roman artefacts and the Roman Theatre, unique in Britain, has a stage as opposed to an amphitheatre. Archaeological excavations in the city centre continue also to reveal evidence of pre-Roman, Saxon and medieval occupation.

The town's significance grew to the extent that it was a signatory and venue for the drafting of the Magna Carta. It was also the scene of major riots during the Peasants' Revolt, the French King John was imprisoned there after the Battle of Poitiers, and heavy fighting took place during the Wars of the Roses.

Previously controlled by the Abbot, the town achieved a Royal Charter in 1553 and City status in 1877. The street market, first established in 1553, is still an important feature of the city, as are many hotels and inns which survive from the days when St Albans was an important coach stop. Tourist attractions include historic churches and houses, and a 15th century clock tower.

The city now contains a wide range of firms, with special emphasis on micro-technology and electronics, particularly in the medical field. In addition, it is the home of the Royal National Rose Society, and of Rothamsted Park, the agricultural research centre.

In 1974 the City and District of St Albans was formed, taking in the town of Harpenden and many villages, and it now covers an area of 63 square miles.

SHEFFIELD

Sheffield (South Yorkshire), the centre of the special steel and cutlery trades, is situated 159 miles north-north-west of London, at the junction of the Sheaf, Porter, Rivelin and Loxley valleys with the River Don.

Sheffield has an area of 91,000 acres (nearly 150 square miles), including 4,619 acres of publicly owned parks and woodland. Though its cutlery, silverware and plate have long been famous, Sheffield has other and now more important industries: special and alloy steels, engineering, tool-making and financial services. Research in glass, metallurgy and other fields is carried out.

The parish church of St Peter and St Paul, founded in the 12th century, became the Cathedral Church of the Diocese of Sheffield in 1914. The Roman Catholic Cathedral Church of St Marie (founded 1847) was created Cathedral for the new diocese of Hallam in 1980. Parts of the present building date from *c.*1435. The principal buildings are the Town Hall (1897, 1923 and 1977), the Cutlers' Hall (1832), the University (1905 and recent extensions, including 19-storey Arts Tower), City Hall (1932), Graves Art Gallery (1934), Mappin Art Gallery and the Crucible Theatre. The restored 19th century Lyceum theatre opened in 1990.

Sheffield was created a city in 1893 and on 1 April 1974 became a Metropolitan District Council incorporating Stocksbridge and most of the Wortley Rural area, and retained city status.

Master Cutler (1992–3) *of the Company of Cutlers in Hallamshire*, R. A. Douglas, MC, TD.

SOUTHAMPTON

Southampton is the leading British deep-sea port on the Channel and is situated on one of the finest natural harbours in the world. The first Charter was granted by Henry II and Southampton was created a county of itself in 1447. In February 1964, The Queen granted city status by Royal Charter. The city has an area of 12,071 acres excluding tidal waters.

There have been Roman and Saxon settlements on the site of the city, which has been an important port since the time of the Conquest due to its natural deep-water harbour. The oldest church is St Michael's (1070) which has a black tournai marble font and an unusually tall spire built in the 18th century as a landmark for navigators of Southampton Water. Other buildings and monuments within the city walls are the Tudor House, God's House Tower, Bargate Museum, the Tudor Merchants Hall, the Weigh-house, West Gate, King John's House, Long House, Wool House, the ruins of Holy Rood Church, St Julien's Church and the Mayflower Memorial. The medieval town walls, built for artillery, are among the most complete in Europe. Public open spaces total over 1,000 acres in extent and comprise 9 per cent of the city's area. The Common covers an area of 328 acres in the central district of the city and is mostly natural parkland.

STOKE-ON-TRENT

Stoke-on-Trent (Staffordshire), familiarly known as The Potteries, stands on the River Trent 157 miles north of London. The present municipal area is 22,916 acres (36 square miles) and the city is the main centre of employment for the population of North Staffordshire.

The city is the largest clayware producer in the world (china, earthenware, sanitary goods, refractories, bricks and tiles) and has a considerable coal mining output drawn from one of the richest coalfields in western Europe. The city has steelworks, foundries, chemical works, engineering plants, rubber works, paper mills, and a very wide range of manufactures. Extensive reconstruction has been carried on in recent years.

The city was formed by the federation in 1910 of the separate municipal authorities of Tunstall, Burslem, Hanley, Stoke, Fenton, and Longton, all of which are now combined in the present City of Stoke-on-Trent.

WINCHESTER

Winchester, the ancient capital of England, is situated on the River Itchen 65 miles south-west of London and 12 miles north of Southampton. Since local government reorganization in 1974, the style of City has been accorded to the whole of the new district of Winchester, which embraces an area of 255 square miles of mid-Hampshire.

Winchester is rich in architecture of all types but the Cathedral takes pride of place. The longest Gothic cathedral in the world, it was built in 1079–93 and exhibits examples of Norman, Early English and Perpendicular styles. Winchester College, founded in 1382, is one of the most famous public schools, the original building (of 1393) remaining largely unaltered. St Cross Hospital, another great medieval foundation, lies one mile south of the city. The Almshouses were founded in 1136 by Bishop Henry de Blois, and Cardinal Henry Beaufort added a new Almshouse of 'Noble Poverty' in 1446. The Chapel and dwellings are of great architectural interest, and visitors may still receive the 'Wayfarer's Dole' of bread and ale.

Recent excavations have done much to clarify the origins and development of Winchester. Part of the forum and several of the streets of the Roman town have been discovered; and excavations in the Cathedral Close have uncovered the entire site of the Anglo-Saxon cathedral (known as the Old Minster) and parts of the New Minster, built by Alfred's son Edward the Elder and the burial place of the Alfredian dynasty. The original burial place of St Swithun, before his remains were translated to a site in the present cathedral, was also uncovered.

Excavations in other parts of the city have thrown much light on Norman Winchester, notably on the site of the Royal Castle, adjacent to which the new Law Courts have been built, and in the grounds of Wolvesey Castle, where the great house built by Bishops Giffard and Henry de Blois in the 12th century has been uncovered. The Great Hall, built by Henry III between 1222 and 1236 survives. It houses the Arthurian Round Table.

YORK

The City of York is a District in the County of North Yorkshire, and is an archiepiscopal seat.

The recorded history of York dates from AD 71, when the Roman Ninth Legion established a base under Petilius Cerealis which later became the fortress of *Eburacum*. In Anglo-Saxon times the city was the royal and ecclesiastical centre of Northumbria, and was captured by a Viking army in AD 866, after which it became the capital of the Viking kingdom of Jorvik. By the 14th century the city had become a great mercantile centre, mainly owing to its control of the wool trade, and was used as the chief base against the Scots. Under the Tudors its fortunes declined, though Henry VIII made it the headquarters of the Council of the North. Recent excavations on many sites, including Coppergate, have greatly expanded knowledge of Roman, Viking and medieval urban life.

With its development as a railway centre in the 19th century the commercial life of York expanded. The principal industries are the manufacture of chocolate, railway coaches, scientific instruments, and sugar. It is the location of several government departments.

The city is rich in examples of architecture of all periods. The earliest church was built in AD 627 and, in the 12th to 15th centuries, the present Minster was built in a succession of styles. Other examples within the city are the medieval city walls and gateways, churches and guildhalls. Domestic architecture includes the Georgian mansions of The Mount, Micklegate and Bootham. Its museums include York Castle Museum, the National Railway Museum and the Jorvik Viking Centre.

English Counties and Shires

LORD LIEUTENANTS AND HIGH SHERIFFS

County or Shire	*Lord Lieutenant*	**High Sheriff, 1992–3*
Avon	Sir John Wills, Bt., TD	F. W. Greenacre
Bedfordshire	S. C. Whitbread	G. James
Berkshire	J. R. Henderson, CVO, OBE	S. W. Smart
Buckinghamshire	Cdr. the Hon. J. T. Fremantle	Lady Popplewell
Cambridgeshire	J. G. P. Crowden	G. R. W. Wright
Cheshire	William Bromley-Davenport	Hon. P. G. Greenall
Cleveland	The Lord Gisborough	Dr G. C. Mitchell
Cornwall	The Viscount Falmouth	E. M. L. Latham
Cumbria	Maj. Sir Charles Graham, Bt.	M. C. R. Sandys
Derbyshire	Col. P. Hilton, MC	D. C. Wigglesworth
Devon	Lt.-Col. the Earl of Morley	Mrs E. A. Eden
Dorset	The Lord Digby	G. P. Sturdy
Durham	D. J. Grant, CBE	Mrs E. A. Jennings
East Sussex	Adm. Sir Lindsay Bryson, KCB	I. D. G. Cox
Essex	The Lord Braybrooke	A. G. Tritton
Gloucestershire	H. W. G. Elwes	Hon. P. R. Smith
Greater London	Field Marshal the Lord Bramall, GCB, OBE, MC	J. A. Lemkin, CBE
Greater Manchester	Col. J. B. Timmins, OBE, TD	S. J. V. Arditti, MBE
Hampshire	Lt.-Col. Sir James Scott, Bt.	A. S. B. Portman
Hereford and Worcester	Capt. T. R. Dunne	Lady Cotterell
Hertfordshire	S. A. Bowes Lyon	H. A. F. Buxton
Humberside	R. A. Bethell	J. W. A. Clugston
Isle of Wight	†The Lord Mottistone, CBE	D. E. J. Guy, MBE
Kent	The Rt. Hon. Robin Leigh-Pemberton	H. H. Villiers
Lancashire	S. Towneley	K. A. Gledhill
Leicestershire	T. G. M. Brooks	J. M. Moubray
Lincolnshire	Capt. Sir Henry N. Nevile, KCVO	J. G. Richardson
Merseyside	H. E. Cotton	A. W. Waterworth
Norfolk	T. J. Colman	A. N. G. Duckworth-Chad
Northamptonshire	J. L. Lowther, CBE	R. P. Seddon
Northumberland	The Viscount Ridley, KG, TD	J. M. Lloyd
North Yorkshire	Sir Marcus Worsley, Bt.	Hon. Sir Richard Storey, Bt.
Nottinghamshire	Sir Andrew Buchanan, Bt.	I. H. Phillipps
Oxfordshire	Sir Ashley Ponsonby, Bt., MC	J. J. Eyston
Shropshire	J. R. S. Dugdale	E. M. A. Thompson
Somerset	Col. G. W. F. Luttrell, MC	E. W. A. Sanford
South Yorkshire	J. H. Neill, CBE, TD	D. B. Clark, CBE
Staffordshire	Sir Arthur Bryan	R. E. Whitfield
Suffolk	Sir Joshua Rowley, Bt.	W. L. G. Jacob
Surrey	R. E. Thornton, OBE	G. E. Lee-Steere
Tyne and Wear	Sir Ralph Carr-Ellison, TD	H. G. Brown
Warwickshire	The Viscount Daventry	Maj. B. C. Bovill
West Midlands	The Earl of Aylesford	J. A. Jefferson
West Sussex	The Duke of Richmond and Gordon	J. F. E. Smith
West Yorkshire	J. Lyles	D. H. Boyle
Wiltshire	Field Marshal Sir Roland Gibbs, GCB, CBE, DSO, MC	G. W. M. Street

* High Sheriffs are nominated by The Queen on 12 November each year and come into office after Hilary Term
† Lord Lieutenant and Governor

COUNTY COUNCILS: Area, Population, Finance

County Council	*Administrative headquarters*	*Area (hectares)*	*Population Census 1991p*	*Total demand upon collection fund 1992*
Avon	Avon House North, St James Barton, Bristol	134,628	919,800	£588,600,000
Bedfordshire	County Hall, Bedford	123,468	514,200	358,275,000
Berkshire	Shire Hall, Reading	125,901	716,500	483,347,000
Buckinghamshire	County Hall, Aylesbury	188,279	619,500	418,926,400
Cambridgeshire	Shire Hall, Cambridge	340,181	640,700	402,114,000
Cheshire	County Hall, Chester	233,325	937,300	619,800,000
Cleveland	Municipal Buildings, Middlesbrough	59,079	541,100	431,836,200
Cornwall	County Hall, Truro	356,442*	469,300	297,087,000
Cumbria	The Courts, Carlisle	682,451	486,900	321,091,000
Derbyshire	County Offices, Matlock	263,098	914,600	586,500,000
Devon	County Hall, Exeter	671,096	998,200	613,855,000
Dorset	County Hall, Dorchester	265,433	645,200	369,776,000
Durham	County Hall, Durham	243,369	589,800	381,537,909
East Sussex	Pelham House, St Andrews Lane, Lewes	179,530	670,600	417,328,000
Essex	County Hall, Chelmsford	367,167	1,495,600	939,029,000
Gloucestershire	Shire Hall, Gloucester	264,270	520,600	320,490,000
Hampshire	The Castle, Winchester	378,022	1,511,900	846,790,000
Hereford and Worcester	County Hall, Worcester	392,650	667,800	397,044,000
Hertfordshire	County Hall, Hertford	163,601	951,500	613,784,000
Humberside	County Hall, Beverley, N. Humberside	351,256	835,200	603,822,000
Isle of Wight	County Hall, Newport, IOW	38,063	126,600	81,831,400
Kent	County Hall, Maidstone	373,063	1,485,100	945,000,000
Lancashire	County Hall, Preston	306,957	1,365,100	960,903,000
Leicestershire	County Hall, Leicester	255,297	860,500	579,013,000
Lincolnshire	County Offices, Lincoln	591,791	573,900	493,000,000
Norfolk	County Hall, Norwich	537,482	736,400	446,002,626
Northamptonshire	County Hall, Northampton	236,721	572,900	374,231,000
Northumberland	County Hall, Morpeth	503,165	300,600	186,881,840
North Yorkshire	County Hall, Northallerton	831,236	698,700	408,500,000
Nottinghamshire	County Hall, Nottingham	216,090	980,600	666,370,000
Oxfordshire	County Hall, Oxford	260,798	553,800	333,800,000
Shropshire	The Shirehall, Shrewsbury	349,013	401,600	258,156,000
Somerset	County Hall, Taunton	345,233	459,100	290,212,000
Staffordshire	County Buildings, Stafford	271,616	1,020,300	625,378,000
Suffolk	County Hall, Ipswich	379,664	629,900	374,986,857
Surrey	County Hall, Kingston upon Thames	167,924	998,000	575,598,000
Warwickshire	Shire Hall, Warwick	198,052	477,000	299,756,500
West Sussex	County Hall, Chichester	198,935	692,800	386,200,000
Wiltshire	County Hall, Trowbridge	347,883	553,300	339,800,000

p preliminary
* Including Isles of Scilly

THE ISLES OF SCILLY

The islands of the Scillies group have an area of 6 square miles (10 square km) and a population of 1,978. They are administered by the Council of the Isles of Scilly, a 21-member non-political body, which combines the powers and duties of a county council and a district council under the Local Government Act 1972 and the Isles of Scilly Orders 1978. Legislation is specifically applied to the Isles of Scilly by Special Order. The Council is responsible for education, fire services, highways, planning and social services. Cornwall County Council provides other services on an agency basis. The police service is administered by the Devon and Cornwall Police Authority, of which the Council is a member. The Isles are part of the St Ives electoral division.

Administrative Headquarters, Town Hall, St Mary's, Isles of Scilly, TR21 OLW.

Chairman of the Council, J. P. Greenlaw.

Clerk and Chief Executive, P. S. Hygate.

Chief Technical Officer, B. M. Lowen.

COUNTY COUNCILS: Officers and Chairman

County Council	*Chief Executive*	*County Treasurer*	*Chairman of County Council*
Avon	B. D. Smith	D. G. Morgan	D. John
Bedfordshire	D. Cleggett	B. Phelps	K. L. White
Berkshire	A. J. Allen	D. J. Bowles	R. J. Day
Buckinghamshire	C. M. Garrett	H. R. H. Springthorpe	Mrs G. M. M. Miscampbell, OBE
Cambridgeshire	A. G. Lister	D. Earle	R. E. Burke
Cheshire	M. E. Pitt	J. E. H. Whiteoak	P. Tyrrell
Cleveland	B. Stevenson	P. Riley†	E. Wood
Cornwall	G. K. Burgess	S. F. Nicol	D. L. C. Roberts
Cumbria	J. E. Burnet	R. F. Mather	J. W. Oswald
Derbyshire	J. S. Raine*	P. Swaby	J. S. Heathcote
Devon	R. D. Clark	B. J. Weston	F. A. C. Pinney, OBE
Dorset	P. K. Harvey	A. P. Peel	Sir Stephen Hammick, Bt.
Durham	K. W. Smith°	J. Kirkby	G. W. Terrans
East Sussex	R. M. Beechey	J. Davies	H. A. Hatcher
Essex	R. W. Adcock, CBE	K. D. Neale	Mrs K. M. Nolan
Gloucestershire	M. Honey	J. R. Cockroft	F. B. Wilton
Hampshire	A. R. Hodgson	J. E. Scotford	R. T. Millard
Hereford and Worcester	G. A. Price	G. A. Price	R. J. Carrington, OBE
Hertfordshire	B. Briscoe	W. D. Ogley‡	H. T. D. Marwood, MBE
Humberside	J. A. Parkes	G. T. Southern‡	G. W. Hobson
Isle of Wight	J. S. Horsnell	J. B. W. Proctor	K. A. G. Lacey
Kent	P. R. Sabin	P. Martin‡	Mrs B. Trench
Lancashire	G. A. Johnson	B. G. Aldred	Mrs J. Farrington
Leicestershire	D. Prince	R. Hale	J. T. Griffiths
Lincolnshire	R. J. D. Procter	M. Spink	W. H. Rawson
Norfolk	B. J. Capon, CBE	C. A. Boar‡	Mrs M. Duigan
Northamptonshire	A. J. Greenwell, CBE	R. Paver‡	T. G. Fordyce
Northumberland	K. Morris	K. Morris‡	K. L. Flaherty
North Yorkshire	R. A. Leyland	D. Martin	Sqn. Ldr. J. Donaldson
Nottinghamshire	M. T. Lyons	R. Latham	G. R. Young
Oxfordshire	J. Harwood	C. Gay	J. Jones
Shropshire	M. N. Davis	M. N. Davis	Mrs J. A. Hayward
Somerset	B. M. Tanner	C. N. Bilsland	H. Hobhouse
Staffordshire	B. A. Price	B. Smith	J. O'Leary
Suffolk	P. F. Bye	P. B. Atkinson	Mrs N. R. Alcock
Surrey	D. J. Thomas	R. Wolstenholme	A. J. Brigstocke
Warwickshire	I. G. Caulfield	S. R. Freer	F. G. Watson, OBE
West Sussex	B. Fieldhouse	D. P. Rigg	M. H. Long, CBE
Wiltshire	I. A. Browning	A. F. Gould	Mrs M. Whitworth

* County Director
° Principal Executive Officer
‡ Director of Finance
† County Finance Officer

English Metropolitan Councils

SMALL CAPITALS denote CITY status

Metropolitan Council	Population Census 1991p	Community charge per head 1992	Chief Executive	(a)	Mayor / Lord Mayor 1992-3
Greater Manchester	2,454,800				
Bolton	253,300	£291.19	B. Collinge		E. Crook
Bury	172,200	315.27	D. J. Burton		W. Ramsey
MANCHESTER	406,900	337.76	G. Hainsworth	(a)	W. Egerton
Oldham	211,400	268.00	C. Smith		N. E. Bennett
Rochdale	196,900	338.00	J. F. D. Pierce		A. Heaford
SALFORD	217,900	328.00	R. C. Rees, OBE		K. Murray
Stockport	276,800	339.00	A. L. Wilson		J. Lloyd, OBE
Tameside	211,700	337.00	M. Greenwood		J. Hughes
Trafford	205,700	249.00	W. A. Lewis		R. A. Tully
Wigan	301,900	307.50	S. M. Jones		A. Wright
Merseyside	1,376,800				
Knowsley	149,100	298.00	D. G. Henshaw		H. Campbell
LIVERPOOL	448,300	400.24	P. Bounds	(a)	Ms R. Cooper
St Helens	175,300	298.47	Mrs C. A. Hudson		J. Caunce
Sefton	282,000	315.00	G. J. Haywood		N. K. Jones
Wirral	322,100	356.00	A. White		F. Jones
South Yorkshire	1,248,500				
Barnsley	217,300	225.47	J. A. Edwards, OBE		K. Young
Doncaster	284,300	240.00	C. B. Jeynes		C. Verrill
Rotherham	247,100	277.00	J. Bell		J. Carr
SHEFFIELD	499,700	281.00	Mrs P. Gordon	(a)	W. Jordan
Tyne and Wear	1,087,000				
Gateshead	196,500	271.00	L. N. Elton		S. Cowans
NEWCASTLE UPON TYNE	263,000	348.97	G. N. Cook	(a)	C. A. Cook
North Tyneside	188,800	340.00	G. A. Aslett; E. D. Nixon*		J. W. Conway
South Tyneside	151,900	283.00	S. Clark		J. Oxley
SUNDERLAND	286,800	277.00	G. P. Key	(a)	W. Craddock
West Midlands	2,499,300				
BIRMINGHAM	934,900	295.00	R. M. W. Taylor	(a)	P. J. Barwell, MBE
COVENTRY	292,500	326.00	I. Roxburgh	(a)	D. Ewart
Dudley	300,400	301.00	A. V. Astling		W. H. Webb
Sandwell	282,000	319.00	N. Summers (*acting*)		P. Sullivan
Solihull	194,100	265.70	J. Scampion		B. Chapple
Walsall	255,600	306.00	D. C. Winchurch		Mrs D. O'Hare
Wolverhampton	239,800	317.00	N. H. Perry, PH.D.		R. Swatman
West Yorkshire	1,984,700				
BRADFORD	449,100	276.00	R. Penn	(a)	B. K. Thorne
Calderdale	187,300	215.97	M. Ellison		B. Carpenter
Kirklees	367,600	249.50	R. V. Hughes		D. A. Wright
LEEDS	674,400	204.00	J. P. Smith	(a)	Ms D. Atkinson
WAKEFIELD	306,300	278.96	R. Mather		F. Hodgson

p preliminary
* Lead Officers

English Non-Metropolitan Councils

SMALL CAPITALS denote CITY status
§ denotes Borough status

District Borough Council	Population Census 1991p	Community charge per head 1992	Chief Executive (*Clerk)	(a) Mayor / (b) Lord Mayor	Chairman 1992-3
Adur, West Sussex	57,400	£280.00	F. M. G. Staden		Mrs S. Bucknall
Allerdale, Cumbria	96,300	246.76	vacant		V. Mulgren
Alnwick, Northumberland	108,029	290.73	L. St Ruth		Mrs S. Bolam

p preliminary

District Borough Council	Population Census 1991*p*	Community charge per head 1992	Chief Executive (*Clerk)		Chairman 1992–3 (*a*) Mayor (*b*) Lord Mayor
§Amber Valley, Derbyshire	26,509	£302.09	F. W. Ellis	(*a*)	Mrs M. Bennett
Arun, West Sussex	127,700	234.14	I. Sumnall		D. Birt
Ashfield, Nottinghamshire	106,800	282.00	S. Beedham		G. Gascoyne
§Ashford, Kent	90,900	242.00	E. H. W. Mexter	(*a*)	Mrs C. M. Rosson
Aylesbury Vale, Bucks.	143,600	216.97	B. J. Quoroll		W. G. Lapham
Babergh, Suffolk	78,500	256.73	D. C. Bishop		C. M. Spence
§Barrow-in-Furness, Cumbria	71,900	303.00	R. H. McCulloch	(*a*)	Mrs J. D. Fleet, BEM
Basildon, Essex	157,500	361.00	J. C. Rosser°		T. G. Leask
§Basingstoke and Deane, Hants.	140,400	233.90	D. W. Pilkington, RD	(*a*)	K. G. Chapman
Bassetlaw, Notts.	103,000	290.00	M. S. Havenham		Ms D. Webster
BATH, Avon	79,900	251.28	N. C. Abbott	(*a*)	E. J. T. Snook
§Berwick-upon-Tweed, Northumberland	26,400	358.10	E. D. Cawthorn	(*a*)	A. J. K. Thompson
§Beverley, Humberside	109,500	307.00	M. Rice	(*a*)	D. B. Leng
Blaby, Leics.	81,900	250.79	E. Hemsley†		W. C. Law
§Blackburn, Lancs.	132,800	331.20	G. L. Davies	(*a*)	Ms E. Entwistle
§Blackpool, Lancs.	144,500	340.00	D. Wardman	(*a*)	Mrs D. Preston
§Blyth Valley, Northumberland	78,000	334.90	D. Crawford	(*a*)	E. Robinson
Bolsover, Derbys.	69,000	248.92	J. R. Fotherby		I. Buggins
§Boothferry, Humberside	63,100	286.87	J. W. Barber	(*a*)	Mrs D. A. Engall
§Boston, Lincs.	52,600	262.00	J. McAusland	(*a*)	Ms J. Dobson
§Bournemouth, Dorset	154,400	269.00	D. Newell	(*a*)	Mrs P. M. Hogarth
§Bracknell Forest, Berks.	93,800	265.00	A. J. Targett	(*a*)	Mrs I. Mattick
Braintree, Essex	115,700	254.00	C. R. Daybell		J. W. C. Perks
Breckland, Norfolk	105,200	247.16	R. Garnett		K. S. Jelly
Brentwood, Essex	68,600	237.00	C. P. Sivell		A. Slaymark
Bridgnorth, Salop	49,700	256.18	A. L. Bain		C. J. Lea
§Brighton, East Sussex	133,400	329.78	G. Jones	(*a*)	Ms G. Sweeting
BRISTOL, Avon	370,300	376.00	M. Robinson	(*b*)	J. Channon
Broadland, Norfolk	104,500	259.48	J. H. Bryant		L. Woolf
Bromsgrove, Hereford and Worcs.	89,800	260.56	R. P. Bradshaw		Miss T. C. Matthews
§Broxbourne, Herts.	79,500	241.77	M. J. Walker	(*a*)	G. F. Batchelor, MBE
§Broxtowe, Notts.	104,600	275.60	M. Brown	(*a*)	Mrs H. Braithwaite
§Burnley, Lancs.	89,000	262.00	B. Whittle	(*a*)	E. C. Ingham
CAMBRIDGE	101,000	349.00	R. Hammond	(*a*)	B. Gardiner
Cannock Chase, Staffs.	87,400	284.78	M. G. Kemp		J. Holston
CANTERBURY, Kent	127,100	258.24	C. Gay	(*b*)	P. Burke
Caradon, Cornwall	75,800	262.12	J. Neal		E. R. Distin
CARLISLE, Cumbria	99,800	333.00	R. S. Brackley	(*a*)	H. Evans
Carrick, Cornwall	82,700	283.77	P. M. Talbot		D. L. G. Hocking
§Castle Morpeth, Northumberland	49,700	318.98	M. Cole	(*a*)	T. J. J. Hulbert
§Castle Point, Essex	84,200	361.00	B. Rollinson	(*a*)	W. J. C. Dick
§Charnwood, Leics.	140,500	292.64	S. M. Peatfield	(*a*)	Dr A. M. Duncan
§Chelmsford, Essex	150,000	256.15	R. M. C. Hartley	(*a*)	E. G. Roberts
§Cheltenham, Glos.	85,900	330.47	C. Nye	(*a*)	B. J. Cassin
Cherwell, Oxon.	115,900	227.50	G. J. Handley		N. A. S. Matthews
CHESTER, Cheshire	115,000	344.38	P. F. Durham	(*b*)	J. Randall
§Chesterfield, Derbyshire	99,700	299.00	D. R. Shaw	(*a*)	T. Kendellen
Chester-le-Street, Co. Durham	51,600	300.97	J. A. Greensmith		K. Potts
Chichester, West Sussex	100,300	212.00	C. E. Evans		Capt. S. A. Stuart, CBE, RN
Chiltern, Bucks.	88,700	275.00	D. G. Sainsbury		P. T. Lole
§Chorley, Lancs.	96,500	306.81	J. W. Davies	(*a*)	B. J. Hodson
§Christchurch, Dorset	40,500	240.16	C. H. Dewsnap	(*a*)	C. R. Bungey
§Cleethorpes, Humberside	67,500	329.39	P. Daniel	(*a*)	K. C. Brookes
§Colchester, Essex	141,100	247.70	J. Cobley	(*a*)	Mrs M. Frank
§Congleton, Cheshire	82,900	312.91	D. N. Mills	(*a*)	Mrs T. E. S. Jones

p preliminary
° Town Manager
† Finance and General Manager

District Borough Council	*Population Census 1991p*	*Community charge per head 1992*	*Chief Executive (*Clerk)*	*(a)* *(b)*	*Chairman 1992–3* *Mayor* *Lord Mayor*
§Copeland, Cumbria	70,700	£277.25	R. G. Smith	(a)	A. Holliday
Corby, Northants.	52,300	275.00	T. S. Simmons		Mrs M. Mawdsley
Cotswold, Glos.	73,000	275.73	D. A. Sketchley		D. F. S. Goodman
Craven, North Yorks	49,700	217.00	H. H. Crabtree††		M. G. Riley
§Crawley, West Sussex	87,100	250.00	M. D. Sander	(a)	I. I. Irvine
§Crewe and Nantwich, Cheshire	101,800	324.64	A. Wenham	(a)	Mrs M. H. Furber
§Dacorum, Herts.	129,200	245.00	K. Hunt	(a)	J. Buteux
§Darlington, Co. Durham	96,700	300.24	H. R. C. Owen	(a)	D. Lyonette
§Dartford, Kent	78,400	268.58	C. R. Shepherd	(a)	E. Huxley
Daventry, Northants.	61,600	265.15	R. J. Symons, RD		J. S. H. Russell, BEM
DERBY	214,000	294.00	R. H. Cowlishaw	(a)	H. Johnson
Derbyshire Dales	67,700	301.91	D. Wheatcroft		Mrs J. A. Twigg
Derwentside, Co. Durham	84,800	276.00	N. F. Johnson		B. Brenkley
Dover, Kent	102,600	258.25	J. P. Moir, TD		R. R. Chesterfield
DURHAM	85,000	301.31	C. G. Firmin	(a)	M. Rochford
Easington, Co. Durham	96,300	247.53	vacant		Mrs J. L. Darwin
§Eastbourne, East Sussex	83,200	320.00	Dr M. Blanch	(a)	M. Skilton
East Cambridgeshire	59,300	254.22	T. T. G. Hardy		L. W. Neal
East Devon	106,200	246.54	F. J. Vallender		F. H. J. Lock
East Dorset	77,200	283.90	A. Breakwell		Sqn. Ldr. P. M. Dunstan
East Hampshire	101,100	273.82	B. P. Roynon		P. F. Ravenscroft
East Hertfordshire	114,200	259.00	R. J. Bailey		R. J. F. Tucker
§Eastleigh, Hants.	103,200	282.58	C. Tapp	(a)	P. Madsen
East Lindsey, Lincs.	115,600	247.22	P. Haigh†		K. J. Holland
East Northamptonshire	65,700	237.46	R. K. Heath		A. R. Mantle
East Staffordshire	96,200	270.28	F. W. Saunders		P. J. Beresford
§East Yorkshire, Humberside	83,700	285.00	J. H. Gibson	(a)	S. M. Burch
Eden, Cumbria	46,300	269.49	I. W. Bruce		E. S. C. Wooff
§Ellesmere Port and Neston, Cheshire	78,800	336.70	S. Ewbank	(a)	K. D. Powell
§Elmbridge, Surrey	109,900	327.00	D. W. L. Jenkins	(a)	A. K. Curran
Epping Forest, Essex	113,100	271.48	J. Burgess		D. Spinks
§Epsom and Ewell, Surrey	67,000	296.00	D. J. Smith	(a)	M. J. C. Staples
§Erewash, Derbyshire	104,000	305.00	R. M. Fletcher	(a)	K. M. Trueman
EXETER, Devon	101,100	256.90	B. Frowd	(a)	Mrs Y. A. C. Henson
§Fareham, Hants.	97,300	227.00	vacant	(a)	Mrs J. Baylis
Fenland, Cambs.	72,900	254.00	E. S. Thompson		Mrs J. Southwell
Forest Heath, Suffolk	57,200	237.59	S. W. Catchpole		Mrs C. F. J. Lynch
Forest of Dean, Glos.	74,200	306.11	R. A. Willis		B. W. Hobman
§Fylde, Lancs.	70,100	279.95	J. P. Johnson	(a)	J. M. Taverner
§Gedling, Notts.	107,600	283.00	W. Brown	(a)	R. Spencer
§Gillingham, Kent	93,300	238.68	J. A. McBride	(a)	Mrs D. M. Chambers
§Glanford, Humberside	70,000	300.00	D. D. H. Cameron	(a)	K. Sills
GLOUCESTER	91,800	309.49	G. Garbutt	(a)	B. Richard
§Gosport, Hants.	72,800	258.00	M. S. Friend	(a)	M. G. Russell
§Gravesham, Kent	90,000	231.00	E. V. J. Seager	(a)	D. W. B. Thomas
§Great Grimsby, Humberside	88,900	338.00	R. S. G. Bennett	(a)	N. G. Perkins
§Great Yarmouth, Norfolk	85,900	292.00	K. G. Ward	(a)	B. Walker
§Guildford, Surrey	121,500	297.00	D. T. Watts	(a)	A. D. Page
§Halton, Cheshire	121,400	346.00	M. Cuff	(a)	J. Weaver
Hambleton, North Yorks.	77,600	214.48	C. Spencer		R. G. Horner
Harborough, Leics.	66,200	280.66	J. Ballantyne		Mrs B. M. Jones
Harlow, Essex	73,500	301.50	D. Byrne‡		Mrs M. Carter
§Harrogate, North Yorks.	141,000	293.00	P. M. Walsh	(a)	B. Hillier
Hart, Hants.	78,700	257.47	D. Hanham		D. W. Cleaton
§Hartlepool, Cleveland	88,200	322.00	B. J. Dinsdale	(a)	V. Burton
§Hastings, East Sussex	78,100	274.00	R. A. Carrier	(a)	Miss J. Fabian

p preliminary
† Director of Central Services
†† Head of Paid Service
‡ General Manager

District Borough Council	Population Census 1991p	Community charge per head 1992	Chief Executive (*Clerk)	(a) (b)	Chairman 1992–3 (a) Mayor (b) Lord Mayor
§Havant, Hants.	117,400	260.00	D. E. Ridley	(a)	G. Tart
HEREFORD	49,800	256.40	C. E. S. Willis	(a)	C. P. C. Davies
§Hertsmere, Hertfordshire	86,100	£259.69	P. Copland†	(a)	E. H. G. Muddle
§High Peak, Derbyshire	83,800	310.85	R. P. H. Brady	(a)	Mrs A. S. Young
§Hinckley and Bosworth, Leics.	93,600	234.73	A. J. Cleary	(a)	Mrs M. Browning
§Holderness, Humberside	49,900	315.32	A. Johnson	(a)	Mrs B. Y. Jefferson
Horsham, West Sussex	107,300	225.26	M. J. Pearson		J. M. Burnham
§Hove, East Sussex	82,500	269.97	J. P. Teasdale	(a)	Mrs A. Rowe
Huntingdonshire, Cambs.	140,700	213.00	T. J. Gee		Mrs H. W. Sneden
§Hyndburn, Lancs.	76,500	278.00	M. J. Wedgeworth	(a)	Mrs K. Thom
§Ipswich, Suffolk	115,500	320.21	J. D. Hehir	(a)	J. E. Cubbin
Kennet, Wilts.	67,500	224.42	P. L. Owens		D. J. Godwin
Kerrier, Cornwall	86,400	278.79	G. G. Cox		Mrs P. H. Clark
§Kettering, Northants.	75,200	257.00	T. P. Williams	(a)	Mrs J. Gosland
§King's Lynn and W. Norfolk	128,400	231.65	A. E. Pask	(a)	J. M. Tilbury
KINGSTON UPON HULL, Humberside	242,200	294.00	D. Stephenson	(b)	D. Barber
§Kingswood, Avon	87,100	300.85	A. Smith	(a)	R. K. Stone
LANCASTER, Lancs.	125,600	310.00	W. Pearson	(a)	H. Towers
§Langbaurgh-on-Tees, Cleveland	141,700	357.06	K. Abigail	(a)	Mrs B. Forster
LEICESTER	270,600	351.00	I. Farookhi	(b)	R. Wigglesworth
Leominster, Hereford and Worcs.	39,000	252.00	G. R. Chilton		T. C. A. Edwards
Lewes, East Sussex	85,400	289.14	J. N. Crawford		Mrs E. M. Hurst
Lichfield, Staffs.	90,700	252.10	J. T. Thompson		J. L. Middleton
LINCOLN	81,900	270.00	C. J. Thomas	(a)	H. Bunnage
§Luton, Beds.	167,300	267.00	J. C. Southwell	(a)	R. M. Sills
§Macclesfield, Cheshire	147,000	298.72	B. W. Longden	(a)	A. Wall
§Maidstone, Kent	133,200	280.83	J. D. Makepeace	(a)	Mrs M. Blackham
Maldon, Essex	50,800	226.00	E. A. P. Plumridge		Mrs M. J. Peel
Malvern Hills, Hereford and Worcs.	87,000	271.20	M. J. Jones		Mrs P. H. Merrick
Mansfield, Notts.	98,800	327.00	R. P. Goad		A. Weaver
§Medina, Isle of Wight	70,100	247.59	J. Sprake‡‡	(a)	B. Wade
§Melton, Leics.	44,500	261.82	P. J. G. Herrick*	(a)	E. A. Stockley
Mendip, Somerset	95,300	295.75	G. Jeffs		O. Pippard
Mid Bedfordshire	108,000	260.46	C. A. Tucker		F. W. Jakes
Mid Devon	63,600	268.68	M. I. R. Bull		Mrs S. M. Meads
§Middlesbrough, Cleveland	141,100	339.22	J. R. Foster	(a)	F. Platt
Mid Suffolk	77,100	254.30	H. McFarlane		Air Cdre. J. B. Wellingham
Mid Sussex	118,800	218.45	B. J. Grimshaw		P. Bailey
§Milton Keynes, Bucks.	172,300	314.75	M. J. Murray	(a)	F. D. W. Smith
Mole Valley, Surrey	77,400	253.00	A. A. Huggins		W. W. Lancaster
Newark and Sherwood, Notts.	103,400	309.12	R. G. Dix††		P. D. Prebble
Newbury, Berks.	136,400	261.00	P. E. McMahon		D. H. T. Lawrence
§Newcastle under Lyme, Staffs.	117,400	281.00	E. Wetherell	(a)	J. Lockett
New Forest, Hants.	157,000	223.39	P. A. D. Hyde		J. E. Coles
§Northampton	178,200	267.00	R. J. B. Morris	(a)	F. Tero
Northavon, Avon	129,600	311.40	F. Maude		C. E. Horton
§North Bedfordshire	132,100	269.84	L. W. Gould	(a)	V. G. Brandon
North Cornwall	73,700	254.96	D. H. Westwell		H. S. Medland
North Devon	85,100	267.49	R. D. Hall		M. J. Edmunds
North Dorset	52,200	226.59	A. J. Bridgeman		G. A. Pitt-Rivers, OBE
North East Derbyshire	95,600	320.00	Mrs C. A. Gilbey		F. Hopkinson
North Hertfordshire	108,600	252.85	S. Philp		G. C. Dumelow

p preliminary
† Head of Paid Service
‡‡ General Manager
†† Managing Director

District Borough Council	Population Census 1991p	Community charge per head 1992	Chief Executive (*Clerk)	(a) (b)	Chairman 1992–3 (a) Mayor (b) Lord Mayor
North Kesteven, Lincs.	78,400	£247.40	S. Lamb		E. A. Robertson
North Norfolk	90,400	219.19	T. V. Nolan		Mrs H. C. Barrow
North Shropshire	52,400	257.00	K. Flood		Mrs S. Lewis
§North Warwickshire	59,800	257.47	D. Monks	(a)	F. A. Paintin
North West Leicestershire	79,400	272.00	J. E. White		B. W. Hall
North Wiltshire	109,600	252.19	H. Miles		A. S. R. Jackson
NORWICH, Norfolk	120,700	305.79	J. R. Packer	(b)	A. Clare
NOTTINGHAM	261,500	316.00	E. F. Cantle	(b)	M. A. Wood
§Nuneaton and Bedworth, Warwicks.	115,300	349.00	J. Walton‡‡	(a)	A. A. Lloyd
§Oadby and Wigston, Leics.	51,500	229.73	Mrs R. E. Hyde	(a)	R. D. Allen
§Oswestry, Shropshire	33,600	279.00	D. A. Towers	(a)	B. W. Case
OXFORD	109,000	311.57	R. S. Block	(b)	Mrs B. Gatehouse
§Pendle, Lancs.	82,700	265.00	F. Wood	(a)	J. David
Penwith, Cornwall	59,400	251.97	M. J. Furneaux†		T. H. E. Laity
PETERBOROUGH, Cambs.	148,800	295.00	W. E. Samuel	(a)	L. Rimes
PLYMOUTH, Devon	238,800	302.00	M. S. Boxall	(b)	R. Simmonds
§Poole, Dorset	130,900	248.00	I. K. D. Andrews*	(a)	H. C. R. Ballam, MBE
PORTSMOUTH, Hants.	174,700	189.95	R. Trist	(b)	J. Patey
§Preston, Lancs.	126,200	307.00	A. Owens	(a)	H. Parker
Purbeck, Dorset	42,600	204.80	P. B. Croft		D. B. Humphry
§Reading, Berks.	122,600	324.00	Ms S. Pierce	(a)	H. Fuad
§Redditch, Hereford and Worcs.	76,900	284.00	Ms S. Manzie	(a)	D. Cartwright
§Reigate and Banstead, Surrey	114,900	270.00	M. Bacon	(a)	E. H. Waller
§Restormel, Cornwall	88,300	254.60	D. Brown	(a)	D. Curnow
§Ribble Valley, Lancs.	51,000	290.00	O. Hopkins	(a)	J. Travis
Richmondshire, North Yorks.	43,800	214.92	H. Tabiner		Mrs M. Rothwell
ROCHESTER UPON MEDWAY, Kent	142,000	97.00	R. I. Gregory	(a)	R. M. Morrad
Rochford, Essex	74,400	242.68	P. W. Hughes		C. R. Morgan
§Rossendale, Lancs.	64,000	265.55	J. S. Hartley	(a)	D. W. Easton
Rother, East Sussex	80,200	270.71	D. F. Powell		R. E. Side
§Rugby, Warwicks.	83,400	325.73	J. S. R. Lawton	(a)	A. C. Webb
§Runnymede, Surrey	71,500	229.00	T. N. Williams	(a)	N. H. Rundell
§Rushcliffe, Notts.	94,900	278.00	J. Saxton	(a)	R. Rodwell
§Rushmoor, Hants.	80,400	252.00	R. Upton	(a)	G. R. J. Kimber
Rutland, Leics.	32,400	269.22	K. R. Emslie		C. H. Forsyth
Ryedale, North Yorks.	90,000	243.10	M. Walker		A. J. Jenkins
ST ALBANS, Herts.	122,400	279.33	E. A. Hackford	(a)	K. M. McCan
§St Edmundsbury, Suffolk	89,100	253.00	G. R. N. Toft	(a)	T. T. F. May
Salisbury, Wilts.	103,200	230.43	D. R. J. Rawlinson		Mrs P. M. Errington-Rycroft
§Scarborough, North Yorks.	107,800	235.21	J. M. Trebble	(a)	J. Warwick
§Scunthorpe, Humberside	60,500	297.00	I. M. Hutchinson	(a)	M. J. Hunt
Sedgefield, Co. Durham	89,200	266.02	A. J. Roberts		Mrs C. Gowton
Sedgemoor, Somerset	97,000	277.28	A. G. Lovell		P. H. Daniel
Selby, North Yorks.	88,200	240.68	J. C. Edwards		T. Limbert
Sevenoaks, Kent	106,100	254.97	B. C. Cova, MBE		Mrs A. E. Dawson
Shepway, Kent	89,200	280.33	R. J. Thompson		P. L. Huxley-Williams
§Shrewsbury and Atcham	90,900	265.00	D. Bradbury	(a)	D. H. P. Davies
§Slough, Berks.	98,600	220.00	A. Bhattacharya*	(a)	D. McCarthy
SOUTHAMPTON, Hants.	194,400	261.00	E. A. Urquhart	(a)	Mrs N. Goss
South Bedfordshire	106,800	392.25	T. D. Rix		D. McVicar
South Bucks.	60,300	233.32	S. R. Jobson		B. W. Learmount
South Cambridgeshire	118,100	218.45	B. J. Hancock		E. W. Bullman
South Derbyshire	71,000	314.51	T. Day		J. Clifton
§Southend-on-Sea, Essex	153,700	239.00	D. Moulson*	(a)	A. J. Cole

p preliminary
‡‡ Borough Manager
† Director of Central Services

District Borough Council	Population Census 1991p	Community charge per head 1992	Chief Executive (*Clerk)		Chairman 1992–3 (a) Mayor (b) Lord Mayor
South Hams, Devon	77,300	£238.45	F. G. Palmer		Mrs D. J. Thomson
South Herefordshire	51,200	234.38	A. Hughes		E. R. Vines
South Holland, Lincs.	66,000	267.98	C. J. Simpkins		W. D. Skells
South Kesteven, Lincs.	107,200	242.51	K. R. Cann		R. Briggs
South Lakeland, Cumbria	101,900	286.79	A. F. Winstanley*		H. S. Lewis
South Norfolk	101,400	238.96	A. G. T. Kellett		E. J. Lines
South Northamptonshire	68,800	257.11	K. Whitehead		S. P. Dunkley
South Oxfordshire	130,900	333.78	R. Watson		Mrs E. A. Ducker
§South Ribble, Lancs.	99,800	294.63	J. B. R. Leadbetter	(a)	J. E. J. Breakell
South Shropshire	37,800	255.00	G. C. Biggs		J. McCormick
South Somerset	139,400	288.86	M. Usher		R. Madelin
South Staffordshire	103,900	250.06	L. Barnfild		Mrs J. Williams
§South Wight, IOW	56,400	266.68	D. W. Jaggar	(a)	A. C. Bartlett
§Spelthorne, Surrey	87,100	272.70	M. B. Taylor	(a)	T. Stubbs, OBE
§Stafford	117,000	234.00	J. K. M. Krawiec*	(a)	Mrs F. S. Dainton
Staffordshire Moorlands	94,000	278.70	A. W. Law		Mrs G. Ferguson
§Stevenage, Herts.	73,700	311.12	H. L. Miller	(a)	B. Woodward
§Stockton-on-Tees, Cleveland	170,200	308.78	F. F. Theobalds*	(a)	S. Smailes
STOKE-ON-TRENT, Staffs.	244,800	305.00	S. W. Titchener	(b)	A. Jones
Stratford-upon-Avon, Warwicks.	103,600	283.33	I. B. Prosser		D. R. Partridge
Stroud, Glos.	108,300	318.58	R. M. Ollin		Mrs S. M. Bruce
Suffolk Coastal	106,800	267.23	T. K. Griffin		G. W. Laing
§Surrey Heath	78,300	271.00	N. M. Pughe	(a)	Mrs J. E. Read
§Swale, Kent	113,700	265.73	W. Croydon, CBE	(a)	B. Groves
§Tamworth, Staffs.	68,900	272.00	G. Morrell	(a)	D. E. Owen
Tandridge, Surrey	75,000	283.00	P. J. D. Thomas		Mrs P. G. Banks
§Taunton Deane, Somerset	93,300	270.34	P. F. Berman	(a)	Mrs M. E. Dickson
Teesdale, Co. Durham	24,200	242.23	C. E. Fell		K. G. Saxby
Teignbridge, Devon	107,100	271.35	P. B. Young		D. Prouse
Tendring, Essex	125,100	240.81	D. Mitchell-Gears		L. Randall
§Test Valley, Hants.	99,000	221.53	G. Blythe	(a)	N. C. Lewis
§Tewkesbury, Glos.	87,400	279.00	R. A. Wheeler	(a)	J. W. Castle
§Thamesdown, Wilts.	167,200	280.99	D. M. Kent	(a)	M. Haines
Thanet, Kent	121,300	241.00	I. G. Gill		Mrs M. Mortlock
Three Rivers, Herts.	74,100	299.23	A. Robertson		C. Whillier
§Thurrock, Essex	124,300	276.00	K. Barnes	(a)	M. Millane
§Tonbridge and Malling, Kent	99,100	261.18	T. Thompson	(a)	D. H. W. Chandler
§Torbay, Devon	122,500	270.00	D. P. Hudson	(a)	D. Lentell
Torridge, Devon	52,100	252.50	R. K. Brasington		W. W. Pillman
§Tunbridge Wells, Kent	98,300	254.37	R. J. Stone	(a)	D. Smith
Tynedale, Northumberland	58,400	310.58	A. Baty		H. J. C. Herron
Uttlesford, Essex	63,900	245.88	K. Ivory		S. W. Neville
Vale of White Horse, Oxon.	109,200	272.70	D. J. Heavens°		J. Francis
§Vale Royal, Cheshire	111,100	330.00	W. R. T. Woods	(a)	A. Walsh
Wansbeck, Northumberland	60,100	283.00	A. G. White		M. G. Ferrigon
Wansdyke, Avon	78,700	317.51	P. May‡		L. G. Sell
§Warrington, Cheshire	179,500	303.89	M. I. M. Sanders	(a)	J. R. Pennington
Warwick	114,900	285.99	J. V. Picking		C. S. Cleaver
§Watford, Herts.	72,100	314.00	D. Plank	(a)	P. Kiely
Waveney, Suffolk	105,500	267.74	M. Berridge		H. H. Ley
§Waverley, Surrey	111,500	272.16	G. W. Nuttall	(a)	H. Denningberg, MBE
Wealden, East Sussex	127,700	272.00	D. R. Holness		Mrs E. M. Gabriel
Wear Valley, Co. Durham	62,100	251.43	Mrs E. M. Ashness°		Mrs M. Land
§Wellingborough, Northants.	71,100	145.00	W. B. Veal	(a)	Mrs E. Higgins

p preliminary
° Director of Administration
‡ General Manager

District Borough Council	Population Census 1991p	Community charge per head 1992	Chief Executive (*Clerk)		Chairman 1992–3 (a) Mayor (b) Lord Mayor
Welwyn Hatfield, Herts.	91,600	£331.87	D. Riddle		Ms A. Hewson
§West Devon	44,400	267.27	J. S. Ligo	(a)	L. J. G. Hockridge
West Dorset	86,300	239.13	R. C. Rennison		Mrs J. D. Cockerill
West Lancashire	106,600	297.79	B. A. Knight		Mrs J. M. White
West Lindsey, Lincs.	72,200	260.34	R. W. Nelsey		G. Greenaway
West Oxfordshire	88,700	240.35	N. J. B. Robson		C. R. M. Fox
West Somerset	34,100	295.55	C. Rockall		K. Ross
West Wiltshire	105,900	260.00	D. G. Latham		Mrs J. M. Stacey
§Weymouth and Portland, Dorset	61,000	273.95	M. N. Ashby	(a)	Revd R. A. Weaver
WINCHESTER, Hants.	95,700	221.50	D. H. Cowan	(a)	Wg. Cdr. J. L. Nunn
§Windsor and Maidenhead, Berks.	128,700	261.56	G. B. Blacker	(a)	A. J. Langdown
§Woking, Surrey	84,000	287.13	P. Russell	(a)	L. C. Prescodd, TD
Wokingham, Berks.	136,300	275.53	N. B. J. Gurney		J. V. E. Trimming
Woodspring, Avon	174,300	320.14	C. A. Stephens		Mrs G. E. Lewis
WORCESTER	81,000	288.00	R. G. Grant	(a)	D. Richards
§Worthing, West Sussex	94,100	230.00	M. J. Ball	(a)	Mrs M. Wilton
Wrekin, Shropshire	137,100	322.60	D. G. Hutchinson		Mrs H. Rhodes
Wychavon, Hereford and Worcs.	99,800	258.61	T. Du Sautoy		G. J. Barnett
Wycombe, Bucks.	154,500	254.00	R. J. Cummins		P. Cartwright
§Wyre, Lancs.	99,700	277.00	M. Brown	(a)	T. Ibison
Wyre Forest, Hereford and Worcs.	93,400	283.05	A. S. Dick		E. C. Higgs
YORK, North Yorks.	100,600	246.00	J. Cairns	(b)	B. Bell

p preliminary

The Cinque Ports

As their name implies, the Cinque Ports were originally five in number: Hastings, New Romney, Hythe, Dover and Sandwich. They existed before the Norman Conquest and were the Anglo-Saxon successors to the Roman system of coast defence organized from the Wash to Spithead to resist Saxon onslaughts. William the Conqueror reconstituted them and granted peculiar jurisdiction, most of which was abolished in 1855. Only jurisdiction in Admiralty still survives.

At some time after the Conquest the 'antient towns' of Winchelsea and Rye were added with equal privileges. The other members of the Confederation, known as Limbs, are Lydd, Faversham, Folkestone, Deal, Tenterden, Margate and Ramsgate.

The Barons of the Cinque Ports have the ancient privilege of attending the Coronation ceremony and are allotted special places in Westminster Abbey.

Lord Warden of the Cinque Ports, HM Queen Elizabeth the Queen Mother

Judge, Court of Admiralty, Gerald Darling, RD, QC

Registrar, I. G. Gill, LVO, PO Box 9, Margate, Kent CT9 1XZ. Tel: 0843-225511

LORD WARDENS OF THE CINQUE PORTS *since* 1904

The Marquess Curzon	1904
The Prince of Wales	1905
The Earl Brassey	1908
The Earl Beauchamp	1913
The Marquess of Reading	1934
The Marquess of Willingdon	1936
Sir Winston Churchill	1941
Sir Robert Menzies	1965
HM Queen Elizabeth the Queen Mother	1978

London

THE CORPORATION OF LONDON

The City of London is the historic centre at the heart of London known as 'the square mile' around which the vast metropolis has grown over the centuries. The City's residential population is 4,000 (1991 Census). The civic government is carried on by the Corporation of the City of London through the Court of Common Council, a body consisting of the Lord Mayor, 24 other Aldermen and 132 Common Councilmen. The legal title of the Corporation is The Mayor and Commonalty and Citizens of the City of London.

The City is the financial and business centre of London and includes the head offices of the principal banks, insurance companies and mercantile houses, in addition to buildings ranging from the historic interest of the Roman Wall and the 15th century Guildhall, to the massive splendour of St Paul's Cathedral and the architectural beauty of Wren's spires.

The City of London was described by Tacitus in AD 62 as 'a busy emporium for trade and traders'. Under the Romans it became an important administration centre and hub of the road system. Little is known of London in Saxon times, when it formed part of the kingdom of the East Saxons. In 886 Alfred recovered London from the Danes and reconstituted it a burgh under his son-in-law. In 1066 the citizens submitted to William the Conqueror who in 1067 granted them a charter, which is still preserved, establishing them in the rights and privileges they had hitherto enjoyed.

The Mayoralty

The Mayoralty was probably established about 1189, the first Mayor being Henry Fitz Ailwyn who filled the office for 23 years and was succeeded by Fitz Alan (1212–14). A new charter was granted by King John in 1215, directing the Mayor to be chosen annually, which has ever since been done, though in early times the same individual often held the office more than once. A familiar instance is that of 'Whittington, thrice Lord Mayor of London' (in reality four times, 1397, 1398, 1406, 1419); and many modern cases have occurred. The earliest instance of the phrase 'Lord Mayor' in English is in 1414. It was used more generally in the latter part of the 15th century and became invariable from 1535 onwards. At Michaelmas the Liverymen in Common Hall choose two Aldermen who have served the office of Sheriff for presentation to the Court of Aldermen, and one is chosen to be Lord Mayor for the following mayoral year.

Lord Mayor's Day

The Lord Mayor of London was previously elected on the feast of St Simon and St Jude (28 October), and from the time of Edward I, at least, was presented to the King or to the Barons of the Exchequer on the following day, unless that day was a Sunday. The day of election was altered to 16 October in 1346, and after some further changes was fixed for Michaelmas Day in 1546, but the ceremonies of admittance and swearing-in of the Lord Mayor continued to take place on 28 and 29 October respectively until 1751. In 1752, at the reform of the calendar, the Lord Mayor was continued in office until 8 November, the 'New Style' equivalent of 28 October. The Lord Mayor is now presented to the Lord Chief Justice at the Royal Courts of Justice on the second Saturday in November to make the final declaration of office, having been sworn in at Guildhall on the preceding day. The procession to the Royal Courts of Justice is popularly known as the Lord Mayor's Show.

Representatives

Aldermen are mentioned in the 11th century and their office is of Saxon origin. They were elected annually between 1377 and 1394, when an Act of Parliament of Richard II directed them to be chosen for life.

The Common Council, elected annually on the first Friday in December, was, at an early date, substituted for a popular assembly called the *Folkmote*. At first only two representatives were sent from each ward, but the number has since been greatly increased.

Officers

Sheriffs were Saxon officers; their predecessors were the *wic-reeves* and *portreeves* of London and Middlesex. At first they were officers of the Crown, and were named by the Barons of the Exchequer; but Henry I (in 1132) gave the citizens permission to choose their own Sheriffs, and the annual election of Sheriffs became fully operative under King John's charter of 1199. The citizens lost this privilege, as far as the election of the Sheriff of Middlesex was concerned, by the Local Government Act 1888; but the Liverymen continue to choose two Sheriffs of the City of London, who are appointed on Midsummer Day and take office at Michaelmas.

The office of Chamberlain is an ancient one, the first contemporary record of which is 1237. The Town Clerk (or Common Clerk) is mentioned in 1274.

Activities

The work of the Corporation is assigned to a number of committees which present reports to the Court of Common Council. These Committees are: City Lands and Bridge House Estates, Policy and Resources, Finance, Planning and Communications, Central Markets, Billingsgate and Leadenhall Markets, Spitalfields Market, Police, Port and City of London Health and Social Services, Libraries, Art Galleries and Records, Boards of Governors of Schools, Music (Guildhall School of Music and Drama), Establishment, Housing, Gresham (City side), Hampstead Heath Management, Epping Forest and Open Spaces, West Ham Park, Privileges, Barbican Residential and Barbican Centre (Barbican Arts and Conference Centre).

The City's estate, in the possession of which the Corporation of London differs from other municipalities, is managed by the City Lands and Bridge House Estates Committee, the chairmanship of which carries with it the title of Chief Commoner. *Chairman* (1992), P. P. Rigby, CBE.

The Honourable the Irish Society (The Irish Chamber, Guildhall Yard, London EC2V 5AE. *Secretary*, B. E. Manning), which manages the Corporation's estates in Ulster, consists of a Governor and five other Aldermen, the Recorder, and 19 Common Councilmen, of whom one is elected Deputy Governor.

The Lord Mayor 1991–2*

The Rt. Hon. the Lord Mayor (1991-2), Sir Brian Jenkins, GBE.

Secretary, Rear-Adm. A. J. Cook, CB.

The Sheriffs 1992–3

R. W. Cork (*Alderman, Tower*) and A. D. Moss; *elected*, 24 June 1992; *assumed office*, 28 September 1992.

Officers

Town Clerk, S. Jones, apptd 1991.
Chamberlain, B. P. Harty, apptd 1983.

* The Lord Mayor for 1992–3 was elected on Michaelmas Day. *See* Stop-press.

THE ALDERMEN

Name and Ward	CC	Ald.	Shff.	Lord Mayor
Cdr. Sir Robin Gillett, Bt., GBE, RD, *Bassishaw*	1965	1969	1973	1976
Sir Peter Gadsden, GBE, *Farringdon Wt.*	1969	1971	1970	1979
Sir Christopher Leaver, GBE, *Dowgate*	1973	1974	1979	1981
Sir Alan Traill, GBE, *Langbourn*	1970	1975	1982	1984
Sir David Rowe-Ham, GBE, *Bridge*		1976	1984	1986
Sir Greville Spratt, GBE, TD, *Castle Baynard*		1978	1984	1987
Sir Christopher Collett, GBE, *Broad Street*	1973	1979	1985	1988
Sir Hugh Bidwell, GBE, *Billingsgate*		1979	1986	1989
Sir Alexander Graham, GBE, *Queenhithe*	1978	1979	1986	1990
Sir Brian Jenkins, GBE, *Cordwainer*		1980	1987	1991
All the above have passed the Civic Chair				
Francis McWilliams, *Aldersgate*	1978	1980	1988	
Paul Newall, TD, *Walbrook*	1980	1981	1989	
Christopher Walford, *Farringdon Wn.*		1982	1990	
Neil Young, *Bread Street*	1980	1982	1991	
Roger Cork, *Tower*	1978	1983		
Bryan Toye, *Lime Street*		1983		
Richard Nichols, *Candlewick*	1983	1984		
Peter Bull, *Cheap*	1968	1984		
Sir Peter Levene, KBE, *Portsoken*	1983	1984		
Leonard Chalstrey, *Vintry*	1981	1984		
Clive Martin, OBE, TD, *Aldgate*		1985		
David Howard, *Cornhill*	1972	1986		
James Oliver, *Bishopsgate*	1980	1987		
Garyn Arthur, *Cripplegate*	1988	1991		
Robert Finch, *Coleman Street*		1992		

THE COMMON COUNCIL OF LONDON

Deputy: Each Common Councilman so described serves as deputy to the Alderman of her/his ward

Angell, E. H. (1991)	*Cripplegate Wt.*
Anstee, N. J. (1987)	*Aldersgate*
Archibald, W. W. (1986)	*Cornhill*
Arthur, G. F. (1988)	*Farringdon Wt.*
Ballard, K. A., MC (1969)	*Castle Baynard*
Balls, *Deputy* H. D. (1970)	*Cripplegate Wt.*
Barker, J. A. (1981)	*Cripplegate Wt.*
Barnes-Yallowley, H. M. F. (1986)	*Coleman Street*
Beale, M. J. (1979)	*Lime Street*
Bird, J. L. (1977)	*Bridge*
Biroum-Smith, P. L. (1988)	*Dowgate*
Blackwood, C. D. (1990)	*Farringdon Wt.*
Block, S. A. A. (1983)	*Cheap*
Bradshaw, D. J. (1991)	*Cripplegate Wn.*
Bramwell, F. M. (1983)	*Langbourn*
Brighton, R. L. (1984)	*Portsoken*
Brooks, W. I. B. (1988)	*Billingsgate*
Brown, *Deputy* D. T. (1971)	*Walbrook*
Cann, T. J. (1988)	*Cripplegate Wn.*
Cassidy, M. J. (1989)	*Coleman Street*
Catt, B. F. (1982)	*Farringdon Wn.*
Challis, G. H., CBE (1978)	*Langbourn*
Clements, *Deputy* G. E. I. (1960)	*Farringdon Wt.*
Cohen, Mrs C. M. (1986)	*Lime Street*
Cole, Lt.-Col. Sir Colin, KCVO, TD (1964)	*Castle Baynard*
Collinson, Miss A. H. (1991)	*Farringdon Wt.*
Cope, Dr J. (1963)	*Farringdon Wt.*
Cotgrove, C. B. (1991)	*Lime Street*
Coven, *Deputy* Mrs E. O., CBE (1972)	*Dowgate*
Currie, Miss S. E. M. (1985)	*Cripplegate Wt.*
Daily-Hunt, R. B. (1989)	*Cripplegate*
Davis, C. B. (1991)	*Bread Street*
Delderfield, D. W. (1982)	*Aldersgate*
de Silva, D., QC (1980)	*Farringdon Wt.*
Donnelly, T. A., MBE (1982)	*Bread Street*
Duckworth, *Deputy* H., CBE (1960)	*Lime Street*
Dunitz, A. A. (1984)	*Portsoken*
Durnin, J. C. (1976)	*Cordwainer*
Edwards, R. D. K. (1978)	*Bassishaw*
Eskenzi, A. N. (1970)	*Farringdon Wn.*
Evans, Mrs J. (1975)	*Farringdon Wt.*
Eve, R. A. (1980)	*Cheap*
Everett, K. M. (1984)	*Candlewick*
Falk, F. A., TD (1984)	*Farringdon Wt.*
Farrow, M. W. W. (1987)	*Bishopsgate*
Farthing, R. B. C. (1981)	*Aldgate*
Fell, J. A. (1982)	*Queenhithe*
FitzGerald, R. C. A. (1981)	*Bread Street*
Floyd-Ewin, *Deputy* Sir David, LVO, OBE (1963)	*Castle Baynard*
Frankenberg, P. B. (1989)	*Cordwainer*
Frappell, *Deputy* C. E. (1973)	*Bread Street*
Fraser, W. B. (1981)	*Vintry*
Frazer, C. M. (1986)	*Farringdon Wt.*
Galloway, A. D. (1981)	*Broad Street*
Gass, *Deputy* G. J. (1967)	*Coleman Street*
Ginsburg, S. (1990)	*Bishopsgate*
Gold, R. (1965)	*Castle Baynard*
Gowman, Miss A. (1991)	*Dowgate*
Graves, A. C. (1985)	*Bishopsgate*
Harding, N. H. (1970)	*Farringdon Wn.*
Hardwick, Dr P. B. (1987)	*Aldgate*
Hart, *Deputy* M. G. (1970)	*Bridge*
Haynes, J. E. H. (1986)	*Cornhill*
Henderson, *Deputy* J. S., OBE (1975)	*Langbourn*
Henderson-Begg, M. (1977)	*Coleman Street*
Holland, *Deputy* J. (1972)	*Aldgate*
Horlock, *Deputy* H. W. S. (1969)	*Farringdon Wn.*
Hughesdon, J. S. (1991)	*Bread Street*
Humphrays, Mrs R. (1976)	*Cripplegate Wt.*
Ide, W. R. (1972)	*Castle Baynard*
Jackson, L. St J. T. (1978)	*Bassishaw*
Jennings, I. G. (1988)	*Cripplegate Wn.*
Keep, Mrs B. (1987)	*Cripplegate Wn.*
Kellett, Mrs M. W. F. (1986)	*Tower*
Kemp, D. L. (1984)	*Coleman Street*
Knowles, S. K. (1984)	*Candlewick*
Lamport, J. C. (1987)	*Cripplegate Wt.*
Langmead, A. D. G., TD (1982)	*Tower*
Lawrence, D. W. O., TD (1979)	*Bridge*
Lawson, G. C. H. (1971)	*Portsoken*
McAuley, *Deputy* C. (1957)	*Bread Street*
MacLellan, A. P. W. (1989)	*Walbrook*
Malins, J. H. (1981)	*Farringdon Wt.*
Martin, R. C. (1986)	*Queenhithe*
Mayhew, Miss J. (1986)	*Queenhithe*
Mills, A. P. (1969)	*Bassishaw*
Minshull-Fogg, J., TD (1986)	*Walbrook*

Mitchell, C. R. (1971)	*Castle Baynard*
Mizen, *Deputy* D. H. (1979)	*Broad Street*
Mobsby, D. J. L. (1985)	*Billingsgate*
Morgan, *Deputy* B. L., CBE (1963)	*Bishopsgate*
Moss, A. D. (1989)	*Tower*
Nash, *Deputy* Mrs J. C. (1983)	*Aldersgate*
Neary, J. E. (1982)	*Aldgate*
Newman, Mrs P. B. (1989)	*Aldersgate*
Northall-Laurie, P. D. (1975)	*Walbrook*
Olson, A. H. F. (1972)	*Dowgate*
Owen, Mrs J. (1975)	*Langbourn*
Owen-Ward, J. R. (1983)	*Bridge*
Packard, Brig. J. J. (1972)	*Cripplegate Wn.*
Pembroke, *Deputy* Mrs A. M. F. (1978)	*Cheap*
Ponsonby of Shulbrede, The Lady (1981)	*Farringdon Wt.*
Pulman, G. A. G. (1983)	*Tower*
Reed, *Deputy* J. L., MBE (1967)	*Farringdon Wn.*
Revell-Smith, P. A., CBE (1959)	*Vintry*
Rigby, P. P. (1972)	*Farringdon Wn.*
Robinson, Mrs D. C. (1989)	*Bishopsgate*
Rodgers, Miss E. H. L. (1987)	*Vintry*
Roney, E. P. T., CBE (1974)	*Bishopsgate*
Samuel, *Deputy* Mrs I. (1971)	*Portsoken*
Sargant, K. A. (1991)	*Cornhill*
Saunders, *Deputy* R. (1975)	*Candlewick*
Savory, M. B. (1980)	*Broad Street*
Scriven, R. G. (1984)	*Candlewick*
Sellon, S. A., TD, OBE (1990)	*Cordwainer*
Shalit, D. M. (1972)	*Farringdon Wn.*
Sharp, *Deputy* Mrs I. M. (1974)	*Queenhithe*
Shindler, *Deputy* A. B. (1966)	*Billingsgate*
Simpson, A. S. J. (1987)	*Aldersgate*
Simpson, Mrs S. G. (1992)	*Aldersgate*
Smithers, H. J. (1986)	*Billingsgate*
Snyder, M. J. (1986)	*Cordwainer*
Spanner, J. H., TD (1984)	*Broad Street*
Stitcher, *Deputy* G. M., CBE (1966)	*Farringdon Wt.*
Swan, N. E. B. (1985)	*Coleman Street*
Taylor, J. A. F., TD (1991)	*Bread Street*
Walsh, S. (1989)	*Farringdon Wt.*
Webb, C. J. (1986)	*Bishopsgate*
White, J. W. (1986)	*Cornhill*
Williams, G. M. E. (1985)	*Aldersgate*
Willoughby, P. J. (1985)	*Bishopsgate*
Wilmot, *Deputy* R. T. D. (1973)	*Cordwainer*
Wilson, A. B., CBE (1984)	*Cheap*
Wixley, G. R. A., TD (1964)	*Bassishaw*
Woodward, *Deputy* C. D., OBE (1971)	*Cripplegate Wn.*
Wooldridge, F. D. (1988)	*Farringdon Wn.*

The City Guilds (Livery Companies)

The Livery Companies of the City of London derive their name from the assumption of a distinctive dress or livery by their members in the 14th century. The order of precedence, omitting extinct companies, is given in parentheses after the name of each company.

Liverymen of the Guilds (23,608 in number) are entitled to vote at elections in Common Hall.

THE TWELVE GREAT COMPANIES

In order of civic precedence

MERCERS (*1*). *Hall*, Ironmonger Lane, London EC2V 8HE. *Livery*, 250. *Clerk*, G. M. M. Wakeford. *Master*, The Hon. H. Palmer.

GROCERS (*2*). *Hall*, Princes Street, London EC2R 8AD. *Livery*, 330. *Clerk*, C. G. Mattingley, CBE. *Master*, Lt.-Col. Sir John Smiley, Bt.

DRAPERS (*3*). *Hall*, Throgmorton Street, London EC2N 2DQ. *Livery*, 232. *Clerk*, R. C. G. Strick. *Master*, P. A. F. Chalk, FRCS, FRCOG.

FISHMONGERS (*4*). *Hall*, London Bridge, London EC4R 9EL. *Livery*, 362. *Clerk*, M. R. T. O'Brien. *Prime Warden*, Lord Camoys.

GOLDSMITHS (*5*). *Hall*, Foster Lane, London EC2V 6BN. *Livery*, 267. *Clerk*, R. D. Buchanan-Dunlop, CBE. *Prime Warden*, Dr A. M. Stirling.

MERCHANT TAYLORS (*6*). *Hall*, 30 Threadneedle Street, London EC2R 8AY. *Livery* 330. *Clerk*, Capt. D. A. Wallis, RN. *Master*, Earl of Stockton.

SKINNERS (*7*). *Hall*, 8 Dowgate Hill, London EC4R 2SP. *Livery*, 360. *Clerk*, Capt. D. H. Dyke, CBE, LVO, RN. *Master*, J. H. Keith.

HABERDASHERS (*8*). *Hall*, Staining Lane, London EC2V 7DD. *Livery*, 320. *Clerk*, Capt. M. E. Barrow, DSO, RN. *Master*, M. A. B. Jenks.

SALTERS (*9*). *Hall*, 4 Fore Street, London EC2Y 5DE. *Livery*, 150. *Clerk*, Col. M. P. Barneby. *Master*, Ven. F. V. Weston.

IRONMONGERS (*10*). *Hall*, Shaftesbury Place, Barbican, London EC2Y 8AA. *Livery*, 119. *Clerk*, J. A. Oliver. *Master*, K. R. Harper.

VINTNERS (*11*). *Hall*, Upper Thames Street, London EC4V 3BJ. *Livery*, 325. *Clerk*, Brig. G. Read, CBE. *Master*, Sir David Mitchell, MP.

CLOTHWORKERS (*12*). *Hall*, Dunster Court, Mincing Lane, London EC3R 7AH. *Livery*, 185. *Clerk*, M. G. T. Harris. *Master*, J. N. Horne.

OTHER CITY GUILDS

In alphabetical order

ACCOUNTANTS, CHARTERED (*86*). *Livery*, 340. *Clerk*, G. H. Kingsmill, The Grove, Hinton Parva, Swindon SN4 0DH. *Master*, F. E. Worsley.

ACTUARIES (*91*). *Livery*, 174. *Clerk*, P. D. Esslemont, 16A Cadogan Square, London SW1X 0JU. *Master*, R. D. Corley.

AIR PILOTS AND AIR NAVIGATORS, GUILD OF (*81*). *Livery*, 400. *Grand Master*, HRH The Prince Philip, Duke of Edinburgh, KG, KT. *Clerk*, Gp Capt J. W. Tritton, 291 Gray's Inn Road, London WC1X 8QF. *Master*, Capt. D. R. Mauleverer.

APOTHECARIES, SOCIETY OF (*58*). *Hall*, Black Friars Lane, London EC4V 6EJ. *Livery*, 1,266. *Clerk*, Lt. Col. R. J. Stringer. *Master*, Dr D. T. D. Hughes.

ARBITRATORS (*93*). *Livery*, 190. *Clerk*, B. W. Vigrass, OBE, VRD, 75 Cannon Street, London EC4N 5BH. *Master*, R. H. Mildred.

ARMOURERS AND BRASIERS (*22*). *Hall*, 81 Coleman Street, London EC2R 5BJ. *Livery*, 120. *Clerk*, Lt.-Col. R. R. F. Cowe. *Master*, H. P. Mason.

BAKERS (*19*). *Hall*, Harp Lane, London EC3R 6DP. *Livery*, 425. *Clerk*, Capt. A. H. Lambourne, RN. *Master*, H. Gould.

BARBERS (*17*). *Hall*, Monkwell Square, London EC2Y 5BL. *Livery*, 223. *Clerk*, Col. A. B. Harfield, CBE. *Master*, Sir Gerard Vaughan, MP.

BASKETMAKERS (*52*). *Livery*, 430. *Clerk*, A. Gillett, 7 Kinghorn Street, London EC1A 7HT. *Prime Warden*, A. K. Brown, MBE, MB, FRCS.

BLACKSMITHS (*40*). *Livery*, 285. *Clerk*, R. C. Jorden, 27 Cheyne Walk, Grange Park, London N21 1DB. *Prime Warden*, C. C. Bates.

BOWYERS (*38*). *Livery*, 100. *Clerk*, A. Black, CBE, 2 Serjeant's Inn, Fleet Street, London EC4Y 1LL. *Master*, C. Ballenden.

BREWERS (*14*). *Hall*, Aldermanbury Square, London EC2V 7HR. *Livery*, 132. *Clerk*, vacant. *Master*, M. G. Delahooke.

BRODERERS (*48*). *Livery*, 148. *Clerk*, P. J. C. Crouch, 11 Bridge Road, East Molesey, Surrey KT8 9EU. *Master*, C. C. Gotto.

BUILDERS MERCHANTS (*88*). *Livery*, 210. *Clerk*, Ms S. Robinson, TD, 14 Charterhouse Street, London EC1M 6AX. *Master*, H. A. Terry.

BUTCHERS (*24*). *Hall*, 87 Bartholomew Close, London EC1A 7EB. *Livery*, 800. *Clerk*, A. H. Emus. *Master*, F. J. Mallion.

CARMEN (*77*). *Livery*, 458. *Clerk*, Lt.-Col. G. T. Pearce, MBE, 35–37 Ludgate Hill, London EC4M 7JN. *Master*, Sir Peter Levene, KBE.

CARPENTERS (*26*). *Hall*, 1 Throgmorton Avenue, London EC2N 2JJ. *Livery*, 150. *Clerk*, Maj.-Gen. P. T. Stevenson, OBE. *Master*, D. V. J. Galbraith.

CHARTERED SECRETARIES AND ADMINISTRATORS (*87*). *Livery*, 230. *Hon. Clerk*, G. H. Challis, CBE, The Irish Chamber, Guildhall Yard, London EC2V 5AE. *Master*, E. S. Kirk.

CLOCKMAKERS (*61*). *Livery*, 286. *Hall*, St Dunstan's House, Carey Lane, London EC2V 8AA. *Clerk*, Air Cdre B. G. Frow, DSO, DFC. *Master*, J. R. Cope.

COACHMAKERS AND COACH-HARNESS MAKERS (*72*). *Livery*, 428. *Clerk*, Maj. W. H. Wharfe, 149 Banstead Road, Ewell, Epsom, Surrey KT17 3HL. *Master*, A. J. D. Ferguson.

COOKS (*35*). *Livery*, 75. *Clerk*, M. C. Thatcher, 35 Great Peter Street, London SW1P 3LR. *Master*, H. E. Taylor.

COOPERS (*36*). *Hall*, 13 Devonshire Square, London EC2M 4TH. *Livery*, 265. *Clerk*, J. A. Newton. *Master*, L. Joughin, OBE.

CORDWAINERS (*27*). *Livery* 150. *Clerk*, Cdr. C. Shears, CVO, OBE, Eldon Chambers, 30 Fleet Street, London EC4Y 1AA. *Master*, L. B. Mainzer.

CURRIERS (*29*). *Livery*, 92. *Clerk*, Gp Capt F. J. Hamilton, Kestrel Cottage, East Knoyle, Salisbury, Wilts. SP3 6AD. *Master*, M. S. Chesterton.

CUTLERS (*18*). *Hall*, Warwick Lane, London EC4M 7GR. *Livery*, 100. *Clerk*, K. S. G. Hinde, TD. *Master*, R. G. Smith.

DISTILLERS (*69*). *Livery*, 231. *Clerk*, C. V. Hughes, 71 Lincoln's Inn Fields, London WC2A 3JF. *Master*, V. Larvan.

DYERS (*13*). *Hall*, Dowgate Hill, London EC4R 2ST. *Livery*, 125. *Clerk*, J. R. Chambers. *Prime Warden*, M. Horton Ledger.

ENGINEERS (*94*). *Livery*, 295. *Clerk*, Cdr. B. D. Gibson, 1 Carlton House Terrace, London SW1Y 5DB. *Master*, J. V. Bartlett, CBE, FEng.

ENVIRONMENTAL CLEANERS (*97*). *Livery*, 203. *Clerk*, S. J. Holt, Whitethorns, Rannoch Road, Crowborough, E. Sussex TN6 1RA. *Master*, Ms I. D. Newell.

FAN MAKERS (*76*). *Livery*, 217. *Clerk*, Lt.-Col. I. R. P. Green, 2 Bolts Hill, Castle Camps, Cambs. CB1 6GL. *Master*, M. B. Phillips.

FARMERS (*80*). *Hall*, 3 Cloth Street, London EC1A 7LD. *Livery*, 300. *Clerk*, C. M. Taylor. *Master*, A. Tritton.

FARRIERS (*55*). *Livery*, 375. *Clerk*, H. W. H. Ellis, 37 The Uplands, Loughton, Essex IG10 1NQ. *Master*, Sir Gordon Shattock.

FELTMAKERS (*63*). *Livery*, 186. *Clerk*, R. M. Peel, 10 Carteret Street, Queen Anne's Gate, London SW1H 9DR. *Master*, W. P. Wright.

FLETCHERS (*39*). *Hall*, 3 Cloth Street, London EC1A 7LD. *Livery*, 105. *Clerk*, J. R. Garnett. *Master*, M. G. Hart.

FOUNDERS (*33*). *Hall*, 1 Cloth Fair, London EC1A 7HT. *Livery*, 170. *Clerk*, A. J. Gillett. *Master*, B. D. Farmer.

FRAMEWORK KNITTERS (*64*). *Livery*, 207. *Clerk*, C. J. Eldridge, Apothecaries' Hall, Black Friars Lane, London EC4V 6EL. *Master*, J. Ridge.

FRUITERERS (*45*). *Livery*, 250. *Clerk*, Cdr. M. T. H. Styles, Denmead Cottage, Chawton, Alton, Hants. GU34 1SB. *Master*, M. B. Sykes.

FUELLERS (*95*). *Livery*, 250. *Clerk*, Wg Cdr. H. F. C. Squire, OBE, 4 Maycross Avenue, Morden, Surrey SM4 4DA. *Master*, G. Stokes.

FURNITURE MAKERS (*83*). *Livery*, 261. *Clerk*, Wg Cdr. G. Acklam, MBE, 30 Harcourt Street, London W1H 2AA. *Master*, D. Ross.

GARDENERS (*66*). *Livery*, 246. *Clerk*, Col. N. G. S. Gray, 25 Luke Street, London EC2A 4AR. *Master*, D. E. Dowlen.

GIRDLERS (*23*). *Hall*, Basinghall Avenue, London EC2V 5DD. *Livery*, 81. *Clerk*, N. Wyldbore-Smith. *Master*, Sir Thomas Crawley-Boevey.

GLASS-SELLERS (*71*). *Livery*, 180. *Hon. Clerk*, B. J. Rawles, 43 Aragon Avenue, Thames Ditton, Surrey KT7 0PY. *Master*, P. S. Northam.

GLAZIERS AND PAINTERS OF GLASS (*53*). *Hall*, 9 Montague Close, London SE1 9DD. *Livery*, 290. *Clerk*, P. R. Batchelor. *Master*, S. M. Lever.

GLOVERS (*62*). *Livery*, 300. *Clerk*, Gp Capt D. G. F. Palmer, OBE, Glovers, Tismans Common, Rudgwick, W. Sussex RH12 3DU. *Master*, C. J. Wood.

GOLD AND SILVER WYRE DRAWERS (*74*). *Livery*, 340. *Clerk*, J. R. Williams, 50 Cheyne Avenue, London E18 2DR. *Master*, G. B. Perkins.

GUNMAKERS (*73*). *Livery*, 230. *Clerk*, F. B. Brandt, The Proof House, 48–50 Commercial Road, London E1 1LP. *Master*, A. McMillan of Cleghorn.

HORNERS (*54*). *Livery*, 328. *Clerk*, S. J. Holt, Whitethorns, Rannoch Road, Crowborough, E. Sussex TN6 1RA. *Master* H. Kleeman, CBE.

INNHOLDERS (*32*). *Hall*, College Street, Dowgate Hill, London EC4R 2SY. *Livery*, 123. *Clerk*, J. R. Edwardes Jones. *Master*, M. Vass.

INSURERS (*92*). *Hall*, 20 Aldermanbury, London EC2V 7HY. *Livery*, 354. *Clerk*, V. D. Webb. *Master*, R. C. W. Bardell, OBE.

JOINERS AND CEILERS (*41*). *Livery*, 134. *Clerk*, D. A. Tate, Parkville House, Bridge Street, Pinner, Middx. HA5 3JD. *Master*, J. W. Farrar.

LAUNDERERS (*89*). *Hall*, 9 Montague Close, London SE1 9DD. *Livery*, 195. *Clerk*, P. E. Coombe. *Master*, M. F. H. Rogers.

LEATHERSELLERS (*15*). *Hall*, 15 St Helen's Place, London EC3A 6DQ. *Livery*, 150. *Clerk*, Capt. N. MacEacharn, CBE, RN. *Master*, C. G. Daniels.

LIGHTMONGERS (*96*). *Livery*, 115. *Clerk*, S. H. Birch, 53 Leithcote Gardens, London SW16 2UX. *Master*, B. J. Castlo.

LORINERS (*57*). *Livery*, 370. *Clerk*, J. R. Williams, 50 Cheyne Avenue, London E18 2DR. *Master*, L. Jessel, MBE.

MARKETORS (*90*). *Livery*, 220. *Clerk*, B. F. Catt, 42 Tottenham Lane, London N8 7EA. *Master*, G. Darby.

MASONS (*30*). *Livery*, 111. *Clerk*, H. J. Maddocks, 9 New Square, London WC2R 3QN. *Master*, R. G. St J. Rowlandson.

MASTER MARINERS, HONOURABLE COMPANY OF (*78*). HQS *Wellington*, Temple Stairs, London WC2R 2PN. *Livery*, 264. *Clerk*, J. A. V. Maddock. *Admiral*, HRH The Duke of Edinburgh, KG, KT. *Master*, Capt. F. E. Holmes, RN.

MUSICIANS (*50*). *Livery*, 300. *Clerk*, M. J. G. Fletcher, 1 The Sanctuary, Westminster, London SW1P 3JT. *Master*, H. Willis.

NEEDLEMAKERS (*65*). *Livery*, 250. *Clerk*, M. G. Cook, 17 Southampton Place, London WC1A 2EH. *Master*, D. S. Anslow-Wilson.

PAINTER STAINERS (*28*). *Hall*, 9 Little Trinity Lane, London EC4V 2AD. *Livery*, 390. *Clerk*, Wg Cdr. B. C. Pratt. *Master*, C. Fisher.

PATTENMAKERS (*70*). *Livery*, 200. *Clerk*, P. Merritt, 25 Wellesley Road, London W4 4BU. *Master*, R. P. Shepherd.

PAVIORS (*56*). *Livery*, 267. *Clerk*, R. F. Coe, Cutlers' Hall, Warwick Lane, London EC4M 7BR. *Master*, A. W. D. Marshall.

PEWTERERS. (*16*). *Hall*, Oat Lane, London EC2V 7DE. *Livery*, 108. *Clerk*, Maj.-Gen. J. S. Grey, CB. *Master*, C. J. M. Hull.

PLAISTERERS (*46*). *Hall*, 1 London Wall, London EC2Y 5JU. *Livery*, 208. *Clerk*, H. Mott. *Master*, R. D. M. Jordan.

PLAYING CARDS, MAKERS OF (*75*). *Livery*, 148. *Clerk*, M. J. Smyth, 6 The Priory, Godstone, Surrey RH9 8NL. *Master*, D. C. Warner.

PLUMBERS (*31*). *Livery*, 350. *Clerk*, Cdr. A. J. Roberts, OBE, 49 Queen Victoria Street, London EC4N 4SE. *Master*, G. W. Bambrough, CBE.

POULTERS (*34*). *Livery*, 180. *Clerk*, Lt.-Col. R. R. F. Cowe, 23 Orchard Drive, Chorleywood, Herts. WD3 5QN. *Master*, Dr C. P. Juniper.

SADDLERS (*25*). *Hall*, 40 Gutter Lane, London EC2V 6BR. *Livery*, 70. *Clerk*, Gp Capt K. M. Oliver. *Master*, K. D. Luxford.

SCIENTIFIC INSTRUMENT MAKERS (*84*). *Hall*, 9 Montague Close, London SE1 9DD. *Livery*, 218. *Clerk*, F. G. Everard. *Master*, Dr D. T. Hughes.

SCRIVENERS (*44*). *Livery*, 218. *Clerk*, H. J. W. Harman, Westminster Bank Chambers, 11 Bridge Road, East Molesey, Surrey KT8 9EU. *Master*, A. H. Cope.

SHIPWRIGHTS (*59*). *Livery*, 450. *Clerk*, Capt. R. F. Channon, RN, Ironmongers' Hall, Barbican, London EC2Y 8AA. *Permanent Master*, HRH The Duke of Edinburgh, KG, KT. *Prime Warden*, D. I. Moor.

SOLICITORS (*79*). *Livery*, 366. *Clerk*, Miss S. M. Robinson, TD, 14 Charterhouse Square, London EC1M 6AX. *Master*, J. A. Rowson.

SPECTACLE MAKERS (*60*). *Livery*, 330. *Clerk*, C. J. Eldridge, Apothecaries' Hall, Black Friars Lane, London EC4V 6EL. *Master*, J. L. Bankes.

STATIONERS AND NEWSPAPER MAKERS (*47*). *Hall*, Ave Maria Lane, London EC4M 7DD. *Livery*, 450. *Clerk*, Capt. P. Hames, RN. *Master*, G. T. Mandl, MBE.

SURVEYORS, CHARTERED (*85*). *Livery*, 325. *Clerk*, Mrs A. L. Jackson, 16 St Mary-at-Hill, London EC3R 8EE. *Master*, T. J. L. Robertson.

TALLOW CHANDLERS (*21*). *Hall*, 4 Dowgate Hill, London EC4R 2SH. *Livery*, 180. *Clerk*, Brig. W. K. L. Prosser, CBE, MC. *Master*, Lt.-Col. P. W. S. Boult, TD.

TIN PLATE WORKERS Alias Wire Workers (*67*). *Livery*, 181. *Clerk*, S. J. Holt, Whitethorns, Rannoch Road, Crowborough, E. Sussex TN6 1RA. *Master*, J. F. R. Hayes.

TOBACCO PIPE MAKERS AND TOBACCO BLENDERS (*82*). *Livery*, 178. *Clerk*, I. J. Kimmins, Bouverie House, 154 Fleet Street, London EC4A 2HX. *Master*, G. H. Challis, CBE.

TURNERS (*51*). *Livery*, 160. *Clerk*, R. G. Woodwark, DSC, 33A Hill Avenue, Amersham, Bucks. HP6 5BX. *Master*, E. W. Sawney.

TYLERS AND BRICKLAYERS (*37*). *Livery*, 130. *Clerk*, F. A. G. Rider, 6 Martin Lane, Cannon Street, London EC4R 0DP. *Master*, C. J. N. Ward.

UPHOLDERS (*49*). *Livery*, 200. *Clerk*, W. R. Wallis, Charrington House, The Causeway, Bishops Stortford CH23 2EW. *Master*, Judge R. Cole.

WAX CHANDLERS (*20*). *Hall*, Gresham Street, London EC2V 7AD. *Livery*, 80. *Clerk*, T. Wood. *Master*, M. Herbert, CBE.

WEAVERS (*42*). *Livery*, 125. *Clerk*, J. G. Ouvry, 1 The Sanctuary, Westminster, London SW1P 3JT. *Upper Bailiff*, Sir Brooke Fairbairn, Bt.

WHEELWRIGHTS (*68*). *Livery*, 246. *Clerk*, M. R. Francis, Greenup, Milton Avenue, Gerrards Cross, Bucks. SL9 8QW. *Master*, R. W. Codling.

WOOLMEN (*43*). *Livery*, 125. *Clerk*, F. Allen, Hollands, Hedsor Road, Bourne End, Bucks. SL8 5EE. *Master*, B. H. Jefferson.

PARISH CLERKS (*No livery*). (*Members*, 100). *Clerk*, B. J. N. Coombes, 1 Dean Trench Street, London SW1P 3HB. *Master*, L. L. Brace.

WATERMEN AND LIGHTERMEN (*No livery*). (*Craft Owning Freemen*, 350). *Hall*, 16 St Mary-at-Hill, London EC3R 8EE. *Clerk*, Lt.-Col. C. P. Cameron, MC. *Master*, A. T. Woods.

In certain companies the election of Master or Prime Warden for the year does not take place till the autumn. In such cases the Master or Prime Warden for 1991–2 is given.

LONDON BOROUGHS

City/Borough §Inner London Borough	Municipal Offices	Population Census 1991p	Community charge per head 1992	Chief Executive (a) Managing Director	Mayor (a) Lord Mayor 1992–3
Barking and Dagenham	°Dagenham, RM10 7BN	139,900	£210.00	W. C. Smith	R. Whitbread
Barnet	†The Burroughs, Hendon, NW4 4BG	283,000	287.00	M. M. Caller	F. Poole
Bexley	‡Bexleyheath, Kent DA6 7LB	211,200	250.00	T. Musgrave	C. L. Tandy
Brent	†Forty Lane, Wembley, HA9 9EZ	226,100	271.00	C. Wood	E. McDonald
Bromley	°Bromley, BR1 3UH	281,700	218.00	N. T. Palk	Mrs D. Laird
§Camden	†Euston Road, NW1 2RU	170,500	374.34	J. Smith	Ms W. Parsons
§CITY OF WESTMINSTER	City Hall, Victoria Street, SW1E 6QP	181,500	36.00	(a) M. C. Montacute	(a) Dr C. Nemeth
Croydon	Taberner House, Park Lane, Croydon CR9 3JS	299,600	220.00	R. Jefferies	I. Croft
Ealing	°Uxbridge Road, W5 2HL	263,600	299.00	Ms J. Hunt	Mrs J. T. Ansell
Enfield	°Enfield, EN1 3XA	248,900	275.00	Ms M. Arnold	Ms D. Mardon
§Greenwich	†Wellington Street, SE18 6PW	200,800	287.00	C. Roberts	B. O'Sullivan
§Hackney	†Mare St, E8 1EA	164,200	378.00	J. White	H. Shaw
§Hammersmith and Fulham	†King St, W6 9JU	136,500	250.00	P. Derrick	D. Filson
Haringey	°Wood Green, N22 4LE	187,300	383.92	G. Singh	R. Rice
Harrow	°Harrow, HA1 2UH	194,300	273.00	A. G. Redmond	G. Harsant
Havering	†Romford, RM1 3BD	224,400	274.00	D. R. Bradley	L. Long
Hillingdon	°Uxbridge, UB8 1UW	225,800	295.00	P. Johnson	A. G. Langley
Hounslow	°Lampton Rd., Hounslow, TW3 4DN	193,400	298.00	R. Kerslake	H. Kanwal
§Islington	†Upper St, N1 2UD	155,200	380.60	E. W. Dear	Ms E. Griffiths
§Kensington and Chelsea (RB)	†Hornton St, W8 7NX	127,600	229.00	R. A. Taylor	Miss E. Christmas
Kingston upon Thames (RB)	Guildhall, Kingston upon Thames KT1 1EU	130,600	256.10	T. Hornsby	D. Edwards
§Lambeth	†Brixton Hill, SW2 1RW	220,100	425.29	H. Ouseley	J. Calinan
§Lewisham	†Catford, SE6 4RU	215,300	197.00	T. Hanafin	J. P. O'Shea
Merton	Crown House, London Rd., Morden, SM4 5DX	161,800	256.00	W. A. McKee	S. Flegg
Newham	†East Ham, E6 2RP	200,200	332.00	D. Stevenson	B. Chapman
Redbridge	†Ilford, IG1 1DD	220,600	250.00	G. U. Price	D. Candy
Richmond upon Thames	°York Street, Twickenham, TW1 3BZ	154,600	278.00	R. L. Harbord	Ms A. Summers
§Southwark	†Peckham Rd., SE5 8UB	196,500	189.00	Ms A. Whyatt	Ms M. Ellery
Sutton	‡St Nicholas Way, Sutton, SM1 1EA	164,300	271.00	Ms P. Hughes	Ms J. Dutton
§Tower Hamlets	†Patriot Square, E2 9LN	153,500	208.00	A. Golding, T. Herbert	K. Appiah
Waltham Forest	†Forest Rd., Walthamstow, E17 4JF	203,400	290.00	A. Tobias	D. Liunberg
§Wandsworth	†Wandsworth, SW18 2PU	237,500	0.00	G. K. Jones	Ms M. Holben

p preliminary
RB Royal Borough
° Civic Centre
† Town Hall
‡ Civic Offices

GREATER LONDON SERVICES

The abolition of the Greater London Council on 1 April 1986 led to the bulk of its work being passed to the London Boroughs, government departments and government-appointed bodies, and to joint boards and committees.

The London Residuary Body (LRB) was established by the Local Government Act 1985, which abolished the GLC. Its brief was to wind up the affairs of the GLC within a maximum life of five years. The LRB's GLC-related tasks were largely completed in 1990 with outstanding matters transferred to the London Borough of Bromley

With the Government's abolition of the Inner London Education Authority, the London Residuary Body was given the task of dealing with residual ILEA affairs as it dealt with the GLC. Its responsibilities included closing ILEA's accounts, disposing of about 200 surplus ILEA pieces of property and land, paying redundancy to ILEA staff and temporarily taking over services such as school transport, adult education, and the payment of grants. The LRB's ILEA-related work has been completed, with outstanding matters transferred to the Royal Borough of Kensington and Chelsea on 30 September 1992. Special arrangements have been made for the LRB's disposal of County Hall.

SOLID WASTE DISPOSAL

Responsibility for the disposal of London's household, commercial and civic amenity refuse lies with 16 waste disposal authorities.

There are four statutory bodies:

West London Waste Authority – Brent, Ealing, Harrow, Hillingdon, Hounslow, Richmond upon Thames

North London Waste Authority – Barnet, Camden, Enfield, Hackney, Haringey, Islington, Waltham Forest

East London Waste Authority – Barking and Dagenham, Havering, Newham, Redbridge

Western Riverside Waste Authority – Hammersmith and Fulham, Kensington and Chelsea, Lambeth, Wandsworth.

Twelve boroughs are waste disposal authorities in their own right and eleven of them have come together in voluntary groupings:

Central London Group – City of London, City of Westminster, Tower Hamlets

South London Group – Bromley, Croydon, Kingston upon Thames, Merton, Sutton

South East London Group – Greenwich, Lewisham, Southwark

Bexley – liaises with Kent County Council.

The London Waste Regulation Authority regulates and controls waste management activities in both the public and private sectors.

LONDON WASTE REGULATION AUTHORITY, Hampton House, 20 Albert Embankment, London SE1 7TJ. Tel: 071-587 3074.

FIRE SERVICE

The authority for London's fire service is the London Fire and Civil Defence Authority (LFCDA). The Fire Brigade is organized into five area commands, which coincide with borough boundaries. The LFCDA's responsibilities also include petroleum licensing.

LONDON FIRE AND CIVIL DEFENCE AUTHORITY, London Fire Brigade Headquarters, 8 Albert Embankment, London SE1 7SD. Tel: 071-582 3811.

Roman Names of English Towns and Cities

Bath	*Aquae Sulis*
Canterbury	*Durovernum Cantiacorum*
Carlisle	*Luguvalium*
Chelmsford	*Caesaromagus*
Chester	*Deva*
Chichester	*Noviomagus Regnensium*
Cirencester	*Corinium Dobunnorum*
Colchester	*Camulodunum*
Doncaster	*Danum*
Dorchester	*Durnovaria*
Dover	*Dubris*
Exeter	*Isca Dumnoniorum*
Gloucester	*Glevum*
Leicester	*Ratae Corieltauvorum*
Lincoln	*Lindum*
London	*Londinium*
Manchester	*Mamucium*
Newcastle upon Tyne	*Pons Aelius*
Pevensey	*Anderetium*
Rochester	*Durobrivae*
St Albans	*Verulamium*
Salisbury (Old Sarum)	*Sorviodunum*
Silchester	*Calleva Atrebatum*
Winchester	*Venta Belgarum*
Wroxeter	*Viroconium Cornoviorum*
York	*Eburacum*

LONDON AND ITS ENVIRONS

For National Art Galleries and Museums in London, *see* Index.

ADELPHI, Strand, London WC2. Adelphi Terrace and district commemorate the four Adam brothers, James, John, Robert and William, who laid out the district (formerly Durham House) at the close of the 18th century, though few 18th century buildings now remain. Four of the streets were formerly called after the brothers but are now Adam Street, John Adam Street, Robert Street and Durham House Street. In the neighbourhood of the Adelphi was York House, built by the Duke of Buckingham in 1625 (the Water Gate of which still stands in Embankment Gardens), the commemorative streets being Charles Street, Villiers Street, Duke Street, Buckingham Street.

ALEXANDRA PALACE AND PARK, Wood Green, London N22 4AY. Set in 200 acres of parkland. The Victorian Palace was severely damaged by fire in 1980 but has been restored and developed and was reopened in January 1988. Alexandra Palace provides modern facilities for exhibitions, sports, conferences and leisure activities. There is an ice rink, open daily.

BALTIC EXCHANGE, St Mary Axe, London EC3. The world market for the chartering of cargo ships. The present Exchange was built in 1903 and the new wing opened by The Queen on 21 November 1956. It was blown up by an IRA bomb on 10 April 1992.

BANK OF ENGLAND, Threadneedle Street, London EC2. The Bank of England, founded in 1694, has always been closely connected with the Government. The present building, completed in 1939 to the designs of Sir Herbert Baker, incorporates features reminiscent of the earlier architects, Sampson (1734), Sir Robert Taylor (1765) and Sir John Soane (1788).
Bank of England Museum (entrance in Bartholomew Lane). The Museum charts the Bank's history since the granting of the Royal Charter in 1694. Open Mon.–Fri. 10–5, Sat., Sun. and Bank Hols. 11–5. Admission free.

BANQUETING HOUSE, Whitehall, London SW1A 2ER. The only important building left of the great Palace of Whitehall. The previous banqueting house was burnt down in 1619, and replaced by the present structure designed by Inigo Jones. In 1635 it was enriched with Rubens' ceiling paintings. Charles I was executed on a scaffold set up just in front of the present entrance. Open Mon.–Sat. 10–5. Closed Sun., Bank Hols. Admission charge.

BARBICAN CENTRE, Silk Street, London EC2Y 8DS. Owned, funded and managed by the Corporation of London, the Barbican Centre was opened on 3 March 1982 by The Queen, and is the largest complex of its kind in western Europe. It houses the 1,166 seat Barbican Theatre, the London base of the Royal Shakespeare Company, along with a smaller 200 seat studio theatre (The Pit), and the 2,026 seat Barbican Hall, the home of the London Symphony Orchestra. There are also three cinemas, an art gallery, a sculpture court, a large lending library, facilities for trade exhibitions and conferences, and bars and restaurants.

BLACKHEATH, London SE10. 272 acres of parkland. Morden College, founded in 1695 as a home for 'decayed Turkey merchants', is near the south-east corner. The building was designed by Wren and its chapel doors have carvings attributed to Grinling Gibbons. Not open to the public. Concerts and poetry recitals are held at Rangers House, a villa built *c*.1700 which houses the Suffolk collection of English portraits from Larkin to Lely, and the Dolmetsch Collection of musical instruments. Open daily 10–5 (Nov.–Jan. 10–4). Closed Good Friday, 24 and 25 Dec. Admission free.

BRIDGES. The bridges over the Thames (from east to west) are: *The Queen Elizabeth II Bridge* (opened Oct. 1991) from Dartford to Thurrock; *Tower Bridge* (built by the Corporation of London and opened in 1894), with its bascules, operated now by new electrically-run machinery, walkway, opened to the public in 1982, and museum, opened in 1983; *London Bridge* (opened after rebuilding in 1831 by Rennie; the new London Bridge was completed in 1973 and opened by The Queen on 16 March 1973); *Southwark Bridge* (opened in 1819; also by Rennie. Rebuilt by the Corporation of London, 1922); *Blackfriars Bridge* (opened in 1769, rebuilt 1869, and widened by the Corporation of London in 1909); *Waterloo Bridge* (Rennie), opened in 1817, commanding a fine view of western London, rebuilt by LCC and reopened 1944; *Hungerford Bridge*, 1863 (railway bridge with a footbridge); *Westminster Bridge* (built in 1750 and then presenting a view that inspired Wordsworth's sonnet; rebuilt and re-opened in 1862; width, 84 ft.); *Lambeth Bridge* (built 1862, rebuilt 1932) leading from Lambeth Palace to Millbank; *Vauxhall Bridge* (built in 1811–16, rebuilt in 1906), leading to Kennington Oval; *Chelsea Bridge*, leading from Chelsea Hospital to Battersea Park (reconstructed and widened, 1937) and *Albert Bridge* (1873); *Battersea Bridge* (opened in 1890); *Wandsworth Bridge* (opened in 1873; rebuilt and re-opened in 1940); *Putney Bridge* (built 1729, rebuilt 1884, widened in 1933), where the Oxford and Cambridge Boat Race starts for Mortlake; *Hammersmith Bridge* (rebuilt 1887); *Barnes Bridge* (for pedestrians only, 1933); *Chiswick Bridge* (opened in 1933); *King Edward VII Bridge*, Kew (rebuilt in 1902, opened 1903), leading to the Royal Botanic Gardens, Kew; *Twickenham Lock Bridge; Twickenham Bridge* (opened 1933); *Richmond Bridge* (opened in 1777); *Kingston Bridge* (built 1828 and widened 1914) and *Hampton Court Bridge* (rebuilt 1933).

BUCKINGHAM PALACE, London SW1A 1AA. Purchased by King George III in 1762 from the heir of the Duke of Buckingham, the Palace has been the London home of the Sovereign since Queen Victoria's accession in 1837. It was altered by Nash for King George IV, and refronted in stone (part of the Queen Victoria Memorial) by Sir Aston Webb in 1913.
The Queen's Gallery, containing a changing selection of the finest pictures and works of art from all parts of the royal collection, was opened to the public on 25 July 1962. Open Tues.–Sat. and Bank Holidays 10–5, Sun. 2–5. Admission charges are payable; enter from Buckingham Palace Road.
The Royal Mews is open to visitors on certain days throughout the year (except in Ascot Week). Admission charges are payable at the entrance. For details, telephone 071–799 2331.

CANONBURY TOWER, London N1. The largest remaining part of a 16th century house originally built by the Priors of St Bartholomew, and since 1952 used as the headquarters of a non-professional theatre company. Contains the 'Spencer' and 'Compton' oak-panelled rooms. Other relics of Canonbury House can be seen nearby.

CATHOLIC CENTRAL LIBRARY, St Francis Friary, 47 Francis Street, London SW1P 1QR. Founded as a private library in 1914, it was taken over in 1959 by the Franciscan

Friars of the Atonement. It is a lending and research library of over 55,000 volumes and 150 periodicals, for the general reader, student and ecumenist. Books are sent by post when required. Open Mon.-Fri. 10–5, Sat. 10–1.30.

CEMETERIES. *Kensal Green Cemetery,* North Kensington, London W10 (70 acres), tombs of Thackeray, Trollope, Sydney Smith, Wilkie Collins, Tom Hood, George Cruikshank, John Leech, Leigh Hunt, I. K. Brunel and Charles Kemble. *Highgate Cemetery,* London N6, tombs of George Eliot, Herbert Spencer, Faraday and Marx. Guided tours only, £2. *Abney Park Cemetery,* Stoke Newington, London N16, tomb of General Booth, founder of the Salvation Army, and memorials to many Nonconformist divines. *South Metropolitan Cemetery,* Norwood, London SE27, tombs of Sir Henry Bessemer, Sir Hiram Maxim, Mrs Beeton, Sir Henry Tate and Joseph Whitaker, FSA (*Whitaker's Almanack*). Churchyard of the former *Marylebone Chapel,* Charles Wesley and his son Samuel Wesley (musician) buried; chapel itself demolished in 1949. Crematoria. *Ilford* (City of London); *Norwood*; *Hendon*; *Streatham Park*; *Finchley* (St Marylebone) and *Golders Green* (12 acres), near Hampstead Heath, with 'Garden of Rest' and memorials to famous men and women.

CENOTAPH, Whitehall, London SW1 (Literally 'empty tomb'.) Monument erected 'To the Glorious Dead', as a memorial to all ranks of the sea, land and air forces who gave their lives in the service of the Empire during the First World War. Designed by Sir Edwin Lutyens. Erected as a temporary memorial in 1919 and replaced by a permanent structure in 1920. Unveiled by King George V on Armistice Day 1920. An additional inscription was added after the Second World War to commemorate those who gave their lives in that conflict.

CHARTERHOUSE, Sutton's Hospital, Charterhouse Square, London EC1M 6AN. A Carthusian monastery from 1371 to 1537, when it came into the possession of Sir Edward (later first Lord) North, who sold it in 1565 to the fourth Duke of Norfolk. After Norfolk's execution in 1572 following the Ridolfi Plot (hatched at Charterhouse), it was eventually granted by Queen Elizabeth I in 1587 to Norfolk's second son, Thomas Howard, later Earl of Suffolk. In 1611 he sold it to Thomas Sutton, who endowed it as a hospital for aged men 'of gentle birth' and a school for poor scholars (removed to Godalming in 1872). The buildings are partly 15th but mainly 16th and 17th century. Parts of the building were damaged by bombing in 1941 but have been largely restored and now accommodate some 40 pensioners. Roger Williams, founder and governor of Rhode Island, was a scholar of the foundation. Among other famous pupils were John Wesley, Lord Baden-Powell, the poets and writers Crashaw, Lovelace and Thackeray, and more recently Lord Beveridge. Visitors are shown round on Wednesdays at 2.15 (April–July). Admission £2.00.
Master, E. E. Harrison, FSA.
Registrar and Clerk to the Governors, Lt.-Col. I. Macdonald.

CHELSEA PHYSIC GARDEN, 66 Royal Hospital Road, London SW3 4HS. A garden of general botanical research, maintaining a wide range of rare and unusual plants. The garden was established in 1673 by the Society of Apothecaries. Open on Wed. and Sun. p.m. during summer months. All enquiries to the Curator at above address.

CITY BUSINESS LIBRARY (Corporation of London), 1 Brewers Hall Garden, London EC2V 5BX. Open Mon.-Fri. 9.30-5.00. Public Information, tel: 071-638 8215.

COLLEGE OF ARMS OR HERALDS' COLLEGE, Queen Victoria Street, London EC4V 4BT. Her Majesty's Officers of Arms (Kings, Heralds and Pursuivants of Arms) were first incorporated by Richard III, and granted Derby House on the site of the present College building by Philip and Mary. The building now in use dates from 1671–88. The powers vested by the Crown in the Earl Marshal (The Duke of Norfolk) with regard to state ceremonial are largely exercised through the College, which is also the official repository of English pedigrees and all Arms granted to subjects of The Queen, except in Scotland and (since 1988) Canada. Enquiry may be made to the officer on duty in the Public Office, Mon.-Fri. 10–4.
The Heralds Museum at the Tower of London (admission charge included in the Tower's own charge) aims to explain what heraldry is about and traces its development over the centuries to its application and use in modern times. Open April–Oct.

COMMONWEALTH INSTITUTE, Kensington High Street, London W8 6NQ. A cultural and educational centre opened on 6 November 1962 by The Queen, replacing the former Imperial Institute opened in 1893 in Kensington. A distinctive feature of the building is its paraboloid copper-sheathed roof. The Institute contains, in 60,000 square feet arranged in three floors of circular galleries, a visual representation of the history, geography and ways of life of the Commonwealth countries and dependencies, as well as educational resource, information and conference centres, a commercial picture library and a restaurant and craft/bookshop (page 338).
Open Mon.–Sat. 10–5, Sun. 2–5. Admission free. Closed Christmas Eve, Christmas Day, Boxing Day, New Year's Day, Good Friday and May Day.

COURTAULD INSTITUTE GALLERIES, Somerset House, Strand, London WC2R 0RN. The galleries of the University of London contain the Lee collection and the Gambier–Parry collections (14th century to 18th century old masters); the Courtauld collection of Impressionist and Post-Impressionist paintings; the Roger Fry collection and the Witt and Spooner collections (old master drawings and English water-colours). A major bequest, the Princes Gate collection of old master paintings and drawings, was received in July 1978, and the Alastair Hunter bequest of modern British works was received in 1983. The galleries moved to Somerset House in June 1990. Open weekdays 10–6, Sun. 2–6. Admission £3, concessions £1.50.
Director, D. L. A. Farr, CBE.

DESIGN MUSEUM, Butlers Wharf, London SE1 2YD. Comprising a study collection, temporary exhibitions, a review of new products, a library and a lecture theatre, the Museum attempts to increase the understanding of design by explaining how mass-produced consumer objects work and why they look as they do. Open Tues.–Sun. and Bank Hols. 11.30–6.30. Admission £3.50, concessions £2.50.

DOWNING STREET, London SW1. Number 10 Downing Street is the official town residence of the Prime Minister, No. 11 of the Chancellor of the Exchequer and No. 12 is the office of the Government Whips. The street was named after Sir George Downing, Bt., soldier and diplomatist, who was MP for Morpeth from 1660 to 1684.
Chequers, a Tudor mansion in the Chilterns, about three miles from Princes Risborough, was presented by Lord and Lady Lee of Fareham in 1917 to serve, from 1 January 1921, as a country residence for the Prime Minister of the day, the Chequers estate of 700 acres being added to the gift by Lord Lee in 1921. The mansion contains a famous collection of Cromwellian portraits and relics.

DULWICH, London SE21. Contains Dulwich College (founded by Edward Alleyn in 1619) and the Dulwich Picture Gallery, built by Sir John Soane to house the collection bequeathed by the artist Sir Francis Bourgeois. The gallery, which is England's oldest public art gallery, was damaged in the Second World War but rebuilt with the aid of a grant from the Pilgrim Trust and reopened in 1953. Open daily (not Mon.); Sun., afternoons only. Dulwich Village retains many of the rural characteristics of the pre-suburban period.

ELTHAM, London SE9. Contains remains of 13th–15th century Eltham Palace, the birthplace of John of Eltham (1316), son of Edward II. The hall, built by Edward IV, has a hammer-beam roof of chestnut. In the churchyard of St John the Baptist is the tomb of Thomas Doggett, the comedian and founder of the Thames Watermen's championship (Doggett's Coat and Badge).

ELY PLACE, Holborn Circus, London EC1. Previously the site of the London house of the Bishop of Ely, Ely Place is a private street (built in 1773) whose affairs are administered by Commissioners under a special Act of Parliament. The 14th century chapel is now St Etheldreda's (RC) Church.

FULHAM PALACE, Bishop's Avenue, London, SW6. The courtyard is 16th century, the remainder 18th and 19th century. Former residence of the Bishop of London.

GEFFRYE MUSEUM, Kingsland Road, London E2 8EA. The Museum is housed in a building erected originally as almshouses in 1713. The exhibits are displayed in a series of period rooms dating from 1600 to 1939, showing the development of decorative art and design. A display of woodworking tools focuses on furniture-making, and the museum has an interesting picture collection. Events and temporary exhibitions are held. Special arrangements exist for children visiting the museum in school parties (which must be booked in advance) and in their leisure time. Open on Tues.–Sat. 10–5, Sun. 2–5. Closed on Christmas Eve, Christmas Day, Boxing Day, New Year's Day and Good Friday and on Mondays except Bank Holidays. Admission free.

GEORGE INN, Borough High Street, London SE1. Near London Bridge Station. Given to the National Trust in 1937. Last galleried inn in London, built in 1677. Now run as ordinary public house.

GREENWICH, London SE10. Greenwich Hospital (since 1873, the Royal Naval College) was built by Charles II, largely from designs by John Webb, and by Queen Anne and William III, from designs by Wren. It stands on the site of an ancient royal palace, and of the more recent Palace of Placentia, an enlarged edition of the palace, constructed by Humphrey, Duke of Gloucester (1391–1447), son of Henry IV. Henry VIII, Queen Mary I and Queen Elizabeth I were born in the Royal Palace (which reverted to the Crown in 1447) and King Edward VI died there. In the principal quadrangle is a marble statue of George II by Rysbraeck. (FOR NATIONAL MARITIME MUSEUM, *see* INDEX.)

Greenwich Park (196½ acres) was enclosed by Humphrey, Duke of Gloucester, and laid out by Charles II, from the designs of Le Nôtre.

Painted Hall and Chapel, open daily (not Thurs.) 2.30–5. Visitors are also admitted to Sunday service in the Chapel at 11 a.m., summer and winter, except during College vacations. The Queen's House, begun in 1616, was designed for Anne of Denmark by Inigo Jones. Open Mon.–Sat. 10–6, Sun. 2–6. Adm. charge.

On a hill in Greenwich Park is the former Royal Observatory (founded 1675). Part of its buildings at Greenwich have been taken over by the Maritime Museum and named Flamsteed House, after John Flamsteed (1646–1719), first Astronomer Royal. Astronomical and navigational equipment is exhibited, and the time ball and zero meridian of longitude can also be seen.

The parish church of Greenwich (*St Alfege*) was rebuilt by Hawksmoor (Wren's pupil) in 1728, and restored after severe damage during the Second World War. General Wolfe and Thomas Tallis are buried in the church. Henry VIII was christened in the former church. *Charlton House* was built in the early 17th century (1607–12) for Adam Newton, tutor to Prince Henry, brother to Charles I. It is largely in the Jacobean style of architecture.

Cutty Sark, the last of the famous tea clippers, which has been preserved as a memorial to ships and men of a past era, is fully restored and re-rigged, with a museum of sail on board. Open weekdays 11–5 (summer 11–6), Sundays and Boxing Day 2.30–5. The yacht *Gipsy Moth IV* in which Sir Francis Chichester sailed single-handed round the world, 1966–7, is preserved alongside the *Cutty Sark*.

GUILDHALL, Gresham Street, London EC2. Centre of civic government for the City for more than a thousand years. Built *c.*1440; façade built 1788–9; damaged in the Great Fire, 1666, and by incendiary bombs, 1940. The main hall and crypt (the most extensive medieval crypt in London) have been restored. Events in Guildhall include the annual election of Lord Mayor, election of Sheriffs, receptions in honour of sovereigns and heads of state, and the meetings of the Court of Common Council. Open weekdays and Sun. (May to Sept.) 10–5. Admission free.

Keeper of the Guildhall, J. H. Lucioni.

The *Guildhall Library* (reference) and the Library and Museum of the Clockmakers' Company are housed in new premises. Library open Mon.–Sat. 9.30–5, Museum open Mon.–Fri. 9.30–4.45. Admission free (entrance in Aldermanbury). The Library contains plans of London, 1570; Deed of Sale with Shakespeare's signature; first, second and fourth folios of Shakespeare's plays etc.

HAMPTON COURT PALACE, East Molesey, Surrey. Sixteenth-century palace built by Cardinal Wolsey, with additions by Sir Christopher Wren for William and Mary. Beautiful gardens with maze and grape vine (planted in 1769). State Apartments and collection of pictures. Tennis Court, built by King Henry VIII in 1530. Collection of Mantegna paintings. Gardens open daily until dusk, Maze and Palace open mid March–mid Oct. daily 9.30–6 (Mon. 10.15–6), mid Oct.–March 9.30–4.30. Admission £5.90, concessions £4.50, £3.90, family ticket £17.90.

HONOURABLE ARTILLERY COMPANY'S HEADQUARTERS, City Road, London EC1Y 2BQ. The HAC received its charter of incorporation from Henry VIII in 1537, and has occupied its present ground since 1641. The Armoury House dates from 1735. The present castellated barracks date from 1860. Four of its members who emigrated in the 17th century, founded in 1638 the Ancient and Honorable Artillery Company of Massachusetts. The HAC is the senior regiment of the Territorial Army Volunteer Reserves, and maintains a headquarters, four squadrons, a gun troop, and two companies of the Home Service Force.

Chief Executive, Brig. M. R. N. Bray, CBE.

HORNIMAN MUSEUM AND LIBRARY, London Road, Forest Hill, London SE23 3PQ. The Museum was presented in 1901 to the London County Council by F. J. Horniman, MP. With the adjoining gardens, it is now an independent charitable trust. The Museum has three main departments: ethnography, musical instruments and natural history. In the ethnography department the large collections include exhibits illustrating man's progress in the arts and crafts from prehistoric times. The natural history department includes an aquarium. Reference library (not Mon.). Free concerts and lectures (autumn and spring). Open Mon.–Sat. 10.30–5.50, Sun. 2–5.50 (not Christmas). Admission free.

Director, D. M. Boston, OBE.

HORSE GUARDS, Whitehall, London SW1. Archway and offices built about 1753. The mounting of the guard (Life Guards, or the Blues and Royals) at 11 a.m. (10 a.m. on Sundays) and the dismounted inspection at 4 p.m. are picturesque ceremonies. Only those on the Lord Chamberlain's list may drive through the gates and archway into *Horse Guard's Parade* (230,000 sq. ft.), where the Colour is 'trooped' on The Queen's Official Birthday.

THE HOUSES OF PARLIAMENT, Westminster, London SW1. An ordinance issued in the reign of Richard II stated that 'Parliament shall be holden or kepid wheresoever it pleaseth the King' and to the present day the Sovereign summons Parliament to meet and prescribes the time and place of meeting. The royal palace of Westminster, originally built by Edward the Confessor (Westminster Hall (*q.v.*) being added by William Rufus), was the normal place of Parliament from about 1340. St Stephen's Chapel was used from about 1550 for the meetings of the House of Commons, which had previously been held in the Chapter House or Refectory of Westminster Abbey. The House of Lords met in an apartment of the royal palace.

The fire of 1834 destroyed much of the palace and the present Houses of Parliament were erected on the site from the designs of Sir Charles Barry and Augustus Welby Pugin between 1840 and 1867. The Chamber of the House of Commons was destroyed by bombing in 1941 and a new Chamber designed by Sir Giles Gilbert Scott was used for the first time on 26 October 1950.

The Victoria Tower of the House of Lords is about 330 ft high, and when Parliament is sitting the Union Flag flies by day from its flagstaff. *The Clock Tower* of the House of Commons is about 320 ft high and contains 'Big Ben', the hour bell said to be named after Sir Benjamin Hall, First Commissioner of Works when the original bell was cast in 1856. This bell, which weighed 16 tons 11 cwt., was found to be cracked in 1857. The present bell (13½ tons) is a recasting of the original and was first brought into use in July 1859. The dials of the clock are 23 ft in diameter, the hands being 9 ft and 14 ft long (including balance piece). A light is displayed from the Clock Tower at night when Parliament is sitting.

For security reasons tours of the Houses of Parliament are available only to those who have made advance arrangements through a Member or Peer.

Admission to the Strangers' Gallery of the House of Lords is arranged by a Peer or by queue via St Stephen's Entrance. Admission to the Strangers' Gallery of the House of Commons is by Members' order (Members' orders should be sought several weeks in advance), or by queue via St Stephen's Entrance. Queues are usually shorter after 6 p.m., Mon.–Thurs. Overseas visitors may obtain cards of introduction from their Embassy or High Commission.

INNS OF COURT. The *Inner* and *Middle Temple*, Fleet Street/Victoria Embankment, London EC4, have occupied (since the early 14th century) the site of the buildings of the Order of Knights Templars. *Inner Temple Hall* (rebuilt in 1955 after bomb damage) is open Mon.–Fri. 10.30–11.30 and 3–4 on application to Treasurer's Office during law sittings. *Middle Temple Hall* (1562–70) is open when not in use, Mon.–Fri. 10–12 and 3–4. Closed on public holidays. In Middle Temple Gardens (not open to the public) Shakespeare (Henry VI, Part I) places the incident which led to the 'Wars of the Roses' (1455–85).

Temple Church, EC4, was restored in 1958 after severe damage by bombing. The nave formed one of five remaining round churches in England (the others being at Cambridge, Northampton, Little Maplestead (Essex) and Ludlow Castle). Open weekdays 10–4. Services: 8.30 and 11.15 a.m. except in August and September. *Master of the Temple*, Revd Canon J. Robinson.

Lincoln's Inn, Chancery Lane/Lincoln's Inn Fields, London WC2, occupies the site of the palace of a former Bishop of Chichester and of a Black Friars monastery. Records show the Society as being in existence in 1422. The Hall and Library Buildings are of 1845, although the Library is first mentioned in 1474; the old Hall (early 16th century) and the Chapel were rebuilt *c.*1619–23. Halls open by appointment, Chapel and Gardens, Mon.–Fri. 12–2.30. Chapel services Sunday 11.30 a.m. during law terms. *Lincoln's Inn Fields* (7 acres). The Square, laid out by Inigo Jones, contains many fine old houses with handsome interiors.

Gray's Inn, Holborn/Gray's Inn Road, London WC1. Early 14th century. Hall 1556–60. Chapel largely rebuilt after bomb damage in the Second World War. Services 11.15 a.m. (during Law Dining Terms only.) Holy Communion 1st Sunday in every month except Aug.–Sept. Gardens open to the public Mon.–Fri.

No other 'Inns' are active, but what remains of *Staple Inn* is worth visiting as a relic of Elizabethan London; though heavy damage was done by a flying-bomb, it retains a picturesque gabled front on Holborn (opposite Gray's Inn Road). *Clement's Inn* (near St Clement Danes' Church), *Clifford's Inn*, Fleet Street, and *Thavies Inn*, Holborn Circus, are all rebuilt. *Serjeant's Inn*, Fleet Street (damaged by bombing) and another (demolished 1910) of the same name in Chancery Lane, were composed of Serjeants-at-Law, the last of whom died in 1922.

JEWISH MUSEUM, Woburn House, Tavistock Square, London WC1H OEP. Tel: 071-388 4525. Opened in 1932, the Museum contains a rich collection of ceremonial art, portraits and antiquities, illustrating Jewish life, history and religion. Open Tues.–Thurs. and Sun. (and Fri. in summer) 10–4, Fri. in winter 10–12.45. Closed on public and Jewish holidays. Group visits by arrangement with Secretary.

KENSINGTON PALACE, London W8 4PX. The original house was bought by William III in 1689 and enlarged by Christoper Wren. The State Apartments contain pictures and furniture from the Royal Collections. A suite of rooms devoted to the memory of Queen Victoria is also shown. The *Royal Ceremonial Dress Collection* is also open, and includes three restored rooms: the Red Saloon, the Teck Saloon and the room where Queen Victoria is said to have been born in 1819. Open weekdays 9–5.30, Sun. 11–5.30. Admission £3.75, concessions £2.80, £2.50.

KENWOOD, London NW3 7JR. Nearly 200 acres forming the northern part of Hampstead Heath. Open air symphony concerts each summer. The Iveagh Bequest, in an Adam villa, includes Old Master paintings and English neoclassical furniture. Recitals and poetry readings in the Orangery. House open daily, except Good Friday and Dec. 24, 25. Times vary seasonally. Admission free.

KEW, Surrey. A favourite home of the early Hanoverian monarchs. Kew House, the residence of Frederick, Prince of Wales, and later of his son, George III, was pulled down in 1803, but the earlier Dutch House, now known as *Kew Palace*, survives. It was built in 1631 and acquired by George III as an annexe to Kew House in 1781. Open April–Sept., 11–5.30. The famous Kew Gardens (*see* Index) were originally laid out as a private garden for Kew House for George III's mother in 1759 and were much enlarged in the 19th century, notably by the inclusion of the grounds of the former Richmond Lodge. *Queen Charlotte's Cottage* is also open at the weekends. Admission £1.10, concessions 80p, 60p.

KNELLER HALL, Twickenham, London TW2 7DU. Royal

Military School of Music. A band of up to 120 instrumentalists gives concerts in the grounds on Wednesdays in June and July, commencing at 8 p.m. Admission charge. Season tickets and party bookings available.

LAMBETH PALACE, London SE1. The official residence of the Archbishop of Canterbury, on the south bank of the Thames; the oldest part is 13th century, the house itself being early 19th century. For leave to visit the historical portions, applications should be made by letter to the Archbishop's Chaplain.

LIVERY COMPANIES' HALLS. The principal Companies (*see* Index) have magnificent halls but admission to view them has generally to be arranged beforehand. The following are among the finest or more interesting. *Goldsmiths' Hall,* Foster Lane. The present hall was completed in 1835, and contains some magnificent rooms. *Fishmongers' Hall,* London Bridge (built 1831–3), restored after severe bomb damage, also contains fine rooms. *Apothecaries' Hall,* Black Friars Lane, was rebuilt in 1670 after the Great Fire, and has library, hall and kitchen which are good examples of the period. *Vintners' Hall,* Upper Thames Street, was also rebuilt after the Great Fire, and its hall has late 17th century panelling. The Watermen and Lightermen's Company is not, strictly speaking, a livery company, but its *Hall,* in St Mary-at-Hill, is a good example of a smaller 18th century building, with pilastered façade. It was completed in 1780. *Stationers' Hall,* in Stationers' Hall Court, behind Ludgate Hill, has a particularly fine carved screen; its façade dates from 1800. *Barbers' Hall,* Monkwell Street, with a Hall attributed to Inigo Jones, was completely destroyed by bombing, but has been rebuilt. The new hall was built some 30 ft. from the old site to enable one of the bastions and part of the wall of the Roman fort to remain exposed to view.

LLOYD'S, Lime Street, London EC3M 7HA. Society of private underwriters which evolved during the 18th century from Lloyds Coffee House. Housed in the Royal Exchange for 150 years and in Leadenhall Street and Lime Street from 1928 to 1986. The present building was opened for business in May 1986, and houses the Lutine Bell. Underwriting is on four floors with a total area of 114,000 sq. ft. A visitors' gallery is open Mon.–Fri. for pre-booked groups, and incorporates an exhibition showing the history and operation of the insurance market at Lloyd's.

LONDON PLANETARIUM, Marylebone Road, London NW1 5LR. Open daily (except Christmas Day), star show and Space Trail 12.20–4.40. Admission charge.

LONDON TRANSPORT MUSEUM, Covent Garden, London WC2E 7BB. Housed in the former Flower Market, the Museum contains a collection of buses, trams, trolleybuses, trains, working displays and London Transport paraphernalia. There is a research library and lecture theatre. Open daily 10–6 (except 24, 25, 26 Dec.). The museum will be closed 7 March–December 1993. Admission £3.20, concessions £1.60, family £7.50.

LORD'S CRICKET GROUND, St John's Wood Road, London NW8 8QN. The headquarters (since 1814) of the Marylebone Cricket Club, the premier cricket club in England (founded 1787), Lord's is the scene of some of the principal matches of the season and Middlesex County headquarters. Real tennis court and squash courts in building behind members' pavilion.

The MCC Museum is open on match days (Mon.-Sat. 10.30–5, Sun. 1–5). Admission £1, concessions 50p. Conducted tours on most days throughout the year can be arranged in advance with the Tours Manager.

MADAME TUSSAUD'S, Marylebone Road, London NW1 5LR. Waxwork exhibition. Open daily (except Christmas Day) 10–5.30. Admission charge.

MANSION HOUSE, London EC4. Built 1739–53, reconstructed 1930–1. The official residence of the Lord Mayor; the Egyptian Hall and Ballroom are the chief attractions. Group visits only by arrangement with the Principal's Assistant.

MARKETS. The London markets (administered by the Corporation of the City of London) provide foodstuffs for 8–9 million people. *Central Meat, Fish, Fruit, Vegetable, and Poultry Markets, Smithfield* (built 1866) the largest meat market in the world and site of St Bartholomew's Fair from 9th to 19th century; *Leadenhall Market* (meat and poultry), built 1881, part recently demolished; *Billingsgate* (fish), Thames Street, built 1875, part recently demolished, a market site for over 1,000 years (moved to the Isle of Dogs, January 1982); *Spitalfields,* E1 (vegetables, fruit, etc.), enlarged 1928 (moved to Leyton, May 1991); *London Fruit Exchange,* Brushfield Street, built by Corporation of London 1928–9; *Covent Garden* (vegetables, fruit, flowers, etc.), (now moved to Nine Elms) established under a charter of Charles II, in 1661; *Borough Market,* SE1 (vegetables, fruit, flowers, etc.).

MARLBOROUGH HOUSE, Pall Mall, London SW1A 2AF. Built by Wren for the first Duke of Marlborough and completed in 1711, the house finally reverted to the Crown in 1835. Prince Leopold lived there until 1831, and Queen Adelaide from 1837 until her death in 1849. In 1863 it became the London house of the Prince of Wales and was the London home of Queen Mary until her death in 1953. The Queen's Chapel, Marlborough Gate, begun in 1623 from the designs of Inigo Jones for the Infanta Maria of Spain, and completed for Queen Henrietta Maria, is open to the public for services on Sundays at 8.30 a.m. and 11.15 a.m. between Easter Day and end July (*see* St James's Palace for winter services in The Chapel Royal). In 1959 Marlborough House was given by The Queen as a centre for Commonwealth government conferences and it was opened as such in March 1962.

LONDON MONUMENT (commonly called The Monument), Monument Street, London EC3. Built from designs of Wren, 1671–7, to commemorate the Great Fire of London, which broke out in Pudding Lane on 2 September 1666. The fluted Doric column is 120 ft. high (the moulded cylinder above the balcony supporting a flaming vase of gilt bronze is 42 ft. in addition), and is based on a square plinth 40 ft. high, with fine carvings on the west face (making a total height of 202 ft.). Splendid views of London from gallery at top of column (311 steps). As total refurbishment planned for 1993 onwards, check with Town Clerk's office for access. Tel: 071-606 3030.

MONUMENTS (sculptor's name in parenthesis). *Albert Memorial,* South Kensington; *Royal Air Force,* Victoria Embankment; *Beaconsfield,* Parliament Square; *Beatty, Jellicoe* and *Cunningham,* Trafalgar Square; *Belgian Gratitude* (Reginald Blomfield), Victoria Embankment; *Boadicea* (or Boudicca), Queen of the Iceni (Thomas Thornycroft), Westminster Bridge; *Brunel* (Marochetti), Victoria Embankment; *Burghers of Calais* (Rodin), Victoria Tower Gardens, Westminster; *Burns,* Embankment Gardens; *Carlyle* (Boehm), Cheyne Walk, Chelsea; *Cavalry,* Hyde Park; *Edith Cavell* (Frampton), St Martin's Place; *Cenotaph* (Lutyens), Whitehall; *Charles I,* Trafalgar Square; *Charles II,* inside the Royal Exchange; *Churchill,* Parliament Square; *Cleopatra's Needle* (68½ ft. high, *c.*1500 BC, erected on the Thames Embankment in 1877–8; the Sphinxes are Victorian); *Clive,* Whitehall; *Captain Cook* (Brock), The Mall; *Crimean,* Broad Sanctuary; *Oliver Cromwell* (Thornycroft), outside Westminster Hall; *Lord Dowding* (Faith Winter), between Australia House and St Clement Danes, Strand; *Duke of Cambridge,* Whitehall; *Duke of York* (124 ft.), Carlton House Terrace; *Edward VII*

(Mackennal), Waterloo Place; *Elizabeth I* (1586, oldest outdoor statue in London; from Ludgate), Fleet Street; *Eros* (Shaftesbury Memorial) (Gilbert), Piccadilly Circus; *Marechal Foch,* Grosvenor Gardens; *Charles James Fox,* Bloomsbury Square; *George III,* Cockspur Street; *George IV* (Chantrey), riding without stirrups, Trafalgar Square; *George V,* Old Palace Yard; *George VI,* Carlton Gardens; *Gladstone,* facing Australia House, Strand; *Guards'* (Crimea), Waterloo Place; (Great War), Horse Guards' Parade; *Haig* (Hardiman), Whitehall; *Sir Arthur (Bomber) Harris* (Faith Winter), St Clement Danes, Strand; *Irving* (Brock), north side of National Portrait Gallery; *James II,* Trafalgar Square; *Samuel Johnson,* opposite St Clement Danes; *Kitchener,* Horse Guards' Parade; *Abraham Lincoln,* Parliament Square; *Milton,* St Giles, Cripplegate; *The Monument* (*see* above); *Mountbatten*, Foreign Office Green; *Nelson* (170 ft. 2 in.), Trafalgar Square, with Landseer's lions (cast from guns recovered from the wreck of the *Royal George*); *Florence Nightingale,* Waterloo Place; *Palmerston,* Parliament Square; *Peel,* Parliament Square; *Pitt* (Chantrey), Hanover Square; *Portal,* Embankment Gardens; *Prince Consort,* Holborn Circus; *Raleigh,* Whitehall; *Richard Coeur de Lion* (Marochetti), Old Palace Yard; *Roberts,* Horse Guards' Parade; *Franklin D. Roosevelt* (Reid Dick), Grosvenor Square; *Royal Artillery* (South Africa), The Mall; (Great War), Hyde Park Corner; *Captain Scott* (Lady Scott), Waterloo Place; *Shackleton,* Kensington Gore; *Shakespeare,* Leicester Square; *Smuts* (Epstein), Parliament Square; *Sullivan,* Victoria Embankment; *Trenchard,* Victoria Embankment; *Victoria Memorial,* in front of Buckingham Palace; *George Washington* (Houdon copy), Trafalgar Square; *Wellington,* Hyde Park Corner; *Wellington* (Chantrey) riding without stirrups, Royal Exchange; *John Wesley,* City Road; *William III,* St James's Square; *Wolseley,* Horse Guards' Parade.

PERCIVAL DAVID FOUNDATION OF CHINESE ART, 53 Gordon Square, London WC1H 0PD. Set up in 1950, the Foundation contains the collection of Chinese ceramics formed by Sir Percival David and his important library of books on Chinese art. To these was added a gift from the Hon. Mountstuart Elphinstone of part of his collection of Chinese monochrome porcelains. The Foundation is administered on behalf of the University of London by the School of Oriental and African Studies. Galleries, Mon.–Fri. 10.30–5. Closed weekends and Bank Holidays. Library available to ticket holders only; applications in writing to the Curator. *Curator*, Miss R. Scott.

PORT OF LONDON. The Port of London covers the tidal portion of the River Thames from Teddington to the seaward limit (Tongue light vessel), a distance of 150 km. The governing body is the Port of London Authority (PLA), whose head office is at Devon House, 58–60 St Katherine's Way, London E1 9LB.

Eighty-eight per cent of the total port traffic is handled at riverside berths between Vauxhall and Canvey Island, the rest at the enclosed dock at Tilbury, 40 km below London Bridge. The docks perform every type of cargo-handling operation. Tilbury is principally used by vessels to and from Australia, the Americas, India, Middle and Far East, Scandinavia, Russia and continental Europe.

Passenger vessels and cruise liners can be handled at moorings at Greenwich, Tower Bridge and Tilbury. The latter provides accommodation for liners at all states of the tide.

RICHMOND, Surrey. Contains the red brick gateway of Richmond Palace (Henry VII, 1485–1509) and buildings of the Jacobean, Queen Anne, and early Georgian periods, including White Lodge in Richmond Park, the former home of Queen Mary's mother (the Duke of Windsor was born there, 23 June 1894), and now the home of the Royal Ballet Lower School. The Star and Garter Home for Disabled Soldiers, Sailors, and Airmen (the Women's Memorial of the Great War) was opened by Queen Mary in 1924. Richmond Park (2,469 acres) contains herds of fallow and red deer.

ROMAN LONDON. Although visible remains from this period are few, excavations carried out in the City on sites due for redevelopment often reveal Roman features. Sections of the city wall are the most striking remains to be seen of Roman *Londinium*, although even these are largely medieval because of the Roman wall being rebuilt during the medieval period. Sections may be seen near the White Tower in the Tower of London; at Tower Hill; at Coopers' Row; at All Hallows, London Wall, its vestry being built on the remains of a semi-circular Roman bastion; at St Alphage, London Wall, showing a striking succession of building repairs from the Roman until the late medieval period, and at St Giles, Cripplegate. Excavations in the Cripplegate area have revealed that a Roman fort was built there *c.* AD 100–120. It was later incorporated into the city wall when this was built *c.* AD 200.

The administrative centre of the Roman city was the great forum and basilica, more than 165 metres square, sections of which have been encountered during excavations in the area of Leadenhall, Gracechurch Street and Lombard Street. Excavations during the past few years have revealed Roman activity along the river. Traces of a massive riverside wall, built in the late Roman period, have been found and a succession of Roman timber quays have been excavated along Lower and Upper Thames Street, helping to prove that Roman London was a thriving commercial centre.

Other major buildings found are the Provincial Governor's Palace in Cannon Street; remains of a bath-building, preserved in Lower Thames Street; and the Temple of Mithras in Walbrook. The fine sculptures from this temple are displayed in the Museum of London (*see* Index) where many other relics from the Roman city may be seen. There is also an Ordnance Survey map of Roman London.

ROYAL ALBERT HALL, Kensington Gore, London SW7 2AP. The elliptical hall, one of the largest in the world, was completed in 1871, and since 1941 has been the venue each summer for the Promenade Concerts founded in 1895 by Sir Henry Wood. Other events include pop concerts, sporting events, conferences and banquets for up to 2,500 people.

Chief Executive, P. Deuchar.

ROYAL EXCHANGE, London EC3V 3LS. Founded by Sir Thomas Gresham, 1566, opened as 'The Bourse' and proclaimed 'The Royal Exchange' by Queen Elizabeth I, 1571, rebuilt 1667–9 and 1842–4. The building is the corporate head office of the Guardian Royal Exchange Assurance. It is administered by the Gresham Committee. *Clerk,* Mercers' Hall, Ironmonger Lane, London EC2.

ROYAL GEOGRAPHICAL SOCIETY, Kensington Gore, London SW7 2AR. Map room open to public, admission free. Advice for scientific expeditions abroad, by appointment only.

ROYAL HOSPITAL, CHELSEA, Royal Hospital Road, London SW3 4SL. Founded by Charles II in 1682, and built by Wren; opened in 1692 for old and disabled soldiers. Open Mon.–Sat. 10–12, daily 2–4. The extensive grounds include the former Ranelagh Gardens, and are the venue for the Chelsea Flower Show held each May by the Royal Horticultural Society.

Governor, General Sir Roland Guy, GCB, CBE, DSO.

Lt.-Governor and Secretary, Maj.-Gen. F. G. Sugden, CB, CBE.

ROYAL OPERA HOUSE, Covent Garden, London WC2E 7DD.

Home of The Royal Ballet (1931), The Royal Opera (1946) and the Birmingham Royal Ballet (1990), formerly Sadler's Wells Royal Ballet (1946). The Royal Opera House is the third theatre to be built on the site, opening 15 May 1858: the first was opened 7 December 1732. The season of the resident companies runs mid September to August.

General Director, J. Isaacs.

St James's Palace, Pall Mall, London SW1. Built by Henry VIII; the Gatehouse and Presence Chamber remain; later alterations were made by Wren and Kent. The Chapel Royal is open for services on Sundays at 8.30 a.m. and 11.15 a.m. between the beginning of October and Good Friday (*see* Marlborough House for summer services in The Queen's Chapel). Representatives of Foreign Powers are still accredited 'to the Court of St James's'. *Clarence House* (1825) in the palace precinct is the home of The Queen Mother.

St Paul's Cathedral, London EC4M 8AD. Built 1675–1710, cost £747,660. The cross on the dome is 365 ft. above the ground level, the inner cupola 218 ft. above the floor. 'Great Paul' in the south-west tower weighs nearly 17 tons. Organ by Father Smith (enlarged by Willis and rebuilt by Mander) in a case carved by Grinling Gibbons (who also carved the choir stalls). The choir and high altar were restored in 1958 after war damage and the North Transept in 1962. The American War Memorial Chapel was consecrated in November 1958. The chapel of the Order of the British Empire in the Crypt of the Cathedral was dedicated in 1960. Nave and transepts free. Open weekdays 9–4.15. Admission: £2.50, children £1.50; Galleries £2.50/£1.50. Services: Sundays, 8 a.m., 10.30 a.m., 11.30 a.m. and 3.15 p.m. Weekdays, 7.30 a.m., 8 a.m., 12.30 p.m. and 5 p.m.

Sherlock Holmes Museum, 221B Baker Street, London NW1 6XE. Looks at the 'life and times' of Sherlock Holmes as portrayed by Sir Arthur Conan Doyle. Run by the Sherlock Holmes International Society. Open daily 10–6, admission £5.00, children £3.00.

Sir John Soane's Museum, 13 Lincoln's Inn Fields, London WC2A 3BP. The house and galleries, built 1812–24, are the work of the founder, Sir John Soane (1753–1837) and contain his collections, arranged as he left them, in pursuance of an Act procured by him in 1833. Exhibits include the Sarcophagus of Seti I (*c*.1290 BC), Classical vases and marbles, Hogarth's *Rake's Progress* and *Election* series, paintings by Canaletto, Reynolds, Turner, Lawrence, etc., and sculpture by Chantrey, Flaxman, etc. Soane's library of 8,000 volumes, and collection of 40,000 architectural drawings are available for study by appointment. Open Tues.–Sat. 10–5. Closed Bank Holidays. Open 6–9 p.m., first Tuesday in the month. Tours must be booked in advance.

Curator, P. Thornton, FSA.

Somerset House, Strand and Victoria Embankment, London WC2. The beautiful river façade (600 ft. long) was built in 1776–86 from the designs of Sir William Chambers; the eastern extension, which houses part of King's College, was built by Smirke in 1829. Somerset House was the property of Lord Protector Somerset, at whose attainder in 1552 the palace passed to the Crown, and it was a royal residence until 1692.

South Bank, London SE1. The arts complex on the south bank of the River Thames includes the South Bank Centre, owned and managed by the South Bank Board, and consisting of the 2,903-seat *Royal Festival Hall* (opened in 1951 for the Festival of Britain), a major venue for concert and ballet seasons, with the adjacent 1,056-seat *Queen Elizabeth Hall* and 368-seat *Purcell Room*, accommodating smaller-scale performances.

The *National Film Theatre* (opened 1958), administered by the British Film Institute, has three auditoria showing almost 2,000 films a year. The London Film Festival is held here every November.

The *National Theatre* opened in 1976 and stages classical, modern, new and neglected plays in its three auditoria: the 1,160-seat Olivier theatre (open stage), the 890-seat Lyttelton theatre (proscenium stage) and the experimental Cottesloe theatre (adaptable stage) which seats up to 400.

The *Museum of the Moving Image* charts the history of the moving image in cinema and television from the earliest devices through to disc technology. Open daily 10–6 (not 24–26 Dec.). Admission £5.00, concessions £4.00 and £4.70.

Southwark Cathedral, London SE1 9DA. Mainly 13th century, but the nave is largely rebuilt. The tomb of John Gower (1330–1408) is between the Bunyan and Chaucer memorial windows in the north aisle; Shakespeare's effigy backed by a view of Southwark and the Globe Theatre in the south aisle; the altar screen (erected 1520) has been restored; the tomb of Bishop Andrews (died 1626) is near the screen. The Early English Lady Chapel (behind the choir), restored 1930, was the scene of the Consistory Courts of the reign of Mary (Gardiner and Bonner) and is still used as a Consistory Court. John Harvard, after whom Harvard University is named, was baptized here in 1607, and the Chapel by the North Choir Aisle is his memorial chapel. Open 8.30–6, admission free. Services: Sundays, 11, 3. Weekdays, 12.45, 5.30 (sung on Tuesdays and Fridays), Saturdays, 12 noon.

Stock Exchange, London EC2. The market floor of the new Stock Exchange building in London opened for trading in June 1973. Since 'Big Bang' in 1986, the floor has been used solely by the London Traded Options Market. A tower, 331 feet high, and the new Market replace the complex of buildings started in 1801 on the same site. The new building is the headquarters of the Stock Exchange, following the amalgamation of all the Stock Exchanges in Great Britain and Ireland on 25 March 1973.

Information on how the Exchange works can be obtained from Public Information, The London Stock Exchange, Old Broad Street, London EC2N 1HP. Tel: 071-797 1000.

Thames Embankments. The *Victoria Embankment*, on the north side (from Westminster to Blackfriars), was constructed by Sir Joseph Bazalgette for the Metropolitan Board of Works, 1864–70 (the seats, of which the supports of some are a kneeling camel, laden with spicery, and of others a winged sphinx, were presented by the Grocers' Company and by Rt. Hon. W. H. Smith, MP, in 1874); the *Albert Embankment*, on the south side (from Westminster Bridge to Vauxhall), 1866–9; the *Chelsea Embankment*, 1871–4. The total cost exceeded £2,000,000. Bazalgette (1819–91) also inaugurated the London main drainage system, 1858–65. A medallion has been placed on a pier of the Victoria Embankment to commemorate the engineer of the Thames waterside improvements (*Flumini vincula posuit*). County Hall includes an embankment on the Surrey side.

Thames Flood Barrier. Officially opened in May 1984, though first used in February 1983, the barrier consists of ten rising sector gates which span 570 yards from bank to bank of the Thames at Woolwich Reach. When not in use the gates lie horizontally, allowing shipping to navigate the river normally; when the barrier is closed, the gates turn through 90 degrees to stand vertically more than 50 feet above the river bed. The barrier took eight years to complete and can be raised within about 30 minutes.

Thames Tunnels. The *Rotherhithe Tunnel*, opened in

1908 at a cost of £1,506,914, connects Commercial Road, London E14, with Lower Road, Rotherhithe; it is 1 mile 332 yards long, of which 474 yards are under the river. The first *Blackwall Tunnel* (vehicles) opened in 1897 at a cost of £1,323,663, connects East India Dock Road, Poplar, with Blackwall Lane, East Greenwich. A second tunnel (for southbound vehicles only) was opened in 1967 at a cost of £9,750,000 and the old tunnel was improved at a cost of £1,350,000 and made one-way northbound. Both tunnels are now for vehicles only. The relative lengths of the tunnels measured from East India Dock Road to the Gate House on the south side are 6,215 ft. (old tunnel) and 6,152 ft. *Greenwich Tunnel* (pedestrians only), opened in 1902 at a cost of £180,000, connects the Isle of Dogs, Poplar, with Greenwich. It is 406 yards long. The *Woolwich Tunnel* (pedestrians only), opened in 1912 at a cost of £86,000, connects North and South Woolwich below the passenger and vehicular ferry from North Woolwich Station, London E16, to High Street, Woolwich, London SE18. The tunnel is 552 yards long.

TOWER BRIDGE WALKWAY AND MUSEUM, London SE1 2UP. Owned by the Bridge House Trust of the Corporation of London and open daily from 10 a.m. Admission £2.50, concessions £1. Closed January to June 1993 for new exhibition installation. Tel: 071–403 3761 for further information. Attractions include exhibitions, video, the observation platform and walkway, engine rooms, working models and souvenir gift shop.

TOWER OF LONDON, London EC3. Admission to a general view of the Tower, the White Tower, the History, Oriental, Ordnance and 18th–19th century Galleries, the Royal Armouries (National Museum of Arms and Armour), and the Wall Walk Phases I and II.

The White Tower is the oldest and central building of the Royal Palace and Fortress of the Tower of London. It was built at the order of William I and constructed by Gundulph, Bishop of Rochester, in the years 1078–98. The Inner Wall, with thirteen towers, was constructed by Henry III in the 12th century. The moat was extended and completed by Richard I and the wharf is first mentioned in 1228. The Outer Wall was completed in the reign of Edward I and now incorporates six towers and two bastions. The last Monarch to reside in the Tower of London was James I. The Crown Jewels came to the Tower in the reign of Henry III. All coinage used in Great Britain was minted in the Outer Ward of the Tower of London until 1810 when the Royal Mint was formed. The Tower of London has had a military garrison since 1078. The Chapel Royal of St John the Evangelist, within the White Tower (1080–8) is the oldest Norman church in London. The chapel of St Peter ad Vincula was built in the early 16th century.

Open weekdays March–Oct., 9.30–6, Nov.–Feb., 9.30–5; Sundays, March–Oct., 10–6. Closed Sundays Nov.–Feb. Tower closed Christmas Eve, Christmas Day, Boxing Day, New Year's Day and Good Friday. On Sundays throughout the year (except August) the public is admitted to Holy Communion, 9.15 a.m., and Morning Service, 11 a.m. Admission £6.40, concessions £4.80, £3.90, family ticket £17.50 (reduced rate when Jewel House closed for cleaning in January).

Constable, Field Marshal Sir John Stanier, GCB, MBE.

Lieutenant, Lt.-Gen. Sir Robert Richardson, KCB, CVO, CBE.

Resident Governor and Keeper of the Jewel House, Maj.-Gen. C. Tyler, CB.

Master of the Armouries, G. Wilson.

Chaplain at the Chapel Royal of St Peter ad Vincula and St John the Evangelist, Revd Canon G. Murphy.

WALTHAM ABBEY (or WALTHAM HOLY CROSS), Essex. The Abbey ruins, 'Harold's' Bridge (14th century), the nave of the former cruciform Abbey Church *c.*1120 and the traditional burial place of King Harold II (1066), and a Guild Chapel of Edward II, with crypt below, which houses a visitors centre with permanent exhibition. New evidence of four former churches on the site, and the shape of the east end of Harold's church, have been revealed in recent excavations. Lee Valley Regional Park Authority has a country centre in the Abbey grounds. At Waltham Cross, one mile from the Abbey, is one of the crosses (partly restored) erected by Edward I to mark a resting place of the corpse of Queen Eleanor on its way to Westminster Abbey. (Ten crosses were erected, but only those at Geddington, Northampton and Waltham survive; 'Charing' Cross originally stood near the spot now occupied by the statue of Charles I at Whitehall.)

WELLINGTON MUSEUM, Apsley House, 149 Piccadilly, at Hyde Park Corner, London W1. Known as 'No. 1 London', Apsley House was designed by Robert Adam for Lord Bathurst, the first Baron Apsley, and built 1771–8. It was bought in 1817 by the Duke of Wellington, who in 1828–9 employed Benjamin Wyatt to enlarge it, face it with Bath stone and add the Corinthian portico. The museum contains many fine paintings, sculptures, services of porcelain and silver plate and personal relics of the 1st Duke of Wellington (1769–1852). The House was given to the nation by the 7th Duke and was first opened to the public in 1952, under the administration of the Victoria and Albert Museum. Closed 1993 for major refurbishment.

WESTMINSTER ABBEY, London SW1. Built 1050–1745. Chapel of Henry VII, Chapter House and Cloisters; King Edward the Confessor's shrine, AD 1269, tombs of kings and queens (Henry III, Edward I, Edward III, Henry V, Mary Queen of Scots, Elizabeth I), and many other monuments and objects of interest, including the grave of 'The Unknown Warrior' and Poets' Corner. The Coronation Chair encloses the 'Stone of Scone', which was removed from Scotland by Edward I in 1296. Open on weekdays 9.20–6 (9.20–7.45 Wed.). Admission to the Royal Chapels, Poets' Corner, Quire and Statesmen's Aisle £3, concessions £1.50/60p. Last admission Mon.–Fri. 4 p.m., Sat. 5 p.m. Wed. 6–8 p.m. free. Nave open on Sundays between services. Services: Sundays, 8, 10, 11.15, 3, 6.30 (generally preceded by an organ recital). Monday–Friday, 7.30, 8, 12.30, 5. Saturdays, 8, 9.20, 3.

WESTMINSTER CATHEDRAL, Ashley Place, London SW1P 1QW. Built 1895–1903 from the designs of J. F. Bentley. The campanile is 283 feet high. Cathedral open 6.45 a.m.–8 p.m. Masses: Sundays, 7, 8, 9, 10.30 (sung), 12, 5.30 and 7; Solemn Vespers and Benediction 3.30. Monday–Friday, 7, 8, 8.30, 9, 10.30, 12.30, 1.05 and 5.30 (sung). Morning Prayer 7.40, Vespers 5. Saturdays 7, 8, 8.30, 9, 10.30 (sung), 12.30 and 6, Morning Prayer 7.40, Vespers 5.30. Holy days of obligation, Low Masses 7, 8, 8.30, 9, 10.30, 12.30, 1.05, 5.30 (sung) and 7.

WESTMINSTER HALL, London SW1A 0AA. The only part of the old Palace of Westminster to survive the fire of 1834, Westminster Hall is adjacent to and incorporated in the Houses of Parliament. Westminster Hall was built by William Rufus from 1097–9 and altered by Richard II, 1394–9. It is about 240 ft. long, 68 ft. wide and 92 ft. high; the hammerbeam roof of carved oak dates from 1396–8. The Hall was the scene of the trial of Charles I. Westminster Hall is included on the route followed by those who have arranged a visit to the Houses of Parliament with their MP.

WHITECHAPEL ART GALLERY, Whitechapel High Street, London E1 7QX. Opened in 1901; administered by a charitable trust. There is no permanent collection;

temporary exhibitions, mainly of modern art, are presented, and community and educational projects are run. Open Tues.–Sun. 11–5; Wed. 11–8. Adm. free.

WIMBLEDON LAWN TENNIS MUSEUM, London SW19 5AE. Exhibits include fashion, trophies, replicas and memorabilia representing the history of lawn tennis. A theatre shows films of great matches. Tea room for refreshments. Open Tues.–Sat. 11–5, Sun. 2–5. Admission £2.00, concessions £1.00.

WINDSOR CASTLE, Begun by William the Conqueror, AD 1066–87. The Castle precincts are open daily. Admission free. The State Apartments of Windsor Castle are open throughout the year unless The Queen is in official residence. Admission charge. *Queen Mary's Dolls' House*, the *Exhibition of The Queen's Presents and Royal Carriages* and *The Gallery* can be seen on the same days as the State Apartments; admission charge. When the State Apartments are closed, the other exhibitions remain open to the public. The *Albert Memorial Chapel* is open throughout the year (closed on Sundays). Admission free. A fee is charged to visit *St George's Chapel*.
The *Royal Mausoleum*, Frogmore Gardens, Home Park, is open annually on two days in early May in conjunction with the opening of Frogmore Gardens in aid of the National Gardens Scheme. Also open on the Wednesday nearest to 24 May (Queen Victoria's birthday). Admission free. Tel: 0753–831118 for recorded information.

ZOOLOGICAL GARDENS (London Zoo), Regent's Park, London NW1. Opened in 1828. Open daily (except Christmas Day) March–September 10–5.30, 10–4 in winter. Admission £6.00, children £3.70, senior citizen £4.70.

LONDON TOURISM BOARD AND CONVENTION BUREAU, Tourist Information Centre, Victoria Station Forecourt, London SW1V 1JU. Tel: 071–730 3488.

PARKS, SPACES AND GARDENS

The principal parks and open spaces in the Metropolitan area are maintained as under:

By the Crown

BUSHY PARK (1,099 acres), Surrey. Adjoining Hampton Court, contains avenue of horse-chestnuts enclosed in a fourfold avenue of limes planted by William III. 'Chestnut Sunday' (when the trees are in full bloom with their 'candles') is usually about 1 to 15 May.

GREEN PARK (49 acres), London W1. Between Piccadilly and St James's Park with Constitution Hill, leading to Hyde Park Corner.

GREENWICH PARK (196½ acres), London SE10.

HAMPTON COURT GARDENS (54 acres), Surrey.

HAMPTON COURT GREEN (17 acres), Surrey.

HAMPTON COURT PARK (622 acres), Surrey.

HYDE PARK (341 acres), London W1/W2. From Park Lane to Kensington Gardens, containing the Serpentine. Fine gateway at Hyde Park Corner, with Apsley House, the Achilles Statue, Rotten Row and the Ladies' Mile. To the north-east is the Marble Arch, originally erected by George IV at the entrance to Buckingham Palace and re-erected in the present position in 1851.

KENSINGTON GARDENS (275 acres), London W2. From the western boundary of Hyde Park to Kensington Palace, containing the Albert Memorial.

KEW, ROYAL BOTANIC GARDENS *see* Index.

REGENT'S PARK and PRIMROSE HILL (464 acres), London NW1. From Marylebone Road to Primrose Hill surrounded by the Outer Circle and divided by the Broad Walk leading to the Zoological Gardens.

RICHMOND PARK (2,469 acres), Surrey.

ST JAMES'S PARK (93 acres), London SW1. From Whitehall to Buckingham Palace. Ornamental lake of 12 acres. The original suspension bridge built in 1857 was replaced in 1957. The Mall leads from the Admiralty Arch to the Queen Victoria Memorial and Buckingham Palace, Birdcage Walk from Storey's Gate, past Wellington Barracks, to Buckingham Palace.

By the Corporation of London

ASHTEAD COMMON (500 acres), Surrey.

BURNHAM BEECHES and FLEET WOOD (540 acres), Bucks. Purchased by the Corporation for the benefit of the public in 1880, Fleet Wood (65 acres) being presented in 1921.

COULSDON COMMON (133 acres), Surrey.

EPPING FOREST (6,000 acres), Essex. Purchased by the Corporation and thrown open to the public in 1882. The present Forest is 12 miles long by 1 to 2 miles wide, about one-tenth of its original area.

FARTHING DOWNS (121 acres), Surrey.

HAMPSTEAD HEATH (789 acres), London NW3. Including Golders Hill (36 acres) and Parliament Hill (271 acres), this was transferred to the Corporation on 1 April 1989.

HIGHGATE WOOD (70 acres), London.

KENLEY COMMON (138 acres), Surrey.

QUEEN'S PARK (30 acres), London.

RIDDLESDOWN (90 acres), Surrey.

SPRING PARK (51 acres), Kent.

WEST HAM PARK (77 acres), London.

WEST WICKHAM COMMON (25 acres), Kent.

WOODREDON AND WARLIES PARK ESTATE (740 acres), Waltham Abbey.

Also smaller open spaces within the City of London, including FINSBURY CIRCUS GARDENS.

Wales

Position and extent

The Principality of Wales (Cymru) occupies the extreme west of the central southern portion of the island of Great Britain, with a total area of 8,018 sq. miles (20,766 sq. km): land 7,968 sq. miles (20,636 sq. km); inland water 50 sq. miles (130 sq. km). It is bounded on the north by the Irish Sea, on the south by the Bristol Channel, on the east by the English counties of Cheshire, Shropshire, Hereford and Worcester, and Gloucestershire, and on the west by St George's Channel.

Across the Menai Straits is the Welsh island of Ynys Môn (Anglesey) (276 sq. miles), communication with which is facilitated by the Menai Suspension Bridge (1,000 ft. long) built by Telford in 1826, and by the tubular railway bridge (1,100 ft. long) built by Stephenson in 1850. Holyhead harbour, on Holy Isle (north-west of Anglesey), provides accommodation for ferry services to Dublin (70 miles).

Population

The population at the Census of 1981 was 2,791,851 (males 1,352,639; females 1,439,212). The preliminary report of the 1991 census put the population at 2,798,500. The average density of population in 1981 was 343 per square mile.

Relief

Wales is a country of extensive tracts of high plateau and shorter stretches of mountain ranges deeply dissected by river valleys. Lower-lying ground is largely confined to the coastal belt and the lower parts of the valleys. The highest mountains are those of Snowdonia in the north-west (Snowdon, 3,559 ft), Berwyn (Aran Fawddwy, 2,971 ft), Cader Idris (Pen y Gadair, 2,928 ft), Dyfed (Plynlimon, 2,467 ft), and the Black Mountain, Brecon Beacons and Black Forest ranges in the south-east (Carmarthen Van, 2,630 ft, Pen y Fan, 2,906 ft, Waun Fâch, 2,660 ft).

Hydrography

The principal river rising in Wales is the Severn (*see* page 529), which flows from the slopes of Plynlimon to the English border. The Wye (130 miles) also rises in the slopes of Plynlimon. The Usk (56 miles) flows into the Bristol Channel, through Gwent. The Dee (70 miles) rises in Bala Lake and flows through the Vale of Llangollen, where an aqueduct (built by Telford in 1805) carries the Pontcysyllte branch of the Shropshire Union Canal across the valley. The estuary of the Dee is the navigable portion, 14 miles in length and about five miles in breadth, and the tide rushes in with dangerous speed over the 'Sands of Dee'. The Towy (68 miles), Teifi (50 miles), Taff (40 miles), Dovey (30 miles), Taf (25 miles) and Conway (24 miles), the last named broad and navigable, are wholly Welsh rivers.

The largest natural lake in Wales is Bala (Llyn Tegid) in Gwynedd, nearly four miles long and about one mile wide; Lake Vyrnwy is an artificial reservoir, about the size of Bala, and forms the water supply of Liverpool; and Birmingham is supplied from a chain of reservoirs in the Elan and Claerwen valleys.

Welsh language

According to the 1981 Census results, the percentage of persons of three years and over able to speak Welsh was:

Clwyd	18.7	Powys	20.2
Dyfed	46.3	S. Glamorgan	5.8
Gwent	2.5	W. Glamorgan	16.4
Gwynedd	61.2		
Mid Glamorgan	8.4	Wales	18.9

The 1981 figure represents a slight decline from 20.8 per cent in 1971 (1961, 26 per cent; 1951, 28.9 per cent).

Flag

A red dragon on a green and white field (per fess argent and vert a dragon passant gules). The flag was augmented in 1953 by a royal badge on a shield encircled with a riband bearing the words *Ddraig Goch Ddyry Cychwyn* and imperially crowned. Only the unaugmented flag is flown on Government offices in Wales and, where appropriate, in London. Both flags continue to be used elsewhere.

EARLY HISTORY

Celts and Romans

The earliest inhabitants of whom there is any record appear to have been subdued or exterminated by the Goidels (a people of Celtic race) in the Bronze Age. A further invasion of Celtic Brythons and Belgae followed in the ensuing Iron Age. The Roman conquest of southern Britain and Wales was for some time successfully opposed by Caratacus (Caractacus or Caradog), chieftain of the Catuvellauni and son of Cunobelinus (Cymbeline). South-east Wales was subjugated and the legionary fortress at Caerleon-on-Usk established by about AD 75–77; the conquest of Wales was completed by Agricola about AD 78. Communications were opened up by the construction of military roads from Chester to Caerleon-on-Usk and Caerwent, and from Chester to Conwy (and thence to Carmarthen and Neath). Christianity was introduced during the Roman occupation, in the fourth century.

The Anglo-Saxon Attacks

The Anglo-Saxon invaders of southern Britain drove the Celts into the mountain stronghold of Wales, and into Strathclyde (Cumberland and south-west Scotland) and Cornwall, giving them the name of *Waelisc* (Welsh), meaning 'foreign'. The West Saxons' victory of Deorham (AD 577) isolated Wales from Cornwall and the battle of Chester (AD 613) cut off communication with Strathclyde and northern Britain. In the eighth century the boundaries of the Welsh were further restricted by the annexations of Offa, King of Mercia, and counter-attacks were largely prevented by the construction of an artificial boundary from the Dee to the Wye (Offa's Dyke).

In the ninth century Rhodri Mawr (844–878) united the country and successfully resisted further incursions of the Saxons by land and raids of Norse and Danish pirates by sea, but at his death his three provinces of Gwynedd (north), Powys (mid) and Deheubarth (south) were divided among his three sons, Anarawd, Mervyn and Cadell. Cadell's son Hywel Dda ruled a large part of Wales and codified its laws but the provinces were not united again until the rule of Llewelyn ap Seisyllt (husband of the heiress of Gwynedd) from 1018 to 1023.

The Norman Conquest

After the Norman conquest of England, William I created palatine counties along the Welsh frontier, and the Norman barons began to make encroachments into Welsh territory. The Welsh princes recovered many of their losses during the civil wars of Stephen's reign and in the early 13th century Owen Gruffydd, prince of Gwynedd, was the dominant figure in Wales. Under Llywelyn ap Iorwerth (1194–1240) the Welsh united in powerful resistance to English incursions and Llywelyn's privileges and *de facto* independence were recognized in Magna Carta. His grandson, Llywelyn ap Gruffydd, was the last native prince; he was killed in 1282 during hostilities between the Welsh and English, allowing Edward I of England to establish his authority over the country. On 7 February 1301, Edward of Caernarvon, son of Edward I, was created Prince of Wales, a title which has subsequently been borne by the eldest son of the sovereign.

Strong Welsh national feeling continued, expressed in the early 15th century in the rising led by Owain Glyndŵr, but the situation was altered by the accession to the English throne in 1485 of Henry VII of the Welsh House of Tudor. Wales was politically assimilated to England under the Act of Union of 1535, which extended English laws to the Principality and gave it parliamentary representation for the first time.

Eisteddfod

The Welsh are a distinct nation, with a language and literature of their own, and the national bardic festival (Eisteddfod), instituted by Prince Rhys ap Griffith in 1176, is still held annually (for date, *see* page 12). These *Eisteddfodau* (sessions) form part of the *Gorsedd* (assembly), which is believed to date from the time of Prydian, a ruling prince in an age many centuries before the Christian era.

PRINCIPAL CITIES

CARDIFF

Cardiff (South Glamorgan), at the mouth of the Rivers Taff, Rhymney and Ely, is the capital city of Wales and one of Britain's major administrative, commercial and business centres. It has many industries, including steel and cigars, and is a flourishing port with a substantial and varied trade.

There are many fine buildings in the civic centre started early this century, including the City Hall, the National Museum of Wales, University Buildings, Law Courts, Welsh Office, County Hall, Police Headquarters and the Temple of Peace and Health. Also in the city are Llandaff Cathedral, the Welsh National Folk Museum at St Fagans, Cardiff Castle, the New Theatre, the Sherman Theatre and the Cardiff College of Music and Drama. New buildings include St David's Hall, a 2,000-seat concert and conference hall, and the Welsh National Ice Rink.

SWANSEA

Swansea (*Abertawe*) is a city and a seaport of West Glamorgan. The Gower peninsula was brought within the city boundary under local government reform in 1974. The trade of the port includes coal, ores, and the import and export of oil. The municipal area is 60,511 acres.

The principal buildings are the Norman Castle (rebuilt *c.* 1330), the Royal Institution of South Wales, founded in 1835 (including Library), the University College at Singleton, and the Guildhall, containing the Brangwyn panels. New buildings include the Industrial and Maritime Museum, the new Maritime Quarter and Marina and the leisure centre.

Swansea was chartered by the Earl of Warwick, *c.*1158–84, and further charters were granted by King John, Henry III, Edward II, Edward III and James II, Cromwell (two) and the Marcher Lord William de Breos.

Welsh Counties

LORD LIEUTENANTS AND HIGH SHERIFFS

County	*Lord Lieutenant*	*High Sheriff, 1992–3*
Clwyd	Sir William Gladstone, Bt.	R. G. Hughes
Dyfed	D. C. Mansel Lewis	G. M. Green
Gwent	R. Hanbury-Tenison	Maj. C. A. Harding-Rolls
Gwynedd	R. E. Meuric Rees, CBE	Mrs A. Carey-Evans
Mid Glamorgan	M. A. McLaggan	K. M. D. Johns, OBE
Powys	M. L. Bourdillon	I. Gray
South Glamorgan	Capt. N. Lloyd-Edwards	A. O. Golley
West Glamorgan	Lt.-Col. Sir Michael Llewellyn, Bt.	W. I. James, MBE

COUNTY COUNCILS: AREA, POPULATION, FINANCE

County Council	*Administrative Headquarters*	*Area (hectares)*	*Population Census 1991p*	*Total demand upon collection fund 1992*
Clwyd	Shire Hall, Mold	243,015	401,900	£40,062,000
Dyfed	County Hall, Carmarthen	576,575	341,600	31,575,000
Gwent	County Hall, Cwmbran	137,652	432,300	33,780,000
Gwynedd	County Offices, Caernarfon	386,331	238,600	19,180,890
Mid Glamorgan	County Hall, Cathays Park, Cardiff	101,749	526,500	47,891,872
Powys	County Hall, Llandrindod Wells	507,716	116,500	8,966,459
South Glamorgan	County Hall, Atlantic Wharf, Cardiff	41,622	383,300	29,176,000
West Glamorgan	County Hall, Swansea	81,960	357,800	33,313,000

p preliminary

COUNTY COUNCILS: Officials and Chairman

County Council	*Chief Executive* **County Clerk*	*County Treasurer*	*Chairman of County Council*
Clwyd	M. H. Phillips, CBE	A. Dalby	D. R. Parry
Dyfed	W. J. Phillips	H. Morse	Revd R. G. Ball
Gwent	M. J. Perry	J. P. Walsh	A. J. Huntley
Gwynedd	H. V. Thomas	T. D. Heald	G. Roberts
Mid Glamorgan	D. H. Thomas, CBE*	L. M. James	E. J. Davies
Powys	A. J. Barnish	J. Wrightson†	E. Kinsey-Pugh, MBE
South Glamorgan	B. Davies	R. G. Tettenborn	P. Perkins
West Glamorgan	A. G. Corless	S. G. Dunster°	D. F. Bevan, CBE

† County Finance Officer
° Director of Finance

District Councils

Small Capitals denote city status
§ denotes Borough status

District Borough Council	*Population Census 1991p*	*Community charge per head 1992*	*Chief Executive*	*Chairman 1992–3* *(a) Mayor* *(b) Lord Mayor*
§Aberconwy, Gwynedd	54,100	£149.34	J. E. Davies	(*a*) B. B. Bertola
Alyn and Deeside, Clwyd	71,700	152.38	W. E. Rogers	D. Messham
§Arfon, Gwynedd	54,600	137.77	D. L. Jones	(*a*) Mrs M. Williams
§Blaenau Gwent, Gwent	74,700	147.00	R. Leadbeter	(*a*) G. Griffiths
§Brecknock, Powys	41,300	133.63	R. O. Doylend	(*a*) M. Griffiths
Cardiff, South Glamorgan	272,600	158.83	R. E. Paine	(*b*) D. Allinson
Carmarthen, Dyfed	54,800	138.27	R. R. Morgan	D. W. Edwards
Ceredigion, Dyfed	63,600	138.21	D. Morgan	L. L. Jones
§Colwyn, Clwyd	54,900	158.90	W. N. Breeze	(*a*) Mrs E. M. Wynne
§Cynon Valley, Mid Glamorgan	63,600	106.22	T. B. Roberts	(*a*) G. I. Jones
§Delyn, Clwyd	66,200	155.20	P. J. McGreevy	(*a*) Mrs E. G. Smith
§Dinefwr, Dyfed	38,000	114.27	E. W. Harries	(*a*) Mrs M. H. Thomas
Dwyfor, Gwynedd	28,600	132.80	E. M. Royles	E. H. Griffith
Glyndŵr, Clwyd	41,500	167.00	J. H. Parry	W. O. Jones
§Islwyn, Gwent	64,900	114.25	B. Bird	(*a*) T. A. G. Harris
§Llanelli, Dyfed	73,500	133.52	D. B. Parry-Jones	(*a*) Mrs E. G. Lloyd
§Lliw Valley, West Glamorgan	61,700	118.53	J. C. Howells	(*a*) B. F. Elliott
Meirionnydd, Gwynedd	33,400	136.27	G. W. Hughes	E. Pugh
§Merthyr Tydfil, Mid Glamorgan	59,300	145.83	R. V. Morris	(*a*) D. L. Jarrett
§Monmouth, Gwent	75,000	154.00	G. Cummings	(*a*) T. J. Cleary
Montgomeryshire, Powys	52,000	122.35	N. J. Bardsley	D. R. Jones
§Neath, West Glamorgan	64,100	109.26	S. Penny	(*a*) D. W. T. Davies
§Newport, Gwent	129,900	152.00	R. D. Blair	(*a*) A. Perry
§Ogwr, Mid Glamorgan	130,500	121.53	J. G. Cole	(*a*) W. B. Evans
§Port Talbot, West Glamorgan	49,900	145.57	I. K. Lewis	(*a*) C. Owen
Preseli Pembrokeshire, Dyfed	69,600	140.88	I. W. R. David	D. E. Pritchard
Radnoshire, Powys	23,200	121.70	G. C. Read	R. C. Bagley
§Rhondda, Mid Glamorgan	76,300	82.32	G. Evans	(*a*) H. S. Blight
§Rhuddlan, Clwyd	54,000	163.79	E. O. Lake	(*a*) Mrs N. Fletcher-Williams
Rhymney Valley, Mid Glamorgan	101,400	138.21	P. A. Bennett	Mrs A. Morgan
South Pembrokeshire, Dyfed	42,100	116.03	G. H. James	J. S. Allen-Mirehouse
Swansea, West Glamorgan	182,100	164.00	A. K. B. Boatswain	(*b*) C. Birss
§Taff-Ely, Mid Glamorgan	95,400	142.92	D. Gethin	(*a*) Mrs M. J. Henderson
§Torfaen, Gwent	88,200	144.50	M. B. Mehta	(*a*) T. Davies
§Vale of Glamorgan, South Glamorgan	110,700	137.93	M. P. A. Smith	(*a*) D. B. Leddington
§Wrexham Maelor, Clwyd	113,600	177.42	R. J. Dutton, CBE	(*a*) D. J. Roberts
§Ynys Môn (Isle of Anglesey), Gwynedd	67,800	137.78	E. L. Gibson	(*a*) H. R. M. Hughes

p preliminary

Scotland

Position and Extent

The Kingdom of Scotland occupies the northern portion of the main island of Great Britain and includes the Inner and Outer Hebrides, and the Orkney, Shetland, and many other islands. It lies between 60° 51′ 30″ and 54° 38′ N. latitude and between 1° 45′ 32″ and 6° 14′ W. longitude, with England to the south, the Atlantic Ocean on the north and west, and the North Sea on the east.

The greatest length of the mainland (Cape Wrath to the Mull of Galloway) is 274 miles, and the greatest breadth (Buchan Ness to Applecross) is 154 miles. The customary measurement of the island of Great Britain is from the site of John o' Groats house, near Duncansby Head, Caithness, to Land's End, Cornwall, a total distance of 603 miles in a straight line and (approximately) 900 miles by road.

The total area of Scotland is 30,420 sq. miles (78,789 sq. km): land 29,767 sq. miles (77,097 sq. km); inland water 653 sq. miles (1,692 sq. km).

Population

The population (1981 Census) was 5,130,735 (males 2,466,437; females 2,664,298). The preliminary report of the 1991 Census put the population at 4,957,289. The average density of the population in 1981 was 168 persons per square mile.

Relief

There are three natural orographic divisions of Scotland. The southern uplands have their highest points in Merrick (2,766 ft), Rhinns of Kells (2,669 ft), and Cairnsmuir of Carsphairn (2,614 ft), in the west; and the Tweedsmuir Hills in the east (Hartfell 2,651 ft, Dollar Law 2,682 ft, Broad Law 2,756 ft).

The central lowlands, formed by the valleys of the Clyde, Forth and Tay, divide the southern uplands from the northern Highlands, which extend almost from the extreme north of the mainland to the central lowlands, and are divided into a northern and a southern system by the Great Glen.

The Grampian Mountains, which entirely cover the southern Highland area, include in the west Ben Nevis (4,406 ft), the highest point in the British Isles, and in the east the Cairngorm Mountains (Cairn Gorm 4,084 ft, Braeriach 4,248 ft, Ben Macdui 4,296 ft). The north-western Highland area contains in the mountains of Wester and Easter Ross Carn Eige (3,880 ft) and Sgurr na Lapaich (3,775 ft).

Created, like the central lowlands, by a major geological fault, the Great Glen (60 miles long) runs between Inverness and Fort William, and contains Loch Ness, Loch Oich and Loch Lochy. These are linked to each other and to the north-east and south-west coasts of Scotland by the Caledonian Canal, providing a navigable passage between the Moray Firth and the Inner Hebrides.

Hydrography

The western coast of Scotland is fragmented by peninsulas and islands, and indented by fjords (sea-lochs), the longest of which is Loch Fyne (42 miles long) in Argyll. Although the east coast tends to be less fractured and lower, there are several great drowned inlets (firths), e.g. Firth of Forth, Firth of Tay, Moray Firth, as well as the Firth of Clyde in the west.

The lochs are the principal hydrographic feature of Scotland. The largest in Scotland and in Great Britain is Loch Lomond (27 square miles), in the Grampian valleys; the longest and deepest is Loch Ness (24 miles long and 800 feet deep), in the Great Glen; and Loch Shin (20 miles long) and Loch Maree in the northern Highlands.

The longest river in Scotland is the Tay (117 miles), noted for its salmon. It flows into the North Sea, with Dundee on the estuary, which is spanned by the Tay Bridge (10,289 ft) opened in 1887 and the Tay Road Bridge (7,365 ft) opened in 1966. Other noted salmon rivers are the Dee (90 miles) which flows into the North Sea at Aberdeen, and the Spey (110 miles), the swiftest flowing river in the British Isles, which flows into Moray Firth. The Tweed, which gave its name to the woollen cloth produced along its banks, marks in the lower stretches of its 96-mile course the border between Scotland and England.

The most important river commercially is the Clyde (106 miles), formed by the junction of the Daer and Portrail water, which flows through the city of Glasgow to the Firth of Clyde. During its course it passes over the picturesque Falls of Clyde, Bonnington Linn (30 ft), Corra Linn (84 ft), Dundaff Linn (10 ft) and Stonebyres Linn (80 ft), above and below Lanark. The Forth (66 miles), upon which stands Edinburgh, the capital, is spanned by the Forth (Railway) Bridge (1890), which is 5,330 feet long, and the Forth (Road) Bridge (1964), which has a total length of 6,156 feet (over water) and a single span of 3,000 feet.

The highest waterfall in Scotland, and the British Isles, is Eas a'Chùal Aluinn with a total height of 658 feet (200 m), which falls from Glas Bheinn in Sutherland. The Falls of Glomach, on a head-stream of the Elchaig in Wester Ross, have a drop of 370 feet.

Gaelic Language

According to the 1981 Census, 82,620 people, mainly in the Highlands and western coastal regions, were able to speak, read or write the Scottish form of Gaelic.

Flag

The cross of St Andrew, the patron saint of Scotland (saltire argent in a field azure).

THE SCOTTISH ISLANDS

The Hebrides did not become part of the Kingdom of Scotland until 1266, when they were ceded to Alexander III by Magnus of Norway. Orkney and Shetland fell to the Scottish Crown as a pledge for the unpaid dowry of Margaret of Denmark, wife of James III, in 1468, the Danish claims to suzerainty being relinquished in 1590 when James VI married Anne of Denmark.

Orkney

The Orkney Islands (total area 375½ sq. miles) lie about six miles north of the mainland, separated from it by the Pentland Firth. Of the 90 islands and islets (holms and skerries) in the group, about one-third are inhabited.

The total population at the 1981 Census was 19,040; the 1981 populations of the islands shown here include those of smaller islands forming part of the same civil parish.

Mainland, 14,299	Shapinsay, 345
Eday, 154	South Ronaldsay, 1,188
Hoy and Graemsay, 80	Stronsay, 462
Papa Westray, 94	Walls and Flotta, 761
Rousay and Egilsay, 264	Westray, 741
Sanday and North Ronaldsay, 652	

The islands are rich in Pictish and Scandinavian remains, the most notable being the Stone Age village of Skara Brae, the burial chamber of Maeshowe, the many brochs (Pictish towers) and St Magnus Cathedral. Scapa Flow, between the Mainland and Hoy, was the war station of the British Grand Fleet from 1914 to 1919 and the scene of the scuttling of the surrendered German High Seas Fleet (21 June, 1919).

Most of the islands are low-lying and fertile, and farming (principally beef cattle) is the main industry. Flotta, to the south of Scapa Flow, is now the site of the oil terminal for the Piper, Claymore and Tartan fields in the North Sea.

The capital is Kirkwall (population 6,881) on Mainland.

SHETLAND

The Shetland Islands have a total area of 551 sq. miles and a population at the 1981 Census of 27,271. They lie about 50 miles north of the Orkneys, with Fair Isle about half-way between the two groups. Out Stack, off Muckle Flugga, one mile north of Unst, is the most northerly part of the British Isles (60° 51′ 30″ N. lat.).

There are over 100 islands, of which 16 are inhabited. Populations at the 1981 census were:

Mainland, 22,184	Muckle Roe, 101
Bressay, 335	Out Skerries, 79
East and West Burra and Trondra, 930	Papa Stour, 29
Fair Isle, 69	Unst, 1,206
Fetlar, 102	Whalsay, 1,026
Foula, 39	Yell, 1,168

Shetland's many archaeological sites include Jarlshof, Mousa and Clickhimin, and its long connection with Scandinavia has resulted in a strong Norse influence on its place-names and dialect.

Industries include fishing, knitwear and farming. In addition to the fishing fleet there are fish processing factories, while the traditional handknitting of Fair Isle and Unst is supplemented now with machine knitted garments. Farming is mainly crofting, with sheep being raised on the moorland and hills of the islands. Latterly the islands have become an important centre of the North Sea oil industry, with pipelines from the Brent and Ninian fields running to the terminal at Sullom Voe, the largest of its kind in Europe. Lerwick is the main centre for supply services for offshore oil exploration and development.

The capital is Lerwick (population 7,901) on Mainland.

THE HEBRIDES

Until the closing years of the 13th century the Hebrides included other Scottish islands in the Firth of Clyde, the peninsula of Kintyre (Argyllshire), the Isle of Man, and the (Irish) Isle of Rathlin. The origin of the name is stated to be the Greek *Eboudai*, latinized as *Hebudes* by Pliny, and corrupted to its present form. The Norwegian name *Sudreyjar* (Southern Islands) was latinized as *Sodorenses*, a name that survives in the Anglican bishopric of Sodor and Man.

There are over 500 islands and islets, of which about 100 are inhabited, though mountainous terrain and extensive peat bogs mean that only a fraction of the total area is under cultivation. Stone, Bronze and Iron Age settlement has left many remains, including those at Callanish on Lewis, and Norse colonization has influenced language, customs and place-names. Occupations include farming (mostly crofting and stock-raising), fishing and the manufacture of tweeds and other woollens. Tourism is also an important factor in the economy.

The Inner Hebrides lie off the west coast of Scotland and relatively close to the mainland. The largest and best-known is Skye (area 643 sq. miles; pop. 8,139; chief town, Portree), which contains the Cuillin Hills (Sgurr Alasdair 3,257 ft), the Red Hills (Beinn na Caillich 2,403 ft) as well as Bla Bheinn (3,046 ft) and The Storr (2,358 ft). Skye is also famous as the refuge of the Young Pretender in 1746. Other islands in the Highland Region include Raasay (pop. 182) Rum, Eigg and Muck.

Islands in the Strathclyde Region include Arran (pop. 4,726) containing Goat Fell (2,868 ft); Coll and Tiree (pop. 933); Colonsay and Oronsay (pop. 137); Islay (area 235 sq. miles; pop. 3,997); Jura (area 160 sq. miles; pop. 239) with a range of hills culminating in the Paps of Jura (Beinn-an-Oir, 2,576 ft, and Beinn Chaolais, 2,477 ft); Mull (area 367 sq. miles; pop. 2,605; chief town Tobermory) containing Ben More (3,171 ft).

The Outer Hebrides, separated from the mainland by the Minch, now form the Western Isles Islands Council area (area 1,119 sq. miles; population at the 1981 Census 31,842). The main islands are Lewis with Harris (area 770 sq. miles, pop. 23,390), whose chief town, Stornoway (pop. 13,409), is the administrative headquarters; North Uist (pop. 1,454); South Uist (pop. 2,223); Benbecula (pop. 1,988) and Barra (pop. 1,232). Other inhabited islands include Bernera (292), Berneray (134), Eriskay (219), Grimsay (206), Scalpay (461) and Vatersay (108).

EARLY HISTORY

PREHISTORIC INHABITANTS

The Picts, believed to be of non-Aryan origin, seem to have inhabited the whole of northern Britain and to have spread over the north of Ireland. Remains are most frequent in Caithness and Sutherland and the Orkney Islands.

Celts arrived from Belgic Gaul during the latter part of the Bronze Age and in the early Iron Age, and except in the extreme north of the mainland and in the islands, the civilization and speech of the people were definitely Celtic at the time of the Roman invasion of Britain.

THE ROMAN INVASION

In AD 79–80 Julius Agricola extended the Roman conquests in Britain by advancing into Caledonia and building a line of fortifications across the isthmus between the Forth and Clyde, but after a victory at Mons Graupius he was recalled. Hadrian's Wall, mostly complete by AD 130, marked the frontier until about AD 143 when the frontier moved north to the Forth–Clyde isthmus and was secured by the Antonine Wall. From about AD 155 the Antonine Wall was damaged by frequent attacks and by the end of the second century the northern limit of Roman Britain had receded to Hadrian's Wall.

THE SCOTS

After the withdrawal (or absorption) of the Roman garrison of Britain there were many years of tribal warfare between the Picts and Scots (the Gaelic tribe then dominant in Ireland), the Brythonic Waelisc (Welsh) of Strathclyde (south-west Scotland and Cumberland), and the Anglo-Saxons of Lothian. The Waelisc were isolated from their kinsmen in Wales by the victory of the West Saxons at Chester (613), and towards the close of the ninth century the Scots under Kenneth Macalpine became the dominant power in Caledonia. In the reign of Malcolm I (943–954) Strathclyde was brought into subjection, the English lowland kingdom (Lothian) being conquered by Malcolm II (1005–1034).

From the late 11th century until the mid 16th century there were constant wars between Scotland and England, the outstanding figures in the struggle being William Wallace, who defeated the English at Stirling Bridge (1297) and Robert Bruce, who won the victory of Bannockburn (1314). James IV and many of his nobles fell at the disastrous battle of Flodden (1513).

THE JACOBITE REVOLTS

In 1603 James VI of Scotland succeeded Elizabeth I on the throne of England (his mother, Mary Queen of Scots, was the great-granddaughter of Henry VII), his successors reigning as sovereigns of Great Britain, although political union of the two countries did not occur until 1707. After the abdication (by flight) in 1688 of James VII and II, the crown devolved upon William III (grandson of Charles I) and Mary (daughter of James VII and II). In 1689 Graham of Claverhouse roused the Highlands on behalf of James VII and II, but died after a military success at Killiecrankie.

After the death of Anne (second daughter of James VII and II), the throne devolved upon George I (great-grandson of James VI and I). In 1715, armed risings on behalf of James Stuart (the Old Pretender) led to the indecisive battle of Sheriffmuir, but the Jacobite movement died down until 1745, when Charles Stuart (the Young Pretender) defeated the Royalist troops at Prestonpans and advanced to Derby in England (1746). From Derby, the adherents of 'James VIII and III' (the title claimed for his father by Charles Stuart) fell back on the defensive, and the movement was finally crushed at Culloden (16 April 1746).

PRINCIPAL CITIES

ABERDEEN

Aberdeen, 130 miles north-east of Edinburgh, received its charter as a Royal Burgh from William the Lion in 1179. Scotland's third largest city, Aberdeen is the second largest Scottish fishing port and the main European centre for offshore oil exploration. It is also an ancient university town and distinguished research centre. Other industries include engineering, shipbuilding, food processing, textiles, paper manufacturing and chemicals.

Places of interest include King's College and Visitor Centre, St Machar's Cathedral, Brig o' Balgownie, Duthie Park and Winter Gardens, the Kirk of St Nicholas, Mercat Cross, Marischal College and Marischal Museum, Provost Skene's House, Art Gallery, James Dun's House (children's museum), Satrosphere Hands-On Discovery Centre, and Provost Ross's House (maritime museum).

DUNDEE

Dundee, a Royal Burgh, is situated on the north bank of the Tay estuary. The city's port and dock installations are important to the offshore oil industry and the airport also provides servicing facilities. Principal industries include textiles, computers and other electronic industries, lasers, printing, tyre manufacture, food processing, carpets, engineering and clothing manufacture. Six sites have Enterprise Zone status, including the Technology Park, airport and port.

The unique City Churches – three churches under one roof, together with the 15th century St Mary's Tower – are the most prominent architectural feature. RRS *Discovery*, the ship which took Captain Scott to the Antarctic and which was built in Dundee in 1901, is berthed in Discovery Quay.

EDINBURGH

Edinburgh is the capital of and seat of government in Scotland. The city is built on a group of hills and contains in Princes Street one of the most beautiful thoroughfares in the world.

The principal buildings are the Castle, which includes St Margaret's Chapel, the oldest building in Edinburgh, and near it, the Scottish National War Memorial; the Palace of Holyroodhouse; Parliament House, the present seat of the judicature; two universities (Edinburgh and Heriot-Watt); St Giles' Cathedral (restored 1879–83); St Mary's (Scottish Episcopal) Cathedral (Sir Gilbert Scott); the General Register House (Robert Adam): the National and the Signet Libraries; the National Gallery; the Royal Scottish Academy; and the National Portrait Gallery.

GLASGOW

Glasgow, a Royal Burgh, is the principal commercial and industrial centre in Scotland. The city occupies the north and south banks of the Clyde, formerly one of the chief commercial estuaries in the world. The principal industries include engineering, electronics, finance, chemicals and printing. The city has also developed recently as a tourism and conference centre.

The chief buildings are the 13th century Gothic Cathedral, the University (Sir Gilbert Scott), the City Chambers, the Royal Concert Hall, Pollok House, the School of Art (Mackintosh), Kelvingrove Art Galleries, the Burrell Collection museum and the Mitchell Library. The city is home to the Scottish National Orchestra, Scottish Opera and Scottish Ballet.

LORD LIEUTENANTS IN SCOTLAND

Region	*Title*	*Name*
Borders	Berwickshire	Maj.-Gen. Sir John Swinton, KCVO, OBE
	Roxburgh, Ettrick and Lauderdale	The Duke of Buccleuch and Queensberry, KT, VRD
	Tweeddale	Lt.-Col. A. M. Sprot of Haystoun, MC
Central	Clackmannan	The Earl of Mar and Kellie
	Stirling and Falkirk	Lt.-Col. J. Stirling of Garden, CBE, TD
Dumfries and Galloway	Dumfries	Capt. R. C. Cunningham-Jardine
	The Stewartry of Kirkcudbright	Sir Michael A. R. Y. Herries, OBE, MC
	Wigtown	Maj. E. S. Orr Ewing
Fife	Fife	The Earl of Elgin and Kincardine, KT
Grampian	Aberdeenshire	Capt. C. A. Farquharson
	Banffshire	J. A. S. McPherson, CBE
	Kincardineshire	The Viscount of Arbuthnott, CBE, DSC, FRSE
	Morayshire	Capt. Sir Iain Tennant, KT

Highland	Caithness	The Viscount Thurso
	Inverness	Lt.-Cdr. L. R. D. Mackintosh of Mackintosh, OBE
	Nairn	The Earl of Leven and Melville
	Ross and Cromarty	Capt. R. W. K. Stirling of Fairburn, TD
	Sutherland	Maj.-Gen. D. Houston, CBE
Lothian	East Lothian	Sir Hew Hamilton-Dalrymple, Bt., KCVO
	Midlothian	Capt. G. W. Burnett, LVO
	West Lothian	The Earl of Morton
Strathclyde	Argyll and Bute	The Marquess of Bute
	Ayrshire and Arran	Maj. R. Y. Henderson, TD
	Dunbartonshire	Brig. D. D. G. Hardie, TD
	Lanarkshire	H. B. Sneddon, CBE
	Renfrewshire	Maj. J. D. M. Crichton Maitland
Tayside	Angus	The Earl of Airlie, KT, GCVO, PC
	Perth and Kinross	Maj. Sir David Butter, KCVO, MC
Orkney	Orkney	Brig. M. G. Dennison
Shetland	Shetland	M. M. Shearer
Western Isles	Western Isles	The Earl Granville, MC

The Lord Provosts of the four city districts of Aberdeen, Dundee, Edinburgh and Glasgow are Lord Lieutenants for those districts *ex officio*

Scottish Regions and Islands

REGIONAL AND ISLANDS COUNCILS: Area, Population, Finance

Region	*Administrative Headquarters*	*Area (hectares)*	*Population (latest estimate)*	*Regional community charge per head 1992*	*Community water charge per head 1992*
Borders	Newtown St Boswells	471,253	102,700	£156.00	£41.00
Central	Stirling	263,455	271,023	233.00	20.00
Dumfries and Galloway	Dumfries	639,561	148,400	171.00	36.00
Fife	Glenrothes	131,201	345,900	214.00	25.00
Grampian	Aberdeen	869,772	502,600	153.00	40.00
Highland	Inverness	2,539,759	204,300	165.00	38.00
Lothian	Edinburgh	171,595	749,600	280.00	30.00
Orkney	Kirkwall	97,581	19,570	180.00	57.00
Shetland	Lerwick	143,268	23,214	201.00	46.00
Strathclyde	Glasgow	1,350,283	2,273,051	233.00	34.00
Tayside	Dundee	749,165	394,000	204.00	28.00
Western Isles	Stornoway, Lewis	289,798	30,660	122.00	58.00

REGIONAL AND ISLAND COUNCILS: Officers and Conveners

Region	*Chief Executive*	*Director of Finance*	*Convener*
Borders	K. J. Clark, CBE	P. Jeary	The Earl of Minto, OBE
Central	D. Sinclair	S. C. Craig	Mrs A. Wallace
Dumfries and Galloway	N. W. D. McIntosh, CBE	J. C. Stewart	D. R. Robinson
Fife	Dr J. A. Markland	A. E. Taylor	R. Gough, CBE
Grampian	A. G. Campbell	A. McLean	R. Middleton
Highland	R. H. Stevenson	J. W. Bremner	D. J. McPherson
Lothian	G. M. Bowie, CBE	D. B. Chynoweth	E. Milligan
Orkney	R. H. Gilbert	R. H. Gilbert	J. A. Tait
Shetland	M. E. Green	J. E. Cornick (*acting*)	E. Thomason, OBE
Strathclyde	N. McIntosh	A. Gillespie	Dr D. Sanderson
Tayside	R. W. Black	I. B. McIver	Dr G. W. Buckman
Western Isles	Dr G. Macleod	R. Bennie	D. Macleod

District Councils

District	Administrative Headquarters	Population (latest estimate)	District community charge per head 1992	Chief Executive	Chairman (a) Convener (b) Provost (c) Lord Provost
Aberdeen City (5)	Aberdeen	205,370	£69.00	D. MacDonald	(c) J. Wyness
Angus (9)	Forfar	95,370	32.00	P. B. Regan	(b) B. M. C. Milne
Annandale and Eskdale (3)	Annan	36,805	58.00	W. J. Davidson	(a) D. T. R. Wilson
Argyll and Bute (8)	Lochgilphead	66,150	78.00	M. A. J. Gossip, CBE	G. McMillan
Badenoch and Strathspey (6)	Kingussie	11,190	37.00	Mrs J. M. Fraser	A. Gordon
Banff and Buchan (5)	Banff	85,920	42.00	R. M. Blackburn	(a) W. R. Cruickshank
Bearsden and Milngavie (8)	Bearsden	40,900	60.00	I. C. Laurie	(b) I. J. Miller
Berwickshire (1)	Duns	19,070	21.00	R. A. Christie	Capt. J. Evans
Caithness (6)	Wick	26,560	25.00	A. Beattie	(a) J. M. Young, OBE
Clackmannan (2)	Alloa	47,470	85.00	I. F. Smith	(a) J. Watson
Clydebank (8)	Clydebank	46,920	98.00	J. T. McNally	(b) A. Macdonald
Clydesdale (8)	Lanark	58,440	89.00	P. W. Daniels	(a) Mrs E. Logan
Cumbernauld and Kilsyth (8)	Cumbernauld	63,100	55.00	J. Hutton	(b) C. Combe
Cumnock and Doon Valley (8)	Cumnock	42,000	59.00	K. W. Inch	(a) E. Ross
Cunninghame (8)	Irvine	137,717	61.00	B. Devine	(a) S. Dewar
Dumbarton (8)	Dumbarton	79,750	167.00	M. J. Watters‡	(b) P. O'Neill
Dundee City (9)	Dundee	172,860	87.00	A. Stephen	(c) T. M. McDonald
Dunfermline (4)	Dunfermline	129,049	52.00	G. Brown	(b) Ms M. Millar
East Kilbride (8)	East Kilbride	82,380	91.00	D. Liddell	(b) S. Crawford
East Lothian (7)	Haddington	84,130	73.00	M. Duncan	G. M. Wanless
Eastwood (8)	Giffnock	61,010	25.00	M. D. Henry	(b) L. M. Rosin
Edinburgh City (7)	Edinburgh	434,520	116.00	P. Lowenberg	(c) Rt. Hon. N. Irons
Ettrick and Lauderdale (1)	Galashiels	33,939	37.00	C. M. Anderson	(b) W. Hardie
Falkirk (2)	Falkirk	139,038	22.00	W. Weir	(b) J. Constable
Glasgow City (8)	Glasgow	696,577	120.00	T. J. Monaghan	(c) Rt. Hon. R. Innes
Gordon (5)	Inverurie	75,500	29.50	M. C. Barron	(b) R. G. Bisset
Hamilton (8)	Hamilton	106,404	93.00	A. Baird	(b) S. Casserly
Inverclyde (8)	Greenock	93,470	79.00	R. McPherson	(b) A. Robertson
Inverness (6)	Inverness	61,748	31.00	B. Wilson	(b) W. A. E. Fraser
Kilmarnock and Loudoun (8)	Kilmarnock	79,000	57.00	R. W. Jenner	(b) D. Coffey
Kincardine and Deeside (5)	Stonehaven	50,920	16.00	T. Hyder	(a) Mrs D. Ewing
Kirkcaldy (4)	Kirkcaldy	148,870	55.00	D. A. Watt§	(a) R. King, OBE
Kyle and Carrick (8)	Ayr	113,000	106.00	I. R. D. Smillie†	(b) G. T. Macdonald
Lochaber (6)	Fort William	19,500	35.00	D. A. B. Blair	D. Purdon
Midlothian (7)	Dalkeith	77,969	54.00	T. Muir	(a) D. Molloy
Monklands (8)	Coatbridge	106,187	92.00	M. V. P. Hart	(b) R. Gilson
Moray (5)	Elgin	85,230	25.00	L. Morgan	(a) E. Aldridge
Motherwell (8)	Motherwell	147,760	65.00	J. Bonomy	(b) W. Wilson
Nairn (6)	Nairn	11,000	42.00	A. M. Kerr†	(b) J. Cattanach
Nithsdale (3)	Dumfries	57,820	57.00	T. Orr	(b) Mrs J. McMurdo
North-East Fife (4)	Cupar	68,260	59.00	R. G. Brotherton	Mrs I. M. Carter
Perth and Kinross (9)	Perth	126,842	49.00	H. Robertson	(b) Mrs J. McCormack
Renfrew (8)	Paisley	193,622	110.00	A. I. Cowe*	(b) W. Orr
Ross and Cromarty (6)	Dingwall	48,910	56.00	R. Mair	(a) Maj. A. Cameron
Roxburgh (1)	Hawick	34,990	38.00	K. W. Cramond	Mrs M. S. Turnbull
Skye and Lochalsh (6)	Portree	11,820	47.00	D. H. Noble	J. F. Munro
Stewartry (3)	Kirkcudbright	23,520	33.00	J. C. Howie	(a) J. Nelson, MBE, TD
Stirling (2)	Stirling	81,318	93.00	G. Bonner	(a) Mrs P. Greenhill
Strathkelvin (8)	Kirkintilloch	87,509	97.00	C. Mallon	(b) C. O'Neill
Sutherland (6)	Golspie	13,000	38.00	J. Allison†	Mrs A. Magee
Tweeddale (1)	Peebles	15,470	26.00	G. H. T. Garvie	D. Suckling
West Lothian (7)	Bathgate	150,334	33.00	A. M. Linkston	(a) J. McGinley
Wigtown (3)	Stranraer	22,310	52.00	A. Geddes	W. Service

‡ District Secretary
§ General Manager
* Managing Director
† Director of Administration

Regions

(1) Borders
(2) Central
(3) Dumfries and Galloway
(4) Fife
(5) Grampian
(6) Highland
(7) Lothian
(8) Strathclyde
(9) Tayside

Northern Ireland

The usually resident population of Northern Ireland according to the 1981 Census was 1,532,198 (males, 749,485; females, 782,713) compared with a total population of 1,536,065 at the Census of 1971. The estimated figure for the population following the 1991 census was 1,583,000.

In 1981 the number of persons in the various religious denominations (expressed as percentages of the total usually resident population) were: Roman Catholic, 28.0; Presbyterian, 22.9; Church of Ireland, 19.0; Methodist, 4.0; others 7.6; not stated, 18.5.

Northern Ireland has a total area of 5,452 sq. miles (14,121 sq. km): land, 5,206 sq. miles (13,483 sq. km); inland water and tideways, 246 sq. miles (638 sq. km). There was a density of population of 282 persons per sq. mile in 1981.

PRINCIPAL CITIES

BELFAST

Belfast, the administrative centre of Northern Ireland, is situated at the mouth of the River Lagan at its entrance to Belfast Lough. The city grew, owing to its easy access by sea to Scottish coal and iron, to be a great industrial centre.

The principal buildings are of a relatively recent date and include the Parliament Buildings at Stormont, the City Hall, the Law Courts, the Public Library and the Museum and Art Gallery.

Belfast received its first charter of incorporation in 1613 and was created a city in 1888; the title of Lord Mayor was conferred in 1892.

LONDONDERRY

Londonderry, situated on the River Foyle, was reputedly founded in 546 by St Columba. Londonderry (formerly Derry) has important associations with the City of London. The Irish Society, under its royal charter of 1613, fortified the city and was for long closely associated with its administration.

The city is famous for the great siege of 1688–9, when for 105 days the town held out against the forces of James II until relieved by sea. The city walls are still intact and form a circuit of almost a mile around the old city.

Interesting buildings are the Protestant Cathedral of St Columb's (1633) and the Guildhall, reconstructed in 1912 and containing a number of beautiful stained glass windows, many of which were presented by the livery companies of London.

CONSTITUTION AND GOVERNMENT

As part of the United Kingdom, Northern Ireland is subject to the same fundamental constitutional provisions which apply to the rest of the United Kingdom. However, the Northern Ireland Constitution Act 1973 and the Northern Ireland Act 1982 provide for a measure of devolved government in Northern Ireland. This arrangement was last in force in January 1974, following agreement between the Northern Ireland political parties to form a power-sharing executive. However, this arrangement collapsed in May 1974 and there has been no devolution since.

In the interim, Northern Ireland continues to be governed by direct rule under the provisions of the Northern Ireland Act 1974. This allows Parliament to approve all laws for Northern Ireland and places the Northern Ireland departments under the direction and control of the Secretary of State for Northern Ireland.

Attempts have been made by successive governments to find a means of restoring a widely acceptable form of devolved government to Northern Ireland. A 78-member Assembly was elected by proportional representation in 1982. However, four years later it was dissolved after it ceased to discharge its responsibilities of making proposals for the resumption of devolved government and of monitoring the work of the Northern Ireland Departments.

In January 1990 further dialogue between the Government and the constitutional political parties in Northern Ireland was established as a means of exploring the extent of the common ground which existed between them at that time. A formula, known as the three stranded approach, for political talks about the future of Northern Ireland and its relationship with the United Kingdom and the Republic of Ireland was agreed in 1991. Strand 1 of the talks between the Government and the four main local constitutional political parties began in April 1992. Strand 2, involving the government of the Republic of Ireland, began in June 1992. The Government remains committed to the objective of finding a means of transferring substantial power and responsibility to local elected representatives on a widely acceptable basis within a framework of stable relationships among the people of Ireland and between the two Governments. (*See also* Events of the Year.)

FLAG

The white star in the centre of the flag of Northern Ireland (cross gules in a field argent) has six points representing the counties of Northern Ireland. It encloses a red hand and stands below a crown.

FINANCE

Taxation in Northern Ireland is largely imposed and collected by the United Kingdom government. After deducting the cost of collection and of Northern Ireland's contributions to the European Community the balance, known as the Attributed Share of Taxation, is paid over to the Northern Ireland Consolidated Fund. Northern Ireland's revenue is insufficient to meet its expenditure and is supplemented by a grant in aid.

	1991–2*	1992–3**
Public income	£5,011,203,933	£5,375,800,000
Public expenditure	5,023,338,825	5,375,700,000

* Outturn
** Estimate

PRODUCTION

INDUSTRIES

The products of the engineering, shipbuilding and aircraft industries, which employed 28,600 persons in 1985, were valued at £856 million. The textile industries, employing about 10,500 persons, produced products valued at approximately £273 million. The food and drink industry, employing about 20,000 persons, produced goods valued at £2,575 million.

MINERALS

In 1990 1,299 persons were employed in mining and quarrying operations in Northern Ireland and the minerals raised (18,543,043 tonnes) were valued at £34,394,432.

COMMUNICATIONS

SEAPORTS

The total tonnage handled by Northern Ireland ports in 1991 was 16.5m. Regular ferry, freight and container services operate to ports in Great Britain and Europe from 18 ports including Belfast, Coleraine, Larne, Londonderry and Warrenpoint.

ROAD AND RAIL

The Northern Ireland Transport Holding Company is largely responsible for the supervision of the subsidiary companies, Ulsterbus and Citybus (which operate the public road passenger services) and Northern Ireland Railways. Road freight services are also provided by a large number of hauliers operating competitively under licence.

AIR

Belfast International Airport is run by Northern Ireland Airports Ltd, a subsidiary of the Northern Ireland Transport Holding Company and provides scheduled and chartered services on domestic and international routes.

Scheduled services also operate from Belfast Harbour Airport to 13 British destinations and from Eglinton, Co. Londonderry, to Manchester, Glasgow and Dublin.

Northern Ireland Counties

‡ denotes County Borough

Counties	*Area* (sq. miles)*	*Lord Lieutenant*	*High Sheriff, 1992*
Antrim	1,093	Sir Richard Dobbs, KCVO	R. G. Reade
‡Belfast City	25	Col. J. E. Wilson, OBE	T. W. S. Patton, OBE
Armagh	484	The Earl of Caledon	J. R. Nelson, FRCGP
Down	945	Col. W. S. Brownlow	M. W. S. Maclaran
Fermanagh	647	The Earl of Erne	E. A. Aiken
†Londonderry	798	Col. M. W. McCorkell, OBE, TD	W. R. L. Moore
‡Londonderry City	3.4	J. T. Eaton, CBE, TD	Dr A. J. Keegan, FRCPEd., FRCPI
Tyrone	1,211	The Duke of Abercorn	R. W. L. Scott

* Excluding inland waters and tideways
† Excluding the City of Londonderry

District and Borough Councils

§ denotes Borough Council

District and Borough Councils	*Population (30 June 1990)*	*Net Annual Value*	*Council Clerk*	*Chairman †Mayor 1992*
§Antrim, Co. Antrim	47,600	£6,476,824	S. J. Magee	†J. Graham
§Ards, Co. Down	65,400	7,574,057	D. J. Fallows	†D. F. Smyth
Armagh, Co. Armagh	49,100	5,050,395	D. R. D. Mitchall	W. G. McCartney
§Ballymena, Co. Antrim	57,300	8,124,254	M. G. Rankin	†S. Spence, MBE
§Ballymoney, Co. Antrim	24,100	2,545,226	W. J. Williamson, MBE	†J. A. Gaston
Banbridge, Co. Down	32,100	3,565,897	R. Gilmore	A. Nelson
Belfast, Co. Antrim and Co. Down	295,100	54,319,405	S. McDowell	H. Ditty (*Lord Mayor*)
§Carrickfergus, Co. Antrim	31,000	4,354,685	R. Boyd	†S. C. Dicksen
§Castlereagh, Co. Down	58,100	7,932,124	J. White	†Mrs I. Robinson
§Coleraine, Co. Londonderry	48,600	7,478,368	W. E. Andrews	†W. H. King
Cookstown, Co. Tyrone	27,700	3,049,678	M. McGuckin	S. A. Glasgow
§Craigavon, Co. Armagh	78,200	10,387,559	E. A. McKinley	†F. E. Crowe
Derry, Co. Londonderry	100,500	11,645,072	J. Keanie	†W. Hay
Down, Co. Down	57,700	5,948,731	O. O'Connor	S. Osborne
Dungannon, Co. Tyrone	43,800	4,410,024	W. J. Beattie	V. Currie
Fermanagh, Co. Fermanagh	50,600	5,275,496	G. Burns, MBE	C. McClaughry
§Larne, Co. Antrim	29,000	3,945,642	G. McKinley	Mrs R. G. Armstrong
§Limavady, Co. Londonderry	29,900	2,779,643	J. K. Stevenson	†N. W. Reynolds

§Lisburn, Co. Antrim and Co. Down	98,700	12,901,509	M. S. Fielding	†I. Davis
Magherafelt, Co. Londonderry	33,200	3,501,565	W. R. S. McMaster, MBE	Mrs M. K. McSorley
Moyle, Co. Antrim	15,000	1,454,276	R. G. Lewis	A. McPherson
Newry and Mourne, Co. Down and Co. Armagh	89,700	8,076,820	K. O'Neill	P. J. Bradley
§Newtownabbey, Co. Antrim	72,900	11,056,714	J. Campbell	†A. M. Templeton
§North Down, Co. Down	72,600	9,225,903	J. McKimm	†Mrs E. McKay
Omagh, Co. Tyrone	45,800	4,375,765	J. P. McKinney	B. P. J. McGowlan, MBE
Strabane, Co. Tyrone	35,700	3,041,430	Dr R. Eakin	E. Turner
Northern Ireland	1,589,400	208,497,782		

Since the reorganization of local government, rates in Northern Ireland are collected by the Department of the Environment and consist of two rates, a regional rate made by the Department of Finance and a district rate made by individual District Councils.

Patron Saints

ST GEORGE
Patron Saint of England

St George is believed to have been born in Cappadocia, of Christian parents, in the latter part of the third century and to have served with distinction as a soldier under the Emperor Diocletian, including a visit to England on a military mission. When the persecution of Christians was ordered, St George sought a personal interview to remonstrate with the Emperor and after a profession of faith resigned his military commission. Arrest and torture followed and he was martyred at Nicomedia on 23 April 303, a day ordered to be kept in remembrance as a national festival by the Council of Oxford in 1222, although it was not until the reign of Edward III that he was made patron saint of England.

St George's connection with a dragon seems to date from the close of the sixth century and to be due to the transfer of his remains from Nicomedia to Lydda, close to the scene of the legendary exploit of Perseus in rescuing Andromeda and slaying the sea monster, credit for which became attached to the Christian martyr.

ST DAVID
Patron Saint of Wales

St David is believed to have been born near the beginning and to have died towards the end of the sixth century. St David was an eloquent preacher, who founded the monastery at Menevia, now St David's. He became the patron of Wales, but there is no record of any papal canonization before 1181. His annual festival is observed on 1 March.

ST ANDREW
Patron Saint of Scotland

St Andrew, one of the Christian Apostles and brother of Simon Peter, was born at Bethsaida on the Sea of Galilee and lived at Capernaum. He preached the Gospel in Asia Minor and in Scythia along the shores of the Black Sea and became the patron saint of Russia. It is believed that he suffered crucifixion at Patras in Achaea, on a *crux decussata* (now known as St Andrew's Cross) and that his relics were removed from Patras to Constantinople and thence to St Andrews, probably in the eighth century, since which time he has been the patron saint of Scotland. The festival of St Andrew is held on 30 November.

ST PATRICK
Patron Saint of Ireland

St Patrick was born, probably in England, about 389 and was carried off to Ireland as a slave about sixteen years later, escaping to Gaul at the age of 22. He was ordained deacon at Auxerre and having been consecrated Bishop in 432 was despatched to Wicklow to reorganize the Christian communities in Ireland. He founded the see of Armagh and introduced Latin into Ireland as the language of the Church. He died *c.* 461 and his festival is celebrated on 17 March.

The Isle of Man

(ELLAN VANNIN)

The Isle of Man is an island situated in the Irish Sea, in lat. 54° 3′–54° 25′ N. and long. 4° 18′–4° 47′ W., nearly equidistant from England, Scotland and Ireland. Although the early inhabitants were of Celtic origin, the Isle of Man was part of the Norwegian Kingdom of the Hebrides until 1266, when this was ceded to Scotland. Subsequently granted to the Stanleys (Earls of Derby) in the 15th century and later to the Dukes of Atholl, it was brought under the direct administration of the Crown in 1765. The island forms the bishopric of Sodor and Man.

The total land area is 221 sq. miles (354.1 sq. km). The report on the 1991 Census showed a resident population of 69,788 (males, 33,693; females, 36,095). In 1991 births numbered 892 and deaths 982. The main language in use is English. There are no remaining native speakers of Manx Gaelic but 643 people are able to speak the language.

CAPITAL – ΨDouglas; population (1991), 22,214. ΨCastletown (3,152) is the ancient capital; the other towns are ΨPeel (3,829) and ΨRamsey (6,496).

FLAG – Three legs in white and gold armed conjoined on a red ground.

TYNWALD DAY – 5 July.

GOVERNMENT

The Isle of Man is a self-governing Crown dependency, having its own parliamentary, legal and administrative system; the Crown is responsible for international relations and defence. The Lieutenant-Governor is The Queen's personal representative in the island.

The legislature, Tynwald, is the oldest parliament in the world in continuous existence. It has two branches: the Legislative Council and the House of Keys. The Council consists of the President of Tynwald, the Bishop of Sodor and Man, the Attorney-General (who does not have a vote) and eight members chosen by the House of Keys. The House of Keys consists of 24 members, elected by universal adult suffrage. The branches sit separately to consider legislation and sit together, as Tynwald Court, for other parliamentary purposes.

The presiding officer in Tynwald Court is the President of Tynwald, elected by the members, who also presides over sittings of the Legislative Council. The presiding officer of the House of Keys is Mr Speaker, who is elected by members of the House.

The principal members of the Manx Government are the Chief Minister and nine departmental ministers, who comprise the Council of Ministers.

Lieutenant-Governor, His Excellency Air Marshal Sir Laurence Jones, KCB, AFC.
ADC to the Lieutenant-Governor, Capt. C. P. Dawson.
President of Tynwald, The Hon. Sir Charles Kerruish, OBE.
Speaker, House of Keys, The Hon. J. C. Kain.
The First Deemster and Clerk of the Rolls, His Honour J. W. Corrin.
Clerk of Tynwald, Secretary to the House of Keys and Clerk of Legislative Council, T. A. Bawden
Counsel to the Speaker, Prof. T. St J. N. Bates.
Attorney-General, T. W. Cain, QC.
Chief Minister, The Hon. M. R. Walker.
Chief Secretary, J. F. Kissack.
Chief Financial Officer, J. A. Cashen.

ECONOMY

Most of the income generated in the island is earned in the services sector with financial and business services being considerably larger than the traditional industry of tourism. Manufacturing industry is also a major generator of income whilst the island's other traditional industries of agriculture and fishing now play a smaller role in the economy.

Under the terms of the island's special relationship with the European Community, the Island has free access to EC markets.

A twenty-acre freeport has been developed adjacent to the main airport at Ronaldsway.

The island's unemployment rate is approximately 1 per cent and price inflation is around 7 per cent per annum.

FINANCE

The island's Budget for 1992–3 provided for gross expenditure of £194,468,030. The principal sources of government revenue are taxes on income and expenditure. Income tax is payable at a rate of 15 per cent on the first £26,000 of taxable income of resident individuals and 20 per cent on the balance. The rate of income tax is 20 per cent on the whole taxable income of non-residents and companies. By agreement with the United Kingdom Government, the island keeps most of its rates of indirect taxation (Value Added Tax and duties) the same as those in the United Kingdom, but this agreement may be terminated by either party. A reciprocal agreement on national insurance benefits and pensions exists between the Governments of the Isle of Man and the United Kingdom. Taxes are also charged on property (rates), but these are comparatively low.

The major government expenditure items are health, social security and education, which account for 57 per cent of the Government budget. The island makes a voluntary annual contribution to the United Kingdom for defence and other external services.

Although the island has a special relationship with the European Community, it neither contributes money to nor receives funds from the EC Budget.

The Channel Islands

The Channel Islands, situated off the north-west coast of France (at distances of from ten to thirty miles), are the only portions of the Dukedom of Normandy now belonging to the Crown, to which they have been attached ever since the Conquest. The islands consist of Jersey (28,717 acres/11,630 ha), Guernsey (15,654 acres/6,340 ha), and the dependencies of Guernsey: Alderney (1,962 acres/795 ha), Brechou (74/30), Great Sark (1,035/419), Little Sark (239/97), Herm (320/130), Jethou (44/18) and Lihou (38/15) – a total of 48,083 acres/19,474 ha, or 75 square miles/121 square km. In 1991 the population of Jersey was 84,082; and of Guernsey, 58,867; Alderney, 2,297 and Sark, 575.

GOVERNMENT

The islands are Crown dependencies with their own legislative assemblies (the States in Jersey, Guernsey and Alderney, and the Court of Chief Pleas in Sark), and systems of local administration and of law, and their own courts. Acts passed by the States require the sanction of The Queen-in-Council. The British Government is responsible for defence and international relations.

In both Bailiwicks the Lieutenant-Governor and Commander-in-Chief, who is appointed by the Crown, is the personal representative of The Queen and the channel of communication between the Crown (via the Privy Council) and the island's government.

The Bailiffs of Jersey and Guernsey, also appointed by the Crown, are President of the States and of the Royal Courts of their respective islands.

The government of each Bailiwick is conducted by committees appointed by the States. Justice is administered by the Royal Courts of Jersey and Guernsey, each consisting of the Bailiff and 12 elected Jurats.

Each Bailiwick constitutes a deanery under the jurisdiction of the Bishop of Winchester (*see* INDEX).

ECONOMY

A mild climate and good soil have led to the development of intensive systems of agriculture and horticulture, which form a significant part of the economy of the Channel Islands. Equally important are invisible earnings, principally from the tourist trade and from banking and finance, the low rate of income tax (20p in the £ in Jersey and Guernsey; no tax of any kind in Sark) and the absence of super-tax and death duties making the Channel Islands a popular tax-haven.

Principal exports are agricultural produce and flowers; imports are chiefly machinery, manufactured goods, food, fuel and chemicals. Trade with the UK is regarded as internal trade.

British currency is legal tender in the Channel Islands but each Bailiwick issues its own coins, and some notes, of the same values as those of the UK. They also issue their own postage stamps; UK stamps are not valid.

LANGUAGE

The official languages are English and French, but French is gradually being supplanted by English, which is the language in daily use. In country districts of Jersey and Guernsey and throughout Sark a Norman-French *patois* is also in use, though to a declining extent.

JERSEY

Lieutenant-Governor and Commander-in-Chief of Jersey, His Excellency Air Marshal Sir John Sutton, KCB, apptd 1990.
Secretary and ADC, Cdr. D. M. L. Braybrooke, LVO.
Bailiff of Jersey, Sir Peter Crill, CBE.
Deputy Bailiff, vacant.
Attorney-General and Receiver-General, P. M. Bailhache, QC.
Solicitor-General, T. C. Sowden, QC.
Greffier of the States, G. H. C. Coppock.
States Treasurer, G. M. Baird.

FINANCE

Year to 31 Dec.	1990	1991
Revenue	£327,059,999	£354,010,485
Revenue expenditure	258,931,630	297,812,924
Capital expenditure	60,673,000	62,701,000
Public debt	174,640	0

CHIEF TOWN – ΨSt Helier, on the south coast of Jersey.
FLAG – A white field charged with a red saltire, and coat of arms.

GUERNSEY AND DEPENDENCIES

Lieutenant-Governor and Commander-in-Chief of the Bailiwick of Guernsey and its Dependencies, His Excellency Lt.-Gen. Sir Michael Wilkins, KCB, OBE, apptd 1990.
Secretary and ADC, Capt. D. P. L. Hodgetts.
Bailiff of Guernsey, G. M. Dorey.
Deputy Bailiff, de V. G. Carey.
HM Procureur and Receiver-General, A. C. K. Day, QC.
HM Comptroller, G. R. Rowland.
States Supervisor, F. N. Le Cheminant, ISO.

FINANCE

Year to 31 Dec.	1990	1991
Revenue	£138,532,424	£149,453,687
Expenditure	126,047,752	132,621,840

CHIEF TOWNS – ΨSt Peter Port, on the east coast of Guernsey; St Anne on Alderney.

FLAG – White, bearing a red cross of St George, with an argent a cross gules superimposed on the cross.

ALDERNEY

President of the States, J. Kay-Mouat.
Clerk of the States, D. V. Jenkins.
Clerk of the Court, A. Johnson.

SARK

Seigneur of Sark, J. M. Beaumont.
The Seneschal, L. P. de Carteret.
The Greffier, J. P. Hamon.

OTHER DEPENDENCIES

Brechou, Lihou and Jethou are leased by the Crown. Herm is leased by the States of Guernsey.

Government Finance

GENERAL GOVERNMENT RECEIPTS

£ billion

	Outturn 1990–1	Budget forecast 1991–2	Latest forecast
Tax, community charge and royalty receipts	167.1	175.2	174.4
Social security receipts	34.9	36.7	36.6
Interest and dividends	6.4	6.1	5.7
Other receipts	8.3	8.4	8.7
Total general government receipts	216.7	226.5	225.4
of which:			
North Sea revenues	2.5	1.4	1.2

Source: HM Treasury - Autumn Statement 1991

GENERAL GOVERNMENT EXPENDITURE AND PLANNING TOTAL

£ million

	Estimated outturn 1991–2	Plans 1992–3*
Central government expenditure	156,700	168,600
Central government support for local authorities	53,200	58,600
Financing requirements of nationalized industries	2,680	3,450
Reserve	—	4,000
Privatization proceeds	−8,000	−8,000
Adjustment	300	
Planning total	204,900	226,600
Local authority self-financed expenditure	10,200	8,500
Central government debt interest	16,700	16,500
Accounting adjustments	4,300	4,500
General government expenditure	236,100	256,300
†GGE excluding privatization proceeds as a percentage of GDP	41½%	42%

*Rounded to the nearest £10 million
†Adjusted to remove the distortion caused by the abolition of domestic rates
Source: HM Treasury - Autumn Statement 1991

CENTRAL GOVERNMENT EXPENDITURE BY DEPARTMENT

£ million

	Estimated outturn 1991–2	Plans 1992–3*
Defence	22,850	24,180
Foreign Office	1,050	1,120
Overseas Development	2,010	2,150
Agriculture, Fisheries and Food	2,380	2,310
Trade and Industry	1,030	1,000
ECGD	250	120
Energy	490	490
Employment	3,210	3,460
Transport	2,450	2,620
DOE – Housing	3,070	2,840
DOE – Environment	750	610
DOE – PSA	90	70
DOE – Local government	250	270
Home Office	2,210	2,260
Legal departments	1,660	1,760
Education and Science	4,570	4,860
Arts and Libraries	560	610
Health	25,540	27,940
Social Security	61,200	66,000
Scotland	5,960	6,340
Wales	2,530	2,720
Northern Ireland	6,420	6,970
Chancellor of the Exchequer's departments	4,800	5,030
Cabinet Office, etc.	400	450
European Communities	910	2,460
Total	156,700	168,600
of which		
Financing requirements of trading funds and public corporations	1,200	1,070

*Rounded to the nearest £10 million
Source: HM Treasury - Autumn Statement 1991

FINANCING REQUIREMENTS OF NATIONALIZED INDUSTRIES

BY DEPARTMENT AND INDUSTRY

£ million

	Estimated outturn 1991–2	Plans 1992–3*
Trade and Industry	−70	−70
Post Office	−70	−70
Energy	460	120
British Coal	540	400
Nuclear Electric	−80	−280
Transport	2,270	3,320
British Rail	1,520	2,040
Civil Aviation Authority	40	70
London Transport	710	1,210
DOE – Environment	50	50
British Waterways Board	50	50
Scotland	−20	30
Electricity (Scotland)	−30	10†
Caledonian MacBrayne Ltd	10	10
Total	2,680	3,450

*Rounded to the nearest £10 million
†Scottish Nuclear
Source: HM Treasury – Autumn Statement 1991

PUBLIC SECTOR BORROWING REQUIREMENT

£ billion

	Outturn 1990–1	Budget forecast 1991–2	Latest forecast
PSBR	−0.5	7.9	10.5
Percentage of GDP	−¼	1¼	1¾
PSBR excluding privatization proceeds	4.8	13.4	18.5
Percentage of GDP	¾	2¼	3¼

Source: HM Treasury – Autumn Statement 1991

CENTRAL GOVERNMENT SUPPORT FOR LOCAL AUTHORITIES

£ million

	Estimated outturn 1991–2	Plans 1992–3*
CURRENT		
Aggregate External Finance and community charge grant		
England		
National non-domestic rate payments	12,410	12,310
Revenue support grant	9,670	16,540
Community charge grant	4,350	300
Specific grants	4,130	4,250
Total	30,560	33,400
Scotland		
Non-domestic rate payments	1,350	
Revenue support grant	2,690	
Community charge grant	440	
Specific grants	310	
Total	4,790	5,070†
Wales		
National non-domestic rate payments	520	540
Revenue support grant	1,240	1,610
Community charge grant	270	30
Specific grants	180	200
Total	2,210	2,380
TOTAL	37,600	40,800
Current grants outside AEF		
Transitional relief	1,140	1,300
Other current grants	8,800	10,200
TOTAL CURRENT	47,500	52,300
CAPITAL		
Capital grants	1,370	1,650
Credit approvals	4,320	4,600
Total capital	5,680	6,250
TOTAL	53,200	58,600

*Rounded to the nearest £10 million
†Breakdown of total not available
Source: HM Treasury – Autumn Statement 1991

HOUSEHOLDS AND THEIR EXPENDITURE[1] UNITED KINGDOM

	1986	1987	1988	1989
NUMBER OF HOUSEHOLDS SUPPLYING DATA	7,178	7,396	7,265	7,410
Total number of persons	18,330	18,735	18,280	18,590
Total number of adults[2]	13,554	13,902	13,640	13,850
HOUSEHOLD PERCENTAGE DISTRIBUTION BY TENURE				
Rented unfurnished	*33.9*	*32.5*	*30.3*	*30.3*
Rented furnished	*3.0*	*3.3*	*2.8*	*3.0*
Rent-free	*2.0*	*2.1*	*1.7*	*1.4*
Owner-occupied	*61.1*	*62.2*	*65.1*	*65.3*
AVERAGE NUMBER OF PERSONS PER HOUSEHOLD				
All persons	2.554	2.533	2.516	2.509
Males	1.236	1.223	1.229	1.217
Females	1.317	1.310	1.288	1.292
Adults[2]	1.888	1.880	1.877	1.869
Persons under 65	1.526	1.512	1.504	1.500
Persons 65 and over	0.362	0.368	0.374	0.369
Children[2]	0.665	0.653	0.639	0.640
Children under 2	0.073	0.078	0.073	0.085
Children 2 and under 5	0.118	0.118	0.111	0.117
Children 5 and under 18	0.474	0.457	0.455	0.439
Persons working	1.160	1.161	1.168	1.167
Persons not working	1.394	1.372	1.348	1.342
Men 65 and over, women 60 and over	0.403	0.408	0.406	0.401
Others	0.991	0.965	0.942	0.940
AVERAGE WEEKLY HOUSEHOLD EXPENDITURE ON COMMODITIES AND SERVICES (£)				
Housing[3]	29.92	30.42	35.81	38.44
Fuel, light and power	10.43	10.55	10.48	10.58
Food	34.97	35.79	38.28	41.67
Alcoholic drink	8.21	8.70	9.19	9.53
Tobacco	4.55	4.67	4.45	4.77
Clothing and footwear	13.46	13.32	14.52	15.25
Household goods	13.67	13.48	15.01	19.17
Household services	8.50	8.23	9.80	9.73
Personal goods and services	6.40	7.02	8.13	8.48
Motoring expenditure	21.22	23.80	25.31	30.42
Fares and other travel costs	4.21	4.60	4.88	5.35
Leisure goods	8.54	9.03	9.65	10.97
Leisure services	13.18	18.11	18.13	19.02
Miscellaneous	0.74	0.88	0.78	0.93
Total	178.10	188.62	204.41	224.32
EXPENDITURE ON COMMODITY OR SERVICE AS A PERCENTAGE OF TOTAL EXPENDITURE (PER CENT)				
Housing[3]	*16.8*	*16.1*	*17.5*	*17.1*
Fuel, light and power	*5.9*	*5.6*	*5.1*	*4.7*
Food	*19.6*	*19.0*	*18.7*	*18.6*
Alcoholic drink	*4.6*	*4.6*	*4.5*	*4.2*
Tobacco	*2.6*	*2.5*	*2.2*	*2.1*
Clothing and footwear	*7.5*	*7.1*	*7.1*	*6.8*
Household goods	*7.7*	*7.1*	*7.3*	*8.5*
Household services	*4.8*	*4.4*	*4.8*	*4.3*
Personal goods and services	*3.6*	*3.7*	*4.0*	*3.8*
Motoring expenditure	*11.9*	*12.6*	*12.4*	*13.6*
Fares and other travel costs	*2.4*	*2.4*	*2.4*	*2.4*
Leisure goods	*4.8*	*4.8*	*4.7*	*4.9*
Leisure services	*7.4*	*9.6*	*8.9*	*8.5*
Miscellaneous	*0.4*	*0.5*	*0.4*	*0.4*
Total	*100.0*	*100.0*	*100.0*	*100.0*

[1] Information derived from the Family Expenditure Survey
[2] Adults = all persons 18 and over and married persons under 18
Children = all unmarried persons under 18
[3] Excludes mortgage payments but includes imputed expenditure (i.e. the weekly equivalent of rateable value)

Source: HMSO - Annual Abstract of Statistics 1992

GROSS DOMESTIC PRODUCT BY INDUSTRY BEFORE DEPRECIATION BUT AFTER STOCK APPRECIATION

	1985	1986	1987	1988	1989	£ million 1990
Agriculture, forestry and fishing	5,725	6,193	6,299	6,149	6,965	7,102
Energy and water supply	32,696	24,098	24,901	22,542	22,474	24,334
Manufacturing	73,432	79,010	84,589	93,504	101,015	106,995
Construction	17,904	20,277	23,760	28,512	32,365	36,085
Distribution; hotels and catering; repairs	40,839	45,492	49,618	57,378	63,429	70,151
Transport and communication	21,725	23,511	25,792	28,684	31,262	34,031
Banking, finance, insurance, business services and leasing	44,758	52,058	59,386	67,021	80,561	87,260
Ownership of dwellings	18,175	19,501	21,013	23,255	25,154	30,719
Public administration, national defence and compulsory social security	21,466	23,069	24,984	27,058	28,622	31,524
Education and health services	26,567	30,035	33,136	37,170	41,094	45,143
Other services	18,602	20,774	23,379	26,573	29,274	30,983
Total	321,889	344,018	376,866	417,846	462,215	504,327
Adjustment for financial services	15,029	17,153	17,555	19,668	25,401	26,740
Statistical discrepancy (income adjustment)	−144	−683	−1,014	−886	−634	160
Gross domestic product (average estimate)	306,716	326,182	358,297	397,292	436,180	477,747

Source: HMSO – Annual Abstract of Statistics 1992

Labour

UNEMPLOYMENT IN THE UNITED KINGDOM
at mid-June each year

	1988	1989	*Thousands* 1990
Total	2,299	1,791	1,618
Males	1,603	1,280	1,194
Females	696	512	425

Source: HMSO – Annual Abstract of Statistics 1992

RATES OF UNEMPLOYMENT BY STANDARD REGIONS Seasonally adjusted

Annual averages	1988	1989	*Percentages* 1990
United Kingdom	8.1	6.3	5.8
North	11.9	9.9	8.7
Yorkshire and Humberside	9.3	7.4	6.7
East Midlands	7.1	5.4	5.1
East Anglia	5.2	3.6	3.7
South East	5.4	3.9	4.0
South West	6.2	4.5	4.4
West Midlands	8.9	6.6	6.0
North West	10.4	8.5	7.7
England	8.0	6.2	5.8
Wales	9.8	7.3	6.6
Scotland	11.3	9.3	8.1
Northern Ireland	15.6	14.6	13.4

NOTE: Percentages calculated using mid-year estimates of total employees in employment, unemployed, self-employed and HM Forces, and participants in work-related government training schemes
Source: HMSO – Annual Abstract of Statistics 1992

Trade

BALANCE OF PAYMENTS £ MILLION

	1986	1987	1988	1989	1990
CURRENT ACCOUNT					
Visible trade					
Exports (fob)	72,627	79,153	80,346	92,389	102,038
Imports (fob)	82,186	90,735	101,970	116,987	120,713
Visible balance	−9,559	−11,582	−21,624	−24,598	−18,675
Invisibles					
Credits	77,253	79,896	88,041	108,465	117,350
Debits	67,507	72,473	81,937	104,271	113,055
Invisibles balance	9,747	7,423	6,103	4,195	4,295
of which:					
Services balance	6,808	6,745	4,574	4,685	5,201
Interest, profits and dividends balance	5,096	4,078	5,047	4,088	4,029
Transfers balance	−2,157	−3,400	−3,518	−4,578	−4,935
CURRENT BALANCE	−187	−4,159	−15,520	−20,404	−14,380
*TRANSACTIONS IN EXTERNAL ASSETS AND LIABILITIES					
Investment overseas by UK residents					
Direct	−12,038	−19,215	−20,880	−21,521	−11,702
Portfolio	−22,095	7,201	−8,600	−31,283	−12,587
Total UK investment overseas	−34,133	−12,014	−29,480	−52,804	−24,289
Investment in the UK by overseas residents					
Direct	4,987	8,478	10,236	17,145	18,997
Portfolio	11,785	19,210	14,387	13,239	5,070
Total overseas investment in UK	16,772	27,688	24,623	30,384	24,067
Foreign currency lending abroad by UK banks	−47,861	−45,787	−14,890	−24,113	−33,327
Foreign currency borrowing abroad by UK banks	58,568	43,143	20,403	33,012	34,000
Net foreign currency transactions of UK banks	10,707	−2,644	5,513	8,899	673
Sterling lending abroad by UK banks	−5,817	−4,640	−4,625	−2,919	−3,919
Sterling borrowing and deposit liabilities abroad of UK banks	5,559	9,457	13,815	10,875	12,179
Net sterling transactions of UK banks	−258	4,817	9,190	7,956	8,260
Deposits with and lending to banks abroad by UK non-bank private sector	−3,109	−4,632	−3,980	−9,473	−5,722
Borrowing from banks abroad by:					
UK non-bank private sector	3,817	2,035	3,971	7,081	7,916
Public corporations	−31	−166	−253	−1,132	−127
General government	100	104	−10	−65	−461
Official reserves (additions to − drawings on +)	−2,891	−12,012	−2,761	5,440	−77
Other external assets of:					
UK non-bank private sector and public corporations	1,656	254	1,201	1,611	−3,740
General government	−509	−796	−891	−942	−1,227
Other external liabilities of:					
UK non-bank private sector and public corporations	567	1,448	1,682	13,710	5,649
General government	78	1,725	841	2,251	1,158
NET TRANSACTIONS IN ASSETS AND LIABILITIES	−7,234	5,810	9,645	12,916	12,081
BALANCING ITEM	7,047	−1,651	5,875	7,488	2,299

* Assets: increase −/decrease +
Liabilities: increase +/decrease −

Source: HMSO - Annual Abstract of Statistics 1992

VALUE OF UNITED KINGDOM IMPORTS (cif) 1990* BY SECTIONS AND DIVISIONS

	£ million 1990*
TOTAL UK IMPORTS	126,165.8
Food and live animals chiefly for food	10,409.2
Live animals chiefly for food	290.7
Meat and meat preparations	1,887.8
Dairy products and birds' eggs	913.7
Fish, crustaceans and molluscs, and preparations thereof	969.0
Cereals and cereal preparations	785.1
Vegetables and fruit	2,964.9
Sugar, sugar preparations and honey	639.2
Coffee, tea, cocoa, spices, and manufactures thereof	904.4
Feeding-stuff for animals (not including unmilled cereals)	624.6
Miscellaneous edible products and preparations	429.9
Beverages and tobacco	1,907.0
Beverages	1,529.8
Tobacco and tobacco manufactures	377.2
Crude materials, inedible, except fuels	5,721.2
Hides, skins and furskins, raw	100.5
Oil seeds and oleaginous fruit	273.0
Crude rubber (including synthetic and reclaimed)	244.9
Cork and wood	1,410.0
Pulp and waste paper	777.3
Textile fibres (other than wool tops) and their wastes (not manufactured into yarn or fabric)	548.9
Crude fertilizers and crude minerals (excluding coal, petroleum and precious stones)	344.7
Metalliferous ores and metal scrap	1,479.2
Crude animal and vegetable materials	542.7
Mineral fuels, lubricants and related materials	7,840.0
Petroleum, petroleum products and related materials	6,254.9
Coal, coke, gas and electric current	1,585.0
Animal and vegetable oils, fats and waxes	377.4
Total manufactured goods	98,275.3
Chemicals and related products	10,834.6
Organic chemicals	2,593.1
Inorganic chemicals	1,000.2
Dyeing, tanning and colouring materials	651.3
Medicinal and pharmaceutical products	1,157.8
Essential oils and perfume materials; toilet, polishing and cleansing materials	756.1
Fertilizers, manufactured	286.2
Plastics in primary forms	2,215.5
Plastics in non-primary forms	1,014.9
Chemical materials	1,162.5

*provisional
nes not elsewhere specified

	£ million 1990*
Manufactured goods classified chiefly by material	21,899.0
Leather, leather manufactures, nes, and dressed furskins	240.7
Rubber manufactures, nes	880.4
Cork and wood manufactures (excluding furniture)	949.1
Paper, paperboard, and articles of paper pulp, of paper or of paperboard	4,016.6
Textile yarn, fabrics, made-up articles, nes, and related products	3,936.2
Non-metallic mineral manufactures, nes	3,602.1
Iron and steel	2,676.7
Non-ferrous metals	3,003.6
Manufactures of metal, nes	2,593.5
Machinery and transport equipment	47,289.6
Power generating machinery and equipment	3,518.4
Machinery specialized for particular industries	3,522.1
Metalworking machinery	993.4
General industrial machinery and equipment, nes, and machine parts, nes	4,359.2
Office machines and automatic data processing equipment	7,714.6
Telecommunications, sound recording and reproducing apparatus and equipment	3,486.4
Electrical machinery, apparatus and appliances, nes, and electrical parts thereof (including non-electrical counterparts, nes, of electrical household type equipment)	6,924.2
Road vehicles (including air cushion vehicles)	12,586.8
Other transport equipment	4,184.5
Miscellaneous manufactured articles	18,252.1
Sanitary, plumbing, heating and lighting fixtures and fittings, nes	394.5
Furniture and parts thereof	1,112.0
Travel goods, handbags and similar containers	309.1
Articles of apparel and clothing accessories	3,905.9
Footwear	1,169.1
Professional, scientific and controlling instruments and apparatus, nes	2,482.1
Photographic apparatus, equipment and supplies and optical goods, nes, watches and clocks	1,589.3
Miscellaneous manufactured articles, nes	7,290.1
Commodities and transactions not classified elsewhere	1,635.6

Source: HMSO – Annual Abstract of Statistics 1992

VALUE OF UNITED KINGDOM EXPORTS (fob) 1990* BY SECTIONS AND DIVISIONS

	(£ million) 1990*
TOTAL UK EXPORTS	103,911.0
Food and live animals chiefly for food	4,324.6
Live animals chiefly for food	258.0
Meat and meat preparations	609.2
Dairy products and birds' eggs	458.1
Fish, crustaceans and molluscs, and preparations thereof	505.3
Cereals and cereal preparations	1,045.5
Vegetables and fruit	263.7
Sugar, sugar preparations and honey	240.3
Coffee, tea, cocoa, spices and manufactures thereof	438.7
Feeding-stuff for animals (not including unmilled cereals)	238.9
Miscellaneous edible products and preparations	266.9
Beverages and tobacco	2,770.2
Beverages	2,112.8
Tobacco and tobacco manufactures	657.5
Crude materials, inedible, except fuels	2,162.6
Hides, skins and furskins, raw	188.8
Oil seeds and oleaginous fruit	67.3
Crude rubber (including synthetic and reclaimed)	221.9
Cork and wood	27.7
Pulp and waste paper	53.1
Textile fibres (other than wool tops) and their wastes (not manufactured into yarn or fabric)	494.5
Crude fertilizers and crude minerals (excluding coal, petroleum and precious stones)	369.9
Metalliferous ores and metal scrap	633.5
Crude animal and vegetable materials	105.9
Mineral fuels, lubricants and related materials	7,801.4
Petroleum, petroleum products and related materials	7,477.6
Coal, coke, gas and electric current	323.7
Animal and vegetable oils, fats and waxes	87.7
Total manufactured goods	84,505.9
Chemicals and related products	13,182.5
Organic chemicals	3,351.1
Inorganic chemicals	952.2
Dyeing, tanning and colouring materials	1,193.5
Medicinal and pharmaceutical products	2,258.1
Essential oils and perfume materials; toilet, polishing and cleansing materials	1,161.8
Fertilizers, manufactured	110.2
Plastics in primary forms	1,342.4
Plastics in non primary forms	781.7
Chemical materials	2,031.4

	£ million 1990*
Manufactured goods classified chiefly by material	15,821.0
Leather, leather manufactures, nes, and dressed furskins	311.8
Rubber manufactures, nes	872.8
Cork and wood manufactures (excluding furniture)	114.2
Paper, paperboard, and articles of paper pulp, of paper or of paperboard	1,539.4
Textile yarn, fabrics, made-up articles, nes, and related products	2,447.0
Non-metallic mineral manufactures, nes	3,191.3
Iron and steel	3,036.0
Non-ferrous metals	2,193.2
Manufactures of metal, nes	2,115.4
Machinery and transport equipment	42,155.4
Power generating machinery and equipment	5,251.4
Machinery specialized for particular industries	4,232.4
Metalworking machinery	912.5
General industrial machinery and equipment, nes, and machine parts; nes	4,545.7
Office machines and automatic data processing equipment	6,341.2
Telecommunications and sound recording and reproducing apparatus and equipment	2,687.5
Electrical machinery, apparatus and appliances, nes, and electrical parts thereof (including non-electrical counterparts, nes, of electrical household type equipment)	5,648.5
Road vehicles (including air cushion vehicles)	7,300.6
Other transport equipment	5,235.7
Miscellaneous manufactured articles	13,347.0
Sanitary, plumbing, heating and lighting fixtures and fittings, nes	260.4
Furniture and parts thereof	533.2
Travel goods, handbags and similar containers	69.9
Articles of apparel and clothing accessories	1,699.4
Footwear	274.4
Professional, scientific and controlling instruments and apparatus, nes	2,941.7
Photographic apparatus, equipment and supplies and optical goods, nes, watches and clocks	1,167.1
Miscellaneous manufactured articles, nes	6,401.0
Commodities and transactions not classified elsewhere	2,258.5

Source: HMSO - Annual Abstract of Statistics 1992

*provisional
nes not elsewhere specified

Transport

GOODS TRANSPORT IN GREAT BRITAIN

	1985	1986	1987	1988	1989	1990
TOTAL TONNE KILOMETRES (thousand millions)	187.1	187.1	195.2	218.8	222.6	215.5
Road	102.9	105.4	113.3	130.2	137.8	136.2
Rail (British Rail only)	15.4	16.5	17.3	18.2	17.3	15.8
Water: coastwise oil products*	39.4	34.4	31.6	34.3	34.3	32.3†
Water: other*	18.2	20.4	22.5	25.0	23.4	20.2†
Pipelines (except gases)	11.2	10.4	10.5	11.1	9.8	11.0
TOTAL (million tonnes)	1,797	1,835	1,909	2,163	2,206	2,160
Road	1,445	1,471	1,542	1,758	1,812	1,749
Rail (British Rail only)	122	140	141	150	146	141
Water: coastwise oil products*	50	46	43	47	46	44†
Water: other*	92	99	100	109	109	105†
Pipelines (except gases)	89	79	83	99	93	121

*'Coastwise' includes all sea traffic within the UK, Isle of Man and Channel Islands. 'Other' means other coastwise plus inland waterway traffic and one-port traffic

†provisional

Source: HMSO – Annual Abstract of Statistics 1992

SEAPORT TRAFFIC OF GREAT BRITAIN Million gross tonnes

	1985	1986	1987	1988	1989	1990
FOREIGN TRAFFIC: *Imports*						
Bulk fuel traffic	57.2	61.7	57.3	62.9	64.2	75.1
Other bulk traffic	36.7	37.3	42.0	45.0	47.0	45.1
Container and roll-on traffic	29.8	31.1	34.0	38.0	40.9	40.7
Semi-bulk traffic	14.5	15.8	16.9	18.9	18.1	18.2
Conventional traffic	1.7	1.5	1.6	1.6	1.2	2.2
All imports	139.9	147.4	151.8	166.4	171.4	181.3
FOREIGN TRAFFIC: *Exports*						
Bulk fuel traffic	103.1	101.9	100.2	91.1	72.9	80.3
Other bulk traffic	17.7	21.1	20.4	18.5	19.5	19.0
Container and roll-on traffic	21.3	22.1	23.9	26.5	29.4	30.9
Semi-bulk traffic	4.1	4.0	5.0	4.6	4.6	4.4
Conventional traffic	1.6	1.2	1.2	1.0	0.7	1.5
All exports	147.8	150.4	150.6	141.7	127.1	136.3
DOMESTIC TRAFFIC						
Bulk fuel traffic	119.9	112.2	108.1	115.3	108.3	97.9
Other bulk traffic	31.7	32.7	34.8	41.1	45.5	44.3
Container and roll-on traffic	5.9	6.2	7.3	7.6	8.1	8.0
Semi-bulk traffic	0.3	0.2	0.2	0.3	0.3	0.3
Conventional traffic	0.3	0.3	0.3	0.3	0.4	0.3
Non-oil traffic with UK offshore installations	3.6	3.3	3.5	3.9	4.2	5.5
All domestic traffic	161.6	154.8	154.2	168.6	166.8	156.3
TOTAL FOREIGN AND DOMESTIC TRAFFIC	449.3	452.6	456.7	476.7	465.2	473.8

Source: HMSO – Annual Abstract of Statistics 1992

PASSENGER TRANSPORT IN GREAT BRITAIN Thousand million passenger kilometres (estimated)

		1985	1986	1987	1988	1989	1990†
TOTAL		536	557	588	618	654	660
Air		4	4	4	5	5	5
Rail*		36	37	39	41	40	41
Road:	Public service vehicles	42	41	41	41	41	41
	Cars and taxis	440	462	490	519	556	561
	Motorcycles	8	8	7	7	7	7
	Pedal cycles	6	5	6	5	5	5

*Including London Regional Transport and Passenger Transport Executive railway systems

†provisional

Source: HMSO – Annual Abstract of Statistics 1992

AIR PASSENGERS BY TYPE OF OPERATOR, 1991

	Total terminal & transit	*Scheduled		*Charter	
		Terminal	*Transit*	*Terminal*	*Transit*
ALL UK AIRPORTS: TOTAL	97,293,213	72,193,667	1,216,163	23,574,739	308,644
LONDON AREA AIRPORTS: TOTAL	63,204,125	52,179,927	340,251	10,593,967	89,980
Battersea Heliport	3,868	—	—	3,868	—
Gatwick	18,813,993	10,341,415	78,657	8,348,916	45,005
Heathrow	40,494,457	40,130,988	248,161	113,807	1,501
London City	171,899	167,355	—	4,544	—
Luton	1,975,711	538,805	874	1,418,664	17,368
Southend	20,815	799	—	20,003	13
Stansted	1,723,382	1,000,565	12,559	684,165	26,093
OTHER UK AIRPORTS: TOTAL	34,089,088	20,013,740	875,912	12,980,772	218,664
Aberdeen	2,042,830	1,092,305	22,128	865,422	699
Barrow-in-Furness	646	84	—	562	—
Belfast	2,181,121	1,833,023	207	335,203	12,688
Belfast City	537,538	535,720	608	1,210	—
Bembridge	489	—	—	480	9
Benbecula	32,519	30,023	1,507	985	4
Birmingham	3,396,060	1,908,255	138,050	1,338,272	11,483
Blackpool	121,076	73,932	754	46,390	—
Bournemouth	130,531	60,176	1,353	64,385	4,617
Bristol	819,396	300,947	20,819	481,823	15,807
Cambridge	26,005	19,739	11	6,244	11
Cardiff	541,891	100,670	18,636	412,589	9,996
Carlisle	1,362	96	—	1,238	28
Coventry	6,480	4,095	322	2,063	—
Dundee	16,360	8,026	6,948	1,275	111
East Midlands	1,149,106	481,395	742	663,167	3,802
Edinburgh	2,431,316	2,166,571	87,392	172,967	4,386
Exeter	170,499	94,048	1,998	70,026	4,427
Glasgow	4,261,555	3,008,409	87,638	1,145,604	19,904
Gloucester/Cheltenham	4,485	760	454	3,259	12
Hawarden	669	—	—	649	20
Humberside	125,009	70,087	16,733	37,949	240
Inverness	208,643	195,739	9,399	3,454	51
Islay	20,385	19,872	247	266	—
Isle of Man	490,661	465,894	16,936	6,982	849
Isles of Scilly–St Mary's	101,673	101,401	—	272	—
–Tresco	21,098	20,517	483	78	20
Kirkwall	113,881	96,791	9,813	5,640	1,928
Leeds/Bradford	656,126	487,095	14,235	150,861	3,935
Lerwick (Tingwall)	12,420	8,133	1,688	2,554	45
Liverpool	478,829	422,311	19,915	34,535	2,068
Londonderry	37,213	35,714	—	1,499	—
Lydd	29,820	25,185	—	4,602	33
Manchester	10,463,584	4,363,440	307,839	5,737,981	54,324
Manston	4,793	424	163	3,990	216
Newcastle	1,579,883	735,977	29,590	790,565	23,751
Norwich	181,435	140,056	5,936	34,824	619
Penzance Heliport	96,846	96,773	73	—	—
Plymouth	95,821	84,094	10,560	1,167	—
Prestwick	59,616	2,166	530	32,795	24,125
Scatsta	14,690	282	20	14,345	43
Shoreham	1,453	—	—	1,395	58
Southampton	429,995	417,448	1,457	10,552	538
Stornoway	80,692	79,832	2	393	465
Sumburgh	449,771	76,458	118	356,101	17,094
Swansea	60	—	—	60	—
Teesside	332,320	249,866	31,950	49,982	522
Tiree	6,245	5,032	935	278	—
Unst	85,230	1,979	—	83,251	—
Wick	38,962	30,624	7,723	588	27
CHANNEL IS. AIRPORTS: TOTAL	2,534,302	2,352,273	62,171	117,153	2,705
Alderney	83,794	83,579	—	215	—
Guernsey	784,116	742,251	35,749	5,931	185
Jersey	1,666,392	1,526,443	26,422	111,007	2,520

*UK and overseas

Source: Civil Aviation Authority

AERODROMES/AIRPORTS

The following aerodromes in the UK, the Isle of Man and the Channel Islands are either state owned or licensed for use by civil aircraft. A number of unlicensed aerodromes not included in this list are also available for private use by special permission. Aerodromes designated as Customs airports are printed in small capitals. Customs facilities are available at certain other aerodromes by special arrangement.

BAA Owned by BAA PLC
H Licensed for helicopters
HIAL Operated by Highland and Islands Airports Ltd
J Military aerodromes – civil availability by prior permission
M Owned by municipal authority
P Private ownership
S Government owned and operated

England and Wales

Aberporth, Dyfed J
Andrewsfield, Essex
Barrow (Walney Island), Cumbria
Bedford/Thurleigh J
Bembridge, IOW
Benson, Oxon J
Beverley/Linley Hill, N. Humberside
BIGGIN HILL, Kent P
BIRMINGHAM, W. Midlands P
Blackbushe, Hants
BLACKPOOL, Lancs P
Bodmin, Cornwall
Bourn, Cambridge
BOURNEMOUTH, Dorset P
BRISTOL, Avon P
Brize Norton, Oxford J
Brough, N. Humberside
Caernarfon, Gwynedd
CAMBRIDGE P
CARDIFF, S. Glamorgan P
Carlisle, Cumbria M
Chichester (Goodwood), Sussex
Chivenor, Devon J
Church Fenton, N. Yorks J
Clacton, Essex
Compton Abbas, Dorset
Cosford, Wolverhampton J
COVENTRY, W. Midlands M
Cranfield, Beds
Cranwell, Lincs J
Crowfield, Suffolk
Culdrose, Cornwall J
Denham, Bucks
Dishforth, N. Yorks J
Doncaster, S. Yorks
Dunkeswell, Devon
Dunsfold, Surrey M
Duxford, Cambs M
Eaglescott, Devon
Earls Colne, Halstead
EAST MIDLANDS, Derbys P
Elstree, Herts
EXETER, Devon
Fairoaks, Surrey
Farnborough, Hants S
Fenland, Lincs
Filton, Bristol
Finningley, S. Yorks J
Fowlmere, Cambs
Gloucestershire (Staverton) P
Great Yarmouth (North Denes), Norfolk H
Halfpenny Green, Staffs
Halton, Bucks J
Hatfield, Herts
Haverfordwest, Dyfed M
Hawarden, Clywd
Hucknall, Notts
HUMBERSIDE P
Ipswich, Suffolk
Isle of Wight/Sandown
Land's End (St Just), Cornwall
Lashenden, Headcorn, Kent
Leavesden, Herts
LEEDS/BRADFORD, Yorks P
Lee-on-Solent, Hants J
Leicester, Leics
Linton-on-Ouse, Yorks J
Little Gransden, Beds
LIVERPOOL, Merseyside P
Llanbedr, Gwynedd J
LONDON/CITY
LONDON/GATWICK BAA
LONDON/HEATHROW BAA
LONDON/STANSTED BAA
London/Westland Heliport H
LUTON, Beds P
LYDD, Kent
Lyneham, Wilts J
MANCHESTER P
Manchester (Barton)
MANSTON, Kent J
Marston Moor, York
Mona, Gwynedd J
Montgomeryshire/Welshpool, Powys
Netherthorpe, S. Yorks
NEWCASTLE, Tyne and Wear P
Newton, Notts J
Northampton (Sywell), Northants
Northolt, Middx J
NORWICH, Norfolk M
Nottingham, Notts
Old Sarum, Wilts
Oxford (Kidlington), Oxfordshire
Panshanger, Herts
Penzance, Cornwall H
Perranporth, Cornwall
Peterborough (Conington)
Peterborough (Sibson), Cambs
PLYMOUTH (ROBOROUGH), Devon
Portland Naval, Dorset JH
Redhill, Surrey
Retford/Gamston, Notts
Rochester, Kent
St Mawgan, Cornwall J
Sandtoft, Humberside
Scilly Isles (St Mary's) M
Seething, Norfolk
Shawbury, Shropshire J
Sherburn-in-Elmet, N. Yorks
Shipdham, Norfolk
Shobdon, Herefordshire
SHOREHAM, W. Sussex P
Silverstone, Northants
Skegness (Ingoldmells), Lincs
Sleap, Shropshire
SOUTHAMPTON/Eastleigh, Hants P
SOUTHEND, Essex P
Stapleford, Essex
Sturgate, Lincs
Swansea, W. Glam M
TEESSIDE, Cleveland P
Thruxton, Hants
Tresco, Isles of Scilly H
Turweston, Northants
Valley, Gwynedd J
Warton, Lancs
Wattisham, Suffolk J
Wellesbourne Mountford, Warwick
Weston, Avon H
White Waltham, Berks
Wickenby, Lincs
Woodford, Gtr Manchester
Woodvale, Merseyside J
Wycombe Air Park (Booker), Bucks
Yeovil, Somerset
Yeovilton, Somerset J

Scotland

ABERDEEN (DYCE) BAA
Barra, Hebrides
Benbecula, Hebrides HIAL
Cumbernauld, Strathclyde
Dounreay (Thurso) S
Dundee, Angus M
Eday M
EDINBURGH BAA
Fair Isle
Fife/Glenrothes M
Flotta, Orkneys
GLASGOW BAA
Inverness (Dalcross) HIAL
Islay (Port Ellen) HIAL
Kirkwall HIAL
Lerwick (Tingwall) M
Leuchars, Fife J
Machrihanish, Kintyre J
North Ronaldsay, Orkneys M
Papa Westray, Orkneys M
Perth (Scone)
PRESTWICK, BAA
Sanday, Orkneys M
Scatsta
Stornoway, Hebrides HIAL
Stronsay, Orkneys M
SUMBURGH, Shetlands HIAL
Tiree HIAL
Unst, Shetlands M
West Freugh, Dumfries S
Westray, Orkneys M
Whalsay, Shetlands
Wick HIAL

Northern Ireland

BELFAST (ALDERGROVE) S
Belfast (City)
Enniskillen (St Angelo) P
Londonderry (Eglinton) M
Newtownards

Islands

ALDERNEY, CI S
GUERNSEY, CI S
JERSEY, CI S
RONALDSWAY, IOM S

BRITISH RAILWAYS

The British Railways Board was set up by the Transport Act 1962, and assumed its responsibilities on 1 January 1963. (For members, *see* Government Departments and Public Offices section.)

Management of the railways has been reorganized into the business sectors of InterCity, Network SouthEast, Regional Railways, Trainload Freight and Railfreight Distribution. The former geographical regions of London Midland, Western, Eastern, Anglia, Scottish and Southern no longer exist. A new organization, European Passenger Services Ltd, has been set up to manage international rail services through the Channel Tunnel.

Financial Results

The profit and loss account for 1991–2 showed a deficit of £176.1 million, £144.7 million after interest and extraordinary items, compared with a deficit of £10.9 million after interest in 1990–1. The railway operating deficit was £101.4 million compared with a deficit of £42.4 million for the previous year.

	£ million
Railways	1991–2
Gross receipts	
Passenger (including grants)	3,020.8
Freight (incl. parcels and mails)	781.7
Other	145.7
Total	3,802.5
Working expenses	
Train services	1,620.2
Terminals	405.0
Miscellaneous traffic expenses	178.1
Track and signalling	916.7
General expenses	525.4
Capital renewal provision	127.3
Other expenses	131.2
Total Expenditure	3,903.9
Railway net deficit	(101.4)
Loss from property sales and interest charges	(43.3)
Group Operating Deficit	(144.7)

Staff

On 31 March 1992 British Rail employed 133,060 staff (131,430 at 31 March 1991). Including subsidiaries, the group total at 31 March 1992 was 138,001 (136,277 at 31 March 1991).

Operating Statistics

At 31 March 1992, British Rail had 23,462 miles of standard gauge lines and sidings in use, representing 10,289 miles of route of which 3,036 miles were electrified. Standard rail on main line has a weight of 110 lb per yard. British Rail had 2,093 locomotives (2 diesel, 1,831 diesel-electric and 262 electric); 2,074 diesel multiple-unit vehicles, 6,909 electric multiple-unit vehicles and 2,842 locomotive-hauled vehicles.

Loaded train miles run in passenger service totalled 231.3 million. Passenger journeys made during the year totalled 739.7 million, including 360.7 million made by holders of season tickets. The average distance of each passenger journey on ordinary fare was 36.1 miles; and on season ticket, 17.3 miles. Passenger stations in use in 1992 numbered 2,473 and freight terminals 83.

Freight

There were 19,877 freight vehicles and 1,253 other vehicles in the non-passenger-carrying stock. Train miles run in freight service totalled 55 million.

Accidents on Railways

	1989	1990
Train accidents: total	1,434	1,283
Persons killed: total	18	4
Passengers	6	0
Railway staff	6	1
Others	6	3
Persons injured: total	404	243
Passengers	311	157
Railway staff	71	73
Others	22	13
Other accidents through movement of railway vehicles		
Persons killed	41	37
Persons injured	2,759	2,658
Other accidents on railway premises		
Persons killed	10	4
Persons injured	7,628	6,815
Trespassers and suicides		
Persons killed	293	285
Persons injured	92	123

ROADS

Highway Authorities

The powers and responsibilities of highway authorities in England and Wales are set out in the Highways Acts 1980; for Scotland there is separate legislation.

Responsibility for trunk road motorways and other trunk roads in Great Britain rests in England with the Secretary of State for Transport, in Scotland with the Secretary of State for Scotland, and in Wales with the Secretary of State for Wales. The costs of construction, improvement and maintenance are paid for by central government. The highway authority for non-trunk roads in England and Wales is, in general, the county council, metropolitan district council or London borough council in whose area the roads lie, and in Scotland the regional or islands council. In Northern Ireland the Northern Ireland Department of the Environment is responsible for public roads and their maintenance and construction.

Expenditure

Transport Supplementary Grant (TSG) is a block grant and was introduced in England and Wales on 1 April 1975 to replace a variety of specific grants paid towards local transport expenditure.

In England grant was paid towards capital and current spending on transport by county councils and the GLC from 1975–6 to 1984–5. From 1 April 1985 TSG has only been paid towards capital spending on highways and the regulation of traffic, current expenditure having been subsumed by rate support grant. Since the abolition of the GLC and the metropolitan county councils on 1 April 1986, grant has been paid to London boroughs, the Common Council of the City of London and metropolitan district councils. From 1 April 1991 TSG has also been paid towards capital spending on bridge assessment and strengthening, and from 1 April 1992 TSG has been paid to carry out structural maintenance on the Primary Route Network. In Wales grant was also paid to the Welsh county councils towards current and capital expenditure on transport. In April 1982 TSG became payable on capital expenditure only, current expenditure having been subsumed by rate support grant. On 1 April 1990 the grant for Wales was renamed Transport Grant.

Grant rates are determined by the respective Secretaries of State; at present, grant is paid at 50 per cent of expenditure accepted for grant in England and Wales.

For the financial year 1992–3 local authorities in England will receive £370 million in TSG. Total expenditure on building and maintaining motorways and trunk roads in 1991–2 was £1.75 billion in England.

In the financial year 1992–3, local authorities in Wales will receive £37 million in TG. Total expenditure on roads in Wales in 1990–1 was £264 million.

Total expenditure on roads during the financial year 1990–1 was £130 million in Scotland.

ROAD LENGTHS (in miles) as at April 1991

	Total roads	*Trunk roads (incl. motorways)*	*Motorways**
England	170,792	6,552	1,691
Wales	20,729	1,054	74
Scotland	32,198	1,955	160
N. Ireland	15,011	1,375†	69
UK	238,730	10,936	1,995

*There were in addition 42 miles of local authority motorway in England and 15 miles in Scotland
†Renamed Class 1 Roads in 1984

MOTORWAYS

The network in England and Wales is based on five main routes:

M1 London to Yorkshire
M4 London to South Wales
M5 Birmingham, Bristol, Exeter
M6 Birmingham to Carlisle
M62 Lancashire to North Humberside

Other important motorways in use include:
M2 Medway towns
M3 London to Winchester
M11 London to Cambridge
M18 Rotherham to Goole
M20 London to Folkestone
M25 London orbital route
M40 London to Birmingham
M56 North Cheshire
M180 South Humberside

Motorways in use in Scotland include:
M8 Edinburgh, Glasgow, Greenock
M9 Edinburgh to Stirling
M73 Maryville to Mollisburn
M74 Millbank to Maryville
M80 Stirling to Haggs
M85 Perth to Friarton Bridge
M90 Perth to Inverkeithing
M876 M80 to Kincardine Bridge

DRIVING TESTS

The number of driving tests conducted in Great Britain in 1991 was 1,788,630, of which 50.81 per cent resulted in a pass. In addition a total of 71,704 LGV/PCV (Large goods vehicle/Passenger carrying vehicle) tests were undertaken, of which 53 per cent were successful.

MOTOR VEHICLES

The number of vehicles in Great Britain with current licences in 1990 was:

Private and light goods	21,952,000
Motor cycles, scooters, mopeds	750,000
Public transport vehicles	109,000
Heavy goods vehicles	449,000
Agricultural tractors	346,000
Others	65,000
Total	24,511,000

This total includes 840,000 Crown vehicles and vehicles exempt from licensing.

BUSES AND COACHES Great Britain 1990–1

Number of vehicles (31 March 1991)	72,100
Vehicle kilometres (millions)	3,838
Passenger journeys (millions)	5,470
Passenger receipts (£ million)	2,853

ROAD ACCIDENTS 1990

Road accidents	258,441
Vehicles involved:	
Pedal cycles	27,108
Motor vehicles	427,625
Total casualties	341,141
Pedestrians	60,230
Vehicle users	280,911
Killed*	5,217
Pedestrians	1,694
Pedal cycles	256
All two-wheeled motor vehicles	659
Cars and taxis	2,371
Others	237

*Died within 30 days of accident

	Killed	*Injured*
1965	7,952	389,985
1970	7,499	355,869
1975	6,366	318,584
1980	6,010	323,000
1985	5,165	312,359
1988	5,052	317,253
1989	5,373	336,219
1990	5,217	335,924

LICENCES

VEHICLE LICENSES

Since 1 October 1974 registration and first licensing of vehicles has been through local offices (known as Vehicle Registration Offices) of the Department of Transport's Driver and Vehicle Licensing Centre in Swansea. The records of existing vehicles are held at Swansea. Local facilities for relicensing are available as follows:

(i) with a licence reminder (form V11) in person at any post office which deals with vehicle licensing, or post it to the post office shown on the form
(ii) with a vehicle licence renewal (form V10). You may normally apply in person at any licensing post office. You will need to take your vehicle registration document with you; if this is not available you must complete form V62 which is held at post offices. Postal applications can be made to the post offices shown on form V100, available at any post

office. This form also provides guidance on registering and licensing vehicles.

Details of the present duties chargeable on motor vehicles are available at post offices and Vehicle Registration Offices. The Vehicles (Excise) Act 1971 provides *inter alia* that any vehicle kept on a public road but not used on roads is chargeable to excise duty as if it were in use.

Rates of duty for motor car and motor cycle licences are shown below.

Type	12 months £	6 months £
Motor Cars		
Those first constructed before 1 January 1947	60.00	33.00
Others	110.00	60.50
Motor Cycles		
With or without sidecar, not exceeding 150 cc	15.00	—
With or without sidecar, 150–250 cc	30.00	—
With or without sidecar, exceeding 250 cc	50.00	27.50
Those first constructed before 1 January 1947, exceeding 250 cc and weighing not more than 101.6 kg	30.00	—
Three Wheelers		
Not over 150 cc	15.00	—
Others	50.00	27.50
Hackney Carriages		
Seating less than 9 persons	110.00	60.50
Seating 9–16 persons	130.00	71.50
Seating 17–35 persons	200.00	110.00
Seating 36–60 persons	300.00	165.00
Seating over 60 persons	450.00	247.50

DRIVING LICENCES – FEES

	On or after 1.2.92
FULL LICENCE	
First full licence	£21.75
Changing a provisional to a full licence after passing a driving test	free
Renewal of licence issued after 30 Sept. 1982	£6.00
Medical renewal	free
Removing endorsements	£6.00
New licence after a period of disqualification	£12.00
PROVISIONAL LICENCE	
First provisional licence	£21.75
Renewal of provisional licence issued before 1 Oct. 1982	£21.75
DUPLICATE LICENCE	£6.00
EXCHANGE LICENCE	£6.00

The minimum age for driving motor cars, light goods vehicles and motor cycles is 17 (moped, 16).

DRIVING TEST FEES	weekday rate/Saturday rate
For cars	£23.50/£35
For motor cycles, part I*	n/a
part II	£34.00/£44
For lorries, buses	£55.50/£75

*Part I of the motor cycle test, now known as Basic Training, is no longer conducted by the Department of Transport but by appointed motor cycle training organizations, who conduct the majority of part I tests within the framework of their own training courses and are free to set their own fee. Part II is now known as the Accompanied Motor Cycle test.

An extended driving test has been introduced from 1 July 1992 for those convicted of dangerous driving. The fee is £47 (car) or £57 (motorcyle).

Driving tests for invalid carriages are free.

MOT TESTING

Cars, motor cycles, motor caravans, light goods and dual-purpose vehicles more than three years old must be covered by a current MoT test certificate. Copies of the legislation governing MoT testing can be obtained from any bookshop which stocks HMSO publications. The legislation comprises The Road Traffic Act 1988 (Sections 45 and 46), The Motor Vehicles (Test) Regulations 1981, and subsequent amendments.

PRINCIPAL MERCHANT FLEETS OF THE WORLD

Flag	1981		1986		1990		1991	
	No.	*Gross tonnage*	*No.*	*Gross tonnage*	*No.*	*Gross tonnage*	*No.*	*Gross tonnage*
Liberia	2,281	74,906,390	1,658	52,649,444	1,688	54,699,564	1,605	52,426,516
Panama	4,461	27,656,573	5,252	41,305,009	4,748	39,298,123	4,953	44,949,330
Japan	10,422	40,835,681	10,011	38,487,773	10,000	27,077,943	10,063	26,406,930
USSR	7,867	23,492,898	6,726	24,960,888	7,383	26,737,418	7,377	26,405,044
Norway	2,409	21,674,886	2,107	9,294,630	2,557	23,429,000	2,577	23,585,661
Greece	3,710	42,004,990	2,255	28,390,800	1,814	20,521,561	1,863	22,752,919
Cyprus	588	1,818,997	940	10,616,809	1,270	18,335,929	1,359	20,297,661
*USA	5,869	18,908,281	6,263	18,300,337	6,348	21,328,131	6,222	20,290,520
China, People's Republic of	1,051	7,653,195	1,562	11,566,974	1,948	13,899,448	2,382	14,298,912
China, Republic of (Taiwan)	498	1,887,836	587	4,272,795	660	5,766,283	644	5,888,100
Bahamas	106	196,682	302	5,985,011	807	13,626,335	973	17,541,196
Philippines	827	2,539,817	1,131	6,922,499	1,420	8,514,876	1,465	8,625,561
Singapore	828	6,888,452	716	6,267,627	774	7,927,866	854	8,488,172
Italy	1,677	10,641,242	1,569	7,896,569	1,616	7,991,404	1,652	8,121,595
Korea (South)	1,634	5,141,505	1,837	7,183,617	2,110	7,783,075	2,136	7,820,532
Malta	77	231,353	246	2,014,947	524	4,518,682	702	6,916,325
United Kingdom	2,975	25,419,427	2,256	11,567,117	1,998	6,716,325	1,949	6,610,633
India	620	6,019,902	736	6,540,121	855	6,475,615	890	6,516,780
Germany, Federal Republic of	1,820	7,708,227	1,752	5,565,214	1,179	4,300,786	1,522	5,971,254†
Brazil	627	5,133,224	697	6,212,287	691	6,015,684	669	5,882,528
Hong Kong	223	2,580,492	416	8,179,670	375	6,564,987	355	5,875,825
Denmark	1,169	5,047,734	1,063	4,651,224	1,260	5,188,105	1,290	5,870,589
Iran	234	1,201,667	359	2,911,359	393	4,738,202	401	4,583,179
Turkey	532	1,663,679	825	3,423,745	869	3,718,641	880	4,107,075
France	1,199	11,455,033	984	5,936,268	900	3,832,388	910	3,988,072
Netherlands	1,271	5,467,486	1,334	4,324,135	1,227	3,784,767	1,249	3,872,301
Romania	355	2,031,524	426	3,233,906	483	4,004,625	469	3,828,034
Spain	2,678	8,133,658	2,397	5,422,002	2,338	3,807,103	2,305	3,617,151
Poland	827	3,579,081	749	3,457,242	698	3,369,183	673	3,348,443
Yugoslavia	483	2,540,592	490	2,872,613	501	3,815,980	462	3,293,447
Sweden	706	4,033,893	660	2,516,614	679	2,774,808	684	3,174,274
Bermuda	75	499,029	97	1,208,276	105	4,258,282	100	3,036,987
St Vincent	33	25,442	103	509,878	521	1,936,814	698	2,709,794
Canada	1,300	3,158,864	1,249	3,160,043	1,224	2,744,221	1,204	2,684,614
Australia	527	1,767,930	673	2,368,462	721	2,511,785	714	2,571,867
Indonesia	1,260	1,744,958	1,707	2,085,635	1,884	2,178,646	1,991	2,336,880
Vanuatu	9	5,837	47	164,953	273	2,163,618	287	2,172,621
Malaysia	258	879,468	498	1,743,629	498	1,717,479	508	1,755,279
Argentina	521	2,306,760	454	2,117,017	479	1,889,999	490	1,708,565
Luxembourg	—	—	—	—	2	3,338	51	1,703,482
Gibraltar	10	40,136	100	1,612,948	57	2,008,456	44	1,410,271
Kuwait	231	2,317,275	239	2,580,924	225	1,854,583	197	1,372,976
Bulgaria	188	1,193,853	205	1,385,009	200	1,360,488	226	1,366,792
Saudi Arabia	286	3,121,821	380	2,978,016	311	1,682,752	309	1,321,464
Egypt	307	599,012	422	1,063,020	435	1,257,145	444	1,256,641
Mexico	456	1,134,625	642	1,520,246	640	1,319,589	649	1,195,517
Finland	341	2,444,504	276	1,469,927	269	1,069,020	266	1,052,980
Myanmar	96	85,439	106	125,524	142	827,382	154	1,046,029

*Including ships of the United States Reserve Fleet
†Including the former German Democratic Republic

Classification with Lloyd's Register of Shipping: Ships classed or to be classed with Lloyd's Register at 30 June 1991, totalled 8,644 with an aggregate gross tonnage of over 95 million

Source: Lloyd's Register of Shipping

MERCHANT SHIPS COMPLETED IN THE WORLD DURING 1991

Country of Build	Total No.	Total Gross tonnage	For Registration in	Total No.	Total Gross tonnage
Japan	602	7,282,756	Panama	138	3,634,487
Korea, South	112	3,496,693	Liberia	88	3,522,335
*China, People's Republic of	35	309,823	Japan	383	1,245,322
China, Republic of (Taiwan)	11	513,764	Norway	50	778,745
Germany, Federal Republic of	82	774,502	Cyprus	33	693,970
Italy	28	499,896	Bahamas	33	659,412
Denmark	26	441,051	Singapore	49	620,846
Yugoslavia	22	355,173	China, People's Republic of	21	97,032
Spain	59	317,422	China, Republic of (Taiwan)	8	402,061
*USSR	106	254,797	Denmark	30	490,688
Brazil	6	230,659	Sweden	16	450,264
Netherlands	84	210,837	Italy	28	438,663
Poland	47	193,842	Germany, Federal Republic of	61	433,214
United Kingdom	31	185,470	USSR	136	295,650
*Romania	14	175,522	Korea (South)	36	267,327
Finland	7	156,466	Netherlands	49	256,074
Norway	40	124,247	Poland	17	222,106
Singapore	52	114,325	Bermuda	5	155,701
France	27	108,836	Hong Kong	13	132,048
Turkey	23	79,939	Greece	9	127,597
Bulgaria	9	59,629	Israel	3	111,627
Sweden	6	38,276	Spain	28	104,718
Australia	17	21,396	India	14	98,845
Portugal	14	21,171	United Kingdom	29	98,477
Egypt	6	19,800	France	32	79,040
Malaysia	9	18,049	Malaysia	16	76,987
Malta	2	12,790	Romania	5	73,289
Austria	5	12,445	Australia	14	64,399
Czechoslovakia	4	12,344	St Vincent	3	63,657
USA	17	9,335	Philippines	3	61,019
Belgium	8	8,127	Brazil	4	52,213
Other countries	63	35,723	Other countries	220	287,292
World Total	1,574	16,095,105	World Total	1,574	16,095,105

*Information incomplete

Source: Lloyd's Register of Shipping

Of the ships completed in the world during the year 3,289,913 gross tonnage (20.4 per cent) was to be classed with Lloyd's Register

Communications

Postal Services

On 1 October 1969 the Post Office ceased to be a government department. The responsibility for running postal services was transferred to a public authority called the Post Office, which also administered telecommunications in the United Kingdom. The British Telecommunications Act 1981 separated the postal and telecommunications functions and gave the Secretary of State for Trade and Industry powers to suspend the monopoly of the Post Office in certain areas and to issue licences to other bodies to provide an alternative service. Non-Post Office bodies are now permitted to transfer mail between document exchanges and to deliver letters, provided that a minimum fee of £1 per letter is charged. Charitable organizations are allowed to carry and deliver Christmas and New Year cards.

INLAND POSTAL SERVICES AND REGULATIONS

Inland Letter Post Rates

Not over	*1st class*	*2nd class*
60 g	24p	18p
100 g	36p	28p
150 g	45p	34p
200 g	54p	41p
250 g	64p	49p
300 g	74p	58p
350 g	85p	66p
400 g	96p	75p
450 g	£1.08	84p
500 g	£1.20	93p
600 g	£1.50	£1.15
700 g	£1.80	£1.35
750 g	£1.95	£1.40 (not
800 g	£2.05	admissible
900 g	£2.25	over 750 g)
1,000 g	£2.40	
Each extra 250 g or part thereof	60p	

Postcards travel at the same rates.

UK Parcel Rates

Not over	
1 kg	£2.50
2 kg	£3.15
4 kg	£4.10
6 kg	£4.65
8 kg	£5.35
10 kg	£6.25
30 kg	£7.80

Stamps

There is a two-tier postal delivery system in the UK with first class letters normally being delivered the following day and second class post within three days.

Postage stamps are sold in values of 1p, 2p, 3p, 4p, 5p, 6p, 10p, 18p, 20p, 24p, 28p, 30p, 33p, 34p, 35p, 39p, 50p, 75p, £1, £1.50, £2.00, and £5.00.

Books of stamps costing 50p or £1 are available from electronic vending machines at some main post offices. At post office counters books are sold containing ten first class stamps (£2.40) and ten second class stamps (£1.80). Rolls of 24p and 18p stamps are also sold. Mixed value rolls are only available on special order from post offices. The sale of postage stamps has been extended to outlets other than post offices, including stationers and newsagents.

Prepaid Stationery

Aerogrammes to all destinations, 32p.

Forces Aerogrammes, free to certain destinations. Other mail charged at a concessionary rate.

Registered Letter Envelopes, printed with a £1.75 stamp (£1.55 for registration and 20p for postage), come in three sizes.

G, 156 × 95mm, £2.30
H, 203 × 120mm, £2.35
K, 292 × 152mm, £2.45

Printed postage stamps cut from envelopes, postcards, newspaper wrappers, etc., may be used as stamps in payment of postage, provided that they are not imperfect or defaced.

Postal Orders

Postal Orders (British pattern) are issued and paid at nearly all post offices in the UK. They are also paid in the Irish Republic, and issued and/or paid in many other countries overseas.

Postal orders are printed with a counterfoil for denominations of 50p and £1, followed by £1 steps to £10, £15 and £20. Postage stamps may be affixed in the space provided to increase the value of the postal order by up to 49p.

Charges (in addition to the value of the postal order): Up to £1, 25p; £2–£4, 40p; £5–£7, 50p; £8–£10, 60p; £15, 70p; £20, 80p.

The name of the payee must be inserted on the postal order. If not presented within six months of the last day of the month of issue, orders must be sent to the local customer services manager of Post Office Counters Ltd (the address and telephone number can be found in the telephone directory), to ascertain whether the order may still be paid, although if the counterfoil has been retained postal orders not more than four years out of date may be paid when presented with the counterfoil at a post office.

Other Services

Cash on Delivery Service

(Inland, excluding Irish Republic and HM ships). A trade charge (amount to be collected) up to £350 can, under certain conditions, be collected from addresses and remitted to the sender of a parcel containing an invoice. Invoice values of over £50 are only collectable at Post Office premises.

Charge per parcel (exclusive of postage and registration): Customers under contract, £1.20; other customers, £1.60; COD enquiry, £1.20.

Certificate of Posting

Issued free on request at time of posting.

Compensation

(Royal Mail inland only). Compensation up to a maximum of £24 may be paid where it can be shown that a letter was damaged or lost in the post due to the fault of the Post Office, its employees or agents. The onus of making up properly any parcel sent by post lies with the sender. The Post Office does not accept any responsibility for loss arising from faulty packing.

Parcelforce. Compensation up to £20 per parcel will be paid for loss or damage if a certificate of posting has been obtained. A Compensation Fee Certificate of Posting can also be obtained; 60p, up to £150 compensation, £1.10, up to £500 compensation.

Newspaper Post

Copies of newspapers registered at the Post Office may be posted by the publisher or their agents in wrappers open at both ends, in unsealed envelopes approved by the Post Office, or without covers and tied by string which can be removed without cutting. Wrappers and envelopes must be prominently marked 'newspaper post' in the top left-hand corner. No writing or additional printing is permitted, other than the words 'with compliments', name and address of sender, request for return if undeliverable and a reference to a page. Items receive first class letter service.

Newspapers posted by the public, or supplements to registered newspapers despatched apart from their ordinary publications, are transmitted under the conditions governing the first or second class letter services.

Prohibited Articles

Prohibitions include offensive or dangerous articles, packets likely to impede Post Office sorters, and certain kinds of advertisement.

Recorded Delivery

The recorded delivery service provides a record of posting and delivery of inland letters. No compensation is available for money or jewellery sent by this service. Charge, 30p; advice of delivery, a further 31p. It is only available at the time of posting.

Redirection

(i) By agent of addressee – mail other than parcels, business reply and freepost items may be reposted free not later than the day after delivery (not counting Sundays and public holidays) if unopened and if original addressee's name is unobscured. Parcels may be redirected free of charge within the same time limits only if the original and substituted address are in the same local parcel delivery area (or within the London postal area). Registered packets, which must be taken to a post office, are re-registered free only up to the day after delivery.

(ii) By the Post Office – requests for redirection of mail should be made on printed forms obtainable from the Post Office and must be signed by the person to whom the letters are to be addressed. A fee is payable for each different surname on the application form.

Charges: Up to 1 calendar month, £3.50; up to 3 calendar months, £7.75; up to 12 calendar months, £18.75; up to 12 calendar months where redirection has already been in operation for 12 months or more, £65.00.

Registration

(Inland first class letters only). All packets intended for registration must be handed to the post office and a certificate of posting obtained.

Compensation up to	*Standard fee in addition to postage*
£950	£1.90
£1,850	£2.10
£2,220	£2.30

For an extra fee, Consequential Loss Insurance provides cover up to £10,000 for items worth more than their material value.

Compensation in respect of currency or other forms of monetary worth is given only if money is sent by registered letter post in one of the special envelopes sold officially (*see* Prepaid Stationery). Compensation cannot be paid in the case of any packet containing anything not legally transmissible by post. Compensation is paid for fragile articles only if they have been adequately packed. No compensation is paid for deterioration due to delay of perishable articles or for damage to exceptionally fragile articles.

Undelivered Mail

Undelivered mail is returned to the sender provided the return address is indicated either on the outside of the envelope or inside. If the sender's address is not available, items not containing property are destroyed. If the packet contains something of value it is retained for up to three months. Exceptionally, items in the minimum weight step on which a rebate of postage has been allowed are destroyed unopened unless there is a return address shown on the outside of the cover. In addition, undeliverable second class mail which contains newspapers, magazines or commercial advertising is destroyed.

Unpaid Mail

All unpaid or underpaid letters are treated as second class mail. The recipient is charged the amount of underpayment plus 13p per item. The same rates apply to parcels.

SPECIAL DELIVERY SERVICES

Datapost

A guaranteed service for the delivery of documents and packages: (i) Datapost Sameday offers same-day collection and delivery in many areas; (ii) Datapost 10 and Datapost 12 offer next day delivery nationwide. Datapost 10 for delivery before 10 a.m. and Datapost 12 for delivery before noon are available to certain destinations only. Items may be collected or handed in at post offices. There are also Datapost links with a number of overseas countries.

Express Delivery

This service is by special messenger from the office of delivery and is available to or from the Isle of Man or the Channel Islands. Charge (in addition to postage), £1.95.

Royal Mail Special Delivery

This service offers special messenger treatment, where necessary, to ensure next day delivery of first class letters and packets. The fee of £1.95 is refunded if next working day delivery is not achieved, provided that items are posted before latest recommended posting times.

Swiftair

Express delivery of air mail letters and packets anywhere in the world. Items normally arrive at least one day in advance of normal air mail. Charge (in addition to postage), £1.95.

OVERSEAS POSTAL SERVICES AND REGULATIONS

OVERSEAS SURFACE MAIL RATES

Letters and Postcards

Not over		*Not over*	
20 g	28p	450 g	£2.44
60 g	48p	500 g	£2.70
100 g	69p	750 g	£4.00
150 g	92p	1,000 g	£5.30
200 g	£1.18	1,250 g	£6.60
250 g	£1.42	1,500 g	£7.90
300 g	£1.66	1,750 g	£9.20
350 g	£1.92	2,000 g	£10.50
400 g	£2.18		

AIRMAIL LETTER RATES

Europe: Letters and Postcards

Not over		*Not over*	
20 g	24p	260 g	£1.60
20 g non EC	28p	280 g	£1.71
40 g	39p	300 g	£1.82
60 g	50p	320 g	£1.93
80 g	61p	340 g	£2.04
100 g	72p	360 g	£2.15
120 g	83p	380 g	£2.26
140 g	94p	400 g	£2.37
160 g	£1.05	420 g	£2.48
180 g	£1.16	440 g	£2.59
200 g	£1.27	460 g	£2.70
220 g	£1.38	480 g	£2.81
240 g	£1.49	*500 g	£2.92

* Max. 2 kg.

Outside Europe: Letters

	Not over 10 g	*Not over 20 g*	*Each extra 20 g*
Zone 1	39p	57p	32p
Zone 2	39p	57p	42p

For Airmail Letter Zones outside Europe, *see* pages 598–9.

OTHER SERVICES

Cash on Delivery

Applicable to parcels only, but not to all countries, nor to British naval, military and RAF forces serving overseas.

A charge starting at £3.70 per parcel must be prepaid in addition to the postage for outward parcels. The trade charge (amount to be collected) may not exceed £1,500 but to most non-European countries the limit is lower. The addressee has also to pay on delivery, besides Customs charges if any, a further charge which is not prepayable. If the trade charge cannot be collected special rules apply for undeliverable COD parcels.

Compensation

If a certificate of posting is produced, compensation may be given for loss or damage in the UK to uninsured parcels to or from most overseas countries. No compensation will be paid for any loss or damage due to the action of The Queen's Enemies.

Export Restrictions

Under Department of Trade and Industry regulations the exportation of some goods by post is prohibited except under Department of Trade licence. Enquiries should be addressed to the Export Data Branch, Overseas Trade Divisions, Department of Trade and Industry, 1 Victoria Street, London SWIH OET. Tel: 071-215 5000.

Insurance

Packets containing valuable papers, documents or articles such as jewellery can be insured as letters, or as parcels if the country of destination does not accept dutiable goods in the letter post. For HM ships abroad and also members of the Army and RAF overseas using BFPO numbers, parcels only are insurable up to £140 at a fee of £1.20.

Charges: Cover up to £150, £1.90; up to £300, £2.15; up to £450, £2.40; up to £600, £2.65; to a limit of £3.90 for £1,500 coverage.

International Reply Coupons

Coupons are used to prepay replies to letters. They are exchangeable abroad for stamps representing the minimum surface mail letter rate from the country concerned to the UK. Charge, 60p each.

Poste Restante

Solely for the convenience of travellers and for three months only in any one town. A packet may be addressed to any post office, except town sub-offices, and should have the words 'Poste Restante' or 'to be called for' in the address. Redirection from a Poste Restante is undertaken for up to three months. Letters at a seaport for an expected ship are kept for two months; otherwise letters are kept for two weeks, or for one month if originating from abroad. At the end of this period mail is treated as undeliverable, unless bearing a request for return.

Registration

(Except for parcels and printed paper items posted in bulk). Registration is available to all countries except the British Indian Ocean Territory and the Republic of the Maldives. No compensation is payable for loss or damage to valuable articles sent in an unregistered letter. Charge in addition to postage, £1.90.

Small Packets Post

This service permits the transmission of goods up to 2 kg to all countries, in the same mails as printed papers (NB: To Australia, Cuba, Myanmar (Burma) and Papua New Guinea there is a limit of 500 g). Packets can be sealed and can contain personal correspondence if it relates to the contents of the packet. Registration is allowed as insurance as long as the item is packed in a way which complies with appropriate insurance regulations. A customs declaration is required and the packet must be endorsed 'small packet' and marked with a return address.

Instructions for the disposal of undelivered packets must be given at the time of posting. A parcel which cannot be delivered will be returned to the sender at his expense.

SMALL PACKETS POST RATES

Surface Mail: World-wide

Not over		*Not over*	
100 g	45p	450 g	£1.50
150 g	60p	500 g	£1.65
200 g	75p	750 g	£2.30
250 g	90p	1,000 g	£2.95
300 g	£1.05	1,500 g	£4.15
350 g	£1.20	2,000 g	£5.35
400 g	£1.35		

Public Telecommunications Services

Under the British Telecommunications Act 1981 the functions of the Post Office were divided between two separate organizations. The Post Office retained control of postal services and BT (formerly British Telecom) was created to provide a telecommunications service. The Act also provided for a limited relaxation of the telecommunications monopoly. This was further advanced by the Telecommunications Act 1984, which removed BT's monopoly on running the public telecommunications system. British Telecom was privatized as a public limited company in 1984.

The Telecommunications Act 1984 also established the Office of Telecommunications (Oftel) as the independent regulatory body for the telecommunications industry. (*See also* Government and Public Offices.)

Public Telecommunications Operators

There are three licensed fixed-link public telecommunications operators (PTOs) in the UK: BT, Mercury Communications Ltd, and Kingston Communications (Hull) PLC. In 1988 the Government announced its intention to license up to six other operators to provide one-way satellite communications systems; during 1989 three of these operators were granted temporary licences and the Government announced that such operators could offer services throughout Europe, rather than in the UK only, as previously indicated. In November 1990, the Government began a formal review of the two major fixed-link operators as part of a wider review of UK telecommunications provision and competition arrangements.

BT's obligations under its operating licence include the provision of a universal telecommunications service; a service in rural areas; and essential services, such as public call boxes and emergency services.

Mercury Communications is licensed to provide national and international public telecommunications services for residential and business customers. These services utilize the digital network created by Mercury. Mercury can also provide the following services: (i) public and private telephone services; (ii) national and international telex; (iii) international packet data services; (iv) electronic messaging (electronic mail and access to telex via a personal computer); (v) data network services; and (vi) customer equipment.

Private Telephone Services

There are over 260 private telephone companies which offer information on a variety of subjects such as the weather, stock market analysis, horoscopes, etc., on the BT network. Other services are available on Mercury's network.

The lines and equipment are provided by BT under condition that services adhere to the codes of practice of the Independent Committee for the Supervision of Standards of Telephone Information Practice. All services are charged at 48p per minute (peak and standard rate) or 36p per minute (cheap rate).

Mobile Telephone Systems

Cellular telephone network systems, in existence since 1985, allow calls to be made to and from mobile telephones. The two companies licensed by the Department of Trade and Industry to provide competing cellular telephone systems are Cellnet, jointly owned by BT and Securicor, and Racal Vodafone Ltd, owned by the Racal Electronics Group. Cellular phones can be identified by the number prefixes 0860, 0850, 0831, 0881 or 0836 and calls to them are charged at the 'm' rate.

INLAND TELEPHONES

Since December 1986 an individual customer can install an extension telephone socket or apparatus in their own home without the need to buy the items from any of the licensed public telecommunications operators. However, it is necessary to possess a special style of master-socket which must be supplied by the public network operator. Although an individual need not buy or rent an apparatus from a PTO, a telephone bought from a retail outlet must be of an approved standard compatible with the public network (indicated by a green disc on the label).

BT CHARGES

Exchange Line Rentals	*Per quarter (excl. VAT)*
Residential, exclusive	£18.46
Supportline, exclusive	£9.23
Business, exclusive	£29.90
Telephone apparatus rental	
Residential	from £3.80
Business	from £4.70
Private payphone	from £36.50

Exchange Line Connection and Take-over Charges (incl. VAT)

	Residential	*Business*
New customer	£163.75	£179.49
Removing customer	£140.35	£156.10
Take-over of existing lines	£0.00	£0.00
Non-simultaneous take-over of lines	£36.78	£36.78

Local and dialled national calls are charged in 4.2p units when made from ordinary lines and in 10p units when made from payphones. All charges are subject to VAT except those from payphones which are VAT inclusive. VAT charges on ordinary lines are calculated as a percentage of the total quarterly bill.

The length of time per unit depends on the distance of the call and the time of day:

**Local rate*

'a' rate – up to 35 miles (56 km).
'b1' rate – frequently used routes over 35 miles (56 km).
'b' rate – over 35 miles (56 km) (incl. Channel Islands and Isle of Man).
'm' rate – dialled calls to mobile phones.
'p1' rate – calls to Callstream service.

*Greater London has an exceptionally large 'local' call area.

Peak rate: Monday to Friday, 9 a.m.–1 p.m.
Standard rate: Monday to Friday, 8 a.m.–9 a.m and 1 p.m.–6 p.m.
Cheap rate: Monday to Friday, 6 p.m.–8 a.m. All day Saturday and Sunday and also Christmas Day, Boxing Day and New Year's Day.

DIALLED CALL UNIT TIME

	Seconds per unit at 4.2p (excl. VAT)
Local rate	
Peak	57.5
Standard	80
Cheap	220
'a' rate	
Peak	27
Standard	36.15
Cheap	80.8
'b1' rate	
Peak	23.9
Standard	32
Cheap	50.35
'b' rate	
Peak	19.2
Standard	32
Cheap	50.35
'm' rate	
Peak	7.16
Standard	7.16
Cheap	11.4
'p1' rate	
Peak	6.2
Standard	6.2
Cheap	8.25

PREFIXED CALL CHARGES

0800 – free.
0345 – charged at the local rate.
0860, 0831 and Callstream 0077 services – charged at 'm' rate (and some 0836 calls also).
0898, 0839 and 08364 – charged at 'p1' rate.

OPERATOR-CONNECTED CALLS

Operator-connected calls from ordinary lines are generally subject to a three-minute minimum charge (and thereafter by the minute) which varies with distance and time of day. Operator-connected calls from payphones are charged in three-minute periods at the payphone tariff. For calls that have to be placed through the operator because a dialled call has failed, the charge is equivalent to the dialled rate, subject normally to the three-minute minimum.

Higher charges apply to other operator-connected calls, including special services calls and those to mobile phones, the Irish Republic and the Channel Islands.

PHONECARDS

Phonecards to the value of £2, £4, £10 and £20 are available from post offices and other outlets for use in specially designated public telephone boxes. Each phonecard unit is equivalent to a 10p coin in a payphone.

Special public payphones at major railway stations and airports also accept commercial credit cards.

INTERNATIONAL TELEPHONES

All UK customers have access to International Direct Dialling (IDD) and can dial direct to numbers on most exchanges in 201 countries world-wide. Details about how to make calls are given in dialling code information and in the International Telephone Guide.

For countries without IDD, calls have to be made through the International Operator. All operator-connected calls are subject to a three-minute minimum charge. Thereafter the call is charged by the minute.

Countries which can be called on IDD fall into one of 13 international charge bands depending on location. Charges in each band also vary according to the time of day; cheap rate dialled calls are available to all countries at certain times, but there is no reduced rate for operator-connected calls. Details of current international telephone charges can be obtained from the International Operator.

For International Dialling Codes, *see* pages 598–9.

OTHER TELECOMMUNICATIONS SERVICES

Telex Service

There are now 208 countries that can be reached by the BT telex service from the UK, over 200 of them by direct dialling.

For most customers, direct dialled calls to international destinations are charged in six-second units. Units cost between 4.5p and 13.5p depending upon the country called. Calls via the BT operator are charged in one-minute steps with a three-minute minimum, plus a surcharge of £1.30 a call. Operator-connected calls are charged at between 39p and £1.60 a minute depending upon the country called.

Calls made via BT's Telex Plus store and forward facility attract normal telex charges and a handling charge of 13p for inland delivered messages and 30p for international delivered messages.

Telemessage

Telemessages can be sent by telephone or telex within the UK for 'hard copy' delivery the next working day, including Saturdays. To achieve this, a telemessage must be telephoned/telexed before 10 p.m. Monday to Saturday (7 p.m. Sundays and Bank Holidays). Dial 100 (190 in London, Birmingham and Glasgow) and ask for the Telemessage Service or see the telex directory for codes.

A telemessage costs £5 for the first 50 words and £2.75 for each subsequent group of 50 words – the name and address are free. A sender's copy costs 85p. A selection of cards is available for special occasions at 80p per card. All prices are subject to VAT.

International Telemessage

Telemessage is also available to the USA. For next working day delivery a telemessage must be filed by 10 p.m. UK time Monday to Saturday (7 p.m. Sundays and Bank Holidays). US addresses must include the ZIP code. Charges are £7.25 for the first 50 words and £3.60 for each subsequent group of 50 words. The name and address are free but all charges are subject to VAT.

BT SERVICES

OPERATOR SERVICES – 100

For difficulties

For the following call services: alarm calls (booking charge £2.15); advice of duration and charge (charge 75p); charge card calls (charge 25p); freefone calls; international personal calls (charge £2.15–£4.30); transferred charge calls (charge 40p); subscriber controlled transfer. (All charges exclude VAT.)

INTERNATIONAL OPERATOR – 155
DIRECTORY ENQUIRIES
For numbers in the London postal area, 142.
For numbers outside the London postal area, including the Irish Republic, 192.
INTERNATIONAL DIRECTORY ENQUIRIES – 153
EMERGENCY SERVICES – 999
Services include fire service; police service; ambulance service; coastguard; lifeboat; cave rescue; mountain rescue.
FAULTS – 151
TELEMESSAGE – 100 (190 in London, Birmingham and Glasgow).
INTERNATIONAL TELEMESSAGE – 100 (190 in London, Birmingham and Glasgow). The service is only available to the USA.
INTERNATIONAL TELEGRAMS – 100 (190 in London, Birmingham and Glasgow). The service is available world-wide.
MARITIME SERVICES – 100. Includes Ship's Telegram Service and Ship's Telephone Service.
BT INMARSAT SATELLITE SERVICE – 155
ALL OTHER CALL ENQUIRIES – 191

Weathercall Service

To obtain local weather forecasts, dial the prefix code 0895 500 followed by the appropriate regional code

Greater London	401
Kent, Surrey and Sussex	402
Dorset, Hampshire and IOW	403
Devon and Cornwall	404
Wiltshire, Glos., Avon and Somerset	405
Berks., Bucks. and Oxfordshire	406
Beds., Herts. and Essex	407
Norfolk, Suffolk and Cambridgeshire	408
West, Mid and South Glamorgan and Gwent	409
Salop, Hereford and Worcester	410
Central Midlands	411
East Midlands	412
Lincolnshire and Humberside	413
Dyfed and Powys	414
Gwynedd and Clwyd	415
North-west England	416
West and South Yorkshire	417
North-east England	418
Cumbria and the Lake District	419
South-west Scotland	420
West Central Scotland	421
Edinburgh, South Fife, Lothian and Borders	422
East Central Scotland	423
Grampian and East Highlands	424
North-west Scotland	425
Caithness, Orkney and Shetland	426
Northern Ireland	427
Yorkshire Dales	748

Calls are charged at 36p per minute cheap rate, 48p at all other times, as at July 1992

Marinecall Service

To obtain information about weather conditions up to twelve miles off the coast, dial the prefix code 0891 500, followed by the appropriate area code

Scotland North	451
Scotland East	452
North-east	453
East	454
Anglia	455
Channel East	456
Mid-Channel	457
South-west	458
Bristol Channel	459
Wales	460
North-west	461
Clyde	462
Caledonia	463
Minch	464
Ulster	465
Southern North Sea	991
English Channel	992

Calls are charged at 36p per minute cheap rate, 48p at all other times, as at July 1992

Inland Letter Post

Year	*Basic rate*
1840	1d
1918	1½d
1940	2½d
1957	3d
1965	4d
*1968	5d
1971	3p
1973	3½p
1974	4½p
1975	7p
1975 September	8½p
1977	9p
1979	10p
1980	12p
1981	14p
1982	15½p
1983	16p
1984	17p
1986.	18p
1988	19p
1989	20p
1990	22p
1991	24p

*Two-tier postal system introduced – subsequent figures are for 1st class letter post

Airmail and IDD Codes

Airmail Zones (AZ)

The table includes airmail letter zones for countries outside Europe, and destinations to which European and European Community airmail letter rates apply (*see also* page 594). (*Source: Post Office*)

1 airmail zone 1
2 airmail zone 2
e Europe
ec European Community

International Direct Dialling (IDD)

International dialling codes are composed of four elements which are dialled in sequence:

(i) the international code
(ii) the country code (*see* below)
(iii) the area code
(iv) the customer's telephone number

Calls to some countries must be made via the international operator. (*Source: BT*)

† Calls must be made via the international operator
p A pause in dialling is necessary whilst waiting for a second tone
**p* Only in Bruges, Ostende and Veurne
° Second tone may not always be audible
* Varies in some areas

Country	AZ	IDD from UK	IDD to UK
Afghanistan	1	010 93	†
Albania	*e*	010 355	†
Algeria	1	010 213	00*p*44
Andorra	*ec*	010 33 628	0*p*44
Angola	1	010 244	†
Anguilla	1	010 1 809	001 44
Antigua and Barbuda	1	010 1 809	011 44
Argentina	1	010 54	00 44
Aruba	1	010 297	†
Ascension Island	1	010 247	
Australia	2	010 61	00 11 44
Austria	*e*	010 43	00 44
Azores	*ec*	010 351	00 44
Bahamas	1	010 1 809	011 44
Bahrain	1	010 973	0 44
Bangladesh	1	010 880	00 44
Barbados	1	010 1 809	011 44
Belgium	*ec*	010 32	00*p*44*
Belize	1	010 501	†
Benin	1	010 229	00*p*44
Bermuda	1	010 1 809	1 44
Bhutan	1	010 975	00 44
Bolivia	1	010 591	00 44
Bosnia-Hercegovina	*e*	010 38	99 44
Botswana	1	010 267	00 44
Brazil	1	010 55	00 44
British Virgin Islands	1	010 1 809 49	011 44
Brunei	1	010 673	00 44
Bulgaria	*e*	010 359	00 44
Burkina Faso	1	010 226	
Burundi	1	010 257	90 44
Cambodia	1	†	†
Cameroon	1	010 237	00 44
Canada	1	010 1	011 44
Canary Islands	*ec*	010 34	07*p*44
Cape Verde	*e*	010 238	†
Cayman Islands	1	010 1 809	0 44
Central African Republic	1	010 236	†
Chad	1	010 235	†
Chile	1	010 56	00 44
China	2	010 86	00 44
CIS	*e*	010 7	810 44
Colombia	1	010 57	90 44
Comoros	1	010 269	†
Congo	1	010 242	00 44
Cook Islands	2	010 682	00 44
Costa Rica	1	010 506	00 44
Côte d'Ivoire	1	010 225	00 44
Croatia	*e*	010 38	99 44
Cuba	1	010 53	
Cyprus	*e*	010 357	00 44
Czechoslovakia	*e*	010 42	00 44
Denmark	*ec*	010 45	009 44
Djibouti	1	010 253	00 44
Dominica	1	010 1 809	011 44
Dominican Republic	1	010 1 809	†
Ecuador	1	010 593	00 44
Egypt	1	010 20	00 44
Equatorial Guinea	1	010 240	†
Estonia	*e*	010 7	810 44
Ethiopia	1	010 251	
Falkland Islands	1	010 500	01 44
Faroe Islands	*e*	010 298	009 44
Fiji	2	010 679	05 44
Finland	*e*	010 358	990 44
France	*ec*	010 33	19*p*44°
French Guiana	1	010 594	†
French Polynesia	2	010 689	00 44
Gabon	1	010 241	00 44
The Gambia	1	010 220	00 44
Germany	*ec*	010 49	00 44
Ghana	1	010 233	
Gibraltar	*ec*	010 350	00 44
Greece	*ec*	010 30	00 44
Greenland	*e*	010 299	009 44
Grenada	1	010 1 809	011 44
Guadeloupe	1	010 590	†
Guam	2	010 671	00 44
Guatemala	1	010 502	00 44
Guinea	1	010 224	†
Guinea-Bissau	1	010 245	†
Guyana	1	010 592	011 44
Haiti	1	010 509	†
Honduras	1	010 504	00 44
Hong Kong	1	010 852	001 44
Hungary	*e*	010 36	00 44
Iceland	*e*	010 354	90 44
India	1	010 91	00 44
Indonesia	1	010 62	00 44
Iran	1	010 98	00 44
Iraq	1	010 964	00 44
Ireland, Republic of	*ec*	010 353	00 44
Dublin		0001	
Israel	1	010 972	00 44
Italy	*ec*	010 39	00 44
Jamaica	1	010 1 809	†
Japan	2	010 81	001 44
Jordan	1	010 962	00 44*
Kenya	1	010 254	000 44
Kiribati	2	010 686	09 44
Korea, North	2	010 850	†
Korea, South	2	010 82	001 44

Country	AZ	IDD from UK	IDD to UK
Kuwait	1	010 965	00 44
Laos	1	†	†
Latvia	*e*	010 7	810 44
Lebanon	1	010 961	00 44
Lesotho	1	010 266	00 44
Liberia	1	010 231	00 44
Libya	1	010 218	00 44
Liechtenstein	*e*	010 41 75	00 44
Luxembourg	*ec*	010 352	00 44
Macao	1	010 853	00 44
Madagascar	1	010 261	†
Madeira	*ec*	010 351 91	00 44*
Malawi	1	010 265	101 44
Malaysia	1	010 60	00 44
Maldives	1	010 960	
Mali	1	010 223	00 44
Malta	*e*	010 356	00 44
Mariana Islands, Northern	2	010 670	
Marshall Islands	2	010 692	
Martinique	1	010 596	†
Mauritania	1	010 222	†
Mauritius	1	010 230	
Mayotte	1	010 269	
Mexico	1	010 52	98 44
Micronesia, Federated States of	2	010 691	
Monaco	*ec*	010 33 93	19*p*44
Mongolia	2	†	†
Montserrat	1	010 1 809	†
Morocco	1	010 212	00*p*44
Mozambique	1	010 258	†
Myanmar	1	010 95	†
Namibia	1	010 264	091 44
Nauru	2	010 674	00 44
Nepal	1	010 977	00 44
Netherlands	*ec*	010 31	09*p*44
Netherlands Antilles	1	010 599	00 44
New Caledonia	2	010 687	00 44
New Zealand	2	010 64	00 44
Nicaragua	1	010 505	00 44
Niger	1	010 227	00 44
Nigeria	1	010 234	009 44
Niue	2	010 683	
Norfolk Island	2	010 672	
Norway	*e*	010 47	095 44
Oman	1	010 968	00 44
Pakistan	1	010 92	00 44
Palau	2	010 6809	
Panama	1	010 507	00 44
Papua New Guinea	2	010 675	31 44
Paraguay	1	010 595	002 or 003 44
Peru	1	010 51	00 44
Philippines	2	010 63	00 44
Poland	*e*	010 48	0*p*044
Portugal	*ec*	010 351	00 44
Puerto Rico	1	010 1 809	135 44
Qatar	1	010 974	044
Réunion	1	010 262	19*p*44
Romania	*e*	010 40	
Rwanda	1	010 250	†
St Helena	1	010 290	†
St Kitts and Nevis	1	010 1 809	†
St Lucia	1	010 1 809	0 44
St Pierre and Miquelon	1	010 508	†
St Vincent and the Grenadines	1	010 1 809	0 44
El Salvador	1	010 503	00 44
Samoa, American	2	010 684	144
San Marino	*ec*	010 39 549	00 44
São Tomé and Príncipe	1	010 23 912	†
Saudi Arabia	1	010 966	00 44
Senegal	1	010 221	00*p*44
Seychelles	1	010 248	0 44
Sierra Leone	1	010 232	†
Singapore	1	010 65	005 44
Slovenia	*e*	010 38	99 44
Solomon Islands	2	010 677	00 44
Somalia	1	010 252	†
South Africa	1	010 27	09 44
Spain	*ec*	010 34	07*p*44
Sri Lanka	1	010 94	00 44
Sudan	1	010 249	†
Suriname	1	010 597	001 44
Swaziland	1	010 268	00 44
Sweden	*e*	010 46	009 44*p*
Switzerland	*e*	010 41	00 44
Syria	1	010 963	00 44
Taiwan	2	010 886	002 44
Tanzania	1	010 255	†
Thailand	1	010 66	001 44
Togo	1	010 228	
Tonga	2	010 676	0 44
Trinidad and Tobago	1	010 1 809	01 44
Tristan da Cunha	1	†	
Tunisia	1	010 216	00 44
Turkey	*e*	010 90	9*p*944
Turks and Caicos Islands	1	010 1 809	†
Tuvalu	2	010 688	†
Uganda	1	010 256	†
United Arab Emirates	1	010 971	00 44
Uruguay	1	010 598	00 44
USA	1	010 1	011 44
Alaska		010 1 907	
Hawaii		010 1 808	
USSR (former)	*e*	010 7	810 44
Vanuatu	2	010 678	†
Vatican City State	*ec*	010 39 66982	
Venezuela	1	010 58	00 44
Vietnam	1	010 84	†
Virgin Islands (US)	1	010 1 809	011 44
Western Samoa	2	010 685	†
Yemen, North	1	010 967	00 44
South	1	010 969	00 44
Yugoslavia	*e*	010 38	99 44
Zaire	1	010 243	00 44
Zambia	1	010 260	00 44
Zimbabwe	1	010 263	110 44

British Currency

COIN

Gold Coins	*Nickel-Brass Coins*
†One hundred pounds £100	Two pounds £2
†Fifty pounds £50	One pound £1
†Twenty-five pounds £25	*Cupro-Nickel Coins*
†Ten pounds £10	Crown £5 (1990)
Five pounds £5	50 pence 50p
Two pounds £2	Crown 25p (pre-1990)
Sovereign £1	20 pence 20p
Half-Sovereign 50p	10 pence 10p (old)
	10 pence 10p (new)
Silver Coins	§5 pence 5p
‡*Maundy Money*	*Bronze Coins*
Fourpence 4p	2 pence 2p
Threepence 3p	1 penny 1p
Twopence 2p	*Copper-plated Steel Coins*
Penny 1p	2 pence 2p
	1 penny 1p

†Britannia gold bullion coins, introduced in October 1987.
‡Gifts of special money distributed by the Sovereign annually on Maundy Thursday to the number of aged poor men and women corresponding to the Sovereign's own age.
§New 5 pence coin introduced on 27 June 1990.

GOLD COIN

Gold ceased to circulate during the First World War. An Order of 27 April 1966 made it illegal for UK residents to continue holding more than four gold coins minted after 1837, or to acquire such coins unless they had been licensed as genuine collectors by the Bank of England. This Order was revoked on 1 April 1971 by the Exchange Control (Gold Coins Exemption) Order 1971, whereby residents of the United Kingdom, Channel Islands and the Isle of Man may freely buy and sell and hold gold coins.

The 1971 Order was revoked on 15 April 1975 by the Exchange Control (Gold Coins Exemption) Order 1975. Under this Order, Section 1 of the Exchange Control Act 1947 (which prohibits dealings in gold or foreign currency except with Treasury permission) was exempted for gold coins minted in or before 1837. The import of gold coins minted after 1837 was prohibited except by authorized dealers in gold with individual import licences from the Department of Trade and Industry, and dealing between other UK residents was restricted to coins already held in the UK.

Under an amendment, dated 16 December 1977, the exemptions contained in the 1975 Order were extended to cover gold coins minted in or before 1937.

The 1975 controls over the import of and dealing in gold coins were abolished on 13 June 1979 under the Exchange Control (Gold Coins Exemption) Order 1979. Gold coins may now be imported and exported without restriction, except gold coins which are more than fifty years old and valued at a sum in excess of £8,000; these cannot be exported without specific authorization from the Department of Trade and Industry.

On 1 April 1982 the Government introduced VAT (currently 17.5 per cent) on sales of all gold coin.

SILVER COIN

Prior to 1920 silver coins were struck from sterling silver, an alloy of which 925 parts in 1,000 were silver. In 1920 the proportion of silver was reduced to 500 parts. From 1 January 1947 all 'silver' coins, except Maundy money, have been struck from cupro-nickel, an alloy of copper 75 parts and nickel 25 parts, except for the 20p, composed of copper 84 parts, nickel 16 parts. Maundy coins continue to be struck from sterling silver.

BRONZE COIN

Bronze, introduced in 1860 to replace copper, is currently an alloy of copper 97 parts, zinc 2.5 parts and tin 0.5 part. These proportions have been subject to slight variations in the past.

The 'remedy' is the amount of variation from standard permitted in weight and fineness of coins when first issued from the Mint.

LEGAL TENDER

Gold, dated 1838 onwards, if not below least current weight, is legal tender to any amount. £5 (Crown 1990), £2 and £1 coins are legal tender to any amount; 50p and 20p coins are legal tender up to £10; 10p and 5p coins are legal tender up to £5, and bronze coins are legal tender for amounts up to 20p.

Farthings ceased to be legal tender on 31 December 1960, the halfpenny on 1 August 1969, the halfcrown on 1 January 1970, the threepence and penny on 31 August 1971, the sixpence on 30 June 1980, the decimal halfpenny on 31 December 1984 and the old 5p on 31 December 1990. The old 10p will cease to be legal tender on 30 June 1993.

The decimal system was introduced on 15 February 1971. Since 1982 the word 'new' in 'new pence' displayed on decimal coins has been dropped.

The Channel Islands and the Isle of Man issue their own coinage, which are legal tender only in the island of issue. For denominations, *see* below.

	Metal	*Standard weight* (g)	*Standard diameter* (cm)
Penny	bronze	3.56400	2.0320
Penny	copper-plated steel	3.56400	2.0320
2 pence	bronze	7.12800	2.5910
2 pence	copper-plated steel	7.12800	2.5910
5p	cupro-nickel	3.25	1.80
10p (new)	cupro-nickel	6.5	2.45
10p (old)	cupro-nickel	11.31036	2.8500
20p	cupro-nickel	5.0	2.14
25p Crown	cupro-nickel	28.27590	3.8608
50p	cupro-nickel	13.5	3.0
£1	copper/nickel/zinc	9.5	2.25
£2	copper/nickel/zinc	15.98	2.84
£5 Crown	cupro-nickel	28.28	3.861

BANKNOTES

Bank of England notes are currently issued in denominations of £5, £10, £20 and £50 for the amount of the Fiduciary Note Issue, and are legal tender in England and Wales.

The old white notes for £10, £20, £50, £100, £500 and £1,000, which were issued until 22 April 1943, ceased to be legal tender in May 1945, and the old white £5 note in March 1946.

The white £5 note issued between October 1945 and September 1956, the £5 notes issued between 1957 and 1963, bearing a portrait of Britannia and the first series to bear a portrait of The Queen, issued between 1963 and 1971, ceased to be legal tender on 14 March 1961, 27 June 1967 and 1 September 1973 respectively. The series of £1 notes issued during the years 1928 to 1960 and the 10*s*. notes of the same type issued from 1928 to 1961 (those without the royal portrait) ceased to be legal tender on 29 May and 30 October 1962 respectively. The £1 note first issued in March 1960 (bearing on the back a representation of Britannia) and the £10 note first issued in February 1964 (bearing a lion on the back) both bearing a portrait of The Queen on the front ceased to be legal tender on 1 June 1979. The £1 note first issued in 1978 ceased to be legal tender on 11 March 1988. The 10*s*. note was replaced by the 50p coin in October 1969, and ceased to be legal tender on 21 November 1970. Banknotes which are no longer legal tender are payable when presented at the head office of the Bank of England in London.

The first of the D series of banknotes was a £20 note issued on 9 July 1970. This was followed by the £5 note on 11 November 1971, which ceased to be legal tender on 29 November 1991. The D series £10 note was issued on 20 February 1975, £1 note on 9 February 1978 and £50 note on 20 March 1981. The £1 coin was introduced on 21 April 1983 to replace the £1 note. The predominant identifying feature of each note is the portrayal on the back of a prominent figure from Britain's history, namely:

£5	The Duke of Wellington
£10	Florence Nightingale
£20	William Shakespeare
£50	Sir Christopher Wren

A new series of notes was introduced in June 1990 when a new £5 was issued, followed by a £20 note in June 1991 and the £10 note on 29 April 1992. This new series will eventually replace the D series. The historical figures portrayed in this series to date are:

£5	George Stephenson
£10	Charles Dickens
£20	Michael Faraday

The £50 note will be issued within the next two years to commemorate the tercentenary of the Bank of England, and will carry a portrait of Sir John Houblon, the first governor.

Note Circulation

Note circulation is highest at the two peak spending periods of the year—around Christmas and during the summer holiday period. A peak of £18,720 million was reached immediately prior to Christmas 1991, a 1.7 per cent increase on the previous year.

The proportion of the total value of £1 notes in circulation at end February 1992 compared with the previous year, remained constant at 0.4 per cent. £5 notes fell from 8.9 per cent to 7.2 per cent. £10 notes decreased from 37.8 per cent to 35.6 per cent. £20 and £50 notes increased from 31.5 per cent and 15.4 per cent to 32.8 per cent and 15.6 per cent respectively.

On 28 February 1992 the values of notes in circulation were:

£1	£59,363,872
£5	£1,165,687,610
£10	£5,743,547,400
£20	£5,287,825,840
£50	£2,515,070,300

Other Banknotes

Scotland – Banknotes are issued by three Scottish banks. The Royal Bank of Scotland and the Bank of Scotland issue notes for £5, £10, £20 and £100. The Royal Bank of Scotland also issues £1 notes. The Clydesdale Bank issues notes for £5, £10, £20, £50, £100. Scottish notes are not legal tender in Scotland but they enjoy there a status comparable to that of the Bank of England note.

Northern Ireland – Banknotes are issued by four banks in Northern Ireland. The Northern Bank and the Ulster Bank issue notes for £5, £10, £20, £50 and £100. The Allied Irish Bank and the Bank of Ireland issue notes for £5, £10, £20 and £100. Northern Irish notes are not legal tender in Northern Ireland but they circulate widely and enjoy a status comparable to that of Bank of England notes.

Channel Islands – The States of Jersey issues its own currency notes and coinage. The note denominations are for £1, £5, £10, £20 and £50. Seven denominations of coins are issued: 1p, 2p, 5p, 10p, 20p, 50p and £1. The States of Guernsey issues its own currency notes and coinage. The notes are for £1, £5, £10 and £20. The denomination of coins are 1p, 2p, 5p, 10p, 20p, 50p, £1 and £2.

The Isle of Man – The Isle of Man Government issues notes for £1, £5, £10, £20 and £50. Although these notes are only legal tender in the Isle of Man they are accepted at face value in branches of the clearing banks in the United Kingdom. The Isle of Man issues coins for 1p, 2p, 5p, 10p, 20p, 50p, £1, £2 and £5.

Although none of the series of notes specified above is legal tender in the United Kingdom they are generally accepted by the banks irrespective of their place of issue. At one time the banks made a commission charge for handling Scottish and Irish notes but this was abolished some years ago.

Slang Terms for Money

(Reproduced from *Whitaker's Almanack* 1891)

In addition to the ordinary terms there are others which, although puzzling to a foreigner, are tolerably well understood in this country. In Scotland, a man who flies 'kites' may not be worth a 'bodle', and in England not worth a 'mag' – coins which no one ever saw. Such a man will toss you for a 'bob'. He, of course, would be shunned by the lady who lost a 'pony' on last year's Oaks, and by her husband who lost a 'monkey' on the Derby at Epsom a day or two previously. A gentleman who is worth a 'plum' (£100,000) need never be short of 'tin'; while the outcast who begs a few 'coppers' in order to procure a bed generally has no 'blunt'. The following words are commonly in use:

A Joey = 4*d*.
A Tanner = 6*d*.
A Bob = 1*s*.
Half a Bull = 2*s*. 6*d*.
A Bull = 5*s*.
A Quid = £1.
A Pony = £25.
A Monkey = £500.
A Kite = An accommodation Bill.
Browns = Copper or bronze.
Tin = Money generally.
Blunt = Silver, or money in general.

Banking

Deposit-taking institutions may be broadly divided into two sectors: the monetary sector, which is predominantly banks and is supervised by the Bank of England; and those institutions outside the monetary sector, of which the most important are the building societies and the National Savings Bank.

The main institutions within the British banking system are the Bank of England (the central bank), the clearing banks (the major retail banks), the merchant banks, the overseas banks, and the discount houses.

The Banking Act 1987 established a single category of authorized institutions eligible to carry out banking business. Under the 1987 Act, the Bank of England exercises a regulatory role over the banking system, and ensures the efficient functioning of payment and settlement systems and efficient services. In its role as the central bank, the Bank of England also acts as banker to the Government and as a note-issuing authority. It is responsible for executing monetary policy and therefore sets the base rates.

BANK BASE RATES 1991–2 (*see also* Stop-press)

12 July 1991	11.0%
4 September 1991	10.5%
5 May 1992	10.0%

CLEARING BANKS

The clearing banks are Abbey National, Bank of Scotland, Barclays, Clydesdale, Co-operative, Coutts, Girobank, Lloyds, Midland, National Westminster, The Royal Bank of Scotland Group, the TSB and the Yorkshire Bank.

Banking hours differ throughout Great Britain. Many banks in England and Wales are experimenting with longer hours and Saturday morning opening, and hours vary from branch to branch. Current minimum opening hours are:

ENGLAND AND WALES: Monday–Friday 9.30–3.30 (City of London town clearers 9.30–3).

SCOTLAND: Monday–Wednesday, Friday, 9.15–4.45; Thursday 9.15–5.30.

NORTHERN IRELAND: Open four days a week 10–3; open 9.30–5 one day a week.

CLEARING SERVICES

The Association for Payment Clearing Services (APACS) manages the payment clearing systems and oversees money transmission in the UK. It is an umbrella organization for three separate companies:

BACS Ltd provides an automated service for inter-bank clearing of payment and collection transactions in the UK (e.g. standing orders, direct debits).

The Cheque and Credit Clearing Company Ltd operates bulk clearing systems for inter-bank cheques and paper credit items.

CHAPS and Town Clearing Company Ltd provides same-day clearing for high value electronic funds transfers and cheques.

Membership of APACS and the operational clearing companies is open to any appropriately regulated financial institution providing payment services and meeting the relevant membership criteria. As at June 1991, APACS had 21 members, comprising the major banks and building societies.

ASSOCIATION FOR PAYMENT CLEARING SERVICES (APACS), Mercury House, Triton Court, 14 Finsbury Square, London EC2A 1BR. Tel: 071-711 6200. *Head of Public Affairs*, R. Tyson-Davies

BACS LTD, De Havilland Road, Edgware, Middlesex HA8 5QA. *Chief Executive*, A. E. Robinson

CHEQUE AND CREDIT CLEARING COMPANY LTD, Mercury house, Triton Court, 14 Finsbury Square, London EC2A 1BR. *Chief Inspector*, E. W. Stubbs

CHAPS AND TOWN CLEARING COMPANY LTD, Mercury House, Triton Court, 14 Finsbury Square, London EC2A 1BR. *Chief Inspector*, E. W. Stubbs

FINANCIAL RESULTS 1991

Bank Group	P/L. *before taxation* £m	P/L. *after taxation* £m	*Total assets* £m	*Number of UK branches*
Abbey National	618	414	57,405,000	678
†Bank of Scotland	140.7	89.4	27,741	500
Barclays	533	296	138,108	2,600
Clydesdale	64.02	42.19	5,123.2	346
Co-operative	−5,972	−2,629	2,758.19	107
Coutts & Co.	−15.17	−10.88	5,062.33	18
*Girobank	48.8	35.1	2,478.9	20,000
Lloyds	645	449	51,306	1,900
Midland	36	−33	59,408	1,830
National Westminster	110	52	122,569	2,816
The Royal Bank of Scotland Group	57.7	90.8	32,200	800
*Yorkshire Bank	107.03	71.8	4,413.4	261

*Nine months only
†For year ended 29 February 1992

AUTHORIZED INSTITUTIONS

As at 29 February 1992, a total of 518 institutions were authorized to undertake banking business, of which 263 were UK-incorporated and 255 were incorporated outside the UK.

Authorized institutions as at 7 August 1992 are listed below.

Incorporated in UK

(Including partnerships formed under the law of any part of the UK)

*In administration
†Provisional liquidator appointed

ABC International Bank PLC
ANZ Grindlays Bank PLC
AY Bank Ltd
Abbey National PLC
Abbey National Treasury Services PLC
Adam & Company PLC
Afghan National Credit & Finance Ltd
Airdrie Savings Bank
Aitken Hume Bank PLC
Ak International Bank Ltd
Albaraka International Bank Ltd
Alexanders Discount PLC
Alliance Trust (Finance) Ltd
Allied Bank Philippines (UK) PLC
Allied Trust Bank Ltd
Anglo Irish Asset Finance PLC
Anglo-Romanian Bank Ltd
Henry Ansbacher & Co. Ltd
Assemblies of God Property Trust
Associates Capital Corporation Ltd
Avco Trust PLC

BNL Investment Bank PLC
Bank Leumi (UK) PLC
Bank of America International Ltd
Bank of Boston Ltd
Bank of Cyprus (London) Ltd
The Bank of Edinburgh PLC
Bank of Scotland
Bank of Scotland Treasury Services PLC
Bank of Tokyo International Ltd
Bank of Wales PLC
Bankers Trust International PLC
Banque Belge Ltd
Banque de la Méditerranée (UK) Ltd
Banque Nationale de Paris PLC
The Baptist Union Corporation Ltd
Barclays Bank PLC
Barclays Bank Trust Company Ltd
Barclays de Zoete Wedd Ltd
Baring Brothers & Co. Ltd
Belmont Bank Ltd
Beneficial Bank PLC
Birmingham Capital Trust PLC
Boston Safe Deposit and Trust Company (UK) Ltd
*British and Commonwealth Merchant Bank PLC
The British Bank of the Middle East
The British Linen Bank Ltd
British Railways Savings Company Ltd
Brown, Shipley & Co. Ltd
Bunge Finance Ltd

CLF Municipal Mutual Bank PLC
Caledonian Bank PLC
Cater Allen Ltd
Central Hispano Bank UK Ltd
Chancery PLC
The Charities Aid Foundation Money Management Company Ltd
Chartered Trust PLC
Chartered West LB Ltd
Charterhouse Bank Ltd
Chase Investment Bank Ltd
Chemical Investment Bank Ltd
Chesterfield Street Trust Ltd
Citibank Trust Ltd
Citicorp Investment Bank Ltd
City Merchants Bank Ltd
City Trust Ltd
Clive Discount Company Ltd
Close Brothers Ltd
Clydesdale Bank PLC
Clydesdale Bank Finance Corporation Ltd
Combined Capital Ltd
Commercial Bank Trust PLC
Commercial Bank of London PLC
Confederation Bank Ltd
Consolidated Credits Bank Ltd
Co-operative Bank PLC
County Nat West Ltd
Coutts & Co.
Credito Italiano International Ltd
Credit Suisse Financial Products

DG Investment Bank Ltd
Daiwa Europe Bank PLC
Dalbeattie Finance Co. Ltd
Dao Heng Bank PLC
Darlington Merchant Credits Ltd
Dartington & Co. Ltd
Davenham Trust PLC
Den norske Bank PLC
The Dorset, Somerset & Wilts. Investment Society Ltd
Dryfield Finance Ltd
Dunbar Bank PLC
Duncan Lawrie Ltd

Eccles Savings and Loans Ltd
*Edington PLC
Enskilda Securities-Skandinaviska Enskilda Ltd
Equatorial Bank PLC
Exeter Bank Ltd

FIBI Bank (UK) Ltd
Fairmount Trust Ltd
Family Finance Ltd
FennoScandia Bank Ltd
Financial & General Bank PLC
James Finlay Bank Ltd
First National Bank PLC
First National Commercial Bank PLC
The First Personal Bank PLC
Robert Fleming & Co. Ltd
Ford Credit PLC
Foreign & Colonial Management Ltd
Forward Trust Ltd
Forward Trust Personal Finance Ltd
Robert Fraser & Partners Ltd
Frizzell Banking Services Ltd

Gartmore Money Management Ltd
Gerrard & National Ltd
Girobank PLC
Goldman Sachs Ltd

Granville Trust Ltd
Gresham Trust PLC
Greyhound Bank PLC
Guinness Mahon & Co. Ltd

HFC Bank PLC
Habibsons Bank Ltd
Hambros Bank Ltd
Hampshire Trust PLC
The Hardware Federation Finance Co. Ltd
Harrods Bank Ltd
Harton Securities Ltd
Havana International Bank Ltd
The Heritable & General Investment Bank Ltd
Hill Samuel Bank Ltd
Hill Samuel Personal Finance Ltd
C. Hoare & Co.
Julian Hodge Bank Ltd
Holdenhurst Securities PLC
Hongkong Bank London Ltd
Humberclyde Finance Group Ltd
Hungarian International Bank Ltd

3i PLC
3i Group PLC
IBJ International PLC
Independent Trust and Finance Ltd
International Mexican Bank Ltd
Iran Overseas Investment Bank Ltd
Italian International Bank PLC

Jordan International Bank PLC
Leopold Joseph & Sons Ltd

KDB Bank (UK) Ltd
KEXIM Bank (UK) Ltd
King & Shaxson Ltd
Kleinwort Benson Ltd
Kleinwort Benson Investment Management Ltd
Korea Long Term Credit Bank International Ltd

LTCB International Ltd
Lazard Brothers & Co. Ltd
Lloyds Bank PLC
Lloyds Bank (BLSA) Ltd
Lloyds Bowmaker Ltd
Lloyds Merchant Bank Ltd
Lloyds Private Banking Ltd
Lombard Bank Ltd
Lombard & Ulster Ltd
Lombard North Central PLC
London Scottish Bank PLC
London Trust Bank PLC
Lordsvale Finance PLC

McDonnell Douglas Bank Ltd
McNeill Pearson Ltd
Manchester Exchange and Investment Bank Ltd
W. M. Mann & Co. (Investments) Ltd
Marks and Spencer Financial Services Ltd
Mase Westpac Ltd
Matheson Bank Ltd
Matlock Bank Ltd
Meghraj Bank Ltd
Mercury Provident PLC
Merrill Lynch International Bank Ltd
The Methodist Chapel Aid Association Ltd
Midland Bank PLC
Midland Bank Trust Company Ltd
Minories Finance Ltd
Minster Trust Ltd
Samuel Montagu & Co. Ltd
Morgan Grenfell & Co. Ltd

Moscow Narodny Bank Ltd
Mount Banking Corporation Ltd
Mutual Trust and Savings Ltd
Mynshul Bank PLC

NIIB Group Ltd
NWS Bank PLC
The National Mortgage Bank PLC
National Westminster Bank PLC
NationsBank Europe Ltd
The Nikko Bank (UK) PLC
Noble Grossart Ltd
Nomura Bank International PLC
Nordbanken UK Ltd
Northern Bank Ltd
Northern Bank Executor & Trustee Company Ltd
Norwich General Trust Ltd
Nykredit Mortgage Bank PLC

Omega Trust Co. Ltd

PaineWebber International Bank Ltd
People's Bank Ltd
Pointon York Ltd
The Private Bank and Trust Company Ltd
Provincial Bank PLC

Ralli Investment Company Ltd
R. Raphael & Sons PLC
Rathbone Bros. & Co. Ltd
Rea Brothers Ltd
Reliance Bank Ltd
Riggs AP Bank Ltd
N. M. Rothschild & Sons Ltd
Roxburghe Bank Ltd
Royal Bank of Canada Europe Ltd
The Royal Bank of Scotland PLC
Royal Trust Bank
RoyScot Trust PLC

Sanwa International PLC
Saudi International Bank (Al-Bank Al-Saudi Al-Alami Ltd)
Schroder Leasing Ltd
J. Henry Schroder Wagg & Co. Ltd
Scotiabank (UK) Ltd
Scottish Amicable Money Managers Ltd
Seccombe Marshall & Campion PLC
Secure Homes Ltd
Security Pacific Trust Ltd
Singer & Friedlander Ltd
Smith & Williamson Securities
Société Générale Merchant Bank PLC
Southsea Mortgage & Investment Co. Ltd
Standard Bank London Ltd
Standard Chartered Bank
Standard Chartered Bank Africa PLC
Sterling Bank & Trust Ltd
Svenska International PLC

TSB Bank PLC
TSB Bank Northern Ireland PLC
TSB Bank Scotland PLC
Tokai Bank Europe Ltd
Turkish Bank (UK) Ltd
Tyndall & Co. Ltd

UBAF Bank Ltd
UCB Bank PLC
ULC Trust Ltd
Ulster Bank Ltd
Unibank PLC
Union Discount Company Ltd

The United Bank of Kuwait PLC
United Dominions Trust Ltd
Unity Trust Bank PLC

Wagon Finance Ltd
S. G. Warburg & Co. Ltd
Western Trust & Savings Ltd
Whiteaway Laidlaw Bank Ltd
Wimbledon & South West Finance Co. PLC
Wintrust Securities Ltd
Woodchester Bank UK PLC

Yamaichi Bank (UK) PLC
Yorkshire Bank PLC
H. F. Young & Co. Ltd

INCORPORATED OUTSIDE THE UK

(Including partnerships or other unincorporated associations formed under the law of any member state of the European Community other than the UK)

†Provisional liquidator appointed

ABN AMRO Bank NV
ABSA Bank Ltd
AIB Capital Markets PLC
AIB Finance Ltd
ASLK – CGER Bank
Allied Bank of Pakistan Ltd
Allied Irish Banks PLC
American Express Bank Ltd
Anglo Irish Bank Corporation PLC
Arab African International Bank
Arab Bank PLC
Arab Banking Corporation BSC
Arab National Bank
Ashikaga Bank Ltd
Australia & New Zealand Banking Group Ltd

BfG Bank AG
BSI – Banca della Svizzera Italiana
Banca Cassa di Risparmio di Torino SpA
Banca Commerciale Italiana
Banca di Roma SpA
Banca Nazionale dell'Agricoltura SpA
Banca Nazionale del Lavoro
Banca Popolare di Milano
Banca Popolare di Novara
Banca Serfin SA
Banco Ambrosiano Veneto SpA
Banco Bilbao–Vizcaya
Banco Central Hispanoamericano SA
Banco de la Nación Argentina
Banco de Sabadell
Banco di Napoli SpA
Banco di Sicilia SpA
Banco do Brasil SA
Banco do Estado de São Paulo SA
Banco Espanõl de Crédito SA
Banco Espirito Santo e Comercial de Lisboa
Banco Exterior Internacional SA
Banco Mercantil de São Paulo SA
Banco Nacional de México SNC
Banco Nacional Ultramarino SA
Banco Português do Atlântico
Banco Real SA
Banco Santander
Banco Totta & Açores SA
Bancomer SA
Bangkok Bank Ltd
Bank Julius Baer & Co. Ltd
Bank Bumiputra Malaysia Berhad
Bank Ekspor Impor Indonesia
Bank Handlowy w Warszawie SA
Bank Hapoalim BM
Bank Mees & Hope NV
Bank Mellat
Bank Melli Iran
Bank Negara Indonesia 1946
Bank of America NT & SA
Bank of Baroda
The Bank of N. T. Butterfield & Son Ltd
Bank of Ceylon
Bank of China
The Bank of East Asia Ltd
The Bank of Fukuoka Ltd
Bank of India
The Bank of Ireland
Bank of Montreal
The Bank of New York
Bank of New Zealand
The Bank of Nova Scotia
Bank of Oman Ltd
Bank of Seoul
The Bank of Tokyo Ltd
The Bank of Yokohama Ltd
Bank Saderat Iran
Bank Sepah-Iran
Bank Tejarat
Bankers Trust Company
Banque Arabe et Internationale d'Investissement
Banque Banorabe
Banque Bruxelles Lambert SA
Banque Française de l'Orient
Banque Française du Commerce Extérieur
Banque Indosuez
Banque Internationale à Luxembourg SA
Banque Nationale de Paris
Banque Paribas
Banque Worms
Bayerische Hypotheken-und Wechsel-Bank AG
Bayerische Landesbank Girozentrale
Bayerische Vereinsbank AG
Beirut Riyad Bank SAL
Belgolaise SA
Berliner Bank AG
Berliner Handels-und Frankfurter Bank
Boston Safe Deposit and Trust Company
Byblos Bank SAL

CARIPLO – Cassa di Risparmio delle Provincie Lombarde SpA
CBI-TDB Union Bancaire Privée
Caisse Nationale de Crédit Agricole
Canadian Imperial Bank of Commerce
Canara Bank
The Chase Manhattan Bank NA
Chemical Bank
The Chiba Bank Ltd
Cho Hung Bank
Christiania Bank og Kreditkasse
The Chuo Trust & Banking Co. Ltd
Citibank NA
Commercial Bank of Korea Ltd
Commerzbank AG
Commonwealth Bank of Australia
Compagnie Financière de CIC et de l'Union Européenne
Confederacion Española de Cajas de Ahorros
Continental Bank, National Association
CoreStates Bank NA

Crédit Commercial de France
Crédit du Nord
Crédit Lyonnais
Crédit Lyonnais Bank Nederland NV
Crédit Suisse
Creditanstalt-Bankverein
Credito Italiano
Cyprus Credit Bank Ltd
The Cyprus Popular Bank

The Dai-Ichi Kangyo Bank Ltd
The Daiwa Bank Ltd
Den Danske Bank Aktieselskab
Den norske Bank A/S
Deutsche Bank AG
Deutsche Genossenschaftsbank
The Development Bank of Singapore Ltd
Discount Bank and Trust Company
Dresdner Bank AG

Fidelity Bank NA
First Bank of Nigeria PLC
First Commercial Bank
First Interstate Bank of California
The First National Bank of Boston
The First National Bank of Chicago
Fleet Bank of Massachusetts, NA
French Bank of Southern Africa Ltd
The Fuji Bank Ltd

Generale Bank
Ghana Commercial Bank
Girocredit Bank Aktiengesellschaft der Sparkassen
Gota Bank
Gulf International Bank BSC

Habib Bank AG Zurich
Habib Bank Ltd
Hamburgische Landesbank Girozentrale
Hanil Bank
Harris Trust and Savings Bank
Hessische Landesbank-Girozentrale
The Hiroshima Bank, Ltd
The Hokkaido Takushoku Bank Ltd
The Hokuriku Bank Ltd
The Hongkong and Shanghai Banking Corporation Ltd

The Industrial Bank of Japan Ltd
Internationale Nederlanden Bank NV
Istituto Bancario San Paolo di Torino SpA

The Joyo Bank Ltd
Jyske Bank

Kansallis-Osake-Pankki
Korea Exchange Bank
Korea First Bank
Kredietbank NV
The Kyowa Saitama Bank, Ltd

The Long-Term Credit Bank of Japan, Ltd

Malayan Banking Berhad
Mellon Bank NA
Merchants National Bank & Trust Company of Indianapolis
Middle East Bank Ltd
The Mitsubishi Bank, Ltd
The Mitsubishi Trust and Banking Corporation
The Mitsui Trust & Banking Co. Ltd
Monte dei Paschi di Siena
Morgan Guaranty Trust Company of New York
Multibanco Comermex SNC

NBD Bank, NA
National Australia Bank Ltd
National Bank of Abu Dhabi
National Bank of Canada
The National Bank of Dubai Ltd
National Bank of Egypt
National Bank of Greece SA
The National Bank of Kuwait SAK
National Bank of Pakistan
NationsBank of North Carolina, NA
Nedcor Bank Ltd
The Nippon Credit Bank, Ltd
Nordbanken
Norddeutsche Landesbank Girozentrale
The Norinchukin Bank
The Northern Trust Company

Oversea-Chinese Banking Corporation Ltd
Overseas Trust Bank Ltd
Overseas Union Bank Ltd

Philippine National Bank
Postipankki Ltd

Qatar National Bank SAQ

The R&I Bank of Western Australia Ltd
Rabobank Nederland (Coöperatieve Centrale Raiffeisen-Boerenleenbank BA)
†Rafidain Bank
Raiffeisen Zentralbank Osterreich AG
Republic National Bank of New York
Reserve Bank of Australia
The Riggs National Bank of Washington, DC
Riyad Bank
Royal Bank of Canada

The Sakura Bank, Ltd
The Sanwa Bank, Ltd
Saudi American Bank
Scandinavian Bank (Skandinaviska Enskilda Banken)
Shanghai Commercial Bank Ltd
Shinhan Bank
The Siam Commercial Bank Ltd
Société Générale
Sonali Bank
State Bank of India
State Bank of New South Wales Ltd
State Bank of South Australia
State Street Bank and Trust Company
Südwestdeutsche Landesbank Girozentrale
The Sumitomo Bank, Ltd
The Sumitomo Trust & Banking Co. Ltd
Svenska Handelsbanken
SwedBank
Swiss Bank Corporation
Swiss Volksbank
Syndicate Bank

TC Ziraat Bankasi
The Thai Farmers Bank Ltd
The Tokai Bank, Ltd
The Toronto-Dominion Bank
The Toyo Trust & Banking Company, Ltd
Türkiye Iş Bankasi AŞ

Uco Bank
Ulster Investment Bank Ltd
Union Bank of Finland Ltd
Union Bank of Nigeria PLC
Union Bank of Switzerland
United Bank Ltd
United Mizrahi Bank Ltd
United Overseas Bank (Banque Unie pour les Pays d'Outre Mer)

United Overseas Bank Ltd
Westdeutsche Landesbank Girozentrale
Westpac Banking Corporation
Wirtschafts- und Privatbank
The Yasuda Trust & Banking Co., Ltd
Z-Länderbank Bank Austria AG
Zambia National Commercial Bank Ltd
Zivnostenská Banka National Corporation

The National Debt

Net central government borrowing each year represents an addition to the National Debt. At the end of March 1991 the National Debt amounted to some £198,700 million of which about £8,300 million was in currencies other than sterling. Of the £190,400 million sterling debt, £123,900 million consisted of gilt-edged stock; of this, 29 per cent had a maturity of up to five years, 46 per cent a maturity of over five years and up to 15 years, and 25 per cent a maturity of over 15 years or undated. The remaining sterling debt was made up mainly of national savings (£31,100 million), certificates of tax deposits, Treasury bills, and Ways and Means advances (very short-term internal government borrowing).

Sizeable Trust Funds have been established over the past fifty years for the purpose of reducing the National Debt. The National Fund was established in 1927 with an original gift of £499,878. At 31 March 1991 it was valued at £77,718,411; it is administered by Baring Brothers & Co. Ltd. The Elsie Mackay Fund was established in 1929 with an original gift of £527,809 to run for 45–50 years. It was wound up on 19 January 1979, when it was valued at £4,902,864. The John Buchanan Fund was established in 1932 with gifts totalling £36,702 to run for 50 years. It was wound up on 28 February 1982, when it was valued at £204,138.

The Cost of Living

The first cost-of-living index to be calculated in Great Britain was the one which took July 1914 as 100 and was based on the pattern of expenditure of working class families in 1904. Since 1947 the General Index of Retail Prices has superseded the cost-of-living index, although the older term is still often popularly applied to it. This index is designed to reflect the month-by-month changes in the average level of retail prices of goods and services purchased by the 'majority' of households in the United Kingdom, including practically all wage-earners and most small and medium salary-earners. For spending coming within the scope of the index, a representative list of items is selected and the prices actually charged for these items are collected at regular intervals. In working out the index figure, the price changes are 'weighted' – that is, given different degrees of importance – in accordance with the pattern of consumption of the average family.

A more widely used guide when considering changes in the average level of prices of all consumer goods and services, particularly over a number of years, is the consumer price index, now renamed the consumers' expenditure deflator. This index, which has been calculated back to 1938, covers the expenditure of all consumers as defined for national income purposes, and compares the price of goods and services actually purchased in a given year with the prices of the same goods and services in a base year.

During 1973 the Central Statistical Office constructed an annual index of prices of consumer goods and services over the period 1914 to 1972. This index has been constructed by linking together the pre-war cost-of-living index for the period 1914–38, the consumers' expenditure deflator for the period 1938 and 1946–62 and the General Index of Retail Prices for the period 1962–72.

In August 1979, the tax and price index (TPI) was introduced in order to provide a statistic which incorporates the effects of direct and indirect taxation, as well as prices, on taxpayers. The TPI is not directly concerned with the purchasing power of money, however, but with the purchasing power of pre-tax income. The General Index of Retail Prices thus retains its function of measuring the changes in the prices of goods and services purchased by households (from their post-tax income), and therefore as an indicator of the purchasing power of money.

	Long term index of consumer goods and services (Jan. 1987=100)	Comparable purchasing power of £1 in 1991
1914	2.8	47.68
1915	3.5	38.14
1920	7.0	19.08
1925	5.0	26.70
1930	4.5	29.67
1935	4.0	33.38
1938	4.4	30.34
There are no official figures for 1939–45		
1946	7.4	18.04
1950	9.0	14.80
1955	11.2	11.91
1960	12.6	10.60
1965	14.8	9.02
1970	18.5	7.20
1975	34.2	3.90
1976	39.8	3.35
1977	46.1	2.90
1978	50.0	2.67
1979	56.6	2.36
1980	66.8	2.00
1981	74.8	1.78
1982	81.2	1.64
1983	84.9	1.57
1984	89.2	1.50
1985	94.6	1.41
1986	97.8	1.37
1987	101.9	1.31
1988	106.9	1.25
1989	115.2	1.16
1990	126.1	1.06
1991	133.5	1.00

By employing this table an annual purchasing power of the pound index may be derived by taking the inverse of the price index. So, for example, if the purchasing power of the pound is taken to be 100p in 1975, then its comparable purchasing power in 1991 would be:

$$100 \times \frac{34.2}{133.5} = 25.6\text{p}$$

It should be noted that these figures can only be approximate.

Mutual Societies

FRIENDLY SOCIETIES IN GREAT BRITAIN

Friendly societies are voluntary mutual organizations, the main purposes of which are the provision of relief or maintenance during sickness, unemployment or retirement, and the provision of life assurance. Many of the older traditional societies complement their business activities by social activity and a general care for individual members in ways normally outside the scope of a purely commercial organization. There are three main categories of friendly societies: societies with separately registered branches, commonly called orders; centralized societies, which conduct business directly with members (having no separately registered branches); and collecting societies. Collecting societies conduct industrial assurance business and are subject to the requirements of the Industrial Assurance Acts in addition to the Friendly Societies Acts. Industrial assurance is life assurance for which the premiums are payable at intervals of less than two months and are received by means of collectors who make house-to-house visits for the purpose.

Long before the term 'friendly society' came into use, the seeds of voluntary mutual insurance had been sown in the ancient religious and trade guilds. Guilds had become widespread in Britain by the 14th century. By then, the purely charitable character of the original guilds had largely changed with the emergence of numerous small institutions adopting primitive mutual insurance methods of a regular flat rate contribution to insure relief when sick or in old age and a payment to the widow in the event of death. The present register of friendly societies includes several societies which have been in existence for upwards of 200 years, the oldest, operating in Scotland, being the Incorporation of Carters in Leith, established as long ago as 1555.

The first Act for the encouragement and protection of friendly societies in this country was not passed until 1793, but various amending Acts were passed during the next century as the result of the recommendations of successive select committees (including a Royal Commission in 1871). The rules and other documents of societies deposited with local justices passed into the custody of the Registrar of Friendly Societies following the Act of 1846. Those relating to some societies no longer on the register have been transferred to the Public Record Office for permanent preservation.

The Friendly Societies Act 1974 allows three other main classes of society to be registered: benevolent societies, working men's clubs and specially authorized societies. Benevolent societies are established for any charitable or benevolent purpose, to provide the same type of benefits as would be permissible for a friendly society, but in contrast the benefits must be for persons who are not members instead of, or in addition to, members. Working men's clubs provide social and recreational facilities for members. Specially authorized societies are registered for any purpose authorized by the Treasury as a purpose to which some or all of the provisions of the 1974 Act ought to be extended. Examples are societies for the promotion of science, literature and the fine arts, or to enable members to pursue an interest in sports and games.

The most recent legislation, the Friendly Societies Act 1992, creates a new legislative framework for friendly societies, enabling them to provide a wider range of services to their members and allowing them to compete on more equal terms with other financial institutions. At the same time it provides for more flexible prudential supervision to safeguard members of societies.

The Act enables friendly societies to incorporate and establish subsidiaries to provide various financial and other services to their members and the public. The activities which subsidiaries will be able to conduct as the relevant provisions come into force under subordinate legislation include those: to establish and manage unit trust schemes and Personal Equity Plans; to arrange for the provision of credit, whether as agents or providers; to carry on long-term or general insurance business; to provide insurance intermediary services; to provide fund management services for trustees of pension funds; to administer estates and execute trusts of wills; and to establish and manage sheltered housing, residential homes for the elderly, hospitals and nursing homes.

The Act establishes a new framework to oversee friendly societies, including a Friendly Societies Commission, whose principal functions will be to regulate the activities of friendly societies, promote their financial stability and protect members' funds. All friendly societies carrying on insurance or non-insurance business will require authorization by the Commission, which will have a broad range of prudential powers. Friendly societies will also be brought within the scope of the Policyholders Protection Act 1975, the statutory investor protection scheme covering insurance policyholders.

The principal statistics at the end of 1990 are given in the table below.

	No. of societies	*No. of members* 000s	*Benefits paid* £000s	*Total funds* £000s
Orders and branches	1,480*	361†	5,463†	172,059†
Collecting societies	30	14,036‡	206,928	2,627,787
Other centralized societies	407	2,844	194,189	2,273,064
Benevolent societies	80	336	3,752	24,228
Working men's clubs	2,397	1,274	n/a	162,793
Specially authorized societies				
Loans	9	15	n/a	568
Others	139	95	641	18,530
Other	1	–	–	5

* 20 orders, 1,460 branches
† 1989 figure
‡ Assurances

INDUSTRIAL AND PROVIDENT SOCIETIES IN GREAT BRITAIN

The familiar 'Co-op' societies are amongst the wide variety which are registered under the Industrial and Provident Societies Act 1965. This consolidating Act, which is administered by the Chief Registrar of Friendly Societies, provides for the registration of societies and lays down the broad framework within which they must operate. Internal relations of societies are governed by their registered rules.

Registration under the Act confers upon a society corporate status by its registered name with perpetual succession and a common seal, and limited liability. A society qualifies for registration if it is carrying on an industry, business or trade, and it satisfies the Registrar either (a) that it is a bona fide co-operative society, or (b) that in view of the fact that its business is being, or is intended to be, conducted for the benefit of the community, there are special reasons why it should be registered under the Act rather than as a company under the Companies Act.

The Credit Unions Act 1979 added a new class of society registerable under the 1965 Act. It also made provision for the supervision of these savings and loan bodies. Unlike other classes, where the role of the Registry is solely that of a registration authority, it is for credit unions the prudential supervisor, seeking to encourage the prudent safekeeping of investors' money.

During 1990 the number of registered societies of all classes increased by 149 to 11,392. The largest single group was the 4,630 housing societies. The largest group in terms of turnover was that consisting of the retail societies, which includes those trading under the 'Co-op' sign, with sales in 1990 of £4,974 million. The principal statistics at the end of 1990 are given in the table below.

	No. of societies	*No. of members* 000s	*Funds of members* £000s	*Total assets* £000s
Retail	195	7,750	1,177,239	2,315,635
Wholesale and productive	202	58	534,553	1,393,402
Agricultural	1,079	343	208,321	556,403
Fishing	97	8	5,196	13,419
Social and recreational clubs	3,779	1,952	205,084	331,916
General service	1,135	496	5,111,085	5,855,015
Housing	4,630	171	11,121,968	16,524,287
Credit unions	275	54	14,378	17,274
TOTAL	11,392	10,830	18,377,824	27,007,352

BUILDING SOCIETIES IN THE UK

The Building Societies Act 1986 gave building societies a completely new legal framework, the first since the initial comprehensive building society legislation in 1874. The new Act replaced both the 1962 Act and the 1967 Act covering Northern Ireland, and therefore applies to societies based throughout the United Kingdom.

The 1986 Act made provision for a Building Societies Commission to promote the protection of shareholders and depositors, the financial stability of societies, and to administer the system of regulation of building societies provided under the Act. The First Commissioner and Chairman of the Commission is also Chief Registrar of Friendly Societies (*see* Index). Much of the Act is concerned with the powers of control of the Commission and provision in relation to the management of societies, accounts, audit and so on. But the greatest impact flowed from the new powers which societies could adopt, leading to an increased range of services which they might provide. There were also some significant changes in relation to members' rights.

Under the 1962 Act, raising funds to make loans was the only purpose for which a building society could exist. Under the 1986 Act that has only to be its principal purpose. The constitutional provisions include the right of members to have access to the register of members, entitlement to have notices of meetings and to vote, and the right of members to have a resolution circulated.

In addition to traditional mortgage business, the power of societies to lend in respect of shared ownership, index-linked and equity-linked schemes is given. Societies may also lend the deposit, lend on registered land before the borrower is registered as the owner and on other equitable interests. Provision is also made for societies to make advances secured on land outside the United Kingdom. Larger societies were able, for the first time, to make unsecured loans, and make loans on mobile homes.

Under the 1962 Act building societies could only hold land for the purposes of running their business. The 1986 Act gave building societies power to hold and develop land as a commercial asset. However, the land has to be primarily for residential purposes, or adjoining land, or for purposes incidental to the holding of residential land.

An Investor Protection Scheme and the Investor Protection Board which administers it were established under the Act. The Scheme comes into operation on the insolvency of a building society and protects the first £20,000 of a person's shares. Joint holdings are split between the holders so that, for example, a husband and wife can each have £20,000 of protected investments. The Board determines the percentage of protected investment in each case; there is a stautory maximum of 90 per cent.

Societies were also empowered to offer for the first time the following services:

(a) Money transmission services
(b) Foreign exchange services
(c) Making or receiving of payments as agents
(d) Management, as agents, of mortgage investments
(e) Management, as agents, of land (larger societies only)
(f) Arranging for the provision of services relating to the acquisition or disposal of investments for individuals
(g) Establishment and management of personal equity plans
(h) Arranging for the provision of credit to individuals
(i) Establishment and management of unit trust schemes for the provision of pensions (through a subsidiary)
(j) Establishment and administration of pension schemes
(k) Arranging for the provision of insurance of any description
(l) Giving advice on insurance of any description
(m) Estate agency service (through a subsidiary)
(n) Surveys and valuations of land
(o) Conveyancing services.

Technical problems emerged in relation to these services and in June 1988 Parliament made Orders which allowed societies to have the power to own up to 100 per cent of a life assurance company, 15 per cent of a general insurance company, 100 per cent of a stockbroking company and to offer an additional range of financial services including executorship and trusteeship, hire purchase and leasing and safe deposit facilities. The Orders also included an increase in the limit on unsecured personal loans from £5,000 to £10,000.

On mergers, the main difference is that borrowers have a vote. For a merger to be approved at least 50 per cent of borrowers who exercise their right to vote must vote in favour, as well as 75 per cent of qualifying share investors who vote. Provision is also made for a society to convert to company status. During 1989 the Abbey National became the first and, as yet, the only building society to complete the process of conversion to a company. During the year ended 31 March 1992 six mergers between societies were completed.

Ombudsman Scheme

Societies must belong to an ombudsman scheme for the investigation of complaints. Matters to be covered by the scheme include operation of share and deposit accounts, loans (but not the making of new loans), money transmission services, foreign exchange services, agency payments and receipts, and the provision of credit. Grounds for complaint include breach of the Act or contract, unfair treatment or maladministration, and where the complainant has suffered pecuniary loss or expense or inconvenience. A society must agree to be bound by decisions of the adjudicator unless it agrees to give notice to its members and the public of its reasons for not doing so. For address of the Building Societies Ombudsman scheme, *see* Index.

Building Societies 1990–1

	1990	1991
No. of societies	117	110
No. of shareholders (000s)	36,948	37,925
No. of depositors (000s)	4,299	4,698
No. of borrowers (000s)	6,724	6,998
Share balances (£m)	160,538	177,519
Deposit balances (£m)	40,696	49,517
Mortgage balances (£m)	175,745	196,946
Total assets (£m)	216,848	243,980
Advances during year		
No. (000s)	1,397	1,492
Amount (£m)	43,081	42,948
Average mortgage rate (%)	15.12	12.84

Mortgage Arrears and Repossessions

The deepest economic recession since the Second World War has resulted in a sharp rise in mortgage arrears and repossessions. During 1991, more than 75,000 properties were repossessed by building societies and at the end of the year 275,000 borrowers were six months or more in arrears with their mortgage payments. The figures for 1991 again showed a large increase on those for the previous year and at the end of 1991 this level of arrears existed in around 3 per cent of the total of nearly 10 million loans outstanding. Details of loans outstanding and properties repossessed for recent years are shown below.

	1985	1986	1987	1988	1989	1990	1991
No. of loans at end year (000s)	7,717	8,138	8,283	8,564	9,125	9,415	9,815
Properties repossessed in year							
No.	19,300	24,090	26,390	18,510	15,810	43,890	75,540
%	0.25	0.30	0.32	0.22	0.17	0.47	0.77

Interest Rates – Mortgage and Share

The interest rates prevailing on mortgage lending and share investment vary to a degree from society to society and in relation to the type or amount of loan or investment. General rate changes are made in response to market conditions and recent rates, with the dates of change, are given below.

The interval between the payments or compounding of interest is crucial in determining the competitiveness of particular societies' accounts. In order to make a true comparison of interest rates, the annual percentage rate or APR, which should appear in all advertisements and leaflets, must be used.

	Oct. '89	Feb. '90	April '90	Oct. '90	Feb. '91	May '91	July '91	Sept. '91	Jan. '92
Gross average rate for all share accounts %	12.36	13.41	14.35	14.19	13.47	11.16	10.20	9.77	9.73
Predominant mortgages rate %	13.50	14.50	15.40	14.50	13.75	12.45	11.95	11.50	10.95

SOCIETIES WITH TOTAL ASSETS EXCEEDING £1 MILLION

AT END OF FINANCIAL YEAR 1991

Est.	*Name of Society (abbreviated) and head office address*	*Share investors*	*Total assets £'000*
1985	Alliance and Leicester, 49 Park Lane, London WIY 4EQ	3,386,942	20,479,300
1853	Barnsley, Regent Street, Barnsley, South Yorks S70 2EH	28,642	115,104
1953	Bath Investment, 20 Charles Street, Bath BAI IHY	12,380	47,385
1866	Beverley, 57 Market Place, Beverley, N. Humberside HU17 8AA	5,923	31,166
1914	Bexhill-on-Sea, 2 Devonshire Square, Bexhill-on-Sea, Sussex TN40 IAE	2,821	15,677
1889	Birmingham Midshires, PO Box 81, 35–49 Lichfield Street, Wolverhampton WVI IEL	648,310	3,745,154
1851	Bradford and Bingley, Crossflatts, Bingley, West Yorks. BD16 2UA	1,040,237	11,910,260
1850	Bristol and West, Broad Quay, Bristol BS99 7AX	n/a	7,140,774
1856	Britannia, Newton House, Cheadle Road, Leek, Staffs. ST13 5RG	1,051,725	8,523,811
1907	Buckinghamshire, High Street, Chalfont St Giles, Bucks. HP8 4QB	6,005	40,359
1850	Cambridge, 32 St Andrew's Street, Cambridge CB2 3AR	40,500	266,065
1960	Catholic, 7 Strutton Ground, London SWIP 2HY	3,206	20,188
1899	Century, 23 Albany Street, Edinburgh EHI 3QW	1,211	9,332
1875	Chelsea, Thirlestaine Hall, Thirlestaine Road, Cheltenham, Glos. GL53 7AL	224,971	2,277,400
1850	Cheltenham and Gloucester, Barnett Way, Gloucester GL4 7RL	1,144,000	14,789,300
1845	Chesham, 12 Market Square, Chesham, Bucks. HP5 IER	9,161	59,900
1870	Cheshire, Castle Street, Macclesfield, Chesire SKII 6AH	227,374	1,101,107
1859	Chorley and District, 49–51 St Thomas's Road, Chorley, Lancs. PR7 IJL	7,480	48,457
1946	City and Metropolitan, 219 High Street, Bromley, Kent BRI IPR	10,108	84,740
1859	Clay Cross Benefit, 42 Thanet Street, Clay Cross, Chesterfield S45 9JT	3,200	13,277
1884	Coventry, PO Box 9, High Street, Coventry CVI 5QN	413,715	2,369,912
1850	Cumberland, Cumberland House, Castle Street, Carlisle CA3 8RX	143,776	482,813
1946	Darlington, Tubwell Row, Darlington, Co. Durham DLI IMX	40,828	225,028
1859	Derbyshire, Duffield Hall, Duffield, Derby DE5 IAG	250,853	1,350,609
1858	Dudley, Dudley House, Stone Street, Dudley DYI INP	15,187	65,666
1869	Dunfermline, 12 East Port, Dunfermline, Fife KY12 7LD	127,434	644,111
1857	Earl Shilton, 22 The Hollow, Earl Shilton, Leicester LE9 7NB	9,467	49,179
1980	Ecology, 18 Station Road, Cross Hills, Keighley, West Yorks BD20 7EH	2,349	8,067
1865	Furness, 51–55 Duke Street, Barrow-in-Furness LA14 IRT	61,127	304,029
1911	Gainsborough, 26 Lord Street, Gainsborough, Lincs. DN 2DB	4,383	20,063
1852	Greenwich, 279–283 Greenwich High Road, London SEIO 8NL	27,177	139,508
1853	Halifax, Trinity Road, Halifax, West Yorks HXI 2RG	8,686,731	58,710,200
1854	Hanley Economic, Granville House, Festival Park, Hanley, Stoke-on-Trent, Staffs. STI 5TB	27,384	151,231
1953	Harpenden, 14 Station Road, Harpenden, Herts. AL5 4SE	8,784	37,025
1890	Haywards Heath, 33 Boltro Road, Haywards Heath, W. Sussex RH16 IBQ	20,194	124,904
1863	Heart of England, Olympus Avenue, Tachbrook Park, Warwick CV34 6NQ	178,045	1,015,430
1865	Hinckley and Rugby, Upper Bond Street, Hinckley, Leics. LEIO IDG	41,160	226,773
1855	Holmesdale, 43 Church Street, Reigate, Surrey RH2 OAE	5,745	54,064
1853	Ilkeston P., 24–26 South Street, Ilkeston, Derby DE2 5HQ	4,095	15,956
1849	Ipswich, 44 Upper Brook Street, Ipswich IP4 IDP	28,680	151,643
1888	Kent Reliance, Reliance House, Manor Road, Chatham, Kent ME4 6AF	46,667	217,004
1852	Lambeth, 118–120 Westminster Bridge Road, London SEI 7AX	51,764	516,995
1875	Leeds and Holbeck, 105 Albion Street, Leeds LSI 5AS	278,155	2,236,472
1848	Leeds P., Permanent House, The Headrow, Leeds LSI INS	3,224,406	10,210,800
1863	Leek United, 50 St Edward Street, Leek, Staffs. ST13 5DH	47,490	283,957
1876	Londonderry Provident, 7 Castle Street, Londonderry BT48 6HQ	1,016	5,021
1867	Loughborough, 6 High Street, Loughborough, Leics. LEII 2PY	12,469	78,572
1922	Manchester, 18–20 Bridge Street, Manchester M3 3BU	8,281	71,238
1870	Mansfield, Regent House, Regent Street, Mansfield, Notts. NG18 ISS	17,779	90,583
1870	Market Harborough, Welland House, The Square, Market Harborough, Leics. LE16 7PB	26,995	181,628
1860	Marsden, 6–20 Russell Street, Nelson, Lancs. BB9 7NJ	41,900	218,440
1874	Melton Mowbray, 39 Nottingham Street, Melton Mowbray, Leics. LE13 INR	30,817	168,934
1966	Mercantile, 75 Howard Street, North Shields, Tyne and Wear NE30 IAQ	20,411	115,939
1880	Mid-Sussex, Mid-Sussex House, 66 Church Road, Burgess Hill, Sussex RH15 9AU	4,592	23,976
1869	Monmouthshire, John Frost Square, Newport, Gwent NP9 IPX	17,500	125,419
1869	National and Provincial, Provincial House, Bradford BDI INL	2,062,213	10,707,642
1896	National Counties, National Counties House, Church Street, Epsom, Surrey KT17 4NL	22,204	339,868
1884	Nationwide, Nationwide House, 136 High Holborn, London WCIV 6PW	6,209,939	34,119,058
1856	Newbury, 17–20 Bartholomew Street, Newbury, Berks. RG14 5LY	32,708	203,557
1863	Newcastle, Grainger Chambers, Hood Street, Newcastle upon Tyne NEI 6JP	131,962	971,457

Est.	**Name of Society (abbreviated) and head office address*	*Share investors*	*Total assets £'000*
1877	North of England, 50 Fawcett Street, Sunderland SR1 1SA	250,234	1,224,302
1850	Northern Rock, Northern Rock House, Gosforth, Newcastle upon Tyne NE3 4PL	743,524	4,414,803
1860	Norwich and Peterborough, Peterborough Business Park, Lynchwood, Peterborough PE2 6WZ	190,979	1,276,945
1850	Nottingham, 5–13 Upper Parliament Street, Nottingham NG1 2BX	131,813	652,753
1935	Nottingham Imperial, Imperial Building, 29 Bridgford Road, West Bridgford, Nottingham NG2 6AU	7,566	32,284
1877	Penrith, 7 King Street, Penrith, Cumbria CA11 7AR	6,728	42,263
1846	Portman, Portman House, Richmond Hill, Bournemouth, Dorset BH2 6EP	461,421	2,594,035
1860	Principality, PO Box 89, Principality Buildings, Queen Street, Cardiff CF1 1UA	240,060	1,030,864
1914	Progressive, 33–37 Wellington Place, Belfast BT1 6HH	36,824	256,291
1849	Saffron Walden, Herts. and Essex, 1A Market Street, Saffron Walden, Essex CB10 1HX	33,382	188,799
1937	St Pancras, 200 Finchley Road, London NW3 6DA	10,810	95,065
1846	Scarborough, Prospect House, 442/444 Scalby Road, Scarborough, Yorks. YO12 6EE	57,752	371,039
1848	Scottish, 23 Manor Place, Edinburgh EH3 7XE	16,507	91,809
1879	Shepshed, Bull Ring, Shepshed, Loughborough, Leics. LE12 9QD	6,643	28,479
1853	Skipton, The Bailey, Skipton, Yorks. BD23 1DN	284,190	2,717,270
1877	Stafford Railway, 4 Market Square, Stafford ST16 2JH	7,408	37,372
1902	Staffordshire, Jubilee House, PO Box 66, 84 Salop Street, Wolverhampton WV3 0SA	176,344	847,979
1875	Standard, 64 Church Way, North Shields, Tyne and Wear NE29 0AF	2,284	13,818
1850	Stroud and Swindon, Rowcroft, Stroud, Glos. GL5 3BG	86,639	493,578
1903	Surrey, Sentinel House, 10–12 Massetts Road, Horley, Surrey RH6 7DE	8,974	78,339
1923	Swansea, 11 Cradock Street, Swansea SA1 3EW	3,150	23,856
1966	Teachers, Allenview House, Wimborne, Dorset BH21 1AG	8,878	110,362
1901	Tipton and Coseley, 57–60 High Street, Tipton, West Midlands DY4 8HG	15,594	73,483
1855	Tynemouth, 53–55 Howard Street, North Shields, Tyne and Wear NE30 1AF	6,047	44,678
1863	Universal, 41 Pilgrim Street, Newcastle upon Tyne NE1 6BT	24,531	157,388
1924	Vernon, 19 St Petersgate, Stockport, Cheshire SK1 1HF	23,016	99,581
1849	West Bromwich, 374 High Street, West Bromwich, West Midlands B70 8LR	259,645	1,110,205
1882	West Cumbria, Cumbria House, Murray Road, Workington CA14 2AD	6,527	31,586
1847	Woolwich Corporate Headquarters, Watling Street, Bexley Heath, Kent DA6 7RR	2,964,000	20,164,800
1885	Yorkshire, Yorkshire House, Westgate, Bradford BD1 2AU	708,558	4,184,821

* 'Building Society' are the last words in every society's name
B Benefit
P Permanent

National Savings

National Savings Bank

On 31 May 1992, there were about 15,807,000 active accounts with the sum of approximately £1,439 million due to depositors in ordinary accounts and about 4,909,000 active accounts with the sum of approximately £8,940.6 million due to depositors in investment accounts.

Interest is earned at 5 per cent per year on each ordinary account for every complete calendar month in which the balance is £500 or more, provided the account is kept open for the whole of 1992 (31 December 1991 to 1 January 1993); and at 2.5 per cent per year for other months or for accounts opened or closed during 1992. The minimum deposit is £5; maximum balance £10,000 plus interest credited. On 31 May 1992 the average amount held in ordinary accounts was approximately £91.

The investment account pays a higher rate of interest (the current rate can be found at any post office). The minimum deposit is £5; maximum balance £25,000 plus interest credited. On 31 May 1992 the average amount held in investment accounts was approximately £1,821.

Premium Bonds

Premium Bonds are a Government security which were first introduced on 1 November 1956. Premium Bonds enable savers to enter a regular draw for tax-free prizes, while retaining the right to get their money back. A sum equivalent to interest on each bond is put into a prize fund and distributed by weekly and monthly prize draws. (The rate of interest is 6.5 per cent a year from 1 July 1988). The prizes are drawn by ERNIE (electronic random number indicator equipment) and are free of all UK income tax and capital gains tax.

Bonds are in units of £1, with a minimum purchase of £100; above this, purchases must be in multiples of £10, up to a maximum holding limit of £10,000 per person. The exception to this is that the minimum purchase by parents, guardians and grandparents for children under 16 is £10. Winners of £50 prize warrants will be invited to return their prize warrants to the Bonds and Stock Office if they wish to reinvest. This transaction cannot be made through the Post Office. Bonds can only be held in the name of an individual and not by organizations.

Bonds become eligible for prizes once they have been held for three clear calendar months following the month of purchase. Each £1 unit can win only one prize per draw, but it will be awarded the highest for which it is drawn. Bonds remain eligible for prizes until they are repaid. When a holder dies, bonds remain eligible for prizes up to and including the twelfth monthly draw after the month in which the holder dies.

By April 1992 bonds to the value of £5,189 million had been sold. Of these £2,761 million had been cashed, leaving £2,427 million still invested. By the April 1993 prize draw, 39.81 million prizes totalling £2,330 million had been distributed since the first prize draw in June 1957.

Income Bonds

National Savings Income Bonds were introduced in 1982. They are particularly suitable for those who want to receive regular monthly payments of interest while preserving the full cash value of their capital. The bonds are sold in multiples of £1,000. The minimum holding is £2,000 and the maximum £50,000 (£100,000 jointly).

Interest is calculated on a day-to-day basis and paid monthly. Interest is taxable, but is paid without deduction of tax at source. The bonds have a guaranteed life of ten years, but may be repaid at par before maturity on giving three months' notice. If repayment of a bond is made within the first year of purchase, interest from the date of purchase to the date of repayment is earned at half rate. If the sole or sole surviving holder dies, however, no formal period of notice is required and there is no loss of interest for repayment made within the first year.

Net investment in National Savings Income Bonds was £9,751 million at the end of April 1992.

Indexed Income Bonds

Indexed Income Bonds were withdrawn from sale on 28 August 1987. Existing holders will continue to receive monthly income in accordance with the prospectus.

Children's Bonus Bonds

Children's Bonus Bonds (Issue A) were introduced in July 1991 and replaced by Issue B in May 1992. They can be bought for any child under 16 and will go on growing in value until he or she is 21. The bonds are sold in multiples of £25. The minimum holding is £25, the maximum £1,000 per child (excluding interest and bonuses) in all issues. Bonds for children under 16 must be held by a parent or guardian.

Children's Bonus Bonds (Issue A) earn 5 per cent a year over five years. A substantial bonus (40.1 per cent) of the purchase price is added at the fifth anniversary. This is equal to 10.9 per cent a year compound. All returns are totally exempt from UK income tax. No interest is earned on bonds cashed in before the first anniversary of purchase. Bonuses are only payable if the bond is held until the next bonus date. Bonds over five years old continue to earn interest and bonuses until the holder is 21, when they should be cashed in. If bonds are not cashed in on the holder's 21st birthday, they earn no interest after that birthday.

FIRST Option Bonds

FIRST (Fixed Interest Rate Savings Tax-paid) Option Bonds were introduced in July 1992. They offer guaranteed rates without the need for long-term commitment for personal savers over 16. They can be held indefinitely and will continue to grow in value at rates of interest fixed for 12 months at a time. Tax is deducted from the interest at source. The minimum purchase is £1,000 and the maximum holding is £250,000. Withdrawals can be made without penalty at any anniversary date and there is no formal notice period for repayment. No interest is earned on repayments before the first anniversary.

Capital Bonds

National Savings Capital Bonds were introduced in January 1989. The latest series, Series D, was introduced in May 1992. Capital Bonds offer capital growth over five years with guaranteed returns at fixed rates. The interest is taxable each year (for those who pay income tax) but is not deducted at source. The minimum purchase is £100, with larger purchases in multiples of £100. There is a maximum holding limit of £100,000 from Series B onwards.

Capital Bonds will be repaid in full with all interest gained at the end of five years. No interest is earned on bonds repaid in the first year.

Deposit Bonds

National Savings Deposit Bonds were withdrawn from sale on 19 November 1988. All Deposit Bonds purchased on or before that date may continue to be held until the tenth anniversary of purchase. They will continue to earn interest until then.

Yearly Plan

The National Savings Yearly Plan was introduced on 2 July 1984. It offers a guaranteed tax-free return. Applicants agree to make 12 monthly payments, leading to the issue of a Yearly Plan Certificate. The maximum guaranteed rate of interest is earned if the certificate is held for a full four years. Applications may be made by any individuals aged 7 or over; in the name of children under 7; and by not more than two trustees for a sole beneficiary.

Payments must be made on the same date every month by standing order from a bank or other acceptable account. Only one payment may be made in any one month and must be in multiples of £5. Minimum monthly contribution is £20, maximum £400. Net investment in National Savings Yearly Plan was £492,925,971 at 30 April 1992.

Gilts on the National Savings Stock Register

Government stock or 'Gilts' are Stock Exchange securities issued by the Government. They usually have a life of between five and 20 years and most pay a guaranteed fixed rate of interest twice a year throughout this period. When they reach the end of this period they are 'redeemed' (which means repaid) at their face value.

The National Savings Stock Register enables investors to buy and sell Gilts by post. It is now possible to have most new issues of Gilts registered on the National Savings Stock Register. Interest on Gilts held on the National Savings Stock Register, although taxable, is paid in full without deduction of tax at source.

NATIONAL SAVINGS CERTIFICATES

Recent Issues

The amount, including accrued interest, index-linked increase or bonus remaining to the credit of investors in National Savings Certificates on 30 April 1992 was approximately £14,789.2 million. In 1991–2, approx. £3,628.8 million was subscribed and £1,616 million (excluding interest, index-linked increase or bonus) was repaid. Interest, index-linked increase, bonus or other sum payable is free of UK income tax (including investment income surcharge) and capital gains tax.

Index-linked Retirement Issue

2 June 1975–15 November 1980
Maximum holding: 120 units
Unit cost: £10

Interest per unit: unlike conventional issues where interest is accrued periodically, the repayment value of Index-Linked Certificates, subject to their being held a year, is related to the movement of the UK General Index of Retail prices.**

Second Index-linked Issue

17 November 1980–29 June 1985
Maximum holding: 1,000 units
Unit cost: £10

Interest per unit: the repayment value, subject to their being held a year, is related to the movement of the UK General Index of Retail Prices.**

Third Index-linked Issue

1 July 1985–31 July 1986
Maximum holding: 200 units
Unit cost: £25

Interest per unit: the repayment value, subject to their being held for one year, is related to the movement of the UK General Index of Retail Prices.**

In addition, there is guaranteed extra interest of 2.5 per cent for the first year; 2.75 per cent for the second year; 3.25 per cent for the third year; 4 per cent for the fourth year, and 5.25 per cent for the fifth year. This interest is worth 3.54 per cent compound over a full five years. Certificates held beyond the fifth anniversary earn index-linking plus half a per cent interest on each following anniversary.*

Fourth Index-linked Issue

1 August 1986–30 June 1990
Maximum holding: 200 units
Unit cost: £25

Interest per unit: the repayment value, subject to their being held for one year, is related to the movement of the UK General Index of Retail Prices.**

In addition, there is guaranteed extra interest of 3 per cent for the first year; 3.25 per cent for the second year; 3.5 per cent for the third year; 4.5 per cent for the fourth year, and 6 per cent for the fifth year. This interest is worth 4.04 per cent compound over a full five years. Certificates held beyond the fifth anniversary earn index-linking plus half a per cent interest on each following anniversary.*

Thirty-third Index-linked Issue

1 May 1987–21 July 1988
Maximum holding: 40 units, plus special facilities to hold up to a further 200 units
Unit cost: £25
Value after five years: £35.06

Interest per unit: after one year the repayment value increases by 5.5 per cent for ordinarily held 33rd Issue. However, 33rd Issue Reinvestment Certificates earn interest during the first year at a rate of 5.5 per cent per annum for each three-month period. Thereafter, all 33rd Issue earn 5.75 per cent after two years; 6 per cent after three years; 6.5 per cent after four years, and 7 per cent after five years.*

Thirty-fourth Index-linked Issue

22 July 1988–16 June 1990
Maximum holding: 40 units, plus facilities to hold up to a further 400 units
Unit cost: £25
Value after five years: £35.89

Interest per unit: after one year the repayment value increases by 6 per cent for ordinarily held 34th Issue. However, 34th Issue Reinvestment Certificates earn interest during the first year at a rate of 6 per cent per annum for each three-month period. Thereafter, all 34th Issue earn 6.25 per cent after two years; 6.5 per cent after three years; 7 per cent after four years, and 7.5 per cent after five years.*

Thirty-fifth Index-linked Issue

18 June 1990–14 March 1991
Maximum holding: 40 units, plus special facilities to hold up to a further 400 units
Unit cost: £25
Value after five years: £39.36

Interest per unit: after one year the repayment value increases by 6.5 per cent for ordinarily held 35th Issue. However, 35th Issue Reinvestment Certificates earn interest during the first year at a rate of 6.5 per cent per annum. Thereafter, all 35th Issue earn 7 per cent after two years; 7.75 per cent after three years; 8.5 per cent after four years, and 9.5 per cent after five years.

FIFTH INDEX-LINKED ISSUE
2 July 1990–
Maximum holding: 200 units, plus special facilities to hold up to a further 400 units
Unit cost: £25
Interest per unit: the repayment value, subject to their being held for one year, is related to the movement of the UK General Index of Retail Prices. In addition, there is guaranteed extra interest which is paid from the date of purchase for each full year the certificates are held. For the first year the return is the Retail Price Index (RPI) only. For the second, the RPI plus 0.5 per cent; for the third, the RPI plus 1 per cent; for the fourth, the RPI plus 2 per cent, and at the fifth anniversary, RPI plus 4.5 per cent.

THIRTY-SIXTH INDEX-LINKED ISSUE
2 April 1991–2 May 1992
Maximum holding: 200 units, plus special facilities to hold up to a further 400
Unit cost: £25
Value after five years: £37.59
Interest per unit: after one year the repayment value increases by 5.5 per cent for ordinarily held 36th Issue. However, 36th Issue Reinvestment Certificates earn interest during the first year at a rate of 5.5 per cent per annum. Thereafter, all 36th Issue earn 6 per cent after two years; 6.75 per cent after three years; 7.5 per cent after four years, and 8.5 per cent after five years

THIRTY-SEVENTH INDEX-LINKED ISSUE
13 May 1992–
Maximum holding: 300 units, plus special facilities to hold up to a further 400
Unit cost: £25
Value after five years: £36.74
Interest per unit: after one year the repayment value increases by 5.5 per cent for ordinarily held 37th Issue. However, 37th Issue Reinvestment Certificates earn interest during the first year at a rate of 5.5 per cent per annum. After one year, £1.38 is added; during the second year, 41 pence per completed three months; during the third year, 56 pence per completed three months; during the fourth year, 71 pence per completed three months, and during the fifth year, 91 pence per completed three months.

*As announced by the Treasury.
†From June 1982, savings certificates of the 7th to 14th, 16th, 18th, 19th, 21st, 23rd to 33rd Issues will be extended on general extension rates as they reach the end of their existing extension periods. The percentage interest rate is determined by the Treasury and any change in this general extension rate will be applicable from the first of the month following its announcement.
Under the new system, a certificate earns interest for each complete period of three months beyond the expiry of the previous extension terms. Within each three-month period interest is calculated separately for each month at the rate applicable from the beginning of that month. The interest for each month is one-twelfth of the annual rate (i.e. it does not vary with the number of days in the month) and is capitalized annually on the anniversary of the date of purchase. The current rate of interest under the general extension rate is given in leaflets available at Post Offices.
**Index-linked certificates of the 1st and 2nd Issues were eligible for an annual supplement of 1.5 per cent for the year to 1 August 1989. There have been six previous annual supplements. No further bonuses will be payable. At the fifth anniversary there is a bonus of 4 per cent of the purchase price and at the tenth anniversary there is a second bonus of 4 per cent of the capitalized value. All supplements and bonuses are fully index-linked once earned.

Insurance

AUTHORIZATION OF INSURANCE COMPANIES

Section Three of the Insurance Companies Act 1982 empowers the Department of Trade and Industry (Insurance Division, 10–18 Victoria Street, London SW1H 0NN) to authorize corporate bodies to transact insurance in the United Kingdom provided they comply with the financial and other regulations detailed in the Act.

At the end of 1991 there were 836 insurance companies with authorization to transact one or more classes of insurance business in the UK.

REGULATION OF INSURANCE COMPANIES

Under the Financial Services Act 1986, the Securities and Investments Board (SIB) is empowered to make, monitor and enforce rules about the conduct of investment business.

The SIB has, in turn, set up a number of self-regulating organizations dealing with different sectors of the investment market. Insurance companies offering long-term contracts like life insurance, pensions, unit trusts and annuities can either obtain authorization directly from SIB or from the main SRO dealing with the marketing of life insurance and pensions, the Life And Unit Trust Regulatory Organization (LAUTRO). Insurance companies may offer other investment services, which may mean authorization by other SROs such as the Investment Management Regulatory Organization (IMRO). For addresses, see Investment Business Regulation section.

Early in 1991 the Securities and Investment Board (SIB) announced a review of retail regulation. In the consultation period many insurance companies have supported the view that a single retail SRO replacing LAUTRO, FIMBRA, and some parts of IMRO and other organizations, would be the way forward. Discussions and consultation continued throughout the year.

ASSOCIATION OF BRITISH INSURERS

Ninety per cent of the world-wide business of insurance companies is transacted by the 450 members of the Association of British Insurers, a trade association which represents both life and general insurers. On general insurance (motor, household, holiday, etc.), ABI acts as a regulatory organization for insurance intermediaries who do not qualify to be registered brokers.

INSURANCE BROKERS

The Insurance Brokers Registration Act 1977 empowers the Insurance Brokers Registration Council (15 St Helen's Place, London EC3A 6DS) as the statutory body responsible for the registration of insurance brokers. The Council is responsible for the registration and training of insurance brokers, conduct of business, and discipline, and it lays down rules relating to such matters as accounting practice, staff qualifications, advertising, etc.

It is possible to act as an insurance intermediary without being registered with the IBRC but unregistered intermediaries are forbidden to use the words 'Insurance Broker' as a title.

IBRC Registered Brokers

	1992
Registered individuals	13,501
Limited companies registered	2,161
Sole traders and partnerships (containing 1,331 partners and directors)	2,888

INVISIBLE EARNINGS OF INSURANCE

	1989	1990
Insurance	£2,927m	£2,152m

GENERAL INSURANCE

The gloom in the general insurance market continued in 1991, with increases in the number of claims made and the average amount claimed. The result was a world-wide trading loss of £3.3 billion.

In the UK for every £1 of premium collected, insurance companies paid out £1.30 in claims and expenses, leading the Association of British Insurers to predict that an average family would face premium increases on motor, home and contents cover totalling about £10 per month.

Both motor and fire and accident insurance results worsened, and the falling housing market meant mortgage indemnity losses of over £1,200 million, dwarfing the premium income of around £200 million.

All forms of crime jumped, with motor theft costing 36 per cent more than in 1990 and domestic theft claims up 75 per cent. Another dry summer meant subsidence costs also continued to rise, reaching a new record of £540 million, over four times the average figure during the 1980s.

Overseas the results were little better, with losses in both the European and United States markets. Reinsurance was also badly hit by natural disasters like Hurricane Bob, the Californian bush fires and the worst ever hail storms in Calgary.

BRITISH INSURANCE COMPANIES IN 1991

The following insurance company figures refer to members of the Association of British Insurers, and also to certain non-members.

CLAIMS STATISTICS

	1990 £m	1991 £m
Fire claims		
Commercial fires	783.9	774.6 (−1.2%)
Domestic fires	223.5	243.5 (+8.9%)
Theft claims		
Commercial theft (inc. money)	232.9	316.6 (+36.9%)
Domestic theft	363.9	590.7 (+62.3%)

WORLD-WIDE GENERAL BUSINESS TRADING RESULT

	1990 £m	1991 £m
Net written premiums	25,491	27,573
Underwriting profit/loss for one year account business		
Motor	−1,439	−1,515
Fire and Accident	−2,605	−3,989
Transfer to profit and loss account for other business		
Marine, Aviation, Transport	−379	−605
Other	−530	−714
Total underwriting result	−4,953	−6,823
Investment income	3,479	3,514
Overall trading profit	−1,474	−3,309
Profit as % of premium income	−5.8%	−12.0%

WORLD-WIDE GENERAL BUSINESS UNDERWRITING RESULT

	1990				1991			
	UK	USA	Other	Total	UK	USA	Other	Total
Fire and Accident								
Premiums (£m)	8,805	1,689	3,017	13,511	9,709	1,614	3,021	14,345
Profit/loss (£m)	−1,939.5	−236.3	−493.6	−2,669.5	−3,306	−241	−441	−3,989
% of premiums	−22.0	−14.0	−16.4	−19.8	−34.1	−14.9	−14.6	−27.8
Motor								
Premiums (£m)	4,839	1,203	2,387	8,428	5,098	1,271	2,555	8,924
Profit/loss (£m)	−904.3	−184.2	−324.6	−1,413.1	−1,171	−135	−210	−1,515
% of premiums	−18.7	−15.3	−13.6	−16.8	−23.0	−10.6	−8.2	−17.0

NET PREMIUM INCOME BY TERRITORY 1991

	UK £m	Other EC countries £m	USA £m	Other overseas £m	Total (world-wide) £m	Increase %
Fire and Accident (non-motor)	10,477	1,355	1,698	3,143	16,673	+8.5
Motor	5,195	1,169	1,272	1,429	9,065	+6.0
Marine, Aviation and Transport	1,408	177	133	117	1,835	+17.3
Total general business	17,080	2,701	3,103	4,689	27,573	+8.2
Ordinary long-term	38,148	2,366	1,965	3,141	45,620	+17.6
Industrial long-term	1,378				1,378	+0.5
Total long-term business	39,526	2,366	1,965	3,141	46,998	+17.0
Total	56,606	5,067	5,068	7,830	74,571	+13.6

LLOYD'S OF LONDON

Lloyd's of London is an incorporated society of private underwriters who provide an international market for almost all types of insurance.

Lloyd's currently earns a gross premium income of around £7,000 million for underwriters each year. Much of this business comes from outside Great Britain and makes a valuable contribution to the balance of payments.

Today, as it was three centuries ago, a policy is underwritten at Lloyd's by private individuals with unlimited liability. Now that Lloyd's members are numbered in their thousands, however, the method of underwriting is the same only in principle. Specialist underwriters accept insurance risks at Lloyd's on behalf of members (often referred to as 'names') grouped in syndicates. There are currently over 20,000 members in some 390 syndicates of varying sizes, some with over 2,000 names, each managed by an underwriting agent approved by the Council of Lloyd's.

Lloyd's membership is drawn from many sources. Industry, commerce and the professions are strongly represented, while many members work at Lloyd's either for brokerage firms or for underwriting agencies. Underwriting membership of Lloyd's is open to anyone provided they meet the stringent financial requirements of the Corporation of Lloyd's. Assets of up to £250,000 have to be shown and a deposit lodged with the Corporation as security for underwriting liabilities. This deposit, which must be in the form of approved securities, is determined at 30 per cent of the member's annual premium income and showing nominal means.

Lloyd's is incorporated by an Act of Parliament (Lloyd's Acts 1871–1982) and currently governed by a Council of 28 members, 12 of which are elected from and by underwriting members working at Lloyd's and eight from and by the external membership. Eight Council members are nominated by the Council subject to confirmation by the Governor of the Bank of England.

The Council is a legislative body responsible for deciding on major policy matters, regulating the market, the election of new underwriting members, and establishing the requirements of membership and the rules governing the financial security to be provided by those doing business at Lloyd's. The role of the Council is currently under scrutiny from a number of internal enquiries charged with investigating whether changes should be made in the way the market is governed and regulated.

The Corporation is a non-profit making body chiefly financed by its members' subscriptions. It provides the premises, administrative staff and services enabling Lloyd's underwriting syndicates to conduct their business. It does not, however, assume corporate liability for the risks accepted by its members, who remain responsible to the full extent of their personal means for their underwriting affairs.

Lloyd's syndicates have no direct contact with the public. All business is transacted through about 250 firms of insurance brokers accredited by the Corporation of Lloyd's. In addition, non-Lloyd's brokers in the United Kingdom, when guaranteed by Lloyd's brokers, are able to deal directly with Lloyd's motor syndicates, a facility which has made the Lloyd's market more accessible to the insuring public.

Lloyd's also provides the most comprehensive shipping intelligence service available in the world. The enormous volume of shipping and other information received from Lloyd's agents, shipowners, news agencies and other sources throughout the world, is collated and distributed to the media as well as to the maritime and commercial communities in general. *Lloyd's List* is London's oldest daily newspaper and contains news of general commercial interest as well as shipping information. *Lloyd's Shipping Index*, also published daily, lists some 25,000 ocean-going vessels in alphabetical order and gives the latest known report of each.

Developments in 1991

A series of reforms, likely to be the most far-reaching in the history of the market, were begun in 1991.

Over 2,000 names were involved in various forms of legal action, many alleging negligence by their underwriting agents. The latest available figures, which are for 1989 because of Lloyd's three-year accounting period, show losses amounting to a record £1,373 billion (compared with a profit of £431 million in 1988). More names also decided to leave the market, bringing to 10,000 the number who have left since 1988. For many names the results meant having to sell property or other assets to meet the growing underwriting losses of their syndicates.

Allegations were also made in Parliament that names who worked in the market were avoiding losses by diverting the worst loss-making risks to syndicates that contained 'outside' names. Subsequent internal market reports have, however, found that, although changes in regulation are needed, there is no evidence to support this.

Catastrophe reinsurance and US legal liability claims were two major causes of loss but, unlike the insurance companies, Lloyd's did underwrite aviation and motor insurance profitably.

Calls for a radical overhaul of the market continued throughout the year, including, among other recommendations, a change to the principle of unlimited liability for individual names and the mixing of corporate interests and individuals in syndicates.

Lloyd's Global Accounts as at 31 December 1990

	1988 £'000	1989 £'000
Gross premiums	5,899,545	7,074,348
Premiums in respect of reinsurance ceded	2,185,891	3,108,827
Net premiums	3,713,654	3,965,521
Reinsurance premiums received from previous accounts	4,862,115	6,183,897
	8,575,769	10,149,418
Gross claims	7,532,872	13,599,934
Reinsurance recoveries	4,462,662	9,368,961
Net claims	3,070,210	4,230,973
Reinsurance premiums paid to close the accounts	6,054,797	7,820,489
	9,125,007	12,051,462
Underwriting result	(549,238)	(1,902,044)
Gross investment income	615,195	554,794
Gross investment appreciation	173,477	181,188
Gross investment return	788,672	735,982
Profit/(loss) on currency exchange	5,673	(56,769)
	794,345	679,213
Result before syndicate expenses	245,107	(1,222,831)
Syndicate expenses	391,297	548,499
Closed year of account loss/profit	(146,190)	(1,771,330)
Names' personal expenses	363,483	291,836
(Loss attributable) profit available to Names before tax	(509,673)	(2,063,166)

Lloyd's Membership and Capacity

	1989	1990	1991
Membership	31,329	28,770	26,539
Of which Brokers	260	254	256
Gross Market capacity	£10,956m	£11,070m	£11,382m
Average capacity per member	£350,000	£385,000	£455,000

THE EUROPEAN COMMUNITY

In 1986 the European Community's Heads of Government signed the Single European Act, which set out a programme of over 300 EC directives which are intended to achieve the removal of barriers to a free market within the community.

Progress on the establishment of a single European insurance market was very slow. Sir Leon Brittan, the EC Commissioner responsible for financial services and competition, outlined in November 1989 plans to introduce a number of directives which will help insurance catch up with other financial sectors in the preparation for a single European market.

In November 1989 Sir Leon announced his proposals for a 'single licence' system (already applying to banks and investment services) for the insurance sector. He also announced a timetable for draft directives to give effect to these plans. The single licence concept envisages the supervisor in the insurer's home country carrying out all the financial supervision necessary. This would mean a UK insurer, authorized by the Department of Trade, would automatically satisfy the supervisory authority in all other EC countries. Considerable progress towards a single market in insurance was made in 1991. It now looks as if the essential directives will have been adopted by the end of 1992 at the latest, although implementation may take a further couple of years.

During the year, Ministers agreed on the text of the Non-Life Framework Directives. Its life equivalent is now being considered. These directives, once adopted, will supersede the Non-Life Services Directive for Large Risks, which came into force in July 1990, and the Motor Services and Life Services (Own Initiatives) Directives, which were adopted in November 1990.

At the end of 1991 the EC Insurance Accounts Directive was adopted and insurers are also watching the progress of the draft EC Data Protection Directive. This goes much

Lloyd's Results 1989

	Marine 1988	Marine 1989	Non-Marine 1988	Non-Marine 1989	Aviation 1988	Aviation 1989	Motor 1988	Motor 1989
	£m	£m	£m	£m	£m	£m	£m	£m
Net premiums	1,263.5	1,326	1,583.8	1,762	320.9	281	545.5	597
Underwriting result	(609.4)	(821)	(154.0)	(1,149)	112.2	16	102.0	52

further than the UK Data Protection Act, particularly in its proposed application to records held manually.

At the end of 1991, a recommendation on the regulation of insurance intermediaries was adopted. This is designed to bring together member states' rules and to provide guidelines for the introduction of rules in those member states which do not currently regulate insurance intermediaries, with the aim of providing a minimum level of regulation. It is not, currently, binding but the EC Commission has said it will become a directive in five years' time if member states do not give effect to it.

LIFE INSURANCE AND PENSIONS

Despite the recession and general economic uncertainty, UK life and pension companies performed well during 1991. Total premium income in the UK increased by 18 per cent to £39.5 billion.

A large part of the increase was due to single premium business where both life insurance and personal pension figures showed increases in excess of 40 per cent, while annuities increased by almost 80 per cent.

Personal pensions continued to prove popular, with banks and building societies selling more personal pensions as independent intermediaries or tied agents of insurance companies than their own deposit-based schemes.

Two issues have dominated the pensions industry during the year. First, equalization of pension ages. Insurers and pension providers were relieved that the Maastricht protocol to the Treaty of Rome suggested that the decision in the case of Barber v. GRE could not be backdated. This removes a lot of uncertainty about the case.

The second issue is the scandal which emerged after the death of the publisher Robert Maxwell. Although none of the Maxwell pension funds were insurance-based schemes, both insured and self-administered schemes have come under close scrutiny by the Government; any resulting changes in pension legislation are likely to affect both types of pension schemes.

PREMIUM INCOME FOR WORLD-WIDE LONG-TERM INSURANCE BUSINESS

	1990 £m	1991 £m
Ordinary Branch:		
Yearly premiums for life insurances, annuities and pensions in the UK	17,137	18,207 (+5.9%)
Single premiums for life insurances, annuities and pensions in the UK	14,692	19,610 (+33.5%)
Premiums for permanent health and other long-term insurances in the UK	311	331 (+7.5%)
Overseas premium income	6,595	7,472 (+13.3%)
Industrial Branch:		
Premium income (UK only)	1,363	2,127 (+7.4%)

WORLD-WIDE LONG-TERM INSURANCE BUSINESS – OUTGO

	1990 £m	1991 £m
Ordinary Branch:		
Total payments made to UK policyholders	19,141	21,576 (+12.7%)
Total payments made to overseas policyholders	3,219	3,924 (+22.2%)
Industrial Branch:		
Total payments made to UK policyholders	1,962	2,127 (+7.4%)

Percentages shown are increases of 1991 figures over those for 1990.

NB: Payments to policyholders include death claims, maturities, annuities, surrenders (including planned cashing-in of linked and other similar savings policies and surrenders of bonus and bonuses in cash), refunds under pension schemes and payments under PHI and other long-term contracts.

INDIVIDUAL PENSIONS: NEW BUSINESS 1990–1

Personal or self-employed pensions	New annual premiums £m			New single premiums £m			DSS rebates* £m	
	Non-linked	Linked	Total	Non-linked	Linked	Total	Non-linked	Linked
1990								
1st quarter	109	153	262	382	342	724	74	104
2nd quarter	130	177	307	497	378	875	81	115
3rd quarter	94	136	230	371	365	736	69	100
4th quarter	111	142	253	365	384	749	106	117
1991								
1st quarter	130	134	264	446	407	853	64	82
2nd quarter	174	164	338	593	526	1,119	64	76
3rd quarter	137	128	265	518	538	1,056	44	56
4th quarter	131	136	267	575	561	1,136	39	50
12 months to:								
31 December 1990	444	608	1,052	1,617	1,468	3,085	330	435
31 December 1991	572	562	1,133	2,132	2,032	4,164	212	264

*The figures shown here are the best estimate of one year's DSS rebates and incentives to be received under policies effected in the quarter, whether received or not.

INVESTMENTS OF INSURANCE COMPANIES 1991

Investment of funds	Long-term business £m	General business £m
Index-linked British Government securities	3,676	239
British Government authority securities (excluding those in line 1)	32,438	5,706
Other government, provincial and municipal stocks	17,132	9,221
Debentures, loan stocks, preference and guaranteed stocks and shares	24,660	7,981
Ordinary stocks and shares	154,923	13,076
Mortgages	14,085	1,246
Real property and ground rents	34,810	3,944
Other invested assets	18,919	8,080
'Net current assets'	616	6,353
Total net assets	301,979	55,846
Gross income for year on investment holdings (gross of tax and interest paid)	19,049	3,877
Interest payable in year	435	363

DIRECTORY OF INSURANCE COMPANIES

Classes of Insurance undertaken

A Accident (which includes Motor, Employers' Liability, etc.)
F Fire (including Burglary)
L Life
M Marine
Re Reinsurance

GROUP MEMBERSHIP

(ES) Eagle Star
(CU) Commercial Union
(GRE) Guardian Royal Exchange
(GA) General Accident
(NU) Norwich Union
(R) Royal
(SA) Sun Alliance & London

Nature of business	*Name of company*	*Head Office address*
L	Abbey Life	80 Holdenhurst Road, Bournemouth BH8 8AL
AFLM Re	AGF Holdings (UK)	41 Botolph Lane, London EC3R 8DL
AFM Re	Albion	9–13 Fenchurch Buildings, London EC3M 5HR
AFLM	Alliance Assurance (SA)	1 Bartholomew Lane, London EC2N 2AB
L	Allied Dunbar	Allied Dunbar Centre, Swindon
L	American Life	2–8 Altyre Road, Croydon CR9 2LG
AF	Ansvar	31 St Leonards Road, Eastbourne BN21 3UR
AFM	Atlas (GRE)	Royal Exchange, London EC3V 3LS
AFL Re	Avon	Arden Street, Stratford-upon-Avon CV37 6WA
AF	Baptist	1 Merchant Street, London E3 4LY
L	Barclays	94 St Paul's Churchyard, London EC4
AFM	Bedford General	Zurich House, Stanhope Road, Portsmouth
AFLM Re	Black Sea and Baltic	65 Fenchurch Street, London EC3M 4EV
AFLM	Bradford	North Park, Halifax HX1 2TU
L	Britannia Life	190 West George Street, Glasgow
AFL	Britannic	Moor Green, Moseley, Birmingham B13 8QF
M	British & Foreign Marine (R)	New Hall Place, Liverpool
Engineering	British Engine (R)	Longridge House, Manchester M60 4DT
AFLM	British Equitable (GRE)	Royal Exchange, London EC3V 3LS
L	British Life Office	Reliance House, Mount Ephraim, Tunbridge Wells, Kent TN4 8BL
FM	British Oak (GRE)	Royal Exchange, London EC3V 3LS
A	Builders' Accident	Inigo Place, 31–33 Bedford Street, London, WC2E 9EL
L	Caledonian (GRE)	Royal Exchange, London EC3V 3LS
AFM	Cambrian (GRE)	Royal Exchange, London EC3V 3LS
L	Canada Life	Canada Life House, Potters Bar, Herts. EN6 5BA
L	Cannon Lincoln	1 Olympic Way, Wembley HA9 0NB
AFM	Car & General (GRE)	Royal Exchange, London EC3V 3LS
AL	Cigna Employee Benefits	PO Box 42, Greenock, Renfrewshire PA15 1AB
L	Citibank Life	Perrymount Road, Haywards Heath, W. Sussex RH16 3TP
L	City of Glasgow Friendly	200 Bath Street, Glasgow G2 4HJ
L	Clerical, Medical Group	10–14 John Adam Street, London WC2N 6HA
L	Colonial Mutual	Chatham Maritime, Kent ME4 4YY
AFLM Re	Commercial Union	St Helen's, 1 Undershaft, London EC3P 3DQ
L	Confederation	Lytton Way, Stevenage, Herts SG1 2NN
AF	Congregational and General	Currer House, Currer Street, Bradford BD1 5BA
AFLM	Co-operative	Miller Street, Manchester M60 0AL
AFLM Re	Cornhill	32 Cornhill, London EC3V 3LJ
L	Crown Financial Management	Crown House, Crown Square, Woking GU21 1XW
A	Crusader	Woodhatch, Reigate, Surrey RH2 8BL

Nature of business	*Name of company*	*Head Office address*
AFM	Dominion	52–54 Leadenhall Street, London EC3A 2AQ
AFLM Re	Eagle Star	60 St Mary Axe, London EC3A 8JQ
AFL	Ecclesiastical	Beaufort House, Brunswick Road, Gloucester
AFL	Economic	Economic House, 25 London Road, Sittingbourne ME10 1PE
AFM	Employers' Liability (CU)	St Helen's, 1 Undershaft, London EC3
Animal Ins.	Equine and Livestock	PO Box 100, Ouseburn, York YO5 9SZ
L	Equitable Life	4 Coleman Street, London EC2R 5AP
L	Equity & Law	Amersham Road, High Wycombe, Bucks HP13 5AL
AFM	Essex & Suffolk (GRE)	Royal Exchange, London EC3V 3LS
A	Federation	29 Linkfield Lane, Redhill, Surrey RH1 1JH
AF	Fine Art & General (CU)	St Helen's, 1 Undershaft, London EC3
L	Friends' Provident	Pixham End, Dorking, Surrey
L	FS Assurance	190 West George Street, Glasgow
AFM Re	General Accident	Pitheavlis, Perth, Scotland
L Re	General Accident Life	2 Rougier Street, York YO1 1HR
AF	Gresham Fire & Accident	11 Queen Victoria Street, London EC4N 4XP
L	Gresham Life	2–6 Prince of Wales Road, Bournemouth
AFM	Guarantee Society (GA)	36–37 Old Jewry, London EC2
L	Guardian Assurance (GRE)	Royal Exchange, London EC3V 3LS
AFLM Re	Guardian Royal Exchange (GRE)	Royal Exchange, London EC3V 3LS
AFM	Hibernian	Haddington Road, Dublin 4
L	Hill Samuel	NLA Tower, Addiscombe Road, Croydon
FL	Ideal	Pitmaston, Birmingham B13
AFLM Re	Insurance Corporation of Ireland	Burlington Road, Dublin 4
L	Irish Life	Lower Abbey Street, Dublin 2
AF	Iron Trades	Iron Trades House, 21–24 Grosvenor Place, London SW1V 7JA
L	LAS Group	113 Dundas Street, Edinburgh EH3 5EB
L	Laurentian Life	Laurentian House, Barnwood, Glos GL4 7RZ
AFLM Re	Legal and General	Temple Court, 11 Queen Victoria Street, London EC4N 4TP
L	Liberty Life	Liberty House, Station Road, New Barnet
AF	Licenses & General	15 Bonhill Street, London EC2A 4BY
AFM	Liverpool Marine & General	4–5 King William Street, London EC4
L	Liverpool Victoria Friendly	Victoria House, Southampton Row, London WC1B 4DB
AFM	Local Government Guarantee (GRE)	Royal Exchange, London EC3V 3LS
AFM Re	Lombard Continental Insurance	77 Gracechurch Street, London EC3
AFM	London & Edinburgh	The Warren, Worthing, W. Sussex BN14 9QD
AFM	London & Lancashire	New Hall Place, Liverpool
L	London & Manchester	Winslade Park, Exeter, Devon EX5 1DS
AFM	London & Scottish (CU)	St Helen's, 1 Undershaft, London EC3
L	London Life	100 Temple Street, Bristol
L	M & G Assurance	M & G House, Victoria Road, Chelmsford
L	Manufacturers Life	St George's Way, Stevenage
M	Marine (R)	34–36 Lime Street, London EC3
M	Maritime (NU)	Surrey Street, Norwich
L	Medical, Sickness, Annuity and Life	7–10 Chandos Street, Cavendish Square, London W1A 2LN
Re	Mercantile & General	Moorfields House, Moorfields, London EC2Y 9AL
L	Merchant Investors (MI Group)	91 Wimpole Street, London W1M 7DA
M	Merchants' Marine (CU)	St Helen's, 1 Undershaft, London EC3
AF	Methodist	Brazennose House, Brazennose Street, Manchester M2 5AS
L	MGM Assurance	MGM House, Heene Road, Worthing BN11 2DY
AFM	Minster	Minster House, Arthur Street, London EC4
AF	Motor Union (GRE)	Royal Exchange, London EC3V 3LS
AFL	Municipal Mutual	25–27 Old Queen Street, London SW1
FL	Nalgo Insurance Association	137 Euston Road, London NW1 2AU
Fidelity Guar.	National Guarantee & Suretyship (CU)	St Helen's, 1 Undershaft, London EC3
L	National Mutual Life	The Priory, Hitchin, Herts. SG5 2DW
L	National Provident Institution	NP House, Tunbridge Wells, Kent TN1 2UE
Machinery	National Vulcan Eng. Ins. Group (SA)	Empire House, St Martin's-le-Grand, London EC1
Naval Officers' risks, etc.	Navigators & General (ES)	113 Queens Road, Brighton BN1 3XN
L	NEL Britannia	Milton Court, Dorking, Surrey RH4 3LZ
AFL Re	NFU Mutual	Tiddington Road, Stratford-upon-Avon CV37 7BJ
AF	Nig Skandia	Crown House, 145 City Road, London EC1V 1LP
L	NM Financial Management	Enterprise House, Isambard Brunel Road, Portsmouth PO1 2AW
AFLM	North British & Mercantile (CU)	St Helen's, 1 Undershaft, London EC3
AFLM	Northern (CU)	St Helen's, 1 Undershaft, London EC3
AFM Re	Norwich Union Fire	Surrey Street, Norwich

Nature of business	*Name of company*	*Head Office address*
L	Norwich Union Life	Surrey Street, Norwich
Re	NRG Victory Reinsurance	Castle Hill Avenue, Folkestone CT20 2TF
AFM	Ocean Accident (CU)	St Helen's, 1 Undershaft, London EC3
M	Ocean Marine (CU)	Room 115, ILU, Leadenhall Street, London EC3
AFM Aviation	Orion	Orion House, Bouverie Road West, Folkestone, Kent CT20 2RW
AFM Re	Palatine	77 Leadenhall Street, London EC3
AFLM Re	Pearl	The Pearl Centre, Lynchwood, Peterborough PE2 6FY
A L Sickness	Permanent	7–10 Chandos Street, Cavendish Square, London W1
AFLM	Phoenix (SA)	1 Bartholomew Lane, London EC2N 2AB
L	Prolific Life and Pensions	Bridge Mills, Stramongate, Kendal LA9 4UB
L	Property Growth	Leon House, High Street, Croydon
L	Provident Life Association	Provident Way, Basingstoke, Hampshire RG21 2SZ
L	Provident Mutual Life	25–31 Moorgate, London EC2R 6BA
F	Provincial	Stramongate, Kendal, Cumbria LA9 4BE
AFLM Re	Prudential	1 Stephen Street, London W1P 2AP
L	Prudential Holborn	30 Old Burlington Street, London W1
AF	Railway Passengers (CU)	St Helen's, 1 Undershaft, London EC3
AFL	Refuge	Refuge House, Alderley Road, Wilmslow, Cheshire SK9 1PF
AFM	Reliance Marine (GRE)	Royal Exchange, London EC3V 3LS
L	Reliance Mutual	Reliance House, Mount Ephraim, Tunbridge Wells, Kent
AF	Road Transport & General (GA)	Pitheavlis, Perth
AF	Royal Exchange	Royal Exchange, London EC3V 3LS
L	Royal Heritage Life	Royal Ins. House, Business Park, Peterborough PE2 6GG
L	Royal Life	PO Box 30, New Hall Place, Liverpool L69 3HS
L	Royal Liver Friendly	Royal Liver Building, Pier Head, Liverpool L3 1HT
AFL	Royal London	Royal London House, Middleborough, Colchester CO1 1RA
L	Royal National Pension Fund for Nurses	Burdett House, 15 Buckingham Street, Strand, London WC2N 6ED
F	Salvation Army	117–121 Judd Street, London WC1H 9NN
L	Save & Prosper	1 Finsbury Avenue, London EC2M
L	Scottish Amicable	150 St Vincent Street, Glasgow G2 5NQ
Engineering	Scottish Boiler (GA)	Pitheavlis, Perth, Scotland
L	Scottish Equitable	28 St Andrew Square, Edinburgh EH2 1YF
M	Scottish General (GA)	100 West Nile Street, Glasgow G12
L	Scottish Legal	95 Bothwell Street, Glasgow G2 7HY
L	Scottish Life	19 St Andrew Square, Edinburgh EH2 2YA
L	Scottish Mutual	109 St Vincent Street, Glasgow G2 5HN
L	Scottish Provident Institution	6 St Andrew Square, Edinburgh EH2 2YA
AFLM	Scottish Union & National (NU)	Surrey Street, Norwich
L	Scottish Widows'	15 Dalkeith Road, Edinburgh EH16 5BU
AFM	Sea (SA)	1 Bartholomew Lane, London EC2N 2AB
L	Sentinel Life	2 Eyre Street Hill, London EC1
L	Stalwart Assurance	Stalwart House, 142 South Street, Dorking RH4 2EV
L	Standard Life	3 George Street, Edinburgh EH2 2X2
AFM	State Assurance (GRE)	Royal Exchange, London EC3V 3LS
AFLM	Sun Alliance and London	1 Bartholomew Lane, London EC2N 2AB
AFM	Sun Insurance Office (SA)	1 Bartholomew Lane, London EC2N 2AB
L	Sun Life Assurance Group	Sun Life Court, Bristol BS99 7SL
L Re	Sun Life of Canada	Basing View, Basingstoke, Hants. RG21 2DZ
AL	Swiss Pioneer Life	16 Crosby Road North, Waterloo, Liverpool L22 0NY
FL	Teacher's Assurance	12 Christchurch Road, Bournemouth BH1 3LW
L	Tunstall & District	Station Chambers, Tunstall, Stoke-on-Trent ST6 6DU
M	Ulster Marine (GA)	Pitheavlis, Perth
AFM	Union Assurance (CU)	St Helen's, 1 Undershaft, London EC3
AFM	Union Insurance Society of Canton (GRE)	Royal Exchange, London EC3V 3LS
M	Union Marine	4–5 King William Street, London EC4
AFL	United Friendly	42 Southwark Bridge Road, London SE1
L	UK Life Assurance	UK House, Worthing Road, Horsham
L	University	4 Coleman Street, London EC2R 5AP
AF	Welsh Insurance Corporation (CU)	St Helen's, 1 Undershaft, London EC3
AFL Re	Wesleyan Assurance	Colmore Circus, Birmingham B4 6AR
AFLM	Western Australian	Swan Court, Mansel Road, Wimbledon, London SW19
AF	West of Scotland (CU)	26 George Street, Edinburgh 2
AF	White Cross (CU)	St Helen's, 1 Undershaft, London EC3
AL	Windsor Life	Windsor House, Telford, Salop TF3 4NB
AFM	World Marine & General (CU)	Dunster House, Mark Lane, London EC3
AFM Re	Zurich	Zurich House, Stanhope Road, Portsmouth

The Stock Exchange

The International Stock Exchange of the United Kingdom and Republic of Ireland Ltd serves the needs of government, industry and investors by providing facilities for raising capital and a central market-place for securities trading. There are 7,300 securities listed on the London Stock Exchange, which have a value of approximately £2,054,926.1 million. In 1991 securities worth some £1,821,828.8 million changed hands. This central market-place covers not only government stocks (called gilts) and UK and overseas company shares (called equities and fixed interest stocks) but other investment instruments such as traded options on equities and indices.

Big Bang

During 1986 the London Stock Exchange went through the greatest period of change in its two-hundred-year history. In March 1986 it opened its doors for the first time to overseas and corporate membership of the Exchange, allowing banks, insurance companies and overseas securities houses to become members of the Exchange and to buy existing member firms. On 27 October 1986, three major reforms took place, changes which became known as 'Big Bang':

1. abolition of scales of minimum commissions, allowing clients to negotiate freely with their brokers about the charge for their services
2. abolition of the separation of member firms into brokers and jobbers. Under the new system, firms are broker/dealers, able to act as agents on behalf of clients; to act as principals buying and selling shares for their own account; and to become registered market makers, making continuous buying and selling prices in specific securities
3. the introduction of the Stock Exchange Automated Quotations (SEAQ) system. Market makers input their buying and selling prices into SEAQ, which displays the competing quotations on a composite page onscreen. For all but the smallest, least frequently traded UK companies, the volume of shares traded is also updated continuously throughout the day.

Of all these changes, the implementation of SEAQ has had perhaps the most visible effect. Dealing in stocks and shares now takes place via the telephone in the firms' own dealing rooms, rather than face to face on the floor of the Exchange. The new systems also provide increased investor protection. All deals taking place via the Exchange's SEAQ system are recorded on a database which can be used to resolve disputes or to carry out investigations.

Members of the London Stock Exchange buy and sell shares on behalf of the public, as well as institutions such as pension funds or insurance companies. In return for transacting the deal, the broker will charge a commission, which is usually based upon the value of the transaction. The market makers, or wholesalers, in each security do not charge a commission for their services, but will quote the broker two prices, a price at which they will buy and a price at which they will sell. It is the middle of these two prices which is published in lists of Stock Exchange prices in newspapers.

Regulatory Bodies

On 12 November 1986 members of the Exchange agreed to merge with members of the international broking community in London, based outside the Exchange, in order to form two new bodies: the International Stock Exchange of the United Kingdom and Republic of Ireland Ltd, and the Securities and Futures Authority. These two regulatory bodies were formed under the provisions of the Financial Services Act 1986, which requires investment businesses to be authorized and regulated by a self-regulating organization (SRO) of which the Securities and Futures Authority is one. The Act also requires business to be conducted through a recognized investment exchange (RIE). The London Stock Exchange is an RIE, regulating three main markets: UK equities, international equities and gilts.

Primary Markets

The Exchange serves the needs of industry by providing a mechanism where companies can raise capital for development and growth through the issue of listed securities. For a company entering the market for the first time there are two possible Stock Exchange markets, depending upon the size, history and requirements of the company. The first is the listed market, which exists for well-established companies which must comply with stringent criteria relating to all aspects of their operations. At present, companies coming to this market require a three-year trading record with a minimum of 25 per cent of the shares held in public hands. The Unlisted Securities Market was established in 1980 with less rigorous entry requirements designed with the smaller and newer company in mind. Companies at present are required to provide a two-year trading record and a minimum of 10 per cent of the shares must be in public hands.

Once admitted to the Exchange, all companies are obliged to keep their shareholders informed of their progress, making announcements of a price-sensitive nature through the Exchange's company announcements department.

The Governing Board

The International Stock Exchange has its headquarters in London, and administrative centres around the UK and the Republic of Ireland. At present there are 395 member firms.

The interests of the membership of the London Stock Exchange are reflected in the governing Board, whose members are responsible for overall policy and the strategic direction of the Exchange. The Board consists of representatives drawn from listed companies, investors and other major users, elected at the annual general meeting, and the Government Broker, the Chief Executive and up to five senior executives of the Stock Exchange.

The London Stock Exchange, Old Broad Street, London EC2N 1HP. Tel: 071-588 2355.

Chairman, Sir Andrew Hugh Smith.

Chief Executive of Stock Exchange, P. J. Rawlins.

Investment Business Regulation

The growth of Britain's financial services industry in the 1970s and 1980s left the regulatory structure existing at that time inadequate to deal with the new competitive climate or to provide the necessary safeguards for the investing public. Under the Financial Services Act 1986, a new supervisory framework was set up to regulate companies conducting investment business and new criminal offences were created. The Act came into force on 29 April 1988, when it became a criminal offence to conduct investment business without authorization, unless specifically exempt from needing authorization.

SECURITIES AND INVESTMENTS BOARD LTD

Gavrelle House, 2–14 Bunhill Row, London EC1Y 8RA
Tel 071-638 1240

The Securities and Investments Board (SIB) is the designated agency under the Financial Services Act 1986 for regulating the activities of investment businesses in the UK. Although not a statutory body, the SIB has statutory powers under the Act to recognize self-regulating organizations, professional bodies, investment exchanges and clearing houses, and directly to authorize firms to undertake investment business in the UK.

It oversees the regulation of all investment business in the UK. It is not responsible for areas involving public issues, takeovers and mergers, and insider dealing investigation. Its area of authority overlaps with that of the Bank of England, the Department of Trade and Industry (for insurance companies) and the Building Societies Commission where their respective member bodies are carrying out investment business.

The regulatory sanctions of the SIB are as follows:

1. It may issue public or private reprimands
2. It may restrict business
3. It may suspend authorization
4. It may withdraw authorization
5. In certain cases it may take out a civil injunction
6. It may petition the Courts for the winding up of companies.

Central Register

Checkline 071-929 3652

The SIB maintains a register of all firms who are authorized to carry on investment business, known as the Central Register. The entry for each firm gives the name, address and telephone number; an SIB reference number; authorization status; appropriate regulatory body; and whether it can handle client money.

Investors Compensation Scheme

The Investors Compensation Scheme, run by a management company as part of the overall investor protection offered by the SIB, comes into play when authorized firms become insolvent owing money to private investors. It is funded by means of a levy on all member firms, according to their size and category.

SELF-REGULATING ORGANIZATIONS

The SIB recognizes self-regulating organizations (SROs), which are responsible to the SIB for ensuring financial supervision in their respective sectors of investment business. Most members of the financial services industry obtain their authorization by being members of an SRO.

The following are recognized by the SIB as being able to provide proper regulation of the investment business carried out by their members, and the necessary standard of investor protection:

FIMBRA (Financial Intermediaries, Managers and Brokers Regulatory Organization), Hertsmere House, Hertsmere Road, London E14 4AB. Tel: 071-538 8860.

IMRO (Investment Management Regulatory Organization), Broadwalk House, Appold Street, London EC2A 2LL. Tel: 071-628 6022.

LAUTRO (Life Assurance and Unit Trust Regulatory Organization), Centre Point, 103 New Oxford Street, London WC1A 1QH. Tel: 071-379 0444.

SFA (Securities and Futures Authority), The Stock Exchange Building, Old Broad Street, London EC2N 1EQ. Tel: 071-256 9000.

IMRO and LAUTRO also regulate the activities of friendly societies.

There are plans to reduce the number of SROs to four with the creation of a new SRO for the private investor, to be called PIA (Personal Investment Authority). This new SRO, replacing FIMBRA and LAUTRO, should become operational in April 1993.

RECOGNIZED PROFESSIONAL BODIES

The SIB also authorizes recognized professional body (RPB) status for companies which undertake investment business but not as their main business activity. The member companies of the RPB must apply for recognition and a certificate will be issued to a particular person.

INSTITUTE OF CHARTERED ACCOUNTANTS IN ENGLAND AND WALES, Chartered Accountants Hall, PO Box 433, Moorgate Place, London EC2P 2BJ. Tel: 071-628 7060.

INSTITUTE OF CHARTERED ACCOUNTANTS OF SCOTLAND, 27 Queen Street, Edinburgh EH2 1LA. Tel: 031-225 5673.

INSTITUTE OF CHARTERED ACCOUNTANTS IN IRELAND, 11 Donegall Square South, Belfast BT1 5JE. Tel: 0232-321600.

CHARTERED ASSOCIATION OF CERTIFIED ACCOUNTANTS, 29 Lincoln's Inn Fields, London WC2A 3EE. Tel: 071-242 6855.

THE LAW SOCIETY, 50–52 Chancery Lane, London WC2A 1SX. Tel: 071-242 1222.

LAW SOCIETY OF SCOTLAND, 26 Drumsheugh Gardens, Edinburgh EH3 7YR. Tel: 031-226 7411.

LAW SOCIETY OF NORTHERN IRELAND, Law Society House, 98 Victoria Street, Belfast BT1 3JZ. Tel: 0232-231614.

INSTITUTE OF ACTUARIES, Staple Inn Hall, High Holborn, London WC1V 7QJ. Tel: 071-242 0106.

INSURANCE BROKERS REGISTRATION COUNCIL, 15 St Helen's Place, London EC3A 6DS. Tel: 071-588 4387.

RECOGNIZED INVESTMENT EXCHANGES

Investment exchanges are exempt from needing authorization from the SIB as an investment business. However, to be a recognized investment exchange (RIE), each must fulfil the following requirements:

1 Adequate financial resources
2 Proper conduct of business rules
3 A proper and reasonable liquid market in its products
4 Procedures of recording transactions
5 Effective monitoring and enforcement of rules
6 Proper arrangements for the clearing and performance of contracts.

INTERNATIONAL PETROLEUM EXCHANGE (IPE), International House, 1 St Katharine's Way, London E1 9UN. Tel: 071-481 0643.

INTERNATIONAL STOCK EXCHANGE OF THE UNITED KINGDOM AND THE REPUBLIC OF IRELAND (ISE), Old Broad Street, London EC2N 1HP. Tel: 071-588 2355.

LONDON COMMODITY EXCHANGE LTD (LONDON FOX), 1 Commodity Quay, St Katharine Docks, London E1 9AX. Tel: 071-481 2080.

LONDON INTERNATIONAL FINANCIAL FUTURES EXCHANGE (LIFFE), Royal Exchange, London EC3V 3PJ. Tel: 071-623 0444.

LONDON METAL EXCHANGE (LME), 4th Floor, E Section, Plantation House, Fenchurch Street, London EC3M 3AP. Tel: 071-626 3311.

OM LONDON LTD, 107 Cannon Street, London EC4N 5AD. Tel: 071-283 0678.

The following overseas exchanges are recognized by the DTI as offering adequate investor protection:

CHICAGO MERCANTILE EXCHANGE, 27 Throgmorton Street, London EC2N 2AN. Tel: 071-920 0722.

NATIONAL ASSOCIATION OF SECURITIES DEALERS AUTOMATED QUOTATIONS SYSTEMS (NASDAQ), 43 London Wall, London EC2M 5TB. Tel: 071-538 5656.

SYDNEY FUTURES EXCHANGE LTD, 30–32 Grosvenor Street, Sydney, NSW 2000, Australia. Tel: 010–2 256 0555.

RECOGNIZED CLEARING HOUSES

A recognized clearing house (RCH) must satisfy the same kind of criteria to obtain recognition as the RIEs. There is one RCH which acts as a clearing house for some of the above RIEs:

LONDON CLEARING HOUSE LTD (LCH), Roman Wall House, 1–2 Crutched Friars, London EC3N 2AN. Tel: 071-265 2000.

DESIGNATED INVESTMENT EXCHANGES

The SIB has drawn up a list of 42 overseas exchanges (known as DIEs) who appear to have operating procedures broadly equivalent to those of the RIEs. Designation merely shows that an exchange meets certain basic criteria but carries no guarantee.

OMBUDSMEN SCHEMES

Independent ombudsmen schemes have been set up for banks, building societies, and insurance companies. They provide an independent and impartial method of resolving disputes that arise between a company and its customer. In each ombudsman scheme there is a council which appoints and supervises the Ombudsman. The Ombudsman Council is composed of people representing public and consumer interests and member companies. The schemes are funded in various ways: annual subscription from member companies, a levy on member companies according to the size of their assets, a charge for each complaint handled against a particular company.

The Investment Management Regulatory Organization (IMRO) has also appointed an independent ombudsman, known as the Investment Ombudsman. The Ombudsman is responsible for resolving disputes that arise between a customer and a member company of IMRO. The Investment Ombudsman scheme is funded by IMRO, but operates independently.

The Pensions Ombudsman is appointed by the Secretary of State for Social Security under the Social Security Act 1990. He attempts to resolve disputes between an individual and his pension scheme, and is responsible to Parliament. The scheme is funded by a statutory levy on pension schemes based on the number of members therein.

THE OFFICE OF THE BANKING OMBUDSMAN, Citadel House, 5–11 Fetter Lane, London EC4A 1BR. Tel: 071-583 1396. *Banking Ombudsman*, L. Shurman.

THE OFFICE OF THE BUILDING SOCIETIES OMBUDSMEN, 35–37 Grosvenor Gardens, London SW1X 7AW. Tel: 071-931 0044. *Building Societies Ombudsmen*, S. Edell, B. Murphy, Ms J. Woodhead.

THE INSURANCE OMBUDSMAN BUREAU, City Gate One, 135 Park Street, London SE1 9EA. Tel: 071-928 7600. *Insurance Ombudsman*, Dr J. T. Farrand. *Deputy Ombudsman*, L. Slade.

INVESTMENT OMBUDSMAN, 6 Frederick Place, London EC2R 8BT. Tel: 071-796 3065. *Investment Ombudsman*, R. Youard.

THE PENSIONS OMBUDSMAN, 11 Belgrave Road, London SW1V 1RB. Tel: 071-834 9144. *Pensions Ombudsman*, M. Platt.

THE TAKEOVER PANEL

PO Box 226, The Stock Exchange Building, London EC2P 2JX
Tel 071-382 9026

The Takeover Panel was set up in 1968 in response to concern about practices unfair to shareholders in takeover bids for public and certain private companies. Its principal objective is to ensure equality of treatment, and fair opportunity for all shareholders to consider on its merits an offer that would result in the change of control of a company. It is a non-statutory body that operates the City Code on Takeovers and Mergers.

The chairman, deputy chairmen and two lay members of the panel are appointed by the Bank of England. The remainder are representatives of the following: British Bankers' Association; Association of British Insurers; Association of Investment Trust Companies; British Merchant Banking and Securities House Association; Confederation of British Industry; IMRO; Institute of Chartered Accountants in England and Wales; London Stock Exchange; National Association of Pension Funds; SFA; Unit Trust Association.
Chairman, Sir David Calcutt, QC.

Taxation

INCOME TAX

Income tax is charged on the total income of individuals for a year of assessment commencing on 6 April and ending on the following 5 April. The rates of tax and the calculation of liability will frequently differ, sometimes substantially, as between one year of assessment and another. The following information is confined to the year of assessment 1992–3, ending on 5 April 1993.

Liability to income tax is determined by establishing the taxable income for a year of assessment. The income will be reduced by an individual's personal allowances and other reliefs. The first £2,000 of taxable income remaining is assessable to income tax at the lower rate of 20 per cent and the next £21,700 at the basic rate of 25 per cent. Should any excess remain over £23,700 (£2,000 plus £21,700) this will be taxable at the higher rate of 40 per cent.

The three rates apply to the assessment of both earned and investment income. Indeed, there is little distinction between the two classes, although the receipt of earned income may produce an entitlement to some allowances not available against investment income.

The tables on the following page show the income tax payable for 1992–3 by an individual on the amount of income specified, after deducting the personal allowance and married couple's allowance also, where appropriate. Elderly persons over the age of 74 years may pay less tax. The taxpayer may also be entitled to transitional allowances and other reliefs which reduce the tax payable below the amount shown by the tables.

Trustees administering settled property are chargeable to income tax at the basic rate of 25 per cent. Where the trustees retain discretionary powers, or income is accumulated, there will also be liability to the additional rate of 10 per cent. Companies residing in the United Kingdom are not liable to income tax but suffer corporation tax on income, profits and gains.

The charge to income tax broadly arises on all taxable income accruing from sources in the United Kingdom. Individuals who are resident in this territory may also become liable on income arising overseas. An individual is resident in the United Kingdom if he or she normally resides here. Persons not normally residing in the United Kingdom may become resident if they visit this territory for periods which average three months or more throughout a period of years, or are present for at least 183 days in a particular year. The existence of a place of abode in the United Kingdom may be sufficient to indicate residence if visits of any duration are made during the year of assessment.

Income arising overseas will often incur liability to foreign taxation. If that income is also chargeable to United Kingdom income tax, excessive liability could well arise. The United Kingdom has concluded double taxation agreements with many overseas territories and these ensure that the same slice of income is not doubly assessed. In the absence of such an agreement, foreign tax suffered can usually be relieved under the domestic code when calculating liability to United Kingdom income tax.

Independent Taxation

For many years the income of a married woman 'living with' her husband was treated as that of the husband for income tax purposes. This did not generally apply in the year of marriage and it remained possible for the couple to exercise the right of separate assessment or for the wife to be separately assessed as a single person on her earned income. However, the husband was usually responsible for submitting income tax returns, for discharging income tax on the combined incomes and dealing generally with taxation matters.

This practice ceased to apply on 6 April 1990 with the introduction of independent taxation. From this date a husband and wife are independently taxed, with each entitled to a personal allowance. In most situations any unused personal allowance available to one spouse cannot be transferred to the other. A married man 'living with' his wife can obtain a married couple's allowance. This allowance must, if possible, be set against the husband's income but where that income is insufficient, any balance of the married couple's allowance may be transferred to the wife. From 6 April 1993 it will be possible for a married woman to claim half the basic married couple's allowance. The entire allowance may be obtained by the wife, if her husband so agrees.

Each spouse may obtain other allowances and reliefs where the underlying conditions are satisfied. Income must be accurately allocated between a husband and wife by reference to the individual beneficially entitled to that income. Where income arises from jointly-held assets, this must be apportioned equally between husband and wife. However, in those cases where the beneficial interests in jointly-held assets are not equal, a special declaration can be made to apportion income by reference to the actual interests in that income.

Income Taxable

Income tax is assessed and collected under several Schedules. Each Schedule determines the extent of liability and establishes the amount to be included in taxable income. In some instances the actual income arising in a year of assessment will be charged to income tax for that year. A different basis of assessment may arise for income taxable under Cases I to V of Schedule D. Frequently, income assessable under these Cases will be that arising in a previous year or period but there are special rules where a new source is acquired or an existing source discontinued.

Following the withdrawal of income tax liability for most commercial woodlands in the United Kingdom, Schedule B no longer applies. The contents of the remaining schedules are shown below.

Schedule A

Tax is charged on annual profits arising from the ownership or occupation of land in the United Kingdom. This will include rents, ground rents and other income from land. Expenditure incurred by the landlord on maintenance, repairs, insurance and management can be subtracted from the annual profits. This Schedule does not include profits from farming, market gardening or woodlands, nor does it extend to mineral rents and royalties. Premiums arising on the grant of a lease for a period not exceeding fifty years are assessed to income tax as rent. However, the amount of the taxable premium may be reduced by 2 per cent for each complete year, after the first year, of the leasing period. Income from furnished lettings is assessable under Case VI of Schedule D, unless an option is exercised for such income to be assessed under Schedule A. Where income arises from

SINGLE PERSONS AND MARRIED WOMEN

Income	Persons under 65		Persons 65 or over*	
£	Income tax £	Average rate %	Income tax £	Average rate %
4,000	111	2.8	—	—
5,000	311	6.2	160	3.2
6,000	539	9.0	360	6.0
7,000	789	11.3	600	8.6
8,000	1,039	13.0	850	10.6
9,000	1,289	14.3	1,100	12.2
10,000	1,539	15.4	1,350	13.5
12,000	2,039	17.0	1,850	15.4
14,000	2,539	18.1	2,350	16.8
16,000	3,039	19.0	3,039	19.0
18,000	3,539	19.7	3,539	19.7
20,000	4,039	20.2	4,039	20.2
25,000	5,289	21.2	5,289	21.2
30,000	6,967	23.2	6,967	23.2
40,000	10,967	27.4	10,967	27.4
50,000	14,967	29.9	14,967	29.9
60,000	18,967	31.6	18,967	31.6
100,000	34,967	35.0	34,967	35.0

* Persons aged 75 or over suffer rather less tax on income falling below £16,000 on this table

MARRIED MEN

Income	Couples under 65		Couples 65 or over†	
£	Income tax £	Average rate %	Income tax £	Average rate %
6,000	167	2.8	—	—
7,000	367	5.2	67	1.0
8,000	609	7.6	267	3.3
9,000	859	9.5	484	5.4
10,000	1,109	11.1	734	7.3
12,000	1,609	13.4	1,235	10.3
14,000	2,109	15.1	1,734	12.4
16,000	2,609	16.3	2,459	15.4
18,000	3,109	17.3	3,109	17.3
20,000	3,609	18.0	3,609	18.0
25,000	4,859	19.4	4,859	19.4
30,000	6,279	20.9	6,279	20.9
40,000	10,279	25.7	10,279	25.7
50,000	14,279	28.6	14,279	28.6
60,000	18,279	30.5	18,279	30.5
100,000	34,279	34.3	34,279	34.3

† Persons aged 75 or over suffer rather less tax on income falling below £18,000 on this table

furnished holiday lettings, additional expenditure may be included in calculating income chargeable to tax. Income from furnished holiday lettings is treated as earned income.

For 1992–3 and future years, receipts not exceeding £3,250 annually and received by an individual from letting property furnished in his or her own home are no longer chargeable to tax.

Schedule C

This Schedule is confined to interest or dividends on government or public authority funds and certain payments made out of the public revenues of overseas countries.

Schedule D

This Schedule is divided into six Cases, as follows:

Cases I and II – Profits arising from trades, professions and vocations, including farming and market gardening. Capital expenditure incurred on assets used for business purposes will often produce an entitlement to capital allowances which reduce the profits chargeable. These profits may also be reduced following the submission of claims for loss relief and other matters.

Case III – Interest on government stocks not taxed at source (e.g. War Loan and British Savings Bonds), interest on National Savings Bank deposits and discounts. Interest up to £70 on ordinary National Savings Bank deposits is exempt from income tax. The exemption applies to both husband and wife separately. Interest on National Savings Bank Special Investment accounts is not exempt.

Cases IV and V – Interest from overseas securities, rents, dividends and all other income accruing outside the United Kingdom. Assessment is based on the full amount of income arising, whether remitted to the United Kingdom or retained overseas, but individuals who are either not domiciled in the United Kingdom or who are ordinarily resident overseas may be taxed on a remittance basis. Overseas pensions are taxable but the amount arising may be reduced by 10 per cent for assessment purposes.

Case VI – Sundry profits and annual receipts not assessed under any other Case or Schedule. These may include insurance commissions, post-cessation receipts, income from furnished lettings, and numerous other receipts specifically charged under Case VI.

Schedule E

All emoluments from an office or employment are assessable under this Schedule. There are three Cases, as follows:

Case I – This applies to all emoluments of an individual resident and ordinarily resident in the United Kingdom.

Case II – Of application where the individual is not resident or not ordinarily resident and extends to emoluments for duties undertaken in the United Kingdom.

Case III – Applies in rare situations to other emoluments remitted to the United Kingdom.

Although earnings for overseas duties may be assessable under Case I where the employee is resident and ordinarily resident in the United Kingdom, a foreign earnings deduction of 100 per cent may be available, which reduces the overseas assessable earnings to nil. This deduction can be obtained where duties are performed overseas for a continuous period reaching or exceeding 365 days and is confined to earnings from the overseas activity.

A 'receipts basis' applies for determining the year of assessment in which earnings must be taxed. Where emoluments are assessable under Case I or Case II, the date of receipt will comprise the earlier of:

(a) the date of payment
(b) the date entitlement arises

In the case of company directors it is the earliest of the two dates given above with the addition of the following three which establish the time of receipt:

(c) the date emoluments are credited in the company's books
(d) where emoluments for a period are determined after the end of that period, the date of determination
(e) where emoluments for a period are determined in that period, the last day of that period

The emoluments assessable under Schedule E include all salaries, wages, director's fees and other money sums. In addition, there are a wide range of benefits which must be added to taxable emoluments. These include the provision of living accommodation on advantageous terms and advantages arising from the use of vouchers.

Further taxable benefits accrue to directors and employees receiving emoluments of £8,500 or more in the year of assessment. These benefits include the reimbursement of expenses, the availability of motor cars for private motoring, the provision of petrol or other fuel for private motoring, the provision of interest-free loans, and other benefits provided at the employer's expense. The cost of providing a limited range of child care facilities may be excluded.

In arriving at the amount to be assessed under Schedule E, all expenses incurred wholly, exclusively and necessarily in the performance of the duties may be deducted. This includes fees and subscriptions paid to certain professional bodies and learned societies. Fees paid to managers by entertainers, actors and others assessable under Schedule E may be deducted, up to a maximum of 17.5 per cent of earnings.

Compensation for loss of office and other sums received on the termination of an office or employment are assessable to tax. However, the first £30,000 may be excluded with only the balance remaining chargeable, unless the compensatory payment is linked with the retirement of the recipient.

Earnings received from an approved profit-related pay scheme are exempt from income tax.

Schedule F

This Schedule is concerned with company dividends and distributions. A United Kingdom resident company paying a dividend or making a distribution must account to the Inland Revenue for advance corporation tax at the rate equal to one-third of the sum paid to shareholders in 1992–3. A shareholder residing in the United Kingdom receives the dividend or distribution, together with a tax credit equal to the amount of advance corporation tax. The dividend or distribution is regarded as having suffered income tax, equal to the tax credit, at the basic rate of 25 per cent. Where the shareholder is not liable, or not fully liable, at this rate a repayment can be obtained. Individuals liable at the higher rate of 40 per cent will incur further liability. Some payments made by an unquoted trading company to redeem or purchase its own shares are not treated as distributions.

Building society interest and bank interest

From 6 April 1991 many payments of building society and bank interest are received after the deduction of income tax at the basic rate of 25 per cent. However, those not liable to income tax at the basic rate may arrange to receive interest gross, with no tax being deducted on payment. Others who suffer income tax by deduction can obtain a repayment in whole or in part if they are not fully liable at the basic rate.

Income Not Taxable

This includes interest on National Savings Certificates, most scholarship income, bounty payments to members of the armed services and annuities payable to the holders of certain awards. Dividend income arising from investments in personal equity plans may be exempt from tax. Income received under most maintenance agreements and court orders made after 30 June 1988 will not be liable to tax. Nor will payments made under many deeds of covenant executed after 14 March 1988 be recognized for tax purposes, unless the recipient is a charity. Interest arising on a Tax Exempt Special Savings Account (TESSA) opened with a building society or bank will be exempt from tax, if the account is maintained throughout a five-year period.

Social Security Benefits

Many social security benefits are not liable to income tax. These include income support, family credit, maternity allowance, long-term sickness benefit, child benefit, war widow's pension, disability living allowance and numerous others. Among the limited range of benefits which are taxable is the retirement pension, widow's allowance, widowed mother's allowance, and unemployment benefits. Short-term sickness benefit and maternity pay payable by an employer are also chargeable to tax.

Pay As You Earn

The Pay As You Earn system is not an independent form of taxation but has been designed to collect income tax by deduction from most emoluments. When paying emoluments to employees, an employer is usually required to deduct income tax and account for that tax to the Inland Revenue. In many cases this deduction procedure will fully exhaust the individual's liability to income tax, unless there is other income. The date of 'receipt' used for assessment purposes (*see* above) also identifies the date of 'payment' when establishing liability for PAYE.

Allowances

The allowances available to individuals for 1992–3 are outlined below.

Personal allowance

Each individual receives a basic personal allowance of £3,445. This is increased to £4,200 for individuals over the age of 64 on 5 April 1993, and further increased to £4,370 for those over the age of 74 on the same date. The increased allowance is available for those who died during the year of assessment but who would otherwise have achieved the appropriate age not later than 5 April 1993.

The amount of the increased personal allowance for older taxpayers will be reduced by one-half of total income in excess of £14,200. This reduction in the allowance will continue until it has been reduced to the basic personal allowance of £3,445.

Apart from limited transitional matters mentioned below, any unused part of the personal allowance of one spouse cannot be transferred to the other.

Married couple's allowance

A married man who was 'living with' his wife at any time in the year ending on 5 April 1993 is entitled to a married couple's allowance. The basic allowance is £1,720. This may be increased to £2,465 if either the husband or the wife is 65 years or over at any time in the year ending on 5 April 1993. A further increase to £2,505 can be obtained where either party to the marriage was 75 or over on 5 April 1993. Where an individual would otherwise have reached either age by 5 April 1993, but who died earlier in the year, the increased allowance is given.

The amount of the increased married couple's allowance may be reduced where the income of the husband (excluding the income of the wife) exceeds £14,200. The reduction will comprise:

(a) one-half of the husband's total income in excess of £14,200, less
(b) the amount of any reduction made when calculating the husband's increased personal allowance

This reduction in the married couple's allowance cannot reduce that allowance below the basic amount of £1,720.

If husband and wife were married during 1992–3 the married couple's allowance of £1,720, or any increased sum, must be reduced by one-twelfth for each complete month commencing on 6 April 1992, and preceding the date of marriage.

Where a husband cannot utilize all or any part of the married couple's allowance due to an absence of income, he may transfer the unused portion to his wife. The decision whether or not to transfer remains with the husband and he cannot be compelled to act.

A different basis may apply when allocating the married couple's allowance for 1993–4 and future years. By filing an election the wife may obtain one-half the basic allowance, leaving the husband with the balance. Alternatively, the couple may jointly elect that the entire allowance should be allocated to the wife only. Except in the year of marriage the election must be made before the commencement of the year of assessment to which it is to apply. It will be possible to transfer any part of the unused allowance to the other spouse.

Additional personal allowance

An allowance of £1,720 is available to a single person who has a qualifying child resident with him or her in 1992–3. The allowance can also be obtained by a married man whose wife is totally incapacitated by physical or mental infirmity throughout the year.

A 'qualifying child' for 1992–3 must be born during the year, be under the age of 16 years at the commencement of the year, or be over the age of 16 at the commencement of the year and either receiving full-time instruction at a university, college, school or other educational establishment or undergoing training for a trade, profession or vocation throughout a minimum period of two years. It is also necessary that the child is the claimant's own, a stepchild of the claimant, an illegitimate child if the parents married after the child's birth, or an adopted child under the age of 18 at the time of adoption. Alternatively it must be shown that the child was either born during 1992–3 or under the age of 18 at the commencement of the year and maintained by the claimant at his or her own expense during the whole of the succeeding twelve-month period.

Only one additional personal allowance of £1,720 can be obtained by an individual notwithstanding the number of children involved. Where an unmarried couple are living together as husband and wife, it is not possible for both to obtain the additional personal allowance.

Widow's bereavement allowance

For the year of assessment in which a husband dies his surviving widow may obtain a widow's bereavement allowance which is £1,720 for 1992–3. It is a requirement that the parties were 'living together' immediately before the husband's death. A similar allowance will be available in the year following death, unless the widow remarried in the year of death. No widow's bereavement allowance can be obtained for future years.

Blind person's allowance

An allowance of £1,080 is available to an individual if at any time during the year ending on 5 April 1993, he or she was registered as blind on a register maintained by a local authority. If the individual is 'living with' a wife or husband, any unused part of the blind person's allowance can be transferred to the other spouse.

Transitional allowances

There are three limited transitional allowances which are intended to ensure that the introduction of independent taxation does not increase liability to income tax. These allowances comprise:

(a) an increased personal allowance available to a wife where the husband cannot fully use that allowance in 1992–3
(b) a special personal allowance available to a husband where his wife falls into a higher age group, namely over 64 or over 74
(c) a married couple's allowance available to a separated husband not 'living with' his wife if the separation occurred before 6 April 1990

Life Assurance Relief

Life assurance deduction relief is limited to premiums paid on policies made before 14 March 1984. No relief is available for policies issued after this date. Where the terms of a policy made before 14 March 1984 are subsequently varied or extended to produce increased benefits, future premiums paid may no longer qualify for relief.

When paying premiums under a qualifying policy made before 14 March 1984, the payer will deduct and retain income tax at the rate of 12.5 per cent. The ability to retain deductions made in this manner is not affected by the payer's liability to income tax on taxable income. No restriction to the deduction procedure arises if aggregate premiums paid during a year of assessment do not exceed £1,500 (calculated before deducting tax). Should premiums exceed this amount, relief will be confined to £1,500 or one-sixth of total income, whichever is the greater. Where sums deducted exceed the maximum limit, the excess must be accounted for to the Inland Revenue.

Other Deductions

In addition to personal and other allowances, which reduce taxable income, further deductions may be available to an individual. These include payments of interest.

In some instances, interest paid by a business proprietor may be included when calculating profits chargeable to income tax under Case I or Case II of Schedule D. Many private individuals cannot obtain relief in this manner and must satisfy stringent requirements before relief will be forthcoming. In general terms, before interest can qualify for relief it must be annual, as opposed to short, interest or paid to a bank, stockbroker or discount house. Relief will not be available to the extent that interest exceeds a reasonable commercial rate and no relief is forthcoming for interest on an overdraft.

For 1992–3 relief will be available on the following payments:

(a) Interest on a loan to purchase, develop or improve an interest in land owned by the individual and used as the only or main residence of that individual. 'Land' includes large houseboats and also caravans used for a similar purpose. No relief is available for interest on loans applied after 5 April 1988 for the development or improvement of land, unless the work involves the construction of a new building. Relief is available for interest paid on a loan applied to acquire a property which is the only or main residence of a dependent relative, a separated spouse or a divorced former spouse, but only where that person occupied the property before 6 April 1988. Relief may also be forthcoming for interest on a loan used to acquire some other property, perhaps to be used as the only or main residence on retirement, by an individual who is compelled to occupy property by reason of his or her work. If the loan, or aggregate of several loans, exceeds £30,000, relief is restricted to interest on that amount. Where two or more persons apply loans after 31 July 1988 to acquire interests in a single building, those persons cannot, collectively, obtain relief for interest on more than £30,000 in relation to that building. For interest paid after 5 April 1991, relief is confined to income tax at the basic rate. There can be no relief at the higher rate in excess of 25 per cent

(b) Interest on a loan to purchase or improve an interest in land which is let or available for letting at a commercial rent. This interest is only capable of being deducted from rental income
(c) Interest on a loan made to acquire an interest in a close company or in a partnership, or to advance money to such a person
(d) Interest on a loan to a member of a partnership to acquire machinery or plant for use in the partnership business
(e) Interest on a loan to an employed person to acquire machinery or plant for the purposes of his/her employment
(f) Interest on a loan made for the purpose of contributing capital to an industrial co-operative
(g) Interest on a loan applied for investment in an employee-controlled company
(h) Interest on a loan made to elderly persons for the purchase of an annuity where the loan is secured on land. If the loan exceeds £30,000, relief is limited to interest on this amount. This relief also is restricted to income tax at the basic rate for payments made after 5 April 1991
(i) Interest on a loan to personal representatives to provide funds for the payment of capital transfer tax or inheritance tax

Relief for many payments of mortgage interest is obtained through a special scheme known as MIRAS (mortgage interest relief at source). This applies to interest paid to a building society, bank, insurance company and certain other approved persons. When making payments of this nature the payer will deduct and retain income tax at the basic rate. This will provide the payer with full relief at the basic rate and no other relief will be necessary. Qualifying payments of interest outside the MIRAS scheme continue to produce relief by deduction from income chargeable to income tax at the basic rate. Where mortgage interest is payable by a husband and/or his wife 'living together', the parties may allocate the interest payment between themselves in whatever manner is most tax-efficient. With the withdrawal of relief at the higher rate little advantage now arises from this facility.

Many employees pay contributions to an approved occupational pension scheme. The amount of their contributions may be deducted when establishing emoluments assessable under Schedule E. Relief should also be available for any additional voluntary contributions paid.

Self-employed individuals and those receiving earnings not covered by an occupational pension scheme may contribute under personal pension scheme arrangements. These individuals may also pay premiums under retirement annuity schemes, if the arrangements were concluded before 1 July 1988. Contributions paid under both headings may obtain income tax relief, subject to maximum limits.

Subject to a maximum of £40,000 in any one year, the cost of subscribing for shares in an unquoted company may qualify as a deduction from taxable income under the Business Expansion Scheme. Many requirements must be satisfied before this relief can be obtained, but husband and wife may each take advantage of the £40,000 annual maximum. The relief is being withdrawn and will cease to be available for subscriptions made after 31 December 1993.

CAPITAL GAINS TAX

A person is chargeable to capital gains tax on chargeable gains which accrue to him or her during a year of assessment ending on 5 April. The application of the tax has been amended substantially in recent years and the following information is confined to the year of assessment 1992–3, ending on 5 April 1993.

Liability extends to persons who are either resident or ordinarily resident for the year but special rules apply where a person permanently leaves the United Kingdom or comes to this territory for the purpose of acquiring residence. Non-residents are not liable to capital gains tax unless, exceptionally, they carry on a business in the United Kingdom through a branch or agency.

Chargeable gains accruing to companies are assessable to corporation tax and not to capital gains tax.

Capital gains tax is chargeable on the total of chargeable gains which accrue to a person in a year of assessment, after subtracting allowable losses arising in the same year. Unused allowable losses brought forward from some earlier year may be offset against current chargeable gains but in the case of individuals this must not reduce the net chargeable gains for 1992–3 below £5,800. It is possible to utilize trading losses in this manner for 1991–2 and future years where those losses have not been offset against income.

Rate of Tax

Where the net chargeable gains accruing to an individual during 1992–3 do not exceed £5,800 there will be no liability to capital gains tax. If the net gains exceed £5,800 the excess is chargeable at the taxpayer's marginal rate of income tax. This is achieved by adding to the amount of income chargeable to income tax the excess net chargeable gains. The rate attributable to this top slice will disclose the rate of capital gains tax payable, which may be at 20 per cent, 25 per cent, 40 per cent or a combination of the three. Although income tax rates are used, capital gains tax remains a separate tax.

Capital gains tax for 1992–3 normally falls due for payment on or before 1 December 1993. If the return or other information recording chargeable gains is delayed, interest may become chargeable.

Husband and Wife

For 1989–90 and earlier years only one aggregate annual exemption was available for a husband and wife 'living together'. In addition, apart from the year of marriage, chargeable gains of a married woman 'living with' her husband were assessed and charged on the husband, unless an election for separate assessment was made. This election did not reduce the aggregate tax payable but merely apportioned liability between the spouses on an equitable basis.

This treatment of a married woman's gains ceased to apply on 6 April 1990. For the future, each spouse is independently assessed on his or her gains, with each being separately entitled to the annual exemption of £5,800 for 1992–3.

No liability to capital gains tax arises from the transfer of assets between spouses 'living together'.

Disposal of Assets

Before liability to capital gains tax can arise a disposal, or deemed disposal, of an asset must take place. This occurs not only where assets are sold or exchanged but applies on the making of a gift. There is also a disposal of assets where any capital sum is derived from assets, for example, where compensation is received for loss or damage to an asset.

The date on which a disposal must be treated as having taken place will determine the year of assessment into which the chargeable gain or allowable loss falls. In those cases where a disposal is made under an unconditional contract, the time of disposal will be that when the contract was entered into and not the subsequent date of conveyance or transfer. A disposal under a conditional contract or option is treated as taking place when the contract becomes unconditional or the option is exercised. Disposals by way of gift are undertaken when the gift becomes effective.

Valuation of Assets

The amount actually received as consideration for the disposal of an asset will be the sum from which very limited outgoings must be deducted for the purpose of establishing the gain or loss. In some cases, however, the consideration passing will not accurately reflect the value of the asset and a different basis must be used. This applies, in particular, where an asset is transferred by way of gift or otherwise than by a bargain made at arm's length. Such transactions are deemed to take place for a consideration representing market value, which will determine both the disposal proceeds accruing to the transferor and the cost of acquisition to the transferee.

Market value represents the price which an asset might reasonably be expected to fetch on a sale in the open market. In the case of unquoted shares or securities, it is to be assumed that the hypothetical purchaser in the open market would have available all the information which a prudent prospective purchaser of shares or securities might reasonably require if he were proposing to purchase them from a willing vendor by private treaty and at arm's length. This is an important consideration as the amount of information deemed to be available to a hypothetical purchaser may materially affect the price 'reasonably' offered in an open market situation. The market value of unquoted shares or securities will usually be established following negotiations with the Shares Valuation Division of the Capital Taxes Office. The valuation of land and interests in land in the United Kingdom will be dealt with by the District Valuer.

Special rules apply to determine the market value of shares quoted on the Stock Exchange.

Deduction for Outgoings

Once the actual or notional disposal proceeds have been determined, it only remains to subtract eligible outgoings for the purpose of computing the gain or loss. There is the general rule that any outgoings deducted, or which are available to be deducted, when calculating income tax liability must be ignored. Subject to this, deductions will usually be limited to:

(a) the cost of acquiring the asset, together with incidental costs wholly and exclusively incurred in connection with the acquisition
(b) expenditure incurred wholly and exclusively on the asset in enhancing its value, being expenditure reflected in the state or nature of the asset at the time of the disposal, and any other expenditure wholly and exclusively incurred in establishing, preserving or defending title to, or a right over, the asset
(c) the incidental costs of making the disposal

Where the disposal concerns a leasehold interest having less than 50 years to run, any expenditure falling under (a) and (b) must be written off throughout the duration of the lease. This recognizes that a lease is a wasting asset which, at the termination of the leasing period, will retain no value.

Assets held on 31 March 1982

Where the disposal of assets held on 31 March 1982 takes place after 5 April 1988, the actual cost of acquisition will not usually enter into the calculation of gain. It is to be assumed that such assets were acquired on 31 March 1982 for a consideration representing market value on that date. The increase in value, if any, occurring before 31 March 1982 will not be assessable to capital gains tax.

Indexation Allowance

An indexation allowance will be available when calculating the chargeable gain or allowable loss. This allowance is based on percentage increases in the retail prices index between the month of March 1982 or, if later, the month in which expenditure is incurred, and the month of disposal. The increase is applied to the items of expenditure in (a) and (b) above to determine the amount of the indexation allowance. However, if the asset was acquired before 31 March 1982 and the disposal occurs after 5 April 1988, the allowance will be based on market value at 31 March 1982.

The amount of the indexation allowance will be subtracted from the gain, or added to the loss, to calculate the chargeable gain or allowable loss arising on disposal.

Exemptions

There is a general exemption from liability to capital gains tax where the net gains of an individual for 1992–3 do not exceed £5,800. This general exemption applies separately to a husband and to his wife where the parties are 'living together'.

The disposal of many assets will not give rise to chargeable gains or allowable losses and these include:

(a) private motor cars
(b) government securities
(c) loan stock and other securities (but not shares)
(d) options and contracts relating to securities within (b) and (c)
(e) National Savings Certificates, Premium Bonds, Defence Bonds and National Development Bonds
(f) currency of any description acquired for personal expenditure outside the United Kingdom
(g) decorations awarded for valour
(h) betting wins and pools, lottery or games prizes
(i) compensation or damages for any wrong or injury suffered by an individual in his/her person or in his/her profession or vocation
(j) life assurance and deferred annuity contracts where the person making the disposal is the original beneficial owner
(k) dwelling-houses and land enjoyed with the residence which is an individual's only or main residence
(l) tangible movable property, the consideration for the disposal of which does not exceed £6,000
(m) certain tangible movable property which is a wasting asset having a life not exceeding 50 years
(n) assets transferred to charities and other bodies
(o) works of art, historic buildings and similar assets
(p) assets used to provide maintenance funds for historic buildings
(q) assets transferred to trustees for the benefit of employees

Dwelling-houses

Exemption from capital gains tax will usually be available for any gain which accrues to an individual from the disposal of, or of an interest in, a dwelling-house or part of a dwelling-house which has been his/her only or main residence. The exemption extends to land which has been occupied and enjoyed with the residence as its garden or grounds. Some restriction may be necessary where the land exceeds half a hectare.

The gain will not be chargeable to capital gains tax if the dwelling-house, or part, has been the individual's only or main residence throughout the period of ownership, or throughout the entire period except for all or any part of the last three years (or two years for disposals before 19 March 1991). A proportionate part of the gain will be exempt if the dwelling-house has been the individual's only or main residence for part only of the period of ownership. In the case of property acquired before 31 March 1982, the period of ownership is treated as commencing on this date.

Where part of the dwelling-house has been used exclusively for business purposes, that part of the gain attributable to business use will not be exempt. It will be comparatively unusual for any part to be used exclusively for such a purpose, except perhaps in the case of doctors' or dentists' surgeries.

In those cases where part of a qualifying dwelling-house has been used to provide rented residential accommodation this non-personal use may frequently be ignored when calculating exemption from capital gains tax, unless relatively substantial sums are involved.

Dwellings occupied by dependent relatives or separated or divorced former spouses, may also qualify for the exemption, but only where occupation commenced before 6 April 1988.

Roll-over Relief

Persons carrying on business will often undertake the disposal of an asset and use the proceeds to finance the acquisition of a replacement asset. Where this situation arises a claim for roll-over relief may be available. The broad effect of such a claim is that all or part of the gain arising on the disposal of the old asset may be disregarded. The gain or part is then subtracted from the cost of acquiring the replacement asset. As this cost is reduced, any gain arising from the future disposal of the replacement asset will be correspondingly increased, unless of course a further roll-over situation then develops.

It remains a requirement that both the old and the replacement asset must be used for the purpose of the taxpayer's business. Relief will only be available if the acquisition of the replacement asset takes place within a period commencing twelve months before, and ending three years after, the disposal of the old asset, although the Board of Inland Revenue retain a discretion to extend this period where the circumstances were such that it was impossible for the taxpayer to acquire the replacement asset before the expiration of the normal time limit.

Whilst many business assets qualify for roll-over relief there are exceptions.

Gifts

The gift of an asset is treated as a disposal made for a consideration equal to market value, with a corresponding acquisition by the transferee at an identical value. In the case of gifts made by individuals and a limited range of trustees after 13 March 1989, and to a transferee resident in the United Kingdom, a form of hold-over relief may be available. Relief is limited to the transfer of certain assets only including the following:

(a) assets used for the purposes of a trade or similar activity carried on by the transferor or his/her family company
(b) shares or securities of a trading company which is neither quoted on a stock exchange nor dealt in on the Unlisted Securities Market
(c) shares or securities of a trading company which is quoted or listed but which is the transferor's family company
(d) many interests in agricultural property qualifying for business property relief or agricultual property relief for inheritance tax purposes
(e) assets involved in transactions which are lifetime transfers for inheritance tax purposes, other than potentially exempt transfers

The effect of the claim is similar to that following a claim for roll-over relief, but adjustments will be necessary where some consideration is given for the transfer, the asset has not been used for business purposes throughout the period of ownership, or not all assets of a company are used for business purposes.

Retirement Relief

Retirement relief is available to an individual who disposes by way of sale or gift of the whole or part of a business. It does not necessarily follow that the isolated disposal of assets will represent the disposal of the whole or part of a business. The main condition for granting this relief is that throughout a period of at least one year the business has been owned either by the individual or by a trading company in which the individual retained a sufficient shareholding interest. The relief extends also to cases where an individual disposes by way of sale or gift of shares or securities of a company. It must be demonstrated that the company was a trading company, that the individual retained a sufficient shareholding interest, and that he/she was engaged as a full-time working director.

An individual who has attained the age of 55 years at the time of a disposal may obtain retirement relief up to a maximum of £375,000 for disposals taking place after 18 March 1991. The amount of this relief must be reduced if the conditions have not been satisfied throughout a ten-year period. With a single exception no retirement relief can be obtained if the disposal occurs before the individual's 55th birthday. This exception arises where an individual is compelled to retire early on the grounds of ill-health. The normal retirement relief may then be obtained. Any retirement relief must be subtracted from the net gains arising on disposal, leaving the balance remaining, if any, chargeable to capital gains tax in the normal manner.

Death

No capital gains tax is chargeable on the value of assets retained at the time of death. However, the personal representatives administering the deceased's estate are deemed to acquire those assets for a consideration representing market value on death. This ensures that any increase in value occurring before the date of death will not be chargeable to capital gains tax. If a legatee or other person acquires an asset under a will or intestacy no chargeable gain will accrue to the personal representatives, and the person taking the asset will also be treated as having acquired it at the time of death for its then market value.

INHERITANCE TAX

Throughout a period of some 90 years estate duty was payable on the value of an individual's estate at the time of death. Liability did not extend to lifetime gifts other than those made shortly before death and a limited range of further gifts where the donor continued to retain some benefit from the assets gifted. Estate duty ceased to apply for deaths occurring after 12 March 1975 following the introduction of capital transfer tax. This tax was not limited to the value of an estate at the time of death but applied to many gifts made during lifetime. Although the broad framework of capital transfer tax remains, very substantial changes were introduced for events occurring after 17 March 1986. In recognition of these changes the tax was renamed inheritance tax and now bears many characteristics of the former estate duty.

The nature and scope of inheritance tax is outlined below, but the comments made have little application to events occurring before 18 March 1986 when capital transfer tax applied.

Liability to inheritance tax may arise on a limited range of lifetime gifts and other dispositions and also on the value of assets retained, or deemed to be retained, at the time of death. An individual's domicile at the time of any gift or on death is an important matter. Domicile will generally be determined by applying normal rules, although special considerations may be necessary where an individual was previously domiciled in the United Kingdom but subsequently acquired a domicile of choice overseas. Where a person was domiciled in the United Kingdom at the time of a disposition or on death the location of assets is immaterial and full liability to inheritance tax arises. Individuals domiciled outside the United Kingdom are, however, chargeable to inheritance tax only on transactions affecting assets located in the United Kingdom.

The assets of husband and wife are not merged for inheritance tax purposes. Each spouse is treated as a separate individual entitled to receive the benefit of his or her exemptions, reliefs and rates of tax. Where husband and wife retain similar assets, for example shares in the same family company, special 'related property' provisions may require the merger of those assets for valuation purposes only.

Lifetime Gifts and Dispositions

Gifts and dispositions made during lifetime fall under four broad headings, namely:

(a) dispositions which are not transfers of value
(b) exempt transfers
(c) potentially exempt transfers
(d) chargeable transfers

Dispositions which are not transfers of value

Several lifetime transactions are not treated as transfers of value and may be entirely disregarded for inheritance tax purposes. These include transactions not intended to confer gratuitous benefit, the provision of family maintenance, the waiver of the right to receive remuneration or dividends, and the grant of agricultural tenancies for full consideration.

Exempt transfers

Certain other transfers are treated as exempt transfers and incur no liability to inheritance tax. The main exempt transfers are listed below:

Transfers between spouses – Transfers between husband and wife are usually exempt. However, if the transferor is, but the transferee spouse is not, domiciled in the United Kingdom, transfers will be exempt only to the extent that the total does not exceed £55,000. Unlike the requirement used for income tax and capital gains tax purposes, it is immaterial whether husband and wife are living together.

Annual exemption – The first £3,000 of gifts and other dispositions made in a year ending on 5 April is exempt. If the exemption is not used, or not wholly used, in any year the balance may be carried forward to the following year only. The annual exemption will only be available for a potentially exempt transfer if that transfer subsequently becomes chargeable by reason of the donor's death.

Small gifts – Outright gifts of £250 or less to any person in one year ending 5 April are exempt.

Normal expenditure – A transfer made during lifetime and comprising normal expenditure is exempt. To obtain this exemption it must be shown that:

(a) the transfer was made as part of the normal expenditure of the transferor
(b) taking one year with another, the transfer was made out of income
(c) after allowing for all transfers of value forming part of normal expenditure the transferor was left with sufficient income to maintain his or her usual standard of living

Gifts in consideration of marriage – These are exempt if they satisfy certain requirements. The amount allowed will be governed by the relationship between the donor and a party to the marriage. The allowable amounts comprise:

(a) gifts by a parent, £5,000
(b) gifts by a grandparent, £2,500
(c) gifts by a party to the marriage, £2,500
(d) gifts by other persons, £1,000

Gifts to charities – Gifts to charities are exempt from liability.

Gifts to political parties – Gifts to political parties which satisfy certain requirements are generally exempt.

Gifts for national purposes – Gifts made to an extensive list of bodies are exempt from liability. These include, among others:

(a) the National Gallery
(b) the British Museum
(c) the National Trust
(d) the National Art Collections Fund
(e) the National Heritage Memorial Fund
(f) the Historic Buildings and Monuments Commission for England (English Heritage)
(g) any local authority
(h) any university or university college in the United Kingdom

A number of other gifts made for the public benefit are also exempt.

Potentially exempt transfers

Lifetime gifts and dispositions which are neither to be ignored nor comprise exempt transfers incur possible liability to inheritance tax. However, relief is available for a range of potentially exempt transfers. These comprise gifts made by an individual to:

(a) a second individual
(b) trustees administering an accumulation and maintenance trust
(c) trustees administering a disabled person's trust

The accumulation and maintenance trust mentioned in (b) must provide that on reaching a specified age, not exceeding twenty-five years, a beneficiary will become absolutely entitled to trust assets or obtain an interest in possession in the income of those assets.

Further additions were made to the list of potentially exempt transfers. These affect settled property administered by trustees where an individual, or individuals, retain an interest in possession. The transfer of assets to, the removal of assets from, or the rearrangement of interests in such property comprise potentially exempt transfers if the person transferring an interest and the person benefiting from the transfer are both individuals.

No immediate liability to inheritance tax will arise on the making of a potentially exempt transfer. Should the donor survive for a period of seven years, immunity from liability will be confirmed. However, the donor's death within the seven-year *inter vivos* period produces liability, as explained later, if the amounts involved are sufficiently substantial.

Chargeable transfers

Any remaining lifetime gifts or dispositions which are neither to be ignored nor represent exempt transfers or potentially exempt transfers, incur liability to inheritance tax. The range of such chargeable transfers is severely limited and is broadly confined to transfers made to or affecting certain trusts, transfers to non-individuals and transfers involving companies.

Gifts with Reservation

A lifetime gift of assets made at any time after 17 March 1986 may incur additional liability to inheritance tax if the donor retains some interest in the subject matter of the gift. This may arise, for example, where a parent transfers a dwelling-house to a son or daughter and continues to occupy the property or to enjoy some benefit from that property. The retention of a benefit may be ignored where it is enjoyed in return for full consideration, perhaps a commercial rent, or where the benefit arises from changed circumstances which could not have been foreseen at the time of the original gift. The gift with reservation provisions will not usually apply to most exempt transfers.

There are three possibilities which may arise where the donor reserves or enjoys some benefit from the subject matter of a previous gift and subsequently dies, namely:

(a) if no benefit is enjoyed within a period of seven years before death there can be no further liability
(b) if the benefit ceased to be enjoyed within a period of seven years before the date of death, the original donor is deemed to have made a potentially exempt transfer representing the value of the asset at the time of cessation
(c) if the benefit is enjoyed at the time of death, the value of the asset must be included in the value of the deceased's estate on death

It must be emphasized that the existence of a benefit enjoyed at any time within a period of seven years before death will establish liability to tax on gifts with reservation, notwithstanding that the gift may have been made many years earlier, providing it was undertaken after 17 March 1986.

Death

Immediately before the time of death an individual is deemed to make a transfer of value. This transfer will comprise the value of assets forming part of the deceased's estate after subtracting most liabilities. Any exempt transfers may, however, be excluded. These include transfers for the benefit of a surviving spouse, a charity and a qualifying political party, together with bequests to approved bodies and for national purposes.

Death may also trigger three additional liabilities, namely:

(a) A potentially exempt transfer made within the period of seven years ending on death loses its potential status and becomes chargeable to inheritance tax
(b) The value of gifts made with reservation may incur liability if any benefit was enjoyed within a period of seven years preceding death
(c) Additional tax may become payable for chargeable lifetime transfers made within seven years before death

Valuations

The valuation of assets is an important matter as this will establish the value transferred for lifetime dispositions and also the value of a person's estate at the time of death. The value of property will represent the price which might reasonably be expected from a sale in the open market. This price cannot be reduced on the grounds that, should the whole property be placed on the market simultaneously, values would be depressed.

In some cases it may be necessary to incorporate the value of 'related property'. This will include property comprised in the estate of the transferor's spouse and certain property previously transferred to charities. The purpose of the related property valuation rules is not to add the value of the property to the estate of the transferor. Related property must be merged to establish the aggregate value of the respective interests and this value is then apportioned, usually on a *pro rata* basis, to the separate interests.

The value of shares and securities quoted on the Stock Exchange will be determined by extracting figures from the daily list of official prices.

Where quoted shares and securities are sold within a period of twelve months following the date of death, a claim may be made to substitute the proceeds for the value on death. This claim will only be beneficial if the gross proceeds realized are lower than market value at the time of death. A similar claim may be available for interests in land sold within a period of three years following death.

Relief for Assets

Special relief is made available for certain assets, notably woodlands, agricultural property and business property. The effect of this relief is summarized below.

Woodlands

Where woodlands pass on death the value will usually be included in the deceased's estate. However, an election may be made in respect of land in the United Kingdom on which trees or underwood is growing to delete the value of those assets. Relief is confined to the value of trees or underwood and does not extend to the land on which they are growing. Liability to inheritance tax will arise if and when the trees or underwood are sold on a future occasion.

Agricultural property

Relief is available for the agricultural value of agricultural property. Such property must be occupied and used for agricultural purposes and relief is confined to the agricultural value.

The value transferred, either on a lifetime gift or on death, must be determined. This value may then be reduced by a percentage. The percentage has changed from time to time but for events taking place after 9 March 1992 a 100 per cent deduction will be available if the transferor retained vacant possession or could have obtained that possession within a period of twelve months following the transfer. In other cases, notably including land let to tenants, a lower deduction of 50 per cent is available.

It remains a requirement that the agricultural property was either occupied by the transferor for the purposes of agriculture throughout a two-year period ending on the date of the transfer, or was owned by him/her throughout a period of seven years ending on that date and also occupied for agricultural purposes.

Business property

Where the value transferred is attributable to relevant business property, that value may be reduced by a percentage. The reduction in value applies to:

(a) property consisting of a business or an interest in a business
(b) shares or securities of an unquoted company which provided the transferor with control
(c) unquoted shares or securities not falling within (b) which provided the transferor with more than 25 per cent of voting rights
(d) other unquoted shares or securities not falling within (c)
(e) shares or securities of a quoted company which provided the transferor with control
(f) any land, building, machinery or plant which, immediately before the transfer, was used wholly or mainly for the purposes of a business carried on by a company of which the transferor had control
(g) any land, building, machinery or plant which, immediately before the transfer, was used wholly or mainly for

the purposes of a business carried on by a partnership of which the transferor was a partner

(h) any land, building, machinery or plant which, immediately before the transfer, was used wholly or mainly for the purposes of a business carried on by the transferor and was then settled property in which he retained an interest in possession

Here also the percentage deductions have changed, but for events occurring after 9 March 1992 a deduction of 100 per cent is available for assets falling within (a), (b) or (c). A reduced deduction of 50 per cent can be obtained for assets within (d) to (h).

It is a general requirement that the property must have been retained for a period of two years before the transfer or death and restrictions may be necessary if the property has not been used wholly for business purposes. The same slice of property cannot obtain both business property relief and the relief available for agricultural property.

Calculation of Tax Payable

The calculation of inheritance tax payable adopts the use of a cumulative total. Each chargeable lifetime transfer is added to the total with a final addition made on death. The top slice added to the total for the current event determines the rate at which inheritance tax must be paid. However, the cumulative total will only include transfers made within a period of seven years before the current event and those undertaken outside this period must be excluded. Although inheritance tax was only introduced on 18 March 1986, the seven-year cumulative total will include chargeable lifetime gifts made before that date, subject to the seven-year limitation.

Lifetime chargeable transfers

The value transferred by the limited range of lifetime chargeable transfers must be added to the seven-year cumulative total to calculate the amount of inheritance tax due. The tax is imposed at one-half of the rate shown below. However, if the donor dies within a period of seven years from the date of the chargeable lifetime transfer, additional tax may be due. This is calculated by applying tax at the full rate (in substitution for the one-half rate previously used). The amount of tax is then reduced to a percentage by applying tapering relief. This percentage is governed by the number of years from the date of the lifetime gift to the date of death and is as follows:

Period of years before death	
Not more than 3	100%
More than 3 but not more than 4	80%
More than 4 but not more than 5	60%
More than 5 but not more than 6	40%
More than 6 but not more than 7	20%

Should this exercise produce liability greater than that previously paid at the one-half rate on the lifetime transfer, additional tax, representing the difference, must be discharged. Where the calculation shows an amount falling below tax paid on the lifetime transfer, no additional liability can arise nor will the deficiency become repayable.

Potentially exempt transfers

Where a potentially exempt transfer loses immunity from liability, due to the donor's death within the seven-year *inter vivos* period, the value transferred becomes liable to inheritance tax. Liability is calculated by applying the full rate shown below, reduced to the percentage governed by tapering relief if the original transfer occurred more than three years before death.

Death

The final addition to the seven-year cumulative total will comprise the value of an estate on death. Inheritance tax will be calculated by applying the full rate shown below. No tapering relief can be obtained.

Rates of Tax

In earlier times there were several rates of inheritance tax which progressively increased as the value transferred grew in size. However, for events taking place after 14 March 1988, a nil rate applies to the initial slice. The size of this slice has been increased on several occasions and for events occurring after 9 March 1992 is £150,000. Any excess is charged at the single positive rate of 40 per cent.

Only one-half of the 40 per cent rate (namely 20 per cent) will be applicable for chargeable lifetime transfers.

The above rate and rateband is likely to be amended on future occasions.

Payment of Tax

Inheritance tax usually falls due for payment six months after the end of the month in which the chargeable transaction takes place. Where a transfer, other than that made on death, occurs after 5 April and before the following 1 October, tax falls due on the following 30 April, although there are some exceptions to this general rule.

Inheritance tax attributable to the transfer of certain land, controlling shareholding interests, unquoted shares, businesses and interests in businesses, together with agricultural property, may usually be satisfied by instalments spread over ten years. Except in the case of non-agricultural land, where interest is charged on outstanding instalments, no liability to interest arises where tax is paid on the due date. In all cases, delay in the payment of tax may incur liability to interest.

Settled Property

Complex rules apply to establish inheritance tax liability on settled property. Where a person is beneficially entitled to an interest in possession, that person is effectively deemed to own the property in which the interest subsists. It follows that where the interest comes to an end during the beneficiary's lifetime and some other person becomes entitled to the property or interest, the beneficiary is treated as having made a transfer of value. However, this will usually comprise a potentially exempt transfer. In addition, no liability will arise where the property vests in the absolute ownership of the previous beneficiary. The death of a person entitled to an interest in possession will require the value of the underlying property to be added to the value of the deceased's estate.

In the case of other settled property where there is no interest in possession (e.g. discretionary trusts), liability to tax will arise on each ten-year anniversary of the trust. There will also be liability if property ceases to be held on discretionary trusts before the first ten-year anniversary date is reached or between anniversaries. The rate of tax suffered will be governed by several considerations, including previous dispositions made by the settlor, transactions concluded by the trustees, and the period throughout which property has been held in trust.

Accumulation and maintenance settlements which require assets to be distributed, or interests in income to be created, not later than a beneficiary's twenty-fifth birthday may be exempt from any liability to inheritance tax.

CORPORATION TAX

Profits, gains and income accruing to companies resident in the United Kingdom incur liability to corporation tax. Non-resident companies are immune from this tax unless they carry on a trade in the United Kingdom through a permanent establishment, branch or office. Companies residing outside the United Kingdom may be liable to income tax at the basic rate on other income arising in the United Kingdom, perhaps from letting property. The following comments are confined to companies resident in the United Kingdom and have little application to those residing overseas.

Liability to corporation tax is governed by the profits, gains or income for an accounting period. This is usually the period for which financial accounts are made up, and in the case of companies preparing accounts to the same accounting date annually will comprise successive periods of twelve months.

Rate of Tax

The amount of profits or income for an accounting period must be determined on normal taxation principles. The special rules which apply to individuals where a source of income is acquired or discontinued are ignored and consideration is confined to the actual profits or income for an accounting period.

The rate of corporation tax is fixed for a financial year ending on 31 March. Where the accounting period of a company overlaps this date and there is a change in the rate of corporation tax, profits and income must be apportioned.

In recent years the rate of corporation tax has been as follows:

Financial year	
12 months ending 31 March 1987, 1988	
1989, 1990	35%
31 March 1991	34%
31 March 1992, 1993	33%

Small Companies Rate

Where the profits of a company do not exceed stated limits, corporation tax becomes payable at the small companies rate. It is the amount of profits and not the size of the company which governs the application of this rate.

The level of profits which a company may derive without losing the benefit of the small companies rate has been frequently changed. In recent years the following small companies rate applies where profits do not exceed £250,000 for the year ending 31 March 1993 and the year ending 31 March 1992, £200,000 for the year ending 31 March 1991, £150,000 for the year ending 31 March 1990 or £100,000 for earlier years:

Financial year	
12 months ending 31 March 1987	29%
31 March 1988	27%
31 March 1989, 1990	
1991, 1992, 1993	25%

If profits do exceed £250,000 for the year to 31 March 1993 or the year to 31 March 1992 but fall below £1,250,000, marginal small companies rate relief applies. The broad effect of marginal relief is that the first £250,000 of profits is taxed at the appropriate small companies rate. Profits falling in the margin then incur liability at the marginal rate of 35 per cent. Different upper limits and marginal rates applied for earlier years. However, where the accounting period of a company overlaps 31 March, profits must be apportioned to establish the appropriate rate for each part of those profits.

The lower limit of £250,000 and the upper limit of £1,250,000 applies for a period of twelve months in duration and must be proportionately reduced for shorter periods. Some restriction in the small companies rate and the marginal rate may be necessary if there are two or more associated companies, namely companies under common control.

The small companies rate is not available for close investment-holding companies. These are mainly investment companies, other than those receiving most of their income from letting land and property.

Capital Gains

Chargeable gains arising to a company are calculated in a manner similar to that used for individuals. However, companies cannot obtain the annual exemption of £5,800, nor are they assessed to capital gains tax. In place of this tax companies suffer liability to corporation tax on chargeable gains.

For disposals taking place before 17 March 1987 only a fraction of the chargeable gain was assessable to corporation tax at the full rate. The fraction selected ensured that companies effectively suffered corporation tax at the rate of 30 per cent on the full chargeable gain. This does not apply to subsequent disposals as the full chargeable gain, and not a fraction, becomes assessable to corporation tax. However, unlike the previous system, the chargeable gain is treated as ordinary profit, thereby obtaining the benefit of the small companies rate where figures are sufficiently low.

Distributions

Dividends and other qualifying distributions made by a United Kingdom resident company are not satisfied after deduction of income tax. However, when making a distribution a company is required to account to the Inland Revenue for an amount of advance corporation tax. For distributions made in the year ending 5 April 1993, the amount of advance corporation tax will represent one-third of the distribution. Thus a cash dividend of £75 paid to a shareholder will also require satisfaction of advance corporation tax amounting to £25.

Advance corporation tax accounted for in this manner for distributions made in an accounting period may usually be set against a company's corporation tax liability for the same period. Some restrictions are imposed on the amount which can be offset but any surplus may be carried forward, or carried backwards, and set against corporation tax due for other accounting periods.

A United Kingdom resident shareholder receiving a qualifying distribution also obtains a tax credit, which for the year ending 5 April 1993, is equal to one-third of the distribution made. Therefore, the total income of the individual comprises the aggregate of the distribution and the tax credit. If the individual is not liable, or not fully liable, to income tax at the basic rate, all or part of the tax credit can be refunded by the Inland Revenue. Individuals with substantial incomes incur liability to income tax at the higher rate of 40 per cent on the aggregate of the distribution and the tax credit, although as tax is deemed to have been suffered at the rate of 25 per cent the additional liability will be limited to the excess of 15 per cent.

Payment of Tax

Corporation tax, less any relief for advance corporation tax, usually falls due for payment nine months following the end of the accounting period to which the tax relates. Companies which were carrying on business before 1966 previously had a later due and payable date, but this has now been phased out to achieve a common nine-month period for all companies.

Interest

On making many payments of interest a company is required to deduct income tax at the basic rate and account for the tax deducted to the Inland Revenue. The gross amount of interest paid will usually comprise a charge on income to be offset against profits on which corporation tax becomes payable.

Groups of Companies

Each company within a group is separately charged to corporation tax on profits, gains and income. However, where one group member realizes a loss, other than a capital loss, a claim may be made to offset the deficiency against profits of some other member of the same group.

Claims are also available to avoid the payment of advance corporation tax on distributions, or the deduction of income tax on the payment of interest, for transactions between members of a group of companies. The transfer of capital assets from one member of a group to a fellow member will incur no liability to tax on chargeable gains.

Pay and File

It is anticipated that from the autumn of 1993 a new 'pay and file' system will affect all companies. Under this system tax will have to be paid nine months following the end of the accounting period involved, with accounts and returns being submitted three months later. Failure to satisfy corporation tax, or to submit documents within these time limits will result in a liability to interest and penalties.

VALUE ADDED TAX

Unlike income tax, capital gains tax, inheritance tax and corporation tax, which are collected and administered by the Inland Revenue, value added tax is the responsibility of Customs and Excise. Value added tax was introduced in 1973 and is charged on the value of supplies made in the United Kingdom by a registered trader and extends both to the supply of goods and to the supply of services. Liability also arises on the value of goods imported into the United Kingdom.

Registration

All traders, including professional men and women, together with companies, making taxable supplies of a value exceeding stated limits are required to register for value added tax purposes. Taxable supplies represent the supply of goods and services potentially chargeable with value added tax. The limits which govern mandatory registration are amended annually but from 10 March 1992, an unregistered trader must register:

(a) at any time, if there are reasonable grounds for believing that the value of taxable supplies in the next 30 days will exceed £36,600
(b) at the end of any month if the value of taxable supplies in the last 12 months then ending has exceeded £36,600.

Liability to register under (b) may be avoided if it can be shown that the value of supplies in the period of 12 months then beginning will not exceed £35,100. There may, however, be liability to register immediately where a business is taken over from another trader as a 'going concern'.

Where the limits governing mandatory registration have been exceeded, it is necessary for the trader to notify Customs and Excise. Failure to provide prompt notification may have unfortunate results as the person concerned will be required to account for value added tax from the proper registration date.

A trader whose taxable supplies do not reach the mandatory registration limits may apply for voluntary registration. This step may be thought advisable to recover input tax or to compete with other registered traders.

A registered trader may submit an application for de-registration if the value of taxable supplies subsequently falls. From 1 May 1992, an application for de-registration can be made if the value of taxable supplies for the year beginning on the application date is not expected to exceed £35,100.

Input Tax

A registered trader will both suffer tax (input tax) when obtaining goods or services for the purposes of his business and also become liable to account for tax (output tax) on the value of goods and services which he supplies. Relief can usually be obtained for input tax suffered, either by setting that tax against output tax due or by repayment. Most items of input tax can be relieved in this manner but there are exceptions including the prohibition of relief for the cost of business entertaining. Where a registered trader makes both exempt supplies and also taxable supplies to his customers or clients, there may be some restriction in the amount of input tax which can be recovered.

Output Tax

When making a taxable supply of goods or services a registered trader must account for output tax, if any, on the value of the supply. Usually the price charged by the registered trader will be increased by adding value added tax but failure to make the required addition will not remove liability to account for output tax.

Exempt Supplies

No value added tax is chargeable on the supply of goods or services which are treated as exempt supplies. These include the provision of burial and cremation facilities, insurance, finance and education. The granting of a lease to occupy land or the sale of land will usually comprise an exempt supply, but there are numerous exceptions. In particular, the sale of new non-domestic buildings or certain buildings used by charities cannot be treated as exempt supplies.

A taxable person may elect to tax rents and other supplies of buildings and agricultural land not used for residential or charitable purposes.

Exempt supplies do not enter into the calculation of taxable supplies which governs liability to mandatory registration. Such supplies made by a registered trader may, however, limit the amount of input tax which can be relieved. It is for this reason that the election may be useful.

Rates of Tax

Two rates of value added tax have applied since 1 April 1991, namely:

(a) a zero, or nil, rate
(b) a standard rate of 17.5 per cent

Although no tax is due on a zero-rated supply, this does comprise a taxable supply which must be included in the calculation governing liability to register.

Zero-rating

A large number of supplies are zero-rated, including, among others:

(a) the supply of many items of food and drink for human consumption. This does not include ice creams, chocolates, sweets, potato crisps and alcoholic drinks. Nor does it extend to supplies made in the course of catering, e.g. at a wedding reception or other social function, or to items supplied for consumption in a restaurant or café. Whilst the supply of cold items, e.g. sandwiches, for consumption away from the supplier's premises, is zero-

rated, the supply of hot food, for example fish and chips, is not
(b) animal feeding stuffs
(c) sewerage and water, unless supplied for industrial purposes
(d) books, brochures, pamphlets, leaflets, newspapers, maps and charts
(e) talking books for the blind and handicapped and wireless sets for the blind
(f) electricity, gas and coal, but supplies are limited to domestic use
(g) supplies of services, other than professional services, when constructing a new domestic building or a building to be used by a charity. The supply of materials for such a building is also zero-rated, together with the sale or the grant of a long lease for these buildings. Alterations to some protected buildings are also zero-rated
(h) the transportation of persons in a vehicle, ship or aircraft designed to carry not less than twelve persons
(i) supplies of drugs, medicines and other aids for the handicapped
(j) supplies of clothing and footwear for young persons
(k) exports

This list is not exhaustive but indicates the wide range of supplies which may be zero-rated.

Collection of Tax

Registered traders submit value added tax returns for accounting periods. Each accounting period is usually three months in duration but arrangements can be made to submit returns on a monthly basis. Very large traders must account for tax on a monthly basis from October 1992 but this does not affect the three-monthly return. The return will show both the output tax due for supplies made by the trader in the accounting period and also the input tax for which relief is claimed. If the output tax exceeds input tax the balance must be remitted with the value added tax return. Where input tax suffered exceeds the output tax due the registered trader may claim recovery of the excess from Customs and Excise.

This basis for collecting tax explains the structure of value added tax. Where supplies are made between registered traders the supplier will account for an amount of tax which will usually be identical to the tax recovered by the person to whom the supply is made. However, where the supply is made to a person who is not a registered trader there can be no recovery of input tax and it is on this person that the final burden of value added tax eventually falls.

Until 31 December 1992 tax on all imports into the United Kingdom must be satisfied at the time of importation or perhaps later where special arrangements have been agreed. Whilst this continues to apply for imports from non-EEC countries, it will no longer apply to imports from within the EEC. The importer from an EEC supplier will in future account for tax with his/her normal VAT return. This is a result of the 'single market' within the European Community which comes into effect from 1 January 1993.

An optional scheme is available for registered traders having an annual turnover of taxable supplies not exceeding £300,000. Such traders may, if they wish, render returns annually. Nine equal payments of value added tax will be paid on account, with a final balancing payment accompanying submission of the return.

Bad Debts

Many retailers operate special retail schemes for calculating the amount of value added tax due. These schemes are, broadly, based on the volume of consideration received in an accounting period. Should a customer fail to pay for goods or services supplied, there will be no consideration on which value added tax falls to be calculated.

To avoid the problem of bad debts incurred by traders not operating a special retail scheme, an optional system of cash accounting is available. This scheme, confined to traders with annual taxable supplies not exceeding £300,000, enables returns to be made on a cash basis, in substitution for the normal supply basis. Traders using such a scheme will not, of course, include bad debts in the calculation of cash receipts.

Where neither the cash accounting arrangements nor the special retail scheme applies, output tax falls due on the value of the supply and liability is not affected by failure to receive consideration. However, where a debt is more than 12 months old and is written off in the supplier's books, relief for bad debts will be forthcoming.

Other Special Schemes

In addition to the schemes for retailers, there are several special schemes applied to calculate the amount of value added tax due and which also limit the ability to recover input tax. These schemes apply to the supply of second-hand motor cars, motor cycles, caravans, boats, electronic organs, aircraft and firearms, together with works of art, antiques and collectors' pieces.

Stamp Duties

Stamp duty is a tax on documents. There are a number of separate duties, under different heads of charge. The Finance Act 1990 included provisions abolishing all the stamp duty charges on transactions in shares from a date to be fixed by Treasury order (which has not yet been made). The Finance Act 1991 removed the stamp duty charges on documents relating to all other types of property except land and buildings, again from a date to be specified (no date yet specified). In the list of documents which follows, those which will be affected by the above provisions are indicated with an asterisk*.

AGREEMENT FOR LEASE, *see* LEASES

AGREEMENT FOR SALE OF PROPERTY

Charged with *ad valorem* duty as if an actual conveyance on sale, with certain exceptions, e.g. agreements for the sale of land, stocks and shares, goods, wares or merchandise, or a ship (*see* S. 59 (1), Stamp Act 1891). If *ad valorem* duty is paid on an agreement in accordance with this provision, the subsequent conveyance or transfer is not chargeable with any *ad valorem* duty and the Commissioners will upon application either place a denoting stamp on such conveyance or transfer or will transfer the *ad valorem* duty thereto. Further, if such an agreement is rescinded, not performed, etc., the Commissioners will return the *ad valorem* duty paid.

AGREEMENT UNDER SEAL

Subject to exemptions, 50p

ASSIGNMENT

By way of sale, *see* CONVEYANCE
By way of gift, *see* VOLUNTARY DISPOSITION

ASSURANCE, *see* INSURANCE POLICIES

*BEARER INSTRUMENT

Inland bearer instrument, i.e. share warrant, stock certificate to bearer or any other instrument to bearer by which stock can be transferred, issued by a company or body formed or established in UK, 1.5%

Overseas bearer instrument, i.e. such an instrument issued in Great Britain by a company formed out of the UK, 1.5%

BILL OF SALE, ABSOLUTE, *see* CONVEYANCE ON SALE

CAPITAL DUTY

This was charged at 1 per cent on every £100 or fraction of £100 of the actual value of assets contributed by the members of a company provided the place of effective management of the company was in Great Britain, or its registered office was in Great Britain but the place of its effective management was outside the EC (Finance Act 1973). The tax was abolished by the Finance Act 1988 in respect of transactions entered into on or after 16 March 1988.

CONTRACT, *see* AGREEMENT

*CONTRACT OR GRANT FOR PAYMENT OF A SUPERANNUATION ANNUITY

For every £10 or fractional part of £10, 5p

CONVEYANCE OR TRANSFER ON SALE

(In the case of a Voluntary Disposition, *see* below)

Conveyance or transfer on sale of any property (except stock or marketable securities), where the Conveyance or Transfer contains a certificate of value certifying that the transaction does not form part of a larger transaction or a series of transactions in respect of which the aggregate amount or value of the consideration exceeds £30,000, *nil*

Exceeds £30,000 (for every £100 or fraction of £100), £1

If the Conveyance or Transfer on Sale does not contain the appropriate statement, duty at the full rate of £1 for every £100 or fraction of £100 will be payable whatever the amount of the consideration.

However, if the consideration does not exceed £500, and the instrument does not contain a certificate of value, there are graduated duties ranging from 50p to £5.

Conveyances to charities are exempt from duty under this head provided the instrument is stamped with a denoting stamp.

CONVEYANCE OR TRANSFER OF ANY OTHER KIND

Fixed duty, 50p

However, under the Stamp Duty (Exempt Instruments) Regulations 1987, instruments which would otherwise fall under this head are exempt from stamp duty provided that the document is duly certified. The certificate must contain a sufficient description of the category into which the instrument falls, and must be signed by the transferor, his solicitor or agent. 'I/We hereby certify that this instrument falls within category . . . in the Schedule to the Stamp Duty (Exempt Instruments) Regulations 1987.'

COVENANT, for original creation and sale of any annuity, *see* CONVEYANCE

DECLARATION OF TRUST

Not being a Will or Settlement, 50p

DEMISE, *see* LEASES

DUPLICATE OR COUNTERPART

Same duty as original, but not to exceed, 50p

GIFT, *see* VOLUNTARY DISPOSITION

*GUARANTEE

If under seal, 50p

INSURANCE POLICIES, LIFE

Exceeding £50 and not exceeding £1,000, for every £100 or part of £100, 5p

Exceeding £1,000, for every £1,000 or any fractional part of £1,000, 50p

Made after 1 August 1966 for period not exceeding two years, 5p

The Finance Act 1989 abolished this charge for policies made after 31 December 1989.

LEASES (INCLUDING AGREEMENTS FOR LEASES)

Lease or tack for any definite term less than a year of any furnished dwelling-house or apartments where the rent for such term exceeds £500, £1

Of any lands, tenements, etc., in consideration of any rent, according to the following:

Annual rent not exceeding	†*Term not exceeding* 7 yrs	35 yrs	100 yrs	*Exceeding* 100 yrs
£	£ p	£ p	£ p	£ p
5	Nil	0.10	0.60	1.20
10	Nil	0.20	1.20	2.40
15	Nil	0.30	1.80	3.60
20	Nil	0.40	2.40	4.80
25	Nil	0.50	3.00	6.00
50	Nil	1.00	6.00	12.00
75	Nil	1.50	9.00	18.00
100	Nil	2.00	12.00	24.00
150	Nil	3.00	18.00	36.00
200	Nil	4.00	24.00	48.00
250	Nil	5.00	30.00	60.00
300	Nil	6.00	36.00	72.00
350	Nil	7.00	42.00	84.00
400	Nil	8.00	48.00	96.00
450	Nil	9.00	54.00	108.00
500	Nil	10.00	60.00	120.00
Exceeding 500, *for every* £50 *or fraction thereof*	0.50	1.00	6.00	12.00

†If the term is indefinite the same duty is payable as if the term did not exceed seven years.

Where a consideration other than rent is payable, the same rule applies where the consideration does not exceed £30,000 as under Conveyance or Transfer on Sale (except stock or marketable securities), provided that any rent payable does not exceed £300 a year and a certificate of value is included in the Conveyance or Transfer.

Leases to charities are exempt from duty under this head provided the instrument is stamped with a denoting stamp.

MORTGAGES, exempt.

RECEIPTS FOR SALARIES, WAGES AND SUPERANNUATION, AND OTHER LIKE ALLOWANCES, exempt.

*TRANSFER OF STOCK AND SHARES BY SALE, 0.5%

*UNIT TRUST INSTRUMENT

Any trust instrument of a unit trust scheme, for every £100 or fraction of £100, of the amount or value of the property subject to the trusts created or recorded by the instrument, 25p

By the Finance Act 1989, the transfer of units in certain authorized unit trusts is no longer subject to duty.

VOLUNTARY DISPOSITION, *inter vivos*, 50p

The Commissioners as a general rule allow deeds, etc., to be stamped after execution:

WITHOUT PENALTY, ON PAYMENT OF DUTY ONLY

Deeds and instruments not otherwise excepted, within 30 days of first execution.

NB. Where wholly executed abroad, the period begins to run from the date of arrival here.

PENALTIES ENFORCEABLE ON STAMPING IN ADDITION TO DUTY

Instruments presented after the proper time (subject to special provisions in some cases and subject to the Commissioner's power to mitigate) a penalty equal to the duty, £10

Legal Notes

IMPORTANT

The purpose of these notes is to outline some of the more common parts of the law as they may affect the average person. They are believed to be correct at the time of going to press. However, the law is constantly developing and changing, and it is always best to take expert advice. Anyone who does not have a solicitor already, and is unable to find one through the recommendation of a friend, can contact the Citizens' Advice Bureau (whose address can be obtained from the telephone directory or from any post office or town hall). Each CAB has a list of solicitors in the area who deal with particular types of problem. Alternatively, assistance can be sought from The Law Society, 113 Chancery Lane, London WC2A 1PL or The Law Society of Scotland, 26 Drumsheugh Gardens, Edinburgh EH3 7YR.

The legal aid and legal advice and assistance schemes exist to make the help of the trained lawyer available to those who would not otherwise be able to afford legal advice. The best policy is to go to a solicitor without delay; timely advice will set your mind at rest but sitting on your rights can mean that you lose them.

It is not necessary for a dispute to have arisen before advice is sought from a solicitor; the legal advice and assistance scheme enables a solicitor to advise you on your rights, for instance under a tenancy agreement, the estate of a deceased person or in connection with matrimonial and consumer matters, and to write letters or take other steps on your behalf. Your entitlement to take advantage of the scheme depends on your means (*see* page 662) but a solicitor or Citizens' Advice Bureau will be able to advise about entitlement.

BRITISH CITIZENSHIP

There are three types of citizenship: British Citizenship; Citizenship of the British Dependent Territories; and British Overseas Citizenship.

Acquisition of citizenship on change of law

The British Nationality Act 1981 which came into force on 1 January 1983 made substantial changes to the law of citizenship, which before that date did not distinguish between the three types of citizenship referred to above. Almost all persons who were then both citizens of the UK and colonies and who had a right of abode in the UK became British citizens when the Act came into force. Most UK and colonies citizens who did not have a right of abode in the UK became Citizens of the British Dependent Territories. This type of citizenship was, broadly speaking, conferred on citizens of the UK and colonies by birth, naturalization or registration in dependent territories. Dependent territories include Hong Kong, Gibraltar, the Falkland Islands, and St Helena and its dependencies. Any UK and colonies citizen who, on 1 January 1983, did not acquire either British or British Dependent Territories' Citizenship became a British Overseas Citizen.

Later acquisition of British citizenship

British citizenship is acquired automatically by those born in the UK (including, for this purpose, the Channel Islands and the Isle of Man) who have a parent who is a British citizen or a parent who is settled in the UK. Certain other categories of children born in the UK also acquire this type of citizenship, i.e. foundlings, those whose parents subsequently settle in the UK, those who live in the UK for ten years from birth and those adopted in the UK.

A person born outside the UK may acquire British citizenship in the following ways:

(a) if one of his/her parents is a British citizen otherwise than by descent, e.g. parent was born in the UK
(b) if one of his/her parents is a British citizen serving the Crown overseas
(c) if the Secretary of State consents to his/her registration while he/she is a minor
(d) if he/she is a Citizen of the British Dependent Territories, a British Overseas Citizen, a British subject or a British Protected Person (these last two are residual categories of people who have not acquired one of the three new types of citizenship) and has been lawfully resident in the UK for five years without any time restriction
(e) if he/she is a British Dependent Territories Citizen who is a national of the UK for the purposes of the EC (i.e. a Gibraltarian)
(f) if he/she is naturalized. Naturalization may be applied for only by adults and the Secretary of State has a discretion whether to permit it. The basic requirements are five years' residence, good character, sufficient knowledge of the English or Welsh language, and an intention to reside in the UK permanently. The requirements are somewhat less restrictive in the case of an applicant who is married to a British citizen

Acquisition of British Dependent Territories and British Overseas Citizenship after the Act

These citizenships are intended for persons connected with certain Commonwealth countries other than the UK. In the case of dependent territories the rules are very similar to those for acquiring British citizenship, except that the connection is with the dependent territory rather than with the UK. British Overseas Citizenship may be acquired by the wife and minor children of a British Overseas Citizen in certain circumstances.

Retention of nationality by persons born in or who are citizens of the Republic of Ireland

By the Ireland Act 1949, a person who was born before 6 December 1922 in what is now the Republic of Ireland (Eire) and was a British subject immediately before 1 January 1949, is not deemed to have ceased to be a British subject unless either he/she (a) was domiciled in the Irish Free State on 6 December 1922, (b) was on or after 10 April 1935 and before 1 January 1949 permanently resident there, or (c) had before 1 January 1949 been registered as a citizen of Eire under the laws of that country.

In addition, by the British Nationality Act 1948, any citizen of Eire who immediately before 1 January 1949, was also a British subject can retain that status by submitting at any time a claim to the Home Secretary on any of the following grounds:

(a) he/she has been in the service of the United Kingdom government
(b) he/she holds a British passport issued in the United Kingdom or in any colony, protectorate, United Kingdom mandated or trust territory

(c) he/she has associations by way of descent, residence or otherwise with any such place; or on complying with similar legislation in any of the 'dominions'

The British Nationality Act 1981 provides that persons who have made a claim may continue to be British subjects. Any citizen of Eire who was a British subject before 1 January 1949 and who has not yet made a claim may do so provided that:

(a) he/she is or has been in Crown service under the government of the United Kingdom
(b) he/she has associations by way of descent, residence or otherwise with the United Kingdom or any dependent territory

Renunciation and resumption

A person may cease to be a British citizen by renouncing his/her citizenship (with the consent of the Secretary of State in wartime). The renunciation is required to be registered with the Secretary of State and will be revoked if no new citizenship or nationality is acquired within six months. Once renounced, citizenship may be reacquired if the renunciation was necessary to retain or acquire some other citizenship or nationality. Similar rules as to renunciation and reacquisition apply in the case of British Dependent Territories Citizenships and of renunciation (but not reacquisition) in the case of British Overseas Citizenship.

Status of aliens

Property may be held by an alien in the same manner as by a natural-born British subject, but he/she may not hold public office, exercise the franchise or own a British ship or aircraft. The Republic of Ireland Act 1949 declares that the Republic, though not part of HM Dominions, is not a foreign country, and any reference in an Act of Parliament to foreigners, aliens, foreign countries, etc., shall be construed accordingly.

CONSUMER LAW

THE SUPPLY OF GOODS AND SERVICES

(1) The Sale of Goods Act 1979 provides protection to the purchaser of goods, by implying certain terms into every contract for the sale of goods. These implied terms are:

(a) A condition that the seller will pass good title to the buyer (unless the seller agrees to transfer only such title as he or his principal has) and warranties that the goods will be free from undisclosed encumbrances, and that the buyer will enjoy quiet possession of the goods.
(b) Where there is a sale of goods by description, a condition that the goods will correspond with that description, and where the sale is by sample and description, a condition that the bulk of the goods shall correspond with both sample and description.
(c) Where the seller sells goods in the course of a business, a condition that the goods will be of merchantable quality, unless before the contract is made, the buyer has examined the goods and ought to have noticed the defect, bearing in mind the purchaser's knowledge of the goods and the extent of the examination, or unless the seller has specifically drawn the attention of the buyer to the defect. Merchantable quality means fit for the purpose for which goods of the kind are commonly bought, taking into account any description applied to them, the price and other relevant circumstances.
(d) A condition that where the seller sells goods in the course of a business, the goods are reasonably fit for any purpose made known to the seller by the buyer, unless the buyer does not rely on the seller's skill and judgment, or it would be unreasonable for him to do so.
(e) Where there is a sale of goods by sample, conditions that the bulk of the goods shall correspond with the sample in quality, that the buyer will have a reasonable opportunity of comparing the bulk with the sample, and that the goods are free from any defect rendering them unmerchantable, which would not be apparent from the sample.

For these purposes, the broad difference between a condition and a warranty is that the remedy for a breach of an implied condition may enable the buyer to reject the goods and recover damages if he has suffered loss, whereas the remedy for a breach of warranty will only enable the buyer to recover damages.

It is possible for a seller to exclude some of the above terms from a contract, subject to restrictions imposed by the Unfair Contract Terms Act 1977 as given below. These restrictions give more protection where the buyer 'deals as consumer'. In a contract of sale of goods, a buyer 'deals as consumer' where there is a sale by a seller in the course of a business, where the goods are of a type ordinarily bought for private use or consumption, and where the goods are sold to a person who does not buy or hold himself out as buying them in the course of a business. A buyer in a sale by auction or competitive tender never 'deals as consumer'.

The 1977 Act prohibits the exclusion of the implied terms given in (b) to (e) above, where the buyer 'deals as consumer'. In sales where the buyer does not 'deal as consumer', terms purporting to exclude these implied terms may be relied upon only to the extent that it would be reasonable to allow reliance. The Act provides guidelines for determining whether it would be reasonable to allow reliance. The implied terms in (a) above cannot be excluded whether the buyer 'deals as consumer' or not.

(2) Similar terms to those implied in contracts of sale of goods are implied into contracts of hire-purchase by the Supply of Goods (Implied Terms) Act 1973, and the 1977 Act limits the exclusion of these implied terms in a similar manner.

(3) Under the Supply of Goods and Services Act 1982, terms similar to those in the Sale of Goods Act relating to quiet possession, compliance with description, merchantable quality, fitness for purpose and correspondence with sample are implied into other types of contract under which ownership of goods passes (e.g. a contract for 'work and materials' such as a supply of new parts during the servicing of a motor car) and also into contracts for the hire of goods. In the case of contracts under which ownership of goods is to pass, there is also an implied condition as to title.

The 1977 Act limits the exclusion of these implied terms in a similar manner to the implied terms in the Sale of Goods Act.

(4) The Supply of Goods and Services Act 1982 also implies into a contract for the supply of services terms that the supplier will use reasonable care and skill, carry out the service within a reasonable time (unless the time is agreed) and make a reasonable charge (unless the charge is agreed).

(5) The Trade Descriptions Act 1968 provides that it is a criminal offence for a trader or businessman to apply a false trade description to any goods, or to supply or offer to supply any goods to which a false trade description has been applied. A trade description includes a description as to quantity, size, method, place and date of manufacture, other history, composition, other physical characteristics, fitness for purpose, behaviour or accuracy, testing or approval. It is also an offence to give a false indication as to the price of goods. Prosecutions are brought by trading standards inspectors.

(6) The Fair Trading Act 1973 is also designed to protect the consumer. It provides for the appointment of a Director-General of Fair Trading, whose duties include keeping under review commercial activities in the UK relating to the supply of goods or services to consumers, and to collect information to discover practices that may adversely affect the economic interests of the consumer. He may refer certain consumer trade practices to the Consumer Protection Advisory Committee, or of his own initiative take proceedings against firms that are trading unfairly. He may also publish information and advice to consumers. Examples of practices which have been prohibited by virtue of references made under this Act include the use of certain void exclusion clauses in contracts for the sale of goods and hire-purchase, and advertisements by traders appearing to sell as private persons.

(7) The Consumer Protection Act 1987 makes the producer of a product liable for any damage exceeding £275 caused by a defect in that product, subject to certain defences.

(8) The Consumer Protection (Cancellation of Contracts Concluded away from Business Premises) Regulations 1987 allow consumers a seven-day period in which to cancel most contracts for supply of goods or services exceeding £35 in cost, where these contracts have been made following an unsolicited visit to the consumer's home or workplace.

Scotland

The Sale of Goods Act 1979, a consolidating Act, applies with some modification to Scotland. For example, it is not necessary in Scotland to distinguish between the words condition and warranty. The remedies of the buyer in both cases are the same, i.e. the buyer can either within a reasonable time reject the goods and treat the contract as repudiated, or retain the goods and treat the failure to perform such material part as a breach which may give rise to a claim for compensation or damages.

Consumer Credit

The Consumer Credit Act 1974 provides a system for the protection of the consumer, of licensing and control of all matters relating to the provision of credit or to the supply of goods on hire or hire-purchase, administered by the Director-General of Fair Trading. A licence is required to carry on a consumer credit or consumer hire business, or to deal in credit brokerage, debt adjusting, counselling or collecting, for which group licences are available. Any 'fit' person may apply to the Director-General of Fair Trading for a licence which is normally renewable after ten years. A licence is not necessary if such types of business are only transacted 'occasionally' or if exempt agreements only are involved.

For the Act's provisions to apply, the agreement must be 'regulated', i.e. be to individuals or partnerships only; must not be exempt, e.g. certain loans by local authorities or building societies; and the total credit must not exceed £15,000. The terms of a regulated agreement can be varied by the creditor, but only if the agreement gives him the right to do so and the debtor receives notice in the prescribed form.

To be enforceable the agreement must be properly executed, and the specified information must be given during the antecedent negotiations for the contract. These are conducted by the creditor, credit broker or supplier (these being the creditor's agents) and begin when the parties first begin discussions.

The agreement must state certain information such as the amount of credit, the annual percentage rate of interest, and the amount and timing of repayments.

An agreement is cancellable under the Act if oral representations were made in the debtor's presence during antecedent negotiations and the debtor signed the agreement other than at the creditor's (or credit-broker's or negotiator's) place of business. Time for cancellation expires five clear days after the debtor receives a second copy of the agreement. The agreement must inform the debtor of his right to cancel and how to cancel.

Where there are arrangements or connections between the creditor and supplier, the former is generally liable for any misrepresentation or breach of contract by the latter, and will thus be liable to indemnify the debtor.

If the debtor is in arrears or is otherwise in breach of the agreement, the creditor may not enforce the agreement, e.g. by repossessing goods, without serving a default notice on the debtor. This notice will give the debtor a chance to remedy the default. Even if the default is not remedied by the debtor, if the agreement is a hire-purchase or conditional sale agreement, the creditor cannot repossess the goods without an order of the court if the debtor has paid one-third of the total price of the goods.

Where the agreement requires the debtor to make grossly exorbitant payments or is contrary to the ordinary principles of fair dealing, the court can reopen it either at the debtor's request or during enforcement proceedings and (*inter alia*) alter the terms of the contract or set aside any obligations it imposes so as to do justice between the parties. Whether an agreement is such an extortionate credit bargain is decided by reference (*inter alia*) to interest rates prevailing at the date of agreement, the pressure for finance the debtor was under, etc.

If a credit reference agency was used to check the debtor's financial standing the creditor must give the agency's name to the debtor, who is entitled to see the agency's file on him on payment of a fee of £1.

Scotland

The Consumer Credit Act also extends to Scotland and goes far in assimilating the Scots law on this topic with English law. The Supply of Goods (Implied Terms) Act 1973 also applies to Scotland. Parts II and III only of the Unfair Contract Terms Act 1977 apply to Scotland. The Sale of Goods Act 1979 applies with some modification to Scotland.

Receipts

The law on receipts in Scotland is governed by the Prescription and Limitations (Scotland) Act 1973, which for this purpose came into force on 25 July 1976. Receipts need only be kept for a period of five years and if a creditor does not make a relevant claim within that period no action can be raised.

THE CROWN – PROCEEDINGS AGAINST

Before 1947, proceedings against the Crown were generally possible only by a procedure known as a petition of right, which placed the litigant at a considerable disadvantage. However, by the Crown Proceedings Act 1947, which came into operation on 1 January 1948, the Crown, in its public capacity, is largely placed in the same position as a subject, although some procedural disadvantages remain, e.g. the enforcement of judgments against the Crown.

Scotland

The Act as amended extends to Scotland and has the effect of bringing the practice of the two countries as closely together as the different legal systems will permit. While formerly actions against the Crown, when permissible, were confined to the Court of Session, proceedings may now be brought in the Sheriff Court.

The Act lays down that arrestment of money in the hands of the Crown or of a government department is competent in any case where arrestment in the hands of a subject would have been competent, but an exception is made in respect of National Savings Bank deposits. Section 2 (1) of the Law Reform (Miscellaneous Provisions) (Scotland) Act 1966 removes the privilege whereby the wages of Crown servants, other than serving members of the armed forces, are exempt from arrestment in execution.

DEATHS

Registration

(For Certificates, *see* pages 651–2)

England and Wales

When a death takes place, information of it must be given in person to the local Registrar of Births and Deaths, and the register signed in his/her presence, by a relative of the deceased present at the death, or in attendance during the last illness; or by some other relative of the deceased; in default of any relatives by (a) a person present at the death, or the occupier of the house in which the death happened, or (b) an inmate of the house; or (c) the person arranging the disposal of the body.

The registration must be made within five days of the death, or within the same time written notice of the death must be sent to the Registrar. If the deceased was attended during his/her last illness by a registered medical practitioner, a certificate of cause of death must be sent by the doctor to the Registrar. The doctor must give to the informant of the death a written notice of the signing of the certificate, which must be delivered to the Registrar.

If the death is not registered within five days (or fourteen days if written notice of the occurrence of the death is sent to him/her), the Registrar may require any one of the above-mentioned persons to attend to register at a stated time and place. Failure to comply involves a penalty. The registration of a death is free of charge. After twelve months no death can be registered without the Registrar-General's consent.

Whenever the death of a child is registered, particulars of the name and occupation of the mother are to be entered in the register.

It is essential that a certificate for disposal should be obtained from the Registrar before the funeral or cremation. No fee is chargeable for this certificate. A body must not be disposed of until: either the Registrar has given a certificate to the effect that he/she has registered or received notice of the death; or until the Coroner has made a disposal order.

A person disposing of a body must within ninety-six hours deliver to the Registrar a notification as to the date, place, and means of the disposal of the body.

Still births: see page 651.

Death at sea: the master of a British ship must record any death on board and send particulars to the Registrar-General of Shipping.

Death abroad: consular officers are authorized to register deaths of British subjects occurring abroad. Certificates are obtainable at the Registrar-General's Office, London. If the deceased was of Scottish domicile, particulars are sent to the Registrar-General for Scotland.

With regard to the registration of deaths of members of the armed forces, and deaths occurring on HM ships and aircraft, *see* the Registration of Births, etc. Act 1957.

Scotland

The Registration of Births, Deaths and Marriages (Scotland) Act 1965 supersedes provisions in former Acts.

Personal notification within eight days must be given to the Registrar of either the registration district in which the death took place, or any registration district in which the deceased was ordinarily resident immediately before his death. When a body is found and the place of death is not known, notification must be given to the Registrar of either the registration district in which the body was found or any other registration district appropriate by virtue of the preceding sentence. When a person dies (in or out of Scotland) in a ship, aircraft or land vehicle during a journey and the body is conveyed therein to any place in Scotland the death shall, unless the Registrar-General otherwise directs, be deemed to have occurred at that place.

The register must be signed in the presence of the Registrar by one of the following: (a) any relative of the deceased; (b) any person present at the death; (c) the deceased's executor or other legal representative; (d) the occupier, at the time of the death, of the premises where the death took place; (e) if these fail, any other person having knowledge of the particulars to be registered. Failure to comply involves a penalty.

The medical practitioner who attended the deceased during the last illness must sign a certificate of the cause of death within seven days. If there is no such medical practitioner, any medical practitioner who is able to do so may sign the certificate. At the time of registering the death the Registrar shall, without charge, give the informant a certificate of registration, and the person to whom the certificate is given must hand it to the undertaker before cremation. A body may, however, be interred before the death is registered, in which case the undertaker must deliver a certificate of burial to the Registrar within three days.

Burial

The duty of burial is placed on the deceased person's executors (if any appointed); it is also a recognized obligation of the parent of a child, and of a householder where the body lies. Funeral expenses of a reasonable amount will be repayable out of the deceased's estate in priority to any other claims. Directions as to place and mode of burial are frequently contained in the deceased's will, in some memorandum placed with private papers, or may have been communicated verbally to a relative. Consequently, steps should immediately be taken to ascertain the deceased's wishes from the above sources. If the wishes are considered objectionable, they are not necessarily enforceable; legal advice should be taken. A person may legally leave directions for the anatomical examination of his/her body. As to the place of burial, the parish churchyard is the normal burying place for parishioners or any person dying in the parish, but nowadays this will apply only in villages and smaller towns. In populous districts cemeteries and crematoria have been established, either by the local council or a private company, and burials will take place there in accordance with the regulations. For an exclusive right to a burial space in the churchyard, a faculty is required from the Ecclesiastical Court. Poor persons may be buried at the public expense by the local authority. As to the necessity for obtaining a Registrar's certificate or authority from the Coroner for disposal, *see* above.

Cremation

Under the Cremation Acts 1902 and 1952, regulations are made by the Home Secretary dealing fully with the cremation of a body, disposal of ashes, etc., and containing numerous safeguards.

If cremation is desired it is advisable for instructions to be left in writing to that effect. However, in Scotland, even if the deceased wished his/her body to be cremated or anatomically dissected, relatives can still veto his/her wishes.

To arrange for cremation, the executor or near relative should instruct the undertaker to that effect and obtain from him the forms required by statute.

INTESTACY

As regards deaths on or after 15 March 1977, the position is governed by the Administration of Estates Act 1925, as amended by the Intestates' Estates Act 1952, the Family Provision Act 1966 and Orders made thereunder. If the intestate leaves a spouse and issue, the spouse takes:

(a) the 'personal chattels'
(b) £75,000 with interest at 6 per cent from death until payment
(c) a life interest in half of the rest of the estate

This life interest can be capitalized at the option of the spouse. Personal chattels are articles of household use or ornament (including motor cars), not used for business purposes. The rest of the estate goes to the issue.

If the intestate leaves a spouse and no issue, but leaves a parent or brother or sister of the whole blood or issue of such brothers and sisters the spouse takes

(a) the 'personal chattels'
(b) £125,000 with interest at 6 per cent from death until payment
(c) half of the rest of the estate absolutely

The other half of the rest of the estate goes to the parents, equally if more than one, or, if none, to the brothers and sisters of the whole blood or issue of such brothers and sisters.

If the intestate leaves a spouse, but no issue, no parents and no brothers or sisters of the whole blood or their issue, the spouse takes the whole estate absolutely.

If resident therein at the intestate's death, the surviving spouse may generally require the personal representatives to appropriate the interest of the intestate in the matrimonial home in or towards satisfaction of any absolute interest of the spouse, including the capitalized value of a life interest. In certain cases, leave of court is required. On a partial intestacy any benefit (other than personal chattels specifically bequeathed) received by the surviving spouse under the will must be brought into account against the statutory legacy of £75,000 or £125,000, as the case may be. If there is no surviving spouse, the estate is distributed among those who survive the intestate in the following order (those entitled under earlier numbers taking to the exclusion of those entitled under later numbers):

(1) children
(2) father or mother (equally, if both alive)
(3) brothers and sisters of the whole blood
(4) brothers and sisters of the half blood
(5) grandparents (equally, if more than one alive)
(6) uncles and aunts of the whole blood
(7) uncles and aunts of the half blood
(8) the Crown

In cases (1), (3), (4), (6) and (7), the persons entitled lose their interests unless they or their issue not only survive the intestate, but also attain eighteen or marry under that age, their shares going to the persons (if any) within the same group who do attain eighteen or marry. Moreover, in the same cases, succession is not *per capita*, but *per stirpes*, i.e. by stocks or families. Thus, if the intestate leaves one child and two grandchildren, being the children of a child of the intestate who predeceased the intestate, the two grandchildren represent their deceased parent and take between them one-half of the issue's share, the remaining half going to the surviving child. Similarly, nephews and nieces represent a deceased brother, and so on.

When the deceased died partially intestate (i.e. leaving a will which disposed of only part of his/her property), the above rules apply to the intestate part.

Children must bring into account (hotchpot) any substantial advances received from the intestate during his/her lifetime before claiming any further share under the intestacy. Special hotchpot provisions apply to partial intestacy.

In respect of deaths occurring on or after 4 April 1988, Section 18 of the Family Law Reform Act 1987 provides that references to any relationship between two persons shall, unless the contrary intention appears, be construed without regard to whether or not the father and mother of either of them, or the father and mother of any person through whom the relationship is deduced, have or had been married to each other at any time.

In respect of deaths after March 1976 the provisions of the Inheritance (Provision for Family and Dependants) Act 1975 may allow other persons to claim provision out of the estate. *See* page 647.

For personal application for letters of administration, *see* page 648.

Scotland

The Succession (Scotland) Act 1964, provides that the whole estate of any person dying intestate shall devolve without distinction between heritable and moveable property. By that Act the surviving spouse of an intestate may, as a prior right (in addition to legal rights, *see* below), claim the matrimonial home to a maximum of £65,000, or a choice of one matrimonial home if more than one (or in certain circumstances the value thereof), with its furniture and plenishings not exceeding £12,000 in value, plus the sum of £21,000 if the deceased left issue or, if no issue, the sum of £35,000. These figures have applied since 1 May 1988 and may be increased from time to time by order of the Secretary of State.

The fact that a person was born illegitimate no longer has any effect in their rights of succession as against a legitimate child, by virtue of the Law Reform (Parent and Child) (Scotland) Act 1986.

Legal rights, referred to above, are:

Jus relicti(ae) – the right of a surviving spouse to one half of the deceased's net moveable estate after satisfaction of prior rights if there are no surviving children, or to one-third if there are any surviving children

Legitim – the right of surviving children to one-half of the net moveable estate of deceased parents if no surviving spouse, or one-third of the net moveable estate of deceased parents after satisfaction of prior rights where there is a surviving spouse.

There are no legal rights in heritage.

In general, the lines of succession are: (1) descendants; (2) collaterals; (3) ascendants and their collaterals, and so on in the ascending scale. The Crown is *ultimus haeres*. The right of representation, i.e. the right of the issue of a person who would have succeeded if he/she had survived the intestate, is open to any line of succession where previously it was limited to apply only when there were next of kin or the issue of predeceasing next of kin. The surviving mother of an intestate now has equal rights of succession with the surviving father, where formerly these were restricted. The intestate's maternal relations, who prior to the Act had no rights of succession, are now on an equal footing with the paternal relations. Where the intestate is survived only by parents and by brothers and sisters (collaterals), half of the estate is taken by the parents and the other half by the brothers and sisters, those of the whole blood being preferred to those of the half blood. Where, however, succession opens to collaterals (which expression can include the brothers and sisters of an ancestor of the intestate) of the half blood, they shall rank equally amongst themselves, whether related to the intestate (or his/her ancestor) through their father or their mother.

WILLS

The following notes and those on intestacy must be read subject to the provisions of the Inheritance (Provision for Family and Dependants) Act 1975, which can affect the estate of anyone dying domiciled in England and Wales after March 1976. Very broadly, a spouse, former spouse who has not remarried, a child of the deceased or one treated by the deceased as a child of his/her family, or any person maintained by him/her at his/her death may apply to the Court under the Act. If the Court thinks that the will or the law of intestacy or both do not make reasonable provision for the applicant, it may order payment out of the net estate of maintenance or a lump sum. It may also order the transfer of property or vary certain trusts, and the powers can affect property disposed of by the deceased in his/her lifetime intending to defeat the Act. It is up to the applicant to take the initiative, and the application must generally be made within six months of the grant of probate or letters of administration.

Making a Will

Every person over the age of 18 should make a will. However small the estate, the rules of intestacy (*see* above) may not reflect a person's wishes as to his/her property. In any case a will can do more than just deal with property. It can in particular appoint executors, give directions as to the disposal of the body and appoint guardians to take care of children in the event of the parents' death. For the wealthier person an appropriately drawn will can operate to reduce the burden of inheritance tax.

It is considered desirable for a will to be properly drawn up by a solicitor. Although normally the making of a will is not one of the services which can be provided under the legal advice and assistance scheme, it can be provided for certain special categories of person such as the aged and infirm (*see* below).

In no circumstances should one person prepare a will for another person where the former is to take any benefit under it. This can easily lead to a suggestion of undue influence, which may cause the will to be held bad.

Assuming a lawyer is not employed, a person having resolved to make a will must remember that it is only after a person is dead, and cannot explain his/her meaning, that his/her will can be open to dispute. It is the more necessary, therefore, to express what is meant in language of the utmost clarity, avoiding the use of any word or expression that admits of another meaning than the one intended. Avoid the use of legal terms, such as heirs and issue, when the same thing may be expressed in plain language. If in writing the will a mistake is made, it is better to rewrite the whole. Before a will is executed (*see* below), an alteration may be made by striking through the words with a pen, but opposite to such alteration the testator and witnesses should write their names or place their initials. Never scratch out a word with a knife or other instrument; no alteration of any kind whatever must be made after the will is executed. If the testator afterwards wishes to change the disposition of his/her estate, it is best to make a new will, revoking the old one. The use of codicils should be left to a lawyer.

A will should be written in ink and very legibly, on a single sheet of paper. Although forms of wills must vary to suit different cases, the following forms may be found useful to those who, in cases of emergency, are called upon to draw up wills, either for themselves or others. Nothing more complicated should be attempted. The forms should be studied in conjunction with the following notes:

This is the last will and testament of me [*Thomas Smith*] of [*Vine Cottage, Silver Street, Reading, Berks.*] which I make this [*thirteenth*] day of [*February* 1993] and whereby I revoke all previous wills and testamentary dispositions.

1. I hereby appoint [*John Green of* _______ *and Richard Brown of* _______] to be the executor(s) of this my will.

2. I give all my property real and personal to [*my wife Mary* or *my sons Raymond and David equally* or as the case may be].

Signed by the testator in the presence of us both present at the same time who, at his request, in his presence and in the presence of each other have hereunto set our names as witnesses.

Thomas Smith
Signature of Testator;

William Jones (*signed*)
of Green Gables, South Street, Reading, tailor.

Henry Morgan (*signed*)
of 16 North Street, Reading, butcher.

Should it be desired to give legacies and/or gifts of specific property, instead of giving the whole estate to one or more persons, the form above should be used with the substitution for clause 2 of the following clauses:

2. I give to _______ of _______ the sum of £_______ and to _______ of _______ the sum of £_______ and to _______ of _______ all my books [*or as the case may require*].

3. All the residue of my property real and personal I give to _______ of _______.

Terms

Real property includes freehold land and houses, while personal property includes debts due, arrears of rents, money, leasehold property, house furniture, goods, assurance policies, stocks and shares in companies, and the like. The words 'my money', apart from the context, will normally only include actual real money. The expression 'goods and chattels' should not be used. In giving particular property, ordinary language is sufficient, e.g. my house, Vine Cottage, Silver Street, Reading, Berks. Such specific gifts fail if not owned by the testator at his death.

Residuary legatees

It is well in all cases where legacies or specific gifts are made, to leave to some person or persons 'the residue of my property', although it may be thought that the whole of the property has been disposed of in legacies, etc., already mentioned in the will. It should be remembered that a will operates on property owned at the time of death.

Execution of a will, and witnesses

The testator should sign his/her name at the foot or end of the will, in the presence of two witnesses, who will immediately afterwards sign their names in the testator's and in each other's presence. A person who has been left any gift or share of residue in the will, or whose wife or husband has been left such a gift, should not be an attesting witness. Their attestation would be good, but they would forfeit the gift. It is better that a person named as executor should not be a witness. Husband and wife may both be witnesses, provided neither is a legatee. If a solicitor be appointed executor, it is lawful to direct that his/her ordinary fees and charges shall be paid; but in this case the solicitor (as an interested party) must not be a witness to the will.

It is desirable that the witnesses should be fully described, as they may possibly be wanted at some future time. If the testator should be too ill to sign, even by a mark, another person may sign the testator's name to the will for him/her, in his/her presence and by his/her direction, and in this case it should be shown that the testator knew the contents of the document. The attestation clause should therefore be worded:

> Signed by Thomas Brown, by the direction and in the presence of the testator, Thomas Smith, in the joint presence of us, who thereupon signed our names in his presence and in the presence of each other, the will having been first read over to the testator, who appeared fully to understand the same.

Where there is any suspicion that the testator is not, by reason of age or infirmity, fully in command of his faculties it is desirable to ask his/her doctor to act as a witness (*see* Testamentary capacity below).

A blind person may make a will in braille. If the testator is blind the will should be read aloud to him/her in the presence of the witnesses, and the fact mentioned in the attestation clause. A blind person cannot witness a will.

If by inadvertence the testator should have signed his/her will without the witnesses being present, then the attestation should be: 'The testator acknowledged his signature already made as his signature to his last will and testament, in the joint presence,' etc. Any omission in the observance of these details may invalidate the will. The stringency of the law as to signature and witnessing of a will is only relaxed in favour of soldiers, sailors and airmen in certain circumstances.

Executors

It is usual to appoint two executors, although one is sufficient; any number up to and including four may be appointed. The name and address of each executor should be given in full. An executor may be a legatee. Thus a child of full age or wife to whom the whole or a portion of the estate is left may be appointed sole executor, or one of two executors. The addresses of the executors are not essential, but it is desirable here as elsewhere, to avoid ambiguity or vagueness.

Lapsed legacies

If a legatee dies in the lifetime of the testator, the legacy generally lapses and falls into the residue. Where a residuary legatee predeceases the testator, his/her share of the residuary estate will not generally pass to the other residuary legatees, but will pass to the persons entitled on the deceased's intestacy. In all such cases it is desirable to make a new will.

An important exception to the general rule of lapse stated above is contained in the Administration of Justice Act 1982, where there is a gift to a child or remoter issue of the testator who dies before the testator leaving issue who survive the testator. In such a case the gift will pass to the issue of the deceased child.

Testamentary capacity

A person under the age of 18 cannot make a will (except for soldiers, sailors and airmen in exceptional circumstances).

So far as mental capacity is concerned the testator must be able to understand and appreciate the nature and effect of making a will, the property of which he can dispose and the claims to which he ought to give effect. If a person is not mentally able to make a will, provision exists (under the Mental Health Act 1983) for the Court to do this for him/her.

Revocation

A later will revokes an earlier will if it expressly says so, or is completely inconsistent with it. Otherwise the earlier one is revoked only in so far as it is inconsistent with the later one. A will may also be revoked by burning, tearing or otherwise destroying the will with the intention of revoking it. Such destruction must either be by the testator or by some other person in the testator's presence and at his/her direction. It is not sufficient to obliterate the will with a pen. Marriage in every case acts as the revocation of a will, except that under the Administration of Justice Act 1982, there is a provision to the effect that if it appears from a will that at the time it was made the testator was expecting to be married to a particular person and that he/she intended that the will (or a disposition in the will) should not be revoked by the marriage to that person, the will will not be revoked by marriage to that person. The Act also provides that where after a testator has made a will the testator's marriage is terminated by a decree of divorce or nullity, any gift to a spouse shall lapse and any appointment of the spouse as executor shall be omitted from the will unless the will shows a contrary intention.

Probate or Letters of Administration

Application for probate or for letters of administration may be made in person at the Personal Application Department of the Principal Registry of the Family Division, a district probate registry or sub-registry, or a probate office, by the executors or persons entitled to a grant of administration. Applicants should bring (a) the will, if any; (b) a certificate of death; (c) particulars of all property and assets left by the deceased; and (d) a list of debts and funeral expenses.

Intending applicants, before attending at a registry or probate office, should write or telephone to the nearest probate registry or sub-registry for the necessary forms. Postal or telephone applications cannot be dealt with at the local probate offices, which are part-time only.

Certain property can be disposed of on death without a grant of probate or administration, or in pursuance of a nomination made by the deceased, provided the amount involved does not exceed £5,000. *See* The Administration of Estates (Small Payments) Act 1965.

Where to Find a Proved Will

A will proved since 1858 must have been proved either at the Principal Registry at Somerset House, or a district registry. In the former case the original will itself is preserved at Somerset House, the copy of which probate has been granted is in the hands of the executors who proved the will, and another copy for Parliament is bound up in a folio volume of wills made by testators of that initial and date. The indices to these volumes may be examined at Somerset House and a copy of any will read. In the latter case, the original will proved in the district registry is kept there and may be seen or a copy obtained, but a copy is sent to and filed at Somerset House, where also it may be seen. A general index of grants, both probates and administrations, is prepared and printed annually in lexicographical form, and may be seen at either the Principal Registry or a district registry. This index is usually ready by about October of the following year.

Recent deaths

A system introduced in 1975 enables a person to discover when a grant of probate or letters of administration is made which may be invaluable to a creditor of the deceased or applicant under the Inheritance (Provision for Family and Dependants) Act 1975 (*see* page 647). A standing search may be made by sending a request in the form set out below to the Record Keeper at the Principal Registry of the Family

Division with a small fee. The searcher will receive particulars of any grant made in the previous twelve months or the following six months, including names and addresses of the executors or administrators and the registry in which the grant was made.

Form of search

In the High Court of Justice
Family Division
The Principal Registry (Probate)
I/We apply for the entry of a standing search so that there shall be sent to me/us an office copy of every grant of representation in England and Wales in the estate of:
Full name of deceased:
Alternative or alias name
Full address
Exact date of death

Which either has issued not more than twelve months before the entry of this application or issues within six months hereafter
Signed ______ (full address).

SCOTLAND

A domiciled Scotsman, unlike a domiciled Englishman, cannot in certain circumstances dispose effectively of the entirety of his estate. If he leave a widow and children, the widow is entitled to a one-third share in the whole of the moveable estate (her *jus relictae*), and the children are entitled to another one-third share equally between them (their *legitim*). If he leave a widow but no children, or children but no widow, the *jus relictae* or *legitim* is increased to a one-half share of the net moveable estate. The remaining portion is known as the dead's part. A surviving husband and children have comparable rights (*jus relicti* and *legitim*) in the wife's estate. The dead's part is the only portion of which the testator can freely dispose. Legacies and bequests are payable only out of the dead's part. All debts are payable out of the whole estate before any division.

Pupils, i.e. a girl up to the age of twelve or a boy up to the age of fourteen, cannot make wills. Formerly a minor could dispose only of moveables but since the passing of the Succession (Scotland) Act 1964, a minor has a like capacity to test on heritable property.

A will must be in writing and may be typewritten or even in pencil. A will may be either:

(a) holograph, i.e. written, dated and subscribed by the testator himself/herself, in which case no witnesses are necessary; a printed form filled up by the testator or a typewritten document is not necessarily a holograph but may become so if the testator writes, in hand, at the foot of the form or document the words 'adopted as holograph' followed by his/her signature and the date. Words written on erasure or marginal additions or interlineations in holograph writings, if proved to be in the handwriting of the maker of the deed, are valid

(b) attested, i.e. signed in presence of two witnesses. It is not necessary that these witnesses should sign in the presence of one another, or even that they should see the testator signing so long as the testator acknowledges his/her signature to the witnesses

The Conveyancing and Feudal Reform (Scotland) Act 1970, whilst altering generally the rules for the subscription of deeds, specifically (s. 44 (2)) makes no change in the rules applying to wills, which must still be signed by the testator on every page. If the testator cannot write or is blind, the will may be authenticated by a law agent, notary public or justice of the peace and two witnesses. It is better that the will is not witnessed by a beneficiary thereunder, although this circumstance will not invalidate the attestation of the will or (as it would in England) the gift. A parish minister may act as a notary for the purpose of subscribing a will in his own parish.

Wills may be registered in the Books of the Sheriffdom in which the deceased died domiciled, or in the Books of Council and Session, HM General Register House, Edinburgh. The original deed may be inspected on payment of a small fee and a certified official copy may be obtained. A Scottish will is not revoked by the subsequent marriage of the testator. The subsequent birth of a child for whom no testamentary provision has been made may revoke a will. A will may be revoked by a subsequent will, either expressly or by implication; but in so far as the two can be read together, both wills have effect. If a subsequent will is revoked, the earlier will is revived.

CONFIRMATION

Confirmation, the Scottish equivalent of probate, is obtained in the Sheriff Court of the sheriffdom in which the deceased was domiciled at the date of his/her death or, where the deceased had no fixed domicile or died abroad, in the Commissariat of Edinburgh. Executors are either 'nominate' or 'dative'. An executor nominate is one nominated by the deceased in the will or, where such person has predeceased the testator, by the residuary beneficiary. An executor dative is one appointed by the Court in the case of intestacy or where the deceased had failed to name an executor in the will and there is no residuary beneficiary. In the former case the deceased's next-of-kin are all entitled to be declared executors dative. An inventory of the deceased's estate and a schedule of debts, together with an affidavit, must first be given up. In estates under £17,000 gross, confirmation is obtained under a simplified procedure at reduced fees.

PRESUMPTION OF SURVIVORSHIP

The Succession (Scotland) Act 1964 provides, by s. 31, that where two persons die in circumstances indicating that they died simultaneously or if it is uncertain which was the survivor, the younger will be deemed to have survived the elder unless the elder person left testamentary provision in favour of the younger, whom failing in favour of a third person, the younger person having died intestate (partially or wholly); but if the persons so dying were husband and wife, neither shall be presumed to have survived the other.

EMPLOYMENT

WAGES AND SICK PAY

Under the Wages Act 1986, subject to certain exceptions, employers may not make deductions from an employee's wages unless authorized by statute or contract or with the employee's prior written consent. There is an upper limit of one-tenth of gross pay for deductions from retail workers' wages on account of cash or stock shortages.

Under the Social Security and Housing Benefits Act 1982 as amended, an employee absent from work because of illness or injury is entitled to receive Statutory Sick Pay from the employer for a maximum period of 28 weeks in any period of three years. No payment is made for the first three days of any period of illness. The employer can recoup the payments from his National Insurance contributions.

The Equal Pay Act 1970, which extends to Scotland, prevents discrimination as regards terms and conditions of employment between men and women employed on like work in the same employment.

Particulars of Terms of Employment

Under the Employment Protection (Consolidation) Act 1978, an employer must give each full-time employee within 13 weeks of the beginning of the employment a written statement containing the following particulars of the contract between them:

(a) the date when the employment began (when continuous employment began if previous work counts as continuous with this job)
(b) the rate of remuneration (or how it is calculated)
(c) the intervals at which wages are paid
(d) the hours of work
(e) the employee's entitlement to holidays (including public holidays) and holiday pay
(f) the title of the employee's job
(g) terms relating to sickness, injury and sick pay
(h) details of any pension scheme
(i) the length of notice which the employee should give and receive in order to terminate the contract

In addition, the written particulars must specify any disciplinary rules; and also must identify the person to whom the employee can apply if dissatisfied with any disciplinary decision or to seek redress of any grievance, and what further steps may ensue.

Termination of Employment

An employee may be dismissed without notice if guilty of gross breach of contract, such as disobedience to a lawful order or dishonesty. The employee is then entitled only to wages accrued due at the date of dismissal.

In other cases, the employee is entitled to reasonable notice which, under the Employment Protection (Consolidation) Act 1978, must not be less than one week if he/she has been continuously employed for four weeks, but less than two years; after two years it is two weeks' notice, increasing by one week's notice for each further full year worked up to a maximum of twelve weeks' notice after twelve years' service.

An employer who wrongfully dismisses an employee (i.e. with less than the length of notice to which he/she is entitled) is generally liable to pay wages for the period of proper notice.

An employee who has a fixed term contract has no claim against his/her employer for breach of contract (wrongful dismissal) if the contract is not renewed when it expires. If he/she is wrongfully dismissed before the contract expires, he/she is generally entitled to remuneration payable over the full period of the contract.

An employee may be entitled to a redundancy payment or to compensation for unfair dismissal if the employment has been terminated by the employer (with or without proper notice) or he/she has a fixed term contract which expires without being renewed or the employment has been terminated by the employee by reason of the employer's breach of contract.

Under the Employment Protection (Consolidation) Act 1978, an employee who satisfies the foregoing conditions and has been continuously employed for two years and who is dismissed by reason of redundancy may be entitled to a redundancy payment calculated by reference to his/her age, pay and length of service.

The Employment Protection (Consolidation) Act 1978 also enables an employee who is unfairly dismissed to complain to an industrial tribunal (generally within three months of dismissal). The onus will then be on the employer to prove that the dismissal was due to capability, conduct, redundancy, illegality or some other substantial reason justifying dismissal. The tribunal must decide whether the employer acted reasonably in dismissing the employee. If the employer fails to prove that the dismissal was due to one or more of the above five reasons, or the tribunal decides that the employer did not act reasonably in dismissing the employee, the dismissal will be unfair, in which case the tribunal can:

(a) order re-engagement or reinstatement
(b) award compensation consisting of a basic and a compensatory award

For an employee to bring himself/herself within the unfair dismissal provisions, he/she must have been continuously employed for a period of two years.

All complaints of unfair dismissal are referred to a conciliation officer or the Department of Employment and a very high proportion of complaints are disposed of in this way.

Discrimination

Discrimination on the grounds of sex or marital status is made unlawful by the Sex Discrimination Act 1975. The provisions of the Sex Discrimination Act are similar to those of the Race Relations Act 1976 which make discrimination on 'racial grounds' unlawful. 'Racial grounds' include colour, race, nationality, or ethnic or national origins. The Equal Opportunities Commission and the Commission for Racial Equality have the function of eliminating such discriminations and may provide assistance in pursuing allegations of discrimination.

FAMILY LAW

ADOPTION OF CHILDREN

In England and Wales the adoption of children is mainly governed by the Adoption Act 1976, as amended by the Children Act 1989. A court order is necessary to legalize the adoption, which, when completed, has the effect of making the adopted child the child of the adopter as if he or she had been born to the adopter in lawful wedlock, and the original rights and duties of the natural parents are thereby cut. The adopter has full rights as to residence, education, etc., and the child is treated as his/hers for the purpose of any devolution of property on an intestacy occurring or under any disposition made after the adoption order. The application may be made to the High Court (Family Division) or to a county court or magistrates' court.

Orders may be made in favour of married couples, single, widowed or divorced persons, but not of one party to a marriage alone unless the other spouse cannot be found, is physically or mentally incapable of making an application, or they are separated in circumstances likely to be permanent. A person aged under 21 cannot adopt.

The child's parents or guardians must consent unconditionally to the making of the order unless the court dispenses with the consent, which it may do if the parent cannot be found or is incapable of giving consent, is withholding consent unreasonably, or has neglected or ill-treated the child.

Restrictions are placed on societies which may arrange adoptions.

An adopted person aged over 18 may apply to the Registrar-General for information to enable him/her to obtain a full certificate of his/her birth, but before being supplied with the information he/she will be informed that counselling services are available to him/her. The 1989 Act provides for the creation of a new register (the Adoption Contact Registrar) in which details of those who have had their children adopted, and of adopted persons themselves, may be recorded.

An adopter and the adopted child are within the prohibited degrees for the purposes of marriage to one another.

All adoptions in Great Britain are registered in the Registers of Adopted Children kept by the Registrars-General in London and Edinburgh respectively. Certificates from these registers, including short certificates which contain no reference to adoptions, can be obtained on conditions similar to those relating to birth certificates (*see* below).

Scotland

The law is consolidated in the Adoption (Scotland) Act 1978 as amended by the Children Act 1989. The law relating to fostering is consolidated in the Foster Children (Scotland) Act 1984. A petition for adoption is presented either to the Sheriff Court or the Court of Session. As in England, the petitioner(s) must be 21 or over and may be a married couple or one person who, if married, is living apart permanently from his or her spouse. The consent of the child's natural parents/guardians is required unless dispensed with, or the child is already free for adoption.

The Succession (Scotland) Act 1964 gives the adopted child the same rights of succession as a child born to the adopter in wedlock but deprives him/her of any such rights in the estates of his natural parents.

BIRTHS (REGISTRATION)

When a birth takes place, personal information of it must be given to the Registrar of Births and Deaths for the sub-district in which the birth occurred, and the register signed in his/her presence by the father or mother of the child; or, if they fail, by (a) the occupier of the house in which the birth happened; (b) a person present at the birth; or (c) the person having charge of the child. The duty of attending to the registration therefore rests firstly on the parents. The mother is responsible for the registration of the birth of an illegitimate child.

The registration is required to be made within 42 days of the birth. Failure to do this without reasonable cause involves liability to a penalty. The registration of a birth is free. In England or Wales, the informant, instead of attending before the registrar of the sub-district where the birth occurred, may make a declaration of the particulars required to be registered in the presence of any registrar. Under the National Health Service Act 1977, notice of every birth must be given by the father, or person in attendance on the mother, to the district medical officer of health by post within 36 hours of the birth. This is in addition to the registration already mentioned.

Still birth: a still birth must be registered, and a certificate signed by the doctor or midwife who was present at the birth or who has examined the body of the child must be produced to the registrar. The certificate must, where possible, state the cause of death and the estimated duration of the pregnancy. A still birth may only be registered within three months of the birth.

Re-registration: the re-registration of the birth of a person legitimated by the subsequent marriage of the parents is provided for in the Births and Deaths Registration Act 1953, as amended by the Family Law Reform Act 1987. Special provisions apply to the registration and re-registration of births of abandoned children, and the re-registration of births of illegitimate children showing the father's name; the mother must normally be party to the latter application.

Birth at sea: the master of a British ship must record any birth on board and send particulars to the Registrar-General of Shipping.

Birth abroad: consular officers are authorized to register births of British subjects occurring abroad. Certificates are obtainable in due course at the Registrar-General's Office, London.

The registration of births occurring out of the United Kingdom among members of the armed forces, or occurring on board HM ships and aircraft, is provided for by the Registration of Births, Deaths and Marriages (Special Provisions) Act 1957, applicable also to Scotland.

Scotland

The Registration of Births, Deaths and Marriages (Scotland) Act 1965 supersedes former Acts. Personal notification within 21 days of any birth must be given to the registrar of either the registration district in which the birth took place, or any registration district in which the mother of the child was ordinarily resident at the time of the birth. In the case of a foundling child, dead or alive, when the place of birth is not known, notification must be given to the registrar of the registration district in which the child, or the body, was found, within two months from the date on which the child was found. When a child is born (in or out of Scotland) in a ship, aircraft or land vehicle during a journey and the child is conveyed therein to any place in Scotland, the birth shall, unless the Registrar-General otherwise directs, be deemed to have occurred at that place.

The register must be signed in the presence of the registrar by the father or mother of the child; or, if they fail, by (a) any relative of either parent who has knowledge of the birth; (b) the occupier of the premises in which the child was, to the knowledge of that occupier, born; (c) any person present at the birth; (d) any person having charge of the child. Failure without reasonable cause involves a penalty.

The name of the father of a child born out of wedlock may be entered in the register of births at the time of registration if jointly requested by the mother and father, and the latter's name may also be recorded at a later date on declaration by both parents. A free abbreviated certificate of birth will be issued to the informant at the time of registration.

Still birth: a still birth must be registered and a certificate, signed by the doctor or certified midwife present at the birth or who has examined the body of the child, must be produced.

Re-registration: provision is made for the re-registration of the birth of a person made legitimate by the subsequent marriage of the parents or whose birth entry is affected by any matter respecting status or paternity, or has been so made as to imply that he/she is a foundling.

CERTIFICATES OF BIRTHS, MARRIAGES, OR DEATHS

Certificates of births, deaths, or marriages in England and Wales can be obtained at the Office of Population Censuses and Surveys, St Catherine's House, 10 Kingsway, London WC2B 6JP, or from the Superintendent Registrar having the legal custody of the register containing the entry of which a certificate is required. Certificates of marriage can also be obtained from the incumbent of the church in which the marriage took place, or from the Nonconformist minister (or other authorized person) where the marriage takes place in a registered building.

A standard certificate of birth, death or marriage may be obtained from the Superintendent Registrar for a fee of £5.50 or from the registrar for a fee of £2.00. One short birth certificate is issued free of charge at registration. The fee for the issue of a short birth certificate by the Superintendent Registrar is £2.50 and by a registrar, £1.50. Certificates of birth, death or marriage for special purposes cost £1.50.

When a certificate is required, the nearest register office will be able to advise on the best way of obtaining it and any fees payable. For a general search in the indexes of not more than six successive hours and where the object is not stated, the fee is £14.00. No fee is payable for a search in the indexes when a particular entry in the register is specified.

Records of births, deaths and marriages registered in England and Wales since 1837 are kept at the Office of Population Censuses and Surveys, St Catherine's House, 10 Kingsway, London WC2B 6JP. The Society of Genealogists, 14 Charterhouse Buildings, Goswell Road, London ECIM 7BA, possesses many records of baptisms, marriages and deaths prior to 1837, including copies in whole or in part of about 4,000 parish registers.

Scotland

Certificates of births, deaths or marriages registered from 1855 (when compulsory registration commenced in Scotland) can be obtained personally at the General Register Office, New Register House, Edinburgh EH1 3YT, or from the appropriate local registrar, on payment of the fee of £8.00 for a full extract entry of birth, death, or marriage (£10.50 by post), and £8.00 for an abbreviated certificate of birth (£10.50 by post). An abbreviated certificate of registration of death is issued free of charge for National Insurance purposes in certain cases. A Register of Divorces (which includes decrees of declaration of nullity of marriage) is kept by the Registrar-General at the General Register Office. The fee for an extract decree is £8.00 (£10.50 by post).

There are also available at the General Register Office old parish registers of the date prior to 1855, which were formerly kept under the administration of the established Church of Scotland. An extract of an entry in these registers may be obtained on payment of the appropriate fee. A fee of £15.00 per day is payable for a general search of all the Scottish registers.

The Registration of Presumed Deaths (Prescription of Particulars) (Scotland) Regulations 1978 as read with Presumption of Death (Scotland) Act 1977 prescribe the particulars to be notified by the Clerk of Court to the Registrar-General after a decree or variation order has been granted in an action of declarator of death of a missing person.

DIVORCE, SEPARATION AND ANCILLARY MATTERS

Matrimonial suits may be conveniently divided into two classes: those in which it is sought to annul the marriage because of some defect; and those in which, the marriage being admitted, it is sought to end the marriage or the duties arising from it. By virtue of the Matrimonial and Family Proceedings Act 1984, all matrimonial causes are commenced in one of the divorce county courts designated by the Lord Chancellor or in the Divorce Registry in London. If the suit becomes defended, it may be transferred to the High Court.

Nullity of Marriage

Nullity of marriage is now mainly governed as to England and Wales by the Matrimonial Causes Act 1973. A marriage is void *ab initio* if the parties were within the prohibited degrees of affinity; or were not male and female; if it was bigamous; if one of the parties was under the age of consent, i.e. 16; or, in the case of a polygamous marriage entered into outside England and Wales, if either party was at the time of the marriage domiciled in England or Wales. Where the formalities of the marriage were defective, the marriage is generally void if both parties knew of the defect (e.g. where marriage took place otherwise than in an authorized building). However, absence of the consent of parents or guardians (or of the Court or other authority, in lieu thereof) in the case of minors does not invalidate the marriage.

A marriage is voidable (i.e. a decree of nullity may be obtained but until such time the marriage remains valid) on the following grounds:

(a) incapacity of either party to consummate
(b) respondent's wilful refusal to consummate
(c) that either party did not validly consent to the marriage, whether in consequence of duress, mistake, unsoundness of mind or otherwise
(d) that either party at the time of marriage was a mentally disordered person
(e) that at the time of marriage the respondent was suffering from communicable venereal disease
(f) that at the time of the marriage the respondent was pregnant by another man

In cases (e) and (f), the petitioner must have been ignorant of the grounds at the date of the marriage. In cases (c), (d), (e) and (f) proceedings must be instituted within three years of the marriage, although leave may be obtained to petition outside this period in the case of certain persons suffering from mental illness. In all cases the court shall not grant a decree where the petitioner has led the respondent to believe that he/she would not seek a decree and it would be unjust for it to be granted.

The 1973 Act provides that a decree of nullity in a voidable marriage only annuls the marriage from the date of the decree. The marriage remains valid until the decree, and any children of the marriage are legitimate. Children of a void marriage are illegitimate unless the father was domiciled in England or Wales at the child's birth (or father's death, if earlier), and at the time of conception (or marriage if later) both or either of the parents reasonably believed the marriage was valid.

A spouse's insistence upon the use of contraceptives will not constitute wilful refusal to consummate within (b) above, even though there has been no normal intercourse, but it may in certain circumstances constitute unreasonable behaviour for the purpose of divorce (*see* below). Further, it has been allowed as a defence to a charge of desertion against the aggrieved party.

Judicial Separation and Divorce

The second class of suit includes a suit for judicial separation (which does not dissolve a marriage) and a suit for divorce (which, if successful, dissolves the marriage altogether and leaves the parties at liberty to marry again). Either spouse may petition for judicial separation. It is not necessary to prove that the marriage has broken down irretrievably and the facts listed under Divorce below are grounds for judicial separation.

Divorce

The sole ground on which a divorce is obtained by either husband or wife is the irretrievable breakdown of the marriage. However, the court is precluded from holding that a marriage has irretrievably broken down unless it is satisfied of one or more of the following facts:

(a) that the respondent has committed adultery since the marriage and the petitioner finds it intolerable to live with the respondent
(b) that the respondent has behaved in such a way that the petitioner cannot reasonably be expected to continue cohabitation
(c) desertion by the respondent for two years immediately before the petition
(d) five years' separation immediately before the petition

(but only two years where the respondent consents to the decree). Matrimonial Causes Act 1973

The foregoing is subject to a clause prohibiting any petition for divorce (but not for judicial separation) before the lapse of one year from the date of the marriage.

Desertion may be defined as a voluntary withdrawal from cohabitation by one spouse without just cause and against the wishes of the other. Where one spouse is guilty of conduct of a serious nature which forces the other to leave, the party at fault is said to be guilty of constructive desertion.

Encouragement of reconciliation

The 1973 Act requires the solicitor for the petitioner in certain cases to certify whether the possibility of a reconciliation has been discussed with the petitioner and whether or not the solicitor has given the petitioner the names and addresses of persons qualified to help effect a reconciliation.

A total period of less than six months during which the parties have resumed living together is to be disregarded in determining whether the prescribed period of desertion or separation has been continuous. Similar provision for effecting a reconciliation exists in relation to the other proofs of breakdown, but a petitioner cannot rely on an act of adultery by the other party if they have lived together for more than six months after discovery of that act of adultery.

Obtaining the decree nisi

Where the suit is defended, i.e. the respondent opposes the dissolution or the fact/ground on which the petitioner seeks it, the petition will be heard by a judge in open court, the parties giving oral evidence. Where the suit is undefended, the evidence will normally take the form of a sworn written statement made by the petitioner which will be sent to the court and read over by a district judge. If the district judge is satisfied that the petitioner has proved the contents of the petition, he/she will simply fix a date for the pronouncement of the decree nisi in open court, it being unnecessary for either party to attend. Only if the district judge is not satisfied as above will he/she order that the petition be heard formally by the judge.

Children

After giving his/her certificate in relation to the decree nisi, the district judge must consider whether he/she should exercise any of his/her powers under the Children Act 1989. If there is already an application pending for an order in relation to children the district judge can in exceptional circumstances delay the grant of the decree absolute.

Decree absolute

Every decree of divorce or nullity is in the first instance a decree nisi, and the marriage subsists until the decree is made absolute, usually six weeks after decree nisi on the petitioner's application. After the decree absolute either party is free to remarry.

Maintenance, etc

The court has wide powers to order either party to the marriage to make financial provision (e.g. periodical payments, a lump sum, the transfer of property) for the other party or any child of the family, having regard to the party's means, the recipient's needs and all the important aspects of the case. These so-called ancillary matters often present more difficulty than the divorce itself, especially affecting the home, and may go on long after the marriage is dissolved. There is, however, nothing to stop financial matters being negotiated by the parties through their solicitors before the divorce goes through.

The court may, where the husband has neglected to provide reasonable maintenance for the wife or children, order the husband to make provision for them, even though no matrimonial suit is pending between the parties to the marriage, and while such an order is in force the court may also make orders relating to the children.

Orders Regarding Children

The Court may make orders in respect of children in connection with a suit for divorce, nullity or judicial separation (above), or with an application to the magistrates (below) whether the suit succeeds or not. In addition, if there is no other matrimonial suit involved, a parent may apply for orders under the Children Act 1989, and any person interested may apply to the High Court for the child to be made a ward of court.

In all cases the welfare of the child is the paramount consideration. The categories of child who may be covered by any particular type of proceedings differ according to the nature of those proceedings and to the nature of the particular relief sought, but it should be borne in mind that in connection with divorce, nullity and judicial separation a child which has been treated by the spouses as a child of the family may be included as a 'child of the family' as well as the children of the spouses themselves. This also applies to most maintenance cases in the magistrates' court (*see* below). It should be borne in mind that where there is financial need (because of continuing education or disability, for instance), maintenance may be ordered for children even beyond the age of majority.

Any dispute relating to the above matters should be placed in the hands of a solicitor without delay.

Separation by Agreement

Husband and wife may enter into an agreement to separate and live apart but the agreement, to be valid, must be followed by an immediate separation. It is most desirable to consult a solicitor in every such case, who will often advise obtaining a court order by consent.

Family Proceedings Court

For many years the law relating to domestic proceedings in magistrates' courts (now family proceedings courts) was out of line with the divorce law which was reformed in 1969. The Domestic Proceedings and Magistrates' Courts Act 1978 took effect in early 1981 and now contains the relevant law.

A husband or wife can apply to a family proceedings court for a matrimonial order on the grounds that the other spouse: (a) has failed to pay reasonable maintenance for the applicant; (b) has failed to make a proper contribution towards the reasonable maintenance of a child of the family; (c) has deserted the applicant; or (d) has behaved in such a way that the applicant cannot reasonably be expected to live with the respondent.

If the case is proved the court can order: (a) periodical payments for the applicant; (b) periodical payments for a child of the family; or (c) a lump sum (not exceeding £1,000) for the benefit of the applicant and for any child of the family.

In deciding what orders (if any) to make, the magistrates must consider a number of guidelines which are similar to those governing financial orders on divorce. There are also special provisions relating to consent orders and separation by agreement. The court also has powers to make orders relating to a child of the family and these orders together with orders for child maintenance can be made even though the court makes no order for spouse maintenance. Other provisions of the Act relate to interim orders, and variation, discharge and revival of orders. An order may be enforceable even though the parties are living together, but in some cases it will cease to have effect if they continue to do so for six months. The hearing of matrimonial disputes is separate from ordinary court business, and the public are not admitted.

Domestic Violence

The Domestic Violence and Matrimonial Proceedings Act 1976, the Domestic Proceedings and Magistrates' Courts Act 1978 (the former not being applicable to Scotland and the latter only to a limited extent; *see* below) and the Matrimonial Homes Act 1983 have made it easier for one spouse who has been subjected to violence by the other to obtain an order to restrain further violence and if need be to have the other excluded from the home. Such orders can be obtained very quickly, and a person disobeying them is liable to be imprisoned for contempt of court. There are some differences of detail between the three Acts; in particular the 1976 Act also applies to unmarried couples. Such orders may also be obtained in the course of suits for divorce and judicial separation.

SCOTLAND

Nullity of Marriage

A declaration of nullity of marriage may be obtained on the ground of any impediment, such as consanguinity and affinity, subsistence of a previous marriage, nonage of one of the parties, incapacity or insanity of one of the parties, or by the absence of genuine consent. The financial provisions on divorce contained in the Family Law (Scotland) Act 1985 also apply to an action for declaration of nullity of marriage.

Judicial Separation

Under the Divorce (Scotland) Act 1976, a decree of judicial separation can be obtained by proof of the same facts necessary to obtain decree of divorce, except that for the principle of irretrievable breakdown there is substituted that of grounds justifying separation. This type of action is competent in both the Court of Session and the Sheriff Court.

Divorce

Actions of divorce could formerly only be raised in the Court of Session, having jurisdiction to entertain such actions only if either of the parties to the marriage in question is domiciled in Scotland on the date when the action is begun, or was habitually resident in Scotland throughout the period of one year ending with that date. As from 1 May 1984, however, when the Divorce Jurisdiction, Court Fees and Legal Aid (Scotland) Act 1983 came into force, actions of divorce may also be raised in the sheriff courts provided the above conditions are complied with, and provided either party to the marriage was resident in the Sheriffdom for a period of forty days ending with the date the action was begun, or was resident in the Sheriffdom for a period of not less than forty days ending not more than forty days before the date the action was begun.

The Scots law of divorce is now governed by the Divorce (Scotland) Act 1976, which for the purposes of divorce came into force on 1 January 1977. The sole ground of divorce is now irretrievable breakdown of the marriage. This can be established only in one of the following ways:

(a) The defending spouse has committed adultery since the date of the marriage. It is not necessary for the pursuing spouse to prove that the fact of adultery made it intolerable to live with the defending spouse
(b) The defending spouse has behaved in such a way that the pursuing spouse cannot reasonably be expected to cohabit with him or her. It is immaterial whether or not the conduct founded upon is active or passive
(c) The defending spouse has deserted the pursuing spouse for a continuous period of two years. There must be no question of the pursuing spouse having refused a genuine and reasonable offer to adhere. Nor is irretrievable breakdown established if cohabitation is resumed for a period of more than three months after the two-year period has expired
(d) There has been no cohabitation at any time during a continuous period of two years immediately preceding the action between the parties to the action, and the defending spouse consents to the divorce being granted
(e) There has been no cohabitation at any time during a continuous period of five years, as in (d), except that on the expiry of the five-year period, the consent of the defending spouse is not required

The facts of desertion and separation are not interrupted by the parties cohabiting for a period or periods not exceeding six months. However, such a period or periods of cohabitation would not be included in the calculation of the two-year or five-year periods.

Encouragement of reconciliation

The burden of promoting a reconciliation between spouses in a divorce action in Scotland falls upon the Court by virtue of the 1976 Act. Where an action of divorce has been raised, it may be postponed by the Court to enable the parties to seek to effect a reconciliation, if the Court feels that there may be a reasonable prospect of such reconciliation. If the parties do cohabit during such postponement, no account shall be taken of such cohabitation if the action later proceeds.

Maintenance, etc

The 1976 Act also provides that either party to a marriage can apply to the Court at any time prior to decree being granted for: (a) an order for interim custody of all or some of the children of the marriage under 16 years of age; (b) an order for access to all or some of the children of the marriage under 16 years of age in the custody of the other party.

The financial provisions on divorce in the 1976 Act have been superseded by the Family Law (Scotland) Act 1985, which allows either party to the marriage to apply to the court for an order for payment of a capital sum or for a periodical allowance or for an incidental order. The Act sets out principles to be applied by the Court, one of these being that the financial provisions awarded to a party who has been dependent for financial support on the other party should be given over a period of not more than three years.

The Act also defines the rights and obligations of aliment between parents and children, thereby excluding aliment between grandparents and grandchildren and of children to parents, and provides that a child is entitled to aliment up to the age of 18 or to 25 if in full-time further education, and for the claiming of aliment whether in connection with an action of divorce, etc., or independently.

Procedure

Appearance in Court at a Proof in an undefended divorce action has been rendered unnecessary since April 1978. A full Proof is still necessary if the action is defended in any respect. In place of court appearance, affidavits (statements sworn before a Notary Public) by the pursuer and any witnesses are lodged in the Court together with a Minute by the solicitor craving decree.

A new simplified procedure for 'do-it-yourself' divorce was introduced in January 1983 for certain divorces. Thus, if the action is based on (d) or (e) above and will not be opposed, and if there are no children under 16 and no financial claims, then the applicant can write directly to the local sheriff court or to the Court of Session, Divorce Section (SP), Parliament House, Edinburgh, for the appropriate forms to enable him or her to proceed. The fee is £40 unless the applicant receives Income Support, Family Credit or legal advice and assistance, in which case there is no fee.

Custody of Children

In actions for divorce and separation, the Court has a discretion in awarding the custody of the children of the parties. The welfare of the children is the paramount consideration, and the mere fact that a spouse, by reason of his or her behaviour, brought about the breakdown of the marriage does not of itself preclude him or her from being awarded custody. The Children Act 1975, as amended, also applies to Scotland.

Domestic Violence

The Matrimonial Homes (Family Protection) (Scotland) Act 1981, as amended, provides that one spouse, whether or not he or she has title to the matrimonial home, can obtain an exclusion order suspending the other spouse's occupancy rights in the matrimonial home. The Court (either Court of Session or Sheriff Court) is empowered to make such an order if satisfied that it is necessary to protect the applicant or any child of the family from any conduct, actual or threatened or reasonably apprehended, of the other spouse which would be injurious to the physical or mental health of the applicant or child. In making the order the Court may include a warrant for the summary ejection of the non-applicant spouse from the matrimonial home and for an interdict prohibiting him/her from entering it.

ILLEGITIMACY AND LEGITIMATION

The Children Act 1989 gives the mother parental responsibility for her child when not married to the father. The father can acquire parental responsibility by agreement with her (in prescribed form) or by court order.

Prima facie every child born of a married woman during a marriage is legitimate; and this presumption can only be rebutted by strong evidence. However, under the Family Law Reform Act 1969, any presumption of law as to the legitimacy (or illegitimacy) of any person may in civil proceedings be rebutted by evidence showing that it is more probable than not that the person is illegitimate (or legitimate) and in any proceedings where paternity is in question, blood tests may be ordered. If, however, the husband and wife are separated under an Order of the Court, a child conceived by the wife during such separation is presumed not to be the husband's child.

Legitimation

The Legitimacy Act 1976 consolidates earlier legislation dating back to 1 January 1927. Where the parents of an illegitimate person marry, or have married, whether before or after that date, the marriage, if the father is at the date thereof domiciled in England or Wales, renders that person, if living, legitimate as from 1 January 1927, or from the date of the marriage, whichever last happens. Marriage legitimates a person even though the father or mother was married to a third person at the time when the illegitimate person was born. It is the duty of the parents to supply to the Registrar-General information for re-registration of the birth of a legitimate child.

Declarations of Legitimacy

A person claiming that he, his parents, or any remoter ancestor has become legitimated, may petition the High Court or the county court for the necessary declaration.

Rights and Duties of Legitimated Persons

A legitimated person, his/her spouse or children may take property under an intestacy occurring after the date of legitimation, or under any disposition (e.g. a will) coming into operation after such date, as if he/she had been legitimate. He/she must maintain all persons whom he/she would be bound to maintain had he/she been born legitimate, and he/she is entitled to the benefit of any Act of Parliament which confers rights on legitimate persons to recover damages or compensation. The Act specially provides that nothing therein contained is to render any person capable of succeeding to or transmitting a right to any dignity or title.

Property Rights of Illegitimate Children

By the Family Law Reform Act 1969 the rights of an illegitimate child on an intestacy were broadly equated with those of a legitimate child, and in any disposition made after 31 December 1969, any reference to children or other relatives was, unless the contrary intention appears, to be construed as including any person who is illegitimate or who is related through another person who is illegitimate. However, these provisions of the 1969 Act have been replaced by the general provision of the Family Law Reform Act 1987 (*see* page 646).

SCOTLAND

The Law Reform (Parent and Child) Scotland Act 1986 implements the Scottish Law Commission's report on illegitimacy. The Act contains a general provision granting equal status to all persons whatever the marital status of their parents. The mother of an illegitimate child may raise an action of affiliation and aliment against the father, either in the Court of Session or, more usually, in the Sheriff Court. Where in any such action the Court finds that the defender is the father of the child, the Court shall, in awarding expenses, or aliment, have regard to the means of the parties and the whole circumstances of the case. The Court may, upon application by the mother or by the father of any illegitimate child, or in any action for aliment for an illegitimate child, make such order as it may think fit regarding the custody of such child and the right of access thereto of either parent, having regard to the welfare of the child and to the conduct of the parents and to the wishes as well of the mother as of the father and may on the application of either parent recall or vary such order. The obligation of the mother and of the father of an illegitimate child to provide aliment for such child shall (without prejudice to any obligation attaching at common law) endure until the child attains the age of sixteen.

Legitimation

By Scottish law an illegitimate child is legitimated by and on the date of the subsequent marriage of its parents and there is no objection to there having been an impediment to the marriage of the parents at the time of the child's conception – *see* the Legitimation (Scotland) Act 1968, which came into operation on 8 June 1968, on which date thousands of existing illegitimate children were regarded as legitimated. By the Registration of Births, Deaths and Marriages (Scotland) Act 1965, a child so legitimated, who has already been registered as illegitimate, may be re-registered as legitimate. The consent of the father of an illegitimate child to its adoption is not required unless he has been awarded parental rights by the court.

MARRIAGE

Marriage According to Rites of the Church of England

Marriage by Banns

The Marriage Act 1949 prescribes audible publication according to the rubric, on three Sundays preceding the ceremony during morning service or, if there is no morning service on a Sunday on which the banns are to be published, during evening service. Where the parties reside in different parishes, the banns must be published in both. Under the Act, banns may be published and the marriage solemnized in the parish church, which is the usual place of worship of the persons to be married or either of them, although neither of such persons dwells in such parish; but this publication of banns is in addition to any other publication required by law and does not apply if the church or the residence of either party is in Wales. The Act provides specially for the case where one of the parties resides in Scotland and the other in England, the publication being then in the parish in England in which one party resides, and, according to the law and custom in Scotland, in the place where the other party resides. After the lapse of three months from the last time of publication, the banns become useless, and the parties must either obtain a licence (*see* below), or submit to the republication of banns.

Marriage by Licence

Marriage licences are of two kinds:

Common Licence: a common licence, dispensing with the necessity for banns, is granted by the Archbishops and Bishops through their surrogates, for marriages in any church or chapel duly licensed for marriages. A common licence can be obtained in London by application at the Faculty Office (1 The Sanctuary, Westminster, London SW1) and (for marriages in London) at the Bishop of London's Diocesan Registry (1 The Sanctuary, Westminster, London SW1), by one of the parties about to be married. In the country they may be obtained at the offices of the Bishop's registrars, but licences obtained at the Bishop's diocesan registry only enable the parties to be married in the diocese in which they are issued; those procured at the Faculty Office are available for all England and Wales. No instructions, either verbal or in writing, can be received, except from one of the parties. Affidavits are prepared from the personal instructions of one of the parties about to be married, and the licence is delivered to the party upon payment of a fee (*see* page 658). Before a licence can be granted one of the parties must make an affidavit that there is no legal impediment to the intended marriage; and also that one of such parties has had his or her usual place of abode for the space of fifteen days immediately preceding the issuing of the licence within the parish or ecclesiastical district of the church in which the marriage is to be solemnized, or that the church in which the marriage is to be solemnized is the usual place of worship of the parties or one of them. In the country there may generally be found a parochial clergyman (surrogate) before whom the affidavit may be taken, and whose office it is to deliver the licence personally to the applicant. (In some dioceses it is necessary for the surrogate to procure the licence from the Bishop's registry.) The licence continues in force for three months from its date.

Special Licence: a special licence is granted by the Archbishop of Canterbury, in special circumstances, for marriage at any place with or without previous residence in the district, or at any time, etc.; but the reasons assigned must meet with the Archbishop's approval. Application must be made to the Faculty Office. For fee, *see* page 658.

Marriage under Superintendent Registrar's Certificate

A marriage may be performed in church on the Superintendent Registrar's Certificate (*see* below) without banns, provided that the incumbent's consent is obtained. One of the parties must be resident within the ecclesiastical parish of the church in which the marriage is to take place unless the church is the usual place of worship of the parties or one of them.

Marriage under Superintendent Registrar's Certificate

The following marriages may be solemnized on the authority of a Superintendent Registrar's certificate (either with or without a licence):

(a) a marriage in a registered building, e.g. a Nonconformist church registered for the solemnization of marriages therein
(b) a marriage in a register office
(c) a marriage according to the usages of the Society of Friends (commonly called Quakers)
(d) a marriage between two persons professing the Jewish religion according to the usages of the Jews
(e) a marriage according to the rites of the Church of England (*see* above – in this case the marriage can only be without licence)
(f) a marriage of a person who is housebound or is detained at the place where he or she normally resides (*see* page 657)

Notice of the intended marriage must be given as follows:

Marriage by certificate (without licence): if both parties reside in the same registration district, they must both have resided there for seven days before the notice can be given. It may then be given by either party. If the parties reside in different registration districts, notice must be given by each to the Superintendent Registrar of the district in which he or she resides, and the preliminary residential qualification of seven days must be fulfilled by each before either notice can be given.

Marriage by certificate (with licence): one notice only is necessary, whether the parties live in the same or in different registration districts. Either party may give the notice, which must be given to the Superintendent Registrar of any registration district in which one of the parties has resided for the period of fifteen days immediately preceding the giving of notice, but both parties must be resident in England or Wales on the day notice is given.

The notice (in either case) must be in the prescribed form and must contain particulars as to names, marital status, occupation, residence, length of residence, and the building in which the marriage is to take place. The notice must also contain or have added at the foot thereof a solemn declaration that there is no legal impediment to the marriage, and, in the case of minors, that the consent of the person whose consent to the marriage is required by law (*see* Minors, page 658) has been duly given, and that the residential qualifications mentioned above have been complied with. A person making a false declaration renders himself or herself liable to prosecution for perjury. The notice is entered in the marriage notice book.

Issue of Certificate

Without licence: the notice (or an exact copy thereof) is affixed in some conspicuous place in the Superintendent Registrar's office for 21 days next after the notice was entered in the marriage notice book. After the lapse of this period the Superintendent Registrar may, provided no impediment is shown, issue his certificate for the marriage which can then take place at any time within three months from the date of the entry of the notice.

With licence: the notice in this case is not affixed in the office of the Superintendent Registrar. After the lapse of one whole day (other than a Sunday, Christmas Day or Good Friday) from the date of entry of the notice, the Superintendent Registrar may, provided no impediment is shown, issue his certificate and licence for the marriage, which can then take place on any day within three months from the date of entry of the notice.

Solemnization of the Marriage

In a registered building

The marriage must generally take place at a building within the district of residence of one of the parties, but if the usual place of worship of either is outside the district of his or her residence, it may take place in such usual place of worship. Further, if there is not within the district of residence of one of the parties a registered building within which marriages are solemnized according to the rites and ceremonies which the parties desire to adopt in solemnizing their marriage, it may take place in an appropriate registered building in the nearest district.

The presence of a Registrar of Marriages is not necessary at marriages at registered buildings which have adopted the provisions of section 43 of the Marriage Act 1949. This section provides for the appointment of an authorized person (a person, usually the minister or an official of the building, certified by the trustees or governing body as having been duly authorized for the purpose) who must be present and must register the marriage.

The marriage must be solemnized between the hours of 8 a.m. and 6 p.m., with open doors in the presence of two or more witnesses. The parties must at some time during the ceremony make the following declaration: 'I do solemnly declare that I know not of any lawful impediment why I, A. B., may not be joined in matrimony to C. D.' Also each of the parties must say to the other: 'I call upon these persons here present to witness that I, A. B., do take thee, C. D., to be my lawful wedded wife [or husband],' or, if the marriage is solemnized in the presence of an authorized person without the presence of a Registrar, each party may say in lieu thereof: 'I, A. B., do take thee, C. D., to be my wedded wife [or husband].'

In a register office

The marriage may be solemnized in the office of the Superintendent Registrar to whom notice of the marriage has been given. The marriage must be solemnized between the hours of 8 a.m. and 6 p.m., with open doors in the presence of the Superintendent Registrar or a Registrar of the registration district of that Superintendent Registrar, and in the presence of two witnesses. The parties must make the following declaration: 'I do solemnly declare that I know not of any lawful impediment why I, A. B., may not be joined in matrimony to C. D.,' and each party must say to the other: 'I call upon these persons here present to witness that I, A. B., do take thee, C. D., to be my lawful wedded wife [or husband].'

No religious ceremony may take place in the register office, though the parties may, on production of their marriage certificate, go through a subsequent religious ceremony in any church or persuasion of which they are members.

Other cases

If both parties are members of the Society of Friends (Quakers), or if, not being in membership, they have been authorized by the Society of Friends to solemnize their marriage in accordance with its usages, they may be married in a Friends' meeting-house. The marriage must be registered by the registering officer of the Society appointed to act for the district in which the meeting-house is situated. The presence of a Registrar of Marriages is not necessary.

If both parties are Jews they may marry according to their usages in a synagogue which has a certified marriage secretary, or in a private dwelling-house at any hour; the building may be situated within or without the district of residence. The marriage must be registered by the secretary of the synagogue of which the man is a member. The presence of a Registrar of Marriages is not necessary.

Marriage under Registrar-General's Licence

The main purpose of the Marriage (Registrar-General's Licence) Act 1970, which came into force on 1 January 1971, is to enable non-Anglicans to be married in unregistered premises where one of the persons to be married is seriously ill, is not expected to recover, and cannot be moved to registered premises.

Detained and Housebound Persons

The Marriage Act 1983 (which does not extend to Scotland) enables marriages of detained persons and housebound persons to be solemnized at their place of residence . The Act came into operation on 1 May 1984.

Marriage in England or Wales when one party lives in Scotland or Northern Ireland

Notice for a marriage by a Superintendent Registrar's certificate in a register office or registered building may be given in the usual way by the party resident in England. As regards Scotland, the party there should give notice of intention to marry to the Registrar. As regards Northern Ireland, the party there, after a residence of seven days, must give notice to the District Registrar of Marriages. Notice cannot be given for such marriages to take place by certificate with licence of the Superintendent Registrar.

Marriage of such parties may take place in a church of the Church of England after the publication of banns, or by ecclesiastical licence.

Civil Fees from 1 April 1992

Marriage by Superintendent Registrar's certificate

If both parties live in same district
- In register office, £33.00
- In a registered building when presence of Registrar is required, £44.00

If the parties live in different districts
- In register office, £49.00
- In a registered building when presence of Registrar is required, £60.00

Marriage by Superintendent Registrar's licence

- In register office, £76.00
- In a registered building when presence of Registrar is required, £87.00

Total fees for the preliminaries to marriage by Registrar-General's licence, £15.00

Marriage of a housebound or detained person

For attendance of Superintendent Registrar at residence of housebound or detained person to attest notice of marriage, £30.00

For attendance of Superintendent Registrar at residence of housebound or detained person, £30.00

For attendance of Registrar at residence of house-bound or detained person, £28.00

In the case of a registered building, further fees may be payable to the Minister or the authorities of the building.

ECCLESIASTICAL FEES from 1 April 1992

Marriage after Banns

Parties residing in same parish, £61.00
Parties residing in different parishes, £72.00

Marriages by Common Licence

Fee for licence varies, but usually, £42.00
Fee to Church authorities for ceremony, £54.00

Marriage on the authority of the Superintendent Registrar's certificate

Parties residing in same registration district, £70.00
Parties residing in different districts, £86.00

Marriage by special licence

Fee payable at Faculty Office, £75.00

Marriage of a housebound or detained person

For attendance of a Superintendent Registrar at residence of a housebound or detained person to attest marriage, £30.00
For entering notice of marriage*, £16.00

*Two notices are required to be given if the parties reside in different registration districts.
Further fees may be payable for additional facilities at the marriage, e.g. the organist's fee.
Some of the above fees may not apply to the Church in Wales.

MISCELLANEOUS NOTES

Consanguinity and affinity

A marriage between persons within the prohibited degrees of consanguinity or affinity is void. Relaxations have, however, been made by various statutes which have now been replaced by the Marriage Act 1949 (see 1st Schedule to the Act) and the Marriage (Enabling) Act 1960. It is now permitted to contract a marriage with:

(a) Sister, aunt or niece of a former wife (whether living or not)
(b) Former wife of brother, uncle or nephew (whether living or not)

No clergyman can be compelled to solemnize any of the foregoing marriages, but he may allow his church to be used for the purpose by another minister.

The Marriage (Prohibited Degrees of Relationship) Act 1986 makes further provision with regard to the marriage of persons related by affinity, e.g. after section 1 of the Act came into force, a marriage between a man and the daughter or granddaughter of his former wife will not be void by reason only of that relationship if both parties have attained 21 at the time of the marriage and the younger party has not at any time before attaining 18 been a child of the family in relation to the other party.

Minors

Persons under 18 years of age are generally required to obtain the consent of certain persons (Marriage Act 1949, section 3 and 2nd Schedule as amended by the Children Act 1989). Where both parents are living, both must consent. Where one is dead, the survivor, or, if there is a guardian appointed by the deceased parent, the guardian and the survivor must consent. (For the position where the parents of the child were not married to each other at the time of the birth, see Schedule 12, paragraph 5 to the Children Act 1989.) No consent is required in the case of a minor's second marriage. In certain exceptional cases consent may be dispensed with, e.g. the insanity of a parent.

If consent is refused the Court may, on application being made, consent to the marriage; application can be made for this purpose to the High Court, the county court, or a court of summary jurisdiction. The Act prohibits any marriage where either party is under 16 years of age.

SCOTLAND

According to the law of Scotland, marriage is a contract which is completed by the mutual consent of parties. The Marriage (Scotland) Act 1977, which came into force on 1 January 1978, states or restates the law in convenient form. References in this section are to that Act.

IMPEDIMENTS TO MARRIAGE

These are: (a) nonage, i.e. where either party is under the age of 16; (b) forbidden degrees of relationship (Section 2) as amended by the Marriage Prohibited Degrees of Relationship Act 1986; (c) subsisting previous marriage; (d) incapacity to understand the nature of the contract; (e) both parties of the same sex; (f) non-residence, i.e. if the requirements of prior residence of one or other of the parties in Scotland have not been complied with.

The Act also states the grounds on which certain marriages may be declared void, but this is amended by the Law Reform (Miscellaneous Provisions) (Scotland) Act 1980 which prevents a marriage being rendered void solely due to the failure to comply with certain formalities, provided the particulars of that marriage are entered in a register of marriages by or at the behest of an appropriate registrar.

Marriages may be regular or irregular.

REGULAR MARRIAGES

A regular marriage is one which is celebrated by a minister of religion or authorized registrar or other celebrant specified in the Act. The parties must submit to the District Registrar a statutory notice of intention to marry, the fee for which is £8.00 each. The Registrar will then enter the parties' names and particulars in the marriage notice book which must also show the intended date of the marriage. The Registrar must then display the notice of intention to marry in a prominent public place until the intended date, and any person claiming an interest may lodge written objections thereto with the Registrar (Section 5). The Registrar, after fourteen days of receipt of the marriage notice and on being satisfied that there are no legal impediments to the marriage, will issue to either or both parties a marriage schedule. The fourteen-day period may be shortened in exceptional circumstances. The marriage schedule must be produced to the celebrant of the marriage. The fee for the solemnization ceremony in a register office is £17.00. After the ceremony the marriage must be registered within three days with the Registrar-General for inclusion in the Register of Births, Deaths and Marriages. Within one month of the ceremony, the fee for an extract marriage certificate is £5.50; thereafter it is £8.00.

IRREGULAR MARRIAGES

Since the Marriage (Scotland) Act 1939 the only form of irregular marriage to be recognized by law, marriage by habit and repute, remains competent under the 1977 Act. If the parties live together constantly as husband and wife and are held to be such by the general repute of the neighbourhood and among their friends and relations, then there may arise a presumption from which marriage can be inferred. Before such a marriage can be registered, however, a decree of declarator of marriage must be obtained from the Deputy Principal Clerk of the Court of Session. It is the duty of the Deputy Principal Clerk to register the decree as soon as it is granted.

JURY SERVICE

Every local or parliamentary elector between the ages of 18 and 70 who has resided in the United Kingdom, Channel Islands or Isle of Man for at least five years since he/she attained the age of 13 will be qualified to serve on a jury unless he/she is ineligible or disqualified.

Ineligible persons include those who have at any time been judges, magistrates and certain senior court officials, those who within the previous ten years have been concerned with the law (such as barristers and solicitors and their clerks, court officers, coroners, police, prison and probation officers); priests of any religion and vowed members of religious communities; and certain sufferers from mental illness.

Disqualified persons are those who have at any time been sentenced by a court in the United Kingdom, Channel Islands or Isle of Man, to a term of imprisonment of five years or more, or a person who in the last ten years has (a) served any part of a sentence of imprisonment, youth custody or detention; (b) been detained in a Borstal institution; (c) had passed on him/her or made in respect of him/her a suspended sentence of imprisonment or order for detention; or (d) had made in respect of him/her a community service order. A person who at any time in the last five years has been placed on probation is also disqualified.

Some others are excusable as of right. These include persons over 65, members and officers of the Houses of Parliament, full-time serving members of the armed forces, registered and practising members of the medical, dental, nursing, veterinary and pharmaceutical professions, and any person who has served on a jury in the two years before he/she is summoned. In other cases the court may excuse a juror at its discretion, e.g. where the service would be a hardship to the juror.

If a person serves on a jury knowing himself/herself to be disqualified or ineligible, he/she is liable to be fined up to £2,000 or £400 respectively.

A juror is entitled to subsistence and travelling expenses, compensation for other expenses incurred in consequence of attendance for jury service, loss of earnings and loss of national insurance benefits, but certain maximum figures (which are revised from time to time) are laid down.

A verdict of a jury must normally be unanimous but after two hours' consideration (or such longer period as the court thinks reasonable), a majority verdict is acceptable if ten jurors agree to it (or nine if the size of the jury has been reduced to ten, e.g. by illness during the trial).

Jury trial is now very unusual in civil cases but a person charged with any but the least serious crimes is entitled to be tried by a jury. The defendant may object to any juror if he/she can show that that juror ought not to be on the jury, e.g. because he/she is ineligible or is biased against him/her.

The Coroners' Juries Act 1983 (which does not extend to Scotland) makes provision in relation to qualification to serve on coroners' juries.

Scotland

It is the duty of the sheriff principal of each sheriffdom, in respect of each sheriff court district in the sheriffdom, to maintain a book (the general jury book) containing the names and designations of persons within the district who are qualified and liable to serve as jurors. The book, which is compiled from information which every householder is required to provide, is kept open for the inspection by any person, upon payment of a nominal fee, at the sheriff clerk's office for the district.

Under s.1 of the Law Reform (Miscellaneous Provisions) (Scotland) Act 1980, every man or woman between the ages of 18 and 65 who is for the time being registered as a parliamentary or local government elector and who has been ordinarily resident in the United Kingdom, the Channel Islands or the Isle of Man for any period of at least five years since attaining the age of 13 years, is qualified to serve on a jury.

Ineligible persons include those who at any time within the past ten years have been judges of the supreme courts, sheriffs and certain other senior court officials, those who at any time within the past five years have been concerned with the administration of justice (such as advocates and their clerks, solicitors, court staff, police officers, prison officers, sheriff officers, procurator fiscals, and members of parole boards and children's panels), and certain sufferers from mental illness.

The same rules for disqualified persons operate in Scotland as in England.

Those excusable as of right are members and officers of the Houses of Parliament, full-time serving members of the armed forces, registered and practising members of the medical, dental, nursing, veterinary and pharmaceutical professions, ministers of religion and other persons in holy orders, and any person who has attended for jury service in the past five years.

If a person serves on a jury knowing himself/herself to be disqualified or ineligible, he/she is liable to be fined up to £2,000 or £400 respectively. Jurors failing to attend without good cause are liable to a maximum fine of £200.

Part II of the Juries Act 1949 (amended by regulations following thereon and by the Law Reform (Miscellaneous Provisions) (Scotland) Act 1980) applies only to Scotland and provides, *inter alia*, for the payment of travelling expenses and subsistence allowances to jurors and for loss of earnings.

The number of a jury in a civil cause in the Court of Session is twelve and in the Sheriff Court seven. In a criminal trial the number is fifteen.

LANDLORD AND TENANT

Although basically the relationship between the parties to a lease is governed by the lease itself, the position is complicated by numerous statutory provisions. The few points dealt with may show the desirability of seeking professional assistance in these matters. Important provisions include the following:

(1) The Agricultural Holdings Act 1986, among other things, regulates the length of notice necessary to determine an agricultural tenancy, the tenant's right to remove fixtures on the land, his right to compensation for damage done by game, for improvements and for disturbance, and his right to require the consent of the Agricultural Land Tribunal to the operation of a notice to quit.

(2) The Landlord and Tenant Acts 1927 and 1954, as amended: Part II of the 1954 Act gives security of tenure to the tenant of most business premises, and in effect the tenant can only be ousted on one or more of the seven grounds set out in the Act. In some cases, where the landlord can resume possession, the tenant is entitled to compensation.

(3) The complicated mass of legislation regarding dwelling-houses is embodied in the Rent Act 1977 and the Housing Act 1988.

If a tenancy of a house is within the Rent Act, the tenant has a personal right to reside there, and may only be ousted on certain grounds. Tenancies with full Rent Act protection are known as regulated tenancies. The maximum rent recoverable under such a tenancy is the rent agreed between the landlord and tenant, unless a fair rent has been registered, in which case that is the maximum. Application for the registration of a fair rent may be made by either the landlord or tenant, to the local rent officer, and appeal against his decision lies to the rent assessment committee.

Since the Housing Act 1988 came into force on 15 January 1989, it has not generally been possible to create a new regulated tenancy, although the above protection remains for existing regulated tenancies. Tenancies granted on or after 15 January 1989 are known as assured tenancies provided they satisfy certain conditions, which are broadly the same as those for regulated tenancies under the 1977 Act. However, the rent payable by an assured tenant is either that agreed with the landlord or the open market rent fixed by the Rent Assessment Committee.

(4) The Rent Act 1974 gave tenants of dwellings let furnished the same security of tenure as those of unfurnished dwellings unless the landlord lived in part of the house. In the latter case, and in the case of a tenancy of a dwelling granted by a resident landlord after 13 August 1974, the tenancy will usually be outside full Rent Act protection, but may fall within the restricted contract provisions of the Rent Act 1977. In this event, the landlord or the tenant may apply to the Rent Tribunal for a reasonable rent to be registered and once registered, this is the maximum rent recoverable. No new restricted contracts can be created after 15 January 1989.

(5) The Protection from Eviction Act 1977, as amended by the Housing Act 1988, provides that if any person with intent to cause the residential occupier of any premises to give up the occupation thereof does any act calculated to interfere with the peace or comfort of the residential occupier or members of the household, that person shall be guilty of an offence. A further provision prevents a landlord enforcing without a court order a right to possession against a tenant who is not protected by any security of tenure legislation, and there are special rules in such cases relating to agricultural employees.

(6) A notice to quit any dwelling-house must be given at least four weeks before it is to take effect, and must be in writing and in the prescribed statutory form.

(7) Part I of the Landlord and Tenant Act 1954 applies to most tenancies of houses for over 21 years at a ground rent. Where it applies, the contractual tenancy is continued until brought to an end in the manner prescribed by the Act, and in effect the landlord can only get possession on limited grounds.

Further, under the Leasehold Reform Act 1967, tenants of houses under leases for over 21 years at a rent less than two-thirds of the rateable value of the house are in most cases given a right to purchase the freehold or to take an extended lease for a term of fifty years, provided the tenant at the time when he/she seeks to exercise the right has been occupying the house as his/her residence for the last three years or for periods amounting to three years in the last ten years.

(8) Full Rent Act or Housing Act protection is available only if a house is let on a tenancy. If the occupier of a house has a mere licence to occupy, he/she does not have protection. Further, even if he/she has a tenancy, he/she will not be protected if the rent payable is less than two-thirds of the rateable value of the house. For these reasons, many occupants of houses owned by farmers and occupied by farm workers did not enjoy full security of tenure. The Rent (Agriculture) Act 1976 contains detailed provisions conferring security of tenure on certain agricultural workers housed by their employers and on their successors on death.

(9) Under the Landlord and Tenant Act 1985 (which does not extend to Scotland), in a lease of a dwelling-house granted for a term of less than seven years, there is implied a covenant by the landlord (a) to keep in repair the structure and exterior of the house and (b) to keep in repair and proper working order the installations in the house for the supply of water, gas and electricity, for sanitation, and for space heating or heating water.

(10) The Housing Act 1985 gives security of tenure to many tenants of local authorities and certain other bodies. Further, and subject to certain conditions, such tenants may have the right to purchase their houses or to take a long lease of their flats.

(11) Tenants of flats and other dwellings are given a number of special rights by the Landlord and Tenant Act 1987, as amended by the Housing Act 1988.

Scotland

A lease is a contract, the relationship of the parties being governed by the terms thereof. As is also the case in England, legislation has played an important part in regulating that relationship. Thus, what at common law was an agreement binding only the parties to the deed, becomes in virtue of the Leases Act 1449, a contract binding the landlord's successors, as purchasers or creditors, provided the following four conditions are observed: (a) the lease, if for more than one year, must be in writing; (b) there must be a rent; (c) there must be a term of expiry; and (d) the tenant must have entered into possession.

It would be impracticable to enter here upon a general discussion of this branch of the law. A few important provisions include:

(1) The Agricultural Holdings (Scotland) Act 1991 is a consolidating Act applicable to Scotland. It contains provisions similar to those in the English Act, alluded to in the preceding section.

The Small Landholders Act 1911 provided for the setting up of the Land Court, which has jurisdiction over a large proportion of agricultural and pastoral land in Scotland.

(2) In Scotland business premises are not controlled by statute to so great an extent as in England, but the Tenancy of Shops (Scotland) Act 1949 gives a measure of security to tenants of shops. This Act enables the tenant of a shop who is threatened with eviction to apply to the Sheriff for a renewal of the tenancy. If the landlord has offered to sell the property to the tenant at an agreed price the application for a renewal of the tenancy may be dismissed. Reference should be made to Section 1 (3) of the 1949 Act for particulars of other circumstances in which the Sheriff has a discretion to dismiss an application. The Act extends to premises held by the Crown or government departments, either as landlord or tenant.

(3) Many leases contain references to the term and quarter days in connection with the expiry of the lease payment dates or for rent reviews. At common law these days and dates are respectively Candlemas (2 February), Whitsunday (15 May), Lammas (1 August) and Martinmas (11 November). The Term and Quarter Days (Scotland) Act 1990 amends these dates to 28 February, 28 May, 28 August and 28 November respectively, with effect from 13 July 1991, unless, in the case of a deed executed before that date an application had been made to a Sheriff for a declaration that a date other than the statutory date should apply. Where a pre-existing deed contains a reference to a specific date instead of or in addition to a day, then it is that date which shall apply.

(4) The Housing (Scotland) Act 1987 consolidates previous legislation in regard to the extensive powers and duties to

local authorities in relation to housing. Included therein is the general provision regarding the rights of public sector tenants to purchase the houses which they occupy and the restrictions regarding this right in certain circumstances where the house has been designed or adapted for occupation by the elderly. This Act also makes provision for secure tenancies for public sector tenants.

(5) The Housing (Scotland) Act 1988 creates, with certain exceptions, two new forms of tenancy for tenancies created after 2 January 1989: assured tenancies, and short assured tenancies. The assured tenancy significantly reduces the concept of security of tenure and abolishes any method of regulating rent other than market forces. The short assured tenancy lasts for at least six months and if properly constituted will allow the landlord to recover possession on its expiry. Provision is made for a tenant to apply to the Rent Assessment Committee to fix a rent based on the rent a landlord might reasonably expect for a short assured tenancy of the property.

(6) For most tenancies created before 2 January 1989, the Rent (Scotland) Act 1984 will continue to apply. It defines regulated tenancies, which may be either furnished or unfurnished, and lays down the system by which a landlord or tenant may obtain from the Rent Office registration of a fair rent. The Act gives to tenants of either furnished or unfurnished lets a substantial degree of security of tenure. There are, however, certain exceptions; they do not apply to tenancies where the interest belongs to the Crown or to a government department or to a local authority, a development corporation of a new town or a housing corporation. There must be a true tenancy for the Act to apply. It does not apply to licencees such as lodgers or persons allowed to occupy houses on a grace and favour basis or to services occupiers.

The Act regulates the short tenancy, a category of let under which, on compliance with certain conditions, the landlord can be assured of recovering possession on the expiry of the stipulated period of let. The Act defines the circumstances in which generally a landlord may apply for increased rent as a consequence of having carried out improvements to the property, and also lays down the system of phasing such rent increases. On the death of a statutory successor to a tenancy, the tenancy may pass for a second time to a member of the family or a relative who has been in residence in the house for a period of at least six months. The Act further lays down the duties and functions of rent officers and rent assessment committees with regard to unfurnished accommodation and of rent tribunals for furnished accommodation.

The Secretary of State for Scotland is given power in the 1988 Act to repeal or amend those sections of the 1984 Act relating to the phasing of rent increases. The other major features of the 1988 Act are to establish Scottish Homes, and to permit public sector properties to be transferred to Scottish Homes or a landlord approved by Scottish Homes.

LEGAL AID

The Legal Aid Act 1988 (as amended) is designed to make legal aid and advice more readily available for persons of small and moderate means. The main structure of the service is contained in the Act itself and the Regulations made thereunder, administered by the Legal Aid Board.

Civil Proceedings

Legal aid is available for proceedings (including matrimonial causes) in the House of Lords, Court of Appeal, High Court, County Courts, Lands Tribunal, Employment Appeal Tribunal, Restrictive Practices Court, before the Commons Commissioners, and civil proceedings in magistrates' courts. In any event, an application for legal aid will not be approved if it appears that the applicant would gain only a trivial advantage from the proceedings. Further, proceedings wholly or partly in respect of defamation are excepted from the scheme, as are also relator actions and election petitions. Legal aid is not available for proceedings before tribunals, other than those mentioned above. It is generally not available for obtaining the decree in undefended divorce and judicial separation, although the legal advice and assistance scheme (*see* below) is, and legal aid is still available to deal with property, disputes over children, etc., arising in the suit.

Where a person is concerned in proceedings only in a representative, fiduciary or official capacity, his/her personal resources are not to be taken into account in considering eligibility for legal aid. In certain public law proceedings under the Children Act 1989, non-means tested legal aid is available. Apart from this, eligibility in civil proceedings depends upon an applicant's disposable income and disposable capital. The figures change frequently; particulars can be obtained from a solicitor, the Law Society or a Citizens' Advice Bureau. Disposable income is calculated by making deductions from gross income in respect of certain matters such as dependants, interest on loans, income tax, rent and other matters for which the applicant must or reasonably may provide. Disposable capital is calculated by excluding from gross capital part of the value of the house in which the applicant resides, furniture and household possessions; allowances are made in respect of dependants. Except in cases where they are living apart or have a contrary interest, any resources of a person's wife or husband or cohabitee are to be treated as that person's resources. These figures will be assessed by the Department of Social Security and will be referred to the Legal Aid Board, who will determine whether reasonable grounds exist for the grant of a civil aid certificate. Appeal from refusal of a certificate lies to an area committee. A person resident in England or Wales desiring legal aid should apply for a certificate to the appropriate area director for the area in which he or she resides; if resident elsewhere, application should be made to an area director in London. If a certificate is granted, the applicant may select his/her solicitor, and, if necessary, counsel from a panel. The costs of the assisted person's solicitor and counsel will be paid out of the legal aid fund. When, however, damages or property are recovered or preserved by the assisted person, the legal aid fund has a charge over them in respect of these costs less any contribution towards costs recovered from the unsuccessful party. In matrimonial cases, maintenance is exempt, as is the first £2,500 of any property settlement. The court may order that the costs of a successful unassisted party shall be paid out of the legal aid fund.

In an urgent case, e.g. domestic violence or to restrain the kidnapping abroad of a child, legal aid may be granted without the applicant's means being fully investigated beforehand. If on a full examination later he/she is found financially ineligible, he/she is liable to pay all the costs incurred on his/her behalf.

Legal Advice and Assistance

The scheme is governed by the Legal Aid Act 1988.

Under the legal advice and assistance scheme a client may obtain such advice or assistance as is normally provided by a solicitor. If necessary, the advice of a barrister may be obtained but, with the exception of domestic proceedings in a magistrates' court and certain other proceedings (*see* below), the scheme does not extend to taking any step in any proceedings before any court or tribunal. Where legal aid is available for civil proceedings (*see* above) or in criminal cases (*see* below), the scheme covers work done in making application for such legal aid.

A person (other than one receiving advice and assistance at a police station or from a duty solicitor) is eligible for advice or assistance under the scheme provided his/her disposable capital and his/her disposable income do not exceed limits in force from time to time or if he/she is eligible for Income Support or Family Credit. In calculating disposable income, income tax and National Insurance contributions are deducted. For a married man or person with children or other dependants, further deductions will be made from both income and capital. It is intended that the financial limits shall approximate to those applying for legal aid in civil proceedings (*see* above). Except when they are separated or have conflicting interests, the means of husband and wife or cohabiting couple will be aggregated for the purpose of determining financial eligibility. As in the case of legal aid, depending on his/her means, a person may be called upon to pay a contribution towards the costs of work done for him/her. Particulars may be obtained from a solicitor, the Law Society or a Citizens' Advice Bureau.

A solicitor cannot do more than two hours' work, or three hours' in the case of divorce, etc., without leave of the area legal aid committee. The solicitor's costs are paid out of the client's contribution and any monies recovered in respect of costs or damages from another party (although this may be waived by leave of the area committee in cases of hardship) and the balance will be paid by the legal aid fund.

The Act also extends the scheme to cover the costs of a solicitor who is present within the precincts of a magistrates' court or county court and is requested by the court to advise or represent a person who is in need of help.

In April 1980 the scheme was enlarged to cover the cost of representation in domestic proceedings in a magistrates' court. It has since been extended to cover the representation of patients before Mental Health Review Tribunals. Subject to financial eligibility limits, application is made to the area or local committee for 'approval of assistance by way of representation' which will replace legal aid for such proceedings. However, the two-hour limit referred to above will not apply. An applicant who is outside the financial limits but eligible for legal aid will still have to apply for a legal aid certificate as before. Free advice and assistance, and assistance by way of representation from a duty solicitor, is also available in limited circumstances to persons appearing before a magistrates' court charged with a criminal offence.

In January 1986 the scheme was further extended to provide free advice and assistance to all suspects detained at a police station, whether arrested or merely helping police with their enquiries, and free representation for all arrested persons who are the subject of an application for a warrant of further detention under the Police and Criminal Evidence Act 1984. Such persons may instruct a solicitor of their choice or take advantage of the duty solicitor scheme which has now been extended to cover police stations.

Criminal Proceedings

The Legal Aid Act 1988 provides for legal aid in criminal proceedings. A criminal court (e.g. magistrates' court, Crown Court) has power to order legal aid to be granted where it appears desirable to do so in the interests of justice. The court shall make an order in certain cases, e.g. where a person is committed for trial on a charge of murder. However, the court may not make an order unless it appears to the court that the person's disposable income and capital are such that he/she requires assistance in meeting the costs of the particular proceedings in question. Application should be made to the appropriate court where proceedings are to take place.

An applicant shall be required to make a contribution towards the costs of his/her case if his/her disposable income and capital exceed certain prescribed limits. Persons in receipt of Income Support are automatically exempt. In order to ascertain the amount of this contribution an applicant will have to produce written evidence of his/her means. Investigation of means will be carried out by the court. Any person who falls into arrears with the payment of contribution is liable to have the order revoked.

Any practising barrister or solicitor may act for a legally aided person in criminal proceedings unless excluded by reason of misconduct. In general, where legal aid is given it will normally include representation by both counsel and solicitor. However, in connection with magistrates' courts, representation will be by solicitor alone unless the offence is a serious one.

Where any doubt arises about the grant of a legal aid order, that doubt is to be resolved in favour of the applicant. The court also has power to amend or revoke a legal aid order. Legal aid may also be granted in connection with appellate proceedings, e.g. on appeal to the Criminal Division of the Court of Appeal under the Criminal Appeal Act 1968.

SCOTLAND

Legal aid in Scotland is now governed by the Legal Aid (Scotland) Act 1986 and the Regulations made thereunder. This Act established the Scottish Legal Aid Board which has the general function of securing that legal aid and legal advice and assistance are available in accordance with the Act, and of administering the Scottish Legal Aid Fund.

Civil Proceedings

Civil legal aid is available in relation to civil proceedings in the House of Lords in appeals from the Court of Session, in the Court of Session, the Lands Valuation Appeal Court, the Scottish Land Court, the Sheriff Court, the Lands Tribunal for Scotland, the Employment Appeals Tribunal and to the European Court of Human Rights. Civil legal aid is granted if, on application to the Board, the Board is satisfied that there is *probabilis causa litigandi* and that it is reasonable in the particular circumstances of the case that legal aid should be awarded. As in England, eligibility and any contribution required from an applicant is dependent on their disposable income and disposable capital. Information on current financial limits can be obtained from the Scottish Legal Aid Board, a solicitor, or a Citizens' Advice Bureau.

A person believing himself/herself to be eligible may instruct any solicitor of his/her own choice. If a court action is not immediately contemplated, application will be made for legal advice and assistance which operates in a similar manner to the legal advice and assistance scheme in England. If proceedings are contemplated then a formal application for civil legal aid will be made and there are special provisions for emergency applications in appropriate circumstances.

If proceedings are decided against a person in receipt of legal aid the court shall determine a reasonable sum in the circumstances as an appropriate award of expenses to be made against the applicant. The court may make an award out of the fund only if proceedings were instituted by the legally assisted person and the court is satisfied that the resisting party would suffer severe financial hardship unless the order is made, and if the court is satisfied that in all the circumstances it is just and equitable that an award be made. If monies are recovered by a legally assisted person these fall to be paid to the Scottish Legal Aid Board who will then determine the appropriate level of contribution from the sums received which should be made to the expenses of their litigation.

Criminal Proceedings

Legal aid in criminal causes is also administered under the Legal Aid (Scotland) Act 1986. The procedure for application for criminal legal aid is dependent on the circumstances of each case. In serious cases heard before a jury under solemn procedure it is for the court to decide whether to grant legal aid. Applications for legal aid must normally be made on the prescribed forms to the clerk of the court in question and an applicant is required to provide therein particulars of the merits of his/her case and his/her financial circumstances. In summary criminal causes, however, the procedure is dependent on whether the applicant is in custody; if so he/she is entitled to automatic free legal aid from the duty solicitor. If the applicant is not in custody and wishes to plead guilty, he/she is ineligible for full legal aid but may be entitled to criminal legal advice and assistance, and in some circumstances may qualify for assistance by way of representation which will enable his/her solicitor to appear and make a plea in mitigation on his/her behalf. If he/she is not in custody and wishes to plead not guilty, he/she can apply to the Scottish Legal Aid Board for criminal legal aid on the prescribed form not later than fourteen days after the first court appearance at which he/she made the plea, and legal aid shall be granted only if the Board is satisfied that the accused cannot meet the expenses of the case without undue hardship and that it is in the interest of justice as defined by the 1986 Act.

TOWN AND COUNTRY PLANNING

The Town and Country Planning Act 1990 (consolidating earlier Acts) as amended by the Planning and Compensation Act 1991, contains far-reaching provisions affecting the liberty of an owner of land to develop and use it at will. A person has generally to get planning permission from the local planning authority before carrying out any development on the land.

Development includes:

(a) carrying out of building, engineering, mining or other operations
(b) making a material change in use

It is expressly provided that if one dwelling-house is converted into two or more dwelling-houses, this involves a material change in use.

The following do not constitute 'development':

(a) maintaining, improving or altering the interior of a building, provided there is no material change to the exterior, with the exception that any expansion, or works begun for the expansion, of a building below ground level constitutes development
(b) changing the use of property within the curtilage of a dwelling-house for a purpose incidental to the use of the dwelling-house as such. (It will, however, be development if building operations are carried out)

Application can be made to the local planning authority to determine whether or not an operation or change of use constitutes development.

Planning Permission

Application for planning permission is not always necessary, as the Secretary of State may make development orders giving general permission for a specified type of development, e.g. enlargement of a dwelling-house (including erection of a garage), so long as the cubic content of the original dwelling (external measurement) is not exceeded by more than 70 cubic metres or 15 per cent, whichever is greater, subject to a maximum of 115 cubic metres. However, in the case of a terraced house, the limitation is 50 cubic metres or 10 per cent, whichever is the greater, subject to the maximum of 115 cubic metres.

Appeal against refusal of permission lies to the Secretary of State and from his decision, in limited circumstances, to the High Court. If the result of the appeal is unsatisfactory, an applicant may in certain circumstances require the local authority to purchase the land.

SCOTLAND

The Town and Country Planning (Scotland) Act 1972 consolidates the statute law relating to town and country planning in Scotland.

The uses of buildings are classified by the Town and Country Planning (Use Classes) (Scotland) Order 1988. Changes in use prior to 31 December 1984 are immune from enforcement proceedings.

Development normally requires to be commenced within five years from the date of granting permission.

The 1972 Act contains provisions for an appeal to the Secretary of State against the refusal of planning permission. The decision of the Secretary of State is final.

Sections 87 and 92 of the Local Government, Planning and Land Act 1980 contain important provisions on planning applications and, unlike certain parts of this Act, extend to Scotland.

VOTERS' QUALIFICATIONS

The franchise is governed by the Representation of the People Acts 1983 and 1985. Those entitled to vote as electors at a parliamentary election in any constituency are all persons resident there on the qualifying date who, at that date and on the date of the poll, are Commonwealth citizens or citizens of the Republic of Ireland and who are not subject to any legal incapacity to vote and who on the date of the poll are at least 18 years of age. However, a person is not entitled to vote at a parliamentary election in any constituency in Northern Ireland unless he/she was resident in Northern Ireland during the whole of the period of three months ending on the qualifying date for that election. Also, no person can use his/her vote unless he/she is on the register of electors kept for the constituency. A person who is of voting age on the date of the poll at a parliamentary or local government election is entitled to vote, whether or not he/she was of voting age on the qualifying date. Accordingly, a qualified person will be entitled to be registered in a register of parliamentary electors or a register of local government electors if he/she will attain voting age within twelve months from the date on which the register is required to be published. Subject to certain conditions, the 1985 Act extends the franchise to British citizens overseas.

The register is prepared by the registration officer in each constituency in Great Britain. It is the registration officer's duty to have a house-to-house or other official inquiry made as to the persons entitled to be registered and to publish preliminary electors' lists showing the persons appearing to him/her to be entitled to be registered. Any person whose name is omitted may claim registration, and any person on the list may object to the inclusion therein of other persons' names; the registration officer determines the claims and objections.

Voters at a parliamentary or local government election must generally vote in person at the allotted polling station, except for those entitled to vote by post or at any polling station, and those for whom proxies have been appointed.

Certain people can apply to be treated as absent voters at a parliamentary election and thus able to vote by post; among these are registered service voters, those unable by reason of blindness or other physical incapacity to go in person to the polling station, and those unable to go in person from their qualifying address to the polling station without making a journey by air or sea.

Unless entitled to vote by post, a person registered as a service voter may vote by proxy at a parliamentary or local government election. A proxy may also be appointed by a registered elector, where the registration officer is satisfied that the applicant's circumstances on the date of the poll are likely to be such that he/she cannot reasonably be expected to vote in person at the allotted polling station. The appointment of a person to vote as proxy at parliamentary elections has effect also for the purposes of local government elections.

The Probation Service

ENGLAND AND WALES

The Probation Service is employed in each area (55 in total) by an independent committee of justices and it provides a professional social work agency in the courts, with responsibility for a wide range of duties which include:

(a) a social enquiry service for the criminal courts
(b) provision of a range of non-custodial measures involving the supervision of offenders in the community
(c) supervisory aftercare for offenders released from custody, together with social work in penal establishments and help for the families of those serving sentences
(d) an enquiry, conciliation and supervision service in the divorce and domestic courts
(e) support for and promotion of preventive and containment measures in the community designed to reduce the level of crime and domestic breakdown

It is a direct grant service funded 80 per cent from the Home Office and 20 per cent from the relevant local authority.

Its national representative bodies are:

THE CENTRAL COUNCIL OF PROBATION COMMITTEES, 38 Belgrave Square, London SWIX 8NT. Tel: 071–245 9364. *Secretary*, I. Miles.

THE ASSOCIATION OF CHIEF OFFICERS OF PROBATION, 20–30 Lawefield Lane, Wakefield WF2 8SP. Tel: 0924–361156. *General Secretary*, W. R. Weston.

THE NATIONAL ASSOCIATION OF PROBATION OFFICERS, 3 Chivalry Road, London SW11 1HT. Tel: 071–223 4887. *General Secretary*, W. Beaumont.

SCOTLAND

The probation service in Scotland is a statutory duty of local authorities under s. 27 of the Social Work (Scotland) Act 1968. Social workers have to supervise and provide advice, guidance and assistance to those persons living in their area who are subject to a court's supervision order. This is done by social workers as part of their normal duties and not by a separate probation staff.

The Media

Broadcasting

TELEVISION

The British Broadcasting Corporation (*see* page 293) is responsible for public service broadcasting in the United Kingdom. Its constitution and finances are governed by Royal Charter and by a Licence and Agreement. Its role is to provide high-quality programmes with wide-ranging appeal that educate, inform and entertain.

The Independent Television Commission (*see* page 325) is the regulator and licenser for independent television companies. The ITV franchises for the 15 regional companies and for breakfast television came up for renewal at the end of 1992; applications for new ten-year licences from January 1993 were received by the ITC in May 1991 and allocated in October 1991. The following regional companies had their licences renewed: Anglia TV, Border TV, Central TV, Channel TV, Grampian, Granada TV, HTV, LWT, Scottish TV, Tyne Tees, Ulster TV and Yorkshire. The new franchise-holders are: Carlton TV (won the London weekday licence from Thames TV); Meridian (won the south and south-east England licence from TVS); GMTV (formerly Sunrise TV) (won the breakfast television licence from TV-am); and Westcountry TV (won the south-west England licence from TSW).

A new independent national television channel is due to be established by the autumn of 1993.

All channels are broadcast in colour on 625 lines UHF from a network of transmitting stations which are owned and operated by National Transcommunications Ltd. Transmissions are available to more than 99 per cent of the population.

BBC TELEVISION

Television Centre, Wood Lane, London W12 7RJ
Tel 081-743 8000

The BBC's experiments in television broadcasting started in 1929 and in 1936 the BBC began the world's first public service of high-definition television from Alexandra Palace.

The BBC broadcasts two national television services, BBC 1 and BBC 2 (outside England these services are designated BBC Scotland on 1, BBC Scotland on 2, BBC 1 Northern Ireland, BBC 2 Northern Ireland, BBC Wales on 1 and BBC Wales on 2).

INDEPENDENT TELEVISION COMPANIES

ITV Network Chief Executive, A. Quinn

ANGLIA TELEVISION (*eastern England*), Anglia House, Norwich. Tel: 0603-615151

BORDER TELEVISION (*the Borders*), Television Centre, Carlisle. Tel: 0228-25101

CARLTON TELEVISION LTD (*London* (*weekdays*)), 101 St Martin's Lane, London WC2N 4AZ. Tel: 071-240 4000

CENTRAL INDEPENDENT TELEVISION (*the Midlands*), Central House, Broad Street, Birmingham. Tel: 021-643 9898

CHANNEL FOUR TELEVISION COMPANY LTD, 60 Charlotte Street, London W1. Tel: 071-631 4444. Provides a service to the UK except Wales, and is charged to cater for interests under-represented by the ITV companies

CHANNEL TELEVISION (*Channel Islands*), The Television Centre, St Helier, Jersey. Tel: 0534-73999

GMTV LTD (*breakfast television*), The London Television Centre, Upper Ground, London SE1 9LT. Tel: 071-827 7000

GRAMPIAN TELEVISION (*northern Scotland*), Queen's Cross, Aberdeen. Tel: 0224-646464

GRANADA TELEVISION (*north-west England*), Granada TV Centre, Manchester. Tel: 061-832 7211

HTV (*Wales and western England*), HTV Wales, Television Centre, Cardiff CF5 6XJ. Tel: 0222-590590

INDEPENDENT TELEVISION NEWS LTD, ITN House, 200 Gray's Inn Road, London WC1. Tel: 071-833 3000

LONDON WEEKEND TELEVISION (*London* (*weekends*)), London Television Centre, Upper Ground, London SE1 9LT. Tel: 071-620 1620

MERIDIAN BROADCASTING LTD (*south and south-east England*), 8 Montague Close, London SE1 9RD. Tel: 071-378 7898

SCOTTISH TELEVISION (*central Scotland*), Cowcaddens, Glasgow. Tel: 041-332 9999

TELETEXT UK LTD, 101 Farm Lane, London SW6 1QJ. Tel: 071-386 5000. Provides teletext services for the ITV companies and Channel 4 (from Jan. 1993)

TYNE TEES TELEVISION (*north-east England*), The Television Centre, City Road, Newcastle upon Tyne. Tel: 091-261 0181

ULSTER TELEVISION (*Northern Ireland*), Havelock House, Ormeau Road, Belfast. Tel: 0232-228122

WELSH FOURTH CHANNEL AUTHORITY (Sianel Pedwar Cymru), Parc Ty Glas, Llanishen, Cardiff. Tel: 0222-747444. S4C schedules Welsh language programmes and also relays most Channel 4 programmes

WESTCOUNTRY TELEVISION LTD (*south-west England*), c/o Brittany Ferries, Millbay Docks, Plymouth PL1 3EW. Tel: 0752-253322

YORKSHIRE TELEVISION (*Yorkshire*), The Television Centre, Leeds. Tel: 0532-438283

INDEPENDENT TELEVISION ASSOCIATION, Knighton House, 56 Mortimer Street, London W1N 8AN. Tel: 071-612 8000. *Director*, D. Shaw

BBC WORLD SERVICE TELEVISION

80 Wood Lane, London W12 0TT
Tel 081-576 2000

BBC World Service Television Ltd is a wholly-owned subsidiary of the BBC incorporated in March 1991 and initially financed by BBC Enterprises. The company took over responsibility for all the BBC's satellite television broadcasting services and brought together the BBC's European subscription channel, formerly known as BBC TV EUROPE, and the BBC World Service's plans for a global television news service. The new channel was launched in April 1991 and offers a range of programmes from BBC 1 and BBC 2, the global television news service and English language teaching programmes. The World Service Television News is also sold in English and other languages to television channels and networks throughout the world.

BBC World Service Television is entirely self-funding; it receives no revenue from the British licence fee or the World Service parliamentary grant-in-aid.

DIRECT BROADCASTING BY SATELLITE TELEVISION

British Sky Broadcasting, 6 Centaurs Business Park, Grant Way, Isleworth, Middx. TW7 5QD. Tel: 071-782 3000. Broadcasts six channels (*Sky 1, Sky News, Sky Sports, The Movie Channel, Sky Movies Plus* and *Sky Movies Gold*)

RADIO

The BBC provides both national and local radio services. The Radio Authority (*see* page 350) is the regulator and licenser for independent radio companies.

Under the Broadcasting Act 1990, the Radio Authority was empowered to allocate licences for three national radio stations. The first national licence was awarded to Classic FM in September 1991 and the second was awarded to Independent Music Radio in April 1992. Twenty-five new independent local radio licences were also offered by the Radio Authority in 1991–2, of which 18 have so far been awarded.

BBC RADIO

Broadcasting House, Portland Place, London W1A 1AA
Tel 071-580 4468

BBC Radio broadcasts five national services to the United Kingdom, Isle of Man and the Channel Islands; a 24-hour radio news network will be broadcast on Radio 4's long-wave frequency from 1994. There is also a tier of national regional services in Wales, Scotland and Northern Ireland and 39 local radio stations in England and the Channel Islands. In Wales there are two regional services based on the Welsh and English languages respectively.
The national services are:

Radio 1 (Pop and rock music) – 24 hours a day. *Frequencies:* FM 97.6–99.8 MHz, coverage 96%; MW 1053 kHz/285m and 1089 kHz/275m, plus two local fillers, 6 a.m. to 12 midnight only

Radio 2 (Popular music, entertainment, comedy and the arts) – 24 hours a day. *Frequency:* FM 88–90.2 MHz, coverage 98%

Radio 3 (Classical music, drama, documentaries, poetry, and cricket in season) – 6.55 a.m.–12.35 a.m. daily. *Frequencies:* FM 90.2–92.4 MHz, coverage 98%

Radio 4 (News, documentaries, drama and entertainment) – 5.55 a.m. to 12.40 a.m. daily. *Frequencies:* FM in England 92.4–94.6 MHz, elsewhere 92.4–96.1 and 103.5–105 MHz, coverage 97%; LW 198kHz/1515m, plus eight local fillers on MW

Radio 5 (Speech radio for the family, with sport, education, children and youth programmes and elements of World Service) – 6 a.m.–12.05 a.m. daily. *Frequencies:* MW 693 kHz/433m and 909 kHz/330m, plus one local filler

The national regional services are:

Radio Scotland *Frequencies:* MW 810 kHz/370m plus two local fillers; FM 92.4–96.1 and 103.5–105 MHz, coverage 94%. Local programmes on FM as above: Radio Aberdeen (also MW 990 kHz/303m); Radio Highland; Radio nan Gaidheal; Radio Orkney; Radio Shetland; Radio Solway (also MW 585 kHz/513m); Radio Tweed

Radio Ulster *Frequencies:* MW 1341 kHz/224m, plus two local fillers; FM 92.4–96.1 MHz, coverage 96%. Local programmes on Radio Foyle *Frequencies:* MW 792 kHz/379m; FM 93.1 MHz

Radio Wales *Frequency:* MW 882 kHz/340m plus two local fillers, coverage 96% (day) and 63% (night). Local programmes on Radio Clwyd *Frequency:* MW 657 kHz/457m

Radio Cymru (Welsh-language) *Frequencies:* FM 92.4–96.1 and 103.5–105 MHz, coverage 96%

BBC LOCAL RADIO STATIONS

There are 39 local stations serving England and the Channel Islands:

Bedfordshire, PO Box 476, Hastings Street, Luton LU1 5BA. Tel: 0582-459111. *Frequencies:* 258/476m, 1161/630 kHz, 95.5/103.8 FM

Berkshire, Broadcasting House, 42A Portman Road, Reading, Berks. RG3 1NB. Tel: 0734-567056. *Frequencies:* 94.6/95.4/104.1/104.4 FM

Bristol, 3 Tyndalls Park Road, Bristol BS8 1PP. Tel: 0272-741111. *Frequencies:* 194m, 1548 kHz, 94.9/95.5/104.6 FM

Cambridgeshire, Broadcasting House, 104 Hills Road, Cambridge CB2 1LD. Tel: 0223-315970. *Frequencies:* 207/292m, 1449/1026 kHz, 96.0/95.7 FM

Cleveland, PO Box 1548, Broadcasting House, Newport Road, Middlesbrough, Cleveland TS1 5DG. Tel: 0642-225211. *Frequencies:* 95.0/95.8 FM

Cornwall, Phoenix Wharf, Truro, Cornwall TR1 1UA. Tel: 0872-75421. *Frequencies:* 476/457m, 630/657 kHz, 95.2/96.0/103.9 FM

Cumbria, Hilltop Heights, London Road, Carlisle CA1 2NA. Tel: 0228-31661. *Frequencies:* 397/206/358m, 756/1458/837 kHz, 95.2/95.6/96.1/104.2 FM

CWR (Coventry and Warwickshire Radio), 25 Warwick Road, Coventry CV1 2WR. Tel: 0203-559911. *Frequencies:* 94.8/103.7 FM; 104 FM (Nuneaton area)

Derby, 56 St Helen's Street, Derby DE1 3HY. Tel: 0332-361111. *Frequencies:* 269m, 1116 kHz, 94.2/95.3/104.5 FM

Devon, PO Box 100, Walnut Gardens, St David's, Exeter EX4 4DB. Tel: 0392-215651. *Frequencies:* 351/303/206/375m, 855/990/1458/801 kHz, 103.4/96.0/95.8/94.8 FM

Essex, 198 New London Road, Chelmsford CM2 9AB. Tel: 0245-262393. *Frequencies:* 392/196/412m, 765/729/1530 kHz, 103.5/95.3 FM

Gloucestershire, London Road, Gloucester GL1 1SW. Tel: 0452-308585. *Frequencies:* 95.0/95.8/104.7 FM

GLR (Greater London Radio), 35C Marylebone High Street, London W1A 4LG. Tel: 071-224 2424. *Frequencies:* 206m, 1458 kHz, 94.9 FM

GMR (Greater Manchester Radio), New Broadcasting House, Oxford Road, Manchester M60 1SJ. Tel: 061-200 2000. *Frequencies:* 206m, 1458 kHz, 95.1 FM

Guernsey, Commerce House, Les Banques, St Peter Port, Guernsey. Tel: 0481-728977. *Frequencies:* 269m, 1116 kHz, 93.2 FM

Hereford and Worcester, 43 Broad Street, Hereford HR4 9HH; and Hylton Road, Worcester WR2 5WW. Tel: 0905-748485. *Frequencies:* 738 kHz, 104.0/94.7 FM

Humberside, 9 Chapel Street, Hull HU1 3NU. Tel: 0482-23232. *Frequencies:* 202m, 1485 kHz, 95.9 FM

Jersey, Broadcasting House, Rouge Bouillon, St Helier, Jersey. Tel: 0534-70000. *Frequencies:* 292m, 1026 kHz, 88.8 FM

Kent, Sun Pier, Chatham, Kent ME4 4EZ. Tel: 0634-830505. *Frequencies:* 290/388/187m, 1035/774/1602 kHz, 96.7/104.2 FM

LANCASHIRE, 20–26 Darwen Street, Blackburn BB2 2EA. Tel: 0254-62411. *Frequencies:* 351/193m, 855/1557 kHz, 95.5/104.5/103.9 FM

LEEDS, Broadcasting House, Woodhouse Lane, Leeds LS2 9PN. Tel: 0532-442131. *Frequencies:* 388m, 774 kHz, 92.4/95.3 FM

LEICESTER, Epic House, Charles Street, Leicester LE1 3SH. Tel: 0533-516688. *Frequencies:* 358m, 837 kHz, 104.9 FM

LINCOLNSHIRE, Radion Buildings, Newport, Lincoln LN1 3BU. Tel: 0522-511411. *Frequencies:* 218m, 1368 kHz, 94.9 FM

MERSEYSIDE, 55 Paradise Street, Liverpool L1 3BP. Tel: 051-708 5500. *Frequencies:* 202m, 1485 kHz, 95.8 FM

NEWCASTLE, Broadcasting Centre, Barrack Road, Fenham, Newcastle upon Tyne NE99 1RN. Tel: 091-232 4141. *Frequencies:* 206m, 1458 kHz, 95.4/104.4/96.0 FM

NORFOLK, Norfolk Tower, Surrey Street, Norwich NR1 3PA. Tel: 0603-617411. *Frequencies:* 95.1/104.4 FM

NORTHAMPTON, Broadcasting House, Abington Street, Northampton NN1 2BH. Tel: 0604-239100. *Frequencies:* 104.2/106.3 FM

NOTTINGHAM, York House, Mansfield Road, Nottingham NG1 3JB. Tel: 0602-415161. *Frequencies:* 189m, 1584 kHz, 103.8/95.5 FM

OXFORD, 269 Banbury Road, Oxford OX2 7DW. Tel: 0865-311444. *Frequency:* 95.2 FM

SHEFFIELD, Ashdell Grove, 60 Westbourne Road, Sheffield S10 2QU. Tel: 0742-686185. *Frequencies:* 290m, 1035 kHz, 104.1/88.6 FM

SHROPSHIRE, 2–4 Boscobel Drive, Shrewsbury SY1 3TT. Tel: 0743-248484. *Frequencies:* 189m, 1584 kHz, 95.0/96.0 FM

SOLENT, Broadcasting House, Havelock Road, Southampton SO1 0XR. Tel: 0703-631311. *Frequencies:* 300m, 999 kHz, 221m, 999 kHz, 1359 kHz, 96.1 FM

STOKE-ON-TRENT, Conway House, Cheapside, Hanley, Stoke-on-Trent ST1 1JJ. Tel: 0782-208080. *Frequencies:* 200m, 1503 kHz, 94.6 FM

SUFFOLK, Broadcasting House, St Matthew's Street, Ipswich IP1 3EP. Tel: 0473-250000. *Frequencies:* 95.5/103.9/104.6 FM

SURREY, Broadcasting House, Guildford, Surrey GU2 5AP. Tel: 0483-306306. *Frequency:* 104.6 FM

SUSSEX, Marlborough Place, Brighton BN1 1TU. Tel: 0273-680231. *Frequencies:* 202/258/219m, 1485/1161/1368 kHz, 95.1/95.3/104.5/104.0 FM

WILTSHIRE SOUND, Broadcasting House, 56–58 Prospect Place, Swindon SN1 3RW. Tel: 0793-513626. *Frequencies:* 225/219m, 1332/1368 kHz, 103.6/104.3/103.5 FM

WM (WEST MIDLANDS), Pebble Mill Road, Birmingham B5 7SD. Tel: 021-414 8484. *Frequencies:* 1458 kHz, 95.6 FM

YORK, 20 Bootham Row, York YO3 7BR. Tel: 0904-641351. *Frequencies:* 450/238m, 666/1260 kHz, 103.7/104.3/95.5 FM

BBC WORLD SERVICE

Bush House, Strand, London WC2B 4PH
Tel 071-240 3456

The BBC World Service broadcasts 820 hours of programmes a week in 38 languages including the English Service. Ninety-one transmitters are used, 37 of them in the UK and 54 at relay stations overseas. In addition the World Service supplies many recorded programmes to other radio stations.

WORLD SERVICE IN ENGLISH, 24 hours a day, directed to all parts of the world, and with additional streams of programmes specially designated for audiences in Africa, south-east Asia, Europe, the Caribbean and the Falklands at appropriate peak listening times

AFRICAN SERVICE, which broadcasts in Swahili, Somali and Hausa

ARABIC SERVICE, on the air for ten and a half hours a day to the Middle East and North Africa

CENTRAL EUROPEAN SERVICE, in Czech, Slovak, Hungarian, Polish and Finnish

EASTERN SERVICE, which broadcasts in Bengali, Burmese, Hindi, Nepali, Pashto, Persian, Sinhalese, Tamil and Urdu

FAR EASTERN SERVICE, in Chinese (Cantonese and Mandarin), Indonesian, Thai and Vietnamese

FRENCH AND PORTUGUESE SERVICE, directed to Europe and Africa

GERMAN SERVICE, directed to Germany, Austria, and German-speaking Switzerland

LATIN AMERICAN SERVICE, in Spanish and Portuguese

RUSSIAN AND UKRAINIAN SERVICE, on the air for eight and a quarter hours a day in Russian to the CIS, and one hour a day in Ukrainian

SOUTH-EAST EUROPEAN SERVICE, in Bulgarian, Romanian, Serbian, Croatian, Slovene, Greek and Turkish

BBC ENGLISH teaches English to learners outside Britain through radio, television and a wide range of published courses

BBC MONITORING provides regional summaries and a teleprinted news service from the output of overseas radio and television stations

TOPICAL TAPES provides a variety of programmes on tape for overseas radio stations and produces the twice-weekly 'Calling the Falklands' programme

BBC TRANSCRIPTION produces and sells to overseas radio stations recorded programmes drawn from the whole range of BBC Radio

INDEPENDENT NATIONAL RADIO STATIONS

CLASSIC FM (from autumn 1992), Academic House, 24–28 Oval Road, London NW1 7DQ. Tel: 071-284 3000. *Frequencies:* 99.9–101.9 FM

INDEPENDENT MUSIC RADIO (from spring 1993), c/o TV-am, Hawley Crescent, London NW1 8EF. Tel: 071-288 4347. *Frequencies:* 1215/1197 kHz

INDEPENDENT LOCAL RADIO STATIONS

AIRE FM, PO Box 2000, Leeds LS3 1LR. Tel: 0532-452299. *Frequency:* 96.3 FM

BAY RADIO, Emmanuel House, Haverbreaks, Lancaster LA1 5BN (from early 1993)

BEACON RADIO, 267 Tettenhall Road, Wolverhampton WV6 0DQ. Tel: 0902-757211. *Frequency:* 97.2/103.1 FM

BREEZE AM, PO Box 300, Southend-on-Sea, Essex SS1 1SY. Tel: 0702-430966. *Frequency:* 1359/1431 kHz

BRMB FM, Aston Road North, Birmingham B6 4BX. Tel: 021-359 4481. *Frequency:* 96.4 FM

BRUNEL CLASSIC GOLD, PO Box 2000, Swindon SN4 7EX. Tel: 0793-853222; PO Box 2000, Bristol BS99 7SN. Tel: 0272-279911. *Frequencies:* 1260 kHz (Bristol); 1161 kHz (Swindon); 936 kHz (West Wilts)

BUZZ FM, The Spencers, 20 Augusta Street, Jewellery Quarter, Birmingham B18 6JA. Tel: 021-236 4888. *Frequency:* 102.4 FM

CAPITAL RADIO PLC, Euston Tower, London NW1 3DR. Tel: 071-608 6080. *Frequencies:* 194m, 1548 kHz, 95.8 FM

CD 603, PO Box 2, Cheltenham, Glos. GL53 7YA. Tel: 0242-255023. *Frequency:* 603 kHz

CENTRAL FM, PO Box 96.7, Stirling FK7 7RP. Tel: 0786-51188. *Frequency:* 96.7 FM

CHANNEL RADIO, Windsor House, St Lawrence, Jersey JE3 1FB (from early 1993)

CHILTERN RADIO PLC, Broadcast Centre, Chiltern Road, Dunstable, Bedfordshire LU6 1HQ. Tel: 0582-666001. *Frequencies:* 362m, 828 kHz (Luton), 379m, 792 kHz (Bedford)

CHOICE FM, 16–18 Trinity Gardens, London SW9 8DP. Tel: 071-738 7969. *Frequency:* 96.9 FM

CITY FM, PO Box 967, Liverpool L69 1TQ. Tel: 051-227 5100. *Frequency:* 96.7 FM

CLASSIC TRACKS BCR, Russell Court, Claremont Street, Lisburn Road, Belfast BT9 6JX. Tel: 0232-438500. *Frequency:* 96.7 FM

CLYDE 1 AND 2, Clydebank Business Park, Clydebank, Glasgow G81 2RX. Tel: 041-306 2200. *Frequencies:* 261m, 1152 kHz, 102.5 FM

CN FM (Cambridge and Newmarket), PO Box 1000, The Vision Park, Chivers Way, Histon, Cambridge CB4 4WW. Tel: 0223-235255. *Frequencies:* 103.0/97.4 FM

COLCHESTER FM, East Anglian Radio, Colegate, Norwich NR3 1DB (from early 1993)

COOL FM, Newtownards, Co. Down BT23 4ES. Tel: 0247-815555. *Frequency:* 97.4 FM

COUNTY SOUND RADIO AM, Broadfield House, Brighton Road, Crawley, W. Sussex RH11 9TT. Tel: 0293-519161. *Frequencies:* 1476, 1521 kHz

DEVONAIR RADIO, 35–37 St David's Hill, Exeter EX4 4DA. Tel: 0392-430703. *Frequencies:* 666 kHz, 97.0 FM (Exeter); 954 kHz, 96.4 FM (Torbay); 103 FM (East Devon)

DOWNTOWN RADIO, Kiltonga Industrial Estate, Newtownards, Co. Down BT23 4ES. Tel: 0247-815555. *Frequencies:* 293m, 1026 kHz, 96.6/96.4/102.4 FM

ESSEX RADIO PLC, Radio House, Clifftown Road, Southend-on-Sea, Essex SS1 1SX. Tel: 0702-333711. *Frequencies:* 96.3 FM (Southend), 102.6 FM (Chelmsford)

FOX FM, Brush House, Pony Road, Horspath Estate, Cowley, Oxford OX4 2XR. Tel: 0865-748787. *Frequencies:* 102.6 FM (Oxford); 97.4 FM (Banbury)

GALAXY RADIO, 25 Portland Square, Bristol BS2 8RZ. Tel: 0272-240111. *Frequency:* 97.2 FM

GEM-AM, 29–31 Castle Gate, Nottingham NG1 7AP. Tel: 0602-581731. *Frequencies:* 1260 kHz (Leicester); 999 kHz (Nottingham); 945 kHz (Derby)

GREAT NORTH RADIO, Newcastle upon Tyne NE99 1BB. Tel: 091-496 0377. *Frequencies:* 1152 kHz (Tyne and Wear); 1170 kHz (Teesside)

GREAT YORKSHIRE RADIO, PO Box 777, Sheffield, Hull and Bradford. Tel: 0742-852121. *Frequencies:* 1548/1305/990 kHz (S. Yorks); 1278/1530 kHz (W. Yorks); 1161 kHz (Humberside)

GWR FM (EAST), PO Box 2000, Swindon SN4 7EX. Tel: 0793-853222. *Frequencies:* 96.5 FM (Marlborough); 97.2 FM (Swindon); 102.2 FM (West Wilts)

GWR FM (WEST), PO Box 2000, Bristol BS99 7SN. Tel: 0272-279900. *Frequency:* 96.3/103.0 FM

HALLAM FM, Radio House, 900 Herries Road, Hillsborough, Sheffield S6 1RH. Tel: 0742-853333. *Frequencies:* 97.4 FM (Sheffield); 96.1 FM (Rotherham); 102.9 FM (Barnsley); 103.4 FM (Doncaster)

HEARTLAND FM, Lower Oakfield, Pitlochry, Perthshire PH16 2DS. Tel: 0796-474040. *Frequency:* 97.5 FM

HEREWARD RADIO LTD, PO Box 225, Queensgate Centre, Peterborough PE1 1XJ. Tel: 0733-46225. *Frequency:* 102.7 FM

HORIZON RADIO, Broadcast Centre, Crownhill, Milton Keynes, Bucks. MK8 0AB. Tel: 0908-269111. *Frequency:* 103.3 FM

INVICTA FM, Radio House, John Wilson Business Park, Whitstable, Kent CT5 3QX. Tel: 0227-772004. *Frequencies:* 1242/603 kHz, 102.8/95.9/97.0/96.1/103.1 FM

ISLAND FM, Cedar Hill, Mount Durand, St Peter Port, Guernsey (from early 1993)

ISLE OF WIGHT RADIO, Dodnor Park, Newport, Isle of Wight PO30 5XE. Tel: 0983-822557. *Frequency:* 1242 kHz

JAZZ FM, 26–27 Castlereagh Street, London W1H 5YR. Tel: 071-706 4100. *Frequency:* 102.2 FM

KCBC (Kettering), PO Box 1530, Kettering, Northants. NN16 8PU. Tel: 0536-412413. *Frequency:* 1530 kHz

KISS 100 FM, Kiss House, 80 Holloway Road, London N7 8JG. Tel: 071-700 6100. *Frequency:* 100.0 FM

KL.FM, PO Box 77, 18 Blackfriars Street, King's Lynn, Norfolk PE30 1NN. Tel: 0553-772777. *Frequency:* 96.7 FM

LANTERN RADIO, Light House, 17 Market Place, Bideford, N. Devon EX39 2DR. Tel: 0237-424444. *Frequency:* 96.2 FM

LBC NEWSTALK (London Broadcasting Company Ltd), Crown House, 72 Hammersmith Road, London W14 8YE. Tel: 071-603 2400. *Frequency:* 97.3 FM

LEICESTER SOUND FM, Granville House, Granville Road, Leicester LE1 7RW. Tel: 0533-551616. *Frequency:* 103.2 FM

LINCS FM, Witham Park, Waterside South, Lincoln LN5 7JN. Tel: 0522-549900. *Frequency:* 102.2 FM

LONDON GREEK RADIO, Florentia Village, Vale Road, London N4 1TD. Tel: 081-800 8001. *Frequency:* 103.3 FM

LONDON TALKBACK RADIO, Crown House, 72 Hammersmith Road, London W14 8YE. Tel: 071-333 0003. *Frequency:* 1152 kHz

MAGIC 828, PO Box 2000, Leeds LS3 1LR. Tel: 0532-452299. *Frequency:* 828 kHz

MARCHER GOLD, The Studios, Mold Road, Wrexham, Clwyd LL11 4AF. Tel: 0978-752202. *Frequencies:* 238m, 1260 kHz

MAX AM, Forth House, Forth Street, Edinburgh EH1 3LF. Tel: 031-556 9255. *Frequency:* 1548 kHz

MELLOW 1557, 21–23 Walton Road, Frinton-on-Sea, Essex CO13 0AA. Tel: 0255-675303. *Frequency:* 1557 kHz

MELODY RADIO, 180 Brompton Road, London SW3 1HF. Tel: 071-584 1049. *Frequency:* 104.9 FM

MERCIA FM, Hertford Place, Coventry CV1 3TT. Tel: 0203-633933. *Frequencies:* 97.0/102.9 FM

METRO FM, Long Rigg, Swalwell, Newcastle upon Tyne NE99 1BB. Tel: 091-488 3131. *Frequencies:* 97.1/103.0 FM

MFM, The Studios, Mold Road, Wrexham, Clwyd LL11 4AF. Tel: 0978-752202. *Frequencies:* 103.4/97.1 FM

MINSTER FM, PO Box 123, Dunnington, York YO1 5ZX. Tel: 0904-488888. *Frequency:* 104.7 FM

MORAY FIRTH RADIO, PO Box 271, Inverness IV3 6SF. Tel: 0463-224433. *Frequencies:* 271m, 1107 kHz, 97.4 FM

NORTHANTS RADIO, Broadcast Centre, The Enterprise Park, Boughton Green Road, Northampton NN2 7AH. Tel: 0604-792411. *Frequencies:* 1557 kHz, 96.6 FM

NORTH SOUND RADIO, 45 Kings Gate, Aberdeen AB2 6BL. Tel: 0224-632234. *Frequencies:* 290m, 1035 kHz, 96.9 FM

OCEAN SOUND CLASSIC HITS, Radio House, Whittle Avenue, Segensworth West, Fareham, Hants. PO15 5PA. Tel: 0489-589911. *Frequencies:* 97.5/96.7 FM

ORCHARD FM, Haygrove House, Shoreditch, Taunton TA3 7BT. Tel: 0823-338448. *Frequencies:* 102.6/97.1 FM

PICCADILLY RADIO LTD, 127-131 The Piazza, Piccadilly Plaza, Manchester M1 4AW. Tel: 061-236 9913. *Frequencies:* 261m, 1152 kHz, 103.0 FM

PIRATE FM, Carn Brea Studios, Wilson Way, Redruth, Cornwall TR15 3XX. Tel: 0209-314400. *Frequencies:* 102.2/102.8 FM

PLYMOUTH SOUND LTD, Earl's Acre, Alma Road, Plymouth PL3 4HX. Tel: 0752-27272. *Frequencies:* 261m, 1152 kHz, 97.0 FM

POWERFM, Radio House, Whittle Avenue, Segensworth West, Fareham, Hants. PO15 5PA. Tel: 0489-589911. *Frequency:* 103.2 FM.

THE PULSE, PO Box 3000, Bradford BD1 5NE. Tel: 0274-731521. *Frequencies:* 97.5/102.5 FM

Q96, 26 Lady Lane, Paisley PA1 2LG. Tel: 041-887 9630. *Frequency:* 96.3 FM

RADIO BORDERS, Tweedside Park, Galashiels TD1 3TD. Tel: 0896-59444. *Frequencies:* 96.8/97.5/103.1/103.4 FM

RADIO BROADLAND, St George's Plain, 47–49 Colegate, Norwich NR3 1DB. Tel: 0603-630621. *Frequencies:* 260m, 1152 kHz, 102.4 FM

RADIO CEREDIGION, Unit 6E, Science Park, Cefnllan, Aberystwyth. Tel: 0970-626626. *Frequencies:* 103.3/96.6 FM

RADIO CITY GOLD, PO Box 967, Liverpool L69 1TQ. Tel: 051-227 5100. *Frequency:* 1548 kHz

RADIO FORTH RFM, Forth House, Forth Street, Edinburgh EH1 3LF. Tel: 031-556 9255. *Frequencies:* 97.3/97.6 FM

RADIO HARMONY, Ringway House, Hill Street, Coventry CV1 4AN. Tel: 0203-525656. *Frequency:* 102.6 FM

RADIO IN TAVISTOCK, Earls Acre, Plymouth PL3 4HX. Tel: 0752-227272. *Frequency:* 96.6 FM

RADIO MALDWYN, c/o Davies Memorial Gallery, Newtown, Powys SY16 2NZ. Tel: 0686-626220. *Frequency:* 756 kHz

RADIO MERCURY (EAST), Broadfield House, Brighton Road, Crawley, W. Sussex. Tel: 0293-519161. *Frequency:* 102.7 FM

RADIO MERCURY (WEST), The Friary, Guildford, Surrey GU1 4YX and 11 Lower Street, Haslemere, Surrey GU27 2NJ. Tel: 0428-61019. *Frequencies:* 96.4/97.1 FM

RADIO TAY, PO Box 123, 6 North Islast, Dundee DD1 9UF. Tel: 0382-200800. *Frequencies:* 258m, 1161 kHz, 102.8 FM (Dundee); 189m, 1584 kHz, 96.4 FM (Perth)

RADIO TFM, Yale Crescent, Thornaby, Stockton-on-Tees, Cleveland TS17 6AA. Tel: 0642-615111. *Frequency:* 96.6 FM

RADIOWAVE, 965 Mowbray Drive, Blackpool, Lancs. FY3 7JR. Tel: 0253-304965. *Frequency:* 96.5 FM

RADIO WYVERN, 5–6 Barbourne Terrace, Worcester WR1 3JZ. Tel: 0905-612212. *Frequencies:* 314m, 954 kHz, 97.6 FM (Hereford), 196m, 1530 kHz, 102.8 FM (Worcester)

RED DRAGON FM, Radio House, West Canal Wharf, Cardiff CF1 5XJ. Tel: 0222-384041. *Frequencies:* 97.4/103.2 FM

RED ROSE GOLD, PO Box 999, St Paul's Square, Preston, Lancashire PR1 1XR. Tel: 0772-556301. *Frequencies:* 301m, 999 kHz, 97.4 FM

RTM, 19 Tavy Bridge, Thamesmead, London SE2 9UG. Tel: 081-311 3112. *Frequency:* 103.8 FM

SEVERN SOUND, Old Talbot House, 67 Southgate Street, Gloucester GL1 2DQ. Tel: 0452-423791. *Frequencies:* 774 kHz, 103.0/102.4 FM

SGR-FM (BURY), Long Brackland, Bury St Edmunds, Suffolk IP33 1JY. Tel: 0284-701511. *Frequencies:* 240m, 1251 kHz, 96.4 FM

SGR-FM (IPSWICH), Electric House, Lloyds Avenue, Ipswich IP1 3HZ. Tel: 0473-216971. *Frequencies:* 1170 kHz, 97.1 FM

SIBC, Market Street, Lerwick, Shetland ZE1 0JN. Tel: 0595-5299. *Frequency:* 96.2 FM

SIGNAL CHESHIRE, Regent House, Heaton Lane, Stockport SK4 1BX. Tel: 061-480 5445. *Frequencies:* 104.9/96.4 FM

SIGNAL RADIO, Studio 257, Stoke Road, Stoke-on-Trent ST4 2SR. Tel: 0782-747047. *Frequencies:* 257m, 1170 kHz, 102.6/96.9 FM

SOUTH COAST RADIO, Radio House, Whittle Avenue, Segensworth West, Fareham, Hants. PO15 5PA. Tel: 0489-589911; Radio House, PO Box 2000, Brighton BN41 2SS. Tel: 0273-430111. *Frequencies:* 1170/1557/1323 kHz

SOUTHERN SOUND CLASSIC HITS, Radio House, PO Box 2000, Brighton BN41 2SS. Tel: 0273-430111. *Frequencies:* 103.5 FM (Brighton); 96.9 FM (Newhaven); 102.4 FM (Eastbourne); 102.0 FM (Hastings)

SOUTH WEST SOUND, Campbell House, Bankend Road, Dumfries DG1 4TH. Tel: 0387-50999. *Frequency:* 97.2 FM

SPECTRUM INTERNATIONAL RADIO, Endeavour House, Brent Cross, London NW2 1JT. Tel: 081-905 5000. *Frequency:* 558 kHz

SPIRE FM, City Hall Studios, Malthouse Lane, Salisbury, Wilts. Tel: 0722-416644. *Frequency:* 102.0 FM

SUNRISE FM, 30 Chapel Street, Little Germany, Bradford BD1 5DN. Tel: 0274-735043. *Frequency:* 103.2 FM

SUNRISE RADIO, Cross Lances Road, Hounslow, Middx. TW3 2AD. Tel: 081-569 6666. *Frequency:* 1413 kHz

SUNSET RADIO, 23 New Mount Street, Manchester M4 4DE. Tel: 061-953 5353. *Frequency:* 102.0 FM

SUNSHINE 819, South Shropshire Communications Ltd, Highridge House, The Sheet, Ludlow, Shropshire SY8 4JT. Tel: 0584-873795. *Frequency:* 819 kHz

SWANSEA SOUND, Victoria Road, Gowerton, Swansea SA4 3AB. Tel: 0792-893751. *Frequencies:* 257m, 1170 kHz, 96.4 FM

1332 THE WORLD'S GREATEST MUSIC STATION, PO Box 225, Queensgate Centre, Peterborough PE1 1XJ. Tel: 0733-34622. *Frequency:* 1332 kHz

TOUCH AM, PO Box 99, Cardiff CF1 5YJ. Tel: 0222-237878. *Frequencies:* 1359 kHz (Cardiff); 1305 kHz (Newport)

TRENT-FM (DERBY), The Market Place, Derby DE1 3AA. Tel: 0332-292945. *Frequency:* 102.8 FM

TRENT-FM (NOTTINGHAM), 29–31 Castle Gate, Nottingham NG1 7AP. Tel: 0602-581731. *Frequencies:* 96.2/96.5 FM

TRISTAR BROADCASTING, c/o Cable House, Waterside Drive, Langley, Berks. SL3 6EZ (from early 1993)

2CR CLASSIC GOLD, 5 Southcote Road, Bournemouth BH1 3LR. Tel: 0202-294881. *Frequencies:* 362m, 828 kHz, 102.3 FM

210 CLASSIC GOLD RADIO, PO Box 2020, Reading, Berks. RG3 5RZ. Tel: 0734-413131. *Frequency:* 1431 kHz

210 FM, PO Box 210, Reading, Berks. RG3 5RZ. Tel: 0734-413131. *Frequency:* 97.0 FM (Reading); 102.9 FM (Basingstoke and Andover)

VIKING FM, Commercial Road, Hull HU1 2SG. Tel: 0482-25141. *Frequency:* 96.9 FM

WABC, 267 Tettenhall Road, Wolverhampton WV6 0DQ. Tel: 0902-757211. *Frequencies:* 990 kHz (Wolverhampton); 1017 kHz (Shrewsbury and Telford)

WEAR FM, Forster Building, Chester Road, Sunderland SR1 3SD. Tel: 091-515 2103. *Frequency:* 103.4 FM

WEST SOUND RADIO, Radio House, 54 Holmston Road, Ayr KA7 3BE. Tel: 0292-283662. *Frequencies:* 290m, 1035 kHz, 96.7 FM

WEY VALLEY RADIO, 74 Queens Road, Alton, Hants. GU34 1HX (from early 1993)

WNK, 185B High Road, Wood Green, London N22 6BA. Tel: 081-889 1547. *Frequency:* 103.3 FM

XTRA-AM, Aston Road North, Birmingham B6 4BX. Tel: 021-359 4481. *Frequencies:* 1152 kHz (Birmingham); 1359 kHz (Coventry)

ASSOCIATION OF INDEPENDENT RADIO COMPANIES, 46 Westbourne Grove, London W2 5SH. Tel: 071-727 2646. *Director*, B. West

THE BROADCASTING COMPLAINTS COMMISSION

Grosvenor Gardens House, 35–37 Grosvenor Gardens, London SW1W 0BS
Tel 071-630 1966

The Broadcasting Complaints Commission's function and authority derive from the Broadcasting Act 1990. Its task is to consider and adjudicate upon complaints of unjust or unfair treatment in sound or television programmes broadcast by the BBC, S4C, the Independent Television Commission, the Radio Authority or their licensees as appropriate. This function extends to all sound, television and cable advertisements and teletext transmissions, and programmes broadcast by the BBC's World Services.

The Members of the Commission are appointed by the Secretary of State for National Heritage.

Chairman, Canon P. Pilkington
Members, D. Allen, CB; T. Christopher, CBE; D. Holmes; R. S. Row; Mrs B. Wells
Legal Adviser, Sir Basil Hall, KCB, MC, TD
Secretary, R. D. Hewlett

SERVICES SOUND AND VISION CORPORATION (Incorporating BFBS)

Chalfont Grove, Gerrards Cross, Bucks. SL9 8TN
Tel 0494-874461

The Services Sound and Vision Corporation (SSVC) is the official organization providing the Ministry of Defence, HM Forces and their families with radio and television broadcasting, audio-visual and electronic training and educational support, training film production, and entertainment. The SSVC is a private limited company and registered charity with 1,100 employees and an annual turnover approaching £47 million; financial surpluses are donated to Services' welfare.

The Corporation's radio arm, British Forces Broadcasting Service, operates stations in London, Germany, Gibraltar, Cyprus, the Falklands, Hong Kong, Brunei and Belize. BFBS provides programmes from London for inclusion with local input by its overseas staff, and broadcasts to overseas stations by satellite throughout the year.

SSVC television broadcasts its own, BBC and ITV programmes in Germany, Cyprus and the Falkland Islands. Up to 60 isolated detachments of HM Forces (including ships at sea and the Service Children's Education Authority schools overseas), receive daily TV programmes on cassette.

All SSVC services are available to other organizations and are provided to overseas governments and many UK companies.

Managing Director, A. Protheroe, CBE, TD

The Press

The newspaper and periodical press in the UK is large and diverse, catering for a wide variety of views and interests. There is no state control or censorship of the press, though it is subject to the laws on publication and the Press Complaints Commission (*see* below) was set up by the industry as a means of self-regulation.

The press is not state-subsidized and receives few tax concessions. The income of most newspapers and periodicals is derived largely from sales and from advertising; the press is the largest advertising medium in Britain.

THE PRESS COMPLAINTS COMMISSION

1 Salisbury Square, London EC3Y 8AE
Tel 071-353 1248

The Press Complaints Commission was founded by the newspaper and magazine industry in January 1991 to succeed the Press Council (established in 1953). It is a voluntary, non-statutory body set up to operate the press's self-regulation system, but if the voluntary system is not successful the Commission might be converted into a statutory body. The Commission is funded by the industry through the Press Standards Board of Finance.

The Commission's objects are to consider, adjudicate, conciliate, and resolve complaints of unfair treatment or unwarranted infringement of privacy by the press; and to ensure that the press maintains the highest professional standards, and respects and defends generally recognized freedoms, including freedom of expression, the public's right to know, and the right of the press to operate free from improper pressure. The Commission judges newspaper and magazine conduct by a code of practice drafted by editors and agreed by the industry.

Seven of the Commission's 16 members are editors of national, regional and local newspapers and magazines, three are former editors, and six, including the chairman, are drawn from other fields.

Chairman, Lord McGregor of Durris
Members, W. Anderson, CBE; Lady Elizabeth Cavendish, LVO; Ms P. Chapman; D. Chipp; M. Clayton; The Lord Colnbrook, KCMG, PC; Dame Mary Donaldson, GBE; Sir Richard Francis, KCMG; B. Hitchen, CBE; A. Hughes; G. McKechnie; K. Parker; Sir Edward Pickering; Prof. R. Pinker; P. Preston; Prof. L. Rees, FRCP, FRPath; R. Ridley
Deputy Director, M. Bolland

NEWSPAPERS

Newspapers are usually financially independent of any political party, though most adopt a political stance in their editorial comments, usually reflecting proprietorial influence. Ownership of the national and regional daily newspapers is concentrated in the hands of large corporations whose interests cover publishing and communications. However, there are strict rules on cross-media ownership to prevent undue concentration of newspaper ownership.

There are 15 daily national papers and 10 Sunday national papers, about 80 regional daily papers, and several hundred local papers that are published weekly or twice-weekly. Scotland, Wales and Northern Ireland all have at least one daily and one Sunday national paper.

Newspapers are usually published in either broadsheet or tabloid format. The 'quality' daily papers, i.e. those providing detailed coverage of a wide range of public matters, have a broadsheet format. The tabloid papers take a more popular approach and are more illustrated.

NATIONAL DAILY NEWSPAPERS

DAILY EXPRESS, Ludgate House, 245 Blackfriars Road, London SE1 9UX. Tel: 071-928 8000.
DAILY MAIL, Northcliffe House, 2 Derry Street, London W8 5TT. Tel: 071-938 6000.
DAILY MIRROR, Holborn Circus, London EC1P 1DQ. Tel: 071-353 0246.
DAILY SPORT, 19 Great Ancoats Street, Manchester M60 4BT. Tel: 061-236 4466.
DAILY TELEGRAPH, Peterborough Court at South Quay, 181 Marsh Wall, London E14 9SR. Tel: 071-538 5000.
FINANCIAL TIMES, 1 Southwark Bridge, London SE1 9HL. Tel: 071-873 3000.
THE GUARDIAN, 119 Farringdon Road, London EC1R 3ER. Tel: 071-278 2332.
THE INDEPENDENT, 40 City Road, London EC1Y 2DB. Tel: 071-253 1222.
MORNING STAR, 1–3 Ardleigh Road, London N1 4HS. Tel: 071-254 0033.
RACING POST, 112–120 Coombe Lane, London SW20 0BA. Tel: 081-879 3377.
THE SPORTING LIFE, Orbit House, 1 New Fetter Lane, London EC4A 1AR. Tel: 071-822 3291.
THE STAR, Ludgate House, 245 Blackfriars Road, London SE1 9UX. Tel: 071-928 8000.
THE SUN, 1 Pennington Street, London E1 9XN. Tel: 071-782 4000.
THE TIMES, 1 Pennington Street, London E1 9XN. Tel: 071-782 5000.
TODAY, 1 Virginia Street, London E1 9BD. Tel: 071-782 4600.

REGIONAL DAILY NEWSPAPERS

Aberdeen: PRESS AND JOURNAL, and EVENING EXPRESS, PO Box 43, Lang Stracht, Mastrick, AB9 8AF.
Ashford, Kent: KENT TODAY, 67 Middle Row, Maidstone ME14 1TJ.
Barrow-in-Furness: NORTH-WEST EVENING MAIL, Newspaper House, Abbey Road, LA14 5QS.
Bath: BATH EVENING CHRONICLE, 33–34 Westgate Street, BA1 1EW.
Belfast: BELFAST TELEGRAPH, 124–144 Royal Avenue, BT1 1EB; IRISH NEWS AND BELFAST MORNING NEWS, 113–117 Donegall Street, BT1 2GE; NEWS LETTER, 51–59 Donegall Street, BT1 2GB.
Birmingham: THE BIRMINGHAM POST, and BIRMINGHAM EVENING MAIL, 28 Colmore Circus, Queensway, B4 6AX.
Blackburn: LANCASHIRE EVENING TELEGRAPH, Telegraph House, High Street, BB1 1HT.
Blackpool: WEST LANCASHIRE EVENING GAZETTE, PO Box 20, FY4 4AU.
Bolton: BOLTON EVENING NEWS, Newspaper House, Churchgate, BL1 1DL.
Bournemouth: EVENING ECHO, Richmond Hill, BH2 6HH.
Bradford: TELEGRAPH AND ARGUS, Hall Ings, BD1 1JR.
Brighton: EVENING ARGUS, Argus House, 89 North Road, BN1 4AU.

Bristol: BRISTOL EVENING POST, and WESTERN DAILY PRESS, Temple Way, BS99 7HD.
Burton-on-Trent: BURTON MAIL, 65–68 High Street, DE14 1LE.
Cambridge: CAMBRIDGE EVENING NEWS, 51 Newmarket Road, CB5 8EJ.
Cardiff: SOUTH WALES ECHO, and WESTERN MAIL, Thomson House, Havelock Street, CF1 1WR.
Cheltenham: GLOUCESTERSHIRE ECHO, 1 Clarence Parade, GL50 3NZ.
Colchester: EVENING GAZETTE, Oriel House, 43–44 North Hill, CO1 1TZ.
Coventry: COVENTRY EVENING TELEGRAPH, Corporation Street, CV1 1FP.
Darlington: NORTHERN ECHO, Priestgate, DL1 1NP.
Derby: DERBY EVENING TELEGRAPH, Northcliffe House, Meadow Road, DE1 2DW.
Dundee: COURIER AND ADVERTISER, and EVENING TELEGRAPH AND POST, 2 Albert Square, DD1 9QJ.
Edinburgh: THE SCOTSMAN, and EVENING NEWS, 20 North Bridge, EH1 1YT.
Exeter: EXPRESS AND ECHO, Sidwell House, 160 Sidwell Street, EX4 6RS.
Glasgow: DAILY RECORD, 40 Anderston Quay, G3 8DA; HERALD, and EVENING TIMES, 195 Albion Street, G1 1QP.
Gloucester: THE GLOUCESTERSHIRE CITIZEN, St John's Lane, GL1 2AY.
Greenock: GREENOCK TELEGRAPH, 2 Crawford Street, PA15 1LH.
Grimsby: GRIMSBY EVENING TELEGRAPH, 80 Cleethorpe Road, DN31 3EH.
Guernsey: GUERNSEY EVENING PRESS AND STAR, PO Box 57, Braye Road, Vale.
Halifax: EVENING COURIER, PO Box 19, Courier Buildings, HX1 2SF.
Hartlepool: HARTLEPOOL MAIL, Clarence Road, TS24 8BU.
Huddersfield: HUDDERSFIELD DAILY EXAMINER, PO Box A26, Queen Street South, HD1 2TD.
Hull: HULL DAILY MAIL, Blundell's Corner, Beverley Road, HU3 1XS.
Ipswich: EAST ANGLIAN DAILY TIMES, and EVENING STAR, 30 Lower Brook Street, IP4 1AN.
Jersey: JERSEY EVENING POST, PO Box 582, Five Oaks, St Saviour.
Kettering: NORTHAMPTONSHIRE EVENING TELEGRAPH, Northfield Avenue, NN16 9TT.
Leeds: YORKSHIRE EVENING POST, and YORKSHIRE POST, PO Box 168, Wellington Street, LS1 1RF.
Leicester: LEICESTER MERCURY, St George Street, LE1 9FQ.
Lincoln: LINCOLNSHIRE ECHO, Brayford Wharf East, LN5 7AT.
Liverpool: DAILY POST, and LIVERPOOL ECHO, PO Box 48, Old Hall Street, L69 3EB.
London: THE EVENING STANDARD, Northcliffe House, 2 Derry Street, W8 5EE.
Maidstone: KENT EVENING POST, 67 Middle Row, ME14 1TJ.
Manchester: MANCHESTER EVENING NEWS, 164 Deansgate, M60 2RR.
Middlesbrough: EVENING GAZETTE, Gazette Building, Borough Road, TS1 3AZ.
Newcastle upon Tyne: EVENING CHRONICLE, and THE JOURNAL, Thomson House, Groat Market, NE1 1ED.
Newport: SOUTH WALES ARGUS, Cardiff Road, Maesglas, NP9 1QW.
Northampton: CHRONICLE AND ECHO, Upper Mounts, NN1 3HR.
Norwich: EASTERN DAILY PRESS, and EASTERN EVENING NEWS, Prospect House, Rouen Road, NR1 1RE.
Nottingham: EVENING POST, Forman Street, NG1 4AB.
Nuneaton: NUNEATON EVENING TRIBUNE, 1 New Century Way, CV11 5NE.
Oldham: EVENING CHRONICLE, 172 Union Street, OL1 1EQ.
Oxford: OXFORD MAIL, Newspaper House, Osney Mead, OX2 0EJ.
Paisley: PAISLEY DAILY EXPRESS, 195 Albion Street, Glasgow G1 1QP.
Peterborough: PETERBOROUGH EVENING TELEGRAPH, Telegraph House, 57 Priestgate, PE1 1JW.
Plymouth: WESTERN MORNING NEWS, and EVENING HERALD, 65 New George Street, PL1 1RE.
Portsmouth: THE NEWS, The News Centre, Hilsea, PO2 9SX.
Preston: LANCASHIRE EVENING POST, Oliver's Place, Fulwood, PR2 4ZA.
Reading: EVENING POST, 8 Tessa Road, RG1 8NS.
Scarborough: SCARBOROUGH EVENING NEWS, 17–23 Aberdeen Walk, YO11 1BB.
Scunthorpe: SCUNTHORPE EVENING TELEGRAPH, Telegraph House, Doncaster Road, DN15 7RE.
Sheffield: THE STAR, York Street, S1 1PU.
South Shields: SHIELDS GAZETTE, Chapter Row, NE33 1BL.
Southampton: SOUTHERN EVENING ECHO, 45 Above Bar, SO9 7BA.
Stoke-on-Trent: EVENING SENTINEL, Sentinel House, Etruria, ST1 5SS.
Sunderland: SUNDERLAND ECHO, Pennywell Industrial Estate, SR4 9ER.
Swansea: SOUTH WALES EVENING POST, Adelaide Street, SA1 1QT.
Swindon: EVENING ADVERTISER, Newspaper House, 100 Victoria Road, SN1 3BE.
Telford: SHROPSHIRE STAR, Ketley, TF1 4HU.
Torquay: HERALD EXPRESS, Harmsworth House, Barton Hill Road, TQ2 8JN.
Weymouth: DORSET EVENING ECHO, 57 St Thomas Street, DT4 8EU.
Wolverhampton: EXPRESS AND STAR, 51–53 Queen Street, WV1 3BU.
Worcester: EVENING NEWS, Hylton Road, WR2 5JX.
York: YORKSHIRE EVENING PRESS, PO Box 29, 76–86 Walmgate, YO1 1YN.

WEEKLY NEWSPAPERS

AL MAJALLA, Arab Press House, 184 High Holborn, London WC1V 7AP. Tel: 071-831 8181.
ASIAN TIMES, Tower House, 139–149 Fonthill Road, London N4 3HF. Tel: 071-281 1191.
CARIBBEAN TIMES, Tower House, 139–149 Fonthill Road, London N4 3HF. Tel: 071-281 1191.
THE EUROPEAN, Orbit House, 5 New Fetter Lane, London EC4A 1AP. Tel: 071-822 2002.
THE GUARDIAN WEEKLY, 119 Farringdon Road, London EC1R 3ER. Tel: 071-278 2332.
THE INDEPENDENT ON SUNDAY, 40 City Road, London EC1Y 2DB. Tel: 071-253 1222.
INDIA TIMES, Suites F and G, 2nd Floor, Liberty Shopping Centre, 14 South Road, Southall, Middx. UB1 1RT. Tel: 081-843 1605.
THE MAIL ON SUNDAY, Northcliffe House, 2 Derry Street, London W8 5TS. Tel: 071-938 6000.
NEWS OF THE WORLD, 1 Pennington Street, London E1 9XN. Tel: 071-782 4000.
THE OBSERVER, Chelsea Bridge House, Queenstown Road, London SW8 4NN. Tel: 071-627 0700.

THE PEOPLE, Holborn Circus, London EC1P 1DQ. Tel: 071-353 0246.
SCOTLAND ON SUNDAY, 20 North Bridge, Edinburgh EH1 1YT. Tel: 031-225 2468.
THE SCOTSMAN, 20 North Bridge, Edinburgh EH1 1YT. Tel: 031-225 2468.
SUNDAY EXPRESS, Ludgate House, 245 Blackfriars Road, London SE1 9UX. Tel: 071-928 8000.
SUNDAY MAIL, 40 Anderston Quay, Glasgow G3 8DA. Tel: 041-248 7000.
SUNDAY MIRROR, Holborn Circus, London EC1P 1DQ. Tel: 071-353 0246.
SUNDAY NEWS, 51–59 Donegall Street, Belfast BT1 2GB. Tel: 0232-244411.
SUNDAY POST, Courier Place, Dundee DD1 9QJ. Tel: 0382-23131.
SUNDAY SPORT, 3rd Floor, Marten House, 39–47 East Road, London N1 6AH. Tel: 071-251 2544.
SUNDAY TELEGRAPH, Peterborough Court at South Quay, 181 Marsh Wall, London E14 9SR. Tel: 071-538 5000.
THE SUNDAY TIMES, 1 Pennington Street, London E1 9XN. Tel: 071-782 5000.
THE VOICE, 370 Coldharbour Lane, London SW9 8PL. Tel: 071-737 7377.
WALES ON SUNDAY, Thomson House, Havelock Street, Cardiff CF1 1WR. Tel: 0222-223333.
WEEKLY NEWS, Courier Place, Dundee, Angus DD1 9QJ. Tel: 0382-23131.
WEEKLY TELEGRAPH, Peterborough Court at South Quay, 181 Marsh Wall, London E14 9SR. Tel: 071-538 5000.

RELIGIOUS PAPERS

Alt. = Alternate; *M.* = Monthly; *Q.* = Quarterly; *W.* = Weekly

BAPTIST TIMES, PO Box 54, 129 The Broadway, Didcot, Oxon OX11 8XB. *W.*
CATHOLIC HERALD, Herald House, Lamb's Passage, Bunhill Row, London EC1Y 8TQ. *W.*
CHALLENGE: THE GOOD NEWS PAPER, Revenue Buildings, Chapel Road, Worthing, W. Sussex BN11 1BQ. *M.*
CHRISTIAN HERALD, Herald House, 96 Dominion Road, Worthing, W. Sussex BN14 8JP. *W.*
CHRISTIAN SCIENCE MONITOR, 20 Beulah Road, London SW19 3SU. *W.*
CHURCH OF ENGLAND NEWSPAPER, 77–79 Farringdon Road, London EC1M 3JY. *W.*
CHURCH OF IRELAND GAZETTE, 36 Bachelor's Walk, Lisburn, Co. Antrim, BT28 1XN. *W.*
CHURCH TIMES, 33 Upper Street, London N1 0PW. *W.*
ENGLISH CHURCHMAN, Mill Lane House, Margate, Kent CT9 1ND. *Alt. W.*
THE FRIEND, Drayton House, 30 Gordon Street, London WC1H 0BQ. *W.*
THE INQUIRER, 1–6 Essex Street, London WC2R 3HY. *Alt. W.*
JEWISH CHRONICLE, 25 Furnival Street, London EC4A 1JT. *W.*
JEWISH GAZETTE, 27 Bury Old Road, Prestwich, Manchester M25 8EY. *W.*
JEWISH TELEGRAPH, Telegraph House, 11 Park Hill, Bury Old Road, Prestwich, Manchester M25 8HH. *W.*
LIFE AND WORK, Church of Scotland, 121 George Street, Edinburgh EH2 4QS. *M.*
METHODIST RECORDER, 122 Golden Lane, London EC1Y 0TL. *W.*
ORTHODOX NEWS, 64 Prebend Gardens, London W6 0XU. *Alt. M.*
PRESBYTERIAN HERALD, Church House, Fisherwick Place, Belfast BT1 6DW. *M.*
QUAKER MONTHLY, Friends House, Euston Road, London NW1 2BJ. *M.*
REFORM, 86 Tavistock Place, London WC1H 9RT. *Eleven times a year.*
SIKH MESSENGER, 43 Dorset Road, London SW19 3EZ. *Q.*
THE TABLET, 1 King Street Cloisters, Clifton Walk, London W6 0QZ. *W.*
THE UNIVERSE, 1st Floor, St James Building, Oxford Street, Manchester M1 6FP. *W.*
THE WAR CRY, 101 Queen Victoria Street, London EC4P 4EP. *W.*

PERIODICALS

There are about 6,700 periodicals published in Britain. These are classified as consumer, i.e. general interest, or as trade, professional or academic.

CONSUMER PERIODICALS

Alt. = Alternate; *M.* = Monthly; *Q.* = Quarterly; *W.* = Weekly

AMATEUR PHOTOGRAPHER, King's Reach Tower, Stamford Street, London SE1 9LS. *W.*
ANGLING TIMES, Bretton Court, Bretton, Peterborough, Cambs. PE3 8DZ. *W.*
ANNABEL, 80 Kingsway East, Dundee, Angus DD4 8SL. *M.*
THE ANTIQUE COLLECTOR, National Magazine House, 72 Broadwick Street, London W1V 2BP. *M.*
APOLLO MAGAZINE, 3 St James's Place, London SW1A 1NP. *M.*
ARENA, 3rd Floor, Block A, Exmouth House, Pine Street, London EC1R 0JL. *Alt. M.*
THE ARTIST, Caxton House, 63–65 High Street, Tenterden, Kent TN30 6BD. *M.*
ASTRONOMY NOW, 193 Uxbridge Road, London W12 9RA. *M.*
ATHLETICS WEEKLY, Bretton Court, Bretton, Peterborough, Cambs. PE3 8DZ. *W.*
AUTOCAR AND MOTOR, 38–42 Hampton Road, Teddington, Middx. TW11 0JE. *W.*
BBC GARDENER'S WORLD, 101 Bayham Street, London NW1 0AG. *M.*
BBC GOOD FOOD, 101 Bayham Street, London NW1 0AG. *M.*
BBC WILDLIFE MAGAZINE, Hyde Park House, Manfred Road, London SW15 2RS. *M.*
BELFAST GAZETTE (*Official*), 129 IDB House, 64 Titchester Street, Belfast BT1 4PS. *W.*
BELLA, 2nd Floor, Shirley House, 25–27 Camden Road, London NW1 9LL. *W.*
BEST, 10th Floor, Portland House, Stag Place, London SW1E 5AU. *W.*
BIRDS, RSPB, The Lodge, Sandy, Beds. SG19 2DL. *Q.*
BIRD WATCHING, Bretton Court, Bretton, Peterborough, Cambs. PE3 8DZ. *W.*
BOXING NEWS, PO Box 300, London SW15 5QF. *W.*
BRIDES & SETTING UP HOME, Vogue House, Hanover Square, London W1R 0AD. *Alt. M.*
BRITISH BOOK NEWS, The British Council, 65 Davies Street, London W1Y 2AA. *M.*
THE BURLINGTON MAGAZINE, 6 Bloomsbury Square, London WC1A 2LP. *M.*
CAMPING & CARAVANNING, Greenfields House, Westwood Way, Coventry CV4 8JH. *M.*

CAR, Bushfield House, Orton Centre, Peterborough, Cambs. PE2 0UW. *M.*

CAT WORLD, 10 Western Road, Shoreham-by-Sea, W. Sussex BN43 5WD. *M.*

CD REVIEW, Media House, Boxwell Road, Berkhamsted, Herts. HP4 3ET. *M.*

CHAT, King's Reach Tower, Stamford Street, London SE1 9LS. *W.*

CITY LIMITS, 66–67 Wells Street, London, W1P 3RB. *W.*

CLASSICAL MUSIC, 241 Shaftesbury Avenue, London WC2H 8EH. *Alt. W.*

CLASSIC AND SPORTSCAR, 60 Waldegrave Road, Teddington, Middx. TW11 8LG. *M.*

CLOTHES SHOW MAGAZINE, 101 Bayham Street, London NW1 0AG. *M.*

COARSE ANGLER, 281 Ecclesall Road, Sheffield S11 8NX. *M.*

COIN NEWS, 84 High Street, Honiton, Devon EX14 8JW. *M.*

COMPANY, 72 Broadwick Street, London W1V 2BP. *M.*

COMPETITORS JOURNAL, PO Box 300, London SW15 5QF. *Alt. W.*

COMPUTER AND VIDEO GAMES, Priory Court, 30–32 Farringdon Road, London EC1R 3AU. *M.*

COSMOPOLITAN, 72 Broadwick Street, London W1V 2BP. *M.*

COUNTRY HOMES AND INTERIORS, King's Reach Tower, Stamford Street, London SE1 9LS. *M.*

COUNTRY LIFE, King's Reach Tower, Stamford Street, London SE1 9LS. *W.*

COUNTRY LIVING, 72 Broadwick Street, London W1V 2BP. *Alt. M.*

THE COUNTRYMAN, Link House, Dingwall Avenue, Croydon, Surrey CR9 2TA. *Alt. M.*

CRICKETER INTERNATIONAL, Beech Hanger, Ashurst, Tunbridge Wells, Kent TN3 9ST. *M.*

CYCLING WEEKLY, King's Reach Tower, Stamford Street, London SE1 9LS. *W.*

THE DALESMAN, Dalesman Publishing Company Ltd, Clapham, Lancaster LE2 8EB. *M.*

DALTONS WEEKLY, CI Tower, St George's Square, New Malden, Surrey KT3 4JA. *W.*

DANCE AND DANCERS, 214 Panther House, 38 Mount Pleasant, London WC1X 0AP. *M.*

DANCING TIMES, Clerkenwell House, 45–47 Clerkenwell Green, London EC1R 0BE. *M.*

DOGS TODAY, 10 Sheet Street, Windsor, Berks. SL4 1BG. *M.*

DOG WORLD, 9 Tufton Street, Ashford, Kent TN23 1QN. *W.*

DO IT YOURSELF, Link House, Dingwall Avenue, Croydon, Surrey CR9 2TA. *M.*

THE ECOLOGIST, 1st Floor, Corner House, Station Road, Sturminster Newton, Dorset DT10 1BB. *Alt. M.*

THE ECONOMIST, 25 St James's Street, London SW1A 1HG. *W.*

EDINBURGH GAZETTE (*Official*), HMSO, PO Box 276, London SW8 5DT. *Twice a week.*

ELLE, Rex House, 4–12 Lower Regent Street, London SW1Y 4PE. *M.*

EMPIRE, Meed House, 21 John Street, London WIN 2BP. *M.*

ESQUIRE, 72 Broadwick Street, London W1V 2BP. *M.*

ESSENTIALS, Garden House, 57–59 Long Acre, London WC2E 9JL. *M.*

EVERYWOMAN, 34 Islington Green, London N1 8DU. *M.*

EXCHANGE AND MART, Link House, West Street, Poole, Dorset BH15 1LL. *W.*

THE FACE, 3rd Floor, Block A, Exmouth House, Pine Street, London EC1R 0JL. *M.*

FAMILY CIRCLE, King's Reach Tower, Stamford Street, SE1 9LS. *Thirteen times a year.*

THE FIELD, 10 Sheet Street, Windsor, Berks. SL4 1BG. *M.*

FILM REVIEW, 214 Panther House, 38 Mount Pleasant, London WC1X 0AP. *M.*

FOR HIM, 9–11 Curtain Road, London EC2A 3LT. *Ten times a year.*

GARDEN NEWS, Apex House, Oundle Road, Peterborough PE2 0UW. *W.*

GAY TIMES, 283 Camden High Street, London NW1 7BX. *M.*

GEOGRAPHICAL MAGAZINE, Hyde Park House, 5 Manfred Road, London SW15 2RS. *M.*

GIBBONS STAMP MONTHLY, 5 Parkside, Christchurch Road, Ringwood, Hants. BH24 3SH. *M.*

GOLF ILLUSTRATED WEEKLY, 37 Millharbour, London E14 9TX. *W.*

GOLF WORLD, Advance House, 37–39 Millharbour, London E14 9TX. *M.*

GOOD HOLIDAY MAGAZINE, 1–2 Dawes Court, 93 High Street, Esher, Surrey KT10 9QD. *Q.*

GOOD HOUSEKEEPING, 72 Broadwick Street, London W1V 2BP. *M.*

GQ, Vogue House, Hanover Square, London W1R 0AD. *M.*

GRAMOPHONE, 177–179 Kenton Road, Harrow, Middx. HA3 0HA. *M.*

GRANTA, 2–3 Hanover Yard, Noel Road, London N1 8BE. *Q.*

GREEN MAGAZINE, PO Box 381, London E14 9TW. *M.*

GUIDING, 17–19 Buckingham Palace Road, London SW1W 0PT. *M.*

HANSARD, *see* Parliamentary Debates.

HARPERS AND QUEEN, 72 Broadwick Street, London W1V 2BP. *M.*

HELLO, 30–34 New Bridge Street, London EC4V 6HH. *W.*

HOMES AND GARDENS, King's Reach Tower, Stamford Street, London SE1 9LS. *M.*

HORSE AND HOUND, King's Reach Tower, Stamford Street, London SE1 9LS. *W.*

HOUSE AND GARDEN, Vogue House, Hanover Square, London W1R 0AD. *M.*

HOUSE BEAUTIFUL, 72 Broadwick Street, London W1V 2BP. *M.*

i-D MAGAZINE, 134–146 Curtain Road, London EC4A 3AR. *M.*

IDEAL HOME, King's Reach Tower, Stamford Street, London SE1 9LS. *M.*

ILLUSTRATED LONDON NEWS, 20 Upper Ground, London SE1 9PF. *Alt. M.*

IN BRITAIN, 3rd Floor, Greater London House, Hampstead Road, London NW1 7QQ. *M.*

INDIAMAIL, Heron House, 109 Wembley Hill, Wembley, Middx. HA9 8DH. *W.*

INVESTORS CHRONICLE, Greystoke Place, Fetter Lane, London EC4A 1ND. *W.*

IRISH POST, 464 Uxbridge Road, Hayes, Middx. UB4 0SP. *W.*

JACKIE, 2 Albert Square, Dundee, Angus DD1 9QJ. *W.*

JAZZ JOURNAL INTERNATIONAL, 113–117 Farringdon Road, London EC1R 3BT. *M.*

JUST 17, 52–55 Carnaby Street, London W1V 1PF. *W.*

LABOUR RESEARCH, 78 Blackfriars Road, London SE1 8HF. *M.*

THE LADY, 39–40 Bedford Street, London WC2E 9ER. *W.*

LAND AND LIBERTY, 177 Vauxhall Bridge Road, London SW1V 1EU. *Alt. M.*

LITERARY REVIEW, 51 Beak Street, London W1R 3LF. *M.*

LIVING, King's Reach Tower, Stamford Street, London SE1 9LS. *Thirteen times a year.*

LONDON GAZETTE (*Official*) Room 413, HMSO, 51 Nine Elms Lane, London SW8 5DR. *Five times a week.*

London Review of Books, Tavistock House South, Tavistock Square, London WC1H 9JZ. *Alt. W.*

London Weekly Advertiser, 137 George Lane, London E18 1AJ. *W.*

Majesty, 26–28 Hallam Street, London W1N 5LF. *M.*

Marie Claire, 195 Knightsbridge, London SW1. *M.*

Me, 57–59 Long Acre, London WC2E 9JL. *W.*

Melody Maker (MM), King's Reach Tower, Stamford Street, London SE1 9LS. *W.*

Meteorological Magazine, HMSO, PO Box 276, London SW8 5DT. *M.*

Metropolitan Home, 141–143 Drury Lane, London WC2B 5TB. *Alt. M.*

Mizz, King's Reach Tower, Stamford Street, London SE1 9LS. *Alt. W.*

Model Boats, Argus House, Boundary Way, Hemel Hempstead, Herts. HP2 7ST. *M.*

Moneywise, Berkeley Square House, Berkeley Square, London W1X 6AB. *M.*

More!, Meed House, 21 John Street, London W1N 2BP. *W.*

Mother and Baby, Victory House, 14 Leicester Place, London WC2H 7BP. *M.*

Motor Cycle News, Bushfield House, Orton Centre, Peterborough PE2 0UW. *W.*

Motoring News, Standard House, Bonhill Street, London EC2A 4DA. *W.*

Motor Sport, Standard House, Bonhill Street, London EC2A 4DA. *M.*

My Weekly, 80 Kingsway East, Dundee DD4 8SL. *W.*

National Student, Bleaklow House, Howard Town Mill, Mill Street, Glossop, Derbys. SK13 8PT. *Three times a year.*

Nature, 4 Little Essex Street, London WC2R 3LF. *W.*

Needlecraft, Beaufort Court, 30 Monmouth Street, Bath BA1 2BW. *M.*

New Internationalist, 55 Rectory Road, Oxford OX4 1BW. *M.*

New Scientist, King's Reach Tower, Stamford Street, London SE1 9LS. *W.*

New Statesman and Society, Foundation House, Perseverance Works, 38 Kingsland Road, London E2 8DQ. *W.*

Newsweek International, 25 Upper Brook Street, London W1Y 2AB. *W.*

New Woman, Fanum House, 48 Leicester Square, London WC2H 7FB. *M.*

19, King's Reach Tower, Stamford Street, London SE1 9LS. *M.*

NME, King's Reach Tower, Stamford Street, London SE1 9LS. *M.*

The Oldie, 26 Charlotte Street, London W1P 1HJ. *Alt. W.*

Opera, 1A Mountgrove Road, London N5 2LU. *M.*

Opera Now, 9 Grape Street, London WC2H 8DR. *M.*

Options, King's Reach Tower, Stamford Street, London SE1 9LS. *M.*

Our Dogs, 5 Oxford Road, Station Approach, Manchester M60 1SX. *W.*

Parents, Victory House, 14 Leicester Place, London WC2H 7BP. *M.*

Parliamentary Debates (Commons) (Hansard), HMSO, PO Box 276, London SW8 5DT. *Daily or weekly during Session.*

Parliamentary Debates (Lords) (Hansard), HMSO, PO Box 276, London SW8 5DT. *Daily or weekly during Session.*

People's Friend, 80 Kingsway East, Dundee DD4 8SL. *W.*

Plays and Players, Media House, 55 Lower Addiscombe, Croydon, Surrey CR0 6PQ. *M.*

Poetry Review, 21 Earl's Court Square, London SW5 9DE. *Q.*

Pony, 296 Ewell Road, Surbiton, Surrey KT6 7AQ. *M.*

Practical Boat Owner, Westover House, West Quay Road, Poole, Dorset BH15 1JG. *M.*

Practical Caravan, 38–42 Hampton Road, Teddington, Middx. TW11 0JE. *M.*

Practical Gardening, Apex House, Oundle Road, Peterborough PE3 8DZ. *M.*

Practical Health, King's Reach Tower, Stamford Street, London SE1 9LS. *Alt. M.*

Practical Parenting, King's Reach Tower, Stamford Street, London SE1 9LS. *Alt. W.*

Practical Photography, Apex House, Oundle Road, Peterborough PE2 9NP. *M.*

Prima, Portland House, Stag Place, London SW1E 5AU. *M.*

Private Eye, 6 Carlisle Street, London W1V 5RG. *Alt. W.*

Progress (*Braille type*), RNIB, Orton, Southgate, Peterborough PE2 0XU. *M.*

The Puzzler, Glenthorne House, Hammersmith Grove, London W6 0LG. *M.*

Q, Meed House, 21 John Street, London W1N 2BP. *M.*

Racing Calendar, The Jockey Club, Weatherbys, Sanders Road, Wellingborough, Northants. NN8 4BX. *W.*

Radio Times, 35 Marylebone High Street, London W1M 4AA. *W.*

Railway Magazine, King's Reach Tower, Stamford Street, London SE1 9LS. *M.*

Railway Modeller, Peco Publications, Beer, Seaton, Devon EX12 3NA. *M.*

Reader's Digest, Berkeley Square House, Berkeley Square, London W1X 6AB. *M.*

Riding, Corner House, Foston, Grantham, Lincs. NG32 2JU. *M.*

Rugby Leaguer, Martland Mill, Martland Mill Lane, Wigan, Lancs. WN5 0LX. *W.*

Rugby World and Post, Weirbank, Bray, Maidenhead, Berks. SL6 2ED. *M.*

Scots Magazine, 7 Bank Street, Dundee, Angus DD1 9HU. *M.*

Scottish Field, 7th Floor, The Plaza Tower, East Kilbride, Glasgow G74 1LW. *M.*

Scouting, Baden-Powell House, Queen's Gate, London SW7 5JS. *M.*

Sea Angler, Bretton Court, Bretton, Peterborough, Cambs. PE3 8DZ. *M.*

She, 72 Broadwick Street, London W1V 2BP. *M.*

Shoot, King's Reach Tower, Stamford Street, London SE1 9LS. *W.*

Shooting Times and Country Magazine, 10 Sheet Street, Windsor, Berks. SL4 1BG. *W.*

Sky Magazine, 27 Swinton Street, London WC1X 9MW. *M.*

Slimming Magazine, Victory House, 14 Leicester Place, London WC2H 7BP. *Alt. M.*

Smash Hits, Meed House, 21 John Street, London W1N 2BP. *Alt. M.*

Spare Rib, 27 Clerkenwell Close, London EC1R 0AT. *M.*

The Spectator, 56 Doughty Street, London WC1N 2LL. *W.*

The Strad, 214 Panther House, 38 Mount Pleasant, London WC1X 0AP. *M.*

Tatler, Vogue House, Hanover Square, London W1R 0AD. *Ten times a year.*

Tennis World, The Spendlove Centre, Enstone Road, Charlbury, Oxon. OX7 3PQ. *Ten times a year.*

This England, Alma House, Rodney Road, Cheltenham, Glos. GL50 1YQ. *Q.*

Time International, Time Life Building, 153 New Bond Street, London W1Y 0AA. *W.*

TIME OUT, Tower House, Southampton Street, London WC2E 7HD. *W.*

THE TIMES EDUCATIONAL SUPPLEMENT, Priory House, St John's Lane, London ECIM 4BX. *W.*

THE TIMES HIGHER EDUCATION SUPPLEMENT, Priory House, St John's Lane, London ECIM 4BX. *W.*

THE TIMES LITERARY SUPPLEMENT, Priory House, St John's Lane, London ECIM 4BX. *W.*

TRIBUNE, 308 Gray's Inn Road, London WCIX 8DY. *W.*

TROUT AND SALMON, Bretton Court, Bretton, Peterborough PE3 8DZ. *M.*

TRUE ROMANCES, 2–4 Leigham Court Road, London SW16 2PD. *M.*

TRUE STORY, 2–4 Leigham Court Road, London SW16 2PD. *M.*

TV TIMES, King's Reach Tower, Stamford Street, London SEI 9LS. *W.*

VACHER'S PARLIAMENTARY COMPANION, 113 High Street, Berkhamsted, Herts. HP4 2DJ. *Q.*

VANITY FAIR, Vogue House, Hanover Square, London WIR OAD. *M.*

THE VEGETARIAN, The Vegetarian Society, Parkdale, Dunham Road, Altrincham, Cheshire WA14 4QG. *Alt. M.*

VIZ COMIC, PO Box 1PT, Newcastle upon Tyne NE99 IPT. *Alt. M.*

VOGUE, Vogue House, Hanover Square, London WIR OAD. *M.*

VOX, King's Reach Tower, Stamford Street, London SEI 9LS. *Alt. M.*

WEATHER, James Glaisher House, Grenville Place, Bracknell, Berks. RG12 IBX. *M.*

WELSH NATION, 51 Cathedral Road, Cardiff CFI 9HD. *Alt. M.*

WHICH?, 2 Marylebone Road, London NWI 4DX. *M.*

WOMAN, King's Reach Tower, Stamford Street, London SEI 9LS. *W.*

WOMAN AND HOME, King's Reach Tower, Stamford Street, London SEI 9LS. *M.*

WOMAN'S JOURNAL, King's Reach Tower, Stamford Street, London SEI 9LS. *M.*

WOMAN'S OWN, King's Reach Tower, Stamford Street, London SEI 9LS. *W.*

WOMAN'S REALM, King's Reach Tower, Stamford Street, London SEI 9LS. *W.*

WOMAN'S WEEKLY, King's Reach Tower, Stamford Street, London SEI 9LS. *W.*

WORLD OF INTERIORS, Vogue House, Hanover Square, London WIR OAD. *Eleven times a year.*

YACHTING MONTHLY, King's Reach Tower, Stamford Street, London SEI 9LS. *M.*

TRADE, PROFESSIONAL AND ACADEMIC PERIODICALS

Alt. = Alternate; *M.* = Monthly; *Q.* = Quarterly; *W.* = Weekly

ACCOUNTANCY, Institute of Chartered Accountants, 40 Bernard Street, London WCIN ILD. *M.*

ACCOUNTANCY AGE, 32–34 Broadwick Street, London WIA 2HG. *W.*

ACCOUNTANTS' MAGAZINE, Institute of Chartered Accountants of Scotland, 27 Queen Street, Edinburgh EH2 ILA. *M.*

THE ACTUARY, Staple Inn Hall, High Holborn, London WCI. *M.*

AGRICULTURE INTERNATIONAL, Yew Tree House, Horne, Horley, Surrey RH6 9JP. *M.*

ANTIQUARIES JOURNAL, Oxford University Press, Pinkhill House, Southfield Road, Eynsham, Oxford OX8 IJJ. *Twice a year.*

ANTIQUE DEALER AND COLLECTORS' GUIDE, PO Box 805, London SEIO 8TD. *M.*

ANTIQUES TRADE GAZETTE, 17 Whitcomb Street, London WC2H 7PL. *W.*

ARCHITECTS' JOURNAL, 33–35 Bowling Green Lane, London ECIA ODA. *W.*

ARCHITECTURAL REVIEW, 33–35 Bowling Green Lane, London ECIA ODA. *M.*

ARMED FORCES DEFENCE INTERNATIONAL, 21 Hawley Road, London NWI 8RP.

THE AUTHOR, Society of Authors, 84 Drayton Gardens, London SWIO 9SB. *Q.*

THE BANKER, Greystoke Place, Fetter Lane, London EC4A IND. *M.*

BANKING WORLD (Chartered Institute of Bankers), Greater London House, Hampstead Road, London NWI 7QQ. *M.*

THE BIOCHEMIST, The Biochemist Society, 59 Portland Place, London WIN 3AJ. *Alt. M.*

BIOLOGIST, Institute of Biology, 20 Queensberry Place, London SW7 2DZ. *Five times a year.*

THE BOOKSELLER, 12 Dyott Street, London WCIA IDF. *W.*

BRAIN, Oxford University Press, Pinkhill House, Southfield Road, Eynsham, Oxford OX8 IJJ. *Alt. M.*

BREWING AND DISTILLING INTERNATIONAL, Peel House, Lichfield Street, Burton-on-Trent, Staffs. DE14 3RH. *M.*

BRITISH BAKER, PO Box 109, Maclaren House, 19 Scarbrook Road, Croydon CR9 IQH. *W.*

BRITISH DENTAL JOURNAL, BMA House, Tavistock Square, London WCIH 9JR. *Alt. W.*

BRITISH FOOD JOURNAL, MCB University Press Ltd, 62 Toller Lane, Bradford BD8 9BY. *Nine times a year.*

BRITISH JEWELLER, Wentworth House, Wentworth Street, Peterborough PEI IDS. *M.*

BRITISH JOURNAL FOR THE PHILOSOPHY OF SCIENCE, Oxford University Press, Pinkhill House, Southfield Road, Eynsham, Oxford OX8 IJJ. *Q.*

BRITISH JOURNAL OF PHOTOGRAPHY, 58 Fleet Street, London EC4Y IJU. *W.*

BRITISH JOURNAL OF PSYCHIATRY, Royal College of Psychiatrists, 17 Belgrave Square, London SWIX 8PG. *M.*

BRITISH JOURNAL OF PSYCHOLOGY, British Psychological Society, 13A Church Lane, London N2 8DX. *Q.*

BRITISH JOURNAL OF SOCIAL WORK, Oxford University Press, Pinkhill House, Southfield Road, Eynsham, Oxford OX8 IJJ. *Six times a year.*

BRITISH MEDICAL JOURNAL, British Medical Association, BMA House, Tavistock Square, London WCIH 9JR. *W.*

BRITISH PRINTER, Maclean Hunter House, Chalk Lane, Cockfosters Road, Barnet, Herts. EN4 OBU. *M.*

BRITISH TAX REVIEW, South Quay Plaza, 183 Marsh Wall, London E14 9FT. *Alt. M.*

BRITISH VETERINARY JOURNAL, 24–28 Oval Road, London NWI 7DX. *Alt. M.*

BUILDING, Builder House, 1 Millharbour, London E14 9RA. *W.*

BUILDING TRADE & INDUSTRY, 131–133 Duckmoor Road, Bristol BS3 2BH. *M.*

BUSINESS CONNECTIONS, Node Court, Drivers End, Codicote, Hitchin, Herts. SG4 8TR. *Alt. M.*

BUSINESS EDUCATION TODAY, 128 Long Acre, London WC2E 9AN. *M.*

CABINET MAKER AND RETAIL FURNISHER, Sovereign Way, Tonbridge, Kent TN9 IRW. *W.*

CAMPAIGN, 22 Lancaster Gate, London W2 3LY. *W.*

CARPET AND FLOORCOVERINGS REVIEW, Sovereign Way, Tonbridge, Kent TN9 IRW. *Alt. W.*

CATERER AND HOTELKEEPER, Quadrant House, The Quadrant, Sutton, Surrey SM2 5AS. *W.*
CHEMIST AND DRUGGIST, Sovereign Way, Tonbridge, Kent TN9 1RW. *W.*
CHEMISTRY AND INDUSTRY, 14 Belgrave Square, London SW1X 8PS. *Alt. W.*
CHEMISTRY IN BRITAIN, Royal Society of Chemistry, Thomas Graham House, Science Park, Milton Road, Cambridge CB4 4WF. *M.*
CHILD EDUCATION, Marlborough House, Holly Walk, Leamington Spa, Warks. CV32 4LS. *M.*
CLASSICAL QUARTERLY, Oxford University Press, Pinkhill House, Southfield Road, Eynsham, Oxford OX8 1JJ. *Twice a year.*
CLASSICAL REVIEW, Oxford University Press, Pinkhill House, Southfield Road, Eynsham, Oxford OX8 1JJ. *Twice a year.*
COMPUTER SHOPPER, 19 Bolsover Street, London W1. *M.*
COMPUTER WEEKLY, Quadrant House, The Quadrant, Sutton, Surrey SM2 5AS. *W.*
COMPUTING, VNU House, 32–34 Broadwick Street, London W1A 2HG. *W.*
CONSTRUCTION NEWS, Morgan-Grampian House, Calderwood Street, London SE18 6QH. *W.*
CONSTRUCTION WEEKLY, Morgan-Grampian House, Calderwood Street, London SE18 6QH. *W.*
CONTAINERISATION INTERNATIONAL, 72 Broadwick Street, London W1V 2BP. *M.*
CONTRACT JOURNAL, Quadrant House, The Quadrant, Sutton, Surrey SM2 5AS. *W.*
CONTROL AND INSTRUMENTATION, Morgan-Grampian House, 30 Calderwood Street, London SE18 6QH. *M.*
CRAFTS MAGAZINE, Crafts Council, 44A Pentonville Road, London N1 9BY. *Alt. M.*
CRIMINOLOGIST, East Row, Little London, Chichester, W. Sussex PO19 1PG. *Q.*
DAIRY FARMER AND DAIRY BEEF PRODUCER, Wharfedale Road, Ipswich IP1 4LG. *M.*
DAIRY INDUSTRIES INTERNATIONAL, Wilmington House, Church Hill, Wilmington, Dartford, Kent DA2 7EF. *M.*
THE DENTIST, 174 High Street, Guildford, Surrey GU1 3HW. *Eleven times a year.*
DESIGN, The Design Council, 28 Haymarket, London SW1Y 4SU. *M.*
DESIGN WEEK, Giles House, 49–50 Poland Street, London W1V 4AX. *W.*
DIRECTOR, Institute of Directors, Mountbarrow House, 6–20 Elizabeth Street, London SW1W 9RB. *M.*
DR THE FASHION BUSINESS, Greater London House, Hampstead Road, London NW1 7QZ. *W.*
ECONOMIC JOURNAL, 108 Cowley Road, Oxford OX4 1JF. *Q.*
EDUCATION, 21–27 Lamb's Conduit Street, London WC1N 3NJ. *W.*
ELECTRICAL AND RADIO TRADING, Quadrant House, The Quadrant, Sutton, Surrey SM2 5AS. *W.*
ELECTRICAL REVIEW, Quadrant House, The Quadrant, Sutton, Surrey SM2 5AS. *Alt. W.*
ELECTRICAL TIMES, Quadrant House, The Quadrant, Sutton, Surrey SM2 5AS. *Ten times a year.*
ELECTRONIC ENGINEERING, Morgan-Grampian House, 30 Calderwood Street, London SE18 6QH. *M.*
ENERGY MANAGEMENT, Maclean Hunter House, Chalk Lane, Cockfosters Road, Barnet, Herts. EN4 0BU. *Alt. M.*
THE ENGINEER, Morgan-Grampian House, 30 Calderwood Street, London SE18 6QH. *W.*
ENGINEERING, 28 Haymarket, London SW1Y 4SU. *M.*
ENGINEER'S DIGEST, Convex House, 43 Dudley Road, Tunbridge Wells, Kent TN1 1LE. *Ten times a year.*
ENGLISH HISTORICAL REVIEW, Longman House, Burnt Mill, Harlow, Essex CM20 2JE. *Q.*
ENGLISH TODAY, Cambridge University Press, The Edinburgh Building, Shaftesbury Road, Cambridge CB2 2RU. *Q.*
THE ENVIRONMENTALIST, 12 Clarence Road, Kew, Surrey TW29 3NL. *Q.*
EQUITY JOURNAL, 8 Harley Street, London W1N 2AB. *Q.*
ESTATES GAZETTE, 151 Wardour Street, London W1V 4BN. *W.*
FAIRPLAY INTERNATIONAL SHIPPING WEEKLY, 20 Ullswater Crescent, Coulsdon, Surrey CR5 2HR. *W.*
FARMERS WEEKLY, Quadrant House, The Quadrant, Sutton, Surrey SM2 5AS. *W.*
FASHION WEEKLY, Greater London House, Hampstead Road, London NW1 7SD. *W.*
FIRE, Queensway House, 2 Queensway, Redhill, Surrey RH1 1QS. *M.*
FIRE PREVENTION, 140 Aldersgate Street, London EC1A 4HX. *Ten times a year.*
FISH, Institute of Fisheries Management, 151 Cove Road, Farnborough, Hants. GU14 0HQ. *Q.*
FISH TRADER, Queensway House, 2 Queensway, Redhill, Surrey RH1 1QS. *Alt. W.*
FLIGHT INTERNATIONAL, Quadrant House, The Quadrant, Sutton, Surrey SM2 5AS. *W.*
FOOD TRADE REVIEW, Station House, Hortons Way, Westerham, Kent TN16 1BZ. *M.*
FORESTRY AND BRITISH TIMBER, Sovereign Way, Tonbridge, Kent TN9 1RW. *M.*
FOUNDRY TRADE JOURNAL, Queensway House, 2 Queensway, Redhill, Surrey RH1 1QS. *Alt. W.*
FROZEN AND CHILLED FOODS, Queensway House, 2 Queensway, Redhill, Surrey RH1 1QS. *M.*
FUEL, Linacre House, Jordan Hill, Oxford OX2 8DP. *M.*
GARDEN TRADE NEWS, Apex House, Oundle Road, Peterborough PE2 9NP. *M.*
GAS WORLD, PO Box 105, 25–31 Ironmonger Row, London EC1V 3PN. *Q.*
GEOGRAPHY, Geographical Association, 343 Fulwood Road, Sheffield S10 3BP. *Q.*
GEOLOGICAL MAGAZINE, Cambridge University Press, The Edinburgh Building, Shaftesbury Road, Cambridge CB2 2RU. *Alt. M.*
GLASS AND GLAZING PRODUCTS, 33–35 Bowling Green Lane, London EC1R 0DA. *M.*
GREECE AND ROME, Oxford University Press, Pinkhill House, Southfield Road, Eynsham, Oxford OX8 1JJ. *Twice a year.*
THE GROCER, Broadfield Park, Crawley, West Sussex RH11 9RJ. *W.*
THE GROWER, 50 Doughty Street, London WC1N 2LS. *W.*
HAIRDRESSERS' JOURNAL INTERNATIONAL, Quadrant House, The Quadrant, Sutton, Surrey SM2 5AS. *W.*
THE HEALTH SERVICE JOURNAL, 4 Little Essex Street, London WC2R 3LF. *W.*
HEALTH VISITOR, BMA House, Tavistock Square, London WC1H 9JR. *M.*
HEATING, VENTILATING AND PLUMBING, PO Box 13, Hereford House, Bridle Path, Croydon, Surrey CR9 4NL. *M.*
HISTORY TODAY, 83–84 Berwick Street, London W1V 2BP. *M.*
INDEPENDENT RETAILER, 14 Pierpoint Street, Worcester WR1 1TA. *M.*
INDUSTRIAL EXCHANGE AND MART, Link House, West Street, Poole, Dorset BH15 1LL. *M.*
INDUSTRIAL RELATIONS JOURNAL, 108 Cowley Road, Oxford OX4 1JF. *Q.*

INTERNATIONAL AFFAIRS, Cambridge University Press, The Edinburgh Building, Shaftesbury Road, Cambridge CB2 2RU. *Q.*

JANE'S DEFENCE WEEKLY, Sentinel House, 163 Brighton Road, Coulsdon, Surrey CR5 2NH. *W.*

THE JOURNALIST, National Union of Journalists, Acorn House, 314 Gray's Inn Road, London WC1X 8DP. *M.*

JOURNAL OF ALTERNATIVE AND COMPLEMENTARY MEDICINE, 53A High Street, Bagshot, Surrey GU19 5AH. *M.*

JOURNAL OF THE BRITISH ASTRONOMICAL ASSOCIATION, Burlington House, Piccadilly, London W1V 9AG. *Alt. M.*

JOURNAL OF THE CHEMICAL SOCIETY, Thomas Graham House, Science Park, Milton Road, Cambridge CB4 4WF. *Five parts each M.*

JUSTICE OF THE PEACE, East Row, Little London, Chichester, W. Sussex PO19 1PG. *W.*

THE LANCET, 42 Bedford Square, London WC1B 3SL. *W.*

LAW QUARTERLY REVIEW, South Quay Plaza, 183 Marsh Wall, London E14 9FT. *Q.*

THE LAW REPORTS, 3 Stone Buildings, Lincoln's Inn, London WC2A 3XN. *M.*

LAW SOCIETY GAZETTE, 50 Chancery Lane, London WC2A 1SX. *W.*

LEATHER, Sovereign Way, Tonbridge, Kent TN9 1RW. *M.*

LIBRARY ASSOCIATION RECORD, 7 Ridgemount Street, London W1V 7AE. *M.*

LLOYD'S LOADING LIST, Sheepen Place, Colchester, Essex CO3 3LP. *W.*

LLOYD'S SHIPPING INDEX, Sheepen Place, Colchester, Essex CO3 3LP. *Daily.*

LOCAL GOVERNMENT CHRONICLE, 122 Minories, London EC3N 1NT. *W.*

MACHINERY AND PRODUCTION ENGINEERING, Franks Hall, Franks Lane, Horton Kirby, Dartford, Kent DA4 9LL. *Alt. W.*

MACHINERY MARKET, 6 Blyth Road, Bromley, Kent BR1 3RX. *W.*

MANAGEMENT ACCOUNTING, Chartered Institute of Management Accountants, 29 Princes Street, London W1R 7RG. *M.*

MANAGEMENT NEWS, British Institute of Management, 2 Savoy Court, London WC2R 0EZ. *Ten times a year.*

MANAGEMENT TODAY, 22 Lancaster Gate, London W2 3LY. *M.*

MANUFACTURING CHEMIST, Morgan-Grampian House, 30 Calderwood Street, London SE18 6QH. *M.*

MARKETING, 22 Lancaster Gate, London W2 3LY. *W.*

MARKETING WEEK, Giles House, 49–50 Poland Street, London W1V 4AX. *W.*

MATERIALS RECLAMATION WEEKLY, PO Box 109, Maclaren House, 19 Scarbrook Road, Croydon CR9 1QH. *W.*

MEAT TRADES' JOURNAL, Greater London House, Hampstead Road, London NW1 7QZ. *W.*

MEDIA WEEK, 33–35 Bowling Green Lane, London EC1R 0DA. *W.*

METALS AND MATERIALS, Institute of Metals, 1 Carlton House Terrace, London SW1Y 5DB. *M.*

METALS INDUSTRY NEWS, Queensway House, 1 Queensway, Redhill, Surrey RH1 1QS. *M.*

MIDWIFE AND HEALTH VISITOR, Greater London House, Hampstead Road, London NW1 7SD. *M.*

MIND, Oxford University Press, Pinkhill House, Southfield Road, Eynsham, Oxford OX8 1JJ. *Q.*

MINING JOURNAL, 60 Worship Street, London EC2A 2HD. *W.*

MOTOR TRANSPORT, Quadrant House, The Quadrant, Sutton, Surrey SM2 5AS. *W.*

MUNICIPAL JOURNAL, 32 Vauxhall Bridge Road, London SW1V 2SS. *W.*

MUNICIPAL REVIEW AND AMA NEWS, 35 Great Smith Street, London SW1P 3BJ. *Ten times a year.*

MUSEUMS JOURNAL, Museums Association, 34 Bloomsbury Way, London WC1A 2SF. *M.*

THE MUSICAL TIMES, 214 Panther House, 38 Mount Pleasant, London WC1X 0AP. *M.*

MUSIC AND LETTERS, Oxford University Press, Pinkhill House, Southfield Road, Eynsham, Oxford OX8 1JJ. *Q.*

MUSIC WEEK, Ludgate House, 245 Blackfriars Road, London SE1 9UR. *W.*

NATIONAL BUILDER, 82 New Cavendish Street, London W1M 8AD. *M.*

NATURAL GAS, Sovereign Way, Tonbridge, Kent TN9 1RW. *Alt. M.*

NOTES AND QUERIES, Oxford University Press, Pinkhill House, Southfield Road, Eynsham, Oxford OX8 1JJ. *Q.*

NUCLEAR ENGINEERING INTERNATIONAL, Quadrant House, The Quadrant, Sutton, Surrey SM2 5AS. *M.*

NURSING TIMES & NURSING MIRROR, 4 Little Essex Street, London WC2R 3LF. *W.*

OFF-LICENCE NEWS, Broadfield Park, Crawley, W. Sussex RH11 9RJ. *W.*

OPTICIAN, Quadrant House, The Quadrant, Sutton, Surrey SM2 5AS. *W.*

OPTOMETRY TODAY, 11 Somerset Place, Glasgow G3 7JT. *Alt. W.*

PACKAGING WEEK, Sovereign Way, Tonbridge, Kent TN9 1RW. *W.*

PAPER, Sovereign Way, Tonbridge, Kent TN9 1RW. *Nineteen times a year.*

PC PLUS, 30 Monmouth Street, Bath BA1 2BW. *M.*

PERSONAL COMPUTER WORLD, 32–34 Broadwick Street, London W1A 2HG. *M.*

PERSONNEL MANAGEMENT (Institute of Personal Management), 57 Mortimer Street, London W1N 7TD. *M.*

PHARMACEUTICAL JOURNAL, 1 Lambeth High Street, London SE1 7JN. *W.*

PHILOSOPHY, Cambridge University Press, The Edinburgh Building, Shaftesbury Road, Cambridge CB2 2RU. *Q.*

THE PHOTOGRAPHER, Fox Talbot House, Anwell End, Ware, Herts. SG12 9HN. *M.*

PHYSICS WORLD, Techno House, Redcliffe Way, Bristol BS1 6NX. *M.*

PLUMBING AND HEATING EQUIPMENT NEWS, Peterson House, Northbank, Berryhill Industrial Estate, Droitwich, Worcs. WR9 9BL. *M.*

POLICE REVIEW, South Quay Plaza 2, 183 Marsh Wall, London E14 9FZ. *W.*

POWER FARMING, Quadrant House, The Quadrant, Sutton, Surrey SM2 5AS. *M.*

THE PRACTITIONER, Morgan-Grampian House, 30 Calderwood Street, London SE18 6QH. *M.*

PRINTING WORLD, Sovereign Way, Tonbridge, Kent TN9 1RW. *W.*

PROBATION JOURNAL, 3–4 Chivalry Road, London SW11 1HT. *Q.*

THE PSYCHOLOGIST, The British Psychological Society, St Andrews House, 48 Princess Road East, Leicester LE1 7DR. *M.*

QUARRY MANAGEMENT, 7 Regent Street, Nottingham NG1 5BY. *M.*

RAILWAY GAZETTE INTERNATIONAL, Quadrant House, The Quadrant, Sutton, Surrey SM2 5AS. *M.*

RATING & VALUATION REPORTER, 4 Breams Buildings, London EC4A 1AQ. *M.*

RETAIL NEWSAGENT TOBACCONIST CONFECTIONER, Robert Taylor House, 11 Angel Gate, City Road, London EC1V 2PT. *W.*

RETAIL WEEK, 33–35 Bowling Green Lane, London EC1R ODA. *W.*

THE REVIEW, Audit House, Field End Road, Eastcote, Ruislip, Middx. HA4 9LT. *M.*

REVIEW OF ENGLISH STUDIES, Oxford University Press, Pinkhill House, Southfield Road, Eynsham, Oxford OX8 1JJ. *Q.*

RUSI JOURNAL, Royal United Services Institute for Defence Studies, Whitehall, London SW1A 2ET. *Q.*

SHIPPING WORLD & SHIPBUILDER, 4 Hubbard Road, Houndsmill, Basingstoke, Hants. RG21 2UH. *M.*

SHOE & LEATHER NEWS, Greater London House, Hampstead Road, London NW1 7QZ. *W.*

SMALLHOLDER, High Street, Stoke Ferry, King's Lynn, Norfolk PE33 9SF. *M.*

SOCIOLOGICAL REVIEW, 108 Cowley Road, Oxford OX4 1JF. *Q.*

SOLICITORS' JOURNAL, 21–27 Lamb's Conduit Street, London WC1N 3NJ. *W.*

SPORTS RETAILING, Bullen Lane, East Peckham, Tonbridge, Kent TN12 5RT. *M.*

THE STAGE AND TELEVISION TODAY, 47 Bermondsey Street, London SE1 3XT. *W.*

STRUCTURAL ENGINEER, 11 Upper Belgrave Street, London SW1X 8BH. *M. (Part A), Q. (Part B).*

SURVEYOR, Quadrant House, The Quadrant, Sutton, Surrey SM2 5AS. *W.*

TAXATION PRACTITIONER, Institute of Taxation, 12 Upper Belgrave Street, London SW1X 8BB. *M.*

TAXI, 9–11 Woodfield Road, London W9 2BA. *Alt. W.*

THE TEACHER, National Union of Teachers, Hamilton House, Mabledon Place, London WC1H 9BD. *Eight times a year.*

TEACHING HISTORY, 108 Cowley Road, Oxford OX4 1JF. *Q.*

TELEVISION, Quadrant House, The Quadrant, Sutton, Surrey SM2 5AS. *M.*

TEXTILE HORIZONS, 10 Blackfriars Street, Manchester M3 5DR. *M.*

TEXTILE MONTH, Caidan House, Canal Road, Timperley, Altrincham, Cheshire WA14 1TD. *M.*

TIMBER TRADES JOURNAL & WOOD PROCESSING, Sovereign Way, Tonbridge, Kent TN9 1RW. *W.*

TOBACCO, Queensway House, 2 Queensway, Redhill, Surrey RH1 1QS. *Alt. M.*

TOWN AND COUNTRY PLANNING, 17 Carlton House Terrace, London SW1Y 5AH. *M.*

TOWN PLANNING REVIEW, Liverpool University Press, PO Box 147, Liverpool L69 3BX. *Q.*

TOY TRADER, 177 Hagden Lane, Watford, Herts. WD1 8LN. *M.*

TRADE MARKS JOURNAL, Patent Office, 25 Southampton Buildings, London WC2A 1AY. *W.*

THE TRADER, Link House, West Street, Poole, Dorset BH15 1LL. *M.*

TRAVEL TRADE GAZETTE (UK and Ireland)—Morgan-Grampian House, 30 Calderwood Street, London SE18 6QH. *W.*

UK PRESS GAZETTE, Maclean Hunter House, Chalk Lane, Cockfosters Road, Barnet, Herts. EN4 0BU. *W.*

WEEKLY LAW REPORTS, 3 Stone Buildings, Lincoln's Inn, London WC2A 3XN. *W.*

WOODWORKING TODAY, 166 High Street, Lewes, E. Sussex BN7 1XU. *Ten times a year.*

WORLD'S FAIR, 2 Daltry Street, Oldham OL1 4BB. *W.*

NEWS AGENCIES IN LONDON

News agencies provide general, business, sport and television news to a variety of subscribers including the press, other media, and industrial, commercial, financial and business users.

THE ASSOCIATED PRESS LTD, 12 Norwich Street, London EC4A 4BP. Tel: 071–353 1515.

CENTRAL PRESS FEATURES LTD, 20 Spectrum House, 32 Gordon House Road, London NW3 1LP. Tel: 071–284 1433.

EXTEL FINANCIAL LTD, 13 Epworth Street, London EC2A 4DL. Tel: 071–251 3333.

HAYTERS, 4–5 Gough Square, EC4A 3DE. Tel: 071–353 0971.

PARLIAMENTARY AND EEC NEWS SERVICE, 19 Douglas Street, London SW1P 4PA. Tel: 071–233 8283.

PRESS ASSOCIATION LTD, 85 Fleet Street, London EC4P 4BE. Tel: 071–353 7440.

REUTERS LTD, 85 Fleet Street, London EC4P 4AJ. Tel: 071–250 1122.

UNITED PRESS INTERNATIONAL (UK) LTD, 2 Greenwich View, Millharbour, London E14 9NN. Tel: 071–538 0932.

UNIVERSAL NEWS SERVICE LTD, 210 Old Street, London EC1V 9AH. TEL: 071-490 8111.

Book Publishers

More than 15,000 firms, individuals and societies have published one or more books in recent years. The list which follows is a selective one comprising, in the main, those firms whose names are most familiar to the general public. An interleaved list, *Publishers in the United Kingdom and Their Addresses*, containing some 2,300 names and addresses is published annually in April by the publishers of *Whitaker's Almanack*.

ACCENT EDUCATIONAL PUBLISHERS, 17 Isbourne Way, Winchcombe, Cheltenham GL54 2NS. Tel: 0242-604466.

ALLAN (IAN), Terminal House, Station Approach, Shepperton, Middx. TW17 8AS. Tel: 0923-228950.

ALLEN (J. A.), 1 Lower Grosvenor Place, London SW1W OEL. Tel: 071-834 0090.

ALLEN (W. H.), *see* Virgin Publishing.

ANAYA PUBLISHERS, 44–50 Osnaburgh Street, London NW1 3ND. Tel: 071-383 2997.

APPLE PRESS, 6 Blundell Street, London N7 9BH. Tel: 071-700 6700.

ARGUS BOOKS, Argus House, Boundary Way, Hemel Hempstead, Herts. HP2 7ST. Tel: 0442-66551.

ARMADA BOOKS, 77 Fulham Palace Road, London W6 8JB. Tel: 081-741 7070.

ARMS & ARMOUR PRESS, 41 Strand, London WC2N 5JE. Tel: 071-839 4900.

ARNOLD (EDWARD), Mill Road, Dunton Green, Sevenoaks TN13 2YA. Tel: 0732-450111.

ARROW BOOKS, 20 Vauxhall Bridge Road, London SW1V 2SA. Tel: 071-973 9700.

ATHLONE PRESS, 1 Park Drive, London NW11 7SG. Tel: 081-458 0888.

AURUM PRESS, 10 Museum Street, London WC1A 1JS. Tel: 071-379 1252.

BBC BOOKS, 80 Wood Lane, London W12 OTT. Tel: 081-576 2536.

BAILLIÈRE TINDALL, 24 Oval Road, London NW1 7DX. Tel: 071-267 4466.

BANTAM BOOKS, 61 Uxbridge Road, London W5 5SA. Tel: 081-579 2652.

BARRIE & JENKINS, 20 Vauxhall Bridge Road, London SW1V 2SA. Tel: 071-973 9710.

BARTHOLOMEW, 12 Duncan Street, Edinburgh EH9 1TA. Tel: 031-667 9341.

BATSFORD (B. T.), 4 Fitzhardinge Street, London W1H OAH. Tel: 071-486 8484.

BINGLEY (CLIVE), 7 Ridgmount Street, London WC1E 7AE. Tel: 071-636 7543.

BLACK (A. & C.), 35 Bedford Row, London WC1R 4JH. Tel: 071-242 0946.

BLACKWELL PUBLISHERS, 108 Cowley Road, Oxford OX4 1JF. Tel: 0865-791100.

BLANDFORD PRESS, 41 Strand, London WC2N 5JE. Tel: 071-839 4900.

BLOOMSBURY PUBLISHING, 2 Soho Square, London W1V 5DE. Tel: 071-494 2111.

BODLEY HEAD, 20 Vauxhall Bridge Road, London SW1V 2SA. Tel: 071-973 9730.

BOXTREE, 21 Broadwall, London SE1 9PL. Tel: 071-928 9696.

BOYARS (MARION), 24 Lacy Road, London SW15 1NL. Tel: 081-788 9522.

BRITISH MUSEUM PRESS, 46 Bloomsbury Street, London WC1B 3QQ. Tel: 071-323 1234.

BUTTERWORTH & CO., Borough Green, Sevenoaks TN15 8PH. Tel: 0732-884567.

CALDER PUBLICATIONS, 9–15 Neal Street, London WC2H 9TU. Tel: 071-497 1741.

CAMBRIDGE UNIVERSITY PRESS, The Edinburgh Building, Cambridge CB2 2RU. Tel: 0223-312393.

CAPE (JONATHAN), 20 Vauxhall Bridge Road, London SW1V 2SA. Tel: 071-973 9730.

CASSELL, 41 Strand, London WC2N 5JE. Tel: 071-839 4900.

CENTAUR PRESS, Fontwell, Arundel, W. Sussex BN18 OTA. Tel: 0243-543302.

CENTURY PUBLISHING CO., *see* Random House UK.

CHAMBERS (W. & R.), 43 Annandale Street, Edinburgh EH7 4AZ. Tel: 031-557 4571.

CHAPMAN & HALL, 2 Boundary Row, London SE1 8HN. Tel: 071-865 0066.

CHAPMAN (GEOFFREY), 41 Strand, London WC2N 5JE. Tel: 071-839 4900.

CHAPMANS PUBLISHERS, 141 Drury Lane, London WC2B 5TB. Tel: 071-379 9799.

CHATTO & WINDUS, 20 Vauxhall Bridge Road, London SW1V 2SA. Tel: 071-973 9740.

CHIVERS PRESS, Windsor Bridge Road, Bath BA2 3AX. Tel: 0225-335336.

CHURCH HOUSE PUBLISHING, Church House, Great Smith Street, London SW1P 3NZ. Tel: 071-222 9011.

CHURCHILL LIVINGSTONE, 1–3 Baxter's Place, Leith Walk, Edinburgh EH1 3AF. Tel: 031-556 2424.

COLLINS (WILLIAM), *see* HarperCollins Publishers.

CONSTABLE & CO., 3 The Lanchesters, 162 Fulham Palace Road, London W6 9ER. Tel: 081-741 3663.

CONSUMERS' ASSOCIATION, 2 Marylebone Road, London NW1 4DF. Tel: 071-486 5544.

CORGI BOOKS, 61 Uxbridge Road, London W5 5SA. Tel: 081-579 2652.

DARTON, LONGMAN & TODD, 89 Lillie Road, London SW6 1UD. Tel: 071-385 2341.

DAVID & CHARLES, Brunel House, Newton Abbot, Devon TQ12 4PU. Tel: 0626-61121.

DENT (J. M.) & SONS, 5 Upper St Martin's Lane, London WC2H 9EA. Tel: 071-240 3444.

DEUTSCH (ANDRE), 105 Great Russell Street, London WC1B 3LJ. Tel: 071-580 2746.

DORLING KINDERSLEY, 9 Henrietta Street, London WC2E 8PS. Tel: 071-836 5411.

DOUBLEDAY, 61 Uxbridge Road, London W5 5SA. Tel: 081-579 2652.

DUCKWORTH & CO., 48 Hoxton Square, London N1 6PB. Tel: 071-729 5986.

ELLIOT RIGHT WAY BOOKS, Kingswood Building, Kingswood, Tadworth, Surrey KT20 6TD. Tel: 0737-832202.

ENCYCLOPAEDIA BRITANNICA INTERNATIONAL, Carew House, Station Approach, Wallington, Surrey SM6 ODA. Tel: 081-669 4355.

EPWORTH PRESS, c/o SCM Press, 26 Tottenham Road, London N1 4BZ. Tel: 071-249 7262.

EVANS BROS, 2A Portman Mansions, Chiltern Street, London W1M 1LE. Tel: 071-935 7160.

EVERYMAN'S LIBRARY, 79 Berwick Street, London W1V 3PF. Tel: 071-287 0035.

FABER & FABER, 3 Queen Square, London WC1N 3AU. Tel: 071-465 0045.

FONTANA, 77 Fulham Palace Road, London W6 8JB. Tel: 081-741 7070.

FOULIS (G. T.), Sparkford, Yeovil, Somerset BA22 7JJ. Tel: 0963-40635.

FOULSHAM (W.) & CO., Yeovil Road, Slough SL1 4JH. Tel: 0753-562769.

FRENCH (SAMUEL), 52 Fitzroy Street, London W1P 6JR. Tel: 071-387 9373.

Gaia Books, 20 High Street, Stroud GL5 1AS. Tel: 0453-752985.
Gibbons (Stanley), 5 Parkside, Christchurch Road, Ringwood, Hants. BH24 3SH. Tel: 0425-472363.
Gibson (Robert), 17 Fitzroy Place, Glasgow G3 7SF. Tel: 041-248 5674.
Ginn & Co., Prebendal House, Parson's Fee, Aylesbury, Bucks. HP20 2QZ. Tel: 0296-88411.
Glasgow (Mary), 131 Holland Park Avenue, London W11 4UT. Tel: 071-603 4688.
Gollancz (Victor), 14 Henrietta Street, London WC2E 8QJ. Tel: 071-836 2006.
Gower Publishing Co., Croft Road, Aldershot, Hants. GU11 3HR. Tel: 0252-331551.
Grafton Books, 77 Fulham Palace Road, London W6 8JB. Tel: 081-741 7070.
Graham (Frank), 10 Blythswood North, Osborne Road, Jesmond, Newcastle NE2 2AZ. Tel: 091-281 3067.
Granta Books, 2 Hanover Yard, London N1 8BE. Tel: 071-704 9776.
Green (W.), 21 Alva Street, Edinburgh EH2 4PS. Tel: 031-225 4879.
Guinness Publishing, 33 London Road, Enfield, Middx. EN2 6DJ. Tel: 081-367 4567.
Hale (Robert), 45 Clerkenwell Green, London EC1R 0HT. Tel: 071-251 2661.
Hamilton (Hamish), 27 Wright's Lane, London W8 5TZ. Tel: 071-416 3100.
Hamlyn (Paul), 81 Fulham Road, London SW3 6RB. Tel: 071-581 9393.
Harcourt Brace Jovanovich, 24 Oval Road, London NW1 7DX. Tel: 071-267 4466.
HarperCollins Publishers, 77 Fulham Palace Road, London W6 8JB. Tel: 081-741 7070.
Harrap, 43 Annandale Street, Edinburgh EH7 4AZ. Tel: 031-557 4571.
Harvester Wheatsheaf, Campus 400, Maylands Avenue, Hemel Hempstead HP2 7EZ. Tel: 0442-881900.
Haynes (J. H.), Sparkford, Yeovil, Somerset BA22 7JJ. Tel: 0963-40635.
Headline Book Publishing, 79 Great Titchfield Street, London W1P 7FN. Tel: 071-631 1687.
Heinemann (William), 81 Fulham Road, London SW3 6RB. Tel: 071-581 9393.
Hippo Books, 7 Pratt Street, London NW1 0AE. Tel: 071-284 4474.
HMSO, PO Box 276, London SW8 5DT. Tel: 071-873 0011.
Hodder & Stoughton, 47 Bedford Square, London WC1B 3DP. Tel: 071-636 9851.
Hogarth Press, 20 Vauxhall Bridge Road, London SW1V 2SA. Tel: 071-973 9740.
Holmes McDougall, 137 Leith Walk, Edinburgh EH6 8NS. Tel: 031-554 9444.
Hutchinson, *see* Random House UK.
Jane's Information Group, 163 Brighton Road, Coulsdon, Surrey CR5 2NH. Tel: 081-763 1030.
Jarrold Publishing, Barrack Street, Norwich NR3 1TR. Tel: 0603-763300.
Johnston & Bacon, PO Box 1, Stirling. Tel: 0786-841867.
Jordan & Sons, 21 St Thomas Street, Bristol BS1 6JS. Tel: 0272-230600.
Joseph (Michael), 27 Wright's Lane, London W8 5TZ. Tel: 071-937 7255.
Kaye & Ward, 38 Hans Crescent, London SW1X 0LZ. Tel: 071-581 9393.
Kegan Paul International, PO Box 256, London WC1B 3SW. Tel: 071-580 5511.
Kelly's, East Grinstead House, East Grinstead, W. Sussex RH19 1XB. Tel: 0342-326972.
Kimpton Medical, 82 Great King Street, Edinburgh EH3 6QY. Tel: 031-332 8764.
Kingsway Publications, Lottbridge Drove, Eastbourne BN23 6NT. Tel: 0323-410930.
Kogan Page, 120 Pentonville Road, London N1 9JN. Tel: 071-278 0433.
Ladybird Books, Beeches Road, Loughborough LE11 2NQ. Tel: 0509-268021.
Lawrence & Wishart, 144A Old South Lambeth Road, London SW8 1XX. Tel: 071-820 9281.
Lennard Publishing, Windmill Cottage, Mackerye End, Harpenden AL5 5DR. Tel: 0582-715866.
Letts (Charles), Parkgate Road, London SW11 4NQ. Tel: 071-407 8891.
Lincoln (Frances), 5 Charlton Kings Road, London NW5 2SB. Tel: 071-482 3302.
Lion Publishing, Peter's Way, Oxford OX4 5HG. Tel: 0865-747550.
Little, Brown & Co., 165 Great Dover Street, London SE1 4YA. Tel: 071-334 4800.
Longman Group, Burnt Mill, Harlow, Essex CM20 2JE. Tel: 0279-426721.
Lund Humphries, 1 Russell Gardens, London NW11 9NN. Tel: 081-458 6314.
Lutterworth Press, PO Box 60, Cambridge CB1 2NT. Tel: 0223-350865.
Macdonald & Evans, 128 Long Acre, London WC2E 9AN. Tel: 071-379 7383.
McGraw-Hill, Shoppenhangers Road, Maidenhead, Berks. SL6 2QL. Tel: 0628-23432.
Macmillan Publishers, 4 Little Essex Street, London WC2R 3LF. Tel: 071-836 6633.
MacRae (Julia), 20 Vauxhall Bridge Road, London SW1V 2SA. Tel: 071-973 9750.
Mammoth, 38 Hans Crescent, London SW1X 0LZ. Tel: 071-581 9393.
Mandala, *see* HarperCollins Publishers.
Mandarin, 81 Fulham Road, London SW3 6RB. Tel: 071-581 9393.
Marshall Cavendish, 58 Old Compton Street, London W1V 5PA. Tel: 071-734 6710.
Methodist Publishing, 20 Ivatt Way, Peterborough PE3 7PG. Tel: 0733-332202.
Methuen London, 7 Kendrick Mews, London SW7 3HG. Tel: 071-581 9393.
Mills & Boon, 18 Paradise Road, Richmond, Surrey TW9 1SR. Tel: 081-948 0444.
Mitchell Beazley, 81 Fulham Road, London SW3 6RB. Tel: 071-581 9393.
Mowbray, 41 Strand, London WC2N 5JE. Tel: 071-839 4900.
Muller (Frederick), 20 Vauxhall Bridge Road, London SW1V 2SA. Tel: 071-973 9680.
Murray (John), 50 Albemarle Street, London W1X 4BD. Tel: 071-493 4361.
National Christian Education Council, Robert Denholm House, Nutfield, Redhill RH1 4HW. Tel: 0737-822411.
Nelson (Thomas), Mayfield Road, Walton-on-Thames KT12 5PL. Tel: 0932-246133.
New English Library, 47 Bedford Square, London WC1B 3DP. Tel: 071-636 9851.
Nisbet & Co., 78 Tilehouse Street, Hitchin, Herts. SG5 2DY. Tel: 0462-438331.
Novello & Co., 8 Lower James Street, London W1R 3PL. Tel: 071-287 5060.
Octopus Books, 81 Fulham Road, London SW3 6RB. Tel: 071-581 9393.
Oliver & Boyd, Longman House, Burnt Mill, Harlow, Essex CM20 2JE. Tel: 0279-426721.

O'Mara (Michael) Books, 9 Lion Yard, 11 Tremadoc Road, London SW4 7NQ. Tel: 071-720 8643.
Orchard Books, 96 Leonard Street, London EC2A 4RH. Tel: 071-739 2929.
Owen (Peter), 73 Kenway Road, London SW5 0RE. Tel: 071-373 5628.
Oxford University Press, Walton Street, Oxford OX2 6DP. Tel: 0865-56767.
Paladin Books, *see* HarperCollins Publishers.
Pan Books, 18 Cavaye Place, London SW10 9PG. Tel: 071-373 6070.
Pelham Books, 27 Wright's Lane, London W8 5TZ. Tel: 071-937 7255.
Penguin Books, Harmondsworth, Middx. UB7 0DA. Tel: 081-759 1984.
Pergamon Press, Headington Hill Hall, Oxford OX3 0BW. Tel: 0865-794141.
Phaidon Press, 140 Kensington Church Street, London W8 4BN. Tel: 071-221 5656.
Pharmaceutical Press, 1 Lambeth High Street, London SE1 7JN. Tel: 071-735 9141.
Philip (George), 59 Grosvenor Street, London W1X 9DA. Tel: 071-493 5841.
Piatkus Books, 5 Windmill Street, London W1P 1HF. Tel: 071-631 0710.
Piccadilly Press, 5 Castle Road, London NW1 8PR. Tel: 071-267 4492.
Pitkin Pictorials, Healey House, Dene Road, Andover, Hants. SP10 2AA. Tel: 0264-334303.
Pitman Publishing, 128 Long Acre, London WC2E 9AN. Tel: 071-379 7383.
Putnam & Co., 101 Fleet Street, London EC4Y 1DE. Tel: 071-583 2412.
Quartet Books, 27 Goodge Street, London W1P 1FD. Tel: 071-636 3992.
Quiller Press, 46 Lillie Road, London SW6 1TN. Tel: 071-499 6529.
Random House UK, 20 Vauxhall Bridge Road, London SW1V 2SA. Tel: 071-973 9000.
Ravette Books, 3 Glenside Estate, Star Road, Partridge Green, Horsham, W. Sussex RH13 8RA. Tel: 0403-710392.
Reader's Digest, 25 Berkeley Square, London W1X 6AB. Tel: 071-629 8144.
Religious & Moral Education Press, St Mary's Works, St Mary's Plain, Norwich NR3 3BH. Tel: 0603-616563.
Rider & Co., *see* Random House UK.
Routledge, 11 New Fetter Lane, London EC4P 4EE. Tel: 071-583 9855.
SCM Press, 26 Tottenham Road, London N1 4BZ. Tel: 071-249 7262.
SPCK, Holy Trinity Church, Marylebone Road, London NW1 4DU. Tel: 071-387 5282.
St Andrew Press, 121 George Street, Edinburgh EH2 4YN. Tel: 031-225 5722.
Scripture Union, 130 City Road, London EC1V 2NJ. Tel: 071-782 0013.
Secker & Warburg, 81 Fulham Road, London SW3 6RB. Tel: 071-581 9393.
Serpent's Tail Publishing, 4 Blackstock Mews, London N4 2BT. Tel: 071-354 1949.
Severn House, 35 Manor Road, Wallington, Surrey SM6 0BW. Tel: 081-773 4161.
Sheed & Ward, 2 Creechurch Lane, London EC3A 5AQ. Tel: 071-283 6330.
Sheldon Press, Holy Trinity Church, Marylebone Road, London NW1 4DU. Tel: 071-387 5282.
Sidgwick & Jackson, Cavaye Place, London SW10 9PG. Tel: 071-373 6070.
Simon & Schuster, Campus 400, Maylands Avenue, Hemel Hempstead HP2 7EZ. Tel: 0442-881900.
Sinclair-Stevenson, 7 Kendrick Mews, London SW7 3HG. Tel: 071-581 1645.
Smythe (Colin), PO Box 6, Gerrards Cross, Bucks. SL9 8XA. Tel: 0753-886000.
Souvenir Press, 43 Great Russell Street, London WC1B 3PA. Tel: 071-580 9307.
Spon (E. & F. N.), 2 Boundary Row, London SE1 8HN. Tel: 071-865 0066.
Stephens (Patrick), Sparkford, Yeovil BA22 7JJ. Tel: 0963-40635.
Stevens & Sons, 183 Marsh Wall, London E14 9FT. Tel: 071-538 8686.
Sweet & Maxwell, 183 Marsh Wall, London E14 9FT. Tel: 071-538 8686.
Thames & Hudson, 30 Bloomsbury Street, London WC1B 3QP. Tel: 071-636 5488.
Thorsons, 77 Fulham Palace Road, London W6 8JB. Tel: 081-741 7070.
Times Books, 77 Fulham Palace Road, London W6 8JB. Tel: 081-741 7070.
University of Wales Press, Gwennyth Street, Cardiff CF2 4YD. Tel: 0222-231919.
Vallentine Mitchell, 11 Gainsborough Road, London E11 1RS. Tel: 081-530 4226.
Viking, 27 Wright's Lane, London W8 5TZ. Tel: 071-938 2200.
Virago Press, 20–23 Mandela Street, London NW1 0HQ. Tel: 071-383 5150.
Virgin Publishing, 26 Grand Union Centre, 338 Ladbroke Grove, London W10 5AH. Tel: 081-968 7554.
Walker Books, 87 Vauxhall Walk, London SE11 5HJ. Tel: 071-793 0909.
Ward Lock, 41 Strand, London WC2N 5JE. Tel: 071-839 4900.
Ward Lock Educational Co., 1 Christopher Road, East Grinstead, W. Sussex RH19 3BT. Tel: 0342-318980.
Warne (Frederick), 27 Wright's Lane, London W8 5TZ. Tel: 071-938 2200.
Watts (Franklin), 96 Leonard Street, London EC2A 4RH. Tel: 071-739 2929.
Webb & Bower, 5 Cathedral Close, Exeter EX1 1EZ. Tel: 0392-435362.
Weidenfeld & Nicolson, 5 Upper St Martin's Lane, London WC2H 9EA. Tel: 071-240 3444.
Whitaker (J.), 12 Dyott Street, London WC1A 1DF. Tel: 071-836 8911.
Wildwood House, Gower House, Croft Road, Aldershot, Hants. GU11 3HR. Tel: 0252-331551.
Wisden (John), 25 Down Road, Merrow, Guildford GU1 2PY. Tel: 0483-570358.
Witherby (H. F. & G.), 14 Henrietta Street, London WC2E 8QJ. Tel: 071-836 2006.
World's Work, *see* Heinemann (William).

Annual Reference Books

If the address of the editorial office of a publication differs from the address to which orders should be sent, the address given is usually the one for orders.

ADVERTISER'S ANNUAL, East Grinstead House, East Grinstead, W. Sussex RH19 1XA. 3v, £155.00.
ALLIED DUNBAR INVESTMENT GUIDE, PO Box 88, Harlow, Essex CM19 5SR. £17.99.
ALLIED DUNBAR TAX GUIDE, PO Box 88, Harlow, Essex CM19 5SR. £17.99.
ANNUAL REGISTER OF WORLD EVENTS, PO Box 88, Harlow, Essex CM19 5SR. £84.00.
ANTIQUE SHOPS OF BRITAIN, GUIDE TO THE, 5 Church Street, Woodbridge, Suffolk IP12 1DS. £14.50.
ART SALES INDEX, 1 Thames Street, Weybridge, Surrey KT1 8JG. £92.00.
ASSOCIATION OF CONSULTING ENGINEERS DIRECTORY OF MEMBERS FIRMS, Alliance House, 12 Caxton Street, London SW1H 0QL. £10.00.
ASTRONOMICAL ALMANAC, HMSO, PO Box 276, London SW8 5DT. (Aug.) £15.00.
AUTOMOBILE YEAR, Unit 6, Pilton Estate, Croydon, Surrey CR0 3RY. £27.95.
BAILY'S HUNTING DIRECTORY, 10 Sheet Street, Windsor, Berks. SL4 1BG. (Oct.) £27.50.
BANKER'S ALMANAC AND YEAR BOOK, East Grinstead House, East Grinstead, W. Sussex RH19 1XE. (Feb.) 2 v. £212.00.
BENEDICTINE AND CISTERCIAN MONASTIC YEAR BOOK, Ampleforth Abbey, York YO6 4EN. £1.00.
BENN'S HOUSEWARES, DO-IT-YOURSELF, GARDENS, PO Box 20, Sovereign Way, Tonbridge, Kent TN9 1RQ. £60.00.
BENN'S MEDIA DIRECTORY, PO Box 20, Sovereign Way, Tonbridge, Kent TN9 1RQ. 3v. £225.00.
BIRMINGHAM POST AND MAIL YEAR BOOK AND WHO'S WHO, 137 Newhall Street, Birmingham B3 1SF. (Sept.) £18.90.
BRITAIN: AN OFFICIAL HANDBOOK, HMSO, PO Box 276, London SW8 5DT. (Jan.) £17.95.
BRITANNICA BOOK OF THE YEAR, Carew House, Station Approach, Wallington, Surrey SM6 0DA. (April) £52.00.
BRITISH CLOTHING INDUSTRY YEAR BOOK, Westbury House, 701–705 Warwick Road, Solihull B91 3DA. £49.00.
BRITISH EXPORTS, East Grinstead House, East Grinstead, W. Sussex RH19 1XB. £115.00.
BRITISH MUSIC WORLDWIDE, 241 Shaftesbury Avenue, London WC2H 8EH. £20.00, £15.00.
BRITISH PLASTICS AND RUBBER DIRECTORY, Catalyst House, 159 Clapham High Street, London SW4 7SS. £10.00.
BROWN'S NAUTICAL ALMANACK DAILY TIDE TABLES, 4–10 Darnley Street, Glasgow G41 2SD. (Sept.) £30.00.
BUILDING SOCIETIES YEAR BOOK, South Quay Plaza, 183 Marsh Wall, London E14 9FS. £52.00.
BUSES YEARBOOK, Terminal House, Station Approach, Shepperton, Middx. TW17 8AS. £9.95.
CARPET ANNUAL, PO Box 20, Sovereign Way, Tonbridge, Kent TN9 1RQ. £67.00.
CATHOLIC DIRECTORY OF ENGLAND AND WALES, 18 Crosby Road North, Liverpool L22 4QF. £17.50.
CHARITIES DIGEST, 501–505 Kingsland Road, London E8 4AU. £14.95.
CHEMICAL INDUSTRY DIRECTORY, PO Box 20, Sovereign Way, Tonbridge, Kent TN9 1RQ. £99.00.
CHEMIST AND DRUGGIST DIRECTORY, PO Box 20, Sovereign Way, Tonbridge, Kent TN9 1RQ. £78.00.
CHRISTIES' REVIEW OF THE SEASON, Musterlin House, Jordan Hill Road, Oxford OX2 8DP. (Dec.) £30.00.
CHURCH OF ENGLAND YEAR BOOK, Church House, Dean's Yard, Westminster, London SW1P 3NZ. (Jan.) £15.00.
CHURCH OF SCOTLAND YEAR BOOK, 121 George Street, Edinburgh EH2 4YN. (April) £9.95.
CITY OF LONDON DIRECTORY AND LIVERY COMPANIES GUIDE, Seatrade House, 42–48 North Station Road, Colchester, Essex CO1 1RB. £18.50, £16.50.
CIVIL SERVICE YEAR BOOK, HMSO, PO Box 276, London SW8 5DT. (Feb.) £18.50.
COMMONWEALTH UNIVERSITIES YEAR BOOK, 36 Gordon Square, London WC1H 0PF. (Sept.) £118.00.
COMMONWEALTH YEAR BOOK, HMSO, PO Box 276, London SW8 5DT. (May) £22.00.
COMPUTER USERS' YEAR BOOK, 32–34 Broadwick Street, London W1A 2HG. £136.50.
CONCRETE YEAR BOOK, Thomas Telford House, 1 Heron Quay, London E14 9XF. 2v. £55.00.
CURRENT LAW YEAR BOOK, South Quay Plaza, 183 Marsh Wall, London E14 9FT. £90.00.
DIPLOMATIC SERVICE LIST, HMSO, PO Box 276, London SW8 5DT. (April) £18.00.
DIRECTORY OF DIRECTORS, East Grinstead House, East Grinstead, W. Sussex RH19 1XE. (April) £152.50.
DIRECTORY OF OFFICIAL ARCHITECTURE AND PLANNING, PO Box 88, Harlow, Essex CM19 5SR. £59.00.
DIRECTORY OF OPPORTUNITIES FOR GRADUATES, Newpoint House, St James's Lane, London N10 3DF. 7v. each £7.95.
DOD'S PARLIAMENTARY COMPANION, Hurst Green, Etchingham, E. Sussex TN19 7PX. £65.00.
EDUCATION AUTHORITIES' DIRECTORY AND ANNUAL, Derby House, Bletchingley Road, Merstham, Surrey RH1 3DN. (Jan.) £58.00, £52.00.
EDUCATION YEAR BOOK, PO Box 88, Harlow, Essex CM19 5SR. £63.00.
ELECTRICAL AND ELECTRONICS TRADES DIRECTORY, Michael Faraday House, Six Hills Way, Stevenage, Herts. SG1 2AY. (Feb.) £66.00.
ELECTRICITY SUPPLY HANDBOOK, Quadrant House, The Quadrant, Sutton, Surrey SM2 5AS. (Feb.) £30.00.
ENGINEER BUYERS' GUIDE, 40 Beresford Street, London SE18 6BQ. £48.00.
EUROPA WORLD YEAR BOOK, 18 Bedford Square, London WC1B 3JN. 2v. £265.00.
EUROPEAN FOOD TRADES DIRECTORY, 32 Vauxhall Bridge Road, London SW1V 2SS. 2v. £105.00.
EUROPEAN GLASS DIRECTORY AND BUYER'S GUIDE, 2 Queensway, Redhill, Surrey RH1 1QS. £76.00.
FAIRPLAY WORLD SHIPPING YEARBOOK, PO Box 96, Coulsdon, Surrey CR5 2TE. £79.00.
FLIGHT INTERNATIONAL DIRECTORY, PO Box 1315, Potters Bar, Herts. EN6 1PU. 2v. £36.00; £40.00.
FROZEN AND CHILLED FOODS YEAR BOOK, 2 Queensway, Redhill, Surrey RH1 1QS. £64.00.
FURNISHING TRADE, DIRECTORY TO THE, PO Box 20, Sovereign Way, Tonbridge, Kent TN9 1RQ. £85.00.
GAS INDUSTRY DIRECTORY, PO Box 20, Sovereign Way, Tonbridge, Kent TN9 1RQ. (Jan.) £70.00.
GIBBONS' STAMPS OF THE WORLD CATALOGUE, 5 Parkside, Christchurch Road, Ringwood, Hants. BH24 3SH. (Oct.) 3v. each £18.00.

GOOD FOOD GUIDE, PO Box 6, Mill Road, Dunton Green, Sevenoaks, Kent TN13 2YA. £14.99.
GOOD HOTEL GUIDE, Brunel Road, Houndmills, Basingstoke, Hants. RG21 2XS. £14.99.
GOVERNMENT AND MUNICIPAL CONTRACTORS REGISTER, 55 High Street, Epsom, Surrey KT19 8DW. (Jan.) £45.00.
GUINNESS BOOK OF ANSWERS, 33 London Road, Enfield EN2 6DJ. £12.99.
GUINNESS BOOK OF RECORDS, 33 London Road, Enfield EN2 6DJ. (Oct.) £13.99.
HISTORIC HOUSES, CASTLES AND GARDENS IN GREAT BRITAIN AND IRELAND, Star Road, Partridge Green, Horsham, W. Sussex RH13 8LD. (Feb.) £6.95.
HOLLIS PRESS AND PR ANNUAL, Contact House, Lower Hampton Road, Sunbury-on-Thames TW16 5HG. (Oct.) £84.50.
HOSPITALS AND HEALTH SERVICES YEARBOOK AND DIRECTORY OF HOSPITAL SUPPLIERS, 75 Portland Place, London W1N 4AN. £70.00.
HOTEL, RESTAURANT AND CATERING SUPPLIES, 55 High Street, Epsom, Surrey KT19 8DW. £40.00.
HUTCHINS' PRICED SCHEDULES, 33 Station Road, Bexhill-on-Sea, E. Sussex TN40 1RG. £35.00.
INDEPENDENT SCHOOLS YEAR BOOK, 35 Bedford Row, London WC1R 4JH. £19.99.
INTERNATIONAL PAPER DIRECTORY, PHILIPS', PO Box 20, Sovereign Way, Tonbridge, Kent TN9 1RQ. £100.00.
INTERNATIONAL WHO'S WHO, 18 Bedford Square, London WC1R 4JH. (Sept.) £125.00.
INTERNATIONAL YEARBOOK AND STATESMAN'S WHO'S WHO, East Grinstead House, East Grinstead, W. Sussex RH19 1XE. (April) £132.00.
JANE'S ALL THE WORLD'S AIRCRAFT, Sentinel House, 163 Brighton Road, Coulsdon, Surrey CR3 2NX. (Oct.) £135.00.
JANE'S ARMOUR AND ARTILLERY, Sentinel House, 163 Brighton Road, Coulsdon, Surrey CR3 2NX. (Nov.) £135.00.
JANE'S CONTAINERIZATION DIRECT, Sentinel House, 163 Brighton Road, Coulsdon, Surrey CR3 2NX. (Nov.) £135.00.
JANE'S FIGHTING SHIPS, Sentinel House, 163 Brighton Road, Coulsdon, Surrey CR3 2NX. £135.00.
JANE'S HIGH SPEED MARINE CRAFT AND AIR CUSHION VEHICLES, Sentinel House, 163 Brighton Road, Coulsdon, Surrey CR3 2NX. £135.00.
JANE'S INFANTRY WEAPONS, Sentinel House, 163 Brighton Road, Coulsdon, Surrey CR3 2NX. (Aug.) £135.00.
JANE'S NAVAL WEAPON SYSTEMS, Sentinel House, 163 Brighton Road, Coulsdon, Surrey CR3 2NX. £250.00.
JANE'S WORLD RAILWAYS, Sentinel House, 163 Brighton Road, Coulsdon, Surrey CR3 2NX. £135.00.
JEWISH YEAR BOOK, 25 Furnival Street, London EC4A 1JT. (Jan.) £14.00.
KELLY'S BUSINESS DIRECTORY, East Grinstead House, East Grinstead, W. Sussex RH19 1XB. £130.00.
KEMPE'S ENGINEERS YEAR BOOK, 40 Beresford Street, London SE18 6BQ. £95.00.
KEMP'S INTERNATIONAL FILM AND TV YEAR BOOK, Windsor Court, East Grinstead House, East Grinstead, W. Sussex RH19 1XA. £50.00.
KEMP'S INTERNATIONAL MUSIC BOOK, 12 Felix Avenue, London N8 9TL. £28.00.
KIME'S INTERNATIONAL LAW DIRECTORY, PO Box 88, Harlow, Essex CM19 5SR. (Dec.) £45.00.
LAXTON'S BUILDING PRICE BOOK, East Grinstead House, East Grinstead, W. Sussex RH19 1XE. £79.50.
LIBRARY ASSOCIATION YEARBOOK, 7 Ridgmount Street, London WC1E 7AE. (May) £29.50.
LLOYD'S LIST OF SHIPOWNERS, 71 Fenchurch Street, London EC3M 4BS. (Sept.) £70.00.
LLOYD'S MARITIME DIRECTORY, Sheepen Place, Colchester CO3 3LP. (Jan.) £130.00.
LLOYD'S NAUTICAL YEAR BOOK, Sheepen Place, Colchester CO3 3LP. (Sept.) £32.00.
LLOYD'S REGISTER OF SHIPS, 71 Fenchurch Street, London EC3M 4BS. (July). £275.00.
LONDON TRADE DIRECTORY, 3rd Floor, Albany House, Hurst Street, Birmingham B5 4BD. (Sept.) £75.00.
LYLE'S OFFICIAL ANTIQUES REVIEW, Glenmayne, Galashiels TD1 3NR. £16.95.
LYLE'S OFFICIAL ARTS REVIEW, Glenmayne, Galashiels TD1 3NR. £16.95.
MACMILLAN AND SILK CUT NAUTICAL ALMANACK, Brunel Road, Houndmills, Basingstoke, Hants. RG21 2XS. £21.95.
MAGISTRATES' COURT GUIDE, Borough Green, Sevenoaks, Kent TN15 8PH. £17.95.
MEDICAL ANNUAL, Falcon House, Queen Square, Lancaster LA1 1RN. £25.00.
MEDICAL DIRECTORY, PO Box 88, Harlow, Essex CM19 5SR. (April) 3v. £135.00.
MEDICAL REGISTER, 44 Hallam Street, London W1N 6AE. (March) 3v. £90.00.
MIDDLE EAST AND NORTH AFRICA, 18 Bedford Square, London WC1B 3JN. (Oct.) £130.00.
MILLER'S ANTIQUES PRICE GUIDE, The Cellars, 5 High Street, Tenterden, Kent TN30 6BN. £19.99.
MINING ANNUAL REVIEW, PO Box 10, Edenbridge, Kent TN8 5NE. £50.00.
MINING INTERNATIONAL YEAR BOOK, PO Box 88, Harlow, Essex CM19 5SR. (June) £115.00.
MOTOR INDUSTRY OF GREAT BRITAIN WORLD AUTOMOTIVE STATISTICS, Forbes House, Halkin Street, London SW1X 7DS. (Oct.) £75.00.
MOTOR SHIP DIRECTORY, Quadrant House, The Quadrant, Sutton, Surrey SM2 5AS. £80.00.
MUNICIPAL YEARBOOK AND PUBLIC SERVICES DIRECTORY, 32 Vauxhall Bridge Road, London SW1V 2SS. (Dec.) 2v. £110.00.
MUSEUMS AND GALLERIES IN GREAT BRITAIN AND IRELAND, Star Road, Partridge Green, Horsham, W. Sussex RH13 8LD. (Nov.) £6.40.
NAUTICAL ALMANAC, HMSO, PO Box 276, London SW8 5DT. (Oct.) £16.50.
OWEN'S AFRICA BUSINESS DIRECTORY, 18 Farndon Road, Oxford OX6 2RT. £60.00.
OWEN'S GULF DIRECTORY, 18 Farndon Road, Oxford OX6 2RT. £90.00.
PACKAGING INDUSTRY DIRECTORY, PO Box 20, Sovereign Way, Tonbridge, Kent TN9 1RQ. £62.00.
PEARS CYCLOPEDIA, 27 Wright's Lane, London W8 5TZ. £13.99.
PHOTOGRAPHY YEAR BOOK, Queensborough House, 2 Claremont Road, Surbiton, Surrey KT6 4QU. £18.95.
POLYMERS, PAINT AND COLOUR YEAR BOOK, 2 Queensway, Redhill, Surrey RH1 1QS. £82.00.
PORTS OF THE WORLD, Sheepen Place, Colchester, Essex CO3 3LP. £125.00.
PRINTERS' YEAR BOOK, 11 Bedford Row, London WC1R 4DX. £40.00.
PRINTING TRADES DIRECTORY, PO Box 20, Sovereign Way, Tonbridge, Kent TN9 1RQ. £82.00.
PUBLISHING, DIRECTORY OF, Artillery House, Artillery Row, London SW1P 1RT. (Oct.) £40.00.

RAC EUROPEAN HOTEL GUIDE, PO Box 100, RAC House, Lansdowne Road, Croydon CR9 2JA. (Jan.) £8.95.
RAC HOTEL GUIDE, PO Box 100, RAC House, Lansdowne Road, Croydon CR9 2JA. (Nov.) £15.99, £12.99.
RAILWAY DIRECTORY AND YEAR BOOK, Quadrant House, The Quadrant, Sutton, Surrey SM2 5AS. (Dec.) £50.00.
RETAIL DIRECTORY OF THE UNITED KINGDOM, 32 Vauxhall Bridge Road, London SW1V 2SS. £116.00.
RIBA DIRECTORY OF PRACTICES, Royal Institute of British Architects, 39 Moreland Street, London EC1V 8BB. (Oct.) £45.00.
ROTHMANS FOOTBALL YEAR BOOK, Headline House, 79 Great Titchfield Street, London W1P 7FN. (Aug.) £19.99, £14.99.
ROYAL SOCIETY YEAR BOOK, 6 Carlton House Terrace, London SW1Y 5AG. (Feb.) £15.00.
RUFF'S GUIDE TO THE TURF AND SPORTING LIFE ANNUAL, Orbit House, 1 New Fetter Lane, London EC4A 1AR. (Jan.) £50.00.
RUSI AND BRASSEY'S DEFENCE YEAR BOOK, 50 Fetter Lane, London EC4A 1AA. £38.50.
SALVATION ARMY YEAR BOOK, 117–121 Judd Street, London WC1H 9NN. (April) £8.95, £4.25.
SCOTTISH CURRENT LAW YEAR BOOK, 2 St Giles Street, Edinburgh EH1 1PU. £290.00.
SCOTTISH LAW DIRECTORY, 59 George Street, Edinburgh EH2 2LQ. £29.00.
SCREEN WORLD, Random Century House, 20 Vauxhall Bridge Road, London SW1V 2SA. £17.99.
SELL'S AEROSPACE EUROPE, 55 High Street, Epsom, Surrey KT19 8DW. £50.00.
SELL'S BRITISH EXPORTERS, 55 High Street, Epsom, Surrey KT19 8DW. £40.00.
SELL'S BUILDING INDEX, 55 High Street, Epsom, Surrey KT19 8DW. £45.00.
SELL'S DIRECTORY OF PRODUCTS AND SERVICES, 55 High Street, Epsom, Surrey KT19 8DW. (July) £65.00.
SELL'S HEALTH SERVICE BUYERS GUIDE, 55 High Street, Epsom, Surrey KT19 8DW. £65.00.
SHEET METAL INDUSTRIES YEAR BOOK, 2 Queensway, Redhill, Surrey RH1 1QS. £51.00.
SOLICITORS AND BARRISTERS DIRECTORY, 4 Durham Road, Borehamwood, Herts. WD6 1LW. £43.00.
SPON'S ARCHITECTS' AND BUILDERS' PRICE BOOK, 2–6 Boundary Row, London SE1 8HN. £52.50.
SPON'S MECHANICAL AND ELECTRICAL SERVICES PRICES BOOK, 2–6 Boundary Row, London SE1 8HN. £55.00.
STATESMAN'S YEARBOOK, Brunel House, Houndmills, Basingstoke, Hants. RG21 2XS. (Aug.) £37.50.
STOCK EXCHANGE OFFICIAL YEAR BOOK, Brunel House, Houndmills, Basingstoke, Hants. RG21 2XS. £180.00.
STONE'S JUSTICES' MANUAL, Borough Green, Sevenoaks, Kent TN15 8PH. 3v. (May) £165.00.
TANKER REGISTER, 12 Camomile Street, London EC3A 7BP. (May) £140.00.
TIMBER TRADES JOURNAL TELEPHONE ADDRESS BOOK, Sovereign Way, Tonbridge, Kent TN9 1RQ. £42.00.
TRAINING DIRECTORY, 120 Pentonville Road, London N1 9JN. £25.00.
TRAVEL TRADE DIRECTORY, 40 Beresford Street, London SE18 6BQ. (July) £45.00.
UK KOMPASS REGISTER, East Grinstead House, East Grinstead, W. Sussex RH19 1XD. 5v. £615.00.
UNITED KINGDOM MINERALS YEARBOOK, British Geological Survey, Keyworth, Nottingham NG12 5GG. £27.50.
UNITED REFORMED CHURCH YEAR BOOK, 86 Tavistock Place, London WC1H 9RT. (Sept.) £7.50.
UNIT TRUST YEAR BOOK, 7th Floor, 50–64 Broadway, London SW1H 0DB. (March) £95.00.
VETERINARY ANNUAL, Osney Mead, Oxford OX2 0EL. £59.50.
WATER SERVICES YEAR BOOK, 2 Queensway, Redhill, Surrey RH1 1QS. (Oct.) £52.00.
WHITAKER'S ALMANACK, 12 Dyott Street, London WC1A 1DF. (Nov.) £40.00, £25.00.
WHITAKER'S BOOKS IN PRINT, 12 Dyott Street, London WC1A 1DF. (Sept.) £215.00.
WHITAKER'S CONCISE ALMANACK, 12 Dyott Street, London WC1A 1DF. (Nov.) £9.95.
WHITAKER'S PUBLISHERS IN THE UNITED KINGDOM AND THEIR ADDRESSES, 12 Dyott Street, London WC1A 1DF. (March) £8.50.
WHO OWNS WHOM? – Holmers Farm Way, High Wycombe, Bucks. HP12 4UL. 2v. £239.00.
WHO'S WHO, 35 Bedford Row, London WC1R 4JH. £85.00.
WILLING'S PRESS GUIDE, East Grinstead House, East Grinstead, W. Sussex RH19 1XE. (Feb.) 2v. £125.00.
WISDEN CRICKETERS' ALMANACK, 13–14 Eldon Way, Lineside Estate, Littlehampton, W. Sussex BN17 7HE. (April) £21.50, £18.50.
WORLD HOTEL DIRECTORY, PO Box 88, Harlow, Essex CM19 5SR. £85.00.
WORLD INSURANCE, PO Box 88, Harlow, Essex CM19 5SR. £115.00.
WORLD MINERAL STATISTICS, British Geological Survey, Keyworth, Notts. NG12 5GG. (Sept.) £50.00.
WORLD OF LEARNING, 18 Bedford Square, London WC1B 3JN. (Jan.) 2v. £165.00.
WRITERS' AND ARTISTS' YEAR BOOK, 35 Bedford Row, London WC1R 4JH. (Oct.) £8.99.

Employers' and Trade Associations

At the end of 1991 there were 131 employers' associations listed by the Certification Officer (*see* page 297). Most national employers' associations are members of the Confederation of British Industry (CBI). For ACAS, the Certification Office, the Commission for Racial Equality, the Equal Opportunities Commission, the Health and Safety Commission, the Industrial Tribunals and Review Bodies, *see* Index.

CONFEDERATION OF BRITISH INDUSTRY

Centre Point, 103 New Oxford Street, London WC1A 1DU
Tel 071-379 7400

The Confederation of British Industry was founded in 1965 and is an independent non-party political body financed by industry and commerce. It exists primarily to ensure that the Government understands the intentions, needs and problems of British business. It is the recognized spokesman for the business viewpoint and is consulted as such by the Government.

The CBI represents, directly and indirectly, some 250,000 companies, large and small, from all sectors as well as state-run companies.

The governing body of the CBI is the 400-strong Council, which meets monthly in London under the chairmanship of the President. It is assisted by some 27 expert standing committees which advise on the main aspects of policy. There are 13 regional councils and offices covering the administrative regions of England, Wales, Scotland and Northern Ireland. There is also an office in Brussels.

President, Sir Michael Angus.
Director-General, H. Davies.
Secretary, M. W. Hunt.

ASSOCIATIONS

ADVERTISING ASSOCIATION, Abford House, 15 Wilton Road, London SW1V 1NJ. Tel: 071-828 2771. *Director-General*, R. L. Wade.

AEROSPACE COMPANIES LTD, SOCIETY OF BRITISH, 29 King Street, London SW1Y 6RD. Tel: 071-839 3231. *Director*, Sir Barry Duxbury, KCB, CBE.

BAKERS, FEDERATION OF, 20 Bedford Square, London WC1B 3HF. *Director*, A. Casdagli, CBE.

BANKERS' ASSOCIATION, BRITISH, 10 Lombard Street, London EC3V 9EL. Tel: 071-623 4001. *Secretary-General*, The Lord Inchyra.

BLIND AND DISABLED INC., NATIONAL ASSOCIATION OF INDUSTRIES FOR THE, Triton House, 43A High Street South, Dunstable, Beds. LU6 3RZ. Tel: 0582-606796. *Hon. Secretary*, G. J. Entwistle.

BREWERS' SOCIETY, 42 Portman Square, London W1H 0BB. Tel: 071-486 4831. *Director-General*, A. G. Tilbury, CBE.

BUILDING EMPLOYERS' CONFEDERATION, 82 New Cavendish Street, London W1M 8AD. Tel: 071-580 5588. *Director-General (acting)*, I. A. Deslandes.

BUILDING MATERIAL PRODUCERS, NATIONAL COUNCIL OF, 26 Store Street, London WC1E 7BT. Tel: 071-323 3770. *Director-General*, N. M. Chaldecott, OBE.

BUS AND COACH COUNCIL, Sardinia House, 52 Lincoln's Inn Fields, London WC2A 3LZ. Tel: 071-831 7546. *Director-General*, Mrs A. V. M. Palmer, MBE.

CHAMBER OF SHIPPING LTD, Minories House, 2–5 Minories, London EC3N 1BJ. Tel: 071-283 2922. *Director-General*, Adm. Sir Nicholas Hunt, GCB, LVO.

CHEMICAL INDUSTRIES ASSOCIATION LTD., Kings Buildings, Smith Square, London SW1P 3JJ. Tel: 071-834 3399. *Director-General*, J. C. L. Cox.

CLOTHING INDUSTRY ASSOCIATION LTD, BRITISH, British Apparel and Textiles Centre, 7 Swallow Place, London W1R 7AA. Tel: 071-408 0020. *Director* J. R. Wilson.

DAIRY TRADE FEDERATION, 19 Cornwall Terrace, London NW1 4QP. Tel: 071-486 7244. *Director-General*, J. P. Price.

ELECTROTECHNICAL AND ALLIED MANUFACTURERS' ASSOCIATIONS, FEDERATION OF BRITISH (BEAMA), Leicester House, 8 Leicester Street, London WC2H 7BN. Tel: 071-437 0678. *Director-General*, J. G. Gaddes.

ENGINEERING EMPLOYERS' FEDERATION, Broadway House, Tothill Street, London SW1H 9NQ. Tel: 071-222 7777. *Director-General*, N. A. Johnson, OBE.

FARMERS' UNION, NATIONAL (NFU), 22 Long Acre, London WC2E 9LY. Tel: 071-235 5077. *Director-General*, D. Evans, CBE.

FARMERS' UNION OF SCOTLAND, NATIONAL, Rural Centre-West Mains, Ingliston, Newbridge, Midlothian EH28 8LT. Tel: 031-335 3111. *Chief Executive*, D. S. Johnston, OBE.

FARMERS' UNION, ULSTER, Dunedin, 475–477 Antrim Road, Belfast BT15 3DA. Tel: 0232-370222. *General Secretary*, J. V. Smyth.

FINANCE AND LEASING ASSOCIATION, 18 Upper Grosvenor Street, London W1X 9PB. Tel: 071-491 2783. *Director*, N. A. D. Grant, CBE.

FOOD AND DRINK FEDERATION, 6 Catherine Street, London WC2B 5JJ. Tel: 071-836 2460. *Director-General*, M. P. Mackenzie.

FREIGHT TRANSPORT ASSOCIATION LTD., Hermes House, 157 St John's Road, Tunbridge Wells, Kent TN4 9UZ. Tel: 0892-26171. *Director-General*, G. Turvey, CBE.

INSURERS, ASSOCIATION OF BRITISH, 51 Gresham Street, London EC2V 7HQ. Tel: 071-600 3333. *Chief Executive*, M. A. Jones.

KNITTING INDUSTRIES FEDERATION LTD., 7 Gregory Boulevard, Nottingham NG7 6NB. Tel: 0602-621081. *Director*, J. P. Harrison.

LEATHER CONFEDERATION, BRITISH, Leather Trade House, Kings Park Road, Moulton Park, Northampton NN3 1JD. Tel: 0604-494131. *Chief Executive*, Dr K. T. W. Alexander.

LEATHER PRODUCERS' ASSOCIATION, Leather Trade House, Kings Park Road, Moulton Park, Northampton NN3 1JD. Tel: 0604-494131. *National Secretary*, J. Purvis.

MANAGEMENT CONSULTANCIES ASSOCIATION, 11 West Halkin Street, London SW1X 8JL. Tel: 071-235 3897. *Executive Director*, B. O'Rorke.

MARINE INDUSTRIES FEDERATION, BRITISH, Meadlake Place, Thorpe Lea Road, Egham, Surrey TW20 8HE. Tel: 0784-473377. *Chief Executive*, P. V. Wagstaffe.

MOTOR MANUFACTURERS AND TRADERS LTD., SOCIETY OF, Forbes House, Halkin Street, London SWIX 7DS. Tel: 071-235 7000. *Chief Executive*, Sir Hal Miller.

NEWSPAPER PUBLISHERS ASSOCIATION LTD., 34 Southwark Bridge Road, London SEI 9EU. Tel: 071-928 6928. *Director*, D. Pollock.

OFFICE SYSTEMS AND STATIONERY FEDERATION, BRITISH, 6 Wimpole Street, London WIM 8AS. Tel: 071-637 7692. *Director*, D. F. Hall.

PAPER AND BOARD INDUSTRY FEDERATION, BRITISH, Papermakers House, Rivenhall Road, Westlea, Swindon SN5 7BD. Tel: 0793-886086. *Director-General*, W. J. Bartlett.

PLASTICS FEDERATION, BRITISH, 5 Belgrave Square, London SWIX 8PD. Tel: 071-235 9483. *Director*, D. R. Jones.

PORTS FEDERATION, BRITISH, Victoria House, Vernon Place, London WCIB 4LL. Tel: 071-242 1200. *Managing Director*, J. Sharples.

PRINTING INDUSTRIES FEDERATION, BRITISH, 11 Bedford Row, London WCIR 4DX. Tel: 071-242 6904. *Director-General*, C. Stanley.

PUBLISHERS ASSOCIATION, THE, 19 Bedford Square, London WCIB 3HJ. Tel: 071-580 6321. *Chief Executive*, C. Bradley.

RADIO COMPANIES LTD, ASSOCIATION OF INDEPENDENT, Radio House, 46 Westbourne Grove, London W2 5SH. Tel: 071-727 2646. *Chief Executive*, B. West.

RETAIL CONSORTIUM, BRITISH, Bedford House, 69–79 Fulham High Street, London SW6 3JW. Tel: 071-371 5185. *Director-General*, J. N. W. May.

RETAIL NEWSAGENTS, NATIONAL FEDERATION OF, Yeoman House, Sekforde Street, London ECIR OHD. Tel: 071-253 4225. *Chief Executive*, K. E. J. Peters.

ROAD FEDERATION, BRITISH, Pillar House, 194–202 Old Kent Road, London SEI 5TG. Tel: 071-703 9769. *Director*, R. Diment.

ROAD HAULAGE ASSOCIATION LTD., Roadway House, 35 Monument Hill, Weybridge, Surrey KT13 8RN. Tel: 0932-841515. *Director-General*, D. B. H. Colley, CB, CBE.

RUBBER MANUFACTURERS' ASSOCIATION LTD, BRITISH, 90 Tottenham Court Road, London WIP OBR. Tel: 071-580 2794. *Director*, W. R. Pollock.

SPORTS AND ALLIED INDUSTRIES FEDERATION LTD, BRITISH, 23 Brighton Road, Croydon CR2 4EA. Tel: 081-681 1242. *Chief Executive*, L. F. Standen.

TELEVISION ASSOCIATION, INDEPENDENT, Knighton House, 56 Mortimer Street, London WIN 8AN. Tel: 071-612 8000. *Director*, D. Shaw.

TEXTILE CONFEDERATION, BRITISH, British Apparel and Textiles Centre, 7 Swallow Place, London WIR 7AA. Tel: 071-491 9702. *Director*, C. M. Purvis.

TIMBER GROWERS' UNITED KINGDOM, 5 Dublin Street, Lane South, Edinburgh EHI 3PX. Tel: 031-557 0944. *Chief Executive*, A. J. Murray (P. H. Wilson from February 1993).

TIMBER MERCHANTS' ASSOCIATION, BRITISH, Stocking Lane, Hughenden Valley, High Wycombe, Bucks. HP14 4JZ. Tel: 0494-563602. *Secretary*, R. T. Allcorn.

TIMBER TRADE FEDERATION, Clareville House, 26–27 Oxendon Street, London SWIY 4EL. Tel: 071-839 1891. *Director-General*, P. G. Harris.

UK OFFSHORE OPERATORS ASSOCIATION LTD., 3 Hans Crescent, London SWIX OLN. Tel: 071-589 5255. *Director-General*, Dr H. W. D. Hughes, OBE.

UK PETROLEUM INDUSTRY ASSOCIATION LTD., 9 Kingsway, London WC2B 6XH. Tel: 071-240 0289. *Director-General*, D. Parker.

WHOLESALE AND INDUSTRIAL DISTRIBUTORS, FEDERATION OF, The Old Post Office, Dunchideock, Exeter EX2 9TU. Tel: 0392-832559. *Director*, vacant.

Trade Unions

At the end of 1991 there were 309 trade unions listed by the Certification Officer (*see* page 297). In 1990 9,810,019 people were members of listed trade unions, representing about 34.5 per cent of the total labour force. Over 80 per cent of trade union members belong to the 73 unions affiliated to the TUC (*see* below).

The Central Arbitration Committee arbitrates in disclosure of information disputes between trade unions and employers. The Commissioner for the Rights of Trade Union Members provides assistance to individuals taking action against their trade union when they have not been afforded their statutory rights or when specific union rules have been breached. For ACAS, the Certification Office, the Commission for Racial Equality, the Equal Opportunities Commission, the Health and Safety Commission, the Industrial Tribunals and Review Bodies, *see* Index.

THE CENTRAL ARBITRATION COMMITTEE, 39 Grosvenor Place, London SW1X 7BD. Tel: 071-210 3737. *Chairman*, Prof. Sir John Wood, CBE.

THE COMMISSIONER FOR THE RIGHTS OF TRADE UNION MEMBERS, 1st Floor, Bank Chambers, 2A Rylands Street, Warrington, Cheshire WA1 1EN. Tel: 0925-415771. *Commissioner*, Mrs G. Rowlands.

TRADES UNION CONGRESS (TUC)

Congress House, 23–28 Great Russell Street,
London WC1B 3LS
Tel 071-636 4030

The Trades Union Congress, founded in 1868, is a voluntary association of trade unions, the representatives of which meet annually to consider matters of common concern to their members. The Congress has met annually since 1871 and in recent years has met normally on the first Monday in September, its sessions extending through the succeeding four days. Congress is constituted by delegates of the affiliated unions on the basis of one delegate for every 5,000 members, or fraction thereof, on whose behalf affiliation fees are paid. Affiliated unions (in 1991–2) totalled 73 with an aggregate membership of 7,757,000.

The main business of the annual Congress is to consider the report of its General Council dealing with the activities of the Congress year, along with motions from affiliated societies on questions of policy and organization.

The standing committees of the General Council are serviced by a full time staff appointed by the General Secretary, who is himself elected by Congress.

Through the General Council and its committees the trade union movement maintains systematic relations with the Government and government departments, with the Confederation of British Industry and with a large number of other bodies both in the UK, European Community and further afield. It is represented on the Health and Safety Commission, the council of the Advisory Conciliation and Arbitration Service and a number of other bodies in Britain and abroad.

Among powers vested in the General Council by consent of the unions in Congress is the responsibility of intervening in disputes and differences between affiliated organizations; if possible, this is done through informal conciliation meetings under TUC auspices but where necessary a Disputes Committee adjudicates. The TUC is affiliated to the International Confederation of Free Trade Unions and the European TUC.

Unions retain full control of their own affairs and the only sanctions which Congress can apply are suspension or exclusion from membership.

President (1992–3), A. D. Tuffin (UCW).
General Secretary, N. D. Willis.

SCOTTISH TRADES UNION CONGRESS

16 Woodlands Terrace, Glasgow G3 6DF
Tel 041-332 4946

The Congress was formed in 1897 and acts as a national centre for the trade union movement in Scotland. In 1992 it consisted of 52 unions with a membership of 807,740 and 41 directly affiliated Trades Councils.

The Annual Congress in April elects a 34-member General Council on the basis of 8 industrial sections.

Chairperson, C. Binks.
General Secretary, C. Christie.

TRADE UNIONS AFFILIATED TO TUC

A list follows of the trade unions affiliated to the Trades Union Congress at 1 September 1992. The number of members of each union is shown in parenthesis.

AMALGAMATED ASSOCIATION OF BEAMERS, TWISTERS AND DRAWERS (HAND AND MACHINE), THE (490), 27 Every Street, Nelson, Lancs. BB9 7NE. Tel: 0282-614181. *General Secretary*, A. Brindle.

AMALGAMATED ENGINEERING UNION (AEU) (now part of Amalgamated Engineering and Electrical Union) (702,228), 110 Peckham Road, London SE15 5EL. Tel: 071-703 4231. *General Secretary*, G. H. Laird, CBE.

AMALGAMATED SOCIETY OF TEXTILE WORKERS AND KINDRED TRADES (2,300), Foxlowe, Market Place, Leek, Staffs. ST13 6AD. Tel: 0538-382068. *General Secretary*, A. Hitchmough.

ASSOCIATED SOCIETY OF LOCOMOTIVE ENGINEERS AND FIREMEN (ASLEF) (18,866), 9 Arkwright Road, London NW3 6AB. Tel: 071-431 0275. *Secretary*, D. Fullick.

ASSOCIATION OF FIRST DIVISION CIVIL SERVANTS (9,642), 2 Caxton Street, London SW1H 0QH. Tel: 071-222 6242. *General Secretary*, Ms E. Symons.

ASSOCIATION OF UNIVERSITY TEACHERS (31,000), United House, 1 Pembridge Road, London W11 3JY. Tel: 071-221 4370. *General Secretary*, vacant.

BAKERS, FOOD AND ALLIED WORKERS' UNION (34,328), Stanborough House, Great North Road, Stanborough, Welwyn Garden City, Herts. AL8 7TA. Tel: 0707-260150. *General Secretary*, J. R. Marino.

BANKING, INSURANCE AND FINANCE UNION (162,429), Sheffield House, 1B Amity Grove, London SW20 0LG. Tel: 081-946 9151. *General Secretary*, L. A. Mills.

BRITISH ACTORS' EQUITY ASSOCIATION (45,000), 8 Harley Street, London W1N 2AB. Tel: 071-636 6367. *General Secretary*, I. McGarry.

BRITISH AIR LINE PILOTS ASSOCIATION, THE (5,391), 81 New Road, Harlington, Hayes, Middx. UB3 5BG. Tel: 081-759 9331. *General Secretary*, C. Darke.
BRITISH ASSOCIATION OF COLLIERY MANAGEMENT, THE (6,694), BACM House, 317 Nottingham Road, Old Basford, Nottingham NG7 7DP. Tel: 0602-785819. *General Secretary*, J. D. Meads.
BROADCASTING, ENTERTAINMENT AND CINEMATOGRAPH TECHNICIANS' UNION (BECTU) (60,000), 181–185 Wardour Street, London W1V 4BE. Tel: 071-439 7585; 111 Wardour Street, London W1V 4AY. Tel: 071-437 8506. *General Secretary*, D. A. Hearn.
CARD SETTING MACHINE TENTERS' SOCIETY (88), 48 Scar End Lane, Staincliffe, W. Yorks. WF12 4NY. Tel: 0924-400206. *Secretary*, A. Moorhouse.
CERAMIC AND ALLIED TRADES UNION, THE (25,929), Hillcrest House, Garth Street, Stoke-on-Trent ST1 2AB. Tel: 0782-272755. *General Secretary*, A. W. Clowes.
CIVIL AND PUBLIC SERVICES ASSOCIATION, THE (124,566), 160 Falcon Road, London SW11 2LN. Tel: 071-924 2727. *General Secretary*, B. Reamsbottom.
COMMUNICATION MANAGERS' ASSOCIATION (18,200), CMA House, Ruscombe Road, Twyford, Reading RG10 9JD. Tel: 0734-342300. *General Secretary*, T. L. Deegan.
CONFEDERATION OF HEALTH SERVICE EMPLOYEES (COHSE) (201,993), Glen House, High Street, Banstead, Surrey SM7 2LH. Tel: 0737-353322. *General Secretary*, H. MacKenzie.
EDUCATIONAL INSTITUTE OF SCOTLAND, THE (46,000), 46 Moray Place, Edinburgh EH3 6BH. Tel: 031-225 6244. *General Secretary*, J. B. Martin.
ELECTRICAL AND PLUMBING INDUSTRIES UNION (4,000), Park House, 64–66 Wandsworth Common North Side, London SW18 2SH. Tel: 081-874 0458. *General Secretary*, J. Aitkin.
ENGINEERING AND FASTENERS TRADE UNION (430), 42 Galton Road, Warley, West Midlands, B67 5JU. Tel: 021-429 2594. *General Secretary*, J. Burdis.
ENGINEERS' AND MANAGERS' ASSOCIATION (39,678), Station House, Fox Lane North, Chertsey, Surrey KT16 9HW. Tel: 0932-564131. *General Secretary*, D. A. Cooper.
FILM ARTISTES' ASSOCIATION (1,937) 61 Marloes Road, London W8 6LE. Tel: 071-937 4567. *Secretary*, M. Reynel.
FIRE BRIGADES UNION, THE (48,223), Bradley House, 68 Coombe Road, Kingston upon Thames, Surrey KT2 7AE. Tel: 081-541 1765. *General Secretary*, K. Cameron.
FURNITURE, TIMBER AND ALLIED TRADES UNION (38,349), Fairfields, Roe Green, London NW9 0PT. Tel: 081-204 0273. *General Secretary*, C. A. Christopher.
GENERAL UNION OF ASSOCIATIONS OF LOOM OVERLOOKERS, THE (687), Overlookers Institute, 9 Wellington Street, St Johns, Blackburn, Lancs. BB1 8AF. Tel: 0254-51760. *President*, D. J. Rishton.
GMB (formerly GENERAL, MUNICIPAL, BOILERMAKERS AND ALLIED TRADES UNION) (860,000), 22–24 Worple Road, London SW19 4DF. Tel: 081-947 3131. *General Secretary*, J. Edmonds.
GRAPHICAL, PAPER AND MEDIA UNION (274,980), 63–67 Bromham Road, Bedford MK40 2AG. Tel: 0234-351521. *General Secretary*, A. D. Dubbins.
HEALTH VISITORS' ASSOCIATION SECTION (Manufacturing, Science and Finance Union) (15,000), 50 Southwark Street, London SE1 1UN. Tel: 071-378 7255. *General Secretary*, Ms C. Burns.
HOSPITAL CONSULTANTS AND SPECIALISTS ASSOCIATION, THE (2,346), 1 Kingsclere Road, Overton, Hants. RG25 3JP. Tel: 0256-771777. *Chief Executive*, S. J. Charkham.
INLAND REVENUE STAFF FEDERATION (57,000), Douglas Houghton House, 231 Vauxhall Bridge Road, London SW1V 1EH. Tel: 071-834 8254. *General Secretary*, C. Brooke.
INSTITUTION OF PROFESSIONALS, MANAGERS AND SPECIALISTS (90,434), 75–79 York Road, London SE1 7AQ. Tel: 071-928 9951. *General Secretary*, W. Brett.
IRON AND STEEL TRADES CONFEDERATION, THE (39,161), Swinton House, 324 Gray's Inn Road, London WC1X 8DD. Tel: 071-837 6691. *General Secretary*, R. L. Evans.
MANUFACTURING, SCIENCE AND FINANCE UNION (MSF) (653,000), Park House, 64–66 Wandsworth Common North Side, London SW18 2SH. Tel: 081-871 2100. *General Secretary*, R. Lyons.
MILITARY AND ORCHESTRAL MUSICAL INSTRUMENT MAKERS' TRADE SOCIETY (43), 2 Whitehouse Avenue, Borehamwood, Herts. WD6 1HD. *General Secretary*, F. McKenzie.
MUSICIANS' UNION (37,500), 60–62 Clapham Road, London SW9 0JJ. Tel: 071-582 5566. *General Secretary*, D. Scard.
NATIONAL AND LOCAL GOVERNMENT OFFICERS' ASSOCIATION (NALGO) (759,735), 1 Mabledon Place, London WC1H 9AJ. Tel: 071-388 2366. *General Secretary*, A. Jinkinson.
NATIONAL ASSOCIATION OF COLLIERY OVERMEN, DEPUTIES AND SHOTFIRERS (6,395), Simpson House, 48 Nether Hall Road, Doncaster DN1 2PZ. Tel: 0302-368015. *Secretary*, P. McNestry.
NATIONAL ASSOCIATION OF CO-OPERATIVE OFFICIALS (4,364), Coronation House, Arndale Centre, Manchester M4 2HW. Tel: 061-834 6029. *General Secretary*, L. W. Ewing.
NATIONAL ASSOCIATION OF LICENSED HOUSE MANAGERS (11,000), 9 Coombe Lane, London SW20 8NE. Tel: 081-947 3080. *General Secretary*, J. Madden.
NATIONAL ASSOCIATION OF PROBATION OFFICERS (7,232), 3–4 Chivalry Road, London SW11 1HT. Tel: 071-223 4887. *Secretary*, W. L. Beaumont.
NATIONAL ASSOCIATION OF SCHOOLMASTERS/UNION OF WOMEN TEACHERS (NAS/UWT) (121,142), Hillscourt Education Centre, Rose Hill, Rednal, Birmingham B45 8RS. Tel: 021-453 6150. *General Secretary*, N. De Gruchy.
NATIONAL ASSOCIATION OF TEACHERS IN FURTHER AND HIGHER EDUCATION (80,000), 27 Britannia Street, London WC1X 9JP. Tel: 071-837 3636. *General Secretary*, G. Woolf.
NATIONAL COMMUNICATIONS UNION (154,783), Greystoke House, 150 Brunswick Road, London W5 1AW. Tel: 081-998 2981. *General Secretary*, A. I. Young.
NATIONAL LEAGUE OF THE BLIND AND DISABLED, THE (2,600), 2 Tenterden Road, London N17 8BE. Tel: 081-808 6030. *Secretary*, M. A. Barrett.
NATIONAL UNION OF CIVIL AND PUBLIC SERVANTS (NUCPS) (112,761), 124–130 Southwark Street, London SE1 0TU. Tel: 071-928 9671. *General Secretary*, L. Christie.
NATIONAL UNION OF DOMESTIC APPLIANCES AND GENERAL OPERATIVES, THE (3,000), 6–8 Imperial Buildings, Corporation Street, Rotherham, S. Yorks. S60 1PB. Tel: 0709-382820. *General Secretary*, A. McCarthy.

NATIONAL UNION OF INSURANCE WORKERS (18,190), 27 Old Gloucester Street, London WC1N 3AF. Tel: 071-405 6798. *General Secretary*, K. Perry.

NATIONAL UNION OF JOURNALISTS (NUJ) (30,000), Acorn House, 314–320 Gray's Inn Road, London WC1X 8DP. Tel: 071-278 7916. *General Secretary*, J. Foster.

NATIONAL UNION OF KNITWEAR, FOOTWEAR AND APPAREL TRADES (64,588), The Grange, Northampton Road, Earls Barton, Northampton NN6 0JH. Tel: 0604-810326. *General Secretary*, Mrs H. McGrath.

NATIONAL UNION OF LOCK AND METAL WORKERS (4,666), Bellamy House, Wilkes Street, Willenhall, W. Midlands WV13 2BS. Tel: 0902-366651. *General Secretary*, M. Bradley.

NATIONAL UNION OF MARINE, AVIATION AND SHIPPING TRANSPORT OFFICERS, THE (18,470), Oceanair House, 750–760 High Road, London E11 3BB. Tel: 081-989 6677. *General Secretary*, J. Newman.

NATIONAL UNION OF MINEWORKERS (NUM) (44,352), Holly Street, Sheffield S1 2GT. Tel: 0742-766900. *General Secretary*, vacant.

NATIONAL UNION OF PUBLIC EMPLOYEES (NUPE) (551,165), Civic House, 20 Grand Depot Road, London SE18 6SF. Tel: 081-854 2244. *Secretary*, R. K. Bickerstaffe.

NATIONAL UNION OF RAIL, MARITIME AND TRANSPORT WORKERS (RMT) (110,000), Unity House, Euston Road, London NW1 2BL. Tel: 071-387 4771. *General Secretary*, J. Knapp.

NATIONAL UNION OF SCALEMAKERS (750), Queensway House, 57 Livery Street, Birmingham B3 1HA. Tel: 021-236 8998. *General Secretary*, A. F. Smith.

NATIONAL UNION OF TEACHERS (NUT) (214,675), Hamilton House, Mabledon Place, London WC1H 9BD. Tel: 071-388 6191. *General Secretary*, D. McAvoy.

NORTHERN CARPET TRADES' UNION (721), 22 Clare Road, Halifax HX1 2HX. Tel: 0422-360492. *General Secretary*, K. Edmondson.

PATTERN WEAVERS SOCIETY (60), 38 St Paul's Road, Kirkheaton, Huddersfield HD5 0EY. Tel: 0484-424988. *General Secretary*, K. Bradley.

POWER LOOM CARPET WEAVERS' AND TEXTILE WORKERS' UNION, THE (2,160), Carpet Weavers Hall, Callows Lane, Kidderminster, Worcs. DY10 2JG. Tel: 0562-823192. *General Secretary*, R. White.

PRISON OFFICERS' ASSOCIATION, THE (27,667), Cronin House, 245 Church Street, London N9 9HW. Tel: 081-803 0255. *General Secretary*, D. Evans.

ROSSENDALE UNION OF BOOT, SHOE AND SLIPPER OPERATIVES, THE (2,329), Taylor House, 7 Tenterfield Street, Waterfoot, Rossendale, Lancs. BB4 7BA. Tel: 0706-215657. *General Secretary*, M. Murray.

SCOTTISH PRISON OFFICERS' ASSOCIATION (4,099) 21 Calder Road, Edinburgh EH11 3PF. Tel: 031-443 8105. *General Secretary*, W. Goodall.

SCOTTISH UNION OF POWER-LOOM OVERLOOKERS (70), 3 Napier Terrace, Dundee DD2 2SL. Tel: 0382-612196. *Secretary*, J. D. Reilly.

SHEFFIELD WOOL SHEAR WORKERS' UNION (16), 50 Bankfield Road, Malin Bridge, Sheffield S9 4RD. Tel: 0742-333688. *Secretary*, J. H. R. Cutler.

SOCIETY OF SHUTTLEMAKERS (19), 211 Burnley Road, Colne, Lancs. BB8 8JD. Tel: 0282-866716. *General Secretary*, L. Illingworth.

SOCIETY OF TELECOM EXECUTIVES (27,151), 1 Park Road, Teddington, Middx. TW11 0AR. Tel: 081-943 5181. *General Secretary*, S. Petch.

TRANSPORT AND GENERAL WORKERS' UNION (TGWU) (1,126,631), Transport House, Smith Square, London SW1P 3JB. Tel: 071-828 7788. *General Secretary*, B. Morris.

TRANSPORT SALARIED STAFFS' ASSOCIATION (40,030), Walkden House, 10 Melton Street, London NW1 2EJ. Tel: 071-387 2101. *General Secretary*, R. A. Rosser.

UNION OF COMMUNICATION WORKERS, THE (UCW) (202,500), UCW House, Crescent Lane, London SW4 9RN. Tel: 071-622 9977. *General Secretary*, A. D. Tuffin.

UNION OF CONSTRUCTION, ALLIED TRADES AND TECHNICIANS (UCATT) (207,000), UCATT House, 177 Abbeville Road, London SW4 9RL. Tel: 071-622 2442. *Secretary*, G. Brumwell.

UNION OF SHOP, DISTRIBUTIVE AND ALLIED WORKERS (USDAW) (341,349), Oakley, 188 Wilmslow Road, Fallowfield, Manchester M14 6LJ. Tel: 061-224 2804. *Secretary*, D. G. Davies.

UNITED ROAD TRANSPORT UNION (18,000), 76 High Lane, Chorlton, Manchester M21 1FD. Tel: 061-881 6245. *General Secretary*, D. Higginbottom.

WIRE WORKERS' SECTION (Iron and Steel Trades Confederation) (4,500), Prospect House, Alma Street, Sheffield S3 8SA. Tel: 0742-721674. *National Secretary*, A. M. Ardron.

WRITERS' GUILD OF GREAT BRITAIN, THE (2,000), 430 Edgware Road, London W2 1EH. Tel: 071-723 8074. *General Secretary*, W. J. Jeffrey.

YORKSHIRE ASSOCIATION OF POWER LOOM OVERLOOKERS (450) Inveresk House, 31 Houghton Place, Bradford BD1 3RG. Tel: 0274-727966. *General Secretary*, A. D. Barrow.

MERGERS, ETC, 1991–2

The Electrical, Electronics, Telecommunications and Plumbing Union (EETPU) (*see* below) merged with the Amalgamated Engineering Union in May 1992 to form the Amalgamated Engineering and Electrical Union (AEEU). Members of the whole union will vote in April 1993 on whether the EEPTU wing should re-affiliate the TUC.

MERGERS UNDER CONSIDERATION

The Civil and Public Services Association (CPSA) and the National Union of Civil and Public Servants (NUCPS) have abandoned merger talks.

The Confederation of Health Service Employees (COHSE), the National and Local Government Officers' Union (NALGO) and the National Union of Public Employees (NUPE) will each vote at the end of 1992 on whether to amalgamate and form a new union, UNISON. If each union approves, UNISON will be formed on 1 July 1993, with a membership of 1.4 million.

Negotiations between the National Union of Mineworkers and the Transport and General Workers Union about the possible amalgamation of the two unions have been abandoned.

EXPELLED FROM THE TUC, September 1988

ELECTRICAL, ELECTRONIC, TELECOMMUNICATION AND PLUMBING UNION (EETPU) (now part of Amalgamated Engineering and Electrical Union) (357,175), Hayes Court, West Common Road, Bromley BR2 7AU. Tel: 081-462 7755. *General Secretary*, P. Gallagher.

National Academies of Scholarship

THE BRITISH ACADEMY (1901)

20–21 Cornwall Terrace, London NW1 4QP
Tel 071-487 5966

The British Academy is an independent, self-governing learned society for the promotion of historical, philosophical and philological studies. It supports advanced academic research in the humanities and social sciences, and is the recognized channel outside the universities for the Government's support of research in the humanities and social sciences.

The Fellowship of the Academy is limited to 350 under the age of 70. The Fellows are scholars who have attained distinction in one of the branches of study that the Academy exists to promote. Candidates must be nominated by existing Fellows. At 1 June 1992 there were 573 Fellows, 16 Honorary Fellows, and 293 Corresponding Fellows overseas.

President, Sir Anthony Kenny, KBE, FBA.
Treasurer, Dr E. A. Wrigley, FBA.
Foreign Secretary, Prof. J. B. Trapp, FBA.
Publications Officer, Prof. D. E. Luscombe, FBA.
Secretary, P. W. H. Brown.

THE ROYAL ACADEMY (1768)

Burlington House, London W1V ODS
Tel 071-439 7438

The Royal Academy of Arts is an independent, self-governing society devoted to the encouragement and promotion of the fine arts.

Membership of the Academy is limited to 74 Royal Academicians, all being painters, engravers, sculptors or architects. Candidates are nominated and elected by the existing Academicians. There is also a limited class of honorary membership and there were 9 honorary members as at mid-1992.

President, Sir Roger de Grey, KCVO, PRA.
Treasurer, Sir Philip Powell, CH, OBE, RA.
Keeper, Prof. N. Adams, RA.
Secretary, P. Rodgers.

THE ROYAL ACADEMY OF ENGINEERING (1976)

2 Little Smith Street, London SW1P 3DL
Tel 071-222 2688

The Royal Academy of Engineering was established as the Fellowship of Engineering in 1976. It was granted a Royal Charter in May 1983 and its present title in 1992. It is an independent, self-governing body whose object is the pursuit, encouragement and maintenance of excellence in the whole field of engineering, in order to promote the advancement of the science, art and practice of engineering for the benefit of the public.

Election to the Fellowship is by invitation only from nominations supported by the body of Fellows. Fellows are chosen from among chartered engineers of all disciplines. The Royal Charter states that the total number of Fellows may not exceed 1,000. At July 1992 there were 906 Fellows, six Honorary Fellows and 43 Foreign Members. The Duke of Edinburgh is the Senior Fellow and the Duke of Kent is a Royal Fellow.

President, Sir William Barlow, FEng.
Past Presidents, The Viscount Caldecote, KBE, DSC, FEng; Sir Denis Rooke, CBE, FRS, FEng.
Senior Vice-President, B. F. Street, FEng.
Vice-Presidents, Dr A. Denton, FEng; Dr A. M. Neville, MC, FEng, FRSE; B. W. Manley, FEng.
Hon. Treasurer, G. A. Lee, FEng.
Hon. Secretaries, R. Garrick, CBE, FEng, FRSE (*Mechanical Engineering*); R. H. Rooley, FEng. (*Civil Engineering*); D. G. Jefferies, CBE, FEng (*Electrical Engineering*); Dr G. S. G. Beveridge, FEng, FRSE (*Process Engineering*); Dr A. A. Denton, FEng. (*Overseas Affairs*); B. W. Manley, FEng. (*Education, Training and Competence to Practise*).
Executive Secretary, G. A. Atkinson.

THE ROYAL SCOTTISH ACADEMY (1838)

The Mound, Edinburgh EH2 2EL
Tel 031-225 6671

The Scottish Academy was founded in 1826 to arrange exhibitions for contemporary paintings and to establish a society of fine art in Scotland. The Academy was granted a Royal Charter in 1838.

Members are elected from the disciplines of painting, sculpture, architecture and printmaking. Elections are from nominations put forward by the existing membership. At mid-1992 there were 14 Senior Academicians, 36 Academicians, 40 Associates, three non-resident Associates and 20 Honorary Members.

President, W. J. L. Baillie, PRSA.
Secretary, I. McKenzie Smith, RSA.
Treasurer, J. Morris, RSA.
Librarian, P. Collins, RSA.
Administrative Secretary, W. T. Meikle.

ROYAL SOCIETY (1660)

6 Carlton House Terrace, London SW1Y 5AG
Tel 071-839 5561

The Royal Society is the United Kingdom's national academy of science. It is an independent, self-governing body under a Royal Charter, promoting and advancing all fields of physical and biological sciences, of mathematics and engineering, medical and agricultural sciences, their applications and place in society.

Election to Fellowship of the Royal Society is limited to those distinguished for original scientific work. Each year up to 40 new Fellows and six Foreign Members are elected from the most distinguished scientists. In addition, the Council can recommend for election members of the Royal family and, on average, one person each year for conspicuous service to the cause of science. At July 1992, there were 1,080 Fellows and 100 Foreign Members.

President, Sir Michael Atiyah, FRS.
Treasurer, Sir Robert Honeycombe, FRS.
Biological Secretary, Prof. Sir Brian Follett, FRS.
Physical Secretary, Sir Francis Graham-Smith, FRS.
Foreign Secretary, Dr A. L. McLaren, FRS.
Executive Secretary, Dr P. T. Warren.

THE ROYAL SOCIETY OF EDINBURGH (1783)
22–24 George Street, Edinburgh EH2 2PQ
Tel 031-225 6057

The Royal Society of Edinburgh is Scotland's premier learned society. The Society was founded by Royal Charter in 1783 for 'the advancement of Learning and Useful Knowledge', and its principal role is the promotion of scholarship in all its branches. It provides a forum for broadly-based interdisciplinary activity in Scotland, including organizing public lectures, conferences and specialist research seminars; providing advice to Parliament and government; administering a range of research fellowships held in Scotland; and publishing learned journals.

Fellows are elected by ballot after being nominated by at least four existing Fellows. At 4 June 1992 there were 1,017 Ordinary Fellows and 68 Honorary Fellows.

President, Sir Alastair Currie, FRCP, FRCPE, FRCPG, FRCSE, FRCPath.
Treasurer, The Lord Balfour of Burleigh.
General Secretary, Prof. V. B. Proudfoot.
Executive Secretary, Dr W. Duncan.

Royal Academicians

The category of Associate was abolished in June 1991 and all the Associates became Royal Academicians.
*Senior Academician

1991 Abrahams, Ivor
1991 Ackroyd, Norman
1972 Adams, Norman
1988 Aitchison, Craigie
1991 Armfield, Diana
1991 Ayres, Gillian, OBE
1991 Bellany, John
1976 Blackadder, Elizabeth, OBE
1981 Blake, Peter, CBE
1975 *Blamey, Norman
1978 Blow, Sandra
1975 Bowey, Olwyn
1981 Bowyer, William
1972 Brown, Ralph
1972 Butler, James
1975 *Cadbury-Brown, H. T., OBE
1984 Camp, Jeffery
1970 *Casson, Sir Hugh, CH, KCVO
1989 Christopher, Ann
1976 Clarke, Geoffrey
1973 Clatworthy, Robert
1972 Coker, Peter
1972 Cooke, Jean
1990 Crosby, Theo
1991 Cullinan, Edward, CBE
1974 Cuming, Frederick
1992 Cummins, Gus
1983 Dannatt, Trevor
1969 de Grey, Sir Roger, KCVO
1976 Dickson, Jennifer
1985 Dowson, Sir Philip, CBE
1991 Draper, Kenneth
1968 Dunstan, Bernard
1986 Eyton, Anthony
1992 *Fedden, Mary
1991 Flanagan, Barry, OBE
1991 Foster, Sir Norman
1985 Fraser, Donald Hamilton
1991 Freeth, Peter
1977 Frink, Dame Elisabeth, DBE
1992 *Frost, Terry
1972 *Gore, Frederick, CBE
1977 Green, Anthony
1970 Hayes, Colin
1961 *Hepple, Norman
1990 *Herman, Josef, OBE
1991 Hockney, David
1984 Hogarth, Paul
1992 Hopkins, Michael, CBE
1991 Howard, Ken
1991 Hoyland, John
1991 Huxley, Paul
1991 Jacklin, Bill
1991 *Jellicoe, Sir Geoffrey
1986 Jones, Allen
1986 Kenny, Michael
1991 Kiff, Ken
1988 King, Phillip, CBE
1991 Kitaj, R. B.
1974 Kneale, Bryan
1991 Koralek, Paul, CBE
1991 *Lasdun, Sir Dennis, CBE
1991 Lawson, Sonia
1986 *Lessore, Helen
1986 Levene, Ben
1991 McComb, Leonard
1956 *Machin, Arnold, OBE
1979 Manasseh, Leonard, OBE
1985 *Martin, Sir Leslie
1985 *Medley, Robert
1991 Mistry, Dhruva
1991 Nolan, Sir Sidney, OM, CBE
1979 Paolozzi, Sir Eduardo, CBE
1988 Partridge, John, CBE
1983 *Pasmore, Victor, CH, CBE
1989 Phillips, Tom
1977 Powell, Sir Philip, CH, OBE
1973 *Roberts-Jones, Ivor, CBE
1984 Rogers, Sir Richard
1991 Rooney, Michael
1969 *Rosoman, Leonard, OBE
1983 *Rothenstein, Michael
1961 *Sanders, Christopher
1989 Sandle, Michael
1969 *Soukop, Willi
1986 Stephenson, Ian
1988 Sutton, Philip
1991 Symons, Patrick
1991 Tilson, Joe
1979 Tindle, David
1991 Titchell, John
1992 Tucker, William
1965 Ward, John, CBE
1965 *Weight, Carel, CBE
1989 Whishaw, Anthony
1974 Williams, Kyffin, OBE
1991 Wilson, Colin St J.
1991 Wragg, John

The Research Councils

The Government funds basic and applied civil science research mostly through the five research councils, which are supported by the Office of Public Service and Science (OPSS) at the Cabinet Office. The councils conduct research through their own establishments (listed below) and by supporting selected research, study and training in universities and other higher education establishments. They also receive income for research commissioned by government departments and the private sector.

AGRICULTURAL AND FOOD RESEARCH COUNCIL

AFRC INSTITUTE FOR ANIMAL HEALTH

Director of Research, Prof. F. J. Bourne, Ph.D., Compton, Newbury, Berks. RG16 0NN. Tel: 0635-578411

COMPTON LABORATORY, Compton, Newbury, Berks. RG16 0NN. Tel: 0635-578411. *Head of Division in Charge*, Dr P. Jones.

HOUGHTON LABORATORY, Houghton, Huntingdon, Cambs. PE17 2DA. Tel: 0480-64101. *Head* (*acting*), L. N. Payne, Ph.D., D.Sc.

PIRBRIGHT LABORATORY, Ash Road, Woking, Surrey GU24 0NF. Tel: 0483-232441. *Head*, Dr A. I. Donaldson.

AFRC AND MRC NEUROPATHOGENESIS UNIT, Ogston Building, West Mains Road, Edinburgh EH9 3JF. Tel: 031-667 5204/5. *Head*, vacant.

AFRC INSTITUTE OF ANIMAL PHYSIOLOGY AND GENETICS RESEARCH

Director of Research, R. B. Heap, Ph.D., Sc.D., FRS, Babraham Hall, Babraham, Cambridge CB2 4AT. Tel: 0223-832312

CAMBRIDGE RESEARCH STATION, Babraham, Cambridge CB2 4AT. Tel: 0223-832312. *Head*, Dr R. G. Dyer.

EDINBURGH RESEARCH STATION, Roslin, Midlothian EH25 9PS. Tel: 031-440 2726. *Head*, Prof. G. Bulfield, Ph.D.

AFRC INSTITUTE OF ARABLE CROPS RESEARCH

Director of Research (*acting*), Prof. T. Lewis, CBE, Rothamsted Experimental Station, Harpenden, Herts. AL5 2JQ. Tel: 0582-763133

LONG ASHTON RESEARCH STATION, Long Ashton, Bristol BS18 9AF. Tel: 0275-392181. *Director*, Prof. P. R. Shewry.

ROTHAMSTED EXPERIMENTAL STATION, Harpenden, Herts. AL5 2JQ. Tel: 0582-763133. *Head*, Prof. T. Lewis, Ph.D., D.Sc.

BROOM'S BARN EXPERIMENTAL STATION, Higham, Bury St Edmunds, Suffolk IP28 6NP. Tel: 0284-810363. *Head*, T. H. Thomas, Ph.D., D.Sc.

AFRC SILSOE RESEARCH INSTITUTE

Director of Research, Prof. B. J. Legg, Wrest Park, Silsoe, Bedford MK45 4HS. Tel: 0525-860000

AFRC INSTITUTE OF FOOD RESEARCH

Director of Research, D. L. Georgala, CBE, Ph.D., Earley Gate, Whiteknights Road, Reading RG6 2EF. Tel: 0734-357000

NORWICH LABORATORY, Colney Lane, Norwich NR4 7UA. Tel: 0603-56122. *Head*, Prof. P. Richmond, D.Sc.

READING LABORATORY, Earley Gate, Whiteknights Road, Reading RG6 2EF. Tel: 0734-357000. *Head*, Prof. B. E. B. Moseley, Ph.D.

AFRC INSTITUTE OF GRASSLAND ENVIRONMENTAL RESEARCH

Director of Research, Prof. J. L. Stoddart, Ph.D., D.Sc., Plas Gogerddan, Aberystwyth, Dyfed SY23 3EB. Tel: 0970-828255

Plant Science and Plant Breeding Division:

WELSH PLANT BREEDING STATION, Plas Gogerddan, Aberystwyth, Dyfed SY23 3EB. Tel: 0970-828255. *Director and Head of Division*, D. Wilson, Ph.D.

Grassland and Ruminant Division:

NORTH WYKE RESEARCH STATION, Okehampton, Devon EX20 2SB. Tel: 0837-82558. *Head*, Dr R. J. Wilkins.

AFRC INSTITUTE OF PLANT SCIENCE RESEARCH

Director, Prof. R. B. Flavell, John Innes Institute, Colney Lane, Norwich NR4 7UH. Tel: 0603-52571

JOHN INNES INSTITUTE, Colney Lane, Norwich NR4 7UH. Tel: 0603-52571. *Director*, Prof. R. B. Flavell.

IPSR CAMBRIDGE LABORATORY, Colney Lane, Norwich NR4 7UH. Tel: 0603-52571. *Head*, C. N. Law, Ph.D.

IPSR NITROGEN FIXATION LABORATORY, University of Sussex, Brighton BN1 9RQ. Tel: 0273-678252. *Head*, Prof. B. E. Smith, Ph.D.

AFRC COMPUTING DIVISION, West Common, Harpenden, Herts. AL5 2JE. Tel: 0582-762271. *Head*, A. Windram.

SCOTTISH AGRICULTURAL RESEARCH INSTITUTES

HANNAH RESEARCH INSTITUTE, Ayr KA6 5HL. Tel: 0292-76013. *Director*, Prof. M. Peaker.

MACAULAY LAND USE RESEARCH INSTITUTE, Craigiebuckler, Aberdeen AB9 2QJ. Tel: 0224-318611; Bush Estate, Penicuik, Midlothian EH26 0PY. Tel: 031-445 3401. *Director*, Prof. T. J. Maxwell, Ph.D.

MOREDUN RESEARCH INSTITUTE, 408 Gilmerton Road, Edinburgh EH17 7JH. Tel: 031-664 3262. *Director*, I. D. Aitken, Ph.D.

ROWETT RESEARCH INSTITUTE, Greenburn Road, Bucksburn, Aberdeen AB2 9SB. Tel: 0224-712751. *Director*, Prof. W. P. T. James.

SCOTTISH CROP RESEARCH INSTITUTE, Invergowrie, Dundee DD2 5DA; Pentlandfield, Roslin, Midlothian EH25 9RF. Tel: 0382-562731. *Director*, Prof. J. Hillman, Ph.D., FRSE.

SCOTTISH AGRICULTURAL STATISTICS SERVICE, University of Edinburgh, James Clerk Maxwell Building, The King's Buildings, Mayfield Road, Edinburgh EH9 3JZ. Tel: 031-650 4901. *Director*, R. A. Kempton.

ECONOMIC AND SOCIAL RESEARCH COUNCIL

CAMBRIDGE GROUP FOR THE HISTORY OF POPULATION AND SOCIAL STRUCTURE, 27 Trumpington Street, Cambridge CB2 1QA. Tel: 0223-333181. *Director*, Dr R. Schofield.

CENTRE FOR ECONOMIC PERFORMANCE, London School of Economics, Houghton Street, London WC2A 2AE. Tel: 071-405 7686. *Director*, Prof. R. Layard.

CENTRE FOR ECONOMIC POLICY RESEARCH, 25–28 Old Burlington Street, London W1X 1LB. Tel: 071-734 9110. *Director*, Prof. R. Portes.

CENTRE FOR EDUCATIONAL SOCIOLOGY, University of Edinburgh, 7 Buccleuch Place, Edinburgh EH8 9LW. Tel: 031-650 4187. *Directors*, Prof. A. McPherson; Prof. D. Raffe.

CENTRE FOR HOUSING RESEARCH, 25 Bute Gardens, Hillhead, The University, Glasgow G12 8LE. Tel: 041-339 8855. *Director*, Prof. D. MacLennan, Ph.D.

CENTRE FOR INSTRUCTION, TRAINING AND LEARNING, University of Nottingham, Nottingham NG7 2RD. Tel: 0602-484848. *Director*, Prof. D. Wood.

CENTRE FOR RESEARCH IN ETHNIC RELATIONS, University of Warwick, Gibbet Hill Road, Coventry CV4 7AL. Tel: 0203-523523. *Director*, Prof. M. Anwar, Ph.D.

CENTRE FOR SCIENCE TECHNOLOGY AND ENERGY POLICY, Science Policy Research Unit, University of Sussex, Mantell Building, Falmer, Brighton BN1 9RF. Tel: 0273-686758. *Director*, Prof. M. Gibbons.

SOCIAL WORK RESEARCH CENTRE, University of Stirling, Stirling FK9 4LA. Tel: 0786-73171. *Director*, Prof. J. Cheetham.

ESRC DATA ARCHIVE, University of Essex, Wivenhoe Park, Colchester, Essex CO4 3SQ. Tel: 0206-872001. *Director*, Prof. D. Lievesley.

INDUSTRIAL RELATIONS RESEARCH UNIT, School of Industrial Business Studies, University of Warwick, Gibbet Hill Road, Coventry CV4 7AL. Tel: 0206-872001. *Director*, Prof. K. Sisson.

MRC/ESRC SOCIAL AND APPLIED PSYCHOLOGY UNIT, Department of Psychology, University of Sheffield, Sheffield S10 2TN. Tel: 0742-756600. *Director*, Prof. P. Warr.

NORTHERN IRELAND ECONOMIC RESEARCH CENTRE, 46–48 University Road, Belfast BT7 1NJ. Tel: 0232-225594. *Director*, Dr G. Gudgin.

RESEARCH CENTRE IN HUMAN COMMUNICATION, University of Edinburgh, 2 Buccleuch Place, Edinburgh EH8 9LW. Tel: 031-650 4665. *Director*, Prof. K. Stenning.

RESEARCH CENTRE IN MICRO-SOCIAL CHANGE, University of Essex, Wivenhoe Park, Colchester, Essex CO4 3SQ. Tel: 0206-872957. *Director*, vacant.

CENTRE FOR FISCAL POLICY, The Institute for Fiscal Studies, 7 Ridgmount Street, London WC1E 7AE. Tel: 071-636 3784. *Director*, Prof. R. Blundell.

CENTRE FOR SOCIAL AND ECONOMIC RESEARCH ON THE GLOBAL ENVIRONMENT, University of East Anglia, Norwich NR4 7TJ. Tel: 0603-56161. *Director*, R. Kerry Turner.

MEDICAL RESEARCH COUNCIL

NATIONAL INSTITUTE FOR MEDICAL RESEARCH, The Ridgeway, Mill Hill, London NW7. Tel: 081-959 3666. *Director*, J. Skehel, Ph.D., FRS.

CLINICAL RESEARCH CENTRE, Watford Road, Harrow, Middx. HA1 3UJ. Tel: 081–864 3232. *Administrative Director*, Dr K. E. Kirkham.

RESEARCH UNITS

ANATOMICAL NEUROPHARMACOLOGY UNIT, Mansfield Road, Oxford OX1 3TH. Tel: 0865-271865. *Hon. Director*, Prof. A. D. Smith, D.Phil.

APPLIED PSYCHOLOGY UNIT, 15 Chaucer Road, Cambridge CB2 2EF. Tel: 0223-355294. *Director*, A. D. Baddeley, Ph.D.

MRC BIOCHEMICAL AND CLINICAL MAGNETIC RESONANCE UNIT, University Dept. of Biochemistry, South Parks Road, Oxford OX1 3QU. Tel: 0865-275274. *Hon. Director*, Prof. G. K. Radda, D.Phil., FRS.

BIOSTATISTICS UNIT, Institute of Public Health, University Forvie Site, Robinson Way, Cambridge CB2 2SR. Tel: 0223-330366. *Hon. Director*, N. E. Day, Ph.D.

BLOOD GROUP UNIT, University College, London, Wolfson House, 4 Stephenson Way, London NW1 2HE. Tel: 071-388 7752. *Director*, Ms P. Tippett, Ph.D.

BLOOD PRESSURE UNIT, Western Infirmary, Glasgow G11 6NT. Tel: 041-339 8822 ext. 4065. *Director*, A. F. Lever, FRCP, FRSE.

BRAIN METABOLISM UNIT, University Dept. of Pharmacology, 1 George Square, Edinburgh EH8 9JZ. Tel: 031-650 3548. *Director*, Prof. G. Fink, MD, D.Phil.

CELL MUTATION UNIT, University of Sussex, Falmer, Brighton BN1 9RR. Tel: 0273-678123. *Director*, Prof. B. A. Bridges, Ph.D.

CELLULAR IMMUNOLOGY UNIT, Sir William Dunn School of Pathology, Oxford OX1 3RE. Tel: 0865-275594. *Director (acting)*, D. W. Mason.

CHILD PSYCHIATRY UNIT, Institute of Psychiatry, De Crespigny Park, Denmark Hill, London SE5 8AF. Tel: 071-703 5411. *Hon. Director*, Prof. Sir Michael Rutter, KBE, MD, FRCP.

CLINICAL ONCOLOGY AND RADIOTHERAPEUTICS UNIT, MRC Centre, Hills Road, Cambridge CB2 2QH. Tel: 0223-245133. *Hon. Director*, Prof. N. M. Bleehen, FRCP, FRCR.

CLINICAL PHARMACOLOGY UNIT, University Department of Clinical Pharmacology, Radcliffe Infirmary, Woodstock Road, Oxford OX2 6HE. Tel: 0865-311188 ext. 24524. *Hon. Director*, Prof. D. G. Grahame-Smith, Ph.D., FRCP.

COGNITIVE DEVELOPMENT UNIT, 17 Gordon Street, London WC1. Tel: 071-387 4692. *Director*, Prof. J. Morton, Ph.D.

MRC COLLABORATIVE CENTRE, 1–3 Burtonhole Lane, Mill Hill, London NW7 1AD. Tel: 081-906 3811. *Director*, C. C. G. Hentschel, Ph.D.

CYCLOTRON UNIT, Hammersmith Hospital, Du Cane Road, London W12. Tel: 081-743 2030. *Administrative Director*, K. I. Gibson, Ph.D.

DENTAL RESEARCH UNIT, The London Hospital Medical College, 30–32 Newark Street, London E1 2AA. Tel: 071-377 0444. *Hon. Director*, Prof. N. W. Johnson, Ph.D.

DUNN NUTRITION UNIT, Downhams Lane, Milton Road, Cambridge CB4 1XJ. Tel: 0223-426356. *Director*, R. G. Whitehead, CBE, Ph.D.

ENVIRONMENTAL EPIDEMIOLOGY UNIT, Southampton General Hospital, Southampton SO9 4XY. Tel: 0703-777624. *Director*, Prof. D. J. P. Barker, MD, Ph.D, FRCP.

EPIDEMIOLOGY AND MEDICAL CARE UNIT, Wolfson Institute of Preventive Medicine, St Bartholomew's Medical College, Charterhouse Square, London EC1M 6BQ. Tel: 071-982 6000. *Director*, Prof. T. W. Meade, DM, FRCP.

EPIDEMIOLOGY UNIT (SOUTH WALES), Llandough Hospital, Penarth, South Glamorgan CF6 1XX. Tel: 0222-711404. *Director*, P. C. Elwood, MD, FRCP.

EXPERIMENTAL EMBRYOLOGY AND TERATOLOGY UNIT, St George's Hospital Medical School, Cranmer Terrace, London SW17 0RE. Tel: 081-672 9944 ext. 56309. *Director*, D. G. Whittingham, D.Sc.

HUMAN BIOCHEMICAL GENETICS UNIT, The Galton Laboratory, University College London, Wolfson House, 4 Stephenson Way, London NW1. Tel: 071-387 7050. *Director*, D. A. Hopkinson, MD.

HUMAN GENETICS UNIT, Western General Hospital, Crewe Road, Edinburgh EH4 2XU. Tel: 031-332 2471. *Director*, Prof. H. J. Evans, Ph.D., FRSE.

MRC HUMAN MOVEMENT AND BALANCE UNIT, Institute of Neurology, National Hospital, Queen Square, London WC1 3BG. Tel: 071-387 3611. *Hon. Director*. Prof. C. D. Marsden, FRS.

IMMUNOCHEMISTRY UNIT, University Department of Biochemistry, South Parks Road, Oxford OX1 3QU. Tel: 0865-275354. *Director*, K. B. M. Reid, Ph.D.

INSTITUTE OF HEARING RESEARCH, University of Nottingham, Nottingham NG7 2RD. Tel: 0602-223431. *Director*, M. P. Haggard, Ph.D.

MRC LABORATORIES, THE GAMBIA, Fajara, near Banjul, The Gambia, W. Africa. *Director*, vacant.

MRC LABORATORIES, JAMAICA, University of the West Indies, Mona, Kingston, Jamaica. *Director*, Prof. G. R. Serjeant, CMG, MD, FRCP.

MRC/LRF LEUKAEMIA UNIT, Royal Postgraduate Medical School, Du Cane Road, London W12 0NN. Tel: 081-743 2030. *Hon. Director*, Prof. L. Luzzatto, MD, FRCP.

MRC MAGNETIC RESONANCE SPECTROSCOPY UNIT, John Radcliffe Hospital, Headington, Oxford OX3 9DU. *Hon. Director*, Prof. G. K. Radda, D.Phil., FRS.

MEDICAL SOCIOLOGY UNIT, 6 Lilybank Gardens, Glasgow G12 8QQ. Tel: 041-357 3949. *Director*, Ms S. Macintyre, Ph.D.

LABORATORY OF MOLECULAR BIOLOGY, Hills Road, Cambridge CB2 2QH. Tel: 0223-248011. *Director*, Prof. Sir Aaron Klug, Ph.D., FRS.

MOLECULAR HAEMATOLOGY UNIT, Institute of Molecular Medicine, John Radcliffe Hospital, Headington, Oxford OX3 9DU. Tel: 0865-222359. *Director*, Prof. Sir David Weatherall, MD, FRCP, FRS.

MRC MOLECULAR IMMUNOPATHOLOGY UNIT, University Medical School, Hills Road, Cambridge CB2 2QH. Tel: 0223-245133. *Hon. Director*, Prof. P. J. Lachmann, PRCPath., FRS.

MRC MUSCLE AND CELL MOTILITY UNIT, Division of Biomolecular Sciences, King's College London, 26–29 Drury Lane, London WC2B 5RL. Tel: 071-836 8851. *Hon. Director*, Prof. R. M. Simmons, Ph.D.

NEUROCHEMICAL PATHOLOGY UNIT, Newcastle General Hospital, Westgate Road, Newcastle upon Tyne NE4 6BE. Tel: 091-273 5251. *Director*, Prof. J. A. Edwardson, Ph.D.

AFRC/MRC NEUROPATHOGENESIS UNIT, Ogston Building, West Mains Road, Edinburgh EH9 3JF. Tel: 031-667 5204. *Director*, vacant.

MRC PROTEIN FUNCTION AND DESIGN UNIT, Dept. of Chemistry, University of Cambridge, Lensfield Road, Cambridge CB2 1EW. Tel: 0223-336341. *Hon. Director*, A. R. Fersht, Ph.D., FRS.

MRC PROTEIN PHOSPHORYLATION UNIT, Department of Biochemistry, University of Dundee, Dundee DD1 4HN. Tel: 0382-307238. *Hon. Director*, Prof. P. Cohen, Ph.D., FRS, FRSE.

RADIOBIOLOGY UNIT, Chilton, Didcot, Oxon. OX11 0RD. Tel: 0235-834393. *Director*, Prof. G. E. Adams, Ph.D., D.Sc.

REPRODUCTIVE BIOLOGY UNIT, Centre for Reproductive Biology, 37 Chalmers Street, Edinburgh EH3 9EW. Tel: 031-229 2575. *Director*, D. W. Lincoln, D.Sc.

MSC/ESRC SOCIAL AND APPLIED PSYCHOLOGY UNIT, Dept. of Psychology, University of Sheffield S10 2TN. Tel: 0742-756600. *Director*, Prof. P. B. Warr, Ph.D.

SOCIAL AND COMMUNITY PSYCHIATRY UNIT, Institute of Psychiatry, De Crespigny Park, Denmark Hill, London SE5 8AF. Tel: 071-703 5411. *Director*, Prof. J. P. Leff, MD, FRCPsych.

TOXICOLOGY UNIT, MRC Laboratories, Woodmansterne Road, Carshalton, Surrey SM5 4EF. Tel: 081-643 8000. *Director*, Dr L. Smith.

TUBERCULOSIS AND RELATED INFECTIONS UNIT, RPMS, Hammersmith Hospital, Du Cane Road, London W12 0HS. Tel: 081-743 2030. *Director*, Dr J. Ivanyi, MD, Ph.D.

VIROLOGY UNIT, Institute of Virology, Church Street, Glasgow G11 5JR. Tel: 041-330 4017. *Hon. Director*, Prof. J. H. Subak-Sharpe, CBE, Ph.D, FRSE.

NATURAL ENVIRONMENT RESEARCH COUNCIL

RESEARCH INSTITUTES AND UNITS

BRITISH ANTARCTIC SURVEY, Madingley Road, Cambridge CB3 0ET. Tel: 0223-61188. *Director*, Dr D. J. Drewry.

BRITISH GEOLOGICAL SURVEY, Nicker Hill, Keyworth, Nottingham NG12 5GG. Tel: 0602-363100. *Director*, Dr P. Cook.

INSTITUTE OF OCEANOGRAPHIC SCIENCES, DEACON LABORATORY, Wormley, nr. Godalming, Surrey GU8 5UB. Tel: 042868-4141. *Director*, Dr C. Summerhayes.

PLYMOUTH MARINE LABORATORY, Prospect Place, The Hoe, Plymouth PL1 3DH; Citadel Hill, Plymouth PL1 2PB. Tel: 0752-222772. *Director*, Dr B. L. Bayne; *Assistant Director*, Dr P. N. Claridge.

PROUDMAN OCEANOGRAPHIC LABORATORY, Bidston, Birkenhead L43 7RA. Tel: 051-653 8633. *Director*, Dr B. S. McCartney.

SEA MAMMAL RESEARCH UNIT, c/o British Antarctic Survey. Tel: 0223-311354. *Head*, J. Harwood, Ph.D.

DUNSTAFFNAGE MARINE LABORATORY, PO Box 3, Oban, Argyll PA34 4AD. Tel: 0631-62244. *Director*, Prof. J. B. L. Matthews.

JAMES RENNELL CENTRE FOR OCEAN CIRCULATION, Gamma House, Chilworth Research Centre, Chilworth, Southampton SO1 7NS. Tel: 0703-766184. *Head of Centre*, Dr R. Pollard.

INSTITUTE OF HYDROLOGY, Maclean Building, Crowmarsh Gifford, Wallingford, Oxon. OX10 8BB. Tel: 0491-38800. *Director*, Prof. W. B. Wilkinson.

INSTITUTE OF TERRESTRIAL ECOLOGY (NORTH), Bush Estate, Penicuik, Midlothian EH26 0QB. Tel: 031-445 4343. *Director*, Prof. O. W. Heal.

INSTITUTE OF TERRESTRIAL ECOLOGY (SOUTH), Monks Wood, Abbots Ripton, Huntingdon PE17 2LS. Tel: 04873-381/8. *Director*, Dr T. M. Roberts.
INSTITUTE OF VIROLOGY AND ENVIRONMENTAL MICROBIOLOGY, Mansfield Road, Oxford OX1 3SR. Tel: 0865-512361. *Director*, Prof. D. H. L. Bishop.
INSTITUTE OF FRESHWATER ECOLOGY, The Ferry House, Far Sawrey, Ambleside, Cumbria LA22 OLP. Tel: 05394-42468. *Director*, Prof. J. G. Jones.
UNIT OF COMPARATIVE PLANT ECOLOGY, Department of Animal and Plant Biology and Ecology, Sheffield University, Sheffield S10 2TN. Tel: 0742-768555. *Head of Unit*, Prof. J. P. Grime.
INTERDISCIPLINARY CENTRE FOR POPULATION BIOLOGY, Imperial College, Silwood Park, Ascot, Berks. SL5 7PY. Tel: 0344-294346. *Director*, Prof. J. Lawton.
NERC UNIT FOR THEMATIC INFORMATION SYSTEMS, Department of Geography, Reading University, Whiteknights, PO Box 227, Reading RG6 2AB. Tel: 0734-318741. *Officer in Charge*, Prof. R. Gurney.

SCIENCE AND ENGINEERING RESEARCH COUNCIL

RESEARCH ESTABLISHMENTS

DARESBURY LABORATORY, Keckwick Lane, Daresbury, Warrington, Cheshire WA4 4AD. Tel: 0925-603000. *Director*, Prof. A. J. Leadbetter. (The Nuclear Structure Facility at Daresbury is due to close at the end of 1992.)
ROYAL GREENWICH OBSERVATORY, Madingley Road, Cambridge CB3 OEZ. Tel: 0223-374700. *Director*, Prof. A. Boksenberg, FRS.
ROYAL OBSERVATORY, EDINBURGH, Blackford Hill, Edinburgh EH9 3HJ. Tel: 031-668 8100. *Director*, Dr P. Murdin, OBE.
RUTHERFORD APPLETON NUCLEAR PHYSICS LABORATORY, Chilton, Didcot, Oxon OX11 OQX. Tel: 0235-821900. *Director*, Dr P. R. Williams.

Research Associations

The following industrial and technological research bodies are members of the Association of Independent Research and Technology Organizations (AIRTO), PO Box 330, Cambridge CB5 8DU. Tel: 0223-467831.

AIRCRAFT RESEARCH ASSOCIATION LTD, Manton Lane, Bedford MK41 7PF. Tel: 0234-350681. *Chief Executive*, Dr J. E. Green.
ADVANCED MANUFACTURING TECHNOLOGY RESEARCH INSTITUTE, Hulley Road, Macclesfield, Cheshire SK10 2NE. Tel: 0625-425421. *Chief Executive (acting)*, I. G. Bruce.
BHR GROUP LTD (BRITISH HYDRO-MECHANICS RESEARCH GROUP), Cranfield, Bedford MK43 OAJ. Tel: 0234-750422. *Chief Executive*, I. Cooper.
BNF-FULMER, Wantage Business Park, Denchworth Road, Wantage, Oxon. OX12 9BJ. Tel: 0235-772992. *Chief Executive*, Dr W. H. Bowyer.
BRITISH CERAMIC RESEARCH LTD, Queen's Road, Penkhull, Stoke-on-Trent ST4 7LQ. Tel: 0782-45431. *Chief Executive*, Dr N. E. Sanderson.
BRITISH GLASS, Northumberland Road, Sheffield S10 2UA. Tel: 0742-686201. *Research Director*, Dr G. J. Copley.
BRITISH LEATHER CONFEDERATION, Leather Trade House, Kings Park Road, Moulton Park, Northants. NN3 1JD. Tel: 0604-494131. *Technical Director*, Dr K. Alexander.
BRITISH MARITIME TECHNOLOGY LTD, Orlando House, 1 Waldegrave Road, Teddington, Middx. TW11 8LZ. Tel: 081-943 5544. *Chief Executive*, D. Goodrich.
BRITISH TEXTILE TECHNOLOGY GROUP, Wira House, West Park Ring Road, Leeds LS16 6QL. Tel: 0532-781381. *Managing Director*, Dr D. N. Munro.
BUILDING SERVICES RESEARCH AND INFORMATION ASSOCIATION, Old Bracknell Lane West, Bracknell, Berks. RG12 4AH. Tel: 0344-426511. *Chief Executive*, G. J. Baker.
CAMBRIDGE CONSULTANTS LTD (*Product and process development of technology applications in business*), Science Park, Milton Road, Cambridge CB4 4DW. Tel: 0223-420024. *Managing Director*, Dr J. P. Auton.
CAMPDEN FOOD AND DRINK RESEARCH ASSOCIATION, Chipping Campden, Glos. GL55 6LD. Tel: 0386-840319. *Director-General*, Prof. C. Dennis.
CIRIA (THE CONSTRUCTION INDUSTRY RESEARCH AND INFORMATION ASSOCIATION), 6 Storey's Gate, London SW1P 3AU. Tel: 071-222 8891. *Director-General*, Dr P. L. Bransby.
CUTLERY AND ALLIED TRADES RESEARCH ASSOCIATION, Henry Street, Sheffield S3 7EQ. Tel: 0742-769736. *Director of Research*, R. C. Hamby.
ERA TECHNOLOGY LTD (*Electronic and electrical engineering*), Cleeve Road, Leatherhead, Surrey KT22 7SA. Tel: 0372-374151. *Chief Executive*, M. J. Withers.
FURNITURE INDUSTRY RESEARCH ASSOCIATION, Maxwell Road, Stevenage, Herts. SG1 2EW. Tel: 0438-313433. *Director and Chief Executive*, Dr C. A. Aitkenhead.
INTERNATIONAL RESEARCH AND DEVELOPMENT LTD (*Electronics and mechanical and electrical engineering*), Fossway, Newcastle upon Tyne NE6 2YD. Tel: 091-265 0451. *General Manager*, W. Carpenter.
LAMBEG INDUSTRIAL RESEARCH ASSOCIATION (*Textiles*), Lambeg, Lisburn, Co. Antrim, N. Ireland BT27 4RJ. Tel: 0846-662255. *Director of Operations*, T. J. Edgar.
LEATHERHEAD FOOD RESEARCH ASSOCIATION, Randalls Road, Leatherhead, Surrey KT22 7RY. Tel: 0372-376761. *Director*, Dr M. P. J. Kierstan.
MOTOR INDUSTRY RESEARCH ASSOCIATION, Watling Street, Nuneaton, Warks. CV10 OTU. Tel: 0203-348541. *Managing Director*, J. R. Wood.
THE NATIONAL COMPUTING CENTRE LTD, Oxford Road, Manchester M1 7ED. Tel: 061-228 6333. *Chief Executive*, J. Lloyd.
PAINT RESEARCH ASSOCIATION, 8 Waldegrave Road, Teddington, Middx. TW11 8LD. Tel: 081-977 4427. *Managing Director*, J. A. Bernie.
PERA INTERNATIONAL (*Multi-disciplinary research, design, development and consultancy*), Melton Mowbray, Leics. LE13 OPB. Tel: 0664-501501. *Director-General*, R. A. Armstrong.
PIRA INTERNATIONAL (*Paper and board, printing, publishing and packaging*), Randalls Road, Leatherhead, Surrey KT22 7RU. Tel: 0372-376161. *Managing Director*, B. W. Blunden.
RAPRA TECHNOLOGY LTD (*Polymer materials*), Shawbury, Shrewsbury SY4 4NR. Tel: 0939-250383. *Chief Executive*, Dr M. Copley.

SATRA FOOTWEAR TECHNOLOGY CENTRE, Satra House, Rockingham Road, Kettering, Northants. NN16 9JH. Tel: 0536-410000. *Chief Executive*, R. E. Whittaker.
SHIPOWNERS REFRIGERATED CARGO RESEARCH ASSOCIATION, 140 Newmarket Road, Cambridge CB5 8HE. Tel: 0223-65101. *Technical Director*, R. D. Heap.
SIRA LTD (*Instrumentation and systems technology*), South Hill, Chislehurst, Kent BR7 5EH. Tel: 081-467 2636. *Managing Director*, R. A. Brook.
SMITH SYSTEM ENGINEERING LTD, Surrey Research Park, Guildford, Surrey GU2 5YP. Tel: 0483-505565. *Chairman*, Dr B. G. Smith.
SPRING RESEARCH AND MANUFACTURERS' ASSOCIATION, Henry Street, Sheffield S3 7EQ. Tel: 0742-760771. *Director*, D. Saynor.
TIMBER RESEARCH AND DEVELOPMENT ASSOCIATION, Stocking Lane, Hughenden Valley, High Wycombe, Bucks. HP14 4ND. Tel: 0494-563091. *Director*, C. J. Gill.
TWI (WELDING), Abington Hall, Abington, Cambridge CB1 6AL. Tel: 0223-891162. *Chief Executive*, A. B. M. Braithwaite, OBE.
WRC (WATER RESEARCH) PLC, Henley Road, Medmenham, PO Box 16, Marlow, Bucks. SL7 2HD. Tel: 0491-571531. *Managing Director*, M. J. Rouse.

Chemical Elements

Element	*Symbol*	*Atomic Number*	*Element*	*Symbol*	*Atomic Number*	*Element*	*Symbol*	*Atomic Number*
Actinium	Ac	89	Hafnium	Hf	72	Promethium	Pm	61
Aluminium	Al	13	Helium	He	2	Protactinium	Pa	91
Americium	Am	95	Holmium	Ho	67	Radium	Ra	88
Antimony	Sb	51	Hydrogen	H	1	Radon	Rn	86
Argon	Ar	18	Indium	In	49	Rhenium	Re	75
Arsenic	As	33	Iodine	I	53	Rhodium	Rh	45
Astatine	At	85	Iridium	Ir	77	Rubidium	Rb	37
Barium	Ba	56	Iron	Fe	26	Ruthenium	Ru	44
Berkelium	Bk	97	Krypton	Kr	36	Samarium	Sm	62
Beryllium	Be	4	Lanthanum	La	57	Scandium	Sc	21
Bismuth	Bi	83	Lawrencium	Lr	103	Selenium	Se	34
Boron	B	5	Lead	Pb	82	Silicon	Si	14
Bromine	Br	35	Lithium	Li	3	Silver	Ag	47
Cadmium	Cd	48	Lutetium	Lu	71	Sodium	Na	11
Caesium	Cs	55	Magnesium	Mg	12	Strontium	Sr	38
Calcium	Ca	20	Manganese	Mn	25	Sulphur	S	16
Californium	Cf	98	Mendelevium	Md	101	Tantalum	Ta	73
Carbon	C	6	Mercury	Hg	80	Technetium	Tc	43
Cerium	Ce	58	Molybdenum	Mo	42	Tellurium	Te	52
Chlorine	Cl	17	Neodymium	Nd	60	Terbium	Tb	65
Chromium	Cr	24	Neon	Ne	10	Thallium	Tl	81
Cobalt	Co	27	Neptunium	Np	93	Thorium	Th	90
Copper	Cu	29	Nickel	Ni	28	Thulium	Tm	69
Curium	Cm	96	Niobium	Nb	41	Tin	Sn	50
Dysprosium	Dy	66	Nitrogen	N	7	Titanium	Ti	22
Einsteinium	Es	99	Nobelium	No	102	Tungsten (Wolfram)	W	74
Erbium	Er	68	Osmium	Os	76	Uranium	U	92
Europium	Eu	63	Oxygen	O	8	Vanadium	V	23
Fermium	Fm	100	Palladium	Pd	46	Xenon	Xe	54
Fluorine	F	9	Phosphorus	P	15	Ytterbium	Yb	70
Francium	Fr	87	Platinum	Pt	78	Yttrium	Y	39
Gadolinium	Gd	64	Plutonium	Pu	94	Zinc	Zn	30
Gallium	Ga	31	Polonium	Po	84	Zirconium	Zr	40
Germanium	Ge	32	Potassium	K	19			
Gold	Au	79	Praseodymium	Pr	59			

Societies and Institutions

ABBEYFIELD SOCIETY, 186–192 Darkes Lane, Potters Bar, Herts. EN6 1AB. Tel: 0707-44845. Housing for elderly people. *Chief Executive*, F. Murphy

ACCOUNTANTS, INSTITUTE OF CHARTERED, IN ENGLAND AND WALES (1880), PO Box 433, Chartered Accountants' Hall, Moorgate Place, London EC2P 2BJ. Tel: 071-628 7060. *Secretary*, A. J. Colquhoun

ACCOUNTANTS, CHARTERED ASSOCIATION OF CERTIFIED (1904), 29 Lincoln's Inn Fields, London WC2A 3EE. Tel: 071-242 6855. *Secretary*, A. W. Sansom

ACCOUNTANTS OF SCOTLAND, THE INSTITUTE OF CHARTERED (1854), 27 Queen Street, Edinburgh EH2 1LA. Tel: 031-225 5673. *Chief Executive*, P. W. Johnston

ACCOUNTANTS IN IRELAND, INSTITUTE OF CHARTERED (1888), Chartered Accountants House, 87–89 Pembroke Road, Dublin 4. Tel: Dublin 680400/ Belfast 321600. *Director*, R. F. Hussey

ACCOUNTANTS, INSTITUTE OF COMPANY (1974), 40 Tyndalls Park Road, Bristol BS8 1PL. Tel: 0272-738261. *Director-General*, B. T. Banks

ACCOUNTANTS, INSTITUTE OF FINANCIAL (1916), Burford House, 44 London Road, Sevenoaks, Kent TN13 1AS. Tel: 0732-458080. *Chief Executive*, D. Gurney

ACCOUNTING TECHNICIANS, ASSOCIATION OF (1980), 154 Clerkenwell Road, London EC1R 5AD. Tel: 071-837 8600. *Secretary*, J. Hanson

ACE STUDY TOURS (formerly Association for Cultural Exchange), Babraham, Cambridge CB2 4AP. Tel: 0223-835055. *General Secretary*, P. B. Barnes

ACTION RESEARCH (1952), Vincent House, North Parade, Horsham, W. Sussex RH12 2DA. Tel: 0403-210406. *Director-General*, Mrs A. Luther

ACTORS' BENEVOLENT FUND (1882), 13 Short's Gardens, London WC2H 9AT. Tel: 071–836 6378. *General Secretary*, Mrs R. Stevens

ACTORS' CHARITABLE TRUST (1896), 19–20 Euston Centre, London NW1 3JH. Tel: 071-608 6212. *General Secretary*, Ms A. Stewart

ACTORS' CHURCH UNION (1899), St Paul's Church, Bedford Street, London WC2E 9ED. Tel: 071-836 5221. *Senior Chaplain*, Canon W. Hall

ACTUARIES IN SCOTLAND, THE FACULTY OF (1856), 23 St Andrew Square, Edinburgh EH2 1AQ. Tel: 031-557 1575. *Secretary*, W. W. Mair

ACTUARIES, INSTITUTE OF (1848), Staple Inn Hall, High Holborn, London WC1V 7QJ. Tel: 071-242 0106. *Secretary-General*, A. G. Tait

ADMINISTRATIVE MANAGEMENT, INSTITUTE OF (1915), 40 Chatsworth Parade, Petts Wood, Kent BR5 1RW. Tel: 0689-875555. *Chief Executive*, Ms C. Hayhurst

ADULT SCHOOL ORGANIZATION, NATIONAL (1899), Masu Centre, Gaywood Croft, Cregoe Street, Birmingham B15 2ED. Tel: 021-622 3400. *General Secretary*, W. J. Scarle

ADVERTISING BENEVOLENT SOCIETY, NATIONAL (1913), 199–205 Old Marylebone Road, London NW1 5QP. Tel: 071-723 8028. *Director*, Mrs D. Larkin

ADVERTISING, INSTITUTE OF PRACTITIONERS IN (1927), 44 Belgrave Square, London SW1X 8QS. Tel: 071-235 7020. *Director-General*, N. Phillips

ADVERTISING STANDARDS AUTHORITY (1962), Brook House, 2–16 Torrington Place, London WC1E 7HN. Tel: 071-580 5555. *Director-General*, Mrs M. Alderson

AERONAUTICAL SOCIETY, ROYAL (1866), 4 Hamilton Place, London W1V 0BQ. Tel: 071-499 3515. *Director*, R. J. Kennett

AFRICAN INSTITUTE, INTERNATIONAL (1926), London School of Economics, Connaught House, Houghton Street, London WC2A 2AE. Tel: 071-831 3068. *Hon. Director*, Prof. P. Lloyd

AFRICAN MEDICAL AND RESEARCH FOUNDATION, 11 Waterloo Street, Clifton, Bristol BS8 4BT. Tel: 0272-238424. *Executive Director*, Mrs E. Young

AGE CONCERN ENGLAND (1940), Astral House, 1268 London Road, London SW16 4ER. Tel: 081-679 8000. *Director*, Ms S. Greengross

AGE CONCERN NORTHERN IRELAND (1976), 6 Lower Crescent, Belfast BT2 7BG. Tel: 0232-245729. *Director*, C. J. Common

AGE CONCERN SCOTLAND (1943), 54A Fountainbridge, Edinburgh EH3 9PT. Tel: 031-228 5656. *Director*, M. Cairns

AGE CONCERN WALES, 4th Floor, 1 Cathedral Road, Cardiff CF1 9SD. Tel: 0222-371566. *Manager*, R. W. Taylor

AGED POOR SOCIETY, *see* ST JOSEPH'S SOCIETY FOR THE RELIEF OF THE AGED POOR

AGEING, CENTRE FOR POLICY ON (1947), 25–31 Ironmonger Row, London EC1V 3QP. Tel: 071-253 1787. *Director*, Ms K. Herbst, Ph.D.

AGEING, RESEARCH INTO (1978), 49 Queen Victoria Street, London EC4N 4SA. Tel: 071-236 4365. *Director*, Ms E. Mills

AGRICULTURAL BENEVOLENT INSTITUTION, ROYAL (1860), Shaw House, 27 West Way, Oxford OX2 0QH. Tel: 0865-724931. *Chief Executive*, Brig. A. G. Staniforth, CBE

AGRICULTURAL BENEVOLENT INSTITUTION, ROYAL SCOTTISH (1897), Ingliston, Edinburgh, EH28 8NB. Tel: 031-333 1023. *Director*, I. C. Purves-Hume

AGRICULTURAL ENGINEERS ASSOCIATION (1875), Samuelson House, Paxton Road, Orton Centre, Peterborough PE2 0LT. Tel: 0733-371381. *Director-General*, J. Vowles

AGRICULTURAL SOCIETY, EAST OF ENGLAND, East of England Showground, Peterborough PE2 0XE. Tel: 0733-234451. *Chief Executive*, R. W. Bird, MBE

AGRICULTURAL SOCIETY OF ENGLAND, ROYAL (1838), National Agricultural Centre, Stoneleigh Park, Warks. CV8 2LZ. Tel: 0203-696969. *Chief Executive*, J. Hearth

AGRICULTURAL SOCIETY OF THE COMMONWEALTH, ROYAL (1957), 55 Sleaford Street, London SW8 5AB. Tel: 071-627 2111. *Hon. Secretary*, F. R. Francis, LVO, MBE

AGRICULTURAL SOCIETY, ROYAL ULSTER (1826), The King's Hall, Balmoral Show Grounds, Belfast BT9 6GW. Tel: 0232-665225. *Chief Executive*, W. H. Yarr

AIR LEAGUE, THE (1909), 4 Hamilton Place, London W1V 0BQ. Tel: 071-491 0740. *Secretary-General*, Air Cdre J. C. Atkinson, CBE

ALCOHOLICS ANONYMOUS (1947), PO Box 1, Stonebow House, Stonebow, York YO1 2NJ. Tel: 0904-644026. *General Secretary*, J. Keeney

ALEXANDRA ROSE DAY (1912), 1 Castelnau, Barnes, London SW13 9RP. *Director*, Mrs G. Greenwood

ALLOTMENT AND LEISURE GARDENERS LIMITED, NATIONAL SOCIETY OF (1930), Hunters Road, Corby, Northants. NN17 1JE. Tel: 0536-66576. *National Secretary*, G. W. Stokes

ALMSHOUSES, NATIONAL ASSOCIATION OF (1946), Billingbear Lodge, Wokingham, Berks. RG11 5RU. *Director*, D. M. Scott

ALZHEIMER'S DISEASE SOCIETY (1979), 158–160 Balham High Road, London SW12 9BN. Tel: 081-675 6557. *Director*, H. Cayton

AMNESTY INTERNATIONAL (1961), International Secretariat, 1 Easton Street, London WC1X 8DJ. Tel: 071-278 6000. *Director*, D. Bull

ANAESTHETISTS OF GREAT BRITAIN AND IRELAND, ASSOCIATION OF (1932), 9 Bedford Square, London WC1B 3RA. Tel: 071-631 1650. *Hon. Secretary*, Dr R. S. Vaughan

ANCIENT BUILDINGS, SOCIETY FOR THE PROTECTION OF (1877), 37 Spital Square, London E1 6DY. Tel: 071-377 1644. *Secretary*, P. Venning

ANCIENT MONUMENTS SOCIETY (1924), St Ann's Vestry Hall, 2 Church Entry, London EC4V 5HB. Tel: 071-236 3934. *Secretary*, M. Saunders

ANGLO-ARAB ASSOCIATION (1961), The Arab British Centre, 21 Collingham Road, London SW5 0NU. Tel: 071-373 8414. *Executive Director*, A. Lee

ANGLO-BELGIAN SOCIETY (1982). *Hon. Secretary*, Mrs A. M. Woodhead, 45 West Common, Haywards Heath, W. Sussex RH16 2AJ. Tel: 0444-452183

ANGLO-BRAZILIAN SOCIETY (1943), 32 Green Street, London W1Y 3FD. Tel: 071-493 8493. *Secretary*, C. H. Seaward, MBE

ANGLO-DANISH SOCIETY (1924), 25 New Street Square, London EC4A 3LN Tel: 0753-884846. *Chairman*, Sir Andrew Stark, KCMG, CVO

ANGLO-NORSE SOCIETY (1918), 25 Belgrave Square, London SW1X 8QD. Tel: 071-235 7151. *Chairman*, Mrs A. Dixon

ANGLO-THAI SOCIETY (1962). *Hon. Secretary*, J. A. Bradstreet, 500 Grovely Lane, Birmingham B45 8PD

ANIMAL CONCERN (SCOTLAND) (1988), 62 Old Dumbarton Road, Glasgow G3 8RE. Tel: 041-334 6014. *Organizing Secretary*, J. F. Robins

ANIMAL HEALTH TRUST (1942), PO Box 5, Newmarket, Suffolk CB8 7DW. Tel: 0638-661111. *Director*, A. J. Higgins, Ph.D

ANTHROPOLOGICAL INSTITUTE, ROYAL (1843), 50 Fitzroy Street, London W1P 5HS. Tel: 071-387 0455. *Director*, J. C. M. Benthall

ANTHROPOSOPHICAL SOCIETY IN GREAT BRITAIN (1923), Rudolf Steiner House, 35 Park Road, London NW1 6XT. Tel: 071-723 4400. *General Secretary*, N. C. Thomas

ANTIQUARIES OF LONDON, SOCIETY OF (1717), Burlington House, Piccadilly, London W1V 0HS. Tel: 071-734 0193. *General Secretary*, H. P. A. Chapman, Ph.D

ANTIQUARIES OF SCOTLAND, SOCIETY OF (1780), Royal Museum of Scotland, Queen Street, Edinburgh EH2 1JD. Tel: 031-225 7534, ext. 327. *Secretary*, Mrs F. Ashmore

ANTI-SLAVERY INTERNATIONAL FOR THE PROTECTION OF HUMAN RIGHTS (1839), 180 Brixton Road, London SW9 6AT. Tel: 071-582 4040. *Director*, Miss L. Roberts

ANTI-VIVISECTION: BRITISH UNION FOR THE ABOLITION OF VIVISECTION (1898), 16A Crane Grove, London N7 8LB. Tel: 071-700 4888. *General Secretary*, C. Fisher

ANTI-VIVISECTION SOCIETY, THE NATIONAL (1875), 261 Goldhawk Road, London W12 9PE. Tel: 081-846 9777. *Director*, Ms J. Creamer

APOSTLESHIP OF THE SEA (1920), Stella Maris, 66 Dock Road, Tilbury, Essex RM18 7BX. Tel: 0375-845641. For active and retired seafarers. *National Director*, Revd J. Maguire

APOTHECARIES OF LONDON, SOCIETY OF (1617), Black Friars Lane, London EC4V 6EJ. Tel: 071-236 1189. *Clerk*, Maj. J. C. O'Leary; *Registrar*, D. H. C. Barrie

ARBITRATORS, THE CHARTERED INSTITUTE OF (1915), International Arbitration Centre, 24 Angel Gate, City Road, London EC1V 2RS. Tel: 071-837 4483. *Secretary*, K. R. K. Harding

ARCHAEOLOGICAL ASSOCIATION, BRITISH, *see* LOCAL HISTORY, BRITISH ASSOCIATION FOR

ARCHAEOLOGICAL ASSOCIATION, CAMBRIAN (1846). *General Secretary*, Dr J. M. Hughes, The Laurels, Westfield Road, Newport, Gwent NP9 4ND. Tel: 0633-262449

ARCHAEOLOGICAL INSTITUTE, ROYAL (1843), c/o Society of Antiquaries of London, Burlington House, Piccadilly, London W1V 0HS. *Secretary*, J. G. Coad

ARCHAEOLOGY, COUNCIL FOR BRITISH (1944), 112 Kennington Road, London SE11 6RE. Tel: 071-582 0494. *Director*, R. K. Morris

ARCHITECTS, THE ROYAL INSTITUTE OF BRITISH (1834), 66 Portland Place, London W1N 4AD. Tel: 071-580 5533. *President*, R. MacCormac; *Director-General*, The Lord Rodgers of Quarry Bank, PC

ARCHITECTS AND SURVEYORS, INCORPORATED ASSOCIATION OF (1925), Jubilee House, Billing Brook Road, Weston Favell, Northampton NN3 4NW. Tel: 0604-404121. *Administrator*, B. D. Hughes

ARCHITECTS AND SURVEYORS INSTITUTE (1926), 15 St Mary Street, Chippenham, Wilts. SN15 3JN. Tel: 0249-444505. *Chief Executive*, B. A. Hunt

ARCHITECTS BENEVOLENT SOCIETY (1850), 66 Portland Place, London W1N 4AD. *Hon. Secretary*, R. J. Double

ARCHITECTS IN SCOTLAND, ROYAL INCORPORATION OF (1922), 15 Rutland Square, Edinburgh EH1 2BE. Tel: 031-229 7545. *Secretary*, C. A. McKean, FRSA

ARCHITECTS REGISTRATION COUNCIL OF THE UNITED KINGDOM (1931), 73 Hallam Street, London W1N 6EE. Tel: 071-580 5861. *Registrar*, D. W. G. Smart

ARCHITECTURAL ASSOCIATION (INC.) (1847), 34–36 Bedford Square, London WC1B 3EG. *Secretary*, E. Le Maistre

ARCHITECTURAL HERITAGE FUND, THE (1976), 27 John Adam Street, London WC2N 6HX. Tel: 071-925 0199. *Secretary*, Lady Weir

ARCHIVISTS, SOCIETY OF (1947). *Executive Secretary*, P. S. Cleary, Information House, 20–24 Old Street, London EC1V 9AP. Tel: 071-253 5087 ext. 65

ARK ENVIRONMENTAL FOUNDATION, THE (1988), 498 Harrow Road, London W9 3QA. Tel: 0763-263132. *Chairman*, G. Jephcott

ARMY BENEVOLENT FUND (1944), 41 Queen's Gate, London SW7 5HR. Tel: 071-581 8684. *Controller*, Maj.-Gen. G. M. G. Swindells, CB

ARMY CADET FORCE ASSOCIATION (1930), E Block, Duke of York's HQ, London SW3 4RR. Tel: 071-730 9733. *General Secretary*, Brig. R. B. MacGregor-Oakford, CBE, MC

ART, THE ROYAL CAMBRIAN ACADEMY OF (1882), Plas Mawr, High Street, Conwy, Gwynedd LL32 8DE. Tel: 0492-593413. *Curator and Secretary*, L. H. S. Mercer

ART COLLECTIONS FUND, NATIONAL (1903), 20 John Islip Street, London SW1P 4JX. Tel: 071-821 0404. *Director*, D. Barrie

ARTHRITIS AND RHEUMATISM COUNCIL FOR RESEARCH (1936), Copeman House, St Mary's Court, St Mary's Gate, Chesterfield, Derbys. S41 7TD. Tel: 0246-558033. *General Secretary*, J. Norton

ARTHRITIS CARE (1949), 18 Stephenson Way, London NW1 2HD. Tel: 071-916 1500. *Secretary*, J. R. Collins

ARTISTS' GENERAL BENEVOLENT INSTITUTION (1814) AND ARTISTS' ORPHAN FUND (1871), Burlington House, Piccadilly, London W1V 0DJ. Tel: 071-734 1193. *Secretary*, Mrs C. M. Rees

ARTISTS, ROYAL SOCIETY OF BRITISH, 17 Carlton House Terrace, London SW1Y 5BD. Tel: 071-930 6844. *President*, T. Coates

ART LIBRARIES SOCIETY, BRITAIN AND EIRE (ARLIS) (1969). *Administrator*, Ms S. French, 18 College Road, Bromsgrove, Worcs. B60 2NE. Tel: 0527-579298

ART WORKERS' GUILD (1884), 6 Queen Square, London WC1N 3AR. Tel: 071-837 3474. *Secretary*, H. Krall

ASLIB (The Association for Information Management) (1924), Information House, 20–24 Old Street, London EC1V 9AP. Tel: 071-253 4488. *Chief Executive*, R. Bowes

ASSISTANT MASTERS AND MISTRESSES ASSOCIATION, *see* TEACHERS AND LECTURERS, ASSOCIATION OF

ASTHMA CAMPAIGN, NATIONAL (1927), 300 Upper Street, London N1 2XX. Tel: 071-226 2260. *Chairman*, Sir Peter Emery, MP

ASTRONOMICAL ASSOCIATION, BRITISH (1890), Burlington House, Piccadilly, London W1V 9AG. Meetings at 23 Savile Row, London W1X 1AB. *Assistant Secretary*, Miss P. M. Barber

ASTRONOMICAL SOCIETY, ROYAL (1820), Burlington House, Piccadilly, London W1V 0NL. Tel: 071-734 3307. *President*, Prof. Sir Martin Rees, FRS; *Executive Secretary*, J. E. Lane

ATS AND WRAC BENEVOLENT FUNDS (1964), Queen Elizabeth Park, Guildford, Surrey GU2 6QH. Tel: 0252-355562. *Secretaries*, Mrs A. H. S. Matthews; Lt.-Col. D. Dunn

AUDIT BUREAU OF CIRCULATIONS LTD (1931), Black Prince Yard, 207–209 High Street, Berkhamsted, Herts. HP4 1AD. Tel: 0442-870800. *Secretary*, J. Beadell

AUTHORS, THE SOCIETY OF (1884), 84 Drayton Gardens, London SW10 9SB. Tel: 071-373 6642. *General Secretary*, M. Le Fanu

AUTOMOBILE ASSOCIATION (1905), Fanum House, Basingstoke, Hants. RG21 2EA. Tel: 0256-20123. *Director-General*, S. Dyer

AVICULTURAL SOCIETY (1894), c/o Bristol Zoological Gardens, Clifton, Bristol BS8 3HA. *Hon. Secretary*, G. R. Greed

AYRSHIRE CATTLE SOCIETY OF GREAT BRITAIN AND IRELAND (1877), PO Box 8, 1 Racecourse Road, Ayr KA7 2DE. Tel: 0292-267123. *General Secretary*, S. J. Thomson

BALTIC AIR CHARTER ASSOCIATION (1949), 6 The Office Village, Romford Road, London E15 4EA. Tel: 081-519 3909. *Hon. Executive*, D. Shepherd

BALTIC EXCHANGE LTD (1903), 19–21 Bury Street, London EC3A 5AU. Tel: 071-623 5501. *Secretary*, J. Buckley

BALTIC EXCHANGE CHARITABLE SOCIETY (1978), 14–20 St Mary Axe, London EC3A 8BU. Tel: 071-623 5501. *Secretary*, D. A. Painter

BALZAN FOUNDATION, INTERNATIONAL (1956), Piazzetta U. Giordano 4, Milan 20122, Italy. Tel: 02-7600 2212. *Secretary-General*, Dr F. M. Tedeschi

BANKERS, THE CHARTERED INSTITUTE OF (1879), 10 Lombard Street, London EC3V 9AS. Tel: 071-623 3531. *Secretary-General*, E. Glover

BANKERS IN SCOTLAND, THE CHARTERED INSTITUTE OF (1875), 19 Rutland Square, Edinburgh EH1 2DE. Tel: 031-229 9869. *Chief Executive*, Dr C. W. Munn

BAPTIST MISSIONARY SOCIETY (1792), Baptist House, PO Box 49, 129 Broadway, Didcot, Oxon. OX11 8RT. Tel: 0235-512077. *General Secretary*, Revd R. G. S. Harvey

BAR ASSOCIATION FOR LOCAL GOVERNMENT AND THE PUBLIC SERVICE (1945). *Chairman*, P. G. Stivadoros, 23 Wentworth Way, Bletchley, Milton Keynes MK3 7RW. Tel: 0908-682205

BARNARDO'S (1866), Tanners Lane, Barkingside, Ilford, Essex IG6 1QC. Tel: 081-550 8822. *Senior Director*, R. Singleton

BARONETAGE, STANDING COUNCIL OF THE (1898), The Church House, Bibury, Cirencester, Glos. GL7 5NR. *Hon. Secretary*, R. B. Snow, ISO

BARRISTERS' BENEVOLENT ASSOCIATION, THE (1873), 14 Gray's Inn Square, London WC1R 5JP. Tel: 071-242 4761. *Secretary*, Mrs A. Ashley

BCMS CROSSLINKS (1922), 251 Lewisham Way, London SE4 1XF. Tel: 081-691 6111. *General Secretary*, Canon J. M. Ball

BEECHAM TRUST, SIR THOMAS (1946), Denton House, Denton, Harleston, Norfolk IP20 0AA. Tel: 098 686-780. *Secretary*, Shirley, Lady Beecham

BEE-KEEPERS' ASSOCIATION, BRITISH (1874), National Agricultural Centre, Stoneleigh Park, Warks. CV8 2LZ. Tel: 0203-696679. *General Secretary*, J. K. Law

BIBLE SOCIETY, BRITISH AND FOREIGN (1804), Stonehill Green, Westlea, Swindon SN5 7DG. Tel: 0793-513713. *Executive Director*, N. Crosbie

BIBLIOGRAPHICAL SOCIETY (1892), British Library, Great Russell Street, London WC1B 3DG. *Hon. Secretary*, Dr M. M. Foot

BIBLIOGRAPHICAL SOCIETY, EDINBURGH (1890), c/o New College Library, Mound Place, Edinburgh EH1 2LU. Tel: 031-225 8400, ext. 256. *Hon. Secretary*, Dr M. C. T. Simpson

BIOCHEMICAL SOCIETY (1911), 59 Portland Place, London W1N 3AJ. Tel: 071-580 5530. *Executive Secretary*, G. D. Jones

BIOLOGICAL ENGINEERING SOCIETY (1960), Royal College of Surgeons, Lincoln's Inn Fields, London WC2A 3PN. Tel: 071-242 7740. *Hon. Secretary*, Dr R. E. Trotman

BIOLOGY, THE INSTITUTE OF (1950), 20–22 Queensberry Place, London SW7 2DZ. Tel: 071-581 8333. *General Secretary*, Dr. R. H. Priestley

BIRD PRESERVATION, INTERNATIONAL COUNCIL FOR (BRITISH SECTION) (1922), c/o RSPB, The Lodge, Sandy, Beds. SG19 2DL. Tel: 0767-680551. *Executive Secretary*, A. Gammell

BIRMINGHAM AND MIDLAND INSTITUTE (1854) and PRIESTLEY LIBRARY (1779), Margaret Street, Birmingham B3 3BS. Tel: 021-236 3591. *Administrator*, J. Hunt

BIRTHDAY TRUST FUND, NATIONAL (1928), 27 Sussex Place, London NW1 4RG.Tel: 071-706 3903. For extension of maternity services

BLIND, GUIDE DOGS FOR THE, *see* GUIDE DOGS FOR THE BLIND ASSOCIATION

BLIND PEOPLE, ACTION FOR (1857), 14–16 Verney Road, London SE16 3DZ. Tel: 071-732 8771. *Director*, A. Kent

BLIND, NATIONAL LIBRARY FOR THE (1882), Cromwell Road, Bredbury, Stockport, Cheshire SK6 2SG. Tel: 061-494 0217. *Director-General*, A. Leach

BLIND, ROYAL LONDON SOCIETY FOR THE (1838), 105–9 Salusbury Road, London NW6 6RH. Tel: 071-624 8844. *Chief Executive*, R. J. Pocock

BLIND, ROYAL NATIONAL COLLEGE FOR THE (1872), College Road, Hereford HR1 1EB. Tel: 0432-265725. *Principal*, C. Housby-Smith, Ph.D

BLIND, ROYAL NATIONAL INSTITUTE FOR THE, *see* ROYAL NATIONAL INSTITUTE FOR THE BLIND

BLIND, ROYAL SCHOOL FOR THE (1799), Highlands Road, Leatherhead, Surrey KT22 8NR. Tel: 0372-373086. *Chief Executive*, R. M. Perkins

BLOOD TRANSFUSION ASSOCIATION, SCOTTISH NATIONAL (1940), Erskine House, 68–73 Queen Street, Edinburgh EH2 4NH. Tel: 031-226 4488. *Secretary*, P. C. Taylor

BLOOD TRANSFUSION SERVICE, NATIONAL (1948), National Directorate, Gateway House, Piccadilly South, Manchester M60 7LP. *National Director*, Dr H. H. Gunson

BLUE CROSS (1897), Shilton Road, Burford, Oxon. OX18 4PF. Tel: 0993-822651. *Secretary*, A. Kennard, MBE

BODLEIAN, FRIENDS OF THE (1925), Bodleian Library, Oxford OX1 3BG. Tel: 0865-277022. *Secretary*, G. Groom

BOOKSELLERS ASSOCIATION OF GREAT BRITAIN AND IRELAND (1895), 272–274 Vauxhall Bridge Road, London SW1V 1BA. Tel: 071-834 5477. *Director*, T. E. Godfray

BOOK TRADE BENEVOLENT SOCIETY (1967), Dillon Lodge, The Retreat, Kings Langley, Herts. WD4 8LT. Tel: 0923-263128. *Executive Secretary*, Mrs A. R. Brown

BOOK TRUST (1986), Book House, 45 East Hill, London SW18 2QZ. Tel: 081-870 9055. *Chief Executive*, K. McWilliams

BOTANICAL SOCIETY OF THE BRITISH ISLES (1836), Dept. of Botany, The Natural History Museum, Cromwell Road, London SW7 5BD. Tel: 0509-215598. *Hon. General Secretary*, Mrs M. Briggs, MBE

BOTANICAL SOCIETY OF SCOTLAND, Royal Botanic Garden, Inverleith Row, Edinburgh EH3 5LR. Tel: 031-552 7171. *Hon. General Secretary*, B. Galt

BOY SCOUTS ASSOCIATION, *see* SCOUT ASSOCIATION

BOYS' BRIGADE, THE (1883), Felden Lodge, Felden, Hemel Hempstead HP3 0BL. Tel: 0442-231681. *Brigade Secretary*, S. Jones.

BOYS' CLUBS, NATIONAL ASSOCIATION OF (1925), 369 Kennington Lane, London SE11 5QY. Tel: 071-793 0787. *National Director*, D. P. Harris

BOYS' CLUBS OF NORTHERN IRELAND (1940), 2nd Floor, 38 Dublin Road, Belfast BT2 7HN. Tel: 0232-241924. *General Secretary*, K. Culbert

BREWING, INSTITUTE OF (1886), 33 Clarges Street, London W1Y 8EE. Tel: 071-499 8144. *Chief Executive*, P. W. E. Istead

BRIDEWELL ROYAL HOSPITAL (1553), Witley, Surrey GU8 5SG. Tel: 0428-682572. *Registrar*, Mrs J. Benyon

BRITAIN-NEPAL SOCIETY (1960). *Hon. Secretary*, Mrs J. Thomas, 24 Carthew Villas, London W6 0BS

BRITAIN-RUSSIA CENTRE (1959), 14 Grosvenor Place, London SW1X 7HW. Tel: 071-235 2116. *Director*, J. C. Q. Roberts

BRITISH AND FOREIGN SCHOOL SOCIETY (1808), Richard Mayo Hall, Eden Street, Kingston upon Thames, Surrey KT1 1HZ. Tel: 081-546 2379. *Secretary*, S. M. A. Banister

BRITISH ATLANTIC COMMITTEE (1952), 5 St James's Place, London SW1A 1NP. *Director*, A. Lee Williams

BRITISH INSTITUTE IN EASTERN AFRICA (1959), 1 Kensington Gore, London SW7 2AR. Tel: 071-584 4653. *London Secretary*, Mrs J. Moyo

British Institute of Archaeology at Ankara (1948), c/o British Academy, 20–21 Cornwall Terrace, London NW1 4QP. Tel: 071–727 6167. *London Secretary*, Mrs F. Ligonnet

British Institute of Persian Studies (1961), 13 Cambrian Road, Richmond, Surrey TW10 6JQ. Tel: 081-940 0647. *Secretary*, Mrs M. E. Gueritz, MBE

British Interplanetary Society (1933), 27–29 South Lambeth Road, London SW8 1SZ. Tel: 071-735 3160. *Executive Secretary*, S. A. Jones

British Israel World Federation (1919), 8 Blades Court, Deodar Road, London SW15 2NU. Tel: 081-877 9010. *Secretary*, A. E. Gibb

British Legion, The Royal (1921), 48 Pall Mall, London SW1Y 5JY. Tel: 071-973 0633. *General Secretary*, Lt.-Col. P. C. E. Creasy, OBE

British Legion Scotland, Royal (1921), New Haig House, Logie Green Road, Edinburgh EH7 4HR. Tel: 031-557 2782. *General Secretary*, Brig. R. W. Riddle, OBE

British Medical Association (1832), BMA House, Tavistock Square, London WC1H 9JP. Tel: 071-387 4499. *President*, Sir John Reid, KCMG, CB; *Secretary*, Dr I. T. Field

British Red Cross (1870), 9 Grosvenor Crescent, London SW1X 7EJ. Tel: 071-235 5454. *Director-General*, M. Whitlam

British School of Archaeology in Jerusalem (1919), The British Academy, 20–21 Cornwall Terrace, London NW1 4QP. Tel: 031-650 3975. *Director*, P. R. S. Moorey, Ph.D, FBA

British Technology Group, 101 Newington Causeway, London SE1 6BU. Tel: 071-403 6666. *Chief Executive*, I. A. Harvey

Brush Manufacturers' Association, British (1908), 35 Billing Road, Northampton NN1 5DD. Tel: 0604 22023. *Secretary*, A. N. Nisbet

BTCV (British Trust for Conservation Volunteers) (1970), 36 St Mary's Street, Wallingford, Oxon. OX10 0EU. Tel: 0491-39766. *Chief Executive*, R. Morley

Buddhist Society, The (1924), 58 Eccleston Square, London SW1V 1PH. Tel: 071-834 5858. *General Secretary*, R. C. Maddox

Budgerigar Society, The (1925), 49–53 Hazelwood Road, Northampton NN1 1LG. *General Secretary*, A. C. Crook

Building, Chartered Institute of (1834), Englemere, Kings Ride, Ascot, Berks. SL5 8BJ. Tel: 0344-23355. *Chief Executive*, K. Banbury

Building Services Engineers, Chartered Institution of (1897), Delta House, 222 Balham High Road, London SW12 9BS. Tel: 081-675 5211. *Secretary*, A. V. Ramsay

Building Societies Association (1936), 3 Savile Row, London W1X 1AF. Tel: 071-437 0655. *Director-General*, M. J. Boléat

Business and Professional Women, United Kingdom Federation of (1938), 23 Ansdell Street, London W8 5BN. Tel: 071-938 1729. *Secretary*, Mrs R. Bangle

Business Archives Council (1934), 185 Tower Bridge Road, London SE1 2UF. Tel: 071-407 6110. *Secretary-General*, W. S. Quinn-Robinson

Business Education, The Faculty of (1872), 1 The Old School, Pant Glas, Oswestry SY10 7HS. Tel: 0691-654019. *General Secretary*, L. Garner

Cadet Force Association, Combined (1952), 'E' Block, The Duke of York's HQ, London SW3 4RR. Tel: 071-730 9733. *Secretary*, Brig. R. B. MacGregor-Oakford, CBE, MC

CAFOD (Catholic Fund for Overseas Development) (1962), 2 Romero Close, Stockwell Road, London SW9 9TY. Tel: 071-733 7900. *Director*, J. Filochowski

Calouste Gulbenkian Foundation (1956), 98 Portland Place, London W1N 4ET. *Director*, B. Whitaker

Cambridge Preservation Society (1929), Wandlebury Ring, Gog Magog Hills, Babraham, Cambridge CB2 4AE. Tel: 0223-243830. *Secretary*, G. Brewster

Cameron Fund, The (1971), Tavistock House North, Tavistock Square, London WC1H 9JP. Tel: 071-388 0796. *Secretary*, Mrs J. Martin

Campaign for Nuclear Disarmament (CND) (1958), 162 Holloway Road, London N7 8DQ. Tel: 071-700 2393. *General Secretary*, G. Lefley

Cancer Relief Macmillan Fund (1911), Anchor House, 15–19 Britten Street, London SW3 3TZ. Tel: 071-351 7811. *Chief Executive*, D. Scott

Cancer Research Campaign, 6–10 Cambridge Terrace, London NW1 4JL. Tel: 071-224 1333. *Director-General*, D. de Peyer

Cancer Research Fund, Imperial (1902), PO Box 123, Lincoln's Inn Fields, London WC2A 3PX. Tel: 071-242 0200. *Secretary*, Miss M. J. Craggs

Cancer Research, the Institute of, Royal Cancer Hospital, 17A Onslow Gardens, London SW7 3AL. Tel: 071-352 8133. *Chief Executive*, Dr P. Garland

Cancer United Patients, British Association of (BACUP) (1985), 121–123 Charterhouse Street, London EC1M 6AA. Tel: 071-696 9003. *Chairman*, Dr M. Slevin

Career Teachers, Association of (1975), Hillsborough, Castledine Street, Loughborough, Leics. LE11 2DX. Tel: 0509-214617. *General Secretary*, Miss R. Yaffé

Carers National Association (1988), 29 Chilworth Mews, London W2 3RG. *Director*, Ms J. Pitkeathley

Carnegie Dunfermline Trust (1903), Abbey Park House, Dunfermline KY12 7PB. Tel: 0383-723638. *Secretary*, F. Mann

Carnegie Hero Fund Trust (1908). Abbey Park House, Dunfermline KY12 7PB. Tel: 0383-723638. *Secretary*, F. Mann

Carnegie United Kingdom Trust (1913), Comely Park House, Dunfermline KY12 7EJ. Tel: 0383-721445. *Secretary*, G. Lord, OBE

Cathedrals Fabric Commission for England (1949), 83 London Wall, London EC2M 5NA. Tel: 071-638 0971. *Secretary*, Dr. R. Gem

CATHOLIC MARRIAGE ADVISORY COUNCIL (1946), Clitherow House, 1 Blythe Mews, Blythe Road, London W14 0NW. Tel: 071-371 1341. *Chief Executive*, Mrs J. C. Judge

CATHOLIC RECORD SOCIETY (1904), c/o 114 Mount Street, London W1Y 6AH. *Hon. Secretary*, Miss R. Rendel

CATHOLIC TRUTH SOCIETY (1868), 38–40 Eccleston Square, London SW1V 1PD. Tel: 071-834 4392. *General Secretary*, D. Murphy

CATHOLIC UNION OF GREAT BRITAIN (1872), St Maximilian Kolbe House, 63 Jeddo Road, London W12 9EE. Tel: 081-749 1321. *President*, The Duke of Norfolk, KG, GCVO, CB, CBE, MC; *Hon. Secretary*, Mrs J. Stuyt, MBE

CATTLE BREEDERS' ASSOCIATION, NATIONAL. *Secretary*, R. W. Kershaw-Dolby, Lawford Grange, Lawford Heath, Rugby, Warks. CV23 9HG. Tel: 0788-565264

CATTLE BREEDER'S CLUB LTD, BRITISH (1945), Lavenders, Isfield, Uckfield, E. Sussex TN22 5TX. Tel: 0825-750356. *Secretary*, C. R. Stains

CECIL HOUSES (Housing Association) (1926), 2 Priory Road, Kew, Richmond, Surrey TW9 3DG. Tel: 081-940 9828. *Secretary*, G. Brighton

CENTRAL BUREAU (for educational visits and exchanges) (1948), Seymour Mews House, Seymour Mews, London W1H 9PE. Tel: 071-486 5101. *Director* A. H. Male

CERAMICS, INSTITUTE OF (1955), Shelton House, Stoke Road, Shelton, Stoke-on-Trent ST4 2DR. *President*, Dr. D. W. F. James

CHADWICK TRUST (1895), Department of Civil Engineering, University College London, Gower Street, London WC1E 6BT. For the promotion of health and prevention of disease. *Secretary to the Trustees*, I. K. Orchardson Ph.D

CHANTREY BEQUEST (1875), Royal Academy of Arts, Burlington House, Piccadilly, London W1V 0DS. Tel: 071-439 7438. *Secretary*, P. Rodgers

CHARITIES AID FOUNDATION (1974), 48 Pembury Road, Tonbridge, Kent TN9 2JD. Tel: 0732-771333. *Director*, M. Brophy

CHARTERED SECRETARIES AND ADMINISTRATORS, INSTITUTE OF (1891), 16 Park Crescent, London W1N 4AH. Tel: 071-580 4741. *Secretary*, M. J. Ainsworth

CHEMICAL ENGINEERS, INSTITUTION OF (1922), The Davis Building, 165–171 Railway Terrace, Rugby, Warks. London CV21 3HQ. Tel: 0788-758214. *General Secretary*, Dr. T. J. Evans

CHEMISTRY, THE ROYAL SOCIETY OF, Burlington House, Piccadilly, London W1V 0BN. Tel: 071-437 8656. *Secretary-General*, Dr. J. S. Gow, FRSE

CHESHIRE (LEONARD) FOUNDATION, *see* LEONARD CHESHIRE FOUNDATION

CHESS FEDERATION, BRITISH (1904), 9A Grand Parade, St Leonards-on-Sea, E. Sussex TN38 0DD. Tel: 0424-442500. *General Secretary*, Mrs G. White

CHEST, HEART AND STROKE ASSOCIATION, *see* STROKE ASSOCIATION, THE

CHIEF EMERGENCY PLANNING OFFICERS' SOCIETY (1966). *Hon. Secretary*, N. B. Knocker, OBE, Emergency Planning Department, County Hall, Trowbridge, Wilts. BA14 8JE. Tel: 0225-753641, ext. 3510

CHILDBIRTH TRUST, NATIONAL (1956), Alexandra House, Oldham Terrace, London W3 6NH. Tel: 081-992 8637. *Chief Executive*, Ms S. Dobson

CHILDMINDING ASSOCIATION, NATIONAL (1977), 8 Masons Hill, Bromley, Kent BR2 9EY. Tel: 081-464 6164. *Director*, Mrs J. Burnell

CHILDREN'S HOME, NATIONAL (1869), 85 Highbury Park, London N5 1UD. Tel: 071-226 2033. *Principal*, T. White, CBE

CHILDREN'S SOCIETY, THE (1881), Edward Rudolf House, Margery Street, London WC1X 0JL. Tel: 071-837 4299. *Director*, I. Sparks

CHINA ASSOCIATION (1889), Swire House, 59 Buckingham Gate, London SW1E 6AJ. Tel: 071-821 3220/1. *Executive Director*, Brig. B. G. Hickey, OBE, MC

CHIROPODISTS, SOCIETY OF (1945), 53 Welbeck Street, London W1M 7HE. Tel: 071-486 3381. *General Secretary*, J. G. C. Trouncer

CHOIRS SCHOOLS ASSOCIATION (1921), The Cathedral Choir School, Whitcliffe Lane, Ripon, N. Yorks. HG4 2LA. Tel: 0765-602134. *Hon. Secretary*, R. J. Shephard

CHRISTIAN ACTION, St Peter's House, 308 Kennington Lane, London SE11 5HY. Tel: 071-735 2372. *Hon. Director*, Revd Canon E. James

CHRISTIAN AID (1945), PO Box 100, London SE1 7RT. Tel: 071-620 4444. *Director*, Revd M. H. Taylor

CHRISTIAN EDUCATION COUNCIL, NATIONAL (1809), Robert Denholm House, Nutfield, Redhill RH1 4HW. Tel: 0737-822411. *Executive Officer*, vacant

CHRISTIAN EDUCATION MOVEMENT (1965), Royal Buildings, Victoria Street, Derby DE1 1GW. Tel: 0332-296655. *General Secretary*, Revd Dr. S. Orchard

CHRISTIAN EVIDENCE SOCIETY (1870), St Stephen's House, St Stephen's Crescent, Brentwood, Essex CM13 2AT. *Hon. Secretary*, Mrs G. M. Ryeland

CHRISTIAN KNOWLEDGE, SOCIETY FOR PROMOTING (SPCK) (1698), Holy Trinity Church, Marylebone Road, London NW1 4DU. Tel: 071-387 5282. *General Secretary*, P. Chandler

CHRISTIANS AND JEWS, COUNCIL OF (1942), 1 Dennington Park Road, London NW6 1AX. Tel: 071-794 8178. *Executive Director*, M. Latham

CHURCH ARMY (1882), Independents Road, London SE3 9LG. Tel: 081-318 1226. *Chief Secretary*, Capt. P. Johanson

CHURCH BUILDING SOCIETY, INCORPORATED (1818), Fulham Palace, London SW6 6EA. Tel: 071-736 3054. *Secretary*, Capt. R. H. C. Heptinstall, RN

CHURCH EDUCATION CORPORATION, Bedgebury School, Goudhurst, Cranbrook, Kent TN17 2SH. Tel: 0580-211630. *Secretary*, C. G. Champion

CHURCH HOUSE, THE CORPORATION OF (1888), Dean's Yard, London SW1P 3NZ. Tel: 071-222 5261. *Secretary*, C. D. L. Menzies

CHURCH LADS' AND CHURCH GIRLS' BRIGADE (1891), 2 Barnsley Road, Wath upon Dearne, Rotherham, S. Yorks. S63 6PY. Tel: 0709-876535. *General Secretary*, Wg Cdr. J. S. Cresswell (retd)

CHURCH MISSIONARY SOCIETY (1799), 157 Waterloo Road, London SE1 8UU. Tel: 071-928 8681. *General Secretary*, Rt. Revd M. Nazir-Ali

CHURCH MUSIC, ROYAL SCHOOL OF (1927), Addington Palace, Croydon CR9 5AD. Tel: 081-654 7676. *Chief Executive*, R. Lawrence

CHURCH OF ENGLAND PENSIONS BOARD (1926), 7 Little College Street, London SW1P 3SF. Tel: 071-222 2091. *Secretary*, R. G. Radford

CHURCH UNION (1859), Faith House, 7 Tufton Street, London SW1P 3QN. Tel: 071-222 6952. *General Secretary*, A. Leggatt

CHURCHES, COUNCIL FOR THE CARE OF (1921), 83 London Wall, London EC2M 5NA. *Secretary*, Dr. T. Cocke

CHURCHES FOR BRITAIN AND IRELAND, COUNCIL OF (1942), Inter-Church House, 35–41 Lower Marsh, London SE1 7RL. Tel: 071-620 4444. *General Secretary*, Revd J. P. Reardon

CHURCHES, FRIENDS OF FRIENDLESS (1957), 12 Edwardes Square, London W8 6HG. Tel: 071-602 6267. *Hon. Director*, I. Bulmer-Thomas

CHURCHES MAIN COMMITTEE (1941), Fielden House, Little College Street, London SW1P 3JZ. Tel: 071-222 4984. *Secretary*, J. D. Taylor Thompson, CB

CHURCHES TOGETHER IN ENGLAND (1990), Inter-Church House, 35-41 Lower Marsh, London SE1 7RL. Tel: 071-620 4444. *General Secretary*, Canon M. Reardon

CHURCHES TOGETHER IN SCOTLAND, ACTION OF (1990), Scottish Churches House, Kirk Street, Dunblane FK15 0AJ. Tel: 0786-823588. *General Secretary*, Revd M. Craig

CITIZENS' ADVICE BUREAUX, NATIONAL ASSOCIATION OF (1931), Myddelton House, 115–123 Pentonville Road, London N1 9LZ. Tel: 071-833 2181. *Chief Executive* A. Abraham

CITY PAROCHIAL FOUNDATION (1891), 6 Middle Street, London EC1A 7PH. Tel: 071-606 6145. *Clerk*, T. Cook

CIVIC TRUST, THE (1957), 17 Carlton House Terrace, London SW1Y 5AW. Tel: 071-930 0914. *Director*, M. C. Bradshaw

CIVIL DEFENCE AND DISASTER STUDIES, INSTITUTE OF (1938), Bell Court House, 11 Blomfield Street, London EC2M 7AY. Tel: 071-588 3700. *Hon. General Secretary*, V. G. B. Atwater

CIVIL ENGINEERS, INSTITUTION OF (1818), Great George Street, London SW1P 3AA. Tel: 071-222 7722. *Secretary*, R. S. Dobson, OBE

CIVIL LIBERTIES, NATIONAL COUNCIL FOR, *see* LIBERTY

CLASSICAL ASSOCIATION (1903). *Hon. Treasurer*, R. Wallace, Department of Classics, University of Keele, Keele, Newcastle under Lyme, Staffs. ST5 5BG. Tel: 0782-621111, ext. 3231

CLEAN AIR AND ENVIRONMENTAL PROTECTION, NATIONAL SOCIETY FOR (1899), 136 North Street, Brighton BN1 1RG. Tel: 0273-26313. *Secretary-General*, Dr R. N. Crossett

CLERGY ORPHAN CORPORATION (1749), 57B Tufton Street, London SW1P 3QL. Tel: 071-222 1812. *Secretary*, Miss J. Buncher

CLERKS OF WORKS OF GREAT BRITAIN INC., INSTITUTE OF (1882), 41 The Mall, London W5 3TJ. Tel: 081-579 2917/8. *Secretary*, A. P. Macnamara

COACHING CLUB (1871), West Compton House, West Compton, Shepton Mallet, Somerset BA4 4PD. Tel: 0749-890633. *Secretary*, D. H. Clarke

COMMERCE, ASSOCIATION OF BRITISH CHAMBERS OF (1860), 9 Tufton Street, London SW1P 3QB. Tel: 071-222 1555. *Director-General*, R. G. Taylor, CBE

COMMERCE, ASSOCIATION OF SCOTTISH CHAMBERS OF, 30 George Square, Glasgow G2 1EQ. Tel: 041-204 2121. *Director*, E. Marwick

COMMERCE AND INDUSTRY, LONDON CHAMBER OF (1881), 69 Cannon Street, London EC4N 5AB. Tel: 071-248 4444. *Chief Executive*, M. Stephens, CB

COMMERCE AND MANUFACTURERS, EDINBURGH CHAMBER OF (1786), 3 Randolph Crescent, Edinburgh EH3 7UD. Tel: 031-225 5851. *Chief Executive*, I. Brown

COMMERCE AND MANUFACTURERS, GLASGOW CHAMBER OF (1783), 30 George Square, Glasgow G2 1EQ. Tel: 041-204 2121. *Chief Executive*, E. Marwick

COMMERCE, CANADA UNITED KINGDOM CHAMBER OF (1921), 3 Regent Street, London SW1Y 4NZ. Tel: 071-930 7711. *Executive Director*, G. F. Bacon

COMMERCIAL AND INDUSTRIAL EDUCATION, BRITISH ASSOCIATION FOR (BACIE) (1919), 16 Park Crescent, London W1N 4AP. *Director*, B. V. Murphy

COMMERCIAL TRAVELLERS' BENEVOLENT INSTITUTION (1849). *Secretary*, M. N. Bown, Gable End, Mill Hill Road, Arnesby, Leics. LE8 3WG. Tel: 0533-478647

COMMISSIONAIRES, THE CORPS OF (1859), Market House, 85 Cowcross Street, London EC1M 6BP. Tel: 071-490 1125. Divisions in Belfast, Birmingham, Bristol, Edinburgh, Glasgow, Leeds, Liverpool, London, Manchester, Newcastle upon Tyne. *Managing Director*, C. J. Salt

COMMONWEALTH TRUST (linking the Royal Commonwealth Society and the Victoria League for Commonwealth Friendship), Commonwealth House, 18 Northumberland Avenue, London WC2N 5BJ. *Director-General*, Maj.-Gen. Sir David Thorne, KBE

COMPLEMENTARY AND ALTERNATIVE MEDICINE, COUNCIL FOR (1985), 179 Gloucester Place, London NW1 6DX. Tel: 071-724 9103. *Secretary*, Ms C. Daglish

COMPLEMENTARY MEDICINE, INSTITUTE FOR (1856), 4 Tavern Quay, Plough Way, Surrey Quays, London SE16 1QZ. Tel: 071-237 5165. *Director*, A. Baird

COMPOSERS' GUILD OF GREAT BRITAIN (1945), 34 Hanway Street, London W1P 9DE. Tel: 071-436 0007. *General Secretary*, Ms E. Yeoman

COMPUTER SOCIETY, BRITISH (1957), 13 Mansfield Street, London W1M 0BP. *Chief Executive*, J. R. Brookes

CONSERVATION OF HISTORIC AND ARTISTIC WORKS, INTERNATIONAL INSTITUTE FOR (1950), 6 Buckingham Street, London WC2N 6BA. Tel: 071-839 5975. *Secretary-General,* Prof. H. W. M. Hodges

CONSULTING ECONOMISTS' ASSOCIATION, INTERNATIONAL (1986), 16A Barnes High Street, London SW13 9LW. Tel: 081-876 2299. *Chairman,* P. Prynne

CONSULTING ENGINEERS, ASSOCIATION OF (1913), Alliance House, 12 Caxton Street, London SW1H 0QL. Tel: 071-222 6557. *Secretary,* Brig. H. Woodrow

CONSULTING SCIENTISTS, ASSOCIATION OF (1958), 2-3 Bosworth House, High Street, Thorpe-le-Soken, Essex CO16 0EA. Tel: 0255-862412. *Hon. Secretary,* W. G. Simpson

CONSUMERS' ASSOCIATION (1957), c/o The Association for Consumer Research, 2 Marylebone Road, London NW1 4DX. Tel: 071-486 5544. *Director.,* Dr J. Beishon

CONTEMPORARY APPLIED ARTS (1948), 43 Earlham Street, London WC2H 9LD. Tel: 071-836 6993. *Director,* Ms T. Peters

CONVEYANCERS, COUNCIL FOR LICENSED (1986), Suite 3, Cairngorm House, 203 Marsh Wall, London E14 9YT. Tel: 071-537 2953. *Secretary,* A. Viner

CO-OPERATIVE PARTY, 342 Hoe Street, London E17 9PX. Tel: 081-520 3580. *Secretary,* D. Wise, OBE

CO-OPERATIVE UNION LTD (1869), Holyoake House, Hanover Street, Manchester M60 0AS. Tel: 061-832 4300. *Chief Executive,* D. L. Wilkinson

CO-OPERATIVE WHOLESALE SOCIETY LTD (CWS) (1863), PO Box 53, New Century House, Manchester M60 4ES. Tel: 061-834 1212. *Chief Executive,* D. Skinner

CO-OPERATIVE WOMEN'S GUILD (1883), 342 Hoe Street, London E17 9PX. Tel: 081-520 4902. *General Secretary,* Mrs S. Bell

CO-OPERATIVE STUDIES, PLUNKETT FOUNDATION FOR (1919), 23 Hanborough Business Park, Long Hanborough, Oxford OX8 8LH. Tel: 0993-883636. *Director,* E. Parnell

COPYRIGHT COUNCIL, BRITISH (1953), 29–33 Berners Street, London W1P 4AA. *Secretary,* G. V. Adams

CORONERS' SOCIETY OF ENGLAND AND WALES (1846). *Hon. Secretary,* Dr. J. D. K. Burton, CBE, 7 Orchard Rise, Richmond, Surrey TW10 5BX. Tel: 071-371 9938

CORPORATE TREASURERS, ASSOCIATION OF (1979), 12 Devereux Court, London WC2R 3JJ. Tel: 071-936 2354. *Secretary,* Ms G. Pierpoint

CORPORATE TRUSTEES, ASSOCIATION OF (1974), 2 Withdean Rise, Brighton BN1 6YN. Tel: 0273-504276. *Secretary,* L. C. Howes

CORRESPONDENCE COLLEGES, ASSOCIATION OF BRITISH (1955), 6 Francis Grove, London SW19 4DT. *Secretary,* Mrs M. Coren

CORRYMEELA COMMUNITY (1965), Corrymeela House, 8 Upper Crescent, Belfast BT7 1NT. Tel: 0232-325008. *Director,* Revd J. Morrow

COTTON GROWING ASSOCIATION, BRITISH (1904), 13 Upper High Street, Thame, Oxon. OX9 3HL. Tel: 0844-261447. *Managing Director,* M. Maynard

COUNCIL FOR THE PROTECTION OF RURAL ENGLAND (CPRE), *see* RURAL

COUNSEL AND CARE (1954), Twyman House, 16 Bonny Street, London NW1 9PG. Tel: 071-485 1550. *General Manager,* J. Smith

COUNTRY HOUSES ASSOCIATION LTD (1955), 41 Kingsway, London WC2B 6UB. Tel: 071-836 1624. *Chief Executive,* R. D. Bratby

COUNTRY LANDOWNERS ASSOCIATION (1907), 16 Belgrave Square, London SW1X 8PQ. Tel: 071-235 0511. *Director-General,* J. Anderson

COUNTY CHIEF EXECUTIVES, ASSOCIATION OF (1974). *Hon. Secretary,* I. G. Caulfield, Shire Hall, Warwick CV34 4RR. Tel: 0926-410410

COUNTY COUNCILS, ASSOCIATION OF (1890), Eaton House, 66A Eaton Square, London SW1W 9BH. Tel: 071-235 1200. *Secretary,* R. G. Wendt

COUNTY EMERGENCY PLANNING OFFICERS' SOCIETY, *see* CHIEF

COUNTY SECRETARIES, SOCIETY OF (1974). *Hon. Secretary,* G. D. Gordon, County Hall, Chester CH1 1SF. Tel: 0244-602262

COUNTY SURVEYORS' SOCIETY (1884). *Hon. Secretary,* D. A. Hutchinson, County Hall, Dorchester DT1 1XJ. Tel: 0305-204741

COUNTY TREASURERS, SOCIETY OF (1903). *Hon. Secretary,* B. Smith, County Buildings, Eastgate Street, Stafford ST16 2NF. Tel: 0785-223121, ext. 6310

CRISIS (1967), 7 Whitechapel Road, London E1 1DV. Tel: 071-377 0489. *Executive Chair,* Ms J. Wade

CRUEL SPORTS, THE LEAGUE AGAINST (1924), 83 Union Street, London SE1 1SG. Tel: 071-407 0979. *Executive Director,* J. Barrington

CRUELTY TO ANIMALS, SOCIETY FOR THE PREVENTION OF, *see* ROYAL and SCOTTISH

CRUELTY TO CHILDREN, SOCIETY FOR THE PREVENTION OF, *see* NATIONAL and ROYAL SCOTTISH

CRUSE – BEREAVEMENT CARE (1959), 126 Sheen Road, Richmond, Surrey TW9 1UR. Tel: 081-940 4818. *Director,* R. Pearce

CURWEN INSTITUTE (1875), 17 Primrose Avenue, Chadwell Heath, Romford RM6 4QB. Tel: 081-599 8230. *General Secretary,* H. Jones

CWMNI URDD GOBAITH CYMRU (1922), Swyddfa'r Urdd, Aberystwyth, Dyfed SY23 1EN. Tel: 0970-623744. *Director,* J. E. Williams

CYCLISTS' TOURING CLUB (1878), Cotterell House, 69 Meadrow, Godalming, Surrey GU7 3HS. Tel: 0483-417217. *Director,* A. Harlow

CYMMRODORION, THE HONOURABLE SOCIETY OF (1751), 30 Eastcastle Street, London W1N 7PD. *Hon. Secretary,* Dr. T. Wyn Jones

CYSTIC FIBROSIS RESEARCH TRUST (1964), Alexandra House, 5 Blyth Road, Bromley BR1 3RS. Tel: 081-464 7211. *Director,* G. J. Edkins

CYTUN (CHURCHES TOGETHER IN WALES) (1990), 21 St Helen's Road, Swansea SA1 4AP. Tel: 0792-460876. *General Secretary,* Revd N. A. Davies

DAIRY ASSOCIATION, UNITED KINGDOM (1950), Giggs Hill Green, Thames Ditton, Surrey KT7 0EL. Tel: 081-398 4101, ext. 2436. *Secretary,* Mrs J. M. Newton

DAIRY FARMERS, ROYAL ASSOCIATION OF BRITISH (1876), 55 Sleaford Street, London SW8 5AB. Tel: 071-627 2111. *Chief Executive*, P. M. Gilbert

DAIRY TECHNOLOGY, SOCIETY OF (1943), 72 Ermine Street, Huntingdon, Cambs. PE18 6EZ. Tel: 0480-450741. *National Secretary*, Mrs R. Gale

DATA (Design and Technology Association), 16 Wellesbourne House, Walton Road, Wellesbourne, Warks. CV35 9JB. Tel: 0789-470007. *Director*, G. Warren

D-DAY AND NORMANDY FELLOWSHIP (1968). *Hon. Secretary*, Mrs L. R. Reed, 9 South Parade, Southsea, Hants. PO5 2JB. Tel: 0705-812180

DEAF, COMMONWEALTH SOCIETY FOR THE (1959), Dilke House, Malet Street, London WC1E 7JA. Tel: 071-631 5311. *Chairman*, C. Holborow, OBE, TD, MD, FRCS

DEAF ASSOCIATION, BRITISH (1890 *formerly* BRITISH DEAF AND DUMB ASSOCIATION), 38 Victoria Place, Carlisle CA1 1HU. Tel: 0228-48844. *Chief Executive*, Ms E. Wincott

DEAF CHILDREN, ROYAL SCHOOL FOR (1792), Victoria Road, Margate, Kent CT9 1NB. Tel: 0843-227561. *Secretary*, D. E. Downs

DEAF PEOPLE, FOLEY HOUSE RESIDENTIAL HOME FOR (1851), Foley House, 115 High Garrett, Braintree, Essex CM7 5NU. Tel: 0376-326652. *Director*, Mrs N. Hartard

DEAF PEOPLE, ROYAL ASSOCIATION IN AID OF (1841), 27 Old Oak Road, London W3 7HN. Tel: 081-743 6187. *Chief Executive*, Ms R. Brotherwood

DEAF PEOPLE, ROYAL NATIONAL INSTITUTE FOR (1911), 105 Gower Street, London WC1E 6AH. Tel: 071-387 8033. *Chief Executive*, S. Etherington

DEER MANAGEMENT SOCIETIES, THE FEDERATION OF (1975). *Chairman*, J. Hotchkis, Stede Court, Biddenden, Ashford, Kent TN27 8JG. Tel: 0580-291235

DEFENCE STUDIES, ROYAL UNITED SERVICES INSTITUTE FOR (1831), Whitehall, London SW1A 2ET. Tel: 071-930 5854. *Director*, Gp. Capt. D. Bolton

DEMOCRATIC LEFT (1991), 6 Cynthia Street, London N1 9BR. Tel: 071-278 4443. *General Secretary*, Ms N. Temple.

DENTAL ASSOCIATION, BRITISH (1880), 64 Wimpole Street, London W1M 8AL. Tel: 071-935 0875. *Chief Executive*, N. H. Whitehouse

DENTAL COUNCIL, GENERAL (1956), 37 Wimpole Street, London W1M 8DQ. Tel: 071-486 2171. *Registrar*, N. T. Davies, MBE

DENTAL HOSPITALS OF THE UNITED KINGDOM, ASSOCIATION OF (1942). *Hon. Secretary*, Mrs P. Harrington, Birmingham Dental Hospital, St Chad's Queensway, Birmingham B4 6NN

DESIGN AND INDUSTRIES ASSOCIATION (1915), 17 Lawn Crescent, Kew Gardens, Surrey TW9 3NR. Tel: 081-940 4925. *Secretary-General*, N. Chamberlain

DESIGNERS FOR INDUSTRY, FACULTY OF ROYAL (1936), RSA, 8 John Adam Street, London WC2N 6EZ. Tel: 071-930 5115. *Secretary*, C. Lucas

DESIGNERS, THE CHARTERED SOCIETY OF (1930), 29 Bedford Square, London WC1B 3EG. Tel: 071-631 1510. *Director*, B. Lymbery

DIABETIC ASSOCIATION, BRITISH (1934), 10 Queen Anne Street, London W1M 0BD. Tel: 071-323 1531. *Director*, M. Cooper

DICKENS FELLOWSHIP (1902), Dickens House, 48 Doughty Street, London WC1N 2LF. Tel: 071-405 2127. *Hon. General Secretary*, E. Preston

DIRECTORS OF PUBLIC HEALTH, ASSOCIATION OF (1982). *Hon. Secretary*, Dr. M. Spencely, South Manchester Health Authority, 293A Upper Brook Street, Manchester M13 0FW. Tel: 061-257 3459.

DIRECTORS, INSTITUTE OF (1903), 116 Pall Mall, London SW1Y 5ED. Tel: 071-839 1233. *Director-General*, P. Morgan

DISPENSING OPTICIANS, ASSOCIATION OF BRITISH (1925), 6 Hurlingham Business Park, Sulivan Road, London SW6 3DU. Tel: 071-736 0088. *Registrar*, D. S. Baker

DISTRESSED GENTLEFOLKS' AID ASSOCIATION (1897), Vicarage Gate House, Vicarage Gate, London W8 4AQ. Tel: 071-229 9341. *General Secretary*, N. B. M. Clack

DISTRICT COUNCILS, ASSOCIATION OF (1974), 26 Chapter Street, London SW1P 4ND. Tel: 071-233 6868. *Secretary*, G. Filkin

DISTRICT SECRETARIES, ASSOCIATION OF (1974), 9 Margaret Road, Bishopsworth, Bristol BS13 9DQ. Tel: 0272-647299. *Hon. Secretary*, E. Richards

DITCHLEY FOUNDATION, Ditchley Park, Enstone, Chipping Norton, Oxon. OX7 4ER. Tel: 0608-677346. *Director*, Sir Michael Quinlan, GCB

DOCKLAND SETTLEMENTS (1895), Rotherhithe Street, London SE16 1LJ. *Chief Executive*, J. B. Faul

DOMESTIC SERVANTS' BENEVOLENT INSTITUTION (1846), Royal Bank of Scotland PLC, 7 Burlington Gardens, London W1A 3DD. *Secretary*, A. J. Gibson

DOWNS SYNDROME ASSOCIATION (1970), 155 Mitcham Road, London SW17 9PG. Tel: 081-682 4001. *Director*, Ms A. Khan.

DOWSERS, BRITISH SOCIETY OF (1933). *Secretary*, M. D. Rust, Sycamore Cottage, Tamley Lane, Hastingleigh, Ashford, Kent TN25 5HW. Tel: 0233-750253

DRAINAGE AUTHORITIES, ASSOCIATION OF (1937). *Secretary*, D. Noble, The Mews, 3 Royal Oak Passage, High Street, Huntingdon, Cambs. PE18 6EA. Tel: 0480-411123

DRINKING FOUNTAIN AND CATTLE TROUGH ASSOCIATION, METROPOLITAN (1859). *Secretary*, D. R. W. Randall, 105 Wansunt Road, Bexley, Kent DA5 2DN. Tel: 0322-528062

DRIVING SOCIETY, BRITISH (1957), 27 Dugard Place, Barford, Warwick CV35 8DX. Tel: 0926-624420. *Secretary*, Mrs J. M. Dillon

DRUG DEPENDENCE, INSTITUTE FOR THE STUDY OF (1968), 1–4 Hatton Place, London EC1N 8ND. Tel: 071-430 1991. *Director*, J. Woodcock, OBE

DUKE OF EDINBURGH'S AWARD SCHEME (1956), Gulliver House, Madeira Walk, Windsor, Berks. SL4 1EU. Tel: 0753-810753. *Director*, Maj.-Gen. M. F. Hobbs, CBE

DYERS AND COLOURISTS, SOCIETY OF (1884), Perkin House, PO Box 244, 82 Grattan Road, Bradford BD1 2JB. Tel: 0274-725138. *General Secretary,* J. D. Watson

EARL HAIG'S (BRITISH LEGION) APPEAL FUND, *see* BRITISH LEGION, ROYAL

EARLY CHILDHOOD EDUCATION, BRITISH ASSOCIATION FOR (1923), 111 City View House, 463 Bethnal Green Road, London E2 9QY. Tel: 071-739 7594. *Secretary,* Mrs B. Boon

ECCLESIASTICAL HISTORY SOCIETY (1961). *Secretary,* Dr R. Swanson, School of History, University of Birmingham, Edgbaston B15 2TT. Tel: 021-414 5748

ECCLESIOLOGICAL SOCIETY (1839). *Hon. Secretary,* Prof. K. H. Murta, Underedge, Back Lane, Hathersage, Derbys. S30 1AR

EDUCATION IN ART AND DESIGN, NATIONAL SOCIETY FOR (1888), The Gatehouse, Corsham Court, Corsham, Wilts. SN13 0BZ. Tel: 0249-714825. *General Secretary,* J. Steers

EDUCATION OFFICERS, SOCIETY OF (1971), 20 Bedford Way, London WC1H 0AL. Tel: 071-612 6388. *General Secretary,* D. J. Hatfield, CBE

EDUCATION OFFICERS' SOCIETY, COUNTY (1889). *Hon. Secretary,* S. Sharp, Education Department, County Hall, Aylesbury, Bucks. Tel: 0296-382105

EDUCATIONAL CENTRES ASSOCIATION (1921), Chequer Centre, Chequer Street, London EC1Y 8PL. *General Secretary,* D. Delahunt

EDUCATIONAL RESEARCH IN ENGLAND AND WALES, NATIONAL FOUNDATION FOR (1946), The Mere, Upton Park, Slough SL1 2DQ. Tel: 0753-574123. *Director,* Ms C. Burstall, PH.D., D.SC

EGYPT EXPLORATION SOCIETY (1882), 3 Doughty Mews, London WC1N 2PG. Tel: 071-242 1880. *Secretary,* Dr P. A. Spencer

ELECTORAL REFORM SOCIETY OF GREAT BRITAIN AND IRELAND, 6 Chancel Street, London SE1 0UU. Tel: 071-928 1622. *President,* The Lord Blake, FBA

ELECTRICAL ENGINEERS, INSTITUTION OF (1871), Savoy Place, London WC2R 0BL. Tel: 071-240 1871. *Secretary,* J. C. Williams, PH.D., FEng

ELGAR FOUNDATION (1973). *Secretary to the Trustees,* J. G. Hughes, 23 Meadow Hill Road, Birmingham B38 8DE. Tel: 021-458 2747

ELGAR SOCIETY (1951). *Secretary,* Mrs C. Holt, 20 Geraldine Road, Malvern, Worcs. WR14 3PA. Tel: 0684-568822

ENERGY ASSOCIATION, BRITISH (1924), 34 St James's Street, London SW1A 1HD. Tel: 071-930 1211. *Director,* M. Jefferson.

ENERGY, INSTITUTE OF (1927), 18 Devonshire Street, London W1N 2AU. Tel: 071-580 7124. *Secretary,* C. Rigg, TD

ENGINEERING COUNCIL, THE (1981), 10 Maltravers Street, London WC2R 3ER. Tel: 071-240 7891. *Secretary,* L. Chelton

ENGINEERING DESIGNERS, INSTITUTE OF (1945), Courtleigh, Westbury Leigh, Westbury, Wilts. BA13 3TA. Tel: 0373-822801. *Secretary,* M. J. Osborne

ENGINEERING INDUSTRIES ASSOCIATION (1941), 16 Dartmouth Street, London SW1H 9BL. Tel: 071-222 2367. *Director-General,* Col. W. T. Williams

ENGINEERS, INSTITUTION OF BRITISH (1928), Royal Liver Building, 6 Hampton Place, Brighton BN1 3DD. Tel: 0273-734274. *Secretary,* Mrs D. Henry

ENGINEERS, SOCIETY OF (INCORPORATED) (1854), Parsifal College, 527 Finchley Road, London NW3 7BG. Tel: 071-435 5600. *Secretary,* P. A. Lancaster

ENGLISH ASSOCIATION, THE (1906), The Vicarage, Priory Gardens, London W4 1TT. Tel: 081-995 4236. *Secretary,* Dr R. Fairbanks-Joseph

ENGLISH FOLK DANCE AND SONG SOCIETY (1932), Cecil Sharp House, 2 Regent's Park Road, London NW1 7AY. Tel: 071-485 2206. *Executive Officer,* Mrs B. Godrich

ENGLISH PLACE-NAME SOCIETY (1923). *Hon. Director* Prof. K. Cameron, CBE, FBA, Department of English, The University, Nottingham NG7 2RD. Tel: 0602-484848, ext. 2892

ENGLISH-SPEAKING UNION OF THE COMMONWEALTH, THE (1918), 37 Charles Street, London W1X 8AB. Tel: 071-493 3328. *Director-General,* D. Thorp

ENTOMOLOGICAL SOCIETY OF LONDON, ROYAL (1833), 41 Queen's Gate, London SW7 5HR. Tel: 071-584 8361. *Registrar,* G. G. Bentley

ENVIRONMENTAL HEALTH OFFICERS, INSTITUTION OF (1883), 16 Great Guildford Street, London SE1 0ES. Tel: 071-928 6006. *Secretary,* T. Blunt

ENVIRONMENT COUNCIL (1969), 80 York Way, London N1 9AG. Tel: 071-278 4736. *Chief Executive,* S. Robinson

EPILEPSY ASSOCIATION, BRITISH (1949), Anstey House, 40 Hanover Square, Leeds LS3 1BE. Tel: 0532-439393. *Chief Executive,* T. J. O'Leary

EPILEPSY, THE NATIONAL SOCIETY FOR (1892), Chalfont Centre for Epilepsy, Chalfont St Peter, Gerrards Cross, Bucks. SL9 0RJ. Tel: 0494-873991. *Chief Executive,* Col. D. W. Eking

EQUESTRIAN FEDERATION, BRITISH (1972), Stoneleigh, Kenilworth, Warks. CV8 2LR. Tel: 0203-696697. *Director-General,* Maj. M. Wallace

ESPERANTO ASSOCIATION OF BRITAIN (1977), 140 Holland Park Avenue, London W11 4UF. Tel: 071-727 7821. *Hon. Secretary,* W. Green

ESTATE AGENTS, NATIONAL ASSOCIATION OF (1962), Arbon House, 21 Jury Street, Warwick CV34 4EH. Tel: 0926-496800. *General Secretary,* A. B. Clark

ESTATE AGENTS, OMBUDSMAN FOR CORPORATE (1990), PO Box 1114, Salisbury, Wilts. SP1 1YQ. Tel: 0722-331810. *Ombudsman,* D. Quayle, CB.

EUGENICS SOCIETY, *see* GALTON INSTITUTE

EVANGELICAL ALLIANCE (1846), Whitefield House, 186 Kennington Park Road, London SE11 4BT. Tel: 071-582 0228. *General Director,* Revd C. R. Calver

EVANGELICAL LIBRARY, THE (1928), 78A Chiltern Street, London W1M 2HB. Tel: 071-935 6997. *Librarian,* S. J. Taylor

EXECUTIVES ASSOCIATION OF GREAT BRITAIN LTD (1929), Suite 87–89, The Hop Exchange, 24 Southwark Street, London SE1 1TY. Tel: 071-403 3653. *Secretary,* Lt.-Col. J. J. Langdon-Mudge

EXPORT, INSTITUTE OF, Export House, 64 Clifton Street, London EC2A 4HB. Tel: 071-247 9812. *Secretary,* I. J. Campbell

EX-SERVICES LEAGUE, BRITISH COMMONWEALTH (1921), 48 Pall Mall, London SW1Y 5JY. Tel: 071-973 0633. *Secretary-General*, Brig. M. J. Doyle, MBE

EX-SERVICES MENTAL WELFARE SOCIETY (1919), Broadway House, The Broadway, London SW19 1RL. Tel: 081-543 6333. *General Secretary*, Brig. A. K. Dixon

FABIAN SOCIETY (1884), 11 Dartmouth Street, London SW1H 9BN. Tel: 071-222 8877. *General Secretary*, S. Crine

FAIR ISLE BIRD OBSERVATORY TRUST (1948), 21 Regent Terrace, Edinburgh EH7 5BT. Tel: 031-556 6042. *Hon. Secretary*, Miss V. M. Thom

FAMILY HISTORY SOCIETIES, FEDERATION OF (1974). *Administrator*, Mrs P. A. Saul, c/o The Benson Room, Birmingham and Midland Institute, Margaret Street, Birmingham B3 3BS

FAMILY MEDIATION (National Association of Family Mediation and Conciliation Services) (1982), Shaftesbury Centre, Percy Street, Swindon SN2 2AZ. Tel: 0793-514055. *Chairman*, Prof. B. Hoggett, QC

FAMILY PLANNING ASSOCIATION (1939), 27–35 Mortimer Street, London W1N 7RJ. Tel: 071-636 7866. *Director*, Ms D. E. Massey

FAMILY WELFARE ASSOCIATION (1869), 501–505 Kingsland Road, London E8 4AU. Tel: 071-254 6251. *Director*, Ms L. Berry

FAUNA AND FLORA PRESERVATION SOCIETY (1903), 1 Kensington Gore, London SW7 2AR. Tel: 071-823 8899. *Administrator*, Miss A. Hillier

FELLOWSHIP HOUSES TRUST (1937), Clock House, 192 High Road, Byfleet, Surrey KT14 7RN. Tel: 0932-343172. *Secretary*, Mrs A. J. Elliot

FIELD ARCHAEOLOGISTS, INSTITUTE OF, (1982), Metallurgy and Materials Building, University of Birmingham, Edgbaston, Birmingham B15 2TT. Tel: 021-471 2788. *Secretary*, S. M. Walls

FIELD SPORTS SOCIETY, BRITISH (1930), 59 Kennington Road, London SE1 7PZ. Tel: 071-928 4742. *Director*, Maj.-Gen. J. Hopkinson, CB

FIELD STUDIES COUNCIL (1943), Preston Montford, Montford Bridge, Shrewsbury SY4 1HW. Tel: 0743-850674. *Director*, A. D. Thomas

FILM CLASSIFICATION, BRITISH BOARD OF (1912), 3 Soho Square, London W1V 5DE. Tel: 071-439 7961. *Director*, J. Ferman

FIRE ENGINEERS, INSTITUTION OF (1918), 148 New Walk, Leicester LE1 7QB. Tel: 0533-553654. *General Secretary*, Mrs C. E. Mackwood

FIRE PROTECTION ASSOCIATION (1946), 140 Aldersgate Street, London EC1A 4HX. Tel: 071-606 3757. *Director*, A. S. Kidd

FIRE SERVICES ASSOCIATION, BRITISH (1949), 86 London Road, Leicester LE2 0QR. Tel: 0533-542879. *General Secretary*, D. Stevens

FIRE SERVICES NATIONAL BENEVOLENT FUND (1943), Marine Court, Fitzalan Road, Littlehampton, W. Sussex BN17 5NF. Tel: 0903-717185. *General Manager*, R. A. Spackman

FLEET AIR ARM OFFICERS ASSOCIATION (1957), 94 Piccadilly, London W1V 0BP. Tel: 071-499 0360. *Chairman*, Capt. A. J. Leary, CBE, RN (retd)

FOLKLORE SOCIETY, c/o University College London, Gower Street, London WC1E 6BT. Tel: 071-387 5894. *Hon. Secretary*, Ms M. Bowman

FOOD AND FARMING INFORMATION SERVICE (1991), European Business Centre, 460 Fulham Road, London SW6 1BY. Tel: 071-610 0402. *General Secretary*, J. Whelan

FOOD FROM BRITAIN (1983), 301–344 Market Towers, New Covent Garden Market, London SW8 5NQ. *Chairman*, P. R. Judge

FOOD SCIENCE AND TECHNOLOGY, INSTITUTE OF (1964), 5 Cambridge Court, 210 Shepherd's Bush Road, London W6 7NL. Tel: 071-603 6316. *Executive Secretary*, Ms H. G. Wild

FORCES HELP SOCIETY AND LORD ROBERTS WORKSHOPS (1899), 122 Brompton Road, London SW3 1JE. Tel: 071-589 3243. *Comptroller and Secretary*, Col. A. W. Davis, MBE

FOREIGN PRESS ASSOCIATION IN LONDON (1888), 11 Carlton House Terrace, London SW1Y 5AJ. Tel: 071-930 0445. *Secretaries*, Mrs D. Crole; Ms C. Flury

FORENSIC SCIENCE SOCIETY, THE (1959), Clarke House, 18A Mount Parade, Harrogate, HG1 1BX. Tel: 0423-506068. *Hon. Secretary*, B. W. J. Rankin

FORENSIC SCIENCES, BRITISH ACADEMY OF (1959). *Secretary-General*, Dr P. J. Flynn, Anaesthetic Unit, The London Hospital Medical College, Turner Street, London E1 2AD. Tel: 071-377 9201

FORESTERS, INSTITUTE OF CHARTERED (1982), 22 Walker Street, Edinburgh EH3 7HR. *Secretary*, Mrs M. W. Dick

FORESTRY ASSOCIATION, COMMONWEALTH (1921), c/o Oxford Forestry Institute, South Parks Road, Oxford OX1 3RB. Tel: 0865-275072. *Chairman*, R. L. Newman

FORESTRY SOCIETY OF ENGLAND, WALES AND NORTHERN IRELAND, ROYAL (1882), 102 High Street, Tring, Herts. HP23 4AF. Tel: 044 282-2028. *Director*, J. E. Jackson, Ph.D

FORESTRY SOCIETY, ROYAL SCOTTISH (1854), Camsie House, Charlestown, Dunfermline, Fife KY11 3EE. Tel: 0383-873014. *Director*, M. Osborne

FOUNDRYMEN, INSTITUTE OF BRITISH (1904), 3rd Floor, Bridge House, 121 Smallbrook Queensway, Birmingham B5 4JP. Tel: 021-643 4523. *Secretary*, G. A. Schofield

FRANCO-BRITISH SOCIETY (1924), Room 623, Linen Hall, 162–168 Regent Street, London W1R 5TB. Tel: 071-734 0815. *Executive Secretary*, Mrs M. Clarke

FREE CHURCH FEDERAL COUNCIL (1940), 27 Tavistock Square, London WC1H 9HH. Tel: 071-387 8413. *General Secretary*, Revd D. Staple

FREEDOM ASSOCIATION (1975), 35 Westminster Bridge Road, London SE1 7JB. Tel: 071-928 9925. *Chairman*, Mrs P. North

FREEMASONS, GRAND LODGE OF ANTIENT FREE AND ACCEPTED MASONS OF SCOTLAND (1736), Freemasons' Hall, 96 George Street, Edinburgh EH2 3DH. Tel: 031-225 5304. *Grand Master Mason of Scotland*, Brig. Sir Gregor MacGregor of MacGregor, Bt.; *Grand Secretary*, A. O. Hazel

FREEMASONS, UNITED GRAND LODGE OF ENGLAND (1717), Freemasons' Hall, Great Queen Street, London WC2B 5AZ. Tel: 071-831 9811. *Grand Master,* HRH The Duke of Kent, KG, GCMG, GCVO; *Grand Secretary,* Cdr. M. B. S. Higham

FREEMEN OF ENGLAND AND WALES (1966). *Secretary,* R. J. M. Bishop, 10 Wyngate Road, Hale, Altrincham, Cheshire WA15 0LZ. Tel: 061-904 9304

FREEMEN'S GUILDS:

City of Coventry Freemen's Guild (1946). *Hon. Clerk,* J. H. Bradbury, 5 Adare Drive, Styvechale, Coventry CV3 6AD. Tel: 0203-501801

Guild of Freemen of the City of London (1908), PO Box 153, 40A Ludgate Hill, London EC4M 7DE. Tel: 071-223 7638. *Clerk,* Col. D. Ivy

Guild of Freemen of the City of York (1953). *Hon. Clerk,* R. Lee, 29 Albemarle Road, York YO2 1EW. Tel: 0904-653698

FRIENDLY SOCIETIES, NATIONAL CONFERENCE OF (1887), Room 313, Victoria House, Vernon Place, London WC1B 4DP. Tel: 071-242 1923. *Secretary,* P. M. Madders

FRIENDS OF CATHEDRAL MUSIC (1956), c/o Addington Palace, Croydon, Surrey CR9 5AD. Tel: 071-638 1621. *Hon. General Secretary,* V. Waterhouse

FRIENDS OF THE CLERGY CORPORATION, THE (1972), 27 Medway Street, London SW1P 2BD. Tel: 071-222 2288. *Secretary,* J. M. Greany

FRIENDS OF THE EARTH (1971), 26–28 Underwood Street, London N1 7JQ. Tel: 071-490 1555.

FRIENDS OF THE ELDERLY AND GENTLEFOLK'S HELP (1905), 42 Ebury Street, London SW1W 0LZ. Tel: 071-730 8263. *General Secretary,* Revd J. Schofield

FRIENDS OF THE NATIONAL LIBRARIES (1931), The British Library, London WC1B 3DG. Tel: 071-323 7559. *Hon. Secretary,* J. F. Fuggles

FURNITURE HISTORY SOCIETY (1964), 1 Mercedes Cottages, St John's Road, Haywards Heath, W. Sussex RH16 4EH. Tel: 0444-413845. *Membership Secretary,* Dr B. Austen

GALLIPOLI ASSOCIATION (1915). *Hon. Secretary,* J. C. Watson Smith, Earlydene Orchard, Earlydene, Ascot, Berks. SL5 9JY. Tel: 0344-26523

GALTON INSTITUTE, THE (formerly The Eugenics Society) (1907), 19 Northfields Prospect, London SW18 1PE. Tel: 081-874 7257. *General Secretary,* Mrs L. Brooks

GAMBLERS ANONYMOUS (1954), PO Box 88, London SW10 0EU. Tel: 081-741 4181

GAME CONSERVANCY, THE (1969), Fordingbridge, Hants. SP6 1EF. Tel: 0425-652381. *Director-General,* R. M. Van Oss

GARDEN HISTORY SOCIETY (1965), 5 The Knoll, Hereford HR1 1RU. Tel: 0432-354479. *Hon. Membership Secretary,* Mrs A. Richards

GARDENERS' ASSOCIATION, THE GOOD (1968), Pinetum, Churcham, Glos. GL2 8AD. Tel: 01452-750402. *Hon. Director,* S. Cooper

GARDENERS' ROYAL BENEVOLENT SOCIETY (1839), Bridge House, 139 Kingston Road, Leatherhead, Surrey KT22 7NT. Tel: 0372-373962. *Secretary-Administrator,* C. R. C. Bunce

GAS CONSUMERS COUNCIL (1986), 6th Floor, Abford House, 15 Wilton Road, London SW1V 1LT. Tel: 071-931 0977. *Director,* I. W. Powe

GAS ENGINEERS, INSTITUTION OF (1863), 17 Grosvenor Crescent, London SW1X 7ES. Tel: 071-245 9811. *Secretary,* D. J. Chapman

GEMMOLOGICAL ASSOCIATION OF GREAT BRITAIN (1931), 1st Floor, 27 Greville Street, London EC1N 8SU. Tel: 071-404 3334. *Secretary,* A. Klein

GENEALOGICAL RESEARCH SOCIETY, IRISH (1936). *Hon. Secretary,* Miss R. McCutcheon, c/o The Irish Club, 82 Eaton Square, London SW1W 9AJ

GENEALOGISTS AND RECORD AGENTS, ASSOCIATION OF (1968), *Secretaries,* Mr and Mrs D. R. Young, 28 Badgers Close, Horsham, W. Sussex RH12 5RU

GENEALOGISTS, SOCIETY OF (1911), 14 Charterhouse Buildings, Goswell Road, London EC1M 7BA. Tel: 071-251 8799. *Director,* A. J. Camp

GENERAL PRACTITIONERS, ROYAL COLLEGE OF (1952), 14 Princes Gate, Hyde Park, London SW7 1PU. Tel: 071-581 3232. *Secretary,* Dr M. McBride

GENTLEPEOPLE, GUILD OF AID FOR (1904), 10 St Christopher's Place, London W1M 6HY. Tel: 071-935 0641. *Secretary,* Mrs G. A. Burgess

GEOGRAPHICAL ASSOCIATION, 343 Fulwood Road, Sheffield S10 3BP. Tel: 0742-670666. *Senior Administrator,* Miss F. Soar

GEOGRAPHICAL SOCIETY, ROYAL (1830), 1 Kensington Gore, London SW7 2AR. Tel: 071-589 5466. *President,* Sir Crispin Tickell, GCMG, KCVO

GEOGRAPHICAL SOCIETY, ROYAL SCOTTISH (1884), 10 Randolph Crescent, Edinburgh EH3 7TU. Tel: 031-225 3330. *Secretary,* A. B. Cruickshank

GEOLOGICAL SOCIETY (1807), Burlington House, Piccadilly, London W1V 0JU. Tel: 071-434 9944. *President,* Prof. A. L. Harris; *Executive Secretary,* R. M. Bateman

GEOLOGISTS' ASSOCIATION (1858), Burlington House, Piccadilly, London W1V 9AG. Tel: 071-434 9298. *Hon. General Secretary,* Mrs M. E. Pugh

GEORGIAN GROUP (1937), 37 Spital Square, London E1 6DY. Tel: 071-377 1722. *Director,* M. Cudlipp

GIFTED CHILDREN, NATIONAL ASSOCIATION FOR (1966), Park Campus, Boughton Green Road, Northampton NN2 7AL. Tel: 0604-792300. *Director,* M. Short

GILBERT AND SULLIVAN SOCIETY (1924). *Hon. Secretary,* Miss B. Dove, 31A Kenmere Gardens, Wembley, Middx. HA0 1TD

GINGERBREAD, AN ASSOCIATION FOR ONE PARENT FAMILIES (1970), 35 Wellington Street, London WC2E 7BN. Tel: 071-240 0953. *Chief Executive,* Ms M. Honeyball

GIRL GUIDES ASSOCIATION, *see* GUIDES ASSOCIATION

GIRLS' BRIGADE, THE, Girls' Brigade House, 62 Foxhall Road, Didcot, Oxon. OX11 7BQ. Tel: 0235-510425. *Brigade Secretary*, Miss D. M. Cosser

GIRLS' FRIENDLY SOCIETY AND TOWNSEND FELLOWSHIP (1875), 126 Queens Gate, London SW7 5LQ. Tel: 071-589 9628. *General Secretary*, Mrs H. Crompton

GIRLS' VENTURE CORPS AIR CADETS (1964), Redhill Aerodrome, Kings Mill Lane, South Nutfield, Redhill RH1 5JY. Tel: 0737-823345. *Secretary-General*, Miss H. P. Prosper

GLASS ENGRAVERS, THE GUILD OF (1975). *Secretary*, Mrs J. Orsler, 8 Rathcoole Avenue, London N8 9NA. Tel: 081-348 8772

GLASS TECHNOLOGY, SOCIETY OF (1916), Thornton, 20 Hallam Gate Road, Sheffield S10 5BT. Tel: 0742-663168. *Manager*, Miss J. Costello

GLIDING ASSOCIATION, BRITISH (1930), Kimberley House, Vaughan Way, Leicester LE1 4SE. Tel: 0533-531051. *General Secretary*, B. Rolfe

GOAT SOCIETY, BRITISH (1879), 34–36 Fore Street, Bovey Tracey, Newton Abbot, Devon TQ13 9AD. Tel: 0626-833168. *Secretary*, Mrs S. Knowles

GRAPHIC FINE ART, SOCIETY OF (1919), 9 Newburgh Street, London W1V 1LH. *Secretary*, Ms J. Caesar

GRAPHOLOGISTS, THE BRITISH INSTITUTE OF (1983), 4th Floor, Bell Court House, 11 Blomfield Street, London EC2M 7AY. *Chairman*, Dr C. Molander

GREEK INSTITUTE (1969), 34 Bush Hill Road, London N21 2DS. Tel: 081-360 7968. *Director*, Dr K. Tofallis

GREEN PARTY, THE (1973), 10 Station Parade, Balham High Road, London SW12 9AZ. Tel: 081-673 0045. *Office Manager*, J. Bishop

GREENPEACE UK (1971), Canonbury Villas, London N1 2PN. Tel: 071-354 5100. *Executive Director*, The Lord Melchett

GROCERS ASSOCIATION, BRITISH INDEPENDENT (1890), Federation House, 17 Farnborough Street, Farnborough, Hants. GU14 8AG. Tel: 0252-515001. *National Secretary*, A. Taylor

GUIDE DOGS FOR THE BLIND ASSOCIATION (1931), Hillfields, Burghfield, Reading RG7 3YG. Tel: 0734-835555. *Director-General*, J. C. Oxley

GUIDES ASSOCIATION (1910), 17–19 Buckingham Palace Road, London SW1W OPT. Tel: 071-834 6242. *Chief Commissioner*, Mrs J. Garside

GULBENKIAN FOUNDATION, *see* CALOUSTE GULBENKIAN FOUNDATION

HAEMOPHILIA SOCIETY, THE (1950), 123 Westminster Bridge Road, London SE1 7HR. Tel: 071-928 2020. *General Secretary*, D. G. Watters

HAKLUYT SOCIETY (1846), c/o Map Library, The British Library, Great Russell Street, London WC1B 3DG. Tel: 0986-86359. *Joint Hon. Secretaries*, Dr W. F. Ryan; Mrs S. Tyacke

HANSARD SOCIETY FOR PARLIAMENTARY GOVERNMENT, THE (1944), 16 Gower Street, London WC1E 6DP. Tel: 071-323 1131. *Director*, D. Harris

HARD OF HEARING, BRITISH ASSOCIATION OF THE (1948), 7–11 Armstrong Road, London W3 7JL. Tel: 081-743 1110. *Chairman*, P. J. Phillips

HARVEIAN SOCIETY OF EDINBURGH (1782), Department of Medicine, The Royal Infirmary, Edinburgh EH3 9YW. Tel: 031-229 2477, ext. 3166. *Joint Secretaries*, A. B. MacGregor; Dr A. D. Toft

HARVEIAN SOCIETY OF LONDON (1831), 11 Chandos Street, London W1M OEB. Tel: 071-580 1043. *Executive Secretary*, M. Griffiths

HEAD TEACHERS, NATIONAL ASSOCIATION OF (1897). *General Secretary*, D. M. Hart, OBE, 1 Heath Square, Boltro Road, Haywards Heath, W. Sussex RH16 1BL. Tel: 0444-458133

HEALTH AUTHORITIES AND TRUSTS, NATIONAL ASSOCIATION OF (1974), Birmingham Research Park, Vincent Drive, Birmingham B15 2SQ. Tel: 021-471 4444. *Director*, P. Hunt

HEALTH CARE ASSOCIATION, BRITISH (1931), 24A Main Street, Garforth, Leeds LS25 1AA. Tel: 0532-320903. *National Secretary*, Ms C. Bell

HEALTH EDUCATION, INSTITUTE OF (1962). *Hon. Secretary*, Prof. L. Baric, PH.D., 14 High Elm Road, Hale Barns, Altrincham, Cheshire WA15 OHS. Tel: 061-980 8276

HEALTH, GUILD OF (1904), Edward Wilson House, 26 Queen Anne Street, London W1M 9LB. Tel: 071-580 2492. *National Director*, W. R. Booth

HEALTH SERVICES MANAGEMENT, INSTITUTE OF (1902), 75 Portland Place, London W1N 4AN. Tel: 071-580 5041. *Director*, Ms P. Charlwood

HEART FOUNDATION, BRITISH (1963), 14 Fitzhardinge Street, London W1H 4DH. Tel: 071-935 0185. *Director-General*, Maj.-Gen. L. F. H. Busk, CB

HEDGEHOG PRESERVATION SOCIETY, BRITISH (1982), Hedgehog House, Dhustone, Clee Hill, Ludlow, Shropshire SY8 3PL. *Secretary*, Mrs A. Jenkins

HELLENIC STUDIES, SOCIETY FOR THE PROMOTION OF (1879), 31–34 Gordon Square, London WC1H OPP. Tel: 071-387 7495. *Secretary*, Dr H. W. Catling

HELP THE AGED (1960), St James's Walk, Clerkenwell Green, London EC1R OBE. Tel: 071-253 0253. *Director-General*, Col. J. Mayo, OBE

HERALDIC AND GENEALOGICAL STUDIES, INSTITUTE OF (1961), 79–82 Northgate, Canterbury, Kent CT1 1BA. *Registrar*, Ms J. Carter

HERALDRY SOCIETY, THE (1947), 44–45 Museum Street, London WC1A 1LY. Tel: 071-430 2172. *Secretary*, Mrs M. Miles, MBE, RD

HERALDRY SOCIETY OF SCOTLAND (1977), PO Box 1, Roslin, Midlothian EH25 9TB

HERPETOLOGICAL SOCIETY, BRITISH (1947), c/o Zoological Society of London, Regent's Park, London NW1 4RY. Tel: 081-452 9578. *Secretary*, Mrs M. Green

HIGHWAYS AND TRANSPORTATION, INSTITUTION OF (1930), 3 Lygon Place, Ebury Street, London SW1W OJS. Tel: 071-370 5245. *Secretary*, Dr M. R. Cragg

HISPANIC AND LUSO BRAZILIAN COUNCIL (1943), Canning House, 2 Belgrave Square, London SW1X 8PJ. Tel: 071-235 2303. *Director-General*, Sir Michael Simpson-Orlebar, KCMG

HISTORICAL ASSOCIATION, THE (1906), 59A Kennington Park Road, London SE11 4JH. Tel: 071-735 3901. *Secretary*, Mrs M. Stiles

HISTORICAL SOCIETY, ROYAL (1868), University College London, Gower Street, London WCIE 6BT. Tel: 071-387 7532. *President*, Prof. F. M. L. Thompson, CBE; *Executive Secretary*, Mrs J. N. McCarthy

HOMOEOPATHIC ASSOCIATION, BRITISH (1902), 27A Devonshire Street, London WIN IRJ. Tel: 071-935 2163. *General Secretary*, Mrs E. Segall

HONG KONG ASSOCIATION (1961), Swire House, 59 Buckingham Gate, London SWIE 6AJ. Tel: 071-821 3220. *Executive Director*, Brig. B. G. Hickey, OBE, MC

HOROLOGICAL INSTITUTE, BRITISH (1858), Upton Hall, Upton, Newark, Notts. NG23 5TE. Tel: 0636-813795. *Secretary*, W. M. G. Evans

HOROLOGICAL SOCIETY, ANTIQUARIAN (1953), New House, High Street, Ticehurst, Wadhurst, E. Sussex TN5 7AL. Tel: 0580-200155. *Secretary*, Mrs M. A. Collins

HORSE SOCIETY, BRITISH (1947) (incorporating The Pony Club), British Equestrian Centre, Kenilworth, Warks. CV8 2LR. Tel: 0203-696697. *Chief Executive*, Col. T. Eastwood

HOSPITAL FEDERATION, INTERNATIONAL (1947), 4 Abbotts Place, London NW6 4NP. Tel: 071-372 7181. *Director-General*, Dr E. N. Pickering

HOSPITAL SATURDAY FUND, THE (1873), 24 Upper Ground, London SEI 9PQ. Tel: 071-928 6662. *Chief Executive*, K. R. Bradley

HOSPITAL SAVING ASSOCIATION, THE, Hambleden House, Andover, Hants. SPIO ILQ. Tel: 0264-353211. *General Secretary*, J. A. Young

HOSPITALITY ASSOCIATION, BRITISH (1907), 40 Duke Street, London WIM 6HR. Tel: 071-499 6641. *Chief Executive*, R. Lees, CB, MBE

HOTEL, CATERING AND INSTITUTIONAL MANAGEMENT ASSOCIATION (1971), 191 Trinity Road, London SW17 7HN. *Director*, Miss E. Gadsby

HOUSE OF ST BARNABAS-IN-SOHO (1846), 1 Greek Street, London WIV 6NQ. Tel: 071-437 1894. For homeless women in London. *Director*, D. G. Saunders

HOUSING, INSTITUTE OF, Octavia House, Westwood Business Park, Westwood Way, Coventry CV4 8JP. Tel: 0203-694433. *Director*, P. McGurk

HOUSING AID SOCIETY, CATHOLIC (1956), 189A Old Brompton Road, London SW5 OAR. Tel: 071-393 4961. *Director*, Ms R. Rafferty

HOUSING AND TOWN PLANNING COUNCIL, NATIONAL (1900), 14–18 Old Street, London ECIV 9AB. Tel: 071-251 2363. *Director*, R. Walker

HOUSING ASSOCIATION FOR OFFICERS' FAMILIES (1916), Alban Dobson House, Green Lane, Morden, Surrey SM4 5NS. Tel: 081-648 0335. *General Secretary*, J. B. Holt

HOVERCRAFT SOCIETY, THE (1971), 24 Jellicoe Avenue, Alverstoke, Gosport, Hants. PO12 2PE. Tel: 0705-822351, ext. 41432. *Chairman*, M. J. Cox

HOWARD LEAGUE FOR PENAL REFORM, THE (1866), 708 Holloway Road, London N19 3NL. Tel: 071-281 7722. *Director*, Ms F. Crook

HUGUENOT SOCIETY OF GREAT BRITAIN AND IRELAND (1885), The Huguenot Library, University College, Gower Street, London WCIE 6BT. Tel: 071-380 7094. *Secretary*, Mrs M. Bayliss

HUMANE RESEARCH TRUST, (1974), Brook House, 29 Bramhall Lane South, Bramhall, Cheshire SK7 2DN. Tel: 061-439 8041. *Chairman*, K. Cholerton

HYDROGRAPHIC SOCIETY (1972), c/o University of East London, Longbridge Road, Dagenham, Essex RM8 2AS. Tel: 081-597 1946. *Hon. Secretary*, V. J. Abbott

HYMN SOCIETY OF GREAT BRITAIN AND IRELAND (1936). *Secretary*, Revd M. Garland, St Nicholas Rectory, Glebe Fields, Curdworth, Sutton Coldfield, W. Midlands B76 9ES. Tel: 0675-470384

IMMIGRANTS ADVISORY SERVICE, UK (1970), 190 Great Dover Street, London SEI 4YB. Tel: 071-357 6917. *Director*, S. Choudhury

INDEPENDENT BRITAIN, CAMPAIGN FOR AN (1976), 81 Ashmole Street, London SW8 INF. Tel: 081-340 0314. *Hon. Secretary*, Sir Robin Williams, Bt.

INDEPENDENT SCHOOL BURSARS' ASSOCIATION (1933). *Secretary*, D. J. Bird, Woodlands, Closewood Road, Denmead, Portsmouth PO7 6JD. Tel: 0705-264506

INDEPENDENT SCHOOLS CAREERS ORGANIZATION (1942), 12A–18A Princess Way, Camberley, Surrey GU15 3SP. Tel: 0276-682587. *Director* G. W. Searle

INDEPENDENT SCHOOLS INFORMATION SERVICE (ISIS) (1972), 56 Buckingham Gate, London SWIE 6AG. Tel: 071-630 8793. *Director*, D. J. Woodhead

INDEPENDENT SCHOOLS JOINT COUNCIL (1974), 35–37 Grosvenor Gardens, London SWIW OBS. Tel: 071-630 0144. *General Secretary*, Dr A. G. Hearnden, OBE

INDEXERS, SOCIETY OF (1957), 38 Rochester Road, London NWI 9JJ. Tel: 071-916 7809. *Secretary*, Mrs C. Troughton

INDUSTRIAL CHRISTIAN FELLOWSHIP (1877), Dukes Meadow, 1 One Tree Lane, Beaconsfield, Bucks. HP9 2BU. Tel: 071-283 6120. *Director*, Revd R. Holloway

INDUSTRIAL EDITORS, BRITISH ASSOCIATION OF, (1949), 3 Locks Yard, High Street, Sevenoaks, Kent, TN13 ILT. Tel: 0732-459331. *Chief Executive*, C. Pedersen

INDUSTRIAL MANAGERS, INSTITUTION OF (1931), Management House, Cottingham Road, Corby, Northants. NN17 ITT. Tel: 0536-407600. *Chief Executive*, J. R. Dixon

INDUSTRIAL MARKETING RESEARCH ASSOCIATION (IMRA) (1963), 11 Bird Street, Lichfield, Staffs. WS13 6PW. Tel: 0543-263448. *Executive Officer*, M. Berry

INDUSTRIAL SOCIETY, THE (1918), Robert Hyde House, 48 Bryanston Square, London WIH 7LN. Tel: 071-262 2401. *Director*, Mrs R. Chapman

INDUSTRY AND PARLIAMENT TRUST, 1 Buckingham Place, London SWIE 6HR. Tel: 071-976 5311. *Director*, F. R. Hyde-Chambers

INDUSTRY TRAINING ORGANIZATIONS, NATIONAL COUNCIL OF (1988), 5 George Lane, Royston, Herts. SG8 9AR. Tel: 0763-247285. *Administrator*, Mrs C. Armstrong

INFANT DEATHS, THE FOUNDATION FOR THE STUDY OF (1971), 35 Belgrave Square, London SWIX 8QB. Tel: 071-235 0965. *Secretary-General*, Mrs J. Epstein

INFORMATION SCIENTISTS, INSTITUTE OF (1958), 44–45 Museum Street, London WC1A 1LY. Tel: 071-831 8003. *Executive Secretary*, Mrs S. A. Carter

INNER WHEEL CLUBS IN GREAT BRITAIN AND IRELAND, ASSOCIATION OF (1934), 51 Warwick Square, London SW1V 2AT. Tel: 071-834 4600. *General Secretary*, Miss J. Dobson

INSURANCE AND INVESTMENT BROKERS' ASSOCIATION, BRITISH, BIIBA House, 14 Bevis Marks, London EC3A 7NT. Tel: 071-623 9043. *Director-General*, Mrs R. Rooley

INSURANCE BROKERS REGISTRATION COUNCIL, 15 St Helen's Place, London EC3A 6DS. Tel: 071-588 4387. *Registrar*, Miss E. J. Rees

INSURANCE INSTITUTE, CHARTERED (1897), 20 Aldermanbury, London EC2V 7HY. Tel: 071-606 3835. *Director-General*, Dr D. E. Bland

INSURERS, ASSOCIATION OF BRITISH (1985), 51 Gresham Street, London EC2V 7HQ. Tel: 071-600 3333. *Chief Executive*, M. A. Jones

INTERCON (INTERCONTINENTAL CHURCH SOCIETY) (1823), 175 Tower Bridge Road, London SE1 2AQ. Tel: 071-407 4588. *General Secretary*, Deaconess P. K. L. Schmiegelow

INTERNATIONAL AFFAIRS, ROYAL INSTITUTE OF (1920), Chatham House, 10 St James's Square, London SW1Y 4LE. Tel: 071-957 5700. *Director*, Prof. L. Martin

INTERNATIONAL FRIENDSHIP LEAGUE (1931), 3 Creswick Road, London W3 9HE. Tel: 081-992 0221. *Secretary*, Mrs B. Macdonald

INTERNATIONAL LAW ASSOCIATION (1873), Charles Clore House, 17 Russell Square, London WC1B 5DR. Tel: 071-323 2978. *Hon. Secretary-General*, B. Mauleverer, QC

INTERNATIONAL POLICE ASSOCIATION (British Section) (1950), 1 Fox Road, West Bridgford, Nottingham NG2 6AJ. Tel: 0602-813638. *Chief Executive Officer*, K. H. Robinson

INTERNATIONAL SHIPPING FEDERATION (1909), 2–5 Minories, London EC3N 1BJ. Tel: 071-702 1100. *Secretary*, D. A. Dearsley

INTERNATIONAL STUDENTS HOUSE (1962), 229 Great Portland Street, London W1N 5HD. Tel: 071-631 3223. *Secretary*, G. Rates

INTERNATIONAL TIN RESEARCH INSTITUTE (1932), Kingston Lane, Uxbridge, Middx. UB8 3PJ. Tel: 0895-72406. *Director*, Dr B. T. K. Barry

INTERNATIONAL VOLUNTARY SERVICE (1920), 162 Upper New Walk, Leicester LE1 7QA. *General Secretaries*, P. Ticher; D. T. Huggins

INTERSERVE (1852), Whitefield House, 325 Kennington Road, London SE11 4QH. Tel: 071-735 8227. *General Director*, A. M. S. Pont

INTER VARSITY CLUBS, ASSOCIATION OF (1946), 26 Chesswood Road, Worthing, W. Sussex BN11 2AD. *Secretary*, M. A. Rooke-Matthews

INVALID CHILDREN'S AID NATIONWIDE (I CAN)(1888), 10 Bowling Green Lane, London EC1R 0BD. Tel: 071-253 9111. *Director*, B. J. Jones

INVALIDS-AT-HOME (1966), 17 Lapstone Gardens, Kenton, Harrow HA3 0EB. Tel: 081-907 1706. *Executive Officer*, Ms S. Lomas

INVISIBLES, BRITISH (1983), Windsor House, 39 King Street, London EC2V 8DQ. Tel: 071-600 1198. *Director-General*, Mrs A. Wright

INVOLVEMENT AND PARTICIPATION ASSOCIATION (1884), 42 Colebrook Row, London N1 8AF. Tel: 071-354 8040. *Director*, B. C. Stevens

IRAN SOCIETY (1936), 2 Belgrave Square, London SW1X 8PJ. Tel: 071-235 5122. *Hon. Secretary*, J. R. H. James, OBE

JACQUELINE DU PRE MEMORIAL FUND (1988), 14 Ogle Street, London W1P 7LG. Tel: 071-436 3173. *Chairman*, Lord Goodman, CH

JAPAN ASSOCIATION (1950), Swire House, 59 Buckingham Gate, London SW1E 6AJ. Tel: 071-821 3220. *Executive Director*, Brig. B. G. Hickey, OBE, MC

JERUSALEM AND THE MIDDLE EAST CHURCH ASSOCIATION, THE (1887), 1 Hart House, The Hart, Farnham, Surrey GU9 7HA. Tel: 0252-726994. *Secretary*, Mrs V. Wells

JEWISH HISTORICAL SOCIETY OF ENGLAND (1893), 33 Seymour Place, London W1H 5AP. Tel: 081-723 4044. *Hon. Secretary*, C. M. Drukker

JEWISH YOUTH, ASSOCIATION FOR (1899), 128 East Lane, North Wembley, Middx. HA0 3NL. Tel: 081-908 4747. *Executive Director*, M. Shaw

JEWS, CHURCH'S MINISTRY AMONG THE (1809), 30C Clarence Road, St Albans, Herts. AL1 4JJ. Tel: 0727-833114. *General Director*, Revd J. M. V. Drummond

JOURNALISTS, THE CHARTERED INSTITUTE OF (1883), 2 Dock Offices, Surrey Quays, Lower Road, London SE16 2XL. Tel: 071-252 1187. *Joint General Secretaries*, W. Tadd, C. Underwood

JUSTICE (British Section of the International Commission of Jurists) (1957), 95A Chancery Lane, London WC2A 1DT. Tel: 071-405 6018. *Director*, Ms A. Owers

JUSTICES' CLERKS' SOCIETY (1839), The Law Courts, Petters Way, Yeovil, Somerset BA20 1SW. Tel: 0935-26281. *Hon. Secretary*, L. G. C. Cramp

KING EDWARD'S HOSPITAL FUND FOR LONDON (THE KING'S FUND) (1897), 14 Palace Court, London W2 4HT. Tel: 071-727 0581. *Director*, Dr R. J. Maxwell

KING GEORGE'S FUND FOR SAILORS (1917), 1 Chesham Street, London SW1X 8NF. Tel: 071-235 2884. *Director-General*, Hon. H. Lawson

KIPLING SOCIETY, THE (1927), 2nd Floor, Schomberg House, 80–82 Pall Mall, London SW1 5HF. Tel: 0428-652709. *Hon. Secretary*, N. Entract

LADIES IN REDUCED CIRCUMSTANCES, SOCIETY FOR THE ASSISTANCE OF (1886), Lancaster House, 25 Hornyold Road, Malvern, Worcs. WR14 1QQ. Tel: 0684-574645

LANDSCAPE INSTITUTE (1929), 6–7 Barnard Mews, London SW11 1QU. Tel: 071-738 9166. *Registrar*, P. R. Broadbent, OBE

LAND-VALUE TAXATION AND FREE TRADE, INTERNATIONAL UNION FOR, 177 Vauxhall Bridge Road, London SW1V 1EU. Tel: 071-834 4266. *President*, Mrs B. P. Sobrielo

LANGUAGE LEARNING, ASSOCIATION FOR (1990), 16 Regent Place, Rugby CV21 2PN. Tel: 0788-546443. *General Secretary*, Mrs C. Wilding

LAW REPORTING FOR ENGLAND AND WALES, INCORPORATED COUNCIL OF (1865), 3 Stone Buildings, Lincoln's Inn, London WC2A 3XN. Tel: 071-242 6471. *Secretary*, B. Symondson

LEAGUE OF THE HELPING HAND (1908), Baileys, Church Street, Charlbury, Oxford OX7 3PR. Tel: 0608-810411. *Secretary*, Mrs D. R. Colvin

LEAGUE OF WELLDOERS (1893), 119–121 Limekiln Lane, Liverpool L5 8SN. Tel: 051-207 1984. *Warden and Secretary*, K. H. Stanton

LEATHER AND HIDE TRADES' BENEVOLENT INSTITUTION (1860), 60 Wickham Hill, Hurstpierpoint, Hassocks, W. Sussex BN6 9NP. Tel: 0273-843488. *Secretary*, Mrs G. M. Stapleton, MBE

LEGAL EXECUTIVES, INSTITUTE OF (1892), Kempston Manor, Kempston, Bedford MK42 7AB. Tel: 0234-841000. *Secretary-General*, L. A. Evans

LEONARD CHESHIRE FOUNDATION (1955), Leonard Cheshire House, 26–29 Maunsel Street, London SW1P 2QN. Tel: 071-828 1822. *Director*, J. Stanford

LEPROSY MISSION, THE (England and Wales) (1874), Room 8, Orton Goldhay, Peterborough PE2 0GZ. *Chairman*, Dr D. Moore

LEUKAEMIA RESEARCH FUND (1962), 43 Great Ormond Street, London WC1N 3JJ. Tel: 071-405 0101. *Director*, D. L. Osborne

LIBERTY (formerly NATIONAL COUNCIL FOR CIVIL LIBERTIES) (1934), 21 Tabard Street, London SE1 4JA. Tel: 071-403 3888. *General Secretary*, A. Puddephatt

LIBRARY ASSOCIATION (1877), 7 Ridgmount Street, London WC1E 7AE. Tel: 071-636 7543. *Chief Executive*, R. Shimmon

LIFEBOATS, *see* ROYAL NATIONAL LIFEBOAT INSTITUTION

LIGHT HORSE BREEDING SOCIETY, NATIONAL (1885), 96 High Street, Edenbridge, Kent TN8 5AR. Tel: 0732-866277. *Secretary*, G. W. Evans

LINGUISTS, INSTITUTE OF (1910), 24A Highbury Grove, London N5 2EA. Tel: 071-359 7445. *General Secretary*, E. Ostarhild

LINNAEAN SOCIETY OF LONDON (1788), Burlington House, Piccadilly, London W1V 0LQ. Tel: 071-434 4479. *Executive Secretary*, Dr J. C. Marsden

LIONS CLUBS INTERNATIONAL (British Isles and Ireland) (1949), 5 Vine Terrace, The Square, Harborne, Birmingham B17 9PU. Tel: 021-428 1909. *General Secretary*, P. Jay

LLOYD'S OF LONDON, 1 Lime Street, London EC3M 7HA. Tel: 071-623 7100. *Chief Executive*, B. C. Johnson

LLOYD'S PATRIOTIC FUND (1803), Lloyd's, Lime Street, London EC3M 7HA. Tel: 071-327 5062. *Secretary*, Mrs J. H. Bright

LOCAL AUTHORITY CHIEF EXECUTIVES, SOCIETY OF (1974). *Hon. Secretary*, A. Taylor, Kensington Town Hall, Hornton Street, London W8 7NX. Tel: 071-938 3400

LOCAL COUNCILS, NATIONAL ASSOCIATION OF (1947), 108 Great Russell Street, London WC1B 3LD. Tel: 071-637 1865. *Secretary*, J. Clark

LOCAL GOVERNMENT INTERNATIONAL BUREAU (1913), *also* COUNCIL OF EUROPEAN MUNICIPALITIES AND REGIONS (British Section) (1951), 35 Great Smith Street, London SW1P 3BJ. Tel: 071-222 1636. *Secretary-General*, P. N. Bongers

LOCAL HISTORY, BRITISH ASSOCIATION FOR (1843), 24 Lower Street, Harnham, Salisbury, Wilts. SP2 8EY. Tel: 0722-320115. *Hon. Secretary*, M. Cowan

LONDON APPRECIATION SOCIETY (1932), 17 Manson Mews, London SW7 5AF. *Hon. Secretary*, H. L. B. Peers, Ph.D

LONDON BOROUGHS ASSOCIATION (1964), College House, Great Peter Street, London SW1P 3LN. Tel: 071-799 2477. *Secretary*, J. Hall

LONDON CITY MISSION (1835), 175 Tower Bridge Road, London SE1 2AH. Tel: 071-407 7585. *General Secretary*, Revd J. McAllen

LONDON COURT OF INTERNATIONAL ARBITRATION (1892), 2–5 Minories, London EC3N 1BJ. Tel: 071-702 9599. *President*, The Rt. Hon. Sir Michael Kerr; *Registrar*, B. W. Vigrass, OBE, VRD

LONDON FLOTILLA (1937). *Hon. Secretary*, Lt. Cdr. P. A. G. Norman, RD, RNR, Marden Rise, 81 Lower Road, Fetcham, Leatherhead, Surrey KT22 9HG. Tel: 0372-453059

LONDON LIBRARY, THE (1841), 14 St James's Square, London SW1Y 4LG. Tel: 071-930 7705. *Librarian*, D. Matthews

LONDON MAGISTRATES' CLERKS' ASSOCIATION (1889). *Hon. Secretary*, K. W. Burman, c/o Juvenile Court, 185 Marylebone Road, London NW1 5QJ. Tel: 071-262 3211, ext. 6478

LONDON PLAYING FIELDS SOCIETY, THE (1890), Boston Manor Playing Field, Boston Gardens, Brentford, Middx. TW8 9LR. *Secretary*, T. W. Syms

LONDON SOCIETY, THE (1912), 4th Floor, Senate House, Malet Street, London WC1E 7HU. Tel: 071-580 5537. *Hon. Secretary*, Mrs B. Jones

LORD'S DAY OBSERVANCE SOCIETY, THE (1831), 6 Sherman Road, Bromley, Kent BR1 3JH. Tel: 081-313 0456. *General Secretary*, J. G. Roberts

LORD'S TAVERNERS, THE (1950), 22 Queen Anne's Gate, London SW1H 9AA. Tel: 071-222 0707. *Director*, Capt. P. Shervington

LOTTERIES COUNCIL, THE (1979), 81 Mansel Street, Swansea SA1 5TT. Tel: 0792-462845. *Hon. Secretary*, J. H. Solly

MAGISTRATES' ASSOCIATION, THE (1920), 28 Fitzroy Square, London W1P 6DD. Tel: 071-387 2353. *Secretary*, T. R. P. Rudin

MAIL USERS' ASSOCIATION (1976), 3 Pavement House, The Pavement, Hay-on-Wye HW3 5BU. Tel: 0497-821357. *Chairman*, J. Blackwell

MALAYSIAN RUBBER PRODUCERS' RESEARCH ASSOCIATION (1938), Tun Abdul Razak Laboratory, Brickendonbury, Hertford SG13 8NL. Tel: 0992-584966. *Director*, Dr C. S. L. Baker

MALCOLM SARGENT CANCER FUND FOR CHILDREN (1968). *General Administrator*, Miss S. Darley, OBE, 14 Abingdon Road, London W8 6AF. Tel: 071-937 4548

MALONE SOCIETY (for the publication of scholarly editions and facsimiles of early English dramatic texts). *Executive Secretary*, Prof. J. Creaser, Royal Holloway and Bedford New College, Egham Hill, Egham, Surrey TW20 0EX

MANAGEMENT, BRITISH INSTITUTE OF (1947), 3rd Floor, 2 Savoy Court, Strand, London WC2R 0EZ. Tel: 071-497 0580. *Director-General*, R. Young

MANAGEMENT AND PROFESSIONAL STAFFS, ASSOCIATION OF (1972), Parkgates, Bury New Road, Prestwich, Manchester M25 8JX. Tel: 061-773 8621. *Executive Secretary*, A. J. Casey

MANAGEMENT SERVICES, INSTITUTE OF, 1 Cecil Court, London Road, Enfield, Middx. EN2 6DD. Tel: 081-363 7452. *General Secretary*, F. O'Connolly

MANIC DEPRESSION FELLOWSHIP (1983), 13 Rosslyn Road, Twickenham, Surrey TW1 2AR. Tel: 081-892 2811. *Director*, Ms M. Fulford

MANORIAL SOCIETY OF GREAT BRITAIN (1906), 104 Kennington Road, London SE11 6RE. Tel: 071-735 6633. *Hon. Chairman*, R. A. Smith

MANPOWER SOCIETY (1969). *Administrator*, Mrs H. Gale, 39 Apple Tree Walk, Littlehampton, W. Sussex BN17 5QN. Tel: 0903-731728

MARIE CURIE MEMORIAL FOUNDATION (1948), 28 Belgrave Square, London SW1X 8QG. Tel: 071-235 3325. *Scottish Office*, 21 Rutland Street, Edinburgh EH1 2AH. *Director-General*, Maj.-Gen. M. E. Carleton-Smith, CBE

MARINE ARTISTS, ROYAL SOCIETY OF (1939), 17 Carlton House Terrace, London SW1Y 5BD. Tel: 071-930 6844. *Secretary*, M. Myers

MARINE BIOLOGICAL ASSOCIATION OF THE UK (1884), Citadel Hill, Plymouth PL1 2PB. Tel: 0752-222772. *Secretary*, Dr M. Whitfield

MARINE BIOLOGICAL ASSOCIATION, SCOTTISH (1914), PO Box 3, Oban, Argyll PA34 4AD. Tel: 0631-62244. *Director*, Prof. J. B. L. Matthews

MARINE ENGINEERS, THE INSTITUTE OF (1889), The Memorial Building, 76 Mark Lane, London EC3R 7JN. Tel: 071-481 8493. *Secretary*, J. E. Sloggett

MARINE SOCIETY, THE (1756), 202 Lambeth Road, London SE1 7JW. Tel: 071-261 9535. *General Secretary*, Lt. Cdr. R. M. Frampton

MARIO LANZA EDUCATIONAL FOUNDATION (for singers) (1976), *Hon. Secretary*, Miss P. Barron, 7 Lionfields Avenue, Allesley Village, Coventry CV5 9GN

MARKET AUTHORITIES, NATIONAL ASSOCIATION OF BRITISH (1948). *Secretary*, B. Ormshaw, 19 Derwent Avenue, Milnrow, Rochdale, Lancs. OL16 3UD. Tel: 0706-57740

MARKETING, CHARTERED INSTITUTE OF (1911), Moor Hall, Cookham, Maidenhead, Berks. SL6 9QH. Tel: 0628-524922. *Director-General*, J. McAinsh

MARKET TRADERS' FEDERATION, NATIONAL (1899), Hampton House, Hawshaw Lane, Hoyland, Barnsley S74 0HA. Tel: 0226-749021. *General Secretary*, D. E. Feeny

MARK MASTER MASONS, GRAND LODGE OF (1856), Mark Masons' Hall, 86 St James's Street, London SW1A 1PL. Tel: 081-839 5274. *Grand Master*, HRH Prince Michael of Kent; *Grand Secretary*, P. G. Williams

MASONIC BENEVOLENT INSTITUTION, ROYAL (1842), 20 Great Queen Street, London WC2B 5BG. Tel: 071-405 8341. *Chief Executive*, Ms J. Reynolds

MASONIC BENEVOLENT INSTITUTIONS IN IRELAND, 17–19 Molesworth Street, Dublin 2. Tel: 0001-679 6799. *Secretary*, M. R. McWilliam

MASONIC TRUST FOR GIRLS AND BOYS (1985), 31 Great Queen Street, London WC2B 5AG. Tel: 071-405 2644. *Secretary*, Col. R. K. Hind

MASTER BUILDERS, FEDERATION OF (1941), Gordon Fisher House, 14–15 Great James Street, London WC1N 3DP. *Director-General*, J. D. Maiden

MASTERS OF FOXHOUNDS ASSOCIATION (1881). *Secretary*, A. H. B. Hart, Parsloes Cottage, Bagendon, Cirencester, Glos. GL7 7DU

MASTERS OF WINE, THE INSTITUTE OF (1955), Five Kings House, 1 Queen Street Place, London EC4R 1QS. Tel: 071-236 4427. *Executive Director*, D. F. Stevens

MATERNAL AND CHILD WELFARE, NATIONAL ASSOCIATION FOR (1911), 40–42 Osnaburgh Street, London NW1 3ND. Tel: 071-383 4115. *Administrator*, Mrs F. N. Kapadia

MATERNITY ALLIANCE, THE (1980), 15 Britannia Street, London WC1X 9JP. Tel: 071-837 1265. *Secretary*, Ms A. Sedley

MATHEMATICAL ASSOCIATION (1871), 259 London Road, Leicester LE2 3BE. Tel: 0533-703877. *Executive Secretary*, Ms H. Whitby

MATHEMATICS AND ITS APPLICATIONS, INSTITUTE OF (1964), 16 Nelson Street, Southend-on-Sea SS1 1EF. Tel: 0702-354020. *Registrar*, Miss C. M. Richards

MECHANICAL ENGINEERS, INSTITUTION OF (1847), 1 Birdcage Walk, London SW1H 9JJ. Tel: 071-222 7899. *Secretary*, R. W. Mellor, CBE

MEDIC-ALERT FOUNDATION, 17 Bridge Wharf, 156 Caledonian Road, London N1 9UU. Tel: 071-833 3034. *Secretary-General*, Mrs M. L. Stanton

MEDICAL COUNCIL, GENERAL (1858), 44 Hallam Street, London W1N 6AE. Tel: 071-580 7642. *Registrar*, P. L. Towers

MEDICAL SOCIETY OF LONDON (1773), 11 Chandos Street, London W1M 0EB. Tel: 071-580 1043. *Registrar*, M. Griffiths, TD

MEDICAL WOMEN'S FEDERATION (1917), Tavistock House North, Tavistock Square, London WC1H 9HX. *Hon. Secretary*, Dr I. Weinreb

MEMORIAL FUND FOR DISASTER RELIEF, 3 Throgmorton Avenue, London EC2N 2WW. Tel: 071-638 6442. *Director*, R. Kandt

MENCAP (1946), 123 Golden Lane, London EC1Y 0RT. Tel: 071-454 0454. *Chief Executive*, F. Heddell

MEN OF THE TREES, *see* TREE FOUNDATION, INTERNATIONAL

MENTAL AFTER CARE ASSOCIATION (1879), Bainbridge House, Bainbridge Street, London WC1A 1HP. Tel: 071-436 6194. *Director*, B. G. Garner

MENTAL HEALTH FOUNDATION, THE (1949), 8 Hallam Street, London W1N 6DH. Tel: 071-580 0145. *Director-General*, Ms J. McKerrow

MERCHANT NAVY WELFARE BOARD (1948), 19–21 Lancaster Gate, London W2 3LN. Tel: 071-723 3642. *General Secretary*, J. I. K. Walker

METALS, THE INSTITUTE OF (1985), 1 Carlton House Terrace, London SW1Y 5DB. Tel: 071-839 4071. *Secretary*, Dr J. A. Catterall

METAL TRADES BENEVOLENT SOCIETY, ROYAL (1843), Kelvin House, 1 Totteridge Avenue, High Wycombe, Bucks. HP13 6XG. Tel: 0494-530430. *General Secretary*, A. Whittle, MBE

METEOROLOGICAL SOCIETY, ROYAL (1850), 104 Oxford Road, Reading, Berks. RG1 7LJ. Tel: 0734-568500. *Executive Secretary*, R. P. C. Swash

METROPOLITAN AND CITY POLICE ORPHANS FUND (1870), 30 Hazlewell Road, London SW15 6LH. Tel: 081-788 5140. *Secretary*, R. Duff-Cole, BEM

METROPOLITAN AUTHORITIES, ASSOCIATION OF (1974), 35 Great Smith Street, London SW1P 3BJ. Tel: 071-222 8100. *Secretary*, R. Brooke

METROPOLITAN HOSPITAL-SUNDAY FUND (1872), 40 High Street, Teddington, Middx. TW11 8EW. Tel: 081-977 4154. *Secretary*, D. A. B. Lynch

MIDDLE EAST ASSOCIATION, THE (1961), Bury House, 33 Bury Street, London SW1Y 6AX. Tel: 071-839 2137. *Director-General*, J. R. Grundon

MIDWIVES, ROYAL COLLEGE OF (1881), 15 Mansfield Street, London W1M 0BE. Tel: 071–580 6523. *General Secretary*, Miss R. M. Ashton, OBE

MIGRAINE ASSOCIATION, BRITISH (1958), 178A High Road, West Byfleet, Surrey KT14 7ED. Tel: 0932-352468. *Director*, Mrs J. Liddell

MIGRAINE TRUST (1965), 45 Great Ormond Street, London WC1N 3HZ. Tel: 071-278 2676. *Director*, P. Hodgkins

MILITARY HISTORICAL SOCIETY, National Army Museum, Royal Hospital Road, London SW3 4HT. Tel: 081-460 7341. *Hon. Secretary*, J. Gaylor

MIND (National Association for Mental Health), 22 Harley Street, London W1N 2ED. Tel: 071-673 0741. *Director*, Ms J. Clements

MINERALOGICAL SOCIETY (1876), 41 Queen's Gate, London SW7 5HR. Tel: 071-584 7516. *Hon. General Secretary*, Dr G. M. Manby

MINES OF GREAT BRITAIN, FEDERATION OF SMALL, 29 King Street, Newcastle under Lyme, Staffs. ST5 1ER. Tel: 0782-614618. *Secretary*, R. W. Bladen

MINIATURE PAINTERS, SCULPTORS AND GRAVERS, ROYAL SOCIETY OF (1895). *Executive Secretary*, Mrs S. M. Burton, Burwood House, 15 Union Street, Wells, Somerset BA5 2PU. Tel: 0749-674472

MINING AND METALLURGY, THE INSTITUTION OF (1892), 44 Portland Place, London W1N 4BR. Tel: 071-580 3802. *Secretary*, M. J. Jones

MINING ENGINEERS, INSTITUTION OF (1889), Danum House, 6A South Parade, Doncaster, S. Yorks. DN1 2DY. Tel: 0302-320486. *Secretary*, W. Bourne, OBE

MISSION TO DEEP SEA FISHERMEN, ROYAL NATIONAL (1881), 43 Nottingham Place, London W1M 4BX. Tel: 071-487 5101. *Chief Executive*, A. D. Marsden

MISSIONS TO SEAMEN, THE (1856), St Michael Paternoster Royal, College Hill, London EC4R 2RL. Tel: 071-248 5202. *General Secretary*, Revd Canon G. Jones

MODERN CHURCHPEOPLE'S UNION (1898). *Hon. Secretary*, Revd R. C. Truss, The Rectory, Church Square, Shepperton, Middx. TW17 9JY. Tel: 0932-220511

MONUMENTAL BRASS SOCIETY (1887). *Hon. Secretary*, W. Mendelsson, 57 Leeside Crescent, London NW11 0HA

MORAVIAN MISSIONS, LONDON ASSOCIATION IN AID OF (1817), Moravian Church House, 5–7 Muswell Hill, London N10 3TJ. Tel: 081-883 3409. *Secretary*, Revd F. Linyard

MOTHERS' UNION, THE (1876), Mary Sumner House, 24 Tufton Street, London SW1P 3RB. Tel: 071-222 5533. *Central Secretary*, Mrs M. Chapman

MOTOR INDUSTRY, THE INSTITUTE OF THE, Fanshaws, Brickendon, Hertford SG13 8PQ. Tel: 0992-86521. *Secretary*, F. W. Janes

MOUNTBATTEN MEMORIAL TRUST (1979), 1 Grosvenor Crescent, London SW1X 7EF. Tel: 071-235 5231, ext. 255. *Director*, J. Boyd-Brent

MOUNTBATTEN TRUST, THE EDWINA (1960), 1 Grosvenor Crescent, London SW1X 7EF. Tel: 071-235 5231, ext. 255. *Secretary*, J. Boyd-Brent

MULTIPLE SCLEROSIS SOCIETY (1953), 25 Effie Road, London SW6 1EE. Tel: 071-736 6267. *General Secretary*, J. Walford

MUNICIPAL ENGINEERS, ASSOCIATION OF, 1–7 Great George Street, London SW1P 3AA. Tel: 071-839 9977. *Director*, K. J. Marchant

MUSEUMS ASSOCIATION (1889), 34 Bloomsbury Way, London WC1A 2SF. Tel: 071-404 4767. *Director*, M. Taylor

MUSIC HALL SOCIETY, BRITISH (1963), Brodie and Middleton Ltd, 68 Drury Lane, London WC2B 5SP. Tel: 071-836 3289. *Hon. Secretary*, Mrs J. D. Masterton

MUSICIANS BENEVOLENT FUND (1921), 16 Ogle Street, London W1P 7LG. Tel: 071-636 4481. *Secretary*, M. B. M. Williams

MUSICIANS, INCORPORATED SOCIETY OF (1882), 10 Stratford Place, London W1N 9AE. Tel: 071-629 4413. *Chief Executive*, N. Hoyle

MUSICIANS OF GREAT BRITAIN, ROYAL SOCIETY OF (1738), 10 Stratford Place, London W1N 9AE. Tel: 071-629 6137. *Secretary*, Mrs M. E. Gleed, MBE

MUSIC INFORMATION CENTRE, BRITISH (1967), 10 Stratford Place, London W1N 9AE. Tel: 071-499 8567. *Administrator*, Ms E. Yeoman

MUSIC SOCIETIES, NATIONAL FEDERATION OF (1935), Francis House, Francis Street, London SW1P 1DE. Tel: 071-828 7320. *Director*, R. Jones

MYALGIC ENCEPHALOMYELITIS ASSOCIATION (1976), Stanhope House, High Street, Stanford-le-Hope, Essex SS17 0HA. Tel: 0375-642466. *Manager*, P. Brown

NACRO (NATIONAL ASSOCIATION FOR THE CARE AND RESETTLEMENT OF OFFENDERS) (1966), 169 Clapham Road, London SW9 0PU. Tel: 071-582 6500. *Director*, V. Stern

NATIONAL AND UNIVERSITY LIBRARIES, STANDING CONFERENCE OF (SCONUL) (1950), 102 Euston Street, London NW1 2HA. Tel: 071-387 0317. *Secretary*, Miss G. M. Pentelow

NATIONAL BENEVOLENT INSTITUTION (1812), 61 Bayswater Road, London W2 3PG. Tel: 071-723 0021. *Secretary*, Gp. Capt. D. St J. Homer, MVO

NATIONAL COUNCIL FOR VOLUNTARY ORGANIZATIONS (1919), Regent's Wharf, 8 All Saints Street, London N1 9RL. Tel: 071-713 6161. *Director*, Ms J. Weleminsky

NATIONAL COUNCIL OF WOMEN OF GREAT BRITAIN (1895), 36 Danbury Street, London N1 8JU. Tel: 071-354 2395. *President*, Mrs P. Purdy

NATIONAL LISTENING LIBRARY, 12 Lant Street, London SE1 1QH. Tel: 071-407 9417. *Executive Director*, G. A. Hepworth

NATIONAL SOCIETY, THE, (1811), Church House, Great Smith Street, London SW1P 3NZ. Tel: 071-222 1672. For promoting religious education. *General Secretary*, G. Duncan

NATIONAL SOCIETY FOR THE PREVENTION OF CRUELTY TO CHILDREN (NSPCC) (1884), 67 Saffron Hill, London EC1N 8RS. Tel: 071-242 1626. *Director*, C. Brown

NATIONAL TRUST, THE (1895), 36 Queen Anne's Gate, London SW1H 9AS. Tel: 071-222 9251. *Chairman*, Lord Chorley; *Director-General*, A. Stirling

NATIONAL TRUST FOR SCOTLAND (1931), 5 Charlotte Square, Edinburgh EH2 4DU. Tel: 031-226 5922. *Director*, Rear-Adm. D. Dow, CB

NATIONAL UNION OF STUDENTS (1922), Nelson Mandela House, 461 Holloway Road, London N7 6LJ. Tel: 071-272 8900. *National President*, Ms L. Fitzsimons

NATIONAL VIEWERS' AND LISTENERS' ASSOCIATION (1964). *President*, Mrs M. Whitehouse, CBE, Ardleigh, Colchester, Essex CO7 7RH. Tel: 0206-230123

NATIONAL WOMEN'S REGISTER (1960), 9 Bank Plain, Norwich, Norfolk NR2 4SL. Tel: 0603-765392. *National Organizer*, Mrs A. Dickinson

NATION'S FUND FOR NURSES (1917), 3 Albemarle Way, London EC1V 4JB. Tel: 071-490 4227. *Administrator*, Mrs S. D. Andrews

NATURALISTS' ASSOCIATION, BRITISH (1905). *Hon. Membership Secretary*, Mrs Y. H. Griffiths, 23 Oak Hill Close, Woodford Green, Essex IG8 9PH

NATURE CONSERVATION, ROYAL SOCIETY FOR (1912), The Green, Witham Park, Lincoln LN5 7JR. Tel: 0522-544400. *Chief Executive*, T. S. Cordy

NAUTICAL RESEARCH, SOCIETY FOR (1911), c/o National Maritime Museum, Greenwich, London SE10 9NF. Tel: 071-873 2139. *Hon. Secretary*, D. G. Law

NAVAL, MILITARY AND AIR FORCE BIBLE SOCIETY (1780), Radstock House, 3 Eccleston Street, London SW1W 9LZ. Tel: 071-730 2155. *General Secretary*, R. Kennedy

NAVAL ARCHITECTS, ROYAL INSTITUTION OF (1860), 10 Upper Belgrave Street, London SW1X 8BQ. Tel: 071-235 4622. *Secretary*, J. Rosewarn

NAVIGATION, ROYAL INSTITUTE OF (1947), 1 Kensington Gore, London SW7 2AT. Tel: 071-589 5021. *Director*, Gp Capt D. W. Broughton, MBE

NAVY RECORDS SOCIETY (1893), c/o Barclays Bank PLC, Murray House, 1 Royal Mint Court, London EC3N 4HH. Tel: 071-382 5400. *Hon. Secretary*, A. J. McMillan

NEEDLEWORK, ROYAL SCHOOL OF (1872). *Principal*, Mrs E. Elvin, Apt. 12A, Hampton Court Palace, East Molesey, Surrey KT8 9AU. Tel: 081-943 1432

NEWCOMEN SOCIETY (1920), Science Museum, London SW7 2DD. Tel: 071-589 1793. For the study of the history of engineering and technology. *Executive Secretary*, C. Ellam

NEWSPAPER EDITORS, GUILD OF BRITISH (1946), Bloomsbury House, Bloomsbury Square, 74–77 Great Russell Street, London WC1B 3DA. Tel: 071-636 7014. *Secretary*, J. K. Bradbury

NEWSPAPER PRESS FUND (1864), Dickens House, 35 Wathen Road, Dorking, Surrey RH4 1JY. Tel: 0306-887511. *Director*, P. W. Evans

NEWSPAPER SOCIETY (1836), Bloomsbury House, Bloomsbury Square, 74–77 Great Russell Street, London WC1B 3DA. Tel: 071-636 7014. *Director*, D. Nisbet-Smith

NEWSVENDORS' BENEVOLENT INSTITUTION (1839), PO Box 306, Dunmow, Essex CM6 1HY. Tel: 0371-874198. *Director*, vacant

NOISE ABATEMENT SOCIETY (1959), PO Box 8, Bromley BR2 0UH. Tel: 081-460 3146. *Chairman*, J. Connell, OBE

NON-SMOKERS, NATIONAL SOCIETY OF, *see* QUIT

NORWOOD CHILD CARE (1795), Stuart Young House, 221 Golders Green Road, London NW11 9DL. Tel: 081-458 3282. *Executive Director*, S. Brier

NOTARIES' SOCIETY (1907), 7 Lower Brook Street, Ipswich IP4 1AF. Tel: 0473-214762. *Secretary*, A. G. Dunford

NUCLEAR ENERGY SOCIETY, BRITISH (1962), 1–7 Great George Street, London SW1P 3AA. Tel: 071-222 7722. *Executive Officer*, P. Bacos

NUFFIELD FOUNDATION (1943), 28 Bedford Square, London WC1B 3EG. Tel: 071-631 0566. *Director*, R. Hazell

NUFFIELD PROVINCIAL HOSPITALS TRUST (1939), 3 Prince Albert Road, London NW1 7SP. Tel: 071-485 6632. *Secretary*, Dr M. Ashley-Miller

NUMISMATIC SOCIETY, BRITISH (1903). *Hon. Secretary*, G. P. Dyer, Royal Mint, Llantrisant, Pontyclun, Mid Glamorgan CF7 8YT. Tel: 0443-222111, ext. 521

NUMISMATIC SOCIETY, ROYAL (1836), c/o Department of Coins and Medals, The British Museum, Great Russell Street, London WC1B 3DG. Tel: 071-323 8585. *Hon. Secretaries*, J. E. Cribb; R. G. Bland

NURSES', RETIRED, NATIONAL HOME (1934), Riverside Avenue, Bournemouth BH7 7EE. Tel: 0202 396418. *Chairman*, E. V. Cornell

NURSES, ROYAL NATIONAL PENSION FUND FOR, Burdett House, 15 Buckingham Street, London WC2N 6ED. Tel: 071-839 6785. *Chief Executive*, V. G. West

NURSING, MIDWIFERY AND HEALTH VISITING, UK CENTRAL COUNCIL FOR, 23 Portland Place, London W1N 3AF. Tel: 071-637 7181. *Registrar and Chief Executive*, C. Ralph

England, Victory House, 170 Tottenham Court Road, London WIP OHA. Tel: 071-388 3131. *Chief Executive Officer,* A. P. Smith

Wales, Floor 13, Pearl Assurance House, Greyfriars Road, Cardiff CFI 3AG. Tel: 0222-395535. *Chief Executive Officer,* D. A. Ravey

Scotland, 22 Queen Street, Edinburgh EH2 IJX. Tel: 031-226 7371. *Chief Executive Officer,* Mrs L. Mitchell

N. Ireland, RAC House, 79 Chichester Street, Belfast BTI 4JE. Tel: 0232-238152. *Chief Executive Officer,* J. J. Walsh

NURSING, ROYAL COLLEGE OF (1916), 20 Cavendish Square, London WIM OAB. Tel: 071-409 3333. *General Secretary,* Miss C. Hancock

NUTRITION FOUNDATION, BRITISH (1967), 15 Belgrave Square, London SWIX 8PG. Tel: 071-235 4904. *Director-General,* Dr D. M. Conning

NUTRITION SOCIETY (1941), Grosvenor Gardens House, 35–37 Grosvenor Gardens, London SWIW OBS. *Hon. Secretary,* Dr R. F. Grimble

OBSTETRICIANS AND GYNAECOLOGISTS, ROYAL COLLEGE OF (1929), 27 Sussex Place, London NWI 4RG. Tel: 071-262 5425. *President,* S. Simmons; *Secretary,* P. A. Barnett

OCCUPATIONAL PENSIONS ADVISORY SERVICE (1982), 11 Belgrave Road, London SWIV IRB. Tel: 071-233 8080. *Chief Executive,* D. Hall

OCCUPATIONAL SAFETY AND HEALTH, INSTITUTION OF (1946), 222 Uppingham Road, Leicester LE5 OQG. Tel: 0533-768424. *Chief Executive,* J. R. Barrell

OFFICERS' ASSOCIATION, THE (1920), 48 Pall Mall, London SWIY 5JY. Tel: 071-930 0125. *General Secretary,* Brig. P. D. Johnson

OFFICERS' PENSIONS SOCIETY LTD (1946), 68 South Lambeth Road, London SW8 IRL. Tel: 071-820 9988. *General Secretary,* Maj.-Gen. Sir Laurence New, CB, CBE

OIL PAINTERS, ROYAL INSTITUTE OF (1883), 17 Carlton House Terrace, London SWIY 5BD. Tel: 071-930 6844

OILSEED, OIL AND FEEDINGSTUFFS TRADES BENEVOLENT ASSOCIATION, 14–20 St. Mary Axe, London EC3A 8BU. Tel: 071-623 5501. *Secretary,* D. A. Painter

ONE PARENT FAMILIES, NATIONAL COUNCIL FOR, 255 Kentish Town Road, London NW5 2LX. Tel: 071-267 1361. *Director,* Miss S. Slipman

OPEN-AIR MISSION, THE (1853), 19 John Street, London WCIN 2DL. Tel: 071-405 6135. *Secretary,* A. J. Greenbank

OPEN SPACES SOCIETY (1865), 25A Bell Street, Henley-on-Thames, Oxon. RG9 2BA. Tel: 0491-573535. *General Secretary,* Miss K. Ashbrook

OPERATIC AND DRAMATIC ASSOCIATION, NATIONAL (1899), NODA House, 1 Crestfield Street, London WCIH 8AU. Tel: 071-837 5655. *General Administrator,* B. Clarke

OPTICAL COUNCIL, GENERAL (1958), 41 Harley Street, London WIN 2DJ. Tel: 071-580 3898. *Registrar,* R. Wilshin

OPTOMETRISTS, BRITISH COLLEGE OF, 10 Knaresborough Place, London SW5 OTG. Tel: 071-373 7765. *General Secretary,* P. D. Leigh

ORDERS AND MEDALS RESEARCH SOCIETY (1942). *General Secretary,* N. G. Gooding, 123 Turnpike Link, Croydon CRO 5NU. Tel: 081-680 2701

ORIENTAL CERAMIC SOCIETY (1921), 31B Torrington Square, London WCIE 7LJ. Tel: 071-636 7985. *Secretary,* vacant

ORNITHOLOGISTS' CLUB, SCOTTISH (1936), 21 Regent Terrace, Edinburgh EH7 5BT. Tel: 031-556 6042. *Secretary,* M. H. Murphy

ORNITHOLOGISTS' UNION, BRITISH (1858), c/o Natural History Museum, Sub-dept. of Ornithology, Tring, Herts. HP23 6AP. Tel: 0442-890080. *Administrative Secretary,* Mrs G. Bonham

ORNITHOLOGY, BRITISH TRUST FOR (1932) National Centre for Ornithology, The Nunnery, Thetford, Norfolk IP24 2PU. Tel: 0842-750050. *Director of Services,* A. Elvin

ORTHOPAEDIC ASSOCIATION, BRITISH (1918), The Royal College of Surgeons, 35–43 Lincoln's Inn Fields, London WC2A 3PN. Tel: 071-405 6507. *Hon. Secretary,* M. K. d'A. Benson, FRCS

OSTEOPATHIC MEDICINE, LONDON COLLEGE OF, 8–10 Boston Place, London NWI 6QH

OSTEOPOROSIS SOCIETY, THE NATIONAL (1986), PO Box 10, Radstock, Bath BA3 3YB. Tel: 0761-432472. *Director,* Mrs L. Edwards

OUTWARD BOUND TRUST LTD (1941), Chestnut Field, Regent Place, Rugby, Warks. CV21 2PJ. Tel: 0788-560423. *Director,* I. L. Fothergill

OVERSEAS DEVELOPMENT INSTITUTE (1960), Regent's College, Inner Circle, Regent's Park, London NWI 4NS. Tel: 071-487 7413. *Director,* Dr J. Howell

OVERSEAS SERVICE PENSIONERS' ASSOCIATION (1960), 138 High Street, Tonbridge, Kent TN9 IAX. Tel: 0732-363836. *Secretary,* D. LeBreton, CBE

OVERSEAS SETTLEMENT, CHURCH OF ENGLAND BOARD FOR SOCIAL RESPONSIBILITY (1925), Great Smith Street, London SWIP 3NZ. Tel: 071-222 9011. *Administration Secretary,* Miss P. J. Hallett

OXFAM (1942), 274 Banbury Road, Oxford OX2 7DZ. Tel: 0865-311311. *Director,* D. Bryer

OXFORD PRESERVATION TRUST (1927), 10 Turn Again Lane, St Ebbes, Oxford OXI IQL. Tel: 0865-242918. *Secretary,* Mrs M. Haynes

OXFORD SOCIETY (1932), 41 Wellington Square, Oxford OXI 2HY. Tel: 0865-270088. *Secretary,* Dr H. A. Hurren

PAEDIATRIC ASSOCIATION, BRITISH (1928), 5 St Andrew's Place, London NWI 4LB. Tel: 071-486 6151. *Hon. Secretary,* Dr R. MacFaul

PAINTER-PRINTMAKERS, ROYAL SOCIETY OF (1880), Bankside Gallery, 48 Hopton Street, London SEI 9JH. Tel: 071-928 7521. *Secretary,* J. Winkelman

PAINTERS IN WATER COLOURS, ROYAL INSTITUTE OF (1831), 17 Carlton House Terrace, London SWIY 5BD. Tel: 071-930 6844

PALAEONTOGRAPHICAL SOCIETY (1847) c/o British Geological Survey, Keyworth, Nottingham NG12 5GG. *Secretary*, S. P. Tunnicliff

PALAEONTOLOGICAL ASSOCIATION (1957). *Secretary*, Dr J. A. Crame, c/o British Antarctic Survey, High Cross, Madingley Road, Cambridge CB3 0ET. Tel: 0223-61188, ext. 261

PARKINSON'S DISEASE SOCIETY (1969), 22 Upper Woburn Place, London WC1H 0RA. Tel: 071-383 3513. *Executive Director*, M. Whelan

PARLIAMENTARY AND SCIENTIFIC COMMITTEE (1939), 16 Great College Street, London SW1P 3RX. Tel: 071-222 7085. *Secretary*, A. Butler

PASTORAL PSYCHOLOGY, GUILD OF (1936). *Hon. Secretary*, Miss J. Whale, 5 Kilmeny House, 36 Arterberry Road, London SW20 8AQ. Tel: 081-946 3172

PATENT AGENTS, CHARTERED INSTITUTE OF (1882), Staple Inn Buildings, High Holborn, London WC1V 7PZ. Tel: 071-405 9450. *Secretary*, M. C. Ralph

PATENTEES AND INVENTORS, INSTITUTE OF (1919), Triumph House, 189 Regent Street, London W1R 7WF. Tel: 071-242 7812. *Secretary*, J. R. Kay

PATHOLOGISTS, ROYAL COLLEGE OF, 2 Carlton House Terrace, London SW1Y 5AF. Tel: 071-930 5863. *Secretary*, K. Lockyer

PATIENTS ASSOCIATION (1963), 18 Victoria Park Square, London E2 9PF. Tel: 081-981 5676. *Chairman*, M. Healy

PEACE COUNCIL, NATIONAL (1908), 88 Islington High Street, London N1 8EG. Tel: 071-354 5200. *Co-ordinators*, A. McLeod; Ms L. Peck

PEAK AND NORTHERN FOOTPATHS SOCIETY (1894). *Hon. General Secretary*, D. Taylor, 15 Parkfield Drive, Tyldesley, Manchester M29 8NR. Tel: 061-790 4383

PEARSON'S HOLIDAY FUND, 18–20 Kingston Road, London SW19 1JZ. Tel: 081-542 5550. *General Secretary*, G. P. Holloway

PEDESTRIANS ASSOCIATION (1929), 1 Wandsworth Road, London SW8 2XX. Tel: 071-735 3270. *Chairman*, Ms F. Lawson

PEN, INTERNATIONAL (1921), 9–10 Charterhouse Buildings, Goswell Road, London EC1M 7AT. Tel: 071-253 4308. World association of writers. *International Secretary*, A. Blokh

PENSION FUNDS LTD, NATIONAL ASSOCIATION OF (1923), 12–18 Grosvenor Gardens, London SW1W 0DH. *Director-General*, M. A. Elton

PEOPLE'S DISPENSARY FOR SICK ANIMALS (PDSA) (1917), Whitechapel Way, Priorslee, Telford, Shropshire TF2 9PQ. Tel: 0952-290999. *General Secretary*, M. R. Curtis, MBE

PERFORMING RIGHT SOCIETY LTD (1914), 29–33 Berners Street, London W1P 4AA. Tel: 071-580 5544. *Chief Executive*, M. J. Freegard

PERIODICAL PUBLISHERS ASSOCIATION LTD (1913), Imperial House, 15–19 Kingsway, London WC2B 6UN. Tel: 071-379 6268. *Chief Executive*, I. Locks

PESTALOZZI CHILDREN'S VILLAGE TRUST (1959), Sedlescombe, Battle, E. Sussex TN33 0RR. Tel: 0424-870444. *Director*, C. C. Wagstaff

PETROLEUM, INSTITUTE OF (1913), 61 New Cavendish Street, London W1M 8AR. Tel: 071-636 1004. *Director-General*, I. Ward

PHARMACEUTICAL SOCIETY OF GREAT BRITAIN, ROYAL (1841), 1 Lambeth High Street, London SE1 7JN. *Secretary and Registrar*, J. Ferguson

PHARMACOLOGICAL SOCIETY, BRITISH (1931). *Hon. General Secretary*, Dr J. Maclagan, Medical College, Charterhouse Square, London EC1M 6BQ. Tel: 071-982 6171

PHILOLOGICAL SOCIETY (1842). *Hon. Secretary*, Prof. T. Bynon, School of Oriental and African Studies, University of London, Thornhaugh Street, London WC1H 0XG. Tel: 071-637 2388, ext. 6361

PHILOSOPHY, ROYAL INSTITUTE OF (1925), 14 Gordon Square, London WC1H 0AG. Tel: 071-387 4130. *Director*, Prof. A. Phillips Griffiths

PHOTOGRAMMETRIC SOCIETY (1952). *Hon. Secretary*, Dr A. S. Walker, Kern Instruments Ltd, Revenge Road, Lordswood, Chatham, Kent ME5 8TE

PHOTOGRAPHY, BRITISH INSTITUTE OF PROFESSIONAL (1901), Fox Talbot House, Amwell End, Ware, Herts. SG12 9HN. Tel: 0920-464011. *Chief Executive*, A. M. Berkeley

PHYSICAL RECREATION, CENTRAL COUNCIL OF (1935), Francis House, Francis Street, London SW1P 1DE. Tel: 071-828 3163/4. *General Secretary*, P. Lawson

PHYSICIANS, ROYAL COLLEGE OF (1518), 11 St Andrew's Place, London NW1 4LE. Tel: 071-935 1174. *Secretary*, D. B. Lloyd

PHYSICIANS AND SURGEONS, ROYAL COLLEGE OF (Glasgow) (1599), 234–242 St Vincent Street, Glasgow G2 5RJ. Tel: 041-221 6072. *Hon. Secretary*, Dr B. Williams

PHYSICIANS OF EDINBURGH, ROYAL COLLEGE OF (1681), 9 Queen Street, Edinburgh EH2 1JQ. Tel: 031-225 7324. *Secretary*, Dr J. L. Anderton

PHYSICS, INSTITUTE OF (1874), 47 Belgrave Square, London SW1X 8QX. Tel: 071-235 6111. *Chief Executive*, Dr A. Jones

PHYSIOLOGICAL SOCIETY (1876). *Hon. Secretary*, Dr D. Cotterell, PO Box 506, Oxford OX1 3XE. Tel: 0865-798498

PHYSIOTHERAPY, THE CHARTERED SOCIETY OF (1894), 14 Bedford Row, London WC1R 4ED. Tel: 071-242 1941. *Secretary*, T. Simon

PIG ASSOCIATION, BRITISH (1884), 7 Rickmansworth Road, Watford, Herts. WD1 7HE. Tel: 0923-234377. *Chief Executive*, G. E. Welsh

PILGRIM TRUST, THE (1930), Fielden House, Little College Street, London SW1P 3SH. Tel: 071-222 4723. *Secretary*, Hon. A. H. Millar

PILGRIMS OF GREAT BRITAIN, THE (1902), Savoy Hotel, London WC2R 0EU. *Hon. Secretary*, M. P. S. Barton

PLANT ENGINEERS, INSTITUTION OF, 77 Great Peter Street, London SW1P 2EZ. Tel: 071-233 2855. *Secretary-General*, R. S. Pratt

PLAYING CARD SOCIETY, THE INTERNATIONAL (1972), 188 Sheen Lane, London SW14 8LF. *Secretary*, C. C. Rayner

PLAYING FIELDS ASSOCIATION, NATIONAL (1925), 25 Ovington Square, London SW3 1LQ. Tel: 071-584 6445. *General Secretary*, Mrs H. Hays

POETRY SOCIETY (1909), 22 Betterton Street, London WC2H 9BU. Tel: 071-240 4810. *Director and General Secretary*, C. Green

POLICY STUDIES INSTITUTE (1978), 100 Park Village East, London NW1 3SR. Tel: 071-387 2171. *Director*, W. W. Daniel

POLIO FELLOWSHIP, BRITISH (1939), Bell Close, West End Road, Ruislip, Middx. HA4 6LP. Tel: 0895-675515. *General Secretary*, L. P. Jackson

POLYTECHNICS, COMMITTEE OF DIRECTORS OF (1970), Kirkman House, 12–14 Whitfield Street, London W1P 6AX. Tel: 071-637 9939. *Secretary*, R. P. Blows

PORTRAIT PAINTERS, ROYAL SOCIETY OF (1891), 17 Carlton House Terrace, London SW1Y 5BD. Tel: 071-930 6844. *President*, G. D. Bruce

POST OFFICE USERS' NATIONAL COUNCIL (1970), Waterloo Bridge House, Waterloo Road, London SE1 8UA. Tel: 071-928 9458. *Secretary*, K. Hall

POULTRY CLUB OF GREAT BRITAIN, THE (1877). *General Secretary*, Mrs E. A. Aubrey-Fletcher, Cliveden, Sandy Bank Farm, Chipping, Preston, Lancs. PR3 2GA

PRAYER BOOK SOCIETY, THE (1975), St James Garlickhythe, Garlick Hill, London EC4V 2AL. Tel: 081-958 8769. *Hon. Secretary*, Mrs. M. Thompson

PRECEPTORS, COLLEGE OF, (1846), Coppice Row, Theydon Bois, Epping, Essex CM16 7DN. Tel: 0992-812727. *Chief Executive Officer*, T. Wheatley

PRE-SCHOOL PLAYGROUPS ASSOCIATION, 61–63 Kings Cross Road, London WC1X 9LL. Tel: 071-833 0991. *Chief Executive Officer*, Ms M. Lochrie

PRESS ASSOCIATION (1868), 85 Fleet Street, London EC4P 4BE. *Secretary*, R. C. Henry

PRESS UNION, COMMONWEALTH (1909), Studio House, 184 Fleet Street, London EC4A 2DU. Tel: 071-242 1056. *Director*, R. Mackichan

PREVENTION OF ACCIDENTS, ROYAL SOCIETY FOR THE (1916), Cannon House, Priory Queensway, Birmingham B4 6BS. Tel: 021-200 2461. *Director-General*, vacant

PRINCESS LOUISE SCOTTISH HOSPITAL (Erskine Hospital) (1916), Bishopton, Renfrewshire PA7 5PU. Tel: 041-812 1100. For disabled ex-servicemen and women. *Commandant*, Col. W. K. Shepherd

PRINCE'S SCOTTISH YOUTH BUSINESS TRUST, THE (1989), 6th Floor, Mercantile Chambers, 53 Bothwell Street, Glasgow G2 6TS. Tel: 041-248 4999. *Director*, D. W. Cooper

PRINCE'S TRUST, THE (1976) and the Royal Jubilee Trusts (1935, 1977), 8 Bedford Row, London WC1R 4BA. Tel: 071-430 0524. *Director*, T. Shebbeare

PRINCE'S YOUTH BUSINESS TRUST, THE, 5 Cleveland Place, London SW1Y 6JJ. Tel: 071-321 6500. *Chief Executor*, J. Pervin

PRINTERS' CHARITABLE CORPORATION (1827), Victoria House, Harestone Valley Road, Caterham, Surrey CR3 6HY. Tel: 0883-345331. *Secretary*, H. J. Court

PRINTING HISTORICAL SOCIETY (1964), St Bride Institute, Bride Lane, London EC4Y 8EE. *Hon. Secretary*, Dr M. Smith

PRINTING, INSTITUTE OF (1961), 8 Lonsdale Gardens, Tunbridge Wells, Kent TN1 1NU. Tel: 0892-538118. *Secretary-General*, C. F. Partridge

PRISON VISITORS, NATIONAL ASSOCIATION OF (1922), 46B Hartington Street, Bedford MK41 7RP. Tel: 0234-359763. *General Secretary*, Mrs A. G. McKenna

PRIVATE LIBRARIES ASSOCIATION (1957). *Hon. Secretary*, F. Broomhead, Ravelston, South View Road, Pinner, Middx. HA5 3YD

PROCURATORS IN GLASGOW, ROYAL FACULTY OF (1600), 12 Nelson Mandela Place, Glasgow G2 1BT. Tel: 041-204 3213. *Clerk*, J. H. Sinclair

PROFESSIONAL CLASSES AID COUNCIL (1921), 10 St Christopher's Place, London W1M 6HY. Tel: 071-935 0641. *Secretary*, Mrs G. A. Burgess

PROFESSIONAL ENGINEERS, UK ASSOCIATION OF (1969), Hayes Court, West Common Road, Bromley BR2 7AU. Tel: 081-462 7755. *Secretary*, J. M. Dalgleish

PROFESSIONAL FOOTBALLERS' ASSOCIATION, 2 Oxford Court, Bishopsgate, Manchester M2 3WQ. Tel: 061-236 0575. *Secretary*, G. Taylor

PROFESSIONS SUPPLEMENTARY TO MEDICINE, THE COUNCIL FOR, Park House, 184 Kennington Park Road, London SE11 4BU. Tel: 071-582 0866. *Registrar*, R. Pickis

PROTECTION OF THE UNBORN CHILD, SOCIETY FOR THE (1967), 7 Tufton Street, London SW1P 3QN. Tel: 071-222 5845. *Director*, Mrs P. Bowman

PROTESTANT ALLIANCE, THE (1845), 77 Ampthill Gardens, Flitwick, Bedford MK45 1BD. Tel: 0525-712348. *General Secretary*, Revd A. G. Ashdown

PSORIASIS ASSOCIATION (1968), 7 Milton Street, Northampton NN2 7JG. Tel: 0604-711129. *National Secretary*, Mrs L. Henley

PSYCHIATRISTS, ROYAL COLLEGE OF (1971), 17 Belgrave Square, London SW1X 8PG. Tel: 071-235 2351. *Secretary*, Mrs V. Cameron

PSYCHICAL RESEARCH, SOCIETY FOR (1882), 49 Marloes Road, London W8 6LA. Tel: 071-937 8984. *President*, Prof. A. E. Roy

PSYCHOLOGICAL SOCIETY, THE BRITISH (1901), St Andrews House, 48 Princess Road East, Leicester LE1 7DR. Tel: 0533-549568. *Executive Secretary*, C. V. Newman, Ph.D

PUBLIC ADMINISTRATION, ROYAL INSTITUTE OF (1922), 3 Birdcage Walk, London SW1H 9JH. Tel: 071-222 2248. *Director-General*, D. Falcon

PUBLIC FINANCE AND ACCOUNTANCY, CHARTERED INSTITUTE OF (1885), 3 Robert Street, London WC2N 6BH. Tel: 071-895 8823. *Director*, N. P. Hepworth, OBE

PUBLIC HEALTH AND HYGIENE, THE ROYAL INSTITUTE OF (1937), 28 Portland Place, London W1N 4DE. Tel: 071-580 2731. *Secretary*, Gp Capt R. A. Smith (retd)

PUBLIC HEALTH ENGINEERS, INSTITUTION OF, *see* WATER AND ENVIRONMENTAL MANAGEMENT

PUBLIC RELATIONS, THE INSTITUTE OF (1948), The Old Trading House, 15 Northburgh Street, London EC1V 0PR. Tel: 071-253 5151. *Executive Director*, J. B. Lavelle

Public Teachers of Law, Society of (1908). *Hon. Secretary*, Prof. P. B. H. Birks, All Souls College, Oxford OX1 4AL. Tel: 0865-279379

Purchasing and Supply, Institute of (1967), Easton House, Easton on the Hill, Stamford, Lincs. PE9 3NZ. Tel: 0780-56777. *Director-General*, P. Thomson

Pure Water Association, National (1960). *Secretary*, N. Brugge, Meridan, Cae Goody Lane, Ellesmere, Shrops. SY12 9DW. Tel: 0691-623015

Quality Assurance, Institute of, 10 Grosvenor Gardens, London SW1 0DQ. Tel: 071-730 7154. *Secretary-General*, Dr J. Davies

Quarrier's Homes (1871), Bridge of Weir, Renfrewshire PA11 3SA. Tel: 0505-612224. *Director-General*, J. Rea, OBE

Quarrying, Institute of (1917), 7 Regent Street, Nottingham NG1 5BY. Tel: 0602-411315. *Secretary*, M. J. Arthur

Queen Elizabeth's Foundation for the Disabled (1967), Leatherhead, Surrey KT22 0BN. Tel: 0372-842204. *Director*, M. B. Clark, Ph.D

Queen Victoria Clergy Fund (1897), Church House, Dean's Yard, London SW1P 3NZ. Tel: 071-222 5261. *Secretary*, C. D. L. Menzies

Queen Victoria School (1908), Dunblane, Perthshire FK15 0JY. Tel: 0786-822288. *Headmaster*, J. D. Hankinson

Queen's English Society, The (1972). *Hon. Membership Secretary*, M. Plumbe, 104 Drive Mansions, Fulham Road, London SW6 5JH. Tel: 071-731 1664

Queen's Nursing Institute (1887), 3 Albemarle Way, London EC1V 4JB. Tel: 071-490 4227. *Director*, Mrs S. Andrews

Quekett Microscopical Club (1865). *Hon. Business Secretary*, B. Scott, 237 Petts Hill, Northolt, Middx. UB5 4NR

Quit (National Society of Non-Smokers) (1926), 102 Gloucester Place, London W1H 3DA. Tel: 071-487 2858. *Director*, Ms S. Wilson

RADAR (The Royal Association for Disability and Rehabilitation) (1977), 25 Mortimer Street, London W1N 8AB. Tel: 071-637 5400. *Director*, B. Massie, OBE

Radiologists, Royal College of (1934), 38 Portland Place, London W1N 3DG. Tel: 071-636 4432. *Secretary*, A. J. Cowles

Radiology, British Institute of (1897), 36 Portland Place, London W1N 4AT. Tel: 071-580 4085. *General Secretary*, Ms M-A. Piggott

Railway and Canal Historical Society. *Hon. Secretary*, G. H. R. Gwatkin, 17 Clumber Crescent North, The Park, Nottingham NG7 1EY. Tel: 0602 414844

Railway Benevolent Institution (1858), 67 Ashbourne Road, Derby DE22 3FS. Tel: 0332-363067. *Director*, R. B. Boiling

Rainer Foundation (1876), 89 Blackheath Hill, London SE10 8TJ. Tel: 081-694 9497. Provides community-based services for young people who are homeless, offending or in difficulty with their families. *Director*, Dr R. Kay

Ramblers' Association (1935), 1–5 Wandsworth Road, London SW8 2XX. Tel: 071-582 6878. *Director*, A. Mattingly

Ranfurly Library Service (1954), 2 Coldharbour Place, 39–41 Coldharbour Lane, London SE5 9NR. Tel: 071-733 3577. *Director*, Mrs S. Harrity

Rare Breeds Survival Trust (1973), National Agricultural Centre, Kenilworth, Warks. CV8 2LG. Tel: 0203-696551. *Executive Director*, L. Alderson

Rathbone Society, The (1919), 1st Floor, Princess House, 105–107 Princess Street, Manchester M1 6DD. Tel: 061-236 5358. Helps people with learning difficulties. *Chief Executive*, Ms A. Weinstock

Record Society, Scottish (1897), Department of Scottish History, University of Glasgow, Glasgow G12 8QQ. Tel: 041-339 8855, ext. 5682. *Hon. Secretary*, Dr J. Kirk

Records Association, British (1932), 18 Padbury Court, London E2 7EH. Tel: 071-729 1415. *Hon. Secretary*, T. Davies

Red Cross Society, British, *see* British Red Cross

Red Poll Cattle Society (1888), The Market Hill, Woodbridge, Suffolk IP12 4DU. Tel: 0394-380643. *Secretary*, P. Ryder-Davies

Refrigeration, Institute of (1899), Kelvin House, 76 Mill Lane, Carshalton, Surrey SM5 2JR. Tel: 081-647 7033. *Secretary*, M. J. Horlick

Refugee Council, British (1981), Bondway House, 3–9 Bondway, London SW8 1SJ. Tel: 071-582 6922. *Director*, A. Dubs

Regional Studies Association (1965), Wharfdale Projects, 15 Micawber Street, London N1 7TB. Tel: 071-490 1128. *Director*, Mrs S. Hardy

Regular Forces Employment Association (1885), 25 Bloomsbury Square, London WC1A 2LN. Tel: 071-637 3918. *General Manager*, Maj.-Gen. D. T. Crabtree, CB

Relate: Marriage Guidance (1938), Herbert Gray College, Little Church Street, Rugby, Warks. CV21 3AP. Tel: 0788-573241. *Director*, D. French

Rent Officers, Institute of (1966). *Hon. Secretary*, A. E. Corcoran, 6th Floor, Grosvenor House, Cumberland Place, Southampton SO1 2BD. Tel: 0703-225900

Research Defence Society (1908), 88 Great Marlborough Street, London W1V 1DD. Tel: 071-287 2818. *Executive Director*, Dr M. Matfield

Residents' Associations, National Union of (1921). *Hon. General Secretary*, Mrs B. Reith, 35 Clement Way, Upminster, Essex RM14 2NX

Retail Book, Stationery and Allied Trades Employees' Association (1919), 8–9 Commercial Road, Swindon SN1 5RB. Tel: 0793-615811. *General Secretary*, J. Windust

Retirement Pensions Associations, National Federation of (1938), 14 St Peter Street, Blackburn BB2 2HD. Tel: 0254-52606. *General Secretary*, R. Stansfield

Revenues, Rating and Valuation Institute of (1882), 41 Doughty Street, London WC1N 2LF. Tel: 071-831 3505. *Director*, C. Farrington

RICHARD III SOCIETY (1924), 4 Oakley Street, London SW3 5NN. *Secretary*, Miss E. M. Nokes

ROAD SAFETY OFFICERS, INSTITUTE OF (1971). *Secretary*, B. Wilkinson, 31 Heather Grove, Hollingworth, via Hyde, Cheshire SK14 8JL. Tel: 0457-62170

ROAD TRANSPORT ENGINEERS, INSTITUTE OF (1945), 1 Cromwell Place, London SW7 2JF. Tel: 071-589 3744. *Executive Secretary*, A. F. Stroud

ROMAN STUDIES, SOCIETY FOR PROMOTION OF (1910), 31–34 Gordon Square, London WC1H OPP. Tel: 071-387 8157. *Secretary*, Dr H. M. Cockle

ROTARY INTERNATIONAL IN GREAT BRITAIN AND IRELAND (1914), Kinwarton Road, Alcester, Warks. B49 6BP. Tel: 0789-765411. *Secretary*, G. S. Large

ROUND TABLES OF GREAT BRITAIN AND IRELAND, NATIONAL ASSOCIATION OF (1927), Marchesi House, 4 Embassy Drive, Calthorpe Road, Edgbaston, Birmingham B15 1TP. Tel: 021-456 4402. *General Secretary*, R. H. Renold

ROYAL AFRICAN SOCIETY (1901), 18 Northumberland Avenue, London WC2N 5BJ. Tel: 071-930 1662. *Secretary*, Mrs L. Allan

ROYAL AIR FORCE BENEVOLENT FUND (1919), 67 Portland Place, London W1N 4AR. Tel: 071-580 8343. *Controller*, Air Chief Marshal Sir Thomas Kennedy, GCB, AFC

ROYAL AIR FORCES ASSOCIATION (1943), 43 Grove Park Road, London W4 3RX. Tel: 081-994 8504. *Secretary-General*, M. G. Tomkins, MBE

ROYAL ALEXANDRA AND ALBERT SCHOOL (1758), Gatton Park, Reigate, Surrey RH2 OTW. Tel: 0737-642576. *Secretary*, Capt. A. J. Walsh, RN

ROYAL ALFRED SEAFARERS' SOCIETY (1865), Weston Acres, Woodmansterne Lane, Banstead, Surrey SM7 3HB. Tel: 0737-352231. *General Secretary*, A. R. Quinton

ROYAL ARMOURED CORPS WAR MEMORIAL BENEVOLENT FUND (1946), c/o RHQ RTR, Bovington, Wareham, Dorset BH20 6JA. Tel: 0929-403331. *Secretary*, Maj. R. Clooney (retd)

ROYAL ARTILLERY ASSOCIATION, Artillery House, Old Royal Military Academy, London SE18 4DN. *General Secretary*, Lt.-Col. M. J. Darmody

ROYAL ASIATIC SOCIETY (1823), 60 Queen's Gardens, London W2 3AF. Tel: 071-724 4741/2. *Secretary*, Miss L. Collins

ROYAL CALEDONIAN SCHOOLS (1815), Aldenham Road, Bushey, Watford, Herts. WD2 3TS. Tel: 0923-226642. *Master*, Capt. D. F. Watts, RN

ROYAL CELTIC SOCIETY (1820), 23 Rutland Street, Edinburgh EH1 2RN. Tel: 031-228 6449. *Secretary*, J. G. Cameron

ROYAL CHORAL SOCIETY (1871), 8 Wendell Road, London W12 9RT. Tel: 081-740 4273. *General Manager*, M. Heyland

ROYAL ENGINEERS ASSOCIATION, RHQ Royal Engineers, Brompton Barracks, Chatham, Kent ME4 4UG. Tel: 0634-847005. *Controller*, Maj. C. F. Cooper, MBE (retd)

ROYAL ENGINEERS, THE INSTITUTION OF (1875), Brompton Barracks, Chatham, Kent ME4 4UG. Tel: 0634-842669. *Secretary*, Col. R. I. Reive, OBE

ROYAL HIGHLAND AND AGRICULTURAL SOCIETY OF SCOTLAND (1784), Royal Highland Centre, Ingliston, Edinburgh EH28 8NF. Tel: 031-333 2444. *Secretary*, J. R. Good

ROYAL HORTICULTURAL SOCIETY (1804), PO Box 313, 80 Vincent Square, London SW1P 2PE. Tel: 071-834 4333. *Secretary*, D. P. Hearn

ROYAL HOSPITAL AND HOME, PUTNEY (1854), West Hill, London SW15 3SW. Tel: 081-788 4511. *Chief Executive*, Col. B. E. Blunt

ROYAL HUMANE SOCIETY (1774), Brettenham House, Lancaster Place, London WC2E 7EP. Tel: 071-836 8155. *Secretary*, Maj. A. J. Dickinson

ROYAL INSTITUTION, THE (1799), 21 Albemarle Street, London W1X 4BS. Tel: 071-409 2992. *Director*, Prof. P. Day, FRS; *Secretary*, Prof. D. C. Bradley, FRS

ROYAL LIFE SAVING SOCIETY, UK (1891), Mountbatten House, Studley, Warks. B80 7NN. Tel: 0527-853943. *Director*, Ms C. J. Godsall

ROYAL LITERARY FUND (1790), 144 Temple Chambers, Temple Avenue, London EC4Y ODA. Tel: 071-353 7150. *Secretary*, Mrs F. M. Clark

ROYAL MEDICAL BENEVOLENT FUND (1836), 24 King's Road, London SW19 8QN. Tel: 081-540 9194. *Secretary*, Mrs G. A. R. Wells

ROYAL MEDICAL SOCIETY (1737), Students Centre, 5-5 Bristo Square, Edinburgh EH8 9AL. Tel: 031-650 2672. *Secretary*, Mrs P. Strong

ROYAL MICROSCOPICAL SOCIETY (1839), 37–38 St Clements, Oxford OX4 1AJ. Tel: 0865-248768. *Administrator*, P. B. Hirst

ROYAL MUSICAL ASSOCIATION (1874). *Secretary*, E. West, 135 Purves Road, London NW10 5TH

ROYAL NATIONAL INSTITUTE FOR THE BLIND (1868), 224 Great Portland Street, London W1N 6AA. Tel: 071-388 1266. *Director-General*, I. Bruce

ROYAL NATIONAL LIFEBOAT INSTITUTION (1824), West Quay Road, Poole, Dorset BH15 1HZ. Tel: 0202-671133. *Chairman*, M. Vernon

ROYAL NAVAL AND ROYAL MARINES CHILDREN'S TRUST (1834), HMS *Nelson*, Portsmouth, PO1 3HH. Tel: 0705-817435. *Secretary*, Mrs M. Bateman

ROYAL NAVAL ASSOCIATION (1950), 82 Chelsea Manor Street, London SW3 5QJ. Tel: 071-352 6764. *General Secretary*, Capt. J. W. Rayner, RMR

ROYAL NAVAL BENEVOLENT SOCIETY (1739), 1 Fleet Street, London EC4Y 1BD. Tel: 071-353 4080. *Secretary*, Cdr P. J. F. Moore, RN

ROYAL NAVAL BENEVOLENT TRUST (1922), 1 High Street, Brompton, Gillingham, Kent ME7 5QZ. Tel: 0634-842743. *General Secretary*, Lt.-Cdr. D. C. Lawrence (retd)

ROYAL NAVY OFFICERS, ASSOCIATION OF (1920), 70 Porchester Terrace, London W2 3TP. Tel: 071-402 5231. *Secretary*, Lt.-Cdr. I. M. P. Coombes

ROYAL OVER-SEAS LEAGUE (1910), Over-Seas House, Park Place, St James's Street, London SW1A 1LR. Tel: 071-408 0214. *Director-General*, R. F. Newell

ROYAL PATRIOTIC FUND CORPORATION (1854), Golden Cross House, Duncannon Street, London WC2 4JR. *Secretary*, Brig. T. G. Williams, CBE

ROYAL PHILATELIC SOCIETY, LONDON, THE (1869), 41 Devonshire Place, W1H 1PE. Tel: 071-486 1044. *General Secretary*, Miss M. Simmonds

ROYAL PHOTOGRAPHIC SOCIETY (1853), Milsom Street, Bath BA1 1DN. Tel: 0225-462841. *Secretary*, Ms A. Nevill

ROYAL PINNER SCHOOL FOUNDATION, 110 Old Brompton Road, London SW7 3RB. Tel: 071-373 6168. *Secretary*, D. Crawford

ROYAL SAILORS' RESTS (1876), 2A South Street, Gosport, Hants. PO12 1ES. Tel: 0705-589551. *Secretary*, A. A. Lockwood

ROYAL SCOTTISH SOCIETY FOR PREVENTION OF CRUELTY TO CHILDREN (1884), Melville House, 41 Polwarth Terrace, Edinburgh EH11 1NU. Tel: 031-337 8539. *General Secretary*, A. M. M. Wood, OBE

ROYAL SIGNALS INSTITUTION (1950), 56 Regency Street, London SW1P 4AD. Tel: 071-414 8421. *Secretary*, Col. A. N. de Bretton-Gordon

ROYAL SOCIETY FOR ASIAN AFFAIRS (1901), 2 Belgrave Square, London SW1X 8PJ. Tel: 071-235 5122. *Secretary*, Miss M. FitzSimons

ROYAL SOCIETY FOR THE ENCOURAGEMENT OF ARTS, MANUFACTURES AND COMMERCE (RSA) (1754), 8 John Adam Street, London WC2N 6EZ. Tel: 071-930 5115. *Chief Executive*, C. Lucas

ROYAL SOCIETY FOR THE PREVENTION OF CRUELTY TO ANIMALS (1824), Causeway, Horsham, W. Sussex RH12 1HG. Tel: 0403-64181. *Chief Executive*, P. R. Davies, CB

ROYAL SOCIETY FOR THE PROTECTION OF BIRDS (1889), The Lodge, Sandy, Beds. SG19 2DL. Tel: 0767-680551. *Chief Executive*, Ms B. Young

ROYAL SOCIETY OF HEALTH, THE (1876), RSH House, 38A St George's Drive, London SW1V 4BH. Tel: 071-630 0121. *Secretary*, D. Goad

ROYAL SOCIETY OF LITERATURE (1823), 1 Hyde Park Gardens, London W2 2LT. Tel: 071-723 5104. *Secretary*, Ms M. Parham

ROYAL SOCIETY OF MEDICINE (1805), 1 Wimpole Street, London W1M 8AE. Tel: 071-408 2119. *Executive Director*, R. N. Thomson

ROYAL SOCIETY OF ST GEORGE, (1894), Dartmouth House, 37 Charles Street, London W1X 8AB. Tel: 071-499 5430. *Chairman*, G. Andrews

ROYAL STAR AND GARTER HOME FOR DISABLED SAILORS, SOLDIERS AND AIRMEN (1916), Richmond, Surrey TW10 6RR. Tel: 081-940 3314. *Chief Executive*, I. Lashbrooke

ROYAL STATISTICAL SOCIETY (1834), 25 Enford Street, London W1H 2BH. Tel: 071-723 5882. *Executive Secretary*, I. Goddard

ROYAL TANK REGIMENT BENEVOLENT FUND (1919), RHQ RTR Centre, Bovington, Wareham, Dorset BH20 6JA. Tel: 0929-403331. *Regimental Secretary*, Maj. R. Clooney (retd)

ROYAL TELEVISION SOCIETY (1927), Tavistock House East, Tavistock Square, London WC1H 9HR. Tel: 071-387 1970. *Hon. Secretary*, A. Pilgrim

ROYAL UNITED KINGDOM BENEFICENT ASSOCIATION (1863), 6 Avonmore Road, London W14 8RL. Tel: 071-602 6274. *Director*, W. Rathbone

RURAL ENGLAND, COUNCIL FOR THE PROTECTION OF (CPRE) (1926), Warwick House, 25 Buckingham Palace Road, London SW1W 0PP. Tel: 071-976 6433. *Director*, Ms F. Reynolds

RURAL SCOTLAND, ASSOCIATION FOR THE PROTECTION OF (1926), Charleston, Dalguise, Dunkeld PH8 0JX. Tel: 0350-728712. *Director*, R. L. Smith, OBE

RURAL WALES, CAMPAIGN FOR THE PROTECTION OF (1928), Tŷ Gwyn, 31 High Street, Welshpool, Powys SY21 7JP. Tel: 0938-556212. *Director*, Dr N. Caldwell

SAILORS' FAMILIES' SOCIETY, THE (1821), Newland, Hull HU6 7RJ. Tel: 0482-42331. *General Secretary*, Lt.-Cdr. C. G. R. Streatfeild-James

SAILORS' SOCIETY, BRITISH (1818), Orchard Place, Southampton, SO9 7SS. Tel: 0703-337333. *General Secretary*, G. Chambers

ST DEINIOL'S LIBRARY (1902), Hawarden, Deeside, Clwyd CH5 3DF. Tel: 0244-532350. *Warden and Chief Librarian*, Revd Dr P. J. Jagger

ST DUNSTAN'S, PO Box 4XB, 12–14 Harcourt Street, London W1A 4XB. Tel: 071-723 5021. For men and women blinded on war service. *Secretary*, W. C. Weisblatt

ST JOHN AMBULANCE (1887), 1 Grosvenor Crescent, London SW1X 7EF. Tel: 071-235 5231. *Executive Director*, T. Gauvain

ST JOSEPH'S SOCIETY FOR THE RELIEF OF THE AGED POOR (1708), St Joseph's House, 42 Brook Green, London W6 7BW. Tel: 071-603 9817. *Secretary*, S. Dolan

SALES AND MARKETING MANAGEMENT, INSTITUTE OF (1966), 31 Upper George Street, Luton LU1 2RD. Tel: 0582-411130. *Director-General*, K. Williams

SALMON AND TROUT ASSOCIATION (1903), Fishmongers' Hall, London Bridge, London EC4R 9EL. Tel: 071-283 5838. *Director*, Col. J. Ferguson

SALTIRE SOCIETY (1936), 9 Fountain Close, 22 High Street, Edinburgh EH1 1TF. Tel: 031-556 1836. *Administrator*, Mrs K. Munro

SAMARITANS, THE (1953), 10 The Grove, Slough, Berks. SL1 1QP. Tel: 0735-532713. Tel. numbers in local telephone directories. *Chief Executive*, S. Armson

SAMUEL PEPYS CLUB (1903). *Secretary*, P. L. Gray, 26 Gloucester Street, Faringdon, Oxon. SN7 7HY

SANE: SCHIZOPHRENIA A NATIONAL EMERGENCY (1986), 2nd Floor, 199–205 Marylebone Road, London NW1 5QP. Tel: 071-724 6520. *Saneline:* 071-724 8000. *Executive Director*, Ms M. Wallace

SAVE BRITAIN'S HERITAGE (1975), 68 Battersea High Street, London SW11 3HX. Tel: 071-228 3336. *Secretary*, Ms M. Watson-Smyth

SAVE THE CHILDREN FUND, THE (1919), Mary Datchelor House, 17 Grove Lane, London SE5 8RD. Tel: 071-703 5400. *Director-General*, N. J. Hinton, CBE

SCHIZOPHRENIA FELLOWSHIP, NATIONAL (1970), 28 Castle Street, Kingston upon Thames, Surrey KT1 1SS. Tel: 081-547 3937. *Chief Executive*, M. Eede

SCHOOL LIBRARY ASSOCIATION (1937), Liden Library, Barrington Close, Liden, Swindon SN3 6HF. Tel: 0793-617838. *Executive Secretary*, Ms V. Fea

SCHOOL NATURAL SCIENCE SOCIETY (1903). *Hon. General Secretary*, Miss D. S. Jackson, 153 Fernside Avenue, Hanworth, Middx. TW13 7BQ

SCHOOLMASTERS, SOCIETY OF (1798). *Secretary*, Mrs M. S. Freeburn, 29 Corrib Court, Fox Lane, London N13 4BG

SCHOOLMISTRESSES AND GOVERNESSES BENEVOLENT INSTITUTION (1843), Queen Mary House, Manor Park Road, Chislehurst, Kent BR7 5PY. Tel: 081-468 7997. *Director*, R. W. Hayward

SCIENCE AND LEARNING, SOCIETY FOR THE PROTECTION OF (1933), 20–21 Compton Terrace, London N1 2UN. *Secretary*, Ms E. Fraser

SCIENCE AND TECHNOLOGY, BRITISH ASSOCIATION FOR THE PROMOTION OF (1831), Fortress House, 23 Savile Row, London W1X 1AB. Tel: 071-494 3326. *Executive Secretary*, Dr P. Briggs

SCIENCE EDUCATION, ASSOCIATION FOR (1963), College Lane, Hatfield, Herts. AL10 9AA. Tel: 0707-267411. *General Secretary*, Dr D. S. Moore

SCOTCH WHISKY ASSOCIATION, THE (1919), 20 Atholl Crescent, Edinburgh EH3 8HF. Tel: 031-229 4383. *Director-General*, Col. H. F. O. Bewsher, OBE

SCOTTISH CHURCH HISTORY SOCIETY (1922). *Hon. Secretary*, Revd Dr P. H. Donald, St Serf's Manse, 1 Denham Green Terrace, Edinburgh EH5 3PG. Tel: 031-552 4059

SCOTTISH CORPORATION, THE ROYAL (1611), 37 King Street, London WC2E 8JS. Tel: 071-240 3718. *Chief Executive*, Wg Cdr. A. Robertson

SCOTTISH COUNTRY DANCE SOCIETY, ROYAL (1923), 12 Coates Crescent, Edinburgh EH3 7AF. Tel: 031-225 3854. *Secretary*, Mrs J. A. Moore

SCOTTISH GENEALOGY SOCIETY (1953), Library and Family History Centre, 15 Victoria Terrace, Edinburgh EH1 2JL. Tel: 031-220 3677. *Hon. Secretary*, Miss J. P. S. Ferguson

SCOTTISH HISTORY SOCIETY (1886). *Hon. Secretary*, Dr E. P. D. Torrie, Department of Scottish History, University of Edinburgh EH8 9YL. Tel: 031-650 4030

SCOTTISH LANDOWNERS' FEDERATION (1906). *Director*, S. Fraser, 25 Maritime Street, Edinburgh EH6 5PN. Tel: 031-555 1031

SCOTTISH LAW AGENTS SOCIETY, 3 Albyn Place, Edinburgh EH2 4NQ. Tel: 031-225 7515. *Secretary*, R. M. Sinclair

SCOTTISH LIFE OFFICES, ASSOCIATED (1841), 23 St Andrew Square, Edinburgh EH2 1AQ. *Secretary*, W. W. Mair

SCOTTISH NATIONAL INSTITUTION FOR THE WAR BLINDED (1915), PO Box 500, Gillespie Crescent, Edinburgh EH10 4HZ. Tel: 031-229 1456. *Secretary*, J. B. M. Munro

SCOTTISH NATIONAL WAR MEMORIAL (1927), The Castle, Edinburgh EH1 2YT. Tel: 031-226 7393. *Secretary*, T. C. Barker

SCOTTISH SECONDARY TEACHERS' ASSOCIATION (1946), 15 Dundas Street, Edinburgh EH3 6QG. Tel: 031-556 5919. *General Secretary*, A. A. Stanley

SCOTTISH SOCIETY FOR THE PREVENTION OF CRUELTY TO ANIMALS (1950), 19 Melville Street, Edinburgh EH3 7PL. Tel: 031-225 6418. *Chief Executive*, J. Morris, CBE

SCOTTISH SOCIETY FOR THE PROTECTION OF WILD BIRDS (1927), Foremount House, Kilbarchan, Renfrewshire PA10 2EZ. Tel: 05057-2419. *Secretary*, Dr J. A. Gibson

SCOTTISH WILDLIFE TRUST (1964), Cramond House, Kirk Cramond, Cramond Glebe Road, Edinburgh EH4 6NS. Tel: 031-312 7765. *Director*, D. J. Hughes Hallett

SCOUT ASSOCIATION, THE (1907), Baden-Powell House, Queen's Gate, London SW7 5JS. Tel: 071-584 7030. *Chief Scout*, W. G. Morrison; *Chief Executive Commissioner*, A. E. N. Black, OBE

SCRIBES AND ILLUMINATORS, THE SOCIETY OF (1921), 54 Boileau Road, London SW13 9BL. Tel: 081-748 9951

SCRIPTURE GIFT MISSION INCORPORATED (1888), Radstock House, 3 Eccleston Street, London SW1W 9LZ. Tel: 071-730 2155. *General Secretary*, R. Kennedy

SCRIPTURE UNION (1867), 130 City Road, London EC1V 2NJ. Tel: 071-782 0013. *General Director*, Revd D. M. S. Cohen

SCULPTORS, ROYAL SOCIETY OF BRITISH (1904), 108 Old Brompton Road, London SW7 3RA. Tel: 071-373 5554. *President*, Ms P. Davidson Davis

SEA CADETS, (1895), 202 Lambeth Road, London SE1 7JF. Tel: 071-928 8978. *General Secretary*, Cdr G. J. A. Shaw, OBE (retd)

SEAMEN'S BOYS' HOME, BRITISH (1863), Berry Head Road, Brixham, Devon TQ5 9AE. Tel: 0803-882129. *Secretary*, Capt. E. M. Marks, RD, RNR

SEAMEN'S CHRISTIAN FRIEND SOCIETY (1846), PO Box 60, Wilmslow, Cheshire SK9 1QX. Tel: 0625-586300. *Administrator*, M. J. Wilson

SEAMEN'S PENSION FUND, ROYAL (1919), 65 High Street, Ewell, Epsom, Surrey KT17 1RX. Tel: 081-393 5873. *Secretary*, D. Barker

SECONDARY HEADS ASSOCIATION (1978), 130 Regent Road, Leicester LE1 7PG. Tel: 0533-471797. *General Secretary*, J. Sutton

SECULAR SOCIETY LTD, NATIONAL (1866), 702 Holloway Road, London N19 3NL. Tel: 071-272 1266. *General Secretary*, T. Mullins

SELDEN SOCIETY (1887), Faculty of Laws, Queen Mary and Westfield College, Mile End Road, London E1 4NS. Tel: 071-975 5136. To encourage the study and advance the knowledge of the history of English law. *Secretary*, V. Tunkel

SELF EMPLOYED AND SMALL BUSINESSES, NATIONAL FEDERATION OF, *see* SMALL BUSINESSES, FEDERATION OF

SENSE (The National Deaf-Blind and Rubella Association) (1955), 11–13 Clifton Terrace, London N4 3SR. Tel: 071-278 1005. *Chief Executive*, R. Clark

SHAFTESBURY HOMES AND *Arethusa* (1843), 3 Rectory Grove, London SW4 0EG. Tel: 071-720 8709. *Director*, Capt. N. C. Baird-Murray, CBE, RN

SHAFTESBURY SOCIETY, THE (1844), 18–20 Kingston Road, London SW19 1JZ. Tel: 081-542 5550. Cares for physically and mentally handicapped, elderly and socially deprived people. *Chief Executive*, G. Holloway

SHELLFISH ASSOCIATION OF GREAT BRITAIN (1904), Fishmongers' Hall, London Bridge, London EC4R 9EL. Tel: 071-283 8305. *Director*, E. Edwards, OBE, Ph.D

SHELTER (National campaign for homeless people) (1966), 88 Old Street, London EC1V 9HU. Tel: 071-253 0202. *Director*, Ms S. McKechnie

SHERLOCK HOLMES SOCIETY OF LONDON (1951). *Hon. Secretary*, Cdr. G. S. Stavert, MBE (retd), 3 Outram Road, Southsea, Hants. PO5 1QP. Tel: 0705-812104

SHIPBROKERS, INSTITUTE OF CHARTERED (1911), 3 Gracechurch Street, London EC3V 0AT. Tel: 071-283 1361. *Secretary*, J. H. Parker

SHIRE HORSE SOCIETY (1878), East of England Showground, Peterborough PE2 6XE. Tel: 0733-390696. *Secretary*, S. A. Stagg

SHRIEVALTY ASSOCIATION (1971), Express Buildings, 17–29 Parliament Street, Nottingham NG1 2AQ. Tel: 0602-350350. *Secretary*, R. Bullock

SIGHT SAVERS (Royal Commonwealth Society for the Blind) (1950), PO Box 191, Haywards Heath, W. Sussex RH16 4YF. Tel: 0444-412424. *Executive Director*, A. W. Johns, CMG, OBE

SIMPLIFIED SPELLING SOCIETY (1908). *Chairman*, C. J. H. Jolly, Clare Hall, Chapel Lane, Chigwell, Essex IG7 6JJ. Tel: 081-501 0405

SIR OSWALD STOLL FOUNDATION (1916), 446 Fulham Road, London SW6 1DT. Tel: 071-385 2110. *Director*, R. C. Brunwin

SMALL BUSINESSES, FEDERATION OF (1974), Parliamentary Office, 140 Lower Marsh, London SE1 7AE. Tel: 071-928 9272. *National Chairman*, J. Harris

SMALL FARMERS' ASSOCIATION, THE (1979), PO Box 18, Woodbridge, Suffolk IP13 0QP. *Chairman*, J. Morford

SOCIALIST PARTY OF GREAT BRITAIN (1904), 52 Clapham High Street, London SW4 7UN. Tel: 071-622 3811. *General Secretary*, P. Hope

SOCIAL RESPONSIBILITY AND EDUCATION, QUAKER, Friends House, Euston Road, London NW1 2BJ. Tel: 071-387 3601. *General Secretary*, Ms B. Smith

SOCIAL WORKERS, BRITISH ASSOCIATION OF (1970), 16 Kent Street, Birmingham B5 6RD. *General Secretary*, D. N. Jones

SOLDIERS' AND AIRMEN'S SCRIPTURE READERS ASSOCIATION, THE (1838), Havelock House, Barrack Road, Aldershot, Hants. GU11 3NP. Tel: 0252-310033. *General Secretary*, Lt.-Col. M. Hitchcott

SOLDIERS', SAILORS' AND AIRMEN'S FAMILIES ASSOCIATION (1885), 19 Queen Elizabeth Street, London SE1 2LP. Tel: 071-403 8783. *Controller*, Maj.-Gen. C. R. Grey, CBE; *Secretary*, Mrs B. R. Best, OBE

SOLDIERS, SAILORS AND AIRMEN'S HELP SOCIETY, *see* FORCES HELP SOCIETY

SOLDIERS' WIDOWS, ROYAL CAMBRIDGE HOME FOR (1851), 82–84 Hurst Road, East Molesey, Surrey KT8 9AH. Tel: 081-979 3788. *Superintendent*, Mrs A. M. Webb

SOLICITORS IN THE SUPREME COURTS OF SCOTLAND, SOCIETY OF (1784). *Secretary*, A. R. Brownlie, OBE, 2 Abercromby Place, Edinburgh EH3 6JZ. Tel: 031-556 4070

SOROPTIMIST INTERNATIONAL OF GREAT BRITAIN AND IRELAND (1923), 127 Wellington Road South, Stockport SK1 3TS. Tel: 061-480 7686. *Executive Officer*, Ms K. Hindley

SOS SOCIETY, THE, *see* 2CARE

SOUTH AMERICAN MISSIONARY SOCIETY (1844), Allen Gardiner House, Pembury Road, Tunbridge Wells, Kent TN2 3QU. Tel: 0892-538647. *General Secretary*, Rt. Revd J. W. H. Flagg

SOUTH WALES INSTITUTE OF ENGINEERS (1857), Empire House, Mount Stuart Square, Cardiff CF1 6DN. Tel: 0222-481726. *Hon. Secretary*, R. E. Lindsay

SPASTICS SOCIETY, THE (1952), 12 Park Crescent, London W1N 4EQ. Tel: 071-636 5020. *Chief Executive*, R. Limb

SPEAKERS CLUBS, THE ASSOCIATION OF (1971). *National Secretary*, F. W. P. Dawkins, 3 Leawood Croft, Holloway, Matlock, Derbyshire DE4 5BD. Tel: 0629-534619

SPINA BIFIDA AND HYDROCEPHALUS, ASSOCIATION FOR (ASBAH), 42 Park Road, Peterborough PE1 2UQ. Tel: 0733-555988. *Executive Director*, A. Russell

SPORTS MEDICINE, INSTITUTE OF (1963), Burlington House, Piccadilly, London W1V 0LQ. Tel: 071-287 5269. *Hon. Secretary*, Dr W. T. Orton

SPURGEON'S CHILD CARE (1867), 30 Mill Street, Bedford MK40 3HD. Tel: 0234-261843. *Director*, D. C. Culwick

STATISTICIANS, INSTITUTE OF (1948), 43 St Peters Square, Preston PR1 7BX. Tel: 0772-204237. *Secretary*, D. A. Holland

STATUTE LAW SOCIETY (1968), Onslow House, 9 The Green, Richmond, Surrey TW9 1PU. Tel: 081-940 0017. *Hon. Secretary*, N. Frudd

STEWART SOCIETY (1899), 314 Leith Walk, Edinburgh EH6 5BU. Tel: 031-555 4640. *Hon. Secretary*, Mrs M. Walker

STRATEGIC PLANNING SOCIETY, THE (1967), 17 Portland Place, London W1N 3AF. Tel: 071-636 7737. *General Secretary*, Ms E. Wooldridge

STRATEGIC STUDIES, THE INTERNATIONAL INSTITUTE FOR (1958), 23 Tavistock Street, London WC2E 7NQ. Tel: 071-379 7676. *Director*, Dr B. Huldt

STROKE ASSOCIATION, THE (1899), CHSA House, Whitecross Street, London EC1Y 8JJ. Tel: 071-490 7999. *Director-General*, Sir David Atkinson

STRUCTURAL ENGINEERS, INSTITUTION OF (1908), 11 Upper Belgrave Street, London SW1X 8BH. Tel: 071-235 4535. *Secretary*, D. J. Clark

STUDENT CHRISTIAN MOVEMENT (1889), 186 St Paul's Road, Balsall Heath, Birmingham B12 8LZ. Tel: 021-440 3000. *General Secretary*, vacant

SUFFOLK HORSE SOCIETY (1878), The Market Hill, Woodbridge, Suffolk IP12 4DU. Tel: 0394-380643. *Secretary*, P. Ryder-Davies

SURGEONS OF EDINBURGH, ROYAL COLLEGE OF (1505), Nicolson Street, Edinburgh EH8 9DW. Tel: 031-556 6206. *Secretary*, Prof. A. C. B. Dean

SURGEONS OF ENGLAND, ROYAL COLLEGE OF (1800), 35–43 Lincoln's Inn Fields, London WC2A 3PN. Tel: 071-405 3474. *Secretary*, R. H. E. Duffett

SURVEYORS, ROYAL INSTITUTION OF CHARTERED (1868), Surveyor Court, Westwood Way, Coventry CV4 8JE. Tel: 071-222 7000. *Secretary-General*, M. Pattison

SUSSEX CATTLE SOCIETY (1887), Station Road, Robertsbridge, E. Sussex TN32 5DG. *Manager*, Miss S. G. Kennedy

SWEDENBORG SOCIETY (1810), 20–21 Bloomsbury Way, London WC1A 2TH. Tel: 071-405 7986. *Secretary*, Ms M. G. Waters

TALKING BOOKS FOR THE HANDICAPPED AND HOSPITAL PATIENTS, *see* NATIONAL LISTENING LIBRARY

TAVISTOCK INSTITUTE, THE (1947), 120 Belsize Lane, London NW3 5BA. Tel: 071-435 7111. *Secretary*, N. Barnes

TAXATION, INSTITUTE OF (1930), 12 Upper Belgrave Street, London SW1X 8BB. Tel: 071-235 9381. *Secretary*, R. J. Ison

TEACHERS AND LECTURERS, ASSOCIATION OF (1978), 7 Northumberland Street, London WC2N 5DA. Tel: 071-930 6441. *General Secretary*, P. Smith

TEACHERS OF HOME ECONOMICS AND TECHNOLOGY, NATIONAL ASSOCIATION OF (1896), Hamilton House, Mabledon Place, London WC1H 9BJ. Tel: 071-387 1441. *General Manager*, P. G. Higgins

TEACHERS OF MATHEMATICS, ASSOCIATION OF (1952), 7 Shaftesbury Street, Derby DE3 8YB. Tel: 0332-46599. *Hon. Secretary*, Ms C. Hopkins

TEACHERS OF THE DEAF, BRITISH ASSOCIATION OF (1977). *Hon. Secretary*, Ms S. Dowe, Icknield High School HIU, Riddy Lane, Luton LU3 2AH. Tel: 0582-596599

TEACHERS' UNION, ULSTER (1919), 94 Malone Road, Belfast BT9 5HP. Tel: 0232-662216. *General Secretary*, D. Allen

TELECOMMUNICATIONS USERS' ASSOCIATION (1965), 48 Percy Road, London N12 8BU. Tel: 081-445 0996. *Chief Executive*, Ms V. Peters

TEMPERANCE SOCIETIES:

British National Temperance League (1834), Room 4, Shirley House, 31 Psalter Lane, Sheffield S11 8YL. Tel: 0742-500713. *Secretary*, L. Swales

Church of England National Council for Social Aid, 38 Ebury Street, London SW1W 0LU. Tel: 071-730 6175. *General Secretary*, Revd E. W. F. Agar

National United Temperance Council (1880), 176 Blackfriars Road, London SE1 8ET. Tel: 071-928 1538. *General Secretary*, Revd B. Kinman

Order of the Sons of Temperance (1855), 5 Ashbourne Road, Derby DE22 3FQ. Tel: 0332-41672. *Secretary*, D. Newbury

Royal Naval Temperance Society (1876) (auxiliary of Royal Sailors' Rests), 2A South Street, Gosport, Hants. PO12 1ES. Tel: 0705-589551. *Secretary*, A. A. Lockwood

United Kingdom Alliance (1863), 176 Blackfriars Road, London SE1 8ET. Tel: 071-928 1538. *General Secretary*, Revd B. Kinman

TEMPLETON FOUNDATION (1973), 16 Kingfisher Lane, Turners Hill, Crawley, W. Sussex RH10 4QP. Tel: 0342-715750. *UK Representative*, Mrs N. Pearse

TERRENCE HIGGINS TRUST (1982), 52–54 Grays Inn Road, London WC1X 8JU. Tel: 071-831 0330. *Helpline*, 071-242 1010. *Chairman*, N. Partridge

TERRITORIAL, AUXILIARY AND VOLUNTEER RESERVE ASSOCIATIONS, COUNCIL OF (1908), The Chapel, Duke of York's HQ, London SW3 4SG. Tel: 071-730 6122. *Secretary*, Maj.-Gen. M. Matthews, CB

TEXTILE INSTITUTE, THE (1910), International HQ, 10 Blackfriars Street, Manchester M3 5DR. Tel: 061-834 8457. *General Secretary*, R. G. Denyer

THEATRE RESEARCH, SOCIETY FOR (1948), c/o The Theatre Museum, 1E Tavistock Street, London WC2E 7PA. *Joint Hon. Secretaries*, Ms E. Cottis; Ms F. Dann

THEATRES TRUST, THE (1976), 22 Charing Cross Road, London WC2H 0HR. Tel: 071-836 8591. *Chairman*, G. L. Harbottle; *Director*, J. Earl

THEATRICAL FUND, ROYAL (1839), 11 Garrick Street, London WC2E 9AR. Tel: 071-836 3322. *Secretary*, R. Coutts Smith

THEATRICAL LADIES' GUILD OF CHARITY (1892), 49 Endell Street, London WC2H 9AJ. Tel: 071-497 3030. *Adminstrative Secretary*, Mrs K. Nichols

THEOSOPHICAL SOCIETY IN ENGLAND (1875), 50 Gloucester Place, London W1H 3HJ. Tel: 071-935 9261. *General Secretary*, A. Warcup

THISTLE FOUNDATION, THE (1945), 27A Walker Street, Edinburgh EH3 7HX. Tel: 031-225 7282. *Director*, P. Croft

THOMAS CORAM FOUNDATION FOR CHILDREN (formerly The Foundling Hospital) (1739), 40 Brunswick Square, London WC1N 1AZ. Tel: 071-278 2424. *Director and Secretary*, C. P. Masters

TIDY BRITAIN GROUP, THE (1953), The Pier, Wigan WN3 4EX. Tel: 0942-824620. *Director-General*, Prof. G. Ashworth, CBE

TOC H (1915), Headquarters, 1 Forest Close, Wendover, Aylesbury, Bucks. HP22 6BT. Tel: 0296-623911. *Executive Secretary*, S. Casimir

TOURIST BOARD, ENGLISH, Thames Tower, Black's Road, London W6 9EL. *Chief Executive*, M. Medlicott

TOURIST BOARD, NORTHERN IRELAND, St Anne's Court, North Street, Belfast BT1 1ND. Tel: 0232-231221. *Chief Executive*, I. Henderson

TOURIST BOARD, SCOTTISH (1969), 23 Ravelston Terrace, Edinburgh EH4 3EU. *Chief Executive*, T. M. Band

TOURIST BOARD, WALES, Brunel House, 2 Fitzalan Road, Cardiff CF2 1UY. *Chief Executive*, P. Loveluck

TOWN AND COUNTRY PLANNING ASSOCIATION (1899), 17 Carlton House Terrace, London SW1Y 5AS. Tel: 071-930 8903. *Director*, D. Hall

TOWN PLANNING INSTITUTE, THE ROYAL (1914), 26 Portland Place, London W1N 4BE. Tel: 071-636 9107. *Secretary-General*, D. Fryer

TOWNSWOMEN'S GUILDS, (1929), Chamber of Commerce House, 75 Harborne Road, Birmingham B15 3DA. Tel: 021-456 3435. *National Secretary*, Ms R. Styles

TOYNBEE HALL, The Universities' Settlement in East London (1884), 28 Commercial Street, London E1 6LS. Tel: 071-247 6943. *Warden and Chief Executive* (*acting*), A. Prescott

TRADE, NATIONAL CHAMBER OF (1897), Enterprise House, 59 Castle Street, Reading, Berks. RG1 7SN. Tel: 0734-566744. *Chief Executive*, B. Tennant

TRADE MARK AGENTS, INSTITUTE OF (1934), 4th Floor, Canterbury House, 2–6 Sydenham Road, Croydon CR0 9XE. Tel: 081-684 3839. *Secretary*, Mrs M. J. Tyler

TRADING STANDARDS ADMINISTRATION, THE INSTITUTE OF (1881), 4–5 Hadleigh Business Centre, 351 London Road, Hadleigh, Essex SS7 2BT. Tel: 0702-559922. *Director of Administration and PR*, vacant

TRANSLATION AND INTERPRETING, INSTITUTE OF (1986), 377 City Road, London EC1V 1NA. Tel: 071-713 7600. *Chairman*, R. Fletcher

TRANSPORT ADMINISTRATION, INSTITUTE OF (1944), 32 Palmerston Road, Southampton SO1 1LL. Tel: 0703-631380. *Director*, Wg Cdr. P. F. Green

TRANSPORT, CHARTERED INSTITUTE OF (1919), 80 Portland Place, London W1N 4DP. Tel: 071-636 9952. *Director-General*, R. P. Botwood

TRANSPORT CONSULTATIVE COMMITTEE, CENTRAL (1948), 1st Floor, Golden Cross House, Duncannon Street, London WC2N 4JF. Tel: 071-839 7338. *Secretary*, M. Patterson

TRAVEL AGENTS, ASSOCIATION OF BRITISH (ABTA) (1950), 55–57 Newman Street, London W1P 4AH. Tel: 071-637 2444. *President*, J. Dunscombe

TREE COUNCIL (1974), 35 Belgrave Square, London SW1X 8XN. Tel: 071-235 8854. *Director*, R. Osborne

TREE FOUNDATION, INTERNATIONAL (1922), Sandy Lane, Crawley Down, W. Sussex RH10 4HS. Tel: 0342-712536. *Secretary*, Mrs I. Driver

TROPICAL MEDICINE AND HYGIENE, ROYAL SOCIETY OF (1907), Manson House, 26 Portland Place, London W1N 4EY. Tel: 071-580 2127. *Hon. Secretaries*, Dr D. C. Barker; Dr S. G. Wright

TURNER SOCIETY (1975), BCM Box Turner, London WC1N 3XX. *Chairman*, E. Shanes

2CARE (formerly The SOS Society) (1929), 13 Harwood Road, London SW6 4QP. Tel: 071-371 0118. Residential homes for the elderly, and psychiatric rehabilitation centres. *Chief Executive*, Miss E. C. R. O'Sullivan

UFAW (Universities Federation for Animal Welfare) (1926), 8 Hamilton Close, South Mimms, Potters Bar, Herts. EN6 3QD. Tel: 0707 58202. *Secretary*, M. Lawson

UNITED NATIONS ASSOCIATION OF GREAT BRITAIN AND NORTHERN IRELAND (1945), 3 Whitehall Court, London SW1A 2EL. Tel: 071-930 2931. *Director*, M. C. Harper

UNITED REFORMED CHURCH HISTORY SOCIETY (1972), 86 Tavistock Place, London WC1H 9RT. Tel: 071-837 7661. *Hon. Secretary*, Revd Dr C. Orchard

UNITED SOCIETY FOR CHRISTIAN LITERATURE (1799), Robertson House, Leas Road, Guildford, Surrey GU14 4QW. Tel: 0483-577877. *General Secretary*, Revd A. Gilmore

UNITED SOCIETY FOR THE PROPAGATION OF THE GOSPEL (USPG) (1701), Partnership House, 157 Waterloo Road, London SE1 8XA. Tel: 071-928 8681. *Secretary*, Canon P. Price

UNIVERSITIES CENTRAL COUNCIL ON ADMISSIONS (1961), PO Box 28, Cheltenham, Glos. GL50 3SA. Tel: 0242-222444 *General Secretary*, P. A. Oakley, MBE

UNIVERSITIES OF THE UNITED KINGDOM, COMMITTEE OF VICE-CHANCELLORS AND PRINCIPALS OF THE (1918), 29 Tavistock Square, London WC1H 9EZ. Tel: 071-387 9231. *Secretary*, T. U. Burgner

UNIVERSITY AND COLLEGE LECTURERS, ASSOCIATION OF (1973), 104 Albert Road, Southsea, Hants. PO5 2SN. Tel: 0705-818625. *Chief Executive*, Ms C. Cheesman

UNIVERSITY WOMEN, BRITISH FEDERATION OF (1907) for all women graduates, Crosby Hall, Cheyne Walk, London SW3 5BA. Tel: 071-352 5354. *Vice-President*, Ms C. Moor

VALUERS AND AUCTIONEERS, INCORPORATED SOCIETY OF (1968), 3 Cadogan Gate, London SW1X 0AS. Tel: 071-235 2282. *Chief Executive*, H. Whitty

VEGAN SOCIETY, THE (1944), 7 Battle Road, St Leonards-on-Sea, E. Sussex TN37 7AA. Tel: 0424-427393. *General Secretary*, R. Farhall

VEGETARIAN SOCIETY OF THE UNITED KINGDOM LTD, Parkdale, Dunham Road, Altrincham, Cheshire WA14 4QG. Tel: 061-928 0793. *Director*, C. Cottom

VENEREAL DISEASES, MEDICAL SOCIETY FOR THE STUDY OF (1922). *Hon. Secretary*, Dr T. McManus, Department of GU Medicine, King's College Hospital, 15–22 Caldecot Road, London SE5 9RS. Tel: 071-326 3470

VERNACULAR ARCHITECTURE GROUP (1953). *Hon. Secretary*, R. Meeson, 16 Falna Crescent, Coton Green, Tamworth, Staffs. B79 8JS. Tel: 0827-69434

VETERINARY ASSOCIATION, BRITISH (1881), 7 Mansfield Street, London W1M 0AT. Tel: 071-636 6541. *Chief Executive*, J. H. Baird

VETERINARY SURGEONS, ROYAL COLLEGE OF, 32 Belgrave Square, London SW1X 8QP (1844). *Registrar*, A. R. W. Porter, CBE

VICTIM SUPPORT (1979), Cranmer House, 39 Brixton Road, London SW9 6DZ. Tel: 071-735 9166. *Director*, Ms H. Reeves, OBE

VICTORIA CROSS AND GEORGE CROSS ASSOCIATION, Room 04, Archway Block South, Old Admiralty Building, Whitehall, London SW1A 2BE. *Chairman*, Rear-Adm. B. C. G. Place, VC, CB, CVO, DSC

VICTORIA INSTITUTE, THE (Philosophical Society of Great Britain), Latchell Hall, Latchett Road, London E18 1DL. Tel: 081-505 5224. *Hon. Treasurer*, B. H. T. Weller

VICTORIAN SOCIETY (1958), 1 Priory Gardens, Bedford Park, London W4 1TT. Tel: 081-994 1019. *Secretary*, Mrs T. Sladen

VICTORY (SERVICES) ASSOCIATION LTD AND CLUB (1907), 63–79 Seymour Street, London W2 2HF. Tel: 071-723 4474. *General Manager*, G. F. Taylor

VIKING SOCIETY FOR NORTHERN RESEARCH (1892), Department of Scandinavian Studies, University College London, Gower Street, London WC1E 6BT. Tel: 071-387 7176. *Hon. Secretary*, Prof. M. P. Barnes

VITREOUS ENAMELLERS, INSTITUTE OF (1935), Ripley, Derby DE5 3EB. Tel: 0773-743136. *Secretary*, J. D. Gardom

VOLUNTARY AGENCIES, NATIONAL COUNCIL FOR (1919), Regent's Wharf, 8 All Saints Street, London N1 9RL. Tel: 071-713 6161. *General Secretary*, Ms J. Weleminsky

VSO (Voluntary Service Overseas) (1958), 317 Putney Bridge Road, London SW15 2PN. Tel: 081-780 2266. *Director*, D. Green

WAR ON WANT (1952), 37–39 Great Guildford Street, London SE1 0ES. Tel: 071-620 1111. *Director*, G. Alhadeff

WATER AND ENVIRONMENTAL MANAGEMENT, INSTITUTION OF (1987), 15 John Street, London WC1N 2EB. Tel: 071-831 3110. *Executive Director*, H. R. Evans

WATERCOLOUR SOCIETY, ROYAL (1804), Bankside Gallery, 48 Hopton Street, London SE1 9JH. Tel: 071-928 7521. *President*, L. Worth; *Secretary*, M. Spender

WELDING INSTITUTE, THE, Abington Hall, Cambridge CB1 6AL. Tel: 0223-891162. *Chief Executive*, A. B. M. Braithwaite

WELFARE OFFICERS, INSTITUTE OF (1945), 254 The Corn Exchange, Hanging Ditch, Manchester M4 3ES. *Secretary*, Mrs M. Maclean-Ives

WELLCOME TRUST (1936), 1 Park Square West, London NW1 4LJ. *Director*, Dr P. O. Williams

WELLS SOCIETY, H. G., (1961). *Hon. Secretary*, Dr S. Hardy, English Dept., Nene College, Moulton Park, Northampton NN2 7AL. Tel: 0604-735500, ext. 2133

WESLEY HISTORICAL SOCIETY (1893). *General Secretary*, Dr E. D. Graham, 34 Spiceland Road, Northfield, Birmingham B31 1NJ. Tel: 021-475 4914

WEST LONDON MISSION (1887), 19 Thayer Street, London W1M 5LJ. Tel: 071-935 6179. *Superintendent*, Revd D. S. Cruise

WILDFOWL AND WETLANDS TRUST (1946), The New Grounds, Slimbridge, Gloucester GL2 7BT. Tel: 0453-890333. *Director-General*, Dr M. Owen

WILLIAM MORRIS SOCIETY AND KELMSCOTT FELLOWSHIP (1918), Kelmscott House, 26 Upper Mall, London W6 9TA. Tel: 081-741 3735. *Hon. Secretary*, J. Purkis

WINE AND SPIRIT ASSOCIATION OF GREAT BRITAIN AND NORTHERN IRELAND (*c.* 1825), Five Kings House, 1 Queen Street Place, London EC4R 1XX. *Director*, P. Lewis

WOMEN, CAREERS FOR (1933), 2 Valentine Place, London SE1 8QH. Tel: 071-401 2280. *Director*, Miss K. M. Menon

WOMEN, SOCIETY FOR PROMOTING THE TRAINING OF (1859). *Secretary*, Revd B. Harris, The Rectory, Great Casterton, Stamford, Lincs. PE9 4AP. Tel: 0780-64036

WOMEN ARTISTS, SOCIETY OF (1855), Westminster Gallery, Westminster Central Hall, Storey's Gate, London SW1H 9NU. *President*, Ms B. Tate

WOMEN'S ENGINEERING SOCIETY (1920), Imperial College of Science and Technology, Department of Civil Engineering, Imperial College Road, London SW7 2BU. Tel: 071-589 5111 ext. 4731. *Secretary*, Ms G. Maxwell

WOMEN'S INSTITUTES, NATIONAL FEDERATION OF (1915), 104 New Kings Road, London SW6 4LY. Tel: 071-371 9300. *General Secretary*, Ms H. Mayall

WOMEN'S INSTITUTES OF NORTHERN IRELAND, FEDERATION OF (1932), 209–211 Upper Lisburn Road, Belfast BT10 0LL. Tel: 0232-301506. *General Secretary*, Mrs I. A. Sproule

WOMEN'S INTERNATIONAL LEAGUE FOR PEACE AND FREEDOM (British Section) (1915), 157 Lyndhurst Road, Worthing, W. Sussex BN11 2DG. Tel: 0903-205161

WOMEN'S NATIONWIDE CANCER CONTROL CAMPAIGN (1964), 128 Curtain Road, London EC2A 3AR. Tel: 071-729 4688. *Helpline*, 071-729 2229. *Administrator*, Ms J. Harding

WOMEN'S ROYAL NAVAL SERVICE BENEVOLENT TRUST (1942), 1A Chesham Street, London SW1X 8NL. Tel: 071-235 5846. *General Secretary*, Mrs J. Y. Ellis

WOMEN'S ROYAL VOLUNTARY SERVICE (WRVS), *see* Government Departments and Public Offices section

WOMEN'S RURAL INSTITUTES, SCOTTISH (1917), 42 Heriot Row, Edinburgh EH3 6ES. *General Secretary*, Mrs E. Nicol

WOMEN'S TRANSPORT SERVICE (1907), FANY HQ, Duke of York's HQ, London SW3 4RX. Tel: 071-730 2058. *Corps Commander*, Mrs A. Whitehead

WOODLAND TRUST, THE (1972), Autumn Park, Dysart Road, Grantham, Lincs. NG31 6LL. Tel: 0476-74297. *Executive Director*, J. D. James

WOOD PRESERVING ASSOCIATION, BRITISH (1930), 6 The Office Village, 4 Romford Road, London E15 4EA. Tel: 081-519 2588. *Director of Administration*, M. J. Tuck

WORKERS' EDUCATIONAL ASSOCIATION, Temple House, 9 Upper Berkeley Street, London W1H 8BY. Tel: 071-402 5608. *General Secretary*, R. Lochrie

WORKING MOTHERS ASSOCIATION, THE (1985), 77 Holloway Road, London N7 8JZ. Tel: 071-700 5771. *Director*, Mrs L. Daniels

WORLD EDUCATION FELLOWSHIP (1921), 33 Kinnaird Avenue, London W4 3SH. Tel: 081-994 7258. *General Secretary*, Mrs R. Crommelin

WORLD ENERGY COUNCIL (1924), 34 St James's Street, London SW1A 1HD. Tel: 071-930 3966. *Secretary-General*, I. D. Lindsay

WORLD MISSION, COUNCIL FOR (1977), Livingstone House, 11 Carteret Street, London SW1H 9DL. Tel: 071-222 4214. *General Secretary*, Dr D. P. Niles

WORLD SHIP SOCIETY (1946). *Secretary*, S. J. F. Miller, 35 Wickham Way, Haywards Heath, W. Sussex RH16 1UJ. Tel: 0444-413066

WORLD SOCIETY FOR THE PROTECTION OF ANIMALS (1981), Park Place, 10 Lawn Lane, London SW8 1UD. Tel: 071-793 0540. *Director-General*, A. Dickson

WORLD-WIDE EDUCATION SERVICE (1888), Canada House Business Centre, 272 Field End Road, Ruislip, Middx. HA4 9NA. Tel: 081-866 4400. *Head of Consultancy*, Mrs T. Mulder-Reynolds

WRITERS TO HM SIGNET, SOCIETY OF (1532), 16 Hill Street, Edinburgh EH2 3LD. Tel: 031-226 6703. *Clerk*, A. M. Kerr

WWF UK (World Wide Fund for Nature) (1961), Panda House, Weyside Park, Godalming, Surrey GU7 1XR. Tel: 0483-426444. *Director*, G. J. Medley, OBE

YEOMANRY BENEVOLENT FUND (1902), 10 Stone Buildings, Lincoln's Inn, London WC2A 3TG. Tel: 071-831 6727. *Secretary*, Mrs C. W. Chrystie

YORKSHIRE AGRICULTURAL SOCIETY (1837), Great Yorkshire Showground, Hookstone Oval, Harrogate HG2 8PW. Tel: 0423-561536. *Chief Executive*, R. Keigwin

YORKSHIRE SOCIETY, THE (1812), 27 Kensington Park, Milford-on-Sea, Hants. SO41 0WD. Tel: 0590-644725. Educational trust making grants to students of all ages. *Secretary*, G. G. Prince, TD.

YOUNG FARMERS' CLUBS, NATIONAL FEDERATION OF, The YFC Centre, National Agricultural Centre, Kenilworth, Warks. CV8 2LG. Tel: 0203-696544. *Secretary*, T. Shields

YOUNG MEN'S CHRISTIAN ASSOCIATION (YMCA) (1844), National Council of YMCAs, 640 Forest Road, London E17 3DZ. Tel: 081-520 5599. *National Secretary*, C. J. Naylor

YOUNG WOMEN'S CHRISTIAN ASSOCIATION OF GREAT BRITAIN (YWCA) (1855), 52 Cornmarket Street, Oxford OX1 3EJ. Tel: 0865-726110. *Executive Director*, Miss F. E. Sharples

YOUTH ACTION (1944), Hampton, Glenmachan Park, Belfast BT4 2PJ. Tel: 0232-760067. *Director*, P. Graham

YOUTH CLUBS UK (1911), 11 Bride Street, London EC4A 4AS. Tel: 071-353 2366. *Chief Executive*, D. Stickels

YOUTH HOSTELS ASSOCIATION (ENGLAND AND WALES) (1930), Trevelyan House, 8 St Stephens Hill, St Albans, Herts. AL1 2DY. Tel: 0727-55215. *Chief Executive*, C. Logan

YOUTH HOSTELS ASSOCIATION OF NORTHERN IRELAND (1931), Bradbury Buildings, 56 Bradbury Place, Belfast BT7 1RU. Tel: 0232-324733. *Hon. Secretary*, N. O'Reilly

YOUTH HOSTELS ASSOCIATION, SCOTTISH (1931), 7 Glebe Crescent, Stirling FK8 2JA. Tel: 0786-51181. *General Secretary*, J. Martin

ZOO CHECK (1984), Cherry Tree Cottage, Coldharbour, Dorking, Surrey RH5 6HA. Tel: 0306-712091. *Director*, W. Travers

ZOOLOGICAL SOCIETY, NORTH OF ENGLAND (Chester Zoo) (1934), Upton by Chester CH2 1LH. Tel: 0244-380280. *Director*, Dr M. Brambell

ZOOLOGICAL SOCIETY OF LONDON (1826), Regent's Park, London NW1 4RY. Tel: 071-722 3333. *President*, Field Marshal Sir John Chapple, GCB, CBE

ZOOLOGICAL SOCIETY OF SCOTLAND, ROYAL (1913), Scottish National Zoological Park, Murrayfield, Edinburgh EH12 6TS. Tel: 031-334 9171. *Director*, R. J. Wheater, OBE, FRSE.

Sports Bodies

SPORTS COUNCILS

THE SPORTS COUNCIL, 16 Upper Woburn Place, London WC1H 0QP. Tel: 071-388 1277. *Director-General*, D. Pickup.

THE SCOTTISH SPORTS COUNCIL, Caledonia House, South Gyle, Edinburgh EH12 9DQ. Tel: 031-317 7200. *Chief Executive*, F. A. L. Alstead, CBE.

THE SPORTS COUNCIL FOR WALES, Sophia Gardens, Cardiff CF1 9SW. Tel: 0222-397571. *Chief Executive*, L. Tatham.

THE SPORTS COUNCIL FOR NORTHERN IRELAND, House of Sport, Upper Malone Road, Belfast BT9 5LA. Tel: 0232-381222. *Director*, J. E. Miller.

CENTRAL COUNCIL OF PHYSICAL RECREATION, Francis House, Francis Street, London SW1P 1DE. Tel: 071-828 3163. *General Secretary*, P. Lawson.

ANGLING

NATIONAL FEDERATION OF ANGLERS, Halliday House, 2 Wilson Street, Derby DE1 1PG. Tel: 0332-362000. *Chief Administration Officer*, K. E. Watkins.

ARCHERY

GRAND NATIONAL ARCHERY SOCIETY, 7th Street, National Agricultural Centre, Stoneleigh, Kenilworth, Coventry CV8 2LG. Tel: 0203-696631. *Chief Executive*, J. S. Middleton.

ASSOCIATION FOOTBALL

THE FOOTBALL ASSOCIATION, 16 Lancaster Gate, London W2 3LW. Tel: 071-262 4542. *Chief Executive*, R. H. G. Kelly.

FOOTBALL LEAGUE LTD, 319 Clifton Drive South, Lytham St Annes, Lancs. FY8 1JG. Tel: 0253-729421. *Secretary*, D. Dent.

SCOTTISH FOOTBALL ASSOCIATION, 6 Park Gardens, Glasgow G3 7YF. Tel: 041-332 6372. *Chief Executive*, J. Farry.

SCOTTISH FOOTBALL LEAGUE, 188 West Regent Street, Glasgow G2 4RY. Tel: 041-248 3844. *Secretary*, P. Donald.

FOOTBALL ASSOCIATION OF WALES, Plymouth Chambers, 3 Westgate Street, Cardiff CF1 1DD. Tel: 0222-372325. *Secretary*, A. E. Evans.

IRISH FOOTBALL ASSOCIATION, 20 Windsor Avenue, Belfast BT9 6EG. Tel: 0232-669458. *General Secretary*, D. I. Bowen.

IRISH FOOTBALL LEAGUE, 96 University Street, Belfast BT7 1HE. Tel: 0232-242888. *Chief Executive*, M. D. G. Brown.

WOMEN'S FOOTBALL ASSOCIATION, 448–450 Hanging Ditch, The Corn Exchange, Manchester M4 3ES. Tel: 061-832 5911. *Chief Executive*, Ms L. Whitehead.

ATHLETICS

BRITISH ATHLETICS FEDERATION, Edgbaston House, 3 Duchess Place, Hagley Road, Birmingham B16 8NM. Tel: 021-456 4050. *Chief Executive*, M. Jones.

AMATEUR ATHLETIC ASSOCIATION OF ENGLAND, Edgbaston House, 3 Duchess Place, Hagley Road, Birmingham B16 8NM. Tel: 021-456 4050. *Chief Executive*, M. Jones.

BADMINTON

BADMINTON ASSOCIATION OF ENGLAND LTD, National Badminton Centre, Loughton Lodge, Bradwell Road, Milton Keynes MK8 9LA. Tel: 0908-568822. *Chief Executive*, G. Snowdon.

SCOTTISH BADMINTON UNION, Cockburn Centre, 40 Bogmoor Place, Glasgow G51 4TQ. Tel: 041-445 1218. *Chief Executive*, Miss A. Smillie.

WELSH BADMINTON UNION, Fourth Floor, 3 Westgate Street, Cardiff CF1 1DD. Tel: 0222-222082. *Chief Executive*, L. Williams.

BASEBALL

BRITISH BASEBALL FEDERATION, 19 Troutdale Grove, Southcoates Lane, Hull HU9 3SD. Tel: 0482-792337. *Secretary*, Mrs R. Collinson.

BASKETBALL

ENGLISH BASKETBALL ASSOCIATION, 48 Bradford Road, Leeds LS28 6DF. Tel: 0532-361166. *Chief Executive*, D. Ransom.

SCOTTISH BASKETBALL ASSOCIATION, Caledonia House, South Gyle, Edinburgh EH12 9DQ. Tel: 031-317 7260. *Technical Director*, K. Johnston.

BASKETBALL ASSOCIATION OF WALES, 327 Cowbridge Road East, Canton, Cardiff CF5 1JD. Tel: 0222-238180. *Administrator*, L. Beck.

BILLIARDS

WORLD PROFESSIONAL BILLIARDS AND SNOOKER ASSOCIATION, 27 Oakfield Road, Clifton, Bristol BS8 2AT. Tel: 0272-744491. *Chief Executive*, D. Harrison.

WORLD LADIES BILLIARDS AND SNOOKER ASSOCIATION, 3 Sywell Grove, Elm, Wisbech, Cambs. PE14 0BN. Tel: 0945-860545. *Secretary*, Ms M. Fisher.

BOBSLEIGH

BRITISH BOBSLEIGH ASSOCIATION, Springfield House, 7 Woodstock Road, Coulsdon, Surrey CR5 3HS. Tel: 0737-555152. *Secretary*, P. Pruszynski.

BOWLS

BRITISH ISLES BOWLING COUNCIL, *Hon. Secretary*, A. R. McKay, 43 Belfast Road, Ballynure, Ballyclare, Co. Antrim BT39 9TZ. Tel: 0960-352334.

BRITISH ISLES INDOOR BOWLING COUNCIL, 8/2 Back Dean, Ravelston Terrace, Edinburgh EH4 3UA. Tel: 031-343 3632. *Secretary*, M. Conlin.

BRITISH ISLES WOMEN'S BOWLING COUNCIL, *Hon. Secretary*, Ms N. Colling, Darracombe, The Clays, Market Lavington, Devizes, Wilts SN10 4AY. Tel: 0380-813774.

BRITISH ISLES WOMEN'S INDOOR BOWLS COUNCIL, *Hon. Secretary*, Ms J. Johns, 16 Windsor Crescent, Radyr, Cardiff CF4 8AE. Tel: 0222-842391.

ENGLISH BOWLING ASSOCIATION, Lyndhurst Road, Worthing, W. Sussex BN11 2AZ. Tel: 0903-820222. *Secretary*, D. Johnson.

ENGLISH WOMENS BOWLING ASSOCIATION, *Hon. Secretary*, Ms N. Colling, Darracombe, The Clays, Market Lavington, Devizes, Wilts. SN10 4AY. Tel: 0380-813774.

Boxing

Amateur Boxing Association of England, Francis House, Francis Street, London SW1P 1DE. Tel: 071-976 5361. *Hon. Secretary*, J. H. Lewis.

British Boxing Board of Control, Jack Petersen House, 52A Borough High Street, London SE1 1XW. Tel: 071-403 5879. *General Secretary*, J. Morris.

British Amateur Boxing Association, 96 High Street, Lochee, Dundee DD2 3AY. Tel: 0382-611412. *Chief Executive*, F. Hendry.

Canoeing

British Canoe Union, Adbolton Lane, West Bridgford, Nottingham NG2 5AS. Tel: 0602-821100. *Director*, P. Owen.

Clay Pigeon Shooting

Clay Pigeon Shooting Association, 107 Epping New Road, Buckhurst Hill, Essex IG9 5TQ. Tel: 081-505 6221. *Director*, B. G. Carter.

Cricket

MCC, Lords, London NW8 8QN. Tel: 071-289 1611. *President* D. R. W. Silk; *Secretary*, Lt.-Col. J. R. Stephenson, OBE.

Test and County Cricket Board, Lord's, London NW8 8QZ. Tel: 071-286 4405. *Chairman* (1992–3), W. R. F. Chamberlain; *Chief Executive*, A. C. Smith.

Cricket Council, Lord's, London NW8 8QZ. Tel: 071-286 4405. *Chairman*, W. R. F. Chamberlain; *Secretary*, A. C. Smith.

Croquet

Croquet Association, c/o The Hurlingham Club, Ranelagh Gardens, London SW6 3PR. Tel: 071-736 3148 *Secretary*, L. W. D. Antenen.

Cycling

British Cycling Federation, 36 Rockingham Road, Kettering, Northants. NN16 8HG. Tel: 0536-412211. *Chief Executive*, J. Hendry.

Road Time Trials Council, Dallacre, Mill Road, Yarwell, Peterborough PE8 6PS. Tel: 0780-782464. *Secretary*, D. E. Roberts.

Equestrianism

British Equestrian Federation, British Equestrian Centre, Kenilworth, Warks. CV8 2LR. Tel: 0203-696697. *Director-General*, Maj. M. Wallace.

Eton Fives

Eton Fives Association. *Hon. Secretary*, M. P. Powell, Welches, Bentley, Farnham, Surrey. Tel: 0420-22107

Fencing

Amateur Fencing Association, 1 Barons Gate, 33–35 Rothschild Road, London W4 5HT. Tel: 081-742 3032. *Secretary*, Miss G. Kenneally.

Gliding

British Gliding Association, Kimberley House, Vaughan Way, Leicester LE1 4SE. Tel: 0533-531051. *Secretary*, B. Rolfe.

Golf

Royal and Ancient Golf Club, St Andrews, Fife KY16 9JD. Tel: 0334-72112. *Secretary*, M. F. Bonallack, OBE.

Ladies' Golf Union, The Scores, St Andrews, Fife KY16 9AT. Tel: 0334-75811. *Administrator*, Mrs A. Robertson.

Greyhound Racing

The National Greyhound Racing Club Ltd, 24–28 Oval Road, London NW1 7DA. Tel: 071-267 9256. *Senior Stipendiary Steward*, F. Melville.

Gymnastics

British Amateur Gymnastics Association, Ford Hall, Lilleshall National Sports Centre, nr. Newport, Shropshire TF10 9NB. Tel: 0952-820330. *Marketing Director*, D. Minnery.

Hockey

Hockey Association, 16 Northdown Street, London N1 9BG. Tel: 071-837 8878. *Chief Executive*, S. P. Baines.

All England Women's Hockey Association, 51 High Street, Shrewsbury SY1 1ST. Tel: 0743-233572. *Executive Director*, Miss T. Morris.

Scottish Hockey Union, Caledonia House, South Gyle, Edinburgh EH12 9DQ. Tel: 031-317 7254. *Chairman*, E. Raistrick.

Welsh Hockey Association, 1 White Hart Lane, Caerleon, Gwent NP6 1AB. Tel: 0633-420326. *Secretary*, J. G. Williams.

Welsh Women's Hockey Association, Welsh Hockey Office, Deeside Leisure Centre, Chester Road West, Deeside, Clwyd CH5 1SA. Tel: 0244-812311. *President*, Miss A. Ells, MBE.

Horse-racing

The Jockey Club (incorporating National Hunt Committee), 42 Portman Square, London W1H 0EN. Tel: 071-486 4921. *Stewards*, Marquess of Hartington (*Senior Steward*); A. J. Struthers (*Deputy Senior Steward*); Brig. A. H. Parker Bowles; Maj. M. C. Wyatt; Col. Sir Piers Bengough; Capt. W. H. Bulwer-Long; C. J. Spence. *Chief Executive*, C. J. M. Haines.

Ice Hockey

British Ice Hockey Association, Second Floor Offices, 517 Christchurch Road, Boscombe, Bournemouth BH1 4AG. Tel: 0202-303946. *General Secretary*, D. Pickles.

Ice Skating

National Skating Association of Great Britain, 15–27 Gee Street, London EC1V 3RE. Tel: 071-253 3824. *President*, C. J. L. Jones, OBE.

Judo

British Judo Association, 7A Rutland Street, Leicester LE1 1RB. Tel: 0533-559669. *Office Manager*, Ms S. Startin.

Lacrosse

English Lacrosse Union, *Hon. Secretary*, R. Balls, 70 High Road, Rayleigh, Essex SS6 7AD. Tel: 0268-770758

All England Women's Lacrosse Association, 4 Western Court, Bromley Street, Digbeth, Birmingham B9 4AN. Tel: 021-773 4422. *Administrator*, Miss A. Mason.

Lawn Tennis

Lawn Tennis Association, The Queen's Club, London W14 9EG. Tel: 071-385 2366. *Secretary*, J. C. U. James.

LUGEING

THE GREAT BRITAIN LUGE ASSOCIATION, 89 Tenison Road, Cambridge CBI 2DG. Tel: 0223-358438. *Secretary*, C. Dyason.

MARTIAL ARTS

MARTIAL ARTS COMMISSION, Broadway House, 15–16 Deptford Broadway, London SE8 4PE. Tel: 081-691 8711. *Chairman*, D. Passmore.

MOTOR SPORTS

AUTO-CYCLE UNION, ACU House, Wood Street, Rugby, Warks. CV21 2YX. Tel: 0788-540519. *Chief Executive*, D. R. Barnfield.

RAC MOTOR SPORTS ASSOCIATION LTD, Motor Sports House, Riverside Park, Colnbrook, Slough SL3 OHG. Tel: 0753-681736. *Chief Executive*, J. R. Quenby.

SCOTTISH AUTO CYCLE UNION LTD, Block 2, Unit 6, Whiteside Industrial Estate, Bathgate, West Lothian EH48 2RX. Tel: 0506-630262. *Secretary*, A. M. Brownlie.

MOUNTAINEERING

BRITISH MOUNTAINEERING COUNCIL, Crawford House, Precinct Centre, Booth Street East, Manchester M13 9RZ. Tel: 061-273 5835. *General Secretary*, D. Walker.

MULTI-SPORT BODIES

BRITISH OLYMPIC ASSOCIATION, I Wandsworth Plain, London SW18 IEH. Tel: 081-871 2677. *General Secretary*, R. Palmer, OBE.

COMMONWEALTH GAMES FEDERATION, Walkden House, 3–10 Melton Street, London NWI 2EB. Tel: 071-383 5596. *Hon. Secretary*, A. de O. Sales, CBE.

BRITISH COLLEGES SPORTS ASSOCIATION, 11 Allcock Street, Birmingham B9 4DY. Tel: 021-766 8855. *Hon. Administrative Secretary*, P. Rhodes.

BRITISH POLYTECHNIC SPORTS ASSOCIATION, 11 Allcock Street, Birmingham B9 4DY. Tel: 021-766 8855. *Administrator*, S. Fairhall.

BRITISH UNIVERSITIES SPORTS FEDERATION, 11 Allcock Street, Birmingham B9 4DY. Tel: 021-766 8855. *General Secretary*, P. Rhodes.

NETBALL

ALL ENGLAND NETBALL ASSOCIATION, Netball House, 9 Paynes Park, Hitchin, Herts. SG5 IEH. Tel: 0462-442344. *Chief Executive*, Mrs E. M. Nicholl.

SCOTTISH NETBALL ASSOCIATION, Kelvin Hall Sports Complex, Argyle Street, Glasgow G3 8AW. Tel: 041-334 3650. *Administrator*, Ms A. Murray.

WELSH NETBALL ASSOCIATION, 82 Cathedral Road, Cardiff CFI 9LN. Tel: 0222-237048. *Chairman*, Mrs T. J. Lane.

ORIENTEERING

BRITISH ORIENTEERING FEDERATION, Riversdale, Dale Road North, Darley Dale, Matlock, Derbyshire DE4 2HX. Tel: 0629-734042. *Manager*, Mrs. H. Gregson.

POLO

THE HURLINGHAM POLO ASSOCIATION, Winterlake, Kirtlington, Oxford OX5 3HG. Tel: 0869-50044. *Secretary*, J. W. M. Crisp.

RACKETS AND REAL TENNIS

TENNIS AND RACKETS ASSOCIATION, c/o The Queen's Club, Palliser Road, London W14 9EQ. Tel: 071-381 4746. *Chief Executive*, Brig. A. D. Myrtle, CB, CBE.

RIFLE SHOOTING

NATIONAL RIFLE ASSOCIATION, Bisley Camp, Brookwood, Woking GU24 OPB. Tel: 0483-797777. *Chief Executive*, C. A. Ewing, OBE.

NATIONAL SMALL-BORE RIFLE ASSOCIATION, Lord Roberts House, Bisley Camp, Brookwood, Woking GU24 ONP. Tel: 0483-76969. *Secretary*, Gp Capt D. King, MBE.

ROWING

AMATEUR ROWING ASSOCIATION LTD, The Priory, 6 Lower Mall, London W6 9DJ. Tel: 081-748 3632. *Senior Administrative Officer*, Mrs R. E. Webb.

HENLEY ROYAL REGATTA, Regatta Headquarters, Henley-on-Thames, Oxon. RG9 2LY. Tel: 0491-572153. *Secretary*, R. S. Goddard.

SCOTTISH AMATEUR ROWING ASSOCIATION, 11 Spottiswode Street, Edinburgh EH9 IEP. Tel: 031-229 2366. *Secretary*, N. MacFarlane.

WELSH AMATEUR ROWING ASSOCIATION, *Hon. Secretary*, Dr G. R. H. Greaves, 30 Lady Mary Road, Cardiff CF2 5NT. Tel: 0222-754259.

RUGBY FIVES

RUGBY FIVES ASSOCIATION, 10 Lovelace Road, London SE21 8JX. Tel: 081-670 3298. *Secretary*, Mrs J. Fuller.

RUGBY LEAGUE

THE RUGBY FOOTBALL LEAGUE, 180 Chapeltown Road, Leeds LS7 4HT. Tel: 0532-624637. *Chief Executive*, D. S. Oxley, OBE.

BRITISH AMATEUR RUGBY LEAGUE ASSOCIATION, West Yorkshire House, 4 New North Parade, Huddersfield HDI 5JP. Tel: 0484-544131. *Chief Executive*, M. F. Oldroyd.

RUGBY UNION

RUGBY FOOTBALL UNION, Twickenham TWI IDZ. Tel: 081-892 8161. *Secretary*, D. E. Wood.

SCOTTISH RUGBY UNION, Murrayfield, Edinburgh EH12 5PJ. Tel: 031-337 2346. *Secretary*, I. A. L. Hogg.

WELSH RUGBY UNION, Cardiff Arms Park, PO Box 22, Cardiff CFI IJL. Tel: 0222-390111. *Secretary*, D. P. Evans.

IRISH RUGBY FOOTBALL UNION, 62 Lansdowne Road, Dublin 4, Republic of Ireland. Tel: 0001-684601. *Secretary*, P. J. O'Donoghue.

WOMEN'S RUGBY FOOTBALL UNION, Meadow House, Springfield Farm, Shipston-on-Stour, Warks. CV36 4HQ. Tel: 0608-663336. *Secretary*, Ms R. Golby.

SKIING

BRITISH SKI FEDERATION, 258 Main Street, East Calder, Livingston, West Lothian EH53 OEE. Tel: 0506-884343. *Chairman*, J. Blyth.

SNOOKER

WORLD PROFESSIONAL BILLIARDS AND SNOOKER ASSOCIATION, 27 Oakfield Road, Clifton, Bristol BS8 2AT. Tel: 0272-744491. *Chief Executive*, D. Harrison.

WORLD LADIES BILLIARDS AND SNOOKER ASSOCIATION, 3 Sywell Grove, Elm, Wisbech, Cambs. PE14 OBN. Tel: 0945-860545. *Secretary*, Ms M. Fisher.

SPEEDWAY

THE SPEEDWAY CONTROL BOARD, 57 Villa Crescent, Bulkington, Nuneaton CV12 9NF. Tel: 0203-643336. *Manager*, J. Eglese.

SQUASH RACKETS

SQUASH RACKETS ASSOCIATION, Westpoint, 33–34 Warple Way, London W3 0RQ. Tel: 081-746 1616. *Chief Executive*, C. J. Gotla.

SCOTTISH SQUASH, Caledonia House, South Gyle, Edinburgh EH12 9DQ. Tel: 031-317 7343. *Secretary*, N. Brydon.

WELSH SQUASH RACKETS FEDERATION, 7 Kymin Terrace, Penarth, South Glamorgan CF6 1AP. Tel: 0222-704096. *Chairman*, A. Price.

SWIMMING

AMATEUR SWIMMING ASSOCIATION, Harold Fern House, Derby Square, Loughborough, Leics. LE11 0AL. Tel: 0509-230431. *Secretary*, D. A. Reeves.

SCOTTISH AMATEUR SWIMMING ASSOCIATION, Holmhills Farm, Greenlees Road, Cambuslang, Glasgow G72 8DT. Tel: 041-641 8818. *General Secretary*, W. Black.

WELSH AMATEUR SWIMMING ASSOCIATION, Empire Pool, Wood Street, Cardiff CF1 1PP. Tel: 0222-342201. *Hon. General Secretary*, G. Robins.

BRITISH SUB-AQUA CLUB, Telfords Quay, Ellesmere Port, South Wirral, Cheshire L65 4FY. Tel: 051-357 1951. *Chairman*, D. Ellerby.

TABLE TENNIS

ENGLISH TABLE TENNIS ASSOCIATION, Queensbury House, Havelock Road, Hastings TN34 1HF. Tel: 0424-722525. *Chief Executive*, Miss E. Shaw.

VOLLEYBALL

ENGLISH VOLLEYBALL ASSOCIATION, 27 South Road, West Bridgford, Nottingham NG2 7AG. Tel: 0602-816324. *National Director*, G. Bulman.

SCOTTISH VOLLEYBALL ASSOCIATION, 48 The Pleasance, Edinburgh EH8 9TJ. Tel: 031-556 4633. *Director*, N. Moody.

WELSH VOLLEYBALL ASSOCIATION, 6 Redwood Close, St Mellons, Cardiff CF3 9BX. Tel: 0222-798110. *Chairperson*, Ms J. Cleeves.

WALKING

RACE WALKING ASSOCIATION. *Hon. Secretary*, P. J. Cassidy, Hufflers, Heard's Lane, Shenfield, Brentwood, Essex CM15 0SF. Tel: 0277-220687.

WATER SKIING

BRITISH WATER SKI FEDERATION, 390 City Road, London EC1V 2QA. Tel: 071-833 2855. *Secretary*, Ms G. Hill.

WEIGHTLIFTING

BRITISH AMATEUR WEIGHTLIFTERS ASSOCIATION. *Hon. Secretary*, W. Holland, OBE, 3 Iffley Turn, Oxford OX4 4DU. Tel: 0865-778319.

WRESTLING

BRITISH AMATEUR WRESTLING ASSOCIATION, 41 Great Clowes Street, Salford, Manchester M7 9RQ. Tel: 061-832 9209. *Secretary*, Mrs C. Barfoot.

YACHTING

ROYAL YACHTING ASSOCIATION, RYA House, Romsey Road, Eastleigh, Hants. SO5 4YA. Tel: 0703-629962. *Secretary-General*, R. Duchesne, OBE.

Clubs

LONDON CLUBS

ALPINE CLUB (1857), 55 Charlotte Road, London EC2A 3QT. Tel: 071-613 0755. *Hon. Secretary*, Dr M. J. Esten.

AMERICAN WOMEN'S CLUB (1899), Connaught Rooms, Great Queen Street, London WC2B 5DA. Tel: 071-831 6660. *Secretary*, Ms K. Fales.

ANGLO-BELGIAN CLUB (1955), 60 Knightsbridge, London SW1X 7LF. Tel: 071-235 2121. *Secretary*, Baronne van Havre.

ARMY AND NAVY CLUB (1837), 36–39 Pall Mall, London SW1Y 5JN. Tel: 071-930 9721. *Secretary*, vacant.

ARTS CLUB (1863), 40 Dover Street, London W1X 3RB. Tel: 071-499 8581. *Secretary*, Mrs J. Downing.

ARTS THEATRE CLUB (1927), 50 Frith Street, London W1V 5TE. Tel: 071-287 9236. *Secretary*, R. Thornton.

THE ATHENAEUM (1824), 107 Pall Mall, London SW1Y 5ER. Tel: 071-930 4843. *Secretary*, R. R. T. Smith.

AUTHORS' CLUB (1892), 40 Dover Street, London W1X 3RB. Tel: 071-499 8581. *Secretary*, Mrs H. Ridgway.

BEEFSTEAK CLUB (1876), 9 Irving Street, London WC2H 7AT. Tel: 071-930 5722. *Secretary*, E. Pool, MC.

BOODLE'S (1762), 28 St James's Street, London SW1A 1HJ. Tel: 071-930 7166. *Secretary*, R. J. Edmonds.

BROOKS'S (1764), St James's Street, London SW1A 1LN. Tel: 071-493 4411. *Secretary*, vacant.

BUCK'S CLUB (1919), 18 Clifford Street, London W1X 1RG. Tel: 071-734 6896. *Secretary*, Capt. P. Murison, RN.

CALEDONIAN CLUB (1891), 9 Halkin Street, London SW1X 7DR. Tel: 071-235 5162. *Secretary*, P. J. Varney.

CANNING CLUB (1910), 42 Half Moon Street, London W1Y 8DS. Tel: 071-499 5163. *Secretary*, T. M. Harrington.

CARLTON CLUB (1832), 69 St James's Street, London SW1A 1PJ. Tel: 071-493 1164. *Secretary*, R. N. Linsley.

CAVALRY AND GUARDS CLUB (1893), 127 Piccadilly, London W1V 0PX. Tel: 071-499 1261. *Secretary*, N. J. Walford.

CHELSEA ARTS CLUB (1891), 143 Old Church Street, London SW3 6EB. Tel: 071-376 3311. *Secretary*, Mrs K. Paltenghi.

CITY LIVERY CLUB (1914), Sion College, Victoria Embankment, London EC4Y 0DN. Tel: 071-353 2431. *Hon. Secretary*, B. L. Morgan, CBE.

CITY OF LONDON CLUB (1832), 19 Old Broad Street, London EC2N 1DS. Tel: 071-588 7991. *Secretary*, G. S. Chisholm.

CITY UNIVERSITY CLUB (1895), 50 Cornhill, London EC3V 3PD. Tel: 071-626 8571. *Secretary*, Miss R. C. Graham.

EAST INDIA CLUB (1849), 16 St James's Square, London SW1Y 4LH. Tel: 071-930 1000. *Secretary*, J. G. F. Stoy.

FARMERS CLUB (1842), 3 Whitehall Court, London SW1A 2EL. Tel: 071-930 3751. *Secretary*, Lt.-Col. G. B. Murray.

FLYFISHERS' CLUB (1884), 24A Old Burlington Street, London W1X 1RG. Tel: 071-734 9229. *Secretary*, Cdr. N. T. Fuller retd.

GARRICK CLUB (1831), 15 Garrick Street, London WC2E 9AY. Tel: 071-379 6478. *Secretary*, M. J. Harvey.

GREEN ROOM CLUB (1877), 9 Adam Street, London WC2N 6AA. Tel: 071–836 7453. *Secretary*, J. Booth.

GROUCHO CLUB (1985), 45 Dean Street, London W1V 5AP. Tel: 071-439 4685. *Company Secretary*, Ms Z. Brand.

HUNTERS CLUB (1981), 3 London Wall Buildings, London EC2M 5PD. Tel: 071-638 0363. *Secretary*, R. A. Sanders.

HURLINGHAM CLUB (1869), Ranelagh Gardens, London SW6 3PR. Tel: 071-736 8411. *Secretary*, P. H. Covell.

KEMPTON PARK CLUB (1878), Kempton Park Racecourse, Sunbury-on-Thames, Middx., TW16 5AQ. Tel: 0932-782292. *Secretary*, Mrs C. Milburn-Lee.

KENNEL CLUB (1873), 1–5 Clarges Street, London W1Y 8AB. Tel: 071-493 6651. *Secretary*, Maj.-Gen. M. H. Sinnatt, CB.

LANSDOWNE CLUB (1934), 9 Fitzmaurice Place, London W1X 6JD. Tel: 071-629 7200. *Secretary*, Lt.-Cdr. T. P. Havers retd.

LONDON ROWING CLUB (1856), Embankment, Putney, London SW15 1LB. Tel: 081-788 1400. *Hon. Secretary*, N. A. Smith.

MCC (MARYLEBONE CRICKET CLUB) (1787), Lord's Cricket Ground, London NW8 8QN. Tel: 071-289 1611. *Secretary*, Lt.-Col. J. R. Stephenson, OBE.

NATIONAL CLUB (1845), 234 Kilburn High Road, London NW6 4JR. Tel: 071-328 3141. *Secretary*, I. E. Nash.

NATIONAL LIBERAL CLUB (1882), Whitehall Place, London SW1A 2HE. Tel: 071-930 9871. *Secretary*, G. Snell.

NAVAL AND MILITARY CLUB (1862), 94 Piccadilly, London W1V 0BP. Tel: 071-499 5163. *Secretary*, Cdr. J. A. Holt, MBE.

NAVAL CLUB (1946), 38 Hill Street, London W1X 8DP. Tel: 071-493 7672. *Chief Executive*, Capt R. J. Husk, CBE, RN retd.

NEW CAVENDISH CLUB (1984), (formerly VAD), 44 Great Cumberland Place, London W1H 8BS. Tel: 071-723 0391. *Secretary*, J. Malone-Lee.

DEN NORSKE KLUB (1924), Norway House, 21–24 Cockspur Street, London SW1Y 5DA. Tel: 071-930 4084. *Secretary*, Mrs V. J. Southwood.

ORIENTAL CLUB (1824), Stratford House, Stratford Place, London W1N 0ES. Tel: 071-629 5126. *Secretary*, S. C. Doble.

PORTLAND CLUB (1816), 42 Half Moon Street, London W1Y 7RD. Tel: 071-499 1523. *Secretary*, R. B. Little.

PRATT'S CLUB (1841), 14 Park Place, London SW1A 1LP. Tel: 071-493 0397. *Secretary*, Capt. P. W. E. Parry, MBE.

QUEEN'S CLUB, THE (1886), Palliser Road, London W14 9EQ. Tel: 071-385 3421. *Secretary*, J. A. S. Edwardes.

RAILWAY CLUB (1899), Room 208, 25 Marylebone Road, London NW1 5JS. *Hon. Secretary*, A. G. Wells.

REFORM CLUB (1836), 104–105 Pall Mall, London SW1Y 5EW. Tel: 071-930 9374. *Secretary*, R. A. M. Forrest.

ROEHAMPTON CLUB (1901), Roehampton Lane, London SW15 5LR. Tel: 081-876 5505. *Chief Executive.*, M. Yates.

ROYAL AIR FORCE CLUB (1918), 128 Piccadilly, London W1V 0PY. Tel: 071-499 3456. *Secretary*, P. N. Owen.

ROYAL AUTOMOBILE CLUB (1897), 89–91 Pall Mall, London SW1Y 5HS. Tel: 071-930 2345. *General Secretary*, M. J. Limb.

ROYAL OCEAN RACING CLUB (1925), 20 St James's Place, London SW1A 1NN. Tel: 071-493 2248. *General Manager*, D. J. Minords, OBE.

ROYAL OVER-SEAS LEAGUE (1910), Over-Seas House, Park Place, St James's Street, London SW1A 1LR. Tel: 071–408 0214. *General Manager*, Capt. J. Rumble.

ROYAL THAMES YACHT CLUB (1775), 60 Knightsbridge, London SW1X 7LF. Tel: 071-235 2121. *Secretary*, Capt. A. R. Ward, CBE, RN.

St Stephen's Constitutional Club (1870), 34 Queen Anne's Gate, London SW1H 9AB. Tel: 071-222 1382. *Secretary*, L. D. Mawby.

Savage Club (1857), 1 Whitehall Place, London SW1A 2HD. Tel: 071-930 8118. *Hon. Secretary*, D. Stirling.

Savile Club (1868), 69 Brook Street, London W1Y 2ER. Tel: 071-629 5462. *Secretary*, N. Storey.

Ski Club of Great Britain (1903), 118 Eaton Square, London SW1W 9AF. Tel: 071-245 1033. *Chief Executive*, Ms I. Grimsey.

Thames Rowing Club (1860), Embankment, Putney, London SW15 1LB. Tel: 081-788 0676. *Hon. Secretary*, Mrs S. Thomas.

Travellers' Club (1819), 106 Pall Mall, London SW1Y 5EP. Tel: 071-930 8688. *Secretary*, M. S. Allcock.

Turf Club (1868), 5 Carlton House Terrace, London SW1Y 5AQ. Tel: 071-930 8555. *Secretary*, Col. J. G. B. Rigby, OBE.

United Oxford and Cambridge University Club (1972), 71 Pall Mall, London SW1Y 5HD. Tel: 071-930 5151. *General Secretary*, D. McDougall.

University Women's Club (1886), 2 Audley Square, London W1Y 6DB. Tel: 071-499 2268. *Secretary*, Mrs P. A. Burtwell.

Victoria Club (1863), 1 North Court, Great Peter Street, London SW1P 3LL. Tel: 071-222 2357. *Secretary*, Ms H. David.

Victory Services Club (1907), 63–79 Seymour Street, London W2 2HF. Tel: 071-723 4474. *General Manager*, Capt. G. F. Taylor.

White's Club (1693), 37–38 St James's Street, London SW1A 1JG. Tel: 071-493 6671. *Secretary*, D. C. Ward.

Wig and Pen Club (1908), 229–230 Strand, London WC2R 1BA. Tel: 071-583 7255. *Administrator*, J. Reynolds.

CLUBS OUTSIDE LONDON

Aldershot: Royal Aldershot Officers Club (1856), Farnborough Road, Aldershot, Hants. Tel: 0252-24036. *Secretary*, Lt.-Col. A. F. J. Channon, MBE (retd).

Bath: Bath and County Club (1865), Queens Parade, Bath, BA1 2NJ. Tel: 0225-423732. *Secretary*, Mrs G. M. Jones.

Birmingham: Birmingham Club (1872), Winston Churchill House, 8 Ethel Street, Birmingham B2 4BG. Tel: 021-643 3357. *Hon. Secretary*, T. R. Pepper.
St Paul's Club (1859), 34 St Paul's Square, Birmingham B3 1QZ. Tel: 021-236 1950. *Hon. Secretary*, E. A. Fellowes.

Bishop Auckland: The Club (1868), 1 Victoria Avenue, Bishop Auckland, Co. Durham DL14 7JH. Tel: 0388-603219. *Hon. Secretary*, R. W. Dennis.

Bristol: Clifton Club (1882), 22 The Mall, Clifton, Bristol BS8 4DS. Tel: 0272-735527. *Secretary*, H. B. Peckham.

Cambridge: Amateur Dramatic Club (1855), ADC Theatre, Park Street, Cambridge CB5 9AS. Tel: 0223-359547. *Secretary*, Ms L. Taylor.
The Union (1815), Bridge Street, Cambridge CB2 1UB. Tel: 0223-61521. *Chief Clerk*, B. Thoday.

Canterbury: Kent and Canterbury Club (1868), 17 Old Dover Road, Canterbury CT1 3JB. Tel: 0227-462181. *Secretary*, F. T. Bedingham.

Cheltenham: New Club (1874), Montpellier Parade, Cheltenham GL50 1UD. Tel: 0242-523285. *Hon. Secretary*, J. A. Warhurst, OBE.

Chester: City Club (1807), St Peter's Churchyard, Chester CH1 2AG. *Secretary*, C. Hodkinson.

Chichester: West Sussex County Club (1872), 5 Stirling Road, Chichester, W. Sussex PO19 2EW. *Secretary*, Mrs P. Green.

Colchester: The Colchester Club (1874), 3–5 Culver Street, Colchester, Essex CO1 1LE.

Devizes: Devizes and District Club (1932), 27 St John Street, Devizes, Wilts. SN10 1BN. *Secretary*, D. J. J. Cox.

Durham: County Club (1890), 52 Old Elvet, Durham. *Secretary*, Mrs C. Arnot.
Durham Union Society (1842), Palace Green, Durham DH1 3EP. Tel: 091-384 3724. *Secretary*, Mrs E. M. Hardcastle.

Eastbourne: Devonshire Club (1872), Hartington Place, Eastbourne, Sussex BN21 3RN. *Hon. Secretary*, D. G. Matthews.

Guildford: County Club, 158 High Street, Guildford GU1 3HF. Tel: 0483-575370. *Hon. Secretary*, R. W. D. Hemingway.

Harrogate: The Club (1857), 36 Victoria Avenue, Harrogate, N. Yorks. *Hon. Secretary*, C. L. Leslie.

Henley-on-Thames: Leander Club (1818), Henley-on-Thames, Oxon. RG9 2LP. Tel: 0491-575782. *Hon. Secretary*, K. Hylton-Smith.
Phyllis Court Club (1906), Marlow Road, Henley, Oxon. RG9 2HT. Tel: 0491-574366. *Secretary*, D. M. Brockett.

Hove: Hove Club (1882), 28 Fourth Avenue, Hove, E. Sussex BN3 2PJ. Tel: 0273-730872. *Hon. Secretary*, Sqn. Ldr. G. A. Inverarity, DFC.

Leamington: Tennis Court Club (1846), 50 Bedford Street, Leamington, Warks. CV32 5DT. Tel: 0926-424977. *Hon. Secretary*, O. D. R. Dixon.

Leeds: Leeds Club (1850), 3 Albion Place, Leeds LS1 6JL. *Administrator*, Mrs D. Kavanagh.

Leicester: Leicestershire Club (1873), 9 Welford Place, Leicester LE1 6ZH. *Manager*, J. A. Evans.

Liverpool: The Athenaeum (1797), Church Alley, Liverpool L1 3DD. Tel: 051-709 7700. *Hon. Secretary*, R. B. Brown.

Macclesfield: Old Boys' and Park Green Club, 7 Churchside, Macclesfield, Cheshire SK10 1HG. Tel: 0625-423292. *Hon. Secretary*, Dr P. R. Baker, MBE.

Manchester: St James's Club, St James's House, Charlotte Street, Manchester M1 4DZ. Tel: 061-236 2235. *Hon. Secretary*, C. R. I. Estridge.

Newcastle upon Tyne: Northern Constitutional Club (1882), 37 Pilgrim Street, Newcastle upon Tyne NE1 6QE. Tel: 091-232 0884. *Hon. Secretary*, J. L. Browne.

Northampton: Northampton and County Club (1873), George Row, Northampton NN1 1DF. Tel: 0604-32962. *Secretary*, J. Coley.

Norwich: Norfolk Club (1770), 17 Upper King Street, Norwich NR3 1RB. Tel: 0603-610652. *Secretary*, A. J. M. Williamson.

Nottingham: Nottingham and Notts. United Services Club (1920), Newdigate House, Castle Gate, Nottingham NG1 6AF. Tel: 0602-472138. *Hon. Secretary*, A. C. Ready.

Oxford: Frewen Club (1869), 98 St Aldate's, Oxford OX1 1BT. Tel: 0865-243816. *Hon. Secretary*, W. H. Miller, BEM.
Oxford Union Society (1823), Frewin Court, Oxford OX1 3JB. *Secretary*, S. Green.
Vincent's Club (1863), 1A King Edward Street, Oxford OX1 4HS. Tel: 0865-722984. *Secretary*, P. M. Blackman

Paignton: PAIGNTON CLUB (1882), The Esplanade, Paignton, Devon TQ4 6ED. Tel: 0803-559682. *Hon. Secretary*, P. Grafton.
Peterborough: CITY AND COUNTIES CLUB (1867), Priestgate, Peterborough PE6 7LT. *Secretary*, J. R. Fillingham.
Reading: BERKSHIRE ATHENAEUM CLUB (1972), 53 Blagrave Street, Reading, Berks. *Hon. Secretary*, W. J. Stuck.
Rye: DORMY HOUSE CLUB (1896), Rye, E. Sussex TN31 7LD. Tel: 0797-222338. *Hon. Secretary*, P. G. Armitage.
Shrewsbury: SALOP CLUB (1974), The Old House, Dogpole, Shrewsbury SY1 1EP. Tel: 0743-362182. *Secretary*, J. W. Rouse.
Stourbridge: STOURBRIDGE OLD EDWARDIAN CLUB (1898), Drury Lane, Stourbridge, West Midlands DY8 1BL. Tel: 0384-395635. *Hon. Secretary*, J. V. Sanders.
Teddington: ROYAL CANOE CLUB (1866), Trowlock Island, Teddington, Middx. TW11 9QZ. Tel: 081-977 5269. *Hon. Secretary*, Mrs J. S. Evans.
Worcester: UNION AND COUNTY CLUB (1861), 40 Foregate Street, Worcester. *Secretary*, M. G. Maton.
York: YORKSHIRE CLUB (1839), 17 Museum Street, York YO1 2DW. Tel: 0904-624611. *Hon. Secretary*, D. E. Gabbitas.

WALES

Cardiff: CARDIFF AND COUNTY CLUB (1866), Westgate Street, Cardiff CF1 1DA. Tel: 0222-220846. *Hon. Secretary*, Cdr. J. E. Payn, RD.

SCOTLAND

Aberdeen: ROYAL NORTHERN AND UNIVERSITY CLUB (1979), 9 Albyn Place, Aberdeen AB1 1YE. Tel: 0224-583292. *Secretary*, Miss R. A. Black.
Ayr: COUNTY CLUB (1872), Savoy Park Hotel, Ayr KA7 2XA. *Hon. Secretary*, J. K. Templeton.
Edinburgh: CALEDONIAN CLUB (1825), 32 Abercromby Place, Edinburgh EH3 6QE. Tel: 031-557 2675. *Secretary*, Ms F. Fowler.
NEW CLUB (1787), 86 Princes Street, Edinburgh EH2 2BB. Tel: 031-226 4881. *Secretary*, A. D. Orr Ewing.
Glasgow: GLASGOW ART CLUB (1867), 135 Wellington Street, Glasgow G2 2XE. Tel: 041-248 3904. *Secretary*, L. J. McIntyre.
ROYAL SCOTTISH AUTOMOBILE CLUB (1899), 11 Blythswood Square, Glasgow G2 4AG. Tel: 041-221 3850. *Secretary*, J. C. Lord.
WESTERN CLUB (1825), 32 Royal Exchange Square, Glasgow G1 3AB. Tel: 041-221 2016. *Secretary*, D. H. Gifford.

NORTHERN IRELAND

Belfast: ULSTER REFORM CLUB (1885), 4 Royal Avenue, Belfast BT1 1DA. Tel: 0232-323411. *Secretary*, Miss M. P. Mackintosh.
Enniskillen: FERMANAGH COUNTY CLUB (1883), 20 Church Street, Enniskillen, N. Ireland BT74 6DF. *Hon. Secretary*, P. Little.

CHANNEL ISLANDS

Guernsey: UNITED CLUB (1870), St Peter Port, Guernsey. Tel: 0481-725722. *Secretary*, J. G. Doggart.
Jersey: VICTORIA CLUB (1853), Beresford Street, St Helier, Jersey. Tel: 0534-23381. *Secretary*, Miss C. Rynd.

YACHT CLUBS

Bembridge: BEMBRIDGE SAILING CLUB (1886), Embankment Road, Bembridge, IOW, PO35 5NR. Tel: 0983-872237. *Hon. Secretary*, B. J. B. Sloley.
Birkenhead: ROYAL MERSEY YACHT CLUB (1844), Bedford Road East, Rock Ferry, Birkenhead, Merseyside L42 1LS. Tel: 051-645 3204. *Hon. Secretary*, A. Tetley.
Bridlington: ROYAL YORKSHIRE YACHT CLUB (1847), 1 Windsor Crescent, Bridlington, N. Humberside YO15 3HX. Tel: 0262-672041. *Secretary*, J. H. Evans.
Burnham-on-Crouch: ROYAL CORINTHIAN YACHT CLUB (1872), Burnham-on-Crouch, Essex CM0 8AX. Tel: 0621-782105. *Hon. Secretary*, K. W. Bushell.
Cowes: ROYAL YACHT SQUADRON (1815), The Castle, Cowes, IOW, PO31 7QT. Tel: 0983-292191. *Secretary*, Maj. R. P. Rising.
ROYAL LONDON YACHT CLUB (1838), The Parade, Cowes, IOW, PO31 7QS. Tel: 0983-299727. *Secretary*, Lt.-Col. R. J. Freeman-Wallace (retd).
Dover: ROYAL CINQUE PORTS YACHT CLUB (1872), 5 Waterloo Crescent, Dover, Kent CT16 1LA. Tel: 0304-206262. *Secretary*, Mrs H. Moors.
Fishbourne: ROYAL VICTORIA YACHT CLUB (1844), Fishbourne Lane, Ryde, IOW, PO33 4EU. Tel: 0983-882325. *Hon. Secretary*, Ms H. Vrba.
Fowey: ROYAL FOWEY YACHT CLUB (1881), Fowey, Cornwall PL23 1BH. Tel: 0726-833573. *Hon. Secretary*, E. P. Warren.
Harwich: ROYAL HARWICH YACHT CLUB (1843), Woolverstone, Ipswich IP9 1AT. Tel: 0473-780319. *Secretary*, I. A. Murdoch.
Kingswear: ROYAL DART YACHT CLUB (1866), Priory Street, Kingswear, Dartmouth, Devon TQ6 0AB. Tel: 080 425-496. *Hon. Secretary*, T. M. Goodearl.
Leigh-on-Sea: ESSEX YACHT CLUB (1890), HQS Bembridge, Foreshore, Leigh-on-Sea, Essex SS9 1BD. Tel: 0702-78404. *Hon. Secretary*, A. Manning.
London: THE CRUISING ASSOCIATION (1908), Ivory House, St Katharine Dock, London E1 9AT. Tel: 071-481 0881. *General Secretary*, Mrs L. Hammett.
ROYAL CRUISING CLUB (1880), c/o Royal Thames Yacht Club, 60 Knightsbridge, London SW1X 7LF. Tel: 071-235 2121. *Hon. Secretary*, C. Buckley.
Lowestoft: ROYAL NORFOLK AND SUFFOLK YACHT CLUB (1859), Royal Plain, Lowestoft, Suffolk NR33 0AQ. Tel: 0502-566726. *Hon. Secretary*, J. M. Brown.
Lymington: ROYAL LYMINGTON YACHT CLUB (1922), Bath Road, Lymington, Hants. SO41 9SE. Tel: 0590-672677. *Secretary*, Gp Capt J. D. Hutchinson (retd).
Plymouth: ROYAL WESTERN YACHT CLUB (1827), Queen Anne's Battery, Plymouth PL4 0TW. Tel: 0752-660077. *Secretary*, Cdr. R. J. Harvey.
ROYAL PLYMOUTH CORINTHIAN YACHT CLUB (1877), Madeira Road, Plymouth PL1 2NY. Tel: 0752-664327. *Hon. Secretary*, V. J. De Boo.
Poole: EAST DORSET SAILING CLUB (1875), 352 Sandbanks Road, Poole, Dorset BH14 8HY. *Hon. Secretary*, P. Neely.
PARKSTONE YACHT CLUB (1895), Pearce Avenue, Parkstone, Poole, Dorset BH14 8EH. Tel: 0202-743610. *Secretary*, J. Shore.
POOLE HARBOUR YACHT CLUB (1949), 38 Salterns Way, Lilliput, Poole, Dorset BH14 8JR. Tel: 0202-707321. *Secretary*, J. N. J. Smith.
POOLE YACHT CLUB (1865), New Harbour Road West, Hamworthy, Poole, Dorset BH15 4AQ. Tel: 0202-672687. *Secretary/Manager*, Miss L. Clark.

Portsmouth: ROYAL NAVAL CLUB AND ROYAL ALBERT YACHT CLUB (1867), 17 Pembroke Road, Portsmouth PO1 2NT. Tel: 0705-824491. *Secretary*, Lt.-Cdr. C. J. Howe.

Ramsgate: ROYAL TEMPLE YACHT CLUB (1857), 6 Westcliff Mansions, Ramsgate, Kent CT11 9HY. Tel: 0843-591766. *Hon. Secretary*, G. F. Randell.

Southampton: ROYAL AIR FORCE YACHT CLUB (1932), Riverside House, Rope Walk, Hamble, Southampton SO3 5HD. Tel: 0703-452208. *Secretary*, Miss A. R. Prees.

ROYAL SOUTHAMPTON YACHT CLUB, 1 Channel Way, Ocean Village, Southampton SO1 1XE. Tel: 0703-223352. *Hon. Secretary*, R. Higgs.

ROYAL SOUTHERN YACHT CLUB (1837), Hamble, Southampton SO3 5HB. Tel: 0703-453271. *Secretary*, Mrs J. A. Atkins.

Southend: ALEXANDRA YACHT CLUB (1873), Clifton Terrace, Southend-on-Sea SS1 1DT. *Hon. Secretary*, D. C. Osborn.

Torquay: ROYAL TORBAY YACHT CLUB (1863), Beacon Hill, Torquay, Devon TQ1 2BQ. Tel: 0803-292006. *Secretary*, A. E. Hinkins.

Westcliff on Sea: THAMES ESTUARY YACHT CLUB (1895), 3 The Leas, Westcliff on Sea, Essex SS0 7ST. Tel: 0702-345967. *Hon. Secretary*, G. R. Noble.

Weymouth: ROYAL DORSET YACHT CLUB (1875), 11 Custom House Quay, Weymouth, Dorset DT4 8BG. Tel: 0305-786258. *Secretary*, Mrs J. B. Cannon.

Windermere: ROYAL WINDERMERE YACHT CLUB (1860), Fallbarrow Road, Bowness-on-Windermere, Cumbria LA23 3DJ. Tel: 05394-43106. *Hon. Secretary*, M. C. Bentley.

Yarmouth: ROYAL SOLENT YACHT CLUB (1878), Yarmouth, IOW, PO41 0NS. Tel: 0983-760256. *Secretary*, Mrs S. Tribe.

WALES

Beaumaris: ROYAL ANGLESEY YACHT CLUB (1802), 6–7 Green Edge, Beaumaris, Gwynedd LL58 8AL. Tel: 0248-810295. *Hon. Secretary*, V. G. Keep.

Caernarvon: ROYAL WELSH YACHT CLUB (1847), Porth-Yr-Aur, Caernarvon, Gwynedd LL55 1SW. Tel: 0286-672599. *Hon. Secretary*, G. Tecwyn Evans.

Penarth: PENARTH YACHT CLUB (1880). The Esplanade, Penarth, S. Glamorgan CF6 2AU. Tel: 0222-708196. *Hon. Secretary*, R. S. McGregor.

Swansea: BRISTOL CHANNEL YACHT CLUB (1875), 744 Mumbles Road, Mumbles, Swansea SA3 4EL. Tel: 0792-366000. *Hon. Secretary*, B. G. T. Rees.

SCOTLAND

Dundee: ROYAL TAY YACHT CLUB (1885), 34 Dundee Road, Broughty Ferry, Dundee DD5 1LX. Tel: 0382-77516. *Hon. Secretary*, Dr G. R. Foster.

Edinburgh: ROYAL FORTH YACHT CLUB (1868), Middle Pier, Granton Harbour, Edinburgh EH5 1HF. Tel: 031-552 8560. *Hon. Secretary*, D. Skinner.

Glasgow: ROYAL WESTERN YACHT CLUB (1875). *Hon. Secretary*, D. G. M. Watson, Lochaber, 20 Barclay Drive, Helensburgh, Dunbartonshire G84 9RB.

Oban: ROYAL HIGHLAND YACHT CLUB (1881). *Secretary*, Mrs J. D. Carr, West Manse House, Kilchrenan, Taynuilt, Argyll PA35 1HG.

Rhu: ROYAL NORTHERN AND CLYDE YACHT CLUB (1978), Rhu, Helensburgh, Dunbartonshire G84 8NG. Tel: 0436-820322. *Hon. Secretary*, B. C. Staig.

NORTHERN IRELAND

Bangor: ROYAL ULSTER YACHT CLUB (1866), 101 Clifton Road, Bangor, Co. Down BT20 5HY. Tel: 0247-270568. *Hon. Secretary*, T. O'Hara.

CHANNEL ISLANDS

Jersey: ROYAL CHANNEL ISLANDS YACHT CLUB (1862), Le Boulevard, Bulwarks, St Aubin, Jersey. Tel: 0534-41023. *Hon. Secretary*, D. C. Dale.

Conservation and Heritage

Countryside Conservation

NATIONAL PARKS

England and Wales

The ten National Parks of England and Wales were established in the 1950s under the provisions of the National Parks and Access to the Countryside Act 1949. The National Parks were set up to conserve and protect scenic landscapes from inappropriate development and to provide access to the land for public enjoyment.

The Countryside Commission is the statutory body which has the power to designate National Parks in England and the Countryside Council for Wales is responsible for National Parks in Wales. The designation of National Parks in England is considered and confirmed by the Secretary of State for the Environment, and the designation of National Parks in Wales by the Secretary of State for Wales. The designation of a National Park does not affect the ownership of the land, nor does it remove the rights of the local community. Although the parks are administered through local government, the majority of the land is owned by private landowners (74 per cent) or by other bodies like the National Trust (7 per cent) and the Forestry Commission (7 per cent). The National Park Authorities own only 2.3 per cent of the land in the National Parks.

Under the Local Government Act 1972, National Park Authorities (NPAs) are the authorities responsible for park administration. They also influence land use and development, and deal with planning applications.

Two-thirds of the members of each authority are appointed by the county and district councils within whose boundaries the parks lie. One-third of the members are appointed by the Secretary of State for the Environment or the Secretary of State for Wales with advice from the Countryside Commission or the Countryside Council for Wales.

In the Peak District and the Lake District the NPAs are special boards: the Peak Park Joint Planning Board and the Lake District Special Planning Board. These are autonomous authorities which are financially independent, unlike the authorities in the other eight parks which are county council committees. The NPAs appoint the National Park Officer for the National Park they administer.

Central government provides 75 per cent of the funding for the parks through the National Park Supplementary Grant. The remaining 25 per cent is supplied by the local authorities concerned. Forecast expenditure for 1992–3 was £25,646,000.

The Countryside Commission has stated that other areas are regarded as being worthy of National Parks status. A special statutory authority, the Broads Authority, was established in 1989 to develop, conserve and manage the Norfolk and Suffolk Broads (*see* Government and Public Offices). The Government has announced its intention of giving the New Forest a status equivalent to that of a National Park by declaring it 'an area of national significance'.

The National Parks in England and Wales are (with date designation confirmed):

Brecon Beacons (1957), 1,351 sq. km/522 sq. miles – The park lies in Powys (66 per cent), Dyfed, Gwent and Mid Glamorgan. The park is centred on the Beacons, Pen y Fan, Corn Du and Cribyn, but also includes the valley of the Usk, the Black Mountains to the east and the Black Mountain to the west. There are information centres at Brecon, Craig-y-nos Country Park, Abergavenny and Llandovery, a study centre at Danywenallt and a day visitor centre near Libanus.
Information Office, 7 Glamorgan Street, Brecon, Powys LD3 7DP. Tel: 0874-624437. *National Park Officer,* M. Fitton.

Dartmoor (1951), 954 sq. km/368 sq. miles – Dartmoor lies wholly in Devon. Dartmoor consists of moorland and rocky granite tors, and is rich in prehistoric remains. There are information centres at Newbridge, Tavistock, Bovey Tracey, Steps Bridge, Princetown and Postbridge.
Information Office, Parke, Haytor Road, Bovey Tracey, Devon TQ13 9JQ. Tel: 0626-832093. *National Park Officer,* N. Atkinson.

Exmoor (1954), 693 sq. km/268 sq. miles – Exmoor lies in Somerset (71 per cent) and Devon. Exmoor is a moorland plateau inhabited by wild ponies and red deer. There are many ancient remains and burial mounds. There are information centres at Lynmouth, County Gate, Dulverton and Combe Martin.
Information Office, Exmoor House, Dulverton, Somerset TA22 9HL. Tel: 0398-23665. *National Park Officer,* K. Bungay.

Lake District (1951), 2,292 sq. km/885 sq. miles – The Lake District lies wholly in Cumbria. The Lake District includes England's highest mountains (Scafell Pike, Helvellyn and Skiddaw) but it is most famous for its glaciated lakes. There are information centres at Keswick, Waterhead, Hawkshead, Seatoller, Bowness, Grasmere, Coniston, Glenridding and Pooley Bridge, an information van at Gosforth and a park centre at Brockhole, Windermere.
Information Office, Busher Walk, Kendal, Cumbria LA9 4RH. Tel: 0539-724555. *National Park Officer,* J. Toothill.

Northumberland (1956), (1,049 sq. km/405 sq. miles) – The Northumberland National Park lies wholly in Northumberland. The park is an area of hill country stretching from Hadrian's Wall to the Scottish Border. There are information centres at Ingram, Once Brewed, Rothbury, Housesteads, Harbottle and Kielder, and an information caravan at Cawfields.
Information Office, Eastburn, South Park, Hexham, Northumberland NE46 1BS. Tel: 0434-605555. *National Park Officer,* G. Taylor.

North York Moors (1952), 1,436 sq. km/554 sq. miles – The North York Moors lie in North Yorkshire (96 per cent) and Cleveland. The park consists of woodland and moorland, and includes the Hambleton Hills and the Cleveland Way. There are information centres at Danby, Pickering, Sutton Bank, Ravenscar, Helmsley and Hutton-le-Hole, and a day study centre at Danby.
Information Office, The Old Vicarage, Bondgate, Helmsley, York YO6 5BP. Tel: 0439-70657. *National Park Officer,* D. Statham.

Peak District (1951), 1,438 sq. km/555 sq. miles – The Peak District lies in Derbyshire (64 per cent),

Staffordshire, South Yorkshire, Cheshire, West Yorkshire and Greater Manchester. The Peak District is composed of the gritstone moors of the 'dark peak' and the limestone dales of the 'white peak'. There are information centres at Bakewell, Edale, Fairholmes and Castleton, and information points at Torside (in the Longdendale Valley) and at Hartington (former station).
Information Office, Aldern House, Baslow Road, Bakewell, Derbyshire DE4 1AE. Tel: 0629-814321.
National Park Officer, C. Harrison.

PEMBROKESHIRE COAST (1952), 584 sq. km/225 sq. miles – The Pembrokeshire Coast National Park lies wholly in Dyfed. The park consists of cliffs, open moorland and Skomer Island. There are information centres at Tenby, St David's, Pembroke, Newport, Kilgetty, Haverfordwest and Broad Haven.
Information Office, County Offices, Haverfordwest, Dyfed SA61 1QZ. Tel: 0437-764591. *National Park Officer*, N. Wheeler.

SNOWDONIA (1951), 2,142 sq. km/817 sq. miles – Snowdonia lies wholly in Gwynedd. It is an area of deep valleys and rugged mountains in northern Wales. There are information centres at Aberdovey, Bala, Betws y Coed, Blaenau Ffestiniog, Conwy, Harlech, Dolgellau and Llanberis.
Information Office, Penrhyndeudraeth, Gwynedd LL48 6LS. Tel: 0766-770274. *National Park Officer*, A. Jones.

YORKSHIRE DALES (1954), 1,769 sq. km/683 sq. miles – The Yorkshire Dales National Park lies in North Yorkshire (88 per cent) and Cumbria. The Yorkshire Dales are composed primarily of limestone overlaid in places by millstone grit. The three peaks of Ingleborough, Whernside and Pen-y-Ghent are within the park. There are information centres at Clapham, Grassington, Hawes, Aysgarth Falls, Malham and Sedbergh.
Information Office, Yorebridge House, Bainbridge, Leyburn, North Yorkshire DL8 3BP. Tel: 0969-50456. *National Park Officer*, R. Harvey.

SCOTLAND AND NORTHERN IRELAND

The National Parks and Access to the Countryside Act 1949 dealt only with England and Wales, and made no provision for Scotland or Northern Ireland. Although there are no national parks in these two countries, there is power to designate them in Northern Ireland under the Amenity Lands Act 1965 and the Nature Conservation and Amenity Lands Order (Northern Ireland) 1985; and in 1989 the Scottish Office asked Scottish Natural Heritage to report on whether national parks should be designated in Scotland.

AREAS OF OUTSTANDING NATURAL BEAUTY

ENGLAND AND WALES

Under the National Parks and Access to the Countryside Act 1949, provision was made for the designation of Areas of Outstanding Natural Beauty (AONBs) by the Countryside Commission. The Countryside Act 1968 further defines the role of AONBs, suggesting that they should show due regard for the interests of other land users, such as agriculture and forestry groups. The Countryside Commission continues to be responsible for AONBs in England but since April 1991 the Countryside Council for Wales has been responsible for the Welsh AONBs. Designations in England are confirmed by the Secretary of State for the Environment and those in Wales by the Secretary of State for Wales.

Although less emphasis is placed upon the provision of open-air enjoyment for the public than in the national parks, AONBs are seen as areas which are no less beautiful and require the same degree of protection to conserve and enhance the natural beauty of the countryside. This includes protecting flora and fauna, geographical and other landscape features.

In AONBs planning and management responsibilities are split between county and district councils (there are 17 which cross county boundaries). Finance for the AONBs is provided by grant-aid.

Thirty-nine Areas of Outstanding Natural Beauty have been designated since 1956. They are (with date designation confirmed):

ANGLESEY (1967), 221 sq. km/85 sq. miles – The designated area extends along the entire coastline of the island, except for breaks around the urban areas and in the vicinity of Wylfa.

ARNSIDE AND SILVERDALE (1972), 75 sq. km/29 sq. miles – The area embraces the upper half of Morecambe Bay, the Kent estuary, and includes extensive tidal flats in the Bay.

BLACKDOWN HILLS (1991), 370 sq. km/143 sq. miles – An area of greensand ridges of Devon and Somerset extending from Cullompton in the west to Chard in the east, south of Taunton to north of Honiton.

CANNOCK CHASE (1958), 68 sq. km/26 sq. miles – An area of high heathland in Staffordshire. Deer continue to roam over the Chase.

CHICHESTER HARBOUR (1964), 74 sq. km/29 sq. miles – The area extends from Hayling Island to Apuldram and includes Thorney Island.

CHILTERNS (1965; extended 1990), 833 sq. km/322 sq. miles – Chalk downlands running from South Oxfordshire northeastwards to Bedfordshire, including the outlying group of hills beyond Luton.

CLWYDIAN RANGE (1985), 157 sq. km/61 sq. miles – A prominent ridge extending southwards from Prestatyn on the north Wales coast. Offa's Dike runs along the crest of the range.

CORNWALL (1959; Camel Estuary 1983), 958 sq. km/370 sq. miles – A number of separate areas including Bodmin Moor; most of the Land's End peninsula; the coast between St Michael's Mount and St Austell (with Falmouth omitted); the Fowey Estuary; in north Cornwall most of the coast to Bedruthan Steps and between Perranporth and Godrevy Towans, plus the Camel Estuary.

COTSWOLDS (1966; extended 1990), 2,038 sq. km/787 sq. miles – The area of limestone hills above the Vales of Gloucester and Evesham.

CRANBORNE CHASE AND WEST WILTSHIRE DOWNS (1983), 983 sq. km/379 sq. miles – A chalkland area covering parts of Wiltshire, Dorset, Hampshire and Somerset, including the wooded remnants of the ancient Chase.

DEDHAM VALE (1970; extended 1978, 1991), 90 sq. km/35 sq. miles – The area on the Essex/Suffolk border where John Constable painted.

EAST DEVON (1963), 268 sq. km/103 sq. miles – The coastline between Exmouth and Lyme Regis, with Sidmouth, Beer and Seaton omitted. Inland, Gittisham Hill, East Hill and Woodbury and Aylebeare Commons are included.

NORTH DEVON (1960), 171 sq. km/66 sq. miles – Includes most of the North Devon coastline, from just north of Bude to the boundary of the Exmoor National Park.

SOUTH DEVON (1960), 337 sq. km/130 sq. miles – Includes the coast between Bolt Head and Bolt Tail, Salcombe,

Slapton Sands and Dartmouth, and the estuaries and valleys of the Yealm, Erme, Avon and Dart.

DORSET (1959), (1,129 sq. km/436 sq. miles – The coastline between Lyme Regis and Poole, with the Isle of Portland and Weymouth omitted, stretching inland to include the Purbeck Hills and the downs of Hardy country.

FOREST OF BOWLAND (1964), 802 sq. km/310 sq. miles – A moorland area mostly in Lancashire running westward from the River Ribble, with a small outlying area east of the Ribble which includes Pendle Hill.

GOWER (1956), 188 sq. km/73 sq. miles – A peninsula in West Glamorgan, South Wales, known for its coastline.

EAST HAMPSHIRE (1962), 383 sq. km/148 sq. miles – A chalkland area stretching from the outskirts of Winchester to the Sussex border at a distance of about 10 miles inland.

SOUTH HAMPSHIRE COAST (1967), 77 sq. km/30 sq. miles – 14 miles of coastline between Hurst Castle and Calshot Castle, extending inland up the Beaulieu River for about six miles.

HIGH WEALD (1983), 1,460 sq. km/564 sq. miles – The area covers parts of East and West Sussex, Kent and Surrey. It is predominantly wooded, and includes larger heathland areas like Ashdown Forest, the remnants of the old Wealden forests.

HOWARDIAN HILLS (1987), 204 sq. km/79 sq. miles – Wooded hills which rise above the Vales of York and Pickering.

KENT DOWNS (1968), 878 sq. km/339 sq. miles – Running east and south-east from the Surrey border near Westerham to the coast near Dover and Folkestone, with a coastal outlier at South Foreland and a narrow strip of the old sea cliff escarpment west of Hythe overlooking Romney Marsh.

LINCOLNSHIRE WOLDS (1973), 558 sq. km/215 sq. miles – The area extends in a south-east direction from Laceby and Caistor in the north to the region of Spilsby, about ten miles west of the coast.

LLEYN (1957), 161 sq. km/62 sq. miles – The peninsula forming the westernmost part of the county of Gwynedd.

MALVERN HILLS (1959), 105 sq. km/40 sq. miles – The whole range of the Malvern Hills in the county of Hereford and Worcester, just touching Gloucestershire.

MENDIP HILLS (1972; extended 1989), 198 sq. km/76 sq. miles – Comprising over half of the Mendip Hills, the area stretches from Bleadon Hill to the A39 road north of Wells and includes Cheddar Gorge and Wookey Hole.

NORFOLK COAST (1968), 451 sq. km/174 sq. miles – An almost continuous coastal strip three to five miles in depth from Hunstanton to Bacton, with a further small strip between Sea Palling and Winterton-on-Sea. The area includes part of the Sandringham estate.

NORTH PENNINES (1988), 1,993 sq. km/766 sq. miles – The northern limit of the Pennine chain and largest AONB, covering parts of Cumbria, Co. Durham and Northumberland.

NORTHUMBERLAND COAST (1958), 135 sq. km/52 sq. miles – Stretches from just south of Berwick to Amble and includes Holy Island and the Farne Islands.

QUANTOCK HILLS (1957), 99 sq. km/38 sq. miles – A range of sandstone hills in Somerset.

ISLES OF SCILLY (1976), 16 sq. km/6 sq. miles – About 140 islands and skerries in the Scillies group of which only five are inhabited. There are a number of Sites of Special Scientific Interest.

SHROPSHIRE HILLS (1959), 804 sq. km/310 sq. miles – Most of south-west Shropshire between the Welsh border and the boundary with Hereford and Worcester, including the region around Clun, the area of the Stiperstones, the Long Mynd and Wenlock Edge, with the tongues of land running north-east to the Wrekin and south towards Ludlow.

SOLWAY COAST (1964), 115 sq. km/44 sq. miles – A stretch of coastline in Cumbria from Maryport to the estuaries of the Rivers Eden and Esk (with Silloth omitted) backed by the Solway Plain.

SUFFOLK COAST AND HEATHS (1970), 403 sq. km/156 sq. miles – The area includes 38 miles of coastline and parts of the Stour and Orwell estuaries, while the Deben, Alde and Blyth flow through it.

SURREY HILLS (1958), 419 sq. km/162 sq. miles – An area of hills to the east and south of Guildford, including the Hog's Back and the ridge of the North Downs.

SUSSEX DOWNS (1966), 983 sq. km/379 sq. miles – The area includes the chalk escarpment of the South Downs from Beachy Head to the Hampshire border, and stretches down to the coast between Eastbourne and Seaford.

NORTH WESSEX DOWNS (1972), 1,730 sq. km/668 sq. miles – An upland area in Hampshire, Wiltshire, Oxfordshire and Berkshire, bounded by the Marlborough and Lambourn Downs in the west, the Chiltern Hills in the east and Salisbury Plain in the south.

ISLE OF WIGHT (1963), 189 sq. km/73 sq. miles – A number of separate areas comprising stretches of coastline, the Yar Valley, the high downland behind Ventnor and the chalk ridge which runs from Newport to Culver Cliff and Foreland.

WYE VALLEY (1971), 326 sq. km/126 sq. miles – The river valley running through the counties of Gwent, Gloucestershire, and Hereford and Worcester.

Proposals for further designations include: the Tamar Valley, Devon/Cornwall and Nidderdale, North Yorkshire.

NORTHERN IRELAND

The Department of the Environment for Northern Ireland, with advice from the Council for Nature Conservation and the Countryside, designates Areas of Outstanding Natural Beauty in Northern Ireland. At present there are nine and these cover a total area of approximately 284,948 hectares (704,121 acres).

ANTRIM COAST AND GLENS, Co. Antrim, 70,600 ha/ 174,452 acres.
CAUSEWAY COAST, Co. Antrim, 4,200 ha/10,378 acres.
LAGAN VALLEY, Co. Down, 2,072 ha/5,119 acres.
LECALE COAST, Co. Down, 3,108 ha/7,679 acres.
MOURNE, Co. Down, 57,012 ha/140,876 acres.
NORTH DERRY, Co. Londonderry, 12,950 ha/31,999 acres.
RING OF GULLION, Co. Armagh, 15,353 ha/37,938 acres.
SPERRIN, Co. Tyrone/Co. Londonderry, 101,006 ha/ 249,585 acres.
STRANGFORD LOUGH, Co. Down, 18,647 ha/46,077 acres.

NATIONAL SCENIC AREAS

No Areas of Outstanding Natural Beauty are designated in Scotland. However, National Scenic Areas have a broadly equivalent status.

Scottish Natural Heritage recognizes areas of national scenic significance. At present there are 40, covering a total area of 1,017,300 hectares (2,513,748 acres).

Development within National Scenic Areas is dealt with by the local planning authority, who are required to consult Scottish Natural Heritage for certain categories of development within these areas. Land management uses can also be modified in the interest of scenic conservation. The Secretary of State for Scotland has limited powers of intervention should a planning authority and Scottish Natural Heritage disagree.

	hectares	*acres*
BORDER		
Eildon and Leaderfoot	3,600	8,896
Upper Tweeddale	12,300	30,393
CENTRAL		
Loch Lomond*	13,900	34,347
Loch Rannoch and Glen Lyon*	1,300	3,212
The Trossachs	4,600	11,367
DUMFRIES AND GALLOWAY		
East Stewartry Coast	5,200	12,849
Fleet Valley	5,300	13,096
Nith Estuary	9,300	22,980
GRAMPIAN		
The Cairngorm Mountains*	29,800	73,636
Deeside and Lochnagar*	32,200	79,566
HIGHLAND		
Assynt-Coigach	90,200	222,884
Ben Nevis and Glen Coe*	69,600	171,982
The Cairngorm Mountains*	37,400	92,415
The Cuillin Hills	21,900	54,115
Dornoch Firth	7,500	18,532
Glen Affric	19,300	47,690
Glen Strathfarrar	3,800	9,390
Kintail	16,300	40,277
Knoydart	39,500	97,604
Kyle of Tongue	18,500	45,713
Loch Shiel	13,400	33,111
Morar, Moidart and Ardnamurchan	15,900	39,289
North-west Sutherland	20,500	50,655
The Small Isles	15,500	38,300
Trotternish	5,000	12,355
Wester Ross	145,300	359,036
ORKNEY ISLANDS		
Hoy and West Mainland	14,800	36,571
SHETLAND ISLANDS		
Shetland	15,600	38,548
STRATHCLYDE		
Ben Nevis and Glen Coe*	17,500	43,242
Jura	21,800	53,868
Knapdale	19,800	48,926
Kyles of Bute	4,400	10,872
Loch Lomond*	30,300	74,871
Loch na Keal, Isle of Mull	12,700	31,382
Lynn of Lorn	4,800	11,861
Scarba, Lunga and the Garvellachs	1,900	4,692
TAYSIDE		
Ben Nevis and Glen Coe*	4,500	11,119
Deeside and Lochnagar*	7,800	19,274
Loch Rannoch and Glen Lyon*	47,100	116,384
Loch Tummel	9,200	22,733
River Earn	3,000	7,413
River Tay	5,600	13,838
WESTERN ISLES		
St Kilda	900	2,224
South Lewis, Harris and North Uist	108,600	268,351
South Uist Machair	6,100	15,073
TOTAL	1,017,300	2,513,748

*National Scenic Areas in more than one region

Nature Conservation Areas

SITES OF SPECIAL SCIENTIFIC INTEREST

Site of Special Scientific Interest (SSSI) is a legal designation applied to land in England, Scotland or Wales which English Nature (EN), Scottish Natural Heritage (SNH), or the Countryside Council for Wales (CCW) identifies as being of special interest because of its flora, fauna, geological or physiographical features. In some cases, SSSI are managed as nature reserves.

EN, SNH and CCW must notify SSSI to the local planning authority, every owner/occupier of the land, and the Secretary of State for the Environment (or Secretary of State for Scotland or for Wales where applicable). Forestry and agricultural departments and a number of other bodies are also informed of this notification.

Objections to the designation of SSSI can be made and ultimately heard at a full meeting of the Council of EN or CCW. In Scotland an objection will be dealt with by the appropriate regional board or the main board of SNH, depending on the nature of the objection. Unresolved objections on scientific grounds must be referred to the Advisory Committee for SSSI.

The protection of these sites depends on the co-operation of individual landowners and occupiers. Owner/occupiers must consult the EN, SNH or CCW and gain written consent before they can undertake certain listed activities on the site. Funds are available through management agreements and grants to assist owners and occupiers in conserving sites' interests. As a last resort a site can be purchased.

As at 31 March 1992 there were 5,866 SSSI in Britain, covering 1,825,076 hectares (4,507,938 acres).

	no.	*hectares*	*acres*
England	3,675	809,525	1,999,527
Scotland	1,350	816,600	2,017,002
Wales	841	195,951	491,409

NORTHERN IRELAND

In Northern Ireland 36 Areas of Special Scientific Interest (ASSIs) have been established by the Department of the Environment for Northern Ireland. These cover a total area of 7,443 hectares (18,392 acres).

NATIONAL NATURE RESERVES

National Nature Reserves are defined in the National Parks and Access to the Countryside Act 1949 as land designated for the study and preservation of flora and fauna, or of geological or physiographical features.

EN, SNH or CCW can designate as a National Nature Reserve land which is being managed as a nature reserve under an agreement with one of the statutory nature conservation agencies; land held and managed by the EN, SNH or CCW; or land held and managed as a nature reserve by another approved body. EN, SNH or CCW can turn to the appropriate Secretary of State to impose by-laws for the protection of the reserves from undesirable development.

As at 31 March 1992 there were 253 National Nature Reserves in Britain, covering 172,057 hectares (424,982 acres).

	no.	*hectares*	*acres*
England	135	46,804	115,606
Scotland	69	112,288	277,352
Wales	49	12,965	32,024

NORTHERN IRELAND

National Nature Reserves are established and managed by the Department of the Environment for Northern Ireland, with advice from the Council for Nature Conservation and the Countryside. There are 44 National Nature Reserves covering 4,506 hectares (11,135 acres).

LOCAL NATURE RESERVES

Local Nature Reserves are defined in the National Parks and Access to the Countryside Act 1949 as land designated for the study and preservation of flora and fauna, or of geological or physiographical features. The Act gives local authorities in England and Wales and district councils in Scotland the power to acquire, declare and manage local nature reserves in consultation with English Nature, Scottish Natural Heritage and the Countryside Council for Wales. Conservation trusts can also own and manage non-statutory local nature reserves.

As at 31 March 1992 there were 305 designated Local Nature Reserve areas in Britain, covering 18,888 hectares (46,654 acres).

	no.	*hectares*	*acres*
England	278	12,599	31,120
Scotland	8	2,866	7,079
Wales	19	3,423	8,455

An additional 17.19 km of linear trails are designated as LNRs.

FOREST NATURE RESERVES

Forest Enterprise has created Forest Nature Reserves from conservation sites within its estate. These are like other nature reserves in that their purpose is to protect and conserve special forms of natural habitat, flora and fauna existing in forested areas.

Forest Enterprise has 340 SSSI on its estates and has chosen 46 as Forest Nature Reserves. They extend in size from under 50 hectares (124 acres) to 500 hectares (1,236 acres). The largest include the Black Wood of Rannoch, by Loch Rannoch; Cannop Valley Oakwoods, Forest of Dean; Culbin Forest, near Forres; Glen Affric, near Fort Augustus; Kylerhea, Skye; Pembrey, Carmarthen Bay; Starr Forest, in Galloway Forest Park; Wyre Forest, near Kidderminster.

NORTHERN IRELAND

There are 36 Forest Nature Reserves in Northern Ireland, covering 1,759 hectares (4,346 acres). They are designated and administered by the Forest Service, a division of the Department of Agriculture for Northern Ireland. There are also 15 National Nature Reserves on Forest Service-owned property.

MARINE NATURE RESERVES

The Wildlife and Countryside Act 1981 gives the Secretary of State for the Environment (and the Secretaries of State for Wales and for Scotland where appropriate) power to designate Marine Nature Reserves, and EN, SNH and CCW powers to select and manage these reserves. Interested parties at a local and at a national level are consulted prior to the confirmation of an area.

Marine Nature Reserves provide protection for marine flora and fauna, and geological and physiographical features on land covered by tidal waters or parts of the sea in or adjacent to Great Britain. Reserves also provide opportunities for study and research.

Statutory Marine Nature Reserves are:

LUNDY (1986), Bristol Channel.
SKOMER (1990), Dyfed.

Other areas proposed for designation as reserves are: the Isles of Scilly; Bardsey Island and part of the Lleyn peninsula, Gwynedd.

A number of non-statutory marine reserves have been set up by conservation groups.

Wildlife Conservation

PROTECTED SPECIES

The Wildlife and Countryside Act 1981 gives legal protection to a wide range of animals and wild plants.

Animals, etc.

Under Schedule 5 of the Act it is illegal without a licence to kill, injure, take, possess or sell any of the animals mentioned below (whether alive or dead) and to disturb its place of shelter and protection or to destroy that place.

†Adder (*Vipera berus*)
§Allis shad (*alosa alosa*)
Anemone, Ivell's Sea (*Edwardsia ivelli*)
Anemone, Startlet Sea (*Nematosella vectensis*)
Apus (*Triops cancriformis*)
Bat, Horseshoe (*Rhinolophidae*, all species)
Bat, Typical (*Vespertilionidae*, all species)
Beetle, Rainbow Leaf (*Chrysolina cerealis*)
Beetle, Violet Click (*Limoniscus violaceus*)
Burbot (*Lota lota*)
*Butterfly, Adonis Blue (*Lysandra bellargus*)
*Butterfly, Black Hairstreak (*Strymonidia pruni*)
*Butterfly, Brown Hairstreak (*Thecla betulae*)
*Butterfly, Chalkhill Blue (*Lysandra coridon*)
*Butterfly, Chequered Skipper (*Carterocephalus palaemon*)
*Butterfly, Duke of Burgundy Fritillary (*Hamearis lucina*)
*Butterfly, Glanville Fritillary (*Melitaea cinxia*)
Butterfly, Heath Fritillary (*Mellicta athalia* (or *Melitaea athalia*))
*Butterfly, High Brown Fritillary (*Argynnis adippe*)
Butterfly, Large Blue (*Maculinea arion*)
*Butterfly, Large Copper (*Lycaena dispar*)
*Butterfly, Large Heath (*Coenonympha tullia*)
*Butterfly, Large Tortoiseshell (*Nymphalis polychloros*)
*Butterfly, Lulworth Skipper (*Thymelicus acteon*)
*Butterfly, Marsh Fritillary (*Eurodryas aurinia*)
*Butterfly, Mountain Ringlet (*Erebia epiphron*)
*Butterfly, Northern Brown Argus (*Aricia artaxerxes*)
*Butterfly, Pearl-bordered Fritillary (*Boloria euphrosyne*)
*Butterfly, Purple Emperor (*Apatura iris*)
*Butterfly, Silver Spotted Skipper (*Hesperia comma*)
*Butterfly, Silver-studded Blue (*Plebejus argus*)
*Butterfly, Small Blue (*Cupido minimus*)
Butterfly, Swallowtail (*Papilio machaon*)
*Butterfly, White Letter Hairstreak (*Stymonida w-album*)
*Butterfly, Wood White (*Leptidea sinapis*)
Cat, Wild (*Felis silvestris*)
Cicada, New Forest (*Cicadetta montana*)
**Crayfish, Atlantic Stream (*Austropotamobius pallipes*)
Cricket, Field (*Gryllus campestris*)
Cricket, Mole (*Gryllotalpa gryllotalpa*)
Dolphin (*Cetacea*)
Dormouse (*Muscardinus avellanarius*)
Dragonfly, Norfolk Aeshna (*Aeshna isosceles*)
*Frog, Common (*Rana temporaria*)
Grasshopper, Wart-biter (*Decticus verrucivorus*)

---

*the offence relates to 'sale' only.
**the offence relates to 'taking' and 'sale' only.
†the offence relates to 'killing and injuring' only.
‡the offence relates to 'killing, injuring and sale'.
§the offence relates to 'killing, injuring and taking'.

Leech, Medicinal (*Hirudo medicinalis*)
Lizard, Sand (*Lacerta agilis*)
‡Lizard, Viviparous(*Lacerta vivipara*)
Marten, Pine (*Martes martes*)
Moth, Barberry Carpet (*Pareulype berberata*)
Moth, Black-veined (*Siona lineata* (or *Idaea lineata*))
Moth, Essex Emerald (*Thetidia smaragdaria*)
Moth, New Forest Burnet (*Zygaena viciae*)
Moth, Reddish Buff (*Acosmetia caliginosa*)
Moth, Viper's Bugloss (*Hadena irregularis*)
Mussel, Freshwater Pearl (*Margaritifera margaritifera*)
Newt, Great Crested (or Warty) (*Triturus cristatus*)
*Newt, Palmate (*Triturus helveticus*)
*Newt, Smooth (*Triturus vulgaris*)
Otter, Common (*Lutra lutra*)
Porpoise (*Cetacea*)
Sandworm, Lagoon (*Armandia cirrhosa*)
Sea-Mat, Trembling (*Victorella pavida*)
Shrimp, Fairy (*Chirocephalus diaphanus*)
Shrimp, Lagoon Sand (*Gammarus insensibilis*)
‡Slow-worm (*Anguis fragilis*)
Snail, Glutinous (*Myxas glutinosa*)
Snail, Sandbowl (*Catinella arenaria*)
‡Snake, Grass (*Natrix natrix* (*Natrix helvetica*))
Snake, Smooth (*Coronella austriaca*)
Spider, Fen Raft (*Dolomedes plantarius*)
Spider, Ladybird (*Eresus niger*)
Squirrel, Red (*Sciurus vulgaris*)
*Toad, Common (*Bufo bufo*)
Toad, Natterjack (*Bufo calamita*)
Turtle, Marine (*Dermochelyidae* and *Cheloniidae*, all species)
Vendace (*Coregonus albula*)
Walrus (*Odobenus rosmarus*)
Whale (*Cetacea*)
Whitefish (*Coregonus lavaretus*)

Plants

Under Schedule 8 of the Wildlife and Countryside Act 1981, it is illegal without a licence to pick, uproot, sell or destroy any of the plants mentioned below and, unless authorized, to uproot any wild plant.

Adder's tongue, Least (*Ophioglossum lusitanicum*)
Alison, Small (*Alyssum alyssoides*)
Broomrape, Bedstraw (*Orobanche caryophyllacea*)
Broomrape, Oxtongue (*Orobanche loricata*)
Broomrape, Thistle (*Orobanche reticulata*)
Cabbage, Lundy (*Rhynchosinapis wrightii*)
Calamint, Wood (*Calamintha sylvatica*)
Catchfly, Alpine (*Lychnis alpina*)
Cinquefoil, Rock (*Potentilla rupestris*)
Club-rush, Triangular (*Scirpus triquetrus*)
Colt's-foot, Purple (*Homogyne alpina*)
Cotoneaster, Wild (*Cotoneaster integerrimus*)
Cottongrass, Slender (*Eriophorum gracile*)
Cow-wheat, Field (*Melampyrum arvense*)
Crocus, Sand (*Romulea columnae*)
Cudweed, Jersey (*Gnaphalium luteoalbum*)
Cudweed, Red-tipped (*Filago lutescens*)
Diapensia (*Diapensia lapponica*)
Eryngo, Field (*Eryngium campestre*)
Fern, Dickie's bladder (*Cystopteris dickieana*)
Fern, Killarney (*Trichomanes speciosum*)
Fleabane, Alpine (*Erigeron borealis*)
Fleabane, Small (*Pulicaria vulgaris*)

Galingale, Brown (*Cyperus fuscus*)
Gentian, Alpine (*Gentiana nivalis*)
Gentian, Fringed (*Gentianella ciliata*)
Gentian, Spring (*Gentiana verna*)
Germander, Cut-leaved (*Teucrium botrys*)
Germander, Water (*Teucrium scordium*)
Gladiolus, Wild (*Gladiolus illyricus*)
Goosefoot, Stinking (*Chenopodium vulvaria*)
Grass-poly (*Lythrum hyssopifolia*)
Hare's-ear, Sickle-leaved (*Bupleurum falcatum*)
Hare's-ear, Small (*Bupleurum baldense*)
Hawk's-beard, Stinking (*Crepis foetida*)
Heath, Blue (*Phyllodoce caerulea*)
Helleborine, Red (*Cephalanthera rubra*)
Helleborine, Young's (*Epipactis youngiana*)
Horsetail, Branched (*Equisetum ramosissimum*)
Hound's-tongue, Green (*Cynoglossum germanicum*)
Knawel, Perennial (*Scleranthus perennis*)
Knotgrass, Sea (*Polygonum maritimum*)
Lady's-slipper (*Cypripedium calceolus*)
Lavender, Sea (*Limonium paradoxum*) (*Limonium recurvum*)
Leek, Round-headed (*Allium sphaerocephalon*)
Lettuce, Least (*Lactuca saligna*)
Lily, Snowdon (*Lloydia serotina*)
Marsh-mallow, Rough (*Althaea hirsuta*)
Marshwort, Creeping (*Apium repens*)
Milk-parsley, Cambridge (*Selinum carvifolia*)
Naiad, Holly-leaved (*Najas marina*)
Orchid, Early Spider (*Ophrys sphegodes*)
Orchid, Fen (*Liparis loeselii*)
Orchid, Ghost (*Epipogium aphyllum*)
Orchid, Late Spider (*Ophrys fuciflora*)
Orchid, Lizard (*Himantoglossum hircinum*)
Orchid, Military (*Orchis militaris*)
Orchid, Monkey (*Orchis simia*)
Pear, Plymouth (*Pyrus cordata*)
Pennyroyal (*Mentha pulegium*)
Pigmyweed (*Crassula aquatica*)
Pink, Cheddar (*Dianthus gratianopolitanus*)
Pink, Childling (*Petroraghia nanteuilii*)
Ragwort, Fen (*Senecio paludosus*)
Ramping-fumitory, Martin's (*Fumaria martinii*)
Restharrow, Small (*Ononis reclinata*)
Rock-cress, Alpine (*Arabis alpina*)
Rock-cress, Bristol (*Arabis stricta*)
Sandwort, Norwegian (*Arenaria norvegica*)
Sandwort, Teesdale (*Minuartia stricta*)
Saxifrage, Drooping (*Saxifraga cernua*)
Saxifrage, Tufted (*Saxifraga cespitosa*)
Solomon's-seal, Whorled (*Polygonatum verticillatum*)
Sow-thistle, Alpine (*Cicerbita alpina*)
Spearwort, Adder's-tongue (*Ranunculus ophioglossifolius*)
Speedwell, Fingered (*Veronica triphyllos*)
Speedwell, Spiked (*Veronica spicata*)
Spurge, Purple (*Euphorbia peplis*)
Star-of-Bethlehem, Early (*Gagea bohemica*)
Starfruit (*Damasonium alisma*)
Stonewort, Foxtail (*Lamprothamnium papulosum*)
Strapwort (*Corrigiola litoralis*)
Violet, Fen (*Viola persicifolia*)
Viper's-grass (*Scorzonera humilis*)
Water-plantain, Ribbon-leaved (*Alisma gramineum*)
Wood-sedge, Starved (*Carex depauperata*)
Woodsia, Alpine (*Woodsia alpina*)
Woodsia, Oblong (*Woodsia ilvensis*)
Wormwood, Field (*Artemisia campestris*)
Woundwort, Downy (*Stachys germanica*)
Woundwort, Limestone (*Stachys alpina*)
Yellow-rattle, Greater (*Rhinanthus serotinus*)

Wild Birds

The Wildlife and Countryside Act 1981 lays down a close season for wild birds (other than game birds) from 1 February to 31 August inclusive, each year. Exceptions to these dates are made for:

Capercaillie and (except Scotland) *Woodcock* – 1 February–30 September.
Snipe – 1 February–11 August.
Wild Duck and *Wild Goose* (below high water mark) – 21 February–31 August.

Birds which may be killed or taken outside the close season (except on Sundays and on Christmas Day in Scotland, and on Sundays in prescribed areas of England and Wales) are the above-named and coot, certain wild duck (gadwall, goldeneye, mallard, pintail, pochard, shoveler, teal, tufted duck, wigeon), certain wild geese (Canada, greylag, pink-footed, white-fronted (in England and Wales only)), moorhen, golden plover and woodcock.

Certain wild birds may be killed or taken at any time by authorized persons: crow, collared dove, gull (great and lesser black-backed or herring), jackdaw, jay, magpie, pigeon (feral or wood), rook, sparrow (house), and starling.

All other British birds are fully protected by law throughout the year.

Proposed Changes

Following recommendations made by the Joint Nature Conservation Committee (JNCC) and consultation with other bodies, it is proposed (subject to Parliamentary approval) to add the following species of animals to Schedule 5 (protected animals) of the Wildlife and Countryside Act 1981 and to amend Schedule 8 (protected plants) of the Act as follows:

Animals, etc.

Three species of beetle (*Graphoderus zonatus*, *Hypebaeus flavipes* and *paracymus aeneus*)
Lesser silver water beetle
Mire pill beetle
High Brown Fritillary Butterfly (already partially protected)
Northern hatchet shell
Lagoon snail
De Folin's snail
Tentacled lagoon worm
Sussex emerald moth
Pink sea fan
Lagoon sea slug
Sturgeon

Plants

Blackwort
Snow caloplaca
Tree carapyrenium
Laurer's catillaria
Slender centaury
Upright mountain cladonia
Meadow clary
Lizard crystalwort
Broad leaved cudweed
Shore dock
Marsh earwort
Norfolk flapwort
Pointed frostwort
Dune gentian
Early gentian
Blunt leaved grimmia
Elm gyalecta
Northroe hawkweed
Shetland hawkweed

Weakleaved hawkweed
Churchyard lecanactis
Tarn lecanora
Copper lecidea
Arctic kidney lichen
Ciliate strap lichen
Coralloid rosette lichen
Earlobed dog lichen
Forked hair lichen
Golden hair lichen
Orange fruited elm lichen
River jelly lichen
Scaly breck lichen
Stary breck lichen
Lindenberg's leafy liverwort
Alpine copper moss
Baltic bog moss
Blue dew moss
Blunt leaved bristle moss
Bright green cave moss
Cordate beard moss
Cornish path moss
Derbyshire feather moss
Dune thread moss
Glaucous beard moss
Green shield moss
Hair silk moss
Large yellow feather moss
Multifruited river moss
Millimetre moss
Knothole moss
Nowell's limestone moss
Rigid apple moss
Round leaved feather moss
Schleicher's thread moss
Triangular pygmy moss
Vaucher's Feather moss
Welsh mudwort
Stalked orache
Lapland marsh orchid
Caledonia pannaria
New Forest parmelia
Oil stain parmentaria
Perfoliate penny cress
Alpine moss pertusaria
Southern grey physcia
Ground pine
Ragged pseudocyphellaria
Rusty alpine psora
Spiked rampion
Western rustwort
Serpentine solenopsora
Bearded stonewort
Turpswort

Plants To Be Deleted From Schedule 8

Recurved sea lavender
St David's sea lavender
Purple spurge

Further consideration is being given to three other recommendations made by the JNCC concerning the giant goby, the basking shark, and the wild cat hybrid.

CLOSE SEASONS AND TIMES

Game Birds

In each case the dates are inclusive:

Black game – 11 December–19 August (31 August in Somerset, Devon and New Forest).
**Grouse* – 11 December–11 August.
**Partridge* – 2 February–31 August.
**Pheasant* – 2 February–30 September.
**Ptarmigan* – (Scotland only) 11 December–11 August.

It is also unlawful in England and Wales to kill the game marked * above on a Sunday or Christmas Day.

Hunting and Ground Game

There is no statutory close time for fox-hunting or rabbit-shooting, nor for hares. However, by an Act passed in 1892 the sale of hares or leverets in Great Britain is prohibited from 1 March to 31 July inclusive under a penalty of £1. The recognized date for the opening of the fox-hunting season is 1 November, and it continues till the following April.

Deer

The statutory close seasons for deer (all dates inclusive) are:

	England and Wales	*Scotland*
Fallow deer		
Male	1 May–31 July	1 May–31 July
Female	1 Mar.–31 Oct.	16 Feb.–20 Oct.
Red deer		
Male	1 May–31 July	21 Oct.–30 June
Female	1 Mar.–31 Oct.	16 Feb.–20 Oct.
Roe deer		
Male	1 Nov.–31 Mar.	21 Oct.–31 Mar.
Female	1 Mar.–31 Oct.	1 April–20 Oct.
Sika deer		
Male	1 May–31 July	21 Oct.–30 June
Female	1 Mar.–31 Oct.	16 Feb.–20 Oct.
Red/Sika hybrids		
Male	—	21 Oct.–30 June
Female	—	16 Feb.–20 Oct.

Angling

Where local by-laws neither specify nor dispense with an annual close season, the following are statutory close times (dates inclusive):

Coarse fishing - 15 March–15 June.
Game fishing - Trout, 1 October–end February; Salmon, 1 November–31 January.

Close seasons vary in accordance with local by-laws. It is now necessary in all cases to check with the National Rivers Authority regional office covering the area (details can be found in the local telephone directory).

Anglers can now purchase an annual national rod licence for £12.50 from the NRA. It allows anglers to fish in fresh water with two rods where local by-laws permit and replaces more than 100 regional licences, removing the need for separate licences for game and coarse fish.

Historic Monuments

ENGLAND

The following is a select list of monuments in the care of English Heritage.

Charges for admission represent the figures obtaining in 1992–3. Concessionary rates are available for children, etc. Annual membership passes are available at £15 for adults, £10.50 for pensioners and £7 for children upon application to English Heritage Membership Department, PO Box 1BB, London W1A 1BB. Membership fees will increase on 1 April 1993.

Standard hours of opening (marked *) are as follows:

1 April–30 September	Daily 10–6
1 October–31 March	Tues.–Sun. 10–4

Monuments not marked * are open from 1 April to 30 September only.

All monuments are closed on 24–26 December and 1 January. Some smaller sites may close for the lunch-hour, which is normally 1–2 p.m. During the winter season, many monuments are closed on Mondays.

BATTLE ABBEY, E. Sussex. £2.50*. Remains of the abbey founded by William the Conqueror on the site of the Battle of Hastings.

BEESTON CASTLE, Cheshire. £1.80*. Thirteenth-century inner ward with gatehouse and towers, and considerable remains of large outer ward.

BOLSOVER CASTLE, Derbyshire. £1.80*. Notable for its interesting 17th century buildings.

BOSCOBEL HOUSE, Shropshire. £2.80*. Timber-framed early 17th century hunting lodge with later alterations. Charles II's 'Royal Oak' is nearby.

BRINKBURN PRIORY, Northumberland. £1.10. A house of Augustinian canons; the church (*c.*1200, repaired 1858) and parts of the cloister buildings survive.

BROUGHAM CASTLE, Cumbria. £1.10. Extensive remains of the 13th century keep, and of other buildings of periods up to the 17th century.

BYLAND ABBEY, North Yorkshire. £1.10*. Considerable remains of church and conventual buildings date from the abbey's foundation in 1177 by the Cistercians.

CARISBROOKE CASTLE, Isle of Wight. £3.00*. Norman castle, the prison of Charles I from 1647–8.

CARLISLE CASTLE, Cumbria. £1.80*. Medieval castle, prison of Mary Queen of Scots. Inner and outer wards enclosing a 12th century keep.

CASTLE ACRE PRIORY, Norfolk. £1.80*. Extensive remains include the 12th century church and the prior's lodgings.

CASTLE RISING CASTLE, Norfolk. £1.10*. A 12th century keep standing in a massive earthwork with its gatehouse and bridge.

CHESTERS ROMAN FORT, Northumberland. £1.60*. Fine example of a bath house.

CHYSAUSTER ANCIENT VILLAGE, Cornwall. £1.20*. Romano-Cornish village, 2nd and 3rd century AD, probably on a late Iron Age site.

CLEEVE ABBEY, Somerset. £1.50*. Much of the claustral buildings survive including timber-roofed frater, but only foundations of the church.

CORBRIDGE ROMAN SITE, Northumberland. £1.80*. Excavations have revealed the central area of a Roman town and successive military bases.

DEAL CASTLE, Kent. £1.80*. The largest and most complete of the forts erected by Henry VIII for coastal defence.

DOVER CASTLE, Kent. £4.50*. One of the strongest British castles, with Roman, Saxon and Norman features.

DUNSTANBURGH CASTLE, Northumberland. £1.10*. The 14th century castle standing on a cliff above the sea has a substantial gatehouse-keep.

FARLEIGH HUNGERFORD CASTLE, Somerset. £1.10*. Late 14th century castle of two courts. The chapel contains fine tomb of Sir Thomas Hungerford.

FARNHAM CASTLE KEEP, Surrey. £1.40. Built by the Bishops of Winchester, the motte of the castle is enclosed by a large 12th century shell keep. Foundations of a Norman tower.

FINCHALE PRIORY, Durham. 95p* (free in winter). Benedictine priory on banks of River Wear with considerable 13th century remains.

FRAMLINGHAM CASTLE, Suffolk. £1.50*. Impressive castle (*c.*1200) with high curtain walls enclosing a poorhouse of 1639.

FURNESS ABBEY, Cumbria. £1.80*. Founded in 1123 by Stephen, afterwards King of England; extensive remains of church and conventual buildings.

GOODRICH CASTLE, Hereford and Worcester. £1.50*. Extensive remains of 13th and 14th century castle incorporating 12th century keep.

GRIMES GRAVES, Norfolk. £1.10*. Extensive group of flint mines dating from the Neolithic period. Several shafts can be inspected.

HAILES ABBEY, Gloucestershire. £1.60*. Ruins of a Cistercian monastery founded in 1246. Museum contains some fine architectural fragments.

HELMSLEY CASTLE, North Yorkshire. £1.50*. Twelfth century keep and curtain wall with 16th century domestic buildings. Spectacular earthwork defences.

HOUSESTEADS ROMAN FORT, Northumberland. £1.80*. Excavation has exposed this infantry fort on Hadrian's Wall with its extra-mural civilian settlement.

KENILWORTH CASTLE, Warwickshire. £1.50*. One of the most extensive castles in Britain, showing many styles of building from 1155 to 1649.

LANERCOST PRIORY, Cumbria. 75p. The nave of the Augustinian priory church, *c.*1166, is still used and there are remains of other claustral buildings.

LINDISFARNE PRIORY, Northumberland. £1.80* (subject to tide). The bishopric of the Northumbrian kingdom destroyed by the Danes; re-established in 11th century as a Benedictine priory, now ruined.

LULLINGSTONE ROMAN VILLA, Kent. £1.50*. A large villa occupied through much of the Roman period; fine mosaics.

MIDDLEHAM CASTLE, North Yorkshire. £1.10*. Childhood home of Richard III. The 12th century keep stands within later fortifications and domestic buildings.

MOUNT GRACE PRIORY, North Yorkshire. £1.80*. Carthusian monastery, founded 1398, with remains of monastic buildings.

NETLEY ABBEY, Hampshire. £1.10* (weekends only in winter). Extensive remains of Cistercian abbey, founded 1239, with ruined Tudor house.

OLD SARUM, Wiltshire. £1.20*. Large earthworks enclosing the excavated remains of the castle and the first Salisbury cathedral, begun in 1078.

ORFORD CASTLE, Suffolk. £1.50*. Circular keep of *c.*1170 and remains of coastal defence castle built by Henry II.
PENDENNIS CASTLE, Cornwall. £1.80*. Well-preserved castle erected by Henry VIII for coastal defence.
PEVENSEY CASTLE, East Sussex. £1.50*. Walls of a 4th century Roman fort enclosing remains of an 11th century castle.
PEVERIL CASTLE, Derbyshire. £1.10*. In a picturesque and nearly impregnable position, this 12th century castle is defended on two sides by precipitous rocks.
PORTCHESTER CASTLE, Hampshire. £1.50*. Walls of a late Roman fort enclosing a Norman keep and an Augustinian priory church.
RECULVER TOWERS and ROMAN FORT, Kent. Adm. free. Remains of Saxon and Norman church with 12th century towers, standing in a Roman fort.
RICHBOROUGH CASTLE, Kent. £1.50*. The landing-site of the Claudian invasion in AD 43, with massive 3rd century stone walls.
RICHMOND CASTLE, North Yorkshire. £1.50*. This 12th century keep, with 11th century curtain wall and gatehouse, commands Swaledale.
RIEVAULX ABBEY, North Yorkshire. £1.80*. Founded *c.*1132. Extensive remains include an early Cistercian nave and fine 13th century choir and claustral buildings.
ROCHESTER CASTLE, Kent. £1.50*. Eleventh century castle partly founded on the Roman city wall, with a square keep of *c.*1130.
ST AUGUSTINE'S ABBEY, Kent. £1.10*. Remains of Benedictine monastery, with Norman church, on site of abbey founded by St Augustine in 598.
ST MAWES CASTLE, Cornwall. £1.20*. Coastal defence castle built by Henry VIII consisting of central tower and three bastions.
SCARBOROUGH CASTLE, North Yorkshire. £1.50*. Remains of 12th century keep and curtain walls dominating the town.
STONEHENGE, Wiltshire. £2.50*. Prehistoric monument consisting of a series of concentric stone circles surrounded by a ditch and bank.
TILBURY FORT, Essex. £1.80*. One of Henry VIII's coastal forts, extended by Charles II.
TINTAGEL CASTLE, Cornwall. £1.80*. 12th century castle on cliff top. Dark Age settlement site.
TYNEMOUTH PRIORY and CASTLE, Tyne and Wear. £1.10*. Remains of a Benedictine priory, founded 1090, on Saxon monastic site. Coastal batteries with reconstructed First World War magazine.
WALMER CASTLE, Kent. £2.50*. (Closed when Lord Warden is in residence.) One of Henry VIII's coastal defence castles, now the residence of the Lord Warden of the Cinque Ports.
WARKWORTH CASTLE, Northumberland. £1.10*. 15th century keep amidst earlier ruins with a 14th century hermitage upstream.
WHITBY ABBEY, North Yorkshire. £1.10*. 13th and 14th century Benedictine church on site of monastery founded in 657.
WROXETER ROMAN CITY, Shropshire. £1.50*. The 2nd century public baths and part of the forum remain of the Roman town of Viroconium.

WALES

The following is a select list of monuments under the control of Cadw: Welsh Historic Monuments. Charges for admission (subject to alteration) are given below. Concessionary rates are available for children, etc.

Standard hours of admission:

	Weekdays	*Sundays*
29 March–24 October	9.30–6.30	2.00–6.30
25 October–28 March	9.30–4.00	2.00–4.00

All monuments are closed on Christmas Eve, Christmas Day, Boxing Day and New Year's Day.

BEAUMARIS CASTLE, Anglesey, Gwynedd. £1.50. The finest example of the concentrically planned castle in Britain, it is still almost intact.
CAERLEON ROMAN AMPHITHEATRE, Gwent. £1.25. Late 1st century oval arena surrounded by bank for spectators.
CAERLEON ROMAN FORTRESS BATHS, Gwent. £1.25, joint ticket £2.50 (with National Museum of Wales). Rare example of a legionary bath-house.
CAERNARFON CASTLE, Gwynedd. £3.00, family ticket £9.00. The most important of the Edwardian castles, built together with the town wall between 1283 and 1330.
CAERPHILLY CASTLE, Mid-Glamorgan. £1.75. Concentrically planned castle (*c.*1270) notable for its great scale and use of water defences.
CASTELL COCH, S. Glamorgan. £1.75. Rebuilt 1875–90 on medieval foundations.
CHEPSTOW CASTLE, Gwent. £2.50, family ticket £7.00. Fine rectangular keep in the middle of extensive fortifications.
CONWY CASTLE, Gwynedd. £2.50, family ticket £7.00. Built by Edward I to guard the Conwy ferry.
CRICCIETH CASTLE, Gwynedd. £1.75. A native Welsh castle of the early 13th century, much altered by Edward I.
DENBIGH CASTLE, Clwyd. £1.25. The remains of the castle, which dates from 1282–1322, include an unusual triangular gatehouse.
HARLECH CASTLE, Gwynedd. £2.50, family ticket £7.00. Well preserved Edwardian castle with a concentric plan sited on a rocky outcrop above the former shore-line.
RAGLAN CASTLE, Gwent. £1.75. Extensive remains of 15th century castle with moated hexagonal keep.
ST DAVID'S, BISHOP'S PALACE, Dyfed. £1.50. Extensive remains of principal residence of Bishop of St David's dating from 1280–1350.
TINTERN ABBEY, Gwent. £2.00, family ticket £6.00. Extensive remains of 13th century church and conventual buildings of this Cistercian monastery.
TRETOWER COURT, Powys. £1.50. Medieval house with remains of castle nearby.

SCOTLAND

The following is a select list of monuments under the control of Historic Scotland.

Except where indicated differently, charges are: adults £1.00, concessions (con.) 50p.

Monuments open at any reasonable time are indicated by A. Standard hours of opening (marked S.) are as follows:

	Weekdays	*Sundays*
April–September	9.30–6.30	2.00–6.30
October–March	9.30–4.30	2.00–4.30

ABERLEMNO SCULPTURED STONES, Tayside. A. Closed in winter. Adm. free. Four Pictish stones.

ANTONINE WALL, Central and Strathclyde regions. A. Adm. free.

BLACKHOUSE ARNOL, Western Isles. S. Closed Sun. Traditional Lewis thatched house.

BONAWE IRONWORKS, Strathclyde. S. Closed in winter. Charcoal-fuelled ironworks. £1.50, con. 80p.

BROCH OF BIRSAY, Orkney. A. Remains of Norse church. Adm. free.

CAERLAVEROCK CASTLE, Dumfries and Galloway. S. £1.20, con. 60p.

CAIRNPAPPLE HILL, Lothian. S. Closed in winter. A prehistoric ritual complex and Bronze Age cairn.

CALLANISH, Western Isles. A. Adm. free. Standing stones.

CATERTHUNS (BROWN AND WHITE), Tayside. A. Adm. free. Iron Age hill forts.

CLAVA CAIRNS, Highland. A. Adm. free.

DRYBURGH ABBEY, Borders. S. £1.70, con. 90p.

EARLS AND BISHOPS PALACES, Kirkwall, Orkney. S. Closed in winter. Family ticket £4.50.

EDINBURGH CASTLE, including Scottish National War Memorial, Scottish United Services Museum and Historic apartments. Open April–September 9.30–6, October–March 9.30–5. Adm. to War Memorial, free; to all other areas £3.40, con. £1.70, family ticket £8.50.

EDZELL CASTLE, Tayside. S. Closed Tuesday p.m. and Friday in winter. £1.50, con. 80p.

ELGIN CATHEDRAL, Grampian. S. Closed Thursday p.m. and Friday in winter.

FORT GEORGE, Highland. S. £2.00, con. £1.00, family ticket £5.00.

GLASGOW CATHEDRAL, Strathclyde. S. Adm. free.

GLENELG BROCHS, Highland. A. Adm. free.

HERMITAGE CASTLE, Borders. S. Closed weekdays in winter.

HUNTLY CASTLE, Grampian. S. Closed Thursday p.m. and Friday in winter. £1.50, con. 80p.

JARLSHOF, Shetland. S. Closed all winter. Remains of Bronze Age village. £1.50, con. 80p.

JEDBURGH ABBEY, Borders. S. £1.70, con. 90p, family ticket £4.50.

KELSO ABBEY, Borders. S. Adm. free.

LINLITHGOW PALACE, Lothian. S. £1.50, con. 80p, family ticket £4.00.

LOANHEAD STONE CIRCLE, Grampian. A. Adm. free.

MAES HOWE, Orkney. S. £1.50, con. 80p, family ticket £4.00. Prehistoric tomb.

MEIGLE MUSEUM, Tayside. S. Closed all winter. Pictish stones.

MELROSE ABBEY, Borders. S. £1.70, con. 90p, family ticket £4.50.

MOUSA BROCH, Shetland. A. Adm. free.

NETHER LARGIE CAIRNS, Strathclyde. A. Adm. free.

NEW ABBEY CORN MILL, Dumfries and Galloway. S. Closed Thursday p.m. and Friday in winter. £1.20, con. 60p.

RING OF BROGAR, Orkney. A. Adm. free.

RUTHWELL CROSS, Dumfries and Galloway. A. Adm. free.

ST ANDREWS CASTLE AND CATHEDRAL, Fife. S. Separate adm. fee for Cathedral; £1.20, con. 60p.

SKARA BRAE, Orkney. S. £1.70, con. 90p, family ticket £4.50. Prehistoric village.

SMAILHOLM TOWER, Borders. S. Closed in winter.

STIRLING CASTLE, Central. Open April–September 9.30–6, October–March 9.30–5. £2.30, con. £1.20, family ticket £6.00.

TANTALLON CASTLE, Lothian. S. £1.50, con. 80p, family ticket £4.00. Closed Thursday p.m. and Friday in winter.

THREAVE CASTLE, Dumfries and Galloway. S. Adm. includes ferry trip. Closed in winter.

Historic Houses and Castles

Dates of opening and admission fees shown are those which obtained in 1992, and are subject to modification. Specific opening hours are not given but may be checked by telephone. Most houses have concessionary rates for certain categories of visitor.

Space permits only a selection of some of the more noteworthy houses in the UK which are open to the public.

*Property of the National Trust
Adm. admission
PM. = open in afternoons only

*A LA RONDE, Exmouth. Good Friday–31 Oct. Sun.–Thurs. Adm. charge. Tel: 0395–265514.

ALNWICK CASTLE, Northumberland. April–Oct. 11–4.30 PM (not Sat. except July–Aug.). Open Bank Hol. weekends. Adm. £3.00. Tel: 0665–510777.

ALTHORP, Northampton. Opening times and prices subject to change. Contact Lord Spencer.

*ANGLESEY ABBEY, Cambs. 28 March–18 Oct. Wed.–Sat. PM. Adm. £4.50. Gardens only Adm. £2.25. Tel: 0223–811200.

ARUNDEL CASTLE, W. Sussex. 29 March–30 Oct. daily (not Sat.). PM. Adm. charge. Tel: 0903–883136.

*BASILDON PARK, Berks. April–Oct. (not Mon. except Bank Hols; not Tues., not Good Friday). Adm. £3.00. Grounds £2.00. Tel: 0734–843040.

BEAULIEU, Hants. Daily (not Christmas). Adm. charge. Tel: 0590–612345. (*See also* page 750.)

*BELTON HOUSE, Grantham. April–Oct. Wed.–Sun. and Bank Hol. Mons. (not Good Friday). PM. Adm. £3.80. Tel: 0476–66116.

BELVOIR CASTLE, nr. Grantham. 1 April–1 Oct. daily (not Mon., Fri. except Bank Hols.) Rest of Oct., Sun. only. Adm. £3.20. Tel: 0476–870262.

BERKELEY CASTLE, Glos. April, Sept. daily (not Mon. except Bank Hols.). PM only except May–Aug., Tues.–Sat. and Bank Hols. 11–5. Oct. Sun. only. Adm. £3.40. Tel: 0453–810332.

BLAIR CASTLE, Tayside. April–30 Oct. daily (Sun. April, May and Oct PM.). Adm. £4.00. Tel: 0796–481207.

BLENHEIM PALACE, Oxon. Mid-March–31 Oct. daily. Adm. charge. Tel: 0993–811325.

BOUGHTON HOUSE, Northants. Aug.–1 Sept. daily. Grounds (excl. gardens) daily (not Fri.) 25 April–27 Sept. PM. Adm. charge. Tel: 0536–515731.

BOWHILL, Selkirk. House 1 July–31 July daily; Grounds 28 April–28 Aug. (not Fri.). daily PM. Adm. £3, Grounds only, £1. Tel: 0750–20732.

BROADLANDS, Hants. 15 April–27 Sept. daily (not Fri. except Aug. and Good Friday). Adm. £4.75. Tel: 0794–516878.

BRONTË PARSONAGE, Haworth, West Yorks. Daily, April–Sept. (not Christmas or 13 Jan.–7 Feb.). Adm. £2.50. Tel: 0535–642323.

BROUGHTON CASTLE, Oxon. 30 May–13 Sept. Wed., Sun. (also Thurs. in July and Aug.) and Bank Hol. Suns and Mons. PM. Adm. £2.80. Tel: 0295–262624.

*BUCKLAND ABBEY, Devon. 1 April–1 Nov. daily except Thurs. Nov.–March Wed., Sat., Sun. PM. Adm. £3.80. Tel: 0822–853607.

BURGHLEY HOUSE, Stamford. Good Friday–4 Oct. (closed 12 Sept) daily. Adm. £4.10. Tel: 0780–52451.

*CALKE ABBEY, Derbyshire. 1 April–end Oct., Sat.–Wed. PM. Adm. £4.00. Tel: 0332–863822.

CARDIFF CASTLE . Daily (not Christmas, New Year). Adm. charge. Tel: 0222–822086.

*CARLYLE'S HOUSE, Chelsea, London. April–end Oct. Wed.–Sun. and Bank Hol. Mons. (not Good Friday). Adm. £2.50. Tel: 071–352 7087.

*CASTLE COOLE, Enniskillen. Easter period, daily; June, July, Aug. daily (not Thurs.); Sat., Sun. and Bank Hols. in April, May, Sept. PM. Adm. £2.20, Grounds April–Sept. free. Tel: 0365–322690.

*CASTLE DROGO, Devon. April–1 Sept. daily except Fri. Adm. £4.40. Grounds £2.00. Tel: 064743–3306.

CASTLE HOWARD, N. Yorks. 25 March–1 Nov., daily. Adm. £5.50. Tel: 065384–333.

CAWDOR CASTLE, Inverness. May–4 Oct., daily. Adm. £3.50, Grounds £1.80. Tel: 06677–615.

*CHARTWELL, Kent. Open three days each week. Times vary. Adm. £3.80, Grounds £1.90. Tel: 0732–866368.

CHATSWORTH, Derbyshire. 21 March–1 Nov. daily. Grounds 29 March–4 Oct., daily. Adm. charge. Tel: 0246–582204.

CHICHELEY HALL, Newport Pagnell. 19 April–31 May, Aug. Sun. and Bank Hols. PM. Adm. £3.00. Tel: 023065–252.

*CLIVEDEN, Maidenhead. House, April–31 Oct., Thurs. and Sun. PM. Gardens March–Dec. daily. Adm. £3.00, £1.00 extra for House. Tel: 0628–605069.

*COMPTON CASTLE, nr. Paignton. April–1 Nov. Mon., Wed., Thurs. daily. Adm. £2.40. Tel: 0803–872112.

*CROFT CASTLE, Herefordshire. Easter Bank Hol. weekend (not Fri.), May–Sept. Wed.–Sun., Bank Hol. Mons., April and Oct. weekends. PM. Adm. £2.70. Tel: 056885–246.

DICKENS HOUSE, London, WC1. Daily (not Sun. and Bank Hols.). Adm. £2.00. Tel: 071–405 2127.

DR JOHNSON'S HOUSE, London, EC4. Daily (not Sun. and Bank Hols.). Adm. £2.00. Tel: 071–353 3745.

DRUMLANRIG CASTLE, Dumfries. May–Aug., daily (not Thurs.). Grounds open May–Sept. Adm. charge. Tel: 0848–31682.

HADDON HALL, Derbyshire. 1 April–30 Sept. Tues.–Sun., and Bank Hols. Closed Sun. in July and Aug. (except Bank Hol. weekends). Adm. £3.20. Tel: 0629–812855.

*HAM HOUSE, Richmond, Surrey. House closed for restoration until 1994. Garden all year (except Mon). Adm. free. Tel: 081–940 1950.

*HARDWICK HALL, Derbyshire. 1 April–31 Oct. House Wed., Thurs., Sat., Sun., Bank Hol. Mons. Garden daily to end Oct. (not Good Friday). PM. Adm. £5.00, Garden only, £2.00. Tel: 0246–850430.

HAREWOOD HOUSE, Leeds. 5 April–31 Oct. daily. Adm. charge. Tel: 0532–886225.

HATFIELD HOUSE, Herts. 25 March–11 Oct. daily (not Mon. except Bank Hols., not Good Friday). PM. except Bank Hols. Grounds, times vary. Adm. £4.30. Tel: 0707–262823.

HEVER CASTLE, Kent. 17 March–8 Nov., daily PM, Grounds 11–6. Adm. charge. Tel: 0732–865224.

HOLKER HALL, Cumbria. 1 April–31 October daily (not Sat.). Adm. charge. Tel: 05395–58328.

HOLKHAM HALL, Norfolk. 24 May–30 Sept. Sun.–Thurs. and Easter, Spring and Summer Bank Holidays. PM, except Bank Hols. Adm. £2.70. Tel: 0328–710227.

HOPETOUN HOUSE, nr. Edinburgh. 17 April–4 October, daily. Adm. £3.30. Tel: 031–331 2451.

HOUGHTON HALL, Norfolk. Easter Sun.–27 Sept., Sun., Thurs. and Bank Hols. PM. Adm. £4.00. Tel: 0485–528569.

*HUGHENDEN MANOR, High Wycombe. April–end Oct. (not Good Friday), Wed.–Sun. and Bank Hol. Mons. PM. March, weekends only. Adm. £3.00. Tel: 0494–532580.

INVERARAY CASTLE, Argyll. 1st Sat. in April–2nd Sun. in

Oct. daily (not Fri., except July–Aug.), Sun., PM. Woods open all year. Tel: 0499–2203.

JANE AUSTEN'S HOUSE, Chawton, Hants. April–Oct. daily, Jan. and Feb. weekends, Nov., Dec. and March, Wed.–Sun. (not Christmas). Adm. £1.50. Tel: 0420–83262.

KEATS HOUSE, Hampstead, London. All year, daily, PM (except Sat.). (Not Christmas, New Year, Good Friday, Easter Eve., 4 May.) Adm. free. Tel: 071–435 2062.

KELMSCOTT MANOR, nr. Lechlade, Glos. April–Sept., Wed. only. Thurs., Fri. by written application. Adm. £4.00.

*KINGSTON LACY HOUSE, Dorset. 1 April–1 Nov., PM. Sat.–Wed. Adm. £4.80, Grounds only £1.70. Tel: 0202–883402.

KNEBWORTH HOUSE, Herts. 4 April–17 May, Sat., Sun., School and Bank Hols., 23 May–6 Sept. daily (not Mon.). PM. Weekends only to 4 Oct. Adm. £4.00, Grounds only, £2.50. Tel: 0438–812661.

*KNOLE, Kent. April–Oct. Wed.–Sat. and Bank Hol. Mons. Sun., PM. Adm. £3.50, Garden 50p. Tel: 0732–450608.

LEEDS CASTLE, Kent. 16 March–end Oct. daily. Nov.–March, weekends only. Adm. charge. Tel: 0622–765400.

*LITTLE MORETON HALL, Cheshire. April–30 Sept., Wed.–Sun. and Bank Hol. Mon., Oct. weekends, Wed. PM. Adm. £2.50 Weekends and Bank Hols. £3.00. Tel: 0260–272018.

LONGLEAT HOUSE, Warminster. House daily (not Christmas). Safari Park mid-March–Oct. Adm. charge. Tel: 0985–844551.

LUTON HOO, Beds. 14 April–18 Oct., daily, PM (not Mon. except Bank Hols.). Adm. £4.30. Tel: 0582–22955.

MARBLE HILL HOUSE, Twickenham, Middx. All year, daily (not 24, 25 Dec.). Adm. free. Tel: 081–892 5115.

MICHELHAM PRIORY, E. Sussex. 25 March–31 Oct. daily. Nov., Feb. and March, Sun. only. Adm. £3.00. Tel: 0323–844224.

*MONTACUTE HOUSE, Yeovil. 1 April–3 Nov. daily (not Tues.) PM. Grounds open all year. Adm. £4.40, Grounds only £2.20. Tel: 0935–823289.

*MOUNT STEWART, Co. Down. Times vary. Adm. House, Garden, Temple £3.30, Garden and Temple only £2.70. Tel: 024774–387.

OSBORNE HOUSE, IOW. 1 April–31 Oct. daily 10–5. Adm. £2.00. Tel: 0983–200022.

*OSTERLEY PARK HOUSE, Isleworth, Middx. March, weekends, April–Oct. Wed.–Sat. PM Sun., Bank Hol. Mon. 11–5. (Closed Good Fri.). Adm. £3.00, Grounds free. Tel: 081–560 3918.

*PENRHYN CASTLE, Bangor. 1 April–1 Nov. daily (not Tues.) PM. Adm. £3.80, Garden £2.00. Tel: 0248–353084.

PENSHURST PLACE, Kent. 1 April–4 Oct. daily PM. Adm. charge. Tel: 0892–870307.

*PETWORTH HOUSE, W. Sussex. April–Oct. Tues.–Sun., Bank Hol. Mons., Good Friday. PM. Adm. £3.80. Tel: 0798–42207.

PORTMEIRION, Gwynedd. All year daily. Adm. £2.90 (April–Oct.) £1.45 (Nov.–March). Tel: 0766–770228.

POWDERHAM CASTLE, Exeter. 17 May–1 Oct. Sun.–Thurs. 11–6. Adm. charge. Tel: 0626–890243.

*POWIS CASTLE, Powys. 1 April–30 June, 1 Sept.–1 Nov. Wed.–Sun. and Bank Hol. Mons.; July and Aug. daily 11–6 (Mon. PM only). Adm. £5.40, Museum, garden £3.20. Tel: 0938–554336.

RABY CASTLE, Durham. Easter (Sat.–Wed.), 3 May–30 June, Wed. and Sun., July–Sept. daily (not Sat.). Also Bank Hol. Sat.–Tues., PM. Adm. £2.75, Grounds £1.00. Tel: 0833–60202.

RAGLEY HALL, Warks. 18 April–27 Sept. daily (not Mon., Fri.), PM. Open Bank Hols. Adm. £4.00, Garden £3.00. Tel: 0789–762090.

ROCKINGHAM CASTLE, Corby. Easter Sunday–30 Sept., Sun., Thurs., (also Bank Hol. Mon. and Tues. and Tues. in Aug.), PM. Adm. £3.30, Gardens only £2.00. Tel: 0536–770240.

*RUFFORD OLD HALL, Lancashire. 1 April–1 Nov. daily (not Fri.), PM. Adm. £2.60. Tel: 0704–821254.

SANDRINGHAM, Norfolk. 19 April–1 Oct. (closed 20 July–8 Aug.) Mon.–Thurs.; Sun. PM. Closed when Royal Family in residence. Adm. £2.50, Grounds only £2.00. Tel: 0553–772675.

SCONE PALACE, Perth. 17 April–12 Oct., daily. Sun., PM. Adm. £3.70. Tel: 0738–52300.

SHERBORNE CASTLE, Dorset. Easter Sat.–end Sept. Thurs., Sat., Sun. and Bank Hol. Mons. PM. Adm. charge. Tel: 0935–813182.

*SHUGBOROUGH, Staffs. 27 March–30 Oct., daily. Adm. £7.50 (House, Museum, Farm; House only, £3.00). Tel: 0889–881388.

SKIPTON CASTLE, N. Yorks. Open all year (not Christmas Day). Daily. (Sun., PM). Adm. £2.40. Tel: 0756–792442.

*SMALLHYTHE PLACE, Kent. April–Oct. Sat.–Wed. PM. Open Good Friday. Adm. £2.00. Tel: 05806–2334.

STANFORD HALL, Leics. Easter Saturday–end Sept. Sat., Sun., Bank Hols. (Mon. and Tues.). PM. Adm. £2.80. Tel: 0788–860250.

STONELEIGH ABBEY, Warks. Open by prior appointment only, Mon.–Fri. Tel: 0926–52116.

STONOR PARK, Oxon. Times vary. Adm. £3.25. Tel: 049163–587.

*STOURHEAD, Wilts. 1 April–1 Nov., Sat.–Wed. PM. Gardens all year, daily. Adm. House £4.00, Gardens £3.60. Tel: 0747–840348.

STRATFIELD SAYE HOUSE, Reading. 1 May–last Sun. in Sept. daily (not Fri.). Grounds March–Oct. daily, Nov.–Feb. weekends only. Adm. charge. Tel: 0256–882882.

SUDELEY CASTLE, Glos. April–Oct. daily, PM. Adm. £4.75. Tel: 0242–602308.

SULGRAVE MANOR, Northants. March–31 Dec., daily (not Wed.), Closed Christmas. Adm. £2.50. Tel: 0295–760205.

SYON HOUSE, Brentford, Middx. 1 April–29 Sept., Sat.–Thurs., and Sun. in Oct. PM. Adm. charge. Tel: 081–560 0881.

*TRERICE, Cornwall. 1 April–1 Nov. daily (not Tues.). Adm. £3.40. Tel: 0637–875404.

TYN-Y-RHOS HALL, and Shrine of St George, Shropshire. Sun. PM. Morning prayers 11.30. Tel: 0691–777898.

WARWICK CASTLE. Daily (not Christmas Day). Adm. charge. Tel: 0926–495421.

WILTON HOUSE, Wilts. Open daily 11–6, Sun. PM. Adm. £5.00. Tel: 0722–743115.

WOBURN ABBEY, Beds. 29 March–1 Nov. daily. 28 Dec.–28 March, weekends only. Adm. £5.50. Tel: 0525–290666.

Museums and Galleries

For National Art Galleries and Museums in London and Merseyside Museums, *see* Index.

Adm. admission; con. concessionary rate (prices are mostly those obtaining in 1992)

BARNARD CASTLE, Co. Durham – *The Bowes Museum.* European art from the late medieval period to 19th century. Fine porcelain and glass, tapestries and furniture. Music and costume galleries. English period rooms from Elizabeth I to Victoria; French decorative arts of 18th and 19th centuries; local antiquities. Temporary exhibitions. Open weekdays: May–Sept., 10–5.30, March, April, Oct., 10–5, Nov.–Feb., 10–4. Sun., 2–5 (summer); 2–4 (winter). Adm. charge.

BATH – *Roman Baths Museum.* Roman Baths complex of 1st century AD. Open daily, 9–6. Adm. (including adjoining 18th century Pump Room), £3.80, con. £1.85.
Museum of Costume, Assembly Rooms. Fashion from 16th century to date. Adm. £2.30, con. £1.30.
American Museum in Britain, Claverton Manor. American decorative arts from late 17th to mid 19th centuries. Open 28 March–1 Nov., daily (not Mon.), 2–5, Bank Hol. Mons. and preceding Suns. 11–5. During winter only on application. Adm. charge.
Victoria Art Gallery, Bridge Street. Open Mon.–Fri. 10–6, Sat. 10–5. Closed Sun., Bank Hols. Adm. free.

BEAMISH – *The North of England Open Air Museum*, Beamish, Co. Durham. Re-creates Northern life *c.*1900. Local buildings have been rebuilt and furnished, including the Town with houses, shops, etc., the Colliery Village, the Railway Station and Home Farm complete with agricultural machinery, animals and exhibitions. Open daily (not Mon. in winter), summer 10–6, winter 10–5. Check for Christmas opening.

BEAULIEU – *National Motor Museum.* Displays of vehicles dating from 1895 to present. Open daily (not Christmas Day), 10–6 (winter, 10–5). Adm. charge.

BELFAST – *Ulster Museum*, Botanic Gardens. Collections of Irish antiquities, natural and local history, fine and applied arts. Open Mon.–Fri. 10–5, Sat. 1–5, Sun. 2–5.
Ulster Folk and Transport Museum, Holywood. Indoor and outdoor exhibits. Open Oct.–March, weekdays 9.30–4, weekends 12.30–4.30 (April–Sept. 9.30–5, Sat. 10.30–6, Sun. 12–6). July, Aug. 10.30–6, Sun. 12–6. Adm. £2.50, con. £1.20.
Transport Museum, Holywood and Witham Street. History of land, sea and air transport in Ireland. Holywood site – open as for Folk Museum. Witham Street site open weekdays 10–5. Adm. 70p, children 40p. Special arrangements at Christmas and Easter.

BEVERLEY, N. Humberside. – *Museum of Army Transport.* Exhibits include field workshop, amphibious assault landing, railway section and aircraft. Open 10–5. Closed Christmas period. Adm. charge.

BIRMINGHAM – *City Museum and Art Gallery.* European art 14th to 20th centuries (particularly Pre-Raphaelites), sculpture, European gold, silver and jewellery, metalwork, glass, pottery and porcelain, furniture, textiles and costume, archaeology, local and natural history. Open Mon.–Sat. 9.30–5, Sun. 2–5. Closed Christmas Day, Boxing Day and New Year's Day. Adm. free.
Museum of Science and Industry, Newhall Street. From the Industrial Revolution to the present; many working machines. Open Mon.–Sat. 9.30–5, Sun. 2–5. Adm. free.
Also *Aston Hall, Blakesley Hall, Birmingham Nature Centre, Sarehole Mill*, and *Weoley Castle.*

BRADFORD – *Cartwright Hall Art Gallery*, Lister Park. British 19th and 20th century fine art.
Bolling Hall, off Wakefield Road, a furnished period house, mainly 17th and 18th century.
Industrial and Horses at Work Museum, Moorside Road, illustrates the local industries and transport in an old mill, with mill owner's and workers' houses and stables with shire horses.
Cliffe Castle, Keighley. Natural history, minerals and folk life material, and period rooms.
Manor House, Ilkley. Archaeology, local history and contemporary fine art. Open 10–5 (April–Sept. 10–6, except Industrial Museum). Closed Good Friday, Christmas Day, Boxing Day and Mon. (except Bank Hols.). Adm. free.

BRIGHTON – *The Royal Pavilion*, Palace of George IV. Chinoiserie interiors with much of the original furniture. Open daily 10–5 (June–Sept. 10–6). Closed Christmas Day and Boxing Day. Adm. charge.
Museum and Art Gallery, Church Street. Old master paintings; Willett pottery and porcelain collection, 20th century art and furniture, ethnography, archaeology, local history, musical instruments, costume gallery. Open Mon.–Sat. 10–5.45, Sun. 2–5. Closed Wed., Christmas Day, Boxing Day, Good Friday and 1 Jan. Adm. free.
Preston Manor, Preston Park. Thomas-Stanford/Macquoid bequests of English period furniture, china and silver. Servants quarters. Open Tues.–Sat. and Bank Hol. Mon. 10–5, Sun. 2–5. Closed Mon., Christmas Day, Boxing Day, Good Friday. Adm. charge.
The Booth Museum of Natural History, Dyke Road. Open 10–5, Sun. 2–5. Closed Thurs., Christmas Day, Boxing Day, Good Friday, and 1 Jan. Adm. free.

BRISTOL – *City Museum and Art Gallery.* Collections include geology, natural history, archaeology, Egyptology, ethnography, Bristol ceramics and the Bristol school of artists, silver, French paintings and Chinese ceramics. Glass collection.
Bristol Industrial Museum, Prince's Wharf. Collections connected with the Bristol region's industrial history, including an early working model railway and Bristol-built aero-engines.
Maritime Heritage Centre. Includes SS *Great Britain*, adm. charge.
Also *Red Lodge, Blaise Castle House Museum, Kings Weston Roman Villa, Georgian House.* Adm. charges. Times vary, tel: 0272–223571.

CAMBRIDGE – *Fitzwilliam Museum.* Egyptian, Greek, Near Eastern and Roman antiquities, coins and medals, medieval manuscripts, paintings and drawings, prints, sculpture, Oriental and Occidental fans, pottery and porcelain, textiles, arms and armour, medieval and renaissance objects of art, and a library. Open Tues.–Sat., Lower Galleries 10–2, Upper Galleries 2–5; Sun. 2.15–5. Closed 24 Dec.–1 Jan., Good Friday, Mon. incl. May Day Bank Hol. but not Easter and Bank Hol. Mons. Adm. free.

CANTERBURY – *Royal Museum and Art Gallery*, and *Buffs Regimental Museum.* Military artefacts and pictures. Open Mon.–Sat. 10–5. Adm. free.
Canterbury Heritage, a museum of the city's history in the medieval Poor Priest's Hospital, Stour Street. Open Mon.–Sat. 10.30–5, Sun. (June–Oct.) 1.30–5. Adm. £1.20, con. 90p.
Roman Mosaic Museum. Closed for redevelopment.
West Gate Museum. Arms and armour and display of city gate-house with battlements.

CARLISLE – *Tullie House Museum and Art Gallery*, Castle Street. Collections of archaeology, natural and social

history, fine and decorative arts in Jacobean house with Victorian and modern extensions. Open Mon.–Sat. 10–5, Sun. 12–5.
Guildhall Museum, Greenmarket. Civic and guild history and artefacts. Contact Tullie House Museum for information. Tel: 0228–34781.

CHESTER – *Grosvenor Museum*, Grosvenor Street. Roman collections, silver gallery, natural history, art and folk-life. Open weekdays 10.30–5, Sun. 2–5.
Chester Heritage Centre, St Michael's Church, Bridge Street Row. Displays Chester's history and architecture. Open weekdays 11–5, Sun. 12–5. Adm. charge.
King Charles Tower, City Walls. Civil War displays.
Water Tower, City Walls. Camera obscura. Open Mon.–Sat. 11–5, Sun. 12–5. Adm. charge.

COLCHESTER – *Colchester Castle.* Local archaeological antiquities, especially from Roman Colchester. Tours of Roman vaults, castle walls, chapel and prisons. Open Mon.–Sat. 10–5, Sun. April–Sept. 2–5. Closed Christmas period. Adm. £1.50, con. 75p (June–Sept. £2.00, con. £1.00).
Hollytrees Museum. 18th and 19th century costume, toys and social history. Open Mon.–Sat. 10–5. Closed Good Friday and Christmas period. Adm. free.
Natural History Museum, All Saints Church. Open as Hollytrees.
Social History Museum, Holy Trinity Church. Domestic life and crafts. Open as Hollytrees.
Tymperleys Clock Museum. Open Mon.–Sat., April–Oct. 10–5. Adm. free.

COVENTRY – *Herbert Art Gallery and Museum*, Jordan Well. 'Coventry Kid' special exhibition, natural history gallery, fine and decorative art. Open weekdays 10–5.30, Sun. 2–5. Closed Good Friday and Christmas period.
Museum of British Road Transport, St Agnes Lane, Hales Street. Open daily 10–5. Adm. £2.50, children £1.50.
Lunt Roman Fort, Baginton. June–Sept., 12–6 (closed Mon. and Thurs.). Adm. £1.00, children 50p.
Whitefriars Museum, London Road/Gulson Road. Open Thurs.–Sat., and some Bank Hols., 10–5.

CRICH, nr. Matlock, Derbyshire – *National Tramway Museum.* Open-air working museum with tram-rides. Open April–Oct. weekends and Bank Hols. 10–6.30. April–Sept., open daily (not Fri. except during school holidays) 10–5.30.

DERBY – *Museum and Art Gallery*, The Strand. Archaeology, geology, military, natural history, paintings by Joseph Wright of Derby, Derby porcelain. Open Mon. 11–5, Tues.–Sat. 10–5, Sun. and Bank Hols. 2–5. Adm. free.
Industrial Museum, Silk Mill, Full Street. Rolls-Royce collection of aero engines, a railway engineering gallery. Open as above. Adm. 30p, con. 10p.
Pickford's House, Friargate. 18th and 19th century period room settings, social history, decorative arts, costume and textiles. Open as above. Adm. 30p, con. 10p.

DORCHESTER – *Dorset County Museum.* Geology, archaeology, local and natural history and rural crafts of Dorset. Collection of Thomas Hardy's manuscripts, books, notebooks and drawings. Open Mon.–Sat. 10–5, closed Christmas Day, Boxing Day and Good Friday. Adm. £2.00, con. £1.00.

DURHAM – *Light Infantry Museum and Art Gallery.* Display of County regiment's 200-year history, arts and crafts exhibitions. Open weekdays (except Mon.) 10–5, Sun. and Bank Hol. Mon. 2–5. Closed Christmas Day and Boxing Day. Adm. 75p, con. 35p.
Oriental Museum, Elvet Hill. Collections ranging from Ancient Egypt to China and Japan.
Cathedral Treasury. Relics of St Cuthbert, church plate, medieval seals, manuscripts and vestments. Open weekdays 10–4.30, Sun. 2–4.30. Adm. 80p, con. 20p.
Old Fulling Mill Museum. Archaeological material from local excavations. Open Nov.–March, daily 12.30–3, April–Oct., daily 11–4. Adm. 50p, con. 25p.

EDINBURGH – *City Art Centre*, 2 Market Street. Late 19th and 20th century art, mostly Scottish, and temporary exhibitions. Open weekdays 10–5 (June–Sept. 10–6). Adm. free.
People's Story, Canongate Tolbooth, Canongate. Courthouse and prison, now museum of Edinburgh life. Open weekdays 10–5 (June–Sept. 10–6). Adm. free.
Huntly House, Canongate. Local history, collections of Edinburgh silver, glass and Scottish pottery. Open weekdays 10–5 (June–Sept. 10–6). Adm. free.
Lady Stair's House, Lawnmarket. Mon.–Sat. 10–5 (June–Sept. 10–6).
Lauriston Castle, Cramond Road South. April–Oct. daily (except Fri.), 11–5; Nov.–March, weekends only.
Museum of Childhood, High Street. Open weekdays 10–5 (June–Sept. 10–6). Adm. free.

EXETER – *Exeter Maritime Museum*, The Haven. Collection of boats. 'Cruel Sea' exhibition. Open daily 10–5. Adm. charge.
Royal Albert Memorial Museum and Art Gallery, Queen Street. Fine art, Exeter silver, ceramics, ethnography, natural and local history. Open Tues.–Sat. 10–5.30. Adm. free.
Underground Passages, High Street. Medieval water supply.
Rougemont House Museum. Costume and lace displayed in Georgian rooms. Castle Street. Open Mon.–Sat. 10–5.30.
St Nicholas' Priory. Norman priory.

FORT WILLIAM – *West Highland Museum*, Cameron Square. Historical, natural history and folk exhibits, including those of the 1745 Rising. Daily (except Sun.) 10–5; July and Aug. 9.30–6, Sun 2–5.

GLASGOW – *Art Gallery and Museum*, Kelvingrove. Old Masters, 19th century French paintings, archaeology and natural history, collection of armour.
People's Palace, Glasgow Green. History of city from 1175 to present.
The Burrell Collection, Pollok Park. Textiles, furniture, ceramics, stained glass, silver and paintings, especially 19th century French.
Pollok House, Pollok Park. Spanish paintings, furniture, silver, ceramics.
Haggs Castle Museum, St Andrews Drive. Children's museum with activity workshops.
Provand's Lordship, Castle Street. Oldest house in Glasgow, period furniture displays.
Rutherglen Museum, King Street. History of former royal burgh of Rutherglen.
Museum of Transport, Kelvin Hall.
All open Mon.–Sat. 10–5, Sun. 11–5. Adm. free.
Also *McLellan Galleries*, Sauchiehall Street. Major exhibition venue for large-scale temporary exhibitions. Adm. charge.

HULL – *Ferens Art Gallery.* European art, especially Dutch 17th century, British portraits from 17th–20th centuries, Humberside marine paintings, live art space and changing exhibitions.
Wilberforce House. Jacobean merchant's house, birthplace of Wilberforce; slavery relics, period furniture, costume and ceramics.
Streetlife. Museum of Transport; public service vehicles from the stage-coach to the last surviving Hull tram.

Hull and East Riding Museum. Archæology and transport; Celtic world, Iron Age Hasholme Boat, mosaics.
Town Docks Museum. Whaling, fishing, trawling, ships and shipping.
Old Grammar School. Hull's oldest secular building with story of Hull displays.
Spurn Lightship, built 1927, restored 1986. Closed Mon. and Tues. in winter.
All open Mon.–Sat. 10–5, Sun. 1.30–4.30.

HUNTINGDON – *Cromwell Museum.* Remaining portion of the 12th century Hospital of St John; portraits of Cromwell, his family and Parliamentary notables, and Cromwelliana. Open April–Oct., Tues.–Fri. 11–5, Sat, Sun. 11–4 (closed 1–2); Nov.–March, Tues.–Fri. 1–4, Sat. 11–1, 2–4, Sun. 2–4. Closed Bank Hols. other than Good Friday. Adm. free.

IPSWICH – *Ipswich Museum.* Suffolk geology, archaeology, natural history and ethnology. Temporary exhibitions. Open Tues.–Sat. 10–5.
Christchurch Mansion. Tudor house containing furniture, Suffolk portraits, English porcelain, pottery and glass. Collections of paintings (local artists, Gainsborough, Constable). Victorian room displays.
Wolsey Art Gallery, temporary exhibitions. Open Tues.–Sat. 10–5, Sun. 2.30–4.30. Closed Good Friday, Dec. 24, 25, 26. Adm. free.

LEEDS – *City Art Gallery.* English watercolours. British and European painting, modern sculpture, Henry Moore gallery, Print Room. Open Mon.–Fri. 10–6, Sat. 10–4, Sun. 2–5.
Temple Newsam House. Tudor/Jacobean house, furnished in style of 17th and 18th centuries; silver, European porcelain and pottery, pictures, etc. Open daily (not Mon. except Bank Hols.) 10.30–6.15, Weds. (May–Sept.) 10.30–8.30. Adm. £1.00, con. 45p.
Lotherton Hall, Gascoigne art and silver collection, oriental gallery, costume collection, 19th century furniture, ceramics; park and gardens. Open daily (not Mon. except Bank Hols.) 10.30–6.15, Thurs. (May–Sept.) 10.30–8.30. Adm. £1.00, con. 45p.
Abbey House Museum. Folk museum including three full-sized streets.
City Museum. Geology, archaeology, ethnography and natural history.
Also *Industrial Museum.*

LEICESTER – *Leicestershire Museum and Art Gallery*, New Walk. Natural history, geology, Egyptology, 18th–20th century European paintings, ceramics, silver.
Newarke Houses, The Newarke. Social history of Leicestershire from 1500, musical instruments, local clocks.
Jewry Wall Museum, St Nicholas Circle. Archaeology, Roman Jewry Wall and Baths, mosaics.
Belgrave Hall, Church Road. Queen Anne house with furniture and garden, coaches and agricultural collection.
Museum of the Royal Leicestershire Regiment, Oxford Street.
Museum of Technology, Corporation Road. Knitting industry and Power galleries. Horse-drawn and motor vehicles, beam engines.
Wygston's House Museum of Costume, Applegate. Costume from 1789–present.
All museums open weekdays 10–5.30, Sun. 2–5.30. Closed Christmas Day, Boxing Day and Good Friday.

LEWES – *Museum of Sussex Archaeology*, Barbican House, near Castle. Open weekdays, 10–5.30, Sun. 11–5.30. Adm. (including Castle and Lewes Living History Model) £2.50, con. £1.25.
Museum of Local History, Anne of Cleves House, Southover. Local history and folk museum. Open April–Oct., weekdays 10–5.30, Sun. 2–5.30. Adm. £1.60, con. 80p.

LINCOLN – *Usher Gallery.* Watches, miniatures, porcelain, silver, etc., Peter de Wint collection of oils and watercolours, Lincolnshire topographical drawings, *personalia* associated with Tennyson family. Open weekdays 10–5.30, Sun. 2.30–5.
City and County Museum, The Greyfriars. Geology and archaeology of Lincolnshire. Open weekdays 10–5.30, Sun. 2.30–5.
Museum of Lincolnshire Life. Covers the last 200 years; large agricultural collection. Open weekdays 10–5.30, Sun. 2–5.30.
National Cycle Museum, Brayford Wharf North. Vintage cycles. Open daily, except Christmas week, 10–5.
Lincoln Castle, 11th century, features Victorian Silent System Prison Chapel, Magna Carta. Open daily.

MANCHESTER – *City Art Galleries*, Mosley Street and Princess Street. Old Masters, Turner, Pre-Raphaelites; sculpture, furniture, porcelain, silver. Changing exhibitions. Weekdays 10–5.45, Sun. 2–5.45.
Whitworth Art Gallery, University of Manchester, Oxford Road. Watercolours, drawings, prints, textiles and wallpaper collections, 20th century British art. Mon.–Sat. 10–5 (Thurs. 10–9), closed Suns, Good Friday and Christmas week. Adm. free.
Museum of Science and Industry, Liverpool Road, Castlefield. Working machinery and displays in world's oldest passenger railway station. Open daily 10–5.
Gallery of English Costume, Platt Hall, Platt Fields, Rusholme. Exhibits from 16th century to present. Times vary.
Also *Heaton Hall*, Prestwich, *Wythenshawe Hall*, Northenden. Times vary, tel: 061–236 5244.

NEWCASTLE UPON TYNE – *Laing Art Gallery*, Higham Place. Fine art from 17th century, pottery, glass, silver and metalwork. Open Tues.–Fri. 10–5.30, Sat. 10–4.30, Sun. 2.30–5.30.
Castle Keep, St Nicholas Street. Oct.–March, Tues.–Sun. 9.30–4 (April–Sept. 9.30–5).
Trinity Maritime Centre and *Trinity House*, Broad Chare. Centre open April–Oct. Mon.–Fri. 11–4; Nov.–March, by arrangement. Trinity House, April–Nov. (chapel and entrance hall only; tour of house by appointment.)
John George Joicey Museum, City Road. Military and social history. Open Tues.–Fri. 10–5.30 (Sat. 10–4.30).
Museum of Science and Engineering, West Blandford Square. Tues.–Fri. 10–5.30, Sat. 10–4.30.
Newburn Hall Motor Museum, Townfield Gardens. Tues.–Sat. 10–8, Sun. 10–6.

NEWMARKET – *National Horseracing Museum.* Six galleries of displays relating to horseracing, horses and people connected with the sport. Sporting art galleries. Equine Tours. Open April–Dec., Tues.–Sat. 10–5, Sun. 12–5. Closed Mon. except Bank Hols, July, Aug. Adm. £2.50, con. £1.50/75p.

NORWICH – *Castle Museum.* Exhibits of art (including Norwich School), archaeology, natural history, silver and glass, Twining teapot gallery. Open Mon.–Sat., 10–5, Sun. 2–5.
Strangers' Hall, Charing Cross. Medieval mansion with period room settings from Tudor to Victorian times, toy display and costumes. Open Mon.–Sat. 10–5.
Bridewell Museum of Local Industries, Bridewell Alley. Open Mon.–Sat. 10–5.
St Peter Hungate Church Museum, Princes Street. 15th century church used for display of church art and antiquities. Brass rubbing centre. Open Mon.–Sat. 10–5.

NOTTINGHAM – *Castle Museum and Art Gallery*. Paintings and drawings 17th–20th centuries. Selection of decorative arts, history of Nottingham gallery with working models and Sherwood Foresters' regimental collection. Conducted tours of Mortimer's Hole caves.
Industrial Museum, Wollaton Park. Lacemaking machinery, steam engines, transport.
Canal Museum, Canal Street. History of local canals and river transport.
Natural History Museum, Wollaton Hall. Tudor building and park.
Museum of Costumes and Textiles, Castlegate.
Brewhouse Yard Museum, Castle Boulevard. Everyday life from the 17th century to present.
Green's Mill and Science Centre, Sneinton. Working windmill and interactive science centre.
Also *The Lace Hall* and the *Robin Hood Centre*.

OAKHAM – *Rutland County Museum*, Catmos Street. – Archaeology, local history, craft tools and agricultural implements. Open Tues.–Sat. 10–1, 2–5, Sun. (April–Oct.) 2–5, and Bank Hol. Mons.

OXFORD – *Ashmolean Museum*, Beaumont Street. The University's collections of European and Oriental fine and applied arts, Classical and Near-Eastern archaeology and numismatics. Open Tues.–Sat. 10–4, Sun. 2–4. Bank Hol. Mons. 2–5. Adm. free.

PLYMOUTH – *City Museum and Art Gallery*, Drake Circus. Fine art including Reynolds' portraits, Plymouth porcelain, archaeology, local and natural history. Tues.–Sat. 10–5.30, Sun. 2–5. Also Bank Holiday Mons. Adm. free.
Elizabethan House, 32 New Street.
Merchant's House, 33 St Andrew's Street. 16th century.
The Dome, the Hoe. Maritime history museum.

PORTSMOUTH – *City Museum and Art Gallery*, Museum Road.
Natural Science Museum and Butterfly House, Eastern Parade.
Southsea Castle and Museum, D-Day Museum, Clarence Esplanade. All open daily 10.30–5.30, except 24–26 Dec. Adm. charge.
Charles Dickens' Birthplace Museum, Old Commercial Road. Open 1 March–31 Oct., daily 10.30–5.30. Adm. charge.
Eastney Industrial Museum, Henderson Road. Open PM April–Sept. weekends, Bank Hols.; Oct.–March 1st Sun. of month. Adm. charge.
Naval Heritage Area. Tells the story of the Royal Navy using Henry VIII's *Mary Rose*, HMS *Victory* and the ironclad HMS *Warrior* (1860).
Royal Naval Museum. Open daily (except Christmas Day). Adm. charge.

ST ALBANS – *Museum of St Albans*, Hatfield Road. Story of St Albans since Roman times. Open weekdays 10–5, Sun. 2–5.
Verulamium Museum, St Michael's. Iron Age and Roman Verulamium including wall plasters, jewellery, mosaics. Open weekdays 10–5.30, Sun. 2–5.30. Adm. £2.00, con. £1.00.

SHEFFIELD – *City Museum*, Weston Park. Includes the Bateman Collection of antiquities from Peak District, cutlery and old Sheffield plate, local geology and wildlife.
Mappin Art Gallery, Weston Park. Paintings and sculpture of 18th–20th centuries (mainly British School) and contemporary works.
Abbeydale Hamlet, Abbeydale Road South. A late 18th–early 19th century scythe and steel works with associated housing.
Kelham Island Industrial Museum. Sheffield's industrial past.
Shepherd Wheel, Whiteley Wood. Water-powered cutlery grinding establishment.
Bishops' House, Meersbrook Park. Museum of local history in Tudor yeoman's house. Opening times vary. Tel: 0742–768588.

STOKE-ON-TRENT – *City Museum and Art Gallery*, Bethesda Street, Hanley. Major ceramic collections. Open daily 10–5, Sun. 2–5.
Chatterley Whitfield Mining Museum, Tunstall. Guided tours underground. Open daily.
Gladstone Pottery Museum, Longton. A working Victorian pottery.
Pottery factory tours are available Mon.–Fri., except during factory holidays, at the following: *Royal Doulton*, Nile Street, Burslem; *Spode*, Church Street, Stoke; *Beswick*, Gold Street, Longton; *Royal Grafton China*, Marlborough Road, Longton; *Coalport*, Park Street, Fenton, *Wedgwood's*, Barlaston; *Aynsley*, Uttoxeter Road, Longton.

STRATFORD-UPON-AVON – *Shakespeare's Birthplace*. Period furniture, rare books, MSS and memorabilia; Shakespeare Centre nearby.
Anne Hathaway's Cottage, Shottery. Home of Shakespeare's wife.
Mary Arden's House, Wilmcote. Tudor farmhouse home of Shakespeare's mother.
New Place, where Shakespeare died.
Hall's Croft. Shakespeare's daughter's home.
Grammar School attended by Shakespeare.
Royal Shakespeare Theatre. Burnt down 1926, rebuilt 1932. New *Swan Theatre*, opened in 1986.

STYAL – *Quarry Bank Mill*, Cheshire. History of the cotton industry, weaving demonstrations at water-powered cotton mill. Restored Apprentice House. Open all year. Closed Mon., Oct.–March. Open Bank Hols. Adm. charge.

WINCHESTER – *City Museum*. Weekdays 10–5, Sun. 2–5 (closed Mon. in winter).
Cathedral Library and *Triforium Gallery*. Illuminated manuscripts, sculpture, wood- and metalwork from 12th to 19th centuries. Times vary. Closed Mon. morning and Suns. Adm. charge.

WORCESTER – *City Museum and Art Gallery*. Natural history of Worcestershire, changing art exhibitions; also military museum. Open Mon.–Wed., Fri. 9.30–6, Sat. 9.30–5. Closed Thurs., Sun.
The Commandery, Sidbury. Civil War centre. Weekdays 10.30–5, Sun. 1.30–5.
Tudor House Museum, Friar Street. Local history. Mon.–Wed., Fri., Sat. 10.30–5.
Dyson Perrins Museum and Royal Worcester Porcelain Works, Severn Street. Mon.–Fri. 9.30–5, Sat. 10–5.

YORK – *Castle Museum*. Everyday life of the last three centuries. Open weekdays 9.30–5.30, Sun. 10–5.30 (closes 6.30 April–Oct., 4.45 Nov.–March). Adm. £3.50, con. £2.50.
Jorvik Viking Centre, Coppergate. Reconstruction of Viking York. Open daily. Adm. £3.50, con. £1.75.
Yorkshire Museum and Gardens, Museum Street, Roman Life gallery, archaeology, decorative arts, geology, natural history. Open weekdays 10–5, Sun. 1–5. Adm. £2.50, con. £1.25, family ticket £6.00. Gardens, Roman, Anglian and medieval ruins. Open weekdays 7.30–dusk (summer 7.30–8), Sun. 10–dusk.
Art Gallery, Exhibition Square. European paintings, 14th to 20th century; watercolours and prints of Yorkshire; modern English stoneware pottery. Open weekdays 10–5, Sun. 2.30–5. Adm. free.
Treasurer's House (National Trust), Chapter House Street. Open April–Oct. 10.30–5. Adm. £2.70, con. £1.20.

Hallmarks

Hallmarks are the symbols stamped on gold, silver or platinum articles to indicate that they have been tested at an official Assay Office and that they conform to one of the legal standards. With certain exceptions, all gold, silver, or platinum articles are required by law to be hallmarked before they are offered for sale. Hallmarking was instituted in England in 1300 under a statute of Edward I.

MODERN HALLMARKS

Normally a complete modern hallmark consists of four symbols – the sponsor's mark, the assay office mark, the standard mark and the date letter. Additional marks have been authorized from time to time.

Sponsor's Mark

Instituted in England in 1363, the sponsor's mark was originally a device such as a bird or fleur-de-lis. Now it consists of the initial letters of the name or names of the manufacturer or firm. Where two or more sponsors have the same initials, there is a variation in the surrounding shield or style of letters.

Standard Mark

The standard mark indicates that the content of the precious metal in the alloy from which the article is made, is not less than the legal standard. The legal standard is the minimum content of precious metal by weight in parts per thousand, and the standards are:

Gold	916.6	(22 carat)
	750	(18 carat)
	585	(14 carat)
	375	(9 carat)
Silver	958.4	(Britannia)
	925	(sterling)
Platinum	950	

The metals are marked as follows, if they are manufactured in the United Kingdom:

Gold – a crown followed by the millesimal figure for the standard, e.g. 916 for 22 carat (see table above).

Silver – Britannia silver: a full-length figure of Britannia. Sterling silver: a lion passant (England) or a lion rampant (Scotland).

Britannia Silver

Sterling Silver (England)

Sterling Silver (Scotland)

Platinum – an orb.

Assay Office Mark

This mark identifies the particular assay office at which the article was tested and marked. The existing assay offices in Britain are:

London, Goldsmiths' Hall, London EC2V 8AQ. Tel: 071-606 8975.

Birmingham, Newhall Street, Birmingham B3 1SB. Tel: 021-236 6951.

Gold and platinum

Silver

Sheffield, 137 Portobello Street, Sheffield S1 4DS. Tel: 0742-755111.

Edinburgh, 9 Granton Road, Edinburgh EH5 3QJ. Tel: 031-551 2189.

Assay offices formerly existed in other towns, e.g. Chester, Exeter, Glasgow, Newcastle, Norwich and York, each having its own distinguishing mark.

Date Letter

The date letter shows the year in which an article was assayed and hallmarked. Each alphabetical cycle has a distinctive style of lettering or shape of shield. The date letters were different at the various assay offices and the particular office must be established from the assay office mark before reference is made to tables of date letters.

The table on page 755 shows specimen shields and letters used by the London Assay Office on silver articles in each period from 1498. The same letters are found on gold articles but the surrounding shield may differ. Since 1 January 1975, each office has used the same style of date letter and shield for all articles.

OTHER MARKS

Foreign Goods

Since 1842 foreign goods imported into Britain have been required to be hallmarked before sale. The marks consist of the importer's mark, a special assay office mark, the figure denoting fineness (fineness mark) and the annual date letter.

The following are the assay office marks for gold imported articles. For silver and platinum the symbols remain the same but the shields differ in shape.

London

Birmingham

Sheffield

Edinburgh

Convention Hallmarks

Special marks at authorized assay offices of the signatory countries of the International Convention (Austria, Denmark, Finland, Ireland, Portugal, Norway, Sweden, Switzerland and the UK) are legally recognized in the United Kingdom as approved hallmarks. These consist of a sponsor's mark, a common control mark, a fineness mark (arabic numerals showing the standard in parts per thousand), and an assay office mark. There is no date letter.

The fineness marks are: for gold, 750 (18 carat), 585 (14 carat) and 375 (9 carat); for silver, 925 (sterling); and for platinum, 950. The common control marks are:

Gold (18 carat)

Silver

Platinum

Duty Marks

In 1784 an additional mark of the reigning sovereign's head was introduced to signify that the excise duty had been paid. The mark became obsolete on the abolition of the duty in 1890.

Commemorative Marks

There are three other marks to commemorate special events, the Silver Jubilee of King George V and Queen Mary in 1935, the Coronation of Queen Elizabeth II in 1953, and her Silver Jubilee in 1977.

LONDON (GOLDSMITHS' HALL) DATE LETTERS FROM 1498

---

	from	*to*
Black letter, small	1498–9	1517–8
Lombardic	1518–9	1537–8
Roman and other capitals	1538–9	1557–8
Black letter, small	1558–9	1577–8
Roman letter, capitals	1578–9	1597–8
Lombardic, external cusps	1598–9	1617–8
Italic letter, small	1618–9	1637–8
Court hand	1638–9	1657–8
Black letter, capitals	1658–9	1677–8
Black letter, small	1678–9	1696–7
Court hand	1697	1715–6
Roman letter, capitals	1716–7	1735–6
Roman letter, small	1736–7	1738–9
Roman letter, small	1739–40	1755–6
Old English, capitals	1756–7	1775–6
Roman letter, small	1776–7	1795–6
Roman letter, capitals	1796–7	1815–6
Roman letter, small	1816–7	1835–6
Old English, capitals	1836–7	1855–6
Old English, small	1856–7	1875–6
Roman letter, capitals [A to M *square* shield N to Z as shown]	1876–7	1895–6
Roman letter, small	1896–7	1915–6
Black letter, small	1916–7	1935–6
Roman letter, capitals	1936–7	1955–6
Italic letter, small	1956–7	1974
Italic letter, capitals	1975	

Countries of the World

WORLD AREA AND POPULATION

The total population of the world in mid-1990 was estimated at 5,292 million, compared with 3,019 million in 1960 and 2,070 million in 1930.

Continent, etc.	Area sq. miles '000	Area sq. km '000	Estimated population mid-1990
Africa	11,704	30,313	642,000,000
North America[1]	8,311	21,525	276,000,000
Latin America[2]	7,933	20,547	448,000,000
Asia[3]	10,637	27,549	3,113,000,000
Europe[4]	1,915	4,961	498,000,000
Former USSR	8,649	22,402	289,000,000
Oceania[5]	3,286	8,510	26,500,000
TOTAL	52,435	135,807	5,292,000,000

[1] Includes Greenland and Hawaii
[2] Mexico and the remainder of the Americas south of the USA
[3] Includes European Turkey, excludes former USSR
[4] Excludes European Turkey and former USSR
[5] Includes Australia, New Zealand and the islands inhabited by Micronesian, Melanesian and Polynesian peoples
Source: UN Demographic Yearbook 1990 (pub. 1992)

A United Nations report (*The Future Growth of World Population*) in 1958, pointed out that the population of the world had increased since the beginning of the 20th century at an unprecedented rate: in 1850 it was estimated at 1,094,000,000 and in 1900 at 1,500,000,000, an increase of 42 per cent in 50 years. By 1925 it had risen to 1,907,000,000 (23 per cent in 25 years) and by 1950 it had reached 2,500,000,000, an increase of 31 per cent in 25 years. Levels of population and the trend in distribution of the population by continents as forecast for the year 2000 were:

Continents, etc.	Estimated population	per cent
Africa	517,000,000	8.2
North America	312,000,000	5.0
Latin America†	592,000,000	9.4
Asia (excluding USSR)	3,870,000,000	61.8
Europe (including USSR)	947,000,000	15.1
Oceania	29,000,000	0.5
TOTAL	6,267,000,000	100

† Mexico and the remainder of the Americas south of USA

No complete survey of many countries has yet been achieved and consequently accurate area figures are not always available. Similarly, many countries have not recently, or have never, taken a Census. The areas of countries given below are derived from estimated figures published by the United Nations. The conversion factors used are:

(i) to convert square miles to square km, multiply by 2·589988

(ii) to convert square km to square miles, multiply by 0·3861022

Population figures for countries are derived from the most recent estimates available. Accurate and up-to-date data for the populations of capital cities are scarce, and definitions of cities' extent differ. The figures given below are the latest estimates available, and where it is known that the figure applies to an urban agglomeration this is indicated.

* latest Census figure
Ψ seaport
u.a. urban agglomeration

AFRICA

Country	Area sq. miles	Area sq. km	Population	Capital	Population of Capital
Algeria	919,595	2,381,741	24,960,000	Ψ Algiers	3,250,000
Angola	481,354	1,246,700	10,020,000	Ψ Luanda	2,000,000
Benin	43,484	112,622	4,736,000	Ψ Porto Novo	208,258
Botswana	224,607	581,730	1,300,000	Gaborone	128,500
Burkina	105,869	274,200	9,001,000	Ouagadougou	400,000
Burundi	10,747	27,834	5,458,000	Bujumbura	215,243
Cameroon	183,569	475,442	11,833,000	Yaoundé	635,670
Cape Verde Islands	1,557	4,033	370,000	Ψ Praia	57,748*
Central African Rep.	240,535	622,984	3,039,000	Bangui	473,817
Chad	495,755	1,284,000	5,678,000	Ndjaména	402,000
Comoros	838	2,171	550,000	Moroni	17,267*
Congo	132,047	342,000	2,271,000	Brazzaville	596,200*
Côte d'Ivoire	124,503	322,463	11,997,000	Ψ Abidjan	3,500,000
Djibouti	8,494	22,000	520,000	Ψ Djibouti	340,700
Egypt	386,662	1,001,449	53,513,000	Cairo	14,000,000
Equatorial Guinea	10,830	28,051	348,000	Ψ Malabo	30,418
Ethiopia	471,778	1,221,900	49,240,000	Addis Ababa	1,793,000
Gabon	103,347	267,667	1,172,000	Ψ Libreville	251,000
Gambia	4,361	11,295	861,000	Ψ Banjul (*u.a.*)	109,986

Country	Area sq. miles	Area sq. km	Population	Capital	Population of Capital
Ghana	92,100	238,537	15,028,000	Ψ Accra (*u.a.*)	1,781,100
Guinea	94,926	245,857	5,755,000	Ψ Conakry	763,000
Guinea-Bissau	13,948	36,125	964,000	Ψ Bissau	109,214*
Kenya	224,961	582,646	24,032,000	Nairobi	1,400,000
Lesotho	11,720	30,355	1,774,000	Maseru	288,951*
Liberia	43,000	111,369	2,607,000	Ψ Monrovia	425,000
Libya	679,362	1,759,540	4,545,000	Ψ Tripoli	1,000,000
Madagascar	226,669	587,041	11,197,000	Antananarivo	1,000,000
Malawi	45,747	118,484	8,289,000	Lilongwe	233,973*
Mali	478,791	1,240,000	8,156,000	Bamako	646,163*
Mauritania	397,955	1,030,700	2,024,000	Nouakchott	500,000
Mauritius	790	2,045	1,022,456	Ψ Port Louis	141,870
Mayotte (*Fr.*)	144	372	67,000	Mamoundzou	12,000
Morocco	172,414	446,550	27,575,000	Ψ Rabat	1,123,000
Western Sahara	102,703	266,000	178,000	Laayoune	96,784*
Mozambique	309,495	801,590	15,656,000	Ψ Maputo	1,150,000
Namibia	318,261	824,292	1,781,000	Windhoek	110,000
Niger	489,191	1,267,080	7,731,000	Niamey	410,000
Nigeria	356,669	923,768	108,542,000	Abuja	378,671
Réunion (*Fr.*)	969	2,510	598,000	St Denis	122,000
Rwanda	10,169	26,338	7,181,000	Kigali	156,000
St Helena (*UK*)	47	122	5,644	Ψ Jamestown	1,332
Ascension Island	34	88	1,192	Ψ Georgetown	—
Tristan da Cunha	38	98	288	Ψ Edinburgh	—
São Tomé & Príncipe	372	964	121,000	Ψ São Tomé	25,000
Senegal	75,750	196,192	7,327,000	Ψ Dakar	1,000,000
Seychelles	108	280	67,378	Ψ Victoria	24,733
Sierra Leone	27,699	71,740	4,151,000	Ψ Freetown	470,000
Somalia	246,201	637,657	7,497,000	Ψ Mogadishu	1,000,000
South Africa	471,445	1,221,031	35,282,000	Pretoria (*u.a.*) Ψ Cape Town (*u.a.*)	822,925 1,911,521
Sudan	967,500	2,505,813	25,203,000	Khartoum (*u.a.*)	3,000,000
Swaziland	6,704	17,363	768,000	Mbabane	38,290
Tanzania	364,900	945,087	25,635,000	Dodoma	85,000
Togo	21,925	56,785	3,531,000	Ψ Lomé	366,476
Tunisia	63,170	163,610	8,180,000	Ψ Tunis	1,394,749
Uganda	91,259	236,036	18,794,000	Kampala (*u.a.*)	750,000
Zaire	905,567	2,345,409	35,562,000	Kinshasa	2,778,281*
Zambia	290,586	752,614	8,073,000	Lusaka (*u.a.*)	1,000,000
Zimbabwe	150,804	390,580	9,369,000	Harare	681,000

AMERICA

Country	Area sq. miles	Area sq. km	Population	Capital	Population of Capital
North America					
Canada	3,849,646	9,970,537	27,296,859	Ottawa (*u.a.*)	313,987*
Greenland (*Den.*)	840,004	2,175,600	55,558	Ψ Godthab	8,425
Mexico	761,605	1,972,547	86,000,000	Mexico City (*u.a.*)	14,987,051
St Pierre and Miquelon (*Fr.*)	93	242	6,300	Ψ St Pierre	—
United States	3,536,338	9,155,579	248,709,873*	Washington, DC	606,900
Central America and the West Indies					
Anguilla (*UK*)	35	91	8,800	The Valley	1,400
Antigua and Barbuda	170	440	65,962	Ψ St John's	30,000
Aruba (*Neth.*)	75	193	60,000	Ψ Oranjestad	20,000
Bahamas	5,380	13,935	254,000	Ψ Nassau	171,000*
Barbados	166	431	255,000	Ψ Bridgetown	7,466
Belize	8,867	22,965	191,000	Belmopan	5,000
Bermuda (*UK*)	20	53	60,000	Ψ Hamilton	2,000
Cayman Islands (*UK*)	100	259	27,000	Ψ George Town	12,921
Costa Rica	19,575	50,700	3,000,000	San José (*u.a.*)	1,068,206
Cuba	42,804	110,861	10,608,000	Ψ Havana	2,100,000

Country	Area sq. miles	Area sq. km	Population	Capital	Population of Capital
Dominica	290	751	82,000	Ψ Roseau	11,000
Dominican Republic	18,816	48,734	7,170,000	Ψ Santo Domingo (*u.a.*)	1,313,172*
Grenada	133	344	86,000	Ψ St George's	10,000
Guadeloupe (*Fr.*)	687	1,779	386,600	Ψ Basse-Terre	14,000
Guatemala	42,042	108,889	9,467,000	Guatemala City	1,675,589
Haiti	10,714	27,750	5,693,000	Ψ Port au Prince	1,000,000
Honduras	43,277	112,088	5,105,000	Tegucigalpa	640,900
Jamaica	4,244	10,991	2,420,000	Ψ Kingston (*u.a.*)	696,300
Martinique (*Fr.*)	425	1,102	359,800	Ψ Fort de France	100,576
Montserrat (*UK*)	38	98	13,000	Ψ Plymouth	3,000
Netherlands Antilles (*Neth.*)	371	961	188,000	Ψ Willemstad	50,000
Nicaragua	50,193	130,000	3,871,000	Managua	615,000
Panama	29,762	77,082	2,370,000	Ψ Panama City	1,063,565
Puerto Rico (*US*)	3,435	8,897	3,522,037	Ψ San Juan (*u.a.*)	1,816,300
St Christopher and Nevis	101	261	44,000	Ψ Basseterre	15,000
St Lucia	238	616	150,000	Ψ Castries	56,000
St Vincent and the Grenadines	150	388	116,000	Ψ Kingstown	33,694
El Salvador	8,124	21,041	5,252,000	San Salvador (*u.a.*)	2,000,000
Trinidad and Tobago	1,981	5,130	1,227,000	Ψ Port of Spain	59,649
Turks and Caicos Is. (*UK*)	166	430	9,000	Ψ Grand Turk	4,500
Virgin Islands:					
British (*UK*)	59	153	10,985*	Ψ Road Town	2,479
US (*US*)	132	342	101,809	Ψ Charlotte Amalie	11,756
South America					
Argentina	1,068,302	2,766,889	32,370,298*	Ψ Buenos Aires	2,955,002
Bolivia	424,165	1,098,581	7,400,000	La Paz	1,000,000
Brazil	3,286,488	8,511,965	150,368,000	Brasilia	1,803,478
Chile	292,258	756,945	13,173,000	Santiago	4,172,293
Colombia	439,737	1,138,914	32,987,000	Bogotá	5,000,000
Ecuador	109,484	283,561	10,782,000	Quito	1,387,887
Falkland Islands (*UK*)	4,700	12,173	2,121*	Ψ Stanley	1,643*
French Guiana (*Fr.*)	35,135	91,000	114,900	Ψ Cayenne	41,000
Guyana	83,000	214,969	796,000	Ψ Georgetown	187,056
Paraguay	157,048	406,752	4,277,000	Asunción (*u.a.*)	729,307
Peru	496,225	1,285,216	22,332,000	Lima (*u.a.*)	6,415,000
South Georgia (*UK*)	1,580	4,092	—	—	—
Suriname	63,037	163,265	422,000	Ψ Paramaribo (*u.a.*)	182,100
Uruguay	68,037	176,215	3,094,000	Ψ Montevideo	1,355,312
Venezuela	352,144	912,050	19,735,000	Caracas (*u.a.*)	2,784,000

ASIA

Country	Area sq. miles	Area sq. km	Population	Capital	Population of Capital
Afghanistan	250,000	647,497	16,121,000	Kabul	2,000,000
Bahrain	240	622	503,000	Ψ Manama	108,684*
Bangladesh	55,598	143,998	108,000,000	Dhaka	6,000,000
Bhutan	18,147	47,000	1,516,000	Thimphu	15,000
Brunei	2,226	5,765	260,863	Bandar Seri Begawan	46,229
Cambodia	69,898	181,035	8,246,000	Ψ Phnom Penh	500,000
China[1]	3,705,408	9,596,961	1,143,330,000	Beijing (Peking) (*u.a.*)	10,860,000
Hong Kong (*UK*)	416	1,074	5,800,000	Ψ Victoria	—
India	1,269,346	3,287,590	843,930,861	Delhi	8,375,188
Indonesia	735,358	1,904,569	179,300,000	Ψ Jakarta	7,885,519
Iran	636,296	1,648,000	54,607,000	Tehran	6,042,584
Iraq	167,925	434,924	18,920,000	Baghdad	3,205,665
Israel[2]	8,019	20,770	5,090,000	Tel Aviv	1,624,100
Japan	145,834	377,708	123,537,000	Tokyo (*u.a.*)	11,935,700
Jordan	37,738	97,740	2,910,000	Amman	1,100,000
Kazakhstan	1,049,155	2,716,626	16,464,000	Alma Ata	1,134,000

Country	Area sq. miles	Area sq. km	Population	Capital	Population of Capital
Korea, DPR (North)	46,540	120,538	21,773,000	Pyongyang	1,500,000
Korea, Rep. of (South)	38,025	98,484	42,793,000	Seoul	9,991,089
Kuwait	6,880	17,818	1,000,000	Ψ Kuwait (city)	400,000
Kyrgyzstan	76,642	198,426	4,258,000	Biskek	646,000
Laos	91,429	231,800	4,139,000	Vientiane	120,000
Lebanon	4,015	10,400	2,701,000	Ψ Beirut	702,000
Macao (*Port.*)	6	16	479,000	Ψ Macao	—
Malaysia	127,317	329,749	17,861,000	Kuala Lumpur	1,103,200
Maldives	115	298	215,000	Ψ Malé	46,334
Mongolia	604,250	1,565,000	2,190,000	Ulan Bator	530,000
Myanmar (Burma)	261,218	676,552	41,675,000	Ψ Yangon (Rangoon) (*u.a.*)	3,973,872
Nepal	54,342	140,747	18,916,000	Kathmandu	235,160
Oman	82,030	212,457	1,502,000	Ψ Muscat	400,000
Pakistan	307,374	746,045	112,049,000	Islamabad (*u.a.*)	350,000
Philippines	115,831	300,000	61,480,000	Ψ Manila	1,876,195
Qatar	4,247	11,000	368,000	Ψ Doha	220,000
Saudi Arabia	830,000	2,149,640	14,870,000	Riyadh	1,500,000
Singapore	241	626	3,002,800	—	—
Sri Lanka	25,332	65,610	17,243,000	Ψ Colombo	1,963,000
Syria	71,498	185,180	12,116,000	Damascus	1,378,000
Tajikistan	54,019	139,855	5,093,000	Dushanbe	596,000
Taiwan	13,800	35,742	20,536,233	Taipei	2,702,678
Thailand	198,457	514,000	57,196,000	Ψ Bangkok	5,400,000
Turkey[3]	301,382	780,576	56,473,035	Ankara	3,236,626
Turkmenistan	188,417	487,811	3,523,000	Ashkhabad	390,000
United Arab Emirates	32,278	83,600	1,909,000	Abu Dhabi	798,000
Uzbekistan	172,742	447,229	19,810,000	Tashkent	2,216,000
Vietnam	127,242	329,556	66,200,000	Hanoi	1,089,000
Yemen	203,850	527,696	7,770,000	Sana'a	427,150

[1] Including Tibet
[2] Including East Jerusalem, the Golan Heights and Israeli citizens on the West Bank
[3] Including Turkey in Europe

EUROPE

Country	Area sq. miles	Area sq. km	Population	Capital	Population of Capital
Albania	11,099	28,748	3,250,000	Tirana	239,381
Andorra	175	453	52,000	Andorra La Vella	19,003
Armenia	11,306	29,271	3,305,000	Erevan	1,186,000
Austria	32,374	83,849	7,860,000	Vienna	1,533,176
Azerbaijan	33,436	86,565	7,021,000	Baku	1,772,000
Belarus	80,300	207,897	10,152,000	Minsk	1,583,000
Belgium	11,781	30,513	9,928,000	Brussels (*u.a.*)	970,501
Bosnia-Hercegovina	19,735	51,129	4,100,000	Sarajevo	447,000
Bulgaria	42,823	110,912	9,010,000	Sofia	1,136,875
Croatia	21,823	56,538	4,600,000	Zagreb	763,000
Cyprus	3,572	9,251	702,000	Nicosia	168,800
Czechoslovakia	49,370	127,869	15,662,000	Prague	1,209,149
Denmark	16,629	43,069	5,135,000	Ψ Copenhagen (*u.a.*)	1,495,736
Faroe Islands	540	1,399	47,485	Ψ Thorshavn	10,726
Estonia	17,413	45,082	1,576,000	Talinn	480,000
Finland	137,851	337,032	4,986,000	Ψ Helsinki	488,777
France	211,208	547,026	56,614,000	Paris (*u.a.*)	9,060,000
Georgia	26,911	69,673	5,401,000	Tbilisi	1,211,000
Germany	137,738	365,755	79,753,000	Berlin	3,376,800
Gibraltar (*UK*)	2	6	31,265	Ψ Gibraltar	—
Greece	50,944	131,944	10,256,464	Athens (*u.a.*)	3,096,775
Hungary	35,919	93,030	10,335,000	Budapest	2,016,000
Iceland	39,768	103,000	253,482	Ψ Reykjavik (*u.a.*)	95,811
Ireland, Republic of	27,136	70,283	3,523,401*	Ψ Dublin	477,675*
Italy	116,304	301,225	57,663,000	Rome (*u.a.*)	2,828,692
Latvia	24,695	63,935	2,677,000	Riga	900,000
Liechtenstein	61	157	2,667,000	Vaduz	4,874

Country	Area sq. miles	Area sq. km	Population	Capital	Population of Capital
Lithuania	26,173	67,761	3,723,000	Vilnius	592,500
Luxembourg	998	2,586	378,400	Luxembourg	77,500
Macedonia	9,925	25,713	1,900,000	Skopje	503,000
Malta	122	316	359,517	Ψ Valletta	9,199
Moldova	13,912	36,018	4,335,000	Kishinev	684,000
Monaco	0.4	1	28,000	Monaco-Ville	1,234
Montenegro	5,331	13,812	600,000	Titograd	95,000
Netherlands	15,770	40,844	15,009,000	Ψ Amsterdam (*u.a.*)	1,034,562
Norway[1]	125,181	324,219	4,242,000	Ψ Oslo	454,927
Poland	120,725	312,677	38,900,000	Warsaw	1,655,063
Portugal[2]	35,553	92,082	10,525,000	Ψ Lisbon	2,128,000
Romania	91,699	237,500	23,200,000	Bucharest	2,036,894
Russia[3]	593,391	17,070,289	147,022,000	Moscow	8,879,000
San Marino	23	61	24,000	San Marino	—
Serbia	34,175	88,538	9,300,000	Belgrade	1,455,000
Slovenia	7,816	20,251	1,800,000	Ljubljana	253,000
Spain[4]	194,897	504,782	38,959,000	Madrid (*u.a.*)	4,731,224
Sweden	173,732	449,964	8,559,000	Ψ Stockholm (*u.a.*)	669,485
Switzerland	15,943	41,293	6,712,000	Berne	135,543
Ukraine	252,046	652,547	51,471,000	Kiev	2,577,000
United Kingdom[5]	94,227	244,046	55,701,000	Ψ London (*u.a.*)	6,377,900
England	50,363	130,439	46,161,000	—	—
Wales	8,018	20,768	2,799,000	Ψ Cardiff	272,600
Scotland	30,414	78,772	4,957,000	Ψ Edinburgh	421,213
Northern Ireland	5,452	14,121	1,583,000	Ψ Belfast (*u.a.*)	295,223
Vatican City State	0.2	0.44	1,000	Vatican City	—

[1] Excludes Svalbard and Jan Mayen Islands (approx. 24,101 sq. miles (62,422 sq. km) and 3,000 population)
[2] Includes Madeira (314 sq. miles) and the Azores (922 sq. miles)
[3] Includes Russia in Asia
[4] Includes Balearic Islands, Canary Islands, Ceuta and Melilla
[5] Includes Isle of Man (227 sq. miles (588 sq. km), 64,282 population), and Channel Islands (75 sq. miles (195 sq. km), 137,196 population)

OCEANIA

Country	Area sq. miles	Area sq. km	Population	Capital	Population of Capital
Australia	2,967,909	7,686,848	17,335,900	Canberra	303,200
Norfolk Island	14	36	1,912	Ψ Kingston	—
Fiji	7,055	18,274	764,000	Ψ Suva	69,665
French Polynesia (*Fr.*)	1,544	4,000	206,000	Ψ Papeete	24,200
Guam (*US*)	212	549	132,152	Agaña	—
Kiribati	281	728	68,000	Tarawa	17,921
Marshall Islands	70	181	42,018	Majuro	20,000
Micronesia, Fed. States of	271	701	100,000	Palikir	—
Nauru	8	21	8,042	Ψ Nauru	—
New Caledonia (*Fr.*)	7,358	19,058	167,000	Ψ Noumea	65,000
New Zealand	103,736	268,676	3,435,000	Ψ Wellington (*u.a.*)	325,700
Cook Islands	91	236	17,185*	Avarua	—
Niue	100	259	2,239	Alofi	—
Ross Dependency†	286,696	750,310	—	—	—
Tokelau	5	12.9	1,578	—	—
Northern Mariana Islands (*US*)	184	476	43,555	Saipan	39,090
Palau (*US*)	192	497	15,105	Koror	10,493
Papua New Guinea	178,260	461,691	3,699,000	Ψ Port Moresby	173,500
Pitcairn Islands (*UK*)	1.9	5	66	—	—
Samoa, Eastern (*US*)	76	197	46,773	Ψ Pago Pago	3,075
Solomon Islands	10,983	28,446	320,000	Ψ Honiara	30,499*
Tonga	270	699	95,000	Ψ Nuku'alofa	30,000
Tuvalu	10	25	9,000	Ψ Funafuti	2,856
Vanuatu	4,706	12,190	142,900	Ψ Port Vila	19,400
Wallis and Futuna Islands (*Fr.*)	106	274	14,000	Ψ Mata-Utu	—
Western Samoa	1,097	2,842	164,000	Ψ Apia	33,100*

† Includes permanent shelf ice

THE ANTARCTIC

The Antarctic is generally defined as the area lying within the Antarctic Convergence, the zone where cold northward-flowing Antarctic sea water sinks below warmer southward-flowing water. This zone is at about latitude 50° S. in the Atlantic Ocean and latitude 55°–62° S. in the Pacific Ocean. The continent itself lies almost entirely within the Antarctic Circle, an area of about 14.25 million square km (5.5 million square miles), 99 per cent of which is permanently ice-covered. The average thickness of the ice is 2,450 m (7,100 ft) but in places exceeds 4,500 m (14,500 ft). Some mountains protrude, the highest being Vinson Massif, 4,897 m (16,067 ft). The ice amounts to some 30 million cubic km (7.2 million cubic miles) and represents more than 90 per cent of the world's fresh water.

Along one-third of the Antarctic coastline, land-ice flowing outwards forms extensive ice shelves, fragments of which break off to form tabular icebergs, leaving ice-cliffs up to 50 m (150 ft) high. Much of the sea freezes in winter, forming fast ice which breaks up in summer and drifts north as pack ice.

The most conspicuous physical features of the continent are its high inland plateau (much of it over 3,000 m (10,000 ft)), the Transantarctic Mountains (which together with the large embayments of the Weddell Sea and Ross Sea mark the approximate boundary between East and West Antarctica), and the mountainous Antarctic Peninsula and off-lying islands which extend northwards towards South America. The continental shelf averages about 32 km (20 miles) in width (half the global mean, and in places it is non-existent) and reaches exceptional depths (390–780 m (1,300–2,600 ft), which is three to six times the global mean).

Climate

On land, summer temperatures range from just below freezing around the coast to −34° C (about −30° F) on the plateau, and in winter from −20° C (about −4° F) on the coast to −65° C (about −85° F) inland. Over a large area the maxima do not exceed −15° C (+5° F).

Precipitation is scanty over the plateau but amounts to 25–76 cm (10–30 in) (water equivalent) along the coast and some scientific stations are permanently buried by snow. Some rain falls over the more northerly areas in summer. Gravity winds on the plateau slopes and cyclonic storms further north can both exceed 160 km/h (100 m.p.h.) and gusts have been known to reach 240 km/h (150 m.p.h.). Visibility can be reduced to zero in blizzards.

Flora and Fauna

Although a small number of flowering plants, ferns and clubmosses occur on the sub-Antarctic islands, only two (a grass and a pearlwort) extend south of 60° S. Antarctic vegetation is dominated by lichens and mosses, with a few liverworts, algae and fungi. Most of these occur around the coast or on islands, but lichens and some mosses also occur inland.

The only land animals are tiny insects and mites with nematodes, rotifers, and tardigrades in the mosses, but large numbers of seals, penguins and other sea-birds go ashore to breed in the summer. The emperor penguin is the only species which breeds ashore throughout the winter. By contrast, the Antarctic seas abound with life, a wide variety of invertebrates (including krill) and fish providing food for the seals, penguins and other birds, and a residual population of whales.

Potential Resources

In the 180 years from Captain James Cook's circumnavigation of the Antarctic in 1772–5 to the mid-1950s, expeditions to the Antarctic made major contributions to geographical and scientific knowledge of the area.

Increasing pressure on the world's food and mineral supplies has stimulated interest in the potential resources even in the extremely hostile polar environment. Minerals may be present in great variety but not in commercially exploitable concentrations in accessible localities. There are indications that off-shore hydrocarbons may be present but mostly below great depths of stormy, ice-infested seas.

Currently, the chief interest is in marine protein, including the shrimp-like krill already fished commercially by Japan, Poland and the Commonwealth of Independent States. Research to ensure rational management of stocks of this organism is being continued by international groups, but it is estimated that they could sustain a yield equal to the present total annual world fish catch.

The Antarctic Treaty

The International Geophysical Year 1957–8 gave great impetus to Antarctic research, increasing the number of stations from 17 to 44 and the number of nations involved in research from four to 12 by 1957. The co-operative scientific effort proved so fruitful that the 12 nations involved (Argentina, Australia, Belgium, Chile, France, Japan, New Zealand, Norway, South Africa, the USSR, the UK and the USA), pledged themselves to promote scientific and technical co-operation unhampered by politics. Hence the Antarctic Treaty was negotiated and signed by the 12 states on 1 December 1959 in Washington DC.

The 12 signatories to the treaty agreed to establish free use of the Antarctic continent for peaceful scientific purposes; to freeze all territorial claims and disputes in the Antarctic; to ban all military activities in the area; and to prohibit nuclear explosions and the disposal of radioactive waste. Since then additional agreements have been reached to promote conservation and restrict tourism, waste disposal and pollution.

The Antarctic Treaty was defined as covering areas south of latitude 60° S., excluding the high seas but including the ice shelves, and came into force in 1961. It has since been signed by a further 28 states, 14 of which are active in the Antarctic and have therefore been accorded consultative status. In 1991 a protocol to the treaty was adopted by the signatory states which introduced a range of measures to protect Antarctica's environment and prohibits mineral exploitation and mining for at least 50 years.

Territorial Claims

Under the provisions of the Antarctic Treaty of 1959 all territorial claims and disputes were frozen without the acceptance or denial of the claims of the various claimants. The US and Soviet governments also made it clear that although they had not made any specific territorial claims, they did not relinquish the right to make such claims.

Seven states have made claims in the Antarctic: Argentina claims the part of Antarctica between 74° W. and 25° W., and Chile that part between 90° W. and 53° W.; Britain claims the British Antarctic Territory, an area of 1,810,000 square km (700,000 square miles) between 20° and 80° W. longitude; France claims Adélie Land, 432,000 square km (166,800 square miles) between 136° and 142° E.; Australia claims the Australian Antarctic Territory, 6,120,000 square km (2,320,000 square miles) between 160° and 45° E. longitude excluding Adélie Land; Norway claims Queen Maud Land between 20° W. and 45° E.; and New Zealand claims the Ross Dependency, 450,000 square km (175,000 miles) between 160° E. and 150° W. longitude. The Argentinian, British and Chilean claims overlap while the part of the continent between 90° W. and 150° W. is unclaimed by any state.

Scientific Research

There are over 40 permanently occupied stations operated by the following nations: Argentina (6), Australia (4), Brazil (1), Chile (3), China (2), Commonwealth of Independent States (7), France (4), Germany (2), India (1), Japan (2), New Zealand (2), Poland (1), South Africa (3), South Korea (1), Uruguay (1), UK (5), USA (3, including one at the South Pole).

The staff of these stations and summer field-workers are the only people present on the continent and off-lying islands. There are no indigenous inhabitants.

LARGEST CITIES OF THE WORLD

In most cases figures refer to urban agglomerations.

	Population		Population
MEXICO CITY, Mexico	14,987,051	MOSCOW, Russia	8,879,000
CAIRO, Egypt	14,000,000	DELHI, India	8,375,188
Ψ Shanghai, China	12,760,000	Ψ JAKARTA, Indonesia	7,885,519
Ψ Bombay, India	12,571,720	Ψ New York, USA	7,322,564
TOKYO, Japan	11,718,720	Manila, Philippines	6,720,050
Ψ Calcutta, India	10,916,272	Rio de Janiero, Brazil	6,603,388
BEIJING, China	10,860,000	Karachi, Pakistan	6,500,000
São Paulo, Brazil	10,063,110	LIMA, Peru	6,415,000
SEOUL, South Korea	9,991,089	Ψ LONDON, UK	6,377,900
PARIS, France	9,060,000	TEHRAN, Iran	6,042,000

Currencies of the World

AND EXCHANGE RATES AGAINST £ STERLING

Franc CFA = Franc de la Communauté financière africaine
Franc CFP = Franc des Comptoirs français du Pacifique

COUNTRY	MONETARY UNIT	AVERAGE RATE TO £ 3 September 1991	AVERAGE RATE TO £ 1 September 1992
Afghanistan	Afghani (Af) of 100 puls	Af 99.25	Af 99.25
Albania	Lek (Lk) of 100 qindarka	Lk 10.0850	Lk 218.00
Algeria	Algerian dinar (DA) of 100 centimes	DA 30.5920	DA 40.05
Andorra	French and Spanish currencies are both in use	—	—
Angola	Kwanza (Kz) of 100 lwei	Kz 99.8395	Kz 1079.95
Antigua and Barbuda	East Caribbean dollar (EC$) of 100 cents	EC$ 4.5510	EC$ 5.3515
Argentina	Peso of 10,000 australes	A 16767.5	Pesos 19620
Armenia	Rouble of 100 kopeks	—	Roubles 1.0494
Aruba	Aruban florin	Florins 3.0170	Florins 3.5475
Australia	Australian dollar ($A) of 100 cents	$A 2.1485	$A 2.7595
Austria	Schilling of 100 Groschen	Schilling 20.695	Schilling 19.645
Azerbaijan	Roubles of 100 kopeks	—	Roubles 1.0494
Azores	Currency is that of Portugal	Esc 252$00	Esc 243$25
Bahamas	Bahamian dollar (B$) of 100 cents	B$ 1.6850	B$ 1.9820
Bahrain	Bahrain dinar (BD) of 1,000 fils	BD 0.6343	BD 0.7475
Balearic Isles	Currency is that of Spain	Pesetas 183.00	Pesetas 180.95
Bangladesh	Taka (Tk) of 100 poisha	Tk 57.60	Tk 77.95
Barbados	Barbados dollar (BD$) of 100 cents	BD$ 3.39	BD$ 3.9865
Belarus	Rouble of 100 kopeks	—	Roubles 1.0494
Belgium	Belgian franc (or frank) of 100 centimes (centiemen)	Francs 60.55	Francs 57.45
Belize	Belize dollar (BZ$) of 100 cents	BZ$ 3.3710	BZ$ 3.9640
Benin	Franc CFA	Francs 499.63	Francs 475.125
Bermuda	Bermuda dollar of 100 cents	$ 1.6850	$ 1.9820
Bhutan	Ngultrum of 100 chetrum (Indian currency is also legal tender)	Ngultrum 43.25	Ngultrum 56.55
Bolivia	Boliviano ($b) of 100 centavos	$b 6.1099	$b 7.3890
Bosnia-Hercegovina	Dinar of 100 paras	—	Dinars 396.4
Botswana	Pula (P) of 100 thebe	P 3.4730	P 4.0545
Brazil	Cruzeiro (BRC) of 100 centavos	BRC 664.475	BRC 9964.80
British Virgin Islands	US dollar (US$) (£ sterling and EC$ also circulate)	US$ 1.6850	US$ 1.9820
Brunei	Brunei dollar of 100 sen (fully interchangeable with Singapore currency)	$ 2.8948	$ 3.1660
Bulgaria	Lev of 100 stotinki	Leva 31.014	Leva 40.10
Burkina	Franc CFA	Francs 499.63	Francs 475.125
Burundi	Burundi franc of 100 centimes	Francs 290.50	Francs 393.25
Cambodia	Riel of 100 sen	Riel 1348.40	Riel 1640.00
Cameroon	Franc CFA	Francs 499.63	Francs 475.125
Canada	Canadian dollar (C$) of 100 cents	C$ 1.9225	C$ 2.3715
Canary Islands	Currency is that of Spain	Pesetas 183.00	Pesetas 180.95
Cape Verde	Escudo Caboverdiano of 100 centavos	Esc 125$70	Esc 124$15
Cayman Islands	Cayman Islands dollar (CI$) of 100 cents	CI$ 1.3990	CI$ 1.6845
Central African Republic	Franc CFA	Francs 499.63	Francs 475.125
Chad	Franc CFA	Francs 499.63	Francs 475.125
Chile	Chilean peso of 100 centavos	Pesos 594.70	Pesos 759.75
China	Yuan of 10 jiao or 100 fen	Yuan 9.0773	Yuan 10.7805
Colombia	Colombian peso of 100 centavos	Pesos 1048.40	Pesos 1535.95
Comoros	Franc CFA	Francs 499.63	Francs 475.125
Congo	Franc CFA	Francs 499.63	Francs 475.125
Costa Rica	Costa Rican colón (₡) of 100 céntimos	₡ 225.02	₡ 268.55
Côte d'Ivoire	Franc CFA	Francs 499.63	Francs 475.125
Croatia	Dinar of 100 paras	—	Dinars 396.4
Cuba	Cuban peso of 100 centavos	Pesos 2.2515	Pesos 1.5010

Country	Monetary Unit	Average Rate to £ 3 September 1991	Average Rate to £ 1 September 1992
Cyprus	Cyprus pound (C£) of 100 cents	C£ 0.8050	C£ 0.8110
Czechoslovakia	Koruna (Kčs) of 100 haléřu	Kčs 51.45	Kčs 26.8163
Denmark	Danish krone of 100 øre	Kroner 11.3575	Kroner 10.7775
Djibouti	Djibouti franc of 100 centimes	Francs 295.00	Francs 347.00
Dominica	East Caribbean dollar (EC$) of 100 cents	EC$ 4.5510	EC$ 5.3515
Dominican Republic	Dominican Republic peso (RD$) of 100 centavos	RD$ 21.3720	RD$ 25.33
Ecuador	Sucre of 100 centavos	Sucres 1835.75	Sucres 2886.65
Egypt	Egyptian pound (£E) of 100 piastres or 1,000 millièmes	£E 5.57	£E 6.55
Equatorial Guinea	Franc CFA	Francs 499.63	Francs 475.125
Estonia	Rouble of 100 kopeks	—	Roubles 1.0494
Ethiopia	Ethiopian birr (EB) of 100 cents	EB 3.4595	EB 4.0775
Falkland Islands	Falkland pound of 100 pence	(at parity with £ sterling)	
Faroe Islands	Currency is that of Denmark	Kroner 11.3575	Kroner 10.7775
Fiji	Fiji dollar (F$) of 100 cents	F$ 2.5082	F$ 2.9255
Finland	Markka (Mk) of 100 penniä	Mk 7.1528	Mk 7.6945
France	Franc of 100 centimes	Francs 9.9925	Francs 9.5025
French Guiana	Currency is that of France	Francs 9.9925	Francs 9.5025
French Polynesia	Franc CFP	Francs 180.00	Francs 170.00
Gabon	Franc CFA	Francs 499.63	Francs 475.125
Gambia	Dalasi (D) of 100 butut	D 15.9045	D 16.7085
Georgia	Rouble of 100 kopeks	—	Roubles 1.0494
Germany	Deutsche Mark (DM) of 100 Pfennig	DM 2.9400	DM 2.7875
Ghana	Cedi of 100 pesewas	Cedi 637.50	Cedi 832.45
Gibraltar	Gibraltar pound of 100 pence	(at parity with £ sterling)	
Greece	Drachma of 100 leptae	Drachmae 324.425	Drachmae 346.95
Greenland	Currency is that of Denmark	Kroner 11.3575	Kroner 10.7775
Grenada	East Caribbean dollar (EC$) of 100 cents	EC$ 4.5510	EC$ 5.3515
Guadeloupe	Currency is that of France	Francs 9.9925	Francs 9.5025
Guam	Currency is that of USA	US$ 1.6850	US$ 1.9820
Guatemala	Quetzal (Q) of 100 centavos	Q 8.5370	Q 10.4650
Guinea	Guinea franc of 100 centimes	Francs 505.65	Francs 1609.95
Guinea-Bissau	Guinea-Bissau peso of 100 centavos	Pesos 1095.55	Pesos 9910.00
Guyana	Guyana dollar (G$) of 100 cents	G$ 214.05	G$ 248.70
Haiti	Gourde of 100 centimes	Gourdes 8.4275	Gourdes 9.82
Honduras	Lempira of 100 centavos	Lempiras 8.9610	Lempiras 11.4560
Hong Kong	Hong Kong dollar (HK$) of 100 cents	HK$ 13.0685	HK$ 15.3065
Hungary	Forint of 100 fillér	Forints 128.68	Forints 150.25
Iceland	Icelandic króna (Kr) of 100 aurar	Kr 103.25	Kr 104.35
India	Indian rupee (Rs) of 100 paisa	Rs 43.25	Rs 56.55
Indonesia	Rupiah (Rp) of 100 sen	Rp 3311.75	Rp 4033.90
Iran	Rial of 100 dinars	Rials 113.10	Rials 121.2
Iraq	Iraqi dinar (ID) of 1,000 fils	ID 0.5936	ID 0.5936
Ireland, Republic of	Punt (IR£) of 100 pence	IR£ 1.0995	IR 1.0570
Israel	Shekel of 100 agora	Shekels 3.9120	Shekels 4.7910
Italy	Lira of 100 centesimi	Lire 2193.00	Lire 2134.50
Jamaica	Jamaican dollar (J$) of 100 cents	J$ 17.53	J$ 45.1895
Japan	Yen of 100 sen	Yen 230.25	Yen 244.25
Jordan	Jordanian dinar (JD) of 1,000 fils	JD 1.1482	JD 1.3180
Kazakhstan	Rouble of 100 kopeks	—	Roubles 1.0494
Kenya	Kenya shilling (Ksh) of 100 cents	Ksh 48.9638	Ksh 65.2080
Kiribati	Australian dollar ($A) of 100 cents	$A 2.1485	$A 2.7595
Korea, North	Won of 100 jun	Won 1.6350	Won 4.2615
Korea, South	Won of 100 jeon	Won 1236.90	Won 1558.25
Kuwait	Kuwaiti dinar (KD) of 1,000 fils	KD 0.49105	KD 0.5758
Kyrgyzstan	Rouble of 100 kopeks	—	Roubles 1.0494
Laos	Kip (K) of 100 at	K 1179.85	K 1417.15
Latvia	Rouble of 100 kopeks	—	Roubles 1.0494
Lebanon	Lebanese pound (L£) of 100 piastres	L£ 1503.10	L£ 4748.20
Lesotho	Loti (M) of 100 lisente	M 4.8408	M 5.4315
Liberia	Liberian dollar (L$) of 100 cents	L$ 1.6850	L£ 1.9820
Libya	Libyan dinar (LD) of 1,000 dirhams	LD 0.4895	LD 0.5118

Country	Monetary Unit	Average Rate to £ 3 September 1991	Average Rate to £ 1 September 1992
Liechtenstein	Swiss franc of 100 Rappen (or centimes)	Francs 2.5825	Francs 2.4950
Lithuania	Rouble of 100 kopeks	—	Roubles 1.0494
Luxembourg	Luxembourg franc (LF) of 100 centimes (Belgian currency is also legal tender)	LF 60.55	LF 57.45
Macao	Pataca of 100 avos	Pataca 13.5130	Pataca 15.8285
Macedonia	Dinar of 100 paras	—	Dinars 396.4
Madagascar	Franc malgache (FMG) of 100 centimes	FMG 2218.00	FMG 3036.50
Madeira	Currency is that of Portugal	Esc 252.00	Esc 243.35
Malawi	Kwacha (K) of 100 tambala	K 4.8130	K 7.5175
Malaysia	Malaysian dollar (ringgit) (M$) of 100 sen	M$ 4.6882	M$ 4.9365
Maldives	Rufiyaa of 100 laaris	Rufiyaa 16.9660	Rufiyaa 20.8905
Mali	Franc CFA	Francs 499.63	Francs 475.125
Malta	Maltese lira (LM) of 100 cents or 1,000 mils	LM 0.5640	LM 0.5752
Marshall Islands	Currency is that of USA	—	US$ 1.9820
Martinique	Currency is that of France	Francs 9.9925	Francs 9.5025
Mauritania	Ouguiya (UM) of 5 khoums	UM 145.90	UM 153.75
Mauritius	Mauritius rupee of 100 cents	Rs 27.00	Rs 28.5210
Mayotte	Currency is that of France	Francs 9.9925	Francs 9.5025
Mexico	Peso of 100 centavos	Pesos 5132.15	Pesos 5947.95
Moldova	Rouble of 100 kopeks	—	Roubles 1.0494
Monaco	French franc of 100 centimes	Francs 9.9925	Francs 9.5025
Mongolia	Tugrik of 100 möngö	Tugriks 5.4500	Tugriks 79.28
Montenegro	Dinar of 100 paras	—	Dinars 396.4
Montserrat	East Caribbean dollar (EC$) of 100 cents	EC$ 4.5510	EC$ 5.3515
Morocco	Dirham (DH) of 100 centimes	DH 14.95	DH 14.8085
Mozambique	Metical (MT) of 100 centavos	2549 MT 75	MT 5424.7
Myanmar (Burma)	Kyat (K) of 100 pyas	K 10.5879	K 11.2275
Namibia	South African rand (R) of 100 cents	R 4.8408	R 5.4315
Nauru	Australian dollar ($A) of 100 cents	$A 2.1485	$A 2.7595
Nepal	Nepalese rupee of 100 paisa	Rs 71.95	Rs 92.4205
Netherlands	Gulden (guilder) or florin of 100 cents	Guilders 3.3125	Guilders 3.1450
Netherlands Antilles	Netherlands Antilles guilder of 100 cents	Guilders 3.0170	Guilders 3.5475
New Caledonia	Franc CFP	Francs 180.00	Francs 170.00
New Zealand	New Zealand dollar (NZ$) of 100 cents	NZ$ 2.9345	NZ$ 3.6645
Nicaragua	Córdoba (C$) of 100 centavos	C$ 8.4275	C$ 10.6630
Niger	Franc CFA	Francs 499.63	Francs 475.125
Nigeria	Naira (N) of 100 kobo	N 18.4560	N 36.5480
Norway	Krone of 100 øre	Kroner 11.5050	Kroner 11.0400
Oman	Rial Omani (OR) of 1,000 baiza	OR 0.6478	OR 0.7629
Pakistan	Pakistan rupee of 100 paisa	Rs 40.50	Rs 49.65
Panama	Balboa of 100 centésimos (US notes are also in circulation)	Balboa 1.6850	Balboa 1.9820
Papua New Guinea	Kina (K) of 100 toea	K 1.6040	K 1.8975
Paraguay	Guaraní (Gs) of 100 céntimos	Gs 2217.05	Gs 3004.70
Peru	New Sol of 100 cénts	New Sol 1.3400	New Sol 2.56
Philippines	Philippine peso (P) of 100 centavos	P 43.00	P 44.90
Poland	Złoty of 100 groszy	Złotys 19043.00	Złotys 26628.0
Portugal	Escudo (Esc) of 100 centavos	Esc 252.00	Esc 243.35
Puerto Rico	Currency is that of USA	US$ 1.6850	US$ 1.9820
Qatar	Qatar riyal of 100 dirhams	Riyals 6.1243	Riyals 7.2135
Réunion	Currency is that of France	Francs 9.9925	Francs 9.5025
Romania	Leu (Lei) of 100 bani	Lei 102.61	Lei 760.83
Russia	Rouble of 100 kopeks	—	Roubles 1.0494
Rwanda	Rwanda franc of 100 centimes	Francs 215.84	Francs 266.50
St Christopher and Nevis	East Caribbean dollar (EC$) of 100 cents	EC$ 4.5510	EC$ 5.3515
St Helena	St Helena pound (£) of 100 pence	At parity with £ sterling	
St Lucia	East Caribbean dollar (EC$) of 100 cents	EC$ 4.5510	EC$ 5.3515
St Pierre and Miquelon	Currency is that of France	Francs 9.9925	Francs 9.5025
St Vincent and the Grenadines	East Caribbean dollar (EC$) of 100 cents	EC$ 4.5510	EC$ 5.3515

Country	Monetary Unit	Average Rate to £ 3 September 1991	Average Rate to £ 1 September 1992
El Salvador	El Salvador colón (₡) of 100 centavos	₡ 13.4635	₡ 16.8865
San Marino	Italian currency is in circulation	Lire 2193.00	Lire 2134.50
São Tomé and Príncipe	Dobra of 100 centavos	Dobra 315.20	Dobra 475.68
Saudi Arabia	Saudi riyal (SR) of 20 qursh or 100 halala	SR 6.3103	SR 7.4255
Senegal	Franc CFA	Francs 499.63	Francs 475.125
Serbia	Dinar of 100 paras	—	Dinars 396.4
Seychelles	Seychelles rupee of 100 cents	Rs 8.95	Rs 9.65
Sierra Leone	Leone (Le) of 100 cents	Le 520.00	Le 981.10
Singapore	Singapore dollar (S$) of 100 cents	S$ 2.8948	S$ 3.1660
Slovenia	Dinar of 100 paras	—	Dinars 396.4
Solomon Islands	Solomon Islands dollar (SI$) of 100 cents	SI$ 4.6300	SI$ 5.7700
Somalia	Somali shilling of 100 cents	Shillings 4416.00	Shillings 5192.85
South Africa	Rand (R) of 100 cents	R 4.8408	R 5.4315
Spain	Peseta of 100 céntimos	Pesetas 183.00	Pesetas 180.95
Sri Lanka	Sri Lankan rupee of 100 cents	Rs 69.00	Rs 86.45
Sudan	Sudanese dinar (SD) of 10 pounds	£S 19.2990	SD 19.82
Suriname	Suriname guilder of 100 cents	Guilders 3.0085	Guilders 3.5380
Swaziland	Lilangeni (E) of 100 cents (South African currency also in circulation)	E 4.8408	E 5.4315
Sweden	Swedish krona of 100 öre	Kronor 10.6925	Kronor 10.1975
Switzerland	Swiss franc of 100 Rappen (or centimes)	Francs 2.5825	Francs 2.4950
Syria	Syrian pound (S$) of 100 piastres	S£ 35.40	S£ 41.6220
Taiwan	Taiwan dollar (T$) of 100 cents	T$ 44.95	T$ 49.85
Tajikistan	Rouble of 100 kopeks	—	Roubles 1.0494
Tanzania	Tanzanian shilling of 100 cents	Shillings 385.65	Shillings 633.45
Thailand	Baht of 100 satang	Baht 42.50	Baht 49.80
Togo	Franc CFA	Francs 499.63	Francs 475.125
Tonga	Pa'anga (T$) of 100 seniti	T$ 2.1485	T$ 2.7595
Trinidad and Tobago	Trinidad and Tobago dollar (TT$) of 100 cents	TT$ 7.1635	TT$ 8.4235
Tunisia	Tunisian dinar of 1,000 millimes	Dinars 1.6335	Dinars 1.6080
Turkey	Turkish lira (TL) of 100 kurus	TL 7753.07	TL 13954.50
Turkmenistan	Rouble of 100 kopeks	—	Roubles 1.0494
Tuvalu	Australian dollar ($A) of 100 cents	$A 2.1485	$A 2.7595
Uganda	Uganda shilling of 100 cents	Shillings 1350.70	Shillings 2343.25
Ukraine	Rouble of 100 Kopeks	—	Roubles 1.0494
United Arab Emirates	UAE dirham of 100 fils	Dirham 6.1790	Dirham 7.2720
United Kingdom	Pound sterling (£) of 100 pence	£ 1.00	£ 1.00
United States of America	US dollar (US$) of 100 cents	US$ 1.6850	US$ 1.9820
Uruguay	New Uruguayan peso of 100 centésimos	Pesos 3606.60	Pesos 6302.75
Uzbekistan	Rouble of 100 kopeks	—	Roubles 1.0494
Vanuatu	Vatu of 100 centimes	Vatu 187.50	Vatu 225.50
Vatican City State	Italian currency is legal tender	Lire 2193.00	Lire 2134.50
Venezuela	Bolívar (Bs) of 100 céntimos	Bs 92.2560	Bs 135.20
Vietnam	Dông of 10 hào or 100 xu	Dông 15186.35	Dông 21544.35
Virgin Islands (US)	Currency is that of USA	US$ 1.6850	US$ 1.9820
Western Samoa	Tala (WS$) of 100 sene	WS$ 4.0315	WS$ 4.8435
Republic of Yemen	Yemeni dinar (YD) of 1,000 fils	YD 0.7770	YD 0.9216
	Riyal of 100 fils	Riyals 20.3945	Riyals 32.7030
Zaire	Zaïre of 100 makuta	Zaïre 25175.00	Zaïre 1312000
Zambia	Kwacha (K) of 100 ngwee	K 116.45	K 178.507
Zimbabwe	Zimbabwe dollar (Z$) of 100 cents	Z$ 6.5905	Z$ 4.6975

Time Zones

Standard time differences from the Greenwich meridian

+	hours ahead of GMT
–	hours behind GMT
*	varies from standard time at some part of the year (Summer Time or Daylight Saving Time)
h	hours
m	minutes

	h m
Afghanistan	+ 4 30
*Albania	+ 1
Algeria	+ 1
Andorra	+ 1
Angola	+ 1
Anguilla	– 3
Antigua and Barbuda	– 4
Argentina	– 3
*Jujuy	– 4
*Mendoza	– 4
Armenia	+ 3
Aruba	– 4
Ascension Island	0
*Australia	+10
Broken Hill area (NSW)	+ 9 30
Northern Territory	+ 9 30
*South Australia	+ 9 30
Western Australia	+ 8
*Austria	+ 1
Azerbaijan	+ 3
*Azores	– 1
*Bahamas	– 5
Bahrain	+ 3
Bangladesh	+ 6
Barbados	– 4
Belarus	+ 2
*Belgium	+ 1
Belize	– 6
Benin	+ 1
*Bermuda	– 4
Bhutan	+ 6
Bolivia	– 4
Botswana	+ 2
Brazil	
Acre	– 5
*eastern, including all coast and Brasilia	– 3
*western	– 4
British Antarctic Territory	– 3
South Georgia	– 2
British Indian Ocean Territory	+ 5
Diego Garcia	+ 6
British Virgin Islands	– 4
Brunei	+ 8
*Bulgaria	+ 2
Burkina	0
Burundi	+ 2
Cambodia	+ 7
Cameroon	+ 1
Canada	
*Alberta	– 7
*British Columbia	– 8
*Labrador	– 4
*Manitoba	– 6
*New Brunswick	– 4
*Newfoundland	– 3 30
*Northwest Territories	
E. of 68° W.	– 4
68° W. to 85° W.	– 5
85° W. to 102° W.	– 6
W. of 102° W.	– 7
*Nova Scotia	– 4
*Ontario	
E. of 90° W.	– 5
W. of 90° W.	– 6
*Prince Edward Island	– 4
*Quebec	
E. of 63° W.	– 4
W. of 63° W.	– 5
*Saskatchewan	– 6
*Yukon	– 8
*Canary Islands	0
Cape Verde	– 1
Cayman Islands	– 5
Central African Republic	+ 1
Chad	+ 1
*Chile	– 4
China	+ 8
Christmas Island (Indian Ocean)	+ 7
Cocos Keeling Islands	+ 6 30
Colombia	– 5
Comoros	+ 3
Congo	+ 1
Cook Islands	– 10
*Costa Rica	– 6
Côte d'Ivoire	0
*Cuba	– 5
*Cyprus	+ 2
*Czechoslovakia	+ 1
*Denmark	+ 1
*Djibouti	+ 3
Dominica	– 4
Dominican Republic	– 4
Ecuador	– 5
*Egypt	+ 2
Equatorial Guinea	+ 1
Estonia	+ 2
Ethopia	+ 3
*Falkland Islands	– 4
*Faroe Islands	0
Fiji	+12
*Finland	+ 2
*France	+ 1
French Guiana	– 3
French Polynesia	–10
Gabon	+ 1
The Gambia	0
Georgia	+ 3
*Germany	+ 1
Ghana	0
*Gibraltar	+ 1
*Greece	+ 2
Greenland	
*Angmagssalik and west coast	– 3
Danmarkshavn	0
Mesters Vig	0
*Scoresby Sound	– 1
Thule area	– 4
Grenada	– 4
Guadeloupe	– 4
Guam	+ 10
*Guatemala	– 6
Guinea	0
Guinea-Bissau	0
Guyana	– 3
*Haiti	– 5
Honduras	– 6
Hong Kong	+ 8
*Hungary	+ 1
Iceland	0
India	+ 5 30
Indonesia	
Bali	+ 8
Irian Jaya	+ 9
Java	+ 7
Kalimantan (south and east)	+ 8
Kalimantan (west and central)	+ 7
Molucca Islands	+ 9
Sulawesi	+ 8
Sumatra	+ 7
Timor	+ 8
*Iran	+ 3 30
*Iraq	+ 3
*Ireland, Republic of	0
*Israel	+ 2
*Italy	+ 1
Jamaica	– 5
Japan	+ 9
*Jordan	+ 2
Kazakhstan	+ 5
Kenya	+ 3
Kiribati	
Banaba	+11 30
Gilbert Islands	+12
Kiritimati Island	–10
Phoenix Islands	–11
Korea, North	+ 9
Korea, South	+ 9
Kuwait	+ 3
Kyrgyzstan	+ 5
Laos	+ 7
Latvia	+ 2
*Lebanon	+ 2
Lesotho	+ 2
Liberia	0
Libya	+ 2
*Liechtenstein	+ 1
Lithuania	+ 2
*Luxembourg	+ 1
Macao	+ 8
Madagascar	+ 3
*Madeira	0
Malawi	+ 2
Malaysia	+ 8
Maldives	+ 5
Mali	0
*Malta	+ 1

	h	m
Marshall Islands	+12	
Eniwetok	−12	
Kwajalein	−12	
Martinique	− 4	
Mauritania	0	
Mauritius	+ 4	
Mexico	− 6	
central	− 7	
western	− 8	
Micronesia		
Caroline Islands	+10	
Kosrae	+11	
Pohnpei	+11	
Moldova	+ 2	
*Monaco	+ 1	
*Mongolia	+ 8	
Montserrat	− 4	
Morocco	0	
Mozambique	+ 2	
Myanmar	+ 6	30
Namibia	+ 2	
Nauru	+12	
Nepal	+ 5	45
Netherlands	+ 1	
Netherlands Antilles	− 4	
New Caledonia	+11	
*New Zealand	+12	
Nicaragua	− 6	
Niger	+ 1	
Nigeria	+ 1	
Norfolk Island	+11	30
*Norway	+ 1	
Oman	+ 4	
Pakistan	+ 5	
Palau	+ 9	
Panama	− 5	
Papua New Guinea	+10	
*Paraguay	− 4	
Peru	− 5	
Philippines	+ 8	
*Poland	+ 1	
*Portugal	0	
Puerto Rico	− 4	
Qatar	+ 3	
Réunion	+ 4	
*Romania	+ 2	
*Russia		
Zone 1	+ 2	
Zone 2	+ 3	
Zone 3	+ 4	
Zone 4	+ 5	
Zone 5	+ 6	
Zone 6	+ 7	
Zone 7	+ 8	
Zone 8	+ 9	
Zone 9	+10	
Zone 10	+11	
Rwanda	+ 2	
St Helena	0	
St Kitts and Nevis	− 4	
St Lucia	− 4	
*St Pierre and Miquelon	− 3	
St Vincent and the Grenadines	− 4	
El Salvador	− 6	
Samoa, American	−11	
San Marino	+ 1	
São Tomé and Príncipe	0	
Saudi Arabia	+ 3	
Senegal	0	
Seychelles	+ 4	
Sierra Leone	0	
Singapore	+ 8	
Solomon Islands	+11	
Somalia	+ 3	
South Africa	+ 2	
*Spain	+ 1	
Sri Lanka	+ 5	30
Sudan	+ 2	
Suriname	− 3	
Swaziland	+ 2	
*Sweden	+ 1	
*Switzerland	+ 1	
*Syria	+ 2	
Taiwan	+ 8	
Tanzania	+ 3	
Thailand	+ 7	
Togo	0	
Tonga	+13	
Trinidad and Tobago	− 4	
Tristan da Cunha	0	
Tunisia	+ 1	
*Turkey	+ 2	
*Turks and Caicos Islands	− 5	
Tuvalu	+12	
Uganda	+ 3	
Ukraine	+ 2	
United Arab Emirates	+ 4	
*Uruguay	− 3	
United States		
Alaska, E. of 169° 30′ W.	− 9	
Aleutian Islands, W. of 169° 30′ W.	−10	
eastern time	− 5	
central time	− 6	
Hawaii	−10	
mountain time	− 7	
Pacific time	− 8	
Uzbekistan	+ 4	
*Vanuatu	+11	
Vatican City State	+ 1	
Venezuela	− 4	
Vietnam	+ 7	
Virgin Islands (US)	− 4	
Western Samoa	−11	
Yemen	+ 3	
*Yugoslav republics	+ 1	
Zaire	+ 2	
Kinshasa	+ 1	
Mbandaka	+ 1	
Zambia	+ 2	
Zimbabwe	+ 2	

Countries of the World: A–Z

AFGHANISTAN
Da Afghanistan Jamhuriat

AREA – Afghanistan is bounded on the west by Iran, on the south by Pakistan, on the north by Tadjikistan, Uzbekistan and Turkmenistan, and on the east by Pakistan and China. Its ancient name was Aryana, by which title it is referred to by Strabo, the Greek geographer who lived in the first century BC. The estimated area is 250,000 sq. miles (647,497 sq. km).

Mountains, chief among which are the Hindu Kush, cover three-quarters of the country, the elevation being generally over 4,000 feet. There are three great river basins, the Oxus, Helmand, and Kabul. The climate is dry, with extreme temperatures.

POPULATION – The population is 16,121,000 (1990 UN estimate). It is estimated that over four million have become refugees in Pakistan and over one million in Iran since the Soviet invasion. The population is very mixed. The most numerous race is the Pushtuns who predominate in the south and west, the Tadjiks, a Persian-speaking people, Uzbeks and Turkomans in the north, Hazaras in the centre, Baluchis in the south-west and Nuristanis, who live near the Chitral border. All are Sunni Muslims, except the Hazaras and Kizilbashes, who belong to the Shia sect.

CAPITAL – Kabul (1988, 1,424,400). The chief commercial centres are Kabul and Kandahar (225,500). Other provincial capitals are (UN estimates) Herat (177,300), Mazar-i-Sharif (130,600), Jalalabad (55,000).

CURRENCY – Afghani (Af) of 100 puls.

FLAG – Black, red and green horizontal stripes with a device in top left-hand corner.

NATIONAL ANTHEM – Soroud-e-Melli.

NATIONAL DAY – 27 April.

GOVERNMENT

The constitutional monarchy, introduced by the 1964 Constitution, was overthrown by a coup on 17 July 1973. The country was ruled by presidential decree until February 1977 when a constitution was approved by a *Loya Jerga* (Grand Tribal Council). Mohammad Daoud was elected President but was overthrown on 27 April 1978 by the Armed Forces and power was handed to the People's Democratic Party of Afghanistan (PDPA). In December 1979 Soviet troops invaded Afghanistan and installed Babrak Karmal as Head of State. Karmal was replaced by Najibollah in May 1986. A peace agreement in April 1988 led to the withdrawal of Soviet troops which was completed by February 1989. A new Constitution, approved in November 1987 and amended in 1990, provides for a President, a Council of Ministers, a National Assembly and a Senate.

Following a party congress in late June 1990, the PDPA was renamed Hezb-e-Watan (Homeland Party) and its Politburo and Central Committee were abolished and replaced by an Executive Council and Central Council. Najibollah was elected Chairman of the Party for a four-year term.

Following widespread defections from the armed forces to the Islamic resistance groups, President Najibollah was forced to step down on 16 April 1992 and was replaced initially by an army-dominated council of his former colleagues. However, anti-government forces overran Kabul on 25 April. A new government was installed under Sebghatullah Mujaddedi, previously leader of a Pakistan-based government-in-exile. Mujaddedi remained as an interim President until 28 June when he was succeeded by Burnahuddin Rabbani, another former exiled leader. Rabbani has also been appointed on an interim basis until new constitutional arrangements are worked out.

Afghanistan has been declared an Islamic State. The former ruling Homeland Party has been dissolved.

HEAD OF STATE

President of the Islamic State of Afghanistan, Prof. Burnahuddin Rabbani.

PROVISIONAL GOVERNMENT as at July 1992

Prime Minister, Ostad Abdol Sabur Farid.
Defence, Gen. Ahmad Shah Massoud.
National Security, Gen. Khoydadad Khan.
Finance, Lt.-Gen. Hamidollah Rahimi.
Foreign Affairs, Sayyid Solayman Gaelani.
Home Affairs, Ahmed Shah.
Construction Affairs, Amir Mohammad Yaser.
Water and Electricity, Dr Faruq.
Justice, Maulvi Jalaluddin Haqqani.
Head of Supreme Court of the Islamic State of Afghanistan, Maulvi Abdollah.
Higher Education, Dr Musa Tawana.
Education and Training, Prof. Abdul Qayum.
Commerce, Wakil Shahbaz.
Industries and Mines, Yaqub Lali.
Development, Dr Sarabi.
Planning, Sayd Mohammad Ali Jawed.
Martyrs and the Disabled, Cdr Muhammad Anwar.
Border Affairs, Abdol Ahad Khan Karzay.
Rural Construction and Development, Zabihollah Hadi.
Information and Culture, Mohammad Siddique Chakri.
Communication, Mohammad Akram.
Islamic Affairs and Endowments, Maulvi Arsala.
Public Health, Dr Najibollah Mujaddedi.
Returnee Affairs, Cdr Rahmotollah Wahedyar.
Social Affairs, Maulvi Abdol Manan.
Light Industries and Foodstuffs, Haji Solayman.
Head of Supreme Prosecution Office, Maulvi Mohammad Qasem Khan.
Minister-Counsellor of Islamic State of Afghanistan, Maulvi Muhammad Mir.
City Construction, Haji Abdol Hafez Beg.
Governor of Kabul Province, Cdr Muhammad Musa.
Mayor of Kabul City, Fazl Karim.
Commander of Police and Gendarmerie, Cdr Abdol Haq.

EMBASSY OF THE ISLAMIC STATE OF AFGHANISTAN
31 Prince's Gate, London SW7 1QQ
Tel 071-589 8891

Minister-Counsellor and Chargé d'Affaires, Taza Khan Wial.

BRITISH EMBASSY
Karte Parwan, Kabul
Tel: Kabul 30511/3

Staff were withdrawn from post in February 1989.

LOCAL GOVERNMENT

The country is divided into 30 provinces. At present, only a few have governors appointed by the new government in Kabul.

JUDICIARY

The Constitution introduced in 1965 provided for the creation of a legal code, and for the complete separation of executive and judiciary, but was abolished in July 1973. In late 1976 and early 1977 new penal and civil codes were published.

Few major changes were made to the operation of the judicial system by the 1987 Constitution and subsequent amendments under the Najibollah regime. The new government in Kabul has, however, announced its intention to introduce Islamic law. A new constitution is also expected to be drawn up in the coming months.

DEFENCE

Before the fall of the Najibollah government, the army numbered about 50,000, supplemented by other security agencies and irregular militias. A small air force was also maintained. The current government is seeking to merge the remnants of some of these forces with the Islamic resistance fighters to form a new national army.

ECONOMY

Agriculture and sheep raising are the principal industries. There are generally two crops a year, one of wheat (the staple food), barley, or lentils, the other of rice, millet, maize, and dal. Sugar beet and cotton are grown. Afghanistan is rich in fruits. Sheep, including the Karakuli, and transport animals are bred. Silk, woollen and hair cloths and carpets are manufactured. Salt, silver, copper, coal, iron, lead, rubies, lapis lazuli, gold, chrome, barite, uranium, and talc are found.

TRADE

Exports are mainly Persian lambskins (Karakul), dried fruits, nuts, cotton, raw wool, carpets, spice and natural gas, while the imports are chiefly oil, cotton yarn and piece goods, tea, sugar, machinery and transport equipment.

Trade with UK	1990	1991
Imports from UK	£7,816,000	£6,956,000
Exports to UK	9,194,000	5,207,000

COMMUNICATIONS

Main roads run from Kabul to Kandahar, Herat, Maimana via Mazari-Sharif and Faizabad via Khanabad. The road from Kabul to the north was shortened by the completion in 1964 of the Salang pass. Roads cross the border with Pakistan at Chaman and via the Khyber Pass, and there are roads from Herat to the borders of Central Asia and Iran. A network of minor roads fit for motor traffic in fine weather links up all important towns and districts.

In 1982 the Afghan and Uzbek shores of the River Oxus were linked by a road and rail bridge which joins the Afghan port of Hairatan and the Uzbek port of Termez. A network of internal air services operates between the main towns.

CULTURE

The principal languages of the country are Dari (a form of Persian) and Pushtu, although a number of minority languages are also spoken in various provinces. All schoolchildren learn both Persian and Pushtu. Education is free and nominally compulsory, elementary schools having been established in most centres; there are secondary schools in large urban areas and two universities, one in Kabul (established 1932) and one in Jalalabad (established early 1970s).

ALBANIA

Republika Shqipërisë

Situated on the Adriatic Sea, Albania is bounded on the north by Montenegro, on the east by Serbia and Macedonia and on the south by Greece. The area of the Republic is estimated at 11,099 sq. miles (28,748 sq. km), with a population (1990 estimate) of 3,250,000.

CAPITAL – Tirana, population (1989) 239,381.
CURRENCY – Lek (Lk) of 100 qindarka.
FLAG – Black two-headed eagle on a red field.
NATIONAL DAY – 11 January.

GOVERNMENT

Albania was under Turkish suzerainty from 1468 until 1912, when independence was declared. After a period of unrest, a republic was declared in 1925, and in 1928 a monarchy. The King went into exile in 1939 when the country was occupied by the Italians; Albania was liberated in November 1944. Elections in 1945 resulted in a Communist-controlled Assembly; the King was deposed in absentia and a republic declared in January 1946.

From 1946 to 1991 Albania was a one-party, Communist state. In March 1991 multi-party elections were held and were won by the Socialist Party (the renamed Party of Labour). Following labour unrest, a coalition government was formed in June 1991.

In December 1991 the Democratic Party withdrew from the government and a non-party government was established which continued in office until new elections were held in March 1992. These elections were won overwhelmingly by the Democratic Party which formed a coalition government with the much smaller Social Democrat and Republican parties. In April 1992 the Democratic Party leader Dr Sali Berisha was elected by parliament as Albania's first non-communist President.

HEAD OF STATE

President, Dr Sali Berisha, *elected* April 1992.

COUNCIL OF MINISTERS as at 13 April 1992

Prime Minister, Aleksander Meksi.
Deputy Chairman of the Council of Ministers and Minister of Agriculture and Food, Rexhep Uka (DP).
Deputy Chairman of the Council of Ministers and Minister of Order, Bashkim Kopliku (DP).
General Secretary, Vullnet Ademi (SDP).
Finances and Economy, Genc Ruli (DP).
Foreign Affairs, Alfred Serreqi (DP).
Justice, Kudred Cela (Ind).
Industry, Mining and Energy Sources, Abdyl Xhaja (Ind).
Foreign Economic Trade and Relations, Artan Hoxha (DP).
Defence, Safet Xhulali (DP).
Transport and Communications, Fatos Bitncka (RP).
Construction, Housing and Territory Adjustments, Ilir Manushi (DP).
Health and Environmental Protection, Tritan Shehu (DP).
Education, Ylli Vejsiu (DP).
Culture, Youth and Sports, Dhimiter Anagnosti (DP).
Tourism, Osman Shehu (DP).
Labour, Emigration, Social Assistance and Political Persecutors, Dashamir Shehu (DP).
Chairman of the Committee of Science and Technology, Maksim Konomi (DP).
Chairman of the Control Commission, Blerim Cela (DP).

DP: Democratic Party; SDP: Social Democrat Party; RP: Republican Party.

ALBANIAN AMBASSADOR TO LONDON
no accreditation as yet.

BRITISH AMBASSADOR – His Excellency Sir Stephen Egerton, KCMG (resident in Rome).

ECONOMY

Much of the country is mountainous and nearly a half is covered by forest. There are fertile areas along the Adriatic coast and the Koritza Basin and there have been land reclamation and irrigation programmes. The main crops are wheat, maize, sugar-beet, potatoes and fruit.

All industry is nationalized. The principal industries are agricultural product processing, textiles, oil products and cement. Exports include crude oil, minerals (bitumen, chrome, nickel, copper), tobacco, fruit and vegetables. The government is now committed to economic reform, privatization and the creation of a market economy. Privatization and redistribution of land is under way.

Trade with UK	1990	1991
Imports from UK	£413,000	£3,179,000
Exports to UK	9,000	274,000

ALGERIA

Al-Jumhuriya al-Jazairiya ad-Dimuqratiya ash-Shabiya

Algeria lies between 8° 45′ W. to 12° E. longitude, 27° 6′ N. to a southern limit about 19° N. and has an area of 919,595 sq. miles (2,381,741 sq. km). The population (1987 Census) was 22,971,558. A 1990 UN estimate gives a figure of 24,960,000.

CAPITAL – ΨAlgiers, population 3,250,000 (approx). It is one of the principal ports of the Mediterranean as well as an important industrial centre. Other towns include ΨOran; Constantine; ΨAnnaba; Blida; Setif; Sidi-Bel-Abbès; Tlemcen; ΨMostaganem; ΨSkikda; ΨBejaia and Tizi Ouzou.

CURRENCY – Algerian dinar (DA) of 100 centimes.

FLAG – Divided vertically green and white with a red crescent and star over all in the centre.

NATIONAL ANTHEM – Qassaman.

NATIONAL DAY – 1 November.

GOVERNMENT

Algiers surrendered to a French force on 5 July 1830, and Algeria was annexed to France in 1842. From 1881 the three northern departments of Algiers, Oran and Constantine formed an integral part of France. The Southern Territories of the Sahara, formerly a separate colony, became an integral part of Algeria on the attainment of independence. An armed rebellion led by the Muslim Front de Liberation Nationale (FLN) against French rule broke out on 1 November 1954. French control of Algeria came to an end when President de Gaulle declared Algeria independent on 3 July 1962; by October 1963 all agricultural land held by foreigners had been expropriated and by 1965 more than 80 per cent of the French population had left Algeria.

Ben Bella was elected President of the Republic in September 1963, but was deposed; a Council of the Revolution presided over by Col. Boumediène assumed power on 19 June 1965. A new constitution was established by referendum on 19 November 1976, and in December 1976 President Boumediène was elected for a six-year term of office. Following President Boumediène's death in December 1978, Chadli Bendjedid was elected President in February 1979.

A new Constitution was agreed by referendum in February 1989 which moves Algeria away from a one-party socialist system to a more pluralist political system. Local elections, held in June 1990, were won by the opposition Islamic Salvation Front (FIS). Following extensive unrest, the government declared a state of siege in June 1991 and postponed multi-party elections until the end of the year.

The first round of the legislative elections were held in December 1991 with the FIS emerging as the clear winner. However before the second round of the elections were held, President Bendjedid resigned and the elections were abandoned. A Higher Committee of State (HCS) was formed, backed by the armed forces, to govern the country. The former FLN veteran Mohammed Boudiaf returned from twenty-five years in exile to head the HCS. The HCS declared a state of emergency in February 1992 and the FIS was banned in March, but continues its activities underground. Clashes between security forces and fundamentalists continued, culminating in the assassination of President Boudiaf on 29 June 1992 by suspected FIS supporters. Boudiaf was replaced by HCS member Ali Kafi.

HEAD OF STATE

President of the Higher Committee of State, Acting Head of State, Ali Kafi, *appointed* July 1992.

HIGHER COMMITTEE OF STATE as at July 1992

President, Ali Kafi.
Members, Maj.-Gen. Khaled Nezzar; Ali Haroun; Tedjini Hadam; Reda Malek.

GOVERNMENT as at July 1992

Prime Minister, Economy, Belaid Abdesselam.
National Defence, Maj.-Gen. Khaled Nezzar.
Foreign Affairs, Lakhdar Brahimi.
Minister Adviser to the Prime Minister, Messaoud Ait Chellal.
Justice, Abdelhamid Mahi Behi.
Interior and Local Authorities, Mohamed Hardi.
National Education, Ahmed Djebbar.
Mines and Industries, Abdemour Keramane.
War Veterans, Brahim Chibout.
Agriculture, Mohamed Elias Mesli.
Religious Affairs, Sassi Lamouri.
Housing, Farouk Tebbal.
Health and Population, Mohamed Seghir Babes.
Labour and Social Affairs, Maamar Benguerba.
Vocational Training, Djelloul Baghli.
Tourism and Handicraft, Abdelwahab Bekri.
Culture and Communications, Habib Chaouki Hamraoui.
Youth and Sport, Abdelkader Khomri.
Post and Telecommunications, Tahar Allane.
Transport, Mokhtar Meherzi.
Energy, Hacene Mefti.
Equipment, Mokdad Sifi.

ALGERIAN EMBASSY
54 Holland Park, London W11 3RS
Tel 071-221 7800

Ambassador Extraordinary and Plenipotentiary, His Excellency Abdelkrim Gheraieb (1989).

BRITISH EMBASSY
7 Chemin des Glycines,
El-Mouradia, Algiers
Tel: Algiers 605601

Ambassador Extraordinary and Plenipotentiary, His Excellency Christopher Charles Richard Battiscombe, CMG (1990).

Cultural Attaché, British Council Representative, D. Munro, 6 Avenue Souidani Boudjemaa, Algiers.

ECONOMY

Development in Algeria is regulated by a series of national development plans. The 1980–4 Plan concentrated on housing, water supply and agriculture. The 1985–9 Plan continued with these objectives and also included food and processing industries. Agrarian reform started in 1987. The 4,000 state farms have been broken up into 23,000 units. Following riots in October 1988, economic reform was speeded up and now endorses the industrial and financial sectors. The aim is to decentralize planning and devolve management. The private sector is also receiving official encouragement.

Algeria's main industry is the hydrocarbons industry. Oil and natural gas are pumped from the Sahara to terminals on the coast before being exported; the gas is first liquefied at liquefaction plants at Skikda and Arzew, although pipelines serve Libya and Italy direct.

Other major industries being developed include a steel industry, motor vehicles, building materials, paper making, chemical products and metal manufactures. Most major industrial enterprises are still under State control.

Trade with UK	1990	1991
Imports from UK	£73,831,000	£55,685,000
Exports to UK	259,959,000	194,874,000

Algeria's main exports are crude oil and liquefied natural gas. Principal imports from the United Kingdom are capital plant, equipment for industrial use and foodstuffs.

COMMUNICATIONS

Algeria has a rapidly expanding network of roads and railways. Considerable sums are also being spent on the development of the State airline, the national shipping company and telecommunications.

ANDORRA

Principat d'Andorra

A small, neutral principality (formed by a treaty in 1278), situated on the southern slopes of the Pyrenees between Spain and France, with an approximate area of 175 sq. miles (453 sq. km), and population (UN estimate 1990) of 52,000, less than one-quarter of whom are native Andorrans. The language of the country is Catalan, but French and Spanish (Castilian) are also spoken. It is surrounded by mountains of 6,500 to 10,000 feet.

CAPITAL – Andorra la Vella (population 19,003).
CURRENCY – French francs and Spanish pesetas are both in use.
FLAG – Three vertical bands, blue, yellow, red; Andorran coat of arms frequently imposed on central (yellow) band but not essential.
NATIONAL DAY – 8 September.

GOVERNMENT

Andorra is divided into seven Parishes, each of which has four Councillors elected by vote to the Valleys of Andorra Council of twenty-eight. The Council appoints the head of the executive government, who designates the members of his government. Constitutionally, the sovereignty of Andorra is vested in two co-Princes, the President of the French Republic and the Spanish Bishop of Urgel. These two co-princes can veto certain decisions of the Council of the Valleys but cannot impose their own decisions without the consent of the Council. They are represented by Permanent Delegates of whom one is the French Prefect of the Pyrenees Orientales Department at Perpignan and the other is the Spanish Vicar-General of the Diocese of Urgel. They are in turn represented in Andorra la Vella by two resident Viguiers known as the Viguier Français and the Viguier Episcopal, who have a joint responsibility for law and order and overall administration policy, together with judicial powers as members of the Supreme Court.

Viguier Français, Jean-Pierre Courtois.
Viguier Episcopal, Francesc Badia.
Head of Government, Oscar Ribas Reig.

HM CONSUL-GENERAL, D. Joy, CBE (resident in Barcelona, Spain) (Tel 3-322 2151).

ECONOMY

The Budget is expressed in pesetas. The estimated national revenue (1989) was US$895 million, with a per capita income of US$17,596. The climate is cold for six months, but mild in spring and summer. Potatoes are produced in the highlands and tobacco in the valleys. The mountain slopes have been developed for skiing, and it is estimated that 10,000,000 tourists visit the valleys during the year. The economy is largely based on tourism, commerce, tobacco, construction and forestry; a third of the country is classified as forest in which pine, fir, oak, birch and box-tree predominate. Andorra has negotiated a customs union with the European Community which came into force on 1 July 1991.

COMMUNICATIONS

A good road into the valleys from Spain is open all year round, and that from France is closed only occasionally in winter. An airport at Seo d'Urgell just outside Andorra provides very limited air connections. There are two radio stations in Andorra, one privately-owned and one operated by a French Government corporation. Both pay dues to the Council of the Valleys.

TRADE WITH UK

	1990	1991
Imports from UK	£15,763,000	£14,188,000
Exports to UK	9,000	36,000

ANGOLA

República de Angola

Angola, which has an area of 481,354 sq. miles (1,246,700 sq. km), lies on the western coast of Africa; its population in 1990 was estimated by the UN at 10,020,000.

CAPITAL – ΨLuanda, population estimate 1990, 2 million.
CURRENCY – New Kwanza (Kz) of 100 lwei.
FLAG – Red and black with a yellow star, machete and cog-wheel.
NATIONAL ANTHEM – Angola Avante.
NATIONAL DAY – 11 November (Independence Day).

GOVERNMENT

After a Portuguese presence of five centuries, and an anti-colonial war since 1961, Angola became independent on 11 November 1975 in the midst of civil war. Soviet-Cuban military assistance to the Popular Movement for the

Liberation of Angola (MPLA) enabled it to defeat its rivals early in 1976. However, the MPLA government remained under pressure from the UNITA guerrilla movement (led by Dr Jonas Savimbi) which by the late 1980s was operating freely. On 8 August 1988 it was announced that a ceasefire between South African, Cuban and Angolan forces had taken place pending talks on withdrawal of South African troops from Angola. The ceasefire agreement was signed, and came into effect, on 22 August. In December 1988 an agreement providing for the withdrawal of the 50,000 Cuban troops by July 1991 was signed in New York. On 31 May 1991 a peace agreement was signed between the government and UNITA. Multi-party presidential and legislative elections are to take place in September 1992.

The MPLA, formerly but no longer a Marxist-Leninist party, was the sole legal party until early 1991 when a multi-party system was adopted. The Constitution provides for a President, who appoints a Council of Ministers to assist him, and a National People's Assembly.

HEAD OF STATE
President, Jose Eduardo Dos Santos.

COUNCIL OF MINISTERS as at 30 May 1992

Prime Minister, Fernando Joe Franca Van Dunem.
Interior, Lt.-Gen. Francisco Magalhaes Paiva.
Territorial Administration, Col. Antonio Paulo Kassoma.
Defence, Col.-Gen. Pedro Tonha.
Foreign Affairs, Col. Pedro de Castro Van-Dunem.
Planning, Emmanuel Carneiro.
Trade, Ambrosio Silvestre.
Industry, Justino Fernandes.
Justice, Dr L. M. Dias.
Petroleum, J. L. Landoite.
Health, Flavio Joao Fernandes.
Labour and Social Security, Diogo Jorge de Jesus.
Public Works, J. H. Garcia.
Fisheries, Maria de Fatima Jardin.
Agriculture, Issac Dos Anjos.
Transport and Communications, Andre Luis Brandao.
Education, Antonio da Silva Neto.
Finance, Mario Monteiro.
Youth and Sport, Osvaldo Senua Van Dunem.
Information, B. de Cardosa.

EMBASSY OF ANGOLA
98 Park Lane, London W1
Tel 071-495 1752

Ambassador Extraordinary and Plenipotentiary, His Excellency José Primo (1991).

BRITISH EMBASSY
Rua Diogo Caõ 4 (Caixa Postal 1244), Luanda
Tel: Luanda 334582/3

Ambassador Extraordinary and Plenipotentiary, His Excellency John Gerard Flynn (1990).

ECONOMY

Angola has valuable oil and diamond deposits and exports of these two commodities account for over 90 per cent of total exports.

Principal agricultural crops are cassava, maize, bananas, coffee, palm oil and kernels, cotton and sisal. Coffee, sisal, maize and palm oil are exported; exports also include mahogany and other hardwoods from the tropical rain forests in the north of the country.

TRADE WITH UK

	1990	1991
Imports from UK	£29,284,000	£34,812,000
Exports to UK	5,142,000	65,078,000

ANTIGUA AND BARBUDA
State of Antigua and Barbuda

AREA, ETC – Antigua and Barbuda comprises the islands of Antigua (108 sq. miles (279 sq. km)), Barbuda (62 sq. miles (160 sq. km)) 25 miles north of Antigua, and Redonda (½ sq. mile; 1.2 sq. km) 25 miles south-west of Antigua. Antigua is part of the Leeward Islands in the Eastern Caribbean and lies 17° 3′ N. and 61° 48′ W. It is distinguished from the rest of the Leeward group by its absence of high hills and forest, and a drier climate than most of the West Indies. Barbuda, formerly a possession of the Codrington family, is very flat, mainly scrub-covered, with a large lagoon.
POPULATION – The total population (official census 1991) is 65,962; Antigua had a population of 64,562, Barbuda 1,400, and Redonda was uninhabited.

CAPITAL – ΨSt John's. Population, 30,000. The town of Barbuda is Codrington.
CURRENCY – East Caribbean dollar (EC$) of 100 cents.
FLAG. – Red with an inverted triangle divided black over blue over white, with a rising gold sun on the white band.
NATIONAL ANTHEM – Fair Antigua and Barbuda.
NATIONAL DAY – 1 November (Independence Day).

GOVERNMENT

Antigua was first settled by the English in 1632, and was granted to Lord Willoughby by Charles II. Antigua became internally self-governing in 1967 and fully independent on 1 November 1981, as a constitutional monarchy with The Queen as Head of State, represented by the Governor-General. There is a Senate of 17 appointed members and a House of Representatives elected every five years. The Attorney-General may be appointed.

The Antigua Labour party led by Mr Vere Bird won the general election of 9 March 1989 and a fourth successive term of office.

Governor-General, Sir Wilfred Ebenezer Jacobs, GCMG, GCVO, OBE, QC.

CABINET as at June 1992

Prime Minister, Rt. Hon. Dr Vere C. Bird, sen.
Legal Affairs and Attorney-General, Hon. Keith Ford, QC.
Finance, Hon. Molwyn Joseph.
Home Affairs and Social Services, Hon. Christopher O'Mard.
Economic Development, Industry and Tourism, Hon. Dr Rodney Williams.
Agriculture, Fisheries, Lands and Housing, Hon. Hilroy Humphreys.
Education, Culture, and Youth Affairs, Hon. Bernard Percival.
Labour and Health, Hon. Adolphus Freeland.
Public Utilities, Transportation and Energy, Hon. Robin Yearwood.
Public Works and Communications, Hon. Eustace Cochrane.
External Affairs, Planning and Trade, Hon. Lester Bird.
Information, Hon. John St Luce.

HIGH COMMISSION FOR ANTIGUA AND BARBUDA
15 Thayer Street, London W1M 5LD
Tel 071-486 7073

High Commissioner, His Excellency James Thomas (1987).

BRITISH HIGH COMMISSION
11 Old Parham Road (PO 483), St John's
Tel: St John's 462 0008/9

High Commissioner, (resides at Bridgetown, Barbados).
Resident Representative, I. D. Marsh (*First Secretary*).

ECONOMY

Tourism is the main sector of the economy. Tourism and related services account for 60 per cent of GDP and employ 40 per cent of the workforce; Antigua was one of the first Caribbean islands to attract tourists.

For many years sugar was the dominant crop but is now produced only for local consumption. Agricultural production includes livestock, sea island cotton, mixed market gardening and fishing.

FINANCE

	1989*	1990*
Revenue	EC$236,720,991	EC$249,560,916
Expenditure (recurrent)	263,579,351	271,730,204

*estimated

TRADE WITH UK

	1990	1991
Imports from UK	£17,890,000	£19,687,000
Exports to UK	2,931,000	5,764,000

ARGENTINA

República Argentina

Argentina occupies the greater portion of the southern part of the South American Continent, and extends from Bolivia to Cape Horn, a total distance of nearly 2,300 miles; its greatest breadth is about 930 miles. It is bounded on the north by Bolivia, on the north-east by Paraguay, Brazil and Uruguay, on the south-east and south by the Atlantic, and on the west by Chile, from which it is separated by the Cordillera de los Andes. On the west the mountainous Cordilleras, with their plateaux, extend from the northern to the southern boundaries; on the east are the great plains.

The Republic consists of 23 provinces and one federal district (Buenos Aires), comprising in all an area of 1,068,302 sq. miles (2,766,889 sq. km.), with a population (Census 1991) of 32,370,298.

CAPITAL – ΨBuenos Aires, population (1990), metropolitan area 2,955,002; with suburbs, 10,881,381. Other large towns are: ΨRosario (1,071,384), Córdoba (1,134,086), ΨLa Plata (630,260), ΨMar del Plata (503,779), San Miguel de Tucumán (603,331), ΨSanta Fé (329,814) and Mendoza (706,909).

CURRENCY – Austral (A) of 100 cents.

FLAG – Horizontal bands of blue, white, blue; gold sun in centre of white band.

NATIONAL ANTHEM – Oid Mortales! (Hear, oh mortals!).

NATIONAL DAY – 25 May.

GOVERNMENT

The estuary of La Plata was discovered in 1515 by Juan Díaz de Solís, but it was not until 1536 that Pedro de Mendoza founded Buenos Aires. This city was abandoned and later re-founded by Don Juan de Garay in 1580. In 1810 Spanish rule was defied, and in 1816, after a long campaign of liberation conducted by General José de San Martín, the independence of Argentina was declared by the Congress of Tucumán.

In 1946 Juan Domingo Perón became President until overthrown in 1955. There followed eighteen years of political and economic instability, and eventually in 1973, Perón was recalled from exile. Elected President he died within a year and was succeeded by his widow, Vice President María Estela Martínez de Perón. However, warring factions in the Perónist movement and increasing terrorist activity eventually led to a coup by the armed forces on 24 March 1976. A Junta, consisting of the three commanders of the Armed Forces, was established with one of their number as President. Following the Falkland Islands defeat in 1982 the President, Gen. Galtieri, resigned and the Army appointed Gen. Bignone as President. The Navy and Air Force withdrew from the Junta but this was reconstituted shortly afterwards. Elections for a civilian government to replace the military one were held on 30 October 1983 and the Radical Party's candidate, Raúl Alfonsín, was elected President. Presidential elections in May 1989 were won by the Peronist candidate Carlos Menem. The government has embarked upon privatization of several state-owned corporations.

HEAD OF STATE

President, Dr Carlos Saúl Menem, *took office* 8 July 1989.
Vice President, Dr Eduardo Alberto Dunalde.

CABINET as at June 1992

Interior, José Luis Manzano.
Foreign Affairs, Dr Guido Di Tella.
Labour, Jorge Diaz.
Economy and Public Works, Dr Domingo Cavallo.
Education, Dr Antonio Salonia.
Defence, Dr Antonio Ermán González.
Health and Social Welfare, Dr Julio Ceson Araoz.
Justice, Leon Arslanaim.

EMBASSY FOR ARGENTINA

53 Hans Place, London SWIX OLA
Tel 071-584 6494

Ambassador Extraordinary and Plenipotentiary, His Excellency Mario Cámpora (1990).

BRITISH EMBASSY

Dr Luis Agote 2412, 1425 Buenos Aires
Tel: Buenos Aires 803-7070/1

Ambassador Extraordinary and Plenipotentiary, His Excellency The Hon. Humphrey Maud, CMG (1990).

BRITISH CHAMBER OF COMMERCE, Av. Corrientes 457, 10 piso, 1043 Buenos Aires.

ECONOMY

AGRICULTURE

Of a total land area of approximately 700 million acres, farms occupy about 425 million. About 60 per cent of the farmland is pasture, 10 per cent annual crops, 5 per cent permanent crops and the remaining 25 per cent forest and wasteland. A large proportion of the land is still held in large estates devoted to cattle raising but the number of small farms is increasing. The principal crops are wheat, maize, oats, barley, rye, linseed, sunflower seed, alfalfa, sugar, fruit and cotton. Argentina is pre-eminent in the production of beef, mutton and wool, and pastoral and agricultural products provide about 85 per cent of Argentina's exports.

MINERAL PRODUCTION

Oil is found in various parts of the Republic and the production of oil is of first importance to Argentina's industries and, to some extent, to its economic and financial development. Total petroleum output for 1991 was 484,000 b.p.d. There is a refinery in San Lorenzo (Santa Fé province). Natural gas is also produced in a number of provinces.

Coal, lead, zinc, tungsten, iron ore, sulphur, mica and salt are the other chief minerals being exploited. There are small worked deposits of beryllium, manganese, bismuth, uranium, antimony, copper, kaolin, arsenate, gold, silver and tin. Coal is produced at the Rio Turbio mine in the province of Santa Cruz. The output of other materials is not large but greater attention is now being paid to the development of these natural resources, especially copper for which the Government and private companies are carrying out exploration.

Industries

Meat-packing is one of the principal industries; flour-milling, sugar-refining, and the wine industry are also important. In recent years progress has been made by the textile, plastic and machine tool industries and engineering, especially in the production of motor vehicles and steel manufactures.

Trade with UK

	1990	1991
Imports from UK	£35,953,000	£69,671,000
Exports to UK	144,205,000	135,512,000

COMMUNICATIONS

There are 25,386 miles of railways, which are State property. Plans are in hand for complete re-organization of the railways in order to improve their operating efficiency and reduce a very large financial deficit. The combined national and provincial road network totals approximately 137,000 miles of which 23,180 miles are surfaced. There are air services between Argentina and all the neighbouring republics, Europe, Asia, Canada, the USA and South Africa.

DEFENCE

The Army consists of four corps organized into 12 brigades, including mountain, jungle, airborne and armoured troops. It numbers about 45,000, including about 10,000 conscripts who serve for between six months and one year.

The Navy consists of 1 aircraft carrier, 6 destroyers, 7 corvettes, 4 submarines, 6 minesweepers and ancillary craft, 41 combat aircraft and 22 helicopters. Strength is about 25,000, including 3,000 conscripts.

The Air Force consists of 9 brigades and a training force, with a strength of 13,000, including 3,000 conscripts, 176 combat aircraft and 14 armed helicopters.

EDUCATION

Education is compulsory for the 7 grades of primary school (6 to 13). Secondary schools (14 to 17+) are available in and around Buenos Aires and in most of the important towns in the interior of the country. Most secondary schools are administered by the Central Ministry of Education in Buenos Aires, while primary schools are administered by the Central Ministry or by Provincial Ministries of Education. Private schools, of which there are many, are also loosely controlled by the Central Ministry. The total number of universities is over 50 with 24 national, 25 private and a small number of provincial universities.

CULTURE

Spanish is the language of the Republic and the literature of Spain is accepted as an inheritance by the people. There is little indigenous literature before the break from Spain, but all branches have flourished since the latter half of the nineteenth century. About 450 daily newspapers are published in Argentina, including seven major ones in the city of Buenos Aires. The English language newspaper is the *Buenos Aires Herald* (daily). There are several other foreign language newspapers.

AUSTRALIA

The Commonwealth of Australia

AREA AND POPULATION*

States and Territories	*Area (sq. km)*	*Resident population 30 June 1991p*
New South Wales (NSW)	801,600	5,901,100
Queensland (Qld.)	1,727,200	2,972,000
South Australia (SA)	984,000	1,456,700
Tasmania (Tas.)	67,800	460,500
Victoria (Vic.)	227,600	4,427,400
Western Australia (WA)	2,525,500	1,665,900
Australian Capital Territory (ACT)	2,400	293,500
Northern Territory (NT)	1,346,200	158,800
Total	7,682,300	17,335,900

* estimated
p preliminary

Population of Aboriginal and Torres Strait Islander Origin as at June 1986

	Number	*% of state population*
New South Wales	59,011	1.1
Queensland	61,268	2.4
South Australia	14,291	1.1
Tasmania	6,716	1.5
Victoria	12,611	0.3
Western Australia	37,789	2.7
Australian Capital Territory	1,220	0.5
Northern Territory	34,739	22.4
Total	227,645	1.5

Births, Deaths, Marriages and Divorces

(Year ended 30 June)

	1988	1989	1990
Births	246,200	250,853	260,662
Deaths	120,463	124,232	119,391
Marriages	114,350	120,121	114,341
Divorces†	41,007	41,383	42,635

† year ended 31 December.

Migration

(Year ended 30 June)

	1989	1990	1991
Permanent arrivals	145,320	121,320	121,690
Permanent departures	21,650	27,860	31,130

GEOGRAPHY

Australia, including Tasmania, comprises a land area of 7,682,300 sq. km lying between latitudes 10°41′S (Cape York) and 43°39′S (South East Cape, Tasmania) and longitudes 113°09′E (Steep Point) and 153°39′E (Cape Byron). The latitudinal distance between Cape York and South East Cape is about 3,680 kilometres and the longitudinal distance between Steep Point and Cape Byron is about 4,000 kilometres. (The latitudinal distance between Cape York and the most southerly point on the mainland South Point, Wilson's Promontory, is about 3,180 kilometres.)

Australia has three major landforms: the western plateau, the interior lowlands and the eastern uplands. The western half of the continent consists mainly of a great plateau of altitude 300–600 metres. The interior lowland includes the channel country of south-west Queensland (drainage to Lake Eyre) and the Murray-Darling river system to the south. The eastern uplands consist of a broad belt of varied width extending from north Queensland to Tasmania and composed largely of tablelands, ranges and ridges with only limited mountain areas above 1,000 metres. The highest point is Mt. Kosciusko (2,228 m) and the lowest, Lake Eyre (−15 m).

Australia's large area and latitudinal range have resulted in climatic conditions ranging from the alpine to the tropical. Two-thirds of the continent is arid or semi-arid although good rainfalls (over 800 mm annually) occur in the northern monsoonal belt under the influence of the Australian–Asian monsoon and along the eastern and southern highland regions under the influence of the great atmospheric depressions of the Southern Ocean. The effectiveness of the rainfall is greatly reduced by marked alternations of wet and dry seasons, unreliability from year to year, high temperatures and high potential evaporation.

Fifty per cent of the area of Australia has a medium rainfall of less than 300 mm per year and 80 per cent has less than 600 mm. Extreme minimum temperatures are not as low as those recorded in other continents because of the absence of extensive mountain masses and because of the expanse of ocean to the south. However, extreme maxima are comparatively high, reaching 50°C over the inland, mainly due to the great east–west extent of the continent in the vicinity of the Tropic of Capricorn.

Only one-third of the Australian land mass drains directly to the ocean, mainly on the coastal side of the Main Divide and inland with the Murray–Darling system. With the exception of the Murray–Darling system, most rivers draining to the ocean are comparatively short and account for the majority of the country's average annual discharge.

FEDERAL CAPITAL – Canberra, in the Australian Capital Territory. Estimated population at 30 June 1989 was 303,200. It is the seat of government and the location of most government department headquarters.

CURRENCY – Australian dollar ($A) of 100 cents.

FLAG – The British Blue Ensign with five stars of the Southern Cross in the fly and the white Commonwealth Star of seven points beneath the Union Jack.

NATIONAL ANTHEM – Advance Australia Fair.

NATIONAL DAY – 26 January (Australia Day).

GOVERNMENT

The Commonwealth of Australia was constituted by an Act of the Imperial Parliament dated 9 July 1900, and was inaugurated 1 January 1901. The government is that of a Federal Commonwealth within the British Commonwealth of Nations, the executive power being vested in the Sovereign (through the Governor-General), assisted by a Federal Ministry of Ministers of State. Under the Constitution the Federal Government has acquired and may acquire certain defined powers as surrendered by the States, residuary legislative power remaining with the States. The right of a State to legislate on any matter is not abrogated except in connection with matters exclusively under Federal control, but where a State law is inconsistent with a law of the Commonwealth the latter prevails to the extent of the inconsistency.

GOVERNOR-GENERAL AND STAFF

Governor-General, His Excellency the Hon. Bill Hayden, AC, *born* 23 January 1933; *assumed office*, 16 February 1989.

Official Secretary, R. D. Sturkey.
Deputy Official Secretary, Ms H. Storey.

CABINET as at 27 May 1992

Prime Minister, Hon. Paul Keating.
Deputy PM and Health, Housing and Community Services, Hon. Brian Howe.
Industry, Technology and Commerce, Senator Hon. John Button.
Foreign Affairs and Trade, Senator Hon. Gareth Evans.
Treasurer, Hon. John Dawkins.
Finance, Hon. Ralph Willis.
Attorney-General, Hon. Michael Duffy.
Employment, Education and Training, Hon. Kim Beazley.
Social Security, Hon. Neil Blewett.
Defence, Senator Hon. Robert Ray.
Immigration, Local Government and Ethnic Affairs, Hon. Gerry Hand.
Arts, Sport, the Environment and Territories, Hon. Ros Kelly.
Industrial Relations, Senator Hon. Peter Cook.
Administrative Services, Senator Hon. Nick Bolkus.
Primary Industries and Energy, Hon. Simon Crean.
Tourism, Hon. Alan Griffiths.
Transport and Communications, Senator Hon. Bob Collins.
Veterans' Affairs, Hon. Ben Humphreys.

JUNIOR MINISTERS

Land Transport, Hon. Robert Brown.
Justice, Immigration, Local Government and Ethnic Affairs, Senator Hon. Michael Tate.
Small Business, Construction, and Customs, Hon. David Beddall.
Aboriginal Affairs, Hon. Robert Tickner.
Aged, Family and Health Services, Hon. Peter Staples.
Higher Education and Employment Services, Hon. Peter Baldwin.
Defence Science and Personnel, Hon. Gordon Bilney.
Local Government and Family Support, Hon. David Simmons.
Resources, Hon. Alan Griffiths.
Arts and Territories, Hon. Wendy Fatin.
Science and Technology, Hon. Ross Free.
Trade and Overseas Development, Hon. John Kerin.
Consumer Affairs, Hon. Jeannette McHugh.

AUSTRALIAN HIGH COMMISSION

Australia House, Strand, London WC2B 4LA
Tel 071-379 4334

High Commissioner, His Excellency The Hon. Richard Smith (1991).
Deputy High Commissioner, R. Greet.
Official Secretary, D. Connors.
Ministers, Ms K. Campbell (*Political*); P. Tormey (*Economic*); Dr D. de Souza (*Health*).
Defence Adviser and Head of Defence Staff, Cdre G. P. Kable.

BRITISH HIGH COMMISSION

Commonwealth Avenue, Canberra, ACT 2600
Tel: Canberra (06) 270 6666

High Commissioner, His Excellency Brian L. Barder (1991).
Deputy High Commissioner, Head of Chancery, I. Mackley, CMG.
Defence and Naval Adviser and Head of British Defence Liaison Staff, Cdre A. C. G. Wolstenholme.
Counsellor, T. N. Young (*Director, Trade Promotion*).
First Secretaries, D. Moorhouse (*Management*); D. Blunt, LVO; G. Minter, MVO (*Commercial, Agriculture*);

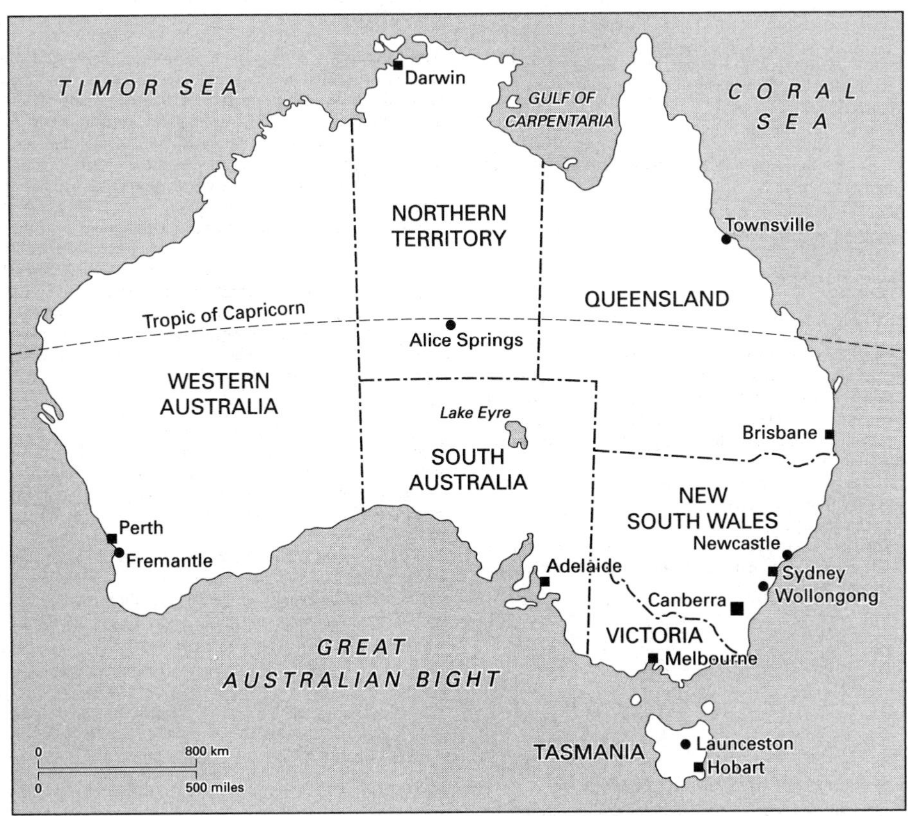

W. C. Patey; M. R. Eastburn (*Information*); M. R. Maiden (*Defence Exports*); M. Neve (*Defence Research*); K. Harding.
Military Adviser, Col. G. A. Morris, OBE.
Air Adviser, Gp. Capt. J. G. Sheldon.
Consuls-General, B. S. Jones, LVO (*Brisbane*); S. D. R. Brown (*Melbourne*); J. B. Noss (*Perth*); R. S. Reeve (*Sydney*).
Cultural Adviser and British Council Representative, M. C. Foot, OBE, Edgecliff Centre, 203–233 New South Head Road (PO Box 88), Edgecliff, Sydney 2027.

LEGISLATURE

Parliament consists of The Queen, the Senate and the House of Representatives. The Constitution provides that the number of members of the House of Representatives shall be, as nearly as practicable, twice the number of Senators. Members of the Senate are elected for six years by universal suffrage, half the members retiring every third year. Each of the six States returns an equal number of 12 Senators, and the Australian Capital Territory and the Northern Territory two each. The House of Representatives, similarly elected for a maximum of three years, contains members proportionate to the population, with a minimum of five members for each State. There are now 148 members in the House of Representatives, including one member for the Northern Territory and two for the Australian Capital Territory.

President of the Senate, Senator Hon. Kerry Sibraa.
Speaker, House of Representatives, Hon. Leo McLeay.

JUDICATURE

HIGH COURT OF AUSTRALIA as at 31 May 1992

Chief Justice, Hon. Sir Anthony Frank Mason, AC, KBE.
Justices, Hons. Sir Gerard Brennan, AC, KBE; Sir William Deane, AC, KBE; Sir Daryl Dawson, AC, KBE, CB; John Toohey, AC; Mary Gaudron; Michael McHugh, AC.
Registrar, F. W. D. Jones.

FEDERAL COURT OF AUSTRALIA as at 1 June 1992

Chief Justice, Hon. M. E. J. Black.
Judges, Hons. C. A. Sweeney, CBE; R. M. Northrop; J. A. Keely; J. F. Gallop; J. D. Davies; J. S. Lockhart; I. F. Sheppard, AO; T. R. Morling; K. J. Jenkinson; A. R. Neaves; B. A. Beaumont; M. R. Wilcox; J. E. J. Spender; P. R. A. Gray; J. C. S. Burchett; J. A. Miles; D. M. Ryan; W. M. C. Gummow; R. S. French; M. R. Einfeld; M. L. Foster; A. B. Nicholson; M. C. Lee; H. W. Olney; J. W. von Doussa; D. G. Hill; M. F. O'Loughlin; D. F. O'Connor; T. J. Higgins; P. C. Heerey; D. P. Drummond; R. E. Cooper.
Registrar, J. T. Howard, RFD, ED.

SUPREME COURT OF THE AUSTRALIAN CAPITAL TERRITORY as at 1 June 1992

Judges, Hons. J. A. Miles (*Chief Justice*); J. F. Gallop; T. J. Higgins (*Resident Judges*); R. M. Northrop;

J. D. Davies; J. S. Lockhart; I. F. Sheppard; T. R. Morling; K. J. Jenkinson; B. A. Beaumont; M. R. Wilcox; J. E. J. Spender; M. L. Foster; D. M. Ryan; J. W. von Doussa (*Additional Judges*).
Master, A. E. Hogan.
Registrar, A. G. Towill.

SUPREME COURT OF THE NORTHERN TERRITORY as at 1 June 1992
Chief Justice, Hon. K. J. A. Asche.
Judges, Hons. Sir William Kearney; B. F. Martin; D. N. Angel; D. Mildren.
Master, P. G. Lefevre.

DEFENCE

A single Department of Defence was created in 1973, though the separate identities of the three services have been retained. The Chief of Defence Force Staff is responsible for command of the Defence Force through the three Service Chiefs of Staff and is also the principal military adviser to the Minister.

The Secretary to the Department of Defence is responsible to the Minister for Defence for advice on policy, resources and organization.

Total defence expenditure was $A9,310,000,000 in 1990.

The personnel strengths of the Permanent Defence Force at 30 June 1992 were:

	Males	*Females*
Navy	13,737	1,919
Army	27,716	2,617
Air Force	18,624	3,228
Total	60,177	7,764

FINANCE

COMMONWEALTH GOVERNMENT FINANCE

Outlays and revenue of the Commonwealth Government were ($Amillion):

	1989–90	1990–1†
Current outlays	85,305	93,242
Capital outlays	11,813	12,009
Revenue and grants received	97,491	101,498
Financing transactions	−372	3,754

† estimate

STATE GOVERNMENT FINANCE 1989–90* ($A million)

	Outlay (current and capital)	*Revenue and grants received*	*Financing trans-actions*
NSW	20,990	19,605	1,385
Victoria	17,420	13,902	3,519
Queensland	9,857	10,197	−339
S. Australia	5,660	4,829	830
W. Australia	7,011	6,112	899
Tasmania	2,122	1,955	167
NT	1,384	1,227	157
ACT	942	990	−48
Total	65,386	58,817	6,570

* preliminary

BANKING

In June 1990 the trading banks had total liabilities of $A268,022 million including total deposits of $A183,430 million securities.

ECONOMY

AGRICULTURE – In 1985, 63.6 per cent of the Australian land area consisted of agricultural establishments, with the remainder being urban areas, State forests, mining leases and unoccupied land. Crop-growing areas constituted up to 4.32 per cent of the total agricultural establishments, emphasizing the relative importance of the livestock industries in Australia (sheep in the warm, temperate, semi-arid lands and beef cattle in the tropics).

The wide range of climatic and soil conditions over the agricultural regions of Australia has resulted in a diversity of crops being grown throughout the country. Generally, cereal crops (excluding rice and sorghum) are grown in all States over wide areas, while other crops are confined to specific locations in a few States. However, scanty or erratic rainfall, limited potential for irrigation and unsuitable soils or topography have restricted intensive agriculture.

MINES AND MINERALS – Significant mineral resources comprise bauxite, coal, copper, crude petroleum, gems, gold, ilmenite, iron ore, lead, limestone, manganese, nickel, rutile, salt, silver, tin, tungsten, uranium, zinc and zircon. Recently, geological exploration has significantly increased the mineral resources of the nation and a number of oilfields are in production.

In 1989–90 the total value of all minerals produced was $A23,294 million. In 1989–90 mine production of black coal was 160,459,000 tonnes, crude oil (including condensate) was 31,700 megalitres and natural gas 15,354 gigalitres. Production of principal metals in 1989 was:

Iron ore	106,000,000	tonnes
Copper	289,000	"
Lead-Zinc concentrate	130,900	"
Gold	203	"

* 1985–6 figures

GROSS VALUE OF AGRICULTURAL COMMODITIES 1990–1p

	$A million
Crops	8,965.4
Livestock slaughterings and other disposals	5,613.6
Livestock products	6,318.3
Total agriculture	20,906.2

p preliminary

LIVESTOCK NUMBERS AT 31 MARCH 1991

	Thousands
Cattle	23,662
Sheep	163,238
Pigs	2,531
Poultry	52,472

GROSS VALUE OF CROPS 1990–1p

	$A million
Cereals for grain	2,996.7
Cotton	821.0
Crops for hay	98.6
Fruit and nuts	1,451.2
Legumes for grain	283.9
Nursery production	473.0
Oilseeds	89.0
Peanuts	23.7
Sugar cane for crushing	698.5
Tobacco	76.3
Vegetables	1,355.7
Pastures and grasses	597.8
Total crops	8,965.4

p preliminary

Manufactures

In 1988–9 there were in Australia 31,249 industrial establishments, employing 1,072,634 persons; wages paid amounted to $A25,599m; and turnover $A151,857m.

TRADE

Of Australia's total exports in the year 1989–90, the largest category was metalliferous ores and metal scrap, worth $A7,188.9m. This was followed by coal, coke and briquettes, $A5,942.2m; textile fibres and their wastes, $A4,680.5m; and non-ferrous metals, $A3,880.2m. Cereals and cereal preparations to the value of $A3,607m were exported, and meat and meat preparations worth $A2,881.4m.

The largest category of Australia's imports was road vehicles, worth $A5,061.7m. This was followed by miscellaneous manufactured articles, $A6,880.1m; office and automatic data processing machines, $A3,557.1m; general industrial machinery and equipment, $A2,975.1m; specialized machinery for particular industries, $A2,757.0m; and electrical machinery, $A2,716.7m.

	1988–9	1989–90
Imports	$A47,039m	$A51,323m
Exports	43,522m	48,746m

In 1989–90, 26.2 per cent of Australia's total exports went to Japan. The USA received 10.8 per cent, Republic of Korea 5.5, New Zealand 5.3, Singapore 4.0, Taiwan 3.7, UK 3.6 and Hong Kong 2.7.

Of Australia's total imports in 1989–90, 24.1 per cent came from the USA, 19.2 from Japan, 6.7 West Germany, 6.5 UK, 4.2 New Zealand, 3.8 Taiwan and 3.2 Italy.

Trade with UK

	1990	1991
Imports from UK	£1,645,620,000	£1,355,127,000
Exports to UK	1,039,080,000	870,823,000

COMMUNICATIONS

Railways – There are six government owned railway systems, operated by the State Rail Authority of NSW, Victorian Railways, Queensland Government Railways, Western Australian Government Railways, the State Transport Authority of Southern Australia, and the Australian National Railways Commission. The ANRC incorporates the former Commonwealth Railways system, and the Tasmanian and non-metropolitan South Australian railways (urban rail services in Southern Australia remain the responsibility of the State Transport Authority). In 1989 there were 35,763 route-kilometres open.

Gross earnings 1988–9 were:	$A million
New South Wales	1,114.1
Victoria	n.a.
Queensland	1,107.1
*South Australia	17.6
Western Australia	306.2
ANRC	315.8
Total	n.a.

*Includes urban rail operations only

In 1988–9 there were 417m rail passenger journeys on government railways and 179m tonnes of goods and livestock carried.

Shipping – Total arrivals and departures of vessels engaged in overseas trade at the various Australian ports in 1988–9 were: arrivals 11,831 (455,162,000 deadweight tonnes); departures 11,727 (448,130,000 deadweight tonnes).

Broadcasting and Television – On 30 June 1984, the Australian Broadcasting Corporation operated 144 stations. Privately owned commercial broadcasting stations totalled 137. On 30 June 1984, 276 national and 152 commercial television and translator stations were in operation.

Motor Vehicles – At 30 June 1990, there were 9,776,600 motor vehicles registered in Australia and 304,000 motor cycles.

Civil Aviation – Figures for domestic and overseas services in 1989–90p are as follows:

	Domestic	*Overseas*
Paying passengers	9,878,000	n.a.
Freight (tonnes)	99,000	n.a.

p=preliminary

THE NORTHERN TERRITORY

The Northern Territory has a total area of 519,770 sq. miles (1,346,200 sq. km), and lies between 129°–138° east longitude and 11°–26° south latitude. The estimated population in the Northern Territory at 30 June 1992 was 166,700, of which about a quarter are Aboriginals.

Government

The administration was taken over by the Commonwealth on 1 January 1911 from the government of the State of South Australia.

The Northern Territory (Self-Government) Act 1978 established the Northern Territory as a body politic as from 1 July 1978, with Ministers having control over and responsibility for Territory finances and the administration of the functions of government as specified by the Federal Government by regulations made pursuant to the Act. Proposed laws passed by the Legislative Assembly in relation to a transferred function require the assent of the Administrator. Proposed laws in all other cases may be assented to by the Administrator or reserved by the Administrator for the Governor-General's pleasure. The Governor-General may disallow any laws assented to by the Administrator within six months of the Administrator's assent.

The Northern Territory has federal representation electing one member to the House of Representatives and two members to the Senate.

Seat of Administration – Darwin.

Administrator, His Hon. the Honourable J. H. Muirhead, AC, QC.

Chief Minister, Hon. Marshall Perron.

Aboriginal Lands

Various Aboriginal Land Trusts hold title to land previously called Reserves, totalling about one-fifth of the Northern Territory.

The Aboriginal Land Rights (NT) Act of 1976 provides for the investigation and determination of Aboriginal traditional claims to vacant Crown land or land already owned by or on behalf of Aboriginals. Successful land claims to date have increased Aboriginal ownership to 34 per cent of the Northern Territory whilst a further 13 per cent is the subject of claims.

A number of major Aboriginal communities previously administered by Church Mission Societies and the Federal Government are now controlled by the Aboriginal people themselves, through local Aboriginal Councils. A recent phenomenon is the voluntary movement of some Aboriginals to their traditional homeland areas where they feel that their culture will be better preserved.

Economy

Northern Territory's economy is based on the exploitation of its natural resources of minerals, land, fisheries and tourist attractions. Following the introduction of a number of government measures designed to expand and diversify primary production, the Territory's agricultural and horticultural industries are also beginning to contribute an increasing amount to Territory rural output. The beef cattle industry continues to be the major user of pastoral lands.

Mining and energy resource development has played a major part in the development of the Northern Territory and in 1991 the total value of production was $A1.83 billion. The Territory is a leading uranium producer, extracting 3,126,676 kg of uranium oxide in 1991 with a value of $A212 million. The Northern Terrritory contains 20 per cent of the Western World's low cost uranium reserves. Large scale production of zinc-lead concentrate is planned to commence in 1994. In 1991 more than one million tonnes of manganese was sold, with a total value of about $A165 million. Gold production for 1991 was estimated at $A298 million. The value ex mines of bauxite sales exceeded $A128 million and alumina production was valued at $A566 million. The value of oil and gas production for 1990 was $A358 million.

Tourism is of importance to the Territory's economy. It is a major growth industry and generates over $A481 million annually.

Communications

The Northern Territory has three main ports; Darwin, managed by the Darwin Port Authority, and the private mining ports of Gove and Groote Eylandt.

The standard gauge rail link between Southern Australia and Alice Springs was officially opened in October 1980. The link between Alice Springs and Darwin is provided by a fully co-ordinated rail-road service.

The main population centres are linked by the Stuart Highway, which connects Alice Springs to Darwin via Tennant Creek and Katherine. Of special interest to the Northern Territory is the operation of 'road trains'. These are basically massive trucks hauling two or three trailers, having a net capacity of about 100 tonnes and measuring up to 45 metres in length.

EXTERNAL TERRITORIES

Ashmore and Cartier Islands

Ashmore Islands (known as Middle, East and West Islands) and Cartier Island are situated in the Indian Ocean some 850 km and 790 km west of Darwin respectively. The islands lie at the outer edge of the continental shelf. They are small and low and are composed of coral and sand. Vegetation consists mainly of grass. Turtles are plentiful at certain times of the year and beche-de-mer is abundant. The islands are uninhabited.

Great Britain took formal possession of the Ashmores in 1878 and Cartier was annexed in 1909. By Imperial Order in Council of 23 July 1931 the islands were placed under the authority of the Commonwealth of Australia, and were accepted in 1933 under the name of the Territory of Ashmore and Cartier Islands. The territory was annexed to the Northern Territory of Australia. With the granting of self-government to the Northern Territory on 1 July 1978 responsibility for the administration of Ashmore and Cartier Islands became a direct responsibility of the Commonwealth Government. In 1983 Ashmore Reef was declared a national nature reserve.

In accordance with an agreement between the governments of Indonesia and Australia, Indonesian fishermen who have traditionally plied the area may engage in limited fishing activity within the territory but are prohibited from taking any products from the nature reserve. They can land to collect water from West Island.

The Australian Antarctic Territory

The Australian Antarctic Territory was established by an Order in Council, dated 7 February 1933, which placed under the government of the Commonwealth of Australia all the islands and territories, other than Adélie Land, which are situated south of the latitude 60° S. and lying between 160° E. longitude and 45° E. longitude. The Order came into force on 24 August 1936, after the passage of the Australian Antarctic Territory Acceptance Act 1933. The boundaries of Terre Adélie were definitely fixed by a French Decree of 1 April 1938, as the islands and territories south of 60° S. latitude lying between 136° E. longitude and 142° E. longitude. The Australian Antarctic Territory Act 1954 declared that the laws in force in the Australian Capital Territory are, so far as they are applicable, in force in the Australian Antarctic Territory. The territory is administered by the Antarctic Division of the Department of Science, which, since its inception in 1947, has organized yearly expeditions to Antarctica, known as Australian National Antarctic Research Expeditions (ANARE).

On 13 February 1954 ANARE opened Mawson Station in Mac-Robertson Land at latitude 67° 36′ S. and longitude 62° 53′ E. Scientific research conducted at Mawson includes upper atmosphere physics, cosmic ray physics, meteorology, earth sciences, biology and medical science. Mawson is also a centre for coastal and inland exploration.

Davis Station was opened on the coast of Princess Elizabeth Land on 13 January 1957, at latitude 68° 35′ S. and longitude 77° 58′ E. Scientific programmes carried out at Davis include meteorology, biology, upper atmosphere physics, with field investigations in biology.

Casey Station, on the coast of Wilkes Land at latitude 66°17′S and longitude 110°32′E, was established in 1969 to replace the American-built Wilkes Station a few miles away. A new station 0.7 miles away was opened in 1988. Scientific research conducted out of Casey includes glaciology (deep ice drilling), meteorology, upper atmosphere physics and botanical studies.

Since 1948 ANARE has operated a station on Macquarie Island, a dependency of Tasmania, situated at 54° 30′ S. and 158° 57′ E., about 900 miles north of the Antarctic Continent.

Summer stations have been established in the Bunger Hills, 200 miles west of Casey, at Cape Denison in Commonwealth Bay, in the Larsemann Hills and on Heard Island.

Christmas Island

Christmas Island was administered as part of the Colony of Singapore until the end of 1957. On 1 October 1958 it became an Australian territory. It is situated in the Indian Ocean about 1,408 km NW of North West Cape in Western Australia, and has an area of 135 sq. km. Population (estimated, 30 June 1990) is 1,300, consisting of former employees of the Phosphate Mining Corporation, and present employees of the Christmas Island Administration, the Christmas Island Shire Council, and their families. There is no indigenous population.

The island is densely wooded and had extensive deposits of phosphates, the extraction of which has traditionally been the major economic activity. An Australian government company, the Phosphate Mining Corporation of Christmas Island, which carried out the mining operation ceased operating in 1987. Extensive deposits of low grade phosphate ore still remain but alternative economic development is being encouraged. The principal current development is a hotel complex.

On 1 July 1992 the Australian Government introduced major reforms to the laws of the island with the application of the Western Australian legal regime.

The Administrator is responsible to the Australian Minister for Arts and Territories in Canberra. The Christmas Island Shire Council has nine elected members. The Council is responsible for municipal functions and services on the island.

Administrator, M. Grimes.

Cocos (Keeling) Islands

The Cocos (Keeling) Islands were declared a British possession in 1857. All land in the islands was granted to George Clunies-Ross and his heirs by Queen Victoria in 1886. In 1955 the islands, which had been governed through the British colonies of Ceylon (from 1878), the Straits Settlements (1886) and Singapore (1903), were accepted as a Territory of Australia.

In 1978 the Australian Government purchased all Clunies-Ross land and property interests except for the family home and grounds. In 1979 ownership of the kampong area of Home Island was transferred to the Cocos (Keeling) Islands Council, the local government body established in 1979. Title to most of the remaining land purchased from Clunies-Ross in 1978 was transferred to the Council in 1984.

The Cocos (Keeling) Islands Act 1955 provides the legal framework for the present political and administrative arrangements in the territory. On 6 April 1984 the Cocos community, in a UN supervised Act of Self-Determination, chose to integrate with Australia. The Government's major commitment was that living standards would reach comparable mainland levels by 1994. The Commonwealth Grants Commission monitors the progress.

The islands are two separate atolls (North Keeling Island and, 24 km to the south, the main atoll) comprising some 27 small coral islands with a total area of about 14 sq. km, situated in the Indian Ocean in latitude 12° 5′ South and longitude 96° 53′ East. The main islands of the southern atoll are West Island (the largest, about 9 km from north to south) on which are the administrative centre, the aerodrome, and the Australia-based employees of government departments; Home Island, where the Cocos Malay community and the Clunies-Ross family live; Direction Island, Horsburgh and South Island.

The territory has no viable economic base at present. In 1986–7 the copra industry suffered severe losses and in 1987 ceased production. Tourism is being developed as a likely successor to the copra industry.

A weekly air charter service operates between Perth, the Cocos (Keeling) Islands and Christmas Island. Population (30 June 1990), 613. The islands are administered by the Australian Government through the Department of the Arts, Sport, the Environment and Territories in Canberra.

Administrator, Barry Cunningham.

Coral Sea Islands Territory

The Coral Sea Islands Territory lies east of Queensland between the Great Barrier Reef and longitude 156° 06′ E., and between latitudes 12° and 24° S. It comprises scattered islands, spread over a sea area of 780,000 sq. km. The islands are formed mainly of coral and sand. Some have grass or scrub cover but most are extremely small, with no permanent fresh water.

There is a manned metereological station in the Willis Group but the remaining islands are uninhabited. Large populations of sea birds nest and breed in the area, and two national nature reserves were designated in the Territory in 1982.

The Australian Government bases its claim to the islands on numerous acts of sovereignty since early this century and enacted the Coral Sea Islands Act 1969 which declares the islands a territory of the Commonwealth of Australia. The Department of the Arts, Sport, the Environment and Territories, Canberra, is responsible for the administration of the territory.

Heard Island and McDonald Islands

The Heard and McDonald islands, about 4,100 km south-west of Fremantle, comprise all the islands and rocks lying between 52° 30′ and 53° 30′ S. latitude and 72° and 74° 30′ E. longitude. Sovereignty over the islands was transferred by the UK to the Commonwealth of Australia in 1947. The Heard Island and McDonald Islands Act 1953 provides for the government of the islands as one territory. Under this Act the law operating there is that of the Australian Capital Territory. The islands are administered by the Department of the Arts, Sport, the Environment and Territories. Under the Environment Protection and Management Ordinance 1987, a permit system regulates entry to the territory and a range of activities there.

Norfolk Island

Norfolk Island is situated in the South Pacific Ocean at latitude 29° 02′ S. and longitude 167° 57′ E., being about 1,676 km NE of Sydney and 1,063 km north of Auckland. It is about 8 km long by 5 km wide, with an area of 3,455 hectares. The climate is mild and sub tropical. Resident population at the 1991 Census was 1,912.

The island, discovered by Capt. Cook in 1774, served as a penal colony from 1788 to 1814 and 1825 to 1855. In 1856, 194 descendants of the *Bounty* mutineers accepted an invitation to leave Pitcairn and settle on Norfolk Island, which led to Norfolk Island becoming a separate settlement under the jurisdiction of the Governor of New South Wales. In 1897 Norfolk Island became a dependency of NSW, and in 1914, pursuant to the Norfolk Island Act 1913, a territory of Australia. From that date, Norfolk Island has been regarded as an integral part of Australia.

In 1979 Norfolk Island gained a substantial degree of self-government, enabling the island to run its affairs to the greatest practical extent. Wide powers are exercised by a nine-member Legislative Assembly. The Act preserves the Commonwealth's responsibility for Norfolk Island as a territory under its authority, with the Minister for the Arts and Territories as the responsible Minister.

The island is a popular tourist resort, and a large proportion of the population depends on tourism and its ancillaries for employment. In 1990–1 there were 28,891 tourist arrivals on the Island. Regular air services operate from mainland Australia and New Zealand.

The seat of government and administration offices are in Kingston.

Administrator, A. G. Kerr.

AUSTRALIAN STATES

NEW SOUTH WALES

The State of New South Wales is situated entirely between the 28th and 38th parallels of S. lat. and 141st and 154th meridians of E. long., and comprises an area of 309,433 sq. miles (801,427 sq. km) (exclusive of 939 sq. miles of Australian Capital Territory which lies within its borders).

Population – Preliminary estimated resident population at 30 June 1991 was 5,731,441.

Births, deaths and marriages of usually resident population were:

	1989	1990
Births	87,274	90,534
Deaths	42,695	43,813
Marriages	44,379	41,450

The annual rate per 1,000 of estimated resident population in 1988 was births 14.8; deaths 7.8; marriages 7.2. Deaths under 1 year per 1,000 live births, 9.0.

RELIGIONS – The members of the Roman Catholic Church in New South Wales, according to the Census of 1986, numbered 1,529,176, Anglican Church 1,519,806, Uniting (including Methodist) 327,360, Presbyterian 227,663, Orthodox 165,659, Baptist 67,187, Lutheran 31,890, other Christian 288,865, Muslim 57,551, Hebrew 28,236 and other religions 57,079. The religion of 1,101,409 persons was either not stated in the census schedules or was stated as 'none'.

STATE CAPITAL – ΨSydney, the largest city in Australia, stands on the shores of Port Jackson. Sydney Harbour extends inland for 21 km; the total area of water is about 55 sq. km. The preliminary estimated resident population in 1991 of the Sydney Statistical Division was 3,539,024. The Newcastle and Wollongong Statistical subdivisions contain populations of 427,568 and 235,913 respectively.

TOWNS – The populations of other principal municipalities are: Albury 39,610, Dubbo 31,290, Greater Taree 36,960, Hastings 42,220, Lismore 38,130, Orange 32,520, Shoalhaven 59,470, Tamworth 33,830, Wagga Wagga 50,930.

GOVERNMENT

New South Wales was first colonized as a British possession in 1788, and after progressive settlement a partly elective legislature was established in 1843. In 1855 responsible government was granted, the present Constitution being founded on the Constitution Act of 1902. New South Wales federated with the other States of Australia in 1901. The executive authority of the State is vested in a Governor (appointed by the Crown), assisted by a Council of Ministers.

Governor of New South Wales, His Excellency Rear-Adm. Peter Sinclair, AO, RAN, *assumed office* August 1990.

Lt.-Governor and Chief Justice of NSW, The Hon. Mr Justice Gleeson, AC.

Premier, Hon. John Fahey.

AGENT-GENERAL IN LONDON, N. E. W. Pickard, 75 King William Street, London EC4N 7HA.

LEGISLATURE

The Legislative Council consists of 42 members, elected by popular vote and the Legislative Assembly consists of 99 members elected for a maximum period of four years.

President of the Legislative Council, Hon. M. Willis, MLC.

Speaker, Legislative Assembly, Hon. K. R. Rozzoli, MP.

JUDICATURE

The judicial system includes a Supreme Court, Industrial Commission, District Court, Land and Environment Court, Compensation Court, and Local Courts (Magistrates).

Chief Justice, Supreme Court, The Hon. Mr Justice Gleeson, AC.

President, Court of Appeal, Hon. Mr Justice Kirby, CMG.

EDUCATION

Education is compulsory between the ages of 6 and 15 years. It is non-sectarian and free at all government schools. The enrolment in 1991 in 2,181 government and 850 non-government schools was 1,030,623. The six universities, together with advanced education colleges, had an enrolment of 160,651 in 1991. Students enrolled in technical and further education colleges in 1990 numbered 316,475.

PRODUCTION AND INDUSTRY

LIVESTOCK AND LIVESTOCK PRODUCTS – A large area is suitable for sheep-raising, the principal breed of sheep being the merino, which was introduced in 1797.

MINING INDUSTRY – The principal minerals are coal, lead, zinc, gold, rutile, copper and zircon. The total value of minerals extracted in 1988–9 was $A3,690 million. The average number of persons employed in the mining industry during 1988–9 was 19,883. In 1988–9, 81,272,000 tonnes of coal were produced.

MANUFACTURING INDUSTRY – In 1989 there were 10,469 manufacturing establishments (employing four or more persons). The number of persons employed at 30 June 1988 was 361,636. Production of raw steel in 1989–90 was 5,333,000 tonnes.

LORD HOWE ISLAND

Lord Howe Island, which is part of New South Wales, is situated 702 kilometres north-east of Sydney. Lat. 31° 33′ 4″ S., Long. 159° 4′ 26″ E. Area 6.37 sq. miles (16.5 sq. km.). Population, 1991, 377. The island is of volcanic origin with Mount Gower reaching an altitude of 866 m. The affairs of the Island are administered by the Lord Howe Island Board.

QUEENSLAND

This State, situated in lat. 9° 14′–29° S. and long. 138°–153° 30′ E., comprises the whole north-eastern portion of the Australian continent. Queensland possesses an area of 666,798 sq. miles (1,727,000 sq. km).

POPULATION – At 30 June 1991 the estimated resident population numbered 2,966,090. Births, deaths and marriages were:

	1990	1991
Births	44,868	44,160
Deaths	19,321	19,175
Marriages	19,671	19,844

The annual rate per 1,000 of estimated resident population in 1991 was – births 14.9; deaths 6.5; marriages 7.0. Deaths under 1 year per 1,000 live births, 7.5.

RELIGIONS – At the Census of 1986, there were 640,867 Anglican, 628,906 Catholics, 255,287 Uniting Church, 120,239 Presbyterians, 56,910 Lutherans, 39,098 Baptists, and 211,316 other Christians.

STATE CAPITAL – ΨBrisbane is situated on the Brisbane River, which is navigable by large vessels to the city, over 23 kilometres from Moreton Bay. The estimated resident population of the Brisbane Statistical Division at 30 June 1991 was 1,327,006. This area includes the cities of Brisbane (753,375), Ipswich (76,673), Logan (153,427) and Redcliffe (49,389).

CITIES – Other cities with population over 30,000 at 30 June 1991, are: ΨTownsville 84,138; Gold Coast 139,899; Toowoomba 83,776; ΨRockhampton 59,505; ΨCairns 44,021; ΨCaloundra 50,609; ΨThuringowa 39,292; Ψ Bundaberg 33,300.

GOVERNMENT

Queensland was constituted a separate colony with responsible government in 1859, having previously formed part of New South Wales. The executive authority is vested in a Governor (appointed by the Crown), aided by an Executive Council of 18 members.

Governor of Queensland, Her Excellency Mrs Mary Marguerite Leneen Forde.

Premier, Hon. W. K. Goss.

AGENT-GENERAL IN LONDON, R. T. Anderson, 392 Strand, London WC2R OLZ.

LEGISLATURE

Parliament consists of a Legislative Assembly of 89 members, elected by all persons aged 18 years and over. The Assembly,

as at 30 June 1990, was composed of: Australian Labor Party, 54; National Party of Australia, 26; Liberal Party of Australia, 9.
Speaker, Hon. D. Fouras.
Chairman of Committees, C. B. Campbell.
Leader of the Opposition, R. E. Borbidge.

Judicature

There are a Supreme Court; District Courts; Children's Courts; an Industrial Court; a Land Court and a Medical Assessment Tribunal; a Local Government Court; the Industrial Conciliation and Arbitration Commission; Inferior Courts at all the principal towns, presided over by Stipendiary Magistrates; a Small Claims Tribunal; Small Debts Court; a Licensing Court and a Mining Warden's Court.
Chief Justice, Supreme Court, Hon. J. M. Macrossan.

Education

Education is compulsory, secular and free between the ages of 5 and 15. At July 1991, there were 1,004 government primary schools, 72 primary/secondary, and 179 secondary schools with 254,397 primary students, and 143,628 secondary students.

Post-secondary education involves technical and further education (TAFE) and higher education. During 1990, 158,402 students were enrolled in TAFE courses, excluding 78,890 enrolled in adult education courses. At 30 April 1991 there were 50,531 full-time, 20,504 part-time, and 13,986 external students enrolled in higher education courses.

Production and Industry

Forestry – Total Australian grown timber processed in 1989–90 amounted to 1,529,057 cubic metres (gross volume measure).
Minerals – There are rich deposits of both metallic and non-metallic minerals. Coal is mined extensively in Central Queensland and on a lesser scale in the Ipswich district.
Manufacturing – In 1990–1 there were 6,201 establishments with four or more workers, employing 125,500 persons, and producing goods and services worth $A23,841 million. Much of the production was the processing of foodstuffs, minerals and chemical, petroleum and coal products. Included in other factory production were the products from engineering, transport equipment, timber, basic and fabricated metal, cement, paper and textile mills and oil refineries.

SOUTH AUSTRALIA

The State of South Australia is situated between 26° and 38° S. lat. and 129° and 141° E. long., the total area being 380,070 sq. miles (984,376 sq. km).
Population – At 30 June 1991, the resident population was estimated to be 1,454,000. Births, deaths and marriages were:

	1990	1991
Births	19,863	19,728
Deaths	10,938	11,188
Marriages	9,609	9,392

The annual rate per 1,000 of estimated resident population in 1991 was births 13.6; deaths 7.7; marriages 6.5. Deaths under 1 year per 1,000 live births, 5.6.
Religions – Religion is free and receives no State aid. At the 1986 Census, the persons belonging to the principal religious denominations were as follows: Catholic 267,137; Anglican 242,722; Uniting Church 176,980; Lutheran 64,851; Orthodox 37,149; Baptist 21,415; Presbyterian 18,566; Church of Christ 16,629; and Pentecostal 14,997.

State Capital – ΨAdelaide, the chief city and capital, estimated resident population on 30 June 1991, 1,062,874 inclusive of suburbs. Other centres (with 1991 populations) are: ΨWhyalla (27,189); ΨMt Gambier (22,447); ΨPort Pirie (15,216); ΨPort Augusta (15,629).

Government

South Australia was proclaimed a British Province in 1836, and in 1851 a partially elective legislature was established. The present Constitution rests upon a Law of 24 October 1856, the executive authority being vested in a Governor appointed by the Crown, aided by a Council of 13 Ministers.
Governor of South Australia, Her Excellency the Hon. Dame Roma Mitchell, AC, DBE (1991).
Lt.-Governor, The Hon. Dr Basil Hetzel, AC (1992).
Premier, Hon. John Bannon.

Agent-General in London, G. Walls, South Australia House, 50 Strand, London WC2N 5LW.

Legislature

Parliament consists of a Legislative Council of 22 members elected for eight years, one half retiring every four years; and a House of Assembly of 47 members, elected for a maximum duration of four years. Election is by ballot, with universal adult suffrage for both the Legislative Council and the House of Assembly.

The representation in the House of Assembly is 22 Labor, 22 Liberals, 2 Labor Independents and 1 National Party.
President of the Legislative Council, Hon. G. L. Bruce.
Speaker of the House of Assembly, Hon. N. T. Peterson.

Judicature

The Supreme Court is presided over by the Chief Justice and 13 Puisne Judges.

Education

Education at the primary and secondary level is available at government schools controlled by the Education Department and at non-government schools, most of which are denominational. In 1991 there were 696 government schools with 186,814 students, and 184 independent schools with 60,019 students. Tertiary education is available through universities, and technical and further education colleges.

The three universities had, in 1990, a total enrolment of 47,164 full-time students.

TASMANIA

Tasmania is an island state of Australia situated in the Southern ocean off the south-eastern extremity of the mainland. It is separated from the Australian mainland by Bass Strait and incorporates King Island and the Furneaux group of islands which are in the Strait. It lies between 40° 38′–43° 39′ S. lat. and 144° 36′–148° 23′ E. long., and contains an area of 26,383 sq. miles (68,331 sq. km). Macquarie Island, situated at 54° 30′ S. and 158° 57′ E., about 900 miles north of the Antarctic Continent, is a dependency of Tasmania.
Population – The estimated resident population at 30 June 1991 was 460,470. Births, deaths and marriages were:

	1990	1991p
Births	7,001	6,827
Deaths	3,690	3,544
Marriages	3,026	3,067

p preliminary

The annual rate per 1,000 of estimated resident population in 1991 was births 14.6; deaths 7.6; marriages 6.6. Deaths under 1 year per 1,000 live births, 7.9.

RELIGIONS – In 1986 there were 154,748 members of the Anglican Church of Australia, 80,479 Catholics, 36,724 Uniting Church of Australia, 12,084 Presbyterians and 8,092 Baptists.

STATE CAPITAL – ΨHobart, founded 1804. Population (30 June 1991) (metropolitan area), 181,838. Other towns (with population at 30 June 1991) are ΨLaunceston (metropolitan area, 93,520), ΨDevonport (24,622), Burnie-Somerset (20,483).

GOVERNMENT

The island was first settled by a British party from New South Wales in 1803, becoming a separate colony in 1825. In 1851 a partly elective legislature was inaugurated, and in 1856 responsible government was established. In 1901 Tasmania became a State of the Australian Commonwealth. The State executive authority is vested in a Governor (appointed by the Crown), but is exercised by Cabinet Ministers responsible to the Legislature, of which they are members.

Governor of Tasmania, His Excellency Gen. Sir Phillip Bennett, AC, KBE, DSO.
Premier, Hon. Raymond J. Groom.

LEGISLATURE

Parliament consists of two Houses, a Legislative Council of 19 members, elected for six years (three retiring annually, in rotation, except in every sixth year, when four retire) and a House of Assembly of 35 members, elected by proportional representation for four years in five seven-member constituencies, the electors for both Houses being all Tasmanians of 18 years and over who have resided continuously in the State for at least six months. Elections for the Assembly are held every four years.

The election of February 1992 resulted in a victory for the Liberal Party, with 19 Liberal, 11 Labor and 5 Independent members of the House of Assembly. The state of the parties in the Legislative Council following the election was Independent 17, Liberal 1, Labor 1.

Speaker of the House of Assembly, Hon. G. R. Page.
President of the Legislative Council, Hon. E. J. C. Stopp.

JUDICATURE

The Supreme Court of Tasmania, with civil, criminal ecclesiastical, admiralty and matrimonial jurisdiction, was established by Royal Charter in 1823.

Local Courts are held before Commissioners who are legal practitioners. Courts of General Sessions, constituted by a chairman who is a Justice of the Peace and at least one other Justice, are established in the municipalities and Courts of Petty Sessions are constituted by Magistrates sitting alone, or by two or more justices. A single justice may hear and determine certain matters.

Chief Justice, Supreme Court, Hon. Sir Guy Green, KBE.

EDUCATION

Government schools are of three main types: primary, secondary and secondary colleges. On 1 July 1991 there were 65,662 students enrolled in 247 government schools. There were also 65 independent schools with an enrolment of 19,952. The University of Tasmania at Hobart, established 1890, had 4,249 full-time students and 1,628 part-time (including external) students in 1990. The Tasmanian State Institute of Technology, offering degree and diploma courses, was established in 1972. In 1990 4,192 students were enrolled.

PRODUCTION AND INDUSTRY

ENERGY – Tasmania, the smallest Australian state, ranks fourth as a producer of electrical energy. Most of it is derived from water power, with a total installed generator capacity of 2,315,000 kW at 30 June 1991. By reason of its low-cost electrical energy, Tasmania has large plants producing ferro-manganese and newsprint. A large aluminium plant is situated at Bell Bay and Tasmania is the source of the bulk of Australian requirements of zinc and fine papers.

FORESTRY – The quantity of timber (excluding firewood) of various species cut in 1990–1 was 4,281,200 cubic metres, including 3,516,200 cubic metres for woodchip and wood-pulp.

MINERALS – The chief ores mined are those containing copper, tin, iron, silver, zinc and lead.

MANUFACTURES – The chief manufactures for export are refined metals, preserved fruit and vegetables, butter, cheese, textiles, paper, confectionery, wood chips and sawn timber. In 1988–9, 962 manufacturing establishments employed 7,532 persons, including working proprietors.

VICTORIA

The State of Victoria comprises the south-east corner of Australia, at the part where its mainland territory projects furthest into the southern latitudes; it lies between 34°–39° S. latitude and 141°–150° E. longitude. Its extreme length from east to west is about 493 miles, its greatest breadth is about 290 miles, and its extent of coast-line is about 1,043 geographical miles, including the length around Port Phillip Bay, Western Port and Corner Inlet, the entire area being 87,876 sq. miles (227,597 sq. km).

POPULATION – The estimated resident population at 30 June 1991 was 4,427,400. Births, deaths and marriages were:

	1990p
Births	67,166
Deaths	30,988
Marriages	30,120

p preliminary

The annual rate per 1,000 of mean estimated resident population in 1991 was births 15.3; deaths 7.0; marriages 6.9. Deaths under 1 year per 1,000 live births, 7.8.

RELIGIONS – At the Census in 1986, members of the Catholic Church numbered 1,104,044, Anglican 715,414, Uniting (union of Presbyterian, Congregationalist and Methodist) 280,262, Presbyterian 138,000, Orthodox 177,565, and Baptist 39,784. The number of persons who did not state their religion was 589,132.

STATE CAPITAL – ΨMelbourne had a resident population at 30 June 1991 estimated at 3,153,500. Other urban centres are ΨGeelong 152,780; Ballarat 82,330; Bendigo 70,360; Shepparton-Mooroopna 41,450.

GOVERNMENT

Victoria was originally known as the Port Phillip District of New South Wales and was created a separate colony in 1851, with a partially elective legislature. In 1855 Responsible Government was conferred. The executive authority is vested in a Governor, appointed by the Crown, aided by an Executive Council of Ministers.

The Legislative Assembly (elected 1 October 1988) consists of Australian Labor Party 46, Liberal Party 33, and National Party 9.

Governor of Victoria, His Excellency the Honourable Richard E. McGarvie, *assumed office* 23 April 1992.
Lt.-Governor, The Hon. Sir John McIntosh Young, KCMG, AO (1974).
Premier, Hon J. Kirner.

AGENT-GENERAL IN LONDON, L. T. Baldock, Victoria House, Melbourne Place, Strand, London WC2B 4LG.

LEGISLATURE

Parliament consists of a Legislative Council of 44 members, elected for the 22 Provinces for two terms of the Legislative Assembly, one half retiring every four years at a General Election; and a Legislative Assembly of 88 members, elected for a maximum duration of four years. Voting is compulsory.
President of the Legislative Council, Hon. A. J. Hunt.
Speaker of the Legislative Assembly, Hon. Dr K. A. Coghill.

JUDICATURE

There is a Supreme Court with a Chief Justice and 24 Puisne Judges, a County Court and Magistrates' Courts.

Chief Justice, Supreme Court, Hon. Mr Justice John Phillips.
Chief Judge, County Court, Hon. G. R. D. Waldron, AO.

EDUCATION

Primary education is compulsory, secular and free between the ages of 6 and 15. At 12 July 1989 there were 2,059 government schools, attended by 527,700 students. In addition there are technical and further education institutions and colleges of advanced education. At 12 July 1989, 257,407 pupils attended non-government schools. There are four state-aided universities.

PRODUCTION AND INDUSTRY

MINERALS – Minerals raised include oil and natural gas, brown coal, limestone, clays and stone for construction material. Production of brown coal in 1989–90 was valued at $A327,438,400 and gold $A48,557,400.
CRUDE OIL AND NATURAL GAS – In 1965 natural gas was discovered in commercial quantities in the offshore waters of the Gippsland Basin in eastern Victoria and in 1966–7, three more valuable oilfields were located in the same general area. These fields are still the largest yet found in Australia. Production from Victorian natural gas and crude oil fields during 1989 was 5,244,959 Mg. litres.
SECONDARY INDUSTRY – At 30 June 1989 there were 9,771 manufacturing establishments in which total employees numbered 367,376.

WESTERN AUSTRALIA

Western Australia includes all that portion of the continent west of 129° E. long., the most westerly point being in 113° 9′ E. long. and from 13° 44′ to 35° 8′ S. lat. Its extreme length is 1,480 miles, and 1,000 miles from east to west; total area 975,920 sq. miles (2,527,621 sq. km).
POPULATION – At 30 June 1990 the estimated resident population was 1,633,900. Births, deaths and marriages were:

	1989	1990p
Births	25,123	25,019
Deaths	9,513	9,567
Marriages	10,578	10,739

p preliminary

The annual rate per 1,000 of estimated resident population in 1989 was births 15.7; deaths 6.0; marriages 6.7. Deaths under 1 year per 1,000 live births, 7.8.
RELIGIONS – The Census of 1986 gave the following: Anglican Church 371,302, Roman Catholics 347,695, Uniting Church 82,876, and Presbyterians 31,641.

STATE CAPITAL – ΨPerth, on the right bank of the Swan River estuary, 12 miles from Fremantle. Estimated resident population (30 June 1990) of Perth Statistical Division, including the port of ΨFremantle, 1,193,130.

GOVERNMENT

Western Australia was first settled by the British in 1829, and in 1870 it was granted a partially elective legislature. In 1890 responsible government was granted, and the administration vested in a Governor, a Legislative Council, and a Legislative Assembly. The present constitution rests upon the Constitution Act 1889, the Constitution Acts Amendment Act 1899, and amending Acts. The Executive is vested in a Governor appointed by the Crown and aided by a Council of responsible Ministers.
Governor of Western Australia, His Excellency the Hon. Sir Francis Burt, AC, KCMG, QC.
Lt.-Governor and Administrator, Hon. D. K. Malcolm.
Premier, Hon. Dr Carmen Lawrence.

AGENT-GENERAL IN LONDON, D. Fischer, Western Australia House, 115 Strand, London WC2R OAJ.

LEGISLATURE

Parliament consists of a Legislative Council and a Legislative Assembly, elected by adult suffrage subject to qualifications of residence and registration. The qualifying age for electors for both the Legislative Council and Legislative Assembly is 18 years. There are 34 members in the Legislative Council elected for a period of four years. The Legislative Assembly has 57 members, who are elected for a term of four years. The Legislative Assembly (elected 4 February 1989) is composed of Australian Labor Party 31, Liberal Party 20, National Party of Australia 6.
President of the Legislative Council, Hon. C. E. Griffiths.
Speaker of the Legislative Assembly, Hon. M. Barnett.

JUDICATURE

Chief Justice, Hon. D. K. Malcolm.
Senior Puisne Judge, Hon. A. R. A. Wallace.
Puisne Judges, Hons. P. F. Brinsden; G. A. Kennedy; W. P. Pidgeon; B. W. Rowland; E. M. Franklyn; P. L. Seaman; R. D. Nicolson; T. A. Walsh; D. A. Ipp; H. A. Wallwork; M. J. Murray.

EDUCATION

In 1990 there were 760 government and 244 non-government primary and secondary school campuses with 215,311 and 69,575 full-time students respectively. The principal higher education institutions are the University of Western Australia (10,815 enrolments in 1990), Murdoch University (6,223), Curtin University (16,642) and Edith Cowan University (14,641).

PRODUCTION AND INDUSTRY

MANUFACTURING INDUSTRIES – There were 3,439 manufacturing establishments operating in the State at 30 June 1989. The total number of persons employed (including working proprietors) by these establishments at the end of June 1989 was 74,500.
FORESTRY – The forests contain some of the finest hardwoods in the world. The total quantity of sawn timber produced during 1989–90 was 324,083 cubic metres.
MINERALS – The State has large deposits of a wide range of minerals, many of which are being mined or are under development for production. The ex-mine value of all minerals (excluding construction materials, clays and limestone) produced during 1988–9 was $A6,243,729,000.

AUSTRIA
Republik Österreich

Austria is a country of central Europe bounded on the north by Czechoslovakia, on the south by Italy and Slovenia, on the east by Hungary, on the north-west by Germany and on the west by Switzerland and Liechtenstein. Its area is 32,367 sq. miles (83,855 sq. km), and its population is 7,860,800 (official estimate 1991). The predominant religion is Roman Catholicism.

CAPITAL – Vienna, on the Danube, population 1,533,176. Other larger towns are Graz (232,155), Linz (202,855), Innsbruck (114,966), Salzburg (143,971), and Klagenfurt (89,502).
CURRENCY – Schilling of 100 Groschen.
FLAG – Three equal horizontal stripes of red, white, red.
NATIONAL ANTHEM – Land der Berge, Land am Strome (Land of mountains, land on the river).
NATIONAL DAY – 26 October.

GOVERNMENT

The Republic of Austria comprises nine provinces (Vienna, Lower Austria, Upper Austria, Salzburg, Tyrol, Vorarlberg, Carinthia, Styria and Burgenland) and was established in 1918 on the break-up of the Austro-Hungarian Empire. On 13 March 1938, as a result of the *Anschluss*, Austria (*Österreich*) was incorporated into the *Deutsches Reich* under the name *Ostmark*. After the liberation of Vienna in 1945, the Republic of Austria was reconstituted within the frontiers of 1937 and a freely-elected Government took office on 20 December 1945. The country was divided at this time into four zones occupied respectively by the UK, USA, USSR and France, while Vienna was jointly occupied by the four Powers. On 15 May 1955 the Austrian State Treaty was signed in Vienna by the Foreign Ministers of the four Powers and of Austria. This Treaty recognized the re-establishment of Austria as a sovereign, independent and democratic state, having the same frontiers as on 1 January 1938.

There is a national assembly of 183 Deputies. After the elections of 7 October 1990, the Socialists formed a coalition with the People's Party. The state of the parties in the Nationalrat (Lower House) was:

Socialist Party (Social Democrat)	80
People's Party (Conservative)	60
Freedom Party (Liberal)	33
Green	10

In the Bundesrat (Upper House) in March 1990 the People's Party held 30 seats, the Socialist Party 29 and the Liberal Party 5.

HEAD OF STATE
President of the Republic of Austria, Dr Thomas Klestil, *took office* 8 July 1992.

CABINET as at July 1992

Chancellor, Dr Franz Vranitzky (SPÖ).
Vice-Chancellor, Science and Research, Dr Erhard Busek.
Minister for Federalism and Administrative Reform, Juergen Weiss (ÖVP).
Women's Affairs, Johanna Dohnal (SPÖ).
Foreign Affairs, Dr Alois Mock (ÖVP).
Economic Affairs, Dr Wolfgang Schüssel (ÖVP).
Employment and Social Affairs, Josef Hesoun (SPÖ).
Finance, Ferdinand Lacina (SPÖ).
Health, Consumer Protection and Sport, Dr Michael Ausserwinkler (SPÖ).
Interior, Dr Franz Löschnak (SPÖ).
Justice, Dr Nikolaus Michalek (Indep.)
Defence, Dr Werner Fasslabend (ÖVP).
Agriculture and Forestry, Dr Franz Fischler (ÖVP).
Environment, Youth and Family Affairs, Ruth Feldgrill-Zankel (ÖVP).
Education and Arts, Dr Rudolf Scholten (SPÖ).
Public Economy and Transport, Vicktor Klima (SPÖ).
Ministers of State, Brigitte Ederer (SPÖ) (*European Questions*); Dr Peter Kostelka (SPÖ) (*Public Service*); Dr Johannes Ditz (ÖVP) (*Finance*); Dr Maria Fekter (ÖVP) (*Economic Affairs, Construction and Tourism*).

SPÖ: Socialists; ÖVP: People's Party (Conservatives).

AUSTRIAN EMBASSY
18 Belgrave Mews West, London SW1X 8HU
Tel 071-235 3731

Ambassador Extraordinary and Plenipotentiary, His Excellency Dr Walter F. Magrutsch (1987).

BRITISH EMBASSY
Jauresgasse 12, 1030 Vienna
Tel: Vienna 7131575

Ambassador Extraordinary and Plenipotentiary, His Excellency Terence Wood (1992).
Counsellor, Consul General and Head of Chancery, R. P. Nash, LVO.
Counsellors, N. H. McMillan, OBE; P. A. S. Wise; J. Franklin.
First Secretaries, S. J. O'Flaherty; S. G. Ratcliffe (*Commercial*); J. Moorby, MBE (*HM Consul*); A. N. King, LVO (*Administration*); R. Dear (*Chancery/Information*).
Defence Attaché, Lt.-Col. P. W. L. Hughes, MBE.

BRITISH CONSULAR OFFICES – There is a consular office at *Vienna*, and Honorary Consulates at *Bregenz, Graz, Innsbruck* and *Salzburg*.

BRITISH COUNCIL REPRESENTATIVE, John Green, OBE, Schenkenstrasse 4, A-1010 Vienna.

EDUCATION

Education is free and compulsory between the ages of 6 and 15 and there are good facilities for secondary, technical and professional education. There are 12 state-maintained universities and six colleges of art.

CULTURE

The language of Austria is German, but the rights of the Slovene- and Croat-speaking minorities in Carinthia, Styria and Burgenland are protected.

COMMUNICATIONS

Internal communications in Austria are partly restricted because of the mountainous nature of the country, although there has been an extensive programme to increase the number of motorways (*Autobahn*), many of which are tunnelled through the mountains. There is a network of *Autobahn* between major cities which also links up with the West German and Italian networks. The railways in Austria (ÖBB) are state-owned and in 1989 had 5,641 km of track, 57.4 per cent of which is electrified. Of the 425 km of waterways, 350 km are navigable and there is considerable trade through the Danube ports by both local and foreign shipping. There are six commercial airports catering for 7,004,141 passengers in 1989.

ECONOMY

The origin of Gross Domestic Product in 1991 was as follows (in AS billion):

Agriculture and forestry	52.5
Manufacturing and mining	509.3
Energy and water supply	48.0
Construction	138.9
Commerce, hotels, restaurants	313.6
Transport and communications	117.5
Asset management	323.5
Other services and producers	91.5
Import duties and other items	180.1

The total value of GDP in 1991 was Schilling 1,916.8 billion.

AGRICULTURE – The arable land produces wheat, rye, barley, oats, maize, potatoes, sugar beet, turnips, and miscellaneous crops. Many varieties of fruit trees flourish and the vineyards produce excellent wine. The pastures support horses, cattle and pigs. Timber forms a valuable source of Austria's indigenous wealth, about 45 per cent of the total land area consisting of forest areas. Coniferous species predominate (75 per cent of afforested area).

TOURISM – In 1991, 25,737,088 tourists visited Austria. Foreign exchange receipts from tourism were Schilling 162,000 million, a major contribution to the balance of payments.

FINANCE

	1989	1990
		Schilling, million
Federal Budget		
Revenue	477,583	425,110
Expenditure	602,300	564,424
Gross Budget Deficit	124,717	139,314

TRADE

Main exports are processed goods (iron and steel, textiles, paper and cardboard products), machinery and transport equipment, other finished goods (including clothing), raw materials and foodstuffs. Main imports are machinery and transport equipment, processed goods, chemical products, foodstuffs, fuel and energy.

	1990	1991
		Schilling, million
Imports	516,622	548,962
Exports	436,797	450,458

Over 80 per cent of all trade is with other European countries, EC countries accounting for about 75 per cent, eastern Europe for about 11 per cent and EFTA members for 9 per cent.

TRADE WITH UK

	1990	1991
Imports from UK	£705,850,000	£766,734,000
Exports to UK	957,789,000	916,265,000

THE BAHAMAS
The Commonwealth of The Bahamas

AREA, POPULATION, ETC – The Bahama Islands are an archipelago lying in the North Atlantic Ocean between 20° 55′–25° 22′ N. lat. and 72° 35′–79° 35′ W. long. They extend from the coast of Florida on the north-west almost to Haiti on the south-east. The group consists of 700 islands, of which 30 are inhabited and 2,400 cays comprising an area of more than 5,832 sq. miles. The population (Census 1990) is 254,000. The principal islands include: Abaco, Acklins, Andros, Berry Islands, Bimini, Cat Island, Crooked Island, Eleuthera, Exumas, Grand Bahama, Harbour Island, Inagua, Long Island, Mayaguana, New Providence (on which is located the capital, Nassau), Ragged Island, Rum Cay, San Salvador and Spanish Wells. San Salvador was the first landfall in the New World of Christopher Columbus on 12 October 1492.

CAPITAL – ΨNassau, population (Census 1990) 171,000.
CURRENCY – Bahamian dollar (B$) of 100 cents.
FLAG – Horizontal stripes of aquamarine, gold and aquamarine, with a black equilateral triangle on the hoist.
NATIONAL ANTHEM – March on, Bahamaland.
NATIONAL DAY – 10 July (Independence Day).

GOVERNMENT

The Bahamas were settled by British subjects when the islands were deserted. The ownership of The Bahamas was taken over in 1782 by the Spanish, but the Treaty of Versailles in 1783 restored them to the British. The Bahamas gained independence on 10 July 1973. The Head of State is HM Queen Elizabeth II, represented in the islands by a Governor-General. There is a Senate of 16 members and an elected House of Assembly of 49 members. A general election is scheduled to take place on 19 August 1992.

Governor-General, His Excellency Sir Clifford Darling (1992).

CABINET as at June 1992

Prime Minister and Minister of Tourism, Rt. Hon. Sir Lynden Pindling, KCMG.
Deputy PM, Minister of Foreign Affairs and of Public Personnel, Hon. Sir Clement Maynard.
National Security and Government Leader in the House of Assembly, Hon. Darrell Rolle.
Finance, Hon. Paul L. Adderley.
Works and Lands, Hon. Philip M. Bethel.
Employment and Immigration, Hon. Alfred T. Maycock.
Transport and Leader of the Senate, Senator Hon. Peter J. Bethell.
Housing and National Insurance, Hon. George W. Mackey.
Agriculture, Trade and Industry, Hon. Perry Christie.
Health, Hon. E. Charles Carter.
Education, Hon. Dr Bernard J. Nottage.
Youth, Sports and Community Affairs, Hon. Dr Norman Gay.
Consumer Affairs, Hon. Vincent A. Peet.
Local Government, Hon. Marvin B. Pinder.
Attorney-General, Senator Hon. Sean G. McWeeney.

President of the Court of Appeal, Kenneth Henry.
Chief Justice, J. C. Gonsalves-Sabola.

BAHAMAS HIGH COMMISSION
Bahamas House, 10 Chesterfield Street, London W1X 8AH
Tel 071-408 4488

High Commissioner, Her Excellency Dr Patricia Rodgers (1988).

BRITISH HIGH COMMISSION
PO Box N-7516, Nassau
Tel: Nassau 325-7471

High Commissioner, His Excellency Brian Attewell (1992).
Deputy High Commissioner, R. G. Church (*Head of Chancery*).

ECONOMY

Tourism is the economic mainstay of The Bahamas, employing about two-thirds of the labour force. It provides about two-thirds of Government revenue and about half the country's foreign exchange earnings. The second main industry is international banking and trust business. The Bahamas' absence of any direct taxation and internal stability have enabled the country to become one of the world's leading financial centres.

Agricultural production is mainly of fresh vegetables, fruit, meat and eggs for the domestic market, and crawfish, mostly for export. There are large reserves of aragonite, and reserves of limestone and salt, all of which are being commercially exploited. Freeport is the country's leading industrial centre, with a pharmaceutical and chemicals plant, an oil trans-shipment and storage terminal, and port and bunkering facilities. There are also a brewery and a rum distillery on New Providence.

Finance	1989p	1990p
Public revenue	B$448.1m	B$489.1m
Expenditure	561.6m	532.1m

p provisional

TRADE

The imports are chiefly foodstuffs, manufactured articles, building materials, vehicles and machinery, chemicals and petroleum. The chief exports are rum, petroleum, hormones, salt, crawfish and aragonite.

Trade with UK	1990	1991
Imports from UK	£22,917,000	£19,631,000
Exports to UK	15,053,000	37,142,000

EDUCATION

Education is compulsory between the ages of 5 and 14. More than 59,500 students are enrolled in Ministry of Education and independent schools in New Providence and the Family Islands.

COMMUNICATIONS

The main ports are Nassau (New Providence), Freeport (Grand Bahama), Mathew Town (Inagua). International air services are operated from Abaco, Bimini, Eleuthera, Exuma, Grand Bahama and New Providence. About 50 smaller airports and landing strips facilitate services between the islands, the services being mainly provided by Bahamasair, the national carrier. There are roads on the larger islands, and roads are under construction on the smaller islands. There are no railways. Wireless and telephone services are in operation to all parts of the world.

BAHRAIN

Dawlet al-Bahrein

AREA – Bahrain consists of a group of low-lying islands situated about half-way down the Gulf, some 20 miles off the east coast of Arabia. The largest of these, Bahrain island itself, is about 30 miles long and 10 miles wide at its broadest. The capital, Manama, is situated on the north shore of this island. The next largest, Muharraq, with the town and Bahrain International Airport, is connected to Manama by a causeway 1½ miles long.

CLIMATE – The climate is humid all the year round, with rainfall of about 3 in. concentrated in the mild winter months, December to March; in summer, May to October, temperatures can exceed 110°F (44°C).

POPULATION – The population (1990 UN estimate) is 503,000, of whom 68.4 per cent are Bahraini. About 35 per cent of the Bahrainis are Sunni Muslims, the remaining 65 per cent being Shias; the ruling family and many of the most prominent merchants are Sunnis.

CAPITAL – ΨManama, population (1981 Census) 108,684. In 1990, it was estimated that 32 per cent of Bahrain's population lives in Manama.

CURRENCY – Bahrain dinar (BD) of 1,000 fils.

FLAG – Red, with vertical serrated white bar next to staff.

NATIONAL DAY – 16 December.

GOVERNMENT

Bahrain has been a fully independent state since 1971. Government takes the form of a constitutional monarchy, in which traditional consultative procedures continue to play an important role.

HEAD OF STATE

Amir, HH Shaikh Isa bin Sulman Al Khalifa, GCMG, *born* 1932; *acceded* 16 December 1961.

Crown Prince and C.-in-C., Bahrain Defence Force, HE Shaikh Hamad bin Isa Al Khalifa, KCMG.

CABINET as at June 1992

Prime Minister, HE Shaikh Khalifa bin Sulman Al Khalifa.
Foreign Affairs, Shaikh Mohammed bin Mubarak Al Khalifa.
Defence, Maj.-Gen. Shaikh Khalifa bin Ahmed Al Khalifa.
Justice and Islamic Affairs, Shaikh Abdullah bin Khalid Al Khalifa.
Development and Industry, and Cabinet Affairs, Yusuf Ahmad Shirawi.
Education, Dr Ali Fakhro.
Health, Jawad Salim Al-Arayyed.
Transportation, Ibrahim Mohammed Humaidan.
Interior, Shaikh Mohammed bin Khalifa Al Khalifa.
Information, Tariq Abdulrahman Al Moayed.
Labour and Social Affairs, Shaikh Khalifa bin Sulman bin Mohammed Al Khalifa.
Works, Power and Water, Majid Jawad Al-Jishi.
Housing, Shaikh Khalid bin Abdullah Al Khalifa.
Finance and National Economy, Ibrahim Abdul Karim.
Commerce and Agriculture, Habib Ahmed Kassim.
Minister of State, Legal Affairs, Dr Hussain Al-Baharna.

EMBASSY OF THE STATE OF BAHRAIN
98 Gloucester Road, London SW7 4AU
Tel 071-370 5132

Ambassador Extraordinary and Plenipotentiary, His Excellency Karim Ebrahim Al Shakar (1990).

BRITISH EMBASSY
21 Government Avenue, Manama 306, PO Box 114
Tel: Manama 534404

Ambassador Extraordinary and Plenipotentiary, His Excellency Hugh Tunnell (1992).
First Secretaries, W. I. Rae, OBE (*Commercial and Head of Chancery and Consul*); J. C. A. Rundall.
Second Secretary, D. J. Holder (*Commercial*).
Third Secretary, S. Harrison.

BRITISH COUNCIL REPRESENTATIVE, J. Wright, West Wing, A A'ali Building, Building No. 146, Sh. Salman Highway, Manama 356.

ECONOMY

The largest sources of revenue are oil production and refining. The Bahrain field, discovered in 1932, is wholly owned by the Bahrain National Oil Co. Production in 1988 stood at about 42,000 b.p.d. The Sitra refinery derives about 70 per cent of its crude oil by submarine pipeline from Saudi Arabia. Bahrain also has a half share with Saudi Arabia in the profits of the offshore Abu Sa'afa field. A reservoir of unassociated gas has recently been developed on Bahrain island.

Heavy industry is currently limited to the Aluminium Bahrain (ALBA) smelter, producing 183,000 tonnes in 1988; the Gulf Petrochemical Industries Co. (GPIC) producing 375,000 tonnes of ammonia and 395,000 tonnes of methanol in 1988, the Gulf Aluminium Rolling Mill (GARMCO), and the Arab Shipbuilding and Repair Yard (ASRY), operating dry dock facilities up to 500,000 tons.

There are a number of small to medium sized industrial units.

The state has developed as a financial centre. Apart from commercial banks, led by the National Bank of Bahrain, the Standard Chartered Bank, the British Bank of the Middle East and the Bank of Bahrain and Kuwait, many international banks have been licensed as offshore banking units; there are also money brokers and merchant banks.

Trade with UK	1990	1991
Imports from UK	£127,309,000	£147,494,000
Exports to UK	48,459,000	39,120,000

COMMUNICATIONS

Bahrain International airport is one of the main air traffic centres of the Gulf; it is the headquarters of Gulf Air, and a stopping point on routes between Europe and Australia and the Far East for other airlines. A causeway linking Bahrain to Saudi Arabia was opened in November 1986.

A world-wide telephone and telex service, by satellite and cable, is operated by Bahrain Telecommunications Company.

BANGLADESH

Ghana Praja Tantri Bangladesh

AREA, POPULATION, ETC. – The People's Republic of Bangladesh consists of the territory which was formerly East Pakistan (the old province of East Bengal and the Sylhet district of Assam), covering an area of 55,598 sq. miles (143,998 sq. km) in the region of the Gangetic delta, and has a population (1991 Census) of 108,000,000.

The country is crossed by a network of navigable rivers, including the eastern arms of the Ganges, the Jamuna (Brahmaputra) and the Meghna, flowing into the Bay of Bengal. The climate is tropical and monsoon; hot and extremely humid during the summer, and mild and dry during the short winter. The rainfall is heavy, varying from 50 inches to 135 inches in different districts and the bulk of it falls during monsoon season from June to September.

RELIGION – The faith of over 90 per cent of the population is Islam. Islam has been constitutionally declared the state religion of Bangladesh.

LANGUAGE – The state language is Bengali. Use of Bengali is compulsory in all government departments. English, however, is understood and is used widely as an unofficial second language.

CAPITAL – Dhaka, population (estimate) 6,000,000.

CURRENCY – Taka (Tk) of 100 poisha.

FLAG – Red circle on a bottle-green ground.

NATIONAL ANTHEM – Amar Sonar Bangla.

NATIONAL DAY – 26 March (Independence Day).

GOVERNMENT

Prior to becoming East Pakistan, the territory had been part of British India. It acceded to Pakistan in October 1947, which became a Republic on 23 March 1956.

By a proclamation of 26 March 1971, Bangladesh purported to secede from the central government, and a government-in-exile was set up which formally declared independence on 17 April. Bangladesh achieved its independence on 16 December 1971, following the conclusion of the Indo-Pakistan war. Pakistan and Bangladesh accorded one another mutual recognition in February 1974.

From 1975 a non-political administration ran the country under martial law. A Presidential election was held in June 1978 and President Zia was elected. Martial law was subsequently lifted. Zia was assassinated in May 1981 in an unsuccessful coup. He was replaced by Justice Abdus Sattar, who won presidential elections in October 1981, but was overthrown in 1982, in a coup led by the then Chief of Army Staff, Gen. Ershad. Following elections held in May 1986, which were boycotted by several opposition parties, a civilian cabinet was appointed and Gen. Ershad was elected as President in October 1986. Further elections, again boycotted by the opposition, were held in March 1988. Popular unrest forced Gen. Ershad's resignation on 6 December 1990. A caretaker government was formed and parliamentary elections were held on 27 February 1991. The Bangladesh Nationalist Party (BNP) won the largest number of seats but failed to gain a majority. After gaining support from Islamic deputies, the BNP leader, Begum Khaleda Zia, was sworn in as Prime Minister on 21 March 1991.

On 7 August 1991, Parliament approved a constitutional amendment reverting Bangladesh to parliamentary rule after 16 years of presidential government. Under the new system, the parliament elected Abdur Rahman Biswas as President.

HEAD OF STATE
President, Abdur Rahman Biswas, *sworn in* 9 October 1991.

CABINET as at June 1992
Prime Minister, and Minister for Information, Mineral Resources, Establishment, Home Affairs, Begum Khaleda Zia.
Law and Justice, Mirza Golam Hafiz.
Education, Dr Badruddoza Chowdhury.
Agriculture, Irrigation, Flood Control and Water Resources, Maj.-Gen. Majedul Huq (retd.).
Foreign Affairs, A. S. M. Mustafizur Rahman.
Finance and Planning, Saifur Rahman.
Local Government, Rural Development and Co-operatives, Abdus Salam Talukder.
Communication, Col. Oli Ahmed (retd.).
Commerce, M. Keramat Ali.
Shipping, M. K. Anwar.
Industry, Shamsul Islam Khan.
Health and Family Planning, Chowdhury Kamal Ibne Yusuf.

BANGLADESH HIGH COMMISSION
28 Queen's Gate, London SW7 5JA
TEL 071-584 0081

High Commissioner, His Excellency Dr A. F. M. Yusuf (1992).

BRITISH HIGH COMMISSION
Abu Bakr House, Plot 7, Road 84, Gulshan Dhaka, 12
PO Box 6079
Tel: Dhaka 600133/7

High Commissioner, His Excellency Colin Henry Imray, CMG (1989).
Deputy High Commissioner, G. Finlayson.

BRITISH COUNCIL REPRESENTATIVE, J. Mayatt, 5 Fuller Road (PO Box 161), Dhaka 1000.

EDUCATION

Primary education is free and planned to be universal by the year 2000. There are about 46,144 primary schools, mostly managed by the Government. There are about 10,576 secondary schools and 947 colleges offering general and technical education. There are nine universities including two for engineering and technology, one for agriculture and another for Islamic education and research. In 1990 the literacy rate was estimated to be 24 per cent (of which 31 per cent male and 16 per cent female).

COMMUNICATIONS

Principal seaports are Chittagong and Mongla. The Bangladesh Shipping Corporation has been set up by the Government to operate the Bangladesh merchant fleet. The principal airports are Dhaka (Zia International) and Chittagong. The international airline, Bangladesh Biman, serves Europe, the Middle East, South and South-East Asia, and an internal network.

There are about 6,880 miles of roads in Bangladesh; 4,724 miles are metalled. There are 2,798 miles of railway track.

Radio Bangladesh is the main national broadcasting service. A television service was introduced in 1965 and colour transmissions began in 1980.

ECONOMY

Bangladesh is a principal producer of raw jute. Other agricultural products are rice, tea, oil seeds, pulses and sugar cane. The chief industries are jute, cotton, tea, leather, pharmaceuticals, fertilizer, sugar, prawn fishing, natural gas and garment manufacture. Remittances sent home by Bangladeshi workers abroad have been of considerable support to the economy in recent years.

AID – Bangladesh is a major recipient of bilateral and multilateral development aid. The total annual development plan for 1991–2 is budgeted at US$2,095 million of which US$1,797 million will be financed from external sources.

Trade with UK	1990	1991
Imports from UK	£70,534,000	£39,086,000
Exports to UK	72,515,000	80,568,000

BARBADOS

AREA, ETC. – Barbados, the most easterly of the Caribbean islands, is situated in latitude 13° 14′ N. and longitude 59° 37′ W. The island has a total area of 166 sq. miles, (430 sq. km), the land rising in a series of tablelands marked by terraces to the highest point, Mt Hillaby (1,116 ft). It is nearly 21 miles long by 14 miles broad. The climate is equable with annual average temperature 26.6°C (79.8°F) and rainfall varying from a yearly average of 75 inches in the high central district to 50 inches in some of the low-lying coastal areas.

POPULATION – The population of Barbados (1990 UN estimate) was 255,000. There are eleven administrative areas (parishes): St Michael, Christ Church, St Andrews, St George, St James, St John, St Joseph, St Lucy, St Peter, St Philip and St Thomas.

CAPITAL – ΨBridgetown (population, estimated April 1980, 7,466) in the parish of St Michael. There are three other towns, Oistins in Christ Church, Holetown in St James and Speightstown in St Peter.
CURRENCY – Barbados dollar (BD$) of 100 cents.
FLAG – Three vertical stripes, dark blue, gold and dark blue, with a trident head on gold stripe.
NATIONAL ANTHEM – In Plenty and in Time of Need.
NATIONAL DAY – 30 November (Independence Day).

GOVERNMENT

The first inhabitants of Barbados were Arawak Indians but the island was uninhabited when first settled by the British in 1627. It was a Crown Colony from 1652 until it became an independent state within the Commonwealth on 30 November 1966. The Legislature consists of the Governor-General, a Senate and a House of Assembly. The Senate comprises 21 Senators appointed by the Governor-General, of whom 12 are appointed on the advice of the Prime Minister, two on the advice of the Leader of the Opposition and seven by the Governor-General at his discretion to represent religious, economic or social interests in the Island or such other interests as the Governor-General considers ought to be represented. The House of Assembly comprises 28 members elected every five years by adult suffrage. The last General Election took place on 22 January 1991 and, as a result, seats in the House of Assembly were distributed as follows: Democratic Labour Party 18, Barbados Labour Party 10.

Governor-General, Dame Nita Barrow, GCMG, DA (1990).

CABINET as at June 1992
Prime Minister, Minister of Finance and Economic Affairs, Civil Service, Rt. Hon. L. Erskine Sandiford.
Deputy Prime Minister, Leader of the House of Assembly, Minister of International Transport, Telecommunications and Immigration, Transport and Works, Hon. Philip M. Greaves, QC.

Attorney-General and Minister of Foreign Affairs, Hon. Maurice A. King.
Health, Hon. Brandford M. Taitt.
Housing and Lands, Hon. E. Evelyn Greaves.
Minister of State, Ministry of Finance and Economic Affairs, Hon. Harold A. Blackman.
Labour, Consumer Affairs and the Environment, Hon. Warwick O. Franklyn.
Tourism and Sports, Hon. Wesley W. Hall.
Justice and Public Safety, Hon. Keith Simmons.
Education, Hon. Cyril V. Walker.
Community Development and Culture, Hon. David J. H. Thompson.
Agriculture, Food and Fisheries and Leader of the Senate, Sen. Hon. L. V. Harcourt Lewis.
Trade, Industry and Commerce, Hon. Dr Carl Clarke.

BARBADOS HIGH COMMISSION
1 Great Russell Street, London WC1B 3NH
TEL 071-631 4975

High Commissioner, His Excellency the Rt. Hon. Sir William Douglas, KCMG (1991).

BRITISH HIGH COMMISSION
Lower Collymore Rock, PO Box 676, Bridgetown
Tel: Bridgetown 426 6694

High Commissioner, His Excellency Emrys Thomas Davies, CMG (1991).

JUDICATURE

There is a Supreme Court of Judicature consisting of a High Court and a Court of Appeal. In certain cases a further appeal lies to the Judicial Committee of the Privy Council. The Chief Justice and Puisne Judges are appointed by the Governor-General on the recommendation of the Prime Minister and after consultation with the Leader of the Opposition.

Chief Justice, The Hon. Sir Denys Ambrose Williams.

EDUCATION

Primary and secondary education is free in government schools. There are 105 primary schools, 21 government secondary schools and 15 approved government secondary schools.

COMMUNICATIONS

Barbados has some 965 miles of roads, of which about 917 miles are asphalted. The Grantley Adams International airport is situated at Seawell, 12 miles from Bridgetown, and frequent scheduled services connect Barbados with the major world air routes. Bridgetown, the only port of entry, has a deep-water harbour with berths for eight ships, but oil is pumped ashore at Spring Gardens and at an Esso installation on the West Coast. Barbados has a colour television service, three radio broadcasting services, and a wired broadcasting service.

ECONOMY

The economy of the island is based on tourism, sugar and light manufacturing. In 1990, 432,092 tourists visited Barbados and 362,611 cruise ship passengers. Chief exports are sugar and its by-products, chemicals, electronic components and clothing.

Finance	1989–90*
Current revenue	BD$960,700,000
Current expenditure	1,050,500,000
Capital expenditure	231,000,000

*estimated.

Trade with UK	1990	1991
Imports from UK	£35,811,000	£33,454,000
Exports to UK	24,294,000	13,316,000

BELGIUM
Royaume de Belgique

AREA – A Kingdom of western Europe, with a total area of 11,781 sq. miles (30,513 sq. km), Belgium is bounded on the north by the Netherlands, on the South by France, on the east by Germany and Luxembourg, and on the west by the North Sea.

Belgium has a frontier of 898 miles, and a seaboard of 41 miles. The Meuse and its tributary, the Sambre, divide it into two distinct regions, that in the west being generally level and fertile, while the table-land of the Ardennes, in the east, has for the most part a poor soil. The polders near the coast, which are protected by dykes against floods, cover an area of 193 sq. miles. The highest hill, Signal de Botranges, rises to a height of 2,276 feet, but the mean elevation of the whole country does not exceed 526 feet. The principal rivers are the Scheldt and the Meuse.

POPULATION – The population (1989) was 9,928,000 (Greater Brussels 971,000; Flanders 5,722,000; Wallonia 3,169,000, of whom 66,000 are German-speaking). The majority of Belgians are Roman Catholics.

CAPITAL – Brussels, has a population (1989) of 970,501. Other towns are ΨAntwerp, the chief port (473,082); ΨGhent (230,822); Liège (199,020); Charleroi (208,021); Bruges (117,653); ΨOstend (68,370); Malines (75,514).

CURRENCY – Belgian franc of 100 centimes (centiemen).

FLAG – Three vertical bands, black, yellow, red.

NATIONAL ANTHEM – La Brabançonne.

NATIONAL DAY – 21 July (Accession of King Leopold I, 1831).

GOVERNMENT

The kingdom formed part of the Low Countries (Netherlands) from 1815 until 14 October 1830, when a National Congress proclaimed its independence, and on 4 June 1831,

Prince Leopold of Coburg was chosen hereditary king. The separation from the Netherlands and the neutrality and inviolability of Belgium were guaranteed by a Conference of the European Powers, and by the Treaty of London (19 April 1839), the famous 'Scrap of Paper', signed by Austria, France, Great Britain, Prussia, The Netherlands, and Russia. On 4 August 1914 the Germans invaded Belgium, in violation of the terms of the treaty. The kingdom was again invaded by Germany on 10 May 1940. The whole kingdom eventually fell and was occupied by Nazi troops until liberated by the Allies in September 1944.

According to the Constitution of 1831 the form of government is a constitutional representative and hereditary monarchy with a bicameral legislature, consisting of the King, the Senate and the Chamber of Deputies. The parliamentary term is four years.

The last general election was held on 24 November 1991. The results were as follows (seats):

Chamber of Deputies: CVP 39; PS 35; SP 28; PVV (Flemish Freedom and Progress Party) 26; PRL (Liberal Reform Party (Francophone)) 20; PSC 18; Vlaams Blok (Flemish Nationalist Party) 12; VU 10; Ecolo (Francophone Ecology Party) 10; Agalev (Flemish Environmental Party) 7; FDF (Francophone Democratic Front) 3; ROSSEM 3; National Front (FN/NF) 1.

Senate: CVP 20; PS 18; SP 14; PVV 13; PRL 9; PSC 9; VlaansBlok 5; VU 5; Ecolo 6; Agalev 5; ROSSEM 1; FDF 1.

Besides these directly elected representatives the Senate also includes 51 members who are elected by the Provincial Councils and 26 who are co-opted in the proportions of the directly elected seats. HRH Prince Albert is a *sénateur de droit*.

HEAD OF STATE

King of the Belgians, HM King Baudouin, KG, *born* 7 Sept. 1930; *succeeded* 17 July 1951, on the abdication of his father, King Leopold III, after having acted as Head of the State since 11 August 1950; *married* 15 Dec. 1960, Doña Fabiola de Mora y Aragòn.

Heir Presumptive, HRH Prince Albert, *born* 6 June 1934, *brother* of the King; *married* 2 July 1959, Donna Paola Ruffo di Calabria, and has *issue* Prince Philippe Léopold Louis Marie, *b.* 15 April 1960; Princess Astrid Josephine-Charlotte Fabrizia Elisabeth Paola Marie, *b.* 5 June 1962; Prince Laurent, *b.* 20 Oct. 1963.

CABINET as at June 1992

Prime Minister, Jean-Luc Dehaene (CVP).
Deputy Prime Minister, Transport and Public Enterprises, Guy Coëme (PS).
Deputy Prime Minister, Foreign Affairs, Willy Claes (SP).
Deputy Prime Minister, Justice, Economic Affairs, Melchoir Wathelet (PSC).
Finance, Philippe Maystadt (PSC).
Social Affairs, Phillipe Moureaux (PS).
Scientific Policy, Jean-Maurice Dehousse (PS).
Foreign Trade and European Affairs, Robert Urbain (PS).
Small and Medium-Sized Enterprises and Agriculture, André Bourgeois (CVP).
Defence, Leo Delcroix (CVP).
Social Integration, Public Health and the Environment, Laurette Onkelinckx (PS).
Pensions, Freddy Wilcockx (SP).
Internal Affairs and the Civil Service, Louis Tobback (SP).
Employment and Equality, Miet Smet (CVP).
Budget, Mieke Offeciers-Van de Wierle (CVP).
Development Co-operation, Erik Derycke (SP).

CVP Christian Social Party (Flemish); PS Socialist Party (Francophone); SP Socialist Party (Flemish); PSC Christian Social Party (Francophone); VU Flemish Peoples' Union.

BELGIAN EMBASSY
103 Eaton Square, London SW1W 9AB
Tel 071-235 5422

Ambassador Extraordinary and Plenipotentiary, His Excellency Herman Dehennin (1991).
Minister-Counsellor, M. Den Doncker.
Minister-Counsellor (Economic), J. Maricou.
Military, Naval and Air Attaché, Capt. M. Lavaert.

BRITISH EMBASSY
Britannia House, 28 rue Joseph II, 1040 Brussels
Tel: Brussels 2179000

Ambassador Extraordinary and Plenipotentiary, His Excellency Robert (Robin) James O'Neill, CMG (1989).
Counsellors, N. M. McCarthy, OBE (*Head of Chancery*); B. Attewell (*Commercial*).
Defence and Military Attaché, Col. J. M. Craster.
Naval and Air Attaché, Wing Cdr. B. A. Horton.
BRITISH CONSULAR OFFICES – There are offices at *Brussels, Antwerp* and *Liège.*
BRITISH COUNCIL REPRESENTATIVE TO BELGIUM AND LUXEMBOURG – K. McGuinness (*Cultural Attaché*).

BRITISH CHAMBER OF COMMERCE FOR BELGIUM AND LUXEMBOURG (INC.), 30 rue Joseph II, 1040 Brussels.

REGIONAL GOVERNMENT

The 1980 regionalization law made provision for the establishment of three Regional Community Parliaments (Assemblies) with executive councils which were set up in November 1981 and became effective in January 1982. The executives are autonomous from the central government, and their members are elected by the members of the Assemblies to whom they are responsible. They prepare Bills within the limits of their regional/community competences, and once these Bills have been passed by the regional assembly and published in the *Moniteur Belge*, they have the force of law.

The Flemish Community Assembly (186 members) and Executive (a President and eight Regional Ministers) covers the provinces of Antwerp, East and West Flanders, Limbourg and the Flemish *arrondissements* (Halle, Vilvoorde, Leuven) in the province of Brabant, and is also responsible for the Flemish population of Brussels.

The Walloon Regional Assembly (104 members) and Executive (a President and six Regional Ministers) covers the provinces of Hainaut, Liège, Luxembourg and Namur, and the *arrondissement* of Nivelles in the province of Brabant.

The French Community Assembly (132 members) and Executive (a President and three Community Ministers) has no fixed territory but is responsible for the Francophone population of Brussels and, in concert with the Walloon Regional Assembly, deals with certain Walloon regional affairs. The German-speaking community (about 66,000) also has an Assembly, which gained autonomy in 1984. It is based in Eupen.

Since June 1989 there has been a 75-member Brussels Regional Council with a five-member Executive: two Flemings, two Francophones and a President.

An Arbitration Court was set up in 1984 to resolve conflicts between laws made by the various legislative bodies.

CULTURE

Belgium is divided between those who speak Dutch (the Flemings) and those who speak French (the Walloons). Dutch is spoken in the provinces of West Flanders, East Flanders, Antwerp, Limburg, and the northern half of Brabant, and French in the provinces of Hainaut, Namur,

Luxembourg, Liège and the southern half of Brabant. Dutch is recognized as the official language in the northern areas and French in the southern (Walloon) area and there are guarantees for the respective linguistic minorities. Brussels is officially bi-lingual. There is a small German-speaking area (Eupen and Malmedy) along the German border, east of Liège.

The literature of France and the Netherlands is supplemented by an indigenous Belgian literary activity, in both French and Dutch. Maurice Maeterlinck (1862–1949) was awarded the Nobel Prize for Literature in 1911. Emile Verhaeren (1855–1916) was a poet of international standing. Of contemporary Belgian writers, perhaps the most celebrated was Georges Simenon (1903–89). There are 39 daily newspapers in Belgium (23 in French, 15 in Dutch and one in German).

EDUCATION

The nursery schools provide free education for the 2½ to 6 age group. There are over 8,000 primary schools (6 to 12 years) of which approximately 5,000 are administered by the local Communities, on authority delegated to them by the State. The remainder are free institutions (predominantly Roman Catholic). There are more than 1,100 secondary schools offering a general academic education slightly over half of which are free institutions (predominantly Roman Catholic but subsidized by the State) and the remainder official institutions. The official school leaving age is 18.

ECONOMY

Belgium is a manufacturing country. With no natural resources except coal, production of which has now ceased, industry is based largely on the processing for re-export of imported raw materials. Gross National Product per capita in 1988 was BFr.520,600. Principal industries are steel and metal products, chemicals and petrochemicals, textiles, glass, and foodstuffs.

FINANCE

Budget	1988	1989
Revenue	BFr.1,505,500m	BFr.1,037,000m
Expenditure	1,901,600m	1,409,600m

TRADE

External trade figures relate to Luxembourg as well as Belgium since the two countries formed an Economic Union in 1921.

	1987	1988
Total Imports	US$83,523m	US$92,250m
Total Exports	83,288m	92,103m

Trade with UK (Belgium and Luxembourg)

	1990	1991
Imports from UK	£5,648,625,000	£5,870,876,000
Exports to UK	5,732,427,000	5,472,663,000

COMMUNICATIONS

In 1983, there were 3,920 kilometres of normal gauge railways operated by the Belgian National Railways, of which 1,763 kilometres were electrified. The Belgian National Light Railways (SNCV) also operated 27,671 kilometres of regular bus routes.

Ship canals include Ghent-Terneuzen (18 miles, of which half is in Belgium and half in the Netherlands) which permits the passage to Ghent of ships up to 60,000 tons; the Canal of Willebroek Rupel-Brussels (20 miles, by which ships drawing 18 ft reach Brussels from the sea; opened in 1922); and Bruges (from Zeebrugge on the North Sea to Bruges, 6¼ miles). The Albert Canal (79 miles), links Liège with Antwerp; it was completed in 1939 and accommodates barges up to 1,350 tons. The modernization of the port of Antwerp is well advanced. Inland waterway approaches to Antwerp are also to be improved. The river Meuse from the Dutch to the French frontiers, the river Sambre between Namur and Monceau, the river Scheldt from Antwerp to Ghent and the Brussels-Charleroi Canal are being widened or deepened to take barges up to 1,350 tons. Most of the maritime trade of Belgium is carried in foreign shipping.

In 1986 there were 14,260 km of trunk roads of which about 1,550 km were motorways.

The Belgian National Airline Sabena operates regular services between Brussels and London, and many continental centres, as well as overseas services to Northern and Central America, Africa, Middle East, Far East, etc. Many foreign airlines call at Brussels.

BELIZE

AREA, ETC – Belize lies on the east coast of Central America, bounded on the north and north-west by Mexico, and on the west and south by Guatemala. The total area (including offshore islands) is about 8,867 sq. miles (22,965 sq. km.), with a length and breadth of 174 miles and 68 miles respectively. The climate is sub-tropical, with a mean annual temperature of 20°C, but is tempered by sea breezes. There are two dry seasons, the main one from March to May and the other (the Maugre season) from August to September. The country is occasionally affected by hurricanes.

The coastal areas are mostly flat and swampy but the country rises gradually towards the interior. The northern and western districts are hilly, and in the south the Maya Mountains and the Cockscombs form the backbone of the country, reaching a height of 3,800 feet at Victoria Peak.

POPULATION – The population is 191,000 (1991 estimate), of which the main racial groups are Creole, Mestizo (Maya-Spanish) and Carib, plus a number of East Indian and Spanish descent. The races are now heavily inter-mixed. The majority of the population is Christian, about 60 per cent Catholic and most of the remainder Protestant.

CAPITAL – Belmopan (estimated population, 1990, 5,000). The largest city and the former capital is ΨBelize City (population, 1980 census, 39,771). Other towns are Corozal (6,899), San Ignacio (5,616), Dangriga (6,661), Orange Walk (8,439), Punta Gorda (2,396).

CURRENCY – Belize dollar (BZ$) of 100 cents. The Belize dollar is tied to the US dollar, BZ$2 = US$1.

FLAG – Blue ground with red band along top and bottom edges, and in centre a white disc containing the coat of arms surrounded by a green garland.

NATIONAL ANTHEM – Land of the Free.

NATIONAL DAY – 21 September (Independence Day).

GOVERNMENT

The early history of Belize is little known, although the numerous ruins in the area indicate that it was heavily populated by the Maya Indians. The first British settlement was established in 1638 but was subject to repeated attacks by the Spanish, who claimed sovereignty over the area, until the decline of Spanish power in the Americas in the 19th century. In 1862 the area was recognized by Britain as a colony and called British Honduras. On 1 June 1973 the colony was officially renamed Belize, and was granted independence on 21 September 1981. The long-standing territorial dispute with Guatemala, which had delayed independence earlier, remains unresolved despite efforts to reach a settlement.

The Queen is Head of State, represented in Belize by a Governor-General, who is a citizen of the country, appointed in consultation with the Prime Minister of Belize. There is a National Assembly, comprising a House of Representatives (28 members elected for five years) and a Senate (eight members appointed by the Governor-General). Executive power is vested in the Cabinet, which is responsible to the National Assembly.

In elections held in September 1989, the People's United Party defeated the incumbent United Democratic Party.

Governor-General, Her Excellency Dame Minita Elmira Gordon, GCMG, GCVO.

THE CABINET as at June 1992

Prime Minister and Minister of Finance, Home Affairs and Defence, Trade and Commerce, Rt. Hon. George Price.
Deputy PM and Minister of Natural Resources, Hon. Florencio Marin.
Foreign Affairs, Economic Development, Education, Hon. Said Musa.
Labour, Local Government and the Public Service, Hon. Valdemar Castillo.
Works, Hon. Samuel Waight.
Health, Urban Development, Hon. Dr Theodore Aranda.
Attorney-General, Minister of Tourism and the Environment, Hon. Glenn Godfrey.
Social Services, Community Development, Hon. Remijio Montejo.
Agriculture and Fisheries, Hon. Michael Espat.
Housing, Co-operatives and Industry, Hon. Leopoldo Briceño.
Energy and Communications, Hon. Carlos Diaz.
Ministers of State, Finance, Home Affairs and Defence, Trade and Commerce, Hon. Ralph Fonseca, Hon. Daniel Silva.
Minister of State, Foreign Affairs, Economic Development, Education, Hon. Vildo Marin.
Minister of State, Natural Resources, Hon. Guadalupe Pech.
Minister of State, Energy and Communications, Hon. Miguel Ruiz.

BELIZE HIGH COMMISSION
10 Harcourt House, 19A Cavendish Square, London W1M 9AD
Tel 071-499 9728

High Commissioner, His Excellency Robert Leslie (1991).

BRITISH HIGH COMMISSION
PO Box 91, Belmopan
Tel: Belmopan 22146/7

High Commissioner, His Excellency David McKilligin (1991).
Deputy High Commissioner, G. H. Morgan.

ECONOMY

About 42 per cent of the population is engaged in agriculture. Corn (maize), rice, red kidney beans, root crops and fruit are the main food crops, although main agricultural exports are sugar, bananas and citrus products. The country is more or less self-sufficient in fresh beef, pork and poultry, but processed meat and dairy products are imported. About 25 per cent of timber production (mostly mahogany) is exported, and there is a large US market for lobster, conch and scale fish. Tourism is also a valuable source of income.

Finance	1990–1
Revenue	BZ$215.8m
Expenditure	205.8m
Surplus	10.0m

Trade	1988	1989
Total imports	BZ$361.9m	BZ$431.4m
Total exports	232.5m	248.1m

Trade with UK	1990	1991
Imports from UK	£12,439,000	£14,574,000
Exports to UK	22,734,000	20,849,000

EDUCATION

Education is compulsory from 5 to 14 years of age. In 1985 primary education was provided by 225 schools, most of which are government aided. Enrolment totalled 38,512. Secondary education is provided by 29 secondary and post-secondary institutions with an enrolment of 7,441. A University College of Belize has been established. The Government also offers scholarships for students to go abroad. There is an extra-mural faculty of the University of the West Indies, with a resident tutor.

COMMUNICATIONS

There is a government-operated radio service and a privately-owned radio station. However, there is no official television service in the country. An automatic telephone service operated by Belize Telecommunications Ltd covers the whole country.

The principal airport is at Belize City and various airlines operate international flights to the USA and other Central American states. The main port is also Belize City, where construction of deep water quays was recently completed. There are 1,865 miles of road, including four main highways, but there is no railway system.

BENIN
République du Benin

A republic situated in West Africa, between 2° and 3° W. and 6° and 12° N., Benin (formerly known as Dahomey) has a short coastline of 78 miles on the Gulf of Guinea but extends northwards inland for 437 miles. It is flanked on the west by Togo, on the north by Burkina and Niger and on the east by Nigeria. It is divided into four main regions running horizontally; a narrow sandy coastal strip, a succession of inter-communicating lagoons, a clay belt and a sandy plateau in the north. It has an area of 43,484 sq. miles (122,622 sq. km), and a population of 4,736,000 (UN 1990 estimate). The official language is French. Although poor in resources, Benin is one of the most heavily populated areas in West Africa, with a high standard of education.

CAPITAL – ΨPorto Novo, population (1982 estimate) 208,258. Principal commercial town and port, ΨCotonou (487,020).
CURRENCY – Franc CFA of 100 centimes.
FLAG – Two horizontal stripes of yellow over red with a vertical green band in the hoist.
NATIONAL DAY – 30 November.

GOVERNMENT

The first treaty with France was signed by one of the kings of Abomey in 1851 but the country was not placed under French administration until 1892. Benin became an independent republic within the French Community in December 1958; full independence outside the Community was proclaimed on 1 August 1960. In October 1963 a popular revolution led to the fall of the government and the Army held power until a civilian government was formed. In subsequent years successive governments were overthrown by the military after only short terms in office until a coup d'état on 26 October 1972 brought to power a Marxist-Leninist Military Revolutionary Government, headed by Lt.-Col. Kerekou.

In response to mounting unrest, the government agreed to drop Marxism-Leninism as the official ideology in December 1989. Following a 'National Conference of Active Forces of the Nation,' the Constitution was revoked on 1 March 1990 and the country's official name was changed from the People's Republic of Benin to the Republic of Benin. The Revolutionary National Assembly (legislature) was dissolved and replaced by a High Council of the Republic (HCR). This, in conjunction with a new 15-member civilian government, is implementing a political transition programme; a new pluralistic Constitution was adopted by referendum in December 1990. Legislative and presidential elections were held in February and March 1991. Nicéphore Soglo was sworn in as the new President on 4 April 1991 and appointed a provisional government. The lack of a clear majority in the legislature for the Union for the Triumph of Democratic Renewal coalition of President Soglo has meant the government has had to rely on an unstable alliance of independents.

HEAD OF STATE

President and Head of the Armed Forces, HE Nicéphore Soglo.

CABINET as at June 1992

The President.
Minister of State and Secretary-General to the President, Desire Vieyra.
Defence, Florentin Feliho.
Interior, Public Security and Territorial Administration, Richard Adjaho.
Foreign Affairs and Co-operation, Théodore Hollo.
Finance, Paul Dossou.
Planning and Statistics, Robert Tagnon.
Rural Development and Co-operatives, Mama Adamou N'Diaye.
Public Works and Transport, Florentin Mito-Baba.
Industry, Small and Medium Enterprises, Sylvain Ladikpo.
Energy, A. Houessou.
Information and Communications, Paulin Hountondji.
National Education, Karim Dramane.
Youth and Sports, Théophile Natta.
Civil Service, Antoine Gbegan.
Employment and Social Affairs, Véronique Attoyo.
Public Health, Véronique Lawson.
Environment, Eustache Sarré.
Parliamentary Relations, Marius Francisco.
Handicrafts and Tourism, Bernard Houégnon.
Justice, Yves Yéhouessi.
Culture, Mr Alabi.

EMBASSY OF THE REPUBLIC OF BENIN
87 Avenue Victor Hugo, 75116 Paris, France
Tel: Paris 45009840

Ambassador Extraordinary and Plenipotentiary, His Excellency Cyrille Sagbo (resident in Paris).

HONORARY CONSULATE, 125/129 High Street, Stanmore, Middlesex HA8 7HS. Tel: 081-951 1234. *Honorary Consul*, L. Landau.

BRITISH AMBASSADOR (resident in Lagos, Nigeria).

TRADE

The principal exports are cotton, palm products, ground nuts, shea-nuts, and coffee. Small deposits of gold, iron and chrome have been found; oil production started in 1983.

Trade with UK	1990	1991
Imports from UK	£6,130,000	£10,716,000
Exports to UK	1,197,000	889,000

BHUTAN
Druk-yul

AREA – Bhutan is a small Himalayan kingdom situated between Tibet (to the north) and India (to the west, south and east). The total area is about 18,147 sq. miles (47,000 sq. km), with a mountainous northern region which is infertile and sparsely populated, a central zone of upland valleys where most of the population and cultivated land is found, and in the south the densely forested foothills of the Himalayas, which are mainly inhabited by Nepalese settlers and indigenous tribespeople.

POPULATION – The population of Bhutan is estimated at 1,516,000 (UN estimate 1990), about 70 per cent of whom are Buddhists. The remainder (mostly the Nepali Bhutanese) are Hindu. The official language, for administrative and religious purposes, is Dzongkha, a variant of Tibetan, which functions as a lingua franca amongst a variety of languages and dialects. From 1990 it has been government policy to make the study of Dzongkha compulsory in schools. This measure and edicts concerning national dress and the immigration status of many of the settlers in the south, have caused an exodus of those of Nepali descent, and there are currently 50,000 living in camps in Nepal. However, English remains the medium of instruction and has become widely used within the administration.

CAPITAL – Thimphu, population estimate (1987) 15,000.

CURRENCY – Ngultrum (Nu) of 100 chetrums. Indian currency is also legal tender.

FLAG – Saffron yellow and orange-red divided diagonally, with dragon device in centre.

NATIONAL DAY – 17 December.

GOVERNMENT

Bhutan has a 150-member National Assembly which meets twice a year. The ten-member Royal Advisory Council, nominated by the King and the National Assembly, acts as a consultative body when the National Assembly is not in session. The King is also assisted by a Council of Ministers. There are no political parties.

In 1949 a treaty was concluded with the Government of India under which the Kingdom of Bhutan agreed to be guided by the advice of the Government of India in regard to its external relations. It has its own diplomatic representatives and is a member of the UN and other international and regional organizations. It also receives from the Government of India an annual payment of Rs500,000 as compensation for portions of its territory annexed by the British Government in India in 1864.

HEAD OF STATE

King of Bhutan, HM Jigme Singye Wangchuk, *born* 11 Nov. 1955; *succeeded his father*, July 1972; *crowned*, 2 June 1974.

Heir, Crown Prince Jigme Gesar Namgyal Wangchuk, *designated*, 31 Oct. 1988.

COUNCIL OF MINISTERS as at 30 June 1991
Chairman of Council of Ministers, HM The King.
HM Representative in Ministry of Finance, HRH Ashi Sonam Chhoden Wangchuk.
HM Representative in Ministry of Agriculture, HRH Ashi Dorji W. Wangchuk.
Home Affairs, HRH Namgyel Wangchuk.
Finance, Dorji Tshering.
Foreign Affairs, Dawa Tshering.
Communications, Social Services and Tourism, Dr T. Tobgyel.
Trade and Industries, Om Pradhan.
Deputy Minister of Defence, Chief Operations Officer of Royal Bhutan Army, Maj.-Gen. Lam Dorji.
Speaker of the National Assembly, Chief Justice, Sangye Penjor.

ECONOMY

The seventh five-year Plan (1992–7) envisages a doubling of internal revenues to Nu2,000m. Economic emphasis is on the infrastructure, especially roads and telecommunications, and hydro-electric power. The economy is based on agriculture and animal husbandry, which engage over 90 per cent of the workforce in what is largely a self-sufficient rural society. The principal food crops are rice, wheat, maize and barley. Vegetables and fruit are also produced. Bhutan is the world's largest producer of cardamon, which forms its principal export to countries other than India. Mineral resources include dolomite and small amounts of coal, which are exported to India. A modest industrial base is being developed. A distillery and cement, chemicals and food processing plants are in production; a forestry industries complex is being expanded. Tourism and postage stamps are increasingly important sources of foreign exchange.

Over 90 per cent of foreign trade is with India. Principal exports are agricultural products, timber, cement and coal; main imports are textiles, cereals and consumer goods. Bhutan's airline, Druk Air, flies between Paro and Calcutta.

Trade with UK	1990	1991
Imports from UK	£778,000	£565,000
Exports to UK	111,000	231,000

BOLIVIA
República de Bolivia

The land-locked Republic of Bolivia extends between lat. 10° and 23° S. and long. 57° 30′ and 69° 45′ W. It has an area estimated at 424,165 sq. miles (1,098,581 sq. km), with a population (UN estimate 1990) of 7,400,000. The Republic derives its name from its liberator, Simon Bolivar (1783–1830).

The chief topographical feature is the great central plateau (65,000 square miles) over 500 miles in length, at an average altitude of 12,500 feet above sea level, between the two great chains of the Andes, which traverse the country from south to north. The total length of the navigable streams is about 12,000 miles, the principal rivers being the Itenez, Beni, Mamore and Madre de Dios.

LANGUAGE – The official language of the country is Spanish, but many of the Indian inhabitants (about two-thirds of the population) speak Quechua or Aymará, the two linguistic groups being more or less equal in numbers.

RELIGION – The Roman Catholic religion was disestablished in 1961.

CAPITAL – La Paz (population, 1,000,000). Other large centres are Cochabamba (250,000), Oruro (180,000), Santa Cruz (380,000), Potosí (90,000), Sucre, the legal capital and seat of the judiciary (80,000) and Tarija (45,000).

CURRENCY – Boliviano ($b) of 100 centavos.

FLAG – Three horizontal bands; red, yellow, green.

NATIONAL ANTHEM – Bolivianos, El Hado Propicio (Oh Bolivia, our long-felt desires).

NATIONAL DAY – 6 August (Independence Day).

HEAD OF STATE
President of the Republic, Jaime Paz Zamora, *inaugurated* 6 August 1989.
Vice President, Luis Ossio Sanjines.

CABINET as at 18 March 1992
Foreign Affairs, Ronald Maclean Abaroa.
Finance, Jorge Quiroga Ramirez.
Transport and Communications, Carlos Aponte Pinto.
Agriculture, Oswaldo Antezana.
Industry, Commerce and Tourism, Fernando Campero Prudencio.
Health, Dr Carlos Dabdoub Arrien.
Mining and Metallurgy, Alvaro Rejas Villarroel.
Information, Jaime Cespedes Toro.
Interior, Carlos Saavedra Bruno.
Minister of the Presidency, Gustavo Fernandez.
Defence, Alberto Saenz.
Planning and Co-ordination, Samuel Doria Medina.
Education and Culture, Hedim Cespedes.
Labour, Oscar Zamora.
Energy and Hydrocarbons, Herbert Mueller.
Urban Development and Housing, Fernando Kieffer.

BOLIVIAN EMBASSY
106 Eaton Square, London SW1W 9AD
Tel 071–235 2257/4248
Ambassador Extraordinary and Plenipotentiary, His Excellency Maj.-Gen. Gary Prado Salmon (1990).

BRITISH EMBASSY
Avenida Arce 2732–2754, (Casilla 694) La Paz
Tel: La Paz 391063
Ambassador Extraordinary and Plenipotentiary, His Excellency Richard Michael Jackson, CVO (1991).
First Secretary, A. W. Shave, OBE (*Commercial and Deputy Head of Mission*).

There is an Honorary Consulate at *Santa Cruz*.

EDUCATION

Elementary education is compulsory and free and there are secondary schools in urban centres. Provision is also made for higher education; in addition to St Francisco Xavier's University at Sucre, founded in 1624, there are six other universities, the largest being the University of San Andres at La Paz. There are nine principal daily newspapers in Bolivia.

ECONOMY

Mining, natural gas, petroleum and agriculture are the principal industries. The ancient silver mines of Potosí are now worked chiefly for tin, but gold, partly dug and partly washed, is obtained on the Eastern Cordillera of the Andes; the tin output is one of the largest in the world, and together with other minerals (copper, antimony, lead, zinc, asbestos, wolfram, bismuth salt and sulphur), provides over half of Bolivia's exports.

In 1982 Bolivia produced 1.4 million cubic metres of oil, sufficient for internal consumption. Gas (currently providing about a quarter of Bolivia's export income) is piped to Argentina and there are plans to build a pipeline to São Paulo, Brazil. Bolivia's agricultural produce consists chiefly of rice, barley, oats, wheat, sugar-cane, maize, cotton, indigo, rubber, cacao, potatoes, cinchona bark, medicinal herbs, brazil nuts etc.

The economy has deteriorated since 1977, with disappointing petroleum reserves, a large external debt, and the collapse of world tin prices in 1985. Tin prices began to increase once more from April 1989.

The peso was replaced in January 1987 with the Boliviano of 1,000,000 old pesos in an effort to stem inflation. The inflation rate in 1991 was 14 per cent. Gross Domestic Product in 1987 was US$5,824 m.

Trade with UK	1990	1991
Imports from UK	£6,234,000	£5,787,000
Exports to UK	12,387,000	9,303,000

Mineral exports represent about 94 per cent of these totals. A large part of Bolivia's minerals were shipped to UK for smelting and re-export, but Bolivia is now developing her own smelters and will in future be exporting metals. The chief imports are wheat and flour, iron and steel products, machinery, vehicles and textiles.

COMMUNICATIONS

There are 2,200 miles of railways in operation including the lines from Corumbá to Santa Cruz (312 miles). There are about 10,950 miles of telegraphs, and microwave telephone communications between La Paz, Santa Cruz, Cochabamba, Oruro and Sucre. Most other towns have radio/telephone communication with the main cities. There is direct railway communication to the sea at Antofagasta (32 hours), Arica (10 hours), and Mollendo (2 days), and also to Buenos Aires (3½ days). Communication with Peru is by road from La Paz via Copacabana and thence to the railhead at Puno.

Commercial aviation in Bolivia is conducted by the national airline, Lloyd Aereo Boliviano and Transporte Aereo Militar between the major towns, and Lloyd Aereo Boliviano and a number of foreign airlines provide international flights to the USA, South and Central America and Europe.

Bolivia is without a coastline, having been deprived of the ports of Tocopilla, Cobija, Mejillones and Antofagasta by the Pacific War of 1879–84.

BOTSWANA
The Republic of Botswana

AREA, ETC – Botswana (formerly the British Protectorate of Bechuanaland) lies between latitudes 18° and 26° S. and longitudes 20° and 28° W. and is bounded by the Cape and Transvaal Provinces of South Africa on the south and east, by Zimbabwe, the Zambezi and Chobe (Linyanti) Rivers on the north and north-east, and by Namibia on the west. Botswana has a total area of 224,607 sq. miles (581,730 sq. km). The climate of the country is generally sub-tropical, but varies considerably with latitude and altitude. A plateau at a height of about 4,000 feet divides Botswana into two main topographical regions. To the east of the plateau streams flow into the Marico, Notwani and Limpopo Rivers; to the west lies a flat region comprising the Kgalagadi Desert, the Okavango Swamps and the Northern State Lands area. Large areas of the country support only herds of game. Elephant numbers have been estimated at 55,000–60,000.

POPULATION – Botswana has an estimated population (1991) of 1,300,000. The eight principal Botswana tribes are Bakgatla, Bakwena, Bangwaketse, Bamalete, Bamangwato, Barolong, Batawana and Batlokwa. The principal languages in use in Botswana are Setswana and English.

CAPITAL – Gaborone, estimated population (1990) 128,500. Other centres are Francistown (60,000), Lobatse (25,000), and Selebi-Phikwe (46,000).

CURRENCY – Pula (P) of 100 thebe.

FLAG – Light blue with a horizontal black stripe fimbriated in white across the centre.

NATIONAL ANTHEM – Fatshe La Rona.

NATIONAL DAY – 30 September.

GOVERNMENT

On 30 September 1966, Bechuanaland became a Republic within the Commonwealth under the name Botswana. The President of Botswana is Head of State and appoints as Vice President a member of the National Assembly who is his principal assistant and leader of Government business in the National Assembly. The Assembly consists of the President, 34 members elected on a basis of universal adult suffrage, four specially elected members, the Attorney-General (non-voting) and the Speaker. Presidential and legislative elections are held every five years. There is also a 15-member House of Chiefs.

HEAD OF STATE
President, His Excellency Dr Q. K. J. Masire, *sworn in* 10 October 1989 for a second five-year term.

CABINET as at June 1992
Vice President, Finance and Development Planning, Festus Mogae.
Presidential Affairs, Public Administration, Lt.-Gen. Mompati Merafhe.
Local Government, Lands and Housing, Chapson Butale.
External Affairs, Dr Gaositwe Chiepe.
Mineral Resources and Water, Archibald Mogwe.
Commerce and Industry, Ponatshego Kedikilwe.
Agriculture, Kebatlamang Morake.
Works and Communications, David Magang.
Health, Bahiti Temane.
Education, Ray Molomo.
Home Affairs, Patrick Balopi.
Assistant Ministers: Finance, Ronald Sebego; *Local Government and Lands*, M. Mokgothu, Geoffrey Oteng; *Agriculture*, Roy Blackbeard.

BOTSWANA HIGH COMMISSION
6 Stratford Place, London W1N 9AE
TEL 071–499 0031
High Commissioner, Her Excellency Mrs Margaret Nasha (1989).

BRITISH HIGH COMMISSION
Private Bag 0023, Gaborone
Tel: Gaborone 352841
High Commissioner, His Excellency John Edwards (1992).

BRITISH COUNCIL REPRESENTATIVE, T. A. Jones, MBE (*Cultural Attaché*).

ECONOMY

Botswana is predominantly a pastoral country. The national herd is normally around 3 million cattle and 1 million sheep and goats but recent drought conditions have reduced the number of cattle to around 2.5 million.

Cattle rearing accounts for about 85 per cent of agricultural output and livestock products, particularly beef, are a major source of foreign exchange earnings. The Government has a number of programmes to improve land use and cattle and crop production, and schemes to provide financial assistance for farmers.

Mineral extraction and processing is now the major source of income for the country following the opening of large mines for diamonds and copper-nickel. Botswana is one of the largest producers of diamonds in the world. Large deposits of coal have been discovered and are being mined on a small scale. Much of the country has yet to be fully prospected. Manufacturing industry is growing and will continue to do so as communications improve but it is still a small sector of the economy.

FINANCE

	1990–1	1991–2e
Revenue	P3,318m	P3,183m
Expenditure	2,899m	3,318m

e = estimate

TRADE

Principal exports are diamonds, copper-nickel matte, and beef and beef products.

	1989p	1990
Imports	P2,136m	P3,483m
Exports	3,613m	3,262m

p preliminary

Trade with UK	1990	1991
Imports from UK	£24,777,000	£35,233,000
Exports to UK	18,854,000	22,662,000

EDUCATION

There are over 654 primary schools (enrolment approx. 308,840), 146 community junior secondary schools (enrolment approx. 48,624) and 23 government and government-aided senior secondary schools (enrolment 19,308). There are four teacher training establishments (total enrolment 1,365), two colleges of education (enrolment 340), one polytechnic with 558 students and the University of Botswana with 2,862 undergraduates. Further expansion of the technical education system is planned via a network of vocational training centres.

COMMUNICATIONS

The railway from Cape Town to Zimbabwe passes through eastern Botswana. The main roads in the country are the north–south road, which closely follows the railway, and the road running east–west that links Francistown and Maun. A new road from Nata to Kazungula provides a direct link to Zambia from Botswana. Air services are provided on a scheduled basis between the main towns.

BRAZIL

República Federativa do Brasil

AREA AND POPULATION – Brazil, discovered in 1500 by Portuguese navigator Pedro Alvares Cabral, is bounded on the north by the Atlantic Ocean, the Guianas, Colombia and Venezuela; on the west by Peru, Bolivia, Paraguay, and Argentina; on the south by Uruguay; and on the east by the Atlantic Ocean. Brazil extends between lat. 5° 16′ N. and 33° 45′ S. and long. 34° 45′ and 73° 59′22″ W. The Republic comprises an area of 3,286,488 sq. miles (8,511,965 sq. km), with a population (official estimate 1990) of 150,368,000.

The northern States of Amazonas and Pará are mainly wide, low-lying, forest-clad plains. The central states of Mato Grosso are principally plateau land and the eastern and southern States are traversed by successive mountain ranges interspersed with fertile valleys. The principal ranges are Serra do Mar, the Serra da Mantiqueira and the Serra do Espinhaco along the east coast.

The River Amazon with a total length of some 4,000 miles has tributaries which are themselves great rivers, and flows from the Peruvian Andes to the Atlantic. Its principal northern tributaries are the Rio Branco, Rio Negro, and Japurá; its southern tributaries are the Juruá, Purus, Madeira and Tapajós, while the Xingú meets it within 200 miles of its outflow into the Atlantic. The Tocantins and Araguaia flow northwards from Mato Grosso and Goiás to the Gulf of Pará. The Parnaiba flows from Piaui into the Atlantic. The São Francisco rises in the South of Minas Gerais and flows to the eastern coast. The Paraguai, rising in the south-west of Mato Grosso, flows through Paraguay to its confluence with the Paraná, which rises in the mountains of that name and divides Brazil from Paraguay.

CAPITAL – Brasilia (inaugurated on 21 April 1960). Population (1990 estimate) 1,803,478. Other important centres are São Paulo (10,063,110); the former capital ΨRio de Janeiro (6,603,388); Belo Horizonte (2,114,429); ΨRecife (1,287,623); ΨSalvador (1,804,438); ΨPorto Alegre (1,272,121); ΨFortaleza (1,582,414); and Belem (1,116,578).

CURRENCY – Cruzeiro (BRC) of 100 centavos.

FLAG – Green with a yellow lozenge containing a blue sphere studded with white stars, and crossed by a white band with the motto *Ordem e Progresso*.

NATIONAL ANTHEM – Ouviram do Ipirangas Margens Placidas (From peaceful Ypiranga's banks).

NATIONAL DAY – 7 September (Independence Day).

GOVERNMENT

Brazil was colonized by Portugal in the early part of the sixteenth century, and in 1822 became an independent empire under Dom Pedro, son of the refugee King Joao VI of Portugal. On 15 November 1889, Dom Pedro II, second of the line, was dethroned and a republic was proclaimed.

The Federative Republic of Brazil is made up of the Federal District and 26 States.

The constitution of October 1988 draws on the same conceptual basis as that of the United States, and envisages an equal distribution of power between the executive, the legislature and the judiciary. Under the existing constitutional provisions the President, who heads the executive, is directly elected for a five-year term.

The Congress consists of a Senate (three Senators per state elected for an eight-year term) and a Chamber of Deputies which is elected every four years. The number of Deputies per state depends upon the state's population. Each state has a Governor, and a Legislative Assembly with a four-year term.

HEAD OF STATE

President, Fernando Collor de Mello, *inaugurated* 15 March 1990.

Vice President, Itamar Franco.

CABINET as at June 1992

Agriculture and Land Reform, Antonio Cabrera.
Air Force, Brig. Sócrates da Costa Monteiro.
Army, Gen. Carlos Tinoco Ribeiro Gomes.
Economy, Marcílio Marques Moreira.
Education, vacant.

Foreign Affairs, Prof. Celso Lafer.
Health, Dr Adib Jatene.
Armed Forces Chief of General Staff, Gen. Antonio Luiz Rocha Veneu.
Justice, Celio Borja.
Labour and Administration, João Mellão Neto.
Mining and Energy, Marcus Vinicius Pratini de Moraes.
Navy, Adm. Mario Cesar Flores.
Social Security, Reinhold Stephanes.
Social Action, Ricardo Fiuza.
Transport and Communication, Alfonso Camargo.

BRAZILIAN EMBASSY
32 Green Street, London W1Y 4AT
TEL 071-499 0877

Ambassador Extraordinary and Plenipotentiary, His Excellency Paulo-Tarso Flecha de Lima (1990).

There is also a Brazilian Consulate-General in *London* and honorary consular offices at *Cardiff* and *Glasgow*.

BRITISH EMBASSY
Setor de Embaixadus Sul, Quadra 801, Conjunto K, 70.408 Brasilia DF
Tel: Brasilia 225–2710

Ambassador Extraordinary and Plenipotentiary, His Excellency Michael John Newington, CMG (1987).

There are British Consulates-General at *Rio de Janeiro* and *São Paulo*.

BRITISH COUNCIL REPRESENTATIVE, Raymond Newberry, OBE, SCR, 708/9-BLF Nos 1/3 (Caixa Postal 6104), 70.740 Brasilia DF. Regional Directors in *Recife*, *Rio de Janeiro* and *São Paulo*.

BRITISH AND COMMONWEALTH CHAMBER OF COMMERCE IN SÃO PAULO, Rua Barão de Itapetininga 275, 7th Floor, 01042, São Paulo (*Postal Address*, PO Box 1621, 01000 São Paulo) and Rua Real Grandeza 99, 22281 Rio de Janeiro.

ECONOMY

There are large and valuable mineral deposits including iron ore (hematite), manganese, bauxite, beryllium, chrome, nickel, tungsten, cassiterite, lead, gold, monazite (containing rare earths and thorium) and zirconium. Diamonds and precious and semi-precious stones are also found. The mineral wealth is being exploited to an increasing extent. The iron ore deposits of Minas Gerais are exceeded by those of the Amazon region, principally in the Carajás areas where deposits are estimated at 35,000 million tonnes. Mining operations began in February 1985.

Electric power production in 1989 was 243,034 Gwh. In the same year, the total output of steel was 24,600 million tonnes and production of oil was 34.6 million cubic metres.

Agriculture production was (tonnes):

	1989
Black Beans	2,327,973
Cassava	23,701,158
Cocoa	394,616
Coffee	1,412,000
Cotton	1,797,446
Maize	26,568,776
Peanuts	155,913
Potatoes	2,134,807
Rice	11,043,228
Soya	24,085,193
Tobacco	448,689
Wheat	5,295,335

FINANCE

	1989	1990
Revenue	NCz$515,193m	Cr$3,146,420m
Expenditure	529,882m	3,146,420m

In 1989 Brazil's total external public debt stood at US$112,000 million.

TRADE

Principal imports are fuel and lubricants, machinery, chemicals, wheat, metals and metal manufactures. Principal exports are coffee, iron ore, soya, meat, steel and orange juice. In 1987 the Brazilian automobile industry produced 920,300 vehicles. Of these, 339,900 vehicles were exported.

	1988	1989
Total imports	US$16,055 m	US$18,263 m
Total exports	33,786 m	34,406 m

Trade with UK	1990	1991
Imports from UK	£328,234,000	£339,442,000
Exports to UK	719,849,000	765,102,000

DEFENCE

The peace-time strength of the Army is 196,000, including 126,000 conscripts. The strength of the Navy is 50,000 personnel, including 2,000 conscripts, and 18 principal surface combatant vessels. The Air Force has a strength of 50,700 personnel (all professional) and 313 combat aircraft.

EDUCATION

Primary education is compulsory and is the responsibility of state governments and municipalities. At this level approximately 12 per cent attend private schools. Secondary education is largely the responsibility of State and municipal governments, although a small number of very old foundations (the Pedro II Schools) remain under direct federal control. Over 33 per cent of all pupils at this level attend private schools. Higher education is available in Federal, State, municipal and private universities and faculties.

CULTURE

Portuguese is the language of the country, but Italian, Spanish, German, Japanese and Arabic are also spoken by minorities, and newspapers of considerable circulation are produced in those languages.

Public libraries have been established in urban centres and there is a flourishing national press with widely circulated daily and weekly newspapers.

COMMUNICATIONS

In 1989 there were 1,663,987 km of highways. The route-length of railways in 1987 was 29,833 km. Internal air services are highly developed. There are 21,944 miles of navigable inland waterways. Rio de Janeiro and Santos are the two leading ports.

BRUNEI
Negara Brunei Darussalam

Brunei is situated on the north-west coast of the island of Borneo, total area of 2,226 sq. miles (5,765 sq. km), population 260,863 (1991), of whom 68 per cent are of Malay, 18 per cent Chinese and 5 per cent other indigenous races. The country has a humid tropical climate.

CAPITAL – Bandar Seri Begawan, with a population of 46,229 (1991).
CURRENCY – Brunei dollar (B$) of 100 sen. It is fully interchangeable with the currency of Singapore.
FLAG – Yellow with diagonal stripes of white over black and the arms in red all over the centre.
NATIONAL ANTHEM – Ya Allah Lanjutkan Lah Usia Kebawah Duli Yang Maha Mulia (O God, long live our Majesty the Sultan).
NATIONAL DAY – 23 February.

GOVERNMENT

In 1959 the Sultan of Brunei promulgated the first written Constitution, which provides for a Privy Council, a Council of Ministers and a Legislative Council. On 1 January 1984 Brunei resumed full independence. A ministerial system of government was established at independence, the seven Ministers being appointed by the Sultan and responsible to him. The Sultan presides over the Privy Council and the Council of Ministers. The Legislative Council was disbanded in February 1984.

HEAD OF STATE
Sultan, HM Sultan Haji Hassanal Bolkiah Mu'izzaddin Waddaulah, Sultan and Yang Di-Pertuan, *acceded* 1967, *crowned* 1 August 1968.

THE COUNCIL OF MINISTERS as at June 1992
Prime Minister, Minister of Defence, HM The Sultan.
Foreign Affairs, HRH Prince Mohammed.
Finance, HRH Prince Jefri.
Special Adviser to the Sultan and Minister for Home Affairs, Pehin Dato Haji Isa.
Education, Pehin Dato Abdul Aziz.
Law, Pengiran Bahrin.
Industry and Primary Resources, Pehin Dato Abdul Rahman.
Religious Affairs, Pehin Dato Mohammed Zain.
Development, Pengiran Dato Dr Ismail.
Culture, Youth and Sports, Pehin Dato Haji Hussein.
Health, Dato Dr Johar.
Communications, Dato Haji Zakaria.

BRUNEI DARUSSALAM HIGH COMMISSION
19–20 Belgrave Square, London SW1X 8PE
TEL 071-581 0521

High Commissioner, Pengiran Dato Haji Mustapha (1990).

BRITISH HIGH COMMISSION
Hong Kong and Shanghai Bank Building (3rd Floor), Jalan Pemancha, P.O. Box 2197 Bandar Seri Begawan
Tel: Bandar Seri Begawan 222231

High Commissioner, His Excellency Adrian Sindall (1991).

BRITISH COUNCIL REPRESENTATIVE, J. Semple, PO Box 3049, Bandar Seri Begawan 1930.

FINANCE

	1991
Revenue	B$2,686m
Expenditure	2,760m

TRADE WITH UK

	1990	1991
Imports from UK	£224,562,000	£215,222,000
Exports to UK	158,516,000	147,666,000

BULGARIA
Republika Bulgaria

The Republic of Bulgaria is bounded on the north by Romania, on the west by Serbia and Macedonia, on the east by the Black Sea, and on the south by Greece and Turkey. The total area is 42,823 sq. miles (110,912 sq. km), with a UN estimated population of 9,010,000 in 1990. The largest religion of the Bulgarians is the Bulgarian Orthodox Church.
LANGUAGE – Bulgarian is a Southern Slavonic tongue, closely allied to Serbo-Croat and Russian with local admixtures of modern Greek, Albanian and Turkish words. The alphabet is Cyrillic.

CAPITAL – Sofia, population (1989), 1,136,875, at the foot of the Vitosha Range, the capital and commercial centre is on the main railway line to Istanbul, 338 miles from the Black Sea port of ΨVarna (316,897); ΨBourgas (224,081) is also a Black Sea port. Other important trading and industrial centres are Plovdiv (374,004), Rousse (210,219), Pleven (168,014), Stara Zagora (186,736), Pernik (120,335), Sliven (149,643), Yambol (98,651), Khaskovo (116,808) and Tolbukhin (112,582).
CURRENCY – Lev of 100 stotinki.
FLAG – 3 horizontal bands, white, green, red.
NATIONAL DAY – 3 March.

HISTORY

A Principality of Bulgaria was created by the Treaty of Berlin (13 July 1878) and in 1885 Eastern Roumelia was added to the newly-created principality. In 1908 the country was declared to be an independent kingdom. In 1912–13 a successful war of the Balkan League against Turkey increased the size of the kingdom, but in August 1913 a short campaign against the remaining members of the League reduced the acquired area and led to the surrender of Southern Dobrudja to Romania. In October 1915, Bulgaria entered the war on the side of the Central Powers by declaring war on Serbia. Involved in the defeats of 1918, Bulgaria made an unconditional surrender to the Allied Powers in September 1918, and in November 1919, signed the Treaty of Neuilly, which ceded to the Allies the Thracian territories (later handed over to Greece) and some territory on the western frontier to Yugoslavia.

Nazi troops entered the country on 3 March 1941, and occupied Black Sea ports. On 26 August 1944, the government declared Bulgaria to be neutral in the Russo-German war and sought terms of peace from Britain and the United States. The Soviet Union refused to recognize the so-called neutrality and called upon Bulgaria to declare war against Germany, and no satisfactory reply being received on 5 September 1944, the USSR declared war on Bulgaria. Bulgaria then asked for an armistice and on 7 September declared war on Germany, hostilities with USSR ending on 10 September. The armistice with the Allies was signed in Moscow, 28 October 1944. The Peace Treaty with Bulgaria was signed on 22 February 1947, and came into force on 15 September 1947. It recognized the return of Southern Dobrudja to Bulgaria.

On 9 September 1944 a coup d'état gave power to the Fatherland Front, a coalition of Communists, Agrarians, Social Democrats and officers and intellectuals. In August 1945, the main body of Agrarians and Social Democrats left the Government. On 8 September 1946 a referendum was held, which led to the abolition of the monarchy and the setting up of a Republic.

The post-war political scene was dominated by the Communist Party (BCP), led by Todor Zhivkov. After he was forced to resign in November 1989, further leadership changes and reforms culminated, in January 1990, in the National Assembly voting to abolish the BCP's constitutional guarantee of power. Multi-party elections to a 400-seat Grand National Assembly (parliament) were held in June 1990. The BCP, renamed the Bulgarian Socialist Party in April, emerged as the majority party. A BSP-dominated government formed in September 1990 was brought down two months later by a combination of industrial strikes and opposition pressure. A multi-party government was formed in December 1990 which began to implement a radical programme of economic and political reform.

GOVERNMENT

A new constitution, enshrining democracy, the free market and a directly elected Presidency, was adopted by the Grand National Assembly on 12 July 1991.

Parliamentary elections were held on 13 October 1991, the UDF emerging as the largest party in the new National Assembly. The UDF won 111 of the total of 240 seats, the BSP 106 seats and the ethnic Turkish Movement for Rights and Freedom Party (MRF) 24 seats. The UDF formed a new government, which took office in November with MRF support under Filip Dimitrov, and declared its priorities to be the economic stabilization of the country and strong anti-inflationary policies.

Head of State

President, Zhelyu Zhelev, *elected* 1 August 1990, *re-elected* 19 January 1992.
Vice-President, Blaga Dimitrova.

Cabinet as at June 1992

Prime Minister, Filip Dimitrov.
Deputy Prime Minister, Justice, Svetoslav Louchnikov.
Deputy Prime Minister, Health, Nikola Vassilev.
Deputy Prime Minister, Economics, Ilko Eskenazi.
Deputy Prime Minister, Education and Science, Nikolai Vassilev.
Industry, Roumen Bikov.
Trade, Alexander Pramatarski.
Agricultural Development, Land Use and Land Restitution, Georgi Stoyanov.
Defence, Alexander Staliyski.
Foreign Affairs, Stoyan Ganev.
Transport, Alexander Alexandrov.
Environment, Valentin Vassilev.
Culture, Elka Konstantinova.
Labour and Social Welfare, Vekil Vanov.
Finance, Ivan Kostov.
Interior, Yordan Sokolov.
Territorial Development, Housing Policy and Construction, Nikola Karadimov.

Embassy of the Republic of Bulgaria

186–188 Queen's Gate, London SW7 5HL
Tel 071–584 9400/9433

Ambassador Extraordinary and Plenipotentiary, Ivan Stancioff (1991).

British Embassy

Boulevard Marshal Tolbukhin 65–67, Sofia
Tel: Sofia 879575

Ambassador Extraordinary and Plenipotentiary, His Excellency Richard Thomas, CMG (1989).

British Council Representative, David Stokes, Todor Strashimirov 7, 1504, Sofia.

ECONOMY

Until 1939 Bulgaria was a predominantly agricultural country, but subsequently pursued an elaborate programme of industrialization. About 90 per cent of the country's agriculture was turned over to co-operatives, and a smaller proportion mechanized. The principal crops are wheat, maize, beet, tomatoes, tobacco, oleaginous seeds, fruit, vegetables and cotton. The livestock includes cattle, sheep, goats, pigs, horses, asses, mules and water buffaloes.

There is now a substantial engineering industry and considerable production of ferrous and non-ferrous metals. There are mineral deposits of varying importance. Bulgaria's heavy industry includes the Kremikovtsi Steel Plant near Sofia and the steel mill at Pernik, the chemical complex at Devnia, the petro-chemical plant at Bourgas and various other chemical and metallurgical works situated around the country. The Soviet-designed nuclear power station at Kozlodui, comprising four reactors, each with a capability of producing 800 million kilowatt-hours and a fifth, 1,000 MW unit, accounts for over 40 per cent of Bulgaria's electrical generating capacity.

Finance

Planned public expenditure for 1991 was 70,476.5 million leva, while the internal budget deficit was expected to reach 7,509.5 m leva.

DEFENCE

Bulgaria has a total active armed forces strength of 107,000 including 70,000 conscripts. Conscripts serve for 18 months. The Army has a strength of 75,000 personnel, including 49,000 conscripts. The Navy has a strength of 10,000 personnel (5,000 conscripts), two principal surface combatant vessels and three submarines. The Air Force has a strength of 22,000 (16,000 conscripts), 266 combat aircraft and 44 armed helicopters.

EDUCATION

Free basic education is compulsory for children from 7 to 15 years inclusive. Government policy emphasizes the need to democratize the education system, to remove the former ideological basis and to encourage private education. There are three universities (at Sofia, Plovdiv and Veliko Turnovo) and 21 higher educational establishments.

TRADE

Since 1989, political and economic developments in Bulgaria and in some of her principal trading partners have had a substantial impact on the volume and pattern of foreign trade. In 1988, 79 per cent of Bulgaria's foreign trade was within the CMEA, including approximately 57 per cent with the Soviet Union. Trade with both the former CMEA member countries and with the industrialized West declined sharply in 1990. Figures for the first quarter of 1991 indicate that over 38 per cent of Bulgaria's exports by value went to the developed industrial countries, some 35 per cent to the former CMEA and 26 per cent to the developing countries. The Soviet Union retained its position as Bulgaria's largest supplier, accounting for approximately 50 per cent of Bulgarian imports by value.

The principal imports are fuels, minerals and metals, engineering goods and industrial equipment. The principal exports are engineering goods and industrial equipment, industrial consumer goods, chemicals and fuels, minerals and metals.

Trade with UK	1990	1991
Imports from UK	£45,022,000	£35,647,000
Exports to UK	32,787,000	36,786,000

BURKINA FASO
République Populaire de Burkina

Burkina Faso (formerly Upper Volta) is an inland savanna state in West Africa, situated between 9° and 15°N. and 2°E. and 5°W. with an area of 105,869 sq. miles (274,200 sq. km), and a population of 9,001,000 (UN estimate 1990). It has common boundaries with Mali on the west, Niger and Benin on the east and Togo, Ghana and the Côte d'Ivoire on the south. The largest tribe is the Mossi whose king, the Moro Naba, still wields a certain moral influence. The official language is French.

CAPITAL – Ouagadougou (400,000). Other principal towns; Bobo-Dioulasso (211,538) and Koudougou (30,000).
CURRENCY – Franc CFA.
FLAG – Equal bands of red over green, with a yellow star in centre.
NATIONAL DAY – 4 August.

HISTORY

Burkina Faso was annexed by France in 1896 and between 1932 and 1947 was administered as part of the Colony of the Ivory Coast. It decided on 11 December 1958 to remain an autonomous republic within the French Community; full independence outside the Community was proclaimed on 5 August 1960.

GOVERNMENT

The 1960 constitution provided for a presidential form of government with a single chamber National Assembly, but in January 1966 the Army assumed power. A new constitution allowing for a partial return to civilian rule but with the Army still in effective control was adopted in 1970, but in 1974 this was suspended. Full legislative and presidential elections were held again in 1978. Following a number of military coups, Capt. Blaise Compaoré took power in October 1987, also by coup. The present government, a broad-based coalition (the Popular Front), held a congress in March 1990 which decided to appoint a committee to draft a 'Constitution leading to democratization'. The Constitution was adopted by referendum on 2 June 1991. Presidential elections were held in December 1991 and won by Capt. Compaoré in the face of a boycott by the main opposition parties, who were unhappy with the new constitution. Opposition parties then boycotted the legislative elections held in May 1992, which were consequently won by Compaoré's Organization for Popular Democracy-Labour Movement (ODP-MT) party, which formed the government.

HEAD OF STATE
President of the Popular Front, Head of State, Capt. Blaise Compaoré, *assumed office*, October 1987, elected December 1991.

COUNCIL OF MINISTERS as at 21 June 1992
Prime Minister, Youssouf Ouedraogo.
Minister of State, Finance and Planning, Rock Marc Christian Kabore.
Ministers of State, Kanidoua Naboho; Herman Yameogo.
Presidential Special Envoy, Salif Diallo.
Defence, Yarga Larba.
Foreign Affairs, Thomas Sanon.
Territorial Administration, Raogo Antoine Sawadogo.
Public Works, Housing and Urban Areas, Joseph Kabore.
Industry, Commerce and Mines, Zéphírin Diabre.
Secondary and Higher Education, Scientific Research, Mélégué Traore.
Justice, Timothée Some.
Communications, Government Spokesman, Kilimité Theordore Hien.
Water, Séni Macaire Nare.
Employment, Works and Social Security, Jean Léonard Compaore.
Transport, Mamadou Simpore.
Parliamentary Relations, Idrissa Zampalegre.
Primary Education and Literacy, Alice Tiendrebeogo.
Environment and Tourism, Anatole Tiendrebeogo.
Agriculture and Animal Husbandry, Albert Djigma.
Civil Service and Administrative Reform, Juliette Bonkoungou.
Health, Social Action and the Family, Christophe Dabire.
Youth and Sport, Ibrahim Traore.
Culture, Ouala Koutiebou.
Secretary-General of the Government and of the Council of Ministers, Tingnimian Sere.

EMBASSY OF BURKINA FASO
16 Place Guy d'Arezzo, 1060 Brussels, Belgium
Tel: Brussels 3459911
Ambassador Extraordinary and Plenipotentiary, His Excellency Salifou Rigobert Kongo (resident in Brussels).
HONORARY CONSULATE, 5 Cinnamon Row, Plantation Wharf, London SW11 3TW. Tel: 071–738 1800. *Honorary Consul*, S. G. Singer.

BRITISH AMBASSADOR (resident in Abidjan, Côte d'Ivoire).

ECONOMY

The 1988 Budget totalled Franc CFA 90,300 million. The principal industry is the rearing of cattle and sheep and the chief exports are livestock, groundnuts, millet and sorghum. Small deposits of gold, manganese, copper, bauxite and graphite have been found. Trade in 1991 was valued at imports, CFA 149,704m, exports, CFA 77,843m.

Trade with UK	1990	1991
Imports from UK	£6,557,000	£6,472,000
Exports to UK	967,000	285,000

BURUNDI
République de Burundi

Formerly a Belgian trusteeship under the United Nations, Burundi was proclaimed independent on 1 July 1962. Situated on the east side of Lake Tanganyika, the state has an area of 10,747 sq. miles (27,834 sq. km) and a population (UN estimate 1990) of 5,458,000. The majority of the population are of the Hutu ethnic group, but power rests in the hands of the minority Tutsi ethnic group. Official languages are Kirundi, a Bantu language, and French. Kiswahili is also used.

CAPITAL – Bujumbura (formerly Usumbura), with 215,243 (1987 estimate) inhabitants. Kitega (18,000 inhabitants) is the only other sizeable town.
CURRENCY – Burundi franc of 100 centimes.

FLAG – Divided diagonally by a white saltire into red and green triangles; on a white disc in the centre three red six-pointed stars edged in green.
NATIONAL DAY – 1 July.

GOVERNMENT

Burundi became independent as a constitutional monarchy but this was overthrown on 28 November 1966 and the country became a republic. On 1 Nov. 1976, the government of President Micombero was overthrown and a Supreme Revolutionary Council led by Col. Jean-Baptiste Bagaza took power. In 1980 the SRC was replaced by a political bureau and central committee as part of a process of political normalization, which continued with elections to the National Assembly, a 65-member legislature. In September 1987 the government of President Bagaza was overthrown by a Military Committee of National Redemption led by Major Pierre Buyoya. The Party of National Unity and Progress (UPRONA), the ruling party, adopted a National Unity Charter to unify the Hutu and Tutsi tribal groups; the Charter was approved by a referendum in February 1991. Following violence and unrest throughout 1991 and early 1992, a further referendum was held in March 1992 which approved the adoption of multiparty politics, an executive President directly elected for five-year terms, and the banning of tribally-based parties. Legislative elections have been scheduled for the end of 1992.

HEAD OF STATE
President, Major Pierre Buyoya, *elected* 9 Sept. 1987, *sworn in* 2 Oct. 1987.

COUNCIL OF MINISTERS as at May 1992
Prime Minister, Adrien Sibomana.
Foreign Affairs and Co-operation, Libere Bararunyeretse.
Agriculture and Animal Husbandry, Jumaine Hussein.
Defence, Lt.-Col. Leonidas Maregarege.
Finance, Gerard Niyibigira.
Rural Development and Handicrafts, Gabriel Toyi.
Justice, Sebastien Ntahuga.
Interior and Local Government, François Ngeze.
Commerce and Industry, Astere Girukwigomaba.
Transport, Posts and Telecommunications, Lt.-Col. Simon Rusuku.
Public Works and Urban Development, Evariste Simbarakiye.
Energy and Mines, Bonaventure Bangurambona.
Public Health, Norbert Ngendabanyikwa.
Civil Service, Charles Karikurubu.
Labour and Social Policy, Julie Ngiriye.
Women's Advancement and Social Protection, Victoire Ndikumana.
Communication, Culture and Sports, Frederick Ngenzebuhoro.
Tourism, Land Use and Environment, Louis Nduwimana.
Higher Education and Scientific Research, Gilbert Midende.
Primary and Secondary Education, Gamariel Ndarunzaniye.
Professional Training and Youth, Adolphe Nahayo.
Secretaries of State, Salvator Sahinguvu (*Planning*); Fridolin Hatungimana (*Economic Planning*); Laurent Kagimbi (*Interior*).

EMBASSY OF THE REPUBLIC OF BURUNDI
Square Marie Louise 46, 1040 Brussels, Belgium
Tel: Brussels 2304535

Ambassador Extraordinary and Plenipotentiary, His Excellency Balthazar Habonimana (1992) (resident in Brussels).
BRITISH AMBASSADOR (resident in Kinshasa, Zaire).

ECONOMY

The chief crop is coffee, representing about 80 per cent of Burundi's export earnings. Cotton is the second most important crop. Mineral, tea, hide and skin exports are also important.

Trade with UK	1990	1990
Imports from UK	£2,804,000	£3,817,000
Exports to UK	224,000	2,341,000

CAMBODIA

AREA AND POPULATION – Situated between Thailand and the south of Vietnam and extending from the border with Laos on the north to the Gulf of Thailand, Cambodia covers an area of 69,898 sq. miles (181,035 sq. km). It has a population (UN estimate 1990) of 8,246,000. The climate is tropical monsoon with a rainy season from May to October.

Fifty per cent of the total land area is forest or jungle. Around the Tonlé Sap lake in the centre of the country and along the Mekong river, which traverses the country, there is ample fertile land for the support of the population in times of peace.

RELIGION – The state religion was Buddhism of the 'Little Vehicle'. The constitution guaranteed religious freedom, but in practice Buddhism was suppressed by the Khmer Rouge. There has been some revival recently and Buddhism has been re-established as the state religion. There were also small Muslim and Christian communities, but many members of them died or fled the country during Khmer Rouge rule.
LANGUAGE – The national language is Khmer.

CAPITAL – Phnom Penh, population 500,000 (1983 estimate).
CURRENCY – Riel of 100 sen.
FLAG – (SNC) United Nations blue with a white silhouette map of Cambodia containing the name of the state in blue letters.
NATIONAL DAY – (NGC) 17 April; (SOC) 7 January.

HISTORY

Once a powerful kingdom, which, as the Khmer Empire, flourished between the tenth and fourteenth centuries, Cambodia became a French protectorate in 1863 and was granted independence within the French Union as an Associate State in 1949. Full independence was proclaimed on 9 November 1953. From 1955 the political life of the country was dominated by Prince Norodom Sihanouk, first as King, then as Head of Government after he had abdicated in favour of his father and finally (following his father's death in 1960) as Head of State. On 18 March 1970, during his absence from the country, Prince Sihanouk was deposed as Head of State by a vote of the National Assembly. A Republic was declared on 9 October 1970 and the name of the country changed to the Khmer Republic.

In April 1970 a civil war began between Communist insurgents and government forces. In April 1975 Phnom Penh fell to the North Vietnamese-backed Khmer Rouge. Prince Sihanouk returned to Cambodia on 9 September as nominal Head of State. A new Constitution was promulgated in 1976 and elections to a People's Representative Assembly were held in March. Prince Sihanouk resigned as Head of State in April, and Khieu Samphan was elected President of the State Presidium. A government led by Pol Pot, the leader of the Khmer Rouge (Communist) party, was appointed and the state was renamed Democratic

Kampuchea. During the years of Khmer Rouge rule hundreds of thousands of Cambodians died or fled into exile.

In December 1978 Vietnamese troops invaded Cambodia in support of an uprising. The Cambodian capital, Phnom Penh, fell on 7 January 1979. The following day the Cambodian National United Front for National Salvation established a People's Revolutionary Council, recognized by Vietnam, USSR and by other, chiefly Soviet-aligned, countries. The state was renamed The People's Republic of Kampuchea (PRK).

With strong support from the Vietnamese army the PRK gained control of most of the country, containing the challenge from the guerrilla forces of the Coalition Government of Democratic Kampuchea (CGDK), which was formed in June 1982 by the Khmer Rouge and two non-Communist groups. Following the final withdrawal of Vietnam's main fighting units in September 1989, the resistance forces have regained ground inside Cambodia.

Encouraged by the five permanent members of the UN Security Council and other interested parties, the four Cambodian factions agreed to the general principles of a peace settlement, including the ending of external military support and the holding of free and fair elections under international supervision. In September 1990, the four Cambodian factions established a Supreme National Council, as provided for in the Permanent Five draft agreement, to embody Cambodian sovereignty and to help finalize and implement a comprehensive settlement. The first meeting took place in Bangkok on 17 September. A temporary ceasefire began on 1 May 1991 and became permanent on 23 June.

The peace agreements were finally signed in Paris on 23 October 1991 and Prince Sihanouk returned to Phnom Penh in November. In mid-March 1992 the United Nations Transitional Authority for Cambodia (UNTAC) began its task of implementing the peace agreements. After initial progress UNTAC encountered problems as the Khmer Rouge launched attacks in the north and west of the country and refused to disarm its fighters according to the agreed schedule because it claimed Vietnamese forces were still supporting the Phnom Penh government. Meanwhile UNTAC continued to take over gradually the administration of the country from the Phnom Penh (SOC) government until free elections can be held.

SUPREME NATIONAL COUNCIL

Members, Prince Sihanouk (S); Hun Sen (SOC); Dit Munti (SOC); Nor Nam Hong (SOC); Ieng Mouly (BLDP); Im Chhunlim (SOC); Khieu Samphan (KR); Norodam Ranariddh (S); Sin Sen (SOC); Son Sann (BLDP); Son Sen (KR); Tea Banh (SOC).

BLDP: Buddhist Liberal Democratic Party, KR: Khmer Rouge (Party of Democratic Kampuchea), S: Sihanoukist, SOC: State of Cambodia.

UNITED NATIONS TRANSITIONAL AUTHORITY FOR CAMBODIA

Administrator, Yasushi Akashi (*Japan*).
Military Commander, Lt.-Gen John Sanderson (*Australia*).

STATE OF CAMBODIA

Chairman of Council of Ministers, Hun Sen.
Chairman of National Assembly, Chea Sim.

HEAD OF BRITISH MISSION TO THE SUPREME NATIONAL COUNCIL, David Burns.

ECONOMY

Cambodia has an economy based on agriculture, fishing and forestry, the bulk of its people being rice-growing farmers. In addition to rice, which is the staple crop, the major products are rubber, livestock, maize, timber, pepper, palm sugar, fresh and dried fish, kapok, beans, soya and tobacco. Rice and rubber used to be the main exports though production was brought to a standstill by the hostilities. Following the Khmer Rouge victory, the populations of Phnom Penh and other towns were forcibly evacuated to the country to work on the land, and re-establish the plantations producing such crops as cotton, rubber and bananas. Following the Vietnamese invasion of 1978 the towns were repopulated and commerce revived; currency was reintroduced. Factories, in particular textile mills, iron smelting works and cement works were put back in production.

Trade with UK	1990	1991
Imports from UK	£478,000	£409,000
Exports to UK	56,000	29,000

COMMUNICATIONS

The country had over 5,000 kilometres of roads, of which nearly half were hard-surfaced and passable in the rainy season, although now in a state of disrepair. There are two railways, one from Phnom Penh to the Thai border; the other from Phnom Penh to Kampot and Kompong Som, but operations and repairs are hindered by the continuing fighting. Phnom Penh is on a river capable of receiving ships of up to 2,500 tons all the year round. The deep water port at Kompong Som on the Gulf of Thailand can receive ships up to 10,000 tons. The port is linked to Phnom Penh by a modern highway.

EDUCATION

In the years preceding the civil war considerable efforts were devoted to the development of education and new schools, colleges and technical institutes had been established. Until April 1975 there was a Buddhist University in Phnom Penh, and several residential teachers' training colleges were in operation. However, most of the country's educated elite died under the Khmer Rouge regime, which closed all institutions of higher education. The university was re-opened in 1988.

CAMEROON
République du Cameroun

The Republic of Cameroon lies on the Gulf of Guinea between Nigeria to the west, Chad and the Central African Republic to the east and Congo and Gabon and Equatorial Guinea to the south. It has an area of 183,569 sq. miles (475,442 sq. km) and a population of 11,833,000 (UN estimate 1990).

LANGUAGES – Cameroon is the only country in Africa where French and English are both official languages enjoying equal status, and the government's declared long-term objective is to achieve complete bilingualism and biculturalism.

CAPITAL – Yaoundé, population estimate (1986) 653,670. ΨDouala (1,029,736) is the commercial centre.
CURRENCY – Franc CFA of 100 centimes.
FLAG – Vertical stripes of green, red and yellow with single five-pointed yellow star in centre of red stripe.
NATIONAL ANTHEM – O Cameroun, Berceau de Nos Ancêtres (O Cameroon, thou cradle of our forefathers).
NATIONAL DAY – 20 May.

GOVERNMENT

The whole territory was administered by Germany from 1884 to 1916. From 1916 to 1959, the former East Cameroon was administered by France as a League of Nations (later UN) trusteeship. On 1 January 1960 it became independent as the Republic of Cameroon. The Republic was joined on 1 October 1961 by the former British administered trust territory of the Southern Cameroons, after a plebiscite held under United Nations auspices. Cameroon became a Federal Republic with separate East and West Cameroon state governments. Subsequently, after a plebiscite held in May 1972, Cameroon became a unitary Republic and a one-party state; after extensive unrest, multi-party elections were promised by the end of 1991. These were finally held in March 1992, with the ruling People's Democratic Movement emerging just short of a majority in the parliament and forming a coalition government with a small opposition party, the Movement for the Defence of the Republic.

HEAD OF STATE

President and Commander in Chief of the Armed Forces, His Excellency Paul Biya, *acceded* 6 Nov. 1982, *elected* 14 Jan. 1984, *re-elected* 24 April 1988, *sworn in* 13 May 1988.

MINISTRY as at June 1992

Prime Minister, Simon Achidi Achu.
Deputy Prime Minister, Mining, Water and Energy, Marcel Niat-Njifenjou.
Posts and Telecommunications, Dakole Daissala.
Territorial Administration, Gilbert Andze Tsoungui.
Minister-Delegate at the Presidency Responsible for Defence, Eduard Akame Mfoumou.
External Relations, Jaques-Roger Booh-Booh.
Justice, Douala Moutome.
Livestock, Fisheries and Animal Industries, Dr Hamadjoda Adjoudji.
Higher Education, Titus Edzoa.
Public Health, Joseph Mbede.
Labour and Social Welfare, Jean-Bosco Samgba.
Industrial and Commercial Development, Réné Owona.
Finance, Justin Ndioroa.
Public Service and Administrative Reform, Garga Haman Adji.
Planning and Regional Development, Tchouta Moussa.
Social and Women's Affairs, Aissatou Yaou.
Communications, Augustin Kontchou Kouomegni.
Minister for Special Duties at the Presidency, John Ebong Ngole.
Agriculture, John Niba Ngu.
Town Planning and Housing, Henri Ebeye Ayissi.
Public Works and Transport, Jean-Baptiste Bokam.
Scientific Research and Technology, Ayuk Takern.
Tourism, Pierre Souman.
Environment and Forestry, Bava Djingoer.
Youth and Sport, Lando Théodore.
National Education, Robert Mbella Mbappe.

EMBASSY OF THE REPUBLIC OF CAMEROON
84 Holland Park, London W11 3SB
Tel: 071–727 0771

Ambassador Extraordinary and Plenipotentiary, His Excellency Dr Gibering Bol-Alima (1987).

BRITISH EMBASSY
Avenue Winston Churchill, BP 547 Yaoundé
Tel: Yaoundé 220545

Ambassador Extraordinary and Plenipotentiary, His Excellency William E. Quantrill (1991).

BRITISH COUNCIL REPRESENTATIVE, Harley Brookes, Immeuble Christo, Rue Charles de Gaulle (BP 818), Yaoundé.

ECONOMY

The main economic emphasis is on agricultural development, both through encouraging small-scale peasant agriculture, and through the development of large-scale agro-industrial complexes, with the aim of making the country agriculturally self-sufficient and a major food exporter.

Principal products are cocoa, coffee, bananas, cotton, timber, ground-nuts, aluminium, rubber and palm products. There is an aluminium smelting plant at Edéa with an annual capacity of 50,000 tons. Oil is now also one of Cameroon's principal products with an estimated production of 7.31 m. tonnes during 1989.

TRADE

	1987	1988
	CFA million	
Total imports	526,186	378,726
Total exports	487,849	468,683

Trade with UK	1990	1991
Imports from UK	£20,652,000	£23,813,000
Exports to UK	8,241,000	6,135,000

CANADA

AREA AND POPULATION

Provinces or Territories (with official contractions)	Area (sq. miles)	Population Census 1991
Alberta (Alta.)	255,285	2,545,553*
British Columbia (BC)	365,946	3,282,061
Manitoba (Man.)	250,946	1,091,942
New Brunswick (NB)	28,355	723,900
Newfoundland and Labrador (Nfld.)	156,648	568,474
Nova Scotia (NS)	21,425	899,942
Ontario (Ont.)	412,579	10,084,885
Prince Edward Island (PEI)	2,185	129,765
Quebec (Que.)	594,857	6,895,963
Saskatchewan (Sask.)	251,865	988,928
Yukon Territory (YT)	186,660	27,797
Northwest Territories (NWT)	1,322,902	57,649
Total	3,849,653	27,296,859

Area figures include land and water area.
*Excludes 1991 Census data for one or more incompletely enumerated Indian reserves or Indian settlements.

BIRTHS, DEATHS AND MARRIAGES, 1990

Province	*Births*	*Deaths*	*Marriages*
Alberta	43,004	14,068	19,806
British Columbia	45,617	23,577	25,216
Manitoba	17,352	8,863	7,666
New Brunswick	9,824	5,426	5,044
Newfoundland	7,604	3,884	3,791
Nova Scotia	12,870	7,388	6,386
Ontario	150,923	70,818	80,097
PEI	2,014	1,143	996
Québec	98,048	48,420	32,060
Saskatchewan	16,090	8,044	6,229
Yukon	555	115	218
NW Territories	1,585	227	228
Total	405,486	191,973	187,737

Canada's birth rate per 1,000 population (1990) 15.3; death rate 7.2; marriage rate 7.1. Divorces were 78.152 in 1990.

Of the total immigration of 230,291 in 1991, 12,874 were from the Caribbean, 7,340 from the United Kingdom and Ireland, and 6,577 from the United States of America.

MOTHER TONGUES OF THE POPULATION

	1986
Single Responses	
English	15,334,085
French	6,159,740
Non-official languages	2,860,570
Cree	57,645
Inuktitut	21,050
Ojibway	16,380

Multiple Responses	
English and French	332,610
English and non-official language(s)	525,720
French and non-official language(s)	36,310
English, French and non-official language(s)	46,585
Non-official languages	13,715
Total Population	25,309,330

PHYSIOGRAPHY

Canada was originally discovered by Cabot in 1497, but its history dates only from 1534, when the French took possession of the country. The first permanent settlement at Port Royal (now Annapolis), Nova Scotia, was founded in 1605, and Quebec was founded in 1608. In 1759 Quebec was captured by the British forces under General Wolfe, and in 1763 the whole territory of Canada became a possession of Great Britain by the Treaty of Paris of that year. Nova Scotia was ceded in 1713 by the Treaty of Utrecht, the Provinces of New Brunswick and Prince Edward Island being subsequently formed out of it. British Columbia was formed into a Crown colony in 1858, having previously been a part of the Hudson Bay Territory, and was united to Vancouver Island in 1866.

Canada occupies the whole of the northern part of the North American continent (with the exception of Alaska), from 49° North latitude to the North Pole, and from the Pacific to the Atlantic Ocean. In Eastern Canada, the southernmost point is Middle Island in Lake Erie, at 41° 41′.

Relief - The relief of Canada is dominated by the mountain ranges running north and south on the west side of the continent, by the pre-Cambrian shield on the east, with, in between, the northern extension of the North American Plain. From the physiographic point of view Canada has six main divisions. These are: (1) Appalachian-Acadian Region, (2) the Canadian Shield, (3) the St Lawrence-Great Lakes Lowland, (4) the Interior Plains, (5) the Cordilleran Region and (6) the Arctic archipelago. The first region occupies all that part of Canada lying south-east of the St Lawrence. In general, the relief is an alternation of highlands and lowlands and is hilly rather than mountainous. The great Canadian Shield comprises more than half the area. The interior as a whole is an undulating, low plateau (general level 1,000 to 1,500 feet), with the more rugged relief lying along the border between Northern Quebec and Labrador. Throughout the whole area water or muskeg-filled depressions separate irregular hills and ridges, 150 to 200 feet in elevation. Newfoundland, an outlying portion of the shield, consists of glaciated, low rolling terrain broken here and there by mountains.

The flat relief of the St Lawrence-Great Lakes lowland varies from 500 feet in the east to 1,700 feet south of Georgian Bay. The most striking relief is provided by the eastward facing scarp of the Niagara escarpment (elevation 250 to 300 feet). The interior plains, comprising the Pacific Provinces, slope eastward and northward a few feet per mile. The descent from west to east is made from 5,000 feet to less than 1,000 feet in three distinct levels, with each new level being marked by an eastward facing conteau or scarp. Five fairly well-developed topographic divisions mark out the Cordilleran region of western Canada. These are: (1) coastal ranges, largely above 5,000 feet with deep fjords and glaciated valleys, (2) the interior plateau, around 3,500 feet and comparatively level, (3) the Selkirk ranges, largely above 5,000 feet, (4) the Rocky Mountains with their chain of 10,000 to 12,000 feet peaks, and (5) the Peace River or Tramontane region with its rolling diversified country.

The Arctic archipelago, with its plateau-like character has an elevation between 500 and 1,000 feet, though in Baffin Land and Ellesmere Island the mountain ranges rise to 8,500 and 9,500 feet. Two tremendous waterway systems, the St Lawrence and the Mackenzie, providing thousands of miles of water highway, occupy a broad area of lowland with their dominant axis following the edge of the shield.

Climate - The climate of the eastern and central portions presents greater extremes than in corresponding latitudes in Europe, but in the south-western portion of the prairie region and the southern portions of the Pacific slope the climate is milder. Spring, summer and autumn are of about seven to eight months' duration, and the winter four to five months.

FEDERAL CAPITAL - Ottawa, on the banks of the Ottawa river, 111 miles west of Montreal and 247 miles north-east of Toronto. Ottawa is connected with Lake Ontario by the Rideau Canal. The city was chosen as the capital of the Province of Canada in 1857 and was later selected as the Dominion capital. The city population was 313,987 at the Census of 1991; and the population of the metropolitan area of Ottawa–Hull was 920,857.

CURRENCY - Canadian dollar (C$) of 100 cents.

FLAG - Red maple leaf with 11 points on white square, flanked by vertical red bars one-half the width of the square.

NATIONAL ANTHEM - O Canada.

NATIONAL DAY - 1 July (Dominion Day).

GOVERNMENT

The Constitution of Canada had its source in the British North America Act of 1867 which formed a Dominion, under the name of Canada, of the four provinces of Ontario, Quebec, New Brunswick and Nova Scotia; to this federation the other provinces have subsequently been admitted. Under this Act, Canada came into being on 1 July 1867, and under the Statute of Westminster, which received the royal assent on 11 December 1931, Canada and the provinces were exempted (in common with other self-governing Dominions of the Commonwealth of Nations) from the operation of the Colonial Laws Validity Act, the Statute of Westminster having removed all limitations with regard to the legislative autonomy of the Dominions, except that the British North America Act could be amended in important respects only by Acts of the British Parliament.

Provinces admitted since 1867 are: Manitoba (1870), British Columbia (1871), Prince Edward Island (1873), Alberta and Saskatchewan (1905) and Newfoundland (1949).

The election of a separatist Parti Quebecois government in Quebec in 1976 led to a referendum in 1980 on whether the province should conduct negotiations with the federal government on a new 'sovereignty-association'; the proposal was rejected.

Agreement was reached in November 1981 between the federal and provincial governments (except Quebec) to patriate the Constitution so that it was amendable only in Canada. The inclusion in the Constitution of a Charter of Rights was also agreed. At the request of the Canadian Parliament, legislation was passed at Westminster and the Constitution formally patriated on 17 April 1982.

To reconcile Quebec to the new constitution the Canadian federal government and the ten provincial governments signed the Meech Lake Accord on 3 June 1987. This transferred certain powers to the provinces and specifically recognized Quebec as 'a distinct society'. The provincial legislatures of Manitoba and Newfoundland refused to approve the Accord by the deadline for its ratification on 22 June 1990. In September 1992 agreement on a new federal constitution was reached between the federal government

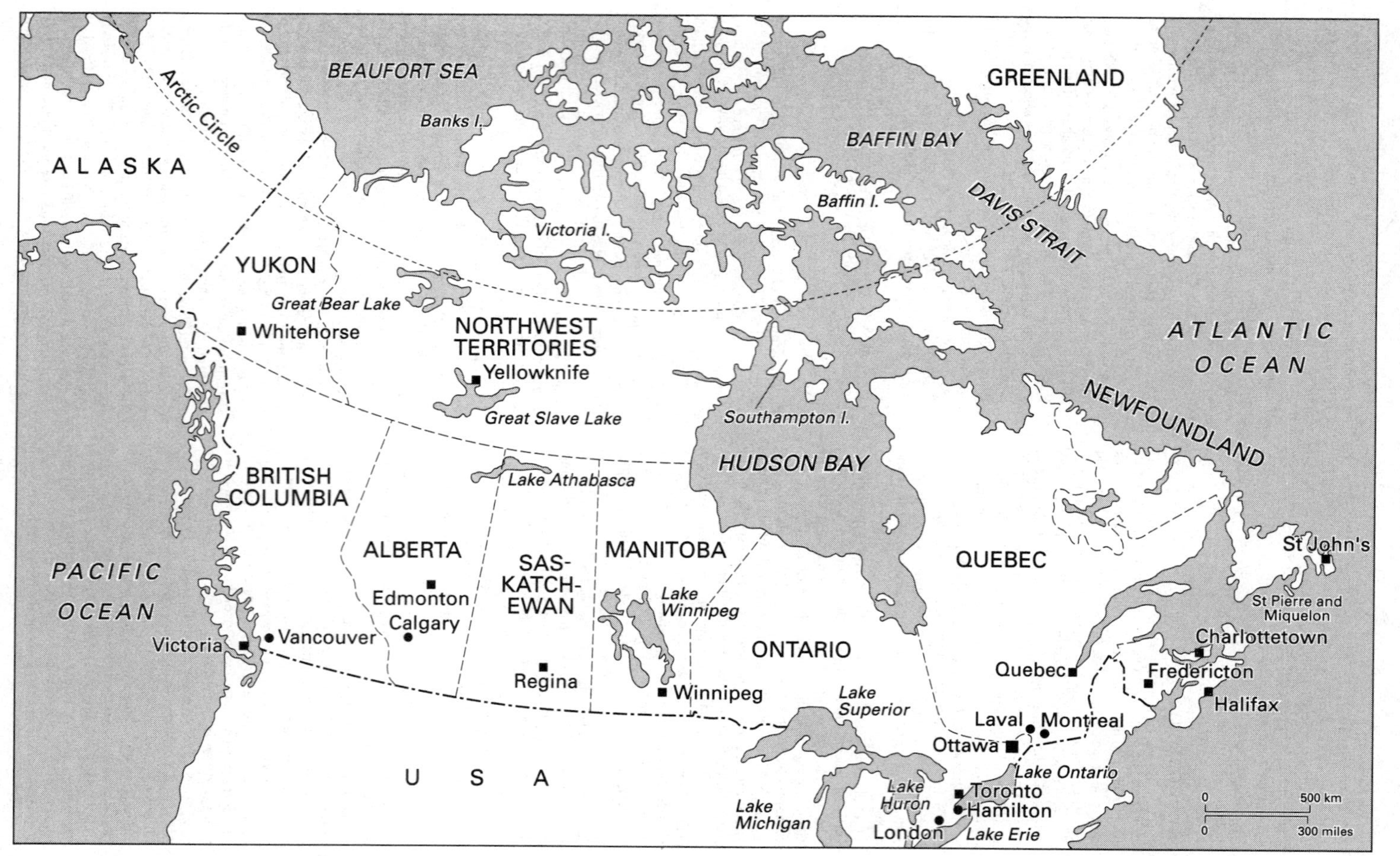
ALASKA
Arctic Circle
BEAUFORT SEA
Banks I.
GREENLAND
BAFFIN BAY
Baffin I.
DAVIS STRAIT
Victoria I.
YUKON
Great Bear Lake
Whitehorse
NORTHWEST
TERRITORIES
Yellowknife
Great Slave Lake
Southampton I.
ATLANTIC
OCEAN
NEWFOUNDLAND
HUDSON BAY
BRITISH
COLUMBIA
Lake Athabasca
ALBERTA
SAS-
KATCH-
EWAN
MANITOBA
QUEBEC
St John's
PACIFIC
OCEAN
Edmonton
Calgary
Lake
Winnipeg
St Pierre and
Miquelon
Victoria
Vancouver
ONTARIO
Charlottetown
Quebec
Fredericton
Regina
Winnipeg
Lake
Superior
Halifax
Laval
Montreal
Ottawa
Lake Ontario
U S A
Lake
Huron
Toronto
Hamilton
Lake
Michigan
London
Lake Erie
0 500 km
0 300 miles

and the provincial governments, and this is to be put to a national referendum on 26 October 1992.

Executive power is vested in a Governor-General appointed by the Sovereign on the advice of the Canadian Ministry, and aided by a Privy Council.

GOVERNOR-GENERAL

Governor-General and Commander-in-Chief, His Excellency the Rt. Hon. Ramon John Hnatyshyn, PC, CC, CMM, CD, QC.

Secretary to the Governor-General, J. A. LaRocque, CVO.

CABINET as at 10 June 1992

Prime Minister, Rt. Hon. Brian Mulroney
Minister responsible for Constitutional Affairs, President of Queen's Privy Council, Rt. Hon. Joe Clark
Fisheries and Oceans, Minister for the Atlantic Canada Opportunities Agency, Hon. John Crosbie.
Deputy Prime Minister, Minister of Finance, Hon. Don Mazankowski.
Public Works, Hon. Elmer Mackay.
Energy, Mines and Resources, Hon. Jake Epp.
Secretary of State, Hon. Robert de Cotret
Communications, Hon. Perrin Beatty
Industry, Science and Technology, International Trade, Hon. Michael Wilson
Minister of State and Government House Leader, Hon. Harvie Andre
National Revenue, Hon. Otto Jelinek
Indian Affairs and Northern Development, Hon. Tom Siddon
Western Economic Diversification, Minister of State (Grains and Oilseeds), Hon. Charles Mayer
Agriculture, Hon. Bill McKnight
Health and Welfare, Hon. Benoit Bouchard
Defence, Hon. Marcel Masse
External Affairs, Hon. Barbara McDougall
Veterans Affairs, Hon. Gerald Merrithew
Minister of State (Employment and Immigration), Minister of State (Seniors), Hon. Monique Vezina
Forestry, Hon. Frank Oberle
Government Leader in the Senate, Hon. Lowell Murray
Supply and Services, Hon. Paul Dick
Minister of State (Fitness, Youth and Amateur Sport), Deputy House Leader, Hon. Pierre Cadieux
Environment, Hon. Jean Charest
Minister of State (Small Business and Tourism), Hon. Tom Hockin
External Relations and Minister of State (Indian Affairs and Northern Development), Hon. Monique Landry
Employment and Immigration, Hon. Bernard Valcourt
Multiculturalism and Citizenship, Hon. Gerry Weiner
Solicitor-General, Hon. Doug Lewis
Consumer and Corporate Affairs and Minister of State (Agriculture), Hon. Pierre Blais
Minister of State (Finance and Privatization), Hon. John McDermid
Minister of State (Transport), Hon. Shirley Martin
Associate Defence Minister, Minister Responsible for the Status of Women, Hon. Mary Collins
Science, Hon. William Winegard
Justice Minister and Attorney-General, Hon. Kim Campbell
Transport, Hon. Jean Corbeil
President of Treasury Board, Minister of State (Finance), Hon. Gilles Loiselle
Labour, Hon. Marcel Danis
Minister of State (Environment), Hon. Pauline Browes

CANADIAN HIGH COMMISSION
Macdonald House, 1 Grosvenor Square, London W1X OAB
Tel 071-629 9492

High Commissioner, His Excellency Frederik Eaton (1991).
Deputy High Commissioner, Gaétan Lavertu.
Ministers, J. T. Boehm (*Political and Public Affairs*); R. J. L. Berlet (*Commercial/Economic*).
Minister-Counsellor, R. Girard (*Immigration*).

BRITISH HIGH COMMISSION
80 Elgin Street, Ottawa K1P 5K7
Tel: Ottawa 237 1530

High Commissioner, His Excellency Sir Nicholas Bayne KCMG.
Deputy High Commissioner, P. M. Newton.
Counsellors, R. J. Fell (*Economic and Commercial*); M. G. B. Greig.
Defence and Military Adviser, Brig. T. D. V. Bevan.
Naval Adviser, Capt. P. J. Bootherstone, DSC.
Air Adviser, Gp Capt J. R. Legh-Smith.
First Secretaries, R. V. Welborn (*Administration*); A. Jordan; I. D. Kydd (*Commercial*); J. Welsh; D. Scrafton.

BRITISH COUNCIL REPRESENTATIVE, M. Evans (Cultural Attaché).

BRITISH COUNCIL REPRESENTATIVE IN QUEBEC, S. Dawbarn, c/o British Consulate-General, 1155 University Street, Montreal, Quebec H3B 3A7.

LEGISLATURE

Parliament consists of a Senate and a House of Commons. The Senate consists of 107 members, nominated by the Governor-General (age limit 75), the seats being distributed between the various provinces. Each Senator must be at least thirty years old, a resident in the province for which he is appointed, a natural-born or naturalized subject of The Queen, and the owner of a property qualification amounting to $4,000. The Speaker of the Senate is chosen by the Government of the day.

The House of Commons has 295 members and is elected every five years at longest. Representation by provinces is at present as follows: Newfoundland 7, Prince Edward Island 4, Nova Scotia 11, New Brunswick 10, Quebec 75, Ontario 99, Manitoba 14, Saskatchewan 14, Alberta 26, British Columbia 32, Yukon 1, Northwest Territories 2.

The state of the parties in the Senate as at June 1992 was Progressive Conservatives 53, Liberals 45, Independent 5, Vacant 3.

Speaker of the Senate, Hon. Guy Charbonneau, QC.
Clerk of the Senate and Clerk of the Parliaments, Gordon Barnhart.

The state of parties in the House of Commons as at June 1992, was Progressive Conservatives 158, Liberals 81, New Democratic Party 44, Independent 11, Reform Party 1.

Speaker of the House of Commons, Hon. John A. Fraser.
Deputy Speaker, Andrée Champagne.
Clerk of the House of Commons, Robert Marleau.

JUDICATURE

The judicature is administered by judges following the civil law in Quebec Province and common law in other Provinces. Each Province has its Court of Appeal. All Superior, County and District Court Judges are appointed by the Governor-General, the others by the Lieutenant-Governors of the Provinces.

The highest federal court is the Supreme Court of Canada, composed of a Chief Justice and eight puisne judges, which exercises general appellate jurisdiction throughout Canada in civil and criminal cases, and which usually holds three sessions each year. There is one other federally constituted Court, the Federal Court of Canada, which has jurisdiction on appeals from its trial division, from federal tribunals and reviews of decisions and references by federal boards and commissions. The trial division has jurisdiction in claims by or against the Crown, its officers or servants or federal bodies. It also deals with inter-provincial and federal-provincial disputes.

SUPREME COURT OF CANADA

Chief Justice of Canada, Rt. Hon. A. Lamer, PC.
Puisne Judges, Hons. G. V. LaForest; Claire L'Heureux-Dube; J. Sopinka; C. Gonthier; P. Cory; Beverley McLachlin; W. A. Stevenson; F. Iacobucci.

FEDERAL COURT OF CANADA

Chief Justice, vacant.
Associate Chief Justice, Hon. J. A. Jerome.
Appeal Division Judges, Hons. L. Pratte; D. V. Heald; P. M. Mahoney, PC; L. Marceau; J. K. Hugesson; A. J. Stone; M. MacGuigan; Alice Desjardins; R. Décary; A. M. Linden.
Trial Division Judges, Hons. J.-E. Dubé; P. U. C. Rouleau; F. C. Muldoon; B. L. Strayer; Barbara J. Reed; P. Denault; Y. Pinard; L. M. Joyal; B. Cullen; L. A. Martin; M. A. Teitelbaum; W. A. MacKay.

FINANCE

Federal Government gross general revenue and expenditure was:

	1990–1	1991–2
Total Revenue	C$128,894m	C$137,654m
Total Expenditure	159,285m	168,062m

DEBT

	1989–90	1990–1
Gross Public Debt	C$408,483m	C$443,278m
Net Public Debt	354,439m	385,047m

BANKING

There were 65 chartered banks on 31 December 1991, with assets of C$491,329m (booked in Canada). Deposits were C$369,916m.

DEFENCE

The Minister of National Defence has the control and management of the Canadian armed forces and all matters relating to National Defence establishments and works for the defence of Canada.

The Canadian forces are organized on a functional basis to reflect the major commitments assigned by the government and are formed into National Defence Headquarters and five major Commands reporting to the Chief of the Defence Staff. The roles of the five Commands are:

Mobile Command – provision of ground forces for the protection of Canadian territory, combat forces in Canada for support of overseas commitments, and forces for support of United Nations or other peace-keeping operations
Maritime Command – provision of sea forces for the defence of Canada, anti-submarine defence in support of NATO. Maritime Command also has operational control of Maritime aircraft
Air Command – provision of operationally ready air forces to national, continental and international commitments
Canadian Forces Communications Command – manages, operates and maintains strategic communications for the Canadian Forces
Canadian Forces Europe – Canadian Forces allocated to support NATO in Europe consisting of land and air elements.

It was announced by the Canadian Government in February 1992 that all Canadian forces would leave Europe by 1994.

National Defence expenditure for the year 1991 was C$13,203 million. Canadian armed forces strength at March 1991: 84,792 authorized force.

EDUCATION

Education is under the control of the provincial governments, the cost of the publicly controlled schools being met by local taxation, aided by provincial grants. In 1991–2 there were 15,521 publicly controlled elementary and secondary schools with 5,236,200 pupils. Of these, 1,377 were private schools with 247,200 pupils; 387 federal schools with 52,600 pupils and 20 special schools for the blind and deaf with 2,400 pupils.

In 1991–2 there were 69 degree-granting universities with a full-time enrolment of 547,800, as well as 330,860 students in 204 other post-secondary, non-university institutions.

ECONOMY

AGRICULTURE – About 7 per cent of the total land area of Canada is farmed land. Over 60 per cent of this is under cultivation, the remainder being predominantly classified as unimproved pasture. More than 80 per cent of the land now cultivated is found in the prairie region of western Canada.

Farm cash receipts from the sale of farm products in 1991 were C$21,286 m. Livestock and animal products contributed C$10,740m; field crops C$8,280m.

Grain crop production ('000 metric tonnes):

	1990	1991p
Wheat	32,709.2	32,822.3
Oats	2,851.3	1,894.2
Barley	13,924.7	12,462.9
Rye	712.7	354.2
Flaxseed	935.3	691.2
Canola	3,281.1	4,303.2
Total	54,414.3	52,528.0

p preliminary

Livestock – In January 1991 the livestock included 11,197,500 cattle, 10,608,000 pigs, 541,300 sheep and lambs and 21,136,000 chickens (layers).

FUR PRODUCTION – Canada in 1990–1 produced pelts valued at C$42m. Wildlife pelts made up 36.3 per cent of the total, with a value of C$15m.

FISHERIES – The marketed value of catches in 1990 was C$3,302m (preliminary).

FORESTRY – About 43 per cent of the total land area is considered as inventoried forest area. The value of shipments and other revenue from forestry related industries in 1989 was: logging $8,697m; sawmill and planing mill products $9,237m; shingle and shake $237m; veneer and plywood $1,068m; and paper and allied products $25,847.5m.

MINERALS – In 1990, Canada was the world's largest producer of zinc and uranium, and the second largest of asbestos, potash, nickel and gypsum. The country is also rich in many other minerals, including gold, silver, copper, lead, molybdenum, platinum group metals, elemental sulphur, cobalt, titanium concentrate, aluminium and cadmium (refined production).

Mineral production ('000 tonnes):

	1990	1991p
Copper	771.4	773.6
Nickel	195.0	189.2
Lead	233.4	239.6

Molybdenum	12.2	11.3
Zinc	1,179.4	1,079.9
Iron Ore	35,670.0	35,961.0
Asbestos	686.0	670.0
Gypsum	7,978.0	7,305.0
Cement	11,745.0	9,396.0
Lime	2,341.0	2,336.0
Salt	11,191.0	11,585.0
Potash	7,345.0	7,012.0

p preliminary

Production of gold was 176,720,000 grams in 1991 and of silver 1,240,000 kg. Uranium production in 1991 was 7,813,000 kilograms.

TRADE

Merchandise imports into Canada in 1991 were valued at C$134,323m and merchandise exports (including re-exports) at C$141,701m. The main exports in 1991 were passenger automobiles and chassis, motor vehicle parts (except engines), trucks, truck tractors and chassis, wood pulp and similar pulp, newsprint paper, softwood lumber, crude petroleum and other telecommunications and related equipment (excluding televisions, radio sets, phonographs).

Trade with the USA accounts for about 69.9 per cent of total trade in merchandise, although efforts are being made to develop alternative markets. Value of trade with Canada's largest trading partners in 1991 was as follows (C$ million):

	**Domestic Exports*	*Imports*
United States	*103,449*	*86,235*
Japan	*7,111*	*10,249*
United Kingdom	*2,920*	*4,182*
Germany	*2,125*	*3,734*
South Korea	*1,861*	*2,110*
China	*1,844*	*1,852*
The Netherlands	*1,655*	*599*
USSR	*1,465*	*233*
France	*1,350*	*2,670*
Belgium	*1,073*	*427*
Taiwan	*1,050*	*2,212*

**Excluding re-exports*

Trade with UK

	1990	*1991*
Imports from UK	*£1,901,939,000*	*£1,701,051,000*
Exports to UK	*2,259,099,000*	*1,922,549,000*

COMMUNICATIONS

Railways – The total track of railways in operation on 31 December 1990, was 86,880 km. In 1990 freight transportation was 248 billion tonne-kilometres, and the balance of property accounts at end 1990 was C$19,053m.

Shipping – The registered shipping on 1 January 1990 including inland vessels, was 43,169 vessels with gross tonnage 4,987,362. The volume of international shipping handled at Canadian ports in 1990 was 159,039,270 metric tonnes loaded and 73,296,005 metric tonnes unloaded.

Canals – The bulk of canal shipping in Canada is handled through the two sections of the St Lawrence Seaway, which provide access to the Great Lakes for ocean-going ships. In 1991, transits on the Montreal-Lake Ontario section numbered 2,859 for a total of 34,900,000 cargo tonnes; transits in the Welland Canal section numbered 3,570 for a total of 36,900,000 cargo tonnes. Principal commodities carried were iron ore, wheat, corn, barley, soybeans, fuel oil, manufactured iron and steel, coal and coke.

Civil Aviation – The number of passengers carried in 1990 (all major Canadian carriers) was 36,785,000; 1,679,361,000 tonne-km of freight was carried in 1989.

Motor Vehicles – Total motor vehicle registrations numbered 16,981,130 in 1990.

Post – Post office revenue in the fiscal year 1991–2 was C$3,800 m; total expenditure C$3,900 m.

Source: for financial and economic statistics, Statistics Canada.

YUKON TERRITORY

The area of the Territory is 186,660 sq. miles (483,450 sq. km), with a population (1991 census) of 27,797. Minerals and tourism are the chief industries, followed closely by transportation, communications and other utilities industry.

Seat of Government – Whitehorse, population (1991 census) 17,925.

The Yukon Act 1970, as amended, provides for the administration of the Territory by a Commissioner acting under instructions from time to time given by the Governor-in-Council or the Minister of Indian Affairs and Northern Development. Legislative powers, analogous to those of a provincial government, are exercised by a Legislative Assembly of 16 members elected from electoral districts in the Territory. The Executive Council of the Assembly consists of the government leader as chairman and four elected members.

Commissioner, J. K. McKinnon.
Premier, Hon. Tony Penikett.

NORTHWEST TERRITORIES

The area of the Northwest Territories is 1,322,900 sq. miles (3,426,389 sq. km), with a population (1991 census) of 57,649. The chief industry is mining, with a total value of $987,900,000 in 1990. Lead, zinc, gold, silver, oil exploration and natural gas contributed about 22 per cent of the 1991 GDP of the Northwest Territories.

The Northwest Territories are subdivided into the regions of Baffin, Forty Smith, Inuvik, Keewatia, Kitikmeot.

Seat of Government – Yellowknife, population (1991 census) 15,179.

The Northwest Territories Act 1979, as amended, provides for a Legislative Assembly of 24 elected members, of which the Executive Council under the chairmanship of the government leader is the senior decision-making body of the government in the Territory.

Commissioner, D. L. Norris.
Government Leader, Hon. Dennis Patterson.

CANADIAN PROVINCES

ALBERTA

Area and Population – The Province of Alberta has an area of 661,185 sq. km (255,285 sq. miles), including about 6,485 sq. miles of water (16,796 sq. km), with a population (1 April 1992) of 2,558,200.

Capital – Edmonton, city population (1991) 616,741, metropolitan area, 839,924. Other centres are Calgary (710,677), Lethbridge (60,974), Red Deer (58,134), Medicine Hat (43,625), St Albert (42,146).

Government

The Government is vested in a Lieutenant-Governor and Legislative Assembly composed of 83 members, elected for

five years, representing 83 electoral districts in the Province. At a provincial election held on 20 March 1989, the Progressive Conservative Party took 59 seats, the New Democratic Party 16 seats and the Liberal Party 8 seats.
Lt.-Governor, The Hon. Gordon Towers.
Premier, President of Executive Council, Hon. Don Getty

AGENT-GENERAL IN LONDON, Mary LeMessurier, Alberta House, 1 Mount Street, London W1Y 5AA.

JUDICATURE

Court of Appeal of Alberta, Chief Justice, Hon. J. H. Laycraft.
Court of Queen's Bench of Alberta, Chief Justice, Hon. W. K. Moore.
Associate Chief Justice, Hon. T. H. Miller

ECONOMY

The total GDP at factor cost in 1990 amounted to C$69,221 million. Preliminary estimates for mineral production in 1991 came to C$16,148 million. Of this total, crude oil amounted to C$8,784 million, and natural gas and its by-products to C$6,351 million.

The total value of manufacturing shipments (1991) was C$19,279 million. Number of industrial establishments 2,966 (1988), total employees 63,532 (1988). The leading industrial products are refined petroleum and coal products, meat and meat products, chemicals and chemical products, fabricated metal products, non-metallic mineral products and primary metals.

FINANCE

Budgetary Estimates

	1990–1	1991–2
Revenue	C$11,766m	C$12,618m
Expenditure	12,995	12,484
Deficit	1,229	—
Surplus	—	134

NOTE: The Budgetary revenue figure does not include funds allocated to the Alberta Heritage Savings Trust Fund.

BRITISH COLUMBIA

AREA AND POPULATION – British Columbia has a total area estimated at 952,263 sq. km (367,669 sq. miles), with a population of 3,282,061 (June 1991).

PROVINCIAL CAPITAL – ΨVictoria, metropolitan population (1991) 287,897. Other principal cities are ΨVancouver (metropolitan population (1991) 1,602,502), Prince George, Kamloops, Kelowna and Nanaimo.

GOVERNMENT

The Government consists of a Lieutenant-Governor and an Executive Council together with a Legislative Assembly of 75 members.

The New Democratic Party formed a government after a General Election on 17 October 1991. The present standing in the Assembly is New Democratic Party 51, Liberal Party 17, Social Credit Party 7.
Lt.-Governor, His Honour Dr David See-Chai Lam
Premier, Hon. Mike Harcourt

AGENT-GENERAL IN LONDON, G. Gardom, QC, British Columbia House, 1 Regent Street, London SW1 4NR.

JUDICATURE

Court of Appeal, Chief Justice of British Columbia, Hon. A. McEachern
Supreme Court, Chief Justice, Hon. W. A. Esson
Associate Chief Justice, Hon. D. H. Campbell

FINANCE

	1991–2	1992–3
Estimated Revenue	C$16,150.0m	C$16,191m
Estimated Expenditure	16,565.0m	17,980m
Net Guaranteed Debt	5,663.3m	7,528m

ECONOMY

Manufacturing activity is based largely on the processing of the output of the logging, mineral, fishing and agriculture industries. The principal manufacturing centres are Vancouver, New Westminster, Victoria, North Vancouver, Kelowna and Prince George. Forestry and forest-based industries form the most important economic activity, accounting for approximately 40 per cent of total production. British Columbia is the leading province of Canada in the quantity and value of its timber and sawmill products. Mining, the second most important non-service economic activity, is based on copper, zinc, lead, iron concentrates, molybdenum, coal, natural gas, crude petroleum, asbestos, gold and silver. Molybdenum production is approximately 99 per cent of the Canadian total.

The production levels for important industries for 1991 were as follows:

Lumber	31,406,000 cu. metres
Paper	2,684,000 tonnes
Pulp	6,702,000 tonnes
Coal	25,379,000 tonnes
Natural gas	14,353,000,000 cu. metres

Mineral production for 1991 is estimated to be valued at C$3,623.6 million.

The most important agricultural products are livestock, eggs and poultry, fruits and dairy products. Salmon accounts for approximately 60 per cent of the value of fisheries. Other species include halibut, herring, sole, cod, flounder, perch, tuna and shellfish. In 1991 farm cash receipts were valued at C$1,229.4 million.

The economy is dependent upon markets outside the province for the disposal of most of the products of industry. An estimated 55–60 per cent of production is exported to foreign markets. Manufacturing shipments in 1991 were valued at C$22,821 million.

TRANSPORT

The Province has deep water harbours which are well serviced by railways and modern highways. Vancouver has one of the finest natural harbours in the world, servicing a variety of vessels, including large bulk cargo carriers. Vancouver is also the base for regular scheduled air routes to other parts of Canada, the United States, Europe, Mexico, South America, Hawaii, Fiji, Australia, Japan, Hong Kong and the Middle East.

MANITOBA

AREA AND POPULATION – Manitoba, originally the Red River settlement, is the central province of Canada. The province has a considerable area of prairie land but is also a land of wide diversity combining 645 kilometres (401 miles) of coastline on Hudson Bay, large lakes and rivers covering an area of 101,592 sq. km (39,225 sq. miles) and pre-Cambrian rock which covers about three-fifths of the province. The total area is 649,947 sq. km (250,946 sq. miles), with a population (1991 census) of 1,091,942.

PROVINCIAL CAPITAL – Winnipeg, population 647,100 (1990 estimate). Other cities are Brandon (39,366), Thompson (14,379), Portage la Prairie (13,522) and Flin Flon (7,708).

Government

The Lieutenant-Governor is The Queen's personal representative in Manitoba. There is a Legislative Assembly of 57 members, of which the Executive Council of Ministers are all members.

The Progressive Conservatives formed a majority government after a General Election held on 11 September 1990. The standing in the House at 30 June 1991 was: Progressive Conservatives 30, New Democratic Party 20, Liberal 7.

Lt.-Governor, His Honour George Johnson
Premier, Hon. Gary A. Filmon

Judicature

Court of Appeal, Chief Justice, Hon. Richard J. Scott
Queen's Bench Division, Chief Justice, Hon. B. Hewak
Associate Chief Justices, Hon. J. J. Oliphant (*QBD*), Hon. A. C. Hamilton (*Family Division*)

Economy

Finance – The projected revenue for the province in the fiscal year 1991–2 was C$4,917 million while expenditures were forecast at C$5,241 million.

Agriculture – The total land area in Manitoba is 135,342,565 acres, of which 19,126,517 acres are in occupied farms. The gross value of agriculture production in 1990 was estimated at C$2,400 million.

Manufactures – Manufacturing enterprises employed about 55,000 persons on average in 1990. The chief manufacturing centres are Winnipeg, Brandon, Selkirk and Portage la Prairie. The largest manufacturing industry is the food and beverage industry, followed by the machinery and metal fabricating industries.

NEW BRUNSWICK

Area and Population – New Brunswick is situated between 45°–48° N. lat. and 63° 47′–69° W. long. and comprises an area of 73,439 sq. km (28,355 sq. miles), with a population (June 1991) of 723,900. It was first colonized by British subjects in 1761, and in 1783 by inhabitants of New England, who had been dispossessed of their property in consequence of their loyalty to the British Crown. New Brunswick entered Confederation in 1867.

Provincial Capital – Fredericton, population (1991), 71,869. Other cities are ΨSaint John (124,981); Moncton (106,503); Bathurst (36,167); Edmundston (22,478); Campbellton (17,183).

Government

Government is administered by a Lieutenant-Governor, an Executive Council, and a Legislative Assembly of 58 members elected by the people. The present Legislative Assembly of the Province was elected on 23 September 1991 and has 58 members; 46 from the Liberal Party, 8 from the Confederation of Regions (COR), 3 from the Progressive Conservative Party and one from the New Democratic Party.

Lt-Governor, His Honour Gilbert Finn
Premier, Hon. Frank McKenna

Judicature

Court of Appeal, Chief Justice, Hon. S. G. Stratton
Queen's Bench Division, Chief Justice, Hon. G. A. Richard

Economy

Finance – The estimated revenue for the year ending 31 March 1991 was C$3,701,900,000 and ordinary expenditure, $3,733,300,000.

Manufactures – New Brunswick's largest manufacturing group, in terms of shipments, is the paper and allied industries, followed by the food and wood industries. Together these industries accounted in 1991 for 52.9 per cent of the total value of manufacturing shipments of C$5,405 million. Saint John has a major ice-free port and is the principal manufacturing centre of the Province.

Agriculture – Total land area 27,633 sq. miles; farms numbered 3,252 and averaged 285 acres each in 1991. Dairy products and potatoes are the leading agricultural products. Both industries together accounted for 43.6 per cent of total farm cash receipts in 1991. Farm cash receipts in 1991 totalled C$254,066,000.

Fisheries – Fishing is an important industry, employing about 7,550 fishermen. The chief commercial fish are lobsters, herring, tuna, crab and cod. Landings reached 105,770 tonnes valued at C$88,072,000 in 1991.

Minerals – Extensive zinc, lead and copper deposits are now being mined in the north-eastern part of the province with New Brunswick being the third largest producer of zinc in Canada. A lead smelter, fertilizer plant and port facilities have been constructed at Belledune. Canada's only primary antimony producer is located at Lake George. There is exploration and development near Sussex and Salt Springs, where potash production continues to escalate. A potash terminal has been built at the port of St John. Coal is mined at Grand Lake and exploration for other deposits is being undertaken. Total mineral production was valued at C$88,072,000 in 1991.

Tourism – Tourism is of increasing value to the economy.

NEWFOUNDLAND AND LABRADOR

Area and Population – The Island of Newfoundland is situated between 46° 37′–51° 37′ N. latitude and 52° 44′–59° 30′ W. longitude, on the north-east side of the Gulf of St Lawrence, and is separated from the North American continent by the Straits of Belle Isle on the north-west and by Cabot Strait on the south-west. The island is about 510 km long and 508 km broad and is triangular in shape. It comprises an area of 111,390 sq. km (43,008 sq. miles), with a population (1991 Census) (inclusive of Labrador) of 568,474.

Labrador – Labrador forms the most easterly part of the North American continent, and extends from Point St Charles, at the north-east entrance to the Straits of Belle Isle, on the south, to Cape Chidley, at the eastern entrance to Hudson's Straits on the north. It has an area of 294,328 sq. km (113,641 sq. miles), with a population (1986 Census) of 28,741. Labrador is noted for its cod fisheries and also possesses valuable salmon, herring, trout and seal fisheries.

Provincial Capital – ΨSt John's (population 1991 Census, Greater St John's 171,859) is North America's oldest city, and thus of historical interest and is the seat of the provincial legislature, the site of most provincial and federal government offices and the principal port for the island of Newfoundland. Newfoundland's second city of Corner Brook (population 1991 Census, 22,410) is situated on the west coast.

Government

On 31 March 1949 Newfoundland became the tenth Province of the Dominion of Canada. The Government is administered by a Lieutenant-Governor, aided by an Executive Council and a Legislative Assembly of 52 members elected for a term of five years. A General Election was held on 20 April 1989. The standings in the current House of Assembly are: Liberals 34; Progressive Conservatives 17, New Democrats 1.

Lt.-Governor, His Honour Frederick W. Russell
Premier, Hon. Clyde Wells

Judicature

Court of Appeal, Chief Justice, Hon. Noel H. A. Goodridge
Trial Division, Chief Justice, Hon. T. A. Hickman

ECONOMY

FINANCE – The estimated gross capital and current account revenues for 1992–3 are C$3,297,191,000 and the gross current and capital account expenditures C$3,536,925,000.
PRODUCTION AND INDUSTRY – The main primary industries are fishing, forestry and mining. In 1987 shipments of fish products were valued at C$822 million. In 1991 newsprint shipments from the three pulp and paper mills were valued at C$499 million, mining plus structural materials shipments were estimated at C$793 million, of which C$783 million was from the two iron ore mines in Labrador. Total manufacturing shipments were valued at C$1,647 million in 1991. The hydro-electric plant on the Churchill river is the largest underground plant in the world, with a capacity of 5,225,000 Kw.
PETROLEUM AND NATURAL GAS – Over 139 wells have been drilled off Newfoundland since 1965. Discovery of oil was made in 1979 on the Grand Banks. Oil production is expected to begin in the 1990s, with a peak production of 110,000 barrels of oil a day. In 1991 offshore exploration expenditure was approximately C$12 million

TRANSPORT

The island portion of the province utilizes the Trans-Coastal Highway and other roadways to access most communities. There is a coastal boat service that operates on the southern portion of the island and on the coast of Labrador linking otherwise isolated communities. The Quebec-North shore and Labrador Railway is operated in Labrador, linking the interior with Sept-Iles, Quebec. The island is connected to mainland Canada by a ferry service that runs from Sydney, Nova Scotia, to Port Aux Basques and Argentia.

NOVA SCOTIA

AREA AND POPULATION – Nova Scotia is a peninsula between 43° 25′–47° N. lat. and 59° 40′–66° 25′ W. long., and is connected to New Brunswick by a low fertile isthmus about 28 km wide. It comprises an area of 55,490 sq. km (21,425 sq. miles), including 2,650 sq. km of lakes and rivers and 10,424 km of shoreline. No place is more than 56 km from the Atlantic Ocean. Population (June 1992 estimate) 899,942.
CAPE BRETON ISLAND – This has been part of Nova Scotia since 1819. It is the centre of the steel manufacturing and coal mining industries, and is also noted for its lakes and coastal scenery, making it a tourist attraction in Canada.

PROVINCIAL CAPITAL – ΨHalifax, including the neighbouring city of Dartmouth, has a population of 182,253. The harbour, ice-free all year round, is the main Atlantic winter port of Canada. Other cities and towns include ΨSydney (26,063), ΨGlace Bay (19,501).

GOVERNMENT

The Government consists of a Lieutenant-Governor and a 52-member elected Legislative Assembly, from which the Executive Council is selected. The state of the parties in June 1992 was Conservatives 27, Liberals 21, New Democratic Party 3, Independent 1.

The Lieutenant-Governor represents The Queen and is appointed by the Governor-in-Council.

Lt.-Governor, His Honour Lloyd R. Crouse, PC
Premier, Hon. Donald W. Cameron
Speaker of the House of Assembly, Hon. Ronald S. Russell

NOVA SCOTIA TRADE AND INVESTMENT OFFICE, Raymond Vaudry, 14 Pall Mall, London SW1Y 5LU.

JUDICATURE

Supreme Court, Appeal Division, Chief Justice, Hon. L. O. Clarke
Supreme Court, Trial Division, Chief Justice, Hon. Constance R. Glube

ECONOMY

FINANCE – The revenue for the fiscal year ending 31 March 1992 was C$3,895,486 and expenditure was C$4,057,607.
MANUFACTURING – Manufacturing constitutes the most important goods producing sector of the economy. Manufacturing plants provide employment for 10.7 per cent of the labour force.
UTILITIES – Electric power in Nova Scotia is supplied by the Nova Scotia Power Corporation. The Corporation's generating stations, which are predominantly coal fired, have a nameplate capacity of 2,129,300 kilowatts.
PETROLEUM ACTIVITY – There was one well drilled onshore in 1989–90. Canada's first offshore oil well went into production on 6 June 1992.
MINING – The total value of mineral production in 1991 (preliminary) was estimated at C$488 million. Dollar value of coal production was C$244 million, and salt production C$58 million.
FISHING – A total of 463,181 tonnes of fish and shellfish was harvested in 1990 for a landed value of C$427 million.
FORESTRY – Forest lands total 10,000,000 acres or 73 per cent of the land area. About 73 per cent of forest land is privately owned. Forest based industries employed an average of 9,000 in 1989, and contributed C$800 million to the Nova Scotia economy.
TOURISM – Between 15 May and 31 October 1990, about 1.15 million visitors spent about C$300 million in the Province.

ONTARIO

AREA AND POPULATION – The Province of Ontario contains a total area of 1,068,572 sq. km (412,578 sq. miles), with a population (1991 estimate) of 9,919,400.

PROVINCIAL CAPITAL – ΨToronto (metropolitan, estimate 1991, 2,275,771) has a wide range of manufacturing and service industries and is a centre of education, business and finance. Other major urban areas are: Ottawa, the national capital (313,987); ΨHamilton (318,499), with iron and steel industry, metal fabrication, machinery, electrical and chemical industries; London (303,165), a business and manufacturing centre; ΨWindsor (191,435); Kitchener (168,282) and Sudbury (92,884).

GOVERNMENT

The Government is vested in a Lieutenant-Governor and a Legislative Assembly of 130 members elected for five years.

After the last election on 6 September 1990, there were 74 New Democrats, 36 Liberals, and 20 Progressive Conservatives.

Lt.-Governor, Hon. Henry N. R. Jackman.
Premier, Hon. Bob Rae

JUDICATURE

Chief Justice of the Court of Appeal for Ontario, Hon. C. L. Dubin
Chief Justice of the Ontario Court-General Division, Hon. F. W. Callaghan
Chief Justice of the Ontario Court-Provincial Division, Hon. Sidney B. Linden

ECONOMY

AGRICULTURE – Ontario has the highest total of agricultural production in Canada with a gross value of C$5,404 million and a total net farm income of C$737 million.
FORESTRY – Productive forested lands cover 39.9 million

hectares. Paper and allied industries are by far the most important sector of Ontario's forest industry.
MINERALS – Ontario's natural resources include 30 basic minerals, such as copper, iron ore, zinc, sulphur, gold, nickel and platinum. Total value of the mineral production in 1991 was estimated at C$5,000 million.
ENERGY – Total electrical energy generated in Ontario in 1991 was 136,966 million kWh.
MANUFACTURE – Ontario is the chief manufacturing province in Canada, producing 50 per cent of all manufactured goods. During 1991 Ontario's exports totalled C$70,744 million.

PRINCE EDWARD ISLAND

AREA AND POPULATION – Prince Edward Island lies in the southern part of the Gulf of St Lawrence, between 46°–47° N. lat. and 62°–64° 30′ W. long. It is about 225 km in length, and from 6 to 64 km in breadth; its area is 5,659 sq. km (2,185 sq. miles), and its population (1991 Census) 129,765.

PROVINCIAL CAPITAL – ΨCharlottetown (30,000), on the shore of Hillsborough Bay, which forms a good harbour.

GOVERNMENT

The Government is vested in a Lieutenant-Governor, an Executive Council, and Legislative Assembly of 32 members elected for a term of up to five years, 16 as Councillors and 16 as Assemblymen. After the election of 29 May 1989 there were 30 Liberals and 2 Progressive Conservatives.
Lt.-Governor, Her Honour Marion L. Reid
Premier, Hon. Joseph A. Ghiz, QC
Speaker of the Legislative Assembly, Hon. Edward W. Clark

JUDICATURE

Appeal Division, Chief Justice, Hon. Norman H. Carruthers.
Trial Division, Chief Justice, Hon. K. R. MacDonald.

ECONOMY

FINANCE – The ordinary revenue of the Province in 1989–90 was C$656.6 million and the expenditure C$654.3 million.
AGRICULTURE – Approximately 48 per cent of the total area of the Province is farmland. The value of farm cash receipts in 1989 was C$253.8 million, of which 46.9 per cent was from the sale of potatoes. Dairy, beef and hogs are also important agriculture products.
FISHERIES – Fish landings were valued at C$72.4 million in 1989 of which 63.7 per cent was of lobster.
MANUFACTURING – The total value of manufacturing shipments was C$366.1 million in 1989, of which 69.4 per cent was in the food products industries and 21.4 per cent in the fish products industries.
TOURISM – A major summer economic activity is tourism. Non-resident tourists spent C$98.3 million in the Province in 1989.
EDUCATION – A university and a college of applied arts and technology were established in 1969, estimated full- and part-time enrolment for 1989–90 being 3,181 (University of Prince Edward Island), and 912 for the college of applied arts and technology (Holland College).

QUEBEC

AREA AND POPULATION – The Province of Quebec contains an area estimated at 1,540,667 sq. km (594,855 sq. miles) with a population (1991 Census) of 6,895,963.

PROVINCIAL CAPITAL – ΨQuebec. Population (Census 1991) 167,517; historic city visited annually by thousands of tourists, and one of the great seaport towns of Canada. Ψ Montreal (1,017,666) is the commercial centre. Other important cities are Laval (314,398); Sherbrooke (76,429), Montreal-Nord (86,516) and La Salle (73,804).

GOVERNMENT

The Government of the Province is vested in a Lieutenant-Governor, a Council of ministers and a National Assembly of 125 members elected for five years. At June 1991, there were 90 Liberals, 31 Parti Quebecois, 3 Equality members and one Independent.
Lt.-Governor, His Honour Martial Asselin
Prime Minister, Hon. Robert Bourassa

AGENT-GENERAL IN LONDON, vacant, 59 Pall Mall, London SW1Y 5JH.

JUDICATURE

Court of Appeal, Chief Justice of Quebec, Hon. Claude Bisson
Superior Court, Chief Justice of Quebec (Montreal), Hon. Pierre Coté

ECONOMY

FINANCE – The revenue for the year 1989–90 was C$31,073,900,000; expenditure amounted to C$32,733,300,000.
PRODUCTION AND INDUSTRY – The principal manufacturing centres are Montreal, Montreal East, Quebec, Trois-Rivières, Sherbrooke, Shawinigan Drummondville and Lachine. Forest lands cover 912,123 sq. km, of which 734,316 sq. km are productive.

Total estimated value of shipments in the manufacturing industries in 1991 was C$67,162 million. Value of 1991 shipments in the chief industries was accounted for by food, C$9,410 million; paper and allied industries, C$6,914m; primary metal industries, C$5,771m, and transport equipment, C$4,938m.
AGRICULTURE AND FISHERIES – In 1990 total farm receipts were:

Crops	C$685,712,000
Livestock and livestock products	2,584,202,000
Other farm receipts	455,551,000

In 1990 72,885 tonnes of fish, to the value of C$71,554,000 were landed.
MINERAL PRODUCTION – Minerals to the value of C$2,920,159,000 were mined in 1990. This included copper, C$301,462,000; asbestos, C$177,135,000; and gold, C$567,778,000.

SASKATCHEWAN

AREA AND POPULATION – The Province of Saskatchewan lies between Manitoba to the east and Alberta to the west and has an area of 652,324 sq. km (251,864 sq. miles) (of which the land area is 570,269 sq. km, or 220,182 sq. miles), with a population (estimated 1991) of 1,013,500. Saskatchewan extends along the Canada–USA boundary for 632 km (393 miles) and northwards for 1,224 km (761 miles). Its northern width is 440 km (276 miles).

PROVINCIAL CAPITAL – Regina. Population (1991 estimate), 179,178. Other cities: Saskatoon (186,058), Moose Jaw (33,593); Prince Albert (34,181) and Yorkton (15,315).

GOVERNMENT

The Government is vested in the Lieutenant-Governor, with a Legislative Assembly of 66 members. There is an Executive Council of 12 members. The Legislative Assembly is elected for five years and the state of the parties in June 1992 was: New Democratic Party 55; Progressive Conservative 10; Liberal 1.
Lt.-Governor, Her Honour Sylvia O. Fedoruk
Premier, Hon. Roy Romanow, QC

JUDICATURE

Court of Appeal, Chief Justice, Hon. E. D. Bayda
Queen's Bench, Chief Justice, Hon. D. K. MacPherson
Provincial Court, Chief Judge, Hon. B. P. Carey

FINANCE

Consolidated Fund and Heritage combined revenue for year ending March 1993 is C$4,491,500,000 and expenditure C$5,008,800,000.

CAPE VERDE

República de Cabo Verde

Cape Verde, off the west coast of Africa, consists of two groups of islands, Windward (Santo Antão, São Vicente, Santa Luzia, São Nicolau, Boa Vista and Sal) and Leeward (Maio, São Tiago, Fogo and Brava) with a total area of 1,557 sq. miles (4,033 sq. km). The population (UN estimate 1909) was 370,000 the majority of whom are Roman Catholic.

CAPITAL – ΨPraia, population (1980) 57,748.
CURRENCY – Escudo Caboverdiano of 100 centavos.
FLAG – Horizontal band of yellow over green, with a vertical red band in the hoist charged with a black star over a garland of maize sheaves, two corn cobs and a clam shell.
NATIONAL DAY – 5 July (Independence Day).

GOVERNMENT

The islands, colonized *c.*1460, achieved independence from Portugal on 5 July 1975 under the nationalist party of Guinea Bissau and Cape Verde. A federation of the islands with Guinea Bissau was planned (till 1879 Guinea-Bissau and the islands were a single administrative unit) but this was dropped following the 1980 coup in Guinea Bissau.

The Republic was a one-party (the PAICV) state until the constitution was amended in September 1990. Multi-party elections, held on 14 January 1991, were won by the opposition Movement for Democracy (MPD) which won 56 seats in the 79-seat National Assembly. The Independent António Mascarenhas Monteiro was elected as President on 17 February 1991.

HEAD OF STATE

President, António Mascarenhas Monteiro *assumed office*, 22 March 1991.

COUNCIL OF MINISTERS as at January 1992

Prime Minister and Minister of Defence, Carlos Veiga.
Foreign Affairs, Jorge Fonseca.
Justice and Labour, Eurico Monteiro.
Finance and Planning, José Veiga.
Fisheries, Agriculture and Rural Animation, Gualberto Rosário.
Infrastructure and Transport, Teofilo Silva.
Health, Rui Soares.
Education, Manuel Fautino.
Culture and Communication, Leão Lopes.
Tourism, Industry and Trade, Manuel Chantre.

EMBASSY OF THE REPUBLIC OF CAPE VERDE
44 Konninginnegracht, 2514 AD, The Hague,
The Netherlands
Tel: The Hague 469623

Ambassador Extraordinary and Plenipotentiary, His Excellency Terêncio Gregorio Alves (1992).
BRITISH AMBASSADOR (resident in Dakar, Senegal).

ECONOMY

The islands have had little rain since 1969, and agriculture is mostly confined to irrigated inland valleys, the chief products being bananas and coffee (for export), maize, sugarcane and nuts. Fish and shellfish are important exports. Salt is obtained on Sal, Boa Vista and Maio; volcanic rock is also mined for export. The main ports are Praia and Mindelo, and there is an international airport on Sal.

TRADE WITH UK

	1990	1991
Imports from UK	£1,537,000	£1,908,000
Exports to UK	336,000	193,000

CENTRAL AFRICAN REPUBLIC

(République Centrafricaine)

The Republic lies just north of the Equator between the Cameroon Republic, the Republic of Chad, the southern part of Sudan, and Zaire. The Republic has an area of 240,535 sq. miles (622,984 sq. km), and a population (UN estimate 1990) of 3,039,000.

CAPITAL – Bangui, near the border with Zaire, population (1984 estimate) 473,817.
CURRENCY – Franc CFA of 100 centimes.
FLAG – Four horizontal stripes, blue, white, green, yellow, crossed by central vertical red stripe with a yellow five-pointed star in top left-hand corner.
NATIONAL DAY – 1 December.

GOVERNMENT

On 1 December 1958 the French colony of Ubanghi Shari elected to remain within the French Community and adopted the title of the Central African Republic. It became fully independent on 17 August 1960. The first President of the Central African Republic, David Dacko, held office from 1960 until 1 January 1966, when he was replaced by the then Col. Bokassa after a coup d'état. On 4 Dec. 1976, President Bokassa proclaimed himself Emperor and a new constitution was introduced, the country being known as the Central African Empire. On 20 Sept. 1979 Emperor Bokassa was deposed by David Dacko in a bloodless coup and the country reverted to a republic. President Dacko surrendered power on 1 September 1981 to army commander Gen. André Kolingba in a bloodless coup. In September 1985 President Kolingba dissolved the Military Committee for National Recovery (CMRN) and appointed a civilian-dominated cabinet. Moves towards democratization have been made and in November 1986 a referendum was held whereby voters approved a new Constitution and the establishment of a one-party state.

Strikes and unrest occurred throughout 1991 and 1992 as opposition groupings and unions have pressurized the government for a national conference to discuss the ending of one-party rule and the implementation of multi-party politics.

HEAD OF STATE

President and General of the Armed Forces, Gen. André Kolingba, *assumed office* 1 Sept. 1981, *re-elected* 21 Nov. 1986.

COUNCIL OF MINISTERS as at June 1992

Prime Minister, Edouard Frank.
Economy, Finance, Planning and International Co-operation, Thierry Bingaba.

Social Security and Territorial Administration, Ismaila Nimaga.
Justice, Jean Kpwoka.
Foreign Affairs, Christian Lingama Toleque.
Primary, Secondary and Technical Education, Youth and Sports, Etienne Goyemide.
Higher Education, Jean-Marie Bassia.
Transport and Civil Aviation, Posts and Telecommunications, Pierre Gonifei Gaibounanou.
Civil Service, Labour, Social Security and Professional Training, Christian-Bernard Yamale.
Public Health and Social Affairs, Genevieve Lombilo.
Rural Development, Casimir Amakpio.
Public Works and Territorial Development, Dieudonné Nana.
Energy, Mines, Geology and Water Resources, Edouard Akapekabou.
Water, Forests, Fish, Wildlife and Tourism, Raymond Mbitikon.
Finance, Commerce, Industry, Small and Medium Enterprises, Auguste Tene-Koyzoa.
Minister in charge of the General Secretariat and Relations with Parliament, Timothée Marboua.
Communications, Arts and Culture, Tony Da Silva.

EMBASSY OF THE CENTRAL AFRICAN REPUBLIC
30 rue des Perchamps, 75016, Paris
Tel: Paris 42244256

Ambassador Extraordinary and Plenipotentiary, new appointment awaited.
BRITISH AMBASSADOR (resident in Yaoundé, Cameroon).

ECONOMY

In an effort to revive an ailing economy, the Government launched a structured adjustment programme in 1986, streamlining the civil service, increasing tax revenues, and reducing price controls. Cotton, diamonds, coffee and timber are the major exports.

TRADE WITH UK

	1990	1991
Imports from UK	£1,669,000	£502,000
Exports to UK	58,000	37,000

CHAD REPUBLIC

Republique du Tchad

Situated in north-central Africa, the Chad Republic extends from 23° N. latitude to 7° N. latitude and is flanked by the Republics of Niger and Cameroon on the west, by Libya on the north, by the Sudan on the east and by the Central African Republic on the south. It has an area of 495,755 sq. miles (1,284,000 sq. km) and a population (UN estimate 1990) of 5,678,000.

CAPITAL – Ndjaména (formerly known as Fort Lamy) south of Lake Chad (402,000).
CURRENCY – Franc CFA of 100 centimes.
FLAG – Vertical stripes, blue, yellow and red.
NATIONAL DAY – 13 April.

GOVERNMENT

Chad became a member state of the French Community on 28 November 1958, and was proclaimed fully independent on 11 August 1960. On 14 April 1962, a new Constitution was adopted involving a presidential-type regime. This was suspended on 13 April 1975 when President Tombalbaye was killed in a military coup. The country was run by a Supreme Military Council, under General Felix Malloum until his overthrow in February 1979. A Transitional Government of National Unity, headed by Goukouni Oueddei, was replaced in June 1982 by the government of Hissène Habré. A ceasefire between Chad and Libya was agreed in September 1987 and on 3 October 1988 they reopened diplomatic relations. The ceasefire was reaffirmed and they said that they would settle the Aouzou dispute peacefully, respecting UN and OAU charters. On 1 September 1990 Chad and Libya presented their territorial claims for the Aouzou Strip to the International Court of Justice.

In December 1990 Idriss Déby launched a successful coup in Chad and the Habré government fell. Déby announced that he would adopt a multi-party system in Chad and that a national conference would be held in 1992 to draw up a constitution and to organize presidential and general elections. Throughout 1992 the national conference has been repeatedly postponed, although an increasing number of political parties have been recognized as legal.

HEAD OF STATE
President, Idriss Déby.

COUNCIL OF MINISTERS as at June 1992

Prime Minister, Joseph Yodoyman.
National Defence Minister, Nadjita Beassoumal.
Foreign Affairs, Mahamat Ali Adoum.
Interior, Djimastra Koibla.
Justice, Youssouf Togoimi.
Planning and Co-operation, Ibni Oumar Mahamat Saleh.
Finance, Mohiadine Salah.
Commerce and Industrial Development, Beade Toira Jeremie.
Public Works and Transport, Abas Koty Yacoub.
Post and Telecommunications, Saleh Makki.
Mines, Energy and Water Resources, Mahamat Habib Doutoum.
Agriculture, Bambe Dansala.
Stockbreeding, Safi Abdelkadar.
National Education, Youth and Sports, Dr Fidele Moungar.
Higher Education and Scientific Research, Ousman Djidda.
Public Health and Social Affairs, Ali Mahamat Zene.
Tourism and Environment, Pierre Tokinon.
Civil Service and Labour, Ndali Nabia.
Information and Culture, Djidi Bichara.

EMBASSY OF THE REPUBLIC OF CHAD
Boulevard Lambermont 52, 1030 Brussels, Belgium
Tel: Brussels 2151975

Ambassador Extraordinary and Plenipotentiary, new appointment awaited.
BRITISH AMBASSADOR (resident in Yaoundé, Cameroon).
Honorary Consul, E. Abtour, BP877, Avenue Moukhtar Ould Dada, Ndjaména.

ECONOMY

About 90 per cent of the workforce is occupied in agriculture, fishing and forestry. There is an oilfield in Kanem and salt is mined around Lake Chad, but the most important activities are cotton growing (mostly in the south) and animal husbandry (in central areas). Raw cotton and meat are the main exports.

TRADE WITH UK

	1990	1991
Imports from UK	£1,567,000	£1,789,000
Exports to UK	369,000	1,477,000

CHILE

República de Chile

A state of South America lying between the Andes and the shores of the South Pacific, Chile extends coastwise from just north of Arica to Cape Horn south, between lat. 17° 15′ and 55° 59′ S. and long. 66° 30′ and 75° 48′ W. The extreme length of the country is about 2,800 miles, with an average breadth, north of 41°, of 100 miles. The great chain of the Andes runs along its eastern limit, with a general elevation of 5,000 to 15,000 feet above sea level; but numerous summits attain a greater height. The chain lowers considerably towards its southern extremity.

The Andes form a boundary with Argentina, and at the head of the pass where the international road from Chile to Argentina crosses the frontier, has been erected a statue of Christ the Redeemer, 26 feet high, made of bronze from old cannon, to commemorate the peaceful settlement of a boundary dispute in 1902. The disputed boundary with Argentina in the Beagle Channel was settled by a treaty ratified in 1985.

There are no rivers of great size, and none of them is of much service as a navigable highway. In the north the country is arid. The total area of the Republic is 292,258 sq. miles (756,945 sq. km), with a population (UN estimate 1990) of 13,173,000.

Among the island possessions of Chile are the Juan Fernandez group (three islands) about 360 miles distant from Valparaiso. One of these islands is the reputed scene of Alexander Selkirk's (Robinson Crusoe) shipwreck. Easter Island (27° 8′ S. and 109° 28′ W.), about 2,000 miles distant in the South Pacific Ocean, contains stone platforms and hundreds of stone figures, the origin of which has not yet been determined. The area of the island is about 45 sq. miles (116.5 sq. km).

POPULATION – The Chilean population has four main sources: indigenous Araucanian Indians, Fuegians, and Changos; Spanish settlers and their descendants; mixed Spanish Indians; and European immigrants. Only the few remaining indigenous Indians and some originally Bolivian Indians in the north are racially separate. Following extensive intermarriage there is no effective distinction among the remainder.

CAPITAL – Santiago, population 4,132,293 (Greater Santiago). Other large towns are: ΨValparaiso (500,000), Concepción (170,000), Temuco (110,000), ΨAntofagasta (110,000), Chillán (79,461), ΨTalcahuano (75,643), Talca (75,354); ΨValdivia (70,000), ΨIquique (50,000), ΨPunta Arenas (50,000). Punta Arenas on the Straits of Magellan, is the southernmost city in the world.

CURRENCY – Chilean peso of 100 centavos.

FLAG – Two horizontal bands, white, red; in top sixth a white star on blue square, next staff.

NATIONAL ANTHEM – Canción Nacional de Chile.

NATIONAL DAY – 18 September (National Anniversary).

GOVERNMENT

Chile was discovered by Spanish adventurers in the 16th century and remained under Spanish rule until 1810, when a revolutionary war, culminating in the Battle of Maipu (5 April 1818), achieved the independence of the nation.

At a general election held in September 1970, the Marxist candidate Dr Allende was elected President by a narrow margin. After severe industrial unrest and widespread violent incidents, Allende was overthrown on 11 September 1973 in a coup carried out by leaders of the armed forces and national police.

After a national plebiscite, the Constitution of 1925 was replaced early in 1981 and General Pinochet was sworn in as President, to serve until 1989. Pinochet was defeated in a plebiscite of 5 October 1988 regarding his term of office being extended for a further eight years. He resisted calls for his resignation. Another plebiscite on 30 July 1989 was held on changes to the 1980 Constitution. Presidential and Congressional elections were held in December 1989. Patricio Aylwin was elected President of the Republic for four years, thus beginning a gradual transition to full democracy.

Executive power is held by the President, legislative power is exercised by a Parliament which comprises an Upper Chamber of 47 Senators and a Lower Chamber of 120 Deputies.

Chile is divided into 12 regions and the Metropolitan Area.

HEAD OF STATE

President of the Republic, Patricio Aylwin Azócar, *assumed office* 11 March 1990.

CABINET as at June 1992

Interior, Enrique Krauss.
Foreign Affairs, Enrique Silva Cimma.
Defence, Patricio Rojas.
Trade and Industry, Carlos Ominami.
Finance, Alejandro Foxley.
Education, Ricardo Lagos.
Justice, Francisco Cumplido.
Public Works, Carlos Hurtado.
Agriculture, Juan Agustin Figueroa.
National Properties, Luis Alvarado.
Labour, Rene Cortazar.
Public Health, Jorge Jimenez.
Mining, Juan Hamilton.
Housing, Alberto Etchegaray.
Transport, German Correa.
General Secretary of Government, Enrique Correa.
General Secretary of Presidency, Edgardo Boeninger.
Central Planning, Sergio Molina.
National Commission for Energy, Jaime Toha.
Corporation for Promotion of Production (CORFO), Rene Abeliuk.

EMBASSY OF CHILE
12 Devonshire Street, London WIN 2DS
Tel 071-580 6392/7

Ambassador Extraordinary and Plenipotentiary, His Excellency German Riesco (1990).

BRITISH EMBASSY
La Concepcion 177, Santiago 9
Tel: Santiago 2319771

Ambassador Extraordinary and Plenipotentiary, His Excellency Richard A. Nielson, CMG, LVO (1990).
Counsellor, Head of Chancery and Consul-General, R. Lavers.
Defence Attaché, Capt. J. Finnigan, RN.
Air Attaché, Gp. Capt. B. Hoskins.

BRITISH CONSULAR OFFICES – There are British Consular Offices at *Arica, Concepción, Santiago, Punta Arenas, Valparaiso*.

BRITISH COUNCIL REPRESENTATIVE – W. Campbell (*Cultural Attaché*), Eliodoro Yañez 832, Santiago, Casilla 15-T Tajamar.

The Council supplies books to the libraries of the Instituto Chileno-Britanico in *Santiago*, *Viña del Mar/Valparaiso* and *Concepción*.

BRITISH-CHILEAN CHAMBER OF COMMERCE, Av. Suecia 155-C, Casilla 536, Santiago.

ECONOMY

Cereals, legumes, sugar beet, vegetables, fruit, tobacco, hemp and vines are grown extensively (especially in the central zone) and livestock accounts for nearly 40 per cent of agricultural production. Sheep farming predominates in the extreme south. There are large timber tracts in the central and southern zones of Chile, some types of which are exported, along with wood derivatives such as cellulose and pulp. Industrial-scale fishing, which exceeded 6.5 million tonnes in 1989, makes Chile the fifth largest nation in terms of catch. The principal end product is fish meal.

The mineral wealth is considerable, the country being particularly rich in copper-ore, iron-ore and nitrates. Chile also produces iodine, manganese ore, coal, mercury, molybdenum, zinc, lead and a small quantity of gold. Uranium is also said to have been discovered in small quantities. The rainless north is the scene of the only commercial production of nitrate of soda (Chile saltpetre) from natural resources in the world. The country has also large deposits of high grade sulphur, but mostly around high extinct volcanoes in the Andes Cordillera, difficult of access. Oil was struck in Magallanes (Tierra del Fuego) in 1945, and oil and natural gas are produced in the Magallanes area from on- and off-shore wells. This domestic production, now declining, covers less than 30 per cent of total oil requirement, and imported crude oil is refined at Concon and San Vicente in the central part of the country. There is a steel plant at Huachipato, near Concepción.

Provisional production figures for 1990 were:

Coal (tonnes)	2,515,189
Copper (tonnes)	1,603,205
Crude oil (cu. metres)	1,137,900
Natural gas (cu. metres)	4,198,300,000
Steel ingots (tonnes)	760,100*

*1989

Industry is based on the processing of mineral, forestry, fish and agricultural products, and the manufacture of consumer goods.

FINANCE

	1987	1988
Total revenue	US$8,469.8 m	US$8,967.1 m
Total expenditure	8,421.6 m	9,452.4 m

Foreign debt at 31 December 1990 was US$18,602 million, including Central Bank obligations with the IMF of US$1,151 million.

COMMUNICATIONS

Chilean ships have a virtual monopoly in the coastwide trade, though, with the improvement of the roads, an increasing share of internal transportation is moving by road and rail. The Chilean mercantile marine numbers 73 vessels (of over 100 tons gross) with a total deadweight tonnage of 820,965 (1990).

There are 6,575 miles of railway track. A metre-gauge line (*the Longitudinal*) runs from La Calera, just north of Santiago, to Iquique. However, road transport has caused considerable reduction in rail traffic along this route. The wide gauge railway runs from Valparaiso through La Calera, 60 miles inland, and after passing through Santiago ends at Puerto Montt.

With the completion of a section of 435 miles from Corumba, Brazil, to Santa Cruz, Bolivia, the Trans-Continental Line will link the Chilean Pacific port of Arica with Rio de Janeiro on the Atlantic. Another line from Antofagasta to Salta (Argentina) was opened in 1948.

Chile is served by over 20 international airlines. Domestic traffic is carried by Linea Aerea Nacional (LAN) and LADECO, which also operate internationally, and smaller regional carriers.

Chile's road system is about 65,000 kilometres in length.

DEFENCE

Military service is compulsory for two years but not all those who are liable are required. Recruitment for the Navy is mostly voluntary, but there are some conscripts. The Navy consists of 1 cruiser, 9 destroyers, frigates and escorts, 6 patrol vessels and FPBs and 4 submarines. There is a support force of transports, tankers, 1 submarine depot ship and ancillary small craft. The strength of the Navy is 25,000 (3,000 conscripts) including men of the Marine Force. The Army's total strength is 54,000, which includes 3,000 officers and 27,000 conscripts. In addition, there is a police force of Carabineros of 27,000 officers and men. The Air Force total strength is 12,800 (800 conscripts) with a strength of 107 aircraft.

EDUCATION

Elementary education is free, and has been compulsory since 1920. There are eight universities (three in Santiago, two in Valparaiso, one each in Antofagasta, Concepción and Valdivia). The religion is Roman Catholic.

CULTURE

Spanish is the language of the country, with admixtures of local words of Indian origin. Recent efforts have reduced illiteracy and have thus afforded access to the literature of Spain, to supplement the vigorous national output. The Nobel Prize for Literature was awarded in 1945 to Señorita Gabriela Mistral, for Chilean verse and prose, and in 1971 to the poet Pablo Neruda. There are over 100 newspapers and a large number of periodicals.

TRADE

The principal exports are metallic and non-metallic minerals (copper represented 45.5 per cent of total export earnings in 1990), sawn timber, cellulose and other wood derivatives, some metal products, fish products, vegetables, fruit and wool. The principal imports are sugar and other food products, industrial raw materials, machinery, equipment and spares, oil fuels, lubricants and transportation equipment.

Trade	1989	1990
Total imports	US$6,734.2 m	US$7,272.1 m
Total exports	8,190.4 m	8,580.3 m

Trade with UK	1990	1991
Imports from UK	£128,056,000	£106,640,000
Exports to UK	222,469,000	177,876,000

CHINA

Zhonghua Renmin Gongheguo – The People's Republic of China

AREA AND POPULATION – The area of China is 3,705,408 sq. miles, (9,596,961 sq. km). A nationwide census (the fourth) was held in July 1990, which recorded a total population of 1,130,000,000. The estimated population for 1991 was 1,143,330,000.

Population of the Provinces (1990 estimates)

Anhui	56,750,000
Beijing	10,860,000
Fujian	30,370,000
Gansu	22,550,000
Guangdong	63,460,000
Guangxi Zhuang Autonomous Region	42,610,000
Guizhou	32,640,000
Hainan	6,630,000
Hebei	61,590,000
Heilongjiang	35,430,000
Henan	86,490,000
Hubei	54,390,000
Hunan	61,280,000
Jiangsu	67,670,000
Jiangxi	38,100,000
Jilin	24,830,000
Liaoning	39,670,000
Nei Monggol Autonomous Region	21,630,000
Ningxia Hui Autonomous Region	4,700,000
Qinghai	4,480,000
Shaanxi	33,160,000
Shangdong	84,930,000
Shanghai	13,370,000
Shangxi	28,990,000
Sichuan	108,040,000
Tianjin	8,840,000
Tibet Autonomous Region	2,220,000
Xinjiang Uygur Autonomous Region	15,290,000
Yunnan	37,310,000
Zhejiang	41,680,000
Armed Forces	3,000,000

China is anxious to control the growth of the population and has introduced stringent policies intended to result in a population of 1,250 million by the year 2000. About 6 per cent of the population belong to around 55 ethnic minorities. Among the largest are the Zhuang of Guangxi, the Uygurs of Xinjiang, the Tibetans and the Mongols.

Capital – Beijing (Peking), population (metropolitan area, 1990) 10,860,000 (excluding temporary residents). Population of major cities in 1989:

ΨShanghai*	12,670,000	Harbin	2,800,000
Tianjin	5,700,000	Chengdu	2,780,000
Shenyang	4,500,000	Xian	2,710,000
Wuhan	3,710,000	Nanjing	2,470,000
Guangzhou (Canton)	3,540,000	Taiyuan	1,900,000
		Kunming	1,500,000
Chongqing	2,960,000	Lanzhou	1,480,000

*metropolitan area

Currency – The currency is called Renminbi (RMB). The unit of currency is the yuan of 10 jiao or 100 fen.

Flag – Red, with large gold five-point star and four small gold stars in crescent, all in upper quarter next staff.

National Anthem – March of the Volunteers.

National Day – 1 October (Founding of People's Republic).

GOVERNMENT

On 10 October 1911, the party of reform forced the Imperial dynasty to a 'voluntary' abdication, and a Republic was proclaimed at Wuchang.

On 30 September 1949 the Chinese People's Political Consultative Conference (CPPCC) met in Beijing (Peking) and appointed the National People's Government Council under the chairmanship of Mao Zedong (Mao Tse-tung). On 1 October Mao proclaimed the inauguration of the Chinese People's Republic.

The regime was recognized by all the Communist bloc countries in quick succession, and soon after by the Asian countries of the Commonwealth, the United Kingdom and by a number of other countries. Others, led by the United States, continued to recognize the Chiang Kai-shek regime of Taiwan as the rightful Government of China. In 1971 the People's Republic won acceptance into the United Nations on the expulsion of Taiwan. Since then many more countries have accorded recognition.

Constitution

A new Constitution was adopted in December 1982, under which the National People's Congress is the highest organ of state power. It is elected for a term of five years and is supposed to hold one session a year. It is empowered to amend the Constitution, make laws, select the President and Vice-President and other leading officials of the state, approve the national economic plan, the state budget and the final state accounts, and to decide on questions of war and peace. The State Council is the highest organ of the state administration. It is composed of the Premier, the Vice-Premiers, the State Councillors, heads of Ministries and Commissions, the Auditor-General and the Secretary-General. Command over the armed forces is vested in the Central Military Commission, of which Jiang Zemin is the Chairman.

Deputies to Congresses at the primary level are 'directly elected' by the voters 'through a secret ballot after democratic consultation'. This is now extended to county level. These Congresses elect the deputies to the Congress at the next higher level. Deputies to the National People's Congress are elected by the People's Congresses of the provinces, autonomous regions and municipalities directly under the central government, and by the armed forces.

Local government is conducted through People's Governments at provincial, municipal and county levels. Autonomous regions, prefectures and counties exist for national minorities and are described as self-governing. The system prevailing is that found elsewhere, i.e. People's Congresses and People's Governments. Beijing, Shanghai and Tianjin continue to come directly under the central government.

Recent Events

Following the deaths of Mao Zedong and Zhou En-lai in 1976, the disgraced Deng Xiaoping was recalled. At the 11th Party Congress in 1977 Deng was elected Vice-Chairman and became the dominant force within the Party by eliminating leftist influence, rehabilitating fallen leaders and adjusting Maoist policies to permit economic liberalization. Deng's policies were reaffirmed at the 12th Congress in 1982. The Congress also elected a new Party leadership dominated by Deng and his supporters. The post of Chairman of the Party was abolished. The Party leader now holds the post of General Secretary. The 13th Party Congress in 1987 reaffirmed open-door policies. Most of the old revolutionary generation were removed, in elections, from the top posts.

Student-led pro-democracy demonstrations throughout April and May ended on 3–4 June 1989 when the People's Liberation Army took control of Beijing, killing thousands of protesters. Political control swung into the hands of the hardline elements of the leadership, who adopted policies of recentralization based on Marxist ideology, while simultaneously pledging commitment to reform under the influence of Deng Xiaoping. Deng retired from his last official post as Chairman of the Central Military Commission in November 1989 but is still the ultimate arbiter on policy decisions. At Deng's instigation during 1992 the emphasis has again

RUSSIA
Lake Baykal
KAZAKHSTAN
Lake Balkhash
UZBEKISTAN
KYRGYZSTAN
TADJIKISTAN
MONGOLIA
Darkhan
Ulan Bator
Choibalsan
Erdenet
Harbin
Shenyang
Beijing (Peking)
Tianjin
Taiyuan
Lanzhou
Xian
CHINA
Nanjing
Shanghai
Chengdu
Wuhan
Lhasa
Kunming
Guangzhou (Canton)
MACAO (PORT.)
HONG KONG (BR.)
N. KOREA
S. KOREA
JAPAN
YELLOW SEA
EAST CHINA SEA
Taipei
TAIWAN
SOUTH CHINA SEA
NEPAL
BHUTAN
BANGLADESH
INDIA
MYANMAR (BURMA)
VIETNAM
LAOS
Bay of Bengal
0 800 km
0 500 miles

switched back to market economic reform in government policy and the power of the hardline elements has begun to wane.

President of the People's Republic of China, Yang Shangkun, *elected* April 1988.
Vice President, Wang Zhen.
Chairman of the Standing Committee of the Seventh National People's Congress, Wan Li.
Chairman of the Central Military Commission, Jiang Zemin.

STATE COUNCIL as at June 1992

Premier, Li Peng.
Vice-Premiers, Yao Yilin; Tian Jiyun; Wu Xueqian; Zhu Rongji; Zou Jiahua.
State Councillors, Li Tieying; Qin Jiwei; Wang Bingqian; Song Jian; Wang Fang; Zou Jiahua; Li Guixian; Chen Xitong; Chen Junsheng; Qian Qichen.

MINISTERS

Aeronautics and Astronautics Industry, Lin Zongtang.
Agriculture, Liu Zhongyi.
Chemical Industry, Gu Xiulian.
Civil Affairs, Cui Naifu.
Commerce, Hu Ping.
Communications, Huang Zhendong.
Construction, Hon Jie.
Culture, He Jingzhi.
Energy Resources, Huang Yicheng.
Finance, Wang Bingqian.
Foreign Affairs, Qian Qichen.
Foreign Economic Relations and Trade, Zheng Tuobin.
Forestry, Gao Dezhan.
Geology and Mineral Resources, Zhu Xun.
Justice, Cai Cheng.
Labour, Ruan Chongwu.
Light Industry, Zeng Xianlin.
Machine Building and Electronics Industry, He Guangyuan.
Materials, Liu Suinian.
Metallurgical Industry, Qi Yuanjing.
National Defence, Qin Jiwei.
Personnel, Zhao Dongwan.
Posts and Telecommunications, Yang Taifang.
Public Health, Chen Minzhang.
Public Security, Tao Siju.
Radio, Film and Television, Ai Zhisheng.
Railways, Li Senmao.
State Security, Jia Chunwang.
Supervision, Wei Jianxing.
Textile Industry, Wu Wenying.
Water Resources, Yang Zhenhuai.

MINISTERS IN CHARGE OF STATE COMMISSIONS

Education, Li Tieying.
Family Planning, Peng Peiyun.
Nationalities Affairs, Ismail Amat.
Physical Culture and Sports, Wu Shaozu.
Planning, Zou Jiahua.
Restructuring Economy, Chen Jinhua.
Science, Technology and Industry for National Defence, Ding Henggao.
Science and Technology, Song Jian.
Auditor-General, Lu Peijian.
Secretary-General, Luo Gan.

President of the People's Bank of China, Li Guixian.

THE CHINESE COMMUNIST PARTY

General Secretary, Jiang Zemin.
Politburo Standing Committee, Jiang Zemin; Li Peng; Qiao Shi; Yao Yilin; Li Ruihuan; Song Ping.
Politburo of the Central Committee, Wan Li; Tian Jiyun; Qiao Shi; Jiang Zemin; Li Tieying; Li Ruihuan; Li Ximing; Yang Rudai; Yang Shangkun; Wu Xueqian; Song Ping; Yao Yilin; Qin Jiwei; Li Peng (*full members*); Ding Guangen (*alternate member*).
Secretariat of the Central Committee, Li Ruihuan; Ding Guangen; Qiao Shi; Yang Baibing (*full members*); Wen Jiabao (*alternate member*).
Advisory Commission, Chen Yun (*Chairman*); Bo Yibo; Song Renqiong (*Vice Chairmen*).
Discipline Inspection Commission, Qiao Shi (*Secretary*); Chen Zuolin; Li Zhengting; Xiao Hongda; Wang Deying (*Deputy Secretaries*).
Membership, 50,320,000 (1991).

EMBASSY OF THE PEOPLE'S REPUBLIC OF CHINA
49–51 Portland Place, London WIN 3AH
Tel 071–636 9375

Ambassador Extraordinary and Plenipotentiary, His Excellency Ma Yuzhen (1991).

BRITISH EMBASSY
11 Guang Hua Lu, Jian Guo Men Wai, Beijing
Tel: Beijing 5321961/5

Ambassador, His Excellency Sir Robin McLaren, KCMG (1991).
Minister, Consul-General and Deputy Head of Mission, P. A. McLean.
Counsellors, D. Coates (*Political*); A. Kerfoot (*Commercial*); A. D. Johnson, CBE (*Cultural, and British Council Representative*).
Defence, Military and Air Attaché, Col. M. T. P. M. Hyland, OBE.
First Secretaries, Dr J. E. Hoare (*Head of Chancery and Consul-General*); G. R. Duff (*Management and Consul*); P. Davies (*Chancery and Consul*); P. Clark (*Chancery*); J. Riordan (*Chancery*); L. Bristow-Smith (*Commercial*); J. E. Rogan (*Chancery*); J. M. Candlish (*Energy*); J. Stoddart (*Cultural ELO*); Dr G. Alexander (*Cultural/ Science*); C. Edwards (Cultural).
There is also a Consulate-General in *Shanghai.*

ARMED FORCES

All three military arms in China are parts of the People's Liberation Army (PLA). The size of this body has not been formally given, but it is estimated that China has approximately 3 million men under arms (1,350,000 conscripts), with a further 12 million (or perhaps many more) reserves who take part in militia activities. In 1955 compulsory military service was introduced for all men between the ages of 18 and 40. This service was on a selective basis. The present length of service for those conscripted is three years in the Army, four years in the Air Force and the Navy. The rank structure, abolished in 1965, was reinstated in 1988. China has eight intercontinental and 60 intermediate range land-based, and 12 submarine-launched nuclear ballistic missiles. The Army has a strength of 2,300,000 (around 1,100,000 conscripts). The Navy has a strength of 260,000 (35,000 conscripts), 94 submarines, 56 principal surface combatant vessels, and 880 combat aircraft. The Air Force numbers 470,000 (160,000 conscripts) and some 4,970 combat aircraft.

RELIGION

The indigenous religions of China are Confucianism (which includes ancestor worship), Taoism (originally a philosophy rather than a religion) and, since its introduction in the first century of the Christian era, Buddhism. There are also Chinese Muslims (officially estimated at about 12 million) and Christians (unofficially estimated at about 50 million).

Religious freedoms, severely curtailed during the Cultural Revolution, are reviving slightly under more liberal policies. Ethnic unrest in Buddhist Tibet and Muslim Xinjiang could threaten such liberalization.

EDUCATION

The Cultural Revolution caused considerable disruption to the educational system and since 1976 attempts have been made to raise academic standards. Primary education now lasts five years, and enrolment (1990) was 122,414,000 including kindergarten. Secondary education lasts five years (three years in junior middle school and two years in senior middle school). There were 51,054,000 middle school pupils in 1990. There are 220 million illiterates; efforts are being made to expand secondary education, particularly in the rural areas. Particular attention is being paid to higher education where there are over 1,000 universities, colleges and institutes with an enrolment (1990) of 2 million students. In May 1985 the Central Committee of the Party announced the abolition of free higher education except for teacher training, and the aim of providing all children with junior secondary education within 10 years.

LANGUAGE AND LITERATURE

The Chinese language has many dialects, notably Cantonese, Hakka, Amoy, Foochow, Changsha, Nanchang, Wu (Shanghai) and the northern dialect. The Common Speech or *Putonghua* (often referred to as Mandarin) which is taught throughout the country is based on the northern dialect. The Communists have promoted it as the national language and made intensive efforts to propagate it throughout the country. Since the most important aspect of this policy is the use of the spoken language in writing, the old literary style and ideographic form of writing has fallen into disuse.

In 1956 the Government decided to introduce 230 simplified characters with a view to making reading and writing easier. The list was enlarged and there are now over 2,000 simplified characters in use. In January 1956 all Chinese newspapers and most books began to appear with the characters printed horizontally from left to right, instead of vertically reading from right to left, as previously.

In February 1958 the National People's Congress adopted a system of romanization, known as pinyin, using 25 of the letters of the Latin alphabet (not v). This has been used within the country largely for assisting schoolchildren and others to learn the pronunciation of characters in *Putonghua*, and is now used for Chinese names in foreign-language publications.

Chinese literature is one of the richest in the world. Paper has been employed for writing and printing for nearly 2,000 years. The Confucian classics which formed the basis of the traditional Chinese culture date from the Warring States period (4th–3rd centuries BC) as do the earliest texts of the rival tradition, Taoism. Histories, philosophical and scientific works, poetry, literary and art criticism, novels and romances survive from most periods. Many have been translated into English. In the past all this considerable literature was available only to a very small class of literati, but with the spread of literacy in the 20th century, a process which has received enormous impetus since the Communists took over in 1949, the old traditional literature has been largely superseded by modern works of a popular kind and by the classics of Marxism and modern developments from them.

The most important among the newspapers and magazines are the *People's Daily* and the twice-monthly *Qiushi*, which replaced *Red Flag* as the CCP's mouthpiece in August 1989.

ECONOMY

China is essentially an agricultural and pastoral country; peasants constitute about 80 per cent of the population. People's communes gave way to townships as the basic level of State administration in rural districts under the 1982 Constitution.

New agricultural policies, designed to give greater incentives to the rural population, have meant that the responsibility for agricultural production has been devolved down to individual households, whereas previously work was generally assigned on a collective basis.

Wheat, barley, maize, millet and other cereals, with peas and beans, are grown in the northern provinces, and rice and sugar in the south. Rice is the staple food of the inhabitants. Cotton (mostly in valleys of the Yangtze and Yellow Rivers), tea (in the west and south), with hemp, jute and flax, are the most important crops.

Livestock is raised in large numbers. Silkworm culture is one of the oldest industries. Cottons, woollens and silks are manufactured in large quantities. The mineral wealth of the country is great. Coal, iron ore, tin, antimony, wolfram, bismuth and molybdenum are abundant. Oil is produced in several northern provinces, particularly in Heilongjiang and Shandong, and off-shore deposits are being sought in co-operation with Western and Japanese companies.

The Chinese State Statistical Bureau issues production figures annually. The following are of note for 1991:

Grain (tons)	446,240,000
Pork, beef, mutton (tons)	25,135,000
Tea (tons)	540,000
Cotton (tons)	4,508,000
Timber (cu. metres)	55,710,000
Crude oil (tons)	138,310,000
Steel (tons)	66,350,000
Electric power (kWh)	621,200,000
Machine tools	117,800
Motor vehicles	514,000

The State Statistical Bureau valued the national income for 1990 at Yuan 1,430 billion, an increase of 4.8 per cent over 1989. The Gross National Product in 1990 was Yuan 1,740 billion, a 5 per cent increase over 1989. The total value of agricultural output rose by 6.9 per cent over the 1989 figure to Yuan 738.2 billion. The total value of industrial output rose by 7.6 per cent to Yuan 2,385.1 billion in 1990.

In 1982 China set itself the aim of quadrupling the 1980 gross agricultural and industrial output value by the year 2000. The focus of its reform programme was switched to industry in 1984. Wide-ranging reforms have been introduced to make the industrial sector more efficient by narrowing the scope of central planning and broadening enterprise decision-making, material incentives and the role of the market.

TRADE

Foreign trade and external economic relations have expanded quickly since the open-door policy, adopted in the late 1970s. The principal articles of export are animals and animal products, oil, textiles, ores, metals, tea and manufactured goods. The principal imports are motor vehicles, machinery, chemical fertilizer plants, aircraft, books, paper and paper-making materials, chemicals, metals and ores, and dyes.

Trade with UK	1990	1991
Imports from UK	£465,585,000	£321,935,000
Exports to UK	583,425,000	706,585,000

COMMUNICATIONS

Of the total area of China over half consists of tableland and mountainous areas where communications and travel are generally difficult. The country has more than 53,400 kilometres of railway trunk and branch lines and some 1,028,300 kilometres of highway (1990). In addition, internal civil aviation has been developed, with routes now totalling more than 471,900 kilometres. As a result the communications network now covers most of the country.

In the past where roads did not exist the principal means of communication east to west was provided by the rivers, the most important of which are the Yangtze (Changjiang) (3,400 miles long), the Yellow River (Huanghe) (2,600 miles long) and the West River (Xihe) (1,650 miles). These, together with the network of canals connecting them are still much used, but their overall importance is less than it was. Coastal port facilities are being improved and the merchant fleet expanded. In the past ten years great progress has been made in developing postal services and telecommunications. It is claimed that 95 per cent of all rural townships are on the telephone and that postal routes reach practically every production brigade headquarters.

TIBET

Tibet is a plateau seldom lower than 10,000 feet, which forms the northern frontier of India (boundary imperfectly demarcated), from Kashmir to Burma, but is separated therefrom by the Himalayas. The area is estimated at 463,000 square miles with a population of 2,220,000 in 1990.

From 1911 to 1950, Tibet was virtually an independent country though its status was never officially so recognized. In October 1950, Chinese Communist forces invaded Eastern Tibet. On 23 May 1951 an agreement was reached whereby the Chinese army was allowed entry into Tibet. A Communist military and administrative headquarters was set up. In 1954 the Government of India recognized that Tibet was an integral part of China, in return for the right to maintain trade and consular representation there.

A series of revolts against Chinese rule over several years culminated on 17 March 1959 in a rising in Lhasa. Heavy fighting continued for several days before the rebellion was suppressed by Chinese troops and military rule imposed. The Dalai Lama fled to India where he and his followers were granted political asylum. On 28 March 1959 the Tibetan government was dissolved. In its place the 16-member Preparatory Committee for the Tibetan Autonomous Region, originally set up in 1955 with the Dalai Lama as Chairman, was to administer Tibet under the State Council; the Preparatory Committee was to have the Panchen Lama as Acting Chairman.

In December 1964 the Dalai Lama was declared to be a traitor, and both he and the Panchen Lama were dismissed. The position of Acting Chairman of the Preparatory Committee was assumed by Ngapoi Ngawang Jigmi. This move marked the end of the period of co-operation by the Chinese Government with the traditional religious authorities, and the eclipse of the latter. The Preparatory Committee completed its work with the setting up of Tibet as an Autonomous Region of China on 9 Sept. 1965. The Panchen Lama was rehabilitated as an official of the CPPCC, but died in 1989. The Chinese have invited the Dalai Lama to return from exile, but suggested negotiations between the Chinese and the Dalai Lama have failed to materialize. Sporadic outbursts of unrest continue in Tibet. Meanwhile, The Dalai Lama was awarded the Nobel Peace Prize in 1990.

COLOMBIA
República de Colombia

The Republic of Colombia lies in the extreme north-west of South America, having a coastline on both the Caribbean Sea and Pacific Ocean. It is situated between 4° 13′ S. to 12° 30′ N. lat. and 68° to 79° W. long., with an area of 440,714 sq. miles (1,141,748 sq. km), and a population (UN estimate 1990) of 32,987,000.

The country is divided into a narrow coastal strip in the west and extensive plains in the east by the Cordillera de los Andes. The Eastern Cordillera consists of a series of vast tablelands. This temperate region is the most densely peopled portion of the Republic. The principal rivers are the Magdalena, Guaviare, Cauca, Atrato, Caquetá, Putumayo and Patia.

CAPITAL – Bogotá, population (1990 estimate) 5,000,000. Bogotá is an inland city in the Eastern Cordilleras, at an elevation of 8,600 to 9,000 ft above sea level. Other centres are Medellin (2,400,000); Cali (1,800,000); Ψ Barranquilla (1,400,000); ΨCartagena (700,000); Bucaramanga (350,000); ΨBuenaventura (130,000) is the country's major port.

CURRENCY – Colombian peso of 100 centavos.

FLAG – Broad yellow band in upper half, surmounting equal bands of blue and red.

NATIONAL ANTHEM – Oh gloria inmarcesible.

NATIONAL DAY – 20 July (National Independence Day).

GOVERNMENT

The Colombian coast was visited in 1502 by Christopher Columbus, and in 1536 a Spanish expedition under Jiménez de Quesada penetrated to the interior and established on the site of the present capital a government which continued under Spanish rule until the revolt of the Spanish–American colonies of 1811–24. In 1819 Simón Bolívar (1783–1831) established the Republic of Colombia, consisting of the territories now known as Colombia, Panama, Venezuela and Ecuador. In 1829–30 Venezuela and Ecuador withdrew from the association of provinces, and in 1831 the remaining territories were formed into the Republic of New Granada. In 1858 the name was changed to the Granadine Confederation and in 1861 to the United States of Colombia. In 1866 the present title was adopted. In 1903 Panama seceded from Colombia, and became a separate Republic.

During the early 1950s Colombia suffered a period of virtual civil war between the supporters of the traditional political parties, the Conservatives and the Liberals. From 1957–74 the country was governed under the 'National Front' agreement with the presidency alternating between the two parties every four years and ministerial posts being shared equally by the parties. The alternation of the presidency was ended in 1974 and parity in appointments in 1978. Thereafter, the constitution lays down that Government portfolios and administrative appointments shall be divided among the two majority parties in Congress in an adequate and equitable manner. However, after a General Election in 1986, the Liberal Party won a large majority. Elections to a constitutional convention were held in November 1990, in which the former guerrilla movement M19 gained 30 per cent of the vote, ending the dominance of the traditional parties. The Convention began meeting in February and a new constitution was promulgated on 4 July 1991.

Congressional elections to the Senate and House of Representatives were held on 27 October 1991 with the

Liberal Party emerging as the largest party in both houses after the Conservative Party had split into three parties. The Liberal Party formed a coalition government with the Social Conservative and New Democratic Force parties.

HEAD OF STATE

President, César Gaviria Trujillo, *assumed office*, 7 August 1990.

CABINET as at July 1992

Interior, Humberto de la Calle.
Foreign Affairs, Noenú Sanú Posada.
Finance and Public Credit, Rudolf Hommes Rodríguez.
Justice, Andrés González.
National Defence, Rafael Pardo Rueda.
Public Works and Transport, Jorge Bendeck Olivella.
Labour and Social Security, Luis Fernando Ramírez.
Agriculture, Alfonso López Caballero.
Health, Gustavo Roux.
Mines and Energy, Guido Nule Amin.
Communications, William Jarmillo Gómez.
National Education, Carlos Holmes Trujillo.
Economic Development, Luis Alberto Moreno.
Foreign Trade, Juan Manuel Santos Calderón.

COLOMBIAN EMBASSY
3 Hans Crescent, London SW1X 0LR
Tel 071–589 9177

Ambassador Extraordinary and Plenipotentiary, His Excellency Dr Virgilio Barco Vargas (1990).

BRITISH EMBASSY
Torre Propaganda Sancho, Calle 98 No. 9–03 Piso 4, Bogotá
Tel: Bogota 2185111

Ambassador Extraordinary and Plenipotentiary, His Excellency Keith E. H. Morris, CMG, (1990).

There are British Consular Offices at *Barranquilla, Bogotá, Cali* and *Medellin*.

BRITISH COUNCIL REPRESENTATIVE, J. Coope, Calle 87 No. 12–79, Bogotá DE.

COLOMBO-BRITISH CHAMBER OF COMMERCE, Apartado Aereo 054 728, Calle 106 No. 25-41, Bogotá DE.

DEFENCE

The Army's strength is some 115,000 (38,000 conscripts). The Navy, with 12,000 personnel including 6,000 marines and 500 conscripts, has five principal surface combatant vessels and two submarines. The Air Force, with 7,000 personnel (1,900 conscripts), has a strength of 68 combat aircraft and 51 armed helicopters.

PRODUCTION

Much of Colombia's natural resources in coal, natural gas and hydro-electricity remain largely unexploited. Development of coal is being given priority but no new hydro projects are likely to be started for the next four to five years. Annual coal production is 12.5 million tonnes now that the Cerrejón Norte coalfield is being fully worked. This is essentially for export. Proven coal reserves stand at 16,000 million tonnes. Estimated natural gas reserves are 3,788,000 million cu. ft, with daily use at 381,772 million BTU. Proven crude oil reserves stand at 1,300 million barrels. Colombia is again a net exporter of oil. In 1991 exports averaged 472,000 b.p.d.

The hydrocarbon sector accounts for over half of the mining output with precious metals (gold, platinum and silver) and iron ore accounting for the remainder. Other mineral deposits include nickel (a processing plant started operating in 1982), bauxite, copper, gypsum, limestone, phosphates, sulphur and uranium. Colombia is also the world's largest producer of emeralds and has deposits of other precious and semi-precious stones.

AGRICULTURE – Because of the range of climate, a wide variety of crops can be grown, and the country is close to self-sufficiency in food. The principal agriculture product is coffee (Colombia is second only to Brazil as the world's largest coffee producer) and other major cash crops are sugar, bananas, cut flowers and cotton. Cattle are raised in large numbers, and meat and cured skins and hides are also exported.

INDUSTRY – The Government has encouraged diversification to reduce dependence on coffee as the major export and this has led to the growth of new export-orientated industries, particularly textiles, paper products and leather goods. Stimulus to the economy has been provided by large loans from the World Bank and IADB for project development, particularly in the power sector (in which hydroelectric projects have predominated) and for telecommunications.

TRADE

Colombia's principal export is still coffee although other products, principally bananas, cut flowers, clothing and textiles, ferro-nickel and coal are important exports. Principal trading partners are USA, the EC and Latin America.

Trade with UK	1990	1991
Imports from UK	£60,469,000	£56,428,000
Exports to UK	82,507,000	110,122,000

COMMUNICATIONS

The massive ranges of the Andes make surface transport difficult so air transport is used extensively. There are daily passenger and cargo air services between Bogotá and all the principal towns, as well as daily services to the USA, frequent services to other countries in South America, and to Europe. The 'Atlantic Railway' links the departmental lines running down to the river, and completes the connection between Bogotá and Santa Marta. Although the railways generally are in a poor state there are about 2,600 miles of rail in use at present. The total road network (1985) consists of 105,201 km of roads of all types, of which 21,800 km are classified as main trunk and transversal roads.

Large appropriations have been made for modernization of the country's telecommunication system. There are 485 radio stations (1983) and two national television channels with several regional ones.

CULTURE

Spanish is the language of the country and education has been free since 1870. Great efforts have been made in reducing illiteracy and estimates (1990) put the literacy rate at 87 per cent of those over 10 years of age. In addition to the National University with headquarters at Bogotá there are 26 other universities. There is a flourishing press in urban areas and a national literature supplements the rich inheritance from the time of Spanish rule.

Roman Catholicism is the established religion.

THE COMOROS

Republique Fédérale Islamique des Comores

The Comoro archipelago includes the islands of Great Comoro, Anjouan, Mayotte and Moheli and certain islets in the Indian Ocean with an area of 838 sq. miles (2,171 sq. km) and a population (UN estimate 1990) of 550,000, most of whom are Muslim.

CAPITAL – Moroni, on Great Comoro (pop. 17,267).
CURRENCY – Comorian franc of 100 centimes. The Comoros also use the Franc CFA of 100 centimes.
FLAG – Green with a white crescent and four white stars in the centre, tilted towards the lower fly.
NATIONAL DAY – 6 July (Independence Day).

GOVERNMENT

The islanders voted for independence from France in December 1974 and three islands became independent on 6 July 1975. (The island of Mayotte was against independence and has remained under French administration.)

A new constitution was adopted by referendum on 7 June 1992 which provides for a President, directly elected for a five-year term renewable once only; an elected legislative assembly with a four-year term; a 15-member Senate chosen by an electoral college; and the appointment of a Prime Minister from the largest party in the legislative assembly. On 10 May 1992 President Djohar appointed a government of national unity to govern until new elections are held.

Each island is administered by a Governor, assisted by up to four Commissioners whom he appoints, and has an elected Legislative Council.

HEAD OF STATE
President, Said Mohamed Djohar, *sworn in* 20 March 1990.

NATIONAL UNITY GOVERNMENT as at May 1992
Head of Government Action, Mohammed Abdoul Karim.
Foreign Affairs and Co-operation, Said Hassan Said Hachim.
Finance, Commerce and Planning, Mohammed Abdallah Mchangama.
Transport and Tourism, Ibouroi Mbae.
Public Health and Population, Ibrahim Allaoui.
National Education, Mohammed El Arif Oukacha.
Energy, Posts and Telecommunications, Ahmed Islam.
Interior and Administration, Ali Mohammed Bacar.
Justice and Employment, Ben Ali Mohammed.
Information, Culture, Youth and Sport, Ahmed Arif Hamid.

BRITISH AMBASSADOR (resident in Madagascar).

ECONOMY

The most important products are vanilla, copra, cloves and essential oils, which are the principal exports; cacao, sisal and coffee are also cultivated. Great Comoro is well forested and produces some timber.

TRADE WITH UK

	1990	1991
Imports from UK	£236,000	£796,000
Exports to UK	54,000	228,000

CONGO
République du Congo

The Republic lies on the Equator between Gabon on the west and Zaire on the east, the River Congo and its tributary the Ubangui forming most of the eastern boundary of the state. The Congo has a short Atlantic coastline. The area of the Republic of Congo is 132,047 sq. miles (342,000 sq. km), with a population of 2,271,000 (UN estimate 1990).

CAPITAL – Brazzaville (600,000); ΨPointe Noire (350,000).
CURRENCY – Franc CFA of 100 centimes.
FLAG – Divided diagonally into green, yellow and red bands.
NATIONAL DAY – 15 August.

GOVERNMENT

Formerly the French colony of Middle Congo, it became a member state of the French Community on 28 November 1958, and was proclaimed fully independent on 17 August 1960.

In 1968, conduct of affairs was assumed by a National Council of army officers. The Parti Congolais du Travail (PCT) was created by the Congress of 29–31 December 1969 and the People's Republic of the Congo was established. After popular pressure, the PCT abandoned its monopoly of power and renounced Marxism in July 1990. A transitional government was formed in January and a national conference of all political forces convened in February 1991. The national conference suspended the constitution, stripping President Sassou-Nguesso of all powers and forming itself into the Higher Council of the Republic (CSR), the transitional legislative body. On 22 December 1991 the CSR adopted a new multiparty constitution with a directly-elected President and bicameral parliament, the President appointing the Prime Minister from the majority party in parliament. The new constitution was approved by a referendum in March 1992 and a Transitional Government formed in May 1992 to govern the country until elections are held in the second half of 1992.

HEAD OF STATE
President, Pascal Lissouba, *elected* 2 August 1992.

TRANSITIONAL GOVERNMENT as at May 1992
Prime Minister, André Milongo.
Defence, Gen. Raymond Ngollo.
Foreign Affairs, Posts and Telecommunications, Dieudonné Ganga.
Interior and Decentralization, Alphonse Nzoungou.
Finance, Planning and Economy, Jean-Luc Malekat.
National Education, Science and Technology, Youth and Sports, Culture and Arts, Justin Koumba.
Justice, Labour and Civil Service, Jean Pierre Mika.
Industry, Commerce and Small and Medium-Sized Enterprises, Crafts, Mines and Energy, Delphin Luembe.
Agriculture, Water, Forestry, Animal Husbandry and Environment, Réné-Lambert Nuane.
Public Works, Transport, Town Planning and Housing, Tourism, François Lounga.
Health and Social Affairs, Médard Mdoya.

EMBASSY OF THE REPUBLIC OF CONGO
37 bis rue Paul Valery, 75116 Paris, France
Tel: Paris 45006057

Ambassador Extraordinary and Plenipotentiary, His Excellency Jean-Marie Ewengue (1986).
HONORARY CONSULATE, Livingstone House, 11 Carteret Street, London SW1H 9DJ. Tel: 071–222 7575. *Honorary Consul and Head of Mission*, L. Muzzu.

BRITISH AMBASSADOR, (resident in Zaire).

ECONOMY

Congo has its own oil deposits, producing about 8 million tonnes annually. It also produces lead, zinc and gold. The principal agricultural products are timber, cassava, sugar cane and yams. Imports are mainly of machinery.

TRADE WITH UK

	1990	1991
Imports from UK	£9,211,000	£9,190,000
Exports to UK	2,563,000	2,407,000

COSTA RICA
República de Costa Rica

The Republic of Costa Rica in Central America extends across the isthmus between 8° 17′ and 11° 10′ N. lat. and from 82° 30′ to 85° 45′ W. long., has an area of 19,575 sq. miles (50,700 sq. km), and a population (1990 estimate) of 3,000,000. The population is basically of European stock, in which Costa Rica differs from most Latin American countries. The Republic lies between Nicaragua and Panama, and between the Caribbean Sea and the Pacific Ocean. The coastal lowlands by the Caribbean Sea and Pacific have a tropical climate but the interior plateau, with a mean elevation of 4,000 feet, enjoys a temperate climate.

CAPITAL – San José, population (estimate 1989) 1,068,206; Alajuela (519,351); Cartago (328,259); Heredia (235,700); Guanacaste (234,962); ΨPuntarenas (326,163); ΨLimón (209,731). (Populations shown are of provinces, cantons and districts.)
CURRENCY – Costa Rican colón (₡) of 100 céntimos.
FLAG – Five horizontal bands, blue, white, red, white, blue (the red band twice the width of the others with emblem near staff).
NATIONAL ANTHEM – Himno Nacional de Costa Rica.
NATIONAL DAY – 15 September.

GOVERNMENT

For nearly three centuries (1530–1821) Costa Rica formed part of the Spanish American dominions, the seat of government being at Cartago. In 1821 the country obtained its independence, although from 1824 to 1839 it was one of the United States of Central America.

On 1 December 1948, the Army was abolished, the President declaring it unnecessary.

HEAD OF STATE
President, Rafael Angel Calderón Fournier, *took office*, 8 May 1990.

MINISTERS as at July 1992
Vice-Presidents, G. Serrano Pinto; A. López Echandi.
Minister for the Presidency, Rolando Lacle.
Foreign Affairs and Worship, B. Niehaus Quesada.
Interior and Police, Public Security, L. Fishman Zonzinski.
Justice, Elizabeth Odio Benito.
Finance, Rodolfo Mendez.
Agriculture, J. R. Lizano Sáenz.
Economy, Industry and Commerce, G. Fajardo Salas.
Natural Resources, Energy and Mines, H. Bravo Trejos.
Public Works and Transport, G. Madriz de Mezerville.
Education, H. Herrera Araya.
Health, C. Castro Charpentier.
Culture, Youth and Sports, Aida de Fishman.
Labour and Social Security, Carlos Monge Rodríguez.
Planning, H. Fallas Venegas.
Housing and Urban Development, C. Zawadzki Wojtasiak.
Foreign Trade, R. Rojas López.
Science and Technology, O. Morales Matamores.
Information and Press, Guillermo Fernández.
Tourism, Luis M. Chacón.

COSTA RICAN EMBASSY
5 Harcourt House, 19A Cavendish Square, London W1M 9AD
Tel 071-495 3985
Ambassador Extraordinary and Plenipotentiary, his Excellency Luis Rafael Tinoco Alvarado (1990).

BRITISH EMBASSY
Apartado 815, Edificio Centro Colon 1007, San José
Tel: San José 215566
Ambassador Extraordinary and Plenipotentiary and Consul-General, His Excellency William Marsden, CMG (1989).

ECONOMY

Agriculture is the chief industry and the principal products are coffee, bananas, sugar and cattle (for meat), all of which are important exports. Other crops are cocoa, rice, maize, potatoes, hemp, pineapple, casava, ginger, chaw chaw, melon and flowers. Industrial activity is principally in the manufacturing sector and manufactured goods are the largest category of exports. The main goods are foodstuffs, textiles and clothing, plastic goods, pharmaceuticals, fertilizers and electrical equipment. Tourism is of growing importance and became the main source of foreign exchange revenue in 1992.

FINANCE

	1988
Revenue	₡54,200.0m
Expenditure	58,790.3m

TRADE

The chief exports are manufactured goods and other products, coffee, bananas, cocoa and sugar. The chief imports are machinery, including transport equipment, manufactures, chemicals, fuel and mineral oils and foodstuffs.

	1990	1991*
Total imports	US$2,026.2m	US$1,932.8m
Total exports	1,369.4m	1,505.2m

*preliminary

Trade with UK	1990	1991
Imports from UK	£14,556,000	£11,312,000
Exports to UK	17,468,000	21,823,000

COMMUNICATIONS

The chief ports are Limón, on the Atlantic coast, through which passes most of the coffee exported, and Caldera on the Pacific coast, currently under construction with Japanese aid. The railway system is nationalized. About 500 miles of railroad are open. LACSA is the national airline, operating flights throughout Central and South America, the Caribbean and USA, besides internal flights to local airports by SANSA.

CULTURE

Spanish is the language of the country. Education is compulsory and free. The literacy rate is the highest in Latin America.

CÔTE D'IVOIRE
République de Côte d'Ivoire

Côte d'Ivoire is situated on the Gulf of Guinea between 5° and 10° N. and 3° and 8° W. It is flanked on the west by Guinea and Liberia, on the north by Mali and Burkina, and on the east by Ghana. It has an area of 124,503 sq. miles (322,463 sq. km), mostly tropical rain forest in the southern half and savanna in the northern. The population of 11,997,000 (UN estimate, 1990) is divided into a large number of ethnic and tribal groups. The official language is French.

CAPITAL – ΨAbidjan (population, 3,500,000) which is also the main port. In March 1983 the National Assembly ratified a decision to transfer the political and administrative capital from Abidjan to Yamoussoukro.
CURRENCY – Franc CFA of 100 centimes.
FLAG – Three vertical stripes, orange, white and green.
NATIONAL ANTHEM – L'Abidjanaise.
NATIONAL DAY – 7 December.

GOVERNMENT

Although French contact was made in the first half of the 19th century, Côte d'Ivoire became a colony only in 1893 and was finally pacified in 1912. It decided on 5 December 1958 to remain an autonomous republic within the French Community; full independence outside the Community was proclaimed on 7 August 1960. Special agreements with France, covering financial and cultural matters, technical assistance, defence, etc., were signed in Paris on 24 April 1961.

Côte d'Ivoire has a presidential system of government modelled on that of the United States and the French Fifth Republic. The single-chamber National Assembly has 175 members. Although the Constitution provides for a multi-party system, it was not until May 1990 that any party other than the ruling PDCI party was authorized. Defeating an opposition candidate, President Houphouët-Boigny was re-elected for a further five-year term in October 1990; the PDCI won multi-party elections held in November 1990. Amid allegations of electoral fraud, opposition protests continue.

HEAD OF STATE
President, Félix Houphouët-Boigny, *elected* for five years in 1960; *re-elected* 1965, 1970, 1975, 1980, 1985 and 1990.

CABINET as at July 1992
Prime Minister, Minister of Economy and Finance, Alassane D. Ouattara.
Ministers assisting the PM; Daniel Kablan Duncan (*Economy, Finance, Trade and Planning*); Guy-Alain Emmanuel Gause (*Raw Materials*).
Defence, Leon Konan Koffi.
Foreign Affairs, Amara Essy.
Interior, Emile Constant Bombet.
Justice, Jacqueline Lohoues-Oble.
National Education, Vamoussa Bamba.
Higher Education and Scientific Research, Alassane Salif N'Diaye.
Agriculture and Animal Resources, Lambert Kouassi Konan.
Industry and Commerce, Ferdinard Kacou Angora.
Mines and Energy, Posts and Telecommunications, Yed Esaie Angoran.
Health and Social Welfare, Frederic F. Alain Ekra.
Communication, Auguste Severin Miremont.
Equipment, Transport and Tourism, Adama Coulibaly.
Environment, Construction and Town Planning, Ezan Akele.
Employment and Civil Service, Patrice Kouame.
Security, Col. Lassana Palenfo.
Culture, Henriette Dagri Diabate.
Promotion of Women, Claire Therese Elisabeth Grah.
Youth and Sports, Rene Djedjemel Diby.

EMBASSY OF THE REPUBLIC OF CÔTE D'IVOIRE
2 Upper Belgrave Street, London SW1X 8BJ
Tel 071-235 6991
Ambassador Extraordinary and Plenipotentiary, His Excellency Gervais Yao Attoungbre (1989).

BRITISH EMBASSY
Immeuble Les Harmonies, 01 BP 2581, Abidjan 01
Tel: Abidjan 226850
Ambassador Extraordinary and Plenipotentiary, Her Excellency Margaret I. Rothwell, CMG (1990).
Head of Chancery and Consul, D. Flanagan.
First Secretary (Cultural) and British Council Representative, C. Stevenson.

BUDGET

	1990
Current Expenditure	CFA609,400 billion
Investment and Equipment	129,600 billion

TRADE

The principal exports are coffee, cocoa, timber, palm oil, pineapples, bananas, and cotton. There are a few deposits of diamonds and minerals including manganese and iron.

Trade	1988	1989
Imports	US$1,907m	US$1,781m
Exports	2,354m	2,588m

Trade with UK	1990	1991
Imports from UK	£26,941,000	£24,131,000
Exports to UK	69,849,000	45,630,000

CUBA
Republica de Cuba

Cuba, the largest island in the Caribbean, lies between 74° and 85° W. long., and 19° and 23° N. lat., with a total area of 42,804 sq. miles (110,861 sq. km). The country is divided into 14 provinces. The population in June 1990 was 10,608,000.

CAPITAL – ΨHavana, population estimate (1986) 2,100,000; other towns are ΨSantiago (429,800), Santa Clara (198,800), Camagüey (279,800), Holgüin (254,300), and ΨCienfuegos (124,600).
CURRENCY – Cuban peso of 100 centavos.
FLAG – Five horizontal bands, blue and white (blue at top and bottom) with red triangle, close to staff, charged with five-point star.
NATIONAL ANTHEM – Al Combate, Corred Bayameses (To battle, men of Bayamo).
NATIONAL DAY – 1 January (Day of Liberation).

HISTORY

The island of Cuba was visited by Christopher Columbus during his first voyage, on 27 Oct. 1492, and was then believed to be part of the western mainland of India. Early in the 16th century the island was conquered by the Spanish, to be used later as a base of operations for the conquest of Mexico and Central America, and for almost four centuries Cuba remained under a Spanish Captain-General. (The island was under British rule for one year, 1762–3, when it was returned to Spain in exchange for Florida.) Separatist agitation culminated in the closing years of the 19th century in open warfare. In 1898 the government of the United States intervened and on 20 April 1898 demanded the evacuation of Cuba by the Spanish forces. A short Spanish–American war led to the abandonment of the island, which was occupied by US troops. Cuba was under US military rule from 1 January 1899 until 20 May 1902, when an autonomous

government was inaugurated with an elected President, and a legislature of two houses.

GOVERNMENT

A revolution led by Dr Fidel Castro overthrew the government of General Batista on 1 January 1959. In October 1965 the Communist Party of Cuba was formed to succeed the United Party of the Socialist Revolution. It is the only authorized political party. The new Socialist Constitution came into force on 24 February 1976 and indirect elections to the National Assembly of People's Power were subsequently held.

President of Council of State and Head of Government, Dr Fidel Castro Ruz, *appointed* 2 November 1976.

COUNCIL OF STATE as at 30 June 1992

President, Dr Fidel Castro Ruz.
First Vice-President, Raúl Castro Ruz.
Vice-Presidents, Juan Almeida Bosque; Osmany Cienfuegos Gorriarán; José Ramón Machado Ventura; Pedro Miret Prieto; Carlos Rafael Rodríguez.
Secretary, José M. Miyar Barrueco.

COUNCIL OF MINISTERS

President, Dr Fidel Castro Ruz.
First Vice-President, Raúl Castro Ruz.
Vice-Presidents, Dr Carlos Rafael Rodríguez; Pedro Miret Prieto; José Ramón Fernández Alvarez; Osmany Cienfuegos Gorriarán; Ramiro Valdés Menéndez; Joel Domenech Benítez; Antonio Rodriguez Maurell; Jaime Crombet Hernández-Baquero; Aldofo Diaz Suárez; Lionel Soto Prieto.
Secretary, Osmany Cienfuegos Gorriarán.
Presidents of State Committees: Antonio Rodriguez Maurell (*Central Planning Board*); Hector Rodriguez Llompart (*National Bank*); Ernesto Melendez Bachs (*Economic Co-operation*); Rodrigo J. Garcia Leon (*Finance*); Francisco Linares Calvo (*Labour and Social Security*); Sonia Rodriguez Cardona (*Material and Technical Supply*); Arturo Guzman Pascual (*Prices*); Ramón Darias Rodés (*Standardization*); Fidel Emilio Vasco Gonzalez (*Statistics*).
Ministers, Carlos Pérez León (*Agriculture*); Marcos J. Portal Leon (*Basic Industry*); Manuel Castillo Rabasa (*Communications*); Homero Crabb (*Construction*); José M. Cañete Alvarez (*Construction Materials Industry*); Armando Enrique Hart Davalos (*Culture*); Manuel Vila

Sosa (*Domestic Trade*); Luis Ignacio Gomez Gutierrez (*Education*); Jorge A. Fernandez Cuervo-Vinent (*Fishing*); Alejandro Roca Iglesias (*Food Industry*); Ricardo Alarcón de Quesada (*Foreign Relations*); Ricardo Cabrisas Ruiz (*Foreign Trade*); Fernando Vecino Alegret (*Higher Education*); Gen. Abelardo Colomé Ibarra (*Interior*); Carlos Amat Fores (*Justice*); Eddie Fernandez Boada (*Light Industry*); Julio Jesus Teja Pérez (*Public Health*); Raul Castro Ruz (*Revolutionary Armed Forces*); Roberto Ignacio Gonzalez Planas (*Steel Industry*); Juan Ramon Herrera Machado (*Sugar Industry*); Gen. Senén Casas Regueiro (*Transport*); Jose Alberto Naranjo Morales; Joaqin Benavides Rodrioguez (*Ministers without Portfolio*).

EMBASSY OF THE REPUBLIC OF CUBA
167 High Holborn, London WC1V 6PA
Tel 071-240 2488

Ambassador Extraordinary and Plenipotentiary, Her Excellency Maria A. Flores (1990).
Councillor, vacant.

BRITISH EMBASSY
Edificio Bolívar, Cárcel 101-103, e Morro y Prado, Apartado 1069, Havana.
Tel: Havana 623071

Ambassador Extraordinary and Plenipotentiary, His Excellency A. Leycester S. Coltman (1991).
Counsellor, N. R. Jarrold (*Deputy Head of Mission*).
First Secretary, R. Daly (*Commercial and HM Consul*).

ECONOMY

The Government has carried out programmes of land and urban reform and of nationalization; by March 1968, virtually all industrial and commercial enterprises were nationalized. About 85 per cent of the cultivated land is in state farms or state-controlled co-operatives. Private smallholders, who own the remainder, have to sell all their produce to the state.

Although efforts are being made to diversify the economy, sugar is still its mainstay and principal source of foreign exchange. In 1989-90 the harvest was 8.04 million tons. Cuba's other main exports are oil, nickel, seafood, citrus fruits, tobacco and rum.

The tourism industry has expanded since 1986. In 1990 340,000 tourists visited Cuba generating US$250 million in gross income.

TRADE

The demise of socialism in eastern Europe has disrupted Cuba's traditional pattern of trade. A limited one-year trade agreement, instead of the normal five-year one, was signed with the USSR at the end of 1990. The new agreement envisages a transition to hard currency dealings.

	1987	1988
Imports	Pesos 7,611.5m	7,579.4m
Exports	5,401.0	5,518.3

Trade with UK	1990	1991
Imports from UK	£37,568,000	£28,413,000
Exports to UK	30,294,000	17,869,000

There are 12,700 km of railway track, of which 5,000 km are in public service. In 1986 there were 13,247 km of road. At present scheduled international air services run to North, Central and South American countries and Europe.

CULTURE

Spanish is the language of the island. English, formerly widely understood, is now spoken less. Education is compulsory and free. In 1964 illiteracy was officially declared to be completely eliminated. The press and broadcasting and television are under the control of the Government.

CYPRUS
Kypriaki Dimokratia/Kibris Cumhuriyeti

AREA – Cyprus, with an area of 3,572 sq. miles (9,251 sq. km), is the third largest island in the Mediterranean Sea. Its greatest length is 140 miles and greatest breadth 60 miles, situated at latitude 35°N. and longitude 33° 30′E. It is about 40 miles distant from the nearest point of Asia Minor, 60 miles from Syria and 240 miles from Port Said.
CLIMATE – Cyprus has a Mediterranean climate with a hot dry summer and a variable warm winter, while the intermediate seasons are short and transitional.
POPULATION – In 1990 the population (UN estimate) was 702,000. There are two major communities, Greek Cypriots (80.1 per cent) and Turkish Cypriots (18.6 per cent); and minorities of Armenians, Maronites and others.

CAPITAL – Nicosia, near the centre of the island, with a population of 168,800 (in the Government controlled area); the other principal towns are ΨLimassol, ΨFamagusta, ΨLarnaca, Paphos and Kyrenia.
CURRENCY – Cyprus pound (C£) of 100 cents.
FLAG – White with a gold map of Cyprus above a wreath of olive.
NATIONAL ANTHEM – Ode to Freedom.
NATIONAL DAY – 1 October (Independence Day).

GOVERNMENT

Cyprus passed under British administration from 1878, and was formally annexed to Great Britain in November 1914, on the outbreak of war with Turkey. From 1925 to 1960 it was a Crown Colony. Following the launching in April 1955 of an armed campaign by EOKA in support of union with Greece, a state of emergency was declared in November 1955, which lasted for four years. After a meeting at Zürich between the Prime Ministers of Greece and Turkey, a conference was held in London and an agreement was signed on 19 February 1959 between the United Kingdom, Greece, Turkey, and the Greek and Turkish Cypriots which provided that Cyprus would be an independent republic.

Under the Cyprus Act 1960, the island became an independent sovereign republic on 16 August 1960. The constitution provided for a Greek Cypriot President and a Turkish Cypriot Vice-President elected for a five-year term by the Greek and Turkish communities respectively. The House of Representatives, elected for five years by universal suffrage of each community separately, was to consist of 35 Greek and 15 Turkish members. The 1960 Constitution proved unworkable in practice and led to intercommunal troubles. The UN Peace Keeping Force in Cyprus (UNFICYP) was set up in March 1964; its mandate was last renewed on 15 June 1990.

DIVISION

In July 1974, mainland Greek officers of the Greek Cypriot National Guard launched a coup d'état against President Makarios and installed a former EOKA member, Nikos Sampson, in his place. Turkey reserved to itself the right to maintain constitutional order and the independence and territorial integrity of the island, invaded Northern Cyprus and occupied over a third of the island. In February 1975 a 'Turkish Federated State of Cyprus' under Mr Rauf Denktash was declared in this area, its constitution being approved by referendum in July 1975. In November 1983 a 'Declaration of Statehood' was issued which purported to establish the 'Turkish Republic of Northern Cyprus'. The declaration was condemned by the UN Security Council and only Turkey has recognized the new 'state'. In May 1985 a referendum in the north of Cyprus approved a constitution for the 'Turkish Republic of Northern Cyprus'. In June 1985 Mr Denktash was elected President of the 'state' and a General Election was held. Mr Denktash was re-elected in April 1990, and a General Election was held in May 1990.

Since 1974 attempts to reach a settlement have focused on intercommunal talks under the auspices of the UN.

A general election was held for the Cyprus House of Representatives on 19 May 1991, resulting in the parties gaining the following number of seats: Democratic Rally-Liberal Party 20; AKEL (Communist) 18; Democratic Party (Centre) 16; EDEK (Socialist) 7.

President, George Vassiliou, *elected* 21 February 1988.

COUNCIL OF MINISTERS as at July 1992

Foreign Affairs, George Iacovou.
Interior, Christodoulos Veniamin.
Finance, George Syrimis.
Education, Christophoros Christofides.
Justice, Nicos Papaioannou.
Defence, Andreas Aloneftis.
Communications and Works, Renos Stavrakis.
Health, Panicos Papageorghiou.
Commerce and Industry, Takis Nemitsas.
Labour and Social Insurance, Iacovos Aristidou.
Agriculture and Natural Resources, Andreas Gavrielides.

CYPRUS HIGH COMMISSION
93 Park Street, London W1Y 4ET
Tel 071-499 8272

High Commissioner, His Excellency Angelos Angelides (1990).

BRITISH HIGH COMMISSION
Alexander Pallis Street (PO Box 1978), Nicosia
Tel: Nicosia 2-473131

High Commissioner, His Excellency David John Michael Dain (1990).

BRITISH COUNCIL REPRESENTATIVE, C. Mogford, PO Box 5654, 3 Museum Street, Nicosia.

BRITISH SOVEREIGN AREAS

The United Kingdom retained full sovereignty and jurisdiction over two areas of 99 square miles in all: Akrotiri–Episkopi–Paramali and Dhekelia–Pergamos–Ayios Nicolaos–Xylophagou. This includes use of roads and other facilities. The British Administrator of these areas is appointed by The Queen and is responsible to the Secretary of State for Defence.

Administrator of the British Sovereign Areas, Air Vice-Marshal A. F. C. Hunter, CBE, AFC.

ECONOMY

Although agriculture still occupies a prime position in the Cyprus economy it is unlikely to expand further. Main products are citrus fruits, grapes and vine products, potatoes and other vegetables. Manufacturing, construction, distribution and other service industries are other major employers. Tourism is the main growth industry with over 1.2 million long-stay tourists producing C£490 million in foreign exchange earnings in 1989. Over 5,000 foreign firms and individuals have registered as offshore companies in Cyprus, which supports Cyprus's claim to be a centre for Middle East trade.

Britain continues to be the country's most important trading partner, taking some 23.4 per cent of its exports in 1989 and supplying 11.4 per cent of its imports. Cyprus is seeking to diversify its export markets and until recently sold almost half its exports to the Middle East. However, these traditional markets are now drying up, and Cyprus is looking more towards Europe. A Customs Union between Cyprus and the EC came into force in January 1988.

FINANCE

	1988	1989
Total Revenue	C£535.0m	C£632.7m
Ordinary Expenditure	598.4m	663.8m

TRADE

There is a large visible trade deficit (C£737.2 million in 1989), which is offset by invisible earnings, particularly from tourism. The current account in 1989 showed a deficit of C£72.8m, which includes the cost of one aircraft amounting to C£80.7m.

Trade	1988	1989
Imports	C£866.8m	C£1,130.3m
Exports (including re-exports)	330.9m	393.0m

Trade with UK	1990	1991
Imports from UK	£204,857,000	£209,877,000
Exports to UK	154,065,000	141,138,000

CZECHOSLOVAKIA
Česká a Slovenská Federativní Republika

At the time of going to press, Czechoslovakia was undergoing a transitional process towards a separation of its two constituent parts, the Czech Republic and the Slovak Republic, into two independent, sovereign states (*see* below).

AREA AND POPULATION – Czechoslovakia, formerly part of the Austro-Hungarian Empire, declared its independence on 28 October 1918. It has an area of 49,370 sq. miles (127,869 sq. km). The population (UN estimate 1990) is 15,662,000.

CURRENCY – Koruna (Kčs) or Czechoslovak crown of 100 Haléřů (Heller).

FLAG – Two equal horizontal stripes, white (above) and red; a blue triangle next to staff.

NATIONAL ANTHEM – Kde Domov Můj (Where is my Motherland) (Czech); Nad Tatrom sa blýska (Storm over the Tatras) (Slovak).

NATIONAL DAYS – 8 May, 5 July, 28 October.

HISTORY

The Communist Party came to power in Czechoslovakia in February 1948, and remained in power until December 1989.

In 1968 the Czechoslovak Communist Party, under the then General Secretary Alexander Dubček, embarked on a political and economic reform programme. The implications for the internal development of the other Communist regimes in the Soviet bloc alarmed the Soviet Union. On the night of 20 August Czechoslovakia was invaded by Soviet, Polish, East German, Hungarian and Bulgarian troops, the capital and all major towns being occupied. The Czechoslovak leadership was forced to modify its policies and to legalize the presence of Soviet troops on Czechoslovak territory. The reforms of 1968 were abandoned when Gustáv Husák became leader of the Communist Party in April 1969 (President 1975–89).

Opposition to Communist Party rule gathered pace in the late 1980s and mass protests in November 1989 led to the resignation of the Communist Party Central Committee. The Communist Party was forced to concede its monopoly of power and on 10 December a new government was appointed in which only half the Ministers were Communist Party members. Gustáv Husák resigned as President and was replaced by Václav Havel. Free elections were held in June 1990. The government's attempts to proceed with the conversion to a market economy were hampered by continued debate over a new constitution which will satisfy both Czechs and Slovaks.

GOVERNMENT

Under the present constitution, Czechoslovakia (renamed the Czech and Slovak Federative Republic in April 1990) consists of the Czech Republic and the Slovak Republic, each of which has its own government responsible to its legislative body, the National Council. Areas such as the constitution, defence, foreign affairs and currency are the responsibility of the federal administration. The Federal Government is responsible to the Federal Assembly, which is composed of two Chambers, the Chamber of the People, whose deputies are elected throughout the federation, and the Chamber of the Nations, consisting of an equal number of Czech and Slovak deputies.

Legislative elections were held in early June 1992 which returned the Civic Democratic Party and the Movement for a Democratic Slovakia as the dominant parties in the Czech and Slovak republics respectively. Talks between Czech and Slovak leaders on continuing the Federation then broke down because of the insistence of Vladimir Meciar, the Movement for a Democratic Slovakia leader, on a declaration of Slovak sovereignty. Meciar agreed with Civic Democratic Party Leader Vaclav Klaus on forming an interim transitional government for the federation with much reduced powers, and this was approved by President Havel and sworn in on 1 July 1992.

The re-election of President Havel was blocked by members of the Movement for a Democratic Slovakia and other Slovak nationalist deputies in the Federal Parliament vote on 3 July 1992, causing tension between Czech and Slovak politicians. Slovak deputies voted by 113 to 24 in Bratislava on 17 July 1992 to declare Slovakia a sovereign state, causing President Havel to resign on 20 July 1992. Czech and Slovak leaders plan to finalize arrangements for a separation of the two republics by 1 January 1993, subject to parliamentary approval.

TRANSITIONAL FEDERAL GOVERNMENT
Prime Minister, Jan Strasky.

EMBASSY OF THE CZECH AND SLOVAK FEDERATIVE REPUBLIC
25 Kensington Palace Gardens, London W8 4QY
Tel 071-229 1255

Ambassador Extraordinary and Plenipotentiary, vacant.

BRITISH EMBASSY
Thunovská 14, 125 50 Prague
Tel: Prague 533347

Ambassador Extraordinary and Plenipotentiary, His Excellency David Brighty, CMG, CVO (1991).
Counsellor, J. S. Laing (*Head of Chancery*).
Defence and Military Attaché, Col. W. J. Chesshyre.
Air Attaché, Wing Cdr. R. Foster.
Cultural Attaché, W. Jefferson, OBE (*British Council Representative*).

ECONOMY

Under Communist rule industry was state-owned and nearly all agricultural land was cultivated by state or co-operative farms. An economic reform programme was begun in 1990 aimed at producing a free-market economy in Czechoslovakia. New laws passed in the spring of 1990 provided a legal basis for private enterprise, joint ventures and foreign investment.

Czechoslovakia is not rich in minerals, although significant quantities of coal and lignite are mined. Principal agricultural products are sugar-beet, potatoes and cereal crops; the timber industry is also very important. The country has long been highly industrialized, and machinery, industrial consumer goods and raw materials are major exports.

TRADE WITH UK

	1990	1991
Imports from UK	£133,158,000	£129,378,000
Exports to UK	135,988,000	131,441,000

LANGUAGE AND LITERATURE

Czech and Slovak are the official languages, each having its own literature. The Reformation gave a wide-spread impulse to Czech literature, the writings of Jan Hus (martyred in 1415 as a religious and social reformer) familiarizing the people with Wyclif's teaching. This impulse endured to the close of the 17th century when Jan Amos Komensky or Comenius (1592–1670) was expelled from the country. Under Austrian rule and with the persistent pursuit of Germanization, there was a period of stagnation until the national revival in the first half of the 19th century. Authors of international reputation include Jaroslav Hašek (1883–1923), Jaroslav Seifert (1901–86, Nobel Prize for Literature, 1985), Václav Havel (b. 1936) and Milan Kundera (b. 1929).

EDUCATION

Education is compulsory and free for all children from the ages of 6 to 16. There are five universities in Czechoslovakia of which the most famous is Charles University in Prague (founded 1348), the others being situated at Bratislava, Brno, Olomouc and Košice. In addition there are a considerable number of other institutions of university standing, technical colleges, agricultural colleges, etc.

CZECH REPUBLIC

The Czech Republic, composed of Bohemia and Moravia, has an area of 30,441 sq. miles (78,864 sq. km) and a population of 10,400,000, of which 94 per cent is Czech and 4 per cent Slovak.

CAPITAL – Prague (Praha) on the Vltava (Moldau) with a population (1985) of 1,190,576. Other towns are Brno (Brüm) (381,000), Ostrava (324,000) and Plzeň (Pilsen) (174,000).

The elections of June 1992 returned the Civic Democratic Party (ODS), led by Vaclav Klaus, as the largest party in the Czech part of the Federation. The ODS has formed a coalition government with the smaller Christian Democrat Party and is determinedly pressing ahead with the market economy reforms and privatizations instigated by the previous federal government in which Vaclav Klaus was a

Minister. It is likely that a parliamentary bill will be passed to introduce the position of President of the Czech Republic, which may be filled by Vaclav Havel.

Prime Minister, Vaclav Klaus.

SLOVAK REPUBLIC

The Slovak Republic has an area of 18,298 sq. miles (49,035 sq. km) and a population of 5,300,000, of which 86.6 per cent are Slovak, 10.9 per cent Hungarian and 1.2 per cent Czech.

CAPITAL – Bratislava, with a population of 401,000. Other main town Košice (214,000).

The elections of June 1992 returned the nationalist Movement for a Democratic Slovakia (HZDS), led by Vladimir Meciar, as the largest party in Slovakia, with other nationalist parties and the ex-Communists emerging strongly as well. Meciar and the HZDS effectively blocked the continuation of the federation by their insistence on Slovak sovereignty (*see* above).

Slovakia has a much higher unemployment rate and is in a much worse economic situation than the Czech Republic because all the heavy industry built by the Communists (arms factories, forges, rolling mills) are dependent on state subsidies which the free-market reforms of the federal government were phasing out. The HZDS government, many of whom are ex-Communists, can be expected to halt market economic reforms, but Slovakia will be worse off economically when independent, as it was a large beneficiary from federal funds.

Prime Minister, Vladimir Meciar.

DENMARK
Kongeriget Danmark

AREA AND POPULATION – A Kingdom of Northern Europe, consisting of the islands of Zeeland, Funen, Lolland, etc., the peninsula of Jutland, and the outlying island of Bornholm in the Baltic, the Faröes and Greenland. Denmark is situated between 54° 34′ and 57° 45′ N. lat., 8° 5′–15° E. 12′ long., with an area of 16,629 sq. miles (43,069 sq. km), and a population (official estimate 1990) of 5,135,000.

CAPITAL – ΨCopenhagen, population (1988) 467,850; Greater Copenhagen 1,495,736. ΨAarhus 259,493; ΨOdense 174,948; ΨAalborg 154,547; ΨEsbjerg 81,480; ΨRanders 61,094; ΨKolding 57,128; ΨHelsingør 56,754; ΨHorsens 54,940; ΨVejle 50,879; Roskilde 48,996; ΨFredericia 45,992.

CURRENCY – Danish krone (Kr) of 100 øre.

FLAG – Red, with white cross.

NATIONAL ANTHEM – Kong Kristian.

NATIONAL DAY – 16 April (The Queen's Birthday).

GOVERNMENT

Under the Constitution of the Kingdom of Denmark Act of 5 June 1953, the legislature consists of one chamber, the *Folketing*, of not more than 179 members, including two for the Faröes and two for Greenland. The voting age is 18.

The coalition government of Poul Schlüter was formed in December 1990 after the General Election on 12 December.

HEAD OF STATE

Queen, Margrethe II, KG, eldest daughter of King Frederik IX, *born* 16 April 1940, *succeeded* 14 Jan. 1972, *married* 10 June 1967, Count Henri de Monpezat (Prince Henrik of Denmark), and *has issue* Crown Prince Frederik *born* 26 May 1968; and Prince Joachim, *born* 7 June 1969.

CABINET as at June 1992

Prime Minister, Poul Schlüter (C).
Foreign Affairs, Uffe Ellemann-Jensen (V).
Finance, Henning Dyremose (C).
Economic and Fiscal Affairs, Anders Fogh Rasmussen (V).
Defence, Knud Enggaard (V).
Education and Research, Bertel Haarder (V).
Justice, Hans Engell (C).
Interior and Nordic Affairs, Thor Pedersen (V).
Housing, Svend Erik Hovmand (V).
Agriculture, Laurits Tørnæs (V).
Cultural Affairs, Grethe Rostbøll (C).
Environment, Per Stig Møller (C).
Social Affairs, Else Winther Anderson (V).
Ecclesiastical Affairs and Communications, Torben Rechendorff (C).
Transport, Kaj Ikast (C).
Fisheries, Kent Kirk (C).
Labour, Knud Erik Kirkegaard (C).
Industry and Energy, Anne Birgitte Lundholt (C).
Health, Ester Larsen (V).

C Conservative Party; V Venstre (Liberals).

ROYAL DANISH EMBASSY
55 Sloane Street, London SW1X 9SR
Tel 071–333 0200

Ambassador Extraordinary and Plenipotentiary, His Excellency R. A. Thorning-Petersen (1989).
Minister Counsellors, F. N. Christensen; P. Essemann (*Commercial*); J. Benthiem (*Press and Culture*); Peter Biering (*Economic and Consular Affairs*).
Defence Attaché, Capt. S. Lund.

BRITISH EMBASSY
36–40 Kastelsvej, DK-2100 Copenhagenø
Tel: Copenhagen 35 264600

Ambassador Extraordinary and Plenipotentiary, His Excellency Nigel Christopher Ransome Williams, CMG (1989).
Counsellors, P. S. Astley (*Head of Chancery*); A. Layden (*Commercial*).
Defence Attaché, Cmdr. R. Kirkwood, RN.
There are Consulates at *Aabenraa*, *Aalborg*, *Aarhus*, *Esbjerg*, *Fredericia*, *Herning*, *Odense*, *Rønne* (Bornholm); at *Tórshavn* (Faröe Islands); and *Nuuk* (Godthåb) (Greenland).

BRITISH COUNCIL REPRESENTATIVE, Michael Holcroft, Møntergade 1, 1116 Copenhagen K.

EDUCATION

Education is free and compulsory. Special schools are numerous, commercial, technical and agricultural predominating. There are universities at Copenhagen (founded in 1479), Aarhus (1933), Odense (1966), Roskilde (1972) and Aalborg (1974). A further university at Esbjerg is planned.

LANGUAGE AND LITERATURE

The Danish language is akin to Swedish and Norwegian. Danish literature, ancient and modern, embraces all forms of expression, familiar names being Hans Christian Andersen (1805–75), Søren Kierkegaard (1813–55) and Karen Blixen (1885–1962). Some 48 newspapers are published in Denmark; two daily papers are published in Copenhagen.

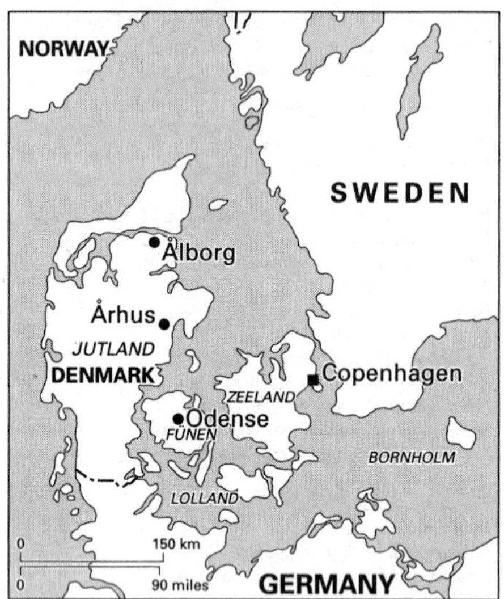

ECONOMY

Of the labour force, in 1988, 1.8 per cent was engaged in agriculture, fishing, forestry, etc.; 27.5 per cent in manufacturing, building and construction; 15.4 per cent in commerce, 0.2 per cent in liberal professions and 53.2 per cent in administration, transport and the financial services. The chief agricultural products are pigs, cattle, dairy products, poultry and eggs, seeds, cereals and sugar beet; manufactures are mostly based on imported raw materials but there are also considerable imports of finished goods.

FINANCE

Budget Estimates	1988	1989
Revenue	Kr201,280m	Kr221,008m
Expenditure	212,823m	222,179m

Denmark's balance of payments on current account showed a deficit for 1988 of Kr12,200 million (1987, Kr20,700 million).

TRADE

The principal imports are industrial raw materials, consumer goods, construction inputs, machinery, raw materials, vehicles and textile products. The chief exports are miscellaneous manufactured articles, agricultural and dairy products.

	1988	1989
Total Imports	Kr178,269m	Kr194,567m
Total Exports	187,381m	204,834m

Trade with UK	1990	1991
Imports from UK	£1,413,713,000	£1,408,549,000
Exports to UK	2,278,569,000	2,226,706,000

COMMUNICATIONS

Mercantile marine (ships above 100 gross tonnage) at beginning of 1988, totalled 618 ships. In 1985 there was 2,471 km of state-owned railway and 494 km of privately-owned railway systems.

THE FARÖES

The Faröes, or Sheep Islands have an area of 540 sq. miles (1,399 sq. km) and a population (1990) of 47,485. The capital is Tórshavn.

The islands are governed by a *Lagting* of 26 members, a *Landsstyre* of four members which deals with special Faröes affairs, and send two representatives to the *Folketing* at Copenhagen. On 14 Sept. 1946 the Lagting, with the consent of the Danish Government, for its own guidance held a plebiscite on the Faröes. About one-third of the electors did not, however, take part in the voting; of the rest, a little more than half the votes cast were in favour of separation from Denmark and the establishment of a republic. At the subsequent general election for the Lagting a great majority voted in favour of remaining part of the Kingdom of Denmark with a certain measure of home rule and in 1948 the Faröes received this. The Faröes are not part of the EC.
Prime Minister, Alti Dam.

Trade with UK	1990	1991
Imports from UK	£7,882,000	£7,330,000
Exports to UK	34,396,000	32,515,000

GREENLAND

Greenland has a total area 2,175,600 sq. km, of which approx. 16 per cent is ice-free, and a population (1990) of 55,558. It is divided into three provinces (West, North and East). The capital is Nuuk (Godthåb)). Greenland has a *Landsraad* of 17 members and sends two representatives to the *Folketing* at Copenhagen. Greenland attained a status of internal autonomy on 1 May 1979. Following a plebiscite Greenland negotiated its withdrawal from the EC, but without discontinuing relations with Denmark, and left on 1 February 1985.

Mineral and oil prospecting revealed deposits of lead, zinc, iron ore, oil, gas and uranium. Commercial exploitation of these resources has already begun. The trade of Greenland is mainly under the management of the Grønlands Handel. The United States of America has acquired certain rights to maintain air bases in Greenland.
Premier, Lars Emil Johansen.

Trade with UK	1990	1991
Imports from UK	£2,256,000	£635,000
Exports to UK	10,322,000	5,039,000

DJIBOUTI
Jumhouriyya Djibouti

Djibouti is situated on the north-east coast of Africa (i.e. the Horn of Africa) and has an area of 8,494 sq. miles (22,000 sq. km.). It has a population (1991 census) of 520,000. The climate is harsh and much of the country is semi-arid desert.

CAPITAL – Ψ Djibouti, population (1991) 340,700.
CURRENCY – Djibouti franc of 100 centimes.
FLAG – Blue over green with white triangle in the hoist containing a red star.
NATIONAL DAY – 27 June (Independence Day).

GOVERNMENT

Formerly known as French Somaliland and then the French Territory of the Afars and the Issas, the Republic of Djibouti became independent on 27 June 1977. The most recent elections to the 65-member Chamber of Deputies took place in April 1987. The sole legal party is *Rassemblement Populaire pour le Progrès* (RPP, the Popular Rally for Progress).

HEAD OF STATE
President, Hassan Gouled Aptidon, *elected* 1977, *re-elected* 1981 and 1987.

CABINET as at June 1992

Prime Minister, Barkat Gourad Hamadou.
Justice and Islamic Affairs, Ougure Hassan Ibrahim.
Foreign Affairs and Co-operation, Moumin Bahdon Farah.
Interior, Posts and Telecommunications, Ahmed Bulaleh Barreh.
Defence, Ismail Ali Youssouf.
Finance and National Economy, Moussa Bouraleh Robleh.
Ports and Shipping, Ahmed Aden Youssouf.
Commerce, Transport and Tourism, Ahmed Ibrahim Abdi.
Education, Omar Chirdon Abass.
Youth and Sports and Culture, Hussein Barkad Siraj.
Public Health and Social Affairs, Idriss Harbi Farah.
Labour, Elaf Orbis Ali.
Civil Service and Administrative Reform, Attehey Waiss.
Public Works, Construction and Housing, Ibrahim Idris Mohamed.
Industry, Salem Abdou Yaya.
Agriculture and Rural Development, Mohamed Moussa Chehem.

EMBASSY OF THE REPUBLIC OF DJIBOUTI
26 rue Emile Ménier, 75116 Paris, France
Tel: Paris 47274922

Ambassador Extraordinary and Plenipotentiary, His Excellency Ahmed Omar Farah (1991).

BRITISH CONSULATE
PO Box 81, 9–11 Rue de Geneve, Djibouti

Honorary Consul, P. Lievin.

The French continue to maintain army, navy and air force bases. Djibouti has an excellent port, international airport and a railway line runs to Addis Ababa.

TRADE WITH UK

	1990	1991
Imports from UK	£14,962,000	£21,889,000
Exports to UK	174,000	119,000

DOMINICA

The Commonwealth of Dominica

AREA, POPULATION, ETC – Dominica, the loftiest of the Lesser Antilles, lies in the Windward Group, between 15° 12′ and 15° 39′ N. lat. and 61° 14′ and 61° 29′ W. long., 95 miles south of Antigua. It is about 29 miles long and 16 broad comprising an area of 289 sq. miles (748.5 sq. km). The island is of volcanic origin and very mountainous, and the soil is very fertile. The temperature varies, according to the altitude, from 13°–29°C. The climate is healthy. The population is 82,000 (1990 UN estimate).

CAPITAL – ΨRoseau, on the south-west coast, population 11,000. The other principal town is Portsmouth, population 2,220.

CURRENCY – East Caribbean dollar (EC$) of 100 cents.

FLAG – Green ground with a cross overall of yellow, white and black stripes, and in the centre a red disc charged with a Sisserou parrot in natural colours within a ring of 10 green stars.

NATIONAL ANTHEM – Dominica Day Song.

NATIONAL DAY – 3 November (Independence Day).

GOVERNMENT

The island was discovered by Columbus in 1493, when it was a stronghold of the Caribs, who remained virtually the sole inhabitants until the French established settlements in the 18th century. It was captured by the British in 1759 but passed back and forth between France and Britain until 1805, after which British possession was not challenged. From 1871 to 1939 Dominica was part of the Leeward Islands Colony, then from 1940 the island was a unit of the Windward Islands group. Internal self-government from 1967 was followed on 3 November 1978 by independence as a republic with the name The Commonwealth of Dominica.

Executive authority is vested in the President, who is elected by the House of Assembly for not more than two terms of five years. Parliament consists of the President and the House of Assembly (representatives elected by universal adult suffrage) and nine Senators, who may be appointed by the President or elected. Parliament has a life of five years.

At the general election of May 1990, the Dominica Freedom Party won 11 seats, the Dominica United Workers' Party 6, and the Labour Party of Dominica the remaining 4.

HEAD OF STATE

President, His Excellency Sir Clarence Seignoret, GCB, OBE.

CABINET as at June 1992

Prime Minister, Minister for Finance and Economic Affairs, Dame M. Eugenia Charles, DBE.
Legal Affairs, Information and Public Relations, Hon. Jenner Armour.
External Affairs and OECS Unity, Hon. Brian Alleyne.
Trade, Industry and Tourism, Hon. Charles Maynard.
Education and Sports, Hon. Rupert Sorhaindo sen.
Community Development and Social Affairs, Hon. Henry George.
Health and Social Security, Hon. Allan Guye.
Labour and Immigration, Hon. Heskeith Alexander.
Communications, Works and Housing, Hon. Alleyne Carbon.
Agriculture, Hon. Maynard Joseph.
Minister without Portfolio, Prime Minister's Office, Hon. Dermott Southwell sen.
Parliamentary Secretary in the Ministry of Agriculture, Trade, Industry and Tourism, Hon. Ossie Walsh.
Parliamentary Secretary in the Ministry of Communications, Works and Housing, Hon. Clem Shillingford.

HIGH COMMISSION FOR THE COMMONWEALTH OF DOMINICA
1 Collingham Gardens, London SW5 0HW
Tel 071-370 5194/5

High Commissioner, His Excellency Franklin A. Baron (1986) (resident in Roseau).
Minister Counsellor (London), Ashworth Elwin.

BRITISH HIGH COMMISSION
High Commissioner (resides at Bridgetown, Barbados).

FINANCE

	1988–9
Recurrent Revenue	EC$120.8m
Recurrent Expenditure	98.8m

ECONOMY

Agriculture is the principal occupation, with tropical and citrus fruits the main crops. Products for export are bananas, lime juice, lime oil, bay oil, copra and rum. Forestry and fisheries are being encouraged. The only commercially exploitable mineral is pumice, used chiefly for building purposes. Manufacturing consists largely of the processing of agricultural products.

TRADE	1988
Imports	US$87.55m
Exports	55.55m

Trade with UK	1990	1991
Imports from UK	£9,707,000	£11,573,000
Exports to UK	23,483,000	25,221,000

DOMINICAN REPUBLIC
República Dominicana

The Dominican Republic, formerly the Spanish portion of the island of Hispaniola, is the oldest settlement of European origin in America. The western part of the island forms the Republic of Haiti. The island lies between Cuba on the west and Puerto Rico on the east and the Republic covers an area of 18,816 sq. miles (48,734 sq. km), with a population (1990 UN estimate) of 7,170,000. The climate is tropical in the lowlands and semi-tropical to temperate in the higher altitudes.

Spanish is the language of the Republic.

CAPITAL – Ψ Santo Domingo, population of the Capital District (1981 census) 1,313,172. Other centres, with populations (1981 census): Santiago de los Caballeros (550,372); La Vega (385,043); San Francisco De Macoris (235,544); San Juan (239,957); San Cristóbal (446,132).
CURRENCY – Dominican Republic peso (RD$) of 100 centavos.
FLAG – Divided into blue and red quarters by a white cross.
NATIONAL ANTHEM – Quisqueyanos Valientes, Alcemos (Brave men of Quisqueya, let's raise our song).
NATIONAL DAY – 27 February (Independence Day 1844).

GOVERNMENT

Santo Domingo was discovered by Christopher Columbus in December 1492, and remained a Spanish colony until 1821. In 1822 it was subjugated by the neighbouring Haitians who remained in control until 1844 when the Dominican Republic was proclaimed. The country was occupied by American marines from 1916 until the adoption of a new Constitution in 1924. From 1930 until 30 May 1961 (when he was assassinated) Generalissimo Rafael Trujillo ruled the country.

President Juan Bosch held office from December 1962 to September 1963, when he was deposed by a military junta. A revolt in favour of ex-President Bosch in April 1965 developed into civil war lasting until September the same year when a provisional President was elected. On 1 June 1966 Dr Joaquin Balaguer was elected President and in November 1966 a new Constitution was introduced.

Executive power is vested in the President, who is elected by direct vote and serves for four years. The President forms his cabinet without reference to the Congress. Legislative power is exercised by the Congress, which has a term of four years concurrent with the Presidency. The Upper Chamber is the Senate of 27 senators, one for each province and one for Santo Domingo. The lower is the Chamber of Deputies which has 120 members, one for each 50,000 inhabitants in each province, with the provision that no province has less than two members. Judicial power is exercised by the Supreme Court of Justice.

HEAD OF STATE
President, Dr Joaquin Balaguer, *took office*, 16 Aug. 1986, *re-elected* 16 May 1990.
Vice-President, Carlos Morales Troncoso.

CABINET as at July 1992
Presidency, Enrique Perez y Perez.
Finance, Marte de Barrios.
Foreign Affairs, Juan Aristides Guzman.
Education and Culture, Pedro Gil Iturbides.
Agriculture, Agronomo Nicolas Concepción.
Labour, Rafael Alburquerque.
Public Health and Social Welfare, Dr Miguel A. Strepan.
Industry and Trade, Rafael Bello Andino.
Sports, Physical Education and Recreation, Cristobal Marte.
Tourism, Andres Venderhorst.
Interior and Police, Gen. Rafael Peraeta Guerrero.
Armed Forces, Lt.-Gen. Hector Garcia Tejeda.

EMBASSY OF THE DOMINICAN REPUBLIC
2 rue Georges Ville, 75116 Paris, France
Tel: Paris 45018881
Ambassador Extraordinary and Plenipotentiary, new appointment awaited.

HONORARY CONSULATE-GENERAL
539 Martins Building, Water Street, Liverpool L2 3TE
Tel 051-236 0722
Honorary Consul-General, T. V. Anthony.
Honorary Vice-Consul, Mrs Hilary Gatenby.

There are also Consular Offices at *Birmingham*, *Cardiff*, *Grimsby*, *London* (6 Queen's Mansions, Brook Green, London W6 7EB), and *Plymouth*.

BRITISH AMBASSADOR, *(resident in Caracas, Venezuela)*.

BRITISH CONSULATE
Abraham Lincoln 552, Santo Domingo DR
Tel: Santo Domingo 5015/0.
Honorary Consul, M. Tejeda, MBE.

COMMUNICATIONS

According to local classification there are 2,932 miles of first class and 1,392 miles of second class and inter-communal roads in the Republic. There is a direct road from Santo Domingo to Port-au-Prince, the capital of Haiti, but that part of it in the border area has fallen into disuse. The frontier has been closed since September 1967, except for that section crossed by the main road linking the two capitals. A telephone system connects practically all the principal towns of the republic and there is a telegraph service with all parts of the world. There are more than 90 commercial broadcasting stations and six television stations.

The Republic is served by two national and six foreign airlines, and an international airport 18 miles to the east of the capital is in operation. Another has been built near Puerto Plata on the north coast.

ECONOMY

Sugar, coffee, cocoa, and tobacco are the most important crops. Other products are peanuts, maize, rice, bananas, molasses, salt, cement, ferro-nickel, gold, silver, cattle, sisal products, honey and chocolate. There is a growing number of light industries producing beer, tinned foodstuffs, glass products, textiles, soap, cigarettes, construction materials, plastic articles, shoes, papers, paint, rum, matches, peanut oil and other products.

FINANCE

	1986
Expenditure	RD$2,251m
Revenue	2,113m

TRADE

The chief imports are machinery, food stuffs, iron and steel, cotton textiles and yarns, mineral oils (including petrol), cars and other motor vehicles, chemical and pharmaceutical products, electrical equipment and accessories, construction material, paper and paper products, and rubber and rubber products. The chief exports are sugar, coffee, cocoa, tobacco, chocolate, molasses, bauxite, ferro-nickel and gold. Tobacco and tobacco manufactures are the principal exports to the UK.

	1984	1985
Imports	RD$1,459,000,000	RD$1,285,900,000
Exports	1,211,100,000	739,300,000

Trade with UK	1990	1991
Imports from UK	£19,668,000	£19,773,000
Exports to UK	17,440,000	22,076,000

ECUADOR

Republica del Ecuador

AREA AND POPULATION – Ecuador is an equatorial state of South America, the mainland extending from lat. 1° 38′ N. to 4° 50′ S., and between 75° 20′ and 81° W. long., comprising an area reduced by boundary settlements with Peru (January 1942) to about 109,484 sq. miles (283,561 sq. km).

It has a population (UN estimate 1990) of 10,782,000, mostly descendants of the Spanish, aboriginal Indians, and Mestizoes. The Republic extends across the Western Andes, the highest peaks in Ecuador being Chimborazo (20,408 ft) and Ilinza (17,405 ft) in the Western Cordillera; and Cotopaxi (19,612 ft) and Cayambe (19,160 ft) in the Eastern Cordillera. Ecuador is watered by the Upper Amazon, and by the rivers Guayas, Mira, Santiago, Chone, and Esmeraldas on the Pacific coast. There are extensive forests.

CAPITAL – Quito, population (1991 estimate) 1,387,887; Ψ Guayaquil (1,531,229) is the chief port; Cuenca (332,117).

CURRENCY – Sucre of 100 centavos.

FLAG – Three horizontal bands, yellow, blue and red (the yellow band twice the width of the others); emblem in centre.

NATIONAL DAY – 10 August (Independence Day).

GOVERNMENT

The former Kingdom of Quito was conquered by the Incas of Peru in the latter part of the 15th century. Early in the 16th century Pizarro's conquests led to the inclusion of the present territory of Ecuador in the Spanish Vice-royalty of Quito. The independence of the country was achieved in a revolutionary war which culminated in the battle of Mount Pichincha (24 May 1822).

After seven years of military rule, Ecuador returned to democracy in 1979. The present constitution, introduced in 1978, provides for an elected President and Vice-President who serve for a four-year term. Neither may stand for re-election. There is a Chamber of Representatives with 72 members elected every four years, 12 of whom are elected on a national basis and the rest by the provinces. The Chamber meets for two months every year (August to October) but can be convoked at any time for extraordinary sessions. Four Legislative Commissions meet through the year.

The Republic is divided into 21 provinces.

Voting is compulsory for all literate and (since 1980) voluntary for all illiterate citizens over the age of 18. Seventeen political parties took part in the 1988 elections.

HEAD OF STATE

President, Sixto Durán Ballén, *took office* 10 August 1992.
Vice-President, Alberto Dahik Garzozi.

CABINET as at August 1992

Government Affairs, Roberto Dunn Barreira.
Foreign Affairs, Dr Diego Paredes.
National Defence, Jose Gallardo Roman.
Education and Culture, Dr Eduardo Pena Trivino.
Finance and Public Credit, Mario Ribadeneira Saenz.
Public Works and Communications, Pedro Lopez Torres.
Energy and Mines, Andres Barreiro Vivas.
Industry, Commerce, Integration and Fisheries, Mauricio Pinto Mancheno.
Labour, Alfredo Corral Borrero.
Agriculture and Livestock, Mariano Gonzalez.
Public Health, Leonardo Viteri Molinari.
Social Welfare, Mariana Argudo Chejin.
Information and Tourism, Pedro Zambrano Izaguirre.
Housing and Urban Development, Francisco Albornoz.
Secretary-General of the Administration, Jose Vicente Maldonado.

EMBASSY OF ECUADOR

Flat 3B, 3 Hans Crescent, London SW1X 0LS
Tel 071-584 1367/2648

Ambassador Extraordinary and Plenipotentiary, new appointment awaited.

BRITISH EMBASSY

Av. Gonzalez Suarez, 111 (Casilla 314), Quito
Tel: Quito 560670

Ambassador Extraordinary and Plenipotentiary, His Excellency Frank Basil Wheeler, CMG (1989).

There are British Consular Offices at *Cuenca, Galapagos* and *Guayaquil*.

BRITISH COUNCIL REPRESENTATIVE, Desmond Lauder, Av. Amazonas 1646 (Casilla 17078829), Quito.

ECONOMY

Agriculture is the most important sector of the economy, supporting nearly 50 per cent of the population (particularly the poorest) and contributing 14.5 per cent of the Gross Domestic Product and 19.5 per cent of exports. The main products for export are fish (mainly shrimps, tuna and sardines), which had become the largest agricultural export by 1982; bananas, which provide a third of agricultural exports; cocoa and coffee. Other important crops are sugar, corn, soya, rice, cotton, African palm (for oil), vegetables, fruit and timber, the temperate crops being produced mostly in the highlands.

The economy was transformed by the discovery in 1972 of major oil fields in the Oriente area, and oil accounted for two-thirds of 1981 export earnings. The economy grew rapidly in the 1970s but is now faced with reduced growth, due mainly to the fall in the price of oil. The oil deposits in the Oriente are estimated at between 10,000 and 15,000 million barrels, and further exploration and development is taking place. The oil is evacuated by a trans-Andean pipeline to the port of Balao (near Esmeraldas City).

FINANCE

The estimated government budget in 1986 was: revenue 186,824 million sucres; expenditure 216,466 million sucres.

TRADE

Import licences are required for all merchandise and these are issued by the Central Bank of Ecuador. Manufactured goods and machinery are the main imports.

	1987	1988
Imports	US$2,229.0m	US$1,713.5m
Exports	1,998.6m	2,192.9m

Trade with UK	1990	1991
Imports from UK	£30,155,000	£45,213,000
Exports to UK	19,572,000	16,284,000

COMMUNICATIONS

There are 23,256 km of permanent roads and 5,044 km of roads which are only open during the dry season. There are about 750 miles of railway, including the railway from Quito to Guayaquil. Ten commercial airlines operate international flights, linking Ecuador with major foreign cities and there are internal services between all important towns.

DEFENCE

The standing Army has a strength of about 50,000. There is an Air Force of some 79 combat aircraft of various kinds and 3,000 personnel. The Navy is 4,800 strong and has two submarines and two principal surface combatant vessels.

CULTURE

Spanish is the principal language of the country but Quechua is also a recognized language and is spoken by the majority of the Indian population. As a result of an intensive national education programme more than 75 per cent of the population are now literate. Elementary education is free and compulsory. There are ten universities (three at Quito, three at Guayaquil, and one each at Cuenca, Machala, Loja and Portoviejo), polytechnic schools at Quito and Guayaquil and eight technical colleges in other provincial capitals. Two daily newspapers are published at Quito and four at Guayaquil.

GALÁPAGOS ISLANDS

The Galápagos (Giant Tortoise) Islands forming the province of the Archipelago de Colón, were annexed by Ecuador in 1832. The archipelago lies in the Pacific, about 500 miles from Saint Elena peninsula, the most westerly point of the mainland. There are 12 large and several hundred smaller islands with a total area of about 3,000 sq. miles and an estimated population (1982) of 6,119. The capital is San Cristobal, on Chatham Island. Although the archipelago lies on the equator, the temperature of the surrounding water is well below equatorial average owing to the Antarctic Humboldt Current. The province consists for the most part of National Park Territory, where unique marine birds, iguanas, and the giant tortoises are conserved. There is some local subsistence farming; the main industry, apart from tourism, is tuna and lobster fishing.

EGYPT

Al-Jumhuriyal Misr al-Arabiya

Area and Population – The total area of Egypt is 386,662 sq. miles (1,001,449 sq. km), only 3 per cent of which is cultivated land, with a population (UN estimate 1990) 53,153,000.

There are three distinct elements in the population. The largest, or 'Egyptian' element, is a Hamito-Semite race, known in the rural districts as *Fellahin* (*fellâh*, ploughman or tiller of the soil). A second element is the *Bedouin*, or nomadic Arabs of the Western and Arabian deserts, of whom about one-seventh are real nomads, and the remainder semi-sedentary tent-dwellers on the outskirts of the cultivated end of the Nile Valley and the Fayüm. The third element is the *Nubian* of the Nile Valley between Aswân and Wadi-Halfa of mixed Arab and Negro blood. Over 90 per cent of the population are Muslims of the Sunni denomination, and most of the rest Coptic Christians.

The territory of Egypt comprises Egypt proper, the peninsula of Sinai and a number of islands in the Gulf of Suez and Red Sea, of which the principal are Jubal, Shadwan, Gafatin and Zeberged (or St John's Island). This territory lies between 22° and 32° N. lat. and 24° and 37° E. long. The northern boundary is the Mediterranean, and Egypt borders the Sudan in the south and Libya in the west. The east boundary follows a line drawn from Rafa on the Mediterranean (34° 15′ E. long.) to the head of the Gulf of 'Aqaba.

The country is mainly flat but there are mountainous areas in the south-west, along the Red Sea coast and in the south of the Sinai peninsula, rising in some places to peaks of over 6,000 ft. The highest mountain in Egypt is Mt Catherina (8,668 ft). Most of the land is desert but the Nile valley and delta are covered by silt 20–30 feet deep, and areas of desert are increasingly being reclaimed by irrigation and fertilization.

The Nile has a total length of 4,145 miles, of which 960 miles runs through Egypt. Since the completion of the Aswan High Dam in 1965 (about a mile upstream from the smaller Aswan Dam, built around the turn of the century), there has been no flood downstream of the dam and the water level remains almost constant throughout the year. The area of fertile land, a 5–15 mile wide strip in the Nile valley and some 6,000 square miles of the Nile delta, has been increased by the opening of the Aswan Dam. This has allowed the reclamation of about 1,300,000 acres, and a further 700,000 acres have been converted from basin to perennial irrigation.

Westward from the Nile Valley stretches the Western desert, containing some depressions, whose springs irrigate small areas known as oases, of which the principal are Kharga, Dakhla, Farafra, Baharia and Siwa. In the Eastern Desert between the Nile and the mountains along the Red Sea coast, are plateaux of sandstones and limestones, dissected by wadis (dry water-courses), often of great length and depth, with some wild vegetation and occasional wells and springs.

Capital – Cairo (population, estimated in 1986 at 14,000,000), stands on the east bank of the Nile, about 14 miles from the head of the delta. Its oldest part is the fortress of Babylon in old Cairo, with its Roman bastions and Coptic churches. The earliest Arab building is the Mosque of 'Amr, dating from AD 643, and the most conspicuous is the Citadel, built by Saladin towards the end of the 12th century and containing in its walls the Mosque of Mohamed Ali built in the 19th century.

ΨAlexandria (estimated population in 1986 of 5,000,000), founded 332 BC by Alexander the Great, was for over 1,000 years the capital of Egypt and a centre of Hellenic culture which vied with Athens itself. Its great *pharos* (lighthouse), 480 feet high, with a lantern burning resinous wood, was one of the Seven Wonders of the World. Other towns are: Ismailia (400,000); ΨPort Said (285,000); Mansura (120,000); Asyût (300,000); Faiyûm (180,000); Tanta (150,000); Mahalla el Kubra (130,000); ΨSuez; ΨDamietta (100,000).

Currency – Egyptian pound (£E) of 100 piastres and 1,000 millièmes.

Flag – Horizontal bands of red, white and black, with an eagle in the centre of the white band.

National Day – 23 July (Anniversary of Revolution in 1952).

HISTORY

The unification of the Kingdoms of Lower and Upper Egypt under the Pharaohs *c.*3100 BC marked the establishment of the Egyptian state, with Memphis as its capital. Egypt was ruled for nearly 2,800 years by a succession of Pharaonic dynasties (31 in all), which built the pyramids at Gizeh. The oldest of these is that of Zoser, built *c.*2700 BC, and the highest the Great Pyramid of Cheops, at 451 feet; nearby is the Sphinx, 189 feet long. A period of Hellenic rule began in 332 BC, after the conquest of Egypt by Alexander the Great, followed by a period of rule by Rome (30 BC to AD 324) and then by the Byzantine Empire. In AD 640 Egypt was subjugated by Arab Muslim invaders, becoming a province of the Eastern Caliphate. In 1517 the country was incorporated in the Ottoman Empire, under which it remained until early in the 19th century.

A British Protectorate over Egypt declared on 18 Dec. 1914, lasted until 28 Feb. 1922, when Sultan Ahmed Fuad was proclaimed King of Egypt. In July 1952, following a military coup d'état, King Farouk abdicated in favour of his infant son, who became King Ahmed Fuad II. In June 1953 however, Gen. Neguib's military council deposed the young King, and Egypt became a Republic.

In 1956, as a result of Egypt's trade agreements with Communist countries, Britain and USA withdrew offers of financial aid and in retaliation President Nasser seized the assets of the Suez Canal Company. Egyptian occupation of the Canal Zone while repulsing an Israeli attack was used as a pretext for military action by Britain and France in support of their Suez Canal Company interests. A ceasefire and Anglo-French withdrawal were negotiated by the UN.

The Israeli invasion of 1956 overran the Sinai peninsula but six months later Israel withdrew and a UN peace-keeping force was established in the area. However, mounting tension culminated in a second invasion of Sinai (the Six Day War of June 1967) and occupation of the peninsula by Israel. Egypt's attempt to recapture the territory (the Yom Kippur War of October 1973) was unsuccessful but Sinai was returned to Egypt in April 1982, under the treaty of 1979 which resulted from the Camp David talks between President Sadat and the Israeli Prime Minister Menachem Begin and formally terminated a 31-year old state of war between the two countries. President Mubarak came to power on 13 October 1981 after the assassination of President Sadat by Muslim fundamentalists.

Egypt benefited considerably, both economically and politically, from its participation in the Gulf War; it has now been fully rehabilitated in the Arab world and has had large amounts of its international debt written off.

GOVERNMENT

The Constitution of 1971 provides for an executive President who appoints Ministers to the Cabinet. The President determines policy which the Cabinet implements and Ministers are responsible to him. The legislature consists of the People's Assembly (454 members, 444 of whom are elected, the remaining ten nominated by the President). The Shura Council, or Consultative Assembly (258 members) has an advisory role. Religious courts were abolished in 1956 and their functions transferred to the national court system.

The ruling National Democratic Party won general elections, boycotted by the major opposition parties, held in November and December 1990.

HEAD OF STATE

President, Muhammad Hosni Mubarak, *elected* 13 Oct. 1981, *re-elected* 1987.

COUNCIL OF MINISTERS as at July 1992

Prime Minister, Dr Atef Muhammad Naguib Sidqi.
Presidential Assistant, Muhammad Abdul Halim Abu Ghazala.
Defence and Military Production, Gen. Hussein Tantawy.
Deputy PM and Minister of Planning and International Co-operation, Dr Kamal Ahmed al-Ganzuri.
Deputy PM and Minister of Agriculture and Land Reclamation, Dr Yussif Amin Wali.
Foreign Affairs, Amre Moussa.
Economy and Foreign Trade, Dr Yussri Ali Mustafa.
Finance, Dr Muhammad Ahmed el-Razzaz.
Interior, Maj.-Gen. Mohammed Abdul Halim Mousa.
Oil and Mineral Wealth, Dr Hamdy El Bambi.
Tourism and Civil Aviation, Fouad Abdul Latif Sultan.
Justice, Farouq Saif al-Nasr.
Culture, Farouq Hosni.
Industry, Muhammad Mahmoud Abdul Wahhab.
Parliamentary and Shura Council Affairs, Dr Ahmed Salama.
Supply and Internal Trade, Dr Mohammed Galaleddin Abdul-Dahab.
Public Works and Water Resources, 'Issam Abdul Hamid Radi.
Manpower and Vocational Training, Assem Abdul Haq.
Education, Dr Hussein Kamal Baha El-Din.
Transport, Communications and Marine Transport, Suliman Metwalli Suliman.
Scientific Research, Dr Adel Abul-Hamid 'Ezz.
Health, Dr Mohammed Ragheb Dawidar.
Information, Muhammad Safwat al-Sharif.
Cabinet Affairs and Administrative Development, Dr 'Atif Mohammad 'Ebeid.
Religious Affairs (*Waqfs*), Dr Muhammad Ali Mahgoub.
Social Affairs and Social Insurance, Dr Amal Abdul Rahim Osman.
Electricity and Energy, Mohammad Mahir Osman Abaza.
Housing, New Communities and Public Utilities, Hasaballah Mohammad al-Kafrawi.
Local Government, Dr Mahmmoud Sherif.
Ministers of State, Gamal al-Sayyid Ibrahim (*Military Production*); Dr Mouris Makramallah (*International Co-operation*).

EMBASSY OF THE ARAB REPUBLIC OF EGYPT
26 South Street, London W1Y 8EL
Tel 071-499 2401

Ambassador Extraordinary and Plenipotentiary, His Excellency Mohamed I. Shaker (1988).

BRITISH EMBASSY
Ahmed Ragheb Street, Garden City, Cairo
Tel: Cairo 354-0850

Ambassador Extraordinary and Plenipotentiary, His Excellency Christopher Long (1992).

BRITISH COUNCIL REPRESENTATIVE, J. Barnett, OBE, 192 Sharia el Nil, Agouza, Cairo. There is also a library in *Alexandria*.

ECONOMY

AGRICULTURE – Despite increasing industrialization, agriculture remains the most important economic activity, employing over 45 per cent of the labour force and contributing to 17 per cent of the country's exports. Agricultural output has been increased as a result of land reclamation programmes and the introduction of more efficient methods, e.g. the change from basin to perennial irrigation which yields two to three crops per year instead of one, the pivotal sprinkling irrigation system which uses water more efficiently, and the increasing mechanization and use of fertilizers. Egypt is still a net importer of foodstuffs, especially grain, and a food security programme has been set up with the aim of achieving self-sufficiency through the use of more advanced technology. Estimates suggest that an additional three million acres of land could be reclaimed by the end of the century.

The main cash crop is cotton, of which Egypt is one of the world's main producers. Other important summer crops are maize, rice and sugar cane. Important winter crops are wheat and beans. Citrus fruit and other fruits and vegetables are also grown.

ENERGY – With its considerable reserves of petroleum and natural gas in Sinai, the Nile delta and the Western Desert, and the hydro-electric power produced by the Aswan and High Dams, Egypt is self-sufficient in energy. Electricity has been provided to almost all of the country and there are plans to extend the natural gas network to all major cities.

INDUSTRY – The production of petroleum provides Egypt with its major export (60–65 per cent of total exports), and supports a growing refining industry. Steel production is another important heavy industry. The major manufacturing industries are in food processing, motor cars and electrical goods, chemical products and yarns and textiles.

FINANCE

	1986–7	1987–8
Estimated revenue	£E12.4m	£E14.2m
Total expenditure	19.9m	21.7m

TRADE

The main imports are wheat and flour, wood and trucks. The main exports are crude petroleum, cotton, cotton yarn, oranges, rice and cotton textiles.

	1986–7
Imports	£E7.8m
Exports	2.6m

Trade with UK	1990	1991
Imports from UK	£290,262,000	£282,928,000
Exports to UK	145,323,000	136,406,000

COMMUNICATIONS

The road and rail networks link the Nile valley and delta with the main development areas to east and west of the river.

The Suez Canal was re-opened in 1975 and a two-stage development project begun to widen and deepen the canal to allow the passage of larger shipping and to permit two-way traffic. Port Said and Suez have been reconstructed and the port of Alexandria is being improved.

EQUATORIAL GUINEA

República de Guinea Ecuatorial

Equatorial Guinea (formerly Spanish Guinea) consists of the island of Biogo (formerly Macias Nguema), in the Bight of Biafra about 20 miles from the west coast of Africa, Pagalu Island (formerly Annobon) in the Gulf of Guinea, the Corisco Islands (Corisco, Elobey Grande and Elobey Chico) and Rio Muni, a mainland area between Cameroon and Gabon. It has a total area of 10,830 sq. miles (28,051 sq. km), and a population (UN estimate 1990) of 348,000.

CAPITAL – ΨMalabo on the island of Bioco, population (1983 estimate) 30,418. ΨBata is the principal town and port of Rio Muni.

CURRENCY – Franc CFA of 100 centimes.

FLAG – Three horizontal bands, green over white over red; blue triangle next staff; coat of arms in centre of white band.

NATIONAL DAY – 12 October.

GOVERNMENT

Formerly colonies of Spain, the territories now forming the Republic of Equatorial Guinea were constituted as two provinces of Metropolitan Spain in 1959, became autonomous in 1963 and fully independent in 1968. Serious disorders in Rio Muni early in 1969 caused many of the Spanish community to leave.

In August 1979, President Macias was deposed by a revolutionary military council headed by his nephew, Col. T. Obiang Nguema. The first parliamentary elections since 1968 were held in August 1983, under a new constitution approved by a referendum in August 1982. The most recent elections to the 41-member National Assembly took place in July 1988. All candidates were nominated by the President and elected unopposed for a five-year term.

The introduction of a multi-party political system was approved by a referendum in November 1991, but at present only the ruling Equatorial Guinea Democratic Party (PDGE) operates legally inside the country. The President has appointed a transitional government to rule until multi-party elections are held.

President of the Supreme Military Council and Minister of Defence, Brig.-Gen. Teodoro Obiang Nguema Mbasogo, *took office*, Aug. 1979, *re-elected* June 1989.

MINISTERS as at August 1992

Prime Minister, Silvestre Siale Bileka.
Deputy PM, Education, Youth and Sport, Isidoro Eyi Monsuy Andeme.
Minister of State, Minister Secretary-General to the Presidency, Casto Nvono Akele.
Ministers of State at the Presidency, Eloy Elo Nve Mbengono; Alejandro Evuna Asangono.
Minister Deputy Secretary-General to the Presidency, Martin Nka Esono Nsing.
Minister of State, Economy, Trade and Planning, Marcelino Nguemo Ongueme.
Justice and Religion, Mariano Nsue Nguema.
Public Works, Urban Development and Transport, Alejandro Envoro Ovono.
Agriculture, Fishing and Forestry, Angel Alogo Nchama.
Industry and Energy, Severino Obiang Bengono.
Labour and Social Development, Juan Balboa Boneke.
Ministers Delegate:
Economic and Financial Affairs, vacant.
Mines and Hydrocarbons, Juan Olo Mba Nseng.
Culture, Tourism and Handicrafts, Leandro Mbomio Nsue.
Foreign Affairs and Francophone Affairs, Benjamin Mba Ekua Miko.
National Defence, Maj. Melanio Ebendeng Nsomo.
Territorial Administration and Communications, Segundo Munoz Italo.
Health, Alejandro Masoko Bengono.
Women's Development, Purificaçion Angue Ondo.

EMBASSY OF THE REPUBLIC OF EQUATORIAL GUINEA
6 Rue Alfred de Vigny, 75008, Paris
Tel: Paris 47664433

Ambassador Extraordinary and Plenipotentiary, new appointment awaited.

BRITISH AMBASSADOR (resident in Yaoundé, Cameroon).

BRITISH CONSULATE
World Bank Compound, Apartado 801, Malabo
Tel: Malabo 2400
Honorary Consul, vacant.

ECONOMY

The chief products are cocoa, coffee and wood (which is exported almost entirely from Rio Muni). Production has declined and except for cocoa, there is little commercial agriculture and the economy is now heavily dependent on outside aid, principally from Spain. Equatorial Guinea entered the 'Franc zone' in 1985.

TRADE WITH UK

	1990	1991
Imports from UK	£1,159,000	£1,967,000
Exports to UK	10,000	33,000

ESTONIA

The Republic of Estonia

GEOGRAPHY

The Republic of Estonia is situated in northern Europe on the eastern coast of the Baltic Sea. To the north, across the Gulf of Finland, lies Finland, to the east the Russian Federation, and to the south Latvia. Estonia lies between 57°30′ and 59°49′N., and between 21°46′ and 28°13′E.
AREA – 45,125 square km (17,420 square miles).
TOPOGRAPHY – The country is relatively flat. It includes 1,500 islands in the Baltic Sea and the Gulf of Riga. Forests cover roughly 20 per cent of the country, which also has many lakes.
CLIMATE – Mild and maritime.

POPULATION

The total population of Estonia is 1,576,000.
ETHNIC GROUPS – 61.5 per cent Estonian, 30.3 per cent Russian, 3.1 per cent Ukrainian, 1.8 per cent Belarussian.
LANGUAGES – 61.5 per cent have Estonian as their first language, and 30.3 per cent Russian. Since regaining its independence, Estonia has introduced stringent language qualifications, making it necessary to be proficient in Estonian to gain Estonian citizenship.
RELIGIONS – Lutheran (majority), Russian Orthodox, Baptist.
MAJOR CITIES – Tallinn (population 480,000), Tartu, Pärnu, Narva.

CAPITAL – Tallinn.
FLAG – Three horizontal stripes of blue, black, white.
NATIONAL ANTHEM – Pacius (My Fatherland).
NATIONAL DAY – 24 February (Independence Day).
CURRENCY – Kroon.
TIME ZONE – 2 hours ahead of GMT.

HISTORY

Estonia, a former province of the Russian Empire, declared its independence from Russia on 24 February 1918. A war of independence was fought against the German army until the end of the First World War in November 1918, and then against Soviet forces until the peace treaty of Tartu was signed on 2 February 1920. By this treaty the Soviet Union recognized Estonia's independence.

The Soviet Union annexed Estonia in 1940 under the terms of the Molotov-Ribbentrop pact with Germany. Estonia was invaded and occupied when Germany invaded the Soviet Union during the Second World War. In 1944 the Soviet Union recaptured the country from Germany and confirmed its annexation, though this was never accepted as legal by most states.

Due to mounting public pressure, the Estonian Supreme Soviet in November 1989 declared the republic to be sovereign and its 1940 annexation by the Soviet Union to be illegal. In February 1990 the leading role of the Communist Party was abolished, and following multi-party elections in March 1990 the Supreme Soviet inaugurated a period of transition to independence. Full independence was supported by an overwhelming majority in a referendum held in March 1991 and was declared on 20 August 1991. The State Council of the Soviet Union recognized the independence of Estonia on 10 September 1991.

GOVERNMENT

Estonians voted in a referendum in June 1992 to adopt a new constitution under which Estonia is a parliamentary democracy. Elections to the legislative, the *Riigikogu*, are held every four years. The President is elected by the Riigikogu.
EXECUTIVE – Executive authority is vested in a Prime Minister and government formed from a governing majority within the parliament.
LEGISLATURE – Legislative power is exercised by the Riigikogu.

CURRENT POLITICAL SITUATION
The situation in Estonia remains unsettled. The first post-independence government led by Edgar Savisaar resigned on 23 January 1992 because, faced with enormous economic problems, it no longer had the support of a majority in parliament. Legislative elections have been scheduled for autumn 1992. In the mean time, a 16-member government of technocrats and civil servants led by Tiit Vähi has been appointed by the Riigikogu.

HEAD OF STATE
President, Arnold Ruutel, *elected* March 1990

GOVERNMENT
Prime Minister, Tiit Vähi

MEMBERSHIP OF INTERNATIONAL ORGANIZATIONS – UN, CSCE, EBRD, IBRD, IMF, IMO, UNESCO.

EMBASSY OF THE REPUBLIC OF ESTONIA
18 Chepstow Villas, London W11 2RB
Tel 071-229 6700
Ambassador Extraordinary and Plenipotentiary, no accreditation as yet.

BRITISH EMBASSY
Tallinn
Ambassador Extraordinary and Plenipotentiary, His Excellency Brian Low, *apptd* 1991.

DEFENCE

Since its independence from the Soviet Union, Estonia has begun to form a small army and national guard, and border guard units.

ECONOMY

Estonia's economic position is one of extreme turmoil caused by attempts to move towards a market economy and the collapse of the centralized Soviet economic system. Imports of raw materials and foodstuffs from the former Soviet Union, on which Estonia was dependent, are no longer guaranteed.

PRIMARY RESOURCES – Agriculture and dairy-farming are a major sector of the Estonian economy, the main products being rye, oats, barley, flax, potatoes, butter and eggs.
INDUSTRY – Light industry is the other major area of the economy, concentrating on textiles, clothing and footwear, and food processing.
TRADE – Estonia still remains dependent on trade with the other republics of the former Soviet Union, most notably the Russian Federation.

EDUCATION

Estonia has a three-tier education system, consisting of primary level (eight years), secondary level (four years) and university level (five years).

ETHIOPIA
Ityopia

AREA AND POPULATION – Ethiopia is in north-eastern Africa, bounded on the north-west by the Sudan, on the south by Kenya, on the east by Djibouti and the Republic of Somalia, and on the north-east by the Red Sea. The area is 471,778 sq. miles (1,221,900 sq. km), with a population (UN estimate 1990) of 49,240,000. About one-third are of Semitic origin (Amharas and Tigrayans) and the remainder mainly Oromos (about 40 per cent of the population), Somalis and Afar.

Ethiopia has a large central plateau (average height, 6,000–7,000 ft) which rises to nearly 15,000 ft at Ras Dashan in the north. The plateau drops to the Nile basin in the west and the Red Sea in the east. To the north (Eritrea) and east (Ogaden) the land is mostly desert. The chief river is the Blue Nile, issuing from Lake Tana; the Atbara and many other tributaries of the Nile also rise in the Ethiopian highlands.
RELIGION – Those of Semitic origin (Amharas and Tigrayans), and many of the Oromos, are Christians of the Ethiopian Orthodox Church, which was formerly led by the head of the Coptic Church, the Patriarch at Alexandria. Since 1959, however, the Ethiopian Church has been autocephalous; the most recent Patriarch, Abuna Merkurios, who was enthroned in Sept. 1988, retired due to ill health in 1991. A successor has not yet been appointed. The Afar people, who inhabit lowland Eritrea, Wollo, Hararghe and Bale provinces, and the Somalis, in the south-east, are Muslim. The Falashas, adherents of Judaism, formerly found principally in Gonder and Tigray provinces, were airlifted to Israel in 1984–5 and 1991.

CAPITAL – Addis Ababa (population, 1989 estimate, 1,739,130), also capital of the province of Shoa; Asmara (population 275,000) is the capital of Eritrea. Dire Dawa is the most important commercial centre after Addis Ababa and Asmara, ΨMassawa and ΨAssab are the two main ports. There are ancient architectural remains at Aksum, Gondar, Lalibela and elsewhere.
CURRENCY – Ethiopian birr (EB) of 100 cents.
FLAG – Three horizontal bands: green, yellow, red.
NATIONAL ANTHEM – Ityopya, Ityopya Kidemi.
NATIONAL DAY – Under review.

HISTORY

The basic Hamitic culture was heavily influenced by Semitic immigration from Arabia in the centuries about the time of Christ. Christianity was introduced in the fourth century. The empire expanded sporadically, attaining a zenith in the sixth century under the Axum rulers, but subsequently checked by Islamic expansion from the east. Modern Ethiopia dates from 1855 when Theodore succeeded in establishing supremacy over the various tribes. The last Emperor was Haile Selassie who reigned from 1930, though in exile from 1936–41 during the Italian occupation. After considerable military and civil unrest the armed forces assumed power in September 1974 and deposed the Emperor. After ten years of military rule, a Workers' Party on the Soviet model was formed in September 1984, with Mengistu Haile Mariam as General Secretary.

GOVERNMENT

The civilian government of the People's Democratic Republic of Ethiopia was established under a new constitution in Sept. 1987 with Lt.-Col. Mengistu being elected the first President. Armed insurgencies by the Eritrean People's Liberation Front (EPLF) and the Ethiopian People's Revolutionary Democratic Front (EPRDF), originating in Tigray, brought down Mengistu's government in May 1991. At a national conference, held in July 1991, an 81-member Transitional Council was formed, comprising the EPRDF and a number of other opposition groups. The transitional government, headed by Meles Zenawi, drew up plans dividing Ethiopia into 14 regions based as closely as possible on the 13 different ethnic groups that were recognized. Elections to the 13 regional councils were held on 21 June 1992, with these councils having a great amount of power devolved to them. The central government in Addis Ababa remains in control of foreign affairs, defence and economic policy, and continues to prepare for national elections.

ERITREA

Eritrea, formerly an Italian colony, was administered by Great Britain from the end of the Second World War until 15 September 1952, when it was federated with Ethiopia. It was incorporated as a province of Ethiopia in 1962. An armed campaign for independence started in 1962 and gathered momentum throughout the 1970s and 1980s. By May 1991, the EPLF had established complete control of the territory and created their own administration. The central government has granted Eritrea a referendum on independence and negotiated an agreement for access to the sea via the port of Assab. The referendum is due to take place in April 1993.

President, Meles Zenawi.

CABINET as at June 1992

Prime Minister, Tamirat Layne.
Justice, Shiferaw Wolde Michael.
Information, Dima Nego.
Foreign Affairs, Seyoum Mesfin.
Health, Dr Adanech Kidane Mariam.
Education, Ibsa Gutema.
Industry, Bekele Tadessa.
Interior, Kuma Demeksa.
Mines and Energy, Isedin Ali.
Commerce, Ahmed Hussen.
State Farms, Hassan Abdella.
Defence, Seye Abraha.
Agriculture and Environmental Protection, Zegeye Asfaw.
Housing and Construction, Aragaw Tiruneh.
Culture and Sports, Lieule Selassie Timamo.
Labour and Social Affairs, Dr Legaso Gidada.
Transport, Belachaw Mekbib.
Finance, vacant.

EMBASSY OF ETHIOPIA
17 Prince's Gate, London SW7 1PZ
Tel 071-589 7212

Ambassador Extraordinary and Plenipotentiary, His Excellency Dr Solomon Gidada (1992).

BRITISH EMBASSY
Fikre Mariam Abatechan Street (PO Box 858), Addis Ababa
Tel: Addis Ababa 612354

Ambassador Extraordinary and Plenipotentiary, His Excellency Michael John Carlisle Glaze, CMG (1990).

BRITISH COUNCIL REPRESENTATIVE, B. Nightingale, Artistic Building, Adwa Avenue (PO Box 1043), Addis Ababa. There is also a library in *Asmara*.

ECONOMY

The principal pursuit is agriculture, which accounts for approximately 40 per cent of GDP, 85 per cent of exports and 80 per cent of total employment. Land was nationalized in 1975 and tenants given rights of use to the land they had tilled; large private holdings became state farms. The major food crops are teff, maize, barley, sorghum, wheat, pulses and oil seeds. Coffee, the principal export crop, generates over 50 per cent of the country's export earnings.

Famine conditions, which attracted world attention in 1984-5, again prevail in 1992. As before, the situation has been exacerbated by guerrilla activity and the recent civil war.

Manufacturing industry accounts for less than 9 per cent of GDP and is heavily dependent on agriculture. Ethiopia's known, but as yet largely unexploited, natural resources include gold, platinum, copper and potash. Traces of oil and natural gas have been found.

FINANCE

	1987-8
Revenue	US$1,709.5m
Expenditure	2,226.4m

TRADE

The chief imports by value are machinery and transport equipment, manufactured goods and chemicals (from UK); the principal exports by value being coffee, oil seeds, hides and skins, and pulses.

	1987-8
Total Imports	US$1,083.6m
Total Exports	393.7m

Trade with UK	1990	1991
Imports from UK	£41,403,000	£29,773,000
Exports to UK	19,465,000	14,660,000

COMMUNICATIONS

With the aid of loans from the IBRD, China and the African Development Bank, a network of roads has been built in rural areas and link the major cities with each other, and with the Sudanese and Kenyan borders and the Red Sea coast. Transport links suffered during the secessionist wars and under the heavy burden of famine relief traffic.

There is a railway link from Addis Ababa to Djibouti although this has been vulnerable to guerrilla activity. The narrow gauge line in Eritrea has been closed by conflict. Ethiopian Airlines maintains regular services from Addis Ababa to many provincial towns. External services are operated throughout Africa and to Europe.

DEFENCE

Ethiopia's considerable military forces (over 300,000 men) failed to contain the rebel forces and were disbanded by the post-Mengistu government. The EPRDF forces, numbering some 100,000 became the national army.

EDUCATION

Elementary education is provided without religious discrimination by Government schools in the main centres of population; there are also Mission schools, and cadet-schools for the Army, Navy, Air Force and Police. Government secondary schools are found mainly in Addis Ababa, but also in most of the provincial capitals. The National University (founded 1961) co-ordinates the institutions of higher education (University College, Engineering, Building and Theological Colleges in Addis Ababa, and Public Health Centre in Gondar, etc.). There are separate universities at Alemaya (agricultural) and Asmara (Eritrea).

Amharic was the official language of instruction, with English as the first foreign language and main language of instruction from secondary level upwards. Arabic is taught in Koran Schools; and Ge'ez (the ancient Ethiopic) in Christian Church Schools, which abound. Language policy is now under review by the post-Mengistu government.

FIJI

Matanitu Ko Viti - Republic of Fiji

AREA, ETC – Fiji is made up of about 332 islands and over 500 islets (including numerous atolls and reefs) in the South Pacific Ocean, about 1,100 miles north of New Zealand. About 100 islands are permanently inhabited. The gross area of the group, which extends 300 miles from east to west, and 300 north to south, between 15° 45′ and 21° 10′ S. lat., and 176° E. and 178° W. long., is 7,055 sq. miles (18,274 sq. km). The International Date Line has been diverted to the east of the island group. The largest islands are Viti Levu and Vanua Levu. The main groups of islands are Lomaiviti, Lau and Yasawas. Most of the larger islands are mountainous with sharp peaks and crags, but also have conspicuous areas of flat land and many of the rivers have built extensive deltas. The climate is tropical, without extremes of heat, and temperatures rarely exceed 32°C and seldom fall below 15°C.

POPULATION – The population (Census 1986) was 715,373, comprising 48.6 per cent Indians, 46.2 per cent Fijians, and 5.2 per cent other races. A UN estimate (1990) gives a total figure of 764,000.

CAPITAL – ΨSuva, on the island of Viti Levu. Population (1986) 69,665.

CURRENCY – Fiji dollar (F$) of 100 cents.

FLAG – Light blue ground with Union flag in top left quarter and the shield of Fiji in the fly.

NATIONAL ANTHEM – God Bless Fiji.

NATIONAL DAY – 12 October (Fiji Day).

GOVERNMENT

Fiji was a British colony from 1874 until 10 October 1970 when it became an independent state and a member of the Commonwealth.

A coalition of the left under Dr Timoci Bavadra defeated the Alliance Party of Ratu Sir Kamisese Mara in a General Election on 12 April 1987. The new government, drawing its support mainly from the Indian population, was overthrown in a military coup on 14 May by Lt.-Col. Sitiveni

Rabuka. In the wake of the constitutional crisis an Advisory Council of 19 members was set up by the Governor-General as an interim government to consider constitutional reform.

A second coup occurred on 25 September 1987. On 7 October Rabuka declared Fiji to be a republic; the Governor-General resigned on 15 October and Fiji's Commonwealth membership lapsed. An Executive Council of Ministers, with Rabuka at its head, assumed control until 5 December when Ratu Sir Penaia Ganilau was appointed President. The President called upon Ratu Sir Kamisese Mara to form another interim administration to work for a resolution to the political crisis.

A new constitution, promulgated on 25 July 1990, established the political dominance of the minority Melanesian community within the judiciary and a bicameral parliament; an amnesty was granted to participants in the 1987 coups. Elections due to be held in 1991 were postponed until boundary changes were completed in 1992. The elections were held during the last week of May 1992, with 37 seats reserved for the Melanesian population, 27 for the Indians and six for other groups (Europeans and Chinese). The Fijian Political Party led by Rabuka formed a coalition government with the General Voters Party.

HEAD OF STATE

President, Ratu Sir Penaia Ganilau, GCMG, KCVO, KBE, DSO, *appointed* 5 Dec. 1987.

CABINET as at June 1992

Prime Minister, Minister for Home Affairs and Immigration, Maj.-Gen. Sitiveni Rabuka, OBE
Deputy Prime Minister and Minister for Foreign Affairs and Civil Aviation, Filipe Bole, CBE
Deputy Prime Minister and Minister for Fijian Affairs and Regional Development, Ratu Timoci Vesikula
Attorney-General and Minister for Justice, Apaitia Seru
Education, Miss Taufa Vakatale
Energy and Rural Electrification, Mesulame Narawa
Finance and Economic Planning, Paul Manueli, OBE
Health, Leo Smith
Housing and Urban Development, Jonetani Kaukimoce
Information, Broadcasting, Television and Telecommunication, Ilai Kuli
Infrastructure, Public Works and Maritime, Apisalome Biuvakaloloma
Labour and Industrial Relations, Militoni Leweniqila
Lands and Mineral Resources, Ratu Ovini Bokini
Primary Industries, Forestry and Co-operatives, Koresi Matatolu
Tourism, Ratu Viliame Dreunimisimisi
Trade and Commerce, Harold Powell
Women, Culture and Multi-ethnic Affairs, Jo Nacola
Youth, Employment and Sports, Ratu Inoke Kubuabola

EMBASSY OF THE REPUBLIC OF FIJI
34 Hyde Park Gate, London SW7 5BN
Tel 071-584 3661/2

Ambassador Extraordinary and Plenipotentiary, His Excellency Brig.-Gen. Ratu Epeli Nailatikau, LVO, OBE (1988).

BRITISH EMBASSY
Victoria House, 47 Gladstone Road, PO Box 1355, Suva
Tel: Suva 311033

Ambassador Extraordinary and Plenipotentiary, His Excellency Timothy David (1992).

FINANCE

	1987	1988
Public Income	F$342m	F$358m
Public Expenditure	416m	399m

ECONOMY

The economy is primarily agrarian, with about 600,000 acres under cultivation. The principal cash crop is sugar cane, which is the main export, followed by coconuts, ginger and copra. A variety of other fruit, vegetables and root crops are also grown, and self-sufficiency in rice is a major aim. Forestry, fishing and beef production are being encouraged in order to diversify the economy. The processing of agricultural, marine and timber products are the main industries, along with gold mining. A policy of tax concessions for export-oriented manufacturing has encouraged expansion of the garment industry.

Tourism is also a major factor in the economy, second only to sugar as a money-earner.

TRADE

The chief imports are foodstuffs, machinery, mineral fuels, chemicals, beverages, tobacco and manufactured articles. Chief exports are sugar, coconut oil, gold, lumber, garments, molasses, ginger and canned fish.

	1988	1989
Total Imports	F$570,700,000	F$961,870,139
Total Exports	493,800,000	598,201,244
Trade with UK	1990	1991
Imports from UK	£8,168,000	£8,268,000
Exports to UK	61,863,000	81,540,000

COMMUNICATIONS

Fiji is one of the main aerial crossroads in the Pacific, providing services to New Zealand, Australia, Tonga, Western Samoa, Vanuatu, the Solomon Islands, Kiribati, Tuvalu, New Caledonia and American Samoa.

Fiji has three ports of entry, at Suva, Lautoka and Levuka.

FINLAND

Suomen Tasavalta

AREA AND POPULATION – A country situated on the Gulfs of Finland and Bothnia, with a total area of 137,851 sq. miles (337,032 sq. km), of which 65 per cent is forest, 8 per cent cultivated land and 9 per cent lakes. The population (1990 UN estimate) is 4,986,000; population density is 16 inhabitants per square km. The population is predominantly Lutheran.

The Åland Archipelago (Ahvenanmaa), a group of small islands at the entrance to the Gulf of Bothnia, covers about 572 square miles, with a population (December 1985) of 23,600 (95.2 per cent Swedish-speaking). The islands have a semi-autonomous status.

CAPITAL – ΨHelsinki (Helsingfors), population (1987) 488,777; other towns are Tampere (Tammerfors), 169,153; ΨTurku (Åbo), 161,508; Espoo (Esbo), 156,851; Vantaa (Vanda), 143,986; ΨOulu (Uleåborg), 97,329; Lahti (Lahtis), 94,467; ΨPori (Björneborg), 78,365.
CURRENCY – Markka (Mk) of 100 penniä.
FLAG – White with blue cross.
NATIONAL DAY – 6 December (Independence Day).

GOVERNMENT

Under the Constitution there is a single Chamber (*Eduskunta*) composed of 200 members, elected by universal suffrage. The legislative power is vested in the Chamber and the President. The highest executive power is held by the President who is elected for a period of six years.

The present government came into office in April 1990,

the first government for 25 years not to include left-wing parties. The four parties in the coalition are the National Coalition Party (conservative), the Centre Party, the Swedish People's Party of Finland, and the Finnish Christian Union Party.

After much discussion and national debate, the Parliament voted by 108 to 55 to apply for membership of the European Community on 18 March 1992 and the application was presented in Brussels at the end of that month.

HEAD OF STATE

President, Dr Mauno Koivisto, *born*, 1923, *elected*, 26 January 1982, *re-elected*, 1 March 1988.

CABINET as at July 1992

Prime Minister, Esko Aho (CP).
Deputy Prime Minister, Minister of Labour and Minister at the Ministry of Finance, Ilkka Kanerva (NCP).
Foreign Affairs, Paavo Vayrynen (CP).
Social Affairs and Health, Eeva Kuuskoski (CP).
Foreign Trade, Pertti Salolainen (NCP).
Transport and Communications, Ole Norrback (SPP).
Defence, Elisabeth Rehn (SPP).
Trade and Industry, Kauko Juhantalo (CP).
Justice, Hannele Pokka (CP).
Interior, Mauri Pekkarinen (CP).
Finance, Iiro Viinanen (NCP).
Education, Riitta Uosukainen (NCP).
Cultural Affairs, Tytti Isohookana-Asunmaa (CP).
Environment, Sirpa Pietikainen (NCP).
Housing, Pirjo Rusanen, (NCP).
Development Co-operation, Toimi Kankaanniemi (FCU).
Agriculture and Forestry, Martti Pura (CP).

NCP National Coalition Party, CP Centre Party, FCU Finnish Christian Union, SPP Swedish People's Party.

FINNISH EMBASSY AND CONSULATE
38 Chesham Place, London SW1W 8HW
Tel 071-235 9531

Ambassador Extraordinary and Plenipotentiary, His Excellency Leif Blomquist (1991).
Minister Counsellor, E. Ulfstedt.
Counsellors, Dr H. Markala; A. Puura-Märkälä.
Defence Attaché, Cdr. P. Kaskeala.

BRITISH EMBASSY
Itäinen Puistotie 17, 00140 Helsinki
Tel: Helsinki 661293

Ambassador Extraordinary and Plenipotentiary, His Excellency Neil Smith, CMG (1989).
Counsellor (Commercial), N. A. Thorne.
First Secretaries, V. J. Henderson (*Head of Chancery*); R. M. F. Kelly; W. Hamilton; R. Norton.
Defence, Naval, Military and Air Attaché, Lt.-Col. F. A. B. Clement.

There are British Consular offices at *Helsinki, Jyväskylä, Kotka, Kuopio, Oulu, Pori, Tampere, Turku, Vaasa* and *Mariehamn*.

BRITISH COUNCIL REPRESENTATIVE, G. Coe, Hakaniemenkatu 2, 00530 Helsinki.

DEFENCE

By the terms of the Peace Treaty (10 February 1947) with UK and USSR, the Army is limited to a force not exceeding 34,400. The Navy is limited to a total of 10,000 tons displacement with personnel not exceeding 4,500. The Air Force, including naval air arm, is limited to 60 machines with a personnel not exceeding 3,000. Bombers or aircraft with bomb-carrying facilities are expressly forbidden. The Defence Forces contain a cadre of regular officers and NCOs, but their bulk is provided by conscripts who serve for 8–11 months. Total strength of trained and equipped reserves is over 700,000, 16,500 of whom have served in the UN peacekeeping force.

EDUCATION

Primary education (co-educational comprehensive school) is compulsory for children from 7 to 16 years, and free of charge. In the autumn of 1986, there were 678,463 in comprehensive schools and 113,117 in vocational institutions of senior level. There are 21 universities or other schools of academic level, and enrolment was (1985) 92,230.

CULTURE

There are two official languages in Finland: 93.6 per cent of the population speak Finnish as their first language, 6.2 Swedish (1986). The remaining 0.2 per cent speak other languages (mainly Lapps who number about 2,500 and live in the far north). Both Finnish and Swedish are used for administration and education; newspapers, books, plays and films appear in both languages.There is a vigorous modern literature. F. E. Sillanpää, who died in 1964, was awarded the Nobel prize for Literature in 1939. In 1988 there were 103 daily newspapers (12 Swedish).

ECONOMY

Finland is a highly industrialized country producing a wide range of capital and consumer goods. Timber and tne products of the forest-based industries remain the backbone of the economy, but the importance of the metal-working, shipbuilding and engineering industries has been growing. The textile industry is well developed and Finland's glass, ceramics and furniture industries enjoy international reputations. Other important industries are rubber, plastics, chemicals and pharmaceuticals, footwear, foodstuffs and electronic equipment. The Finnish economy has been adversely affected by declining trade with eastern Europe and the former Soviet Union.

TRADE

The principal imports are raw materials, machinery and manufactured goods. In 1988 more than half of all industrial production was exported. The value of exports was broken down as follows: paper 33.4 per cent, wood 8.2 per cent, metal and engineering products 31 per cent, basic metal industry 8.3 per cent, chemicals 9 per cent, textiles and clothing 4.6 per cent.

	1987	1988
Total Imports	Mk86,696m	Mk88,192m
Total Exports	87,564m	90,861m

Trade with UK	1990	1991
Imports from UK	£1,041,739,000	£847,671,000
Exports to UK	1,775,766,000	1,522,337,000

COMMUNICATIONS

There are 9,000 kilometres of railroad, a railway connection with Sweden and Russia, passenger boat connection with Sweden, Germany, Poland, Russia and the Baltic States. Vessels on the London to Leningrad route call at Helsinki. There are also passenger/cargo services between Britain and Helsinki, Kotka and other Finnish ports. External civil air services are maintained by most European airlines. The merchant fleet at the end of 1986 totalled 1,900,000 tons gross.

FRANCE

La République Française

AREA AND POPULATION – France extends from 42° 20′ to 51° 5′ N. lat., and from 7° 85′ E. to 4° 45′ W. long. Its area is estimated at 211,208 sq. miles (547,026 sq. km), divided into 95 departments, including the island of Corsica, in the Mediterranean off the west coast of Italy. The population, according to the 1990 census results, is 56,614,000 (Metropolitan France).

POPULATION OF THE REGIONS 1990
Names of Departments in brackets

Alsace (Bas-Rhin, Haut-Rhin)	1,624,000
Aquitaine (Dordogne, Gironde, Landes, Lot-et-Garonne, Pyrénées-Atlantiques)	2,796,000
Auvergne (Allier, Cantal, Haute-Loire, Puy-de-Dôme)	1,321,000
Basse-Normandie (Calvados, Manche, Orne)	1,391,000
Bourgogne (Côte-d'Or, Nièvre, Saône-et-Loire, Yonne)	1,609,000
Bretagne (Côtes-du-Nord, Finistère, Ille-et-Vilaine, Morbihan)	2,796,000
Centre (Cher, Eure-et-Loir, Indre, Indre-et-Loire, Loir-et-Cher, Loiret)	2,371,000
Champagne-Ardenne (Ardennes, Aube, Marne, Haute-Marne)	1,348,000
Corse (Corse-du-Sud, Haute-Corse)	250,000
Franche-Comté (Doubs, Haute-Saône, Jura, Territoire-de-Belfort)	1,097,000
Haute-Normandie (Eure, Seine-Maritime)	1,737,000
Île-de-France (Essonne, Hauts-de-Seine, Seine-et-Marne, Seine-St-Denis, Val-de-Marne, Val-d'Oise, Ville de Paris, Yvelines)	10,660,000
Languedoc-Roussillon (Aude, Gard, Hérault, Lozère, Pyrénées-Orientales)	2,115,000
Limousin (Corrèze, Creuse, Haute-Vienne)	723,000
Lorraine (Meurthe-et-Moselle, Meuse, Moselle, Vosges)	2,306,000
Midi-Pyrénées (Ariège, Aveyron, Haute-Garonne, Gers, Lot, Hautes-Pyrénées, Tarn, Tarn-et-Garonne)	2,431,000
Nord-Pas-de-Calais (Nord, Pas-de-Calais)	3,965,000
Pays de la Loire (Loire-Atlantique, Maine-et-Loire, Mayenne, Sarthe, Vendée)	3,059,000
Picardie (Aisne, Oise, Somme)	1,811,000
Poitou-Charentes (Charente, Charente-Maritime, Deux-Sèvres, Vienne)	1,595,000
Provence-Alpes-Côte d'Azur (Alpes-de-Haute-Provence, Alpes-Maritimes, Bouches-du-Rhône, Hautes-Alpes, Var, Vaucluse)	4,258,000
Rhône-Alpes (Ain, Ardèche, Drôme, Isère, Loire, Rhône, Savoie, Haute-Savoie)	5,351,000

CAPITAL – Paris, on the Seine. Population (census 1990) 2,152,000 (town); 9,060,000 (incl. suburbs).
The largest conurbations (populations 1990) are ΨMarseilles (1,087,000); Lyon (1,262,000); Toulouse (608,000); Lille (950,000) and ΨBordeaux (685,000).
The chief towns of Corsica are ΨAjaccio (55,279) and ΨBastia (45,081).

CURRENCY – French franc of 100 centimes.

FLAG – The tricolour, three vertical bands, blue, white, red (blue next to flagstaff).

NATIONAL ANTHEM – La Marseillaise.

NATIONAL DAY – 14 July (Bastille Day 1789).

HISTORY

There are dolmens and menhirs in Brittany, prehistoric remains and cave drawings in Dordogne and Ariège, and throughout France various megalithic monuments erected by primitive tribes, predecessors of Iberian invaders from Spain (now represented by the Basques), Ligurians from northern Italy and Celts or Gauls from the valley of the Danube. Julius Caesar found Gaul 'divided into three parts' and described three political groups; Aquitanians south of the Garonne, Celts between the Garonne and the Seine and Marne, and Belgae from the Seine to the Rhine. Roman remains are plentiful throughout France in the form of aqueducts, arenas, triumphal arches, etc., and the celebrated Norman and Gothic Cathedrals, including Notre Dame in Paris, and those of Chartres, Reims, Amiens (where Peter the Hermit preached the First Crusade for the recovery of the Holy Sepulchre), Bourges, Beauvais, Rouen, etc., have survived invasions and bombardments with only partial damage, and many of the Renaissance and the 17th- and 18th-century chateaux survived the French Revolution.

LANGUAGE AND LITERATURE

French is the official language. The work of the French Academy, founded by Richelieu in 1635, has established *le bon usage*, equivalent to 'The Queen's English' in Great Britain. French authors have been awarded the Nobel Prize for Literature on twelve occasions, including R. F. A. Sully-Prudhomme (1901), Anatole France (1921), André Gide (1947), François Mauriac (1952), Albert Camus (1957), Jean Paul Sartre (1964) and Claude Simon (1985).

GOVERNMENT

The legislature consists of the National Assembly of 577 deputies (555 for Metropolitan France and 22 for the overseas departments and territories) and the Senate composed of 321 Senators (298 for Metropolitan France, 13 for the overseas departments and territories and 10 for French dependencies). The normal session of Parliament is confined to five and a half months each year and it may also meet in extraordinary

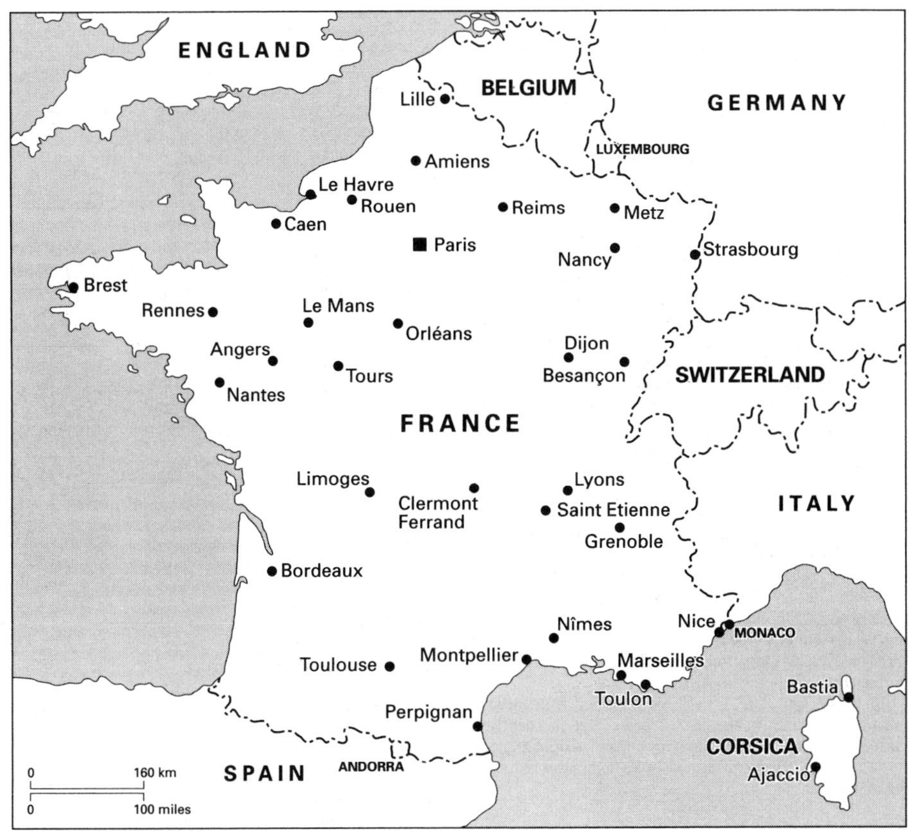

session for 12 days at the request of the Prime Minister or a majority of the Assembly.

The Prime Minister is appointed by the President, as is the Cabinet on the Prime Minister's recommendation. They are responsible to Parliament, but as the executive is constitutionally separate from the legislature Ministers may not sit in Parliament.

A Constitutional Council is responsible for supervising all elections and referenda and must be consulted on all constitutional matters and before the President of the Republic assumes emergency powers.

HEAD OF STATE

President of the French Republic, François Mitterrand, *elected* 10 May 1981, *re-elected* 8 May 1988.

COUNCIL OF MINISTERS as at 3 June 1992

Prime Minister, Pierre Bérégovoy.
National Education and Culture, Jack Lang.
Foreign Affairs, Roland Dumas.
Civil Service and Reforms of the Administration, Michel Delebarre.
Justice, Michel Vauzelle.
Interior, Public Security, Paul Quiles.
Defence, Pierre Joxe.
Economy and Finance, Michel Sapin.
Budget, Michel Charasse.
Environment, Ségolène Royal.
Public Works, Transport and Housing, Jean-Louis Bianco.
Industry and Foreign Trade, Dominique Strauss-Kahn.
Labour, Employment and Vocational Training, Martine Aubry.
Agriculture and Forestry, Louis Mermaz.
Social Affairs and Integration, René Teulade.
Health and Humanitarian Policy, Bernard Kouchner.
Overseas Departments and Territories, Louis Le Peusec.
Research and Space, Hubert Curien.
Postal Services and Telecommunications, Emile Zuccarelli.
Youth and Sport, Frédérique Bredin.

FRENCH EMBASSY
58 Knightsbridge, London SW1X 7JT
Tel 071-235 8080

Ambassador Extraordinary and Plenipotentiary, His Excellency Bernard Dorin (1991).

BRITISH EMBASSY
35 rue du Faubourg St Honoré, 75383 Paris Cedex 08
Tel: Paris 42 66 91 42

Ambassador Extraordinary and Plenipotentiary, His Excellency Sir Ewen Alastair John Fergusson, KCMG (1987).
Minister, T. R. Young.
Defence and Air Attaché, Air Cdre C. R. Adams, AFC.
Counsellor and Head of Chancery, J. M. Macgregor.
Consul-General, M. Hunt.
Counsellors: B. P. Noble; P. A. McDermott (*Management*); Dr R. A. Pullen (*Technology*); R. D. Wilkinson (*Information*); C. D. Crabbie (*Financial and EC*); R. A. Kelly, CMG (*Trade Promotion and Investment*).

British Consular Offices. There are British Consulates-General in Metropolitan France at *Bordeaux, Lille, Lyon, Marseille* and *Paris*.

British Council Representative, D. Ricks, OBE, 9 rue de Constantine, 75007 Paris.

Franco-British Chamber of Commerce, 8 rue Cimarosa, 75116 Paris. *President*, R. Lyon. *Vice-President*, B. Cordery, OBE.

DEFENCE

The total armed forces in 1991 numbered 453,100 (228,800 conscripts). Strategic nuclear forces consist of 64 submarine-launched ballistic missiles on four nuclear-powered submarines, 18 land-based intermediate range ballistic missiles, and 25 nuclear-capable Mirage IVP aircraft with medium-range nuclear air-to-surface missiles.

The Army has a strength of 280,300 (173,500 conscripts) with some 40 Pluton short-range nuclear missile launchers, 1,350 main battle tanks, 4,500 armoured personnel carriers and armoured infantry fighting vehicles, 1,403 artillery pieces and 704 helicopters.

The Navy has a strength of 65,300 (19,000 conscripts) with some 13 submarines, two aircraft carriers and 39 other principal surface combatant vessels, 156 combat aircraft and 52 armed helicopters.

The Air Force has a strength of 92,900 (34,000 conscripts) and some 845 combat aircraft. Conscripts in all services usually serve 12 months. France deploys some 75,600 armed forces personnel abroad; 43,700 in Germany; 23,100 in French Overseas Departments and Territories; and 8,800 in former French colonies in Africa.

In April 1992 the French government announced a planned reduction in the armed forces over the next five years including a reduction in Army personnel from 280,000 to 220,000 and an overall armed forces manpower reduction of 25 per cent.

EDUCATION

The educational system is highly centralized and is administered by the Ministry of National Education. Local administration comprises 25 Territorial Academies, with inspecting staff for all grades, and Departmental Councils presided over by the *Préfet*, and charged especially with primary education.

Primary and secondary education are compulsory, free and secular, the school age being from 6 to 16. Schools may be single-sex or co-educational. Primary education is given in nursery schools, primary schools and *collèges d'enseignement général* (four-year secondary modern course); secondary education in *collèges d'enseignement technique, collèges d'enseignement secondaire* and *lycées* (seven-year course leading to one of the five *baccalauréats*). Special schools are numerous.

There are many *Grandes Ecoles* in France which award diplomas in many subjects not taught at university, especially applied science and engineering. Most of these are state institutions but have a competitive system of entry, unlike the universities. There are universities in twenty-four towns in France, two or three in some major provincial towns, and thirteen in Paris and the immediate surrounding district.

In 1989–90 enrolment in pre-school and primary schools was 6,699,116; in secondary schools 5,390,646, and in post-secondary education 1,421,408.

COMMUNICATIONS

Roads – The length of roads in use at the end of 1989 was 805,000 km of which 7,000 km were motorways.

Railways – The system of railroads in France is very extensive. The length of lines open for traffic at the end of 1989 was 34,322 km, of which 12,430 km were electrified.

Shipping – The French mercantile marine consisted in 1991 of 220 ships of over 100 tons gross, of which 29 were passenger vessels (228,000 tons gross), 56 tankers (2,084,000 tons gross) and 135 cargo vessels (1,407,000 tons gross). The principal rivers of France are the Seine, Loire, Garonne, and Rhône.

ECONOMY

Budget – Government expenditure (ordinary and capital) by function in the 1991 general Budget, was:

	F million
Agriculture and Forestry	38,367
Co-operation and Development	7,865
Culture and Communications	12,105
Defence	238,458
Economy, Finance and Budget	309,212
Education	248,320
Equipment, Housing, Transport and the Sea	125,344
Foreign Affairs	13,074
Industry, Local Planning and Tourism	21,130
Interior	67,933
Justice	18,177
Labour and Employment	67,669
Overseas Departments	2,185
Prime Ministerial	5,526
Research and Technology	25,833
Solidarity, Health, Social Protection	38,879
Veterans	27,232
Youth and Sports	2,576
Other	2,209
Total	1,272,094

Agriculture – Approximately 31,338,000 hectares of land is used for agricultural purposes, 13,944,000 hectares is forested. Production in 1989 included wheat, 31,800,000 tonnes; maize, 12,900,000 tonnes; barley, 9,800,000 tonnes; and potatoes 5,800,000 tonnes.

The vine is extensively cultivated, regions famous for their wines including Bordeaux, Burgundy and Champagne. Production of wine in 1989 was 5,900,000 tonnes. Cognac, liqueurs and cider are also important products.

Energy – France produces its own oil, the greater part coming from fields in the Landes area, but is a net importer of crude oil, for processing by its important oil-refining industry. Natural gas is produced in the foothills of the Pyrenees. Electricity production was 407,000m kW in 1989.

Industry – France's heavy industries include oil-refining and the production of iron and steel, and aluminium. In 1989 production of steel was 19,300,000 tonnes and cement 25,900,000 tonnes. Other important industries produce chemicals, tyres, aluminium, textiles, paper products and processed food. Engineering products include motor vehicles, and television and radio sets.

Trade

The principal imports are raw materials for the heavy and manufacturing industries (e.g. oil, minerals, chemicals), machinery and precision instruments, agricultural products and vehicles. Raw materials, semi-manufactured and manufactured goods are also France's principal exports. Other member countries of the EC are France's main trading partners.

Trade	1989	1990
Imports	F1,408,000m	F1,469,400m
Exports	1,425,000m	1,467,000m

Trade with UK	1990	1991
Imports from UK	£10,885,803,000	£11,591,139,000
Exports to UK	11,758,481,000	11,066,081,000

OVERSEAS DEPARTMENTS

Legislation passed in December 1982 by the French Parliament granted greater powers of self-government to four of the five overseas departments, French Guiana, Guadeloupe, Martinique and Réunion. These former colonies had enjoyed departmental status since 1947 and the status of regions of France since 1974. Their directly-elected Assemblies operate in parallel with the existing, indirectly constituted Regional Councils. The French government is represented by a Commissioner (a Prefect in French Guiana).

French Guiana – Situated on the north-eastern coast of South America, French Guiana is flanked by Suriname on the west and by Brazil on the south and east. Area, 34,749 sq. miles (90,000 sq. km). Population (1990) 114,900. Capital, ΨCayenne (41,000). Under the administration of French Guiana is a group of islands (St Joseph, Ile Royal and Ile du Diable), known as Iles du Salut. On Devil's Isle, Captain Dreyfus was imprisoned from 1894 to 1899.

Prefect, J.-P. Lacroix.

Guadeloupe – A number of islands in the Leeward Islands group of the West Indies, consisting of the two main islands of Guadeloupe (or Basse-Terre) and Grande-Terre, with the adjacent islands of Marie-Galante, La Désirade and Îles des Saintes, and the islands of St Martin and St Barthélemy over 150 miles to the north-west. Area, 687 sq. miles (1,779 sq. km). Population (1990) 386,600. Capital ΨBasse Terre (14,000) in Guadeloupe. Other towns are ΨPointe à Pitre (26,000) in Grande-Terre and ΨGrand Bourg (6,611) in Marie Galante.

Commissioner, J-P. Proust.

Martinique – An island situated in the Windward Islands group of the West Indies, between Dominica in the north and St Lucia in the south. Area, 425 sq. miles (1,102 sq. km). Population (1990) 359,800. Capital ΨFort de France (100,576). Other towns are ΨTrinité (11,214) and ΨMarin (6,104).

Commissioner, J.-C. Roure.

Réunion – Réunion, which became a French possession in 1638, lies in the Indian Ocean, about 569 miles east of Madagascar and 110 miles south-west of Mauritius. Area, 969 sq. miles (2,510 sq. km). Population (1990 estimate) 598,000. Capital, St Denis (122,000).

Also lying in the Indian Ocean adjacent to Madagascar are the smaller, uninhabited islands of Bassas da India, Europa, Îles Glorieuses, Juan de Nova and Tromelin, which are administered from Réunion.

Commissioner, D. Constantin.

TERRITORIAL COLLECTIVITÉS

Mayotte – Area, 144 sq. miles (372 sq. km). Population (1987 estimate) 67,000. Capital, Mamoundzou (12,000). Part of the Comoros Islands group, Mayotte remained a French dependency when the other three islands became independent as the Comoros Republic in 1975. Since 1976 the island has been a *collectivité territoriale*, an intermediate status between Overseas Department and Overseas Territory.

Commissioner, A. Khider.

St Pierre and Miquelon – Area 93 sq. miles (242 sq. km). Population (1990) 6,300. Two small groups of islands off the coast of Newfoundland. Became a *collectivité territoriale* in June 1985.

Commissioner, J.-P. Marquie.

OVERSEAS TERRITORIES

French Polynesia – Five archipelagos in the south Pacific, comprising the Society Islands (Windward Islands group includes Tahiti, Moorea, Makatea, Mehetia, Tetiaoroa, Tubuai Manu, etc; Leeward Islands group includes Huahine, Raiatea, Tahaa, Bora-Bora, Maupiti, etc.), the Tuamotu Islands (Rangiroa, Hao, Turéia, etc.), the Gambier Islands (Mangareva, etc.), the Tubuai Islands (Rimatara, Rurutu, Tubuai, Raivavae, Rapa, etc.) and the Marquesas Islands (Nuku-Hiva, Hiva-Oa, Fatu-Hiva, Tahuata, Ua Huka, etc.). Area, 1,544 sq. miles (4,000 sq. km). Population (1990 UN estimate) 206,000. Capital, ΨPapeete (24,200) in Tahiti. Economy based on tourism and exports of copra, coffee, vanilla, citrus fruits and cultured pearls.

High Commissioner, J. Montpezat.

New Caledonia – A large island in the western Pacific, 700 miles east of Queensland. Dependencies are the Isles of Pines, the Loyalty Islands (Mahé, Lifou, Urea, etc.), the Bélep Archipelago, the Chesterfield Islands, the Huon Islands and Walpole. New Caledonia was discovered in 1774 and annexed by France in 1854; from 1871 to 1896 it was a convict settlement. A referendum in 1987 on the question of independence for New Caledonia was boycotted by the indigenous Kanaks, and New Caledonia therefore voted to remain French. However, a new independence referendum has been promised for 1998. Area, 7,358 sq. miles (19,058 sq. km). Population (1990 UN estimate) 167,000. Capital Ψ Noumea (65,000). It is one of the world's largest producers of nickel.

High Commissioner, B. Grasset.

Southern and Antarctic Territories – Created in 1955 from the former Réunion dependencies, the territory comprises the islands of Amsterdam (25 sq. miles) and St Paul (2.7 sq. miles), the Kerguelen Islands (2,700 sq. miles) and Crozet Islands (116 sq. miles) archipelagos and Adélie Land (116,800 sq. miles) in the Antarctic continent. The only population are members of staff of the scientific stations.

Wallis and Futuna Islands – Two groups of islands (the Wallis Archipelago and the Îles de Hooru) in the central Pacific, north-east of Fiji. Area, 106 sq. miles (274 sq. km). Population (1990 census) 14,000. Capital, Mata-Utu on Uvea, the main island of the Wallis group.

THE FRENCH COMMUNITY

The Constitution of the fifth French Republic promulgated on 6 Oct. 1958, envisaged the establishment of a French Community of States. A number of the former French states in Africa have seceded from the Community but for all practical purposes continue to enjoy the same close links with France as those that remain formally members of the French Community. With the exception of Guinea, all the former French African colonies are closely linked to France by a series of financial, technical and economic agreements.

Francophone Countries

In the following countries French is either the official or national language or the language of instruction; where there is another national language the name of it is shown after the name of the country: Algeria (*Arabic*); Belgium (*Flemish*); Benin; Burkina; Burundi (*Kirundi*); Cambodia (*Khmer*); Cameroon (*English*); parts of Canada (Quebec, parts of Ontario and New Brunswick) (*English*); Central African Republic (*Sangho*); Chad; Congo; Côte d'Ivoire; France; Gabon; Guinea; Haiti (*Creole*); Laos (*Laotian*); Lebanon (*Arabic*); Luxembourg (*German and Letzeburgesch*); Madagascar (*Malagasy*); Mali; Morocco (*Arabic*); Mauritania (*Arabic*); Niger; Rwanda (*Kinyarwanda*); Senegal;

Switzerland (1,000,000 French-speaking); Togo; Tunisia (*Arabic*); Vietnam (*Vietnamese*); Zaire. French is also spoken in the Overseas Departments (*see* above).

GABON

République Gabonaise

Gabon lies on the Atlantic coast of Africa at the Equator and is flanked on the north by Equatorial Guinea and Cameroon, and on the east and south by the People's Republic of Congo. It has an area of 103,347 sq. miles (267,667 sq. km) and a population (UN estimate 1990) of 1,172,000

CAPITAL – ΨLibreville (251,000).
CURRENCY – Franc CFA of 100 centimes.
FLAG – Horizontal bands, green, yellow and blue.
NATIONAL ANTHEM – La Concorde.
NATIONAL DAY – 17 August.

GOVERNMENT

Gabon elected on 28 November 1958 to remain an autonomous republic within the French Community and was proclaimed fully independent on 17 August 1960. The Constitution provides for an Executive President directly elected for a seven-year term, who appoints the Council of Ministers. There is a unicameral National Assembly comprising 120 members.

Following widespread unrest, a national conference was called in March 1990 and delegates forced President Bongo to legalize opposition parties. Several rounds of multi-party elections were held in September, October and November 1990 and eventually won by the ruling Parti democratique gabonais (PDG), amid allegations of fraud. The PDG formed a coalition government with several opposition parties but retained the most important portfolios. Opposition parties left the government in June 1991 in protest at the dominating power of the PDG. Multi-party presidential elections are scheduled for December 1993.

HEAD OF STATE
President, El Hadj Omar Bongo, *assumed office*, Dec. 1967, *re-elected*, Feb. 1973, Dec. 1979 and Nov. 1986.

COUNCIL OF MINISTERS as at July 1992
Prime Minister, Casimir Oyé Mba.
Public Works, Construction and Territorial Administration, Zacharie Myboto.
Justice, Michel Anchouey.
Foreign Affairs and Co-operation, Pascaline Bongo.
Commerce, Consumption and Industry, Relations with Parliament, André Dieudonné Berre.
Town Planning, Housing, Adrien Nkoghe Essingone.
National Defence, War Veterans, Public Security and Immigration, Martin Fidèle Magnaga.
Territorial Administration and Local Collectives, Antoine Mboumbou-Miyakou.
Civil Service and Administrative Reform, Paulette Moussavou.
Finance, Budget and State Holdings, Paul Toungui.
Planning and Economic Development, Marcel Doupamby-Matoka.
Information, Posts and Telecommunications, and Government Spokesman, Jean Rémy Pendy-Bouyiki.
Mines, Hydrocarbons, Energy and Hydraulic Resources, Hervo Akendengue.
National Education, Higher Education and Scientific Research, Marc Ropivia.
Public Health, Population, Social Affairs and National Solidarity, Eugène Kakou Mayaza.
Employment, Human Resources and Professional Training, Serge Mba.
Agriculture, Livestock and Rural Economy, Emmanuel Ondo Methogo.
Water, Forests and Environment, Eugène Capito.
Youth, Sports, Culture and Popular Education, in charge of Francophone Affairs, Pierre Claver Nzeng.
Transport, Jerome Ngoua Bekalé.
State Control and Para-Public Sector Reform, Jean-Baptiste Obiang Etoughe.
Tourism, National Parks and Leisure, Pépin Mongoskodji.
Small and Medium-Sized Enterprises and Handicrafts, Victor Mapangou Moucani Mietsa.

EMBASSY OF THE REPUBLIC OF GABON
27 Elvaston Place, London SW7 5NL
Tel 071-823 9986

Ambassador Extraordinary and Plenipotentiary, His Excellency Vincent Boulé (1991).

BRITISH AMBASSADOR (resident in Zaire).

ECONOMY

Gabon's economy remains heavily dependent on oil, and, to a much lesser extent, other mineral resources, including manganese and uranium. Gabon has considerable timber reserves (particularly Okoumé) although production in this industry has stagnated in recent years.

The economy, which experienced considerable growth in real terms from the mid-1970s onwards, had since 1986 been adversely affected by the fall in oil prices. Revenue is expected to increase in the 1990s following major oil exploitation at Rabi-Kounga.

Gabon is a full member of OPEC.

TRADE WITH UK

	1990	1991
Imports from UK	£17,563,000	£30,597,000
Exports to UK	1,809,000	3,221,000

THE GAMBIA

The Republic of the Gambia

AREA, ETC – The Gambia takes its name from the Gambia River, which it straddles for over 200 miles inland from the west coast of Africa. It is a narrow strip, surrounded by the Republic of Senegal, except at the coast, lying between 13° 10′–13° 45′ N. and 13° 90′–16° 50′ W. The area is 4,361 sq. miles (11,295 sq. km), of which one-fifth is the river. The climate is typically Sahelian, with a dry season between October and May and heavy rainfall during the months of July and August (32–40 inches a year).
POPULATION – The population comprises mainly Wolof, Mandinka and Fula peoples who originally migrated there from the north and east. Population (1990 UN estimate) was 861,000.

CAPITAL – ΨBanjul. Population (1983 Census) of the island of Banjul was 44,536, and of adjacent Kombo St Mary district 102,858. Total population of Banjul/Kombo St Mary, 147,394.
CURRENCY – Dalasi (D) of 100 butut.
FLAG – Horizontal stripes of red, blue and green, separated by narrow white stripes.
NATIONAL ANTHEM – For The Gambia, Our Homeland.
NATIONAL DAY – 18 February (Independence Day).

HISTORY

The Gambia River basin was part of the region dominated in the tenth to 16th centuries by the strong Songhai and Mali kingdoms centred on the upper Niger. The first recorded Europeans to reach the Gambia River were the Portuguese in 1447. In 1588 Queen Elizabeth I gave the first charter to English merchants to trade along the river. Merchants from France, Courland (now part of Latvia) and the Netherlands also established trading posts there. The English presence was strongly challenged by the French, who were dominant further north up the coast, but in 1783 the Treaty of Versailles acknowledged English rights. In 1816, after the Napoleonic Wars, and in order to enforce abolition of the slave trade, the British stationed a garrison on a low sandy island called Banjul at the river mouth. Renamed Bathurst, this became the capital of a small British-administered colony, initially under the Governor of Sierra Leone. Negotiations with France continued sporadically until 1889 when it was agreed that the British rights along the upper river should extend 10 km on either bank. British administration was extended from the Colony to this Protectorate. The Gambia became independent within the Commonwealth on 18 February 1965, and a Republic on 24 April 1970.

The Gambia's relationship with Senegal has always been an important factor in political and economic policy. Moves towards a closer association were accelerated after an abortive coup in The Gambia in July 1981 was put down with the help of Senegalese troops. In February 1982 the Senegambia Confederation was formally instituted based on certain joint institutions and integration of policies, with each country remaining sovereign and independent. However, following disagreements it was decided to dissolve the confederation, and formal dissolution took place on 31 December 1989. A treaty of friendship and co-operation was signed with Senegal in January 1991.

GOVERNMENT

The constitution is democratic and parliamentary, with an executive President elected for five years. The House of Representatives has 35 elected members, five elected Chiefs Representatives and up to eight nominated members plus the Attorney-General (ex-officio). The Vice-President and other Ministers are appointed by the President. Parliament must be dissolved after five years. The last general elections were held in April 1992. The present state of the parties for elected members is PPP (People's Progressive Party) 25; NCP (National Convention Party) 6; Gambian People's Party 2; Independents 3.

President and Cabinet as at July 1992

President, His Excellency Alhaji Sir Dawda Kairaba Jawara, GCMG.
Vice-President and Minister of Defence, Civil Service and Women's Affairs, Hon. Alhaji Saihou Sabally.
Attorney-General and Minister of Justice, Hon. Hassan B. Jallow.
Finance and Economic Affairs, Hon. Bakary Bunja Darbo.
External Affairs, Hon. Alhaji Omar Sey.
Interior, Hon. Lamin Kiti Jabang.
Agriculture, Hon. Omar A. Jallow.
Education, Hon. Alieu Ebrima Wula Fala Badjie.
Local Government and Lands, Hon. Yaya Ceesay.
Natural Resources and the Environment, Hon. Sarjo Touray.
Health, Hon. Landing Jallow Sanko.
Works and Communications, Hon. Matthew Yaya Baldeh.
Trade, Industry, Hon. Mbemba Jatta.
Information and Tourism, Hon. Alkali James Gaye.
Youth, Sports and Culture, Hon. Bubacarr Michael Baldeh.
Chief Justice, Hon. E. Olayinka Ayoola.
Speaker, Alhaji Hon. M. B. N'Jie.

Gambia High Commission

57 Kensington Court, London W8 5DG
Tel 071-937 6316

High Commissioner, His Excellency Mohammadou N. Bobb (1992).

British High Commission

48 Atlantic Road, Fajara (PO Box 507), Banjul
Tel: Banjul 95133

High Commissioner, His Excellency Alan J. Pover, CMG (1991).

COMMUNICATIONS

There is an international airport at Yundum, 17 miles from Banjul, with scheduled services flying to other West African states and to the UK and Belgium. Banjul is the main port. Internal communication is by road and river. There is no railway system. There are two broadcasting stations and a UHF telephone service linking Banjul with the principal towns in the provinces. There is no television service.

EDUCATION

There are 24 secondary schools (eight high and 16 technical) with a total enrolment of 15,635 students. Two High Schools provide A-level education. Gambia College provides post-secondary courses in education, agriculture, public health and nursing. There are seven vocational training institutions with a total enrolment of 1,400. Higher education and advanced training courses are taken outside The Gambia, currently by over 200 students.

ECONOMY

Seventy-five per cent of the population depend for their livelihood on agriculture (40 per cent of GDP). The chief product, groundnuts, is also the most important export item, forming over 80 per cent of all domestic exports. Other crops are rice, millet, sorghum, maize and cotton. Fishing and livestock industries are being developed. Thirty per cent of the country's basic food requirements are imported. There are no significant deposits of minerals. Manufactures are limited to groundnut processing, minor metal fabrications, paints, furniture, soap and bottling. Tourism is developing quickly. The entrepôt trade through The Gambia, re-exporting imported goods to neighbouring countries, is an important element in the national economy.

Finance

	1990–1*
Recurrent Revenue	D623,000,000
Recurrent Expenditure	633,000,000

*Estimate.

Over 80 per cent of capital expenditure comes from external aid grants and loans. In 1987–8 there was a GDP growth rate of 5.4 per cent.

Trade

	1987–8	1988–9
Total imports	D844,900,000	D940,000,000
Total exports	576,600,000	311,400,000

Trade with UK	1990	1991
Imports from UK	£17,815,000	£19,141,000
Exports to UK	3,158,000	2,865,000

GERMANY

Bundesrepublik Deutschland – Federal Republic of Germany

AREA AND POPULATION – The area of the Federal Republic is approximately 138,000 square miles (357,050 km²). The estimated population of the Federal Republic (end 1990) was 79,753,000. The distribution of the population among the *Länder* at the end of 1990 was:

Baden-Württemberg	9.5m
Bavaria	11.2m
Berlin	3.4m
Brandenburg	2.6m
Bremen	0.65m
Hamburg	1.6m
Hesse	5.6m
Lower Saxony	7.2m
Mecklenburg–Western Pomerania	2.1m
North Rhine Westphalia	16.9m
Rhineland Palatinate	3.7m
Saarland	1.1m
Saxony	4.9m
Saxony-Anhalt	3.0m
Schleswig-Holstein	2.6m
Thuringia	2.5m

There were 10.4 live births per 1,000 inhabitants in the Federal Republic in 1990 (11.3 in West and 6.6 in East).

RELIGION (West Germany only) – In 1987 there were 25.2 million Protestants in the Federal Republic, 26.2 million Roman Catholics, and 1.6 million Muslims. The number of Jews was 27,711 in 1988.

CAPITAL – Berlin. By decision of the Bundestag, the seat of government is to be transferred from Bonn, Federal Germany's post-war provisional capital to the historical capital, Berlin. The move will take many years to complete. The *Bundesrat* (upper house) will remain in Bonn.

The population of the principal cities and towns in the Federal Republic in 1989–90 was:

Berlin	3,376,800	Duisberg	529,200
Hamburg	1,606,600	Dresden	515,900
Munich	1,218,300	Hanover	502,400
Cologne	940,200	Nuremberg	481,900
Frankfurt am Main	628,800	Chemnitz	309,600
		Magdeburg	290,400
Essen	620,900	Bonn	283,700
Dortmund	589,200	Rostock	254,800
Düsseldorf	570,200	Halle	234,800
Stuttgart	565,700	Erfurt	220,000
Leipzig	538,900	Potsdam	143,000
Bremen	537,600	Schwerin	130,700

CURRENCY – Deutsche Mark (DM) of 100 Pfennig.

FLAG – Horizontal bars of black, red and gold.

NATIONAL ANTHEM – Einigkeit und Recht und Freiheit (Unity and right and freedom).

NATIONAL DAY – 23 May.

HISTORY

The term 'deutsch' (German) probably began to be used in the eighth century and initially described the language spoken in the eastern part of the Frankish realm which reached its apogee in Charlemagne's reign, subsequently being divided into an eastern and western realm whose political and linguistic borders coincided. Then the term was transferred from the language to its speakers, and ultimately to the region they lived in. The first German realm was the Holy Roman Empire, established in AD 962 when Otto I of Saxony was crowned Emperor. The Empire endured until 1806, but from as early as the 12th century the achievement of a national state was prevented by territorial fragmentation into small principalities and dukedoms, the gradually increasing autonomy of their rulers weakening the central power.

The Holy Roman Empire was replaced by a loose association of the individual sovereign states known as the German Confederation, which survived until 1866 when it was dissolved and replaced by the Prussian-dominated North German Federation. Prussia, directed by its Prime Minister (later Chancellor) Otto von Bismarck, had translated its earlier economic predominance amongst the German states into political hegemony by the annexation of the duchies of Schleswig and Holstein from Denmark in 1864 and a decisive defeat of Austria in 1866 (the Seven Weeks' War) which ended Austrian influence over German politics. After the Franco-Prussian War of 1870–1 resulted in the defeat of France and the cession of Alsace and Lorraine, the south German principalities united with the northern federation to form a second German Empire, the King of Prussia being proclaimed Emperor at Versailles on 18 January 1871.

Germany's defeat in the 1914–18 War led to the abdication of the Emperor and the princes, and the country became a republic. The 1919 Treaty of Versailles returned Alsace and Lorraine to France, large areas in the east of the country were lost to the newly created state of Poland, and all German colonies placed under the administration of other countries. The world economic crisis of 1929 led to the collapse of the Weimar Republic and the subsequent rise to power of the National Socialist movement of Adolf Hitler, who became Chancellor in 1933.

After concluding a Treaty of Non-Aggression with Soviet Russia in August 1939, Germany invaded Poland (1 Sept. 1939), thus precipitating World War II, which lasted until 1945. Hitler committed suicide on 30 April 1945. On 8 May 1945, the unconditional surrender of all German forces was accepted by representatives of the Western Allied and Soviet Supreme Commanders.

THE POST WAR PERIOD

After the unconditional surrender, the Four Powers (France, UK, USA, USSR) assumed supreme authority in Germany. Policy was agreed at the Potsdam Conference (July/August 1945) between the UK, USA and USSR. Germany was divided into American, French, British and Soviet zones of occupation. Supreme authority was exercised by the Commanders-in-Chief, each in his own zone of occupation and, in matters affecting Germany as a whole, jointly through the Control Council comprising the four Commanders. Berlin was placed under the joint administration of the four occupying powers.

No central German government was permitted but several German central administrations were established as support organs for the Control Council. A peace treaty with Germany was envisaged as concluding the occupation period. However, quadripartite control failed when differences with the USSR over the implementation of the Postdam Agreement could not be resolved; and against a background of growing international tension, the USSR withdrew from the Control Council in March 1948. The rift divided Germany *de facto* into East and West.

The Federal Republic of Germany (FRG) was created out of the three Western zones in 1949 when, following general elections, a federal government took office in Bonn. A Communist government was meanwhile established in the Soviet zone (henceforth the German Democratic Republic

(GDR)). The Bonn/Paris Conventions in May 1955 terminated the occupation regime in West Germany and restored federal German autonomy subject to the reservation of Three Power rights and responsibilities relating to Berlin and to Germany as a whole, including the reunification of Germany and a peace settlement. The GDR became an ostensibly sovereign state in the same year.

In August 1961 the Soviet zone was sealed off, and the Berlin Wall was built along the zonal boundary, partitioning the western sectors of the city from the eastern.

In the course of the Brandt government's policy of Ostpolitik, normalizing relations with eastern Europe, the FRG established relations of a special kind with the GDR in 1972. This step did not constitute recognition by the FRG of the GDR, which in international law would have conceded the *de jure* division of Germany (as the GDR maintained). The FRG, however, recognized the GDR as a separate and independent state (the two states/one nation theory). The status of Berlin as a city under Four Power occupation remained unchanged, although the GDR claimed East Berlin as its capital and held West Berlin to be a separate political entity.

Soviet-initiated reform in eastern Europe during the late eighties brought unrest to the GDR. The mass exodus of its citizens via the open borders to the west culminated in the opening of the Berlin Wall in November 1989 and the collapse of Communist government there. The 'Treaty on the Final Settlement with respect to Germany', concluded between the FRG, GDR and the four former occupying powers on 12 September 1990, unified Germany with effect from 3 October 1990 as a fully sovereign state and NATO member occupying the territory of the former two Germanies and Berlin. Economic and monetary union preceded formal union on 1 July 1990. Unification is constitutionally the accession of Berlin and the five re-formed *Länder* of the GDR to the FRG which remains in being. The first government of the new Germany took office in January 1991 following the first all-German elections since 1933 on 2 December 1990. Early setbacks revealed the formidable problems of translating German unity into political, social and economic reality.

GOVERNMENT

The Basic Law provides for a President, elected for a five-year term, a lower house (*Bundestag*), with a four-year term of office, elected by direct universal suffrage, and an upper house (*Bundesrat*) composed of 68 delegates of the *Länder*, without a fixed term of office.

The results of the elections held for the Bundestag on 2 December 1990, were as follows:

	Seats
Christian Democratic Union	258
Social Democrats	239
Christian Social Union	51
Free Democrats	79
Democratic Socialists	17
The Greens/Alliance 90	8

HEAD OF STATE

Federal President, Dr Richard von Weizsäcker, *born* 1920, *elected President of West Germany* 22 May 1984, *re-elected* 23 May 1989, *sworn in*, 1 July 1989, *for five years.*

CABINET as at July 1992

Federal Chancellor, Dr Helmut Kohl (CDU).
Economy and Deputy Chancellor, Jürgen Möllemann (FDP).
Federal Chancellery, Friedrich Böhl (CDU).
Interior, Rudolf Seiters (CDU).
Foreign Affairs, Dr Klaus Kinkel (FDP).
Justice, Sabine Leutheusser-Schnarrenberger (FDP).
Finance, Dr Theodor Waigel (CSU).
Agriculture, Ignaz Kiechle (CSU).
Labour and Social Affairs, Dr Norbert Blüm (CDU).
Defence, Volker Rühe (CDU).
Health, Horst Seehofer (CSU).
Women and Youth, Dr Angela Merkel (CDU).
Family and Elderly, Hannelore Rönsch (CDU).
Transport, Dr Günther Krause (CDU).
Environment, Dr Klaus Töpfer (CDU).
Posts and Telecommunications, Dr Christian Schwarz-Schilling (CDU).
Housing and Construction, Dr Irmgard Adam-Schwätzer (FDP).
Research, Dr Heinz Riesenhuber (CDU).
Education, Dr Rainer Ortleb (FDP).
Economic Co-operation, Carl-Dieter Spranger (CSU).

CDU: Christian Democratic Union; CSU: Christian Social Union; FDP: Free Democratic Party.

EMBASSY OF THE FEDERAL REPUBLIC OF GERMANY
23 Belgrave Square, London SW1X 8PZ
Tel 071-235 5033

Ambassador Extraordinary and Plenipotentiary, His Excellency Baron Hermann von Richthofen (1988).
Minister Plenipotentiary, Helmut Wegner.
Minister-Counsellor, Gerhard Kunz.
First Counsellors, F. Gröning (*Head of Press Dept.*); Dr R. Huber (*Head of Economic Dept.*); Dr J. Bakenhus (*Defence Research*); D. Greineder (*Scientific Affairs*); C-J. Weiers (*Agriculture*).

BRITISH EMBASSY
Friedrich-Ebert-Allee 77, 5300 Bonn 1
Tel: Bonn 23 40 61

Ambassador Extraordinary and Plenipotentiary, His Excellency Sir Christopher Mallaby, KCMG (1988).
Minister, J. A. Shepherd, CMG.
Counsellors, C. Budd, CMG (*Political*); E. J. Mitchell (*Bilateral Relations*); Miss A. Walker (*Defence Supply*); D. S. Broucher (*Economic*); D. E. Lyscom (*Science and Technology*); P. V. Rollitt (*Management*); J. Franklin (*Labour*).
First Secretaries, J. I. Link; R. E. Brinkley; R. W. Barnett; V. Evans; D. J. Grieg; T. H. Carter; J. Darby; D. R. Todd; J. E. T. Lewis; P. Cunningham; S. Wordsworth.
Legal Adviser, P. Waterworth.
Defence Attaché, Brig. A. P. Simm.
Military Attaché, Col. N. S. Hunter.
Naval Attaché, Capt. J. McLees.
Air Attaché, Air Cdre W. M. Craghill.
Head of Visa Section (Düsseldorf), M. Carbine.
Chaplain, Revd J. Newsome.

BERLIN OFFICE
Olympic Stadium, Hanns-Braun Strasse, 1000 Berlin 19
International Trade Centre, Georgenstrasse, 1028 Berlin

Minister and Head of Mission, M. St E. Burton, CMG, CVO.
Counsellors, Sir John Ramsden, Bt. (*Deputy Head of Mission*); M. J. Reynolds.
First Secretaries, S. G. Atwood (*Management*); H. R. Mortimer (*Political*); O. J. Traylor; P. J. Laing (*Political*); B. Brett Rooks (*Information*); A. R. Nuttall (*Director of Trade Promotion for Eastern Germany*); D. J. Peate, OBE (*Commercial*); R. H. Sharpe (*Economic*).

There are British Consulates-General at *Berlin*, *Düsseldorf*, *Frankfurt*, *Hamburg*, *Munich* and *Stuttgart*.

BRITISH COUNCIL REPRESENTATIVE, M. Ward, Hahnenstrasse 6, 5000 Köln 1. Offices at *Berlin*, *Hamburg* and *Munich* and British Council libraries at all four centres.

BRITISH CHAMBER OF COMMERCE, Neumarkt 14, D-5000 Köln 1. *Director*, Herr Heumann.

The Ministers-President (Prime Ministers) of the *Länder* governments in July 1991, were:
Baden-Württemberg - Erwin Teufel (CDU).
Bavaria - Max Streibl (CSU).
Berlin - Eberhard Diepgen (CDU) (*Governing Mayor*).
Brandenburg - Manfred Stolpe (SPD).
Bremen - Klaus Wedemeier (*Mayor*) (SPD).
Hamburg - Henning Voscherau (*First Mayor*) (SPD).
Hesse - Hans Eichel (SPD).
Lower Saxony - Gerhard Schröder (SPD).
Mecklenburg-Western Pomerania - Bernt Seite (CDU).
North Rhine-Westphalia - Johannes Rau (SPD).
Rhineland-Palatinate - Rudolf Scharping (SPD).
Saarland - Oskar Lafontaine (SPD).
Saxony - Kurt Biedenkopf (CDU).
Saxony-Anhalt - Werner Münch (CDU).
Schleswig-Holstein - Björn Engholm (SPD).
Thuringia - Bernhardt Vogel (CDU).

JUDICATURE

Judicial authority is exercised by the Federal Constitutional Court, the Federal courts provided for in the Basic Law and the courts of the Länder.

The death sentence has been abolished.

DEFENCE

Under the terms of the Treaty of Unification the German armed forces are to be reduced from the present active total of 476,300 to 370,000 by the end of 1994, at which time the last of the former Soviet Armed Forces will leave Germany. Germany at present is in the process of absorbing the former GDR armed forces, for which separate totals are shown because they remain non-NATO forces.

The Army has a strength of 335,000 including 163,300 conscripts, 64,600 territorials and 51,400 Eastern Command. It deploys 7,000 main battle tanks, 4,600 artillery pieces, 13,500 armoured personnel carriers and infantry fighting vehicles, and 832 helicopters. The Navy has a strength of 37,600 including 8,900 conscripts and 5,200 Eastern Command, with 24 submarines, 14 principal surface combatants and 142 aircraft and 41 helicopters. The Air Force has a strength of 103,700 including 30,800 conscripts and 12,200 Eastern Command, with 638 combat aircraft.

There remain some 365,100 NATO personnel in Germany (USA 222,500; UK 63,400). The number is to be reduced to around 160,000 by the end of the decade, while the present 338,000 former Soviet personnel should all leave by the end of 1994.

ECONOMY

Despite the division of Germany, which cut off from the Federal Republic the main food-producing areas of eastern Germany and some of the principal centres of light industry, the Federal Republic restored Germany's position as the main industrial power in Europe. It is the most economically powerful member of the European Community.

Unification has, however, imposed a severe strain on the federal economy. Large-scale West German investment in the former GDR (estimated at DM180 billion for 1992) resulted in the first federal budgetary and trade deficits for ten years, tax increases, rising interest rates and serious inflationary pressures (4.6 per cent in May 1992 in West Germany). East German demand, however, initially generated growth conditions in the old FRG with gross national product at DM2615.2 billion in 1991, up 3.1 per cent after 4.5 per cent growth in 1990.

In East Germany the immediate price of integration has been high. In particular, the task of transforming eastern Germany into a market economy sharply reduced output to about one-third of pre-unification levels and brought high inflation and unemployment levels (nearly 15 per cent in mid-1992). Two key factors were the unexpected loss of East Germany's traditional trading outlets in eastern Europe following all-German currency reform in July 1990 and the rapid rise of wages to West German levels without a corresponding increase in productivity. Financing East German recovery is expected to require government funding at present levels for at least the next ten years.

INDUSTRIAL PRODUCTION

The Federal Republic has a predominantly industrial economy. Principal industries are coal mining, iron and steel production, machine construction, the electrical industry, the manufacture of steel and metal products, chemicals and textiles, and the processing of foodstuffs. The index of industrial net production adjusted for irregularities of the calendar (1985 = 100) is as follows:

West Germany	1990	1991
Mining	85.1	82.6
Manufacturing industry	118.3	122.3
Basic materials	110.9	112.2
Capital goods	123.0	126.1
Consumer goods	118.8	123.4
Foodstuffs	119.7	129.5
Power (electricity and gas)	111.8	114.8
Construction	124.1	127.8
Total industry	117.7	121.0

Annual production figures were ('000 tonnes):

West Germany	1990	1991
Hard coal	70,159	66,438
Brown coal	107,525	111,676
Crude petroleum	3,606	3,424
Pig iron	28,875	28,792
Raw steel	38,055	38,445
Rolled steel	29,728	29,305
Fuel oils	30,780	31,362
Petrol	21,424	21,484
Chemical fibres	838	810
Cement	30,433	31,816

AGRICULTURE

In 1990 total area of farmland was 14m hectares, of which 7.3m hectares (West Germany) and 4.7 million (East Germany) were arable land. Forest areas cover 7.4m hectares (West Germany only).

Crop yields were ('000 tonnes):

West Germany	1989	1990
Rye	1,797.0	1,944.0
Wheat	11,065.0	11,053.0
Barley	9,757.0	9,195.0
Oats	1,552.0	1,535.0
Potatoes	7,811.0	7,233.0
Sugar beet	20,767.0	23,310.0
Rape seed	1,377.0	1,720.0
East Germany	1989	1990
Rye	2,103.0	2,043.0
Wheat	3,477.0	4,189.0
Barley	4,683.0	4,797.0
Oats	476.0	570.0
Potatoes	9,167.0	6,806.0
Sugar beet	6,220.0	7,290.0
Rape seed	419.0	368.0

Milk production in 1990 was 23,672,000 tonnes (West Germany) and 8,193,000 tonnes (East Germany). Total yield of fisheries in 1990 (West Germany) was 154,146 tonnes, valued at DM234,480,000.

LABOUR

Labour figures, in annual averages, were:

West Germany	1990	1991
Employment	28,453,000	28,886,000
Unemployed	1,883,000	1,689,000
East Germany	1990	1991
Employment	8,115,378	8,864,077
Unemployed	642,182	913,000
Short-time workers	1,795,264	1,616,000

FINANCE

East and West Germany

	1991	1992
Expenditure	DM401.8 billion	DM426.0 billion
Revenue	348.6	385.0

The 1991 plan included expenditure of DM122.6 billion on social welfare, DM52.5 billion on defence, DM35.5 billion on transport and DM13.9 billion on agriculture.

TRADE

East and West Germany

	1990	1991
Total imports	DM573,479m	DM645,422m
Total exports	680,857	666,166

Of 1991 imports, 10.6 per cent were foodstuffs, 5.6 per cent raw materials and 72.4 per cent manufactured goods. Main trading partners in 1991 were (figures shown as percentage of total trade):

	Imports	Exports
France	12.2	13.1
Netherlands	9.7	8.4
Italy	9.3	9.2
Belgium/Luxembourg	7.1	7.3
USA	6.7	6.3
UK	6.6	7.6
Japan	6.1	2.5

Trade with UK	1990	1991
Imports from UK	£13,169,405,000	£14,653,972,000
Exports to UK	19,907,062,000	17,741,093,000

COMMUNICATIONS

At the end of 1989 the state-owned railways of the Federal Republic (*Deutsche Bundesbahn*) measured 27,053 kilometres of which 11,680 kilometres were electrified, and the privately owned railways totalled approximately 2,795 kilometres. In 1989 the railways handled 315.4 million tonnes of goods. The former GDR (*Deutsche Reichsbahn*) had 14,482 kilometres of track in 1989, of which 3,829 kilometres were electrified.

Classified roads measured 220,853 kilometres (West and East) in 1990, of which motorways were 10,571 kilometres. The total number of motor vehicles registered at the beginning of 1991 was 43 million.

Ocean-going shipping under the German flag in Dec. 1989, amounted to 5,822,000 tons gross. Inland waterways handled 234.8m tonnes of goods in 1989.

SOCIAL WELFARE

There is compulsory insurance against sickness, accident, old age and unemployment. Children's allowances, child rearing benefits and parental leave of absence are available in respect of all children. Pension schemes for widows and orphans of public servants are in operation. Public assistance is given to persons unable to earn their living, or with insufficient income to maintain a decent standard of living.

EDUCATION

School attendance is compulsory for all children and juveniles between the ages of six and 18 and comprises nine years full-time compulsory education at primary and main schools (*Grund und Hauptschulen*) and three years of compulsory vocational education on a part-time basis. In 1989 (West Germany only) there were 20,598 primary and main schools (*Grund und Hauptschulen*) with 3,703,772 pupils. Secondary modern schools (*Realschulen*) numbered 2,573 with 857,218 pupils. There were 2,884 other general secondary schools (*Gymnasien* including *Gesamtschulen*) with 1,818,578 pupils.

There were also 2,762 special schools (*Sonderschulen*) for physically and mentally handicapped and socially maladjusted children in the Federal Republic with 246,278 pupils.

The secondary school leaving examination (*Abitur*) entitles the holder to a place of study at a university or another institution of higher education.

Children below the age of 18 who are not attending a general secondary or a full-time vocational school have compulsory day-release at a vocational school. In 1989 (West Germany only) there were 2,683 full- and part-time vocational schools (*Berufsschulen*) with 1,660,355 pupils and 276 vocational extension schools (*Berufsaufbauschulen*) with 8,207 pupils, 2,365 full-time vocational schools (*Berufsfachschulen*) with 262,206 pupils, 1,022 schools for secondary technical studies (*Fachoberschulen/Fachgymnasien*) with 201,204 students.

In 1990–1 there were a total of 1,585,167 students at institutions of higher education, of whom 1,050,396 were attending universities. The largest universities are in Munich, Berlin, Hamburg, Bonn and Cologne.

CULTURE

Modern (or New High) German has developed from the time of the Reformation to the present day, with differences of dialect in Austria, Alsace and the German-speaking cantons of Switzerland.

The literary language is usually regarded as having become fixed by Luther and Zwingli at the Reformation, since which time many great names occur in all branches, notably philosophy, from Leibnitz (1646–1716) to Kant (1724–1804), Fichte (1762–1814), Schelling (1775–1854) and Hegel (1770–1831); the drama from Goethe (1749–1832) and Schiller (1759–1805) to Gerhart Hauptmann (1862–1946); and in poetry, Heine (1797–1856). German authors have received the Nobel Prize for Literature on seven occasions: Theodor Mommsen (1902), R. Eucken (1908), P. Heyse (1909), Gerhart Hauptmann (1912), Thomas Mann (1929), N. Sachs (1966) and Heinrich Böll (1972).

GHANA

The Republic of Ghana

AREA – Ghana (formerly known as the Gold Coast) is situated on the Gulf of Guinea, between 3° 07′ W. long. and 1° 14′ E. long. (about 334 miles), and extends 441 miles north from Cape Three Points (4° 45′ N.) to 11° 11′ N. It is bounded on the north by Burkina, on the west by the Côte d'Ivoire, on the east by Togo, and on the south by the Atlantic Ocean. Although a tropical country, Ghana is cooler than many countries within similar latitudes. Ghana has a total area of 92,099 sq. miles (238,537 sq. km).

POPULATION – The population was (UN estimate) 15,028,000 in 1990. Most Ghanaians are Sudanese Negroes, although Hamitic strains are common in northern Ghana. The official language is English. The principal indigenous language group is Akan, of which Twi and Fanti are the most commonly used. Ga, Ewe and languages of the Mole-Dagbani group are common in certain regions.

CAPITAL – ΨAccra. Population of the Greater Accra Region (including Tema) was (1990 estimate) 1,781,100. Other towns are Kumasi, Tamale, ΨSekondi-Takoradi, ΨCape Coast, Sunyani, Ho, Koforidua, Tarkwa and ΨWinneba.

CURRENCY – Cedi of 100 pesewas.

FLAG – Equal horizontal bands of red over gold over green; five-point black star on gold stripe.

NATIONAL ANTHEM – Hail the Name of Ghana.

NATIONAL DAY – 6 March (Independence Day).

GOVERNMENT

There is no recorded history of the Gold Coast region before the coming of Europeans in the fifteenth century. The constituent parts of the state came under British administration at various times, the original Gold Coast Colony (the coastal and southern areas) being first constituted in 1874; Ashanti in 1901; and the Northern Territories Protectorate in 1901. The territory of Trans-Volta-Togoland, part of the former German colony of Togo, was mandated to Britain by the League of Nations after the First World War, and remained under British administration as a United Nations Trusteeship after the Second World War. After a plebiscite in May 1956, under the auspices of the United Nations, the territory was integrated with the Gold Coast Colony.

The former Gold Coast Colony and associated territories became the independent state of Ghana and a member of the British Commonwealth on 6 March 1957 and adopted a Republican constitution on 1 July 1960.

Since 1966 Ghana has experienced long periods of military rule divided by short-lived civilian governments. A coup in June 1979 led to the formation of an Armed Forces Revolutionary Council chaired by Flt. Lt. Jerry Rawlings. Civilian rule was restored in September 1979 but overthrown on 31 December 1981, when another coup brought back into power Flt. Lt. Rawlings.

PROVISIONAL NATIONAL DEFENCE COUNCIL

Chairman and Head of State, Flt. Lt. Jerry Rawlings.
Chairman, National Commission for Democracy, Mr Justice D. F. Annan.
General Duties, Dr Mary Grant.
Defence, Alhaji Mahamad Iddrissu.
Chairman of the Committee of Secretaries, P. V. Obeng.
Chairman, National Development Planning Committee, Lt.-Gen. A. Quainoo.
Labour, Ebo Tawiah.
Security and Foreign Affairs, Capt. Kojo Tsikata (retd).

PNDC SECRETARIES as at August 1992

Agriculture, Ibrahim Adams.
Education and Culture, Dr Alex Ababio.
Finance and Economic Planning, Dr Kwesi Botchwey.
Foreign, Obed Y. Asamoah.
Energy, Ato Ahwoi.
Health, Cdr. S. G. Obimpeh.
Industries, Science and Technology, Capt. K. Butah.
Information, Kofi Totobi Quakyi.
Interior, Col. E. M. Osei-Owusu.
Justice and Attorney-General, Nana Kwesi Obuadum.
Transport and Communications, Kwame Peprah.
Local Government and Rural Development, Kwamena Ahwoi.
Mobilization and Social Welfare, D. S. Boateng.
Roads and Highways, Col. Laud Attivor.
Trade and Tourism, John Bawa.
Lands and Natural Resources, J. A. Danso.
Works and Housing, K. Ampratwum.
Youth and Sports, Lt.-Gen. A. Quainoo.

GHANA HIGH COMMISSION

104 Highgate Hill, London N6 5HE
Tel 081-342 8686

High Commissioner, His Excellency K. B. Asante (1991).

BRITISH HIGH COMMISSION

PO Box 296, Osu Link, Accra
Tel: Accra 221665

High Commissioner, His Excellency Anthony Michael Goodenough, CMG (1989).

BRITISH COUNCIL REPRESENTATIVE, J. M. Day, Liberia Road (PO Box 771), Accra. There is also an office in *Kumasi.*

ECONOMY

AGRICULTURE – Agriculture forms the basis of Ghana's economy, employing 70 per cent of the working population. Crops of the forest zone include cocoa, which is the largest single source of revenue, rice and a variety of other foodstuff crops grown on mixed-crop farms. Fruits such as avocado pears, oranges and pineapples are grown. Cassava is the most important crop of the coastal savannas zone, of the lower Volta area. Production of pulses such as groundnuts is widespread. Near the Togo border oil palms, yams, maize, cassava, fruit and vegetables are produced. Livestock is raised in the uncultivated areas. The northern savanna zone is Ghana's principal cattle rearing area and other livestock production there is important for home consumption. Corn and millet crops are produced in the far north and maize, yams, rice and groundnut crops in more southerly parts of the zone.

Attempts are being made to diversify agricultural production, with cash crops being extensively cultivated for export and to provide raw materials for local industry.

FISHERIES – Fishing is important in coastal areas and in the Volta itself. However, production cannot meet demand and there are considerable imports of fish products. About 80 per cent of home supply is obtained from sea fisheries, but production from the Volta Lake and other inland fisheries is increasing.

MINERAL PRODUCTION – The area within a 60 mile radius of Dunkwa produces 90 per cent of Ghana's mineral exports. Manganese production from Nsuta ranks among the world's highest and gold, industrial diamonds and bauxite are also produced. Some 30,000 persons are employed by the mining companies.

MANUFACTURES – Examples of the small-scale traditional industries are tailoring, goldsmithing and carpentry. Priority has been given in recent years to the establishment of a number of 'Pioneer Industries' including timber products, vehicle and refrigerator assembly, cigarettes, boatbuilding, food processing, cotton textiles, clothing, footwear, printing and other light industries. A modern industrial complex is growing in the Accra-Tema area.

VOLTA RIVER PROJECT – Since 1966 the Volta Dam at Akosombo has generated hydro-electric power for the processing of bauxite and fed a power transmission network for the Accra-Kumasi-Takoradi area. Electricity is now also sent to Togo and Benin.

TRADE

Principal exports are cocoa, timber and gold. Principal imports are road vehicles, manufacturing equipment, petroleum and raw materials.

Trade with UK	1990	1991
Imports from UK	£162,057,000	£169,296,000
Exports to UK	105,118,000	77,345,000

COMMUNICATIONS

The Kotoka Airport at Accra is an international airport and Ghana Airways Corporation is the national airline. There are also internal airports at Takoradi, Kumasi, Sunyani, and Tamale.

There are 20,000 miles of motorable roads, of which 2,335 miles are bitumenized. There are 600 miles of railway, linking Accra and the principal ports of Takoradi and Tema with their hinterlands, and with each other.

Takoradi Harbour consists of seven quay berths – one is leased specially for manganese exports. Tema Harbour has ten berths for larger ocean going vessels and the largest dry dock on the West African coast. An oil berth has also been built to serve the Ghaip refinery which has been constructed at Tema.

GREECE
Elliniki Dimokratia

Greece is a maritime state in the south-east of Europe, bounded on the north by Albania, Macedonia and Bulgaria, on the south and west by the Ionian and Mediterranean seas, and on the east by Turkey. It has an estimated area of 50,944 sq. miles (131,944 sq. km).

The main areas of Greece are: *Macedonia* (which includes Mt Athos and the island of Thasos), *Thrace* (including the island of Samothrace), *Epirus, Thessaly, Continental Greece* (which includes the island of Euboea and the Sporades or 'scattered islands' of which the largest is Skyros), the *Peloponnese* (or *Morea*), the *Dodecanese* or *Southern Sporades* (12 islands occupied by Italy in 1911 during the Italo-Turkish War and ceded to Greece by Italy in 1947) consisting of Rhodes, Astypalaia, Karpathos, Kassos, Nisyros, Kalymnos, Leros, Patmos, Kos, Symi, Khalki and Tilos, the *Cyclades* (a circular group numbering about 200, with a total area of 923 sq. miles; the chief islands are Syros, Andros, Tinos, Naxos, Paros, Santorini, Milos and Serifos), the *Ionian Islands* (Corfu, Paxos, Levkas, Ithaca, Cephalonia, Zante and Cerigo), the *Aegean Islands* (Chios, Lesbos, Limnos and Samos). In *Crete* there was for over 1,500 years (3000 to 1400 BC) a flourishing civilization which spread its influence far and wide throughout the Aegean, and the ruins of the palace of Minos at Knossos afford evidence of astonishing comfort and luxury.

POPULATION – The population at the 1991 census was 10,256,464.

RELIGION – Over 97 per cent of the people are adherents of the Greek Orthodox Church, which is the state religion, all others being tolerated and free from interference. The Church of Greece recognizes the spiritual primacy of the Oecumenical Patriarch of Constantinople, but is otherwise a self-governing body administered by the Holy Synod under the presidency of the Archbishop of Athens and All Greece. It has no jurisdiction over the Church of Crete, which has a degree of autonomy under the Œcumenical Patriarch, nor over the monastic community of Mount Athos and the Church in the Dodecanese, both of which come directly under the Œcumenical Patriarch.

CAPITAL – Athens, population (including ΨPiraeus and suburbs), 3,096,775 (1991 Census). Other large towns are (1991) ΨSalonika (977,528); ΨPatras (172,763); ΨVolos (115,732); Larissa (269,300); and ΨKavalla (135,747). Larger towns in the islands are: in Crete, ΨHeraklion or Candia (263,868), ΨCanea (133,060), and ΨRethymnon (69,290); in the Ionian Islands, ΨCorfu (36,901); in the Dodecanese, ΨRhodes (43,619); in the Cyclades, ΨSyros Hermoupolis (16,008); in Lesbos, ΨMytilene (25,440); in Chios, ΨChios (27,405).

CURRENCY – Drachma of 100 leptae.

FLAG – Blue and white stripes with a white cross on a blue field in the canton.

NATIONAL ANTHEM – Imnos Eis Tin Eleftherian (Hymn to Freedom).

NATIONAL DAY – March 25 (Independence Day).

GOVERNMENT

A military coup on 21 April 1967 suspended parliamentary government and, following an unsuccessful royal counter-coup on 13 December 1967, King Constantine went into voluntary exile in Rome. On 1 June 1973 the monarchy was abolished and a republic established under the Presidency of George Papadopoulos.

The overthrow of Archbishop Makarios, President of Cyprus, on 15 July 1974, by a military coup led by Greek officers of the Cypriot National Guard caused an international crisis, in the wake of which the heads of the Greek armed forces decided, on 23 July, to relinquish power. Konstantinos Karamanlis, Prime Minister between 1955 and 1963, returned from his self-imposed exile in Paris to form a provisional government, and the first elections for ten years were held on 17 November 1974.

The constitutional position of the King, who was still in exile, remained unsettled until 8 December, when by a referendum, the Greek people rejected 'crowned democracy' by 69.2 per cent to 30.8 per cent and Greece became a republic. A new constitution came into force on 11 June 1975.

The unicameral 300-member Chamber of Deputies is elected for a four-year term by universal adult suffrage under a system of proportional representation. The most recent general election was held on 8 April 1990.

HEAD OF STATE

President of the Hellenic Republic, Constantine Karamanlis, *elected* 4 May 1990.

CABINET as at 30 April 1992

Prime Minister, Constantine Misotakis.
Deputy PM, Tzannis Tzannetakis.
Minister for the Aegean, Giorgos Missailidis.
Minister to the PM, Sotiris Kouvelas.
Foreign Affairs, Michalis Papaconstantinou.
Interior, Nikolaos Kleitos.
National Defence, Justice, Ioannis Varvitsiotis.
National Economy, Finance, Stephanos Manos.
Merchant Marine, Aristotelis Pavlidis.
Agriculture, Sotiris Hadzigakis.
Labour, Aristides Kalantzakos.
Health, Welfare and Social Security, George Sourlas.
Education and Religious Affairs, Georg Souflias.
Culture, Anna Psarouda-Benaki.
Public Order, Theodore Anagnostopoulos.
Macedonia and Thrace, Panayiotis Hadzinikolaou.
Environment, Town Planning and Public Works, Achileas Karamanlis.
Industry and Commerce, Andreas Andrianopoulos.
Transport and Communications, Nikolaos Gelestathis.
Tourism, vacant.

EMBASSY OF GREECE
1A Holland Park, London W11 3TP
Tel 071-727 8040
Ambassador Extraordinary and Plenipotentiary, His Excellency George D. Papoulias (1990).
Defence Attaché, Capt. H. Zevelakis.
There are Honorary Consulates at *Belfast, Birmingham, Edinburgh, Falmouth, Glasgow, Leeds* and *Southampton.*

BRITISH EMBASSY
1 Ploutarchou Street, 10675 Athens
Tel: Athens 7236211/9
Ambassador Extraordinary and Plenipotentiary, His Excellency Sir David Miers, KBE, CMG (1989).
Deputy Head of Mission and Consul-General, R. N. Culshaw, MVO.
Counsellors, W. V. Fell; Dr J. L. Munby, OBE (*Cultural Affairs*).

Defence and Military Attaché, Brig. G. Bulloch, MBE.
Naval and Air Attaché, Capt. J. J. Pearson.
Hon. Attaché, Elizabeth Bayard French (*Director, British School of Archaeology*).

BRITISH CONSULAR OFFICES – There are British Consular Offices at *Athens, Corfu, Samos, Rhodes, Salonika, Heraklion* (Crete), *Syros* and *Volos*.

BRITISH COUNCIL, 17 Plateia Philikis Etairias (PO Box 3488), Kolonaki Square, Athens 10210. *Representative*, Dr J. L. Munby.
There is also an office at *Salonika* and British Council libraries at both centres.

BRITISH-HELLENIC CHAMBER OF COMMERCE, 25 Vas. Sofias Avenue, GR-106 74 Athens. Tel: 72 10 361.

DEFENCE

The strength of the Army is 113,000, including 100,000 conscripts; in addition there are some 34,000 in the National Guard. The Navy consists of 19,500 (11,400 conscripts) men and is equipped with 10 submarines and 18 principal surface combatant vessels. The Air Force consists of 26,400 (14,400 conscripts) men and is equipped with aircraft disposed in 19 combat squadrons supported by the necessary transport, training, helicopter and reconnaissance squadrons, a total of 375 combat aircraft. National service is two years on average.

COMMUNICATIONS

The 2,650 kilometres of Greek railways are state-owned with the exception of the Athens–Piraeus Electric Railway. Greek roads total somewhat over 35,500 kilometres, of which about 25 per cent are classified as national highways and just under 30,000 km are classified as provincial roads. The road connection with Albania was reopened in 1985.

On 31 December 1986 the Greek mercantile fleet numbered 2,138 ships with a total tonnage of 24,792,516 tons gross. On the same day Greek-owned ships over 100 tons gross and registered under foreign flags numbered 276 with a total tonnage of 5,176,347 tons gross. Athens has direct airline links with Australasia, North America, most countries in Europe, Africa and the Middle East.

EDUCATION

Education is free and compulsory from the age of six to 15 and is maintained by state grants. There are six universities, Athens, Salonika, Patras, Thrace, Ioannina and Crete. There are several other institutes of higher learning, mostly in Athens.

ECONOMY

Though there has in recent years been a substantial measure of industrialization, agriculture still employs about a quarter of the working population. The most important agricultural products are tobacco, wheat, cotton, sugar and rice. The most important of the fruit trees are the olive, peach, vine, orange, lemon, fig, almond and currant-vine. Exports of fresh fruit and vegetables have established themselves as an important contributor to the economy and have considerable growth potential. Currants, grown mainly around Patras, remain one of Greece's main exports, the United Kingdom being the principal purchaser.

The principal minerals mined in Greece are nickel, bauxite, iron ore, iron pyrites, manganese magnesite, chrome, lead, zinc and emery, and prospecting for petroleum is being carried on. Oil refineries are in operation near Athens and at Salonika, where there is also a petro-chemical plant.

The chief industries are textiles (cotton, woollen and synthetics), chemicals, cement, glass, metallurgy, shipbuilding, domestic electrical equipment and footwear. In recent years new factories have been opened for the production of aluminium, nickel, iron and steel products, tyres, chemicals, fertilizers and sugar (from locally-grown beet). Food processing and ancillary industries have also grown up throughout the country.

The development of the country's electric power resources, irrigation and land reclamation schemes and the exploitation of Greece's lignite resources for fuel and industrial purposes are also being carried out. Tourism has developed rapidly, but is now slowing down.

TRADE

	1986	1987
Total imports	Drs 1,587,214.0m	Drs 1,758,951.1m
Total exports	789,994.6m	880,958.2m

Trade with UK	1990	1991
Imports from UK	£682,887,000	£667,741,000
Exports to UK	400,476,000	378,146,000

CULTURE

Greek civilization emerged about 1300 BC and the poems of Homer, the blind poet of Chios, which were probably current about 800 BC, record the ten-year struggle between the Achaeans of Greece and the Phrygians of Troy (1194 to 1184 BC).

The spoken language of modern Greece is descended by a process of natural development from the Common Greek of Alexander's empire. *Katharevousa*, a conservative literary dialect evolved by Adamantios Corais (Diamant Coray), who lived and died in Paris (1748–1833) and used for official and technical matters, has been phased out. Novels and poetry are mostly composed in *dimotiki*, a progressive literary dialect which owes much to John Psycharis (1854–1929). The poets Solomos, Palamas, Cavafis, Sikelianos, Seferis and Elytis have won a European reputation.

GRENADA

The State of Grenada

AREA, ETC – Grenada is situated between the parallels of 12° 13′–11° 58′ N. lat. and 61° 20′–61° 35′ W. long., and is about 90 miles north of Trinidad, 68 miles south-south-west of St Vincent, and about 120 miles south-west of Barbados. The island is about 21 miles in length and 12 miles in breadth, with an area of 133 sq. miles (344 sq. km). Also included in the territory of Grenada are some of the Grenadines islets, the largest of which is Carriacou, 13 square miles in area. The country is mountainous and very picturesque, and the climate is healthy.

POPULATION – The population is estimated at 86,000 (1990 UN estimate).

CAPITAL – ΨSt George's (population 10,000) lies on the south-west coast, and possesses a good harbour.

CURRENCY – East Caribbean dollar (EC$) of 100 cents.

FLAG – Divided diagonally into yellow and green triangles within a red border containing six yellow stars, a yellow star on a red disc in the centre and a nutmeg on the green triangle in the hoist.

NATIONAL DAY – 7 February (Independence Day).

GOVERNMENT

Grenada was discovered by Columbus in 1498, and named Conception. It was originally colonized by the French, and was ceded to Great Britain by the Treaty of Versailles in 1783. It became an Associated State in 1967 and an independent nation within the Commonwealth on 7 February 1974.

The government was overthrown on 13 March 1979 by the New Jewel Movement and a People's Revolutionary Government was set up. Disagreements within the PRG led, in October 1983, to violence and the death of the Prime Minister, whose government was replaced by a Revolutionary Military Council. These events prompted the intervention of Caribbean and US forces. The Governor-General installed an advisory council to act as an interim government until a General Election was held, on 3 December 1984. A phased withdrawal of US forces was completed by June 1985.

The Queen is Head of State and is represented by a Governor-General. Legislative power is vested in a bicameral parliament consisting of an elected House of Representatives and a 13-member Senate. The most recent General Election was held in March 1990. Nicholas Brathwaite of the National Democratic Congress was sworn in as Prime Minister on 16 March 1990.

Governor-General, Sir Paul Scoon, GCMG, GCVO, OBE (1978).

CABINET (as at May 1992)

Prime Minister, Minister for External Affairs, Finance and Planning, National Security, Carriacou and Petit Martinique Affairs, Rt. Hon. Nicholas Brathwaite, OBE.
Agriculture, Trade, Industry and Production, Hon. George Brizan.
Attorney-General, Minister for Legal Affairs, Local Government, Dr the Hon. Francis Alexis.
Communications, Works, Public Utilities, Hon. Phinsley St Louis.
Tourism, Civil Aviation, Women's Affairs, Social Development, Youth Affairs, Sports and Culture, Hon. Joan Purcell.
Health, Housing, the Environment, Hon. Michael Andrew.
Labour, Co-operatives, Social Security, Community Development, Hon. Edzel Thomas.
Education, Information, Sen. the Hon. Carlyle Glean.
Minister of State (Finance), Sen. Tillman Thomas.

GRENADA HIGH COMMISSION
1 Collingham Gardens, London SW5 0HW
Tel 071-373 7808

High Commissioner, His Excellency Lynton C. Noel (1990).

BRITISH HIGH COMMISSION
14 Church Street, St George's
Tel: St George's 440-3222

High Commissioner (resides at Bridgetown, Barbados).
Resident Representative, A. H. Drury (*First Secretary*).

ECONOMY

The economy is principally agrarian, with cocoa, nutmegs and bananas the major crops. Fruit and vegetables are grown and a little livestock raised for domestic consumption. The fishing industry is being developed. Manufacturing is mostly confined to processing agricultural products.

Tourism has prospered since the opening in 1984 of the Point Salines International Airport. British Airways began regular weekly flights in April 1987. A hotel expansion programme is planned. The number of cruise ships visiting Grenada in 1988 was 234.

TRADE

Total value of imports in 1988 was EC$248.6 million. Principal domestic exports for 1988 were nutmeg (EC$31.3m), cocoa (EC$8.75m), mace (EC$7.3m) and fruit (EC$3.8m).

Trade with UK	1990	1991
Imports from UK	£7,822,000	£7,730,000
Exports to UK	4,778,000	4,236,000

GUATEMALA

República de Guatemala

Guatemala, in Central America, is situated in N. lat. from 13° 45′ to 17° 49′, and in W. long. from 88° 12′ 49″ to 92°13′ 43″, and has an area of 42,042 sq. miles (108,889 sq. km), and a population (estimate 1991) of 9,467,000.

The Republic is traversed from west to east by an elevated mountain chain, containing several volcanic summits rising to 13,000 feet above sea level; earthquakes are frequent. The country is well watered by numerous rivers; the climate is hot and malarial near the coast, temperate in the higher regions. The rainfall in the capital averages 57 in per annum. The chief seaports are San José de Guatemala and Champerico on the Pacific and Santo Tomás de Castilla and Puerto Barrios on the Atlantic side.

LANGUAGE AND LITERACY – Spanish is the language of the country, but 40 per cent of the population speak an Indian language. Since the establishment of the university in the capital, education has received a marked impulse and the high figure of illiteracy is being reduced. The national library contains about 80,000 volumes in Spanish.

CAPITAL – Guatemala City, population estimate, 1,675,589. Quezaltenango has a population of over 100,000. Other towns are ΨPuerto Barrios (23,000), Mazatenango (21,000), and Antigua (30,000).

CURRENCY – Quetzal (Q) of 100 centavos.

FLAG – Three vertical bands, blue, white, blue; coat of arms on white stripe.

NATIONAL ANTHEM – Guatemala Feliz (Guatemala be praised).

NATIONAL DAY – 15 September.

GOVERNMENT

The constitutionally elected president, Gen. Miguel Ydigoras Fuentes, was overthrown on 31 March 1963 by the Army, which handed executive and legislative powers to the Minister of Defence, Col. Enrique Peralta Azurdia. Elections for a new Congress and for President and Vice-President took place on 6 March 1966.

The constitution was suspended 'for as long as the situation demands' following a military coup in March 1982. An amnesty for guerrillas was unsuccessful and the Army was fully occupied dealing with the proliferating subversive groups throughout the country.

Elections for a Constituent Assembly were held on 1 July 1984, as promised by Gen. Mejía Víctores when he overthrew Gen. Ríos Montt in 1983. The Assembly drew up a new constitution, promulgated in June 1985, and a new electoral law, paving the way for presidential, governmental and municipal elections which were won by the Christian Democratic Party. Presidential elections, held in November 1990, were won by Jorge Serrano Elias, the leader of the Solidarity Action Movement (MAS). MAS failed to win Congressional elections and a government of national unity was formed.

The republic is divided into 22 departments.

HEAD OF STATE

President Jorge Serrano Elias, *inaugurated*, January 1991.

CABINET as at June 1992

Minister of Government, Fernando Hurtado Prem.
Foreign Affairs, Gonzalo Menéndez Park.
National Defence, General José Luis Samayoa.
Finance, Richard Aitkenhead Castillo.
Communications, Alvaro Heredía.
Education, María Luisa Beltranena Padilla.
Agriculture, Adolfo José Boppel Carrera.
Economy, Juan Luís Mirón.
Public Health and Social Welfare, Dr Eusebio del Cid Peralta.
Labour and Social Welfare, Dr Mario Solorzano Martínez.
Energy and Mines, Cesar Fernández.
Special Affairs, Antulio Castillo Barajas.
Urban and Rural Development, Ricardo Castillo Sinibaldi.
Culture and Sport, Eunice Lima Shaul.
Minister without portfolio, Antulio Castillo Barajas.

EMBASSY OF GUATEMALA

13 Fawcett Street, London SW10 9HN
Tel 071 351 3042

Ambassador Extraordinary and Plenipotentiary, His Excellency Edmundo Nanne (1992).

BRITISH EMBASSY

Centro Financiero Torre II (7th Floor), Seventh Avenue 5–10 Zone 4, Guatemala City
Tel: Guatemala City 321601

Ambassador Extraordinary and Plenipotentiary, His Excellency Justin Nason, OBE (1990).

FINANCE

The central government revenue in 1989 was Quetzales 2,253 million, and expenditure Quetzales 2,775 million.

TRADE

The principal export is coffee, other articles being manufactured goods, sugar, bananas, cotton, beef and essential oils. The chief imports are petroleum, vehicles, machinery and foodstuffs.

	1990
Imports (c.i.f.)	US$1,407.0m
Exports (f.o.b.)	1,211.0m

Trade with UK	1990	1991
Imports from UK	£17,551,000	£16,224,000
Exports to UK	42,034,000	10,458,000

GUINEA

République de Guinée

Formerly part of French West Africa, Guinea has a coastline on the Atlantic Ocean between Guinea-Bissau and Sierra

Leone, and in the interior is adjacent to Senegal, Mali, Côte d'Ivoire, Liberia and Sierra Leone. Area, 94,926 sq. miles (245,857 sq. km). The population (UN estimate 1990) is 5,755,000, mostly the Fullah, Malinké and Soussou tribes.

CAPITAL – ΨConakry (763,000). Other towns are Kankan, which is connected with Conakry by a railway, Kindia, N'Zérékoré, Mamou, Siguiri and Labé.

CURRENCY – Guinea franc of 100 centimes.

FLAG – Three vertical stripes of red, yellow and green.

NATIONAL DAY – 2 October (Anniversary of Proclamation of Independence).

GOVERNMENT

Guinea was separated from Senegal in 1891 and administered by France as a separate colony until 1958. In a referendum held in September 1958, Guinea rejected the new French Constitution and on 2 October 1958 became an independent republic governed by a Constituent Assembly. M. Sékou Touré, Prime Minister in the Territorial Assembly, assumed office as head of the new Government, and was elected President in 1961.

Under a provisional constitution, adopted in November 1958, powers of government are exercised by a president assisted by the Cabinet. The President, eligible for a term of seven years and for re-election, is head of state and of the armed forces. President Sékou Touré died in March 1984; a few days later there was a military coup. Guinea was ruled by a military government, which was directed by a Military Committee for National Recovery (CMRN). A new constitution, providing for the end of military rule and the introduction of a two-party system within five years, was approved by referendum in December 1990.

In January 1991 the CMRN was dissolved and a mixed civilian-military Transitional Committee for National Recovery (CTRN) was established. This appointed a new government in February 1991. Disturbances throughout 1991 led by trade unions and opposition parties caused the government to announce in October that a full multiparty system would be introduced in April 1992. Seventeen opposition parties were legalized in April 1992 but no date has been set for any elections.

HEAD OF STATE

President and Minister of Defence, Maj. Gen. Lansana Conté, *took power*, 3 April 1984.

COUNCIL OF MINISTERS as at June 1992

Foreign Affairs and Co-operation, Maj. Ibrahima Sylla.
Minister at the Presidency in charge of National Defence, Maj. Abdourahmane Diallo.
Interior and Security, René Alseny Gomez.
Planning and Finance, Soriba Kaba.
Justice, Salifou Sylla.
Agriculture and Animal Resources, Ibrahima Sory Sow.
Natural Resources, Energy and Environment, Toumani Dakoum Sako.
Territorial Development, Maj. Ibrahima Diallo.
Higher Educational and Vocational Training, Charles Pascal Tollo.
Public Health and Social Affairs, Madigbe Fofana.
Communication, Capt. Jean-Claude Fassou.
Youth, Culture, Arts and Sports, Assifat Dorank.
Administrative Reform, Civil Service and Labour, René Loua Fassou.
Industry, Small- and Medium-sized Enterprises, Mamadou Boyé Barry.
Commerce, Transport and Tourism, Nantenin Camara.

EMBASSY OF THE REPUBLIC OF GUINEA
51 rue de la Faisanderie, 75061 Paris, France
Tel Paris 47048148

Ambassador Extraordinary and Plenipotentiary, new appointment awaited.

BRITISH AMBASSADOR (resident in Dakar, Senegal).

ECONOMY

The principal products of Guinea are bauxite, alumina, iron-ore, palm kernels, millet, rice, coffee, bananas, pineapples and rubber. At Sangaredi in the mountainous hinterland, where the rivers Senegal, Gambia and Niger have their sources, large deposits of bauxite are mined. Deposits of iron ore, gold, diamonds and uranium have also been discovered. Principal imports are cotton goods, manufactured goods, tobacco, petroleum products, sugar, rice, flour and salt; exports, bauxite, alumina, iron-ore, diamonds, coffee, hides, bananas, palm kernels and pineapples.

TRADE WITH UK

	1990	1991
Imports from UK	£11,368,000	£7,800,000
Exports to UK	11,508,000	5,854,000

GUINEA-BISSAU
Repûblica da Guiné-Bissau

Guinea-Bissau, formerly Portuguese Guinea, lies in Western Africa, between Senegal and Guinea; it has an area of 13,948 sq. miles (36,125 sq. km), and has a population (UN estimate 1990) of 964,000. The main ethnic groups are the Balante, Malinké, Fulani, Mandjako and Pepel.

CAPITAL – ΨBissau, population (Census 1979) 109,486, is also the chief port.

CURRENCY – Guinea-Bissau peso of 100 centavos.

FLAG – Horizontal bands of yellow over green with vertical red band in the hoist charged with a black star.

NATIONAL DAY – 24 September (Independence Day).

GOVERNMENT

Guinea-Bissau achieved independence on 24 September 1974. Luis Cabral was ousted in a coup led by Maj. (now Brig.-Gen.) Vieira in November 1980. Following the coup the Assembly was suspended, and a Revolutionary Council was established. Under a new constitution adopted in April 1984 the Revolutionary Council became a 15-member Council of State, and a parliament was set up. The ruling African Party for the Independence of Guinea and Cape Verde (PAIGC) voted to introduce a multi-party system in January 1991. Three opposition parties were legalized in November and December 1991 and presidential and legislative elections, under Portugese supervision, are scheduled for November and December 1992 respectively.

Chairman of the Council of State, *C.-in-C. of the Armed Forces*, Brig.-Gen. João Bernardo Vieira, *took power*, Nov. 1980; *elected for a five-year term*, June 1989.

COUNCIL OF MINISTERS as at June 1992

Prime Minister, Carlos Correia.
Minister of State for the Armed Forces, Col. Iafai Camara.
Minister without Portfolio, Vasco Cabral.
Justice, Joao Cruz Pinto.
Defence, Samba Lamine Mane.
Interior, Abubacar Balde.
Rural Development and Agriculture, Mario Cabral.

Minister of State for Social Affairs, Carmen Pereira.
Finance, Filinto de Barros.
Minister of State at the Presidency, Fidelis Cabral de Almada.
Women's Affairs, Francisca Pereira.
Natural Resources and Industry, Manuel Santos.
Foreign Affairs, Julio Semedo.
Civil Service, Labour, Pedro Gomes.
Commerce and Tourism, Luis Oliveira Sanca.
Fisheries, Freire Monteiro.
International Co-operation, Bernardino Cardoso.
Public Health, Henriqueta Godinho Gomes.
Transport, Avito Jose da Silva.
Public Works, Construction and Town Planning, Alberto Antonio Voss Lima Gomes.
Information and Telecommunications, Malam Bacai Sanha.
Regional Ministers, Mario Mendes (*Eastern Province*); Vasco Salvador Corneia (*Southern Province*); Zeca Martins (*Northern Province*).
Minister-Governor of the Central Bank, Pedro Godinho Gomes.
Education, Alexandre Funtado.

EMBASSY OF THE REPUBLIC OF GUINEA-BISSAU
Avenue Franklin Roosevelt 70, 1050 Brussels, Belgium
Tel: Brussels 6470890

Ambassador Extraordinary and Plenipotentiary, new appointment awaited.

BRITISH AMBASSADOR, (resident in Dakar, Senegal).

ECONOMY

The country produces rice, coconuts, ground-nuts and palm oil products. Cattle are raised, and there are bauxite deposits in the south.

TRADE WITH UK

	1990	1991
Imports from UK	£924,000	£1,201,000
Exports to UK	833,000	36,000

GUYANA
The Co-operative Republic of Guyana

AREA, POPULATION, ETC – Guyana, the former colony of British Guiana, which includes the counties of Demerara, Essequibo and Berbice, is situated on the north-east coast of South America, bordering Venezuela, Brazil and Suriname. It has a total area of 83,000 sq. miles (214,969 sq. km), and a population (1990 UN estimate) of 796,000.

There are three distinct areas. A narrow alluvial coastal belt ten to 40 miles deep, the eastern part of which is intensively cultivated and contains some 90 per cent of the population. Much of this is below the level of the sea and is drained and irrigated by an intricate system of canals constructed by the Dutch.

A mountainous area of dense rain forest lies behind the coastland. Still partly unexplored, it reaches its highest point at Mount Roraima (9,000 ft) on the junction of the Guyana–Brazil–Venezuela borders.

The open savanna country of the Rupununi in the south-west is the third area. Here cattle ranching is practised and oil deposits have been discovered.

The entire country is intersected by numerous large rivers, though these are of limited navigational use because of rapids and waterfalls, the most notable of which are the Kaieteur Fall on the Potaro River with a sheer drop of 741 ft, the Horse Shoe Falls on the Essequibo and the Marina Fall on the Ipobe River.

CLIMATE – The two dry seasons normally last from mid February to end April, and from mid August to end November. In the August to October period it is hot. The mean temperature is 27°C, the usual extremes being 21°C and 32°C. In the interior the mean temperature is higher, at 28°C, its extremes ranging from 19°C to 40°C. The yearly rainfall is subject to marked variation, its mean on the coast lands averaging about 90 inches with an average of 58 inches on the savannas.

CAPITAL – ΨGeorgetown. Estimated population, including environs, 185,000. Other towns are: Linden (29,000); ΨNew Amsterdam (23,000); Corriverton (17,000).

CURRENCY – Guyana dollar (G$) of 100 cents.

FLAG – Green with a yellow, white-bordered triangle based on the hoist and surmounted by a red, black-bordered triangle.

NATIONAL ANTHEM – Dear Land of Guyana.

NATIONAL DAYS – 26 May (Independence Day); 23 February (Republic Day).

GOVERNMENT

Guyana became independent on 26 May 1966, with a Governor-General appointed by The Queen. It became a Co-operative Republic on 23 February 1970. Under the Independence Constitution the Prime Minister and Cabinet were responsible to a National Assembly elected by secret ballot every five years. The last election under this Constitution was in 1973 and the term of that Assembly was later extended to October 1980.

A new Constitution was passed into law in February 1980 and promulgated in October 1980. It provides for an Executive President, a National Assembly of 65 members, and also for a National Congress of Local Democratic Organs responsible for local government. The Supreme Congress of the People consists of all members of these two assemblies. The electoral system is a proportional representation or 'single list' system, each voter casting his vote for a party list of candidates. The voting age is 18.

A general election was scheduled for the end of 1991 but has been postponed because of the failure of the all-party Elections Commission to establish electoral machinery free from fraud and large-scale voter registration irregularities. The election is now scheduled for 5 October 1992.

HEAD OF STATE
Executive President, H. Desmond Hoyte, *took office* Aug. 1985, *sworn in* 12 December 1985 for five-year term.

CABINET as at June 1992
The Executive President.
Prime Minister and Minister of Health, Hamilton Green.
Deputy PM and Minister of Public Works, Communications and Regional Development, Robert Corbin.
Deputy PM and Minister of Trade, Tourism and Industry, Winston Murray.
Finance, Carl Greenidge.
Attorney-General and Minister of Legal Affairs, Keith Massiah.
Senior Minister of Public Works, Communications and Regional Development, Richard Kranenburg.
Senior Minister of Labour, Human Services and Social Security, Rabbian Ali-Khan.
Minister of Labour, Human Services and Social Security, Jean Persico.
Senior Minister of Education and Cultural Development, Deryck Bernard.
Minister in the Office of the President, Gowkarran Sharma.
Minister in the Office of the President responsible for the Public Service, Faith Harding.

GUYANA HIGH COMMISSION
3 Palace Court, Bayswater Road, London W2 4LP
Tel 071-229 7684

High Commissioner, His Excellency Cecil Stanley Pilgrim (1986).

BRITISH HIGH COMMISSION
44 Main Street (PO Box 10849), Georgetown
Tel: Georgetown 65881/4

High Commissioner, His Excellency Robert Douglas Gordon (1990) (also Ambassador to Suriname).

JUDICATURE

The Supreme Court of Judicature consists of a Court of Appeal and a High Court. There are also Courts of Summary Jurisdiction. The Court of Appeal consists of the Chancellor as President, the Chief Justice and such number of Justices of Appeal as may be prescribed by Parliament.

The High Court consists of the Chief Justice, as President, and nine Puisne Judges. It is a court with unlimited jurisdiction in civil matters and exercises exclusive jurisdiction in probate, divorce and admiralty, and certain other matters.
Chancellor, K. M. George.
Chief Justice, R. Harper.

ECONOMY

The economy is based almost entirely on the main export items of sugar, rice, bauxite and alumina. Diamonds and gold are also mined, timber and rum are produced and there is some cattle ranching. The fishing industry is being expanded. Industry is fairly small-scale.

TRADE WITH UK

	1990	1991
Imports from UK	£15,294,000	£19,275,000
Exports to UK	53,892,000	50,479,000

COMMUNICATIONS

Georgetown and New Amsterdam are the principal ports, though bauxite ships also sail to Linden, on the River Demerara, and Everton, on the River Berbice. There are no public railways and the few roads are confined mainly to the coastal areas. Air transport is the easiest form of communication between the coast and the interior.

There is a state-owned radio broadcasting station which operates two channels and a fledgling television service.

EDUCATION

The Government assumed total control of the education system in September 1976 and made education free from nursery to university level. The Government trains teachers for primary and secondary schools at its own institutions.

Approximately 1,800 students were enrolled at the University of Guyana in degree programmes and certificate and diploma courses in 1990.

There are several technical and vocational institutions, as well as some 30 adult education schools (with an enrolment of 13,500). There are also a number of technical and vocational institutions not under the aegis of the Ministry of Education.

HAITI
République d'Haiti

The Republic of Haiti occupies the western third of the island of Hispaniola, which, after Cuba, is the largest island in the West Indies. The area of the Republic, including off-shore islands, is 10,714 sq. miles (27,750 sq. km) (of which about three-quarters is mountainous), with a population (UN estimate 1990) of 5,693,000.
CLIMATE – The climate is tropical with comparatively little difference in the temperatures between the summer (March–Oct.) and the winter (Nov.–Feb.). Humidity is high, especially in the autumn.
LANGUAGE – Following the new constitution of March 1987 both French and Creole are regarded as the official languages of Haiti. French is the language of the government and the press, but it is only spoken by the educated minority. The usual language of the people is Creole.

CAPITAL – ΨPort-au-Prince. Population estimated at about 1 million. Other centres are: ΨCap Haitien (54,691); Gonaives (36,736); Les Cayes (27,222); Jérémie (25,117); St Marc (20,504); Jacmel (16,449); ΨPort de Paix (21,733).
CURRENCY – Gourde of 100 centimes.
FLAG – Horizontally blue over red.
NATIONAL ANTHEM – La Dessalinienne.
NATIONAL DAY – 1 January.

GOVERNMENT

Haiti was a French colony under the name of Saint-Domingue from 1697. The slave population, estimated at 500,000, revolted in 1791 under the leadership of Toussaint L'Ouverture, who was born a slave and made himself Governor-General of the colony. He capitulated to the French in 1802 and died in captivity in 1803. Resistance was continued by Jean Jacques Dessalines, also a former Negro slave, who, on 1 January 1804, declared the former French colony to be an independent state. It was at this time that the name Haiti, an aboriginal word meaning mountainous, was adopted. Dessalines became Emperor of Haiti, but was assassinated in 1806.

Dr Duvalier was installed as President in 1957 and held the position until his death in 1971. He was succeeded as President for life on the same day by his son, Jean Claude Duvalier, whom he had nominated as his successor. President Duvalier fled to France in February 1986 in the face of sustained popular unrest, and a council headed by Gen. Henri Namphy assumed power. In March 1987, by popular referendum, a new Constitution was agreed and Presidential elections scheduled for November; these were aborted following violence in the capital. The elections held in January 1988 were boycotted by a number of leading candidates but Leslie Manigat eventually won after a very low turnout. President Manigat was inaugurated in February 1988, but he and his government were ousted on 19 June by Gen. Henri Namphy. Manigat was deported to the Dominican Republic and Namphy set up a military government until he in turn was replaced in a coup by Lt.-Gen. Prosper Avril on 18 September 1988. Following growing government opposition in 1990, Prosper Avril resigned on 10 March. The presidency devolved upon Ertha Pascal-Trouillot, advised by a 19-member Council of State. Father Jean-Bertrand Aristide, leader of the National Front for Change and Democracy, won a free presidential election, held on 16 December 1990.

Father Aristide launched a wide-scale anti-corruption campaign, including removing from power the last supporters of the Duvalier dictatorships and purging the military leadership. This led to a military coup on 30 September 1992 which ousted Aristide and installed a provisional government under President Joseph Nerette. Aristide escaped to the USA via Venezuela. The Organization of American States imposed a trade embargo on Haiti to force the military to accept the return of Aristide as President, but the military and Provisional Government have refused, causing the country great economic hardship.

Presidency, vacant.

PROVISIONAL GOVERNMENT as at July 1992

Prime Minister, Marc Bazin.
Interior and Defence, Gen. Carl Michel Nicolas.
Social Affairs, André Brutus.
Justice, Moise Senatus.
Economy and Finance, Wilner Fort.
Planning and Co-ordination, Jean André Victor.
Public Health and Population, Andrien Westerband.
Agriculture, Jacques Becker.
Public Works, Transport and Communications, Jean Carmelo Piérre-Louis.
Foreign Affairs, François Benoit.
Information, André Calixte.
Industry and Commerce, Jean Robert Delsoin.
Education, Max Carré.

The London Embassy of the Republic of Haiti closed on 30 March 1987.
BRITISH AMBASSADOR (resident in Kingston, Jamaica).

ECONOMY

In recent years measures for agricultural rehabilitation have been taken with the aim of a gradual restoration of productivity, which had declined after the ending of the colonial plantation system. The main project is a scheme for the irrigation of more than 70,000 acres of the Artibonite valley.

Coffee accounts for about 32 per cent of total exports, worth approximately US$55 million in 1986. Cocoa is the second largest export earner at US$4.5 million. Corn, 110,000 tonnes (1985), sorghum, 108,000 tonnes (1985), and rice are also grown. Increased production of tropical fruits and vegetables is being encouraged.

Export assembly industries account for about 30 per cent of the total manufacturing industry in Haiti, employing an estimated 40,000 people. Items such as leather goods, textiles, electronic components and sports equipment are manufactured, using imported raw materials, for re-export, primarily to the USA. Principal imports are raw materials for the export assembly sector, foodstuffs, machinery, vehicles, mineral oils and textiles.

TRADE WITH UK

	1990	1991
Imports from UK	£6,807,000	£7,280,000
Exports to UK	1,271,000	1,253,000

COMMUNICATIONS

The main roads are asphalted and secondary roads are fair. Internal air services are maintained between the capital and the principal provincial towns. International air-services connect Port-au-Prince with the USA and other Caribbean and South American cities. The principal towns and villages are connected by telephone and/or telegraph. The telephone company is state owned (51 per cent) and the service both in Port-au-Prince and inter-urban has been greatly improved. External telegraph, telephone and postal services are normal. There are several commercial radio stations and two television stations at Port-au-Prince.

Regular passenger liner services to New York have ceased, but cruise ships call occasionally. Freight sailings are frequent for the USA, Canada, Europe, Latin America (except Cuba) and the main Caribbean ports.

EDUCATION

Education is free but estimates of illiteracy are as high as 85 per cent.

HOLY SEE *see* VATICAN CITY STATE

HONDURAS

Republica de Honduras

Honduras, in Central America, lies between lat. 13° and 16° 30′ N. and long. 83° and 89° 41′ W. with a seaboard of about 375 miles on the Caribbean Sea and an outlet, consisting of a small strip of coast 63 miles in length on the Pacific. Its frontiers are contiguous with those of Guatemala, Nicaragua and El Salvador.

The republic contains a total area of approximately 43,277 sq. miles (112,088 sq. km) and is very mountainous, being traversed by the Cordilleras, with peaks rising to 1,500 and 2,400 metres above sea level. Most of the soil is poor and acidic, except for the coastal plains of the north and some areas of the interior. Three-quarters of the territory is covered by pine forests which contribute to much of the country's wealth in natural resources. Rainfall is seasonal, May to October being wet and November to April dry.

POPULATION – The population, 5,105,000 (1990 UN estimate) is of mixed Spanish and Indian blood. Garifunas in Northern Honduras are of West Indian origin.

LANGUAGE – The language of the country is Spanish, although English is the first language of many in the islands and on the north coast.

CAPITAL – Tegucigalpa, population (1987 estimate) 640,900; other towns are San Pedro Sula (429,300), ΨLa Ceiba (66,000), ΨPuerto Cortes (42,100), Choluteca (64,500) and ΨTela (27,800).
CURRENCY – Lempira of 100 centavos.
FLAG – Three horizontal bands, blue, white, blue (with five blue stars on white band).
NATIONAL ANTHEM – Tu Bandera Es Un Lampo De Cielo (Your flag is a heavenly light).
NATIONAL DAY – 15 September.

GOVERNMENT

Originally discovered and settled by the Spanish at the beginning of the 16th century, Honduras formed part of the Spanish American dominions for nearly three centuries until 1821 when independence was proclaimed. Under military government from 1972 to 1981, and after two terms of Liberal administration, the most recent legislative election in November 1989 was won by the Partido Nacional (National Party). The new Government took office in January 1990.

The Republic is divided into 18 departments, the newest of which, Gracias a Dios, formed in 1957, is now the home of thousands of Miskito Indian refugees from Nicaragua.

HEAD OF STATE
President of the Republic, Rafael Leonardo Callejas, *assumed office*, 27 January 1990.

CABINET as at July 1992

Interior and Justice, Francisco Cardona Arguelles.
Foreign Affairs, Mario Carias Zapata.
Defence, Col. Alvaro Antonio Romero.
Education, Jaime Martinez Guzman.
Finance, Benjamin Villanueva.
Economy, Ramon Medina Luna.
Communications, Public Works and Transport, Mauricio Membreno.
Health, Dr Cesar Castellanos.
Labour and Social Security, Carlos Torres Lopez.

Natural Resources, Mario Nufio Gamero.
Culture and Tourism, Sonia Canales De Mendieta.
Economic Planning, Manlio Martinez Cantor.
Director of National Agrarian Institute, Juan Ramon Martinez.

EMBASSY OF HONDURAS
115 Gloucester Place, London W1H 3PJ
Tel 071-486 4880

Ambassador Extraordinary and Plenipotentiary, His Excellency Carlos Zeron (1991).

BRITISH EMBASSY
Apartado Postal 290, Tegucigalpa
Tel: Honduras 32-0612/18

Ambassador Extraordinary and Plenipotentiary, His Excellency Peter John Streams, CMG (1989).

ECONOMY

Agriculture is mainly confined to the large and fertile valleys on the wide Caribbean plain, and the extensive valleys found in the Comayagua and Olancho regions of the interior. Reaching inland from the Caribbean towards the eastern border with Nicaragua a vast tropical forest area called the Mosquitia provides valuable reserves of timber. Lead, zinc and silver are mined on a small scale. There are large tracts of uncultivated land.

TRADE

The chief exports are coffee, bananas and timber, the most important woods being pine, mahogany and cedar. Cattle raising and the exporting of frozen meat is an important industry, and exports of shrimps and lobsters are increasing. Other products are tobacco, beans, maize, rice, cotton, palm oil, sugar cane, cement and tropical fruits.

		1987	1988
Imports	Lempiras	2,646.1m	2,786.2m
Exports		1,986.9m	2,057.5m

Trade with UK	1990	1991
Imports from UK	£7,345,000	£6,784,000
Exports to UK	11,661,000	9,065,000

EDUCATION

Primary and secondary education is free, primary education being compulsory, and the Government has launched a campaign to eradicate illiteracy.

COMMUNICATIONS

There are about 1,004 km of railway in operation, chiefly to serve the banana plantations and the Caribbean ports. There are 17,947 km of roads, of which 2,173 km are paved, excluding some 250 km of new major highways recently inaugurated. Improvements are being made and new roads built. There are 33 smaller airstrips and three international airports, Tegucigalpa, San Pedro Sula and La Ceiba.

Ψ The chief ports are Puerto Cortes, Tela and La Ceiba on the north coast, through which passes the bulk of the trade with the United States and Europe. Puerto Castilla is being developed as a deep-water container port, and San Lorenzo is also experiencing rapid growth.

HUNGARY

Magyar Köztársaság

AREA AND POPULATION – The area of Hungary is 35,919 sq. miles (93,030 sq. km) with a population (1991) of 10,335,000.

CAPITAL – Budapest, on the Danube; population (1990) 2,016,000. Other large towns are: Miskolc (196,449); Debrecen (212,247); Szeged (175,338) and Pécs (170,119).
CURRENCY – Forint of 100 fillér.
FLAG – Red, white, green (horizontally).
NATIONAL ANTHEM – Isten Aldd Meg A Magyart (God Bless the Hungarians).
NATIONAL DAYS – 15 March, 20 August, 23 October.

GOVERNMENT

Hungary, reconstituted a kingdom in 1920 after having been declared a republic on 17 November 1918, joined the Anti-Comintern Pact in February 1939 and entered the 1939–45 War on the side of Germany in 1941. On 20 January 1945 a Hungarian provisional government of liberation, which had been set up during the preceding December, signed an armistice under the terms of which the frontiers of Hungary were withdrawn to the limits existing in 1937, set under the Treaty of Trianon in 1919.

After the liberation, a coalition of the Smallholder, National Peasant, Social Democrat and Communist parties carried out major land reform and mines, heavy industry, banks and schools were nationalized. By 1949 the Communists had succeeded in gaining a monopoly of power and by 1952 practically the entire economy had been 'socialized'. The Party formulated policy and the function of the Government was mainly executive.

The period from July 1956 to the outbreak of the national revolution on 23 October was marked by growing ferment in intellectual circles and increased discord within the Party. The withdrawal of Soviet troops from the country and free elections were among the demands put forward. Fighting broke out on the night of 23 October between demonstrators, who had been joined by large numbers of factory workers, and the State Security Police. Soviet forces intervened in strength early the next morning. By 30 October Soviet troops had withdrawn from Budapest and on 3 November an all-party coalition government under Imre Nagy was formed. This government was overthrown and the revolution suppressed as the result of a renewed attack by Soviet forces on Budapest in the early hours of 4 November. The formation of a new Hungarian Revolutionary Worker Peasant Government under the leadership of Mr Kádár was announced.

From 1963, the government gradually introduced economic reforms and some political liberalization. Kádár was forced to resign in May 1989. In October 1989 the National Assembly (*Országgyülés*) approved an amended Constitution which described Hungary as an independent, democratic state. Multi-party elections took place in March and April 1990. The majority of seats were won by the Hungarian Democratic Forum, followed by the Alliance of Free Democrats. In May 1990 a coalition government was installed. The former ruling Communist Party, reconstituted as the Hungarian Socialist Party, is now in opposition.

HEAD OF STATE
President, Arpad Göncz, *sworn in* 3 August 1990.

CABINET as at June 1992

Prime Minister, Dr József Antall.
Interior, Dr Péter Boross.
Agriculture, Elemér Gergácz.
Justice, Dr István Balsai.
Industry and Commerce, Iván Szabó.
Environmental Protection, Sándor Keresztes.
Transport and Communications, Csaba Siklós.
Foreign Affairs, Géza Jeszenszky.
Defence, Lajos Für.
Labour, Dr Gyula Kiss.
Education and Culture, Dr Bertalan Andrásfalvy.
Public Welfare, László Surján.
International Economic Relations, Béla Kádár.
Finance, Mihály Kupa.
Ministers without Portfolio, Ferenc Mádl; Ernö Pungor; Tamás Szabó; Ferenc József Nagy; Balázs Horváth; Tibor Füzessy.
State Secretaries:
International Economic Relations, László Bogár.
Finance, Tibor Pongrácz.
PM's Office, Géza Entz; Balázs Bárdos; Miklós Lukáts; Tamás Katona; Dr Miklós Palós.
Justice, Dr Tamás Isépy.
Foreign Affairs, András Kelemen.
Social Welfare, Erzsébet Pusztai.
Transport, Telecommunications, Zsolt Rajkai.
Agriculture, László Sárossy.
Labour, György Schamschula.
Environment, Mrs László Tarján.

EMBASSY OF THE REPUBLIC OF HUNGARY
35 Eaton Place, London SW1X 8BY
Tel 071-235 4048/7191

Ambassador Extraordinary and Plenipotentiary, His Excellency Tibor Antalpéter (1990).
Minister Plenipotentiary, József Hajgató.
Counsellors, A. Gerelyes (*Consul*); T. Vajda (*Press*); E. Sziklai (*Commercial*); J. G. Turi (*Culture*).
Defence and Military Attaché, Col. P. Szücs.

BRITISH EMBASSY
Harmincad Utca 6, Budapest V
Tel: Budapest 118-2888

Ambassador Extraordinary and Plenipotentiary, His Excellency John Allan Birch, CMG (1989).
Counsellor and Deputy Head of Mission, H. J. Pearce.
Defence and Military Attaché, Col. W. Ibbotson.
Air Attaché, Wg.-Cdr. M. Gaynor.
First Secretary and British Council Representative, D. J. Harvey.
Consul, F. A. Blogg.

DEFENCE

Hungary has a total armed forces active strength of 86,500 (including 45,900 conscripts). Conscripts serve for 12 months. The Army has a strength of 66,400 (36,400 conscripts) with 1,482 main battle tanks, 1,760 armoured personnel carriers and armoured infantry fighting vehicles, 1,087 artillery pieces and 110 surface-to-air missiles. The Air Force has a strength of 20,100 (9,500 conscripts) and 111 combat aircraft and 39 attack helicopters. As Hungary is landlocked it has no navy but the Army maintains a small Danube Flotilla with six mine countermeasures vessels.

ECONOMY

Since 1968 the Hungarian economy had been run according to a system which allowed more decentralized decision-making than in some other eastern European countries, although central control in vital areas such as the allocation of fuels and raw materials remained. The new government has embarked upon the privatization of state-owned concerns and the return of nationalized land to its former owners.

Industrialization has made considerable progress in the last decade and now produces 68 per cent of national income. Industry is mainly based on imported raw materials but Hungary has its own coal (mostly brown), bauxite, considerable deposits of natural gas (some not yet under full exploitation), some iron ore and oil. Output figures in 1991 (1,000 tons): coal 16,974; aluminium 6,316; rolled steel 1,532; crude oil 1,893. Natural gas production totalled 5,041 million cubic metres.

Agriculture still occupies an important place in the Hungarian economy. In 1990 10½ per cent of the entire land area was owned by state farms and a further 63.8 per cent was within co-operative farms. Co-operative farms will remain a feature of Hungarian agriculture. Production in 1989 was (tons):

Maize	6,700,000
Wheat	6,500,000
Sugar beet	5,300,000
Barley	854,000
Rye	261,000
Oats	145,000

GDP per capita in 1990 was US$3,175.

TRADE

	1991
Imports	Forints 924,100m
Exports	801,900m

Trade with UK	1990	1991
Imports from UK	£121,837,000	£132,448,000
Exports to UK	102,741,000	103,869,000

RELIGION

About two-thirds of the population are Roman Catholics, and the remainder mostly Calvinist.

EDUCATION

There are five types of schools under the Ministry of Education: kindergartens for age three to six, general schools for age six to 14 (compulsory), vocational schools (15–18), secondary schools (15–18), universities and adult training schools (over 18).

CULTURE

Magyar, or Hungarian, is one of the Finno-Ugrian languages. Hungarian literature began to flourish in the second half of 16th century. Among the greatest writers of the 19th and 20th centuries are Mihály Vörösmarty (1800–55), Sándor Petöfi (1823–49), János Arany (1817–82), Imre Madách (1823–64), Kálmán Mikszáth (1847–1910), Endre Ady (1877–1918), Attila József (1905–37), Mihály Babits (1883–1941) and Dezsö Kosztolányi (1885–1936).

ICELAND
Island

Iceland is a large volcanic island in the North Atlantic Ocean, extending from 63° 23′ to 66° 33′ N. lat., and from 13° 22′ to

24° 35′ W. long., with an estimated area of 39,768 sq. miles (103,000 sq. km). The population was 253,482 on 1 December 1989.

CAPITAL – ΨReykjavík, population (1 Dec. 1989), 95,811. Other centres in approximate order of importance are Ψ Akureyri, Kópavogur, ΨHafnarfjördur, Keflavík, Westmann Islands, Akranes, Isafjördur and ΨSiglufjördur.
CURRENCY – Icelandic króna (Kr) of 100 aurar.
FLAG – Blue, with white-bordered red cross.
NATIONAL ANTHEM – O Gud Vors Lands (Our Country's God).
NATIONAL DAY – 17 June.

HISTORY

Iceland was uninhabited before the ninth century, when settlers came from Norway. For several centuries a form of republican government prevailed, with an annual assembly of leading men called the *Althing*, but in 1241 Iceland became subject to Norway, and later to Denmark. During the colonial period, Iceland maintained its cultural integrity but a deterioration in the climate, together with frequent volcanic eruptions and outbreaks of disease, led to a serious fall in the standard of living and to a decline in the population to little more than 40,000. In the nineteenth century a struggle for independence began which led first to home rule for Iceland under the Danish Crown (1918), and later to complete independence under a republican form of rule in 1944.

GOVERNMENT

The parliamentary (*Althing*) elections in April 1991 gave the Independence Party 28 seats, Progressives 13, Social Democratic Party 10, People's Alliance 9 and Women's Alliance 6. David Oddsson formed a new coalition government on 30 April 1991.

HEAD OF STATE
President, Vigdís Finnbogadóttir, *born* 1930, *elected* 29 June 1980, *re-elected*, July 1984, June 1988 and June 1992.

CABINET as at 30 April 1992
Prime Minister, Minister for the Statistical Bureau of Iceland, David Oddsson (IP).
Foreign Affairs and Trade, Jón Baldvin Hannibalsson (SDP).
Finance, Fridrik Sophusson (IP).
Fisheries, Justice and Ecclesiastical Affairs, Thorsteinn Pálsson (IP).
Education and Culture, Ólafur Einarsson (IP).
Social Affairs, Jóhanna Sigurthardóttir (SDP).
Health and Social Security, Sighvatur Björgvinsson (SDP).
Commerce, Industry and Nordic Co-operation, Jón Sigurthsson (SDP).
Agriculture and Communications, Halldór Blöndal (IP).
Environmental Affairs, Eidur Gudnason (SDP).

IP Independence Party
SDP Social Democrat Party

EMBASSY OF ICELAND
1 Eaton Terrace, London SW1W 8EY
Tel 071-730 5131

Ambassador Extraordinary and Plenipotentiary, His Excellency Helgie Ágústsson, GCVO (1989).

BRITISH EMBASSY
Laufásvegur 49, 101 Reykjavik
Tel: Reykjavik 15883/4

Ambassador Extraordinary and Plenipotentiary and Consul-General, His Excellency P. F. M. Wogan, CMG (1991).
Deputy Head of Mission, Second Secretary and Consul, A. Mehmet, MVO.

BRITISH CONSULAR OFFICES – There are Consular Offices at *Akureyri* and *Reykjavík*.

CULTURE

The ancient Norraena (or Northern tongue) presents close affinities to Anglo-Saxon and as spoken and written in Iceland today differs little from that introduced into the island in the ninth century. There is a rich literature with two distinct periods of development, from the mid-11th to the late 13th century and from the early 19th century to the present.

ECONOMY

Iceland has considerable resources of hydro-electric and geothermal energy. It is estimated that exploited water power (4,000 Gigawatt hours/a) represents only about 9 per cent of that economically exploitable, whereas only 5 per cent of the estimated 80,000 Gigawatt hours/a of available geothermal power has so far been harnessed. Energy-intensive heavy industry includes an aluminium smelter, a nitrogen fertilizer factory, a diatomite plant and a ferro-silicone plant.

FINANCE

	1988	1989
Revenue	Kr63,091m	Kr77,100m
Expenditure	55,198m	67,651m

TRADE

The principal exports are frozen fish fillets, salt fish, stock fish, fresh fish on ice, frozen scampi, fishmeal and oil, skins and aluminium; the imports consist of almost all the necessities of life, the chief items being petroleum products, transport equipment, textiles, foodstuffs, animal feeds, timber, and alumina.

	1988	1989
Exports	Kr61,674m	Kr80,072m
Imports	68,971m	80,250m

Trade with UK	1990	1991
Imports from UK	£88,537,000	£96,615,000
Exports to UK	259,438,000	238,428,000

COMMUNICATIONS

At 1 January 1990, the mercantile marine consisted of 622 vessels of under 100 gross tons and 345 ships of 100 gross tons and over; a total of 967 vessels (178,314 gross tons), of which 842 (116,011 gross tons) are decked fishing vessels. There are regular shipping services between Reykjavík and Felixstowe, Humber ports and the Continent.

A regular air service is maintained between Glasgow and London and Reykjavík. There are also air services from the island to Scandinavia, USA, Germany, France and Luxembourg.

Road communications are adequate in summer but greatly restricted by snow in winter. Only roads in town centres and key highways are metalled, the rest being of gravel, sand and lava dust. The climate and terrain make first-class surfaces for highways out of the question. There are no railways.

INDIA
The Republic of India

AREA – The Republic of India has an area of 1,269,346 sq. miles (3,287,590 sq. km), composed of three well-defined regions: the mountain range of the Himalayas, the Indo-Gangetic plain, and the southern peninsula. The main

mountain ranges are the Himalayas in the north (over 29,000 feet) and the Western and Eastern Ghats (over 8,000 feet). Major rivers include the Ganges, Indus, Krishna, Godavari and Mahanadi.

CLIMATE – There are four seasons: the cold season (December–March); the hot season (April–May); the rainy season (June–September); and the season of the retreating south-west monsoon (October–November). Temperatures vary over the whole country, between averages of about 10°C and 33°C, reaching over 38°C in some parts during the hot season. There are similar variations in rainfall, from only a few inches a year falling in the western Thar Desert to over 400 inches in Meghalaya.

POPULATION – India is the second most populous country in the world. The population at the 1991 Census was 843,930,861, of which more than 20 per cent was urban. The majority of the population is Hindu (82 per cent), the rest being Muslim (11 per cent), Christian (2.5 per cent), Sikh (1.8 per cent), Buddhist (0.7 per cent) and Jain (0.5 per cent).

LANGUAGES – The official languages are Hindi in the Devanagari script and English, though 14 regional languages also are recognized for adoption as official state languages.

CAPITAL – Delhi (population in 1991 was 8,375,188). Populations of other principal cities (1991 figures) were Ahmedabad 3,297,655; Bangalore 4,086,548; ΨBombay (Mumbai) 12,571,720; ΨCalcutta 10,916,272; Hyderabad 4,280,261; Kanpur 2,111,284; Lucknow 1,642,134; Ψ Madras 5,361,468; Pune 2,485,014.
CURRENCY – Indian rupee (Rs) of 100 paisa.
FLAG – The National Flag is a horizontal tricolour with bands of deep saffron, white and dark green in equal proportions. In the centre of the white band appears an Asoka wheel in navy blue.
NATIONAL ANTHEM – Jana-gana-mana.
NATIONAL DAY – 26 January (Republic Day).

HISTORY

The Indus civilization was fully developed by *c.*2500 BC but collapsed *c.*1750 BC, subsequently being replaced by an Aryan civilization spread from the west. The first Arab invasions of the north-west began in the seventh century and Muslim, Hindu and Buddhist states developed until the establishment of the Mogul dynasty in 1526. The British East India Company established settlements throughout the 17th century; clashes with the French and native princes led to the British government taking control of the company in 1784. The separate dominions of India and Pakistan became independent within the Commonwealth in 1947 and India became a Republic in 1950.

GOVERNMENT

The Constitution of India came into force in 1950. Executive power is vested in the President, who is elected for a five year term by an electoral college consisting of the elected members of the Union and State Legislatures. He appoints the Prime Minister and, on the latter's advice, the Ministers, and can dismiss them. The Council of Ministers is collectively responsible to the *Lok Sabha* (lower house). The Vice-President is ex-officio chairman of the *Rajya Sabha* (upper house).

Legislative power rests with the President, the Rajya Sabha (which has up to 250 members) and the Lok Sabha (which has up to 544 members). Twelve members of the Rajya Sabha are nominated by the President, the rest are indirectly elected representatives of the State and Union Territories. They hold office for six years. The 525 members of the Lok Sabha representing the States are directly elected by universal adult franchise, and 17 representatives of the Union Territories are chosen, for a maximum term of five years. Subject to the provisions of the Constitution, the Union Parliament can make laws for the whole of India and the State legislatures for their respective units.

HEAD OF STATE
President of the Republic of India, Dr Shankar Dayal Sharma, *elected* 16 July 1992.
Vice-President, vacant.

CABINET as at July 1992
Prime Minister, Minister of Personnel, Public Grievances, Science and Technology, Electronics, Atomic Energy, Chemical and Fertilizers, Rural Development, Civil Supplies and Public Distribution, Space, Ocean Development, Defence and Industry, P. V. Narasimha Rao.
Finance, Dr Manmohan Singh.
Agriculture, Balram Jakhar.
Human Resources Development, Arjun Singh.
Urban Development, Sheila Kaul.
Railways, C. K. Jaffer Sharief.
Petroleum and Natural Gas, B. Shankaranand.
Law, Justice and Company Affairs, K. Vijaya Bhaskara Reddy.
Home Affairs, S. B. Chavan.
External Affairs, Madhavsinh Solanki.
Welfare, Sitaram Kesri.
Health and Family Welfare, M. L. Fotedar.
Water Resources, V. C. Shukla.
Civil Aviation and Tourism, Madhav Rao Scindia.
Parliamentary Affairs, Ghulam Nabi Azad.
In addition there are 13 ministers of state (independent charge), 26 ministers of state and eight deputy ministers, making a total of 62 in the Council of Ministers.

INDIAN HIGH COMMISSION
India House, Aldwych, London WC2B 4NA
Tel 071–836 8484

High Commissioner, His Excellency Dr L. M. Singhvi (1991).
Deputy High Commissioner, K. V. Rajan.

BRITISH HIGH COMMISSION
Chanakyapuri, New Delhi 21, 1100–21.
Tel: New Delhi 601371

High Commissioner, His Excellency Sir Nicholas Fenn, KCMG (1991).
Deputy High Commissioner and Minister, P. J. Fowler, CMG.
Minister for Cultural Affairs and British Council Representative in India, R. Arbuthnott, CBE. Offices also at *Bombay*, *Calcutta* and *Madras*. There are British Council libraries at these four centres and British libraries at *Ahmedabad, Bangalore, Bhopal, Hyderabad, Lucknow, Patna, Pune, Ranchi* and *Trivandrum*.

STATES AND TERRITORIES OF THE UNION

There are 25 States and seven Union Territories. Each State is governed by a Governor appointed by the President who holds office for five years, and by a Council of Ministers. All States have a Legislative Assembly, and some have also a Legislative Council, elected directly by adult suffrage for a maximum period of five years. The judges of the High Court of a State are appointed by the President.

The Union Territories are administered, except where otherwise provided by Parliament, by the President acting through an Administrator or Lieutenant-Governor, or other authority appointed by him.

JUDICATURE

The Supreme Court consists of the Chief Justice and not more than 17 other judges, appointed by the President. It is the highest court in respect of all constitutional matters and the final Court of Appeal.

DEFENCE

The supreme command of the armed forces is vested in the President. Administrative and operational control resides in the Army, Navy and Air Headquarters under the supervision of the Ministry of Defence.

The Army has five commands, Southern, Eastern, Northern, Western and Central, and a total strength of some 1,100,000, with some 3,100 main battle tanks of Soviet and indigenous manufacture; 1,250 armoured infantry fighting vehicles and armoured personnel carriers; over 4,000 artillery pieces and 120 helicopters.

The Indian Navy consists of two aircraft carriers, 17 submarines and 26 destroyers and frigates organized into a number of frigate squadrons, including some of the latest type of anti-submarine and anti-aircraft frigates, a squadron of anti-submarine patrol vessels and minesweeping squadrons. A Naval aviation wing deploys some 46 combat aircraft and 75 armed helicopters. India has started building her own naval craft.

The Indian Air Force has a strength of some 110,000 with 630 combat aircraft and 36 armed helicopters. It is organized in seven major formations, the Western, Eastern, Central, Southern and South-Western Air Commands, and the Training and Maintenance Commands. Aircraft in use include SU-7, Hunter, Gnat, MiG 21 and MiG 23, Canberra bomber, Jaguar and Mirage-2000, helicopter and training planes.

ECONOMY

AGRICULTURE – Agriculture is the chief industry, supporting about 70 per cent of the population, and providing nearly 40 per cent of the Gross Domestic Product. The area under cultivation has been increased by irrigation schemes, but most holdings are less than five acres. Production has grown by 3 per cent each year since 1951, remaining slightly ahead of the 2 per cent increase necessary to keep pace with the rising population. Food crops occupy three-quarters of the total cropped area and production of food grains amounted to 176 million tonnes in 1990–1. In 1991–2 foodgrains production was expected to reach about 182 million tonnes following good rains. The main food crops are rice, cereals (principally wheat) and pulses. The major cash crops include sugar cane, jute, cotton and tea. Other products include oil seeds, spices, groundnuts, tobacco, rubber and coffee. Livestock is raised, principally for dairy purposes or for the hides: cattle (an estimated 181 million), goats (71 million), sheep (41 million) and pigs (9.9 million).

INDUSTRY – India's major industries are based on the exploitation and processing of her mineral resources,

States and Territories (Capitals)	*Area (sq. km)*	*Population (1991 Census)*	*Governor*	*Chief Minister*
STATES				
Andhra Pradesh (Hyderabad)	275,100p	53,549,673	K. Kant	N. Janardhan Reddy
Arunachal Pradesh (Itanagar)	83,700p	631,839	S. Dwivedy	Gegong Apang
Assam (Dispur)	78,400	24,456,000	Loknath Misra	Hiteshwar Saika
Bihar (Patna)	173,900p	86,338,853	M. S. Quershi	Lalu Prasad
Goa (Panaji)	3,701	1,000,000†	B.P. Singh	R. S. Naik
Gujarat (Gandhinagar)	196,000p	41,174,060	Sarup Singh	Chimanbhai Patel
Haryana (Chandigarh)	44,200p	12,922,618	D. L. Mandal	Bhajan Lal
Himachal Pradesh (Shimla)	55,700	4,280,818	V. Verma	Shanta Kumar
Jammu and Kashmir* (Srinagar/Jammu)	222,200p	5,987,389	Girish Chandra Saxena	(Governor's rule)
Karnataka (Bangalore)	191,800	44,817,398	K. A. Khan	S. Rangarappa
Kerala (Trivandrum)	38,900p	25,453,680	B. Rachiah	K. Karunakaran
Madhya Pradesh (Bhopal)	443,500p	66,135,862	K. M. Ali	Sunderlal Patwa
Maharashtra (Bombay-Mumbai)	307,700p	62,784,171	C. Subramaniam	S. Naik
Manipur (Imphal)	22,300	1,420,953	C. Panigrahi	R. K. D. Singh
Meghalaya (Shillong)	22,400p	1,335,819	M. Dighe	B. B. Lyngdoh
Mizoram (Aizawl)	21,100	686,217	S. Kaushal	Lal Thanhawla
Nagaland (Kohima)	16,600	1,215,573	M. M. Thomas	vacant
Orissa (Bhubaneswar)	155,700	26,370,271	Y. D. Sharma	J. B. Patnaik
Punjab (Chandigarh)	50,400	16,788,915	Surindra Nath	Beaut Singh
Rajasthan (Jaipur)	342,200	34,261,862	Dr Sarup Singh	Bhairon Singh Shekhawat
Sikkim (Gangtok)	7,100	403,612	Adm. R. H. Tahiliani	N. B. Bhandari
Tamil Nadu (Madras)	130,100p	48,408,077	Bhishma Marain Singh	J. Jayalalitha
Tripura (Agartala)	10,500	2,744,807	R. Reddy	S. R. Majumdar
Uttar Pradesh (Lucknow)	294,400p	110,862,013	B. S. Reddy	Kalyan Singh
West Bengal (Calcutta)	88,800p	67,782,732	Prof. N. Hasan	Jyoti Basu
UNION TERRITORIES			*Lt.-Governor*	
Andaman and Nicobar Is. (Port Blair)	8,200	188,741	Lt.-Gen. R. S. Dyal	
Chandigarh	100	451,610	Surindra Nath	
Dadra and Nagar Haveli (Silvassa)	500	103,676	B. P. Singh	
Daman and Diu	112	78,981†	B. P. Singh	
Delhi	1,500	6,220,406	vacant	
Lakshadweep (Kavaratti)	30	51,681	S. P. Agrawal	
Pondicherry	500	789,416	Harswarup Singh	S. Vaithalingam

p provisional figure
† estimated figure

* Jammu and Kashmir is an area disputed between India, Pakistan and China, all three controlling a part of the territory. The area figure includes those parts occupied by Pakistan and China, which are claimed by India, but the population figure excludes the population of these areas, where the Census was not taken. The state's capital is at Srinagar in summer and Jammu in winter.

principally coal, oil and iron. The coal industry, nationalized in the early 1970s, reached an output in 1989–90 of 213 million tonnes. Production of crude oil from the main fields in Assam and from offshore drilling was about 25.6 million tonnes in 1989–90. Steel production is mainly in the hands of the public sector, with five public and one private sector integrated steel plants producing 10.5 million tonnes of ingot steel in 1989–90. The engineering industry, heavy and light, is also primarily in the hands of the public sector. The manufacture of chemicals, fertilizers, petrochemicals, motor vehicles and commercial vehicles has been expanded.

Other principal manufactures are those derived from agricultural products, textiles, jute goods, sugar, leather, which along with tea, fish, and iron ore and concentrates are India's major exports.

Faced with the need to obtain loans from the World Bank and assistance from the IMF, India has abandoned centralized planning, after 40 years; subsidies are to be cut, state corporations privatized and the economy opened up to foreign companies.

FINANCE

The budget estimates for 1989–90 placed current expenditure (on revenue account) at Rs.596,420 million. Current revenue (excluding States' shares) was estimated at Rs.518,950 million.

TRADE WITH UK

	1990	1991
Imports from UK	£1,264,189,000	£1,017,398,000
Exports to UK	799,438,000	776,976,000

COMMUNICATIONS

CIVIL AVIATION – Five international airports – Palam (Delhi), Sahar (Bombay), Dum Dum (Calcutta), Meenambakkam (Madras) and Trivandrum – are managed by the International Airports Authority. The other 88 aerodromes are controlled and operated by the Civil Aviation Department of the Government. The national airlines are Indian Airlines (internal) and Air India (international).

RAILWAYS – The railways are grouped into nine administrative zones, Southern, Central, Western, Northern, North-Eastern, North-East Frontier, Eastern, South-Eastern and South-Central with a total track length of 62,211 km, about 15 per cent of which is electrified.

Gross traffic receipts (1990–1), crores of rupees, 12,096. Working expenses, 11,153. Net railway revenues, 943.

PORTS – The chief seaports are Bombay (Mumbai), Calcutta, Haldia, Madras, Mormugao, Cochin, Visakhapatnam, Kandla, Paradip, Mangalore and Tuticorin. There are 139 minor working ports with varying capacity.

SHIPPING – In March 1990, 408 ships totalling 5,980,000 gross tons were on the Indian Register.

INDONESIA
Republik Indonesia

Situated between latitudes 6° N. and 11° S. and between longitudes 95° and 141° E., Indonesia comprises the islands of Java, Madura, and Sumatra, the Riouw-Lingga Archipelago (which with Karimon, Anambas, Natuna Islands, Tambelan, and part of Sumatra, forms the province of Riau), the islands of Bangka and Billiton, part of the island of Borneo (Kalimantan), Sulawesi (formerly Celebes) Island, the Molucca Islands (Ternate, Tidore, Halmahera, Buru, Seram, Banda, Timor-Laut, Larat, Bachiam, Obi, Kei, Aru, Babar, Leti and Wetar), the island of Bali and the islands of Lombok, Sumbawa, Sumba, Flores, Timor and others comprising the provinces of East and West Nusa Tenggara and the western half of the island of New Guinea (Irian Jaya), with a total area of 735,358 sq. miles (1,904,569 sq. km), and a population (UN estimate 1990) of 179,300,000.

CAPITAL – ΨJakarta (population 7,885,519). Other important centres are: (Java) ΨSurabaya (2,027,913), ΨSemarang (1,026,671), Bandung (1,462,637); (Sumatra) Palembang (787,187), Medan (1,378,955); (Sulawesi) ΨUjung Pandang (formerly *Makassar*) (709,038); (Kalimantan) Banjarmasin (381,286), ΨPontianak (304,778), ΨBalikpapan (280,675); (Moluccas) Ambon (208,898); (Bali) Denpasar, Singaraja (for whole island 2,174,105); (Nusa Tenggara) Kupang (329,371); (Irian Jaya) Jayapura (107,164).

CURRENCY – Rupiah (Rp) of 100 sen.

FLAG – Equal bands of red over white.

NATIONAL ANTHEM – Indonesia Raya (Great Indonesia).

NATIONAL DAY – 17 August (Anniversary of Proclamation of Independence).

HISTORY

From the early part of the 17th century much of the Indonesian Archipelago was under Netherlands rule. Following the Second World War, during which the Archipelago was occupied by the Japanese, a strong nationalistic movement manifested itself and after sporadic fighting the formal transfer of sovereignty by the Netherlands of all the former Dutch East Indies except western New Guinea took place on 27 December 1949.

Western New Guinea became part of Indonesia in 1963 under the name West Irian (now Irian Jaya), this interpretation being confirmed in an 'Act of Free Choice' in July 1969, of which the United Nations took note in November 1969. Following a unilateral declaration of independence by the Fretilin in November 1975, Indonesia took over the former Portuguese colony of East Timor, which in July 1976 was declared the 27th province of Indonesia.

Following a three-week period of unrest and violent student demonstrations the Minister of the Army, General Suharto, took over effective political power in March 1966.

General Suharto was made Acting President with full powers on 11 March 1967, and on 28 March 1968 appointed full President for a period of five years.

GOVERNMENT

In the general election of June 1992, Golkar obtained 281 seats, the Muslim United Development Party 63 seats and the Indonesian Democratic Party 56 seats.

HEAD OF STATE

President, General Suharto, *born* 9 June 1921. *Acting President*, 12 March 1967; *confirmed as President*, 28 March 1968, *re-elected for a term of five years*, March 1973, March 1978, March 1983 and March 1988.

Vice-President, Lt.-Gen. Sudharmono, *elected* March 1988.

CABINET as at July 1992

Co-ordinating Ministers, Adm. Sudomo (*Political and Security Affairs*); Dr Radius Prawiro (*Economy, Finance, Industry and Development Supervision*); Gen. Supardjo Rustam (*Public Welfare*).

Ministers, Gen. Rudini (*Internal Affairs*); Ali Alatas (*Foreign Affairs*); Gen. L. B. Murdani (*Defence and Security*); Lt.-Gen. Ismail Saleh (*Justice*); Mr Harmoko (*Information*); Dr J. B. Sumarlin (*Finance*); Dr Arifin

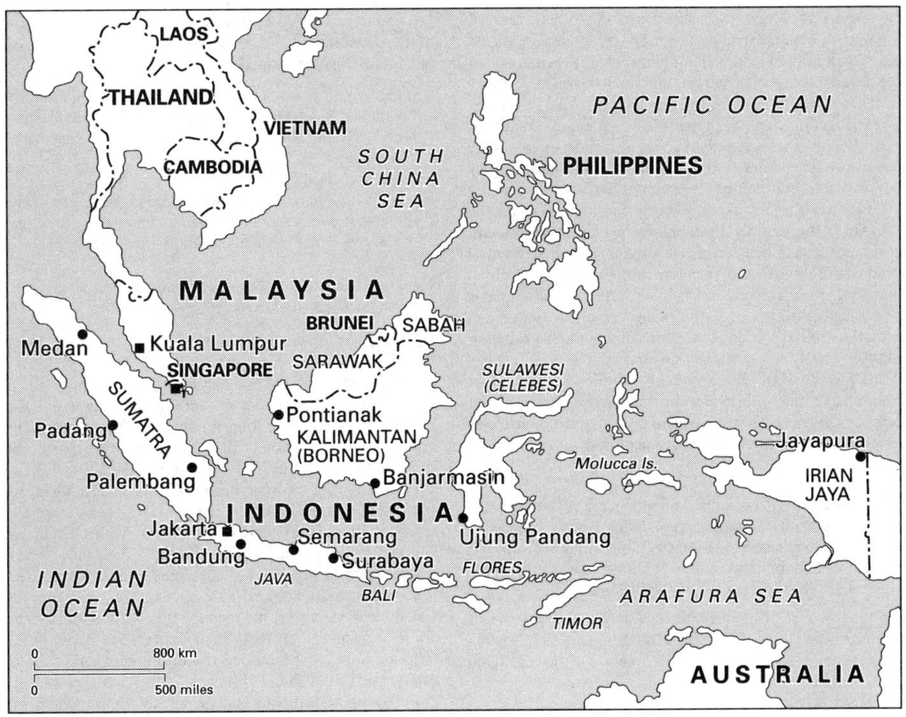

Siregar (*Trade*); Mr Hartarto (*Industry*); Mr Wardoyo (*Agriculture*); Air Vice-Marshal Ginandjar Kartasasmita (*Mines and Energy*); Radinal Mochtar (*Public Works*); Maj.-Gen. Azwar Anas (*Communications*); Maj.-Gen. Bustanil Arifin (*Co-operatives*); Cosmas Batubara (*Manpower*); Lt.-Gen. Sugiarto (*Transmigration*); Gen. Susilo Sudarman (*Tourism, Posts and Telecommunications*); Prof. Fuad Hassan (*Education and Culture*); Dr Adhyatma (*Health*); Haji Munawir Sjadzali (*Religious Affairs*); Prof. Haryati Subadio (*Social Affairs*); Hasjrul Harahap (*Forestry*).

Ministers of State, Maj.-Gen. Murdiono (*State Secretary*); Dr Saleh Afif (*National Development Planning*); Siswono Judo Husodo (*Housing*); Prof. Emil Salim (*Population and Environment*); Sarwono Kusumaatmadja (*Administrative Reform*); Prof. B. J. Habibie (*Research and Technology*); Mrs A. Sulasikin Murpratomo (*Women's Affairs*); Akbar Tandjung (*Sport and Youth Affairs*).

INDONESIAN EMBASSY
38 Grosvenor Square, London W1X 9AD
Tel 071-499 7661

Ambassador Extraordinary and Plenipotentiary, His Excellency Teuku Mohammad Hadi Thayeb (1990).
Minister, Herijanto Soeprapto (*Deputy Chief of Mission*).

BRITISH EMBASSY
Jalan M. H. Thamrin 75, Jakarta 10310
Tel: Jakarta 330904

Ambassador Extraordinary and Plenipotentiary, His Excellency Roger Carrick, CMG, LVO (1990).

BRITISH CONSULAR OFFICES – There are British Consular Offices at *Jakarta*, *Medan* and *Surabaya*.

BRITISH COUNCIL REPRESENTATIVE, Howard Thompson, OBE, S Widjojo Centre, Jalan Jenderal Sudirman 71, Jakarta 12190. There are also libraries at *Bandung* and *Medan*.

INDONESIA BRITAIN ASSOCIATION, c/o R. A. M. Ramsay, Lippo Life Building, 7th Floor, Jl. HR Rasuna Said, Jakarta 12910.

DEFENCE

The Armed Forces have a total active strength of 278,000 with selective conscription of two years. The Army has a strength of 212,000 with some 150 light tanks, 630 armoured personnel carriers, 200–50 artillery pieces and 65 surface-to-air missile launchers. The Navy has 42,000 personnel (including 12,000 marines), 2 submarines, 17 principal surface combatant vessels, 18 combat aircraft and 15 armed helicopters. The Air Force has 24,000 personnel and some 81 combat aircraft of US and British manufacture.

ECONOMY

Nearly 70 per cent of the population of Indonesia is engaged in agriculture and related production. Copra, kapok, nutmeg, pepper and cloves are produced, mainly by smallholders; palm oil, sugar, fibres and cinchona are produced by large estates. Rubber, tea, coffee and tobacco are also produced by both in large quantities. Rice is a traditional staple food for the people of Indonesia and the islands of Java, Sulawesi and Sumatra are important producers. Production has risen rapidly in recent years to 25 million tons and the country is now self-sufficient.

Oil and liquefied natural gas are the most important assets, the export of which constitutes around 80 per cent of Indonesia's export earnings, but more recent developments have underscored the vulnerability of the economy to depressed international markets and weak oil prices. Timber is the second largest foreign exchange earner after oil. Strenuous efforts have been made to develop non-oil exports, and, although these recently reached about 56 per cent, they have since fallen back to below 50 per cent of total exports but, in real terms, their value continues to rise.

Indonesia is rich in minerals, particularly tin, of which the country is the world's third biggest producer; petroleum, coal, nickel and bauxite are the other principal mineral products. There are also considerable deposits of gold, silver, manganese phosphates and sulphur. Aid to Indonesia is channelled through the Inter-Governmental Group on Indonesia (IGGI). Indonesia received about US$4.6 billion in 1991.

Indonesia's Fifth Development Programme started in 1984 and its main objectives are the diversification of the economy to reduce dependence on crude oil, with particular emphasis on agriculture and manufacturing.

Trade with UK

Principal exports to the United Kingdom are rubber, timber, non-ferrous metals, clothing, tea, coffee, spices, vegetable oils and fats, and crude oil for refinement. Imports from the United Kingdom are mainly of machinery, transport equipment, electrical equipment and chemicals.

	1990	1991
Imports from UK	£194,274,000	£197,991,000
Exports to UK	327,877,000	415,340,000

COMMUNICATIONS

In Java a main railway line connects Jakarta with Surabaya in the east of Java and there are several branches. In Sumatra the important towns of Medan, Padang and Palembang are the centres of short railway systems.

Sea communications in the archipelago are maintained by the state-run shipping companies Djakarta-Lloyd (ocean-going) and Pelni (coastal and inter-island) and other small concerns. Transport by small craft on the rivers of the larger islands plays an important part in trade.

Air services in Indonesia are operated by Garuda Indonesian Airways and other local airlines, and Jakarta is served by various international services. There are approximately 50,000 miles of roads.

IRAN

Jomhori-e-Islami-e-Iran

Area and Population – Iran has an area of 636,296 sq. miles (1,648,000 sq. km), with a population of 54,607,000 (1990 UN estimate). It is mostly an arid table-land, encircled, except in the east, by mountains, the highest in the north rising to 18,934 ft. The central and eastern portion is a vast salt desert.

Religion – The Iranians are mostly Shia Muslims but among them are Zoroastrians, Bahais, Sunni Muslims and Armenian and Assyrian Christians. Emigration has much reduced the once substantial Jewish community.

Language and Literature – Persian, or Farsi, the language of Iran, and of some other areas formerly under Persian rule, is an Indo-European tongue with many Arabic elements added; the alphabet is mainly Arabic, with writing from right to left. Among the great names in Persian literature are those of Abu'l Kásim Mansúr, of Firdausi (AD 939–1020), Omar Khayyám, the astronomer-poet (died AD 1122), Muslihu'd-Din, known as Sa'di (born AD 1184), and Shems-ed-Din Muhammad, or Hafiz (died AD 1389).

Capital – Tehran, population (1990 UN estimate) 6,042,584. Other large towns are Tabriz, Isfahan, Meshed, Shiraz, Resht, Kerman, Hamadan, Yazd, Kermanshah and Ahwaz.

Currency – Rial of 100 dinars.

Flag – Three horizontal stripes of green, white, red, with the slogan *Allahu Akbar* repeated 22 times along the edges of the green and red stripes, and the national emblem in the centre.

National Anthem – Sorood-e Jomhoori-e Eslami.

National Day – 11 February.

GOVERNMENT

Iran was ruled from the end of the 18th century by Shahs of the Qajar dynasty. A nationalist movement became active in December 1905, and in August 1906 Shah Muzaffer-ud-Din granted a Constitution. After the war of 1914–18, the subsequent troubles and the signature of the Soviet-Iranian Treaty of 1921, a vigorous Prime Minister, Reza Khan, re-established general order. On 31 Oct. 1925 the last representative of the Qajar dynasty, Sultan Ahmed Shah, was deposed in his absence by the National Assembly, which handed over the government to Prime Minister Reza Khan. Reza Khan was elected Shah on 13 Dec. 1925 by the Constituent Assembly, and took the title Reza Shah Pahlavi. On 16 September 1941 Reza Shah abdicated in favour of the Crown Prince, who ascended the throne under the title of Mohammed Reza Shah Pahlavi.

Following widespread and persistent opposition to his regime, the Shah departed from Iran in January 1979. Ayatollah Khomeini, the main spiritual leader of the Shia Muslims, returned to Iran from exile on 1 February. Following a national referendum, Iran was declared an Islamic Republic on 1 April 1979. A new constitution, providing for a President, Prime Minister and Consultative Assembly, and also for overall leadership by Ayatollah Khomeini, was approved by referendum in December 1979. The government's severe measures suppressed violent opposition. In June 1989 Khomeini died and President Khamenei was appointed Leader of the Islamic Republic. Rafsanjani was elected President in July 1989, and the post of prime minister was abolished. In April 1992 elections to the Majlis (consultative assembly), moderates supporting President Rafsanjani were overwhelmingly elected, winning over 200 of the 270 seats.

Iran was at war with Iraq following the Iraqi invasion of Iran in September 1980. International efforts to end the fighting focused on United Nations Security Council Resolution 598 of July 1987, and a ceasefire came into effect on 20 August 1988. In August 1990 Iraq accepted Iran's conditions for settling the conflict, including return to the 1975 border, but a formal peace treaty has not been signed.

Leader of the Islamic Republic, Ayatollah Seyed Ali Khamenei, *appointed* June 1989.

President, Hojjatoleslam Ali Akbar Hashemi Rafsanjani, *elected* 28 July 1989.

Cabinet as at 30 June 1992

Agriculture, Issa Kalantari.
Commerce, Abdol-Hossein Vahaji.
Construction Crusade, Gholamreza Forouzesh.
Higher Education, Mostafa Moin.
Defence and Armed Forces Logistics, Akbar Torkan.
Economy and Finance, Mohsen Nourbakhsh.
Education, Mohammad Ali Najafi.

Energy, Bizhan Namdar Zanganeh.
Islamic Guidance, Mohammad Khatami.
Foreign Affairs, Ali Akbar Velayati.
Health, Reza Malekzadeh.
Heavy Industries, Mohammad Hadi Nezhad-Hosseinian.
Housing and Urban Development, Serajuddin Kazerouni.
Industries, Mohammad Reza Nematzadeh.
Intelligence, Ali Fallahian.
Interior, Abdollah Nouri.
Justice, Esmail Shoushtari.
Labour and Social Affairs, Hossein Kamali.
Mines and Metals, Mohammad Hossein Mahloujchi.
Oil, Gholamreza Aghazadeh.
Posts, Telephones and Telegraphs, Mohammad Gharrazi.
Roads and Transport, Mohammad Saidi-Kia.
Co-operatives, Gholem Reza Shafei.

EMBASSY OF THE ISLAMIC REPUBLIC OF IRAN
27 Prince's Gate, London SW7 1PX
Tel 071-584 8101

Chargé d'Affaires, S. Sh. Khareghani.

BRITISH EMBASSY
143 Ferdowsi Avenue, PO Box 11365-4474, Tehran 11344
Tel: Tehran 675011

Chargé d'Affaires, D. N. Reddaway, MBE.

DEFENCE

Since the end of the war with Iraq the Iranian armed forces have been significantly reduced in size and now number some 528,000 active personnel. The conscription term is 24 months, with conscripts serving almost exclusively in the Army. The Army has a strength of 305,000 (including 250,000 conscripts) with one special forces, four armoured and seven infantry divisions, some 700 main battle tanks, 750 armoured personnel carriers and armoured infantry fighting vehicles, 1,000 artillery pieces and 300 helicopters.

The Navy is 18,000 strong, with eight principal surface combatant vessels, numerous patrol and support craft, and nine armed helicopters. The Air Force has 35,000 personnel, with some 213 combat aircraft. However, only around 50 per cent of these are serviceable due to the US armaments embargo, in operation since 1979.

The Islamic Revolutionary Guards Corps numbers some 170,000, of which 150,000 are ground and 20,000 naval forces.

EDUCATION

Since 1943 primary education has been compulsory and free, but there is some absenteeism, particularly outside the towns. There are 22 universities in Iran (eight in Tehran, 14 in the provinces). The educational system has been reformed following the revolution.

ECONOMY

Agriculture has suffered from a lack of investment during the Iran–Iraq war, but output is rising. Under the current Five-Year Development Plan, an attempt is being made to reduce Iran's dependence on food imports.

Wheat is the principal crop; other important crops are barley, rice, cotton, sugar beet, fruit, nuts and vegetables. Wool is also a major product. There are extensive forests in the north and west, the conservation of which is a continuing problem.

INDUSTRY – Apart from oil, the principal industrial products are carpets, textiles, sugar, cement and other construction materials, ginned cotton, vegetable oil and other food products, leather and shoes, metal manufactures, pharmaceuticals, motor vehicles, fertilizers and plastics. Industrial output was severely curtailed by the 1979 revolution, as a result of which many industrialists left the country, and by the Iran–Iraq war, but the private sector is now being encouraged again and prospects for industry are quite good.

ENERGY – The oilfields, which lie in south-western Iran, were nationalized in 1951. From 1957 until the 1979 revolution a consortium of eight oil companies (one British, one French, one Dutch, and five American) was responsible for the production, refining and sale of oil. In July 1979 the National Iranian Oil Company assumed full control of the oil industry. In addition to that extracted from the onshore wells, oil is also produced from a number of off-shore oilfields. Oil production is over 3 million b.p.d., of which some 2.3 million b.p.d. is exported. Iran is a member of OPEC.

FINANCE

	1990
Revenue	Rials 4,009,700m
Expenditure	5,595,800m

TRADE

Some 90 per cent of Iran's export earnings come from oil though an effort is being made to increase non-oil exports. The level of finance for imports depends largely on the international oil price, but with foreign investment being encouraged and restrictions on the private sector eased, the market has become more buoyant over the last two years.

Imports into Iran consist mainly of industrial and agricultural machinery, motor vehicles and motor vehicle components for assembly, iron and steel (including manufactures), electrical machinery and goods, meat, various other foods, and certain textile fabrics and yarns.

The principal exports, apart from oil, are cotton, carpets, dried fruit, nuts, hides and skins, mineral ores, wool, gums, caviare, cumin seed and spices. Germany and Japan are Iran's leading suppliers.

Trade with UK	1990	1991
Imports from UK	£384,713,000	£511,532,000
Exports to UK	279,135,000	158,354,000

COMMUNICATIONS

Tehran is at the centre of a network of highways linking the capital with other major towns, the ports and the frontiers with Turkey, Armenia, Azerbaijan, Turkmenistan, Afghanistan and Pakistan, and with the Caspian Sea.

The Trans-Iranian Railway runs from Bandar Turcoman, on the Caspian Sea, via Tehran to Bandar Khomeini, on the Persian Gulf. Other lines link Tehran with Tabriz and with Mashad. There are also railways from Tabriz to Julfa and from Zahedan to Quetta, and a branch line from Ahwaz to Khorramshahr. An extension from Qom to Kerman is now in operation, as is one from Bandar Turcoman to Gorgan. The Iranian rail system is linked to the Turkish system via Van, and is to be linked also to Turkmenistan.

There is an international airport at Tehran (Mehrabad), and airports at all the major provincial centres. The national airline, Iranair, is government-owned and operates international and domestic routes.

IRAQ

Al-Jumhouriya al-'Iraqia

AREA, ETC – Traversed by the Rivers Euphrates and Tigris, Iraq extends from Turkey on the north and north-east to the

Gulf on the south and south-east, and from Iran on the east to Syria and Arabian Desert on the west. The approximate position being between 37½° to 48½° E. long., and 37½° to 30° N. lat. The area of Iraq is 167,925 sq. miles (434,924 sq. km), of which 37 per cent is desert land. About 35 to 40 per cent of the remainder is potentially cultivable either by rainfall or by irrigation.

The Euphrates (which has a total length of 1,700 miles from its source to its outflow in the Persian Gulf) is formed by two arms, of which the Murad Su (415 miles) rises in eastern Erzurum, and flows westwards to a junction with the Kara Su, or Frat Su (275 miles); the other arm rises in the north-west of Erzurum in the Dumlu Dagh. The River Tigris has a total length of 1,150 miles from its source to its junction with the Euphrates at Qurna, 70 miles from the Gulf, and rises in two arms south of the Taurus mountains, in Kurdistan, uniting at Til, where the boundaries of the districts of Diarbekir, Van and Bitlis conjoin.

POPULATION – At the Census of October 1987 Iraq had a total population of 16,278,316. A 1990 UN estimate gives a figure of 18,920,000.

LANGUAGE – The official language is Arabic. Minority languages include Kurdish (about 15 per cent), Turkic and Aramaic.

CAPITAL – Baghdad. Population of the governorate (Census 1977) 3,205,645. Other towns of importance are ΨBasra, Mosul and Kirkuk.

CURRENCY – Iraqi dinar (ID) of 1,000 fils.

FLAG – Three horizontal stripes of red, white, black; on the white stripe three stars and the slogan *Allahu Akbar* all in green.

NATIONAL DAY – 17 July (Revolution Day).

HISTORY

In 1944 excavations at Tell Hassuna, near Shura (on the Tigris in north Iraq) unearthed abundant traces of culture dating back to 5000 BC. Excavations in 1948 at Tel Abu Shahrain, south of 'Ur of the Chaldees,' confirm Eridu's claim to be the most ancient city of the Sumerian world. Hillah, the ancient city on the left bank of the Shatt el Hillah, a branch of the Euphrates, about 70 miles south of Baghdad, is near the site of Babylon and of the 'house of the lofty-head' or 'gate of the god' (Tower of Babel). Mosul governorate covers a great part of the ancient kingdom of Assyria, the ruins of Nineveh, the Assyrian capital, being visible on the banks of the Tigris, opposite Mosul. Qurna, at the junction of the Tigris and Euphrates, is traditionally supposed to be the site of the Garden of Eden.

Under the Treaty of Lausanne (1923), Turkey renounced sovereignty over Mesopotamia. A provisional Arab Government was set up in November 1920, and in August 1921 the Emir Faisal was elected King of Iraq. The country was a monarchy until July 1958, when King Faisal II was assassinated. From 1958 Iraq has been under Presidential rule.

GOVERNMENT

According to the Provisional Constitution, the highest state authority is the Revolutionary Command Council (RCC), which elects the President from among its own members. The President appoints the Council of Ministers. Legislative authority is shared by the RCC and the 250-member National Assembly, which is elected every four years by universal adult suffrage. Following general elections in April 1989 the Arab Ba'ath Socialist Party holds the majority of the Assembly seats, the remainder being held by the state-sponsored National Progressive Patriotic Front.

Iraq invaded Kuwait on 2 August 1990. The subsequent announcement of annexation was declared void by the UN Security Council. In August 1990 Iraq accepted Iran's conditions for a peace treaty, thus formally ending hostilities in which the two states had been involved since September 1980.

SECCESSION

Following the allied victory in Kuwait in February 1991, rebellion against the government broke out in both Kurdish northern Iraq and Shiite southern Iraq. Although the revolt was suppressed by the end of April, the plight of the resultant Kurdish refugees led Western governments to set up a security zone in northern Iraq to protect them. Allied forces were withdrawn in July. The Kurds have since established a *de facto* administration in certain northern areas. In May 1992 the Kurds voted in free elections for a 100 seat parliament and a 'political leader'. The Kurdish Democratic Party and the Patriotic Union of Kurdistan both gained 50 seats and a Kurdish government was formed in July with party leaders Masoud Barzani and Jalal Talabani as joint leaders.

HEAD OF STATE

President, Chairman of the Revolutionary Command Council, Saddam Hussein, *assumed office* 16 July 1979.
Vice President, Taha Yassin Ramadhan.

CABINET as at June 1992

Prime Minister, Muhammad Hamza al-Zubaidi.
Deputy Prime Minister, Tariq Aziz.
Interior, Wathban Hassan Ibrahim.
Defence, Ali Hassan al-Majid.
Foreign Affairs, Mohammed Saaed al-Sahhaf.
Finance, Ahmad Hussein al-Khodair.
Culture and Information, Hamad Youssef Hammadi.
Justice, Shabib al-Malki.
Agriculture and Irrigation, Abdul Wahab Mahmoud Abdullah.
Industry and Minerals, Amer Hammadi As-Saadi.
Oil, Usama Abdul Ar-Razzaq Hammadi.
Education, Hikmat Abdullah al-Bazzaz.
Labour and Social Affairs, Umeed Madhat Mubarak.
Health, Abdul As-Salem Muhammad Saeed.
Planning, Samal Majid Faraj.
Higher Education and Scientific Research, Humam Abdel-Khaliq.
Housing and Construction, Mahmoud Diyab Al-Ahmad.
Transport and Communications, Abdul As-Sattar Ahmad Al-Maini.
Religious Endowments and Religious Affairs, Abdullah Fadel-Abbas.
Trade, Muhammed Mahdi Salih.
Minister of State for Military Affairs, Gen. Abdul Al-Jabbar Khalil.
Minister of State for Foreign Affairs, Muhammad Saeed As-Sahaf.

IRAQI DIPLOMATIC MISSION IN LONDON

Since Iraq's breach of diplomatic relations with Britain in February 1991, the Jordanian Embassy has handled Iraqi interests in this country.

BRITISH DIPLOMATIC REPRESENTATION

The British Embassy was closed in January 1991.

DEFENCE

The Iraqi armed forces were decimated in the defeat by the Allied coalition which drove them from Kuwait but remained strong enough to suppress the Kurdish and Shiite rebellions. Estimates of the size and strength of the armed forces can only be vague but total active personnel is in the region of 380,000, from a pre-war total of one million. The Army has a strength of around 350,000, with around 2,300 main battle tanks (5,300 pre-war); 2,900 armoured personnel carriers and armoured infantry fighting vehicles (4,800 pre-war); 1,000 artillery pieces (3,150 pre-war) and 120 armed helicopters. The Navy has a strength of around 2,500 with six corvettes. The Air Force has a strength of around 30,000 with some 260 combat aircraft and a further 115 still in Iran, where they were flown during the war. The Allies destroyed 135 aircraft.

Since the end of the war, UN weapons inspection teams have searched Iraq, destroying and dismantling nuclear, chemical and biological weapons, Scud missiles and their launchers, and the Superguns. However, it is believed that Iraq has successfully hidden some weapons of mass destruction and the means of producing them.

COMMUNICATIONS

Facilities at the port of Basra have been improved but the port has not been used since the outbreak of hostilities with Iran in September 1980. Continuous dredging of the Shatt-al-Arab has also been suspended by hostilities and the channel has seriously silted. The port of Um Qasr near the Kuwaiti border has been developed for freight and sulphur handling and a container terminal is ready for operation but not in use due to the port's proximity to the war zone. All external borders, except that of Jordan, are closed to Iraqi traffic.

There is an international airport at Baghdad. Iraqi Airways provided flights between Baghdad and London, and other international airlines operated to Europe. Iraqi Republican Railways provided regular passenger and goods services between Basra, Baghdad and Mosul. There is also a metre gauge line connecting Baghdad with Khanaqin, Kirkuk and Arbil.

Iraqi communications were greatly affected by the Gulf War; large numbers of bridges were destroyed and the railway system extensively disrupted.

ECONOMY

Apart from the valuable revenues to be derived from oil, agricultural development makes a valuable contribution to the wealth of the country and two harvests can usually be gathered in the year. Production fluctuates from year to year according to rainfall. The Government's concern with agricultural development is shown in the large financial allocations made to the sector. Salinity and soil erosion, caused by a high water table, inadequate irrigation and drainage and traditional farming methods, are the major problems now being addressed by development planners.

Increasing industrialization is taking place but industrial production has been greatly reduced because of war damage.

Iraq's major industry is oil production. It was nationalized on 1 June 1972 and accounts for approximately 98 per cent of the total government revenue and 45 per cent of the Gross National Product. Production was some 3.5 million barrels per day in 1979 but the effects of war damage on the Basra terminals and the closure of the trans-Syria pipeline reduced production until new pipelines were built via Turkey and Saudi Arabia. Total revenues from oil were estimated at $11,000–14,000 million in 1988.

In August 1990, the UN imposed mandatory economic sanctions on Iraq, including a world-wide ban on its oil exports. Sanctions were modified in August 1991 to allow the sale of 20 per cent of pre-war oil production; the proceeds are to be allocated to a special UN account for the purchase of food and other essential supplies, and for the funding of war reparations, but Iraq has refused to make use of this.

TRADE

The principal imports in normal times would be iron and steel, cement and other building materials, mechanical and electrical machinery, motor vehicles, textiles and clothing, essential foodstuffs, grain, tinned foods and raw industrial materials. The chief exports would be crude petroleum, dates, raw wool, raw hides and skins and raw cotton.

Trade with UK	1990	1991
Imports from UK	£293,393,000	£4,399,000
Exports to UK	101,557,000	2,548,000

IRELAND

POSITION AND EXTENT – Ireland lies in the Atlantic Ocean, to the west of Great Britain. It is separated from Scotland by the North Channel and from Wales by the Irish Sea and St George's Channel. The area of the island is 32,588 sq. miles (84,402 sq. km), and its geographical position between 51° 26′ and 55° 21′ N. latitude and from 5° 25′ to 10° 30′ W. longitude. The greatest length of the island, from north-east to south-west (Torr Head to Mizen Head), is 302 miles, and the greatest breadth, from east to west (Dundrum Bay to Annagh Head), is 174 miles.

On the north coast of Achill Island (Co. Mayo) are the highest cliffs in the British Isles, 2,000 feet sheer above the sea. Ireland is occupied for the greater part of its area by the central plain, with an elevation 50 to 350 ft above mean sea level, with isolated mountain ranges near the coastline. The principal mountains, with their highest points, are the Sperrin Mountains (Sawel 2,240 ft) of Co. Tyrone; the Mountains of Mourne (Slieve Donard 2,796 ft) of Co. Down, and the Wicklow Mountains (Lugnaquilla 3,039 ft); the Derryveagh Mountains (Errigal 2,466 ft) of Co. Donegal; the Connemara Mountains (Twelve Pins 2,695 ft) of Co. Galway; Macgillicuddy's Reeks (Carrantuohill 3,414 ft, the highest point in Ireland); and the Galtee Mountains (3,018 ft) of Co. Tipperary, and the Knockmealdown (2,609 ft) and Comeragh Mountains (2,470 ft) of Co. Waterford.

The principal river of Ireland (and the longest in the British Isles) is the Shannon (240 miles), rising in Co. Cavan and draining the central plain; the Shannon flows through a chain of loughs to the city of Limerick, and thence to an estuary on the western Atlantic seaboard. The Slaney flows into Wexford Harbour, the Liffey to Dublin Bay, the Boyne to Drogheda, the Lee to Cork Harbour, the Blackwater to Youghal Harbour, and the Suir, Barrow and Nore to Waterford Harbour.

The principal hydrographic feature is the Loughs, of which Lough Neagh (150 sq. miles) in the north-east is the largest in Ireland and the British Isles, others being the Shannon Chain of Allen, Boderg, Forbes, Ree and Derg, and the Erne Chain of Gowna, Oughter, Lower Erne, and Erne; Melvin, Gill, Gara and Conn in the north-west; and Corrib and Mask (joined by a hidden channel) in the west. In Co. Kerry, to the east of Macgillicuddy's Reeks, are the famous lakes of Killarney.

EARLY HISTORY – Although little is known concerning the earliest inhabitants of Ireland, there are many traces of

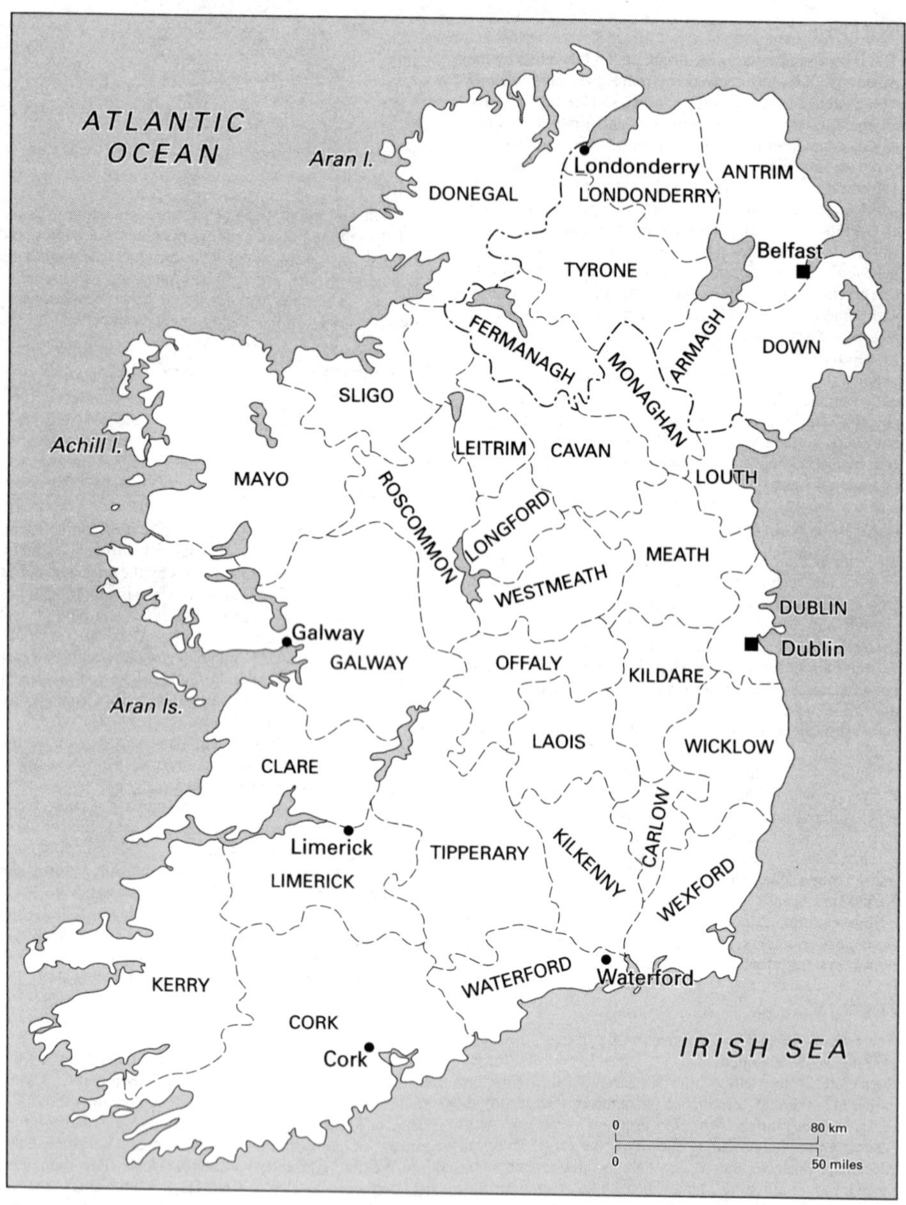

neolithic man throughout the island; a grave containing a polished stone axehead assigned to 2500 BC was found at Linkardstown, Co. Carlow, in 1944, and the use of bronze implements appears to have become known about the middle of the 17th century BC. In the later Bronze Age a Celtic race of Goidels appears to have invaded the island, and in the early Iron Age Brythons from South Britain are believed to have effected settlements in the south-east, while Picts from North Britain established similar settlements in the north. Towards the close of the Roman occupation of Britain, the dominant tribe in the island was that of the Scoti, who afterwards established themselves in Scotland.

According to Irish legends, the island of Ierne was settled by a Milesian race, who came from Scythia by way of Spain, and established the Kingdom of Tara, about 500 BC. The supremacy of the Ardri (high king) of Tara was acknowledged by eight lesser kingdoms (Munster, Connaught, Ailech, Oriel, Ulidia, Meath, Leinster and Ossory) ruled by descendants of the eight sons of Miled. The basalt columns on the coast of Antrim, eight miles from Portrush, known as the Giant's Causeway, are connected with the legendary history of Ireland as the remnants of a bridge built in the time of Finn M'Coul (Fingal) to connect Antrim with Scotland (Staffa).

Hibernia was visited by Roman merchants but never by Roman legions, and little is known of the history of the country until the invasions of Northmen (Norwegians and Danes) towards the close of the eighth century AD. The Norwegians were distinguished as Findgaill (White Strangers) and the Danes as Dubgaill (Black Strangers), names which survive in Fingall, MacDougall and MacDowell, while the name of the island itself is held to be derived from the Scandinavian *Ira-land* (land of the Irish), the names of the provinces being survivals of Norse dialect forms (Ulaidstir, Laiginstir, Mumans-tir and Kunnak-tir). The outstanding events in the encounters with the Northmen are the Battle of Tara (980), at which the Hy Neill king Maelsechlainn II defeated the Scandinavians of Dublin and the Hebrides under the king Amlaib Cuarán; and the Battle of Clontarf (1014) by which the Scandinavian power was completely broken.

After Clontarf the supreme power was disputed by the O'Briens of Munster, the O'Neills of Ulster, and the O'Connors of Connaught, with varying fortunes. In 1152 Dermod MacMurrough (Diarmit MacMurchada), the deposed king of Leinster, sought assistance in his struggle with Rauidhri O'Connor (the high king of Ireland), and visited Henry II of England. Henry authorized him to obtain armed support in England for the recovery of his kingdom, and Dermod enlisted the services of Richard de Clare, the Norman Earl of Pembroke, afterwards known as Strongbow, who landed at Waterford (23 Aug. 1170) with 200 knights and 1,000 other troops for the reconquest of Leinster, where he eventually settled after marriage with Dermod's daughter.

In 1172 (18 Oct.) Henry II himself landed in Ireland. He received homage from the Irish kings and established his capital at Dublin. The invaders subsequently conquered most of the island and a feudal government was created. In the 14th and 15th centuries, the Irish recovered most of their lands, while many Anglo-Irish lords became virtually independent, royal authority being confined to the Pale, a small district round Dublin. Though, under Henry VII, Sir Edward Poynings, as Lord Deputy, had passed at the Parliament of Drogheda (1494) the act later known as Poynings' Law, subordinating the Irish legislature to the Crown, the Earls of Kildare retained effective power until Henry VIII began the reconquest of Ireland in 1534. Parliament in 1541 recognized him as King of Ireland and by 1603 English authority was supreme.

REPUBLIC OF IRELAND
Poblacht Na hEireann

AREA – The Republic has a land area of 27,136 sq. miles (70,283 sq. km), divided into the four Provinces of *Leinster* (Carlow, Dublin, Kildare, Kilkenny, Laoighis, Longford, Louth, Meath, Offaly, Westmeath, Wexford and Wicklow); *Munster* (Clare, Cork, Kerry, Limerick, Tipperary and Waterford); *Connacht* (Galway, Leitrim, Mayo, Roscommon and Sligo); and part of *Ulster* (Cavan, Donegal and Monaghan).

POPULATION – The preliminary population of the Republic in 1991 census was 3,523,401. Figures also showed 52,690 births, 16,859 marriages and 31,498 deaths in the year 1991 (provisional).

LANGUAGES – The Irish language, being the national language, is the first official language. The English language is recognized as a second official language.

RELIGION

At the Census of 1981 religious adherence was:

Catholic, 3,204,476;
Church of Ireland, 95,366;
Presbyterians, 14,255;
Methodists, 5,790;
Others, 123,518.

CAPITAL – ΨDublin (*Baile Atha Cliath*) is a city and county borough on the River Liffey at the head of Dublin Bay. In April 1991 the population (1991 Census, preliminary) was 477,675.

Other county boroughs, with their preliminary population figures at the 1991 Census, are ΨCork (127,024); Ψ Limerick (52,040); ΨWaterford (40,345); and Ψ Galway (50,842).

NATIONAL ANTHEM – Amhrán na BhFiann (The Soldier's Song).

NATIONAL DAY – 17 March (St Patrick's Day).

GOVERNMENT

The Constitution, approved by a plebiscite on 1 July 1937 came into operation on 29 December 1937. The Constitution declares the national territory to be the whole island of Ireland, its islands and the territorial seas. Pending the reintegration of the national territory, and without prejudice to the right of the Parliament and the Government established by the Constitution to exercise jurisdiction over the whole of the national territory, the laws enacted by that Parliament shall have the like area and extent of application as those of the Irish Free State, which did not include the six counties of Northern Ireland.

The President (*Uachtarán na hEireann*) is elected by direct vote of the people for a period of seven years, and is eligible for a second term. The President, in the exercise and performance of certain of her constitutional powers and functions, is aided and advised by a Council of State.

The National Parliament (*Oireachtas*) consists of the President and two Houses: a House of Representatives (*Dáil Éireann*) and a Senate (*Seanad Éireann*).

Dáil Éireann is composed of 166 members elected by adult suffrage on a basis of proportional representation by means of the single transferable vote. The voting age is 18 years. Each Dáil may continue for a period not exceeding five years from the date of election.

Seanad Éireann is composed of 60 members, of whom 11 are nominated by the Taoiseach and 49 are elected; six by institutions of higher education, and 43 from panels of candidates, established on a vocational basis.

The executive authority is exercised by the Government subject to the Constitution. The Government is responsible to the Dáil, meets and acts as a collective authority, and is collectively responsible for the departments of state administered by the Ministers.

The Taoiseach is appointed by the President on the nomination of the Dáil. The other members of the government are appointed by the President on the nomination of the Taoiseach with the previous approval of the Dáil. The Taoiseach appoints a member of the Government to be the *Tánaiste*, who acts for all purposes in the place of the Taoiseach in the event of the death, permanent incapacitation, or temporary absence of the Taoiseach. The Taoiseach, the Tánaiste and the Minister for Finance must be members of the Dáil. The other members of the Government must be members of the Dáil or the Seanad, but not more than two may be members of the Seanad.

The composition of the Dáil Eireann in July 1992 was as follows: Fianna Fáil 77; Fine Gael 55; Labour 16; Democratic Left 6; Progressive Democrats 6; Independent 6. Total membership including the *Ceann Comhairle* (chairman), 166.

The present coalition Government was formed by the Fianna Fail Party (FF) and the Progressive Democrat Party (PD) following a general election on 15 June 1989.

HEAD OF STATE
President, Mary Robinson, *born* 1944, *assumed office*, 3 Dec. 1990.

CABINET as at July 1992
Taoiseach, Albert Reynolds (FF).
Tánaiste, Minister for Defence and for the Gaeltacht, John P. Wilson (FF).
Foreign Affairs, David Andrews (FF).
Finance, Bertie Ahern (FF).
Industry and Commerce, Des O'Malley (PD).
Labour, Brian Cowen (FF).
Justice, Padraig Flynn (FF).
Energy, Bobby Molloy (PD).
Agriculture and Food, Joe Walsh (FF).
Social Welfare, Charlie McGeevy (FF).
Environment, Michael Smith (FF).
Health, John O'Connell (FF).
Education, Seamus Brennan (FF).
Marine, Michael Woods (FF).
Tourism, Transport and Communications, Máire Geoghegan-Quinn (FF).

IRISH EMBASSY
17 Grosvenor Place, London SW1X 7HR
Tel 071-235 2171

Ambassador Extraordinary and Plenipotentiary, His Excellency Joseph Small (1991).

BRITISH EMBASSY
31 Merrion Road, Dublin 4
Tel: Dublin 695211

Ambassador Extraordinary and Plenipotentiary, His Excellency David E. S. Blatherwick, CMG, OBE (1991).
Counsellor and Head of Chancery, J. Thorp.
First Secretaries, D. F. B. Edye (*Commercial*); I. R. Whitting (*Economic*); T. A. Gallagher (*Political/Information*); J. S. McKervill; D. Harris.
BRITISH COUNCIL REPRESENTATIVE, Dr Ken Churchill, 22 Lower Mount Street, Dublin 2.

JUDICIAL SYSTEM

The judicial system comprises Courts of First Instance and a Court of Final Appeal called the Supreme Court (*Cúirt Uachtarach*). The courts of First Instance include a High Court (*Ard-Chúirt*) and courts of local and limited jurisdiction, with a right of appeal as determined by law. The High Court alone has original jurisdiction to consider the question of the validity of any law having regard to the provisions of the Constitution. The Supreme Court has appellate jurisdiction from decisions of the High Court.

Chief Justice (IR£75,512), Hon. Thomas A. Finlay.
President of the High Court (IR£67,786), Hon. Liam Hamilton.
Attorney-General, Harold Whelehan.

DEFENCE

Establishments provide at present for a Permanent Defence Force of approximately 12,900 all ranks, including the Air Corps and the Naval Service. Recruitment is on a voluntary basis. Minimum term of enlistment is three years in the Permanent Defence Force followed by six years in the Reserve Defence Force. Establishments also provide for a Reserve Defence Force of 16,100 all ranks. Recruitment is also on a voluntary basis; minimum term of enlistment is three years. The Defence Estimate for the year ending 31 December 1991 provides for an expenditure of IR£317,435,000.

FINANCE

	1991*	1992†
Total current revenue	IR£8,776m	IR£9,312m
Total current expenditure	9,076	9,648
Current revenue		
Customs	IR£120m	IR£128m
Excise Duties	1,722	1,718
Capital Taxes	103	77
Stamp Duties	250	260
Income Tax	3,231	3,406
Income Levy	–	–
Corporation Tax	593	678
Value-Added Tax	2,010	2,230
Agricultural Levies (EC)	10	10
Motor Vehicle Duties	184	217
Employment and Training Levy	134	142
Total tax revenue	8,357	8,866
Non-tax revenue	419	446
Current expenditure		
Debt Service	IR£2,353m	IR£2,411m
Industry and Labour	236	264
Agriculture	254	255
Fisheries	19	25
Forestry	5	6
Tourism	26	28
Roads and Transport	19	25
Sanitary Services	2	1
Health	1,346	1,402
Education	1,200	1,343
Social Welfare	1,798	1,941
Housing	8	5
Subsidies	167	167
Defence	369	372
Garda	325	338
Prisons	78	81
Legal, etc.	48	54
Other	813	915
Total	9,066	9,633

*provisional outturn
†post-Budget estimate

The Gross Debt at end 1989 was IR£24,827.8m.

EDUCATION

Primary education is directed by the state, with the exception of 85 private primary schools with an enrolment of 8,784 in 1990–1. There were 3,352 state-aided primary schools with an enrolment of 543,744.

In 1990–1 there were 476 recognized secondary schools with 212,966 pupils under private management (mainly religious orders), and 248 vocational schools with 86,428 pupils. Vocational schools are controlled by 38 statutory local Vocational Education Committees. There were 16 state comprehensive schools in 1990–1 with a total enrolment of 8,861 students, and 52 community schools with an enrolment of 34,080 students. There were also other miscellaneous second-level schools and the total full-time enrolment at second-level for 1990–1 was 345,941.

Third-level education is catered for by seven University Colleges, and also by third-level courses offered by the Technical Colleges and Regional Technical Colleges and other miscellaneous third-level institutions. There were 69,988 full-time third-level students in 1990–1, of whom 39,837 were attending university courses.

The estimated state expenditure on education in 1992, excluding administration and inspection, is first-level education IR£540,510,000; second-level education IR£526,122,000. The vote for third-level education amounted to IR£274,505,000.

MINERALS AND FISHERIES

Minerals – Metal content of ores raised (1991): lead, 39,800 tonnes; zinc, 187,500 tonnes; silver 10,500,000 grammes.
Sea Fisheries – An estimated 7,750 persons were employed in the fisheries in 1987. Total value of all fish landed in 1989 was IR£89.3 million.

COMMUNICATIONS

RAILWAYS – In the year ended 31 December 1990, there were 1,944 km of railway; 25,010,000 passengers and 3,278,000 tonnes of merchandise were conveyed; the receipts were IR£76,511,000 and expenditure IR£164,651,000. These figures are in respect of railway working by *Iarnród Eireann.*
ROAD MOTOR SERVICES – In 1990 road motor vehicles carried 228,709,000 passengers, the gross receipts being IR£135,742,000.
SHIPPING – In 1990 the number of ships with cargo which arrived at Irish ports was 12,521 (31,769,000 net registered tons); of these 2,579 (7,023,000 net registered tons) were of Irish nationality.
CIVIL AVIATION – Shannon Airport, 15 miles west of Limerick, is on the main transatlantic air route. In 1991 the airport handled 1,542,899 passengers.

Dublin Airport, six miles north of Dublin, serves the cross-channel and European services operated by the Irish national airline Aer Lingus and other airlines. In 1991 the airport handled 5,278,534 passengers.

Cork Airport, five miles south of Cork serves the cross-channel and European services operated by Aer Lingus and other airlines. In 1991 the airport handled 644,896 passengers.

TRADE

	1990
Imports	IR£12,468,818,545
Exports	14,336,714,521
Trade balance	1,867,895,976

Trade with UK	1990	1991
Imports from UK	£5,311,539,000	£5,295,949,000
Exports to UK	4,498,571,000	4,416,151,000

ISRAEL
Medinat Israel

AREA – Israel lies on the western edge of the continent of Asia at the eastern extremity of the Mediterranean Sea, between lat. 29° 30′ to 33° 15′ N. and longitude 34° 15′ to 35° 40′ E. Its political neighbours are Lebanon on the north, Syria on the north and east, Jordan on the east and the Egyptian province of Sinai on the south-west. The area is estimated at 8,019 sq. miles (20,770 sq. km).

Israel comprises four main regions: the hill country of Galilee and Judea and Samaria, rising in places to heights of nearly 4,000 ft.; the coastal plain from the Gaza strip to north of Acre, including the plain of Esdraelon running from Haifa Bay to the south-east, and cutting in two the hill region; the Negev, a semi-desert triangular-shaped region, extending from a base south of Beersheba, to an apex at the head of the Gulf of 'Aqaba; and parts of the Jordan valley, including the Hula region, Tiberias and the south-western extremity of the Dead Sea.

The principal river is the Jordan, which rises from three main sources in Israel, the Lebanon and Syria, and flows through the Hula valley and the canals which have replaced Lake Hula, drained in 1958. Between Hulata and Tiberias (Sea of Galilee) the river falls 926 ft. in 11 miles and becomes a turbulent stream. Lake Tiberias is 696 ft. below sea-level and liable to sudden storms. Between it and the Dead Sea the Jordan falls 591 ft. The other principal rivers are the Yarkon and Kishon.

The largest lake is the Dead Sea (shared between Israel and Jordan); area 393 sq. miles, 1,286 feet below sea-level, 51.5 miles long, with a maximum width of 11 miles and a maximum depth of 1,309 ft.; it receives the waters of the Jordan and of six other streams, and has no outlet, the surplus being carried off by evaporation. The water contains an extraordinarily high concentration of mineral substances.

The highest mountain peak is Mount Meron, 3,962 ft. above sea-level, near Safad, Upper Galilee.
CLIMATE – The climate is variable, similar to that of Lower Egypt but modified by altitude and distance from the sea. The summer is hot but tempered in most parts by daily winds from the Mediterranean. The winter is the rainy season lasting from November to April, the period of maximum rainfall being January and February.
POPULATION – The population (estimate 1992) including East Jerusalem and Jewish settlers in the Occupied Territories is 5,090,000. Of these 4,175,000 are Jewish (82 per cent); 700,000 are Arab Muslims (13.8 per cent); 130,000 Arab Christians (2.5 per cent); and 85,000 are Druze (1.7 per cent). During the upheavals of 1948–9 a large number of Arabs left the country as refugees and settled in neighbouring countries.
IMMIGRATION – The Declaration of Independence of 14 May 1948, laid down that 'the State of Israel will be open to the immigration of Jews from all countries of their dispersion.' The Law of Return, passed by the *Knesset* on 5 July 1950, provides that an immigrant visa shall be granted to every Jew who expresses his desire to settle in Israel. From the establishment of the state until 1988, about 1.8 million immigrants had entered Israel from over 100 different countries. Since 1990, a further 250,000 Jews have arrived in Israel from the Soviet Union, eastern Europe, and Ethiopia.
LANGUAGES – Hebrew and Arabic are the official languages of Israel. Arabs are entitled to transact all official business with government departments in Arabic, and provision is made in the *Knesset* for the simultaneous translation of all speeches into Arabic.
CAPITAL – Most of the Government departments are in Jerusalem, population (1989) 498,800. A resolution proclaiming Jerusalem as the capital of Israel was adopted by the *Knesset* on 23 January 1950. It is not, however, recognized as the capital by the United Nations because East Jerusalem is part of the Occupied Territories captured as a result of the 1967 war. Other principal towns (1986) are ΨTel Aviv and district (1,624,100); ΨHaifa and district (393,000) and Beersheba and district (115,000).
CURRENCY – New Shekel of 100 agora.
FLAG – White, with two horizontal blue stripes, the Shield of David in the centre.
NATIONAL ANTHEM – Hatikvah (The Hope).

ANTIQUITIES

The following are among the principal historic sites in Israel:
Jerusalem – the Church of the Holy Sepulchre; the Al Aqsa Mosque and Dome of the Rock, standing on the remains of

the Temple Mount of Herod the Great, of which the Western (wailing) Wall is a fragment; the Church of the Dormition and the Coenaculum on Mount Zion; Ein Karem; Church of the Visitation, Church of St John the Baptist. *Galilee*; the Sea; Church and Mount of the Beatitudes; ruins of Capernaum and other sites connected with the life of Christ. *Mount Tabor*: Church of the Transfiguration. *Nazareth*: Church of the Annunciation, and other Christian shrines associated with the childhood of Christ. There are also numerous sites dating from biblical and medieval days, such as Ascalon, Caesarea, Atlit, Massada, Megiddo and Hazor. Other antiquities in the West Bank of Jordan and the Golan Heights at present occupied by Israel can now be visited from Israel.

THE OCCUPIED TERRITORIES

As a result of the 1967 war, Israel gained control of East Jerusalem, the Gaza Strip and the West Bank of the Jordan River. East Jerusalem was subsequently annexed by Israel, although this move has not gained international recognition. Extreme Jewish groups began a programme of settlement in the Occupied Territories, later encouraged by the Israeli government. This heightened tension with the resident Palestinian population, now estimated at 1,450,000, whose protests were paralleled by Palestinian Liberation Organization attacks around the world. Frustration at the continued Israeli occupation led to the start of the *Intifada* in 1987, a campaign of sustained unrest in the Occupied Territories.

In accordance with the terms of the peace treaty signed between Egypt and Israel on 26 March 1979, Israel withdrew in April 1982 to the pre-1967 boundary, returning the Sinai area to Egyptian sovereignty.

GOVERNMENT

There is a Cabinet and a single-chamber Parliament (*Knesset*) of 120 members. A general election is held at least once every four years. The general election in November 1988 resulted in the formation of a 'national unity' coalition government. Disputes between Labour and Likud, the two main partners, led to the collapse of the coalition in March 1990.

The present government coalition of the Labour, Meretz and Shas parties came to power after the general election of June 1992 and immediately reduced the planned building of Jewish settlements in the Occupied Territories in an attempt to move towards a peace settlement with Arab states.

HEAD OF STATE
President of Israel, Chaim Herzog, *born* 1918, *elected* 1983, *re-elected* 20 Feb. 1988, *inaugurated*, 8 May 1988.

CABINET as at July 1992
Prime Minister, Defence, Religious Affairs and Welfare, Yitzhak Rabin (L).
Deputy Prime Minister, Foreign Affairs, Shimon Peres (L).
Deputy Prime Minister, Transport, Yisrael Kessar (L).
Communications and Police, Moshe Shahal (L).
Education, Shulamit Aloni (M).
Health, Haim Ramon (L).
Industry, Micha Harish (L).
Finance, Auraham Shohat (L).
Economics, Shimon Shitreet (L).
Interior, Aryeh Deri (S).
Agriculture, Yaacov Tsur (L).
Immigration Absorption, Yair Tsaban (M).
Tourism, Uzi Baram (L).
Justice, David Libai (L).
Energy, Amnon Rubinstein (M).
Housing, Binyamin Ben-Eliezer (L).
Environment, Ora Namir (L).
L Labour Party
M Meretz
S Shas.

EMBASSY OF ISRAEL
2 Palace Green, Kensington, London W8 4QB
TEL 071-957 9500
Ambassador Extraordinary and Plenipotentiary, His Excellency Yoav Biran (1988).

BRITISH EMBASSY
192 Hayarkon Street, Tel Aviv 63405
Tel: Tel Aviv 5249171

Ambassador Extraordinary and Plenipotentiary, His Excellency Mark Elliott, CMG (1988).
Counsellor, T. R. V. Phillips (*Head of Chancery, Consul-General and Counsellor*).
Defence and Military Attaché, Col. E. C. Loden.

BRITISH COUNCIL REPRESENTATIVE, P. Sandiford, 140 Hayarkon Street, Tel Aviv 61032. There is a library in *Tel Aviv* and in *West Jerusalem*.

ISRAEL-BRITISH CHAMBER OF COMMERCE, 76 IBN Guirol Street, Tel Aviv 64162.

DEFENCE

The Israeli defence forces have a total active strength of some 141,000 (including 110,000 conscripts). Since its inception, however, Israel has based its defence capabilities on a large and highly-trained reserve, and a truer picture of armed forces strength is given by the size of the reserve forces, at present 504,000 personnel. Conscripts serve for periods of four years (officers), three years (men) and two years (women). Reserves serve for one month a year and are eligible for call-up until age 54 (men) and age 24 (women). Israel is widely believed to have a nuclear capacity of around 100 warheads which could be delivered by Jericho I and II missiles.

The Army has an active strength of 104,000 (88,000 conscripts) and a strength of 598,000 on mobilization, with some 4,500 main battle tanks, 5,900 armoured personnel carriers, 1,400 artillery pieces. The Navy has an active strength of 9,000 (3,000 conscripts) and 10,000 on mobilization, with three submarines and an array of patrol craft. The Air Force has a strength of 28,000 (19,000 conscripts) and 37,000 on mobilization, with some 591 combat aircraft of US and home manufacture and 94 armed helicopters.

EDUCATION

Elementary education for all children from five to 15 years is free, though secondary education is not compulsory. The law also provides for working youth age 15–18, who for some reason have not completed their primary education, to be exempted from work in order to do so.

In 1985–6 enrolment in all educational establishments was 1,383,838: kindergartens 277,200; elementary education 622,056; secondary education 348,262; post-secondary 98,420.

COMMUNICATIONS

Israel State Railways started operating in August 1949. Towns now served are Haifa, Tel Aviv, Jerusalem, Lod, Nahariya, Beersheba, Dimona, Ashdod and intermediate stations. In 1986 the total railway network amounted to 528 km. There were 12,823 km of paved road and in 1986 819,102 licensed vehicles.

Israel's merchant marine had reached a total of 2,805,000 tons deadweight by December 1985. The chief ports are Haifa, a modern harbour, with a depth of 30 ft. alongside the main quay; the harbour on the Red Sea at Eilat, inaugurated in September 1965, has a capacity of 10,000 tons a day; Acre has an anchorage for small vessels; the deep-water port at Ashdod, 20 miles south of Tel Aviv, which started operations at the end of 1965, handled 8,006,000 tons of cargo in 1986. In the same year Israel's three main ports handled 17,048,000 tons of cargo.

In 1986, 3,098,000 passengers passed through Ben Gurion airport, of which 230,146 arrived by charter flight.

ECONOMY

FINANCE – Government expenditure in 1989 was 25,953,000,000 new Shekels at market prices. GNP at market prices was 81,880,000,000 new Shekels.

AGRICULTURE – The country is generally fertile and climatic conditions vary so widely that a large variety of crops can be grown, ranging from temperate crops, such as wheat and cherries, to subtropical crops such as sorghum, millet and mangoes. The famous 'Jaffa' orange is produced in large quantities mostly in the coastal plain for export. High-profit and specialized glasshouse crops for export, such as flowers, tomatoes and strawberries, are becoming increasingly popular. Olives are cultivated, mainly for the production of oil used for edible purposes and for the manufacture of soap. The main winter crops are wheat and barley and various kinds of pulses, while in summer sorghum, millet, maize, sesame and summer pulses are grown. Large areas of seasonal vegetables are planted. Beef, cattle and poultry farming have been developed and the production of mixed vegetables and dairy produce has greatly increased. Tobacco and medium staple cotton are now grown. Fishing production (mostly from fish farms) was 14,958 tons in 1985–6. All kinds of summer fruits such as figs, grapes, plums and apples are produced in increasing quantities for local consumption.

Water supply for irrigation is the principal limiting factor to greater production. The area under cultivation is 4,370,000 dunams, of which 2,370,000 is under irrigation.

The Israel land measure is the *dunam*, equivalent to 1,000 square metres (approximately a quarter of an acre).

INDUSTRY – In value polished diamonds account for about one quarter of Israel's total exports. Amongst the most important exporting industries are textiles, foodstuffs, chemicals (mainly fertilizers and pharmaceuticals). Metal-working and science-based industries are highly sophisticated and technologically advanced. These include the aircraft and military industries. Other important manufacturing industries include plastics, rubber, cement, glass, paper and oil refining.

TRADE

The principal imports are foodstuffs, crude oil, machinery and vehicles, iron, steel and manufactures thereof, and chemicals. The principal exports are citrus fruits and by-products, polished diamonds, plywood, cement, tyres, minerals, finished and semi-finished textiles.

	1988	1989
Imports	US$12,287.2m	US$12,736.5m
Exports	9,445.4m	10,334.9m

Trade with UK	1990	1991
Imports from UK	£567,712,000	£529,484,000
Exports to UK	506,106,000	455,765,000

ITALY
Repubblica Italiana

Italy is a republic in the south of Europe, consisting of a peninsula, the large islands of Sicily and Sardinia, the island of Elba and about 70 other small islands. Italy is bounded on the north by Switzerland and Austria, on the south by the Mediterranean, on the east by the Adriatic and Slovenia, and on the west by France and the Ligurian and Tyrrhenian Seas. The total area is about 116,304 sq. miles (301,225 sq. km).

The peninsula is for the most part mountainous, but between the Apennines, which form its spine, and the east coastline are two large fertile plains: Emilia/Romagna in the north and Apulia in the south. The Alps form the northern limit of Italy, dividing it from France, Switzerland, Austria and Slovenia. Mont Blanc (15,771 ft.), the highest peak, is in the French Pennine Alps, but partly within the Italian borders are Monte Rosa (15,217 ft.), Matterhorn (14,780 ft.) and several peaks from 12,000 to 14,000 ft.

The chief rivers are the Po (405 miles), which flows through Piedmont, Lombardy and the Veneto, and the Adige (Trentino and Veneto) in the north, the Arno (Florentine plain) and the Tiber (flowing through Rome to Ostia).

POPULATION – In February 1986 Italy's population was 57,193,708. A 1990 UN estimate gives a figure of 57,663,000.

CAPITAL – Rome. Population of the commune (1986) 2,821,420.

Estimates of the population of the communes of the principal cities and towns in 1986 are Milan 1,511,193; ΨNaples 1,204,959; Turin 1,034,007; ΨGenoa 733,990; Bologna 436,570; Florence 429,865; *Sicily*, ΨPalermo 719,960; *Sardinia*, ΨCagliari 223,021.

CURRENCY – Lira of 100 centesimi.

FLAG – Vertical stripes of green, white and red.

NATIONAL ANTHEM – Inno di Mameli.

NATIONAL DAY – 2 June.

HISTORY

Italian unity was accomplished under the House of Savoy, after a struggle from 1848 to 1870, in which Mazzini (1805–72), Garibaldi (1807–82) and Cavour (1810–61) were the principal figures. It was completed when Lombardy was ceded by Austria in 1859 and Venice in 1866, and through the evacuation of Rome by the French in 1870. In 1871 the King of Italy entered Rome, and that city was declared to be the capital.

Benito Mussolini, known as *Il Duce* (The Leader) was continuously in office as Prime Minister from 30 October 1922 until 25 July 1943, when the fascist regime was abolished. He was captured by Italian partisans while attempting to escape across the Swiss frontier and killed on 28 April 1945.

In fulfilment of a promise given in April 1944 that he would retire when the Allies entered Rome, a decree was signed on 5 June 1944, by King Victor Emmanuel III under which Prince Umberto, the King's son, became Lieutenant-General of the Realm. The King remained head of the House of Savoy and retained the title King of Italy until his abdication on 9 May 1946, when he was succeeded by the Crown Prince. A general election was held on 2 June 1946, together with a referendum on the future of the monarchy. The result showed a majority in favour of replacing the monarchy with a republic. The Royal Family left the country on 13 June and on 28 June 1946 a provisional President was elected.

GOVERNMENT

The constitution of the Republic of Italy, approved by the Constituent Assembly on 22 December 1947, provides for the election of the President by an electoral college which consists of the two houses of the parliament (the Chamber of Deputies and the Senate) sitting in joint session together with three delegates from each region (one in the case of the Valle d'Aosta). The President, who must be over 50 years of age, holds office for seven years. He has numerous carefully defined powers, the main one of which is the right to dissolve one or both houses after consultation with the Speakers.

With 50 governments since 1947, there is growing public pressure for constitutional reform This led to a large loss of support for the four-party (Christian Democrat, Socialist, Social Democrat, Liberal) government in 1990 and 1991, forcing it to resign amid a welter of corruption scandals in January 1992. The ensuing general election in April was seen as a defeat for the established parties of the government and the Democratic Left (reformed Communists) as it produced a large increase in support for Northern League and anti-Mafia parties. The four-party coalition failed to persuade any other parties to join them and formed a new government in June with a small majority in parliament and the avowed intent to pursue constitutional and economic reform.

HEAD OF STATE

President of the Italian Republic, Oscar Luigi Scalfaro, *elected* 25 May 1992.

COUNCIL OF MINISTERS as at August 1992

Prime Minister, Guiliano Amato (PSI).
Foreign Affairs, Emilio Colombo (DC).
Interior, Sen. Nicola Mancino (PSI).
Justice, Claudio Martelli (PSI).
Defence, Salvo Ando (PSI).
Treasury and Public Administration, Prof. Piero Barucci (DC).
Finance, Giovanni Goria (DC).

Budget and Southern Development, Sen. Franco Reviglio (PSI).
Health, Francesco De Lorenzo (PLI).
Education, Sen. Rosa Russo Jervolino (DC).
Industry and State Holdings, Prof. Giuseppe Guarino (DC)
Agriculture, Sen. Gianni Fontana (DC).
Employment and Social Welfare, Nino Cristofori (DC).
Transport and Merchant Marine, Dr Giancarlo Tesini (DC).
Public Works, Sen. Francesco Merloni (DC).
Posts and Telecommunications, Maurizio Pagani (PSDI).
Foreign Trade, Sen. Claudio Vitalone (DC).
Tourism, Sen. Margherita Boniver (PSI).
Environment, Dr Carlo Ripa Di Meana (PSI).
Culture, Dr Alberto Ronchey (IND).
Universities and Research, Sen. Alessandro Fontana (DC).

DC Christian Democrat Party
PSI Socialist Party
PLI Liberal Party
PSDI Social Democratic Party.

ITALIAN EMBASSY
14 Three Kings Yard, Davies Street,
London W1Y 2EH
Tel 071-629 8200

Ambassador Extraordinary and Plenipotentiary, His Excellency Giacomo Attolico (1991).
Minister-Counsellor, Livio Muzi-Falconi.
First Counsellors, A. V. de Mohr; F. Pigliapoco; N. Cappello; L. Visconti di Modrone; S. Ronca.

There are also consular offices in *Bedford*, *Edinburgh* and *Manchester*.

BRITISH EMBASSY
Via XX Settembre 80A, 00187 Rome
Tel: Rome 482-5441

Ambassador Extraordinary and Plenipotentiary, His Excellency Sir Patrick Fairweather, KCMG (1992).
Ministers, T. C. Wood, CMG; J. R. Goldsack, MBE (*FAO*).
Defence and Military Attaché, Brig. A. R. Jones.
Naval Attaché, Capt. W. C. McKnight, LVO.
Air Attaché, Gp Capt. A. R. Tolcher, RAF.
Counsellors, C. L. Fransella (*Political*); G. M. Gowlland, LVO (*Political/Management*); C. R. L. de Chassiron (*Commercial/Economic*).

First Secretaries, C. W. G. Edmonds-Brown (*Management*); D. J. Hollamby (*Social Affairs*); N. K. Darroch (*Economic*); G. Roberts (*Consul*); H. Kershaw (*Commercial*); M. E. Smith (*Agriculture and Environment*); S. W. Gregson (*Information*); R. J. C. Allen (*Political*); J. A. Towner (*Economic*); J. Ashton (*Political*).

BRITISH CONSULAR OFFICES – There are offices at *Milan*, *Rome*, *Naples*, *Genoa*, *Florence*, *Venice*, *Trieste*, *Brindisi*, *Bari* and *Turin*.

BRITISH COUNCIL REPRESENTATIVE, Keith Hunter, OBE, Palazzo del Drago, Via Quattro Fontane 20, 00184 Rome. There are *British Council Offices* at *Milan* and *Naples*, each with a library.

BRITISH CHAMBER OF COMMERCE, Via San Paolo 7, 20121 Milan.

DEFENCE

Total active armed forces personnel number some 361,400 (including 216,000 conscripts who serve 12 months). The Army has a strength of 234,200 (170,000 conscripts), with some 1,220 main battle tanks, 3,879 armoured personnel carriers, 1,952 artillery pieces, 60 aircraft and 320 helicopters. The Navy has a strength of 49,000 (including 20,000 conscripts), with nine submarines, one helicopter carrier, two cruisers and 29 destroyers and frigates with 36 armed helicopters. The Air Force has a strength of 78,200 (26,000 conscripts) with 449 combat aircraft.

In addition to the regular armed forces there is the paramilitary Carabinieri, who are part of the Ministry of Defence and number some 111,400, with some 230 armoured personnel carriers and 75 helicopters.

There are several NATO bases in Italy with some 14,100 US armed forces personnel stationed in the country.

REGIONS OF ITALY

ROME AND CENTRAL ITALY – Rome was founded, according to legend, by Romulus in 753 BC. It was the focal point of Latin civilization and dominion under the Republic and afterwards under the Roman Empire, and became the capital of Italy when the Kingdom was established in 1871. The capital is concerned mainly with tourism and government, but its importance as a business centre is steadily increasing, and it is reportedly the third largest industrial centre in the country.

LOMBARDY AND MILAN – In the Lombardy region are to be found some 15.7 per cent of Italy's commercial and banking services and some 21.9 per cent of the manufacturing industry. The whole range of Italian industry is represented, most important being the steel, machine tool and motor car factories.

TURIN AND PIEDMONT – Turin between 1861 and 1865 was Italy's first capital as the home of the Piedmontese royal family. Now it is the headquarters of Europe's largest manufacturer of motor cars, produces 75 per cent of Italy's motor vehicles and over 80 per cent of its roller bearings. Turin is also Italy's second largest steel producing city. Piedmont is the centre of the Italian textile industry based mainly on Biella.

GENOA AND THE LIGURIAN RIVIERA – Genoa has been one of Europe's major ports since the Middle Ages, and handles one-third of Italy's foreign trade. About 80 per cent of the goods handled are imports.

VENICE AND THE NORTH-EAST – Venice is primarily a tourist attraction of unique beauty. It was founded in the middle of the fifth century by refugees from the mainland fleeing attacks, and by the 16th century it was one of the strongest and richest states of Europe, dominating Eastern Mediterranean trade. It lost its independence in 1797 when Napoleon handed it over to Austria. Industry (paper and stationery, mechanical equipment, consumer goods, electrical appliances, woollens) is now developing in the Venice area, particularly on the autostrada linking Venice with Verona, Vicenza, Padua and in the areas around Treviso and Pordenone. Near Trieste, is the modern Monfalcone shipyard.

TUSCANY, EMILIA AND ROMAGNA – Florence, the capital of Tuscany, was one of the greatest cities in Europe from the 11th to the 16th centuries, and the cradle of the Renaissance. Under the Medici family in the 15th century flourished many of the greatest names in Italian art, including Filippo Lippi, Botticelli, Donatello and Brunelleschi, and in the 16th century great Florentine artists like Michelangelo and Leonardo da Vinci. These regions were the agricultural centre of Italy but the post-war period has seen the development of large industrial centres at Bologna, Florence, Modena, Pistoia and Ravenna. The footwear industry is based in Florence, textiles in Prato, reproduction furniture at Cascina and Poggibonsi, ceramics at Sassuolo, and glass and pottery at Empoli and Montelupo. Bologna is an important centre for the food industry.

NAPLES AND THE TOE OF ITALY – Naples, formerly the capital and administrative centre of the Kingdom of Naples and Sicily, remains the dominant city in the area, but it is beset with great problems of unemployment and the need for modernization. Around it, however, helped by government incentives, industry is slowly developing, northwards to Caserta, southwards to Salerno and eastwards to Benevento.

PUGLIA – Bari has always been a commercial centre and now industrial development is also taking place in the areas of Taranto, Brindisi and Foggia. At Taranto there are a highly-mechanized steel-works and a modern oil refinery. The Bari industrial zone has factories producing electronic and pneumatic valves, specialized vehicle bodies and tyres, etc. The main industry of Brindisi is a petro-chemical plant. At Foggia there is a textile factory.

SICILY – The main source of income is agriculture, particularly citrus fruits, almonds and tomatoes. Oil in small quantities has been found off the southern shore of the island and drilling continues, while onshore there are growing oil-refining, natural gas and petrochemical industries. Small and medium sized industries, benefiting from the Government's incentives, are developing, and tourism is bringing an increasing amount of revenue to the island.

SARDINIA – Sardinia is an autonomous region, with its capital at Cagliari. Six main industrial development areas have been officially designated. The major industries are aluminium production (there is a smelting plant at Porto Vesme), petrochemicals, lead and zinc mining; and the tourist industry is flourishing.

ECONOMY

Italian gross domestic product in 1989 was US$859,996 million. One of the economy's major problems is the large budget deficit which is now nearing 10 per cent of GDP. The rate of inflation in 1989 was 6.5 per cent.

INDUSTRY – The general index of industrial production (1980=100) stood at +2.7 per cent in 1985–6. The state-owned sector of Italian industry is important, dominated by the holding companies IRI (mechanical, steel, airlines), ENI (petro-chemicals) and ENEL (electricity).

MINERAL PRODUCTION – Italy is generally poor in mineral resources but since the war deposits of natural methane gas and small deposits of oil have been discovered and rapidly exploited. Production of lignite has also increased. Other minerals produced in significant quantities include iron ores and pyrites, mercury (over one-quarter of the world production), lead, zinc and aluminium. Marble is a traditional product of the Massa Carrara district.

AGRICULTURE – Agriculture accounted for 5.2 per cent of gross domestic product in 1984. The agricultural labour force was 2,242,000 in 1986.

TOURISM – In 1987 an estimated 52 million foreign tourists visited Italy, spending an estimated L15,782,808 million.

TRADE

The balance of trade in 1987 showed a deficit of 11,138 billion lira, compared with 3,722 billion lira in 1986.

The main markets for Italian exports in 1987 were the OECD countries, which accounted for almost 80 per cent of the total, and the EC markets with 56 per cent of the total. Imports came principally from the Federal Republic of Germany, France and the USA.

Trade with UK	1990	1991
Imports from UK	£5,612,751,000	£6,145,014,000
Exports to UK	6,735,496,000	6,378,908,000

COMMUNICATIONS

The main railway system is state-run by the *Ferrovia dello Stato*. A network of motorways (*autostrade*) covers the country, built and operated mainly by the IRI state-holding company and ANAS the state highway authority. Alitalia, the principal international and domestic airline, is also state-controlled by the IRI group. Other smaller companies, including ATI (an Alitalia subsidiary) and Air Mediterranea operate on domestic routes. The Italian mercantile marine totalled 7,587,117 tons in December 1985.

CULTURE

Italian is a Romance language derived from Latin. It is spoken in its purest form in Tuscany, but there are numerous dialects, showing variously French, German, Spanish and Arabic influences. Sard, the dialect of Sardinia, is accorded by some authorities the status of a distinct Romance language.

Italian literature (in addition to Latin literature, which is the common inheritance of Western Europe) is one of the richest in Europe, particularly in its golden age (Dante, 1265–1321; Petrarch, 1304–74; Boccaccio, 1313–75) and in the Renaissance (Ariosto, 1474–1533; Machiavelli, 1469–1527; Tasso, 1544–95). Modern Italian literature has many noted names in prose and verse, notably Manzoni (1785–1873), Carducci (1835–1907) and Gabriele d'Annunzio (1864–1938). The Nobel Prize for Literature has been awarded to Italian authors on five occasions: G. Carducci (1906), Signora G. Deledda (1926), Luigi Pirandello (1934), Salvatore Quasimodo (1959) and Eugenio Montale (1975).

In 1987, there were 72 daily newspapers published in Italy, of which 14 were published in Rome and seven in Milan.

EDUCATION

Education is free and compulsory between the ages of six and 14; this comprises five years at primary school and three in the 'middle school', of which there are about 8,000. Pupils who obtain the middle school certificate may seek admission to any 'senior secondary school', which may be a lyceum with a classical or scientific or artistic bias, or an institute directed at technology (of which there are eight different types), trade or industry (including vocational schools), or teacher-training. Courses at the lyceums and technical institutes usually last for five years and success in the final examination qualifies for admission to university.

There are 35 state and 14 private universities, some of ancient foundation; those at Bologna, Modena, Parma and Padua were started in the 12th century. University education is not free, but entrants with higher qualifications are charged reduced fees according to a sliding scale.

In general, schools, lyceums and universities are financed by local taxation and central government grants.

ISLANDS

PANTELLERIA ISLAND (part of Trapani Province) in the Sicilian Narrows, has an area of 31 sq. miles and a population of 9,601.

THE PELAGIAN ISLANDS (Lampedusa, Linosa and Lampione) are part of the Province of Agrigento and have an area of 8 sq. miles, pop. 4,811.

THE TUSCAN ARCHIPELAGO (including Elba), area 293 sq. km, pop. 31,861.

PONTINE ARCHIPELAGO, including Ponza, area 10 sq. km, pop. 2,515.

FLEGREAN ISLANDS, including Ischia, area 60 sq. km, pop. 51,883.

CAPRI.

EOLIAN ISLANDS, including Lipari, area 116 sq. km, pop. 18,636.

TREMITI ISLANDS, area 3 sq. km, pop. 426.

JAMAICA

AREA, ETC. – Jamaica is situated in the Caribbean Sea south of the eastern extremity of Cuba and lies between latitudes 17° 43′ and 18° 32′ N., and longitude 76° 11′ and 78° 21′ W. Jamaica is 4,244 sq. miles (10,991 sq. km) in area and is divided into three counties (Surrey, Middlesex and Cornwall) and 14 parishes. The greatest length from east to west (Morant Point to Negril Point) is 146 miles and the extreme breadth 51 miles.

The topography consists mainly of coastal plains, divided by the Blue Mountain Range in the east, and the hills and limestone plateaux which occupy the central and western areas of the interior. The central chain of high peaks of the Blue Mountains is over 6,000 feet above sea level, and the Blue Mountain Peak, the highest of these, reaches an elevation of 7,402 feet.

POPULATION – In 1990 the population was estimated at 2,420,00 by the UN.

CAPITAL – The seat of government is ΨKingston, the largest town and seaport (estimated population of the corporate area of Kingston and St Andrew in 1982, 696,300). Other main towns are ΨMontego Bay, Ocho Rios, Spanish Town, Mandeville and May Pen.

CURRENCY – Jamaican dollar (J$) of 100 cents.

FLAG – Gold diagonal cross forming triangles of green at top and bottom, triangles of black at hoist and in fly.

NATIONAL ANTHEM – Jamaica, Land We Love.

NATIONAL DAY – First Monday in August (Independence Day).

GOVERNMENT

The island was discovered by Columbus on 4 May 1494, and occupied by the Spanish from 1509 until 1655 when a British expedition, sent out by Oliver Cromwell, under Admiral Penn and General Venables, attacked the island, which capitulated after a token resistance. In 1670 it was formally ceded to England by the Treaty of Madrid. Jamaica became independent state within the Commonwealth on 6 August 1962.

The legislature consists of a Senate of 21 nominated members and a House of Representatives consisting of 60 members elected by universal adult suffrage. The constitution provides for a Leader of the Opposition.

At the General Election of 9 February 1989, the People's National Party won 45 seats and the Jamaica Labour Party won 15.

Governor-General, His Excellency Howard Felix Hanlon Cooke, *apptd* 1991.

CABINET as at July 1992

Prime Minister, Hon. Percival J. Patterson, QC.
Finance and Planning, Hon. Hugh Small.
Agriculture, Hon. Seymour Mullings.
Production, Mining and Commerce, Sen. the Hon. Carlyle Dunkley.
Public Utilities, Transport and Energy, Hon. Robert Pickersgill.
Tourism and the Environment, Hon. John Junior.
Foreign Affairs and Foreign Trade, Sen. the Hon. David Coore.
Education and Culture, Hon. Burchell Whiteman.
Health, Hon. Easton Douglas.
Labour, Welfare and Sport, Hon. Portia Simpson.
Construction, Hon. O. D. Ramtaillie.
Public Service and Information, Sen. the Hon. Dr Paul Robertson.
Local Government, Youth and Community Development, Hon. Desmond Leakey.
National Security and Justice, Hon. K. D. Knight.
Minister without Portfolio in the Office of the Prime Minister, Sen. the Hon. Dr Peter Phillips.

JAMAICAN HIGH COMMISSION
1–2 Prince Consort Road, London SW7 2BZ
Tel 071–823 9911

High Commissioner, Her Excellency Mrs Ellen Gray Bogle (1989).

BRITISH HIGH COMMISSION
PO Box 575, Trafalgar Road, Kingston 10
Tel: Kingston 926 9050

High Commissioner, His Excellency Derek Francis Milton, CMG (1989).

BRITISH COUNCIL REPRESENTATIVE IN THE CARIBBEAN, Gillian Roche, 3rd Floor, First Life Building, 64 Knutsford Boulevard, Kingston 5.

JUDICATURE

Chief Justice and Keeper of Records, Hon. E. Zacca.
Judges of the Court of Appeal, Hons. I. D. Rowe, B. H. Carey; M. L. Wright; I. X. Forte; H. E. Downer; M. E. Morgan.

COMMUNICATIONS

There are several excellent harbours, Kingston being the principal port. The island has 2,944 miles of main roads and over 7,000 miles of subsidiary roads.

There are two international airports capable of handling the largest civil jet aircraft, the Norman Manley International Airport on the south coast serving Kingston, and Sangster Airport on the north coast serving the major tourist areas. In addition there are licensed aerodromes at Port Antonio, Ocho Rios, Mandeville and Negril. There are 16 privately owned, seven public and two military airstrips.

Air Jamaica, the national airline, operates international services; Trans-Jamaica Airlines operates scheduled internal services.

ECONOMY

Jamaica is a popular tourist resort, attracting 1,340,506 visitors during 1991. Actual foreign exchange receipts from tourism amounted to US$764m in 1991.

Alumina, bananas, bauxite and sugar are the four major Jamaican exports. Earnings from sugar in 1991 amounted to US$87.5m, bauxite US$113m, alumina US$543m and bananas US$45.1m. Less traditional exports include garments, processed food products, limestone and ornamental horticultural products.

FINANCE

	1990	1991
Revenue	US$2,401.6m	US$908m
Expenditure	2,537.5m	1,091.7m

TRADE

	1990	1991
Total imports	US$1,850.7m	US$1,799.5m
Total exports	1,126.1m	1,145.0m

Trade with UK	1990	1991
Imports from UK	£58,702,000	£54,669,000
Exports to UK	136,535,000	123,773,000

JAPAN

Nihon Koku - Land of the Rising Sun

AREA AND POPULATION – Japan consists of four large islands: *Honshū* (or Mainland), 230,448 sq. km (88,839 sq. m), *Shikoku*, 18,757 sq. km (7,231 sq. m), *Kyūshū*, 42,079 sq. km (16,170 sq. m), *Hokkaido*, 78,508 sq. km (30,265 sq. m), and many small islands situated in the North Pacific Ocean between longitude 128° 6′ and 145° 49′ E. and between latitude 26° 59′ and 45° 31′ N., with a total area of 145,834 sq. miles (377,708 sq. km), and a population estimated by the UN in 1990 at 123,537,000. In 1988 the birth rate was 10.8 per 1,000, and the death rate 6.5 per 1,000.

PHYSIOGRAPHY – The coastline exceeds 17,000 miles and is deeply indented, so that few places are far from the sea. The interior is very mountainous, and crossing the mainland from the Sea of Japan to the Pacific is a group of volcanoes, mainly extinct or dormant. Mount Fuji, the loftiest and most sacred mountain of Japan, about 60 miles from Tokyo, is 12,370 ft. high and has been dormant since 1707, but there are other volcanoes which are active, including Mount Aso in Kyūshū. There are frequent earthquakes, mainly along the Pacific coast near the Bay of Tokyo. Japan proper extends from sub-tropical in the south to cool temperate in the north. Heavy snowfalls are frequent on the western slopes of Hokkaidō and Honshū, but the Pacific coasts are warmed by the Japan current. There is a plentiful rainfall and the rivers are short and swift-flowing, offering abundant opportunities for the supply of hydro-electric power.

RELIGION – All religions are tolerated. The principal religions of Japan are Mahayana Buddhism and Shinto. About 1 per cent of Japanese are Christians.

CAPITAL – Tokyo, population (December 1989) 11,718,720. The other chief cities had the following populations: Ψ Osaka (2,633,000); Ψ Nagoya (2,152,000); Ψ Yokohama (3,197,000); Kyoto, the ancient capital (1,471,000); Ψ Kobé (1,464,000); Kita-Kyushu (1,034,000); Sapporo (1,652,000); Ψ Kawasaki (1,159,000); Ψ Fukuoka (1,220,000).

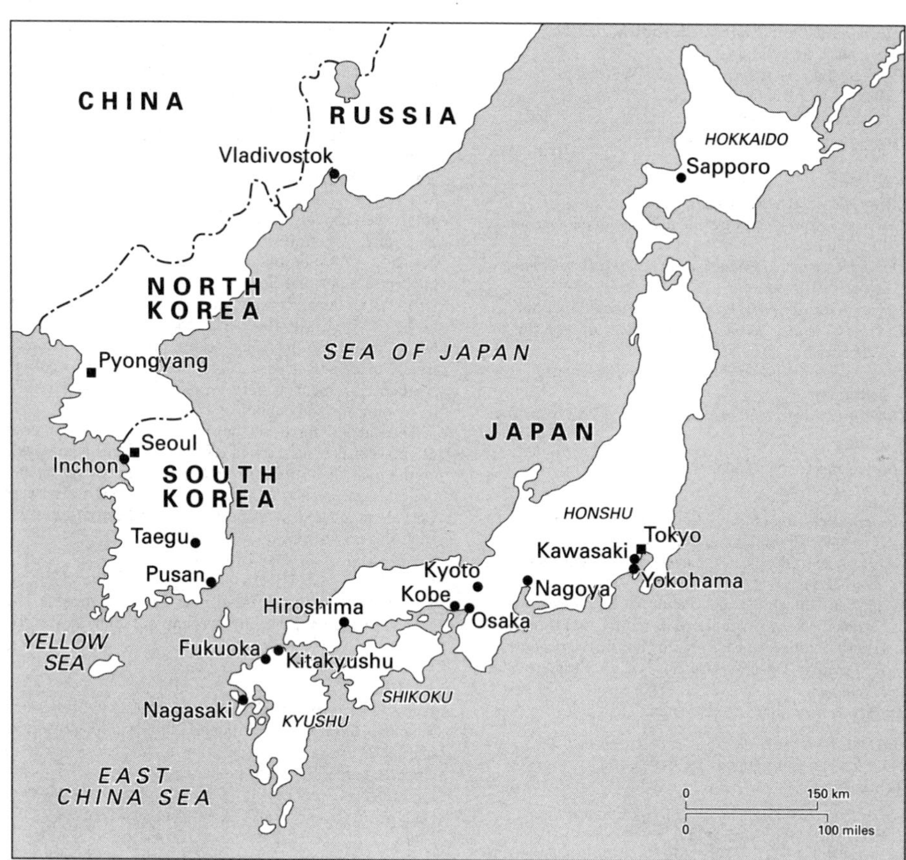

CURRENCY – Yen of 100 sen.
FLAG – White, charged with sun (red).
NATIONAL ANTHEM – Kimigayo.
NATIONAL DAY – 23 December (the Emperor's Birthday).

GOVERNMENT

According to Japanese tradition, Jimmu, the first Emperor of Japan, ascended the throne on 11 February 660 BC. Under the *Meiji* constitution of 11 February 1889, the monarchy was hereditary in the male heirs of the Imperial house.

After the unconditional surrender to the Allied Nations (14 August 1945), Japan was occupied by Allied forces under General MacArthur (15 September 1945). A Japanese peace treaty conference held in San Francisco in September 1951 led to 48 nations signing the treaty, which became effective on 28 April 1952. Japan then resumed her status as an independent power.

A new constitution came into force on 3 May 1947. Legislative authority rests with the Diet, which is bicameral, consisting of a House of Representatives and a House of Councillors, both houses being composed of elected members. Executive authority is vested in the Cabinet which is responsible to the legislature.

The conservatives have governed Japan almost without interruption since World War II. Since 1955, when it was formed, the Liberal Democratic Party has maintained an absolute majority in the House of Representatives. In June 1991 the strength of the parties was: Liberal Democratic Party 286; Japan Socialist Party 139; Komeito 46; Japan Communist Party 16; Democratic Socialist 14; Independents, 6; Social Democratic Federation 4; others 1.

The House of Councillors, whose powers are subordinate to the House of Representatives, re-elects half of its members every three years. In June 1992 the strength of the parties was: Liberal Democratic Party 107; Japan Socialist Party 71; Komeito 24; Other, 20; Rengo 12; Japan Communist Party 11; Democratic Socialist 6.

HEAD OF STATE

Emperor of Japan, His Imperial Majesty the Emperor Akihito, *born* 23 December 1933; *succeeded* 8 January 1989; *enthroned* 12 November 1990; *married* 10 April 1959, Miss Michiko Shoda, and has *issue* Prince Naruhito Hironomiya (*Crown Prince*), *born* 23 February 1960, Prince Akishino, *born* 30 November 1965, and Princess Sayako, *born* 18 April 1969.

CABINET as at June 1992

Prime Minister, Kiichi Miyazawa.
Deputy PM, Foreign Affairs, Michio Watanabe.
Justice, Takashi Tawara.
Finance, Tsutomu Hata.
Education, Kunio Hatoyama.
Health and Welfare, Tokuo Yamashita.
Agriculture, Forestry and Fisheries, Masami Tanabu.

International Trade and Industry, Kozo Watanabe.
Transport, Keiwa Okuda.
Posts and Telecommunications, Hideo Watanabe.
Labour, Tetsuo Kondo.
Construction, Taku Yamasaki.
Home Affairs, Masajuro Shiokawa.

MINISTERS OF STATE

Chief Cabinet Secretary, Koichi Kato.
Director-General of Management and Co-ordination Agency, Junzo Iwasaki.
Director-General of Hokkaido and Okinawa Development Agencies, Tomoo Ie.
Director-General of the Defence Agency, Johei Miyashita.
Director-General of Science and Technology Agency, Kanzo Tanigawa.
Director-General of Environment Agency, Shozaburo Nakamura.
Director-General of National Land Agency, Yoshiyuki Toya.

EMBASSY OF JAPAN
101–104 Piccadilly, London W1V 9FN
TEL 071-465 6500

Ambassador Extraordinary and Plenipotentiary, His Excellency Hiroshi Kitamura (1991).
Ministers, Isao Ohtsuka (*Financial*); Iamon Kitabatake (*Commercial*).
Counsellors, Hitoshi Tanaka (*Political*); Yasuo Nozaka (*Information and Cultural*); Makoto Mizutani (*Economic*); Hiroshi Ueno (*Financial*); Kozo Konishi (*Agriculture*); Dr Yasuhiko Tatsumi (*Medical Attaché*); Yoshikiyo Ono (*Transport*).
Defence Attaché, Capt. Osamu Izuka.

BRITISH EMBASSY
No. 1 Ichiban-cho, Chiyoda-ku, Tokyo 102
Tel: Tokyo 3265-5511

Ambassador Extraordinary and Plenipotentiary, His Excellency John Boyd, (1992).
Minister, E. J. Field, CMG (*Deputy Head of Mission*); J. E. W. Kirby (*Financial*).
Counsellors, P. Dimond (*Commercial*); C. Humfrey (*Economic*); G. H. Fry (*Head of Chancery*); Dr R. Hinder (*Science and Technology*); C. Loughlin (*Atomic Energy*); R. Seeley (*Chancery*); J. Kirby (*Financial*); D. Pragnell, LVO, OBE (*Management*).
First Secretaries, N. Hook, MVO, S. Plater (*Commercial*); D. H. Powell, P. W. Sprunt (*Chancery*); J. Alderson, P. Madden, S. McNeil-Ritchie, S. J. Smith (*Economic*); T. Salusbury (*Science and Technology*); R. E. Coghlan (*Information*); P. V. Baines (*Consul*).
Defence and Naval Attaché, Capt. C. Crawford.
Air Attaché, Gp Capt. A. Terrett.

There is a British Consulate-General at *Osaka* and Honorary Consulates at *Fukuoka*, *Hiroshima* and *Nagoya*.

BRITISH COUNCIL REPRESENTATIVE, R. P. Joscelyne, 2 Kagurazaka 1-Chome, Shinjuku-ku, Tokyo 162. There is also an office and library in *Kyoto*.

BRITISH CHAMBER OF COMMERCE, No. 16 Kowa Building, 1–9–20 Akasaka, Minato-ku, Tokyo 107.

ECONOMY

AGRICULTURE – Owing to the mountainous nature of the country not more than one-sixth of its area is available for cultivation. The forest land includes Cryptomeria japonica, Pinus massoniana, Zeikowaskeaki, and Paulownia imperialis, in addition to camphor trees, mulberry, vegetable wax tree and a lacquer tree which furnishes the celebrated lacquer of Japan. The soil is only moderately fertile, but intensive cultivation secures good crops. Tobacco, tea, potato, rice, wheat and other cereals are all cultivated. Rice is the staple food of the people, about 10,627,000 tonnes being produced in 1987. Fruit is abundant, including the mandarin, persimmon, loquat and peach. European fruits such as apples, strawberries, pears, grapes and figs are also produced. There is a small-scale beef industry and pigs and chickens are widely reared.

MINERALS – The country has mineral resources, including gold, silver, copper, lead, zinc, iron chromite, white arsenic, coal, sulphur, petroleum, salt and uranium. However, iron ore, coal and crude oil are among the principal post-war imports to supply deficiencies at home.

INDUSTRY – Japan is the most highly industrialized nation in the Far East, with the whole range of modern light and heavy industries, including motor vehicles, electronics, metals, machinery, chemicals, textiles (cotton, silk, wool and synthetics), cement, pottery, glass, rubber, lumber, paper, oil refining and shipbuilding.

The labour force of Japan in 1988 (average) was 61,700,000, of which around 2.5 per cent were unemployed. Of the total labour force, over 15 per cent are over 65 and this rate is increasing. Industrial, manufacturing and services workers numbered 53,430,000 and agricultural, forestries and fisheries workers 5,090,000 in 1985.

FINANCE

The Budget for the financial year 1990 for revenue and expenditure on the general account was Yen 66,236,700 million.

TRADE

Being deficient in natural resources, Japan has had to develop a complex foreign trade. Principal imports in 1988 consisted of mineral oils (20.5 per cent), raw materials (8.7 per cent) e.g. metal ores and scrap, 4.5 per cent, timber, 3.8 per cent, foodstuffs (15.5 per cent) (e.g. wheat and sugar), machinery (14.2 per cent), chemicals (7.9 per cent) and textiles (5.7 per cent).

Principal exports consist of non-electric machinery (21.2 per cent), motor vehicles (18.4 per cent), electric machinery and appliances (18.4 per cent), steel (5.8 per cent), chemicals (4.5 per cent), textile goods (2.6 per cent) and ships (1.5 per cent).

	1987 (US$'000)	1988
Total imports	149,515,113	187,353,686
Total exports	229,221,230	264,916,803

Trade with UK	1990	1991
Imports from UK	£2,631,326,000	£2,257,552,000
Exports to UK	6,761,592,000	6,753,642,000

COMMUNICATIONS

There were 1,120,051 km of road and 44,297 km of rail road (steam and electric) in 1984. Also new Shinkansen (bullet train) tracks are currently being expanded. Japan National Railways was privatized on 1 April 1987 and is known as Japan Railways (JR). There are six regional companies and one goods company. The opening in 1988 of the Seikan rail tunnel and the Seto Ohashi rail bridge means that the four major islands are now linked for the first time.

The merchant fleet had a shipping capacity of 38.5 million gross tons in 1986.

DEFENCE

After the unconditional surrender of August 1945 the Imperial Army and Navy were disarmed and disbanded. Although the constitution of Japan prohibits the maintenance of armed forces, internal security forces came into being in 1950 and 1952. In July 1954, the mission of the forces was extended to include the defence of Japan against direct and indirect aggression. The government in June 1992 managed to force a bill through parliament allowing for a maximum of 2,000 troops to take part in UN peacekeeping missions overseas, limited to non-front line activities.

The defence budget allocated for 1991 was Yen 4,402,300 million. The authorized uniformed strength was: Ground Self-Defence Force (GSDF) 180,000 (Reserve 43,000); Maritime Self-Defence Force (MSDF) 43,897 (Reserve 600); Air Self-Defence Force (ASDF) 46,204. The actual strength of the active armed forces is 246,400 (all professional).

The GSDF has a strength of 156,100 and is organized into five regional armies, totalling thirteen divisions, one of which is an armoured division. Equipment includes 1,200 main battle tanks, 770 armoured personnel carriers, 850 artillery pieces and 440 helicopters. Equipment is now largely manufactured in Japan.

The MSDF has a strength of 44,000 personnel, with 17 submarines and 66 principal surface combatants, 99 combat aircraft and 72 armed helicopters.

The ASDF has a strength of 46,300 personnel with 422 combat aircraft of US and Japanese manufacture.

The US at present stations 45,100 personnel in Japan: Army 1,800; Navy 6,300; Marines 22,000; Air Force 15,000.

EDUCATION

Under the Education Law of 1947, education at elementary (six-year course) and lower secondary (three-year course) schools is free, compulsory and co-educational. The (three-year) upper secondary schools are attended by 94 per cent of the age group. They have courses in general, agricultural, commercial, technical, mercantile marine, radio-communication and home economics education, etc.

Of the population aged between 18 and 21, 33 per cent were enrolled in higher education in 1984. There are two- or three-year junior colleges and four-year universities. Some of the universities have graduate schools. In 1987 there were 1,003 universities and junior colleges, the vast majority of which are privately maintained. The most prominent universities are the seven state universities of Tokyo, Kyoto, Tohoku (Sendai), Hokkaido (Sapporo), Kyushu (Fukuoka), Osaka and Nagoya, and the two private universities, Keio and Waseda.

CULTURE

Japanese is said to be one of the Uro-Altaic group of languages and remained a spoken tongue until the fifth to seventh centuries AD, when Chinese characters came into use. Japanese who have received school education (99.8 per cent of the population) can read and write the Chinese characters in current use (about 1,800 characters) and also the syllabary characters called Kana. English is the best known foreign language. It is taught in all middle and high schools and universities. There are 125 daily newspapers in Japan.

JORDAN

Al-Mamlaka al Urduniya al-Hashemiyah

AREA – The Hashemite Kingdom of the Jordan, which covers 37,738 sq. miles (97,740 sq. km), is bounded on the north by Syria, on the west by Israel, on the south by Saudi Arabia and on the east by Iraq. Since the hostilities of June 1967, that part of the country lying to the west of the Jordan River has been under Israeli occupation.

POPULATION – Total population on the East Bank of the Jordan was estimated (1988) to be 2,910,000.

RELIGION – The majority of the population are Sunni Muslims and Islam is the religion of the State; freedom of belief is, however, guaranteed by the Constitution.

CAPITAL – Amman, population (1988 estimate) 1,100,000.

CURRENCY – Jordanian dinar (JD) of 1,000 fils.

FLAG – Three horizontal stripes of black, white, green and a red triangle based on the hoist, containing a seven-pointed white star.

NATIONAL ANTHEM – Long Live the King.

NATIONAL DAY – 25 May (Independence Day).

HISTORY

After the defeat of Turkey in the First World War the Amirate of Transjordan was established in the area east of the River Jordan as a state under British mandate. The mandate was terminated after the Second World War and the Amirate, still ruled by its founder, the Amir Abdullah, became the Hashemite Kingdom of Jordan. Following the 1948 war between Israel and the Arab states, that part of Palestine remaining in Arab hands (but excluding Gaza) was incorporated into the Hashemite Kingdom. King Abdullah was assassinated in 1951; his son Talal ruled briefly but abdicated in favour of the present King, Hussein, in 1952.

THE WEST BANK

All of Jordan west of the River has been under Israeli occupation since 1967. In 1988 Jordan severed its legal and administrative ties with the occupied West Bank, but did not formally renounce sovereignty over the area. As a result of the wars of 1948 and 1967 there are about 991,000 refugees and displaced persons living in East Jordan, about 200,000 of whom live in refugee and displaced persons camps established by the UN Relief and Works Agency (UNRWA). In addition there are some 300,000 entirely self-supporting Palestinian members of the East Jordanian community.

GOVERNMENT

The present constitution of the Kingdom came into force in 1952. It provides for a senate of 40 members (all appointed by the King) and an elected House of Representatives. Until 1988, the House of Representatives had 60 members representing both the East and West Banks. Legislation passed in 1989 stipulated that in future elections, seats would be contested on the East Bank only. The first parliamentary elections since 1967 to the new 80-member House of Representatives took place in November 1989.

The King appoints the members of the Council of Ministers. Crown Prince Hassan normally acts as Regent when King Hussein is away from Jordan. In June 1991 a new National Charter was agreed between the King and political parties in which the ban on political parties was lifted in return for allegiance to the monarchy.

HEAD OF STATE

King of the Jordan, Hussein, GCVO, *born* 14 November 1935, *succeeded* on the deposition of his father, King Talal, 11 Aug. 1952, *assumed constitutional powers*, 2 May 1953, on coming of age.

Crown Prince, Prince Hassan, third son of King Talal of Jordan, *born* 1947, *appointed Crown Prince*, 1 April 1965.

COUNCIL OF MINISTERS as at July 1992

Prime Minister and Minister of Defence, Sharif Zeid Bin Shaker.
Deputy PM, Education, Thugan Al-Hindawi.
Deputy PM, Transportion, Ali Sukeimat.
Foreign Affairs, Dr Kamel Abu Jaber.
Industry and Trade, Dr Abdullah Nassour.
Higher Education, Dr Awad Khleifat.
Tourism, Yanal Hikmat.
Minister of State for Prime Ministry Affairs, Ibrahim Izzedin.
Finance, Basel Jardaneh.
Planning, Dr Ziad Fariz.
Justice, Yousef Mubaideen.
Labour, Abdul Karim Kabariti.
Communications and Post, Jamal Sarairah.
Housing and Public Works, Sa'ad Hayel Al-Srour.
Water and Irrigation, Samir Kawar.
Minister of State, Jamel Khreishah.
Interior, Jawdat Sboul.
Energy and Mineral Resources, Ali Abu Ragheb.
Youth, Saleh Rsheidat.
Awqaf and Islamic Affairs, Sheikj Izzedin Al-Tamimi.
Municipal, Rural and Environmental Affairs, Dr Abdul Razzak Tubeishat.
Information, Mahmoud Sharif.
Minister of State for Parliamentary Affairs, Atef Al-Btoush.
Minister of State, Sultan Al-Idwan.
Culture, Dr Mahmoud Samra.
Supplies, Mohammed Assaqaf.
Health, Aref Bataineh.
Agriculture, Dr Faiz Al-Khasawneh.
Social Development, Dr Awin Mashaqba.

EMBASSY OF THE HASHEMITE KINGDOM OF JORDAN
6 Upper Phillimore Gardens, London W8 7HB
Tel 071-937 3685/7

Ambassador Extraordinary and Plenipotentiary, His Excellency Fouad Ayoub.
Minister Counsellor, Dr Abdulla Madadha.
Defence Attaché, Brig. H. Al-Rusan.
Service Office: 16 Upper Phillimore Gardens, London W8. Tel: 071-937-9611.

BRITISH EMBASSY
Abdoun (PO Box 87), Amman
Tel: Amman 823100

Ambassador Extraordinary and Plenipotentiary, His Excellency P. H. C. Eyers, CMG, LVO.
Counsellors, H. G. Hogger (*Deputy Head of Mission and Consul-General*); M. S. Allen.
Defence Attaché, Col. P. A. Goddard.
First Secretaries, C. E. Cooper (*Consul and Management*); T. Ellis (*Commercial and Development*).

BRITISH COUNCIL REPRESENTATIVE, M. Roddis, Rainbow Street, (PO Box 634), Jebel Amman, Amman.

ECONOMY

The main agricultural areas are the Jordan Valley, the hills overlooking the valley and the flatter country to the south of Amman and around Madaba and Irbid, though several large farms, which depend for irrigation on water pumped from deep aquifers, have been established in the southern desert area. The rest of the country is desert and semi-desert. The principal crops are wheat, barley, vegetables, olives and fruit (mainly grapes and citrus fruits). Agricultural production has increased considerably in recent years due to improvements in production and irrigation techniques, and exports to Europe and elsewhere are increasing.

Important industrial products are raw phosphates (1988, 5.6 million tons) and potash (1988, 1.3 million tons), most of which is exported. The Trans-Arabian oil pipeline (Tapline) runs through North Jordan on its way from the eastern province of Saudi Arabia to the Lebanese port of Sidon. A branch pipeline, together with oil trucked by road from Iraq, feeds a refinery at Zerqa (production 1988, 2.3 million tons) which meets most of Jordan's requirements for refined petroleum products. Sufficient reserves of natural gas have been discovered in the north-east to produce electricity for the national grid (generators were commissioned in May 1989). Despite extensive efforts no significant reserves of oil have been found.

Tourism has steadily developed. International-class hotels cater for businessmen and tourists in Amman and Aqaba. A spa hotel has been opened by hot springs close to the Dead Sea and a hotel complex is planned at the Dead Sea.

FINANCE

	1987	1988
	(JD'000)	
Revenue	869,969	917,562
Expenditure	965,808	1,045,680
Surplus/Deficit	−95,839	−128,118

TRADE WITH UK

	1990	1991
Imports from UK	£109,483,000	£89,411,000
Exports to UK	14,788,000	10,984,000

COMMUNICATIONS

The trunk road system is good. Amman is linked to Aqaba, Damascus, Baghdad and Jeddah by roads which are of considerable importance in the overland trade of the Middle East.

The former Hejaz Railway enters Jordan from Syria east of Ramtha and runs through Zerqa and Amman to Ma'an with a spur to the top of the Ras al-Naqb escarpment. It is little used, mainly for freight between Amman and Damascus. The Aqaba railway carries phosphate rock from the mines of al Hasa and al Abiad to Aqaba. A total of 2,583 vessels called at Aqaba in 1988, and 20,096,200 tons of cargo were handled.

The Royal Jordanian Airline operates from Amman to Aqaba and has an extensive network of routes to the Middle East, Europe, North America and the Far East.

KENYA

Jamhuri ya Kenya

AREA, ETC – Kenya is bisected by the equator and extends approximately from latitude 4° N. to latitude 4° S. and from longitude 34° E. to 41° E. From the coast of the Indian Ocean in the east, the borders of Kenya are with Somalia in the east and Ethiopia and Sudan in the north and north-west. To the west lie Uganda and Lake Victoria. On the south is Tanzania. The total area is 224,961 sq. miles (582,646 sq. km), including 5,171 square miles of water. The country is divided into eight provinces (Central, Coast, Eastern, Nairobi, Nyanza, North Eastern, Rift Valley, Western).

POPULATION – The population is 24,032,000 (1990 UN estimate). The main tribal groups are the Kikuyu, Luhya, Luo, Kalenjin, Kamba and Masai.

LANGUAGES – The official languages are Swahili, which is generally understood throughout Kenya, and English; numerous indigenous languages are also spoken.

CAPITAL – Nairobi, population 1,400,000 (1989 estimate).
CURRENCY – Kenya shilling (Ksh) of 100 cents.
FLAG – Horizontally black, red and green with the red fimbriated in white, and with a shield and crossed spears all over in the centre.
NATIONAL ANTHEM – Kenya, Land of the Lion.
NATIONAL DAY – 12 December (Independence Day).

GOVERNMENT

Kenya became an independent state and a member of the British Commonwealth on 12 December 1963 after six months of internal self-government. Kenya became a Republic on 12 December 1964. In 1982 the government introduced amendments to the constitution and election law, making the country a one-party state. The Kenya African National Union (KANU) was the sole legal political organization. In December 1991 the government yielded to internal and international pressure and introduced a multi-party democracy through parliamentary legislation. Elections for a multi-party parliament are due by March 1993. There is a uni-cameral National Assembly of 202 members.

HEAD OF STATE

President and C.-in-C. Armed Forces, Hon. Daniel T. arap Moi, *took office*, 14 October 1978, returned for a third five-year term on 29 February 1988.

CABINET as at July 1992

Vice-President and Minister for Finance, Hon. Prof. George Saitoti.
Environment and Natural Resources, Hon. Phillip Leakey.
Lands and Housing, Hon. Darius Mbela.
Water Development, Hon. John Okwanyo.
Home Affairs and National Heritage, Hon. Davidson Kuguru.
Planning and National Development, Hon. Dr Z. Onyonka.
Transport and Communications, Hon. Dalmas Otieno.
Energy, Hon. John Kyalo.
Local Government, Hon. William Ntimama.
Foreign Affairs and International Co-operation, Hon. Wilson Ndolo Ayah.
Commerce, Hon. Arthur K. Magugu.
Tourism and Wildlife, Hon. Katana Ngala.
Culture and Social Services, Hon. James Njiru.
Agriculture, Hon. Elijah W. Mwangale.
Health, Hon. Jeremiah Nyagah.
Public Works, Hon. Timothy Mibei.
Co-operative Development, Hon. John Cheruiyot.
Labour, Hon. Phillip Masinde.
Education, Hon. Joseph J. Kamotho.
Information and Broadcasting, Hon. Burundi Nabwera.
Livestock Development, Hon. James K. Muregi.
Industry, Hon. Francis Ole Kaparo.
Research, Science and Technology, Hon. Kurugi M'Mukindia.
Supplies and Marketing, Hon. Wycliffe Musalia Mudavadi.
Technical Training and Applied Technology, Hon. Prof. Sam K. Ongeri.
Manpower Development and Employment, Hon. Archbishop Stephen Ondiek.
Reclamation and Development of Arid, Semi-Arid and Waste Land, Hon. George Ndoto.
Regional Development, Hon. Onyango Midika.
Attorney-General, Hon. Amos Wako.

KENYA HIGH COMMISSION

45 Portland Place, London WIN 4AS
Tel 071-636 2371
High Commissioner, His Excellency Simon Bullet (1992).

BRITISH HIGH COMMISSION

Bruce House, Standard Street, PO Box 30465 Nairobi
Tel: Nairobi 335944

High Commissioner, His Excellency Sir Roger Tomkys, KCMG (1990).

BRITISH COUNCIL REPRESENTATIVE, T. Edmundson, (PO Box 40751) ICEA Building, Kenyatta Avenue, Nairobi. There are offices at *Kisumu* and *Mombasa*.

ECONOMY

Agriculture provides about 52 per cent of total export earnings (excluding processed oil products). The great variation in altitude and ecology provide conditions under which a wide range of crops can be grown. These include wheat, barley, pyrethrum, coffee, tea, sisal, coconuts, cashew nuts, cotton, maize and a wide variety of tropical and temperate fruits and vegetables. The total area of well-farmed land on which concentrated mixed farming can be practised is small and the remainder is arid or semi-arid country but population pressure and the need to increase agricultural production for export has led to attempts to develop such areas.

Prospecting and mining are carried on in some parts of the country, the principal minerals produced being soda ash, salt and limestone.

Hydro-electric power has been developed, particularly on the Upper Tana River. Kenya is now almost self-sufficient in electric power generation but the connection with Owen Falls in Uganda is still in being.

There has been considerable industrial development over the last 15 years and Kenya has a wide variety of industries processing agricultural produce and manufacturing an increasing range of products from local and imported raw materials. New industries have recently come into being such as steel, textile mills, dehydrated vegetable processing and motor tyre manufacture as well as many smaller schemes which have added to the country's already considerable consumer goods. There is an oil refinery in Mombasa supplying both Kenya and Uganda, and a fuel pipeline now connects Mombasa and Nairobi.

TRADE

Principal exports are coffee and tea, which account for 33 per cent of total export earnings. Also exported are fruit, vegetables, and crude animal and vegetable material. Petroleum products account for about 37 per cent of imports; other imports are manufactured goods, particularly machinery, transport equipment, metals, pharmaceuticals and chemicals.

Trade with UK	1990	1991
Imports from UK	£223,080,000	£206,927,000
Exports to UK	149,474,000	141,996,000

COMMUNICATIONS

The Kenya Railways Corporation has 1,700 miles of railway open to traffic. There are also 39,000 miles of road, of which 5,000 are bitumen surfaced. Trans-border links with Tanzania were re-opened in 1985 with rail services for freight and steamer services for passengers and freight.

The principal port is Mombasa, operated by the Kenya Ports Authority.

International air services operate from airports at Nairobi and Mombasa.

KIRIBATI

Ribaberikin Kiribati

AREA, POPULATION, ETC – Kiribati, the former Gilbert Islands, became an independent Republic in 1979. Kiribati comprises 36 islands, the Gilberts Group (17) including Banaba (formerly Ocean Island), the Phoenix Islands (8), and the Line Islands (11), which are situated in the south-west central Pacific around the point at which the International Date Line cuts the Equator. The total land area of 281 sq. miles (728 sq. km) is spread over some 2 million square miles of ocean. Few of the atolls are more than half a mile in width or more than 12 feet high. The vegetation consists mainly of coconut palms, breadfruit trees and pandanus. The population (UN estimate 1990) is 66,000, and predominantly Christian.

CAPITAL – Tarawa, population estimated at 17,921.

CURRENCY – Kiribati uses the Australian dollar ($A) of 100 cents.

FLAG – Red, with blue and white wavy lines in base, and in the centre a gold rising sun and a flying frigate bird.

NATIONAL ANTHEM – Teirake Kain Kiribati (Stand Kiribati).

NATIONAL DAY – 12 July (Independence Day).

GOVERNMENT

The President is Head of State as well as Head of Government and is elected nationally. There is an elected House of Assembly of 41 members. Executive authority is vested in the Cabinet.

CABINET as at July 1992

President and Minister of Foreign Affairs and International Trade, HE Teatao Teannaki.
Vice-President and Minister of Finance and Economic Planning, Hon. Taomati T. Iuta.
Health, Family Affairs and Social Welfare, Hon. Baitika Toum.
Line and Phoenix Development, Hon. Boanereke Boanereke.
Home Affairs and Decentralization, Hon. Binata Tetaeka.
Transport, Communications and Tourism, Hon. Inatoa Tebania.
Education, Science and Technology, Hon. Anterea Kaitaake.
Commerce, Industry and Employment, Hon. Remuera Tateraka.
Works and Energy, Hon. Tamwi Naotarai.

HONORARY CONSULATE
c/o Faith House, 7 Tufton Street, London SW1P 3QN
Tel 071-222 6952

Honorary Consul, Hon. Maurice Chandler, CBE.

BRITISH HIGH COMMISSION
PO Box 61, Bairiki, Tarawa
Tel: Bairiki 21327

High Commissioner, His Excellency Derek White (1990).

ECONOMY

Most people still practise a semi-subsistence economy, the main staples of their diet being coconuts and fish.

Estimated recurrent revenue for 1988 is $A24.9m. The principal imports are foodstuffs, consumer goods, machinery and transport equipment. The principal exports are copra, which earned $A4,203,000, and fish, income from which was around $A1,606,000 in 1988. Total value of exports in 1988 was $A6,670,000.

TRADE WITH UK

	1990	1991
Imports from UK	£604,000	£253,000
Exports to UK	21,000	9,000

COMMUNICATIONS

Air communication exists between most of the islands, and is operated by Air Tungaru, a statutory corporation. Air Marshall Islands operates a weekly service between Majuro, Tarawa, Funafuti and Nandi, and Air Nauru between Tarawa, Nauru and Nandi. Inter-island shipping is operated by a statutory corporation, the Shipping Corporation of Kiribati.

SOCIAL WELFARE

The Government maintains a teacher training college and a secondary school. Five junior secondary schools are maintained by missions. Throughout the Republic there are about a hundred primary schools. The total enrolment of children of school age is about 16,000.

The Marine Training School at Tarawa trains seamen for service with overseas shipping lines.

There is a general hospital at Tarawa. The other inhabited islands have dispensaries.

KOREA

Korea is situated between 124° 11″ and 130° 57′ E. long., and between 33° 7′ and 43° 1″ N. lat. It has an area of 84,565 sq. miles (219,022 sq. km), with a population (UN estimate 1990) of 64,566,000, of whom 42,793,000 million live south of the present dividing line. The southern and western coasts are fringed with innumerable islands, of which the largest, forming a province of its own, is Cheju.

LANGUAGE AND LITERATURE

Despite the great cultural influence of the Chinese, Koreans have developed and preserved their own cultural heritage. The Korean language is of the Ural-Altaic Group. Its script, Hangul, was invented in the 15th century; prior to this Chinese characters alone were used. Also invented around this time was the first metal movable printing type.

HISTORY

The last native dynasty (Yi) ruled from 1392 until 1910, in which year Japan formally annexed Korea. The country remained an integral part of the Japanese Empire until the defeat of Japan in 1945, when it was occupied by troops of the USA and the USSR, the 38th parallel being fixed as the boundary between the two zones of occupation.

The US Government endeavoured to reach agreement with the Soviet Government for the creation of a Korean Government for the whole country and the withdrawal of all Russian and American troops. These efforts met with no success, and in September 1947 the US Government laid the whole question of the future of Korea before the General Assembly of the United Nations. The Assembly in November 1947 resolved that elections should be held in Korea for a National Assembly under the supervision of a temporary Commission formed for that purpose by the United Nations and that the National Assembly when elected should set up a Government. The Soviet Government refused to allow the Commission to visit the Russian-occupied zone and in consequence it was only able to discharge its function in that part of Korea which lies to the south of the 38th parallel.

A general election was held on 10 May 1948, and the first National Assembly met in Seoul on 31 May. The Assembly passed a constitution on 12 July and on 15 August 1948 the Republic was formally inaugurated and American Military Government came to an end.

Meanwhile, in the Russian-occupied zone north of the 38th parallel the Democratic People's Republic had been set up with its capital at Pyongyang. A Supreme People's Soviet was elected in September 1948, and a Soviet-style Constitution adopted.

THE KOREAN WAR

The country remained effectively divided into two along the line of the 38th parallel until June 1950, when the North Korean forces invaded South Korea. In response to Security Council recommendations that United Nations members should furnish assistance to repel the attack, 16 nations, including the USA and the UK, came to the aid of the Republic of Korea. China entered the war on the side of North Korea in November 1950. The fighting was ended by an Armistice Agreement signed on 27 July 1953. By this Agreement (which was not signed by the representatives of the Republic of Korea), the line of division between North and South Korea remained in the neighbourhood of the 38th parallel.

Talks between North and South Korea on the reunification of the country have taken place intermittently. A non-aggression accord was signed between the North and South in December 1991 and an agreement on the Denuclearization of the Korean peninsula was reached in February 1992.

REPUBLIC OF KOREA
Daehanminkuk

The Republic of Korea has been officially recognized by the governments of the United States, France, United Kingdom, and most other countries but, until recently, not by any Communist bloc country. Since 1989 diplomatic relations have been established with all eastern European countries.

RELIGION – There is freedom of religion. Buddhism has the most followers (13 million) followed by Protestantism (8 million) and Confucianism (4.7 million). Catholics number 2.2 million.

CAPITAL – Seoul, population (Nov. 1987) 9,991,089. Other main centres are ΨPusan (3,654,097), Taegu (2,165,954) and ΨInchon (1,526,435).

CURRENCY – Won of 100 jeon.

FLAG – White with a red and blue yin-yang in the centre, surrounded by four black trigrams.

NATIONAL ANTHEM – Aegukka.

NATIONAL DAY – 15 August (Independence Day).

GOVERNMENT

Following extensive political unrest in 1987, a new Constitution was adopted in February 1988. The President, who is Head of State, Chief of the Executive and Commander-in-Chief of the Armed Forces, is directly elected for a single term of five years. He appoints the Prime Minister with the consent of the National Assembly, and members of the State Council (Cabinet) on the recommendation of the Prime Minister. The President is also empowered to take wide-ranging measures in an emergency, including the declaration of martial law, but must obtain the agreement of the National Assembly. The National Assembly of 299 members is directly elected for a four-year term.

The most recent elections to the National Assembly were held in March 1992. The ruling Democratic Liberal Party (DLP) lost its parliamentary majority, winning 149 out of 299 seats, but then regained a majority by persuading independent members to join the party.

HEAD OF STATE

President, Roh Tae Woo, *took office* 24 February 1988.

CABINET as at 25 June 1992

Prime Minister, Chung Won Shik.
Deputy Prime Minister, Economic Planning Board, Choi Gak Joong.
Deputy Prime Minister, National Unification, Choi Young Choul.
Foreign Affairs, Lee Sang Ock.
Home Affairs, Lee Dong Hoo.
Finance, Rhee Yong Man.
Justice, Kim Ki Choon.
Defence, Choi Sae Chang.
Education, Yoon Hyoung Sup.
Youth and Sports, Lee Jin Sam.
Agriculture and Fisheries, Kang Hyon Ock.
Energy and Resources, Jin Nyum.
Environment, Lee Jai Chang.
Trade and Industry, Hahn Bong Soo.
Construction, Seo Yeong Taek.
Health and Social Affairs, Ahn Pil Joon.
Labour, Lee Yon Taek.
Transport, Roh Kon Il.
Communications, Song Eon Jong.
Culture, Lee Soo Jung.
Information, Son Chu Whan.
Government Administration, Lee Moon Suk.
Science and Technology, Kim Jin Hyun.
First Minister for Political Affairs, Kim Dong Young.
Second Minister for Political Affairs, Kim Kap Hyun.
Director, Office of Legislation, Han Young Sok.
Director, Patrons and Veterans' Administration, Min Kyung Bae.
Director, National Security Planning Agency, Lee Sang Yeon.

KOREAN EMBASSY
4 Palace Gate, London W8 5NF
Tel 071-581 0247

Ambassador Extraordinary and Plenipotentiary, His Excellency Dr Hong Koo Lee (1991).
Minister, Yang Chun Park.

BRITISH EMBASSY
No. 4, Chung-Dong, Chung-Ku, Seoul 100
Tel: Seoul 735-7341/3

Ambassador Extraordinary and Plenipotentiary, His Excellency David John Wright, CMG, LVO (1990).
Counsellor, P. Longworth (*Commercial*).
Defence and Military Attaché, Brig. D. P. de C. Morgan, OBE.
First Secretaries, Dr M. D. Reilly (*Head of Chancery and Consul*); D. M. Gray (*Commercial/Information*); P. S. Guest (*Defence Supply*).

There is an Honorary British Consul at *Pusan*.

BRITISH COUNCIL REPRESENTATIVE, T. White, MBE, Anglican Church Annex, 3-7 Chung Dong, Choong-ku, Seoul.

BRITISH CHAMBER OF COMMERCE, c/o Chartered Bank, 1st and 2nd Floors, Samsung Building, 50, 1-Ka Ulchi Ro, Chung-Ku, Seoul.

DEFENCE

The Republic of Korea has total armed forces of some 750,000 personnel. The Army has a strength of 650,000 active personnel divided into eight corps, with 1,550 main battle tanks, 2,100 armoured personnel carriers and armoured infantry fighting vehicles, 4,000 artillery pieces and 98 combat aircraft. The Navy has a strength of 60,000 (19,000 conscripts) including 25,000 marines, with four submarines and 35 principal surface combatants, 24 combat aircraft and 35 armed helicopters. The Air Force has a strength of 40,000, with 405 combat aircraft, almost all of US manufacture, organized into seven combat and two transport wings.

Conscripts in all services serve between 30 and 36 months and then serve in the reserve forces until age 35.

The US maintains 41,800 personnel in the Rebublic of Korea divided into 31,500 Army and 10,300 Air Force personnel.

EDUCATION

Primary education is compulsory for six years from the age of seven. Secondary and higher education is extensive. The national illiteracy rate is among the lowest in Asia.

ECONOMY

The soil is fertile but the arable land is limited by the mountainous nature of the country. Staple agricultural products are rice, barley and other cereals, beans, tobacco and hemp. Fruit-growing and sericulture are also practised. Ginseng, a medicinal root much used by both the Chinese and Koreans, forms a useful source of revenue. The Korean fishing industry is a major contributor to both food supply and exports.

The Republic of Korea is deficient in mineral resources, except for deposits of coal on the east coast and tungsten. There are some prospects of discovering oil in the sea between Korea and Japan.

FINANCE

The budget for 1990 totals Won 22,689,000. Since the beginning of 1962 a series of successful five-year plans have resulted in real economic growth averaging around 10 per cent a year. The sixth economic development plan (1987–91) envisages a growth rate of 7.5 per cent. Annual per capita GNP is US$4,400 (1989).

TRADE

Since the 1960s the Republic of Korea has industrialized rapidly on the basis of greatly expanded exports. Important exports include cars, electrical and electronic equipment, footwear, ships, railway rolling stock and iron and steel products.

	1989	1990
Imports	US$56,312m	US$65,091m
Exports	61,409m	63,236m

Trade with UK	1990	1991
Imports from UK	£620,690,000	£786,162,000
Exports to UK	963,829,000	924,615,000

COMMUNICATIONS

In 1989 there were 37,493 km of paved road. Seoul and Pusan have subway systems and there are national railway and airline systems. Korean Air operates regular flights to Europe, the United States, the Middle East and South East Asia. Pusan and Inchon are the major ports with Pusan serving the industrial areas of the south-east. Inchon, 28 miles from Seoul, serves the capital, but development and operation at Inchon are hampered by a tidal variation of 9–10 metres.

DEMOCRATIC PEOPLE'S REPUBLIC OF KOREA

Chosun Minchu-chui Inmin Kongwa-guk

The area of North Korea is 46,540 sq. miles (120,538 sq. km), with a population of 21,773,000 (UN estimate 1990).

CAPITAL – Pyongyang, approximate population, 1,500,000.
CURRENCY – Won of 100 chon.
FLAG – Red with white fimbriations and blue borders at top and bottom; a large red star on a white disc near the hoist.
NATIONAL ANTHEM – A Chi Mun Bin No Ra I Gang San (Shine bright, oh dawn, on this land so fair).
NATIONAL DAY – 8 September.

GOVERNMENT

The Constitution of the Democratic People's Republic of Korea provides for a Supreme People's Assembly, presently consisting of 687 deputies, which is elected every four years by universal suffrage. The Assembly elects a President, and the Central People's Committee. In turn, the Central People's Committee directs the Administrative Council which implements the policy formulated by the Committee. The Administrative Council (51 members), formally the government of North Korea, includes the Prime Minister and various ministers. In practice however, the country is ruled by the Korean Workers' Party which elects a Central Committee; this in turn appoints a Politburo. The senior ministers of the Administrative Council are all members of the Communist Central Committee and the majority are also members of the Politburo. Kim Il-sung was elected President for a fifth four-year term on 24 May 1990.

Politburo of the Central Committee, Kim Il-sung; Kim Chong-il; O Chin-u (*full members and members of the presidium*); Yi Chong-ok; Pak Song-chol; Kim Yong-nam; Yon Hyong-muk; Kye Ung-tae; Kang Song-san; So Yun-sok; Chon Pyong-ho; Choe Kwang; Han Song-yong (*full members*). Cho Se-ung; Kang Hui-won; Kim Pok-sin; Hong Si-hak; Hong Song-nam; Choe Tae Pok; Kim Chol-man; Choe Yong-nim (*alternate members*).

Secretariat of the Central Committee, Kim Il-sung (*General Secretary*); Kim Chong-il; Hwang Chang-yop; So Kwan-hui; Pak Nam-ki; Kim Chung-nin; Kye Ung-tae; Chon Pyong-ho; Choe Tae-pok; Han Song-yong; Yun Ki-pok; Kim Yong-sun.

ECONOMY

North Korea is rich in minerals and industry has been developed, but the economy has stagnated in recent years because of poor planning and a shortage of foreign exchange. The armed forces are believed to number about 890,000 men.

TRADE WITH UK

	1990	1991
Imports from UK	£4,774,000	£5,503,000
Exports to UK	373,000	349,000

KUWAIT
Dowlat al- Kuwait

AREA AND POPULATION – Kuwait extends along the shore of the Persian Gulf from Iraq to Saudi Arabia, with an area of 6,880 sq. miles (17,818 sq. km). Kuwait has a dry, desert climate with a summer season extending from April to September. The mean temperature varies between 29–45°C in summer, and 8–18°C in winter. Humidity rarely exceeds 60 per cent except in July and August. At the 1985 census the population was 1,695,128, of which about 40 per cent were Kuwaiti citizens, the remainder being other Arabs, Iranians, Indians and Pakistanis. The total European and American population was about 12,500. The gross population growth rate is 6.4 per cent, a growth rate of 3.5 per cent for Kuwaiti citizens. The Iraqi occupation of Kuwait led to a substantial emigration of nationals and foreign residents. The population was estimated to have returned to over one million in January 1992, including 425,000 foreigners. It is the government's intention to keep the proportion of foreigners down to 40 per cent.

The official language is Arabic, and English is widely spoken as a second language. Islam is the official religion, though religious freedom is constitutionally guaranteed.

CAPITAL – Ψ Kuwait, population (excluding suburbs) 400,000.

CURRENCY – Kuwaiti dinar (KD) of 1,000 fils.

FLAG – Three horizontal stripes of green, white and red, with black trapezoid next to staff.

NATIONAL DAY – 25 February.

GOVERNMENT

Although Kuwait had been independent for some years, the 'exclusive agreement' of 1899 between the Sheikh of Kuwait and the British Government was formally abrogated by an exchange of letters dated 19 June 1961.

Under the Constitution legislative power is vested in the Amir and the 50-member National Assembly, and executive power in the Amir and the Cabinet. The sixth National Assembly was dissolved in July 1986. Iraq invaded Kuwait on 2 August 1990 and a government-in-exile was established in Saudi Arabia. In October 1990, the Kuwaiti Prime Minister confirmed the al-Sabahs' commitment to the 1962 constitution. Kuwait was liberated in February 1991.

A new National Council was established in April 1990 with 50 elected members and an additional 25 members appointed by the Amir. Having boycotted the elections in June 1990, the opposition maintained their demands for the restoration of the National Assembly. The restored government has promised elections to a restored National Assembly in October 1992.

HEAD OF STATE

Amir, HH Sheikh Jabir al-Ahmad al Jabir Al-Sabah, *born* 1928; acceded 1 Jan. 1978.

CABINET as at June 1992

Crown Prince and Prime Minister, HH Sheikh Saad al-Abdullah al-Salim al-Sabah.
Deputy Prime Minister and Minister for Foreign Affairs, Sheikh Salem al-Sabah al-Salim al-Sabah.
Education, Dr Sulaiman Sa'adoun al-Badr.
Social Affairs and Labour, Sheikh Nawaf al-Ahmed al-Sabah.
Public Works, Abdullah al-Qattami.
Defence, Sheikh Ali al-Sabah al-Salim al-Sabah.
Justice, Legal and Administrative Affairs, Ghazi Obeid al-Sammar.
Communications, Habib Jawhar Hayat.
Information, Dr Badr Jassim al-Yacoub.
Public Health, Dr Abdul Wahab Suleiman al-Fouzan.
Planning, Dr Ahmed Ali al-Jasser.
Electricity and Water, Ahmed Mohammed al-Adasani.
Oil, Dr Hamoud al-Roqobah.
Finance, Nasser al-Rawdhan.
Awqaf and Islamic Affairs, Mohammed Saqr al-Mosharji.
Interior, Sheikh Ahmed Hmoud al-Jaber al-Sabah.
Trade and Industry, Abdullah Hassan al-Jarallah.
Higher Education, Dr Ali Abdullah al-Shamlan.
Minister of State for Cabinet Affairs, Dhari Abdullah al-Othman.
Minister of State for Housing, Mohammed al-Asfour.
Minister of State for Municipal Affairs, Dr Ibrahim Majed al-Shahine.

EMBASSY OF THE STATE OF KUWAIT
45–46 Queen's Gate, London SW7 5JN
Tel 071-589 4533

Ambassador Extraordinary and Plenipotentiary, His Excellency Ghazi M. A. Al-Rayes (1980).

BRITISH EMBASSY
PO Box 2 Safat, Arabian Gulf Street, Kuwait
Tel: Kuwait 2403326

Ambassador Extraordinary and Plenipotentiary, His Excellency Sir Michael Weston, KCMG, CVO (1990).
Counsellor, F. X. Gallagher, OBE.
First Secretaries, R. D. Lamb (*Political*); C. R. Winter, OBE (*Commercial*); P. Wallis (*Political*); A. Young (*Defence*).

BRITISH COUNCIL REPRESENTATIVE, Dr N. Taylor, 2 al Arabi Street (PO Box 345), Mansouriyah.

EDUCATION

The Kuwait Government invested its considerable oil revenues in comprehensive social services. Education and medical treatment are free. Kuwait University was opened in 1966, and in 1987–8 had 15,602 students. In 1987–8 there were over 489,000 pupils at government and private schools. These numbers have declined along with the total population since the Iraqi invasion and a number of schools did not re-open after Kuwait's liberation.

COMMUNICATIONS

Kuwait's ports and airport were damaged during the Iraqi occupation, but have re-opened since liberation. There is a network of dual-carriageway roads and more are under construction. Telecommunications and postal services are conducted by the Kuwait Government. Its earth satellite station and telecommunications network were severely damaged during the Iraqi occupation but domestic and international telephone services were restored in the early months following liberation.

PUBLIC UTILITIES

Before the Iraqi invasion Kuwait had six power stations capable of generating 7,200 Mw of electricity. Associated desalination capacity, on which the country largely depends for water, was 118 million gallons a day; reserves stored up to 2,000 million barrels. All six power stations were damaged during the Iraqi occupation. Essential services were restored after liberation but it will take several years and substantial investment to restore electricity and water distillation capacity to pre-invasion levels.

Finance

Expected revenue for the financial year 1991–2 was KD870m and expenditure KD6,237m. This compares with revenue of KD2,405m and expenditure of KD3,634m in the pre invasion budget for 1990–1. Oil revenues constitute about 80 per cent of total revenue. There are a large number of investment banks in some of which the Government holds equity. The banking system is controlled by the Central Bank of Kuwait.

The GDP of Kuwait in 1989 was estimated at KD6,779 million.

Production

Despite the desert terrain, 8.4 per cent of land is under cultivation, fruit and vegetables being the main crops. Shrimp fishing is becoming important.

The government of Kuwait began to participate in the ownership of the British- and American-owned Kuwait Oil Company in 1974 and an agreement was signed in November 1975 which brought 100 per cent government ownership. After a reorganization of the national oil industry in 1980, all the business was taken over by the Kuwait Petroleum Corporation.

The centre of Kuwait oil production is at Burgan, south of Kuwait City. Oil is also lifted in the Kuwait/Saudi Arabia Partitioned Zone (Wafra) south of the state. Oil is exported through a specially constructed port at Mina al Ahmadi.

Oil installations were extensively damaged during the Iraqi occupation. Oil exports were resumed in July 1991 and production (including output from the neutral zone) reached 1,000,000 barrels per day in June 1992, on schedule to reach the government's target of 1,500,000 barrels per day by the end of 1992 (compared to a production capacity of 2,200,000 barrels per day before the Iraqi invasion). By June 1992, half of Kuwait's pre-invasion refining capacity had been restored to working order.

Trade

Oil constitutes Kuwait's major export. Non-oil exports, mainly to Asian countries and the Indian sub-continent, have included chemical fertilizers, ammonia and other chemicals, metal pipes, shrimps and building materials. Re-exports to neighbouring states traditionally accounted for a major proportion of non-oil exports but were brought to a halt by the Iraqi invasion. Major trading partners are Japan, the USA and Western Europe.

Trade with UK	1990	1991
Imports from UK	£181,480,000	£178,336,000
Exports to UK	108,970,000	29,886,000

LAOS

Satharanarath Pasathipatai Pasason Lao

The People's Democratic Republic of Laos is in the northerly part of Indo-China, with China and Vietnam on the north and east, and Myanmar (Burma) and Thailand on the west. Laos has a common boundary with Cambodia to the south. The area of the country is 91,429 sq. miles (231,800 sq. km), with a population (UN estimate 1990) of 4,139,000.

Capital – Vientiane, population (estimated 1984) 120,000.
Currency – Kip (K) of 100 at.
Flag – Blue background with a central white circle, framed by two horizontal red stripes.
National Day – 2 December.

GOVERNMENT

The Kingdom of Lane Xang, the Land of a Million Elephants, was founded in the 14th century, but broke up at the beginning of the 15th century into the separate kingdoms of Luang Prabang and Vientiane and the Principality of Champassac, which together came under French protection in 1893. In 1945 the Japanese executed a coup and suppressed the French administration. Under a Constitution of 1947 Laos became a constitutional monarchy under King Sisvang Vong of the House of Luang Prabang, and an independent sovereign state in 1949. The next twenty-five years in Laos were marked by power struggles and civil war.

The Lao People's Democratic Republic was proclaimed in December 1975 following victory by the Communist Lao Patriotic Front and the abdication of the King. A President and Council of Ministers were installed, and a 45-member Supreme People's Council was appointed to draft a Constitution. A draft Constitution was approved by the People's Supreme Assembly in August 1991. The Lao People's Revolutionary Party (LPRP) is the sole legal political organization.

Head of State

President, Kaysone Phomvihane.
President of the Supreme People's Assembly, Nouhak Phoumsavan.

Council of Ministers as at June 1992

Prime Minister, Gen. Khamtai Siphandon.
Deputy PM and Minister for Economy, Planning and Finance, Khamphoui Keoboualapha.
Foreign Affairs, Phoune Sipraseuth.
National Defence and Supreme Commander of the Lao People's Army, Lt.-Gen. Choummali Saignason.
Minister, and Head of the Office of the Party Central Committee and of the Office of the Council of Ministers, Maisouk Saisompheng.
Minister to the PM's Office, Chanmi Douangboutdi.
Interior, Asang Laoli.
Justice, Kou Souvannamethi.
Public Health, Kambou Sounisai.
Agriculture, Sisavat Keobounphan.
Industry and Handicraft, Soulivong Daravong.
Communications, Transport, Posts and Construction, Bouathong.
Trade and Tourism, vacant.
Education and Sport, Lt.-Gen. Saman Vignaket.
Economic Relations with Foreign Countries, Phao Bounaphon.
Information and Culture, Mounkeo Olaboun.
Chairwoman of the State Bank, Pani Yathotou.
Chairman of the Party and State Inspection Committee, Maychantan Sengmani.
Science and Technology, Souli Nanthavong.

Embassy of the Lao People's Democratic Republic

74 Avenue Raymond-Poincaré 75116 Paris
Tel: Paris 45530298

Ambassador Extraordinary and Plenipotentiary, new appointment awaited.

British Ambassador, resident in Bangkok, Thailand.

ECONOMY

There is no significant industrial base in Laos, an estimated 85 per cent of the work force being engaged in agriculture, largely concerned with rice cultivation. Rice production in

1984 amounted to 1.3 million tonnes, thus rendering the country theoretically self-sufficient in this staple food.

In 1984, exports amounted to US$36.2m and imports to US$98.4m. Hydro-electric power was 88.3 per cent of exports, timber 8.5 per cent and coffee 1.2 per cent. Clearing agreements have been signed with certain socialist countries and the trade gap is largely financed by foreign aid, of which some 60 per cent is provided by socialist countries.

Laos' economic performance so far has been poor and shows no signs of early recovery. The free market rate for the dollar is much higher than the official rate and prices of consumer items continue to increase.

TRADE WITH UK

	1990	1991
Imports from UK	£1,261,000	£1,173,000
Exports to UK	54,000	39,000

LATVIA
The Republic of Latvia

The republic of Latvia is situated in northern Europe on the eastern coast of the Baltic sea. To the north lie Estonia and Finland, to the south Lithuania and Belarus, and to the east the Russian Federation.

AREA – 66,000 square km (25,000 square miles).

TOPOGRAPHY – Latvia is low-lying with occasional chains of hills. Forests cover 20 per cent of the total territory.

CLIMATE – Moderately continental.

POPULATION – The total population of Latvia is 2,667,000 (1989).

ETHNIC GROUPS – 51.8 per cent Latvian, 33.8 per cent Russian, 4.5 cent Belarussian, small Ukrainian and Polish minorities.

LANGUAGES – 51.8 per cent have Latvian as their first language and 33.8 per cent Russian. Education is now only in Latvian and all employees must pass language tests in Latvian. The right of minorities to use their mother tongue has been acknowledged.

MAJOR CITIES – Riga (population 900,000), Liepaja, Ventspils.

CAPITAL – Riga.

FLAG – Crimson, with a white horizontal stripe across the centre.

NATIONAL ANTHEM – Dievs, sveti Latviju (God bless Latvia).

NATIONAL DAY – 18 November.

NATIONAL CURRENCY – Rouble (likely to be changed to the Lat).

TIME ZONE – 2 hours ahead of GMT.

HISTORY

Latvia came under the control of the German Teutonic Knights at the end of the thirteenth century. During the next few centuries the country endured sporadic invasions by the Swedes, Poles and Russians. By 1795 Latvia was entirely under Russian control. On 18 November 1918 Latvia declared its independence and this was confirmed by the Versailles Treaty in 1919. Several years of fighting with the new Soviet Union ensued until a peace treaty was signed under which the Soviet Union renounced all claims to Latvian territory.

The Soviet Union annexed Latvia in 1940 under the terms of the Molotov-Ribentrop pact with Germany. Latvia was invaded and occupied when Germany invaded the Soviet Union during the Second World War. In 1944 the Soviet Union recaptured the country from Germany and confirmed its annexation, though this was never accepted as legal by most states.

In October 1988 the Popular Front of Latvia was formed to campaign for greater sovereignty and democracy for Latvia. The Popular Front convincingly won elections to the Latvian Supreme Soviet in 1989, and on 4 May 1990 the Supreme Soviet declared the independent Republic of Latvia to be, *de jure*, still in existence. Agitation in Latvia against Soviet rule led in 1990 and early 1991 to clashes between independence supporters and Latvian Communists and the Soviet military. Violence reached a peak in January 1991 with deaths caused by soviet Interior Ministry troops and attacks on Baltic border posts. A national referendum was held in March 1991 in which 73 per cent of voters declared in favour of independence, and this was declared on 21 August 1991. The State Council of the Soviet Union recognized the independence of Latvia on 10 September 1991.

CONSTITUTION

The present governing system is transitional and is intended to restore democratic government to Latvia.

EXECUTIVE – Executive authority is vested in a Prime Minister and Cabinet of Ministers.

LEGISLATURE – Legislative power is exercised by the Supreme Council of the Republic of Latvia, which consists of 210 deputies. The deputies elect from amongst their number a President of the Supreme Council, who also acts as the President of the Republic.

CURRENT POLITICAL SITUATION – Of the 210 seats in the Supreme Council, 128 are held by the Popular Front, which forms the government and has nominated the President.

HEAD OF STATE
President, Anatolijs Gorbunovs, *elected* March 1990
First Deputy President, Dainis Ivans

GOVERNMENT
Prime Minister, Ivars Godmanis
First Deputy Prime Minister, Ilmars Bisers
Deputy Prime Minister, Arnis Kalnins
Agriculture, Dainis Gegeris
Architecture and Construction, Aivars Prusis
Culture, Raimonds Pauls
Economy, Janis Aboltins
Energy, Anseklis Silins
Foreign Affairs, Janis Jurkans
Governmental Affairs, Karlis Licis
Health, Edvins Platkajis
Interior, Aloizs Vaznis
Material Resources, Edgars Zasujevs
Trade, Armands Plaudis
Transport, Janis Janovskis

MEMBERSHIP OF INTERNATIONAL ORGANIZATIONS – UN, CSCE, EBRD, IBRD, IMF, UNESCO.

EMBASSY OF THE REPUBLIC OF LATVIA
72 Queensborough Terrace, London W2 3SP
Tel 071-727 1698

Ambassador Extraordinary and Plenipotentiary, no accreditation as yet.

BRITISH EMBASSY
Riga

Ambassador Extraordinary and Plenipotentiary, His Excellency Richard Samuel, CMG, CVO, *apptd* 1991

ECONOMY

Since the former Latvian Supreme Soviet declared the *de jure* independence of Latvia on 4 May 1990, Latvia has pressed ahead with transition from a command economy to a market economy system. It has also attempted to achieve economic independence from the rest of the former Soviet Union. The Latvian governnment has initiated a privatization process which has made many industrial facilities available for purchase both by Latvian and foreign private investors.

PRIMARY RESOURCES – Latvia is an agricultural exporter, specializing in cattle and pig breeding, dairy farming and crops, including sugar beet, flax and potatoes. Latvia's natural resources include limestone, gypsum, peat and timber.

INDUSTRY – Latvian industry was organized to contribute to the centralized Soviet command economy and is specialized in certain areas. These include the production of electric and diesel trains, telephones, telephone exchange equipment, agricultural machinery, and timber and paper products.

SERVICE INDUSTRY – Tourism is being developed in Latvia, capitalizing on its beach resorts, nature reserves and parks. Latvia is also geographically well-placed for the development of transport services.

TRADE – The Russian Federation remains by far the most important trading partner for Latvia. Over 70 per cent of Latvian trade is with the other former Soviet republics; Latvia imports most of its raw materials from the former Soviet republics and exports its finished industrial products to them. However, Latvia is expanding its trade links with the other Baltic states and western nations, to try to offset any decline in exports to the former Soviet republics.

COMMUNICATIONS

Latvia has a reasonably well-developed railway and road system, along which a significant proportion of exports from former Soviet republics are transported to western Europe. Latvia is also being developed as a transportation route from Scandinavia to central and southern Europe. Several warm-water ports exist, of which two, Riga and Ventspils, are developed for commercial transport.

CULTURE

The Latvian language belongs to the Baltic branch of the Indo-European languages, and as such is distinct from Russian. The Latin alphabet is used.

LEBANON
Al-Jumhouriya al-Lubnaniya

AREA AND POPULATION – Lebanon forms a strip about 120 miles in length and varying in width from 30 to 35 miles, along the Mediterranean littoral, and extending from the Israel frontier in the south to the Nahr al Kebir (15 miles north of Tripoli) in the north; its eastern boundary runs down the Anti-Lebanon range and then down the great central depression, the *Beqaa*, from which flow the rivers Orontes and Litani. It is divided into five districts, North Lebanon, Mount Lebanon, Beirut, South Lebanon and Beqaa. The seaward slopes of the mountains have a Mediterranean climate and vegetation. The inland range of Anti-Lebanon has the characteristics of steppe country.

There is a mixed Arabic-speaking population of Christians, Muslims and Druses. The total area of Lebanon is 4,015 sq. miles, (10,400 sq. km), population (UN estimate 1990) 2,701,000.

LANGUAGE AND LITERATURE – Arabic is the official language, and French and English are also widely used.

CAPITAL – Ψ Beirut (population 702,000). Other towns are Ψ Tripoli (175,000), Zahlé (46,800), ΨSidon (24,740), Ψ Tyre (14,000).

CURRENCY – Lebanese pound (£L) of 100 piastres.

FLAG – Horizontal bands of red, white and red with a green cedar of Lebanon in the centre of the white band.

NATIONAL ANTHEM – Kulluna Lil Watan Lil'ula Lil'alam (We all belong to the homeland).

NATIONAL DAY – 22 November.

GOVERNMENT

Lebanon became an independent state in September 1920, administered under French mandate until 22 November 1943. Powers were transferred to the Lebanese Government from January 1944, and French troops were withdrawn in 1946.

In April 1975, serious fighting broke out in Beirut between members of the predominantly Christian Phalangist Party and mainly Muslim militias later supported by Palestinian guerrillas based in Lebanon.

In the autumn of 1976 the Arab Deterrent Forces, composed mainly of Syrian troops, imposed an effective ceasefire. In March 1978 Israeli forces invaded but withdrew some months later, handing over their positions, except for a belt in the south, to the UN Interim Force in Lebanon (UNIFIL). In the summer of 1982 Israeli forces again invaded the country, penetrating as far as Beirut. Following negotiations, Palestinian officials and fighters left Beirut for various Arab countries. Although the bulk of Israeli troops withdrew from southern Lebanon in 1985, a buffer zone controlled by Israeli-backed Christian militias has been established along the Israeli-Lebanon border. Syrian forces are deployed in west Beirut and in the north and the east of the country.

In September 1988 outgoing President Gemayel appointed a transitional Christian-led military government under Gen. Michel Aoun to replace the Muslim-led government of Selim al-Hoss. Each party claimed to represent the constitutional government of Lebanon, and refused to accept the other's authority. The Taif Accord 'for national conciliation', drawn up by an Arab League-appointed committee, gained the approval of a majority of Lebanese MPs in October 1989, but was rejected by Michel Aoun, who insisted on an immediate Syrian troop withdrawal. Following an outbreak of fighting between Gen. Aoun and the dominant Christian militia, the Lebanese Government acted with the backing of Syrian troops to oust Gen. Aoun in October 1990. A new Government, which included the main militia leaders, was formed in December 1990. Since then the Government has moved to clear the militias from the Greater Beirut area and has restored its authority throughout the former Christian enclave. The Lebanese Army moved into surrounding areas during 1991, extending the control of the Government to virtually all areas not under Syrian and Israeli control and disarming all the militias apart from Hezbollah. Further, since July 1992 the Army has been enforcing the government's policy of retaking all public buildings from the militias.

In May 1991 Lebanon and Syria signed a Treaty of Brotherhood, Co-operation and Co-ordination aimed at regulating the relationship between the two countries, as laid down in the Taif Accord.

Partly as a result of overt popular discontent with chronic economic difficulties the government resigned and was replaced with a broadly similar cabinet in May 1992. The first parliamentary elections since the beginning of the civil war were being held in August and September 1992, but there was a total boycott of the polls in Christian areas because of the continued Syrian military presence, in breach of the Taif Accord.

In October 1991 Lebanon began to participate in the bilateral sessions of the Middle East peace talks, but so far has, with Syria, boycotted the multilateral rounds.

HEAD OF STATE

President of the Republic of Lebanon, Elias Hrawi, *took office*, 25 November 1989.

CABINET as at June 1992

Prime Minister, Rashid al-Solh.
Deputy PM and Minister of Defence, Michel Murr.
Foreign and Expatriate Affairs, Fares Bouez.
Justice, Nasri Ma'aluf.
Health and Social Affairs, Marwan Hamadeh.
Labour, Abdullah al-Amin.
Posts and Telecommunications, Georges Saadeh.
Finance, As'ad Diyab.
Education and Fine Arts, Zaki Mazboudi.
Hydroelectric Resources, Muhammad Beydoun.
Economy and Trade, Dr Samir Makdisi.
Information, Michel Samaha.
Agriculture, Mohsen Dalloul.
Public Works and Transport, Shawki Fakhury.
Industry and Oil, Shahi Barsumian.
Interior, Maj. Gen. Sami al-Khatib.
Housing and Co-operatives, Sleiman Tony Frangieh.
Tourism, Brig.-Gen. Ahmed Minkara.
Ministers of State, Nabih Berri; Nazih Bizri; Walid Jumblatt; Asad Hardan; Elie Hobeika (Refugee Affairs).

LEBANESE EMBASSY
21 Kensington Palace Gardens, London W8 4QM
Tel 071-229 7265/6

Ambassador Extraordinary and Plenipotentiary, His Excellency Mahmoud Hammoud (1990).
Consular Section, 15 Palace Gardens Mews, London W8. Tel: 071-727 6696.

BRITISH EMBASSY
Shamma Building, Raouché, Ras Beirut, Beirut
Tel: Beirut 812849

Ambassador Extraordinary and Plenipotentiary, His Excellency David Tatham, CMG (1989).

COMMUNICATIONS

The railways are not functioning as a result of the civil war. There is an international airport at Beirut, served by the national carrier MEA, Air France, Cyprus Air and other Arab and European airlines. An internal service operates from Beirut to Tripoli.

ARCHAEOLOGY

Lebanon has some important historical remains, notably Baalbek (Heliopolis) which contains the ruins of first to third century Roman temples and Jbeil (Byblos), one of the oldest continuously inhabited towns in the world, and ancient Tyre.

EDUCATION

There are six universities in Beirut, the American and the French Universities established in the last century, and the Lebanese National University, the Beirut University College, the Kaslik Saint Esprit University and the Arab University, with the University of Balamond situated near Tripoli. There are several institutions for vocational training, and there is a good provision throughout the country of primary and secondary schools, among which are a great number of private schools. Education at all levels has been severely disrupted by the civil war.

ECONOMY

Fruits are the most important products and include citrus fruit, apples, grapes, bananas and olives. There is some light industry, mostly for the production of consumer goods, but most factories were adversely affected by the civil war. Reconstruction is now under way.

FINANCE

No reliable statistics have been published for some time. The country is known to have a deficit, and the Lebanese pound has lost much of its value against foreign currencies. At its May 1990 summit meeting, the Arab League agreed to set up an international fund for Lebanon's reconstruction, but progress in establishing the fund was halted by the Kuwait crisis. Reconstruction has been slow to take off and the hoped for economic recovery has yet to materialize.

TRADE

Principal imports are gold and precious metals, machinery and electrical equipment, textiles and yarns, vegetable products, iron and steel goods, and motor vehicles. There has been a gradual decline in the overall amount of imports, as a result of continued instability.

Principal exports include gold and precious metals, fruits and vegetables, textiles, building materials, furniture, plastic goods, foodstuffs, tobacco and wine.

At one time there was a considerable transit trade through

Beirut into the Arab hinterland. Lebanon is the terminal for two oil pipe lines, one formerly belonging to the Iraq Petroleum Company, debouching at Tripoli, the other belonging to the Trans Arabian Pipeline Company, at Sidon. These lines have not functioned for some years.

Trade with UK	1990	1991
Imports from UK	£53,266,000	£87,760,000
Exports to UK	6,249,000	8,465,000

LESOTHO

'Muso oa Lesotho

Lesotho is a landlocked mountainous state entirely surrounded by the Republic of South Africa. Of the total area of 11,720 sq. miles (30,355 sq. km), a belt between 20 and 40 miles in width lying across the western and southern boundaries and comprising about one-third of the total is classed as lowlands, being between 5,000 and 6,000 ft. above sea level. The remaining two-thirds are classed as foothills and highlands, rising to 11,425 ft. The population (UN estimate 1990) is 1,774,000.

CAPITAL – Maseru, population (1986 Census) 288,951.
CURRENCY – Loti (M) of 100 lisente.
FLAG – Diagonally white over blue over green with the white of double width, and an assegai and knobkerrie on a Basotho shield in brown in the upper hoist.
NATIONAL ANTHEM – Pina ea Sechaba.
NATIONAL DAY – 4 October (Independence Day).

GOVERNMENT

Lesotho (formerly Basutoland) became a constitutional monarchy within the Commonwealth on 4 October 1966. The independence constitution was suspended in January 1970, when the country was governed by a Council of Ministers until the establishment of a nominated National Assembly in April 1974.

The Government was overthrown in January 1986, and executive and legislative powers were conferred upon the King, to be advised by the Military Council and Council of Ministers led by Maj.-Gen. Justin Lekhanya. In March 1990 King Moshoeshoe III's powers were formally revoked and vested in the Chairman of the Council of Ministers. In November 1990 the King was deposed and replaced by his son, who assumed the title of Letsie III. Maj.-Gen. Lekhanya was overthrown in a coup on 30 April 1991, led by Col. Elias Ramaema. Elections were promised for 1992.

The country is divided into 11 administrative districts. In each district there is a District Secretary who co-ordinates all Government activity in the area, working in co-operation with hereditary chiefs.

HEAD OF STATE
King, HM King Letsie III.

MILITARY COUNCIL

Chairman, HE Maj.-Gen. Elias P. Ramaema.
Members, HE Col. Blyth R. Ntsohi; HE Lt.-Col. William M. Khuele; HE Lt.-Col. Ernest M. Mokete; HE Lt.-Col. Tseliso Lehohla; HE Lt.-Col. Maoabi Mothibeli.

COUNCIL OF MINISTERS as at June 1992

Chairman of the Council of Ministers, HE Maj.-Gen. Elias Ramaema.
Finance, Planning and Economic Development, Hon. Abel. L. Thoahlane.
Foreign Affairs, Hon. Tokonye Kotelo.
Water, Energy and Mining, Hon. Col. Alexander L. Jane.
Works, Transport and Communications, Hon. Col. Valentius M. Mokone.
Highlands Water, Hon. Maj. Reentseng Habi.
Education, Hon. Dr L. B. B. J. Machobane.
Justice, Prisons, Law and Constitutional Affairs, Hon. Albert K. Maope.
Trade and Industry, Hon. Chief Moletsane Mokoroane.
Tourism, Sports and Culture, Hon. Chief Lechesa Mathealira.
Information and Broadcasting, Hon. Patrick J. Molapo.
Interior, Chieftainship Affairs and Rural Development, Hon. Chief Mohlalefi Bereng.
Health, Hon. Col. Obed L. Matel.
Employment, Social Welfare and Pensions, Hon. Leonard P. Mothakathi.

LESOTHO HIGH COMMISSION
10 Collingham Road, London SW5 0NR
Tel 071-373 8581

High Commissioner, His Excellency M. K. Tsekoa (1989).

BRITISH HIGH COMMISSION
PO Box 521, Maseru 100
Tel: Maseru 313961

High Commissioner, His Excellency John Coates Edwards, CMG (1988).

BRITISH COUNCIL REPRESENTATIVE, D. Bates, Hobson's Square, PO Box 429, Maseru 100.

JUDICIARY

The Lesotho Courts of Law consist of the Court of Appeal, the High Court, Magistrates' Courts, Judicial Commissioners' Court, Central and local Courts. Magistrates' and higher courts administer the laws of Lesotho. They also adjudicate appeals from the Judicial Commissioner's and Subordinate Courts.
Chief Justice, Hon. B. P. Cullinan.

EDUCATION

Most schools are mission-controlled, the Government providing grants for salaries and buildings. There are over 1,000 primary and over 100 secondary schools; few areas lack a school and there is a high literacy rate of about 70 per cent. Increasing emphasis is being laid on agricultural and vocational education. The National University of Lesotho at Roma was established in 1975.

COMMUNICATIONS

A tarred road links Maseru to several of the main lowland towns, and this is being extended in the south of the country. The mountainous areas are linked by gravelled and earth roads and tracks. Roads link border towns in South Africa with the main towns in Lesotho. Maseru is connected by rail with the main Bloemfontein–Natal line of the South African Railways. Scheduled international air services are operated daily between Maseru and Johannesburg and other scheduled international flights are to Gabarone, Harare, Manzini and Maputo. There are around 30 airstrips. Internal scheduled services are operated by the Lesotho Airways Corporation.

The telephone network is fully automated in all urban centres. Radio telephone communication is used extensively in the remote rural areas.

ECONOMY

The economy of Lesotho is based on agriculture and animal husbandry, and the adverse balance of trade (mainly consumer and capital goods) is offset by the earnings of the large numbers of the population who work in South Africa. Apart from some diamonds, Lesotho has few natural resources and only small-scale industrial development. The Lesotho National Development Corporation was set up to promote the development of industry, mining, trade and tourism. Work has commenced on the Highlands Water Scheme designed to provide water for the Vaal industrial zone in South Africa and hydro-electricity for Lesotho. Drilling is being carried out for oil. A National Park has been established at Sehlabathebe in the Maluti mountains. A number of light manufacturing and processing industries have recently been established.

FINANCE

The main sources of revenue are customs and excise duty. Estimates of expenditure and revenue (1986) are recurrent revenue M241.2 million; recurrent expenditure M265.3 million; capital revenue M144 million; capital expenditure M198 million.

Trade with UK	1990	1991
Imports from UK	£642,000	£3,258,000
Exports to UK	1,288,000	2,799,000

LIBERIA
Republic of Liberia

An independent republic of West Africa, occupying that part of the coast between Sierra Leone and the Côte d'Ivoire, which is between the rivers Mano in the north-west and Cavalla in the south-east, a distance of about 350 miles, with an area of about 43,000 sq. miles (111,369 sq. km), and extending to the interior to latitude 8° 50′, a distance of 150 miles from the seaboard. It was founded by the American Colonization Society in 1822 as a colony for freed American slaves, and has been recognized since 1847 as an independent state. The population at the Census of 1974 was 1,481,524; a 1990 UN estimate put the figure at 2,607,000. The official language is English. Over 16 ethnic languages are spoken.

CAPITAL – ΨMonrovia, population estimate (1984) 425,000. Other ports are ΨBuchanan, ΨGreenville (Sinoe) and ΨHarper (Cape Palmas).
CURRENCY – Liberian dollar (L$) of 100 cents.
FLAG – Alternate horizontal stripes (five white, six red), with five-pointed white star on blue field in upper corner next to flagstaff.
NATIONAL ANTHEM – All Hail, Liberia, Hail.
NATIONAL DAY – 26 July.

GOVERNMENT

William V. S. Tubman, President since 1944, died in 1971 and was succeeded by Dr Tolbert. The constitution was suspended following a military coup on 12 April 1980, during which Tolbert was killed. M/Sgt. Samuel Doe assumed power as chairman of a military council. A new constitution was endorsed by a referendum in July 1984. Doe and his party, the National Democratic Party of Liberia (NDPL) won the elections held in October 1985, amid allegations of electoral fraud, and a civilian government was formally installed in January 1986.

CIVIL WAR

A rebel incursion launched in December 1989 by the National Patriotic Front of Liberia (NPFL) led by Charles Taylor developed into a full-scale civil war. By July 1990 most members of the government had left the country, and foreigners were airlifted to safety by US Marines. A five-nation ECOWAS peacekeeping force landed in Monrovia in an effort to end the conflict but in September President Doe was killed, having refused to step down. The Interim Government (IGNU) was formed in August in Banjul, The Gambia, and arrived in Monrovia in November. A ceasefire agreement was signed in Bamako, Mali on 28 November 1990 as efforts to reach a political settlement continued. After months of stalemate, slow progress is being made in returning the country to normality. ECOMOG forces have been tasked with supervising disarmament and the opening of roads.

FACTIONS

There are two competing claims to the leadership of Liberia; that of Interim President Amos Sawyer of the Interim Government of National Unity (IGNU), based in Monrovia and supported by ECOMOG (Economic Community of West African States Ceasefire Monitoring Group); and that of Charles Taylor, leader of the National Patriotic Reconstruction Assembly Government (NPRAG), supported by the National Patriotic Front of Liberia (NPFL) and based in Gbarnga, which controls a large part of the territory of Liberia. After lengthy negotiations, agreement was reached between the two sides that legislative elections would be held under international supervision. These are scheduled for late 1992. However, the timetable is likely to slip, as it has in the past.

EMBASSY OF THE REPUBLIC OF LIBERIA
2 Pembridge Place, London W2 4XB
Tel 071-221 1036

Minister Plenipotentiary, George Bardell Cooper.
Chargé d'Affaires, Rudolf P. Von Ballmoos.

BRITISH EMBASSY
The British Embassy in Monrovia was closed in March 1991.

COMMUNICATIONS

The artificial harbour and free port of Monrovia was opened on 26 July 1948. There are nine ports of entry, including three river ports. Robertsfield International Airport is under NPFL control and not yet in use. Spriggs Payne airfield, on the outskirts of Monrovia, normally used for internal flights, is currently being used for flights to other West African countries.

ECONOMY

In December 1990 the UN launched an appeal for $13.8 m in emergency aid to finance the enormous task of reconstruction. Of the country's 2.5 million population, an estimated 500,000 to one million are refugees in neighbouring countries and it is estimated that up to 20,000 have died. Liberia is receiving relief aid from a number of countries including the United Kingdom, the EC and various international agencies.

TRADE

Before the unrest began principal exports were iron ore, crude rubber, timber, uncut diamonds, palm kernels, cocoa and coffee, but the civil war has resulted in the suspension of most economic activity.

Trade with UK	1990	1991
Imports from UK	£8,639,000	£8,865,000
Exports to UK	13,240,000	972,000

LIBYA

Al-Jamahiriya Al-Arabiya
Al-Libya Al-Shabiya Al-Ishtirakiya Al-Uthma

Libya, on the Mediterranean coast of Africa, is bounded on the east by Egypt and Sudan, on the south by the Republics of Chad and Niger, and on the west by Algeria and Tunisia. It consists of the three former provinces of Tripolitania, Cyrenaica and the Fezzan, with a combined area of 679,362 sq. miles (1,759,540 sq. km) and a population (UN estimate 1990) of 4,545,000. The people of Libya are principally Arab with some Berbers in the west and some Tuareg tribesmen in the Fezzan. Islam is the official religion of Libya, but other religions are tolerated. The official language is Arabic.

Vast sand and rock deserts, almost completely barren, occupy the greater part of Libya. The southern part of the country lies within the Sahara Desert. There are few rivers and as rainfall is irregular outside parts of Cyrenaica and Tripolitania, good harvests are rare.

The ancient ruins in Cyrenaica, at Cyrene, Ptolemais (Tolmeta) and Apollonia, are outstanding, as are those at Leptis Magna, 70 miles east, and at Sabratha, 40 miles west of Tripoli. An Italian expedition found in the south-west of the Fezzan a series of rock-paintings more than 5,000 years old.

CAPITAL – ΨTripoli, population estimate (1991) 1,000,000. The principal towns are: ΨBenghazi (500,000); ΨMisurata (200,000); Sirte (100,000).

CURRENCY – Libyan dinar (LD) of 1,000 dirhams.

FLAG – Libya uses a plain emerald green flag.

NATIONAL DAY – 1 September.

GOVERNMENT

Libya was occupied by Italy in 1911–12 in the course of the Italo-Turkish War, and under the Treaty of Ouchy (October 1912) the sovereignty of the province was transferred by Turkey to Italy. In 1939 the four provinces of Libya (Tripoli, Misurata, Benghazi and Derna) were incorporated in the national territory of Italy as *Libia Italiana*. After the Second World War Tripolitania and Cyrenaica were placed provisionally under British and the Fezzan under French administration, and in conformity with a resolution of the UN General Assembly in November 1949, Libya became on 24 December 1951 the first independent state to be created by the United Nations. The monarchy was overthrown by a revolution in September 1969, and the country was declared a republic. It was ruled by the Revolutionary Command Council (RCC) under the leadership of Colonel Muammar Gadaffi.

In March 1977 a new form of direct democracy, the 'Jamahiriya' (state of the masses) was promulgated and the official name of the country was changed to Socialist People's Libyan Arab Jamahiriya. At local level authority is now vested in about 1,500 Basic and 14 Municipal People's Congresses which appoint Popular Committees to execute policy. Officials of these congresses and committees, together with representatives from unions and other organizations, form the General People's Congress, which normally meets for about a week early each year. In addition, a number of extraordinary sessions are held throughout the year. This is the highest policy-making body in the country.

The General People's Congress appoints its own General Secretariat and the General People's Committee, whose members head the 13 government departments which execute policy at national level. The Secretary of the General People's Committee has functions similar to those of a Prime Minister.

Since a reorganization in March 1979 neither Col. Gadaffi nor his former RCC colleagues have held formal posts in the administration. Gadaffi continues to hold the ceremonial title 'Leader of the Revolution'.

Leader of the Revolution and Supreme Commander of the Armed Forces, Col. Muammar al-Gadaffi.

SECRETARIAT OF THE GENERAL PEOPLE'S CONGRESS as at June 1992

Secretary, Abd al-Raziq Sawsa.
Assistant Secretary, Mahmud Hamid al-Khafifi.
Secretary (Affairs of People's Congresses), Abd al-Hamid al-Fayturi Ammar.
Secretary (Affairs of People's Committees), Sulayman Sasi al-Shuhumi.
Secretary (Affairs of Professional Congresses), Bashir Huwayj Humaydi.

GENERAL PEOPLE'S COMMITTEE

Secretary-General, Abu Zayd 'Umar Durda.
Foreign Liaison, Ibrahim Muhammad Bishari.
Petroleum, Abdullah Salem al-Badri.
Communications and Transport, Izz al-Din al-Hinshari.
Higher Education, Ibrahim Misbah Bukhzam.
Planning and Economy, Umar Mustafa al Muntasir.
Health, Dr Zaydan Badr Zaydan.
Strategic Industries, Jadallah Azzuz al-Talhi.
Treasury, Muhammad al Madani al Bukhari.
Information and Culture, Al Milad Abu Jaziyah.
Marine Wealth, Miftah Muhammad Ku'aybah.
Vocational Training, Ma'tuq Muhammad Ma'tuq.
Scientific Research, Nuri al-Fayturi al Madani.
Agrarian Reform and Land Reclamation, Abd al-Majid al-Qa'ud.
Justice, Ibrahim Muhammad Bakkar.
Education, Madani Ramadhan Abu al-Tuwayrat.
Light Industries, Dr Fathi Hamad bin Shatwan.
Electricity, Jum'a Salim al-Arbash.
Amenities and Public Works, Dr Salim Ahmad Funayr.
Social Security, Ishma'il Miftah bin Sharadah.
Youth and Sport, Bukhari Salim Hawdah.
Supervision and Follow-Up, Ammar al-Mabruk Litayf.
Arab Maghreb Union, Muhammad al-Zarruq Rajab.
Integration with Egypt, Muhammad Mahmud al-Hijazi.
Integration with Sudan, Jum'a al-Mahdi al-Fazzani.

LIBYAN DIPLOMATIC MISSION IN LONDON

Since the break of diplomatic relations with Libya in April 1984, the Royal Embassy of Saudi Arabia has handled Libyan interests in Britain.

BRITISH EMBASSY

Diplomatic relations between the UK and Libya were broken in April 1984. British interests are currently handled by the British Interests Section of the Italian Embassy, Sharia Uahram 1, (PO Box 4206), Tripoli.

DEFENCE

Libya has a total active armed forces of some 85,000, with selective conscription of two to four years. The Army has a strength of 55,000, with 2,150 main battle tanks, 2,650 armoured infantry fighting vehicles and armoured personnel carriers, and some 1,100 artillery pieces. The Navy has a strength of 8,000 personnel, with six submarines, three frigates, 45 patrol and coastal vessels, and 31 armed helicopters. The Air Force has some 22,000 personnel, with 409 combat aircraft and 45 armed helicopters.

COMMUNICATIONS

Besides the coastal road running from the Tunisian frontier through Tripoli to Benghazi, Tobruk and the Egyptian border, which serves the main population centres, main roads now link the provincial centres, and the oil-producing areas of the south with the coastal towns.

There are airports at Tripoli and Benghazi (Benina), Tobruk, Mersa Brega, Sebha, Ghadames and Kufra regularly used by commercial airlines, and military airfields near Tobruk, near Tripoli and at Al Watiya, south of Zuara.

ECONOMY

Agriculture is confined mainly to the coastal areas of Tripolitania and Cyrenaica, where barley, wheat, olives, almonds, citrus fruits and dates are produced, and to the areas of the oases, many of which are well supplied with springs supporting small fertile areas. Among the important oases are Jaghbub, Ghadames, Jofra, Sebha, Murzuq, Brak, Ghat, Jalo and the Kufra group in the south-east.

The main industry is oil and gas production. There are pipelines from Zelten to the terminal at Mersa Brega, from Dahra to Ras-es-Sider, from Amal to Ras Lanuf, and from the Intisar field to Zuetina. Since 1984 average production of crude oil has been about 1.2 million barrels per day. A major petrochemical complex has been built at Ras Lanuf where a refinery and ethylene plant began operations in early 1985. The construction of an iron and steel plant at Misurata has been completed. Economic constraints have delayed some projects, particularly since Libya decided in 1983 to go ahead with a major irrigation scheme, the 'Great Man-Made River'.

Libya has technical assistance agreements with a number of countries, and also employs large numbers of foreign labourers and experts.

TRADE

Exports from Libya are dominated by crude oil, but some wool, cattle, sheep and horses, olive oil, and hides and skins are also exported. Principal imports are foodstuffs, including sugar, tea and coffee, and most constructional materials and consumer goods. In recent years the private sector has been virtually eliminated and Libya is now a state trading country with imports controlled by state monopolies. In early 1988, however, reforms were implemented which have allowed a small private sector to be re-established.

Trade with UK	1990	1991
Imports from UK	£244,850,000	£255,719,000
Exports to UK	151,605,000	121,220,000

LIECHTENSTEIN
Fürstentum Liechtenstein

Liechtenstein is a principality on the Upper Rhine, between Vorarlberg (Austria) and Switzerland, with an area of 61 sq. miles (158 sq. km), and a population in 1989 of 28,452. The language of the principality is German.

CAPITAL – Vaduz, population (1990) 4,874.
CURRENCY – Swiss franc of 100 rappen (or centimes).
FLAG – Equal horizontal bands of blue over red; gold crown on blue band near staff.
NATIONAL ANTHEM – Oben am Jungen Rhein (High on the Rhine).
NATIONAL DAY – 15 August.

GOVERNMENT

At the General Election on 5 March 1989 the Patriotic Union Party won 13 seats and Progressive Citizens' Party 12.

HEAD OF STATE

Prince, Hans Adam II, *born* 14 Feb. 1945; *succeeded* 13 November 1989; *married* 30 July 1967, Countess Marie Kinsky; and has *issue*, Prince Alois, *b.* 11 June 1968; Prince Maximilian, *b.* 16 May 1969; Prince Constantin, *b.* 15 March 1972; Princess Tatjana, *b.* 10 April 1973.

MINISTRY as at June 1992

Prime Minister, Hans Brunhart (*Head of Government 'Presidium', Foreign Affairs, Education, Finance, Construction*).
Deputy PM, Dr Herbert Wille (*Interior, Agriculture, Forestry and Environment, Culture, Youth and Sport, Justice*).
Government Councillors, René Ritter (*Economy*), Dr Peter Wolff (*Social and Health Services*), Wilfried Büchel (*Communications*).

DIPLOMATIC REPRESENTATION

Liechtenstein is represented in diplomatic and consular matters in the United Kingdom by the Swiss Embassy.

BRITISH CONSUL GENERAL, T. Bryant, CMG (*office* at Dufourstrasse 56, 8008 Zürich).

ECONOMY

The main industries are high and ultra-high vacuum engineering, semi-conductor industry, roller bearings, fastenings and securing systems, artificial teeth, heating and hot water equipment, synthetic fibres, woollen and homespun fabrics.

In May 1991 Liechtenstein became a member of the European Free Trade Association, and as such is a party to the European Economic Area (EEA) Agreement with the EC, due to come into force on 1 January 1993.

FINANCE

	1989	1990
Revenue	F371,867,639	F405,409,370
Expenditure	367,249,600	400,801,399

LITHUANIA
Lietuva

The Republic of Lithuania lies on the eastern coast of the Baltic Sea between 53° 54′ and 56° 27′ N., and 20° 56′ and 20° 51′ E. To the north lies Latvia, to the east and south lies Belarus, to the south-west lie Poland and the Kaliningrad region of the Russian Federation.

AREA – 65,200 square km (25,170 square miles).
TOPOGRAPHY – Lithuania lies in the middle and lower basin of the river Nemunas. Along the coast is a lowland plain 15–20 km (9–13 miles) wide, which rises inland to form uplands in east and central Lithuania. These uplands, the Middle Lowlands, give way to the Baltic Highlands in east and south-east Lithuania; the highest point is 294 m (965 ft). The country has a network of rivers and over 2,800 lakes, which mainly lie in the east of the country.
CLIMATE – Varies between maritime and continental. The mean average temperature is 8.1°C (47°F), the average in January being −4.9°C (23°F) and in July 17°C (63°F). The average annual rainfall varies between 540 mm (21 inches) in the Middle Lowlands and 930 mm (37 inches) in the south-west.
POPULATION – The total population of Lithuania is

3,723,000 (1990). Population density is 56 persons per square km (145 persons per square mile). The rate of increase of population is 4.8 per cent. Male life expectancy is 67.7 years, and female 76.6 years (1989).

ETHNIC GROUPS – 79.6 per cent Lithuanian, 9.4 per cent Russian, 7.0 per cent Polish, 1.7 per cent Belarussian, 1.2 per cent Ukrainian.

RELIGIONS – Roman Catholic (majority), Russian Orthodox, Lutheran.

LANGUAGES – 80 per cent Lithuanian, with Russian, Polish and Belarussian minorities.

MAJOR CITIES – Vilnius (population 592,500), Kaunas (430,000), Klaipéda (206,000), Siauliai (148,000).

CAPITAL – Vilnius.

CURRENCY – Rouble.

FLAG – Three horizontal stripes of yellow, red, green.

NATIONAL ANTHEM – Tautiška Giesmé (The National Song).

NATIONAL DAY – 16 February (Restoration of the Lithuanian State).

TIME ZONE – 2 hours ahead of GMT.

HISTORY

The first independent Lithuanian state emerged as the Kingdom of Lithuania in 1251, and over the next few centuries acted as a buffer state between Germans to the west and Mongols and Tartars to the east. After forming a joint Commonwealth and Kingdom with Poland in 1569, Lithuania was taken over by the Russian Empire in the partitions of Poland that occurred in 1772, 1792 and 1795.

Lithuania declared its independence from the Russian Empire on 16 February 1918 and then fought against German and Soviet forces until its independence was recognized by the Versailles Treaty in 1919 and the peace treaty signed with the Soviet Union on 12 July 1920. The Soviet Union annexed Lithuania in 1940 under the terms of the Molotov-Ribbentrop pact with Germany. Lithuania was invaded and occupied when Germany invaded the Soviet Union during the Second World War. In 1944 the Soviet Union recaptured the country and confirmed its annexation, though this was never accepted as legal by most states.

On 20 December 1989 public pressure forced the Lithuanian Communist Party to agree to multi-party elections, which were held in February 1990. These were won by the nationalist Sajudis movement, which declared the independence of Lithuania on 11 March 1990. Clashes occurred throughout 1990 between the Lithuanian population and Soviet military forces, culminating in January 1991 with the killing of Lithuanians at the television centre in Vilnius. Over 90 per cent of the population voted for independence in a referendum in February 1991. The State Council of the Soviet Union recognized the independence of Lithuania on 10 September 1991.

CONSTITUTION

Under the Provisional Fundamental Law (i.e. constitution) adopted on 11 March 1990, the Republic of Lithuania is a sovereign democratic state. Sovereign power is vested in the people of Lithuania and is exercised by the Supreme Council, the government and the Court of the Republic of Lithuania.

EXECUTIVE – Executive authority is vested in the government, consisting of the Prime Minister, who is appointed on the recommendation of the President, and ministers appointed upon the recommendation of the Prime Minister. The government is accountable to the Supreme Council.

LEGISLATURE – Legislative power is exercised by the Supreme Council, which is a one-chamber parliament of 141 deputies. The Chairman of the Supreme Council is also the President of the Republic, and is elected by deputies for a five-year term (with a maximum of two consecutive terms).

CURRENT POLITICAL SITUATION

The situation in Lithuania has been unstable since independence. In April 1992 government ministers criticized the dictatorial attitude of the Prime Minister and asked the Supreme Council for a clarification of Prime Ministerial and ministerial powers. Meanwhile, the President has tried to introduce a presidential system of government.

HEAD OF STATE

President, Vytautas Landsbergis

GOVERNMENT

Prime Minister, Alexandras Abisala
Deputy Prime Minister, Zigmas Vaisvila
Deputy Prime Minister and Social Welfare, Algis Dobrovolskas
Agriculture, Rimvydas Survila
Housing and Urban Development, Algimantas Nasvytis
Communication and Information, A. Basevicius
Culture and Education, Darius Kuolys
Economics, Albertas Simenas
Energy, Vaidotas Asmantas
Finance, vacant
Foreign Affairs, Algirdas Saudargas
International Economic Relations, Vytenis Aleskaitis
Forestry, Jonas Klimas
Health, Juozas Olekas
Interior, Petras Valiukas
Justice, Vytautas Pakalniskis
Material Resources and Trade, Vilius Zidonis
Transportation, Jonas Birziskis
Defence, Audrius Butkevicius

MEMBERSHIP OF INTERNATIONAL ORGANIZATIONS – UN, CSCE, EBRD, IBRD, IMF, UNESCO.

EMBASSY OF THE REPUBLIC OF LITHUANIA
17 Essex Villas, London W8 7BP
Tel 071-938 2481

Ambassador Extraordinary and Plenipotentiary, His Excellency Vincas Balickas (1992).

BRITISH EMBASSY
Vilnius

Ambassador Extraordinary and Plenipotentiary, His Excellency Michael Peart, LVO, *apptd* 1991

LOCAL GOVERNMENT

Lithuania is divided into 11 cities and 44 rural districts. Each has a municipal council elected by the local population for a period of five years.

JUDICIAL SYSTEM

The judicial system comprises the Supreme Court and district and city courts composed of judges, who are elected by the Supreme Council for a ten-year period, and of assessors, who are elected by the Supreme Council and district councils for a five-year term. Supreme legal supervision is exercised by the Prosecutor-General of the Republic.

ECONOMY

The economy is basically an agricultural one that was heavily and rapidly industrialized by the Soviet Union in the 1940s and 1950s. The economy is in turmoil at present because of attempts to switch to a market economy from the centralized

Soviet command economy. Moreover, the economy has yet to recover from the Soviet economic blockade of 1990–1, imposed to try to halt moves to independence.

PRIMARY RESOURCES – Agriculture and forestry are still major sectors of the economy, the chief products being rye, oats, wheat, flax, barley, sugar beet and potatoes.

INDUSTRY – The main industries are chemicals and petrochemicals, food processing, wood products, building materials, textiles, machine tools and household appliances.

SERVICES – Lithuania is capitalizing on its clean beaches and picturesque countryside to develop a tourism industry attractive to Western visitors.

TRADE – Lithuania's main trading partners remain the republics of the former Soviet Union.

COMMUNICATIONS

Lithuania has a relatively well developed railway system running east-west and north-south and linking the major towns with Vilnius and Klaipéda, the main international port. Vilnius has an international airport and there is a smaller one at Kaunas.

CULTURE

Lithuanian culture and literature is closely linked to the national liberation movements of the nineteenth and early twentieth century, and the underground literature of the Soviet occupation era.

EDUCATION

Lithuania re-established a national education system in 1990 with instruction predominantly in Lithuanian, but there are also Russian and Polish schools. Tuition begins at six years of age with elementary, then intermediate and secondary schools. Lithuania has three universities.

SOCIAL WELFARE

HEALTH SERVICES – In 1989 there were 192 hospitals with 46,000 beds, 16,900 physicians and 45,500 paramedical personnel.

SOCIAL SERVICES – A national social security system exists which comprises compulsory state social insurance, and social benefits provided by the state.

LUXEMBOURG

Grand-Duché de Luxembourg

Luxembourg is a Grand Duchy in western Europe, bounded by Germany, Belgium and France. The area is 998 sq. miles (2,586 sq. km), the population of 378,400 (1990) is nearly all Roman Catholic. The country is well wooded, with many deer and wild boar. The language is Letzeburgesch but French is the official language; most speak German.

CAPITAL – Luxembourg, population (1987) 77,500, is a dismantled fortress.

CURRENCY – Luxembourg franc (LF) of 100 centimes. Belgian currency is also legal tender. The Luxembourg franc has at present the same value as the Belgian franc.

FLAG – Three horizontal bands, red, white and blue.

NATIONAL ANTHEM – Ons Hémécht (Our homeland).

NATIONAL DAY – 23 June.

HISTORY

Established as an independent state under the sovereignty of the King of the Netherlands as Grand Duke by the Congress of Vienna in 1815, Luxembourg formed part of the Germanic Confederation 1815–66, and was included in the German 'Zollverein'. In 1867 the Treaty of London declared it a neutral territory. On the death of the King of the Netherlands in 1890 it passed to the Duke of Nassau.

The territory was invaded and overrun by the Germans at the beginning of the war in 1914, but was liberated in 1918. By the Treaty of Versailles, 1919, Germany renounced its former agreements with Luxembourg and in 1921 an economic union was made with Belgium. The Grand Duchy was again invaded and occupied by Germany on 10 May 1940.

GOVERNMENT

There is a Chamber of 60 Deputies, elected by universal suffrage for five years. Legislation is submitted to the Council of State.

HEAD OF STATE

Grand Duke, HRH Jean, KG, *born* 5 Jan. 1921, *married*, 9 April 1953, Princess Joséphine-Charlotte of Belgium, and has *issue*, three sons and two daughters; *succeeded* (on the abdication of his mother) 12 Nov. 1964.

Heir Apparent, Prince Henri, *born* 16 April 1955, *married* 14 February 1981, Maria Teresa Mestre, and has *issue*, Prince Guillaume, *b.* 11 Nov. 1981; Prince Felix, *b.* 3 June 1984; Prince Louis, *b.* 3 Aug. 1986; Princess Alexandra, *b.* 2 Feb. 1991; Prince Sébastien, *b.* 16 April 1992.

CABINET as at June 1992

Christian Socialists:

President of the Government, Minister of State, Minister of the Treasury and Cultural Affairs, Jacques Santer.
Interior, Housing and Town Planning, Jean Spautz.
The Family and Middle Classes, and Tourism, Fernand Boden.
Budget, Finance and Labour, Jean-Claude Juncker.
Education, Justice and the Civil Service, Marc Fischbach.
Agriculture and Viticulture, Rene Steichen.

Socialists:

Vice-President of the Government, Minister of Foreign Affairs, Foreign Trade and Aid, and Defence, Jacques Poos.
Health, Social Security, Sport and Youth, Johny Lahure.
Economy and Trade, Transport and Public Works, Robert Goebbels.
Environment, Territorial Administration, Posts and Telecommunications and Energy, Alex Bodry.
State Secretary for Social Security, Health, Sport and Youth, Mady Delvaux.
State Secretary for Foreign Affairs, Overseas Trade, Aid and Defence, Georges Wohlfart.

EMBASSY OF LUXEMBOURG

27 Wilton Crescent, London SW1X 8SD
Tel 071-235 6961

Ambassador Extraordinary and Plenipotentiary, His Excellency Edouard Molitor, KCMG (1989).

BRITISH EMBASSY

14 Boulevard F. D. Roosevelt, L-2018 Luxembourg Ville
Tel: Luxembourg 229864

Ambassador Extraordinary and Plenipotentiary, His Excellency The Hon. Michael Pakenham (1992).

INTERNATIONAL RELATIONS

The constitution of the Grand Duchy was modified on 28 April 1948, and the stipulation of permanent neutrality was then abandoned. Luxembourg is now a signatory of the Brussels and North Atlantic Treaties, and also a member of the European Communities. Luxembourg is a member of the Belgium-Netherlands-Luxembourg Customs Union (Benelux 1960).

The Court of the European Communities has its seat in Luxembourg, as does the Secretariat of the European Parliament, the European Investment Bank, the European Audit Court and the European Monetary Co-operation Fund.

ECONOMY

The Grand Duchy possesses an important iron and steel industry. Government revenue for 1990 was estimated at LF 97,300 million, expenditure LF 94,500 million.

TRADE WITH UK
(Belgium and Luxembourg)

	1990	1991
Imports from UK	£5,648,625,000	£5,870,876,000
Exports to UK	5,732,427,000	5,472,663,000

MADAGASCAR
Repoblika n'i Madagaskar

Madagascar lies 240 miles off the east coast of Africa and is the fourth largest island in the world. France has recognized Madagascar's claim to the islands of Juan de Nova, Glorieuses, Isle de l'Europe, Bassa da India and Tromelin which had remained integral parts of the French Republic after independence. It has an area of 226,669 sq. miles (587,041 sq. km), and a population (UN estimate 1990) of 11,197,000. The people are of mixed Polynesian, Arab and African origin. The official languages are Malagasy and French. There are sizeable French, Chinese and Indian communities.

CAPITAL – Antananarivo, population estimate 1,000,000. Other main towns are the chief port Ψ Toamasina (55,000); Ψ Mahajanga (50,000); Fianarantsoa (47,000); Ψ Antsiranana (41,000).

CURRENCY – Franc Malgache (Malagasy franc) (FMG) of 100 centimes.

FLAG – Equal horizontal bands of red (above) and green, with vertical white band by staff.

NATIONAL DAY – 26 June (Independence Day).

GOVERNMENT

Madagascar (known from 1958 to 1975 as the Malagasy Republic) became a French protectorate in 1895, and a French colony in 1896 when the former queen was exiled. Republican status was adopted on 14 October 1958, and independence was proclaimed on 26 June 1960.

The post-independence civilian government was replaced by a military government in January 1975 and the following month martial law was declared. A Supreme Council of the Revolution of 18 members under Capitaine de Frégate (subsequently Admiral) Didier Ratsiraka was established on 15 June 1975.

In December 1975 a new constitution was approved in a referendum, which vested executive power in the President. He appointed a Council of Ministers to assist him. The Revolutionary Supreme Council and the National People's Assembly were dissolved in November 1991.

The situation in Madagascar remains confused, as it has been for most of 1991 and 1992. After six months of strikes and agitation against his one-party Communist rule, which had made the country ungovernable, President Ratsiraka in November 1991 relinquished executive power to a new Prime Minister, Guy Razanamasy. However, the President retained his official position and the main opposition grouping, the *Forces Vives*, established a rival government led by Albert Zafy. In December 1991 a transitional government including Forces Vives and Razanamasy supporters was formed to draft a new constitution to be put to a referendum in May 1992. However, the inability of the government to assert any control over the country because of quarrels between Forces Vives and Razanamasy supporters, together with attempts by the President to regain executive power, meant that the referendum was not held until 19 August 1992, when the new constitution was approved. Presidential and legislative elections are due to be held by November 1992.

EMBASSY OF THE REPUBLIC OF MADAGASCAR
4 avenue Raphael, 75016 Paris, France
Tel: Paris 45046211

Ambassador Plenipotentiary and Extraordinary, His Excellency François de Paul Rabotoson (1987) (resident in Paris).

HONORARY CONSULATE OF THE REPUBLIC OF MADAGASCAR
16 Lanark Mansions, Pennard Road, London W12 8DT
Tel 071-746 0133

Honorary Consul, Stephen Hobbs.

BRITISH EMBASSY
BP 167, Antananarivo
Tel: Antananarivo 277 49

Ambassador Extraordinary and Plenipotentiary, His Excellency Dennis Oldgrieve Amy, OBE (1990).
Second Secretary, C. G. R. Poole.

ECONOMY

The island's economy is still largely based on agriculture, which accounts for three-quarters of its exports. Development plans have placed emphasis on increasing agricultural and livestock production, the improvement of communications, the exploitation of mineral deposits and the creation of small industries.

TRADE

	1985	1986
Imports	US$ 400.54m	US$ 441.54m
Exports	274.23m	351.18m

Trade with UK	1990	1991
Imports from UK	£16,093,000	£6,946,000
Exports to UK	5,952,000	7,707,000

MALAWI
Dziko La Malawi

AREA, ETC – Malawi comprises Lake Malawi (formerly Lake Nyasa) and its western shore, with the high tableland separating it from the basin of the Luangwa River, the watershed forming the western frontier with Zambia; south of the lake, Malawi reaches almost to the Zambezi and is surrounded by Mozambique, the frontier lying on the west on the watershed of the Zambezi and Shire Rivers, and to the east on the Ruo, a tributary of the Shire, and Lakes Chiuta and Chirwa. This boundary reaches the eastern shore of Lake Malawi and extends up to the mid-point of the lake for about half its length where it returns to the eastern and northern shores to form a frontier with Tanzania. Malawi has a total area of 45,747 sq. miles (118,484 sq. km).

POPULATION – The population according to the Census held in 1987 was 7,982,607. According to a UN estimate (1990), the population was 8,289,000. The official languages are Chichewa and English.

CAPITAL – Lilongwe, population (1987) 223,973. The city of Blantyre in the Southern Region, incorporating Blantyre and Limbe (population (1987) 331,588), is the major commercial and industrial centre. Other main centres are: Mzuzu, Thyolo, Mulanje, Mangochi, Salima, Dedza and Zomba, the former capital.

CURRENCY – Kwacha (K) of 100 tambala.

FLAG – Horizontal stripes of black, red and green, with rising sun in the centre of the black stripe.

NATIONAL ANTHEM – O God Bless Our Land of Malawi.

NATIONAL DAY – 6 July (Independence Day).

GOVERNMENT

Malawi (formerly Nyasaland) became a republic on 6 July 1966, having assumed internal self-government on 1 February 1963, and achieved independence on 6 July 1964.

There is a Cabinet consisting of the Life President and other Ministers. The Parliament consists of 112 members, each elected by universal suffrage. Under the 1981 Amendment to the Constitution, the Life President has the power to nominate as many Members of Parliament as he wishes. Being a one-party state (the Malawi Congress Party), all elected members are required to be members of the Party. The Parliament, which usually meets three times a year, is presided over by a Speaker.

During late 1991 and the first half of 1992 the President has come under increasing internal and international pressure to move towards a multi-party democratic system of government. In February 1992 exiled opposition leaders formed a United Front for Multiparty Democracy and in May 1992 aid donors tied new loans to improvements in the country's human rights record and moves to multi-party democracy. Strikes and riots in May and June 1992, which left many dead, signalled growing internal unrest.

President, Minister of External Affairs, Agriculture, Justice, Works, Supplies, Women and Children's Affairs and Community Services, Dr H. Kamuzu Banda, *elected* 1966, *sworn in as President for Life*, 6 July 1971.

CABINET as at June 1992

Minister without Portfolio, Wadson Bini Deleza.
Transport and Communications, Robson Chirwa.
Local Government, Katola Phiri.
Finance, Louis Chimango.
Trade and Industry, Dalton Katopola.
Information and Tourism, Mfunjo Mwakikunga.
Education and Culture, Michael Mlambala.
Health, Pitakuti Ntaba.
Minister of State in the President's Office, John Tembo.
Labour, William Binali.
Forestry and Natural Resources, Edson Sambo.
Energy and Mines, Bernard Mshabala.

MALAWI HIGH COMMISSION
33 Grosvenor Street, London W1X 0DE
Tel 071-491 4172

High Commissioner, His Excellency P. T. S. Kandiero (1990).

BRITISH HIGH COMMISSION
PO Box 30042, Lilongwe 3
Tel: Lilongwe 731544

High Commissioner, His Excellency Nigel Wenban Smith, CMG (1990).

BRITISH COUNCIL REPRESENTATIVE, S. Newton, PO Box 30222, Lilongwe 3. There is also a library at *Blantyre*.

JUDICIARY

Chief Justice, Hon. F. L. Makuta.

EDUCATION

Primary education is the responsibility of local authorities in both urban and rural areas, although policy, curricula and inspection are the responsibility of the Ministry of Education and Culture. The Ministry is also responsible for secondary schools, technical education and primary teacher training. Religious bodies, with Government assistance, still play an important part in these fields. The University of Malawi was opened in 1965 and has five constituent colleges. The total number of students in 1988–9 was 1.2 million in primary schools, 28,000 in secondary schools and 2,330 at university.

COMMUNICATIONS

A single-track railway runs from Mchinji on the Zambian border, through Lilongwe and Salima on Lake Malawi (itself served by two passenger and a number of cargo boats) through to Blantyre. The route south to the Mozambique port of Beira is severed at the Zambesi, but the route to Nacala in Mozambique has recently re-opened. There are 12,215 km of roads in Malawi of which about 21.8 per cent are bituminized.

There is an international airport 26 km from Lilongwe, which handles regional and inter-continental flights.

ECONOMY

The economy is largely agricultural, with maize the main subsistence crop. Tobacco, sugar, tea, groundnuts and cotton are the main cash crops and principal exports. There are two sugar mills and total production in 1989 was 157m kg. A number of light manufacturing industries have been established, mainly in agricultural processing, clothing/textiles and building materials.

FINANCE
excluding Development Account

	1987–8	1988–9
Revenue	K583m	K752m
Expenditure	823m	1071m

TRADE

	1987	1988
Imports	K654m	K1080m
Exports	602m	742m

Trade with UK	1990	1991
Imports from UK	£33,575,000	£31,462,000
Exports to UK	24,666,000	25,381,000

MALAYSIA
Persekutuan Tanah Malaysia

AREA – Malaysia, comprising the 11 states of peninsular Malaya plus Sabah and Sarawak, forms a crescent well over 1,000 miles long between latitudes 1° and 7° N. and longitudes 100° and 119° E. It occupies two distinct regions, the Malay peninsula which extends from the isthmus of Kra to the Singapore Strait, and the north-west coastal area of the island of Borneo. Each is separated from the other by the South China Sea. The total area of Malaysia, including the Federal Territories of Kuala Lumpur and Labuan, is about 127,317 sq. miles, (329,749 sq. km).

CLIMATE – The year is commonly divided into the south-west and north-west monsoon seasons. Rainfall averages about 100 inches throughout the year. The average daily temperature throughout Malaysia varies from 21° C to 32° C, though in higher areas temperatures are lower and vary widely.

POPULATION – Population was 16,921,300 (1988 Census), 17,861,000 UN estimate (1990).

ETHNIC GROUPS – The principal racial groups are the Malays, the Chinese and those of Indian and Sri Lankan origin, as well as the indigenous races of Sarawak and Sabah.

LANGUAGES – Bahasa Malaysia (Malay) is the sole official language, but English, various dialects of Chinese, and Tamil are also widely spoken. There are a few indigenous languages widely spoken in Sabah and Sarawak.

RELIGION – Islam is the official religion of Malaysia, each ruler being the head of religion in his state, though the heads of state of Sabah and Sarawak are not heads of the Muslim religion in their states. The Yang di-Pertuan Agung is the head of religion in Melaka and Penang. The Constitution guarantees religious freedom.

CAPITAL – Kuala Lumpur was proclaimed Federal Territory on 1 February 1974. Its population (1985) is 1,103,200.
CURRENCY – Malaysian dollar (ringgit) (M$) of 100 sen.
FLAG – Equal horizontal stripes of red (seven) and white (seven); 14-point yellow star and crescent in blue canton.
NATIONAL ANTHEM – Negara-Ku.
NATIONAL DAY – 31 August (*Hari Kebangsaan*).

GOVERNMENT

The Federation of Malaya became an independent country within the Commonwealth on 31 August 1957, as a result of an agreement between HM The Queen and the rulers of the Malay States. On 16 September 1963 the Federation was enlarged by the accession of the states of Singapore, Sabah (formerly British North Borneo) and Sarawak, and the name of Malaysia was adopted from that date. On 9 August 1965 Singapore seceded from the Federation.

The Constitution was designed to ensure the existence of a strong federal government and also a measure of autonomy for the state governments. It provides for a constitutional Supreme Head of the Federation (HM the *Yang di-Pertuan Agung*) to be elected for a term of five years by the rulers from among their number, and for a Deputy Supreme Head (HRH *Timbalan Yang di-Pertuan Agung*) to be similarly elected. The Malay rulers are either chosen or succeed to their position in accordance with the custom of the particular state. In other states of Malaysia, choice of the Head of State is at the discretion of the Yang di-Pertuan Agung after consultation with the Chief Minister of the State.

The Federal Parliament consists of two houses, the Senate and the House of Representatives. The Senate (*Dewan Negara*) consists of 68 members, under a President (*Yang di-Pertua Dewan Negara*), 26 elected by the Legislative Assemblies of the States (two from each) and 42 appointed by the Yang di-Pertuan Agung. The House of Representatives (*Dewan Rakyat*), consists of 180 members. Members are elected on the principle of universal adult suffrage with a common electoral roll.

The Constitution provides that each state shall have its own constitution not inconsistent with the federal constitution, with the ruler or Governor acting on the advice of an Executive Council appointed on the advice of the Chief Minister and a single chamber Legislative Assembly. The State Secretary, the State Legal Adviser and the State Financial Officer sit in the Executive Council as *ex-officio* members. The Legislative Assemblies are fully elected on the same basis as the Federal Parliament.

Dr Mahathir Muhammad won a third term in office in a general election held on 21 October 1990.

HEAD OF STATE
Supreme Head of State, HM Sultan Azlan Muhibuddin Shah Ibni-Almarhum Sultan Yusuff Izzuddin Ghafarullahu-Lahu Shah (Sultan of Perak), sworn in 26 April 1989.
Deputy Supreme Head of State, HRH Tuanku Jaafar Ibni Al-Marhum Tuanku Abdul Rahman (Yang Dipertuan Besar of Negeri Sembilan).

MINISTRY as at June 1992
Prime Minister, Minister of Home Affairs, Hon. Datuk Seri Dr Mahathir Muhammad.
Deputy Prime Minister, Minister for Rural Development, Hon Abdul Ghafar Baba.
Transport, Hon. Datuk Seri Dr Ling Liong Sik.
Energy, Telecommunications and Posts, Hon. Datuk Seri S. Samy Vellu.
Primary Industries, Hon. Datuk Seri Dr Lim Keng Yaik.
Works, Hon. Datuk Leo Moggie Anak Irok.
International Trade and Industry, Hon. Datuk Seri Rafidah Aziz.
Education, Hon. Datuk Dr Haji Sulaiman bin Haji Daud.
Agriculture, Hon. Datuk Seri Sanusi bin Junid.
Finance, Hon. Datuk Seri Anwar bin Ibrahim.
Domestic Trade and Consumer Affairs, Hon. Datuk Haji Abu Hassan bin Haji Omar.
Health, Hon. Datuk Lee Kim Sai.
Foreign Affairs, Hon. Datuk Abdullah bin Haji Ahmad Badawi.
Defence, Hon. Datuk Sri Haji Mohd Najib bin Tun Haji Abdul Razak.
Information, Hon. Datuk Mohamed bin Rahmat.
Culture, Arts and Tourism, Hon. Datuk Sabbaruddin bin Chik.
National Unity and Community Development, Hon. Datuk Napsiah binti Omar.
Public Enterprises, Hon. Datuk Dr Mohammad Yusof bin Haji Mohamed Nor.
Human Resources, Hon. Datuk Lim Ah Lek.
Science, Technology and Environment, Hon. Law Hieng Ding.
Housing and Local Government, Hon. Dr Ting Chew Peh.
Land and Co-operative Development, Hon. Tan Sri Datuk Haji Sakaran bin Dandai.
Justice, Hon. Syed Hamid bin Syed Jaafar Albar.
Youth and Sports, Sen. the Hon. Haji Annuar bin Musa.

NOTE: Tunku/Tengku, Tun, Tan Sri, and Datuk are titles. Tunku/Tengku is equivalent to Prince. Tun denotes membership of a high Order of Malaysian Chivalry and Tan Sri and Datuk (Datuk Seri in Perak and Datu in Sabah) are each the equivalent of a knighthood. The wife of a Tun is styled Toh Puan, that of a Tan Sri is styled Puan Sri and of a Datuk, Datin. The honorific Tuan or Encik is equivalent to Mr and the honorific Puan is equivalent to Mrs. Al-Haj or Haji indicates that the person so named has made the pilgrimage to Mecca.

MALAYSIAN HIGH COMMISSION
45 Belgrave Square, London SW1X 8QT
Tel 071-235 8033

High Commissioner, His Excellency Tan Sri Wan Sidek (1990).

British High Commission
185 Jalan Ampang (PO Box 11030), 50732 Kuala Lumpur
Tel: Kuala Lumpur 03-2482122

High Commissioner, His Excellency Duncan Slater, CMG (1992).

British Council Representative, Dr G. Howell, PO Box 10539, Jalan Bukit Aman, Kuala Lumpur 50916. There are also offices at *Kota Kinabalu* (Sabah) and *Kuching* (Sarawak), and a library in *Penang*.

STATES OF THE FEDERATION

The 13 States of the Federation of Malaysia (State capitals in brackets) and their populations at the 1988 Census are:

ΨJohore (Johore Bahru)	2,007,300
Kedah (Alor Setar)	1,353,500
Kelantan (Kota Bahru)	1,150,400
ΨMelaka (Melaka)	560,700
Negri Sembilan (Seremban)	694,100
ΨPahang (Kuantan)	1,001,200
ΨPenang (Georgetown)	1,103,200
Perak (Ipoh)	2,143,200
Perlis (Kangar)	179,700
ΨSabah (Kota Kinabalu)	1,371,000
ΨSarawak (Kuching)	1,591,000
ΨSelangor (Shah Alam)	1,878,300
ΨTerengganu (Kuala Terengganu)	705,200

Federal Territories

The two Federal Territories and their population at the 1988 Census are:

Kuala Lumpur Labuan	1,182,700

JUDICATURE

The judicial system consists of a Supreme Court and two High Courts, one in peninsular Malaysia and one for Sabah and Sarawak (sitting alternately in Kota Kinabalu and Kuching).

The Supreme Court comprises a President, the two Chief Justices of the High Courts and other judges. It possesses appellate, original and advisory jurisdiction.

Each of the High Courts consists of a Chief Justice and not less than four other judges. The Federal Constitution allows for a maximum of twelve such judges for Malaya and eight for Borneo. In peninsular Malaysia the subordinate courts consist of the Sessions Courts and the Magistrates' Courts. In Sabah/Sarawak the Magistrates' Courts constitute the subordinate courts.

DEFENCE

The Malaysian armed forces consist of the Army, Navy and Air Force, together with volunteer forces for each arm. The defence of the country is largely borne by the Army in its role of providing defence against external threat and counter-insurgency operations and also to assist the police in the performance of public order duties. The Royal Malaysian Navy (RMN) has the responsibility of defending the 3,000 miles of the country's coastline and maintaining constant patrol of the seas that separate Sabah and Sarawak from the mainland. The Royal Malaysian Air Force (RMAF) is capable of providing close strategic and tactical support to the Army and police in the defence and internal security of the country.

The Army has a strength of 105,000 personnel, with 26 light tanks, 300 reconnaissance vehicles, 670 armoured personnel carriers and 200 artillery pieces. The RMN has a strength of 10,500, with four frigates, 37 patrol and coastal craft and six armed helicopters. The Air Force has a strength of 67 combat aircraft and 12,400 personnel.

ECONOMY

Finance

	1988	1989
Revenue	M$22.0 billion	M$24.7 billion
Expenditure	25.9 billion	29.7 billion

Manufacturing has overtaken agriculture as the largest single contributor to the economy, though rice, the staple food, is produced throughout the country and efforts are being made to achieve self-sufficiency.

Trade

Malaysia is the largest exporter of natural rubber, tin, palm oil and tropical hardwoods. Other major export commodities are manufactured and processed products, petroleum, oil, and other minerals, palm kernel oil, tea and pepper.

Exports of major commodities were (percentage of total exports):

	1988	1989
Manufactured goods	48.5	54.1
Agriculture	33.4	28.3
Minerals	16.7	16.9

Imports consist mainly of machinery and transport equipment, manufactured goods, foods, mineral fuels, chemicals and inedible crude materials.

	1988	1989
Imports	M$42.8 billion	M$60.9 billion
Exports	54.4 billion	67.8 billion

Trade with UK	1990	1991
Imports from UK	£601,909,000	£582,239,000
Exports to UK	775,667,000	930,036,000

THE MALDIVES

Divehi Jumhuriya

Area, etc – The Maldives are a chain of coral atolls, some 400 miles to the south-west of Sri Lanka, stretching from just south of the equator for about 600 miles to the north. There are about 20 coral atolls comprising over 1,200 islands, 202 of which are inhabited. Total area of the islands is 115 sq. miles (298 sq. km). No point in the entire chain of islands is more than 8 feet above sea-level.

Population – The population of the islands (UN estimate 1990) is 215,000. The people are Sunni Muslims and the Maldivian (Dhivehi) language is akin to Elu or old Sinhalese.

Capital – ΨMalé, population (1985) 46,334. There is an international airport at Malé.

Currency – Rufiyaa of 100 laaris.

Flag – Green field bearing a white crescent, with wide red border.

National Anthem – Qawmee Salaam.

National Day – 26 July.

GOVERNMENT

Until 1952 the islands were a Sultanate under the protection of the British Crown. Internal self-government was achieved in 1948 and full independence in 1965. In 1982 the Republic of The Maldives became a special member of the Commonwealth, and a full member in 1985.

The Maldives form a republic which is elective. There is a

legislature (the *Citizens' Majlis*) with representatives elected from all the atolls. The life of the Majlis is five years. The Government consists of a Cabinet, which is responsible to the Majlis.

HEAD OF STATE

President, His Excellency Maumoon Abdul Gayoom, *elected* 1978, 1983, *re-elected* September 1989 (also *Minister of Defence and National Security, and Minister of Finance*).

CABINET as at June 1992

Foreign Affairs, Hon. Fathulla Jameel.
Justice, Hon. Mohamed Rasheed Ibrahim.
Home Affairs and Sports, Hon. Umar Zahir.
Education, Hon. Abdulla Hameed.
Health and Welfare, Hon. Abdul Sattar Moosa Didi.
Fisheries and Agriculture, Hon. Abbas Ibrahim.
Atolls Administration, Hon. Ilyas Ibrahim.
Trade and Industries, Hon. Ahmed Mujuthaba.
Tourism, Hon. Abdulla Jameel.
Public Works and Labour, Hon. Abdulla Kamaludeen.
Planning and Environment, Hon. Ismail Shafeen.
Transport and Shipping, Ahmed Zahir.
Minister at the President's Office and Acting Attorney-General, Hon. Mohamed Zahir Hussain.

BRITISH HIGH COMMISSION

High Commissioner (resides at Colombo, Sri Lanka).

ECONOMY

The vegetation of the islands is coconut palms with some scrub. Hardly any cultivation of crops is possible and nearly all food to supplement the basic fish diet has to be imported. The principal industry is fishing and considerable quantities of fish are exported to Japan. Dried fish is exported to Sri Lanka, where it is a delicacy. The tourist industry is expanding rapidly (131,000 visitors in 1987). Maldives Shipping Ltd has a fleet of some 30 merchant ships.

TRADE WITH UK

	1990	1991
Imports from UK	£3,458,000	£2,862,000
Exports to UK	6,573,000	7,909,000

MALI

République du Mali

The Republic of Mali, an inland state in north-west Africa, has an area of 478,791 sq. miles (1,240,000 sq. km), and a population (UN estimate 1990) of 8,156,000. The principal rivers are the Niger and the Senegal.

CAPITAL – Bamako (600,000). Other towns are Gao, Kayes, Mopti, Sikasso, Segou and Timbuktu (all regional capitals).
CURRENCY – Franc CFA of 100 centimes.
FLAG – Vertical stripes of green (by staff), yellow and red.
NATIONAL DAY – 22 September.

GOVERNMENT

Formerly the French colony of Soudan, the territory elected on 24 November 1958 to remain as an autonomous republic within the French Community. It associated with Senegal in the Federation of Mali which was granted full independence on 20 June 1960. The Federation was effectively dissolved on 22 August by the secession of Senegal. The title of the Republic of Mali was adopted in September 1960.

The regime of Modibo Keita was overthrown on 19 November 1968 by a group of Army officers who formed a National Liberation Committee and appointed a Prime Minister. Moussa Traoré assumed the functions of Head of State. A new civil constitution came into being in 1979.

After several months of pro-reform protests and strikes, often leading to bloody riots, President Traoré was overthrown in March 1991 by troops led by Lt.-Col. Amadou Toumani Toure. A joint civilian/military National Reconciliation Committee, later replaced by the Transitional Committee for the Salvation of the People, suspended the constitution and dissolved the Mali People's Democratic Union (UPDM), formerly the sole party. A transitional government was formed under Soumana Sacko in April. In August, a new constitution was approved by a national conference and approved by a national referendum in January 1992. The new constitution provided for a multiparty political system, and legislative elections were held in February and March 1992 with the Alliance for Democracy in Mali (ADEMA) emerging victorious. Alpha Konare, the ADEMA leader, won the presidential elections in April 1992 and appointed a Prime Minister and Cabinet in June dominated by ADEMA members.

HEAD OF STATE

President, Alpha Oumar Konare, *elected* 28 April 1992, *sworn in* 8 June 1992.

CABINET as at June 1992

Prime Minister, Younoussi Toure.
Minister of State, Territorial Administration and Security, Mohamed Traore.
Minister of State, National Education, Baba Haidara.
Minister of State, Justice, Human Rights, Idrissa Traore.
Minister of State, Defence, Abdoulaye Sow.
Civil Service, Labour and Administration Modernization, Dioncounda Traore.
Foreign Affairs, Alhousseini Toure.
Culture and Scientific Research, Issa N'Diaye.
Economics, Finance and Planning, Mahamar Maiga.
Equipment and Housing, Samba Sidibe.
Youth and Sports, Mohamed Erlaf.
Tourism and Crafts, Ambadjo Kassogue.
Health, Solidarity and Pensioners, Cmdt Modibo Sidibe.
Communications, Boubacar Karamoko Coulibaly.
Mines, Industry and Energy, Abdoulaye Camara.
Rural Development and Environment, Seydon Traore.
Employment and Professional Training, Fatou Haidara.
Malians Abroad, Mamadou Diarra.

EMBASSY OF THE REPUBLIC OF MALI
Avenue Molière 487, 1060 Brussels, Belgium
Tel: Brussels 3457432

Ambassador Extraordinary and Plenipotentiary, His Excellency N'Tji Trané (1991) (resident in Brussels).

BRITISH AMBASSADOR, resident in Dakar, Senegal.

ECONOMY

Mali's principal exports are groundnuts (raw and processed), cotton fibres, meat and dried fish. The Republic rejoined the CFA Franc Zone on 1 June 1984.

TRADE WITH UK

	1990	1991
Imports from UK	£8,819,000	£9,589,000
Exports to UK	1,835,000	1,631,000

MALTA

Repubblika Ta'Malta

AREA, ETC. – Malta lies in the Mediterranean Sea, 58 miles (93 km) from Sicily and about 180 miles (288 km) from the African coast, about 17 miles (27 km) in length and 9 miles (14.5 km) in breadth, and having an area of 94.9 square miles (246 km²). Malta includes also the adjoining islands of Gozo (area 25.9 sq. miles (67 km²)), Comino and minor islets.

POPULATION – The estimated population in 1991 was 359,517. The Maltese are mainly Roman Catholic.

LANGUAGES – The Maltese language is of Semitic origin and held by some to be derived from the Carthaginian and Phoenician tongues. Maltese and English are the official languages of administration and Maltese is ordinarily the official language in all the courts of law and the language of general use in the islands.

CAPITAL – ΨValletta. Population (Census 1990), 9,199. Valletta Grand Harbour is very deep and large vessels can anchor alongside the shore. It is an important port of call and ship repairing centre for vessels, being half-way between Gibraltar and Port Said.

CURRENCY – Maltese lira (LM) of 100 cents and 1,000 mils.

FLAG – Two equal vertical stripes, white at the hoists and red at the fly. A representation of the George Cross is carried edged with red in the canton of the white stripe.

NATIONAL ANTHEM – L-Innu Malti.

NATIONAL DAY – 21 September (Independence Day).

HISTORY

Malta was in turn held by the Phoenicians, Carthaginians, Romans and Arabs. In 1090 it was conquered by Count Roger of Normandy. In 1530 it was handed over to the Knights of St John, who made it a stronghold of Christianity. In 1565 it sustained the famous siege, when the last great effort of the Turks was successfully withstood by Grandmaster La Valette. The Knights expended large sums in fortifying the island and carrying out many magnificent works, until they were expelled by Napoleon in 1798. The Maltese rose against the French garrison soon afterwards, and the island was subsequently blockaded by the British fleet. The Maltese people freely requested the protection of the British Crown in 1802 on condition that their rights and privileges would be preserved and respected. The islands were finally annexed to the British Crown by the Treaty of Paris in 1814.

Malta was again closely besieged in the Second World War. From June 1940 to the end of the war, 432 members of the garrison and 1,540 civilians were killed by enemy aircraft, and about 35,000 houses were destroyed or damaged. The island was awarded the George Cross for gallantry on 15 April 1942.

GOVERNMENT

On 21 September 1964 Malta became an independent state within the Commonwealth; on 13 December 1974, Malta became a republic within the Commonwealth.

Elections are held for the unicameral Parliament of 65 members every five years by a system of proportional representation. Seats are obtained by the highest number of votes in the respective districts. The party with the highest number of votes forms the government, with extra members being co-opted if necessary.

HEAD OF STATE
President, Dr Vincent Tabone, *took office* 4 April 1989.

CABINET as at July 1992
Prime Minister, Hon. Dr Edward Fenech Adami.
Deputy PM and Minister of Foreign Affairs, Hon. Dr Guido De Marco.
Education and Human Resources, Hon. Dr Ugo Mifsud Bonnici.
Home Affairs and Social Development, Hon. Dr Louis Galea.
Economic Services, Hon. Dr G. Bonello Du Puis.
Environment, Hon. Michael Falzon.
Food, Agriculture and Fisheries, Hon. Lawrence Gatt.
Social Security, Hon. George Hyzler.
Justice, Hon. Joseph Fenech.
Youth and the Arts, Hon. Michael Frendo.
Transport and Communications, Hon. Francis Dimech.
Gozo, Hon. Anton Tabone.
Finance, Hon. John Dalli.

MALTA HIGH COMMISSION
16 Kensington Square, London W8 5HH
Tel 071-938 1712

High Commissioner, His Excellency Saviour Stellini (1991).

BRITISH HIGH COMMISSION
7 St Anne Street, Floriana
Tel: 233134/8

High Commissioner, His Excellency Peter Wallis, CMG (1991).

BRITISH COUNCIL REPRESENTATIVE, G. Graves, 89 Archbishop Street, Valletta.

EDUCATION

In June 1990 there were 118 government primary schools with 37,016 pupils and 43 secondary schools and new lyceums, with a total of 24,800 pupils.

The government also runs 27 technical/trade schools (with an enrolment of 6,880 students). Schools of art, music, secretarial studies, catering, nursing and dramatic art are sponsored by the government. Tertiary education is available at the University of Malta, which had 2,525 students in 1990.

A number of private schools offer more or less the same facilities that exist in Government schools. All state education is free.

ECONOMY

AGRICULTURE – Agriculture plays a significant role in the economy. There are 3,000 full time farmers and about 13,000 part time farmers. Crop production consists mainly of tomatoes, potatoes, onions, cabbages and cauliflowers, marrows, carrots and fruit. Grape is the largest fruit crop. Flowers and cuttings are produced for export markets.

INDUSTRY – The island's leading industry is the state-owned Malta Drydocks, employing about 4,300 people. The main port of Grand Harbour handled traffic of 13,140,007 tonnes in 1990.

At the end of 1991 manufacturing firms employed some 32,374 people. The wide range of produce includes food processing, textiles and clothing, plastics and chemical products, electronic equipment and components. The gross output of the manufacturing industry in 1991 was LM590.6 million, of which LM371 million were export sales.

Tourism has assumed primary importance, with over 892,547 tourists visiting the island in 1991, and Marsamxett Harbour is being further developed by the extension of a yacht centre. Gross income from this industry stood at LM175.3 million in 1991.

FINANCE

	1990	1991
Revenue	LM385,606,000	LM411,793,000
Expenditure	381,690,000	417,403,000

TRADE

The principal imports for home consumption are foodstuffs (mainly wheat, meat and bullocks, milk and fruit), fodder, beverages and tobacco, fuels, chemicals, textiles and machinery (industrial, agricultural and transport). The chief domestic exports are processed food, electronics, textiles, and other manufactures.

	1990	1991
Imports	LM617,500,000	LM683,200,000
Exports	357,000,000	404,100,000

Trade with UK	1990	1991
Imports from UK	£141,298,000	£162,454,000
Exports to UK	50,541,000	40,771,000

MARSHALL ISLANDS

Republic of the Marshall Islands

AREA –The Republic of the Marshall Islands consists of 29 atolls and five islands in the central Pacific Ocean. The state lies between 4° and 19°N., and 160° and 175°E. The islands and atolls are scattered over 1,294,500 square km (500,000 square miles), forming two parallel chains running northwest-southeast: the Ratak (Sunrise) chain and the Ralik (Sunset) chain. The total land area is 181 square km (70 square miles). The largest atoll is Kwajalein in the Ralik chain.

TOPOGRAPHY – The atolls are coral and the islands are volcanic. Each atoll is formed by a cluster of many small islands circling a lagoon. None of the islands rises more than a few metres above sea level.

CLIMATE – Hot and humid. The average annual temperature is 27°C (81°F), with little seasonal variation. Annual average rainfall varies from 1,780 mm (70 inches) in the north to 4,320 mm (170 inches) in the south. The typhoon season lasts from December to March.

POPULATION – The population of the Marshall Islands is 42,018 (1989). There is an annual rate of increase of 4.29 per cent and over half the population is under 15. About 60 per cent of the population is concentrated on the two atolls of Majuro and Kwajalein.

ETHNIC GROUPS – 99 per cent Micronesian.

LANGUAGES – Marshallese and English are the official languages.

RELIGIONS – Christian, primarily Protestant but with a substantial Catholic minority. The principal Protestant denomination is the United Church of Christ.

MAJOR TOWNS – Majuro (population 20,000), Ebeye (9,200).

CAPITAL – Majuro.

CURRENCY – US Dollar.

FLAG – Blue with a diagonal ray divided white over orange running from the lower hoist to the upper fly; in the canton a white sun.

NATIONAL DAY – 21 October (Compact Day).

TIME ZONE – 12 hours ahead of GMT.

HISTORY

The Marshall Islands were claimed by Spain in 1592, but were left undisturbed by the Spanish Empire for 300 years. In 1885 the Marshall Islands formally became a protectorate of the German Empire under colonial German administration. On the outbreak of the First World War in 1914, Japan took control of the islands on behalf of the Allied powers, and after the war administered the territory as a League of Nations mandate. During the Second World War United States armed forces took control of the islands from the Japanese after intense fighting. In 1947 the United States entered into agreement with the UN Security Council to administer the Micronesia area, of which the Marshall Islands are a part, as the UN Trust Territory of the Pacific Islands.

The US Trusteeship administration of the Marshall Islands came to an end on 21 October 1986, when a Compact of Free Association between the United States and the Republic of the Marshall Islands came into effect. By this agreement the USA recognized the Republic of the Marshall Islands as a fully sovereign and independent state. However, the Soviet Union used its veto to prevent the UN Security Council from terminating the UN Trust Territory of the Pacific for the Marshall Islands until December 1990, when the independence of the Republic of the Marshall Islands was finally recognized by the UN.

CONSTITUTION

The Republic of the Marshall Islands is a democracy based on a parliamentary system of government. The electorate ratified in a referendum in 1979 a constitution drafted by a constitutional convention, at which time the nation became internally self-governing. The constitution draws on British and US concepts and consists of executive, legislative and judicial branches.

EXECUTIVE – The executive is under the leadership of the President, who is elected by the Nitijela from among its members. The President serves for a four-year term.

LEGISLATURE – The legislature has two chambers, the Council of Iroij of 12 members and the Nitijela of 33 members. The Nitijela is the law-making chamber, to which the President and government are accountable. The Council of Iroij has an advisory role.

HEAD OF STATE

President, Hon. Amata Kabua, *elected* 1979, *re-elected* 1984, 1988, 1992.

THE GOVERNMENT as at January 1992

Finance, Hon. Ruben Zackras
Foreign Affairs, Hon. Tom Kijiner
Transport and Communications, Hon. Kunio Lemari
Resources and Development, Hon. Amsa Jonathan
Education, Hon. Phillip Muller
Social Services, Hon. Christopher Loeak
Public Works, Hon. Antonio Eliu
Health and Environment, Hon. Henchi Balos
Justice, Hon. Luckner Abner
Internal Affairs, Hon. Brenson Wase

MEMBERSHIP OF INTERNATIONAL ORGANIZATIONS – UN, WHO, ICAO.

REPUBLIC OF THE MARSHALL ISLANDS' AMBASSADOR IN LONDON, no accreditation as yet

BRITISH AMBASSADOR, His Excellency Derek White (resident in Kiribati)

LOCAL GOVERNMENT

There are 24 local government districts, each of which usually consists of an elected council, a mayor and appointed local officials.

JUDICIAL SYSTEM

There are four court levels; the Supreme Court; the High Court; the District and Community Courts; and the Traditional Rights Courts. Trial is by jury. Jurisdiction of the traditional Rights Court is limited to cases involving titles or land rights and other disputes arising from customary law and traditional practice.

DEFENCE

The Republic of the Marshall Islands has no defence forces. The Compact of Free Association places full responsibility for defence of the Marshall Islands on the USA. The US Department of Defence controls islands within Kwajalein Atoll where it has a missile test range.

ECONOMY

The economy is a mixture of a large subsistence sector and a modern service-based sector. About half the working population is engaged in agriculture and fishing, with coconut oil and copra production comprising 90 per cent of total exports. The modern service sector is based in Majuro and Ebeye and concentrated in banking and insurance, construction, transportation and tourism. Direct US aid under the Compact accounts for two-thirds of the islands budget. The USA and Japan are the major trading partners.
GDP – US$68 million (1988). GDP growth was 6.3 per cent in 1981.
GDP PER HEAD – US$1,600 (1988).

COMMUNICATIONS

Air Marshall Islands provides air services within the islands and to Hawaii. Continental Air Micronesia serves Majuro and Kwajalein with flights to Hawaii and Guam. Majuro also has shipping links to Hawaii, Australia, Japan and throughout the Pacific.

CULTURE

The Marshallese culture revolves around a complex clan system of matrilineal structure. The sea has traditionally been the major source of food and thoroughfare among the atolls, and remains important to the Marshallese culture.

EDUCATION

The state school system provides education up to age 18, but only 25 per cent of students proceed beyond elementary level because of inadequate resources.

SOCIAL WELFARE

Majuro and Ebeye have hospitals run by the government with aid from the US Public Health Service. Each outer island community has a health assistant.

MAURITANIA
République Islamique de Mauritanie

Mauritania lies on the north-west coast of Africa immediately to the north of Senegal. It is bounded on the east by the Republic of Mali. To the north it is bounded by Morocco, Algeria and the Western Sahara. Area 397,955 sq. miles (1,030,700 sq. km). The population (UN estimate 1990) is 2,024,000. The official languages are French and Arabic.

CAPITAL – Nouakchott (500,000).
CURRENCY – Ouguiya of 5 khoums.
FLAG – Yellow star and crescent on green ground.
NATIONAL DAY – 28 November.

GOVERNMENT

The Republic of Mauritania elected on 28 November 1958 to remain within the French Community as an autonomous republic. It became fully independent on 28 November 1960. In 1972 Mauritania left the Franc Zone.

Mauritania and Morocco took possession of the Western Sahara territory in February 1976 when Spain formally relinquished all right to it and in April 1976 agreed on a new frontier dividing the territory between them. In August 1979, Mauritania relinquished all claim to the southern sector of the Western Sahara after a three-year war against the Polisario front guerrilla army.

After a military coup deposed the first President in 1978, Mauritania was ruled by a Military Committee for National Salvation (CMSN).

Having previously rejected reform, in April 1991 President Taya announced a political amnesty, a referendum on the constitution and the calling of multi-party elections thereafter for a reconvened Senate and National Assembly. The constitution was approved by a large majority in July. Multi-party elections to the Senate and National Assembly were held in March 1992 and won by the Republican Democratic and Social Party (PRDS) led by President Taya. The President appointed a cabinet of PRDS members in April 1992, but the legitimacy of the new government was undermined by the boycotting of the elections by the main opposition grouping, the Union of Democratic Forces (UDF).

Conflict continues between the Arab-dominated government and the African minority in the south of the country.

HEAD OF STATE
President, Col. Maaouya Ould Sidi Ahmed Taya, *took power* 12 Dec. 1984.

CABINET as at June 1992
Prime Minister, Sidi Mohammed Ould Boubaker.
Foreign Affairs and Co-operation, Mohammed Abdrahmane Abou Ould Moine.
Defence, Col. Ahmed Ould Minnih.
Justice, Sow Adema Samba.
Interior, Posts and Telecommunications, Hasni Ould Didi.
Finance, Kan Acheikh.
Planning, Mohammed Ould Michel.
Fisheries and Maritime Economy, Ahmed Ould Ghanahallah.

EMBASSY OF THE ISLAMIC REPUBLIC OF MAURITANIA
5 rue de Montevideo, Paris XVIe, France
Tel: Paris 45048854

Ambassador Extraordinary and Plenipotentiary, His Excellency Muhammad Al-Hanchi Ould Muhammad Saleh (1989) (resident in Paris).

BRITISH AMBASSADOR – resident in Rabat, Morocco.

ECONOMY

Mauritania's main source of potential wealth lies in rich deposits of iron ore around Zouérate, in the north of the country.

TRADE WITH UK

	1990	1991
Imports from UK	£2,997,000	£2,336,000
Exports to UK	14,525,000	15,313,000

MAURITIUS

AREA, ETC. – Mauritius is an island group lying in the Indian Ocean, 550 miles east of Madagascar, between 57° 17′ and 57° 46′ E. long. and 19° 58′ and 20° 33′ S. lat. Mauritius and Rodrigues with the other outer islands comprise an area of 790 square miles (2,045 sq. km).
CLIMATE – Mauritius enjoys a sub-tropical maritime climate, with a wide range of rainfall and temperature resulting from the mountainous nature of the island. Humidity is rather high throughout the year and rainfall is sufficient to maintain a green cover of vegetation, except for a brief period in the driest districts.
POPULATION – The population (1990 estimate, excluding Rodrigues and the outer islands) was 1,022,456, made up of Asiatic races (Hindus 52.6 per cent, Muslims 16.5 per cent), and persons of European (mainly French) extraction, mixed and African descent (28.3 per cent).
LANGUAGES – English is the official language but French may be used in the Legislative Assembly and lower law courts. However, Creole is the mostly commonly used language.

CAPITAL – ΨPort Louis, population (1989) 141,870; other centres are Beau Bassin-Rose Hill (94,236); Curepipe (66,260); Vacoas-Phoenix (56,630) and Quatre Bornes (65,759).
CURRENCY – Mauritius rupee of 100 cents.
FLAG – Red, blue, yellow and green horizontal stripes.
NATIONAL ANTHEM – Glory to the Motherland.
NATIONAL DAY – 12 March.

HISTORY

Mauritius was discovered in 1511 by the Portuguese; the Dutch visited it in 1598 and named it Mauritius, after Prince Maurice of Nassau. From 1638 to 1710 it was held as a small Dutch colony and in 1715 the French took possession but did not settle it until 1721. Mauritius was taken by a British Force in 1810. A British garrison remained on the island until June 1960. The French language and French law were preserved under British rule.

GOVERNMENT

A Crown Colony for 158 years, Mauritius became an independent state within the Commonwealth on 12 March 1968. After 24 years of constitutional monarchy, Mauritius became a republic on 12 March 1992 with a President as Head of State. The President of the Republic is elected by a simple majority of all the members of the National Assembly.

The Constitution defined by the Mauritius Independence Order of 1968 and amended by the Constitutional Amendment Acts of 1969 and 1991 provides for a Council of Ministers consisting of the Prime Minister and not more than 24 other Ministers. The Prime Minister, appointed by the President, is the member of the National Assembly who appears to the President best able to command the support of the majority of members of the Assembly. Other ministers are appointed by the President acting in accordance with the advice of the Prime Minister.

The National Assembly has a normal term of five years and consists of 62 elected members (the Island of Mauritius is divided into 20 three-member constituencies and Rodrigues returns two members), and eight specially-elected members. Of the latter, four seats go to the 'best loser' of whichever communities in the island are under-represented in the Assembly after the General Election and the four remaining seats are allocated on the basis of both party and community.

At the General Election held on 15 September 1991, the ruling alliance of the Mouvement Socialiste Militant (MSM), Mouvement Militant Mauricien (MMM) and the Mouvement Travailliste Democrate (MTD) gained 57 of the 62 seats available and formed the government.

HEAD OF STATE
President, Sir Veerasamy Ringadoo, GCMG, QC.

COUNCIL OF MINISTERS as at May 1992
Prime Minister, Minister of Defence and Internal Security, Information, Internal and External Communications and the Outer Islands, Rt. Hon. Sir Anerood Jugnauth, KCMG, QC.
Deputy PM, Minister for Health, Hon. Prem Nababsing.
External Affairs, Hon. Paul Raymond Berenger.
Economic Planning and Development, Hon. Jean-Claude de l'Estrac.
Education and Science, Hon. Armoogum Parsuramen.
Trade and Shipping, Hon. Anil Kumar Bachoo.
Energy, Water Resources and Postal Services, Hon. Mahyendrah Utchanah.
Housing, Lands and Town and Country Planning, Hon. Jayen Cuttaree.
Social Security, Hon. Karl Auguste Offman.
Women's Rights and Family Welfare, Hon. Sheilabai Bappoo.
Youth and Sports, Hon. Michael Glover.
Rodrigues, Hon. Serge Clair.
Co-operatives and Handicrafts, Hon. Jagdishwar Goburdhun.
Agriculture, Fisheries and Natural Resources, Hon. Murlidas Dulloo.
Industry and Industrial Technology, Hon. Cassam Uteem.
Works, Hon. Dwarkanath Gungah.
Local Government, Hon. Regis Finnette.
Civil Service Affairs and Employment, Hon. Keertee Coomar Ruhee.
Environment and Quality of Life, Hon. Swaley Kasenally.
Manpower Resources, Vocational and Technical Training, Hon. Ramduthsing Jaddoo.
Attorney-General and Minister of Justice, Hon. Alan Ganoo.
Finance, Hon. Ramakrishna Sithanen.
Tourism, Hon. Noe Ah-Quret Lee Cheong Lem.
Arts, Culture, Leisure and Reform Institutions, Hon. Mookhesswur Choonee.

MAURITIUS HIGH COMMISSION
32–33 Elvaston Place, London SW7 5NW
Tel 071-581 0294

High Commissioner, His Excellency Babooram Mahadoo (1992).

BRITISH HIGH COMMISSION
King George V Avenue, Floreal
Tel: Floreal 6865795/9

High Commissioner, His Excellency Michael Edward Howell, CMG, OBE.

BRITISH COUNCIL REPRESENTATIVE, M. Bootle, PO Box 111, Foondun Building, 2nd Floor, Royal Road, Rose Hill.

EDUCATION

Primary education is free and in 1991 was provided for 135,233 children at 280 primary schools. Although education is not compulsory it is estimated that about 90 per cent of children of primary age attend school. At post-primary level there were a total of 81,090 students attending secondary schools; fees and teachers' salaries in the private secondary schools are paid by government. There are a number of training facilities offering training in engineering and mechanical trades, nursing, building, seamanship, hotel and catering etc. The Institute of Education is responsible for training primary and secondary schoolteachers and for curriculum development. The University of Mauritius consists of Schools of Agriculture, Engineering, Law, Management and Social Studies, and Science. Estimated expenditure on education in 1990–1 was Rs.1,318,00,000.

COMMUNICATIONS

Port Louis, on the north-west coast, handles the bulk of the island's external trade. A bulk sugar terminal capable of handling the total crop began operating in 1980. The international airport is located at Plaisance in the south-east of the island about five miles from Mahébourg. There are five daily newspapers and 15 weeklies, mostly in French, and two Chinese daily papers and one weekly paper. The Mauritius Broadcasting Corporation has a monopoly of radio broadcasting in the country; television was introduced in 1965. There is a satellite communications ground station near Port Louis.

ECONOMY

In September 1991 the manufacturing sector employed 108,528, while the sugar industry employed 41,377.

About 55 per cent of the total sugar crop is produced on a plantation scale, while smaller owners (cultivating less than ten acres) cultivate about 24 per cent of the land under cane. Tea and tobacco are also grown commercially but on a smaller scale than sugar.

	1990	1991
Sugar	624,302 tonnes	611,340 tonnes
Tea (manufactured)	5,751	5,934
Tobacco (leaves)	799	876

In 1991 production of molasses, mainly for export, was 170,000 tonnes. Other products include alcohol, rum, denatured spirits, perfumed spirits and vinegar.

The bulk of the island's requirements in manufactured products still has to be imported. However, the Mauritius Export Processing Zone (MEPZ) scheme, introduced in 1971, has attracted investment from overseas and the number of export-orientated enterprises has risen from ten in 1971 to 586 at the end of 1991, employing 90,000 people. The biggest firms are in clothing manufacture, particularly woollen knitwear, but the range of goods produced includes toys, plastic products, leather goods, diamond cutting and polishing, watches, television sets and telephones.

Tourism is a major source of income for Mauritius, with an estimated 300,670 tourists in 1991. Earnings from tourism in 1991 are estimated to be Rs.3,875 million. The neighbouring French island of Réunion is the most important source of tourists, followed closely by mainland France.

FINANCE

The main sources of Government revenue are private and company income tax, customs and excise duties, mainly on imports, but also on sugar exports.

	1990–1	1991–2*
Public revenue	Rs.9,899m	Rs.10,981m
Public expenditure (recurrent)	9,230m	10,070m

*estimate

TRADE

Most foodstuffs and raw materials have to be imported from abroad. Apart from local consumption (about 36,500 tonnes per annum), the sugar produced is exported, mainly to Britain.

	1990	1991
Total imports	Rs.24,019m	Rs.24,672m
Total exports	18,246m	19,273m

Trade with UK	1990	1991
Imports from UK	£50,746,000	£52,363,000
Exports to UK	233,936,000	250,218,000

RODRIGUES AND DEPENDENCIES OF MAURITIUS

Rodrigues, formerly a dependency but now part of Mauritius, is about 350 miles east of Mauritius, with an area of 40 square miles. Population (1990) 34,204. Cattle, salt fish, sheep, goats, pigs, maize and onions are the principal exports. The island is administered by an Island Secretary.
Island Secretary, J. Cunden.

The islands of Agalega and St Brandon are dependencies of Mauritius. Total population (1989) 500. Other small islands, formerly Mauritian dependencies, have since 1965 constituted the British Indian Ocean Territory (*see* British Dependent Territories section).

MEXICO
Estados Unidos Mexicanos

AREA – Mexico occupies the southern part of the continent of North America, with an extensive seaboard to both the Atlantic and Pacific Oceans, extending from 14° 33′ to 32° 43′ N. lat. and 86° 46′ to 117° 08′ W. long., and comprising one of the most varied zones in the world. It contains 31 states and the federal district of Mexico, making in all 32 political divisions, covering an area of 761,605 sq. miles (1,972,547 sq. km).

The two great ranges of North America, the Sierra Nevada and Rocky Mountains, are prolonged from the north to a convergence towards the narrowing isthmus of Tehuantepec, their course being parallel to the west and east coasts. The surface of the interior consists of an elevated plateau between the two ranges, with steep slopes both to the Pacific and Atlantic (Gulf of Mexico). In the west is the peninsula of Lower California, with a mountainous surface, separated from the mainland by the Gulf of California. The Sierra Nevada, known in Mexico as the Sierra Madre, terminates in a transverse series of volcanic peaks, from Colima on the west to Citlaltepetl (El Pico de Orizaba) on the east.

The low-lying lands of the coasts form the Tierra Caliente, or tropical regions (below 3,000 ft.), the higher levels form the Tierra Templada, or temperate region (from 3,000 to 6,000 ft.), and the summit of the plateau with its peaks is known as Tierra Fria, or cold region (above 6,000 ft.). The main rivers are the Rio Grande del Norte which forms part of the northern boundary, and is navigable for about 70 miles from its mouth in the Gulf of Mexico, and the Rio Grande de Santiago, the Rio Balsas and Rio Papaloapan. The largest fresh-water lakes are Chapala (70 miles long and 20 miles wide), and Pátzcuaro.

POPULATION – At the 1990 Census, the total population was 81,140,922; a 1991 estimate gives a figure of 86,000,000.

LANGUAGES – Spanish is the official language of Mexico and is spoken by about 95 per cent of the population. In addition to Spanish, there are five basic groups of Indian languages spoken in Mexico. The 1970 Census showed that of the

3,111,415 inhabitants speaking an Indian language, 25.7 per cent spoke Náhuatl; 14.6 per cent Maya; 9.1 per cent Zapotec; 7.1 per cent Otomí; 7.5 per cent Mixtec and 36 per cent one or other of the 59 dialects derived from these basic languages. The poet Octavio Paz won the Nobel Prize for Literature in 1991.

CAPITAL – Mexico City, population of metropolitan area (1990 census) 14,987,051. Other cities (1990 census) are:

Guadalajara	2,846,000	Puebla	1,454,526
Monterrey	2,521,697	León	956,070
Torréon	876,456	Ciudad Juarez	797,679
Toluca	827,339	Tijuana	742,686

CURRENCY – Peso of 100 centavos.

FLAG – Three vertical bands in green, white, red, with the Mexican emblem (an eagle on a cactus devouring a snake) in the centre.

NATIONAL ANTHEM – Mexicanos, Al Grito De Guerra (Mexicans, to the war cry).

NATIONAL DAY – 16 September (Proclamation of Independence).

HISTORY

The present Mexico and Guatemala were once the centre of a remarkable indigenous civilization, which flowered in the periods from AD 500 to 1100 and 1300 to 1500 and collapsed before the little army of Spanish adventurers under Hernán Cortés in the years following 1519.

Pre-Columbian Mexico was divided between different but connected Indian cultures, each of which has left distinctive archaeological remains. The best-known of these are Chichén Itzá, Uxmal, Bonampak and Palenque, in Yucatán and Chiapas (Maya); Teotihuacon, renowned for the Pyramid of the Sun (216 feet high) in the Valley of Mexico (Teotihuacáno); Monte Albán and Mitla, near Oaxaca (Zapotec); El Tajín in the state of Veracruz (Totonac); and Tula in the state of Hidalgo (Toltec). The last and most famous Indian culture of all, the Aztec, based on Tenochitlán, suffered more than the others from the Spanish and very few Aztec monuments remain.

A few years after the conquest, the Spanish built Mexico City on the ruins of Tenochitlán, and appointed a Viceroy to rule their new dominions, which they called New Spain. The country was largely converted to Christianity, and a distinctive colonial civilization, representing a marriage of Indian and Spanish traditions, developed and flourished, notably in architecture and sculpture. In 1810 a revolt began against Spanish rule. This was finally successful in 1821, when a precarious independence was proclaimed.

Friction with the United States in Texas led to the war of 1845–8, at the end of which Mexico was forced to cede the northern provinces of Texas, California and New Mexico. In 1862 Mexican insolvency led to invasion by French forces which installed Archduke Maximilian of Austria as Emperor. The empire collapsed with the execution of the Emperor in 1867 and the austere reformer, Juárez, restored the republic. Juárez's death was followed by the dictatorship of Porfirio Diaz, which saw an enormous increase of foreign, particularly British and United States, investment in the country. In 1910 began the Mexican Revolution which reformed the social structure and the land system, curbed the power of foreign companies and ushered in the independent industrial Mexico of today. In 1986 Mexico joined GATT and began a liberalization programme of large-scale privatization and administrative reform.

GOVERNMENT

Under the Constitution of 1917 (as subsequently amended), Congress consists of a Senate of 64 members, elected for six years, and of a Chamber of Deputies, at present numbering 500, elected for three years. Presidents, who wield full executive powers, are elected for six years; they cannot be re-elected.

There are nine political parties registered in Mexico, of which the largest and most influential is the Partido Revolucionario Institucional (PRI) which has for more than 60 years constituted the governing party, despite constant allegations of electoral fraud. The main opposition parties are Partido de Acción Nacional (PAN) and Partido de la Renovación Democratica (PRD) In June 1992 the state of the parties in the Chamber of Deputies was: PRI 320, PAN 89, PRD and allied parties 91.

HEAD OF STATE

President (1988–94), Carlos Salinas de Gortari, *elected*, 4 June 1988, *took office*, 1 Dec. 1988.

CABINET as at June 1992

Interior, Fernando Gutiérrez Barrios.
Foreign Affairs, Fernando Solana Morales.
Finance and Public Credit, Dr Pedro Aspe Armella.
Defence, Gen. Antonio Riviello Bazán.
Navy, Adm. Luis Carlos Ruano Angulo.
Energy, Mines and Parastatal Industries, Fernando Hiriart Balderrama.
Trade and Industrial Development, Dr Jaime Serra Puche.
Agriculture and Water Resources, Carlos Hank González.
Communications and Transport, Andrés Caso Lombardo.
Education, Dr Ernesto Zedillo Ponce de León.
Social Development and Ecology, Luis Donaldo Colosio.
Health, Dr Jesús Kumate Rodríguez.
Labour and Social Security, Arsenio Farell Cubillas.
Agrarian Reform, Victor Cervera Pacheco.
Tourism, Pedro Joaquin Coldwell.
Fisheries, Guillermo Jiménez Morales.
Attorney-General, Ignacio Morales Lechuga.
Attorney-General of Federal District, Diego Valadez Ríos.
Comptroller-General, María Elena Vazquez Nava.
Mayor of Mexico City, Manuel Camacho Solís.

MEXICAN EMBASSY
42 Hertford Street, London W1Y 7TF
Tel 071-499 8586

Ambassador Extraordinary and Plenipotentiary, His Excellency Bernardo Sepulveda (1989).

BRITISH EMBASSY
Calle Río Lerma 71, Colonia Cuauhtémoc,
06500 Mexico City, DF
Tel: Mexico City 207 20 89

Ambassador Extraordinary and Plenipotentiary, His Excellency Sir Roger Hervey, KCVO, CMG (1992).

There are British Consular Offices at *Mexico City, Acapulco, Guadalajara, Mérida, Monterrey, Tampico, Veracruz,* and *Cuidad Juarez*.

BRITISH COUNCIL REPRESENTATIVE, Dr Brian Lavercombe, Maestro Antonio Caso 127, Col. San Rafael (PO Box 30-588), Mexico 06470 DF.

BRITISH CHAMBER OF COMMERCE, British Trade Centre, Rio de la Plata 30, Col. Cuauhtemoc, CP 06500, Mexico City DF, *Manager*, Stephen Grant.

COMMUNICATIONS

Veracruz, Tampico and Coatzacoalcos are the chief ports of the Atlantic, and Guaymas, Mazatlán, Puerto Lázaro Cárdenas, Acapulco, Salina Cruz and Puerto Madero on the Pacific. Work is proceeding on the reorganization and re-equipment of the whole system; help in this has been forthcoming from the World Bank, the Export-Import Bank and private sources in the United States. Total track length of the railways was 240,186 kms in 1990.

Mexico City may be reached by at least three highways from the United States, and from the south from Yucatán as well as on two principal highways from the Guatemalan border.

International telegraph services to the United States frontier are provided by the government-owned Mexican Telegraph Company and then through the United States to Canada and Europe.

Teléfonos de México, now privatized, controls about 98 per cent of all telephone services. Satélite Latinoamericano (SATELAT) is a joint government/private sector venture disseminating television programmes to Latin America through Intelsat IV satellite facilities leased by the Mexican Government.

There are 1,113 airports and landing fields in Mexico, of which eighteen are equipped to handle long-distance flights. There are 166 airline companies, including two of the major, now private, national airlines, Mexicana de Aviación and Aeroméxico. The total number of air passengers in 1990 was 21,825,000.

ECONOMY

In 1991 26 per cent of Mexican Gross Domestic Product (GDP) was produced by commerce, 23 per cent by manufacturing, 33.6 per cent by services, 5 per cent by construction, 7.4 per cent by agriculture, 3.5 per cent by mining and 1.5 per cent by public utilities. Direct foreign investment at the end of 1991 was a cumulative US$33.9 billion, of which over 60 per cent was American. Privatization has been successful with only 208 public enterprises remaining in 1991 (1,155 in 1982). The main trading partners are the USA (65.6 per cent), EC (15 per cent), Latin America (5.2 per cent) and Japan (5 per cent).

AGRICULTURE – The principal crops are maize, beans, rice, wheat, sugar cane, coffee, cotton, tomatoes, chili, tobacco, chick-peas, groundnuts, sesame, alfalfa, vanilla, cocoa and many kinds of fruit, both tropical and temperate. The maguey, or Mexican cactus, yields several fermented drinks, mezcal and tequila (distilled) and pulque (undistilled). Another species of the same plant supplies sisal-hemp (henequen). The forests contain mahogany, rosewood, ebony and chicle trees. Agriculture employs an estimated 20 per cent of the working population.

INDUSTRY – The principal industries are mining and petroleum, although there has been considerable expansion of both light and heavy industries. Exports of manufactured goods now average about 56 per cent of total exports. The steel industry expanded steadily until recently and current production is around 7.9m tons. In 1991, 989,000 motor vehicles were produced of which 365,000 were for export.

The mineral wealth is great, and principal minerals are gold, silver, copper, lead, zinc, quicksilver, iron and sulphur. Substantial reserves of uranium have been found. In the non-metals sector, Mexico continues to produce 25 per cent of the world's supply of fluorspar.

The total proven petroleum reserves were 72 billion barrels in 1983. Oil exports were 1.37 million barrels per day in 1991. Daily production of natural gas is approximately 3 billion cubic feet. Oil reserves have increased substantially due to important discoveries in the Gulf of Campeche. A new refinery at Tula, State of Hidalgo, is the nation's largest; and new refineries in Monterrey, State of Nuevo Leon, and Salina Cruz, State of Oaxaca, are under construction.

Electricity generating capacity was 27.4 million KW in 1991.

Textile production is led by the artificial fibres sector, which comprised 66 per cent of the industry's output in 1983.

TRADE

Major imports include computers, auto assembly material, electrical parts, auto and truck parts, powdered milk, corn and sorghum, transport, sound-recording and power-generating equipment, chemicals, industrial machinery, pharmaceuticals and specialized appliances. Principal exports include oil, automobiles, auto engines, fruits and vegetables, shrimps, coffee, computers, cattle, glass, iron and steel pipes, and copper.

Trade with UK	1990	1991
Imports from UK	£262,952,000	£276,557,000
Exports to UK	172,144,000	147,214,000

DEFENCE

Supreme command is vested in the President, exercised through the Ministries of Defence (for Army and Air Force) and Marine.

The total armed forces number some 175,000, including 60,000 conscripts. Conscription is decided by lottery and is for a one-year period. The Army has a strength of 130,000 (including 60,000 conscripts), with some 310 reconnaissance vehicles, 110 armoured personnel carriers, 120 artillery pieces. The Navy has a strength of 37,000 personnel, with three destroyers, 97 patrol and coastal craft, and nine combat aircraft. The Air Force is 8,000 strong, with 113 combat aircraft and 25 armed helicopters.

EDUCATION

Education is divided into primary, secondary and superior levels. In 1990 there were 18,061,000 in the first level, 6,599,000 in the second and 1,236,000 in the third.

FEDERATED STATES OF MICRONESIA

The Federated States of Micronesia comprise more than 600 islands extending 2,900 km (1,800) miles) across the archipelago of the Caroline Islands in the western Pacific Ocean. The islands are located between the Equator and 9°N., and 138° and 168°E. Pohnpei island is 4,670 km (2,900 miles) south-west of Honolulu and 1,610 km (1,100 miles) south-east of Guam.

AREA – 700 square km (270 square miles).

TOPOGRAPHY – The islands vary geologically from mountainous islands to low coral atolls.

CLIMATE – Tropical. The average annual temperature is 27°C (81°F). Annual rainfall is consistently high; Pohnpei receives the highest rainfall, averaging 8,900 mm (350 inches) annually. Storms are common between August and December, and typhoons between July and November.

POPULATION – The population of the Federated States of Micronesia was approximately 100,000 in 1988: Pohnpei 31,000; Chuuk (formerly Truk) 52,000; Yap 12,000; Kosrae 6,500.

ETHNIC GROUPS – Micronesian.

LANGUAGES – English (official) and eight other languages are used in different parts of the Federated States: Yapese, Ulithian, Woleaian, Ponapean, Nukuoran, Kapingamarangi, Trukese and Kosraen.

RELIGIONS – Predominantly Christian.

CAPITAL – The Federal capital is Palikir, on Pohnpei island.
FLAG – United Nations blue with four white stars in the centre.
TIME ZONES – Yap and Chuuk 10 hours ahead of GMT; Pohnpei and Kosrae 11 hours ahead of GMT.

HISTORY

The Spanish Empire claimed sovereignty over the Caroline Islands until 1899, when Spain withdrew from her Pacific territories and sold her possessions in the Caroline Islands to Germany. The Caroline Islands became a protectorate of the German Empire under colonial German administration until the outbreak of the First World War in 1914, when Japan took control of the islands on behalf of the Allied powers. After the war Japan continued to administer the territory under a League of Nations mandate. During the Second World War, United States armed forces took control of the islands from the Japanese. In 1947 the United States entered into agreement with the UN Security Council to administer the Micronesia area, of which the Federated States of Micronesia were a part, as the UN Trust Territory of the Pacific Islands.

The US Trusteeship Administration of the Federated States of Micronesia came to an end on 3 November 1986, when a Compact of Free Association between the USA and the Federated States of Micronesia came into effect. By this agreement the USA recognized the Federated States of Micronesia as a fully sovereign and independent state. However, the Soviet Union used its veto to prevent the UN Security Council from terminating the UN Trust territory of the Pacific Islands for the Federated States of Micronesia until December 1990, when the independence of the Federated States of Micronesia was finally recognized by the UN.

CONSTITUTION

The Federated States of Micronesia is a federal democracy. The constitution separates the executive, legislative and judicial branches. There is a bill of rights and provision for traditional rights.

EXECUTIVE – The executive comprises a federal President and Vice-President, both of whom must be chosen from amongst the four nationally-elected senators.

LEGISLATURE – There is a one-chamber legislature of 14 members, four members elected on a nation-wide basis and ten members elected from congressional districts apportioned by population.

HEAD OF STATE
President, Bailey Olter (Pohnpei)
Vice-President, Jacob Nina (Kosrae)

MEMBERSHIP OF INTERNATIONAL ORGANIZATIONS – UN, UNESCO.

FEDERATED STATES OF MICRONESIA AMBASSADOR TO LONDON, no accreditation as yet

BRITISH AMBASSADOR, His Excellency Derek White (resident in Kiribati)

LOCAL GOVERNMENT

The Federated States of Micronesia is a federal republic of four constituent states. Each state has its own government and legislative system.

Pohnpeo: *population*, 31,000; *capital*, Kolonia; *Governor*, Rasio Moses
Chuuk (Truk): *population*, 52,000; *capital*, Moen; *Governor*, Sasao Gouland
Yap: *population*, 12,000; *capital*, Colonia; *Governor*, Petrus Tun
Kosrae: *population*, 6,500; *capital*, Lelu; *Governor*, Yosivo George

JUDICIAL SYSTEM

The judiciary is headed by the Supreme Court, which is divided into trial and appellate divisions. Below this, each state has its own judicial system.

DEFENCE

The Compact of Free Association places full responsibility for the defence of the Federted States of Micronesia on the USA.

ECONOMY

The economy is dependent mainly on subsistence agriculture and government spending. Copra and fish are the two main exports. The majority of the working population is engaged in government administration, subsistence farming, fishing, copra production and the growing tourist industry.

CULTURE

Each of the four states has an indigenous culture, and these differ considerably from one another. Recognition of the role of traditional leaders and customs is common to all, though Kosrae has no traditional leaders.

MONACO
Principauté de Monaco

A small principality on the Mediterranean, with land frontiers joining France at every point, Monaco is divided into the districts of Monaco-Ville, La Condamine, Fontvielle and Monte Carlo. The principality comprises a narrow strip of country about two miles long (area approx. 195 hectares), with approximately 28,000 inhabitants (1990) and a yearly average of over 250,000 visitors.

CAPITAL – Monaco-Ville, population (1982) 1,234.
CURRENCY – Monaco uses the French franc of 100 centimes as legal tender.
FLAG – Two equal horizontal stripes, red over white.
NATIONAL ANTHEM – Hymne Monegasque.
NATIONAL DAY – November 19.

GOVERNMENT

The principality, ruled by the Grimaldi family since the late 13th century, was abolished during the French Revolution and re-established in 1815 under the protection of the Kingdom of Sardinia. In 1861 Monaco came under French protection.

The 1962 Constitution, which can be modified only with the approval of the National Council, maintains the traditional hereditary monarchy and guarantees freedom of association, trade union freedom and the right to strike. Legislative power is held jointly by the Prince and a uni-cameral, 18-member National Council elected by universal suffrage. Executive power is exercised by the Prince and a four-member Council of Government, headed by a Minister of State. The judicial code is based on that of France.

HEAD OF STATE
Sovereign Prince, HSH Rainier III Louis-Henri-Maxence Bertrand, *born* 31 May 1923, *succeeded* 9 May 1949; *married* 19 April 1956, Miss Grace Patricia Kelly (died 14 Sept. 1982) and *has issue* Prince Albert Alexandre Louis Pierre,

born 14 March 1958, Princess Caroline Louise Marguerite, *born* 23 January 1957; and Princess Stephanie Marie Elisabeth, *born* 1 Feb. 1965.

President of the Crown Council, Jean-Charles Marquet.
President of the National Council, Jean-Charles Rey.
Minister of State, Jacques Dupont, *appointed* 1991.

CONSULATE GENERAL OF MONACO
4 Audley Square, London W1Y 5DR
Tel 071-629 0734

Consul-General, I. B. Ivanovic.

HM Consul-General, John Illman (1990), resident in Marseilles, France.

ECONOMY

The whole available ground is built over, so that there is no cultivation, though there are some notable public and private gardens. Monaco has a small harbour (30 ft. alongside quay) and the import duties are the same as in France.

MONGOLIA

Republic of Mongolia

AREA AND POPULATION – The Republic of Mongolia is a large and sparsely populated country to the north of China. Its area is 604,250 sq. miles (1,565,000 sq. km). Its population (UN estimate 1990) is 2,190,000. However, this total constitutes only part of the Mongolians of Asia, a number of whom are to be found in China and in the neighbouring regions of the Russian Federation (especially the Mongolian Buryat Autonomous Region).

Mongolia, which is almost nowhere below 1,000 metres above sea level, forms part of the central Asiatic plateau and rises towards the west in the high mountains of the Mongolian Altai and Khanggai Ranges. The Khentai Mountain Range, situated to the north-east of the capital Ulan Bator, is less high. The Gobi region covers much of the southern half of the country. It contains some sand deserts, but between these less hospitable areas there is semi-desert which provides pasture for great numbers of sheep, goats, camels and horses (the latter is still the characteristic means of transport for the rural population) and some cattle. In the steppe areas to the north pasturage is better and livestock more abundant. Even further north, in the better watered provinces, grain, fodder and vegetable crops are increasingly grown. There are several long rivers and many lakes, but good water is scarce since much of the lake water is salty. The climate is harsh, with a short mild summer giving way to a long winter when temperatures can drop as low as minus 50°C.

CAPITAL – Ulan Bator, population (1989) 530,000.
CURRENCY – Tugrik of 100 möngö.
FLAG – Vertical tri-colour red, blue, red and in the hoist the traditional Soyombo symbol in gold.
NATIONAL DAY – 11 July.

HISTORY

Mongolia, under Genghis Khan the conqueror of China and much of Asia, was for many years a buffer state between Tsarist Russia and China, although it was under general Chinese suzerainty. The outbreak of the Chinese Revolution in 1911 led to a declaration of autonomy under Chinese suzerainty which was confirmed by the Sino-Russian Treaty of Kiakhta (1915), but cancelled by a unilateral Chinese declaration in 1919. Later the country became a battleground of the Russian civil war, and Soviet and Mongolian troops occupied Ulan Bator in 1921; this was followed by another declaration of independence. However, in 1924 the Soviet Union in a treaty with China again recognized the latter's sovereignty over Mongolia; but this was never properly exercised because of China's preoccupation with internal affairs, and later by the war with Japan.

The Mongolian People's Republic was formally established in 1924. Under the Yalta Agreement, Chiang Kai-shek agreed to a plebiscite, held in 1945, in which the Mongolians declared their desire for independence and this was formally recognized by Nationalist China. The country entered the United Nations in 1961.

GOVERNMENT

The Mongolian People's Revolutionary Party (MPRP) has been the ruling party since 1924. A series of demonstrations in favour of political and economic reform began in December 1989 and led to changes in the MPRP leadership in March 1990. The MPRP's constitutionally guaranteed monopoly of power was subsequently relinquished, and the introduction of a multi-party system was approved by the Great People's Hural. In May 1990 the formation of a Small Hural was approved. While the Great Hural was still the supreme body, the Small Hural was now the permanent legislative body. The MRRP won the first multi-party elections, held in July and August 1990. Since then, and following Moscow's lead, Mongolia has embarked on an ambitious programme of political and economic reforms. A coalition government was formed in October 1990.

A new constitution was approved in January 1992 which enshrines the concepts of democracy, a mixed economy, free speech, and neutrality in foreign affairs. The Small Hural was abolished, a smaller Great Hural becoming the legislative body of the country. Elections were held in June 1992 which were won by the MPRP by a landslide.

The country, and three city districts (Ulan Bator, Darkhan and Erdenet), is today divided into 18 *aimaks* (provinces) and beneath these into 258 *somons* (districts), and these form the basis of the state organization of the country.

HEAD OF STATE
President, Punsalmaagiyn Ochirbat.
Vice President, Radnaasumbereliyn Gonchigdorji.

CABINET as at July 1992
Prime Minister, Puntsagiin Jasray.
First Deputy PM, Davaadorjiyn Ganbold.
Deputy PMs, Dambiyn Dorligyav; Choyjilsurengiyn Purevdorj.
Defence, Maj.-Gen. Shagalyn Jadambaa.
Agriculture, Dandzangiyn Radnaaragchaa.
Education, Nonovyn Urtnasan.
Foreign Relations, Tserenpiliyn Gombosuren.
Finance, Ayuurdzanyn Badzarhuu.
National Development, Jamyangiyn Batsuur.
Trade and Industry, S. Bayarbaatar.
Labour, Choyjamtsyn Badamhaamb.
Justice, Jugneegiyn Amarsanaa.
Health and Policy Plans, Pagvajavyn Nyamdavaa.
State Control Committee for Nature and the Environment, Dzardin Batjargal.

EMBASSY OF MONGOLIA
7 Kensington Court, London W8 5DL
Tel 071-937 0150

Ambassador Extraordinary and Plenipotentiary, His Excellency Choisurengyn Baatar (1991).

British Embassy
30 Enkh Taivny Gudamzh (PO Box 703), Ulan Bator 13
Tel: Ulan Bator 51033/4

Ambassador Extraordinary and Plenipotentiary, His Excellency A. B. N. Morey (1989).
Second Secretary, N. Hart (*Head of Chancery*).

ECONOMY

The total of Mongolia's livestock was 25 million in 1991. Traditionally the Mongolians lead a nomadic life tending flocks of sheep, goats and horses, cows and camels. With the coming of the Communist regime and especially since 1952, great efforts have been made to settle the population, but a proportion still live nomadically or semi-nomadically in the traditional *ger* (circular tent). The pastoral population was collectivized at the end of the 1950s into huge *negdels* (co-operatives) and state farms which have hastened the process of settlement, but within these the herdsmen and their families still move with their *gers* from pasture to pasture as the seasons change.

Membership of the Communist bloc brought Mongolia considerable quantities of aid from other socialist countries, especially from the Soviet Union, but this has now been halted; the aid hastened industrialization while it lasted. For although the economy remains predominantly based on the herds of animals, and the principal exports of the country are still animal by-products (especially wool, hides and furs) and cattle, factories serving the needs of the country have been started up and the coal and electricity industries are being developed to provide an industrial base. A joint Mongolian/Soviet enterprise for copper and molybdenum mining was opened in 1978, at Erdenet in northern Mongolia. It is now in full production and processes 16 million tonnes of ore annually. Coal production in 1980 was 4.5 m tons, and had risen to 8.04 m tons by 1990.

Ulan Bator, which contains over a quarter of the country's population, is the main seat of industry. The second largest industrial centre is at Darkhan, north of the capital, near the Soviet frontier. Its industries include lime, cement and building materials, a flour mill and a power station. Choibalsan, in the east, is also being developed industrially. Communication is still difficult in the country as there are very few tarmac roads. The trans-Mongolian railway, following the line of the old north-south trade route, was opened in 1955 and links Mongolia with both China and Russia. Mongolia's fundamental difficulty is its very small population and labour force.

Trade

Foreign trade was formerly dominated by the Soviet Union and other eastern bloc countries. Following the collapse of the CMEA, trade with western countries, Japan and South Korea is increasing. The country experienced transitional problems in its attempt to establish a market economy by the end of 1991, such as food and fuel shortages, and unemployment; since January 1991, trade is no longer in transferable roubles but in hard currency, causing particular strain. Mongolia joined the IMF, the World Bank and the Asian Development Bank in February 1991.

Trade with UK	1990	1991
Imports from UK	£1,636,000	£1,148,000
Exports to UK	1,674,000	1,430,000

MOROCCO
Al-Mamlaka Al-Maghrebia

Area and Population – Morocco is situated in the north-west of the African continent between latitude 27° 40′ and 36° N. and longitude 1° and 13° W. with an area estimated at 172,414 sq. miles (446,550 sq. km).

It is traversed in the north by the Rif mountains and in a general south-west to north-east direction, by the Middle Atlas, the High Atlas, the Anti-Atlas and the Sarrho ranges. The northern flanks of the Middle and High Atlas mountains are well wooded but their southern slopes, exposed to the dry desert winds, are generally arid and desolate. The north-westerly point of Morocco is the peninsula of Tangier which is separated from the continent of Europe by the narrow strait of Gibraltar. The Jebel Mousa dominates the promontory and, with the rocky eminence of Gibraltar, was known to the ancients as the Pillars of Hercules, the western gateway of the Mediterranean.

Climate – The climate of Morocco is generally good and healthy, especially on the Atlantic coast (where a high degree of humidity is prevalent), the country being partially sheltered by the Atlas mountains from the hot winds of the Sahara. The rainy season may last from November to April. The plains of the interior are intensely hot in summer. Average summer and winter temperatures for Rabat are 27°C and 7°C.

Population – The population (1990 estimate) is 27,575,000.

Language – Arabic is the official language. Berber is the vernacular mainly in the mountain regions. French and Spanish are also spoken mainly in the towns.

Capital – ΨRabat, population (including Salé) 1,123,000. Regional capitals, with municipal population figures as at 1989, are: ΨCasablanca (2,904,000); Marrakesh (1,425,000); Fez (933,000); Oujda (895,000); Meknes (1,425,000); ΨAgadir (700,000). The towns of Fez, Marrakesh and Meknes were capitals at various times in Morocco's history.

Currency – Dirham (DH) of 100 centimes.

Flag – Red, with green pentagram (the Seal of Solomon).

National Day – 3 March (Anniversary of the Throne).

GOVERNMENT

Morocco became an independent sovereign state in 1956, following joint declarations made with France on 2 March 1956, and with Spain on 7 April 1956. The Sultan of Morocco, Sidi Mohammad ben Youssef, adopted the title of King Mohammad V.

The constitution of 1972 provides that not only political parties, but trade unions, chambers of commerce and professional bodies will participate in the organization of the state and representation of the people; specifies that the King is the supreme representative of the people; makes changes in the composition of the Regency Council and the Sovereign's rights and establishes a unicameral legislature. The Chamber has 306 members, 204 elected by direct universal suffrage (including five representing overseas workers) and 102 members elected by electoral colleges representing local government, industry, agriculture and working class groups.

There were elections in September 1984 and the new Parliament began its six year term on 12 October. A new government was named in April 1985 which included members of three political parties, though over half the portfolios went to non-political appointees. The term of the current Chamber of Representatives has been extended by two years, following a referendum held in December 1989.

WESTERN SAHARA

Formerly the Spanish Sahara, the territory was split between Morocco and Mauritania in 1976 after Spain withdrew in December 1975. In 1979 Mauritania renounced its claim to its share of the territory, which was added by Morocco to its area. Morocco's annexation has been opposed by Polisario guerrillas, who want the territory to become an independent state. On 30 August 1988, Morocco and the Polisario Front accepted a UN peace plan. Under the plan a ceasefire is to come into effect, and a referendum to determine the future of the area was to have been held in January 1992. However, the referendum has been repeatedly postponed because the Moroccan government and Polisario cannot agree on the referendum terms, and Polisario has threatened to resume hostilities.

HEAD OF STATE

King, HM King Hassan II (Moulay Hassan Ben Mohammed), *born* 9 July 1929; *acceded* 3 March 1961.
Heir, Crown Prince Sidi Mohamed, *born* 21 August 1963.

MINISTERS as at July 1992

Prime Minister, Dr Azeddine Laraki.
Minister of State, Moulay Ahmed Alaoui.
Minister of State in charge of Foreign Affairs and Co-operation, Abdellatif Filali.
Justice, Moulay Mustapha Belarbi Alaoui.
Interior and Information, Driss Basri.
National Education, Prof. Taieb Chkili.
Health, Tayeb Bencheikh.
Religious Endowments and Islamic Affairs, Abdelkebir Alaoui M'Daghri.
Public Works, Vocational and Executive Training, Mohamed Kabbaj.
Finance, Mohamed Berrada.
Tourism, Abdelkadar Ben Slimane.
Handicrafts, Industries, and Social Affairs, Mohamed Abied.
Transport, Mohamed Bouamoud.
Energy and Mines, Moulay Driss Alqoui M'Daghri.
Youth and Sport, Abdellatif Semlali.
Sea Fisheries and the Merchant Marine, Bensalem Smili.
Secretary-General of the Government, Abbès Kaissi.
Culture, Mohamed Benaissa.
Housing, Abderrahmane Boufettass.
Posts and Telecommunications, Mohamed Laensar.
Agriculture and Agricultural Reform, Othman Demnati.
Trade and Industry, Abdellah Al Azmani.
Employment, Hassan Abbadi.
Overseas Trade, Hassan Abouyoub.
Equipment, Senior Grades and Vocational Training, Mohammed Kabbaj.
Prime Minister's Office, Moulay Zine Zahidi (*Economic Affairs*); Khali Hanna Ould Errachid (*Saharan Affairs*); Rachidi Ghazouani (*Planning*); Abdeslem Baraka (*Relations with Parliament*); Abderrahim Ben Abdeljalil (*Administrative Affairs*).

EMBASSY OF THE KINGDOM OF MOROCCO
49 Queen's Gate Gardens, London SW7 5NE
Tel 071-581 5001/4

Ambassador Extraordinary and Plenipotentiary, His Excellency Khalil Haddaoui (1991).
Military, Naval and Air Attaché, Col. M. Jabrane.

BRITISH EMBASSY
17 Boulevard de la Tour Hassan (BP 45), Rabat
Tel: Rabat 720905

Ambassador Extraordinary and Plenipotentiary, His Excellency John Esmond Campbell Macrae, CMG (1990).
First Secretary, G. A. Pirie (*Head of Chancery/Commercial, and Consul*).
Defence Attaché, Lt.-Col. C. Le Hardy.
Vice-Consul (*Tangier*) W. W. Page.
There is a British Consulate-General/Commercial Office at *Casablanca* and an Honorary Consul at *Agadir*.

BRITISH COUNCIL REPRESENTATIVE, J. Weston, BP 427, 36 rue Tanger, Rabat.

BRITISH CHAMBER OF COMMERCE, 1st Floor, 185 Boulevard Zerktouni, Casablanca. Tel: 256920.

DEFENCE

The armed forces have a total active strength of 195,500, including conscripts who serve 18 month terms. The Army has a strength of some 175,000, the majority of which has been deployed in southern Morocco and Western Sahara fighting the Polisario Front. It is equipped with 280 main battle tanks, 160 light tanks, 325 reconnaissance vehicles, 850 armoured infantry fighting vehicles and armoured personnel carriers, and 290 artillery pieces. The Navy has a strength of 7,000, with one frigate, and 27 patrol and coastal combatant craft. The Air Force has a strength of 13,500, with 90 combat aircraft and 24 armed helicopters.

ECONOMY

Morocco's main sources of wealth are agricultural and mineral. The Five Year Plan (1981-5) for economic development placed particular emphasis on social improvement. Other priority sectors were industrial development, fisheries, agriculture and tourism. The next development plan (1987 onwards) is similar to the last. The world recession and high energy prices, coupled with a fall in the price of phosphates and poor harvests due to low rainfall have created problems for the economy since the end of the 1970s. However, rains in the winter of 1985-6 ended the long drought and the 1986 harvest was good. Similarly the fall in oil prices, the value of the dollar and interest rates have helped.

Agriculture employs more than 40 per cent of the working population and accounts for about 36 per cent of Morocco's exports. The main agricultural exports are fruit and vegetables. Cork and wood-pulp are the most important commercial forest products. Esparto grass is also produced. There is a fishing industry and substantial quantities of canned fish, mainly sardines and fishmeal, are exported. Manufacturing industries are centred in Casablanca, Fez, Tangier and Safi.

Morocco's mineral exports are phosphates, fluorite, barite, manganese, iron ore, lead, zinc, cobalt, copper and antimony. Morocco possesses nearly three-quarters of the world's estimated reserves of phosphates. There are oil refineries at Mohammedia and Sidi Kacem handling about four million tonnes of crude oil per year, but no significant quantities of hydrocarbons have been found.

Tourism is of increasing importance to the Moroccan economy, with development concentrated in Agadir and Marrakesh.

TRADE

Morocco's main import requirements are petroleum products, motor vehicles, building materials, agricultural and other machinery, chemical products, sugar, green tea and other foodstuffs.

	1987	1988
Imports	DH 1,066,711,000	DH 1,154,867,000
Exports	627,664,000	870,246,000

Trade with UK	1990	1991
Imports from UK	£118,599,000	£152,245,000
Exports to UK	106,425,000	95,522,000

COMMUNICATIONS

The railway runs south from Tangier to Sidi Kacem. From this junction, one line runs eastwards through Fez to Oujda, and another continues southwards, through Rabat and Casablanca, to Marrakesh. A line running due south from Oujda skirts the Morocco-Algeria frontier and reaches Bouarfa. Moroccan railroads cover 1,250 miles and traction is electric or diesel. An extensive network of well-surfaced roads covers all the main towns in the kingdom.

There are air services between Casablanca, Tangier, Agadir (seasonal), Marrakesh and London, and also between Tangier and Gibraltar connecting with London. Royal-Air-Maroc operates internal services.

In 1984 there were seven Arabic and five French daily newspapers.

EDUCATION

There are government primary, secondary and technical schools. At Fez there is a theological university of great repute in the Muslim world. There is a secular university at Rabat. Schools for special denominations, Jewish and Catholic, are permitted and may receive government grants. American schools operate in Rabat and Casablanca.

MOZAMBIQUE

República de Moçambique

AREA AND POPULATION – The Republic of Mozambique lies on the east coast of Africa, and is bounded by Swaziland in the south, South Africa in the south and west, Zimbabwe in the west, Zambia and Malawi in the north-west and Tanzania in the north. It has an area of 309,495 sq. miles (801,590 sq. km), with a population (1990 UN estimate) of 15,656,000. The official language is Portuguese.

CAPITAL – Ψ Maputo, estimated population (1990), 1,150,000. Other main ports are ΨBeira and ΨNacala.
CURRENCY – Metical (MT) of 100 centavos.
FLAG – Horizontally green, black, yellow with white fimbriations; a red triangle based on the hoist containing the national emblem.
NATIONAL DAY – 25 June (Independence Day).

GOVERNMENT

Mozambique, discovered by Vasco de Gama in 1498 and colonized by Portugal, achieved complete independence from Portugal on 25 June 1975. The date had been agreed in September 1974 by Portugal and Frelimo (Frente de Libertação de Moçambique), the Marxist liberation movement. Frelimo ceased to be a Marxist-Leninist party in July 1989, but it still has Socialist beliefs.

In August 1990 President Chissano announced government plans to adopt a multi-party system. The new democratic constitution came into force on 30 November 1990, enshrining freedom of association and the free market. The official name of the country was changed from The People's Republic of Mozambique to the Republic of Mozambique. The legislative assembly has between 200 and 250 members.

Negotiations with the rebel Mozambique National Resistance (MNR) continued in 1991–2 to end the war which had devastated much of the country. An Agreement was reached between President Chissano and the Renamo leader Afonso Dhlakama in August 1992 on a ceasefire to come into effect on 1 October 1992. After this date Renamo will act as a political opposition and presidential and legislative elections will be held within one year, on a proportional representation basis.

HEAD OF STATE
President, Joaquim Alberto Chissano, *sworn in*, November 1986.

COUNCIL OF MINISTERS as at June 1992
Prime Minister, Mario da Graca Machungo.
Foreign Affairs, Pascoal Mocumbi.
National Defence, Alberto Joaquim Chipande.
Co-operation, Jacinto Veloso.
Minister in the Presidency, Feliciano Gundana.
State Administration, Aguiar Jonassane Reinaldo Mazula.
Education, Aniceto dos Muchangos.
Interior, Manuel Antonio.
Minister without Portfolio, Mariano de Araujo Matsinha.
Transport and Communications, Armando Emilio Guebuza.
Finance, Eneas Da Conceĭcao Comiche.
Health, Dr Leonardo Simao.
Information, Rafael Maguni.
Construction and Water, Joao Salomao.
Trade, Daniel Gabriel Tembe.
Agriculture, Alexandre Jose Zandamela.
Industry and Energy, Octavio Muthemba.
Mineral Resources, John Kachamila.
Justice, Ossumane Ali Dauto.
Culture, Jose Mateus Katupha.
Labour, Feodato Mondim Da Silva Hunguana.

EMBASSY OF THE REPUBLIC OF MOZAMBIQUE
21 Fitzroy Square, London W1P 5HJ
Tel 071-383 3800

Ambassador Extraordinary and Plenipotentiary, His Excellency Armando Alexandre Panguene (1988).

BRITISH EMBASSY
Av. Vladimir I Lenine 310, CP 55, Maputo
Tel: Maputo 420111/2/5/6/7

Ambassador Extraordinary and Plenipotentiary, Her Excellency Maeve Geraldine Fort, CMG (1989).

BRITISH COUNCIL REPRESENTATIVE, C. ffrench Blake.

ECONOMY

The basis of the economy is subsistence agriculture, but there is an industrial sector based mainly in Beira and Maputo. After giving priority to the development of collective farms and state enterprises in all sectors, the government is now encouraging the private sector and foreign investment, particularly in agriculture and consumer goods production. There are substantial coal deposits in Tete province. Mozambique has a range of aid and co-operation agreements with a number of countries in eastern Europe and in the West. An agreement of non-aggression and good neighbourliness with South Africa was signed on 16 March 1984 (the Nkomati Accord).

TRADE

Main exports are sugar, cashew nuts, prawns, copra, cotton, tea and sisal.

Trade with UK	1990	1991
Imports from UK	£28,992,000	£18,851,000
Exports to UK	10,709,000	2,393,000

MYANMAR

Pyidaungsu Myanma Naingngandaw

AREA AND POPULATION – The Union of Myanmar (Burma) forms the western portion of the Indo-Chinese district of the continent of Asia, lying between 9° 58′ and 28° N. latitude and 92° 11′ and 101° 9′ E. longitude, with an extreme length of approximately 1,200 miles and an extreme width of 575 miles. It has a sea coast on the Bay of Bengal to the south and west, and a frontier with Bangladesh along the Naaf River (defined in 1964) and India to the north-west (defined in 1967). In the north and east the frontier with China was determined by a treaty with the People's Republic in October 1960, and has since been demarcated; there is a short frontier with Laos in the east, while the long finger of Tenasserim stretches southwards along the west coast of the Malay peninsula, forming a frontier with Thailand to the east. The total area of the Union is 261,218 sq. miles (676,552 sq. km).

There are four natural divisions. Arakan (with the Chin Hills region), the Irrawaddy basin, Tenasserim, including the Salween basin and extending southwards to the Myanmar-Thailand peninsula, and the elevated plateau on the east. Mountains enclose the Union on three sides, the highest point being Hka-kabo Razi (19,296 ft.) in the northern Kachin hills. Mt Popa, 4,981 ft., in the Myingyan district is an extinct volcano and a well-known landmark in central Myanmar. The principal river systems are the Kaladan-Lemro in Arakan, the Irrawaddy-Chindwin and the Sittang in central Myanmar, and the Salween which flows through the Shan Plateau.

POPULATION – The population (UN estimate 1990) is 41,675,000.

ETHNIC GROUPS – The indigenous inhabitants who entered the country from the north and east are of similar racial types and speak languages of the Tibeto-Burman, Mon-Khmer and Thai groups. The three important non-indigenous elements are Indians, Chinese and those from the former East Pakistan.

LANGUAGES – Burmese is the official language, but minority languages include Shan, Karen, Chin, Kayah and the various Kachin dialects. English is spoken in educated circles.

RELIGIONS – Buddhism is the religion of 85 per cent of the people, with 5 per cent Animists, 4 per cent Muslims, 4 per cent Hindus and less than 3 per cent Christians.

CAPITAL – The chief city of lower Myanmar and the seat of the government of the Union is ΨYangon (Rangoon). Population (1983): Yangon District 3,973,872; city population 2,458,712.

Mandalay is the chief city of upper Myanmar, population (1983): Mandalay district 4,580,923; city 532,985; Mawlamyine (Moulmein) 219,991 and Pathein (Bassein) 144,092. Pagan, on the Irrawaddy, south-west of Mandalay, contains many sacred buildings.

CURRENCY – Kyat (K) of 100 pyas.

FLAG – The Union flag is red, with a canton of dark blue, inside which are a cogwheel and two rice ears surrounded by 14 white stars.

NATIONAL DAY – 4 January.

GOVERNMENT

The Union of Burma (the name was officially changed to the Union of Myanmar in June 1989) became an independent republic outside the British Commonwealth on 4 January 1948 and remained a parliamentary democracy for 14 years. On 2 March 1962 the army took power and suspended the parliamentary constitution. A Revolutionary Council of senior officers under General Ne Win took measures to create a socialist state.

After months of popular demonstrations and rioting and a series of presidents throughout the summer of 1988, Gen. Saw Maung, leader of the armed forces, assumed power in September 1988. The People's Assembly, the Council of State and the Council of Ministers were abolished and replaced by the State Law and Order Restoration Council (SLORC) headed by Gen. Saw Maung as Prime Minister. The constitution was effectively abrogated.

A People's Assembly Election Law was published in March 1989 committing the SLORC to hold multi-party elections. These were held on 27 May 1990, resulting in a majority for the National League for Democracy (NLD). The SLORC refused to transfer power to a civilian government and large numbers of NLD members were detained, including their leader, Aung San Suu Kyi. However, following the replacement of Saw Maung by Than Shwe as SLORC Chairman and Prime Minister in April 1992, the government announced that it would begin a dialogue with some elements of the opposition. A convention to discuss a future constitution has been established. At the same time, the SLORC has released many political detainees, although Aung San Suu Kyi has not been freed.

A 'National Coalition Government of the Union of Burma', led by Sein Winn, was established in December 1990 at Manerplaw on the Thai border by NLD members and other opposition groups. In 1992 a Burmese Army offensive failed to capture the NCGUB base at Mannerplaw.

POLITICAL DIVISIONS

Myanmar is comprised of seven states (Chin, Kachin, Karen, Kayah, Mon, Rakhine, Shan) and seven divisions (Irrawaddy, Magwe, Mandalay, Pegu, Yangon (Rangoon), Sagaing, Tenasserim).

CABINET as at June 1992

Chairman of SLORC, Prime Minister and Minister of Defence, Gen. Than Shwe.
Agriculture, Maj.-Gen. Myint Aung.
Communications, Posts and Telegraphs, U Soe Tha.
Construction, U Khin Maung Yin.
Co-operatives, Maj.-Gen. Mya Thinn.
Culture, Lt.-Gen. Aung Ye Kyaw.
Transport, Lt.-Gen. Tin Tun.
Energy, U Khin Maung Thein.
Foreign Affairs, U Ohn Gyaw.
Forestry, Lt.-Gen. Chit Swe.
Health and Education, Col. Pe Thein.
Industry, Lt.-Gen. Sein Aung.
Information, Brig.-Gen. Myo Thant.
Labour, Lt.-Gen. Tin Tun.
Livestock Breeding and Fisheries, Brig.-Gen. Maung Maung.
Mines, Vice-Adm. Mg Mg Khin.
Planning and Finance, Brig.-Gen. Abel.
Rail and Transportation, U Win Sein.
Religious Affairs, Maj.-Gen. Myo Nyunt.
Social Welfare, Brig.-Gen. Thaung Myint.
Trade, Brig.-Gen. Abel.

EMBASSY OF THE UNION OF MYANMAR
19A Charles Street, Berkeley Square, London W1X 8ER
Tel 071-629 6966

Ambassador Extraordinary and Plenipotentiary, His Excellency U Hla Maung (1992).

BRITISH EMBASSY
80 Strand Road (Box No. 638), Rangoon
Tel: Rangoon 81700

Ambassador Extraordinary and Plenipotentiary, His Excellency Julian Hartland-Swann (1990).
Deputy Head of Mission, First Secretary (Commercial) and Consul, P. R. Hagart.

Cultural Attaché and British Council Representative, Ralph Isaacs, MBE.

EDUCATION

The literacy rate is high compared to other Asian countries. There is no caste system and women engage freely in social intercourse and play an important part in agriculture and retail trade.

Most children attend primary school, and about four million are currently enrolled; in middle and high schools, enrolment is about 11 million. There are three universities, at Yangon (Rangoon), Mandalay and Mawlamyine (Moulmein), and in 1986–7 the numbers graduating were 9,981. A number of autonomous institutes of university standard award their own degrees. Under the universities are three affiliated degree colleges and the Workers' College, Yangon. There are also 14 two-year colleges affiliated to the universities, spread throughout the country.

There are three teachers' training institutes for middle and primary schools, and 13 teachers' training schools for primary only. Seven government technical institutes offer post-secondary technical training courses and 14 technical high schools train semi-skilled tradesmen. Six agricultural institutes offer training courses in agriculture and veterinary science; nine agricultural high schools train semi-skilled agriculturists. There are 34 vocational schools for weaving, handicrafts, etc.

ECONOMY

FINANCE – The chief sources of revenue are profits on state trading, income tax, customs duties, commercial taxes and excise duties; the chief heads of expenditure are defence, education and police. The budget estimates for 1990–1 were: Revenue K38,270 million; Expenditure, K48,670 million.

AGRICULTURE – Three-quarters of the population depend on agriculture; the chief products are rice, oilseeds (sesamum and groundnut), maize, millet, cotton, beans, wheat, grain, tea, sugarcane, tobacco, jute and rubber. Rice was for many years the mainstay of the economy, but in 1985 teak overtook rice. The quantity of teak available for export in 1989 was 180,000 tons; the quantity of rice and by-products available for export was 160,000 tons.

MINERAL RESOURCES – Myanmar is rich in minerals, including petroleum, lead, silver, tungsten, zinc, tin, wolfram and gemstones. Of these, petroleum products are the most important. Oil is now being produced from oilfields in Myanaung, Prome and Shwepyitha and at Chauk, Yenangyaung, Mann, and Letpando. Production of crude oil in 1986–7 totalled 10,103,000 US barrels. There is a refinery at the main oilfield, Chauk, another at Syriam near Yangon (Rangoon) and a third at Mann. There has been a steady decline in oil production in recent years and the country is no longer self-sufficient. Onshore exploration continues. There has also been some offshore oil exploration on a small scale. Major reserves of natural gas have been discovered in the Martaban Gulf, which Myanmar is hoping to develop.

INDUSTRY – All industrial activity of any size is in the public sector. Under development plans, projects completed or under construction with overseas financial and technical assistance include the production of cement, bricks and tiles, sheet glass, steel sections, jute bags and twine, cotton yarns, cotton and cotton mixture cloth, pharmaceuticals, sugar, paper, plywood, urea fertilizers, soda ash, tractors and tyres; also a hydro-electric scheme and various irrigation works.

Faced with a serious foreign exchange shortage, Myanmar was included in the UN's list of Least Developed Countries in December 1987.

TRADE WITH UK

	1990	1991
Imports from UK	£15,951,000	£8,294,000
Exports to UK	4,582,000	2,771,000

COMMUNICATIONS

The Irrawaddy and its chief tributary, the Chindwin, form important waterways, the main stream being navigable beyond Bhamo (900 miles from its mouth) and carrying much traffic. The chief seaports are Yangon (Rangoon), Mawlamyine (Moulmein), Akyab (Sittwe) and Pathein (Bassein).

The railway network covers 2,764 route miles, extending to Myitkyina, on the Upper Irrawaddy. There were 2,452 miles of Union highways and 11,767 miles of other main roads in 1982–3. The airport at Mingaladon, about 13 miles north of Yangon (Rangoon), only handles limited international air traffic.

NAMIBIA
The Republic of Namibia

AREA, ETC – Namibia stretches from the southern border of Angola (lat. 17° 23′ S.) to the northern (Orange River) and north-western borders of the Cape Province of the Republic of South Africa; and from the Atlantic Ocean in the west to Botswana in the east. The average rainfall over 70 per cent of the country is below 400 mm per annum.

Namibia has an area of 318,261 sq. miles (824,292 sq. km), including the area of Walvis Bay (434 sq. miles) which is claimed by Nambia but remains under South African sovereignty.

POPULATION – The population was estimated by the UN at 1,781,000 in 1990. The main population groups are: Ovambo (587,000), Kavango (110,000), Damara (89,000), Herero (89,000), Whites (78,000), Nama (57,000), Coloured (48,000), Caprivians (44,000), Bushmen (34,000), Rehoboth Baster (29,000), Tswana (7,000).

CAPITAL – Windhoek (population, 1987 estimate, 110,000). The only port of any size is ΨWalvis Bay.

CURRENCY – South African rand (R) of 100 cents is legal tender.

FLAG – Divided diagonally blue, red and green with the red fimbriated in white; a gold twelve-rayed sun in the upper hoist.

NATIONAL DAY – 21 March (Independence Day).

HISTORY

A German protectorate from 1880 to 1915, Namibia, as South West Africa, was administered until the end of 1920 by the Union of South Africa. Under the terms of the Treaty of Versailles, the territory was entrusted to South Africa with full powers of administration and legislation over the territory. After the dissolution of the League of Nations and in the absence of a trusteeship agreement, South Africa informed the United Nations that it would continue to administer South West Africa.

On 21 June 1971 the International Court of Justice at The Hague delivered an advisory opinion as requested by the UN Security Council on the legal consequences for states of the continued presence of South Africa in Namibia (South West Africa). It was the Court's majority opinion that the continued presence of South Africa was illegal, and that it was to withdraw its administration from Namibia immediately, putting an end to its occupation of the territory. The South African Government rejected this opinion, but accepted the principle that the territory should attain independence. In 1977 the five Western members of the UN Security Council drew up a plan, later incorporated into Security Council Resolution 435, for a peaceful settlement.

After a series of talks between Cuba, Angola, South Africa and the USA, agreement was reached in December 1988 for the withdrawal over 27 months of Cuban troops in Angola in exchange for South African withdrawal from Namibia leading to Namibian independence under UN Security Council Resolution 435. Implementation of Resolution 435 began on 1 April 1989. The UN Secretary-General sent his Special Representative to Namibia to oversee the seven-month run-up to elections and a 4,500 strong United Nations Transition Assistance Group (UNTAG) was deployed to monitor South African troop withdrawal and the conduct of the parties.

Elections for 72 seats in Namibia's first nationally elected body took place under UN supervision on 7–11 November 1989. Of voters registered, 95.9 per cent took part. Seats were allocated to parties according to the percentage of the vote won. The South West Africa People's Organization (SWAPO) won 41 seats with 57.32 per cent of the vote, the Democratic Turnhalle Alliance won 21 seats with 28.55 per cent, the United Democratic Front won 4 seats, Action Christian National 3, Namibia Patriotic Front 1, Federal Convention of Namibia 1, and Namibia National Front 1.

The National Assembly met for the first time on 21 November 1989 at the legislative building in Windhoek (the Tintenpalast). The Independence Constitution was adopted unanimously on 9 February 1990, and independence was declared on 21 March 1990. Namibia joined the Commonwealth upon independence.

GOVERNMENT

Constitutionally defined as a multiparty, secular, democratic republic, Namibia has an executive President as head of state who exercises the functions of government with the assistance of a Cabinet headed by a Prime Minister. Legislative authority lies with the National Assembly, which is the lower house of a bicameral parliamentary structure; an upper house (National Council) representing regional councils is to be created in January 1993. Each regional council will appoint two representatives to the National Council. The main function of the National Council will be to review and consider legislation from the National Assembly. Under a system of proportional representation, elections to the National Assembly are to take place every five years, or earlier if decided by the President. Members of the National Council will hold their seats for six years.

HEAD OF STATE
President, Dr Sam Nujoma, *elected*, 16 February 1990.

CABINET as at July 1992
Prime Minister, Rt. Hon. Hage Geingob.
Home Affairs, Hon. Hifikepunye Pohamba.
Foreign Affairs, Hon. Theo-Ben Gurirab.
Defence, Hon. Peter Mueshihange.
Finance, Hon. Gerhard Hanekom.
Education and Culture, Hon. Nahas Angula.
Information and Broadcasting, Hon. Hidipo Hamutenya.
Health and Social Services, Hon. Dr Nicky Iyambo.
Labour, Public Service and Manpower Development, Hon. Hendrik Witbooi.
Mines and Energy, Hon. Andimba Toivo Ya Toivo.
Justice, Hon. Ngarikutuke Tjiriange.
Local Government and Housing, Hon. Libertine Amathila.
Agriculture, Water and Rural Development, Hon. Anton von Wietersheim.
Trade and Industry, Hon. Ben Amathila.
Wildlife and Conservation, and Tourism, Hon. Nico Bessinger.
Works, Transport, and Communication, Hon. Marco Hausiku.
Lands Resettlement and Rehabilitation, Hon. Richard Kabadjani.
Youth and Sport, Hon. Pendukeni Iithana.
Fisheries and Marine Resources, Hon. Helmut Angula.
State Security, Hon. Peter Tshirumbu.

HIGH COMMISSION FOR THE REPUBLIC OF NAMIBIA
34 South Molton Street, London W1Y 2BP
Tel 071-408 2333

High Commissioner, His Excellency Veiccoh K. Nghiwete (1991).

BRITISH HIGH COMMISSION
116A Leutwein Street, Windhoek
Tel: Windhoek 223022

High Commissioner, His Excellency Henry George Hogger (1992).

British Council Representative, J. Utley, PO Box 24224, 74 Bülowstrasse, Windhoek 9000.

ECONOMY

Mining (mainly diamonds and uranium), agriculture and fisheries account for over 40 per cent of Namibia's GDP. Most of the labour force is employed in the agricultural sector.

Trade with UK

	1990	1991
Imports from UK	£4,246,000	£3,981,000
Exports to UK	349,000	19,606,000

REPUBLIC OF NAURU

The Republic of Nauru is an island of 8.2 sq. miles (21 sq. km) in size, situated in 166° 55′ E. longitude and 0° 32′ S. of the Equator. It had a population (Census May 1983) of 8,042 (Nauruans 4,964; other Pacific Islanders 2,134; Asians 682; Caucasians 262). The UN estimated a total population of 9,000 in 1989. About 43 per cent of Nauruans are adherents of the Nauruan Protestant Church and there is a Roman Catholic Mission on the island. The main languages are English and Nauruan.

Currency – Nauru uses the Australian dollar ($A) of 100 cents as legal tender.

Flag – Twelve-point star (representing the 12 original Nauruan tribes) below a gold bar (representing the Equator), all on a blue ground.

National Day – 31 January (Independence Day).

GOVERNMENT

From 1888 until the First World War Nauru was administered by Germany, in 1920 becoming a British mandated territory under the League of Nations administered by Australia. A trusteeship superseding the mandate was approved in 1947 by the UN and Nauru continued to be administered by Australia until it became independent on 31 January 1968. It was announced in November 1968 that a limited form of membership of the Commonwealth had been devised for Nauru at the request of its government.

Parliament has eighteen members including the Cabinet and Speaker. Voting is compulsory for all Nauruans over 20 years of age, except in certain specified instances. Elections are held every three years. The Cabinet is chosen by the President, who is elected by the Parliament from amongst its members, and comprises not fewer than five nor more than six members including the President.

Head of State

President and Minister for External Affairs, Internal Affairs, Island Development and Industry, Civil Aviation Authority and the Public Service, His Excellency Hon. Bernard Dowiyogo.

Cabinet as at June 1992

Works and Community Services and Minister Assisting the President, Hon. Vinson Detenamo.

Finance, Hon. Kinza Clodumar.

Health and Education, Hon. Vinci Clodumar.

Justice, Hon. Nimes Ekwona.

British High Commission

British High Commissioner (resides at Suva, Fiji).

JUDICIARY

A Supreme Court of Nauru is presided over by the Chief Justice. The District Court, which is subordinate to the Supreme Court, is presided over by a Resident Magistrate. Both the Supreme Court and the District Court are Courts of Record. The Supreme Court exercises both original and appellate jurisdiction.

SOCIAL SERVICES

Nauru has a hospital service and other medical and dental services. There is also a maternity and child welfare service.

Education is available in nine primary and two secondary schools on the island with a total enrolment of about 1,600 pupils receiving primary education and 500 secondary education.

ECONOMY

The only fertile areas are the narrow coastal belt and local requirements of fruit and vegetables are mostly met by imports. The economy is heavily dependent on the extraction of phosphate, of which the island has one of the world's richest deposits. About 1.5 million tonnes of phosphate are mined each year, providing employment for over 1,000 people. The industry has been run since 1970 by the Nauru Phosphate Corporation. Considerable investments have been made abroad with the royalties on phosphate exports to provide for a time when production declines.

The Nauru Pacific Line owns six ships; the Government-owned Air Nauru normally operates air services throughout the Pacific region and to Australia, New Zealand, Japan, Singapore and the Philippines.

Trade with UK

	1990	1991
Imports from UK	£1,145,000	£1,189,000
Exports to UK	54,000	718,000

NEPAL

Area – Nepal lies between India and the Tibet Autonomous Region of China on the slopes of the Himalayas, and includes Mount Everest (29,078 ft). It has a total area of 54,342 sq. miles (140,747 sq. km).

The country comprises three distinct horizontal formations. In the south, joining the Indian plains, is the Terai, much of which was covered with jungle. It has recently been more widely cultivated but wild life is preserved in parts. The region represents 23 per cent of the total land area and nearly 44 per cent of the population live there. The central belt of the country is hilly, but with many fertile valleys, leading up to the snowline at about 14,000 feet. The hills account for 42 per cent of the area of the country and about 48 per cent of the population. The remainder of the country, the Himalayan region, consists of high mountains which are sparsely inhabited. The country is drained by three great river systems rising within and beyond the Himalayan mountain ranges and eventually flowing into the Ganges in India.

Population – The population was (UN estimate 1990) 18,916,000. The inhabitants are of mixed stock, with Mongolian characteristics prevailing in the north and Indian in the south.

Religions – The official religion is Hinduism: 89.5 per cent of the population are Hindus and 6 per cent are Buddhist. Gautama Buddha was born in Nepal.

CAPITAL – Kathmandu, population (1981) 235,000. Other towns of importance are Biratnagar (94,000), Lalitpur (81,000) and Bhaktapur (50,500) and Pokhara (48,500).
CURRENCY – Nepalese rupee of 100 paisa.
FLAG – Double pennant of crimson with blue border on peaks; white moon with rays in centre of top peak; white quarter sun, recumbent in centre of bottom peak.
NATIONAL ANTHEM – May Glory Crown Our Illustrious Sovereign.
NATIONAL DAY – 18 February (National Democracy Day).

HISTORY

The country was originally divided into numerous hill clans and petty principalities, but Nepal emerged as a nation in the middle of the 18th century when its component parts were unified by the warrior Raja of Gorkha, Prithvi Narayan Shah, who founded the present Nepalese dynasty. In 1846 power was seized by Jung Bahadur Rana after a massacre of nobles, and he was the first of a line of hereditary Rana Prime Ministers who ruled Nepal for 104 years. During this time the role of the monarchs was mainly ceremonial.

In 1950–1 a revolutionary movement achieved its aim of breaking the hereditary power of the Ranas and restoring the monarchy to its former position. After ten years, during which various parties and individuals tried their hand at government, King Mahendra proscribed all political parties and assumed direct powers on 16 December 1960, with the object of leading a united country to democracy. In 1962 he introduced a new constitution embodying a tiered, partyless system of panchayat (council) democracy. Mass agitation for political reform led in April 1990 to the lifting of the ban on political parties and the abolition of the panchyat system.

GOVERNMENT

A new constitution was promulgated on 9 November 1990, establishing a multi-party, parliamentary system of government and a constitutional monarchy. The monarch retained joint executive power with the Council of Ministers. A bicameral legislature was set up, consisting of a 205-member House of Representatives and a 60-member National Council, including 10 royal nominees. Elections, held on 12 May 1991, were won by the Nepali Congress Party.

HEAD OF STATE
Sovereign, HM King Birendra Bir Bikram Shah Dev, *born* 28 Dec. 1945; *succeeded* 31 Jan. 1972; *crowned* 24 Feb. 1975; *married*, Feb. 1970, HM Queen Aishwara Rajya Laxmi Devi Shah.
Heir, HRH Crown Prince Dipendra Bir Bikram Shah Dev, *born* 27 June 1971.

COUNCIL OF MINISTERS as at June 1992
Prime Minister, Minister of Defence, Foreign Affairs, Royal Palace Affairs, Girija Prasad Koirala.
Housing and Physical Planning, Bal Bahadur Rai.
Land Reform and Management, Jagannath Acharya.
Tourism, Ramhari Joshi.
Agriculture, Shailaja Acharya.
Home Affairs, Sher Bahadur Deupa.
Local Development, Ram Chandra Poudel.
General Administration, Law and Justice, and Parliamentary Affairs, Maheswor Prasad Singh.
Works and Transport, Khum Bahadur Khadka.
Education, Culture and Social Welfare, Govinda Raj Joshi.

ROYAL NEPALESE EMBASSY
12A Kensington Palace Gardens, London W8 4QU
Tel 071-229 1594/6231

Ambassador Extraordinary and Plenipotentiary, His Excellency Maj.-Gen. Bharat Kesher Simha (1988).
Counsellor, Madhab Prasad Khanal.

BRITISH EMBASSY
Lainchaur Kathmandu, PO Box 106
Tel: Kathmandu 410583

Ambassador Extraordinary and Plenipotentiary, His Excellency Timothy George, CMG (1990).
First Secretary, Dr A. R. Hall (*Deputy Head of Mission and Consul*).
Defence and Military Attaché, Col. M. H. Kefford.
Vice-Consul, L. C. Craig.

BRITISH COUNCIL REPRESENTATIVE, R. P. Hale, (PO Box 640), Kantipath, Kathmandu.

ECONOMY

Nepal exports carpets, jute, handicrafts, garments, hides and skins, medicinal herbs, cardamom, pulses etc., and imports textiles, machinery and parts, transport equipment, medicine, construction materials etc. Tourism is the single largest commercial earner of foreign exchange (US$55.9 million in 1986–7).

The budget for the fiscal year 1988–9 was estimated at NRs. 19,520.2 million, of which NRs. 6,152,139 million was allocated to regular and NRs. 13,368,061 million to development expenditures. Revenue was estimated at NRs. 9,300 million, foreign aid and grants NRs. 8,890.2 million, and domestic borrowing NRs. 1,330 million.

TRADE WITH UK

	1990	1991
Imports from UK	£4,099,000	£4,938,000
Exports to UK	7,039,000	4,531,000

COMMUNICATIONS

Kathmandu is connected with India by a road, the mountain section of which was built by India under the Colombo Plan, and to Tibet by a road to Kodari on the border which was built by the Chinese and opened on 26 May 1967. The Indian-aided Sunauli-Pokhara road (128 miles) was inaugurated in April 1972, and a road between Pokhara and Kathmandu, constructed by the Chinese, was opened in 1973. A link road between Mugling and Naryanghat, completed by the Chinese in 1981, has further improved communications between Kathmandu and the Terai. The East–West Highway (Mahendra Raj Marg) running along the entire length of the country is complete except for the Banbasa-Mahahali section. The total length of roads in Nepal in 1987–8 was 6,525 km.

Telecommunication services, both domestic and international, are available from the Central Telegraph Office or hotels. There are international subscriber dialling facilities from Nepal to 35 countries. Nepal television was introduced in 1984.

Royal Nepal Airlines operates an extensive network of domestic flights, and there are international flights to Britain, India, Pakistan, Bangladesh, Myanmar, Singapore, Thailand, West Germany, and the Middle East.

THE NETHERLANDS
Koninkrijk der Nederlanden

AREA – The Kingdom of the Netherlands is a maritime country of western Europe, situated on the North Sea, in lat. 50° 46′ to 53° 34′ N. and long. 3° 22′ to 7° 14′ E., consisting of 12 provinces (Eastern and Southern Flevoland being

amalgamated to form the twelfth province) and containing a total area of 15,770 sq. miles (40,844 sq. km).

The land is generally flat and low, intersected by numerous canals and connecting rivers. The principal rivers are the Rhine, Maas, Yssel and Scheldt.

POPULATION – The population (1990 estimate) is 15,009,000. The live birth rate in 1990 was 19.5 per 1,000 of the population, and the death-rate was 12.7.

LANGUAGE – Dutch is a West Germanic language of Saxon origin, closely akin to Old English and Low German. It is spoken in the Netherlands and the northern part of Belgium. It is also used in the Netherlands Antilles. (Afrikaans, one of the two South African languages, has Dutch as its origin, but differs from it in grammar and pronunciation.) There are six national papers, four of which are morning papers, and there are many regional daily papers.

CAPITAL – ΨAmsterdam, population 1,031,000 (urban agglomeration).

SEAT OF GOVERNMENT – The Hague (Den Haag or, in full, 's-Gravenhage), population 443,456.

Other principal cities ΨRotterdam 571,081; Utrecht, 229,969; Eindhoven, 191,675; Haarlem 151,025; Groningen 168,119; Tilburg 153,812.

CURRENCY – Netherlands guilder or florin of 100 cents.

FLAG – Three horizontal bands of red, white and blue.

NATIONAL ANTHEM – Wilhelmus.

GOVERNMENT

In 1815 the Netherlands became a constitutional Kingdom under King William I, a Prince of Orange-Nassau, a descendant of the house which had taken a leading part in the destiny of the nation since the 16th century.

The States-General consists of the *Eerste Kamer* (First Chamber) of 75 members, elected for four years by the Provincial Council; and the *Tweede Kamer* (Second Chamber) of 150 members, elected for four years by voters of 18 years and upwards. Members of the *Tweede Kamer* are paid. The most recent election to the Second Chamber was held in September 1989, and resulted in the formation of a centre-left coalition.

HEAD OF STATE

Queen of the Netherlands, Her Majesty Queen Beatrix Wilhelmina Armgard, KG, GCVO, *born* 31 Jan. 1938; *succeeded*, 30 April 1980, upon the abdication of her mother Queen Juliana; *married* 10 March 1966, HRH Prince Claus George Willem Otto Frederik Geert of the Netherlands, Jonkheer van Amsberg; and has *issue*, Prince Willem Alexander, *b.* 27 April 1967; Prince Johan Friso, *b.* 25 Sept, 1968; Prince Constantijn Christof, *b.* 11 Oct. 1969.

CABINET as at July 1992

Prime Minister, Minister of General Affairs, Ruud F. M. Lubbers (CDA).
Deputy PM and Minister of Finance, W. Kok (PvdA).
Home Affairs, Mrs C. J. Dales (PvdA).
Foreign Affairs, H. van den Broek (CDA).
Development Co-operation, J. Pronk (PvdA).
Defence, A. L. ter Beek (PvdA).
Economic Affairs, Dr J. E. Andriessen (CDA).
Antillian Affairs and Justice, Prof. E. H. M. Hirsch Ballin (PvdA).
Agriculture and Fisheries, P. Bukman (CDA).
Education and Science, Prof. Dr J. M. M. Ritzen (PvdA).
Social Affairs and Employment, Dr B. de Vries (CDA).
Transport and Public Works, Mrs H. May-Weggen (CDA).
Housing, Physical Planning and Environment, J. G. M. Alders (PvdA).
Welfare, Health and Culture, Mrs H. d'Acona (PvdA).

CDA Christian Democratic Appeal
PvdA Labour Party.

ROYAL NETHERLANDS EMBASSY
38 Hyde Park Gate, London SW7 5DP
Tel 071-584 5040

Ambassador Extraordinary and Plenipotentiary, His Excellency Johan Bernard Hoekman (1990).
Ministers Plenipotentiary, M. H. R. Loudon; A. J. Quanjer.
Counsellors, H. W. de Boer; P. A. Hamoen; G. J. Schulten; R. J. van Vollenhouen.
First Secretaries, O. D. Kervers; P. A. Menkveld.
Defence, Naval and Air Attaché, Capt. W. F. L. van Leeuwen.
Military Attaché, Col. G. C. W. Soetermeer.

BRITISH EMBASSY
Lange Voorhout 10, The Hague, 2514 ED
Tel: The Hague 364 5800

Ambassador Extraordinary and Plenipotentiary, His Excellency Sir Michael Romilly Heald Jenkins, KCMG (1988).
Counsellors, R. P. Flower (*Deputy Head of Mission*); A. D. Sprake (*Commercial/Agriculture*).
Defence and Naval Attaché, Capt. H. W. Rickard, RN.
Military and Air Attaché, Lt.-Col. P. Cook.
First Secretary and Head of Chancery, J. D. Sawyer.

There is a Consulate-General at Amsterdam.

BRITISH COUNCIL REPRESENTATIVE, J. Andrews, Keizersgracht 343, 1016 EH Amsterdam.

NETHERLANDS-BRITISH CHAMBER OF COMMERCE, The Dutch House, 307–308 High Holborn, London WC1V 7LS.

UK OFFICE IN THE HAGUE, Holland Trade House, Bezuidenhoutseweg 181, 2594 AH The Hague.

ECONOMY

The chief agricultural products are potatoes, wheat, rye, barley, sugar beet, cattle, pigs, milk and milk products, cheese, butter, poultry, eggs, beans, peas, vegetables, fruit, flower bulbs, plants and cut flowers and there is an important fishing industry.

Among the principal industries are engineering, both mechanical and electrical, electronics, nuclear energy, petrochemicals and plastics, road vehicles, aircraft and defence equipment, shipbuilding repair, steel, textiles of all types, electrical appliances, metal ware, furniture, paper, cigars, sugar, liqueurs, beer, clothing etc.

Of a total GNP of US$219.6 billion in 1989, industry accounted for around 21 per cent, agriculture for 4 per cent and mining 3 per cent.

Finance

	1989
Budget Revenue	Guilders 147,000m
Budget Expenditure	170,000m

Trade

The Dutch are traditionally a trading nation. Entrepot trade, banking and shipping are of particular importance to the economy. The geographical position of the Netherlands, at the mouths of the Rhine, Meuse and Scheldt, brings a large volume of transit trade to and from the interior of Europe to Dutch ports.

Principal trading partners are Germany and Belgium/Luxembourg. UK supplied 9.2 per cent of Netherlands imports in 1988 and took 7.7 per cent of Netherlands exports.

Excluding the construction industry, the index of industrial production in the Netherlands (1980 = 100) was 109 in 1989. Inflation was 1.3 per cent in 1989.

	1989	1990
Imports	Guilders 221,400m	Guilders 232,000m
Exports	229,400m	234,000m

Trade with UK	1990	1991
Imports from UK	£7,516,576,000	£8,258,475,000
Exports to UK	10,483,576,000	9,969,981,000

DEFENCE

The armed forces are almost entirely committed to NATO. All ground and air units are assigned to the NATO Central Region, and naval forces to the Atlantic and Channel commands. Total armed forces number some 102,000, which includes 45,000 conscripts and 1,700 women. In addition there are 152,000 reservists. There is compulsory military service of 12–15 months.

The Army has a strength of 64,100 (40,500 conscripts) with 913 main battle tanks, 3,200 armoured infantry fighting vehicles and armoured personnel carriers, 824 artillery pieces and 90 armed helicopters. The Navy has a strength of 16,600, including 1,600 naval air arm, 2,800 marines and 1,400 conscripts. It maintains a force of five submarines, four destroyers, 11 frigates with mine warfare, amphibious and support ships, 13 combat aircraft and 22 armed helicopters. The Air Force has a strengh of 16,000 (3,500 conscripts), with some 200 combat aircraft, 180 of which are variants of the US-manufactured F16.

As part of its NATO commitment, the Netherlands maintains 5,700 Army personnel in Germany and is the base for HQ Allied Forces Central Europe, which has 2,750 US personnel.

EDUCATION

Primary and secondary education is given in both denominational and state schools, the denominational schools being eligible for state assistance on equal terms with the state schools. Attendance at primary school is compulsory.

The principal universities are at Leiden, Utrecht, Groningen, Amsterdam (two), Nijmegen and Rotterdam, and there are technical universities at Delft (polytechnic); Eindhoven (polytechnic), Enschede (polytechnic) and Wageningen (agriculture). Illiteracy is practically non-existent.

COMMUNICATIONS

The total extent of navigable rivers including canals, was 4,845 km at 1 Jan. 1985, and of metalled roads 97,189 km. In 1985 the total length of the railway system amounted to 2,867 km, of which 1,810 km were electrified. The mercantile marine in January 1985 consisted of 550 ships of total 3,461,000 gross registered tons. The total length of air routes covered by KLM (Royal Dutch Airlines) in 1985 was 370,640 km.

OVERSEAS TERRITORIES

Aruba

Aruba overs an area of 75 sq. miles (193 sq. km) with a population (1990 UN estimate) of 60,000. The island of Aruba was from 1828 part of the Dutch West Indies and from 1845 part of the Netherlands Antilles. On 1 January 1986 it became a separate territory within the Kingdom of the Netherlands. The 1983 Constitutional Conference agreed that Aruba's separate status would last for ten years from 1986, after which the island would become fully independent.

Governor, F. B. Tromp.

Prime Minister, Nelson Oduber.

Capital – ΨOranjestad (population 20,000); and Sint Nicolaas (17,000).

Currency – Aruban florin.

Economy – The economy of Aruba is based largely on tourism. In 1986 there were over 180,000 tourists.

Trade with UK	1990	1991
Imports from UK	£11,386,000	£18,934,000
Exports to UK	50,000	6,365,000

Netherlands Antilles

The Netherlands Antilles comprise the islands of Curaçao, Bonaire, part of St Martin, St Eustatius, and Saba in the West Indies. The islands cover an area of 308 sq. miles (800 sq. km) with a population (UN 1990 estimate) of 188,000. The Netherlands Antilles (which have a federal parliament) are largely self-governing under the terms of the Realm Statute which took effect on 29 December 1954.

Governor, Dr Jaime Saleh.

Prime Minister, Mrs Maria Liberia Peters.

Capital – ΨWillemstad (on Curaçao) (pop. 50,000).

Currency – Netherlands Antilles guilder of 100 cents.

Economy – The economy of the Netherlands Antilles is based on small manufacturing industries. The soil is too poor to permit large-scale agriculture and most products for consumption, and industrial raw materials must be imported.

Trade with UK	1990*	1991*
Imports from UK	£23,800,000	£18,954,000
Exports to UK	43,552,000	29,049,000

*Curaçao

NEW ZEALAND

AREA AND POPULATION

Islands	*Area (sq. miles)*	*Population at Census March 1991*
North Island	44,281	2,553,400
South Island	58,093	881,500
Other Islands	1,362	
Total	103,736	3,435,000
Territories		
Tokelau	5	1,578
Niue*	100	2,239
Cook Islands*	93	17,185 (a)
Ross Dependency	175,000	

* The Cook Islands have had complete internal self-government since 4 August 1965, as has Niue since 19 October 1974, but Cook Islanders and Niueans remain New Zealand citizens

(a) 1 December 1986

POPULATION BY ETHNIC GROUP

	1986	1991
European	2,612,958	2,514,420*
Maori	294,201	326,325
Chinese	19,206	
Polynesian (other than NZ Maori)	90,612	123,660

* NZ European only.

RELIGIONS

	1981	1986
Church of England	25.7%	24.0%
Presbyterian	16.7	18.0
Roman Catholic	14.3	15.2
Methodist	4.7	4.7
Baptist	1.6	2.1

BIRTHS, DEATHS AND MARRIAGES

	1989	1990
Births	57,438	58,711
Deaths	27,390	26,890
Marriages	22,733	23,341

Infant mortality per 1,000 live births in 1989–90, 10.6.

GEOGRAPHY

New Zealand consists of a number of islands in the South Pacific Ocean, and has also administrative responsibility for the Ross Dependency in Antarctica. The two larger and most important islands, the North and South Islands of New Zealand, are separated by only a relatively narrow strait. The remaining islands are very much smaller and, in general, are widely dispersed over a considerable expanse of ocean. The boundaries, inclusive of the most outlying islands and dependencies, range from 33° to 53° S. latitude, and from 162° E. longitude to 173° W. longitude.

The two principal islands have a total length of 1,040 miles, and a combined area of 102,344 sq. miles (265,069 sq. km). A large proportion of the surface is mountainous in character. The principal range is the Southern Alps, extending over the entire length of the South Island and having its culminating point in Mount Cook (12,349 ft). The North Island mountains include several volcanoes, two of which are active, others being dormant or extinct. Mt Ruapehu (9,175 ft) and Mt Ngauruhoe (7,515 ft) are the most important. Of the numerous glaciers in the South Island, the Tasman (18 miles long by 1¼ wide), the Franz Josef and the Fox are the best known. The North Island is noted for its hot springs and geysers. For the most part the rivers are too short and rapid for navigation. The more important include the Waikato (270 miles in length), Wanganui (180), and Clutha (210). Lakes (Taupo, 234 sq. miles in area; Wakatipu, 113; and Te Anau, 133) are abundant.

New Zealand includes, in addition to North and South Islands:

Chatham Islands, comprising Chatham, Pitt, South East Islands and some rocky islets, in 44° S. lat. and 176° 20′ W. long., have a combined area of 965 sq. km (373 sq. miles). They lie 700 km south-east of Wellington, and are largely uninhabited.

Stewart Island, largely uninhabited, lies 30 km south of South Island and has an area of 1,746 sq. km (674 sq. miles).

The Kermadec Group (population normally 9 or 10) between 29° 10′ to 31° 30′ S. lat., and 177° 45′ to 179° W. long., includes Raoul or Sunday, Macaulay, Curtis Islands, L'Esperance, and some islets. All the inhabitants are government employees at a meteorological station.

Campbell Island, used as a weather station.

The Three Kings (discovered by Tasman on the Feast of the Epiphany), in 34° 9′ S. lat. and 172° 8′ 8″ E. long.

Auckland Islands, about 290 miles south of Bluff Harbour, in 50° 32′ S. lat. and 166° 13′ E. long.

Antipodes Group, 40° 41′ 15″ S. lat. and 178° 43′ E. long.

Bounty Islands, 47° 4′ 43″ S. lat., 170° 0′ 30″ E. long.

Snares Islands and Solander.

All these islands are uninhabited.

CLIMATE – New Zealand has a temperate marine climate, but with abundant sunshine. A very important feature is the small annual range of temperature which permits some growth of vegetation, including pasture, all the year round. Very little snow falls on the low levels even in the South Island. The mean temperature ranges from 15°C in the North to about 9°C in the South. Rainfall over the more settled areas in the North Island ranges from 35 to 70 inches and in the South Island from 25 to 45 inches. The total range is from approximately 13 to over 250 inches.

CAPITAL – ΨWellington, in the North Island. Population (March 1991 census) of Wellington urban area, 325,700. Other large urban areas; ΨAuckland 885,600; ΨChristchurch 307,200; ΨDunedin 109,500; Hamilton 104,100; Ψ Napier-Hastings 107,700.

CURRENCY – New Zealand dollar (NZ$) of 100 cents.

FLAG – Blue ground, with Union Flag in top left quarter, four five-pointed red stars with white borders on the fly. On 20 June 1968, a naval ensign bearing the Southern Cross was adopted, replacing the British white ensign.

NATIONAL ANTHEM – God Save The Queen/God Defend New Zealand.

NATIONAL DAY – 6 February (Waitangi Day).

GOVERNMENT

The discoverers and first colonists of New Zealand were Polynesian people, ancestors of the Maori of today. Whether there was a single colonization, several, or many, is not known but the ninth century is generally considered to be the date of the first settlement. By the 13th or 14th century early exploration was over and there were well established Maori settlements.

The first European to discover New Zealand was a Dutch navigator, Abel Tasman, who sighted the coast on 13 December 1642 but did not land. It was the British explorer

James Cook who circumnavigated New Zealand and landed in 1769. Traders, whalers and sealers made up the majority of Europeans in New Zealand from the end of the 18th century until the late 1830s, when the proportion of permanent European settlers became significant.

Largely as a result of increased British emigration, the country was annexed by the British government in 1840. The British Lieutenant-Governor, William Hobson, RN, proclaimed sovereignty over the North Island by virtue of the Treaty of Waitangi, signed by him and many Maori chiefs, and over the South Island and Stewart Island by right of discovery.

On 3 May 1841 New Zealand was, by letters patent, created a separate colony distinct from New South Wales. Organized colonization on a large scale commenced in 1840 with the New Zealand company's settlement at Wellington. On 26 September 1907 the designation was changed to 'The Dominion of New Zealand'. The constitution rests upon the Constitution Act of 1852, and other Imperial statutes such as the Bill of Rights. A 1986 Constitution Act brought a number of statutory constitutional provisions. The Statute of Westminster was formally adopted by New Zealand in 1947.

The executive authority is entrusted to a Governor-General appointed by the Crown and aided by an Executive Council, within a legislature consisting of one chamber, the House of Representatives.

GOVERNOR-GENERAL

Governor-General and Commander-in-Chief of New Zealand, Her Excellency Dame Catherine Tizard, GCMG, DBE, *sworn in*, November 1990.

THE EXECUTIVE COUNCIL as at July 1992

The Governor-General

Prime Minister, Minister in Charge of the New Zealand Security Intelligence Service, Rt. Hon. J. B. Bolger.
Deputy PM, Minister of External Relations and Trade, Foreign Affairs, Hon. D. C. McKinnon.
Labour, Immigration, State Services, Pacific Island Affairs, Hon. W. F. Birch.
Finance, Hon. Ruth Richardson.
Attorney-General, Hon. Paul East.
Agriculture, Forestry, Hon. John Falloon.
State-Owned Enterprises, Fisheries, Railways, Works and Development, Hon. D. L. Kidd.
Commerce, Hon. Philip Burdon.
Health, the Environment, and Research, Science and Technology, Hon. Simon Upton.
Police, Tourism, Recreation and Sport, Hon. John Banks.
Social Welfare, Women's Affairs, Hon. Jenny Shipley.
Defence, Local Government, Hon. Warren Cooper.
Justice, Disarmament and Arms Control, Arts and Culture, Hon. Douglas Graham.
Education, Hon. Dr Lockwood Smith.
Employment, Hon. Maurice McTigue.
Transport, Statistics, Lands, Hon. Rob Storey.
Maori Affairs, Hon. Douglas Kidd.
Conservation, Science (DSIR), Hon. Denis Marshall.
Housing, Energy, Hon. John Luxton.
Revenue, Customs, Hon. Wyatt Creech.

NEW ZEALAND HIGH COMMISSION
New Zealand House, Haymarket, London SW1Y 4TQ
Tel 071-930 8422

High Commissioner, His Excellency the Hon. George F. Gair (1991).
Deputy High Commissioner, J. P. Larkindale.
Minister, D. Walker (*Commercial*).
Head, Defence Staff, Cdre J. G. Leonard.

BRITISH HIGH COMMISSION
44 Hill Street (PO Box 1812), Wellington 1
Tel: Wellington 4726-049

High Commissioner, His Excellency David Joseph Moss, CMG (1990).
Deputy High Commissioner, I. C. Orr.
Defence Adviser, Gp Capt. D. Angela.
First Secretaries, Mrs E. Blackwell (*Agriculture and Food*); P. Rogan (*Commercial*); J. W. Yapp (*Chancery, Information*).

BRITISH COUNCIL REPRESENTATIVE, D. J. F. King.
BRITISH CHAMBER OF COMMERCE FOR AUSTRALIA AND NEW ZEALAND, PO Box 141, Manuka, ACT 2603, Australia; UK OFFICE, Suite 615, 6th Floor The Linen Hall, 162–168 Regent Street, London W1R 5TB.

LEGISLATURE

House of Representatives consists of 97 members elected for three years. There are four Maori electorates. Women have been entitled to vote since 1893, and to be elected Members of the House of Representatives since the passing of the Women's Parliamentary Rights Act 1919.

Following the General Election of 27 October 1990, the state of the parties in the House of Representatives was National 67, Labour 29 and New Labour 1.
Speaker of the House of Representatives, Hon. Robin Gray.

JUDICATURE

The judicial system comprises a High Court and a Court of Appeal; also District Courts having both civil and criminal jurisdiction.

Chief Justice, Rt. Hon. Sir Thomas Eichelbaum, GBE, PC.
President, Court of Appeal, Rt. Hon. Sir Robin Cooke, KBE.
Judges, Rt. Hon. Sir Ivor Richardson; Rt. Hon. Sir Maurice Casey; Hon. Mr Justice Hardie-Boys; Rt. Hon. Mr Justice Gault; Rt. Hon. Mr Justice McKay.

DEFENCE

The Governor-General, representing the Crown, is Commander-in-Chief of the armed forces. Executive power, however, is vested in the Cabinet. The Chief of Defence Force (CDF) heads the New Zealand Defence Force (NZDF). The Chief of Naval Staff, Chief of General Staff and Chief of Air Staff are directly responsible to the CDF. The Secretary of Defence is the chief executive of the Defence Office, and the CDF and the Secretary of Defence are both directly responsible to the Minister of Defence.

Annual defence expenditure for the year 1989–90 was about 5 per cent of total net government expenditure. In 1991 the total number of armed forces personnel was 11,300.

The Army has a strength of 4,900 personnel, with 26 light tanks, 76 armoured personnel carriers and 44 artillery pieces. The Navy has a strength of 2,500, with four frigates, eight patrol and support craft, and seven armed helicopters. The Air Force has a strength of 3,900 personnel with 41 combat aircraft.

FINANCE

Into the Consolidated Account (New Zealand's main public account) are paid the proceeds of income tax, goods and services tax, customs and excise duties and other taxes, also interest, profits from trading undertakings, and departmental receipts. Revenue from taxation is also paid into the National Roads Fund principally from a tax on motor spirits and registration and licence fees for motor vehicles.

Revenue and expenditure including the National Roads Fund for year ended 31 March:

	1989
Revenue	NZ$25,473.3m
Expenditure (net)	25,460.8m

Taxation receipts in 1989–90 for all purposes amounted to NZ$26,198 million (an average of NZ$7,627 per head of population).

Net expenditure includes:

	1989
Debt services	NZ$1,393m
Education	3,569m
Health	3,639m
Social services	9,123m
Foreign relations	1,679m
Other	6,057.8m
Total	25,460.8m

Banking

The New Zealand financial system comprises a central bank (the Reserve Bank of New Zealand), registered banks and a range of other financial institutions. The number of registered banks is presently 20.

The Reserve Bank is the sole issuer of notes and coin.

EDUCATION

Schools are free and attendance is compulsory between the ages of six and 15. At July 1988 there were 424,400 pupils attending public primary schools, and 12,053 pupils attending registered private primary schools. The secondary education of boys and girls is carried on in 315 state secondary schools, 35 area high schools and 18 registered private secondary schools. The total number of pupils receiving full-time secondary education in July 1988 was 233,603 and in addition there were 124,863 students attending technical classes. Almost all the students attending technical classes are part-time. There are seven universities with a total of 72,313 students in 1988.

ECONOMY

Gross Value of Agricultural Production to year ended March (NZ$ million)

	1986–7	1987–8
Gross output	6,902	7,352
Sheep	646	690
Wool	1,215	1,373
Cattle	974	935
Dairy products	1,130	1,294
Fruit, nuts, oilseeds	531	578
Agricultural services	474	538
Sales of live animals	607	590

Agricultural and Pastoral Production

	1988	1989
*Wheat, metric tons	206,000	135,000
*Wool, metric tons	346,000	341,000
†Butter, metric tons	242,000	246,000
†Cheese, metric tons	128,000	128,000
‡Stock Slaughtered:		
Lambs	30,414,000	30,302,000
Sheep	7,927,000	9,757,000
Cattle	2,222,000	2,289,000
Calves	981,000	876,000
Pigs	782,000	781,000

*Year ended 30 June
†Year ended 31 May
‡Year ended 30 September

Livestock – Livestock on farms at 30 June 1989 included 3,302,377 dairy cattle, 4,526,056 beef cattle and 411,334 pigs. Sheep numbered 60,568,653.

Forestry – The output of sawn timber for 1989 was 1,877,000 cubic metres, of which 1,802,000 cubic metres represented exotic varieties, mainly radiata pine.

Minerals – Non-metallic minerals such as coal, clay, limestone and dolomite are both economically and industrially more important than metallic ones. Coal output in 1988 was 2,400,000 tonnes (provisional). Of the metals, the most important is ironsand. Natural gas deposits in Taranaki are being used for electricity generation and as a premium fuel, piped to all the major North Island centres.

Trade

	1988–9	1989–90
Imports (v.f.d.)	NZ$11,401.7m	NZ$14,420m
Exports (f.o.b.)	14,905.4m	14,589m

New Zealand produce exported to the UK in the 12 months ending June 1989 included butter and cheese, valued at NZ$292,702,000; wool NZ$133,280,000; lamb NZ$272,262,000; hides, skins and leather NZ$55,224,000.

Trade with UK	1990	1991
Imports from UK	£439,608,000	£260,052,000
Exports to UK	483,615,000	391,643,000

COMMUNICATIONS

Railways – The national railway system is owned and operated by the New Zealand Railways Corporation. In March 1989, there were 4,776 route km of government railway in operation.

Motor Vehicles – At 31 March 1990 there were 2,300,231 licensed motor vehicles.

Shipping – During 1989 the vessels entered from overseas ports numbered 3,741 (gross tonnage 30,940,000) and those cleared for overseas 3,730 (gross tonnage 30,190,000).

Civil Aviation – Domestic flights in 1988 carried 4,125,000 passengers and 39,300 tonnes of freight. International flights carried 3,340,000 passengers, 127,981 tonnes of freight and 4,529 tonnes of mail.

TERRITORIES

Tokelau (or Union Islands)

Tokelau is a group of atolls, Fakaofo, Nukunonu and Atafu (population 1,578 at November 1991), which was proclaimed part of New Zealand as from 1 January 1948.

The Ross Dependency

The Ross Dependency, placed under the jurisdiction of New Zealand by Order in Council dated 30 July 1923, is defined as all the Antarctic islands and territories between 160° E. and 150° W. longitude which are situated south of the 60° S. parallel. The Ross Dependency includes Edward VII Land and portions of Victoria Land. Since 1957 a number of research stations have been established in the Dependency.

ASSOCIATED STATES

Cook Islands

Included in the boundaries of New Zealand since June 1901, the Cook Islands group consists of the islands of Rarotonga, Aitutaki, Mangaia, Atiu, Mauke, Mitiaro, Manuae, Takutea, Palmerston, Penrhyn or Tongareva, Manihiki, Rakahanga, Suwarrow, Pukapuka or Danger, and Nassau. The total population of the group was 17,185 at 1 December 1986.

The chief industries of the Cook Islands are tourism, financial services and the production of fruit juice, clothing, copra, bananas, citrus fruit and pulp, and pearl shell. The trade is chiefly with New Zealand, Australia, Japan, the UK and the USA. The New Zealand Government continues to give financial aid to the Cook Islands.

The Queen has a representative on the islands, as does the New Zealand government. Since 4 August 1965, the islands have enjoyed complete internal self-government, executive power being in the hands of a Cabinet consisting of the Premier and five other ministers. The Constitution Act came into force after it had been endorsed by the 22-member Legislative Assembly of the Cook Islands, elected in April 1965.

The New Zealand citizenship of the Cook Islanders is embodied in the Constitution, and assurances have been given that the changed status of the islands will in no way affect the consideration of subsidies or the right of free entry into New Zealand for exports from the group.

HM Representative, Apenera Short, OBE.
New Zealand Representative, T. Caughley.

NIUE

The population of Niue was 2,239 at the November 1991 Census.

A New Zealand Representative is stationed at Niue, which since October 1974 has been self-governing in free association with New Zealand. New Zealand is responsible for external affairs and defence, and continues to give financial aid. Executive power is in the hands of a Premier and a Cabinet of three drawn from the Assembly of 20 members. The Assembly is the supreme lawmaking body.

New Zealand Representative, K. Meyer.

NICARAGUA
República de Nicaragua

Nicaragua is the largest state of Central America, with a long seaboard on both the Atlantic and Pacific Oceans, situated between 10° 45′ and 15° N. lat. and 83° 40′ and 87° 38′ W. long., containing an area of 50,193 sq. miles (130,000 sq. km).

POPULATION – It has a population (UN estimate 1990) of 3,871,000 of whom about three-quarters are of mixed blood. Another 15 per cent are white, mostly of pure Spanish descent, and the remaining 10 per cent are West Indians or Indians. The latter group includes the Misquitos, who live on the Atlantic coast and were formerly under British protection.

CAPITAL – Managua, population 615,000. Other centres are León, 158,577; Granada, 72,640; Masaya, 78,308; Chinandega, 144,291.

CURRENCY – Córdoba (C$) of 100 centavos.

FLAG – Horizontal stripes of blue, white and blue, with the Nicaraguan coat of arms in the centre of the white stripe.

NATIONAL DAY – 15 September.

NATIONAL ANTHEM – Salve A Ti Nicaragua (Hail, Nicaragua).

HISTORY

The eastern coast of Nicaragua was touched by Columbus in 1502, and in 1518 was overrun by Spanish forces under Davila, and formed part of the Spanish Captaincy-General of Guatemala until 1821, when its independence was secured. In 1927 Augusto Cesar Sandino began a guerrilla war against the occupation of Nicaragua by US Marines, which continued until they were expelled in 1933. Sandino was assassinated by Anastasio Somoza, director of the National Guard, and in 1936 Somoza assumed the Presidency. He was succeeded in power by his sons Luis and Anastasio Somoza, until 1979 when the family and the National Guard were overthrown by guerrillas of the Sandinista National Liberation Front. A Junta of National Reconstruction subsequently took power. Elections for President, Vice-President and a National Assembly were held in November 1984, and in January 1985 they replaced the Junta and the Council of State.

GOVERNMENT

After ten years in power, the Sandinistas lost their parliamentary majority in elections held in February 1990. A coalition of former opposition parties, Unión Nacional de Opositora (UNO) now holds the majority.

HEAD OF STATE
President, Minister of Defence, Violeta Barrios de Chamorro, *inaugurated* 25 April 1990.
Vice-President, Virgilio Godoy.

COUNCIL OF MINISTERS as at July 1992
Minister to the Presidency, Antonio Lacayo.
External Relations, Ernesto Leal.
Interior, Carlos Hurtado.
Finance, Emilio Pereira.
Foreign Co-operation, Erwin Krugger.
Construction and Transport, Jaime Icalbalceta Mayorga.
Health, Ernesto Salmerón.
Agriculture, Roberto Rondón Sacasa.
Labour, Francisco Rosales.
Economy and Planning, Julio Cardenas.
Education, Humberto Belli Pereira.

EMBASSY OF NICARAGUA
8 Gloucester Road, London SW7 4PP
Tel 071-584 4365

Ambassador Extraordinary and Plenipotentiary, His Excellency Fernando Zelaya Rojas (1992).

BRITISH EMBASSY
PO Box A-169, El Reparto 'Los Robles', Primera Etapa, Entrada Principal de la Carretera a Masaya, Managua, Nicaragua.
Tel: Managua 70034

British Ambassador and Consul-General, His Excellency R. H. Brown (1992).

ECONOMY

The country is mainly agricultural. The major crops are cotton, coffee (30 per cent of total export earnings), sugar cane, tobacco, sesame and bananas. Beans, rice, maize and ipecacuanha, livestock and timber production are also important. However, fishing, forestry, grain and cattle production have been hit by the civil war in the main growing areas. Nicaragua possesses deposits of gold and silver.

TRADE

Considerable quantities of foodstuffs are imported as well as cotton goods, jute, iron and steel, machinery and petroleum products. The chief exports are cotton, coffee, beef, gold, sugar, cottonseed and bananas.

Trade with UK	1990	1991
Imports from UK	£6,515,000	£8,029,000
Exports to UK	1,899,000	492,000

COMMUNICATIONS

There are 252 miles of railway, all on the Pacific side of the country, and approximately 5,500 miles of telegraph. There are 51 radio stations and two television stations in Managua. An automatic telephone system has been installed in the capital and extended to all major cities. A ground station for satellite communication was inaugurated in 1973.

Transport, except on the Pacific slope, is still attended with difficulty but many new roads have either been opened or are under construction. The Inter-American Highway runs from the Honduras frontier in the north to the Costa Rican border in the south; the inter-oceanic highway runs from the Corinto on the Pacific coast via Managua to Rama, where there is a natural waterway to Bluefields on the Atlantic. The country's main airport is at Managua. The chief port is Corinto on the Pacific.

CULTURE

The official language of the country is Spanish and the majority profess Catholicism, although the English language and the Moravian Church are widespread on the Atlantic coast. There are three daily newspapers published at Managua, apart from the official Gazette (*La Gaceta*). A national literacy campaign in 1980 has reduced illiteracy to 12 per cent. There are universities at León and Managua.

NIGER
République du Niger

Situated in west central Africa, between 12° and 24° N. and 0° and 16° E., Niger has common boundaries with Algeria and Libya in the north, Chad, Nigeria, Benin, Mali and Burkina. It has an area of about 489,191 sq. miles (1,267,000 sq. km). Apart from a small region along the Niger Valley in the south-west near the capital the country is entirely savanna or desert.

POPULATION – The population (UN estimate 1990) is 7,731,000. The main ethnic groups are the Hausa (54 per cent) in the south, the Songhai and Djerma in the south-west, the Fulani, the Beriberi–Manga, and the nomadic Tuareg in the north. The official language is French.

CAPITAL – Niamey, population 410,000.
CURRENCY – Franc CFA of 100 centimes.
FLAG – Three horizontal stripes, orange, white and green with an orange disc in the middle of the white stripe.
NATIONAL DAY – 18 December.

GOVERNMENT

The first French expedition arrived in 1891 and the country was fully occupied by 1914. It decided on 18 December 1958 to remain an autonomous republic within the French Community; full independence outside the Community was proclaimed on 3 August 1960.

The constitution of Niger, adopted on 8 November 1960, provided for a presidential system of government, modelled on that of the United States and the French Fifth Republic, and a single Chamber National Assembly. In April 1974 Lt.-Col. Seyni Kountché seized power, suspended the Constitution, dissolved the National Assembly, and suppressed all political organizations. He then set up a Supreme Military Council with himself as President. President Kountché died on 10 November 1987 and was succeeded peacefully by his cousin, Col. Ali Saibou, who restored a measure of normal political life.

In August 1991, a national conference of all groups voted to suspend the constitution and stripped President Saibou of all powers; he remains nominal head of state. The national conference announced a transitional period to democracy, to last until 31 January 1993, by which time multiparty elections are to be held. On 26 October 1991 it appointed Amadou Cheiffou Prime Minister of a transitional government, and on 3 November 1991 formed a 15-member High Council of the republic to act as the interim legislative body.

HEAD OF STATE
President, Brig.-Gen. Ali Saibou.

MINISTERS as at June 1992
Prime Minister, Minister of National Defence, Amadou Chieffou.
National Education and Research, Albert Wright.
Interior, Daouda Rabiou.
Foreign Affairs and Co-operation, Hassane Hamidou.
Justice, Abdou Tiousso.
Economy and Finance, Laoual Chaffani.
Agriculture and Animal Breeding, Boukar Abba Malam.
Water Resources and Environment, Hassane Abdou.
Mines, Energy, Industry and Cottage Industry, Mahamadou Ouhoumoudou.
Public Health, Souleymane Saidou.
Social Development, Population and Women's Promotion, Aissata Bagna.
Communications, Culture, Youth and Sports, Adam El Back.
Equipment and Territorial Development, Laouali Baraou.
Civil Service and Labour, Mariama Banakoye.

EMBASSY OF THE REPUBLIC OF NIGER
154 rue de Longchamp, 75116, Paris
Tel: Paris 45048060

Ambassador Extraordinary and Plenipotentiary, His Excellency Sandi Yacouba (1990).

British Ambassador (resident in Abidjan, Côte d'Ivoire).

ECONOMY

The cultivation of ground-nuts and the production of livestock are the main industries and provide two of the main exports. A company formed by the Government, the French Atomic Energy Authority and private interests is exploiting uranium deposits at Arlit, and this is the main export. There is also some oil exploration.

FINANCE – The 1989 General Budget allocation was CFA 220,100 million.

TRADE WITH UK

	1990	1991
Imports from UK	£10,780,000	£10,838,000
Exports to UK	1,161,000	382,000

NIGERIA
Federal Republic of Nigeria

AREA, ETC – The Republic of Nigeria is situated on the west coast of Africa. It is bounded on the south by the Gulf of Guinea, on the west by Benin, on the north by Niger and on the east by Cameroon. It has an area of 356,669 sq. miles (923,768 sq. km). A belt of mangrove swamp forest 10–60 miles in width lies along the entire coastline. North of this there is a zone 50–100 miles wide of tropical rain forest and oil-palms. North of the rain forest, the country rises and the vegetation changes to open woodland and savanna. In the

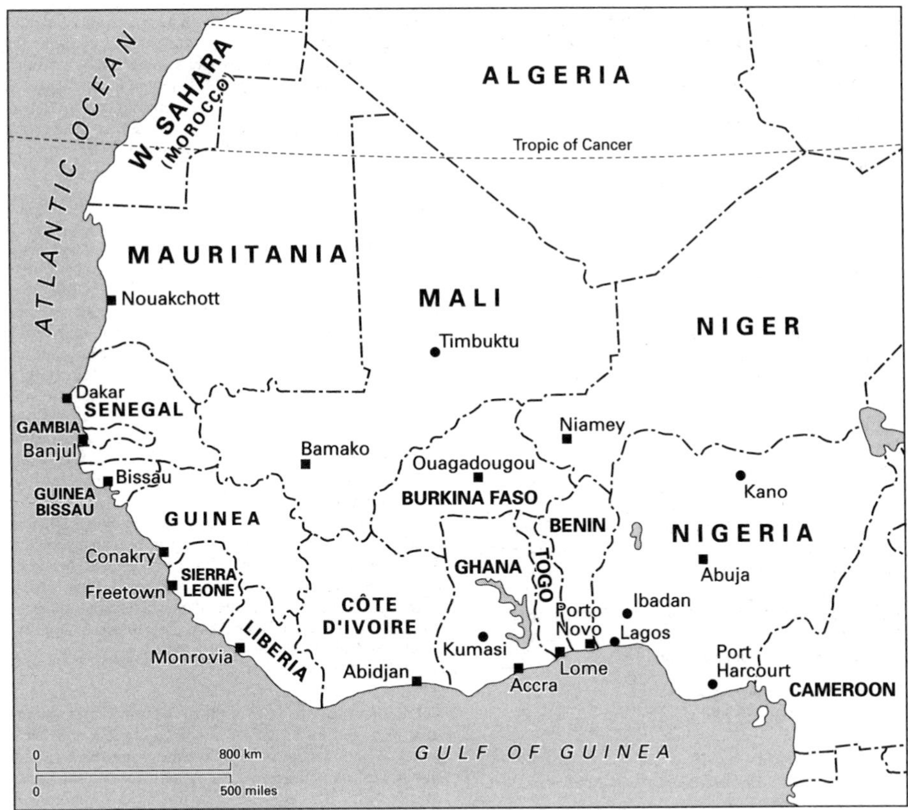

extreme north the country is semi-desert. There are few mountains, but in northern Nigeria the central plateau rises to an average level of 4,000 feet. The Niger, Benue, and Cross are the main rivers.

CLIMATE – The climate varies with the types of country described above, but Nigeria lies entirely within the tropics and temperatures are high. The rainy season is from about April to October; rainfall varies from under 25 inches a year in the extreme north to 172 inches on the coast line. During the dry season the *harmattan* wind blows from the desert; it is cool and laden with fine particles of dust.

POPULATION – The population (UN estimate 1990) is 108,542,000. The population is almost entirely African. The main ethnic groups are Hausa/Fulani, Yoruba and Ibo, and the principal languages are English, Hausa, Yoruba and Ibo.

RELIGIONS – Over half the population are Muslim, these being concentrated in the north and west. In the southern areas in particular there are many Christians.

CAPITAL – ΨAbuja, estimated population, 378,671. Other important towns are the former capital Lagos, Ibadan, Kaduna, Kano, Benin City, Enugu and ΨPort Harcourt.

CURRENCY – Naira (N) of 100 kobo.

FLAG – Three equal vertical bands, green, white and green.

NATIONAL ANTHEM – Arise, O Compatriots.

NATIONAL DAY – 1 October (Republic Day).

GOVERNMENT

The Federation of Nigeria attained independence as a member of the Commonwealth on 1 October 1960 and became a republic in 1963. On 15 January 1966 the military took power, suspended the constitution and dissolved the legislature. In 1979 civil rule was restored under a new constitution similar to that of the United States after elections at national and state level.

After similar elections in 1983 the new administration was removed by the military on 31 December, this regime itself being overthrown in August 1985. A 28-member Armed Forces Ruling Council (AFRC) was sworn in on 30 August; it currently has 19 members. It is the country's most senior decision-making body. The Council of Ministers is the third most senior body after the AFRC and the National Council of States, which comprises the 30 State Governors.

On 3 May 1989 Gen. Babangida promulgated the new draft constitution paving the way for a return to civilian rule by 1992. He also announced that a ban on political parties was to be lifted, leading to the formation in October 1989 of two new parties, the Social Democratic Party and the National Republican Convention. State governorship and assembly elections were held in all 30 states in December 1991, with the National Republican Convention winning 16 state governorship elections and gaining control of 13 state assemblies. The Social Democratic Party won 13 governorships and gained control of 16 state assemblies.

Federal elections to the National Assembly were held on 4 July 1992 and won by the Social Democratic Party, which gained majorities in both the House of Representatives and the Senate. A President is due to be elected in December, with Gen. Babangida and the military handing over power on 2 January 1993.

President, Commander-in-Chief of the Armed Forces, Chairman of the Armed Forces Ruling Council, Gen. Ibrahim Babangida.
Vice-President, Adm. Augustus Aikhomu.

COUNCIL OF MINISTERS as at June 1992

Agriculture, Water Resources and Rural Development, Alhaji A. Hashidu.
Commerce and Tourism, Air Vice-Marshal M. Yahaya (retd).
Defence, Gen. S. Abacha.
Education and Youth Development, Prof. Aliu Fafunwa.
Labour and Productivity, Alhaji Bunu Sherif Musa.
Petroleum and Mineral Resources, Dr Chu Okongwu.
Foreign Affairs, Maj.-Gen. Ike Nwachukwu (retd).
Minister of State for Foreign Affairs, Ambassador Z. Ibrahim.
Health and Human Services, Prof. O. Ransome-Kuti.
Internal Affairs, Dr T. Olagunju.
Industry and Technology, Maj.-Gen. Bagudu Mamman (retd).
Information and Culture, Prof. Sam Ogoubaire.
Justice, Clement Akpamgbo.
Finance, Alhaji Ahmed Abubakar.
Power and Steel, Air Vice-Marshal Nura Imam (retd).
Transport and Communications, Olawale Ige.
Federal Capital Territory, Maj.-Gen. Gado Nasko (retd).
Works and Housing, Maj.-Gen. Mamman Kontagora (retd).
Establishment and Management Services, Chief Gabriel Chiekelu.
Special Duties and National Planning Commission, Senas Ukpanah.
Police Affairs, Alhaji Ismaila Gwarzo.

NIGERIA HIGH COMMISSION
9 Northumberland Avenue,
London WC2 5BX
Tel 071-839 1244

High Commissioner, His Excellency Alhaji Abubakar Alhaji (1992).

BRITISH HIGH COMMISSION
11 Eleke Crescent, Victoria Island, Lagos
Tel: Lagos 619531

High Commissioner, His Excellency Christopher Macrae, CMG (1991).

BRITISH COUNCIL REPRESENTATIVE, P. MacKenzie-Smith, 11 Kingsway Road, Ikoyi (PO Box 3702), Lagos. Branch offices at *Enugu, Kaduna* and *Kano City*.

THE FEDERATION

Originally regional in structure, the Federation was divided into 12 states in 1967. It was divided again into 19 states in 1976, and a further two states were created in 1987. In 1989–90 the Federation was restructured into 30 states and on 12 December 1991 Abuja was declared the federal capital and a separate Federal Capital Territory created.

EDUCATION

A programme was introduced in September 1976 intended to achieve universal primary education. Numbers of pupils in 1982–3 were: 15.4 million in primary schools, 3.5 million in secondary schools, 53,766 in polytechnics and 88,636 in universities. There are 24 universities.

COMMUNICATIONS

The Nigerian railway system, which is controlled by the Nigerian Railway Corporation, is the most extensive in West Africa. There are 2,178 route miles of lines. The principal international airlines operate from Lagos, Kano and Port Harcourt. A network of internal air services connects the main centres. The principal seaports are served by a number of shipping lines, including the Nigerian National Line. A nationwide television and radio network is being developed, with each state eventually having its own television and radio station. There is a network of meteorological reporting stations.

ECONOMY

Nigeria was a predominantly agricultural country until the early 1970s with agriculture contributing over 60 per cent of export revenue and 45 per cent of GNP. Tin and calumbite mining on the Jos plateau, textiles and coal mining were also important. The major exports were ground nuts, palm products, tin, cocoa, rubber and timber. Recently oil has provided over 90 per cent of exports revenue and agricultural exports have greatly declined. Though agriculture still employs half the labour force it contributes only 20 per cent of GNP, exceeded by trading and oil. The construction sector is twice as large as the manufacturing sector and industries dependent on imported raw materials such as vehicle assembly have faltered recently.

Three oil refineries are in operation at Port Harcourt, Warri and Kaduna. A steel plant has been opened near Warri and a larger one is being completed at Ajaokuta. Other projects include natural gas liquifaction, petro-chemicals, fertilizers and several power stations plus the Abuja Federal Capital. Several large irrigation schemes have been completed and more are planned.

TRADE

Oil revenues have fallen over the decade since 1981 and are now restricted by an OPEC production quota and lower prices to half their peak level. Austerity measures such as import curbs and payments restrictions were introduced in March 1982. The present Government is attempting to stimulate greater self-reliance in the economy by encouraging non-oil exports and the use of local rather than imported raw materials.

Trade with UK	1990	1991
Imports from UK	£499,838,000	£544,533,000
Exports to UK	297,436,000	249,254,000

NORWAY
Kongeriket Norge

AREA AND POPULATION – Norway is a kingdom in the northern and western part of the Scandinavian peninsula, and was founded in AD 872. It is 1,752 km in length, its greatest width about 430 km. The length of the coastline is 2,650 km, and the frontier between Norway and the neighbouring countries is 2,542 km (Sweden 1,619 km, Finland 727 km and Russia 196 km). It is divided into 19 counties (*fylker*) and comprises an area of 149,282 sq. miles (386,638 sq. km), of which Svalbard and Jan Mayen have a combined area of 63,080 sq. km, with a total population (1990 UN estimate) of 4,242,000.

The Norwegian coastline is extensive, deeply indented with numerous fjords, and fringed with an immense number of rocky islands. The surface is mountainous, consisting of elevated and barren tablelands, separated by deep and narrow valleys. At the North Cape the sun does not appear to set from the second week in May to the last week in July, causing the phenomenon known as the Midnight Sun;

conversely, there is no apparent sunrise from about 18 November to 23 January. During the long winter nights are seen the multiple coloured Northern Lights or Aurora Borealis, which have a maximum intensity in a line crossing North America from Alaska to Labrador and Northern Europe to the Arctic coast and Siberia.

LANGUAGE AND LITERATURE – Old Norse literature is among the most ancient and richest in Europe. Norwegian in both its present forms is closely related to other Scandinavian languages. Independence from Denmark (1814) and resurgent nationalism led to the development of 'new Norwegian' based on dialects, which now has equal official standing with 'bokmål', in which Danish influence is more obvious. This was formed in the time of the Reformation, and Ludvig Holberg (1684–1754) is regarded as the father of Norwegian literature, though the modern period begins with the patriotic and romantic writings of Henrik Wergeland (1808–45). Some of the famous names are Henrik Ibsen (1828–1906), Bjørnstjerne Bjørnson (1832–1910), Nobel Prizewinner in 1903, and the novelists Jonas Lie (1833–1908), Alexander Kielland (1849–1906), Knut Hamsun (1859–1952) and Sigrid Undset (1882–1949), the latter two also Nobel Prizewinners. In 1990 there were 155 daily newspapers.

CAPITAL – ΨOslo (including Aker), population (Jan. 1987) 450,808. Other towns are ΨTrondheim 135,542; ΨBergen 209,912; ΨStavanger 96,316; ΨKristiansand 63,637; ΨDrammen 51,807; ΨTromsø 49,358.

CURRENCY – Krone of 100 øre.

FLAG – Red, with white-bordered blue cross.

NATIONAL ANTHEM – Ja, Vi Elsker Dette Landet (Yes, we love this country).

NATIONAL DAY – 17 May (Constitution Day).

GOVERNMENT

From 1397 to 1814 Norway was united with Denmark, and from 4 November 1814 with Sweden, under a personal union which was dissolved on 7 June 1905, when Norway regained complete independence.

Under the constitution of 17 May 1814, the *Storting* (Parliament) itself elects one-quarter of its members to constitute the *Lagting* (Upper Chamber), the other three-quarters forming the *Odelsting* (Lower Chamber). Legislative questions alone are dealt with by both parts in separate sittings.

A minority Labour government replaced the previous three-party, centre-right coalition government, which collapsed in October 1990 because of a dispute over whether to apply for membership of the European Community.

HEAD OF STATE

King, HM Harald V, GCVO, *born* 21 Feb. 1937; *succeeded*, 17 Jan. 1991, on death of his father King Olav V; *married* 29 Aug. 1968, Sonja Haraldsen, and has *issue*, Prince Haakon Magnus (*see below*), and Princess Martha Louise, *born* 22 Sept. 1971.

Heir-Apparent, HRH Crown Prince Haakon Magnus, *born* 20 July 1973.

CABINET as at June 1992

Prime Minister, Gro Harlem Brundtland.
Foreign Affairs, Thorvald Stoltenberg.
Petroleum and Energy, Finn Kristensen.
Defence, Johan Jørgen Holst.
Local Government, Kjell Borgen.
Labour and Government Administration, Tove Strand Gerhardsen.
Agriculture, Gunhild Øyangen.
Justice, Kari Gjesteby.
Fisheries, Oddrunn Pettersen.
Industry, Ole Knapp.
Environment, Thorbjørn Berntsen.
Transport and Communications, Kjell Opseth.
Health and Social Affairs, Tove Veierød.
Church, Education and Research, Gudmund Hernes.
Trade and Shipping, Björn Tore Godal.
Family and Consumer Affairs, Grete Berget.
Cultural Affairs, Åse Kleveland.
Finance, Sigbjørn Johnsen.
Development Co-operation, Grete Faremo.

ROYAL NORWEGIAN EMBASSY
25 Belgrave Square, London SW1X 8QD
Tel: 071–235 7151

Ambassador Extraordinary and Plenipotentiary, His Excellency Kjell Eliassen, GCMG (1989).
Minister, Jon Bech.
Counsellors, Paul Moe (*Press and Cultural*); Marius Hauge (*Fisheries*); Harald Tørum (*Economic*); Viggo Smestad (*Commercial*).
First Secretaries, J. A. Knutsen (*Political*); W. Kirkebye (*Consul*); B. Mogard.

BRITISH EMBASSY
Thomas Heftyesgate 8, 0244 Oslo 2
Tel: Oslo 55 24 00

Ambassador Extraordinary and Plenipotentiary, His Excellency David John Edward Ratford, CMG, CVO (1990).
Counsellor, A. J. K. Bailes (*Deputy Head of Mission and Consul General*)
First Secretaries, E. R. M. Davies; S. M. Williams (*Economic and Commercial*); R. H. Tonkin (*Management*); G. M. Walton.
Defence and Air Attaché, Wg Cdr. J. C. W. Marshall.
Naval Attaché, Cdr. G. S. Pearson.
Military Attaché, Lt.-Col. G. Dodgson.

BRITISH CONSULAR OFFICES – There is a British Consular Office at *Oslo* and Honorary Consulates at *Bergen, Tromsø, Alesund, Kristiansund* (North), *Stavanger, Trondheim, Kristiansand* (South), *Haugesund* and *Harstad*.

BRITISH COUNCIL REPRESENTATIVE – D. N. Constable, Fridtjof Nansens Plass 5,0160, Oslo 1.

DEFENCE

Norway is a member of the North Atlantic Treaty Organization, and the headquarters of Allied Forces Northern Europe is situated near Oslo. The period of compulsory national service is 15 months (without refresher training) in the Navy and Air Force, and 12 months (with refresher training) in the Army.

The total active armed forces number some 32,700 (22,800 conscripts), Reserve forces number some 285,000, mobilizable in 24–72 hours. The Army has a strength of 15,900 (13,000 conscripts), with 210 main battle tanks, 200 armoured infantry fighting vehicles and armoured personnel carriers, and 527 artillery pieces. The Navy has a strength of 7,300, including 4,500 conscripts, with 11 submarines, five frigates, and 35 patrol and coastal combatants. The Air Force has a strength of 9,500 (5,300 conscripts), with 85 combat aircraft, mainly US manufactured F16s.

EDUCATION

Education from seven to 16 is free and compulsory in the 'basic schools' maintained by the municipalities with state grants-in-aid. The majority of the pupils receive post-compulsory schooling at 'upper secondary' schools, colleges of education (19), regional colleges akin to polytechnics (12), universities (four) and other university-level specialist institutions.

COMMUNICATIONS

The total length of railways open at the end of 1988 was 4,168 km, excluding private lines. There are 86,838 km of public roads in Norway (including urban streets). At the end of 1988, 2,893,639 road motor vehicles were registered.

Scheduled internal air services are operated by Scandinavian Airlines System (SAS) on behalf of Det Norske Luftfartselskap (DNL), by Braathens South American and Far East Airtransport (SAFE), and by Wideróes Flyveselskap AS.

The Mercantile Marine in 1988 consisted of 1,532 vessels of 12,921,932 gross tons (vessels above 100 gross tons, excluding fishing boats, floating whaling factories, tugs, salvage vessels, icebreakers and similar types of vessel).

ECONOMY

The cultivated area is about 8,636 sq. km, 2.3 per cent of total surface area. Forests cover nearly 25 per cent; the rest consists of highland pastures or uninhabitable mountains.

The Gulf Stream pours from 140 to 170 million cubic feet of warm water per second into the sea around Norway and causes the temperature to be higher than the average for the latitude. It brings shoals of herring and cod into the fishing grounds and causes a warm current of air over the west coast, making it possible to cultivate potatoes and barley in latitudes which in other countries are perpetually frozen. In normal years the quantity of fish caught by Norwegian fishing vessels is greater than that of any other European country except Russia. In 1988 the total catch amounted to 1,750,000 tonnes.

The chief industries are manufactures, agriculture and forestry, fisheries, mining, production of metals and ferro-alloys, and shipping. Also in recent years industries providing both manufactured products and services for the development of North Sea oil and gas resources have assumed growing importance. In 1988, the total workforce was 2,183,000 of which 324,000 persons were employed in Norwegian industry. Manufactures are aided by great resources of hydro-electric power. Actual production in 1988 amounted to 110,063 Gwh.

FINANCE

	1990
Total Revenue	K298,205,000
Total Expenditure	332,217,000

TRADE

The chief imports are raw materials, motor vehicles, chemicals, motor spirit, fuel and other oils; coal, ships and machinery; together with manufactures of silk, cotton and wool. The exports consist chiefly of crude oil and gas, manufactured goods, fish and products of fish (as canned fish, whale oils), pulp, paper, iron ore and pyrites, nitrate of lime, stone, calcium carbide, aluminium, ferro-alloys, zinc, nickel, cyanamides, etc.

	1987	1988
Total imports	K211,794m	K217,455m
Total exports	199,731m	213,117m

Trade with UK	1990	1991
Imports from UK	£1,289,789,000	£1,357,299,000
Exports to UK	4,235,348,000	4,232,827,000

TERRITORIES

SVALBARD

The Svalbard Archipelago lies between 74° and 81° N. lat. and between 10° and 35° E. long., with an estimated area of 24,295 square miles. The archipelago consists of a main island, known as Spitsbergen (15,200 sq. miles); North East Land, closely adjoining and separated by Hinlopen Strait; the Wiche Islands, separated from the mainland by Olga Strait; Barents and Edge Islands, separated from the mainland by Stor Fjord (or Wybe Jansz Water); Prince Charles Foreland, to the west; Hope Island, to the south-east; Bear Island (68 square miles) 127 miles to the south; with many similar islands in the neighbourhood of the main group.

South Cape is 355 miles from the Norwegian coast. Ice Fjord is 520 miles from Tromsø, 650 miles from Murmansk, and 1,300 miles from Aberdeen. Transit from Tromsø to Green Harbour takes two to three days; from Aberdeen five to six days.

By Treaty (9 Feb. 1920) the sovereignty of Norway over the Spitsbergen (Pointed Mountain) Archipelago was recognized by other nations, and on 14 August 1925 Norway assumed sovereignty. In September 1941 Allied forces (British, Canadian and Norwegian) landed on the main island. After destruction of the accumulated stocks of coal and dismantling of mining machinery and the wireless installation, the Norwegian inhabitants (about 600) were evacuated to a British port and the Russians (about 1,500) to the USSR. After the war the Norwegian mining plants were rebuilt. In addition to those engaged in coal-mining, the archipelago is also visited by hunters for seals, foxes and polar bears.

JAN MAYEN ISLAND

Jan Mayen, an island in the Arctic Ocean (70° 49′ to 71° 9′ N. lat. and 7° 53′ to 9° 5′ W. long.) was joined to Norway by law of 27 February 1930.

NORWEGIAN ANTARCTIC TERRITORIES

BOUVET ISLAND (54° 26′ S. lat. and 3° 24′ E. long.) was declared a dependency of Norway by law of 27 Feb. 1930.

PETER THE FIRST ISLAND (68° 48′ S. lat. and 90° 35′ W. long.), was declared a dependency of Norway by resolution of government, 1 May 1931.

PRINCESS RAGNHILD LAND (from 70° 30′ to 68° 40′ S. lat. and 24° 15′ to 33° 30′ E. long.) has been claimed as Norwegian since 17 February 1931.

QUEEN MAUD LAND – On 14 January 1939 the Norwegian Government declared the area between 20° W. and 45° E., adjacent to Australian Antarctica, to be Norwegian territory.

OMAN

The Sultanate of Oman

The independent Sultanate of Oman lies at the eastern corner of the Arabian peninsula. Its seaboard is nearly 1,000 miles long and extends from near Tibat on the west coast of the Musandam peninsula round to Ras Darbat Ali, with the exception of the stretch between Dibba and Kalba on the east coast which belongs to Sharjah and Fujairah of the United Arab Emirates. Ras Darbat Ali marks the boundary between the Sultanate and the southern border of the Republic of Yemen. The Sultanate extends inland to the borders of the Rub al Khali, or Empty Quarter of the Arabian Desert. The area of Oman has been estimated at 82,030 sq. miles (212,457 sq. km).

Physically the north and the south of Oman are divided by a large tract of desert. Northern Oman has three main sections. The Batinah, the coastal plain, varies in width from 30 miles in the neighbourhood of Suwaiq to almost nothing at Muscat where the mountains descend abruptly to the sea. The plain is fertile, with date gardens extending over its full length of 150 miles. The Hajjar is a mountain spine running from north-west to south-east, reaching nearly 10,000 feet in height on Jabal Akhdar. For the most part the mountains are barren, but numerous valleys penetrate the central massif of Jabal Akhdar and in these there is considerable cultivation irrigated by wells or a system of underground canals called *falajs* which tap the water table. The two plateaus leading from the western slopes of the mountains, the Dhahirah in the north and the Sharqia in the south-east, also have centres of settlements and cultivation. They fall from an average height of 1,000 feet into the sands of the Empty Quarter. The north is separated from the south by nearly 400 miles of inhospitable country crossed by one trunk road, the only land link. Dhofar, the southern province, is the only part of the Arabian peninsula to be touched by the south-west monsoon. Temperatures are more moderate than in the north and sugar cane and coconuts are grown on the coastal plain, while cattle are bred on the mountains.

POPULATION – The population (UN estimate 1990) is 1,502,000. The inhabitants of the north are for the most part Arab but there are large communities of Hindus, Khojas and Baluch, in addition to Omanis of Zanzibari origin. In Dhofar there is also a large proportion of Omanis of Zanzibari origin around Salalah, but in the mountains the inhabitants are either of pure Arab descent or belong to tribes of pre-Arab origin, the Qarra and Mahra, who speak their own dialects of semitic origin.

CAPITAL – Ψ Muscat, estimated population 400,000. The commercial centre has grown around Mutrah, three miles away and the main port, and Ruwi. The main towns on the northern coast are ΨSur, ΨBarka and ΨSohar. The main town of Dhofar is Salalah.

CURRENCY – Rial Omani (OR) of 1,000 baiza.

FLAG – Red with a white panel in the upper fly and a green one in the lower fly; in the canton the national emblem in white.

NATIONAL DAY – 18 November.

GOVERNMENT

A State Consultative Council established in 1981 was replaced by Sultanic decree in 1991 by a Majlis A' shura, or State Advisory Council. This body, meeting twice a year, consists of a representative from each of the 59 Wilayats, or Governorates, of the Sultanate. The Council has the right to review legislation, question ministers and make policy proposals.

HEAD OF STATE

Sultan, Prime Minister, Minister of Foreign Affairs, Defence and Finance, HM Qaboos Bin-Said, *succeeded* on deposition of Sultan Said bin Taimur, 23 July 1970.

COUNCIL OF MINISTERS as at June 1992

Personal Representative of HM The Sultan, HH Sayyid Thuwainy bin Shihab Al Said.
Adviser, Office of the Personal Representative of HM The Sultan, HE Sheikh Ahmed bin Mohammed Al Nabhani.
Deputy PM for Security and Defence, HH Sayyid Fahr bin Taimur al Said.
Deputy PM for Legal Affairs, HH Sayyid Fahad bin Mahmood al Said.
Deputy PM for Financial and Economic Affairs, HE Qais bin Abdul Munem al Zawawi.
Minister of State and Governor of Dhofar, HE Sayyid Mussellam bin Ali Al Busaidi.
Minister of State and Governor of Muscat, HE Sayyid Al Mutassim bin Hamoud Al Busaidi.
National Heritage and Culture, HH Sayyid Faisal bin Ali al Said.
Agriculture and Fisheries, HE Mohammed bin Abdallah bin Zaher al Hinai.
Electricity and Water, HE Shaikh Mohammed bin Ali Al Qatabi.
Water Resources, HE Hamed bin Said Al Aufi.
Justice, Awqaf and Islamic Affairs, HE Hamoud bin Abdullah Al Harthi.
Health, HE Dr Ali bin Mohammed bin Moosa.
Petroleum and Minerals, HE Said bin Ahmed bin Said al Shanfari.
Housing, HE Malik bin Suleiman al Ma'amari.
Civil Services, HE Ahmed bin Abdul Nabi Macki.
Communications, HE Salim bin Abdullah Al Ghazali.
Education and Youth Affairs, HE Yahya bin Mahfoodh al Manthri.
Interior, HE Sayyid Badr bin Sa'oud bin Hareb al Busaidi.
Information, HE Abdul Aziz bin Mohammed al Rowas.
Environment, HH Sayyid Shabib bin Taimur bin Faisal al Said.
Regional Municipalities and Environment, HE Shaikh Amer bin Shuwain al Hosni.
Minister of State for Foreign Affairs, HE Yousuf bin Alawi bin Abdullah.
Commerce and Industry, HE Maqbool bin Ali bin Sultan.
Social Affairs and Labour, HE Ahmed bin Mohammed bin Salim Al Isa'ee.
Posts, Telegraphs and Telephones, HE Ahmed bin Sweidan al Baluchi.
Secretary-General at the Ministry of Defence, HE Saif bin Hamad al Batashi.
Diwan of Royal Court, HE Sayyid Saif bin Hamed bin Sa'oud.
Palace Office Affairs, HE Gen. Ali bin Majid Al Ma'amari.

EMBASSY OF THE SULTANATE OF OMAN
44A/B Montpelier Square, London SW7 1JJ
Tel 071-584 6782/3/4

Ambassador Extraordinary and Plenipotentiary, His Excellency Abdulla Mohammed Al-Dhahab (1990).

BRITISH EMBASSY
PO Box 300, Muscat
Tel: Muscat 738501/5

Ambassador Extraordinary and Plenipotentiary, His Excellency Sir Terence Clark, KBE, CMG, CVO (1990).
Counsellor, N. H. S. Armour (*Deputy Head of Mission*).
Defence Attaché, Brig. M. Bremridge, MC.
Naval and Air Attaché, Wg Cdr. C. B. Troke.
First Secretaries, B. Baldwin; N. H. Bates.

BRITISH COUNCIL REPRESENTATIVE, R. A. Steedman, PO Box 7090, Mutrah, Oman.

ECONOMY

Although there is considerable cultivation in the fertile areas and cattle are raised on the mountains, the backbone of the economy is the oil industry. Petroleum Development (Oman) Ltd (owned 60 per cent by Oman Government and 34 per cent by Shell) began exporting oil in 1967. Concessions (off and on shore) are held by several major international companies. The current level of oil production is about 650,000 barrels per day, planned to increase to 700,000.

Development

For many years the Sultanate was a poor country with a total annual income of less than £1,000,000. The advent of oil revenues since 1967 and the change of regime in 1970 led to the initiation of a wide-ranging development programme, especially concerned with health, education and communications. New hospitals have been completed in the main provincial centres and there are now nearly 50 hospitals with around 3,400 beds; 759 schools, with 327,131 pupils, were in operation in 1989. A gas turbine power station operates at Rusail, where there is also a 200 plot industrial estate. There is a power station and a desalination plant near Muscat and flour, animal feed, cement and copper production facilities.

Trade

Trade is mainly with the UAE, UK, Japan, the Netherlands, USA, Germany, France and India. Total imports for the year 1988 were OR846,430,275. Chief imports were machinery, cars, building materials, food and telecommunications equipment.

Trade with UK	1990	1991
Imports from UK	£272,072,000	£237,890,000
Exports to UK	89,446,000	73,574,000

COMMUNICATIONS

Since 1972 ships have been using Port Qaboos at Matrah, where eight deep water berths have been constructed as part of the harbour facilities.

A modern telecommunications service to the main population centres and an international service are operated by the General Telecommunications Organization. There are good tarmac roads linking most main population centres of the country with the coast and with the towns of the UAE. There is now over 4,000 km of asphalted road in the Sultanate.

PAKISTAN
Islami Jamhuriya-e-Pakistan

Area, etc – The Islamic Republic of Pakistan is situated in the north-west of the Indian sub-continent, bordered by Iran, Afghanistan, China, the disputed territory of Kashmir, and India. It covers a total area of 803,950 sq. km. Running through Pakistan are five great rivers, the Indus, Jhelum, Chenab, Ravi and Sutlej. The upper reaches of these rivers are in Kashmir, and their sources in the Himalayas.

Population – The Census in 1981 showed a population figure of 83,780,000 (1990 UN estimate, 112,049,000). Of these, about 95 per cent are Muslims, about 1 per cent Hindus, 3.5 per cent Christians, and 0.5 per cent Buddhists.

Capital – Islamabad, population 350,000. ΨKarachi (estimated population 6,500,000) is the largest city and seaport; Lahore has a population of about 3,500,000.

Currency – Pakistan rupee of 100 paisa.

Flag – Green with a white crescent and star, and a white vertical strip in the hoist

National Anthem – Quami Tarana.

National Days – 23 March (Pakistan Day), 14 August (Independence Day).

GOVERNMENT

Pakistan was constituted as a Dominion under the Indian Independence Act 1947. Until 1972 when East Pakistan seceded, Pakistan consisted of two geographical units, West and East Pakistan, which were separated by about 1,100 miles of Indian territory.

Pakistan became a Republic on 23 March 1956, when a parliamentary constitution came into force. On 7 October 1958, however, this constitution was abrogated and Pakistan came under martial law.

The first general elections held in Pakistan on a basis of 'one man, one vote' were held in December 1970 and January 1971. The Awami League in East Pakistan, led by Sheikh Mujibur Rahman, and the Pakistan People's Party in West Pakistan, led by Zulfikar Ali Bhutto, won large majorities. Following the elections there was total disagreement between the two main parties on the question of a new constitution for Pakistan, Sheikh Mujibur insisting on complete autonomy for East Pakistan. The proposed opening of the National Assembly at Dacca on 25 March 1971 was postponed and civil war broke out. East Pakistan seceded by unilateral declaration the following day. Fighting continued until December 1971 when a ceasefire was arranged, and 'The Democratic Government of Bangladesh' was formally proclaimed on 17 April 1972.

Following general elections in March 1977 and allegations of vote-rigging, the armed forces under Gen. Zia-ul-Haq assumed power on 5 July 1977 and imposed martial law throughout the country. The military government scheduled new general elections for October 1977, but these were postponed. Gen. Zia declared himself President on 16 September 1978. In December 1984 Gen. Zia got a five-year mandate as a civilian President through a national referendum. Martial law was lifted on 30 December 1985. On 29 May 1988, Zia dissolved the National Assembly and the cabinet and announced fresh elections. A caretaker cabinet was announced on 9 June. Zia was killed in a plane crash on 17 August 1988. The Pakistan People's Party won the election to the National Assembly and Benazir Bhutto became Prime Minister on 2 December 1988. The legislature then elected President Ghulam Ishaq Khan as the President. In August 1990, the President dissolved the National Assembly and dismissed the Bhutto cabinet. Elections were held on 24 October 1990 and won by the Islamic Democratic Alliance, led by Mian Muhammad Nawaz Sharif.

Head of State

President, Ghulam Ishaq Khan, *elected* 12 December 1988 *for a four-year term.*

Ministers as at June 1992

Prime Minister, Foreign Affairs, Mian Muhammad Nawaz Sharif.
Defence, Syed Ghous Ali Shah.
Defence Production, Mir Hazar Khan Bijarani.
Information and Broadcasting, Mian Abdul Sattar Laleka.
Interior, Chaudhry Shujat Hussain.
Inter-Provincial Co-ordination, Muhammed Aslam Khan Khattak.
Kashmir and Northern Affairs, Sardar Mehtab Ahmad Khan
Law and Justice, Ch. Abdul Ghafoor.
Railways, Ghulam Ahmad Bilor.
Production, Islam Nabi.
Housing and Works, Syed Tariq Mahmood.
Narcotics Control, Rana Chandar Singh.
Finance and Economic Affairs, Sartaj Aziz.
Environment and Urban Affairs, Anwar Saifullah Khan.
Industries and Culture, Sheikh Rashid Ahmed.

Local Government and Rural Development, Ghulam Dastgir Khan.
Education, Syed Fakhar Imam.
Commerce, Malik Muhammad Naeem Khan.
Petroleum and Natural Resources, Chaudhry Nisar Ali Khan.
Planning and Development, Chaudhry Hamid Nasir Chatta.
Health, Syed Tasneem Nawaz Gardezi.
Food, Agriculture and Co-operatives, Lt.-Gen. Abdul Majid Malik (retd).
Labour, Manpower and Overseas Pakistanis, Muhammad Ijaz-ul-Haq.
Adviser to the Prime Minister, Roedad Khan.
Parliamentary Affairs and Youth Affairs, Ch. Amir Hussain.
Religious Affairs, Maulama Muhammad Abdus Sattar Khan Niazi.
Science and Technology, Illahi Bakksh Soomro.
States and Frontier Regions, Sardar Yaqub Khan Nasser.
Water and Power, Shahzada Muhammad Yousaf.
Adviser to the Prime Minister on Establishment, Muhammad Asad Ali Khan Junejo.

HIGH COMMISSION FOR PAKISTAN
35 Lowndes Square, London SW1X 9JN
Tel 071-235 2044

High Commissioner, His Excellency Dr Humayun M. Khan (1990).

BRITISH HIGH COMMISSION
Diplomatic Enclave, Ramna 5, PO Box 1122, Islamabad
Tel: Islamabad 822131/5

High Commissioner, His Excellency Sir Nicholas Barrington, KCMG, CVO (1987).

There is a British Consulate-General at *Karachi* and a Consulate at *Lahore*.

BRITISH COUNCIL REPRESENTATIVE, L. Phillips, PO Box 1135, Islamabad. There are offices at *Karachi*, *Lahore* and *Peshawar*.

EDUCATION

Formal education in Pakistan is organized into five stages. These are five years of primary education (five to nine years), three years of middle or lower secondary (general or vocational), two years of upper secondary, two years of higher secondary (intermediate) and two to five years of higher education in colleges and universities. Education is free to upper secondary level. It was expected that primary education would become universal for boys by mid-1985 and for girls by mid-1988.

At primary level enrolment had increased to 6.5 million in 1984–5, and the number of schools to 75,000. At the middle level enrolment had increased to 1.7 million in 1984–5, and the number of schools to 6,200. At the upper secondary level enrolment increased to 570,000 in 1984–5.

Provincial governments are responsible for the total financial support of the government institutions and for grants to non-government institutions. But policy making is authorized by the national government, which makes annual grants. In 1986, 24 per cent of adults were estimated as being literate.

COMMUNICATIONS

The main seaport is Karachi. The main airport at Karachi occupies an important position on international trunk routes and is equipped with modern facilities and equipment. Pakistan International Airlines operates air services between the principal cities within the country as well as abroad.

Post and telegraph facilities are available to every country in the world.

ECONOMY

Pakistan's economy is chiefly based on agriculture. The principal crops are cotton, rice, wheat, sugar cane, maize and tobacco. There are large deposits of rock salt. Pakistan has one of the longest irrigation systems in the world. The total area irrigated is 33 million acres.

Pakistan also produces hides and skins, leather, wool, fertilizers, paints and varnishes, soda ash, paper, cement, fish, carpets, sports goods, surgical appliances and engineering goods, including switchgear, transformers, cables and wires.

FINANCE

The 1991–2 Budget anticipated net federal revenues of Rs.258.3 billion.

TRADE

Pakistan imported manufactured goods and raw materials to the value of US$5,792 million in 1986–7 and exported mainly agricultural products valued at US$3,498 million. Principal imports are petroleum products, machinery, fertilizers, transport equipment, edible oils, chemicals and ferrous metals. Principal exports are raw cotton, cotton yarn and cloth, carpets, rice, petroleum products, synthetic textiles, leather, and fish.

Trade with UK	1990	1991
Imports from UK	£251,841,000	£272,068,000
Exports to UK	236,448,000	261,291,000

PANAMA

República de Panama

Panama lies on the isthmus of that name which connects North and South America. The area of the Republic is 29,762 sq. miles (77,082 sq. km), the population (Census 1990) 2,315,047. Spanish is the official language.

CAPITAL – ΨPanama City, population (1990) 1,064,221.
CURRENCY – Balboa of 100 centésimos. US$ notes are also in circulation.
FLAG – Four quarters; white with blue star (top, next staff), red (in fly), blue (below, next staff) and white with red star.
NATIONAL ANTHEM – Alcanzamos Por Fin La Victoria (Victory is ours at last).
NATIONAL DAY – 3 November.

HISTORY

After a revolt in November 1903, Panama declared its independence from Colombia and established a separate government.

After 1968 control of Panama was increasingly taken over by Gen. Omar Torrijos, commander of the National Guard, following a military coup. In 1972 Gen. Torrijos was designated as 'Leader of the Revolution' with wide overriding powers. In October 1978 he withdrew from the government, and Dr Aristides Royo was elected President by the Assembly of Representatives. In a presidential election in May 1984, Dr Nicolas Barletta was elected President. He resigned in September 1985 after disagreements with military leaders and was succeeded by his Vice-President, Eric Arturo Delvalle. An attempt in February 1988 by President Delvalle to remove Gen. Noriega as Commander of the Defence Forces failed. Noriega ousted Delvalle and replaced him with Manuel Solis Palma. Presidential elections were held in

May 1989, but Noriega annulled the results, which had appeared to give victory to the opposition. A US military invasion on 20 December 1989 followed Noriega's formal assumption of power as Head of State on 15 December. Guillermo Endara, believed to have won the May elections, was installed as President following the ousting of Gen. Noriega. Panama is still suffering from the physical destruction and political instability caused by the US invasion.

In December 1991 the Legislative Assembly approved a change to the constitution which abolished the armed forces.

GOVERNMENT

Legislative power is vested in a unicameral Legislative Assembly of 67 members; executive power is held by the President, assisted by two elected Vice-Presidents and an appointed Cabinet. Elections are held every five years under a system of universal and compulsory adult suffrage.

HEAD OF STATE

President, Guillermo Endara Galimany, *sworn in* 27 December 1989.

First Vice-President, Dr Ricardo Arias Calderon.

Second Vice-President and Minister of Planning and Political Economy, Guillermo Ford Boyd.

CABINET as at July 1992

Foreign Affairs, Dr Julio Linares.
Treasury and Finance, Dr Mario Galindo.
Government and Justice, Juan B. Chevalier.
Agricultural Development, Dr Cesar Pereira.
Commerce and Industry, Roberto Alfaro.
Labour and Social Welfare, Jorge Rosas.
Health, Dr Guillermo Rolla Pimental.
Housing, Guillermo E. Quijano.
Education, Marco A. Alarcon.
Presidency, Julio Harris.
Public Works, Alfredo Arias.

EMBASSY OF THE REPUBLIC OF PANAMA
119 Crawford Street, London W1H 1AF
Tel 071-487 5633

Ambassador Extraordinary and Plenipotentiary, His Excellency Teodoro F. Franco (1990).

There are also Consular Offices at *Liverpool* and *London* (24 Tudor Street, London EC4Y 0JD).

BRITISH EMBASSY
Torre Swiss Bank, Calle 53 (Apartado 889 Zona 1), Panama City, Panama 1
Tel: Panama City 69-0866

Ambassador Extraordinary and Plenipotentiary, His Excellency T. H. Malcomson (1992).

Defence, Naval, Military and Air Attaché, Lt.-Col. T. A. Glen.

There is a British consular office at *Panama City*.

ECONOMY

The soil is moderately fertile, but nearly one-half of the land is uncultivated. The chief crops are bananas, sugar, coconuts, cacao, coffee and cereals. The shrimping industry plays an important role in the Panamanian economy. A railway 47 miles in length joins the Atlantic and Pacific oceans.

Education is compulsory and free from seven to 15 years.

TRADE

Imports are mostly manufactured goods, machinery, lubricants, chemicals and foodstuffs. Exports are bananas, petroleum products, shrimps, sugar, meat and fishmeal.

Republic of Panama	1988	1989
Imports	US$712.3m	US$796.0m
Exports	283.0m	297.3m
Colon Free Zone		
Imports	US$1,843m	US$243.8m
Exports	2,119m	249.9m

Trade with UK†	1990	1991
Imports from UK	£35,552,000	£36,656,000
Exports to UK	4,056,000	1,679,000

† Including Colon Free Zone

THE PANAMA CANAL ZONE

With effect from 1 October 1979 the Canal Zone (647 sq. miles) was disestablished, with all areas of land and water within the Zone reverting to Panama. By the 1977 treaty with the USA, the USA is allowed the use of operating bases for the Panama Canal, together with several military bases, but the Republic of Panama is sovereign in all such areas. Control of the Canal will revert to Panama in the year 2000.

DEPENDENCIES OF PANAMA

Taboga Island (area 4 sq. miles) is a popular tourist resort some 12 miles from the Pacific entrance to the Panama Canal.

Tourist facilities have also been developed in the Las Perlas Archipelago in the Gulf of Panama, particularly on the island of Contadora.

There is a penal settlement at Guardia on the island of Coiba (area 19 sq. miles) in the Gulf of Chiriqui.

PAPUA NEW GUINEA

AREA, POPULATION, ETC. – Papua New Guinea extends from the Equator to Cape Baganowa in the Louisiade Archipelago at 11° S. latitude and from the border with Irian Jaya to 160° E. longitude. The total area of Papua New Guinea is 178,260 sq. miles, (461,691 sq. km), of which approximately 152,420 sq. miles form the mainland, on the island of New Guinea.

The country has many island groups, principally the Bismarck Archipelago, a portion of the Solomon Islands, the Trobriands, the D'Entrecasteaux Islands and the Louisade Archipelago. The main islands of the Bismarck Archipelago are New Britain, New Ireland and Manus. Bougainville is the largest of the Solomon Islands within Papua New Guinea.

CLIMATE – Papua New Guinea lies within the tropics and has a typically monsoonal climate. Temperature and humidity are uniformly high throughout the year. The average rainfall is about 80 inches per year but there are wide variations; from 47 inches at Port Moresby to over 200 inches in mountainous western areas.

POPULATION – The population in 1990 (UN estimate) was 3,699,000.

CAPITAL – ΨPort Moresby. Estimated population (1990), 173,500. Other major towns are Lae, Rabaul, Madang, Wewak, Goroka and Mount Hagen.

CURRENCY – Kina (K) of 100 toea.

FLAG – Divided diagonally red (fly) and black (hoist); on the red a soaring Bird of Paradise in yellow and on the black five white stars of the Southern Cross.

NATIONAL ANTHEM – Arise All You Sons.

NATIONAL DAY – 16 September (Independence Day).

HISTORY

New Guinea was sighted by Portuguese and Spanish navigators in the early sixteenth century, but remained largely isolated from the rest of the world. In 1884 a British Protectorate was proclaimed over the southern coast of New Guinea (Papua) and the adjacent islands. British New Guinea, as the Protectorate was called, was annexed outright in 1888. In 1906 the Territory of British New Guinea was placed under the authority of the Commonwealth of Australia. Also in 1884 Germany had formally taken possession of certain northern areas, which later came to be known as the Trust Territory of New Guinea. In 1914 the German areas were occupied by Australian troops and remained under military administration until 1921, when the League of Nations conferred on Australia a mandate for their government. New Guinea was administered under the mandate and Papua under the Papua Act until the invasion by the Japanese in 1942 when the civil administration was suspended until the surrender of the Japanese in 1945.

The first House of Assembly for the whole country met in 1964 and included an elected majority and ten nominated official members. After 1970 there was a gradual assumption of powers by the Papua New Guinea Government, culminating in formal self-government in December 1973. Final reserve powers held by Australia over defence and foreign relations were relinquished to Papua New Guinea in March 1975, and Papua New Guinea achieved full independence on 16 September 1975.

A secessionist movement, the Bougainville Revolutionary Army (BRA), began an insurrection on Bougainville in 1989. In March 1990 the Papua New Guinean security forces withdrew from the island and the BRA declared an independent republic in May 1990. In January 1991, a peace accord was signed between the two sides in Honoria, the Solomon Islands; the question of Bougainville's future status was deferred.

GOVERNMENT

Elections are held every five years. The Parliament comprises 109 elected Members, 20 from Regional electorates, the remainder from Open electorates. There are 19 provinces, which have their own provincial governments with certain legislative and administrative powers.

Governor-General, His Excellency Sir Wiwa Korowi, GCMG.

NATIONAL EXECUTIVE COUNCIL as at August 1992

Prime Minister, Rt. Hon. Paias Wingti.
Deputy PM and Minister of Finance and Planning, Rt. Hon. Sir Julius Chan, KBE.
Provincial Affairs and Village Development, John Nilkare.
Works, Albert Karo.
Transport, Roy Yaki.
Fisheries, Iairo Lasaro.
Public Services, Albert Kipalan.
Lands, Tim Ward.
Foreign Affairs, John Kaputin.
Mining and Petroleum, Masket Iangalio.
Forests, Tim Neville.
Bougainville, Michael Ogio.
Justice, Philemon Embel.
Agriculture, Roy Evara.
Environment and Conservation, Perry Zeipi.
Trade and Industry, David Mai.
Labour and Employment, Castan Maibawa.
Defence, Paul Tohian.
Education, Andrew Baing.
Health, Francis Koimanrea.
Housing, John Jaminan.
Home Affairs and Youth, Andrew Posai.
Communications, Martin Thompson.
Energy and Science, Thomas Pelika.
Police, Avusi Tanao.
Administrative Services, Matthew Yago.

PAPUA NEW GUINEA HIGH COMMISSION
3rd Floor, 14 Waterloo Place, London SW1R 4AR
Tel 071-930 0922/7

High Commissioner, His Excellency Noel Levi (1991).

BRITISH HIGH COMMISSION
PO Box 4778, Boroko, Port Moresby
Tel: Port Moresby 212500

High Commissioner, His Excellency John Westgarth Guy, OBE (1991).

COMMUNICATIONS

Road communications are very limited, the most important road being that linking Lae with the populous highlands.

Air Niugini (the national airline) and Qantas operate regular air services between Port Moresby and Australia. Air Niugini also operates services to Manila (Philippines), Honiara (Solomon Islands), Jayapura (Indonesia), Honolulu and Singapore. Internal air services are operated by Air Niugini, Douglas Airways, and Talair.

Several shipping companies operate cargo services between Papua New Guinea and Australia, Europe, the Far East and USA. There are very limited cargo and passenger services between Papua New Guinea main ports, outports, plantations and missions.

Papua New Guinea is linked by international cable to Australia, Guam, Hong Kong, Kota Kinabalu, the Far East and USA. Telecommunications are widely available.

ECONOMY

Until the 1970s the Papua New Guinea economy was based almost entirely on agriculture. At the beginning of the 20th century copra plantations formed the basis of the cash economy. Further crops which have been introduced over the years are cocoa, tea, coffee, palm oil, rubber, groundnuts, spices and timber. A variety of commercial agricultural developments now co-exist with the traditional informal rural economy. New developments to promote export crops and increase employment, typically involving foreign investment, are planned for the future.

In 1972, Bougainville Copper Pty Ltd (BCL) began mining in the North Solomons Province, producing copper, silver and gold. The Bougainville Copper Mine closed indefinitely in May 1989 but is now scheduled to reopen. There are extensive mineral deposits throughout Papua New Guinea, including nickel, chromite, bauxite and possibly commercial deposits of oil and gas. The most important new development is the exploitation of large copper and gold deposits on the Ok Tedi, in the Western Province.

Industry includes processing of primary products, and brewing, bottling and packaging, paint, plywood, and metal manufacturing and the construction industries.

Although the formal economy is still dominated by non-Papua New Guineans, the participation of Papua New Guineans is increasing.

TRADE WITH UK

	1990	1991
Imports from UK	£8,793,000	£15,446,000
Exports to UK	34,849,000	32,170,000

PARAGUAY

República del Paraguay

AREA AND POPULATION – Paraguay is an inland subtropical state of South America, situated between Argentina, Bolivia and Brazil. The area is estimated at 157,048 sq. miles (406,752 sq. km), with a population (1990 UN estimate) of 4,277,000.

Paraguay is a country of grassy plains and dense forest, the soil being marshy in many parts and liable to floods while the hills are covered for the most part with immense forests. The streams flowing into the Alto Paraná descend precipitously into that river. In the angle formed by the Paraná-Paraguay confluence are extensive marshes, one of which, known as Neembucú (or endless) is drained by Lake Ypoa, a large lagoon south-east of the capital. The Chaco, lying between the rivers Paraguay and Pilcomayo and bounded on the north by Bolivia, formed the subject of a long-standing dispute with that country and led to war between Paraguay and Bolivia from 1932 to 1935. The Chaco is a flat plain, rising uniformly towards its western boundary to a height of 1,140 feet; it suffers much from floods and still more from drought, but the building of dams and reservoirs has converted part of it into good pasture for cattle raising.

LANGUAGE – Spanish is the official language of the country but outside the larger towns Guarani, the language of the largest single unit of original Indian inhabitants, is widely spoken. Four daily and five weekly newspapers are published in Asunción.

CAPITAL – Asunción, about 1,000 miles up the River Paraguay from Buenos Aires. Population (1985 census) 729,307; other centres are Ciudad del Este (98,491); Encarnación (31,445); Concepción (25,607); P. Juan Caballero (41,475).

CURRENCY – Guaraní (Gs) of 100 céntimos.

FLAG – Three horizontal bands, red, white, blue with the National seal on the obverse white band and the Treasury seal on the reverse white band.

NATIONAL ANTHEM – Paraguayos, Republica O Muerte (Paraguayans, republic or death).

NATIONAL DAY – 15 May.

GOVERNMENT

In 1535 Paraguay was settled as a Spanish possession. In 1811 it declared its independence of Spain.

The constitution provides for a two-chamber legislature consisting of a 36-member Senate and a 72-member Chamber of Deputies. Two-thirds of the seats in each chamber are allocated to the majority party and the remaining one-third shared among the minority parties in proportion to the votes cast. Voting is compulsory for all citizens over 18.

The President is elected for five years and may be re-elected for a further term. He appoints the Cabinet, which exercises all the functions of government. During parliamentary recess it can govern by decree through the Council of State, the members of which are representative of the government, the armed forces and various other bodies.

Gen. Alfredo Stroessner, dictator from 1954, was overthrown by Gen. Andrés Rodriguez in February 1989. Gen. Rodriguez was elected President in May 1989. There are moves towards reform; in May 1991, the first free municipal elections were held, and elections to the parliament were held in December 1991 and won by the ruling Colorado Party. Major amendments to the constitution were agreed in Parliament and came into effect in June 1992, including the creation of the post of Vice-President, who will serve five-year terms with the President from 1994 onwards. President Rodriguez has also been barred from standing for re-election in 1994.

HEAD OF STATE

President, General Andrés Rodriguez, *elected* 1 May 1989.

CABINET as at July 1992

Foreign Affairs, Dr Alexis Frutos Vaesken.
Interior, Gen. Orlando Machuca Vargas.
Finance, Juan José Diáz Perez.
Education and Worship, Dr Horacio Galeano Perrone.
Agriculture and Livestock, Raul Torres Segovia.
Public Works and Communications, Gen. Porfirio Pereira Ruiz Diaz.
Defence, Gen. Angel Juan Souto Hernandez.
Public Health and Social Welfare, Cynthia Prieto Conti.
Justice and Labour, Hugo Estigarribia Elizeche.
Industry and Commerce, Ubaldo Scavone.
Without Portfolio, Dr Juan Ramón Cháves.

EMBASSY OF PARAGUAY

Braemar Lodge, Cornwall Gardens, London SW7 4AQ
Tel 071-937 1253

Ambassador Extraordinary and Plenipotentiary, His Excellency Antonio Espinoza (1990).

BRITISH EMBASSY

Calle Presidente Franco 706 (PO Box 404), Asunción
Tel: Asuncíon 444472

Ambassador Extraordinary and Plenipotentiary and Consul-General, His Excellency Michael A. C. Dibben (1991).

ECONOMY

About three-quarters of the population are engaged in agriculture and cattle raising. Cassava, sugar cane, soya, corn, cotton and wheat are the main agricultural products. The forests contain many varieties of timber which find a good market abroad.

Paraguay's hydroelectric power station at Acaray produced 1,118 kWh in 1985, of which a surplus was exported to Argentina and Brazil. At Itaipú the largest hydroelectric dam in the world, a joint project by Paraguay and Brazil, was inaugurated in 1982. It is expected to be completed in 1991 when it will have a capacity of over 12 million kW. Work is also under way on a hydroelectric project with Argentina at Yacyretá which it is hoped will be in operation by the end of the decade.

BUDGET EXPENDITURE 1990

Central Government	Gs 815.6m
Decentralized Bodies	1,600.5m

TRADE

Total value of imports in 1989 was US$660,778,000. The chief imports were machinery (US$211.6m); fuels and lubricants (US$115.0m); transport and accessories (US$61.7m); and drinks and tobacco (US$45.5m). Total value of exports in 1989 was US$660,778,000. The chief exports were soya bean (US$382.9m); cotton fibres (US$306.9m); meat (US$96.1m); and coffee (US$40.3m).

Trade with UK	1990	1991
Imports from UK	£32,035,000	£38,229,000
Exports to UK	10,077,000	1,488,000

COMMUNICATIONS

A railway, 985 miles in length, connects Asunción with Buenos Aires. The journey takes 55 hours. Train ferries enable the run to be accomplished without break of bulk. River steamers also connect Buenos Aires and Asunción (three to five days). This service is liable to cancellation without warning when the river is low or in flood. There are direct shipping services to Asunción from Britain, Western Europe and the USA. Eight airlines operate services from Asunción.

There are 27,741 km (1990) of asphalted roads in Paraguay, connecting Asunción with São Paulo (26 hours) via the Bridge of Friendship and Foz de Yguazú, and with Buenos Aires (24 hours) via Puerto Pilcomayo, and about 4,050 miles of earth roads in fairly good condition, but liable to be closed or to become impassable in wet weather. A 1,000 km road, of which 300 km are paved, links Asunción with the Bolivian border. There are services to Buenos Aires, São Paulo and Paranagua, a port on the Brazilian coast.

DEFENCE

Paraguay has an active armed forces strength of 17,000 (10,300 conscripts). Conscripts serve 18 months in the Army and Air Force and two years in the Navy.

The Army has a strength of 12,500 (8,600 conscripts), with 25 light tanks, 50 armoured personnel carriers and reconnaissance vehicles, and 104 artillery pieces. The Navy has a stength of 3,500 (1,700 conscripts), with seven lake and river patrol vessels, four support vessels and two combat aircraft. The Air Force has a strength of 1,000 (700 conscripts), with 10 combat aircraft.

EDUCATION

Education is free and compulsory. In 1990 there were 4,641 government primary schools with 694,972 pupils and 27,477 teachers. There were 809 secondary schools with 155,339 pupils and 8,112 teachers. The National University in Asunción had 20,343 students in 1984. The Catholic University had 10,971 students.

PERU

República del Peru

AREA AND POPULATION – Peru is a maritime republic of South America, situated between 0° 00′ 48″ and 18° 21′ 00″ S. latitude and between 68° 39′ 27″ and 81° 20′ 13″ W. longitude. The area of the Republic is 496,225 sq. miles (1,285,216 sq. km), with a population (1990 estimate) of 22,332,100.

The country is traversed throughout its length by the Andes, running parallel to the Pacific coast, the highest points in Peru being Huascaran (22,211 ft), Huandoy (20,855 ft), Ausangate (20,235 feet), Misti volcano (18,364 ft), Hualcan (20,000 ft), Chachani (19,037 ft), Antajasha (18,020 ft), Pichupichu (17,724 ft), and Mount Meiggs (17,583 ft).

There are three main regions, the Costa, west of the Andes, the Sierra or mountain ranges of the Andes, which include the Punas or mountainous wastes below the region of perpetual snow, and the Montaña, or Selva, which is the vast area of jungle stretching from the eastern foothills of the Andes to the eastern frontiers of Peru. The coastal area, lying upon and near the Pacific, is not tropical, though close to the Equator, being cooled by the Humboldt Current.

In the mountains, where most of the Indians live, are to be found minerals in great richness and variety, and cattle, sheep, llamas and alpacas are bred there.

LANGUAGE – Spanish, the language of the original Spanish stock from which the governing and professional classes are mainly recruited, was formerly the only official language of the country. However, in May 1975, Quechua was declared the second official language. Quechua and Aymará are spoken by more than half the population of the country.

CAPITAL – Metropolitan Lima (including ΨCallao), population estimate (1990) 6,415,000. Other major cities are: Arequipa (712,279) and Lambayeque (625,553).

CURRENCY – Nuevo Sol 100 cents.

FLAG – Three vertical stripes of red, white, red.

NATIONAL ANTHEM – Somos Libres, Seámoslo Siempre (We are free, let us remain so forever).

NATIONAL DAY – 28 July (Anniversary of Independence).

GOVERNMENT

Peru was conquered in the early 16th century by Francisco Pizarro (1478–1541). He subjugated the Incas (the ruling caste of the Quechua Indians), who had started their rise to power some 500 years earlier, and for nearly three centuries Peru remained under Spanish rule. A revolutionary war of 1821–4 established its independence, declared on 28 July 1821. The constitution rests upon the fundamental law of 18 October 1856 and is that of a democratic Republic.

Peru was afflicted by rampant inflation, but this has gradually been brought under control to an annual rate of around 37 per cent. There remains drug-inspired violence and terroism; the main guerrilla movements are the Maoist Sendero Luminoso (Shining Path) and the Movimiento Revolucionario Tupac Amaru (MRTA). Large areas of the country are under states of emergency.

In April 1992 President Fujimori, with the support of the armed forces, suspended the constitution and dissolved Congress and began to govern with absolute powers. A programme of drastic market-orientated reform, new measures in the anti-terrorist war, and a streamlining of the executive, legislative and judicial institutions was announced. A referendum on constitutional reforms has been scheduled for November 1992, with parliamentary elections and a return to democracy by mid-1993.

HEAD OF STATE

President of the Republic, Alberto Fujimori, *assumed office* 28 July 1990.
First Vice-President, Máximo San Román.
Second Vice-President, Carlos García.

CABINET as at September 1992

Prime Minister and Minister of Foreign Affairs, Dr Oscar de la Puente Raygada.
Economy and Finance, Dr Carlos Boloña Behr.
Interior, Gen. Juan Briones Davilla.
Justice, Dr Fernando Vega Santa Gadea.
Defence, Gen. Victor Malca Villanueva.
Education, Eduardo Varillas Montenegro.
Health, Victor Paredes Guerra.
Labour and Social Promotion, Augusto Antonioлli Vasquez.
Agriculture, Absalon Vasquez Villanueva.
Energy and Mines, Jaime Yoshiyama Tanaka.
Transport and Communications, Housing and Construction, Alfredo Ross Antezana.
Fisheries, Jaime Augustin Sobero Taira.
Industry, Commerce, Tourism and Integration, Jorge Camet.
Minister of the Presidency, Jorge Lau Kon.

EMBASSY OF PERU
52 Sloane Street, London SW1X 9SP
Tel 071–235 1917/2545

Ambassador Extraordinary and Plenipotentiary, new appointment awaited.

Minister, Gilbert Chauny.
Minister-Counsellor, Julio Florián.

BRITISH EMBASSY
Natalio Sánchez 125 Piso 12, Plaza Washington (PO Box 854), Lima 100.
Tel: Lima 334738

Ambassador Extraordinary and Plenipotentiary, His Excellency Keith Haskell, CMG, CVO (1990).
First Secretary, F. R. C. Thomson (*Deputy Head of Mission and Consul*).
Defence Attaché, Col. C. H. Van der Noot, MBE.

There is a British Consular Office at *Lima* and Honorary Consulates in *Arequipa, Cusco, Iquitos, Piura* and *Trujillo*.

BRITISH COUNCIL REPRESENTATIVE J. Harvey, PO Box No. 14-0114, Calle Alberto Lynch 110, San Isidro, Lima 14.

ECONOMY

The chief products of the coastal belt are cotton, sugar and petroleum. There are large tracts of land suitable for cultivation and stock raising on the eastern slopes of the Andes, and in the mountain valleys maize, potatoes and wheat are grown. The jungle area is a source of timber and petroleum. Other major crops are fruit, vegetables, rice, barley, grapes and coffee. Mineral exports include lead, zinc, copper, iron ore and silver. Peru is normally the world's largest exporter of fishmeal.

TRADE

Import trade of Peru in 1989 totalled US$2,370 million and exports US$1,159 million.

The principal imports are machinery and chemicals and pharmaceutical products. The chief exports are minerals and metals, fishmeal, sugar, cotton and coffee.

Trade with UK	1990	1991
Imports from UK	£29,233,000	£33,061,000
Exports to UK	96,654,000	84,034,000

COMMUNICATIONS

In recent years the coastal and sierra zones have been opened up by means of roads and air routes. There is air communication, as well as communication by protracted land routes, with the tropical and eastern zones which lie east of the Andes towards the borders of Brazil. The Andean Highway from the Pacific port of Callao, via Lima to Pucallpa, the river port on the Ucayali, forms a link between the Pacific, the Amazon and the Atlantic. The Panamerican Highway runs along the Peruvian coast connecting it with Ecuador and Chile. The Inter-Ocean Corridor linking the port of Matarani and Buenos Aires will be opened soon.

The first railway was opened in 1850 and the 2,400 miles of track are now administered by the Government. There is also steam navigation on the Ucayali and Huallaga, and in the south on Lake Titicaca. Air services are maintained throughout Peru, and many international services call at Lima.

DEFENCE

The Armed Forces have a total active strength of some 105,000 (73,000 conscripts), with selective conscription of some two years duration. The Army has a strength of 72,000 (52,000 conscripts) and is heavily engaged in combating the Shining Path and MRTA guerilla movements. It has a strength of 13 divisions with some 350 main battle tanks, 110 light tanks, 625 reconnaissance and armoured personnel carriers and 300 artillery pieces. The Navy has some 18,000 personnel (14,000 conscripts), divided into the Pacific, Lake Titicaca and Amazon River force areas. It has a strength of ten submarines, two cruisers and ten destroyers and frigates. The Air Force has a strength of 15,000 personnel (7,000 conscripts), with 113 combat aircraft and ten armed helicopters. In addition there is the paramilitary National Police of some 70,000 who also play a major role in counter-insurgency operations.

EDUCATION

Education is compulsory and free for both sexes between the ages of five and 16.

THE PHILIPPINES
Repúblika ng Pilipinas

AREA – The Philippines are situated between 21° 20′–4° 30′ N. lat. and 116° 55′–126° 36′ E. long., and are about 500 miles from the south-east coast of the continent of Asia.

The total land area of the country is 115,831 sq. miles (300,000 sq. km). There are eleven larger islands and 7,079 other islands.

The principal islands are:

	sq. miles		sq. miles
Luzon	40,422	Mindoro	3,759
Mindanao	36,538	Leyte	2,786
Samar	5,050	Cebu	1,703
Negros	4,906	Bohol	1,492
Palawan	4,550	Masbate	1,262
Panay	4,446		

Other groups in the Republic are the Sulu islands (capital, Jolo), Babuyanes and Batanes; the Catanduanes; and Culion Islands.

POPULATION – The population of the Philippines (UN estimate 1990) is 61,480,000.

ETHNIC GROUPS – The inhabitants, known as Filipinos, are basically of Malay stock, with a considerable admixture of Spanish and Chinese blood in many localities. The Chinese minority is estimated at 500,000, and other much smaller foreign communities include Spanish, American and Indian.

RELIGIONS – About 90 per cent are Christian, predominantly Roman Catholics. Most of the remainder are Muslims, in the south, and Animists and pagans, mainly in the north.

LANGUAGE – The official languages are Filipino and English. Filipino, the national language, is based on Tagalog, one of the Malay–Polynesian languages and the language of the part of Luzon surrounding Metro Manila. Filipino is spoken by 29.66 per cent of the total number of households, but local languages and dialects are strong and Cebuano is spoken by 24.2 per cent of total households. English, which is the language of government and of instruction in secondary and university education, is spoken by at least 44 per cent of the population. Spanish, which ceased to be an official language in 1973, is now spoken by a very small minority. Eighty-nine per cent of the population are literate.

CAPITAL – ΨManila, on the island of Luzon, estimated population (1990) City area 1,876,195; Manila with suburbs (incl. Quezon City, Pasay City, Caloocan City, Makati, Parañaque, San Juan Mandaluyong and Navotas) 6,720,050. The next largest cities are (1989 estimate) ΨCebu (613,184), ΨDavao (819,525), ΨIloilo (287,711), ΨZamboanga (433,328), and Bacolod (328,648).

CURRENCY – Philippine peso (P) of 100 centavos.

FLAG – Equal horizontal bands of blue (above) and red; gold sun with three stars on a white triangle next staff.
NATIONAL ANTHEM – Pambansang Awit.
NATIONAL DAY – 12 June (Independence Day).

GOVERNMENT

The Portuguese navigator Magellan came to the Philippines in 1521 and was killed by the natives of Mactan, a small island near Cebu. In 1565 Spain undertook the conquest of the country, which was named Filipinas after the son of the King of Spain. In 1571 the city of Manila was founded by the conquistador Legaspi, who subdued the inhabitants of almost all the islands, their conversion being undertaken by the Augustinian friars in Legaspi's train. In 1762 Manila was occupied by a British force, but in 1764 it was restored to Spain.

In the Spanish-American War of 1898, Manila was captured by American troops with the help of Filipinos and the islands were ceded to the United States by the Treaty of Paris of 10 December 1898. Despite a rebellion against the US government between 1899 and 1902, the Americans remained in control of the country until 1946. The Republic of the Philippines came into existence on 4 July 1946 with a presidential form of government based on the American system.

Ferdinand Marcos was President from 1965 to 1986. Although he gained a majority of votes in the official count of a presidential election in February 1986, the election was marred by widespread electoral abuse and his rival, Mrs Corazon Aquino, launched a series of non-violent civil disturbance actions which gained wide support. On 25 February Marcos, his family and aides left for Hawaii. Mrs Aquino took over as President and survived several attempts to overthrow her.

Presidential elections were held on 11 May 1992 and were won by former defence secretary Fidel Ramos after President Aquino announced that she would not run for a second term and endorsed Ramos.

A new constitution was approved by referendum in February 1987 and came into force on 27 July 1987. Legislative authority is vested in a bicameral elected Congress comprising a House of Representatives of up to 250 members and a 24-member Senate.

INSURGENCY

There is unrest in many of the islands due to insurgency. Muslim insurgents, the Moro National Liberation Front, operate in western Mindanao and the Sula archipelago. Most of the current activity is due to the Communist New People's Army, which is strongest in eastern Mindanao, Negros, Samar, Bicol, the mountains of northern Luzon, and Bataan.

President, Fidel V. Ramos, *assumed office* 30 June 1992.
Vice-President, Joseph Estrada.

CABINET SECRETARIES as at July 1992
Foreign Affairs, Roberto Romulo.
Finance, Ramon del Rosario jun.
Justice, Franklin Drilon.
Agriculture, Roberto Sebastian.
Public Works and Highways, José de Jesus.
Education, Armand Fabella.
Labour, Nieves Confesor.
National Defence, Renato de Villa.
Health, Dr Juan Flavier.
Trade and Industry, Rizalino Navarro.
Social Welfare and Development (acting), Corazon de Leon.
Agrarian Reform, Ernesto Garilao.
Interior and Local Government, Rafael Alunan.
Tourism, Vicente Carlos.
Environment and Natural Resources, vacant.
Budget, Salvador Enriquez.
Transport and Communications, Jesus Garcia.
Executive Secretary, Edelmiro Amante.
Science and Technology (acting), Ricardo Gloria.
Director-General, National Economic and Development Authority, Cielito Habito.
Press Secretary, Rodolfo Reyes.

EMBASSY OF THE PHILIPPINES
9A Palace Green, London W8 4QE
Tel 071-937 1600/9

Ambassador Extraordinary and Plenipotentiary, His Excellency Manuel T. Yan (1991).
Minister-Counsellor, Estrella Beranguel.

BRITISH EMBASSY
Locsin Building, 6752 Ayala Avenue, Corner Makati Avenue, Makati, Metro Manila (PO Box 1970)
Tel: Manila 816-7116

Ambassador Extraordinary and Plenipotentiary, His Excellency Alan Montgomery (1992).
Counsellor, A. Collins.
Defence Attaché, Col. J. P. Clough.
First Secretary, R. Cork (*Commercial*).

BRITISH COUNCIL REPRESENTATIVE, N. Bisset, 7, 3rd Street, New Manila, PO Box AC 168, Cubao, Quezon City, Metro Manila.

EDUCATION

Secondary and higher education is extensive and there are 37 private universities recognized by the Government, including the Dominican University of Santo Tomas (founded in 1611). There are also 296 state-supported colleges and universities, including the University of the Philippines, founded 1908.

COMMUNICATIONS

The highway system covered 161,709 kilometres in 1985 and there was a total of 1,120,172 registered road vehicles. The Philippine National Railway operates 740 km of track on Luzon Island.

There are 94 ports of entry in the Philippines and 164,404 vessels of various types totalling 50,467,000 tons, are engaged in inter-island traffic.

There 82 national airports and 137 privately operated airports. Philippine Air Lines have regular flights throughout the Far East, to the USA and Europe, in addition to inter-island services.

ECONOMY

The Philippines is a predominantly agricultural country, the chief products being rice, coconuts, maize, sugar-cane, abaca (manila hemp), fruits, tobacco and lumber. There is, however, an increasing number of manufacturing industries and it is the policy of the Government to diversify its economy.

Principal exports are sugar, coconut oil, copper concentrate, lumber and copra.

TRADE

	1987	1988
Total imports	US$6,736,969,000	US$8,159,378,000
Total exports	5,720,238,000	6,994,425,000

Trade with UK	1990	1991
Imports from UK	£158,030,000	£146,571,000
Exports to UK	220,706,000	229,955,000

POLAND

Rzeczpospolita Polska

AREA AND POPULATION – Poland adjoins Germany in the west, the boundary being formed by the rivers Oder and Neisse, Czechoslavakia in the south, and Belarus, Ukraine, Lithuania and the Kaliningrad region of Russia in the east. The present frontiers were established at the end of the Second World War. To the north is the Baltic Sea. The country has an area of 120,725 sq. miles (312,677 sq. km), and a population (official estimate 1991) of 38,900,000. Roman Catholicism is the religion of 95 per cent of the inhabitants.

CAPITAL – Warsaw, on the Vistula, population (1989) 1,655,063. Other large towns are Lódź (851,690); Kraków (748,356); Wroclaw (642,234); Poznan (588,715); Gdansk (464,649); Szczecin (412,000); Katowice (367,041); Bydgoszcz (380,385).

CURRENCY – Zloty of 100 groszy.

FLAG – Equal horizontal stripes of white (above) and red.

NATIONAL ANTHEM – Jeszcze Polska Nie Zginela (Poland has not yet been destroyed).

NATIONAL DAY – 3 May.

GOVERNMENT

The Polish Commonwealth ceased to exist in 1795 after three successive partitions in 1772, 1793 and 1795, in which Prussia, Russia and Austria shared. The Republic of Poland (reconstituted within the limits of the old Polish Commonwealth) was proclaimed at Warsaw in November 1918, and its independence guaranteed by the signatories of the Treaty of Versailles.

German forces invaded Poland on 1 September 1939; on 17 September, Russian forces invaded eastern Poland, and on 21 September 1939 Poland was declared by Germany and Russia to have ceased to exist. A line of demarcation was established between the areas occupied by German and Russian forces. At the end of the war a coalition government was formed in which the Polish Workers' Party played a large part. In December 1948, the Polish Workers' Party and the Polish Socialist Party fused in the new Polish United Workers' Party (PUWP). A new constitution modelled on the Soviet constitution of 1936 was adopted in July 1952, and was modified in February 1976.

In July 1980 steep rises in food prices but static wages led to widespread strikes. The strikes continued throughout August, obliging the government to agree to allow independent trade unions, the right to strike, the easing of censorship and other political and economic demands. The independent trade union movement, Solidarity, led by Lech Walesa, became a powerful force but many of its leaders, including Walesa, were detained and union activity suspended when martial law was declared in December 1981. Initially there was some passive resistance to martial law, which was suspended in December 1982 and finally lifted in July 1983.

Solidarity continued as an underground movement until 1988 when a wave of strikes and the call for the legalization of Solidarity resulted in talks between Walesa and the PUWP early in 1989. By April plans for political and economic reforms had been drawn up. These included the restoration of the legal status of Solidarity (17 April); the introduction of a bicameral parliamentary system comprising an upper house (Senate) and lower house (Sejm), and an executive presidency; multi-party parliamentary elections were held in the summer of 1989.

General Jaruzelski was elected President by Poland's MPs on 20 July and on 20 August 1989 Tadeusz Mazowiecki became the first non-Communist Prime Minister since 1945. Under the new constitution the Prime Minister can appoint all members of the Council of Ministers.

The PUWP, since August 1989 no longer the ruling party, disbanded in January 1990. Lech Walesa was elected President in December 1990. Jan Bielecki became Prime Minister in January 1991, following a policy of rapid introduction of the market economy. Disagreement over a post-Communist constitution continues, especially over the relative powers of Parliament and the President.

Parliamentary elections were held in October 1991 which led to an extremely fragmented Parliament of over 20 parties. Jan Olszewski eventually formed a government in January 1992, but this was voted out of office by Parliament in June 1992. Waldemar Pawlak was appointed Prime Minister but failed to form a government and was replaced by Hanna Suchocka who successfully did so in July 1992.

HEAD OF STATE

President, Lech Walesa, *elected* 9 December 1990 *for a six-year term.*

COUNCIL OF MINISTERS as at 11 July 1992

Prime Minister, Hanna Suchocka.
Deputy Prime Minister (Economy), Henryk Goryszewski.
Deputy Prime Minister (Policy), Pawel Laczkowski.
Head of the Council of Minister's Office, Jan Rokita.
Foreign Affairs, Krzysztof Skabiszewski.
Internal Affairs, Andrzej Milczanowski.
National Defence, Janusz Onyszkiewicz.
Justice and Attorney-General, Zbigniew Dyka.
Head of the Central Planning Office, Jerzy Kropiwnicki.
Finance, Jerzy Osiakynski.
Foreign Economic Relations, Andrzej Arendarski.
Agriculture, Gabriel Janowski.

Transport and Maritime Economy, Zbigniew Jaworski.
Environment Protection, Natural Resources and Forestry, Zygmunt Hortmanowicz.
Labour and Social Policy, Jacek Kuron.
National Education, Zdobyslaw Flisowski.
Culture, Piotr Lukasiewicz.
Health, Andrzej Wojtyla.
Poland-European Community Relations, Krzysztof Bielecki.
Business Enterpreneurship, Zbigniew Eysmont.
Minister without Portfolio, Jerzy Kaminski.
Industry and Trade, Waclaw Niewiarowski.
Land Management and Construction, Andrzej Bratkowski.
Communication, Krzysztof Kilian.
Privatization, Janusz Lewandowski.
Head of Scientific Research Committee, Witold Karczewski.

EMBASSY OF THE REPUBLIC OF POLAND
47 Portland Place, London WIN 3AG
Tel 071-580 4324

Ambassador Extraordinary and Plenipotentiary, His Excellency Tadeusz de Virion (1990).

BRITISH EMBASSY
No. 1 Aleja Róz, 00-556 Warsaw
Tel: Warsaw 6281001

Ambassador Extraordinary and Plenipotentiary, His Excellency Michael J. Llewellyn-Smith, CMG (1991).
Counsellor, R. A. E. Gordon, OBE (*Deputy Head of Mission*).
Defence and Air Attaché, Gp. Capt. H. H. Moses.
Naval and Military Attaché, Lt.-Col. J. R. M. Pitt.

BRITISH COUNCIL REPRESENTATIVE, Charles Chadwick, OBE, Al. Jerozolimskie 59, 00-697 Warsaw.

EDUCATION

Elementary education (ages seven to 15) is compulsory and free. Secondary education is optional and free. There are universities at Kraków, Warsaw, Poznan, Lódź, Wroclaw, Lublin and Toruń and a considerable number of other towns.

CULTURE

Polish is a western Slavonic tongue, the Latin alphabet being used. Polish literature developed rapidly after the foundation of the University of Kraków (a printing press was established there in 1474 and Copernicus died there in 1543). A national school of poetry and drama survived the dismemberment and the former era of romanticism, whose chief Polish exponent was Adam Mickiewicz, was followed by realistic and historical fiction, including the works of Henryk Sienkiewicz (1846–1916), Nobel Prize-winner for Literature in 1905; Boleslaw Prus (1847–1912); Stanislaw Reymont (1868–1925), Nobel Prize-winner in 1924; Czeslaw Milosz, Nobel Prize-winner in 1980.

ECONOMY

On 3 January 1946, a decree was issued to provide for the nationalization of mines, petroleum resources, water, gas and electricity services, banks, textile factories and large retail stores. Until recently over 99 per cent of Polish industry was stated to be 'socialized', but 68 per cent of agricultural land was privately farmed. Legislation passed in July 1990 provides a framework for 80 per cent of the economy to be transferred from the state to the private sector.

TRADE WITH UK

	1990	1991
Imports from UK	£221,536,000	£347,069,000
Exports to UK	357,164,000	313,828,000

PORTUGAL
República Portuguesa

AREA – Continental Portugal occupies the western part of the Iberian Peninsula, covering an area of 34,317 sq. miles (88,880 sq. km). It lies between 36° 58′ and 42° 12″ N. lat. and 6° 11′ 48″ and 9° 29′ 45″ W. long. It is 362 miles in length from north to south, and averages about 117 miles in breadth from east to west.

POPULATION – The population (UN estimate 1990) is 10,525,000 (including the Azores and Madeira).

LANGUAGE – Portuguese is a Romance language with admixtures of Arabic and other idioms. It is the language of Portugal and Brazil, and is the *lingua franca* of Angola, Mozambique, Cape Verde, São Tomé and Principe, East Timor and Guinea-Bissau. Portuguese language and literature reached the culminating point of their development in the *Lusiadas* (dealing with the voyage of Vasco da Gama) and other works of Camoens (Camões) (1524–80). There are four morning and three evening daily newspapers in Lisbon and three morning papers in Oporto, and six main weekly newspapers.

CAPITAL – ΨLisbon, population estimate (1989) 2,128,000. ΨOporto 1,683,000.

CURRENCY – Escudo (Esc) of 100 centavos.

FLAG – Divided vertically into unequal parts of green and red with the national emblem over all on the line of division.

NATIONAL ANTHEM – A Portuguesa.

NATIONAL DAY – 10 June.

HISTORY

From the eleventh century until 1910 the government of Portugal was a monarchy, and for many centuries included the Vice-Royalty of Brazil, which declared its independence in 1822. In 1910 an armed rising in Lisbon drove King Manuel II and the royal family into exile, and the National Assembly of 21 August 1911 sanctioned a republican form of government. A period of great political instability ensued until eventually the military stepped in. The Constitution of 1933 gave formal expression to the corporative 'Estado Novo' (New State) which was personified by Dr Salazar, Prime Minister 1932–68. Dr Caetano succeeded Salazar as Prime Minister in 1968 but his failure to liberalize the regime or to conclude the wars in the African colonies resulted in his government's overthrow by a military coup on 25 April 1974. The next two years were characterized by great political turmoil with no fewer than six provisional governments between April 1974 and July 1976 but with the failure of an attempted coup by the extreme left in November 1975 the situation began to become more stable.

GOVERNMENT

Constitutional reforms in 1982 reduced the President's scope for day-to-day intervention in government but the decision to dissolve the Assembly is still largely the President's. The revisions also ended the military's capacity for political interference, and created two new organs of state, the Constitutional Tribunal and the Council of State, to advise the President. Further constitutional reforms were made in 1989.

The President, elected for a five-year term by universal adult suffrage, appoints the Prime Minister. Legislative authority is vested in the 230-member Assembly of the Republic, elected by a system of proportional representation for a term of up to four years.

In the General Election held on 6 October 1991, the Social Democratic Party (PSD) won 135 seats; the Socialist Party (PS) 72 seats; the Communist Party (PCP) 17 seats, the Christian Democrats (CDS) 5 seats and the National Solidarity Party 1 seat.

HEAD OF STATE
President of the Republic, Dr Mario Soares, *elected*, 16 February 1986, *re-elected*, 13 January 1991.

MINISTERS as at June 1992
Prime Minister, Anibal Cavaco Silva.
Minister of the Presidency, Defence, Joaquim Fernando Nogueira.
Justice, Dr Alvaro Laborinho Lucio.
Parliamentary Affairs, Luis Marques Mendes.
Finance, Jorge Braga de Macedo.
Planning and Territorial Administration, Luis Valente de Oliveira.
Home Affairs, Manuel Dias Loureiro.
Foreign, João de Deus Pinheiro.
Agriculture, Arlindo Marques da Cunha.
Industry and Energy, Luis Mira Amaral.
Education, António Couto dos Santas.
Public Works, Transport and Communications, Joaquim Ferreira do Amaral.
Health, Arlindo Gomes de Carvalho.
Labour and Social Security, José Silva Peneda.
Commerce and Tourism, Fernando Faria de Oliveira.
Environment and Natural Resources, Carlos Borrego.
Sea, Eduardo de Azevedo Soares.

PORTUGUESE EMBASSY
11 Belgrave Square, London SW1X 8PP
Tel 071-235 5331

Ambassador Extraordinary and Plenipotentiary, His Excellency Antonio Vaz-Pereira (1989).
Minister Counsellor, Francisco Seixas-da-Costa.

BRITISH EMBASSY
35-37 Rua de S. Domingos à Lapa, 1200 Lisbon
Tel: Lisbon 3961191

Ambassador Extraordinary and Plenipotentiary, His Excellency Hugh James Arbuthnott, CMG (1989).

There are British Consulates in *Oporto, Portimão, Funchal* (Madeira) and *Ponta Delgada* (Azores).

BRITISH COUNCIL REPRESENTATIVE, J. Mallon, OBE, Rua de Sao Marçal 174, 1294 Lisbon.
BRITISH PORTUGUESE CHAMBER OF COMMERCE, Rua da Estrela 8, 1200 Lisbon and Rua Sa de Bandeira 784-20E, Frente, 4000 Oporto.

DEFENCE

Most physically fit males are liable for military service but conscription is becoming increasingly selective as the armed forces were greatly reduced following the end of the colonial wars, and reorganized and re-equipped for a conventional national defence role. The armed forces have a total active strength of 61,800 (33,300 conscripts) with reserves of 190,000.

The present strength of the Army is 33,100 (23,000 conscripts), with 146 main battle tanks, 415 armoured personnel carriers and reconnaissance vehicles, and 306 artillery pieces. One brigade is earmarked for NATO service. The Navy consists of 15,300 personnel (5,400 conscripts), including 2,500 marines, manning about 60 craft of various types, including three submarines and 10 frigates. The present serving strength of the Air Force is 13,400 (4,900 conscripts), including 2,300 paratroops, with 83 combat aircraft plus helicopters and transport and training aircraft.

EDUCATION

Education is free and compulsory for nine years from the age of six. Secondary education is mainly conducted in state lyceums, commercial and industrial schools, but there are also private schools. There are also military, naval, technical, polytechnic and other special schools. There are old established universities at Coimbra (founded in 1290), Oporto and Lisbon. New universities have been established at Lisbon, Braga, Aveiro, Vila Real, Faro, Evora and in the Azores.

COMMUNICATIONS

There is an international airport at Portela, about six miles from Lisbon, and the airports of Pedras Rubras near Oporto and Faro airport in the Algarve are also used for scheduled international services. There are direct flights between London and Manchester and Faro in the Algarve.

ECONOMY

The chief agricultural products are cork, cereals, rice, vegetables, olives, figs, citrus fruits, almonds, timber, port wine and table wines. There are extensive forests of pine, cork, eucalyptus and chestnut covering about 20 per cent of the total area of the country.

The principal mineral products are pyrites, wolfram, uranium, iron ores, copper and sodium and calcium minerals.

The country is so far only moderately industrialized, but is fairly rapidly extending its industries. The principal manufactures are textiles, clothing and footwear, machinery (including electric machinery and transport equipment), pulp and paper, pharmaceuticals, foodstuffs (tomato concentrates and canned fish), chemicals, fertilizers, wood, cork, furniture, cement, glassware and pottery. There are a modern steelworks and two large shipbuilding and repair yards at Lisbon and Setúbal, working mainly for foreign shipowners. There are several hydro-electric power stations and a new thermal power station.

FINANCE
Portugal is a member of the European Monetary Agreement, the World Bank, the International Monetary Fund and the International Finance Corporation. The country has substantial gold and foreign exchange reserves. The Portuguese Escudo joined the European Community exchange rate mechanism in April 1992.

TRADE
The principal imports are cereals, meat, raw and semimanufactured iron and steel, industrial machinery, chemicals, crude oil, motor vehicles and raw materials for textiles.

The principal exports are textiles, footwear, timber, pulp, automotive parts, cork, electrical and other machinery, and chemicals.

	1988	1989
Total imports	£6,164,627m	£11,535,432m
Total exports	4,230,727m	7,738,209m

Trade with UK	1990	1991
Imports from UK	£1,033,268,000	£1,085,084,000
Exports to UK	1,176,161,000	1,043,511,000

The British share of the Portuguese market was 7.6 per cent in 1990 and the UK was the fourth largest market for Portuguese exports.

OVERSEAS REGIONS

Madeira and The Azores are two administratively autonomous regions of Portugal, having locally elected assemblies and governments.

MADEIRA

Madeira is a group of islands in the Atlantic Ocean about 520 miles south-west of Lisbon, and consists of Madeira, Porto, Santo and three uninhabited islands (Desertas). The total area is 314 sq. miles (813 sq. km), with a population of 271,400 (1989). ΨFunchal in Madeira, the largest island (270 square miles), is the capital, with a population of 44,111; Machico (10,905).

THE AZORES

The Azores are a group of nine islands (Flores, Corvo, Terceira, São Jorge, Pico, Faial, Graciosa, São Miguel and Santa Maria) in the Atlantic Ocean, with a total area of 922 sq. miles (2,387 sq. km), and a population of 255,100 (1989). ΨPonta Delgada, on São Miguel, is the capital of the group; population is 137,700. Other ports are ΨAngra, in Terceira (55,900) and ΨHorta (16,300).

OVERSEAS TERRITORY

MACAO

Macao, situated at the mouth of the Pearl River, comprises a peninsula and the islands of Coloane and Taipa, having an area of six sq. miles (15.5 sq. km), with a population (UN estimate 1990) of 479,000. Portuguese trade with China began early in the 16th century and Macao became a Portuguese colony in 1557; in a Sino-Portuguese treaty of 1887 China recognized Portugal's sovereignty over, and government of, Macao. In 1974 Portugal changed Macao's status from that of an Overseas Province to 'a territory under Portuguese administration'. Following the Sino-British Joint Declaration on Hong Kong in 1984, Sino-Portuguese negotiations on the transfer of administration began in 1986 and an agreement on the transfer of the administration of Macao to the Chinese authorities was signed on 13 April 1987. Macao will become a 'special administrative region' of China when transferred on 20 December 1999.

Macao is subject to Portuguese constitutional law but otherwise enjoys administrative, economic and financial autonomy. The Governor is appointed by the Portuguese President and there is a 23-member legislative assembly, which has a three-year term. The assembly comprises seven members appointed by the Governor; eight directly elected, and eight indirectly elected by business associations. A new electoral system which came into effect 28 February 1984 gave equal voting rights to all residents, thus enfranchising the Chinese population.

Macao's major industry is textile manufacturing which accounts for 62 per cent of all exports. Port Macao is served by British, Portuguese and Dutch shipping lines and has regular services to Hong Kong, some 35 miles away.

Governor, Rocha Vieira.

Trade with UK	1990	1991
Imports from UK	£11,398,000	£15,329,000
Exports to UK	44,809,000	40,010,000

QATAR
Dawlat Qatar

The state of Qatar covers the peninsula of Qatar from approximately the northern shore of Khor al Odaid to the eastern shore of Khor al Salwa. The area is about 4,247 sq. miles (11,000 sq. km).

POPULATION – The population (UN estimate 1990) is 368,000. The great majority of the population is concentrated in the urban district of the capital Doha. Only a small minority still pursue the traditional life of the semi-nomadic tribesmen and fisherfolk.

CAPITAL – ΨDoha, population (estimated) 220,000. Other towns include Khor, Dukhan, Wakra and ΨUmm Said.
CURRENCY – Qatar riyal of 100 dirhams.
FLAG – White and maroon, white portion nearer the mast; vertical indented line comprising 17 angles divides the colours.
NATIONAL DAY – 3 September.

GOVERNMENT

Until 1971, Qatar was one of the nine independent Emirates in the Arabian Gulf in special treaty relations with the UK. In that year, with the withdrawal of British forces from the area, these special treaty relations were terminated. On 2 April 1970 a provisional constitution for Qatar was proclaimed, providing for the establishment of a Council of Ministers and for the formation of a Consultative Council to assist the Council of Ministers in running the affairs of the state. There are no political parties or legislature. Qatar is a member of the Arab League as well as of the United Nations.

HEAD OF STATE

Amir of Qatar and Prime Minister, HH Sheikh Khalifa bin Hamad Al Thani, GCMG, GCB, *assumed power* 22 February 1972.

Heir Apparent, Minister of Defence and Commander-in-Chief of Armed Forces, HH Sheikh Hamad bin Khalifa Al Thani, KCMG.

COUNCIL OF MINISTERS as at June 1992

Interior, HE Sheikh Abdullah bin Khalifa Al Thani.
Finance and Petroleum, HE Sheikh Abdulaziz bin Khalifa Al Thani.
Foreign Affairs, HE Mubarak Ali Al Khater.
Education, HE Abdulaziz Abdullah Turki.
Justice, temporary Minister for Public Health, HE Sheikh Ahmed bin Saif Al Thani.
Economy and Commerce HE Sheikh Hamad bin Jassim bin Hamad Al Thani.
Industry and Public Works, HE Ahmed Mohamed Ali Al Subaie.
Municipal Affairs and Agriculture, temporary Minister for Electricity and Water, HE Sheikh Hamad bin Jassim bin Jabr Al Thani.
Labour, Social Affairs and Housing, HE Abdulrahman Saad Al Dirham.
Communications and Transport, HE Abdulla bin Saleh Al Manei.
Public Health, HE Sheikh Khaled bin Mohamed bin Ali Al Thani.
Information and Culture, HE Sheikh Hamad bin Suhaim Al Thani.
Amiri Diwan Affairs, HE Dr Issa Ghanim Al Kuwari.

EMBASSY OF THE STATE OF QATAR

27 Chesham Place, London SW1X 8HG
Tel 071-235 0851

Ambassador Extraordinary and Plenipotentiary, His Excellency Abdul Rahman Abdulla Al-Wohaibi, KCVO (1989).

BRITISH EMBASSY

PO Box 3, Doha
Tel: Doha 421991

Ambassador Extraordinary and Plenipotentiary, His Excellency Graham Boyce, CMG (1990).
First Secretary, F. G. Geere (*Commercial*).
Second Secretary, R. Davis (*Consul and Administration*).
Vice Consul, F. A. Drayton.

BRITISH COUNCIL REPRESENTATIVE, J. Shorter, Ras Abu Aboud Road (PO Box 2992), Doha.

ECONOMY

Although Qatar is a desert country, there are gardens and smallholdings near Doha and to the north and encouragement is being given to the development of agriculture.

The Qatar General Petroleum Corporation is the state-owned company controlling Qatar's interests in oil, gas and petrochemicals. The corporation is responsible for Qatar's oil production onshore and offshore. The production level for Qatar agreed in OPEC is currently 371,000 b.p.d. Explorations continue for further oil. The large reserves of natural gas in the North Field came into production with the opening of the first phase in September 1991. A 50,000 b.p.d. oil refinery was commissioned in 1984 to increase domestic refinery capacity.

Current industries include a steel mill, a fertilizer plant, a cement factory, a petrochemical complex and two natural gas liquids plants. With the exception of the cement works, which is at Umm Bab, all these industries are at Umm Said, about 30 miles south of Doha. There are tentative plans for new industry, including an aluminium smelter, a second ammonia plant and a methanol plant, downstream of the North Field.

Qatar is also expanding its infrastructure including electrical generation and water distillation, roads, houses, and government buildings, although reduced demand for crude oil in international markets has led to a downturn in the economy and a slower rate of development than hitherto.

TRADE WITH UK

	1990	1991
Imports from UK	£98,504,000	£109,248,000
Exports to UK	5,004,000	5,488,000

COMMUNICATIONS

Regular air services connect Qatar with Bahrain and the United Arab Emirates, Kuwait, Oman, Saudi Arabia, Jordan, Syria, Lebanon, Egypt, the Indian sub-continent, Africa and Europe. The Qatar Broadcasting Service transmits on medium, shortwave, and VHF. Regular television transmissions in colour began in 1974 and a second channel opened in 1982.

ROMANIA
România

AREA AND POPULATION – Romania is a republic of south-eastern Europe, formerly the classical *Dacia* and *Scythia Pontica*. The area of Romania is 91,699 sq. miles (237,500 sq. km) and the population (UN 1990 estimate) is 23,200,000.

LANGUAGE – Romanian is a Romance language with many archaic forms and with admixtures of Slavonic, Turkish, Magyar and French words. There is wealth of folk-songs and folklore, transmitted orally through many centuries and collected in the 19th century.

RELIGION – The leading religion is that of the Romanian Orthodox Church; the Roman Catholics and some Protestant denominations are of importance numerically.

ETHNIC GROUPS – There is a Hungarian minority of around 2.5 million, and a dwindling German minority of around 150,000.

CAPITAL – Bucharest, on the Dimbovita, population (1989 estimate) 2,036,894. Other large towns are:

Braşov	352,640	ΨGalati	238,292
Constanţa	315,917	Craiova	300,030
Cluj-Napoca	317,914	Ploieşti	247,502
Iasi	330,195	ΨBrăila	242,595
Timişoara	333,365		

CURRENCY – Leu (*plural* Lei) of 100 bani.
FLAG – Three vertical bands, blue, yellow, red.
NATIONAL ANTHEM – Trei Culori (Three colours).
NATIONAL DAY – 23 August (Liberation Day, 1944).

HISTORY

Romania has its origin in the union of the Danubian principalities of Wallachia and Moldavia under the Treaty of Paris (April 1856). The principalities remained separate entities under Turkish suzerainty until 1859, when Prince Alexandru Ion Cuza was elected Prince of both, still under the suzerainty of Turkey. Prince Cuza abdicated in 1866 and was succeeded by Prince Charles of Hohenzollern-Sigmaringen, in whose successors the crown was vested. By the Treaty of Berlin (13 July 1878) the principality was recognized as an independent state, and part of the Dobrudja (which had been occupied by the Romanians) was incorporated. On 27 March 1881 it was recognized as a Kingdom. The First World War added Bessarabia, the Bukovina, Transylvania, the Banat and Crisana-Maramures, these additions of territory being confirmed in the Treaty of St Germain, 1919, and the Treaty of Petit Trianon, 1920.

On 27 June 1940, in compliance with an ultimatum from USSR, Bessarabia and Northern Bukovina were ceded to the Soviet government, and in August 1940 Romania ceded to Bulgaria the portion of southern Dobrudja taken from Bulgaria in 1913.

Romania became 'The Romanian People's Republic' in December 1947, on the abdication of King Michael. A new constitution, modelled on the Soviet Constitution of 1936, was adopted unanimously on 24 September 1952, by the Grand National Assembly. The leading political force from the Second World War until 1989 was the Romanian Communist Party.

A revolution in December 1989 led to the overthrow of Nicolae Ceauşescu, President since 1967, and the collapse of his government. A provisional government was formed which abolished the leading role of the Communist Party and promised free elections. In May 1990 presidential and parliamentary elections took place under a system of universal adult suffrage and proportional representation. There is a Senate of 119 members and a 396-member Assembly of Deputies.

The National Salvation Front government was brought down in October 1991 by riots over continuing economic hardship, led by the coalminers. President Iliescu appointed Theodor Stolojan as Prime Minister of an interim transitional coalition government which took office in October 1991. Economic and democratic reforms were speeded up; a new constitution was passed by parliament in November 1991 and affirmed by a referendum in December that year. The constitution formally makes Romania a multi-party democracy and endorses human rights and a market economy. The first free local elections were held in February 1992, in which the Opposition Democratic Convention gained ground at the expense of the National Salvation Front. New presidential and parliamentary elections are scheduled for 27 September 1992.

Head of State
President of the Republic, Ion Iliescu, *elected*, 20 May 1990.

Government as at June 1992
Prime Minister, Theodor Stolojan.
Economy and Finance, George Danielescu.
Foreign Affairs, Adrian Năstase.
National Defence, Lt.-Gen. Constantin Nicolae Spiroiu.
Interior, Victor Babiuc.
Industry, Dan Constantinescu.
Justice, Mircea Ionescu-Quintus.
Education and Science, Mihail Golu.
Labour and Social Protection, Dan Mircea Popescu.
Agriculture and Food, Petru Marculescu.
Trade and Tourism, Constantin Fota.
Transport, Traian Băsescu.
Public Works and Physical Planning, Dan Nicolae.
Culture, Ludovic Spiess.
Communications, Andrei Chirică.
Health, Mircea Maiorescu.
Environment, Marcian Bleahu.
Youth and Sports, Ioan Moldovan.
Budget at the Ministry of Economy and Finance, Florian Bercea.
Relations with Parliament, Ion Aurel Stoica.
Secretary of State at the Ministry of Education, Emil Tocaci.

Embassy of Romania
4 Palace Green, London w8 4QD
Tel 071-937 9666

Ambassador Extraordinary and Plenipotentiary, His Excellency Sergiu Celac (1990).

British Embassy
24 Strada Jules Michelet, 70154 Bucharest
Tel: Bucharest 120 303/4/5/6

Ambassador Extraordinary and Plenipotentiary, His Excellency Andrew Bache, CMG (1992).
Counsellor, Deputy Head of Mission, C. J. Ingham.
Defence, Naval and Military Attaché, Lt.-Col. P. G. Davies.
Cultural Attaché and British Council Representative, C. C. Henning.

ECONOMY

Wallachia, Moldavia and Transylvania are potentially among the most fertile areas in Europe, and agriculture and sheep and cattle raising are the principal industries of Romania, although extreme weather conditions can have adverse effects on crops. These are principally cereal crops, legumes and other vegetables, flax and hemp. Vines and fruits are also grown. The forests of the mountainous regions are extensive, and the timber industry is important.

Socialization of agriculture was completed when collectivization was achieved in the spring of 1962. Since December 1989 agricultural workers have been allocated plots of land and are allowed to sell their produce on the open market. One-third of the arable land is now farmed independently. Of the remaining 6 million hectares, one-third belongs to state farms and two-thirds to co-operative farms. A law on land privatization was adopted in early 1991, allowing for private ownership of plots up to 10 hectares in size. Allocation was to take place in November 1991.

Before the Second World War, petroleum and agriculture were the backbone of the Romanian economy but rapid industrialization since 1948 has meant that they no longer hold the same dominant position. There are plentiful supplies of natural gas, together with various mineral deposits including coal, iron ore, bauxite, lead, zinc, copper and uranium in quantities which allow a substantial part of the requirements of industry to be met from local resources. Production of crude oil was put at about 9,400,000 tonnes in 1988.

The economy has faced increasing problems since the late 1970s, the result of over investment in energy-intensive heavy industry and neglect of agriculture, which has led to food shortages. The effects of these policies were aggravated by the international recession and by high interest rates, and Romania was severely in debt by the early 1980s. The Ceauşescu government sought to alleviate the situation by reducing borrowing and cutting imports. The formerly centrally-planned economy is being transformed into a market economy under the new government. Thirty per cent of state property is to be distributed in the form of vouchers or shares to the population. The rest is to be sold off. Foreign investment and ownership of up to 100 per cent of enterprises is now permitted. Industrial output declined sharply in 1990–1.

Trade

In 1990 imports were 4,374m roubles and $5,132m. The trade deficit was 700m roubles and $1,200m. Imports are chiefly semi-manufactured goods, raw materials, machinery and metals; export consists principally of maize, wheat, barley, oats, petroleum, timber, cattle, meat, machines and industrial equipment.

Trade with UK	1990	1991
Imports from UK	£85,879,000	£58,735,000
Exports to UK	61,215,000	58,531,000

EDUCATION

Education is free and nominally compulsory. There are universities at Bucharest, Iasi, Cluj, Timişoara, Craiova and Braşov, polytechnics at Bucharest, Timişoara, Cluj, Braşov, Galati and Iasi, two commercial academies at Bucharest and Braşov, and agricultural colleges at Bucharest, Iasi, Cluj, Craiova and Timişoara.

COMMUNICATIONS

In 1979 there were 11,113 km of railway open for traffic. The mercantile marine had a gross tonnage of 13,220,000 tons in 1979. The principal ports are Constanta (on the Black Sea), Sulina (on the Danube Estuary), Galati, Braila, Giurgiu and Turnu Severin. The Danube and the Black Sea are linked by a canal completed in 1984. Romania is a member of the Danube Commission whose seat is at Budapest.

RWANDA
Republika y'u Rwanda

Rwanda, formerly part of the Belgian-administered trusteeship of Ruanda-Urundi, has an area of 10,169 sq. miles (26,338 sq. km), and a population (UN estimate 1990) of 7,181,000, mainly of the Hutu tribe, with Tutsi and Twa minorities.

Capital – Kigali (156,000).
Currency – Rwanda franc of 100 centimes.
Flag – Three vertical bands, red, yellow and green with letter R on yellow band.
National Day – 1 July.

GOVERNMENT

A referendum held in September 1961 showed the majority of the population were opposed to the retention of the monarchy which was accordingly abolished on 2 October

1961. Rwanda became an independent Republic on 1 July 1962, with Gregoire Kayibanda as head of state and head of the government. He was deposed in 1973, and replaced by a military government under Maj.-Gen. Juvénal Habyarimana.

In October 1990, Rwanda was invaded by the Rwandan Patriotic Front, composed of members of the minority Tutsi tribe in exile in Uganda. Attempts to reach a binding ceasefire began at talks in June 1992 between the Government and the Rwandan Patriotic Front, and a ceasefire agreement was signed in July 1992. Meanwhile the MRND (National Revolutionary Movement for Development), renamed the National Republican Movement for Democracy and Development, ended its monopoly of power in April 1991. A new multi-party constitution was promulgated in July 1991, introducing the post of prime minister and restricting the tenure of the president. A coalition transitional government was formed in April 1992 by the MRND and four opposition parties. This transitional government reached agreement with the Rwandan Patriotic Front in August 1992 on political reforms and a new interim government.

HEAD OF STATE

President, Maj.-Gen. Juvénal Habyarimana, *assumed office*, 5 July 1973, *elected*, 24 Dec. 1978, *re-elected*, 19 Dec. 1983 and 17 Dec. 1988.

TRANSITIONAL GOVERNMENT as at May 1992

Prime Minister, Dismas Nsengiyaremye.
Foreign Minister, Boniface Ngulinzaira.
Interior, Faustin Munyazesa.
Justice, Stanislas Mbonampeka.
Defence, James Gasana.
Finance, Marc Rugenera.

EMBASSY OF THE REPUBLIC OF RWANDA
1 avenue des Fleurs, Woluwe Saint Pièrre, Brussels 1150, Belgium
Tel: Brussels 7630702

Ambassador Extraordinary and Plenipotentiary, François Ngarukiyintwali (1991).

BRITISH AMBASSADOR (resident in Kinshasa, Zaire).

ECONOMY

Coffee (accounting for 90 per cent of Rwanda's export earnings in 1989), tea and sugar are grown. Tin, hides, bark of quinine and extract of pyrethrum flowers are also exported.

The National University of Rwanda is situated at two campuses, Butare and Ruhengeri.

In 1987 total imports were valued at US$351.7m; total exports, US$112.3m.

TRADE WITH UK

	1990	1991
Imports from UK	£1,915,000	£2,334,000
Exports to UK	2,128,000	2,193,000

ST CHRISTOPHER AND NEVIS

The Federation of St Christopher and Nevis

The State of St Christopher and Nevis is located at the northern end of the eastern Caribbean. It comprises the islands of St Christopher (St Kitts) (68 sq. miles) and Nevis (36 sq. miles); combined population (UN estimate 1990) 44,000.

St Christopher, lat. 17° 18′ N. and long. 62° 48′ W., was the first island in the British West Indies to be colonized (1623). The central area of the island is forest-clad and mountainous, rising to the 3,792 ft. Mount Liamuiga.

Nevis, lat. 17° 10′ N. and long. 62° 35′ W., is separated from the southern tip of St Christopher by a strait two miles wide and is dominated by the central Nevis Peak, 3,232 ft.

CAPITAL – ΨBasseterre (estimated population, 15,000). Chief town of Nevis is ΨCharlestown (population 1,200), which is a port of entry.

CURRENCY – East Caribbean dollar (EC$) of 100 cents.

FLAG – Three diagonal bands, green, black and red; each colour separated by a stripe of yellow. Two white stars on the black band.

NATIONAL ANTHEM – Oh Land of Beauty.

NATIONAL DAY – 19 September (Independence Day).

GOVERNMENT

The Territory of St Christopher and Nevis became a State in Association with Britain on 27 February 1967. The State of St Christopher and Nevis became an independent nation on 19 September 1983, with a new constitution under which Great Britain relinquished its responsibility for defence and external affairs.

Under the constitution, The Queen is head of state, represented in the islands by the Governor-General. There is a central government with a ministerial system, the head of which is the Prime Minister of St Christopher and Nevis, and a National Assembly located on St Christopher. The National Assembly is composed of the Speaker, three senators (nominated by the Prime Minister and the Leader of the Opposition) and 11 elected representatives. On Nevis there is a Nevis Island Administration, the head being styled Premier of Nevis, and a Nevis Island Assembly of five elected and three nominated members.

Governor-General, His Excellency Sir Clement Athelston Arrindell, GCMG, GCVO, QC (1983).

CABINET as at August 1992

Prime Minister and Minister of Finance, Home Affairs and Foreign Affairs, Rt. Hon. Dr Kennedy A. Simmonds.
Deputy PM, Youth and Community Affairs, Communications, Works and Public Utilities, Hon. Sydney E. Morris.
Agriculture, Lands, Housing and Development, Hon. Hugh C. Heyliger.
Health, Labour and Women's Affairs, Hon. Constance Mitcham.
Trade, Industry and Tourism, Hon. Fitzroy P. Jones.
Minister in Ministry of Finance, Hon. Richard L. Caines.
Attorney-General, Hon. S. W. Tapley Seaton, CVO.
Minister in the Office of the Prime Minister, Hon. Joseph Parry.

ST KITTS HIGH COMMISSION
10 Kensington Court, London W8 5DL
Tel 071-937 9522

High Commissioner for the Eastern Caribbean States, His Excellency Richard Gunn, CBE (1987).

BRITISH REPRESENTATIVE, Ian Marsh (resides at Antigua).

ECONOMY

The economy of the islands has been based on sugar for over three centuries. Tourism and light industry are now being developed. The economy of Nevis centres on small peasant farmers, but a sea-island cotton industry is being developed for export.

FINANCE

	1989	1990
Revenue	EC$91,508,604	EC$96,900,000
Expenditure	84,427,961	94,100,000

TRADE WITH UK

	1990	1991
Imports from UK	£6,477,000	£5,755,000
Exports to UK	4,513,000	6,476,000

COMMUNICATIONS

Basseterre is a port of registry and has deep water harbour facilities. Golden Rock airport, on St Kitts, can take most large jet aircraft; Newcastle airstrip on Nevis can take small aircraft and has night landing facilities.

The sea ferry route from Basseterre to Charlestown is 11 miles.

ST LUCIA

St Lucia, the second largest of the Windward group, situated in 13° 54′ N. lat. and 60° 50′ W. long., at a distance of about 21 miles north of St Vincent, and 24 miles south of Martinique, is 27 miles in length, with an extreme breadth of 14 miles. It comprises an area of 238 sq. miles (616 sq. km), with a population (1990 UN estimate) of 150,000. It possesses perhaps the most interesting history of all the smaller islands. Fights raged hotly around it, and it constantly changed hands between the English and the French. It is mountainous, its highest point being Mt Gimie (3,145 ft) and for the most part it is covered with forest and tropical vegetation.

CAPITAL – ΨCastries (population 1989, 56,000) is recognized as being one of the finest ports in the West Indies on account of its reputation as a safe anchorage in the hurricane season.

CURRENCY – East Caribbean dollar (EC$) of 100 cents.

FLAG – Blue, bearing in centre a device of yellow over black over white triangles having a common base.

NATIONAL ANTHEM – Sons and Daughters of Saint Lucia.

NATIONAL DAY – 22 February (Independence Day).

GOVERNMENT

St Lucia became independent within the Commonwealth on 22 February 1979. The head of state is The Queen, represented in the island by a St Lucian Governor-General, and there is a bicameral legislature. The Senate has 11 members, six appointed by the ruling party, three by the Opposition and two by the Governor-General. The House of Assembly, which has a life of five years, has 17 elected Members and a Speaker, who may be elected from outside the House.

Governor-General, His Excellency Sir Stanislaus James, KCMG, OBE.

CABINET as at July 1992

Prime Minister, Minister of Finance, Planning, Development, Information and Broadcasting, Rt. Hon. John G. M. Compton.

Deputy PM and Minister of Home Affairs, Foreign Affairs, Trade and Industry, Hon. George Mallet.

Communications, Works and Transport, Hon. Gregory Avril.

Tourism, Public Utilities and National Mobilization, Hon. Romanus Lansiquot.

Youth, Community Development, Social Affairs, Sports and Co-operatives, Hon. Desmond Braithwaite.

Attorney-General and Minister for Legal Affairs, Hon. Senator Lorraine Williams.

Agriculture, Lands, Fisheries and Forestry, Hon. Ira D'Auvergne.

Education, Culture and Labour, Hon. Louis George.

Health and Local Government, Hon. Stephenson King.

ST LUCIA HIGH COMMISSION
10 Kensington Court, London W8 5DL
Tel 071–937 9522

High Commissioner for the Eastern Caribbean States, His Excellency Richard Gunn, CBE (1987).

OFFICE OF THE BRITISH HIGH COMMISSION
Columbus Square, PO Box 227, Castries
Tel: Castries 2248

High Commissioner (resides at Bridgetown, Barbados).
Resident Representative, P. T. Rouse, MBE.

ECONOMY

The economy is mainly agrarian, with manufacturing based on the processing of agricultural products. Principal crops are bananas, coconuts, cocoa, mangoes, avocado pears, breadfruit, spices, root crops such as cassava and yams, and citrus fruit. Attempts are being made to diversify the economy, in particular through greater industrialization. Tourism is also of increasing importance, with 204,000 visitors to the island in 1989.

TRADE

The principal exports are bananas, coconut products (copra, edible oils, soap), cardboard boxes, beer, and textile manufactures. The chief imports are flour, meat, machinery, building materials, motor vehicles, cotton piece goods, petroleum and fertilizers.

Trade with UK	1990	1991
Imports from UK	£17,573,000	£19,025,000
Exports to UK	£55,737,000	44,852,000

ST VINCENT AND THE GRENADINES

The territory of the State of St Vincent includes certain of the Grenadines, a chain of small islands stretching 40 miles across the Caribbean Sea between Grenada and St Vincent, some of the larger of which are Bequia, Canouan, Mayreau, Mustique, Union Island, Petit St Vincent and Prune Island. The whole territory extends 150 sq. miles (388 sq. km).

The main island, St Vincent, is situated between 13° 6′ and 14° 35′ N. latitude and 61° 6′ and 61° 20′ W. longitude, approximately 21 miles south-west of St Lucia and 100 miles west of Barbados. The island is 18 miles long and 11 miles wide at its extremities comprising an area of 133 sq. miles (344 sq. km), and a population (1990 UN estimate) of 116,000.

CAPITAL – ΨKingstown, estimated population 33,694.

CURRENCY – East Caribbean dollar (EC$) of 100 cents.

FLAG – Three vertical bands, of blue, yellow and green, with three green diamonds in the shape of a 'V' mounted on the yellow band.

NATIONAL ANTHEM – St Vincent, Land So Beautiful.

NATIONAL DAY – 27 October (Independence Day).

GOVERNMENT

St Vincent was discovered by Christopher Columbus in 1498. It was granted by Charles I to the Earl of Carlisle in 1627 and after subsequent grants and a series of occupations alternately by the French and English, it was finally restored to Britain in 1783.

St Vincent achieved full independence within the Commonwealth as St Vincent and the Grenadines on 27 October 1979.

St Vincent has a constitution under which there is a Governor-General who is The Queen's representative. Except where otherwise provided, the Governor-General is required to act in accordance with the advice of the Prime Minister.

The House of Assembly consists of 15 elected members and four Senators appointed by the Government and two by the Opposition. It is presided over by a Speaker elected by the House from within or without it. All 15 seats were won by the governing New Democratic Party at the election held on 16 May 1989.

Governor-General, His Excellency Sir David Jack, GCMG, MBE, *sworn in* 20 September 1989.

CABINET as at August 1992

Prime Minister, Minister of Finance and Planning, Rt. Hon. James Mitchell.
Attorney-General and Minister of Justice and Information, Hon. Parnell Campbell, CVO.
Culture, Education, Youth and Women's Affairs, Hon. John Horne.
Agriculture, Industry and Labour, Hon. Allan Cruickshank.
Foreign Affairs and Tourism, Hon. Herbert Young.
Health and the Environment, Hon. Burton Williams.
Trade and Consumer Affairs, Hon. Jonathan Peters.
Housing, Local Government, Community Development, Hon. Louis Jones.
Communications and Works, Hon. Jeremiah Scott.
Minister of State, Hon. Mrs Yvonne Gibson (*Education, Culture, Youth and Women's Affairs*).

ST VINCENT AND THE GRENADINES HIGH COMMISSION
10 Kensington Court, London W8 5DL
Tel 071-937 9522

High Commissioner for the Eastern Caribbean States, His Excellency Richard Gunn, CBE (1987).

OFFICE OF THE BRITISH HIGH COMMISSION
Granby Street (PO Box 132), Kingstown
Tel: St Vincent 71701

High Commissioner (resides at Bridgetown, Barbados).
Resident Representative, G. Greaves.

ECONOMY

This is based mainly on agriculture but the tourist and manufacturing industries have been expanding. The main products are bananas, arrowroot, coconuts, cocoa, spices and various kinds of food crops. The main imports are foodstuffs (meat, rice, beverages), textiles, lumber, cement and other building materials, fertilizers, motor vehicles and fuel.

TRADE WITH UK

	1990	1991
Imports from UK	£9,514,000	£7,316,000
Exports to UK	37,906,000	29,259,000

EL SALVADOR
República de El Salvador

AREA AND POPULATION – The Republic of El Salvador extends along the Pacific coast of Central America for 160 miles with a general breadth of about 50 miles, and contains an area of 8,124 sq. miles (21,041 sq. km), with a population (1990 estimate) of 5,252,000. The population density is one of the highest in the world with 253 inhabitants per square km. It is divided into 14 Departments.

The surface of the country is very mountainous, many of the peaks being extinct volcanoes. The highest are the Santa Ana volcano (7,700 ft.) and the San Vicente volcano (7,200 ft.). Much of the interior has an average altitude of 2,000 feet. The climate varies from tropical to temperate. The lowlands along the coast are generally hot, but towards the interior the altitude tempers the severity of the heat. There is a wet season from May to October, and a dry season from November to April. Earthquakes have been frequent in the history of El Salvador, the most recent being that of 10 October 1986, when considerable damage was done to San Salvador.

The principal river is the Rio Lempa. There is a large volcanic lake (Ilopango) a few miles to the east of the capital, while farther away and to the west lies the smaller lake of Coatepeque, which appears to have been formed in a vast crater flanked by the Santa Ana volcano.

LANGUAGE – The language of the country is Spanish. There are five daily newspapers published at the capital, and four in the provinces.

CAPITAL – San Salvador. Estimated population of metropolitan area, 2,000,000. Other towns are Santa Ana (417,000), San Miguel (157,838), Ψ La Union (Cutuco), Ψ La Libertad and Ψ Acajutia.

CURRENCY – El Salvador colón (₡) of 100 centavos.

FLAG – Three horizontal bands, sky blue, white, sky blue; coat of arms on white band.

NATIONAL ANTHEM – Saludemos La Patria Orgullosos (Let us proudly hail the Fatherland).

NATIONAL DAY – 15 September.

GOVERNMENT

El Salvador was conquered in 1526 by Pedro de Alvarado, and formed part of the Spanish vice-royalty of Guatemala until 1821.

After two years of government by a junta headed by José Napoleon Duarte, elections for a Constituent Assembly were held in March 1982, ending decades of military rule. Presidential elections, although boycotted by the guerrilla movement (Farabundo Martí National Liberation Front (FMLN)), were held in March 1984 and won by Duarte, the Christian Democrat leader, over the Nationalist Republican Alliance (ARENA) candidate. Alfredo Cristiani (ARENA) won the presidential elections in March 1989.

In elections to an enlarged 84-seat Legislative Assembly, held on 10 March 1991 and boycotted by the FMLN, ARENA won the largest number of seats (39) but failed to gain a majority. Negotiations continued between the government and the FMLN in an attempt to end the violence of both right and left, and culminated in the peace plan agreed in New York on 1 January 1992 and signed in Mexico City on 16 January 1992. A ceasefire took effect on 1 February with the swearing in of a commission to oversee implementation of the peace agreements, and the beginning of a nine-month transition period. During the transition period, the Army and FMLN forces are withdrawing to agreed positions, the

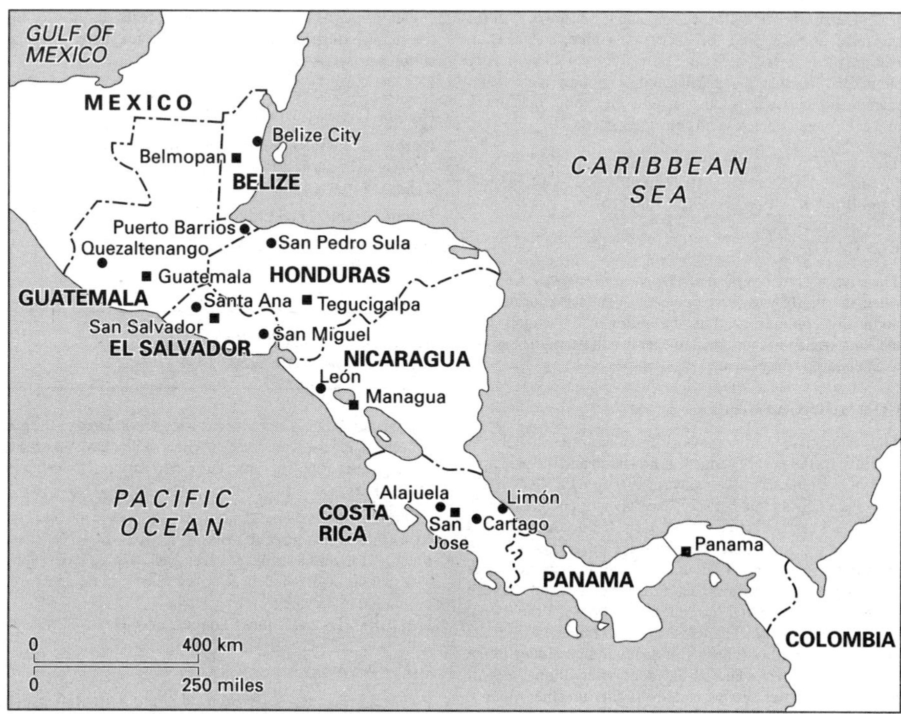

size of the Army is to be halved, a new civilian police force independent of military control is to be created, the FMLN will gradually disarm under UN supervision, and the FMLN will become a legal political party. In May 1991 the UN established the UN Observers for El Salvador (ONUSAL) which will monitor the implementation of the ceasefire and peace agreement.

HEAD OF STATE

President, Alfredo Felix Cristiani Burkard, *elected* 19 March 1989, *assumed office* 1 June 1989.
Vice-President, Francisco Merino.

CABINET as at June 1992

Minister of the Presidency, Dr Oscar Santamaría.
Foreign Affairs, Dr Manuel Pacas Castro.
Planning, Mirna Lievano de Márquez.
Interior, Col. Juan Antonio Martínez Varela.
Justice, Dr René Hernández Valiente.
Finance, Dr Rafael Alvarado Cano.
Economy, Arturo Zablah.
Education, Cecilia Gallardo de Cano.
Defence, Gen. René Emilio Ponce.
Labour and Social Security, Mauricio González.
Agriculture and Livestock, Antonio Cabrales.
Public Health and Social Welfare, Dr Lisandro Vásquez Sosa.
Works, José Castaneda Villacorta.
Secretary of Information, Mauricio Sandoval.

EMBASSY OF EL SALVADOR
5 Great James Street, London WC1N 3DA
Tel 071-430 2141

Ambassador Extraordinary and Plenipotentiary, His Excellency Dr Maurico Rosales-Rivera (1986).

BRITISH EMBASSY
PO Box 1591, San Salvador
Tel: San Salvador 239639

Ambassador Extraordinary and Plenipotentiary, His Excellency M. H. Connor (1992).

ECONOMY

The principal cash crops are coffee, which is grown principally on the slopes of the volcanoes, cotton, which is cultivated on the coastal plains, and sugarcane and shrimps. However, cotton and sugar production have decreased as a result of the civil war. Also cultivated are maize, sesame, indigo, rice, balsam, etc. In the lower altitudes towards the east, sisal is produced and used in the manufacture of coffee and cereal bags. Land reforms announced in March 1980 have largely been implemented. The Salvadorean Coffee Company, sugar exports and the banking system are nationalized but President Cristiani is in the process of privatizing these industries and introducing competition.

Existing factories make textiles, clothing, constructional steel, furniture, cement and household items. In 1989 GDP amounted to US$4,808 million (US$874 per capita). El Salvador is a member of the Central American Common Market. The first trade zone was inaugurated in November 1974 and others are planned.

BUDGET

	1988	1989
Revenue	₡2,843.8m	₡3,330.2m
Expenditure	3,042.2m	3,900.2m

TRADE

There is foreign exchange control. There is also a parallel market in US dollars.

Chief exports are coffee, cotton, sugar, shrimps, sisal (in the form of bags used for exporting coffee, sugar, etc.), balsam, meat, towels, hides and skins. The chief imports are chemicals, fertilizers, pharmaceutical goods, petroleum, manufactured goods, industrial and electronic machinery and equipment, vehicles and consumer goods.

Trade with UK	1990	1991
Imports from UK	£10,415,000	£14,545,000
Exports to UK	1,261,000	4,063,000

EDUCATION

The illiteracy rate has risen to 68.1 per cent (1985) since 1980 when the figure was 30.5 per cent. Primary education is nominally compulsory, but the number of schools and teachers available is too small to enable education to be given to all children of school age.

COMMUNICATIONS

The Executive Autonomous Port Commission (CEPA) administers the port of Cutuco, at La Union and the principal port of Acajutla, and the railways through FENADESAL. There is a railway line between San Salvador and Guatemala City and Puerto Barrios on the Caribbean coast but it is subject to interruption. The roads are paved and in good condition but some bridges are temporary structures following guerrilla action. There are good roads between Acajutla and the capital (60 miles), and between the capital and Guatemala City. The Pan-American Highway from the Guatemalan frontier follows this route and continues to the Honduran frontier. The El Salvador international airport can receive jet aircraft with daily flights to other Central American capitals, Mexico, and five US cities.

There are post and telegraph offices throughout the country. There are 100 broadcasting stations and six television stations.

SAN MARINO

Repubblica di San Marino

A small republic in the hills near Rimini, on the Adriatic, founded, it is said, by a pious stonecutter of Dalmatia in the fourth century. The Republic resisted Papal claims and those of neighbouring dukedoms during the 15th to 18th centuries, and its integrity and sovereignty is recognized and respected by Italy. San Marino became a member of the UN in March 1992. The area is approximately 23 sq. miles (61 sq. km.), the population (1992) is 24,000.

CITY – San Marino, on the slope of Monte Titano, has three towers, a fine church and Government palace, a theatre and museums.
CURRENCY – San Marino and Italian currencies are in circulation.
FLAG – Two horizontal bands, white, blue (with coat of arms of the Republic in centre).
NATIONAL DAY – 3 September.

The Republic is governed by a State Congress of ten members, under the presidency of two Heads of State, who are elected at six-monthly intervals. The Great and General Council, a legislative body of 60 members, is elected by universal suffrage for a term of five years. A Council of Twelve forms in certain cases a Supreme Court of Justice. A coalition government of the Christian Democratic Party and the Socialist Party took office in March 1992, succeeding the Christian Democrat/Communist Party coalition.

The principal products are wine, cereals, and cattle, and the main industries are tourism, ceramics, lime, concrete, cotton yarns, colour and paints.

HEADS OF STATE
Regents, Two 'Capitani Reggenti'.

CONSULATE-GENERAL IN LONDON
166 High Holborn, London WC1V 6SS
Tel 071-836 7744

Consul-General, The Lord Forte.

BRITISH CONSUL-GENERAL, M. Holmes, MBE (resident in Florence, Italy).

SÃO TOMÉ AND PRÍNCIPE

República Democrática de São Tomé e Príncipe

The islands of São Tomé and Príncipe are situated in the gulf of Guinea, off the west coast of Africa. They have an area of 372 sq. miles (964 sq. km), and a population (UN estimate 1990) of 121,000.

CAPITAL – ΨSão Tomé (25,000).
CURRENCY – Dobra of 100 centavos.
FLAG – Horizontal stripes of green, yellow, green, the yellow of double width and bearing two black stars; and a red triangle in the hoist.
NATIONAL DAY – 12 July (Independence Day).

GOVERNMENT

Following Portugal's decision to grant independence, a transitional government was installed in December 1974, and the islands became independent on 12 July 1975.

A multi-party constitution was approved by referendum in August 1990. The Movement for the Liberation of São Tomé and Príncipe (MLSTP), which had been the sole legal party since independence, was defeated by the opposition Democratic Convergence Party (PCD) in legislative elections held on 20 January 1991. Miguel Trovoada, an independent, was elected President on 3 March 1991. The President dismissed the government in April 1992, because of mounting criticism of economic reforms, and appointed a new Prime Minister.

HEAD OF STATE
President and Commander-in-Chief of the Armed Forces, Miguel Trovoada, *elected* 3 March 1991.

COUNCIL OF MINISTERS as at June 1992

Prime Minister, Noberto Costa Alegre.
Foreign Affairs and Co-operation, Albertino Braganca.
Defence, Evaristo Carvalho.
Economy and Finance, Arlindo Carvalho.
Justice and Labour, Olegario Pires Tiny.
Agriculture, Jose Mendes.
Health, Dulce Gomes.
Príncipe, Sylvestre Umbelina.
Commerce and Industry, Arfemiro Prazeres.

EMBASSY OF THE DEMOCRATIC REPUBLIC OF SÃO TOMÉ AND PRÍNCIPE
42 avenue Brugman, Brussels 1060, Belgium
Tel: Brussels 3475375

Ambassador Extraordinary and Plenipotentiary, new appointment awaited.

HONORARY CONSULATE
42 North Audley Street, London W1A 4PY
Tel 071-499 1995

Honorary Consul, Mr Wilder.

BRITISH CONSULATE
c/o Hull Blythe (Angola)Ltd., BP 15, São Tomé

British Ambassador (resident in Luanda, Angola).
Honorary Consul, J. Gomes.

TRADE

Cacao is the main product.

Trade with UK	1990	1991
Imports from UK	£879,000	£1,020,000
Exports to UK	114,000	1,000

SAUDI ARABIA

Al Mamlaka al Arabiya as-Sa'udiyya

The Kingdom of Saudi Arabia is a personal union of two regions, the Sultan of Nejd becoming also King of the Hejaz. Great Britain recognized Abdul Aziz Ibn Saud as an independent ruler, King of the Hejaz and of Nejd and its Dependencies, by the Treaty of Jeddah (20 May 1927). The name was changed to the Kingdom of Saudi Arabia in September 1932.

The total area of the Kingdom is about 830,000 sq. miles (2,149,640 sq. km), with a population (UN estimate 1990) of 14,870,000. Islam is the established and only permitted religion.

Saudi Arabia comprises almost the whole of the Arabian peninsula, with the exception of the Republic of Yemen in the extreme south, Oman and the UAE in the south-east and Qatar in the east. In the north-west it borders Jordan and in the north-east Iraq and Kuwait, while to the west lies the Red Sea and to the east the Gulf. The Nejd ('plateau'), now the Central Province, extends over the centre of the peninsula, including the Nafud and Dahna deserts. The Hejaz ('the boundary'), now the Western Province, extends along the Red Sea coast to Asir and contains the holy towns of Mecca and Medina. Mecca, about 60 km east of Jeddah, is the birthplace of the Prophet Mohammed, and contains the Great Mosque, within which is the Kaaba or sacred shrine of the Muslim religion. This is the focus of the annual Hajj ('pilgrimage'), performed by 1.4 million in 1990. Medina Al Munawwarah ('The City of Light'), some 300 km north of Mecca, is celebrated as the first city to embrace Islam and as the Prophet Mohammed's burial place (he died there on Rabia 12, AH 11, corresponding to 7 June AD 632).

Asir ('inaccessible') is named for its mountainous terrain, and, with the coastal plain of the Tihama, lies along the southern Red Sea coast from Hejaz to the border with Yemen. It is the only region to enjoy substantial rainfall. Water supplies are, however, supplemented by dams and irrigation. The east and south-east of the country are lower-lying and largely desert.

CAPITAL – Riyadh, population (1990) about 1.5 million. Other major centres are Jeddah (estimated population 1 million), Buraydah, Dammam, Hofuf, Mecca, Medina and Tabuk.

CURRENCY – Saudi riyal (SR) of 20 qursh or 100 halala.

FLAG – Green oblong, white Arabic device in centre: 'There is no God but God and Muhammad is the Prophet of God,' and a white scimitar beneath the lettering.

NATIONAL ANTHEM – Long live our beloved King.

HISTORY

In the 18th century Nejd was an independent state governed from Diriya (now in ruins, 25 km from Riyadh) and the stronghold of the Wahhabis, a puritanical Islamic sect. It subsequently fell under Turkish rule; in 1913 Abdul Aziz Ibn Saud threw off Turkish rule and captured the Turkish province of Al Hasa. In 1920 he captured the Asir, and in 1921, by force of arms, he added to his dominions the Jebel Shammar territory of the Rashid family. In 1925 he completed the conquest of the Hejaz.

GOVERNMENT

Saudi Arabia is a hereditary monarchy, ruled by the sons and grandsons of the state's founder, Abdul Aziz Ibn Saud, in accordance with the Sharia law of Wahhabi Islam. The line of succession, unlike in most western monarchies, passes from brother to brother according to age, although several sons of Ibn Saud renounced their right to the throne.

In 1992 King Fahd announced a new Basic Law based on Sharia law, and including rules to protect personal freedoms. A Consultative Council of 60 members appointed by the King was set up to share power with, and question the government, and to make recommendations to the King. The rules of succession have also been changed so that all sons and grandsons of Ibn Saud must be consulted before a new King accedes the throne.

HEAD OF STATE

Custodian of the Two Holy Mosques and King of Saudi Arabia, HM King Fahd bin Abdul Aziz, *born*, 1921, *ascended the throne* 1 June 1982.
Crown Prince, HRH Amir Abdullah bin Abdul Aziz.

COUNCIL OF MINISTERS as at August 1992

Prime Minister, HM King Fahd bin Abdul Aziz.
First Deputy Prime Minister and Commander of the National Guard, HRH Prince Abdullah bin Abdul Aziz.
Second Deputy Prime Minister, Defence and Aviation, HRH Prince Sultan bin Abdul Aziz.
Public Works and Housing, HRH Prince Mit'ab bin Abdul Aziz.
Interior, HRH Prince Naif bin Abdul Aziz.
Foreign Affairs, HRH Prince Saud al-Faisal bin Abdul Aziz.
Finance and National Economy, Muhammad Aba al-Khail.
Agriculture and Water, Dr Abdul Rahman bin Abdul Aziz bin Hassan Al al-Shaikh.
Municipal and Rural Affairs, Muhammad al-Shaikh.
Justice, Sheikh Mohammed bin Ibrahim al Jubeir.
Commerce, Dr Sulaiman al-Solaim.
Communications, Dr Hussain Mansouri.
Petroleum and Mineral Resources, Hisham Nazer.
Planning, Abdul Wahab al-Attar.
Labour and Social Affairs, Dr Mohamed Ali al-Faiz.
Information, Ali Sha'er.
Health, Faisal bin Abdul Aziz al Hejailan.
Pilgrimage and Endowments, Abdul Wahhab Ahmed Abdul Wasi.
Education, Dr Abdul Aziz Al-Abdullah al-Khuwaiter.
Higher Education, Khalid al-Angari.
Posts, Telegraphs and Telecommunications, Dr Alawi Darwish Kayyal.
Industry and Electricity, Abdul Aziz al-Zamil.

ROYAL EMBASSY OF SAUDI ARABIA
30 Charles Street, London W1X 7PM
Tel 071-917 3000

Ambassador Extraordinary and Plenipotentiary, His Excellency Dr Ghazi Al-Ghosaibi (1992).

Ministers Plenipotentiary, Ibrahim M. Mosly; Saud Ahmed M. Alyahya, LVO; Abdullah O. Barry, LVO.

BRITISH EMBASSY
PO Box 94351, Riyadh 11693
Tel: Riyadh 488 0077

Ambassador Extraordinary and Plenipotentiary, His Excellency Sir Alan Gordon Munro, KCMG (1989).
Counsellors, J. S. Laing, CMG (*Deputy Head of Mission*); C. Wilton (*Commercial*).
Defence and Military Attaché, Brig. M. J. Holroyd Smith, OBE.
Naval Attaché, Cdr. T. Waddington.
First Secretaries, M. D. K. Halsey (*Chancery*); P. O. Gooderham (*Economic*); A. Walker (*Commercial*); C. H. Woodland (*Consul-General*); M. Tonnison (*Defence Supply*).
CONSUL-GENERAL, L. E. Walker, OBE, LVO, PO Box 393, Jeddah 21411. There is also a trade office in Dhahran.

BRITISH COUNCIL REPRESENTATIVE, Clive Smith, OBE, Olaya Main Road, Al Mousa Centre, Tower B (PO Box 58012), Riyadh 11594. There is also an office in *Jeddah*.

ECONOMY

Outside the manufacturing centres which have grown up around some of the towns, most of the population are engaged in agriculture. The productivity of traditional dryland farming is increasingly supplemented by irrigation.

Oil was first found in commercial quantities in Dhahran, near Dammam, in 1938. Total production of crude oil peaked at 9.9 million b.p.d. in 1980, and in 1986 was 4.8 million b.p.d. About 97 per cent of the total is extracted by the Arabian-American Oil Company. Recoverable reserves stood at about 167 billion barrels at the end of 1986, equivalent to about 95 years' production at the 1986 rate. Aramco's 66-year lease will terminate in 1999 but the company was effectively nationalized in 1980.

The government actively encourages the establishment of manufacturing industries in the country. Industries have developed in the fields of construction materials, metal fabrication, simple machinery and electrical equipment, food and beverages, chemicals and plastics. Investment in industrial gases, intermediate petrochemicals, light engineering and machinery is encouraged.

Two industrial poles have been established at Jubail and

Yanbu, financed by the state agency Saudi Arabian Basic Industries Corporation. Linked by gas and oil pipelines, both are to have petrochemical complexes producing, initially, ethylene and methanol; six of the seven plants now on-stream are joint ventures with American and Japanese companies. Complete new cities are being built at each pole: Jubail will eventually house 300,000 and Yanbu 190,000.

The state agency Petromin operates three domestic refineries and two lubricant plants and the last of three joint-venture export refineries came on-stream in 1986. Total refining capacity is now approximately 1,950,000 b.p.d.

Trade

Oil remains the main source of receipts in the balance of payments. As a result, government revenues are markedly affected by oil prices and volume of production. The 1990 budget provided for expenditure of SR143,000 million (36 per cent on defence), and a revenue of SR25,000 million.

The leading suppliers of imports are USA, Japan, Germany, the UK, Italy and France and the chief customers for exports are Japan, France, USA and Singapore. There is a total ban on the importation of alcohol, pork products, firearms, and items regarded as non-Islamic or pornographic.

	1988	1989
Total imports	SR81,582m	SR79,219m
Total exports	88,896m	103,892m

Trade with UK	1990	1991
Imports from UK	£2,012,585,000	£2,228,965,000
Exports to UK	794,633,000	963,919,000

COMMUNICATIONS

The railway from the port of Dammam to the oilfields at Abqaiq and through Hofuf to Riyadh was opened in 1951, and a direct Dammam-Riyadh line opened in 1985. An extension to Jeddah via Medina and the reopening of the Hejaz railway are planned. Metalled roads connect all the cities and main towns; the network consisted of 28,500 km in 1985.

The principal port of the Gulf is Dammam which has 39 berths and an annual capacity of 9.1 million tons. Jeddah is the centre of commercial traffic on the Red Sea and has 51 piers, giving an annual capacity of 17 million tons.

The government-owned Saudi Arabian Airlines (Saudia) operate scheduled services to 22 domestic airports. There are international airports at Dhahran, Jeddah and Riyadh. Work on the new King Fahd International Airport in Eastern Province has yet to be completed. Saudia have an extensive overseas operation, and a large number of international airlines operate into the country.

Telecommunications are being rapidly expanded. The government is a major participant in the Arab Satellite Communications Organization.

EDUCATION

With the exception of a few schools for expatriate children, all schools are government supervised and segregated for boys and girls. By mid-1985 there were a total of 1,692,300 schoolchildren in 5,323 primary and 1,219 intermediate and 418 secondary schools.

There are universities in Jeddah, Mecca, Riyadh (branches in Abha and Qassim), Dammam (branch at Hofuf) and Dhahran, and there are Islamic universities in Medina and Riyadh. In addition there is great emphasis on vocational training, provided at 24 literacy and artisan skill training centres and 21 more advanced industrial, commercial and agricultural education institutes. Education in government-owned institutes is free at all levels.

SENEGAL
République du Sénegal

Senegal lies on the west coast of Africa between Mauritania in the north, Mali in the east, and Guinea-Bissau and Guinea in the south. The Gambia lies entirely within Senegal, except for its sea-coast. Senegal has an area of 75,750 sq. miles (196,192 sq. km), and a population (UN estimate 1990) of 7,327,000.

Capital – ΨDakar (1,000,000).
Currency – Franc CFA of 100 centimes.
Flag – Three vertical bands, green, yellow and red; a green star on the yellow band.
National Day – 4 April.

GOVERNMENT

Formerly a French colony, Senegal elected in November 1958 to remain within the French Community as an autonomous republic. A border dispute continues with Mauretania and there is an insurgent separatist movement in the southern Casamance region.

In March 1963 (after an attempted coup d'état by the then Prime Minister in the previous December) a new constitution was approved giving executive powers to the President, on the lines of the present French constitution. The process of political liberalization continued; there are now 16 political parties officially recognized. A general election for the National Assembly of 120 seats is held every five years.

Six parties contested the general election in February 1988. The Parti Socialiste (PS) took 103 seats and the Parti Démocratique Sénégalais (PDS) 17. A new government, including members of the opposition, was formed in April 1991.

In 1982, after an attempted coup in The Gambia in July 1981 had been put down with the aid of Senegalese troops, the Senegambia Confederation was established, but this collapsed in 1989.

Head of State

President and Head of Government, Abdou Diouf, *installed*, 1 Jan. 1981, *elected for a second seven-year term*, 28 Feb. 1988.

Ministers as at September 1992

Prime Minister, Habib Thiam.
Minister of State, Abdoulaye Wade.
Economy, Finance and Planning, Famara Ibrahima Sagna.
Armed Forces, Médoune Fall.
Guardian of the Seals, Minister of Justice, Serigne Lamine Diop.
Foreign Affairs, Djibo Leyti Ka.
Interior, Madieng Khary Dieng.
National Education, André Sonko.
Equipment, Transport and the Sea, Robert Sagna.
Rural Development and Water Resources, Cheikh Abdoul Khadre Cissokho.
Industry, Trade and Handicrafts, Alassane Dialy Ndiaye.
Tourism and Environment, Jacques Baudin.
Town Planning and Housing, Amath Dansokho.
Labour and Vocational Training, Ousmane Ngom.
Communication, Moctar Kebe.
Health and Social Action, Assane Diop.
Culture, Moustapha Ka.
African Economic Integration, Jean-Paul Diaz.
Youth and Sports, Abdoulaye Makhtar Diop.
Women, Children and the Family, Ndioro Ndiaye.

EMBASSY OF THE REPUBLIC OF SENEGAL
11 Phillimore Gardens, London W8 7QG
Tel 071-937 0925/6

Ambassador Extraordinary and Plenipotentiary, His Excellency Seydou Madani Sy (1991).

BRITISH EMBASSY
BP 6025, Dakar
Tel: Dakar 237392

Ambassador Extraordinary and Plenipotentiary, His Excellency Roger Campbell Beetham, LVO (1990).
First Secretary, M. J. Hentley (*Head of Chancery and Consul*).
Third Secretary, K. J. Lynch (*Vice Consul*).

BRITISH COUNCIL REPRESENTATIVE, A. Malamah-Thomas, 34–36 Blvd. de la Republique, Immeuble Sonatel, BP 6232, Dakar.

TRADE

Senegal's principal exports are groundnuts (raw and processed) and phosphates. Tourism is also of growing importance as a revenue earner.

Trade with UK	1990	1991
Imports from UK	£14,884,000	£13,960,000
Exports to UK	5,002,000	5,025,000

SEYCHELLES
The Republic of Seychelles

The Republic of Seychelles, in the Indian Ocean, consists of 115 islands with a total land area of 176 sq. miles, spread over 400,000 square miles of ocean. There is a relatively compact granitic group, 32 islands in all, with high hills and mountains (highest point about 2,972 ft.), of which Mahé is the largest and most populated (90 per cent of the population live on Mahé); and the outlying coralline group, for the most part only a little above sea-level. Although only 4° S. of the Equator, the climate is pleasant though tropical.
POPULATION – The population was estimated (mid 1990) to be 67,378.

CAPITAL – ΨVictoria (population, 1982, 24,733), on the north-east side of Mahé.
CURRENCY – Seychelles rupee (Rs) of 100 cents.
FLAG – Red over green, divided by wavy white band.
NATIONAL ANTHEM – Fyer Seselwa (Proud Seychellois).
NATIONAL DAY – 5 June.

GOVERNMENT

Proclaimed as French territory in 1756, the Mahé group began to be settled as a dependency of Mauritius from 1770, was captured by a British ship in 1794, changed hands several times between 1803 and 1814, when it was finally assigned to Great Britain. By Letters Patent of September 1903, these islands, together with the coralline group, were formed into a separate colony. On 29 June 1976, the islands became an independent republic within the Commonwealth. A coup d'état took place on 5 June 1977.

A new constitution making Seychelles a one-party state came into force in June 1979. The executive power lies with the President, who is elected by universal suffrage for a five-year term. Legislative power lies with the President and the People's Assembly which has 23 elected members and two nominated by the President.

A multi-party democratic system was re-introduced by the President in December 1991, and multi-party elections to a commission to draw up a new constitution were held in July 1992. These were won by the Seychelles People's Progressive Front (SPPF) of President René, who gained 12 seats on the 20-man commission, with the opposition Democratic Party gaining the remaining eight. The new constitution will be drawn up by the end of 1992 and put to a referendum in December, so that multi-party elections can be held under the new constitution soon afterwards.

HEAD OF STATE
President, France Albert René, *assumed office* 5 June 1977; *elected* 26 June 1979; *re-elected* 18 June 1984, and 12 June 1989.

COUNCIL OF MINISTERS as at June 1992
Defence, Tourism, Transport, Legal Affairs, Industry, The President.
Finance and Information, James Michel.
Administration and Manpower, Joseph Belmont.
Community Development, Esme Jumeau.
Environment, Economic Planning and External Relations, Danielle de St Jorre.
Health, Ralph Adam.
Agriculture and Fisheries, Jeremie Bonnelame.
Employment and Social Affairs, William Herminie.
Education, Simone Testa.
Local Government, Culture and Sports, Sylvette Frichot.

SEYCHELLES HIGH COMMISSION
Box No. 4PE, 111 Baker Street, 2nd Floor, Eros House, London W1M 1FE
Tel 071-224 1660

High Commissioner, His Excellency Sylvester Radegonde (1992).

BRITISH HIGH COMMISSION
Victoria House, PO Box 161 Victoria, Mahé
Tel: Victoria 215225

High Commissioner, His Excellency John Sharland (1991).

ECONOMY

The economy is based on tourism, fishing, small-scale agriculture and manufacturing, and the re-export of fuel for aircraft and ships.

Deep sea tuna fishing by foreign fleets under licence, improved trans-shipment and other port facilities at Victoria, exports from a tuna canning factory opened in 1987 and the export of fresh and frozen fish, attract growing revenues.

TRADE

The principal imports are foodstuffs, beverages, tobacco, mineral fuels, manufactured items, building materials, machinery and transport equipment.

	1989	1990
Imports	Rs.925,771,000	Rs.991,500,000
Exports	67,789,000	73,200,000
Re-exports	109,407,000	131,200,000

Trade with UK	1990	1991
Imports from UK	£14,955,000	£10,513,000
Exports to UK	8,353,000	8,457,000

SIERRA LEONE
The Republic of Sierra Leone

AREA, POPULATION, ETC – Sierra Leone, with a total land area of 27,699 sq. miles (71,740 sq. km), is on the west coast of Africa, between Guinea and Liberia. A Census of December 1985 put the population at 3,700,000. The 1990 UN estimate was 4,151,000. The southern half of Sierra Leone is inhabited by peoples whose languages fall into the Mende group; the northern half by the Temne, and smaller groups such as the Limba, Loko, Koranko and Susu.

CAPITAL – ΨFreetown (population at 1985 Census, 470,000).
CURRENCY – Leone (Le) of 100 cents.
FLAG – Three horizontal stripes of leaf green, white and cobalt blue.
NATIONAL ANTHEM – High We Exalt Thee, Realm of the Free.
NATIONAL DAY – 27 April (Independence Day).

GOVERNMENT

The origins of the country date back to the late 18th century when a project was begun to settle destitute Africans from England on Freetown peninsula. In 1808 the settlement was declared a Crown colony and became the main base in West Africa for enforcing the 1807 Act outlawing the slave trade. The colony was also used as a settlement for Africans from North America and the West Indies, and great numbers of Africans rescued from slave ships also settled there. In 1896 a Protectorate was declared over the hinterland.

In 1951 a new constitution was set up that united the colony of Freetown and the Protectorate and on 27 April 1961 Sierra Leone became a fully independent state within the Commonwealth. On 19 April 1971 a republican constitution was adopted and Dr Siaka Stevens became the first Executive President. In June 1978 Sierra Leone became a one-party state, following approval by Parliament and a referendum. The first general election under the one party system was held on 1 May 1982. The Parliament comprised 105 elected members and ten Paramount Chiefs, plus ten nominated members.

The government was overthrown by a coup led by junior army officers on 30 April 1992. Captain Valentine Strasser was named as chairman of a new National Provisional Ruling Council (NPRC) and became head of state. The House of Representatives was dissolved and all political activity was suspended. A cabinet was appointed to govern the country until promised multi-party elections.

HEAD OF STATE
Capt. Valentine Strasser, *sworn in* 3 May 1992.

NATIONAL PROVISIONAL RULING COUNCIL
as at August 1992

Head of State, Chairman of the NPRC, Minister of Defence, Capt. Valentine Strasser.
Vice-Chairman of the NPRC, Lt. Solomon Musa.
Finance, Development and Economic Planning, James Funna.
Foreign Affairs, Ahmed Dumbuya.
Mineral Resources, Lt.-Col. Daniel Kobina Anderson.
Agriculture, Forestry and Fisheries, Maj. Abdul Sesay.
Education, Youth and Sports, Arthur Abraham.
Health and Social Services, Maj. Akim Gibril.
Labour, Energy and Power, Lt. Samuel Kambo.
Public Works, Maj. James Bundu.
Minister of State in the Chairman's Office, John Benjamin.
Transport, Communication and Tourism, Lt. Charles Mbayo.
Internal Affairs and Rural Development, Col. Alimany Kamara.
Trade, Industry and State Enterprises, John Karimu.
Information, Broadcasting and Culture, Lt. Julius Bio.
Attorney-General, Justice, Arnold Gooding.

SIERRA LEONE HIGH COMMISSION
33 Portland Place, London WIN 3AG
Tel 071-636 6483

High Commissioner, new appointment awaited.

BRITISH HIGH COMMISSION
Standard Bank of Sierra Leone Building, Lightfoot Boston Street, Freetown
Tel: Freetown 23961

High Commissioner, His Excellency David Keith Sprague, MVO (1991).

BRITISH COUNCIL REPRESENTATIVE, Theresa Koroma, OBE, PO Box 124, Tower Hill, Freetown.

COMMUNICATIONS

Since the phasing out of the railway system in 1974 the road network has been developed considerably and there are now 5,000 miles of roads in the country, over 2,000 miles being surfaced. A bridge has been constructed over the Mano River linking Sierra Leone and Liberia.

The Freetown international airport is situated at Lungi, across the Sierra Leone River from Freetown. The main port is Freetown, which has one of the largest natural harbours in the world, and where there is a deep water quay providing about six berths for medium sized ships. There are smaller ports at Pepel, Bonthe and Niti.

Radio is operated by the Department of Broadcasting of the Sierra Leone Government. There are two shortwave transmitting and receiving stations in Freetown. Broadcasts are made in several of the more important indigenous languages in addition to English. There is also a weekly broadcast in French.

EDUCATION

In 1989 there were 2,554 primary schools in Sierra Leone and 201 secondary schools. Technical education is provided in the two government technical institutes, situated in Freetown and Kenema, in two trade centres and in the technical training establishments of the mining companies. Teacher training is carried out at the university, six colleges in the provinces and in the Milton Margai Training College near Freetown. The University of Sierra Leone (1967), consists of Fourah Bay College (1827), the Institute of Public Administration and Management (1980), the College of Medicine and Allied Health Sciences (1988) and Njala University College (1964).

ECONOMY

On the Freetown peninsula, farming is largely confined to the production of cassava and garden crops, such as maize and vegetables, for local consumption. In the hinterland, the principal agricultural product is rice, which is the staple food of the country, and cash crops such as cocoa, coffee, palm kernels, and ginger.

The economy depends largely on mineral exports; mainly diamonds, gold, bauxite and rutile. Diamond exports provided Le1,254.5m in 1989. Total imports for 1989 were to the value of Le10,901.8m and exports were Le8,269.5m.

TRADE WITH UK

	1990	1991
Imports from UK	£21,365,000	£17,928,000
Exports to UK	7,011,000	5,616,000

SINGAPORE

AREA, ETC – The Republic of Singapore consists of the island of Singapore and 58 islets, covering a total area of 626.4 sq. km. Singapore island is 26 miles long and 14 miles in breadth and is situated just north of the Equator off the southern extremity of the Malay peninsula, from which it is separated by the Straits of Johore. A causeway, carrying a road, railway and a water pipeline, crosses the three-quarters of a mile to the mainland. The highest point of the island is 581 feet above sea level. The climate is hot and humid and there are no clearly defined seasons. Rainfall averages 240 cm a year and temperature ranges from 24°–32° C (76°–89° F).

POPULATION – In 1990, the population was 3,002,800, which comprised 2,239,700 Chinese, 406,200 Malays, 230,000 Indians (including those of Pakistani, Bangladeshi and Sri Lankan origin) and 126,900 from other ethnic groups. Malay, Mandarin, Tamil and English are the official languages. At least eight Chinese dialects are used.

CURRENCY – Singapore dollar (S$) of 100 cents.
FLAG – Horizontal bands of red over white; crescent with five five-point stars on red band near staff.
NATIONAL ANTHEM – Majulah Singapura.
NATIONAL DAY – 9 August.

GOVERNMENT

Singapore, where Sir Stamford Raffles first established a trading post under the East India Company in 1819, was incorporated with Penang and Malacca to form the Straits Settlements in 1826. The Straits Settlements became a Crown colony in 1867.

Singapore fell into Japanese hands in 1942 and civil government was not restored until 1946, when it became a separate colony. Internal self-government and the title 'State of Singapore' were introduced in 1959. Singapore became a state of Malaysia when the Federation was enlarged in September 1963, but left Malaysia and became an independent sovereign state within the Commonwealth on 9 August 1965. Singapore adopted a Republican constitution from that date, the Yang di-Pertuan Negara being re-styled President. There is a Cabinet collectively responsible to a fully-elected Parliament of 81 members.

After the General Election of 31 August 1991 the People's Action Party (PAP) had 77 seats in Parliament. The Singapore Democratic Party (SDP) won three seats and the Workers' Party won one seat.

HEAD OF STATE
President, Wee Kim Wee, *re-elected* August 1989 for a second five-year term.

CABINET as at August 1992
Prime Minister, Goh Chok Tong.
Senior Minister, PM's Office, Lee Kuan Yew, GCMG, CH.
Deputy PM, Ong Teng Cheong.
Deputy PM and Minister for Trade and Industry, Lee Hsien Loong.
National Development, S. Dhanabalan.
Education, Lee Yock Suan.
Environment and Muslim Affairs, Dr Ahmad Mattar.
Communications, Mah Bow Tan.
Defence, Dr. Yeo Ning Hong.
Law and Home Affairs, Prof. S. Jayakumar.
Finance, Dr Richard Hu Tsu Tau.
Labour, Lee Boon Yang.
Foreign Affairs, Wong Kan Seng.
Health and Community Development, Yeo Cheow Tong.
Information and The Arts, George Yeo.
Speaker of Parliament, Tan Soo Khoon.

SINGAPORE HIGH COMMISSION
9 Wilton Crescent, London SW1X 8SA
Tel 071-235 8315

High Commissioner, His Excellency Abdul Aziz Mahmood (1988).

BRITISH HIGH COMMISSION
Tanglin Road, Singapore 1024
Tel: Singapore 4739333

High Commissioner, His Excellency Gordon Duggan (1990).

BRITISH COUNCIL REPRESENTATIVE, J. Davies, 30 Napier Road, Singapore 1025.

COMMUNICATIONS

Singapore is one of the largest and busiest seaports in the world, with deep water wharves and ship repairing facilities. Ships also anchor in the roads, unloading into lighters. In 1990, the total volume of cargo handled was 188,000,000 tonnes. More than 700 shipping lines use the port, with 44,600 ship arrivals in 1990.

The international airport is at Changi, in the east of the island. There are 67 km of metric gauge railway connected to the Malaysian rail system by the causeway across the Straits of Johore, and 2,882 km of roads.

There are both wireless and wired broadcasting services carrying commercial advertising. There are three television channels. The Singapore Broadcasting Authority Corporation was established in February 1980.

ECONOMY

Historically Singapore's economy was largely based on the sale and distribution of raw materials from surrounding countries and on entrepot trade in finished products. However, new manufacturing industries have been successfully introduced, including ship building and repairing, iron and steel, textiles, footwear, wood products, micro-electronics, scientific instruments, detergents, confectionery, pharmaceuticals, petroleum products, etc. Singapore has also become a financial centre with 137 commercial banks and 71 merchant banks established in the Republic, and an oil-refining centre.

In September 1988 Singapore was promoted by the World Bank to the 'high income' bracket of countries earning at least US$6,000 per capita annually.

FINANCE (estimates)

	1989	1990
Revenue	S$15,508.9m	S$16,424.7m
Expenditure	10,626.4m	13,257.1m

TRADE

	1990	1991
Total imports	S$109,805.8m	S$114,000m
Total exports	95,205.8m	102,000m

Trade with UK	1990	1991
Imports from UK	£1,040,188,000	£1,018,419,000
Exports to UK	1,021,148,000	1,134,365,000

SOLOMON ISLANDS

Forming a scattered archipelago of mountainous islands and low-lying coral atolls, the Solomon Islands stretches about 900 miles in a south-easterly direction from Bougainville in

Papua New Guinea to the Santa Cruz islands. The archipelago covers an area of about 249,000 square nautical miles while the land area is 10,938 sq. miles (28,446 sq. km). Solomon Islands lies between the longitudes 155° 30′ and 170° 30′E. and between latitudes 5° 10′ and 12° 45′S. The six biggest islands are Choiseul, New Georgia, Santa Isabel, Guadalcanal, Malaita and Makira. They are characterized by precipitous, thickly-forested mountain ranges intersected by deep, narrow valleys, and vary between 90 and 120 miles in length and between 20 and 30 miles in width.

POPULATION – The total population was 285,176 at the 1986 Census. The 1990 UN estimate was 320,000. English is the official language; there are over 80 local languages.

CAPITAL – ΨHoniara, population (1986), 30,499.
CURRENCY – Solomon Islands dollar (SI$) of 100 cents.
FLAG – Blue over green divided by a diagonal yellow band, with five white stars in the top left quarter.
NATIONAL ANTHEM – God Bless our Solomon Islands.
NATIONAL DAY – 7 July (Independence Day).

GOVERNMENT

The origin of the present Melanesian inhabitants is uncertain. European discovery of the islands began in the mid-16th century and continued intermittently for about 300 years, when the inauguration of sugar plantations in Queensland and Fiji (which created a need for labour) and the arrival of missionaries and traders led to increased European interest in the region. Great Britain declared a Protectorate in 1893 over the Southern Solomons, adding the Santa Cruz group in 1898 and 1899. The islands of the Shortland groups were transferred by treaty from Germany to Great Britain in 1900.

The Solomon Islands achieved internal self-government in 1976, and became independent in July 1978. The Solomon Islands is a constitutional monarchy, The Queen being represented locally by the Governor-General. Legislative power is vested in a unicameral National Parliament of 38 members, elected for a four-year term. The executive authority is exercised by the Cabinet.

A government of political personalities was formed in October 1990.

Governor-General, His Excellency Sir George Lepping, GCMG, MBE.

CABINET as at August 1992
Prime Minister, Hon. Solomon Mamaloni.
Deputy PM and Minister of Health and Medical Services, Hon. Sir Baddeley Devesi, GCMG, GCVO.
Agriculture and Lands, Hon. George Luialamo.
Education and Human Resource Development, Hon. Sam Alasia.
Finance and Economic Planning, Hon. Christopher Columbus Abe.
Foreign Affairs and Trade Relations, Hon. Job Dudley Tusinga.
Housing and Government Services, Hon. A. Kemakeza.
Natural Resources, Hon. Victor Ngele.
Police and Justice, Hon. Albert Laore.
Post and Communications, Hon. Michael Maina.
Provincial Government, Hon. A. Qurusu.
Tourism and Aviation, Hon. Nathaniel Supa.
Works and Public Utilities, Hon. Ben Gale.
Commerce and Primary Industries, Hon. Alfred Maetia.

DIPLOMATIC REPRESENTATION
High Commissioner, His Excellency Wilson Ifunaoa, CMG (resident in Honiara, Solomon Islands).

HONORARY CONSULATE
17–19 Springfield Road, London SW19 7AL
Tel 071-946 5552
Honorary Consul, E. E. Nielsen, OBE.

BRITISH HIGH COMMISSION
Soltel House, Mendana Avenue (PO Box 676), Honiara
Tel: Honiara 21705
High Commissioner, His Excellency Raymond F. Jones, OBE (1991).

JUDICIARY

The High Court of Solomon Islands, constituted by the Solomon Islands Independence Order, consists of a Chief Justice and not fewer than two nor more than three Puisne Judges. The Court of Appeal Act was enacted on 8 May 1978.

COMMUNICATIONS

A new international air service was started by Solomon Airlines in June 1990. Services are operated from Honiara to Brisbane, Sydney, Auckland, Port Moresby, Vila and Nadi (Fiji). In addition there is a weekly Qantas flight from Brisbane to Honiara and Air Niugini flight Port Moresby–Honiara–Port Moresby.

There are about 52 miles of secondary and minor roads in the urban areas of Honiara, Auki and Gizo. About 18 miles of road in and around Honiara and one mile in Gizo are bitumen sealed, the remainder being coral or gravel surfaced. In the rural areas there are some 800 miles of road, including those in private plantations, forestry areas and roads built and maintained by councils.

Telekom, a company jointly owned by Cable and Wireless Limited and the Solomon Islands government, operates the international and domestic telephone circuits from a ground station in Honiara via the Intelsat Pacific Ocean communication satellite.

TRADE

The main imports are foodstuffs, consumer goods, machinery and transport materials. Principal exports are timber, fish, copra, and palm oil. Fisheries exports for 1989 totalled SI$65.3m, timber SI$41.3m and copra SI$21m. Other exports include cocoa and marine shells.

TRADE WITH UK

	1990	1991
Imports from UK	£523,000	£1,170,000
Exports to UK	6,903,000	6,846,000

SOMALIA
Jamhuuriyadda Diimoqraadiga ee Soomaaliya

The Somali Democratic Republic occupies part of the north-east horn of Africa, with a coast-line on the Indian Ocean extending from the boundary with Kenya (2° S latitude) to Cape Guardafui (12° N.), and on the Gulf of Aden to the boundary with Djibouti. Somalia is bounded on the west by Djibouti, Ethiopia and Kenya and covers an area of approximately 246,201 sq. miles (637,657 sq. km). The population, of which a large proportion is nomadic, is 7,497,000 (UN estimate 1990).

CAPITAL – ΨMogadishu, population (estimated 1987), 1,000,000. Other towns are Hargeisa (20,000), Boroma (65,000), ΨKisimayu (60,000), ΨBerbera (15,000) and Burao (15,000).

CURRENCY – Somali shilling of 100 cents.
FLAG – Five-pointed white star on blue ground.
NATIONAL DAY – 21 October.

GOVERNMENT

The Somali Democratic Republic, consisting of the former British Somaliland Protectorate and the former Italian trust territory of Somalia, was established on 1 July 1960. British rule in Somaliland lasted from 1887 until 1960 except for a short period in 1940–1 when the Protectorate was occupied by Italian forces. Somalia, formerly an Italian colony, was occupied by British forces in 1941. In 1950 it was placed under Italian administration by a resolution of the UN; this trusteeship lasted until independence.

Following the assassination of President Shermake on 15 October 1969, the armed forces, assisted by the police, took over the government without resistance and a Revolutionary Council under Siad Barre assumed control of the country. In July 1990 a referendum on a new constitution, followed by multi-party elections, was promised but Siad Barre was overthrown in January 1991 by rebel movements. One group, the United Somali Congress, took control in Mogadishu and formed an interim administration in February 1991.

In July 1991 the United Somali Congress (USC), met representatives of the rival Somali Salvation Democratic Front (SSDF), the Somali Patriotic Movement (SPM) and the Somali Democratic Movement (SDM) and agreed on the formation of a new coalition government. Acting President Ali Mahdi Mohammed, leader of the USC, was recognized by the other clan-based factions as President of Somalia. Each faction was assigned a number of portfolios in the new government. In the north of the country, the Somali National Movement (SNM) refused to participate in negotiations and formed a government under SNM leader, and acting President, Abourahman Ahmed Ali. Faction fighting erupted in the summer of 1991 between supporters of Interim President Ali Mahdi Mohammed and supporters of General Mohamed Aideed, who had been instrumental in overthrowing Siad Barre. The fighting degenerated into civil war throughout 1991 and 1992, devastating Mogadishu and large parts of the south of the country. The civil war, overlaid with clan fighting, has left Somalia ungovernable and forced the UN to intervene in April 1992 with massive food aid shipments to feed a population on the verge of starvation. In August 1992 the UN Security Council approved the dispatch of 3,000 armed guards to protect relief convoys, while the USA initiated an emergency food airlift.

President, Ali Mahdi Mohammed.
First Vice-President, Abdalqadir Mohammed Aden Gobeh.
Second Vice-President, Omar Maalin Mahamud.

SOMALI DIPLOMATIC REPRESENTATION, The Embassy closed in January 1992.

BRITISH DIPLOMATIC REPRESENTATION, The British Embassy in Mogadishu was closed temporarily in January 1991.

SECESSION

Civil war broke out in May 1988 between the government and the opposition Somali National Movement (SNM) in the north of the country. With the downfall of Siad Barre, the SNM took control of the north and in May 1991 declared unilateral independence as the 'Somaliland Republic'.

ECONOMY

Livestock raising is the main occupation in Somalia and there is a modest export trade in livestock on the hoof, skins and hides. Italy, the Gulf States and Saudi Arabia import the bulk of the banana crop, the second biggest export.

TRADE WITH UK

	1990	1991
Imports from UK	£11,865,000	£3,152,000
Exports to UK	510,000	42,000

SOUTH AFRICA
Republiek van Suid-Afrika

AREA – The Republic, comprising the provinces of the Cape of Good Hope, Natal, the Transvaal and the Orange Free State, occupies the southernmost part of the African continent from the courses of the Limpopo, Molopo and Orange Rivers (34° 50′ 22″ S.) to the Cape of Good Hope, with the exception of Lesotho, Botswana and Swaziland, and part of Mozambique. It has a total area of 471,445 sq. miles (1,221,031 sq. km).

The southernmost province contains many parallel ranges, which rise in steps towards the interior. The south-western peninsula contains the famous Table Mountain (3,582 ft.), while the Great Swartberg and Langeberg run in parallel lines from west to east of the Cape Province. Between these two ranges and the Roggeveld and Nuweveld ranges to the north is the Great Karoo Plateau, which is bounded on the east by the Sneeuberg, containing the highest summit in the province (Kompasberg, 7,800 ft.). In the east are ranges which join the Drakensberg (11,000 ft.) between Natal and the Orange Free State.

The Orange Free State presents a succession of undulating grassy plains with occasional hills or kopjes. The Transvaal is also mainly an elevated plateau with parallel ridges in the Magaliesberg and Waterberg ranges of no great height. The eastern province of Natal has pastoral lowlands and rich agriculture land between the slopes of the Drakensberg and the coast, the interior rising in terraces as in the southern provinces. The Orange, with its tributary the Vaal, is the principal river of the south, rising in the Drakensberg and flowing into the Atlantic between Namibia and the Cape Province. The Limpopo, or Crocodile River, in the north, rises in the Transvaal and flows into the Indian Ocean through Mozambique. Most of the remaining rivers are

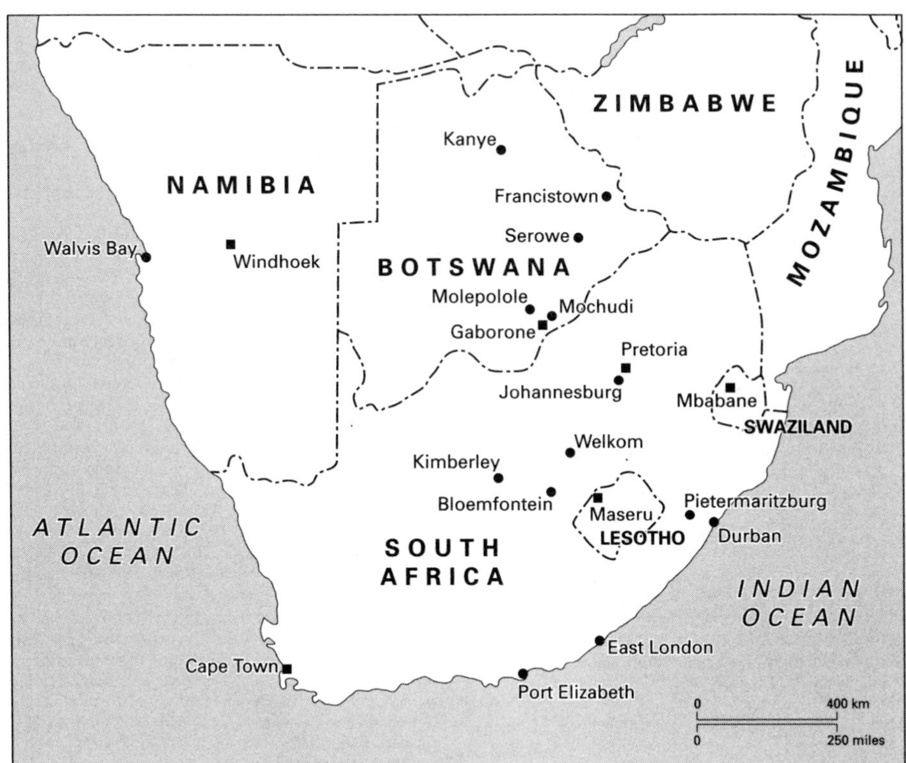

furious torrents after rain, with partially dry beds at other seasons.

POPULATION – The official population estimate for 1990, excluding Bophuthatswana, Ciskei, Transkei and Venda, was 30,788,000, comprising 21,600,000 Blacks, 5,018,000 Whites, 3,214,000 Coloureds, and 956,000 Indians. These figures are not thought to be accurate; the UN (1990) estimate for all of South Africa is 35,282,000.

CAPITAL – The administrative seat of the government is Pretoria, Transvaal; population (1985 estimate) 822,925; the seat of the legislature is ΨCape Town, population (1985) 1,911,521.

Other large towns (1985 figures) are Johannesburg, Transvaal (1,609,408); ΨDurban, Natal, the largest seaport (634,301); ΨPort Elizabeth, Cape (651,993); Bloemfontein, capital of Orange Free State (232,984); Ψ East London, Cape (167,992); and Pietermaritzburg, capital of Natal (192,417).

CURRENCY – Rand (R) of 100 cents.

FLAG – Three horizontal stripes of equal width; from top to bottom, orange, white, blue; in the centre of the white stripe, the old Orange Free State flag hanging vertical, towards the pole the Union Flag horizontal, away from the pole the old Transvaal Vierkleur, all spread full.

NATIONAL ANTHEM – Die Stem Van Suid-Afrika (The Call of South Africa).

NATIONAL DAY – 31 May.

GOVERNMENT

The self-governing colonies of the Cape of Good Hope, Natal, the Transvaal and the Orange River Colony became united on 31 May 1910 in a legislative union under the name of the Union of South Africa, the four colonies becoming provinces of the Union.

A new constitution came into effect in September 1984 which provided for an executive President and a three-chamber Parliament; the House of Assembly (178 members) representing Whites, the House of Representatives (85 members) representing Coloureds, and the House of Delegates (45 members) representing Indians. The majority black population has no representation. There is joint parliamentary responsibility for 'general' affairs (foreign policy, defence, finance, law and order, justice, transport, manpower, commerce and industry, agriculture), and each chamber has separate responsibility for the 'own' affairs of the population group it represents (housing, social welfare, health, education, local government and some aspects of agriculture). Disputes between the chambers may be referred by the President to the President's Council (60 members: 20 White, ten Coloured, five Indian elected by their respective chambers, 15 nominated by the President, 10 nominated by Opposition parties).

The President is chosen by an 88-member electoral college (in the proportion 4 White: 2 Coloured: 1 Indian) of the majority parties of the three chambers. The President appoints the Cabinet from all three communities, and also appoints each community's ministerial council for 'own' affairs.

Elections to the House of Assembly last took place on 6 September 1989. Party representation is as follows: National Party 102; Conservative Party 43; Democratic Party 28; Independents (supporting the ANC) 5.

HEAD OF STATE

State President, Frederick Willem de Klerk, *sworn in* 20 September 1989.

CABINET as at August 1992

Foreign Affairs, Pik Botha.
Minister of State Affairs, Dr Gerrit Viljoen.
Water Affairs and Forestry, Gen. Magnus Malan.
Public Enterprises, Dr Dawie de Villiers.
Justice, National Intelligence Service, Kobie Coetzee.
Defence and Public Works, Gene Louw.
Correctional Services, Adriaan Vlok.
State Expenditure, Amie Venter.
Manpower, National Education, Piet Marais.
Education and Training, Sam J. de Beer.
Mineral and Energy Affairs, George S. Bartlett.
Agriculture, Dr Kraai van Niekerk.
National Health, Dr Rina Venter.
Law and Order, H. J. Kriel.
Regional and Land Affairs, Jacob de Villiers.
Home Affairs, Environment, Louis Pienaar.
Finance, Trade and Industry, Economic Co-Ordination, Derek Keys.
Administration and Tourism, Dr Org Marais.
Transport and Post and Telecommunications, Piet Welgemoed.
Constitutional Development and Communication, Roelf Meyer.
Manpower, Local Government and National Housing, Leon Wessels.

EMBASSY OF THE REPUBLIC OF SOUTH AFRICA
South Africa House, Trafalgar Square, London WC2N 5DP
Tel 071-930 4488

Ambassador Extraordinary and Plenipotentiary, His Excellency K. D. S. Durr (1991).
Minister, R. W. Carter.
Minister (Trade), P. M. Pullen.

BRITISH EMBASSY
255 Hill Street, Pretoria
Tel: Pretoria 433121
91 Parliament Street, Cape Town 8001 (Jan.–June)
Tel: Cape Town 4617220

Ambassador Extraordinary and Plenipotentiary, His Excellency Sir Anthony Reeve, KCMG (1991).
Counsellor, Deputy Head of Mission, Dr D. Carter.
Counsellor, A. A. Rowell, CMG
First Secretaries, R. W. Kyles; G. D. Adams; P. Haggie; D. E. G. Kerly (Management).

Cultural Attaché and British Council Representative, R. B. Timms, 76 Juta Street, (PO Box 30637), Braamfontein 2017, Johannesburg (Tel. 339 3715).

There are British Consular Offices at *Cape Town, Johannesburg* and *Durban*; and Honorary Consuls at *Port Elizabeth* and *East London*.

HOMELANDS

As part of its policy of apartheid, the government established a number of black 'homelands'. Six areas (Gazankulu, Lebowa, KwaNdbele, KaNgwane, Qwaqwa and KwaZulu) are now designated as self-governing states. A further four (Bophuthatswana, Ciskei, Transkei and Venda) are regarded as independent republics by the South African government but are not recognized as such by the UN. Most homelands are now in the process of re-integrating into South Africa.

APARTHEID

From 1948, South Africa's social and political structure was based on the policy of racial segregation, apartheid. Opposition protests at this policy culminated in demonstrations at Sharpeville, near Johannesberg, in 1960, in which 69 protesters were shot dead by police; the African National Congress and other opposition groups were subsequently banned. Largely as a result of world protests, South Africa left the Commonwealth and became a republic on 31 May 1961.

A new wave of opposition to apartheid climaxed in 1976 with uprisings in Soweto, in which hundreds of blacks, including many schoolchildren, were shot dead while protesting at the introduction of Afrikaans as the compulsory medium of instruction.

The promulgation of the new constitution in 1984 coincided with rioting in the black townships and the continuing unrest led to the declaration on 20 July 1985 of a state of emergency in 36 districts. A nationwide state of emergency was declared on 12 June 1986; it was renewed annually until it was finally lifted in the Cape, Transvaal and Orange Free State provinces in June 1990, and in Natal in October 1990.

In September 1989, F. W. de Klerk replaced F. W. Botha as President of South Africa and accelerated the process of reform. In February 1990, the ban on the ANC and restrictions on other anti-apartheid groups were lifted; Nelson Mandela, the main ANC political detainee, was also released. In 1991 apartheid was effectively abolished with the repeal in March of the Land Acts, restricting land ownership by race, and the Group Areas Act, restricting residence by race; the Population Registration Act, classifying people by race, was repealed in June. In March 1992 a referendum was held amongst the white electorate on continued political reform and a new constitution reached by negotiation, and was approved by 69 per cent to 31 per cent.

Negotiations continued between various groups to establish a non-racial democracy. These negotiations led to the opening in Johannesburg on 20 December 1991 of the Convention on a Democratic South Africa (CODESA) talks.

The CODESA talks between the Government, the ANC, the Inkatha Freedom Party and other political, business and church groups continued throughout late 1991 and early 1992, and by June 1992 came close to a potential agreement on an interim executive and assembly to govern the country until multi-racial elections. However, the constitutional talks had been continuing against an escalating level of violence involving mainly ANC and Inkatha supporters, but also the security forces, white extremists and Pan-African Congress supporters. After 39 people were killed at Boipatong in June, the ANC withdrew from the CODESA talks indefinitely, blaming the government and security forces for the continuing political violence, and demanding the immediate formation of an interim multi-racial government. Hardliners in the ANC, led by South African Communist Party (SACP) members, then gained the upper hand in an internal power struggle during the summer and started a rolling campaign of mass action and general strikes which increased political violence and the number of deaths In September the campaign was extended to the nominally-independent homelands, with the ANC leading a march into Ciskei to overthrow its leader, resulting in 28 deaths and over 200 wounded.

At the time of going to press, the situation remained volatile, but signs were emerging that Government–ANC negotiations might be resumed.

COMMUNICATIONS

The previously state-owned and controlled South African Transport Services has been privatized. Independent companies now operate the national railway system, the principal harbours, most long-distance passenger and freight road transport services, the South African Airways airline and a network of pipelines for petroleum products.

There are international airports at Johannesburg (Jan

Smuts), Durban (Louis Botha) and Cape Town (D. F. Malan), with another under construction at La Mercy, Natal. South African Airways operates international services to Europe, South America, the Far East and the Middle East, as well as to neighbouring countries, and it is the principal operator of domestic flights.

The largest sea-port is Durban, Natal. Other major ports are Cape Town, Port Elizabeth, East London, Saldanha Bay and Mossel Bay in Cape Province and Richards Bay, Natal.

ECONOMY

Mining is of great importance to the South African economy. Minerals to the value of R37,899.4 million were produced in 1990. The principal minerals produced are gold, coal, diamonds, copper, iron ore, manganese, lime and limestone, and chrome ore. South Africa is the world's largest producer of gold.

Agriculture, forestry and fishing account for about 5 per cent of GDP. Over 50 per cent of land is pasture so livestock farming is widespread with meat and wool important products. Principal crops are maize, sugar-cane, fruits and vegetables, wheat, sorghum, sunflower seed and groundnuts. Cotton is widely grown because of its suitability to the climate, and viticulture is also widespread.

Industries, concentrated most heavily around Johannesburg, Pretoria and the major ports, process foodstuffs, metals and non-metallic mineral products, and also produce beverages and tobacco, motor vehicles, chemicals and chemical products, machinery, textiles and clothing, and paper and paper products.

TRADE

Principal exports are gold, base metals and metal products, diamonds, food (especially fruit), chemicals, machinery and transport equipment, and wool. Principal imports are machinery, chemicals, motor vehicles, metals and metal products, food, inedible raw materials and textiles.

In 1986 the United States imposed economic sanctions and the EC a trade embargo on South Africa in protest at its apartheid policies. These were lifted in July 1991 and January 1992 respectively, leaving only the longer-standing UN arms and oil embargoes in place.

Trade with UK	1990	1991
Imports from UK	£1,113,397,000	£1,023,469,000
Exports to UK	1,078,546,000	954,676,000

FINANCE

Estimated revenue for 1988–9 was R47,460 million, and estimated expenditure was R56,556 million.

SPAIN
España

AREA AND POPULATION – Situated in the south-west of Europe, between 36° and 43° 45′ N. lat., and 4° 25′ E. and 9° 20′ W. long., Spain is bounded on the south and east by the Mediterranean, on the west by the Atlantic and Portugal, and on the north by the Bay of Biscay and France, from which it is separated by the Pyrenees. Continental Spain occupies about eleven-thirteenths of the Iberian peninsula, the remaining portion forming the Republic of Portugal. Its coast-line extends 1,317 miles, 712 formed by the Mediterranean and 605 by the Atlantic, and it comprises a total area of 194,897 sq. miles (504,782 sq. km), with a population (UN estimate 1990) of 38,959,000.

The interior of the Iberian peninsula consists of an elevated tableland surrounded and traversed by mountain ranges: the Pyrenees, the Cantabrian Mountains, the Sierra Guadarrama, Sierra Morena, Sierra Nevada, Montes de Toledo, etc. The principal rivers are the Duero, the Tajo, the Guadiana, the Guadalquivir, the Ebro and the Miño.

CAPITAL – Madrid, population (1986) 4,731,224. Other large cities are ΨBarcelona (4,597,429), ΨValencia (2,078,812), Seville (1,594,250), Zaragoza (824,781), ΨMálaga (1,137,782), Bilbao (1,179,148); Murcia (1,006,788).

CURRENCY – Peseta of 100 céntimos.

FLAG – Three horizontal stripes of red, yellow, red, with the yellow of double width.

NATIONAL ANTHEM – Marcha Real Española.

NATIONAL DAY – 12 October.

GOVERNMENT

Spain was a monarchy until April 1931, when King Alfonso XIII left the country and a Republic was proclaimed. A provisional government, drawn from the various Republican and Socialist parties, was formed. On 18 July 1936 a counter-revolution broke out in military garrisons in Spanish Morocco and spread rapidly throughout Spain. The principal leader was General Francisco Franco Bahamonde, leader of the Military-Fascist fusion, or *Falange*. On 29 March 1939 the civil war was declared to have ended, the Popular Front governments in Madrid and Barcelona surrendering to the Nationalists (as General Franco's followers were then named). On 5 June 1939 the Grand Council of the *Falange Española Tradicionalista y de las Juntas Ofensivas Nacional-Sindicalistas* met at Burgos to legislate for the reorganization of the country under the presidency of General Franco.

On 22 July 1969 General Franco nominated Prince Juan Carlos (Alfonso) of Bourbon (grandson of the late King Alfonso XIII) to succeed him as head of state at his death or retirement. The nomination was approved in the *Cortes* by a large majority. Following the death of General Franco on 20 November 1975, Juan Carlos acceded to the throne.

Under the constitution drawn up in 1977–8 there is a bicameral *Cortes* comprising a 350-member Congress of Deputies elected for four years by universal adult suffrage, and a Senate consisting of directly elected representatives of the provinces, islands, autonomous regions, and Ceuta and Melilla. At the General Election on 29 October 1989, PSOE (Spanish Socialist Workers' Party) won 175 seats, and the PP (Popular Party) 107.

REGIONS

Since the promulgation of the 1978 constitution, 17 autonomous regions have been established, with their own parliaments and governments. These are Andalucia, Aragon, Asturias, Balearics, the Basque country, Canaries, Castilla-La Mancha, Castilla-Leon, Cantabria, Cataluña, Extremadura, Galicia, Madrid, Murcia, Navarre, La Rioja and Valencia.

HEAD OF THE STATE

King Juan Carlos I de Borbón y Borbón, KG, GCVO, *born* 5 Jan. 1938, *acceded to the throne*, 22 Nov. 1975, *married* 14 May 1962, Princess Sophie of Greece *and has issue*, Infante Felipe Juan Pablo Alfonso y Todos los Santos (Prince of Asturias, *and heir to the throne*), *born* 30 Jan. 1968; Infanta Elena Maria Isabel Dominga, *born* 20 Dec. 1963; and Infanta Cristina Federica Victoria Antonia, *born* 13 June 1965.

CABINET as at August 1992

Prime Minister, Felipe González Márquez.
Deputy PM, Narcís Serra Serra.

Foreign Affairs, Javier Solana Madariaga.
Justice, Tomás de la Quadra-Salcedo Fernández del Castillo.
Defence, Julián García Vargas.
Economy and Finance, Carlos Solchaga Catalán.
Interior, José Luis Corcuera Cuesta.
Public Works and Town Planning and Transport, José Borrell Fontelles.
Education and Science, vacant.
Labour and Social Security, Luis Martínez Noval.
Industry and Energy, Commerce and Tourism, Claudio Aranzadi Martínez.
Agriculture, Food and Fisheries, Pedro Solbes Mira.
Public Administration, Juan Manuel Eguiagaray Ucelay.
Culture, Jordi Solé Tura.
Health and Consumer Affairs, José Antonio Griñán Martínez.
Relations with the Cortes and Government Secretariat, Virgilio Zapatero Gómez.
Social Affairs, Matilde Fernández Sanz.
Government Spokeswoman, Rosa Conde Gutiérrez del Alamo.

SPANISH EMBASSY
16th Floor, Portland House, Stag Place, London SW1E 5SE
Tel 071-235 5555

Ambassador Extraordinary and Plenipotentiary, His Excellency Felipe de la Morena (1990).
Minister-Counsellor, Marques de Torregrosa.

BRITISH EMBASSY
Calle Fernando el Santo, 16, 28010 Madrid
Tel: Madrid 319 0200

Ambassador Extraordinary and Plenipotentiary, His Excellency Sir Robin Fearn, KCMG (1989).
Minister, I. V. Roberts.
Counsellors, D. Ridgway, OBE (*Commercial*); A. Longrigg, CMG (*Economic and Community Affairs*).
Defence and Naval Attaché, Capt. J. Gozzard.
Head of Political Section, T. C. Morris.

There are Consulates General in *Madrid, Barcelona, Bilbao*; Consulates in *Tenerife, Alicante, Seville, Malaga, Palma de Mallorca, Las Palmas*; Vice Consulates in *Algeciras, Ibiza*; Honorary Consulates in *Arecife, Santander, Minorca, Tarragona, Vigo.*

BRITISH COUNCIL REPRESENTATIVE – B. Vale, OBE, Calle Almagro 5, 28010 Madrid. There is a branch library in *Barcelona.*

BRITISH CHAMBER OF COMMERCE – Plaza de Santa Barbara 10, 1st Floor, 28004 Madrid, also Paseo de Gracia 11, Barcelona 7 and Alameda de Mazarredo 5, Bilbao 1.

DEFENCE

There are in Spain one armoured, one mechanized, one motorized and two mountain divisions; one artillery brigade, two cavalry brigades, one air-transportable brigade, one helicopter brigade, one coastal artillery brigade, one Spanish Legion brigade. The *Guardia Civil* operates as a gendarmerie in the rural areas under the control of the Ministry of Defence.

The armed forces have a total active strength of 257,400 (158,000 conscripts) with a 12-month period of conscription. The Army has 182,000 personnel (115,000 conscripts), with 838 main battle tanks, 440 reconnaissance vehicles, 3,500 armoured personnel carriers, 1,355 artillery pieces, and 28 combat helicopters.

The active Spanish Navy has a strength of 39,800 (22,000) conscripts) and consists of eight submarines, one aircraft carrier, four destroyers, 15 frigates and corvettes, and 62 patrol and coastal combatants. The Navy also has 35 armed helicopters and 21 Harrier aircraft.

The Air Force has a strength of 35,600 (21,000 conscripts) and is divided geographically into three regions covering Spain, plus an air zone for the Canaries. There are also functional Combat, Tactical and Transport Commands. The Air Force consists of three fighter/ground attack squadrons, nine air defence squadrons, seven transport squadrons, one maritime squadron, four search and rescue squadrons, eleven training squadrons and six support squadrons, with a total of 247 combat aircraft.

Spain became a member of NATO in May 1982. Continued membership (linked to non-military integration) was confirmed in a referendum in March 1986.

EDUCATION

Education is free for all those aged six to 18, and compulsory up to the age of 14. Under the 1985 Education Law, private schools (30 per cent of primary and 60 per cent of secondary schools) will have to fulfill certain criteria to receive government maintenance grants.

There are 33 public sector universities, the oldest of which, Salamanca, was founded in 1218. Other ancient foundations are Valladolid (1346), Barcelona (1430), Zaragoza (1474), Santiago (1495), Valencia (1500), Seville (1505), Madrid (1508), Granada (1531), Oveido (1604). Private universities are Deusto in Bilbao, Navarra in Pamplona, one in Madrid and one in Salamanca. Student numbers in the universities in 1989–90 totalled 1,067,874.

CULTURE

Castilian is the language of more than three-quarters of the population of Spain. Basque, said to have been the original language of Iberia, is spoken in Vizcaya, Guipuzcoa and Alava. Catalan is spoken in Provençal Spain, and Galician, spoken in the north-western provinces, is akin to Portuguese; the governments of these regions actively encourage use of their local languages.

The literature of Spain is one of the oldest and richest in the world, the *Poem of the Cid*, the earliest of the heroic songs of Spain, having been written about AD 1140. The outstanding writings of its golden age are those of Miguel de Cervantes Saavedra (1547–1616), Lope Felix de Vega Carpio (1562–1635) and Pedro Calderón de la Barca (1600–81). The Nobel Prize for Literature has five times been awarded to Spanish authors: J. Echegaray (1904), J. Benavente (1922), Juan Ramón Jimenez (1956), Vicente Aleixandre (1977) and Camilo José Cela (1989).

ECONOMY

The expansion of the Spanish economy and accession to the EC have led to changes in Spanish agriculture. It accounts for over 5 per cent of GDP and employs over 13 per cent of the working population (down from 28 per cent in 1970). Between 1970 and 1985 the net value of agricultural production increased by 56 per cent in real terms.

The country is generally fertile, and well adapted to agriculture and the cultivation of heat-loving fruits such as olives, oranges, lemons, almonds, pomegranates, bananas, apricots, tomatoes, peppers, cucumbers and grapes. The agricultural products include wheat, barley, oats, rice, hemp and flax. The orange crop is exported mainly to Germany, France and the United Kingdom. The vine is cultivated widely; in the south-west, Jerez, the well-known sherry and tent wines are produced. The fishing industry is important.

Spain's mineral resources of coal, iron, wolfram, copper, zinc, lead and iron ores are variously exploited. Output of coal in 1988 was 15.5 million tonnes; output of steel (1988) 11.9 million tonnes.

The principal goods produced are cars, steel, ships, manufactured goods, textiles, chemical products, footwear and other leather goods. In 1988 an estimated 54,172,000 tourists visited Spain.

TRADE

The principal imports are cotton, tobacco, cellulose, timber, coffee and cocoa, food products, fertilizers, dyes, machinery, motor vehicles and agricultural tractors, wool and petroleum products. The principal exports include cars, petroleum products, iron ore, cork, salt, vegetables, fruits, wines, olive oil, potash, mercury, pyrites, tinned fruit and fish, tomatoes and footwear.

The balance of payments on current account showed a deficit of US$15,717 million in 1990 and reserves stood at US$53,104 million.

	1990	1991
	million pesetas	
Imports	8,914,700	9,672,100
Exports	5,642,800	6,225,700

Trade with UK	1990*	1991*
Imports from UK	£3,750,143,000	£4,278,767,000
Exports to UK	2,884,691,000	2,627,857,000

*Excluding the Canary Islands, Ceuta and Melilla.

ISLANDS

The Balearic Isles form an archipelago off the east coast of Spain. There are four large islands (Majorca, Minorca, Ibiza and Formentera), and seven smaller (Aire, Aucanada, Botafoch, Cabrera, Dragonera, Pinto and El Rey). The islands were occupied by the Romans after the destruction of Carthage and provided contingents of the celebrated Balearic slingers. The total area is 1,935 sq. miles (5,011 sq. km), with a population of 685,088. The archipelago forms a province of Spain, the capital being ΨPalma in Majorca, pop. 304,422; ΨMahon (Minorca), pop. 22,926.

The Canary Islands are an archipelago in the Atlantic, off the African coast, consisting of seven islands and six mostly uninhabited islets. The total area is 2,807 sq. miles (7,270 sq. km), with a population of 1,444,626. The Canary Islands form two provinces of Spain: Las Palmas, comprising Gran Canaria, Lanzarote (38,500), Fuerteventura (19,500) and the islets of Alegranza, Roque del Este, Roque del Oeste, Graciosa, Montaña Clara and Lobos, with seat of administration at ΨLas Palmas (366,454) in Gran Canaria; and Santa Cruz de Tenerife, comprising Tenerife, La Palma (76,000), Gomera (31,829), and Hierro (10,000), with seat of administration at ΨSanta Cruz in Tenerife, population estimate 190,784.

Isla de Faisanes is an uninhabited Franco-Spanish condominium, at the mouth of the Bidassoa in La Higuera bay.

ΨCeuta is a fortified post on the Moroccan coast, opposite Gibraltar. The total area is 5 sq. miles (13 sq. km), with a population of 70,864.

ΨMelilla is a town on a rocky promontory of the Rif coast, connected with the mainland by a narrow isthmus. Melilla has been in Spanish possession since 1492. Population 58,449. Ceuta and Melilla are parts of Metropolitan Spain.

OVERSEAS TERRITORIES

Spanish settlements on the Moroccan seaboard are: *Peñon de Alhucemas*, the bay of that name includes six islands, population 366; *Peñon de la Gomera* (or *Peñon de Velez*) is a fortified rocky islet about 40 miles west of Alhucemas Bay, population 450; the *Chaffarinas* (or Zaffarines) are a group of three islands near the Algerian frontier, about two miles north of Cape del Agua, population 610.

The protectorate of Spanish Morocco was incorporated in Morocco on the latter's independence in 1956. Ifni, the former enclave in Morocco, was incorporated by treaty on 30 June 1969, and the Spanish Sahara came under joint Moroccan and Mauritanian control in November 1975.

SRI LANKA

Sri Lanka Prajatantrika Samajawadi Janarajaya

AREA, ETC – Sri Lanka (formerly Ceylon) is an island in the Indian Ocean, off the southern tip of the peninsula of India and separated from it by a narrow strip of shallow water, the Palk Strait. Situated between 5° 55′ and 9° 50′ N. latitude and 79° 42′ and 81° 52′ E. longitude, it has an area of 25,332 sq. miles (65,610 sq. km), including 33 square miles of inland water. Its greatest length is from north to south, 270 miles; and its greatest width 140 miles, no point in Sri Lanka being more than 80 miles from the sea.

Forests, jungle and scrub cover the greater part of the island, often being intermingled. In areas over 2,000 feet above sea level grasslands (*patanas* or *talawas*) are found. One of the highest peaks in the central massif is Adam's Peak (7,360 ft), a place of pilgrimage for Buddhists, Hindus and Muslims.

CLIMATE – The climate of Sri Lanka is warm throughout the year, with a high relative humidity. In the hills the climate is more temperate. Rainfall is generally heavy, with marked regional variations. The two main monsoon seasons are mid-May to September (south-west) and November to March (north-east).

POPULATION – The 1991 estimated population was 17,243,000. Of these 74 per cent were Sinhalese, 12.6 per cent Sri Lankan Tamils, 5.6 per cent Indian Tamils, 7.1 per cent Sri Lankan Moors and 0.7 per cent Burghers, Malays and others. The religion of the great majority of inhabitants is Buddhism, introduced from India, according to ancient Sinhalese chronicles, in 247 BC. After Buddhism (69.3 per cent), Hinduism has the largest following (15.5 per cent); 7.6 per cent of the population are Muslims and 7.5 per cent Christians. The national languages are Sinhalese, Tamil and English.

CAPITAL – ΨColombo, population (1991) 1,963,000. Other principal towns are ΨJaffna (876,000), Kandy (1,251,000), ΨGalle (946,000), and ΨTrincomalee (316,000).

CURRENCY – Sri Lankan rupee (Rs) of 100 cents.

FLAG – On a dark red field, within a golden border, a golden lion passant holding a sword in its right paw, and a representation of a *bo*-leaf, issuing from each corner; and to its right, two vertical stripes of saffron and green also placed within a golden border, to represent the minorities of the country.

NATIONAL ANTHEM – Namo Namo Matha (We all stand together).

NATIONAL DAY – 4 February (Independence Commemoration Day).

GOVERNMENT

Early in the sixteenth century the Portuguese landed in Ceylon and founded settlements, eventually conquering much of the country. Portuguese rule in Ceylon lasted 150 years but in 1658, following a twenty-year period of decline, Portuguese rule gave way to that of the Dutch East India Company which was to exploit Ceylon with varying fortunes until 1796.

The maritime provinces of Ceylon were ceded by the Dutch to the British on 16 February 1798, becoming a British

Crown Colony in 1802 under the terms of the Treaty of Amiens. With the annexation of the Kingdom of Kandy in 1815, all Ceylon came under British rule.

On 4 February 1948 Ceylon became a self-governing state and a member of the British Commonwealth. A republican constitution was adopted on 22 May 1972, providing for a unicameral legislature, the National State Assembly, which has a six year term, and the country was renamed the Republic of Sri Lanka (meaning 'Resplendent Island'). On 5 September 1978 a new constitution introduced the title the Democratic Socialist Republic of Sri Lanka and a system of proportional representation. Legislative power is exercised by the National State Assembly, the executive power being exercised by the President.

A Bill providing for the holding of the Provincial Council elections was passed on 22 January 1988. President Jayewardene issued a proclamation on 8 September 1988, merging the Northern and Eastern Provinces, as envisaged under the Indo-Sri Lanka Agreement. The Eelam People's Revolutionary Liberation Front (EPRLF) gained a clear majority in the Northern-Eastern Provincial Council, while the ruling United National Party (UNP) gained an absolute majority in elections to the seven other Provincial Councils.

In the General Election of 15 February 1989 the United National Party gained a decisive victory. The results were as follows: United National Party 125 seats, Sri Lanka Freedom Party 67, Independent Tamils 14, Tamil United Liberation Front 10, Sri Lanka Muslim Congress 3, United Socialist Alliance 3, Mahajana Eksath Peramuna 3.

The rebellion by secessionist Tamil groups in the north-east of the country continues.

HEAD OF STATE

President, His Excellency Ranasinghe Premadasa, *elected* 20 Dec. 1988, *sworn in* 2 Jan. 1989 (*also Minister of Buddha Sasana, Education, Higher Education, Defence, and Policy Planning and Implementation*).

CABINET as at August 1992

Prime Minister and Minister of Finance, Labour and Vocational Training, Hon. D. B. Wijetunge.
Transport and Highways, Hon. Wijayapala Mendis.
Justice, Hon. A. C. S. Hameed.
Environment and Parliamentary Affairs, Hon. M. Vincent Perera.
Public Administration, Provincial Councils and Home Affairs, Hon. Festus Perera.
Tourism and Rural Industrial Development, Hon. S. Thondaman.
Industries, Science and Technology, Hon. Ranil Wickramasinghe.
Lands, Irrigation and Mahaweli Development, Hon. Gamini Athukorale.
Fisheries and Aquatic Resources, Hon. Joseph Michael Perera.
Cultural Affairs and Information, Hon. W. J. M. Lokubandara.
Posts and Telecommunications, Hon. A. M. S. Adhikari.
Youth Affairs and Sports, Hon. C. Nanda Mathew.
Trade and Commerce, Hon. A. R. Munsoor.
Handlooms and Textile Industries, Hon. U. B. Wijekoon.
Health and Women's Affairs, Hon. Renuka Herath.
Reconstruction and Rehabilitation, Hon. P. Dayaratne.
Housing and Construction, Hon. B. Sirisena Cooray.
Plantation Industries, Hon. Rupasena Karunatilleke.
Foreign Affairs, Hon. Harold Herat.
Food and Co-operatives, Hon. Weerasinghe Mallimarachchi.
Agricultural Development and Research, Hon. Dharmadasa Banda.
Power and Energy, Hon. K. D. M. Chandra Bandara.
Ports and Shipping, Hon. Alick Aluvihare.

HIGH COMMISSION FOR THE DEMOCRATIC SOCIALIST REPUBLIC OF SRI LANKA
13 Hyde Park Gardens, London W2 2LU
Tel 071-262 1841

High Commissioner, His Excellency Gen. D. S. Attygalle, LVO (1990).

BRITISH HIGH COMMISSION
Galle Road 190, Kollupitiya (PO Box 1433), Colombo 3
Tel: Colombo 437336

High Commissioner, His Excellency E. J. Field, CMG (1991).

BRITISH COUNCIL REPRESENTATIVE, R. A. Jarvis, 49 Alfred House Gardens, Colombo 3. Library also in *Kandy*.

THE JUDICATURE

The judicial system provides for a Supreme Court, a Court of Appeal, a High Court and other Courts of First Instance.

COMMUNICATIONS

There are over 15,660 miles of motorable roads in Sri Lanka and a government-run railway system with 984 miles of lines.

There is a satellite earth station at Padukka, in south-west Sri Lanka, which provides telecommunication links via satellite with any part of the globe.

The principal airports are at Katunayake, 19 miles north of Colombo, and Ratmalana, nine miles south of the capital. Air Lanka operates on 76 flights weekly to the Gulf States, the Maldives, Western Europe and throughout the Far East.

ECONOMY

The staple products of the island are tea, rubber, copra, spices and gems. There is increasing emphasis on local production of food, especially rice, and plans for the large-scale production of sugar cane, cotton and citrus fruits.

Factories are established for the manufacture or processing of ceramic ware, vegetable oils and by-products, paper, tobacco, tanning and leather goods, plywood, cement, chemicals, sugar, flour, salt, textiles, ilmenite, tiles, tyres, fertilizers, clothing, jewellery and hardware and there is a petroleum refinery.

TRADE WITH UK

	1990	1991
Imports from UK	£88,496,000	£128,565,000
Exports to UK	63,362,000	74,460,000

SUDAN

Al-Jamhuryat es-Sudan Al-Democratia

AREA – Sudan extends from the southern boundary of Egypt, 22° N. lat., to the northern boundary of Uganda, 3° 36′ N. lat., and reaches from the Republic of Chad about 21° 49′ E. (at 12° 45′ N.) to the north-west boundary of Ethiopia in 38° 35′ E. (at 18° N.). On the east lie the Red Sea and Ethiopia; on the south lie Kenya, Uganda and Zaire; and on the west the Central African Republic, Chad, and Libya. The greatest length from north to south is approximately 1,300 miles, and east to west 950 miles. The estimated area is about 967,500 sq. miles (2,505,813 sq. km).

The White Nile enters from Uganda at Nimule as the Bahr el Jebel, and leaves Sudan at Wadi Halfa. The Blue Nile flows from Lake Tana on the Ethiopian plateau. Its course in Sudan is nearly 500 miles long, before it joins the White Nile at Khartoum. The next confluence of importance is at Atbara where the main Nile is joined by the River Atbara. Between Khartoum and Wadi Halfa lie five of the six cataracts.

POPULATION – The population is 25,203,000 (UN estimate 1990). Arab and Nubian peoples populate the northern and central two-thirds of Sudan, Nilotic and Negro peoples the southern third. Arabic is the official language and Islam the state religion, although the Nilotics of the Bahr el Ghazal and Upper Nile valleys are generally Animists or Christians.

CAPITAL – Khartoum. The combined population of Khartoum, Khartoum North and Omdurman (excluding refugees and displaced people) is estimated at 3,000,000.
CURRENCY – Sudanese Dinar of 10 pounds.
FLAG – Three horizontal stripes of red, white and black with a green triangle next to the hoist.
NATIONAL ANTHEM – Nahnu Djundullah (We are the army of God).
NATIONAL DAY – 1 January (Independence Day).

GOVERNMENT

The Anglo-Egyptian Condominium over Sudan was established in 1899 and ended when the Sudan House of Representatives, on 19 December 1955, voted unanimously a declaration that Sudan was a fully independent sovereign state. A Republic was proclaimed on 1 January 1956, and was recognized by Great Britain and Egypt, a Supreme Commission being sworn in to take over sovereignty. Sudan was under military rule from November 1958 until 1964 when a civilian government was appointed. Government of the country was taken over on 25 May 1969 by a ten-man revolutionary council headed by Col. Gaafar Mohamed El Nimeri. In February 1972 an agreement was signed at Addis Ababa which brought to an end nearly 17 years of insurrection and civil war in the six southern provinces, and which recognized southern regional autonomy within a unified Sudanese state. Insurrection broke out again in 1983 and continues.

In April 1985 the Army command assumed power after popular demonstrations, deposed Nimeri and appointed a transitional government. In May 1986 power was transferred to a civilian regime following multi-party elections.

The third military coup since Sudan's independence took place on 30 June 1989 when the government of Sadiq al Mahdi was overthrown by Brig.-Gen. Omar Hassan Ahmad al-Bashir. The constitution was suspended and parliament was replaced by a 15-member ruling junta who have de facto control over a cabinet of 21 ministers.

CABINET as at September 1992

Prime Minister and Minister for Defence, Lt.-Gen. Omar Hassan Ahmad al-Bashir.
Deputy PM and Minister of Interior, Maj.-Gen. Zubir Mohammed Saleh.
Presidential Affairs, Lt.-Col. Tayib Ibrahim Mohammed Khayr.
Foreign Affairs, Ali Sahlul.
Justice and Attorney-General, Hassan Ismail al-Billi.
Culture and Information, Abdullah Mohammed Ahmed.
Finance and National Economic Planning, Abdel Rahim Mahmoud Hamdi.
Agriculture and Natural Resources, Ahmad Ali al-Genief.
National Guidance and Orientation, Abdella Deng Danyal.
Local Government and Co-ordination of Provincial Affairs, Natali Yanku Ambu.
Irrigation, Yacoub Abu Shura Musa.
Energy and Mining, Abdel Munim Khujali.
Industry, Dr Taj Al Sir Mustafa.
Education, Abdul Basit Sabdarat.
Housing, Construction and Public Utilities, Osman Abdoul Gadir Abdul Latif.
Higher Education, Dr Ibrahim Ahmed Omer.
Transport and Communications, Col. Salah Ed Din Karer.
Labour and Social Security, George Kinga.
Commerce, Co-operation and Supply, Faruq al-Bushra.
Health and Social Welfare, Dr Hussein Abu Salih.

EMBASSY OF THE REPUBLIC OF THE SUDAN
3 Cleveland Row, London SW1A 1DD
Tel 071-839 8080

Ambassador Extraordinary and Plenipotentiary, new appointment awaited.

BRITISH EMBASSY
(PO Box 801), Khartoum
Tel: Khartoum 70760/7

Ambassador Extraordinary and Plenipotentiary, His Excellency Peter J. Streams, CMG (1990).
Counsellor, Head of Chancery and Consul-General, P. R. Heigh.

BRITISH COUNCIL REPRESENTATIVE, A. Thomas, 14 Abu Sinn Street (PO Box 1253), Khartoum.

EDUCATION

School education is free for most children, but not compulsory, beginning with six years primary education, followed by three years secondary education at general secondary schools, the more academic higher secondary schools or vocational schools. The medium of instruction is Arabic. English is taught as the principal foreign language in all schools.

Khartoum University has ten faculties. There is a branch of Cairo University in Khartoum, an Islamic University at Omdurman and universities at Wad Medani and Juba.

In addition to the universities there are various technical post-secondary institutes as well as professional and vocational training establishments.

ECONOMY

The principal grain crops are *dura* (great millet) and wheat, the staple food of the population. Sesame and ground-nuts are other important food crops, which also yield an exportable surplus and a promising start has been made with castor seed.

The principal export crop is cotton. Traditionally a major producer of long-staple cotton, Sudan has in recent years grown more short and medium-staple cotton. These grades now account for more than half total production. Production in 1987–8 is estimated to have been around 837,000 bales. Sudan also produces the bulk of the world's supply of gum arabic. Sugar is an increasingly important crop, although Sudan still has to achieve self sufficiency in its production.

Livestock is the mainstay of the nomadic Arab tribes of the desert and the Negro tribes of the swamp and wooded grassland country in the south. Production has, however, been affected by drought, famine and flooding.

Sudan's agriculture production provided employment for over 60 per cent of the labour force and contributed 37 per cent to GDP in 1986–7. It is based on large and medium sized public sector irrigation projects with small scale private irrigation schemes providing mostly fruit and vegetables. Mechanized and traditional agriculture is practised in areas of sufficient rainfall.

The manufacturing sector contributed less than 8 per cent to GDP in 1986–7 and provided employment for 4 per cent of the work force. The main manufacturing enterprises are concentrated in the areas of food processing, textiles, shoes, cigarettes and batteries.

FINANCE

	1986–7
Revenue	£S2,741.1m
Expenditure	6,100.7m
Deficit	2,527.6m
Deficit financing	2,527.6m

TRADE

The principal exports are cotton, livestock, gum arabic and other agricultural produce. The chief imports are petroleum goods and other raw materials, machinery and equipment, transport and equipment, medicines and chemicals.

	1989*
Total imports	US$14,532.0m
Total exports	651.5m

*estimated

Trade with UK	1990	1991
Imports from UK	£63,670,000	£75,460,000
Exports to UK	9,016,000	6,168,000

COMMUNICATIONS

The railway system, adversely affected by the civil war, has a route length of about 3,200 miles, linking Khartoum with Wadi Halfa, Karima, Port Sudan, Wad Medani, Sennar, El Damazin, Kosti, El Obeid and Nyala. Nile river services between Khartoum and Juba have been interrupted by the southern insurrection. Port Sudan is the country's main seaport. Sudan Airways fly services from Khartoum to many parts of the Sudan and to other African states, Europe and the Middle East.

SURINAME

Nieuwe Republick van Suriname

Suriname is situated on the north coast of South America and is bounded by French Guiana in the east, Brazil in the south and Guyana in the west. It has an area of 63,037 sq. miles (163,265 sq. km), with a population (UN 1990 estimate) of 422,000.

CAPITAL – ΨParamaribo, population (1971) 110,000.
CURRENCY – Suriname guilder of 100 cents.
FLAG – Horizontal stripes of green, white, red, white, green, with a five-pointed yellow star in the centre.
NATIONAL DAY – 25 November.

GOVERNMENT

Formerly known as Dutch Guiana, Suriname remained part of the Netherlands West Indies until 25 November 1975, when it achieved complete independence. Suriname had received autonomy in domestic affairs on 29 December 1954.

The civilian government was ousted in February 1980 by the military who appointed a predominantly civilian Cabinet in 1982.

According to the constitution approved by referendum in September 1987, a National Assembly of 51 members elects the President. The Army remains the 'vanguard of the people'. President Shankar was overthrown in a military coup, instigated by Lt.-Col. Desi Bouterse, in December 1990; Johan Kraag, a supporter of Bouterse, was installed as President. Elections to the National Assembly were held on 25 May 1991. The New Front for Democracy and Development, a coalition comprising opposition groups, won 30 of the 51 seats, but failed to gain the necessary two-thirds majority to appoint the President. Eventually in September 1991 a special sitting of a United People's Assembly elected New Front leader Ronald Venetiaan as President and he formed a new government which is committed to amending the constitution to limit the power of the military.

HEAD OF STATE

President, Chairman of the State Security Council, Dr Ronald Venetiaan, *elected* 7 September 1991.

CABINET as at July 1992

Vice-President, Prime Minister, Jules Ajodhia.
Labour, Reynold Simons.
Foreign Affairs, Subhas Mungra.
Defence, Siegfried Gilds.
Finance, Humphrey Hildenberg.
Economics, Tjandrikapersad Gobardhan.
Justice and Police, Soeshiel Girjasing.
Natural Resources, Harold Pollack.
Education, Cornelis Pigot.
Public Works, Radj Koemar Randjietsingh.
Planning and Development, Edwin Sedoc.
Regional Affairs, Rufus Nooitmeer.
Agricultural and Fisheries, S. Setroredjo.
Transport, Communications and Tourism, John Defares.
Public Health, Mohamed Khudabux.
Interior, J. Sisal.
Social Affairs, W. Soemita.

EMBASSY OF THE REPUBLIC OF SURINAME
2 Alexander Gogelweg, The Hague, The Netherlands
Tel: The Hague 650844

Ambassador Extraordinary and Plenipotentiary, His Excellency Cyrill Bisoendat Ramkisor (1990) (resident in The Hague).

BRITISH AMBASSADOR (resident in Georgetown, Guyana).
BRITISH CONSULATE, c/o VSH United Buildings, Van't Hogerhuystraat, PO Box 1300, Paramaribo. *Honorary Consul,* J. J. Healy, MBE.

ECONOMY

Suriname has large timber resources. Rice and sugar cane are the main crops. Bauxite is mined, and is the principal export. In 1987, GDP amounted to US$1,080 million. Principal trading partners are the Netherlands, USA and Norway.

TRADE

	1985
Imports	US$359.5m
Exports	337.3m

Trade with UK	1990	1991
Imports from UK	£10,564,000	£7,896,000
Exports to UK	£10,094,000	9,922,000

SWAZILAND

Umbuso we Swatini

AREA, POPULATION, ETC – Surrounded by South Africa on its northern, western and southern borders and by Mozambique to the east, this small land-locked country is geographically and climatically divided into three principal areas. The broken mountainous Highveld along the western border with an average altitude of 4,000 feet is densely forested mainly with conifers and eucalyptus; the Middleveld, averaging about 2,000 feet, is a mixed farming area including cotton and pineapples; and the Lowveld in the east, which was mainly scrubland until the introduction of large sugar cane plantations west of the Lubombo mountain range and the

Mozambique border. Four rivers, the Komati, Usutu, Mbuluzi and Ngwavuma, flow from west to east. The total area of Swaziland is 6,704 sq. miles (17,363 sq. km), and the population (UN estimate 1990) is 768,000.

CAPITAL – Mbabane (population 1986, 38,290), the headquarters of the government, is situated at an average altitude of 3,800 ft. Other main townships are Manzini (estimated population, 30,000), Big Bend, Mhlambanyati, Mhlume, Nhlangano, Pigg's Peak and Simunye.

CURRENCY – Lilangeni (E) of 100 cents. South African currency is also in circulation. Swaziland is a member of the Common Monetary Area and its unit of currency *Emalangeni* (singular *Lilangeni*) has a par value with the South African Rand.

FLAG – Blue with a wide crimson horizontal band bordered in yellow across the centre, bearing a shield and two spears horizontally.

NATIONAL ANTHEM – Ingoma Yesive.

NATIONAL DAY – 6 September (Independence Day).

GOVERNMENT

The Kingdom of Swaziland came into being on 25 April 1967 under a new internal self-government constitution and became an independent kingdom, headed by HM Sobhuza II, in membership of the Commonwealth on 6 September 1968.

A new government system was introduced in 1978, under which the King, assisted by his appointed Cabinet, holds considerable executive, legislative and judicial authority. In addition, there is a bicameral legislative body comprising a Senate and a House of Assembly. Each of the 40 traditional Tinkhundla (chieftaincies) elects two members to the electoral college who elect 40 members to the House of Assembly. The King appoints ten members to the House of Assembly, making 50 in all, who then elect ten members (not of their own number) to the Senate. To these are added ten senators appointed by the King, bringing the full membership of the Senate to 20. All political parties are banned under the 1978 Constitution.

HEAD OF STATE
HM King Mswati III, inaugurated 25 April 1986.

CABINET as at July 1992
Prime Minister, Hon. Obed Dlamini.
Foreign Affairs, Hon. Sir George Mamba.
Justice, Hon. Dr Zonke Khumalo.
Finance, Hon. Barnabas Dlamini.
Home Affairs, Hon. Prince Sobandla.
Education, Hon. Prince Khuzulwandle.
Works and Construction, Hon. Prince Mbilini.
Health, Hon. Dr Fanny Friedman.
Agriculture, Hon. Themba Masaku.
Commerce and Industry, Hon. Barnabas Mhlongo.
Labour and Public Service, Hon. David Motsa.
Natural Resources, Land Utilization and Energy, Hon. Senzenjoni Shabalala.
Housing and Urban Development, Hon. Thomas Stephens.
Economic Planning and Development, Hon. Solomon Dlamini.
Transport and Communications, Hon. Albert Shabangu.
Broadcasting, Information and Tourism, Hon. Douglas N. Ntiwane.

KINGDOM OF SWAZILAND HIGH COMMISSION
58 Pont Street, London SW1X 0AE
Tel 071-581 4976/8

High Commissioner, His Excellency Mboni N. Dlamini (1988).

BRITISH HIGH COMMISSION
Allister Miller Street, Mbabane
Tel: Mbabane 42581

High Commissioner, His Excellency Brian Watkins (1990).

COMMUNICATIONS

Swaziland's railway is about 150 miles long and runs from Ngwenya in the west to the Mozambique border near Goba in the east, and thence to the Mozambique port of Maputo. A southern link from Phuzumoya in central Swaziland joins up with the South African railway network to Richards Bay. A rail link from Mpaka in central Swaziland to the northwest border opened in 1986 and provides a link to Komatipoort.

Most passenger and goods traffic is carried by privately-owned motor transport services. There are daily scheduled air services by Royal Swazi National Airways to Johannesburg and scheduled routes to Durban, Harare, Lusaka, Gaborone, Nairobi and Dar es Salaam. International telecommunications and television services are provided through a satellite earth station opened in 1983. There is also a national telephone network through a series of microwave links.

ECONOMY

In the 1989–90 budget, total expenditure, including debt repayment, was projected at E447,000,000. A surplus of E12,500,000 was predicted due to increase in revenue.

Manufacturing was announced to have replaced agriculture as the dominant sector in 1988.

TRADE WITH UK

	1990	1991
Imports from UK	£2,719,000	£4,336,000
Exports to UK	34,473,000	39,607,000

SWEDEN
Konungariket Sverige

AREA AND POPULATION – Sweden occupies the eastern area of the Scandinavian peninsula in north-west Europe and comprises 24 local government districts (*Län*), with a total area of 173,732 sq. miles (449,964 sq. km), and population of 8,559,000 (1990 UN estimate). In 1986 the birth rate was 12.2 per 1,000 inhabitants, the death rate 11.1 per 1,000 inhabitants and infant mortality rate was 6.8 per 1,000 live births.

RELIGION – The state religion is Lutheran Protestant, to which over 95 per cent of the people officially adhere.

CAPITAL – ΨStockholm. Population (1988): City 669,485; Greater Stockholm, 1,471,242; ΨGothenburg (Göteborg) (430,765); ΨMalmö (231,575); Uppsala (161,828).

CURRENCY – Swedish krona of 100 øre.

FLAG – Yellow cross on a blue ground.

NATIONAL ANTHEM – Du Gamla, Du Fria (Thou ancient, thou freeborn).

NATIONAL DAY – 6 June (Day of the Swedish Flag).

GOVERNMENT

Sweden is a constitutional monarchy, with the monarch retaining purely ceremonial functions as head of state. Under the Act of Succession of 6 June 1809 (with amendments) the throne is hereditary in the House of Bernadotte. Jean-Baptiste Jules Bernadotte, Prince of Ponte Corvo, a Marshal of France, was invited to accept the title of Crown Prince, with succession to the throne. He succeeded Charles XIII in

1818. A 1979 amendment vested the succession in the monarch's eldest child, irrespective of sex.

There is a unicameral legislature (*Riksdag*) of 349 members elected by universal suffrage for three years. The Council of Ministers (*Statsråd*) is responsible to the *Riksdag*. In the General Election held on 15 September 1991, the following seats were won: Social Democrats 138; Moderates 80; Liberals 33; Centre 31; Christian Democrats 26; New Democracy 25; Left Party 16.

On 1 July 1991 Sweden applied to join the European Community.

HEAD OF STATE

King of Sweden, HM Carl XVI Gustaf, KG, *born* 30 April 1946, *succeeded* 15 September 1973, *married* 19 June 1976 Fräulein Silvia Renate Sommerlath and has *issue*, Crown Princess Victoria Ingrid Alice Désirée, Duchess of Västergötland, *born* 14 July 1977; Prince Carl Philip Edmund Bertil, Duke of Värmland, *born* 13 May 1979; Princess Madeleine Thérèse Amelie Josephine, Duchess of Hälsingland and Gästrikland, *born* 10 June 1982.

COUNCIL OF MINISTERS as at July 1992

Prime Minister, Carl Bildt (M).
Deputy Prime Minister, Minister of Social Affairs, Bengt Westerberg (L).
Justice, Gun Hellsvik (M).
Foreign Affairs, Baroness Margaretha of Ugglas (M).
Defence, Anders Björck (M).
Transport and Communications, Mats Odell (CD).
Finance, Anne Wibble (L).
Education, Per Unckel (M).
Agriculture, Karl Erik Olsson (C).
Labour, Börje Hörnlund (C).
Industry and Commerce, Per Westerberg (M).
Public Administration, Inger Davidsson (CD).
Environment, Olof Johansson (C).
Culture, Birgit Friggebo (L).
Constitutional and Civil Law, Reidunn Laurén (Ind).
International Development Co-operation and Human Rights Issues, Alf Svensson (CD).
European Affairs and Foreign Trade, Ulf Dinkelspiel (M).
Health and Social Security, Bo Könberg (L).
Fiscal Affairs and Financial Markets, Bo Lundgren (M).
Schools and Adult Education, Beatrice Ask (M).
Physical Planning, Görel Thurdin (C).

M Moderate Party; L Liberal Party; C Centre Party; CD Christian Democrat Party

SWEDISH EMBASSY
11 Montagu Place, London W1H 2AL
Tel 071-724 2101

Ambassador Extraordinary and Plenipotentiary, His Excellency Lennart Eckerberg, KCMG (1991).
Minister Plenipotentiary, P. O. Jödahl.
Counsellors, L.-O. Lundberg (*Press*); P. Bruce (*International Organizations*); P. Järborg (*Consular and Consul-General*); R. Ängeby (*Political*).
Defence and Naval Attaché, Cmdr. J. Bring.
Military and Air Attaché, Col. E. J. Hjelm.
Trade Commissioner, M. Nilsson, 73 Welbeck Street, London W1M 8AN.

BRITISH EMBASSY
Skarpögatan 6–8, 115 93 Stockholm
Tel: Stockholm 6670140

Ambassador Extraordinary and Plenipotentiary, His Excellency R. L. B. Cormack, CMG (1991).
Counsellor (Political) and Consul-General, M. R. J. Guest.

There are British Consular Offices at *Stockholm* and *Gothenburg*, and Honorary Consuls at *Luleå, Gothenburg, Malmö* and *Sundsvall*.

BRITISH COUNCIL REPRESENTATIVE, Dr S. M. Lewis.
BRITISH-SWEDISH CHAMBER OF COMMERCE, Grevgatan 34, 11453 Stockholm.

ECONOMY

The country's industrial prosperity is based on an abundance of natural resources in the form of forests, mineral deposits and water power. The forests are extensive, covering about half the total land surface, and sustain timber, pulp and paper milling industries. The mineral resources include iron ore, lead, zinc, sulphur, granite, marble, precious and heavy metals (the latter not exploited) and extensive deposits of low grade uranium ore. Industries based on mining, principally iron and steel, aluminium and copper are important but it is the general engineering industry that provides the basis of Sweden's exports. Growth areas are largely in the specialized machinery and systems and chemical industries. About 40 per cent of Sweden's industrial output is exported, mainly in the form of cars, trucks, machinery, electrical and communications equipment. The relative importance of agriculture has declined and in 1992 only 3 per cent of the labour force was engaged in farming.

Apart from water power Sweden has no significant indigenous resources of conventional hydrocarbon fuels and relies to a high degree upon imported oil. Much of Sweden's electricity is generated by nuclear power but as a result of a referendum in 1980 the nuclear programme is to be discontinued by 2010. However, this decision is now being debated once more and could be reversed. Small supplies of natural gas are imported from Denmark into southern Sweden, with the pipeline being extended to Gothenburg.

Finance

	1990–1	1991–2
Revenue	Kronor 407,900m	Kronor 454,928m
Expenditure	408,200m	455,526m

Trade

	1989	1990
Imports	Kronor 315,061.0m	Kronor 322,854m
Exports	332,144.9m	339,772m

Trade with UK	1990	1991
Imports from UK	£2,712,775,000	£2,471,539,000
Exports to UK	3,594,547,000	3,142,449,000

Sweden's main imports from Britain, accounting for 10 per cent of total imports in 1990, are engineering products, semi-manufactures and chemical products. Britain's main imports from Sweden are paper and board, road vehicles, machinery, wood, steel and pulp.

COMMUNICATIONS

The total length of Swedish railroads is 11,745 km. The road network is over 400,000 km in length. The mercantile marine amounted on 31 December 1985 to 2,619,625 gross tonnage.

The Board of Civil Aviation under the control of the Ministry of Communications handles civil aviation matters. Regular domestic air traffic is maintained by the Scandinavian Airlines System and by Linjeflyg. Regular European and inter-continental air traffic is maintained by the Scandinavian Airlines System.

DEFENCE

Based on the policy of non-alignment in peace leading to neutrality in war Sweden maintains a 'total defence' intended to make any attack on her costly. Total defence includes peacetime organizations for civil, economic and psychological defence.

All men aged 18–47 are eligible for conscription, with the initial conscription term being seven to 15 months for the Army and Navy and eight to 12 months for the Air Force. Men are obliged to serve in the reserves until age 47 with a commitment to refresher training lasting between 17 and 31 days every fourth year.

The armed forces have a total active strength of 63,000 (46,800 conscripts), with reserves of 709,000 (Army 550,000; Navy 102,000; Air Force 57,000). The Army has an active strength of 43,500 (35,000 conscripts), and on mobilization a strength of 600,000 with five armoured brigades, one mechanized brigade and 16 infantry and winter warfare brigades. Equipment includes 885 main battle tanks, 200 light tanks, 600 armoured personnel carriers, 1,020 artillery pieces and 20 combat helicopters. The Navy has 12 submarines, 42 fast attack craft, a number of minor craft and auxiliaries, five coast artillery units, 14 combat helicopters and a strength of 12,000 (6,300 conscripts). The Air Force has modern supersonic aircraft of Swedish manufacture forming a standing force of 220 air defence, 100 attack and 55 reconnaissance with support aircraft and a modern air defence radar system. The Air Force has a strength of 7,500 (5,500 conscripts). Facilities exist for rapid dispersal from main bases in war.

CULTURE

Swedish belongs, with Danish and Norwegian, to the North Germanic language group. Swedish literature dates back to King Magnus Eriksson, who codified the old Swedish provincial laws in 1350. With his translation of the Bible, Olaus Petri (1493–1552) formed the basis for the modern Swedish language. Literature flourished during the reign of Gustavus III, who founded the Swedish Academy in 1786. Notable Swedish writers include Almquist (1795–1866), Strindberg (1849–1912) and Lagerlöf (1858–1940), Nobel Prize winner in 1909. Contemporary authors include Lagerquist (1891–1974), Nobel Laureate in 1951, Martinson (1904–78) and Johnson (1900–76), Nobel Laureates jointly in 1974. The Swedish scientist Alfred Nobel (1833–96) founded the Nobel Prizes for literature, science and peace.

EDUCATION

Tuition within the state system, which is maintained by the state and by local taxation, is free. It provides nine years' compulsory schooling from the age of seven to 16 in the comprehensive elementary schools; further education of two to four years' duration in the upper secondary schools and a unified higher education system administered in six regional areas containing one of the universities: Uppsala (founded 1477); Lund (1668); Stockholm (1878); Gothenburg (1887); Umeå (1963) and Linköping (1967). At present there are 33 institutions of higher education including three technical universities in Stockholm, Gothenburg and Luleå, and the Karolinska Institute in Stockholm, which specializes in medicine and dentistry.

SWITZERLAND

Schweizerische Eidgenossenschaft - Confédération Suisse - Confederazione Svizzera

Area and Population – Switzerland, the Helvetia of the Romans, is a federal republic of central Europe, situated between 45° 50′ and 47° 48′ N. lat. and 5° 58′ and 10° 3′ E. long. It is composed of 23 Cantons, three subdivided, making 26 in all, and comprises a total area of 15,943 sq. miles (41,293 sq. km), with a population (1990 UN estimate) of 6,712,000. In 1989 there were 81,180 live births, 60,882 deaths and 45,066 marriages. Of the total population in 1980, 44.3 per cent was Protestant, 47.6 per cent Roman Catholic, 3.2 per cent other religions and 4.9 per cent without religion.

Switzerland is the most mountainous country in Europe. The Alps, covered with perennial snow and from 5,000 to 15,217 feet in height, occupy its southern and eastern frontiers, and the chief part of its interior; the Jura mountains rise in the north-west. The Alps occupy 61 per cent, and the Jura mountains 12 per cent of the country. The highest peak, Mont Blanc, Pennine Alps (15,782 ft.) is partly in France and Italy; Monte Rosa (15,217 ft.) and Matterhorn (14,780 ft.) are partly in Switzerland and partly in Italy. The highest wholly Swiss peaks are Dufourspitze (15,203 ft.), Finsteraarhorn (14,026), Aletschhorn (13,711), Jungfrau (13,671), Mönch (13,456), Eiger (13,040), Schreckhorn (13,385), and Wetterhorn (12,150) in the Bernese Alps, and Dom (14,918), Weisshorn (14,803) and Breithorn (13,685).

The Swiss lakes are famous for their beauty and include Lakes Maggiore, Zürich, Lucerne, Neuchâtel, Geneva, Constance, Thun, Zug, Lugano, Brienz and the Walensee. There are also many artificial lakes.

Capital – Berne, population (1990) 135,543 (city). Other large towns are (1990) Zürich (345,215), Basle (171,888), Geneva (169,491), Lausanne (122,600), Winterthur (85,200), St Gallen (73,200), Lucerne (59,100).

Currency – Swiss franc of 100 centimes or rappen.

FLAG – Square and red, bearing a couped white cross.
NATIONAL ANTHEM – Trittst im Morgenrot Daher (Radiant in the morning sky).
NATIONAL DAY – 1 August.

GOVERNMENT

The legislature consists of two chambers, a National Council (*Nationalrat*) of 200 members, and a States Council (*Ständerat*) of 46 members; both Chambers united are called the Federal Assembly. Members of the National Council are elected for four years, elections taking place in October.

The executive power is in the hands of a Federal Council (*Bundesrat*) of seven members, elected for four years by the Federal Assembly and presided over by the President of the Confederation.

Each year the Federal Assembly elects from the Federal Council the President and the Vice-President. Not more than one of the same canton may be elected member of the Federal Council; on the other hand, there is a tradition that Italian and French-speaking areas should between them be represented on the Federal Council by at least two members.

The Federal Council voted by four votes to three in May 1992 to apply for European Community membership.

FEDERAL COUNCIL

President of the Swiss Confederation (1992) *and Head of Foreign Affairs*, René Felber.
Vice-President (1992) *and Head of Transport, Communications and Energy*, Adolf Ogi.
Military, Kaspar Villiger.
Home Affairs, Flavio Cotti.
Economic Affairs, Jean-Pascal Delamuraz.
Finance, Otto Stich.
Justice and Police, Arnold Koller.

EMBASSY OF SWITZERLAND

16–18 Montagu Place, London W1H 2BQ
Tel 071–723 0701

Ambassador Extraordinary and Plenipotentiary, His Excellency Franz E. Muheim (1989).
Minister, C. M. W. Faessler.
Counsellor, J. Bucher (*Economic and Financial*).
Defence, Military, Naval and Air Attaché, Maj.-Gen. G. de Loës.
Consul-General and Head of Administration, E. Jaun.

There is a Swiss Consulate-General in *Manchester*.

BRITISH EMBASSY

Thunstrasse 50, 3005 Berne
Tel: Berne 445021

Ambassador Extraordinary and Plenipotentiary, His Excellency David Beattie, CMG (1992).
Counsellors, C. C. Bright; C. W. Wainwright.
First Secretary, P. Cole.
Second Secretaries, Dr J. Mitchiner; P. A. Chatt.
Defence, Naval and Military Attaché, Lt.-Col. W. R. Thatcher.
Air Attaché, Wg Cdr. H. W. Hughes.

BRITISH CONSULAR OFFICES – There is a Consular section at the Embassy in Berne; Consulates-General at *Zürich* and *Geneva* and Consular offices at *Lugano, Valais* and *Montreux*. The Directorate of British Export Promotion in Switzerland is in the Consulate-General Office in *Zürich*.

BRITISH-SWISS CHAMBER OF COMMERCE, Freiestrasse 155, 8032 Zürich.
SWISS-BRITISH SOCIETIES: Berne – *President*, Dr H. Beriger. Zürich – *President*, J.-P. Müller. Basle – *President*, Dr C. Grey.

DEFENCE

All Swiss males must undertake military service in the Army or the Air Corps, which is part of the Army. The total active armed forces number some 3,500 regulars with, in addition, two intakes of 18,000 each a year for 17 weeks recruit training. Conscription takes the form of the 17 weeks recruit training at age 20 and regular reservist refresher training up to age 50.

The Army has a strength on mobilization of some 565,000 organized into four corps, with some 870 main battle tanks, 1,350 armoured personnel carriers and armoured infantry fighting vehicles, and 1,370 artillery pieces. The Air Corps has a strength on mobilization of 60,000 with 289 combat aircraft deployed in eight air defence, eight ground attack, one reconnaissance and one liaison squadron with support and training units.

ECONOMY

Agriculture is followed chiefly in the valleys and all over the Mittelland, where cereals, flax, hemp, and tobacco are produced, and nearly all temperate zone fruits and vegetables as well as grapes are grown. Dairying and stock-raising are the principal industries, about 3,000,000 acres being under grass for hay and 2,000,000 acres pasturage. The forests cover about one-quarter of the whole surface.

The chief manufacturing industries comprise engineering and electrical engineering, metal-working, chemicals and pharmaceuticals, textiles, watchmaking, woodworking, foodstuffs and footwear. Banking, insurance and tourism are major industries.

FINANCE

	1989*	1990
Revenue	SFr28,031m	SFr30,324m
Expenditure	27,555m	29,850m

*estimate

TRADE

The principal imports are machinery, electrical and electronic equipment, textiles, motor vehicles, non-ferrous metals, chemical elements, clothing, food, medicinal and pharmaceutical products. The principal exports are machinery, chemical elements, non-ferrous metals, watches, electrical and electronic equipment, textiles, dyeing, tanning and colouring equipment. Switzerland is a member of EFTA.

	1990	1991
Total Imports	SFr96,611m	SFr95,032m
Total Exports	88,257m	87,946m

Trade with UK†	1990	1991
Imports from UK	£2,358,528,000	£2,105,656,000
Exports to UK	4,252,783,000	3,754,586,000

†Including Liechtenstein

COMMUNICATIONS

There were in 1988 5,020 km of railway tracks (Swiss Federal Railways, 2,990 km; Swiss privately owned railways 2,030 km). At the end of 1990 the number of telephones amounted to 3,943,000 and the network was fully automatic throughout the country. At the same time there were 2,670,000 licensed radio receivers and 2,435,000 television receivers.

At the end of 1989 the total length of motorways was 1,495 km. The number of motor vehicles licensed in 1989 was 3,809,000.

A merchant marine, established in 1941, consisted at June 1990 of 20 vessels with a total gross tonnage of 287,487 tonnes. In 1989, goods handled at Basle Rhine ports amounted to 8,845,162 tonnes. In 1987, 163 lake and river vessels (excluding the Rhine) transported 10,608,200 passengers and 500 tonnes of freight.

Swiss airlines have a network covering 347,009 km (1989) and in 1989 carried 8,507,511 passengers. Swissair, the national airline, flies to and from the airports at Zürich, Geneva and Basle.

EDUCATION

Education is controlled by cantonal and communal authorities; there is no central organization. Primary education is free and compulsory. School age varies, generally seven to 14, with secondary education from age 12 to 15. Schools are numerous and well-attended, and there are many private institutions. Special schools make a feature of commercial and technical instruction. Universities are Basle (founded 1460), Berne (1834), Fribourg (1889), Geneva (1873), Lausanne (1890), Zürich (1832), and Neuchâtel (1909), the technical universities of Lausanne and Zürich and the economics university of St Gall.

CULTURE

There are four official languages: French, German, Italian and Romansch. German is the dominating language in 19 of the 26 cantons; French in Fribourg, Jura, Geneva, Neuchâtel, Valais and Vaud; Italian in Ticino, and Romansch in parts of the Grisons.

Many modern authors, alike in the German school and in the Suisse Romande, have achieved international fame. Karl Spitteler (1845–1924) and Hermann Hesse (1877–1962) were awarded the Nobel Prize for Literature, the former in 1919, the latter in 1946.

SYRIA

Al-Jamhouriya Al-Arabia as-Souriya

AREA AND POPULATION – Syria is in the Levant, covering a portion of the former Ottoman Empire. Bounded by the Mediterranean and Lebanon on the west, Israel and Jordan on the south-west, Iraq on the east and Turkey on the north, it has an estimated area of 71,498 sq. miles (185,180 sq. km), and a population (UN 1990 estimate) of 12,116,000, most of whom are Arabic-speaking and Muslim.

The Orontes flows northwards from the Lebanon range across the northern boundary to Antakya (Antioch, Turkey). The Euphrates crosses the northern boundary near Jerablus and flows through north-eastern Syria to the boundary of Iraq.

ARCHAEOLOGY, ETC. – The region is rich in historical remains. Damascus (Dimishq ash-Sham) is said to be the oldest continuously inhabited city in the world (although Aleppo disputes this claim), having existed as a city for over 4,000 years. The city contains the Omayed Mosque, the Tomb of Saladin, and the 'street which is called Straight' (Acts 9:11), while to the north-east is the Roman outpost of Dmeir and further east is Palmyra.

On the Mediterranean coast at Amrit are ruins of the Phoenician town of Marath, and also ruins of Crusaders' fortresses at Markab, Sahyoun, and Krak des Chevaliers. At Tartous (also on the coast) the cathedral of Our Lady of Syria, built by the Knights Templars in the 12th and 13th centuries, has been restored as a museum. One of the oldest alphabets in the world has been discovered at Ugarit (Ras Shamra), a Phoenician village near the port of Latakia.

Hittite cities dating from 2000 to 1500 BC, have been explored on the west bank of the Euphrates at Jerablus and Kadesh.

CAPITAL – Damascus, population (estimated) 1,378,000. Other important towns are Aleppo, Homs and Hama, and the principal port is ΨLatakia.

CURRENCY – Syrian pound (S£) of 100 piastres.

FLAG – Red over white over black horizontal bands, with two green stars on central white band.

NATIONAL DAY – 17 April.

GOVERNMENT

Syria, which had been under French mandate since the 1914–18 war, became an independent republic during the 1939–45 war. The first independently elected Parliament met on 17 August 1943, but foreign troops were in part occupation until April 1946. Syria remained an independent republic until February 1958, when it became part of the United Arab Republic. It seceded from the United Arab Republic on 28 September 1961.

A new constitution was promulgated in March 1973. This declared that Syria is a democratic, popular socialist state, and that the Arab Socialist Renaissance (Ba'ath) Party, which has been the ruling party since 1963, is the leading party in the state and society.

Elections to the expanded 250-seat Peoples' Council in May 1990 resulted in a large majority for the Ba'ath Party, which won 134 seats; its National Progressive Front allies (Arab Socialist Union, Socialist Unionist Movement, Arab Socialist Party, Syrian Communist Party) together won 32 seats. The Independents won 84.

HEAD OF STATE

President, Lt.-Gen. Hafez el Assad, *assumed office* 14 March 1971, *re-elected*, Feb. 1978, 13 March 1985, 3 December 1991.

Vice-Presidents, Abdul Halim Khaddam, Rifaat Al Assad, Zuhair Mashariqa.

MINISTERS as at June 1992

Prime Minister, Mahmoud Al Zubi.
Deputy PM and Minister for Defence, Gen. Mustafa Tlass.
Deputy PM for Public Services, Rashid Akhtarini.
Deputy PM for Economic Affairs, Dr Salim Yassin.
Education, Ghassan Halabi.
Higher Education, Kamal Sharaf.
Interior, Mohammad Harbah.
Transport, Yusuf al-Ahmed.
Information, Mohammad Salman.
Local Administration, Ahmed Diab.
Supply and Internal Trade, Hassan Saqqa.
Economy and Foreign Trade, Mohammad al-Imadi.
Culture, Najah al-Attar.
Foreign Affairs, Farooq ash-Shar'.
Tourism, Adnan Quli.
Health, Iyad al-Shatti.
Waqfs (Religious Endowments), Abdel-Majid Tarabulsi.
Irrigation, Abd ar-Rahman Madani.
Electricity, Kamil al-Baba.
Oil and Mineral Resources, Nadir Nabulsi.
Construction, Marwan Farra.
Housing and Utilities, Mohammad Nur Antabi.
Agriculture and Agrarian Reform, Mohammad Ghabbash.
Finance, Khaled al-Mahayni.
Industry, Antoine Jubran.
Communications, Murad Quwatli.
Justice, Abdullah Tulbah.
Presidential Affairs, Wahib Fadil.
Labour and Social Affairs, Haydar Buzu.

Embassy of the Syrian Arab Republic
8 Belgrave Square, London SW1X 8PH
Tel 071-245 9012

Ambassador Extraordinary and Plenipotentiary, His Excellency Mohammed al Khoder (1991).

British Embassy
Quartier Malki, 11 rue Mohammad Kurd Ali, Imm. Kotob, Damascus
Tel: Damascus 712561

Ambassador Extraordinary and Plenipotentiary, His Excellency Andrew F. Green, CMG.

DEFENCE

The total active armed forces have a strength of 404,000. There is a conscription period of 30 months, with a reserve commitment to age 45. The Army has a strength of some 300,000, with 4,350 main battle tanks, 500 reconnaissance vehicles, 3,750 armoured personnel carriers and infantry fighting vehicles and 2,200 artillery pieces. The Navy has a strength of 4,000 personnel, with three submarines, two frigates, 25 patrol and coastal combatants and 17 armed helicopters. The Air Force (including the Air Defence Command) has a strength of some 100,000, with 651 combat aircraft and 100 armed helicopters of Soviet manufacture organized into 18 air defence, 10 ground attack, six transport, and six reconnaissance squadrons, and training and support units.

Syria maintains a force of some 30,000 men in Lebanon and within Syria has some 4,500 men in armed Palestinian forces and some 1,800 advisers from the former Soviet Union.

ECONOMY

Agriculture is the principal source of production; wheat and barley are the main cereal crops, but the cotton crop is the highest in value. Tobacco is grown in the maritime plain in Sahel, the Sahyoun and the Djebleh district of Latakia. Large new areas are coming under irrigation and cultivation in the north-east of the country as a result of the Thawra dam. Skins and hides, leather goods, wool and silk, textiles, cement, vegetable oil, glass, soap, sugar, plastics and copper and brass utensils are produced. There are an increasing number of light assembly plants as Syria's industrialization programme develops. Oil has been found at Karachuk and other parts in the north-eastern corner of the country and production of high quality reserves is proceeding in the region of Deir ez Zor. Syria produces nearly 400,000 barrels of oil per day at present. A pipeline has been built to the Mediterranean port of Banias, via Homs. Two oil refineries are in production at Homs and Banias. Syria also has gas reserves, deposits of phosphate and rock salt, and produces asphalt.

Trade

The principal imports are foodstuffs (fruit, vegetables, cereals, meat and dairy products, tea, coffee and sugar), mineral and petroleum products, yarn and textiles, iron and steel manufactures, machinery, chemicals, pharmaceuticals, fertilizers and timber. Exports include raw cotton, oil, cereals, fruit, phosphates, cement, livestock and dairy products, other foodstuffs, textiles and raw wool.

Trade with UK	1990	1991
Imports from UK	£38,245,000	£49,791,000
Exports to UK	85,874,000	42,459,000

CULTURE

Arabic is the principal language, but Kurdish, Turkish and Armenian are spoken among significant minorities and a few villages still speak Aramaic, the language spoken by Christ and the Apostles. There are three daily newspapers and several periodicals in Arabic published in Damascus, and also a daily newspaper in English. English has taken over from French as the main foreign language, especially among the young.

EDUCATION

Education in Syria is under state control and although a few of the schools are privately owned, they all follow a common system and syllabus. Elementary education is free at state schools, and is compulsory from the age of seven. Secondary education is not compulsory and is free only at the state schools. Because of the shortage of places, entry to these state schools is competitive. Damascus University, founded in 1924, has nine faculties and a Higher Teachers' Training College. The number of students has risen to over 60,000. There are also about 20,000 students at Aleppo University (founded 1961), over 10,000 at Tishrin University, Latakia (founded 1975) and 6,000 at Ba'ath University, Homs. Approximately 10 per cent of all students receive scholarships, and at the present time Palestinian refugees are admitted free. The rest pay fees.

COMMUNICATIONS

Although railway lines run from Damascus to both Beirut and Amman, train services go only to Amman, as much of the Lebanese line has been dismantled. A track has been opened connecting Homs with Damascus. A track links Homs, Hamah, Aleppo, Deir ez Zor and Qamishliye to the Iraq frontier. Branch lines connect the ports of Tartous and Latakia to the system and another line runs from Aleppo down Euphrates valley to Deir ez Zor and thence north to Qamishliye, with a branch going to the Euphrates Dam. All the principal towns in the country are connected by roads which vary from modern dual carriageways to narrow country lanes.

An internal air service operates between all major towns. The main international airport is at Damascus and there are also flights to Eastern Europe, Turkey, Greece and Armenia from Aleppo.

TAIWAN (REPUBLIC OF CHINA)

Chung-hua Min-kuo

An island of some 13,800 sq. miles (35,742 sq. km) in the China Sea, Taiwan, formerly Formosa, lies 90 miles east of the Chinese mainland in latitude 21° 45′N. to 25° 56′N. The population (20,536,233 in 1991), is almost entirely Chinese in origin. About 2,000,000 mainlanders came to the island with Chiang Kai-shek in 1947–9.

The eastern part of the main island is mountainous and forest covered. Mt Morrison (Yu Shan) (13,035 ft.) and Mt Sylvia (Tz'ukaoshan) (12,972 ft.) are the highest peaks. The western plains are watered by many rivers.

The territories administered by the Chinese Nationalists include the Pescadores Islands (50 sq. miles), some 35 miles west of Taiwan, as well as Quemoy (68 sq. miles) and Matsu (11 sq. miles) which are only a few miles from the mainland.

Capital – Taipei, population (1989) 2,702,678. Other towns are ΨKaohsiung (1,374,231); Tainan (667,622); Taichung (730,376); and ΨKeelung (348,672).

Currency – New Taiwan dollar (NT$) of 100 cents.

Flag – Red, with blue quarter at top next staff, bearing a twelve-point white sun.

National Day – 10 October.

GOVERNMENT

Settled for centuries by the Chinese, the island was administered by Japan from 1895 to 1945. General Chiang Kai-shek withdrew to Taiwan in 1949, towards the end of the war against the Communist regime in mainland China, accompanied by 500,000 Nationalist troops, after which the territory continued under his presidency until his death on 5 April 1975. Martial law was lifted in July 1987, after 38 years. Chiang Kai-shek's son Chiang Ching-kuo died in January 1988 and was succeeded by Vice-President Lee Teng-hui, a native Taiwanese.

On 30 April 1991, President Lee announced that the 'period of Communist rebellion' on the Chinese mainland was over, thus granting *de facto* recognition of the People's Republic. The announcement also ended emergency measures which had frozen political life on Taiwan since 1949. Power is being shifted away from mainlanders to native Taiwanese. Elections for a reformed National Assembly were held in December 1991 and won by the Kuomintang ruling party of President Lee. During 1992 the National Assembly has been deliberating over constitutional reforms before a general election to be held on 19 December 1992.

President, Lee Teng-hui, *elected*, 13 Jan. 1988, *re-elected* 20 May 1990.
Vice-President, Li Yuan-zu.
Premier, Hau Pei-tsun.

ECONOMY

The soil is very fertile, producing sugar, rice, sweet potatoes, tea, bananas, pineapples and tobacco. Mineral resources are meagre. Taiwan produces one-tenth of its coal needs and some natural gas. There are important fisheries. The principal seaports ΨKeelung and ΨKaohsiung are situated in the northern and southern sections of the island.

TRADE WITH UK

	1990	1991
Imports from UK	£430,643,000	£519,821,000
Exports to UK	1,211,968,000	1,271,990,000

TANZANIA

Jamhuri ya Mwungano wa Tanzania

AREA, ETC – Tanganyika, the mainland part of the United Republic of Tanzania (Tanganyika and Zanzibar), occupies the east-central portion of the African continent, between 1° and 11° 45′ S. lat. and 29° 20′ and 40° 38′ E. long. It is bounded on the north by Kenya and Uganda; on the southwest by Lake Malawi, Malawi and Zambia; on the south by Mozambique; on the west it is bounded by Rwanda, Burundi and Zaire; on the east the boundary is the Indian Ocean. Tanzania has an area of 364,900 sq. miles (945,087 sq. km). The greater part of the country is occupied by the central African plateau from which rise, among others, Mt Kilimanjaro (19,340 ft), the highest point on the continent of Africa, and Mt Meru (14,974 ft). The Serengeti National Park, which covers an area of 6,000 sq. miles in the Arusha, Mwanza and Mara Regions, is famous for its variety and number of species of game.

POPULATION – The UN estimated the total population of Tanzania to be 25,635,000 in 1990. Africans form a large majority, while Europeans, Asians, and other non-Africans form the minority. The African population consists mostly of tribes of mixed Bantu race. Swahili is the national and official language. The use of English is widespread both for educational and government purposes.

ZANZIBAR – Formerly ruled by the Sultan of Zanzibar, and a British Protectorate until 10 December 1963, Zanzibar consists of the islands of Zanzibar, Pemba and Latham. The surface area is 2,461 sq. km, and the population (UN estimate 1990), is 663,000. ΨZanzibar (population, 133,000) is the chief town and seaport of the island.

CAPITAL – Dodoma (population 85,000, 1985 estimate). The economic and administrative centre is ΨDar es Salaam (population 1,096,000, 1985 estimate). Other towns (1985 population) are ΨTanga (172,000), Mwanza (252,000), Mbeya (194,000).

CURRENCY – Tanzanian shilling of 100 cents.

FLAG – Green (above) and blue; divided by diagonal black stripe bordered by gold, running from bottom (next staff) to top (in fly).

NATIONAL ANTHEM – Mungu Ibariki Afrika (God Bless Africa).

NATIONAL DAY – 26 April (Union Day).

GOVERNMENT

Tanganyika became an independent state and a member of the British Commonwealth on 9 December 1961, and a republic, within the Commonwealth, on 9 December 1962.

On 10 December 1963, Zanzibar became an independent state within the Commonwealth and on 26 April 1964, Tanganyika united with Zanzibar to form the United Republic of Tanzania.

Tanzania became a one-party state on 10 July 1965 but with the Tanganyika African National Union (TANU) and the Afro-Shirazi Party (ASP) remaining the ruling parties in Tanganyika and Zanzibar respectively. On 5 February 1977 these two parties merged to form the Chama Cha Mapinduzi (CCM) (Revolutionary Party).

A new constitution was introduced on 26 April 1977 and revised in October 1984. There are a President and two Vice-Presidents, one the President of Zanzibar and the other the Prime Minister. The President may only serve two five-year terms and if he comes from Zanzibar the Prime Minister will be the First Vice-President and must come from Tanganyika. If the President comes from Tanganyika the President of Zanzibar will be the First Vice-President.

The National Assembly contains 255 members, of whom 130 are elected from mainland constituencies and 50 from Zanzibar, 25 are ex-officio, 15 nominated and 35 indirectly elected. The Speaker may either be elected from among the members or be an additional member. Constituency members are elected by popular vote at a general election held at a maximum of five-yearly intervals.

A new constitution was also approved in 1984 for Zanzibar providing for an elected President and House of Representatives. Although Zanzibar has its own government and Chief Minister, Tanganyika is governed by the government of the Union. Overall policy has been decided by the CCM whose chairman is President Mwinyi.

In January 1992 President Mwinyi and the CCM leadership agreed to amend the constitution to allow multi-party politics, after internal and international pressure. On 17 June 1992 the constitution was amended when President Mwinyi endorsed a bill legalizing multi-party politics, with the stipulation that all parties must be active in both the mainland and in Zanzibar and that parties must not be formed on tribal or racial grounds.

President of the United Republic, HE Hon. Ali Hassan Mwinyi, *elected* 27 Oct. 1985; *re-elected* 28 Oct. 1990.

First Vice-President of the United Republic and Prime Minister, Hon. John Malecela.
Second Vice-President of the United Republic and President of Zanzibar, HE Salmin Amour.

CABINET as at July 1992

Defence, The President.
Foreign Affairs and International Co-operation, Hon. Hassan Diria.
Agriculture and Livestock Development, Co-operatives, Hon. Amran Mayagila.
Communications and Transport, Hon. Jackson Makwetta.
Works, Hon. Prof. Kighoma Malima.
Education and Culture, Hon. Charles Kabeho.
Energy, Minerals and Water, Hon. Jakaya Kikwete.
Finance, Hon. Steven Kibona.
Health, Hon. Prof. Philemon Sarungi.
Home Affairs, Hon. Augustine Mrema.
Industry and Trade, Hon. Cleopa D. Msuya.
Information and Broadcasting, Hon. Dr William Shija.
Labour and Youth, Hon. Joseph Rwegasira.
Lands, Housing and Urban Development, Hon. Marcel B. Komanya.
Community Development, Women and Children, Hon. Anna Makinda.
Tourism, Natural Resources, Environment, Hon. Abubakar Mugumia.
Science, Technology and Higher Education, Hon. Benjamin Mkapa.
Minister without Portfolio, and CCM Vice-Chairman, Hon. Rashid M. Kawawa.

TANZANIA HIGH COMMISSION
43 Hertford Street, London W1Y 7TF
Tel 071-499 8951

High Commissioner, His Excellency Ali S. Mchumo (1991).

BRITISH HIGH COMMISSION
Hifadhi House, Samora Avenue (PO Box 9200), Dar es Salaam
Tel: Dar es Salaam 29601

High Commissioner, His Excellency Roger Westbrook (1992).

BRITISH COUNCIL REPRESENTATIVE, N. H. Ross, Ohio Samora Avenue (PO Box 9100), Dar es Salaam.

EDUCATION

All Tanzanian secondary schools are expected to include practical subjects in the basic course. All who receive secondary (or equivalent) education are called up for a period of national service. The school system is administered in Swahili but the Government is making efforts to improve English standards for the purposes of secondary and higher education. For higher education Tanzanian students go to the University of Dar es Salaam, Sokoine University of Agriculture in Morogoro, other East African universities, or to universities and colleges outside East Africa, including Britain.

COMMUNICATIONS

The main port is Dar es Salaam, and there are other ports on the coast at Tanga, Mtwara, Zanzibar, Mkoani and Wete, in addition to Mwanza, Musoma and Bukoba on Lake Victoria and Kigoma on Lake Tanganyika. Coastal shipping services connect the mainland to Zanzibar, and lake services are operated on Lake Tanganyika and Lake Malawi with neighbouring countries.

The principal international airports are Dar es Salaam and Kilimanjaro. Other airports include Zanzibar, Arusha, Mwanza and Tanga.

There are two railway systems; one connecting Dar es Salaam to Zambia, and the second having two main lines running from Dar es Salaam, one to northern Tanzania and Kenya and the other to Lake Tanganyika and Victoria.

ECONOMY

The economy is based mainly on the production and export of primary produce and the growing of foodstuffs for local consumption. The islands of Zanzibar and Pemba produce a large part of the world's supply of cloves and clove oil; and coconuts, coconut oil and copra are also produced. The mainland's chief export crops are coffee, cotton, sisal, tea, tobacco, cashew nuts and diamonds. The most important minerals are diamonds. Hides and skins are another valuable export. Industry is at present largely concerned with the processing of raw material for either export or local consumption. There are also secondary manufacturing industries, including factories for the manufacture of leather and rubber footwear, knitwear, razor blades, cigarettes and textiles, and a wheat flour mill.

TRADE WITH UK

	1990	1991
Imports from UK	£84,694,000	£72,822,000
Exports to UK	25,575,000	20,938,000

THAILAND
Prathes Thai

AREA AND POPULATION – The Kingdom of Thailand, formerly known as Siam, has an area of 198,457 sq. miles (514,000 sq. km), with a population (1990 UN estimate) of 57,196,000. The population growth rate averages 2.4 per cent per year. Thailand has a common boundary with Malaysia in the south, is bounded on the west by Myanmar (Burma) and on the north-east and east by Laos and Cambodia. Although there is no common boundary between Thailand and China, the Chinese province of Yunnan is separated from the Thai northern border only by a narrow stretch of Burmese and Laotian territory.

Thailand is divided geographically into four regions: central, north-eastern, northern and southern. The capital, Bangkok, is situated in the south of the central plain area. To the north-east there is a plateau area and to the north-west mountains. The south of Thailand consists of a narrow mountainous peninsula. The principal rivers are the Chao Phraya in the central plains, and the Mekong on the northern and north-eastern borders.

LANGUAGE – Thai is basically a monosyllabic, tonal language, a branch of the Indo-Chinese linguistic family, but its vocabulary has been strongly influenced by Sanskrit and Pali. It is written in an alphabetic script derived from ancient Indian scripts.

RELIGION – The principal religion is Buddhism. In 1988 94.37 per cent of the population were Buddhists, 3.95 per cent Muslims, 0.53 per cent Christians and 1.15 per cent other religions.

CAPITAL – ΨBangkok, at the mouth of the River Chao Phraya, population (1985) 5,400,000. Other centres are Chiang Mai, Phitsanuloke, Chon Buri, Korat, Khon Kaen, Surat Thani, Hat Yai and ΨPhuket but none approaches Bangkok in size or importance.

CURRENCY – Baht of 100 satang.

FLAG – Five horizontal bands, red, white, dark blue, white, red (the blue band twice the width of the others).

NATIONAL ANTHEM – Sanrasern Phra Barami.
NATIONAL DAY – 5 December (The King's Birthday).

GOVERNMENT

Thailand became a constitutional monarchy in 1932. The constitution promulgated in December 1978 provides for a National Assembly consisting of a 261-member Senate appointed by the monarch and a 347-member House of Representatives elected by universal adult suffrage for a term of four years.

The civilian government of Gen. Chatichai Choonhavan was overthrown by a military coup on 23 February 1991. On 6 March 1991 the King approved an interim government, led by Anand Panyarachun; the interim constitution stipulated that elections must be held within one year. Under heavy military pressure, a new constitution was approved in December 1991 under which the military would appoint the members of an expanded 270-member Senate and so enshrine its place in Thai politics. Parties aligned with the military won the general election on 22 March 1992, and Armed Forces Supreme Commander Gen. Suchinda Kraprayoon became Prime Minister on 7 April.

Opposition to the military-controlled government grew and mass demonstrations held in Bangkok from 17 to 20 May eventually, with the help of the King, forced the government from power. Many demonstrators were killed by soldiers before the government fell, and this led to a curbing of military power and the sacking of military chiefs by the new interim government of Anand Panyarachun, who was re-appointed Prime Minister by the King. New parliamentary elections were held on 13 September 1992 which resulted in a parliamentary majority for 'democratic parties', i.e. those not allied with the military. (*See* Stop-press.)

HEAD OF STATE

King, HM Bhumibol Adulyadej, *born* 1927; *succeeded his brother*, 9 June 1946; *married* Princess Sirikit Kitiyakara, 28 April 1950; *crowned* 5 May 1950; and has *issue*, Princess Ubolratana, *born* 6 April 1951; Crown Prince Vajiralongkorn, *born* 28 July 1952; Princess Sirindhorn, *born* 2 April 1955; Princess Chulabhorn *born* 4 July 1957.

ROYAL THAI EMBASSY IN LONDON

29–30 Queen's Gate, London SW7 5JB
Tel 071-589 2944

Ambassador Extraordinary and Plenipotentiary, His Excellency Tongchan Jokitasthira (1991).

BRITISH EMBASSY

Wireless Road, Bangkok 10330
Tel: Bangkok 253 0191

Ambassador Extraordinary and Plenipotentiary, His Excellency C. C. W. Adams, CMG (1992)

BRITISH COUNCIL REPRESENTATIVE, Dr P. Moss, 428 Rama 1 Road, Siam Square Soi 501, Pathumwan, Bangkok 10330.

BRITISH CHAMBER OF COMMERCE, BP Building 18th Floor, Unit 1810, 54 Asoke Road (Sukhumvit 21) Bangkok 10110

EDUCATION

Primary education is compulsory and free and secondary education in government schools is free. In 1988 there were 37,696 schools and training colleges, with a total of 10,699,132 pupils and 562,028 teachers. Private universities and colleges are playing an increasing role in higher education. In 1984 the government agreed to upgrade four private colleges to universities. Out of 43 universities and other similar higher institutes of learning, 21 are private and attended by some 53,708 students. In 1986 their total enrolment was 171,438 students.

ECONOMY

The agricultural sector provides just under half the national income and employs 67.5 per cent of the labour force, which in 1985 was estimated at 26.8 million. Rice remains the most important crop, accounting for 60 per cent of the area planted. After rice the main crops are sugar, maize, rubber, tobacco, kenaf and jute. In recent years the production of livestock and poultry, especially pigs and chickens for export, has gained importance. There is a large fishing industry with more than 20,000 vessels registered. Fish farming is popular in many inland areas. A ban on hardwood export has resulted in the decline of the forestry industry.

The discovery of onshore oil and offshore gas in the late 1970s ushered in a new economic era. Crude oil production which began in 1983 stood at around 1.85 million tonnes in 1989, or about 15 per cent of the country's needs. In 1988, 212,641 million cubic feet of natural gas was produced. The predicted surplus of natural gas has led the Government to designate an area on the east coast as the future centre of the petrochemical industry. Another energy resource becoming more important is lignite which is found mainly in the north and is being used increasingly for electricity production.

Mineral resources are mainly tin, tungsten, lead, antimony and iron. Among these, tin is the most important. In addition, about 60,000 tons of zinc ingots a year are expected to be produced by a zinc refinery which was opened in early 1984.

Industry is divided into two main categories, service and manufacturing. Since 1982 tourism has replaced rice as the country's top foreign exchange earner. There were 4,809,508 overseas visitors in 1989, generating an estimated 96,386 million baht for the country. The banking system is large and contributes much to the economy, especially employment. There are over 1,800 bank branches in the country employing some 72,000 workers.

Since 1960 the government has actively promoted industrial investments by means of tax relief and other incentives to local and foreign investors; in 1985, 74.6 per cent of this investment was in Thai projects. Most of the industries established under this scheme in early years were import-substituting. However, there has been an increasing shift to export-oriented industries, taking advantages of low-wage labour and available domestic resources. Manufacturing now accounts for about 21.8 per cent of the national income. Crops contribute 12.1 per cent of GDP.

TRADE

Thailand's main exports are rice, tapioca and tapioca products, garments, rubber, integrated circuit boards, precious stones, pearls and other ornaments, maize, canned sea food, fabrics, sugar and tin. Main imports are crude oil, chemicals and pharmaceuticals, electrical and non-electrical machinery and spare parts, industrial machinery, iron and steel, diesel oil and other fuel oil, vehicle and transport equipment.

	1989	1990
Total imports	Bhat 650.7bn	Bhat 829.0bn
Total exports	509.9bn	590.0bn

Trade with UK	1990	1991
Imports from UK	£416,648,000	£463,449,000
Exports to UK	484,276,000	625,374,000

COMMUNICATIONS

The importance of rivers and canals as the traditional mode of transportation has been replaced by highways and roads. The existing road and highway network, totalling 44,409 kilometres in 1989, reaches all parts of the country. Most of the smaller towns and bigger villages are now served by paved roads.

Navigable waterways have a length of about 1,100 km in the dry season and 1,600 km in the wet season. About 4,450 km of state-owned railways were open to traffic in 1989. Main lines run from Bangkok to Aranya Prathet on the Cambodian border and to Nong Khai, the ferry terminal on the River Mekong opposite Vientiane, capital of Laos; to Chiang Mai and to Hat Yai, whence lines go down the eastern and western sides of the Malay peninsula to Singapore. A new line to Sattahip on the east coast is being constructed.

Bangkok is an important international air centre and has direct flights to most of the world's major cities. The airports at Chiang Mai, Phuket and Hat Yai also receive international flights. Most major provincial towns have airports. Thai International and Thai Airways merged in April 1988. Now named THAI, the airline is state-owned.

Thailand has an extensive network of telecommunications services, and the telephone service though still poor is being improved. All major cities and towns are linked by direct long-distance calls. Thailand has two mobile telephone networks, AMPS (urban), and NMT (rural) presently covering only the central area but expanding rapidly.

There are two important ports in the country. Bangkok, which is a river port, can serve vessels up to 27 ft. draught. The deep-sea port at Sattahip caters for larger vessels. Phuket and Songkhla deep water ports have already been completed and are the first to be managed privately under a ten-year concession. Construction of Laem Chabang deep water port started in 1988.

TOGO
République Togolaise

The Republic is situated in West Africa between 0° and 2° W. and 6° and 11° N., with a coastline 35 miles long on the Gulf of Guinea. Togo extends northwards inland for 350 miles. It is flanked on the west by Ghana, on the north by Burkina and in the east by Benin. It has an area of 21,925 sq. miles (56,785 sq. km), and a population (UN estimate 1990) of 3,531,000, including people of several African races. The official language is French; Ewe is spoken by about 47 per cent.

CAPITAL – ΨLomé, population (1983) 366,476.
CURRENCY – Franc CFA of 100 centimes.
FLAG – Five alternating green and yellow horizontal stripes; a quarter in red at top next staff bearing a white star.
NATIONAL DAY – 13 January (National Liberation Day).

GOVERNMENT

The first President of Togo, Sylvanus Olympio, assassinated on 13 January 1963, was succeeded by Nicolas Grunitzky, who was himself overthrown by an army coup d'état on 13 January 1967. On 14 April 1967, the Commander-in-Chief of the Togolese army, Lt.-Col. (later promoted General) Eyadéma named himself President.

President Eyadéma has come under increasing popular pressure to introduce reforms. In October 1990 the Rassemblement du peuple togolais (RPT), the sole legal party, approved plans for a new constitutional conference after pro-democracy riots. Bloody riots again broke out in March 1991 in protest at the slow pace of reform, and in April the government was forced to concede a political amnesty, the introduction of a multi-party constitution and a national conference. In August 1991 the national conference stripped President Eyadéma of all powers, banned the RPT and elected Kokou Koffigoh as Prime Minister of an interim government. The national conference set a date of 9 February 1992 for a referendum on a new constitution.

However, throughout the second half of 1991 and early 1992 the political situation became progressively more unstable. Troops loyal to President Eyadéma three times attempted to overthrow Koffigoh and his government (October, November and December 1991) but were frustrated by pro-democracy supporters. Rival armed gangs supporting various new political parties engaged in ambushes and assassination attempts of political leaders in early 1992, resulting in the referendum on a new constitution being postponed first to May 1992 and then to early 1993. The situation remains unstable and legislative and presidential elections planned for summer 1992 were also postponed.

HEAD OF STATE
President, Gen. Gnassingbé Eyadéma, *assumed office*, 14 April 1967; *re-elected for seven-year term*, 23 Dec. 1986.

INTERIM GOVERNMENT as at July 1992
Prime Minister, Defence, Joseph Kokou Koffigoh.
Economy and Finance, Elias Kpetigo.
Foreign Affairs and Co-operation, Abdou Tchiaka.
Planning and Territorial Development, Aimé Gogue.
Equipment and Mines, Joseph Amefia.
Rural Development, Koffi Abotsi.
Justice, Kouma Kouame.
Territorial Administration, Yao Komlanvi.
Communications and Culture, Kougblenou Dzaba.
Environment, Kpandja Fare.
Technical and Professional Training, Issa Affo.
Social Welfare and National Solidarity, Were Gazoro.
Human Rights, Dzodzi Dali.
Tourism and Crafts, Small and Medium-Sized Enterprises, Kokou Afantchao.

EMBASSY OF TOGO – The Embassy of Togo closed in September 1991

BRITISH EMBASSY – *British Ambassador* resident in Accra, Ghana.

ECONOMY

Although the economy of Togo remains largely agricultural, exports of phosphates have superseded agricultural products as the main source of export earnings. Other exports include palm kernels, copra and manioc. The production of phosphates entirely for export was taken over completely by the government in February 1974.

TRADE WITH UK

	1990	1991
Imports from UK	£13,038,000	£20,932,000
Exports to UK	3,545,000	1,820,000

TONGA
Kingdom of Tonga

Tonga, or the Friendly Islands, comprises a group of islands situated in the Southern Pacific some 450 miles east-south-east of Fiji, with an area of 270 sq. miles (699 sq. km), and population (1990 UN estimate) of 95,000. The largest island, Tongatapu, was discovered by Tasman in 1643. Most of the islands are of coral formation, but some are volcanic (Tofua, Kao and Niuafoou or 'Tin Can' Island). The limits of the group are between 15° and 23° 30′ S., and 173° and 177° W.

CAPITAL – ΨNuku'alofa (population estimate 30,000), on Tongatapu.

CURRENCY – Pa'anga (T$) of 100 seniti.

FLAG – Red with a white canton containing a couped red cross.

NATIONAL ANTHEM – E, 'Otua Mafimafi (Oh, Almighty God Above).

NATIONAL DAY – 4 June (Independence Day).

GOVERNMENT

The Kingdom of Tonga is an independent constitutional monarchy within the Commonwealth. Prior to 4 June 1970 it had been a British-protected state for 70 years. The constitution provides for a government consisting of the Sovereign, a privy council which functions as a cabinet, a legislative assembly and a judiciary. The legislative assembly includes the King, privy council, nine hereditary nobles and nine popularly elected representatives (who hold office for three years). The most recent election took place on 15 February 1990.

HEAD OF STATE

King of Tonga, HM King Taufa'ahau Tupou IV, GCMG, GCVO, KBE, *acceded* 16 Dec. 1965.

Heir, HRH Crown Prince Tupouto'a.

CABINET as at July 1992

Prime Minister, Minister of Agriculture, Fisheries, Forests, and Marine, Baron Vaea of Houma.

Deputy Prime Minister, Minister of Education, Works and Civil Aviation, Hon. Dr S. Langi Kavaliku.

Labour, Commerce and Industry, Hon. Tutoatasi Fakafanva.

Police, Prisons and Fire Services, Hon. George 'Akau'ola.

Health, Hon. Dr S. Tapa.

Foreign Affairs and Defence, HRH Crown Prince Tupouto'a.

Finance, Hon. J. Cecil Cocker.

Attorney-General, Justice, Hon. Tevita P. Tupou.

Minister without Portfolio, Hon. Ma'afu Tuku'i'aulahi.

Minister of Lands, Survey, and Natural Resources, Hon. Dr S. Ma'afu Tupou.

Governor of Ha'apai, Hon. Fakafanua.

Governor of Vava'u, Hon. Tu'i'afitu.

TONGA HIGH COMMISSION
36 Molyneux Street, London W1H 6AB
Tel 071-724 5828

High Commissioner, His Excellency Sione Kité (1992).

BRITISH HIGH COMMISSION
PO Box 56, Nuku'alofa
Tel: Nuku'alofa 21020

High Commissioner, His Excellency William Lawson Cordiner (1990).

ECONOMY

The economy is primarily agricultural; the main crops are coconuts, bananas, vanilla, yams, taro, cassava, groundnuts and other fruits. Fish is an important staple food though recent shortfalls have led to canned fish being imported. Industry is based on the processing of agricultural produce, and the manufacture of foodstuffs, clothing and sports equipment.

TRADE

The principal exports are copra, other coconut products, tropical root crops, bananas, knitwear, leather goods and fibreglass boats.

	1985	1989
Total imports	T$58,900,000	T$68,334,194
Total exports	7,700,000	11,517,597

Trade with UK	1990	1991
Imports from UK	£1,296,000	£944,000
Exports to UK	239,000	20,000

TRINIDAD AND TOBAGO

The Republic of Trinidad and Tobago

AREA, ETC – Trinidad, the most southerly of the West Indian islands, lies close to the north coast of South America, the nearest point being Venezuela, seven miles distant. The island is situated between 10° 2′ and 11° 12′ N. lat. and 60° 30′ and 61° 56′ W. long., and is about 50 miles in length by 37 miles in width, with an area of 1,864 sq. miles (4,827 sq. km). Two mountain systems, the Northern and Southern Ranges, stretch across almost its entire width and a third, the Central Range, lies diagonally across its middle portion; otherwise the island is mostly flat.

CLIMATE – The climate is tropical with temperatures averaging 82° F (27.8° C) by day and 74° F (23.3° C) by night, and a rainfall averaging 82 inches a year. There is a well-marked dry season from January to May, and a wet season from June to December broken by a short dry season (the *Petite Careme*) in September and October.

Tobago lies between 11° 9′ and 11° 21′ N. lat. and between 60° 30′ and 60° 50′ W. long., 19 miles north-east of Trinidad. The island is 32 miles long at its widest point, and 11 wide, and has an area of 116 sq. miles (300 sq. km). It is a popular tourist resort. It was ceded to the British Crown in 1814 and amalgamated with Trinidad in 1888.

Corozal Point and Icacos Point, the north-west and south-west extremities of Trinidad, enclose the Gulf of Paria. West of Corozal Point lie several islands, of which Chacachacare, Huevos, Monos and Gaspar Grande are the most important.

POPULATION – In 1989 the population of Trinidad and Tobago was estimated by the UN to be 1,227,000; Tobago's population is about 45,000.

CAPITAL – ΨPort of Spain (population approximately 59,649 in 1985) is the administrative centre of the islands. About 33 miles south of the capital is San Fernando (population approximately 34,300 in 1985), a town of growing importance which is emerging as the industrial centre of Trinidad, and which is in close proximity to a number of large industrial plants. The main town of Tobago is ΨScarborough.

CURRENCY – Trinidad and Tobago dollar (TT$) of 100 cents.

FLAG – Black diagonal stripe bordered with white stripes, running from top by staff, all on a red field.

NATIONAL DAYS – 31 August (Independence Day); 24 September (Republic Day).

GOVERNMENT

Trinidad was discovered by Columbus in 1498, was colonized in 1532 by the Spaniards, capitulated to the British under Abercromby in 1797, and was ceded to Britain under the Treaty of Amiens (25 March 1802).

Tobago was discovered by Columbus in 1498. Dutch colonists arrived in 1632; Tobago subsequently changed hands numerous times until it was ceded to the British Crown by France in 1814 and amalgamated with Trinidad in 1888.

The Territory of Trinidad and Tobago became an independent state and a member of the British Commonwealth on 31 August 1962, and a republic in 1976. The President is elected for five years by all members of the Senate and the House of Representatives. The House of Representatives has 36 members, elected by universal adult suffrage, and the Senate has 31, of whom 16 are appointed on the advice of the Prime Minister, six on the advice of the Leader of the Opposition and nine at the discretion of the President. Legislation was passed in September 1980 which afforded Tobago a degree of self-administration through the 12-member Tobago House of Assembly.

HEAD OF STATE
President, His Excellency Noor Mohammed Hassanali.

CABINET as at July 1992
Prime Minister, Hon. Patrick Manning.
Finance, Hon. Wendell Mottley.
Attorney-General, Hon. Keith Sobion.
Energy and Energy Industries, Hon. Barry Barnes.
Trade, Industry and Tourism, Hon. Brian Tung.
National Security, Hon. Russel Huggins.
Local Government, Hon. Kenneth Valley.
Foreign Affairs, Hon. Ralph Maraj.
Sport and Youth Affairs, Hon. Jean Pierre.
Consumer Affairs and Social Services, Hon. Linda Baboolal.
Works and Transport, Hon. Colm Imbert.
Education, Hon. Augustus Ramrekersingh.
Health, Hon. John Eckstein.
Public Utilities, Hon. Morris Marshall.
Planning and Development, Hon. Lenny Saith.
Labour and Co-operatives, Hon. Kenneth Collis.
Community Development, Culture and Women's Affairs, Hon. Joan Yuille-Williams.
Agriculture, Lands and Marine Resources, Hon. Dr Keith Rowley.
Housing and Settlements, Hon. Dr Vincent Lasse.

HIGH COMMISSION OF THE REPUBLIC OF TRINIDAD AND TOBAGO
42 Belgrave Square, London SW1X 8NT
Tel 071–245 9351

High Commissioner, His Excellency Mr Justice Ulric Cross, DSO, DFC (1990).

BRITISH HIGH COMMISSION
Furness House, 90 Independence Square, (PO Box 778)
Port of Spain
Tel: Port of Spain 6252861

High Commissioner, His Excellency B. Smith, OBE.

EDUCATION

The education system provides for free education at all state-owned and government-assisted denominational schools and certain faculties at the University of the West Indies. In addition there are various private teaching establishments. Attendance is compulsory for children aged six to 12 years, after which attendance at free secondary schools is determined by success in the common entrance examination at 11 years. There are three technical institutes, two teachers' training colleges, and one of the three branches of the University of the West Indies is located in Trinidad, at the St Augustine campus. A medical teaching complex was built at Mt Hope, and operates in collaboration with the University of the West Indies.

COMMUNICATIONS

There are some 6,436 km of all-weather roads in Trinidad and Tobago. The only general cargo port is Port of Spain but there are specialized port facilities elsewhere for landing crude oil, loading refinery products and sugar, and for storing and transmitting bauxite and cement. Regular shipping services call here and many inter-island craft use the port. Another rapidly growing port is at Port Lisas where new industries powered by local natural gas are located.

International scheduled airlines, including the national airline, Trinidad and Tobago Airways (BWIA) Corporation, use Piarco International Airport outside Port of Spain. The airline also flies between Piarco and Crown Point Airport in Tobago.

Three commercial broadcasting stations and one commercial television station operate in Trinidad and Tobago. The internal telephone system and the external telephone and telegraph connections are operated by part-state-owned companies.

ECONOMY

Trinidad and Tobago's main source of revenue is from oil. Production of domestic crude was 55 million barrels in 1990. Trinidad has large reserves of natural gas, and reserves are estimated to be in the region of 100 years at the current rates of production. An integrated steel plant, an anhydrous ammonia plant and a methanol plant have been constructed at Point Lisas.

Fertilizers, tyres, clothing, soap, furniture and foodstuffs are manufactured locally while motor vehicles, radios, TV sets, and electro-domestic equipment are assembled from parts, mainly from Japan.

FINANCE

	1989	1990
Revenue	TT$4,972.5m	TT$5,645.2m
Expenditure	5,776.0m	5,816.2m

TRADE

	1989	1990
Imports	TT$5,190.4m	TT$5,361.8m
Exports	6,706.9m	8,842.0m

Trade with UK	1990	1991
Imports from UK	£49,894,000	£62,491,000
Exports to UK	45,058,000	41,664,000

TUNISIA

Al-Djoumhouria Attunusia

AREA AND POPULATION – Tunisia lies between Algeria and Libya and extends southwards to the Sahara Desert, with a total area of 164,150 sq. km, and a population (UN estimate 1990) of 8,180,000.

CAPITAL – Ψ Tunis, connected by canal with La Goulette on the coast, had a population (1984) of 1,394,749. The ruins of ancient Carthage lie a few miles from the city. Other towns of importance are: Ψ Sfax (577,992); Ψ Sousse (322,491); Ψ Bizerta (394,670); Kairouan; Gabes; Menzel Bourguiba.

CURRENCY – Tunisian dinar of 1,000 millimes.

FLAG – Red with a white disc containing a red crescent and star.

NATIONAL ANTHEM – Himat Al Hima.

NATIONAL DAY – 20 March.

GOVERNMENT

A French Protectorate from 1881 to 1956, Tunisia became an independent sovereign state with the signing on 20 March 1956 of an agreement whereby France recognized Tunisia's independence and right to conduct its own foreign policy and to form an army.

Following a first general election held on 25 March 1956, a Constituent Assembly met for the first time on 8 April. On 25 July 1957 the Constituent Assembly abolished the monarchy and elected M. Bourguiba first President of the Republic. On 1 June 1959 the Constitution was promulgated and on 7 December 1959 the National Assembly held its first session. In March 1975 the National Assembly proclaimed M. Bourguiba as President for life.

On 7 November 1987 M. Bourguiba was deposed and succeeded by President Zine el-Abidine Ben Ali. Presidential and legislative elections were held in April 1989. The RCD (Rassemblement Constitutionnel Democratique) won all 141 seats in the National Assembly. Seven political parties contested the election. President Ben Ali was re-elected with 99 per cent of the vote.

The country is divided into 23 regions (*gouvernorats*) each administered by a governor.

HEAD OF STATE

President, Zine el-Abidine Ben Ali *took office* 7 Nov. 1987, *re-elected* 2 April 1989.

CABINET as at August 1992

Prime Minister, Hamed Karoui.
Minister of State, Interior, Abdallah Kallel.
Justice, Sadok Chaabane.
Director of Presidential Office, Mohamed el Jeri.
Foreign Affairs, Habib ben Yahia.
Defence, Abdelaziz Ben Dhia.
Economy, Sadok Rabah.
Finance, Mouldi Zouaoui.
Planning and Regional Development, Mustapha Nabli.
International Co-operation and Development, Mohammed Ghannouchi.
Agriculture, vacant.
Public Estates, Mustapha Bouaziz.
Equipment and Housing, Ahmed Friaa.
Transport, Faouzi Belkahia.
Tourism and Handicrafts, Mohamed Jegham.
Communications, Habib Lazreg.
Education and Science, Mohamed Charfi.
Culture, Mongi Bousnina.
Health, Daly Jazy.
Social Affairs, Ahmed Smaoui.
Infrastructure and Land Management, Salah Jebali.
Professional Training and Employment, Taoufik Cheikrouhou.
Youth and Childhood Welfare, Mohamed Saad.
Secretary-General of the Government, Mohamed Habib Hadj Said.

TUNISIAN EMBASSY
29 Prince's Gate, London SW7 1QG
Tel 071-584 8117

Ambassador Extraordinary and Plenipotentiary, His Excellency Dr Abdelaziz Hamzaoui (1991).

BRITISH EMBASSY
5 Place de la Victoire, Tunis 1015 RP
Tel: Tunis 245100

Ambassador Extraordinary and Plenipotentiary and Consul-General, His Excellency Michael Tait, CMG, LVO (1992).
First Secretary, A. Holmes, MBE (*Deputy Head of Mission*).

BRITISH COUNCIL REPRESENTATIVE, C. Stevenson.

ECONOMY

The valleys of the northern region support large flocks and herds, and contain rich agricultural areas, in which wheat, barley, and oats are grown. Vines and olives are extensively cultivated.

The chief exports are crude oil, phosphates, olive oil, finished textiles, and fruit. The chief imports are machinery and equipment, foodstuffs, petroleum products, and textiles. Some oil has been discovered and crude oil production in 1989 was 4.8 million tons. Gas has also been discovered off the east coast but exploitation is not viable at present. Tourists numbered almost 3 million in 1989.

TRADE

France remains the main trading partner, supplying 27.6 per cent of the country's imports and purchasing 22.9 per cent of Tunisia's exports.

Tunisia became an associate member of the EC early in 1969, and signed a new agreement with the EC in 1976. Textile exports are the main foreign exchange earner after tourism.

	1988	1989
Total Imports	TD3,167,000	TD4,150,000
Total Exports	2,055,000	2,762,000
Trade with UK	1990	1991
Imports from UK	£40,800,000	£43,651,000
Exports to UK	40,959,000	25,613,000

TURKEY
Türkiye Cumhuriyeti

AREA AND POPULATION – People of Turkic stock are to be found scattered throughout a wide belt extending from China through the central Asian states of the CIS, Afghanistan and Iran to Turkey, and into Bulgaria.

Turkey itself extends from Edirne to Transcaucasia and Iran, and from the Black Sea to the Mediterranean, Syria and Iraq. The surface area of Turkey is 814,578 square km of which 790,200 square km is in Asia and 24,378 is in Europe. Total population at the Census of 1990 was 56,473,035.

Turkey in Europe consists of Eastern Thrace, including the cities of Istanbul and Edirne, and is separated from Asia by the Bosporus at Istanbul and by the Dardanelles (about 40 miles in length with a width varying from one to four miles), the political neighbours being Greece and Bulgaria on the west.

Turkey in Asia comprises the whole of Asia Minor or Anatolia and extends from the Aegean Sea to the western boundaries of Georgia, Armenia and Iran, and from the Black Sea to the Mediterranean and the northern boundaries of Syria and Iraq.

RELIGION – Islam ceased to be the state religion in 1928. However, 98.99 per cent of the population are Muslim. The main religious minorities, which are concentrated in Istanbul and on the Syrian frontier, are Greek Orthodox, Armenian, Syriani Christian, and Jewish.

CAPITAL – Ankara (Angora), an inland town of Asia Minor, about 275 miles east-south-east of Istanbul, with a population (1990) of 3,236,626. Ankara (or Ancyra) was the capital of the Roman Province of *Galatia Prima*, and a marble temple (now in ruins), dedicated to Augustus, contains the *Monumentum* (*Marmor*) *Ancyranum*, inscribed with a record of the reign of Augustus Caesar.

ΨIstanbul (7,309,190), the former capital, was the Roman city of Byzantium. It was selected by Constantine the Great as the capital of the Roman Empire about AD 328 and renamed Constantinople. Istanbul contains the celebrated church of St Sophia, which, after becoming a mosque, was made a museum in 1934. It also contains Topkapi, former Palace of the Ottoman Sultans, which is also a museum.

Other cities are ΨIzmir (2,649,770); Adana (1,934,907); Bursa (1,603,137); Gaziantep (1,140,549); and Konya (1,750,303).

CURRENCY – Turkish lira (TL) of 100 kurus.

FLAG – Red, with white crescent and star.

NATIONAL ANTHEM – Istiklal Marşi (The Independence March).

NATIONAL DAY – 29 October (Republic Day).

GOVERNMENT

On 29 October 1923 the National Assembly declared Turkey a republic and elected Gazi Mustafa Kemal (later known as Kemal Ataturk) President. In 1945 a multi-party system was introduced but in 1960 the government was overthrown by the Turkish armed forces. A new constitution was adopted in July 1961 and, after a general election, a civilian government took office. Civilian governments remained in power until September 1980 when mounting problems with the economy and terrorism led to a military takeover. A civilian technocratic government was appointed later that month.

A new constitution, extending the powers of the President, was approved by a referendum on 7 November 1982. It provided for the separation of powers between the legislature, executive and judiciary, and the holding of free elections to the unicameral Grand National Assembly, which now has 450 members elected every five years. Following the General Election in November 1983 the military leadership handed over power to a newly elected civilian government.

The Motherland Party, led by Turgut Özal, won general elections held in November 1987. The last election was held in October 1991. Süleyman Demirel, leader of the True Path Party, formed a coalition government with the Social Democrat Populist Party.

There is continued Kurdish unrest in the south-east of the country; Kurds are estimated to constitute one-sixth of the population.

Turkey is divided for administrative purposes into 73 *il* with subdivisions into *ilçe* and *nahiye*. Each *il* has a governor (*vali*) and elective council.

HEAD OF STATE

President, Turgut Özal, *elected for a seven-year term*, 31 October 1989.

GOVERNMENT as at July 1992

Prime Minister, Süleyman Demirel (DYP).
Deputy Prime Minister, Prof. Erdal Inönü (SHP).
Ministers of State, Cavit Çağlar; Prof. Tansu Çiller; Ekrem Ceyhun; Akin Gönen; Gökberk Ergenekon; Orhan Killercioğlu; Ömer Barutçu; Mehmet Ali Yilmaz; Şerif Ercan; Mehmet Batalli (DYP); Ibrahim Tez; Türkan Akyol; Mehmet Kahraman; Erman Şahin (SHP).
Justice, Mehmet Seyfi Oktay (SHP).
National Defence, Nevzat Ayaz (DYP).
Interior, Ismet Sezgin (DYP).
Foreign Minister, Hikmet Çetin (SHP).
Finance and Customs, Sümer Oral (DYP).
Education, Köksal Toptan (DYP).
Public Works and Housing, Prof. Onur Kumbaracibaşi (SHP).
Health, Dr Yildirim Aktuna (DYP).
Communications, Yaşar Topçu (DYP).
Labour and Social Security, Mehmet Moğultay (SHP).
Trade and Industry, Tahir Köse (SHP).
Energy and Natural Resources, Ersin Faralyali (DYP).
Culture, Fikri Sağlar (SHP).
Tourism, Prof Abdulkadir Ateş (SHP).
Forestry, Dr Vefa Tanir (DYP).
Environment, Dogancan Akyurek (DYP).
DYP True Path Party; SHP Social Democrat Populist Party.

TURKISH EMBASSY
43 Belgrave Square, London SW1X 8PA
Tel 071-235 5252

Ambassador Extraordinary and Plenipotentiary, His Excellency Candemir Önhon (1991).

BRITISH EMBASSY
Sehit Ersan Caddesi 46/A, Cankaya, Ankara
Tel: Ankara 4274310/4

Ambassador Extraordinary and Plenipotentiary, His Excellency John Goulden (1992).
Counsellor, Deputy Head of Mission, W. B. McCleary.
First Secretaries, S. N. Evans (*Political*); I. F. M. Lancaster (*Chancery*); D. T. Healy (*Commercial*); J. A. Francis (*Management*); A. J. Mounford, Ms R. L. Varley, A. J. F. Pickin (*Cultural Affairs*).
Defence and Military Attaché, Brig. R. D. H. H. Greenwood.
Naval and Air Attaché, Wg Cdr. A. Campbell.

BRITISH CONSULAR OFFICES, There is a British Consulate-General at *Istanbul*, a Vice-Consulate at *Izmir* and Honorary British Consulates at *Antalya, Bodrun, Iskenderun, Mersin* and *Marmaris*.

BRITISH COUNCIL REPRESENTATIVE, Colin Perchard, OBE, Kirklangic Sokak 9, Gazi Osman Pasa, Ankara 06700. There is also a centre and library at *Istanbul*.

BRITISH CHAMBER OF COMMERCE OF TURKEY INC., Mesrutiyet Caddessi No. 34, Tepebasi Beyoğlu, Istanbul (Postal Address, PO Box 190 Karaköy, Istanbul).

EDUCATION

Education is free, secular and compulsory at primary level. There are elementary, secondary and vocational schools.

There are 27 universities in Turkey, including six in Istanbul, five in Ankara, two in Izmir, and one each in Erzurum and Trabzon.

CULTURE

Until 1926, Turkish was written in Arabic script, but in that year a version of the Roman alphabet reflecting Turkish phonetics was substituted for use in official correspondence and in 1928 for universal use, with Arabic numerals as used throughout Europe. The revolution of 1908 led to the introduction of native literature free from foreign influences and adapted to the understanding of the people. The Turkish language is spoken in a large geographical area including in newly independent central Asian states such as Azerbaijan, Turkmenistan, Kazakhstan, Uzbekistan and Kyrgyzstan.

The leading Turkish newspapers are centred in Istanbul and Ankara, although most provincial towns have their own daily papers. There are foreign language papers in French, Greek, Armenian and English and numerous magazines and weeklies.

ECONOMY

In 1985 agricultural production accounted for some 16 per cent of the gross domestic product at constant factor prices. About 50 per cent of the working population are in the rural sector. Production figures for the principal crops in 1989 were ('000 tons):

Wheat	20,000	Olives	1,100
Barley	7,300	Tea (wet leaves)	608
Rice	138	Hazelnuts	375
Tobacco	287	Grapes and figs	3,800
Sugar beet	13,985		

With the important exception of wheat, which is mostly grown on the arid central Anatolian plateau, most of the crops are grown on the fertile littoral. Tobacco, sultana and fig cultivation is centred around Izmir, where substantial quantities of cotton are also grown. The main cotton area is in the Cukurova plain around Adana. The forests which lie between the littoral plain and the Anatolian plateau contain beech, pine, oak, elm, chestnut, lime, plane, alder, box, poplar and maple. In 1990 28 per cent of the land area was forest.

INDUSTRY – After agriculture, Turkey's most important industry is based on the considerable mineral wealth which is, however, comparatively unexploited. The main export minerals are chromite and boron. Production in 1989 was (tons):

Coal	6,259,000
Lignite	50,926,000
Crude petroleum	2,868,000
Crude iron	3,523,000
Boron minerals	1,884,000

The bulk of the country's requirements in sugar, cotton, woollen and silk textiles, and cement, is produced locally, while other industries contributing substantially to local needs include vehicle assembly, paper, glass and glassware, iron and steel, leather and leather goods, sulphur refining, canning and rubber goods, soaps and cosmetics, pharmaceutical products, prepared foodstuffs and a host of minor industries.

Steep rises in oil prices from 1973 onwards led to a succession of economic crises culminating in January 1980 in the introduction of an economic stability programme. Exports have since risen dramatically, topping US$11,846 million in 1988. Inflation, however, remains high (65 per cent in 1991). GNP growth for 1989 was about 3.4 per cent and unemployment remains high.

FINANCE

	1990
Estimated expenditure	TL64,400.4 billion
Estimated revenue	53,860.0 billion

TRADE

The main imports are machinery, crude oil and petroleum products, iron and steel, vehicles, medicines and dyes, chemicals, fertilizers and electrical appliances. Agricultural commodities (cotton, tobacco, fruits, nuts, livestock) represent 47 per cent of total exports. Other exports are minerals, textiles, glass and cement.

	1989	1991
Total imports	US$15,762.6m	US$22,302m
Total exports	11,627.3m	12,959m
Trade with UK	1990	1991
Imports from UK	£606,829,000	£729,988,000
Exports to UK	550,803,000	402,770,000

DEFENCE

The armed forces have a total active strength of 579,200 (498,800 conscripts), with a term of conscription of 18 months. The Army has an active strength of 470,000 (427,000 conscripts) organized into four army groups, with some 3,783 main battle tanks, 3,560 armoured personnel carriers and 4,187 artillery pieces. The Navy has 52,000 personnel (40,000 conscripts) including 4,000 marines, with 15 submarines, 12 destroyers, eight frigates, 47 patrol and coastal craft, 22 combat aircraft and 15 armed helicopters. The Air Force has a strength of 57,200 (31,800 conscripts), with 530 combat aircraft organized into 17 ground attack squadrons, two air defence squadrons, and four transport squadrons with training as support units.

Since its invasion of Cyprus in 1974, Turkey has maintained forces in the north of the island and at present has 30,000 men in two infantry divisions stationed there. As a member of NATO, Turkey is host to the Headquarters Allied Land Forces South-Eastern Europe and the Sixth Allied Tactical Air Force, together with some 4,900 US Army and Air Force personnel.

COMMUNICATIONS

The rail network is a nationalized one, run by the State Railways Administration. The total length of lines in operation (1989) is 10,369 km.

At the end of 1988 there were 59,128 km of roads (31,149 of which were national).

The Bosporus is spanned by two bridges; plans are being drawn up for a third fixed link between the two continents.

By the end of 1988 the number of ships over 18 gross tons was 3,805.

The state airline (THY) operates all internal services and has services to Europe, the Far East, Africa, North America and the Middle East. Most of the leading European airlines operate services to Istanbul and some also to Ankara.

TUVALU

Tuvalu comprises nine coral atolls situated in the south-west Pacific around the point at which the International Date Line cuts the Equator. The total land area is about 10 sq. miles. Few of the atolls are more than 12 ft above sea level or more than half a mile in width. The vegetation consists mainly of coconut palms.

POPULATION – The resident population in 1985 was 8,229, but it is estimated that about 1,500 Tuvaluans work overseas, mostly in Nauru, or as seamen. The UN estimated that the population was 9,000 in 1990. The people are almost entirely Polynesian. The principal languages are Tuvaluan and English. The entire population is Christian and is predominantly Protestant.

CAPITAL – ΨFunafuti, estimated population 2,856. The capital has a grass strip airfield from which a service operates regularly to Fiji and Kiribati, and is also the only port.

CURRENCY – Tuvalu uses the Australian dollar ($A) of 100 cents as legal tender. In addition there are Tuvalu dollar and cent coins in circulation.

FLAG – Blue ground with Union Flag in top left quarter and nine five-pointed gold stars in the fly.

NATIONAL ANTHEM – Tuvalu Mo Te Atua (Tuvalu for the Almighty).

NATIONAL DAY – 1 October (Independence Day).

GOVERNMENT

Tuvalu, formerly the Ellice Islands, formed part of the Gilbert and Ellice Islands Colony until 1 October 1975, when separate constitutions came into force. Separation from the Gilbert Islands was implemented on 1 January 1976.

On 1 October 1978 Tuvalu became fully independent as a sovereign state within the Commonwealth. The constitution provides for a Prime Minister and four other Ministers who must be members of the 12-member elected Parliament. The Prime Minister presides at meetings of the Cabinet, which consists of the five Ministers, and is attended by the Attorney-General. Local government services are provided by elected Island Councils.

Governor-General, His Excellency the Rt. Hon. Toaripi Lauti.

CABINET as at July 1992

Prime Minister, Minister of Foreign Affairs and Economic Planning, Rt. Hon. Bikenibeu Paeniu.
Minister for Finance and Commerce, Hon. Dr Alesana Seluka.
Natural Resources and Home Affairs, Hon. Tomu Sione, OBE.
Works and Communications, Hon. Ionatana Ionatana, CVO, OBE.
Health, Education and Community Affairs, Hon. Naama Latasi.
Secretary to Government, Tauaasa Taafaki.
Attorney-General, Feleti Teo.

BRITISH HIGH COMMISSION
British High Commissioner (resides at Suva, Fiji).

EDUCATION AND WELFARE

There are eight primary schools in Tuvalu and a church secondary school run jointly with the Government. A maritime training school started in 1979 now caters for 60 boys per annum.

There is a 30-bed hospital at Funafuti. All islands are served by a dispensary and a primary school.

ECONOMY

Most people still practise a subsistence economy, the main staples of their diet being coconuts and fish. The main imports are foodstuffs, consumer goods and building materials. The only export is copra, though philatelic sales provide a major source of revenue and handicraft sales are increasing. However, Tuvalu is almost entirely dependent on foreign aid.

TRADE WITH UK

	1990	1991
Imports from UK	£506,000	£107,000
Exports to UK	–	1,000

UGANDA
Republic of Uganda

AREA, POPULATION, ETC – Situated in eastern Africa, Uganda is flanked by Zaire, Sudan, Kenya and on the south by Tanzania and Rwanda. Large parts of Lakes Victoria, Edward and Albert (Mobuto) are within its boundaries, as are Lakes Kyoga, Kwania, George and Bisina (formerly Salisbury) and the course of the River Nile from its outlet from Lake Victoria to the Sudan frontier post at Nimule. Uganda has an area of 91,259 sq. miles (236,036 sq. km) (water and swamp 16,400 sq. miles) and population (1990 UN estimate) of 18,794,000. The official language is English. The main local vernaculars are of Bantu, Nilotic and Hamitic origins. Ki-Swahili is generally understood in trading centres.

Despite its tropical location, the climate is tempered by its situation some 3,000 ft. above sea level, and well over that altitude in the highlands of the Western and Eastern Regions. In South Uganda, temperatures seldom rise above 85° F (29° C) or fall below 60° F (15° C). The rainfall averages about 50 inches a year. Uganda has three National Parks and a fourth (Lake Mburo) has been designated.

CAPITAL – Kampala (estimated population of Greater Kampala, 1990, 750,000). Other principal towns are Jinja (45,000), Mbale (28,000) and Masaka (29,000).
CURRENCY – Uganda shilling of 100 cents.
FLAG – Six horizontal stripes of black, yellow, red, with a white disc in the centre containing the badge of a crested crane.
NATIONAL ANTHEM – Oh Uganda.
NATIONAL DAY – 9 October (Independence Day).

GOVERNMENT

Uganda became an independent state and a member of the Commonwealth on 9 October 1962, after some 70 years of British rule. A republic was instituted on 8 September 1967, under an executive President, assisted by a Cabinet of Ministers.

Early in 1971 an army coup took place and Maj.-Gen. Idi Amin, the Army commander, proclaimed himself head of state. In 1979, following risings and military intervention by Tanzania, President Amin was overthrown. Dr Milton Obote became President in 1980 but was ousted by a military coup in 1985. A military council was installed which attempted to negotiate a power-sharing agreement with the National Resistance Movement led by Yoweri Museveni. However, the National Resistance Army captured Kampala in January 1986, securing control of the rest of the country in the following few months. Yoweri Museveni was sworn in as President in January 1986; subsequently the Prime Minister and a National Resistance Council (NRC) were appointed.

The NRC acts as a legislative body with an interim mandate to form a constitution. Since the most recent elections in February 1989 it consists of 210 elected and 68 presidentially appointed members. In October 1989 the NRC voted to extend its term of office by five years from 26 January 1990. A new constitution is being drafted.

HEAD OF STATE
President, Yoweri Museveni, *sworn in* 29 Jan. 1986.
Vice-President, Dr Samson Kisseka.

CABINET as at June 1992
Minister of Defence, The President.
Internal Affairs, The Vice-President.
Prime Minister, George Cosma Adyebo.
First Deputy PM, Eriya Kategaya.
Second Deputy PM and Minister for Foreign Affairs, Paul Ssemogerere.
Third Deputy PM and Attorney-General, Abu Bakar Mayanja.
Finance and Economic Planning, Joshua Mayanja-Nkangi.
Agriculture, Animal Industry and Fisheries, Mrs Victoria Ssekitoleko.
Commerce, Industry and Co-operatives, Richard Kaijuka.
Local Government, Jaberi Bidandi-Ssali.
Educational and Sports, Amanya Mushega.
Public Services, Sam Sebagereka.
Information, Paul Etiang.
Lands, Housing and Urban Development, Dr E. T. Adriko.
Labour and Social Affairs, Ateke Ejalu.
Works, Transport and Communications, Dr Ruhakana-Rugunda.
Tourism, Wildlife and Antiquities, James Wapakabulo.
Health, James Makumbi.

Water, Energy, Minerals and Environmental Protection, Henry Kajura.

Women in Development, Culture and Youth, Wandira Kazibwe.

UGANDA HIGH COMMISSION
Uganda House, 58–59 Trafalgar Square, London WC2N 5DX
Tel 071–839 5783

High Commissioner, His Excellency Prof. George Kirya (1990).

BRITISH HIGH COMMISSION
10–12 Parliament Avenue, PO Box 7070, Kampala
Tel: Kampala 257054/9

High Commissioner, His Excellency Charles A. K. Cullimore (1989).

BRITISH COUNCIL REPRESENTATIVE, Stan Moss, OBE.

EDUCATION

Education is a joint undertaking by the government, local authorities and, to some extent, voluntary agencies. In 1988 it was estimated that Uganda had 7,905 primary schools with an enrolment of 2,638,100 children. Secondary schools numbered 774 with 240,834 students enrolled; and 7,291 students in various technical training institutions.

The national university is Makerere University, Kampala, founded as a trade school in 1921 and becoming an independent university in 1970. There are universities at Mbale and Mbarara; the Uganda Martyrs University opened in October 1991.

COMMUNICATIONS

There is an international airport at Entebbe, with direct flights to destinations in Africa and Europe. There are eight other airfields in Uganda. Having no sea coast, Uganda is heavily dependent upon rail and road links to Mombasa and Dar es Salaam for its trade. Over 5,000 km of the country's dilapidated roads are currently being rehabilitated. A railway network joins the capital to the western, eastern and northern centres.

ECONOMY

The principal export earner is coffee (over 90 per cent of all exports), which earned US$264 million in 1988. Attempts are being made to increase production of cotton and tea for export. Hydro-electricity is produced from the Owen Falls power station which generated 564 kW in 1988, 110 kW of which was exported to Kenya. The principal food crops are plantains, bananas, cassava, sweet potatoes, potatoes, maize and sorghum.

TRADE WITH UK

	1990	1991
Imports from UK	£39,506,000	£35,718,000
Exports to UK	12,124,000	6,730,000

FORMER UNION OF SOVIET SOCIALIST REPUBLICS

CHRONOLOGICAL SYSTEM – The Gregorian calendar was not introduced until 14 February 1918. Hence the events surrounding the 1917 revolutions are shown here as the Gregorian calendar dates in use in the rest of the world at the time, with the dates the events occurred in the Julian calendar (OS) still in use in Russia in parenthesis.

HISTORY

The geographical extent of what was the Soviet Union was virtually analogous to that of the Russian Empire it replaced. Russia was formally created from the principality of Muscovy and its territories by Tsar Peter I (The Great) (reigned 1682–1725), who initiated its territorial expansion, introduced western ideas of government and state organization and founded St Petersburg. By the end of Peter the Great's reign, the Baltic territories (modern-day Estonia and Latvia) had been annexed from Sweden and Russia had become the dominant military power of north-eastern Europe. In the reign of Catherine the Great (1763–96) the partitions of Poland and wars with Turkey brought the territories of modern-day Lithuania, Belarus, the Ukraine and the Crimea under Russian control. The colonization of the vast expanses of Siberia east of the Urals also began in earnest, with large numbers of Russians settling the sparsely populated area. Catherine's immediate successors overran the Caucasus region (modern-day Armenia, Azerbaijan and Georgia) in the early nineteenth century, seized Finland from Sweden in 1809 and Bessarabia from Turkey in 1812. Throughout the remainder of the nineteenth century Russia subdued and annexed the independent Muslim states which now form the five Central Asian republics.

It was as a multinational empire covering a huge geographical area, in which the monarch and nobility held almost absolute power (an ineffectual parliament, the Duma, was created in 1905), that Russia entered the First World War in 1914. Discontent caused by autocratic rule, the poor conduct of the military campaign and wartime privation led to a revolution which broke out on 12 March (27 February OS) 1917. Tsar Nicholas II abdicated three days later and a provisional government was formed, with a republic being proclaimed on 14 September (1 September OS) 1917. A political power struggle ensued between the provisional government and the Bolshevik Party which controlled the Soviets (councils) set up by workers, soldiers and peasants. This led to a second revolution on 7 November (25 October OS) 1917 in which the Bolsheviks seized power.

The Bolshevik (Communist) Party led by Lenin soon withdrew from the First World War, but under draconian terms. By the Treaty of Brest-Litovsk (March 1918) Estonia, Latvia, Lithuania and Russian Poland were surrendered to Germany and Austria-Hungary, and the independence of Finland, the Ukraine and Georgia was recognized. However, by this time armed resistance to Communist rule had developed into all-out civil war between 'red' Bolshevik forces and 'white' monarchist and anti-Communist forces supported by Britain, France, Japan and the USA. The civil war lasted until the end of 1922 when the 'white' forces were defeated and foreign intervention ended. During the civil war, Russia had been declared a Soviet Republic and other Soviet republics had been formed in the Ukraine, Byelorussia and Transcaucasia. These four republics merged to form the Union of Soviet Socialist Republics (USSR) on 30 December 1922.

By the time of Lenin's death in 1924, all of the former lands of the Russian Empire apart from Finland, eastern Poland and Bessarabia had been brought under Soviet control and incorporated into the USSR. After an internal Communist Party power struggle, Joseph Stalin emerged in 1928 as the undisputed party leader. He initiated a series of reorganizations of the USSR, so that by 1936 there were 11 constituent republics, five having been created in Central Asia, and three from Transcaucasia. Stalin introduced a policy of rapid industrialization under a system of five-year plans, brought all sectors of industry under government control, abolished private ownership and enforced the collectivization of agriculture. A government campaign of terror in 1929–30 against the richest peasant class, the Kulaks, who resisted collectivization, left an estimated half a million dead and millions banished to desolate areas. Collectivization of agriculture caused widespread famine in 1932–3 in which millions died. This was followed by the great purges and show trials of the late 1930s which led to half a million executions and the imprisonment of millions in forced labour camps, where many more died. Total political repression lasted until Stalin's death in March 1953.

The Nazi-Soviet pact of August 1939 and the Second World War caused the next phase of geographic reorganization of the USSR. Soviet troops occupied eastern Poland in September 1939 and incorporated it into the Ukrainian and Belorussian republics. In March 1940 territory ceded by Finland to the USSR was joined to the autonomous Karelia region of Russia to form the Karelo-Finnish republic, which became the twelfth republic of the USSR. In August 1940 the Moldavian republic was formed from the majority of the land of Bessarabia (ceded by Romania in June 1940) and the Moldavian region of the Ukraine. The remainder of Bessarabia, together with Northern Bukovina, was incorporated into the Ukraine. Also in August 1940, Estonia, Latvia and Lithuania were annexed by the USSR to form the 14th, 15th and 16th republics. At the end of the Second World War, the part of German East Prussia around Königsberg (now Kaliningrad) was incorporated into the Russian Republic; Ruthenia was ceded by Czechoslovakia and incorporated into the Ukraine; Petsamo province was ceded by Finland to the USSR; and southern Sakhalin and the Kurile Islands were taken from Japan by agreement with the allies. In July 1956 the Karelo-Finnish Republic lost its republic status and became part of the Russian republic, reducing the number of Soviet republics from 16 to 15.

After Stalin's death, repression was lessened under his successors Khruschev and Brezhnev, but the Communist Party remained dominant in all walks of life. This was the state of affairs when Mikhail Gorbachev became Soviet leader in March 1985. Gorbachev introduced the policies of *perestroika* (complete restructuring) and *glasnost* (openness) in order to revamp the economy, which had stagnated since the 1970s, to root out corruption and inefficiency, and to move towards ending the Cold War and its attendant arms race. Private ownership was allowed, individual expression and limited private enterprise was tolerated, Soviet history was reappraised, political prisoners released and eventually the guaranteed leading role of the Communist Party abolished.

The political openness and the retreat from total control by the Communist Party unleased ethnic and nationalist tensions, especially in the three Baltic republics, Armenia and Azerbaijan. Opposition, democratic and reformist Communist political groupings were also able to build rival power bases within the Russian Republic, particularly under Boris Yeltsin, who was elected President of Russia in June 1991. Events came to a head on 19 August 1991 when a coup was attempted against Soviet President Gorbachev by hardline elements of the Communist Party, the armed forces and the state security service (KGB) in order to reimpose one-party Communist control on the USSR. The coup was defeated by reformist and democratic political groupings supported by the majority of the population, who took to the streets of Moscow and other large cities under the leadership of Yeltsin. The coup leaders were arrested and imprisoned, and Mikhail Gorbachev returned to Moscow to try to form a new Union of Sovereign States to replace the USSR. However, it became clear that effective political power was in the hands of the republican leaders, especially Russian President Yeltsin, who on 29 August 1991 banned the Soviet Communist Party and all its activities.

In September 1991 the three Baltic states of Estonia, Latvia and Lithuania were recognized as independent sovereign states. A referendum in the Ukraine in early December 1991 showed overwhelming support for independence, and this galvanized the other republic leaders. The Russian, Ukrainian and Belorussian leaders concluded an agreement in Minsk on 8 December 1991 on the formation of a new Commonwealth of Independent States (CIS). The leaders declared that the USSR had ceased to exist and renounced the 1922 treaty which established it. On 21 December at a meeting in Alma-Ata, the three founding members of the CIS were joined by Armenia, Azerbaijan, Moldavia (now Moldova), Kazakhstan, Kirghizia (now Kyrgyzstan), Tajikistan, Turkmenistan and Uzbekistan. Mikhail Gorbachev resigned as Soviet President on 25 December 1991 and on 26 December 1991 the USSR formally ceased to exist.

Commonwealth of Independent States

The Commonwealth of Independent States (CIS) is neither a sovereign state nor a supranational organization but a multilateral grouping of sovereign states which were formerly constituent republics of the USSR. Membership of the CIS consists of all the former Soviet republics apart from the Baltic states and Georgia (11 in total). It acts as a co-ordinating mechanism for foreign, defence and economic policies, and is a forum for addressing those problems which have specifically arisen from the break-up of a former sovereign state, the USSR. The affairs of the CIS are addressed in inter-state, multilateral bodies and not by central institutions. Two multilateral CIS councils were formed in January 1992, the Council of Heads of State and the Council of Heads of Government. The Council of Heads of State is the highest organ of the CIS and meets not less than twice yearly; it is chaired by the heads of state of the members in (Russian) alphabetical order. The Council of Heads of Government meets not less than once every three months and carries out the co-ordination of military and economic activity in the Commonwealth.

DEFENCE

On becoming member states of the CIS, the 11 states agreed to recognize their existing borders, respect one another's territorial integrity and reject the use of military force or other forms of coercion to settle disputes between them. Agreement was also reached on fulfilling all the international treaty obligations of the former USSR, and on a unified central control for nuclear weapons and other strategic forces.

However, implementation of these agreements has proved problematic. Armenia and Azerbaijan are engaged in a full-scale war over the disputed Nagorno-Karabakh region. The Russian and Ukrainian governments have clashed repeatedly over control of the Black Sea fleet and the validity of the 1954 transfer of the Crimea, which is the base of the fleet, from Russia to the Ukraine. In August 1992 the Russian and Ukrainian governments agreed on joint command and control of the fleet for a period of three years.

The CIS states agreed on a central CIS command for all nuclear weapons, and when President Gorbachev resigned in December 1991 he handed control of nuclear weapons to the CIS commander-in-chief Marshal Shaposhnikov. All tactical nuclear weapons had been transferred to the Russian republic by May 1992. An agreement was reached with the USA in May 1992 by the four republics with strategic nuclear weapons (Russia, the Ukraine, Belarus, Kazakhstan) on implementing the strategic arms reduction talks (START) treaty previously signed by the USA and USSR. Under this agreement the Ukraine, Belarus and Kazakhstan have agreed to eliminate all their strategic nuclear weapons over a seven year period and Russia has agreed to reduce its strategic nuclear weapons over the same period to such an extent that there will be a 38 per cent reduction in the overall former Soviet arsenal.

As far as non-nuclear forces are concerned, the situation is confused. Although it was hoped that joint armed forces would be retained in some form, this has proved impossible to achieve. All 11 member states have formed, or are in the process of forming their own defence ministries and armed forces, creating competition for the allegiance of particular units, especially between Russia and the Ukraine. The six European CIS states (Russia, the Ukraine, Belarus, Moldova, Armenia and Azerbaijan) have reached agreement on how to implement the reductions required of the former Soviet armed forces by the Conventional Forces in Europe (CFE) Treaty signed by the former USSR. All forces stationed outside the former Soviet Union and in the three Baltic States have been declared Russian. Agreements have been reached to withdraw former Soviet forces from Poland by November 1992, from Cuba and Lithuania by August 1993, and from eastern Germany by October 1994. Forces remain in Estonia and Latvia, but it is planned to have no former Soviet forces outside CIS territory by 1995.

The latest details on CIS armed forces relate to the ex-Soviet Union forces in late 1991 and therefore are only approximate; the forces are subject to large reductions and division among the member states.

In late 1991 the total active armed forces numbered some 3,400,000 (including 2 million conscripts serving for two-year periods and 650,000 Ministry of Defence staff). The strategic nuclear forces had a strength of 280,000 personnel, with 912 missiles in 60 submarines, 1,388 inter-continental ballistic missiles based on land, and 177 long range and 410 medium range bombers.

The Army had a strength of 1,400,000 personnel (1 million conscripts), with 38,400 main battle tanks, 1,000 light tanks, 78,000 armoured infantry fighting vehicles and armoured personnel carriers, 73,200 artillery pieces and 2,050 armed helicopters. The Air Force (including air defence troops) had a strength of 795,000 personnel (500,000 conscripts), with 4,905 combat aircraft and 220 attack helicopters.

The Navy had a strength of 434,000 (270,000 conscripts) with 221 submarines, five aircraft carriers, 38 cruisers, 29 destroyers, 146 frigates, 1,354 combat aircraft and 312 armed helicopters. The Pacific, Northern and Baltic fleets are based in Russia and will all become Russian, whilst the Black Sea fleet is to come under joint Russian and Ukrainian command, and the Caspian Sea flotilla is to be divided between Russia, Azerbaijan, Kazakhstan and Turkmenistan.

The para-military forces numbered 580,000, including 230,000 KGB and 350,000 internal security troops.

ECONOMY

One of the most remarkable aspects of the former Soviet economy was the transformation of an essentially agricultural economy in 1917 into what was by the early 1960s the second strongest industrial power in the world. This rapid industrializaton was achieved through a series of five-year plans. However, by the late 1960s and early 1970s it had become clear that the Western world was continually outperforming the Soviet economy in all areas of the civilian economy. Although the Soviet economy was able to keep pace in the area of military and space technology, it was only by devoting increasing proportions of national income and resources to the military-industrial complex. Consequently, the civilian economy began to stagnate and was further suffocated by the bureaucratic inefficiency of the centrally planned economic system.

Under this system the entire direction of the economy and all industries (which were state-owned and controlled) was planned by the Communist Party leadership in Moscow, according to set production targets. No account was taken of the free market economic principles of supply and demand, and there was no reward for individual enterprise, which stifled economic and technological innovation. The extremely poor distribution system also caused problems, especially with agricultural products, which often rotted before they could reach consumers. Agriculture was also a prime example of the effect of lack of incentive. Peasants were organized into collective farms with set production quotas to reach, never seeing any rewards for their labour. Realizing this, in the 1980s the Soviet authorities allowed peasants to own and cultivate small private plots. These made a significant contribution to production even though the area of private plots was small compared to that of the collective farms.

It was in an attempt to solve the problems of the centrally planned economic system that Gorbachev introduced economic restructuring (perestroika). After attempts to reform the economy within the restraints of the centrally planned system had failed, an increasing number of free market reforms were introduced, including the legalization of small private businesses in August 1990, the reduction of state control over the economy in October 1990, and denationalization and privatization measures in July 1991. However, despite the introduction of these measures, the economy continued to decline rapidly. The abolition of central planning without its replacement by a fully free market system, coupled with continued obstruction of reform by the bureaucracy, the military industrial complex and the Communist Party, led to economic chaos.

As it became clear that the Soviet Union was disintegrating in October 1991, nine republics signed a treaty forming an economic community, and were joined by two other republics in November 1991. The principles of the treaty have been embodied within the CIS and form the basis of its economic co-operation. Members have agreed to refrain from economic actions that would damage each other and to conduct co-ordinated policies in energy production, taxation, customs regulations and tariffs, foreign economic relations, and monetary and banking systems. A single monetary unit, the rouble, was agreed upon by all 11 member states, and the members recognized that the basis of recovery for their economies was private ownership, free enterprise and competition. However, it became clear in early 1992 that economic co-operation was a problem because of the different pace of economic reform in each member state, in particular Russia and the Ukraine. The Russian government is intent on introducing large-scale free market reforms quickly, including mass privatization, the removal of all subsidies to industry and complete price liberalization, to enable free market principles to create a true market mechanism. However, the Ukrainian government was not prepared to accept the political consequences of such moves, which include mass unemployment, inflation and short-term poverty. In an attempt to divorce themselves from Russian measures, the Ukrainian government has introduced coupons to replace the rouble and is planning its own currency, called the hryvnia.

A major advantage of economic co-ordination by the 11 CIS members has been the granting of large amounts of aid by Western countries, as the aid was dependent on co-operation between the former Soviet republics. Western countries and international organizations made it clear that economic aid to the member states to enable them to reform their economies was dependent on the republics accepting reponsibility for the former USSR's debt, abiding by all the former USSR's international obligations (such as nuclear and conventional arms reductions), and having a secure, central control and command of nuclear weapons. These conditions have been accomplished through the CIS mechanisms and enabled the 11 members to gain extensive grants, loans, credits, trade agreements and technological, business and planning expertise and guidance from Western countries individually, the EC, the G7 grouping, the European Bank for Reconstruction and Development, the IMF and the World Bank.

TRADE WITH UK (USSR)

	1990	1991
Imports from UK	£606,013,000	£354,705,000
Exports to UK	917,691,000	901,833,000

COMMUNICATIONS

The European area of the CIS member states is relatively well served by railways, St Petersburg and Moscow being the two main focal points of rail routes. The centre and south have a good system of north-south and east-west lines, but the eastern part (the Volga lands), traversed as it is by trunk lines between Europe and Asia which enter Siberia via Yekaterinburg, Chelyabinsk, Magnitogorsk and Ufa, lacks north-south routes. In Asia, there are still large areas of Russia, notably in the far north and Siberia, with few or no railways. Railways built since 1928 include the Turkestan-Siberian line (*Turksib*) which has made possible a large-scale industrial exploitation of Kazakhstan, a number of lines within the system of the Trans-Siberian Railway (Magnitogorsk-Kartaly-Troitsk, Yekaterinburg-Kurgan, Novosibirsk-Proyektnaya, etc.), which are of great importance for the industrial development in the east, the Petropavlovsk-Karaganda-Balkhash line which has made possible the development of the Karaganda coal basin and of the Balkhash copper mines, and the Moscow-Donbass trunk line. In the northern part of European Russia, the North Pechora Railway has been completed, while in the Far East a recently completed second Trans-Siberian line (the Baikal-Amur Railway) is partially in use; it follows a more northerly alignment than the earlier Trans-Siberian and terminates in the Pacific port of Sovetskaya Gavan.

PORTS AND WATERWAYS – The most important ports (Odessa, Nikolayev, Batumi, Taganrog, Rostov, Kerch, Sevastopol and Novorossiisk) lie around the Black Sea and the Sea of Azov. The northern ports (St Petersburg, Murmansk and Archangel) are, with the exception of Murmansk, icebound during winter. Several ports have been built along the Arctic Sea route between Murmansk and Vladivostok and are in regular use every summer. The far eastern port of Vladivostok, the Pacific naval base of Russia, is kept open by icebreakers all the year round.

Inland waterways, both natural and artificial, are of great importance in the country, although some of them are icebound in winter (from two and a half months in the south to six months in the north). The great rivers of European Russia flow outwards from the centre, linking all parts of the plain with the chief ports, an immense system of navigable waterways which carried about 690 million tons of freight in 1988. They are supplemented by a system of canals which provide a through traffic between the White, Baltic, Black and Caspian Seas. The most notable are the White Sea-Baltic Canal, the Moscow-Volga Canal and the Volga-Don Canal linking the Baltic and the White Seas in the north to the Caspian Sea, the Black Sea and the Sea of Azov in the south.

CIS MEMBER STATES

ARMENIA

Haikakan Hanrapetoutioun

AREA – Armenia has an area of 11,306 sq. miles (29,800 sq. km) and occupies the south-western part of the Caucasus region of the former Soviet Union. It is bordered on the east and south-west by Azerbaijan, on the north by Georgia, on the south by Iran and on the west by Turkey. It is a very mountainous country consisting of several vast tablelands surrounded by ridges.

CLIMATE – Continental, dry and cold, but the Araks valley has a long, hot and dry summer.

POPULATION – According to the 1989 census the population is 3,305,000. The population is concentrated in the low-lying part of Armenia, the Aras valley and the Erevan hollow. Armenians form 93 per cent of the population, Kurds 1.7 per cent and Russians 1.6 per cent. Azerbaijanis formed 2.6 per cent of the population, but most fled or were expelled after the outbreak of the conflict with Azerbaijan.

RELIGION – Armenian Orthodox Christian (Armenian Church centred in Etchmiadzin).

CAPITAL – Erevan. Population 1,186,000 (1988).

CURRENCY – Rouble of 100 kopeks.

FLAG – Three horizontal stripes of red, blue and orange.

GOVERNMENT

Armenia declared independence from the Soviet Union on 23 September 1991 and was admitted to memberhip of the UN in February 1992. The political situation in Armenia is dominated by the war with Azerbaijan and the effects of the 1988 earthquake. The earthquake, which devastated much of the country, left thousands homeless and industry badly affected, and Armenia has neither the money nor the expertise to complete the rebuilding process. The war with Azerbaijan over the disputed region of Nagorno-Karabakh, the Armenian-populated enclave in Azerbaijan, simmered from February 1988 and erupted into all-out war in May 1992, when Armenian forces breached Azerbaijan's defences to form a land bridge to Nagorno-Karabakh.

President, Levon Ter-Petrosyan, *elected* 16 October 1991.
Prime Minister, G. G. Arutyunyan.

ECONOMY

Armenia has a strong agricultural sector in low-lying areas, where industrial and fruit crops are grown. Grain is grown in the hills and the country is also noted for its wine. There are large copper ore and molybdenum deposits and other minerals. The Armenian economy has been crippled by a trade blockade by Azerbaijan, through which supplies of oil and gas used to come.

AZERBAIJAN

Azarbaijchan Respublikasy

AREA – Azerbaijan has an area of 33,436 sq. miles (86,600 sq. km) and occupies the eastern part of the Caucasus region of the former Soviet Union, on the shore of the Caspian Sea. It is bordered on the south by Iran, on the west by Armenia and on the north by Georgia and the Russian Federation. The north-eastern part of the republic is taken up by the south-eastern end of the main Caucasus ridge, its south-western part by the smaller Caucasus hills, and its south-eastern corner by the spurs of the Talysh Ridge. Its central part is a depression irrigated by the Kura and by the lower reaches of its tributary, the Araks. Azerbaijan includes the

ARCTIC OCEAN
Arctic Circle
Murmansk
Archangel
SWEDEN
FINLAND
RUSSIA
St. Petersburg (Leningrad)
Moscow
Nizhny-Novgorod (Gorky)
Yekaterinburg (Sverdlovsk)
Novosibirsk
Minsk
POLAND
Samara
Kiev
Kishinev
ROMANIA
Caspian Sea
Aral Sea
Black Sea
Tbilisi
Erevan
Baku
Bishkek
Alma-Ata
Tashkent
MONGOLIA
Vladivostok
TURKEY
Ashkhabad
Dunshanbe
CHINA
JAPAN
Mediterranean Sea
IRAN
AFGHANISTAN
PAKISTAN
PACIFIC OCEAN
EGYPT
SAUDI ARABIA
INDIA
Arabian Sea
Bay of Bengal
0
1500 km
0
1000 miles

Nakhichevan Autonomous Republic and the Nagorno-Karabakh Autonomous Province.
CLIMATE – Sheltered by the mountains from the humid west winds blowing from the Black Sea, Azerbaijan has a continental climate.
POPULATION – According to the 1989 census, Azerbaijan has a population of 7,021,000, of which 83 per cent are Azerbaijanis, six per cent Russians and six per cent Armenians.
RELIGION – The population is predominantly Shia Muslim.

CAPITAL – ΨBaku. Population 1,772,000 (1988).
CURRENCY – Rouble of 100 kopeks.
FLAG – Three horizontal stripes of blue, red and green with a white crescent and eight-pointed star in the centre.

GOVERNMENT

In January 1990, the Azerbaijani Popular Front took power from the local Communist Party and declared independence from the Soviet Union, partly as a result of the Soviet government's decision in 1989 to take control of the Nagorno-Karabakh region away from Azerbaijan and to impose direct rule upon it to stop Azeri-Armenian fighting there. Soviet troops overthrew the Popular Front regime the day after it took power and re-installed the Communist regime under President Ayaz Mutalibov. This government declared Azerbaijan's independence from the Soviet Union in August 1991 and gained UN membership for Azerbaijan in February 1992. Mutalibov overwhelmingly won the presidential election held on 8 September 1991, but he was forced to resign by widespread civil unrest at his perceived pro-Moscow stance and the poor conduct of the war with Armenia. At the ensuing presidential election the Popular Front leader Abulfaz Elchibey was elected, pledging to withdraw from the CIS and align his country more closely with Turkey. At the time of going to press in September 1992, Azerbaijan was still participating in the CIS, but its parliament had not ratified its membership.

President, Abulfaz Elchibey, *elected* 7 June 1992.
Prime Minister, R. A. Guseinov.

ECONOMY

Azerbaijani industry is dominated by oil and natural gas extraction and related chemical and engineering industries centred on Baku and Sumgait. The republic is also rich in mineral resources, with iron, copper, lead and salt. A large power station on the Araks was completed in 1969, in conjunction with Iran. Azerbaijan is also important as a cotton-growing area.

BELARUS
Respublika Belarus

AREA – Belarus has an area of 80,300 sq. miles (207,600 sq. km) and is situated in the western part of the European area of the former USSR. It is bordered on the north by Latvia and Lithuania, on the east by Russia, on the south by the Ukraine and on the west by Poland. The republic is largely a plain with many lakes, swamps and marshy areas. The main rivers are the upper reaches of the Dnieper, of the Niemen and of the Western Dvina. The republic is divided into six provinces (Brest, Gomel, Grodno, Minsk, Mogilev and Vitebsk).
POPULATION – According to the 1989 census, Belarus has a population of 10,152,000, of which 78 per cent are Belorussians, 13 per cent Russians, 4 per cent Poles and 3 per cent Ukrainians.
RELIGION – Most of the population are Roman Catholics.

CAPITAL – Minsk. Population 1,583,000 (1988). The city is the administrative centre of the CIS.
CURRENCY – Rouble of 100 kopeks.
FLAG – Three horizontal stripes of white, red, white.

GOVERNMENT

Belarus declared its independence from the Soviet Union after the failed coup in Moscow in August 1991. As the former Soviet republic of Belorussia it was a founding member of the UN along with the USSR and the Ukraine. Its independence from the USSR was recognized by the EC and USA in January 1992.

After the failed Moscow coup, the Belorussian leader, Nikolai Dementei, was ousted because of his involvement with the coup leaders. He was replaced by Stanislav Shushkevich at the head of an informal coalition of Communists and democrats. Belarus was one of the three CIS founding members.

Chairman of the Supreme Soviet (*Parliament*), S.S. Shushkevich, *elected* September 1991.
Prime Minister, V. F. Kebich.

ECONOMY

The collapse of the Soviet centrally planned economic system has hit Belarussian industry badly. Belarus had many factories manufacturing products from raw materials sent from the rest of the former USSR. However, the republic cannot afford to pay market prices for the raw materials, causing factories to close.

Belarussian agriculture, based on the meat and dairy industries, is in much better shape and will cushion the republic from the worst of any food shortages. The peat industry is also being developed to make Belarus as self-sufficient as possible in fuel.

KAZAKHSTAN
Kazak Respublikasy

AREA – Kazakhstan has an area of 1,049,155 sq. miles (2,717,300 sq. km) and occupies the northern part of what was Soviet Central Asia. It stretches from the Volga and the Caspian Sea in the west to the Altai and Tienshan mountains in the east. It is bordered on the west by the Caspian Sea and the Russian Federation, on the south by Turkmenistan, Uzbekistan and Kyrgyzstan, on the east by China and on the north by the Russian Federation. Kazakhstan is a country of arid steppes and semi-deserts, flat in the west, hilly in the east and mountainous in the south-east (Southern Altai and Tienshan mountains). The main rivers are the Irtysh, the Ural, the Syr-Darya and the Ili.
CLIMATE – Continental and very dry.
POPULATION – According to the 1989 census the population is 16,464,000, of which 40 per cent are Kazakhs, 38 per cent Russians and 5 per cent Ukrainians.
RELIGION – The majority of ethnic Kazakhs are Muslims, and this is the main religion of the republic.

CAPITAL – Alma-Ata. Population 1,134,000 (1988).
CURRENCY – Rouble of 100 kopeks.
FLAG – Red with a light blue horizontal stripe near the lower edge; in the canton a gold hammer and sickle and red, gold-edged, star.

GOVERNMENT

Kazakhstan was the last of the former USSR republics to declare its independence (16 December 1991), which was recognized by the EC and the USA later that month. UN membership was gained in January 1992.

President Nazarbaev, although genuinely popular with the population, has refused to enter into a coalition government with opposition democratic parties and has restrained Islamic fundamentalist groups who want to repatriate ethnic Russians. A delicate balance was found over the important language law debate, Kazakh being declared the official language, with Russian as the official language of inter-ethnic communication.

President, Nursultan Nazarbaev, *elected* 2 December 1991.
Prime Minister, S. Tereschenko.

ECONOMY

Kazakhstan is very rich in minerals, with copper, lead, zinc, iron ore, coal, oil and natural gas. The main centres of the metal industry are in the Altai mountains, in Chimkent, north of the Balkhash Lake and in central Kazakhstan. Agriculture including stock-raising is highly developed, particularly in the central and south-west of the republic. Grain is grown in the north and north-east, and cotton in the south and south-east.

KYRGYZSTAN
Kyrgyz Respublikasy

AREA – Kyrgyzstan has an area of 76,642 sq. miles (198,500 sq. km) and occupies the central eastern part of the former Soviet Central Asia. The republic's name was changed from Kirghizia in December 1990. It is bordered on the north by Kazakhstan, on the east by China, on the south and south-west by Tajikistan and on the west by Uzbekistan. Kyrgyzstan is a mountainous country, the major part being covered by the ridge of the Central Tienshan, while the mountains of the Pamir-Altai system occupy its southern part. There are a number of spacious mountain valleys, the Alai, Susamyr and others. Kyrgyzstan is divided into two provinces, Issyk-Kul and Osh.
POPULATION – According to the 1989 census the population is 4,258,00, of which 52.4 per cent are Kirghiz (Turkic origin), 21.5 per cent are Russian and 12.9 per cent Uzbek. The majority of the population is concentrated in plains lying at the foot of the mountains.
RELIGION – Islam is the main religion.

CAPITAL – Bishkek. Population 646,000 (1988).
CURRENCY – Rouble of 100 kopeks.
FLAG – Red with a gold sun in the centre containing a representation of a yurt in red.

GOVERNMENT

Kyrgyzstan declared independence from the Soviet Union just after the failed Moscow coup on 31 August 1991, and gained UN membership in January 1992. The Communist Party was already out of power by this time, but nevertheless President Akaev has had trouble introducing economic reforms because of the obstructive bureaucracy. Ethnic tensions between the rural nomadic Kirghiz, the urban Russians and the wealthy Uzbeks who own many businesses, are never far from the surface. Fighting over land between ethnic Kirghiz and Uzbeks in the town of Osh in 1991 left over 500 dead.

President and Prime Minister, Askar Akaev, *elected President* October 1991, *self-appointed Prime Minister* February 1992.

ECONOMY

Agriculture is the major sector of the economy with sugar beet, cotton and sheep being the main products. Industry is concentrated in the food-processing, textiles, timber and mining fields.

MOLDOVA
Republica Moldovenească

AREA – Moldova has an area of 13,912 sq. miles (33,700 sq. km) and occupies the extreme south-western corner of the former USSR. To the north, east and south-east it is bordered by the Ukraine, and to the west by Romania. The border with Romania is formed by the Pruth river, but the main river of the republic is the Dniester, navigable along its whole course. The northern part of the republic consists of flat steppe lands, in the centre there are woody hills, and in the south low-lying steppe lands. Forests skirt the Dniester.
CLIMATE – Moderate.
POPULATION – According to the 1989 census the population is 4,335,000, of which 64 per cent are Moldovan, 14.2 per cent Ukrainian and 12.8 per cent Russian.
RELIGION – Most of the population are adherents of the Romanian Orthodox Church.

CAPITAL – Kishinev. Population 684,000 (1988).
CURRENCY – Rouble of 100 kopeks.
FLAG – Vertical stripes of blue, yellow, red, with the national arms in the centre.

GOVERNMENT

Moldova (formerly Moldavia) was formed from land ceded to the Soviet Union by Romania in 1940 and land taken from the Ukraine east of the river Dniester. When independence from the USSR was declared in August 1991, the majority ethnic Romanian population expressed a wish to rejoin Romania. This alienated the ethnic Ukrainian and Russian populations, who form a majority east of the Dniester. After failed negotiations and several armed clashes, the Ukrainian and Russian populations declared their independence from Moldova as the Transdniester republic in December 1991. The Moldovan government refused to recognize this and throughout 1992 a war has been waged between government forces and Transdniester forces, who have been supported by the former Soviet 14th Army stationed in Transdniester. At the time of going to press, fighting continues and despite negotiating efforts by Russia, Romania and the Ukraine, no settlement has been reached. Moldova was recognized by the EC and USA in January and February 1992 respectively and gained UN membership in February 1992.

President, Mircea Snegur, *elected* December 1991.
Prime Minister, vacant.

ECONOMY

The main sector of the economy is agriculture, especially viniculture, fruit-growing and market gardening. Industry is small and concentrated east of the Dniester, where it has been paralysed by the war.

RUSSIA/RUSSIAN FEDERATION
Rossiiskaya Federatsiya

AREA – Russia has an area of 6,593,391 sq. miles (17,075,000 sq. km) and occupies three-quarters of the land area of the former Soviet Union, making it the largest state in the world. It stretches from well beyond the Arctic Circle in the extreme north to the Northern Caucasus in the south, and from the Kaliningrad enclave on the Baltic Sea in the west to the Bering Strait in the far east. In the west it is bordered by Norway, Finland, Estonia, Latvia, Belarus and the Ukraine (the Kaliningrad enclave borders Lithuania and Poland). To the south Russia is bordered in Europe by Georgia, Azerbaijan, the Black Sea and the Caspian Sea, and in Asia by Kazakhstan, China, Mongolia and North Korea. In the east it meets the North Pacific (where its nearest point is only a few miles from Japan), and the Bering Strait (where its nearest point is only a few miles from Alaska). To the north is the Arctic Ocean and the Barents Sea.

The Russian Federation comprises the following: 49 provinces (Amur, Archangel, Astrakhan, Belgorod, Bryansk, Chelyabinsk, Chita, Irkutsk, Ivanov, Kaliningrad, Kaluga,

Kamchatka, Kemerovo, Kirov, Kostroma, Kurgan, Kursk, Lipetsk, Magadan, Moscow, Murmansk, Nizhny Novgorod, Novgorod, Novosibirsk, Omsk, Orel, Orenburg, Penza, Perm, Pskov, Rostov, Ryazan, St Petersburg, Sakhalin, Samara, Saratov, Smolensk, Tambov, Tomsk, Tula, Tver, Tyumen, Ulyanovsk, Vladimir, Volgograd, Vologda, Voronezh, Yaroslavl, Yekaterinburg); five autonomous territories (Khabarovsk, Krasnodar, Krasnoyarsk, Maritime, Stavropol) containing in their turn three autonomous regions; and 22 autonomous republics (Adygei, Altai, Bashkortostan, Buryaad, Chechen, Chuvash, Dagestan, Ingush, Kabardin-Balkar, Kalmyk, Karachaev-Cherkess, Karelia, Khakassia, Komi, Mari-El, Mordovia, North Ossetia, Tatarstan, Tuva, Udmurt, Yakut-Sakha, Yamal-Nenetsk.

There are three principal geographic areas: a low-lying flat western part stretching eastwards up to the Yenisei and divided in two by the Ural ridge; an eastern part, between the Yenisei and the Pacific, consisting of a number of tablelands and ridges; and a southern mountainous part. Russia has a very long coast-line, including the longest Arctic coastline in the world (about 17,000 miles). The most important rivers are the Volga, the Northern Dvina and the Pechora, the Neva, the Don and the Kuban in the European part, and in the Asiatic part, the Ob, the Irtysh, the Yenisei, the Lena and the Amur, and, further north, Khatanga, Olenek, Yana, Indigirka, Kolyma and Anadyr. Lakes are abundant, particularly in the north-west. The huge Baikal Lake in eastern Siberia is the deepest lake in the world. There are also two large artificial water reservoirs within the Greater Volga canal system, the Moscow and Rybinsk 'Seas'.

CLIMATE – Climatically, Russia extends from Arctic and tundra belts to the subtropical in the south.

POPULATION – According to the 1989 Census, Russia has a population of 147,022,000, of which 82 per cent are Russian, 4 per cent Tatar and 3 per cent Ukrainian. There are another 12 minorities with populations of over half a million.

RELIGION – The Russian Orthodox Church is the predominant religion, though the Tatars are Muslims and there are Jewish communities in Moscow and St Petersburg.

LANGUAGE, LITERATURE AND ARTS – Russian is a branch of the Slavonic family of languages which is divided into the following groups: *eastern*, including Russian, Ukrainian and White Russian; *western*, including Polish, Czech, Slovak and Sorbish (or Lusatian Wendish); and *southern*, including Serbo-Croat, Slovene, Macedonian and Bulgarian. The western group and part of the southern group are written in the Latin alphabet, the others in the Cyrillic, said to have been instituted by SS Cyril and Methodius in the ninth century and largely based on the Greek alphabet.

Before the westernization of Russia under Peter the Great (1682–1725), Russian literature consisted mainly of folk ballads (*byliny*), epic songs, chronicles and works of moral theology. The 18th and particularly the 19th centuries saw a brilliant development of Russian poetry and fiction. Romantic poetry reached its zenith with Alexander Pushkin (1799–1837) and Mikhail Lermontov (1814–41). The 20th century produced great poets like Alexander Blok (1880–1921), the 1958 Nobel Prize laureate Boris Pasternak (1890–1960), Vladimir Mayakovsky (1893–1930) and Anna Akhmatova (1888–1966). Realistic fiction is associated with the names of Nikolai Gogol (1809–52), Ivan Turgenev (1818–83), Fedor Dostoyevsky (1821–81) and Leo Tolstoy (1828–1910), and later with Anton Chekhov (1860–1904), Maxim Gorky (1868–1936), Ivan Bunin (1870–1953) and Alexander Solzhenitsyn (*b.* 1918).

Great names in music include Glinka (1804–57), Borodin (1833–87), Mussorgsky (1839–81), Rimsky-Korsakov (1844–1908), Rubinstein (1829–94), Tchaikovsky (1840–93), Rachmaninov (1873–1943), Skriabin (1872–1915), Prokofiev (1891–1953), Stravinsky (1882–1971) and Shostakovich (1906–75).

CAPITAL – Moscow. Population 8,879,000 (1988). Moscow, founded about AD 1147 by Yuri Dolgoruki, became first the centre of the rising Moscow principality and in the 15th century, the capital of the whole of Russia (Muscovy). In 1325 it became the seat of the Metropolitan of Russia. In 1703 Peter the Great transferred the capital to the newly-built St Petersburg, but on 14 March 1918 Moscow was again designated as the capital. ΨSt Petersburg (from 1914–24 Petrograd and from 1924–91 Leningrad) has a population of 4,948,000 (1 January 1987).

Other towns with populations (1 January 1987) exceeding 1,000,000 are:

Nizhny-Novgorod (Gorky)	1,425,000
Novosibirsk (Novonikolayevsk)	1,423,000
Yekaterinburg (Sverdlovsk)	1,331,000
Samara (Kuibyshev)	1,280,000
Omsk	1,134,000
Chelyabinsk	1,119,000
Ufa	1,092,000
Perm (Molotov)	1,075,000
Kazan	1,068,000
Rostov-on-Don	1,004,000

CURRENCY – Rouble of 100 kopeks.

FLAG – Three horizontal stripes of white, blue, red.

GOVERNMENT

Within the former Soviet Union, Russia was known as the Russian Soviet Federal Socialist Republic. This was changed to the Russian Federation by presidential decree on 25 December 1991, and two official names, 'Russia' and 'the Russian Federation', were adopted by the Congress of People's Deputies on 19 April 1992. Russia was recognized as an independent state by the EC and USA in January 1992, and it inherited the Soviet Union's seat at the UN.

A new Russian Federal Treaty was signed on 13 March 1992 between the central government and the autonomous republics, but Tatarstan and Chenchen have refused to sign it and declared their 'independence'.

The present Russian constitutional system was adopted after changes to the Soviet constitution in 1988 made the establishment of specifically Russian institutions and government possible. Previously Russia was covered by the Soviet institutions. The legislature consists of the Congress of People's Deputies, which is directly elected and has 1,068 members who then elect from among their numbers a smaller Supreme Soviet. The Supreme Soviet is the main law-making and parliamentary body, meeting most of the year. The Congress of People's Deputies meets for only a few days a year, but has the power to amend the constitution and sack government ministers. Under the constitution, the President has only a ceremonial role but Boris Yeltsin has been voted wide-ranging emergency powers by the Congress of People's Deputies.

At present President Yeltsin and democratic political groups are trying to force through constitutional changes to enable the introduction of a western-style constitution with an executive President and a two-chamber legislature. The legislature would consist of a directly-elected State Duma of around 300 members and a Federal Assembly of three delegates from each republic or province. However, constitutional change is difficult because it requires the support of the Congress of People's Deputies, which was elected in March 1990 and has a majority of Communist members, who are ambivalent about reform.

Throughout 1992 President Yeltsin's government has faced continuing opposition to reform from the bureaucracy, some of the military and the influential heads of major state enterprises. In April 1992 a political impasse was reached between the Congress of People's Deputies and the government. The government offered to resign because of the Congress's attempts to limit economic reforms, but President Yeltsin refused to accept the resignations and forced the reforms through the Congress.

In May 1992 the great majority of state subsidies were abolished and price liberalization was introduced. In August 1992 mass privatization was announced and in October 1992 all citizens will receive vouchers so that they can participate in an auction of the majority of Russian state industry. In September 1992 the abolition of the central distribution system was announced, with effect from 1 January 1993.

President, Boris Yeltsin, *elected* 12 June 1991.
Vice-President, Aleksandr Rutskoi, *elected* 12 June 1991.
Acting Prime Minister, Yegor Gaidar.

EMBASSY OF THE RUSSIAN FEDERATION
13 Kensington Palace Gardens, London W8 4QX
Tel 071-229 3628

Ambassador Extraordinary and Plenipotentiary, His Excellency Boris Pankin (1991).
Minister-Counsellors, Vladimir Ivanov; Aleksandr Kudinov.

BRITISH EMBASSY
Naberezhnaya Morisa Toreza 14, Moscow 72
Tel: Moscow 231 8511

Ambassador Extraordinary and Plenipotentiary, His Excellency Sir Brian Fall, KCMG (1992). (Also non-resident Ambassador to Armenia, Azerbaijan, Belarus and Kazakhstan).
Minister and Deputy Head of Mission, F. N. Richards, CVO.
Minister-Counsellor, G. D. G. Murrell, OBE.
Defence and Air Attaché, Air Cdre P. M. Stean.
There is a British Consulate-General in St Petersburg.

BRITISH COUNCIL DIRECTOR, T. Sandell, OBE.

ECONOMY

The Republic has some of the richest mineral deposits in the world. Coal is mined in the Kuznetsk area, in the Urals, south of Moscow, in the Donets basin (its eastern part lies in Russia) and in the Pechora area in the north. Oil is produced in the northern Caucasus, in the area between the Volga and the Ural and in western Siberia, which also has large deposits of natural gas. Coal and gas deposits in Siberia and the Far East (especially Yakutia) are currently being developed, now that some deposits in the western parts of Russia are approaching exhaustion. The Ural mountains contain a unique assortment of minerals: high-quality iron ore, manganese, copper, aluminium, gold, platinum, precious stones, salt, asbestos, pyrites, coal, oil, etc. Iron ore is also mined near Kursk, Tula, Lipetsk, in several areas in Siberia and in the Kola Peninsula. Non-ferrous metals are found in the Altai, in eastern Siberia, in the northern Caucasus, in the Kuznetsk-Basin, in the far east and in the far north. Nine-tenths of all former USSR forests are located in Russia.

The vast area of the republic and the great variety in climatic conditions cause great differences in the structure of agriculture from north to south and from west to east. In the far north reindeer breeding, hunting and fishing are predominant. Further south, timber industry is combined with grain growing. In the southern half of the forest zone and in the adjacent forest-steppe zone, the acreage under grain crops is far larger and the structure of agriculture more complex. In the eastern part of this zone, between the Volga and the Urals, cericulture is predominant (particularly summer wheat), followed by cattle breeding. Beyond the Urals is another important grain-growing and stock-breeding area in the southern part of the western Siberian plain. The southern steppe zone is the main wheat granary of Russia, containing also large acreages under barley, maize and sunflower. In the extreme south cotton is now cultivated. Vine, tobacco and other southern crops are grown on the Black Sea shore of the Caucasus.

Industrially, Russia occupies the first place among the former Soviet republics. Moscow and St Petersburg are still the two largest industrial centres in the country, but new industrial areas have been developed in the Urals, the Kuznetsk basin, in Siberia and the Far East. Most of the oil produced in the former USSR came from Russia; half the annual output comes from Tyumen Oblast in western Siberia. All industries are represented in Russia, including iron and steel and engineering.

TAJIKISTAN
Respublika i Tojikiston

AREA – Tajikistan has an area of 54,019 sq. miles (143,100 sq. km) and occupies the extreme south-east of former Soviet Central Asia. It is bordered on the west and north-west by Uzbekistan, on the north-east by Kyrgyzstan, on the east by China and on the south by Afghanistan. The republic includes the Gorno-Badakhstan Autonomous Province and the Kulyab, Kurgan-Tyubinsk and Khodzhent Provinces. The country is mountainous with the Pamír highlands in the east and the high ridges of the Pamir-Altai system in the centre. Plains are formed by wide stretches of the Syr-Darya valley in the north and of the Amu-Darya in the south.
POPULATION – According to the 1989 census the population is 5,093,000, of which 62 per cent are Tajiks (linguistically and culturally akin to Persian), 23 per cent are Uzbeks and 8 per cent Russians.
RELIGION – Predominantly Sunni Muslim.

CAPITAL – Dushanbe. Population 596,000 (1988).
CURRENCY – Rouble of 100 kopeks.
FLAG – Red with a band divided horizontally white over green running near the lower edge; in the canton a gold hammer and sickle and a red, gold-edged star.

GOVERNMENT

At the time of going to press, the situation in Tajikistan was unstable and very confused. Tajikistan under President Kakhar Makhkamov had declared independence from the Soviet Union on 6 September 1991. At the presidential election on 24 November 1991, the former hardline Communist leader of Tajikistan, Rakman Nabiev, was elected President, but by only a narrow majority. Tension between Nabiev's mainly Communist government and supporters and the opposition Islamic and democratic groups led to demonstrations and armed clashes in the capital Dushanbe in early May 1992 and Nabiev was forced to form a coalition government with opposition groups on 11 May. Clashes erupted again in August 1992, leaving hundreds dead in Dushanbe. Nabiev was forced to resign on 7 September 1992 as he tried to flee the capital. Since then, opposition groups have tried without success to form a government. Tajikistan was recognized as independent by the EC and USA in January and February 1992 respectively, and gained UN membership in February 1992.

ECONOMY

Agriculture is the major sector of the economy, concentrating on cotton-growing and cattle-breeding. Tajikistan also has rich mineral deposits of lead, zinc and oil and is a source of uranium. Industry specializes in the production of clothing and textiles.

TURKMENISTAN
Turkmenostan Respublikasy

AREA– Turkmenistan has an area of 188,417 sq. miles (488,100 sq. km) and occupies the extreme south of the former Soviet Central Asia between the Caspian Sea and the Amu-Darya river. To the west it is bordered by the Caspian Sea, to the south by Iran, to the south-east by Afghanistan, to the east and north by Uzbekistan and to the north-west by Kazakhstan. The republic comprises five provinces: Ashkhabad; Chardjou; Krasnovodsk; Mary; and Tashauz. The country is a low-lying plain fringed by hills in the south. Ninety per cent of the plain is taken up by the Kara-Kum desert.
CLIMATE – Hot and dry.
POPULATION – According to the 1989 census the population is 3,523,000, of which 72 per cent are Turkomans, 9.5 per cent Russians and 9 per cent Uzbeks.
RELIGION – Mainly Sunni Muslim.

CAPITAL – Ashkhabad. Population 390,000 (1988).
CURRENCY – Rouble of 100 kopeks.
FLAG – Green with a vertical strip near the hoist of magenta with a carpet pattern in red, white and black; in the canton a white crescent and five white stars tilted towards the upper hoist.

GOVERNMENT

Turkmenistan declared its independence from the Soviet Union on 27 October 1991; it was recognized by the EC and USA in December 1991 and gained UN membership in February 1992. The new constitution passed on 18 May 1992 makes the President head of state and government and provides for a new legislature, the Majlis, of 50 directly-elected members. There are fears of inter-ethnic tension, as the constitution abolished the use of Russian as the official language of inter-ethnic communication.

President, Saparmurad Niyazov, *elected* 27 October 1990, *re-elected* 21 June 1992, *appointed Head of Government* 18 May 1992.

ECONOMY

Cotton cultivation, stock-raising and mineral extraction are the principal industries, together with natural gas production and the long-established silk industry. Some fisheries exist along the Caspian sea coast.

THE UKRAINE
Ukraina

AREA – The Ukraine has an area of 231,990 sq. miles (603,700 sq. km) and lies in the south west of the European part of the former Soviet Union. It is bordered on the north by Belarus and Russia, on the east by Russia, on the south by the Black Sea, on the south-west by Romania and Moldova and on the west by Hungary, Czechoslovakia (the future Slovakia) and Poland. The area of the present Ukraine is significantly larger than that of the Ukrainian Soviet Republic formed in the 1917–19 period because of the westward territorial expansion of the former Soviet Union in the 1939–45 period and the addition of the Crimea from Russia in 1954 (*see* History). The Ukraine now consists of 25 provinces: Cherkassy, Chernigov, Chernovtsy, Crimea, Dnepropetrovsk, Donetsk, Ivano-Frankovsk, Kharkov, Kherson, Khmelnitsky, Kiev, Kirovograd, Lugansk, Lvov, Nikolayev, Odessa, Poltava, Rovno, Sumy, Ternopol, Transcarpathia, Vinnitsa, Volhynia, Zaporozhye and Zhitomir.

The larger part of the Ukraine forms a plain with small elevations. The Carpathian mountains lie in the south-western part of the republic. The main rivers are the Dnieper with its tributaries, the Southern Bug and the Northern Donets (a tributary of the Don).
CLIMATE – Moderate with relatively mild winters (particularly in the south west) and hot summers.
POPULATION – According to the 1989 census the population was 51,471,000, of which 73 per cent are Ukrainian and 22 per cent Russian.
RELIGION – The two main religions are Roman Catholicism and Orthodox. The Orthodox rite is divided between the Russian Orthodox Church with its Patriarch in Moscow and the Autocephalous Orthodox Church of the Ukraine with its own Patriarch in Kiev. Roman Catholics are concentrated in the west of the country. There are also large numbers of Reformed Protestants in the Transcarpathian region and a sizeable Jewish community in Kiev.

CAPITAL – Kiev. Population 2,577,000 (1988). Other major cities are Kharkov (1,587,000); Dnepropetrovsk (1,182,000); ΨOdessa (1,141,000); Donetsk (1,090,000).
CURRENCY – The rouble has been replaced by coupons as an interim measure until the planned introduction of the hryvna.
FLAG – Divided horizontally blue over yellow.

GOVERNMENT

The Ukraine declared itself independent of the Soviet Union, subject to a referendum, after the failed Moscow coup in August 1991. The referendum was held on 1 December 1991 and 90 per cent of the electorate voted for independence. Simultaneously, the former Ukrainian Communist leader Leonid Kravchuk was elected President of the Republic. The Ukraine was a founding member of the UN, along with Belarus and the former USSR, and its independence was recognized by the EC and USA in December 1991.

Political power in the Ukraine still rests with former Communists led by the President. There has effectively been no democratic revolution because throughout late 1991 and 1992 democratic nationalist parties such as Rukh have supported the President and non-democratic central administration as the best means of preventing perceived Russian attempts to dominate the Ukraine. President Kravchuk and the former Communist government have been able to build themselves a strong position and prevent effective free market reforms.

The relationship with Russia is central to events in the Ukraine and in the CIS. To insulate itself as far as possible from Russian economic reforms, the Ukrainian government is introducing its own currency and establishing customs post on the border with Russia, both in violation of CIS agreements. The Ukraine has also tried to claim as many of the former Soviet conventional armed forces as possible, causing tensions with Russia over keeping 'strategic' conventional forces including the Black Sea fleet under CIS control. The situation of the Crimea with its ethnic Russian majority has also caused concern, as the Crimean parliament first voted to make the Crimea an autonomous republic in September 1991, which was accepted by Kiev, but then voted for independence in May 1992, which was not. Meanwhile, the Russian Parliament voted in January 1992 to re-examine the legality of the Crimea's transfer from Russia to the Ukraine in 1954.

President, Leonid Kravchuk, *elected* 1 December 1991.
Prime Minister, V. P. Fokin.

BRITISH EMBASSY

Room 1008, Zhovtneva Hotel, Ulitza Rozi Luxembourg, 252021 Kiev
Tel: Kiev 291 8907

Ambassador Extraordinary and Plenipotentiary, His Excellency S. N. P. Hemans, CVO (1992).
Consul-General and Deputy Head of Mission, D. G. Martin.

Economy

The southern part of the country contains a major coal-mining and iron and steel industrial area which was the largest in the former Soviet Union. The Ukraine also contains major engineering and chemical industries and ship-building yards on the Black Sea coast.

Ukrainian agricultural production is also good with large areas under cultivation with wheat, cotton, flax and sugar beet; stock-raising is very important. There are large deposits of coal and salt in the Donets Basin, of iron ore in Krivoy Rog and near Kerch in the Crimea, of manganese in Nikopol, and of quicksilver in Nikitovka.

UZBEKISTAN

Ozbekiston Respublikasy

Area – Uzbekistan has an area of 172,742 sq. miles (447,400 sq. km) and occupies the south-central part of former Soviet Central Asia, lying between the high Tienshan Mountains and the Pamir highlands in the east and south-east and sandy lowlands in the west and north-west. It is bordered on the north by Kazakhstan and the Aral Sea, on the east by Kyrgyzstan and Tajikistan, on the south by Afghanistan and Turkmenistan, and on the west by Kazakhstan. Uzbekistan consists of the Kara-Kalpak Autonomous Republic and 12 provinces: Andizhan, Bokhara, Dzhizak, Ferghana, Kashkadar, Khorezm, Namangan, Navoi, Samarkand, Surkhan-Darya, Syr-Darya and Tashkent. The major part of the country is a plain with huge waterless deserts, and several large oases which form the main centres of population and economic life. The largest is the Ferghana valley, watered by the Syr-Darya. Other oases include Tashkent, Samarkand, Bokhara and Khorezm.
Climate – Continental and dry.
Population – According to the 1989 census the population is 19,810,000, of which 71 per cent are Uzbeks, 8 per cent Russians, 5 per cent Tajiks and 4 per cent Kazakhs.
Religion – Predominantly Sunni Muslim.

Capital – Tashkent. Population 2,210,000 (1988). Samarkand (388,000) contains the Gur-Emir (Tamerlane's Mausoleum) completed AD 1400 by Ulugbek, Tamerlane's astronomer grandson.
Currency – Rouble of 100 kopeks.
Flag – Three horizontal stripes of blue, white, green, with the white fimbriated in red; near the hoist on the blue stripe with a white crescent and twelve white stars.

Government

Uzbekistan declared its independence from the Soviet Union on 31 August 1991 after the failed Moscow coup. Its independence was recognized by the EC and USA in December 1991, and it gained UN membership in January 1992.

The government of President Karimov is formed by the former Communist Party, which has renamed itself the People's Democratic Party. Censorship is still widely used and little political opposition is tolerated. Uzbek nationalism has caused violent clashes with Tajiks in the Ferghana valley over the past three years. A knowledge of and ability to speak Uzbek (a form of Turkish) is also now a condition of appointment to government posts, and those not able to speak it are being dismissed. This has severely disrupted the civil service and public sector, mostly staffed by Russians. President Karimov is attempting to form close ties with Turkey in the cultural and business spheres, and this has caused problems with influential religious leaders who look to Iran and Saudi Arabia for support.

President, Islam Karimov, *elected* December 1991.
Prime Minister, A. Mutalov.

Economy

Uzbekistan's economy is based on intensive agricultural production, and especially cotton production, based on extensive irrigation schemes. In addition there are some agricultural and textile machinery plants and several chemical combines. Large and previously underdeveloped mineral resources are to be fully exploited; these include gold, natural gas, oil, copper, lead, zinc and coal.

GEORGIA

Sakartvelos Respublika

Status – Georgia is a former USSR republic but has not joined the CIS.
Area – Georgia has an area of 26,911 sq. miles (69,700 sq. km) and occupies the north-western part of the Caucasus region of the former Soviet Union. It is bordered on the north by Russia, on the south-east by Azerbaijan, on the south by Armenia, on the south-west by Turkey, and on the west by the Black Sea. Georgia contains the two autonomous republics of Abkhazia and Adjaria and the autonomous province of South Ossetia. The latter was abolished by Georgian law in December 1990 but this was not recognized by the Soviet government.

Georgia is very mountainous, with the Greater Caucasus in the north and the Lesser Caucasus in the south. The relatively low-lying land between these two ranges is divided into western and eastern Georgia by the Surz Ridge.
Climate – Western Georgia has a mild and damp climate, eastern Georgia is more continental and dry. The Black Sea shore and the Rioni lowland are subtropical.
Population – According to the 1989 census Georgia has a population of 5,401,000, of which 70 per cent are Georgian, 8 per cent are Armenian, 6 per cent Russian, 6 per cent Azerbaijani and 3 per cent Ossetians.
Religion – Most of the population are adherents of the Georgian Orthodox Church.

Capital – Tbilisi. Population 1,211,000 (1987).
Currency – Rouble of 100 kopeks.
Flag – Crimson, with a canton divided black over white.

Government

In March 1990 the Georgian Supreme Soviet declared illegal the treaties of 1921–2 by which Georgia had joined the Soviet Union. The Communist Party's monopoly on power was abolished in 1990 and in multi-party elections held in October and November 1990 the nationalist leader Zviad Gamsakhurdia was elected President. Georgia declared its independence from the Soviet Union in April 1991. The independence of Georgia was recognized by the EC in March 1992.

The political situation became confused after independence was declared as the increasingly dictatorial attitude of Gamsakhurdia alienated much of the population; by late 1991 armed opposition to Gamsakhurdia's government had begun in earnest. At the same time, the South Ossetians took up arms against Georgian rule in an attempt to join North Ossetia, itself a part of the Russian Federation. By the end of December 1991 there was a savage civil war raging in Tbilisi between supporters and opponents of President Gamsakhurdia. The President was overthrown and fled on 6 January 1992 and a military council took power until March 1992, when a state council was appointed with the former Soviet foreign minister Eduard Shevardnadze as its chairman. Throughout 1992 Gamsakhurdia's followers, allied with Abkhazian separatists, have fought the State Council government, and fighting continues in South Ossetia. Parliamentary elections are planned for October 1992.

Chairman of the State Council, Eduard Shevardnadze.
Prime Minister, Tengiz Sigua.

ECONOMY

Georgia has a strong agricultural sector with viniculture, tea and tobacco-growing the most important activities. There are significant mineral deposits of manganese, coal and oil, and an advanced oil refining industry. The tourist industry, which was very important to the Georgian economy, has been badly affected by fighting on the Abkhazian coast.

UNITED ARAB EMIRATES

Al-Imarat Al-Arabiya Al-Muttahida

AREA AND POPULATION – The approximate area of the UAE is 32,278 sq. miles (83,600 sq. km), and the population (1991 estimate) is 1,909,000.

Six of the emirates lie on the shore of the Gulf between the Musandam peninsula in the east and the Qatar peninsula in the west while the seventh, Fujairah, lies on the Gulf of Oman.

CURRENCY – UAE dirham of 100 fils.

FLAG – Horizontal stripes of green over white over black with vertical red stripe in the hoist.

NATIONAL DAY – 2 December.

GOVERNMENT

The United Arab Emirates (formerly the Trucial States) is composed of seven emirates (Abu Dhabi, Ajman, Dubai, Fujairah, Ras al Khaimah, Sharjah and Umm al Qaiwain) which came together as an independent state on 2 December 1971 when they ended their individual special treaty relationships with the British Government (Ras al Khaimah joined the other six on 10 February 1972).

The British government, by virtue of a treaty made in 1892, had been responsible for the external affairs of the emirates through the British Political Resident in the Persian Gulf and the British Political Agents in each emirate, but on independence the Union Government assumed full responsibility for all internal and external affairs apart from some internal matters that remained the prerogative of the individual emirates. Overall authority lies with the Supreme Council of the seven emirate rulers, each of whom is an absolute monarch in his own territory. The President and Vice-President are elected by the Supreme Council from among its members. The President appoints the Council of Ministers.

HEAD OF STATE

President, Sheikh Zayed bin Sultan al Nahyan (*Abu Dhabi*).
Vice-President, Sheikh Maktoum bin Rashid al Maktoum (*Dubai*).

COUNCIL OF MINISTERS as at July 1992

Finance and Industry, Sheikh Hamdan bin Rashid al Maktoum.
Defence, Sheikh Mohammed bin Rashid al Maktoum.
Interior, Maj.-Gen. Hamouda bin Ali.
Foreign Affairs, Rashid Abdullah al Noami.
Communications, Mohammed Saeed al Mualla.
Planning, Sheikh Humaid bin Ahmed al Mualla.
Islamic Affairs and Endowments, Sheikh Mohammed bin Ahmed al Khazraji.
Water and Electricity, Humaid bin Nasser al Oweis.
Economy and Commerce, Saeed Ghobash.
Agriculture and Fisheries, Saeed al Ragabani.
Labour and Social Affairs, Saif al Jarwan.
Minister of State for Cabinet Affairs, Saeed al Ghaith.
Information and Culture, Khalfan bin Mohammed al Roumi.
Education, Hamad Abdul Rahman al Madfa.
Minister of State for Financial and Industrial Affairs, Ahmed bin Humaid al Tayer.
Minister of State for Foreign Affairs, Sheikh Hamdan bin Zayed al Nahyan.
Minister of State for Supreme Council Affairs, Sheikh Mohammed bin Saqr bin Mohammed al Qassimi.
Higher Education, Sheikh Nahyan bin Mubarak al Nahyan.
Justice, Dr Abdullah bin Omran Taryam.
Health, Ahmed bin Saeed al Badi.
Petroleum and Mineral Resources, Yousuf bin Omeir bin Yousuf.
Public Works and Housing, Rakad bin Salem bin Rakad.
Youth and Sports, Sheikh Faisal bin Khaled bin Mohammed al Qassimi.

EMBASSY OF THE UNITED ARAB EMIRATES
30 Prince's Gate, London SW7 1PT
Tel 071-581 1281

Ambassador Extraordinary and Plenipotentiary, His Excellency Easa Saleh Al-Gurg, CBE (1991).

BRITISH EMBASSIES
PO Box 248, Abu Dhabi
Tel: Abu Dhabi 326600

Ambassador Extraordinary and Plenipotentiary, His Excellency Graham Stuart Burton, CMG (1990).

BRITISH COUNCIL REPRESENTATIVE, J. H. G. Foley, OBE.

PO Box 65, Dubai
Tel: Dubai 521070

Counsellor and Consul-General, R. A. M. Hendrie.

BRITISH COUNCIL REPRESENTATIVE, A. Swales, PO Box 1636, Dubai.

DEFENCE

Security in the area is maintained by the UAE Armed Forces. The Ministry of Defence is located in Dubai with a general headquarters in Abu Dhabi. Most of the separate police forces have also been merged.

TRADE

Revenue is chiefly derived from oil, re-exports and customs dues on imports.

Trade with UK	1990	1991
Imports from UK	£664,724,000	£759,660,000
Exports to UK	181,486,000	231,931,000

ABU DHABI

Abu Dhabi is the largest emirate of the UAE in area, stretching from Khor al Odaid in the west to the borders with Dubai in the Jebel Ali area. It includes six villages in the Buraimi oasis, the other three being part of the Sultanate of Oman, and a number of settlements in the Liwa oasis system. Following negotiations with Saudi Arabia, some adjustment of the border has now been made in the Khor al Odaid region, but the agreement has not yet been ratified. The population of the Emirate is now about 798,000

The Abu Dhabi government controls oil, gas and petrochemical operations in the emirate through the Supreme Petroleum Council. This body in turn issues instructions to the Abu Dhabi National Oil Company (ADNOC) which has majority shareholdings in the several oil operating and gas treatment companies. ADNOC also has majority shareholdings in oil industry-related companies covering drilling, refining, distribution, chemical manufacture and investment.

Offshore production began in 1962, the most important fields being Umm Shaif and Lower Zakum, near Das Island, site of a large associated gas liquefaction plant. The Upper Zakum field came on stream in late 1982, and four other offshore fields are being developed, one near Abu Dhabi city and three near Delma. Production of oil onshore began in 1963 from the Murban field. A large onshore associated gas liquefaction project based at Ruwais started production in 1981. Other large natural gas finds in recent years will consolidate Abu Dhabi's position as a holder of some of the largest reserves of natural gas in the world. Abu Dhabi's crude oil production in 1990 was approximately 1.65 million barrels per day.

With its oil wealth the emirate has seen a period of growth (which is currently slowing down), not only in Abu Dhabi, now a modern city of about 450,000 people, but also in Al Ain in the Buraimi oasis and in the new petro-chemical city at Ruwais. An international airport opened in 1982 at Abu Dhabi and another is under construction at Al Ain. There are airfields on Das Island and at Jebel Dhanna. The port and harbour on Abu Dhabi island are now completed and there are port facilities at Ruwais.

AJMAN AND UMM AL QAIWAIN

Ajman and Umm al Qaiwain are the smallest emirates, having populations of around 76,000 and 27,000 respectively. Both lie on the Gulf coast although Ajman has two inland enclaves at Manama and Masfut. Exploration work continues in both emirates for oil and gas but so far only Umm Al Qaiwain has experienced any success, with the offshore discovery of natural gas, but the field has yet to be commercially developed. The discovery of onshore gas in nearby Sharjah has increased hopes of similar discoveries in both Ajman and Umm Al Qaiwain.

DUBAI

Dubai is the second largest emirate both in size and in population, which is about 501,000. The town of Dubai is the main port for the import of goods into the UAE and has a wide re-export trade to the other Gulf states. Dubai's prosperity was established by this trade long before the discovery of oil. Oil was discovered in 1966 and production began in September 1969. The producer in Dubai's offshore oilfields is Dubai Petroleum Company, operated by CONOCO. Production is in excess of 350,000 b.p.d. In 1982 an ARCO-Britoil joint venture discovered an extensive gas and condensate field onshore. A small amount of condensate is produced from the onshore Margam field.

Oil income has been used to finance Dubai's infrastructure, and major construction projects include an international airport, a dry dock complex and an international trade and exhibition centre. There is also a 66-berth port at Jebel Ali, forming the heart of an industrial complex which includes an aluminium smelter with an associated de-salination plant and a gas processing plant. The port and its immediate area is a free trade zone which is expected to attract more industry.

FUJAIRAH

Fujairah, with a population of 63,000, is the most remote of the seven emirates, lying on the Gulf of Oman coast and only connected by a metal road to the rest of the country since the end of 1975. Largely agricultural, its population is spread between the slopes of the inland Hajar mountain range and the town of Fujairah itself, together with a number of smaller settlements on the comparatively fertile plain on the coast. Although exploration work continues, there have been no hydrocarbon discoveries in the emirate. However, there are some chrome and other mineral deposits. Fujairah has a general cargo port.

RAS AL KHAIMAH

Ras al Khaimah has a population of 130,000 of whom more than half live in the town. An ancient sea-port, near to which archaeological remains have been found, Ras al Khaimah is developing as the most agricultural of the emirates, producing vegetables, dates, fruit and tobacco. In 1982 Ras al Khaimah announced the discovery of oil and gas offshore and this field currently produces approximately 5,000 b.p.d. An industrial area has been developed to the north of the emirate, which includes two cement works. Ras al-Khaimah has an international airport and has also expanded its port. A new international airport is nearing completion. A new trade centre has been completed and it is hoped that more industry will be attracted to the emirate.

SHARJAH

Sharjah, with a population of approximately 314,000, has declined from its former position as principal town in the area. It became the third oil-producing emirate in the summer of 1974, following the discovery of oil offshore. The field declined over the years and by 1982 was yielding less than 6,000 b.p.d. However, new oil and gas discoveries were made in 1982 in the northern emirates and production now stands at about 50,000 b.p.d.

Sharjah is well connected by metalled roads to all the other northern emirates. It experienced a construction boom in the mid-1970s including an ambitious layout of roads and flyovers within the town. A container port has been constructed on the Gulf of Oman at Khor Fakkan. The international airport opened in 1979.

URUGUAY

República Oriental del Uruguay

AREA AND POPULATION – Uruguay is the smallest republic in South America, situated on the east coast of the Rio de la Plata in lat. 30° to 35° S. and long. 53° 15′ to 57° 42′ W., with an area of 68,037 sq. miles (176,215 sq. km). The population (UN estimate 1990) is 3,094,000, almost entirely white and predominantly of Spanish and Italian descent. Many Uruguayans are Roman Catholics. There is complete freedom of religion and no church is established by the state.

The country consists mainly of undulating grassy plains. The principal chains of hills are the Cuchilla del Haedo, which cross the Brazilian boundary and extend southwards to the Cuchilla Grande of the south and east. In no case do the peaks exceed 2,000 feet.

The principal river is the Rio Negro (with its tributary the Yi), flowing from north-east to south-west into the Rio Uruguay. The boundary river Uruguay is navigable from its estuary to Salto, about 200 miles north, and the Negro is also navigable for a considerable distance. Smaller rivers are the Cuareim, Yaguaron, Santa Lucia, Queguay and the Cebollati.

CLIMATE – The summer is warm, but the heat is often tempered by the breezes of the Atlantic. The winter is, on the whole, mild, but cold spells, characterized by winds from the south polar regions, are experienced in June, July and August. Rainfall is regular throughout the year, but there are occasional droughts.

CAPITAL – ΨMontevideo, population (1984) 1,355,312. Other centres are Salto, ΨPaysandu, Mercedes, Minas, Melo, and Rivera.

CURRENCY – New Uruguayan peso of 100 centésimos.

FLAG – Four blue and five white horizontal stripes surcharged with sun on a white ground in the top corner, next flagstaff.

NATIONAL ANTHEM – Orientales, La Patria O La Tumba (Uruguayans, the fatherland or death).

NATIONAL DAY – 25 August (Declaration of Independence, 1825).

GOVERNMENT

Uruguay (or the *Banda Oriental*, as the territory lying on the eastern bank of the Uruguay River was then called) resisted all attempted invasions of the Portuguese and Spanish until the beginning of the 17th century, and 100 years later the Portuguese settlements were captured by the Spanish. From 1726 to 1814 the country formed part of Spanish South America and underwent many vicissitudes during the wars of independence. In 1814 the armies of the Argentine Confederation captured the capital and annexed the province, and it was afterwards annexed by Portugal and became a province of Brazil. In 1825, the country threw off Brazilian rule. This action led to war between Argentina and Brazil which was settled by the mediation of the United Kingdom, Uruguay being declared an independent state in 1828. In 1830 a republic was inaugurated.

According to the constitution the President appoints a council of 11 ministers and a Secretary (Planning and Budget Office), and the Vice-President presides over Congress. The legislature consists of a Chamber of 99 deputies and a Senate of 30 members (plus the Vice-President), elected for five years by a system of proportional representation. General elections held in November 1984 marked the return to civilian rule after 11 years of presidential rule with military support. The first fully free presidential and legislative elections since 1971 were held in November 1989, and were won by the Partido Nacional Blanco.

The Republic is divided into 19 Departments each with a chief of police and a Departmental Council.

HEAD OF STATE

President, Dr Luis Alberto Lacalle, *took office* 1 March 1990.
Vice-President, Dr Gonzalo Aguirre Ramírez.

CABINET as at July 1992

Interior, Dr Juan Andrés Ramírez.
Foreign Affairs, Dr Héctor Gros Espiell.
Economy and Finance, Dr Ignacío De Posadas.
Transport and Public Works, Wilson Elso Goñi.
Public Health, Dr Carlos del Piazzo.
Labour and Social Security, Dr Enrique Alvaro Carbone Rico.
Livestock, Agriculture and Fisheries, Alvaro Ramos.
Education and Culture, Dr Guillermo García Costa.
National Defence, Dr Mariano R. Brito.
Industry and Energy, Dr Augusto Montesdeoca.
Tourism, José Villar.
Housing, Territorial Regulation and Environment, Raul Lago.
Planning and Budget Office, Carlos Alfredo Cat.

EMBASSY OF THE ORIENTAL REPUBLIC OF URUGUAY
2nd Floor, 140 Brompton Road, London SW3 1HY
Tel 071-584 8192; *Consulate* 071-589 8735

Ambassador Extraordinary and Plenipotentiary, His Excellency Dr Luis Alberto Solé-Romeo (1987).

BRITISH EMBASSY
Calle Marco Bruto 1073, Montevideo 11300
Tel: Montevideo 623650

Ambassador Extraordinary and Plenipotentiary, His Excellency Donald Lamont (1991)
First Secretary, A. T. Lovelock (*Deputy Head of Mission and Consul*).

There is a British Consular Office at *Montevideo*.

ANGLO-URUGUAYAN CULTURAL INSTITUTE, San José 1426, Montevideo. There are branch Institutes throughout Uruguay.

BRITISH-URUGUAYAN CHAMBER OF COMMERCE, Avenida Labertador Brig. Gen., Lavalleja 1641, P2-OF 201, Montevideo.

ECONOMY

Wheat, barley, maize, linseed, sunflower seed and rice are cultivated. The wealth of the country is obtained from its pasturage, which supports large herds of cattle and sheep. There are just over 9 million cattle and just under 24 million sheep. In addition to wool, meat packing, other foodstuffs (citrus, wine, beer), fishing and textile industries are of importance.

The development of local industry continues and, in addition to the greatly augmented textile industry, marked expansion in local production is notable in respect of tyres, sheet-glass, three-ply wood, cement, leather-curing, beet-sugar, plastics, household consumer goods, edible oils and the refining of petroleum and petroleum products.

There are some ferrous minerals, not extracted at present. Non-ferrous exploited minerals include clinker, dolomite, marble and granite.

FINANCE

	1988	1989
Revenue	Pesos 456,675.2 m	Pesos 753,573 m
Expenditure	510,651.4 m	918,442 m

The external debt at June 1990 was US$6,117.3 million. Central Bank reserves (December 1989) were US$1,017 million.

COMMUNICATIONS

There are about 9,899 km of national highways, and about 12,083 km of telegraph and 48,375 miles of telephone communications.

There are about 2,987 km of standard gauge railway in use in Uruguay. Passenger rail services were cancelled in January 1988 and services are now limited to cargo transport. A State Autonomous Entity was formed to administer the railway systems purchased by the government from four British companies in 1948.

A state-owned airline, PLUNA, runs daily services to southern Brazil, Paraguay and Argentina, and two flights a week to Spain. The principal capitals of the interior and a limited freight service are connected to Montevideo by TAMU, another state-owned airline, using principally military aircraft and personnel. International passenger and freight services are maintained by American, South American and European airlines. The international airport of Carrasco lies 12 miles outside Montevideo.

EDUCATION

Primary education is compulsory and free, and technical and trade schools and evening courses for adult education are state controlled. There are about 322,053 pupils in the 2,362 state schools. The university at Montevideo (founded in 1849) has about 18,000 students enrolled in its ten faculties.

CULTURE

Spanish is the language of the Republic. Five daily newspapers are published in Montevideo with an estimated total circulation of 150,000. Most of them are distributed throughout the country.

Trade

The major exports are meat and by-products, wool and by-products, hides and bristle and agricultural products. The principal imports are raw materials, construction materials, oils and lubricants, automotive vehicles, kits and machinery. Principal trading partners are Brazil, USA and Argentina.

	1988	1989
Total exports	US$1,404,527 m	US$1,598,800 m
Total imports	1,176,945 m	1,195,900 m
Trade with UK	1990	1991
Imports from UK	£31,192,000	£33,303,000
Exports to UK	51,859,000	47,894,000

The principal export items to the UK are wool and beef, the main imports are chemicals, machinery, raw materials, metals and beverages.

UNITED STATES OF AMERICA

The United States of America occupies nearly all of the North American continent between the Atlantic and Pacific Oceans, in latitude 25° 07′ to 49° 23′ N. and longitude 66° 57′ to 124° 44′ W., its northern boundary being Canada and the southern boundary Mexico. The separate state of Alaska reaches a latitude of 71′ 23° N., at Point Barrow.

The general coastline of the United States has a length of about 2,069 miles on the Atlantic, 7,623 miles on the Pacific, 1,060 miles on the Arctic, and 1,631 miles on the Gulf of Mexico.

The principal river is the Mississippi-Missouri-Red, traversing the whole country from north to south. Its length is 3,710 miles to its mouth in the Gulf of Mexico, with many large affluents, the chief of which are the Yellowstone, Platte, Arkansas, and Ohio rivers. The rivers flowing into the Atlantic and Pacific Oceans are comparatively small; among the former are the Hudson, Delaware, Susquehanna, Potomac, James, Roanoke and Savannah; of the latter, the Columbia-Snake, Sacramento, and Colorado. The Nueces, Brazos, Trinity, Pearl, Mobile-Tombigbee-Alabama, Apalachicola-Chattahoochee, Suwannee and Colorado of Texas fall into the Gulf of Mexico, also the Rio Grande, a long river partly forming the boundary with Mexico.

The chain of the Rocky Mountains separates the western portion of the country from the remainder. West of these, bordering the Pacific coast, the Cascade Mountains and Sierra Nevada form the outer edge of a high tableland, consisting in part of stony and sandy desert and partly of grazing land and forested mountains, and including the Great Salt Lake, which extends to the Rocky Mountains. In the eastern states large forests of valuable timber still exist, the remnants of the forests which formerly extended over all the Atlantic slope.

The highest point is Mount McKinley (Alaska), 20,320 ft. above sea level and the lowest point of dry land is in Death Valley (Inyo, California), 282 ft. below sea-level.

AREA AND POPULATION

	Total Area 1990 (sq. miles)	Population Census 1980
The United States (*a*)	3,536,338	248,709,8873
Puerto Rico	3,426	3,522,037
Palau	177	15,122
Outlying areas under US jurisdiction	598	325,079
Territories	419	281,734
Guam	209	133,152
US Virgin Islands	133	101,809
American Samoa	77	46,773
Northern Mariana Is.	179	43,345
Population abroad (*b*)	–	922,819
Armed Forces	–	529,269
TOTAL	3,541,556	254,631,012

(*a*) the 50 states and the Federal District of Columbia
(*b*) excludes US citizens temporarily abroad on private business.

IMMIGRANTS BY PLACE OF BIRTH, 1971–91

From 1820 to 1989, 55,009,566 immigrants were admitted to the United States. Figures for 1991 include 1,123,162 legalization applicants who gained permanent residence status.

Place of Birth	1971–80	1991
Europe	801,300	135,234
Asia	1,633,800	358,533
North America	1,645,000	1,207,599
Canada	114,800	13,504
Mexico	637,200	946,167
West Indies	759,800	136,835
Central America	132,400	111,093
South America	284,400	79,934
Africa	91,500	36,179
Australia	14,300	1,678
New Zealand	5,300	793
Other countries	17,700	7,217
TOTAL	4,493,300	1,827,167

1971–6, year ends 30 June; from 1977, year ends 30 September

RESIDENT POPULATION BY RACE 1990, Thousands

White	199,686
Black	29,986
*American Indian	1,959.2
Chinese	1,645.5
Filipino	1,406.8
Japanese	847.6
Asian Indian	815.4
Korean	798.8
Vietnamese	614.5
Other Asian or Pacific Islander	1,145
All other races	9,804.8
†Hispanic origin	22,354
Cuban	1,043.9
Mexican	13,495.9
Puerto Rican	2,727.8
Other Hispanic	5,086.4
TOTAL	248,704.9

*Includes Eskimo and Aleut.
†Persons of Hispanic origin may be of any race.

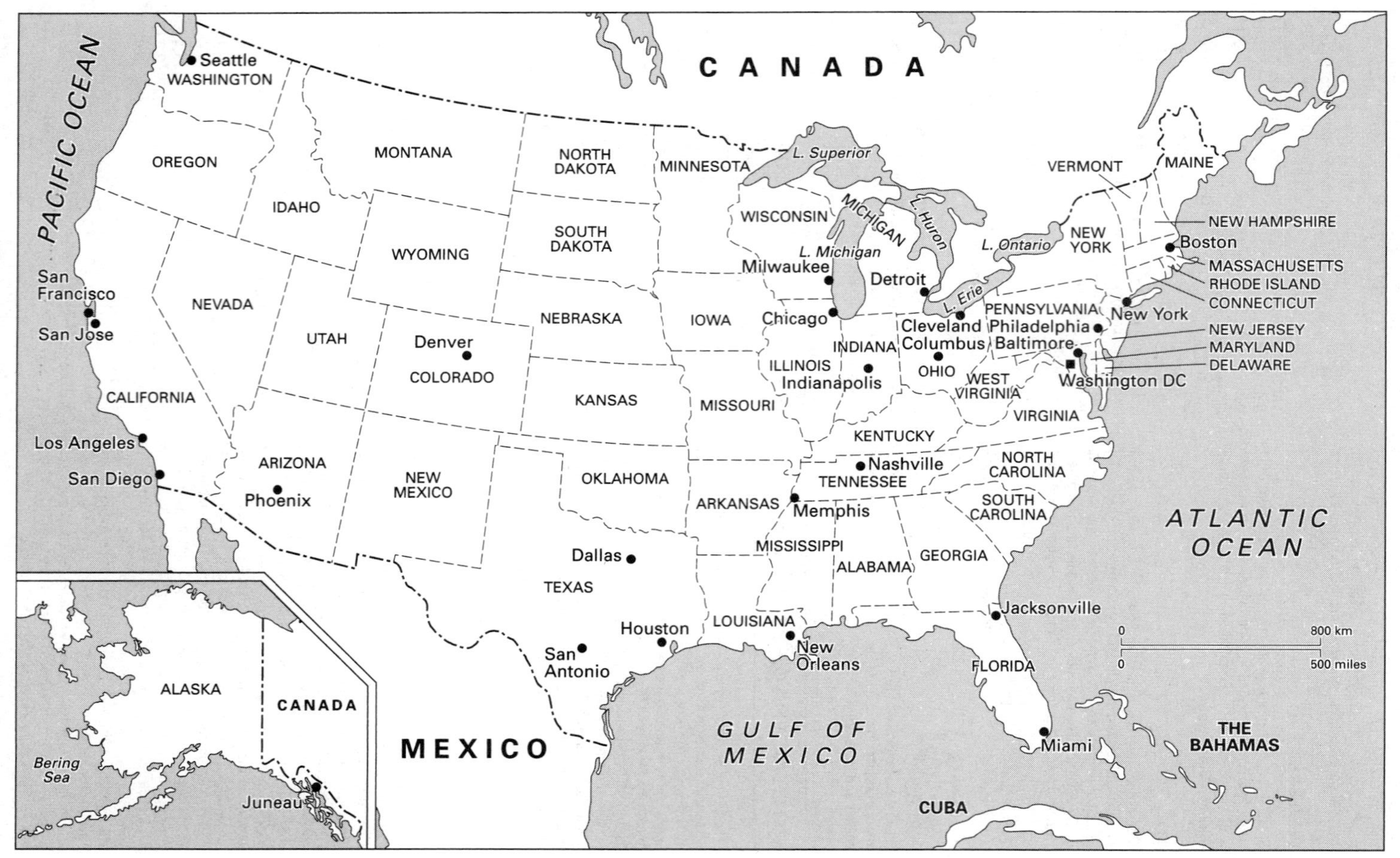
CANADA
PACIFIC OCEAN
ATLANTIC OCEAN
GULF OF MEXICO
MEXICO
THE BAHAMAS
CUBA
0 800 km
0 500 miles
Seattle
WASHINGTON
OREGON
IDAHO
MONTANA
NORTH DAKOTA
MINNESOTA
L. Superior
VERMONT
MAINE
NEW HAMPSHIRE
Boston
MASSACHUSETTS
RHODE ISLAND
CONNECTICUT
WISCONSIN
MICHIGAN
L. Huron
L. Michigan
L. Ontario
NEW YORK
WYOMING
SOUTH DAKOTA
Milwaukee
Detroit
L. Erie
San Francisco
San Jose
NEVADA
UTAH
Denver
COLORADO
NEBRASKA
IOWA
Chicago
PENNSYLVANIA
New York
Cleveland
Philadelphia
NEW JERSEY
INDIANA
Columbus
Baltimore
MARYLAND
ILLINOIS
Indianapolis
OHIO
WEST VIRGINIA
DELAWARE
Washington DC
CALIFORNIA
KANSAS
MISSOURI
VIRGINIA
KENTUCKY
Los Angeles
San Diego
ARIZONA
Phoenix
NEW MEXICO
OKLAHOMA
Nashville
TENNESSEE
NORTH CAROLINA
SOUTH CAROLINA
ARKANSAS
Memphis
MISSISSIPPI
ALABAMA
GEORGIA
Dallas
TEXAS
LOUISIANA
Jacksonville
Houston
San Antonio
New Orleans
FLORIDA
Miami
ALASKA
CANADA
Bering Sea
Juneau

THE STATES OF THE UNION

STATE (with date and *order* of admission)	LAND AREA sq. m.	POPULATION (1990 Census)	CAPITAL	GOVERNOR (term of office in years, and expiry year)	
Alabama (Ala.) (1819) (*22*)	50,767	4,040,587	Montgomery	Harold G. Hunt (*R*)	(4 – 1995)
Alaska (1959) (*49*)	570,833	550,043	Juneau	Walter Hickel (*I*)	(4 – 1994)
Arizona (Ariz.) (1912) (*48*)	113,508	3,665,228	Phoenix	Fife Symington (*R*)	(4 – 1995)
Arkansas (Ark.) (1836) (*25*)	52,078	2,350,725	Little Rock	Bill Clinton (*D*)	(4 – 1995)
California (Calif.) (1850) (*31*)	156,299	29,760,021	Sacramento	Pete Wilson (*R*)	(4 – 1995)
Colorado (Colo.) (1876) (*38*)	103,595	3,294,394	Denver	Roy Romer (*D*)	(4 – 1995)
Connecticut (Conn.)§(1788) (*5*)	4,872	3,287,116	Hartford	Lowell Weicker (*I*)	(4 – 1995)
Delaware (Del.) § (1787) (*1*)	1,932	666,168	Dover	Michael N. Castle (*R*)	(4 – 1993)
Florida (Fla.) (1845) (*27*)	54,153	12,937,926	Tallahassee	Lawton Chiles (*D*)	(4 – 1995)
Georgia (Ga.) § (1788) (*4*)	58,056	6,478,216	Atlanta	Zell Miller (*D*)	(4 – 1995)
Hawaii (1959) (*50*)	6,425	1,108,229	Honolulu	John D. Waihee III (*D*)	(4 – 1994)
Idaho (1890) (*43*)	82,412	1,006,749	Boise	Cecil D. Andrus (*D*)	(4 – 1995)
Illinois (Ill.) (1818) (*21*)	55,645	11,430,602	Springfield	James R. Thompson (*R*)	(4 – 1995)
Indiana (Ind.) (1816) (*19*)	35,932	5,544,159	Indianapolis	Evan Bayh (*D*)	(4 – 1993)
Iowa (1846) (*29*)	55,965	2,776,755	Des Moines	Terry Branstad (*R*)	(4 – 1995)
Kansas (Kan.) (1861) (*34*)	81,778	2,477,574	Topeka	Joan Finney (*D*)	(4 – 1995)
Kentucky (Ky.) (1792) (*15*)	39,669	3,685,296	Frankfort	Wallace G. Wilkinson (*D*)	(4 – 1992)
Louisiana (La.) (1812) (*18*)	44,521	4,219,973	Baton Rouge	Edwin Edwards (*D*)	(4 – 1996)
Maine (Me.) (1820) (*23*)	30,995	1,227,928	Augusta	John R. McKernan, Jr. (*R*)	(4 – 1995)
Maryland (Md.) § (1788) (*7*)	9,837	4,781,468	Annapolis	William D. Schaefer (*D*)	(4 – 1995)
Massachusetts (Mass.) § (1788) (*6*)	7,824	6,016,425	Boston	William Weld (*R*)	(4 – 1995)
Michigan (Mich.) (1837) (*26*)	56,954	9,295,297	Lansing	John Engler (*R*)	(4 – 1995)
Minnesota (Minn.) (1858) (*32*)	79,548	4,375,099	St Paul	Anne Carlson (*R*)	(4 – 1995)
Mississippi (Miss.) (1817) (*20*)	47,233	2,573,216	Jackson	Kirk Fordice (*R*)	(4 – 1996)
Missouri (Mo.) (1821) (*24*)	68,945	5,117,073	Jefferson City	John Ashcroft (*R*)	(4 – 1993)
Montana (Mont.) (1889) (*41*)	145,388	799,065	Helena	Stan Stephens (*R*)	(4 – 1993)
Nebraska (Neb.) (1867) (*37*)	76,644	1,578,385	Lincoln	Ben Nelson (*D*)	(4 – 1995)
Nevada (Nev.) (1864) (*36*)	109,894	1,201,833	Carson City	Robert J. Miller (*D*)	(4 – 1995)
New Hampshire (NH) § (1788) (*9*)	8,993	1,109,252	Concord	Judd Gregg (*R*)	(2 – 1993)
New Jersey (NJ) § (1787) (*3*)	7,468	7,730,188	Trenton	James S. Florio (*D*)	(4 – 1994)
New Mexico (NM) (1912) (*47*)	121,335	1,515,069	Santa Fé	Bruce King (*D*)	(4 – 1995)
New York (NY) § (1788) (*11*)	47,377	17,990,455	Albany	Mario M. Cuomo (*D*)	(4 – 1995)
North Carolina (NC) § (1789) (*12*)	48,843	6,628,637	Raleigh	James G. Martin (*R*)	(4 – 1993)
North Dakota (ND) (1889) (*39*)	69,300	638,800	Bismarck	George A. Sinner (*D*)	(4 – 1993)
Ohio (1803) (*17*)	41,004	10,847,115	Columbus	George Voinovich (*R*)	(4 – 1995)
Oklahoma (Okla.) (1907) (*46*)	68,655	3,145,585	Oklahoma City	David Walters (*D*)	(4 – 1995)
Oregon (Ore.) (1859) (*33*)	96,184	2,842,321	Salem	Neil Goldschmidt (*D*)	(4 – 1995)
Pennsylvania (Pa.) § (1787) (*2*)	44,888	11,881,643	Harrisburg	Robert P. Casey (*D*)	(4 – 1995)
Rhode Island (RI) § (1790) (*13*)	1,055	1,003,464	Providence	Bruce Sundlun (*D*)	(2 – 1993)
South Carolina (SC) § (1788) (*8*)	30,203	3,486,703	Columbia	Carroll A. Campbell, Jr. (*R*)	(4 – 1995)
South Dakota (SD) (1889) (*40*)	75,952	696,004	Pierre	George S. Mickelson (*R*)	(4 – 1995)
Tennessee (Tenn.) (1796) (*16*)	41,155	4,877,185	Nashville	Ned R. McWherter (*D*)	(4 – 1995)
Texas (1845) (*28*)	262,017	16,986,510	Austin	Anne Richards (*D*)	(4 – 1995)
Utah (1896) (*45*)	82,073	1,722,850	Salt Lake City	Norman H. Bangerter (*R*)	(4 – 1993)
Vermont (Vt.) (1791) (*14*)	9,273	562,758	Montpelier	Richard Snelling (*R*)	(2 – 1993)
Virginia (Va.) § (1788) (*10*)	39,704	6,187,358	Richmond	L. Douglas Wilder (*D*)	(4 – 1994)
Washington (Wash.) (1889) (*42*)	66,511	4,866,692	Olympia	Booth Gardner (*D*)	(4 – 1993)
West Virginia (W. Va.) (1863) (*35*)	24,119	1,793,477	Charleston	Gaston Caperton (*D*)	(4 – 1993)
Wisconsin (Wis.) (1848) (*30*)	54,426	4,891,769	Madison	Tommy Thompson (*R*)	(4 – 1995)
Wyoming (Wyo.) (1890) (*44*)	96,989	453,588	Cheyenne	Michael Sullivan (*D*)	(4 – 1995)
Dist. of Columbia (DC) (1791)	63	606,900	—	†	

OUTLYING TERRITORIES AND POSSESSIONS

American Samoa	76	46,773	Pago Pago	Peter Tali Coleman (*D*)	(4 – 1993)
Guam	209	133,152	Agaña	Joseph Ada (*R*)	(4 – 1995)
Northern Mariana Islands	184	43,555	Saipan	Lorenzo I. DeLeon Guerrero (*R*)	(4 – 1994)
Palau	192	15,105	Koror	—	
Puerto Rico	3,421	3,522,037	San Juan	R. Hernandez-Colon (*PDP*)	(4 – 1993)
Virgin Islands	132	101,809	Charlotte Amalie	Alexander Farrelly (*D*)	(4 – 1995)

§The 13 Original States
D Democratic Party; *I* Independent; *PDP* Popular Democratic Party; *R* Republican Party
†The capital territory is governed by Congress through a Commissioner and City Council

REGISTERED BIRTHS AND DEATHS

	1990	1991*
Live births		
Number	4,179,000	4,111,000
Rate per 1,000	16.7	16.2
Deaths		
Number	2,162,000	2,165,00
Rate per 1,000	8.6	8.5

Sample base was 100 per cent
Deaths exclude foetal deaths
Rates are based on the population as estimated on 1 July
*Provisional

MARRIAGE AND DIVORCE

Laws of marriage and of divorce are within the exclusive jurisdiction of each state. Each state legislature enacts its own laws prescribing rules and qualifications pertaining to marriage and its dissolution.

	1990	1991*
Marriages		
Number	2,448,000	2,371,000
Rate per 1,000	9.8	9.4
Divorces (estimated)		
Number	1,175,000	1,187,000
Rate per 1,000	4.7	4.7

Population as estimated on 1 July
*Provisional

LARGEST CITIES 1990 Census

ΨNew York, NY	7,322,564
ΨLos Angeles, California	3,485,398
ΨChicago, Illinois	2,783,726
ΨHouston, Texas	1,630,533
ΨPhiladelphia, Pennsylvania	1,585,577
ΨSan Diego, California	1,110,549
ΨDetroit, Michigan	1,027,974
Dallas, Texas	1,006,877
Phoenix, Arizona	983,403
San Antonio, Texas	935,933
San Jose, California	782,248
*Indianapolis, Indiana	741,952
ΨBaltimore, Maryland	736,014
ΨSan Francisco, California	723,959
*Jacksonville, Florida	672,971
Columbus, Ohio	632,910
ΨMilwaukee, Wisconsin	628,088
Memphis, Tennessee	610,337
Washington, DC	606,900
ΨBoston, Massachusetts	574,283
ΨSeattle, Washington	516,259
El Paso, Texas	515,342
*Nashville-Davidson, Tennessee	510,784
ΨCleveland, Ohio	505,616

Ψ Seaport
*consolidated city

CAPITAL

In 1790 Congress ratified the cession of 100 sq. miles by the states of Maryland and Virginia as a site for a federal city to be the national capital of the United States. In 1791 it was decided to name the capital Washington and in 1793 the foundation-stone of the Capitol building was laid. In 1800 the seat of government was removed to Washington, which was chartered as a city in 1802. In 1846 the Virginia portion was retroceded and the present area of the District of Columbia (with which the City of Washington is considered co-extensive) is 63 sq. miles, with a resident population (mid-1989 estimate) of 604,000.

The District of Columbia is governed by an elected mayor and City Council.

The City of Washington is situated on the west central edge of Maryland, opposite the state of Virginia, on the left bank of the Potomac at its confluence with the Anacostia. The population of the metropolitan area in 1988 was estimated at 3,734,200.

GOVERNMENT

The United States of America is a federal republic consisting of 50 states and the federal District of Columbia and of organized territories. Of the present 50 states, 13 are original states, seven were admitted without previous organization as territories, and 30 were admitted after such organization. Hawaii formally entered the Union as the 50th state on 21 August 1959, and with effect from the following 4 July, the flag of the United States has 13 stripes and 50 stars in nine horizontal rows of six and five alternately.
NATIONAL ANTHEM – The Star-Spangled Banner.
NATIONAL DAY – 4 July (Independence Day).

THE CONSTITUTION

By the Constitution of 17 Sept. 1787 (to which ten amendments were added on 15 Dec. 1791 and 11th to 26th, 8 Jan. 1798, 25 Sept. 1804, 18 Dec. 1865, 28 July 1868, 30 March 1870, 25 Feb. 1913, 31 May 1913, 16 Jan. 1920, 26 Aug. 1920, 6 Feb. 1933, 5 Dec. 1933, 26 Feb. 1951, 29 March 1961, 23 Jan. 1964, 10 Feb. 1967 and 30 June 1971), the government of the United States is entrusted to three separate authorities: the executive, the legislative, and the judicial.

THE EXECUTIVE

The executive power is vested in a President, who is indirectly elected every four years. There is also a Vice-President, who, on the death of the President, becomes President for the remainder of the term. Under the 20th Amendment to the Constitution the terms of the President and Vice-President end at noon on 20 January of the years in which such terms would have ended if the Amendment had not been ratified, and the terms of their successors then begin. In case of the removal or death of both President and Vice-President, a statute provides for the succession. Under the 22nd Amendment to the Constitution, the tenure of the Presidency is limited to two terms.

The President, with the consent of the Senate, appoints the Cabinet officers and all the chief officials.

He makes recommendation of a general nature to Congress, and when laws are passed by Congress he may return them to Congress with a veto. But if a measure so vetoed is again passed by both Houses of Congress by two-thirds majority in each House, it becomes law, notwithstanding the objection of the President. The President must be at least 35 years of age and a native citizen of the United States.

Presidential elections

Each state elects (on the first Tuesday after the first Monday in November of the year preceding the year in which the presidential term expires) a number of electors, equal to the whole number of Senators and Representatives to which the state may be entitled in the Congress. The electors for each state meet in their respective states on the first Monday after the second Wednesday in December following, and vote for a President by ballot. The ballots are then sent to Washington, and opened on 6 January by the President of Senate in presence of Congress. The candidate who has received a majority of the whole number of electoral votes cast is declared President for the ensuing term. If no one has a majority, then from the highest on the list (not exceeding three) the House of Representatives elects a President, the votes being taken by states, the representation from each state having one vote.

President of the United States, George Herbert Walker Bush, *born* 12 June 1924, *sworn in* 20 January 1989. Republican.
Vice-President, Dan Quayle, *born* 4 February 1947, *sworn in* 20 January 1989.

THE CABINET

Acting Secretary of State, Lawrence Eagleburger.
Secretary of the Treasury, Nicholas Brady.
Secretary of Defence, Richard Cheney.
Attorney-General, William Barr.
Secretary of the Interior, Manuel Lujan.
Secretary of Agriculture, Edward Madigan.
Secretary of Commerce, Barbara Fanklin.
Secretary of Labour, Lynn Martin.
Secretary of Health and Human Services, Dr Louis Sullivan.
Secretary of Housing and Urban Development, Jack Kemp.
Secretary of Transportation, Andrew Card.
Secretary of Energy, James Watkins.
Secretary of Education, Andrew Lamar Alexander.
Secretary of Veterans' Affairs, Edward Derwinski.

Other senior positions:
Director of CIA, Robert Gates.
Director, Office of National Drug Control Policy, Bob Martinez.
White House Chief of Staff, James Baker.
National Security Adviser, Brent Scowcroft.
Director, Office of Management and Budget, Richard Darman.
Administrator, Environmental Protection Agency, William Reilly.
US Trade Representative, Carla Hills.

UNITED STATES EMBASSY
24 Grosvenor Square, London W1A 1AE
Tel 071-499 9000

Ambassador Extraordinary and Plenipotentiary, The Honourable Raymond G. H. Seitz (1991).
Minister, Hon. Ronald Woods.
Minister for Economic Affairs, Mrs Ann R. Berry.
Minister Counsellors, Norbert J. Krieg (*Consular Affairs*); Nicholas Baskey (*Administrative Affairs*); Kenneth Moorefield (*Commercial Affairs*); James P. Rudbeck (*Agricultural Affairs*); Bruce G. Burton (*Political Affairs*); Charles E. Courtney (*Public Affairs*).
Defence and Naval Attaché, Capt. Peter Baxter.
Army Attaché, Col. David Smith.
Air Attaché, Col. Chester Garrison.

BRITISH EMBASSY
3100 Massachusetts Avenue NW, Washington DC 20008
Tel: Washington DC 462 1340

Ambassador Extraordinary and Plenipotentiary, His Excellency Sir Robin Renwick, KCMG (1991).
Ministers, D. Peretz (*Economic*); C. V. Balmer (*Defence Equipment*); C. J. R. Meyer, CMG (*Commercial*); W. Marsden, CMG; P. Lo (*Hong Kong Economic and Trade Affairs*).
Head of British Defence Staff and Defence Attaché, Air Vice-Marshal Peter Dodworth, OBE, AFC.
Naval Attaché, Rear-Adm. A. P. Hoddinott, OBE.
Military Attaché, Brig. I. B. R. Fowler.
Air Attaché, Air Cdre S. A. Baldwin, MBE.
Counsellors, R. Ralph, CVO (*Head of Chancery*); A. F. Smith (*Admin. and HM Consul-General*); M. Brown (*Economic*); R. B. Dearlove, OBE; R. M. Graham-Harrison (*Overseas Development*); P. C. Leung (*Hong Kong Commercial Affairs*); R. J. Griffins (*Civil Aviation and Shipping*); D. A. Rolt (*Science, Technology and Energy*); N. W. Browne (*Information*); P. L. Thomas (*Politico/Military*); B. J. Limbert (*Defence Supply*); B. R. Coleman; P. J. Torry (*External Affairs*); R. J. Nicholls; A. P. Vinall (*Trade and Environment*); L. N. Large (*Defence, Science and Equipment*); J. D. Hansen.
Cultural Attaché and British Council Representative, G. Tindale, OBE.

BRITISH CONSULATES-GENERAL – *Atlanta, Boston, Chicago, Houston, Los Angeles, New York* and *San Francisco*.
BRITISH CONSULATES – *Anchorage, Cleveland, Dallas, Kansas City, Miami, New Orleans, Norfolk, Philadelphia, Portland, St Louis, Seattle* and *Puerto Rico*.

BRITISH-AMERICAN CHAMBER OF COMMERCE, 275 Madison Avenue, New York 10016; UK OFFICE, Suite 201, High Holborn, London WC1V 6RR.

THE CONGRESS

The legislative power is vested in two Houses, the Senate and the House of Representatives, the President having a veto power, which may be overcome by a two-thirds vote of each House. The Senate is composed of two Senators from each state, elected by the people thereof for the term of six years, and each Senator has one vote. Representatives are chosen in each State, by popular vote, for two years. The average number of persons represented by each Congressman is one for 575,000.

The Senate consists of 100 members. The House of Representatives consists of 435 Representatives, a resident commissioner from Puerto Rico and a delegate from American Samoa, the District of Columbia, Guam and the Virgin Islands. By the 19th Amendment, sex is no disqualification for the franchise. The Bureau of the Census estimated that there were 185,105,411 persons of voting age, excluding members of the armed forces overseas, as of November 1990.

Members of the 102nd Congress were elected on 8 November 1990. The 102nd Congress is constituted as follows:

Senate – Democrats 57; Republicans 43; total 100.
House of Representatives – Democrats 268; Republicans 166; Independent 1; total 435 (15 June 1992).

President of the Senate, Dan Quayle (*Vice-President of the United States*).
Speaker of the House of Representatives, Thomas S. Foley, *Washington*.
Secretary of the Senate, Walter J. Stewart, *District of Columbia*.
Clerk of the House of Representatives, Donnald K. Anderson, *California*.

THE JUDICATURE

The federal judiciary consists of three sets of federal courts: The Supreme Court at Washington, DC, consisting of a Chief Justice and eight Associate Justices, with original jurisdiction in cases affecting Ambassadors, etc., or where a state is a party to the suit, and with appellate jurisdiction from inferior federal courts and from the judgments of the highest Courts of the states; the United States Courts of Appeals, dealing with appeals from District Courts and from certain federal administrative agencies, and consisting of 168 Circuit Judges within 13 circuits; the 94 United States District Courts served by 575 District Court Judges.

THE SUPREME COURT
US Supreme Court Building, Washington DC 20543

Chief Justice, William H. Rehnquist, *Ariz.*, apptd 1986.

Associate Justices
Byron R. White, *Colo.*, apptd 1962
Harry Blackmun, *Minn.*, apptd 1970
John Paul Stevens, *Ill.*, apptd 1975
Sandra Day O'Connor, *Ariz.*, apptd 1981
Antonin Scalia, *Va.*, apptd 1986
Anthony M. Kennedy, *Calif.*, apptd 1988
David H. Souter, *NH.*, apptd 1990
Clarence Thomas, *Ga.*, apptd 1991

Clerk of the Supreme Court, William K. Suter.

CRIMINAL STATISTICS Number of offences

	1990	1991
Murder and non-negligent manslaughter	23,438	24,700
Forcible rape	102,555	106,590
Robbery	639,271	687,730
Aggravated assault	1,054,863	1,092,740
Burglary	3,073,909	3,157,200
Larceny – theft	7,945,670	8,142,200
Thefts of motor vehicles	1,635,907	1,661,700
Total	14,475,613	14,872,900

DEFENCE

Each military department is separately organized under its own Secretary and functions under the direction, authority and control of the Secretary of Defence.

Commanders of unified and specified commands are responsible to the President and the Secretary of Defence for the accomplishment of military missions assigned to them.

Secretary of Defence (in the Cabinet), Richard B. Cheney.
Secretary of the Army, Michael P. W. Stone.
Secretary of the Navy, H. L. Garrett.
Secretary of the Air Force, D. B. Rice.
Chairman, Joint Chiefs of Staff, Gen. Colin Powell.
Vice-Chairman, Adm. David E. Jeremiah.

COMMANDERS-IN-CHIEF OF UNIFIED COMMANDS

US European Command, Brussels – Gen. John Shalikashvili (*US Army*).
US Southern Command, Quarry Heights, Panama Canal Zone – Gen. George A. Joulwan (*US Army*).
US Atlantic Command, Norfolk, Virginia – Adm. Paul David Miller (*US Navy*).
US Pacific Command, Hawaii. – Adm. Charles R. Larson (*US Navy*).
US Space Command, Gen. Charles Horner (*USAF*).
**US Transportation Command*, Gen. Hansford T. Johnson (*USAF*).
US Special Operations Command, Florida. – Gen. Carl W. Stiner (*US Army*).
US Central Command, Gen. Joseph Hoar (*USMC*).
* A specified command.

Army – The US Army had a strength on 31 March 1992 of 665,643.
Chief of the Staff of the Army, Gen. Gordon R. Sullivan.

Navy – The strength of the Navy on 31 March 1992 was 552,128 active duty personnel.
Chief of Naval Operations, Adm. Frank B. Kelso II.

Marine Corps – Established 1775. Strength on 31 March 1992 was 191,101 active duty personnel.
Commandant, Gen. Carl E. Mundy, jun.

Air – The United States Air Force was established as a separate organization on 18 September 1947. In March 1961 the Air Force was assigned primary responsibility for the Department of Defence space development programmes and projects. On 31 March 1992 there were 498,058 officers and airmen on active duty.
Chief of Staff of the US Air Force, Gen. Merril A. McPeak.

FINANCE

THE BUDGET (US$ billions)

	1990 *actual*	1991 *estimated*
Receipts by source		
Individual income taxes	466.9	467.8
Corporation income taxes	93.5	98.0
Social insurance taxes and contributions	380.1	396.0
Excise taxes	35.3	42.4
Estate and gift taxes	11.5	11.1
Customs duties	16.7	15.9
Miscellaneous	27.3	22.4
TOTAL	1,031.3	1,054.3
Outlays by function		
National defence	299.3	272.5
International affairs	13.8	16.2
Income security	147.3	171.6
Health	57.8	71.2
Medicare	98.1	104.5
Social security	248.6	269.0
Veterans' benefits and services	29.1	31.3
Education, training, employment and social services	38.5	41.5
Commerce and housing credit	67.1	75.6
Transportation	29.5	31.5
Natural resources and environment	17.1	18.7
Energy	2.4	1.7
Community and regional development	8.5	7.4
Agriculture	12.0	14.9
Net interest	184.2	195.0
General science, space and technology	14.4	15.9
General government	10.7	11.4
Administration of justice	10.0	12.3
Undistributed offsetting receipts	−36.6	−39.4
TOTAL	1,251.8	1,322.0

SOCIAL WELFARE EXPENDITURE

Total expenditure by programme (US$ millions)

	1988	1989
Social insurance	434,038	468,055
Education	219,382	238,631
Public aid	118,495	127,475
Health and medical	52,958	56,866
Veterans' programmes	29,254	30,104
Other social welfare	15,479	16,609
Housing	16,556	18,127
TOTAL	886,172	955,866
Expenditure per capita		
Social insurance	US$1,731	US$1,849
Education	878	946
Public aid	474	506
Health and medical	212	226
Veterans' programmes	116	119
Other social welfare	62	66
Housing	66	72
TOTAL	3,540	3,783

PUBLIC DEBT

At the end of September 1991 the total gross federal debt of the United States stood at US$3,598,919 million.

GROSS NATIONAL PRODUCT BY INDUSTRY 1989

	US$ millions
Domestic industries	5,163,200
Private industries	4,561,000
Agriculture, forestry, fisheries	113,500
Mining	80,300
Construction	247,700
Manufacturing	966,000
Durable goods	541,000
Non-durable goods	425,000
Transportation and public utilities	460,900
Transportation	171,500
Communication	133,700
Electric, gas, and sanitary services	155,600
Wholesale trade	339,500
Retail trade	486,000
Finance, insurance, and real estate	896,700
Services	970,500
Government and government enterprises	619,300
Rest of the world	37,600
TOTAL GNP	5,200,800

CURRENCY

The US unit of currency is the dollar ($) of 100 cents.

ECONOMY

AGRICULTURE AND LIVESTOCK

The total number of farms in 1991 was 2,104,560, with a total area of land in farms of 982,576,000 acres, and an average acreage per farm of 467 acres. The total number of people employed on farms during the week of 12–18 January 1992 was 2,572,000, of whom 321,000 were unpaid workers, 703,000 hired workers and 123,000 agricultural service workers.

Principal crops are corn for grain, soybeans, wheat hay, cotton, tobacco, grain sorghums, potatoes, oranges and barley.

Livestock on farms on 1 January 1991 and 1992 was:

	1991	1992
All cattle	98,896,000	100,110,000
Milk cows	10,156,000	9,904,000
Sheep and lambs	11,200,000	10,850,000
Hogs and pigs	54,477,000	56,974,000
Chickens	351,616,000	359,473,000

Gross income from farming in 1991 was US$183,000 million, of which cash receipts from marketing were US$168,000 million and government payments US$8,000 million. Cash income from all crops in 1991 was US$82,000 million and from livestock and livestock products US$86,000 million.

NON-FUEL MINERALS

The value of non-fuel raw mineral production in 1990 totalled an estimated US$33,319 million compared with US$32,225 million in 1989.

Trade	1989	1990
Imports	US$35,537m	US$33,389m
Exports	21,558m	20,868m

Production ('000 metric tons)	1990	1991e
Aluminium	4,048	4,100
Iron Ore	56,400	53,700
Phosphate rock	46,343	47,000
Zinc Ore	515	520
Refined Copper	2,018	2,020
Refined Lead	1,278	1,180

e estimate

ENERGY

Figures expressed in quadrillion (10^{15}) BTU

	1990	1991
Production	67.85	67.49
Coal	22.46	21.55
Natural Gas	18.36	18.42
Crude Oil	15.57	15.61
Consumption	81.29	81.51
Petroleum	33.55	32.72
Coal	19.12	20.16
Natural Gas	19.30	18.81
Imports	18.99	18.35
Crude Oil	12.77	12.55
Petroleum	4.35	3.70
Exports	4.91	5.19
Coal	2.77	2.85

LABOUR

The civilian labour force was 129,002,000 in June 1992. The number of employed persons was 118,907,000. This includes self-employed, wage and salary-earners, and unpaid family workers. Unemployment was estimated at 10,095,000 in June 1992 (7.8 per cent) (6.9 per cent in June 1991).

TRADE

	1989	1990
General imports		
c.i.f. value	US$493,352.0m	US$516,946.1m
customs value	473,396.5	495,259.6
Exports and re-exports		
†f.a.s. value	363,765.5	392,975.8
Trade balance		
f.a.s. exports: c.i.f. imports	−129,586.5	−123,970.3
f.a.s. exports: customs imports	−109,631.0	−102,283.8

† excluding military aid

PRINCIPAL TRADING AREAS/COUNTRIES 1990

Area/Country	*Exports and Re-exports to*	*General Imports from*
Africa	US$7,950.8m	US$16,997.9m
Asia	120,256.8	217,155.2
Japan	48,584.6	93,069.6
Taiwan	11,482.4	23,829.6
Korea, Rep. of	14,398.7	19,287.0
Oceania	9,964.2	6,263.1
Australia	8,534.7	4,792.8
Europe	117,237.4	115,700.5
EC	98,023.5	95,466.3
N. & Central America	121,432.3	132,696.9
Canada	82,966.5	93,780.6
Mexico	28,375.5	30,796.7
S. America	15,612.2	28,172.5

Trade with UK	1990	1991
Imports from UK	£12,998,506,000	£11,340,030,000
Exports to UK	14,357,516,000	13,711,538,000

COMMUNICATIONS

RAILWAYS – Revenue, etc, of Class I line-haul railroads (US$ thousands):

	1988	1989
Operating		
Revenues	27,999,839	27,956,000
Freight	27,154,961	27,956,000
Passenger	84,677	893,300
Total operating expenses	24,889,015	25,038,000
Net working capital	−217,182	−2,119,000
Average number of employees	236,891	228,000

ROADS – In 1990 there were 3.88 million miles of public roads and streets in the United States, of which 3.12 million miles were in rural areas and 757,663 miles were in urban areas. Surfaced roads and streets account for 90.7 per cent of the total.

An estimated total of US$71,573 million was spent in 1990 for roads and streets in the United States. Capital outlay accounts for 49.5 per cent of the total expenditure; 27.6 per cent was spent for maintenance, and 8.9 per cent for administration; 9.7 per cent for highway police and safety; and 4.3 per cent for interest on highway bonds.

In 1990 there were 44,529 deaths caused by motor vehicle accidents. The death rate per 100,000,000 vehicle-miles of travel was 2.07 in 1990 compared with 2.16 in 1989.

SHIPPING – The ocean-going merchant marine of the US on 1 January 1992 consisted of 619 vessels of 1,000 gross tons and over, of which 394 were privately-owned and 225 were government-owned ships. There were 165 ships in the National Defence Reserve Fleet of inactive government-owned vessels.

AIR – According to preliminary figures, United States domestic and international scheduled airlines in 1989 carried 453,000,000 passengers over 432,400,000,000 revenue passenger miles. Air cargo ton-miles were distributed as follows: freight and express 10,275,000,000; and air mail 1,911,000,000.

Total operating revenues of all US scheduled airlines were US$69,141,000,000 in 1989.

Total operating expenses rose to US$67,279,000,000 in 1989. Scheduled operations showed a net operating profit of US$1,868,000,000 in 1989, compared with a net operating profit of US$3,461,000,000 in 1988.

EDUCATION

All the 50 states and the District of Columbia have compulsory school attendance laws. In general, children are obliged to attend school from seven to 16 years of age. Officers of local administrative units, usually known as truant or attendance officers, are charged with enforcing the compulsory attendance laws.

In the autumn of 1991, 47,032,000 children were enrolled in regular elementary and secondary day schools in the United States, of whom 5.17 million or 11.0 per cent attended private schools.

The following percentages of the school-age population were estimated to be enrolled in school in the autumn of 1991: 95 per cent of 5- and 6-year-olds; 100 per cent of 7- to 13-year-olds; 96 per cent of 14- to 17-year-olds, and 38 per cent of 18- to 24-year-olds.

During the 1989–90 school year, the average daily attendance in regular public elementary and secondary day schools was 37,778,512. In the 1989–90 school year 2,320,000 students graduated from regular public high schools and 268,000 graduated from private high school. In addition some 42,000 graduated from evening schools and adult education programmes, and an estimated 410,000 received high school equivalency certificates. Public school teachers numbered 2,357,000, with an average salary of US$31,350.

Most of the revenue for public elementary and secondary school purposes comes from federal, state, and local governments. Less than 0.5 per cent comes from gifts and from tuition and transportation fees. Revenue receipts during 1989–90 amounted to US$207,584,000,000; 6.1 per cent from the federal government, 47.2 per cent from state governments, and 46.6 per cent from local sources. Estimated current expenditure in the 1989–90 school year was US$187,384 million; for sites, buildings, furniture and equipment expenditures, US$17,685 million; for interest on school debt US$3,693 million.

HIGHER EDUCATION

In the autumn of 1991, total enrolment in universities, colleges, professional schools, and two-year schools numbered 14,157,000.

During 1989–90 the major fields for bachelor's degrees were business and management (249,081), social sciences (116,925), education (104,715) and engineering (82,110). First-profession degrees in law (35,567) and medicine (15,454) predominated. Master's degrees were heavily concentrated in education (86,057) and business and management (77,203). The most popular fields of study for doctorates were education (6,922) and engineering (4,965). Total expenditures for colleges and universities during the 1989–90 academic year were US$147,800 million.

Particulars of some of the universities (with opening autumn enrolment figures, 1990) are: *Harvard* (22,851 students, including 10,476 women), founded at Cambridge, Mass. on 28 Oct. 1636, and named after John Harvard of Emmanuel College, Cambridge, England, who bequeathed to it his library and a sum of money in 1638; *Yale* (10,994 students, including 4,847 women), founded at New Haven, Connecticut, in 1701; *Bowdoin*, Brunswick, Me. (founded 1794; 1,399 students including 610 women); *Brown*, Providence, RI (founded 1764; 7,577 students, including 3,527 women); *Columbia*, New York, NY (founded 1754; 18,242 students, including 8,375 women); *Cornell* (founded at Ithaca, NY, 1865; 20,837 students, including 9,008 women); *Dartmouth*, Hanover, NH (founded 1769, 4,859 students, including 2,012 women); *Georgetown*, Washington, DC (founded 1789; 11,525 students, including 5,608 women); *North Carolina*, Chapel Hill, NC (founded in 1789; 23,878 students, including 13,532 women); *Pennsylvania*, Philadelphia, Pa. (founded 1740; 21,868 students, including 9,976 women); *Princeton*, NJ (founded 1746; 6,483 students and 2,533 women); and *William and Mary*, Williamsburg, Va. (founded 1693; 7,672 students, including 4,166 women).

WEIGHTS AND MEASURES

The weights and measures in common use in the United States are of British origin, and date back to the American Revolution when practically all the standards were intended to be equivalent to those used in England at that period. Divergencies in these weights and measures were, however, quite common and because of these discrepancies the system of weights and measures in the United States (US inch-pound system) is not identical with the British system.

The US ton (short) = 2,000 pounds (British Imperial ton = 2,240 pounds, or 1 US long ton). The US gallon = 231 cubic inches (277.42 cubic inches in UK) or 128 fluid ounces (160 fluid ounces in UK). In the British system the units of dry measure are the same as those of liquid measure. In the United States these two are not the same, the gallon and its subdivisions being used in the measurement of liquids, while the bushel, with its subdivisions, is used in the measurement of certain dry commodities. The US gallon is divided into 4 liquid quarts and the US bushel into 32 dry quarts.

In 1975 the US Congress passed the Metric Conversion Act to co-ordinate and plan the increasing use of the metric system in the USA. In 1988 the Omnibus Trade and Competitiveness Act amended the original Metric Conversion Act and designated the metric system as the preferred system of weights and measures for US trade and commerce. It also required that all federal agencies use the metric system in their activities, except where economically unfeasible or likely to cause loss of markets to US firms. The US Department of Commerce's metric programme at the National Institute of Standards and Technology works with the Federal Interagency Council on Metric Policy to identify and help remove barriers that may stand in the way of metric conversion in federal and state or local government rules, standards and codes, and regulations.

US TERRITORIES, ETC

The territories and the principal islands and island groups under the sovereignty of the USA are the Commonwealth of Puerto Rico, the Commonwealth of the Northern Mariana Islands, and the following territories: Guam, American Samoa, US Virgin Islands, Johnston Atoll, Midway Islands, Wake Islands.

Johnston Atoll (formerly Johnston and Sand Islands) comprises two small islands, less than 1 sq. mile in area, to the south-west of Hawaii which are administered by the US Air Force. The two Midway Islands (area, 3 sq. miles), at the western end of the Hawaiian chain, are administered by the US Navy. The Wake Islands have an area of about 3 sq. miles and an average elevation of less than 3 metres. They lie about 2,300 miles west of Hawaii and are administered by the US Air Force.

Under the terms of a Treaty of Friendship between the United States and Kiribati, signed in 1979 and subsequently ratified by the US Senate, the United States renounced its claim to Canton and Enderbury Islands.

There are certain small guano islands, rocks, or keys which, in pursuance of action taken under the Act of Congress, 18 August 1856, subsequently embodied in Sections 5570–8 of the Revised Statutes are considered as appertaining to the United States. Responsibility for territorial affairs generally is centred in the Office of the Assistant Secretary, Territorial and International Affairs, Department of the Interior, Washington DC.

THE COMMONWEALTH OF PUERTO RICO

Puerto Rico (Rich Port) is an island of the Greater Antilles group in the West Indies, and lies between 17° 50′ and 18° 30′ N. lat. and 65° 30′ and 67° 15′ W. long., with a total area of 3,421 sq. miles (8,860 sq. km), and a population (1990 Census) of 3,522,037. The majority of the inhabitants are of Spanish descent and Spanish is the official language. The island is about 111 miles from west to east, and 36 miles from north to south.

Puerto Rico was discovered in 1493 by Christopher Columbus and explored by Ponce de Léon in 1508. It continued as a Spanish possession until 18 October 1898, when the United States took formal possession as a result of the Spanish-American War. It was ceded by Spain to the United States by the treaty ratified on 11 April 1899.

The Constitution approved by the Congress and the President of the United States, which came into force on 25 July 1952, establishes the Commonwealth of Puerto Rico with full powers of local government. Legislative functions are vested in the Legislative Assembly, which consists of two elected houses; the Senate of 27 members (two from each of eight senatorial districts and 11 at large) and the House of Representatives of 51 members (one from each of 40 representative districts and 11 at large). Membership of each house may be increased slightly to accommodate minority representatives. The term of the Legislative Assembly is four years. The selection of the Secretary of State must be approved also by the House of Representatives.

The Governor is popularly elected for a term of four years. A Supreme Court of seven members is appointed by the Governor, with the advice and consent of the Senate. The Governor appoints all judges. Residents of Puerto Rico are US citizens. Puerto Rico is represented in Congress by a Resident Commissioner, elected for a term of four years, who has a seat in the House of Representatives, but not a vote, although he has a right to vote on those committees of which he is a member.

Preliminary 1983 figures for the Commonwealth Government's budget were Receipts, US$4,948 million (of which US$1,180 million were transfers from the Federal Government) and Expenditures, US$4,111 million (including payments of US$135 million to the Federal Government). Manufacturing added US$5,765 million to net Commonwealth income in 1983 (preliminary figures), trade US$1,743 million, finance, insurance and real estate US$1,841 million and agriculture US$435 million. Principal crops are sugar cane, coffee, vegetables, fruits and tobacco. Most valuable areas of manufacturing are chemicals and allied products, metal products and machinery. Public and private schools are established throughout: enrolment in 1985–6 was 686,914. Enrolment in private colleges and universities for 1985–6 was 98,402.

CAPITAL – ΨSan Juan, population of the municipality (1984), 1,816,300; Other major towns are: ΨPonce (234,500); ΨMayagüez (209,800); and ΨArecibo (163,300).

Governor, Rafael Hernández Colón.

TRADE

	1985	1986
Total Imports	US$10,113m	US$10,108m
Total Exports	10,543m	11,588m

Trade with UK	1990	1991
Imports from UK	£69,593,000	£81,637,000
Exports to UK	123,087,000	109,295,000

GUAM

Guam, the largest of the Ladrone or Mariana Islands in the north Pacific Ocean, lies in 13° 26′ N. lat. and 144° 39′ E. long., at a distance of about 1,506 miles east of Manila. The area of the island is estimated at 209 sq. miles (541 sq. km), with an estimated population (1990) of 133,152.

The Guamanians are of Chamorro stock mingled with Filipino and Spanish blood. The Chamorro language belongs to the Malayo-Polynesian family, but with considerable admixture of Spanish. Chamorro and English are the official languages and most residents are bilingual.

Guam was occupied by the Japanese in December 1941 but was recaptured and occupied throughout by US forces before the end of July 1944. Under the Organic Act of Guam of 1 August 1950, Guam has statutory powers of self-government, and Guamanians are United States citizens. A 21-member unicameral legislature is elected biennially. The Governor and Lieutenant-Governor are popularly elected. A non-voting Delegate is elected to serve in the US House of Representatives. There is also a District Court of Guam, with original jurisdiction in cases under federal law.

Guam's two main sources of revenue are tourism and US military spending.

CAPITAL – Agaña. Port of entry, ΨApra.

Governor, Joseph F. Ada.
Lt.-Governor, Frank Blas.

AMERICAN SAMOA

American Samoa consists of the island of Tutuila, Anu'u, Ofu, Olesega, Ta'u, Rose and Swains Islands, with a total area of 76 sq. miles (197 sq. km) and an estimated population of 46,773 in 1990.

Tutuila, the largest of the group, has an area of 52 square miles and contains a magnificent harbour at Pago Pago, the capital. The remaining islands have an area of about 24 square miles. Tuna and copra are the chief exports.

American Samoans are US nationals, but some have acquired citizenship through service in the United States armed forces or other naturalization procedure.

The 1960 Constitution grants American Samoa a measure of self-government, with certain powers reserved to the US Secretary of the Interior. There is a bicameral legislature with popularly elected Representatives and Governors and a popularly elected Governor. A non-voting Delegate is elected to serve in the US House of Representatives.

The constitution of American Samoa designates the village of Fagatogo as the seat of government.

Governor, Peter Tali Coleman.
Lt.-Governor, Galea'i Poumele.

THE VIRGIN ISLANDS

Purchased by the United States from Denmark for the sum of US$25 million, and proclaimed 25 January 1917. The total area of the islands is 132 sq. miles (342 sq. km), with a population (1990) of 101,809. There are three main islands, St Thomas (28 sq. miles), St Croix (84 sq. miles), St John (20 sq. miles) and about 50 small islets or cays, mostly uninhabited.

The government of the Virgin Islands is organized under the provisions of the Revised Organic Act of the Virgin Islands, enacted by the Congress of the United States on 22 July 1954. Legislative power is vested in the Legislature, a unicameral body composed of 15 senators popularly elected for two-year terms. Virgin Islanders are citizens of the United States. From the elections of November 1970, the Governor has been popularly elected. A non-voting Delegate is elected to serve in the US House of Representatives. A referendum is to take place at a future date to determine the future political status of the islands.

The Virgin Islands are now a favourite tourist area in the Caribbean.

CAPITAL – ΨCharlotte Amalie on St Thomas. Population (1980) 11,756.

Governor, Alexander Farrelly.
Lt.-Governor, Derek M. Hodge.

NORTHERN MARIANA ISLANDS

The land area of the Northern Mariana Islands is 184 sq. miles (476 sq. km) with an estimated population (1990) of 43,555. Saipan, the government seat and commerce centre, has an estimated population of 39,090 (1990).

A law enacted by Congress on 24 March 1976 provides a Covenant to establish a Commonwealth of the Northern Mariana Islands. The provisions of the Covenant became fully effective upon termination of the Trusteeship Agreement on 3 November 1986. Most of the residents became US citizens. There is a popularly elected bicameral legislature and a popularly elected Governor.

Governor, Lorenzo D. L. Guerrero.
Lt.-Governor, Benjamin M. Manglona.

REPUBLIC OF PALAU

Palau consists of more than 200 Pacific Ocean islands of which eight are permanently inhabited. The Palau archipelago stretches over 400 miles. The land area is 191 sq. miles (494 sq. km), with an estimated population of 15,105. The major island is Koror with a population of 10,493.

Palau and the USA signed a Compact of Free Association in August 1982, which, when approved by a three-quarters majority of the voters of Palau, will recognize the Republic of Palau as a self-governing state. The USA is responsible for financial support, and for the defence of Palau for 50 years. The Compact is incompatible with the ban on nuclear weapons in the constitution. The status of Palau remains unclear.

Constitutional government was installed in Palau in January 1981 and provides for a bicameral legislature. The President and Vice-President are directly elected.

President, Ngiratkel Etpison.
Vice-President, Kuniwo Nakamura.

THE PANAMA CANAL

As a result of the Panama Canal Treaty 1977, the Canal Zone was disestablished, with all areas of land and water within the former Canal Zone reverting to Panama with effect from 1 October 1979. Under the treaty, the United States is allowed the use of operating areas for the Panama Canal, together with several military bases, although the Republic of Panama is sovereign in all such areas. The Panama Canal Commission, an arm of the US Government, will continue to operate the canal until the year 2000.

The canal is fifty statute miles long (44.08 nautical miles), and the channel is from 500 to 1,000 feet wide at the bottom. It contains 12 locks in twin flights; three steps at Gatun on the Atlantic side, one step at Pedro Miguel and two at Miraflores on the Pacific side. Each lock chamber is 1,000 feet long and 110 feet wide. Transit from sea to sea takes on average eight to ten hours. The least width is in Gaillard Cut, and the greatest in Gatun Lake.

TOTAL OCEAN GOING COMMERCIAL TRAFFIC

Fiscal year	*No. of transits*	*Canal net tons*	*Cargo tons*
1987	12,230	186,488,707	148,690,380
1988	12,234	191,566,065	156,482,641
1989	11,989	185,825,532	151,636,113
1990	11,941	181,689,790	157,072,979
1991	12,572	191,786,895	162,695,886

VANUATU
Ripablik Blong Vanuatu

AREA, ETC – Vanuatu, the former Anglo-French Condominium of the New Hebrides, is situated in the South Pacific Ocean, between 13° and 21° S. and 166° and 170° E. It includes 13 large and some 70 small islands, of coral and volcanic origin, including the Banks and Torres Islands in the north, and has a total land area of 4,706 sq. miles (12,190 sq. km). The principal islands are Vanua Lava, Espiritu Santo, Maewo, Pentecost, Ambae, Malekula,

Ambrym, Epi, Efate, Erromango, Tanna and Aneityum. Most islands are mountainous and there are active volcanoes on several. The climate is oceanic tropical, moderated by the south-east trade winds which blow between May and October. At other times winds are variable and cyclones may occur. Temperatures range between 17° C and 28° C, with annual rainfall averaging 90 in. to the south and 155 in. to the north.

POPULATION – The results of a national census which took place in May 1989 show a population of 142,900. About 95 per cent of the population are Melanesian, the rest being made up largely of Micronesians, Polynesians and Europeans. The national language is Bislama, but English and French are also official languages.

SEAT OF ADMINISTRATION – ΨPort Vila, Efate, population (1989) 19,400. The only other town is Luganville (population, 1989, 6,900), on Espiritu Santo.

CURRENCY – Vatu of 100 centimes.

FLAG – Red over green with a black triangle in the hoist, the three parts being divided by fimbriations of black and yellow, and in the centre of the black triangle a boar's tusk overlaid by two crossed fern leaves.

NATIONAL ANTHEM – Nasonal sing sing blong Vanuatu.

NATIONAL DAY – 30 July (Independence Day).

GOVERNMENT

The Anglo-French Condominium of the New Hebrides became an independent republic within the Commonwealth under the name of Vanuatu on 30 July 1980.

Parliament consists of 46 members elected for a term of four years. A Council of Chiefs advises on matters of custom. Executive power is held by the Prime Minister (elected from and by parliament) and a Council of Ministers who are responsible to parliament. The President is elected for a five-year term by the presidents of the 11 regional councils and the members of parliament.

HEAD OF STATE

President, His Excellency Frederick Karlomuana Timakata, *elected* 1989.

COUNCIL OF MINISTERS as at July 1992

Prime Minister and Minister of Public Service, Planning and Statistics, Police, Media and Language Services, Hon. Maxime Carlot Korman.

Deputy Prime Minister and Minister for Justice, Culture and Women's Affairs, Hon. Sethy John Regenvanu.

Home Affairs, Hon. Charlie Nako.

Finance, Commerce, Industry and Tourism, Hon. Willie Jimmy.

Foreign Affairs, External Trade and Immigration, Hon. Serge Vohor.

Transport, Public Works, Ports and Marine and Urban Water Supply, Hon. Amos Bangabiti.

Natural Resources, Hon. Paul Telukluk.

Education, Hon. Romain Batick.

Health and Rural Water Supply, Hon. Hilda Lini.

Agriculture, Livestock, Forestry and Fisheries, Hon. Onneyn Tahi.

Postal Services, Telecommunications and Meteorology, Dr Edward Tambisari.

Chief Justice, Charles Vaudin D'Imecourt.

Attorney-General, Julian Marc Ala.

High Commissioner to Great Britain, Thomas Duggin (resident in Port Vila, Vanuatu).

BRITISH HIGH COMMISSION
PO Box 567, Port Vila
Tel: Vila 23100

High Commissioner, His Excellency T. J. Duggin (1992).

ECONOMY

Most of the population is employed on plantations or in subsistence agriculture. Subsistence crops include yams, taro, manioc, sweet potato and breadfruit; principal cash crops are copra, cocoa and coffee. Large numbers of cattle are kept on the plantations and beef is the second largest export after copra.

Principal exports are copra, meat (frozen, tinned and chilled), timber and cocoa.

Tourism is an important revenue earner, and the absence of direct taxation has led to growth in the finance and associated industries.

Trade with UK	1990	1991
Imports from UK	£1,796,000	£381,000
Exports to UK	47,000	202,000

VATICAN CITY STATE

Stato della Città del Vaticano

The office of the ecclesiastical head of the Roman Catholic Church (Holy See) is vested in the Pope, the Sovereign Pontiff. For many centuries the Sovereign Pontiff exercised temporal power, but by 1870 the Papal States had become part of unified Italy. The temporal power of the Pope was in suspense until the treaty of 11 February 1929, which recognized the full and independent sovereignty of the Holy See in the City of the Vatican. The area of the Vatican City is 108 acres and its population in 1989 was about 1,000.

CURRENCY – Italian currency is legal tender.

FLAG – Square flag; equal vertical bands of yellow (next staff), and white; crossed keys and triple crown device on white band.

NATIONAL DAY – 22 October (Inauguration of present Pontiff).

Sovereign Pontiff, His Holiness Pope John Paul II (Karol Wojtyla), *born* at Wadowice (Krakow, Poland), 18 May 1920, *elected* Pope (in succession to Pope John Paul I), 16 Oct. 1978.

Secretary of State, Cardinal Angelo Sodano, *appointed* December 1990.

APOSTOLIC NUNCIATURE
54 Parkside, London SW19 5NF
Tel 081–946 1410

Apostolic Pro Nuncio, His Excellency Archbishop Luigi Barbarito (1986).

Counsellor, Mgr Ramiro Ingles Moliner.

BRITISH EMBASSY TO THE HOLY SEE
91 Via Condotti, I-00187 Rome
Tel: Rome 678 9462

Ambassador Extraordinary and Plenipotentiary, His Excellency Andrew Eustace Palmer, CMG, CVO (1991).

First Secretary, F. A. Doherty.

TRADE WITH UK

	1990	1991
Imports from UK	£461,000	£955,000
Exports to UK	16,000	6,000

VENEZUELA
La Republica de Venezuela

AREA AND POPULATION – A South American republic, situated approximately between 0° 45′ S. lat. and 12° 12′ N. lat. and 59° 45′ and 73° 09′ W. long., Venezuela consists of one Federal District, 20 states and two territories. It has a total area of 352,144 sq. miles (912, 050 sq. km) and a population (UN estimate 1990) of 19,735,000.

Venezuela lies on the north of the South American continent, and is bounded on the north by the Caribbean Sea, west by Colombia, east by Guyana, and south by Brazil. Included in the area of the republic are 72 islands off the coast, with a total area of about 14,650 square miles, the largest being Margarita, which is politically associated with Tortuga, Cubagua and Coche to form the state of Nueva Esparta. Margarita has an area of about 400 square miles.

The Eastern Andes from the south-west cross the border and reach to the Caribbean coast, where they are prolonged by the Maritime Andes of Venezuela to the Gulf of Paria on the north-east. The main range is known as the Sierra Nevada de Merida, and contains the highest peaks in the country in Pico Bolivar (16,411 feet) and Picacho de la Sierra (15,420 feet). Near the Brazilian border the Sierras Parima and Pacaraima, and on the eastern border the Sierras de Rincote and de Usupamo, enclose the republic with parallel northward spurs, between which are valleys of the Orinoco tributaries.

The principal river is the Orinoco, with innumerable affluents, the main river exceeding 1,600 miles in length from its rise in the southern highlands of the republic to its outflow in the deltaic region of the north-east. The upper waters of the Orinoco are united with those of the Rio Negro (a Brazilian tributary of the Amazon) by a natural river or canal, known as the Casiquiare.

The coastal regions of Venezuela are much indented and contain many lagoons and lakes, of which Maracaibo, with an area of 8,296 square miles, is the largest lake in South America.

The climate is tropical and, except where modified by altitude or tempered by sea breezes, is unhealthy, particularly in the coastal regions and in the neighbourhood of lowland streams and lagoons. The hot, wet season lasts from April to October, the dry, cooler season from November to March.

LANGUAGE – Spanish is the language of the country.

CAPITAL – Caracas, population 2,784,000. Other principal towns are ΨMaracaibo (1,364,000), Barquisimeto (602,000), Valencia (903,000), Maracay (354,000), San Cristobal (230,000), Cumaná (212,000) and Ciudad Guayana (536,506).

CURRENCY – Bolivar (BS) of 100 céntimos.

FLAG – Three horizontal stripes of yellow, blue, red with an arc of seven white stars on the blue stripe.

NATIONAL ANTHEM – Gloria Al Bravo Pueblo (Glory to the brave people).

NATIONAL DAY – 5 July.

GOVERNMENT

The Republic of Venezuela gained independence from Spain in 1830. According to the 1961 Constitution, executive power is held by the President, who also appoints the Council of Ministers. Legislative power is exercised by a bicameral National Congress, comprising a 196-member Chamber of Deputies and a Senate of 49 elected members plus the former Presidents of constitutional governments as life members. The President and National Congress are directly elected for concurrent five-year terms. The most recent elections were held in December 1988.

HEAD OF STATE

President, Carlos Andrés Pérez, *elected* 4 Dec. 1988, *inaugurated*, 2 Feb. 1989.

COUNCIL OF MINISTERS as at July 1992

Interior, Luis Piñerúa Ordaz.
Foreign Affairs, Dr Humberto Calderón Berti.
Finance, Dr Pedro Rosas Bravo.
Defence, Gen. Fernando Ochoa Antich.
Transport and Communications, Dr Fernando Martínez Mottola.
Urban Development, Dr Diógenes Mujica.
Energy and Mines, Dr Alirio Parra.
Environment and Natural Resources, Enrique Colmenares Finol.
Health and Social Welfare, Dr Rafael Orihuela.
Agriculture and Livestock, Jonathan Coles.
Education, Dr Pedro Augusto Beauperthuy.
Labour, Jesús Rubín Rodríguez.
The Family, Teresa Alvanes.
Justice, Dr José Mendoza Angulo.
Presidential Secretariat, Dr Celestino Armas.
Science and Technology, Dulce Arnao de Uzcátegui.
Culture, José Antonio Abreu.
Co-ordination and Planning, Miguel Rodríguez.
Minister, President of the Venezuelan Investment Fund, Dr José Ignacio Moreno León.
Development, Dr Pedro Vallenilla.

VENEZUELAN EMBASSY
1 Cromwell Road, London SW7 2HW
Tel 071-584 4206/7

Ambassador Extraordinary and Plenipotentiary, His Excellency Dr Ignacio Arcaya (1992).

BRITISH EMBASSY
Apartado 1246, Caracas 1010-A
Tel: Caracas 7511022

Ambassador Extraordinary and Plenipotentiary, His Excellency Giles Eden FitzHerbert, CMG (1987).
Counsellor, M. Hickson (*Deputy Head of Mission*).
Defence Attaché, Capt. R. L. Perrett, RN.

There are British Consular Offices at *Caracas, Maracaibo* and *Mérida*.

BRITISH COUNCIL REPRESENTATIVE, J. A. Coope, OBE.

BRITISH-VENEZUELAN CHAMBER OF COMMERCE, Apartado 5713, Caracas 1010. Torre Británica, Piso 11, Letra E, Av. José Félix Sosa, Altamira Sur, Caracas 1060.

EDUCATION

Education is free and compulsory between the ages of seven and 13. There are ten universities in Venezuela, five in Caracas and the others in Maracaibo, Mérida, Valencia, Cumaná and Barquisimeto.

ECONOMY

Products of the tropical forest region include orchids, wild rubber, timber, mangrove bark, balata gum and tonka beans; of agricultural areas, cocoa beans, coffee, cotton, rice, maize, sugar, sesame, groundnuts, potatoes, tomatoes, other vegetables, sisal and tobacco. There is an extensive beef and dairy farming industry. Despite substantial improvements in agriculture, Venezuela is heavily reliant upon food imports, which constitute about 60 per cent of total consumption. The government has embarked on a policy of economic reform and privatization.

The principal industry is that of petroleum, which in 1986 contributed 83 per cent of Venezuela's foreign exchange income. Daily production in the oilfields (nationalized 1976) has steadily declined since 1973 in line with Venezuela's conservation policies, reaching 1.7m b.p.d. in 1986 (compared with 3.366m in 1973) but has since recovered to around 2.5m. There are refineries at Punta Cardon, Amuay, Caripitó, San Lorenzo, Puerto La Cruz, Tucupeido, El Chaure and El Palito. Development of the Orinoco heavy oil belt is now moving ahead with the inauguration of the Lagovén continuous steam injection pilot plant at El Jobo in southern Monagas. It has been estimated conservatively that there might exist recoverable resources of 70,000 million barrels in the Orinoco region.

Aluminium is the second highest source of foreign exchange after petroleum. The Venezuelan state now holds the majority stake in both the principal producing companies, Venalum and Alcasa, and is moving towards a consolidation of the aluminium industry, with both companies sharing their resources and adopting general policies of marketing and procurement of supplies.

Rich iron ore deposits in eastern Venezuela have been developed. The government-owned steel mill at Matanzas in the Guayana uses local iron ore and obtains its electric power from hydro-electric installations on the Caroni River. It produces seamless steel tubes, billets, wire and profiles. A mill at Ciudad Guayana for the production of centrifugally-cast iron pipe came into operation at the end of 1970, with an annual capacity of 30,000 tons.

Other industries include petrochemicals, gold, diamonds and asbestos; textiles, clothing and footwear; plastics; manufacture or preparation of foodstuffs, alcoholic and non-alcoholic beverages; manufacture of paper, cement, glass, tyres, cigarettes, soap, animal feeding concentrates, simple steel products, tins, jewellery, rope, furniture, sacks, paint and motor-vehicle assembly; preparation of pharmaceutical goods; pearl fishing, sanitary ware, electric home appliances, pumps, toys, agricultural machinery, bicycles, electronic components, cosmetics and many others.

TRADE

	1987	1988
Total imports	US$8,711m	US$10,472m
Total exports	10,843m	10,365m

Trade with UK	1990	1991
Imports from UK	£204,921,000	£166,654,000
Exports to UK	101,717,000	100,210,000

COMMUNICATIONS

There are about 62,449 km of roads, 22,975 km of them paved. The state has now acquired all but a very few of the railway lines, whose total length is only some 372 kilometres. Road and river communications have made railways of negligibile importance in Venezuela except for carrying iron ore in the south-east. However, the government is restoring the Puerto Cabello-Barquisimeto line and expanding it to Turén in the agricultural heartland of Venezuela. A new line connecting Caracas with La Guaira and the Litoral is planned, and in 1983 the Caracas Metro came into operation.

The Orinoco is navigable for large steamers from its mouth for 700 miles, and by smaller vessels as far as the Maipures cataract, some 200 miles farther up-stream. Dredging operations have opened the Orinoco to ocean-going ships, of up to 40 ft. draught, as far as Ciudad Guayana (about 150 miles up-stream). Foreign vessels are not permitted to engage in the coast trade.

British, US and European airlines provide Venezuela with a wide range of services. There are three Venezuelan airlines which between them have a comprehensive network of internal lines and also connect Caracas with the United States, Central and South America, the Caribbean and Europe.

The telegraph, radio-telegraph and radio-telephone services are state-owned. There are four television stations in Venezuela, all in Caracas. Two are government controlled.

VIETNAM

Công Hòa Xã Hôi Chu Nghĩa Viêt Nam

Vietnam, with an area of 127,242 sq. miles (329,556 sq. km), and an estimated population (UN 1990) of 66,200,000, is bordered on the north by China and the west by Laos and Cambodia.

CAPITAL – Hanoi, population (1989) 1,089,000. Other cities are Ho Chi Minh City (3,169,000) and Hai Phong (456,000).

CURRENCY – Dông of 10 hao or 100 xu.

FLAG – Red, with yellow five-point star in centre.

NATIONAL ANTHEM – Tien Quan Ca (The troops are advancing).

NATIONAL DAY – 2 September.

GOVERNMENT

Following the end of the war in Vietnam in 1975, and the establishment of a Provisional Revolutionary Government to administer South Vietnam, a National Assembly representing the whole of Vietnam was elected on 25 April 1976. The Assembly met in Hanoi on 24 June, and on 2 July approved the reunification of North and South Vietnam under the name of the Socialist Republic of Vietnam. The national flag, anthem and capital of North Vietnam were unanimously adopted for the Socialist Republic, and Saigon was renamed Ho Chi Minh City.

Effective power lies with the ruling party, the Vietnamese Communist Party (VCP), its highest executive body being the Central Committee, elected by a Party Congress on a national basis. The Seventh Party Congress of the VCP in June 1991 elected a new Central Committee. It is the Politburo and the Secretariat of the Central Committee which exercises real power and rules Vietnam.

A new constitution was adopted in June 1992 which reaffirmed Communist Party rule but also formalized free market economic reforms. The powers of the President are to be significantly increased and the Council of Ministers is to be replaced by a Prime Minister and Cabinet. A new National Assembly was elected in August 1992 which will convene in September and October 1992 to elect a President and confirm the appointment of a Prime Minister and Cabinet.

HEAD OF STATE

President, General Secretary of VCP, Do Muoi.

COUNCIL OF MINISTERS as at August 1992

Chairman, Vo Van Kiet.
First Vice-Chairman, Phan Van Khai.
Vice-Chairmen, Nguyen Kanh; Tran Duc Luong.
National Defence, Doan Khue.
Foreign Affairs, Nguyen Manh Cam.
Interior, Bui Thieu Ngo.
Chairman of the State Planning Commission, Do Quoc Sam.

Chairman of the State Commission for Co-operation and Investment, Dao Ngoc Xuan.
Finance, Ho Te.
Governor of the State Bank, Cao Sy Kiem.
Commerce and Tourism, Le Van Triet.
Labour, War Invalids and Social Affairs, Tran Dinh Hoan.
Construction, Ngo Xuan Loc.
Communications, Transport and Posts and Telegraphs, Bui Danh Luu.
Heavy Industry, Tran Lum.
Energy, Vu Ngoc Hai.
Light Industry, Dang Vu Chu.
Agriculture, Nguyen Cong Tan.
Forestry, Phan Xuan Dot.
Water Conservancy, Nguyen Canh Dinh.
Marine Products, Nguyen Tien Trinh.
Culture, Information and Sports, Tran Hoan.
Public Health, Pham Song.
Education and Training, Tran Hong Quan.
Justice, Nguyen Dinh Loc.
Population and Family Planning, Mai Ky.

VIETNAMESE COMMUNIST PARTY

Politburo of the Central Committee, Do Muoi (*General Secretary*); Le Duc Anh; Voa Van Kiet; Dao Duy Tung; Doan Khue; Vu Oanh; Le Phuoc Tho; Pham Van Kai; Bui Thien Ngo; Nong Duc Manh; Phan The Duyet; Nguyen Duc Binh; Vo Tran Chi (*full members*).

EMBASSY OF THE SOCIALIST REPUBLIC OF VIETNAM
12–14 Victoria Road, London W8 5RD
Tel 071–937 1912

Ambassador Extraordinary and Plenipotentiary, His Excellency Chau Phong (1990).

BRITISH EMBASSY
16 Pho Ly Thuong Kiet, Hanoi
Tel: Hanoi 4252510

Ambassador Extraordinary and Plenipotentiary, His Excellency Peter Keegan Williams (1990).

ECONOMY

During recent years, Vietnam's economy has faced considerable problems. These include serious agricultural losses because of adverse weather, attempts to collectivize agriculture in the south, major reductions in western aid (as a result of Vietnam's invasion and occupation of neighbouring Cambodia), border hostilities with China, and the continued allocation of resources to military expenditure. Efforts to integrate the economies of the north and south have not been very successful.

Vietnam's overall economic position is not good. Vietnam has been in default of repayments to the international banking world from the IMF to major commercial and merchant banks and therefore has received very few long term credits. Some attempted reforms of the economic system in 1985, including devaluation and a currency change, had adverse effects and inflation increased rapidly in late 1985 and early 1986. Assistance from Russia (formerly the Soviet Union) (estimated at US$2.3 billion p.a. in 1987) has declined sharply. However, economic reforms were instituted in the wake of the Sixth Party Congress (1986) and have begun to take effect. Inflation is down to single figures per month; the exchange rate has been rationalized, subsidies removed and much greater economic activity allowed. The effective creation of free market conditions for agricultural production and petty trading since 1989 has led to a significant improvement in agricultural production, with Vietnam becoming a major rice exporter. Foreign investment is being actively encouraged and is beginning to have effect but the amount of western and international agency investment and aid will remain limited until Vietnam and the United States resolve their differences and resume full diplomatic relations.

TRADE WITH UK

	1990	1991
Imports from UK	£5,802,000	£6,916,000
Exports to UK	1,443,000	6,440,000

WESTERN SAMOA

Malotuto'atasi o Samoa i Sisifo

AREA, ETC – Western Samoa lies in the south Pacific Ocean between latitudes 13° and 15° S. and longitudes 171° and 173° W. It consists of the islands of Savai'i (662 sq. miles) and of Upolu, which, with seven other islands (Apolima, Manono, Fanuatapu, Namua, Nuutele, Nuulua and Nuusafee), has an area of 435 sq. miles (1,714 sq. km). All the islands are mountainous. Upolu, the most fertile, contains the harbours of ΨApia and ΨSaluafata, and Savai'i the harbour of ΨAsau.
POPULATION – The population at the 1981 census was 158,130, the largest numbers being on Upolu (114,980) and Savai'i (43,150); a 1990 UN estimate put the figure at 164,000. The Samoans are a Polynesian people, though the population also includes other Pacific Islanders, Euronesians, Chinese and Europeans. The main languages spoken are Samoan and English. The islanders are Christians of different denominations.

CAPITAL – ΨApia, on Upolu (population, 1981 census, 33,100). Robert Louis Stevenson died and was buried at Apia in 1894.
CURRENCY – Tala (WS$) of 100 sene.
FLAG – Red with a blue canton bearing five white stars of the Southern Cross.
NATIONAL ANTHEM – The Banner of Freedom.
NATIONAL DAY – 1 June (Independence Day).

GOVERNMENT

Formerly administered by New Zealand (latterly with internal self-government), Western Samoa became, on 1 June 1962, the first fully-independent Polynesian state. The state was treated as a member country of the Commonwealth until its formal admission on 28 August 1970.

The 1962 constitution provides for a head of state to be elected by the 49-member legislative assembly, the *Fono*, for a five year term. However, it was decided that initially two of the four Paramount chiefs should jointly hold the office of head of state for life. When one of the chiefs died in April 1963, Malietoa Tanumafili II became the holder of the office of head of state for life. The head of state's functions are analogous to those of a constitutional monarch. Executive government is carried out by a Cabinet of Ministers.

Suffrage, previously confined to 20,000 *Matai* (the male heads of extended families), was made universal following a referendum held in October 1990. After elections held on 7 March 1991, the seats in the *Fono* were as follows: Human Rights Protection Party 30; Samoan National Development Party 16; Independents 3.

Head of State, HH Malietoa Tanumafili II, GCMG, CBE (15 April 1963).
Deputy Head of State, Hon. Mataafa Faasuamaleaui Puela.

Cabinet as at July 1992

Prime Minister, Minister for Foreign Affairs, Hon. Tofilau Eti Alesana.
Finance, Hon. Tuilaepa Sailele.
Justice, Hon. Fuimanono Lotomau.
Education, Hon. Fiame Naomi.
Health, Hon. Sala Vaimili Uili II.
Post and Telecommunications, Hon. Toi Aukuso.
Agriculture, Hon. Jack Netzler.
Public Works, Hon. Leafa Vitale.
Lands and Environment, Hon. Faasooatuloa Pati.

Western Samoa High Commission
Avenue Franklin D. Roosevelt 123, 1050 Brussels
Tel: Brussels 6608454

High Commissioner, His Excellency Afamasaga Toleafoa (1990).

British High Commission
High Commissioner (resides at Wellington, New Zealand).

ECONOMY

Agriculture is the basis of Western Samoa's economy, the principal cash crops (and exports) being coconuts (copra), cocoa and bananas. Other agricultural exports include coffee, timber, tropical fruits and seeds. Efforts are being made to develop fishing on a commercial scale. Manufacturing is very small in scope and concerned largely with processing agricultural products, but is being encouraged by the government. Tourism is increasing rapidly.

Trade with UK

	1990	1991
Imports from UK	£427,000	£671,000
Exports to UK	295,000	16,000

REPUBLIC OF YEMEN
Al-Jamhuriya Al-Yamaniya

Area and Population – The Republic of Yemen comprises that area of the Arabian peninsula formerly occupied by the Yemen Arab republic (North Yemen) and the People's Democratic Republic of Yemen (South Yemen). Bounded on the west by the Red Sea, on the north by Saudi Arabia, on the east by Oman and on the south by the Gulf of Aden, Yemen has an estimated area of 203,850 sq. miles (527,969 sq. km) and a population (1990 UN estimate) of 11,282,000. Included in the state are the offshore islands of Perim and Kamaran in the Red Sea, and Socotra in the Gulf of Aden.

The highlands and central plateau, and the highest portions of the maritime range of what was South Yemen, form the most fertile part of Arabia, with abundant but irregular rainfall. The area of former North Yemen is largely composed of mountains and desert, and rainfall is generally scarce.

Capital – Sana'a, population (1986) 427,150. Ψ Aden (270,000) is the other main city and the former capital of South Yemen.

Currency – Yemeni dinar (YD) of 1,000 fils and Riyals of 100 fils are both legal tender (1 Dinar = 26 Riyals).

Flag – Horizontal bands of red, white and black.

National Day – 22 May.

GOVERNMENT

Turkish occupation of North Yemen (1872–1918) was followed by the rule of the Hamid al-Din dynasty until a revolution in 1962 overthrew the monarchy and the Yemen Arab Republic was declared. The People's Republic of South Yemen was set up in November 1967 when the British government ceded power to the National Liberation Front, thus bringing to an end 129 years of British rule in Aden and some years of protectorate status in the hinterland. The name was changed to the People's Democratic Republic of Yemen in November 1970. Negotiations towards merging the two states began in 1979.

A draft joint constitution, proposing the establishment of a unified multi-party state, was published by the leaders of North and South Yemen in December 1989. Unification was proclaimed on 22 May 1990 following ratification the previous day by both parliaments. The constitution was approved by referendum on 16 May 1991. Elections are to be held in November 1992.

A five-member Presidential Council comprising former senior government figures of the separate states was formed for the period of transition. The former President of North Yemen was declared President of the unified state, with the former President of South Yemen becoming Prime Minister. The parliament of the unified state, the House of Representatives, comprises 270 members, 159 of which were former members of North Yemen's parliament, and 111 of South Yemen's.

President, Gen. Ali Abdullah Saleh, *elected* 22 May 1990.
Vice President, Ali Salim al-Beedh.
Members of Presidential Council, Qadi Abdel-Karim al-Arashi; Abdel Aziz Abdel Ghani; Salim Salih Mohammed.

Council of Ministers as at July 1992

Prime Minister, Haider Abu Bakr al-Attas.
First Deputy PM, Dr Hassan Mohammed Makki.
Deputy PM, Minister for Internal Affairs, Brig.-Gen. Mujahid Yahya Abu Shawarib.
Deputy PM, Security and Defence, Brig.-Gen. Salih Ubayd Ahmed.
Deputy PM, Development of Manpower and Administrative Reform, Mohammed Haider Masdus.
Construction, Abdullah Hussayn al-Kurshumi.
Foreign Affairs, Abdullah al-Karim Ali al-Iryani.
Expatriates' Affairs, Brig.-Gen. Salih Munassar as-Siyayli.
Industry, Mohammed Said al-Attar.
Oil and Mineral Resources, Salih Abu Bakr Bin Hussain.
Supply and Trade, Fadl Mohsin Abdullah.
Legal Administration, Mohammed Said Abdullah Muhsin.
Electricity and Water, Abdul-Wahhab Mahmud Abdul-Hamid.
Civil Service and Administrative Reform, Mohammed al-Khadim al-Wajih.
Planning and Development, Faraj Bin Ghanim.
Telecommunications, Ahmad Mohammed al-Unsi.
Legal Affairs, Ismail Ahmad al-Wazir.
Waqfs (Religious Affairs) and Guidance, Muhsin Mohammed al-Ulufi.
Securities and Social Affairs, Ahmad Mohammed Luqman.
Culture and Tourism, Hasan Ahmad al-Lawzi.
Youth and Sports, Mohammed Ahmad al-Kabab.
Education, Mohammed Abdullah al-Jayfi.
Justice, Abdul Wasi Ahmed Sallam.
Information, Mohammed Ahmed Jirghum.
Transport, Salih Abdullah Muthanna.
Fisheries, Salim Mohammad Jubran.
Housing and Urban Planning, Mohammed Ahmed Salman.
Finance, Alawi Salih al-Salami.
Public Health, Mohammed Ali Muqbil.
Agriculture and Water Resources, Sadiq Amin Abu Ras.
Interior and Security, Col. Ghalib Motahar al-Qomesh.

Defence, Brig.-Gen. Haytham Qasim Tahir.
Labour and Vocational Training, Abdul Rahman Dhiban.
Higher Education and Scientific Research, Ahmad Salim al-Qadi.

In addition there are four Ministers of State.

EMBASSY OF THE REPUBLIC OF YEMEN
41 South Street, London W1Y 5PD
Tel 071-629 9905

Ambassador Extraordinary and Plenipotentiary, His Excellency Dr Shaya Mohsin Mohamed (1991).

BRITISH EMBASSY
PO Box 1287, Sana'a
Tel: Sana'a 215630

Ambassador Extraordinary and Plenipotentiary, His Excellency Mark Anthony Marshall, CMG (1987).
First Secretary, G. Kirby (*Deputy Head of Mission and Aid*).

There is a British Consulate-General at *Aden*.

BRITISH COUNCIL REPRESENTATIVE, A. Lewis, Beit Al-Mottahar, Al-Bonia Street, Harat Handhal (PO Box 2157), Sana'a.

ECONOMY

Exports include cotton, coffee, hides and skins. Agriculture is the main occupation of the inhabitants. This is largely of a subsistence nature, sorghum, sesame and millets being the chief crops, with wheat and barley widely grown at the higher elevations. Oil has been produced at Marib since December 1987; production averages 200,000 b.p.d. and is expected to reach 400,000 b.p.d. by 1992. A new field is being developed at Shabwa in what used to be South Yemen. There is a refinery at Aden. The Aden Free Zone was opened in May 1991 and could help Aden recover its old commercial importance in the region.

TRADE WITH UK

	1990
Imports from UK	£70,835,000
Exports to UK	36,238,000

THE FORMER YUGOSLAVIA

The area of the former Yugoslavia was estimated at 98,766 sq. miles (255,804 sq. km). The population (UN estimate 1990) was 23,809,000; the latest Census (April 1991) broke down the population into 8,320,000 Serbs, 4,520,000 Croats, 2,400,000 Muslims, 1,780,000 Slovenes, 2,210,000 Albanians, 1,430,000 Macedonians and 1,330,000 'Yugoslavs', as well as a variety of other minorities.

Yugoslavia was a federation comprising the Republics of Serbia, Bosnia and Hercegovina, Croatia, Montenegro, Macedonia and Slovenia.

Yugoslavia had been gradually unravelling since President Tito, the wartime partisan leader and post-war Communist President, died in 1980. The Catholic, western-looking, more prosperous republics of Slovenia and Croatia began to break away from the other predominantly Orthodox and Muslim, Balkan republics of the rest of Yugoslavia; Communism was widely rejected. Efforts by the federal presidency and international mediators to end inter-communal conflict and negotiate a new federal or confederal structure for the country failed in 1991.

On 25 June 1991 Slovenia and Croatia both declared their independence from Yugoslavia, causing fighting to begin immediately as the Federal Yugoslav Army (JNA) intervened against local defence forces to prevent the disintegration of the Yugoslav Federation. In Slovenia it soon became clear that the Serb-dominated JNA had failed to stop the secession because it was ill-prepared and a long distance from its Serbian bases. Seeing that Slovenia was virtually ethnically homogeneous with no Serbian minority, the JNA soon withdrew from the republic and within two months Slovenia had negotiated its independence from Yugoslavia.

However, the situation in Croatia differed because its ethnic Serb minority comprised 12 per cent of the population. These ethnic Serbs refused to accept Croatia's independence and formed themselves into armed guerrilla groupss. Bitter fighting erupted in July 1991 between Croat Defence Forces and Serbian guerrillas backed by the JNA. By September 1991 fighting had escalated into an all-out war between Croatia and Serbia, which had taken over control of the JNA. In October the last vestiges of the power of the Federation ended when the federal presidency was usurped by Serbia and its ally Montenegro.

The war in Croatia continued until January 1992 when, after constant attempts, the EC and the UN were able to bring about a ceasefire that held. The JNA and Serbian forces had secured control of virtually all ethnic Serbian areas in Croatia and the two sides were not able to carry on the fighting. The war left an estimated 10,000 people dead, scores of villages and the city of Vukovar destroyed, and badly damaged Dubrovnik. Three UN Protected Areas in Croatia, Krajina and Eastern and Western Slovonia, were created from the Serb-controlled areas in Croatia and 14,000 UN troops arrived to police the areas. The JNA withdrew from Croatia and the local Serbian guerrillas were disarmed. At the time of going to press, the situation in the UN protected areas remains tense, with the Croatian government determined to gain control of the areas, and the Serbs adamant that they will not live under Croatian rule.

While the war continued in Croatia, Bosnia-Hercegovina declared its independence from Yugoslavia on 15 October 1991, and this was affirmed in a referendum on 1 March 1992. Independence was supported by the ethnic Muslims and Croats but rejected by the ethnic Serbs, who formed 33 per cent of the population and wanted to form a Greater Serbia with the Serbian republic. Fighting between Muslims and Serbs broke out on 2 March 1992 and the JNA intervened massively against the poorly-armed Muslims. By May 1992 Serbian forces had overrun over 70 per cent of the republic and Croat forces much of the rest, leaving the legitimate Bosnian Muslim government forces besieged in the capital Sarajevo and a few other cities. By May intense international pressure forced Serbia to withdraw the JNA from Bosnia, but the JNA handed over most of its weapons to Bosnian Serb forces. At the end of May the UN imposed a total trade embargo and economic sanctions on Serbia and Montenegro, but the war in Bosnia continued throughout the summer. As evidence of 'ethnic cleansing' and Serb-run concentration camps emerged in August 1992, the UN first of all authorized the use of troops to keep Sarajevo airport open for relief flights, and then forced all the warring participants to attend a peace conference in London at the end of August.

At the time of going to press, the fighting in Bosnia had abated, but only slightly, with the UN attempting to bring Serb heavy artillery under its supervision and to resume aid flights, and 6,000 UN troops (including 1,800 British) preparing to travel to Bosnia to protect aid convoys. Sarajevo and other Bosnian areas remain under siege, and Sarajevo is without food or water.

BOSNIA-HERCEGOVINA

Bosnia-Hercegovina is bounded by Serbia, Montenegro and Croatia and has an area of 19,735 sq. miles (51,129 sq. km.).

It has a population of 4.1 million, of whom some 40 per cent are Muslims, 33 per cent Serbs and 18 per cent Croats. The capital is Sarajevo with a population (1981) of 447,000. Results of the elections, held in November and December 1990 for the 240-seat bicameral Assembly, were: the (Muslim) Party of Democratic Action 86 seats, the (Serbian) Democratic Party 72, and the Croat Democratic Union 44.

At the time of going to press, 70 per cent of the territory of Bosnia was controlled by Serbian forces, who had declared their own Bosnian Serb republic under the leadership of Dr Radovan Karadzic. A further 20 per cent of the territory of Bosnia was controlled by Croat forces who had announced an independent Croat republic in western Hercegovina. The mainly Muslim forces of the Bosnian government were in an uneasy alliance with Croatian and Bosnian Croat forces, who were trying to cut Serbian supply lines to Serb enclaves in Croatia. Because of Serbian 'ethnic cleansing' of Muslim-populated areas, thousands of Muslims have died and hundreds of thousands of refugees fled to Croatia and the rest of Europe. Bosnia-Hercegovina was recognized as an independent state by the EC and USA on 7 April 1992 and admitted to UN membership in May 1992.

FLAG – White with the shield of arms in the centre.

President, Alija Izetbegovic.

CROATIA

Croatia is bounded by Slovenia, Hungary, Serbia and Bosnia-Hercegovina; it includes the Adriatic coastline of Istria and Dalmatia and has an area of 21,823 sq. miles (56,538 sq. km). It has a population of 4.7 million of whom 75 per cent are Croats and some 12 per cent Serbs. The capital is Zagreb (population (1981) 763,000). Elections held in August 1992 for the three-chamber *Sabor* were won by the Croat Democratic Union. Croatia declared its independence on 25 June 1991. The EC recognized Croatia's independence on 15 January 1992 and it was admitted to UN membership in May 1992. One-third of Croatian territory remains under UN control as UN protected areas. The war has cost Croatia at least 7,000 dead, it is host to 650,000 refugees and the economy is in ruins.

FLAG – Three horizontal stripes of red, white, blue, with the national arms over all in the centre.

President, Franjo Tudjman, *elected* April 1990, *re-elected* 2 August 1992.

OFFICE OF THE CROATIAN REPRESENTATIVE
18–21 Germain Street, London SW1Y 6HP
Tel: 071 434 2946

Representative of the Croatian Republic, Dr D. Stambuk.

Representative of the Croatian Republic, Dr D. Stambuk.

BRITISH EMBASSY
Ilica 12/II, PO Box 434, 41000 Zagreb.
Tel: Zagreb 424888

Ambassador Extraordinary and Plenipotentiary, His Excellency Bryan Sparrow (1992).

There is a British Consulate in Split.

MACEDONIA

Macedonia is a landlocked republic bordered by Serbia, Bulgaria, Greece and Albania, with an area of 9,925 sq. miles (25,713 sq. km). It has a population of 1.9 million, of whom 67 per cent are Macedonian, 20 per cent Albanian and 3 per cent Serbian, with ethnic Greeks, Bulgars and Turks among the remainder. The capital is Skopje, which has a population (1981) of 503,000. Multi-party elections were held in December 1990 for the 120-seat Assembly which produced the first non-Communist government since the Second World War. Macedonia declared its independence from Yugoslavia in April 1992 and the JNA withdrew peacefully soon afterwards. Its independence has not, however, been internationally recognized because of Greece's objections to the state's name and its territorial implications. The inability of the government to secure Macedonia's international recognition caused the downfall of the government by a no-confidence vote in parliament in July 1992 and interim power now rests with the President.

President, Kiro Gligorov.

SLOVENIA

Slovenia is bounded by Italy, Austria, Hungary and Croatia and has an area of 7,816 sq. miles (20,251 sq. km). It has a population of 1.8 million, of whom over 90 per cent are Slovene, are overwhelmingly Roman Catholic and speak Slovenian as their mother tongue. The capital is Ljubljana with a population (1981) of 253,000. The United Democratic Opposition (Demos) won multi-party elections held in April 1990. Slovenia declared its independence on 25 June 1991. Attacks by the federal army followed but failed to coerce the republic and troops were withdrawn by August 1991.

In December 1991 the Demos coalition dissolved itself and formed into four right-wing and centre-right parties. Continuing economic problems caused by independence from the centrally-planned former Yugoslav economy forced the resignation of the government in April 1992 and the appointment of Liberal Democratic Party leader Janez Drnovsek as Prime Minister. Slovenia introduced the tolar in October 1991 to replace the dinar as its currency.

FLAG – Three horizontal stripes of white, blue and red, with the national arms over all in the canton.

President, Milan Kucan.

EMBASSY OF SLOVENIA
49 Conduit Street, London W1R 9FB
Tel 071 734 8870

Ambassador Extraordinary and Plenipotentiary, His Excellency Matjaz Sinkovec.

FEDERAL REPUBLIC OF YUGOSLAVIA

On 27 April 1992 the two remaining republics of the former Socialist Federal Republic of Yugoslavia, namely Serbia and Montenegro, announced the formation of a new Yugoslav federation, which they invited Serbs in Croatia and Bosnia-Hercegovina to join. The new federation remains unrecognized internationally because of continued Serbian aggression in Bosnia, and is seen as a Serbian attempt to inherit the rights of the former Federation. Elections to a new Federal Parliament were held on 31 May 1992 and were won by the Serbian Socialist Party in alliance with the Montenegrin Social Democrats (both parties being the respective republican former Communist parties). The Federal Republic has a bi-cameral parliament with a Chamber of Citizens and a Chamber of Republics. The JNA has become the army of the new federation. The government is headed by Prime Minister Milan Panic, who at the time of going to press had become embroiled in a power struggle with Serbian President Milosevic over the conduct of the war and the worsening economic situation due to the UN trade embargo and economic sanctions.

FLAG – Three horizontal stripes of blue, white, red.

President, Dobrica Cosic.

MONTENEGRO

Montenegro has an area of 5,331 sq. miles (13,812 sq. km) and is bounded by Bosnia-Hercegovina, Serbia, Albania and the Adriatic. It has a population of 650,000, of whom 68 per cent are Montenegrins, 13 per cent Muslims, 6 per cent Albanians and 3 per cent Serbs. The capital is Podgorica with a population (1981) of 95,000. The League of Communists (now renamed Social Democrats) won multi-party elections in December 1990 for the 125-seat assembly. Montenegro remains a close ally of Serbia. Serbo-Croat written in the Cyrillic script is the main language, and the Orthodox religion the main religion.

President, Momir Bulatovic.

SERBIA

Serbia has a total area of 34,175 sq. miles (88,538 sq. km) and has frontiers with all the former Yugoslav republics except Slovenia, as well as with Hungary, Romania and Bulgaria. The capital is Belgrade with a population (1981) of 1,455,000. It has a total population of 9.3 million (Vojvodina 2.0 million, Kosovo 1.6 million), of whom 66 per cent are Serbs. It includes the provinces of Kosovo, of great historic importance to Serbs, and Vojvodina; the autonomy of both was ended in September 1990. Kosovo, with its capital at Priština, is predominantly Albanian (90 per cent). In defiance of the Serbian authorities, ethnic Albanians held parliamentary and presidential elections in May 1992, which were won respectively by the Democratic League of Kosovo and its leader Ibrahim Rugova. Tension between Albanians and Serbs remains very high. Vojvodina, with its capital at Novi Sad, has a large Hungarian minority (21 per cent).

The Socialist Party of Serbia (formerly the League of Communists) won multi-party elections for the 250-seat National Assembly, held in December 1990. Serbia has traditionally been the dominant republic in Yugoslavia. Serbo-Croat written in the Cyrillic script is the dominant language, and Serbian Orthodox is the dominant religion.

President, Slobodan Milosevic.

ECONOMY

The wars in Croatia and Bosnia-Hercegovina have almost completely destroyed the industries and economies of both republics. The Slovene economy has been badly affected by its withdrawal from the federal centrally-planned economy. At the time of going to press, the Serbian and Montenegrin economies were suffering badly because of the UN trade embargo and economic sanctions, with most factories being closed and production ending. The Macedonian economy is also on the verge of collapse because it has effectively been denied the ability to trade, and any foreign loans and investment, because of its lack of international recognition.

The currency in all of the republics except Slovenia is the dinar.

TRADE WITH UK

	1990	1991
Imports from UK	£260,972,000	£193,836,000
Exports to UK	189,421,000	147,876,000

BRITISH EMBASSY
General Ždanova 46, 11000 Belgrade
Tel: Belgrade 645055

Ambassador Extraordinary and Plenipotentiary, His Excellency Peter E. Hall, CMG (1989).
Counsellor, M. J. Robinson.
Defence and Military Attaché, Col. E. D. Powell-Jones.
Naval and Air Attaché, Wg Cdr. R. Parker.

BRITISH COUNCIL REPRESENTATIVE, P. Early, Generala Ždanova 34-Mezanin (Post Fah 248), 11001 Belgrade.

ZAIRE
République du Zaïre

Situated between long. 12° and 31° E. and lat. 5° N. and 13° S., the Republic of Zaire comprises an area of 905,567 sq. miles (2,345,409 sq. km), with a population (1985 Census) of 34,671,607. A 1990 UN estimate gives a figure of 35,562,000.
CLIMATE – Apart from the coastal district in the west which is fairly dry, the rainfall averages between 60 and 80 inches. The average temperature is about 27°C, but in the south the winter temperature can fall nearly to freezing point. Extensive forest covers the central districts.
ETHNIC GROUPS – The population is composed almost entirely of Bantu groups, divided into semi-autonomous tribes, each speaking a Bantu tongue. Minorities include Sudanese, Nilotes, Pygmies and Hamites, as well as refugees from Angola.
LANGUAGES – Swahili, a Bantu dialect with an admixture of Arabic, is the nearest approach to a common language in the east and south, while Lingala is the language of a large area along the river and in the north, and Kikongo of the region between Kinshasa and the sea. French is the language of administration.

CAPITAL – Kinshasa (formerly Leopoldville), population (1985 Census) 2,778,281. Principal towns, Lubumbashi (formerly Elisabethville) (403,623); Kisangani (formerly Stanleyville) (310,705); Likasi (146,394); Kananga (601,239); Ψ Matadi (143,598); and Mbandaka (134,495).
CURRENCY – Zaïre of 100 makuta.
FLAG – Dark brown hand and torch with red flame in yellow roundel on green background.
NATIONAL DAY – 24 November.

GOVERNMENT

The state of the Congo, founded in 1885, became a Belgian colony in November 1908, and was administered by Belgium until independence in 1960, when it became the Democratic Republic of the Congo. In October 1971 the name changed to the Republic of Zaire.

Mobutu Sésé Seko, formerly Commander-in-Chief of the Congolese National Army, came to power in a coup in 1965, and was elected President in 1970. Legislative power is vested in a unicameral National Legislative Council, elected for a five-year term by compulsory direct and universal suffrage. All candidates are proposed by the sole legal political party, Mouvement Populaire de la Révolution (MPR). In 1980 a MPR central committee was formed with powers to overrule the National Legislative Council.

Following mounting social tension, political reforms were announced in April 1990. They include the separation of the roles of head of state and head of government, and the gradual introduction of a three-party system. A transitional government was appointed in May 1990. After mounting opposition pressure, President Mobutu called a national conference, intended to draft a new constitution, in April 1991; the conference convened in August. Violent demonstrations began as soon as the conference opened because the government refused to grant it sovereign status. The main opposition parties formed a 'Sacred Union' to bring down the transitional government, leading to political and economic chaos with violent rioting in Kinshasa. Mobutu eventually accepted an opposition-dominated government under Prime Minister Etienne Tshisekedi in October 1991, but then replaced this with MPR-dominated governments, first under Mungal Diaka, and then in November 1991 under Nguza Karl-I-Bond. In response, the Sacred Union formed a rival government under Etienne Tshisekedi and a political impasse ensued until Nguza Karl-I-Bond resigned in August 1992. The National Conference confirmed the Tshisekedi government as the legitimate one and it took office in August 1992. Mobutu's presidential term ended on 4 December 1991, but he announced he would remain in office indefinitely.

PROVINCES – There are 11 regions, each under a Governor and provincial administration: Bas-Zaire (provincial capital, Matadi); Bandundu (Bandundu); Equateur (Mbandaka); Haut-Zaire (Kisangani); Kinshasa (Kinshasa); Maniema (Kindu); Nord-Kivu (Goma); Sud-Kivu (Bukavu); Shaba, formerly Katanga (Lubumbashi); East Kasai (Mbuji-Mayi); West Kasai (Kananga).

HEAD OF STATE

President of the Republic and National Security, Marshal Mobutu Sésé Séko, *born* 30 Oct. 1930; *assumed office* 25 November 1965; *elected* 5 Nov. 1970; *re-elected for third term*, 28 July 1984.

EXECUTIVE COUNCIL as at July 1992

Prime Minister, Etienne Tshisekedi.
Interior and Territorial Security, Mathieu Bosunga Lombe.
External Relations, Pierre Lumbi.
Justice, Roger Gisanga.
Defence, Paul Bandoma.
National Education, Loka Ne Kongo.
Scientific Research and Technology, Theophile Mbemba Fundu.
Culture and Arts, Gervais Kabamba.
Finance and Budget, Benoit Atale.
Economy, Industry and External Trade, Fernand Tala-Ngai.
Planning, Kirarawumu Isengoma.
Small and Medium Enterprises, Paul Kapita Shabani.
Public Works, Mwitaba Katemwe.
Agriculture and Rural Development, Jean Paul N'Kanga.
Environment and Tourism, Tharcisse Loseke.
Public Health and Social Affairs, Honorine Nabunyi.
Transport and Communications, Baudouin Kabisi.
Mines and Energy, Jean Seka Buhoro.
Posts and Telecommunications, Kumbu Ki Lutete.
Civil Service, Lubaga Wedisonga.
Labour and Social Services, Nbumb Musong.
Youth, Sport and Leisure, Charles Gonghandiki.

EMBASSY OF THE REPUBLIC OF ZAIRE
26 Chesham Place, London SW1X 8HH
Tel 071-235 6137

Ambassador Extraordinary and Plenipotentiary, His Excellency Liloo Nkema (1991).

BRITISH EMBASSY
Avenue des Trois 'Z', Gombe, Kinshasa
Tel: Kinshasa 34775/8

Ambassador Extraordinary and Plenipotentiary, His Excellency Roger Westbrook, CMG (1991).

There are British Consulates at *Lubumbashi, Goma* and *Kisangani*.

ECONOMY

The cultivation of oil palms is widespread, palm oil being the most important agricultural cash product though it is no longer exported. Coffee, rubber, cocoa and timber are the most important agricultural exports. The production of cotton, pyrethrum and copal fell sharply on independence but is now increasing. The country is rich in minerals, particularly Shaba (ex-Katanga) province. Copper is widely exploited, and industrial diamonds and cobalt are also produced. Oil deposits are exploited off the Zaire estuary and reef-gold is mined in the north-east of the country.

There is a wide variety of small secondary industries, the main products being foodstuffs, beverages, tobacco, textiles, leather, wood products, cement and building materials, matallurgy, small river craft and bicycles. There are large reserves of hydro-electric power and the huge Inga dam on the river Zaire supplies electricity to Matadi, Kinshasa and Shaba.

TRADE

The chief exports are copper, crude oil, coffee, diamonds, rubber, cobalt, gold, cassiterite, zinc and other metals.

Trade with UK	1990	1991
Imports from UK	£23,801,000	£15,040,000
Exports to UK	7,337,000	4,733,000

COMMUNICATIONS

There are approximately 20,500 km of roads (earth-surfaced) of national importance, and 6,000 km of railways. The country has four international and 40 principal airports.

ZAMBIA
Republic of Zambia

AREA, POPULATION, ETC – The Republic of Zambia lies on the plateau of Central Africa between the longitudes 22° E. and 33° 33′ E. and between the latitudes 8° 15′ S. and 18° S. It has an area of 290,586 sq. miles (752,614 sq. km) within boundaries 3,515 miles in length and a population (UN estimate, 1990) of 8,073,000.

With the exception of the valleys of the Zambezi, the Luapula, the Kafue and the Luangwa Rivers, and the Luano valley, elevations vary from 3,000 to 5,000 feet above sea level, but in the north-east the plateau rises to occasional altitudes of over 6,000 feet.

Although Zambia lies within the tropics, and fairly centrally in the African land mass, its elevation relieves it from extremely high temperatures and humidity.

CAPITAL – Lusaka, situated in the Central Province. Population (1989 estimate) 1 million. Other centres are Livingstone, Kabwe, Chipata, Mazabuka, Mbala, Kasama, Solwezi, Mongu, Mansa, Ndola, Luanshya, Mufulira,

Chingola, Chililabombwe, Kalulushi and Kitwe, the last six towns being the main centres on the Copperbelt.
CURRENCY – Kwacha (K) of 100 ngwee.
FLAG – Green with three small vertical stripes, red, black and orange (next fly); eagle device on green above stripes.
NATIONAL ANTHEM – Stand and Sing of Zambia, Proud and Free.
NATIONAL DAY – 24 October (Independence Day).

GOVERNMENT

At the dissolution of the Federation of Rhodesia and Nyasaland, on 31 December 1963, Northern Rhodesia (as Zambia was then known) achieved internal self-government under a new constitution. Zambia became an independent republic within the Commonwealth on 24 October 1964, 75 years after coming under British rule and nine months after achieving internal self-government.

In July 1973, a new constitution was introduced, making the United National Independence Party (UNIP) the only party. In July 1990 it was announced that a referendum on introducing a multi-party system would be held in August 1991. After continued pressure from the Movement for Multiparty Democracy, set up in July 1990, and other opposition groups, the referendum was cancelled and multiparty and presidential elections were called for October 1991. The Movement for Multiparty Democracy (MMD) won 125 of the 150 seats in parliament, and MMD candidate Frederick Chiluba defeated Kaunda, who had ruled since independence, in the presidential election.

President, Frederick J. Chiluba, *elected* 31 October 1991.
Vice-President, Levy Patrick Mwanawasa.

CABINET as at July 1992
Defence, Benjamin Mwila.
Foreign Affairs, Vernon Mwaanga.
Finance, Emmanuel G. Kasonde.
Home Affairs, Newstead L. Zimba.
Local Government and Housing, Michael Sata.
Health, Dr Boniface Kawimbe.
Education, Arthur Wina.
Commerce, Trade and Industry, Ronald Penza.
Community Development and Social Welfare, Gabriel Maka.
Labour and Social Security, Dr Ludwig Sondashi.
Communications, Transport and Public Works, Andrew Kashita.
Energy and Water Development, Alfeyo Hambayi.
Agriculture, Food and Fisheries, Dr Guy Scott.
Lands, Dawson Lupunga.
Legal Affairs, Dr Roger Chongwe.
Environment and Natural Resources, Keli Walubita.
Information and Continuing Education, Stan Kristafor.
Mines and Mineral Development, Humphrey Mulemba.
Technical Education and Vocational Training, Akashambatwa Mbikusita-Lewanika.
Youth and Child Development, Baldwin Nkumbula.
Tourism, Gen. Christon Tembo.
Works and Supply, Emphraim Chibwe.
Minister without Portfolio, Brig.-Gen. Godfrey Miyanda.

ZAMBIA HIGH COMMISSION
2 Palace Gate, London W8 5LS
Tel 071-589 6655

High Commissioner, His Excellency Love Mtesa (1992).

BRITISH HIGH COMMISSION
Independence Avenue (PO Box 50050), Lusaka
Tel: Lusaka 228955

High Commissioner, His Excellency Peter Hinchcliffe, CMG, CVO (1990).

BRITISH COUNCIL REPRESENTATIVE, G. Ness, Heroes Place, Cairo Road, (PO Box 34571), Lusaka. There is also a library in *Ndola*.

JUDICATURE

There is a Chief Justice appointed by the President, all other judges being appointed on the recommendation of the Judicial Service Commission consisting of the Chief Justice, the chairman of the Public Service Commission, a senior Justice of Appeal and one Presidential nominee.

ECONOMY

Principal products are maize, sugar, groundnuts, cotton, livestock, vegetables and tobacco.

Mineral production was valued at K8,390,765,000 in 1987, of which copper production (of 483,100 tonnes) accounted for K6,870,386,000.

Gross Domestic Product (current prices) was K18,079.8m in 1987. GDP per capita (current prices) was K2,486.9.

TRADE

	1986	1987
Imports	K4,447,687	K6,627,473
Exports	3,074,357	8,058,595

Trade with UK	1990	1991
Imports from UK	£92,832,000	£62,655,000
Exports to UK	19,308,000	22,468,000

ZIMBABWE
Republic of Zimbabwe

AREA, POPULATION, ETC. – Zimbabwe, the former Southern Rhodesia (named after Cecil Rhodes) comprising eight provinces (Manicaland, Masvingo, Matabeleland North, Matabeleland South, Midlands, Mashonaland West, Central and East), lies south of the Zambezi river. The political neighbours are Zambia and Mozambique on the north, South Africa and Botswana on the south and west, and Mozambique on the east. It has a total area of 150,804 sq. miles (390,580 sq. km), and a population (UN estimate 1990) of 9,369,000.
CAPITAL – Harare (formerly Salisbury) situated on the Mashonaland plateau, population (July 1983) 681,000. Bulawayo is the largest town in Matabeleland, population (July 1983) 429,000. Other centres are, Chitungwiza, Mutare, Gweru, Kadoma, Kwe Kwe, Masvingo and Hwange.
CURRENCY – Zimbabwe dollar (Z$) of 100 cents.
FLAG – Seven horizontal stripes of green, yellow, red, black, red, yellow, green; a white, black-bordered, triangle based on the hoist containing the national emblem.
NATIONAL ANTHEM – Ishe Komborerai Africa.
NATIONAL DAY – 18 April (Independence Day).

GOVERNMENT

Southern Rhodesia was granted responsible government in 1923. An illegal declaration of independence on 11 November 1965 was finally terminated on 12 December 1979. Following elections in February 1980 the country obtained independence on 18 April 1980 as the Republic of Zimbabwe, a member of the British Commonwealth.

A Constitutional Amendment Bill designed to replace the 20 reserved white seats with nominated members from any race, was approved in September 1987. On 30 October 1987 a Constitutional Amendment Bill was passed providing for the creation of an executive presidency. On 30 December

1987 Robert Mugabe was elected by MPs and Senators as the first President. The Bill provides for a President to be popularly elected every six years. The President has the power to appoint a Cabinet and to veto parliamentary bills.

A merger agreement between the ZANU (PF) and ZAPU parties was signed on 22 December 1987 with a view to the eventual creation of a one-party state. The new party is known as ZANU-PF.

The latest general election was held in March 1990. ZANU-PF won 116 of the 120 elective seats, and the legislature became unicameral, comprising a House of Assembly of 160 members.

HEAD OF STATE

Executive President, Hon. Robert Gabriel Mugabe, *elected* 30 Dec. 1987, *re-elected* March 1990.

CABINET as at August 1992

The President.
Vice-President, Hon. Simon Muzenda.
Vice-President, Hon. Dr Joshua Nkomo.
Senior Minister, National Affairs, Employment Creation and Co-operatives, Hon. Didymus Mutasa.
Senior Minister, Economic Ministries, Hon. Dr Bernard Chidzero.
Senior Minister for Local Government, Rural and Urban Development, Hon. Joseph Msika.
Foreign Affairs, Hon. Dr Nathan Shamuyarira.
Justice, Legal and Parliamentary Affairs, Hon. Emmerson Munangagwa.
Defence, Hon. Moven Mahachi.
Higher Education, Hon. Dr Stanslous Mudenge.
Education and Culture, Hon. Dr Witness Mangwende.
Home Affairs, Hon. Dumiso Dabengwa.
Public Construction and National Housing, Hon. Enos Chikowore.
Lands, Agriculture and Water Resources, Hon. Kumbirai Kangai.
Information, Posts and Telecommunications, Hon. David Karimanzira.
Labour, Public Service and Social Welfare, Hon. John Nkomo.
Industry and Commerce, Hon. Dr. Christopher Ushewokunze.
Mines, Hon. Dr Eddison Zvobgo.
Transport and Energy, Hon. Dennis Norman.
Health and Child Welfare, Hon. Dr Timothy Stamps.
Environment and Tourism, Hon. Herbert Murerwa.
Attorney-General, Hon. Patrick Chinamasa.

HIGH COMMISSION OF THE REPUBLIC OF ZIMBABWE
Zimbabwe House, 429 Strand, London WC2R 0SA
Tel 071-836 7755

High Commissioner, S. C. Chiketa (1990).

BRITISH HIGH COMMISSION
Stanley House, Jason Moyo Avenue (PO Box 4490), Harare
Tel: Harare 793781

High Commissioner, His Excellency Sir Kieran Prendergast, KCVO, CMG (1989).

BRITISH COUNCIL REPRESENTATIVE, P. L. Elborn, OBE, 23 Stanley Avenue (PO Box 664), Harare.

EDUCATION

Since independence, a policy of free primary education and accelerated expansion at secondary level has resulted in rapidly expanding enrolment. In 1986 there were 2,260,367 primary school and 545,841 secondary school pupils in both government and government aided-schools. Over 80 per cent of schools are government-aided schools. The University of Zimbabwe was founded in 1955.

ECONOMY

The country is endowed with minerals, water, forests, wildlife and other resources. The agricultural sector is well developed with both commercial and communal farmers. Tobacco remains the most important crop in terms of export and maize the most important for domestic consumption. Other crops include wheat, cotton, and sugar. Beef is exported to the EC. Production can be severely affected by drought.

The manufacturing sector has a high degree of interdependency and many industries depend on the agricultural sector for their raw materials. Industry is dependent on vital imports e.g. fuel oil, steel products and chemicals, as well as heavy machinery and items of transport. The mining sector, although contributing a relatively small portion to GDP (7.6 per cent in 1984) is important to the economy as a foreign exchange earner (26 per cent of total in 1984). Almost all mineral production is exported. Gold is the most important mineral, others are asbestos, silver, nickel, copper, chrome ore, tin, iron ore and cobalt. There is a successful ferrochrome industry and a substantial steel works which has been heavily subsidized by Government.

A high domestic budget deficit combining with a high external debt service ratio has put the economy into decline. Recent droughts have made this worse.

FINANCE

	1984–5	1985–6
Revenue	Z$2,212.3m	Z$2,616.2m
Expenditure	2,923.0m	3,307.8m

TRADE WITH UK

	1990	1991
Imports from UK	£83,718,000	£135,309,000
Exports to UK	86,280,000	103,891,000

British Dependent Territories

ANGUILLA

AREA – Anguilla is a flat coralline island, about 16 miles in length, three and a half miles in breadth at its widest point and its area is about 35 sq. miles (91 sq. km). It lies approximately 18° N. latitude and 63° W longitude, to the north of the Leeward Islands group.

The island is covered with low scrub and fringed with some of the finest white coral-sand beaches in the Caribbean. The climate is pleasant and healthy with temperatures in the range of 24-30°C throughout the year.

POPULATION – The population (1992 Census) is 8,800.
CAPITAL – The Valley (population 1,400).
CURRENCY – East Caribbean dollar (EC$) of 100 cents.

GOVERNMENT

Anguilla has been a British colony since 1650. For most of its history it has been linked administratively with St Christopher, but three months after the Associated State of Saint Christopher (St Kitts)-Nevis-Anguilla came into being in 1967, the Anguillans repudiated government from St Kitts. A Commissioner was installed in 1969 and in 1976 Anguilla was given a new status and separate constitution. Final separation from St Kitts and Nevis was effected on 19 December 1980 and Anguilla reverted to a British dependency. A new Constitution was introduced in 1982, providing for a Governor, an Executive Council comprising four elected Ministers and two ex-officio members (Attorney General and Permanent Secretary, Finance), and an 11-member legislative House of Assembly presided over by a Speaker.

The 1982 Constitution (Amendment) Order 1990 came into operation on 30 May 1990. Among the new constitutional provisions are a Deputy Governor (who replaces the Permanent Secretary (Finance) in the Executive Council and the Legislature), a Parliamentary Secretary, Leader of Opposition and Deputy Speaker.

Governor, His Excellency A. W. Shave, OBE, *apptd* 1992.
Deputy Governor, H. McCrory, *apptd* 1991.

EXECUTIVE COUNCIL

(as at 18 June 1992)
Chief Minister and Minister of Home Affairs, Tourism and Economic Development, Hon. Emile Gumbs.
Social Services and Lands, Hon. Eric Reid.
Communications, Public Utilities and Works, Hon. Kenneth Harrigan.
Finance and Economic Development, Hon. Osbourne Fleming.
Attorney-General, Hon. Kurt De Freitas.

FINANCE	1989	1990
Revenue	EC$32,530,300	EC$34,715,429
Expenditure	28,725,600	32,122,292

ECONOMY

Low rainfall limits agricultural output and export earnings are mainly from sales of lobsters. Tourism has developed rapidly in recent years and accounts for most of the island's economic activity. In 1991 there were 31,002 tourists and a further 59,542 day visitors.

TRADE WITH UK	1990	1991
Imports from UK	£1,853,000	£2,687,000
Exports to UK	122,000	197,000

ASCENSION – *see* St Helena

BERMUDA

AREA – The Bermudas, or Somers Islands, are a cluster of about 100 small islands (about 20 of which are inhabited) situated in the west of the Atlantic Ocean, in 32° 18′ N. lat. and 64° 46′ W. long., the nearest point of the mainland being Cape Hatteras in North Carolina, about 570 miles distant. The total area is approximately 20.59 sq. miles (53 sq. km), which includes 2.3 sq. miles leased to the USA.

POPULATION – The civil population is approximately 60,000 (1990 estimate).
CAPITAL – ΨHamilton (population 1990, 2,000).
CURRENCY – Bermuda dollar of 100 cents.

HISTORY

The colony derives its name from Juan Bermudez, a Spaniard, who sighted it before 1515. No settlement was made until 1609 when Sir George Somers, who was shipwrecked there on his way to Virginia, colonized the islands.

GOVERNMENT

Internal self-government was introduced on 8 June 1968. There is a Senate of 11 members and an elected House of Assembly of 40 members. The Governor retains responsibility for external affairs, defence, internal security and the police, although administrative matters for the Police Service have been delegated to the Minister of Home Affairs.

At the General Election of 9 February 1989 the United Bermuda Party gained 22 seats, the Progressive Labour Party 15 and Independents 2.

Governor and Commander-in-Chief, His Excellency Lord Waddington, PC, QC, *apptd* 1992.
Deputy Governor, John Kelly, MBE.

CABINET

(as at June 1992)
Premier, Hon. Sir John Swan, KBE.
Minister of Delegated and Legislative Affairs, Hon. Sir John Sharpe.
Health, Social Services and Housing, Hon. Quinton Edness.
Labour and Home Affairs, Hon. J. Irving Pearman.
Education, Hon. Gerald D. E. Simons.
Deputy Premier and Minister of the Environment, Hon. A. F. Cartwright DeCouto.
Works and Engineering, Dr the Hon. Clarence Terceira.
Youth, Sport and Recreation, Senator Pamela Gordon.
Community and Cultural Affairs , Hon. Leonard O. Gibbons.
Tourism, Hon. C. V. Jim Woolridge.
Transport, Hon. Ralph Marshall.
Finance, Dr the Hon. David Saul.
Management and Information Services, Hon. Michael Winfield.
President of the Senate, Hon. A. S. Jackson, MBE.
Speaker of the House of Assembly, Hon. D. Wilkinson.
Chief Justice, Hon. Sir James R. Astwood.
Puisne Judges, Hon. L. Austin Ward, QC; Hon. Mrs. N. Wade; Hon. R. W. Ground, OBE, QC.

Finance	1990–1	1991–9
Public revenue	$342,000,000	$361,600,000
Public expenditure	306,081,000	322,526,000

Economy

Locally manufactured concentrates, perfumes, cut flowers and pharmaceuticals are now the colony's leading exports. Little food is produced except vegetables and fish, other foodstuffs being imported.

The islands' economic structure is based on tourism, the major industry, and international company business, attracted by the low level of taxation and sophisticated telecommunications system. In 1991 a total of 512,197 visitors arrived by air and cruise ship. Cruise ships dock at Hamilton, Somerset and St George's.

Trade with UK	1990	1991
Imports from UK	£28,114,000	£16,205,000
Exports to UK	12,849,000	3,559,000

Education

Free elementary education was introduced in 1949. Free secondary education was introduced in 1965 for those children in the aided and maintained schools who were below the upper limit of the statutory school age of 16 (from 1969 onwards).

THE BRITISH ANTARCTIC TERRITORY

The British Antarctic Territory was designated in 1962 and consists of the areas south of 60°S. latitude which were previously included in the Falkland Islands Dependencies. The territory lies between longitudes 20° and 80°W., south of latitude 60°S. and includes the South Orkney Islands, the South Shetland Islands, the mountainous Antarctic Peninsula (highest point Mount Jackson, 13,620ft, in Palmer Land) and all adjacent islands, and the land mass extending to the South Pole. The territory has no indigenous inhabitants and the British population consists of the scientists and technicians who man the British Antarctic Survey stations. The number averages about 60 to 70 in winter, but increases considerably in the summer months with the arrival of field workers. Argentina, Brazil, Chile, China, Korea (South), Poland, USA, Russia and Uruguay also have scientific stations in the territory.

The first two British Antarctic Survey stations were established in the South Shetland Islands in 1944, and by 1956 the number of stations had risen to twelve. Due to the completion of field work in some areas and increased mobility, the number has now been reduced to five. These are Signy (Signy Island, South Orkney Islands), Faraday (Argentine Islands, Graham Coast), Rothera (Adelaide Island), Halley (Caird Coast) and, in summer only, Fossil Bluff (George VI Sound). Fifteen other stations have been established but are at present unoccupied.

The territory is administered by a Commissioner, resident in London.

Commissioner, Peter M. Newton.

THE BRITISH INDIAN OCEAN TERRITORY

The British Indian Ocean Territory was established by an Order in Council in 1965 and included islands formerly administered from Mauritius and the Seychelles. After the independence of both, the territory was redefined in 1976 as comprising only the islands of the Chagos Archipelago.

The Chagos Archipelago consists of six main groups of islands situated on the Great Chagos Bank and covering some 21,000 sq. miles (54,389 sq. km). The largest and most southerly of the Chagos Islands is Diego Garcia, a sand cay with a land area of about 17 square miles approximately 1,100 miles east of Mahé, used as a joint naval support facility by Britain and USA.

The other main island groups of the archipelago, Peros Banhos (29 islands with a total land area of 4 sq. miles) and Salomon (11 islands with a total land area of 2 sq. miles) are uninhabited. The islands have a typical tropical maritime climate, with average temperatures between 25° C and 29° C in Diego Garcia, and rainfall in the whole archipelago of 90–100 inches a year.

Commissioner and Administrator, T. G. Harris.

Trade with UK	1990	1991
Imports from UK	£689,000	£821,000
Exports to UK	118,000	197,000

THE BRITISH VIRGIN ISLANDS

Area – The Virgin Islands are a group of islands at the eastern extremity of the Greater Antilles, divided between Great Britain and the USA. Those of the group which are British number 46, of which 11 are inhabited, and have a total area of about 59 sq. miles, (153 sq. km). The principal are Tortola, the largest (situated in 18° 27′ N. lat. and 64° 40′ W. long., area, 21 sq. miles), Virgin Gorda (8¼ sq. miles), Anegada (15 sq.miles) and Jost Van Dyke (3½ sq. miles).

Apart from Anegada, which is a flat coral island, the British Virgin Islands are hilly, being an extension of the Puerto Rico and the US Virgin Islands archipelago. The highest point is Sage Mountain on Tortola which rises to a height of 1,780 feet.

Climate – The islands lie within the trade winds belt and possess a sub-tropical climate. The average temperature varies from 22°–28° C in winter and 26°–31° C in summer. The summer heat is tempered by sea breezes and the temperature usually falls by about 6° C at night. Average annual rainfall is 53 inches.

Population – The 1980 Census showed a total population of 10,985: Tortola (9,119); Virgin Gorda (1,443); Anegada (169); Jost Van Dyke (136); and other islands (82). A 1989 UN estimate gave a total figure of 13,000.

Capital – ΨRoad Town, on the south-east of Tortola. Population 2,479.

Currency – The US dollar (US$) of 100 cents is legal tender.

Government

Under the 1977 Constitution the Governor, appointed by the Crown, remains responsible for defence and internal security, external affairs and the civil service but in other matters acts in accordance with the advice of the Executive Council. The Executive Council consists of the Governor as Chairman, one ex officio member (the Attorney-General), the Chief Minister and three other ministers. The Legislative Council consists of a Speaker chosen from outside the Council, one ex officio member (the Attorney-General), and nine elected members returned from nine one-member electoral districts.

Governor, Peter Alfred Penfold, OBE, *apptd* 1992.
Deputy Governor, E. Georges, OBE.

THE EXECUTIVE COUNCIL
(as at 30 June 1992)
Chairman, The Governor.
Chief Minister and Minister of Finance, Hon. H. Lavity Stoutt.
Natural Resources and Labour, Hon. Ralph O'Neal, OBE.
Communications and Works, Hon. Terrance Lettsome.
Health, Education and Welfare, Hon. Louis Walters, MBE.
Attorney-General, Hon. Donald Trotman.

Puisne Judge (resident), vacant.

FINANCE	1989	1990
Revenue	US$32,629,000	US$41,400,000
Expenditure	31,038,000	40,600,000

ECONOMY

Tourism is the main industry but the financial centre is growing steadily in importance. Other industries include a rum distillery, three stone-crushing plants and factories manufacturing concrete blocks and paint. The major export items are fresh fish, gravel, sand, fruit and vegetables; exports are largely confined to the US Virgin Islands. Chief imports are building materials, machinery, cars and beverages.

TRADE WITH UK	1990	1991
Imports from UK	£4,454,000	£6,081,000
Exports to UK	1,205,000	1,736,000

COMMUNICATIONS

The principal airport is on Beef Island, linked by bridge to Tortola, and an extended runway of 3,600 ft enables larger aircraft to call. There is a second airfield on Virgin Gorda and a third on Anegada. There are direct shipping services to the United Kingdom and the United States and fast passenger services connect the main islands by ferry.

THE CAYMAN ISLANDS

AREA – The Cayman Islands, between 79° 44′ and 81° 26′ W. and 19° 15′ and 19° 46′ N., consist of three islands, Grand Cayman, Cayman Brac, and Little Cayman, with a total area of 100 sq. miles (259 sq. km). About 150 miles south of Cuba, the islands are divided from Jamaica, 180 miles to the south-east, by the Cayman Trench, the deepest part of the Caribbean. The nearest point on the US mainland is Miami in Florida, 450 miles to the north. Cooled by trade winds, the annual average temperature and rainfall are 27.2° C and 50.7 inches, respectively.

POPULATION – Population (estimate 1991) 27,000, of which the vast majority live on Grand Cayman.

CAPITAL – ΨGeorge Town, in Grand Cayman, population (1989) 12,921.

CURRENCY – Cayman Islands dollar (CI$) of 100 cents, which is fixed at CI$ = US$1.20.

HISTORY

The colony derives its name from the Carib word for the crocodile, 'caymanas', which appeared in the log of the first English visitor to the Cayman Islands, Sir Francis Drake. Although tradition has it that the first settlers arrived in 1658, the first recorded settlers arrived in 1666–71. The first recorded permanent settlers followed the first land grant by Britain in 1734. The islands were placed under direct control of Jamaica in 1863. When Jamaica became independent in 1962, the islands opted to remain under the British Crown.

GOVERNMENT

The constitution provides for a Governor, a Legislative Assembly and an Executive Council, and effectively allows a large measure of self-government. Unless there are exceptional reasons, the Governor accepts the advice of the Executive Council, which comprises three official members and four others elected from the 12 elected members of the Assembly. The official members also sit in the Assembly. The Governor has responsibility for the police, civil service, defence and external affairs. The Governor handed over the presidency of the Legislative Assembly to the Speaker on 15 February 1991. The normal life of the Assembly is four years, with a general election next due in November 1992.

Governor, His Excellency Michael E. J. Gore, CBE, *apptd* 1992.

EXECUTIVE COUNCIL
(as at 30 June 1992)
President, The Governor.
Chief Secretary, Hon. J. L. Hurlston, MBE.
Acting Attorney-General, Hon. A. S. Smellie.
Financial Secretary, Hon. G. A. McCarthy.
Member for Tourism, Aviation and Trade, Hon. W. N. Bodden, OBE.
Member for Education, Environment, Recreation and Culture, Hon. B. O. Ebanks, OBE.
Member for Health and Social Services, Hon. D. E. Miller.
Member for Communications, Works and Agriculture, Hon. L. H. Pierson.
Speaker of Legislative Assembly, Mrs S. I. McLaughlin, MBE.

LONDON OFFICE
Cayman Islands Government Office, 100 Brompton Road, London SW3 1EX
Tel 071-581 9418

Government Representative, T. Russell, CMG, CBE.

FINANCE	1991	1992*
Revenue	CI$127.3m	CI$125.6m
Expenditure	104.4m	109.1m

*estimated

ECONOMY

Based on a complete absence of direct taxation, the Cayman Islands have been successfully promoted over the past 25 years as an offshore financial centre. With representation from 60 countries, there were, at the end of 1991, 544 banks and trust companies, of which local offices were maintained by 72. In addition, there were 367 licensed insurance companies and 23,700 registered companies at the end of 1991.

Promotion of tourism, with an emphasis on scuba diving, has also been successful. There were 237,351 visitors by air and 474,747 cruise ship callers in 1991.

The two industries support a heavy imbalance in trade resulting from the need to import most of what is consumed and used on the islands, and have created a thriving local economy in which the GNP reached US$669.6m (US$25,300 per capita) in 1991. Import duty and fees from financial centre operations have provided revenue enabling the government to undertake heavy investment in education (which is provided free to all 4–16 year olds), health and other social programmes.

TRADE	1990	1991
Total imports	CI$239.7m	CI$222.9m
Total exports	3.1m	2.5m

TRADE WITH UK	1990	1991
Imports from UK	£13,394,000	£6,081,000
Exports to UK	2,262,000	1,736,000

FALKLAND ISLANDS

AREA – The Falkland Islands, the only considerable group in the South Atlantic, lie about 300 miles east of the Straits of Magellan, between 52° 15′–53° S. lat. and 57° 40′–62° W. long. They consist of East Falkland (area 2,610 sq. miles; 6,759 sq. km), West Falkland (2,090 sq. miles; 5,413 sq. km) and upwards of 100 small islands in the aggregate. Mount Usborne (E. Falkland), the loftiest peak, rises 2,312 feet above the level of the sea. The islands are chiefly moorland.

CLIMATE – Cool. At Stanley the mean monthly temperature varies between 9° C in January and 2° C in July.

POPULATION – The population, excluding the British garrison, was 2,121 at 5 March 1991.

CHIEF TOWN – ΨStanley, population 1,643 (1991). Stanley is about 8,103 miles distant from England .

CURRENCY – Falkland pound of 100 pence.

HISTORY

The Falklands were sighted first by Davis in 1592, and by Hawkins in 1594; the first known landing was by Strong in 1690. A settlement was made by France in 1764; this was subsequently sold to Spain, but the latter country recognized Great Britain's title to a part at least of the group in 1771. After Argentina declared independence from Spain, the Argentine government in 1820 proclaimed its sovereignty over the Falklands and a settlement was founded in 1826. The settlement was destroyed by the Americans in 1831. In 1833 occupation was resumed by the British for the protection of the seal-fisheries, and the islands were permanently colonized as the most southerly organized colony of the British Empire. Argentina continued to claim sovereignty over the islands (known to them as las Islas Malvinas), and in pursuance of this claim invaded the islands on 2 April 1982 and also occupied South Georgia. A Task Force despatched from Great Britain recaptured South Georgia on 25 April and after landing at San Carlos Bay on 21 May recaptured the islands from the Argentines, who surrendered on 14 June 1982. A British naval and military presence remains in the area.

GOVERNMENT

Under the 1985 Constitution, the Governor is advised by an Executive Council consisting of three elected members of the Legislative Council and two ex-officio members, the Chief Executive and the Financial Secretary. The Legislative Council consists of eight elected members and the same two ex-officio members.

Governor and Chairman of the Executive Council, His Excellency David Everard Tatham, *apptd* 1992.

Chief Executive, R. Sampson.

Financial Secretary, D. F. Howatt.

Commander, British Forces, Falkland Islands, Rear-Adm. N. E. Rankin, CBE.

Attorney General, D. G. Lang, QC.

LONDON OFFICE

Falkland Islands Government Office, Falkland House, 14 Broadway, London SW1H OBH.

Tel 071-222 2542.

Government Representative, Miss S. Cameron.

FINANCE	1989–90	1990–1
Public Revenue	£44,060,260	£43,327,160
Expenditure	35,911,730	41,138,150

ECONOMY

The economy was formerly based solely on agriculture, principally sheep-farming with a little dairy farming for domestic requirements and crops for winter fodder. Since the establishment of an interim conservation and management zone around the islands and the consequent introduction on 1 February 1987 of a licensing regime for vessels fishing within the zone the economy has diversified and income from the associated fishing activities is now the largest source of revenue. Chief imports are provisions, alcoholic beverages, timber, clothing and hardware.

TRADE WITH UK	1990	1991
Imports from UK	£11,309,000	£16,039,000
Exports to UK	4,817,000	3,379,000

GIBRALTAR

AREA – Gibraltar is a rocky promontory, 2¾ miles in length, three-quarters of a mile in breadth, with a total area of 2¼ sq. miles. It is 1,396 ft. high at its greatest elevation, near the southern extremity of Spain, with which it is connected by a low isthmus. It is about 14 miles distant from the opposite coast of Africa. The town stands at the foot of the promontory on the west side.

POPULATION – The population at the end of 1990 stood at 31,265.

CURRENCY – Gibraltar pound of 100 pence.

HISTORY

Gibraltar was captured in 1704, during the war of the Spanish Succession, by a combined Dutch and English force under Sir George Rooke, and was ceded to Great Britain by the Treaty of Utrecht 1713. Several attempts have been made to retake it, the most celebrated being the great siege of 1779 to 1783, when General Eliott, afterwards Lord Heathfield, held it for three years and seven months against a combined French and Spanish force.

GOVERNMENT

The Constitution of Gibraltar, approved in 1969, made formal provision for certain domestic matters to devolve on Ministers appointed from among elected members of the House of Assembly then set up to replace the former Legislative Council. The House of Assembly consists of an independent Speaker, 15 elected members, the Attorney-General and the Financial and Development Secretary.

Governor and Commander-in-Chief, His Excellency Admiral Sir Derek Reffell, KCB.

Flag Officer, Gibraltar, and Admiral Superintendent, HM Naval Base, Gibraltar, Rear-Adm. J. T. Sanders, OBE.

Deputy Governor, A. Carter.

Financial and Development Secretary, P. Brooke.

Attorney-General, vacant.

Chief Justice, A. Kneller.

Chief Minister, J. Bossano.

Speaker, Mayor R. J. Peliza, OBE.

FINANCE	1989–90	1990–1
Revenue	£87,716,000	£90,820,300
Expenditure	90,158,000	96,133,000

ECONOMY

Gibraltar enjoys the advantages of an extensive shipping trade and is a popular shopping centre. The chief sources of revenue are the port dues, the rent of the Crown estate in the town, and duties on consumer items. The free port tradition of Gibraltar is still reflected in the low rates of import duty. The gradual change from a fortress city to a holiday centre has led to a flourishing tourist trade.

A total of 3,316 merchant ships (61.5 million gross registered tons aggregate) entered the port during 1991. Of these 2,843 were deep-sea ships (60.9 million gross registered tons aggregate). In addition 4,403 yachts called at the port. There are 49.9 km of roads.

TRADE	1990	1991
Total imports	£200,493,000	£266,348,000
Total exports	76,138,000	101,679,000

TRADE WITH UK	1990	1991
Imports from UK	£69,073,000	£80,105,000
Exports to UK	5,048,000	4,289,000

EDUCATION

Education is compulsory and free for children between the ages of 4 and 15 whose parents are ordinarily resident in Gibraltar. Scholarships are available for higher education in Britain. The total enrolment in government schools was 4,690 in December 1991.

HONG KONG

AREA – Hong Kong, consisting of more than 230 islands and of a portion of the mainland (Kowloon and the New Territories), on the south-east coast of China, is situated at the eastern side of the mouth of the Pearl River, between 22° 9′ and 22° 37′ N. lat. and 113° 52′–114° 30′ E. long. The total area of the territory (including recent reclamation) is 416 sq. miles (1,075 sq. km).

The island of Hong Kong is about 11 miles long and from two to five miles broad, with a total area of 29 sq. miles (80 sq. km); at the eastern entrance to the harbour it is separated from the mainland by a narrow strait.

CLIMATE – Hong Kong's climate is sub-tropical, tending towards the temperate for nearly half the year. The mean monthly temperature ranges from 17° C to 30° C. The average annual rainfall is 2,214 mm, of which nearly 80 per cent falls between May and September. Tropical cyclones passing at various distances from Hong Kong occur between May and November, causing high winds and heavy rain.

POPULATION – Population at the beginning of 1992 was 5.8 million.

CAPITAL – ΨVictoria, situated on the island of Hong Kong, is about 81 miles SE of Canton and 40 miles E. of the Portuguese province of Macao at the other side of the Pearl River. It lies along the northern shore of the island and faces the mainland; the harbour (19 sq. miles water area) lies between the city and the mainland.

CURRENCY – Hong Kong dollar (HK$) of 100 cents.

HISTORY

The island was first occupied by Great Britain in January 1841, and formally ceded by the Treaty of Nanking in 1842. Kowloon was subsequently acquired by the Peking Convention of 1860, and the New Territories, consisting of a peninsula in the southern part of the Guangdong province together with adjacent islands, by a 99-year lease signed on 9 June 1898.

GOVERNMENT

Hong Kong is administered by the Hong Kong Government, at the head of which is the Governor, and its administration has developed from the basic pattern applied to all British-governed territories overseas. Under the terms of the Joint Declaration of the British and Chinese Governments, which entered into force on 27 May 1985, Hong Kong will become, with effect from 1 July 1997, a Special Administrative Region of the People's Republic of China. However, the social and economic systems in the SAR will remain unchanged for 50 years. The British and Chinese governments have, since the entry into force of the agreement, been involved in consultations on the implementation of the agreement via the Joint Liaison Group.

The Governor governs aided by an Executive Council and a Legislative Council. The Executive Council consists of four ex-officio and ten appointed members. The Legislative Council includes three ex-officio members, seven official members, 21 appointed members and 18 directly elected members. The first direct elections for 18 of the 60 Legislative Council seats were held in September 1991. It is planned that 21 members of the Legislative Council will be directly elected by 1 July 1997.

There is also an Urban Council which provides services relating to public health and sanitation, culture and recreation in the urban area. A Regional Council was also set up in 1986 to provide similar services in the New Territories. Twelve of the 36 Regional Council seats and 15 of the 40 Urban Council seats were directly elected for the first time in May 1991. Both Councils are financially autonomous. China is demanding an increasing voice in Hong Kong affairs as the handover in 1997 approaches.

Governor, His Excellency The Rt. Hon. Christopher Patten, *apptd* 1992.
Chief Justice, The Hon. Sir Ti Liang Yang.
Chief Secretary, Hon. Sir David Ford, KBE, LVO.
Commander, British Forces, Maj.-Gen. J. P. Foley, CB, OBE, MC.
Financial Secretary, Hon. N. W. H. McLeod, CBE.
Attorney-General, Hon. J. F. Mathews, CMG
Secretary for the Civil Service, Hon. E. B. Wiggham, CBE.
Planning, Environment and Lands, Hon. A. G. Eason.
Transport, Hon. Michael M. K. Leung, CBE.
Education and Manpower, Hon. John C. C. Chan, LVO, OBE.
Economic Services, Hon. Mrs Anson Chan, CBE.
Home Affairs, Michael M. Y. Suen.
Health and Welfare, Hon. Mrs Elizabeth C. L. Wong-Chien, ISO.
Security, Hon. A. P. Asprey, OBE, AE.
Monetary Affairs, D. A. C. Nendick, CBE.
Recreation and Culture, James So, CBE.
Treasury, K. Y. Yeung.
Trade and Industry, T. H. Chau.
Constitutional Affairs, Michael C. Sze, ISO.
Works, James Blake.

BRITISH COUNCIL REPRESENTATIVE, T. Buchanan, Easey Commercial Building, 225 Hennessy Road, Wanchai, Hong Kong.

LONDON OFFICE

Hong Kong Government Office, 6 Grafton Street, London W1X 3LB.
Tel 071-499 9821

Commissioner, Stephen Day, CMG, *apptd* 1992.

FINANCE	1990–1	1991–2*
Public revenue	HK$89,523m	HK$112,020m
Public expenditure	85,556m	96,755m

*estimated

ECONOMY

The manufacturing sector is the mainstay of Hong Kong's economy, contributing about 16.7 per cent to the GDP and accounting for about 25.3 per cent of total employment. Up to 90 per cent of Hong Kong's manufacturing output is eventually exported.

Hong Kong's manufacturing industries produce light consumer goods, such as electronics, plastics, electrical products, watches and clocks, which accounted for 33 per cent of Hong Kong's total domestic exports in 1989. The corresponding share of textiles and clothing, Hong Kong's traditional leading industries, was 39 per cent in 1990.

Diversification in terms of products and markets continues to be the main feature of recent industrial development, as are industrial partnerships with overseas companies. The economy of Hong Kong is based on export rather than the domestic market.

Trade

In 1991, the total value of visible trade (including domestic exports, re-exports and imports) amounted to 244 per cent of the GDP. Hong Kong's visible trade account had in 1991 a deficit of HK$16,200 million. Taking visible and invisible trade together, there was a combined surplus of HK$18,535 million, compared with HK$27,619 million in 1990. In 1991, Hong Kong's principal customers for its domestic products, in order of value of trade, were USA, China, the Federal Republic of Germany, the United Kingdom, Japan, Singapore and Taiwan. China was its principal supplier.

	1990	1991
Exports	HK$641,915m	HK$766,731m
Imports	660,679m	807,674m

Trade with UK	1990	1991
Imports from UK	£1,238,023,000	£1,386,892,000
Exports to UK	1,972,154,000	2,147,611,000

Communications

Hong Kong, one of the world's finest natural harbours, possesses excellent wharves. The Kwai Chung container terminal has 12 berths. A pier at the Ocean Terminal can accommodate large liners and cargo vessels up to 290 metres length and 10 metres draught. Mooring buoys in the harbour are available to vessels of up to 12 metres draught. Available dockyard facilities include three floating drydocks, the largest being capable of docking vessels up to 150,000 tonnes deadweight. In 1991 some 129,300 ocean-going and river-trade vessels called at Hong Kong and loaded and discharged more than 104 million tonnes of cargo.

Hong Kong International Airport, Kai Tak, situated to the east of the Kowloon peninsula, is regularly used by over 47 international airlines, providing some 1,870 frequent scheduled passenger and cargo services each week. During 1991, over 109,700 aircraft on international flights arrived and departed, carrying 19.2 million passengers and 852,000 tonnes of freight. A new international airport is to be built on reclaimed land off Lantau Island at Chek Lap Kok and is planned to become operational by 1997 with an initial capacity to handle 35 million passengers and 1.5 million tonnes of cargo a year.

Education

In October 1991 there were 2,597 day schools with 1,304,806 pupils. Free education for children up to the age of 15 was made compulsory in 1979. Post-secondary education is provided by three universities, two polytechnics, the Hong Kong Baptist College and four approved post-secondary colleges. The Hong Kong Polytechnic and City Polytechnic of Hong Kong have about 10,935 and 7,040 full-time students respectively. The Open Learning Institute of Hong Kong provides university education to about 16,500 students. There are also eight technical institutes and four teacher-training colleges.

MONTSERRAT

Area – Situated in 16° 45′ N. lat. and 61° 15° W. long., 27 miles SW of Antigua, Montserrat is about 11 miles long and seven wide, with an area of 38 sq. miles (98 sq. km). Fertile and green, it is volcanic with several hot springs. About two-thirds of the island is mountainous, the rest capable of cultivation.

Population – Population (UN estimate 1989) was 13,000.

Chief Town – ΨPlymouth, population 3,000.

Currency – East Caribbean dollar (EC$) of 100 cents.

History

Discovered by Columbus in 1493, Montserrat was settled by Irishmen in 1632, conquered and held by the French for some time, and finally assigned to Great Britain in 1783.

Government

A ministerial system was introduced in Montserrat in 1960. The Executive Council is presided over by the Governor and is composed of four elected members (the Chief and three other Ministers) and two ex-officio members (the Attorney-General and the Financial Secretary). The four Ministers are appointed from the members of the political party holding the majority in the Legislative Council. The Legislative Council consists of the Speaker, two ex-officio members (the Attorney General and the Financial Secretary), two nominated unofficial members and seven elected members.

Governor, His Excellency David Taylor, *apptd* 1990.

Executive Council

(as at 8 October 1991)

President, The Governor.
Chief Minister and Minister of Finance and Economic Development, Hon. Reuben T. Meade.
Communications, Works and Sport, Hon. David S. Brandt.
Agriculture, Trade and the Environment, Hon. Charles T. Kirnon.
Education, Health, Community Services and Labour, Hon. Lazelle Howes.
Attorney-General, Hon. Stanley A. Moore.
Financial Secretary, Hon. C. T. John, OBE.

Speaker of the Legislative Council, Dr the Hon. H. A. Fergus, OBE.

Finance	1989	1990
Revenue	EC$35,049,330	EC$39,138,570
Expenditure	34,308,150	38,155,890

Economy

The economy is dominated by tourism, related construction activities and offshore business services. There is some light industry and efforts are being made to increase agricultural exports and establish an agro-processing industry.

Trade with UK	1990	1991
Imports from UK	£3,515,000	£2,720,000
Exports to UK	425,000	39,000

PITCAIRN ISLANDS

Area – Pitcairn, a small volcanic island 1.9 sq. miles (5 sq. km) in area, is the chief of a group of islands situated about midway between New Zealand and Panama in the South Pacific Ocean at longitude 130° 06′ W. and latitude 25° 04′ S. The island rises in cliffs to a height of 1,100 feet and access from the sea is possible only at Bounty Bay, a small rocky cove, and then only by surf boats. The other three islands of the group (Henderson lying 105 miles ENE of Pitcairn, Oeno lying 75 miles NW and Ducie lying 293 miles E.) are all uninhabited. Henderson Island is occasionally visited by the Pitcairn Islanders to obtain supplies of 'miro' wood which is used for their carvings. Oeno is visited for excursions of about a week's duration every two years or so.

CLIMATE – Mean monthly temperatures vary between 66°F (19°C) in August and 75°F (24°C) in February and the average annual rainfall is 80 inches. With an equable climate, the island is very fertile and produces both tropical and sub-tropical trees and crops.

POPULATION – At May 1992 the population was 56.

HISTORY

First settled in 1790 by the Bounty mutineers and their Tahitian companions, Pitcairn was left uninhabited in 1856 when the entire population was resettled on Norfolk Island. The present community are descendants of two parties who, not wishing to remain on Norfolk, returned to Pitcairn in 1859 and 1864 respectively.

GOVERNMENT

Pitcairn became a British settlement under the British Settlement Act, 1887, and was administered by the Governor of Fiji from 1952 until 1970, when the administration was transferred to the British High Commission in New Zealand and the British High Commissioner was appointed Governor. The local Government Ordinance of 1964 provides for a Council of ten members of whom six are elected.

Governor of Pitcairn, Henderson, Ducie and Oeno Islands, His Excellency David Joseph Moss, CMG (*British High Commissioner to New Zealand*).
Island Magistrate and Chairman of Island Council, J. Warren.
Education Officer and Government Adviser, A. R. Washington.

ECONOMY

The islanders live by subsistence gardening and fishing, and their limited monetary needs are satisfied by the manufacture of wood carvings and other handicrafts which are sold to passing ships and to a few overseas customers. Other than small fees charged for gun and driving licences there are no taxes and Government revenue is derived almost solely from the sale of postage stamps. Communication with the outside world is maintained by cargo vessels travelling between New Zealand and Panama which call at irregular intervals; and by means of a satellite service providing telephone, telex and fax facilities.

SOCIAL WELFARE

The New Zealand Ministry of Education provides assistance in recruiting a teacher for the sole-charge school. Education is compulsory between the ages of five and fifteen. Secondary education in New Zealand is encouraged by the Administration which provides scholarships and bursaries for the purpose. Medical care is provided by a registered nurse when a doctor is not present. Since 1887 the islanders have all been adherents of the Seventh-day Adventist Church.

ST HELENA AND DEPENDENCIES

ST HELENA

AREA – Probably the best known of all the solitary islands in the world, St Helena is situated in the South Atlantic Ocean, 955 miles south of the Equator, 702 SE of Ascension, 1,140 from the nearest point of the African Continent, 1,800 from the coast of South America, 1,694 from Cape Town (transit five days), in 15° 55′ S. lat. and 5° 42′ W. longitude. It is 10½ miles long, 6½ broad, and encloses an area of 47 sq. miles (122 sq. km).

St Helena is of volcanic origin, and consists of numerous rugged mountains, the highest rising to 2,700 feet, interspersed with picturesque ravines.

CLIMATE – Although within the tropics, the south-east 'trades' keep the temperature mild and equable.

POPULATION – Population was 5,644 in 1987.

CAPITAL – ΨJamestown. Population (1987) 1,332.

CURRENCY – St Helena pound (£) of 100 pence.

HISTORY

St Helena was discovered by the Portuguese navigator, Juan da Nova Castella, in 1502 (probably on St Helena's Day) and remained unknown to other European nations until 1588. It was used as a port of call for vessels of all nations trading to the East until it was annexed by the Dutch in 1633. It was never occupied by them, however, and the English East India Company seized it in 1659. In 1834 it was ceded to the Crown. During the period 1815 to 1821 the island was lent to the British Government as a place of exile for the Emperor Napoleon Bonaparte who died in St Helena on 5 May 1821. It was formerly an important station on the route to India, but its prosperity decreased after the construction of the Suez Canal. Since the collapse of the New Zealand flax industry in 1965, there have been no significant exports. ΨSt James's Bay, on the north-west of the island, possesses a good anchorage. There is as yet no airport or airstrip.

GOVERNMENT

The government of St Helena is administered by a Governor, with the aid of a Legislative Council, consisting of a Speaker, three ex-officio members (Chief Secretary, Financial Secretary and Attorney-General) and twelve elected members. Five committees of the Legislative Council are reponsible for general oversight of the activities of government departments and have in addition a wide range of statutory and administrative functions. The Governor is also assisted by an Executive Council of the three ex-officio members and the Chairmen of the Council committees.

Governor, His Excellency A. N. Hoole, OBE, *apptd* 1991.
Chief Secretary, M. Hone, MBE.
Financial Secretary, R. Perrott.
Attorney-General, D. Jeremiah.
Chief Medical Officer, Dr N. Nichol.
Chief Agriculture and Forestry Officer, C. Lomas.
Chief Education Officer, B. George.
Chief Engineer, D. Johnston.
Chief Social Services and Employment Officer, Mrs J. Young.

FINANCE	1990–1	1991–2
Local revenue	£2,520,918	£3,544,653
Budgetary	4,136,000	3,424,400
Recurrent expenditure	6,372,496	6,407,445
Development aid	1,494,889	1,058,487

TRADE	1990–1	1991–2
Total imports	£5,906,751	£6,320,224
Total exports	72,303	90,616

TRADE WITH UK	1990	1991
Imports from UK	£7,429,000	£6,980,000
Exports to UK	555,000	820,000

ASCENSION

AREA – The small island of Ascension lies in the South Atlantic (7° 56′ S., 14° 22′ W.) some 700 miles north-west of the island of St Helena. It is a rocky peak of purely volcanic origin. The highest point (Green Mountain), some 2,817 ft., is covered with lush vegetation. Ascension Island Services operate a farm of some 10 acres on the mountain, producing vegetables and livestock. The island is famous for turtles, which land on the beaches from January to May to lay their eggs. It is also a breeding area for the sooty tern, or wideawake, large numbers of which settle on the south-western coastal section every eighth month to hatch their eggs. Other wildlife on the island includes feral donkeys and cats, rabbits and francolin partridge. All wildlife except rabbits and cats is protected by law. The ocean surrounding the island contains shark, barracuda, tuna, bonito and many other fish.

POPULATION – The resident population in March 1992 totalled 1,129, of whom 805 were from St Helena, 229 from the UK, 148 from the USA and 10 from the Republic of South Africa. The residents consist of the employees and families of the British organizations, of the contractors of the US Air Force (Computer Sciences Raytheon) and of the St Helena Government.

British forces returned to the island in April 1982 in support of operations in the Falkland Islands. At present there are over 100 RAF/PSA personnel on the island supporting the air link to the Falklands.

CAPITAL – Georgetown.

HISTORY

Ascension is said to have been discovered by Juan da Nova Castella on Ascension Day 1501 and two years later was visited by Alphonse d'Albuquerque, who gave the island its present name. It was uninhabited until the arrival of Napoleon in St Helena in 1815 when a small British naval garrison was stationed on the island. It remained under the supervision of the Board of Admiralty until 1922, when it was made a dependency of St Helena by Royal Letters Patent.

GOVERNMENT

The British Foreign Secretary appoints the Administrator who is responsible to the Governor resident in St Helena. There is a small Police Force and Post Office. The British organizations through Ascension Island Services (AIS) provide and operate various common services for the island (school, hospital, public works etc).

Administrator, B. N. Connelly.

COMMUNICATIONS

Ascension Island is a main relay point of the coaxial submarine cable system laid between South Africa, Portugal and the United Kingdom, which is operated by the South Atlantic Cable Company. Cable & Wireless PLC operates the international telephone and cable services and maintains an internal telephone service. The BBC opened its Atlantic relay station broadcasting to Africa and South America in 1967.

TRISTAN DA CUNHA

AREA – Tristan da Cunha is the chief island of a group of islands in the South Atlantic which lies in lat. 37° 6′ S. and long. 12° 2′ W., some 1,320 miles (2,124 km) south-south-west of St Helena, about 1,500 miles (2,414 km) west of the Cape of Good Hope, and 3,600 miles (5,794 km) north-east of Cape Horn. Tristan da Cunha has an area of 38 square miles (98 square km). Inaccessible Island lies 20 miles west and has an area of 4 square miles (11 square km), and the three Nightingale Islands lie 20 miles south of Tristan da Cunha and have an area of three-quarters of a square mile (2 square km). Gough Island lies some 250 miles south-south-east of Tristan da Cunha in lat. 40° 20′ S. and long. 9° 44′ W. and has an area of 35 square miles (91 square km).

All the islands are volcanic and steep sided with cliffs or narrow beaches. Tristan itself has a single volcanic cone rising to 6,760 feet (2,060 m) and a narrow north-western coastal plain on which the settlement of Edinburgh is situated.

Inaccessible Island is a lofty mass of rock with sides two miles in length; the island is the resort of penguins and sea-fowl. Cultivation was started in 1937 but has been abandoned.

The Nightingale Islands are three in number, of which the largest is one mile long and three-quarters of a mile wide, and rises in two peaks, 960 and 1,105 feet above sea level respectively. The smaller islands, Stoltenhoff and Middle Isle, are little more than huge rocks. Seals, innumerable penguins, and vast numbers of sea-fowl visit these islands.

Gough Island (or Diego Alvarez) is about eight miles long and four miles broad and is the resort of penguins and sea-elephants and has valuable guano deposits.

CLIMATE – The islands have a warm-temperate oceanic climate which is damp and windy and supports forest and scrub. Rainfall averages 66 inches a year on the coast of Tristan da Cunha.

POPULATION – Population in 1991 was 288, in the settlement of Edinburgh on Tristan da Cunha. In addition, there is a meteorological station maintained on Gough Island by the South African government and manned by South Africans. Inaccessible Island and the Nightingale Islands are uninhabited.

CAPITAL – Edinburgh.

CURRENCY – Pound Sterling.

TIME ZONE – Greenwich Mean Time.

HISTORY

Tristan da Cunha was discovered in 1506 by a Portuguese admiral (Tristão da Cunha) after whom it was named. It was the resort of British and American sealers from the middle of the eighteenth century, and in 1760 a British naval officer visited the group of islands and gave his name to Nightingale Island. On 14 August 1816 the group was annexed to the British Crown and a garrison was placed on Tristan da Cunha, but this force was withdrawn in 1817. Corporal William Glass remained at his own request with his wife and two children. This party, with five others, formed a settlement. In 1827 five women from St Helena, and afterwards others from Cape Colony, joined the party.

Due to its position on a main sailing route the colony thrived, with an economy based on whaling, sealing and barter with passing ships. However, with the replacement of sail by steam in the late nineteenth century, a period of decline set in, with no regular calls by shipping.

In October 1961, a volcano, believed to have been extinct for thousands of years, erupted and the danger of further volcanic activity led to the evacuation of inhabitants to the United Kingdom. An advance party returned to Tristan da Cunha in the spring of 1963, and subsequently the main body of the islanders returned to the island.

Government

In 1938 Tristan da Cunha and the neighbouring islands of Inaccessible, Nightingale and Gough were made dependencies of St Helena and this remains their status today. They are administered by the Foreign and Commonwealth Office through a resident Administrator, with headquarters at the settlement of Edinburgh. Under a new Constitution introduced in 1969, the Administrator is advised by an Island Council of eight elected members, of whom one must be a woman, and three appointed members. There is universal suffrage at 18.

Administrator, Philip Johnson.

Economy and Communications

The main industries on the island are crayfish fishing, fish-processing and agriculture, with the shore-based fishing industry having been developed with the construction of the boat harbour in 1967 and the re-establishment of the crayfish-freezing factory in 1966. There are no taxes on Tristan, with income being derived from the fishing company, and the sales of stamps and handicrafts. Apart from the fishing industry, the other main employer is the Administration itself. There is one hospital, opened in 1971, and a school opened in 1975 catering for those up to age 15.

The island is isolated and scheduled visits are restricted to about six calls a year by fishing vessels from Cape Town and an annual call of the RMS *St Helena* from the UK. A wireless station on the island is in daily contact with Cape Town and a radio-telephone service was established in 1969, the same year that electricity was introduced to all the islanders' homes. A satellite system providing direct dialling telephone and fax facilities is in the process of being installed and will be operational by the end of 1992.

SOUTH GEORGIA AND THE SOUTH SANDWICH ISLANDS

South Georgia is an island 800 miles east-south-east of the Falkland group, with an area of 1,450 sq. miles. The population comprises an army unit and a civilian harbour master at King Edward Point, and staff of the British Antarctic Survey at Bird Island, in the north-west of South Georgia.

The South Sandwich Islands lie some 470 miles SE of South Georgia. The group is a chain of uninhabited, actively volcanic islands about 150 miles long, with a wholly Antarctic climate.

The present constitution came into effect on 3 October 1985. It provides for a Commissioner who, for the time being, shall be the officer administering the Government of the Falkland Islands.

Commissioner for South Georgia and the South Sandwich Islands, David Everard Tatham, CMG, *apptd* 1992.

TURKS AND CAICOS ISLANDS

Area – The Turks and Caicos Islands are situated between 21° and 22° N. latitude and 71° and 72° W. longitude, about 100 miles north of the Dominican Republic and 50 miles south-east of the Bahamas of which they are geographically an extension. There are over 30 islands, of which eight are inhabited, covering an estimated area of 166 sq. miles (430 sq. km). The principal island is Grand Turk.

Climate – The Islands lie in the trade wind belt. The average temperature varies from 24°–27° C in the winter and 29°–32° C in the summer and humidity is generally low. Average rainfall is 21 inches per annum.

Population – The population in 1988 was estimated to be 14,000 (Grand Turk 4,500).

Government

A new Constitution was introduced in 1988, providing for an enlarged Executive Council and Legislative Council. The Executive Council is presided over by the Governor and comprises the Chief Minister and four elected Ministers, together with the Chief Secretary, the Attorney General and the Financial Secretary ex-officio.

At the General Election of 3 April 1991, the People's National Party won 8 seats and the People's Democratic Movement 5 seats in the Legislative Council.

Governor, His Excellency Michael John Bradley, CMG, QC, *apptd* 1987.

Executive Council

(as at 28 May 1992)
President, The Governor.
Chief Secretary, Hon. M. Forrester.
Attorney-General, Hon. L. Agard (*acting*).
Financial Secretary, Hon. A. Robinson, OBE.
Members, Hon. W. Misick (*Chief Minister*); Hon. A. Durham; Hon. A. Smith; Hon. R. Hall; Hon. M. Misick.

Finance	1990–1	1991–2*
Local revenue	US$22,507,881	US$26,580,658
Expenditure	24,377,073	26,074,808
Budgetary aid	Nil	Nil

*estimate

Economy

The most important industries are fishing, tourism and offshore finance.

Trade with UK	1990	1991
Imports from UK	£1,719,000	£1,732,000
Exports to UK	8,000	12,000

Communications

The principal airports are on the islands of Grand Turk, Providenciales and South Caicos. There are direct shipping services to the USA (Miami). There is an air service between Miami, Providenciales and Grand Turk, between South Caicos and the Bahamas, and between Providenciales and Grand Turk and Haiti and the Dominican Republic. An internal air service provides a twice daily service between the principal islands. A comprehensive telephone and telex service is provided by Cable and Wireless (WI) Ltd.

International Organizations

ASSOCIATION OF SOUTH EAST ASIAN NATIONS

70 A. Jl. Sisingamangaraja Kebayoran Baru, Jakarta, Indonesia

Formed in 1967, the main aims of the Association of South East Asian Nations (ASEAN) are the acceleration of economic growth, social progress and cultural development, the promotion of collaboration and mutual assistance in matters of common interest, and the continuing stability of the South East Asian region.

The heads of government of the member countries are the highest authority and give directions to ASEAN as and when necessary. The main policy-making body is the annual meeting of foreign ministers of the member countries. The members of the Association are Brunei, Indonesia, Malaysia, the Philippines, Singapore and Thailand.

Secretary-General, Rusli Noor (*Indonesia*).

BANK FOR INTERNATIONAL SETTLEMENTS

Centralbahnplatz 2, 4002 Basle, Switzerland

The objectives of the Bank for International Settlements (founded in 1930) are to promote the co-operation of central banks; to provide facilities for international financial operations; and to act as trustee or agent in international financial settlements entrusted to it. The London agent is the Bank of England, and the Governor of the Bank of England is a member of the Board of Directors, in which administrative control is vested.

Chairman of the Board of Directors and President of the Bank for International Settlements, B. Dennis (*Sweden*).

CAB INTERNATIONAL

Wallingford, Oxon. OX10 8DE Tel: 0491-32111

CAB International (formerly the Commonwealth Agricultural Bureaux) was founded in 1929. It consists of four institutes and five editorial divisions under the control of an Executive Council comprising representatives of the countries which contribute to its funds. The functions of CABI are to provide a scientific information service, identification of pests, biological control services and mutual assistance. Each institute and editorial division acts as an effective clearing house for the collection, collation and dissemination of information in its particular branch of agricultural science.

Director-General, D. Mentz.

CARIBBEAN COMMUNITY AND COMMON MARKET

PO Box 10827, Georgetown, Guyana

The Caribbean Community and Common Market (Caricom) was established in 1973 with three objectives: economic co-operation through the Caribbean Common Market; the co-ordination of foreign policy among the independent member states; the provision of common services and co-operation in functional matters such as health, education and culture, communications and industrial relations. The principal organs are the Conference of Heads of Government, which determines policy, and the Common Market Council of Ministers, consisting of ministers of government (usually ministers of trade) designated by each member state, which is responsible for the development and smooth running of the Common Market and for the settlement of any problems arising out of its functioning. The principal administrative arm is the Secretariat, based in Guyana.

The 13 member states are Antigua and Barbuda, The Bahamas (which is not a member of the Common Market), Barbados, Belize, Dominica, Grenada, Guyana, Jamaica, Montserrat, St Christopher and Nevis, St Lucia, St Vincent and the Grenadines and Trinidad and Tobago. The British Virgin Islands and the Turks and Caicos Islands are associate members. The Dominican Republic, Haiti, Mexico, Puerto Rico, Suriname and Venezuela have observer status.

Secretary-General, Roderick Rainford (*Jamaica*).

The Commonwealth

The Commonwealth is a free association of 50 sovereign independent states together with their associated states and dependencies. All of the states were formerly parts of the British Empire, or League of Nations (later UN) mandated territories.

The status and relationship of member nations were first defined by the Inter-Imperial Relations Committee of the 1926 Imperial Conference, under the chairmanship of Lord Balfour, when the six existing dominions (Australia, Canada, the Irish Free State, Newfoundland, New Zealand and South Africa) were described as 'autonomous Communities within the British Empire, equal in status, in no way subordinate one to another in any aspect of their domestic or external affairs, though united by a common allegiance to the Crown and freely associated as Members of the British Commonwealth of Nations'. This formula was given legal substance by the Statute of Westminster 1931.

This concept of a group of countries owing allegiance to a single Crown changed in 1949 when India decided to become a republic. Her continued membership of the Commonwealth was agreed by the other members on the basis of her 'acceptance of the King as the symbol of the free association of its independent member nations and as such the head of the Commonwealth'. This paved the way for other republics to join the association in due course. Member nations agreed at the time of the accession of Queen Elizabeth II to recognize Her Majesty as the new Head of the Commonwealth. However, the position is not vested in the British Crown.

The Modern Commonwealth

With the membership of India and Pakistan in 1947, Ceylon (later Sri Lanka) in 1948 and Ghana in 1957, the character of the Commonwealth changed fundamentally. The grouping of all-white dominions gave way to a modern, multi-racial association of equal, sovereign nations and their peoples. The new era was characterized most succinctly by the British Prime Minister Harold Macmillan in his 'wind of change' speech to the South African Parliament in 1960, in which he predicted the independence of Britain's African colonies. In the following decades, Britain granted independence to almost all of her colonies in Africa, Asia, the Caribbean and the Pacific. Virtually all of these newly-independent countries joined the Commonwealth.

In its modern form, the Commonwealth increasingly focused its attention on promoting development and on helping to end racial inequality in southern Africa. The Commonwealth played an important role in the resolution of the Rhodesian crisis ending with the independence of Zimbabwe, strongly supported the independence of Namibia, and from the late 1970s took concerted action, including sporting and economic sanctions, against the South African government over its policy of apartheid.

The Harare Declaration

As progress was made towards ending apartheid and introducing democracy in South Africa, the Commonwealth set itself new goals at its heads of government meeting in Harare, Zimbabwe, in October 1991. Outlined in the Harare Commonwealth Declaration, these goals include the promotion of the Commonwealth's fundamental political values, such as democracy, the rule of law, good government and human rights; the promotion of equality for women; the provision of universal access to education; the promotion of sustainable development and the alleviation of poverty; action against disease and illegal drugs; help for small Commonwealth states; and support of the UN in the quest for international consensus on key issues.

Membership

Membership of the Commonwealth involves acceptance of the association's basic principles and is subject to the approval of existing members. The membership currently stands at 50. (The date of joining the Commonwealth is shown in parenthesis.)

*Antigua and Barbuda (1981)
*Australia (1931)
*The Bahamas (1973)
Bangladesh (1972)
*Barbados (1966)
*Belize (1981)
Botswana (1966)
Brunei (1984)
*Canada (1931)
Cyprus (1961)
Dominica (1978)
The Gambia (1965)
Ghana (1957)
*Grenada (1974)
Guyana (1966)
India (1947)
*Jamaica (1962)
Kenya (1963)
Kiribati (1979)
Lesotho (1966)
Malawi (1964)
Malaysia (1967)
The Maldives (1982)
Malta (1964)
Mauritius (1968)
Namibia (1990)
Nauru (1968)
*New Zealand (1931)
Nigeria (1960)
Pakistan (1947)
*Papua New Guinea (1975)
*St Christopher and Nevis (1983)
*St Lucia (1979)
*St Vincent and the Grenadines (1979)
Seychelles (1976)
Sierra Leone (1961)
Singapore (1965)
*Soloman Islands (1978)
Sri Lanka (1948)
Swaziland (1968)
Tanzania (1961)
Tonga (1970)
Trinidad and Tobago (1962)
*Tuvalu (1978)
Uganda (1962)
*United Kingdom
Vanuatu (1980)
Western Samoa (1970)
Zambia (1964)
Zimbabwe (1980)

*Realms of Queen Elizabeth II

Nauru and Tuvalu are special members, with the right to participate in all functional Commonwealth meetings and activities, but not to attend meetings of Commonwealth heads of government.

Countries which have left the Commonwealth
Fiji (1987)
Republic of Ireland (1949)
Pakistan (1972, rejoined 1989)
South Africa (1961)

Of the 50 member states, 16 have Queen Elizabeth II as head of state, 29 are republics, and five are indigenous monarchies.

In each of the realms where Queen Elizabeth II is head of state (except for the United Kingdom), she is personally represented by a Governor-General, who holds in all essential respects the same position in relation to the administration of public affairs in the realm as is held by Her Majesty in Britain. The Governor-General is appointed by The Queen on the advice of the government of the state concerned.

Intergovernmental and Other Links

The main forum for consultation is the Commonwealth heads of government meetings held biennially to discuss international developments and to consider co-operation among members. Decisions are reached by consensus, and the views of the meeting are set out in a communiqué. There are also annual meetings of finance ministers and frequent meetings of ministers and officials in many other fields, such as education, health, labour. Intergovernmental links are complemented by the activities of some 300 Commonwealth non-governmental organizations linking professionals, sportsmen and sportswomen, and interest groups, forming a 'people's Commonwealth'. The Commonwealth Games take place every four years.

Assistance to other Comonwealth countries normally has priority in the bilateral aid programmes of the association's developed members (Australia, Britain, Canada and New Zealand), who direct some 30 per cent of their aid to other member countries. Developing Commonwealth nations also assist their poorer partners, and many Commonwealth voluntary organizations promote development.

Many of the smaller Commonwealth countries are party to the Lomé Convention, which accords preferential access to the European Community (EC) for developing countries of Africa, the Caribbean and the Pacific, and provides for them to receive EC aid.

Commonwealth Secretariat

The Commonwealth has a secretariat, established in 1965 in London, which is funded by all member governments. This is the main agency for multilateral communication between member governments on issues relating to the Commonwealth as a whole. It promotes consultation and co-operation, disseminates information on matters of common concern, organizes meetings including the biennial summits, co-ordinates Commonwealth activities, and provides technical assistance for economic and social development through the Commonwealth Fund for Technical Co-operation.

Commonwealth Secretariat, Marlborough House, Pall Mall, London SW1Y 5HX. Tel: 071-839 3411. *Secretary-General*, Chief Emeka Anyaoku (Nigeria).

Commonwealth Institute, Kensington High Street, London W8 6NQ. Tel: 071-603 4535. *Director-General*, S. Cox.

CONFERENCE ON SECURITY AND CO-OPERATION IN EUROPE

Thunovska 12, Mala, Strana, 110 00 Prague 1

The Conference on Security and Co-operation in Europe (CSCE) was launched in 1975 under the Helsinki Final Act, which established agreements between NATO members, Warsaw Pact members, and neutral and non-aligned European countries covering security in Europe; economic, scientific, technological and environmental co-operation; and humanitarian principles and co-operation. Further conferences were held at Belgrade (1977–8), Madrid (1980–3), Vienna (1986–9) and Helsinki (1992–).

With the end of the Cold War, it was decided that the CSCE should be revitalized to provide a new security framework for Europe. The Charter of Paris for a New Europe was signed at Paris on 21 November 1990, committing members to support for multi-party democracy, free-market economics and human rights. The signatories also undertook to enhance political consultation, agreeing on regular meetings of heads of government, ministers and officials. The CSCE is underpinned by a new institutional structure; a Secretariat (Prague), a Conflict Prevention Centre (Vienna) and an Office for Democratic Institutions and Human Rights (Warsaw). The European Assembly of member parliamentarians will also be formed. In June 1991 the CSCE agreed upon new crisis prevention mechanisms to prevent violent conflict between and within member countries.

The CSCE has 52 members: Albania, Armenia, Austria, Azerbaijan, Belarus, Belgium, Bosnia-Hercegovina, Bulgaria, Canada, Croatia, Cyprus, Czechoslovakia, Denmark, Estonia, Finland, France, Georgia, Germany, Greece, Hungary, Iceland, Ireland, Italy, Kazakhstan, Kyrgyzstan, Latvia, Liechtenstein, Lithuania, Luxembourg, Malta, Moldova, Monaco, the Netherlands, Norway, Poland, Portugal, Romania, the Russian Federation, San Marino, Slovenia, Spain, Sweden, Switzerland, Tajikistan, Turkey, Turkmenistan, UK, Ukraine, USA, Uzbekistan, the Vatican and Yugoslavia.

Director of Secretariat, Nils Eliasson (*Sweden*).

THE COUNCIL OF EUROPE

67006 Strasbourg, France

The Council of Europe was founded in 1949. Its aim is to achieve greater unity between its members to safeguard their European heritage and to facilitate their economic and social progress through discussion and common action in economic, social, cultural, educational, scientific, legal and administrative matters and in the maintenance and furtherance of pluralist democracy, human rights and fundamental freedoms. The Council of Europe is now making an active contribution to welcoming the new democracies of central and eastern Europe.

The 27 members are Austria, Belgium, Bulgaria, Cyprus, Czechoslovakia, Denmark, Finland, France, Germany, Greece, Hungary, Iceland, the Republic of Ireland, Italy, Liechtenstein, Luxembourg, Malta, Netherlands, Norway, Poland, Portugal, San Marino, Spain, Sweden, Switzerland, Turkey and the UK. 'Special guest status' has been granted to Albania, Croatia, Estonia, Latvia, Lithuania, Romania, the Russian Federation and Slovenia.

The organs are the Committee of Ministers, consisting of the foreign ministers of member countries, who meet twice yearly, and the Parliamentary Assembly of 210 members, elected or chosen by the national parliaments of member countries in proportion to the relative strength of political parties. There is also a Joint Committee of Ministers and Representatives of the Parliamentary Assembly.

The Committee of Ministers is the executive organ of the Council. The majority of its conclusions take the form of international agreements (known as European Conventions) or recommendations to governments. Decisions of the Ministers may also be embodied in partial agreements to which a limited number of member governments are party. Member governments accredit Permanent Representatives to the Council in Strasbourg, who are also the Ministers' Deputies. The Committee of Deputies meets every month to transact business and to take decisions on behalf of Ministers.

The Parliamentary Assembly holds three week-long sessions a year. It debates reports on, *inter alia*, political, economic, agricultural, social, educational, legal and regional planning affairs, and also reports received annually from the OECD, other European organizations and certain specialized agencies of the United Nations. Its 13 permanent committees meet, normally in private, once or twice between each public plenary session of the Assembly. The Standing Conference of Local and Regional Authorities of Europe each year brings together mayors and municipal councillors in the same numbers as the members of the Parliamentary Assembly.

One of the principal achievements of the Council of Europe is the European Convention on Human Rights (1950) under which was established the European Commission and the European Court of Human Rights. Among the other conventions and agreements which have been concluded are the European Social Charter, the European Cultural Convention, the European Code of Social Security, and conventions on extradition, the legal status of migrant workers, torture prevention, conservation, and the transfer of sentenced prisoners. Most recently the specialized bodies of the Venice Commission and Demosthenes have been set up to assist in developing legislative, administrative and constitutional reforms in central and eastern Europe.

Non-member states take part in certain Council of Europe activities on a regular or *ad hoc* basis; thus the Holy See participates in all the educational, cultural and sports activities. The European Youth Centre is an educational residential centre for young people from all over Europe and further afield. The European Youth Foundation provides youth organizations with funds for their international activities.

Secretary-General, Catherine Lalumière (*France*).
Permanent UK Representative, His Excellency Noël Marshall, CMG *apptd* 1990.

THE ECONOMIC COMMUNITY OF WEST AFRICAN STATES

6 King George V Road, PMB 12745, Lagos, Nigeria

The Economic Community of West African States (ECOWAS) was founded at a summit of West African heads of government at Lagos on 28 May 1975, and came into operation in January 1977. It aims to promote the cultural, economic and social development of West Africa through mutual co-operation.

Measures undertaken by ECOWAS include the gradual elimination of barriers to the movement of goods, people and services between member states and the improvement of regional telecommunications and transport.

The supreme authority of ECOWAS is vested in the annual summit of heads of government of all 16 member states. A Council of Ministers, two from each member state, meets biannually to monitor the organization and make recommendations to the summit. ECOWAS operates through a Secretariat, headed by the Executive Secretary. In addition there is a financial controller, an external auditor, the Disputes Tribunal and the Defence Council.

A Fund for Co-operation, Compensation and Development, situated at Lomé, Togo, finances development projects

and provides compensation to member states who have suffered losses as a result of ECOWAS's policies, particularly in relation to trade liberalization.
Executive Secretary, Dr Abbas Bundu.

THE EUROPEAN BANK FOR RECONSTRUCTION AND DEVELOPMENT
122 Leadenhall Street, London EC3

The foundation of a European Bank for Reconstruction and Development (EBRD) was proposed by President Mitterrand of France on 25 October 1989. The charter of the EBRD was signed in Paris by 40 countries, the European Commission and the European Investment Bank on 29 May 1990. The EBRD was inaugurated in London on 15 April 1991.

The aim of the EBRD is to assist the transformation of the states of central and eastern Europe (Albania, Bulgaria, Czechoslovakia, Estonia, Hungary, Latvia, Lithuania, Poland, Romania, the republics of the former USSR and Yugoslavia) from centrally-planned economies to free market economies, with particular regard for strengthening democratic institutions, and respect for human rights and the environment. The EBRD provides technical assistance, training and investment in: the upgrading of infrastructure (energy, telecommunications and transport); the creation of modern financial systems (efficient banks, capital markets); and the restructuring of state industries. The EBRD's assistance is weighted towards the private sector; no more than 40 per cent of its investment can be made in state-owned concerns. It works in co-operation with its members, private companies, and international organizations, such as the OECD, the IMF, the World Bank and the UN specialized agencies.

The EBRD has an initial subscribed capital of ECU10 billion. The major subscribers are: the USA, 10 per cent; Britain, France, Germany, Italy and Japan, 8.5 per cent each; central and eastern European states, 11.9 per cent.

The EBRD has 51 members. The highest authority is the Board of Governors; each member appoints one Governor and one alternate. The Governors delegate most powers to a 23-member Board of Directors; the Directors are responsible for the EBRD's operations and are appointed by the Governors for three-year terms. The Governors also elect the President of the Board of Directors, who acts as the Bank's chief of staff, for a four-year term. A Secretary-General liaises between the Directors and EBRD staff.
President of the Board of Directors, Jacques Attali (*France*).
UK Executive Director, J. A. L. Faint.
Secretary-General, Bart le Blanc (*Netherlands*).

The European Community

The beginnings of the European Community (EC) lie in the desire following the Second World War to replace the European system of competing nation states with a new union. It was partially out of a desire to heal traditional Franco-German enmity that in May 1951 Robert Schuman, the French Foreign Minister of the time, proposed that France and West Germany pool their coal and steel industries under an independent, supranational authority. They were joined by Belgium, Luxembourg, the Netherlands and Italy and the Treaty of Paris was signed in 1951, establishing the European Coal and Steel Community (ECSC) in 1952.

The success of the ECSC led to discussions in 1955 in Messina, Italy, between the foreign ministers of its six member states on proposals for further moves towards European economic integration. As a result of these discussions the Treaty of Rome, establishing the European Economic Community, was signed on 25 March 1957. A second treaty founding the European Atomic Energy Community (EURATOM) was signed on the same day; this pledged the six signatories to co-operate in research into nuclear science, particularly in relation to nuclear energy.

The Treaty of Rome was intended to create a customs union to remove all obstacles to the free movement of capital, goods, people and services between member states. It also established a common external trade policy and common policies for agriculture and fisheries. Other articles of the treaty refer to preventing the distortion of competition within the Common Market; the co-ordination of economic policies; the harmonization of social policy sufficient to enable the functioning of the Common Market; the creation of a European Social Fund to increase employment and raise living standards; and the association of overseas countries and territories with the Community to increase mutual trade and to assist their economic and social development.

In addition, the Treaty of Rome established the Community's institutional structure; the Commission, the Council of Ministers, the Economic and Social Committee, the European Investment Bank, the Parliament, and the Court of Justice. Whereas the Parliament and Court of Justice were common to all three Communities from 1958, each Community had its own executive body and Council of Ministers. The three separate executive bodies and Councils of Ministers were merged in 1967.

In May 1969, the heads of government of the Six met at the Hague and decided both to widen and to deepen the Community. In accordance with the Hague decisions, the Council of Ministers agreed in 1970 that from 1975 the Community would have its own revenue, independent of national contributions; this would be derived from customs duties and agricultural import levies collected at the EC external frontier, and a proportion of national receipts from VAT.

In June 1970, the Six invited Britain, Denmark, Ireland and Norway to open negotiations on their applications to join the EC. The four countries signed a Treaty of Accession in Brussels on 22 January 1972; Norway subsequently withdrew its application after conducting a referendum on EC entry. The enlarged Community of the Nine came into existence on 1 January 1973.

During the 1970s the EC sought to strengthen the democracies of southern Europe; this led to the admission of Greece to the EC on 1 January 1981, and Portugal and Spain on 1 January 1986. Following a plebiscite, Greenland negotiated its withdrawal from the EC and left in 1986. The unification of Germany brought the former German Democratic Republic into the EC in October 1990. Andorra joined the customs union on 1 July 1991, but does not participate in other EC institutions.

Following the completion of the Single Market in 1993, the EC is expected to undergo further enlargement. Applications for EC membership have already been received from Austria, Cyprus, Finland, Malta, Sweden, Switzerland and Turkey, and are expected from a number of other European states. The Commission is developing the concept of affiliate EC membership for the new democracies of eastern Europe.

The Common Agricultural Policy

The Treaty of Rome established the Common Agricultural Policy (CAP) to increase agricultural production, to provide a fair standard of living for farmers and to ensure the availability of food at reasonable prices. This aim is achieved by a number of mechanisms: Import Levies (the EC sets a target price for a particular product in the Community, the world price is monitored and if it falls below the guide price, an import levy can be imposed equivalent to the difference between the two); Intervention Purchase (if the price of a product falls below the level indicated by the Council, member states must purchase supplies of the product, provided that they are of suitable quality); Export Subsidies (the EC pays a food exporter a subsidy equivalent to the difference between the price at which the product is bought in the EC and the lower sale price on the world market).

These measures had the required aim of stimulating production but also placed increasing demands on the EC budget. To surmount this problem, the EC created the system of co-responsibility levies; farm payments to the EC by volume of product sold. This system was supplemented by national quotas for particular products, such as milk. The increase in the number of EC members and the greater use of modern technology has further increased production and exacerbated EC budgetary problems; CAP now accounts for over 50 per cent of EC expenditure. Radical reforms were agreed at the end of May 1992, based on the reduction of target prices for cereals, beef and dairy produce. These are to be reduced by 29 per cent, 15 per cent and 5 per cent respectively. Hence, the amount of money spent by the EC on the three mechanisms of Import Levies, Intervention Purchase and Export Subsidies will fall. Production is expected to fall also because EC prices will be much closer to world price levels. Emphasis is also to be placed on direct grants to farmers to encourage them to take land out of production as a means of reducing surpluses.

European Political Co-operation

The framework for European Political Co-operation (EPC) dates from an initiative at the Hague summit in 1969. In the resultant Luxembourg Report (1970), EC foreign ministers decided to harmonize and co-ordinate their foreign policy positions and achieve common actions where possible. Although the Single European Act obliged EC members to consult each other on foreign policy and the Commission participates in deliberations, EPC is an inter-governmental system operating parallel to, but outside, the Community.

The EPC system is headed by the European Council, which provides general lines of policy. Specific policy decisions are taken by the Council of Foreign Ministers, which meets at least four times a year. The foreign minister of the state holding the EC presidency initiates action, manages EPC and represents it abroad. He is supported by a secretariat based in Brussels and is advised by the past and future holders of the presidency, forming a so-called troika. The Council of Ministers is supported by the Political Committee which meets each month, or within 48 hours if there is a crisis, to prepare for ministerial discussions. A group of correspondents, designated diplomats in each member's foreign ministry, provides day-to-day contact.

The Single Market

Throughout the 1970s and early 1980s, EC members became increasingly concerned at the slow growth of the European economy. Although tariffs and quotas had been removed between member states, the EC was still separated into a number of national markets by a series of non-tariff barriers. It was to overcome these internal barriers to trade that the concept of the Single Market was developed. The measures to be undertaken were outlined in the Cockfield report (1985) and codified in the Single European Act (SEA), signed in 1986 and which came into force in 1987.

The SEA includes articles removing obstacles that distort the internal market: the elimination of frontier controls; the mutual recognition of professional qualifications; the harmonization of product specifications, largely by the mutual recognition of national standards; open tendering for public procurement contracts; the free movement of capital; the harmonization of VAT and excise duties; and the reduction of state aid to particular industries. The SEA changed the legislative process within the EC; particularly with the introduction of qualified majority voting in the Council of Ministers for some policy areas. The SEA also extends EC competence into the fields of technology, the environment, regional policy, monetary policy and external policy. The Single Market is to be completed on 1 January 1993 and is expected to result in at least a 5 per cent increase in the collective GNP of EC member states.

After over four years of negotiations, the EC signed an agreement in May 1992 extending the Single Market to the EFTA states, to form the European Economic Area (EEA). The provisions of the Single Market will apply throughout the EEA from 1 January 1993. The EFTA states will provide a 'cohesion fund' for the poorer regions of the EC of 500 million ECU in grants and 1.5 billion ECU in loans.

New Developments

EC members are engaging in further moves towards European integration. Inter-governmental conferences on political and economic union began in December 1990. The Maastricht European Council in December 1991 agreed a new Treaty on European Union which is divided into an Economic and Monetary Union section and a Political Union section.

In the Economic and Monetary Union section, the treaty provides for a European Central Bank to be established by 1 January 1999, and sets criteria for the economic convergence of national economies necessary for the beginning of stage three of Economic and Monetary Union.

In the Political Union section, the treaty provides for greater powers for the European Parliament over EC legislation and for the Western European Union to become the defence arm of the EC. In addition, two new 'pillars' were introduced into the EC by the Treaty, one to deal with foreign and security policy and one to deal with immigration, asylum and policing. Decision-making in these two areas is to be based on the Council of Ministers, minimizing the roles of the Commission and Parliament. A separate protocol on social policy was also agreed by 11 member states but not the UK.

For the Maastricht Treaty to come into force it must be ratified by all member states, either by referendum or parliamentary vote. Although Ireland, Luxembourg and Greece have ratified the Treaty, its future has been thrown into doubt by its rejection in the Danish referendum.

The Legislative Process

The core of the EC policymaking process is a dialogue between the Commission, which initiates and implements policy, and the Council of Ministers, which takes policy decisions. A degree of democratic control is exercised by the European Parliament.

The original EC legislative process is known as the consultative procedure. The Commission drafts a proposal which it submits to the Council. The Council then consults the ESC and the Parliament; the Parliament may request that amendments are made. With or without these amendments, the proposal is then adopted by the Council and becomes law.

Under the Single European Act, changes were made to the EC legislative process, particularly in strengthening the role of the Parliament in the implementation of the Single

Market, in some areas of social policy, and in research and development. In these areas the new co-operation procedure operates. The Parliament now has a second reading of proposals in these fields, and after the second reading its rejection of a proposal can only be overturned by a unanimous decision of the Council.

The Council issues the following legislation: (a) Regulations, which are binding in their entirety and directly applicable to all member states; they do not need to be incorporated into national law to come into effect; (b) Directives, which are less specific, binding as to the result to be achieved but leaving the method of implementation open to member states; a directive thus has no force until it is incorporated into national law; (c) Decisions, which are also binding but are addressed solely to one or more member states or individuals in a member state; (d) Recommendations; (e) Opinions, which are merely persuasive.

THE COUNCIL OF MINISTERS

170 rue de la Loi, 1048 Brussels, Belgium

The Council of Ministers consists of ministers from the government of each of the member states. It formally comprises the foreign ministers of the member states but in practice the minister depends on the subject under discussion; i.e. when EC environment matters are under discussion, the meeting is informally known as the Environment Council. Council decisions are taken by majority vote, qualified majority vote (in which members' votes are weighted) or by unanimity. Council meetings are prepared by the Committee of Permanent Representatives (COREPER) of the member states, which acts as the 'gatekeeper' between national governments and the supranational EC, often negotiating on proposals with the Commission during the legislative process.

The European Council, comprising the heads of government of the member states, meets twice a year to provide overall policy direction. Established in 1974, the European Council was only formally brought within the EC institutional framework with the SEA.

The Presidency of the EC is held in rotation for six-month periods, setting the agenda for and chairing all Council meetings. The Presidency serves an important function since the incumbent nation has an opportunity to pursue its own particular policy priorities. The European Council holds a summit in the country holding the Presidency at the end of its period in office. The holders of the Presidency for the years 1992–5 are:

1992 Portugal; UK
1993 Denmark; Belgium
1994 Greece; Germany
1995 France; Spain

OFFICE OF THE UNITED KINGDOM PERMANENT REPRESENTATIVE TO THE EUROPEAN COMMUNITIES
Rond-point Robert Schuman 6, 1040 Brussels, Belgium
Ambassador and UK Permanent Representative, Sir John Kerr, KCMG, *apptd* 1990.

THE COMMISSION

200 rue de la Loi, 1049 Brussels, Belgium

The Commission consists of 17 Commissioners, two each from France, Germany, Italy, Spain and the UK, and one each from the remaining member states. The members of the Commission are appointed for four-year renewable terms by the agreement of the member states; the President and Vice-Presidents are appointed from among the Commissioners for two-year terms, also renewable. The Commissioners pledge sole allegiance to the EC.

The Commission initiates and implements EC legislation and is the guardian of the EC treaties. It is the exponent of Community-wide interests rather than the national preoccupations of the Council. Each Commissioner is supported by advisers and oversees whichever of the 23 departments, known as Directorates-General (DGs), assigned to him. Each Directorate-General is headed by a Director-General.

COMMISSIONERS

President

Secretariat-General; Legal Services; Monetary Affairs; Spokesman's Service; Joint Interpreting and Conference Service; Think Tank; Security Office, Jacques Delors (France).

Vice-Presidents

External Relations and Trade Policy; Co-operation with other European Countries, Frans Andriessen (Netherlands).
Economic and Financial Affairs; Co-ordination of Structural Instruments; Statistics Office, Henning Christophersen (Denmark).
Co-operation and Development; Fisheries, Manuel Marin (Spain).
Research and Science; Telecommunications; Information Technology and Innovation; Joint Research Centre, Filippo Maria Pandolfi (Italy).
Internal Market and Industrial Affairs; Relations with the European Parliament, Martin Bangemann (Germany).
Competition Policy; Financial Institutions, Sir Leon Brittan (UK).

Members

Environment; Nuclear Safety; Civil Protection, vacant.
Personnel and Administration; Energy; Euratom Supply Agency; Policy on Small and Medium-Sized Enterprises; Tourism; Social Economy, Antonio Cardoso E. Cunha (Portugal).
Mediterranean Policy; Relations with Latin America; North-South Relations, Abel Matutes (Spain).
Budget; Financial Control, Peter Schmidhuber (Germany).
Taxation; Customs Union; Questions Relating to Obligatory Levies, Christiane Scrivener (France).
Regional Policy, Bruce Millan (UK).
Audio-Visual Policy; Cultural Affairs; Information and Communication Policy; Citizens' Europe; Office for Official Publications, Jean Dondelinger (Luxembourg).
Agriculture; Rural Development, Ray MacSharry (Ireland).
Transport; Credit, Investments and Financial Instruments; Consumer Protection, Karel Van Miert (Belgium).
Social Affairs and Employment; Education and Training; Human Resources, Ioannis Palaiokrassis (Greece).
Secretary-General, D. Williamson (UK).

DIRECTOR-GENERALS

DGI, External Relations, H. G. Krenzler.
DGII, Economic and Financial Affairs, G. Ravasio.
DGIII, Internal Market and Industrial Affairs, R. Perissich.
DGIV, Competition, C.-D. Ehlerman.
DGV, Employment, Industrial Relations and Social Affairs, J. Degimbe.
DGVI, Agriculture, G. Legras.
DGVII, Transport, E. Peña Abizanda.
DGVIII, Development, D. Frisch.

DGIX, Personnel and Administration, F. de Koster.
DGX, Audiovisual, Information, Communication and Culture, C. Flesch.
DGXI, Environment, Consumer Protection and Nuclear Safety, L. J. Brinkhorst.
DGXII, Science and Research and Development, P. Fasella.
DGXIII, Telecommunications, Information Technology and Innovation, M. Carpentier.
DGXIV, Fisheries, J. Almedia Serra.
DGXV, Financial Institutions and Company Law, G. Fitchew.
DGXVI, Regional Policies, E. L. Illarramendi.
DGXVII, Energy, C. S. Maniatopoulos.
DGXVIII, Credit and Investments, E. Cioffi.
DGXIX, Budgets, J.-P. Mingasson.
DGXX, Financial Control, L. de Moor.
DGXXI, Customs Union and Indirect Taxation, P. Wilmott.
DGXXII, Co-ordination of Structural Policies, T. O'Dwyer.
DGXXIII, Enterprise Policy, Commerce, Tourism and Social Economy, H. von Moltke.

THE EUROPEAN PARLIAMENT

The European Parliament originated as the Common Assembly of the ECSC; it acquired its present name in 1962. MEPs were initially appointed from the membership of national parliaments. Direct elections to the Parliament began in 1979. Elections to the Parliament are held on differing bases throughout the EC; British MEPs are elected on a first-past-the-post system, except in Northern Ireland which uses proportional representation. The next elections will be held in 1994.

The Parliament has 518 seats allocated as follows: France, Germany, Italy, UK, 81 each; Spain, 60; the Netherlands, 25; Belgium, Greece and Portugal, 24 each; Denmark, 16; Ireland, 15; Luxembourg, 6. An additional eighteen German observer MEPs represent the länder of the former East Germany. MEPs serve on 19 committees, which scrutinize draft EC legislation and particular directorate-generals. Plenary sessions are held in Strasbourg, committees meet in Brussels and the Secretariat's headquarters are in Luxembourg.

The EP has gradually expanded its influence within the EC. It has general powers of supervision over and consultation with the Commission and the Council; it can dismiss the Commission by a two-thirds majority. It can reject the EC budget as a whole and alter non-compulsory expenditure not specified in the EC primary legislation. Although the EP cannot directly initiate legislation, its reports can spur the Commission into action.

The MEPs in the present Parliament sit in the following political groupings: Socialist (including the British Labour Party), 179; European People's Party (including the British Conservative Party and Official Unionist Party), 162; Liberal Democratic Reformists, 45; European United Left, 29; Greens, 27; European Democratic Alliance, 21; Rainbow Alliance (including Scottish National Party), 15; European Right, 14; Coalition Left, 13; Independents (including the Democratic Unionist Party), 13.

PARLIAMENT, Palais de l'Europe,
67006 Strasbourg Cedex, France; 97–113 rue Belliard, 1040 Bruxelles, Belgium.
SECRETARIAT, Centre Européen, Kirchberg, 2929 Luxembourg.
President, Dr Egon Klepsch (Germany).
(For a full list of British MEPs, *see* pages 275–6).

THE ECONOMIC AND SOCIAL COMMITTEE

2 rue Ravenstein, 1000 Brussels, Belgium

The Economic and Social Committee is an advisory and consultative body. The ESC has 189 members, who are nominated by member states. It is divided into three groups; employers; workers; and other interest groups such as consumers, farmers and the self-employed. It issues opinions on draft EC legislation and can bring matters to the attention of the Commission, Council and Parliament; it has a key role in providing specialist and technical input.

THE COURT OF AUDITORS

12 rue A. de Gasperi, L-1615 Luxembourg

The Court of Auditors, established in October 1977, is responsible for the audit as well as the sound financial management of the resources managed by the European Communities and Community bodies. The Court may also submit observations on specific questions and deliver opinions. It has 12 members appointed by the Council of Ministers.
President, Aldo Angioi (*Italy*).

COURT OF JUSTICE OF THE EUROPEAN COMMUNITIES

L-2925 Luxembourg

The European Court superseded the Court of Justice of ECSC and is common to the three European Communities. It exists to safeguard the law in the interpretation and application of the Community treaties, to decide on the legality of decisions of the Council of Ministers or the Commission, and to determine violations of the Treaties. Cases may be brought to it by the member states, the Community institutions, firms or individuals. Its decisions are directly binding in the member countries. The thirteen judges and six advocates-general of the Court are appointed for renewable six-year terms by the member Governments in concert. During 1991, 326 new cases were lodged at the court and 204 judgments were delivered.

Composition of the Court, in order of precedence, with effect from 10 March 1992:
O. Due (*President*); R. Joliet (*President of the 1st and 5th Chambers*); F. A. Schockweiler (*President of the 2nd and 6th Chambers*); F. Grevisse (*President of the 3rd Chamber*); G. Tesauro (*First Advocate-General*); P. J. G. Kapteyn (*President of the 4th Chamber*); G. F. Mancini; C. N. Kakouris; C. O. Lenz (*Advocate-General*); M. Darmon (*Advocate-General*); J. C. Moitinho de Almeida; G. C. Rodriguez Iglesias; M. Diez de Velasco; M. Zuleeg; W. van Gerven (*Advocate-General*); F. G. Jacobs (*Advocate-General*); C. Gulmann (*Advocate-General*); J. L. Murray; D. A. O. Edward; J.-G. Giraud (*Registrar*).

COURT OF FIRST INSTANCE

L-2925 Luxembourg
Established by a Council decision of 24 October 1988, under powers conferred by the Single European Act, the Court of First Instance took up its duties in 1989 and started to exercise its functions at the end of October. It has jurisdiction to hear and determine certain categories of cases brought by

natural or legal persons, in particular cases brought by European Community officials, or cases on competition law. During 1991, 93 new cases were lodged at the court and 41 judgments were delivered.

Composition of the Court, in order of precedence, with effect from 12 March 1992:

J. L. Cruz Vilaca (*President*); H. Kirschner (*President of the 1st Chamber*); B. Vesterdarf (*President of the 3rd Chamber*); R. García-Valdecasas y Fernandez (*President of the 4th Chamber*); K. Lenaerts (*President of the 5th Chamber*); D. P. M. Barrington; A. Saggio; C. Yeraris; R. Schintgen; C. P. Briët; J. Biancarelli; C. Bellamy; H. Jung (*Registrar*).

THE EUROPEAN INVESTMENT BANK

100 Boulevard Konrad Adenauer
L-2950 Luxembourg

The European Investment Bank (EIB) was set up in 1958 under the terms of the Treaty of Rome to finance capital investment projects promoting the balanced development of the European Community.

It grants long-term loans to private enterprises, public authorities and financial institutions, to finance projects which further: the economic development of less advanced regions (Assisted Areas); improvement of European communications; environmental protection; attainment of the Community's energy policy objectives; modernization of enterprises, co-operation between undertakings in the different member states, and the activities of small and medium-sized enterprises.

EIB activities have also been extended outside member countries as part of the Community's development co-operation policy, under the terms of different association or co-operation agreements with twelve countries in the Mediterranean region, five in eastern Europe and, under the Lomé Conventions, 70 in Africa, the Caribbean and the Pacific.

The Bank's total financing operations in 1991 amounted to 15,339 million ECU, of which 14,423 million were for investments in the European Community and 916 million for outside the Community. Between 1987 and 1991 the EIB had made available a total of 5,530 million ECU for investment in the UK.

The members of the European Investment Bank are the twelve member states of the Community, who have all subscribed to the Bank's capital, of 57,600 million ECU. The bulk of the funds required by the Bank to carry out its tasks are borrowed on the capital markets of the Community and non-member countries, and on the international market.

As it operates on a non-profit-making basis, the interest rates charged by the EIB reflect the cost of the Bank's borrowings and closely follow conditions on world capital markets.

The Board of Governors of the European Investment Bank consists of one government minister nominated by each of the member countries, usually the finance minister, who lay down general directives on the policy of the Bank and appoint members to the Board of Directors (21 nominated by the member states, one by the Commission of the European Communities), which takes decisions on the granting and raising of loans and the fixing of interest rates. A Management Committee, also appointed by the Board of Governors, is responsible for the day-to-day operations of the Bank. The President and Vice-Presidents also preside as Chairman and Vice-Chairmen at meetings of the Board of Directors.

President, Ernst-Günther Bröder.

Vice-Presidents, Lucio Izzo; Alain Prate; José de Oliveira Costa; Ludovicus Meulemans; Roger Lavelle; Hans Duborg.

UK OFFICE: 68 Pall Mall, London SW1Y 5ES Tel: 071-839 3351.

EUROPEAN COMMUNITY INFORMATION

The Commission maintains offices in:

LONDON, 8 Storey's Gate, London SW1P 3AT. Tel: 071-973 1992.

EDINBURGH, 9 Alva Street, Edinburgh EH2 4HP. Tel: 031-225 2058.

CARDIFF, 4 Cathedral Road, Cardiff CF1 9SG. Tel: 0222-371631.

BELFAST, Windsor House, 9–15 Bedford Street, Belfast BT2 7EG. Tel: 0232-240708.

DUBLIN, 39 Molesworth Street, Dublin 2.

WASHINGTON, 2100 M Street NW (Suite 707), Washington DC 20037.

NEW YORK, 1 Dag Hammarskjöld Plaza, 254 East 47th Street, New York, NY 10017.

OTTAWA, Inn of the Provinces, Office Tower (Suite 1110), 350 Sparks Street, Ontario, K1R 7SA.

CANBERRA, 18 Alakana Street, Yarralumia, ACT 2600, and a number of other cities.

UK EUROPEAN PARLIAMENT INFORMATION OFFICE

2 Queen Anne's Gate, London SW1H 9AA. Tel: 071-222 0411.

There are European Information Centres, set up to give information and advice to small businesses, in 24 British towns and cities. A number of universities maintain European Documentation Centres.

EUROPEAN FREE TRADE ASSOCIATION

9–11 rue de Varembé, 1211 Geneva 20, Switzerland

The European Free Trade Association (EFTA) was established on 3 May 1960, by Austria, Denmark, Norway, Portugal, Sweden, Switzerland and the UK. EFTA was subsequently joined by Finland, Iceland and Liechtenstein; Denmark and the UK left EFTA in 1972 and Portugal in 1985; all joined the EC.

The first objective of EFTA was to establish free trade in industrial goods between members; this was achieved in 1966. Its second objective was the creation of a single market in western Europe and in 1972 EFTA signed a free trade agreement with the EC covering trade in industrial goods; the remaining tariffs on industrial products were finally abolished in 1984.

In 1989 exploratory talks began on the free movement of goods, services, capital and labour throughout the EC–EFTA area. The talks also covered co-operation in education, the environment, social policy, and research and development. Formal negotiations on the establishment of a European Economic Area (EEA), encompassing all 19 EC and EFTA countries, began in 1990. These negotiations were concluded when EFTA and EC ministers signed the EEA Agreement on 2 May 1992 in Oporto, Portugal. The aim is to have the EEA enter into force at the same time as the EC single market in 1993.

EFTA has expanded its relations with other non-EC states in recent years, especially in eastern Europe where assisting economic reforms is the priority. Free trade agreements have been signed with Czechoslovakia and Turkey, and negotiations for similar agreements are under way with Hungary, Poland and Israel. In addition, EFTA has signed declarations on economic co-operation with Romania, Bulgaria, Estonia, Latvia, Lithuania and Slovenia.

With the applications of Austria, Finland, Sweden and Switzerland to the EC and the expected applications of other EFTA members, many observers predict the eventual dissolution of EFTA and its fusion with the EC.

The Council of EFTA is the principle organ of the Association. It generally meets once a week at the level of heads of the permanent national delegations to EFTA and twice a year at ministerial level. The chairmanship of the Council rotates every six months. Each state has a single vote and recommendations must normally be unanimous; decisions of the Council are binding on member countries.
Secretary General, Georg Reisch (*Austria*).

EUROPEAN ORGANIZATION FOR NUCLEAR RESEARCH (CERN)

1211 Geneva 23, Switzerland

The Convention establishing the European Organization for Nuclear Research (CERN) came into force in 1954. The organization promotes European collaboration in high energy physics of a purely scientific nature. It is not concerned with research of a military nature.

The member countries are Austria, Belgium, Czechoslovakia, Denmark, Finland, France, Germany, Greece, Hungary, Italy, Netherlands, Norway, Poland, Portugal, Spain, Sweden, Switzerland and the UK. The following have observer status: Israel, the Russian Federation, Turkey, Yugoslavia, the EC Commission and UNESCO.

The Council is the highest policy-making body and is made up of two delegates from each member state. There is also a Committee of the Council comprising a single delegate from each member state (who is also a Council member) and the chairmen of the scientific policy and finance advisory committees. The Council is chaired by a President who is elected by the Council in Session. The Council also elects the Director-General, the person responsible for the internal organization of CERN. The Director-General heads a workforce of approximately 3,100, including physicists, craftsmen, technicians and administrative staff. At present over 5,000 physicists use CERN's facilities.

The member countries contribute to the budget directly in proportion to their net national revenue. The 1990 budget was SFr 908 million.
President of the Council, Sir William Mitchell, CBE, FRS (*UK*).
Director-General (1989–93), C. Rubbia.

EUROPEAN SPACE AGENCY

8–10 rue Mario Nikis, 75738 Paris, France

The European Space Agency (ESA) was set up on 31 May 1975. It was formed from two earlier space organizations—the European Space Research Organization (ESRO) and the European Launcher Development Organization (ELDO). Its aims include the advancement of space research and technology, the implementation of a long-term European space policy and the co-ordination of national space programmes.

The member countries are Austria, Belgium, Denmark, France, Federal Republic of Germany, Republic of Ireland, Italy, Netherlands, Norway, Spain, Sweden, Switzerland and the United Kingdom. Finland is an associate member and Canada a co-operating state.

The agency is directed by a Council composed of the representatives of the member states, and its chief officer is the Director-General.
Director-General, Jean-Marie Luton, *apptd* 1990.

FOOD AND AGRICULTURE ORGANIZATION OF THE UNITED NATIONS

Via della Terme di Caracalla, 00100 Rome, Italy

The Food and Agriculture Organization (FAO) is a specialized UN agency, established on 16 October 1945. It assists rural populations by raising levels of nutrition and living standards, and by encouraging greater efficiency in food production and distribution. In addition, it collects, analyses and disseminates information on agriculture and natural resources. FAO also advises governments on national agricultural policy and planning; its Investment Centre, together with the World Bank and other financial institutions, helps to prepare development projects. FAO's field programme covers a range of activities, including strengthening crop production, rural and livestock development, and conservation.

The FAO keeps a special watch on areas where famine can occur. The Office for Special Relief Operations channels emergency aid from governments and other agencies, and assists in rehabilitation. The Technical Co-operation Programme provides schemes for countries facing agricultural crises.

The FAO had 160 members as at January 1992. It is governed by a biennial Conference of all its members which sets the forthcoming programme and budget. The budget for 1992–3 is US$645,600,000, funded by member countries in proportion to their gross national products. The FAO also receives substantial additional funding from the UN Development Programme, donor governments and other institutions.

The Conference elects a Director-General and a 49-member Council, which governs between Conferences. The Field Programme is administered by a Secretariat, headed by the Director-General, by the Development Department and by five regional offices.
Director-General, Edouard Saouma (*Lebanon*).
UK Representative, J. Goldsack, MBE, British Embassy, Rome.

GENERAL AGREEMENT ON TARIFFS AND TRADE

Centre William Rappard, 154 rue de Lausanne,
1211 Geneva 21, Switzerland

Under an initiative of the UN Economic and Social Council, a committee met in 1947 to draft the charter of a new international trade organization. The charter was never ratified and the General Agreement on Tariffs and Trade (GATT), intended as an interim arrangement with effect from January 1948, became the only regime for the regulation of world trade. Never formalized, GATT has evolved rules and procedures to adapt to changing circumstances. One hundred and three states are now contracting parties and a further 29 apply its rules *de facto*; GATT thus covers nearly 90 per cent of world trade.

GATT is dedicated to the expansion of non-discriminatory international trade. It provides a common code of conduct and a forum for the discussion and solution of international trade problems, and for multilateral negotiations to reduce tariffs and other trade barriers. Special attention is given to assisting the trade of developing countries, which are exempted from some GATT provisions.

Extensions of free trade are made progressively via 'rounds' of multilateral negotiations. Seven have been completed, including the Kennedy Round (1964–7) and the Tokyo Round (1973–9). The average duties on manufactured goods have been reduced from 40 per cent in the 1940s to 5 per cent. The current Uruguay Round was launched in 1986. The 108 participating governments are conducting negotiations covering market access and new trade rules regarding tariffs, non-tariff barriers, tropical products, textiles, agriculture, etc. For the first time new multilateral rules for services, intellectual property and investment are also being discussed.

The Uruguay Round was scheduled to finish in December 1990, but has not been completed because of disagreement between the USA, other members of the Cairns group of New World agricultural producers, and the European Community over the level of Community agricultural subsidies.

A Secretariat performs administrative and intelligence functions, as well as playing an important role in diffusing conflicts between contracting parties. A Council of Representatives convenes usually eight times a year to set the agenda for forthcoming meetings of the parties. Various standing committees and groups of experts address specific issues.

The International Trade Centre, founded in 1964 to help developing countries with export expansion, is operated jointly with the UN Conference on Trade and Development.

Director-General, A. Dunkel (*Switzerland*).

Permanent UK Representative, M. R. Morland, CMG, 37–39 rue de Vermont, 1211 Geneva 20.

INTERNATIONAL ATOMIC ENERGY AGENCY

Vienna International Centre, Wagramerstrasse 5,
PO Box 100, 1400 Vienna, Austria

The International Atomic Energy Agency (IAEA) was established on 29 July 1957 as a consequence of the UN International Conference on the Peaceful Uses of Atomic Energy held the previous year. Although it operates under the aegis of, and reports annually to, the UN, the IAEA is not a specialized agency.

The IAEA aims to accelerate and enlarge the contribution of atomic energy to peace, health and prosperity, and to ensure that any assistance provided by it or under its supervision is not used for military purposes. It establishes atomic energy safety standards and offers services to its member states for the safe operation of their nuclear facilities and for radiation protection. It is the central point for the International Convention on early notification of a nuclear accident. The IAEA also encourages research and training in nuclear power. It is additionally charged with drawing up safeguards and verifying their use in accordance with the Non-Proliferation Treaty of 1968.

Together with the Food and Agriculture Organization and the World Health Organization, the IAEA established an International Consultative Group on Food Irradiation in 1983.

The IAEA had 112 members as at September 1992. A General Conference of all its members meets annually to decide policy, a programme and a budget (1992, US$186 million), as well as electing a Director-General and 35-member Board of Governors. The Board meets four times a year to execute policy which is implemented by the Secretariat under a Director-General.

Director-General, Hans Blix (*Sweden*).

Permanent UK Representative, G. E. Clark, CMG, Jaurésgasse 12, 1030 Vienna, Austria.

INTERNATIONAL CIVIL AVIATION ORGANIZATION

1000 Sherbrooke Street West, Montreal, Quebec,
Canada H3A 2R2

The International Civil Aviation Organization (ICAO) was founded with the signing of the Chicago Convention on International Civil Aviation in December 1944, and became a specialized agency of the United Nations on 4 April 1947. It sets international technical standards and recommended practices for all areas of civil aviation, including airworthiness, air navigation, traffic control and pilot licensing. It encourages uniformity and simplicity in ground regulations and operations at international airports, including immigration and customs control. The ICAO also promotes regional air navigation, plans for ground facilities, and collects and distributes air transport statistics worldwide. It is dedicated to improving safety and to the orderly development of civil aviation throughout the world.

The ICAO had 168 members as at 12 June 1992. It is governed by an assembly of all its members which meets at least once every three years. A Council of 33 members is elected, taking into account the leading air transport nations as well as ensuring representation of less developed countries. The Council elects the President, appoints the Secretary-General and supervises the organization through subsidiary committees, serviced by a Secretariat.

President of the Council, Dr Assad Kotaite (*Lebanon*).

Secretary-General, Dr Philippe Rochat (*Switzerland*).

UK Representative, F. A. Neal, CMG, Suite 928, 1000 Sherbrooke Street West, Montreal, Quebec, Canada H3A 3G4.

INTERNATIONAL CONFEDERATION OF FREE TRADE UNIONS

37–41 rue Montagne aux Herbes Potagères, 1000
Brussels, Belgium

Formed in 1949 the International Confederation of Free Trade Unions (ICFTU) was created to promote free trade unionism worldwide. It aims to establish, maintain and promote free trade unions, and to promote peace with economic security and social justice.

Affiliated to the ICFTU are 154 individual unions and representative bodies in 109 countries and territories. On 24 March 1992 there were nearly 108 million members.

The supreme authority of the organization is the Congress which convenes at least every four years. It is composed of delegates from the affiliated trade union organizations. The Congress elects an Executive Board of 49 members which meets not less than once a year. The Board establishes the budget and receives suggestions and proposals from affiliates as well as acting on behalf of the Confederation. The Congress also elects the General Secretary.

General Secretary, Enzo Friso.

UK Affiliate, TUC, Congress House, 23–28 Great Russell Street, London WC1B 3LS.

INTERNATIONAL CRIMINAL POLICE ORGANIZATION

50 quai Achille Lignon, 69006 Lyon, France

The International Criminal Police Commission (Interpol) was set up in 1923 to establish an international criminal records office and to harmonize extradition procedures. In 1956 a revised Constitution was adopted and the organization adopted its present name. On 1 July 1992 the organization comprised 158 member states.

Interpol's aims are to ensure and promote mutual assistance between all criminal police authorities, and to support government agencies concerned with combating crime, whilst respecting the national sovereignty of members. Interpol is financed by annual contributions from the governments of member states.

Interpol's policy is decided by the General Assembly which meets annually; it is composed of delegates appointed by the member states. The 13-member Executive Committee is elected by the General Assembly from among the member states' delegates, and is chaired by the President, who has a four-year term of office. The permanent administrative organ is the General Secretariat, headed by the Secretary-General, who is appointed by the General Assembly.

Secretary-General, Raymond Kendall, QPM (*UK*).

UK OFFICE, Interpol Bureau, New Scotland Yard, London SW1H OBG.

UK Representative, A. Mullett, QPM.

INTERNATIONAL ENERGY AGENCY

Chateau de la Muette, 2 rue André-Pascal, 75775 Paris, France

The International Energy Agency (IEA), founded in November 1974, is an autonomous agency within the framework of the Organization for Economic Co-operation and Development (OECD). The IEA had 22 member countries at January 1992.

The IEA's objectives include improvement of energy supply and demand worldwide, increased efficiency, development of alternative energy sources and the promotion of relations between oil producing and oil consuming countries. The IEA also maintains an emergency system to alleviate the effects of severe oil supply disruptions.

The main decision-making body is the Governing Board composed of senior energy officials from member countries. Various standing groups and special committees exist to facilitate the work of the Board. The IEA Secretariat, with a staff of energy experts, carries out the work of the Governing Board and its subordinate bodies. The Executive Director is appointed by the Board.

Executive Director, Mrs Helga Steeg (*Germany*).

INTERNATIONAL FUND FOR AGRICULTURAL DEVELOPMENT

107 Via del Serafico, 00142 Rome, Italy

The establishment of the International Fund for Agricultural Development (IFAD) was proposed by the 1974 World Food Conference and IFAD began operations as a UN specialized agency in December 1977. Its purpose is to mobilize additional funds for agricultural and rural development projects in developing countries that benefit the poorest rural populations.

IFAD had 145 members as at June 1991. Membership is divided into three categories: the developed countries (OECD), the oil-exporting developing countries (OPEC) and the remaining developing countries. All powers are vested in a Governing Council of all member countries. It elects an 18-member Executive Board (with 17 alternate members) responsible for IFAD's operations. The Council elects a President who is also chairman of the Board.

President, Idriss Jazairy (*Algeria*).

INTERNATIONAL LABOUR ORGANIZATION

4 route des Morillons, 1211 Geneva 22, Switzerland

The International Labour Organization (ILO) was established in 1919 as an autonomous body of the League of Nations and became the UN's first specialized agency in 1946. The ILO aims to increase productive labour, improve working conditions and raise living standards. It sets minimum international labour standards through the drafting of international conventions. Member countries are obliged to submit these to their domestic authorities for ratification, and thus undertake to bring their domestic legislation in line with the conventions. Members must report to the ILO periodically on how these regulations are being implemented. The ILO also runs a technical assistance programme in developing countries, and conducts research and disseminates information on labour. Through its World Employment Programme, it is attempting to reduce unemployment in developing countries by assisting national and international efforts to provide productive work. It is also developing an international programme to improve working conditions.

The ILO had 157 members as at June 1992. It is composed of the International Labour Conference, the Governing Body and the International Labour Office. The Conference of members meets annually, and is attended by national delegations comprising two government delegates, one worker delegate and one employer delegate. It formulates international labour conventions and recommendations, provides a forum for discussion of world labour and social problems, and approves the ILO's programme and budget (1992–3, US$376,168,000). Additional project funding is provided by the UN Development Programme, the UN Fund for Population Activities and other sources.

The 56-member Governing Body, composed of 28 government, 14 worker and 14 employer members, acts as the ILO's executive council. Ten governments, including Britain, hold seats on the Governing Body because of their industrial importance. There are also various regional conferences and advisory committees. The International Labour Office acts as a secretariat and as a centre for operations, publishing and research.

In 1960 the ILO established the International Institute for Labour Studies in Geneva as a think-tank on labour and social policy.

Director-General, Michel Hansenne (*Belgium*).

UK OFFICE, Vincent House, Vincent Square, London SW1P 2NB. Tel: 071-828 6401.

INTERNATIONAL MARITIME ORGANIZATION

4 Albert Embankment, London SE1 7SR

The International Maritime Organization (IMO) was established as a UN specialized agency in 1948. Due to delays in treaty ratification it did not commence operations until 17 March 1958. Originally it was called the Inter-Governmental Maritime Consultative Organization (IMCO) but changed its name in 1982.

The IMO fosters inter-governmental co-operation in technical matters relating to international shipping, especially with regard to safety at sea. It is also charged with preventing and controlling marine pollution caused by shipping and facilitating marine traffic. The IMO is responsible for calling maritime conferences and drafting marine conventions. Additionally, it provides technical aid to countries wishing to develop their activities at sea.

The IMO had 136 members as at June 1992. It is governed by an Assembly comprising delegates of all its members. It meets biennially to make policy, decide the budget (1992–3, £30 million) and vote on specific recommendations on pollution and maritime safety. It elects the Council and the Maritime Safety Committee. The Council fulfils the functions of the Assembly between sessions and appoints the Secretary-General. It consists of 32 members; eight from the world's largest shipping nations, eight from the nations most dependent on seaborne trade, and 16 other members to ensure a fair geographical representation. The Maritime Safety Committee, working through various sub-committees, makes reports and recommendations to the Council and the Assembly. There are a number of other specialist subsidiary committees, including one for marine environmental protection.

The IMO acts as the secretariat for the London Dumping Convention (1972) which regulates the disposal of land-generated waste at sea.

Secretary-General, William A. O'Neil (*Canada*).

INTERNATIONAL MARITIME SATELLITE ORGANIZATION

40 Melton Street, London NW1 2EQ

Inmarsat (the International Maritime Satellite Organization) was founded in July 1978 and began operations on 1 February 1982. Inmarsat operates a system of satellites to provide global mobile communications at sea, in the air and on land. Inmarsat satellite terminals are used worldwide on ships, in aircraft and on land for global telephone, facsimile, telex, e-mail data, as well as maritime safety and distress communications.

Inmarsat comprises three bodies: the Assembly, the Council and the Directorate. The Assembly is composed of representatives of all member countries, each with one vote. It meets every two years to review activities and objectives, and to make recommendations to the Council. The Council is the main decision-making body and consists of representatives of the 18 members with the largest investment shares. Four others who represent the interests of developing countries are elected to the Council on the basis of geographical representation. The Council meets at least three times a year and oversees the activities of the directorate, the permanent staff of Inmarsat.

As at May 1992 there were 64 member countries.

Director-General, Olof Lundberg (*Sweden*).

INTERNATIONAL MONETARY FUND

700 19th Street NW, Washington DC 20431, USA

The International Monetary Fund (IMF) was established on 22 July 1944, at the UN Monetary and Financial Conference held at Bretton Woods, New Hampshire. Its Articles of Agreement entered into force on 27 December 1945, and the IMF began operations in May 1946. The IMF exists to promote international monetary co-operation, the expansion of world trade, and exchange stability, and to eliminate foreign exchange restrictions. The IMF advises members on their economic and financial policies; promotes policy co-ordination among the major industrial countries; and gives technical assistance in central banking, balance of payments accounting, taxation, and other financial matters.

Upon joining the IMF, a member is assigned a 'quota', based on the member's relative standing in the world economy and its balance of payments position, that determines its capital subscription to the Fund, its access to IMF resources, its voting power, and its share in the allocation of Special Drawing Rights (SDRs). Quotas are reviewed every five years and adjusted accordingly. After the latest review, it was agreed to increase quotas by 50 per cent, from the present total of SDR 91.1 billion to SDR 136.7 billion; ratification of the increase is expected by the end of 1992. The SDR, an international reserve asset issued by the IMF, is calculated daily on a basket of usable currencies and is the IMF's unit of account; on 1 May 1992, SDR 1 equalled US$1.37374. SDRs are allocated at intervals to supplement members' reserves and thereby improve international financial liquidity.

IMF financial resources derive primarily from members' capital subscriptions, which are equivalent to their quotas. In addition, the IMF is authorized to borrow from official lenders. Periodic charges are also levied on financial assistance. At the end of April 1992, total outstanding IMF credits amounted to SDR 26.7 billion; borrowings amounted to SDR 23.7 billion.

The IMF is not a bank and does not lend money; it provides temporary financial assistance by selling a member's SDRs or other members' currencies in exchange for the member's own currency. The member can then use the purchased currency to alleviate its balance of payments difficulties. The IMF disburses this purchased currency in four 'credit tranches', each equal to 25 per cent of the member's quota, either over one to three years (a stand-by arrangement) or over three to four years (an extended arrangement). Drawings beyond the first credit tranch are subject to economic policy conditions. A member is expected to repay or repurchase its currency from the IMF within three and a quarter to five years under a stand-by arrangement, and within four and a half to ten years under an extended arrangement. Repurchase is made with SDRs or currencies acceptable to the Fund.

In addition, members with acute balance of payments problems can draw larger amounts through the enlarged access policy. Members experiencing a temporary balance of payments shortfall have access to the compensatory and contingency financing facility. The IMF also offers credits to low-income countries engaged in economic reform through its structural adjustment facility and enhanced structural adjustment facility.

The IMF is headed by a Board of Governors, comprising representatives of all members, which meets annually. The Governors delegate powers to 22 Executive Directors, six appointed and 16 elected. The Executive Directors operate the Fund on a daily basis under a Managing Director, whom they elect. The appointed directors represent France, Germany, Japan, Saudi Arabia, UK and USA.

Managing Director, Michel Camdessus (*France*).

UK Executive Director, D. Peretz, Room 11-120, IMF, 700 19th Street NW, Washington DC 20431.

INTERNATIONAL RED CROSS AND RED CRESCENT MOVEMENT

17 avenue de la Paix, 1211 Geneva, Switzerland

The International Red Cross and Red Crescent Movement is composed of three elements. The International Committee of the Red Cross (ICRC) is the founding body of the Red Cross and was formed in 1863. It is a neutral intermediary negotiating between warring factions, working throughout the world to protect and assist victims of armed conflict. It also ensures the application of the Geneva Conventions with regard to prisoners of war and detainees.

The International Federation of Red Cross and Red Crescent Societies, founded in 1919, is the body which exists to contribute to the development of the humanitarian activities of national societies, to co-ordinate their relief operations for victims of natural disasters, and to care for refugees outside areas of conflict. There are national Red Cross and Red Crescent Societies in 150 countries with a global membership of 250 million.

The International Conference of the Red Cross and Red Crescent meets every four years, bringing together delegates of the ICRC, the International Federation and the national societies, as well as representatives of nations bound by the Geneva Conventions.

President of the ICRC, Cornelio Sommaruga.

BRITISH RED CROSS, 9 Grosvenor Crescent, London SW1X 7EJ. *Director-General*, Michael R. Whitlam.

INTERNATIONAL TELECOMMUNICATIONS SATELLITE ORGANIZATION

3400 International Drive NW, Washington DC 20008–3098, USA

Formed in 1964, the International Telecommunications Satellite Organization (Intelsat) owns and operates the world-wide commercial communications satellite system. The system is composed of a network of nineteen satellites and more than 1,600 antennas which link together over 170 countries, territories and dependencies.

Intelsat provides an international telephone service; an international television service; the Intelsat Business Service (IBS); Intelnet (a digital service designed for data collection and distribution); domestic telecommunications services and the Vista service providing telecommunications to remote communities.

Each of the 123 member states contributes to the capital costs of the organization in proportion to its investment share. The investment share is based on the relative usage of the system by member countries.

There is a four-tier hierarchy. The Assembly of Parties to the agreement meets every two years to consider long-term objectives and is composed of representatives of the member governments. The Meeting of Signatories annually considers the financial, technical and operational aspects of the system. The Board of Governors has 28 members; the executive organ is the permanent staff of Intelsat and is headed by a Director-General who reports to the Board of Governors.

Director-General, Irving Goldstein (*USA*).

INTERNATIONAL TELECOMMUNICATIONS UNION

Place des Nations, 1211 Geneva 20, Switzerland

The International Telecommunications Union (ITU) was founded in Paris in 1865 as the International Telegraph Union and became a UN specialized agency in 1947. It promotes international co-operation and sets standards and regulations for telecommunications operations of all kinds. It assists the development of telecommunications and provides technical assistance to developing countries. The ITU allocates the radio frequency spectrum and registers radio frequency assignments in order to avoid harmful interference between radio stations of different countries. It also collects and disseminates telecommunications information.

The ITU had 168 members as at 19 May 1992. The supreme authority is the Plenipotentiary Conference, composed of representatives of all the members, which meets not less than once every five years. It elects the Administrative Council of 43 members which meets annually to supervise the Union and set the budget (1992, SFr144 million). The Conference also elects the Secretary-General, who heads the General Secretariat. Four other permanent bodies include the International Frequency Registration Board, the Telecommunications Development Bureau and two consultative committees, one for radio, and one for telephone and telegraph.

Secretary-General, Dr P. Tarjanne (*Finland*).

LEAGUE OF ARAB STATES

Maidane Al-Tahrir, Nile Cornish, Cairo, Egypt

The purpose of the League of Arab States (founded 1945) is to ensure co-operation among member states and protect their independence and sovereignty, to supervise the affairs and interests of Arab countries and to control the execution of agreements concluded among the member states. The League considers itself a regional organization and is an observer at the United Nations.

Member states are Algeria, Bahrain, Djibouti, Egypt, Iraq, Jordan, Kuwait, Lebanon, Libya, Mauritania, Morocco, Oman, Palestine, Qatar, Saudi Arabia, Somalia, Sudan, Syria, Tunisia, United Arab Emirates and the Republic of Yemen.

Secretary-General, Dr Ahmed Asmat Abdel-Meguid (*Egypt*).

UK OFFICE, 52 Green Street, London W1Y 3RH.

NORDIC COUNCIL

Tyrgatan 7, Box 19506, Stockholm 10432, Sweden

The Nordic Council was established in March 1952 as an advisory body on economic and social co-operation, comprising parliamentary delegates from Denmark, Iceland, Norway and Sweden. It was subsequently joined by Finland (1955), and representatives from the Faröes and the Åland Islands (1969/70), and Greenland (1984).

Co-operation is regulated by the Treaty of Helsinki signed in 1962. This was amended in 1971 to create the Nordic Council of Ministers, which discusses all matters except defence and foreign affairs. Matters are given preparatory consideration by a Committee of Co-operation Ministers'

Deputies and joint committees of officials. Decisions of the Council of Ministers, which are taken by unanimous consent, are binding, although if ratification by member parliaments is required, decisions only become effective following parliamentary approval. The Council of Ministers is advised by the Nordic Council, to which it reports annually. There are Ministers for Nordic Co-operation in every member government.

The Nordic Council, comprising 89 voting delegates nominated from member parliaments and about 80 non-voting government representatives, meets annually in plenary sessions. The full Council chooses a ten-member Praesidium, comprising two delegates from each sovereign member, which conducts business between sessions. A Secretariat, headed by a Secretary-General, liaises with the Council of Ministers and provides administrative support, as well as acting as a publishing house and information centre. The Council of Ministers has a separate Secretariat, based in Copenhagen.

Secretary-General, Jostein Osnes (*Norway*).

SECRETARIAT OF NORDIC COUNCIL OF MINISTERS, Store Strandgade 18, 1255 Copenhagen K, Denmark.

NORTH ATLANTIC TREATY ORGANIZATION

Brussels 1110, Belgium

The North Atlantic Treaty was signed on 4 April 1949 by the foreign ministers of twelve nations: Belgium, Canada, Denmark, France, Iceland, Italy, Luxembourg, the Netherlands, Norway, Portugal, the UK and USA. Greece and Turkey acceded to the Treaty in 1952, the Federal Republic of Germany in 1955 (the reunited Germany acceded in October 1990), and Spain in 1982.

The North Atlantic Council, chaired by the Secretary-General, is the highest authority of the Alliance and is composed of permanent representatives of the sixteen member countries. It meets at ministerial level (foreign ministers) at least twice a year. The permanent representatives (Ambassadors) head national delegations of advisers and experts. Defence matters are dealt with in the Defence Planning Committee (DPC), composed of representatives of all member countries, except France.

The Council and DPC are forums for confidential and constant inter-governmental consultation and are the main decision-making bodies within the North Atlantic Alliance. They are assisted by an International Staff, divided into five divisions: Political Affairs; Defence Planning and Policy; Defence Support; Infrastructure, Logistics and Civil Emergency Planning; Scientific Affairs.

The senior military authority in NATO, under the Council and DPC, is the Military Committee composed of the Chief of Defence of each member country, except France and Iceland. The Military Committee, which is assisted by an international military staff, also meets in permanent session with permanent military representatives and is responsible for making recommendations to the Council and Defence Planning Committee on measures considered necessary for the common defence of the NATO area and for supplying guidance on military matters to the major NATO commanders.

The strategic area covered by the North Atlantic Treaty is divided among three Commands (European, Atlantic and Channel) and a Regional Planning Group (Canada and the United States).

The major NATO commanders are responsible for the development of defence plans for their respective areas, for the determination of force requirements and for the deployment and exercise of the forces under their command. The major NATO commanders report to the Military Committee.

At a NATO summit held in London in 1990, NATO heads of state and government redefined the goals and strategy of the organization in the light of the end of the Cold War. At a meeting held in May 1991, defence ministers agreed to create a new rapid reaction corps under British command. A Declaration of Peace and Co-operation was issued at a further summit held in Rome in November 1991 and a new strategic concept was published, introducing major changes in the organization of NATO forces and overall reductions of around 30 per cent. A North Atlantic Co-operation Council was also established within a framework of dialogue and partnership between the member countries of the Alliance and states of eastern Europe and the former Soviet Union.

Secretary-General and Chairman of the North Atlantic Council, Manfred Wörner (*Germany*).

UK Permanent Representative on the North Atlantic Council, Sir John Weston.

Chairman of the Military Committee, Field Marshal Sir Richard Vincent (*UK*).

Supreme Allied Commander, Europe, Gen. John Shalikashvili (*US*).

Supreme Allied Commander, Atlantic, Adm. Leon Edney (*US*).

Commander-in-Chief, Channel, Adm. Sir Jock Slater, KCB, LVO (*UK*).

Commander (*designate*) *Allied Rapid Reaction Corps*, Lt.-Gen. Sir Jeremy MacKenzie (*UK*).

ORGANIZATION FOR ECONOMIC CO-OPERATION AND DEVELOPMENT

2 rue André-Pascal, 75116 Paris

Formed on 30 September 1961, the Organization for Economic Co-operation and Development (OECD) replaced the Organization for European Economic Co-operation. The OECD is the instrument for international co-operation among industrialized member countries on economic and social policies. Its objectives are to assist its member governments in the formulation and co-ordination of policies designed to achieve high, sustained economic growth while maintaining financial stability, to contribute to world trade on a multilateral basis and to stimulate members' aid to developing countries.

The following countries belong to the OECD: Australia, Austria, Belgium, Canada, Denmark, Germany, Finland, France, Greece, Iceland, Republic of Ireland, Italy, Japan, Luxembourg, the Netherlands, New Zealand, Norway, Portugal, Spain, Sweden, Switzerland, Turkey, UK and USA.

The Council is the supreme body of the organization. Composed of one representative for each member country, it meets at permanent representative level under the chairmanship of the Secretary-General, or at ministerial level (usually once a year) under the chairmanship of a minister elected annually. Decisions and recommendations are adopted by mutual agreement of all members of the Council. Fourteen members of the Council are chosen annually to form an executive committee to assist the Council. However, most of the OECD's work is undertaken in over 200 specialized committees and working parties. Five autonomous or semi-autonomous bodies are related in varying degrees to the Organization: the Nuclear Energy Agency, the International Energy Agency, the Development Centre,

the Centre for Educational Research and Innovation, and the European Conference of Ministers of Transport. These bodies, the committees and the Council are serviced by an international Secretariat headed by the Secretary-General of the Organization.
Secretary-General, Jean-Claude Paye (*France*).
UK Permanent Representative, Keith MacInnes, 19 rue de Franqueville, Paris 75116.

ORGANIZATION OF AFRICAN UNITY

PO Box 3243, Addis Ababa, Ethiopia

The Organization of African Unity (OAU) was established in 1963 and has 51 members. It aims to further African unity and solidarity, to co-ordinate political, economic, social and defence policies, and to eliminate colonialism in Africa.

The chief organs are the Assembly of heads of state or government and the Council of foreign ministers. The main administrative body is the Secretariat, based in Addis Ababa.
Secretary-General, Salim Ahmed Salim (*Tanzania*).

ORGANIZATION OF AMERICAN STATES

17th Street and Constitution Avenue NW, Washington DC 20006, USA

Originally founded in 1890 for largely commercial purposes, the Organization of American States (OAS) adopted its present name and charter in 1948. The charter was later amended by the Protocol of Buenos Aires (1967) and the Protocol of Cartagena de Indias (1985). Its aims are to strengthen the peace and security of the continent; to promote and consolidate representative democracy with due respect for the principle of non-intervention; to prevent possible causes of difficulties and to ensure the pacific settlement of disputes that may arise among the member states; to provide for common action on the part of those states in the event of aggression; to seek the solution of political, judicial and economic problems that may arise among them; to promote, by co-operative action, their economic, social and cultural development; and to achieve an effective limitation of conventional weapons that will make it possible to devote the largest amount of resources to the economic and social development of the member states. The OAS is a regional organization within the United Nations.

Policy is determined by the annual General Assembly. Meetings of ministers of foreign affairs consider urgent problems, and advise in cases of armed attack and threats to peace. A Permanent Council, comprised of one representative from each member state, meets at OAS headquarters throughout the year.

The 35 member states are Antigua and Barbuda, Argentina, Bahamas, Barbados, Belize, Bolivia, Brazil, Canada, Chile, Colombia, Costa Rica, Cuba, Dominica, Dominican Republic, Ecuador, Grenada, Guatemala, Guyana, Haiti, Honduras, Jamaica, Mexico, Nicaragua, Panama, Paraguay, Peru, St Christopher and Nevis, St Lucia, St Vincent and the Grenadines, El Salvador, Suriname, Trinidad and Tobago, Uruguay, USA and Venezuela.
Secretary-General, João Clemente Baena Soares (*Brazil*).

ORGANIZATION OF ARAB PETROLEUM EXPORTING COUNTRIES

PO Box 108 Maglis Al-Shaab, 11516 Cairo, Egypt.

The Organization of Arab Petroleum and Exporting Countries (OAPEC) was founded in 1968. The objectives of the organization are to promote co-operation in economic activities; to safeguard members' interests; to unite efforts to ensure the flow of oil to consumer markets; and to create a favourable climate for the investment of capital and expertise.

The Ministerial Council is composed of oil ministers from the member countries and meets twice a year to determine policy, to direct activities and to approve the budgets and accounts of the General Secretariat and the Judicial Tribunal. The Judicial Tribunal is composed of seven part-time judges who rule on disputes between member nations and disputes between nations and oil companies. The executive organ of OAPEC is the General Secretariat.

The member countries of OAPEC are Algeria, Bahrain, Egypt, Iraq, Kuwait, Libya, Qatar, Saudi Arabia, Syria and the United Arab Emirates. Tunisia's membership has been inactive since 1987.
Secretary-General, Abdel-Aziz A. Al-Turki.

ORGANIZATION OF THE PETROLEUM EXPORTING COUNTRIES

Obere Donaustrasse 93, 1020 Vienna, Austria

The Organization of the Petroleum Exporting Countries (OPEC) was created in 1960 as a permanent intergovernmental organization with the aims of unifying and co-ordinating the petroleum policies of members and determining the best means of protecting their interests, individually and collectively.

The supreme authority is the Conference of Ministers of Oil, Mines and Energy of member countries which meets at least twice a year and formulates policy. The Board of Governors, nominated by member countries, directs the management of OPEC and implements Conference resolutions. The Secretariat, based in Vienna, carries out executive functions under the direction of the Board of Governors.

The 13 member countries are Algeria, Ecuador, Gabon, Indonesia, Iran, Iraq, Kuwait, Libya, Nigeria, Qatar, Saudi Arabia, UAE and Venezuela.
Secretary-General, Dr Subroto (*Indonesia*).

SOUTH PACIFIC COMMISSION

BP D5, Nouméa Cedex, New Caledonia

The South Pacific Commission is a technical assistance agency with programmes in agriculture and plant protection, marine resources, rural management and technology, and community and education services. The management committee is involved with the day-to-day running of the organization and is headed by the Secretary-General. The other members are the Director and the Deputy Director of Programmes.

The South Pacific Commission was established in February 1947 following the signing of the Canberra Agreement by the governments of Australia, France, the Netherlands, New Zealand, the UK and the USA. The aim was to promote the economic and social stability of the islands in the region.

In 1983, the South Pacific Conference adopted a resolution that the Conference's 27 governments and administrations should have full and equal membership. Since 1967 the Conference has met annually to discuss the future policy of the Commission, to adopt the budget and to nominate the officers of the Commission.
Secretary-General, Atanraoi Baiteke (*Kiribati*).
Director of Programmes, Hélène Courte (*New Caledonia*).
Deputy Director of Programmes, Vaasatia Poloma Komiti (*Western Samoa*).

The United Nations

UN Plaza, New York, NY 10017, USA

The United Nations is a voluntary association of states, dedicated through signature of the UN Charter to the maintenance of international peace and security and the solution of economic, social and political problems through international co-operation. The UN is not a world government and has no right of intervention in the essentially domestic affairs of states.

The UN was founded as a successor to the League of Nations and inherited many of its procedures and institutions. The name 'United Nations' was first used in the Washington Declaration of January 1942 to describe the 26 states which had allied to fight the Axis powers. The UN Charter developed from discussions at the Moscow Conference of the foreign ministers of China, the United Kingdom, the USA and Soviet Union held in October 1943. Further progress was made at Dumbarton Oaks, Washington, between August and October 1944 during talks involving the same states. The role of the Security Council was formulated at the Yalta Conference of Churchill, Roosevelt and Stalin in January 1945. The Charter was formally drawn up by 50 allied nations at the San Francisco Conference between April and 26 June 1945, when it was signed. Following ratification the UN came into effect on 24 October 1945, which is celebrated annually as United Nations Day. The UN flag is light blue with the UN emblem centred in white.

The principal organs of the UN are the General Assembly, the Security Council, the Economic and Social Council, the Trusteeship Council, the Secretariat and the International Court of Justice. The Economic and Social Council and the Trusteeship Council are auxiliaries, charged with assisting and advising the General Assembly and Security Council. The official languages used are Arabic, Chinese, English, French, Russian and Spanish. Deliberations at the International Court of Justice are in English and French only.

Membership

Membership is open to all countries which accept the Charter and its principle of peaceful co-existence. New members are admitted by the General Assembly on the recommendation of the Security Council. The original membership of 51 states has grown to 178:

Afghanistan
Albania
Algeria
Angola
Antigua and Barbuda
*Argentina
Armenia
*Australia
Austria
Azerbaijan
Bahamas
Bahrain
Bangladesh
Barbados
*Belarus
*Belgium
Belize
Benin
Bhutan
*Bolivia
Bosnia-Hercegovina
Botswana
*Brazil
Brunei
Bulgaria
Burkina
Burundi
Cambodia (Kampuchea)
Cameroon
*Canada
Cape Verde
Central African Rep.
Chad
*Chile
*China
*Colombia
Comoros
Congo
*Costa Rica
Côte d'Ivoire
Croatia
*Cuba
Cyprus
*Czechoslovakia
*Denmark
Djibouti
Dominica
*Dominican Republic
*Ecuador
*Egypt
Equatorial Guinea
Estonia
*Ethiopia
Federated States of Micronesia
Fiji
Finland
*France
Gabon
Gambia
Germany
Ghana
*Greece
Grenada
*Guatemala
Guinea
Guinea-Bissau
Guyana
*Haiti
*Honduras
Hungary
Iceland
*India
Indonesia
*Iran
*Iraq
Ireland, Republic of
Israel
Italy
Jamaica
Japan
Jordan
Kazakhstan
Kenya
Korea, D.P.Rep. (North)
Korea, Rep. of (South)
Kuwait
Kyrgyzstan
Laos
Latvia
*Lebanon
Lesotho
*Liberia
Libya
Liechtenstein
Lithuania
*Luxembourg
Madagascar
Malawi
Malaysia
Maldives
Mali
Malta
Marshall Islands
Mauritania
Mauritius
*Mexico
Moldova
Mongolia
Morocco
Mozambique
Myanmar (Burma)
Namibia
Nepal
*Netherlands
*New Zealand
*Nicaragua
Niger
Nigeria
*Norway
Oman
Pakistan
*Panama
Papua New Guinea
*Paraguay
*Peru
*Philippines
*Poland
Portugal
Qatar
Romania
*Russian Federation
Rwanda
St Christopher and Nevis
St Lucia
St Vincent and the Grenadines
*El Salvador
San Marino
São Tomé and Príncipe
*Saudi Arabia
Senegal
Seychelles
Sierra Leone
Singapore
Slovenia
Solomon Islands
Somalia
*South Africa
Spain
Sri Lanka
Sudan
Suriname
Swaziland
Sweden
*Syria

Tajikistan	*United States of America
Tanzania	*Uruguay
Thailand	Uzbekistan
Togo	Vanuatu
Trinidad and Tobago	*Venezuela
Tunisia	Vietnam
*Turkey	Western Samoa
Turkmenistan	Yemen
Uganda	*Yugoslavia (suspended)
*Ukraine	Zaire
United Arab Emirates	Zambia
*United Kingdom	Zimbabwe

*Original member (i.e. from 1945). From 25 October 1971 'China' was taken to mean the People's Republic of China.

A number of countries are not members, usually due to their small size and limited financial resources. Notable exceptions include Switzerland, which follows a policy of absolute neutrality, and Taiwan, which was replaced by the People's Republic of China in October 1971. The Russian Federation took over the membership of the Soviet Union in the Security Council and all other UN organs on 24 December 1991. Belarus (formerly Belorussia) and the Ukraine on becoming independent sovereign states continued their existing memberships of the UN, both having been granted separate UN membership in 1945 as a concession to the Soviet Union.

OBSERVERS

Permanent observer status is held by the Holy See, Monaco and Switzerland. The Palestinian Liberation Organization has special observer status.

THE GENERAL ASSEMBLY

UN Plaza, New York, NY 10017, USA

The General Assembly is the main deliberative organ of the UN. It consists of all members, each entitled to five representatives but having only one vote. The annual session begins on the third Tuesday of September, when the President is elected, and usually continues until mid-December. Special sessions are held on specific issues and emergency special sessions can be called within 24 hours.

The Assembly is empowered to discuss any matter within the scope of the Charter, except when it is under consideration by the Security Council, and to make recommendations. Under the 'uniting for peace' resolution, adopted in November 1950, the Assembly may also take action to maintain international peace and security when the Security Council fails to do so because of a lack of unanimity of its permanent members. Important decisions, such as those on peace and security, the election of officers, the budget, etc., need a two-thirds majority. Others need a simple majority. The Assembly has effective power only over the internal operations of the UN itself; external recommendations are not legally binding.

The work of the General Assembly is divided among seven main committees, on each of which every member has the right to be represented: Disarmament and related security questions (assisted by a Special Political Committee); Economic and Financial; Social, Humanitarian and Cultural; Decolonization (including non-self governing territories); Administrative and Budgetary; Legal. In addition, the General Assembly appoints *ad hoc* committees to consider special issues, such as human rights, peace-keeping, disarmament and international law. All committees consider items referred to them by the Assembly and recommend draft resolutions to its plenary meeting.

The Assembly is assisted by a number of functional committees. The General Committee co-ordinates its proceedings and operations, while the Credentials Committee verifies the credentials of representatives. There are also two standing committees, the Advisory Committee on Administration and Budgetary Questions and the Committee on Contributions, which suggests the scale of members' payments to the UN.

President of the General Assembly (1991), Samir S. Shihabi (*Saudi Arabia*).

The Assembly has created a large number of specialized bodies over the years, which are supervised jointly with the Economic and Social Council. They are supported by UN and voluntary contributions from governments, non-governmental organizations and individuals. These organizations include:

THE CONFERENCE ON DISARMAMENT (CD)
Palais des Nations, 1211 Geneva 10, Switzerland
Established by the UN as the Committee on Disarmament in 1962, the CD is the single multilateral disarmament negotiating forum. The present title of the organization was adopted in 1984. There were 39 members as at 1 June 1991.

The Conference holds three regular sessions per year, from January to March, May to June, and July to August. The work of the Conference is conducted both in public plenary meetings and in private *ad hoc* committees set up with the consent of all members to deal with specific items of the agenda. Currently under negotiation are a ban on chemical weapons and the prevention of an arms race in outer space.

Secretary-General, HE Miljan Komatina.
UK Representative, Miss T. A. H. Solesby, CMG, 37–39 rue de Vermont, 1211 Geneva 10, Switzerland.

THE UNITED NATIONS CHILDREN'S FUND (UNICEF)
3 UN Plaza, New York, NY 10017, USA
Established in 1947 to assist children and mothers in the immediate post-war period, UNICEF now concentrates on developing countries. It provides primary health-care and health education. In particular, it conducts programmes in oral hydration, immunization against leading diseases, child growth monitoring, and the encouragement of breast-feeding. Its operations are often conducted in co-operation with the World Health Organization (WHO).
Executive Director, James Grant (*USA*).

THE UNITED NATIONS DEVELOPMENT PROGRAMME (UNDP)
1 UN Plaza, New York, NY 10017, USA
Established in 1966 from the merger of the UN Expanded Programme of Technical Assistance and the UN Special Fund, UNDP is the central funding agency for economic and social development projects around the world. Much of its annual expenditure is channelled through UN specialized agencies, governments and non-governmental organizations.
Administrator, William H. Draper III (*USA*).

THE UNITED NATIONS HIGH COMMISSIONER FOR REFUGEES (UNHCR)
Centre William Rappard, 154 rue de Lausanne, PO Box 2500, 1211 Geneva 2, Switzerland
Established in 1951 to protect the rights and interests of refugees, it organizes emergency relief and longer-term solutions, such as voluntary repatriation, local integration or resettlement.
High Commissioner, Sadako Ogata (*Japan*).

UK OFFICE, 36 Westminster Palace Gardens, London SW1P 1RR. Tel: 071-222 3065.

THE UN RELIEF AND WORKS AGENCY FOR PALESTINE REFUGEES IN THE NEAR EAST (UNRWA)
Vienna International Centre, Wagramerstrasse 5, PO Box 100, 1400 Vienna, Austria
Established in 1949 to bring relief to the Palestinians displaced by the Arab-Israeli conflict.
Commissioner-General, Ilter Turkman (*Turkey*).

Other bodies include:

THE UN CENTRE FOR HUMAN SETTLEMENTS (Habitat), PO Box 30030, Nairobi, Kenya
THE UN COMMISSION FOR TRADE AND DEVELOPMENT (UNCTAD), Palais des Nations, 1211 Geneva 10, Switzerland
THE OFFICE OF THE UN DISASTER AND RELIEF CO-ORDINATOR (UNDRO), Palais des Nations, 1211 Geneva 10, Switzerland
THE UN ENVIRONMENT PROGRAMME (UNEP), PO Box 30552, Nairobi, Kenya
THE UN FUND FOR POPULATION ACTIVITIES (UNFPA), 220 East 42nd Street, New York, NY 10017, USA
THE UN INSTITUTE FOR THE ADVANCEMENT OF WOMEN (INSTRAW), PO Box 21747, Santo Domingo, Dominican Republic
THE UN UNIVERSITY (UNU), Toho Seimei Building, 15–1, Shibuya, 2-Chome, Shibuya-ku, Tokyo 150, Japan
THE WORLD FOOD COUNCIL (WFC), Via delle Terme di Caracalla, 00100 Rome, Italy
THE WORLD FOOD PROGRAMME (WFP), Via delle Terme di Caracalla, 00100 Rome, Italy

BUDGET OF THE UNITED NATIONS

The budget adopted for the biennium 1992–3 was US$2,389,234,900. The scale of assessment contributions of 88 UN members is set at the minimum 0.01 per cent. The ten largest assessments are: USA, 25 per cent; Japan, 11.38; Russian Federation, 9.99; Germany, 9.36; France, 6.25; UK, 4.86; Italy, 3.99; Canada, 3.09; Spain, 1.95; Netherlands, 1.65.

THE SECURITY COUNCIL

UN Plaza, New York, NY 10017, USA

The Security Council is the senior arm of the UN and has the primary responsibility for maintaining world peace and security. It consists of 15 members, each with one representative and one vote. There are five permanent members, China, France, the Russian Federation, UK and USA, and ten non-permanent members. Each of the non-permanent members is elected for a two-year term by a two-thirds majority of the General Assembly and is ineligible for immediate re-election. Five of the elective seats are allocated to Africa and Asia, one to eastern Europe, two to Latin America and two to western Europe and remaining countries. Procedural questions are determined by a simple majority vote. Other matters require a majority inclusive of the votes of the permanent members; they thus have a right of veto. The abstention of a permanent member does not constitute a veto. The presidency rotates each month by state in (English) alphabetical order. Parties to a dispute, other non-members and individuals can be invited to participate in Security Council debates but are not permitted to vote. In 1992 the ten non-permanent members were: Austria, Belgium, Ecuador, India and Zimbabwe (*term expires 31 December 1992*); Cape Verde, Hungary, Japan, Morocco and Venezuela (*term expires 31 December 1993*).

The Security Council is empowered to settle or adjudicate in disputes or situations which threaten international peace and security. It can adopt political, economic and military measures to achieve this end. Any matter considered to be a threat to or breach of the peace or an act of aggression can be brought to the Security Council's attention by any member state or by the Secretary-General. The Charter envisaged members placing at the disposal of the Security Council armed forces and other facilities which would be co-ordinated by the Military Staff Committee, composed of military representatives of the five permanent members. The Security Council is also supported by a Committee of Experts, to advise on procedural and technical matters, and a Committee on Admission of New Members. Owing to superpower disunity, the Security Council has rarely played the decisive role set out in the Charter; the Military Staff Committee was effectively suspended from 1948 until 1990, when a meeting was convened during the Gulf Crisis on the formation and control of UN-supervised armed forces.

At an extraordinary meeting of the Security Council on 31 January 1992 attended by heads of government, plans were laid to transform the UN in light of the changed post-Cold War world. The Secretary-General was asked to draw up a report on transforming the UN's peace-keeping ability. The report was produced in June 1992 and centred on the establishment of a UN army composed of national contingents on permanent standby, as envisaged at the time of the UN's formation.

PEACE-KEEPING FORCES

The Security Council has established a number of peace-keeping forces since its foundation, comprising contingents provided mainly by neutral and non-aligned UN members. Current forces include: the UN Truce Supervision Organization (UNTSO), 1948, Israel; the UN Military Observer Group in India and Pakistan (UNMOGIP), 1949; the UN Force in Cyprus (UNFICYP), 1964; the UN Disengagement Observer Force (UNDOF), 1974, Golan Heights, Syria; the UN Interim Force in Lebanon (UNIFIL), 1978; the UN Iraq-Kuwait Observation Mission (UNIKOM), 1991; UN Angola Verification Mission II (UNAVEM II), 1991; UN Observers for El Salvador (ONUSAL), 1991; the UN Mission for the Referendum in Western Sahara (MINURSO), 1991; the UN Protection Force (UNPROFOR), 1992, Croatia and Bosnia-Hercegovina; the UN Transitional Authority in Cambodia (UNTAC), 1992; and the UN Operation in Somalia (UNOSOM), 1992.

THE ECONOMIC AND SOCIAL COUNCIL

UN Plaza, New York, NY 10017, USA

The Economic and Social Council is responsible under the General Assembly for the economic and social work of the UN and for the co-ordination of the activities of the 15 specialized agencies and other UN bodies. It makes reports and recommendations on economic, social, cultural, educational, health and related matters, often in consultation with non-governmental organizations, passing the reports to the General Assembly and other UN bodies. It also drafts conventions for submission to the Assembly and calls conferences on matters within its remit.

The Council consists of 54 members, 18 of whom are elected annually by the General Assembly for a three-year term. Each has one vote and can be immediately re-elected on retirement. A President is elected annually and is also eligible for re-election. Meetings are held biennially and decisions reached by simple majority vote of those present.

The Council has established a number of standing committees on particular issues and several commissions. Commissions include: Statistical, Human Rights, Social Development, Status of Women, Crime Prevention and Criminal Justice, Narcotic Drugs, Science and Technology for Development, and Population; and Regional Economic Commissions for Europe, Asia and the Pacific, Western Asia, Latin America and Africa.

THE TRUSTEESHIP COUNCIL

UN Plaza, New York, NY 10017, USA

The Trusteeship Council supervises the administration of territories within the UN Trusteeship system inherited from the League of Nations. It now consists of the USA, the only remaining administrator, and the four other permanent members of the Security Council. Meetings are held annually and decisions reached by a majority vote of those present. Ten of the original eleven trusteeships have now progressed towards independence or merged with neighbouring states. With the termination of the trust status for the Federated States of Micronesia in December 1990, only the Republic of Palau now remains within the system.

THE SECRETARIAT

UN Plaza, New York, NY 10017, USA

The Secretariat services the other UN organs and is headed by a Secretary-General elected by a majority vote of the General Assembly on the recommendation of the Security Council. He is assisted by an international staff, chosen to represent the international character of the organization. The Secretary-General is charged with bringing to the attention of the Security Council any matter which he considers poses a threat to international peace and security. He may also bring other matters to the attention of the General Assembly and other UN bodies and may be entrusted by them with additional duties. As chief administrator to the UN, the Secretary-General is present in person or via representatives at all meetings of the other five main organs of the UN. He may also act as an impartial mediator in disputes between member states.

The power and influence of the Secretary-General has, to a large extent, been determined by the character of the office-holder and by the state of relations between the superpowers. The thaw in these relations since the mid-1980s has increased the effectiveness of the UN, particularly in its attempts to intervene in international disputes. It helped to end the Iran-Iraq war and sponsored peace in Central America. Following Iraq's invasion of Kuwait in 1990 the UN took its first collective security action since the Korean War. UN action to protect the Kurds in northern Iraq has widened its legal authority by breaching the prohibition on its intervention in the essentially domestic affairs of states. Currently the UN plans to set up a UN-sponsored interim government in Cambodia and is addressing the global problems of AIDS and environmental destruction.

Since he took office on 1 January 1992, the new Secretary-General Boutros Boutros-Ghali has introduced radical change in the Secretariat, reducing the number of departments from 20 to eight, each headed by an Under-Secretary-General.

Secretary-General, Boutros Boutros-Ghali (*Egypt*).
Under-Secretaries-General:
Africa, Asia and the Middle East, James Jonah, (*Sierra Leone*).
Europe, Latin America, Disarmament, the General Assembly and the Security Council, Vladimir Petrovsky (*Russian Federation*).
Peace-keeping Operations, Marrack Goulding (*UK*).
Economic and Social Development, Ji Chaozhu (*China*).
Legal Affairs, Carl-August Fleischhauer (*Germany*).
Humanitarian Affairs, Jan Eliasson (*Sweden*).
Public Information, Eugeniusz Wyzner (*Poland*).
Administration and Budget, Richard Thornburgh (*US*).

INTERNATIONAL COURT OF JUSTICE

The Peace Palace, 2517 KJ The Hague, The Netherlands

The International Court of Justice is the principal judicial organ of the UN. The Statute of the Court is an integral part of the Charter and all members of the UN are *ipso facto* parties to it. The Court is composed of 15 judges, elected by both the General Assembly and the Security Council for nine-year terms which are renewable. Judges may deliberate over cases in which their country is involved. If no judge on the bench is from a country which is a party to a dispute under consideration, that party may designate a judge to participate *ad hoc* in that particular deliberation. If any party to a case fails to adhere to the judgment of the Court, the other party may have recourse to the Security Council.

President, Sir Robert Jennings (*UK*) (2000).
Vice-President, Shigeru Oda (*Japan*) (1994).
Judges, Manfred Lachs (*Poland*) (1994); Bola Ajibola (*Nigeria*) (1994); Roberto Ago (*Italy*) (1997); Stephen M. Schwebel (*USA*) (1997); Mohammed Bedjaoui (*Algeria*) (2000); Ni Zhengyu (*China*) (1994); Jens Evensen (*Norway*) (1997); Nikolai K. Tarassov (*Russian Federation*) (1997); Gilbert Guillaume (*France*) (2000); Mohammed Shahabuddeen (*Guyana*) (1997); Andrés Aguilar Mawdsley (*Venezuela*) (2000); Christopher G. Weeramantry (*Sri Lanka*) (2000); and Raymond Ranjeva (*Madagascar*) (2000).

SPECIALIZED AGENCIES

Fifteen independent international organizations, each with its own membership, budget and headquarters, carry out their responsibilities in co-ordination with the UN under agreements made with the Economic and Social Council. An entry for each appears elsewhere in the International Organizations section. They are as follows: the Food and Agriculture Organization of the UN; International Civil Aviation Organization; International Fund for Agricultural Development; International Labour Organization; International Maritime Organization; the International Monetary Fund; International Telecommunications Union; UN Educational, Scientific and Cultural Organization; UN Industrial Development Organization; Universal Postal Union; World Bank (International Bank for Reconstruction and Development, International Development Agency, International Finance Corporation); World Health Organization; World Intellectual Property Organization; and World Meteorological Organization. The International Atomic Energy Agency and the General Agreement on Tariffs and Trade are linked to the UN but are not specialized agencies.

UK MISSION TO THE UNITED NATIONS
845 Third Avenue, New York, NY 10022, USA
Permanent Representative to the United Nations and Representative on the Security Council, Sir David Hannay, KCMG, *apptd* 1990.
Deputy Permanent Representative, T. L. Richardson, CMG.

UK MISSION TO THE OFFICE OF THE UN AND OTHER INTERNATIONAL ORGANIZATIONS IN GENEVA
37–39 rue de Vermont, 1211 Geneva 20, Switzerland
Permanent UK Representative, M. R. Morland, CMG *apptd* 1990.
Deputy Permanent Representatives, E. G. M. Chaplain, OBE (*Head of Chancery*); Miss A.E.Stoddart (*Economic Affairs*).

UK MISSION TO THE INTERNATIONAL ATOMIC ENERGY AGENCY, THE UN INDUSTRIAL DEVELOPMENT ORGANIZATION AND THE UNITED NATIONS OFFICE AT VIENNA
Jaurésgasse 12, 1030 Vienna, Austria
Permanent UK Representative, G.E.Clark, CMG *apptd* 1987.
Deputy Permanent Representative, Miss M.R.McIntosh.

UN OFFICE AND INFORMATION CENTRE
Ship House, 20 Buckingham Gate, London SW1E 6LB
Tel: 071-630 1981

UNITED NATIONS EDUCATIONAL, SCIENTIFIC AND CULTURAL ORGANIZATION

7 place de Fontenoy, Paris 75700, France

The United Nations Educational, Scientific and Cultural Organization (UNESCO) was established on 4 November 1946, the consequence of an international conference held in London in 1945. It promotes collaboration among its member states in education, science, culture and communication. It aims to further a universal respect for human rights, justice and the rule of law, without distinction of race, sex, language or religion, in accordance with the UN Charter.

UNESCO runs a number of programmes to improve education and extend access to it. It provides assistance to improve the quality of the world's media and maintain cultural heritage in the face of development. It fosters research and study in all areas of the social sciences.

UNESCO had 166 member states as at June 1992. There are three associate members. The General Conference, consisting of representatives of all the members, meets biennially to decide the programme and the budget (1992–3, US$444,704,000). It elects the 51-member Executive Board, which supervises operations, and appoints a Director-General. The Director-General heads a Secretariat responsible for day-to-day functions. In most member states national commissions liaise with UNESCO to execute its programme.

The UK withdrew from UNESCO in 1985. It was granted observer status in 1986.

Director-General, Federico Mayor Zaragoza (*Spain*).

UNITED NATIONS INDUSTRIAL DEVELOPMENT ORGANIZATION

Vienna International Centre, Wagramerstrasse 5,
PO Box 300, 1400 Vienna, Austria

The United Nations Industrial Development Organization (UNIDO) was established as an organ of the UN General Assembly in 1966, replacing the Centre for Industrial Development. It became a UN specialized agency on 1 January 1986 with the aim of promoting the industrialization of developing countries, with special emphasis upon the manufacturing sector. To this end it provides technical assistance and advice, as well as help with planning.

UNIDO had 156 members as at May 1992. It is funded by the UN Development Programme, other UN bodies, governments and non-governmental organizations. A General Conference of all the members meets biennially to discuss policy, set a budget (1992–3, US$181,013,400) and elect the Industrial Development Board. This executive body is composed of 33 members from developing countries, 15 from developed countries and five from centrally planned economies. There is a subsidiary Programme and Budget Committee. A Secretariat administers UNIDO under a Director-General, appointed by the Conference.

Director-General, Domingo L. Siazon jun. (*Philippines*).
Permanent UK Representative, G. E. Clark, CMG, British Embassy, Vienna.

UNIVERSAL POSTAL UNION

Weltpoststrasse 4, 3000 Berne 15, Switzerland

The Universal Postal Union (UPU) was established by the Convention of Berne on 9 October 1874, taking effect from July 1875, and became a UN specialized agency in June 1947. The UPU exists to form a single postal territory of all member countries, for the reciprocal exchange of correspondence without discrimination. It also assists and advises on the improvement of postal services.

The UPU had 171 members as at May 1992. A Universal Postal Congress of all the members meets every five years to review the Convention and to elect a 40-member Executive Council (including one member from the host country) which continues the UPU's work between Congresses. The Congress also elects a 35-member Consultative Council for Postal Studies which meets annually to address specific matters. The Council, together with the Swiss government, supervises the International Bureau, a secretariat headed by a Director-General.

Funding is provided by members according to a scale of contributions drawn up by the Congress. The Council sets the annual budget (1992, SFr27,622,265) within a five-year figure decided by the Congress.

Director-General, A. C. Botto de Barros (*Brazil*).

WESTERN EUROPEAN UNION

9 Grosvenor Place, London SW1X 7HL

The Western European Union (WEU) originated as the Brussels Treaty Organization (BTO). This was established under the Treaty of Brussels, signed in 1948 by Belgium, France, Luxembourg, the Netherlands and UK, to provide collective self-defence and economic, cultural and social collaboration amongst its signatories. With the collapse of the European Defence Community and the decision of NATO to incorporate the Federal Republic of Germany into the Western security system, the BTO was modified to become the WEU in 1954 with the admission of West Germany and Italy.

Owing to the overlap with NATO and the Council of Europe, the Union became largely defunct. From the late 1970s onwards efforts were made to add a security dimension to the EC's European Political Co-operation. Opposition to these efforts from Denmark, Greece and Ireland led the remaining EC countries, all WEU members, to decide to reactivate the Union in 1984. Members committed themselves to harmonizing their views on defence and security and developing a European security identity, while bearing in mind the importance of transatlantic relations. Portugal and Spain joined the WEU in 1988.

The future of the WEU is currently under debate. Some

members want the WEU to strengthen its position as a European pillar of the transatlantic alliance, others want the WEU to be absorbed into the EC as part of a unitary European defence and security policy. In 1991 a study group was established to investigate the creation of a WEU-controlled rapid deployment force. The debate has continued throughout 1992, with the EC Maastricht Treaty designating the WEU as the future defence component of the EC. The formation of a Franco-German corps of 35,000 men, to be operational by 1995 under the umbrella of the WEU, was announced in May. WEU foreign ministers agreed in the Petersburg Declaration of June 1992 to assign forces to WEU command for 'peacemaking' operations in Europe.

A Council of Ministers (foreign and defence) meets biannually in the capital of the presiding country; the presidency rotates annually. A Permanent Council of the signatories' London ambassadors and a senior British official meet regularly in London. An Enlarged Council of political directors and member defence officials was created in 1986. Both the Enlarged Committee and the Permanent Committee are chaired by the Secretary-General and serviced by the Secretariat. The Assembly of the WEU is composed of 108 parliamentarians of member states and meets twice annually in Paris to debate matters within the scope of the Brussels Treaty.

Presidency (1992–3), Italy.

Secretary-General, Dr Willem van Eekelen (*Netherlands*).

ASSEMBLY, 43 avenue du Président Wilson, 75775 Paris Cedex 16, France.

THE WORLD BANK

1818 H Street NW, Washington DC 20433, USA

The World Bank, more formally known as the International Bank for Reconstruction and Development (IBRD), is a specialized agency of the UN, and developed from the international monetary and financial conference held at Bretton Woods, New Hampshire, in 1944. Determined to avoid the financial chaos and depression of the inter-war years, 44 nations established the IBRD on 27 December 1945, to encourage economic growth in developing countries through the provision of loans and technical assistance to their respective governments. The IBRD now has 162 members.

The Bank is owned by the governments of member countries and its capital is subscribed by its members. It finances its lending primarily from borrowing in world capital markets, and derives a substantial contribution to its resources from its retained earnings and the repayment of loans. The interest rate on its loans is calculated in relation to its cost of borrowing. Loans generally have a grace period of five years and are repayable within 20 years. The loans (including IFC loans) made by the Bank since its inception to 30 June 1991, totalled US$203,053,900,000 to 110 countries. Subscribed capital is US$139,120,022,000.

Originally directed towards post-war reconstruction in Europe, the Bank has subsequently turned towards assisting less-developed countries with the establishment of two affiliates, the International Finance Corporation (IFC) in 1956 and the International Development Association (IDA) in 1960. The IFC aids developing member countries by promoting the growth of the private sector of their economies and by helping to mobilize domestic and foreign capital for this purpose. The IFC's subscribed share capital was US$1,177,138,000 at 30 June 1991. It is also empowered to borrow up to two and half times the amount of its unimpaired subscribed capital and accumulated earnings for use in its lending programme. At 30 June 1992, the IFC had committed financing totalling more than US$9,506,082,000 in about 96 countries.

The IDA performs the same function as the World Bank but primarily to less developed countries and on terms that bear less heavily on their balance of payments than IBRD loans. Eligible countries must have a per capita gross national product of less than US$1,195 (1990). Funds (called credits to distinguish them from IBRD loans) come mostly in the form of subscriptions and contributions from the IDA's richer members and transfers from the net income of the IBRD. The terms for IDA credits, which bear no interest and are made to governments only, are ten-year grace periods and 35- or 40-year maturities. By 30 June 1991, the IDA had extended development credits totalling US$64,515,300,000 to 87 countries.

The IBRD and its affiliates are financially and legally distinct but share headquarters. The IBRD is headed by a Board of Governors, consisting of one Governor and one alternate Governor appointed by each member country. Twenty-two Executive Directors exercise all powers of the Bank except those reserved to the Board of Governors. The President, elected by the Executive Directors, conducts the business of the Bank, assisted by an international staff. Membership in both the IFC (144 members) and the IDA (142 members) is open to all IBRD countries. The IDA is administered by the same staff as the Bank; the IFC has its own personnel but draws on the IBRD for administrative and other support. All share the same President.

In 1988 a third affiliate, the Multilateral Investment Guarantee Agency (MIGA) was formed. MIGA encourages foreign investment in developing states by providing investment guarantees to potential investors and advisory services to developing member countries. At 30 June 1992 85 countries were members of MIGA.

President (IBRD, IFC, IDA, MIGA), L. Preston (*USA*).

UK Executive Director, P. Coady, Room D1328, IMF, 1809 G Street NW, Washington DC 20433.

EUROPEAN OFFICE, 66 avenue d'Iena, 75116 Paris, France.

JAPAN OFFICE, Kokusai Building 1-1, Marunouchi 3-Chomse, Chiyoda-ku, Tokyo 100, Japan.

UK OFFICE, New Zealand House, Haymarket, London SW1Y 4TQ.

THE WORLD COUNCIL OF CHURCHES

PO Box 2100, 1211 Geneva 2, Switzerland

The World Council of Churches (WCC) was constituted in Amsterdam in 1948 to promote unity among the many different Christian churches. The 320 member churches of the WCC have adherents in more than 100 countries. With the exception of Roman Catholicism, virtually all Christian traditions are included in the WCC membership.

The policies of the Council are determined by delegates of the member churches meeting in Assembly, about every seven years; the seventh Assembly was held in Canberra, Australia, in February 1991. More detailed decisions are taken by a 151-member Central Committee which is elected by the Assembly and meets, with the eight WCC Presidents, annually. The Central Committee in turn appoints a smaller Executive Committee and also nominates commissions to guide the various programmes.

General Secretary, Dr Emilio Castro (*Uruguay*).

WORLD FEDERATION OF TRADE UNIONS

Branicka 112, Branik, Prague 4, Czechoslovakia

The World Federation of Trade Unions (WFTU) was founded in October 1945. In 1949 a number of members withdrew and founded the International Confederation of Free Trade Unions. The WFTU now has 92 affiliated federations with 188 million members.

The Congress, which is comprised of delegates from member nations, meets every five years to review WFTU's work and to elect the General Council and Bureau. The General Council is elected from members of national federations and meets three times between Congresses. Each affiliated organization has one member and one deputy. The Presidential Council of 20 members is elected by the General Council and carries out the executive work of the WFTU
General Secretary, Alexander Zharikov (*Russia*).

WORLD HEALTH ORGANIZATION

20 avenue Appia, 1211 Geneva 27, Switzerland

The UN International Health Conference held in 1946 established the World Health Organization (WHO) as a UN specialized agency, with effect from 7 April 1948. It is dedicated to attaining the highest possible level of health for all. It collaborates with member governments, UN agencies and other bodies to develop health standards, control communicable diseases and promote all aspects of family and environmental health. It seeks to raise the standards of health teaching and training, and promotes research through collaborating research centres world-wide. Its other services include the *International Pharmacopoeia*, epidemiological surveillance, and the collation and publication of statistics. WHO activities are orientated to achieving 'Health for all by the year 2000', i.e. a level of health allowing the world's citizens to lead socially and economically productive lives.

WHO had 177 members as at June 1992. It is governed by the annual World Health Assembly of members which meets to set policy, approve the budget (1992–3 biennium, US$734,936,000), appoint a Director-General, and adopt health conventions and regulations. It also elects 31 members who designate one health-qualified person to serve in a personal capacity on the Executive Board. The Board effects the programme, suggests initiatives and is empowered to deal with emergencies. A Secretariat, headed by the Director-General, supervises the health activities of six regional offices.
Director-General, Dr H. Nakajima (*Japan*).

WORLD INTELLECTUAL PROPERTY ORGANIZATION

34 chemin des Colombettes, 1211 Geneva 20, Switzerland

The World Intellectual Property Organization (WIPO) was established in 1967 by the Stockholm Convention, which entered into force in 1970, and was intended to replace the Bureau international réuni pour la protection de la propriété intellectuelle (BIRPI). BIRPI was founded in 1893 to represent the joint secretariats of the Paris Convention for the Protection of Industrial Property (1883) and the Berne Convention for the Protection of Literary and Artistic Works (1886). Both conventions maintain separate organizations pending the formal accession of all BIRPI members to WIPO. WIPO became a UN specialized agency in 1974.

WIPO promotes the protection of intellectual property: industrial property (patented inventions and designs, scientific discoveries and trademarks, etc.); and copyright (literary, musical, cinematic and artistic works, etc.). WIPO also assists creative intellectual activity and facilitates technology transfer, particularly to developing countries. It administers various conventions, most importantly the Berne and Paris Conventions.

WIPO had 128 members as at 30 April 1992. The biennial Conference of all its members sets policy, a programme and a budget (1992–3, SFr188,009,000). A General Assembly meets simultaneously, comprising only WIPO members who are also members of BIRPI. The Assembly appoints, instructs and supervises a Director-General, who heads the International Bureau (secretariat) of some 400 people. A Co-ordination Committee represents the organizations of the Berne and Paris Conventions.

A separate International Union for the Protection of New Varieties of Plants (UPOV), established by convention in 1961, is linked to WIPO. It has 19 members.
Director-General, Dr Arpad Bogsch (*USA*).

WORLD METEOROLOGICAL ORGANIZATION

41 avenue Giuseppe Motta, PO Box 2300, 1211 Geneva 20, Switzerland

The World Meteorological Organization (WMO) was established as a UN specialized agency on 23 March 1950, succeeding the International Meteorological Organization which had been founded in 1873. It facilitates co-operation between the world-wide network of meteorological services, standardizes meteorological observations and data, and assists training and research. It also fosters collaboration between meteorological and hydrological services, and furthers the application of meteorology to aviation, shipping, agriculture, etc.

The WMO had 155 member states and five member territories, as at 1 June 1991. The supreme authority is the World Meteorological Congress of member states and member territories, which meets every four years to determine general policy, make recommendations and set a budget (1992–5, SFr236,100,000). It also elects 26 members of the 36-member Executive Council, the other members being the President and three Vice-Presidents of the WMO, and the Presidents of the six Regional Associations. The Council supervises the implementation of Congress decisions, initiates studies and makes recommendations on matters needing international action. The WMO functions through six Regional Meteorological Associations and eight technical commissions. The Secretariat is headed by a Secretary-General, appointed by the Congress.
Secretary-General, G. O. P. Obasi (*Nigeria*).

Presidents of the USA

Name (*with Native State*)	Party	Born	Inaugura-tion	Died	Age
George Washington, *Va.*	Federation	22 February 1732	1789	14 December 1799	67
John Adams, *Mass.*	Federation	30 October 1735	1797	4 July 1826	90
Thomas Jefferson, *Va.*	Republican	13 April 1743	1801	4 July 1826	83
James Madison, *Va.*	Republican	16 March 1751	1809	28 June 1836	85
James Monroe, *Va.*	Republican	28 April 1758	1817	4 July 1831	73
John Quincy Adams, *Mass.*	Republican	11 July 1767	1825	23 February 1848	80
Andrew Jackson, *SC*	Democrat	15 March 1767	1829	8 June 1845	78
Martin Van Buren, *NY*	Democrat	5 December 1782	1837	24 July 1862	79
William Henry Harrison†, *Va.*	Whig	9 February 1773	1841	4 April 1841	68
John Tyler (*a*), *Va.*	Whig	29 March 1790	1841	17 January 1862	71
James Knox Polk, *NC*	Democrat	2 November 1795	1845	15 June 1849	53
Zachary Taylor†, *Va.*	Whig	24 November 1784	1849	9 July 1850	65
Millard Fillmore (*a*), *NY*	Whig	7 January 1800	1850	8 March 1874	74
Franklin Pierce, *NH*	Democrat	23 November 1804	1853	8 October 1869	64
James Buchanan, *Pa.*	Democrat	23 April 1791	1857	1 June 1868	77
Abraham Lincoln†§, *Ky.*	Republican	12 February 1809	1861	15 April 1865	56
Andrew Johnson (*a*), *NC*	Republican	29 December 1808	1865	31 July 1875	66
Ulysses Simpson Grant, *Ohio*	Republican	27 April 1822	1869	23 July 1885	63
Rutherford Birchard Hayes, *Ohio*	Republican	4 October 1822	1877	17 January 1893	70
James Abram Garfield†§, *Ohio*	Republican	19 November 1831	1881	19 September 1881	49
Chester Alan Arthur (*a*), *Vt.*	Republican	5 October 1830	1881	18 November 1886	56
Grover Cleveland, *NJ*	Democrat	18 March 1837	1885	24 June 1908	71
Benjamin Harrison, *Ohio*	Republican	20 August 1833	1889	13 March 1901	67
Grover Cleveland, *NJ*	Democrat	18 March 1837	1893	24 June 1908	71
William McKinley†§, *Ohio*	Republican	29 January 1843	1897	14 September 1901	58
Theodore Roosevelt (*a*), *NY*	Republican	27 October 1858	1901	6 January 1919	60
William Howard Taft, *Ohio*	Republican	15 September 1857	1909	8 March 1930	72
Woodrow Wilson, *Va.*	Democrat	28 December 1856	1913	3 February 1924	67
Warren Gamaliel Harding†, *Ohio*	Republican	2 November 1865	1921	2 August 1923	57
Calvin Coolidge (*a*), *Vt.*	Republican	4 July 1872	1923	5 January 1933	60
Herbert Clark Hoover, *Iowa.*	Republican	10 August 1874	1929	20 October 1964	90
Franklin Delano Roosevelt†‡, *NY*	Democrat	30 January 1882	1933	12 April 1945	63
Harry S. Truman (*a*), *Missouri*	Democrat	8 May 1884	1945	26 December 1972	88
Dwight David Eisenhower, *Texas*	Republican	14 October 1890	1953	28 March 1969	78
John Fitzgerald Kennedy, *Mass.*†§	Democrat	29 May 1917	1961	22 November 1963	46
Lyndon Baines Johnson (*a*), *Texas*	Democrat	27 August 1908	1963	22 January 1973	64
Richard Milhous Nixon, *California*	Republican	9 January 1913	1969		
Gerald Rudolph Ford (*b*), *Nebraska*	Republican	14 July 1913	1974		
James Earl Carter, *Georgia*	Democrat	1 October 1924	1977		
Ronald Wilson Reagan, *Illinois*	Republican	6 February 1911	1981		
George Herbert Walker Bush, *Mass.*	Republican	12 June 1924	1989		

† Died in office
(*a*) Elected as Vice-President
§ Assassinated
‡ Re-elected 5 November 1940, the first case of a third term; re-elected for a fourth term 7 November 1944.
(*b*) Appointed under the provisions of the 25th Amendment

Events of the Year

1 September 1991–31 August 1992

BRITISH AFFAIRS

SEPTEMBER 1991

1. The Prime Minister (John Major) and the Foreign Secretary (Douglas Hurd) visited Moscow for talks with Presidents Gorbachev and Yeltsin. **2.** Mr Major and Mr Hurd arrived in China for an official visit. The Trades Union Congress annual conference opened in Glasgow. Petrol bombs were thrown during a third night of disturbances on the Blackbird Leys estate in Oxford. A third night of rioting took place on the Ely estate in Cardiff. The convener of the Western Isles Council, Revd Donald Macaulay, resigned over the council's loss of £24 million in the collapse of the Bank of Credit and Commerce International (BCCI). **4.** Mr Major arrived in Hong Kong for a two-day visit. **8.** The Liberal Democrat Party annual conference opened in Bournemouth. **9.** The Keith Prowse booking agency went into receivership. Rioting and looting took place overnight on the Meadow Well estate in North Shields, Tyne and Wear. **11.** Petrol bombs were thrown when hundreds of youths rioted in Newcastle upon Tyne. Violence broke out again on the night of 12 September. **18.** The Scottish National Party conference opened in Inverness. **20.** The Green Party conference opened in Wolverhampton. **22.** The Princess of Wales arrived in Pakistan for a five-day official visit. **24.** The British hostage Jackie Mann was released in Beirut; on 25 September he arrived at RAF Lyneham, Wiltshire. **25.** The national executive committee of the Labour Party suspended two Labour MPs, Terry Field (Liverpool Broadgreen) and Dave Nellist (Coventry South East), pending an inquiry into their alleged support of the Militant Tendency. **29.** The Labour Party annual conference opened in Brighton.

OCTOBER 1991

2. The widely-used sleeping pill Halcion was withdrawn by the Department of Health. **3.** The Director of Public Prosecutions, Sir Allan Green, resigned after being stopped by police for alleged kerb-crawling in London on 2 October. **7.** The Queen and the Duke of Edinburgh left London for state visits to Namibia and Zimbabwe. The Princess Royal arrived in Poland for a four-day visit. **8.** The Conservative Party annual conference opened in Blackpool. **9.** The Transport Secretary (Malcolm Rifkind) announced at the Conservative Party conference that the Channel Tunnel rail link route would run to King's Cross, London, via Stratford, despite the preference of British Rail and Eurotunnel for the alternative Kent route. **14.** The Queen opened the Commonwealth heads of government meeting in Harare, Zimbabwe. **22.** Two motions were tabled in the House of Commons calling for an inquiry into alleged links between the newspaper proprietor Robert Maxwell, the foreign editor of the *Daily Mirror*, Nick Davies, and the Israeli intelligence service, Mossad; on 28 October Mr Davies was sacked after he had falsely denied visiting Ohio, where he was alleged to have met an arms dealer. The 1990–1 session of Parliament ended. **23.** The Prince and Princess of Wales flew to Canada for a seven-day official visit. **30.** The Health Secretary (William Waldegrave) launched a 'Patient's Charter', setting out national standards of care for NHS patients. **31.** The Queen opened the new session of Parliament.

NOVEMBER 1991

3. The Confederation of British Industries annual conference opened in Bournemouth. **5.** Trading in shares in Mirror Group Newspapers (MGN) and Maxwell Communication Corporation (MCC) was suspended when proprietor Robert Maxwell was reported missing at sea; his body was later recovered off the Canary Islands. His sons Ian and Kevin became acting chairmen of the two companies. **7.** By-elections took place at Hemsworth, Kincardine and Deeside, and Langbaurgh. **14.** The Lord Advocate (Lord Fraser of Carmyllie) announced, simultaneously with the US Justice Department, that warrants had been issued for the arrest of two Libyan intelligence agents believed to be responsible for the Lockerbie bombing in 1988; Syrian and Iranian involvement was ruled out. **15.** Two people were killed when a bomb they were carrying exploded in a disused building in St Albans near the venue of a concert being given by the band of the Blues and Royals; the IRA later said that the two who died were IRA members. **18.** The British hostage Terry Waite was released in Beirut; on 19 November he arrived at RAF Lyneham, Wiltshire. **21.** At the end of a two-day debate in the House of Commons, MPs voted by 351 votes to 250 to support the Government's negotiating stance on European economic, monetary and political union; during the debate former Prime Minister Margaret Thatcher called for a referendum on the issue. **23.** Ian Richter, a British businessman imprisoned in Iraq since 1986 on bribery charges, was released after Britain agreed to release £70 million of frozen Iraqi assets. **26.** Tesco, Safeway and Asda announced that they would join British Home Stores in opening stores on the four Sundays before

Christmas; on 27 November the Attorney-General (Sir Patrick Mayhew) said that it was the responsibility of local authorities, not the Government, to take action against the stores. **30.** Quantities of Semtex explosive and other bomb-making equipment were discovered in Wanstead, London.

DECEMBER 1991

1. Four stores in central London were damaged by firebombs planted by the IRA. A fifth shop was damaged on 2 December. **2.** The Prime Minister received the Dalai Lama at Downing Street. **3.** Kevin and Ian Maxwell resigned from the boards of Maxwell Communications Corporation and Mirror Group Newspapers after it was disclosed that MGN pension fund assets had been lent to companies privately owned by Robert Maxwell; on 4 December the Serious Fraud Office started an investigation into the pension fund losses. **5.** Kevin and Ian Maxwell asked the High Court to appoint administrators to all the privately-owned Maxwell companies; all the Maxwell family's main assets, including MGN and MCC, were put up for sale. The Church of England Bishops published a report, *Issues on Human Sexuality*, in which it was stated that the clergy cannot claim the liberty to enter into active homosexual relationships. **5.** Terry Fields, MP (Liverpool Broadgreen), was expelled from the Labour Party for being a supporter of Militant Tendency. On 7 December Dave Nellist, MP (Coventry South East), was expelled from the party for the same reason. **7.** Fires started by IRA incendiary devices caused serious damage to shops in Blackpool and Manchester. **9.** The Prime Minister, the Foreign Secretary and the Chancellor of the Exchequer (Norman Lamont) attended the European Community summit meeting in Maastricht. **14.** Three IRA fire bombs caused minor damage to shops in Brent Cross shopping centre, London; another device was found after the centre closed in the evening. **15.** An IRA firebomb caused minor damage in the Sainsbury wing of the National Gallery. **16.** A small IRA bomb exploded on a railway line outside Clapham Junction, London; all London mainline stations were closed for several hours. The chief executive and the financial director of the Western Isles Council were sacked after a council disciplinary hearing into the loss of £24 million in the collapse of BCCI; the chief executive was reinstated on 21 February 1992. **19.** The Chancellor of the Exchequer announced that stamp duty was to be waived on properties up to the value of £250,000 until August 1992. He also confirmed that building societies and banks would be contributing £1,000 million to a scheme for cutting the number of repossessions in 1992. The Education Secretary (Kenneth Clarke) announced the first national curriculum test results for seven-year-olds. **20.** Alison Halford, the assistant chief constable of Merseyside, was found by the High Court to have been unfairly suspended on disciplinary grounds in December 1990. **23.** The London Underground network was shut down after incendiary devices exploded on three trains. Four people died in gales which hit many parts of Britain. **31.** The four British hostages released in Beirut in 1990–1 (Brian Keenan, John McCarthy, Jackie Mann and Terry Waite) were awarded CBEs in the New Year's Honours List.

JANUARY 1992

4. The Education Secretary (Kenneth Clarke) announced that teacher training courses would be changed to place greater emphasis on practical experience in schools. The inaugural session of a Muslim 'parliament' was held at Kensington Town Hall, London. A holdall containing 6 lb of explosives was found near Weeton Barracks, Lancashire. **8.** British Steel announced that the Ravenscraig plant would close in autumn 1992, two years earlier than planned, with the loss of 1,220 jobs. **9.** Merseyside Police Authority voted to reinvoke the suspension of Alison Halford (*see* 20 December) and to continue disciplinary proceedings against her. **10.** A 5 lb bomb planted by the IRA exploded in Whitehall Place, London; no one was injured. **13.** Kevin and Ian Maxwell appeared before the House of Commons social security select committee but refused to answer its questions about the money missing from Maxwell company pension funds on the grounds that their replies could prejudice the chance of a fair trial. **14.** The collapsed Bank of Credit and Commerce International (BCCI) was put into formal liquidation by the High Court. **18.** The Foreign Secretary arrived in Kazakhstan for talks with President Nazarbayev. On 19 January he met President Kravchuk of the Ukraine in Kiev, and on 20 January held talks with President Yeltsin of Russia in Moscow. **20.** The Northern Ireland Secretary (Peter Brooke) offered his resignation to the Prime Minister, who refused it (*see* Northern Ireland). **21.** British Coal announced over 1,100 job losses at four pits in Yorkshire, and that the Selby coalfield would close ten years ahead of schedule. **24.** The Defence Secretary (Tom King) confirmed that 2,750 civilian defence jobs would be lost over the next ten years. **31.** British Coal announced a further 1,158 job losses. The trading floor of the Stock Exchange in London was used by dealers for the last time.

FEBRUARY 1992

4. The European Court of Justice ruled that British Aerospace need not repay the £44.4 million it received from the Government in illegal subsidies as an incentive to buy the Rover Group in 1988. **5.** Paddy Ashdown, the leader of the Liberal Democrats, admitted that he had had an affair with his secretary five years ago, after a document was stolen from his solicitor's office and offered to a newspaper; on 7 February two people were charged with dishonestly handling stolen documents. **6.** A television documentary, *Elizabeth R*, was shown to mark the fortieth anniversary of The Queen's accession to the throne. **7.** The Foreign Secretary signed the Maastricht Treaty on European Union. **10.** The Prince and Princess of Wales arrived in India for a six-day official visit. **11.** The Prime Minister held the first talks for 16 years with leaders of the four main political parties in Northern Ireland at Downing Street. An IRA bomb was defused in Whitehall. **13.** Ford announced a record loss of £590 million in 1991. **14.** Sunderland was accorded city status by The Queen to mark the fortieth anniversary of her accession to the throne. **17.** The Queen and the Duke of Edinburgh left Heathrow for an eight-day visit to Australia. **28.** Twenty-nine people were injured when an IRA bomb exploded at London Bridge station during the morning rush hour; all mainline and Underground stations in London were closed for much of the day. **29.** One person was slightly injured when an IRA bomb exploded outside the offices of the Crown Prosecution Service in London.

March 1992

1. An IRA bomb was defused at White Hart Lane station, London, before a League Cup semi-final match at White Hart Lane stadium. **4.** A Passengers' Charter promising compensation for late or cancelled trains was published by the Transport Secretary and British Rail. **6.** The Home Secretary (Kenneth Baker) announced a proposal for a national lottery to raise money for sport, charities and the arts. Richard Branson sold the Virgin Group to Thorn EMI for £560 million. **9.** BT announced up to 24,000 job losses. **10.** The Chancellor of the Exchequer presented his Budget statement to the House of Commons (*see* pages 1162). A suspected IRA bomb exploded on the track near Wandsworth Common station, south London. **13.** A service of dedication was held at the City Church of Christ the Cornerstone in Milton Keynes, the first purpose-built ecumenical church in Britain. **16.** The 1987–92 Parliament was formally dissolved. **17.** The Hong Kong and Shanghai Banking Corporation announced an agreed takeover of the Midland Bank. Federal Express announced 3,500 job losses in the UK and Ireland. **19.** A statement from Buckingham Palace announced that the Duke and Duchess of York were to separate. **24.** A Labour Party election broadcast on the NHS was attacked by the Conservative Party; the controversy dominated the second week of the election campaign.

April 1992

1. A further 99 NHS hospitals became self-governing trusts. **6.** A 1 lb bomb believed to have been planted by the IRA exploded in Soho, London. **7.** A man was seriously injured when he was savaged by two pit bull terriers in Ealing, London. **9.** The General Election took place; the Conservatives were returned to power with a reduced majority of 21. National Westminster Bank announced 1,900 job losses. **10.** Three people were killed and 91 injured when a 100 lb bomb planted by the IRA exploded outside the Baltic Exchange in the City of London. **11.** A 100 lb bomb planted by the IRA exploded at 1 a.m. at Staples Corner, north-west London, causing extensive damage. The Prime Minister (John Major) announced a reshuffled Cabinet; Kenneth Baker, Tom King, Peter Brooke and Lord Waddington left the Cabinet and John Patten, Virginia Bottomley, Gillian Shephard, Michael Portillo and Sir Patrick Mayhew entered the Cabinet for the first time. Two new Cabinet posts were created: a National Heritage minister (David Mellor) and a Citizen's Charter minister, later renamed Public Service and Science minister (William Waldegrave). **13.** Neil Kinnock announced that he would resign as leader of the Labour Party as soon as a successor had been elected; Roy Hattersley resigned as deputy leader of the party. A soldier was shot near an army careers office in Derby and died on 14 April; the INLA claimed responsibility. **14.** The Prime Minister announced 22 new junior ministerial appointments. **21.** The *Irish Times* published a leaked Metropolitan Police policy committee document which revealed that the force had little intelligence on IRA operations in mainland Britain. In May, ultimate responsibility for gathering intelligence about the IRA was transferred from the Metropolitan Police to MI5. **23.** The Princess Royal was granted an uncontested decree nisi to end her marriage to Capt. Mark Phillips. **24.** Chris Patten, the chairman of the Conservative Party, was appointed governor of Hong Kong from July 1992 until the transfer of power to China at the end of June 1997. **27.** The House of Commons elected Betty Boothroyd as its first woman Speaker. Lord Justice Taylor was sworn in as Lord Chief Justice of England. **28.** Lloyds Bank announced a proposed £3.7 million bid to take over the Midland Bank. **30.** HMS *Vanguard*, the Royal Navy's first Trident submarine, was launched at Barrow-in-Furness by the Princess of Wales.

May 1992

1. British Coal announced the closure of Markham Main colliery, Yorkshire, with the loss of 730 jobs. **6.** The State Opening of Parliament took place. In a debate following The Queen's Speech, the Prime Minister named the head of MI6, Sir Colin McColl, for the first time. **7.** Local government elections took place in England (except London), Wales and Scotland. **10.** Seven firebombs planted by the IRA exploded in the Metro Centre, Gateshead. The Princess of Wales arrived in Egypt for a six-day visit. **12.** The Queen addressed the European Parliament in Strasbourg for the first time. **18.** At the inquest in Oxford into the deaths of nine British soldiers caused by American 'friendly fire' during the Gulf war, the jury returned a verdict of unlawful killing. **19.** The Chancellor of the Duchy of Lancaster (William Waldegrave) announced for the first time the membership of 16 Cabinet committees and ten sub-committees, and published procedural guidelines for ministers. **21.** The bill to ratify the Maastricht Treaty, the European Communities (Amendment) Bill, was given a second reading in the House of Commons by 336 votes to 92. The Prince and Princess of Wales attended the British national day at the Expo '92 World Fair in Seville, Spain. British Telecom announced pre-tax profits of £3 billion for 1991–2, **22.** At least 20,000 people attended an illegal four-day New Age festival at Castlemorton Common, Worcs. **25.** The Archbishop of Canterbury, Dr George Carey, met the Pope for the first time in the Vatican. **26.** The Prime Minister left Britain for a four-day visit to Poland, Czechoslovakia and Hungary. **28.** The Queen and the Duke of Edinburgh arrived in Malta for a three-day state visit. Olympia and York asked the High Court to appoint administrators for the Canary Wharf development in London's Docklands. **31.** Ten people were arrested during demonstrations when Queen Elizabeth the Queen Mother unveiled a statue of Sir Arthur (Bomber) Harris in London.

JUNE 1992

1. The Yugoslav ambassador was ordered to leave Britain as a consequence of UN sanctions against Yugoslavia. **3.** The RAF announced 1,110 redundancies. **5.** Lloyds Bank withdrew its takeover bid for the Midland Bank. **7.** A special constable was shot dead by two IRA gunmen after stopping their car near Tadcaster, North Yorkshire; a regular police constable was also injured. A small IRA bomb exploded near the Royal Festival Hall, London, causing minor damage. The *Sunday Times* began the serialization of a book by Andrew Morton, *Diana: Her True Story*, which led to intense press speculation about the marriage of the Prince and Princess of Wales. **8.** The Social Security Secretary (Peter Lilley) announced a review of UK occupational pension schemes, and said that £2.5 million would be set aside for pensioners affected by Robert Maxwell's theft from his companies' pension funds. **9.** The Queen and the Duke of Edinburgh arrived in France for a four-day state visit. **10.** The Prime Minister arrived in Rio de Janeiro, Brazil, for the Earth Summit. A small bomb believed to have been planted by the IRA exploded in Victoria, London. **15.** An IRA bomb planted in a minicab exploded in London. The Defence Secretary (Malcolm Rifkind) announced that all tactical nuclear weapons on Royal Navy surface ships and maritime aircraft would be scrapped. **17.** The Zoological Society of London announced that London Zoo would close on 30 September 1992 because of financial problems. **18.** Kevin and Ian Maxwell and Larry Trachtenberg, the Maxwells' financial adviser, were arrested and charged with fraud offences. INLA firebombs caused extensive damage to two shops in Leeds. **24.** Lloyd's of London reported record losses of £2.06 billion on 1989 trading. **25.** A Royal Navy minehunter intervened after skirmishes between French and British fishing boats off the Isles of Scilly. A 2 lb IRA car bomb exploded in the City of London, causing minor damage. **30.** The Queen arrived in Canada for a two-day visit to mark the 125th anniversary of the Confederation of Canada.

JULY 1992

1. Britain took over the presidency of the European Community. British Rail announced losses of £144.7 million in 1991–2. **7.** The Government placed an order for a fourth Trident nuclear submarine. **9.** McDermott's, the largest private sector employer in the Scottish Highlands, announced 1,300 redundancies at the oil rig construction yard at Ardersier. **16.** Rioting broke out on the Hartcliffe estate in Bristol after two joyriders who had stolen a police motor bike died while being chased by police; violence continued on the two following nights. Both Houses of Parliament rose for the summer recess. A man was arrested after scaling the walls of Buckingham Palace and entering the building. **17.** Thirteen-year-old Ganesh Sittampalam became the youngest-ever graduate in Britain when he was awarded a degree in mathematics from the University of Surrey. The Foreign Secretary (Douglas Hurd) visited Sarajevo. **18.** John Smith was elected leader of the Labour Party and Margaret Beckett was elected deputy leader. **19.** The National Heritage Secretary (David Mellor) offered his resignation to the Prime Minister because of forthcoming newspaper reports about an extra-marital relationship; the offer was refused. **21.** Alison Halford, the assistant chief constable of Merseyside, agreed to drop a claim of sexual discrimination against the Chief Constable of Merseyside and the Home Secretary; in return, disciplinary charges against her were dropped and she was allowed to take early retirement on medical grounds. **22.** The Cabinet announced that the planning total for public expenditure for 1993–4 (£244.5 billion) could not be exceeded. British Coal announced record profits of £170 million for 1991–2. **23.** Rioting broke out in separate incidents in Blackburn, Burnley and Huddersfield. Labour MPs elected a new Shadow Cabinet. **24.** The Foreign Office expelled three employees at the Iranian embassy who were suspected of plotting to murder Salman Rushdie, the author of *The Satanic Verses*. **30.** ICI announced that it would be restructured into two companies. Two IRA firebombs caused minor damage in the centre of Milton Keynes.

AUGUST 1992

5. Seven nurses at Ashworth top security hospital were suspended after an inquiry into the death of a patient at the hospital in 1988 found evidence of systematic bullying and abuse of patients; the Health Secretary (Virginia Bottomley) announced a review of the role of top security hospitals. **11.** Armed police arrested three men in west London and Hertfordshire following the seizure of a van containing a 300 lb IRA bomb. **14.** The Foreign Office announced that an Iranian diplomat was being expelled from Britain in retaliation for Iran's expulsion of a British diplomat in July. **18.** An emergency Cabinet meeting was held at which ministers agreed to make up to 1,800 troops available to the UN to escort aid convoys in Bosnia-Hercegovina, and to send six RAF Tornado strike aircraft to the Gulf to police an air exclusion zone over southern Iraq intended to protect the Shia Muslims. **20.** The *Daily Mirror* published intimate photographs of the Duchess of York and her friend John Bryan on a private holiday in France after lawyers acting for Mr Bryan failed to obtain an injunction to stop their publication. A Briton, Paul Ride, was sentenced in Iraq to seven years imprisonment for illegally entering the country. **21.** Ratners announced more than 1,000 job losses and the closure of about 180 shops. **24.** Several newspapers published extracts from a tape recording made in 1989 of an intimate conversation allegedly between the Princess of Wales and a male friend. **25.** Four suspected IRA firebombs exploded in Shrewsbury. **26.** The Prime Minister opened the two-day Yugoslav peace conference in London (*see* page 1087). The Chancellor of the Exchequer (Norman Lamont) said that the Government would not devalue the pound, which was near the bottom of its permitted range within the European exchange rate mechanism, and that Britain would not leave the ERM. The Bank of England spent an estimate £300 million in support of sterling. **27.** Six Tornado aircraft left Britain for the Gulf region. **27.** Lord Owen replaced Lord Carrington as the EC's chief mediator on the Yugoslav crisis.

ACCIDENTS AND DISASTERS

September 1991

4. Two fishermen were drowned when their trawler sank after colliding with a cargo vessel in the English Channel. **9.** Floods outside Phnom Penh, Cambodia, killed about 100,000 people and left 300,000 homeless. **13.** Seven people died when their car came off the road and landed in a canal in Dublin. **20.** St James Garlickhythe, a Wren church in the City of London, was badly damaged when a builder's crane collapsed on to it. **23.** Over 200 people were killed by landslides in south-west China.

October 1991

1. Sixteen fishermen drowned when a Spanish trawler sank 200 miles west of the Hebrides. **17.** Sixteen people were killed when two trains crashed at Melun, outside Paris. **20.** At least 1,600 people were killed when an earthquake registering 6.1 on the Richter scale hit the Garhwal Hills in northern India. **21.** Twenty-four people were killed and more than 600 homes destroyed by a bush fire in California. **29.** A typhoon hit the Philippines, killing at least 2,700 people.

November 1991

5. At least 5,400 people were killed and 50,000 left homeless by floods caused by a tropical storm in the central Philippines. **21.** Three seamen were drowned when two cargo ships collided in Dublin Bay.

December 1991

7. Eighty-eight people were injured when two passenger trains collided in the Severn Tunnel. **4.** Up to 476 people were drowned when an Egyptian ferry sank in the Red Sea. **17.** The Fun House funfair in Blackpool was destroyed by fire. **18.** Four crew members died after a freak wave hit the Soviet factory ship *Kartli* off the west coast of Scotland; 47 other people were rescued. **22.** A DC3 aircraft crashed near Heidelberg, Germany, with the loss of 27 lives. **27.** All 129 passengers and crew survived when a DC9 aircraft crash-landed after both engines failed soon after take-off from Stockholm airport. **28.** Nine people were crushed to death outside an arena staging a celebrity basketball game in Harlem, New York. **31.** Over 80 people died in Bombay, India, after drinking poisoned alcohol during New Year celebrations.

January 1992

3. Seven people were killed and 110 injured in a 50-car pile-up on the autostrada between Milan and Piacenza, Italy. **17.** At least 47 people drowned and 150 were missing after a ferry capsized in the Jhelum River, Pakistan. **20.** Eighty-six people were killed when a French Airbus A320 crashed in the Vosges mountains about 25 miles from Strasbourg.

February 1992

1–2. Over 154 people were killed in a series of avalanches in eastern Turkey. Nine people died and more than 25 were injured in car crashes in thick fog throughout Britain. **6.** At least 16 people were killed when a military transport plane crashed into a restaurant and motel complex in Indiana, USA. **8.** Forty-seven people were injured when a train hit a lorry on a level crossing at Dimmocks Cote, Cambs. **9.** Thirty-one people were killed when a plane chartered by a French holiday company crashed in southern Senegal; there were 28 survivors. **13.** Two miners were killed and six injured when a train crashed underground at Wearmouth colliery near Sunderland. **18.** Over 50 people were killed when a hostel for Hindu pilgrims collapsed in Tamil Nadu, India. **29.** At least 23 people were killed and 20 injured when the roof of a café collapsed under the weight of heavy rain in Jerusalem.

March 1992

4. At least 270 miners were killed after a methane explosion at a mine in northern Turkey. **8.** Over 90 people drowned when a ferry was struck by an oil tanker south of Bangkok, Thailand. **13.** At least 376 people were killed when an earthquake registering between 6.2 and 6.8 on the Richter scale struck eastern Turkey. Eleven men were killed when a helicopter ditched in the sea during a short flight from a North Sea oil platform to an accommodation barge. **19.** Over 150 people were killed when a landslide partly destroyed a slum near Belo Horizonte, Brazil. **22.** Twenty-seven people were killed when a jet crashed in Flushing Bay soon after taking off from La Guardia airport, New York, in heavy snow. **24.** At least 60 people were killed when an ammonia tank exploded in a factory in Senegal.

April 1992

5. Three people were killed and two seriously injured when a car hit a train at an unmanned level crossing near Doncaster. **8.** Eight miners were rescued after being trapped underground for 15 hours by a roof fall at the Stillingfleet mine, North Yorkshire. **13.** An earthquake registering 5.6 on the Richter scale and centred on Roermond in the Netherlands caused tremors throughout northern Europe; one person was killed. **18.** Three hundred people were reported missing after two ferries collided off the coast of Nigeria. **23.** Over 220 people were killed and over 1,000 injured in a series of gas explosions in Guadalahara, Mexico. **25.** An earthquake registering 6.9 on the Richter scale hit northern California, USA. **26.** Thirty-nine people were killed when a plane crashed in western Iran.

MAY 1992

5. Ten people were killed and 527 injured when a temporary spectators' stand collapsed at a football match in Bastia, Corsica. **6.** Eleven people were killed and 26 injured when a passenger ferry sank after colliding with another ferry in Dubrovnik harbour. **27.** Five people were killed and three injured in a seven-vehicle pile-up on the M6 in Warwickshire.

JUNE 1992

9. At least 38 miners were killed in a methane explosion at a mine in the Ukraine. **28.** Two earthquakes registering 7.4 and 7.0 on the Richter scale hit southern California, Arizona and Nevada, USA.

JULY 1992

17. A crewman died in an engine-room fire on a cross-Channel ferry, *Quiberon*. **30.** All 292 passengers and crew survived when a TWA Lockheed L1011 aircraft burst into flames during take-off from Kennedy airport, New York. **31.** At least 100 people were killed when a Thai Airlines airbus crashed in the foothills of the Himalayas.

AUGUST 1992

8. The *QE2* was holed when she hit an uncharted object off the north-east coast of the USA; 600 passengers were evacuated and there were no injuries. **12.** Two children were killed by fumes from a faulty sewage system on the Swansea-Cork ferry *Celtic Pride*. **19.** Forty-five people were killed when their coach crashed at Torreblanca, Spain. **22.** Four people were killed when their plane crashed on the island of Jura on a flight from Blackpool to Mull. **24.** Hurricane Andrew hit the Bahamas and the coast of Florida, USA, causing at least 12 deaths and widespread devastation; on 26 August the hurricane hit Louisiana and Mississippi. **25.** Five people were drowned when their speedboat capsized off Llandudno.

ARTS, SCIENCE AND MEDIA

SEPTEMBER 1991

6. An entertainment at Salisbury Cathedral raised £1 million towards the cost of making safe the spire. **8.** Sir Alec Guinness was awarded the fellowship of the British Film Institute. **16.** The Prince of Wales and Crown Prince Naruhito of Japan attended the opening ceremony of the Japan Festival 1991 at the Victoria and Albert Museum. **17.** The Russian writer Alexander Solzhenitsyn said that he would be returning to Russia because charges of treason against him had been dropped.

OCTOBER 1991

14. Vivienne Westwood was named British Fashion Designer of the Year for the second successive year. **16.** The Independent Television Commission announced the winners of the auction for the 16 independent television franchises. **21.** The Royal Opera House cancelled performances until further notice because of a pay dispute with its orchestra; on 1 November the dispute was settled. **29.** Sir Leslie Martin was awarded the Royal Institute of British Architects trustees' medal for his work at the Calouste Gulbenkian Foundation, Lisbon.

NOVEMBER 1991

4. Pierre Combescot was awarded the Prix Goncourt for his novel *Les Filles du Calvaire*. **7.** The Arts Minister (Timothy Renton) announced that the Arts Council grant for 1992–3 would rise by almost 14 per cent to £221.2 million. **9.** Scientists at the Culham Laboratory, Oxon., for the first time produced significant amounts of power from controlled nuclear fusion. **17.** The Scottish Chamber Orchestra won the 1991 Prudential Award. **26.** Anish Kapoor was awarded the Turner Prize for contemporary art.

DECEMBER 1991

12. The employees of *The European* newspaper were made redundant by the administrators of the Maxwell companies (*see also* British Affairs).

JANUARY 1992

6. W. H. Smith announced that it would stop selling LP records by March 1992. The title of *The European* newspaper was bought by David and Frederick Barclay, ensuring its survival. **12.** Paul Simon gave the first major concert in South Africa since the relaxation of UN cultural sanctions against the country. **21.** John Richardson won the 1991 Whitbread Book of the Year award for volume one of his biography *A Life of Picasso*. **30.** The Prince of Wales announced the foundation of his own Institute of Architecture dedicated to restoring the human dimension in building.

FEBRUARY 1992

3. David Plowright, the chairman of Granada Television, was forced to resign after disagreeing with the Granada group about cost-cutting plans.

MARCH 1992

25. Soviet cosmonaut Sergei Krikalyev arrived back on earth after ten months on the space station Mir; his return had been delayed by four months due to the financial problems of the joint Soviet-British mission. The Royal Institute of British Architects awarded its Royal Gold Medal for Architecture to the structural engineer Peter Rice. **31.** At the Academy Awards ceremony in Los Angeles, Anthony Hopkins became the third British actor in three years to win the Best Actor award. The National Gallery bought a Holbein painting, *Lady with a Pet Squirrel and a Starling*, from Lord Cholmondeley for £10 million with the assistance of grants from the National Heritage Memorial Fund and the National Art Collections Fund.

April 1992

2. Independent Music Radio, a Virgin and TV-AM consortium, was awarded the second national independent radio licence by the Radio Authority. **8.** The last edition of the satirical periodical *Punch* was published. **15.** The composer Sir Andrew Lloyd Webber bought Canaletto's *View of the Old Horse Guards London from St James's Park* for £10.25 million at Christie's in order to prevent the painting from being sold abroad. **20.** A tribute to Freddie Mercury, the lead singer of Queen who died of Aids in November 1991, was held at Wembley stadium, London. The Expo '92 World Fair opened in Seville, Spain. **23.** Scientists at the American space agency NASA announced that the Cosmic Background Explorer (COBE) orbiting radio telescope had revealed for the first time how the cosmos developed from the Big Bang into clusters of galaxies.

May 1992

14. Three astronauts fitted a new motor to the stranded Intelsat-6 satellite which was then fired into a new orbit. **26.** The Arts Council announced a biennial British Literature Prize worth £30,000.

June 1992

5. Albert Finney left the cast of *Reflected Glory* at the Vaudeville theatre, London, because he had not been paid; the play closed. **8.** A baby boy weighing 11 oz was born alive at Nottingham City Hospital; he is believed to be the smallest surviving baby to be born in the world since 1938, but died on 27 July. **12.** British scientists staged a one-day strike at the UK Atomic Energy Authority in protest at the disparity in pay between British and foreign scientists working on the Joint European Torus project. **28.** Events were held throughout the UK to mark National Music Day. **30.** A six-month European Arts Festival to mark Britain's presidency of the EC was launched at the National Gallery, London. Tina Brown, the editor of *Vanity Fair* magazine, was appointed editor of the *New Yorker*.

July 1992

14. The director-general of the BBC announced that a 24-hour radio news channel would be launched by January 1994. **24.** The last performance took place at the original opera house at Glyndebourne; a new theatre will be built by 1994.

August 1992

17. The film director Woody Allen said that he was having an affair with the daughter of Mia Farrow, his partner of 12 years. Allen had earlier filed for custody of the couple's three children. **28.** At the Edinburgh Television Festival Michael Grade, the chief executive of Channel 4, delivered a speech critical of the government and management of the BBC.

CRIMES AND LEGAL AFFAIRS

September 1991

2. Four police officers were stabbed by a man in a shop in Wood Green, London. **4.** The trial of Manuel Noriega, former President of Panama, opened in Miami, Florida. **9.** Lynne Rogers, who went missing after arranging to meet a man for a job interview on 4 September, was found murdered at Rotherfield, East Sussex; on 10 October a man was charged with her murder. **13.** Two children and two teenagers were killed at Cheyney Manor, Wiltshire, when a car hit the bench on which they were sitting; another teenager hit by the car died on 14 September. On 17 September a man was charged with causing death by reckless driving. **23.** Fourteen-year-old Norbert McCootie was ordered at the Central Criminal Court to be detained for eight years and seven months for the rape of two women; the judge criticized social services in Lambeth for not placing McCootie in secure accommodation when he was on remand, thus allowing him the opportunity to commit the second rape. **30.** In a civil action brought by the victim's mother, the High Court ruled that Michael Brookes murdered 16-year-old Lynn Siddons in 1978, although no criminal charges had been brought against him.

October 1991

1. The Crown Prosecution Service announced that criminal charges would be brought against four former officers of West Midlands police over their handling of the inquiry into the 1974 Birmingham pub bombings. **23.** The House of Lords ruled that a man can be convicted of raping his wife, upholding the judgment of the Court of Appeal in March 1991. **25.** Record damages of £150,000 were awarded in the High Court to Dr Malcolm Smith after the jury upheld his claim that he had been slandered by Dr Alanah Houston, who had accused him in front of patients of sexual harassment. **30.** Desmond Ellis was acquitted at the Central Criminal Court of conspiring to cause explosions in Britain. A 12-year-old girl was killed when she was hit by a car driven by joyriders in Toxteth, Liverpool; on 31 October two men were charged with manslaughter. On 5 November a nine-year-old boy also hit by the car died. John McGranaghan, who was jailed for life in 1981 for rape and indecent assault, was freed by the Court of Appeal, which found his conviction 'wholly unsafe and unsatisfactory'. **31.** Six-year-old Rebecca Field, who was brain damaged and paralysed when forceps were used with excessive force at her birth, was awarded record damages of £100 million against Hereford Health Authority in a structured settlement in the High Court.

NOVEMBER 1991

1. Dr Michael Prentice and Dr Barry Sullman were convicted at Birmingham Crown Court of the manslaughter of a patient who died after being wrongly injected with a powerful drug. They were sentenced to nine months imprisonment, suspended for a year. **25.** Winston Silcott, sentenced to life imprisonment in 1985 for the murder of PC Keith Blakelock during the Broadwater Farm riot, was cleared by the Court of Appeal after new forensic tests suggested that the police had fabricated evidence. On 27 November Mark Braithwaite and Engin Raghip, who were also jailed for the murder, were released on bail and on 5 December their convictions were formally quashed. **26.** In a unanimous decision, the European Court of Human Rights ruled that the Government was in breach of the European Human Rights Convention in preventing the media from publishing extracts from Peter Wright's book *Spycatcher* when it had been published abroad in 1987. **29.** The Home Secretary (Kenneth Baker) was found guilty of contempt of court by the Court of Appeal for failing to comply with a court order requiring the return to Britain of an asylum-seeker from Zaire who had been deported in May 1991. A policeman was stabbed to death and two others seriously wounded in separate incidents in east and south London. Frank Beck, who was found guilty of sexual and physical abuse of children in his care in Leicestershire children's homes, was sentenced at Leicester Crown Court to five terms of life imprisonment.

DECEMBER 1991

5. John Tanner was sentenced at Birmingham Crown Court to life imprisonment for the murder of his girlfriend Rachel McLean, a student at Oxford University, in April 1991. **11.** William Kennedy Smith, a nephew of Senator Edward Kennedy, was acquitted of rape charges at his trial in West Palm Beach, Florida, USA. **13.** An off-duty police officer was stabbed to death in central London. Pamela Sainsbury was placed on two years probation at Plymouth Crown Court after being convicted of strangling her violent husband and dismembering his body. **16.** Esther Rantzen, the television presenter and chairman of Childline, won £250,000 libel damages in the High Court from the *People* newspaper, which had claimed that she protected an alleged paedophile because he had helped the charity. **19.** A police sergeant was shot and seriously wounded in London, after stopping a car to question the driver.

JANUARY 1992

1. Vernon Reynolds stabbed his estranged wife to death in Llandudno, Gwynedd, wounded five of her relatives, and then died in a car crash which also killed three young men. A man armed with what was later found to be a replica gun was shot dead by police in Rastrick, West Yorkshire. **4.** Four British tourists were shot dead in an ambush in southern Angola. **8.** Carol Withers was sentenced at Wood Green Crown Court to 15 months imprisonment after being convicted in November 1991 of fracturing the skulls of two babies in her care. **10.** Leroy Wade was sentenced at the Central Criminal Court to nine years imprisonment after being convicted of the manslaughter of his five-month-old daughter, whom he threw into the River Thames. **28.** Tommy Sheridan, the leader of the Anti-Poll Tax Federation, was sentenced in Edinburgh to six months imprisonment for defying a court order banning him from attending the first community charge warrant sale in Scotland in October 1991. **29.** Brian Nelson, a British army agent who had infiltrated the Ulster Defence Association, pleaded guilty at Belfast Crown Court to 20 terrorist charges including five of conspiracy to murder people alleged to be connected with the IRA; on 3 February he was sentenced to ten years imprisonment. Rajinder Bisla was given an 18-month suspended prison sentence at the Central Criminal Court after pleading guilty to the manslaughter of his cruel and domineering wife. **30.** Stephanie Slater, an estate agency negotiator, was released after being abducted by a man she had arranged to show round a house in Birmingham on 22 January; the kidnapper escaped with a ransom of £175,000. On 23 February a man was charged with the abduction; on 26 February he was also charged with the murder of Julie Dart in July 1991. **31.** Aileen Wuornos, a prostitute who said that she had killed seven of her clients in self-defence, was sentenced to death in Florida, USA, after being convicted of the murder of one of them.

FEBRUARY 1992

10. Peter Clowes, the former head of the Barlow Clowes investment group, was convicted at the Central Criminal Court of 18 counts of fraud and theft involving over £113 million; on 11 February he was sentenced to ten years imprisonment. The former world champion boxer Mike Tyson was convicted of rape at a court in Indianapolis, USA; on 26 March he was sentenced to six years imprisonment. **11.** Mr Justice Henry discharged the jury in the trial of Roger Seelig and Lord Spens on charges connected with the Guinness takeover of Distillers in 1986, on the grounds of Mr Seelig's ill health. **13.** William McKane was acquitted at the Central Criminal Court of conspiring with members of the IRA to cause explosions in Britain. **14.** Jonathan Cohen, Nicholas Wells, David Reed and Martin Gibbs were convicted at the Central Criminal Court of conspiring to mislead the financial markets about the £837 million Blue Arrow rights issue in 1987; on 17 February they were given suspended sentences but on 16 July the convictions were quashed by the Court of Appeal, which criticized the trial judge and the prosecution for the length and complexity of the charges.

15. Jeffery Dahmer was convicted at Milwaukee, Wisconsin, USA, of murdering and dismembering 17 men and boys; he was sentenced to life imprisonment. **18.** Stefan Kisko, who was sentenced to life imprisonment in 1976 for the murder of 11-year-old Lesley Molseed, was cleared of the murder at the Court of Appeal; the acquittal was based on scientific evidence which had been available at the time of his conviction. **20.** Eberhard Thust and Nicole Meissner were sentenced at a court in Germany to three years and two years imprisonment respectively for blackmailing the father of tennis champion Steffi Graf over an alleged affair. **21.** Cecil Jackson was sentenced at the Central Criminal Court to life imprisonment after being convicted of murdering his wife by strangling her and putting her in a bath of hydrochloric acid. **25.** Christine Dryland, the wife of a British Army major, admitted at a court martial in Verden, Germany, the manslaughter of her husband's mistress Marika Sparfeldt by running her over in her car in July 1991. On 28 February she was given a 12-month community service order and ordered to spend a year in a psychiatric hospital in London. **27.** A man was shot dead by police after he had shot and wounded a police constable and taken a driving instructor hostage in Bury St Edmunds, Suffolk. **28.** Jacqueline Fletcher, who was sentenced to life imprisonment in 1988 for murdering her baby, was released when the Court of Appeal ruled that the baby was almost certainly a cot death victim.

March 1992

5. A 12-year-old girl was convicted at Newcastle Crown Court of the manslaughter of an 18-month-old child she was babysitting in January 1990; on 29 April she was sentenced to five years detention. **9.** Barry McGuigan, the former world featherweight boxing champion, and the Channel 5 video company were ordered to pay libel damages of £450,000 to McGuigan's former manager Barney Eastwood after alleging in a video that Eastwood had forced McGuigan to fight while injured. **11.** The body of Jo Ramsden, a 21-year-old woman with Down's Syndrome who had gone missing in April 1991, was found in woodland near Lyme Regis, Dorset. **23.** June Scotland, who killed her bullying husband with a rolling pin in 1987, was convicted of manslaughter at Luton Crown Court and put on probation for two years. **27.** Rosemary Aberdour was sentenced at the Central Criminal Court to four years imprisonment after being convicted of stealing up to £2.7 million from the National Hospital Development Foundation, a charity of which she was deputy director. **31.** The Isle of Man Parliament voted to decriminalize sexual acts between consenting adult males.

April 1992

1. Albert Dryden was sentenced at Newcastle upon Tyne Crown Court to life imprisonment after being convicted of murdering the chief planning officer of Derwentside District Council, Harry Collinson, in June 1991. PC Alec Mason was sentenced at the Central Criminal Court to two and a half years imprisonment after being convicted of stamping on the head of a black motorist he had arrested, using racially abusive language, and falsifying police records. **2.** John Gotti, the head of the largest mafia family in New York, was convicted on 12 charges of murder and racketeering; on 23 June he was sentenced to life imprisonment without parole. **3.** The pop star Jason Donovan was awarded £200,000 libel damages and costs against the magazine *The Face*, which had published an article which he alleged had implied that he was gay and had lied about his sexual preferences; he later agreed to waive most of the damages in order to save the magazine from closure. **9.** Manuel Noriega, the deposed dictator of Panama, was convicted at a court in Miami, USA, of eight charges of drug trafficking and racketeering. On 10 July he was sentenced to 40 years imprisonment. **16.** Carlo de Benedetti, the chairman of the Olivetti group, was sentenced in Italy to six years and four months imprisonment after being convicted on fraud charges connected with the collapse of the Banco Ambrosiano in 1982; he was released pending an appeal. Paul Taylor, who led the riot at Strangeways prison in April 1990, was sentenced at Manchester Crown Court to ten years imprisonment. **18.** Five people died in a fire in a house in Hove, East Sussex; a man later confessed to arson and committed suicide. **21.** A policeman shot and wounded a gunman who had held a woman hostage for 48 hours in Darlington, Co. Durham.

May 1992

2. The bodies of Matthew Manwaring and his daughter Alison, who had gone missing from their home in Woolwich, London, on 23 April, were found buried in a garden in Abbey Wood, south London. **11.** Judith Ward, who served 18 years in prison after being convicted of the IRA coach bombing on the M62 in 1974, was released on bail by the Court of Appeal. On 4 June her conviction was found to have been 'unsafe and unsatisfactory'. **19.** The Director of Public Prosecutions announced that a two-year investigation by the Police Complaints Authority had concluded that no criminal charges should be brought against members of the disbanded West Midlands Serious Crimes Squad. **22.** Stephen Owen, who shot and wounded the man who had killed his son in a hit-and-run accident, was cleared of attempted murder and five other charges by a jury at Maidstone Crown Court. **23.** A three-year-old boy was found battered to death in undergrowth near his home in Coventry. **24.** A patient at the Royal Free Hospital, London, was shot dead while making a telephone call. **28.** The Australian entrepreneur Alan Bond was sentenced in Perth to two and a half years imprisonment after being convicted of dishonest business dealings; on 27 August the conviction was quashed and he was released on bail pending a retrial.

JUNE 1992

11. Edward Bartley was sentenced at the Central Criminal Court to 20 years imprisonment after being convicted of raping five women in south-west London between 1987 and 1991. **15.** Susan Christie, a former member of the Ulster Defence Regiment, was sentenced at Downpatrick Crown Court to five years imprisonment after being convicted of the manslaughter of Penny McAllister, whose husband, an officer in the regiment, was Christie's lover. **17.** Muhammed Saeed was sentenced at Leeds Crown Court to five years imprisonment after being convicted of defrauding a health authority by practising as a doctor for 30 years when unqualified to do so. **19.** Fred Bushell, the former chairman of the Lotus car company, was fined £2.25 million at Belfast Crown Court and sentenced to three years imprisonment for his part in a £9 million fraud at the De Lorean car company in 1982. **25.** Five law lords overruled a Court of Appeal judgment of April 1991 that local authorities seeking injunctions against shops illegally trading on Sundays would have to compensate the shops if restrictions on Sunday trading were eventually found to be illegal. **29.** Two rangers accused of murdering Julie Ward in the Masai Mara game reserve, Kenya, in 1988, were acquitted in Nairobi.

JULY 1992

6. Shots were fired at police and firefighters in three separate incidents on the Ordsall estate in Salford. **8.** The European Court of Justice ruled that existing restrictions on Sunday trading under British law do not contravene EC law. **10.** A federal jury in New York decided that Pan Am was guilty of wilful misconduct over the bombing of Flight 103 over Lockerbie in 1988. **14.** Wayne and Paul Darvell were released after six years imprisonment when their convictions for the murder of a sex shop manageress in Swansea in 1985 were found to be unsafe and unsatisfactory. **15.** A young woman, Rachel Nickell, was raped and murdered on Wimbledon Common, London, in front of her two-year-old son. **17.** Antony Gecas, who was a platoon commander in a Lithuanian police battalion during the Second World War, lost a libel case against Scottish Television, which had alleged in a programme that he had committed war crimes. **22.** Scott Singleton was sentenced at Lewes Crown Court to life imprisonment after being convicted of the murder of Lynne Rogers (*see* 9 September). Frank Welton was sentenced at Harrow Crown Court to eight years imprisonment for raping a woman in his black taxi in February. **24.** Michelle and Lisa Taylor were sentenced at the Central Criminal Court to life imprisonment after being convicted of the murder of Alison Shaughnessy, the wife of Michelle's lover, in June 1991. **26.** A woman lecturer was found stabbed to death at an Open University summer school in York. **30.** The body of nine-year-old Christopher Stanley, who had gone missing from his home on 29 July, was found on Hounslow Heath. **31.** The High Court imposed a joint fine of £75,000 on Channel 4 and Box Productions for contempt of court after they refused to identify their sources for a programme alleging widespread links between the RUC and loyalist paramilitaries in Northern Ireland.

AUGUST 1992

1. Fifteen-year-old Helen Gorrie was found murdered near her home in Horndean, Hampshire. **5.** In the High Court, the South African journalist Jani Allan lost a libel action against Channel 4 over a programme that she claimed had alleged an affair between her and the South African neo-Nazi leader Eugene Terre Blanche. **13.** A six-month old baby, Farrah Quli, was abducted from her home in London by a woman posing as a childminder. The baby was found safe and well in Limerick, Republic of Ireland, on 15 August. **14.** A bank manager's wife was kidnapped in Cheshire; she was released four hours later after her husband had paid a £40,000 ransom. **17.** Four people were sentenced at the Central Criminal Court to between five and ten years imprisonment after being convicted of plotting to launder the proceeds of the £26 million Brinks-Mat bullion robbery of 1983. Chris Eubank, the boxing champion, was fined £250 with £1,450 costs for driving without due care and attention when his car went off the road and killed a building worker in February 1992.

ENVIRONMENT

OCTOBER 1991

4. A protocol to the 30-year Antarctic Treaty was signed in Madrid, banning exploration for oil and other minerals in Antarctica for 50 years. **17.** The British Government received a letter from the European Environment Commissioner asking that work on seven building projects should stop because the necessary environmental assessments had not been carried out. **29.** The parliament of the Ukraine voted to shut the nuclear power station at Chernobyl by 1993.

NOVEMBER 1991

3. The last of the Kuwaiti oil wells set on fire by the Iraqi army at the end of the Gulf war was extinguished.

DECEMBER 1991

11. A survey published by the National Rivers Authority found that between 500 and 1,000 miles of river in Britain were of poorer quality in 1990 than in 1985. **12.** Middlesbrough was named Environment City of the Year by the Royal Society for Nature Conservation.

JANUARY 1992

4. Thousands of people were forced to stay indoors when a cloud of poisonous gas leaked from a chemical plant at Pyewipe, Grimsby. **13.** Acidic water containing high levels of metals broke out of the abandoned Wheal Jane tin mine in Cornwall, polluting and discolouring the Carnon river estuary.

FEBRUARY 1992

11. President Bush announced that the USA would phase out the production of chlorofluorocarbons (CFCs) by 1995, four years earlier than its original deadline. On 14 February the Environment Secretary (Michael Heseltine) announced that the production of CFCs in Britain would also cease by 1995. **27.** The Environment Secretary and the Minister of Agriculture (John Gummer) announced an Action for the Countryside initiative, a £45 million three-year package of measures aimed at improving the environment and countryside of Britain.

MARCH 1992

4. The EC Commission announced that the production of CFCs and other substances harmful to the ozone layer would cease by the end of 1995, 18 months earlier than the original deadline. **24.** A cloud of radioactive gas leaked from a nuclear power station near St Petersburg, Russia. **25.** The Environment Secretary granted permission for fifteen 80 ft high wind generators to be built on a Site of Special Scientific Interest in Cumbria

APRIL 1992

21. An operation to stem a flow of lava from Mount Etna, Sicily, was successful. **30.** The Prime Minister announced that Britain would freeze carbon dioxide emissions at 1990 levels by the year 2000, five years earlier than the original target. On 8 May the USA announced a similar deadline.

MAY 1992

28. The Pollution Inspectorate ruled that National Power could not burn orimulsion, a bitumen-based fuel, at Pembroke power station, Wales, because it would cause large quantities of acid rain.

JUNE 1992

3. An 11-day UN Conference on Environment and Development, the Earth Summit, opened in Rio de Janeiro, Brazil, with delegates from 178 countries. **15.** The National Rivers Authority ordered the water companies to reduce the amount of water taken from 20 rivers in danger of running dry. **29.** Norway announced its intention to resume commercial whale hunting.

THE EARTH SUMMIT

The Rio Declaration on Sustainable Development:

- Agenda 21: an action plan for promoting development and protecting the Earth's resources
- A UN Sustainable Development Commission to be set up in autumn 1992 to oversee the implementation of Agenda 21
- A funding agreement to provide environmental aid for the Third World; the UN aid target of 0.7 per cent of GNP for developing countries to be reached as soon as possible
- World statement of principles for the sustainable management and conservation of forests

Legally Binding Conventions:

- Convention on climate change (signed by 150 countries)
- Convention on biodiversity (signed by 152 countries, not including the USA)

JULY 1992

31. The EC Commission dropped its legal challenge to the extension of the M3 through Twyford Down, outside Winchester.

NORTHERN IRELAND

(*see also* British Affairs)

SEPTEMBER 1991

3. A Roman Catholic man was shot dead in Belfast. **10.** A Protestant man was shot dead in Belfast. **13.** A man was shot dead in Belfast. **16.** A Sinn Fein councillor was shot dead by the Ulster Freedom Fighters (UFF) at Magherafelt, Co. Londonderry. **17.** A member of the Royal Ulster Constabulary was killed in a mortar attack in Swatragh, Co. Londonderry. **19.** The head of a building supply company was shot dead by the IRA in Belfast. **29.** A student who was mistaken for a terrorist was shot dead by the RUC at Cookstown, Co. Tyrone.

OCTOBER 1991

10. A Protestant man was shot dead in Belfast; later a Roman Catholic taxi driver was shot dead in north Belfast. **13.** A Roman Catholic man was shot dead by the UFF in south Belfast. **15.** A Roman Catholic man was shot dead by the UFF in Belfast. **25.** A Roman Catholic man was shot dead near Pomeroy, Co. Tyrone.

NOVEMBER 1991

2. Two soldiers were killed when an IRA bomb exploded without warning in the military wing of the Musgrave Park Hospital, Belfast. **6.** A UDR soldier was killed in a mortar attack at Bellagny, Co. Londonderry. **9.** A woman and her 16-year-old son died after a firebomb attack on their home in Glengormley, Belfast. **13.** Four Protestant men were shot dead in two separate attacks by the IRA in Belfast; a five-week-old baby was seriously injured in one of the attacks. **14.** Three men were shot dead by the Ulster Volunteer Force (UVF) at Craigavon, Co. Armagh. **24.** A Protestant remand prisoner was killed and eight others injured when an IRA bomb exploded inside Crumlin Road prison in Belfast; on 28 November another prisoner died as a result of the attack. **25.** A Roman Catholic man was shot dead in

Belfast. **27.** The IRA kidnapped and shot dead a member of the UDR. Four members of the INLA forced their way into the house of Laurence Kennedy, the leader of the Conservative Party in Northern Ireland; his wife alerted the police and the men were arrested. The Secretary of State for Defence (Tom King) announced that a battalion was being sent to Northern Ireland in response to a request from the Secretary of State for Northern Ireland (Peter Brooke) for extra troops. **28.** Seven people were injured when two IRA car bombs exploded in the centre of Belfast.

DECEMBER 1991

4. An IRA bomb in Belfast caused severe damage to the Grand Opera House and the Europa Hotel. **12.** Sixteen people were injured and widespread damage caused when a 2,000 lb car bomb exploded outside a police station in Craigavon, Co. Armagh. **21.** In Moy, Co. Tyrone, a student was shot dead as he shielded his father from gunmen. Two men were killed when gunmen opened fire in a loyalist pub in Belfast; later a Roman Catholic man was shot dead in Belfast. **22.** A Roman Catholic man was killed and an eight-year-old boy and another man seriously injured when a gunman opened fire in a pub in Belfast; the UFF claimed responsibility. **23.** The Provisional IRA announced a three-day ceasefire beginning at midnight.

JANUARY 1992

3. A Roman Catholic man was shot dead and another man injured by the UVF in Moy, Co. Tyrone. **5.** A 600 lb IRA bomb exploded in the centre of Belfast, causing extensive damage. Another bomb exploded the following day. **9.** A Roman Catholic man was shot dead by the UFF in Moira, Co. Down. A car bomb exploded outside Londonderry police headquarters, causing extensive damage. UDR reservists were called up for full-time duty to support the increased security measures taken by the RUC in and around Belfast. **11.** A hoard of IRA bombs, guns and ammunition was found by security forces in west Belfast. **12.** An IRA bomb-making factory was found in Belfast and an arms cache in Ballymoney, Co. Antrim; six men and a woman were arrested. **13.** A Roman Catholic man was killed by a bomb placed under his car in Coalisland, Co. Tyrone. The IRA said it had planted the device acting 'on erroneous information'. **14.** A man was shot dead in Dundonald, Co. Down. **17.** Eight building workers were killed and six others injured when their minibus was blown up by an IRA bomb at Teebane Cross, near Carrickmore, Co. Tyrone. The Northern Ireland Secretary (Peter Brooke) appeared on a chat show on Irish television and was persuaded by the show's host to sing a song. This led to accusations of insensitivity on Mr Brooke's part to the Teebane Cross bombing, and demands for his resignation. **18.** The Northern Ireland minister responsible for security (Brian Mawhinney) announced that more than 1,000 extra troops would be sent to the province. **20.** Northern Ireland Secretary Peter Brooke offered his resignation to the Prime Minister, who refused it and expressed his support for Mr Brooke. The Prime Minister visited Northern Ireland. **30.** A Roman Catholic man was shot dead by the UFF in Lisburn, Co. Antrim.

FEBRUARY 1992

2. A Roman Catholic taxi driver was shot dead by the UFF in north Belfast. **3.** A Protestant man was shot dead by the IRA in Dungannon, Co. Tyrone. **4.** Allen Moore, a member of the RUC, shot three people dead and wounded two others in the Sinn Fein office in Belfast; he then shot himself. President Robinson of Ireland made a one-day visit to Belfast. **5.** Five men were killed and nine wounded when loyalist gunmen opened fire in a betting shop in Belfast; the UFF claimed responsibility. A part-time member of the UDR was shot in the leg by gunmen near Belleek, Co. Fermanagh; he returned fire and shot one of the gunmen dead. **10.** Six hundred extra troops were sent to Northern Ireland. **16.** Four members of the IRA were shot dead by security forces after an attack on a police station at Coalisland, Co. Tyrone. **17.** A Protestant man was shot dead in north Belfast. **19.** Joseph Doherty, an IRA member who was convicted of the murder of an SAS officer but escaped from Crumlin Road prison, Belfast, in 1981 before being sentenced to 30 years imprisonment, was flown back to Belfast after fighting extradition from the USA since 1983.

MARCH 1992

3. Two former UDR soldiers were sentenced at Belfast Crown Court to life imprisonment after being convicted of giving intelligence to the UFF in 1989 which resulted in the murder of a Roman Catholic man. **4.** A Roman Catholic man was shot dead by the UVF in Co. Armagh. **5.** A 1,000 lb IRA bomb exploded in the centre of Lurgan, Co. Armagh. **12.** A Roman Catholic man was shot dead at his home in north Belfast. **28.** An RUC officer was killed and another seriously injured when an IRA mortar bomb hit their patrol car in Newry, Co. Down. **29.** A Roman Catholic man was shot dead by the UVF in Portadown, Co. Armagh.

APRIL 1992

2. A canvasser working for a Sinn Fein candidate in the Londonderry East constituency was shot dead by the UFF. In Lurgan, Co. Armagh, the UVF shot dead a man they claimed was a UVF member who had committed 'treason'. **4.** A man who was shot by the UVF in Moy, Co. Tyrone on 3 January died of his injuries. **15.** A Protestant man was shot dead in east Belfast. **18.** A Roman Catholic man who had been a member of the Territorial Army was shot dead by the IRA in Armagh. **28.** A Roman Catholic woman was shot dead in west Belfast. **29.** A member of the Irish People's Liberation Organization (IPLO) was shot dead by the UVF in Belfast.

MAY 1992

1. A soldier was killed by an IRA bomb outside Newry, Co. Down. **5.** A Protestant man was shot dead in Belfast. **12.** Members of the 3rd Battalion The Parachute Regiment allegedly attacked civilians in Coalisland, Co. Tyrone, after a colleague was seriously injured by a landmine in Cappagh, Co. Tyrone, earlier in the day; on 14 May a lieutenant of the regiment was suspended. **17.** A paratrooper shot and injured three civilians during further disturbances in Coalisland; on 18 May the Parachute Regiment was withdrawn from the town. **24.** The Army confirmed that Brig. Tom Longland had been relieved of his duties as commander of 3 Brigade in the Armagh and Tyrone border area of Northern Ireland **25.** A man was shot dead in Coalisland, Co. Tyrone.

JUNE 1992

27. Twenty-one people were injured when a magnetic bomb clamped on to a police car by the IRA exploded in Belfast city centre. **30.** In London leaders of the four main political parties in Northern Ireland and British and Irish government ministers held talks for the first time in 70 years and agreed an agenda for further talks on the political future of Northern Ireland.

JULY 1992

1. The bodies of three men were found in Co. Armagh and, after a tip-off, a woman's body was found in Co. Sligo. The IRA said the men were IRA members who had been killed for colluding with the security forces and murdering the woman in 1991. **5.** A Roman Catholic man was beaten to death by Protestant youths in Belfast. **6.** Negotiations on the political future of Northern Ireland opened in London under the chairmanship of Sir Ninian Stephen, the former governor-general of Australia. **8.** A Roman Catholic man was shot dead by the UFF in east Belfast. **29.** Three former members of the UDR convicted of murdering a Roman Catholic man in 1984 were released by the High Court in Belfast after an investigation found that RUC officers had falsified evidence. The appeal of a fourth man was not upheld.

AUGUST 1992

3. A soldier was shot dead by the IRA in north Belfast. Two car bombs injured 21 people and caused extensive damage in central Belfast. **10.** The Northern Ireland Secretary (Sir Patrick Mayhew) announced that the UDA had been proscribed in Northern Ireland. **11.** A man was shot dead by the IRA in Belfast. **18.** The leader of the IPLO, Jimmy Brown, was shot dead in west Belfast. **21.** A woman from Rochdale, Lancs., was shot dead in an IRA attack on a security patrol in Belfast. **27.** A man was shot dead in west Belfast, the 3,000th victim of violence since 1969. **28.** A soldier was shot dead by the IRA in Crossmaglen, Co. Armagh.

SPORT

SEPTEMBER 1991

18. Liverpool football club played in the first round of the UEFA Cup, their first game in a European competition since the six-year ban imposed by UEFA following the Heysel stadium disaster in 1985. **21.** The boxer Michael Watson was admitted to hospital in London, having collapsed just after the referee stopped his WBO super-middleweight title fight against Chris Eubank in the final round. He underwent two operations to remove a blood clot from his brain.

OCTOBER 1991

12. Kenny Dalglish was appointed manager of Blackburn Rovers football club. **15.** Bertrand Gachot, the French grand prix racing driver imprisoned for 18 months in London on 15 August for assault, was released after the Court of Appeal reduced his sentence to nine months, six months of it suspended. **25.** The French national rugby union coach, Daniel Dubroca, resigned after allegations that he had abused David Bishop, the referee of the World Cup match between France and England in Paris on 19 October. **29.** Colin McMillan won the Lonsdale Belt outright in the record time of 160 days after successfully defending his British featherweight boxing title against Sean Murphy in London. **31.** Two masters of the Quorn Hunt were suspended by the hunt committee after video film secretly shot by the League Against Cruel Sports showed hunt members involved in cruelty to foxes. On 1 November the National Trust revoked the Quorn's licence to hunt on its land in Derbyshire and Leicestershire. On 2 November the chairman and four masters of the Hunt resigned.

NOVEMBER 1991

4. The England captain Bryan Robson announced his retirement from international football. **10.** In Calcutta, South Africa lost to India by three wickets in their first international cricket match for 21 years. **20.** The footballer Gary Lineker announced that he would be playing for the Grampus Eight team in Japan from February 1993. British heavyweight boxer Frank Bruno returned to the ring after an absence of nearly three years and knocked out John Emmen in the first round of the fight in London. **29.** At Great Ormond Street Hospital, London, Gary Lineker's eight-week-old son was diagnosed as suffering from acute myeloid leukaemia. **30.** The inaugural women's football world cup final took place in Canton, China.

DECEMBER 1991

1. France won the Davis Cup (tennis) for the first time since 1932. **9.** Oxford United put its 28 professional footballers up for sale to help clear its

£2 million debt to the family of Robert Maxwell. **17.** The Jockey Club announced proposed reforms to the conduct of racing in Britain, including the establishment of a British Horseracing Board responsible for strategic planning, policy and financial matters. **19.** The Minister for Sport (Robert Atkins) announced details of a sports policy review, including the setting up of an English Sports Council and a UK Sports Commission. **26.** Desert Orchid fell at the third-last fence while attempting to win the King George VI Rank Chase at Kempton Park for a record fifth time; on 27 December he was retired from racing. **27.** The jockey Philip Barnard died from injuries sustained in a fall at Wincanton on 26 December. Hungarian chess player Judit Polgar became the youngest-ever grandmaster at the age of 15 years and five months.

JANUARY 1992

3. Martin Offiah was transferred from Widnes to Wigan for a world record rugby league fee of £440,000. **4.** The football league champions and FA Cup favourites Arsenal were knocked out of the FA Cup by fourth division Wrexham. **13.** Fatima Whitbread, the former world javelin record-holder, announced her retirement due to a persistent shoulder injury. **21.** Tessa Sanderson, the former Olympic javelin champion, announced that she would retire after the Barcelona Olympics.

FEBRUARY 1992

3. In India's match against Australia in Perth, the Indian cricketer Kapil Dev became the second player ever to take 400 wickets in Test cricket. **5.** Dan Maskell announced his retirement as a tennis commentator. **6.** Ian Botham won his 100th Test cap for England in the match against New Zealand in Wellington. **8.** John Wright and Andrew Jones set a record New Zealand second-wicket stand of 241 in the third Test against England in Wellington. The Winter Olympics opened in Albertville, France. **10.** England bowler David Lawrence broke his kneecap in the Test against New Zealand in Wellington; scuffles broke out as players tried to stop him being photographed as he was carried from the pitch. The former world champion boxer Mike Tyson was convicted of rape at a court in Indianapolis, USA; on 26 March he was sentenced to six years imprisonment. **15.** Katrin Krabbe, the German world sprint champion, and her team-mates Silke Moeller and Grit Breuer were suspended for four years by the German Athletics Federation for tampering with drug test samples they had provided in South Africa in January; on 5 April the suspensions were lifted because of anomalies in the testing procedure but further investigations were carried out (*see also* 28 June, 4 August). Two French players, Lascube and Moscato, were sent off in the France v England rugby match in Paris. **16.** Martina Navratilova won a record 158th singles title at the Virginia Slims tennis tournament in Chicago. **20.** The FA Council approved the formation of the new Premier football league from August 1992. **22.** The Swiss speed-skating champion Nicolas Bochatay was killed when he collided with a snow machine in training at the Winter Olympics in Albertville. **26.** John Hebbes, a member of the Oxford University rowing team, died of a heart attack while training for the Boat Race.

MARCH 1992

2. Birmingham City football club was charged with bringing the game into disrepute after a pitch invasion at their ground on 29 February. **5.** Ian Botham took four wickets for no runs in seven balls in England's match against Australia in the cricket World Cup in Sydney. **7.** England won their second successive Five Nations rugby union grand slam. **22.** In the cricket World Cup semi-final in Sydney, England beat South Africa after the controversial 'rain rule' was applied following a 12-minute stoppage caused by rain. **25.** The fourth division football club Aldershot collapsed with debts of £1.2 million and left the Football League.

APRIL 1992

2. One horse died and three jockeys were injured in falls on the first day of the Grand National meeting at Aintree. **4.** The Indian Test batsman Sachin Tendulkar became the first overseas player to join Yorkshire Cricket Club. **6.** Graeme Souness, the manager of Liverpool football club, was admitted to hospital for a heart bypass operation. **8.** The former Wimbledon tennis champion Arthur Ashe announced that he is HIV positive. **15.** The racehorse Nijinsky was put down in Kentucky, USA. **16.** The International Rugby Football Board adopted over forty law changes for the 1992–3 season. **19.** Durham played their first competitive cricket match as a first-class county. **20.** Marcel Albers, a Dutch racing driver, died after crashing at 100 m.p.h. in the British Formula 3 motor racing championship at Thruxton, Hants. **28.** Nigel Short became the first British chess grandmaster to reach the world championship candidates' final when he beat Anatoly Karpov 6–4 in Spain.

MAY 1992

2. Bath clinched the rugby union league and cup double in the Cup final at Twickenham; the match was won with a drop goal in the last seconds of extra time. Wigan clinched the rugby league double in the Challenge Cup final at Wembley. Wigan also won the Premiership Trophy on 17 May, becoming the first team to complete the treble. **5.** UEFA announced that the finals of the 1996 European football championships would be held in England. **9.** Three horses were killed in falls after heavy rain at the Badminton Horse Trials. Twelve yachts capsized in force 8 gales during a regatta in the Bristol Channel. **15.** Peter Shreeves was sacked as manager of Tottenham Hotspur football club. **17.** Nigel Mansell became the first Formula 1 racing driver to win the first five races of the season when he won the San Marino Grand Prix. **18.** The new football Premier League agreed a £304 million deal with British Sky

Broadcasting for the broadcast of live league matches for five years. **19.** The Test and County Cricket Board voted for reforms in county cricket from 1993, including extending the length of county championship matches to four days. **25.** The transfer of Tottenham Hotspur footballer Paul Gascoigne to Lazio, Rome, for £5.5 million was finalized. **31.** Yugoslavia's place in the European football championships in Sweden was awarded to Denmark after the imposition of UN sanctions against Yugoslavia.

JUNE 1992

5. Only two balls were bowled in the first Test match between England and Pakistan because of rain and bad light; spectators protested when no ticket refunds were forthcoming. **6.** Monica Seles won the French Open tennis championship for the third successive year. **11.** Dave McAuley lost the IBF world flyweight title to Rodolfo Blanco in Bilbao in a disputed points decision. **14.** Serious disorder broke out among English football supporters at the European championships in Malmö, Sweden. Disturbances continued on the following two nights and after England had been knocked out of the tournament on 17 June. The match was Gary Lineker's last international match. **26.** Denmark, who had originally failed to qualify, won the European football championships. **28.** An arbitration committee of the International Amateur Athletics Federation lifted the suspensions of Katrin Krabbe, Silke Moeller and Grit Breuer on the grounds that the German Athletics Federation had contravened its constitution (*see* 15 February).

JULY 1992

6. David Gower scored 73 runs in the Test match against Pakistan, taking his total of runs scored for England to a record 8,154 and passing Geoffrey Boycott's previous record of 8,114. **7.** Pakistan fast bowler Aqib Javed was fined half his match fee by the Test referee for bowling a series of short balls to the England number 11 batsman Devon Malcolm in the Test match on 6 June. The Pakistan manager, Intikhab Alam, was severely reprimanded for criticizing the behaviour of umpire Roy Palmer. **8.** The International Cricket Council lifted the five-year Test match ban imposed on former England captain Mike Gatting and 15 other players who toured South Africa in 1990. It also granted Test status to Zimbabwe. **9.** Former Olympic decathlon champion Daley Thompson announced his retirement from international athletics. **10.** The Government confirmed that third and fourth division football clubs would be allowed to retain standing accommodation in their grounds, contrary to the recommendations of the Taylor report on the Hillsborough stadium disaster. **12.** Nigel Mansell set a British record of 28 grand prix wins with his victory in the British grand prix at Silverstone; spectators invaded the track to congratulate him while several cars were still racing. Eight-year-old Luke McShane became the youngest-ever chess master when he won the world under-10 championship in Duisburg, Germany. **19.** Nick Faldo won the Open golf championship for the third time. **25.** The Olympic Games opened in Barcelona, Spain. **26.** The first Sunday race meeting in Britain was held at Doncaster. Adrian Moorhouse retired from swimming after finishing last in the final of the Olympic 100 metres breaststroke. Alan Shearer was transferred from Southampton football club to Blackburn Rovers for a British record fee of £3.2 million. **29.** Chris Boardman became the first British cyclist for 84 years to win an individual gold medal at the Olympic Games. **30.** The British Olympic Association announced that three British competitors, including the sprinter Jason Livingston, had been sent home from the Olympic Games after drugs tests carried out in Britain proved positive. The former chairman of Swindon Town football club, Brian Hillier, was sentenced to one year's imprisonment after being convicted of a tax fraud involving illegal payments to players.

AUGUST 1992

1. Linford Christie won the Olympic 100 metres gold medal. Steve Redgrave won a third consecutive Olympic gold medal in the coxless pairs rowing event with his new partner Matthew Pinset. **2.** Johnny and Greg Searle and Garry Herbert won Olympic gold medals in the coxed pairs rowing event. **3.** The winner of the Olympic 10,000 metres, Khalid Skah of Morocco, was disqualified for allegedly being paced by a team-mate he lapped towards the end of the event; after an appeal the disqualification was rescinded. Two people died in separate accidents during a yachting race at Cowes. **4.** The German Athletic Federation confirmed that out-of-competition drugs tests on Katrin Krabbe and Grit Breuer had proved positive. **5.** Sally Gunnell won the Olympic gold medal in the 400 metres hurdles. **15.** The first matches took place in the new football Premier League. South Africa was beaten 27-24 by New Zealand in their first international rugby match since 1984. **16.** Nigel Mansell became the Formula One drivers' champion after finishing second in the Hungarian Grand Prix in Budapest. **20.** The England cricket team scored 363-7 against Pakistan, the highest total ever recorded in a one-day match. **26.** Allan Lamb, the England batsman, was fined about £2,000 and suspended for two games by his county, Northamptonshire, after writing an unauthorized newspaper article accusing the Pakistani bowlers of cheating in the one-day international against England on 23 August. On 28 August the International Cricket Council said that it would not be disclosing the reason for the ball being changed by the umpires during the match.

APPOINTMENTS AND RESIGNATIONS

In addition to those mentioned above, the following appointments, resignations, etc., were announced:

1991

25 September Prof. Sir Roland Smith resigned as chairman of British Aerospace.
18 October Sir David Nicholas retired as chairman of Independent Television News.
8 December Sir John Quinton was appointed chairman of the new football Premier League.
16 December Mrs Stella Rimington was appointed head of MI5 from February 1992.
20 December Ian Martin resigned as secretary-general of Amnesty International.

1992

10 January Gerald Ratner stepped down as chairman of Ratners but remained chief executive.
6 February Babara Mills, QC, was appointed Director of Public Prosecutions, the first woman to hold the post.
12 February Laurence Cooklin resigned as chief executive of the Burton Group.
13 February Arthur Sandford resigned as chief executive of the Football League.
12 March John Tusa resigned as managing director of the BBC World Service with effect from the end of 1992.
28 April Sir John Quinton resigned as chief executive of Barclays Bank from the end of May 1992 and as chairman from the end of December 1992.
6 May Keith Fletcher was appointed manager of the England cricket team from September 1992.
2 June Gerald Kaufman, the shadow foreign secretary, announced that he would not be seeking re-election to the Shadow Cabinet.
25 June Robert Horton resigned as chairman and chief executive of British Petroleum; Sir Michael Bishop was appointed chairman of Channel 4.
10 July Sir David English was appointed chairman of Associated Newspapers; Paul Dacre was appointed editor of the *Daily Mail*; Stewart Steven was appointed editor of the *Evening Standard;* Jonathan Holborrow was appointed editor of the *Mail on Sunday;* Simon Jenkins announced his intended resignation as editor of *The Times*.
23 July Peter Stothard was appointed editor of *The Times* from October 1992.
30 July Andrew Quinn was appointed the first chief executive of ITV.
13 August Lord Justice Bingham was appointed Master of the Rolls from October 1992.

AFRICA

SEPTEMBER 1991

3. It was reported that Sierra Leone had voted in favour of a new multi-party constitution in a referendum. **4.** The South African government published a draft constitution that would grant the vote to blacks but would not concede majority rule. **5.** The 27-year state of emergency in Zambia was lifted. **6.** In the Western Sahara, a cease-fire between Moroccan forces and Polisario guerrillas came into effect. Fighting was renewed between rival factions in Mogadishu, Somalia. **14.** The South African government, the ANC, *Inkatha* and other political groups signed a peace accord intended to end inter-communal violence. **15.** In Mauritius, the general election was won by the ruling MSM/MMM government. **23.** In Zaire, troops mutinied, causing the worst riots since the 1960s; on 29 September President Mobutu and opposition leaders agreed to form a crisis government led by Etienne Tshisekedi.

OCTOBER 1991

8. Eighteen blacks were killed by gunmen in South Africa. **9.** In Zaire President Mobutu demanded half the seats in the new Tshisekedi government for his supporters. **14.** In Chad an attempted coup was defeated by troops loyal to President Deby. **20.** The Mozambique government and Renamo guerrillas signed in Rome an agreement to end the country's civil war. **21.** President Mobutu of Zaire sacked Etienne Tshisekedi as Prime Minister; rioting broke out in protest. **23.** President Mobutu appointed as Prime Minister Mungul Diaka, who was immediately rejected by the Sacred Union opposition grouping. **25.** Rioting, looting and clashes between troops and Sacred Union supporters spread in Zaire; France and Belgium cut off all aid to President Mobutu's regime. **31.** Presidential and general elections were held in Zambia, the first multi-party poll in 24 years; President Kaunda lost the presidential election to Frederick Chiluba and resigned from office on 1 November.

NOVEMBER 1991

1. Two rival governments were sworn into office in Zaire, one led by Mungal Diaka and the other by Etienne Tshisekedi. **4.** Seventeen people were killed and 44 injured on the eve of a 48-hour general strike in South Africa. **7.** President Chiluba announced that Zambia would open diplomatic relations with South Africa. **16.** Opposition leaders were arrested and a pro-democracy rally broken up by police in Nairobi, Kenya. **24.** Forces loyal to President Ali Muhammed of Somalia exchanged artillery and rocket barrages with rebels in Mogadishu. **25.** President Mobutu of Zaire replaced Prime Minister Diaka with Nguza Karl I-Bond, dividing the Sacred Union opposition grouping of which Nguza was a founder. **28.** Army units in Togo stormed the radio and television stations in an attempt to seize power from the Koffigoh government and halt democratic reforms which reduced the powers of President Eyadema. **29.** In South Africa a preparatory conference between the government and twenty political groupings convened to prepare the ground for constitutional talks.

DECEMBER 1991

3. Prime Minister Koffigoh of Togo was seized by rebel troops in a coup in support of President Eyadema. In Kenya the ruling KANU party voted to allow political pluralism. **4.** Township battles between ANC and *Inkatha* supporters left 16 dead. **9.** In South Africa, 17 were killed in Soweto in continuing clashes between *Inkatha* and ANC supporters. **15.** State governorship and legislative elections were held in Nigeria. **18.** The *Inkatha* leader Chief Buthelezi withdrew from negotiations on South Africa's political future after other political groups rejected his demand for three Zulu delegations. **20.** The Convention for a Democratic South Africa opened in Johannesburg to discuss proposals for an interim multiracial government. **26.** The fundamentalist Islamic Salvation Front (FIS) won 188 of the 231 seats contested in the first round of Algeria's general election.

JANUARY 1992

1. In Chad, forces loyal to deposed President Habre attacked army positions in the Lake Chad area; the army was reported to have defeated the rebels by 7 January. **11.** President Benjedid of Algeria resigned as the armed forces took control in support of the National Liberation Front government and to prevent an Islamic Salvation Front victory at the polls; the National Assembly was dissolved. **12.** The second round of voting in Algeria was cancelled after the *de facto* coup by the armed forces. A five-man Council of State led by Mohammed Boudiaf was formed on 15 January. **20.** In Congo, Prime Minister Andre Milongo was overthrown by the army. **21.** In Algiers youths attacked army road-blocks and security posts in protest at the coup. **22.** The acting leader of the Islamic Salvation Front in Algeria, Abdelkader Hachani, was arrested. **23.** In Zaire troops loyal to President Mobutu crushed a mutiny by rebel soldiers calling for the resumption of the national conference on democracy. The UN Security Council imposed an arms embargo on Somalia to try to end the continuing civil war. **24.** At the opening of parliament in Cape Town, President De Klerk said that white South Africans would have a veto on constitutional changes designed to replace apartheid with a non-racial democracy. **28.** South African police arrested the entire leadership of the paramilitary Afrikaner Resistance Movement.

FEBRUARY 1992

9. The Algerian government declared a state of emergency following two days of clashes between fundamentalists and security forces. **10.** Islamic fundamentalists killed eight policemen in an attack in the Algiers kasbah.

MARCH 1992

3. The Somalian President, Ali Muhammed, and the rebel leader General Muhammed Aidid signed a UN-sponsored truce in the country's civil war. **4.** The South African government, the ANC and 17 other political groups reached agreement on forming an interim multiracial government pending the adoption of a new constitution. **12.** Mauritius became a republic, remaining within the Commonwealth. **18.** The white electorate in South Africa voted by 68 per cent to 32 per cent in favour of constitutional and political reform.

APRIL 1992

13. The ANC president Nelson Mandela announced a separation from his wife Winnie, who was felt to be discrediting the ANC because of allegations that she had been involved in kidnapping and murder. **21.** In South Africa five white Democratic Party MPs defected to the ANC, giving the ANC its first ever representatives in parliament. **23.** President De Klerk proposed the formation of a five-member executive elected by South Africans of all races to replace the presidency. **26.** Nelson Mandela and the *Inkatha* leader Chief Buthelezi both rejected President De Klerk's proposals for a rotating presidency.

MAY 1992

1. Junior army officers seized power and imposed a state of emergency in Sierra Leone; President Momoh fled to Guinea. **15.** General Aidid consolidated his power base in the continuing Somali civil war by capturing the key port of Kismayu. **19.** The Nigerian army sealed off the central state of Kaduna after three days of ethnic and religious clashes left over 300 people dead. **28.** President Compaoré's ruling party defeated opposition groups to win Burkina Faso's first multi-party elections for 14 years. The Sudanese army captured Kapoeta, the capital of rebel-controlled southern Sudan. **29.** In Harare, Zimbabwe riot police clashed with students protesting at the continued rule of President Mugabe and his government.

JUNE 1992

15. The latest phase of constitutional negotiations on South Africa's future collapsed amid inter-party bickering. **18.** Thirty-nine people were killed in Boipatong near Johannesburg, South Africa, allegedly by *Inkatha* supporters. **20.** Police opened fire on black residents of Boipatong who had physically forced President De Klerk to call off a visit to the area after only ten minutes. **23.** The ANC withdrew indefinitely from the talks on a new constitution for South Africa in protest at the Boipatong violence. **29.** President Mohammed Boudiaf of Algeria was assassinated by Islamic fundamentalists.

JULY 1992

2. Ali Kafi became the new President of Algeria. **5.** UN military observers arrived in the Somali capital Mogadishu to help distribute food aid. **6.** The centre-left Social Democratic Party won the Nigerian federal legislative election. **7.** The Goldstone Judicial Commission investigating the Boipatong massacre stated that there was no evidence linking the government to the massacre. **9.** Nelson Mandela effectively ruled out a resumption of constitutional talks in South Africa, saying that the ANC was not interested in power-sharing. **15.** The president and vice-president of the Islamic Salvation Front were sentenced in Algeria to 12 years imprisonment for conspiracy against the state. **17.** The UN Security Council appointed a special representative, Cyrus Vance, to investigate violence in South Africa. **28.** The UN Security Council threatened factions in Mogadishu with UN military intervention in Somalia if they did not co-operate with UN relief efforts.

AUGUST 1992

2. Members of a UN mission arrived in South Africa to monitor the 48-hour general strike campaign by the ANC. **3.** The first day of the ANC's mass action campaign resulted in violence and 36 deaths. **5.** The first direct talks in 15 years of civil war in Mozambique opened in Rome between President Chissano and the Renamo rebel leader Afonso Dhlakama. **6.** The military government of Nigeria announced the annulling of presidential primary elections amid reports of widespread vote-rigging. **7.** An agreement to end the civil war in Mozambique was reached in Rome; a peace accord is to be signed by 1 October 1992. **17.** The UN Security Council authorized the stationing of observers in South Africa to help end violence in the country. **28.** Almost 200 Tunisian Islamic fundamentalists were convicted in Tunis of plotting to take power by force. The UN Security Council voted to provide 3,000 armed guards to protect food convoys in Somalia; on the same day a US military airlift of food for the starving population began.

THE AMERICAS

SEPTEMBER 1991

11. Guatemala established diplomatic relations with Belize, ending a 400-year border dispute. **16.** Criminal proceedings against Oliver North for directing the Irangate cover-up were dropped. **25.** In El Salvador, the government and guerrilla movements signed a peace accord to end the 11-year civil war. **29.** Two Salvadorian army officers were found guilty of murdering six Jesuit priests and two women in 1989. **30.** President Aristide of Haiti was overthrown in a military coup and fled to Venezuela; on 8 October Joseph Nerette was installed as President by the military.

OCTOBER 1991

8. Judge Clarence Thomas, President Bush's nominee to the US Supreme Court, was accused of sexual harassment by Prof. Anita Hill. **11.** The Senate Judiciary Committee hearing to confirm Clarence Thomas's nomination to the Supreme Court heard evidence from Prof. Anita Hill. **15.** Clarence Thomas's appointment as a Supreme Court Judge was confirmed. **16.** A gunman killed 22 people in a Texas restaurant. **27.** In general elections in Colombia, the Liberal Party won majorities in both the Senate and Lower House.

NOVEMBER 1991

9. A delegation from the Organization of American States seeking to restore President Aristide to power in Haiti was prevented from entering the country on arrival at Port-au-Prince airport by protesters supporting the coup leaders. **14.** The Farabundo Martí National Liberation Front (FMLN) announced a unilateral suspension of all offensive operations against the El Salvador government from 16 November. **25.** Negotiations between the ousted President Aristide and Haitian MPs to restore democratic rule in Haiti broke down without agreement.

DECEMBER 1991

3. John Sununu resigned as White House Chief of Staff. A US soldier, Albert Sombolay, was sentenced to 34 years imprisonment for spying for Iraq during the Gulf war. **4.** David Duke, a former Ku Klux Klan leader, announced his intention to challenge President Bush for the Republican presidential nomination. **5.** President Bush appointed Transport Secretary Samuel Skinner as White House Chief of Staff. **10.** Patrick Buchanan announced his intention to challenge President Bush for the Republican presidential nomination. **16.** The ruling National Alliance for Reconstruction Party in Trinidad and Tobago was defeated in the general election by the People's National Movement.

JANUARY 1992

8. President Bush collapsed at a televised state dinner in Tokyo but recovered soon afterwards from suspected gastro-enteritis. **9.** Governor Douglas Wilder of Virginia withdrew from the contest for the Democratic Party presidential nomination. **13.** Cuba appealed for direct talks with the USA to end the 30-year-old US economic embargo. **16.** The accord to end the war between the El Salvador government and the FMNL was officially signed in Mexico City. **21.** Eight people were killed in northern Nicaragua in fighting between former Contra rebels and ex-Sandinista soldiers.

FEBRUARY 1992

1. The UN-mediated cease-fire came into effect in El Salvador. **3.** US coastguard vessels took the first of thousands of Haitian refugees back to Haiti from the

US base at Guantanamo Bay. **4.** Rebel soldiers were defeated in their attempt to mount a coup against President Perez of Venezuela. **11.** In the first US presidential primary, Senator Tom Harkin won 77 per cent of the delegates' votes in the Democratic Party primary in Iowa. **18.** In New Hampshire, President George Bush beat Patrick Buchanan in the Republican Party presidential primary; Paul Tsongas beat Bill Clinton in the Democratic Party primary. **24.** An agreement was reached between ousted President Aristide of Haiti and members of the Haitian parliament that he should return as president and democracy would be restored.

MARCH 1992

5. Senator Bob Kerrey withdrew from the contest for the Democratic Party nomination. **8.** President George Bush and Bill Clinton emerged as front runners for their respective party presidential nominations after the South Carolina primaries. **9.** Senator Tom Harkin withdrew from the contest for the Democratic Party nomination. **10.** Bill Clinton emerged victorious from the Super Tuesday primaries, winning all eight southern states. **18.** Bill Clinton and President George Bush beat Paul Tsongas and Patrick Buchanan respectively in the Illinois and Michigan primaries. **19.** Paul Tsongas withdrew from the contest for the Democratic Party nomination. **28.** Percival Patterson was elected leader of the Jamaican People's National Party and became Prime Minister, succeeding Michael Manley who resigned on health grounds.

APRIL 1992

5. President Alberto Fujimori of Peru suspended the constitution and dissolved the congress with the backing of the military, in an attempt to produce a more efficient administration. **7.** Bill Clinton won Democratic Party primaries in New York, Wisconsin and Kansas. **9.** The former President of Panama, Manuel Noriega, was found guilty in Miami on eight charges, including money-laundering and cocaine-manufacturing, and was later sentenced to 40 years in prison. **10.** The disbanded Peruvian congress elected Vice-President Garcia as President in defiance of President Fujimori, who retained power. **19.** President Bush announced new restrictions on trade with Cuba, tightening the 30-year-old embargo. **22.** President Fujimori promised to return Peru to democracy within 12 months, following international criticism of his takeover of power. **29.** Four white policemen were acquitted in Los Angeles of beating a black motorist, in spite of a videotaped recording of the incident; rioting broke out in the city on 30 April in protest at the acquittals and recurred on the following three nights.

MAY 1992

1. President Bush ordered 1,000 federal law officers and 4,000 regular troops to Los Angeles as rioting and looting continued. **3.** The clear-up began in Los Angeles after the civil unrest, in which 58 people died and thousands were injured. **22.** President Patricio Aylwin of Chile announced plans to reform the constitution to give himself the power to appoint and remove military chiefs.

JUNE 1992

2. The American presidential primary season ended with voting in California and five other states which confirmed President Bush and Governor Clinton as, respectively, the provisional Republican and Democratic nominees. Marc Bazin was appointed Prime Minister of Haiti, a compromise between the military and the business elite.

JULY 1992

5. Sixto Duran Ballen was elected President of Ecuador. **15.** Governor Bill Clinton and Senator Al Gore were formally nominated by the Democratic Party National Convention as the party's presidential and vice-presidential candates. **16.** The potential independent US presidential candidate H. Ross Perot announced that he would not be standing in the November election. **23.** Colombian drug baron Pablo Escobar escaped from house arrest and went on the run as the authorities tried to move him to a military jail.

AUGUST 1992

12. Agreement was reached by the USA, Canada and Mexico on the establishment of a North American Free Trade Agreement. **13.** James Baker resigned as US Secretary of State to become White House Chief of Staff and President Bush's campaign manager. **19.** Sir Lynden Pindling resigned after 25 years as Prime Minister of the Bahamas after he lost the general election. **20.** President George Bush and Vice-President Dan Quayle were formally nominated by the Republican Party National Convention as the party's candidates in the forthcoming presidential elections.

ASIA

SEPTEMBER 1991

2. The Prime Minister (John Major) and Foreign Secretary (Douglas Hurd) arrived in China for an official visit. **3.** Britain and China signed an agreement on the construction of a new airport in Hong Kong. **9.** A Hong Kong businessman who had been imprisoned in China for aiding the escape of dissidents was released. **15.** Pro-democracy parties won 16 of the 18 directly elected seats on the Hong Kong Legislative Council. A referendum in Bangladesh favoured restoring parliamentary rule. **25.** It was reported that the Indian government had accepted plans to reserve 60 per cent of government jobs for people from middle or lower castes.

OCTOBER 1991

2. President Aquino announced that the USA would be given three years to withdraw its armed forces from the Philippines. **8.** Abdur Rahman Biswas was elected President of Bangladesh. **17.** In Sri Lanka, 52 Tamil separatists and 27 government soldiers were reported dead after fierce battles. **23.** The four Cambodian factions signed an agreement in Paris to end 13 years of civil war. North and South Korea agreed to draft an agreement on non-aggression, political reconciliation and economic co-operation. **29.** An agreement was signed by Britain and Vietnam providing for the return, by force if necessary, of boat people from Hong Kong to Vietnam.

NOVEMBER 1991

1. The Indonesian government cancelled a visit by politicians and journalists to East Timor amid widespread riots in the area against Indonesian rule. **5.** Kiichi Miyazawa replaced Toshiki Kaifu as Prime Minister of Japan. A five-day visit to Peking by Vietnamese leaders ended years of enmity between China and Vietnam. **8.** The first enforced repatriation of boat people from Hong Kong to Vietnam took place. **10.** The advance guard of a UN force arrived in Cambodia to start its peace-keeping task, leading to UN supervised general elections. **11.** Talks took place in Moscow between Afghan mujahidin leaders and the Soviet leadership; on 15 November an agreement that the Soviet-backed regime should hand over power to an Islamic interim government was concluded. **12.** A hundred people were reported killed by Indonesian forces in East Timor after protests against Indonesian rule. **14.** Prince Norodom Sihanouk returned to Cambodia to lead the new Supreme National Council. **15.** The US Secretary of State (James Baker) visited Peking to discuss human rights, weapon sales and unfair trade practices. **17.** The Afghan government announced that it was willing to hold peace talks with mujahidin guerrillas. **20.** Prince Norodom Sihanouk was officially declared President of Cambodia by the Phnom Penh government. **22.** The USA and Vietnam opened talks intended to lead to the restoration of full diplomatic ties. **27.** Khieu Samphan, the official leader of the Khmer Rouge, arrived in Phnom Penh for a meeting of the Supreme National Council but had to be rescued by troops and flown to Thailand after being attacked by a crowd. **29.** China announced the release of two prominent dissidents imprisoned after the 1989 Tiananmen Square demonstrations.

DECEMBER 1991

11. Pro-democracy protests broke out in Myanmar, calling for the release of Aung San Suu Kyi. **13.** North and South Korea signed a non-aggression accord. **22.** In the Cambodian capital of Phnom Penh, the army and police restored order after two days of anti-government demonstrations and riots. **27.** The Philippine government stated that US forces must leave the Philippines within one year, after talks on a three-year phased withdrawal collapsed. **30.** Khieu Samphan returned to Phnom Penh under heavy protection for the first meeting of the Supreme National Council.

JANUARY 1992

20. Relief agencies in the Cambodian capital of Phnom Pehn reported that 25 villages had been attacked by the Khmer Rouge.

FEBRUARY 1992

7. A senior Pakistani government official admitted for the first time that his country has the components and expertise to assemble a nuclear bomb. **12.** Pakistani police opened fire on Kashmiri demonstrators to prevent them from marching to the Indian border; five were killed and over 50 wounded. **18.** Seventeen people were murdered in the Punjab, India, by Sikh militants seeking to enforce a boycott of the first state elections for seven years. **28.** The UN Security Council voted to create a UN Transitional Authority in Cambodia and to send 22,000 peace-keeping personnel.

MARCH 1992

5. The Myanmar air force bombed and strafed Mannerplaw, the centre of the resistance movement. **20.** Mujahidin rebels in Afghanistan captured the city of Mazar-i-Sharif. The Vietnamese National Assembly passed a new constitution. **22.** Political parties aligned with the military won the Thai general election with a majority of eight seats. **24.** The ruling Democratic Liberal Party in South Korea lost its parliamentary majority in the general election. **29.** The Phnom Penh government in Cambodia announced an offensive to halt Khmer Rouge gains in the north of the country, hampering UN peace efforts.

APRIL 1992

15. Mujahidin forces captured the Bagram air base north of Kabul. **16.** President Najibullah of Afghanistan was overthrown by a council of four vice-presidents; mujahidin forces closed in on Kabul. **24.** Leaders of ten Afghan mujahidin groups agreed at a meeting in Peshawar, Pakistan, to form a fifty-member interim council. **25.** Mujahidin forces entered and took control of Kabul with the agreement of the outgoing regime. **26.** Fighting broke out in Kabul between rival mujahidin groups. **28.** President Sigbatullah Mojaddedi and the new interim council arrived in Kabul.

MAY 1992

4. Fighting began near Kabul between the forces of the new government and those of Gulbuddin Hekmatyar. **8.** More than 100,000 demonstrators clashed with riot police and troops in Bangkok, Thailand, as they called for the resignation of the unelected Prime Minister, General Kraprayoon. **11.** A presidential election was held in the Philippines. **17.** At least 20 people were killed by security forces in Bangkok as further pro-democracy demonstrations against the government were crushed. Broad agreement was reached between the new Afghan government and Gulbuddin Hekmatyar. **19.** The death toll in demonstrations in Bangkok continued to rise, with hundreds injured and thousands arrested. **20.** The Prime Minister and opposition leaders were summoned to an audience with the King of Thailand, at which amendments to the constitution to allow more democratic government were agreed in return for an end to the demonstrations. **24.** The Thai Prime Minister Suchinda Kraprayoon resigned after he lost the support of the governing parties. **25.** Rival Afghan leaders Ahmad Shah Massoud and Gulbuddin Hekmatyar agreed to withdraw their forces from Kabul and hold elections in six months. **26.** Thailand's parliament endorsed constitutional amendments to curb the political power of the military.

JUNE 1992

2. Fighting began and continued for several days in the Afghan capital Kabul between Saudi-backed and Iranian-backed fundamentalist groups. **10.** Anand Panyarechum was named by the King of Thailand as the new Prime Minister. **16.** Fidel Ramos was declared the winner of the Philippines presidential election and was sworn in on 30 June. **22.** An international conference on Cambodia criticized the Khmer Rouge for jeopardizing the peace process by refusing to disarm or allow UN forces into areas controlled by them.

JULY 1992

7. Abdul Sabbur Fareed became the new Afghan Prime Minister under a reconciliation agreement between rival mujahidin forces. **9.** Chris Patten was sworn in as the 28th Governor of Hong Kong. **16.** Shankar Dayal Sharma was elected President of India. **31.** The Philippines Congress approved an amnesty for Communist and Muslim guerrillas and legalized the Communist party.

AUGUST 1992

10. Hezb-i-Islami guerrillas launched a rocket bombardment on Kabul; continued fighting between rival mujahidin groups left over 1,000 people dead. **12.** Heavy fighting continued in and around Kabul. **16.** Afghan President Burhanuddin sacked Prime Minister Abdul Sabur Fareed because of his membership of Hezb-i-Islmai. **24.** China and South Korea established diplomatic relations.

AUSTRALASIA AND THE PACIFIC

SEPTEMBER 1991

6. Walter Lini, Prime Minister of Vanuatu, resigned; he was replaced by Donald Kalpokas. **24.** The trial of Sir Joh Bjelke-Petersen, the former Prime Minister of Queensland, on charges of corruption began in Australia.

OCTOBER 1991

1. The Governor-General of Papua New Guinea, Sir Serei Eri, resigned after causing a constitutional crisis that had led the Papuan government to ask The Queen to dismiss him.

NOVEMBER 1991

11. The parliament of Papua New Guinea elected Wiwa Korowi, an opposition MP, as Governor-General.

DECEMBER 1991

2. In the general election in Vanuatu the Union of Moderate Parties won 19 of the 46 seats and formed a coalition government on 17 December with the Vanuatu National United Party. **12.** The Australian Prime Minister, Bob Hawke, was told by senior Cabinet ministers that he could no longer count on the support of Labour MPs for his leadership of the party. **19.** Bob Hawke said he was resigning as Labour party leader but would immediately seek re-election to the post; he was defeated by Paul Keating, who became Prime Minister.

JANUARY 1992

10. Rebels on Bougainville island seized a ship and took its crew hostage to force the Papua New Guinea government to end its two-year blockade of the island, imposed after the island's declaration of independence.

FEBRUARY 1992

4. The Papua New Guinea government signed an agreement with the secessionist leaders of Bougainville intended to ensure peace and stability. **27.** The Australian Prime Minister, Paul Keating, accused Britain of abandoning Australia to Japan in the Second World War, amid a continuing republican versus monarchy debate in Australia.

APRIL 1992

8. Papua New Guinea troops killed at least 15 secessionists in a raid on Bougainville island to free trapped villagers. France announced it would suspend all nuclear tests at Mururoa atoll in the South Pacific until the end of 1992.

MAY 1992

20. Papua New Guinea troops landed on Bougainville after a peace agreement with the secessionists had been reached. **30.** A general election was held in Fiji, the first since the coups in 1987; the Fijian Political Party, led by Sitiveni Rabuka, emerged as the largest party.

JUNE 1992

24. The Prime Minister of New South Wales, Nick Greiner, resigned amid allegations of corruption.

JULY 1992

21. Paias Wingti was elected by parliament as the new Prime Minister of Papua New Guinea after a general election which had taken place throughout June.

EUROPE

SEPTEMBER 1991

6. Lothar de Maziere, deputy leader of the ruling German Christian Democratic Party (CDU) and former Prime Minister of East Germany, resigned after being unable to prove that he had not collaborated with the East German secret police. **15.** The ruling Social Democrats lost the general election in Sweden. **26.** Troops were deployed in Bucharest to end two days of rioting by thousands of miners protesting at declining living standards; the Romanian government resigned and Teodore Stolojan became Prime Minister on 1 October. **29.** In Belgium, the Flemish People's Union party withdrew from the coalition government of Wilfried Martens. In the German state of Bremen the ruling Social Democrats were heavily defeated in the Land Assembly election by the extreme right-wing Deutsche Volksunion party, which doubled its vote.

OCTOBER 1991

1. In Sweden a new government was formed by a coalition of the Moderates, Liberals, Centre and Christian Democrat parties. **4.** Belgium's coalition government collapsed because of disputes between Flemish and francophone parties. **6.** In Portugal the ruling Social Democratic party won the general election. **13.** In the Bulgarian general election the Union of Democratic Forces won the most seats and the Bulgarian Socialist Party came second, leaving the Turkish Movement for Rights and Freedom holding the balance of power. **16.** A new Romanian coalition government was formed. **18.** The Irish Prime Minister Charles Haughey survived a no-confidence vote in the Dail prompted by seven weeks of financial scandals. **27.** A general election was held in Poland; the result was inconclusive, as none of the 20 parties had won more than 12 per cent of the vote.

NOVEMBER 1991

7. In Poland, talks between the four main parties and President Walesa failed to agree on a coalition government and choice of prime minister. The Irish Prime Minister, Charles Haughey, sacked finance minister Albert Reynolds because Reynolds had supported no-confidence votes against him in the Dail. On 8 November Haughey sacked environment minister Padraig Flynn for the same reason. President Walesa appointed Bronislaw Geremek as Prime Minister-designate of Poland. The Union of Democratic Forces formed the first wholly non-Communist government in Bulgaria since 1944. **9.** Charles Haughey survived a no-confidence motion in a vote by MPs of his Fianna Fail party. **10.** Austria's radical right-wing Freedom Party made large gains in local elections. **13.** The Irish Prime Minister cancelled the appointment of Dr James McDaid as defence minister after Dr McDaid admitted links with an IRA terrorist. Bronislaw Geremek resigned as Polish Prime Minister-designate after failing to form a coalition. **24.** In the Belgian general election the green and far right parties gained seats at the expense of the traditional political parties. The Prime Minister Wilfried Martens agreed to head a caretaker government. **26.** Wieslaw Chrzanowski was elected Speaker of the Polish parliament.

DECEMBER 1991

5. President Walesa appointed Jan Olszewski as Prime Minister and also took steps to transfer many government powers to the presidency. **6.** The Democratic Party left the coalition government in Albania and Prime Minister Yili Bufi resigned. **8.** Although much of the electorate boycotted the poll at the request of monarchist, opposition and ethnic Hungarian parties, those who did vote overwhelmingly endorsed Romania's first post-Communist constitution. **9.** Rallies held in the Albanian capital called for the resignation of President Alia because of the government's failure to improve living conditions. **12.** Poland's centre-right coalition government collapsed after failing to agree an economic programme. **17.** Polish Prime Minister Jan Olszewski resigned after President Walesa rejected his proposed Cabinet as insufficiently committed to radical market reform. **23.** The Polish parliament voted to accept the Cabinet proposed by Jan Olszewski, overturning the President's wishes, and refused to accept Olszewski's resignation.

JANUARY 1992

12. In the first round of the presidential election in Bulgaria the incumbent president, Zhelyu Zhelev, gained a clear lead; in the second round on 19 January, Zhelev was elected President. **17.** It was announced that the 1948 Soviet-Finnish Mutual Friendship and Co-operation treaty, which had restricted Finnish sovereignty throughout the post-war period, was to be ended. **21.** The Irish Prime Minister was implicated in a telephone-tapping scandal by a former Irish justice minister; on 22 January the Progressive Democrats, the junior partners in the Irish coalition government, called for Mr Haughey's resignation. **23.** The Estonian government resigned because of its inability to combat severe food and fuel shortages. **30.** Charles Haughey announced his decision to resign from office as Prime Minister of Ireland with effect from 6 February. The Italian Prime Minister, Giulio Andreotti, announced the collapse of the coalition government and called a general election for 5 April.

FEBRUARY 1992

6. Albert Reynolds was elected leader of the ruling Fianna Fail party and became Prime Minister of the Irish Republic. Five people were killed and seven injured in Madrid by a car bomb planted by the Basque separatist organization ETA, which announced a campaign to disrupt the Olympic Games and Expo '92 World Trade Fair. **13.** The Swedish Prime Minister, Carl Bildt, stated that his country's foreign and security policies were no longer those of neutrality, and that Sweden was actively interested in security co-operation with the rest of Europe. **22.** The Nationalist Party was re-elected in the Maltese general election. **25.** Rioting broke out in Albania in protest at the lack of food and other goods.

MARCH 1992

5. The Polish government's attempt to ease the country's strict economic reform programme was defeated in the Polish parliament. **7.** A new government led by Jean-Luc Dehaene was sworn into office in Belgium. **13.** The German Bundesrat voted unanimously to require the federal government to include representatives of the Länder in future EC financial negotiations, and threatened to block ratification of the Maastricht treaty if this was not agreed. **22.** France's ruling Socialist Party suffered a crushing defeat in regional elections, winning only 18 per cent of the vote. **23.** The Democratic Party won a landslide victory in the Albanian general election, ending 45 years of Communist rule.

APRIL 1992

2. Edith Cresson resigned as Prime Minister of France and was replaced by Pierre Bérégovoy. **3.** President Ramiz Alia of Albania, a Communist, resigned after the Democratic Party's general election victory. **6.** In the general election in Italy, the established political parties suffered a large-scale defeat at the hands of regionalist and protest parties. **9.** The Albanian parliament elected Dr Sali Berisha as President. **24.** The Italian Cabinet resigned amid continuing political uncertainty following the inconclusive general election of 5 April. **24.** The first large-scale public sector strikes for 18 years began in Germany, with large pay claims prompted by rising inflation and increases in taxes to pay for unification. **26.** President Cossiga of Italy resigned because, with only ten weeks remaining of his term of office, he lacked the authority to broker the formation of a new government. The exiled King Michael of Romania was welcomed by thousands of royalists when he returned to Bucharest for the first time since 1947. **27.** The German government came under increased strain with the resignation of the veteran foreign minister Hans-Dietrich Genscher, and the start of an all-out national public service strike. The strike continued until 7 May, when the unions accepted improved pay offers.

MAY 1992

15. The German federal government agreed with the 16 Länder to amend the constitution to guarantee the Länder a veto on any transfer of sovereignty to the EC. **18.** Czechoslovakia launched a mass privatization campaign of hundreds of state companies. **22.** Poland and Russian signed an agreement providing for the withdrawal of former Soviet troops from Poland by 15 November 1992. **24.** Thomas Klestil, of the People's Party, was elected President of Austria. **25.** Oscar Scalfaro was elected President of Italy.

JUNE 1992

5. The Polish government of Prime Minister Jan Olszewski was voted out of office by the Polish parliament; Waldemar Pawlak became the new Prime Minister. **6.** Federal and republication elections in Czechoslovakia produced a stalemate, pro-independence parties winning in Slovakia and pro-federal parties in the Czech lands. **17.** The Czech leader Vaclav Klaus and the Slovak leader Vladimar Meciar provisionally agreed to form an interim federal government. **19.** Vaclav Klaus and Vladimar Meciar signed an agreement in Bratislavia to dissolve the Czechoslovak state and form two independent states. The member states of the Western European Union agreed to assign forces to WEU command to take part in peace-keeping operations. **28.** Italian Prime Minister-designate Giuliano Amato announced his new Cabinet.

JULY 1992

1. President Havel approved a much smaller federal government in Czechoslovakia, widely seen as an interim administration to oversee the country's division. French lorry drivers used their vehicles to block motorways and main roads throughout France in protest at a new penalty system for driving offences. The blockades lasted for a week, causing chaos. **3.** Slovak nationalist deputies in the Czechoslovak federal parliament prevented the re-election of President Havel. **8.** President Walesa nominated Hanna Suchocka as Prime Minister-designate of Poland after Waldemar Pawlak failed to form a Cabinet. **17.** President Havel of Czechoslovakia resigned after Slovak deputies voted to declare their republic a sovereign state. **26.** The Italian government sent troops to Sicily to reinforce police efforts to combat increased Mafia violence. **28.** The new Italian government forced an emergency bill through parliament to cut the federal budget and raise revenue in order to stop the country from going bankrupt. **29.** Former East German leader Erich Honeker was forced to leave the Chilean Embassy in Moscow and was handed over to German officials. He was flown to Berlin to face manslaughter charges over the killing of people who had tried to escape from East Germany over the Berlin Wall.

AUGUST 1992

26. Czech and Slovak leaders agreed in talks in Brno to divide Czechoslovakia into two separate states on 1 January 1993.

THE FORMER SOVIET UNION

SEPTEMBER 1991

3. In Moldova, the Russian-speaking Dnestr region declared independence as the Dnestr Soviet Socialist Republic. **5.** The Soviet Congress of People's Deputies approved the interim government of a State Council, a reformed parliament and an interim economic committee. **6.** The State Council recognized the independence of Estonia, Latvia and Lithuania. The Russian Soviet confirmed the renaming of Leningrad as St Petersburg. **8.** Ayaz Mutalibov was elected President of Azerbaijan. **9.** Tajikistan declared independence from the Soviet Union. **21.** Armenia voted in a referendum to secede from the Soviet Union; independence was declared on 23 September. **23.** In a Communist counter-coup, Rakhom Nabiyev was declared President of Tajikistan by the republic's parliament. **24.** A state of emergency was declared in Georgia as opposition forces continued to demand the resignation of President Gamsakhurdia.

OCTOBER 1991

9. The Chenchen-Ingush autonomous republic of Russia declared itself independent of Russia after a coup led by Gen. Jokhar Dudayev. **11.** The Council of State of the Soviet Union voted to dissolve the KGB. **18.** Eight of the 12 Soviet republics signed an agreement on economic co-operation. **28.** Unofficial elections in the Chenchen-Ingush autonomous republic of Russia resulted in a landslide victory for Gen. Dudayev.

NOVEMBER 1991

1. President Yeltsin of Russia was granted emergency powers by the Congress of People's Deputies to enable him to introduce radical economic reforms. **5.** The World Bank agreed to advance the Soviet Union £17 million-worth of technical assistance. **6.** The Ukraine and Moldova signed the economic co-operation agreement signed by other republics on 18 October. **8.** President Yeltsin declared emergency rule in the secessionist Chenchen-Ingush region. **9.** President Yeltsin sent paratroopers to Chenchen-Ingush to force Gen. Dudayev to stand down. **10.** After a confrontation in Chenchen-Ingush, the troops sent by President Yeltsin were forced to withdraw. **13.** The dissolution of the Soviet Union continued; it was announced that its gold reserves and national debt would be divided among the republics. **14.** President Gorbachev and seven republican leaders agreed in principle to form a new state, the Union of Sovereign States (USS). **19.** Eduard Shevardnadze was appointed Soviet foreign minister by President Gorbachev. **21.** The eight Soviet republics that had agreed to share responsibility for the Soviet Union's debt were granted emergency financing and debt repayment referral by the G7 countries. **22.** The Russian republic took over the Soviet Central Bank and claimed the sole right to exercise monetary, credit and currency policy in its territory. **24.** Rakman Nabiyev was elected President of Tajikistan. **25.** In Moldova pro-Soviet ethnic Russians and Ukrainians in the self-proclaimed republic of Transdnestr announced that they would hold elections separately from the rest of the republic.

DECEMBER 1991

1. The Ukraine voted for independence from the Soviet Union. **3.** President Gorbachev appealed to the Soviet parliament and people to prevent the disintegration of the Union. **8.** The Soviet Union effectively ceased to exist when the leaders of Russia, the Ukraine and Belarus, meeting in Minsk, created a Commonwealth of Independent States. **9.** President Gorbachev refused to resign and refused to recognize the new Commonwealth. **12.** The Russian Parliament endorsed the new Commonwealth of Independent states. The Ukrainian President, Leonid Kravchuk, declared himself commander-in-chief of all non-strategic forces located in the Ukraine. **13.** Leaders of the five Central Asian republics agreed to join the new Commonwealth. **17.** Presidents Gorbachev and Yeltsin agreed to complete the transfer of remaining Soviet powers to the new Commonwealth of Independent States (CIS) by the end of December. **19.** President Yeltsin issued decrees abolishing the Soviet foreign and interior ministries and creating a Russian ministry of security and the interior. NATO foreign ministers agreed to co-ordinate emergency food, medical and other aid to the Soviet Union. **21.** The presidents of eight ex-Soviet republics signed the accession of their republics to the Commonwealth of Independent States; only Georgia failed to join. **22.** In Tbilisi, Georgia, armed opposition groups attacked the parliament and government buildings in an attempt to oust President Gamsakhurdia. **25.** Soviet President Mikhail Gorbachev resigned and the Soviet Union officially ceased to exist. Control of the Soviet Union's strategic nuclear weapons was handed to Russia. President Gamsakhurdia of Georgia appealed for Western help to lift a siege of the parliament by armed opposition forces as heavy fighting between rebels and troops loyal to the President continued in Tbilisi. **26.** At a meeting in Moscow of the defence ministers of the new Commonwealth, disagreements emerged between Russia and the Ukraine over control of the Black Sea fleet. **30.** Leaders of the CIS agreed to place nuclear weapons under the control of President Yeltsin, and that the Ukraine, Moldova and Azerbaijan would set up their own national armies, while the remaining eight republics would create a joint force.

JANUARY 1992

2. Rebels besieging President Gamsakhurdia in the Georgian parliament building formed a joint military council as part of an attempt to seize full government power. State control of the price of goods ended in Russia and the Ukraine. **3.** In Tbilisi, masked gunmen opened fire on unarmed demonstrators supporting President Gamsakhurdia. **6.** President Gamsakhurdia fled Tbilisi for Armenia. **9.** President Yeltsin of Russia and President Kravchuk of the Ukraine openly disagreed over control of the Black Sea fleet. **16.** President Gamsakhurdia returned to Georgia and called on supporters to take up arms against the ruling military council and provisional government. **23.** In western Georgia troops of the ruling military council clashed with armed supporters of President Gamsakhurdia, leaving 15 dead. **24.** The Russian government presented its first budget, which included an 80 per cent cut in weapons spending and the ending of many large building projects. **26.** The TASS news agency reported that 60 people had been killed in fighting between Armenians and Azerbaijanis over the disputed territory of Nagorno-Karabakh. **31.** Azerbaijani forces launched a land assault against the disputed enclave of Nagorno-Karabakh, causing the CSCE to send a fact-finding mission. President Kravchuk called for the dismissal of the head of the Black Sea fleet, Admiral Kasatonov, after Kasatonov's refusal to put the fleet under Ukrainian control.

February 1992

3. The foreign ministers of Armenia and Azerbaijan agreed in principle to meet in Moscow, as casualties mounted in the fighting in Nagorno-Karabakh. **9.** A march in Moscow of hard-line Communists protesting at economic reforms attracted 20,000 people. **10.** Operation Provide Hope began, airlifting food and medical aid to the former Soviet republics from the West. **14.** At a meeting of republican presidents in Minsk, the Ukraine, Moldova and Azerbaijan made clear their wish not to take part in the joint armed forces, and Belarus and Uzbekistan expressed reservations. **26.** In Nagorno-Karabakh, Armenian forces captured the town of Khodjaly. **28.** The commander-in-chief of the Commonwealth armed forces ordered all former Soviet forces to leave Nagorno-Karabakh as fighting continued between Armenians and Azerbaijanis.

March 1992

2. Western journalists verified Azerbaijani claims that Armenian forces had massacred Azeri civilians fleeing the town of Khodjaly; 100 were reported dead. **3.** In Moldova two people were killed and many injured in fighting between Moldovan troops and Russian and Ukrainian separatists. **10.** The former Soviet foreign minister Eduard Shevardnadze was named chairman of a new Georgian State Council. **13.** Leaders of 18 of the Russian Federation's 20 autonomous regions and republics initialled a new federation treaty granting them increased internal powers; the treaty was signed on 31 March. **15.** In Georgia armed supporters of deposed President Gamsakhurdia attacked provisional government forces. **17.** An attempt by Communist hardliners to reconvene the Soviet Congress of People's Deputies and challenge President Yeltsin's government was unsuccessful. **22.** The population of the autonomous republic of Tatarstan in the Russian Federation voted in a referendum to become an autonomous state. **29.** A state of emergency was declared in Moldova by President Snegur as a confrontation between Romanian and Russian speakers became increasingly likely.

April 1992

1. Moldovan security forces launched an attack on the town of Bendery held by the militia of the Russian-speaking Transdnestr region. **2.** A ceasefire was called in Moldova after Russian troops of the former Soviet army stationed in the republic threatened to intervene in the conflict. **13.** The Russian government offered its resignation to President Yeltsin in protest at the restrictions placed on it by the Communist-controlled Congress of People's Deputies. **15.** The Russian government withdrew its resignation after the Congress of People's Deputies was forced by President Yeltsin to vote for a continuation of radical economic reform. **17.** The Congress of People's Deputies voted to give the republic two names: Russia and the Russian Federation.

May 1992

5. The Crimean parliament declared the independence of the Crimea from the Ukraine, subject to a referendum. **6.** Pro- and anti-government forces fought for control of Dushanbe, capital of Tajikistan; at least 20 people died. The remaining tactical nuclear weapons on Ukrainian, Belarussian and Kazakhstan soil were transferred to the Russian republic. **7.** An alliance of democrats and Muslim fundamentalists overthrew the government of President Nabiyev in Tajikistan. President Yeltsin announced the creation of Russia's own armed forces, with himself as commander-in-chief; he had become defence minister on 16 March. **9.** Armenian forces captured Shusha, the last remaining Azeri stronghold in Nagorno-Karabakh. **15.** The Popular Front movement in Azerbaijan stormed the parliament and the presidential palace in Baku and took power from President Mutalibov. **19.** Armenian forces broke through Azerbaijani defences to create a territorial link between the Nagorno-Karabakh enclave and Armenia. **21.** The Crimean parliament voted to suspend its declaration of independence from the Ukraine; the Russian parliament declared invalid the 1954 transfer of the Crimea from Russia to the Ukraine.

June 1992

7. Abulfaz Elchibey was elected President of Azerbaijan and promised to withdraw the state from the CIS. **22.** President Yeltsin of Russia and President Snegur of Moldova agreed on an immediate ceasefire in the Transdnestr region of Moldova. **23.** Ethnic Russian leaders in the Transdnestr region of Moldova announced they would seek full independence from Moldova. **24.** President Yeltsin of Russia and the Georgian leader Eduard Schevardnadze signed an agreement intended to end the violence in the South Ossetia region of Georgia. An attempt by armed supporters of ex-President Gamsakhurdia to launch a coup in Tbilisi against Eduard Schevardnadze was unsuccessful.

JULY 1992

6. Leaders of the CIS agreed to the formation of a joint peace-keeping force to be deployed in areas of inter-ethnic disputes within the CIS.

AUGUST 1992

3. President Yeltsin of Russia and President Kravchuk of Ukraine reached agreement on joint command and control of the Black Sea Fleet for a period of three years. **7.** The US Congress approved the provision of over £8 billion of aid for Russia. **14.** Azerbaijani forces fired rockets at Stepanakert, the capital of Nagorno-Karabakh, killing and wounding large numbers of people. Government forces in Georgia launched an offensive against armed supporters of ex-President Gamsakhurdia, who had taken control of the Abkhazia region. **19.** President Yeltsin announced a mass privatization programme, involving the distribution of vouchers to the population from 1 October 1992.

THE FORMER YUGOSLAVIA

SEPTEMBER 1991

2. An EC-brokered cease-fire agreement was signed by opposing forces in Yugoslavia. **3.** Lord Carrington was appointed to chair an EC-sponsored peace conference. **7.** The EC-sponsored peace conference opened in the Hague, the Netherlands; sporadic fighting continued in Yugoslavia. **8.** In a referendum, the republic of Macedonia voted in favour of independence but reserved the right to rejoin a renewed Yugoslav federation. **17.** Another cease-fire between Croats and Serbs was negotiated by Lord Carrington but was quickly broken. **20.** Serbian forces launched their largest offensive since serious conflict began in June 1991. The federal defence minister, Veljko Kadijevic, refused to submit his resignation, requested by the federal Prime Minister. **25.** The UN approved a mandatory arms embargo on Yugoslavia.

OCTOBER 1991

2. Federal armed forces bombarded Dubrovnik. **3.** Four members of the federal Presidency (Serbia, Montenegro, Kosovo and Vojvodina) usurped the powers of the Presidency. **8.** Croatia and Slovenia announced full independence from Yugoslavia. **9.** Serbian, Croatian and federal army leaders met in the Hague and agreed another cease-fire. **10.** Fierce fighting continued in the beseiged Croatian town of Vukovar. **11.** An EC relief convoy failed to reach Vukovar after being attacked by Serbian irregulars. **14.** The peace conference resumed in the Netherlands. **15.** Bosnia-Hercegovina declared itself a sovereign state. **25.** Federal armed forces completed their withdrawal from Slovenia. **27.** A federal army ultimatum calling on Croatian forces in Dubrovnik to surrender expired without a Croatian reply. **28.** The EC gave Serbia until 5 November to accept a peace plan or face economic sanctions.

NOVEMBER 1991

1. The federal army stepped up its attack on Dubrovnik. **4.** Serbia rejected an EC ultimatum to agree to the latest peace initiative. **5.** Croatian armed forces launched their first attack on Serbia with an artillery barrage of the town of Sid. **6.** The federal air force in Croatia bombed advancing Croatian forces. **8.** The EC imposed economic and trade sanctions against the whole of Yugoslavia and suspended the peace conference in the Hague. **10.** Croatian authorities appealed for a cease-fire as the federal army and navy bombardment of Dubrovnik continued. **13.** Croatian forces withdrew from Srdj, overlooking Dubrovnik, leaving Dubrovnik indefensible. **14.** Refugees and the EC cease-fire monitors left Dubrovnik by ferry. **17.** After an 86-day battle and siege, Vukovar fell to federal and Serbian forces. **20.** The federal army began to shell Osijek, in eastern Croatia. **23.** The UN special envoy in Yugoslavia, Cyrus Vance, brokered a new cease-fire but Serbian and federal forces continued to bombard Osijek.

DECEMBER 1991

2. The EC dropped its economic and trade sanctions against all Yugoslav republics except Serbia and Montenegro. **6.** Heavy fighting resumed throughout Croatia, ending the cease-fire of 23 November. The USA imposed trade sanctions against all Yugoslav republics. **9.** Representatives of the warring parties met at the Hague to discuss resuming the peace conference. The federal navy lifted its blockade of Dubrovnik to allow aid to reach the town. **12.** The Serbian government resigned after criticism by opposition parties about the conduct and cost of the war. **15.** The UN Security Council voted unanimously to send a group to Yugoslavia to prepare for a peace-keeping operation. **16.** EC foreign ministers announced that they had agreed to recognize the independence of Croatia and Slovenia by 15 January. **20.** The federal Prime Minister, Ante Markovic, a Croat, resigned after 86 per cent of the federal budget for the forthcoming year was allocated to the army to pay for the war. Bosnia-Hercegovina's Presidency voted to ask for EC diplomatic recognition. **26.** The central Croatian town of Karlovac was shelled by Serbian and federal army forces.

JANUARY 1992

1. The UN special envoy Cyrus Vance brokered a new cease-fire and an agreement in principle to the deployment of UN peace-keeping troops. **3.** Fighting across Croatia died down after the UN-brokered cease-fire came into effect. **7.** Five EC observers were killed when their helicopter was shot down by a federal air force jet. **8.** The EC monitoring mission said that the 200 EC cease-fire observers were suspending their activities until the federal army provided guarantees of their safety. **9.** Serbs in Bosnia-Hercegovina declared their own republic, in reaction to the Presidency's decision to seek EC recognition of Bosnia-Hercegovina as an independent state. **15.** The EC recognized Croatia and Slovenia as independent states. **20.** Leaders in the Serbian areas in Croatia refused to accept UN peace-keeping forces in their territory, or to disarm Serbian fighters in the area. **21.** Serbia announced plans to create a new Yugoslav state, inviting to join them any other areas of the former Yugoslavia that wished to. **29.** The UN special envoy Marrick Goulding said that he could not recommend sending peace-keeping troops to Yugoslavia as the agreement of all parties to the peace plan had not been gained.

FEBRUARY 1992

2. Leaders of Serb enclaves in Croatia were persuaded to accept the UN peace plan and the deployment of UN forces. **5.** The UN Secretary-General reported to the Security Council that the conditions for establishing a UN peace-keeping force in Yugoslavia still did not exist. **21.** The UN Security Council voted to send 13,000 UN peace-keeping troops to three Serbian enclaves in Croatia.

MARCH 1992

1. Voters in Bosnia-Hercegovina voted overwhelmingly in a referendum for the republic's independence from Yugoslavia. Voters in Montenegro voted to form a new Yugoslavia in alliance with Serbia. **2.** Violent clashes occurred in the Bosnian capital Sarajevo between militant Serbs, and Muslims and Croats. **9.** In Belgrade 25,000 people attended a rally demanding the resignation of President Milosevic and the Serbian government because of its poor conduct of the war against Croatia. **27.** Nineteen people were killed in clashes between Muslims, Croats and Serbs in northern Bosnia.

APRIL 1992

1. The presidents of all six former Yugoslav republics agreed to end legal and physical trade barriers between them. **3.** President Izetbegovic of Bosnia-Hercegovina appealed for UN intervention to prevent civil war. **5.** In Bosnia-Hercegovina, artillery clashes and air attacks involving Serb, Croat, Muslim and federal armed forces left hundreds of people dead. **7.** The EC formally recognized the independence of Bosnia-Hercegovina; fighting escalated in the republic, with the federal air force aiding Serb forces. **8.** Serb and federal army forces launched an artillery bombardment of Sarajevo as the Bosnian government declared a state of emergency. **10.** President Izetbegovic of Bosnia appealed for international intervention as Serbian forces blockaded Sarajevo. **12.** Ethnic leaders in Bosnia-Hercegovina agreed to a cease-fire in EC-sponsored talks. **21.** Heavy fighting broke out in Sarajevo as Serbian forces attacked Muslims and Croats defending the city. **22.** Serbian forces were driven out of central Sarajevo by Muslim and Croat forces. **27.** Serbia and Montenegro announced the formation of a new Yugoslav state comprising their two republics.

MAY 1992

1. The federal army took President Izetbegovic prisoner and said that he would only be released if a cease-fire was agreed. **3.** After a brief cease-fire to allow the release of President Izetbegovic, fighting continued in Sarajevo. **8.** President Milosevic of Serbia dismissed 38 generals and the acting defence minister in an attempt to gain control of the army. **11.** Heavy fighting throughout Bosnia-Hercegovina left 28 people dead and forced 40,000 Muslim and Croat refugees to flee from Serbian forces. The EC member states agreed to recall their ambassadors from Belgrade and called on the federal army to withdraw from Bosnia-Hercegovina. **14.** The commander of the UN peace-keeping troops in Yugoslavia, General Nambiar, was trapped in Sarajevo by fierce shelling and fighting. **15.** The UN Security Council demanded the withdrawal of all federal and Croatian forces from Bosnia-Hercegovina and a halt to all fighting. **21.** The Yugoslav federal army suspended its withdrawal from eastern Croatia, which it was due to hand over to UN forces, because of alleged Croatian artillery attacks. **22.** Slovenia, Croatia and Bosnia-Hercegovina were formally admitted to membership of the UN. **25.** Ibrahim Rugova was elected president of the Kosovo region of Serbia by the mainly Albanian population, in defiance of the Serbian government. **26.** The EC agreed on a total trade embargo against Serbia. **29.** Serbian and federal forces launched artillery bombardments on Sarajevo and Dubrovnik despite growing international condemnation. **30.** The UN Security Council imposed a ban on trade, air and sporting links and an oil embargo on the new Yugoslav state (i.e. Serbia and Montenegro) because of continuing Serbian aggression in Bosnia-Hercegovina. **31.** The Socialist party of President Milosevic won elections held in the new Yugoslav state; the elections were boycotted by opposition parties.

JUNE 1992

8. Muslim forces under siege in Sarajevo counter-attacked Serbian positions for the first time. **15.** Muslim and Croat forces recaptured the Bosnian city of Mostar from Serbian forces after three months of fighting. **17.** Serbian forces renewed attacks on Sarajevo, breaking the two-day-old cease-fire. **22.** Muslim women and children refugees arrived in central Sarajevo after escaping from the Serbian 'ethnic cleansing' and killing of Muslim men in the suburb of Dobrinja. **23.** The UN commander, General Nambiar, warned that Croatian forces were beginning to seize land in UN-protected areas in Croatia. **26.** The UN Secretary-General told Serbian forces attacking Sarajevo to end hostilities within 48 hours or face possible UN military action. **28.** Crown Prince Alexander, the exiled heir to the Serbian throne, led a rally in Belgrade of 60,000 opposition supporters calling for the Milosevic government to resign. **29.** Serbian forces withdrew from Sarajevo airport as the UN Security Council ordered 1,000 troops from Croatia to Sarajevo to reopen the airport.

JULY 1992

2. UN troops began arriving at Sarajevo airport to secure it for relief flights, which began on 3 June. **5.** Croat leaders in Bosnia-Hercegovina announced the formation of a separate state in western and northern regions called Herceg-Bosnia. **12.** The first UN aid convoy reached the besieged Sarajevo suburb of Dobrinja. **13.** The strategically important eastern Bosnian town of Goradze came under intense artillery and air bombardment by ethnic Serbian forces. **14.** The new Yugoslav Prime Minister, Milan Panic, declared that he would respect the independence of Bosnia-Hercegovina. The UN soldiers defending Sarajevo airport shot dead a Serbian sniper. **15.** Peace negotiations between ethnic Serb, Croat and Muslim Bosnian leaders opened under the chairmanship of Lord Carrington in London; Serbian troops intensified attacks on Goradze. **22.** The Presidents of Bosnia-Hercegovina and Croatia signed a military co-operation pact. **29.** An international conference on the plight of Yugoslav refugees opened in Geneva. **31.** Five UN soldiers were seriously injured in a mortar attack on their observation post outside Sarajevo.

AUGUST 1992

4. Sarajevo airport was closed for three days by Serbian shelling. **6.** Evidence emerged of the execution and beating of Bosnians in Serbian-run camps in Bosnia. **7.** As television pictures publicized conditions in Serbian camps in Bosnia, the Yugoslav Prime Minister Milan Panic promised to use his influence with Bosnian Serb leaders to close the camps within 30 days. **13.** The UN Security Council passed resolution authorizing the use of force to protect aid convoys in Bosnia-Hercegovina and condemning 'ethnic cleansing' as a war crime. **15.** A UN relief convoy reached Goradze, breaking a four-month Serbian siege of the Muslim-held town. **20.** Sarajevo came under intense artillery and mortar attack by Serbian forces. **21.** A UN base in Sarajevo was repeatedly hit during fighting between Serbian and Muslim forces. **25.** Lord Carrington resigned as chairman of the EC peace effect. **26.** The London Conference on Yugoslavia opened with warnings by co-chairmen John Major and Boutros Ghali to Serbia that it faced further sanctions and international isolation unless it renounced territory won by war. **27.** The London Conference closed, having achieved detailed agreements to solve the conflict in stages, including the lifting of the sieges of Sarajevo and other cities, UN supervision of heavy weapons, the return and compensation of refugees, the withdrawal of Bosnian Serbs from substantial portions of occupied territory, and the recognition of Bosnia-Hercegovina and its borders. **28.** Heavy fighting continued in Sarajevo, with no sign of any attempts to comply with the London peace agreements. **30.** Fifteen people were killed and 50 wounded when an artillery shell exploded amid a bread queue in Sarajevo; Serbian forces lifted the siege of Goradze, in line with the London peace agreements.

EUROPEAN COMMUNITY

SEPTEMBER 1991

6. EC plans to reduce tariffs on agricultural imports from Czechoslovakia, Hungary and Poland were vetoed by France. **12.** The Prime Minister (John Major) proposed the extension of full membership of the EC to the states of eastern Europe and eventually the Soviet republics. **21.** EC finance ministers informally agreed to create a single European currency and central bank when the economies of seven member states had converged sufficiently. **26.** The Commission began legal action against the British government for failing to carry out environmental impact assessments on several large construction projects. **30.** EC foreign ministers rejected a Dutch draft treaty on political union.

OCTOBER 1991

4. Britain and Italy presented a paper on future European defence, proposing that the Western European Union should be the defence arm of the EC, while NATO would remain the main guarantor of European security. **7.** The EC agreed an aid package of £14 billion for the Soviet Union. **10.** The European Parliament voted to increase the number of German MEPs from 81 to 99 to take account of German unification. **15.** President Mitterand and Chancellor Kohl called for a more ambitious European defence identity and the incorporation of the WEU into the Community. **22.** The EC and EFTA agreed to extend the single market to include the EFTA states, creating a European Economic Area. **28.** In economic and monetary union negotiations, the UK government secured the right to keep the pound sterling if it so wished.

NOVEMBER 1991

10. The Prime Minister held talks in Bonn with Chancellor Kohl, the first of a series of meetings with European leaders prior to the summit meeting in Maastricht. **13.** EC foreign ministers ended a two-day meeting in the Netherlands with four issues still unresolved: the social charter, majority voting on foreign policy, immigration policy, and the single currency.

DECEMBER 1991

9. The Maastricht summit on European political and monetary union began. The meeting concluded on 11 December with agreement on the political treaty and the economic and monetary treaty (*see* below); a protocol on social and employment policy was agreed by all member states except the UK. The treaties were signed in Maastricht on 7 February 1992. **14.** The European Court of Justice rejected the EC's European Economic Area agreement with the EFTA states as not compatible with the Treaty of Rome. **16.** The EC signed association agreements with Hungary, Poland and Czechoslovakia covering political and trade issues.

MAASTRICHT AGREEMENT

The main points of the agreement were:

Economic and Monetary Union (EMU) Treaty, stage three:

- A majority of EC members' economies to have converged sufficiently by 31 December 1996 for stage three to begin
- European Central Bank to be established by 1 July 1998
- A single EC currency to be introduced by 1 January 1999
- Special protocol agreed allowing the UK to 'opt out' of the single currency if it so wishes in January 1999

Political Union Treaty:

- The word 'federal' dropped from the preamble to the treaty
- Greater powers for the European Parliament over EC legislation
- An agreement to move towards common foreign and defence policies
- The Western European Union to become the defence component of the EC
- The introduction of two new 'pillars' in the Community, one to deal with foreign and security policy and one to deal with immigration, asylum and policing. Decision-making in these two new 'pillars' to be based on the Council of Ministers, minimizing the roles of the Commission, Parliament and European Court in these areas.

JANUARY 1992

1. Portugal took over the presidency of the EC. **15.** The EC recognized the independence of Slovenia and Croatia. **29.** Hungary announced that it would apply for EC membership soon and would like to negotiate entry jointly with Sweden and Austria.

FEBRUARY 1992

12. The President of the European Commission, Jacques Delors, presented a draft budget to the European Parliament, calling for the proposed 30 per cent increase in the Community's budget to be financed by increases in members' contributions. **14.** EC and EFTA negotiators reached a new agreement on a 19-nation single market (*see* 14 December). **28.** The European Court of Justice ruled that almost all EC legislation since 1957 could be invalid because of a technicality over signatures.

MARCH 1992

18. Finland applied to join the EC.

APRIL 1992

5. Portugal joined the exchange rate mechanism of the European monetary system. **7.** The European Parliament voted to accept the Maastricht treaties agreed in December 1991. **10.** The European Court of Justice ruled that the European Economic Area agreement between the EC and EFTA states could go ahead without infringing EC law.

MAY 1992

3. The member states of EFTA and the EC signed the European Economic Area agreement which will extend the single European market to the EFTA states when it comes into force on 1 January 1993. **11.** The UK government rejected the EC Commission's demands that it abandon border controls and insisted on its right to retain passport controls. **12.** The Queen addressed the European Parliament in Strasbourg for the first time. **18.** The Swiss federal government voted to recommend to parliament that the country apply to join the EC. **20.** EC agriculture ministers agreed on a fundamental reform of the Common Agricultural Policy, including extensive cuts in the farm price support system and taking 15 per cent of arable land out of production. **22.** France and Germany announced the creation of a joint military corps of two divisions, 35,000 strong and based in Strasbourg, to provide the EC with its own military capacity.

JUNE 1992

2. In a referendum the Danish electorate voted by a narrow majority to reject the Maastrict treaties on economic and monetary and political union. **3.** A referendum in France on the Maastrict treaties was announced. **9.** EC finance ministers rejected Commission proposals for a large increase in the EC budget. **19.** In a referendum the Irish electorate voted by 69 per cent to 31 per cent in favour of the Maastrict treaties. **27.** The Lisbon heads of government summit ended without agreement on the budget or the EC's enlargement, but Jacques Delors was confirmed in office for a further two-year term. **29.** The EC environment commissioner Carlo Ripa di Meana resigned to join the new Italian cabinet.

JULY 1992

1. The UK took over the presidency of the EC. **2.** The Luxembourg parliament ratified the Maastrict treaties. **27.** The EC finance ministers agreed that the minimum rate of VAT in member states should be 15 per cent until the end of 1996. **31.** The Greek parliament ratified the Maastrict treaties.

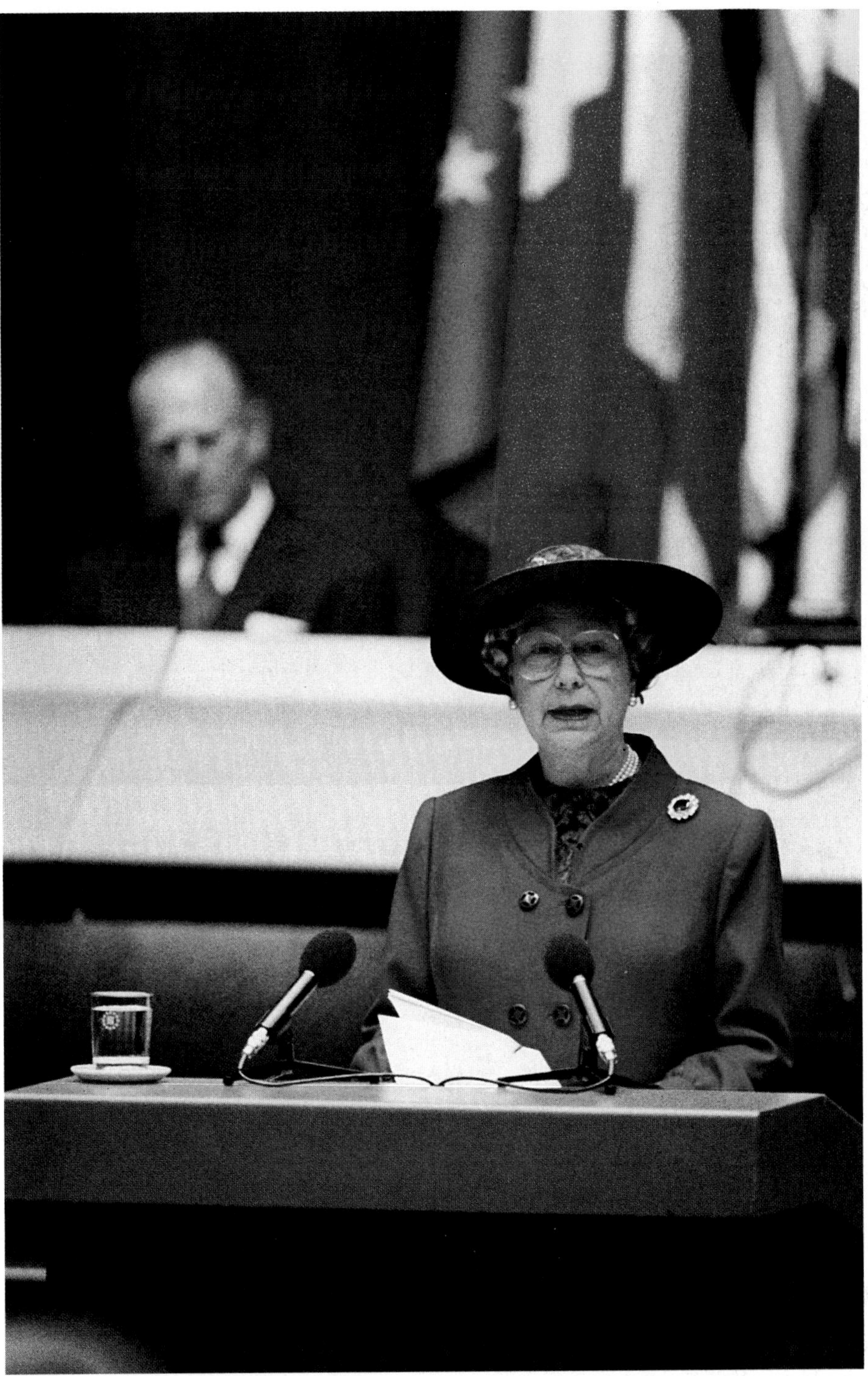

THE QUEEN IN STRASBOURG

In May 1992 The Queen addressed the European Parliament in Strasbourg for the first time since Britain joined the European Community in 1973 *(AFP)*

THE MAASTRICHT SUMMIT

European Community heads of government met in Maastricht, the Netherlands, in December 1991 and reached agreement on the next stages of political, economic and monetary union *(Rex Features)*

Following the General Election in April 1992 John Major (left) was returned to No. 10, and Betty Boothroyd was elected the first woman Speaker of the House of Commons *(Rex Features)*

The Labour Party leader Neil Kinnock (left) stood down and was replaced in July 1992 by John Smith *(Rex Features)*

IRA Bombings

An IRA bomb in the City of London in April 1992 killed three people and destroyed the Baltic Exchange *(Rex Features)*

Financial Troubles

Kevin and Ian Maxwell faced criminal charges after fraud and corruption within Maxwell companies were uncovered following their father's death in November 1991 *(Rex Features)*

Lloyd's 'names' faced heavy losses after the Lloyd's syndicates suffered their worst-ever trading results *(Simon Walker/The Times, London)*

Dr Boutros Ghali (left) became the UN Secretary-General in January 1992. Terry Waite, the last British hostage in Lebanon, was released in November 1991 *(Rex Features)*

Bill Clinton (left), for the Democrats, challenged the incumbent Republican president George Bush in the American presidential election in November 1992 *(Rex Features)*

THE LOS ANGELES RIOTS

Three days of rioting broke out in Los Angeles in April 1992 after white policemen were acquitted of beating a black motorist, in spite of a videotaped recording of the incident *(Rex Features)*

MIDDLE EAST PEACE CONFERENCE

A peace conference on the Middle East, in which all the states in the region participated, met for the first time in Madrid in October 1991 *(Rex Features)*

THE GULF

Tension between Iraq and the West increased in August 1992 when the USA, Britain and France established an air exclusion zone in southern Iraq to protect the Shias. Britain sent six Tornados to police the zone *(Chris Harris/The Times, London)*

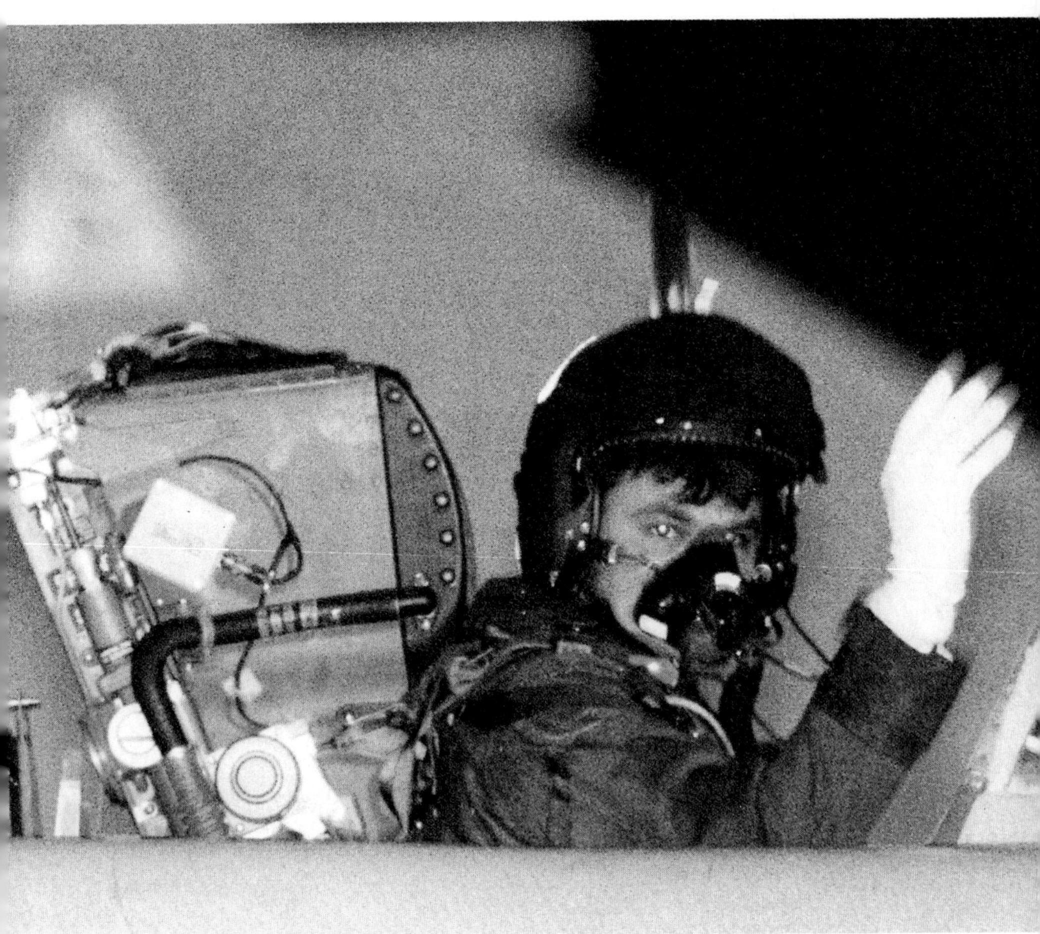

Yugoslavia

Ethnic conflict in Yugoslavia in 1991 led to the dissolution of the country into its constituent republics amid widespread destruction *(Rex Features)*

Yugoslavia

Atrocities by all sides in the Yugoslav conflict included 'ethnic cleansing' and the establishment of concentration camps *(Rex Features)*

SOUTH AFRICA

Attempts to negotiate a racially-integrated democratic constitution in South Africa were disrupted by continuing violence including the Boipatong massacre in June and the Ciskei massacre (below) in September 1992 *(AFP)*

FAMINE IN AFRICA

Famine was widespread in eastern and southern Africa in 1992, aggravated in Somalia by continuing civil war which hampered relief efforts *(Rex Features)*

Deaths during the year included those of Lord Cheshire (top left), Marlene Dietrich (top right), Freddie Mercury (bottom left) and Olivier Messiaen *(Rex Features)*

Sporting Success

Nigel Mansell became the Formula One grand prix champion in August 1992; on his way to the title he became the first driver to win the first five races in a season and notched up a British record number of wins *(Rex Features)*

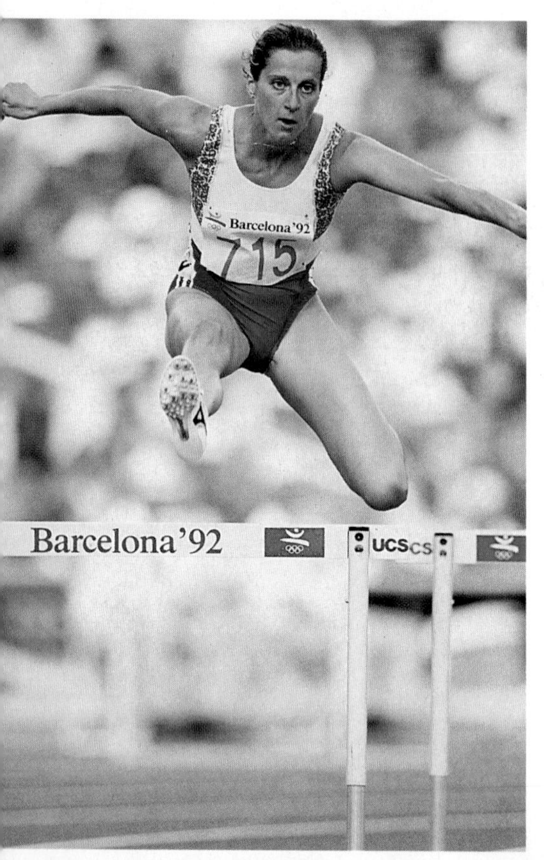

Olympic Success

Sally Gunnell (left), winner of the 400 metres hurdles, and Linford Christie, winner of the 100 metres, were among the British gold medallists in Barcelona *(Allsport/Rex Features)*

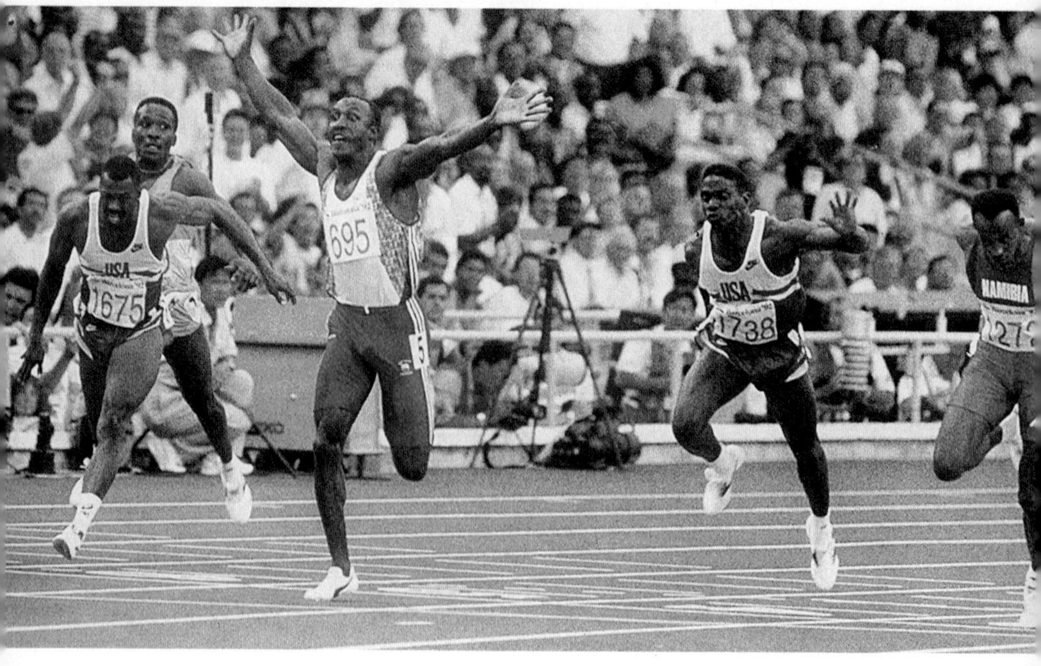

MIDDLE EAST

SEPTEMBER 1991

11. The Israeli government released 51 Muslim guerrillas and the bodies of nine guerrillas killed in fighting with Israeli forces. **12.** President Bush of the USA said that he would veto $10 billion in loans for housing for Soviet Jewish immigrants if the Israelis did not stop the construction of new settlements in the Occupied Territories for 120 days. **14.** Saadoun Hammadi was dismissed as Prime Minister of Iraq and replaced by Muhammad Hamza al Zubaidi. **19.** The UN Security Council voted to authorize the sale of $1 billion of Iraqi oil over the next six months. It also demanded that UN inspection teams be allowed unrestricted access to Iraq. **23.** In Iraq, a UN inspection team found evidence of an Iraqi nuclear weapons programme; the team was arrested by Iraqi troops but later released. **24.** In Iraq, the UN inspection team was detained for a second time in a Baghdad car park. **28.** The Palestine Liberation Organization (PLO) agreed to participate in the Middle East peace conference.

OCTOBER 1991

1. Iraq allowed a new UN inspection team to search for and to destroy Scud missile sites. **11.** The UN Security Council unanimously adopted a resolution prohibiting Iraq from any nuclear activity. The seventh team of UN and IAEA inspectors arrived in Iraq to search for nuclear weapons sites. **18.** Israel and the Soviet Union restored diplomatic relations. **20.** In the Turkish general election the ruling Motherland party was defeated by the True Path party. **21.** Israel released 15 Lebanese Shiite detainees. **25.** Turkey launched three days of commando and air attacks against Kurds in northern Iraq after an alleged Kurdish attack on a Turkish frontier post. **30.** The Middle East peace conference sponsored by the USA and the Soviet Union opened in Madrid, with Israel, Syria, Lebanon, Jordan and the Palestinians the main participants.

NOVEMBER 1991

3. The second phase of the Madrid conference opened with bilateral talks between Israeli delegations and Syrian, Lebanese, and Jordanian-Palestinian delegations. **14.** Arrest warrants were issued in the USA and in Scotland for two Libyans alleged to be responsible for the Lockerbie bombing in 1988. **15.** Libya rejected a British request for the extradition of the two men accused of the Lockerbie bombing. **20.** In Turkey the True Path and Social Democratic parties formed a coalition government. **24.** A British businessman, Ian Richter, was released after being imprisoned in Baghdad in July 1986 for bribery. **29.** Libya announced that it would hold an investigation into British and American charges that Libyans planted the Lockerbie bomb.

DECEMBER 1991

3. President Assad of Syria was re-elected for a fourth term. **4.** The second round of Middle East peace talks opened and closed in 20 minutes in Washington DC because of the refusal of the Israelis to attend until 9 December. **10.** The Middle East peace conference reopened in Washington DC; Israeli delegations met Syrian and Lebanese delegations but refused to meet separate Jordanian and Palestinian delegations. **12.** The two Libyans accused of planting the Lockerbie bomb declared their innocence. **18.** The peace conference in Washington ended. **30.** A car bomb exploded in west Beirut killing at least 30 people and injuring over 100.

JANUARY 1992

2. The Israeli government won a crucial budget vote in parliament, but at the expense of concessions to right-wing and religious parties over extra housing for settlers in the Occupied Territories. **13.** The Middle East peace conference resumed in Washington after a procedural wrangle over Israeli-Palestinian negotiations was solved by the Israelis negotiating with two sub-committees. **15.** The right-wing Tehiya party decided to withdraw from the Israeli coalition government over the peace conference in Washington; the Moledet party followed within a few days, leaving the Israeli government without a majority in the Knesset. **16.** The peace conference in Washington ended after three days of inconclusive talks, the Israeli negotiators' mandate being weakened by the breakdown of the Israeli coalition government. **21.** The UN adopted a resolution calling on Libya to hand over the two men accused of planting the Lockerbie bomb. **28.** The Moscow round of the peace conference opened without the Syrian or Lebanese delegations; it almost collapsed after the Israeli delegation refused to negotiate with Palestinians from outside the Occupied Territories. Libyan officials said that they were prepared to hand over the Lockerbie suspects to an independent international commission. **29.** The peace conference in Moscow reached a stalemate over the membership of the Palestinian delegation.

FEBRUARY 1992

6. Iraq rejected a UN plan for long-term monitoring of its arms industry and refused to resume talks with the UN about using receipts from its oil sales to pay for humanitarian aid. **11.** Kuwait and Britain signed a defence pact. **16.** In southern Lebanon, Israeli helicopters fired rockets at the motorcade of the Hezbollah leader Sheikh Abbas Musawi, killing him and five bodyguards. **19.** Yitzhak Rabin was elected leader of the Israeli Labour party. **20.** Israeli troops advanced into southern Lebanon to destroy rockets fired by Hezbollah guerrillas into northern Israel. Yitzhak Shamir was re-elected Likud party leader. **23.** Fifteen Iraqi opposition leaders met in Saudi Arabia to try to form a united front capable of toppling Saddam Hussein's regime. **24.** The US administration renewed its threat to Israel to veto American loan guarantees if Israel did not stop building homes for Jewish settlers in the Occupied Territories. **24.** The Middle East peace conference reconvened in Washington. **26.** The Palestinian delegation at the peace talks rejected outright an Israeli proposal for Palestinian self-government which did not include ending Jewish settlement in or withdrawing the Israeli military from the Occupied Territories. **28.** Iraq refused to comply with a UN demand to allow UN officials to destroy its Scud missile-making equipment.

MARCH 1992

1. King Fahd of Saudi Arabia announced the establishment of a basic law founded on the Sharia and a consultative council, the Majlis al-Shura, of 60 appointed members. **3.** The Palestinian delegation at the peace talks in Washington presented a plan for interim self-rule in the Occupied Territories leading to a Palestinian state, which was rejected by the Israelis. **4.** The fourth round of Middle East peace talks ended in Washington without agreement between the delegations over when and where to meet next. **11.** The USA, Britain and France warned Iraq in an extraordinary session of the Security Council that they might bomb its nuclear weapons facilities if it continued to refuse to allow destruction of its weapons. **15.** A fleet of over 20 US and Royal Navy ships assembled in the Gulf for a possible air strike against Iraqi weapons production facilities. **17.** President Bush rejected a Congressional compromise allowing the provision of loan guarantees to Israel after the Israeli government refused to stop building new settlements in the Occupied Territories. **20.** Iraq agreed to comply with a UN demand to destroy equipment for making Scud missiles. **31.** The UN Security Council voted to impose sanctions on Libya, including a ban on air links and weapon sales, from 15 April because of its refusal to hand over the two Lockerbie bombing suspects, unless Libya complied before that date.

APRIL 1992

2. The UN Security Council condemned Libya after crowds in Tripoli attacked and burned the Venezuelan, Russian and some Western embassies in response to the UN Security Council vote of 31 March. **10.** In elections to the Iranian parliament, moderate supporters of President Rafsanjani won a landslide victory over Islamic radicals. **14.** The International Court of Justice rejected a Libyan attempt to prevent the UN Security Council imposing sanctions on it for failing to hand over the two Lockerbie bombing suspects. **15.** The UN Security Council's sanctions against Libya began. **16.** The UN boundary commission issued its findings on the Iraqi-Kuwait border, and moved the border some 600 metres north of the line accepted before the Gulf war. **27.** The fifth round of the Middle East peace conference began in Washington; Israel offered to hold municipal elections in the Occupied Territories.

MAY 1992

6. The Lebanese government resigned because of the country's worsening economic situation. **11.** Multilateral Middle East peace talks began on specialized issues of economic co-operation and arms control but were boycotted by the Israeli, Syrian and Lebanese delegations. **19.** The Kurds of northern Iraq elected an assembly and a political leader for the first time. **27.** In elections for the Kuwait Chamber of Commerce, opponents of the government won 24 of the 25 seats, a pointer to the result of the general election to be held in October.

JUNE 1992

2. Four days of rioting in the Iranian city of Mashad ended with 300 arrests. **23.** In the Israeli general election the Labour party won a convincing victory over the ruling Likud party. **25.** Three Israelis and three Palestinians were killed in separate incidents in the Occupied Territories.

JULY 1992

13. The new Labour-led Israeli coalition government was approved by the Knesset at its inaugural session during which the new Prime Minister, Yitzhak Rabin, invited Arab leaders to Jerusalem and offered to travel to Arab capitals. **15.** The US government warned Iraq to stop obstructing the work of UN weapons inspectors in Baghdad or face a resumption of hostilities. **16.** The new Israeli government announced a temporary ban on the signing of new building contracts in the West Bank and Gaza Strip. **21.** Yitzhak Rabin met the Egyptian President Hosni Mubarak in Cairo. **26.** Iraq finally agreed to allow a UN weapons inspection team into the ministry of agriculture building of Baghdad. **30.** The Lebanese army drove Hezbollah forces from a barracks in eastern Lebanon that they had occupied for ten years.

AUGUST 1992

5. The Israeli government announced an indefinite ban on all new private housing construction in the Occupied Territories. **11.** President Bush announced that Israel would receive the $10 billion loan guarantees previously frozen because of building in the Occupied Territories. **13.** The UN Security Council decided to maintain the embargo on air links and armaments imposed on Libya because of its failure to hand over the Lockerbie bombing suspects. **16.** Lebanese Christian leaders announced that they would be boycotting the forthcoming parliamentary elections because of the Syrian refusal to withdraw its troops from the country. **20.** Iraq announced that it had sentenced Paul Ride, a Briton who had gone missing in northern Kuwait, to seven years imprisonment for illegally entering the country. **24.** The sixth round of Middle East peace talks opened in Washington. The Speaker of Lebanon's parliament, Hussein Al-Husseini, resigned after accusing Hezbollah of cheating and ballot-rigging in the first stage of the country's general election. **27.** An air exclusion zone south of the 32nd parallel in southern Iraq was imposed by the USA, Britain and France to protect Shia Muslims from Iraqi air attacks.

RELEASE OF WESTERN HOSTAGES

8 August 1991 John McCarthy (British), after 1,943 days in captivity.
11 August 1991 Jerome Leyraud (French), after 3 days in captivity.
11 August 1991 Edward Tracy (American), after 1,758 days in captivity.
24 September 1991 Jack Mann (British), after 865 days in captivity.
21 October 1991 Jesse Turner (American), after 1,731 days in captivity.
18 November 1991 Thomas Sutherland (American), after 2,353 days in captivity.
18 November 1991 Terry Waite (British), after 1,763 days in captivity.
2 December 1991 Joseph Cicippio (American), after 1,908 days in captivity.
3 December 1991 Alann Steen (American), after 1,774 days in captivity.
4 December 1991 Terry Anderson (American), after 2,454 days in captivity.
17 June 1992 Thomas Kemptner (German), taken captive May 1989.
17 June 1992 Heinrig Struebig (German), taken captive May 1989.

INTERNATIONAL RELATIONS

SEPTEMBER 1991

11. President Gorbachev of the USSR announced that Soviet forces would be withdrawn from Cuba. **13.** The US and Soviet governments agreed to stop supplying arms to forces in Afghanistan. **17.** Estonia, Latvia, Lithuania, Micronesia, the Marshall Islands, North and South Korea became members of the UN. **28.** President Bush announced substantial unilateral cuts in the US nuclear arsenal.

OCTOBER 1991

1. The Soviet Union announced plans to cut its armed forces by almost half. **5.** At the IMF/World Bank annual meeting in Bangkok the Soviet delegation failed to secure any substantial aid but won agreement to full Soviet membership, dependent on the Union economic treaty. **6.** President Gorbachev announced the abolition of the Soviet Union's short-range nuclear weapons arsenal, and reductions of 1,000 strategic warheads and 700,000 men. **14.** The Commonwealth heads of government meeting opened in Zimbabwe. It ended on 21 October with a declaration committing members to the promotion of democracy and human rights, and an agreement to lift sporting, cultural and travel sanctions against South Africa. **17.** NATO defence ministers agreed to scrap 80 per cent of the alliance's nuclear weapons in Europe. **18.** The world's five main arms exporters (the USA, the Soviet Union, the UK, France and China) agreed guidelines for the export of conventional weapons. **29.** Presidents Bush and Gorbachev met in Madrid to discuss Western aid to the Soviet Union and arms cuts proposals.

NOVEMBER 1991

7. A two-day NATO heads of government meeting opened in Rome; the establishment was announced of a North Atlantic Co-operation Council which would include the former Warsaw Pact members and the Baltic states. **13.** The USA and the EC announced that they had reached the basis of an agreement on reducing agricultural subsidies at the GATT negotiatons. **14.** Arrest warrants were issued in Washington DC and Dumfries, Scotland, for two Libyans alleged to be responsible for the Lockerbie bombing in 1988 (*see also* Middle East). **15.** The UN voted in favour of a British proposal to create an international register of conventional arms sales.

DECEMBER 1991

6. The USA ended its ban on the sale of military equipment to Poland, Hungary and Czechoslovakia. NATO defence ministers called for an urgent meeting with Soviet officials to discuss political control of Soviet armed forces and nuclear weapons arsenals. **13.** The UN General Assembly voted unanimously to end the ban on sporting, scientific and academic links with South Africa. **16.** The UN General Assembly voted to repeal its 1975 resolution equating Zionism with racism. **20.** The GATT Secretary-General appealed to negotiators to consider his compromise proposals aimed at averting a final collapse in trade talks, as European and American negotiators failed to reach agreement. **29.** China's parliament agreed to sign the Nuclear Non-Proliferation Treaty. **31.** At a special UN Security Council meeting, President Yeltsin of Russia formally took over the former Soviet Union's seat on the Council.

JANUARY 1992

1. Boutros Boutros Ghali became UN Secretary-General on the retirement of Javier Perez de Cuellar. **21.** The UN Security Council unanimously adopted a resolution calling on Libya to hand over the two men suspected of involvement in the Lockerbie bombing. **22.** President Bush opened a 47-state conference on co-ordinating aid to the newly independent republics of the ex-Soviet Union, calling for a global coalition to sustain freedom and democracy. **27.** The French government announced its decision to sign the 1968 Nuclear Non-Proliferation Treaty. **27.** The ASEAN Free Trade Area came into being; the six member states of ASEAN announced plans to cut tariffs to a maximum of 5 per cent within ten years. **28.** President Bush announced nuclear weapons reductions, dependent on Russian reciprocation, which would leave the USA with only half the nuclear arsenal agreed in the 1991 strategic arms treaty. **29.** President Yeltsin, reacting to President Bush's offer of nuclear arms reductions, announced that 600 strategic missiles were being taken off alert, silos were being destroyed and production of long-range nuclear bombers would be curbed. **30.** Ten former Soviet republics were admitted to membership of the Conference on Security and Co-operation in Europe. **31.** Heads of state and government attended an extraordinary meeting of the UN Security Council and laid plans to transform the UN into a more active world peace-keeping body.

February 1992

3. The Black Sea Economic Co-operation Zone agreement was signed in Ankara by Turkey, Romania, Bulgaria, Russia, the Ukraine, Moldova, Georgia, Armenia and Azerbaijan. **6.** The International Atomic Energy Agency warned that four nuclear power stations, one in Bulgaria, one in Czechoslovakia and two in Russia, were in a very dangerous condition. **7.** The UN Secretary-General announced changes in the UN Secretariat, moving the focus of UN work more towards international security and peace-keeping. **9.** The US Vice-President, Dan Quayle, warned the EC that the US government intended to link progress in the GATT talks to a continued US commitment to NATO in Europe. **26.** The Canadian government announced that it intended to withdraw all of its armed forces from Europe by 1994.

March 1992

2. The former Soviet republics of Armenia, Azerbaijan, Kazakhstan, Kyrgyzstan, Moldova, Tajikistan, Turkmenistan and Uzbekistan were formally admitted to UN membership. **4.** The EC rejected proposals for cuts to agricultural subsidies made by the GATT secretariat, effectively ending any chance of an agreement on the Uruguay round of GATT in 1992. **10.** The Russian foreign minister, Andrei Kozyrev, announced that Russia was prepared to discuss the elimination of all multiple-warhead strategic missiles. **31.** The UN Security Council voted to impose sanctions on Libya, including a ban on air links and weapon sales, from 15 April because of its refusal to hand over the two Lockerbie bombing suspects, unless Libya complied by that date.

April 1992

1. The G7 group of industrialized nations announced a £14 billion aid package for the former Soviet Union. **22.** At a meeting in Washington, US and EC leaders failed to resolve the continuing deadlock in the Uruguay round of GATT talks. **27.** The Baltic states and all the former Soviet republics except Azerbaijan were accepted as members of the IMF.

May 1992

22. The three former Yugoslav republics of Slovenia, Croatia and Bosnia-Hercegovina were formally admitted to membership of the UN. **24.** The USA reached an agreement with Russia, Belarus, the Ukraine and Kazakhstan to eliminate all 3,000 strategic nuclear warheads in the three non-Russian republics in the next seven years and to reduce Russian warheads by the year 2000.

June 1992

3. The UN Conference on Environment and Development opened in Rio de Janeiro (*see* Environment). **4.** NATO foreign ministers agreed to allow the use of NATO troops as peace-keeping forces in conflicts outside member countries. **5.** The states of the former Soviet Union and the former Warsaw Pact undertook to ratify the Treaty on Conventional Forces in Europe signed in 1990. **16.** Presidents Bush and Yeltsin reached an agreement to destroy about two-thirds of US and Russian strategic nuclear arsenals over the next ten years. **17.** President Yeltsin of Russia addressed the US Congress. **19.** UN Secretary-General Boutros Ghali called for the creation of a UN army made up of national contingents on permanent standby.

July 1992

7. The G7 leaders issued a political communique from their Munich summit which stressed the importance of extending the Nuclear Non-proliferation Treaty and strengthening the UN to prevent the spread of nuclear weapons and ethnic conflicts. **8.** President Yeltsin attended the G7 summit, where G7 leaders agreed to reschedule the former Soviet Union's debt repayments and endorse a large credit facility from the IMF to Russia. **10.** The members of the CSCE agreed at their summit in Helsinki to make the organization the main authority for considering threats to European security and authorizing any military response. **13.** President Bush announced that the US would stop producing plutonium and highly-enriched uranium to halt the spread of nuclear weapons. **17.** The Conventional Forces In Europe Treaty (CFE) came into force.

Obituaries

1 SEPTEMBER 1991 – 31 AUGUST 1992

Addison, 3rd Viscount, aged 77 – 23 March 1992.
Agar, Eileen, RA, artist, aged 91 – 17 November 1991.
Allen, Harry, official chief hangman since 1956, aged 80 – 14 August 1992.
Anderson, Dame Judith, DBE, actress, aged 93 – 3 January 1992.
Arbuthnot, Sir John, Bt., MBE, Conservative MP for Dover 1950–64, aged 80 – 18 June 1992.
Arletty, French actress and singer, aged 94 – 24 July 1992.
Arlott, John, OBE, cricket commentator and journalist, aged 77 – 14 December 1991.
Ashburnham-Ruffner, Doreen, GC, aged 86 – 4 October 1991.
Asimov, Isaac, science fiction writer, aged 72 – 6 April 1992.
Audley, Maxine, actress, aged 69 – 23 July 1992.
Babington, John, GC, OBE, former bomb-disposal specialist, aged 81 – 24 March 1992.
Bacon, Francis, artist, aged 82 – 28 April 1992.
Bacon, Dr Francis (Tom), OBE, FRS, fuel cell pioneer, aged 87 – 24 May 1992.
Barbie, Klaus, war-time Gestapo chief in Lyons, aged 77 – 25 September 1991.
Barkat Singh, Subedar, GC, aged 87 – 15 December 1991.
Barnes, Sir Denis, KCB, permanent secretary at the Department of Employment 1968–73, chairman of the Manpower Services Commission 1974–6, aged 77 – 6 May 1992.
Bartholomew, Freddie, child film star, aged 67 – 23 January 1992.
Bath, 6th Marquess, former Conservative MP and safari park pioneer, aged 87 – 30 June 1992.
Beatty, Robert, Canadian actor, aged 82 – 3 March 1992.
Begin, Menachem, Prime Minister of Israel 1977–83 and Nobel Peace Prize winner, aged 78 – 9 March 1992.
Berners, Baroness (15th in line), aged 90 – 20 February 1992.
Bevan, Michael, Lord Lieutenant of Cambridgeshire since 1985, aged 65 – 2 March 1992.
Bingham, His Hon. Richard, TD, QC, circuit judge, and Conservative MP for Garston 1957–66, aged 76 – 26 July 1992.
Black, Sir Cyril, Conservative MP for Wimbledon 1950–70, aged 89 – 29 October 1991.
Blackburn, Richard, GC, aged 79 – 31 January 1992.
Blackburn, Sydney, GC, aged 83 – 15 December 1991.
Boudiaf, Muhammad, President of Algeria since January 1992, aged 73 – assassinated 29 June 1992.
Bovet, Daniele, Italian physiologist and Nobel laureate, aged 85 – 8 April 1992.
Bratby, John, RA, painter and author, aged 64 – 20 July 1992.
Briginshaw, Lord, general secretary of NATSOPA 1951–75, aged 83 – 27 March 1992.
Brooks-Ward, Raymond, equestrian commentator, aged 62 – 22 August 1992.
Brown, Georgia, singer and actress, aged 58 – 5 July 1992.
Broxbourne, Lord (Sir Derek Walker-Smith, Bt.), TD, QC, PC, former Conservative MP, minister, and MEP, aged 81 – 22 January 1992.
Bryceland, Yvonne, South African actress, aged 67 – 13 January 1992.
Buckley, George, MP, Labour MP for Hemsworth since 1987, aged 56 – 14 September 1991.
Buckmaster, Col. Maurice, OBE, head of the French section of the Special Operations Executive 1941–5, aged 90 – 17 April 1992.
Burton of Coventry, Baroness, SDP peer and former Labour MP for Coventry, aged 87 – 6 October 1991.
Butler, Joyce, Labour MP for Wood Green (later Haringey, Wood Green) 1955–79, aged 81 – 2 January 1992.
Cage, John, American composer, philosopher and writer, aged 79 – 12 August 1992.
Capra, Frank, American film director, aged 94 – 3 September 1991.
Carstens, Karl, President of West Germany 1979–84, aged 77 – 30 May 1992.
Carter, Angela, novelist and short story writer, aged 51 – 16 February 1992.
Cessna, Eldon, American aircraft designer, aged 84 – 22 February 1992.
Cheshire, Gp Capt. The Lord, VC, OM, DSO, DFC, wartime pilot, founder of the Leonard Cheshire Foundation Homes and the Memorial Fund for Disaster Relief, aged 74 – 31 July 1992.
Clarke, Mae, American film actress, aged 84 – 30 April 1992.
Clarke, Brig. Terence, CBE, Conservative MP for Portsmouth West 1950–66, aged 88 – May 1992.
Constantine, Air Chief Marshal Sir Hugh, KCB, CB, DSO, aged 83 – 16 April 1992.
Darby, Prof. Sir Clifford, CBE, geographer, aged 83 – 14 April 1992.
d'Aubuisson, Roberto, El Salvador politician, aged 48 – 20 February 1992.
David, Elizabeth, CBE, cookery writer, aged 78 – 22 May 1992.
Davies, Ernest, Labour MP for Enfield 1945–50 and for East Enfield 1950–9, and Foreign Office junior minister 1950–1, aged 89 – 16 September 1991.

Davies of Penrhys, Lord, former Labour MP, aged 78 – 28 April 1992.
Davis, Miles, jazz trumpeter, aged 65 – 28 September 1991.
Delacombe, Maj.-Gen. Sir Rohan, KCMG, KCVO, KBE, CB, DSO, General Officer Commanding (British Sector) Berlin 1959–62, Governor of Victoria 1963–74, aged 85 – 10 November 1991.
Devlin, The Lord, PC, FBA, Lord of Appeal in Ordinary 1961–4 and writer, aged 86 – 9 August 1992.
Dietrich, Marlene, actress and cabaret singer, aged 90 – 6 May 1992.
Dimitrios I, Ecumenical Patriarch of Constantinople since 1972, aged 77 – 2 October 1991.
Ducie, 6th Earl, aged 73 – 12 November 1991.
Dulverton, 2nd Baron, CBE, TD, conservationist and philanthropist, aged 76 – 17 February 1992.
Dunalley, 6th Baron, aged 79 – 26 June 1992.
Eardley, George, VC, MM, aged 79 – 11 September 1991.
Eddison, Robert, actor, aged 83 – 14 December 1991.
Ennals, Martin, former secretary-general of Amnesty International and Nobel Peace Prize winner, aged 64 – 5 October 1991.
Eurich, Richard, OBE, RA, artist, aged 89 – 6 June 1992.
Evans of Claughton, Lord, former president of the Liberal Party, aged 64 – 22 March 1992.
Eyre, Ronald, stage and television director, aged 62 – 8 April 1992.
Ferrer, José, American actor and director, aged *c.*80 – 26 January 1992.
Ferrier, Lord, ED, business, Deputy Speaker of the House of Lords 1970–3, aged 92 – 4 June 1992.
Ffrangcon-Davies, Dame Gwen, DBE, actress, aged 101 – 27 January 1992.
Fieldhouse, Admiral of the Fleet Lord, GCB, GBE, leader of Falklands task force 1982, former Chief of Defence Staff, aged 64 – 17 February 1992.
Fisher, Bernard, GC, aged 80 – 12 April 1992.
Francis, Sir Richard, KCMG, director of the British Council since 1987, aged 58 – 26 June 1992.
Fuller, Roy, poet, novelist and critic, aged 79 – 28 September 1991
Galitzine, Prince George, businessman and Russian historian, aged 75 – 31 March 1992.
Garcia Robles, Alfonso, diplomat, disarmament crusader and Nobel Peace Prize winner, aged 80 – 2 September 1991.
Geisel, Theodore Seuss (Dr Seuss), writer of children's books, aged 87 – 24 September 1991.
Gerard, 4th Baron, aged 74 – 11 July 1992.
Gibbs, Col. Sir Martin, KCVO, CB, DSO, TD, Lord-Lieutenant for Gloucestershire since 1978, aged 74 – 8 February 1992.
Gibbs, Stanley, GC, aged 82 – 3 March 1991.
Gittings, Robert, CBE, poet and biographer, aged 81 – 18 February 1992.
Godfree, Kitty, tennis player and Wimbledon singles champion 1924 and 1926, aged 96 – 19 June 1992.
Godwin, Dame Anne, DBE, trade unionist, aged 94 – 11 January 1992.
Goossens, Marie, OBE, harpist, aged 97 – 18 December 1991.
Greenham, Peter, RA, painter, aged 82 – 11 July 1992.
Groves, Sir Charles, CBE, conductor, aged 77 – 20 June 1992.
Haley, Alex, American author, aged 70 – 10 February 1992.
Hall, Unity, journalist and novelist, aged 63 – 11 April 1992.
Hallifax, Admiral Sir David, KCB, KCVO, KBE, aged 64 – 23 August 1992.
Harpley, Sydney, RA, sculptor aged 64 – 9 March 1992.
Harris, Reg, world champion racing cyclist, aged 72 – 22 June 1992.
Hart of South Lanark, Baroness, DBE, PC (Judith Hart), former Labour MP and Cabinet minister, aged 67 – 8 December 1991.
Havers, Lord, PC, Conservative MP 1970–87, Solicitor-General 1972–4, Attorney-General 1979–87, Lord Chancellor 1987, aged 69 – 1 April 1992.
Hawarden, 8th Viscount, aged 65 – 6 September 1991.
Hawke, 10th Baron, aged 87 – 19 August 1992.
Henreid, Paul, Austrian-born actor, aged over 80 – 29 March 1992.
Hill, Benny, comedian, aged 67 – found dead 20 April 1992.
Hobson, Sir Harold, CBE, drama critic, aged 87 – 12 March 1992.
Hodgson, Alfreda, singer, aged 51 – 17 April 1992.
Holt, Richard, MP, Conservative MP for Langbaurgh since 1983, aged 60 – 21 September 1991.
Hoskins, Prof. W. G., CBE, historian, aged 83 – 11 January 1992.
Houston, Donald, actor, aged 67 – 13 October 1991.
Howerd, Frankie, OBE, comedian, aged 75 – 19 April 1992.
Hulme, Joe, footballer, cricketer and sports journalist, aged 87 – 26 September 1991.
Husák, Gustáv, secretary of the Czechoslovak Communist Party 1969–87 and President of Czechoslovakia 1975–89, aged 78 – 18 November 1991.
Irvine, Rt. Hon. Sir Bryant Godman, Conservative MP for Rye 1955–83 and Deputy Speaker of the House of Commons 1976–82, aged 82 – 3 May 1992.
Iveagh, 3rd Earl, former chairman of Guinness brewing company, aged 55 – 18 June 1992.
James of Rusholme, Lord, High Master of Manchester Grammar School 1945–62 and Vice-Chancellor of York University 1962–73, aged 83 – 16 May 1992.

Jenkins, Peter, journalist, aged 58 – 27 May 1992.
Jones, Allan, American singer and film actor, aged 83 – 27 June 1992.
Jones, Arthur (Bert), Conservative MP for South Northamptonshire (later Daventry) 1962–79, aged 76 – 6 December 1991.
Kearton, Lord, OBE, FRS, industrialist and Chancellor of Bath University since 1980, aged 81 – 2 July 1992.
Kelsey, Jack, footballer, aged 62 – 20 March 1992.
Khoei, Grand Ayatollah, spiritual leader of most Shia Muslims, aged 93 – 8 August 1992.
Kinski, Klaus, German film actor, aged 65 – 24 November 1991.
Kobal, John, film historian and photo archivist, aged 51 – 28 October 1991.
Krenek, Ernst, Austrian-born composer, aged 91 – 23 December 1991.
Lee, Vanessa (Lady Graves), singer and actress, aged 71 – 15 March 1992.
Llewellyn, Sir David, Conservative MP for Cardiff North 1950–9, and journalist, aged 76 – 9 August 1992.
Lucas of Crudwell (10th in line) and Dingwall (7th in line), Lady, aged 72 –31 December 1991.
Lurgan, 5th Baron, OBE, aged 80 – 17 September 1991.
MacBeth, George, poet and novelist, aged 60 – 16 February 1992.
McFadzean of Kelvinside, Lord, industrialist, aged 76 – 23 May 1992.
MacKenzie, Rt. Hon. Gregor, former government minister and Labour MP for Rutherglen 1964–87, aged 64 – 4 May 1992.
McMillan, Edwin, American physicist and Nobel laureate, co-discoverer of neptunium and plutonium, and developer of the synchrocyclotron, aged 83 – 7 September 1991.
MacMurray, Fred, American film actor, aged 83 – 5 November 1991.
McWilliam, F. E., CBE, RA, sculptor, aged 83 – 30 April 1992.
Mark, Herman, Austrian researcher into polymers, aged 96 – 6 April 1992.
Maxwell, Robert, MC, businessman and newspaper proprietor, aged 68 – 5 November 1991.
Mercury, Freddie, rock star and lead singer of Queen, aged 45 – 24 November 1991.
Messiaen, Olivier, French composer, aged 83 – 28 April 1992.
Mills, Air Marshal Sir Nigel, KBE, surgeon-general to the armed forces 1990–1, aged 58 – 18 October 1991.
Mitchell, Dr Peter, FRS, biochemist and Nobel laureate, aged 71 – 10 April 1992.
Molson, Lord, PC, former Conservative MP and minister, aged 88 – 13 October 1991.
Montand, Yves, Italian-born singer and actor, aged 70 – 9 November 1991.
Montrose, 7th Duke, former Rhodesian government minister, aged 84 – 10 February 1992.
Moriarty, Joan, founder of the Irish National Ballet, aged late 70s – 24 January 1992.
Morley, Robert, CBE, actor and playwright, aged 84 – 3 June 1992.
Mortimer, Harry, CBE, musician and brass band leader, aged 89 – 23 January 1992.
Moyne, 2nd Baron (Bryan Guinness), novelist, poet and playwright, aged 86 – 6 July 1992.
Moynihan, 3rd Baron, aged 55 – 24 November 1991.
Mudie, Jackie, footballer, aged 61 – 2 March 1992.
Muirshiel, 1st Viscount, KT, CH, CMG, PC, Secretary of State for Scotland 1957–62, aged 86 – 17 August 1992.
Muldoon, Rt. Hon. Sir Robert, GCMG, CH, Prime Minister of New Zealand 1975–84, aged 71 – 4 August 1992.
Naismith, Laurence, actor, aged 83 – 5 June 1992.
Naughton, Bill, novelist and playwright, aged 81 – 9 January 1992.
Newton, 4th Baron, former Conservative MP and government whip in House of Commons and Lords, aged 77 – 16 June 1992.
Norton, Mary, actress and writer, aged 88 – 29 August 1992.
Nutter, Tommy, fashion designer and tailor, aged 49 – 17 August 1992.
Oliver, Stephen, composer, aged 42 – 29 April 1992.
Ormrod, Rt. Hon. Sir Roger, Lord Justice of Appeal 1974–82, aged 80 – 6 January 1992.
Paling, William, Labour MP for Dewsbury 1945–59, aged 99 – April 1992.
Panufnik, Sir Andrzej, composer and conductor, aged 77 – 27 October 1991.
Pao, Sir Yue-Kong, CBE, Hong Kong shipping and property magnate, aged 72 – 23 September 1991.
Papp, Joseph, American theatrical producer, aged 70 – 31 October 1991.
Philipson, Sir Robin, RA, painter, aged 75 – 26 May 1992.
Phillips, Baroness, aged 82 – 14 August 1992.
Pierrepoint, Albert, official chief hangman 1946–56, aged 87 – 10 July 1992.
Piper, John, CH, painter and writer, aged 88 – 28 June 1992.
Pirie, Gordon, athlete, aged 60 – 7 December 1991.
Pitter, Ruth, CBE, poet and craftswoman, aged 94 – 29 February 1992.
Poett, Gen. Sir Nigel, KCB, DSO, aged 84 – 29 October 1991.
Purvis, James, GC, aged 87 – 12 February 1992.
Ramsay, Margaret (Peggy), theatrical agent, aged 83 – 4 September 1991.
Ray, Satyajit, Indian film director, aged 70 – 23 April 1992.
Rees-Davies, William, QC, Conservative MP for the Isle of Thanet, subsequently West Thanet, 1953–83, aged 75 – 12 January 1992.
Reiach, Alan, OBE, RSA, architect, aged 82 – 23 July 1992.
Richards, Sir James, CBE, architectural historian and critic, aged 84 – 27 April 1992.

Richardson, Tony, stage and film director, aged 63 – 14 November 1991.
Riding, Laura, American poet and writer, aged 90 – 2 September 1991.
Roberts, Dame Shelagh, DBE, Conservative MEP for London South West 1979–89 and a former chairman of the Conservative Party conference (created a life peer in the New Year's Honours list), aged 67 – 16 January 1992.
Roborough, 2nd Baron, Lord Lieutenant of Devon 1958–78, aged 88 – 30 June 1992.
Roddenberry, Gene, creator of the *Star Trek* television series, aged 70 – 24 October 1991.
Rook, Jean, journalist, aged 59 – 5 September 1991.
Rootes, 2nd Baron, former chairman of Rootes car company and Chrysler UK, aged 74 – 16 January 1992.
Rothenstein, Sir John, CBE, director of the Tate Gallery 1938–64, aged 90 – 27 February 1992.
Rothermere, Viscountess ('Bubbles'), society hostess, aged 63 – 12 August 1992.
St Aldwyn, 2nd Earl, GBE, TD, PC, aged 79 – 29 January 1992.
Salmon, Lord, PC, Lord of Appeal 1972–80, aged 87 – 7 November 1991.
Southborough, 4th Baron, aged 70 – 15 June 1992.
Southesk, 11th Earl, KCVO, aged 98 – 16 February 1992.
Spencer, 8th Earl, LVO, aged 68 – 29 March 1992.
Spessivtseva, Olga, Russian ballet dancer, aged 96 – 16 September 1991.
Stansgate, Viscountess (Margaret), religious campaigner and first President of the Congregational Federation 1972–3, aged 94 – 21 October 1991.
Steedman, Air Chief Marshal Sir Alasdair, GCB, CBE, DFC, aged 69 – 2 January 1992.
Stewart, Rt. Hon. Donald, Scottish Nationalist MP for the Western Isles 1970–87, parliamentary leader 1974–87 and President 1982–7, aged 71 – 24 August 1992.
Stigler, Prof. George, American economist and Nobel laureate, aged 80 – 1 December 1991.
Stirling, Sir Jamess, RA, architect, aged 66 – 25 June 1992.
Stone, Sir Richard, CBE, economist and Nobel laureate, aged 78 – 6 December 1991.
Story, Jack Trevor, novelist and screenwriter, aged 74 – 5 December 1991.
Strathspey, 5th Lord, aged 79 – 27 January 1992.
Surridge, Stuart, cricketer, aged 74 – 13 April 1992.
Sutcliff, Rosemary, OBE, FRSL, historical novelist, aged 71 – 23 July 1992.
Tennyson, 4th Baron, aged 72 – 19 October 1991.
Thornton, Ernest, MBE, Labour MP for Farnworth 1952–70, aged 86 – 5 February 1992.
Tierney, Gene, American film actress, aged 70 – 6 November 1991.
Turner, Adm. Sir Francis, KCB, DSC, aged 79 – 26 October 1991.
Villiers, Sir Charles, MC, chairman of British Steel Corporation 1976–80, aged 79 – 22 January 1992.
von Hayek, Friedrich, CH, economist and Nobel laureate, aged 92 – 23 March 1992.
Ward, Gen. Sir Dudley, GCB, KBE, DSO, aged 86 – 28 December 1991.
Wastie, Granville, GC, aged 89 – 24 March 1992.
Welensky, Rt. Hon. Sir Roy, KCMG, Prime Minister of the Federation of Rhodesia and Nyasaland 1956–63, aged 84 – 5 December 1991.
Westwood, 2nd Baron, President of the Football League 1974–81, aged 83 – 8 November 1991.
Winterbottom, Lord, former Labour MP, SDP and Conservative peer, aged 79 – 4 July 1992.
Yerby, Frank, American novelist, aged 75 – 29 November 1991.
Younger, Sir William McEwan, Bt., DSO, brewer, aged 86 – 15 April 1992.

From the First Edition

The first edition, *Whitaker's Almanack 1869*, was published in December 1868. Queen Victoria had been on the throne for 31 years and Gladstone became Prime Minister for the first time that December following the general election in November, the first held after the passing of the Reform Act of 1867.

The chief political controversies of the year centred around Irish matters. The general election was precipitated by the success in the House of Commons of Gladstone's proposal that the Church of Ireland be disestablished, carried against the Government by a majority of 65. Meanwhile, violent Fenian action continued, including the serious wounding of the Duke of Edinburgh, Queen Victoria's second son, who was shot in the back while on a visit to Australia.

Overseas, British troops under the command of Sir Robert Napier secured the release of British prisoners held captive by King Theodore of Abyssinia. On his return to Britain, Napier was raised to the peerage, taking the title of Lord Napier of Magdala. The cost of the expedition lead to a temporary increase in income tax to 6d in the pound.

The following description of events in 1868 is taken from the Remarkable Occurrences section of the first edition of *Whitaker*.

JANUARY 1868

4. Great eruption of Mount Vesuvius, with earthquakes, descent of lava, &c. **7.** Visit of the Prince of

Wales to the patients (at St Bartholomew's hospital) who were injured by the explosion (caused by Fenians) at Clerkenwell prison in December. **17, 18.** Severe gales on all coasts of the United Kingdom, with many wrecks and great loss of life. **18.** Attempted murder by Clancy, a Fenian, of two policeman, in Bedford Square. **18–25.** Heavy gales throughout the Kingdom, with much loss of life and property at sea and on land. Loss of nineteen fishing vessels, and fifty-two lives near the Burry river on the Welsh coast. **19.** Reports of the safety of Dr Livingstone, the celebrated African traveller, reach Plymouth. **28.** Great fire at Chicago, US, with loss of property valued at three million dollars.

FEBRUARY 1868

1. A telegraphic message sent to San Francisco from London, and reply returned, through a distance, in all, of 14,000 miles, in two minutes. **8.** Great damage on the banks of the Thames, through an unusually high tide. **22–29.** Heavy gales on all the British coasts; with numerous wrecks and loss of life. **25.** Resignation of the premiership by the Earl of Derby, and retirement into private life.

MARCH 1868

6. Serious religious and party riots at Rochdale. **12.** Attempted assassination of the Duke of Edinburgh by an Irishman named O'Farrell, at a picnic held at Clontarf, near Port Jackson, New South Wales. O'Farrell was tried on 31 March, found guilty, and executed 21 April. **13.** President Johnson was summoned to appear before the Senate Court of the United States under impeachment. **28.** Gift by Mr Joseph Whitworth (of gun celebrity) of £100,000 to promote technical education. During the month of March, 18,852 persons emigrated from Liverpool to the United States.

APRIL 1868

10. Great battle at Arogee, Abyssinia. **13.** Taking of Magdala by storm, by Sir Robert Napier, and death by supposed suicide of King Theodore. The British and other captives had been previously given up by him. **15.** Assassination of James Howard Fetherstonhaugh, of Bracklyn Castle, on his road home from Dublin, aged 49. **20.** Opening of the cause of Lyon *v.* Home, the spiritualist, for the recovery of £60,000, of which, it was alleged, he had defrauded Mrs Lyon. Serious disturbances at Wigan through strike of colliers. **27.** Conviction and sentence to death of Barrett, for complicity in the Fenian outrage at Clerkenwell, in December 1867. The two Desmonds, English, and Anne Justice, were acquitted. **30.** Resolution passed by the House of Commons, tending to the disestablishment of the Irish Church.

MAY 1868

2. Opening of the Thames Embankment between Lambeth and Westminster Bridges. **8, 9.** Religious riots at Ashton-under-Lyne. **20.** Testimonial, value £1,000, presented to Dr Richardson, in acknowledgment of his investigations into methods of rendering patients insensible of pain during surgical operations, &c.

JUNE 1868

10. Assassination of Prince Michael of Servia (*sic*). **29.** Rejection of Mr Gladstone's Irish Church Suspensory Bill, by the House of Lords.

JULY 1868

1. Public dinner at Willis's Rooms, London, to Cyrus Field, in acknowledgment of the services he had rendered to ocean telegraphy. **8.** Great *fête* at the Crystal Palace in honour of Sir Robert (now Lord) Napier for his successes in Abyssinia. **9.** Settlement of a pension of £2,000 per annum on Sir Robert Napier, in consideration of his services in Abyssinia. **15.** Presentation of the Lancashire Famine Memorial Window to the Corporation of London. Discovery of the one hundredth planet of our system; and a new observation of Encke's comet – its thirteenth periodic return. **23.** Five persons drowned at Pontypool by the upsetting of a pleasure-boat. **25.** Swarms of large gnats at Woolwich, arising from the intense heat (frequently 90° in the shade). These insects subsequently spread into the adjacent marshes and villages, attacking persons with all the effects of the tropical mosquito. Many deaths from sunstroke. **28.** Murder of two children by their father, Ezra Whitcook, a farmer, near Rochdale, Lancashire. **30.** Opening of the north portion of the Thames Embankment, from Westminster to the Temple. Fearful accident at the Victoria Music Hall, Manchester, by a panic, caused through a false alarm of fire. Thirty persons crushed to death, and many others seriously injured.

July to August. Great drought throughout the whole of Europe, accompanied with fires on heaths, moors, corn-lands, &c., with general destruction of green crops.

AUGUST 1868

1. Seizure of a British schooner by the Spanish authorities at Carthagena, on the ground of alleged piracy. **11.** First private execution in the kingdom, at Maidstone, of Wells, a railway-porter, who killed the station-master at Dover. **13–16.** Fearful earthquake in Peru and Ecuador. Immense loss of life and property; the former estimated at 50,000 persons, and the latter incalculable. **16.** Extraordinary motion of the sea in South California. A rise of 60 feet above, and a fall of the same extent below the usual level, being experienced. Doubtless related to the earthquake in Peru and Ecuador at that date. **18.** Great thunderstorm in the West of England, 33 sheep killed by lightning near Tenbury. Great solar eclipse, with complete obscuration of the sun, lasting six minutes; visible in India and adjacent countries. Interesting astronomical results were obtained. Two distinct shocks of an earthquake at Gibraltar, attended with a strong easterly current in the Mediterranean. **20.** Horrible railway accident on the Chester and Holyhead line, near Abergale, through an express train running into a van containing petroleum, causing 34 deaths. **22.** Great gale on the British coast, 100 lives being lost off the Mersey alone. **25.** Great yacht race between the American schooner, the *Sappho*, and English yachts; the *Cambria*, an English yacht, being the victor. **27.** Opening of the tomb of William Rufus, in Winchester Cathedral. The skeleton was nearly perfect. Many interesting relics were discovered. Severe snowstorm and violent gale at Braemar; a remarkable circumstance, because the heat in the south of England was of a tropical character. **30.** Discovery of a rich gold country in the north of Cape Colony, near the Limpopo River, consisting of quartz veined with gold.

SEPTEMBER 1868

3. Resignation by Garibaldi, through infirmity, of his seat in the Italian Parliament. Serious potato riot at Cork, in which 3,000 persons were engaged. **5.** Cab-strike in London, owing to the demands of the cabmen to be admitted generally to railway stations, not being conceded by the directors of the metropolitan lines. It terminated with the defeat of the cabmen on the following Thursday. **5, 6.** 'No popery' riots in Manchester, owing to the arrest of Murphy, an ultra-protestant lecturer. **12.** Great festivities at Cardiff, in Wales, and Rothesay, in Bute, Scotland, in consequence of the coming of age of the Marquis of Bute. The property, which is said to be now worth £300,000 a year, is rapidly improving, and, in less than 20 years, will produce an income of half a million. Poisoning of a whole family at Drax, near Selby, through eating sour or putrid suet. **16.** Potato riots at Cork, several persons severely injured. **16.** *et seq.* Great revolution in Spain, commencing with the fleet off Cadiz, and gradually spreading over the whole peninsula, attended with little bloodshed. Flight of Queen Isabella to France, and the formation of a form of Republican Government under Prim, Serrano, and others at Madrid. **18.** Examination of Byrne at Guildhall for supposed Fenianism, and possession of a large number of guns and other arms. Capture of an albacore, a tropical fish, weighing 5 cwt, and ten feet long, off Dawlish. Disgraceful disturbances in Lombard Street, City, owing to the denunciations of the banking interest by Father Ignatius (Revd J. L. Lyne) whilst preaching. **24.** *et seq.* Second trial of Madame Rachael, the face enameller ('Beautiful for Ever'), for obtaining £1,400 under false pretences from Mrs Barrodaile, ending in her conviction, and sentence of five years' penal servitude. **26.** *et seq.* Great gales all round the coast, with much loss of life and numerous shipwrecks. **30.** Singular discovery of a new eruptive disease, common throughout the country, affecting the feet, and due to the use of stockings dyed of yellow and red colours. Fearful explosion of fire-damp at Green Pit, near Ruabon, Wales, with loss of several lives, caused by carelessness. Discharge of John Surratt, who had been long charged with complicity in the assassination of President Lincoln, US. Renewed Maori disturbances in New Zealand through the escape of 150 prisoners.

OCTOBER 1868

4. Successful submerging of a submarine cable 900 miles long, in a direct line, between Malta and Alexandria. **19.** Alarming explosion of a self-supplying kitchen boiler in the Haymarket, with injury to six persons and much destruction of property. **21.** Severe earthquake throughout California, and great destruction of buildings, property, &c., at San Francisco. **23, 24.** Great gales on the south coast of England, attended with many shipwrecks and much loss of life. **24.** Severe shocks of earthquakes felt at Mallow, Cork, followed by loud noise. **30.** Earthquake shocks felt in many parts of England, but chiefly in the west. Serious riots in Rotherham. Many persons injured and three rioters shot. **31.** Formation of a revolutionary Ministry in Spain under Serrano, Prim, and others. Eruption of Mount Vesuvius.

NOVEMBER 1868

1. Extraordinary recession of the waters of Lake Ontario, near Cobourg, to the extent of nearly 100 feet from the usual water-mark, and accompanied with a rushing sound similar to that of the tide coming in at the sea-coast. The ebbing and flowing was repeated several times for nearly an hour. **1–4.** Election riots at Blackburn, with much damage to property and personal injury; one life lost. **3.** General Grant elected President of the United States; and Schuyler Colfax, Vice-President. **9.** Massacre of European settlers by the natives of Poverty Bay, New Zealand. **14–21.** General election of members of Parliament throughout the Kingdom. **21.** Public funeral of Rossini at the Church of the Trinity, at Paris. **21–28.** Election riots at Tredegar, Blaenavon, Bandon, Barnsley, and other places. **22.** Fenian demonstration in Hyde Park, in memory of 'the martyrdom of Allen, Larkin, and O'Brien,' on 22 November 1867. **24.** Opening of the New City Meat Market at Smithfield. **26.** Terrible colliery explosion at Hindley Green coal pit, near Wigan, with the loss of nearly 60 lives. **28.** Eruption of Mount Etna from the north-east cone. **29.** Removal of the remains of Prince Albert to the Mausoleum, at Frogmore. Mrs Disraeli raised to the peerage as Viscountess Beaconsfield. Discovery of two apartments of a Roman building at Cowes, with various domestic relics.

DECEMBER 1868

2. Resignation of Mr Disraeli and the Conservative Ministry, owing to the result of the elections being adverse to his party. **3.** The Queen sends for Mr Gladstone to form a Ministry. **9.** Mr Disraeli resigns the premiership, and is succeeded by Mr Gladstone. **6.** Great gale in London and the provinces, attended with much loss of life and property on sea and land. **8.** Renewed eruption of Mount Etna. **13.** Dreadful accident on the Brighton line; two railway guards burnt to death by explosion of mineral oil at the Three Bridges station. **16.** Insult to the missionaries in China, and demand for reparation by the British authorities, supported by the fleet, anchored off Nanking. **18.** Robbery of the van of a railway train, at Birmingham; the perpetrator threw naphtha into the eyes of the guard, and thus effected his escape, but being discovered, was sentenced to penal servitude. **24.** Further donation of £100,000 by Mr Peabody, for the benefit of the London poor. This gentleman has since, by his will, left an additional £150,000 for the same purpose, making in all half a million. **27–28.** Much damage done by storms in London, Sheffield, Rochdale, &c. **31.** Explosion of a firework factory at Bethnal-green; one person killed.

Among new scientific discoveries and inventions recorded in the first edition was 'a new blasting powder, invented by M. Nobel' and called dynamite; the introduction of the first electric light in a lighthouse (at Dungeness); the installation of the electric telegraph in the police and fire-engines stations of the metropolis; and the continuing extension of the telegraphic system world-wide.

However, according to *Whitaker*, one of the most important inventions of 1867–8 'in a sanitary and social point of view, was that of the earth-closet system, invented by the Revd H. Moule, and for the use of which in India the Government presented him with a gratuity of £500'.

Excise duties and taxes were charged on the principal means of transport. Railways were charged a duty of £5 per £100 of passenger traffic. Rates for horses and mules varied according to the use to which they were put; the usual rate of 1 guinea for each riding or carriage horse dropped to 10s 6d if only one horse was kept and its use was necessary to the owner's livelihood, e.g. minister of religion, doctor, farmer. Employers also paid a tax of 1 guinea for each male servant employed, and 'every person who shall use hair powder' paid a tax of £1 3s 6d.

LANDMARKS IN THE HISTORY OF WHITAKER'S ALMANACK

1820 Joseph Whitaker born
1868 First edition, *Whitaker's Almanack 1869*, published
1878 *Whitaker's Almanack* for that year placed in the foundations of Cleopatra's Needle when it was set up on the Embankment, London
1895 Joseph Whitaker died; succeeded as editor by his son Cuthbert
1900 William Clowes, Beccles, became printers of *Whitaker's Almanack*
1914 *Whitaker's Almanack* features in a Sherlock Holmes story, *The Valley of Fear*, in which the detective uses the book to decode a message
1927 Concise edition with paper covers first published
1931 First edition to contain over 1,000 pages of editorial matter
1940 Whitaker premises destroyed by incendiary bombs
1950 Sir Cuthbert Whitaker died; succeeded as editor by F. H. C. (Tom) Tatham
1954 First edition to contain a 16-page section of black and white photographs
1960 First edition to have a dust jacket
1981 First edition to be typeset by computer
Tom Tatham succeeded as editor by Richard Blake
1986 Richard Blake succeeded as editor by Hilary Marsden
1993 First edition in new design, the first change of format since 1868

Wedding Anniversaries

First	*Cotton*
Second	*Paper*
Third	*Leather*
Fourth	*Fruit and Flower*
Fifth	*Wood*
Sixth	*Sugar/Iron*
Seventh	*Wool*
Eighth	*Bronze/Electrical appliances*
Ninth	*Copper/Pottery*
Tenth	*Tin*
Eleventh	*Steel*
Twelfth	*Silk and Fine Linen*
Thirteenth	*Lace*
Fourteenth	*Ivory*
Fifteenth	*Crystal*
Twentieth	*China*
Twenty-fifth	*Silver*
Thirtieth	*Pearl*
Thirty-fifth	*Coral*
Fortieth	*Ruby*
Forty-fifth	*Sapphire*
Fiftieth	*Gold*
Fifty-fifth	*Emerald*
Sixtieth	*Diamond*
Seventieth	*Platinum*

Archaeology

The year under review has seen much organizational change, of which the most public aspect was probably the retirement of Lord Montagu as the first chairman of English Heritage. He was succeeded at the end of his extended term on 1 April 1992 by Jocelyn Stevens, rector of the Royal College of Art, who previously pursued a distinguished career in journalism.

Considerable publicity was given to the redundancy of a substantial number of archaeologists employed by the Museum of London, the criticism of the management by an industrial tribunal, the disestablishment of the Department of Greater London Archaeology and the creation of the new Museum of London Archaeology Service. On one level the debate was over the respective powers of English Heritage and the Museum of London in the administration of an archaeological service in Greater London, while on another it reflected the weakness of archaeological investigations dependent upon funding from developers at a time of national economic recession and when the construction industry is especially badly hit.

When financial resources are available, there is no shortage of archaeological sites to investigate, as three English Heritage-sponsored projects demonstrate. Excavations along the route of the A47 by-pass to the south of Norwich produced important discoveries from the prehistoric period onwards, including a highly significant Anglo-Saxon cemetery with 46 graves. At Shepton Mallet, Somerset, excavations near the Fosse Way of a site for the construction of a warehouse complex led to the discovery of a previously unknown and unnamed Romano-British town which existed during the second, third and fourth centuries and possessed a Christian community. Excavations at Westhampnett on the route of the A27 Chichester by-pass revealed much of importance dating from the mesolithic to Romano-British times, including what is believed to be the largest late Iron Age cremation cemetery in south-eastern England.

Warwickshire Palaeolithic Site

In 1984 the late Professor Shotton discovered a former river channel beneath glacial gravels at Waverley Wood Farm Pit, a gravel quarry, near Leamington Spa, Warks. Investigation of this channel has produced much material, amongst which are the remains of insects and molluscs as well as the bones of a number of mammals, including a large straight-tusked elephant. Most significantly, human occupation is demonstrated by the discovery of a number of stone tools including two substantial hand axes. A small display about the site, which is thought to date to about 500,000 years ago, is being mounted at the Warwickshire Museum in Warwick.

The discovery of other palaeolithic sites in recent years, usually as a result of applications to extract sand and gravel, has led to the establishment by English Heritage of the Southern Rivers Palaeolithic Project which began work in March 1991. The aim of this three-year survey is to provide information which will assist in the planning process and to give an opportunity for renewed co-operation between archaeologists and those whose livelihood depends on the extraction of minerals.

Roman Finds

The detailed investigation of Romano-British sites continues apace, but attention is drawn here to three objects of general interest, all of which were noted in *Minerva* (volumes 2 and 3, 1991–2). In 1989 a statuette representing a mounted warrior god was discovered near the Fosse Way and the Roman site of Brough; this Romano-British bronze figure has since been acquired by the British Museum. The warrior, in helmet and tunic, would once have been holding a spear and shield; he rides a horse which, in addition to having a highly decorated harness, has its left foreleg extended and raised, carrying out a high-stepping exercise. This horse and rider represents a Celtic British but Romanized deity whose name is unknown. However, there are a number of other examples, including figures from the temple sites of Brigstock in Northamptonshire and Willingham Fen in Cambridgeshire.

Near Banbury, Oxon., metal detector users are reported as having discovered a fourth-century AD mosaic pavement showing Belerophon killing the three-headed chimera. Claimed as 'the most important Roman mosaic to have come to light in Britain for more than a decade', it dates to about AD 360 and was apparently part of a large previously-unknown villa. The discovery is significant because only three other Belerophon mosaics are known in Britain, two in Dorset and one in Kent. It is noted that 'all three other Belerophon sites also produced early Christian mosaics or wall paintings and there is speculation that the Banbury site may provide similar material'. The Banbury Belerophon rides Pegasus and directs his spear at the three-headed chimera. The chimera in this case is a stranger than usual creature whose three heads are those of a dog or wolf, a duck and a snake, rather than the more traditional heads of a lion, goat and snake.

The retirement of Sir David Wilson as director of the British Museum in December 1991 was marked by the purchase by the British Museum Society for the Museum collections of a small enamelled Roman bronze box or pyxis which had previously been sold at auction for £33,000. The pyxis was found by two amateur archaeologists who had permission to investigate a ploughed field at Elsenham, Essex. Other material was found subsequently which indicated a rich cremation burial that may have been part of a larger cremation cemetery or attached to a settlement site. It is reported that 'the Elsenham pyxis is the first of its kind to be found in Britain; moreover it is the most complete and well-preserved of the nine such vessels so far recorded'. In particular, it is the only example to be found in a clear archaeological context and the finders have presented other pieces from the grave group to the British Museum. Despite the delight at such a fitting tribute to its outgoing director being acquired by the British Museum, the sale of the pyxis by public auction, and the subsequent three-month export licence delay, again raise concern over the inadequacy of the law relating to portable antiquities.

SUTTON HOO

The eight seasons of excavation at Sutton Hoo sponsored by the Society of Antiquaries and the British Museum have now ended and it is appropriate to draw attention to the interview given by the Director, Professor Martin Carver, to *Current Archaeology* (volume 11, number 8, March 1992), from which a brief summary of the results of the excavations is extracted. The site is located near the River Deben in Suffolk and the recent investigations yielded a total of 17 mounds. The last of these, excavated in the autumn of 1991, was probably the first to have been raised in the sixth or seventh century AD by the Anglo-Saxons. Underneath the mound was the grave of an important warrior and alongside was a second grave pit containing the young man's horse. The next mound to be constructed was number 5, which covered a cremation burial of another person of high status who had been cremated with grave goods. Of particular interest was the fact that this grave was surrounded by satellite burials, called 'sandmen' because they survived only as stains in the sands. It is considered that these may have been human sacrifices because 'in some cases their wrists or their ankles have been bound together. Sometimes they were face downwards. Sometimes their hands were bound behind their backs. In several cases the neck was broken or the head was the wrong way round. In some cases the head had been cut off and placed by the foot or the knee or underneath the arm'. Mounds 6, 7, 3 and 4 follow. 'Just beyond mound 5 was a row of three burials, all children or adolescents. The best preserved was a child of about four, buried in an oak coffin with a tiny little spear, a tiny little buckle, and under a tiny mound only about 2 metres in diameter. Adjacent there were two others, adolescents, buried with standard 7th century grave goods. It seems that, by this time, status could be inherited.'

Mound 14 had been a chamber-grave burial, 'with planks set on end all the way around the chamber, with thin planks forming a very delicate chamber'. The finds, little silver buckles from a shoe and a chatelaine, indicated a female grave. Next were the two best-known mounds covering the ship burials, and of these mound 2 was probably raised first; this was a chamber grave with a ship on top of it. In mound 1, by contrast, it was found that the great ship had been hauled up and placed in position first, the burial chamber being erected in the middle of it. This was the ship burial investigated in 1939 and from which were recovered so many of the best-known objects, namely, the buckles, shoulder clasps, purse and sword, together with drinking horns and a lyre. From this mound was recovered the great silver dish stamped with the control mark of Anastasius I (AD 491–518), the three cauldrons, bucket and chain, together with the symbols of royalty, the shield and the helmet, the iron standard and the bronze stag on its whetstone.

The whole cemetery is pagan in character and the final great ship burial has particular significance. 'This then was the final act of defiance of a beleaguered pagan Kingdom. Having established kinship, they continued in the face of ideological pressure from the Christian Merovingiam Empire to emphasize their paganism and to signal their allegiance to Scandinavia by adding these two ship burials, the most extravagant burials of all. But this is the last act. The political argument is lost and the curtain falls. Christianity triumphs, and the cemetery is abandoned. Paganism suffers the fate of losers: it is derided, disparaged – and forgotten.'

WHARRAM PERCY

The 41st and final season of excavations within Wharram Percy deserted medieval village has been completed. The achievements of the Wharram project are explained in a book published by English Heritage, *Wharram Percy Deserted Medieval Village* by Maurice Beresford and John Hirst, with whom the investigation of the area will always be associated.

The Wharram Percy site in North Yorkshire is important because it represents a class of monument, the deserted medieval village, recognition of which is one of the milestones in British archaeology in the post-1945 period. Precisely because these village sites were deserted, and therefore not encumbered with post-medieval building levels, it is possible to investigate by archaeological means (refined over the decades) the way of life of those who lived in these rural communities. Wharram Percy was selected for in-depth investigation over four decades and for preservation as a monument to which the public have access. Two manor houses, the parish church with cemetery, the parsonage houses, the mill and fish-pond were examined, and particular attention was paid to the medieval peasant houses, which enabled a new insight to be gained into the nature of medieval rural settlement. As this project ends, it is appropriate that the widest possible recognition should be given to the significance of Wharram Percy, a classic deserted medieval village site.

Pre-Columbian Syphilis

The commemoration of Christopher Columbus's first voyage to the Americas 1492 has occasioned much debate about whether the outcome was good or bad for mankind. Over the years one of the matters debated has been the origin of syphilis and whether or not Columbus's sailors brought the disease back from the New World to the Old. In a new publication, *The International Journal of Osteoarchaeology* (volume 1, 1991), Ann Stirland in a paper entitled 'Pre-Columbian Treponematosis in Medieval Britain' publishes the skeleton of a young adult male, number 412 from the cemetery of the now demolished St Margaret's Church in Magdalen Street, Norwich. The cemetery was in use from the 1100s to 1468 and this particular burial is thought to be early in the sequence. Having reviewed the evidence, the author is of the opinion that this skeleton does demonstrate the presence of syphilis in medieval Norwich, but state 'whether this is an example of endemic non-venereal syphilis or the acquired, venereal form, however, is another matter'. Of equal interest is the author's observation that other skeletons 'from the same cemetery were suffering from leprosy, although they obviously had not been excluded socially. Perhaps the nature of their disease was not recognized as distinct from syphilis. A re-evaluation of the material in the European leprosy cemeteries is now urgently required'.

Queen Street Mill

Situated in the industrial village of Harle Syke on the edge of Burnley, Lancs., Queen Street Mill began work in 1894 as a co-operative. It is of the greatest importance to industrial archaeologists, as Peter de Lange, writing in *English Heritage Conservation Bulletin* (issue 17, June 1992) makes clear. 'Apart from its importance as a relic of the Lancashire cotton weaving industry of the nineteenth century, it is unique among textile mills in England, and possibly in Europe, in retaining its original machinery *in situ* and in working order. The Mill consists of a large single-storey weaving shed with a north light roof (and 19 valley gutters) and a two-storey block housing the machines for preparing the cotton for weaving. This was originally three-storey, but was partly destroyed in a fire in 1918. At one corner of the building is the boiler and engine house, and the engine – renamed "peace" to celebrate the 1918 Armistice – drives all the machinery in the Mill through a series of drive shafts and belts.'

The future of Queen Street Mill has been under discussion since it closed as a commercial operation in 1982. Fortunately, the problem of what to do with it has been solved by Lancashire County Council's decision to operate it as a working museum. 'The Council already runs the cotton spinning mills at Helmshore about ten miles from Burnley and, with Queen Street, would have the whole story of the Lancashire cotton industry from raw material to finished cloth.' Although the county council is prepared to run the museum, extensive repairs are required which will cost almost £1 million. A grant-aid package has been agreed and English Heritage will provide £600,000, the National Heritage Fund £200,000, and the European Community £100,000. Further help has been received from Burnley Borough Council, which has sold the freehold of the mill (purchased when it closed as a commercial concern) to the county council for a nominal sum, and has agreed to maintain its revenue contribution towards running costs.

Securing the future of an industrial building as large as Queen Street Mill and with such large overheads at a time of economic recession shows what can be done when local authorities and national organizations work closely together.

Medieval Period

A comprehensive summary of work relating to the medieval period was published in *Medieval Archaeology*, volume XXXV for 1991. Amongst the various excavations noted was that of a Saxon cemetery much affected by ploughing at Barrington, Cambs., where 27 skeletons were excavated in 1989 and another 44 examined in 1990. 'Of great interest was the discovery of two 7th-century "bed burials" of women and their grave goods. The first was in a grave that was sufficiently deep to preserve iron fittings (cleats, eyelets and head-rails) of the bed. Grave-goods included an iron-bound bucket, the contents of a probable bag consisting of a bronze buckle, bone comb, glass bead and fossilized sea-urchin, an iron "latch-lifter" and a short sword or weaving baton . . . this woman was a leper. The second "bed burial" was less deeply buried and so had been more disturbed by ploughing, but the iron-work that survived showed that the original bed had been very similar. The woman wore two delicate bronze buckles on her thighs, a ring of twisted silver on her right shoulder and a bronze pin on her left shoulder. Sixth-century burials were accompanied by a total of eleven spears, five shields, assorted iron shield fittings, twelve buckles, two pairs of wrist-clasps, 33 knives and one other "match-lifter". Five women wore necklaces of glass or amber beads, one of whom also had a pair of small-long brooches and another a pair of penannular brooches.'

At Oxborough, Norfolk, excavations disclosed ten Anglo-Saxon graves, some of which cut the upper fills of a possible Bronze Age ring-ditch, taken to be the remains of a barrow. 'One remarkable example was a woman, aged 25–35 years, who had undergone and recovered from trephination. Several other similar healed examples are known from West Norfolk and Suffolk and may represent the work of the same sixth-century surgeon.'

At Barton-upon-Humber rescue excavation was undertaken on a known Anglian inhumation cemetery first found in 1940. 'A total of *c.*106 burials was recorded, including – from the evidence of grave goods – more women than men, and more men than children. About 60 per cent of burials were accompanied by grave goods, dated 550–675. The distribution of burials suggested a polyfocal organization of the cemetery, one focus being the grave of a warrior. The stratigraphic relationship between graves suggested two or three successive periods of cemetery use. Numerous post-holes may have defined the boundary, restated during one of these periods, and some similar evidence was recorded for grave markers or structures. The finds included a sword, javelin head and hanging bowl with the warrior burial; weapons were relatively uncomon. Female grave goods included beads, copper-alloy brooches of annular and cruciform types, pins, bangles, earrings, and a small number of similar objects of silver. Pots accompanied several burials; these included a mammiform vessel with a perforated teat-shaped base from an infant's grave, believed to be the first Anglo-Saxon feeding bottle to be identified by excavation.'

At Flixborough, S. Humberside, rescue excavations in advance of quarrying have revealed a middle Saxon settlement, including buildings and ovens. 'Preservation of finds and animal bone is quite remarkable, due in part to the accumulation of 2 m of sand after settlement abandonment. Many of the finds are of high quality and include numerous silver and copper-alloy pins, some gilded, buckles, strap ends, rings and tweezers. Activities undertaken within the settlement are represented by loom weights, spindle whorls, needles, querns, knives, shears and iron slag. Literacy is indicated by the inscribed lead plaque and over twenty styli of iron, copper-alloy and base silver. Dating evidence from the coins and other finds suggests the settlement was occupied from late 7th to the late 9th century.'

At Newcastle upon Tyne excavations within the area of the medieval castle revealed more of the known Anglian cemetery, producing 114 inhumations. 'Further evidence of continued use of the cemetery after the construction of the Norman Castle in 1080 was shown by the burials in stone-built cists, some marked on the cemetery surface by dressed stone slabs with head and foot markers. One slab, associated with an infant burial in a wooden coffin, was unusual in being covered with a mass of decorative motifs dated on stylistic grounds to between 1080 and *c.* 1100.'

Excavations carried out at Ipswich included one at Franciscan Way, where it was found that in the later ninth century AD 'an extensive iron-working industry was established in the area'. It is noted that 'the evidence for iron-working here is on a much larger scale than on any of the other excavations undertaken in Ipswich. The total amount of slag and industrial waste recovered from the later 9th-century context was 217 kg, from late Saxon contexts over 240 kg and from early medieval contexts 148 kg. The industry then declined rapidly and relatively little slag was recovered from later medieval contexts. This material awaits specialists examination but it appears to represent smithing, rather than smelting, activity. A few post-holes were found around the cobbled area indicating a structure possibly associated with this industry. The single most important artefact from the site also indicates its industrial nature; this is an antler brooch mould which came from a pit of late 9th- or 10th-century date, used for making base metal disc brooches.'

On the line of the Gillingham relief road in Dorset were found 'the remains of two ovens which are believed to be of early medieval date and are tentatively interpreted as iron-ore roasting ovens associated with iron smelting. The ovens lay just inches beneath the surface of a meadow that has remained virtually unploughed since the Norman Conquest.' It is noted that 'although medieval iron working sites are well known from other parts of the country, particularly the Weald, the process of roasting poor quality local ores to improve them prior to smelting is represented by only a few sites in Britain and Europe, and at present there are no known parallels for Gillingham ovens.'

The many excavations in London included one at 78–79 Leadenhall Street in the City, where some 59 burials were recovered associated with the Church of St Katharine Cree and Holy Trinity Priory. 'Finds of note include a late Saxon composite bone comb and case from a pit predating the burials, the second of its kind to be found in London, a late Saxon glass linen smoother and an Anglo-Norman bone skate.' Amongst discoveries at 25–51 St Mary Axe/9 St Helen's Place it is noted that 'deposits from within a 14th-century pit were sieved, yielding a large quantity of scrap from the manufacture of fancy knife handles: these had bone scales inlaid with jet and amber, and sheet copper alloy and iron endcaps and shoulder bolsters. Only one knife of comparable form has been excavated hitherto in London.' At the important site at Vintry House, Vintners Place, 'spoil from the pile holes on the site was metal-detected with the help of members of the Society of Thames Mudlarks, producing a very large assemblage of well-preserved early and late medieval ceramic and inorganic finds. In addition to large quantities of dress fittings, coins, trade seals and waste products of metal working, numerous badges were found commemorating pilgrimage and denoting personal allegiance. Notable in the latter category is a small pewter hart-and-tree badge used by Richard II and his followers, the first example found in London. Deposit in a coffer dam in the river produced a large pewter plate with the letter V on it, possibly signifying its use by the Vintners Company. Other finds from the coffer dam include an elaborate pewter crucifix badge of late 14th-century/15th-century date, a 15th-century Talbot badge of allegiance to the Earls of Shrewsbury and a small lead ingot with the mark of the Plumbers Company, paralleled by one found at Nonsuch Palace, Surrey. A wattle-lined cess pit at the north end of the site contained two almost complete wooden bowls, a large boxwood comb and Spanish and German pottery of late medieval date.'

In Bury St Edmunds, Suffolk, excavations were undertaken in advance of the extension of the Priory Hotel, which stands within the precinct of Babwell Priory, founded by the Franciscans in the late 13th century just outside the medieval town walls. Some 23 articulated skeletons were discovered, together with the remains of what are taken to be disturbed burials. 'Two of the bodies inside the building were buried with gypsum, and one grave was lined with mortar (presumably a cheap imitation of a stone coffin). A more prestigious burial contained a priest interred in a stone coffin with his chalice and paten, confirming the impression that the building was a church.'

In Cheshire, investigations were undertaken at the Holt-Farndon Bridge. 'This bridge across the Dee (which here forms the boundary between England and Wales) joins the villages of Holt and Farndon. It was built in 1338/9 on the ancient salt route between Nantwich and Wrexham. A thorough programme of repair and restoration was undertaken by Cheshire County Highways Service, including repointing all stonework and lowering the carriageway to its original level. A survey of the stonework and watching-brief of the carriageway alterations was maintained. The latter revealed evidence for the gate-tower demolished in the later 18th century. Various phases of masonry repairs were identified as well as much of the original structure of the bridge.'

At Reigate, Surrey, 'on land below Colley Hill a hoard was discovered of *c.*6,701 coins, including 135 of gold, dating to *c.*1460. Two small jugs, both broken, one Tudor Green and one plain, were associated, but it is doubtful whether much of the hoard could have been contained in them, and the remainder may have been originally contained in bags. The hoard was buried *c.*0.5 m beneath the surface of a former sports fields and found during house construction. The field is bordered by a hollow way which formed a medieval route leading north from the west end of the town, which lay *c.*0.5 km distant. The hoard was declared Treasure Trove in July 1991.'

POST-MEDIEVAL PERIOD

Work relating to post-medieval Britain is recorded in *Post-Medieval Archaeology*, volume 25 for 1991. Investigations include those at 50A St Owen's Street, Hereford, 'one of several commercial properties in an unimportant-looking range of buildings just within the site of St Owen's Gate'. A survey in 1990 'established that 50A was just part of a very large and high-status timber-framed building, substantially intact. It was of two storeys, jetted, with dormered attics and stone-lined cellars, and had four bays with a total street frontage of 15 m. On each floor a principal two-bay room was flanked by single bay chambers. The rooms would have been lit by very large windows and the ovolo-moulded wall-plate surviving in an adjacent roof space shows that a rear first floor window was full bay-width and of eight lights. The floors appear to have been reached by an extruding stair tower to the rear of the property, parts of the framing of which survive. Later alterations, refronting and property sub-divisions have obscured the true scale of this important building, in which the basic framework has survived intact. It probably dates to the late 16th or early 17th century.'

Excavations at Marlborough House, London, 'in the grounds and basement of Wren's 1709 redbrick town house revealed extensive remains of two main phases of occupation, pre-dating the house. Foundations of the kitchen ranges of Henry VIII's St James Palace (1538), destroyed by fire in 1809, and associated metalled surfaces were identified, together with a substantial part of the brick boundary wall of the 17th-century Capuchin Friary that originally stood at the east end of Inigo Jones's Queen's Chapel (1627). Inside the house, walls and floors of Wren's original building (altered in the 1770s and again between 1861–3) were recorded beneath later basement floor levels.'

A survey of 18th-century garden features was carried out at Kirkleatham Old Hall, near Middlesbrough. The northern edge of the Old Hall estate is marked by two ornamental round bastions once linked by a water-filled ha-ha; 'each contains a circular vaulted chamber lit by decorated loops, and each originally had an embattled parapet. Nearby is an elaborate crenellated gateway known as the Toasting Gate. Cholmley Turner, the presumed builder of these features, was a close friend of Laurence Sterne and it is has been suggested that the bastions are the prototype of the miniature fortifications built by Uncle Toby in Sterne's *Life and Opinions of Tristram Shandy*.'

At Oriel College, Oxford, the former real tennis court behind 104–105 High Street was investigated before its conversion to college accommodation, and 'four phases of court floors were found, the earliest probably dating from around 1600. A tennis play is recorded here in 1572, and the court is shown roofed in 1675. The second phase of flooring was of 6-inch clay tiles, replaced by 9-inch tiles and subsequently by a surface of York stone slabs which had largely survived. Many of the painted court markings also survived on the ashlar inside walls, and the shape of the penthouse could be traced on the south and west walls. There was clear evidence of a timber predecessor to the stone court, like those depicted on Loggan's map of Cambridge in the later 17th century. The Oriel court is associated with Charles I, who evidently played Prince Rupert here during the siege of Oxford, and who also conducted some of his dealings with Parliament from the court.' At Wheatlands Farm, Redcar, a concrete acoustical mirror of First World War vintage was surveyed. 'This is one of a series of mirrors along the Yorkshire coast which were intended to detect the engine noise of Zeppelin raiders. The structure is built of concrete, cast in corrugated iron shuttering and rendered. The smooth surface of the mirror and the stump of the iron post which supported the collecting microphone survive.'

Architecture

'THE ARK' OFFICE BUILDING
Hammersmith, London

Architect: Ralph Erskine, in collaboration with Lennart Bergström Arkitektkontor and Rock Townsend

The thousands of harried commuters who speed every day along the motorway flyover in Hammersmith, and the thousands more who throng the Underground trains through Barons Court will by now have grown used to one of the most extraordinary new London buildings of recent times. Nicknamed 'The Ark' even from its inception, it is hard not to make a direct comparison with its biblical namesake as its huge hull-like form looms into view.

Yet this is not a huge building, the main office component comprising 15,000 square metres of the highest standard office accommodation on 11 floors, with all the usual trappings of full air-conditioning, raised floors, wallclimbing passenger lifts, central computer-controlled services and basement car parking. It is by virtue of its highly imaginative response to a hostile suburban environment, and the expression of a social awareness inherent in an innovative vision of the role of the individual in the workplace, that this design achieves its distinction.

Both the developer and his architect are of Scandinavian origin and keenly supportive of the management thinking prevalent in more socially advanced companies in Sweden and Norway. They have determined upon an ambitious project to introduce to the English scene a prospect of company management structures aided by appropriate workplace environments in which the workers are treated with intelligence and respect, valued for their potential contribution in a more democratically based organization than is typical of many Western corporate hierarchies.

The physical expression of this intent finds form in the treatment of the internal environment of what, by way of a defensive response to its immediate context, is of necessity an inward-looking building. Inside the protective shell of the 'hull', everything is contrived to maximize the potential for exchange of ideas, chance meetings, social interaction and sharing of experiences in the everyday workplace, with a bewildering variety of forms and spaces designed for complete flexibility in use. It is an intelligent building for use by civilized people. It is all the more remarkable that, rather than being an individual custom response to the needs of a particular forward-looking tenant, this extraordinary building has been developed on a more or less speculative basis, although a part of the space is intended to become the developer's London headquarters.

The distinctive form of the building is generated by a gradual stepping-out of each successive floor plate, coupled with a progressively greater cut-out along the south facing perimeter at the upper levels to allow light to penetrate the interior spaces. All of these are capped by a great sweeping curve of copper-clad roof punctuated by domed rooflights and other curious protuberances. The sloping walls are principally of glass, with three horizontal bands to each storey. A central band of clear glass, actually a triple-glazed composite window for thermal and acoustic insulation purposes, is bordered by a band of brown-tinted glass top and bottom, again triple glazed, the inner pane of bronze-coloured glass effectively defining the central clear band as the window although all three bands are transparent. At each floor level the slab is expressed through a horizontal copper-plated spandrel panel with corrugated copper profiles accentuating the junctions between glazed and solid elements. The floors are of a special 'slim' design with a depth of 300 mm. Each slab overhangs the one below, generating progressively longer cantilevers until at the sixth floor the edges of the slabs are hung by perimeter columns which act in tension.

Through all of these expanding geometries the structural columns and core elements, lifts and escape stairs, remain implacably vertical. The primary structural elements at the perimeter are set out from a mid-point such that higher up the building they disappear to the interior, while at the lower levels they project forward by ever greater amounts as the window planes recede towards the ground. The exposed surfaces of these solid projections are clad in brick, but not the usual facing brick, rather the jaggedly cut face of snapped bricks turned inside out; a device to exploit the potential of simple materials for creating complex and unexpected visual textures and patterns.

The position of the main entrance to the building is defined by a narrow slotted recess driven right through the height and depth of the office floors above. It achieves its final expression within the sweeping curve of the roof where a huge lattice beam slices through the building along the same axis, its faceted form visible on the exterior, and supporting a continuous glazed rooflight. Though the entrance itself is relatively insignificant as a feature in the overall composition, the glazed slot and lattice beam in slicing a clean plane through the complex shapes provide a reassuring means of orientating oneself in a potentially confusing interior.

A small reception area is reached up a flight of steps and gives access to the floor of the atrium. From this point an amazingly complex view unfolds, as the eye takes in what appears to be an enormous stage-set, with projecting balconies and terraces, and bridges crossing the spaces at all angles. The typical floors are in fact conventional 18-metre wide strips of office accommodation, but wrapped around the space in a continuous band on a triangular format with a soft bulbous curve at each apex. As the upper floors move progressively outwards bridges and balconies enter into and withdraw from the space, offering a wealth of visually stimulating shapes and juxtapositions. These seem at first arbitrary and random but while not the result of any self-evident logic are nevertheless finely controlled. At the two sharpest internal corners, cylindrical spaces are carved out through the height of the building.

The majority of the surfaces are white, relieved only by the natural colours of the huge billowing roof and the edges of the ceilings, which are finished with timber slats arranged in a pattern of varying widths, the balcony handrails, redwood with walnut inlay, and the floor finishes. What is absent from the interior, at least at the moment, is the ubiquitous glazed wall, for every floor except the topmost is open to the atrium space.

This has led to the need for a radical approach to fire safety, as the entire building is treated as a single enclosure for the purposes of fire separation, rather than the more usual floor-by-floor compartments. The four main service cores containing lifts and escape stairs are pressurized automatically to keep them free of smoke, while the atrium is designed to provide a smoke reservoir at the highest level, vented through smoke extractor fans sited above the central lattice beam which crosses the building from one side to the other.

The openness of floor to atrium may in any event be compromised by the desire of individual tenants to provide cellular offices overlooking the interior. Care has been taken to ensure that the floors can be subdivided according to a number of different principles for office space planning, ranging from a high degree of cellular compartmentation to open planned burolandschaft schemes.

FITZWILLIAM COLLEGE CHAPEL
Cambridge

Architect: MacCormac Jamieson Prichard

Fitzwilliam College is one of the more recently founded colleges in Cambridge, with its origins in the Non-Collegiates Society of the nineteenth century. It was not until 1966 that it acquired collegiate status, at which time it moved into buildings newly designed by Denys Lasdun on a site off Huntingdon Road, north of the city. The original masterplan prepared by Lasdun had envisaged a phased development on the site taking the form of a spiral of linear residential buildings, with a Chapel at the heart of the spiral and a large freestanding dining hall at the centre of the enclosed landscaped courtyard. When the college first occupied the campus only the first phase of this plan had been completed, extending around the perimeter of the northern half of the site.

This concept was adapted by the architect Richard MacCormac in 1984 when he was asked to prepare an alternative master plan for the completion of the campus, still retaining the nineteenth-century villa on the east side of the site which had once been in the Darwin family's ownership, but developing new proposals for the layout of the residential and social elements required by the College. New residential wings were designed by MacCormac in a variation of Lasdun's three-storey high design of the first phase, and he also planned an extensive cloister linking the different parts of the site, with the social facilities which were to be housed in separate buildings directly accessible from it.

The new Chapel occupies the key position on the cloister route, terminating the eastern end of Lasdun's original projecting wing and facing the retained villa. However, after MacCormac's plans were drawn up the decision was taken to omit the covered cloister, leaving the route as an external walkway only; a change of policy which leaves the Chapel building very much a centrepiece in a varied landscape, visible from and related to the formal courtyard spaces of the residential wings as well as the informal character of the villa garden. The new building grows out of the end of the earlier residential wing, and MacCormac's second phase additions echo Lasdun's choice of materials with a similar colour brick and precast stone strings. Here too the theme is carried on into the new Chapel building, with the addition of a large steel-framed and glazed east window looking out over the garden. The external finishes, as well as the height and width of the original wing are thus respected, but the detailing and finish of the Chapel throughout present a smoother, more elegant and refined architectural vocabulary.

The entry to the Chapel was designed as part of the cloister walkway, with a vestibule opening directly off it, separating the two buildings, but with a bridge link above. The vestibule opens through a range of banded oak doors into a meeting room or 'crypt', while curving stairs lead up from the sides into the Chapel at first floor level. Placing the two primary spaces one over the other enabled the plan to be as compact as possible, and also generated sufficient height to complement and terminate the three-storey bedroom wing from which it springs. The outer brick walls are massive and curved, and, extending the language of the residential wings, circle and protect the Chapel within, like cupped hands protecting a jewel.

The central space of the Chapel is defined by four pairs of square columns arranged on the corners of a perfect square. These are circumscribed by a circular balustrade within the larger flanking circle of the outer walls, a separate structural entity, isolated from the outer world save for the curving stairs that climb around the flanking walls from below. Both in the planning and structural concepts and in the detailing much is derived from the religious symbols of the ship and the ark, and the progression from a worldly darkness to heavenly light. While the crypt is a sombre, private and intense space, almost cave-like with its glimpses of daylight, the Chapel seems suspended in light, floating on air, an efffect achieved and enhanced by the unusual detailing of the Chapel floor. This is profiled on the underside like a ship, with a soft hull-like form curving in three dimensions and finished with varnished American White Oak planking.

From within the vestibule the curving surfaces of the wooden ceiling draw the gaze to the sides, where staircases wind up and out of view apparently within the thickness of the wall, hinting at the major space above. At the base of each stair is a re-entrant glazed rectangular bay which slices through the drum of the curved brick outer walls, separating them from the main structure and providing an interpenetrating special device linking upper and lower levels. The repeated horizontals of the black steel glazing bars echo the steel banding to the oak entrance doors and the expressed horizontal jointing in the coursing of the walls, and develop eventually into the large-scale subtleties of the east window, study of which reveals a pleasing and coolly handled series of variants on the form of the Cross.

Ascending either of the staircases from the vestibule, one begins a circular climb towards the light as gradually the Chapel is revealed to view. Towards the top of the stairs the image of the ship is again evident, as the upper parts of the 'hull' emerge through the glazed margin abutting the concrete inner walls of the crypt, and are transformed into an outward canted balustrade, surmounted by a wide, robust solid oak rail and black painted steel angle handrail, and supported by elegantly curved oak brackets.

On arrival in the body of the Chapel the delicate sail-like forms of the roof are revealed. The four innermost columns are capped by concrete beams which define and support a simple white flat ceiling over the central part of the Chapel. Each of the pairs of outer columns is also surmounted by a concrete beam which acts as the support for a series of tapered oval wooden spars and radiating rafters that carry gently curved oak panels, separated from the flanking outer walls by a strip of glazing that allows light to flood down the curving white surfaces. Looking out over the altar position the huge east window frames a stunning view of a magnificent plane tree in the garden of the villa, its massive natural forms and changing shifts of light and pattern seen in pleasing contrast to the simple rectangular grid of the black steel frame.

The Chapel floor extends back over the entrance and 'cloister' to form a short 'nave', terminated by the display of decorative pipework of the organ case, which in turn conceals an unobtrusive secondary staircase access. This rises directly from the cloister, on the opposite side of the vestibule entrance and assists a quiet entry by latecomers. The nave element of the Chapel floor continues the 'hull' motif and is in effect a bridge over the pedestrian cloister route below. This is emphasised by the large window slots cut into the linking walls, which reveal the curved timber planking of the 'ship's hull' crossing the gap apparently free of support from the walls.

This is an inspiring, and inspired, building. The precision of the detailing, the white concrete structure and the warm honey-coloured wood, impart an air of purity, calm and welcoming enclosure. The black-painted steel windows and the tall radiators with their thin vertical pipes linking the paired columns convey a sense of dignity and purpose. In seeking to create a sense of place appropriate to the best traditions of the Church, the architect has employed a thoroughly modern architectural vocabulary imbued with a highly controlled use of symbolism to interpret the fundamental aspects of human experience and produce a most uplifting environment for contemplation and prayer.

LIVERPOOL STREET STATION
London

Architect: Architecture and Design Group, BR Board

Once one of the gloomiest and shabbiest of London's main line railway termini, Liverpool Street Station has recently emerged from years of complex building operations to rank as perhaps the smartest and most welcoming of all. The £120 million project has been undertaken simultaneously with the massive neighbouring development of Broadgate; indeed, one of the later phases has involved the construction of a huge new office block perched over platforms 11 to 18, along the eastern perimeter, with all the complications that this inevitably created in separating daily users from the construction activities and maintaining safety standards, particularly in the aftermath of the King's Cross disaster.

The original station was opened in 1875 and included a combination of shorter suburban platforms, and longer platforms for long-distance trains. When put together they generated an L-shaped plan, with the Gothic-styled station offices occupying the angle of the L. Such was the success of the suburban services that in 1892–4 the eastern trainshed was constructed, adding seven more platforms. Its new concourse, however, did not align with the original and could be reached only by footbridge. The subsequent addition of access routes to the Underground train system, not originally planned for, served only to exacerbate the confused layout. Not a lot happened to alter this state of affairs until the 1970s, when British Rail announced plans to demolish and build a new station.

As a result of the interest, indeed furore, that the redevelopment proposals unleashed, the western trainshed and the original offices were listed. In the resulting public debate it was agreed that while the eastern trainshed and the neighbouring Broad Street Station would be redeveloped and demolished, the listed structures would be retained, refurbished and extended, in an intriguing mix of conservation, historical replication and some entirely contemporary additions.

Although a lengthy and complex programme of engineering and enabling works was required to facilitate the planned changes to the station's layout and appearance, these are now behind the scenes and of little interest to the average rail passenger. The most obvious change has been the redesign of the main concourse areas into one simple and unified space. Liverpool Street is unusual in that the concourse level is a full story height below the street levels outside. In the old station this often facilitated an excellent view of the trains, and one was always aware of the primary travel function of the building. Now the split in levels between entrance and concourse has been utilized by the designers to provide an upper level of retail space right along the concourse as a bridge deck over the ticket barriers and entrances to the platforms. Yet although this new insertion into the Victorian Gothic of the original trainshed has been carried out in the most transparent of contemporary hi-tech styles, the sight of the trains themselves is completely interrupted and obscured from view from the concourse areas.

The whole phenomenon seems to be part of the general trend towards sanitizing the experience of rail travel so that it conforms to international design norms dictated by the development of air travel. The upper retail level is almost entirely clear-glazed, with slender white mullions curved over the top to create a simple barrel vault profile which does much to soften the intrusion of such a volume within space. Being at street level the pedestrian promenade giving access to the shops offers an easy and enjoyable route from which to experience the delights of the revamped terminus.

However, the modern minimalist structure of the glazed shops pales into insignificance when compared with the glories of the original cast-iron trainshed roof. This was originally constructed with four spans of considerable height supported on cast-iron columns, with tall faceted bases. The spandrels within the principal arches and springing from each column were infilled with decorative filigree cast-iron panels, with further rectangular panels filling the space at roof level between the central double row of columns. The columns themselves are ornamented with mouldings and the original acanthus leaf capitals have been reinstated. It is a magnificent structure, and has not only been thoroughly and sensitively restored, with a new paint colour scheme, but it has also been extended in like manner over the new concourse, all the details being faithfully replicated as far as possible to be indistinguishable from the original.

Recreation of historical detail has not been confined to the roof. The concourse has two primary entrance points, one to the south on to Liverpool Street, the other to the east on to Bishopsgate, and for each of these a completely new entrance structure has been designed. Each combines the latest in glazed technology with full-blown historicism. On Bishopsgate, passengers enter or leave through a barrel-vaulted glazed porch with suspended side canopies, standing as a separate structure in a small square. To the south are the original Victorian Great Eastern Hotel, to the north the massive bulk of new Broadgate buildings. To the rear and acting as a backdrop is a new gabled brick wall punctuated at high level by a range of lancet windows, and flanked by two slender brick towers in an Italianate style, elaborated with traditional clock faces and carved panels and with steeply pitched tapering roofs supporting a small bell stage.

The Liverpool Street entrance has been undertaken with a similar juxtaposition of new and old. Here the extended trainshed roof structure is presented to the outside in all its glory, seen to superb effect through a sheer glass curtain suspended and stiffened by an intricate array of stainless steel rods, ties and trusses. It is interesting to reflect on the engineeering skills of such different ages, the Victorian design solid, reassuring, space-defining, the modern hi-tech design light, taut, shiny and minimalist, both admirable in their own way.

The eastern side of the square formed at this entrance is a recreation of the original 1875 Gothic station offices, though with a number of alterations in design. These are chiefly at ground level where an open arcade of Gothic-style arches in Portland and Bath limestones has been introduced, including clustered columns and ornately carved capitals. On the west side of the square are placed a second pair of the Italianate brick towers, supporting a part of the extended trainshed roof between them as a canopy. The end result is a fascinating mixture of 'new' and 'old', though such is the attention to detail and the quality of finish throughout that to the untrained eye it might not be apparent that for all the Gothic and Italianate styling, everything is in fact as new as the daring hi-tech glass screen hovering over the entrance.

To have produced a clean and understandable plan based on a single large concourse, and to have recreated with such loving care the delicate intricacies of the trainshed roof as well as the reassuring forms and rhythms of the original Victorian buildings can be counted as a triumph.

THE PEARL CENTRE

Lynch Wood, Peterborough

Architect: Chapman Taylor Partners

The dream of an easy and pleasant journey to and from work, a relaxed and healthy countryside environment in which to enjoy a superior quality of life, and a modern, clean and spacious workplace with all the latest computer technology in a place custom-designed for the workforce, has been a potent motivating factor in the trend towards relocation of major company headquarters away from London that developed as long ago as the 1960s.

The Pearl Assurance Company, who are one of the country's largest and oldest life assurance and financial services organizations, made the decision to move to Peterborough in 1987. Following an intensive study of potential locations and sites they decided to proceed with the design and construction of their new headquarters on a 24-acre site in the Lynch Wood Business Park, on the outskirts of Peterborough. The 'lynch' from which the business park gets its name is a belt of mature woodland on the northern boundary of the site, separating it from the River Nene. This dominant landscape feature has inspired an enlightened approach to the development of the building and its services, aimed at enhancing the overall landscape setting and achieving the closest possible relationship between it and the office interiors.

The countryside around Peterborough is the predominantly flat landscape of the Fens. Looking for appropriate architectural references in this understated and peaceful landscape the designers drew inspiration from that classic vernacular symbol of the region, the Maltings at Snape, with its huge expanse of roof, punctuated by ventilation towers. The simple solid ground-hugging forms typical of these buildings proved an eminently suitable thematic framework upon which to develop a solution conforming with Peterborough Development Corporation's planning brief, which imposed a limit on height, required the use of traditional local materials and sought the creation of a parkland ambience.

The new building was required to house 2,200 staff, mainly in flexible open-planned offices, a hall for a main-frame computer, a restaurant to seat 600 people at a sitting, a training centre and parking for 1,500 cars. This large complex was also required to have a single entrance, to maximize security and foster a proper 'front door' image One of the key early decisions was to accommodate the majority of the car parking on two levels underneath the buildings. This enabled the buildings and roads together to cover less than half of the site area and maximized the opportunities for landscaping around the offices.

The office accommodation is arranged in three large square blocks, each three storeys high and arranged around a central atrium, the three being linked together at the corners on a diagonal line to create one continuous building. This arrangement generates a stepped profile defining a number of outdoor spaces which are thus visible from a large proportion of the offices. The available length of window wall is also maximized, while the diagonal linking permits shorter travel distances between different departments and blocks.

The entrance to the building is positioned at one of the free corners of the central office block, or office halls as they are called here. Entry to the building is made via a landscaped square at first floor level and is thus not only at the centre of the plan but also at the mid-point in the height of the building. The open courtyard, on a diagonal axis at right angles to the office halls, is enclosed by the distinctive forms of the restaurant building and computer hall, each flanking the main entrance, while the separate building of the Training Centre completes the other sides of the square. From the first floor entrance hall access to any part of the office areas is therefore only one floor up or down via the staircases within the atrium spaces.

The octagonal-shaped entrance hall is a bright, white-walled space some 10 metres high, capped with an octagonal glazed rooflight. This is supported from a single central column by an impressive array of radiating laminated timber trusses, the whole looking like a huge timber umbrella structure. Around the base of the octagon, an open arcade of round arched openings framed by continuous half round pilasters leads off into the various adjacent spaces and contains the central security control point. The floor is an amazing tour-de-force of geometrically patterned polished marble and granite, predominantly in black and white and betraying a distinctively Arabian influence, a sumptous introduction to the superbly high standards of materials and finish that are carried right through the project.

From the entrance hall, a low vaulted mall leads into the main central atrium of Middle Hall, a spectacular centrepiece bathed in natural light from the huge conical glazed rooflight, here supported simply on long slender timber beams radiating from the apex. The view from the office floors is through an open metal and timber screen, of decidedly Japanese inspiration, as are the two sweeping staircases, with their exaggeratedly chunky timber handrails and newel posts and stylized black metal junction pieces and balustrade screens. The floor is once again an exemplary demonstration of the stone mason's art. All of these superbly crafted elements are set against a background of lush planting.

Each of the other two atria follows a broadly similar pattern but is allowed to develop its own distinctive character, a device that not only adds to the richness and variety of what is a self-contained community but also aids recognition and orientation in relation to the different parts of a potentially confusing building. Throughout the interior, a variety of specially commissioned works of art embellish surfaces, adorn walls, add vibrant colour and interest and provide moments of intellectual uplift in what is already a stimulating environment.

The feeling of community and openness is much assisted by the decision to open up the atria to the office floors by omitting the usual glazed perimeter screens. This has in turn necessitated some innovation in terms of smoke-venting and fire precautions, and is partly instrumental in the requirement for the large ventilation towers, linked to the escape staircases, which form such a dominant feature of the elevations.

Returning to the exterior, the oversailing forms of the huge orange pantiled roofs dominate the vertical faces of the offices, the more so because the office section recedes at ground floor level beneath the overhanging first floor, accentuating the horizontality of the elevational treatment. The office walls are a fully-glazed mahogany-framed curtain wall system, with varying rhythms of mullions on each of the three floors, and different height windows to each generated by the overhang and intermediate sloping roof of the projecting first floor. The framing of the first-floor windows features a decorative spandrel composed of glass panels in alternating colours of bright red, blue, green and yellow.

Each façade is punctuated at the centre by one of the stair towers, clad in buff-coloured handmade bricks and with quoins, strings and dressings in pale cream limestone, St Maximin from France. The ground storey is faced with limestone rubble and smooth ashlar quoins, as is the main entrance portico facing the central courtyard. The towers are capped with shallow pitched lead-covered roofs with deeply overhanging eaves over a louvred base supported on large curved timber brackets. Similar rooftop projections punctuate the main ridge lines at the corners of the squares, and house air-handling plant. Other towers, such as those that flank the main entrance, simply have a hipped pantiled roof. The combination of natural materials and traditional forms lends the building a manifest air of permanence and quality. The varied treatment of each storey in cross section at the perimeter, the heavy oversailing eaves, the intricate rhythms of the timber mullioned panels, and the development of a simple plan concept into a symmetrical but interesting profile, with pavilions extended into the landscape from the corners of the outer squares, contrive a complex and stimulating visual experience, full of life and colour and highlighting the play of light and shade.

The end result is a building of enormous richness and diversity, one with which it is hard to see the inhabitants becoming bored. The distinctive qualities of its component parts working in conjunction with an openness of atmosphere will surely result in a strong sense of community and engender a commonality of purpose often lacking in workforces denied the level of patronage shown here. The £75 million contract started on site in June 1989 and was completed in February 1992. The Pearl Centre, as it is known, can stand scrutiny as a well crafted building, giving the sense of solidity and security that is expected of a major financial institution, and yet meeting the client's demanding requirements for flexibility in use and capability of accommodating the latest in data technology.

WOODLEA PRIMARY SCHOOL

Whitehill, Hampshire

Architect: Hampshire County Architect's Department
Chief Architect: C. Stansfield Smith
Project Architect: N. Churcher

The county of Hampshire has become renowned for the quality and variety of its schools over the last few years, and this project is one of the more recent of a clutch of primary schools to be designed by the county architect's department under the enlightened leadership of Colin Stansfield Smith. It was finished in August 1991 in readiness for the new intake of children in the autumn.

The site chosen for this school was a particularly sensitive one, being heavily wooded and in close proximity to an ancient meadow and some Iron-Age earthworks. The original brief was for two schools, but after a close study of the site the authority was persuaded to proceed only with a new mixed juniors and infants school, comprising three infants and four junior classrooms, with an assembly hall, kitchen facilities and staff areas.

The topography of the area has clearly influenced the siting and the spirit of the new building, which is clustered informally around a natural depression or bowl at the higher, west end of the sloping site. A new flat playing field has been created by a cut and fill process at the lower end of the site, but is very much an open 'field' surrounded by woodland, linked to the school only by grassy slopes winding up through the trees.

The wooded character of the place has been allowed to remain dominant and provides a wonderfully sylvan setting for the activities of the children. The slope of the site has been exploited in several ways and particularly in the cross-sections through the classroom blocks. Where they are cut into the slope at the 'rear', the construction is of brick walls and concrete floors, but on the lower side the construction changes to lightweight timber posts and framing and a suspended timber floor which terminates in a series of wooden slatted balcony terraces projecting forward over the edges of the softly landscaped bowl. These provide a substantial amount of additional outside teaching space for use in fair weather, and simultaneously integrate the complex forms of the classrooms much more closely into their landscape setting. Assisted by numerous stairs and exits, the children are given the maximum encouragement by this device to make use of the landscape as a valuable teaching/learning resource, not only for nature studies but for many other related topics.

The slope of the site has also generated three distinct levels within the building. At the core of the building lies the main entrance and circulation spine, with staff facilities, craft room and library all at the same middle level. To the west, and half a metre higher, lie the assembly hall and music/drama room, while to the east and correspondingly lower lie the separate wings of the junior and infant classrooms, wrapping round the edges of the bowl. The fragmented informal plan layout has been developed by dividing the building into four distinct zones, each with its own structural grid aligned in different directions in response to the prevailing site features and constraints of access and orientation. The various constituent parts of the building, both structural and non-structural, are carefully articulated and expressed both inside and out. Timber is stained in natural colours, with the windows and doors highlighted in different hues from the timber frames, laminated beams and boarded ceilings. The detailing is simple and robust, yet the overall effect is far from rustic.

The three infant classes are provided with a secluded 'base' off each main classroom, small in scale and tucked beneath the lowest part of the pitched roof to provide a sense of security and privacy. The rear brick built part of the classroom, the hard 'outer shell' enclosing and protecting the softer fragmented inner world, has a decorative tiled floor and a sink, while the 'front' end of the classroom has carpet on its timber floor and opens through a screen into a shared area accessible from all three classrooms. This common area in turn opens out on to the timber decks used as external work areas.

The junior classrooms have a similar structural and spacial organization, but without the 'bases' provided for infants. Instead there is a tutorial room provided for small specialist groups, and communal arrangements for lavatories and coats. All the classrooms are roofed with a combination of tall mono-pitched roofs incorporating a high level clerestory for good daylighting and flat or shallow pitched sections with lower headroom and overhanging eaves. The complexity of roof forms that is generated when the typical roof section is applied to a plan form angled and stepped around the site allows the bulk of the building to be visually much reduced in scale. This, together with the natural shingle coverings to the steeper pitches, has ensured that the building settles very gently into its carefully nurtured surroundings.

Woodlea, therefore, adds to the fine tradition of school building in Hampshire. Its image of a cluster of small houses nestling informally round a central hall seems appropriate to its rural setting and it sits picturesquely in the wooded landscape, embodying a view of education in which the potential for self-discovery and chance learning outside the classroom can be exploited to the full, within the more generally ordered processes of education with which we are familiar.

Periods of Gestation or Incubation

The table shows approximate periods of gestation or incubation for some common animals and birds. In some cases the periods may vary and where doubt arises professional advice should be sought.

Species	*Shortest period (days)*	*Usual period (days)*	*Longest period (days)*
Human	240	273	313
Horse	305	336	340
Cow	273	280	294
Goat	147	151	155
Sheep	140	147–50	160
Pig	109	112	125
Dog	55	63	70
Cat	53	56	63
Rabbit	30	32	35
Goose	28	30	32
Turkey	25	28	28
Duck	28	28	32
Chicken	20	21	22
Pigeon	17	18	19
Canary	12	14	14
Guinea Pig	63	–	70
Mouse	18	–	19
Rat	21	–	24
Elephant		21–22 months	
Zebra		56 weeks	
Camel		45 weeks	

Bequests to Charity

The alphabetical list below represents some of the principal charitable bequests from wills published since the last edition. Prior bequests, expenses and inheritance tax have to be deducted from the net figures given for the estate, so that the exact amount left to charities is never known. For the first time, more than half the estates listed are over £1 million.

By far the largest estate in the list is the £29 million estate of Comtesse Barbara de Brye, of Warminster, Wilts. Similar prominent bequests include the residue of the £618,497 estate of Charles Wollaston to the Charles Wollaston Award Fund at the Royal Academy of Arts, the fund he set up in 1978 to make awards for the most distinguished exhibit in each year's Summer Exhibition. Lt.-Col. Alan Hopkins, of Barnstaple, left one third of the residue of his £1.3 million estate to Eton College 'as a gesture of my gratitude'.

Two millionaires, Edgar Borrow and retired London schoolmaster John Tulloch, left their entire estates to a single charity. Baron Molson, the former Conservative MP for High Peak, left a quarter of the residue of his £674,542 estate to the Charities Aid Foundation and the other three-quarters for such charitable purposes as his executors selected. A similar discretion was given to her executors by Margaret Ramsay, the West End literary agent, for half the residue of her £2.7 million estate, and by Edith Hills who left a quarter of the residue in a similar manner. Similar discretionary residuary bequests were made by two brothers, Ronald Raven, the internationally renowned oncologist, and John Raven, a retired Buckinghamshire farmer.

The RNLI received several large bequests, including the residues of the estates of Stanley Barker, Emeritus Town Clerk of Barking and Dagenham, Lady Dora Pechell and Marion Stell. Leslie Middleton left the residue of his £1.3 million estate between the RNLI and the National Trust, the latter also receiving the residues of the estates of John Lewes, and Mary Shafer – she specified that it be used for the Dorset coast, and the Lake District, where she had also lived. Florence Shirlaw left a share of the residue of her estate to the 'Birds Welfare and Protection Association', provided her executors could trace it within a year of her death. Eleanor Pattison requested that 'loving, quiet country private homes' be found for her dogs by the RSPCA, whom she left £160,000 after the income was used for the dogs' upkeep. Ellen Newton made a bequest not mentioned below, of £50,000 to Revd Ian Paisley, to assist Protestants in Northern Ireland in financial distress as a result of terrorist activities within the province as he determined.

Sir Anthony Lincoln, the High Court judge, writer and broadcaster, left part of the residue of his estate to Salisbury Cathedral Spire Appeal, while Winchester Cathedral received a quarter of the residue of the estate of retired Southampton shipbroker Alfred Day. Edward Kelland-Espinosa, the dancer and producer, left most of his estate to the British Ballet Organization and the Espinosa Memorial Fund, while Jean Batters left the residue of her estate to the Actors' Charitable Trust. The actor Alan Wheatley, perhaps best remembered as the Sheriff of Nottingham in the 1950s television series *Robin Hood*, left a fifth of his estate to the Salvation Army. Not included in the list below was Arnold Lawrence, the former Professor of Classical Archaeology at Cambridge, who left the residue of his £434,618 estate to the Seven Pillars of Wisdom Trust, including all material relating to his older brother, better known as Lawrence of Arabia.

Catherine Mary Walker-Alexander, of Ludlow, Salop, £1,628,490 (the residue equally between Parkinson's Disease Society, Cancer Research Campaign, Royal Commonwealth Society for the Blind and the Raynauds Association Trust)

Beryl Catherine Allpress, of Chartfield Square, London SW15, £3,328,817 (£160,000 to the National Trust)

Robert Hammond Rose Archer, of Camberley, Surrey, £1,109,321 (one 25th of the residue each to Help the Aged, the British Red Cross Society, NSPCC, Barnardo's, Cheshire Foundation, Multiple Sclerosis Society, Oxfam, Mencap, RNLI and Salvation Army)

Stanley Watson Barker, of Hornchurch, Essex, £1,815,786 (£200,000 each to the National Asthma Campaign and a charity for research into idiopathic scoliosis, and the residue equally between the Imperial Cancer Research Fund and the RNLI)

Bernard Pawley Barton, of Wilmington, Devon, £1,616,794 (the residue equally between the RNLI, Police Dependants' Trust, Musicians Benevolent Fund and Cancer Relief Macmillan Fund)

Jean Eleanor Batters, of Eastbourne, East Sussex, £708,169 (the residue to the Actors' Charitable Trust, for the benefit of Denville Hall, Northwood)

Margaret Lamplough Bean, of Cotmanthorpe, N. Yorks., £702,866 (the residue equally between St Leonard's Hospice, York, St Dunstan's, Imperial Cancer Research Fund and Guide Dogs for the Blind Association)

Jessie Lilian Caroline Binks, of Woodford Green, Essex, £716,911 (the residue equally between the Distressed Gentlefolk's Aid Association, Animal Health Trust, Help the Aged and Cancer Research Campaign)

Leslie Archbald Borer, of Tring, Herts., £854,240 (half the residue to Christ's Hospital, Horsham)

Edgar Wilfred Borrow, of Cowplain, Hants., £1,967,547 (his entire estate to the Borrow Dental Milk Foundation)

Marjorie Mons Bousfield, of Copford Green, Essex, £1,890,946 (£30,000 and 30 per cent of the residue each to the Guide Dogs for the Blind Association, and St Joseph's Hospice, London E8, 20 per cent of the residue to the Imperial Cancer Research Fund, £20,000 and 10 per cent to the PDSA, and 10 per cent of the residue to the Blue Cross)

Elizabeth Florence Chambers, of Warley, Brentwood,

Essex, £1,404,865 (the residue equally between the RNLI, Barnardo's and Guide Dogs for the Blind Association)

Bernard Eustace Chaplin, of Shermanbury, West Sussex, £1,167, 252 (the residue equally between the Friends of King Edward VII Hospital, Midhurst, the Gun and Allied Trades Benevolent Society, and the Samaritans)

Margaret Chappell, of Fallowfield, Manchester, £1,139,462 (the residue equally between the RNLI and RNIB)

Clarice Elizabeth Chree, of Kingston upon Thames, Surrey, £1,227,836 (the residue to the Christian Science Trust in Great Britain)

Norman Llewellyn Clay, of Worsborough, S. Yorks., £1,032,308 (one 18th of the residue each to Chapeltown Methodist Church, the RNIB, Royal Commonwealth Society for the Blind, International Christian Relief and Salvation Army)

Ronald Inglis Conradi, of Waddington Road, London E15, £793,356 (the residue to the Children's Society)

Zacharias Constantinou, of Park Street, London W1, £1,291,887 (the residue to the Old Poor House of Larnaca)

Francis George Cooke, of Lelant, Cornwall, £1,010,064 (the residue to Brighton College Scholarship and Prize Foundation)

Alfred Edgar Victor Day, of Bitterne, Southampton, £2,658,313 (one quarter of the residue to Winchester Cathedral, and one quarter of the residue equally between the Royal Commonwealth Society for the Blind, British Red Cross, Salvation Army, Cancer Relief Macmillan Fund, London Association for the Blind, Save the Children Fund, Queen Elizabeth's Foundation for the Disabled, Barnardo's, Age Concern England, NSPCC, MIND, Marie Curie Cancer Care, RNID, the RNLI, and the Leukaemia Research Fund, Southampton Branch)

Comtesse Barbara de Brye, of Boyton Manor, Wilts., £29,724,890 (£1,000,000 to Lucy Cavendish College, Cambridge, £250,000 each to Salisbury Cathedral and the Victoria and Albert Museum, and £100,000 each to Boyton Church, Wardour Catholic Church, Tisbury, and the Salisbury and South Wiltshire Museum Trust)

Richard Lionel Lea Priestley Edwards, of Windsor, Berks., £764,442 (the residue to the Leukaemia Research Fund)

Edward John Kelland-Espinosa, of Lonsdale Road, London SW13, £995,370 (£55,000, other bequests and half the residue to the British Ballet Organization, and £10,000 and half the residue to the Espinosa Memorial Fund)

Gilbert Roy Fletcher, of Meole Brace, Shrewsbury, Salop, £4,545,501 (the residue, including the Marrington Estate, to the Roy Fletcher Charitable Trust)

Beatrix Rosalie Elizabeth Ford, of Abergavenny, Gwent, £1,569,352 (two-thirds of the residue to the RSPCA and one third of the residue for such charities for the advancement of relations between Great Britain and France as her trustee thinks fit)

Joyce Campbell Forster, of Darras Hall, Northumberland, £1,883,226 (the residue equally between the Guide Dogs for the Blind Association, North of England Cancer Research Campaign, Marie Curie Cancer Care, Newcastle upon Tyne, the NCPCC, West Northumberland Branch, the RSPCA, Newcastle upon Tyne, Tynemouth Blind Welfare, Northumberland Wildlife Trust, Arthritis Care, Whitley Bay, Age Concern, Newscastle upon Tyne, the Northumbria Deaf Mission, and the Abbeyfield Ponteland Society)

William James Geen, of Spaxton, Somerset, £1,066,955 (£100,000 to Spaxton Village Hall, and the residue equally between St Margaret's Somerset Hospice, Taunton, the Musgrove Grove Hospital Coronary Care Unit, Taunton, the League of Friends of Bridgwater Hospitals, the Bridgwater Society for Mentally Handicapped Children and Adults, Age Concern Somerset, the Kerland Foundation for Brain Damaged Children, and the Royal Agricultural Benevolent Institution, for grants and accommodation in Somerset)

Alexander Golodetz, of West Wittering, W. Sussex, £3,806,946 (£200,000 and one third of the residue as to 20 parts each to the Central British Fund for World Jewish Relief and the Jewish Welfare Board, 14 parts to the Hafetz-Haim Orphanage, Jerusalem, 4 parts each to Battersea Dogs Home, the PDSA and Oxfam, 3 parts to the RSPCA, and 2 parts each to the Donkey Sanctuary, Sidmouth, Greater London Fund for the Blind, Guide Dogs for the Blind Association and LEPRA)

William Rowland Griffiths, of Pembroke, Dyfed, £768,115 (the residue equally between the Cancer Research Campaign, RNLI, Barnardo's, British Heart Foundation, Cheshire Foundation, Guide Dogs for the Blind Association, NSPCC, Royal British Legion, Salvation Army and WRVS)

Alice Ellen Haigh, of Stoneygate, Leicester, £1,235,980 (one fifth of the residue to the National Trust, and one tenth of the residue each to the RSPCA, Imperial Cancer Research Fund, NSPCC, Barnardo's, National Fund for Research into Crippling Diseases, Homes of Rest for Gentlewomen, London, Help the Aged and the Royal Wolverhampton School)

Sheila Rosemary Haldane, of Northwood, Middx, £765,455 (half the residue to Emmanuel Parish Church, Northwood, and one quarter of the residue each to the National Rose Society and St Andrews University, Scotland)

Gladys Muriel Harris, of Yarnton, Oxon., £1,041,570 (the residue equally between the RNIB, RSPCA, Royal Agricultural Benevolent Institution, Help the Aged, the Burcot Cheshire Home, Imperial Cancer Research Fund and BLESMA)

William Leonard Harrison, of Ockley Road, London SW16, £1,033,162 (£50,000 and 14 per cent of the residue each to Barnardo's, British Kidney Patient Association, National Association for Mental Health, Multiple Sclerosis Society and Action Aid)

Joseph William Hetherington, of Blindcrake, Cockermouth, Cumbria, £928,854 (the residue to the Faith Mission Bible College, Edinburgh)

Edith May Hills, of Strood, Kent, £3,155,043 (three-quarters of the residue to the R. G. Hills Charitable Trust, and one quarter of the residue for such charitable purposes in England as her trustees select)

Douglas Bromley Hillyard, of Stratford-upon-Avon, £1,361,942 (the residue to the Warwickshire Masonic Charitable Association, towards the cost of building a retirement home)

Lt.-Col. Alan John Lambert Hopkins, retd, of Roundswell, Barnstaple, Devon, £1,344,908 (one third of the residue to Eton College, and two-ninths of the residue each to the PDSA, Animal Health Trust and Blue Cross)

Amy Howcraft, of Chagford, Devon, £900,512 (the residue to the Children's Society)

Alan Harry Hudson, of Wisbech, Cambs., £2,106,232 (the residue to the Hudson Foundation)

John Faulkner Irving, of Eaton upon Tern, Salop, £2,261,528 (the residue, after a life interest, equally between the RNLI and RNIB)

Elsie Mabel Jowett, of Ilkley, W. Yorks., £1,904,627 (two-thirds of the residue equally between the Bradford Flower Fund Homes, the YWCA, Leeds Branch, Barnardo's and the Missions to Seamen, and one third of the residue equally between the Salvation Army, RNLI, St Dunstan's, and the National Children's Home, for the Leeds/Bramhope branch)

Mary Isabel Jupe, of Cambridge, £862,880 (the residue equally between the Royal College of Surgeons and the Royal College of Radiologists)

Elisabeth Wilhelmine Frieda Anna Kahnweiler, of Gerrards Cross, Bucks., £3,467,324 (£25,000 and one quarter of the residue each to the League of Friends of the Chalfont and Gerrards Cross Hospital, the Arthritis and Rheumatism Council, RNIB and the Council of Christians and Jews)

Ronald Benedict Kaufmann, of Regent's Park, London NW1, £1,111,955 (£100,000 to University College School, London, and the residue equally between the Jewish Welfare Board, the Joint Israel Appeal, Multiple Sclerosis Society and the National Trust)

Thomas James Kelly, of Davyhulme, Manchester, £1,262,134 (half his estate equally between the National Trust, Barnardo's, Age Concern England, the English Martyrs Roman Catholic Church, Urmston, the Sisters of the Convent of Notre Dame, Audenshaw, the Catholic Children's Rescue Society, Manchester, and the Incorporated Benevolent Association of the Chartered Institute of Patent Agents)

Illa Kodicek, of Piccadilly, London W1, £2,388,064 (the residue to the National Association of Boys Clubs)

Thelma Laycock, of Kirkby Overblow, Harrogate, N. Yorks., £1,547,936 (half her estate to the British Heart Foundation)

Ailsey Lazarus, of Trevor Place, London SW7, £1,239, 624 (the residue equally between the Jewish Welfare Board, Imperial Cancer Research Fund, British Council for Aid to Refugees, British Red Cross Society, Central British Fund for Jewish Relief and Rehabilitation, Arthritis and Rheumatism Council, National Trust, Sue Ryder Foundation, Cheshire Foundation and the Winged Fellowship Trust)

Harry Leder, of West Heath Avenue, London NW11, £1,070,821 (the residue equally between the Jewish Welfare Board, Norwood Homes for Jewish Children, Jewish Blind Society, British Friends of Israel War Disabled and the Imperial Cancer Research Fund)

Doris Cecilia Levy, of Liverpool, £1,949,118 (one quarter of the residue each to the Friends of the Hebrew University of Jerusalem and WIZO)

John Powell Ponsonby Lewes, of Ciliau Aeron, Lampeter, Dyfed, £3,148,875 (the residue to the National Trust)

Hon. Sir Anthony Leslie Julian Lincoln, of Upper Woodford, Salisbury, Wilts., £899,052 (the residue equally between Salisbury Cathedral Spire Appeal, the Harrison Homes for the Elderly and Leukaemia Research Fund)

Molly Mary Mackrill, of Hockley Heath, West Midlands, £726,729 (£150,000 for such charitable purposes in the UK as her trustees select, and the residue equally between Greenpeace, the International League for the Protection of Horses, Birmingham Dogs Home, Donkey Sanctuary, Sidmouth, Raystede Animal Centre, Ringmer, the Cats Protection League, Blue Cross, PDSA, National Canine Defence League, National Anti-Vivisection Society, Parkinson's Disease Society, FRAME, Dr Hadwen Trust for Humane Research, International Fund for Animal Welfare, the Acorn Children's Hospice, Birmingham, the Warren Pearl Hospice, Solihull, St Barnabas Hospice, Worthing, Redwings Horse Sanctuary, Norwich, and the RSPCA)

Thelma McLaughlin, of Seaton Delaval, Northumberland, £1,397,137 (the residue equally between Christian Aid, Age Concern, National Children's Home, PDSA, Marie Curie Memorial Foundation, and the Synod of the Northern Province of the United Reformed Church)

Norbert Nathan Magnus, of Eaton Square, London SW1, £1,073,865 (his three pictures by Matisse and one by Georges Rouault to the British Friends of the Art Museums of Israel, and the residue in such proportion as his trustees determine between the City of Westminster Society for Mentally Handicapped Children, the Cancer Research Campaign Clinical Trials Centre, London, the Jewish Blind Society, Jewish Deaf Association, Fight for Sight Fund, Arthritis and Rheumatism Council, Children and Youth Aliyah Committee, the Central British Fund for World Jewish Relief, the Jewish Philanthropic Association, Jewish Welfare Board, and the Ravenswood Foundation)

Margery Matthias, of Moss, Wrexham, Clwyd, £1,082,095 (half the residue to the Maelor General Hospital, Wrexham)

Cecil Robert Mavin, of Shepley, Huddersfield, W. Yorks., £972,893 (half the residue to the National Canine Defence League, and one sixth of the residue each to Kirklees Hospice Society, Jerry Green Foundation and the Arthritis and Rheumatism Council)

Leslie John Middleton, of Maylandsea, Essex, £1,350,947 (the residue equally between the RNLI and National Trust)

Rt. Hon. Arthur Hugh Elsdale, Baron Molson, of Marsham Street, London SW1, £674,542 (three-quarters of the residue for such charitable purposes as his trustees select, and one quarter of the residue to the Charities Aid Foundation)

Frederick John Moore, of Cambridge, £997,427 (the residue equally between St Andrew's Church, Oakington, Cambs., the Province of Cambridgeshire Masonic Benevolent Fund, the Arthur Rank Hospice, Cambridge, Professor Joseph Mitchell's Cancer Research Fund, Cambridge, Ida Darwin Hospital, Fulbourn, the New Masonic Samaritans Fund, NSPCC and RNLI)

Ellen Margaret Newton, of Hindhead, Surrey, £2,791,248 (two 17ths of the residue each to the Salvation Army, National Kidney Research Fund and the RNIB, and one 17th of the residue each to the Distressed Gentlefolk's Aid Association, Society for the Assistance of Ladies in Reduced Circumstances, the Sheppard Trust for Elderly Gentlewomen of Limited Means, the National Trust Enterprise Neptune Fund, the Wildlife Preservation Fund, Institute of Cancer Research, Imperial Cancer Research Fund, Royal Association in Aid of the Deaf and Dumb, National Deaf Children's Society, Cheshire Foundation, and the RNLI)

John Bertram Patston, of Stockerston, Leics., £1,639,871 (the residue to the Jack Patston Charitable Trust)

Eleanor Pattison, of Sarsden, Oxon., £2,161,451 (one quarter of the sale proceeds of freehold property and effects and two 21sts of the residue to the Animal Health Trust, two 21sts of the residue each to the PDSA, National Anti-Vivisection Society and Battersea Dogs Home, one quarter of the above sale proceeds and one 21st of the residue to the Blue Cross, and one 21st of the residue each to the Salvation Army, National Trust, Barnardo's, Distressed Gentlefolk's Aid Association, RNIB, Donkey Sanctuary, Sidmouth, National Canine Defence League, British Union for the Abolition of Vivisection, Guide Dogs for the Blind Association, Council for the Protection of Rural England, World-Wide Fund for Nature, and the Society of the Sacred Mission, Willen Priory, Bucks.)

Lady Dora Constance Pechell, of Felpham, W. Sussex, £706,287 (the residue to the RNLI)

Theophilus George Phillips, of Henlade, Taunton,

Somerset, £944,960 (the residue equally between the RNIB and League Against Cruel Sports)

Eva Victoria Puddephatt, of Wendover, Bucks., £953,366 (the residue equally between the Arthritis and Rheumatism Council, Cheshire Foundation, Imperial Cancer Research Fund, National Kidney Research Fund, British Red Cross Society, and the Chest, Heart and Stroke Association)

Betty Hattersley Pugh, of Hampsthwaite, Harrogate, N. Yorks., £5,088, 950 (one ninth of the residue each to Harrogate Neighbours Housing Association, Barnardo's, Spastics Society, Salvation Army, British Heart Foundation, Arthritis and Rheumatism Council, RNLI and Yorkshire Cancer Research Campaign, and one eighteenth of the residue each to the National Benevolent Fund for the Aged, and the National Benevolent Institution, London)

Margaret Francesca Ramsay, of Redcliffe Square, London SW10, £2,770,196 (half the residue for such charitable objects as her trustees consider will benefit writers and encourage the art of writing)

Fanny Rapaport, of Prestwich, Manchester, £980,053 (half the residue to her Charitable Settlement dated 30 April 1963, £6,000, effects and one quarter of the residue to the Manchester Jewish Home for the Aged, and one eighth of the residue each to the JNF Charitable Trust and the Friends of the Hebrew University of Jerusalem)

John Mason Raven, of Wingrave, Bucks., £1,235,377 (the residue for such charitable institutions in England as his trustees select)

Ronald William Raven, of Harley Street, London W1, £1,468,545 (the residue for such charitable institutions in England as his trustees select)

Winifred Nellie Richards, of Shrewsbury, Salop, £871,887 (two-fifths of the residue to the National Trust, for work in Shropshire, and one fifth of the residue each to the Royal Shrewsbury Hospital, the Shropshire Hospice, Shrewsbury, and the Shropshire Trust for Nature Conservation)

Marjorie Rosefield, of Notting Hill Gate, London W11, £2,417,294 (the residue to the Jewish Welfare Board)

Carol Evelyn May Rygate, of Frenchay Common, Bristol, £736,853 (the residue equally between the Abbeyfield Society and Distressed Gentlefolk's Aid Association)

Jessie Vera Scuffham, of Waddington, Lincs., £946,305 (three-quarters of her estate equally between the RNIB, RNID, Arthritis and Rheumatism Council, and the British Heart Foundation)

Mary Shafer, of Southbourne, Dorset, £756,662 (the residue to the National Trust, for the preservation or acquisition of property in the Lake District and Dorset)

Florence Nightingale Shirlaw, of Walmer, Kent, £1,203,514 (the residue equally between the Bransby Home of Rest for Horses, the Land Heritage, the Cinnamon Trust, Raystede Centre for Animal Welfare, Ringmer, Animal Welfare Trust, the Bird Sanctuary, Sandwich, the Countryside Commission Wildlife Trust, Woodland Trust, Wood Green Animal Shelter, Soil Association and 'the Birds Welfare and Protection Association')

Ernest William Skinner, of St Minver, Wadebridge, Cornwall, £1,160,885 (the residue equally between Mount Edgcumbe Hospice, St Austell, the Cornwall Air Ambulance at RAF St Mawgan, the Imperial Cancer Research Fund, and Royal London Society for the Blind)

William Reuben Sloman, of Saffron Walden, Essex, £652,763 (the residue to such registered charities as his trustees select)

John Smeds, of South Shields, Tyne and Wear, £632,675 (the residue to Lloyds Charities Trust, London)

Arthur Smith, of Grove, Wantage, Oxon., £2,092,546 (£100,000 to the Grovelands Charity and the residue variously to that charity, the Grove Strict Baptist Chapel, Aged Pilgrims Friend Society, Gospel Standard Bethesda Fund, Gospel Standard Publishing Fund, Gospel Standard Magazine Fund, the Gables Care Group, Wantage, Trinitarian Bible Society, Spurgeons Homes, Arthritis Care, Imperial Cancer Research Fund, Mental Health Foundation, Treloar Trust, Save the Children Fund, RNIB, Lord's Day Observance Society, Guide Dogs for the Blind Association, RNLI, Royal Commonwealth Society for the Blind, British Heart Foundation, Help the Aged, and the Friends of Wantage Hospital)

Marion Stell, of Ilkley, W. Yorks., £1,463,974 (the residue to the RNLI)

Kenneth Livsey Sutcliffe, of Beckwithshaw, Harrogate, N. Yorks., £1,526,068 (£5,000 and one 115th of the residue each to St Michael and All Angels Church, Beckwithshaw, Beckwithshaw Village Hall, Harrogate Hospital, SSAFA, Barnardo's, British Heart Foundation, Salvation Army, and the Martin House Hospice, Boston Spa)

Daphne Elizabeth Thompson, of Cambridge, £960,280 (one third of the residue to the National Society for Cancer Relief, and one sixth of the residue each to the Royal Commonwealth Society for the Blind, RNID, Arthritis and Rheumatism Council, and Guide Dogs for the Blind Association)

Eric John Torkington, of Mylor Downs, Falmouth, Cornwall, £1,193,557 (the residue equally between the Imperial Cancer Research Fund, Cancer Research Campaign, and the MacMillan Service, Cornwall)

John William Martin Tulloch, of Kensington Park Road, London W11, £1,273,334 (his entire estate to the RSPCA)

Ilona Tweedy, of Horsell, Surrey, £1,088,287 (20 per cent of the residue to Barnardo's, 15 per cent of the residue to the Salvation Army, and 5 per cent of the residue each to Age Concern England, St Joseph's Hospice, London E8, and the RNLI)

Sidney Arthur Walton, of Upton, W. Yorks., £1,112,970 (the residue to the Yorkshire Cancer Research Campaign)

William Cameron Welsh, of Hilton, Yarm, Cleveland, £2,138,232 (half the residue to the Imperial Cancer Research Fund)

Alan Wheatley, of Bryanston Square, London W1, £698,725 (one fifth of the residue to the Salvation Army)

Marion Humphreys Winstone, of Sheffield, S. Yorks., £1,218,845 (the residue equally between the Yorkshire Cancer Research Campaign, Woodland Trust and the RSPB)

Charles Hannam Gulston Wollaston, of Felpham, W. Sussex, £618,497 (the residue to the Royal Academy of Arts Charles Wollaston Award Fund)

Florence Elsie Woods, of Paignton, Devon, £951,466 (£2,000 and half the residue to Quaker Action on Drink and Drugs, and half the residue to the Salvation Army)

Frances Barbara Young, of Henleaze, Bristol, £917,856 (the residue to the National Trust)

Conservation and Heritage

THE NATURAL ENVIRONMENT

Barn Owls in Decline

The once familiar barn owl has declined seriously in numbers during the past 25 years, and no longer nests over much of central England. An amendment to the Wildlife and Countryside Act has now made it illegal to release captive barn owls under licence and has made the registration and ringing of captive owls compulsory. This measure was prompted by the large number of owls, estimated at 3,000, that are raised and released by amateur enthusiasts each year. They are easy to rear, and a hen bird can be induced to lay several clutches in succession with the use of incubators. There may be as many as 20,000 captive barn owls in Britain, compared with a wild population of only about 4,500 pairs. Although the released birds' chances of survival are low, ornithologists fear that the increased competition for limited food and nesting space may be putting the wild birds at a disadvantage. Interbreeding may also dilute wild genetic strains, thus weakening the owls' ability to survive in the wild.

The main reason for the barn owl's decline seems to be the loss of suitable habitats in which to nest and feed. In many areas there are few suitable old trees or derelict barns, although this deficiency can to some extent be redressed by the thoughtful placement of nest boxes made from tea chests. Barn owls may also be finding it more difficult to catch voles and mice. Agricultural progress has resulted in the loss of hedges and rough ground, and although short grassy field headlands are ideal hunting grounds for owls, the effect of agricultural set-aside policies in increasing such areas has so far been disappointing. Uncultivated grassland is now also frequently infested with brambles, thistle and scrub, making it difficult or impossible for the owl to reach its prey. The impact of new roads, with their slipways, service stations and all-too-enticing grass verges, also threatens barn owls. Research has shown that the decline is not the result of persecution or toxic chemicals, as was once supposed.

Burren Visitor Centre

A proposal by the Irish Government to build an elaborate tourist attraction in the heart of the Burren, Europe's largest limestone 'pavement', has alarmed conservationists. The Burren is celebrated for its rare flowers, combining mountain and coast species with elements of the Mediterranean and North American flora. As planned, the Burren Centre, to be built with EC funds, will cater for up to 60,000 visitors a year, with 30 acres of landscaped walkways, new roads and the probability of 'knock-on' development. Conservationists are not against the centre as such, but argue that it should be more sensitively sited close to existing facilities in a nearby village. They are particularly concerned about the impact of the development on nearby turloughs, seasonal lakes which are particularly vulnerable to disturbance and pollution.

The Irish Office of Public Works granted itself planning permission for the work. However, lobbying of the European Commission by the Burren Action Group helped to secure a delay while an environmental assessment was carried out. The resulting report was criticized by an independent analysis commissioned by the World Wide Fund for Nature, which said the assessment failed adequately to address wildlife and ecology needs.

The Burren Visitor Centre proposal highlights the problems caused when EC funds are available for poorer members of the Community to develop hitherto remote places rich in wildlife. The results of this policy are already evident along the coastline of Portugal and Spain.

Freshwater Pollution

The four-year drought shows no signs of ending. The worst affected freshwater sites continue to be spring-fed rivers on porous bedrocks such as chalk, and shallow lakes and fens. The problem is exacerbated by excessive water abstraction, especially in East Anglia and the Home Counties. Pumping directly from rivers for crop irrigation is still common, although the National Rivers Authority (NRA), which is responsible for regulating water licences, says it is now restricting the issue of new licences.

The effects of water pollution and enrichment become more severe during low flows. A 1990 NRA survey found that only 29 per cent of rivers in England and Wales were 'very clean', compared with 35 per cent in 1985. The main pollutants are phosphate-rich human sewage and farm slurry, and nitrates from leached fertilizers and field run-off. The scheme promoted by the Ministry of Agriculture, Fisheries and Food to designate 'nitrate sensitive areas' has failed in its aim of reducing the use of nitrogen fertilizers. The NRA has so far brought 900 successful prosecutions against companies and farms for illegal pollution, the worst offenders being British Coal, Welsh Water and St Ivel. This is generally acknowledged to be the tip of a large iceberg. A recent report by the Royal Commission on Environmental Pollution recommended making the polluter pay for effluent discharge over certain limits, thus providing a stronger incentive for a factory to reduce its discharges. It also recommended the building of phosphate-stripping plants at sewage works, as is already the practice in Germany and Holland.

The Government have reacted by promising to introduce a new system of statutory water quality objectives in 1993 to ensure that the 'clean river' count does not decline any further. To be effective the system will require regular and frequent monitoring. In the meantime, 15 river systems of outstanding interest for wildlife are to be notified as Sites of Special Scientific Interest (SSSIs) by English Nature.

Major Roads

Two road-building proposals dominated the headlines this year: a major roadway which will destroy part of Oxleas Wood in Greenwich, south-east London; and the final section of the M3 motorway, which will cut through Twyford Down, the last area of undeveloped chalk downland near Winchester. Both proposals have been the subject of a series of public inquiries and the intervention of the European Environment Commissioner.

Oxleas Wood was purchased by public subscription in 1934 and is now both a Local Nature Reserve and an SSSI. The wood and its attractive surroundings lie in the path of the East London River Crossing, an expressway designed to extend the M11 motorway across the Thames and link it with the A2. After a public inquiry in 1985–6 at which 8,000 objections to the proposal were heard, the Inspector recommended a cut-and-cover tunnel to avoid bisecting Oxleas Wood. The Government rejected this proposal on the grounds of cost. The objectors then took their case to the EC on technical grounds, alleging that the Department of Transport had failed to carry out an adequate environmental assessment as required under EC law, and to put forward measures to preserve the village of Plumstead and its adjacent green spaces. In 1991 the Government announced plans to complete the expressway using a box girder bridge, again rejecting the Inspector's recommendation of a tunnel. Legal proceedings against the British Government were begun by the European Commissioner in October 1991.

Twyford Down proved an even more contentious case. After 20 years of debate and three public inquiries held between 1977 and 1988, a route was chosen for a four-lane motorway which will destroy two scheduled ancient monuments, damage two SSSIs and cut a deep cavity through a designated Area of Outstanding Natural Beauty. Again, a tunnel option was rejected on the grounds of cost and delay. The Twyford Down Association, formed largely of local residents, took their case to the High Court, alleging that the Department of Transport had again failed to comply with the EC directive on environmental assessments. Their claim was rejected by the judge, who awarded £100,000 costs against three private individuals and two parish councils. Proceedings against the UK Government were opened by the European Commissioner, although they now appear to have been shelved.

Large numbers of protestors arrived on the site as work on the motorway began in 1992. Although they withdrew peacefully after a court injunction was served, few environmental issues in Britain have seen protest on such a large and vehement scale; local opinion may have contributed towards the loss of the Southampton Itchen parliamentary seat of Christopher Chope, the Transport Minister responsible for the decision. Road construction will continue to be a major environmental issue in Britain as long as the Department of Transport remains in a position to act as both judge and jury in cases where interests other than those of motorists are involved.

Peatland Preservation

In a controversial agreement signed early in 1992, Fisons PLC, the main producer of horticultural peat in Great Britain, donated 2,378 hectares of lowland peat bog to English Nature; however, peat cutting is to continue on more than half of this area. Undisturbed lowland peatland has declined from an estimated 34,500 hectares to only 445 hectares through exploitation and reclamation, and virtually all the intact areas have now been designated as SSSIs. However, planning permission to cut peat generally predates the wildlife legislation and therefore remains unrestricted by SSSI designation. Modern mechanized methods of peat milling are much more destructive of the peatland habitat than peat cutting, and effectively sterilize the bog surface. Several square miles of Thorne and Hatfield Moors in South Yorkshire, by far the largest lowland peat bog in England, are now 'black deserts' of level milled peat, bereft of plant life. Whether or not such areas can ever be restored to living peat bogs is uncertain.

The agreement between English Nature and Fisons was criticized by most major conservation bodies, whose Peatland Campaign Consortium had campaigned to secure better protection for peatlands and had successfully promoted 'environmentally friendly' alternatives to peat. The agreement undoubtedly caused a degree of suspicion between English Nature and the non-governmental conservation organizations, who deplored the secrecy in which the negotiations were held and the lack of consultation with them. On the other hand, English Nature could point to the immediate benefits to relatively intact areas of peat bog through the blocking of drains to raise the water table. The decision was defended 'as a practical answer to an urgent problem' and it was pointed out that to safeguard all peatland SSSIs would involve the Government in enormous compensation claims and the loss of about 200 jobs.

Two months later, Fisons placed their horticultural division, the branch responsible for supplying peat products, up for sale. At the time of writing no buyer has been announced.

Protected Species

Fourteen species of animal and 73 species of plant are to be given complete protection under the Wildlife and Countryside Act 1981 as a result of the Act's second five-year review (for full list, *see* pages 743–4). To qualify for protected status, a species has to be considered 'endangered' or 'vulnerable' to extinction by the Government's wildlife advisory bodies. Other criteria include endemic species, those which have suffered a major decline in numbers or are confined to threatened habitats, and those which are considered rare and threatened throughout Europe. In previous reviews of the Act most protected species have belonged to the more popular groups: birds, wild flowers, butterflies, moths and fish. In recent years, however, new information has been gathered on the distribution and status of the 'lower plants': mosses, liverworts, lichens and stonewort algae, and Red Data Books are in preparation for these groups. Most species of lower plants are recognizable only by specialists, and have no common name. At the request of the Department of the Environment, the Joint Nature Conservation Committee (JNCC) created English names for all the candidate species, introducing such novelties as 'the millimetre moss', 'the earlobed dog lichen' and 'the oil-stain parmentaria'. Also on the protected list for the first time are three 'micro-species' of hawkweeds, one of which (*Hieracium attenuatifolium*) is confined to '12 plants growing on a single rock'. Better known to most naturalists is the high brown fritillary butterfly, a species of open woodland butterfly which has declined to the stage where it may be vulnerable to over-collecting. The sturgeon has also been protected, although it is now rarely seen in British waters. It is threatened throughout Europe by river pollution, over-fishing and dams built across its spawning waters.

Several species recommended by the JNCC for protection were shelved by the Department pending further investigation. They include the basking shark, for which there is a small fishery based in Scotland; protecting the shark therefore has commercial and employment implications. The JNCC also wished to secure protection for the hybrid between the Scottish wild cat and the domestic cat. The hybrid may be almost identical to the true wild cat, and hence a legal loophole exists in which the continued persecution of the protected wild cat can be defended. There is no precedent in wildlife legislation, however, for extending protection to a particular form of hybrid rather than to a species. Three species of wild flower were deleted from the protected list. The purple spurge (*Euphorbia peplis*) has not been seen since 1965 and is presumed extinct. Two sea lavenders were also deleted as they are now considered insufficiently distinctive to be true species.

Scottish Compensation Costs

Nature conservation in the Scottish Highlands is no longer a matter of gentleman's agreements and nominal payments. Under the Wildlife and Countryside Act, landowners are entitled to seek compensation for profits forgone as a result of SSSI designation. Such payment is made from the annual budget of Scottish Natural Heritage (SNH), which is funded by the taxpayer. In a test case last year, John Cameron, one of Europe's biggest sheep farmers, was awarded £568,294 for not planting shelter bells and intensifying farming and deer-stalking on two SSSIs in Glen Lochay, Perthshire. With backdated interest and legal fees, his compensation payment was believed to be about £1 million. His neighbour, a member of the Lands Tribunal which awarded the claim, has himself received a payment reported to be £250,000 from SNH for cancelling a damaging forestry scheme on an SSSI.

When details of the Cameron settlement were announced, other Scottish landowners entered into negotiations with SNH over SSSIs on their estates. Although few of these negotiations have been made public, Lord Kimball of Altnaharra Estate in Sutherland said that he was seeking a settlement that might total £3 million over the future management of four SSSIs. Another large claim has been made by the private owner of at least one National Nature Reserve. If such payments continue to be met, SNH could face bankruptcy and the laws on wildlife conservation in Scotland would be brought into disrepute.

Behind such claims is the resistance of Highland landowners to outside interference with their property rights; the Scottish Office is reportedly sympathetic to such views. Last year a consortium of conservation bodies failed in their bid to acquire Mar Lodge estate in the Cairngorms as a Nature Reserve with money raised largely by public donations, apparently because funds for its future management were not available.

Figures released by Scottish Wildlife and Countryside Link indicate that at least 151 of Scotland's 1,300 SSSIs were damaged between 1985 and 1991. The report suggests, however, that this is an underestimate, as overgrazing, burning and pollution are not officially recorded as 'damage'. Scottish MPs are now calling for urgent changes in the law.

Trees Suffer Die-Back

A condition known as die-back is affecting ash, beech and oak trees across much of eastern England. Symptoms include the early yellowing or shedding of leaves and the death first of fine twigs and later of whole branches, resulting in the gradual thinning of the crown. At the same time, the tree becomes increasingly vulnerable to fungal and insect attack.

During 1992 some 50,000 ash trees in Cambridgeshire were in varying stages of die-back, and the problem seems to be equally severe in neighbouring counties. The cause is believed to be related to drought rather than disease, although many ash standards in this area are 200 years old and close to the end of their natural lives. Hedgerow ashes have long suffered from agricultural practices, notably deep ploughing, herbicides and stubble burning, which result in premature ageing and the die-back of the crowns. Ash trees in woods and in suburban parks and gardens have escaped the worst effects of die-back.

The Forest Authority has identified a bank of beeches in poor health stretching from Devon to Norfolk. In many cases crown-thinning was accompanied by beech bark disease, caused by fungal and aphid attack on the already weakened tree. Imperial College London carried out a four-year monitoring programme which found that about one-third of the beech trees in the area are affected by crown-thinning. Unhealthy trees had lower potassium levels both in the leaves and the surrounding soil, and on acid soils the aluminium content was significantly higher. Although the underlying causes are complex, both drought and air pollution are implicated. High levels of nitrogen dioxide and sulphur dioxide in the atmosphere weaken the tree by reducing its natural defences to frost and fungal and insect attack.

Die-back has affected 40 per cent of oak trees from the 80- to 120-year class at Sherwood Forest, and it has also been noted in at least 30 woods and parks in southern England. It afflicted large parts of mainland Europe from the early 1980s, but there were few instances in England before 1988. Cores taken from the trunks of oaks at Sherwood suggest that growth began to slow in the mid-1980s. Again, no obvious pathogen has been detected and drought is suspected to be the main cause. Oak is, however, prone to occasional severe attacks from caterpillars, mildew and honey fungus, and widespread die-back from these causes is not unknown.

THE BUILT ENVIRONMENT

Although the General Election did not bring a change of Government, there have been many changes of personnel and administration within the higher echelons of those concerned with architectural conservation. The election brought a new Secretary of State for the Environment (Michael Howard) and a new department, the Department of National Heritage (DNH), with its own Secretary of State (David Mellor). The new ministry is more eclectic than its name implies, covering areas such as sport and broadcasting as well as the arts, tourism and historic buildings. It took over responsibility for the works programme of the Royal Household, the Royal Parks, English Heritage, the Redundant Churches Fund, the National Heritage Memorial Fund, the Royal Armouries, the Architectural Heritage Fund, the Royal Fine Arts Commission and the Historic Royal Palaces Agency.

The creation of the new ministry was seen as a mixed blessing by conservationists. On the one hand a ministry with the word 'Heritage' in its title could be expected to fight hard for the cause, but on the other there were fears that dividing responsibilities between the new ministry and the DoE would create friction. A few weeks after the election it was decided that the listing of historic buildings and the scheduling of ancient monuments would go to the new ministry, but that decisions on listed building consent, i.e. what happens to the buildings after they have been listed, would remain with the DoE. Scheduled monument consent applications are to be decided by the DNH.

Outside the Government, there were more new faces. Lord Rothschild took over as chairman of the National Heritage Memorial Fund in the spring, and the Marquess of Anglesey, a member of the Historic Buildings Council for Wales for 39 years and its chairman since 1977, stood down in favour of Thomas Lloyd. Michael Cudlipp became the new director of the Georgian Group, the principal amenity society concerned with the architecture of the 18th century, and Francis Golding succeeded Jane Fawcett as secretary of ICOMOS UK (the domestic branch of the International Committee on Monuments and Sites). The appointment of Jocelyn Stevens, former rector of the Royal College of Art, as the new chairman of English Heritage took effect in July 1992. New commissioners with English Heritage include Roger Suddards, author of the standard volume on listed building law and practice, and Candida Lycett Green.

ENGLISH HERITAGE

English Heritage has decided that from 1 April 1992 all Grade I and II* buildings will be regarded as outstanding for grant purposes (under Section 3A). The only exceptions to this rule will be where a building listed Grade I or II* (or A or B in the case of churches) is clearly overgraded or where a Grade II or unlisted building is clearly undergraded. English Heritage hopes that this will not lead to a flood of fresh applications; the present pool of 19,000 potentially eligible structures elicit only some 400 grant applications a year, and it is considered likely that the increased total of 26,000–27,000 will lead to only a proportionate increase. Partly in order to meet any increased demand; English Heritage plans to raise the total offer limit for the two buildings and monuments and churches grant schemes from £17.7 million in 1992 to £20 million. The assessment for eligibility will be focused more narrowly on the financial need, the means of the applicant and the urgency of the repairs.

One of the earliest decisions of English Heritage after its foundation in 1983 was to appoint a Buildings at Risk Survey Officer. In January 1992 a report on the problem was published. Extrapolating from a sample survey, the report concludes that about 37,000 of England's 500,000 listed buildings are at risk from neglect, and that twice that number are in a vulnerable condition and require repair. English Heritage has the power to grant-aid threatened buildings within conservation areas but not beyond, and the report highlights the need for this anomalous situation to be addressed.

In March 1992 Lord Montagu of Beaulieu, the outgoing chairman, announced funding totalling £5.4 million to assist in urgent repairs and conservation work at English cathedrals over the next three years. Of the 33 cathedrals identified for assistance, five were Roman Catholic, and being built in the 20th century proved no bar to aid: £79,000 went to Guildford, built by Sir Edward Maufe, and £500,000 to Liverpool's Roman Catholic Cathedral, to be used almost exclusively on the crypt by Sir Edwin Lutyens rather than Sir Frederick Gibberd's superstructure. The largest beneficiaries were Salisbury (£870,000 over three years) and Ely (£690,000 over two years) Cathedrals.

European Conservation Scheme

The European Commission moved tentatively into the field of historic buildings with a pilot scheme for the conservation of the architectural heritage. With a total budget of only £1.8 million the allocation is hardly generous, and of 40 British submissions only four were successful in 1991. The theme was projects related to historic 'production activities', and the British winners were Barnham Tower windmill in West Sussex, the Newport transport bridge in Gwent, the Levant mine beam engine and house at Pendean in Cornwall, and the Upper Swaledale and Arkengarthdale conservation area in North Yorkshire. The 1992 scheme covered projects which aimed 'to upgrade public spaces in historic centres'.

Royal Commission on the Historical Monuments of England

In 1991 the archaeological division of the Royal Commission on the Historical Monuments of England (RCHME) recorded sites as diverse as deserted medieval villages, priory ruins, an early 17th-century water garden (at Tackley, Oxfordshire) and the Mulberry Harbour construction site of 1943–4 at Lepe on the Solent. The architectural division has been completing a three-volume work on medieval rural houses in Kent; two books on the Close and the Cathedral in Salisbury are also expected soon. There has been a rapid survey of buildings in the Duke Street area of Liverpool, while the major survey of hospitals built between *c.*1660 and 1948 is now well under way. The second of the new national projects will deal with the architectural development of gentry houses from 1500 to 1700.

The most significant of the acquisitions by the National Buildings Record during the year was the purchase of the negatives and prints of the photographers Millar and Harris, who started work in 1924 and were prodigious recorders of new buildings before and after the Second World War. Four thousand negatives of military structures and Victorian churches taken by the late J. Stanton were also acquired, and about 1,000 large format colour transparencies of medieval church wall paintings taken by Charlotte Stanley. The photographic programmes included a full record of the 19th-century stained glass at Worcester Cathedral, detailed recording of the western towers at Westminster Abbey by Hawksmoor, the quire and vaults at Durham Cathedral, and the monuments and stained glass at Tewkesbury Abbey. The national inventory of war memorials, partly sponsored by the RCHME, is continuing.

The RCHME and the DoE reached agreement early in 1992 on retaining the open access library of the National Buildings Record in London for the medium term, subject to a financial appraisal.

National Heritage Memorial Fund

The NHMF is unique among heritage quangos in being purely an enabler rather than an owner: its funds are distributed to allow others to buy land, buildings, works of art and other treasures for the permanent benefit of the nation. Projects benefiting in the year to March 1991 included the quintessential museum of curiosities known as A La Ronde, built in the late 18th century near Exmouth, Devon, which has now been acquired by the National Trust; the completion of the re-erection in the Bradford Industrial Museum of one of the last unaltered back-to-back terraces of cottages in the city; the acquisition by the National Trust of the Georgian Gothic house known as Plas Dinefwr in Dyfed; the restoration of the octagon and lantern at Ely Cathedral, partly required because of storm damage in 1990; the safeguarding by the Cambridge University Library of 1,000 items in the Hanson collection of documentation relating to the history of shipbuilding and navigation; the purchase by the Imperial War Museum of preliminary sketches by Sir Edwin Lutyens for the Cenotaph in Whitehall; a grant towards the restoration of the St John triptych (1615) in St Mary's Church, Lydiard Tregoze, Wiltshire; the securing by the Lancashire Record Office of the family papers associated with Towneley Hall; the establishment of a working museum in the 1833 Verdant Works in Dundee; and the restoration of murals within the Village Hall at Wood Green in Hampshire, painted in the 1930s by students from the Royal College of Art.

In October 1991 the NHMF played a vital role in saving that most English of houses, Chastleton in Oxfordshire, which is little changed since it was built in 1602. The Fund gave £2 million for the purchase (on behalf of the National Trust) and a further £2 million for endowment. English Heritage is giving a grant of £800,000 and the National has launched a public appeal for a further £500,000.

Redundant Churches

The Redundant Churches Fund reported ten new vestings in its annual report for 1990, the most distinguished being St John Maddermarket in Norwich. The expenditure on repairs in 1990 – £2,700,111 – was a record, the work being spread over nearly 200 churches, also a record. A fire at Bristol St Thomas caused serious damage but insurance is likely to cover the cost of repairs. Wall paintings were conserved at Broughton and at Duxford. Important vestings in 1991 included St Andrew's, Hove, designed by Sir Charles Barry, architect to the Palace of Westminster (1827–8), and William Burges's masterpiece of Christ the Consoler at Skelton in the diocese of Ripon. The Fund is at present financed 70 per cent by the state and 30 per cent by the Church of England. An equivalent body, designed to protect redundant non-Anglican places of worship, is expected to be established soon.

Listing and the Law

The year under review saw some legislative action and the possibility of further changes. From 27 July 1992 the Government introduced powers for local authorities to control the demolition of unlisted houses, and in the course of the year it published a discussion paper on the legal exemption which places of worship in use presently enjoy. The paper proposed to maintain the exemption across the board for internal works but to withdraw it for external changes, unless each denomination introduces a system of internal control to be centred on a body independent of the local congregation or community proposing the works. It further proposed that all structures within the curtilage of ecclesiastical buildings should be subjected to listed building control in the same was as they would in respect of secular buildings.

In the course of 1990 3,574 historic buildings were added to the DoE's list of listed buildings in England, bringing the total to 437,040. By the end of 1991 the total stood at 439,048, of which 6,068 were listed Grade I. By December 1990 there were 7,157 conservation areas, of which 442 had been declared in the preceding 12 months.

Recent listings have included an early gun-making factory in Birmingham; a chemist shop in Ealing; a garrison church in Kent; a tool and watchmaker's workshop at Prescot in Lancashire; and an apiary in Dyfed.

Restoration

Acts of God continued to claim some historic buildings. Prior Park near Bath, Harrington Hall in Lincolnshire and Buckfastleigh church in Devon were gutted by fire in 1991–2, while the Wren church of St James Garlickhythe in the City of London was severely damaged by a collapsing crane. However, repair of the fire damage at the National Trust house at Uppark in Sussex is now well advanced, and some long standing cases of dereliction have been arrested. One of the greatest of the 18th-century Nonconformist chapels, the 1707 Rook Lane Chapel at Frome in Somerset, is being repaired by the Somerset Building Preservation Trust with grant-aid from English Heritage and local authorities.

Organizations established in 1991–2 include a number to further restoration work. The Association of Small Historic Towns and Villages of the United Kingdom (ASHTAV) was launched on 7 March 1992, and SALVO 91, which is intended to co-ordinate activity within the architectural salvage business was set up in 1991. A Building Limes Forum was set up in York to encourage the development of expertise and understanding in the use of lime in building. New building preservation trusts have been established to serve Boston, Bury St Edmunds, Glanford (Lincs.), Ramsgate and Sheffield. The Trust in Manchester ceased to exist.

New Attractions

Attractions opened in the course of the year included the early 18th-century Derwentcote steel furnace in Co. Durham, owned by English Heritage; the early 12th-century ruins of the Bishop of Winchester's Palace at Witney in Oxfordshire, also owned by English Heritage; the Castle at Castle Eden in Cleveland; Stoneyhurst College at Hurst Green in Lancashire, now a boys' Catholic boarding school; Cottesbrooke Hall, Northamptonshire (1702); the Etruria Industrial Museum, Stoke-on-Trent; the Theatre Royal, Margate (1780); and Pitchford Hall at Condover in Shropshire (1473), which sadly was put on the market for the first time in the summer of 1992. Also in 1992 the house known as Goddards at Abinger in Surrey, built in 1898–9 by Sir Edwin Lutyens and given to the Lutyens Trust by its previous owner, was opened to the public for the first time. But other attractions closed, including the virtually unique Ecclesiastical Museum at the former St Nicholas's Church in Bristol; and the recession continued to frustrate efforts to establish a Museum of the London Docklands.

Awards

The 1991 Building Conservation Award offered by the Royal Institution of Chartered Surveyors went to the restoration by the Landmark Trust of the East Banqueting House at Chipping Campden in Gloucestershire. The 1991 winners of the annual *Europa Nostra* awards included seven Medals of Honour and 36 Diplomas of Merit for projects in 14 countries. The seven Medals of Honour went to the conversion into a hotel of the largest water tower in Europe, at Cologne; the restoration of three revolving windmills, in Germany; the conservation of Arendal in Norway; the conservation of the chapel of San Isidro in the Church of San Andres in Madrid; a 15th century mansion in Valencia; the restoration of Inverary County Court-house in Scotland; and the restoration of the Foreign Office in London.

Dance

Looking back on the year 1991–2, the most significant events in the long-term may turn out to be the preparation of a national strategy for the arts, the announcement of a national lottery, and the creation of a new ministry to include responsibility for the arts.

In 1990, the then Minister for the Arts (Richard Luce) asked the arts and media funding bodies (the Arts Council, the British Film Institute, the Crafts Council and the Regional Arts Associations) to draw up a 'national strategy' for the arts. This resulted in the publication of a series of discussion documents in the summer of 1991 and a draft national strategy in the spring of 1992. The final version, published in the autumn of 1992, was intended to set out clear targets for the arts and a framework within which funding bodies could work.

The dance discussion document, written by Susan Hoyle (the Arts Council's dance director), celebrated the wide range of dance forms practised in the United Kingdom, lamented the relatively low profile of dance and the funding accorded to it, and urged positive action by all dance organizations to exploit the public's enthusiasm for dance, whether as artists or audience. It also recommended that a national 'audit' of dance spaces should be commissioned, reiterated the need for a national dance house, and highlighted the problems for accredited vocational dance schools in the face of local authority cuts in discretionary grants to students. The latter situation had already led to urgent demands that grants to accredited schools should be mandatory.

A Foundation for Sport and the Arts was set up in 1991, largely funded by the pools companies, and from this English National Ballet (the only dance recipient in 1991) was allocated £150,000. A similar amount was allocated to London City Ballet in 1992. After the General Election in 1992 the long-awaited national lottery was announced; it is not yet clear whether the Foundation for Sport and the Arts will continue to have a role once the lottery is established. The national lottery could raise up to £1 billion a year from 1994, and is intended to augment rather than replace existing government funding for sport and the arts.

A new ministry, the Department of National Heritage, with responsibility for sport, the arts, the 'national heritage' and the media, was set up following the General Election. Although many welcomed the presence of an arts minister in the Cabinet, there was a certain amount of scepticism as to whether this would actually lead to tangible benefits for the arts. Dance had acquired a surprising boost during the General Election campaign, when the Labour Party became the first political party to launch an official policy on dance; but it continues to be treated as the poor relation of opera in terms of funding and status. The Arts Council took a year to appoint a new chairman of its dance advisory panel after the death of Adrian Ward-Jackson; Prudence Skene's appointment was finally announced in May 1992. And while the English National Opera was given a grant of £10.8 million to enable it to buy the London Coliseum, it is still apparently impossible to find funding for a national dance house. The latest proposals involve a group of 'favoured' dance venues which would receive extra sponsorship from the London Arts Board; a feasibility study is also being carried out to assess the suitability of the Lyceum as a theatre for dance. Meanwhile the redevelopment of the Royal Opera House is now planned to start in 1997, with a public appeal being launched to raise the necessary funds. The redevelopment of Sadler's Wells Theatre, which was only saved from closure by an emergency grants package totalling £280,000 (mainly from the Arts Council and the London Arts Board) in August 1992, has been put on hold because of the recession.

Finance

The total Arts Council budget for dance companies for 1991–2 was £18.4 million, and over £1 million was allocated to dance companies from the Arts Council's enhancement fund. About 90 per cent of both the budget and the enhancement funding was allocated to the six largest companies (The Royal Ballet, Birmingham Royal Ballet, English National Ballet, Rambert Dance Company, London Contemporary Dance Theatre and Northern Ballet Theatre). Franchise funding was offered to DV8 Physical Theatre, Siobhan Davies, Adventures in Motion Pictures and the Cholmondeleys for the first time, but London City Ballet continued to be ignored (the company has finally been offered a touring grant of £250,000 per annum from 1992–3, but is still denied revenue status).

Debate continues on whether the national arts companies should be funded directly by the government, and whether the 'arm's length' principle of funding is in any case really embodied in the Arts Council. The Government's enthusiasm for business sponsorship of the arts also continues unabated; in 1991 the then Minister for the Arts (Timothy Renton) described sponsorship as 'a business transaction between two equal partners with real and tangible benefits'. One company which has responded enthusiastically is Digital Equipment Company, which increased its sponsorship of the arts, and in particular dance, to £550,000 in 1992.

The Royal Opera House increased the sponsorship it received by 22 per cent in 1991–2, to a total of over £8 million, but its cumulative deficit now stands at £3.3 million, which must be cleared by 1995. Its total

Arts Council grant, including money from the enhancement fund, was about £18.5 million (of which about £10.5 million was for the two ballet companies), but this represented less than 40 per cent of its total income. Higher seat prices met with some resistance, and no further rises are planned for 1992–3; in fact some prices will be reduced slightly. The Opera House faces a troubled year, with industrial action threatened over a proposed pay freeze, and mounting criticism of its financial and artistic management.

Classical

The beginning of the Royal Ballet's season was disrupted by an orchestra strike, but once under way its two greatest successes were in works of radically different styles. *Stoics quartet* was created by Jonathan Burrows earlier in 1991. Burrows' choreography is unpredictable, idiosyncratic and non-balletic; it is also highly entertaining and was expertly danced by members of the Royal Ballet who also dance in the Jonathan Burrows Group. At the end of the season, Burrows and several of his dancers left the Royal Ballet to pursue freelance careers. *In the middle, somewhat elevated* was created by William Forsythe for the Paris Opera Ballet in 1987, and demands an aggressive, hard-edged classicism from its dancers. The Royal Ballet cast, led by Sylvie Guillem and Laurent Hilaire, responded magnificently to the challenge and were rewarded by the 1992 Laurence Olivier Award for the most outstanding achievement in dance. The Evening Standard Ballet Award for 1991 had already been won by Sir Kenneth MacMillan for *Winter Dreams*, and in July 1992 Dame Ninette de Valois, founder of the Royal Ballet, was awarded the Society of West End Theatre's Special Award for outstanding achievement, the first person from the dance world to receive the award.

One of the world's finest ballet conductors and de Valois' former colleague, Robert Irving, died in September 1991. As the conductor of Sadler's Wells Ballet/The Royal Ballet from 1949 to 1958, he formed a fruitful collaboration with Frederick Ashton before moving to New York City Ballet. On 9 April 1992 a gala, *Welcome Back St Petersburg*, was held to celebrate, and raise money for, the historic Maryinsky (formerly Kirov) Theatre in St Petersburg. The Royal Ballet's own Russian star, Irek Mukhamedov, led a highly successful independent small-scale regional tour with a group of Royal Ballet dancers. The company also launched an initiative in inner London schools, A Chance to Dance, jointly with dancers from the Dance Theatre of Harlem; its aim is to encourage and help children from all ethnic groups and social backgrounds to take up ballet. The season ended with a successful tour to Japan.

Birmingham Royal Ballet's director, Peter Wright, won the Digital Premier Dance Award in the autumn of 1991, and used the prize money to commission a new work from the company's young choreographer Oliver Hindle. However, the unexpected triumph of the season was a revival of Massine's 1933 work *Choreatium*. Two MacMillan works, a revival of his 1958 ballet *The Burrow* and the first performances of his *Romeo and Juliet* by this company, with new designs by 22-year-old Paul Andrews, provoked considerable interest. Miyako Yoshida was voted Dancer of the Year by readers of *Dance and Dancers* magazine, and Marion Tait, the company's senior ballerina, was awarded an OBE in the New Year's honours list. The company's popularity in Birmingham continues to grow and there are plans to extend its seasons there still further.

English National Ballet, in common with the other classical companies, largely relied on full-length ballets to keep box office returns healthy, and mounted new productions of *The Nutcracker* and *Cinderella*, both by Ben Stevenson. However, it also took a range of shorter ballets to small venues, and presented a programme of works new to the company in London in the summer of 1992. Its biggest coup was the recruitment of the Bolshoi ballerina Ludmila Semenyaka as a principal; although nearing the end of her career she is still a beautiful and much-respected dancer.

Scottish Ballet continued its steady progress under Galina Samsova's direction, and in June 1992 became the first western ballet company to visit Russia and the Ukraine since the political upheavals of the previous year. It also mounted its first-ever production of *Coppélia* in March 1992. Northern Ballet Theatre's new production of *Swan Lake* in February 1992 attracted some lurid pre-publicity but turned out to be a less than successful (but nevertheless popular) re-working of the ballet, directed by Christopher Gable and choreographed by Dennis Wayne. The company did, however, attract a £500,000 three-year sponsorship package from BT. London City Ballet continues to attract large, enthusiastic audiences to its small-scale productions of the classics. It also added works by Ashton and Balanchine to its repertoire, appeared at the Singapore Arts Festival, and recruited ex-Royal Ballet ballerina Bryony Brind as resident guest artist. Brind was also involved in VoltAire (formerly Dance Advance), one of the more interesting small classical ballet groups to perform during the year; its programme *Ballet for Sax* emphasized collaboration between dancers and live music.

Contemporary

The larger contemporary dance companies, Rambert Dance Company and London Contemporary Dance Theatre, are finding it increasingly difficult to fill the medium-sized venues they generally visit. However, while Rambert under Richard Alston have a strong sense of purpose and creative activity within the company, LCDT is facing another crisis with the resignation of its new artistic director, Nancy Dunn, after less than a year in charge. Robert Cohan, the company's founding artistic director, will act as artistic adviser until a new director is appointed. Rambert continued its close association with Siobhan

Davies, and presented the world première of a work by Merce Cunningham in June 1992.

The 1991 Dance Umbrella presented its usual wide range of work, the highlight of which was the return of American dancer and choreographer Trisha Brown and her company to Sadler's Wells Theatre. The other participants ranged from Scottish Ballet to Saburo Teshigawara from Japan with his 'noise dance piece' *dah-dah-sko-dah-dah* (representing the sound of a Japanese festival drum). One of the five £25,000 Prudential Arts Awards for 1992 was awarded to Dance Umbrella's founder, Val Bourne.

Two other major festivals of independent dance were Spring Loaded (at the Queen Elizabeth Hall and The Place, London, from February to April) and the Turning World festival of European contemporary dance at The Place from April to May. The latter was opened by Rosas, the company run by one of Europe's leading young choreographers, Anna Teresa de Keersmaeker, in her latest work *Achterland.* Spring Loaded featured artists including Jacob Marley, Laurie Booth, the Cholmondeleys and the Featherstonehaughs as well as LCDT and Adventures in Motion Pictures. John Ashford of The Place was presented with the Award of Excellence in International Dance by the British International Theatre Institute in recognition of his work.

DV8 Physical Theatre consolidated its reputation for exciting and imaginative work, and its director and choreographer Lloyd Newson was shortlisted for a £5,000 Arts Council Award for innovative work over a five-year period. His latest work, *Strange Fish*, was commissioned by Expo '92, and after its première in April in Budapest it was shown at venues in Europe, Canada and the UK to enormous acclaim. Michael Clark, the self-consciously outrageous ex-Royal Ballet dancer, re-formed a company to present his new work *Modern Masterpiece;* it was a great success, if not perhaps quite living up to its title.

Siobhan Davies also re-formed her company to perform a new work, *Arctic Heart*, in the autumn of 1991. At the same time, the Leeds-based Phoenix Dance Company celebrated its tenth anniversary with a short season at Sadler's Wells Theatre; the company has undergone a metamorphosis from an all-black, all-male outfit to a mixed-sex company including one white woman under a new white female director (Margaret Morris).

The influx of Russian dancers and companies continued throughout 1991–2. Visiting companies included Moscow Festival Ballet, Moscow City Ballet and Moscow La Classique Ballet (whose tour was suspended when its promoter went into liquidation), as well as a group billed as Stars of the Bolshoi Ballet, although this turned out to be something of an exaggeration. More rewarding visits came from the Ballet du Rhin, who presented a reconstruction of the original 1789 production of *La Fille mal gardée* at Sadler's Wells Theatre; the Berlin Ballet, under the directorship of Peter Schaufuss; the Australian Ballet; the White Oak Dance Project, led by Mikhail Baryshnikov in his new guise as a performer and director of modern dance; Pina Bausch and her company, Wuppertal Dance Theatre (at the 1992 Edinburgh Festival); Mark Morris and his company (also in Edinburgh); the Israel Ballet, in its British début season; and Alvin Ailey American Dance Theater in a long-awaited London season at the Coliseum.

A six-month European Arts Festival was launched in July 1992 to mark Britain's presidency of the EC; organized by John Drummond, it covers all parts of the UK, and its dance programme ranges from choreographic workshops to major visiting companies. Looking further forward, the Arts Council has designated 1993 the Year of Dance, as part of a series designed to celebrate all arts forms between 1992 and the year 2000. The Year of Dance will be centred on the East Midlands, and the dance world is looking forward to an ambitious and wide-ranging celebration of its art.

PRODUCTIONS

ROYAL BALLET, founded 1931
Royal Opera House, Covent Garden, London WC2E 9DD

World premières:

(20 November 1991) *Present Histories.* A one-act ballet. Choreography, William Tuckett; music, Schubert; set, Andy Klunder; costumes, Lucy Bevan. Cast, Viviana Durante, William Trevitt, Lynne Bristow, Michael Nunn, Darcey Bussell, Adam Cooper and Dana Fouras.

(19 March 1992) *The Judas Tree.* A one-act ballet. Choreography, Kenneth MacMillan; music, Brian Elias; design, Jock McFadyen. Cast led by Irek Mukhamedov, Viviana Durante, Michael Nunn and Mark Silver.

Company premières:

(4 November 1991) *La Luna.* Choreography, Maurice Béjart; music, Bach. A solo danced by Sylvie Guillem. Solo violinist, Bradley Creswick.

(20 November 1991) *Stoics quartet.* Choreography, Jonathan Burrows (1991); music, Mendelssohn; design, Craig Givens. Cast, Luke Heydon, Deborah Jones, Natalie McCann and Simon Rice.

(20 November 1991) *Symphony in C.* Choreography, George Balanchine (1947); music, Bizet; design, Anthony Dowell. First cast included Lesley Collier, Mark Silver, Sylvie Guillem, Adam Cooper, Fiona Chadwick, Tetsuya Kumakawa, Deborah Bull and Stuart Cassidy.

(13 February 1992) *In the middle, somewhat elevated.* Choreography, William Forsythe (1988); music, Thom Willems; design, William Forsythe. Cast, Sylvie Guillem, Laurent Hilaire, Darcey Bussell, Deborah Bull, Michael Nunn, Bonnie Moore, Peter Abegglen, Deborah Jones and Gillian Revie.

Full-length ballets from the repertoire: *La Fille mal gardée* (Ashton, 1960), *The Nutcracker* (Ivanov/Wright, 1984), *Giselle* (Petipa after Coralli/Perrot, prod. Wright, 1985),

Manon (MacMillan, 1974), *Romeo and Juliet* (MacMillan, 1965), *La Bayadère* (Makarova after Petipa, 1980), *Cyrano* (Bintley, 1991).

One-act ballets and *pas de deux* from the repertoire: *Les Sylphides* (Fokine), *Méditation from Thaïs* (Ashton), *Tchaikovsky pas de deux* (Balanchine), *Winter Dreams* (MacMillan), *Agon* (Balanchine), *Scènes de ballet* (Ashton), *Monotones* (Ashton), *Stravinsky Violin Concerto* (Balanchine), *A Month in the Country* (Ashton), *Elite Syncopations* (MacMillan).

In addition to its performances at the Royal Opera House, the company gave one-week seasons at the Bristol Hippodrome (30 March–4 April) and the Birmingham Hippodrome (6–11 April). It performed *Manon* and a triple bill of *Monotones, Winter Dreams* and *Symphony in C* at both venues. The company also toured Japan (15 May–14 June), performing *The Dream* (Ashton), *Monotones, Diana and Acteon pas de deux* (Vaganova), *Tchaikovsky pas de deux, Grand pas classique* (Gsovsky) and *Elite Syncopations.*

BIRMINGHAM ROYAL BALLET, founded 1946
(formerly Sadler's Wells Royal Ballet)
Birmingham Hippodrome, Thorp Street, Birmingham B5 4AU

World première:

(24 March 1992) *Dark Horizons.* A one-act ballet. Choreography, Oliver Hindle; music, Shostakovich; design, Peter Farley. Cast led by David Yow, Joseph Cipolla and Michael O'Hare.

Company premières:

(25 October 1991) *Choreatium.* Choreography, Léonide Massine (1933); music, Brahms; design, Nadine Baylis. Cast led by Karen Donovan, Joseph Cipolla, Samira Saidi, Sandra Madgwick, Michael O'Hare and Kevin O'Hare.

(31 October 1991) *The Burrow.* Choreography, Kenneth MacMillan (1958, re-worked for this revival); music, Frank Martin; design, Nicholas Georgiadis (re-designed for this revival). Cast, Marion Tait, Michael O'Hare, Jessica Clarke, Paul Bayes-Kitcher, Desmond Kelly and Anita Landa.

(6 March 1992) *Galanteries.* Choreography, David Bintley (1986); music, Mozart; design, Jan Blake. Cast led by Marion Tait, Monica Zamora and Duncan De Gruchy.

(1 June 1992) *Romeo and Juliet.* Choreography, Kenneth MacMillan (1965); music, Prokofiev; design, Paul Andrews. Cast led by Nina Ananiashvili and Kevin O'Hare.

Full-length ballets from the repertoire: *Hobson's Choice* (Bintley, 1989), *Swan Lake* (Petipa/Ivanov, additional choreography by Wright, 1980), *The Nutcracker* (Ivanov/Wright, 1990), *Giselle* (Petipa after Coralli/Perrot, prod. Wright, 1968).

One-act ballets and *pas de deux* from the repertoire: *Divertimento No. 15* (Balanchine), *Petrushka* (Fokine), *Les Sylphides* (Fokine, in a new production by Galina Samsova), *Le Corsaire pas de deux* (after Petipa), *Five Tangos* (Van Manen), *Card Game* (Cranko), *Elite Syncopations* (MacMillan).

In addition to three seasons at the Birmingham Hippodrome, the company toured to Leeds, Plymouth, Liverpool, London (Sadler's Wells Theatre), Eastbourne, Canterbury, Bradford, Oxford, Southampton and Bristol.

ENGLISH NATIONAL BALLET, founded 1950
(formerly London Festival Ballet)
Markova House, 39 Jay Mews, London SW7 2ES

World premières:

(18 February 1992) *A Stranger I Came.* A one-act ballet. Choreography, Robert North; music, Schubert; design, Andrew Storer. Cast led by José Manuel Carreño, Beth Otter and Kevin Richmond.

(23 June 1992) *White Nights.* A one-act ballet. Choreography, Kim Brandstrup; music, Gerard McBurney after Mussorgsky; design, Fotini Dimou. Cast led by Josephine Jewkes and Christopher Powney.

Company premières:

(28 November 1991) *The Nutcracker.* Choreography, Ben Stevenson (1972, adapted for ENB); music, Tchaikovsky; design, Desmond Heeley. Cast led by Agnes Oaks and Thomas Edur.

(29 April 1992) *Cinderella.* Choreography, Ben Stevenson (1970, adapted for ENB); music, Prokofiev; design, David Walker. Cast led by Maria Teresa del Real, José Manuel Carreño and Renata Calderini.

(23 June 1992) *The Envelope.* Choreography, David Parsons (1984); music, Rossini; costumes, Judy Wirkula.

(23 June 1992) *Sleep Study.* Choreography, David Parsons (1984); music, Flim; costumes, David Soar.

(23 June 1992) *L.* Choreography, Ben Stevenson (1973); score, Don Lawson; costumes, David Soar. Cast led by Thomas Edur and José Manuel Carreño.

Full-length ballets from the repertoire: *Onegin* (Cranko, 1965), *The Taming of the Shrew* (Cranko, 1969), *Coppélia* (Hynd, 1985), *Romeo and Juliet* (Ashton, 1955).

One-act ballets and *pas de deux* from the repertoire: *Les Sylphides* (Fokine, prod. Markova), *Anne Frank* (Wainrot), *Polovtsian Dances* from *Prince Igor* (Fokine), *La Bayadère* (The Kingdom of the Shades) (Makarova after Petipa), *Four Last Songs* (Stevenson), *Graduation Ball* (Lichine), *Swansong* (Bruce), *Apollo* (Balanchine), *Aureole* (Taylor), *Three Preludes* (Stevenson), *Our Waltzes* (Nebrada), *Etudes* (Lander), *Don Quixote pas de deux* (Petipa), *Le Spectre de la Rose* (Fokine), *The Dying Swan* (Fokine), *Schéhérazade* (Fokine).

In addition to two seasons at the Royal Festival Hall, London, and one at the London Coliseum, the full company visited Southampton, Bristol, Bradford, Newcastle and Manchester. It split into two smaller groups from February to March 1992, with one group performing in Cambridge, Basildon, Ulverston, Malvern, Poole, Preston and Coventry, and the other visiting Yeovil, Stevenage, Newtown, Hayes, Swindon, Bury St Edmunds, Hexham and Crewe.

The company also performed in Hungary (23–26 March) in a programme comprising *A Stranger I Came, Swansong* and *Etudes.* It gave four performances in Spain in July (Madrid and Seville, the latter at the Expo '92 festival), performing *Our Waltzes, Swansong* and *Etudes* in Madrid, and *Aureole, A Stranger I Came* and *Our Waltzes* in Seville.

RAMBERT DANCE COMPANY, founded 1926
94 Chiswick High Road, London W4 1SH

World premières:

(11 October 1991) *Completely Birdland.* Choreography, Laurie Booth; music, Hans Peter Kuhn; decor, Graham Snow; costumes, Jeanne Spaziani.

(22 November 1991) *Island to Island.* Choreography, Mark Baldwin; sound, Ben Craft.

(13 March 1992) *Winnsboro Cotton Mill Blues.* Choreography, Siobhan Davies; music, Frederic Rzewski.

(16 March 1992) *Still Dance*. Choreography, Paul Old; danced in silence.

(12 June 1992) *Cat's Eye*. Choreography, Richard Alston; music, David Sawer; design, Paul Huxley.

(20 June 1992) *Touchbase*. Choreography, Merce Cunningham (the first Cunningham piece to be created on a British dance company); music, Michael Pugliese; design, Mark Lancaster.

(26 June 1992) *Phillidor's Defence*. Choreography, Guido Severien; music, Glyn Perrin; design, Carolien Scholtes.

Works from the repertoire: *Signature* (Davies, 1990), *Plain Song* (Davies, 1981), *Roughcut* (Alston, 1990), *Four Elements* (Childs, 1990), *Embarque* (Davies, 1988), *Slippage* (Tuckett, 1991), *Wildlife* (Alston, 1984), *Sounding* (Davies, 1989), *Opal Loop* (Brown, 1980), *Strong Language* (Alston, 1987).

The company performed in Billingsgate Old Fish Market, London (a gala performance of *Roughcut* in aid of charity on 26 September), Leicester, Manchester, London (Royalty Theatre), Oxford, Newcastle, Stratford-upon-Avon, Bath, Canterbury, Mold, Exeter, Southampton and Bristol. It also visited Turkey (Istanbul and Izmir) (6–10 July), giving performances of *Winnsboro Cotton Mill Blues, Completely Birdland* and *Roughcut,* and Buenos Aires, Argentina (28 July–1 August), giving performances of *Winnsboro Cotton Mill Blues, Completely Birdland* and *Strong Language*.

LONDON CONTEMPORARY DANCE THEATRE, founded 1967
The Place, 17 Duke's Road, London WC1H 9AB

Company premières:

(15 October 1991) *Wind Devil*. Choreography, Nina Wiener (1983); music, Sergio Cervetti.

(30 October 1991) *Freedom of Information* (Section 3). Choreography, Arnie Zane (1983); music, David Cunningham.

Other works from the repertoire: *White Heat* (Wagoner, 1990), *Hang Up* (Lunn, 1987), *Harmonica Breakdown* (Dudley, 1938), *Rikud* (Dror and Ben Gal, 1991), *Flee As A Bird* (Wagoner, 1986).

The company performed in Plymouth, Southampton, Warwick, Leeds, Bristol, London (Sadler's Wells Theatre), Birmingham, Northampton, Blackpool, Newcastle, Oxford and Sheffield. It performed *Freedom of Information* at the Dance for Life Gala at the London Palladium on 1 December, took part in the Royal Opera's *Turandot* at Wembley Arena, London (29 December–8 January), and gave workshop showings as part of the Spring Loaded season at The Place, London (31 March–4 April). It also visited Denmark (Copenhagen) in September, performing *Orfeo*, and Italy (Turin) in June, performing *Freedom of Information*, *White Heat* and *Rikud*.

THE SCOTTISH BALLET, founded 1956
261 West Princes Street, Glasgow G4 9EE

World premières:

(28 May 1992) *Macbeth*. A one-act ballet. Choreography, André Prokovsky; music, David Earl; design, Robin Don. Cast led by Michael Crooks and Noriko Ohara.

(28 May 1992) *Wildlife 1*. A one-act ballet. Choreography, Neville Campbell; music, Rhythm Street; design, Neville Campbell.

Company premiéres:

(22 August 1991) *Concerto Barocco*. Choreography, George Balanchine (1941); music, Bach. Cast led by Anne Christie, Cecilia Boorman and Robert Hampton.

(22 August 1991) *Troy Game*. Choreography, Robert North (1974); music, Batucada/Bob Downes; costumes, Peter Farmer.

(2 November 1991) *Sea of Troubles*. Choreography, Kenneth MacMillan (1988); music, Webern and Martinů; design, Deborah MacMillan.

(25 January 1992) *Scarlatti and Friends*. Choreography, André Prokovsky (1972); music, Scarlatti; design, André Prokovsky.

(25 January 1992) *That Certain Feeling*. Choreography, André Prokovsky (1984, under the title *The Aquarium*); music, Gershwin; design, The Scottish Ballet.

(12 March 1992) *Coppélia*. Choreography, Peter Wright after Petipa and Cecchetti (1979); music, Delibes: design, Peter Snow. Cast led by Noriko Ohara, Robert Hampton and Christopher Blagdon.

(27 May 1992) *Brief*. Choreography, Amanda Miller (1990); music, Bach; design, Amanda Miller.

Full-length ballets from the repertoire: *Giselle* (Petipa after Coralli/Perrot, prod. Darrell, 1971), *Cinderella* (Darrell, 1979).

One-act ballets and *pas de deux* from the repertoire: *Vespri* (Prokovsky), *Othello* (Darrell), extracts from *The Nutcracker* (Darrrell after Ivanov) and *Swan lake* (Darrell after Petipa and Ivanov), *Laurencia pas de six* (Samsova after Chaboukiani), *Monotones* (Ashton), *Five Brahms Waltzes in the Manner of Isadora Duncan* (Ashton), *Forgotten Land* (Kylian), *Symphony in D* (Kylian), *Who Cares?* (Balanchine), *Esprit* (Paulo Lopes).

The company gave performances in Glasgow, Aberdeen, Inverness, Liverpool, Edinburgh, Hull, Newcastle and Belfast. The small-scale touring company, SB2, visited smaller venues throughout Scotland in the autumn and spring, and also performed near London for the first time (Barking) and in Colchester, Cheltenham, Milford Haven and Carmarthen.

The main company visited Russia and the Ukraine for the first time, performing two triple bills in St Petersburg and Kiev and one in Moscow (3–20 June).

Drama

There were no obvious signs of recovery in the British theatre which continued to feel the effects of the recession in the past year. Attendances in 1991 were down to 10.9 million, from 11.3 million in 1990. The average price of a theatre ticket in the West End rose in 1991 to £17.45, pushed up by the preponderance of musicals, which cost more to produce. Annual figures from the Society of West End Theatre showed that there were more performances of musicals in 1991 than any other type of production, 4,850 (over 2,200 performances more than the next largest category, which was modern drama), and they accounted for 46 per cent of all attendances. In 1991 there were 193 new productions, compared with 187 in 1990, but on average only 37 of 50 London theatres were open at any one time.

Despite a number of expensive flops, the potential financial returns from a long-running West End musical still proved an irresistible lure. There were indications of a move away from plot-based musicals towards musical revues or revivals. Shows such as Jack Good's *Good Rockin' Tonite, The Cotton Club,* Ken Hill's *Phantom of the Opera,* and the celebrations of well-known and established composers, such as *Duke Ellington's Sophisticated Ladies,* Sheridan Morley's celebration of Noël Coward in *Noël and Gertie,* and the Rodgers and Hammerstein *The Sound of Music* hardly broke new ground and met with varying degrees of success.

Shows which attempted to break the mould fared little better. Mike Batt wrote the music, lyrics and book for his adaptation of Lewis Carroll's *The Hunting of the Snark,* a mock heroic nonsense poem. The show was reported to have cost over £2 million to stage, and had been eight years in development. Neither the subject matter nor a cast including Kenny Everett as Billiard Marker and David McCallum as Carroll could save the production from a critical mauling and an early death.

Harpooned

Another casualty was *Moby Dick,* a bizarre musical backed by Cameron Mackintosh which cost £1.2 million. It related the efforts of the girls of the fictional St Godrick's Academy to put on an end-of-term musical based on Melville's *Moby Dick.* With a largely undistinguished cast, featuring Tony Monopoly as headmistress Miss Hyman, the show veered from parody to smut and was comprehensively harpooned by the critics. Mackintosh presciently foretold that the show would run for 'six weeks or six years', with his lower estimate the more accurate.

Tommy Steele's production of *Some Like It Hot* followed *The Hunting of the Snark* into the Prince Edward theatre but enjoyed no more success. It was difficult to understand why Billy Wilder's classic film, which featured masterly performances by Tony Curtis, Jack Lemmon and Marilyn Monroe, should be felt suitable for musical adaptation. Unfortunately, the production provided no solutions, other than as a star vehicle for Tommy Steele, capitalizing on his success with *Singin' in the Rain.* Other productions that failed to establish themselves included *The Cotton Club,* which ran for five months at the Aldwych, and *Sikulu,* 'the new African song and dance sensation' from the creators of *Ipi Tombi,* which was simplistic and uninspired in its presentation of life in black South Africa. More surprising was the failure of *The Blue Angel* to survive its West End move. It was premièred at Stratford's rebuilt The Other Place to good notices before embarking on a provincial tour, but might have fared better at the Barbican Pit in repertory. Andrew Lloyd Webber's *Aspects of Love* also closed.

Ayckbourn Flop

It was not only musicals that suffered; Alan Ayckbourn experienced his first West End flop when *The Revengers' Comedies* closed after only a couple of months. Unlike many of Ayckbourn's works which interlock with other plays or have alternative versions, *The Revengers' Comedies* was best seen as 'a four-act play with a convenient division' as the second play made little sense on its own. Theatregoers were required to attend two separate performances to appreciate the work to the full. Insufficient numbers were prepared to make that commitment. The plays centred around two people who meet on Albert Bridge intent on suicide. Instead they decide to plan revenge on those who had brought them to their present predicaments. The idea was spread too thinly to sustain two plays but the production featured an excellent performance from Lia Williams as Karen, with Griff Rhys Jones and Joanna Lumley in leading roles.

John Osborne's *Déjàvu* was aptly named. By returning to the character of Jimmy Porter, created in *Look Back in Anger* at the Royal Court in 1956, Osborne raised expectations that he was unable to fulfil. The earlier play was a landmark in English theatre and had helped launch a new school of realist drama. Porter, now referred to as 'JP', is described by Osborne as 'a man of gentle susceptibilities constantly goaded by a brutal and coercive world' and he was effectively played by Peter Egan, but a play built around an almost uninterrupted monologue of middle-aged *angst* and nostalgia with no obvious dramatic impetus made for unsatisfactory entertainment.

Ronald Harwood's new play *Reflected Glory* related the story of two brothers. One is a playwright, played by Stephen Moore, who is in dispute with his brother, a restaurateur, played by Albert Finney, about using his family as the basis for his drama. In spite of some good reviews and a fine performance from Finney, the play was reported to be playing to barely one-third capacity audiences. Matters came to a head in early June when Finney announced during a radio interview that he was not going to appear in that night's performance because he had not been paid, thus precipitating the play's closure. Other productions were struggling to survive a poor summer in 1992 with attendances as low as 20 per cent in some cases. Even *The Mousetrap*, now in its 40th year, was down to half-full houses.

Carry on Dreaming

One of the measures that theatres were adopting in the hope of riding out the recession was Sunday opening. Bob Carlton's succesful *Return to the Forbidden Planet* was one of the first shows to replace Monday night performances with Sunday matinées. It was also tried by *The Pocket Dream*, a heavy-handed comedy in which six people attempt to perform *A Midsummer Night's Dream* after most of the cast fail to turn up. Written by Sandi Toksvig and Elly Brewer *The Pocket Dream* failed to become a reality and made little of the abilities of its cast, several of whom had established reputations for improvisational comedy.

Arthur Miller's works continued to be widely performed on the British stage. His new play *The Ride Down Mt Morgan* received its world première at Wyndham's. Featuring Tom Conti as Lyman Felt, a bigamist whose duel life is exposed when he is hospitalized after a car crash, the play surprised some critics by its use of humour to explore serious themes. More successful was the revival of Miller's *All My Sons*, the play with which he made his name in 1947, which continued his fruitful collaboration with the Young Vic. Ian Bannen played Joe Keller, the manufacturer of aeroplane parts who is responsible for the deaths of young pilots when he sends out a defective consignment. Directed by David Thacker, the production benefited from several strong performances, notably Marjorie Yates as Kate Keller and Matthew Marsh as Chris, although performance in the round meant that much of the effect of the portrayals was dissipated for those in the audience seeing the characters' backs at any particular time. Miller's *The Price* was also produced at the Haymarket, Leicester, directed by Sylvia Syms.

Ibsen Successes

There were major productions of several of the works of Henrik Ibsen during the year. Most notable was Deborah Warner's production of *Hedda Gabler*, which was first presented at the Abbey Theatre in Dublin before moving to the Playhouse in London. Fiona Shaw's powerful performance in the leading role was justly acclaimed. *The Pretenders* was produced at the Barbican Pit, directed by Danny Boyle, and a heavily truncated *Brand*, featuring Roy Marsden in the role Ibsen described as 'myself in my best moments', was directed by Roger Williams, appearing at the Aldwych after opening at the Thorndike in Leatherhead. A creditable production of *The Doll's House* appeared at the 70-seater Duke of Cambridge pub theatre after the cast and director Polly Irvin invested their own money and collected donations to finance it. *Hedda Gabler* was also produced at the Citizens, Glasgow, with Robert David Macdonald directing Anne Lambton in his own translation.

There were three versions of *The Dybbuk*, Solomon Anski's powerful drama about a woman possessed by a 'dybbuk' or spirit of a man who had died before he could marry her. Set in a Hassidic Jewish community, Anski's play, written in 1914, poses the question, 'Why does the soul fall from the highest heights to the deepest depths? Within the fall the rising lies'. Bruce Myers attempted to answer the question in his *A Dybbuk for Two People* at Hampstead; the other productions were directed by Julia Pascal at the New End and Katie Mitchell at the Barbican Pit.

Party Piece

A short new play by Harold Pinter, *Party Time*, concerned a woman whose husband had been killed by an unidentified totalitarian regime. It transpires that she is attending a party with members of the same regime. Directed by Pinter and featuring Nicola Pagett, *Party Time* appeared with his 1988 play *Mountain Language*.

More unsettling in its examination of torture and evil was Ariel Dorfman's masterly *Death and the Maiden*, featuring Juliet Stevenson as a woman who, having been raped and tortured by secret police, meets her torturer 15 years later. After opening at the Royal Court Theatre Upstairs during the London International Festival of Theatre, the production transferred to the main theatre and moved to the Duke of York's in early 1992. Miss Stevenson was invited to repeat the role in the Broadway production directed by Mike Nicholls but American Equity would not accept her and the role went to Glenn Close.

At the Royal Court the post of artistic director, held by Max Stafford-Clark since 1979, was re-advertised. Stafford-Clark re-applied but Stephen Daldry, director of the 60-seat Gate Theatre, was appointed to succeed him. However, Stafford-Clark was appointed to run the theatre in tandem with Daldry for 18 months, and as associate director for the following two years. Daldry established his reputation at the Gate through his innovative programme run on a limited budget; in 1991 the Gate featured 16 new productions.

New productions at the Royal Court included Timberlake Wertenbaker's *Three Birds Alighting on a Field*, an examination of the art world which opens with the auction of an apparently blank canvas entitled *No Illusion*, which is sold for £1.2 million. The play was well researched, with obvious parallels with the Greek myth of Philoctetes, but at times the authentic detail sat uneasily with the comic elements. John Guare's *Six Degrees of Separation* was a splendid drama by an American dramatist whose work is not well-known in Britain. It was based on the true story of a man who infiltrated, and became accepted by, Manhattan high society by pretending to be the son of a famous actor. Directed by Phyllida Lloyd, the production featured American actress Stockard Channing as Ouisa, who with her husband Flan is deceived by the young man Paul, brilliantly played by Adrian Lester. Howard Brenton's new play *Berlin Bertie* featured Diana Rigg in her Royal Court début. The play dealt with the collapse of Communism in East Germany following the destruction of the Berlin Wall; although it raised interesting points about how people readjust when the values they believe in have been removed, it was poorly contrived.

Brian Friel's *Dancing at Lughnasa* was both a critical and popular success when it opened a few years ago. The Dublin Abbey Theatre production of his *Faith Healer*, which consisted of four dramatic monologues spoken by three actors, was produced at the Royal Court. It featured Donal McCann as Frank, the travelling faith healer, who, it transpires, has died. His widow, Grace, was played by Sinead Cusack and his manager, Teddy, by Ron Cook. While not reaching the heights achieved by *Dancing at Lughnasa*, *Faith Healer* nevertheless confirmed Friel as an accomplished dramatist.

Mystery Play

The Japanese Festival included fascinating performances of the various forms of the great classical theatre of Japan, as well as one oddity. The Shike Theatrical Company of Tokyo brought their Kabuki-style, Japanese-language version of Rice and Lloyd Webber's *Jesus Christ Superstar* to the Dominion, the apparent justification being that the work could be viewed 'freed from Christian preconceptions'. More notable was *Orin and the Angels with Closed Eyes*, featuring the popular Japanese film actress Ineko Arima in a drama set in early 19th-century Japan about the 'goze', or blind dancing girls. The play, written by Tsutomu Mizukami and directed by Koichi Kimura, was a great success in Japan. Other productions included a Kabuki version of *Hamlet*, a Kyogen (comic style) *Falstaff* based on *The Merry Wives of Windsor*, plus examples of Grand Kabuki, Noh theatre and the traditional puppet theatre Bunraku. Of particular note was the visually superb production of *King Lear* by the Banyu Inryoku Company, directed by J. A. Seazer.

While the well-advertised Japanese Festival may have attracted much attention, Stephen Daldry's small fringe theatre the Gate won plaudits for its excellent season featuring the 'Golden Age' of Spanish drama. Notable productions included Lope de Vega's *The Gentleman from Olmedo* directed by Laurence Boswell, Calderon's *Three Judgments in One* directed by Simon Usher, and Tirso de Molina's *Damned for Despair* directed by Daldry.

The Riverside Studios put on an imaginative production of George Orwell's *Down and Out in Paris and London* adapted by Nigel Gearing. Presented by the Paines Plough Company in association with Centre Régional de Créations Européennes and Salisbury Playhouse, the play featured up to 50 members of the public as homeless extras, with the cast of eight sharing over 50 main roles. The production was well staged and atmospheric in its series of vignettes.

No Beauty

David Hirson's pastiche of Molière *La Bête* was a costly failure on Broadway. At the Lyric, Hammersmith it was less savagely mauled, although some critics felt it was guilty of the very triviality it sought to expose. However, it was notable for an opening half-hour monologue of stunning virtuosity by Alan Cummings as Valère.

There were several productions of plays by George Bernard Shaw during the year. *Caesar and Cleopatra*, directed by Matthew Francis at Greenwich, featured Alec McCowen and Amanda Root. The Hampstead production of *The Philanderer* included for the first time a 'missing' act which dealt with the subject of divorce. Michael Holroyd, Shaw's biographer, found the work in the British Museum while researching his book. The play failed when first performed in 1905 and Shaw later dismissed it as 'mechanical farce and realistic filth which quite disgusts me'. Trevor Nunn directed an all-star cast in *Heartbreak House* at the Haymarket Theatre Royal, with Paul Scofield notable as Captain Shotover, while the Olivier staged Howard Davies's production of *Pygmalion*, with Frances Barber as Eliza Doolittle and Alan Howard as Henry Higgins.

Mary Braddon's *Lady Audley's Secret* was a great success when first published in 1862. Sylvia Freedman's adaptation at the Lyric, Hammersmith, unfortunately dissipated much of the dramatic tension by revealing the heroine's secret at the beginning, and suffered also from uncertainty of tone. Janet Suzman was impressive in Euripides's *Hippolytos* at the Almeida, while his *Medea* was adapted by Steve Carter for a Caribbean setting as *Pecong*. Phyllida Lloyd directed *Medea* at the Royal Exchange, Manchester, with Claire Benedict in the title role, while at the Lilian Baylis Ishia Bennison performed the same part in Clare Venables' production.

Kenneth Branagh's Renaissance Theatre Company brought their production of Chekhov's *Uncle Vanya* to the Lyric, Hammersmith. The play was notable for a fine performance from Richard Briers; Peter Egan assumed directorial control after Branagh was called away for filming after casting the production. Anouilh's *Becket* was presented in a new translation by Jeremy Sams at the Haymarket; there were sound performances from Robert Lindsay as Henry and Derek Jacobi as Beckett although as drama the piece was not impressive and as history it is unsound.

Grand Hotel arrived from Broadway trailing awards and not a little controversy, after disputes between the American and British Equity unions over casting. Based on the novel by Vicki Baum that inspired the well-known film, and set in Berlin in the 1920s, the show represented a triumph for style over content. Directed and choreographed brilliantly by Tommy Tune, *Grand Hotel* marked a notable return to form for the large-scale Broadway musical.

National Theatre

The latest Arts Council grants, announced in November 1991, gave the National Theatre a 10.6 per cent increase of £1 million. A very successful season, with attendances on average 90 per cent, saw several notable productions on the three South Bank stages as well as successful touring productions at home and abroad. Alan Bennett's *The Madness of George III* opened at the Lyttleton, with a fine performance by Nigel Hawthorne as the Lear-like figure of the king, subjected to all the horrors of 18th-century medical ignorance for treatment of a condition now believed to have been porphyria but then diagnosed as madness. Bennett's *Talking Heads*, which featured himself and Patricia Routledge in three monologues first performed on television, was also seen at the Comedy during the year.

Molière's *Le Bourgeois Gentilhomme*, translated by Nick Dear, featured an exuberant performance by Timothy Spall as Monsieur Jourdain, the tradesman's son with aspirations towards joining the aristocracy, although there was criticism that the portrayal was too coarse and vulgar. The production used the original music by Jean-Baptiste Lully which is seldom performed in Britain. Sean Mathias directed a strong cast including Ian McKellen, Antony Sher and Eric Porter in Chekhov's *Uncle Vanya* at the Cottesloe, but Sher appeared miscast as Astrov and the production seemed underrehearsed.

The most controversial production was Shakespeare's *A Misummer Night's Dream* at the Olivier, directed by the Canadian Robert Lepage. Lepage's *Tectonic Plates* was seen the previous year at the Cottesloe, which also staged his *Needles and Opium*, a bold and imaginative account of a trip he had made to Paris for a documentary about jazz musician Miles Davis, in April 1992. It was apparent that his first Shakespeare production in Britain would bring a rare individual talent to bear on a familiar work. His *Dream* was set in a muddy lake, which could be taken to represent the darkness of awakening sexuality, and Michael Levine's design was intelligently conceived and executed. However, there was much justified criticism that the pervasive mud proved a distraction at times, and, more seriously, that the verse was subordinated to the staging to such an extent that much of the rhythm and poetry was lost altogether.

After his much-praised examination of the state of the Church of England in *Racing Demons*, David Hare turned his attention to the judiciary in *Murmuring Judges*, premièred at the Olivier. Although a worthy and thoroughly researched piece, with its story of a man from Northern Ireland imprisoned after a dishonest detective fixed evidence against him, it came across as didactic and dull in Richard Eyre's production. Edward Bond's *The Sea* was revived at the Lyttelton, its first major London production since 1973, with Judi Dench as Mrs Rafi. Also of note was Richard Eyre's production of Tennessee Williams's *Night of the Iguana*, featuring Frances Barber and Alfred Molina, and Jim Cartwright's *The Rise and Fall of Little Voice*, featuring Alison Steadman.

Royal Shakespeare Company

The Royal Shakespeare Company successfully put its past traumas behind it and in August 1991 celebrated the reopening of The Other Place in Stratford. The old theatre had established a reputation for powerful performances in its intimate atmosphere. Rebuilt at a cost of £1.8 million, the new theatre has seating for 250 spectators but manages to retain much of the spirit of the original stage. Its first production was the première of *The Blue Angel*, a new musical by Pam Gems adapted from the 1905 novel *Professor Unrat* by Heinrich Mann. Set in Vienna, it is the story of an elderly schoolmaster, played by Philip Madoc, who becomes infatuated with a nightclub singer, played by Kelly Hunter. The second production was Shakespeare's *Measure for Measure*; both were directed by Trevor Nunn, with Maria Bjørnson's clever set serving both plays. After a season at Stratford, both productions went on tour to 16 different venues. The Other Place also featured Thomas Heywood's *A Woman Killed with Kindness* directed by Katie Mitchell, Derek Walcott's adaptation of Homer's *Odyssey* and Sam Mendes' production of *Richard III*, featuring a strong performance from Simon Russell Beale.

At the Memorial Theatre David Leveaux's production of *Romeo and Juliet* was criticized as overlong, and although Michael Maloney was well received as Romeo the play suffered through the lack of any apparent attraction between him and Clare Holman's Juliet. Steven Pimlott's *Julius Caesar* was also misconceived and poorly staged. More successful was Bill Alexander's *The Taming of the Shrew* which retained and developed the Christopher Sly introduction in which a drunken tinker is deceived into thinking he is a lord who has been out of his mind, and is made to watch the performance of the *Shrew* that follows. Anton Lesser played Petruchio with Amanda Harris as Kate and Rebecca Saire as Bianca.

The Swan's programme included Adrian Noble's *The Thebans*, which consisted of Sophocles' three Oedipus plays translated by Timberlake Wertenbaker. Richard Brome's *A Jovial Crew* was one of what the RSC term their 'discovery' plays. Brome was a servant of Jonson, whose influence is evident in his work, and the play was one of the last performed before the Puritans closed the theatres. Its last known performance was in 1742, although it had later been turned into an operetta. The play was adapted by Stephen Jeffreys, with music by Ian Dury, and marked Max Stafford-Clark's directorial début with the RSC.

Hall's Well

Sir Peter Hall returned to Stratford and the company he founded after a break of 25 years to direct Shakespeare's *All's Well That Ends Well*, his first production of the work. He invited Richard Johnson, one of his original contract players, to return after a 20-year absence from Stratford and 15 years away from the stage, to play the King of France. Hall's first use of the Swan stage was a resounding success with uniformly high standards of acting matched by fine staging from John Gunter.

Having accumulated a £3 million deficit the Royal Shakespeare Company hoped to break even over its 1991–2 season. However, the company was unable to find a sponsor for its tour of *Richard III* starring Simon Russell Beale, which meant that fewer performances could be given and ticket prices had to be raised.

At Chichester, Patrick Garland's appointment as director was renewed for a further two years. Having lost £700,000 over the previous two seasons the Festival Theatre was desperately in need of success. Its 30th season opened promisingly – advance booking was at £1 million – with the Renaissance Theatre Company production of Shakespeare's *Coriolanus* directed by Tim Supple and featuring Kenneth Branagh as Coriolanus, Judi Dench as Volumnia and Richard Briers as Menenius. For its second production Garland revived *Venus Observed*, a poetic drama by the forgotten man of English drama, Christopher Fry. Fry had originally written the play to fulfil a commission for Laurence Olivier at the St James Theatre in 1950. At the time Fry was at the height of his popularity, but his style of drama fell from fashion with the advent of 'kitchen sink' realism in the late 1950s. Fry agreed to the revival on condition that he could rework the play, which he felt he had rushed originally. Accordingly, he changed it from three acts to two, cut come passages and altered some of the characters. Whether this was enough to bring about a renewed interest in his work is debatable. Although well served by Donald Sinden as the Duke of Altair the weaknesses in construction were still evident and the style was dated. Garland also directed Melvyn Bragg's *King Lear in New York* which featured John Stride as an actor attempting a stage comeback in New York as King Lear, his progress paralleling that of the character.

The Glasgow Citizens opened two new theatres in February 1992. The Second Theatre holds 130 seats and the Third Theatre 70, both constructed for performances in the round, and adding to the 650 seats in the main auditorium. The Second Theatre opened with *1953*, a version of Racine's *Andromaque* by Craig Raine starring Patrick O'Kane as Vittorio Mussolini and Greg Hicks as Klaus Maria von Orestes, directed by Philip Prowse. Robert David Macdonald translated, directed and appeared in *Niagara* by Alonso Alegria in the Third Theatre.

At the Sheffield Crucible, Mark Brickman resigned as artistic director in October 1991. Facing a loss of £250,000, the management board had wanted to cancel scheduled productions of *Hedda Gabler* and *The Front Page* for 'quality productions that would be financially viable'. Brickman refused, saying that there was 'little point in having a subsidized theatre which does not put on challenging work'. The Birmingham Repertory Theatre was awarded a grant of £500,000 by the Foundation for Sport and the Arts which would enable it to complete its Centenary Square development, providing new technical and front of house facilities.

Awards

In the Evening Standard Drama Awards, presented in November 1991, best actor went to John Wood for *King Lear* at the RSC; best actress, Vanessa Redgrave as Isadora Duncan in *When She Danced* at the Globe; Brian Friel's *Dancing at Lughnasa* (National) won best play; best comedy was Steven Berkoff's *Kvetch* (King's Head); best musical *Carmen Jones* (Old Vic); Trevor Nunn won best director for *Timon of Athens* (Young Vic) and Rona Munro was most promising playwright for *Bold Girls* (Hampstead).

The main winners of the Laurence Olivier Awards, presented in April 1992 by the Society of West End Theatre, were: best actor Nigel Hawthorne (*The Madness of George III*, National); best actress Juliet Stevenson (*Death and the Maiden*, Royal Court); best play *Death and the Maiden* (Ariel Dorfman, Royal Court); best comedy *La Bête* (David Hirson, Lyric, Hammersmith); best musical *Carmen Jones* (Old Vic); best play director Deborah Warner (*Hedda Gabler*, Playhouse) and best director of a musical Simon Callow for *Carmen Jones*.

PRODUCTIONS

LONDON PRODUCTIONS

16 August 1991 to 15 August 1992

Albery, wc2 (21 November 1991) *The Cabinet Minister* (Pinero) with Maureen Lipman, Derek Nimmo, Sara Kestelman, Gwen Watford; director, Braham Murray; designer, Simon Higlett (Plymouth Theatre Royal production). (3 March 1992) *The Pocket Dream* (Brewer and Toksvig) with Mike McShane, Sandi Toksvig; director, Pip Broughton; designer, Jacqueline Gunn (Nottingham Playhouse production). (21 May) *Body & Soul* (Roy Kendall) with Robert Hardy, Angela Thorne, Nicola Redmond; director, Val May; designer, Tim Shortall. (23 July) *Shades* (Sharman Macdonald) with Pauline Collins, Matthew Steer, Daphne Oxenford, James Cosmo; director, Simon Callow.

Aldwych, wc2 (27 August 1991) *Brand* (Ibsen, trans. Robert David MacDonald) with Roy Marsden, Kim Thomson, Gillian Martell, Ewan Hooper; director, Roger Williams;

designer, Bernard Culshaw (Leatherhead Thorndike production). (24 January 1992) *The Cotton Club* (Douglas Barron) with Richard Lloyd King, Debby Bishop, Brit Wilson; director, Billy Wilson.

ALMEIDA, N1 (17 September 1991) *Hippolytos* (Euripides, trans. David Lan) with Janet Suzman, Duncan Bell, Brenda Bruce, Ian McDiarmid, Ewan Hooper; director, Andrei Serban; designer, Richard Hudson. (6 November) *Party Time* and *Mountain Language* (Harold Pinter) with Nicola Pagett, Dorothy Tutin, Barry Foster, Peter Howitt, Roger Lloyd Pack; director, Harold Pinter; designer, Mark Thompson. (3 January 1992) *The Gigli Concert* (Tom Murphy) with Barry Foster, Tony Doyle, Ruth McCabe; director, Karel Reisz; designer, Ashley Martin-Davis. (3 March) *A Hard Heart* (Howard Barker) with Anna Massey, James Clyde, Angela Down; director, Ian McDiarmid; designer, Anthony Ward. (12 May) *The Rules of the Game* (Pirandello, adapted by David Hare) with Richard Griffiths, Nicola Pagett, David Yelland; director, Jonathan Kent; designer, Peter J. Davison.

AMBASSADORS, WC2 (19 September 1991) *Thunderbirds F.A.B.* (transferred from Mermaid). (26 May 1992) *Mad, Bad and Dangerous to Know* (devised by Jane McCulloch) with Derek Jacobi, Isla Blair; director, Jane McCulloch; music, Donald Fraser; designer, Liz da Costa (English Chamber Theatre/Proscenium production). (20 July) *From a Jack to a King* (Bob Carlton) with Christian Roberts, Matthew Devitt, Robert Dallas, Allison Harding; director, Matthew Devitt (transferred from Boulevard, Soho).

ARTS, W1 (4 September 1991) *Good Golly Miss Molly* (Bob Eaton) with Sarah Mortiner, Steven Glanville, Mark Brignal, Carl Proctor; director, Bob Eaton.

BARBICAN, EC2 (11 September 1991) *Richard II* (Shakespeare) with Alex Jennings, Anton Lesser, Mike Dowling, Bernard Lloyd, Valentina Yakunina; director, Ron Daniels; designer, Antony McDonald. (2 October) *A Woman of No Importance* (Wilde) with Barbara Leigh-Hunt, Cherry Morris, John Carlisle, Nichola McAuliffe, Carol Royle; director and designer, Philip Prowse. (27 November) *The Strange Case of Dr Jekyll and Mr Hyde* (Robert Louis Stevenson, adapted by David Edgar) with Simon Russell Beale, Roger Allam, Pippa Guard, Oliver Ford Davies; director, Peter Wood; designer, Carl Toms. (31 March 1992) *Henry IV, Part 1* (Shakespeare) with Julian Glover, Michael Maloney, Robert Stephens, Owen Teale, Sylvestra le Touzel, Linda Bassett; director, Adrian Noble; designer, Bob Crowley. (15 April) *The Alchemist* (Ben Jonson) with David Bradley, Jonathan Hyde, Joanne Pearce, Philip Voss; director, Sam Mendes; designer, Anthony Ward. (7 May) *Henry IV, Part 2* (Shakespeare) with Julian Glover, Michael Maloney, Robert Stephens, Joanne Pearce, David Bradley; director, Adrian Noble; designer, Bob Crowley. (24 June) *Romeo and Juliet* (Shakespeare) with Michael Maloney, Clare Holman, Tim McInnerny, Sheila Reid, Ian Hughes; director, David Leveaux; designer, Alison Chitty. (22 July) *Columbus and the Discovery of Japan* (Richard Nelson) with Jonathan Hyde, Jane Gurnett, Philip Voss, Christopher Benjamin; director, John Caird; designer, Timothy O'Brien.

BARBICAN PIT (11 September 1991) *Curse of the Starving Class* (Sam Shepard) with John McEnery, Alex Kingston, Susan Fleetwood, George Anton; director, Robin Lefevre; designer, Kenny Miller. (26 September) *The Pretenders* (Ibsen, adapted by Chris Hannan) with Paterson Joseph, David Calder, Alan McNaughtan; director, Danny Boyle; designer, Deirdre Clancy. (20 November) *The Bright and Bold Design* (Peter Whelan) with Clive Russell, Katy Behean, Alex Kingston, Paul Webster; director, Bill Alexander; designer, Kit Surrey. (3 April 1992) *The Virtuoso* (Thomas Shadwell) with Saskia Reeves, Barry Lynch, Sean Murray, Josette Bushell-Mingo, Linda Marlowe, Guy Henry, Richard Bonneville, Christopher Benjamin; director, Phyllida Lloyd; designer, Anthony Ward. (14 April) *A Woman Killed with Kindness* (Thomas Heywood) with Michael Maloney, Saskia Reeves, Sylvestra le Touzel, Jonathan Cullen, Barry Lynch, Valentine Pelka; director, Katie Mitchell; designer, Vicki Mortimer. (6 May) *'Tis Pity She's a Whore* (Ford) with Jonathan Cullen, Saskia Reeves, Jonathan Hyde, Sheila Reid, Tim McInnerny; director, David Leveaux; designers, Kenny Miller and Bob Howell. (14 July) *The Dybbuk* (Solomon Anski, adapted by Mira Rafalowicz) with John Shrapnel, Joanne Pearce, Charles Daish, Rob Edwards, Peter Needham; director, Katie Mitchell; designer, Vicki Mortimer.

BUSH, W12 (2 September 1991) *Blue Night in the Heart of the West* (James Stock) with Tom Mannion, Matthew Zajac; director, Sallie Aprahamian; designer, Anthony Lamble. (18 November) *The Belfry* (Billy Roche) with Des McAleer, Ingrid Craigie, Gary Lydon; director, Robin Lefevre; designer, Andrew Wood. (10 February 1992) *The Cutting* (Maureen O'Brien) with Siân Thomas, Paul Freeman; director, Dominic Dromgoole; designer, Mark Viner.

COMEDY, WC2 (28 October 1991) *It's Ralph* (Hugh Whitemore) with Timothy West, Jack Shepherd, Connie Booth; director, Clifford Williams; designer, Carl Toms. (27 January 1992) *Talking Heads* (Alan Bennett) with Patricia Routledge, Alan Bennett; director, Alan Bennett; designer, Simon Higlett. (4 April) *The Pope and the Witch* (Dario Fo, trans. Ed Emery, adapted by Andy de la Tour) with Clive Merrison, Berwick Kaler, Frances de la Tour, David Horovitch, Paul Venables; director, Jude Kelly; designer, Rob Jones. (10 June) *Déjàvu* (John Osborne) with Peter Egan, Gareth Thomas, Alison Johnson, Eve Matheson; director, Tony Palmer; designer, Geoffrey Scott (Leatherhead Thorndike production). (5 August) *Six Degrees of Separation* (transferred from Royal Court).

DOMINION, WC1 (22 June 1992) *Grand Hotel* (book, Luther Davis; lyrics, Robert Wright and George Forrest; music, Maury Yeston) with Liliane Montevecchi, Brent Barrett, Lynnette Perry, Barry Foster; director and choreographer, Tommy Tune; designer, Tony Walton.

DUCHESS, WC2 (19 December 1991) *An Evening with Gary Lineker* (Arthur Smith and Chris England) with Nick Hancock, Maria McErlane, Audrey Cooke, Chris England, Caroline Quentin, Andy Taylor; director, Arthur Smith.

DUKE OF YORK'S, WC2 (8 October 1991) *The Glory of the Garden* (Stephen Mallatrat) with Russell Dixon, Jill Gascoine, Janine Duvitski, Steven Mackintosh; director, Robin Herford. (3 December) *Noël and Gertie* (Sheridan Morley) with Edward Petherbridge, Susan Hampshire; director, Sean Mathias. (11 February 1992) *Death and the Maiden* (transferred from Royal Court).

GARRICK, WC2 (2 October 1991) *Kvetch* (Steven Berkoff) with Anita Dobson, Steven Berkoff, Henry Goodman, Stanley Lebor; director, Steven Berkoff; designer, Silvia Jahnsons.

GATE, W11 (15 October 1991) *Three Judgments in One* (Calderon, trans. Gwynne Edwards) with Kevin Costello, Bob Barrett, Hermione Norris; director, Simon Usher; designer, Anthony Lamble. (October) *The Gentleman from Olmedo* (Lope de Vega, trans. David Johnston) with James Clyde, Janet Henfry, Richard Hope; director, Laurence Boswell; designer, Jeremy Herbert. (15 November) *Damned for Despair* (Tirso de Molina, trans. Laurence Boswell) with Timothy Walker, Simon Gregor, Lorcan Cranitch; director,

Stephen Daldry; designer, Tim Hartley. (14 December) *The Great Pretenders* (Lope de Vega, trans. Laurence Boswell, David Johnston) with Clara Salaman, John Straiton, Louis Hilyer, Jamie Newall; director, Laurence Boswell. (4 February 1992) *Walpurgis Night* (Venedict Erofeyev, trans. Snoo Wilson) with Nicholas Farrell, Allan Corduner, Patrick Godfrey, George Irving; director, Dalia Ibelhauptaite. (8 May) *Bad Blood* (Grizelda Gambaro) with Peter Marinker, Louis Hilyer, John Padden; director, Kate Rowland; designer, Eve Stewart.

GLOBE, WI (6 January 1992) *Duke Ellington's Sophisticated Ladies* with Jacqueline Dankworth, Jamie Dee, Horace Oliver; director, Roger Haines. (20 May) *The Blue Angel* (Royal Shakespeare Company production).

GREENWICH, SEIO (23 September 1991) *Rookery Nook* (Ben Travers) with Tyler Butterworth, Christopher Godwin, Richenda Carey, Steven Beard; director, Matthew Francis; designer, Di Seymour. (30 January 1992) *Caesar and Cleopatra* (Shaw) with Alec McCowen, Amanda Root, Michael Cronin; director, Matthew Francis; designer, Julian McGowan. (26 March) *Playing Sinatra* (Bernard Kops) with Ian Gelder, Susan Brown, Stefan Bednarczyk; director, Ted Craig; designer, Michael Pavelka. (4 May) *As You Like It* (Shakespeare) with Jemma Redgrave, Philip Franks, Buddug Morgan, John Rogan, Robert Hands, Kate Gartside; director, James Robert Carson; designer, Kathy Strachan. (23 June) *Schippel, the Plumber* (C. P. Taylor) with James Saxon, Richard Freeman, Brian Protheroe, David Bamber, Philip Franks; director, Jeremy Sams; designer, Lez Brotherston. (3 August) *Mother Tongue* (Alan Franks) with Prunella Scales, Gwen Taylor, Bernice Stegers, Robert McBain; director, Richard Cottrell.

HAMPSTEAD, NW3 (4 September 1991) *Bold Girls* (Rona Munro) with Imelda Staunton, Britta Smith, Orla Charlton, Catherine Cusack; director, John Dove; designer, Robert Jones. (25 October) *Carlucco and the Queen of Hearts* (George Rosie) with David Kincaid, Eilidh Fraser, Janet Dye; director, Sandy Neilson (Fifth Estate production). (14 November) *The Philanderer* (Shaw) with Clive Owen, Eleanor David, Caroline Langrishe, Jonathan Coy, Barry Morse, Geoffrey Toone; director, Brian Cox; designer, Tom Piper. (10 January 1992) *A Dybbuk for Two People* (Solomon Anski, adapted by Bruce Myers) with Corinne Jaber, Bruce Myers. (6 February) *Making It Better* (James Saunders) with Jane Asher, Rufus Sewell, Larry Lamb, David de Keyser; director, Michael Rudman; designer, Simon Higlett. (6 April) *Back Up the Hearse and Let Them Smell the Flowers* (William Gaminara) with Danny Webb, Lesley Dunlop, Paul Bown, James Purefoy, Debra Gillett, Christopher Fairbank; director, John Dove; designer, Robert Jones. (19 May) *The Fastest Clock in the Universe* (Philip Ridley) with Con O'Neill, Jonathan Coy, Elizabeth Bradley, Jude Law, Emma Amos; director, Matthew Lloyd; designer, Moggie Douglas. (10 July) *Someone Who'll Watch Over Me* (Frank McGuinness) with Stephen Rea, Alec McCowen, Hugh Quarshie; director, Robin Lefevre; designer, Robin Don.

HAYMARKET THEATRE ROYAL, SWI (7 October 1991) *Becket* (Anouilh, trans. Jeremy Sams) with Derek Jacobi, Robert Lindsay, David Lyon, Ken Bones; director, Elijah Moshinsky; designer, Michael Yeargan. (19 March 1992) *Heartbreak House* (Shaw) with Paul Scofield, Vanessa Redgrave, Felicity Kendal, Daniel Massey, Imogen Stubbs; director, Trevor Nunn; designer, William Dudley. (24 June) *A Woman of No Importance* (Royal Shakespeare Company production).

KING'S HEAD, NI (15 January 1992) *Spread a Little Happiness* (compiled by Sheridan Morley) with Frank Thornton, Rachel Robertson, Fiona Sinnott; director, Dan Crawford. (26 May) *Philadelphia, Here I Come!* (Brian Friel) with Jonathan Arun, Brendan Coyle, Pauline Delany, Frank Dunne, Eamon Kelly; director, Dan Crawford; designer, Nigel Hook.

LILIAN BAYLIS, ECI (2 December 1991) *Lady Windermere's Fan* (Wilde) with Irina Brook, Peter Lindford, Lorna Heilbron; director, Mike Alfreds; designer, Paul Dart (Cambridge Theatre Company). (January 1992) *Medea* (Euripides) with Ishia Bennison, Nick Walker, Martin Gower, Richard Owens; director, Clare Venables.

LYRIC, Hammersmith, W6 (14 August 1991) *Uncle Vanya* (Chekhov, adapted Pam Gems) with Peter Egan, Richard Briers, Siân Thomas, Patrick Godfrey; directors, Kenneth Branagh, Peter Egan; designer, Kenny Miller (Renaissance Theatre Company). (9 September) *The Knickers* (Carl Sternheim) with Philip Whitchurch, Marcia Warren, Caroline Langrishe, Adrian Schiller; director, Phil Young; designer, David Burrows. (21 October) *Lady Audley's Secret* (Mary Braddon, adapted Sylvia Freedman) with Sally Edwards, Robert Bathurst, Michael Simkins; director, Annie Castledine; designer, Martin Johns. (4 December) *As You Like It* (Shakespeare) with Patrick Toomey, Tom Hollander, Joe Dixon, Adrian Lester, Peter Needham; director, Declan Donnellan; designer, Nick Ormerod (Cheek by Jowl Company). (30 January 1992) *La Bête* (David Hirson) with Jeremy Northam, Timothy Walker, Alan Cumming; director, Richard Jones; designer, Richard Hudson. (1 April) *The Winter's Tale* (Shakespeare) with Simon McBurney, Marcello Magni, Kathryn Hunter; director, Annabel Arden; designer, Ariane Gastambide (Théâtre de Complicité production). (7 May) *Loot* (Joe Orton) with Dearbhla Molloy, Ben Walden, David Troughton, Colin Hurley; director, Peter James; designer, Bernard Culshaw. (11 June) *A Judgement in Stone* (Ruth Rendell, adapted Neil Bartlett, Nicholas Bloomfield) with Sheila Hancock, Beverley Klein; directors, Neil Bartlett, Leah Hausman; designer, Mark Bailey (Gloria Company production). (30 July) *Absent Friends* (Alan Ayckbourn) with Cherith Mellor, Gary Bond, Susie Blake, Jane Slavin, Michael Melia, John Salthouse; director, Peter James; designer, Bernard Culshaw (co-production with West Yorkshire Playhouse).

LYRIC STUDIO, W6 (3 September 1991) *Hard Times* (Charles Dickens, adapted Stephen Jeffreys) with Jeffrey Perry, Leonard Kavanagh, Lilian Evans, Deirdre Edwards; director, Giles Block. (13 September) *Oh Hell!* (*The Devil and Billy Markham* – Shel Silverstein, with Steve Frost; *Bobby Gould in Hell* – David Mamet, with Nic D'Avirro, Martin Sadofski, Steven O'Shea); director, Aaron Mullen. (22 October) *The Woman Destroyed* (Simone de Beauvoir, trans. and adapted Diana Quick) with Diana Quick; director, Vanessa Fielding; designer, Michael Vale. (January 1992) *A Killing Passion* (Alby James and Sheena Wrigley) with Anthony Warren, Charlie Folorunshoi, Catherine Coffey; director, Alby James; designer, Andrea Montag (Temba Company). (12 March) *Cabal and Love* (Schiller) with Tim Barker, Sarah Burghard, Christopher Hollis; director, Patrick Wilde; designer, Cecil Hayter (Theatre Manoeuvres production). (14 May) *Dr Faustus* (Marlowe, adapted Max Hafler) with Femi Elufowoju, Max Hafler; director, Tony Hegarty (Commonweal Theatre Company production). (23 July) *No Remission* (Rod Williams) with Pip Donaghy, Rob Spendlove, Daniel Craig; director, Derek Wax.

NATIONAL THEATRE, SEI. COTTESLOE (17 September 1991) *At Our Table* (Daniel Mornin) with Stephen Boxer, Nicholas Woodeson, Cathryn Harrison; director, Jenny Killick; designer, Bunny Christie. (5 December) *The Little Clay Cart* (Shudraka, trans. Jatinder Verma, Ranjit Bolt) with

Stanley Townsend, J. D. Kelleher, Vincent Ebrahim, Shelley King, Cuckoo Parameswaran; director, Jatinder Verma; designer, Magdalen Rubalcava. (17 December) *Blood Wedding* (Lorca, trans. Gurenda Pandolfi) with Mona Hammond, Cyril Nri, Helen McCrory, Gary McDonald; director, Yvonne Brewster; desiogner, Kendra Ullyart. (23 January 1992) *Angels in America* (Tony Kushner) with Sean Chapman, Marcus D'Amico, Felicity Montagu, Nick Reding, Henry Goodman; director, Declan Donnellan; designer, Nick Ormerod. (25 February) *Uncle Vanya* (Chekhov, adapted Pam Gems) with Ian McKellen, Antony Sher, Janet McTeer, Eric Porter; director, Sean Mathias; designer, Stephen Brimson Lewis. (30 April) *Needles and Opium* with Robert Lepage. (16 June) *The Rise and Fall of Little Voice* (Jim Cartwright) with Alison Steadman, Jane Horrocks, Pete Postlethwaite; director, Sam Mendes; designer, William Dudley.

LYTTELTON (28 November 1991) *The Madness of George III* (Alan Bennett) with Nigel Hawthorne, Michael Fitzgerald, Julian Wadham, Charles Kay, Janet Dale; director, Nicholas Hytner; designer, Mark Thompson. (6 December) *The Sea* (Edward Bond) with Judi Dench, Ken Stott, Samuel West, Sarah Woodward, David Thewlis, Alan McNaughtan; director, Sam Mendes; designer, Bob Crowley. (6 February 1992) *Night of the Iguana* (Tennessee Williams) with Frances Barber, Alfred Molina, Eileen Atkins, Robin Bailey; director, Richard Eyre; designer, Bob Crowley. (5 May) *Le Bourgeois Gentilhomme* (Molière, trans. Nick Dear) with Timothy Spall, Cathryn Bradshaw, Adam Kotz, Teddy Kempner, Anita Dobson; director, Richard Jones; designer, the Brothers Quay; choreographer, Michael Popper.

OLIVIER (10 October 1991) *Murmuring Judges* (David Hare) with Michael Bryant, Richard Pasco, Lesley Sharp, Robert Patterson, Alphonsia Emmanuel; director, Richard Eyre; designer, Bob Crowley. (6 March 1992) *The Recruiting Officer* (Farquhar) with Alex Jennings, Desmond Barrit, Ken Stott, Suzanne Burden, Sally Dexter; director, Nicholas Hytner; designer, Ashley Martin-Davis. (9 April) *Pygmalion* (Shaw) with Frances Barber, Alan Howard, Gillian Barge, Robin Bailey, Michael Bryant; director, Howard Davies; designer, William Dudley. (9 July) *A Midsummer Night's Dream* (Shakespeare) with Angela Laurier, Timothy Spall, Sally Dexter, Indra Ove, Rudi Davies, Rupert Graves, Simon Coates, Jeffery Kissoon; director, Robert Lepage; designer, Michael Levine.

NEW END, NW3 (25 June 1992) *The Dybbuk* (Solomon Anski, adapted Julia Pascal) with Kate Margam, Philippe Smolikowski, Thomas Kampe; director, Julia Pascal.

OPEN AIR, Regent's Park, NW1 (1 June 1992) *A Midsummer Night's Dream* (Shakespeare) with Jane Maud, Ken Bones, Dinsdale Landen, Gavin Muir; director, Ian Talbot; designer, Paul Farnsworth. (17 June) *As You Like It* (Shakespeare) with Oliver Parker, Sarah-Jane Holm, Cathryn Harrison, Anna Patrick, John Kane, Bette Bourne; director, Maria Aitken; designer, Bruno Santini. (29 July) *Lady Be Good* (George and Ira Gershwin) with Bernard Cribbins, Joanna Riding, Simon Green, Gillian Rushton; director, Ian Talbot.

PICCADILLY, W1 (28 August 1991) *Tango at the End of Winter* (Kunio Shimuzu, adapted Peter Barnes) with Alan Rickman, Suzanne Bertish; director, Yukio Ninagawa (Edinburgh Festival production). (29 October) *Tovarich* (Jacques Deval, adapted Anthony Wood) with Natalia Makarova, Robert Powell (Chichester Festival Theatre production). (17 March 1992) *Moby Dick* (Robert Longden and Hereward Kaye) with Tony Monopoly, Theresa Kartell, Jayne Collins, Jackie Crawford; director, Robert Longden; designer, Paul Farnsworth.

PLAYHOUSE, WC2 (3 September 1991) *Hedda Gabler* (Ibsen, trans. Una Ellis-Fermor) with Fiona Shaw, Hugh Ross, Maire Hastings, Ingrid Craigie, Garrett Keogh; director, Deborah Warner; designer, Hildegard Bechtler (Dublin Abbey Theatre production). (22 October) *Tartuffe* (Molière, trans. Ranjit Bolt) with Paul Eddington, Felicity Kendal, John Sessions, Dulcie Gray; director, Peter Hall; designer, Timothy O'Brien. (22 January 1922) *Painting Churches* (Tina Howe) with Leslie Phillips, Josie Lawrence, Siân Phillips; director, Patrick Sandford; designer, Carl Toms. (18 March) *Good Rockin' Tonite* (transferred from Strand).

PRINCE EDWARD, W1 (24 October 1991) *The Hunting of the Snark* (Mike Batt) with Kenny Everett, David McCallum, Mark McGann, Philip Quast; director, Mike Batt. (19 March 1992) *Some Like It Hot* (Jule Styne, Bob Merrill) with Tommy Steele, Billy Boyle, Mandy Perryment; director, Tommy Steele; designer, Terry Parsons.

QUEEN'S, W1 (23 September 1991) *Waiting for Godot* (Beckett) with Rik Mayall, Adrian Edmondson, Philip Jackson, Christopher Ryan; director, Les Blair; designers, Madeleine Morris, Derek Jarman.

RIVERSIDE, W6 (25 September 1991) *Lady Day at Emerson's Bar & Grill* (Lanie Robertson) with Chris Calloway, Darryl G. Ivey, Roger Inniss; director, Martin L. Platt. (10 November) *The Dragon's Trilogy* with Marie Brassard, Richard Frechette, Robert Bellefeuille; director, Robert Lepage (Repere Company, Quebec). (December) *Electra* (Sophocles, trans. Kenneth McLeish) with Fiona Shaw, Sheila Gish, Susan Colverd, John Lynch; director, Deborah Warner; designer, Hildegard Bechtler. (11 March 1992) *Down and Out in Paris and London* (George Orwell, adapted Nigel Gearing) with Andy McEwan, Jonathan Burn, Michael Benson, Harley Loudon, Lucinda Curtis, Elaine Claxton; director, Anna Furse; designer, Sally Jacobs (Paines Plough production).

ROYAL COURT, SW1 (10 September 1991) *Three Birds Alighting on a Field* (Timberlake Wertenbaker) with Harriet Walter, Robin Soans, Patti Love, Clive Russell, David Bamber; director, Max Stafford-Clark; designer, Sally Jacobs. (4 November) *Death and the Maiden* (Ariel Dorfman) with Juliet Stevenson, Bill Paterson, Michael Byrne; director, Lindsay Posner; designer, Ian MacNeil (transferred from Theatre Upstairs). (21 January 1992) *Faith Healer* (Brian Friel) with Donal McCann, Sinead Cusack, Ron Cook; director, Joe Dowling; designer, Frank Flood (Dublin Abbey Theatre production). (20 February) *Pygmies in the Ruins* (Ron Hutchinson) with Fiona Victory, Ian McElhinney, Lorcan Cranitch; director, Eoin O'Callaghan; designer, Kathy Strachan (Lyric Belfast production). (14 April) *Berlin Bertie* (Howard Brenton) with Penny Downie, Kevin Allen, Diana Rigg, Nicholas Woodeson, Susan Lynch; director, Danny Boyle; designer, Paul McCauley. (18 May) *Patagonia* with Lis Hughes Jones, Eddie Ladd, Richard Lynch, Mike Pearson, Marc Rees; director, Mike Pearson; designer, Cliff McLucas (Brith Gof Company production). (18 June) *Six Degrees of Separation* (John Guare) with Stockard Channing, Adrian Lester, Paul Shelley; director, Phyllida Lloyd; designer, Mark Thompson.

ROYAL COURT THEATRE UPSTAIRS (22 August 1991) *Talking in Tongues* (Winsome Pinnock) with Nicholas Monu, Cecilia Noble, Joanne Campbell, Pamela Nomvete, Lizzy McInnerny; director, Hettie Macdonald; designer, Ian McNeil. (26 November) *The Woman Who Cooked Her Husband* (Debbie Isitt) with Beverley Klein, Mark Kilmurry, Debbie Isitt; director, Debbie Isitt; designer, Gary Tanner. (7 May 1992) *Karate Billy Comes Home* (Klaus Pohl, trans.

David Tushingham) with David Bamber, Kevin McMonagle, Clare Holman; director, Stephen Unwin; designer, Lucy Weller.

SADLER'S WELLS, EC1 (18 June 1992) *The Sound of Music* (Rodgers and Hammerstein) with Liz Robertson, Christopher Cazenove, Robin Nedwell, Jan Waters, Linda Hubberd; director, Wendy Toye; designer, Terry Parsons.

SHAFTESBURY, WC2 (5 September 1991) *Our Town* (Thornton Wilder) with Alan Alda, Robert Sean Leonard, Jemma Redgrave; director, Robert Allan Ackerman. (18 December) *The Phantom of the Opera* (Ken Hill) with Peter Straker, Christina Collier, Steven Pacey, Reginald Marsh; director, Ken Hill; designer, Sarah-Jane McClelland. (11 May 1992) *A Slip of the Tongue* (Dusty Hughes) with John Malkovich, Clotilde Courau, Ingeborga Dapkunaite, Lizzy McInnerny, Kara Zediker; director, Simon Stokes; designer, Thomas Lynch (Steppenwold Theatre Company, Chicago, production).

STRAND, WC2 (16, 17 October 1991) *Revengers' Comedies, Parts 1 and 2* (Ayckbourn) with Griff Rhys Jones, Joanna Lumley, Jeff Shankley, Lia Williams; director, Alan Ayckbourn; designer, Roger Glossop. (28 January 1992) *Good Rockin' Tonite* with Philip Bird, David Howarth, Tim Whitnall, Michael Dimitri, Gavin Stanley; director, Jack Good.

THEATRE ROYAL, E15 (23 October 1991) *The Invisible Man* (H. G. Wells, adapted Ken Hill) with Jon Finch, Brian Murphy, Toni Palmer; director, Ken Hill. (5 June 1992) *A Better Day* (Sheila Yeger) with Ian Angus Wilkie, Lynn Ferguson; director, Annie Castledine; designer, Jenny Tiramani.

TRICYCLE, NW6 (October 1991) *Pecong* (Steve Carter) with Jenny Jules, Victor Romero Evans, Pat Bowie; director, Paulette Randall. (10 March 1992) *Anna Karenina* (Tolstoy, adapted Helen Edmundson) with Annabelle Apsion, Richard Hope, Pooky Quesnel, Max Gold, Gregory Floy; director, Nancy Meckler (Shared Experience Company production). (5 June) *Love and a Bottle* (Farquhar, adapted Declan Hughes) with Ali White, Helene Montagu, Phelim Drew; director, Lynne Parker (Rough Magic Company, Dublin, production).

VAUDEVILLE, WC2 (3 October 1991) *A Swell Party* with Nickolas Grace, Maria Friedman, Angela Richards, David Kernan; director, David Gilmore. (8 April 1992) *Reflected Glory* (Ronald Harwood) with Albert Finney, Stephen Moore, Nicky Henson; director, Elijah Moshinsky; designer, Saul Radomsky. (13 July) *Murder by Misadventure* (Edward Taylor) with Gerald Harper, William Gaunt, Angela Down, Greg Hicks; director, Val May; designer, Tim Shortall.

WHITEHALL, SW1 (23 June 1992) *Spread a Little Happiness* (King's Head production).

WYNDHAM'S, WC2 (31 October 1991) *The Ride Down Mt Morgan* (Arthur Miller) with Tom Conti, Gemma Jones, Clare Higgins, Marsha Hunt; director, Michael Blakemore; designer, Tanya McCallin. (20 March 1992) *Straight and Narrow* (Jimmie Chinn) with Carmel McSharry, Nicholas Lyndhurst, Neil Daglish, Peter Jonfield; director, Allan Davis; designer, Carl Toms. (21 July) *Philadelphia, Here I Come!* (transferred from King's Head).

YOUNG VIC, SE1 (5 September 1991) *The Winter's Tale* (Shakespeare) with Trevor Eve, Sarah-Jane Fenton, Rudi Davies, Richard Cordery, Ben Miles, Brian Protheroe, Fiona Victory, Barrie Rutter; director, David Thacker; designer, Sheila Keegan. (21 January 1992) *All My Sons* (Arthur Miller) with Ian Bannen, Matthew Marsh, Marjorie Yates, Amanda Boxer, David Westhead, Suzan Sylvester; director, David Thacker; designer, Fran Thompson. (10 March) *Measure for Measure* (Royal Shakespeare Company production).

OUTSIDE LONDON

CHICHESTER: FESTIVAL (4 May 1992) *Coriolanus* (Shakespeare) with Kenneth Branagh, Richard Briers, Judi Dench, Susannah Harker, Iain Glen; director, Tim Supple; designer, Bunny Christie (Renaissance Theatre Company production). (20 May) *Venus Observed* (Christopher Fry) with Donald Sinden, Denis Quilley, Jean Boht, Alexandra Bastedo, Kate O'Mara; director, James Roose-Evans; designer, Poppy Mitchell. (8 July) *King Lear in New York* (Melvyn Bragg) with John Stride, Kate O'Mara, Richard Warwick, Jenny Seagrove, Rosalind Bailey, Maria Miles; director, Patrick Garland; designer, Simon Higlett. (5 August) *She Stoops to Conquer* (Oliver Goldsmith) with Jean Boht, Denis Quilley, Susannah Harker, Iain Glen; director, Peter Wood.

CHICHESTER: MINERVA (20 August 1991) *Adam was a Gardener* (Louise Page) with Sharon Maughan, Simon Dormandy, Petra Markham; director, Caroline Sharman; designer, Paul Farnsworth. (6 July 1992) *Me and My Friend* (Gillian Plowman) with Doon Mackichan, Theresa Fresson, Jonathan Morris; director, Ian Rickson; designer, Lucy Hall.

EDINBURGH: ROYAL LYCEUM (14 October 1991) *The Comedians* (Trevor Griffiths) with Jimmy Logan, Douglas Henshall, Joseph Long, Stuart McQuarrie, Seamus Gubbins, Ron Pember; directors, Ian Wooldridge, Benjamin Twist; designer, Neil Warmington.

GLASGOW: CITIZENS (9 September 1991) *The Playboy of the Western World* (Synge) with Charon Bourke, Patrick O'Kane, Ray Callaghan, Anne Myatt; director, Giles Havergal; designer, Julian McGowan. (15 October) *Hedda Gabler* (Ibsen, trans. Robert David Macdonald) with Anne Lambton, Brian Deacon, Patrick Hannaway, Debra Gillett; director, Robert David Macdonald; designer, Julian McGowan. (18 November) *Design for Living* (Noël Coward) with Roberta Taylor, Greg Hicks, Jonathan Phillips, Ellen Sheean; director, Philip Prowse.

LEICESTER: HAYMARKET (December 1991) *The Price* (Arthur Miller) with Michael J. Shannon, Ed Bishop, Roy Barraclough; director, Sylvia Syms.

MANCHESTER: ROYAL EXCHANGE (12 September 1991) *Blithe Spirit* (Noël Coward) with Miranda Foster, Rosalind March, Martin Turner, Susie Blake; director, James Maxwell; designer, Phoebe de Gaye. (1 November) *Medea* (Euripides, trans. Frederic Raphael, Kenneth McLeish) with Claire Benedict, Ray Jewers, John Southworth, Akim Mogaji; director, Phyllida Lloyd. (8 December) *The Miser* (Molière, adapted Robert Cogo-Fawcett, Braham Murray) with Tom Courtenay, Alex Hardy; director, Braham Murray. (21 May 1992) *The Recruiting Officer* (Farquhar) with Haydn Gwynne, Greg Wise, Derek Griffiths, Matild Ziegler, Tim Wallers, Ewan Hooper; director, Braham Murray; designer, Johanna Bryant.

MOLD: THEATR CLWYD (8 May 1992) *The Seagull* (Chekhov, trans. Susanna Hamnett, adapted Jeremy Brooks) with Dorothy Tutin, Nick Waring, Catherine Cusack, Ian Hogg, Bernard Lloyd; director, Toby Robertson; designer, Paul Edwards.

SCARBOROUGH: STEPHEN JOSEPH (15 April 1992) *Time of My Life* (Ayckbourn) with Terence Booth, Russell Dixon,

Colette O'Neill, Richard Garnett, Karen Drury; director, Alan Ayckbourn.

STRATFORD: MEMORIAL (28 August 1991) *Romeo and Juliet* (Shakespeare) with Michael Maloney, Clare Holman, Sheila Reid, Tim McInnerny; director, David Leveaux; designer, Alison Chitty. (24 October) *Julius Caesar* (Shakespeare) with Jonathan Hyde, Robert Stephens, David Bradley, Owen Teale; director, Steven Pimlott; designer, Tobias Hoheisel. (1 April 1992) *The Taming of the Shrew* (Shakespeare) with Anton Lesser, John McAndrew, Richard McCabe, Amanda Harris, Rebecca Saire, Geoffrey Freshwater; director, Bill Alexander; designer, Tim Goodchild. (22 April) *As You Like It* (Shakespeare) with Samantha Bond, Peter de Jersey, Anthony O'Donnell, Michael Siberry, Phyllida Hancock, Andrew Jarvis; director, David Thacker; designer, Johan Engels. (1 July) *The Winter's Tale* (Shakespeare) with John Nettles, Samantha Bond, Andrew Jarvis, Gemma Jones, Phyllida Hancock, Benjamin Whitrow, Richard McCabe; director, Adrian Noble; designer, Anthony Ward.

STRATFORD: THE SWAN (27 August 1991) *The Alchemist* (Ben Jonson) with David Bradley, Jonathan Hyde, Philip Voss, Joanne Pearce; director, Sam Mendes; designer, Anthony Ward. (2 November) *The Thebans* (*Oedipus Tyrannos*, *Oedipus in Colonus* and *Antigone*) (Sophocles, trans. Timberlake Wertenbaker) with Gerard Murphy, Joanne Pearce, John Shrapnel, Clifford Rose, Linda Bassett; director, Adrian Noble; designer, Ultz; music, Ilona Sekacz. (7 April 1992) *The Beggar's Opera* (Gay) with David Burt, Alan Cox, Elizabeth Renihan, Jenna Russell, Anthony O'Donnell, Paul Jesson; director, John Caird; designer, Kendra Ullyart; music, Ilona Sekacz. (21 April) *A Jovial Crew* (Richard Brome, adapted Stephen Jeffreys) with Rebecca Saire, Paul Jesson, Emily Raymond, Ron Cook, Stephen Casey, Pearce Quigley; director, Max Stafford-Clark; designer, Fotini Dimou. (30 June) *All's Well That Ends Well* (Shakespeare) with Richard Johnson, Toby Stephens, Sophie Thompson, Michael Siberry, Barbara Jefford, Anthony O'Donnell; director, Peter Hall; designer, John Gunter.

STRATFORD: THE OTHER PLACE (27 August 1991) *The Blue Angel* (Pam Gems) with Philip Madoc, Kelly Hunter; director, Trevor Nunn; designer, Maria Bjørnson. (18 September) *Measure for Measure* (Shakespeare) with David Haig, Claire Skinner, Jason Durr, Jonathan Glynn, Desmond McNamara, Philip Madoc, Alan Mitchell; director, Trevor Nunn; designer, Marie Bjørnson. (29 October) *A Woman Killed with Kindness* (Thomas Heywood) with Michael Maloney, Saskia Reeves, Barry Lynch, Sylvestra le Touzel; director, Katie Mitchell; designer, Vicki Mortimer. (24 June 1992) *The Odyssey* (Homer, adapted Derek Walcott) with Ron Cook, Rudolph Walker, Bella Enahoro, Geoffrey Freshwater, Amanda Harris; director, Gregory Doran; designer, Michael Pavelka. (11 August) *Richard III* (Shakespeare) with Simon Russell Beale, Simon Dormandy, Cherry Morris, Stephen Boxer, Annabelle Apsion; director, Sam Mendes.

WATFORD PALACE (February 1992) *Me and Mamie O'Rourke* (Mary Agnes Donoghue) with Diana Hardcastle, Patti Love, Ron Berlglas; director, Robert Chetwyn; designer, Alexandra Byrne.

The Academy Awards 1991

Best Picture	*The Silence of the Lambs*
Best Director	Jonathan Demme *The Silence of the Lambs*
Best Actor	Anthony Hopkins *The Silence of the Lambs*
Best Actress	Jodie Foster *The Silence of the Lambs*
Best Supporting Actor	Jack Palance *City Slickers*
Best Supporting Actress	Mercedes Ruehl *The Fisher King*
Best Original Screenplay	Callie Khouri *Thelma and Louise*
Best Adapted Screenplay	Ted Tally *The Silence of the Lambs*
Best Foreign Language Film	*Mediterraneo* Italy
Best Original Score	Alan Menken *Beauty and the Beast*
Best Original Song	Alan Menken and Howard Ashman, 'Beauty and the Beast' *Beauty and the Beast*
Best Cinematography	Robert Richardson *JFK*
Best Art Direction	Dennis Gassner *Bugsy*
Best Costume Design	Albert Wolsky *Bugsy*
Best Film Editing	Joe Hutshing and Pietro Scalia *JFK*
Best Sound	Tom Johnson, Gary Rydstrom, Garry Summers and Lee Orloff *Terminator 2: Judgement Day*
Best Sound Effects Editing	Gary Rydstrom and Gloria S. Borders *Terminator 2: Judgement Day*
Best Visual Effects	Dennis Muren, Stan Winston, Gene Warren jun. and Robert Skotak *Terminator 2: Judgement*
Best Make-up	Stan Winston and Jeff Dawn *Terminator 2: Judgement Day*
Best Animated Short	*Manipulation*
Best Short Documentary	*Deadly Deception*
Best Documentary Feature	*In the Shadow of the Stars*
Best Live Action Short	*Session Man*
Irving Thalberg Award	George Lucas

Film

Prospects for the British film industry showed some signs of improvement with the Government's announcement in the 1992 Budget of tax concessions. The new measures permit all pre-production costs to be written off against tax immediately, and production costs to be written off over a three-year period following completion of the film. The Government estimated that the measures would cost £5 million in the first year, increasing to £15 million in 1993–4. Although the move was welcomed as easing cash-flow problems for film producers, there was disappointment in the film industry that the Government had not restored the capital allowances for foreign producers that had existed until 1985 or removed the tax levy on foreign stars.

Investment in the British film industry plummeted from £275 million in 1984 to £79 million in 1990, and the figure for 1991 is believed to be even less. There were fewer films in production than for ten years: 12 British-financed films were made in 1991, compared with 19 in 1990.

The shortsightedness of allowing an industry to decline when there is an increasing demand for its product was demonstrated by the rise in cinema attendances to over 100 million in 1991, worth over £300 million in ticket sales, from 98 million in 1990 (£265 million). In the first six months of 1991, attendances totalled 47.8 million, an increase of 11.6 per cent, with June alone 74 per cent up on the previous year. In 1991, 16 new multiplex cinemas opened, bringing the total in Britain to 61 and increasing the number of screens to 1,642.

The three top earning films in the United Kingdom in 1991 were *Robin Hood, Prince of Thieves*, which took £19.8 million, *Terminator 2: Judgment Day* (£18 million) and *The Silence of the Lambs* (£17.1 million). *The Silence of the Lambs* was reported to have broken the world record for cinema takings with its figure of £290,937 for one week in Leicester Square, London. While the increasing popularity of cinema as entertainment, matched by a slight decline in video rentals, was an encouraging sign, less promising was the fact that of the top 100 films only two were wholly British-made and financed: *Truly, Madly, Deeply* at no. 83 and Mike Leigh's *Life is Sweet* at no. 88. Another 11 films had a significant British input, with the British-made but US-financed *The Commitments* tenth in the list. In the USA for the first time in 15 years cinema attendances dropped below 1,000 million.

Silence of the Lambs

Traditionally, films released early in the year miss out in the annual Oscar awards, and other awards preceding the prestigious Academy Awards are taken as indications of which films and actors are in or out of favour. At the 49th Hollywood Golden Globe Awards, Nick Nolte won best actor for *Prince of Tides*, Oliver Stone best Director for *JFK*, Jodie Foster best actress for *The Silence of the Lambs* and Warren Beatty's *Bugsy* was best film. *Bugsy* was also favoured by the Los Angeles critics' circle, while the New York critics preferred *The Silence of the Lambs*.

There were, therefore, no clear favourites for the 64th Academy Awards (Oscars). *The Silence of the Lambs*, based on Thomas Harris's novel about a cannibalistic serial killer, Dr Hannibal Lecter, portrayed in a chilling performance by Anthony Hopkins, received seven nominations; *Bugsy* received ten nominations; and Walt Disney's animated feature *Beauty and the Beast* received six, including for best picture, the first cartoon to be nominated in that category. Oliver Stone's account of the assassination of President Kennedy, *JFK*, was nominated in eight categories, while Barbra Streisand's *Prince of Tides* received seven nominations, although controversially not for best director. John Singleton's impressive directing début in *Boyz N The Hood* earned him a nomination plus the distinction of becoming, at 23, the youngest person nominated in that category. Set in south central Los Angeles, *Boyz N The Hood* portrayed the violent lives of young black gangs, and featured Cuba Gooding jun., Larry Fishburne and Morris Chestnut.

The apparent uncertainty over the outcome of the Oscars made the eventual triumph of *The Silence of the Lambs* all the more unexpected. Despite its unfashionably early release, *Lambs* was voted best picture. Anthony Hopkins won best actor, making it three in a row for British actors following the success of Jeremy Irons and Daniel Day Lewis in the same category in the previous two years. To complete the clean sweep of the major prizes, Jodie Foster won her second best actress award for her role in the film as FBI agent Clarice Starling, Jonathan Demme won best director, and Ted Tally's screenplay received the prize for best adaptation.

Jack Palance received the award for best supporting actor, 39 years after his only previous nomination, for his role as the trail boss Curly, 'a saddlebag with eyes', in Ron Underwood's intelligent and enjoyable comedy *City Slickers*. Written by Lowell Ganz and Babaloo Mandel, the film told the story of three middle-aged men who confront their mid-life crisis by embarking on a cattle drive from New Mexico to Colorado. The 'city slickers' themselves were played by Billy Crystal, Bruno Kirby and Daniel Stern.

Best supporting actress was Mercedes Ruehl in *The Fisher King*, directed by Terry Gilliam and starring Jeff Bridges as a disc jockey and Robin Williams as a professor of medieval history who takes to the streets of New York as a Parsifal-like tramp after personal tragedy. Callie Khouri received the award for best original screenplay for *Thelma and Louise*, 'the world's first feminist road movie', which starred Geena Davis as a bored housewife and Susan Sarandon as a waitress who joins her for a weekend away. Robert Richardson received the Oscar for best cinematography for *JFK*, while best score was won by Alan Menken for *Beauty and the Beast*. *JFK* also received the award for best film editing, while *Bugsy* collected only two awards, for art direction and costume design. The best foreign film was the Italian comedy *Mediterraneo*.

British Awards

At the 23rd British Academy of Film and Television Arts (BAFTA) Awards, the most successful film was *The Commitments*, which won the awards for best film, best director and best adapted screenplay. Adapted by Dick Clement and Ian La Frenais with Roddy Doyle from Doyle's novel of the same name, the film was directed by Alan Parker. This story of a group of young people from Dublin determined to form a soul group was a funny and exuberant film, notable for its cast of unknowns and amateurs who gave uniformly good performances, with 16-year-old Andrew Strong especially notable for his powerful vocal contribution as lead singer Deco. Anthony Hopkins and Jodie Foster foreshadowed their Oscars by taking the BAFTA best actor and actress awards. Anthony Minghella received the award for best original screenplay for *Truly, Madly, Deeply*, which he had also directed. Made for BBC television, the film was an unexpected success in America. It featured an excellent performance from Juliet Stevenson as Nina whose lover Jamie, a musician, has died; distraught at his death, she is at first unable to let him go and she wills his spirit back. An intelligent and sensitive film about love and grief, *Truly, Madly, Deeply* struck a chord already touched by the very successful *Ghost* but handled the issues with greater intelligence and feeling.

Major Features

Oliver Stone's *JFK* was a 190-minute examination of the events surrounding the assassination of President John F. Kennedy in 1963. Stone, who directed and co-wrote the screenplay with Zachary Sklar, focused on the attempts by New Orleans District Attorney Jim Garrison to discover the truth behind the killing, and to prove that Lee Harvey Oswald had not acted alone. With a wealth of detail and 'evidence' the film is superficially convincing in establishing that Kennedy was the victim of a coalition of criminals, government agencies and arms dealers who wanted to ensure that America did not withdraw from involvement in south-east Asia. However, although long on theories the film was criticized for being short on real evidence. Also, although it may be justifiable to raise serious questions about Kennedy's death, the whole exercise becomes suspect when characters, such as Willie O'Keefe, are created for dramatic convenience. Kevin Costner is effective as Garrison, making the character convincing through his decent if dull performance. The climax of the film is the trial of businessman Clay Shaw, played by Tommy Lee Jones, the only trial to be held as a result of the assassination. Even then, Stone further undermines the credibility of the whole enterprise by inventing a 15-minute dramatic and patriotic courtroom speech by Garrison. The film also featured Sissy Spacek, Donald Sutherland and Joe Pesci, with Gary Oldman as Oswald. Also released was *Ruby*, directed by John Mackenzie and based on Stephen Davis's drama *Love Play*. This concentrated on nightclub owner Jack Ruby, played by Danny Aiello, who murdered Oswald before he could be brought to trial. The film *Ruby* suffered from similar faults as *JFK*, with the dramatic device of an amalgam character, Candy Cane, representing the various striptease dancers Ruby had known blurring the line between fact and fiction.

Steven Spielberg was again ignored by Hollywood, his latest film *Hook* receiving only three Oscar nominations in minor categories. In the past Spielberg's treatment has seemed a perverse reaction to the man responsible for some of the most popular and profitable films ever made. However, in the case of *Hook* it was more understandable. After *Terminator 2*, *Hook* was reported to have been the second most costly film ever made, at some $80 million. It used nine Hollywood stages, a 170-foot pirate ship and over half a million gallons of water, plus some of Hollywood's leading stars. Spielberg had long cherished the idea of filming J. M. Barrie's classic children's story, but his decision to update the story proved misguided.

The film opens with Robin Williams as Peter Banning, a 40-year-old New Yorker with little time for his family who is unaware that he was once Peter Pan. In London to see Grandmother Wendy, played by Maggie Smith, his children are kidnapped by Captain Hook, played by Dustin Hoffman, and taken to Never Never Land. Wendy has to convince Banning of his true identity before he can confront and defeat Hook and recover his children. In spite of the special effects from George Lucas's Industrial Light and Magic Company and the array of Hollywood's finest talent, the film lacked the real magic that Spielberg had achieved in such films as *ET – the Extraterrestrial*, and appeared charmless and self-indulgent.

With the current depressed state of American film companies, it seemed likely that *Hook* would mark the end of large-budget Hollywood pictures. Nevertheless, in spite of a cool critical reception and initially discouraging box office returns, indications are that *Hook* should earn at least $300 million world-wide. This sum would more than cover its production and publicity costs and prove the film a sound investment for Spielberg, Hoffman and Williams, who had agreed profit-sharing deals that would repay substantial dividends when the film had passed fixed profit targets. *Hook* also featured Julia Roberts, somewhat out of sorts and miscast, as Tinkerbell and Bob Hoskins as Smee.

Sound Judgement

By way of contrast, *Terminator 2: Judgement Day*, the most expensive film ever made at a cost variously estimated between $90 and $100 million, was a huge success. It recouped its production costs within two weeks of being released in America; in Britain alone, it earned £2.5 million in its first three days. It was made as a follow-up to *Terminator*, which had cost only $6.5 million in 1984 and had helped to launch Arnold Schwarzenegger on his career as the highest-paid film actor of all time. As in the first film, Schwarzenegger played the role of a cyborg sent from the future to determine the course of events. In the first film he was supposed to destroy the infant John Connor, while in *Judgement Day* his mission is to save him, sent by Connor himself and programmed to be his protector. The ingenious plot was backed by superb special effects, generated by computer, which enabled the evil mutating cyborg that intended to destroy Connor to change shape at will in spectacular fashion. The young John Connor was played by Edward Furlong, with Linda Hamilton again playing his mother Sarah, and Robert Patrick as the human part of the terminator T1000. The film was directed by James Cameron.

Another successful sequel was *Lethal Weapon 3*, directed by Richard Donner, reported to have grossed over $140 million. This entertaining all-action thriller once more paired Mel Gibson with Danny Glover as detectives Riggs and Murtaugh, with support from Joe Pesci, as Leo Getz.

Mob Popularity

The failure of *Bugsy* to win any of the major Oscars was a fair reflection on a competent film that failed because it did not confront fully the more unpleasant aspects of the character of Benjamin ('don't call me Bugsy') Siegel. Warren Beatty brought no real depth to the role of the 1940s gangster who was responsible for creating the gambling city of Las Vegas in the Nevada desert. The film over-glamorized some unpleasant characters, with only Ben Kingsley as Meyer Lansky showing the steel beneath the surface gloss. Annette Bening played Bugsy's girlfriend, actress Virginia Hill, with cameo roles from Elliott Gould and Harvey Keitel. James Toback wrote the screenplay and the film was directed by Barry Levinson.

Billy Bathgate, adapted by Tom Stoppard from E. L. Doctorow's novel, was also disappointing. Loren Dean played Billy, who becomes the protégé of gangster Dutch Schultz. Although Billy should provide the dramatic focus as the action is seen through his eyes, Dustin Hoffmann as Schultz shifts the emphasis towards his character through the power of his performance. Nicole Kidman played Drew, Schultz's girlfriend with whom Billy falls in love, with Bruce Willis as Beau, a gangster whose feet are encased in concrete before he is dispatched to a watery grave from a tugboat. The film was directed by Robert Benton.

Barton Fink was the first film to scoop the Palme d'Or at Cannes, winning also the awards for best director and best actor, in 1991. Directed by Joel Coen, produced by his brother Ethan Coen and jointly scripted, it featured John Turturro as Fink, a successful playwright who goes to Hollywood in 1941 to write scripts after the success of his play *Bare Ruined Choirs* on Broadway. Fink, whose character is obviously influenced by left-wing playwright Clifford Odets, finds himself working on a film about wrestling for Wallace Beery. He is a writer out of touch with his world, and the film conveys an artist's struggle to come to terms with the creative process as he faces writer's block in the run-down Hotel Earle. *Barton Fink* works on several levels, as comedy thriller, parody, and a study of one man's mind. Turturro received strong support from John Goodman, Judy Davis and Michael Lerner, with John Mahoney as W. P. Mayhew, an alcoholic writer bearing a strong resemblance to William Faulkner.

Kenneth Branagh's first American film as director was *Dead Again*, a suspense thriller in which he also starred with his wife Emma Thompson. Branagh plays an LA private detective looking after a woman suffering from amnesia, played by Thompson. Under hypnosis by Derek Jacobi, and helped by Robin Williams as a struck-off psychiatrist, the couple discover that they are reincarnations of a German composer and his murdered wife. The film achieved success in America, though the plot suffered from some obvious implausibilities.

Martin Scorsese's remake of J. Lee Thompson's 1962 film *Cape Fear* features cameo performances from both the stars of the earlier film, Robert Mitchum and Gregory Peck. However, the film is dominated by Robert De Niro's extraordinary embodiment of evil in the role of Max Cady, a released prisoner seeking revenge on Sam Bowden, played by Nick Nolte, the lawyer who had defended him. Cady discovers that Bowden withheld from the court evidence that might have saved him from his 14-year jail sentence and on his release tracks down him and his family. Scorsese has altered the balance of the earlier film, so that the moral issues are by no means clear-cut. Both unpleasant and disquieting, *Cape Fear* is a brilliantly executed suspense thriller.

Nick Nolte also starred in *The Prince of Tides*, co-starring and directed by Barbra Streisand. Nolte plays Tom Wingo, a football coach whose sister Savannah, played by Melinda Dillon, is being treated for suicidal tendencies by a New York psychiatrist, Susan Lowenstein, played by Streisand. Both Wingo and Lowenstein have to resolve problems in their own lives before Savannah can be helped. Nolte's fine performance was deservedly nominated for an Oscar, as was the film, surprisingly, Streisand's direction was not nominated.

THRILLERS AND CHILLERS

The year's most controversial film was *Basic Instinct*, directed by Paul Verhoeven and featuring Michael Douglas as a detective hunting a serial killer, with Sharon Stone as a bisexual writer and suspect with whom he has an affair. Joe Eszterhas received a record $3 million for his script but later tried to amend it to accommodate some of the objections from gay groups in America who felt the film was offensive and used stereotypes to confirm anti-gay prejudices. There were protests during filming in San Francisco and at many cinemas after the film opened, which probably brought far more attention than was deserved to what was a superficial, voyeuristic and exploitative thriller.

David Cronenberg succeeded in making a film of the 'unfilmable' 1959 William Burroughs novel *Naked Lunch*, condemned at the time for 'unrelieved perversion' but now attaining the status of a cult classic. The film features Peter Weller as William Lee, a writer based on Burroughs, and uses incidents from Burroughs' own life, such as the accidental killing of his wife, played by Judy Davis, as the starting point for the creative process which led to the writing of the book. With its talking typewriters, alien creatures from a mythical place called Interzone and other manifestations of Lee's drug-induced existence, the film goes some way towards revealing the motivation behind the novel.

The Lawnmower Man, directed by Brett Leonard, was inspired by a Stephen King story and is notable as the first film to use computer-generated 'virtual reality' techniques and images. However, the dazzling special effects were ill-served by a weak script. Pierce Brosnan played Dr Lawrence Angelo, a scientist who transforms a simpleton (Jeff Fahey) into a superhuman genius.

Black Robe, adapted by Brian Moore from his own novel, was the first Canadian and Australian co-production. Directed by Bruce Beresford, this powerful film is set in 17th-century Quebec and features Lothaire Bluteau as Father Laforgue, a Jesuit priest on a mission to convert native Indians to Christianity. Named 'Black Robe' by the Algonquin Indians because of his habit, he is at first driven by belief in the justification of his cause: 'If we do not change them, how can they enter heaven?'. However, after contact with the dignified Algonquins who, Bluteau's assistant Daniel, played by Aden Young, points out, 'are true Christians – they live for each other and they have an afterlife of their own', and then torture by the brutal Iroquois, Laforgue comes to realize the futility of his task and to reappraise his own faith.

Batman Returns is a rare example of a sequel that improves on the original. Michael Keaton once more played the caped crusader and his alter ego Bruce Wayne, Tim Burton again directed, and the film benefited from the absence of Jack Nicholson, whose Joker had overpowered the earlier film. Danny DeVito gave a splendid performance as the Penguin, with Michelle Pfeiffer superb as Catwoman and Michael Gough as Alfred the Butler.

Rambling Rose was adapted by Calder Willingham from his own novel and starred Laura Dern as a free spirit, a 19-year-old innocent raised in Alabama who goes to work as a home-help in Georgia and becomes involved in the sexual awakening of the eldest child Buddy, played by Lukas Haas. Dern is excellent as the uninhibited Rose, a role for which she was nominated for an Oscar. However, in Britain, laws designed to protect children against exploitation on screen had the unfortunate effect of altering and distorting the emphasis of a crucial scene between Rose and Buddy.

Far and Away, directed by Ron Howard and co-written with Bob Dolman, marked a return to the old-style Hollywood epic, magnificently filmed on the grand scale by Mikael Salomon. Husband and wife Tom Cruise and Nicole Kidman played poor farmer Joseph Donelly and rich girl Shannon Christie who leave late 19th-century Ireland for a better life in America. The film includes lavishly filmed action sequences, with a climax based on the Oklahoma land rush, yet suffers from a contrived plot and inadequate script.

Michael Frayn's play about an unsuccessful drama company, *Noises Off*, crossed the Atlantic for the film treatment directed by Peter Bogdanovich, yet remained largely faithful to the original. Michael Caine played Lloyd Fellowes, director of the cast, which included Carol Burnet, Christopher Reeve, John Ritter and Denholm Elliott.

Similarly, Richard Harris set his play *Stepping Out* in America rather than England when he adapted it for the screen. Directed by Lewis Gilbert and starring Liza Minnelli as Mavis Turner, the dance teacher whose class hope to perform at the Centre for the Performing Arts, this slight but charming tale retained much of its appeal on the big screen. The cast included Julie Walters and Shelley Winters.

One of the more unlikely successes in America was *Wayne's World*, directed by Penelope Spheeris, which was reported to have taken over $100 million at the box office in three months. The film featured Mike Myers and Dana Carvey as Wayne and Garth, a pair of heavy metal rock music fans who, in a send-up of public access cable television stations, broadcast a chat show from Wayne's family home. The idea began as a short sketch on a popular US television show *Saturday Night Live* and the film develops the basic idea by introducing Rob Lowe as a televison company executive who gives the pair a slot on network television. Although self-indulgent, featuring its own slang vocabulary and many in-jokes, *Wayne's World* is an entertaining if undemanding comedy.

Charles Addams's bizarre cartoon characters were successfully brought to the screen in a suitably macabre black comedy directed by Barry Sonnenfeld. *The Addams Family* starred Anjelica Huston as Morticia Addams, Raul Julia as Gomez and Christopher Lloyd as Uncle Fester, and was written by Larry Wilson and Caroline Thompson. Its main weakness is the narrative, which fails adequately to connect some splendid set pieces inspired by Addams's original drawings, and the music of M. C. Hammer which seems out of place.

Speaking Volumes

Sir John Gielgud long cherished an ambition to appear as Prospero in a film of *The Tempest.* The opportunity arose in Peter Greenaway's remarkable film *Prospero's Books.* Greenaway took as his starting point a passage in Act I of Shakespeare's play in which Prospero tells Miranda that Gonzalo 'furnish'd me from mine own library with volumes that I prize above my dukedom' for his desert island. The film features two dozen books that Prospero might have taken, covering a wide range of topics, such as architecture and mythology, with actors miming the books. The controlling force is Prospero himself, who in the final volume, which is Shakespeare's 1623 folio, is writing *The Tempest* on 19 blank pages. Until the end of the film, when under Ariel's influence other characters are allowed to speak, Prospero takes all the roles in the play. Gielgud gives a memorable performance and dominates the film, which is a complex visual feast, awash with images and dense with allusions.

Peter Medak's *Let Him Have It* was based on the 1952 case of Craig and Bentley, which resulted in the hanging of the educationally backward Derek Bentley for the murder of a policeman who was shot by the juvenile Craig. Craig was too young to be hanged, but even though Bentley was in police custody when the fatal shot was fired, as an accomplice he was held to be as guilty as Craig. The case aroused great controversy and attempts are still being made to obtain a posthumous pardon for Bentley. The title of the film refers to the ambiguous phrase Bentley was alleged to have said to Craig. At Bentley's trial the words were taken to mean that he should fire the gun; subsequently it has been claimed that Bentley was urging Craig to hand the weapon over and surrender. Recent evidence from Craig himself casts doubt on whether the words were in fact spoken. Whatever the case, the film draws attention to one of the less savoury examples of capital punishment. Christopher Eccleston played Bentley, with Tom Courtenay and Eileen Atkins as his parents and Paul Reynolds as Craig. The sceenplay was written by Neal Purvis and Robert Wade.

Howard's End, adapted from the novel by E. M. Forster, was the latest collaboration between the well-established team of director James Ivory, producer Ismail Merchant and scriptwriter Ruth Prawer Jhabvala, already responsible for highly praised adaptations of *A Room with a View* and *Maurice* by the same author. A strong cast ensured that full justice was done to Forster's work, with Anthony Hopkins as Henry Wilcox, Vanessa Redgrave as Ruth Wilcox, Helena Bonham Carter and Emma Thompson as Helen and Margaret Schlegel and Samuel West as Leonard Bast.

Meeting Venus, a European production produced by David Puttnam and directed by Istvan Szabo, was inspired by Szabo's experiences when he attempted to direct Wagner at the Paris Opera. It was also said to be a metaphor for Puttnam's experiences in Hollywood as head of Columbia Pictures. Co-written by Szabo and Michael Hirst, the film featured Niels Arestrup as a little-known Hungarian conductor, Zoltan Szanto, who is attempting to direct Wagner's *Tannhäuser* for global satellite transmission at Opera Europa in Paris, with Glenn Close as Swedish diva Karin Anderson with whom he has an affair. One of the more intelligent films about opera, the high point of *Meeting Venus* was undoubtedly the music, provided by the Philharmonic Orchestra under Marek Janowski, with Dame Kiri Te Kanawa dubbing Glenn Close's singing voice.

A Franco-British co-production, *The Lover* was adapted by Gerard Brach from Marguerite Duras's Goncourt Prize-winning novel. Directed by Jean-Jacques Annaud, the film featured Jane March as a 15-year-old French girl in French Indo-China in the 1920s who has an erotic love affair with a rich 32-year-old Chinese businessman. The families of both disapprove of the relationship, which is doomed to failure. The action is counter-balanced by Jeanne Moreau's narration, as the girl looking back on her youth. The film achieved a certain notoriety through the explicit nature of some of the love scenes, but it handled its themes with style and sensitivity.

Jacques Rivette's four-hour film *La Belle Noiseuse* was a brilliant study of an artist's creative process and the complex relationship between him and his model. Developed from a 20-page treatment by Pascal Bonitzer and Christine Laurent, the film featured Michel Piccoli as Edouard Frenhofer. Having abandoned a painting for which his wife (played by Jane Birkin) had originally posed, he is persuaded to return to it when a new model, Marianne (Emmanuelle Beart) agrees to pose for him. A two-hour version of the film, *La Belle Noiseuse - Divertimento*, was released which used different takes from the full version for some scenes, giving a different perspective to the relationship. Although inferior to the complete work, it provided an interesting aperitif for it.

Festivals

The 45th Edinburgh Film Festival, directed for the last time by David Robinson (film critic of The Times), featured Derek Jarman's *Edward II*, co-produced by the BBC. One of Jarman's more accessible films, it is based on Marlowe's play although Marlowe is discarded when he does not suit Jarman's purposes, notably at the end, where Edward falls in love with his would-be assassin, thus avoiding his gruesome death at Berkeley Castle. Edward was played by Steven Waddington, with Andrew Tiernan as Gaveston, Tilda Swinton as Isabella and Nigel Terry as Mortimer. The Michael Powell Award for best British film of 1990–1 was awarded to a BBC production, *The Grass Arena*, directed by Gillies Mackinnon. Mark Rylance gave a much-praised performance in this true story based on the life of John Healy, a boxer who became a down-and-out alcoholic and criminal but discovered some point to his life in prison when he took up chess. Jaco Van Dormael received the Charles Chaplin New Director's Award for *Toto le Heros* which he also wrote, an entertaining tale of an old man who is convinced that he was exchanged with a neighbour's baby when an infant. Also featured was Stephen Poliakoff's *Close My Eyes*, the story of an incestuous relationship between a brother and his sister, played by Clive Owen and Saskia Reeves. Filmed by Witold Stok, *Close My Eyes* was visually impressive, even if its message was unclear.

At Venice *(XLVIII Mostra Internazionale d'Arte Cinematografica)*, the festival included the première of Greenaway's *Prospero's Books*, which failed to win any awards. The Golden Lion went to Nikita Michalkov's *Urga*, a visually splendid but weakly scripted story about a sheep-breeder on the Mongolian steppes who is befriended by a Russian lorry driver. The Special Jury Prize was awarded to Manoel de Oliveira for *A Divina Comedia*, set in a madhouse.

The 35th London Film Festival opened with *Enchanted April*, adapted by Peter Barnes from the 1922 novel by Elizabeth von Arnim. It tells the story of two Hampstead women trying to enliven their existence by taking a villa in Italy. Directed by Mike Newell, it featured Miranda Richardson, Josie Lawrence and Joan Plowright. Among the 200 or so films shown over the 16 days of the event, were *Bwana Devil*, a 3-D film made in 1953 and shown as part of a tribute to Arch Oboler, and *Limite*, a Brazilian avant-garde film from 1929 directed by Mario Peixoto at the age of 19; his sole completed film, it was restored in the 1970s. The festival closed with Mark Peploe's *Afraid of the Dark*, featuring James Fox and Fanny Ardant.

At the 42nd Berlin Film Festival the winner of the Golden Bear was Lawrence Kasdan's *Grand Canyon*, featuring Kevin Kline and Danny Glover in a parable about divisions in modern American society set in Los Angeles. Best director was Jan Troell for *Il Capitano*, best actor Armin Mueller-Stahl in *Utz* and best actress Maggie Cheung in *Centre Stage*.

The 1992 Cannes Film Festival saw the end of recent American domination of the main award. The Palme d'Or was awarded to Billie August's *The Best Intentions*, written by Ingmar Bergman and relating the story of his parent's meeting and marriage. Pernilla Ostergren August, who played Bergman's mother, won the prize for best actress. Robert Altman was voted best director for *The Player*, a splendid satire on Hollywood adapted by Michael Tolkin from his own novel. Tim Robbins won the award for best actor for his role in the film as the studio executive Griffin Mill who accidently kills a scriptwriter he suspects of sending him hate mail. The Jury Prize was shared by Victor Erice's *The Dream of Light* and Vitali Kanevski's *An Independent Life*. John Turturro, best actor for his role in *Barton Fink* in 1991, won the prize for best feature, the Camera d'Or, for *Mac*, his directorial début. The Merchant Ivory production of E. M. Forster's *Howard's End* received a special award to mark the festival's 45th anniversary.

Film and Video Certificates

The British Board of Film Classification issues the following categories of film certificates:

- U Universal: suitable for all
- PG Parental guidance: some scenes may be unsuitable for young children
- 12 Passed only for persons of twelve years and over
- 15 Passed only for persons of fifteen years and over
- 18 Passed only for persons of eighteen years and over
- R18 For restricted distribution only (through specially licensed cinemas to which no one under the age of eighteen is admitted)

The classifications of video tapes differ slightly:

- U Universal: suitable for all
- Uc Universal: particularly suitable for children
- PG Parental guidance: general viewing, but some scenes may be unsuitable for young children
- 15 Suitable only for persons of 15 years and over
- 18 Suitable only for persons of 18 years and over
- R18 Restricted: to be supplied only in licensed sex shops to persons of not less than 18 years

Literature

A very public dispute among the judges ensured that the 1991 Booker prize was the most controversial for some years. Nicholas Mosley, whose *Hopeful Monsters* had won the previous year's Whitbread Book of the Year, is the self-confessed dark horse of the literary world, acknowledged for his experimental and metaphysical novels. It was therefore a bold but perhaps risky move to invite Mosley to join the Booker judging panel.

After the judges had worked their way through 109 novels, in itself a daunting task, Mosley resigned from the panel because none of the books he favoured were included on the shortlist. Mosley was the first judge to resign since 1971. 'What was the point of going on to the final judgment when I had nothing to fight for? My top novel was the Allan Massie. Their objection was that it was primarily a novel of ideas and the characters were representative of ideas.'

The judges, led by Jeremy Treglown, former editor of *The Times Literatary Supplement*, had decided by a count of votes on five of the six novels for the shortlist. *Such a Long Journey* was Rohan Mistry's first novel. He is an Indian-born author now resident in Canada, and set the story in Bombay in 1971 at the time of the creation of the state of Bangladesh from former East Pakistan. It relates the struggle of the Parsee family of Gustad Noble to survive in the vast, squalid city of Bombay, which is vividly described. Timothy Mo, twice shortlisted before, set *The Redundancy of Courage* around East Timor's struggle for independence from Indonesia. William Trevor's *Reading Turgenev*, about a woman in a small town in Ireland in the 1950s finding romance, was a novella originally published with another, *My House in Umbria*, in a volume entitled *Two Lives*. Roddy Doyle's *The Van*, set in the imaginary suburb of Barrytown in Dublin, continued the story of the Rabbitte family, previously encountered in *The Commitments* and *The Snapper*. Jimmy and his friend Bimbo buy an old fish and chip van, but find their friendship suffers in its close confines; largely written in local dialogue, *The Van* is a witty and entertaining book. Ben Okri's *The Famished Road* is an imaginative story of Azaro, a spirit child in West Africa growing up in the 1960s. Drifting between the magical spirit world and the strife-torn real world, the child resists his impulse to return to the former and remains 'to bring a smile upon the face of his mother'.

What About Us?

Three novels tied for the last place on the shortlist: *Time's Arrow* by Martin Amis, in which Mosley felt 'there weren't any ideas, just this one trick of everything going backwards. I didn't think the use of that particular trick in that very agonizing context was suitable or admissible'; *The Tax Inspector* by Peter Carey (who won the Booker in 1988 with *Oscar and Lucinda*), the story of the Catchprice family who run a second-hand car lot in Franklin, Sydney. The tax inspector of the title is Maria Takis, a heavily pregnant immigrant Greek who uncovers family problems as well as irregular accounting practices in the bizarre family's business. The final novel was Allan Massie's *The Sins of the Father*, a contemporary novel that ranged from Argentina to England and Israel, and studied the effect on human beings of regimes such as Nazism. Its final words, 'What about me? What about us? What about humanity?' came to encapsulate the disagreement between Mosley and his fellow judges, who were reported to have felt that any book ending on such a note was unfit for the prize; Treglown said that he would prefer the last question to have been asked 'in an imaginatively striking way'. Treglown used his casting vote in favour of Amis's novel, prompting Mosley's resignation.

When published the shortlist provoked further criticism as it included no women writers. Conspicuous by its absence was Angela Carter's *Wise Children*, an entertaining tale of two elderly former chorus girls looking back on their lives and their confused parentage. At the prize-giving ceremony, Treglown praised this 'funny, nostalgic, exuberant, life-loving story', which made its exclusion all the more puzzling.

Suffered A Reverse

Time's Arrow continued to divide the critics and caused widespread controversy. It was the first novel by Martin Amis to reach the Booker shortlist but its chances of winning must have been reduced by the manner of its inclusion, with no judge making it his or her first choice. The title had occurred to Amis previously: in a foreword to his last novel, *London Fields*, he wrote, 'A word about the title. Several alternatives suggested themselves. For a while I toyed with *Times's Arrow*. Then I thought *Millennium* would be wonderfully bold (a common belief: *everything* is called *Millennium* just now).' Amis's central conceit is to tell the whole story in reverse. Starting with the death of Tod T. Friendly 'out of blackest sleep' in America, it traces back his life under various aliases, including Dr Odilo Unverdorben, a Nazi doctor at Auschwitz, to his birth, when he disappears into his mother. The story is told not by Friendly but by an internal parasite with 'no access to his thoughts—but I am awash with his emotions'.

Amis has used the device of time reversal in stories in *Einstein's Monsters*, and Kurt Vonnegut included a memorable sequence in *Slaughterhouse 5* about the bombers sucking up their deadly cargoes from German cities and taking them back to America to be dismantled. However, sustained throughout a whole novel the device frequently becomes tiresome and occasionally the author's control slips. Amis was criticized also for using the Holocaust, and, some felt, trivializing it, when he had no experience himself of the events he used. His purpose in this was to attempt to understand how something as dreadful as the Holocaust could have been allowed to happen. The idea sprang from his realization that the doctors who worked in the Nazi death camps had reversed their principles by causing suffering and death instead of curing it. By reversing time throughout the novel, Amis forces the reader to re-appraise the events. It is shocking to imagine Jews coming into Auschwitz dead or diseased, only to leave healed and repaired, as part of a 'preternatural purpose ... to dream a race. To make a people from the weather'. By realizing that this vision of Utopia is unattainable, Amis succeeds in taking a fresh look at the human condition.

The Booker Prize was awarded to Okri for *The Famished Road*. In the opinion of the judges, 'Ben Okri's beautifully written and moving novel combines fantasy and the vision of a child, the supernatural and the here-and-now to convey Nigerian peasant life in a changing world. It is the most ambitious as well as one of the most fully realized of this year's novels. It brings a distinctively black African way of writing and seeing things into the mainstream of European fiction.' Okri said that winning was 'an extremely beautiful dream. When my first book was published, the elders of my village got together and bought me a pen. This will buy me quite a lot of pens.'

Rushdie

At the Booker prize-giving, Jeremy Treglown reminded the audience of the continuing plight of Salman Rushdie. 'He and the freedom he represents need our support and deserve our support as much as they have ever done', he said. Rushdie's plight continued unresolved, however. In November 1991 a vigil was planned at Central Hall, Westminster, London to mark the 1,000th day since the passing of the *fatwa* (religious decree) that sentenced him to death for blasphemy against Islam. However, after pressure from the Foreign Office, which was concerned that any public demonstration of support for Rushdie would be seen as hostile by Iran and would delay the release of Terry Waite from captivity in Lebanon, the vigil was called off. Rushdie criticized 'the foolishness of establishing a public linkage between two unrelated events, and thus, in effect, inviting the hostage-holders and their patrons to make use of it'.

In December 1990 Rushdie had announced that he had espoused the Muslim faith and that he would restrict future publication of *The Satanic Verses*. Subsequently, Rushdie felt that he had not received the Muslim support that he believed he had been promised and he backtracked on his claim to be a Muslim. In a move guaranteed to inflame opinion against him still further, he called for a paperback edition of the book to be published, saying 'it must be freely available and easily affordable', Dr El-Assawy, leader of the Muslim scholars who met Rushdie in December 1990, said that Rushdie had now 'pushed himself into a corner. He wants to be a martyr for the cause of freedom of speech'.

A paperback edition of *The Satanic Verses* was published in Britain and America in May 1992 by the Consortium, an anonymous collective. Rushdie's original dedication had been replaced by one 'to individuals and organizations who have supported this publication'. Rushdie is still under constant threat of death and there is no foreseeable solution to the situation.

English Nobel?

In May 1992 the Arts Council announced the creation of the British Literature Prize, a new award worth £30,000 to the recipient. It will be administered jointly with Coutts and Co, with the prize money provided by the David Cohen Family Charitable Trust, which was founded in 1980 to support the arts. Lord Palumbo, chairman of the Arts Council, said that 'Literature is ... perhaps our finest gift to the world. Until now, however, there has been no prize which has honoured our major creative writers, not just for a single work but for the achievement of a lifetime'. The award will be made for a writer's *œuvre*, whether fiction, non-fiction, poetry or a combination of forms. The first award will be made in the spring of 1993, and it was hoped that the prize will come to be seen as the supreme accolade for a living British author.

Debate will no doubt continue on the pros and cons of rewarding writers at or past the peak of their careers with large sums of money, rather than encouraging up-and-coming writers who would derive greater benefit from the recognition and the financial rewards. At present, British literary awards tend to be ranked in order of importance in direct relation to their monetary value; only the Booker has reached the point at which the prestige of receiving the prize outweighs its monetary value. The Nobel Prize for Literature, the most valuable prize of all at six million Kronor or some £570,000, has little credibility, whereas in France the Prix Goncourt confers immense prestige and guarantees huge sales, yet is worth only 50 francs (about £5).

Still Life

The 1991 Whitbread Book of the Year was John Richardson's *A Life of Picasso: Volume 1, 1881–1906*, the first of a projected four or five volume biography. Richardson received £20,500, plus £2,000 for winning the biography category. A friend of Picasso during his life, Richardson said that he told his story 'with its shadows, its Spanish darkness and superstitions and all'. He had access to the painter's diaries and papers and was helped by his widow Jacqueline, yet did not allow friendship to blind him to Picasso's faults, or to make him take Picasso at face value. The first volume covers Picasso's early years, particularly his relations with his father Don José, up to the point at which he is about to start work on *Les Demoiselles d'Avignon*, the first Cubist painting.

Jane Gardam's *The Queen of the Tambourine* won the best novel category in the Whitbread awards, with Gordon Burns's *Alma Cogan* best first novel, Michael Longley's *Gorse Fires* best poetry and Diana Hendry's *Harvey Angell* best children's novel.

The NCR Book Award for a work of non-fiction was awarded to Jung Chang for *Wild Swans*, a remarkable account of the upbringing of the author, her mother and her grandmother in China. At the age of 15, her grandmother Yu-fang was made a concubine to a Chinese war-lord, escaping with her child after his death. Chang's parents, although Communist Party members and 'heroes of the revolution', were tortured and sent to labour camps during the Cultural Revolution, yet Chang herself became a Red Guard. After escaping from China, she wrote the book to help 'understanding of how a totalitarian regime works'. The three other short-listed works were *Columbus* by Felipe Fernandez; *Bernard Shaw: The Lure of Fantasy 1918–50* by Michael Holroyd, and John Richardson's *A Life of Picasso*.

The *Irish Times*-Aer Lingus International Fiction Prize was awarded to Louis Begley, a 58-year-old Polish American lawyer, for his first novel, *Wartime Lies*. This accomplished début work told the story of Maciek, a Polish Jew, who, with the help of his aunt Tania, survives the Holocaust through using Aryan papers. This deception, although it saves his life, creates 'a distance between the thing that is inside him and the figure he presents to the world'. Having lived a lie in his childhood, 'our man has no childhood that he can bear to remember; he has had to invent one'. The novel was inspired by Begley's own wartime experiences, although he declines to disclose how much of the book is autobiographical.

The *Irish Times*-Aer Lingus Prize for Fiction, awarded to Irish writers, was won by Colm Tobin for *The South*. The original choice, *Fables of the Irish Intelligentsia* by Nina Fitzpatrick, was found to be ineligible as its author was Polish-born Nina Witoszek, who had written the work under a *nom de plume* to disguise the fact that it draws on her relations with her colleagues.

Michael Frayn's *A Landing on the Sun* was awarded the *Sunday Express* Book of the Year Award: the judges described it as 'a witty and touching meditation on the nature of happiness'. The novel tells the story of Brian Jessel, a clerk in the Cabinet Office, who is told to investigate the death of his predecessor 16 years earlier because a television company is now looking into the event. Jessel discovers that the dead man, Stephen Summerchild, whom he had known in his youth, had been working for the Government's Strategy Unit and trying to establish the nature of happiness through 'the quality of life'. The project was led by Dr Elizabeth Serafin, an Oxford philosophy don with whom Summerchild had an affair which seriously unsettled him. The novel is accomplished and drily amusing, but suffers from implausibilities in the plot and the sense that the reason for Summerchild's death is of minor significance.

The *Guardian* Fiction Prize was awarded jointly to Rachael Anderson for *Paper Faces* and Hilary McKay for *The Exiles*. The Boots Romantic Novel of the Year was won by June Knox-Mawer with *Sandstorm* and the Betty Trask Award by Liane Jones with *The Dreamstone*. The Ian St James Award for short stories, for which 4,000 entries were received, was presented to Faith Addis for *Small Beginnings*, with Alan Dunn second with *French Kisses* and Stephanie Ellyne third with *Me and Renata*. An anthology of the twelve best stories was published under the title *Midnight Oil*.

The Smarties Prize for Children's Books was won by Martin Waddell and Helen Oxenbury for *Farmer Duck*, also the winner of the 0–5 years category. Magdalen Nabb and Pirkko Vainio won the 6–8 age group with *Josie Smith and Eileen*, and Philip Ridley won the 9–11 age group with *Krinklekrax*. The Commonwealth Writers Prize was won by David Malouf with *The Great World*, while the European Prize for Literature and Translation was awarded to Claude Delarue for *Waiting for War*, translated by Vivienne Menkes-Ivry. A gruesome, depressing tale set in a huge nuclear bunker, in Delarue's novel 'The age of mere living is over. The age of survival is just beginning'. In France, the Prix Goncourt was won by Pierre Combescot for *Les Filles du Calvaire* (The Daughters of Calvary), a tale of working class life in Paris.

Benefit to Humanity

The Nobel Prize for Literature was awarded to Nadine Gordimer, considered South Africa's most distinguished living writer and an implacable opponent of apartheid. The citation said, 'Through her magnificent, epic writing she has—in the words of Alfred Nobel—been of very great benefit to humanity'. While the award was widely welcomed, it was noted that Gordimer's name had been on the list for consideration for some 20 years; by making the award after the release of Nelson Mandela and the virtual dismantling of the apartheid system in South Africa, the Nobel Committee avoided making a political issue of the award.

Gordimer has written ten novels and over 200 short stories. Her most recent collection, *Jump and other Stories*, was published during the year. Gordimer was also commissioned to write the autobiography of Nelson Mandela, but it was reported that the African National Congress had objected because she was white; instead, she was an 'informal adviser' on the project.

Gordon Burns's accomplished first novel *Alma Cogan*, which received the Whitbread first novel award, was described in the judges' citation as 'a haunting, ghostlike journey through the darker side of fame'. Narrated in the first person, the novel recreates the language and atmosphere of the late 1950s when Cogan, 'the girl with the giggle in her voice', was Britain's highest paid female singer. Cogan becomes disillusioned with her fame, however, and dreams of killing her famous self so she can be ordinary again. Burns imagines her as a woman in her 60s looking back on her past and obsessed with the minutiae of her life. A darker note enters the novel with references to Moors murderer Myra Hindley; a disturbing connection is revealed, with news that Hindley had killed to the sound of Cogan's voice on the radio.

In *Empire of the Sun*, published in 1985, J. G. Ballard drew on his childhood experiences in Shanghai during the Second World War. The novel was widely praised and showed that Ballard was more than a writer of science fiction, or 'predictive fables' as he called his earlier work. In *The Kindness of Women* Ballard returns to the character of Jim and, in the first person, follows his life from that same period to Cambridge, where he studies medicine, which he gives up to fly with the RAF in Canada. Having married and had children, Jim's wife Miriam dies tragically, as did Ballard's wife Mary. Ballard describes brilliantly the key events that have shaped his life and influenced his writing: 'The kindness of women came to my rescue, at a time when I had almost given up hope.' It was through this kindness that Ballard was able to come to terms with the meaningless deaths he had witnessed and to gain a positive view of the world. 'The happiness I found had been waiting for me within the modest reach of my own arms, in my children and the women I had loved, and in the friends who had made their own way through the craze years.'

Ian McEwan's *Black Dogs* is a powerful account of how two people's lives are irrevocably changed by an incident that symbolizes the evil forces endemic in Europe. Jeremy, a publisher, decides to write the life story of his wife's parents: 'Ever since I lost mine in a road accident when I was eight, I have had my eye on other people's parents'. He discovers that their holiday in southern France in 1946 had been ruined when June was attacked by two black dogs, 'the alien black gums, slack black lips rimmed by salt, a thread of saliva breaking . . .'. The incident assumes religious significance for her, 'my discovery, but of course, it's nothing new, and it's not mine. Everyone has to make it for himself.' She discovers that the dogs had been trained by the Nazis to attack prisoners. She separates from her husband, Bernard, who had not shared the experience. However, these spirit hounds' incarnations do not disappear for good; they are seen as 'black stains in the grey of dawn, fading as they move into the foothills of the mountains from where they will return to haunt us, somewhere in Europe, in another time.' The symbolism is not laboured and McEwan controls the tension with great skill.

Barry Unsworth, the author of such fine novels as *Pascali's Island* and *The Stone Virgin*, has written a splendid maritime saga *Sacred Hunger*. The hunger of the title is for wealth and power, and the story opens in 1752 with the slave trader *Liverpool Merchant*, owned by Kemp, about to sail. Kemp's son Erasmus intends to avenge a childhood slight by his cousin Matthew Paris, the ship's doctor, during the voyage; Paris also falls foul of the brutal captain Saul Thursoe, as if the pair are 'heirs to some ancient feud'. Suspense is created and maintained as the dramatic conflicts are resolved against the brutal background of the trade in human flesh. If the novel has a theme it is that 'Nothing a man suffers will prevent him from inflicting suffering on others. Indeed, it will teach him the way.'

Paradise Lost

Paradise News, David Lodge's ninth novel, is a disappointing account of British tourists on a trip to Hawaii, 'the winterless home of the happy dead'. The main character, Bernard Walsh, is an ex-priest and a theology lecturer at Rummidge University who accompanies his father on a visit to his dying sister. His father is run over in Waikiki by Yolande, who awakens Bernard's dormant sexuality. The plot is contrived, the parallels too obvious and the humour from the clash of cultures predictable, as the author treads a well-worn path he followed with greater skill in *Nice Work* and *Changing Places*.

Timothy Harcombe, the central character in Peter Ackroyd's *English Music* has spiritual powers. In a series of dreams and mystical experiences, he imagines himself with a host of real and imagined characters from the whole range of English culture, the 'music' of the title, including Robinson Crusoe, Hogarth, Dickens and William Byrd. Readers familiar with Ackroyd's penchant for pastiche and 'slipping through time' will sympathize with Harcombe's comment 'Yes. I have returned to the past. I have made the journey.' Whether Ackroyd's theme, that 'the old music never dies . . . It's always the same melody repeated through the centuries, reaching every generation', is valid is open to question, but it is certainly true of his style. While this was original and interesting in *Hawksmoor* it has come to irritate, especially when it permeates even his biographies, such as *Dickens*. According to Ackroyd, a book requires re-reading to be properly understood 'if it be well and artificially made' but few are likely to give this novel a second reading.

Kingsley Amis's latest novel, *The Russian Girl*, is a disappointing lapse from form by one of the great comic writers. Richard Vaisey is Professor of Russian Literature at the London Institute of Slavonic Studies, he declares that 'The only thing I've had, ever really had, is whatever you care to call it, my professional self-respect, my devotion to my subject, my determination to stick to the truth as I see it'. His decision to praise the writing of Russian poet Anna Danilova when she obviously has no talent fails to convince. Further, Vaisey's wife Cordelia, a woman so dreadful that even the female psychiatrist in *Stanley and the*

Women seems reasonable by comparison, so dominates the scenes in which she appears that the balance of the book is disturbed. Also published during the year was *We Are All Guilty*, a curious work by Amis written for 'young adults', a target audience that he seemed not to have identified clearly or succeeded in reaching.

A. N. Wilson's *Daughters of Albion* is the third volume in his sequence 'The Lampitt Papers', following *Incline Our Hearts* and *A Bottle in the Smoke*. The narrator is actor and author Julian Ramsey, foremost in a cast of over 80 characters which Wilson has listed at the front of the book. The story concerns Ramsey's arch rival Raphael Hunter, who is sued for libel by Rice Robey yet triumphs unjustly. The latest chapter in an enjoyable saga, the novel raises many themes, in particular about the creation of myths through story-telling: 'the world of phenomena and of other people is not a fixed set of *things* . . . but rather a story which we tell to ourselves'.

Margaret Drabble's *The Gates of Ivory*, completing the trilogy of *The Radiant Way* and *A Natural Curiosity*, aspires to extend or even depart from the bounds of fiction. It has an extensive bibliography, and opens with the words, 'This is a novel – if novel it be . . .' The title provides the clue, for in Homer's *Odyssey* dreams that come through the ivory gates 'deceive us with false images of what will come to pass'. The novel opens with Liz Headleand, a psychoanalyst, receiving a package from Cambodia which contains some papers belonging to Stephen Cox, a Booker Prize-winning novelist who disappeared some years previously while on a trip to the east in search of spiritual renewal. Her retracing of his journey and discovery of his plight provides the narrative impetus for a thoughtful and ambitious examination of 'the heart of darkness'.

Robert McCrum's fourth novel *Mainland* looks at the complex relationship between an occupied province and its governing mainland, without ever making explicit that the territories are Northern Ireland and Great Britain. The device is effective, with McCrum able to look afresh at an intractable situation. Stephen Mallory, a 'political consultant', visits the province to make a promotional video for Troy, 'the singer who likes to think too much', a project endorsed by the mainland government because it will show that, 'under the umbrella of a military presence . . . it is possible to achieve some semblance of ordinary life there.'

'These are, I should warn you, the words of a dead man' is the opening to Graham Swift's *Ever After*, in which Bill Unwin, having failed in a suicide attempt, examines the question of truth, the nature of existence and the survivial of species, and the effect that Darwin's theories had on those Victorians whose whole system of belief was undermined by them. Swift has said that the book is 'a love story . . . about love and death, and it begins with death and ends with love', but it embraces much wider spiritual and philosophical issues with great dexterity.

SPIRITS ABROAD

Even more dramatic is the opening to Robertson Davies's latest novel, *Murther & Walking Spirits*: 'I was never so amazed in my life as when the Sniffer drew his concealed weapon from its case and struck me to the ground stone dead'. Connor 'Gil' Gilmartin, entertainments editor of *The Colonial Advocate*, had discovered his wife in bed with a colleague, the film critic Going, known as 'The Sniffer'. After being killed, he becomes a walking spirit and accompanies Going to a film festival. Here Gil finds that instead of seeing the programme of movie classics, he sees films depicting the history of his ancestors on their way from Holland and Wales to Canada. Through viewing and appreciating his heritage, in a series of rich and varied episodes, he comes to a fuller understanding of himself.

Anne Tyler's *Saint Maybe*, set in Baltimore, relates the story of the Bledloes, whose comfortable and happy existence is shattered when Ian leads his brother Danny to believe that his wife Lucy has been unfaithful to him; Danny commits suicide, as does Lucy not long afterwards. Ian, bearing the guilt of the deaths, takes on the responsibility of bringing up their children and becomes involved with a sect called the Church of the Second Chance. Tyler writes with skill and sensitivity of how Ian comes to terms with his guilt, of his worries that he is 'squandering his life' and his relationships with the three children, who are particularly well imagined; he eventually meets a 'Clutter Counsellor' whom he marries, a slightly contrived ending to a thoughtful, well-written work.

Thomas Keneally was told the story which forms the basis of *Woman of the Inner Sea* in 1980, the same year he learned about the heroic German factory owner who risked his life to save Jews during the Second World War. Unlike *Schindler's Ark*, however, this novel is artificial, Keneally relying by his own admission on 'cheap devices' which undermine the story and dilute the impact. *Woman of the Inner Sea* tells of the journey, both physical and spiritual, of Kate Kozinski, who moves away from Sydney to the heart of the Australian bush after tragedy befalls her children.

GREAT EXPECTATIONS

It was a good year for the Great American Novel, with the publication of several prime contenders for the title. Harold Brodkey's *The Runaway Soul* was described as 'the most eagerly awaited first novel of all time'; the book was commissioned in 1964 on the strength of a volume of short stories Brodkey had published. During the intervening 27 years, Brodkey acquired a reputation as a great American author, a reputation which might have survived longer had the novel remained unpublished. Perhaps inevitably, this 850-page story of Wiley Silenowicz and his progress towards a career as a writer is a disappointment, as few novels could fulfil such a weight of expectation, but *The Runaway Soul* appears unfinished despite its lengthy gestation. Overwritten, ill-written, self-indulgent and humourless, it does not work. Brodkey said in an interview, 'The problem is the way I write. The book at first reading is not completely acceptable.' Certainly the prose is difficult to accept, laden with portentous statements such as 'At the edge of every statement is what it means further than itself – and what it doesn't mean'.

Norman Mailer at least has earned a literary reputation over the years, but whether his latest novel will enhance it remains to be seen. *Harlot's Ghost* is over 1,100 pages long; ominously, this overblown account of the CIA ends with the words 'to be continued'.

The Reckoning: The Murder of Christopher Marlowe is an excellent attempt to delve into the underside of Elizabethan politics by Charles Nicholl, who questions the official account of the death of the dramatist, supposedly stabbed to death in a tavern brawl in Deptford by one Ingram Friser. Nicholl reveals that Marlowe was probably recruited as a govenment spy when at Cambridge and acted as an *agent provocateur* and conspirator against the Catholics. The Privy Council interceded with the university on Marlowe's behalf when it seemed that his degree might be withheld, saying that he had done 'good service' for the government. However, it would appear that Marlowe became a liability and had to be disposed of, but the motives for his murder are not clear. Nicholl's book brilliantly evokes the 'secret theatre' of intrigue and double-dealing.

LIVES

Almost a Gentleman: An Autobiography, 1955–1966 covers the period in playwright John Osborne's life from the acceptance of *Look Back in Anger*, the play that made his name, by George Devine's English Stage Company to Devine's death. However, Osborne provoked much adverse comment by including a section about his fourth wife, Jill Bennett, whom he did not marry until two years after the volume supposedly ends and who committed suicide in 1990. He describes her death as 'the most perfect act of misanthropy, judged with the tawdry, kindless theatricality she strove to achieve in life. She had no love in her heart for people and only a little more for dogs.' Although the volume contains some good anecdotes, Osborne's desperate striving for unpopularity and settling of old scores leaves a sour taste.

Laurie Lee has continued his memoir, begun so memorably over 30 years ago with *Cider with Rosie* and continued in 1969 with *As I Walked Out One Midsummer Morning.* The third volume, *A Moment of War*, takes up his life story as he goes to Spain to fight in the civil war, 'to make one grand, uncomplicated gesture of personal sacrifice and faith which might never occur again. Lee looks back on his experiences with the advantages of hindsight and detachment, from his nearly having been shot as a spy to his shooting of an enemy, 'an unknown young man in a blur of panic which in no way could affect victory or defeat'. Lee wrote a poem entitled A Moment of War in 1937, when the memory of the events was not filtered by experience: 'your breathing is the blast, the bullet, and the final sky'. Dedicated 'to the defeated', *A Moment of War* is a powerful reminder of the horrors of war, witnessed by an idealist and a poet.

Auberon Waugh's autobiography *Will This Do?* begs the response that it will not; the book fails sufficiently to enlighten readers about the life, though not the opinions, of the journalist and critic, who claims to have the 'gift for making the comment . . . which people least wish to hear'. Of considerable interest, however, is his account of his relationship with his father, the novelist Evelyn Waugh, who wrote of his son that he was 'clumsy and dishevelled, sly, without intellectual, aesthetic or spiritual interest'. Evelyn also said that 'the presence of my children affects me with deep weariness and depression', a feeling that may well have been reciprocated. Auberon describes how, after the war, bananas were supplied for children in each family, who had never enjoyed 'the most delicious taste in the world'; he sat expectantly with his two sisters, only to witness his father eat all three fruits, covered with sugar and cream. The book does contain some amusing anecdotes; Waugh recounts how he agreed to a telephone request to deliver a paper on breast feeding to a conference in Senegal, only to find after his talk to an increasingly confused audience that his topic was meant to be press freedom. Also published was the second volume of Martin Stannard's biography of Evelyn Waugh, *No Abiding City, 1939–1966*, which revealed that apart from his dislike of children, Waugh's political attitudes consisted of 'a network of prejudice and fantasy that few intelligent people could take seriously'.

Antonia White: Diaries 1926–1957, edited by her daughter Susan Chitty, provides interesting insights into the character of the author of *Frost in May*, a complex and frequently disturbed person who said of herself 'I am not a genius with great powerful impulses and rich imagination. I have a very small, limited talent'. White left over one million words of diaries, although she destroyed her earliest volumes. Chitty had edited them down by three-quarters in a curious style that leaves gaps and *non-sequiturs* in the published text.

In *Bernard Shaw: Volume IV, 1950–1991 – The Last Laugh*, Michael Holroyd follows his magisterial three-volume life with an account of what had happened to Shaw's will following his death. Shaw cast 'an eternal curse on whomsoever shall now or at any time hereafter make schoolbooks of my works, and make me hated as Shakespeare is hated'. According to Holroyd, many of the terms and conditions have not been met, particularly his wish to establish a phonetic alphabet.

Roy Jenkins's political memoir, *A Life at the Centre*, rises above the usual attempts at self-justification common among politicians in their twilight years. Well-written, entertaining and at times self-deprecating, Jenkins treats his former colleagues with fairness and generosity, particularly Harold Wilson, although his dislike of David Owen, co-founder of the SDP, cannot be disguised. Jenkins served with distinction in the Cabinet offices of Home Secretary and Chancellor of the Exchequer; he attributes his failure to become Prime Minister to not wanting the job badly enough, so that when an opportunity presented itself, he 'faltered for want of single-minded ruthlessness'.

PUBLIC LENDING

In the 1990–1 payment to authors under the Public Lending Right Scheme, the rate per loan was increased from 1.37 to 1.81 pence. A total of 16,864 authors received some form of payment, with 81 receiving the maximum permissible payment of £6,000 (55 in 1989–90). A total of 41 authors received between £5,000 and £5,999; 185 received £2,500 to £4,999; 501 received £1,000 to £2,499; 705 received to £500 to £999; 3,698 received £100 to £499; 11,653 received £1 to £99, and 3,339 registered authors received no payment.

Booker Prizewinners

1969 *Something to Answer For* P. H. Newby (Faber)
1970 *The Elected Member* Bernice Rubens (Eyre & Spottiswoode)
1971 *In A Free State* V. S. Naipaul (Andre Deutsch)
1972 *G* John Berger (Weidenfeld)
1973 *The Siege of Krishnapur* J. G. Farrell (Weidenfeld)
1974 *The Conservationist* Nadine Gordimer (Cape)
Holiday Stanley Middleton (Hutchinson)
1975 *Heat and Dust* Ruth Prawer Jhabvala (Murray)
1976 *Saville* David Storey (Cape)
1977 *Staying On* Paul Scott (Heinemann)
1978 *The Sea, The Sea* Iris Murdoch (Chatto & Windus)
1979 *Offshore* Penelope Fitzgerald (Collins)
1980 *Rites of Passage* William Golding (Faber)
1981 *Midnight's Children* Salman Rushdie (Cape)
1982 *Schindler's Ark* Thomas Keneally (Hodder & Stoughton)
1983 *Life & Times of Michael K* J. M. Coetzee (Secker & Warburg)
1984 *Hôtel du Lac* Anita Brookner (Cape)
1985 *The Bone People* Keri Hulme (Hodder & Stoughton)
1986 *The Old Devils* Kingsley Amis (Hutchinson)
1987 *Moon Tiger* Penelope Lively (Deutsch)
1988 *Oscar and Lucinda* Peter Carey (Faber)
1989 *The Remains of the Day* Kazuo Ishiguro (Faber)
1990 *Possession* A. S. Byatt (Chatto & Windus)
1991 *The Famished Road* Ben Okri (Cape)

The finalists for the 1992 prize were:

The Butcher Boy Patrick McCabe (Picador), *Black Dogs* Ian McEwan (Cape), *Sacred Hunger* Barry Unsworth (Hamish Hamilton), *The English Patient* Michael Ondaatje (Bloomsbury), *Serenity House* Christopher Hope (Macmillan), *Daughters of the House* Michèle Roberts (Virago)

Nobel Prizes

For prize winners for the years 1901–1988, *see* earlier editions of *Whitaker's Almanack*.

The Nobel Prizes are awarded each year from the income of a trust fund established by the Swedish scientist Alfred Nobel, the inventor of dynamite, who died on 10 December 1896, leaving a fortune of £1,750,000. The prizes are awarded to those who have contributed most to the common good in the domain of:

Physics
awarded by the Royal Swedish Academy of Sciences;
Chemistry
awarded by the Royal Swedish Academy of Sciences;
Physiology or Medicine
awarded by the Karolinska Institute;
Literature
awarded by the Swedish Academy of Arts;
Peace
awarded by a five-person committee elected by the Norwegian Storting;
Economic Sciences (instituted 1969)
awarded by the Royal Swedish Academy of Sciences.

The first awards were made in 1901 on the fifth anniversary of Nobel's death. The prizes are awarded every year on December 10, the anniversary of Nobel's death.

The Trust is administered by the board of directors of the Nobel Foundation, Stockholm, consisting of five members and three deputy members. The Swedish Government appoints a chairman and a deputy chairman, the remaining members being appointed by the awarding authorities.

The awards have been distributed as follows:

Physics
American 55, British 20, German 19 (1948–90, West German 8), French 10, Soviet 7, Dutch 6, Swedish 4, Austrian 3, Danish 3, Italian 3, Japanese 3, Chinese 2, Swiss 2, Canadian 1, Indian 1, Irish 1, Pakistani 1.

Chemistry
American 36, German 27 (1948–90, West German 10), British 23, French 7, Swiss 5, Swedish 4, Canadian 2, Dutch 2, Argentinian 1, Austrian 1, Belgian 1, Czech 1, Finnish 1, Hungarian 1, Italian 1, Japanese 1, Norwegian 1, Soviet 1.

Physiology or Medicine
American 67, British 22, German 13 (1948–90, West German 4), French 7, Swedish 7, Danish 5, Swiss 5, Austrian 4, Belgian 4, Italian 3, Australian 2, Canadian 2, Dutch 2, Hungarian 2, Russian 2, Argentinian 1, Japanese 1, Portuguese 1, South African 1, Spanish 1.

Literature
French 12, American 9, British 8, Swedish 7, German 6 (1948–90, West German 1), Italian 5, Spanish 5, Danish 3, Norwegian 3, Soviet 3, Chilean 2, Greek 2, Irish 2, Polish 2, Swiss 2, Australian 1, Belgian 1, Colombian 1, Czech 1, Egyptian 1, Finnish 1, Guatemalan 1, Icelandic 1, Indian 1, Israeli 1, Japanese 1, Mexican 1, Nigerian 1, South African 1, Yugoslav 1, Stateless 1.

Peace
American 17, Institutions 16, British 9, French 9, Swedish 5, German 4 (1948–90, West German 1), Belgian 3, Swiss 3, Argentinian 2, Austrian 2, Norwegian 2, South African 2, Soviet 2, Burmese 1, Canadian 1, Costa Rican 1, Danish 1, Dutch 1, Egyptian 1, Irish 1, Israeli 1, Italian 1, Japanese 1, Mexican 1, Polish 1, Tibetan 1, Vietnamese 1, Yugoslav 1.

Economics
American 18, British 6, Norwegian 2, Swedish 2, Dutch 1, French 1, Soviet 1.

Prize	1989	1990	1991
Physics	Prof. N. Ramsey (American) Prof. H. Dehmelt (American) Prof. W. Paul (W. German)	Prof. J. Friedman (American) Prof. H. Kendall (American) Prof. R. Taylor (Canadian)	Prof. P.-G. de Gennes (French)
Chemistry	Prof. T. Cech (American) Prof. S. Altman (American)	Prof. E. Corey (American)	Prof. R. Ernst (Swiss)
Physiology or Medicine	Prof. J. M. Bishop (American) Prof. H. E. Varmus (American)	Dr J. Murray (American) Dr E. D. Thomas (American)	E. Neher (German) B. Sakmann (German)
Literature	C. José Cela (Spanish)	O. Paz (Mexican)	N. Gordimer (South African)
Peace	HH the Dalai Lama of Tibet (Tibetan)	Pres. M. Gorbachev (Soviet)	Aung San Suu Kyi (Burmese)
Economics	T. Haavelmo (Norwegian)	Prof. H. Markowitz (American) Prof. M. Miller (American) Prof. W. Sharpe (American)	Prof. R. Coase (British)

Opera

Opera continued to flourish during the period under review, although finance played, as usual, an important part in the operatic scene. Early in November 1991 the Arts Council announced a general increase in arts funding of 14 per cent. Later in the month it became clear that the regional and touring companies would receive substantially larger grants than the London-based companies. Welsh National Opera's grant rose by 120 per cent, Glyndebourne Productions's (the touring company) by 61 per cent, and Scottish Opera's by 20 per cent. By contrast, English National Opera's grant rose by only 9 per cent and the Royal Opera's by 8 per cent. However, ENO was helped to buy the freehold of the London Coliseum for £12.8 million with funds provided by the Office of Arts and Libraries and the Foundation for Sport and the Arts, so securing the future of the company at its present home.

The directorial game of musical chairs which began last year continued without pause. ENO announced that Sian Edwards would become the new music director, while Dennis Marks would take over as general director. Nicholas Payne will succeed Paul Findlay as director of the Royal Opera, while Payne's post as managing director of Opera North is to be taken by Ian Ritchie. David Lloyd-Jones, music director of Opera North since its inception, has already been succeeded by Paul Daniel, while John Mauceri, Scottish Opera's musical director, will not renew his contract when it falls due next year; Richard Armstrong, his successor, will form a strong team with Richard Jarman, the company's new managing director.

Anniversaries

The last months of the bicentenary of Mozart's death showed no abatement in the torrent of new productions of his operas. At Covent Garden *La clemenza di Tito*, which subsequently won the Laurence Olivier Award for the most outstanding achievement in opera, was followed, early in 1992, by *Don Giovanni*, third in the series of Mozart/Da Ponte comedies staged by Johannes Schaaf; these three productions were toured by the Royal Opera to Japan during July. ENO offered a popular new version of *Le nozze di Figaro*, translated by Jeremy Sams as *Figaro's Wedding*. Scottish Opera chose *Don Giovanni*, and WNO presented *Idomeneo*, superbly conducted by Charles Mackerras. The City of Birmingham Touring Opera broke new ground with *Zaïde*, Mozart's unfinished oriental mystery, in a version by the Italian novelist Italo Calvino.

Covent Garden paid welcome if belated tribute to the centenary of Prokofiev's birth in 1891 by staging *The Fiery Angel*, his opera about obsession and demonic possession, in co-production with the Kirov Opera of St Petersburg. Starring two of the Kirov's finest singers, the powerful production was greatly admired in both cities. The Royal Opera also celebrated the bicentenary of Meyerbeer (born 1791) by staging *Les Huguenots*, the work with which the present Covent Garden theatre opened in 1858; once hugely popular, the opera had not been heard there since 1927. Unfortunately, the production, borrowed from the Deutsche Oper, Berlin, updated and relocated the action from Paris at the time of the St Bartholomew's Day massacre in 1572 to Berlin at the height of the Cold War; as the Berlin Wall has come down, this idea fell flat. The first three performances of the run were cancelled owing to a strike by the orchestral musicians.

The bicentenary of Rossini (born 1792) proved more rewarding; in addition to revivals of *Guillaume Tell* and *Il barbiere di Siviglia*, the Royal Opera offered the first British professional production of *Il viaggio a Reims*. Originally a *pièce d'occasion* written to commemorate the coronation of Charles X as King of France in Reims Cathedral, the work easily adapted as a birthday tribute to the great Italian composer. Other Rossini performances included *L'Italiana in Algeri* at Buxton, conducted by Jane Glover, artistic director-elect of the Festival. Opera North staged *La gazza ladra* (*The Thieving Magpie*), an opera not heard in Britain for several years, but undoubtedly the most ambitious project realized by the company during the season was the British stage première of Schreker's *Der ferne Klang* (The Distant Sound), produced by Brigitte Fassbaender, the German mezzo-soprano, in her British directorial début.

Wagner's music-dramas are expensive to mount and extremely difficult to cast. Scottish Opera was forced, through lack of funds, to abandon a long-planned production of *Tristan und Isolde;* however, the company was able to put on *Die Walküre*, the second instalment of its popular *Ring* cycle, produced by Richard Jones. The Royal Opera completed its own *Ring*, staged by Götz Friedrich, with *Das Rheingold*, and then gave two performances of the complete cycle. There was also a new production of *Der fliegende Holländer*, to launch the 21st anniversary of the Covent Garden Proms; during the week-long season 700 opera lovers a night paid £9 for a space in the stalls, where normally seats cost up to £150. The grand finale to the event was a revival of Saint-Saëns' *Samson et Dalila* starring the Spanish tenor Placido Domingo, also celebrating his 21st anniversary at Covent Garden, in the role of Samson. This performance, transmitted live on the Big Screen in the Piazza, was enjoyed free by thousands of opera lovers.

Large and Small

Opera on the grand scale continued in popularity. The Royal Opera's production of *Turandot* filled Wembley Arena for ten performances at the end of December and the beginning of January, when no less than six sopranos shared the title role. At the other end of the spectrum, Scottish Opera-Go-Round toured a mini-version of Donizetti's *Maria Stuarda* to 30 venues the length and breadth of Scotland, while WNO's BP Opera Circuit took the same composer's *Don Pasquale* to 29 towns in Wales and southern England. After successful autumn and spring tours, Opera 80 announced that from October 1992 its name will be English Touring Opera; its policy of bringing high quality opera in English at affordable prices to places not visited by other professional companies remains unchanged.

The performance on 23 July of Tchaikovsky's *The Queen of Spades* with which the 1992 season at Glyndebourne ended, was the last to be given in the old opera house, where the bulldozers had already moved in. There will be no Glyndebourne Festival in 1993, but the new theatre will open on 28 May 1994, 60 years to the day since the original opening, and with the same opera, *Le nozze di Figaro*. The new house, to be built on the present north-west/south-east axis but turned 180° to take full advantage of the slope of the ground, will hold 1,150 people, as opposed to 830 in the old auditorium. It will cost £33 million, more than 85 per cent of which had already been raised by July 1992. Meanwhile, the 1992 season was particularly successful, with new productions of *Peter Grimes* and *The Queen of Spades*, the latter in particular earning the highest praise. Glyndebourne Touring Opera continued as usual, despite a fire in the scenery store during May when sets for *Figaro* and *The Rake's Progress* (both operas included in GTO's programme), as well as some props for the new *Peter Grimes*, were destroyed.

Although the work of Tchaikovsky was one of the main themes of the 1992 Edinburgh International Festival, only one of his operas was actually staged: the one-act *Yolanta*, presented by Opera North in a double bill with the ballet *The Nutcracker*, as the two works were originally performed in 1892. There was also a concert performance by Scottish Opera of *The Oprichnik*, Tchaikovsky's first operatic success.

New Works

New operas performed during the year included *The Bakxai*, John Buller's first opera, based on Euripides's play *The Bacchae*. The work was given its world première by ENO and scored a considerable success even though it was sung mainly in ancient Greek, in contravention of the company's usual practice of singing all operas in the vernacular. Opera North, together with Huddersfield Contemporary Music Festival, commissioned *Caritas*, a chamber opera by Robert Saxton with libretto by Arnold Wesker based on his play of the same name. First performed at Wakefield, *Caritas* was given its London première at the Queen Elizabeth Hall. The Royal Opera's Garden Venture, in co-operation with Birmingham Repertory Theatre, gave the first performance of *Biko*, with music by Pritti Panital and text by Richard Fawkes, in Birmingham, and then presented the work at the Hammersmith Riverside Studios, as part of a revitalized London Opera Festival. Other events in the festival included Rossini's *Semiramide*, ingeniously staged by Nuremberg Pocket Opera at Riverside Studios, and David Freeman's new production of *The Coronation of Poppea* for Opera Factory at the Queen Elizabeth Hall. Freeman's other Monteverdi productions, *Orfeo* and *The Return of Ulysses*, were both revived by ENO during the season.

Almeida Opera, a collaboration between the Almeida Theatre and ENO's Contemporary Opera Studio, gave the world premières of Nigel Osborne's *Terrible Mouth*, with text by Howard Barker based on the life and work of the Spanish artist Goya, and of Nils Vigeland's *False Love/True Love*, a chamber opera dramatizing two episodes from Charlotte Brontë's novel *Jane Eyre*. Almeida Opera also gave the well-received British première of *Mario and the Magician*, a setting of a text based on Thomas Mann's story by Stephen Oliver, who died less than three months previously at the age of 42.

Deaths

Stephen Oliver, an immensely prolific composer, wrote about 50 operas, though some of them, especially those intended for children, last only a few minutes. Perhaps the best known of his full-length operas, *The Duchess of Malfi*, based on John Webster's tragedy, was first performed by Oxford University Opera Club in 1971 (when the composer was only 21) and later given in Sweden and, in revised form, at Santa Fe. *Tom Jones* (1976), based on Fielding's novel, was commissioned and first performed by English Music Theatre, proving extremely popular. Oliver wrote several operas specially for Musica nel Chiostro at Battignano: these included *La bella e la bestia* (1984), a version of the fairy tale *Beauty and the Beast*, as well as *Mario ed il mago* (1988) (*Mario and the Magician*). *Timon of Athens* (1991), commissioned by ENO, was respectfully received by critics and audiences alike in spite of the dauntingly bleak nature of the Shakespeare play upon which it is based.

Other musicians with operatic connections who died during the year included Sir Charles Groves. While chief conductor of the Bournemouth Symphony Orchestra, he conducted numerous operas for WNO (1952–62), including Verdi's *Nabucco*, *The Sicilian Vespers*, *I Lombardi* and *La battaglia di Legnano*, as well as *William Tell* and *Lohengrin*. He was also music director of ENO for two seasons (1977–9). Arthur Hammond, who died at the age of 86, worked for three decades with the Carl Rosa Opera, first as conductor and then as music director, until the company's final disbandment in 1960. A fine scholar, he made performing editions of Berlioz' *Benvenuto Cellini*, Offenbach's *Les Contes d'Hoffmann* and Bizet's *Carmen*, and acted as music consultant to the Royal Opera until his retirement in 1988.

James Johnston, the Belfast-born tenor who died aged 88, sang at Sadler's Wells (1945–51) and Covent Garden (1949–58), where he created Hector in Bliss's *The Olympians* (1949). His ringing Italianate voice was heard to best advantage in roles such as Manrico, Radames, Rodolpho and Calaf, but he was also much admired as Faust and Don José. Ronald Eyre, the distinguished theatre director, staged only a few operas during his career but Berlioz' *Beatrice et Benedict* and Cavalli's *Giasone* for the Buxton Festival, Verdi's *Falstaff* (conducted by Carlo Maria Giulini) in Los Angeles and at Covent Garden, and *Peter Grimes* for Opera North were landmarks in music theatre production.

PRODUCTIONS

In the summaries of the company activities shown below, the dates in brackets indicate the year that the current production entered the company's repertory.

ROYAL OPERA, estab. 1946
Royal Opera House, Covent Garden, London WC2E 9DD

Productions from the repertoire: *Rigoletto* (1988), *Die Walküre* (1989), *Siegfried* (1990), *Götterdämmerung* (1991), *Le nozze di Figaro* (1987), *Così fan tutte* (1989), *Les Contes d'Hoffmann* (1980), *Guillaume Tell* (1990), *L'elisir d'amore* (1975), *La Bohème* (1974), *Salome* (1988), *Samson et Dalila* (1981), *Don Pasquale* (1973).

New productions:

(16 September 1991) *Das Rheingold* (Wagner). Conductor, Bernard Haitink; producer, Götz Friedrich; designer, Peter Sykora.

Gillian Webster (Woglinde), Monica Groop (Wellgunde), Jane Turner (Flosshilde), Ekkehard Wlaschiha (Alberich), Helga Dernesch (Fricka), James Morris (Wotan), Deborah Riedel (Freia), Gwynne Howell (Fasolt), Franz-Josef Selig (Fafner), Kim Begley (Froh), Donald Maxwell (Donner), Kenneth Riegel (Loge), Alexander Oliver (Mime), Anne Gjevang (Erda).

(24 October 1991) *Les Huguenots* (Meyerbeer). Conductor, David Atherton; producer, John Dew; designer, Gottfried Pilz.

Jeffrey Black (Nevers), Richard Leech (Raoul), Gwynne Howell (Marcel), Jennifer Larmore (Urbain), Judith Howarth (Marguerite de Valois), Amanda Thane (Valentine), Richard Van Allan (Saint-Bris).

(12 November 1991) *Simon Boccanegra* (Verdi). Conductor, Georg Solti; producer, Elijah Moshinsky; designers, Michael Yeargan (sets), Peter J. Hall (costumes).

Alan Opie (Paolo), Mark Beesley (Pietro), Alexandru Agache (Simon Boccanegra), Roberto Scandiuzzi (Fiesco), Kiri Te Kanawa (Amelia), Michael Sylvester (Gabriele Adorno).

(5 December 1991) *Mitridate, rè di Ponto* (Mozart). Conductor, Hartmut Haenchen; producer, Graham Vick; designer, Paul Brown.

Jacqelyn Fugelle (Arbate), Ann Murray (Sifare), Yvonne Kenny (Aspasia), Jochen Kowalski (Farnace), Patrick Power (Marzio), Bruce Ford (Mitridate), Lillian Watson (Ismene).

(5 February 1992) *Don Giovanni* (Mozart). Conductor, Bernard Haitink; producer, Johannes Schaaf; designer, Peter Pabst.

Claudio Desderi (Leporello), Carol Vaness (Donna Anna), Thomas Allen (Don Giovanni), Robert Lloyd (Commendatore), Hans Peter Blochwitz (Don Ottavio), Patricia Schuman (Donna Elvira), Marta Marquez (Zerlina), Bryn Terfel (Masetto).

(10 March 1992) *Death in Venice* (Britten). Conductor, Steuart Bedford; producer, Colin Graham; designers, Colin Graham (sets), Charles Knode (costumes).

Philip Langridge (Gustav von Aschenbach), Alan Opie (the Traveller), Michael Chance (Apollo), Giacomo Ciriaci (Tadzio).

(14 April 1992) *The Fiery Angel* (Prokofiev). Conductor, Edward Downes; producer, David Freeman; designer, David Roger.

Sergei Leiferkus (Ruprecht), Galina Gorchakova (Renata), Elizabeth Bainbridge (Hostess), Gillian Knight (Fortune Teller), John Dobson (Jacob Glock), Ian Caley (Agrippa), Bruno Caproni (Mathias), Robert Tear (Mephistopheles), Roderick Earle (Faust), Anne Collins (Mother Superior), Paata Burchuladze (Inquisitor).

(12 May 1992) *I Puritani* (Bellini). Conductor, Daniele Gatti; producer, Andrei Serban; designer, Michael Yeargan.

Dmitri Hvorostovsk (Riccardo), Robert Lloyd (Giorgio), June Anderson (Elvira), Giuseppe Sabbatini (Arturo), Mark Beesley (Walton), Anne Mason (Enrichetta).

(8 June 1992) *Der fliegende Holländer* (Wagner). Conductor, Christoph von Dohnanyi; producer, Ian Judge; designers, John Gunter (sets), Deirdre Clancy (costumes).

Gwynne Howell (Daland), Neill Archer (Steersman), James Morris (the Dutchman), Anne Wilkens (Mary), Julia Varady (Senta), Thomas Sunnegardh (Erik).

(4 July 1992) *Il viaggio a Reims* (Rossini). Conductor, Carlo Rizzo; producer, John Cox; designer, Mark Thompson.

Catherine Wyn-Rogers (Maddalena), Montserrat Caballé (Mme Cortese), Renée Fleming (Comtesse de Folleville), John Aler (Belfiore), Andrew Shore (Baron Trombonok), Gregory Yurisich (Don Profondo), Peter Coleman-Wright (Don Alvaro), Della Jones (Marquise Melibea), Bonaventura Bottone (Count Libenskof), Sylvia NcNair (Corinna), Alastair Miles (Lord Sidney).

ENGLISH NATIONAL OPERA, estab. 1931
London Coliseum, St Martin's Lane, London WC2N 4ES

Productions from the repertoire: *Don Giovanni* (1985), *Werther* (1987), *Billy Budd* (1988), *La Bohème* (1977), *The Mikado* (1986), *A Masked Ball* (1989), *Christmas Eve* (1988), *Xerxes* (1985), *Street Scene* (1989), *The Barber of Seville* (1987), *Orfeo* (1981), *Madam Butterfly* (1984), *The Return of Ulysses* (1989), *Falstaff* (1989).

New productions:

(30 October 1991) *Figaro's Wedding* (Mozart). Conductor, Paul Daniel; producer, Graham Vick; designer, Richard Hudson.

Bryn Terfel (Figaro), Cathryn Pope (Susanna), Joan Rodgers (Countess Almaviva), Anthony Michaels-Moore (Count Almaviva), Diana Montague (Cherubino), Donald Adams (Doctor Bartolo), Eiddwen Harrhy (Marcellina), Sally Harrison (Barbarina), Arwel Huw Morgan (Antonio), Edward Byles (Don Curzio).

(2 December 1991) *Die Fledermaus* (J. Strauss). Conductor, Adam Fischer; producer, Richard Jones; designer, Nigel Lowery.

Vivian Tierney (Rosalinda), Donald Maxwell (Eisenstein), Lesley Garrett (Adèle), Nicholas Folwell (Dr Falke), Anthony Mee (Alfred), Ann Howard (Prince Orlofsky), Andrew Shore (Col. Frank), Frosch (John Carter).

(30 January 1992) *Königskinder* (Humperdinck). Conductor, Mark Elder; producer, David Pountney; designer, Sue Blane.
Cathryn Pope (Goosegirl), Joseph Evans (Prince), Alan Opie (Fiddler), Sally Burgess (Witch), Donald Adams (Woodcutter), Edward Byles (Broomstick-maker), Richard Angas (Innkeeper), Maria Moll (Innkeeper's Daughter).

(2 April 1992) *Don Carlos* (Verdi). Conductor, Mark Elder; producer, David Pountney; designer, David Fielding.
Edmund Barham (Don Carlos), Rosalind Plowright (Elisabeth de Valois), Jonathan Summers (Posa), Gwynne Howell (King Philip), Linda Finnie (Princess Eboli), Christine Bunning (Thibault), Richard Van Allan (Grand Inquisitor), Michael Druiett (Monk).

(5 May 1992) World première of *Bakxai* (John Buller). Conductor, Martin André; producer, Julia Hollander; designers, Hildegard Bechtler (sets), Nicky Gillibrand (costumes).
Thomas Randle (Dionysus), Graeme Matheson-Bruce (Pentheus), Gregory Yurisich (Cadmus), Sarah Walker (Agave), Richard Van Allan (Tiresias).

WELSH NATIONAL OPERA, estab. 1946
John Street, Cardiff CF1 4SP

Productions from the repertoire: *Die Fledermaus* (1987), *Rigoletto* (1991), *The Magic Flute* (1979), *Ernani* (1979), *Madam Butterfly* (1978).

New productions:

(18 September 1991) *Idomeneo* (Mozart). Conductor, Charles Mackerras: producer, Howard Davies; designers, William Dudley (sets), Liz da Costa (costumes).
Dennis O'Neill (Idomeneo), John Mark Ainsley (Idamante), Rebecca Evans (Ilia), Suzanne Murphy (Elettra), Anthony Roden (Arbace), High Priest (Paul Charles Clarke).

(21 February 1992) *Pelléas et Mélisande* (Debussy). Conductor, Pierre Boulez; producer, Peter Stein; designers, Karl Ernst Herrmann (sets), Moidele Bickel (costumes).
Alison Hagley (Mélisande), Penelope Walker (Geneviève), Neill Archer (Pelléas), Donald Maxwell (Golaud), Kenneth Cox (Arkel), Samuel Burkey (Yniold).

(18 May 1992) *Iphigénie en Tauride* (Gluck). Conductor, Charles Mackerras; producers, Patrice Caurier, Moshe Leiser; designers, Christian Ratz (sets), Etienne Couleon (costumes).
Diana Montague (Iphigénie), Peter Bronder (Pylade), Simon Keenlyside (Oreste), Peter Sidhom (Thoas), Alwyn Mellor (Diana).
Performances of the repertoire were given at the New Theatre, Cardiff, and on tour in Liverpool, Birmingham, Swansea, Oxford, Southampton, Bristol, Plymouth, Manchester and Paris-Châtelet.

OPERA NORTH, estab. 1978
Grand Theatre, 46 New Briggate, Leeds LS1 6NU

Productions from the repertoire: *La finta giardiniera* (1989), *Don Giovanni* (1991), *The Jewel Box* (1991), *Masquerade* (1990), *Madama Butterfly* (1982), *Rigoletto* (1979), *Boris Godunov* (1989).

New productions:

(17 September 1991) *L'Etoile* (Chabrier). Conductor, Jean-Yves Ossonce; producer, Phyllida Lloyd; designer Anthony Ward.
Mary Hegerty (Princess Laoula), Pamela Helen Stephen (Lazuli), Kate Flowers (Aloes), Anthony Mee (King Ouf), Mark Curtis (Tapioca), Alan Oke (Herisson), John Hall (Sirocco).

(21 November 1991) The world première of *Caritas* (Robert Saxton). Conductor, Diego Masson; producer, Patrick Mason; designer, Joe Vanek.
Eirian Davies (Christine), Linda Hibbert (Agnes), Linda Ormiston (Matilda), Paul Wilson (Matthew), Christopher Ventris (Robert Lonle), David Gwynne (Richard Lonle), Jonathan Best (Bishop of Norwich), Roger Bryson (William).

(14 January 1992) British première of *Der ferne Klang* (Schreker). Conductor, Paul Daniel; producer, Brigitte Fassbaender; designer, Ultz.
Virginia Kerr (Grete), Linda Ormiston (Grete's Mother), Fiona Kimm (Woman), Kim Begley (Fritz), Philip Sheffield (Chevalier), William Dazeley (Count), Peter Sidhom (Dr Vigelius), Peter Savidge (Actor), Graeme Broadbent (Innkeeper/Baron).

(24 April 1992) *The Thieving Magpie* (Rossini). Conductor, Ivor Bolton; producer, Martin Duncan; designer, Sue Blane.
Anne Dawson (Ninetta), Christine Bryan (Lucia), Elizabeth McCormack (Pippo), Barry Banks (Giannetto), Arwel Huw Morgan (Fabrizio), Matthew Best (Fernando), Andrew Shore (Podesta).

(19 June 1992) *Orpheus in the Underworld* (Offenbach). Co-production with D'Oyly-Carte Opera. Conductor, Wyn Davies; producer, Martin Duncan; designer, Tim Harley.
Linda Kitchen (Eurydice), Margaret Preece (Diana), Shirley Thomas (Venus), Deborah Pearce (Cupid), Linda Ormiston (Public Opinion), Harry Nicoll (Orpheus), Paul Wade (John Styx), Alan Oke (Pluto), Eric Roberts (Jupiter).
Performances of the repertoire were given at the Grand Theatre, Leeds, and toured to Manchester, Hull, Glyndebourne, Nottingham, Wakefield, Stratford-upon-Avon, Sheffield, Bradford, Northampton and Sunderland.

SCOTTISH OPERA, estab. 1962
39 Elmbank Crescent, Glasgow G2 4PT

Productions from the repertoire: *Madama Butterfly* (1987), *Carmen* (1986), *The Marriage of Figaro* (1986), *La traviata* (1981), *Billy Budd* (1987), *Aida* (1987).

New productions:

(29 August 1991) *La clemenza di Tito* (Mozart). Conductor, Nicholas McGegan; producer, Stephen Wadsworth; designers, Thomas Lynch (sets), Dunya Rmicova (costumes).
Glenn Winslade (Titus), Juliana Gondek (Vitellia), Anne Mason (Sextus), Cheryl Barker (Annius), Claire Daniels (Servilia), Robert Poulton (Publius).

(19 October 1991) *Die Walküre* (Wagner). Conductor, John Mauceri; producer, Richard Jones; designer, Nigel Lowery.
Carol Yahr (Sieglinde), John Keyes (Siegmund), Kevin Maynor (Hunding), Willard White (Wotan), Jane Eaglen (Brünnhilde), Sally Burgess (Fricka).

(22 April 1992) *Don Giovanni* (Mozart). Conductor, Robert Dean; producer and designer, Tom Cairns.
Steven Page (Don Giovanni), Linda McLeod (Donna Anna), Gideon Saks (Leporello), Virginia Kerr (Donna Elvira), Glenn Winslade (Don Ottavio, David Gwynne (Commendatore), Rosemary Joshua (Zerlina), Meurig Davies (Masetto).

Performances of the repertoire were given at the Theatre Royal, Glasgow, and on tour at Edinburgh, Belfast, Aberdeen, Birmingham, Newcastle upon Tyne, Bradford and Inverness.

GLYNDEBOURNE FESTIVAL OPERA, estab. 1934
Glyndeborne, Lewes, E. Sussex BN8 5UU

The 1992 Festival ran from 2 May to 23 July. *Così fan tutte* (1991), *Jenůfa* (1989) and *Death in Venice* (1989) were revived.

The new productions were:

(2 May 1992) *Peter Grimes* (Britten). Conductor, Andrew Davis; producer, Trevor Nunn; designer, John Gunter.

Stephan Drakulich (Peter Grimes), Vivian Tierney (Ellen Orford), Alan Opie (Captain Balstrode), Menai Davies (Auntie), John Graham-Hall (Bob Boles), Donald Adams (Swallow), Susan Bickley (Mrs Sedley), Robert Poulton (Ned Keene).

(15 June 1992) *The Queen of Spades* (Tchaikovsky). Conductor, Andrew Davis; producer, Graham Vick; designer, Richard Hudson.

Yuri Marusin (Herman), Sergei Leiferkus (Tomsky), Dimitri Kharitonov (Yeletsky), Felicity Palmer (The Countess), Nancy Gustafson (Lisa), Louise Winter (Pauline), Anne Dawson (Chloe).

Glyndebourne Touring Opera performed *Le nozze di Figaro*, *Kat'a Kabanova* and *The Rake's Progress* at Sadler's Wells, London, Plymouth, Sheffield, Southampton Manchester and Oxford from September to November 1992.

OPERA 80, estab. 1980

The Magic Flute and *Albert Herring* were toured to Wolverhampton, Eastbourne, Ipswich, Buxton, Weston-super-Mare and Dartford in October and November 1991.

Don Giovanni and *Albert Herring* were toured to Swindon, Cheltenham, Exeter, Basildon, Crawley, Poole, Yeovil, Reading, Brighton, Cambridge, Lincoln, Preston, Carlisle, Darlington, Ulverston and Sadler's Wells, London, from February to April 1992.

OPERA FACTORY, estab. 1982
South Bank Centre, London SE1 8XX

Don Giovanni (1991) was revived at the Queen Elizabeth Hall.

(1 May 1991) *The Coronation of Poppea* (Monteverdi). Conductor, Peter Robinson; producer, David Freeman; designer, David Roger.

Marie Angel (Poppea), Nigel Robson (Nero), Janis Kelly (Octavia), Geoffrey Dolton (Otho), Michael Neil (Seneca), Sally Ann Shepherdson (Drusilla), Howard Milner (Arnalta). Performed at the Queen Elizabeth Hall, Londonderry and Cheltenham from May to July 1992.

OPERA NORTHERN IRELAND
Grand Opera House, Belfast

(20 September 1991) *The Bartered Bride* (Smetana). Conductor, Howard Williams; producer, Mike Ashman; designers, Jan Schlubach (sets), Elisabeth Urbancic (costumes).

Gordon Sandison (Krusina), Angela Hickey (Ludmilla), Nova Thomas (Marenka), Gordon Wilson (Jenik), Philip Joll (Kecal), Christopher Gillett (Vasek), Paul Nemeer (Tobias Micha).

(21 September 1991) *Così fan tutte* (Mozart). Conductor, Kenneth Montgomery; producer, Javier Lopez Pinon; designers, Rick Swarte (sets), Carly Everaert (costumes).

Sylvie Valayre (Fiordiligi), Cynthia Buchan (Dorabella), Linda Ormiston (Despina), Philip Sheffield (Ferrando), Johannes Mannov (Guglielmo), Huub Claessens (Don Alfonso).

Masters of the Queen's (King's) Music

'Master of the King's Music' was the title given to the official who presided over the court band during the reign of Charles I. The first Master was appointed in 1626. Today the Master is expected to organize the music for state occasions and to write new music for them, although there are no fixed duties. The post is held for life and the Master receives an annual honorarium of £100.

Nicholas Lanier (1588–1666), appointed 1626
Louis Grabu (?–1674), appointed 1666
Nicholas Staggins (1650–1700), appointed 1674
John Eccles (1668–1735), appointed 1700
Maurice Greene (1695–1755), appointed 1735
William Boyce (1710–79), appointed 1755
John Stanley (1713–86), appointed 1779
Sir William Parsons (1746–1817), appointed 1786
William Shield (1748–1829), appointed 1817
Christian Kramer (?–1834), appointed 1829
François (Franz) Cramer (1772–1848), appointed 1834
George Anderson (?–1870), appointed 1848
Sir William Cusins (1833–93), appointed 1870
Sir Walter Parratt (1841–1924), appointed 1893
Sir Edward Elgar (1857–1934), appointed 1924
Sir Henry Walford Davies (1869–1941), appointed 1934
Sir Arnold Bax (1883–1953), appointed 1941
Sir Arthur Bliss (1891–1975), appointed 1953
Malcolm Williamson (1931–), appointed 1975

Prime Ministers since 1782

Over the centuries there has been some variation in the determination of the dates of appointment of Prime Ministers. Where possible, the date given is that on which a new Prime Minister kissed the Sovereign's hands and accepted the commission to form a ministry. However, until the middle of the 19th century the dating of a commission or transfer of seals could be the date of taking office. Where the composition of the Government changed, e.g. became a coalition, but the Prime Minister remained the same, the date of the change of government is given.

The Marquess of Rockingham, *Whig*, 27 March 1782
The Earl of Shelburne, *Whig*, 4 July 1782
The Duke of Portland, *Coalition*, 2 April 1783
William Pitt, *Tory*, 19 December 1783
Henry Addington, *Tory*, 17 March 1801
William Pitt, *Tory*, 10 May 1804
The Lord Grenville, *Whig*, 11 February 1806
The Duke of Portland, *Tory*, 31 March 1807
Spencer Perceval, *Tory*, 4 October 1809
The Earl of Liverpool, *Tory*, 8 June 1812
George Canning, *Tory*, 10 April 1827
Viscount Goderich, *Tory*, 31 August 1827
The Duke of Wellington, *Tory*, 22 January 1828
The Earl Grey, *Whig*, 22 November 1830
The Viscount Melbourne, *Whig*, 16 July 1834
The Duke of Wellington, *Tory*, 17 November 1834
Sir Robert Peel, *Tory*, 10 December 1834
The Viscount Melbourne, *Whig*, 18 April 1835
Sir Robert Peel, *Tory*, 30 August 1841
Lord John Russell (subsequently the Earl Russell), *Whig*, 30 June 1846
The Earl of Derby, *Tory*, 23 February 1852
The Earl of Aberdeen, *Peelite*, 19 December 1852
The Viscount Palmerston, *Liberal*, 6 February 1855
The Earl of Derby, *Conservative*, 20 February 1858
The Viscount Palmerston, *Liberal*, 12 June 1859
The Earl Russell, *Liberal*, 29 October 1865
The Earl of Derby, *Conservative*, 28 June 1866
Benjamin Disraeli, *Conservative*, 27 February 1868
William Gladstone, *Liberal*, 3 December 1868
Benjamin Disraeli, *Conservative*, 20 February 1874
William Gladstone, *Liberal*, 23 April 1880
The Marquess of Salisbury, *Conservative*, 23 June 1885
William Gladstone, *Liberal*, 1 February 1886
The Marquess of Salisbury, *Conservative*, 25 July 1886
William Gladstone, *Liberal*, 15 August 1892
The Earl of Rosebery, *Liberal*, 5 March 1894
The Marquess of Salisbury, *Conservative*, 25 June 1892
Arthur Balfour, *Conservative*, 12 July 1902
Sir Henry Campbell-Bannerman, *Liberal*, 5 December 1905
Herbert Asquith, *Liberal*, 7 April 1908
Herbert Asquith, *Coalition*, 25 May 1915
David Lloyd-George, *Coalition*, 7 December 1916
Andrew Bonar Law, *Conservative*, 23 October 1922
Stanley Baldwin, *Conservative*, 22 May 1923
Ramsay MacDonald, *Labour*, 22 January 1924
Stanley Baldwin, *Conservative*, 4 November 1924
Ramsay MacDonald, *Labour*, 5 June 1929
Ramsay MacDonald, *Coalition*, 24 August 1931
Stanley Baldwin, *Coalition*, 7 June 1935
Neville Chamberlain, *Coalition*, 28 May 1937
Winston Churchill, *Coalition*, 10 May 1940
Winston Churchill, *Conservative*, 23 May 1945
Clement Attlee, *Labour*, 26 July 1945
Sir Winston Churchill, *Conservative*, 26 October 1951
Sir Anthony Eden, *Conservative*, 6 April 1955
Harold Macmillan, *Conservative*, 10 January 1957
Sir Alec Douglas-Home, *Conservative*, 19 October 1963
Harold Wilson, *Labour*, 16 October 1964
Edward Heath, *Conservative*, 19 June 1970
Harold Wilson, *Labour*, 4 March 1974
James Callaghan, *Labour*, 5 April 1976
Margaret Thatcher, *Conservative*, 4 May 1979
John Major, *Conservative*, 28 November 1990

Speakers of the Commons since 1708

The date of appointment given is the day on which the Speaker was first elected by the House of Commons. The appointment requires Royal approbation before it is confirmed and this is usually given within a few days. The present Speaker is the 155th.

Parliament of Great Britain

Sir Richard Onslow, 16 November 1708
William Bromley, 25 November 1710
Sir Thomas Hanmer, 16 February 1714
Spencer Compton (*Earl of Wilmington*), 17 March 1715
Arthur Onslow, 23 January 1728
Sir John Cust, 3 November 1761
Sir Fletcher Norton, 22 January 1770
Charles Cornwall, 31 October 1780
Hon. William Grenville, 5 January 1789
Henry Addington, 8 June 1789

Parliament of United Kingdom

Sir John Mitford (*Lord Redesdale*), 11 February 1801
Charles Abbot (*Lord Colchester*), 10 February 1802
Charles Manners-Sutton (*Viscount Canterbury*), 2 June 1817
James Abercromby (*Lord Dunfermline*), 19 February 1835
Charles Shaw-Lefevre (*Viscount Eversley*), 27 May 1839
J. Evelyn Denison (*Viscount Ossington*), 30 April 1857
Sir Henry Brand (*Viscount Hampden*), 9 February 1872
Arthur Wellesley Peel (*Viscount Peel*), 26 February 1884
William Gully (*Viscount Selby*), 10 April 1895
James Lowther (*Viscount Ullswater*), 8 June 1905
John Whitley, 27 April 1921
Hon. Edward Fitzroy, 20 June 1928
Douglas Clifton-Brown, 9 March 1943
William Morrison, 31 October 1951
Sir Harry Hylton-Foster, 20 October 1959
Horace King (*Lord Maybray-King*), 26 October 1965
Selwyn Lloyd (*Lord Selwyn-Lloyd*), 12 January 1971
George Thomas (*Viscount Tonypandy*), 2 February 1976
Bernard Weatherill (*Lord Weatherill*), 15 June 1983
Betty Boothroyd, 27 April 1992

Parliament

Both Houses of Parliament returned from the summer recess on 14 October, with speculation rife about the possibility of an autumn election.

On 14 October the Secretary of State for Transport (Malcolm Rifkind) announced that the Government's preference for the Channel Tunnel rail link was the eastern route, terminating at King's Cross, and that it was their intention that the link should be financed by the private sector. The Minister of State at the Foreign Office (Douglas Hogg) reported on the deteriorating situation in Yugoslavia, calling for an end to the fighting and for genuine negotiations. In the annual debate on defence the Parliamentary Under-Secretary for Defence (Kenneth Carlisle) announced a reduction in the number of hours of low-flying to be undertaken by the RAF, the chartering of a vessel to replace HMS *Endurance* as the ice patrol ship in the South Atlantic and that the Government would be ordering replacements for the amphibious landing ships HMS *Intrepid* and HMS *Fearless*. On 15 October the Home Secretary (Kenneth Baker) published a consultation document, *Squatting*, on proposals to change the law relating to the unlawful occupation of private property. In the House of Lords the Government was defeated by 111 votes to 102 on the third reading of the British Technology Group Bill on an amendment moved by an independent peer (Lord Flowers) insisting that universities should be consulted over the proposed sale of the research body, once privatized. On 16 October the Health Secretary (William Waldegrave) announced the details of the second tranche of NHS Trusts; 99 of the 113 hospitals and bodies that had applied would be granted trust status from 1 April 1992. The four London teaching hospitals which had applied would in principle also have the status granted but this would be dependent on the outcome of the Tomlinson Commission on health care in London.

On 21 October the Social Security Secretary (Tony Newton) detailed the annual uprating of social security benefits, with the new rates to come into effect in the first full week of the tax year and mainly being increased in line with the retail price index (4.1 per cent). On 22 October Kenneth Carlisle, replying to a private notice question from the Labour defence spokesman (Martin O'Neill) on the outcome of the fatal accident inquiry involving MV *Antares* and the submarine HMS *Trenchant* in November 1990, announced changes to the safety margins used in submarine exercises.

The Queen's Speech

The 1990–1 Parliamentary session ended on 22 October and The Queen opened the 1991–2 session of Parliament on 31 October. The Queen's Speech outlined twelve bills with three main themes

- implementing key elements of the Citizen's Charter in education, local government and the regulated utilities
- improving further and higher education
- abolishing the local government community charge and replacing it with the council tax, and providing for reforms of local government structure in England

The programme also provided for

- dealing with asylum cases more quickly and efficiently
- creating a new offence to deter prison rioting and increasing the maximum sentence to deter aiding escapes
- modernizing the regulation of charities
- strengthening health and safety legislation covering offshore oil and gas exploration and extraction
- streamlining the way in which transport development schemes are authorized
- providing for the construction of the Cardiff Bay Barrage

The following bills were announced

- Asylum
- Cardiff Bay Barrage
- Charities
- Competition and Service (Utilities)
- Education (Schools)
- Further and Higher Education and Further and Higher Education (Scotland)
- Local Government
- Local Government Finance
- Offshore Safety
- Prison Security
- Transport and Works

Other bills would also be introduced.

Despite the early start to the session, it could not last more than about three quarters of the length of a normal session at its maximum as a general election had to be called by June.

Debate on the Queen's Speech

The Leader of the Opposition (Neil Kinnock) said the speech contained 'proposals . . . which we can welcome', such as a commitment to arms control, combating terrorism and drug trafficking, recognition of the need to keep pressure on Iraq, hope for a successful conclusion of the GATT round and the wish for a constructive UNCED, but there was much more that he could not support, 'nothing in the Queen's Speech can offer better prospects'. He regretted in particular the fact that there was no reference to measures to combat joy-riding, nor to the establishment of an Environmental Protection Agency, nor for better employment conditions for women. He summed up the content as 'not a programme for the future, but a paint job over the past. It is an attempt to cover over the injustices and failures of the Government's making. It will not succeed . . . That is why, whenever the Prime Minister works up the nerve to call the general election, there will be no further extension of Tory power. The Government will be beaten and the British people will give themselves the chance to make a fresh start with a Labour government.' The Liberal Democrat leader (Paddy Ashdown) described the speech as 'half an apology, half a speech in mitigation for what the Government have done in the past . . . it struck me that the Gracious Speech was the programme of a Government who have nothing further to say. It should never have been presented to the House because we should either have had a general election or be in the process of one.' After the usual six days of debate on the speech, a Labour amendment on the economic content was defeated by 323 votes to 193 and a Liberal Democrat amendment on the omissions from the speech was defeated by 320 votes to 19. The speech itself was approved without a division.

On 4 November the Northern Ireland Secretary (Peter Brooke) made a statement on the bombing of Musgrave Park Hospital by the IRA in which two soldiers had been killed and eleven other people injured. On 5 November the Parliamentary Under-Secretary for Energy (Colin Moynihan) launched the 1991 Non-Fossil Fuel Obligation Renewables Order, setting up the biggest contractual requirement to build renewable energy plant ever planned. There would be six technology bands covering wind, hydro-electricity, landfill gas, municipal and general industrial waste, sewerage gas and others. The Minister for Overseas Development (Lynda Chalker) outlined the extent of the Government's relief package to Bangladesh, following the devastating cyclone in April.

Autumn Financial Statement

On 6 November the Chancellor of the Exchequer (Norman Lamont) presented his first autumn financial statement, outlining the spending plans for government departments. The main points were:

- £5,600 million increase in public spending in 1992–3 (total £226,600 million)
- planning totals for 1993–4 to be £244,500 million; for 1994–5, £258,000 million
- ratio of government expenditure to GDP 42 per cent in 1992–3; 41.75 per cent in 1993–4
- privatization proceeds to be £8,000 million in 1992–3
- Public sector borrowing requirement to be £10,500 million in 1991–2 (1.75 per cent of GDP); £19,000 million (3 per cent of GDP) in 1992–3

Departmental plans

- social security expenditure up by £4,250 million
- health spending up by £1,500 million (total £28,150 million)
- transport spending up by £1,400 million (17 per cent)
- local authority spending up by £1,400 million
- education spending increased by £627 million (total £7,950 million)
- £830 million extra (total £24,500 million) for defence
- National Insurance contributions lower earnings limit raised to £54 per week, upper limit to £405 per week

Economic forecast

- rise of 2.25 per cent in Gross Domestic Product in 1992
- RPI inflation to return to 4 per cent by last quarter of 1992
- unemployment to average 2.35 million in 1991–2, and 2.4 million over next three years
- current account deficit predicted to halve to £6,500 million this year; widen to £9,500 million next year
- manufacturing output to rise by 0.5 per cent in second half of 1991
- domestic expenditure to rise by 2.5 per cent in 1992 after 0.75 per cent drop in 1991

Also on 6 November the Severn Bridges Bill to allow for the construction of a new bridge went through all its stages in the House of Commons in one day, without debate.

On 12 November the Prime Minister (John Major) reported to the Commons on the outcome of the NATO summit held in Rome on 7–8 November, where NATO leaders had agreed to adapt its strategy to the changed situation in Europe and to build a new partnership with the countries of central and eastern Europe. On 14 November the Foreign Secretary (Douglas Hurd) made a statement about the progress in the investigations into the Lockerbie air disaster and announced that the Lord Advocate had issued warrants for the arrest of two Libyan intelligence officers in connection with the atrocity. In the House of Lords the Offshore Safety Bill, implementing many of the recommendations of the Cullen report, received its second reading.

On 20–21 November there was a two-day debate seeking approval for the Government's approach to the forthcoming European Community summit at Maastricht. John Major believed it was 'in Britain's interest to continue to be at the heart of the European Community and be able to shape its future and that of Europe as a whole'. Neil Kinnock, attempting to embarrass the Government by highlighting their divisions on this issue, claimed that 'the country cannot be properly served by a Government who pretend they can somehow call a halt to or defer the agreed purpose of the rest of the Community'. The former Prime Minister (Margaret Thatcher) called for a referendum on the issue of monetary union. Norman Lamont hinted that Britain would be prepared to accept arrangements in stage three of the monetary union process under which the proposed European Central Bank would not be subject to political control. The motion was passed by 351 votes to 250 but six Conservative MPs voted against the Government.

On 25 November the Cardiff Bay Barrage Bill, authorizing the construction of a barrage across the estuary of the rivers Taff and Ely in Cardiff Bay and replacing a Private Bill withdrawn in the previous session, was given a second reading by 278 votes to 130, despite Opposition objections that it contained inadequate ground water protection provisions. On 26 November the Secretary of State for the Environment (Michael Heseltine) detailed the level of the local authority financial settlement for England for 1992–3: the expected average community charge rate would be £257; the multiplier for the uniform business rate would be 40.2p; and the overall spend by local authorities would be £41,800 million, an increase of 7.2 per cent. On 27 November the Attorney-General (Sir Patrick Mayhew), replying to a private notice question from a Conservative backbencher (Ivor Stanbrook) on the breach of Sunday trading laws by supermarkets, said that the law had not been suspended but that there was uncertainty over the present state of Community law, which required clarification; meantime it remained the responsibility of local authorities to decide their own course of action. Immediately after this the Minister of State at the Home Office (Angela Rumbold) announced that discussions were still going on over the reform of the law on Sunday trading and it remained the Government's intention to bring forward proposals for reform once the legal position was clear. On 28 November the Welsh Secretary (David Hunt) announced an increase of £186 million (to £1,877 million) on expenditure by the Government on health and personal social services in Wales in the next year. The Welsh Development Agency Bill, increasing the statutory financial limit of the agency to £950 million, completed all its House of Commons stages in one day.

On 2 December William Waldegrave, responding to a private notice question from a Conservative backbencher (David Ashby), announced the setting-up of an inquiry into child abuse in Leicestershire and the establishment of a national inquiry under Norman Warner to look at staff selection procedures for children's homes and to report by July 1992. The Home Secretary (Kenneth Baker) made a statement on the judgment by the Court of Appeal that had found him guilty of contempt of court over the deportation of a Zairean national; he would be appealing to the House of Lords. In the House of Lords the Government was defeated by 62 votes to 55 on an amendment to Clause 8 of the Local Government Bill (Application to Competitive Tendering to Professional Services) moved by a Labour peer (Lord McIntosh of Haringey), designed to take away the power of the Secretary of State to impose competitive tendering.

On 3 December the Scottish Secretary (Ian Lang) announced that he would be approving the applications from three groups of hospitals in Scotland (Foresterhill, Royal Scottish National and South Ayrshire) for NHS trust status. The Labour Scottish spokesman (Donald Dewar) called it 'a betrayal – a victory for prejudice over common sense'. In an adjournment debate the MP for Leicester West (Greville Janner) was able to explain the recent allegations made against him during the trial of a Leicestershire child care officer; the Solicitor-General (Sir Nicholas Lyell) was unable to give an undertaking that press coverage of court proceedings would be altered to prevent such a situation from arising again. On 4 December Ian Lang detailed the level of public expenditure in Scotland for 1992–3: the total allocation would be some £12,400 million for government departments and there would be further expenditure on top of that by local authorities, an increase of 9.2 per cent over the previous year. On 5 December the House of Commons was entertained by the statement made by a junior Foreign Office Minister (Mark Lennox-Boyd) explaining to the Shadow Foreign Secretary (Gerald Kaufman) how a Canadian diplomatic bag had been sent for cleaning at the laundry of Wandsworth prison, still containing diplomatic mail.

On 9 December, in response to a private notice question from a local Conservative backbencher (Sir John Cope), Malcolm Rifkind announced the setting-up of an inquiry by British Rail into the rail crash in the Severn Tunnel on 7 December in which some 90 passengers had been injured. The Aggravated Vehicle-Taking Bill, intended to make sure that everyone who gets involved in the taking of someone else's vehicle is made criminally liable for the consequences and giving the courts power to sentence serious cases in a suitable way, completed all its House of Commons stages in one day. On 10 December the Secretary of State for Defence (Tom King) made a statement about the proposed reduction in the numbers of Britain's reserve forces for the 1990s. On 11 December John Major reported back on the outcome of the EC summit in Maastricht; agreement had been reached on a treaty on European union covering economic and monetary union as well as political union (*see* page 1088). The United Kingdom had negotiated an opt-out clause on economic and monetary union and had come to a similar arrangement over the Social Chapter. He called it 'a good agreement for Europe and a good agreement for the United Kingdom'. Neil Kinnock said, 'it is impossible to regard the Government's actions as effective negotiation when they have simply opted out of the two basic economic and social issues and have left an empty chair in the EC'.

On 16 December in the House of Lords the Paymaster-General (Lord Belstead) offered concessions on the proposals in the Further and Higher Education Bill for power to intervene in the running of universities and other higher education institutions. There was a two-day debate on the Maastricht agreement on 18–19 December. The government motion congratulating the Prime Minister and warmly endorsing the agreement was passed by 339 votes to 253, but seven Conservatives voted against the motion. In the House of Lords a similar motion was approved by 184 votes to 81 on 18 December. On 19 December Norman Lamont made a statement on measures designed to reduce the level of mortgage repossessions, including the suspension of stamp duty for eight months on house purchases below £250,000 and increased mortgage interest payments for people on income support. Tony Newton detailed the proposed revision of arrangements for the paying of income support in respect of mortgage interest, including the speeding-up of adjudication and provision for direct payment to qualifying lenders, after a claim had continued for 16 weeks. On 20 December the Parliamentary Secretary for Agriculture, Fisheries and Food (David Curry) reported the outcome of the EC Fisheries Council meeting earlier in the week, which had dealt with the alternatives to the current eight-day tie-up rule.

On 9 January in the House of Lords, which had returned from the Christmas recess before the House of Commons, the Parliamentary Under-Secretary at the Scottish Office (Lord Strathclyde) made an announcement on the decision by British Steel to close their Ravenscraig works, calling the decision 'hugely disappointing'.

On 13 January, responding to a private notice question from Donald Dewar, Ian Lang also expressed deep disappointment at British Steel's decision to close Ravenscraig and thought that they owed it to their employees to explain and justify the decision. David Hunt detailed the local government finance settlement for Wales, an increase of 8.5 per cent to £2,606.4 million: the average community charge was therefore expected to be around £118; the multiplier for the uniform business rate would be 42.5p. On 15 January the Secretary of State for Employment (Michael Howard), responding to a private notice question from the Labour employment spokesman (Tony Blair), announced that since the establishment of Training and Enterprise Councils his department had ceased to have training contact with the APEX Trust but had given a grant of £500,000 in March 1991; he could offer no more money and the Trust had announced plans to call in the receivers. The Minister for Agriculture, Fisheries and Food (John Gummer) announced upgraded environmentally sensitive area schemes to cover the Broads, the Pennine Dales, the South Downs, the Somerset levels and west Penrith. On 17 January a backbench bill presented by the Conservative MP who had come top of the Private Member's Bill ballot (Ivan Lawrence), the National Lottery Bill, which would create a national lottery to support good causes, was denied a second reading despite the tacit support of the Government because fewer than 100 MPs were present to vote on the closure motion, which had to be passed before the vote could be taken on the second reading itself.

On 20 January Northern Ireland Secretary Peter Brooke made a statement on the murder of seven construction workers by the IRA on 17 January and his own appearance on an Irish television chat show that same evening. The Minister for Defence Procurement (Alan Clark) announced that EURO-DASS, a consortium led by Marconi Defence Systems Ltd, had been chosen to provide the defensive aids subsystem (DASS) for the European Fighter Aircraft (EFA). All Commons stages of the Stamp Duty (Temporary Provisions) Bill implementing the arrangements outlined by the Chancellor before Christmas were completed in one day. On 22 January the House of Commons held their annual debate on the Chancellor's Autumn Statement; a Labour amendment criticizing the Government's financial policy was defeated by 320 votes to 233 and the substantive motion was passed by 317 votes to 227. On 23 January Tom King confirmed that a further order for three Type 23 frigates would be placed with Yarrow Shipbuilders on the Clyde. In the House of Lords the Parliamentary Under-Secretary for Defence (Earl of Arran) announced in reply to a private notice question from a Labour peer (Lord Shackleton) the purchase of the hitherto rented Norwegian logistics support and scientific research ship *Polar Circle* as the permanent replacement for HMS *Endurance* in the South Atlantic.

On 27 January in the House of Lords there was an unusual procedural twist to the British Waterways Bill, a Private Bill. The third reading, normally the final chance to amend a piece of legislation, was agreed but it was also agreed that amendments to the bill could still be tabled and discussed at a later stage, in March, when there would be a separate motion that the bill now pass. On 28 January Michael Howard announced the Government's legislative plans following the responses to the consultation paper *Industrial Relations in the 1990s*, published in July 1991: members of the public would have a right to seek injunctions to halt unlawful action affecting public services; the rights of trade union members would be strengthened against fraud, vote rigging, intimidation and financial mismanagement; union members would have the right to join the union of their choice; seven days notice of strikes and other industrial action would be required. Tony Blair dismissed the proposals as 'not for the sake of better industrial relations but for the sake of the worst prejudices of the Tory party'. On 29 January the Leader of the House (John MacGregor) had to move a closure motion on the Government's Education (Schools) Bill when it became obvious that the Opposition was going to force an all-night sitting. He introduced a guillotine motion the following day. Also on 30 January Colin Moynihan, replying to a private notice question from the Labour energy spokesman (Frank Dobson), explained the Government's decision to authorize further imports of natural gas and announced the setting-up of an independent study under the chairmanship of Sir Geoffrey Chipperfield into the further liberalization of gas trade throughout Europe.

On 3 February John Major reported to the Commons on the visit to London by President Yeltsin of Russia and the subsequent special meeting of the

UN Security Council in New York on 31 January to discuss aid to the emerging states of the former Soviet Union. In the House of Lords the Government suffered two defeats on the third reading of the Further and Higher Education Bill: first, on an amendment moved by the Bishop of Guildford to introduce a new clause to continue the present requirement that a regular act of worship be held in sixth form colleges and that religious education courses be offered to all who sought them, which was carried by 106 votes to 89 – the Lord Chancellor (Lord Mackay of Clashfern) failed to vote; second, on an amendment introduced by a Conservative peer (Lord Belloff) designed to limit the powers of the Secretary of State over the appointment of staff, admissions, students and the duration of courses, which was passed by 86 votes to 72. In two other votes the Government's majority was reduced to one. On 5 February the Social Security (Mortgage Interest Payments) Bill, implementing the proposals announced by the Secretary of State for Social Security before Christmas, completed all its House of Commons stages in one day. On 6 February Peter Brooke made a statement on the security situation in Northern Ireland, where 12 people had been murdered in the first six days of the month, promising that the Government would not 'shirk' its responsibility to deal with terrorism.

On 10 February Malcolm Rifkind announced the publication of proposals for the deregulation of motorway service areas, placing the onus on the private sector rather than the Department of Transport. In the House of Lords on 12 February the Parliamentary Under-Secretary for Employment (Viscount Ullswater) announced during the second reading of a Labour peer's (Baroness Turner) private member's Offshore Safety (Protection Against Victimization) Bill that the Government itself would be willing to introduce the measures intended to end victimization offshore as soon as possible. On 13 February Alan Clark confirmed the decision to replace HMS *Intrepid* and HMS *Fearless* with a new helicopter landing ship. On 14 February the second reading of the Wild Animals (Protection) Bill, introduced by the Labour backbench MP who had come fifth in the Private Members' Bill ballot (Kevin McNamara), which would outlaw the hunting of wild animals by dogs, was defeated by 187 votes to 175.

On 17 February the Secretary of State for Trade and Industry (Peter Lilley) made a statement on the agreement reached between the United Kingdom and the European Commission on the distribution of European regional development funds under the RECHAR programme that had been in dispute for some time. On 19 February Alan Clark announced a number of new equipment projects for the armed forces, including the conversion of VC10 transport aircraft to tanker capability, a further batch of air-launched anti-radar missiles, the continuation of SKYNET IV stage two and the order of new SeaKing helicopters for search and rescue. On 21 February the Referendum Bill, introduced by the Conservative MP who had come sixth in the Private Members' Bill ballot (Richard Shepherd), which would have established the principle of a referendum for issues of national importance such as the ratification of the Maastricht treaty, was denied a second reading because fewer than 100 MPs were present to vote on the closure motion.

On 24 February the Draft Prevention of Terrorism (Temporary Provisions) Act 1989 (Continuance) Order 1992, relating to the role of the security forces in Northern Ireland, was approved by 300 votes to 115. The Parliamentary Corporate Bodies Bill, implementing the recommendations of the Ibbs report on the House of Commons Services completed its Commons stages in one day. In the committee stage of the Education (Schools) Bill in the House of Lords, the Government agreed to give HM Inspectors of Schools greater powers to oversee the appointment by school governors to the newly created private schools inspectors, which could mean the appointment of 40 chief inspectors as opposed to the 20 originally envisaged by the Government. On 25 February Kenneth Baker announced a package of six measures aimed at reducing the number of so-called bail bandits offending on bail. These included more severe penalties for those who commit an offence whilst on bail, legislation to arrest people immediately who breach bail, and greater scope for magisterial guidance on the granting of bail. He also announced an extra £8 million over the following three years for bail accommodation and support. In the House of Lords on 26 February the Government introduced its promised amendments to Baroness Turner's Offshore Safety (Protection Against Victimization) Bill. On 27 February Tony Newton announced the outcome of the five-year review on the level of national insurance rebates for people contracting out of SERPS: the new rates would be 4.8 per cent for 1993 to 1996, split 1.8 per cent for employees and 3 per cent for employers. On 28 February a Conservative MP (John Browne) won the top place in the ballot for the private member's motion and spent over four hours detailing his own grievances against the House of Commons, which had suspended him the previous year, and the circumstances which had led to his being deselected as the Conservative candidate for Winchester. John Gummer made a statement in response to a private notice question from the SNP leader (Alex Salmond) detailing the Government's decision on the new fishery decommissioning scheme.

In the House of Lords on 2 March the Government suffered two defeats in the committee stage of the Education (Schools) Bill: first, on an amendment introduced by a Labour peer (Lord Peston) to allow school governors to be responsible for choosing inspectors, which was passed by 95 votes to 67; second, on an amendment introduced by a Conservative peer (Earl Baldwin of Bewley) deleting proposals to remove from local authorities the right of entry to inspect state schools, which was passed by 97 votes to 63. On 3 March Tom King announced the decision to choose the British Aerospace ASRAAM missile for the RAF's short-range air-to-air missile. David Hunt announced proposals for the future of local government in Wales, which would replace the present eight councils and 37 district councils with twenty-three unitary authorities. On 4 March Peter Brooke made a statement on Lord Colville's report on the management of paramilitary prisoners in Belfast prison, following the explosion in C wing the previous November.

On 9 March Malcolm Rifkind announced the sale of the three trust ports privatized in the Ports Act 1991: Clyde to Clyde Port Holdings Ltd, Medway to Medports Mebo Ltd and Tilbury to International Transport Ltd.

The Budget

On 10 March Norman Lamont presented his second Budget statement. The main points were:

Income tax
- new lower tax band, first £2,000 of taxable earnings to attract 20 per cent rate
- personal allowances rise in line with inflation

Pensions
- pensioners on income support to get an extra £2 (single) or £3 (married) a week

Motor industry
- car tax halved to 5 per cent
- capital allowance limit on business cars raised to £12,000
- taxi firms and driving schools to be able to reclaim VAT
- move towards car price, not engine size, as basis for company car tax scales

Excise duties
- alcohol, diesel and unleaded petrol up in line with inflation
- leaded petrol up by 7.5 per cent
- tobacco, cigarettes up by 10 per cent, pipe tobacco in line with inflation
- duty on matches and mechanical lighters scrapped
- Vehicle Excise Duty up by £10
- Betting Duty cut from 8 per cent to 7.75 per cent

Company taxation
- Corporation tax, no change
- Uniform Business Rate, transitional arrangements changed
- Inheritance tax, many business assets exempted
- Business Expansion Scheme to be abolished

VAT
- penalties for mistakes to be reduced
- deferred payment scheme extended

Small businesses
- action on late payment of bills
- new terms for quarterly PAYE payments

Public sector borrowing requirement (PSBR)
- doubles to £28,100 million (4.5 per cent of GDP) this current fiscal year
- forecast to remain in deficit until 1996–7

Economic forecast
- GDP to grow by 1 per cent this year
- inflation to fall to 3.75 per cent by end of 1992
- consumer spending to grow by 1 per cent this year and by 3 per cent in the first half of 1993
- current account deficit to rise to £6,500 million this year and £9,000 million in 1993

Debate on the Budget

As usual the Leader of the Opposition (Neil Kinnock) congratulated the Chancellor on the way in which he delivered his speech, 'Indeed with rather greater felicity than I usually do because this will be the last speech by a Conservative Chancellor for many years to come'. He was also able to welcome some measures in the speech, 'The step that he made in the direction of radical reform of the Budget process is certainly worth a warm welcome . . . We should also like to welcome several of the changes that the Chancellor is introducing in respect of businesses, large and small . . . for the automobile manufacturing industry . . . the changes in the special car tax must be welcome . . . we also support the modest but welcome steps that he has taken in respect of the British film industry'. But that was where his support ended, 'What our country needed today was a Budget for strengthening Britain and promoting sustainable recovery out of the recession caused by the Government. What we got was a Budget to try to bribe voters with borrowed money which they will have to repay. The borrowing that the Government are raising to finance tax cuts is not, as the Chancellor would insist, prudent economic strategy, it is a panic-stricken pre-election political sweetener.' For the Liberal Democrats Sir David Steel said, 'It will not do the economy any good but it will make people feel better temporarily . . . I believe that that is what it was designed to do.' The debate on the Budget was curtailed due to the calling of the general election and lasted only two days. The Budget resolution was approved by 351 votes to 208. Specific excise motions were passed by 351 votes to 206.

General Election

On 11 March the Leader of the House (John MacGregor) came to the Commons to inform MPs of the Prime Minister's decision to seek the dissolution of the Commons on 16 March for an election on 9 April. On 13 March all stages of a reduced Finance Bill were completed, with only eleven clauses relating mostly to excise duties, betting levies, VAT, car tax and the income tax proposals from the Chancellor's budget included, the other proposals being dropped pending the election. The Government forced a division on the bill in committee so that the Opposition would have to vote against the income tax proposals and they were approved by 325 votes to 143.

On 16 March Parliament met to complete a hurriedly rearranged legislative package, with the Asylum Bill being the only bill to be dropped, the

Charities Bill completing all its Commons stages in one day without debate, and a special motion being passed on the Cardiff Bay Barrage Bill to allow for it to be carried over into the next session of Parliament, and for prorogation and dissolution. The shortened Finance Bill was among 31 bills receiving Royal Assent.

Following the election victory for the Conservative party in the election on 9 April, the new House of Commons met specially on 27 April to elect a new Speaker of the House to replace Mr Speaker Weatherill who had stood down at the election. The MP for West Bromwich West (Betty Boothroyd) was elected by 372 votes to 238, defeating the candidacy of the former Northern Ireland Minister (Peter Brooke). New MPs were also sworn in on 27 April.

The Queen's Speech

The Queen opened the new Parliament on 6 May. The Queen's Speech outlined sixteen bills with two main themes

- implementing measures to provide for more opportunity and choice
- measures to continue the vigorous programme of privatization and deregulation

The programme also provided for

- implementing the Maastricht agreement
- implementing the Budget improvements to the transition arrangements for the non-domestic rate
- establishing an Urban Regeneration Agency
- dealing with asylum applications more quickly and efficiently
- in Scotland, legislation to amend the laws of bankruptcy and to reform the existing arrangements for the early release of determinate sentence prisoners and for the review and release of discretionary life prisoners
- greater recognition of the Welsh language
- facilitating the work of the Boundary Commission
- measures to maintain an additional rebate for holders of personal pensions aged 30 or over

The following bills were announced

- Agriculture (Deregulation and Marketing)
- Asylum Bill
- Bankruptcy (Scotland)
- British Coal and British Rail (Transfer Proposals)
- Coal
- Education
- Employment
- European Communities (Amendment)
- Housing, Land and Urban Development
- National Lottery
- Non-Domestic Rating
- Parliamentary Boundary Commissions
- Prisoners and Criminal Proceedings (Scotland)
- Railways
- Social Security (Contributions)
- Welsh Language

Other bills would also be introduced.

Following the April election this session of Parliament would run from May 1992 until October 1993, some 17 months.

Debate on the Queen's Speech

Neil Kinnock said that he 'naturally welcomed several items in the Queen's Speech', among them the commitments on terrorism and drugs, the search for a peaceful settlement in Yugoslavia and assistance for developments in the former Soviet Union but he regretted that 'there are no changes that will bring sustained and sustainable recovery, because there are no policies that will bring sustained and sustainable improvements in productive performance'. He was concerned at the lack of any mention of the word 'unemployment' in the speech and concluded by saying, '... freedom of choice means nothing when there is little or no provision to choose from ... freedom of opportunity is spurious when they have to take a second-rate treatment in a two-tier service ... the Government's promise of choice and opportunity is fraudulent ... the Government's commitment to a classless society is a pretence ... they are a Government who are not worthy of the country'. Paddy Ashdown, although congratulating the Prime Minister on his electoral victory, was sceptical about the Government's commitment to genuine opportunity and added, 'I fear for much in Britain under this Government. I fear for the cohesion of our social structure, and the underfunded National Health Service. I fear that we shall not do what is necessary to put the economy really right in the long term. But, most of all, I fear for our education system ... There is no evidence of a Government with a clear set of new ideas for our country. Instead I see a Government who intend to stumble on after an election that they did not expect to win ... It has no theme'. There were the usual six days of debate on the speech. Amendments relating to the environment were defeated by 323 votes to 292 and to the economy by 335 votes to 283, whilst the vote at the end was 332 in favour and 18 against, with the official Opposition line being to abstain.

On 8 May the Home Secretary (Kenneth Clarke) made a statement about the division of responsibilities for intelligence and counter terrorism between the Metropolitan Police, Special Branch and the Security Services, with MI5 now to take the lead on intelligence gathering. On 14 May the Secretary of State for the Environment (Michael Howard) announced that ten councils, including three under Conservative control, were to be capped in 1992–3. A new Finance Bill was introduced to implement those measures from the March Budget not included in legislation due to the election.

On 19 May the Secretary of State for Defence (Malcolm Rifkind), in response to a private notice question from Martin O'Neill, made a statement on the outcome of the inquest in Oxford into the deaths of nine British soldiers killed by US air force missiles, so-called friendly fire, during the Gulf war. The House of Commons passed the traditional 'humble address' to The Queen to confer a royal favour on the retiring Speaker of the House (Bernard Weatherill).

MAASTRICHT BILL

On 20–21 May there was a two-day debate on the second reading of the European Communities (Amendment) Bill, which would ratify the Maastricht treaty agreed in December 1991. Opening the debate John Major said, 'At Maastricht we obtained a good deal for the country. We improved the way in which the Community works. We set the basis for the growth and expansion of the Community for years ahead. I believe that that was a good deal for the country and for Europe. I invite the House to have confidence in our future in Europe and to approve the Bill.' Neil Kinnock responded, 'The Labour Party has already made it clear that it broadly supports the treaty concluded at Maastricht because it is a necessary framework for the economic, social and political development of the European Community . . . we cannot, however, extend that support to the Bill. We cannot endorse the Government's action in opting out from the agreements made by the other eleven EC member countries on social policy and on the approach to economic and monetary union. Both of those decisions by the Government will disadvantage the British people.' Paddy Ashdown said, 'We shall not vote for the Bill because we believe that the Prime Minister has, true to his word, put Britain at the heart of Europe, he has not. We shall vote in favour because we believe that the Maastricht treaty is a step forward that must be taken. It would be a disaster for Britain and Europe were it not ratified.' An Opposition amendment declining to give the Bill a second reading because it excluded the United Kingdom from the Social Chapter was defeated by 360 votes to 261. The second reading itself was passed by 336 votes to 92. On this vote the official Opposition line was to abstain; some 22 Conservative backbenchers voted against the Government.

On 21 May in the House of Lords the Community Care (Residential Accommodation) Bill, to allow continued funding of residential care by local authorities in private homes, completed all its stages in one day. On 22 May John Gummer made a statement on the agreement reached in Brussels on reform of the Common Agricultural Policy, including a reduction in cereal prices of nearly 30 per cent.

Returning from the spring recess on 2 June Michael Howard, replying to a private notice question from the Labour environment spokesman (Bryan Gould), announced that his department was actively considering a move of some 2,000 civil servants to a site in London's Docklands, yet to be decided, and that the Canary Wharf development, in the hands of the receivers, was one of those sites. Other departments were also considering such a move. Douglas Hurd announced the details of the UN resolution to impose sanctions on Serbia and Montenegro, passed on 30 May. The Finance Bill implementing those parts of the Budget dropped due to the election received its second reading by 308 votes to 256. Following the Danish referendum result rejecting the Maastricht treaty John Major reported on the implications on 3 June. He said that the Government had decided to postpone further discussion on the British bill to ratify the treaty until the legal and practical implications of the Danish result had been sorted out. He stressed that this was a delay rather than a withdrawal. On 4 June in the House of Lords the Government suffered a defeat in the committee stage of the Prisoners and Criminal Proceedings (Scotland) Bill when an amendment to Clause 31 from a Conservative peer (Lord Campbell of Alloway) to prevent the use of televised evidence in war crime trials in Scotland was passed by 121 votes to 80.

On 8 June the Secretary of State for Social Security (Peter Lilley) announced the setting-up of a committee under Prof. Roger Goode to carry out a thorough review of pension law in the light of the Maxwell affair. He also announced the setting-up of a special unit within his department and a package of repayable grants worth £2.5 million to ease the immediate predicament of the Maxwell pensioners. While welcoming the package as 'ending the Government's six-month long stupor', the Labour social security spokesman (Michael Meacher) felt it did not go nearly far enough. Douglas Hurd reported back on the outcome of the Foreign Affairs Council in Oslo which had discussed the implications of the Danish referendum. On 10 June the Draft Northern Ireland (Emergency and Prevention of Terrorism Provisions) (Continuance) Order 1992 was passed by 281 votes to 170. On 11 June the Minister of Transport in London (Steven Norris) detailed the plans for the extension of the scheme of priority routes in London to include some 300 miles of red routes. In the House of Lords, the Minister of State for Education (Baroness Blatch) announced that the Government would be issuing a consultation document later in the year on the education of children with special needs.

On 15 June John Major reported to the Commons on the outcome of the UN Conference on the Environment and Development (the Earth summit) held in Rio de Janeiro. He had launched three specific British initiatives, the Darwin initiative, an initiative for partnership in global technology, and an initiative for the UK to convene a global forum of the non-governmental organizations community in 1992. On 16 June Norman Lamont announced the decision to abolish the National Economic Development Council (NEDC). The Shadow Chancellor (John Smith) called it 'an act of industrial vandalism'. During the debate on the Armed Forces Discipline Acts (Continuation) Order the Minister for Defence Procurement (Jonathan Aitken) announced that homosexual acts in the armed forces would be decriminalized although those involved in such activities would still be dismissed.

In the House of Lords on 22 June the Lord Privy Seal (Lord Wakeham) replied to a private notice question from a Labour peer (Lord Hatch of Lusby) on the massacre of black Africans in the South African township of Boipatong. On 25 June the Minister of

State for Agriculture, Fisheries and Food (David Curry), replying to a private notice question from a Conservative MP (David Harris), announced that a Royal Navy fisheries protection vessel had been dispatched to the area around the Scilly Isles following an incident involving French and Cornish fishermen.

On 29 June John Major reported to the Commons on the outcome of the European Council meeting in Lisbon on 26–28 June, where the Council had agreed to reappoint the president of the Commission (Jacques Delors) for a further two years. On 30 June approval was given for the setting-up of the departmental select committees for the new Parliament; in particular this meant there was no longer to be an energy committee and new committees would be created to monitor national heritage and the Office of Science and Technology. On 2 July a Labour MP (Dennis Skinner) was ordered to withdraw from the House of Commons for a day for refusing to withdraw the word 'wort' as a description of the Agriculture Minister. There was a debate on the UK presidency of the European Community. In a similar debate in the House of Lords Baroness Thatcher made her maiden speech; she strongly criticized the Maastricht treaty and called for a referendum in Britain.

On 6 July the Secretary of State for Health (Virginia Bottomley), replying to a private notice question from the Labour health spokesman (Robin Cook), said the Government regretted the result of the ballot of dentists on withdrawing in whole or in part from the NHS and assured MPs that the Government would take the necessary steps to safeguard NHS dental services. In the House of Lords the Government suffered a defeat when an independent peer (Lord Henderson of Brompton) moved a motion to amend the Income Support (General) Regulations 1987 to include a small boarder premium (£10 per week) to cover the plight of those who have to live, and feed their children on income support, which was supported by 126 votes to 108. On 7 July Malcolm Rifkind, replying to a private notice question from the Liberal Democrat defence spokesman (Menzies Campbell), confirmed that Germany would not be proceeding with the European Fighter Aircraft (EFA) project. The next step would be to consider with the other EFA partners and with industry how best to take the project forward.

On 13 July John Major reported to the Commons on the outcome of the G7 economic summit in Munich and the summit of the Conference on Security and Co-operation in Europe (CSCE) in Helsinki. At Munich there had been a firm commitment to conclude the Uruguay round of GATT within 1992; at Helsinki discussion had been dominated by events in Yugoslavia. There was a debate on the principle of amending the sittings of the House of Commons following the recommendations of the Jopling report but no definite decisions were taken. Nominations for membership of the departmental select committees were approved, but not without a row over the non-selection of a Conservative backbencher (Nicholas Winterton) to serve on the health committee, following the invoking of a hitherto unknown rule that no MP could serve on a committee for more than three Parliaments. A motion proposing his reinstatement was defeated by 210 votes to 147. In the House of Lords there was an unusual procedural occurrence when the voting on the second reading of a Private Bill (River Usk Barrage Bill) was tied at 24 contents and 24 not contents; in accordance with Standing Order No. 54 which provides that no proposals to reject a bill should be agreed unless there is a majority in favour of such rejection, the second reading was passed. On 14 July Neil Kinnock made his last appearance at Prime Minister's question time as Leader of the Opposition, following his resignation after the election. The Government was defeated over proposed increases in MPs allowances when its motion to increase them by some 7 per cent rather than the 39 per cent recommended by the review body was rejected by an Opposition amendment which was passed by 324 votes to 197. An Opposition amendment to introduce also the full increase for office cost allowances was passed by 317 votes to 186. On 15 July the President of the Board of Trade (Michael Heseltine) announced the decision in principle to privatize the Royal Mail Parcelforce; the Government would be looking for advice on the best way to achieve this. On 16 July both Houses rose for the summer recess. There was a demonstration by five Scottish Labour MPs in an attempt to prevent the closure of the session until Scottish Ministers had made a statement on their intentions for the privatization of Scottish water. Some eight government bills, including the Finance Bill received Royal Assent.

PUBLIC ACTS OF PARLIAMENT

This list of Public Acts commences with one Act of Parliament which obtained the Royal Assent before September 1991. Those Acts which follow were enacted after August 1991. The date stated after each Act is the date on which it came into operation; c. indicates the chapter number of each Act.

Water Industry Act 1991, c. 56, 1 December 1991

Consolidates enactments concerning supply of water and provision of sewerage services with amendments to give effect to recommendations of the Law Commission.

British Technology Act 1991, c. 66, various dates, some to be appointed

Provides for the vesting of the property, rights and liabilities of the National Research Development Corporation and the National Enterprise Board in a company nominated by the Secretary of State and provides for the subsequent dissolution of the Corporation and the Board.

Export and Investment Guarantees Act 1991, c. 67, day or days to be appointed

Makes provision as to the functions exercisable by the Secretary of State through the Export Credits Guarantee Department.

Consolidated Fund (No. 3) Act 1991, c. 68, 19 December 1991

Applies certain sums out of the Consolidated Fund to the service of the years ending on 31 March 1992 and 1993.

Welsh Development Agency Act 1991, c. 69, 19 December 1991

Increases the financial limit under section 18(3) of the 1975 Act.

Consolidated Fund Act 1992, c. 1, 13 February 1992

Applies certain sums to be applied to the service of the years ending 31 March 1992 and 1993.

Stamp Duty (Temporary Provisions) Act 1992, c. 2, 13 February 1992 – retrospective in effect to 20 December 1991

Provides for temporary relief from stamp duty and for the repayment by the Commissioners of Inland Revenue of duty on certain documents already stamped.

Severn Bridges Act 1992, c. 3, various dates, some to be appointed

Provides for a new bridge to be constructed over the Severn Estuary between England and Wales and roads leading to the new bridge and associated works; also provides for the levying of tolls on the existing and the new bridges.

Social Security Contributions and Benefits Act 1992, c. 4, 1 July 1992

Consolidates certain enactments relating to social security contributions and benefits and gives effect to recommendations of the Law Commission and the Scottish Law Commission.

Social Security Administration Act 1992, c. 5, 1 July 1992

Consolidates certain enactments relating to the administration of social security with amendments and gives effect to recommendations of the Law Commission and the Scottish Law Commission.

Social Security (Consequential Provisions) Act 1992, c. 6, 1 July 1992

Provides for repeals, consequential amendments, transitional and transitory matters and savings in connection with the consolidation of the various enactments relating to the Social Security Administration Act 1992 and the Social Security Contributions and Benefits Act 1992.

Social Security Contributions and Benefits (Northern Ireland) Act 1992, c. 7, 1 July 1992

Consolidates certain enactments relating to social security contributions and benefits for Northern Ireland.

Social Security Administration (Northern Ireland) Act 1992, c. 8, 1 July 1992.

Provides for the consolidation of certain enactments relating to social security administration for Northern Ireland.

Social Security (Consequential Provisions) (Northern Ireland) Act 1992, c. 9, 1 July 1992

Provides for repeals, consequential amendments, transitional and transitory matters and savings in connection with the consolidation of enactments relating to the Social Security Administration (Northern Ireland) Act 1992 and the Social Security Contributions and Benefits (Northern Ireland) Act 1992.

Bingo Act 1992, c. 10, 6 May 1992

Amends the Gaming Act 1968 in relation to the advertising of bingo and associated establishments.

Aggravated Vehicle Taking Act 1992, c. 11, day or days to be appointed

Provides for a new offence under the Theft Act 1968 of aggravated vehicle taking, which relates to offences concerning mechanically propelled vehicles where, e.g. the vehicle is damaged or driven dangerously.

Taxation of Chargeable Gains Act 1992, c. 12, 6 April 1992

Consolidates certain enactments relating to the taxation of chargeable gains.

Further and Higher Education Act 1992, c. 13, day or days to be appointed

Makes new provision in relation to further and higher education mainly in relation to those responsible for further education and the types of institutions within the further education sector.

Local Government Finance Act 1992, c. 14, various dates, some to be appointed

Provides for the introduction of a new tax, the council tax, to replace the existing community charge (or poll tax) and provides local authorities with the power to levy and collect the tax.

Offshore Safety Act 1992, c. 15, various dates some to be appointed

Extends Part I of the Health and Safety at Work etc. Act 1974 to cover the safety, health and welfare of persons on offshore installations or engaged on associated pipeline work, covering the safety of the installations, pipelines and their construction and dismantling. The penalties for certain offences under Part I of the 1974 Act are increased; and for purposes connected with security of petroleum and petroleum products.

Nurses, Midwives and Health Visitors Act 1992, c. 16, day or days to be appointed

Amends the 1979 Act.

Coal Industry Act 1992, c. 17, day or days to be appointed

Makes provision for extending the duration of and increasing the limits on grants under the 1987 Act; also repeals the Coal Mines Regulation Act 1908.

Licensing (Amendent) (Scotland) Act 1992, c. 18, day to be appointed

Amends the provisions of the 1976 Act relating to the transfer of licences; and for connected purposes.

Local Government Act 1992, c. 19, various dates, some to be appointed

Gives effect to various proposals contained in the Citizens' Charter (Cm. 1599) relating to publicity and competition, provides for the securing of economy, efficiency and effectiveness in the manner in which local authorities carry on certain activities, and makes new provision relating to structural boundary and electoral changes.

Finance Act 1992, c. 20, 16 March 1922

Grants certain duties and alters others and amends the law relating to the national debt and the public revenue.

Consolidated Fund (No. 2) Act 1992, c. 21, 16 March 1992

Applies certain sums out of the Consolidated Fund for the service of the years ending 31 March 1991 and 1992.

Appropriation Act 1992, c. 22, 16 March 1992

Applies certain sums out of the Consolidated Fund for the years ending 31 March 1992 and 1993; appropriates supplies granted in the last session of Parliament and repeals certain Consolidated Fund and Appropriation Acts.

Access to Neighbouring Land Act 1992, c. 23, day to be appointed

Enables a person to gain access to neighbouring land in order to carry out works which are reasonably necessary for the preservation of his own land.

Offshore Safety (Protection against Victimization) Act 1992, c. 24, 16 March 1992

Protects employees working on offshore installations from victimization when acting as safety representatives or members of safety committees.

Prison Security Act 1992, c. 25, 16 May 1992

Makes provision for a new offence of prison mutiny and amends the existing law in relation to offences relating to assisting the escape of a prisoner.

Tourism (Overseas Promotion) (Wales) Act 1992, c. 26, 16 May 1992

Enables the Welsh Tourist Board to carry on activities abroad to promote tourism to and within Wales.

Parliamentary Corporate Bodies Act 1992, c. 27, 16 March 1992

Establishes corporate bodies to hold land and perform other functions for the benefit of the Houses of Parliament; and allows for the transfer of certain property, rights and liabilities to those bodies.

Medicinal Properties: Prescription by Nurses etc. Act 1992, c. 28, various dates, some to be appointed

Makes provision to authorize certain drugs and medicines to be prescribed by certain categories of nurses, midwives and health visitors.

Still-Birth (Definition) Act 1992, c. 29, various dates

Amends the law in respect of the definition of still-birth to cover a child born in the 24th week of pregnancy.

Traffic Calming Act 1992, c. 30, 16 May 1992

Makes provision about the carrying out of works on highways which affect the movement of vehicular and other traffic for the purpose of promoting safety and of preserving or improving the environment; and for connected purposes.

Firearms (Amendment) Act 1992, c. 31, 16 March 1992

Empowers the Secretary of State to extend the period for which firearm and shotgun certificates are granted or renewed.

Cheques Act 1992, c. 32, 16 June 1992

Amends the law relating to cheques, e.g. where a cheque is crossed 'a/c payee', it ceases to be transferable.

Social Security (Mortgage Interest Payments) Act 1992, c. 33, 16 March 1992

Provides that where mortgage interest is payable by a person (or his partner, etc.) who is entitled to income support, that part of the benefit shall, in certain cases, be paid directly to the lender; and for connected purposes.

Sexual Offence (Amendment) Act 1992, c. 34, various dates, some to be appointed

Extends the principle of anonymity for a victim of a rape to a victim of certain other sexual offences.

Timeshare Act 1992, c. 35, day to be appointed

Provides additional cancellation rights for those entering into an agreement in relation to its cancellation and the recovering of moneys spent.

Sea Fisheries (Wildlife Conservation) Act 1992, c. 36, 16 May 1992

Makes provision requiring appropriate ministers and relevant bodies to have regard in the discharge of their functions to the conservation of flora and fauna under the Sea Fisheries Acts.

Further and Higher Education (Scotland) Act 1992, c. 37, day or days to be appointed

Makes new provision in relation to further and higher education in Scotland; and for connected purposes.

Education (Schools) Act 1992, c. 38, various dates, some to be appointed

Provides with respect to the inspection of schools and with respect to the publication and distribution of information about schools and their pupils.

Army Act 1992, c. 39, 1 July 1992

Provides for serving members of the Ulster Defence Regiment to cease to be members at the end of June 1992; amends the Armed Forces Act 1960, s. 2; and makes provision for connected purposes.

Friendly Societies Act 1992, c. 40, day or days to be appointed

Makes further provision in relation to Friendly Societies.

Charities Act, 1992, c. 41, day or days to be appointed

Amends the 1960 Act; makes further provision in relation to the regulation of fund-raising activities carried on in connection with charities and in relation to public charitable collections; and for connected purposes.

Transport and Works Act 1992, c. 42, day or days to be appointed

Empowers the Secretary of State to make orders relating to the construction or operation of railways, tramways, trolley car vehicle systems, other guided transport systems and inland waterways; and for connected purposes.

Competition and Service (Utilities) Act 1992, c. 43, various dates, some to be appointed

Makes provision relating to the standards of performance and service in relation to the telecommunications, gas supply, water supply and sewerage service industries; makes provision with respect to customer complaints and the powers of the industry regulators; facilitates competition in certain of those industries; and for connected purposes.

Museums and Galleries Act 1992, c. 44, day or days to be appointed

Establishes Boards of Trustees of the National Gallery, Tate Gallery, National Portrait Gallery and the Wallace Collection; makes provision for the transfer of property between them and for their finance and of the Museums and Galleries Commission; and for purposes connected with museums and galleries.

Mauritius Republic Act 1992, c. 45, retrospective to 12 March 1992

Provides for Mauritius becoming a republic within the Commonwealth.

Non-domestic Rating Act 1992, c. 46, day or days to be appointed

Makes provision with respect to non-domestic rating between 11 March 1992 and 31 March 1995; and for connected purposes.

Appropriation Act 1992, c. 47, 16 July 1992

Applies certain funds for the service of the year ending 31 March 1992.

Finance (No. 2) Act 1922, c. 48, 16 July 1992

Grants certain duties, alters others and amends the law relating to the national debt and the public revenue. *Inter alia*, brings in a special income tax relief for those letting out part of their home.

Community Care (Residential Accommodation) Act 1992, c. 49, section 2 on 16 July 1992, section 1 on a day to be appointed

Provides for the amendment of the NHS and Community Care Act 1990 so as to remedy an existing defect in relation to the powers of local authorities to make arrangements for the provision of residential accommodation in hostels, etc.

Carriage of Goods by Sea Act 1992, c. 50, 16 September 1992

Replaces the Bills of Lading Act 1855 with new provisions with respect to bills of lading and other shipping documents; provides for amendments of the rights and liabilities attaching to such documents; and for connected purposes.

Protection of Badgers Act 1992, c. 51, 16 October 1992

Consolidates the law relating to the protection of badgers.

Trade Union and Labour Relations (Consolidation) Act 1992, c. 52, 16 October 1992

Consolidates various enactments relating to collective labour relations, including trades unions and employers' associations.

Tribunals and Inquiries Act 1992, c. 53, 1 October 1992

Consolidates various enactments relating to the construction, practice and procedure of tribunals and inquiries.

Human Fertilization and Embryology (Disclosure of Information) Act 1992, c. 54, 16 July 1992

Amends the Human Fertilization and Embryology Act 1990 in relation to the restriction on disclosure of information by a person to whom a licence under the 1990 Act applies.

WHITE PAPERS

Custody, Caring and Justice: The Way Ahead for the Prison Service in England and Wales, presented to Parliament by the Home Secretary (Kenneth Baker) on 16 September 1991, proposed:

- the establishment of a Criminal Justice Consultative Council to improve co-ordination within the criminal justice system
- the introduction of tighter security measures, including the installation of new security and emergency planning manuals in all prisons
- the introduction of an offence of prison mutiny
- prison governors to take greater responsibility for their own budgets and for some recruitment
- the establishment of a complaints adjudicator to act as an independent appeal body for complaints and disciplinary matters; boards of visitors to be relieved of their disciplinary powers
- the introduction of a training strategy for prison officers
- a pilot scheme for a code of standards covering the details of prison life; slopping-out to end by the end of 1994 and other conditions and facilities to be improved
- overcrowding to be ended by about 1995, after which date a system of ovecrowding certificates to be considered
- separate prison rules for unconvicted remand prisoners
- the acceptance of the principle of community prisons, although fundamental changes would take many years to complete
- the annual publication of an agreement between the Home Secretary and the Director-General of the Prison Service setting out objectives and resources for the coming year

Competing for Quality: Buying Better Public Services, presented to Parliament by the Financial Secretary to the Treasury (Francis Maude) on 18 November 1991, proposed:

- competitive tendering to be increased throughout Civil Service departments and agencies, achieving savings of £5,000 million
- services to be considered for contracting-out to include fisheries surveillance, Royal Marines amphibious training, electronic warfare training for the armed services, elements of national air defence, management of approved hostels, the electronic monitoring of curfew orders, the maintenance of court-houses in Scotland

People, Jobs and Opportunity, presented to Parliament by the Secretary of State for Employment (Michael Howard) on 11 February 1992, proposed:

- individuals to be encouraged to negotiate direct with their employers rather than through trade unions
- proposals to allow employers to seek compensation when newly-trained employees are 'poached' by rivals
- legislation to clarify the law relating to training contracts
- the introduction of vouchers for workers to buy careers guidance and counselling about training
- users of a public service to be enabled to take legal action against unlawful disruption caused by industrial action
- individuals to be allowed to join the trade union of their choice
- salaries of union leaders to be disclosed
- prevention of the abuse of arrangements for union subscriptions to be deducted from workers' pay
- an advisory group to be set up to look at ways of discouraging employers from discriminating against older people seeking jobs

A New Framework for Local Justice, presented to Parliament by the Lord Chancellor (Lord Mackay of Clashfern) and the Home Secretary (Kenneth Baker) on 26 February 1992, proposed:

- the creation of a new magistrates' courts inspectorate with lay members (to be operational by summer 1993)
- a gradual reduction in the number of magistrates' courts' committees in England and Wales from 105 to between 50 and 60
- magistrates' courts' committees to have a maximum of 12 members and to be able to co-opt non-magistrates
- a new corporate management team to be established in each committee area
- regular planning and performance reviews by the committees
- committees to be allowed to seek tenders from the private and public sectors
- further consultation about the courts' structure in London
- performance-related pay and fixed-term contracts for senior management staff
- a commitment to preserving the judicial independence of magistrates

A National Lottery: Raising Money for Good Causes, presented to Parliament by the Home Secretary (Kenneth Baker) on 6 March 1992, proposed:

- a national lottery to be set up by 1994
- tickets to be sold through shops and other outlets
- people over 16 to be allowed to buy tickets
- tickets to cost £1; 33 pence from each ticket sold to go to sport, charities and the arts; 15 pence to be spent on administration; the rest to be divided between prize money and tax
- consultation with charities over the impact of the scheme
- relaxation of the restrictions on football pools advertising
- proceeds not to be used to replace existing public expenditure
- the lottery to be administered by an independent board and run by a private contractor

Budgetary Reform White Paper, presented to Parliament by the Chancellor of the Exchequer (Norman Lamont) on 10 March 1992, proposed:

- from 1993 a combined spending and taxation statement each December to replace the current spring and autumn financial statements

The Health of the Nation, presented to Parliament by the Secretary of State for Health (Virginia Bottomley) on 8 July 1992, proposed the following targets:

- a reduction of 40 per cent in the number of deaths from coronary heart disease and strokes among people under 65 by the year 2000
- a reduction of 30 per cent in deaths from lung cancer among men and of 15 per cent among women by the year 2010
- a reduction of 25 per cent in deaths from breast cancer by the year 2000
- a reduction of at least 20 per cent in the number of deaths from cervical cancer by the year 2000
- a reduction of 15 per cent in the number of deaths from suicide by the year 2000
- a reduction of one third in the number of fatal accidents among children and people over 64 by the year 2005
- a reduction of at least 20 per cent in the incidence of gonorrhoea by 1995
- a reduction of 50 per cent in conceptions among girls under 16 by the year 2000
- a reduction of one third in the number of smokers and of 40 per cent in the number of cigarettes sold by the year 2000
- a reduction of 25 per cent in obesity levels among men and of one third among women by the year 2005
- a reduction of 30 per cent in the number of people drinking to excess by the year 2005
- a reduction in the incidence of drug misuse

New Opportunities for the Railways, presented to Parliament by the Transport Secretary (John MacGregor) on 14 July 1992, proposed:

- franchising, to be negotiated and monitored by a new Franchising Authority, to enable the private

sector to manage and operate passenger services
- the restructuring of British Rail to separate track and infrastructure (to be renamed Railtrack) from a residual operating company which would be responsible for running passenger services until they are franchised
- an independent regulator to be set up to protect passengers' interests and ensure fair pricing by Railtrack
- the sale of British Rail's freight and parcel businesses
- opportunities for railway stations to be sold or leased
- new operators to be given rights of access to the rail network

Choice and Diversity: A New Framework for Schools, published by the Secretary of State for Education (John Patten) on 28 July 1992, proposed:

- all schools to be encouraged to opt out of local authority control and obtain grant-maintained status; the procedure for balloting parents to be simplified; groups of small primary schools to be allowed to opt out together; existing cash incentives for schools to opt out to be reduced
- the Secretary of State for Education to have the power to remove governors from grant-maintained schools
- a Funding Agency for Schools to take over responsibility for allocating funds to grant-maintained schools; regional offices to be established when sufficient numbers of schools have opted out
- the Funding Agency to share overall responsibility for education with the local education authority, should 10 per cent of schools in the area opt out; and to take over most of the responsibilities should 75 per cent opt out
- local education authorities to retain responsibility for children with special needs, school transport, and other areas
- an Education Association, with regional offices, to take over the running of problem schools; the schools then to opt out without the need for a ballot of parents
- the National Curriculum Council and the School Examination and Assessment Council to merge to form the School Curriculum and Assessment Authority
- schools to be encouraged to specialize in particular areas, such as technology, sciences, business studies, languages or music
- efforts to be increased to reduce truancy levels in schools
- a review of religious education in schools to be undertaken by local education authorities; greater emphasis to be laid by teachers on the concepts of right and wrong
- the Office of Her Majesty's Chief Inspector of Schools to oversee independent inspections and identify problem schools; a full survey of schools in England to be completed within four years
- a Special Needs Tribunal to be set up
- the Secretary of State for Wales to establish 23 unitary authorities with responsibility for education and training

The Queen's Awards

The Queen's Award for Export Achievement and The Queen's Award for Technological Achievement were instituted by Royal Warrant in 1976. The two separate awards took the place of The Queen's Award to Industry, which had been instituted in 1965. In 1992 the scheme was extended with the launch of a third award, The Queen's Award for Environmental Achievement.

The awards are designed to recognize and encourage outstanding achievements in exporting goods or services from the United Kingdom and in advancing process or product technology. The purpose of the new award is to recognize and encourage product and process development which has major benefit for the environment and which is commercially successful.

The awards differ from a personal Royal honour in that they are given to a unit as a whole, management and employees working as a team. They may be applied for by any organization within the United Kingdom, the Channel Islands or the Isle of Man producing goods or services which meet the criteria for the awards. Eligibility is not influenced in any way by the particular activities of the unit applying, its location, or size. Units or agencies of central and local government with industrial functions, as well as research associations, educational institutions and bodies of a similar character, are also eligible, provided that they can show they have contributed to industrial efficiency.

Each award is formally conferred by a Grant of Appointment and is symbolized by a representation of its emblem cast in stainless steel and encapsulated in a transparent acrylic block.

Awards are held for five years and holders are entitled to fly the appropriate award flag and to display the emblem on the packaging of goods produced in this country, on the goods themselves, on the unit's stationery, in advertising and on certain articles used by employees. Units may also display the emblem of any previous current awards during the five years.

Awards are announced on 21 April (the actual birthday of The Queen) and published formally in a special supplement to the London Gazette.

Awards Office

All enquiries about the scheme and requests for application forms (completed forms must be returned by 31 October) should be made to: The Secretary, The Queen's Awards Office, Dean Bradley House, 52 Horseferry Road, London SW1P 2AG. Tel 071-222 2277.

EXPORT ACHIEVEMENT

The criterion upon which recommendations for an award for export achievement is based is a substantial and sustained increase in export earnings to a level which is outstanding for the products or services concerned and for the size of the applicant unit's operations. Account will be taken of any special market factors described in the application. Applicants for the award will be expected to explain the basis of the achievement (e.g. improved marketing organization or new initiative to cater for export markets) and this will be taken into consideration. Export earnings considered will include receipts by the applicant unit in this country from the export of goods produced in this country, and the provision of services to non-residents. Account will be taken of the overseas expenses incurred other than marketing expenses. Income from profits (after overseas tax) remitted to this country from the applicant unit's direct investments in its overseas branches, subsidiaries or associates in the same general line of business will be taken into account, but not receipts from profits on other overseas investments or by interest on overseas loans or credits.

In 1992, The Queen's Award for Export Achievement was conferred on the following concerns:

Aegis Group PLC, London SW1
Aerocontracts Ltd, Horley, Surrey
Ano-Coil Ltd, Milton Keynes
APV Crepaco Pumps Ltd, Eastbourne, East Sussex
Associated Timber Services Ltd, Newmarket, Suffolk
J. Barbour & Sons Ltd, South Shields, Tyne and Wear
Baxter Woodhouse & Taylor Ltd, Macclesfield, Cheshire
The Binding Site Ltd, Edgbaston, Birmingham
Bisley Office Equipment Ltd, Woking, Surrey
British Aerospace (Commercial Aircraft) Ltd, Hatfield, Herts
British Gas PLC, On Line Inspection Centre, Cramlington, Northumberland
British Soap Company Ltd, Bicester, Oxon
British Steel, General Steels (a division of British Steel PLC), Rotherham, South Yorkshire
Brittains (T.R.) Ltd, Hanley, Stoke-on-Trent
BWE Ltd, Ashford, Kent
Chase Research PLC, Basingstoke, Hants
Chloride Industrial Batteries Ltd, Swinton, Manchester
Chubb Safe Equipment Company, Wolverhampton
City Technology Ltd, Portsmouth
G. Clancey Ltd, Halesowen, West Midlands
Clerical Medical International Insurance Company Ltd, Douglas, Isle of Man
Colvern Ltd, Romford, Essex
Compaq Computer Manufacturing Ltd, Bishopton, Renfrewshire
Compu Inc. UK Ltd (t/a Computype), Hull
Compugraphics International Ltd, Glenrothes, Fife
Conoco Ltd, London SE1
Contour Seats Ltd, Farnborough, Hants
Coors Ceramics Electronics Ltd, Glenrothes, Fife
Data Connection Ltd, Enfield, Middx
C. Davidson & Sons, Aberdeen
Denge Power Projects Ltd, Milton Keynes
Domino Amjet Ltd, Bar Hill, Cambridge

Dowty Aerospace Gloucester Ltd, Gloucester
Dunlop International Technology Ltd ('DITL'), Birmingham
The Engineering Division of Dussek Campbell Ltd, Crayford, Kent
EBI Foods Ltd, Abingdon, Oxon
EES (Manufacturing) Ltd, Port Talbot, West Glamorgan
Euromoney Publications PLC, London EC4
Europa Scientific Ltd, Crewe, Cheshire
Fabdec Ltd, Ellesmere, Shropshire
The Staffware Division, Financial & Corporate Modelling Consultants PLC, London NW1
Format International Ltd, Woking, Surrey
Fortnum & Mason PLC, London W1
Fryett's Fabrics Ltd, Clifton, Manchester
Fulleon Ltd, Cwmbran, Gwent
GB Glass Engineering (a division of GB Glass Ltd), Chesterfield, Derbyshire
Gloverall PLC, London NW2
Gödel, Escher, Bach Ltd, London W1
GPT Payphone Systems, Liverpool
Gracefern Ltd (t/a Oakwood Design), Letchworth, Herts
Grants of Dalvey Ltd, Alness, Ross-shire
Helena Laboratories (UK) Ltd, Gateshead, Tyne and Wear
Hewitt-Robins International Ltd, Yoker, Glasgow
Hoyland Fox Ltd, Penistone, Sheffield
Huntleigh Technology PLC (Healthcare division), Luton
ICI Katalco Puraspec Purification Processes, Billingham, Cleveland
Imatronic Ltd, Newbury, Berks
International Additives Ltd, Wallasey, Merseyside
International Aerospace Ltd, Cranfield, Beds
International Rectifier Co. (GB) Ltd, Oxted, Surrey
Intersolar Group, High Wycombe, Bucks
Inver House Distillers Ltd, Airdrie, Lanarkshire
JLG Industries (Europe), Cumbernauld, Glasgow
R. G. C. Jenkins & Co, London SW1
Kemble & Company Ltd, Milton Keynes
The Kemble Instrument Company Ltd, Burgess Hill, West Sussex
Kyushu Matsushita Electric (UK) Ltd, Newport, Gwent
Linx Printing Technologies Ltd, Huntingdon, Cambs
London Business School, London NW1
Magnex Scientific Ltd, Abingdon, Oxon
Jim Marshall (Products) Ltd, Milton Keynes
Mayflower Glass Ltd, East Boldon, Tyne and Wear
MediSense Contract Manufacturing Ltd, Abingdon, Oxon
The Michael Ross Group Ltd, Hayes, Middx
More Fisher Brown, London E1
Motchman & Watkins (Theatre) Ltd (t/a Edwards and Edwards), London WC2
Neill Johnstone Ltd, Langholme, Dumfriesshire
Newbridge Networks Ltd, Newport, Gwent
Newman Martin and Buchan Ltd, London EC3
Nissan Motor Manufacturing (UK) Ltd, Sunderland
O.I.L. Ltd, Woking, Surrey
Orbit Valve PLC, Tewkesbury, Glos
Oxford Magnet Technology Ltd, Eynsham, Witney, Oxon
Pall Europe Ltd, Portsmouth, Hants
Pandrol UK Ltd, Worksop, Notts
Partridge Holdings PLC, Wotton-under-Edge, Glos
Pasminco Europe (Impalloy) Ltd, Bloxwich, Walsall
Penny & Giles Data Recorders Ltd, Christchurch, Dorset
Perfecseal Ltd, Londonderry
Peugeot Talbot Motor Company Ltd, Coventry
Phase 3 Ltd, near Skipton, North Yorkshire
Piccadilly Shoes Ltd, Manchester
Poker Plastics Ltd, near Moreton-in-Marsh, Glos
Polymark Futurail, Banbury, Oxon
Remploy Ltd (Knitwear Division), Alfreton, Derbyshire
Renishaw Transducer Systems Ltd, Wotton-under-Edge, Glos
Richard Coulbeck Ltd, Grimsby
Ritrama (UK) Ltd, Eccles, Manchester
Robinson & Hannon Ltd, Blaydon-on-Tyne, Tyne and Wear
Rolls-Royce PLC, Aerospace Group Civil Engine Business, Derby
Ross Breeders Ltd, Newbridge, Midlothian
L.A. Rumbold Ltd, Camberley, Surrey
SBJ Regis Low Ltd, London EC4
Schumacher Filters Ltd, Handsworth, Sheffield
Scotprime Seafoods Ltd, Ayr
Silverts Ltd, London EC1
Specialix Ltd, Byfleet, Surrey
Stakehill Engineering Ltd, Bolton
Starstream Ltd (t/a The Children's Channel), London WC2
Technic Group PLC, Burton-on-Trent, Staffs
Technigraph Products Ltd, Thetford, Norfolk
Thermomax Ltd, Bangor, Northern Ireland
Thorn Secure Science Ltd, Swindon
Thornton Precision Forgings Ltd, Sheffield
Tibbett Ltd, Wellingborough, Northants
Timsons Ltd, Kettering, Northants
Tiphook PLC, London SW1
University of Cambridge Local Examinations Syndicate, Cambridge
The University of Manchester Institute of Science and Technology, Manchester
Valpar Industrial Ltd, Bangor, Northern Ireland
Varn Products Company Ltd, Irlam, Greater Manchester
Vickers PLC, Cosworth Engineering Division, Northampton
Vikoma International Ltd, Cowes, Isle of Wight
Warwick International Ltd, Mostyn Holywell, Clwyd
Williams Fairey Engineering Ltd, Stockport, Cheshire
Xtrac Ltd, Wokingham, Berks
Yamazaki Machinery UK Ltd, Worcester

TECHNOLOGICAL ACHIEVEMENT

The criterion upon which recommendations for an award for technological achievement is based is a significant advance, leading to increased efficiency, in the application of technology to a production or development process in British industry or the production for sale of goods which incorporate new and advanced technological qualities.

In 1992 The Queen's Award for Technological Achievement was conferred on the following concerns:

The Escalator Division of APV Baker Ltd, Peterborough, Cambs – *heavy duty public service escalators*
Acorn Computer Group PLC, Cambridge – *ARM – 32 bit low cost RISC processor*
Amerada Hess Ltd, London W1 – *floating production facility for offshore production of oil and gas*
The Pharmaceutical Division of Amersham International PLC, Amersham, Bucks – *Ceretec, brain imaging agent*
Andergauge Ltd, Aberdeen – *adjustable stabilizer for drilled oil wells*
Babcock Energy Ltd, Renfrew – *low NOx axial swirl burner*
The Engineering Directorate of the British Broadcasting Corporation, London W12 – *stereo sound television (NICAM 728)*
The Midlands Research Station of the Research and Technology Division of British Gas PLC, Solihull – *regenerative burner system for fuel fired furnaces*

Cotswold Pig Development Company Ltd, Rothwell, Lincs – *genetic improvement of litter size in pigs*
Crosfield Electronics Ltd, Hemel Hempstead, Herts – *computerized pagination system*
Optical and Display Science Division of the Electronics Division of the Defence Research Agency, Malvern, Worcs – *advanced mixtures for liquid crystal displays*
Double R Controls Ltd, Heywood, Lancashire – *In-Line certification of magnetic media*
Filtronic Components Ltd, Shipley, West Yorkshire – *microwave switched multiplexer*
Glaxo Group Research Ltd, Greenford, Middx – *Cefuroxime axetil, an orally active broad spectrum β-lactamase resistant antibiotic*
Hotwork Development Ltd, Dewsbury, West Yorkshire – *regenerative burner system for fuel fired furnaces*
IBM United Kingdom Laboratories Ltd, Winchester, Hants – *mathematically-based computer software system*
The Insecticide Project Team of the Research and Development Department of ICI Agrochemicals, Haslemere, Surrey – *synthetic pyrethroid insecticides*
ICI Pharmaceuticals, Macclesfield, Cheshire – *Diprivan, an injectable general anaesthetic*
The Electrical Projects Group of In-Spec Manpower & Inspection Services Ltd, Dyce, Aberdeen – *non-invasive fault diagnosis in AC induction motors*
Lucas Nitrotec Services Ltd, Birmingham – *Nitrotec process to uprate engineering performance of low alloy steels*
The Stanmore Unit of Marconi Electronics Ltd, Stanmore, Middx – *integrated microwave receiver for satellite television*
The Industrial Chemical Division of Merck Ltd, Poole, Dorset – *advanced mixtures for liquid crystal displays*
Mercol Descaling Co. Ltd, Chesterfield, Derbyshire – *epoxy resin process for refurbishing potable water mains*
Ometron Ltd, London SE26 – *vibration pattern imager*
Oxford Lasers Ltd, Oxford – *100W copper laser*
Oxford University Computing Laboratory, Oxford – *mathematically-based computer software system*
Peboc Ltd, Anglesey, Gwynedd – *N-chlorophthalimide, a major pharmaceutical intermediate*
Pilkington Communications Systems Ltd, Rhyl, Clwyd – *optical backplane connector for cable termination*
Portakabin Ltd, York – *Pullman series of relocatable buildings*
Racal Radar Defence Systems Ltd, Chessington, Surrey – *radar identification system for defence purposes*
Rank Taylor Hobson Ltd, Thurmaston, Leicester – *Form Talysurf Series of measuring gauges based on computer technology*
Rover Group, Rover Power Train, Longbridge, Birmingham – *the K Series Engine*
Shelbourne Reynolds Engineering Ltd, Bury St Edmunds, Suffolk – *machinery to harvest small grain and seed crops*
Silsoe Research Institute, Silsoe, Beds – *machinery to harvest small grain and seed crops*
SmithKline Beecham Pharmaceuticals Research and Development, Epsom, Surrey – *Bactroban, an antibiotic for bacterial skin infections and elimination of nasal staphylococci*
TSL Group PLC, Wallsend, Tyne and Wear – *high purity quartz powder and ingots*
Vector Fields Ltd, Kidlington, Oxford – *software for electro-magnetic device research*
VideoLogic Ltd, King's Langley, Herts – *full motion digital video adaptor for personal computers*

ENVIRONMENTAL ACHIEVEMENT

The criterion upon which recommendations for an award for environmental achievement is based is a significant advance in the application by British industry of the development of products, technology or processes which offer major benefits in environmental terms compared to existing products, technology or processes. An award is only granted for products, technology or processes which have achieved commercial success.

The first winners of The Queen's Award for Environmental Achievement will be announced on 21 April 1993.

Science and Discovery

Asteroid Photographed

The first close-up photograph of an asteroid was achieved on 29 October 1991 when the NASA spacecraft *Galileo* flew past the minor planet 951 Gaspra at a distance of 1600 km. Because the main antenna could not be opened fully, communication with the spacecraft was via a small auxiliary antenna and telemetry could only be relayed back at a painfully slow 40 bits per second. To send back all the one billion bits of scientific data at that rate would have taken eight and a half months. Although *Galileo* took a total of 150 pictures, only about thirty are expected to show images of the asteroid. There was some uncertainty about the direction in which to point the camera as the position of the spacecraft along the track relative to the asteroid could only be determined to an accuracy of about 300 km. Consequently, the instruments on board had a wide field of view to ensure that the asteroid was located. The mission directors at the Jet Propulsion Laboratory decided that they would try to obtain only a limited amount of data and were successful in obtaining four images at various wavelengths. These show a heavily cratered body measuring 16 by 12 km, though it is believed that the actual size is about 20 by 12 by 11 km. The smallest details resolved are about 200 metres across but it is thought that the images stored on board the space vehicle have a fourfold improvement. At the press conference the imaging team commented that Gaspra appears to have had a catastrophic history. This is supported by ground-based spectroscopic data which indicates that the asteroid is not an unaltered primitive object but composed primarily of metal-rich silicates.

The bulk of the photographs, multispectral maps and other experimental data stored in the spacecraft will be transmitted back to Earth either when the main antenna is coaxed fully open or when the spacecraft swings past the Earth again at the end of 1992.

Asteroids beyond Uranus?

The normal belt for the asteroids lies between the orbits of Mars and Jupiter. There are many individual objects whose orbits take them inside that of the Earth but fewer have orbits going outside that of Jupiter. Until recently the asteroid with the largest known aphelion distance (point in orbit that is furthest from the Sun) was 2060 Chiron, with an aphelion of 19 astronomical units (Earth-Sun distance). This takes it well beyond the orbit of Saturn. Studies since its discovery show that it has produced comet-like emissions, suggesting that it may be a comet. But this definitely does not apply to an object discovered in 1991.

A faint photographic trail on a plate exposed on 18 February 1991 was discovered by Robert McNaught during a search for asteroids approaching Earth, a project being carried out at Siding Spring, Australia. Its orbit of this object extends from just inside Mars's orbit to well beyond that of Uranus, with an aphelion distance of 22.2 astronomical units. Its orbit was also found to be inclined at 62° to the ecliptic. The orbit was so unusual that observations of the object were made with larger instruments using charge-coupled devices (CCDs) to see if there was any evidence of a coma, the cloud of gas and dust around the nucleus of a comet, but nothing was found. A spectrogram in red light using the 3.9 metre Anglo-Australian Telescope also failed to show any cometary emissions. There are small variations in its brightness suggesting that it is rotating quite rapidly. The object's diameter is estimated to be about 5 km and its starlike image supports the theory that it is a genuine minor planet. Accordingly, it has been given the temporary label 1991DA.

ATP Manufacture

Two American chemists Arthur Broom and Nrusingha Mistra of the University of Utah have found a simple method of making adenosine triphosphate (ATP), a compound that is responsible for driving many of the metabolic processes in plants and animals. Previously the manufacturing process was very laborious, involving an inorganic detergent phosphate. The two chemists discovered the new process by accident when they were trying to make a diphosphate derivative of the nucleoside 1-amino-6-thiosine. The process involved reacting the nucleoside with phosphoryl chloride ($POCl_3$) and then with ordinary phosphate. The reaction did not proceed as expected and the chemists found that they had made 1-amino-6-thiosine 5-triphosphate. The entire process was carried out in a single reaction flask and it was not necessary to separate the intermediate products.

The chemists started by dissolving the nucleoside in trimethyl phosphate, added the reagent $POCl_3$, left the mixture for three hours and then added tributylammonium phosphate. They quenched the reaction with water and separated what they believed would be the diphosphate. They purified the product using a chromatographic technique. However, instead of the expected result they found that the yield was only a few percent of diphosphate but an 85 per cent yield of the triphosphate. They repeated the experiment with adenosine and produced a similar yield of ATP.

Jim Barber, a biochemist at Imperial College, says that the results of this work will be far reaching as ATP is the single most important molecule in biology. The ATP commercially available at present has to be extracted from horse muscle and other living tissues.

Apart from making the manufacture of ATP much easier, the discovery opens the door to making other biological triphosphates.

Beyond Pluto

For many years there has been circumstantial evidence to suggest that another planet lies beyond the orbit of Pluto. This evidence was based on the abnormal behaviour of Neptune and, to a lesser extent, Uranus in their orbit round the Sun. The latest survey of the sky, using data from the Infra-red Astronomical Satellite (IRAS), has provided no evidence to support the theory, even though the most likely area for the position of such a body, in the constellation of Centaurus, was covered by the survey. Although IRAS located about half a million infra-red sources, an orbiting planet would have been detected immediately because the source would have moved between successive scans by the satellite.

Work carried out using the *Voyager 2* spacecraft to Neptune has shown that the apparently abnormal behaviour of Neptune was due to incomplete knowledge of the planet's orbit and not to some external source. In addition, all modern surveys at optical wavelengths have failed to locate any body which could be labelled as the tenth planet. But this does not mean that the region beyond Neptune is empty. Recent theories suggest that the region contains a multitude of icy bodies, just a few kilometres across, which could be the nuclei of comets, and that many of them stray into the region of the known planets. This theory is supported by the outburst of Halley's comet, now thought to have been due to a collision with a small icy body. The surface features of some of the satellites of the outer planets also suggest that they have been bombarded with icy bodies and according to Alan Stern of the University of Colorado in Boulder, the three outermost planets all show signs of collision with an ice dwarf body between 100 and 2,000 km in diameter. A collision with Uranus tipped the planet's axis of rotation. Neptune could have captured its largest satellite, Triton, when Triton collided with another body. It is also thought a possibility that another collision split Pluto and its large moon Charon.

The discovery several years ago of Chiron, a body several hundred kilometres across, orbiting the Sun between Saturn and Uranus more or less puts a limit on the size of objects observers are capable of picking up from the Earth, but the next few years may provide important evidence for these theories.

Big Bang Ripples

The Big Bang theory for the formation of the Universe was established in 1964 when American radio astronomers discovered the background radiation coming from a gas at a temperature of 3°K. The existence of this radiation was predicted and it is thought to have come from the hot gas that filled the Universe soon after the Big Bang, currently thought to have occurred some 15,000 million years ago.

It has been known for a long time that the Universe is expanding. The theory is that all matter was concentrated in one spot at a single instant and that since then the Universe has been expanding at a constant rate. The Universe consisted of sub-atomic particles for about 300,000 years, but by the end of this time the temperature had dropped to about 3000°K and the particles began to combine to form atoms. Before this, the gas was more or less opaque with charged particles absorbing the radiation, but with the formation of neutrons, which are capable of absorbing only a small fraction of the radiation, the radiation was free to travel outwards. As the space expanded, the wavelength of the radiation gradually lengthened, making it appear as though it had come from a much cooler body.

It was this radiation that was recorded in 1964. It had the temperature predicted by theory and it had the same temperature all over the sky, because all directions point back towards the Big Bang. But here lay the problem. The Universe today is very lumpy, with galaxies collecting in clusters. These large formations must have originated from clouds of gas which were not evenly distributed. Therefore, the background radiation, if the theory is correct, should exhibit small temperature variations. A search for this variation has been taking place for the last quarter of a century.

One such search was carried out using NASA's Cosmic Background Explorer Satellite (COBE), which was placed into orbit round the Earth in 1989. It carried three instruments. Two observed the sky at long infra-red wavelengths. The third was designed to look for fluctuations in the background temperature. After much careful analysis, in which radiation from the Milky Way and instrument noise was extracted, a residual signal remained which showed that the temperature of the background radiation is not uniform. Bright spots occur in which the temperature is about 30 millionths of a kelvin warmer than the average, with an error of 5 millionths.

More work needs to be done before these results are accepted generally, but if they are correct the discovery will be one of the most sensational of all time.

Black Hole in our Galaxy

Black holes are believed to be objects where the material from which they are made is condensed to such an extent that the gravitational field set up around the object is so strong that even light cannot escape from it. There is still some doubt about the existence of such objects but recently astronomers have discovered a new candidate in the Milky Way, possibly the best evidence so far. This new object has been discovered in the constellation of Cygnus and is known as V404 Cygni. V404 Cygni lies about 5,000 light years away. The other suspected black holes in the Milky Way are Cygnus X-1 and A0620-00 in Monoceros.

The star system containing the black hole attracted the attention of astronomers in May 1989 when a burst of X-rays was detected by the Japanese satellite

Ginga. Optical studies following this outburst revealed that the star had gone nova and was shining 1,000 times more brightly for a short time. A nova outburst had previously been recorded in 1938. Astronomers from Spain and Britain, using the 4.2 metre William Herschel Telescope in the Canary Islands, identified a yellow star, a little cooler than the Sun, orbiting a dark object with a period of 6.47 days, at a speed of at least 211 km per second. From this data the astronomers have concluded that the dark companion must have a mass of at least 6.3 times that of the Sun, but is most likely to be between eight and 15 times solar mass. Because the dark object's mass greatly exceeds the three times solar mass attributed to neutron stars, it is felt that the object must be a black hole.

However, investigators believe that the situation is not straightforward. They think the system involves three stars. The yellow component is too distant from the black hole to transfer mass to the black hole. The observed periodicity of 5.8 hours in the light from the system indicates that there is a third star, a red dwarf, an object much fainter and cooler than the Sun, very close to and orbiting the black hole in about 5.8 hours. It is this object which is transferring material to it and so producing the outbursts.

The surprising presence of spectral lines representing lithium in the yellow star, usually associated with young stars, can be explained by X-rays from the accretion disc of the black hole smashing into the heavier atoms on the yellow star and splitting them into lighter elements.

Cloud Upsets Cosmologists

A cloud of gas situated towards the edge of the observable Universe and containing molecules of carbon monoxide has presented cosmologists with a problem. They already have difficulty in explaining how galaxies and quasars formed so early in the history of the Universe. The existence of a molecular cloud with a red shift of 2.29 indicates that the cloud was formed when the Universe was less than one tenth of its present age. Such a cloud could only have been formed from atoms synthesized in the interior of an earlier generation of stars and flung into space by events such as supernovae explosions. Current theories do not explain how this could have happened so quickly after the Big Bang, the point at which the Universe was created.

Robert Brown and Paul Vanden Bout of the National Radio Astronomy Observatory at Charlottesville, Virginia, used the 12 metre telescope at Kitt Peak, Arizona, to identify the spectral lines from the carbon monoxide molecule. The frequency of this emission is 345 gigahertz (GHz) but because of the huge red shift, the emission was observed at a frequency of 105 GHz. From the intensity of the spectral lines, the scientists calculated the amount of carbon monoxide in the cloud and, assuming that the ratio of carbon monoxide to hydrogen is the same as that in our own galaxy, showed that the cloud has a mass 100 times greater than that of the Milky Way. The cloud is a diffuse object with a diameter of about 60,000 light years.

Because of the problems that arise with current theories, cosmologists are beginning to think that stars and galaxies are formed more quickly than originally thought and are based on the presence of cold dark matter. Some suggest that a generation of supergiant stars was formed before the first galaxies and that these stars produced the heavy elements found in many stars, but others think this unlikely.

Clover as Natural Fertilizer

Scientists at the Agriculture and Food Research Council's Institute of Grassland Environmental Research have found that clover can be used as an alternative to chemical fertilizers and pesticides in cereal growing.

Clover extracts nitrogen from the air and bacteria in nodules on the clover root convert it into a form suitable for use as a fertilizer. In the past farmers have planted it along with rye-grass to provide good grazing. The latest idea is to exploit its properties by planting it with cereals. The clover not only fertilizes the crop but also acts as a pesticide because beetles and spiders make their homes in the clover, preying on aphids and other insects.

For the last few years Lewis Jones, leader of the team of researchers, has been comparing the crop yields of cereals fertilized by chemical fertilizers with those of cereals sown in ground in which white clover was planted beforehand. He found that a mixture of winter wheat and clover did at least as well as the chemically fertilized wheat. As the cereal grows it cuts off light to the clover, killing some and so releasing nitrogen into the soil. It has been calculated that about 100 kg of nitrogen per hectare is released into the soil by this process, a figure comparable with that from artificial fertilizers. In addition, Jones found that the clover plots had far fewer aphids and slugs than neighbouring land. He also found that by planting the cereal wider apart, some of the clover had enough sunlight to survive beyond the harvest and recolonize the plot in time for the next crop.

The clover-wheat mixture can be used year after year, but leaving the ground without cereal for a year gives more time for the clover to recover. The significant advantage of this discovery, apart from the obvious environmental one, is the negligible cost for the fertilizer and pesticide.

Dinosaurs in Australia

In the summer of 1991 a team of 40 scientists searched an area covering hundreds of square kilometres in Western Australia and in a three-week period found more than 500 shark teeth, 12 jaws from a previously unknown species of elephant shark, three vertebrae from a large marine reptile like a mosasaur, and identified the tracks of stegosaurs. The fossils are thought to be between 120 and 66 million years old.

The marine specimens were found along the Exmouth Gulf, some 1,150 km north of Perth, and the dinosaur footprints near Broome in the extreme north of Western Australia. Amongst the teeth are about thirty which came from the jaw of a single specimen. John Long of the West Australian Museum in Perth, who organized the expedition, is of the opinion that the creature was 4.5 metres in length, similar to the great white whale. Noel Kemp, of the Tasmanian Museum in Hobart, thinks that the shark is a member of the genus *Otodus*. If this is correct it is the earliest appearance of the genus, which has not been recorded elsewhere until the Tertiary period. Long is of the opinion that when the finds have been thoroughly studied, they may find as many as five unknown types of shark. The newly discovered shark fills a major gap in the fossil record and may throw more light on the extinction of so many species 65 million years ago when the Earth was hit by a huge meteoroid or comet.

From the tracks found at Broome, the investigators have identified seven types of dinosaur, including stegosaurs, tyrannosaurs, brontosaurs and iguaodons, which lived in the area between 110 and 120 million years ago. The identification of the stegosaurs has solved the problem of the apparent absence of these creatures in Australia. This was originally thought to have been due to the fact that Australia split away from Antarctica about 100 million years ago, but the discovery shows that the dinosaurs dominated life on Earth for 150 million years on every continent.

Fullerene Chemistry

In the last few years there have been rapid developments in our understanding of the fullerene compounds. The first compound, known as buckminsterfullerene, consists of a regular surface array of 60 carbon atoms. Japanese chemists have produced polymers in which the fullerenes are glued together using palladium atoms. They have made three types, with approximate formulae $C_{60}Pd$, $C_{60}Pd_2$ and $C_{60}Pd_3$, corresponding to one-, two- and three-dimensional polymers. The polymers are electrically neutral and stable in air, in contrast to other metal derivatives. For example, the equivalent three-dimensional with the formula $C_{60}K_3$ is superconducting but unstable in air.

One of the problems in reacting fullerenes with other compounds is that they are hydrophobic, or water-hating, and so it has been impossible to dissolve the molecules in water. This problem has been partially overcome by the work of Swedish scientists at the University of Technology at Gothenburg. They enclosed the fullerene molecules in a large water-soluble host, a doughnut-shaped, cyclic molecule known as cyclodextrin. The cyclodextrins consist of six, seven or eight sugar molecules joined together in a ring. Although γ-cyclodextrin, which has eight sugar molecules, is soluble in water, it has a hydrophobic cavity, which means that the fullerene stays in this hole rather than roaming freely in the water. The Swedes believe that the reaction of fullerenes in water will differ from their reaction in organic solvents, possibly producing new products.

Work at the Universities of Exeter and Nottingham has concentrated on the development of rules to predict the structures of fullerenes containing more than 60 carbon atoms. These rules are based on several requirements. One requirement is that carbon atoms must use up all four of their outermost electrons for a stable structure. Also, using a theory developed by Erich Hucket in the 1930s, it was found that the football structure of buckminsterfullerene was the most stable of 1,760 differing ways in which 60 carbon atoms can combine to form a single cage-shaped molecule. The British scientists also used the theory to develop series of fullerenes with more than 60 carbon atoms. In the case of a closed cage containing 84 atoms, the 30,000 possible combinations were reduced to three stable ones. Of these, one is of great interest because it is chiral, i.e. it is capable of existing in right- and left-hand forms. Recently American chemists have isolated a small amount of C_{84} and work is going on to clarify the structure.

A fullerene with 76 carbon atoms has been isolated by American chemists but unlike the regular outline of the earlier ones, this new one is slightly twisted. In the case of C_{60} all the atoms occupy equivalent positions, which means that its nuclear magnetic resonance (NMR) spectrum has a single peak. The spectrum of the complex C_{70} has five peaks but C_{76} has 19 peaks. This means that there are 19 ways in which a carbon atom can be attached to its neighbours. This compound is also chiral.

Gamma Ray Source Detected

NASA's Gamma Ray Observatory (GRO) was launched in April 1991 and like previous satellites launched to investigate a new region of the electromagnetic spectrum, it has produced some sensational results, many of them completely unexpected. The satellite has on board instruments capable of recording gamma rays of almost all frequencies and in greater detail than earlier experiments. Gamma rays have very high energies and are generated during the most violent events, such as supernova explosions. Before the launch of the satellite, gamma-ray bursts had been recorded coming from across the whole sky.

In early June 1991, the planned survey of the sky was changed to a study of the series of intense flares which had suddenly erupted on the Sun. These eruptions were responsible for the sightings of aurorae at low latitudes. The GRO made high quality measurements of several solar outbursts. After the active region on the Sun responsible for these outbursts had disappeared round the Sun's western limb, the GRO was reprogrammed to its normal mode.

A month later it was announced that the GRO had discovered the most distant and luminous gamma-ray source ever recorded. The source lies in the constellation of Virgo and it was found to be a variable quasar 3C279 at a distance of 7,000 million light years. The quasar is emitting ten million times more energy than the entire Milky Way. Because of the intensity of the outburst, it would have been detected by satellites launched in the 1970s if it had existed then, so in about nine years the quasar has developed from high energy obscurity to the brightest gamma-ray source in the sky.

Many of these discoveries were made from two of the experiments on board the satellite. The Burst and Transient Source Experiment and the Oriented Scintillation Spectrometer Experiment use the fact that low energy gamma rays create tiny flashes of light, which are amplified using photomultipliers. The results obtained do not conform to current theoretical models so ideas about the formation of these rays need to be modified drastically.

Gold from Bacteria

A study of gold grains, known as placer gold, was carried out by John Watterson of the US Geological Survey and he found that the grains were attached to bacteria. He examined gold from Lillian Creek, Alaska, under a scanning electron microscope and found lace-like networks resembling the common bacteria *Pedmicrobium*. It is not certain how the gold particles collect on the surface of the bacteria but one theory suggests it may be a chemical residue which is left after bacteria break down the humic acids in the Alaskan soil; such acids contain gold. Another possibility is that the gold comes from enzyme activity outside the bacterial cell. It is certainly not a purely Alaskan phenomenon because similar lacy particles have been found in China and South Africa, the former on rocks 220 million years old and the latter on rocks 2.8 billion years old. The formation of the gold is a very slow process; it is estimated that a 0.1 mm gold grain takes at least a year to grow.

Another source of microscopic gold is the volcano Mount Erebus, the largest volcano in Antarctica. American geologists have detected particles measuring 0.1 to 20 micrometers across in the volcanic gases, and other particles up to 60 micrometres in the surrounding snow. Although other volcanoes have been found to emit gold, Mount Erebus is the only one known to do so in metallic form. Lava from Mount Erebus emits hot gas which carries the gold, together with other materials which are volatile at 1,000°C. On contact with the air, it quickly cools to 100°C, precipitating metals such as zinc and copper within about a metre of the hot lava. It is thought that the gas contains too little gold to form crystals in the air and so crystallizes at the crusty surface of the lava. Because the gas is emitted slowly, the particles are thought to grow for minutes or even hours before the gas blows them into the atmosphere.

Hydrogen in Earth's Core

Little is known about the composition of the Earth's core. Seismologists have obtained its density by measuring the velocity of waves passing through it. From this they have deduced that the inner core, which has a radius of 1200 km, is made up of pure, solid iron. They know that the outer region of the core is liquid because shear waves cannot pass through it. However, the change in density at the inner-outer core boundary is thought to be too great for a simple change from liquid to solid. It appears that the outer core is not made of pure liquid iron but of iron combined with some lighter elements. Hydrogen is one possibility but little is known about the high temperature–high pressure chemistry of the conditions existing in those regions.

Work carried out by John Badding, Russell Hemley and Ho-Kwang of the Carnegie Institution in Washington suggests that hydrogen is the element responsible. They subjected iron and hydrogen to pressures up to 62 gigapascals, more than 600,000 atmospheres, in a diamond anvil cell. When the pressure reached 3.5 gigapascals, the iron swelled and the hydrogen around it flowed into it suddenly, the metal changing from a smooth shiny state to granular. The hydride formed was found to be stable up to the highest pressures reached. By studying the decrease in volume of the hydride with increasing pressure, the researchers have forecast that it will remain stable for pressures over 100 gigapascals, the pressure thought to exist in the outer regions of the Earth's core. They have also predicted that the density at pressures similar to those found at the inner–outer core boundary, i.e 330 gigapascals, is in agreement with the values obtained by the seismologists.

More research is required before it is clear whether this iron hydride is the answer to the problems involved in studying the inner regions of the Earth.

Iceberg Tracking

During 1986 some 13,000 square kilometres of the Filchner Barrier broke away from the main Antarctic land mass to form a floating island. As the ice broke away, it split into three large detached masses. At the time it was thought that these islands would become trapped close to their original positions because the ice thickness (230–250 metres) was only slightly less than the depth of the fairly shallow water in the area (about 250–300 metres). This was the case until early 1990, when one of the islands, which had an area of about 3,800 square kilometres, started to be carried away by the sea currents. It drifted across the Weddell Sea, along the eastern coast of the Atlantic Peninsula and by August 1991 it had reached the South Atlantic Ocean, about 100 km east of Clarence Island (South Shetland Islands). By this time it had lost about 20 per cent of its original size, now being about 83 km long and 54 km wide.

Between 28 August and 9 September 1991 a large iceberg of about 300 square kilometres broke away and subsequently broke into four smaller fragments, but the main mass continued its motion northwards at a rate of about 5 km per day. In January 1992 it stopped its northward motion and drifted westwards for about a fortnight before recommencing its northerly track. Observations in February and March 1992 indicated that it may have grounded at a position about 51°S. lat. and about 47°W. long., roughly halfway between the Falkland Islands and South Georgia.

The iceberg is monitored constantly by geostationary and polar-orbiting satellites. Apart from the need for accurate information about its position, precise tracking will lead to a better understanding of the sea currents in that part of the Atlantic Ocean.

Ice on Mercury

Mercury is a very difficult planet to study because of its closeness to the Sun. Two important steps in unravelling its mysteries occurred in 1965 and 1974. In 1965, radar observations showed that the rotational period was 59 days, exactly two-thirds its orbital period. In 1974, *Mariner 10* sent back photographs of its surface showing it to be very similar to that of the Moon. Being very near to the Sun, temperatures on the planet's surface are quite high, over 500°C in places. But surprisingly, recent observations suggest that ice may exist in the polar regions.

During its passage through inferior conjunction in August 1991, i.e. when the planet moves between the Earth and the Sun, presenting its dark side to the Earth, radar studies carried out by American astronomers indicate that in the north polar region there exists a feature which is thought to be an ice-cap. The characteristics of this bright patch are exactly the same as those of the south polar cap on Mars. Icesheets found on the Earth's surface absorb microwave energy but if they are cooled sufficiently, they become very good reflectors of radar waves. If the bright patches on Mercury are due to ice, it is necessary to find the conditions which make this possible.

The inclination of the planet's spin axis to its orbital plane is virtually 90° so that Mercury's equator is always directly under the Sun. This means that neither pole of the planet ever sees more than a sliver of the Sun's disc above the horizon. Sunlight would merely graze the surface and any depression would be permanently in shadow. The tidal lock, which causes the planet to rotate exactly one and a half times during the 88-day orbital period also produces circumstances which favour the formation of very cold conditions in selected areas. The eccentric orbit of Mercury round the Sun should theoretically produce an elliptical cap measuring about 400 by 100 km. This seems to match the dimensions of the bright patch observed on the planet. However, there are several factors which suggest that the ice theory is not tenable, so more observations are required before the existence of the ice-cap is confirmed.

Impact Craters in Argentina

In 1989 Ruben Lianza, an Argentine Air Force captain, became curious about a group of elliptically-shaped depressions while flying not far from the city of Rio Cuarto in north central Argentina. Being an amateur astronomer he thought they might have an impact origin and so sent photographs to the editors of *Sky and Telscope*, the American astronomical magazine. After nearly two years of correspondence and discussion, an expedition was organized to study the region in detail. This was led by Peter Schultz of Brown University, Providence, Rhode Island, and included a specialist in crater erosion, John Grant, as well as Lianza.

The expedition found ten elliptical depressions with a 4:1 length to width ratio along a 50 km line running north-east to south-west, eight of which occurred within a corridor 30 km long and only 2 km wide. The most northern one is the largest, 4.5 km long; 11 km to the south west lie two craters side by side, each being 3.5 km long. Three more adjacent craters, less than a kilometre long, are situated some 5 km further along the line. The three largest features have poorly defined rims at the ends of the long axis but the rims are well defined along the sides, reaching 3.7 metres above the surrounding plain. The floors are about 7 metres below the plain. The smaller features are better-preserved than the larger ones.

Amongst the stones picked up in the area were meteorites and impactites. The interior of a larger impactite was found to be laced with deformed grains of quartz, indicating exceedingly high pressures at the time of the impact. Some of the glassy chunks of fused dirt appeared to bear the indentation of the plants they were thrown against at the time they were molten.

It is thought that within the last 10,000 years, a small object (or objects) with a diameter of about 150 metres approached the area from the north east at an angle of less than 15° and produced the main crater. Pieces of the object then ricocheted, causing the secondary and smaller craters. The low angle of the approach and the fact that it happened recently makes the feature exceptionally important. Statistically, an event of this size and approach angle should occur every three million years.

Largest Living Creature

For years pride of place as the largest living organisms has gone to the giant redwood trees of North America and the female blue whale. However, in April 1992 this top position was reported to be challenged by the discovery of a fungus *Armillaria bulbosa*, which infests tree roots. The fungus was found in a forest in north Michigan, USA; it weighs more than 10,000 kg and covers an area of about 15 hectares. A giant redwood can weigh up to ten times as much but most of it is dead wood. According to Myron Smith and James Anderson of Michigan Technical University and Toronto University, the fungus has been growing for the last 1,500 years.

Within two months, a report of an even larger fungus made *A. bulbosa* seem quite small. This new fungus *Armillaria ostayae* is also known as the honey fungus. It is found near Mount Adams in Washington State, USA, and is reported to cover an area of 600 hectares. Terry Shaw of the US Forest Service measured its size several years ago and is of the opinion that it is between 500 and 1,000 years old. It spreads from root to root, passing between trees where they make contact below the ground. It attacks the roots of the conifers, eventually killing them. In the past forest fires kept the forests open, limiting contact between the trees, but settlers curbed the forest fires and the forests grew thicker. Only the largest trees were chopped down but the stumps were left in the ground to decay, speeding up the spread of the fungus. In the early 1970s the practice of removing the stumps was started in order to curb fungal activity. The plan is to keep healthy trees at least six metres from any sign of infection. If these activities are successful in curbing the growth of fungi, then it is possible that such large specimens will not be found in future.

Local Group of Galaxies

A faint galaxy lying in the constellation of Tucana was discovered by American astronomers in the 1980s. Australian astronomers at the Siding Spring Observatory, using the 1 metre and later the 3.8 metre Anglo-Australian Telescope, showed that it belonged to the Local Group of Galaxies. This group contains about 30 members but most can be considered as satellite galaxies to the two largest members, the Andromeda galaxy and our own Milky Way.

The Tucana galaxy is less than 3 million light years away, a little farther than the Andromeda galaxy, which is 2.2 million light years distant. It is a dwarf galaxy, only about half a million times brighter than the Sun, and lies in a region within the Local Group which has few galaxies. Both the Andromeda galaxy and the Milky Way have about ten satellite galaxies but the distance of the Tucana feature from the two main galaxies indicates it is not a satellite of either at present. In fact it lies on the opposite side of the Milky Way from Andromeda.

The brightest stars in the galaxy are very faint, having a magnitude of about 22, some two and a half million times fainter than the faintest star visible to the naked eye. Overall the Tucana dwarf is elliptical in shape, with one axis twice as long as the other. The major axis is only 4,000 light years in length compared with the Milky Way's diameter of 130,000 light years.

The history of the feature within the group is uncertain. It may have escaped from the two large galaxies, alternatively it may have only recently joined the group. More information on its origin may be available when its motion is measured accurately by determining its red (or blue) shift. Because of the faintness of the stars, this will be very difficult.

Lunar Rock in Australia

A small meteorite, 3 cm across and weighing only 19 grams, which was found on the Nullabour Plain in Australia, has been identified as coming from the Moon. This is the first one found outside the Antarctic continent, where 11 lunar meteorites were collected between 1979 and 1989.

Robert Haag of Tucson, Arizona, is well-known for his large private collection of extraterrestrial material and recently he was examining some meteorites which he had purchased some three years earlier. They had been found in 1960 at Calcalong Creek. Although similar in appearance to the rest, one specimen had subtle differences in colour and texture so it was put on one side for further study. Haag cut the fusion crust and ground off a corner to look at the internal structure of the rock. He immediately noticed tiny flecks of white rock within the dark grey matrix, a feature he had seen previously in close-up photographs of lunar rocks. Haag took it to the University of Arizona where it was analysed and found to have iron/manganese and potassium/lanthanum ratios differing from terrestrial rocks but similar to the values found in lunar rocks. The analysis also found a 20 per cent fraction of KREEP (potassium, rare earth elements and phosphorus) similar to that found in the Apollo 14 and Apollo 16 lunar samples. The meteorite is a breccia containing material from both the lunar highlands and the maria.

The specimen is undergoing further studies and comparisons are being made with the lunar meteorites from the Antarctic to see if it was ejected from the Moon at the same time as any of the Antarctic specimens. These studies should also provide information on the transfer of impact ejecta from the Moon to the Earth.

Magellan at Venus

In May 1991 the *Magellan* spacecraft completed its first scan of the planet Venus and then turned its side-looking radar from left to right to scan the planet for a second time from a different angle. This was scheduled for completion on 15 January 1992 but on 4 January a transmitter failure brought the scan to a halt after 95 per cent of it had been completed. Mapping was successfully started again twenty days later but the backup transmitter did not function properly so radar scans were limited to between 18° and 76° northern latitudes. This third scan of the planet is being devoted to obtaining stereo photographs. It is hoped to complete it by September 1992 and then the spacecraft's orbit will be lowered by 100 km. This will improve the 120 metre resolution and permit a study of gravitational anomalies of the planet.

The results from *Magellan* reveal that in the past Venus has been volcanically active, with huge volcanoes, massive lava flows, mountain ranges and chasms, but whether this activity continues is uncertain. The surface is generally quite young and contains craters which are less than 800 million years old. The youngest crustal material has been found at the summit of Maat Mons, a 8 km high peak. The radar-bright lava flows at the top of the peak are not as radar reflective as those on other mountain peaks. It is thought that the material is less than 10 million years old and therefore has not weathered as much as the rocks elsewhere.

Of great interest are the meandering channels. One channel is only 2 km wide but it runs for over 6,800 km. The near constant width implies that it was formed by a fast-flowing liquid, possibly the same lava flows that flooded the plains. Some of the channels flow up and over hills, so it is possible that plains that originally were flat have been tilted subsequently by ground movement.

Magnetic Organic Compounds

A team from Japan, led by Minoru Kinoshita of the University of Tokyo, have produced a magnet made from atoms of carbon, hydrogen, nitrogen and oxygen, constituents common in organic compounds but completely different from those which normally produce ferromagnetic properties. This strong magnetic property is only apparent at a very low temperature, 0.65°K. It is, however, an important step in the search for organic magnets which are stable at room temperatures. Such materials would have numerous applications, from lightweight motors to new methods of data storage. The discovery highlights the modern shift in the manufacture of magnets from the metallurgical to the organic laboratory.

Although there have been past discoveries of magnetism in organic compounds, the magnetism has been very weak. The ferromagnetic behaviour of this new compound (para-nitrophenyl-nitronyl-nitroxide, or, p-NPNN for short) originates from its unpaired electron, but the team say that they are still investigating the magnetic behaviour of the crystal in detail. For the material as a whole to be ferromagnetic, all the unpaired electron spins must interact so that they are all aligned in a common direction.

Other research groups are carrying out similar research with organic compounds which have metals incorporated in their molecules. One team in the USA discovered a compound which was ferromagnetic to a temperature as high as 350°K. This satisfies the room temperature criterion but unfortunately the compound is unstable in air. However, progress is being made and it may not be too long before organic compounds with ferromagnetic properties are commonplace.

Oldest Known Mollusc

Chitons are small marine animals with soft bodies and a shell, and are members of the mollusc family. They were regarded as a minor offshoot of molluscs until the discovery at the Yorke Peninsula in South Australia of a chiton which is at least 550 million years old. This suggests that chitons emerged no later and possibly earlier than other forms of molluscs, including the gastropods and bivalves. Karen Golette-Holmes of the South Australia Museum says that the discovery means that most classes of molluscs were well established by the Cambrian period. The oldest known chiton, prior to the recent find, came from late Cambrian deposits in Queensland and North America and were thought to have ages of about 520 million years. The discovery at Horse Gully near Ardrossan in South Australia was found in marine deposits from the early Cambrian, with ages between 550 and 600 million years.

The chiton had a length of less than a centimetre but the basic structure is no different from the modern-day chitons, which can be as long as 30 cm. The creature had a shell composed of eight overlapping plates, and was initially described by Simon Conway Morris of Cambridge University as operculum-like and given the name *Triplicatella disdoma.* An operculum is a plate which closes the aperture of the shell of some molluscs when the animal is retracted. Later analysis by Gowlett-Holmes and Adam Yates confirmed that the animal was a chiton.

Ötze: Neolithic Man

On 19 September 1991 two German hikers discovered a frozen corpse in a Tyrolean mountain pass at an altitude of some 3,200 metres. At first it was believed to be the remains of a recent climber in the area but an examination of the relics found with the corpse suggested that this was not the case. Rainer Henn, a forensic scientist from Innsbruck University, was asked to examine the body and immediately recognized the importance of the find. The corpse was packed in ice and sent back to Innsbruck, where it was examined by Konrad Spindler, head of the University's Institute of Prehistory. It quickly became apparent that the corpse was probably about 4,000 years old and the body of a man from the Bronze Age.

Political wranglings over the ownership of the body and arguments about the best way to preserve the corpse were sorted out by Christmas 1991.

Studies of the Bronze Age have been mainly via remains found in graves but on this occasion it appears that Ötze, as the body was named, was not buried deliberately but was killed by an accident of some kind. Not only were the skin and internal organs in perfect condition but so were the artifacts that surrounded the body. The wooden handles of his tools were still intact. The body will not be dismembered for scientific tests but the investigators will use all the latest techniques to study it. For example, a few years ago it would have needed 30 grams of tissue for a determination of the age but now just 1 milligram is needed for a carbon dating.

The carbon-dating tests have shown that the body is much older than originally thought. Tests carried out in Sweden and Paris indicate that the body is between 4,600 and 4,800 years old, bringing it out of the early Bronze Age into the late Neolithic. The man was between 20 and 40 years old at his death. Close to the corpse were found animal bones and dried fruit, including small plums. Ötze carried a backpack built around a wooden frame. This and some of his leather clothes have decayed but his leather trousers have survived and are in good condition. They were found to be packed with dry grass for insulation. A quiver was found containing 14 arrows just under a metre long, together with a bow he was making when he died. A fascinating aspect was the discovery of tattoo marking on his body.

A full report of the discovery has yet to be made public.

Potent New Painkiller

For a long time morphines have been one of the most widely used painkillers but this role may be severely curtailed by the discovery of a new drug which is some 200 times more effective than morphine. The new discovery was made by a team of chemists led by John Daly at the National Institute of Health at Bethesda, Maryland. The chemical was extracted from the skin of a frog found in Equador, South America. The team obtained 60 milligrams of material from about 750 frogs and then purified it using chromatographic techniques, to produce 24 milligrams of a chemical called epibatidine (after the frog *Epipedobates tricolor*). The compound was found to have a chemical formula $C_{11}H_{13}N_2Cl$ and to consist of a pyridine ring with a chlorine atom attached to it, the whole attached to another ring of six carbon atoms with a nitrogen bridge across the middle.

This new chemical compound is the first identified member of a completely new class of alkaloids and is of a kind which is rarely found in animals. Its importance lies in the fact that it is a very powerful painkiller. One of the tests used by Daly and his colleagues is the so-called hot plate test. If a rat is dropped on to an electrically heated plate which is too hot, it will normally leap into the air. If the animal is injected with a strong painkiller, it will remain standing on the plate. Most rats will remain on the plate if injected with morphine equivalent to 1 mg per kilogram body weight. With epibatidine, this could be achieved by using only 5 micrograms per kilogram body weight.

Of great interest to the chemists is the function of the chlorine atom attached to the pyridine ring. If it is found that this atom is involved in the compound's analgesic properties, its replacement by other elements may open the door to a class of painkillers even more powerful than epibatidine.

Scorpion Colony in Britain

Scorpions are usually associated with warm climates so the existence of a colony in the Isle of Sheppey comes as a surprise to many people. The cold British winters should have killed them off but they have survived for more than 120 years.

Tim Benton of the University of Cambridge has made a study of these rather elusive creatures, which live in cracks in walls and seem to venture out only at nights, principally for food and sex. He tagged 162 scorpions and watched their noctural habits using an ultraviolet lamp which made the creatures fluoresce bright green. Their main food is the woodlouse but they sometimes prey on each other. They can manage without food for surprisingly long periods. Benton records that one of them lived for 17 months on one housefly. He also found that the females leave the shelter of the cracks no more than ten times a year but the males become more adventurous during the mating season in the summer. Overall night-time activity is controlled mainly by temperature. Any that venture out on winter nights run the risk of dying from the cold.

The scorpions do not seem to have any natural enemies except for humans treading on them. Their lives seem to consist of retreating deep into a crack to survive the cold and then waiting for an unfortunate woodlouse to come along.

Silicon and Oxygen Compounds

Silicates make up 75 per cent of the rock in the Earth's crust. The silicon atom is normally attached to four oxygen atoms to form a tetrahedron, a structure which is mechanically strong, has a high melting point and is very resistant to chemical attack. The widespread existence of silica (silicon dioxide SiO_2) in the form of sand and quartz illustrates its durability. For a long time chemists have tried to overcome the chemical inactivity of silica to produce silicone polymers, organosilicon reagents, semiconductors and ceramics. The usual technique is to heat the silica with carbon to remove the oxygen and then heat the resulting silicon with hydrogen chloride and methyl chloride to produce methyl silicon compounds which are far more reactive.

A new approach has been developed by Richard Laine and colleagues at the University of Michigan. Instead of removing the oxygen, they have developed methods of adding oxygen using the common industrial solvent ethylene glycol. This produced a highly reactive five-coordinate silicate. The silica is dissolved in the glycol using potassium hydroxide. The ethylene glycol displaces the oxygen and attaches itself to the silicon. The mixture is then heated in nitrogen for six hours and when the mixture cools, the compound crystallizes out. If it is then dissolved in methanol and acetonitrile is added, the silicate recrystallizes. X-ray analysis of the crystals has shown that the silicon is bonded to oxygen atoms.

Laine has also shown that similar reactions can produce a six-coordinate silicate. It has been known for some time that such minerals exist. For example, the mineral stishovite has been identified in localities where meteoritic craters exist. In fact the presence of the mineral is a strong indicator of such an impact. Martin Hope, one of Laine's team, recently made six-coordinate silicate from ethylene glycol. It is highly reactive and can be used in silicate polymers, glasses and ceramics. One of the five-coordinate silicates is thought to conduct electricity. The applications for these new products are widespread.

Spiral Galaxy

In almost all cases where a spiral galaxy has been observed face on, it has been found that the spiral arms trail in the direction of rotation. But recently Gene Byrd of the University of Alabama noticed that in a photograph produced in a textbook of the spiral galaxy NGC 4622, there were two sets of arms winding in opposite directions. The galaxy lies about 140 million light years away in the constellation of Centaurus. The photograph shows one arm unwinding counterclockwise, then suddenly changes into two arms unwinding clockwise.

Byrd and his colleagues discussed the matter at a

meeting of the American Astronomical Society in Atlanta. It was explained that NGC 4622 was not actually rotating in two directions at once. They believe that in the recent past a low-mass companion travelled through the galaxy in a retrograde direction and that tidal effects generated the inner arm, causing it to lead the galaxy in the direction of rotation. Byrd's colleagues, Ronald Buta and Debora Crocker, obtained near-infra-red photographs of the galaxy using the 1.5 metre telescope at Cerro Tololo in Chile. At these wavelengths, the astronomers were not troubled by interstellar dust and they were able to see clearly the leading arm against the galaxy's old disc stars.

Work is now being carried out to identify the low-mass companion which produced the unusual spiral pattern. There are several disturbed companions nearby, but the outer trailing arm of NGC 4622 seems undisturbed. Computer simulations have indicated that with an encounter close enough to produce the leading arm, the outer parts of the visible disc would be torn away. A small galaxy about two arcminutes to the east of the spiral is currently thought to have been the body responsible.

Stellar Evolution

Most astronomical processes, like those in geology, take millions of years to evolve, although phrases such as 'in a short time' are frequently used. With stellar evolution, the time spent by a star on the main sequence, i.e. when hydrogen in the core is being converted to helium, depends on the mass of the star. In the case of the Sun this is about 10,000 million years, but for larger stars the period is considerably less because the stars are much hotter and they consume the hydrogen at a much faster rate.

A star in the constellation of Cynus, P Cygni, is about 40 times more massive than the Sun and is therefore consuming its nuclear fuel at a fantastic rate. Observations of the star over the past 50 years have shown that it has varied considerably. Estimates made between 1700 and 1919 have been used to build up a detailed picture of its behaviour. Even earlier observations indicate that it had brightened up considerably in 1600 and again in 1653, but in the early 17th century it could not be seen with the naked eye. Since then it has brightened gradually but irregularly. The star is 6,000 light years distant and is some 700,000 times more luminous than the Sun. Its surface temperature is about 20,000°C.

The increase in brightness is due to a decrease in temperature. P Cygni shines mostly in the ultraviolet part of the spectrum. The fall in temperature means that the peak of the energy distribution has shifted slightly from the ultraviolet to the visible part of the spectrum, so that the ultraviolet brightness has fallen but the visual brightness has increased. The observations indicate a fall in temperature of about 6 per cent per century, although theory suggests about 3 per cent for a star of that size.

Nevertheless the behaviour of the star is roughly in line with current theories. Because the star is in a critical mode, it is forecast that there will be more outbursts of the kind seen earlier. On such occasions it is thought that the star throws off into space masses comparable to the whole mass of the Sun. The difference between the observed and theoretical rate of decrease in temperature could be explained by too high an estimate for the mass of the star.

Superconductors

The aim of researchers working in the field of superconductors is to produce a compound which is superconducting at room temperatures. Over the years progress has been made in achieving higher critical temperatures, i.e. the highest temperature at which the compound remains superconducting. Above this temperature it has a measurable electrical resistance.

Some time ago Peter Edwards of the University of Birmingham and Ru-shi Liu of the University of Cambridge achieved a critical temperature of −165°C with a complex compound involving thallium, strontium, calcium and copper oxides. Since then they have concentrated on a thallium-barium-calcium-copper oxide compound, using it to study the properties needed to produce reliable superconductors. Working with Jeffrey Tallon of the New Zealand DSIR, they have discovered that it is difficult to produce consistent results because the number of holes in the material controls the superconductivity. They have developed a carefully controlled three-stage process which appears to give consistent results. The first stage involved producing the optimum mixture of the oxides for the best results. The second stage involved heating the ceramic to ensure that it contained a single phase. The final step was heating the ceramic again in oxygen at a low temperature under precise conditions. The results of this work produced a critical temperature of −145°C, the highest recorded so far.

Their research showed that the ceramic lost about 5 per cent of its weight due, it is thought, to the loss of thallium. This loss created cation holes in the material, the property which controls the superconductivity. It is believed that even higher temperatures will be achieved in the near future.

Terrestrial Magnetism

Study of the direction of the magnetism in rocks has shown that the Earth's magnetic field changes completely every few hundred thousand years. However, until recently little was known about the rate at which these reversals take place; it had been assumed that a reversal would take place over a few thousand years. Now it is claimed that this supposition was completely wrong and that the reversals take place so rapidly that 'you would virtually be able to watch the compass needle move'.

As molten lava cools it remains magnetized in the prevailing direction of the magnetic field at the time the rocks solidified. There are large gaps in the lava records and during these gaps the magnetic field could have moved as much as 120°, but it was not possible to determine whether the reversals were slow and continuous during the gaps. Now a team of geophysicists from France and the USA has succeeded in filling in two of the gaps in a magnetic reversal that occurred some 15.5 million years ago. They studied in detail lava flows from Steens Mountain in Oregon. One of the flows was 2 metres thick and another 1.5 metres thick. The thicker lava would have taken about two weeks to solidify from its outer surface to the centre. During the solidification, the rock layers would act like a natural compass and it was found that the needle swung through an angle of 50° during the fortnight and 48° in the case of the thinner layer. These values indicate that the magnetic poles were moving between 3 and 8 degrees a day. This implies that material in the Earth's core was flowing at a speed of several kilometres per hour, some 1,000 times faster than the generally accepted value.

Further work is being carried out to see if similar results can be obtained during other reversals. Apart from information gained at the times of the reversals, the results are important for studies of the electrical currents circulating deep within the Earth. These currents arise when material moves in the iron-rich liquid in the Earth's outer core. It is now thought that the flow of the molten minerals forms a chaotic system and out of this chaos comes the periodic magnetic reversals and the wobbling of the magnetic poles.

Titan's Atmosphere

Astronomers have been at a loss to explain why Titan, the largest moon of Saturn, has an atmosphere but Ganymede and Callisto, moons of roughly the same size but orbiting Jupiter, have no atmosphere. The most commonly accepted view has been that the difference is due to the formation of the satellites in different environments, Titan round Saturn and the other two round Jupiter. A team from NASA Ames Research Center, California, and the Institute for Theoretical Astrophysics, Toronto, claims that this explanation is wrong and that the difference can be explained by impacting comets.

They believe that comets coming in from the outer regions of the solar system crashed into Saturn's moons during the formation of the solar system, depositing their frozen gases on the satellites. Titan was large enough to hold on to these gases but the weaker gravitational fields of the smaller satellites allowed the gases to escape. The absence of atmospheres around Jupiter's satellites can be explained by the fact that the comets would hit Titan much more slowly than they did Ganymede and Callisto. Saturn has a mass of only 30 per cent that of Jupiter so the cometary material would not be accelerated as much. In addition, Saturn is nearly twice as far away from the Sun as Jupiter and the comets would be moving far more slowly in the region of Saturn's orbit than in regions closer to the Sun.

The scientists claim that the theory also explains the composition of Titan's atmosphere. Both Titan's atmosphere and comets contain large quantities of nitrogen, and the ratio of deuterium to hydrogen is the same for both bodies. The theory could also explain why Titan's atmosphere is similar to that of Pluto and Triton, a satellite of Neptune, although both of these are only approximately half the size of Titan.

Ulysses at Jupiter

The spacecraft *Ulysses* is intended to fly under the Sun's south pole in 1994 and over the north pole the following year. The way of achieving such an orbit in the most efficient manner is to send the probe to Jupiter and use the gravitational pull of the planet to produce the desired orbit. The craft flew over the north pole of Jupiter on 8 February 1992, passing within 450,000 km of the planet's equator before swinging under the south pole in a direction towards the Sun. This manoeuvre was carried out without any damage to the instruments on board the spacecraft from Jupiter's radiation field.

During the flyby the opportunity was taken to study in detail some of the properties of Jupiter's magnetosphere. The earlier *Voyager* probes sent back details of the equatorial regions but *Ulysses* was able to study the north-south dimension. The spacecraft entered Jupiter's magnetosphere two days earlier than expected and left it again two days earlier than predicted. This indicates that the magnetosphere reaches out to about 50 times the diameter of the planet in the equatorial region but only half that distance in the polar direction. This shape can be explained by a huge electrical current that flows through the gases surrounding Jupiter. The current is carried by atoms of sulphur and oxygen which originated from Io, the innermost of the four large moons and on which volcanic eruptions have been seen. Energetic particles trapped in the magnetic field ionize these atoms to form a plasma which spreads out beyond Io's orbit into a thin sheet. According to the team responsible for the magnetometer on *Ulysses*, the sheet carries an electrical current of about a billion amps. The magnetic field, identified by the earlier *Voyager* probes, was confirmed by *Ulysses* at about 20,000 times stronger than that of the Earth. The magnetosphere extends out twice as far in the equatorial plane as it did in the 1970s. The reason for the variable size is thought to be activity on Io and the instability of the torus around Io, where the atoms reside after they leave Io.

An experiment to measure the impact of dust particles provided interesting data. Before the approach, the spacecraft recorded about one hit a week but as it swept past the planet, it was struck eight times by particles between 1 and 10 micrometres across. It is thought that six of these originated in the dust ring which surrounds the planet but the other two were probably drawn in from interplanetary space by Jupiter's gravitational field.

Venus's Peculiar Craters

The majority of objects in the solar system which have a solid surface show the scars of intense volcanic activity or of meteoritic impact. Venus is no exception, although many of the scars do not show the basic characteristics of an impact explosion. During its radar mapping of the surface of Venus the *Magellan* spacecraft has identified many features which correspond with what is known to occur when a meteoroid hits the surface and explodes. However, there are numerous other cases where the craters have strange shapes or a region containing concentric discs which appear dark in the orbiter's radar images but with a virtual absence of a central crater. In contrast, a typical crater formed by impact is surrounded by debris.

Kevin Zahnle of NASA Ames Research Center, California, has modeled the behaviour of a large meteoroid entering the thick atmosphere of Venus and claims that the features on the planet's surface can be explained by an atmospheric explosion. It is thought that the incoming meteoroid disintegrates due to frictional heating. The spherical blast-wave from the explosion, which could be equivalent to that from a million megaton nuclear explosion, would shatter the surface rocks to a depth of one kilometre and to a radius of between 15 and 31 km. The rocks would be reduced to a fine rubble. This rubble would not respond to the spacecraft's radar and the area would therefore appear dark.

Study of the pictures sent back by *Magellan* show about 400 of these peculiar features but it is thought that there may be as many as 1,000. The extreme density of the atmosphere would produce more atmospheric explosions than occur on the Earth. The Tunguska event of 1908 was most probably the result of an atmospheric explosion, when it is thought that the object exploded at a height of about 10 km. Zahnle does not agree with the generally accepted view that this object was a comet but thinks it more likely to have been a dense stony object, such as an asteroid, entering the atmosphere at a fairly low velocity.

Water from Mars

The present situation on the surface of Mars suggests that the planet is nearly devoid of water. The pictures sent back, however, show strong evidence of dry river beds and canyons, so it is believed that the current conditions may not reflect the conditions of the past and that at some time water flowed freely over the surface. Water may still be present, but beneath the surface of the planet. Detailed examination of meteorites thought to have come from the planet has shed new light on the subject.

A relatively rare type of meteorite, classified as SNC meteorites, are thought to have come from Mars because they contain noble gases in exactly the same ratios as rocks on the Martian surface which were analysed by instruments on board the *Viking* spacecraft. A few grams of these meteorites were heated very gently to collect the water trapped in the micropores of the rock. Care was taken not to release any water held chemically by the silicate material of the rock. Analysis of this water showed that the ratio of the oxygen isotopes eliminated the possibility of the silicates being the source of the water. For example, the 'free water' had a higher concentration of the isotope oxygen-17 than that in the water locked in the silicates. It was therefore concluded that the water came from elsewhere on the planet. The possibility of it originating from an icy comet which had hit the surface was dismissed because the water was present in all the meteorites tested. It could have come from water vapour in the Martian atmosphere, but the most likely source is thought to be an ancient Martian ocean.

Future explorations of the planet include robot explorers with instruments designed to detect the presence of any ice beneath the Martian surface.

Astronomers Royal

Instituted in 1675, the title of Astronomer Royal was given to the director of the Greenwich Observatory until 1975. Currently it is an honorary title for an outstanding astronomer, who receives a stipend of approximately £100 a year.

John Flamsteed (1646–1719), appointed 1675
Edmund Halley (1656–1742), appointed 1720
James Bradley (1693–1762), appointed 1742
Nathaniel Bliss (1700–64), appointed 1762
Nevil Maskelyne (1732–1811), appointed 1765
John Pond (1767–1836), appointed 1811
Sir George Airy (1801–92), appointed 1835
Sir William Christie (1845–1922), appointed 1881
Sir Frank Dyson (1868–1939), appointed 1910
Sir Harold Jones (1890–1960), appointed 1933
Sir Richard Woolley (1906–86), appointed 1955
Sir Martin Ryle (1918–84), appointed 1972
Sir Francis Graham-Smith (1923–), appointed 1982
Arnold Wolfendale (1927–), appointed 1991

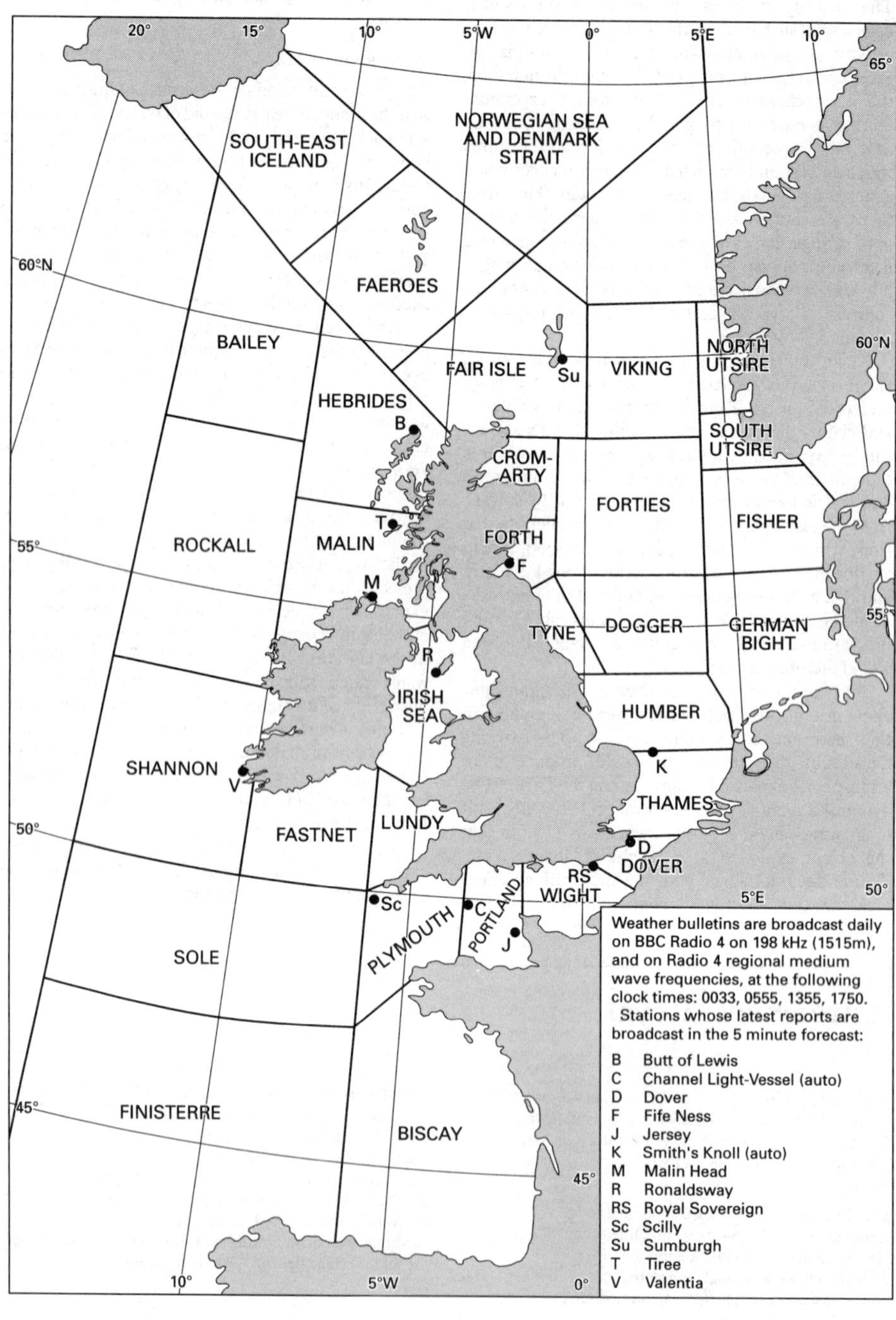

SOUTH-EAST ICELAND
NORWEGIAN SEA AND DENMARK STRAIT
FAEROES
BAILEY
FAIR ISLE
VIKING
NORTH UTSIRE
SOUTH UTSIRE
HEBRIDES
CROMARTY
FORTIES
FISHER
ROCKALL
MALIN
FORTH
TYNE
DOGGER
GERMAN BIGHT
IRISH SEA
HUMBER
SHANNON
THAMES
FASTNET
LUNDY
DOVER
WIGHT
SOLE
PLYMOUTH
PORTLAND
FINISTERRE
BISCAY
Weather bulletins are broadcast daily on BBC Radio 4 on 198 kHz (1515m), and on Radio 4 regional medium wave frequencies, at the following clock times: 0033, 0555, 1355, 1750.
Stations whose latest reports are broadcast in the 5 minute forecast:
B Butt of Lewis
C Channel Light-Vessel (auto)
D Dover
F Fife Ness
J Jersey
K Smith's Knoll (auto)
M Malin Head
R Ronaldsway
RS Royal Sovereign
Sc Scilly
Su Sumburgh
T Tiree
V Valentia

Weather

JULY 1991

Rainfall totals were above average in northern Scotland, parts of southern Scotland, Wales and southern England but below normal elsewhere. Heavy rain fell in parts of Scotland, northern England and Northern Ireland on the 1st. On the 2nd there was rain, with thunder at times, in south-east England, East Anglia and the Midlands. Thunderstorms occurred in northern Wales and north-west England with heavy showers and hail. On the 3rd fog spread over much of East Anglia and became widespread over much of England and Wales on the 4th. Thunderstorms, severe at times, with hail occurred in southern England on the 5th, reaching parts of Wales and the Midlands by the 6th. On the 5th 105 mm (4.1 in) of rain fell at St Mary's (Scilly). There were further thunderstorms in many places on the 6th and 7th. A gust of 51 knots (58.7 mph) was recorded at Culdrose (Cornwall) on the 7th. Thunderstorms on the 8th caused lightning damage in northern Wales and Scotland. Fog was frequent over hills and coasts in southern Wales and southern England between the 11th and 21st. On the 13th a tornado caused damage to roofs and power lines at Castle Bytham (Lincs.). On the 17th–18th there was heavy rain in Wales and southern England; 49 mm (1.93 in) fell at Penmaen (W. Glam.). Thunderstorms over south-west England on the 23rd became widespread by the evening and moved into East Anglia and eastern England on the 24th. There was heavy rain in parts of southern England and the Midlands on the 30th.

Monthly mean temperatures were above normal almost everywhere and Scotland had one of the warmest Julys on record. The temperature reached 27°C (80.6°F) in many places inland and along the south and west coasts of England and Wales on the 4th and 5th, 30°C (86.0°F) being recorded at Southampton (Hants.) and Kinlochewe (Highland) on the 4th. On the 11th temperatures reached 30°C (86.0°F) in East Anglia and eastern England. The highest temperature recorded during the month was 32.1°C (89.8°F) at Cromer (Norfolk) on the 11th and the lowest was 4.1°C (39.4°F) at Glenlee (Dumfries and Galloway) on the 17th.

Sunshine totals were above normal over parts of western Scotland and most of England but below normal elsewhere. The highest daily total was 16.3 hours at Benbecula (Western Isles) on the 3rd and the highest monthly total was 253 hours at Shanklin (IOW).

AUGUST 1991

Rainfall totals were below normal almost everywhere; Hastings (E. Sussex) had only 5 per cent of normal, recording only 3 mm (0.12 in) in the whole month. It was generally the driest August since 1976, and the driest at Coventry since 1947. On the 1st, 24.9 mm (0.98 in) of rain fell in 15 minutes at Wye College (Kent) and thunderstorms occurred in East Anglia and south-east England, causing local flooding with disruption of traffic. Lightning killed one person in Kent and injured two people in Essex and there was structural damage to property in south-east London. On the 7th 23.6 mm (0.93 in) of rain fell at St James's Park, London, and the night of the 8th–9th was very wet in the Welsh Mountains, the Lake District and parts of central Scotland. On the 9th 88 mm (3.46 in) of rain fell at Machynlleth (Powys) and 60 mm (2.36 in) at Moel Cynnedd (Powys), and a gust of 53 knots (61 mph) was recorded at Edinburgh. On the 10th–11th 72 mm (2.83 in) of rain fell at Trawsfynydd (Gwynedd). There were thunderstorms over north-west England on the 16th and over Scotland and north-east England on the 17th. There were also isolated thunderstorms on the 21st, when coloured dust was deposited at Towy Castle (Dyfed). Further thunderstorms occurred over southern Scotland on the 22nd, and over Wales and south-west England on the 22nd and 23rd. A gust of 55 knots (63 mph) was recorded at Culdrose (Cornwall) on the 23rd. On the 30th fog was dense in parts of East Anglia and lightning was observed over Cornwall and the Channel Islands. A gust of 53 knots (61 mph) was recorded at Camborne (Cornwall) on the 30th. On the 31st there were thunderstorms over Cornwall and southern Wales.

Monthly mean temperatures were above normal everywhere in the United Kingdom. Maximum temperatures exceeded 20°C somewhere in the United Kingdom every day except the 7th and 23rd, with 25°C to 27°C (77°F to 81°F) common over England and Wales. The highest temperature recorded during the month was 29.9°C (85.8°F) at St Helier (CI) on the 21st and the lowest was 1.6°C (34.9°F) at Magherally (Co. Down) on the 8th.

Sunshine totals were above average nearly everywhere. The highest daily total was 14.4 hours at Scarborough (N. Yorks.) on the 26th and the highest monthly total was 300 hours at Eastbourne and Hastings (E. Sussex).

SEPTEMBER 1991

Monthly rainfall totals were generally below normal except in north-west Scotland and parts of southern and eastern England. It was mainly dry over much of England and Wales during the first three weeks. Fog was widespread on the 2nd and dense in places between the 2nd and 4th. Hill fog occurred widely on the 5th. There were thunderstorms over eastern Scotland on the 16th and sleet fell at Fair Isle

(Shetland) on the 22nd and 23rd. On the 24th winds reached gale force in places and a gust of 71 knots (81.8 mph) was recorded at Butt of Lewis (Western Isles) with a mean wind speed of 51 knots (58.7 mph). Thunderstorms became widespread over central southern and eastern England on the 26th, bringing the first heavy rain of the month to many areas. Fog was dense in places on the 26th and waterspouts were observed near Llanbedr (Gwynedd) and Pendine (Dyfed). Scattered thunderstorms on the 27th gave further heavy rain in places. There was widespread heavy rain on the 28th and 29th, with thunderstorms over southern England on the night of the 28th–29th and over parts of south-east England and East Anglia on the 29th. A gust of 61 knots (70.2 mph) was recorded at Gwennap Head (Cornwall) on the 28th; on the same day 110 mm (4.33 in) of rain fell at Poole (Dorset), 96 mm (3.78 in) at Velindre (Powys), 85 mm (3.35 in) at Lower Kingcombe (Dorset) and 52 mm (2.01 in) at Coningsby (Lincs.).

Monthly mean temperatures were above normal everywhere except Scotland where they were generally below normal. It was the warmest start to September for 30 years in some places. Temperatures rose to 28°C (82.4°F) in southern areas on the 4th and reached 26°C (78.8°F) in western Scotland. Air frost occurred widely in eastern and central Scotland on the 12th. The highest temperature recorded during the month was 29.8°C (85.6°F) at Marholm (Cambs.) on the 1st and the lowest was −3.7°C (25.3°F)) at Grantown-on-Spey (Highland) on the 12th.

Sunshine totals were above normal nearly everywhere. During the first 12 days of the month daily totals exceeded 10 hours in many places. The highest daily total of the month was 13.1 hours at Newquay (Cornwall) on the 5th and at Morecambe (Lancs.) on the 6th and the highest monthly total was 205.6 hours at Morley St Botolph (Norfolk).

October 1991

Rainfall totals were above average in western and north-eastern areas but below average in central Scotland and central and eastern England. Several places in East Anglia received less than 20 mm (0.79 in) of rain in the whole month. On the 1st there were gales in northern areas when gusts of over 60 knots (69 mph) were recorded in south-east Scotland and north-east England. Thunderstorms occurred in the Manchester area on the 1st and over Orkney and Shetland on the 3rd and 4th. Sleet fell at Wick (Highland) on the 3rd and hail at Cape Wrath (Highland). On the 7th 67 mm (2.64 in) of rain fell at Tredegar (Gwent) and there were thunderstorms over Devon on the 8th and 9th. Fog was dense in south-east England and East Anglia on the 9th and in some central and eastern areas of England on the 11th. From Essex to Merseyside, coloured dust was deposited in rain on the 11th and in several places on the 12th and 13th. On the 16th 75 mm (2.95 in) of rain fell at Cassley (Highland). A gust of 75 knots (86 mph) was recorded at Butt of Lewis (Western Isles) on the 16th and 71 knots (82 mph) at Orlock Head (Co. Down) on the 17th. Snow fell over Orkney and the higher ground of northern England and southern Scotland on the 16th, and hail was widespread between the 16th and 19th. Sleet fell at Fair Isle (Shetland) on the 18th and there was snow at Aviemore (Highland). A waterspout was observed near Alderney (CI) on the 18th and sleet fell in north-east Scotland on the 19th and 20th. Fog was dense over Scotland and inland areas of England on the 22nd and over much of Scotland on the 23rd and 24th. Gusts of 70 knots (81 mph) were recorded at Kilkeel (Co. Down) on the 31st. There was flooding in Birmingham and Bidston (Merseyside) after a short burst of torrential rain on the 31st.

Monthly mean temperatures were below normal nearly everywhere. Maximum temperatures were about 20°C (68°F) in many areas on the 10th but by the 20th ground frost was widespread at night with some air frost in places. On the 21st Bedford had its lowest October temperature, −2.6°C (27.3°F), since 1957. The highest temperature recorded during the month was 24.2°C (75.6°F) at Sellafield (Cumbria) on the 11th and the lowest was −3.5°C (25.7°F) at Brooksby Hall (Leics.) on the 21st.

Sunshine totals were below normal nearly everywhere and it was a particularly dull month near eastern and northern coasts. The highest daily total was 10.6 hours at Everton (Hants) on the 2nd and the highest monthly total was 132 hours at Folkestone (Kent).

November 1991

Rainfall totals were generally near or above normal. On the 1st there were local thunderstorms, and sleet fell in Fair Isle (Shetland) on the 2nd. Snow fell as far south as southern Wales on the 3rd and 3 cm (1.2 in) of snow lay on the Pennines. Thunderstorms were widespread over England and Wales on the 3rd. On the 4th, 6th, 7th and 8th there was sleet and snow over Scotland, and on the 4th and 8th over northern England. The 10th was a particularly wet day over southern Scotland when 72 mm (2.83 in) of rain fell at Clatteringshaws (Dumfries and Galloway). Thunderstorms occurred over western Scotland on the 11th and were widespread over Wales and northern and eastern England between the 11th and 14th. On the 12th 63 mm (2.48 in) of rain fell at Brodick Castle (Strathclyde) and on the 12th–13th there were violent thunderstorms over Cumbria. The 12th was a windy day, and gusts of 81 knots (93 mph) were recorded at Aberporth (Dyfed), 79 knots (91 mph) at Ronaldsway (IOM) and 77 knots (89 mph) at Gwennap Head (Cornwall). Botwnnog School (Gwynedd) sustained extensive structural damage. Also, a tornado was reported at Dullingham (Cambs.). On the 13th sleet and snow fell as far south as Devon and Cornwall and on the 16th sleet fell in many areas. On the 17th there was sleet and snow over Scotland and nothern England. Overnight fog was widespread on the 17th, 21st, 24th and 27th over England and Wales, particularly in eastern areas.

Monthly mean temperatures were normal over Northern Ireland and slightly above normal over the rest of the United Kingdom. The month started warm with temperatures reaching 16°C (60.8°F) on the 1st, but the temperature fell to −3.0°C (26.6°F) at Glasgow on the 5th and there was widespread frost on the 6th and on the 21st. The highest temperature recorded during the month was 16.4°C (61.5°F) at Heathrow (London) on the 1st and the lowest recorded was −8.4°C (16.9°F) at Grantown-on-Spey (Highland) on the 17th.

Sunshine totals were below normal nearly everywhere, but it was often quite sunny in southern areas during the first three weeks of the month. The highest daily total was 9.3 hours at Keele (Staffs.) on the 5th and the highest monthly total was 75.8 hours at Ventnor Park (IOW).

December 1991

Rainfall totals were below normal over the whole of the United Kingdom. Much of southern England and southern Wales received less than half the normal amount, with only 14 per cent falling at Odiham (Hants). Over England and Wales it was the driest December since 1971 but over Northern Ireland it was the wettest since 1986. Overnight fog was frequent from the 1st to 17th and was widespread on the 7th and 9th, becoming dense in places on the 10th and again widespread on the 11th. There was further dense fog in places on the 14th, 15th and 16th. Rain fell in many areas on the 16th and 17th, when much of England and Wales had the first significant rain of the month. On the 18th 58 mm (2.28 in) of rain fell at Loch Bradan (Co. Tyrone). Snow fell as far south as Cambridgeshire and sleet was reported in southern Hampshire on the 20th. On the same day 62 mm (2.44 in) of rain fell at Widdybank Fell (Co. Durham) and there was a thunderstorm at Prestwick (Strathclyde). Hail fell in south-west England and southern Wales on the 20th. Heavy rain and gale force winds on the 21st caused extensive damage, with bridges washed away and railway lines blocked, particularly around Sheffield, in Greater Manchester, the Severn Valley and the Welsh Marches. Snow fell in Scotland on the 21st and sleet fell as far south as the Midlands. On the same day 116 mm (4.57 in) of rain fell at Holme Moss (W. Yorks.), 80 mm (3.15 in) at Malham Tarn (N. Yorks.), 78 mm (3.07 in) at Moel Cynnedd (Powys), 68 mm (2.68 in) at Clatteringshaws (Dumfries and Galloway) and 67 mm (2.64 in) at Slaidburn (Lancs.). Snow fell in northern areas between the 22nd and 24th. The 23rd was a very windy day, with gusts of 60 knots (69 mph) in places from western Wales to Kent and power lines brought down in Shropshire. Winds were very strong over northern areas on the 31st, and at Butt of Lewis (Western Isles) a gust of 96 knots (110.5 mph) equalled the December record set at St Mary's (Scilly Isles) in 1935 and at Stornoway and Benbecula (Western Isles) in 1956.

Monthly mean temperatures were generally below normal in southern and eastern areas but above normal elsewhere. On the 11th temperatures remained below freezing all day over much of England and Wales, and there were some severe night frosts from the 11th to 16th. Parts of the north and the Midlands were badly affected by freezing fog on the 11th. The highest temperature recorded during the month was 15.6°C (60.1°F) at Elmstone (Kent) on the 22nd and the lowest was −13.3°C (8.1°F) at Grendon Underwood (Bucks.) on the 12th.

Sunshine totals were above normal in many eastern areas but generally below normal in northern and western areas. The highest daily total was 7.2 hours at Jersey Airport on the 1st and at Rustington (W. Sussex) on the 6th. The highest monthly total was 80.8 hours at St Helier (CI).

The Year 1991

For the first time this century there was a cold, wet, dull June followed by three very warm months in succession. It was the driest year since 1975 and the eighth driest this century but rainfall was around normal over Cumbria and much of Scotland. The spring was wet in the north and west but dry in the east. The summer was generally dry and the autumn was very warm and the driest since 1904. Thunderstorms were more frequent than usual in many parts of the country and the number of gales during the year was about average. Annual mean temperatures were generally near or above normal.

January was a stormy month and on the 1st heavy rain and melting snow caused flooding in southern Scotland. On the 5th gales driving high tides caused considerable damage along western and southern coasts with extensive flooding and disruption of power supplies and transport. On the 8th heavy snowfall over southern Scotland and northern England caused severe traffic problems. Northern Ireland had its driest January since 1972. February was an unsettled month with frequent snow showers during the first half. Heavy snow on the 7th brought most of Powys to a standstill with depths of 30 cm (11.81 in) in places. On the 7th–8th 20 cm (7.87 in) of snow lying in central London was the greatest depth recorded there since 1962. On the 12th Fylingdales (N. Yorks.) had 45 cm (17.72 in) of level snow and 46 cm (18.11 in) lay at Longframlingham (Northumberland) on the 13th. Temperatures did not rise above freezing between the 5th and 10th. March was generally wet during the first three weeks, especially in western areas. On the 3rd a tornado hit south-west Wales uprooting trees and causing serious damage to property.

April was another unsettled month, with rain or showers followed by hail, sleet and snow. On the 10th the Isle of Rhum (Highland) had its wettest April day since 1958. Heavy rain on the 29th in parts of south-east England gave some places their wettest April day this century. May started with rain in the north followed by sharp overnight frosts. The second half of the month was often cloudy, but very warm around the 21st. It was the driest May in England and Wales since 1896 and in Glasgow since 1868.

June was one of the coolest, dullest and wettest this century. The weather was generally unsettled with outbreaks of rain, drizzle, hail, snow or sleet. On the 23rd torrential rain caused extensive flooding in south-west England. Temperatures were below normal everywhere and the 5th was the coldest June night since records began at a number of stations. Thunderstorms were frequent and sunshine totals were below normal almost everywhere.

July was showery with some longer periods of rain. Temperatures were above normal everywhere and Scotland had one of the warmest Julys on record. Sunshine totals were above normal over western Scotland and most of England. August produced persistent cloud and mist with comparatively low temperatures and little sunshine in the west. Rainfall was mostly below normal and generally it was the driest August since 1976. Temperatures were above normal everywhere and sunshine amounts above normal nearly everywhere. September was a warm month, especially in the south, and generally dry but there was some heavy rainfall in the second half of the month. Temperatures were above normal except in Scotland and it was the warmest start to September for 30 years in some places. Sunshine totals were above normal nearly everywhere.

October was another unsettled month. Temperatures and sunshine were below normal nearly everywhere. November was unsettled during the first two weeks, with rain affecting most areas, but then became quieter. Temperatures were mostly just above normal but sunshine totals were mostly below normal. December started dry with some severe frosts but then became unsettled with some heavy rain.

January 1992

Rainfall totals were below normal everywhere except in central Scotland and parts of central England. Fort Augustus (Highland) had 222 per cent of the normal amount, whereas Bexhill (E. Sussex) received only 16 per cent of normal. On the 1st very heavy rain caused extensive flooding, especially in western Scotland; 120 mm (4.27 in) fell at Inverinan Moor (Strathclyde) and Tyndrum (Perthshire), and 100 mm (3.94 in) at Cassley (Highland). There were also severe gales in northern and western areas, and gusts of 98 knots (112.9 mph) and 95 knots (109.4 mph) were recorded at Sumburgh and Sella Ness (Shetland) respectively. Strong winds were also recorded in northern and western Scotland on the 2nd and 3rd. Sleet fell at Kirkwall (Orkney) and around Glasgow on the 5th, and on the 6th 67 mm (2.64 in) of rain fell at Holme Moss (W. Yorks.) and Crossway (Gwent). There was rain over southern England on the night of the 7th–8th, and on the 8th 65 mm (2.56 in) fell at Llanishen (Gwent) and at Ledbury (Herefordshire). Also on the 8th there was snow in western areas as far south as Cornwall. On the 9th 8 cm (3.15 in) of snow lay at Cwmbargoed (Mid Glam.). There was sleet over Lincolnshire and East Anglia and snow fell at Eskdalemuir (Dumfries and Galloway) on the 11th. On the 11th and 12th fog caused disruption to road and air traffic, particularly in central Scotland. Fog formed again on the 14th–15th, becoming widespread over most of central England on the 16th. Snow and sleet fell in places in the Midlands on the 23rd and over eastern England on the 24th. Sleet fell in northern Scotland on the 25th. On the 26th the atmospheric pressure rose to 1,049 millibars in northern Wales, the highest January pressure recorded in England and Wales for 30 years. During the last week there was frequent overnight fog, and on the 28th dozens of vehicles were involved in multiple collisions on the M8 motorway in Scotland in thick fog. Fog remained widespread over England and Wales until the 31st.

Monthly mean temperatures were generally above normal in northern Scotland and near normal over much of England and Wales but below normal in south-west England. After a very mild start the month gradually became cooler and night frosts were frequent from the 11th onwards. The 21st to 24th was particularly cold with persistent frost in parts of the Midlands and northern England. The highest temperature recorded during the month was 15.1°C (59.2°F) at Dyce (Grampian) on the 2nd and the lowest was −12.3°C (9.9°F) at Barbourne (Worcs.) on the 23rd.

Sunshine totals were above normal over much of eastern Scotland, the eastern side of England, western Wales and the south coast of England, but below normal elsewhere. The highest daily total was 8.3 hours at Moel-y-Crio (Clwyd) on the 31st and the highest monthly total was 95 hours at Dawlish (Devon).

February 1992

Rainfall totals were above normal over most of Scotland and in parts of Wales, Merseyside and Northern Ireland but below normal elsewhere. The Isle of Rhum (Highland) received nearly three times the normal amount for February whereas parts of Cambridgeshire received less than a quarter of the normal amount. On the 1st there was widespread dense fog over England and Wales, freezing in places, and persisting in many places until the afternoon of the 2nd. On the 2nd snow and sleet fell in northern Scotland and thunderstorms occurred around Cape Wrath (Highland). Winds were strong in the north and west of Scotland during the first few days of the month and a gust of 71 knots (81.8 mph) at Benbecula (Western Isles) and one of 62 knots (71.4 mph) at Orlock Head (Co. Down) were recorded on the 2nd. Further falls of snow or sleet occurred over northern Scotland on the 3rd and over northern and eastern Scotland and north-east England on the 4th. Fog became widspread over East Anglia and south-east England overnight on the 7th–8th. Wintry showers in northern Scotland on the 9th and 10th gave a covering of snow on high ground. Hail fell in West Yorkshire on the 10th and there was sleet over Orkney on the 11th. On the 12th there was snow lying on Great Dun Fell (Cumbria) and there was a thunderstorm at Aberporth (Dyfed). There were thunderstorms in the Manchester area on the 13th and snow fell over large areas of the Pennines from the 13th to 15th, spreading to a large area of eastern Scotland and north-east England on the 15th. Heavy snow showers affected many places on the 16th. On the 17th a band of rain, sleet and snow, some of it heavy, spread eastwards across the country, affecting most of Scotland, western England and Wales. On the 18th heavy snow in the Midlands caused severe road conditions. Further snow fell in parts of Humberside, East Anglia, southern Wales and central southern England on the 19th, and in Orkney on the 20th. On the 21st 87 mm (3.43 in) of rain fell at Kinlochewe (Highland). Winds were frequently strong between the 21st and 29th with gusts of over 50 knots (57.6 mph) being recorded at many places in Scotland and northern England. Snow fell over Orkney on the 22nd and 23rd and there was hail over Shetland on the 24th. Occasional snow fell over Orkney and the Western Isles from the 23rd to the end of the month. On the 27th a gust of 54 knots (62.2 mph) was recorded at Aberporth (Dyfed) and a gust of 61 knots (70.2 mph) was recorded at Killough (Co. Down).

Monthly mean temperatures were above normal everywhere. The highest temperature recorded during the month was 15.7°C (60.3°F) at Elmstone (Kent) on the 29th and the lowest was −11.4°C (11.5°F) at Kindrogan (Tayside) on the 19th.

Sunshine totals were above normal in eastern areas and below normal in western areas. The highest daily total was 9 hours at Falmouth (Cornwall) on the 21st and the highest monthly total was 107 hours at Whitby (N. Yorks.).

March 1992

Rainfall totals were above normal everywhere, except parts of the West Midlands and southern England where they were below normal. On the 1st rain occurred in all areas and some snow and hail fell over Orkney. There were strong winds in the north on the 3rd with a gust of 75 knots (86.4 mph) being recorded at Fair Isle (Shetland). The 10th brought hail to Cottesmore (Leics.) and Honnington (Suffolk) and thunderstorms were reported at Benbecula (Western Isles), Prestwick, Machrihanish (Strathclyde) and Shetland. Wintry showers on the 10th produced extensive falls of snow as far south as Wiltshire. Gusts exceeded 60 knots (69.1 mph) over Orkney and Shetland on the 11th, and some sleet fell at Leeds. During the 11th and 12th snow fell over several areas of Scotland with 7 cm (2.76 mph) lying at Wick (Highland) by the 13th. The 12th was a windy day in many areas, with gusts exceeding 70 knots (80.6 mph) over Shetland and 60 knots (69.1 mph) over places as far apart as Orkney and Cornwall. A gust of 122 knots (140.5 mph) was recorded at Cairngorm chairlift (Highland) and of 76 knots (87.5 mph) at Lerwick (Shetland). The 13th was another windy day and snow fell north of a line from Shropshire to Norfolk. There was further snow over Scotland on the 14th, giving a depth of 20 cm (7.87 in) at Wick (Highland). On the 15th wintry showers fell as far south as Essex. The 18th was a wet day almost everywhere and sleet fell over Orkney and Shetland. Snow fell over north-east Scotland on the 20th and there was some very heavy rain over the Welsh hills. On the 21st sleet or snow fell in northern areas and a gust of 64 knots (73.7 mph) was recorded at Valley (Gwynedd). There were thunderstorms over Benbecula (Western Isles) on the 21st and 65 mm (2.56 in) of rain fell at Dolydd (Powys). On the 22nd snow fell at Holme Moss (W. Yorks.), hail at Hemsby (Norfolk) and sleet in parts of Scotland. On the 23rd sleet fell south of a line from the Wirral to north Lincolnshire. On the 26th snow again fell at Holme Moss and over the Scottish Highlands, while sleet fell over Orkney, Shetland and southern Wales. Winds were strong in the west with 78 knots (89.8 mph) recorded at Culdrose (Cornwall), 62 knots (71.4 mph) at Aberporth and Brawdy (Dyfed), and 64 knots (73.7 mph) at Butt of Lewis (Western Isles). There were thunderstorms around Swansea on the 26th. Snow fell at Newcastle upon Tyne on the 27th and over Orkney and Shetland on the 28th. On the 29th there was snow at Dunkerswell (Devon) and over parts of Wales, with 6 cm (2.36 in) lying at Merthyr Tydfil, and there was heavy rain in many other area. On the 30th most places had showers or periods of rain and snow fell on Great Dun Fell (Cumbria). On the 31st very heavy rain fell in Scotland; 57 mm (2.24 in) was recorded at Turnhouse (Lothian) and 52 mm (2.05 in) at Salsburgh (Strathclyde).

Monthly mean temperatures were above normal nearly everywhere. The highest temperature recorded during the month was 18.2°C (64.8°F) at Malvern (Worcs.) on the 16th and the lowest was −9.5°C (14.9°F) at Leith Hall (Grampian) on the 14th.

Sunshine totals were above normal in parts of north-east England but below normal elsewhere. The highest daily total was 10.7 hours at Lyneham (Wilts.) on the 8th and the highest monthly total was 115.3 hours at Tynemouth (Tyne and Wear).

April 1992

Rainfall totals were generally above normal except for Merseyside, parts of central England and parts of eastern Scotland, where totals were below normal. The 1st was a very wet day in north-eastern areas. Hail fell over Cornwall and southern Wales during thunderstorms, and there were gales over southern Scotland and northern England. On the same day 58 mm (2.28 in) of rain fell at Newcastle upon Tyne and 57 mm (2.24 in) at Carterhouse (Borders). Snow was widespread over much of Scotland on the 1st and 2nd and hail fell over East Anglia on the 2nd, which was a wet day in many eastern areas. Wintry showers continued on the 3rd and sleet fell in Lincolnshire and Kent. Hail fell in East Anglia on the 5th and there were further showers in southern counties. The 6th was a wet day everywhere and hail fell over

Devon on the 7th. Sleet fell in several places on the 12th and snow fell at Holme Moss (W. Yorks.). Thunder occurred over Shetland on the 12th and hail showers were frequent and sometimes widespread between the 12th and 18th. On the 13th sleet fell in southern Scotland and on the Pennines, and there was heavy snow in the Scottish Highlands with gales on exposed coasts. On the 14th sleet and snow fell in many parts of Scotland and thunderstorms occurred over southern Wales. Thunderstorms occurred at Wick (Highland) and Gatwick (W. Sussex) on the 15th and on the 18th there were very strong winds over northern and western Scotland. On the 20th 80 mm (3.15 in) of rain fell at Knockanrock (Highland). Fog formed widely over England and Wales on the 22nd. Thunderstorms occurred in the Isle of Man on the 24th and over Leeds and western Scotland on the 25th. There were strong winds over a large area from the 24th to 26th and hail was again frequent and widespread between the 25th and 28th. Thunderstorms occurred in Lincolnshire on the 26th and in parts of Scotland on the 26th and 27th. Rain fell in many areas on the 28th and on the 30th coastal fog was extensive in southern Wales, south-west England and along the south coast.

Monthly mean temperatures were above normal nearly everywhere. The highest temperature recorded during the month was 20.3°C (68.5°F) at Folkestone (Kent) on the 18th and the lowest was −5.3°C (22.5°F) at Santon Downham (Norfolk) on the 1st.

Sunshine totals were below or near normal almost everywhere. The highest daily total was 13.1 hours at Bastreet (Cornwall) on the 9th and the highest monthly total was 184 hours at Bognor Regis (W. Sussex).

May 1992

Rainfall totals were generally below normal, although very heavy rain between the 28th and 30th in many places produced as much rainfall in three days as they normally receive in a month. Amounts ranged from 198 per cent of normal at Heathrow (London) to 16 per cent at Tynemouth (Tyne and Wear). Winds were strong over the Western Isles on the 1st and over Orkney and Shetland on the 7th. Snow fell over the Pennines on the 7th and sleet over Fair Isle (Shetland) and Kirkwell (Orkney). On the 8th there was sleet and snow as far south as the north Midlands and winds were strong from the Midlands northwards. On the 9th winds were strong over southern England and Wales and sleet or snow showers occurred over Scotland. Thunderstorms were frequent between the 8th and 15th. Scattered sleet and snow fell over Scotland on the 10th and 71 mm (2.8 in) of rain fell at Machynlleth (Powys) on the 11th. Winds were strong over northern Scotland on the 15th when a gust of 60 knots (69.1 mph) occurred at Duirinish (Highland). On the 29th heavy rain fell at Gayton (Northants) and Chorleywood (Herts.), and 73 mm (2.87 in) fell at Grendon Underwood (Bucks.), 70 mm (2.76 in) at Northolt (London) and 62 mm (2.44 in) at Heathrow (London). Thunderstorms were widespread during the last few days of the month.

Monthly mean temperatures were above normal in most areas. Over central England it was the warmest May since 1833. On the 14th the temperature rose to 28.9°C (84.0°F) at Edinburgh, the highest temperature recorded in Scotland since 1896. The 14th was also the warmest May day on record at Haydon Bridge (Northumberland). From the 19th 25°C (77.0°F) was exceeded each day somewhere in the United Kingdom. The highest temperature recorded during the month was 29.5°C (85.1°F) at Barbourne (Worcs.) on the 20th and the lowest was −4.7°C (23.5°F) at Aberfoyle (Central Scotland) on the 10th.

Sunshine totals were generally above normal. The highest daily total was 15.2 hours at Stonehaven (Grampian) on the 17th and the highest monthly total was 292 hours at St Helier (CI).

June 1992

Rainfall totals were generally below normal except for some places in the Midlands and eastern parts of England and Scotland. Totals ranged from 14 per cent of normal at Eskdalemuir (Dumfriesshire) to 195 per cent of normal at Finningley (S. Yorks.). The month was notable for periods of intense rain in places. Thunderstorms occurred somewhere on every day up to the 10th and were widespread from the Isle of Man to Essex on the 1st and over eastern Scotland on the 2nd. Thunder was accompanied by hail in the east Midlands on the 3rd, and 65 mm (2.56 in) of rain fell at St Mary's (Scilly). Fog patches formed in southern England on the 3rd and the 8th. On the 5th a gust of 50 knots (57.6 mph) was recorded at Culdrose (Cornwall). On the 8th heavy rain caused flash floods around Lampeter (Dyfed) and during the 9th and 10th storms which had battered parts of Yorkshire, Cheshire, northern Wales and Strathclyde moved southwards. There were flash floods in London, rail travel was disrupted and a school in south-east London was struck by lightning. On the 9th lightning cut power supplies over much of the Fylde area (Lancs.). On the 10th violent storms caused flooding in parts of Greater Manchester and dense fog patches formed in the Midlands, parts of East Anglia and south-east England. From the 11th to the 18th many places had no rain but heavy rain returned in places on the 29th and 30th.

Monthly mean temperatures were above normal everywhere. A mean temperature of 16.4°C (61.5°F) in central England made it the second warmest June this century. The highest temperature recorded during the month was 30.3°C (86.5°F) at Malvern (Worcs.) on the 29th and the lowest was −1.5°C (29.3°F) at Kielder Castle (Northumberland) on the 11th.

Sunshine totals were generally near or above normal. The highest daily total was 16.7 hours at Twist (Devon) on the 18th and the highest monthly total was 295 hours at St Helier (CI).

AVERAGE AND GENERAL VALUES, 1990–2 (JUNE)

	Rainfall (mm) Aver. 1941–70	1990	1991	1992	Temperature (°C) Aver. 1951–80	1990	1991	1992	Bright Sunshine (hrs per day) Aver. 1951–80	1990	1991	1992
ENGLAND AND WALES												
January	86	133	92	48	4.0	7.1	3.9	3.8	1.6	1.8	2.2	1.7
February	65	141	63	45	4.1	7.8	2.0	5.5	2.3	2.8	2.3	2.3
March	59	24	75	85	5.9	8.7	8.1	7.2	3.6	4.4	2.9	2.4
April	58	38	68	72	8.2	8.5	8.3	8.5	5.1	7.1	5.1	4.2
May	67	25	14	49	11.3	12.9	10.9	13.2	6.3	8.2	4.7	8.0
June	61	70	92	38	14.3	14.0	12.4	15.4	6.7	4.4	4.7	7.3
July	73	35	68	–	16.0	17.0	17.0	–	5.9	8.7	6.2	–
August	90	46	31	–	15.9	18.4	17.0	–	5.5	7.1	6.9	–
September	83	53	62	–	14.0	13.6	14.7	–	4.6	5.1	5.9	–
October	83	103	77	–	11.0	12.5	10.2	–	3.3	3.3	2.8	–
November	97	67	95	–	7.1	7.5	6.7	–	2.1	2.2	1.8	–
December	90	97	49	–	5.1	4.9	4.7	–	1.5	1.5	1.5	–
YEAR	912	832	786	–	9.8	11.1	9.7	–	4.1	4.7	3.9	–
SCOTLAND												
January	137	247	146	133	3.5	5.7	3.2	4.1	1.3	1.3	1.7	1.4
February	104	292	83	165	3.4	5.6	2.6	5.0	2.4	2.1	2.3	1.9
March	92	241	128	206	5.1	7.5	6.7	5.7	3.3	3.0	2.7	2.3
April	90	95	121	119	7.1	7.3	7.5	7.0	5.0	5.6	5.2	3.3
May	91	55	43	80	9.9	11.0	10.4	11.1	5.7	6.6	5.1	7.5
June	92	124	121	40	12.7	12.5	11.0	13.8	5.9	4.3	5.2	5.9
July	112	75	91	–	13.9	14.6	15.3	–	4.9	6.8	4.8	–
August	129	119	67	–	13.9	15.1	14.9	–	4.6	4.0	4.8	–
September	137	149	131	–	12.2	11.5	11.9	–	3.7	3.5	5.0	–
October	149	213	165	–	9.8	10.4	8.7	–	2.6	2.4	2.1	–
November	142	102	227	–	6.0	6.0	5.6	–	1.7	1.8	1.5	–
December	156	184	141	–	4.5	4.5	4.7	–	1.1	0.9	0.8	–
YEAR	1431	1896	1464	–	8.5	9.4	8.5	–	3.5	3.5	3.4	–

WEATHER RECORDS

WORLD RECORDS

Maximum air temperature — 57.8°C/136°F
San Louis, Mexico, 11 August 1933

Minimum air temperature — −89.2°C/−128.56°F
Vostok, Antarctica, 21 July 1983

Greatest rainfall in one day — 1870 mm/73.62 in
Cilaos, Isle de Réunion, 16 March 1952

Greatest rainfall in one calendar month — 9300 mm/366.14 in
Cherrapunji, Assam, July 1861

Greatest annual rainfall total — 22,990 mm/905.12 in
Cherrapunji, 1861

Highest gust of wind — 201 knots/231 mph
Mt Washington Observatory, USA, 12 April 1934

UNITED KINGDOM RECORDS

Maximum air temperature — 37.1°C/98.8°F
Cheltenham, Glos., 3 August 1990

Minimum air temperature — −27.2°C/−17°F
Braemar, Grampian, 11 February 1895 and 10 January 1982

Greatest rainfall in one day — 280 mm/11 in
Martinstown, Dorset, 18 July 1955

Greatest annual rainfall total — 6528 mm/257 in
Sprinkling Tarn, Cumbria, 1954

Highest gust of wind — 150 knots/173 mph
Cairngorm, Highland, 20 March 1986

Highest low-level gust* — 123 knots/141.7 mph
Fraserburgh, Grampian, 13 February 1989

Highest mean hourly speed — 92 knots/106 mph
Great Dun Fell, Cumbria, December 1974

Highest low-level mean hourly speed* — 72 knots/83 mph
Shoreham-by-Sea, Sussex, 16 October 1987

* below 200 m/656 ft

WIND FORCE MEASURES

The *Beaufort Scale* of wind force has been accepted internationally and is used in communicating weather conditions. Devised originally by Admiral Sir Francis Beaufort in 1805, it now consists of the numbers 0–17, each representing a certain strength or velocity of wind at 10 m (33 ft) above ground in the open.

Scale no.	Wind Force	mph	knots
0	Calm	1	1
1	Light air	1–3	1–3
2	Slight breeze	4–7	4–6
3	Gentle breeze	8–12	7–10
4	Moderate breeze	13–18	11–16
5	Fresh breeze	19–24	17–21
6	Strong breeze	25–31	22–27
7	High wind	32–38	28–33
8	Gale	39–46	34–40
9	Strong gale	47–54	41–47
10	Whole gale	55–63	48–55
11	Storm	64–72	56–63
12	Hurricane	73–82	64–71
13	–	83–92	72–80
14	–	93–103	81–89
15	–	104–114	90–99
16	–	115–125	100–108
17	–	126–136	109–118

TEMPERATURE, RAINFALL AND SUNSHINE

The following table gives mean air temperature (°C), total monthly rainfall (mm) and mean daily bright sunshine (hours) at a representative selection of climatological reporting stations in the United Kingdom during the year July 1991 to June 1992 and the calendar year 1991. The heights (in metres) of the reporting stations above mean sea level are also given. *Source:* data provided by the Met Office.

		1991 *July*			*August*			*September*			*October*		
	Ht m	Temp. °C	Rain mm	Sun hrs	Temp. °C	Rain mm	Sun hrs	Temp. °C	Rain mm	Sun hrs	Temp. °C	Rain mm	Sun hrs
Aberdeen (Dyce)	65	15.3	60	4.3	15.5	27	6.6	12.1	28	5.3	9.0	105	2.5
Aberporth	134	15.9	80	5.5	16.1	26	6.7	14.9	56	6.1	10.3	142	2.8
Aldergrove	68	16.5	73	4.5	15.9	29	5.5	13.4	54	5.7	9.5	106	2.3
Aspatria	61	16.9	44	6.5	15.8	59	5.9	13.1	62	6.5	9.2	122	2.6
Bala	163	15.6	80	4.4	14.5	46	5.0	12.9	55	4.8	8.9	148	2.1
Birmingham (Elmdon)	98	17.4	109	6.3	16.9	15	7.1	14.7	73	6.1	9.9	47	2.9
Boulmer	23	15.1	32	5.2	15.6	27	6.1	13.0	31	5.8	9.8	53	2.4
Bournemouth (Hurn)	10	16.9	78	7.1	17.3	12	8.4	15.1	66	6.2	10.3	96	2.9
Bradford	134	16.9	31	5.1	16.3	17	5.3	13.9	36	5.1	10.6	65	2.2
Braemar	339	14.9	57	–	14.1	31	–	10.7	58	4.7	6.9	144	–
Buxton	307	16.1	69	5.8	15.5	50	6.1	13.1	44	6.0	8.5	111	2.6
Cambridge	24	18.0	32	6.2	18.2	41	7.0	15.2	47	5.9	10.5	19	2.9
Cheltenham	65	18.0	101	7.1	17.6	11	7.5	16.1	81	5.3	10.9	69	2.2
Clacton-on-Sea	16	17.5	64	5.6	18.7	8	7.9	15.5	43	6.0	10.9	13	3.3
Douglas	85	15.7	60	3.9	15.5	42	3.9	13.7	75	5.2	10.3	147	2.1
Dumfries	49	16.3	56	5.1	15.6	64	4.6	12.8	53	5.8	9.3	162	2.3
Dundee	45	16.1	62	–	16.3	19	6.2	12.9	60	5.7	9.4	61	–
Durham	102	16.2	44	5.9	16.2	21	6.2	12.8	24	5.2	9.2	50	2.5
East Malling	33	17.7	61	7.1	18.4	53	8.8	15.3	37	6.1	10.5	25	3.3
Edinburgh	134	15.4	82	4.4	15.7	15	5.3	10.0	65	5.0	9.1	50	2.1
Glasgow (Abbotsinch)	5	16.6	109	5.1	15.5	39	4.8	12.5	93	5.2	8.9	92	2.1
Gogerddan	31	16.9	109	5.4	15.9	35	7.5	14.5	73	5.8	10.3	140	3.2
Hastings	45	17.0	118	6.8	17.8	3	9.7	16.1	41	6.5	11.7	36	3.8
Hull	2	18.3	19	–	18.1	21	–	15.1	60	–	11.1	33	–
Inverness	4	15.9	73	3.4	16.1	23	5.3	12.9	56	4.5	9.3	52	2.3
Leeming	32	17.3	21	5.9	17.1	25	6.3	13.9	37	5.5	10.1	56	2.5
Lerwick	82	13.2	104	4.3	13.1	57	3.9	10.2	121	4.4	8.2	158	1.6
London (Heathrow)	25	18.8	93	7.1	19.3	26	7.0	16.5	44	6.1	11.1	19	2.8
Long Ashton	51	17.1	95	–	17.1	20	–	15.1	45	–	10.3	105	–
Lowestoft	25	17.7	33	6.5	18.5	10	7.7	15.3	47	5.7	11.1	28	2.5
Manchester (Ringway)	75	17.6	49	5.6	16.7	27	6.0	14.7	53	6.1	10.4	70	2.9
Manston	44	17.4	78	6.9	18.4	11	8.6	15.8	63	6.0	10.9	32	3.6
Melbury	143	15.4	91	4.6	15.5	30	6.3	14.5	99	6.3	9.9	122	2.7
Morecambe	7	17.9	45	5.7	16.7	69	5.9	14.8	66	6.5	10.5	130	2.9
Nottingham (Watnall)	117	17.5	53	6.7	17.3	10	6.8	14.8	51	5.9	10.1	45	2.8
Oxford	63	17.9	93	7.0	18.3	12	7.9	15.3	43	5.5	10.3	34	2.6
Penzance	19	16.1	75	4.1	17.1	34	6.3	16.0	47	5.5	11.8	110	3.4
Plymouth	27	16.1	93	5.1	16.7	31	6.9	15.9	46	6.1	11.1	84	3.5
Prestwick	16	16.7	64	5.3	15.8	42	5.1	13.0	87	6.0	9.7	90	2.5
Rhoose	65	16.6	82	5.8	16.8	24	7.1	15.4	80	6.5	10.3	98	2.9
St Mawgan	103	15.8	87	4.3	16.5	33	6.4	15.8	71	5.8	11.1	108	3.1
Shawbury	72	17.1	72	6.3	16.4	24	6.4	14.1	25	5.6	9.9	49	2.8
Sheffield	131	17.7	51	7.1	17.3	9	7.1	14.5	37	6.2	10.3	54	2.2
Skegness	5	17.5	17	7.8	17.5	12	7.6	14.9	64	6.4	10.5	22	2.6
Southampton	3	17.8	70	7.1	18.7	12	8.1	16.7	44	5.1	11.4	77	2.7
Stornoway	15	14.8	52	5.5	14.3	83	4.1	11.5	104	3.8	8.7	116	1.6
Tenby	5	16.0	89	4.9	15.9	46	6.8	14.5	92	6.3	10.5	151	3.5
Tiree	9	15.3	84	6.3	14.7	70	5.1	12.0	109	5.7	9.7	145	2.1
Torbay (Torquay)	8	16.6	42	6.0	17.3	13	7.6	16.7	93	6.5	11.4	91	3.2
Trawscoed	10	16.7	25	5.6	16.3	33	6.1	15.1	35	6.3	11.1	101	3.2
Ventnor	135	16.3	62	7.4	17.5	5	8.8	16.6	43	6.3	11.7	56	3.4
Waddington	68	17.9	14	7.3	17.7	13	7.2	14.7	73	6.5	10.2	29	2.9
Weymouth	21	16.4	60	7.0	16.9	19	8.0	16.2	76	5.7	11.5	94	2.9
Whitby	41	16.3	31	6.3	16.8	12	6.5	13.7	16	5.0	10.1	65	2.2
Worthing	2	16.9	74	7.3	17.7	5	9.1	15.8	39	6.0	11.1	64	3.5
Writtle	35	17.7	47	6.9	17.9	49	7.9	14.7	43	6.3	10.1	19	3.3

TEMPERATURE, RAINFALL AND SUNSHINE—*contd.*

	1991									1992					
	November			*December*			*Year*			*January*			*February*		
	Temp. °C	Rain mm	Sun hrs	Temp. °C	Rain mm	Sun hrs	Temp. °C	Rain mm	Sun hrs	Temp. °C	Rain mm	Sun hrs	Temp. °C	Rain mm	Sun hrs
Aberdeen (Dyce)	5.6	99	2.1	4.0	20	1.6	8.3	724	3.8	3.7	44	2.5	4.6	31	3.0
Aberporth	7.5	100	1.0	5.9	18	1.1	9.5	770	4.1	4.7	47	2.6	6.5	55	2.1
Aldergrove	6.1	109	1.9	5.7	78	0.9	9.2	802	3.5	4.5	57	1.0	5.2	62	1.9
Aspatria	6.1	168	1.9	4.7	88	1.1	9.0	992	4.0	3.5	39	1.6	5.3	114	2.2
Bala	6.2	168	1.3	4.1	137	1.0	8.5	1230	3.1	3.2	62	1.4	5.5	70	1.6
Birmingham (Elmdon)	6.3	55	1.6	4.0	13	1.2	9.3	614	3.8	3.2	71	1.1	5.3	23	2.2
Boulmer	5.9	77	2.4	4.9	45	2.4	8.7	533	4.1	4.5	11	2.5	5.5	25	3.5
Bournemouth (Hurn)	6.9	51	2.3	5.0	35	1.7	9.7	734	4.5	3.6	20	2.1	5.2	32	2.1
Bradford	6.0	106	1.7	4.7	97	0.5	9.1	810	2.9	3.3	62	1.0	5.5	46	2.0
Braemar	4.0	114	0.9	2.7	51	0.9	6.9	886	–	1.9	62	1.6	3.3	53	1.8
Buxton	5.1	134	1.5	3.9	144	1.1	8.0	995	3.5	2.2	76	1.2	4.3	85	2.3
Cambridge	7.0	55	1.7	4.3	12	1.4	9.9	452	3.7	3.9	68	1.6	5.6	14	1.9
Cheltenham	7.3	95	1.7	4.2	19	1.5	10.0	841	3.9	4.0	82	1.3	5.5	34	2.3
Clacton-on-Sea	7.1	53	–	5.3	25	–	10.0	432	–	4.5	19	2.1	5.2	15	2.5
Douglas	7.4	145	1.3	7.1	78	0.9	9.5	994	3.3	5.6	47	1.3	6.3	98	2.0
Dumfries	6.0	140	2.4	4.3	93	0.7	–	–	–	3.4	60	1.3	5.1	91	1.8
Dundee	5.8	43	1.7	4.3	38	1.4	8.9	648	–	3.7	52	2.1	5.3	28	2.9
Durham	5.3	60	2.1	3.8	45	2.2	8.7	533	3.8	3.5	23	2.1	5.4	34	3.5
East Malling	7.1	57	1.8	4.7	20	2.0	10.0	610	4.3	4.3	10	1.7	5.5	21	2.5
Edinburgh	5.7	50	2.1	4.8	57	1.4	8.5	658	3.6	3.7	62	2.4	5.3	48	3.0
Glasgow (Abbotsinch)	5.7	171	1.9	4.6	126	0.7	8.9	1113	3.7	3.5	110	1.1	5.4	141	1.9
Gogerddan	7.7	121	1.4	5.3	41	1.4	9.6	935	4.0	4.1	55	2.4	6.7	60	1.7
Hastings	7.8	139	2.0	6.3	26	2.3	10.3	737	4.6	4.9	14	2.0	5.9	23	2.9
Hull	6.7	43	–	5.1	36	–	10.1	458	–	4.0	41	–	5.9	23	–
Inverness	6.7	70	1.4	5.8	45	0.7	9.2	648	3.3	5.4	94	1.6	5.9	42	2.4
Leeming	6.2	63	2.1	4.1	31	1.5	9.3	499	3.6	3.0	32	1.8	5.6	22	3.0
Lerwick	5.9	190	1.0	5.1	120	0.2	7.5	1198	2.9	5.2	105	0.9	4.8	147	1.7
London (Heathrow)	7.4	59	2.0	5.0	12	2.0	10.7	535	4.1	4.7	13	1.8	5.9	18	1.7
Long Ashton	7.1	119	–	4.5	33	–	9.8	870	–	3.7	47	–	5.5	41	–
Lowestoft	6.6	61	1.6	4.8	28	1.4	9.7	385	4.1	4.4	50	1.8	4.9	17	2.8
Manchester (Ringway)	6.6	70	1.8	5.3	63	1.3	9.6	577	3.7	3.5	45	1.5	5.7	51	2.4
Manston	7.0	57	1.7	5.3	18	1.9	10.1	486	4.5	4.2	17	1.6	5.1	13	2.7
Melbury	7.7	151	1.4	5.9	68	1.4	9.4	1218	4.0	3.8	53	2.1	6.1	76	1.8
Morecambe	7.1	151	2.0	5.1	103	1.4	9.9	937	3.9	3.5	64	1.8	6.0	77	2.3
Nottingham (Watnall)	6.1	47	1.7	4.3	42	1.3	9.3	527	3.7	3.2	38	1.7	5.3	24	2.2
Oxford	7.2	62	1.9	4.3	16	1.9	10.0	528	4.1	3.7	30	1.5	5.5	22	2.3
Penzance	9.3	100	2.1	8.4	35	1.1	11.2	1048	4.2	6.4	40	1.9	7.7	83	2.7
Plymouth	8.2	79	2.0	7.1	46	1.3	–	–	–	5.1	27	2.1	6.2	69	2.4
Prestwick	6.4	184	2.0	5.5	114	0.8	9.1	989	4.0	4.5	96	1.9	5.9	111	2.0
Rhoose	7.3	87	1.9	5.3	42	1.1	9.8	842	4.2	3.7	42	1.3	5.7	34	1.8
St Mawgan	8.5	97	1.9	7.0	30	1.5	10.3	958	4.3	4.8	40	2.9	6.4	61	2.4
Shawbury	6.3	53	1.7	4.5	16	0.9	9.1	517	3.7	3.0	51	0.9	5.7	21	2.2
Sheffield	6.5	73	1.4	5.3	78	0.9	9.6	667	3.7	3.7	44	1.2	5.9	26	1.8
Skegness	6.4	35	1.9	4.7	29	1.6	9.7	380	4.0	4.3	37	1.9	5.3	20	2.6
Southampton	7.9	56	1.9	5.8	28	1.4	11.0	661	4.0	4.7	21	2.1	6.0	38	2.0
Stornoway	6.5	215	1.2	6.7	85	0.5	9.0	1071	3.0	6.2	73	0.5	5.9	146	1.6
Tenby	7.9	98	2.0	–	–	–	–	–	–	5.2	55	2.0	6.9	65	1.7
Tiree	7.3	200	1.4	7.4	116	0.2	9.0	1282	4.0	6.7	85	0.7	6.8	151	1.8
Torbay (Torquay)	8.7	66	2.0	7.6	29	1.1	–	–	–	5.7	39	1.9	6.9	55	3.1
Valley	8.4	82	1.5	6.9	27	1.8	–	–	–	5.5	41	2.1	6.9	55	2.2
Ventnor	8.5	70	2.5	6.9	53	2.0	10.5	621	4.9	5.2	16	2.5	6.3	27	2.7
Waddington	6.1	43	2.3	4.5	23	1.8	9.5	414	4.1	3.1	61	2.0	5.4	21	2.6
Weymouth	8.6	49	–	6.5	24	–	10.5	691	–	4.7	27	–	6.1	34	–
Whitby	6.4	71	2.0	4.7	46	2.3	9.2	476	3.8	4.2	25	2.3	5.8	30	3.7
Worthing	7.6	79	2.1	5.5	24	1.9	10.1	642	4.6	4.6	14	2.3	5.3	26	2.5
Writtle	6.9	52	1.8	3.9	19	1.2	9.6	526	3.9	3.9	14	1.6	5.3	13	2.4

TEMPERATURE, RAINFALL AND SUNSHINE—*contd.*

1992	*March*			*April*			*May*			*June*		
	Temp. °C	Rain mm	Sun hrs	Temp. °C	Rain mm	Sun hrs	Temp. °C	Rain mm	Sun hrs	Temp. °C	Rain mm	Sun hrs
Aberdeen (Dyce)	6.1	80	2.7	7.2	73	3.4	10.9	54	7.4	13.7	59	5.5
Aberporth	7.3	67	1.9	8.3	69	4.2	12.9	44	7.9	14.3	50	7.1
Aldergrove	6.7	97	2.5	7.7	92	2.6	11.9	33	6.8	14.7	43	5.8
Aspatria	6.4	125	2.7	7.9	112	3.3	12.6	47	8.8	15.1	26	8.1
Bala	6.7	147	1.9	7.5	80	3.2	12.1	82	7.3	13.5	68	5.8
Birmingham (Elmdon)	7.3	55	2.3	8.7	40	3.8	13.5	78	8.3	15.8	74	6.6
Boulmer	6.9	70	3.7	7.8	78	4.7	10.4	16	7.5	13.7	17	7.5
Bournemouth (Hurn)	7.5	60	2.3	8.7	84	5.3	14.7	21	9.0	15.4	28	8.5
Bradford	6.7	95	2.2	8.2	55	3.4	12.5	32	6.6	15.3	31	5.9
Braemar	4.3	116	2.3	5.1	63	3.2	10.1	43	8.5	–	42	–
Buxton	5.5	143	1.8	6.9	113	3.7	11.9	51	7.5	14.6	60	–
Cambridge	7.8	58	2.4	9.0	41	3.9	13.9	34	7.5	16.2	26	6.2
Cheltenham	–	–	–	9.1	–	4.9	14.7	52	8.4	16.7	–	7.3
Clacton-on-Sea	7.1	65	2.3	8.9	61	3.9	13.7	37	8.1	15.7	32	8.0
Douglas	7.1	111	1.6	7.9	119	2.5	12.3	77	8.1	–	–	–
Dumfries	6.5	146	2.5	7.7	101	3.5	12.3	34	7.1	–	–	–
Dundee	6.5	104	–	7.9	38	3.9	11.5	29	7.9	15.0	30	–
Durham	6.7	63	3.2	8.0	95	4.1	11.6	19	7.1	14.6	20	6.5
East Malling	8.1	53	2.3	9.2	60	4.6	14.4	49	8.6	15.9	17	8.1
Edinburgh	6.7	77	2.6	7.3	38	3.4	12.0	34	6.4	14.2	37	5.3
Glasgow (Abbotsinch)	6.7	130	2.7	7.7	66	2.8	12.1	79	6.6	14.9	23	6.3
Gogerddan	7.4	108	1.9	–	18	–	–	–	–	14.7	44	–
Hastings	7.7	52	2.3	9.3	76	5.1	14.3	22	9.3	15.7	22	8.8
Hull	7.6	62	–	9.2	51	–	13.3	24	–	15.9	34	–
Inverness	5.9	74	2.1	7.5	37	3.2	11.0	42	6.5	14.0	28	5.1
Leeming	7.1	47	3.0	8.6	50	3.7	12.6	30	7.7	15.4	21	6.6
Lerwick	4.3	115	2.4	5.7	95	3.5	9.1	75	7.5	11.9	32	7.9
London (Heathrow)	8.3	39	2.0	9.8	57	4.3	15.6	95	8.8	17.4	23	7.1
Long Ashton	7.6	113	–	8.6	87	–	13.5	41	–	15.7	49	–
Lowestoft	7.3	77	2.9	8.9	60	4.6	13.5	43	8.2	15.7	35	7.9
Manchester (Ringway)	7.3	85	2.3	8.5	53	3.8	13.7	57	8.2	15.9	32	7.3
Manston	7.6	60	2.9	8.9	41	4.6	13.9	51	9.2	15.9	15	8.1
Melbury	7.3	79	2.2	8.1	98	4.2	12.5	33	7.9	13.7	27	8.0
Morecambe	7.1	127	2.4	8.7	73	3.9	13.8	57	8.3	16.3	27	8.0
Nottingham (Watnall)	6.9	56	2.3	8.5	41	4.0	13.4	47	8.0	16.3	53	6.5
Oxford	7.9	48	–	9.4	58	4.6	14.4	62	8.5	16.5	43	7.0
Penzance	9.1	58	3.6	9.6	118	5.3	13.2	18	7.9	15.5	19	7.8
Plymouth	8.1	56	2.9	9.0	111	5.1	13.2	22	9.0	15.9	16	8.9
Prestwick	6.9	125	2.7	7.9	57	2.6	12.5	66	8.3	14.9	37	6.9
Rhoose	7.5	68	2.8	8.7	83	4.6	13.5	34	8.2	15.8	27	8.5
St Mawgan	7.8	51	2.4	8.7	95	4.8	13.1	19	8.3	14.9	36	8.2
Shawbury	7.1	53	2.4	8.4	43	4.2	12.9	83	7.9	14.9	56	6.4
Sheffield	7.1	74	2.4	8.8	42	4.2	13.7	58	7.7	16.1	52	6.4
Skegness	–	73	3.1	–	28	4.5	12.9	35	8.3	15.3	15	9.4
Southampton	8.1	37	2.2	9.5	91	4.9	15.0	16	9.0	17.1	49	7.4
Stornoway	5.3	158	2.2	7.0	94	3.5	10.7	50	8.0	12.7	33	6.2
Tenby	7.7	97	2.2	8.5	82	4.5	12.7	32	8.2	16.1	14	7.9
Tiree	6.7	151	2.0	7.6	122	3.7	11.3	48	8.3	13.4	33	6.7
Torbay (Torquay)	8.9	41	3.3	9.9	73	5.6	13.9	18	8.9	16.3	31	9.3
Valley	8.0	78	2.9	8.9	59	4.5	13.0	79	8.4	15.2	50	8.0
Ventnor	7.9	35	2.7	9.3	83	5.9	13.8	26	9.6	16.1	17	8.6
Waddington	6.9	58	2.9	8.7	25	4.5	13.4	34	8.4	15.9	25	6.4
Weymouth	8.1	43	–	9.0	82	–	13.3	13	–	15.5	30	–
Whitby	7.3	71	3.3	8.7	43	4.5	11.6	9	8.3	14.4	49	5.8
Worthing	7.8	43	2.4	8.9	88	5.3	13.9	16	9.3	15.3	19	8.0
Writtle	7.5	60	–	8.9	51	4.2	13.7	53	–	15.7	27	–

METEOROLOGICAL OBSERVATIONS London (Heathrow)

Entries of maximum temperature cover the 24 hour period 9–9 h; minimum temperature the 24 hour period 9–9 h; rainfall is for the 24 hours commencing at 9 h on the day of entry; sunshine is for the 24 hours 0–24 h; mean wind speed is 10 metres above the ground. 100 knots = 115.1 mph; 100 mm = 3.94 in; °F = 9/5°C + 32. Averages are for the period 1951–80 except for mean wind speed which is for 1961–80.

JULY 1991

	Temperature Max. °C	Min. °C	Wind speed knots	Rain-fall mm	Sun-shine hrs
Day 1	20.7	13.8	5.7	0.0	5.4
2	20.0	11.5	3.7	25.1	3.0
3	24.1	13.5	5.4	0.0	9.6
4	27.4	15.6	8.6	0.0	12.4
5	27.6	17.3	10.3	5.5	13.0
6	23.4	17.7	6.3	0.0	13.1
7	26.5	15.9	6.0	0.0	11.5
8	20.8	16.5	9.9	0.0	0.3
9	22.7	14.2	8.7	0.0	9.7
10	25.5	12.1	7.0	0.0	12.3
11	27.6	16.9	6.9	0.0	10.8
12	20.7	13.5	8.0	0.0	1.0
13	29.4	15.2	5.3	0.2	0.0
14	24.1	11.9	4.7	0.0	9.3
15	20.9	14.1	5.4	0.0	5.0
16	21.4	13.7	4.9	0.5	3.6
17	21.2	10.6	3.1	14.2	7.0
18	23.8	12.8	6.6	2.5	4.7
19	19.9	14.2	5.1	0.0	2.5
20	23.8	14.0	3.3	0.0	8.9
21	21.2	14.6	2.0	0.0	3.5
22	24.0	13.0	3.3	0.0	7.5
23	27.1	16.6	4.2	0.7	3.5
24	18.6	13.6	4.5	15.3	1.3
25	21.8	13.2	3.3	0.0	7.4
26	24.1	14.5	2.5	0.0	9.0
27	24.6	14.4	3.2	0.0	10.3
28	25.6	13.2	4.7	0.0	10.1
29	28.5	16.7	8.5	0.0	11.7
30	18.7	17.5	2.4	28.9	0.0
31	23.4	14.1	4.2	0.0	11.2
Total	–	–	–	92.9	218.6
Mean	23.2	14.4	5.4	–	–
Temp. °F	73.8	57.9	–	–	–
Average	22.0	12.9	8.2	51.0	189.7

AUGUST 1991

	Temperature Max. °C	Min. °C	Wind speed knots	Rain-fall mm	Sun-shine hrs
Day 1	23.6	14.3	2.5	14.4	8.8
2	23.7	13.8	3.0	0.0	11.4
3	23.9	16.3	3.3	0.0	2.6
4	24.5	14.0	3.4	0.1	10.1
5	23.5	15.0	5.0	0.0	3.6
6	22.5	16.9	5.4	0.0	1.5
7	19.9	16.1	2.3	7.8	0.0
8	23.9	14.7	3.2	0.0	11.2
9	24.6	11.9	4.8	0.0	9.1
10	26.7	17.9	6.0	0.0	8.0
11	21.7	17.5	4.8	0.1	0.5
12	23.2	13.0	2.8	0.0	10.9
13	23.7	15.2	2.2	0.0	7.5
14	25.1	16.9	2.3	0.0	5.0
15	25.1	14.4	4.2	0.0	12.7
16	24.1	15.1	4.2	0.0	12.1
17	24.0	14.4	5.5	0.0	9.3
18	21.6	9.9	2.4	0.0	9.3
19	24.7	9.9	3.4	0.0	8.7
20	25.2	14.5	2.7	0.0	11.8
21	27.9	15.7	4.8	0.0	8.6
22	24.5	18.3	6.5	1.3	3.4
23	17.8	13.5	8.6	2.3	1.0
24	22.6	12.9	3.2	0.0	4.4
25	24.6	11.5	2.1	0.0	7.6
26	27.0	13.0	2.3	0.0	11.9
27	26.7	13.7	2.8	0.0	11.4
28	24.0	14.3	4.3	0.0	3.0
29	23.7	12.2	5.1	0.0	12.5
30	25.4	13.4	6.4	0.0	11.7
31	26.7	15.0	6.5	0.0	12.1
Total	–	–	–	26.0	241.7
Mean	24.1	14.4	4.1	–	–
Temp. °F	75.4	57.9	–	–	–
Average	21.6	12.7	8.0	58.0	176.4

SEPTEMBER 1991

	Temperature Max. °C	Min. °C	Wind speed knots	Rain-fall mm	Sun-shine hrs
Day 1	29.7	13.6	2.9	0.0	10.1
2	26.3	15.0	2.3	0.0	9.6
3	25.8	14.8	4.2	0.0	9.6
4	27.5	14.1	5.2	0.0	6.8
5	25.0	14.8	3.3	0.0	7.4
6	20.7	14.1	4.3	0.0	10.0
7	21.4	9.1	2.0	0.0	11.8
8	24.7	9.7	1.5	0.0	10.6
9	23.9	11.4	3.4	0.0	8.9
10	24.3	12.1	0.8	0.0	5.8
11	18.8	13.3	5.4	0.0	0.0
12	21.6	12.2	4.9	0.0	8.7
13	23.3	9.5	3.7	0.0	9.4
14	24.6	13.5	6.8	3.6	5.5
15	22.2	14.2	3.3	3.1	6.1
16	20.8	13.5	6.5	2.9	0.1
17	21.8	10.7	5.4	0.0	8.1
18	21.4	12.2	4.0	0.0	1.7
19	19.6	6.6	1.0	0.0	8.3
20	20.2	6.5	2.5	0.0	10.2
21	24.6	9.6	6.5	6.8	7.8
22	18.8	11.3	8.8	0.0	9.0
23	19.6	11.6	8.6	0.0	0.1
24	18.7	14.2	9.0	2.6	0.1
25	18.9	11.7	1.5	0.2	3.6
26	17.7	10.0	1.6	11.2	3.4
27	12.6	10.2	1.7	0.1	0.1
28	14.2	6.6	8.0	12.3	0.7
29	16.9	12.0	2.9	0.9	0.2
30	15.2	7.5	3.1	0.0	9.3
31					
Total	–	–	–	43.7	183.0
Mean	21.4	11.5	4.2	–	–
Temp. °F	70.5	52.7	–	–	–
Average	19.2	10.6	7.9	56.0	144.7

OCTOBER 1991

	Temperature Max. °C	Min. °C	Wind speed knots	Rain-fall mm	Sun-shine hrs
Day 1	17.2	10.3	8.6	0.0	8.3
2	17.9	0.2	4.3	0.0	8.0
3	18.8	11.7	5.6	0.2	1.6
4	17.0	6.0	2.7	0.0	6.0
5	15.4	7.1	2.6	2.8	0.2
6	14.5	3.8	2.5	0.0	10.0
7	16.9	6.9	5.3	0.0	3.5
8	14.6	6.4	3.6	0.0	0.2
9	17.0	10.0	4.2	0.8	1.0
10	20.1	11.5	4.3	0.0	1.9
11	20.7	13.7	5.7	0.2	3.1
12	18.0	12.1	3.0	0.0	3.3
13	17.5	7.5	2.0	0.7	3.4
14	17.0	8.9	2.5	0.0	2.2
15	15.3	10.2	2.3	0.6	1.1
16	16.3	10.8	10.0	1.2	0.9
17	12.0	7.4	12.4	0.0	8.1
18	10.0	7.3	5.8	0.0	0.3
19	9.9	2.8	5.6	0.0	7.1
20	9.8	2.3	3.0	0.0	1.7
21	11.8	1.5	2.5	0.0	7.7
22	11.7	1.5	2.6	0.0	0.5
23	10.6	2.5	2.7	0.0	0.0
24	10.2	7.6	2.4	0.0	0.0
25	10.7	8.5	2.1	0.0	0.1
26	11.5	8.6	3.1	0.0	0.0
27	12.9	8.6	3.1	0.1	0.4
28	13.8	8.2	5.1	0.2	0.0
29	14.3	8.2	7.3	6.9	2.6
30	14.3	9.8	3.4	0.1	3.9
31	15.3	6.3	13.1	4.7	0.0
Total	–	–	–	18.5	87.1
Mean	14.6	7.6	4.6	–	–
Temp. °F	58.3	45.7	–	–	–
Average	15.2	7.6	7.8	56.0	104.4

NOVEMBER 1991

	Temperature Max. °C	Min. °C	Wind speed knots	Rain-fall mm	Sun-shine hrs
Day 1	16.4	11.5	12.6	5.6	0.6
2	14.9	10.3	12.5	5.6	2.3
3	10.6	7.8	10.3	2.9	2.4
4	9.9	3.4	7.8	0.7	4.5
5	7.6	3.5	5.0	0.2	1.8
6	13.0	−0.7	7.3	0.1	2.2
7	13.5	3.6	13.4	1.0	0.0
8	11.5	10.7	7.8	0.7	0.9
9	9.6	2.3	4.8	0.0	7.4
10	11.2	−0.7	6.6	3.6	0.2
11	10.0	2.3	5.9	0.0	0.1
12	10.4	0.1	8.7	4.8	0.2
13	8.9	3.9	6.0	0.1	5.8
14	7.5	0.6	2.3	0.0	1.5
15	9.1	−0.7	2.2	0.0	3.1
16	9.2	2.1	2.0	0.0	5.1
17	8.9	1.0	2.9	0.6	0.0
18	12.6	2.9	3.2	19.9	2.7
19	8.3	4.3	9.1	13.4	0.0
20	8.0	3.8	6.9	0.0	5.9
21	7.4	−1.5	2.0	0.0	4.8
22	9.3	−0.4	2.2	0.0	0.0
23	10.5	6.7	2.6	0.0	2.3
24	10.9	3.8	4.3	0.0	2.6
25	10.6	5.0	6.9	0.1	0.0
26	12.5	6.4	2.3	0.0	0.3
27	11.7	8.4	2.7	0.0	0.0
28	12.3	8.8	3.3	0.0	0.0
29	12.8	9.5	3.6	0.0	2.5
30	9.2	6.5	2.5	0.0	0.0
31					
Total	–	–	–	59.3	59.2
Mean	10.6	5.6	5.7	–	–
Temp. °F	51.1	42.1	–	–	–
Average	10.2	3.9	8.9	62.2	64.0

DECEMBER 1991

	Temperature Max. °C	Min. °C	Wind speed knots	Rain-fall mm	Sun-shine hrs
Day 1	10.8	7.5	2.3	0.0	0.0
2	9.1	6.7	3.5	0.0	0.0
3	8.0	7.5	4.5	0.0	0.0
4	7.7	5.0	5.7	0.0	0.0
5	8.3	5.3	3.2	0.0	0.0
6	7.5	0.9	2.7	0.0	5.2
7	6.0	−2.8	2.2	0.0	2.3
8	6.5	−2.5	2.5	0.0	5.0
9	5.1	−1.9	2.2	0.0	1.8
10	3.5	−0.9	3.5	0.0	5.9
11	1.1	−4.1	2.0	0.0	6.1
12	0.3	−8.0	1.9	0.0	0.0
13	7.4	−7.2	2.0	0.2	4.3
14	−0.9	−3.8	2.0	0.2	0.0
15	7.6	−5.4	2.0	1.6	2.7
16	10.8	−2.0	2.2	1.5	2.4
17	11.9	6.9	6.2	5.6	0.0
18	12.3	3.9	7.7	1.6	3.1
19	13.1	4.9	11.5	0.1	0.0
20	10.6	2.8	10.2	0.5	4.7
21	13.6	3.5	13.5	0.7	0.0
22	13.9	9.4	11.5	0.0	1.5
23	13.5	11.3	12.2	0.0	1.9
24	7.7	1.6	3.3	0.0	6.1
25	9.0	−0.5	3.5	0.0	1.8
26	11.2	−0.4	5.1	0.0	0.1
27	9.1	1.5	2.0	0.0	5.8
28	6.8	0.5	2.5	0.0	0.0
29	8.2	2.0	2.0	0.0	0.0
30	7.5	5.2	2.0	0.0	0.0
31	9.5	4.9	2.7	0.0	0.0
Total	–	–	–	12.0	60.7
Mean	7.8	1.3	4.5	–	–
Temp. °F	46.0	34.3	–	–	–
Average	7.9	2.2	7.0	55.0	43.9

JANUARY 1992

	Temperature Max. °C	Min. °C	Wind speed knots	Rain-fall mm	Sun-shine hrs
Day 1	10.4	4.8	7.6	0.0	0.1
2	11.6	8.5	10.7	0.0	0.0
3	11.8	8.6	12.6	3.1	0.2
4	11.7	6.1	4.2	1.8	0.0
5	13.6	6.7	7.9	0.1	0.0
6	12.3	10.1	5.7	0.0	5.5
7	11.5	6.7	6.3	1.2	0.2
8	12.4	6.8	8.3	1.5	0.0
9	8.9	7.4	7.7	1.9	0.1
10	7.2	2.6	6.2	0.0	6.3
11	5.9	0.3	2.3	0.0	4.9
12	5.7	−2.4	2.0	0.3	0.0
13	6.4	−2.1	2.2	0.0	0.2
14	6.0	1.0	2.0	0.0	0.0
15	6.0	4.6	2.0	0.0	0.0
16	6.9	1.9	2.4	0.0	0.0
17	4.7	−2.4	2.0	0.0	0.6
18	8.7	−0.1	2.1	0.0	3.1
19	8.0	0.4	3.6	0.3	0.0
20	5.4	5.0	7.3	0.0	0.0
21	3.7	−0.2	3.8	0.0	5.7
22	4.2	−3.2	2.3	0.0	7.0
23	3.0	−3.9	2.2	0.0	3.5
24	1.9	−4.5	2.0	0.0	0.0
25	6.4	−4.4	2.0	2.4	0.0
26	7.0	0.3	3.0	0.0	4.0
27	6.1	2.7	2.5	0.0	3.6
28	6.6	0.0	3.5	0.0	5.0
29	7.9	2.6	6.8	0.0	6.0
30	4.0	−1.5	2.1	0.0	0.0
31	4.4	−1.2	2.0	0.0	0.0
Total	–	–	–	12.6	56.0
Mean	7.5	2.0	4.4	–	–
Temp. °F	45.5	35.6	–	–	–
Average	6.7	1.1	8.6	51.0	48.8

FEBRUARY 1992

	Temperature Max. °C	Min. °C	Wind speed knots	Rain-fall mm	Sun-shine hrs
Day 1	2.5	−0.1	2.0	0.0	0.8
2	8.5	−1.8	3.0	1.0	0.0
3	9.5	−0.2	4.7	0.2	1.3
4	13.3	2.8	6.8	0.0	0.3
5	10.8	7.0	3.9	0.0	0.5
6	10.1	7.3	2.5	0.0	0.0
7	9.6	1.8	3.4	0.0	2.8
8	10.3	−1.2	4.0	0.2	2.9
9	10.7	1.8	6.5	1.7	0.5
10	9.4	2.4	4.9	7.7	1.8
11	10.7	4.3	2.4	0.1	0.1
12	12.6	8.7	7.0	2.9	0.0
13	10.5	4.4	4.6	0.0	5.6
14	10.6	3.1	7.0	1.8	0.0
15	10.1	6.0	7.3	0.0	6.3
16	7.5	1.8	7.8	0.0	4.7
17	6.5	−1.4	2.2	0.0	7.5
18	6.7	0.6	3.7	0.0	0.3
19	4.0	0.2	2.0	0.0	0.0
20	5.9	−3.5	2.0	0.0	0.8
21	7.8	−2.1	2.2	0.0	0.7
22	9.2	0.6	7.4	0.0	0.0
23	11.2	5.1	5.0	0.0	0.0
24	10.7	5.5	2.7	0.1	0.9
25	6.5	−0.9	2.3	0.0	0.2
26	12.1	0.6	3.5	0.0	0.3
27	14.2	5.0	6.0	2.0	5.4
28	8.4	6.3	2.5	0.0	0.0
29	14.6	3.8	3.5	0.0	6.6
30					
31					
Total	–	–	–	17.7	50.3
Mean	9.5	2.3	4.2	–	–
Temp. °F	49.1	36.1	–	–	–
Average	7.3	1.3	9.3	38.0	62.2

MARCH 1992

	Temperature Max. °C	Min. °C	Wind speed knots	Rain-fall mm	Sun-shine hrs
Day 1	10.2	3.0	4.9	2.9	0.0
2	10.6	1.3	6.6	0.1	2.6
3	12.3	4.9	7.6	0.0	0.0
4	13.6	5.8	4.8	0.0	5.3
5	11.6	4.4	5.6	0.6	0.1
6	14.0	3.9	6.7	0.0	7.3
7	12.3	6.0	7.1	0.2	0.8
8	10.6	6.0	3.1	0.0	2.3
9	12.2	1.4	4.8	0.1	5.6
10	13.3	5.5	7.9	3.7	1.7
11	10.4	2.7	8.1	0.2	0.4
12	11.1	6.3	12.1	0.4	0.0
13	13.2	8.8	11.5	0.1	2.0
14	11.1	3.0	4.9	0.2	0.2
15	13.4	6.2	4.3	0.9	0.0
16	13.7	7.6	2.1	0.0	0.0
17	13.6	8.2	3.2	0.0	2.7
18	14.3	8.4	5.3	0.0	1.1
19	15.9	2.7	4.1	0.0	2.3
20	14.6	6.4	6.3	0.5	0.1
21	13.3	6.8	10.4	3.0	5.8
22	14.3	7.3	8.7	4.5	2.0
23	9.4	3.9	6.5	2.9	3.2
24	9.5	4.1	12.2	0.4	4.7
25	9.3	4.8	4.7	6.0	0.4
26	9.0	4.8	8.0	0.5	4.3
27	8.3	4.4	9.2	0.0	0.7
28	9.9	2.4	2.2	0.0	0.1
29	10.9	5.0	5.5	5.0	0.0
30	8.7	2.4	3.7	6.2	0.3
31	10.3	4.8	5.7	0.1	5.8
Total	–	–	–	38.5	61.8
Mean	11.8	4.9	6.4	–	–
Temp. °F	53.2	40.8	–	–	–
Average	10.2	2.6	9.5	43.0	110.8

APRIL 1992

	Temperature Max. °C	Min. °C	Wind speed knots	Rain-fall mm	Sun-shine hrs
Day 1	12.4	1.6	4.9	0.0	8.5
2	9.4	4.5	4.6	0.0	0.7
3	8.9	3.5	4.8	0.0	0.9
4	10.0	1.5	3.1	0.0	5.7
5	13.4	−0.5	3.3	0.0	9.6
6	8.9	4.6	6.5	2.4	0.0
7	11.3	5.2	5.8	1.5	0.0
8	17.4	5.0	3.7	0.0	8.1
9	17.3	4.9	3.3	0.0	10.6
10	17.0	2.8	2.1	0.0	7.2
11	18.2	4.2	2.3	0.0	10.3
12	14.3	8.8	5.7	0.4	2.3
13	13.1	4.9	9.5	0.0	5.2
14	10.1	6.9	7.4	15.2	0.0
15	9.3	3.4	7.6	2.7	3.1
16	10.3	2.2	5.9	5.0	6.3
17	16.0	3.9	3.5	0.1	0.2
18	18.5	7.1	4.7	0.0	3.2
19	17.4	8.5	2.6	0.0	3.6
20	18.5	9.6	4.5	0.0	10.6
21	17.3	10.5	3.7	0.0	3.6
22	14.9	7.5	3.3	0.3	1.6
23	15.6	8.2	4.5	0.0	5.0
24	15.0	7.0	8.5	1.1	0.4
25	16.2	8.1	8.1	0.1	8.0
26	13.9	10.1	9.7	0.8	0.4
27	15.5	8.0	8.6	12.4	5.6
28	13.8	7.4	4.7	5.9	3.3
29	13.0	3.4	4.0	0.2	5.7
30	13.4	5.7	5.5	9.0	0.0
31					
Total	–	–	–	57.1	129.7
Mean	14.0	5.6	5.2	–	–
Temp. °F	57.2	42.1	–	–	–
Average	13.2	4.6	8.3	41.0	146.9

MAY 1992

	Temperature Max. °C	Min. °C	Wind speed knots	Rain-fall mm	Sun-shine hrs
Day 1	15.0	8.4	6.0	0.0	8.2
2	13.2	4.7	4.5	0.3	5.8
3	15.6	2.5	2.5	0.0	12.1
4	18.2	5.1	2.4	0.0	9.8
5	13.3	10.0	2.4	0.0	0.6
6	20.3	6.0	3.6	0.0	7.9
7	20.0	10.0	5.7	0.0	10.7
8	15.1	9.5	8.0	2.6	8.1
9	15.8	6.9	5.9	9.0	1.4
10	13.4	4.9	3.1	0.2	1.5
11	16.0	7.8	6.3	1.1	8.0
12	16.7	10.2	8.6	0.0	0.1
13	22.6	8.9	5.4	0.0	10.9
14	26.7	12.7	5.0	1.5	12.8
15	20.4	12.2	2.3	0.0	4.4
16	21.3	10.5	5.2	0.0	13.8
17	18.2	6.8	5.1	0.0	11.5
18	21.6	7.8	7.3	0.0	10.6
19	26.5	11.0	4.7	0.0	13.3
20	26.8	11.5	3.9	0.0	13.6
21	26.8	11.0	2.7	0.0	9.1
22	26.6	12.5	3.6	0.0	13.5
23	25.9	12.5	5.3	0.6	9.0
24	27.3	14.2	4.2	0.0	11.4
25	26.6	14.4	2.5	0.0	12.8
26	26.7	16.0	5.7	0.0	13.4
27	23.4	13.4	6.9	0.0	13.1
28	26.2	16.1	6.0	13.3	5.6
29	20.0	15.1	2.6	61.8	2.5
30	20.7	12.9	4.9	0.0	5.9
31	24.0	11.5	3.6	4.1	10.5
Total	–	–	–	94.5	271.9
Mean	21.0	10.2	4.7	–	–
Temp. °F	69.8	50.4	–	–	–
Average	17.1	7.8	8.5	48.0	196.1

JUNE 1992

	Temperature Max. °C	Min. °C	Wind speed knots	Rain-fall mm	Sun-shine hrs
Day 1	19.5	15.5	2.4	1.4	0.1
2	20.4	12.7	1.8	0.0	3.9
3	21.3	11.1	3.5	0.5	12.2
4	16.1	10.7	2.7	1.1	0.1
5	15.1	10.0	3.7	6.1	0.0
6	23.2	10.5	3.3	1.4	3.3
7	15.8	13.0	1.4	0.0	0.0
8	21.9	13.0	1.7	0.0	9.4
9	23.2	12.0	2.1	1.5	8.6
10	23.6	11.9	1.7	0.0	8.2
11	22.4	11.8	4.9	0.0	10.2
12	24.1	11.4	4.1	0.0	13.3
13	25.9	11.5	1.7	0.0	13.3
14	27.4	13.2	2.4	0.0	14.1
15	28.2	13.0	3.4	0.0	14.4
16	20.9	14.4	7.7	0.0	3.3
17	20.3	10.6	6.8	0.0	9.8
18	19.4	9.2	4.8	0.0	6.5
19	15.4	7.9	4.8	7.2	4.2
20	20.9	9.4	8.0	0.0	13.3
21	22.7	10.1	4.5	0.0	13.1
22	21.8	12.5	1.8	0.0	3.3
23	21.6	14.0	2.0	0.0	2.1
24	22.0	12.9	2.0	0.0	6.2
25	23.6	12.4	0.6	0.0	3.0
26	26.2	12.6	0.8	0.0	6.9
27	25.9	14.7	2.4	0.0	7.0
28	27.8	13.7	2.1	0.0	11.8
29	30.2	16.1	2.3	3.0	9.6
30	23.7	16.9	2.0	0.3	2.1
31					
Total	–	–	–	22.5	213.3
Mean	22.3	12.3	3.1	–	–
Temp. °F	72.1	54.1	–	–	–
Average	20.5	10.9	8.4	51.0	206.0

Source: data provided by the Met Office

Sports Results

ALPINE SKIING

WORLD CUP 1991–2

MEN

Downhill: F. Heinzer (Switzerland), 649 pts
Slalom: A. Tomba (Italy), 820 pts
Giant Slalom: A. Tomba (Italy), 520 pts
Super Giant Slalom: P. Accola (Switzerland), 429 pts
Overall: P. Accola (Switzerland), 1,699 pts

WOMEN

Downhill: K. Seizinger (Germany), 523 pts
Slalom: V. Schneider (Switzerland), 511 pts
Giant Slalom: C. Merle (France), 566 pts
Super Giant Slalom: C. Merle (France), 417 pts
Overall: P. Kronberger (Austria), 1,262 pts

Nations Cup: 1 Austria, 2 Switzerland, 3 Germany

AMERICAN FOOTBALL

XXVI American Superbowl 1992 (Minneapolis, 26 January): Washington Redskins beat Buffalo Bills 37–24
World League of American Football Bowl 1992 (Montreal, 7 June): Sacramento Surge beat Orlando Thunder 21–17
American Bowl 1992 (Wembley, 16 August): San Francisco 49ers beat Washington Redskins 17–15
British League Championship final 1992 (Birmingham, 9 August): London Olympians beat Leicester Panthers 34–6

ANGLING

NATIONAL COARSE CHAMPIONSHIPS 1991

Division: 1
Venue: Trent and Mersey Canal; *no. of teams:* 86
Individual winner: P. Hargreaves (Alrewas AC), 6.600 kg
Team winners: Izaak Walton (Preston), 823 pts

Division: 2
Venue: River Severn; *no. of teams:* 86
Individual winner: J. Cowen (Kings Arms and Cheshunt), 36.270 kg
Team winners: Isis (Oxford), 826 pts

Division: 3
Venue: River Trent; *no. of teams: 8*
Individual winner: G. Egan (Measham and District), 11.760 kg
Team winners: Central AC, 774 pts

Division: 4
Venue: River Welland; *no. of teams:* 83
Individual winner: S. Wolstenholme (Erne Anglers), 22.570 kg
Team winners: Forth Park WML, 847 pts

Division: 5
Venue: Gloucester Canal; *no. of teams:* 68
Individual winner: V. Camilleri (Crawley MG), 7.630 kg
Team winners: Ossett Anglers, 675 pts

Division: 6
Venue: Gloucester Canal; *no. of teams:* 45
Individual winner: V. Sickemore (Papermakers AC), 9.010 kg
Team winners: A1 AC, 436 pts

WORLD CHAMPIONSHIPS 1992

River Erne, Belleek

Individual Champion: D. Wesson (Australia), 9.020 kg, 3 pts
Team Champions: Italy, 39.060 kg, 94 pts

ASSOCIATION FOOTBALL

LEAGUE COMPETITIONS 1991–2

ENGLAND AND WALES

Division 1
1. Leeds Utd, 82 pts
2. Manchester Utd, 78 pts

Relegated: Luton, 42 pts; Notts County, 40 pts; West Ham, 38 pts

Division 2
1. Ipswich, 84 pts
2. Middlesbrough, 80 pts

Third promotion place: Blackburn Rovers
Relegated: Plymouth Argyle, 48 pts; Brighton, 47 pts; Port Vale, 35 pts

Division 3
1. Brentford, 82 pts
2. Birmingham, 81 pts

Third promotion place: Peterborough Utd
Relegated: Bury, 51 pts; Shrewsbury, 47 pts; Torquay, 47 pts; Darlington, 37 pts

Division 4
1. Burnley, 83 pts
2. Rotherham, 77 pts
3. Mansfield, 77 pts

Fourth promotion place: Blackpool
No relegation

GM Vauxhall Conference
Promoted: Colchester Utd, 94 pts
Relegated: Cheltenham, 43 pts; Barrow, 38 pts

Women's Inaugural National League: Doncaster Belles

SCOTLAND

Premier Division
1. Rangers, 72 pts
2. Hearts, 63 pts

Relegated: St Mirren, 24 pts; Dunfermline, 18 pts

Division 1
1. Dundee, 58 pts
2. Partick Thistle, 57 pts

Relegated: Montrose, 27 pts; Forfar, 22 pts

Division 2
1. Dumbarton, 52 pts
2. Cowdenbeath, 51 pts

No relegation

CUP COMPETITIONS 1991–2

England

FA Cup final 1992 (Wembley, 9 May): Liverpool beat Sunderland 2–0
Rumbelows League Cup final 1992: Manchester Utd beat Nottingham Forest 1–0
Zenith Data Systems Cup final 1992: Nottingham Forest beat Southampton 3–2 a.e.t.
Autoglass Trophy final 1992: Stoke City beat Stockport County 1–0
FA Vase final 1992: Wimborne Town beat Guiseley 5–3
FA Trophy final 1992: Colchester Utd beat Witton Albion 3–1
Arthur Dunn Cup final 1992: Old Chigwellians beat Old Etonians 3–1
Women's FA Cup final 1992: Doncaster Belles beat Red Star Southampton 4–0
Charity Shield 1991: Arsenal and Tottenham Hotspur drew 0–0
Charity Shield 1992: Leeds Utd beat Liverpool 4–3

Wales

Welsh FA Cup final 1992: Cardiff beat Hednesford 1–0

Scotland

Scottish FA Cup final 1992 (Hampden Park, 9 May): Rangers beat Airdrieonians 2–1
B & Q Cup final 1991: Hamilton Academicals beat Ayr Utd 1–0
Skol Cup final 1991: Hibernian beat Dunfermline Athletic 2–0

Europe

European Cup final 1992 (Wembley, 20 May): Barcelona beat Sampdoria 1–0 a.e.t.
European Cup-Winners' Cup final 1992 (Lisbon): Werder Bremen beat Monaco 2–0
UEFA Cup final 1992: Ajax Amsterdam 2, Torino 2 on agg. Torino won on away goals rule

EUROPEAN CHAMPIONSHIPS

Qualifying Rounds

1991

16 Oct	*Wembley*	England 1, Turkey 0
	Bucharest	Romania 1, Scotland 0
	Nuremberg	Germany 4, Wales 1
	Belfast	N. Ireland 2, Austria 1
13 Nov	*Poznan*	Poland 1, England 1
	Hampden Park	Scotland 4, San Marino 0
	Cardiff	Wales 1, Luxembourg 0
	Odense	Denmark 2, N. Ireland 1

Finals

Sweden, 10–26 June 1992

Group 1: Sweden 5 pts; Denmark 3 pts; France 2 pts; England 2 pts

Group 2: Holland 5 pts; Germany 3 pts; Scotland 2 pts; CIS 2 pts

Semi-finals
Sweden 2, Germany 3
Holland 2, Denmark 2 a.e.t. Denmark won 5-4 on penalties

Final (Gothenburg)
Denmark 2, Germany 0

INTERNATIONALS 1992

19 Feb	*Wembley*	England 2, France 0
	Hampden Park	Scotland 1, N. Ireland 0
	Lansdowne Rd	Rep. of Ireland 0, Wales 1
25 Mar	*Prague*	Czechoslovakia 2, England 2
	Hampden Park	Scotland 1, Finland 1
29 Apr	*Moscow*	CIS 2, England 2
	Vienna	Austria 1, Wales 1
12 May	*Budapest*	Hungary 0, England 1
17 May	*Wembley*	England 1, Brazil 1
	Denver	USA 0, Scotland 1
21 May	*Toronto*	Canada 1, Scotland 3
30 May	*Utrecht*	Holland 4, Wales 0
2 June	*Bremen*	Germany 1, N. Ireland 1
3 June	*Helsinki*	Finland 1, England 2
	Oslo	Norway 0, Scotland 0
	Gifu	Argentina 1, Wales 0
7 June	*Matsuyama*	Japan 0, Wales 1
9 Sept	*Santander*	Spain 1, England 0

WORLD CUP 1994

Qualifying Rounds

1992

28 Apr	*Belfast*	N. Ireland 2, Lithuania 2
20 May	*Bucharest*	Romania 5, Wales 1
9 Sept	*Geneva*	Switzerland 3, Scotland 1
	Belfast	N. Ireland 3, Albania 0
	Cardiff	Wales 6, Faroes 0

Women's World Cup final 1991: USA beat Norway 2–1
African Nations Cup final 1992: Ivory Coast 0, Ghana 0 a.e.t. Ivory Coast won 11–10 on penalties

---

ATHLETICS

UK CROSS-COUNTRY CHAMPIONSHIPS

Basingstoke, 9 February 1992

Men (12,000 m)	min.	sec.
1 D. Clarke (Hercules–Wimbledon)	36	46
2 A. Bristow (Brighton)	37	02
3 P. Dugdale (Horwich)	37	09

Team result: 1 Scotland, 43 points

Women (6,000 m)		
1 A. Hulley (Leeds)	21	16
2 L. York (Leicester)	21	24
3 V. McPherson (Glasgow University)	21	25

Team result: 1 England, 14 points

WOMEN'S NATIONAL CROSS-COUNTRY CHAMPIONSHIPS

Cheltenham, 15 February 1992

	min.	sec.
1 L. York (Leicester)	19	49
2 A. Whitcombe (Parkside)	19	52
3 S. Rigg (Sale)	19	54

Team result: 1 Parkside, 103 points

AAA INDOOR CHAMPIONSHIPS

Birmingham, 15–16 February 1992

MEN'S EVENTS

metres	min.	sec.
60—J. Drummond (USA)		6.60
200—J. Drummond (USA)		21.40
400—A. Mafe (London Irish)		46.47
800—M. Steele (Longwood)	1	47.78
1,500—J. Chesire (Kenya)	3	43.34
3,000—J. Mayock (Barnsley)	8	01.54
60 *hurdles:* C. Jackson (Brecon)		7.55
		metres
High jump: S. Horn (Norway)		2.25
Pole vault: G. Nikov (Bulgaria)		5.45
Long jump: M. Forsythe (Haringey)		7.85
Triple jump: V. Samuels (Wolverhampton)		11.24
Shot: P. Edwards (Belgrave)		19.15

WOMEN'S EVENTS

metres	min.	sec.
60—S. Douglas (Milton Keynes)		7.31
200—R. Stevens (USA)		23.59
400—J. Richardson (Canada)		52.72
800—D. Gandy (Hounslow)	2	07.80
1,500—C. Cahill (Gateshead)	4	12.34
3,000—K. Hutcheson (Berryhill–Mansfield)	9	11.99
60 *hurdles:* J. Humphrey (USA)		8.23
		metres
High jump: D. Marti (Bromley)		1.91
Long jump: J. Wise (Coventry)		6.27
Triple jump: M. Griffith (Windsor)		13.16
Shot: Y. Hanson-Nortey (Hallamshire)		16.33

EUROPEAN INDOOR CHAMPIONSHIPS

Genoa, 28 February–1 March 1992

MEN'S EVENTS

metres	min.	sec.
60—J. Livingston (GB)		6.53
200—N. Antonov (Bulgaria)		20.41
400—S. Brankovic (Yugoslavia)		46.33
800—L. Gonzales (Spain)	1	46.80
1,500—M. Yates (GB)	3	42.32
3,000—G. di Napoli (Italy)	7	47.24
60 *hurdles:* I. Kazanov (Latvia)		7.55
5,000 *walk:* G. de Benedictis (Italy)	18	19.97
		metres
High jump: P. Sjoberg (Sweden)		2.38
Pole vault: P. Bochkaryev (CIS)		5.85
Long jump: D. Bogrianov (CIS)		8.12
Triple jump: L. Voloshin (CIS)		17.35
Shot: A. Bagach (CIS)		20.75
Heptathlon: C. Plaziat (France)		6,418 points

WOMEN'S EVENTS

metres	min.	sec.
60—Z. Tarnopolskaya (CIS)		7.24
200—O. Stepicheva (CIS)		23.18
400—S. Myers (Spain)		51.21
800—E. Kovacs (Romania)	1	59.98
1,500—Y. Podkopayeva (CIS)	4	06.61
3,000—M. Keszeg (Romania)	8	59.80
60 *hurdles:* L. Narozhilenko (CIS)		7.82
3,000 *walk:* A. Ivanova (CIS)	11	49.99
		metres
High jump: H. Henkel (Germany)		2.02
Long jump: L. Berezhnaya (CIS)		7.00
Triple jump: I. Kravets (CIS)		14.15
Shot: N. Lisovskaya (CIS)		20.70
Pentathlon: L. Nastase (Romania)		4,701 points

MEN'S NATIONAL CROSS-COUNTRY CHAMPIONSHIPS

Newark, 29 February 1992

	min.	sec.
1 E. Martin (Basildon)	40	29
2 W. Dee (Luton)	40	56
3 A. Carey (Warrington)	41	13

Team result: 1 Tipton, 229 points

GREAT BRITAIN v. USA INDOORS

Birmingham, 14 March 1992

MEN'S EVENTS

metres	min.	sec.
60—L. Christie (GB)		6.57
200—L. Christie (GB)		20.74
400—W. Caldwell (USA)		47.04
800—M. Dailey (USA)	1	47.24
Mile: M. Yates (GB)	3	54.77
3,000—R. Denmark (GB)	7	46.60
60 *hurdles:* C. Jackson (GB)		7.62
4 × 400 *relay:* USA	3	06.27
		metres
High jump: B. Stanton (USA)		2.31
Pole vault: D. Volz (USA)		5.60
Long jump: A. Ester (USA)		7.84
Triple jump: V. Samuels (GB)		16.73
Shot: R. Backes (USA)		19.79

Team points: USA 141, Great Britain 129

WOMEN'S EVENTS

metres	min.	sec.
60—T. Neighbours (USA)		7.19
200—D. Webber (USA)		23.56
400—N. Kaiser (USA)		52.08
800—P. Fryer (GB)	2	04.93
Mile: L. York (GB)	4	33.50
3,000—E. McColgan (GB)	8	43.34
60 *hurdles:* K. McKenzie (USA)		8.15
4 × 400 *relay:* USA	3	33.35
		metres
High jump: A. Bradburn (USA)		1.95
Long jump: D. Boone (USA)		6.49
Triple jump: M. Griffith (GB)		13.50
Shot: R. Pagel (USA)		17.78

Team points: USA 133, Great Britain 117

WORLD CROSS-COUNTRY CHAMPIONSHIPS

Boston, USA, 21 March 1992

MEN	min.	sec.
1 J. Ngugi (Kenya)	37	05
2 W. Mutwol (Kenya)	37	17
3 F. Bayisa (Ethiopia)	37	18

Team points: 1 Kenya 46, 2 France 145, 3 Great Britain 147

WOMEN

1	L. Jennings (USA)	21	16
2	C. McKiernan (Ireland)	21	18
3	A. Dias (Portugal)	21	19

Team points: 1 Kenya 47, 2 USA 77, 3 Ethiopia 96

LONDON MARATHON

12 April 1992

MEN		hr.	min.	sec.
1	A. Pinto (Portugal)	2	10	02
2	J. Huruk (Poland)	2	10	07
3	T. Naali (Tanzania)	2	10	08

WOMEN				
1	K. Dörre (Germany)	2	29	39
2	R. Kokówská (Poland)	2	29	59
3	A. Wallace (GB)	2	31	33

GREAT BRITAIN v. HUNGARY v. ITALY
(Field Events Only)

Sheffield, 5 June 1992

MEN'S EVENTS

	metres
High jump: B. Reilly (GB)	2.20
Pole vault: A. Pegoraro (Italy)	5.20
Long jump: F. Frigerio (Italy)	7.70
Triple jump: J. Edwards (GB)	17.26
Shot: P. Dal Soglio (Italy)	19.76
Discus: A. Horvath (Hungary)	60.88
Hammer: E. Sgruletti (Italy)	77.00
Javelin: M. Hill (GB)	78.44

Team points: Great Britain 70½, Italy 61, Hungary 42½

WOMEN'S EVENTS

	metres
High jump: A. Bevilacqua (Italy)	1.83
Long jump: F. May (GB)	6.73
Triple jump: M. Berkeley (GB)	13.56
Shot: A. Maffeis (Italy)	16.88
Discus: A. Maffeis (Italy)	54.50
Javelin: K. Zsigmond (Hungary)	63.90

Team points: Great Britain 49½, Italy 47, Hungary 35½

UNITED KINGDOM CHAMPIONSHIPS

Sheffield, 6–7 June 1992

MEN'S EVENTS

metres	min.	sec.
100—L. Christie (TVH)		10.43
200—M. Adam (Belgrave)		20.75
400—R. Black (Team Solent)		44.84
800—C. Robb (Liverpool)	1	46.95
1,500—S. Crabb (Enfield)	3	46.81
3,000—J. Nuttall (Preston)	7	58.69
5,000—I. Robinson (Preston)	14	03.93
3,000 *steeplechase:* C. Walker (Gateshead)	8	32.66
110 *hurdles:* C. Jackson (Brecon)		13.43
400 *hurdles:* K. Akabusi (Team Solent)		49.00
		metres
High jump: B. Reilly (Corby)		2.30
Pole vault: M. Edwards (Belgrave)		5.30
Long jump: S. Faulkner (Birchfield)		7.86
Triple jump: J. Edwards (Gateshead)		16.51
Shot: P. Edwards (Belgrave)		18.77
Discus: A. Ekoku (Belgrave)		56.42
Hammer: P. Head (Newham)		71.06
Javelin: M. Hill (Leeds)		84.38

WOMEN'S EVENTS

metres	min.	sec.
100—M. Richardson (Windsor)		11.68
200—P. Smith (Wigan)		23.46
400—S. Douglas (Trafford)		52.73
800—L. Robinson (Coventry)	2	04.47
1,500—B. Nicholson (Tipton)	4	13.16
3,000—E. McColgan (Dundee)	8	56.01
100 *hurdles:* K. Morley-Brown (Cardiff)		13.59
400 *hurdles:* G. Retchakan (Thurrock)		55.42
		metres
High jump: D. Marti (Bromley)		1.89
Long jump: Y. Idowu (Oxford City)		6.66
Triple jump: R. Kirby (Hounslow)		13.11
Shot: M. Augee (Bromley)		17.84
Discus: J. McKernan (Lisburn)		55.44
Javelin: A. Liverton (Exeter)		57.22

GREAT BRITAIN v. KENYA
(Track Events Only)

Edinburgh, 19 June 1992

MEN'S EVENTS

metres	min.	sec.
100—L. Christie (GB)		10.20
200—L. Christie (GB)		20.48
400—R. Black (GB)		45.12
800—C. Robb (GB)	1	47.08
1,500—K. McKay (GB)	3	35.94
3,000—P. Bitok (Kenya)	7	49.77
5,000—P. Kirui (Kenya)	13	17.26
3,000 *steeplechase:* T. Hanlon (GB)	8	16.50
110 *hurdles:* C. Jackson (GB)		13.30
400 *hurdles:* K. Akabusi (GB)		49.67
4 × 100 *relay:* Great Britain		39.98
4 × 400 *relay:* Great Britain	3	00.93

Team points: Great Britain 145, Kenya 92

WOMEN'S EVENTS

metres		
400—J. Stoute (GB)		52.29
800—P. Fryer (GB)	2	02.04
1,500—K. Wade (GB)	4	11.60
3,000—Y. Murray (GB)	8	36.63

Team points: Great Britain 62, Kenya 25

AAA CHAMPIONSHIPS

Sheffield, 5–6 June 1992

MEN'S EVENTS

10,000 *metres:* E. Martin (Basildon), 28 min. 02.56 sec.
Decathlon: A. Kruger (Border), 7,582 points

WOMEN'S EVENTS

10,000 *metres:* A. Wallace (Torbay), 32 min. 21.61 sec.
Heptathlon: C. Court (Birchfield), 5,846 points

Birmingham, 27–28 June 1992

MEN'S EVENTS

metres	min.	sec.
100—L. Christie (TVH)		10.09
200—J. Regis (Belgrave)		20.27
400—A. Daniel (Trinidad)		44.84
800—C. Robb (Liverpool)	1	45.16
1,500—K. McKay (Sale)	3	37.51
3,000—F. O'Mara (Ireland)	7	59.97

metres	min.	sec.
5,000—J. Buckner (Charnwood)	13	22.50
3,000 *steeplechase:* C. Walker (Gateshead)	8	25.15
110 *hurdles:* C. Jackson (Brecon)		13.15
400 *hurdles:* K. Akabusi (Team Solent)		49.16
10 km *walk:* M. Rush (Loughborough)	41	46.42
		metres
High jump: S. Smith (Liverpool)		2.31
Pole vault: I. Tullett (Belgrave)		5.30
Long jump: D. Culbert (Australia)		7.85
Triple jump: J. Golley (TVH)		16.81
Shot: P. Edwards (Belgrave)		19.08
Discus: W. Reiterer (Australia)		61.78
Hammer: S. Carlin (Australia)		74.60
Javelin: S. Backley (Cambridge)		88.14

WOMEN'S EVENTS

metres	min.	sec.
100—M. Gainsford (Australia)		11.38
200—M. Gainsford (Australia)		23.04
400—C. Freeman (Australia)		51.14
800—D. Edwards (Sale)	2	00.41
1,500—Y. Murray (Edinburgh)	4	05.87
3,000—L. York (Leicester)	8	50.18
100 *hurdles:* S. Gunnell (Essex Ladies)		13.13
400 *hurdles:* G. Retchakan (Thurrock)		55.04
5,000 *walk:* V. Lupton (Sheffield)	22	12.21
		metres
High jump: L. Haggett (Croydon)		1.89
Long jump: F. May (Derby)		6.70
Triple jump: R. Kirby (Hounslow)		13.09
Shot: M. Augee (Bromley)		17.29
Discus: J. McKernan (Lisburn)		54.48
Javelin: T. Sanderson (Hounslow)		63.26

GRAND PRIX 1992 FINAL RESULTS

MEN'S EVENTS

100 *metres:* D. Mitchell (USA), 53 pts
800 *metres:* N. Kiprotich (Kenya), 55 pts
1 *mile:* W. Kirochi (Kenya), 58 pts
5,000 *metres:* P. Bitok (Kenya), 57 pts
400 *metres hurdles:* K. Young (USA), 63 pts
High jump: P. Sjöberg (Sweden), 56½ pts
Triple jump: M. Conley (USA), 46 pts
Shot: W. Gunthor (Switzerland), 63 pts
Hammer: I. Astapkovich (Belarus), 59 pts
Overall Winner: K. Young (USA)

WOMEN'S EVENTS

200 *metres:* M. Ottey (Jamaica), 61 pts
400 *metres:* S. Richards (Jamaica), 51 pts
1,500 *metres:* L. Rogachova (Russia), 59 pts
5,000 *metres:* S. O'Sullivan (Ireland), 48 pts
100 *metres hurdles:* L. Tolbert (USA), 57 pts
Long jump: H. Drechsler (Germany), 63 pts
Discus: I. Wyludda (Germany), 49 pts
Javelin: T. Hattestad (Norway), 59 pts
Overall Winner: H. Drechsler (Germany)

BADMINTON

ENGLISH NATIONAL CHAMPIONSHIPS 1992

Men's Singles: A. Nielsen beat D. Hall 15–9, 15–9
Women's Singles: F. Smith beat S. Louis 11–6, 11–3
Men's Doubles: A. Goode and C. Hunt beat N. Ponting and D. Wright 15–7, 17–16
Women's Doubles: G. Clark and J. Bradbury beat G. Gowers and S. Sankey 15–9, 15–11
Mixed Doubles: Ms J. Wright and N. Ponting beat Ms S. Sankey and D. Wright 6–15, 15–6, 15–4

SCOTTISH NATIONAL CHAMPIONSHIPS 1992

Men's Singles: K. Scott beat J. Mailer 12–15, 15–7, 15–5
Women's Singles: A. Gibson beat G. Martin 11–4, 11–5
Men's Doubles: R. Hogg and K. Middlemiss beat A. Gatt and G. Haldane 15–0, 8–15, 15–5
Women's Doubles: E. and J. Allen beat J. Haldane and A. Nairn 15–5, 15–9
Mixed Doubles: Ms E. Allen and K. Middlemiss beat Ms A. Nairn and D. Travers 15–11, 15–6

WELSH NATIONAL CHAMPIONSHIPS 1992

Men's Singles: M. Richards beat S. Yates 5–15, 15–4, 17–14
Women's Singles: K. Morgan beat G. Davis 11–2, 11–5
Men's Doubles: L. Williams and C. Rees beat A. Carlotti and R. Burton 15–4, 15–4
Women's Doubles: K. Morgan and R. Phipps beat S. Williams and L. Carpenter 15–14, 17–16
Mixed Doubles: Ms L. Carpenter and C. Rees beat Ms S. Williams and D. Tonks 15–12, 10–15, 15–8

ALL-ENGLAND CHAMPIONSHIPS 1992

Men's Singles: Liu Jun (China) beat Zhao Jinhua (China) 15–13, 15–13
Women's Singles: Tang Jiuhong (China) Beat Bang Soo-Hyan (S. Korea) 9–12, 12–10, 11–1
Men's Doubles: R. Gunawan and E. Hartono (Indonesia) beat J. Paulsen and H. Svarrer (Denmark) 15–0, 15–12
Women's Doubles: Lin Yanfen and Yao Fen (China) beat Guan Weizhen and Nong Qunhua (China) 18–14, 18–17
Mixed Doubles: Ms P. Dupont and T. Lund (Denmark) beat Ms G. Mogensen and J. Holst-Christensen (Denmark) 15–10, 15–11

Thomas Cup final 1992: Malaysia beat Indonesia 3–1
Uber Cup final 1992: China beat South Korea 3–2

BASKETBALL

MEN

Championship play-off final 1992: Kingston beat Thames Valley 84–67
NatWest Trophy final 1992: Kingston beat Leicester City 71–68
National Cup final 1992: Kingston beat Thames Valley 90–71
National League: Kingston

WOMEN

Championship play-off final 1992: Thames Valley beat Sheffield 56–54
National Cup final 1992: Sheffield beat Thames Valley 68–62
National League: Sheffield

BILLIARDS

World Masters Championship 1991: G. Sethi (India) beat N. Dagley (GB) 8–3
World Professional Championship 1992: G. Sethi (India) beat M. Russell (England) 2,529–718

World Amateur Championship 1991: M. Kothari (India)
World Matchplay Championship 1991: M. Russell (England) beat G. Sethi (India) 7–6
UK Championship 1992: R. Foldvari (Australia) beat S. Agarwal (India) 4–1
British Open Championship 1991: N. Dagley beat I. Williamson 7–5

BOWLS (Men)

WORLD CHAMPIONSHIPS 1992

Worthing, August

Fours final: Scotland beat Canada 18–15
Triples final: Israel beat South Africa 23–12
Pairs final: R. Corsie and A. Marshall (Scotland) beat S. Adamson and S. Allan (Ireland) 35–14
Singles final: T. Allcock (England) beat R. Corsie (Scotland) 25–20

NATIONAL CHAMPIONSHIPS 1992

Worthing, September

Fours final: Bournemouth beat Cove 17–15
Triples final: Chandos Park beat Poole Park 19–3
Pairs final: G. Smith and A. Thompson (Blackheath and Greenwich) beat J. Durrant and R. Moses (Hollingbury Park, Brighton) 24–17
Singles final: S. Farish (Wigton) beat H. Duff (West Park, Hull) 21–18

WORLD INDOOR CHAMPIONSHIPS 1992

Singles Championship: I. Schuback (Australia) beat J. Price (Wales) 3–1
Pairs Championship: T. Allcock and D. Bryant (England) beat R. Parrella and I. Schuback (Australia) 3–1

BRITISH ISLES INDOOR CHAMPIONSHIPS 1992

Newton Abbott, Devon, March

Fours final: Northern Ireland beat Scotland 24–18
Triples final: Scotland beat Ireland 24–8
Paris final: A. Thomson and G. Smith (England) beat D. Gourlay and R. McCulloch (Scotland) 29–11
Singles final: A. Thomson (England) beat D. Gourlay jun. (Scotland) 21–16

Middleton Cup (Inter-County Championship) final 1992: Norfolk beat Cornwall 120–112

BOWLS (Women)

WORLD CHAMPIONSHIPS 1992

Ayr, June

Fours final: Scotland beat New Zealand 22–21
Triples final: Scotland beat New Zealand 27–16
Pairs final: Ireland beat Jersey 23–11
Singles final: M. Johnston (Ireland) beat A. Rutherford (Australia) 25–10
Team Trophy: Scotland

NATIONAL CHAMPIONSHIPS 1992

Royal Leamington Spa, August

Fours final: Middlesex beat Nottinghamshire 18–15
Triples final: Oxfordshire beat Cambridgeshire 17–15
Pairs final: Cambridgeshire beat Middlesex 21–18
Singles final (two woods): M. Dyer (Somerset) beat J. Cleet (Durham) 14–9
Singles final (four woods): W. Line (Hampshire) beat E. Shorter (Norfolk) 21–20

WORLD INDOOR CHAMPIONSHIP 1992

Singles Championship: S. Gourlay (Scotland) beat M. Price (England) 3–1

BRITISH ISLES INDOOR CHAMPIONSHIPS 1992

Llanelli, March

Fours final: Wales beat Scotland 20–18
Triples final: Ireland beat Scotland 19–8
Pairs final: E. Shorter and M. Ward (England) beat L. Evans and E. Thomas (Wales) 19–13
Singles final: M. Price (England) beat M. Johnston (Ireland) 21–19

BOXING

PROFESSIONAL BOXING

as at September 1992

World Boxing Council (WBC) Champions

Heavy: E. Holyfield (USA)
Cruiser: A. Wamba (France)
Light-heavy: J. Harding (Australia)
Super-middle: M. Galvano (Italy)
Middle: J. Jackson (USA)
Super-welter: T. Norris (USA)
Welter: J. McGirt (USA)
Super-light: J. C. Chavez (Mexico)
Light: M. A. Gonzalez (Mexico)
Super-feather: A. Nelson (Ghana)
Feather: P. Hodkinson (GB)
Super-bantam: T. Patterson (USA)
Bantam: V. Rabanales (Mexico)
Super-fly: M. Sung-kil (S. Korea)
Fly: M. Kittikasem (Thailand)
Light-fly: H. Gonzalez (Mexico)
Straw: R. Lopez (Mexico)

World Boxing Association (WBA) Champions

Heavy: E. Holyfield (USA)
Cruiser: R. Czyz (USA)
Light-heavy: vacant
Super-middle: M. Nunn (USA)
Middle: R. Johnson (USA)
Super-welter: V. Pazienza (USA)
Welter: M. Taylor (USA)
Super-light: M. East (Philippines)
Light: J. Gamache (USA)
Super-feather: J. Gamache (USA)
Feather: P. Young Kyun (Korea)
Super-bantam: W. Vazquez (Puerto Rico)
Bantam: I. Contreras (Venezuela)
Super-fly: K. Onizuka (Japan)

Fly: A. Guzman (Venezuela)
Light-fly: H. Ioka (Japan)
Straw: C. Hi-yong (S. Korea)

INTERNATIONAL BOXING FEDERATION (IBF) CHAMPIONS

Heavy: E. Holyfield (USA)
Cruiser: J. Warring (USA)
Light-heavy: C. Williams (USA)
Super-middle: I. Barkley (USA)
Middle: J. Toney (USA)
Super-welter: G. Rosi (Italy)
Welter: M. Blocker (USA)
Super-light: P. Whitaker (USA)
Light: vacant
Super-feather: B. Mitchell (S. Africa)
Feather: M. Medina (Mexico)
Super-bantam: W. Ncita (S. Africa)
Bantam: O. Canizales (USA)
Super-fly: R. Quiroga (USA)
Fly: R. Blanco (Colombia)
Light-fly: M. Carbajal (USA)
Straw: M. Melchor (Philipines)

BRITISH CHAMPIONS

Heavy: L. Lewis
Cruiser: C. Thompson
Light-heavy: vacant
Super-middle: H. Wharton
Middle: F. Grant
Light-middle: A. Till
Welter: G. Jacobs
Light-welter: A. Holligan
Light: C. Crook
Super-feather: M. Armstrong
Feather: J. Davison
Bantam: D. Docherty
Fly: R. Regan

COMMONWEALTH CHAMPIONS

Heavy: L. Lewis (GB)
Cruiser: D. Angol (GB)
Light-heavy: G. Waters (Australia)
Super-middle: H. Wharton (GB)
Middle: R. Woodhall (GB)
Light-middle: M. Hughes (GB)
Welter: D. Boucher (Canada)
Light-welter: A. Holligan (GB)
Light: C. Crook (GB)
Super-feather: A. Pep (Canada)
Feather: C. McMillan (GB)
Bantam: J. Armour (GB)
Fly: A. Kotei (Ghana)

EUROPEAN CHAMPIONS

Heavy: vacant
Cruiser: A. Tafer (France)
Light-heavy: vacant
Super-middle: F. Nicotra (France)
Middle: S. Kalambay (Italy)
Light-middle: J. C. Fontana (France)
Welter: P. Oliva (Italy)
Light-welter: V. Kayumba (France)
Light: J-B. Mendy (France)
Super-feather: J. Bredahl (Denmark)
Feather: F. Benichou (France)
Bantam: J. Bredahl (Denmark)
Fly: S. Fanni (Italy)

AMATEUR BOXING

AMATEUR BOXING ASSOCIATION (ABA) CHAMPIONSHIP WINNERS 1992

Super-heavy (91 + kg): M. Hopper
Heavy (91 kg): S. Welch
Light-heavy (81 kg): K. Oliver
Middle (75 kg): L. Woolcock
Light-middle (71 kg): J. Calzaghe
Welter (67 kg): M. Santini
Light-welter (63.5 kg): D. McCarrick
Light (60 kg): D. Amory
Feather (57 kg): A. Temple
Bantam (54 kg): P. Mullings
Fly (51 kg): K. Knox
Light-fly (48 kg): D. Fifield

CHESS

World Champion: G. Kasparov (USSR)
Women's World Champion: Xie Jun (China)
British Championship 1992: J. Hodgson
Women's British Championship 1992: S. Arkell

CRICKET

TEST MATCHES

AUSTRALIA V. INDIA

First Test (Brisbane, 29 November–2 December 1991): Australia won by 10 wickets. India 239 and 156; Australia 340 and 58–0
Second Test (Melbourne, 26–29 December 1991): Australia won by 8 wickets. India 263 and 213; Australia 349 and 128–2
Third Test (Sydney, 2–6 January 1992): Match drawn. Australia 313 and 173–8; India 483
Fourth Test (Adelaide, 25–29 January 1992): Australia won by 38 runs. Australia 145 and 451; India 225 and 333
Fifth Test (Perth 1–5 February 1992): Australia won by 300 runs. Australia 346 and 367–6 dec.; India 272 and 141

PAKISTAN V. SRI LANKA

First Test (Sialkot, 12–17 December 1991): Match drawn. Sri Lanka 270 and 137–5; Pakistan 423–5 dec.
Second Test (Gujranwala, 20–25 December 1991): Match abandoned as a draw. Pakistan 109–2
Third Test (Faisalabad, 2–7 January 1992): Pakistan won by 3 wickets. Sri Lanka 240 and 165; Pakistan 221 and 188–7

NEW ZEALAND V. ENGLAND

First Test (Christchurch, 18–22 January 1992): England won by an innings and 4 runs. England 580–9 dec.; New Zealand 312 and 264
Second Test (Auckland, 30 January–3 February 1992): England won by 168 runs. England 203 and 321; New Zealand 142 and 214
Third Test (Wellington, 6–10 February 1992): Match drawn. England 305 and 359–7 dec.; New Zealand 432–9 dec. and 43–3

West Indies v. South Africa

Test (Bridgetown, 18–23 April 1992): West Indies won by 52 runs. West Indies 262 and 283; South Africa 345 and 148

England v. Pakistan

First Test (Edgbaston, 4–8 June 1992): Match drawn. Pakistan 446–4 dec.; England 459–7 dec.
Second Test (Lord's, 18–21 June 1992): Pakistan won by 2 wickets. England 255 and 175; Pakistan 293 and 141–8
Third Test (Old Trafford, 2–7 July 1992): Match drawn. Pakistan 505–9 dec. and 239–5 dec.; England 390
Fourth Test (Headingley, 23–26 July 1992): England won by 6 wickets. Pakistan 197 and 221; England 320 and 99–4
Fifth Test (The Oval, 6–9 August 1992): Pakistan won by 10 wickets. England 207 and 174; Pakistan 380 and 5–0

Sri Lanka v. Australia

First Test (Colombo, 18–22 August 1992): Australia won by 16 runs. Australia 256 and 471; Sri Lanka 547 and 164
Second Test (Colombo, 29 August–2 September 1992): Match drawn. Australia 247 and 296–6 dec.; Sri Lanka 258–9 dec. and 136–2
Third Test (Colombo, 8–13 September 1992): Match drawn. Australia 337 and 271–8; Sri Lanka 274–9 dec.

ONE-DAY INTERNATIONALS

Pakistan v. Sri Lanka

Sargodha (10 January 1992): Pakistan won by 8 wickets. Sri Lanka 155–6; Pakistan 157–2
Karachi (13 January 1992): Pakistan won by 29 runs. Pakistan 210–5; Sri Lanka 181
Hyderabad (15 January 1992): Pakistan won by 59 runs. Pakistan 241–3; Sri Lanka 182–9
Multan (17 January 1992): Sri Lanka won by 4 wickets. Pakistan 205–5; Sri Lanka 206–6

New Zealand v. England

Auckland (11 January 1992): England won by 7 wickets. New Zealand 178–7; England 179–3
Dunedin (12 February 1992): England won by 3 wickets. New Zealand 186–7; England 188–7
Christchurch (15 February 1992): England won by 71 runs. England 255–7; New Zealand 184–8

England v. Pakistan (Texaco Trophy)

Lord's (20 May 1992): England won by 79 runs. England 278–6; Pakistan 199
The Oval (22 May 1992): England won by 39 runs. England 302–5; Pakistan 263
Trent Bridge (20 August 1992): England won by 198 runs. England 363–7; Pakistan 165
Lord's (22–23 August 1992): Pakistan won by 3 runs. Pakistan 204–5; England 201
Old Trafford (24 August 1992): England won by 6 wickets. Pakistan 254–5; England 255–4

INTERNATIONAL CUPS

World Cup 1992

First Round Final Table

Team	P	W	L	NR	Pts
New Zealand	8	7	1	—	14
England	8	5	2	1	11
South Africa	8	5	3	—	10
Pakistan	8	4	3	1	9
Australia	8	4	4	—	8
West Indies	8	4	4	—	8
India	8	2	5	1	7
Sri Lanka	8	2	5	1	5
Zimbabwe	8	1	7	—	2

Semi-finals

(Auckland, 21 March): Pakistan beat New Zealand by 4 wickets. New Zealand 262–7; Pakistan 264–6
(Sydney, 22 March): England beat South Africa by 20 runs. England 252–6; South Africa 232–6 (target revised to 252 in 43 overs because of rain)

Final:

(Melbourne, 25 March) Pakistan beat England by 22 runs. Pakistan 249–6; England 227

World Series Cup final 1992: Australia beat India 2–0

Wills Trophy 1991: Pakistan

NEW ZEALAND v. ENGLAND 1991–2 (Averages)

New Zealand Batting

Batsmen	I	NO	R	HS	Av.
M. L. Su'a	3	2	56	36	56.00
J. G. Wright	6	0	258	116	43.00
M. D. Crowe	6	1	212	56	42.40
A. H. Jones	6	0	226	143	37.66
D. N. Patel	5	0	155	99	31.00
R. T. Latham	1	0	25	25	25.00
C. L. Cairns	5	0	119	61	23.80
K. R. Rutherford	4	1	68	32	22.66
B. R. Hartland	6	0	88	45	14.66
I. D. S. Smith	3	0	42	21	14.00
C. Pringle	2	1	11	6	11.00
A. C. Parore	2	0	15	15	7.50
W. Watson	2	1	7	5*	7.00
D. K. Morrison	5	2	20	12	6.66

Played in one match: M. J. Greatbatch, 0, 11; S. A. Thomson, 0, 5
*Not out

Bowling

Bowlers	O	M	R	W	Av.
M. L. Su'a	100	31	236	8	29.50
W. Watson	50	23	100	3	33.33
D. N. Patel	143.3	34	374	10	37.40
C. L. Cairns	117	20	429	11	39.00
C. Pringle	36	4	127	3	42.33
D. K. Morrison	116.5	24	361	8	45.12

Also bowled: A. H. Jones, 4–0–15–0; S. A. Thomson, 15–3–47–0

England Batting

Batsmen	I	NO	R	HS	Av.
A. J. Lamb	5	0	338	142	67.60
A. J. Stewart	5	0	330	148	66.00
R. A. Smith	5	0	213	96	42.60
C. C. Lewis	3	0	126	70	42.00
R. C. Russell	5	1	135	36	33.75
G. A. Gooch	5	0	161	114	32.20
G. A. Hick	5	0	134	43	26.80
D. A. Reeve	5	0	124	59	24.80
D. R. Pringle	3	0	53	41	17.66
P. A. J. DeFreitas	4	1	11	7*	3.66
P. C. R. Tufnell	3	3	8	6*	—

Played in one match: I. T. Botham, 1, 15; D. V. Lawrence, 6
*Not out

Bowling

Bowlers	O	M	R	W	Av.
P. C. R. Tufnell	186.1	69	367	16	22.93
C. C. Lewis	100	21	249	10	24.90
I. T. Botham	22	5	76	3	25.33
P. A. J. DeFreitas	106.4	39	235	8	29.37
D. A. Reeve	24.5	8	60	2	30.00
D. R. Pringle	58	16	162	5	32.40
G. A. Hick	87	36	148	4	37.00
D. V. Lawrence	29.1	8	71	1	71.00

Also bowled: R. A. Smith, 4–2–6–0

ENGLAND v. PAKISTAN 1992 (Averages)

England Batting

Batsmen	I	NO	R	HS	Av.
A. J. Stewart	8	1	397	190	56.71
D. I. Gower	5	2	150	73	50.00
G. A. Gooch	8	0	384	135	48.00
R. A. Smith	8	1	314	127	44.85
M. A. Atherton	5	0	145	76	29.00
R. C. Russell	4	2	56	29*	28.00
T. A. Munton	2	1	25	25*	25.00
I. D. K. Salisbury	3	0	66	50	22.00
G. A. Hick	5	0	98	51	19.60
A. J. Lamb	3	0	54	30	18.00
C. C. Lewis	7	0	114	55	16.28
M. R. Ramprakash	5	1	31	17	7.75
I. T. Botham	2	0	8	6	4.00
N. A. Mallender	3	0	8	4	2.66
P. A. J. DeFreitas	2	0	3	3	1.50
D. E. Malcolm	5	0	6	4	1.20
D. R. Pringle	4	1	2	1	0.66

Played in one match: P. C. R. Tufnell, 0, 0*
*Not out

Bowling

Bowlers	O	M	R	W	Av.
G. A. Gooch	51	15	94	5	18.80
N. A. Mallender	74.5	20	215	10	21.50
P. A. J. DeFreitas	59	14	179	7	25.57
D. E. Malcolm	102.5	14	380	13	29.23
C. C. Lewis	188	40	544	12	45.33
D. R. Pringle	70	10	227	5	45.40
T. A. Munton	67.3	15	200	4	50.00
I. D. K. Salisbury	70.1	3	306	5	61.20
P. C. R. Tufnell	34	9	87	1	87.00

Also bowled: M. R. Ramprakash, 1.1–0–8–0; I. T. Botham, 24–8–61–0; G. A. Hick, 18–3–63–0

Pakistan Batting

Batsmen	I	NO	R	HS	Av.
Salim Malik	8	2	488	165	81.33
Javed Miandad	8	2	364	153*	60.66
Shoaib Mohammad	1	0	55	55	55.00
Aamer Sohail	9	1	413	205	51.62
Rashid Latif	1	0	50	50	50.00
Ramiz Raja	9	1	312	88	39.00
Asif Mujtaba	8	0	253	59	31.62
Wasim Akram	7	1	118	45*	19.66
Inzamam-ul-Haq	6	1	66	26	13.20
Waqar Younis	6	2	51	20*	12.75
Moin Khan	6	1	46	15	9.20
Mushtaq Ahmed	6	0	35	11	5.83
Aqib Javed	4	2	5	5*	2.50

*Not out

Bowling

Bowlers	O	M	R	W	Av.
Wasim Akram	168.5	36	462	21	22.00
Ata-ur-Rehman	18	5	69	3	23.00
Waqar Younis	166	29	557	22	25.31
Asif Mujtaba	13	5	30	1	30.00
Mushtaq Ahmed	178.4	37	475	15	31.66
Aqib Javed	104.4	21	366	9	40.66

Also bowled: Salim Malik, 1–0–5–0; Aamer Sohail, 5–2–14–0

COUNTY CHAMPIONSHIP TABLE 1992

Order for 1991 in brackets	P	W	L	D	Bt	Bl	Pts
Essex (1)	22	11	6	5	60	64	300
Kent (6)	22	9	3	10	60	55	259
Northamptonshire (10)	22	8	4	10	62	58	248
Nottinghamshire (4)	22	7	7	8	54	58	224
Derbyshire (3)	22	7	6	9	47	63	222
Warwickshire (2)	22	6	8	8	55	68	219
Sussex (11)	22	6	7	9	60	61	217
Leicestershire (16)	22	7	7	8	40	59	211
Somerset (17)	22	5	4	13	64	62	206
Gloucestershire (13)	22	6	6	9	48	58	202
Middlesex (15)	22	5	3	14	62	60	202
Lancashire (8)	22	4	6	12	75	49	188
Surrey (5)	22	5	7	10	56	50	186
Glamorgan (12)	22	5	4	13	53	49	182
Hampshire (9)	22	4	6	12	61	57	182
Yorkshire (14)	22	4	6	12	56	52	172
Worcestershire (6)	22	3	4	14	54	65	167
Durham	22	2	10	10	46	53	131

BATTING AND BOWLING AVERAGES

First Class Batting Averages 1992

Batsmen	I	NO	R	HS	Av.
Salim Malik	21	6	1,184	165	78.93
M. E. Waugh	24	7	1,314	219*	77.29
D. M. Jones	23	7	1,179	157	73.68
G. A. Gooch	29	3	1,850	160	71.15
M. W. Gatting	36	6	2,000	170	66.66
P. D. Bowler	38	7	2,044	241*	65.93
N. H. Fairbrother	18	7	689	166*	62.63
A. J. Lamb	28	4	1,460	209	60.83
Javed Miandad	17	3	809	153*	57.78
N. J. Speak	36	3	1,892	232	57.33
M. A. Roseberry	41	5	2,044	173	56.77
Asif Mujtaba	25	6	1,074	154*	56.52
R. T. Robinson	33	5	1,547	189	55.25
N. R. Taylor	35	7	1,508	144	53.85
G. A. Hick	27	2	1,337	213*	53.48
M. D. Moxon	28	2	1,385	183	53.26
T. L. Penney	24	7	904	151	53.17
K. J. Barnett	29	5	1,270	160	52.91
Inzamam-ul-Haq	21	7	736	200*	52.57
G. R. Cowdrey	31	6	1,291	147	51.64
M. A. Atherton	37	6	1,598	199	51.54
G. D. Lloyd	37	10	1,389	132	51.44
G. P. Thorpe	41	4	1,895	216	51.21
V. P. Terry	17	2	766	141	51.06
T. S. Curtis	41	5	1,829	228*	50.80

*Not out

First Class Bowling Averages 1992

Bowlers	O	M	R	W	Av.
C. A. Walsh	587.2	138	1469	92	15.96
Wasim Akram	499.5	127	1330	82	16.22
I. R. Bishop	483	116	1118	64	17.46
J. R. Ayling	356.2	78	989	48	20.60
D. J. Millns	468.5	107	1526	74	20.62
R. P. Davis	582	150	1609	74	21.74
A. A. Donald	575.2	139	1647	74	22.25
M. A. Robinson	413.5	79	1134	50	22.68
V. J. Wells	301	93	751	33	22.75
N. A. Mallender	436.3	94	1282	55	23.30
G. J. Parsons	343.2	92	955	39	24.48
Mushtaq Ahmed	614.4	158	1620	66	24.54
Waqar Younis	287.1	50	913	37	24.67
N. G. B. Cook	325.1	90	939	38	24.71
D. R. Pringle	425.5	98	1177	47	25.04
D. J. Capel	446	92	1214	48	25.29
P. M. Such	411.5	126	1015	40	25.37
J. E. Emburey	854.5	249	2069	81	25.54
M. P. Bicknell	628.5	116	1823	71	25.67
P. J. Newport	618.2	130	1770	68	26.02
C. E. L. Ambrose	543.4	151	1307	50	26.14
N. F. Williams	437	86	1283	48	26.72
Aqib Javed	292	58	966	36	26.83
M. J. McCague	457.2	86	1430	53	26.98
A. R. Caddick	587.4	99	1918	71	27.01

Source for averages and county championship table: TCCB/Bull Computer Official Statistics

OTHER RESULTS 1992

Benson and Hedges Cup final: Hampshire beat Kent by 41 runs. Hampshire 253–5; Kent 212

NatWest Trophy final: Northamptonshire beat Leicestershire by 8 wickets. Leicestershire 208–7; Northamptonshire 211–2

Sunday League Champions: Middlesex

Holt Cup (Minor Counties knockout final): Devon beat Staffordshire by 4 wickets. Staffordshire 217–7; Devon 221-6

Minor Counties Championship final: Staffordshire beat Devon by 79 runs. Staffordshire 201–8; Devon 122

National Club Championship final: Optimists beat Kendal by 7 wickets. Kendal 165–9; Optimists 168–3

National Village Championship final: Hursley Park beat Methley by 6 wickets. Hursley Park 154-4; Methley 150–6

Universities: Cambridge beat Oxford by 7 wickets. Cambridge 60–7 dec. and 238–3; Oxford 182–7 dec. and 115–1 dec.

Britannic Challenge 1991: (1 day) Victoria beat Essex by 59 runs. Victoria 274–3; Essex 215; *(4 day)* Match drawn. Essex 343–9 dec.; Victoria 168 and 56–8

CYCLING

Tour of Spain 1992: T. Rominger (Switzerland)
Milk Race 1992: C. Henry (Ireland)
Giro d'Italia 1992: M. Indurain (Spain)
Tour de France 1992: M. Indurain (Spain)
Tour of Britain 1992: M. Sciandri (Italy)
Nissan Classic 1992: P. Anderson (Australia)
World Road Race Championship 1992: G. Bugno (Italy)
World Cyclo-Cross Championship 1992: M. Kluge (Germany)
British Road Race Championship 1992: S. Yates
British Open Cyclo-Cross Championship 1992: D. Baker
Scottish Provident League 1992: C. Lillywhite (Banana-Met)
World Amateur Cyclo-Cross Championship 1992: D. Pontoni (Italy)
British Amateur Road Race Championship 1992: S. Bray
Women's World Road Race Championship 1992 (also the Olympic title): K. Watt (Australia)
Women's National Road Race Championship 1992: M. Purvis

EQUESTRIANISM

SHOW JUMPING

World Cup Final 1992
Del Mar, California

1. T. Fruhmann on Bockman's Genius (Austria)
2. Mrs L. McNaught Mandli on Moet Pirol (Switzerland)
3. M. Fuchs on Interpane Shandor (Switzerland)

British Jumping Derby 1992
Hickstead

1. M. Whitaker on Henderson Monsanta (GB)
2 = J. Whitaker on Henderson Gammon (GB), J. Turi on Vital (GB), N. Pessoa on Loro Piana Vivaldi (Brazil)

THREE-DAY EVENTING

Badminton Horse Trials 1992

1. Ms M. Thomson on King William (GB)
2. Miss V. Leng on Master Craftsman (GB)
3. Ms V. Latta on Chief (NZ)

British Open Horse Trials 1992
Gatcombe Park

1. Miss P. Nolan on Sir Barnaby (GB)
2. F. Bergendorff on Michaelmas Day (Sweden)
3. Mrs L. Green on Up River (GB)

Burghley Horse Trials 1992

1. Ms C. Hollingsworth on The Cool Customer (GB)
2. B. Tait on Delta (New Zealand)
3. T. Randle on Legs Eleven (GB)

ETON FIVES

County Championship 1992: Staffordshire
Amateur Championship (Kinnaird Cup) 1992: M. J. Moore and G. Baker
Holmwoods Schools' Championship 1992: Wolverhampton
Alan Barber Cup 1992: Old Wulfrunians
League Championship (Douglas Keeble Cup): Old Harrovians

FENCING

MEN

BRITISH CHAMPIONSHIPS 1992

Foil: W. Gosbee (Salle Boston)
Epée: J. Llewellyn (Reading)
Sabre: I. Williams (London Thames)

Sporting Record Cup 1992: Salle Boston
Savage Shield 1991: Reading
Martin Edmunds Cup 1992: not fenced
Challenge Martini International Epée 1992: V. Resnitschenko (Germany)
Eden Cup 1991: L. Donzelli (Italy)

WOMEN

BRITISH CHAMPIONSHIPS 1992

Foil: L. Harris (Salle Paul)
Epée: G. Usher (Meadowbank)
Sabre: not fenced

GOLF (Men)

THE MAJOR CHAMPIONSHIPS 1992

US Masters (Augusta, Georgia, 9–12 April): F. Couples (USA), 275
US Open (Pebble Beach, California, 18–21 June): T. Kite (USA), 285
The Open (Muirfield, 16–19 July): N. Faldo (GB and Ireland), 272
US PGA Championship (St Louis, 13–16 August): N. Price (Zimbabwe), 278

PGA EUROPEAN TOUR 1991

International Open (Munich): A. Lyle (GB), 268
World Matchplay Championship (Wentworth): S. Ballesteros (Spain)
Volvo Masters (Valderrama, Portugal): R. Davis (Australia), 280
European Tour Order of Merit 1991: 1. S. Ballesteros (Spain); 2. S. Richardson (GB); 3. B. Langer (Germany)

PGA EUROPEAN TOUR 1992

Asian Classic (Bangkok): I. Palmer (S. Africa), 268
Desert Classic (Dubai): S. Ballesteros (Spain), 272
Turespana Masters (Malaga): V. Singh (Fiji), 277
Tenerife Open: J-M. Olazábal (Spain), 268
Mediterranean Open (El Bosque, Spain): J-M. Olazábal (Spain), 276
Balearic Open (Majorca): S. Ballesteros (Spain), 277
Catalan Open (Girona): J. Rivero (Spain), 280
Portuguese Open (Vila-Sol): R. Rafferty (GB and Ireland), 273
Florence Open: A. Forsbrand (Sweden), 271
Rome Masters: J-M. Canizares (Spain), 286
Jersey Open: D. Silva (Portugal), 277
Moroccan Open (Rabat): D. Gilford (GB and Ireland), 287
Cannes Open: A. Forsbrand (Sweden), 273
Italian Open (Monticello): A. Lyle (GB and Ireland), 270
International Open (St Mellion, Plymouth): P. Senior (Australia), 287
Spanish Open (Madrid): A. Sherborne (GB and Ireland), 271
PGA Championship (Wentworth): T. Johnstone (Zimbabwe), 272
British Masters (Woburn): C. O'Connor jun. (GB and Ireland), 270
Irish Open (Killarney): N. Faldo (GB and Ireland), 274
Austrian Open (Salzburg): P. Mitchell (GB and Ireland), 271
Lyon Open: D. Russell (GB and Ireland), 267
French Open (Paris): M. Martin (Spain), 276
Monte Carlo Open: I. Woosnam (GB and Ireland), 261
Scottish Open (Gleneagles): P. O'Malley (Australia), 262
Dutch Open (Noordwijk): B. Langer (Germany), 277
Scandinavian Masters (Barseback, Sweden): N. Faldo (GB and Ireland), 277
International Open (Munich): P. Azinger (USA), 266
German Open (Dusseldorf): V. Singh (Fiji), 262
English Open (The Belfry): V. Fernandez (Argentina), 283
European Masters (Crans-sur-Sierre, Switzerland): J. Spence (GB and Ireland), 271
European Open (Sunningdale): N. Faldo (GB and Ireland), 262
Lancôme Trophy (Paris): M. Roe (GB and Ireland), 267
Belgian Open (Knokke-le-Zoute): M. A. Jiménez (Spain), 274
German Masters (Stuttgart): B. Lane (GB and Ireland), 272

World Cup 1991: I. Woosnam (GB), 273
PGA Grand Slam 1991: I. Woosnam (GB), 135
Inaugural World Championship 1991: F. Couples (USA), 281

TEAM EVENTS

Dunhill Cup 1991 (St Andrews, 10–13 October): Sweden beat S. Africa 2-1
World Cup of Golf 1991: Sweden, 563
Benson and Hedges Mixed Team Trophy 1991 (Marbella): A. Forsbrand and Miss H. Alfredsson (Sweden), 275

AMATEUR CHAMPIONSHIPS 1992

British Amateur (Carnoustie): S. Dundas (Haggs Castle)
Brabazon Trophy (English Open Strokeplay) (Hollinwell): I. Garrido (Spain), 280
Welsh Open Strokeplay (Royal St Davids): A. Barnett, 278
Scottish Open Strokeplay (Royal Troon): D. Robertson, 281
English Amateur (Deal): S. Cage
Welsh Amateur (Pyle and Kenfig): H. Roberts
Scottish Amateur (Glasgow Gailes): S. Gallacher
Lytham Trophy (Royal Lytham and St Anne's): S. Cage, 294
Berkshire Trophy (The Berkshire): V. Phillips, 274
International match (Royal Lytham and St Anne's): England beat France 18–6
Home International Championship: Ireland
President's Putter (Rye): M. Cox beat C. Nevill 2 and 1
Halford Hewitt Cup (for public schools' old boys) (Deal): Tonbridge beat Malvern 3½–1½
Universities: Oxford beat Cambridge 8½–6½
Eisenhower Trophy 1990 (world amateur team championship): Sweden
European Team Championship 1991: England

GOLF (Women)

US Women's Open 1992 (Oakmont, Pennsylvania): P. Sheehan (USA), 280

WPG EUROPEAN TOUR 1991

Matchplay Championship (Milan): F. Dassu (Italy)
Longines Classic (Cannes): P. Grice-Whittaker (GB), 277
European Tour Order of Merit 1991: 1. C. Dibnah (Australia); 2. H. Alfredsson (Sweden); 3. D. Reid (Scotland)

WPG EUROPEAN TOUR 1992

Ford Classic (Woburn): S. Croce (Italy), 286
AGF French Open (Paris): A. Nicholas (GB and Ireland), 275
European Masters (Bercuit, Belgium): K. Douglas (GB and Ireland), 279
Spanish Classic (La Manga): T. Johnson (GB and Ireland), 274
European Open (Munich): L. Davies (GB and Ireland), 285
Hennessy Cup (Cologne): H. Alfredsson (Sweden), 271
English Open (Tytherington): L. Davies (GB and Ireland), 281
Netherlands Open (Rijswijk): V. Michaud (France), 204
Swedish Open (Haninge): H. Alfredsson (Sweden), 278
Italian Open (Venice): L. Davies (GB and Ireland), 274
British Open (Woburn): P. Sheehan (USA), 207

World Championship 1991 (Cairns, Australia): M. Mallon (USA), 216

TEAM EVENTS

Solheim Cup 1992 (Dalmahoy, Edinburgh, 2–4 October): Europe beat USA 11½–6½
Curtis Cup 1992 (Hoylake): Great Britain and Ireland beat USA 10–8
Mixed Team Trophy 1991: A. Forsbrand and Ms H. Alfredsson (Sweden), 275

AMATEUR CHAMPIONSHIPS 1992

British Open Championship (Saunton): P. Pedersen (Denmark)
English Championship (St Annes Old Links): C. Hall
Welsh Championship (Newport): J. Foster
Scottish Championship (Royal Aberdeen): J. Moodie
British Strokeplay (Frilford Heath): J. Hockley, 287
English Strokeplay (Littlestone): J. Morley, 289
Welsh Strokeplay (Royal Porthcawl): C. Lambert, 218
Espirito Santo Trophy (world amateur team championship) (Vancouver, Canada): Spain, 588
Home International Championship (Hamilton): England

GREYHOUND RACING

Television Trophy 1992 (Manchester): Fortunate Man
Grand National 1992 (Birmingham): Kildare Slippy
Greyhound Derby 1992 (Wimbledon): Farloe Melody
Scurry Gold Cup 1992 (Catford): Glengar Desire

GYMNASTICS

MEN

World Champion: G. Misutin (USSR)
World Team Champions: USSR

WORLD INDIVIDUAL APPARATUS CHAMPIONSHIPS 1992

Floor: I. Korobschinsky (CIS)
Pommel Horse: =V. Scherbo (CIS), Li Jing (China), Pae Gil Su (N. Korea)
Rings: V. Scherbo (CIS)
Vault: Y. Ok Youl (S. Korea)
Parallel Bars: =A. Voropayev (CIS) and Li Jing (China)
High Bar: G. Misutin (CIS)

BRITISH CHAMPIONSHIPS 1992

British Champion: N. Thomas
British Individual Apparatus Champions:
Floor: N. Thomas
Pommel Horse: =N. Thomas, D. Cox, P. Bowler
Rings: =N. Thomas, P. Bowler
Vault: N. Thomas
Parallel Bars: N. Thomas
High Bar: N. Thomas
British Team Champions (Adam Shield): Liverpool

WOMEN

World Champion: K. Zmeskal (USA)
World Team Champions: USSR

WORLD INDIVIDUAL APPARATUS CHAMPIONSHIPS 1992

Beam: K. Zmeskal (USA)
Floor: K. Zmeskal (USA)
Vault: H. Onodi (Hungary)
Assymetric Bars: L. Milosovici (Romania)

World Rythmics Champion: O. Skaldina (USSR)

BRITISH CHAMPIONSHIPS 1992

British Champion: R. Roberts
British Individual Apparatus Champions:
Beam: R. Roberts
Floor: R. Roberts
Vault: L. Redding
Assymetric Bars: S. Mercer
British Open Club Team Champions: Heathrow

British Rythmics Champion: A. Sands

HOCKEY

MEN

County Championship final 1992: Yorkshire beat Buckinghamshire 2–1
National League: Havant
Hockey Association Cup final 1992: Hounslow beat Teddington 3–2
National Indoor Club Championship final 1992: St Albans beat Stourport 3–2
Universities 1992: Oxford beat Cambridge 2–1
European Club Championship 1992: Uhlenhorst (Germany) beat Terrassa (Spain) 7–2
European Indoor Club Championship 1992: St Albans 9, WAC Vienna 9. St Albans won 3–0 on penalties
European Cup final 1992: England beat Germany 2–1
European Cup-Winners Cup 1992: HGC Wassenaar (Holland) beat Hounslow 4–0
Champions Trophy final 1992: Germany beat Australia 4–0

WOMEN

County Championship final 1992: Lancashire 3, Warwickshire 3. Lancashire won 3–1 on penalties
National League: Slough
Hockey Association Cup final 1992: Hightown 3, Slough 3. Hightown won 3–2 on penalties
National Indoor Club Championship final 1992: Hightown beat Chelmsford 4–2
Typhoo Tea Cup final 1992: England beat Spain 1–0
Home Countries Tournament 1992: England
European Club Championship 1992: Amsterdam beat Glasgow Western 4–0
European Indoor Club Championship 1992: Russelsheim beat Atletico Madrid 8–3
European Cup-Winners Cup 1992: Sutton Coldfield 0, MOP Vught (Holland) 0. Sutton Coldfield won 4–2 on penalties

HORSERACING

WINNING OWNERS 1991

Sheikh Mohammed	£1,077,233
Fahd Salman	£975,248
Hamdan Al-Maktoum	£744,137
Khalid Abdulla	£488,379
Maktoum Al-Maktoum	£467,438
R. Sangster	£458,304
Lady Beaverbrook	£371,807
G. Strawbridge	£312,278
E. Fustok	£288,303
W. Gredley	£220,761

WINNING TRAINERS 1991

P. Cole	£1,251,507
R. Hannon	£872,877
M. Stoute	£825,819
C. Brittain	£712,272
H. Cecil	£666,686
J. Dunlop	£616,635
B. Hills	£583,747
L. Cumani	£574,234
J. Berry	£572,635
D. Elsworth	£517,445

LEADING BREEDERS 1991

	Value
Barronstown Stud (Ireland)	£666,155
Hesmonds Stud	£307,485
Marystead Farm Ltd (France)	£265,218
Juddmonte Farms	£245,485
G. Strawbridge jun (USA)	£243,097
Stetchworth Park Stud	£235,649
Swettenham Stud (USA)	£232,063
Buckram Oak Farm (USA)	£231,966
Gainsborough Stud Management	£201,981
Kingstown Park Stud	£175,418

WINNING SIRES 1991

	Horses	*Races won*	*Total value*
Caerleon (1980) by Nijinsky	53	31	£1,159,388
Sadler's Wells (1981) by Northern Dancer	70	44	£800,959
Fairy King (1982) by Northern Dancer	40	29	£708,909
Green Desert (1983) by Danzig	53	46	£643,068
Persian Bold (1975) by Bold Lad	67	38	£597,985
Ahonoora (1975) by Lorenzaccio	54	40	£589,745
Alzao (1980) by Lyphard	67	29	£571,593
Shareef Dancer (1980) by Northern Dancer	46	31	£533,785
Thatching (1975) by Thatch	80	49	£516,229
Sharpen Up (1969) by Atan	24	19	£482,537

WINNING FLAT JOCKEYS 1991

	1st	*2nd*	*3rd*	*Unpl.*	*Total mts*
P. Eddery	165	130	76	436	807
W. Carson	155	130	93	512	890
M. Roberts	114	108	95	532	849
S. Cauthen	107	79	57	229	472
R. Cochrane	102	103	82	420	707
A. Munro	99	83	72	470	724
L. Dettori	93	90	83	432	698
J. Carroll	86	74	66	343	569
R. Quinn	84	78	71	392	625
J. Reid	78	93	72	405	648

WINNING NATIONAL HUNT JOCKEYS 1991–2

	1st	*2nd*	*3rd*	*Unpl.*	*Total mts*
P. Scudamore	175	80	52	206	513
R. Dunwoody	137	128	108	342	715
P. Niven	105	65	46	183	399
G. McCourt	102	75	54	277	508
C. Grant	78	63	55	253	449
J. Osborne	76	66	45	226	413
M. Dwyer	73	46	42	219	380
A. Maguire	71	69	57	305	502
C. Llewellyn	53	41	43	245	382
D. Murphy	48	42	39	196	325

The above statistics are the copyright of *The Sporting Life*

CESAREWITCH

(1839) Newmarket, 2 miles and about 2 f

1989 Double Dutch (5y), (9st 10lb)
1990 Trainglot (3y), (7st 12lb), W. Carson
1991 Go South (7y), (7st 11lb), N. Carlisle

CHAMPION STAKES

(1877) Newmarket, 1 mile, 2 f

1989 Legal Case (3y), (8st 10lb)
1990 In the Grove (3y), (8st 9lb), S. Cauthen
1991 Tel Quel (3y), (8st 12lb), A. Fabre

*HENNESSY GOLD CUP

(1957) Newbury, 3 miles and about 2½ f

1988 Strands of Gold (9y), (10st)
1989 Ghofar (6y), (10st 2lb)
1990 Arctic Call (7y), (11st), J. Osborne
1991 Chatham (7y), (10st 6lb), P. Scudamore

*KING GEORGE VI CHASE

(1937) Kempton, about 3 miles

1988 Desert Orchid (9y), (11st 10lb)
1989 Desert Orchid (10y), (11st 10lb)
1990 Desert Orchid (11y), (11st 10lb), R. Dunwoody
1991 The Fellow (6y), (11st 10lb), A. Kondrat

*National Hunt

THE CLASSICS

ONE THOUSAND GUINEAS

(1814) Rowley Mile, Newmarket, for three year old fillies

Year	*Winner*	*Betting*	*Owner*	*Jockey*	*Trainer*	*No. of Runners*
1989	Musical Bliss	7–2	Sheikh Mohammed	W. Swinburn	M. Stoute	7
1990	Salsabil	6–4	H. Al-Maktoum	W. Carson	J. Dunlop	10
1991	Shadayid	4–6	H. Al-Maktoum	W. Carson	J. Dunlop	14
1992	Hatoof	5–1	M. Al-Maktoum	W. Swinburn	C. Head	14

TWO THOUSAND GUINEAS

(1809) Rowley Mile, Newmarket, for three year olds

Year	*Winner*	*Betting*	*Owner*	*Jockey*	*Trainer*	*No. of Runners*
1989	Nashwan	3–1	H. Al-Maktoum	W. Carson	R. Hern	14
1990	Tirol	9–1	J. Horgan	M. Kinane	R. Hannon	14
1991	Mystiko	13–2	Lady Beaverbrook	M. Roberts	C. Brittain	14
1992	Rodrigo de Triano	6–1	R. Sangster	L. Piggott	P. Chapple-Hyam	16

Record time: 1 minute 35.84 seconds, 1990

THE DERBY

(1780) Epsom, 1 mile and about 4 f, for three year olds

The first winner was Sir Charles Bunbury's Diomed in 1780. The owners with the record number of winners are Lord Egremont, who won in 1782, 1804, 1805, 1807, 1826 (also won five Oaks); and the late Aga Khan, who won in 1930, 1935, 1936, 1948, 1952 (also won two Oaks). Other winning owners are: Duke of Grafton (1802, 1809, 1810, 1815); Mr J. Bowes (1835, 1843, 1852, 1853); Sir J. Hawley (1851, 1858, 1859, 1868); the 1st Duke of Westminster (1880, 1882, 1886, 1899); and Sir Victor Sassoon (1953, 1957, 1958, 1960).

Record times are: 2 min. 33.80 sec. by Mahmoud in 1936; 2 min. 33.84 sec. by Kahyasi in 1988; 2 min. 33.9 sec. by Reference Point in 1987.

The Derby was run at Newmarket from 1915–18 and from 1940–5.

Year	*Winner*	*Betting*	*Owner*	*Jockey*	*Trainer*	*No. of Runners*
1989	Nashwan	5–4	H. Al-Maktoum	W. Carson	R. Hern	12
1990	Quest for Fame	7–1	K. Abdulla	P. Eddery	R. Charlton	18
1991	Generous	9–1	Prince Fahd Salman	A. Munro	P. Cole	13
1992	Dr Devious	8–1	S. Craig	J. Reid	P. Chapple-Hyam	18

THE OAKS

(1779) Epsom, 1 mile and about 4 f, for three year old fillies

Year	*Winner*	*Betting*	*Owner*	*Jockey*	*Trainer*	*No. of Runners*
*1989	Snow Bride	13–2	S. M. Al-Maktoum	S. Cauthen	H. Cecil	9
1990	Salsabil	2–1	H. Al-Maktoum	W. Carson	J.Dunlop	8
1991	Jet Ski Lady	50–1	J. Dunlop	C. Roche	J. Bolger	9
1992	User Friendly	5–1	W. Gredley	G. Duffield	C. Brittain	7

* The Oaks in 1989 was won by HH Aga Khan's Aliysa, but Aliysa was disqualified after a urine test found traces of a prohibited substance, and the Jockey Club awarded the race to Snow Bride

ST LEGER

(1776) Doncaster, 1 mile and about 6 f, for three year olds

Year	*Winner*	*Betting*	*Owner*	*Jockey*	*Trainer*	*No. of Runners*
†1989	Michelozzo	6–4	C. St George	S. Cauthen	H. Cecil	8
1990	Snurge	7–2	M. Abib	R. Quinn	P. Cole	8
1991	Toulon	5–2	K. Abdulla	P. Eddery	A. Fabre	10
1992	User Friendly	7–4	W. Gredley	G. Duffield	C. Brittain	8

†The 1989 St Leger was run at Ayr after the course at Doncaster was ruled unsatisfactory

*CHAMPION HURDLE

(1927) Cheltenham, 2 miles and about ½ f

1989 Beech Road (7y), (12st)
1990 Kribensis (6y), (12st)
1991 Morley Street (7y), (12st), J. Frost
1992 Royal Gait (9y), (12st), G. McCourt

*QUEEN MOTHER CHAMPION CHASE

(1959) Cheltenham, about 2 miles

1989 Barnbrook Again (8y), (12st)
1990 Barnbrook Again (9y), (12st)
1991 Katabatic (8y), (12st), S. McNeill
1992 Remittance Man (8y), (12st), J. Osborne

*CHELTENHAM GOLD CUP

(1924) 3 miles and about 2½ f

1989 Desert Orchid (10y), (12st)
1990 Norton's Coin (9y), (12st)
1991 Garrison Savannah (8y), (12st), M. Pitman
1992 Cool Ground (10y), (12st), A. Maguire

LINCOLN HANDICAP

(1965) Doncaster, 1 mile

1989 Fact Finder (5y), (7st 9lb)
1990 Evichstar (6y), (7st 10lb)
1991 Amenable (6y), (8st 1lb), A. Greaves
1992 High Low (4y), (8st), J. Quinn

*GRAND NATIONAL

(1837) Liverpool, 4 miles and about 4 f

1989 Little Polveir (12y), (10st)
1990 Mr Frisk (11y), (10st 6lb)
1991 Seagram (11y), (10st 6lb), N. Hawke
1992 Party Politics (8y), (10st 7lb), C. Llewellyn

Record times: 8 minutes 47.8 seconds by Mr Frisk in 1990; 9 minutes 1.9 seconds by Red Rum in 1973

*WHITBREAD GOLD CUP

(1957) Sandown, 3 miles and about 5 f

1989 Brown Windsor (7y), (10st)
1990 Mr Frisk (11y), (10st 5lb)
†1991 Docklands Express (9y), (10st 13lb), A. Tory
1992 Topsham Bay (9y), (10st), H. Davies

† Cahervillahow finished first but after an objection and a stewards' inquiry was placed second

JOCKEY CLUB STAKES

(1894) Newmarket, 1½ miles

1989 Unfwain (4y), (8st 10lb)
1990 Roseate Tern (4y), (8st 9lb)
1991 Rock Hopper (4y), (8st 7lb), P. Eddery
1992 Sapience (6y), (8st 12lb), R Cochrane

KENTUCKY DERBY

(1875) Louisville, Kentucky, 1¼ miles

1989 Sunday Silence
1990 Unbridled
1991 Strike the Gold, C. Antley
1992 Lil E Tee, P. Day

PRIX DU JOCKEY CLUB

(1836) Chantilly, 1½ miles

1989 Old Vic
1990 Sanglamore
1991 Suave Dancer (9st 2lb), C. Asmussen
1992 Polytain (9st 2lb), L. Dettori

ASCOT GOLD CUP

(1807) Ascot, 2 miles and about 4 f

1989 Sadeem (6y), (9st)
1990 Ashal (4y), (9st)
1991 Indian Queen (6y), (8st 13lb), W. Swinburn
1992 Drum Taps (6y), (9st 2lb), L. Dettori

IRISH SWEEPS DERBY

(1866) Curragh, 1½ miles, for three year olds

1989 Old Vic (9st)
1990 Salsabil (8st 11lb)
1991 Generous (9st), A. Munro
1992 St Jovite (9st), C. Roche

ECLIPSE STAKES

(1886) Sandown, 1 mile and about 2 f

1989 Nashwan (3y), (8st 8lb)
1990 Elmaamul (3y), (8st 10lb)
1991 Environment Friend (3y), (8st 10lb), G. Duffield
1992 Kooyonga (4y), (9st 4lb), W. O'Connor

KING GEORGE VI AND QUEEN ELIZABETH DIAMOND STAKES

(1952) Ascot, 1 mile and about 4 f

1989 Nashwan (3y), (8st 8lb)
1990 Belmez (3y), (8st 9lb)
1991 Generous (3y), (8st 9lb), A. Munro
1992 St Jovite (3y), (8st 9lb), S. Craine

GOODWOOD CUP

(1812) Goodwood, about 2 miles

1989 Mazzacano (4y), (9st)
1990 Lucky Moon (3y), (7st 10lb)
1991 Further Flight (5y), (9st), M. Hills
1992 Further Flight (6y), (9st 5lb), M. Hills

CAMBRIDGESHIRE HANDICAP

(1839) Newmarket, 1 mile

1989 Rambo's Hall (4y), (8st 6lb)
1990 Risen Moon (3y), (8st 9lb)
1991 Mellottie (6y), (9st 1lb), J. Lowe
1992 Rambo's Hall (7y), (9st 3lb), D. McKeown

PRIX DE L'ARC DE TRIOMPHE

(1920) Longchamp, 1½ miles
1989 Carroll House (4y), (9st 4lb)
1990 Saumarez (3y), (8st 11lb)
1991 Suave Dancer (3y), (8st 11lb), C. Asmussen
1992 Subotica (4y), (9st 4lb), T. Jarnet

*National Hunt

ICE HOCKEY

World Champions 1992: Sweden
British Championship final 1992: Durham Wasps beat Nottingham Panthers 7–6
League Championship 1992:
Premier Division: Durham Wasps
First Division: Fife Flyers
Stanley Cup 1990–1: Pittsburgh Penguins beat Minnesota North Stars 4–2
Stanley Cup 1991–2: Pittsburgh Penguins beat Chicago Blackhawks 4–0
Women's World Championship final 1992: Canada beat USA 8–0

ICE SKATING

BRITISH CHAMPIONSHIPS 1991

Nottingham, November

Men: S. Cousins
Women: J. Conway
Pairs: Ms K. Pritchard and J. Briggs
Ice Dance: Ms M. Bruce and A. Place

EUROPEAN CHAMPIONSHIPS 1992

Lausanne, January

Men: P. Barna (Czechoslovakia)
Women: S. Bonaly (France)
Pairs: Miss N. Mishkutienok and A. Dmitriev (CIS)
Ice Dance: Miss M. Klimova and S. Ponomarenko (CIS)

WORLD CHAMPIONSHIPS 1992

Oakland, California, March

Men: V. Petrenko (CIS)
Women: K. Yamaguchi (USA)
Pairs: Miss N. Mishkutienok and A. Dmitriev (CIS)
Ice Dance: Miss M. Klimova and S. Ponomarenko (CIS)

JUDO

BRITISH CHAMPIONSHIPS 1991

Gateshead, December

MEN

Heavyweight (over 95 kg): E. Gordon
Light heavyweight (95 kg): N. Kokotaylo
Middleweight (86 kg): D. White
Light middleweight (78 kg): R. Birch
Lightweight (71 kg): W. Cusack
Featherweight (65 kg): M. Preston
Bantamweight (60 kg): J. Newton

WOMEN

Heavyweight (over 72 kg): K. Knowles
Light heavyweight (75 kg): K. Howey
Middleweight (66 kg): S. Mills
Light middleweight (61 kg): M. Reveley
Lightweight (56 kg): N. Fairbrother
Featherweight (52 kg): S. Rendle
Bantamweight (48 kg): K. Briggs

LAWN TENNIS

MAJOR CHAMPIONSHIPS 1992

AUSTRALIAN OPEN CHAMPIONSHIPS (Melbourne)

Men's Singles: J. Courier (USA) beat S. Edberg (Sweden) 6–3, 3–6, 6–4, 6–2
Women's Singles: M. Seles (Yugoslavia) beat M.-J. Fernandez (USA) 6–2, 6–3
Men's Doubles: T. Woodbridge (Australia) and M. Woodforde (Australia) beat K. Jones (USA) and R. Leach (USA) 6–4, 6–3, 6–4
Women's Doubles: A. Sanchez Vicario (Spain) and H. Sukova (Czechoslovakia) beat M.-J. Fernandez (USA) and Z. Garrison (USA) 6–4, 7–6
Mixed Doubles: Miss N. Provis (Australia) and M. Woodforde (Australia) beat Miss A. Sanchez Vicario (Spain) and T. Woodbridge (Australia) 6–3, 4–6, 11–9

FRENCH OPEN CHAMPIONSHIPS (Paris)

Men's Singles: J. Courier (USA) beat P. Korda (Czechoslovakia) 7–5, 6–2, 6–1
Women's Singles: M. Seles (Yugoslavia) beat S. Graf (Germany) 6–2, 3–6, 10–8
Men's Doubles: J. Hlasek and M. Rosset (Switzerland) beat D. Adams (Australia) and A. Olhovskiy (CIS) 7–6, 6–7, 7–5
Women's Doubles: G. Fernandez (USA) and N. Zvereva (CIS) beat C. Martinez and A. Sanchez Vicario (Spain) 6–3, 6–2
Mixed Doubles: Miss A. Sanchez Vicario (Spain) and T. Woodbridge (Australia) beat Ms L. McNeil and B. Shelton (USA) 6–2, 6–3

ALL ENGLAND CHAMPIONSHIPS (Wimbledon)

Men's Singles: A. Agassi (USA) beat G. Ivanisevic (Croatia) 6–7, 6–4, 6–4, 1–6, 6–4
Women's Singles: S. Graf (Germany) beat M. Seles (Yugoslavia) 6–2, 6–1
Men's Doubles: J. McEnroe (USA) M. Stich (Germany) beat J. Grabb and R. Reneberg (USA) 7–5, 6–7, 6–3, 6–7, 19–17
Women's Doubles: G. Fernandez (USA) and N. Zvereva (CIS) beat J. Novotna (Czechoslovakia) and L. Savchenko-Neiland (Latvia) 6–4, 6–1
Mixed Doubles: Mrs L. Savchenko-Neiland (Latvia) and C. Suk (Czechoslovakia) beat Ms M. Oremans and J. Eltingh (Holland) 7–6, 6–2

US OPEN CHAMPIONSHIPS (New York)

Men's Singles: S. Edberg (Sweden) beat P. Sampras (USA) 3–6, 6–4, 7–6, 6–2
Women's Singles: M. Seles (Yugoslavia) beat A. Sanchez Vicario (Spain) 6–3, 6–3
Men's Doubles: J. Grabb and R. Reneberg (USA) beat K. Jones and R. Leach (USA) 3–6, 7–6, 6–3, 6–3
Women's Doubles: G. Fernandez (USA) and N. Zvereva (CIS) beat J. Novotna (Czechoslovakia) and L. Savchenko-Neiland (Latvia) 7–6, 6–1
Mixed Doubles: Ms N. Provis and M. Woodforde (Australia) beat Ms H. Sukova (Czechoslovakia) and T. Nijssen (Holland) 4–6, 6–3, 6–3

The Grand Slam Cup 1991: D. Wheaton (USA) beat M. Chang (USA) 7–5, 6–2, 6–4

TEAM CHAMPIONSHIPS

Davis Cup 1991: France beat USA 3–1
Federation Cup 1992: Germany beat Spain 2–1
LTA County Cup 1992:
Men: Yorkshire
Women: Leicestershire

NATIONAL CHAMPIONSHIPS 1991

Men's Singles: A. Castle beat S. Cole 7–6, 2–6, 10–8
Women's Singles: J. Durie beat S. Gomer 6–2, 6–2

Men's Doubles: A. Castle and J. Bates beat D. Sapsford and N. Fulwood 6–4, 6–4
Women's Doubles: J. Durie and C. Wood beat S. Gomer and V. Lake 6–4, 6–2

MOTOR CYCLING

500 cc GRAND PRIX 1992

Japanese (Suzuka): M. Doohan (Honda)
Australian (Eastern Creek): M. Doohan (Honda)
Malaysian (Kuala Lumpur): M. Doohan (Honda)
Spanish (Jerez): M. Doohan (Honda)
Italian (Mugello): K. Schwantz (Suzuki)
Grand Prix of Europe (Catalunya): W. Rainey (Yamaha)
German (Hockenheim): M. Doohan (Honda)
Netherlands (Assen): A. Criville (Honda)
Hungarian (Budapest): E. Lawson (Cagiva)
French (Magny Cours): W. Rainey (Yamaha)
British (Donington Park): W. Gardner (Honda)
Brazilian (Sao Paolo): W. Rainey (Yamaha)
South African (Kyalami): J. Kocinski (Yamaha)
Riders' Championship 1992: 1. W. Rainey, 140 pts; 2. M. Doohan, 136 pts; 3. J. Kocinski, 102 pts

Senior Manx Grand Prix: A. Bennallick (Honda)
Senior TT, Isle of Man: S. Hislop (Norton)
Junior TT, Isle of Man: D. O'Leary (Yamaha)

MOTOR RACING

FORMULA ONE GRAND PRIX 1991

Japanese (Suzuka): 1. G. Berger (McLaren); 2. A. Senna (McLaren); 3. R. Patrese (Williams)
Australian (Adelaide): 1. A. Senna (McLaren); 2. N. Mansell (Williams); 3. R. Patrese (Williams)
Drivers' Championship 1991: 1. A. Senna (McLaren), 96 pts; 2. N. Mansell (Williams), 72 pts; 3. R. Patrese (Williams), 53 pts
Constructors' Championship 1991: 1. McLaren, 139 pts; 2. Williams, 125 pts; 3. Ferrari, 55.5 pts

FORMULA ONE GRAND PRIX 1992

South African (Kyalami): 1. N. Mansell (Williams); 2. R. Patrese (Williams); 3. A. Senna (McLaren)
Mexican (Mexico City): 1. N. Mansell (Williams); 2. R. Patrese (Williams); 3. M. Schumacher (Benetton)
Brazilian (Interlagos): 1. N. Mansell (Williams); 2. R. Patrese (Williams); 3. M. Schumacher (Benetton)
Spanish (Barcelona): 1. N. Mansell (Williams); 2. M. Schumacher (Benetton); 3. J. Alesi (Ferrari)
San Marino (Imola): 1. N. Mansell (Williams); 2. R. Patrese (Williams); 3. A. Senna (McLaren)
Monaco (Monte Carlo): 1. A. Senna (McLaren); 2. N. Mansell (Williams); 3. R. Patrese (Williams)
Canadian (Montreal): 1. G. Berger (McLaren); 2. M. Schumacher (Benetton); 3. J. Alesi (Ferrari)
French (Magny Cours): 1. N. Mansell (Williams); 2. R. Patrese (Williams); 3. M. Brundle (Benetton)
British (Silverstone): 1. N. Mansell (Williams); 2. R. Patrese (Williams); 3. M. Brundle (Benetton)
German (Hockenheim): 1. N. Mansell (Williams); 2. A. Senna (McLaren); 3. M. Schumacher (Benetton)
Hungarian (Budapest): 1. A. Senna (McLaren); 2. N. Mansell (Williams); 3. G. Berger (McLaren)
Belgian (Spa-Francorchamps): 1. M. Schumacher (Benetton); 2. N. Mansell (Williams); 3. R. Patrese (Williams)
Italian (Monza): 1. A. Senna (McLaren); 2. M. Brundle (Benetton); 3. M. Schumacher (Benetton)
Portuguese (Estoril): 1. N. Mansell (Williams); 2. G. Berger (McLaren); 3. A. Senna (McLaren)

MOTOR RALLYING

1991
Lombard RAC Rally: J. Kankkunen (Finland) (Lancia)
World Championship: J. Kankkunen (Finland) (Lancia)

1992
Paris–Cape Town Rally: H. Auriol (France) (Mitsubishi)
Monte Carlo Rally: D. Auriol (France) (Lancia)
Swedish Rally: M. Jonsson (Sweden) (Toyota)
Portuguese Rally: J. Kankkunen (Finland) (Lancia)
Safari Rally (Kenya): C. Sainz (Spain) (Toyota)
Indianapolis 500: A. Unser jun. (USA) (Galmer-Chevrolet)
Acropolis Rally: D. Auriol (France) (Lancia)
New Zealand Rally: C. Sainz (Spain) (Toyota)
Argentine Rally: D. Auriol (France) (Lancia)
Thousand Lakes Rally (Finland): D. Auriol (France) (Lancia)
Australian Rally: D. Auriol (France) (Lancia)
Paris–Peking Rally: M. Perin and P. Lartigue (France) (Citroen)
Le Mans 24-hour race 1992: D. Warwick (GB), Y. Dalmas (France) and M. Blundell (GB) (Peugeot 905)

NETBALL

World Championship final 1991: Australia beat New Zealand 53–52

TEST MATCHES 1991

2 Nov	*Wembley*	England 41, W. Indies 61
6 Nov	*Gateshead*	England 40, W. Indies 40
9 Nov	*Sheffield*	England 40, W. Indies 42

INTERNATIONALS

1991

6 Oct	*Birmingham*	England 63, Canada 28

1992

15 Feb	*Tonbridge*	England 70, Scotland 17
21 Mar	*Cardiff*	Wales 40, England 47

Inter-County Championship final 1992: Surrey beat Middlesex 13–11
National Clubs Championship final 1992: Toucans beat Aquila 48–30
English Counties League Championship 1991–2: Surrey

POLO

Prince of Wales's Trophy final 1992: Ellerston White beat Maple Leaf 11–4
Queen's Cup final 1992: Ellerston White beat Pendell 10–7
Warwickshire Cup final 1992: Los Locos beat Guardacre 12–8
Gold Cup final 1992 (British Open): Black Bears beat Sante Fe 10–9
Westchester Cup 1992: USA beat Great Britain 8–7
Silver Jubilee Cup final 1992: Hurlingham Polo Association beat Spain 6–4
Cowdray Challenge Cup final 1992: Alcatel beat Tramontana 7–6
Guards 26 Goal 1992: Tramontana beat Ellerston White 10–9
Universities 1992: Oxford beat Cambridge 3–2

RACKETS

World Singles Champion: J. Male
World Doubles Champions: S. Hazell and N. Smith
Professional Singles Championship final 1992: N. Smith beat S. Hazell 3–0
Amateur Singles Championship final 1991: J. Prenn beat W. Boone 3–0
Amateur Doubles Championship final 1992: W. Boone and T. Cockcroft beat J. Prenn and A. Robinson 4–1
British Open Singles Championship final 1992: S. Hazell beat W. Boone 4–2
British Open Doubles Championship final 1992: S. Hazell and N. Smith beat J. Prenn and W. Boone 4–1
National League final 1992: Clifton (N. Cooper and G. Palmer) beat Manchester (J. Beaumont and J. Trimble) 2–0
Noel Bruce Cup final 1991: Eton (W. Boone and M. H. Williams) beat Tonbridge (A. Spurling and R. Owen-Browne) 4–0
Public Schools Singles Championship final 1992: Harrow (C. Danby) beat Harrow (H. Foster) 3–2
Public Schools Doubles Championship final 1992: Winchester (N. Hall and M. Segal) beat Marlborough (S. Gidoomal and T. Stewart-Liberty) 4–3
Universities 1992: Oxford beat Cambridge 2–1

REAL TENNIS

World Singles Champion: W. Davies
Professional Singles Championship final 1992: C. Ronaldson beat R. Fahey 3–2
Professional Doubles Championship final 1992: L. Deuchar and R. Fahey beat C. Ronaldson and S. Ronaldson 2–0
Amateur Singles Championship final 1992: J. Snow beat A. Page 3–0
Amateur Doubles Championship final 1992: J. Snow and M. McMurrugh beat A. Lovell and M. Dean 3–1
British Open Singles Championship final 1991: L. Deuchar beat R. Fahey 3–2
British Open Doubles Championship final 1991: M. Gooding and C. Bray beat L. Deuchar and P. Tabley 3–2
British Open Ladies Singles Championship final 1992: C. Cornwallis beat M. Groszek 2–0
British Open Ladies Doubles Championship final 1992: S. Grant and A. Garside beat P. Lumley and C. Cornwallis 2–1
Henry Leaf Cup final 1992: Radley (J. Male and R. Warburg) beat Winchester (A. Lovell and P. Seabrook) 2–0
Universities 1992: Oxford beat Cambridge 6–0

ROAD WALKING

MEN'S NATIONAL 10 MILE WALK

Birmingham, 21 March 1992

		hr.	min.	sec.
1	I. McCombie (Cambridge)	1	09	42
2	M. Bell (Splott)	1	11	00
3	G. Holloway (Splott)	1	12	10

Team result: 1 Splott, 20 points

WOMEN'S NATIONAL 15 KM WALK

Birmingham, 21 March 1992

		hr.	min.	sec.
1	M. Brooke (Nuneaton)	1	16	17
2	S. Brown (Surrey)	1	20	24
3	K. Baird (Dudley and Stourbridge)	1	22	35

Team result: 1 Dudley and Stourbridge, 16 points

MEN'S NATIONAL 50 KM WALK

Redditch, 18 April 1992

		hr.	min.	sec.
1	C. Maddocks (Plymouth)	4	13	25
2	A. King (Leicester)	4	22	53
3	C. Berwick (Leicester)	4	25	51

Team result: 1 Trowbridge, 23 points

MEN'S NATIONAL 20 KM WALK

Lancaster University, 9 May 1992

		hr.	min.	sec.
1	C. Maddocks (Plymouth)	1	23	38
2	A. Penn (Coventry)	1	24	37
3	M. Bell (Splott)	1	25	42

Team result: 1 Coventry, 45 points

WOMEN'S NATIONAL 10 KM WALK

Lancaster University, 9 May 1992

		min.	sec.
1	V. Lupton (Sheffield)	46	04
2	M. Brookes (Nuneaton)	48	18
3	V. Larby (Aldershot)	49	24

Team result: 1 Dudley and Stourbridge, 32 points

MEN'S NATIONAL 35 KM WALK

Colchester, 13 June 1992

		hr.	min.	sec.
1	L. Morton (Sheffield)	2	59	38
2	S. Partington (Manx)	3	08	54
3	M. Easton (Surrey)	3	12	14

Team result: 1 York Postal, 29 points

WOMEN'S NATIONAL 5 KM WALK

Colchester, 13 June 1992

		min.	sec.
1	S. Black (Birchfield)	25	18
2	A. Crofts (Leicester)	26	50
3	K. Smith (Coventry)	26	59

Team result: 1 Steyning, 20 points

ROWING

NATIONAL CHAMPIONSHIPS 1992

Holme Pierrepont, July

MEN

Coxed pairs: Rob Roy
Coxless pairs: Goldie
Coxed fours: London
Coxless fours: Nottingham County
Single sculls: C. Maclennan (Leander)
Double sculls: Molesey
Quad sculls: Nottingham County
Eights: Nottingham County/City of Cambridge/London

WOMEN

Coxless pairs: Thames Tradesmen
Coxed fours: Staines
Coxless fours: Thames Tradesmen/University of London
Single sculls: P. White (Rob Roy)
Double sculls: Runcorn/Staines
Quad sculls: Hollingworth Lake/Tideway Scullers/University of London
Eights: Thames

THE 138th UNIVERSITY BOAT RACE

Putney–Mortlake, 4 miles 1 f, 180 yd

4 April 1992

Oxford beat Cambridge by 1½ lengths; 17m 44s
Cambridge have won 69 times, Oxford 68 and there has been one dead heat. The record time is 16m, 45s, rowed by Oxford in 1984
WOMEN'S BOAT RACE 1992: Cambridge beat Oxford by ⅓ of a length; 6m 20.6s

HENLEY ROYAL REGATTA 1992

Grand Challenge Cup: University of London beat Wannsee (Germany) by 1¾ lengths
Ladies' Challenge Plate: Imperial College London beat Nereus (Holland) by 1 length
Temple Challenge Cup: Imperial College London beat Trinity College Dublin by a canvas
Visitors' Cup: Durham University beat University of British Columbia (Canada) by 1 length
Thames Challenge Cup: Lea beat Goldie by ¾ length
Stewards' Challenge Cup: Notts County beat Malmo and Brudpiga (Sweden) by 1 length
Queen Mother Challenge Cup: Stromstads (Sweden) beat Notts County B by ½ length
Princess Elizabeth Cup: Pangbourne College beat Westminster School by ½ length
Prince Philip Cup: Leander beat Tideway Scullers School by 3 lengths
Silver Goblets and Nickall's Challenge Cup: Gillard and Clarry beat Ashley-Carter and Murray by 3 lengths
Wyfold Cup: Notts County A beat University of London by 3¾ lengths
Britannia Challenge Cup: Goldie beat London by 3¼ lengths
Double Sculls Cup: D. Dickison and T. Hallett (Canada) beat D. Kruyswyk and P. Wiltenburg (Holland) by 1¼ lengths
Diamond Challenge Sculls: R. Henderson beat P. Reedy by 3 lengths

OTHER ROWING EVENTS 1992

Oxford Torpids: Men, Oriel; *Women,* Somerville
Cambridge Lents: Men, Trinity Hall; *Women,* Lady Margaret
Oxford Summer Eights: Men, Oriel; *Women,* Somerville
Cambridge Mays: Men, Trinity Hall; *Women,* Lady Margaret
Head of the River: Men, Molesey I; *Women,* Tideway Scullers
Doggett's Coat and Badge (estab. 1715, 278th race; London Bridge to Chelsea, 4½ miles): J. McCarthy (Blackheath)
Wingfield Sculls: G. Pooley (Cambridge University)

RUGBY FIVES

National Singles Championship 1991: Men, W. Enstone beat N. Roberts 2–0; *Women,* P. Smith beat D. Hall-Witton 1–0
National Doubles Championship 1992: W. Enstone and N. Roberts beat I. Fuller and D. Hebden 2–0
Scottish Open Championship 1992: Singles, N. Roberts; *Doubles,* N. Roberts and J. Guthrie
National Schools Championships 1992: Singles, S. Fraser (Loretto); *Doubles,* I. Purvis and S. Fraser (Loretto)

RUGBY LEAGUE

INTERNATIONAL MATCHES

27 Oct 1991	*Swansea*	Wales 68, Papua New Guinea 0
21 Mar 1992	*Swansea*	Wales 35, France 6

TEST MATCH

7 Mar 1992	*Hull*	Great Britain 36, France 0

WORLD CUP QUALIFYING MATCHES

1991		
9 Nov	*Wigan*	Great Britain 56, Papua New Guinea 4
1992		
16 Feb	*Perpignan*	France 12, Great Britain 30
31 May	*Port Moresby*	Papua New Guinea 14, Great Britain 20
12 June	*Sydney*	Australia 22, Great Britain 6
26 June	*Melbourne*	Australia 10, Great Britain 33
3 July	*Brisbane*	Australia 16, Great Britain 10
12 July	*Auckland*	New Zealand 15, Great Britain 14
19 July	*Auckland*	New Zealand 16, Great Britain 19

The World Cup final is to take place on 24 October 1992 at Wembley between Great Britain and Australia

World Sevens (inaugural): Wigan beat Brisbane 18–6

DOMESTIC COMPETITIONS

Rugby League Challenge Cup final 1992 (Wembley, 2 May): Wigan beat Castleford 28–12
Premiership Trophy final 1992 (Old Trafford, 17 May): Wigan beat St Helens 48–16
Regal Trophy final 1992 (Wigan, 11 January): Widnes beat Leeds 24–0
Divisional Premiership final 1922: Sheffield Eagles beat Oldham 34–20
Stones Bitter Championship: Wigan
Division 2 Championship: Sheffield Eagles
Division 3 Championship: Huddersfield
Lancashire Cup final 1991: St Helens beat Rochdale 24–14
Yorkshire Cup final 1991: Castleford beat Bradford Northern 28–6
Universities 1992: Oxford beat Cambridge 34–22

AMATEUR RUGBY LEAGUE 1991–2

County Championship: Lancashire
National Inter-League Shield Competitions:
Open Age: Wakefield
Under 17: West Cumbria Youth
National Cup Competitions:
Open Age: Hull Dockers
Under 19: Hensingham
National League Champions: Wigan St Patricks
National League Challenge Cup 1992: Wigan St Patricks

RUGBY UNION

WORLD CUP

1 October–2 November 1991

First Round
Pool 1: New Zealand 9 pts; England 7 pts; Italy 5 pts; USA 3 pts
Pool 2: Scotland 9 pts; Ireland 7 pts; Japan 5 pts; Zimbabwe 3 pts
Pool 3: Australia 9 pts; Western Samoa 7 pts; Wales 5 pts; Argentina 3 pts
Pool 4: France 9 pts; Canada 7 pts; Romania 5 pts; Fiji 3 pts

Quarter Finals
France 10, England 19
Scotland 28, Western Samoa 6
Ireland 18, Australia 19
New Zealand 29, Canada 13

Semi-Finals
Scotland 6, England 9
Australia 16, New Zealand 6

Third place play-off
Scotland 6, New Zealand 13

Final (Twickenham)
England 6, Australia 12

INTERNATIONAL MATCHES 1992

18 Jan	*Edinburgh*	Scotland 7, England 25
	Dublin	Ireland 15, Wales 16
1 Feb	*Twickenham*	England 38, Ireland 9
	Cardiff	Wales 9, France 12
15 Feb	*Paris*	France 13, England 31
	Dublin	Ireland 10, Scotland 18
7 Mar	*Twickenham*	England 24, Wales 0
	Edinburgh	Scotland 10, France 6
21 Mar	*Cardiff*	Wales 15, Scotland 12
	Paris	France 44, Ireland 12
30 May	*Dunedin*	New Zealand 24, Ireland 21
6 June	*Wellington*	New Zealand 59, Ireland 6
13 June	*Sydney*	Australia 27, Scotland 12
21 June	*Brisbane*	Australia 37, Scotland 13

FIVE NATIONS' CHAMPIONSHIP 1992

	P	W	D	L	Pts F	Pts A	Total
England	4	4	0	0	118	29	8
France	4	2	0	2	74	62	4
Scotland	4	2	0	2	47	56	4
Wales	4	2	0	2	40	63	4
Ireland	4	0	0	4	46	116	0

DOMESTIC COMPETITIONS

English League: division 1, Bath, 20 pts; *division 2,* London Scottish, 22 pts; *division 3*, Richmond, 21 pts; *division 4*, Aspatria, 22 pts (*north*); Havant, 22 pts (*south*)
County Championship final 1992: Lancashire beat Cornwall 9–6
Scottish League: division 1, Melrose, 23 pts; *division 2*, Kelso, 26 pts; *division 3*, Grangemouth, 23 pts; *division 4*, Morgan Academy, 22 pts; *division 5*, Stewartry, 24 pts; *division 6*, Clydebank, 25 pts; *division 7*, Berwick, 26 pts
Welsh League: division 1, Swansea, 27 pts; *division 2*, South Wales Police, 26 pts; *division 3*, Tenby Utd, 30 pts; *division 4*, Tumble, 30 pts
Irish League: division 1, Garryowen, 14 pts; *division 2*, Dungannon, 16 pts
Pilkington Cup final 1992 (Twickenham, 2 May): Bath beat Harlequins 15–12
Welsh Cup final 1992: Llanelli beat Swansea 16–7
Hospitals' Cup final 1992: St Marys beat UCH-Middlesex 49–0
Services Championship 1992: Army beat Royal Navy 16–9; Royal Navy beat Royal Air Force 22–13; Royal Air Force beat Army 18–6
Universities 1991: Cambridge beat Oxford 17–11
Middlesex Sevens 1992: Western Samoa beat London Scottish 30–6

SHOOTING

BISLEY, 123RD NRA, 1992

Queen's Prize: A. Ringer, 287.27 pts
Grand Aggregate: Mrs M. J. Pugsley, 591.76 pts
Prince of Wales Prize: J. Pugsley, 75.15 pts
St George's Vase: A. D. Le Cheminant, 148 pts
Allcomers Aggregate: P. G. Kent, 323.49 pts
National Trophy: England, 2025.240 pts
Kolapore Cup: Great Britain, 1172.151 pts
Chancellor's Challenge Plate: Cambridge University, 1151.121 pts
Musketeers Cup: University of London 'A', 581.81 pts
Vizianagram Trophy: House of Lords, 680.32 pts
County Long-Range Championship: Norfolk, 287.29 pts
Mackinnon Challenge Cup: England, 1110.96 pts
Hopton Challenge Cup: S. Collings, 965.101 pts

CLAY PIGEON SHOOTING 1992

International Cup (Down-the-Line): Wales, 7,388/7,500
British Open Down-the-Line Championship: K. Bond, 100/300
Mackintosh Trophy: Wales, 7,388/7,500
British Open Skeet Championship: M. Vessey, 100+125
British Open Sporting Championship: S. Whitelock, 88/100

SNOOKER

1991

Rothmans Grand Prix: S. Hendry (Scotland) beat S. Davis (England) 10–6
UK Professional Championship: J. Parrott (England) beat J. White (England) 16–13
World Matchplay Championship: G. Wilkinson (England) beat S. Davis (England) 18–11
Dubai Classic: J. Parrott (England) beat T. Knowles (England) 9–3
Women's British Open Championship: A. Fisher beat K. Corr 3–1
Women's World Championship: A. Fisher (England) beat K. Corr (N. Ireland) 8–2
World Amateur Championship: N. Noppajorn (Thailand) beat D. Dale (Wales) 11–9

1992

Mercantile Credit Classic: S. Davis (England) beat S. Hendry (Scotland) 9–8
Asian Open: S. Davis (England) beat A. McManus (Scotland) 9–3
Benson and Hedges Masters: S. Hendry (Scotland) beat J. Parrott (England) 9–4
Welsh Open: S. Hendry (Scotland) beat D. Morgan (Wales) 9–3
British Open: J. White (England) beat J. Wattana (Thailand) 10–7
European Open: J. White (England) beat M. Johnston-Allen (England) 9–3
Irish Masters: S. Hendry (Scotland) beat K. Doherty (Ireland) 9–6
World Professional Championship: S. Hendry (Scotland) beat J. White (England) 18–14
Scottish Masters: N. Foulds (England) beat G. Wilkinson (England) 10–8
Womens' UK Championship: T. Davidson beat S. Hillyard 4–3

SPEEDWAY

World Individual Championship 1992: G. Havelock (England)
World Pairs Championship 1992: G. Hancock, S. Ermolenko, R. Correy (USA)
World Team Championship 1992: USA, 39 pts
British League Riders' Championship 1991: S. Ermolenko (Wolverhampton)
British League Championship 1991: Wolverhampton
British League Knock-Out Cup 1991: Bradford
Gold Cup final 1992: Wolverhampton beat Reading 91–88
British Champion 1992: G. Havelock (Bradford)

SQUASH

MEN

World Open Championship final 1992: Jansher Khan (Pakistan) beat C. Dittmar (Australia) 3–1
World Team Championship final 1991: Australia beat England 3–0
European Team Championship final 1992: Scotland beat Finland 3–2
European Club Championship final 1992: St Cloud (France) beat Erik Van Der Pluijn (Netherlands) 5–0
British Open Championship final 1992: Jansher Khan (Pakistan) beat C. Robertson (Australia) 3–0
National Championship final 1992: P. Marshall beat B. Beeson 3–1

WOMEN

World Open Championship final 1990; S. Devoy (New Zealand) beat M. Le Moignan (England) 3–0
World Team Championship 1990: England
European Team Championship final 1992: England beat Germany 3–0
European Club Championship final 1992: Victoria (Netherlands) beat Pontefract (England) 2–1
British Open Championship final 1992: S. Devoy (New Zealand) beat M. Le Moignan (England) 3–0
National Championship final 1992: S. Wright beat S. Horner 3–1

SWIMMING

NATIONAL CHAMPIONSHIPS 1992

Sheffield, June

MEN

50m freestyle: M. Foster (Barnet Copthall)
100m freestyle: M. Fibbens (Barnet Copthall)
200m freestyle: P. Howe (City of Birmingham)
400m freestyle: P. Palmer (Lincoln)
1,500m freestyle: I. Wilson (City of Sunderland)
50m backstroke: M. Harris (Barnet Copthall)
100m backstroke: M. Harris (Barnet Copthall)
200m backstroke: G. Robins (Portsmouth Northsea)
50m breastroke: A. Moorhouse (City of Leeds)
100m breastroke: N. Gillingham (City of Birmingham)
200m breastroke: N. Gillingham (City of Birmingham)
50m butterfly: M. Foster (Barnet Copthall)
100m butterfly: R. Leishman (City of Leeds)
200m butterfly: S. Wainwright (Lincoln)
200m medley: J. Davey (Rochdale Aquabears)
400m medley: G. Robins (Portsmouth Northsea)
4 × 100m medley relay: City of Leeds
4 × 100m freestyle relay: Barnet Copthall

WOMEN

50m freestyle: K. Pickering (Ipswich)
100m freestyle: K. Pickering (Ipswich)
200m freestyle: K. Pickering (Ipswich)
400m freestyle: K. Pickering (Ipswich)
800m freestyle: E. Arnold (Nova Centurion)
50m backstroke: K. Read (Barnet Copthall)
100m backstroke: K. Read (Barnet Copthall)

200m backstroke: K. Read (Barnet Copthall)
50m breastroke: Z. Baker (City of Sheffield)
100m breastroke: L. Rogers (Bristol)
200m breastroke: S. Brown (City of Leeds)
50m butterfly: S. Davies (Portsmouth Northsea)
100m butterfly: M. Campbell (Portsmouth Northsea)
200m butterfly: H. Jepson (City of Leeds)
200m medley: S. Davies (Portsmouth Northsea)
400m medley: H. Slatter (Warrington Warriors)
4 × 100m freestyle relay: Nova Centurion
4 × 100m medley relay: Portsmouth Northsea

TABLE TENNIS

World Team Cup final 1991: China beat Sweden 3–0
Women's World Team Cup final 1991: China beat N. Korea 3–1
European Nations Cup final 1992: Germany beat France 3–2

EUROPEAN CHAMPIONSHIPS 1992

Men's Singles: J. Rosskopf (Germany) beat J.-M. Saive (Belgium) 3–1
Women's Singles: B. Vriesekoop (Holland) beat L. Lomas (England) 3–0
Men's Doubles: J. Persson and E. Lindh (Sweden) beat J.-O. Waldner and M. Appelgren (Sweden) 2–0
Women's Doubles: J. Fazlic and G. Perkucin (Yugoslavia) beat C. Batorfi and G. Wirth (Hungary) 2–0
Mixed Doubles: Ms O. Badescu (Romania) and C. Creanga (Greece) beat Ms Wang Xiaoming and J.-P. Gatien (France) 2–1
Men's Team Event: Sweden beat England 4–1
Women's Team Event: Romania beat Holland 3–1

ENGLISH NATIONAL CHAMPIONSHIPS 1992

Men's Singles: C. Xinhua beat C. Prean 3–1
Women's Singles: A. Gordon beat A. Holt 3–1
Men's Doubles: A. Cooke and D. Douglas beat S. Andrew and N. Mason 2–0
Women's Doubles: F. Elliot and L. Lomas beat A. Holt and K. Goodall 2–1
Mixed Doubles: Ms F. Elliot and S. Andrew beat Ms A. Gordon and J. Holland 2–0

VOLLEYBALL

MEN

World Cup 1991: USSR
British Championships 1991: Scotland
National League Championship 1991–2: Mizuno Malory
National Cup final 1992: Mizuno Malory beat Polonia Ealing 3–2

WOMEN

World Cup 1991: Cuba
British Championships 1991: England
National League Championship 1991–2: Brixton
National Cup final 1992: Britannia Music beat Trafford 3–1

YACHTING

AMERICA'S CUP

San Diego, May 1992

America 3 (USA) beat *Il Moro di Venezie* (Italy) 4–1

EUROPE 1 SINGLE-HANDED TRANSATLANTIC RACE

June

L. Peyron (*Fujicolor 11*) in 11 days, one hour, 35 minutes

The Olympic Games 1992

The Winter Olympic Games

Albertville, France, 8–23 February 1992

ALPINE SKIING (Men)

Downhill: P. Ortlreib (Austria)
Slalom: F. Jagge (Norway)
Giant Slalom: A. Tomba (Italy)
Super Giant Slalom: K. Aamodt (Norway)
Combined: J. Polig (Italy)

ALPINE SKIING (Women)

Downhill: K. Lee-Gartner (Canada)
Slalom: P. Kronberger (Austria)
Giant Slalom: P. Wiberg (Sweden)
Super Giant Slalom: D. Compagnoni (Italy)
Combined: P. Kronberger (Austria)

FREESTYLE SKIING (Men)

Moguls: E. Grospiron (France)

FREESTYLE SKIING (Women)

Moguls: D. Weinbrecht (USA)

NORDIC SKIING (Men)

10 *kilometres:* V. Ulvang (Norway)
15 *kilometres:* B. Dahlie (Norway)
30 *kilometres:* V. Ulvang (Norway)
50 *kilometres:* B. Dahlie (Norway)
4 × 10 *kilometres:* Norway

NORDIC SKIING (Women)

5 *kilometres:* M. Lukkarinen (Finland)
10 *kilometres:* L. Yegorova (Unified Team)
15 *kilometres:* L. Yegorova (Unified Team)
30 *kilometres:* S. Belmondo (Italy)
3 × 7.5 *kilometres:* Unified Team

BIATHLON (Men)

10 *kilometres:* M. Kirchner (Germany)
20 *kilometres:* Y. Redkine (Unified Team)
4 × 7.5 *kilometres:* Germany

BIATHLON (Women)

7.5 *kilometres:* A. Restzova (Unified Team)
15 *kilometres:* A. Misersky (Germany)
3 × 7.5 *kilometres:* France

NORDIC COMBINED

Individual: F. Guy (France)
Team: Japan

SKI JUMPING

90 *metres hill:* E. Vettori (Austria)
120 *metres hill:* T. Nieminen (Finland)
Team: Finland

BOBSLEDDING

2-*man:* Switzerland I
4-*man:* Austria

LUGEING (Men)

Singles: G. Hackl (Germany)
2-*man:* Germany I

LUGEING (Women)

Singles: D. Neuner (Austria)

ICE HOCKEY

Winners: Unified Team

FIGURE SKATING

Men: V. Petrenko (Unified Team)
Women: K. Yamaguchi (USA)
Pairs: Ms N. Mishkutienok and A. Dmitriev (Unified Team)
Ice Dance: Ms M. Klimova and S. Ponomarenko (Unified Team)

SPEED SKATING (Men)

500 *metres:* U. Mey (Germany)
1,000 *metres:* O. Zinke (Germany)
1,500 *metres:* J. Koss (Norway)
5,000 *metres:* G. Karlstad (Norway)
10 *kilometres:* B. Veldkamp (Netherlands)

SPEED SKATING (Women)

500 *metres:* B. Blair (USA)
1,000 *metres:* B. Blair (USA)
1,500 *metres:* J. Boerner (Germany)
3,000 *metres:* G. Niemann (Germany)
5,000 *metres:* G. Niemann (Germany)

SHORT TRACK SPEED SKATING (Men)

1,000 *metres:* Ki-Hoon Kim (S. Korea)
Relay (5 *kilometres*)*:* S. Korea

SHORT TRACK SPEED SKATING (Women)

500 *metres:* C. Turner (USA)
Relay (3 *kilometres*)*:* Canada

MEDAL TABLE

	Gold	*Silver*	*Bronze*	*Total*
Germany	10	10	6	26
Unified Team	9	6	8	23
Norway	9	6	5	20
Austria	6	7	8	21
USA	5	4	2	11
Italy	4	6	4	14
France	3	5	1	9
Finland	3	1	3	7
Canada	2	3	2	7
South Korea	2	1	1	4
Japan	1	2	4	7
Netherlands	1	1	2	4

Sweden	1	0	3	4
Switzerland	1	0	2	3
China	0	3	0	3
Luxembourg	0	2	0	2
New Zealand	0	1	0	1
Czechoslovakia	0	0	3	3
North Korea	0	0	1	1
Spain	0	0	1	1
	57	58	56	171

The Olympic Games

Barcelona, 25 July–9 August, 1992
**World record*

ARCHERY (Men)

Individual: S. Flute (France)
Team: Spain

ARCHERY (Women)

Individual: Cho Youn-Jeong (S. Korea)
Team: South Korea

ATHLETICS (Men)	hr.	min.	sec.
100 metres: L. Christie (GB)			9.96
200 metres: M. Marsh (USA)			20.01
400 metres: Q. Watts (USA)			43.50
800 metres: W. Tanui (Kenya)		1	43.66
1,500 metres: F. Cacho (Spain)		3	40.12
5,000 metres: D. Baumann (Germany)		13	12.52
10,000 metres: K. Skah (Morocco)		27	46.70
Marathon: Hwang Young-cho (S. Korea)	2	13	23
110 metres hurdles: M. McKoy (Canada)			13.12
400 metres hurdles: K. Young (USA)			46.78*
3,000 metres steeplechase: M. Birir (Kenya)		8	08.84
20 km walk: D. Plaza (Spain)	1	21	45
50 km walk: A. Perlov (Unified Team)	3	50	13
4 × 100 metres relay: USA			37.40*
4 × 400 metres relay: USA		2	55.74*

	metres
High jump: J. Sotormayor (Cuba)	2.34
Long jump: C. Lewis (USA)	8.67
Triple jump: M. Conley (USA)	18.17
Pole vault: M. Tarasov (Unified Team)	5.80
Shot: M. Stulce (USA)	21.70
Discus: R. Ubartas (Lithuania)	65.12
Hammer: A. Abduvaliyev (Unified Team)	82.54
Javelin: J. Zelezny (Czechoslovakia)	89.66
Decathlon: R. Zmelik (Czechoslavakia)	8,611 pts

ATHLETICS (Women)	hr.	min.	sec.
100 metres: G. Devers (USA)			10.82
200 metres: G. Torrence (USA)			21.81
400 metres: M. Perec (France)			48.83
800 metres: E. Van Langen (Netherlands)		1	55.54
1,500 metres: H. Boulmerka (Algeria)		3	55.30
3,000 metres: Y. Romanova (Unified Team)		8	46.04
10,000 metres: D. Tulu (Ethiopia)		31	06.02
Marathon: V. Yegorova (Unified Team)	2	32	41
100 metres hurdles: V. Patoulidou (Greece)			12.64
400 metres hurdles: S. Gunnell (GB)			53.23
10 km walk: Chen Yueling (China)		44	32
4 × 100 metres relay: USA			42.11
4 × 400 metres relay: Unified Team		3	20.20

	metres
High jump: H. Henkel (Germany)	2.02
Long jump: H. Dreschler (Germany)	7.14
Shot: S. Krivelyeva (Unified Team)	21.06
Discus: M. Marten (Cuba)	70.06
Javelin: S. Renk (Germany)	68.34
Heptathlon: J. Joyner-Kersee (USA)	7,044 pts

BADMINTON (Men)

Singles: A. Kusuma (Indonesia)
Doubles: South Korea

BADMINTON (Women)

Singles: S. Susanti (Indonesia)
Doubles: South Korea

BASEBALL

Team: Cuba

BASKETBALL (Men)

Team: USA

BASKETBALL (Women)

Team: Unified Team

BOXING

Light flyweight (48 kg): R. Garcia (Cuba)
Flyweight (51 kg): Choi Chol-Su (N. Korea)
Bantamweight (54 kg): J. Casamayor (Cuba)
Featherweight (57 kg): A. Tews (Germany)
Lightweight (60 kg): O. De La Hoya (USA)
Light Welterweight (63.5 kg): H. Vinent (Cuba)
Welterweight (67 kg): M. Carruth (Ireland)
Light Middleweight (71 kg): J. Garcia (Cuba)
Middleweight (75 kg): A. Hernandez (Cuba)
Light Heavyweight (81 kg): T. May (Germany)
Heavyweight (91 kg): F. Savon (Cuba)
Super Heavyweight (+91 kg): R. Balado Mendez (Cuba)

CANOEING (Men)

K1 500 *metres:* M. Kolehmainen (Finland)
K2 500 *metres:* Germany
K1 1,000 *metres:* C. Robinson (Australia)
K2 1,000 *metres:* Germany
K4 1,000 *metres:* Germany
C1 500 *metres:* N. Boukhalov (Bulgaria)
C2 500 *metres:* Unified Team
C1 1,000 *metres:* N. Boukhalov (Bulgaria)
C2 1,000 *metres:* Germany

SLALOM
K1: P. Ferazzi (Italy)
C1: L. Pollert (Czechoslavakia)
C2: USA

CANOEING (Women)

K1 500 *metres:* B. Schmidt (Germany)
K2 500 *metres:* Germany
K4 500 *metres:* Hungary

SLALOM
K1: E. Micheler (Germany)

CYCLING (Men)

	hr	min.	sec.
100 km *Team Time Trial:* Germany	2	01	39
Individual Road Race: F. Casartelli (Italy)	4	35	21
Sprint: J. Fiedler (Germany)			
1,000 *metres Individual Time Trial:* J. Moreno (Spain)		1	02.342
Points Race: G. Lombardi (Italy)			
Team Pursuit: Germany		4	08.791
Individual Pursuit: C. Boardman (GB)			

CYCLING (Women)

	hr	min.	sec.
Sprint: E. Salumae (Estonia)			
Individual Road Race: K. Watt (Australia)	2	04	42
3,000 *metres Individual Pursuit:* P. Rossner (Germany)			

DIVING (Men)

Springboard: M. Lenzi (USA) 645.57 pts
Platform: Sun Shuwei (China) 677.31 pts

DIVING (Women)

Springboard: Gao Min (China) 572.40 pts
Platform: Mingxia Fu (China) 461.43 pts

EQUESTRIANISM

Three-Day Event – Team: Australia
Three-Day Event – Individual: M. Ryan (Australia)
Dressage – Team: Germany
Dressage – Individual: N. Uphoff (Germany)
Jumping – Team: Netherlands
Jumping – Individual: L. Beerbaum (Germany)

FENCING (Men)

Foil – Individual: P. Omnes (France)
Sabre – Individual: B. Szabo (Hungary)
Epée – Individual: E. Srecki (France)
Foil – Team: Germany
Sabre – Team: Unified Team
Epée – Team: Germany

FENCING (Women)

Foil – Individual: G. Trillini (Italy)
Foil – Team: Italy

FOOTBALL

Team: Spain

GYMNASTICS (Men)

Team: Unified Team
Individual all-round: V. Shcherbo (Unified Team)
Floor: Li Xiaoshang (China)
Pommel Horse: V. Shcherbo (Unified Team), Gil-Su Pae (N. Korea)
Rings: V. Shcherbo (Unified Team)
Vault: V. Shcherbo (Unified Team)
Parallel Bars: V. Shcherbo (Unified Team)
Horizontal Bar: T. Dimas (USA)

GYMNASTICS (Women)

Team: Unified Team
Individual all-round: T. Goutsou (Unified Team)
Floor: L. Milosovici (Romania)
Vault: H. Onodi (Hungary), L. Milosivici (Romania)
Asymmetrical Bars: Lu Li (China)
Beam: T. Lyssenko (Unified Team)
Rhythmic: A. Timoshenko (Unified Team)

HANDBALL (Men)

Team: Unified Team

HANDBALL (Women)

Team: South Korea

HOCKEY (Men)

Team: Germany

HOCKEY (Women)

Team: Spain

JUDO (Men)

Bantamweight (60 kg): N. Goussinev (Unified Team)
Half-lightweight (65 kg): R. Sampaio (Brazil)
Lightweight (71 kg): T. Koga (Japan)
Half-middleweight (78 kg): H. Yoshida (Japan)
Middleweight (86 kg): W. Legien (Poland)
Half-heavyweight (95 kg): A. Kovacs (Hungary)
Heavyweight (+95 kg): D. Khakhaleichvili (Unified Team)

JUDO (Women)

Bantamweight (48 kg): C. Nowak (France)
Half-lightweight (52 kg): A. Martinez (Spain)
Lightweight (56 kg): M. Blasco (Spain)
Half-middleweight (61 kg): C. Fleury (France)
Middleweight (66 kg): O. Reve (Cuba)
Half-heavyweight (72 kg): Kim Mi Jung (S. Korea)
Heavyweight (+72 kg): Zhuang Xiaoyan (China)

MODERN PENTATHLON

Individual: A. Skrzypaszek (Poland) 5,559 pts
Team: Poland 16,018 pts

ROWING (Men)

Single Sculls: T. Lange (Germany)
Double Sculls: Australia
Quad Sculls: Germany
Coxless Pairs: Great Britain
Coxed Pairs: Great Britain
Coxless Fours: Australia
Coxed Fours: Romania
Eights: Canada

ROWING (Women)

Single Sculls: E. Lipa (Romania)
Double Sculls: Germany
Quad Sculls: Germany
Coxless Pairs: Canada
Coxless Fours: Canada
Eights: Canada

SHOOTING (Men)

Free Pistol: K. Loukachik (Unified Team)
Free Rifle Prone: Lee Eun-chal (S. Korea)
Air Rifle: Y. Fedkin (Unified Team)

Rifle 3 Positions: G. Petikiane (Unified Team)
Rapid Fire Pistol: R. Schumann (Germany)
Running Target: M. Jakosits (Germany)
Air Pistol: Wang Yifu (China)

SHOOTING (Women)

Air Rifle: Yeo Kab Soon (S. Korea)
Sport Pistol: M. Logvinenko (Unified Team)
Air Pistol: M. Logvinenko (Unified Team)
Rifle 3 Positions: L. Melli (USA)

SHOOTING (Open)

Olympic Trap: P. Hrdlicka (Czechoslovakia)
Olympic Skeet: Zhang Shan (China)

SWIMMING (Men)	min.	sec.
50 *metres freestyle:* A. Popov (Unified Team)		21.91
100 *metres freestyle:* A. Popov (Unified Team)		49.02
200 *metres freestyle:* Y. Sadovyi (Unified Team)	1	46.70
400 *metres freestyle:* Y. Sadovyi (Unified Team)	3	45.00*
1,500 *metres freestyle:* K. Perkins (Australia)	14	43.48*
4 × 100 *metres freestyle:* USA	3	16.74
4 × 200 *metres freestyle:* Unified Team	7	11.95*
100 *metres breaststroke:* N. Diebel (USA)	1	01.50
200 *metres breaststroke:* M. Barrowman (USA)	2	10.16*
100 *metres butterfly:* P. Morales (USA)		53.32
200 *metres butterfly:* M. Stewart (USA)	1	56.26
100 *metres backstroke:* M. Tewksbury (USA)		53.98
200 *metres backstroke:* M. Lopez-Zubero (Spain)	1	58.47
200 *metres individual medley:* T. Darnyi (Hungary)	2	00.76
400 *metres individual medley:* T. Darnyi (Hungary)	4	14.23
4 × 100 *metres relay:* USA	3	36.93*

SWIMMING (Women)	min.	sec.
50 *metres freestyle:* Yang Wenyi (China)		24.79*
100 *metres freestyle:* Zhuang Yong (China)		54.64
200 *metres freestyle:* N. Haislett (USA)	1	57.90
400 *metres freestyle:* D. Hase (Germany)	4	07.18
800 *metres freestyle:* J. Evans (USA)	8	25.52
4 × 100 *metres freestyle:* USA	3	39.46*
100 *metres breaststroke:* Y. Roudkovskaya (Unified Team)	1	08.00
200 *metres breaststroke:* K. Iwasaki (Japan)	2	26.65
100 *metres butterfly:* Qian Hong (China)		58.62
200 *metres butterfly:* S. Sanders (USA)	2	08.67
100 *metres backstroke:* K. Egerszegi (Hungary)	1	00.68
200 *metres backstroke:* K. Egerszegi (Hungary)	2	07.06
200 *metres individual medley:* Li Lin (China)	2	11.65*
400 *metres individual medley:* K. Egerszegi (Hungary)	4	36.54
4 × 100 *metres relay:* USA	4	02.54*

SYNCHRONIZED SWIMMING

Solo: K. Babb-Sprague (USA)
Team: USA

TABLE TENNIS (Men)

Singles: J.-O. Waldner (Sweden)
Doubles: China

TABLE TENNIS (Women)

Singles: Deng Yaping (China)
Doubles: China

TENNIS (Men)

Singles: M. Rosset (Switzerland)
Doubles: Germany

TENNIS (Women)

Singles: J. Capriati (USA)
Doubles: USA

VOLLEYBALL (Men)

Team: Brazil

VOLLEYBALL (Women)

Team: Cuba

WATER POLO

Team: Italy

WEIGHTLIFTING

Flyweight (52 kg): I. Ivanov (Bulgaria)
Bantamweight (56 kg): Chun Byung-Kwan (S. Korea)
Featherweight (60 kg): N. Suleymanoglu (Turkey)
Lightweight (67.5 kg): I. Militosian (Unified Team)
Middleweight (75 kg): F. Kassapu (Unified Team)
Light-Heavyweight (82.5 kg): P. Dimas (Greece)
Mid-Heavyweight (90 kg): K. Kakhiashvili (Unified Team)
Under 100 kg: V. Tregubov (Unified Team)
Heavyweight (110 kg): R. Weller (Germany)
Super-Heavyweight (+100 kg): A. Kurlovich (Unified Team)

WRESTLING (Greco–Roman)

Light-flyweight (48 kg): O. Koutcherenko (Unified Team)
Flyweight (52 kg): J. Ronningen (Norway)
Bantamweight (57 kg): An Han-Bong (S. Korea)
Featherweight (62 kg): A. Pirim (Turkey)
Lightweight (68 kg): A. Repka (Hungary)
Welterweight (74 kg): N. Iskandarian (Unified Team)
Middleweight (82 kg): P. Farkas (Hungary)
Light-Heavyweight (90 kg): M. Bullmann (Germany)
Heavyweight (100 kg): H. Perez (Cuba)
Super-Heavyweight (130 kg): A. Kareline (Unified Team)

WRESTLING (Freestyle)

Light-flyweight: Kim Il (N. Korea)
Flyweight: Li Hak-Son (N. Korea)
Bantamweight: A. Diaz (Cuba)
Featherweight: J. Smith (USA)
Lightweight: A. Fadzaev (Unified Team)
Welterweight: Park Jang-Soon (S. Korea)
Middleweight: K. Jackson (USA)
Light-Heavyweight: M. Khadartsdev (Unified Team)
Mid-Heavyweight: L. Khabelov (Unified Team)
Heavyweight: B. Baumgartner (USA)

YACHTING (Men)

Windsurfing: F. David (France)
470: Spain
Finn: J. Van de Ploeg (Spain)

YACHTING (Women)

Windsurfing: B. Kendall (New Zealand)
470: Spain
Europe: L. Andersen (Norway)

YACHTING (Open)

Star: USA
Soling: Denmark
Flying Dutchman: Spain
Tornado: France

MEDAL TABLE

	Gold	*Silver*	*Bronze*	*Total*
Unified Team	45	38	29	112
USA	37	34	37	108
Germany	33	21	28	82
China	16	22	16	54
Cuba	14	6	11	31
Spain	13	7	2	22
South Korea	12	5	12	29
Hungary	11	12	7	30
France	8	5	16	29
Australia	7	9	11	27
Italy	6	5	8	19
Canada	6	5	7	18
Great Britain	5	3	12	20
Romania	4	6	8	18
Czechoslovakia	4	2	1	7
North Korea	4	0	5	9
Japan	3	8	11	22
Bulgaria	3	7	6	16
Poland	3	6	10	19
Holland	2	6	7	15
Kenya	2	4	2	8
Norway	2	4	1	7
Turkey	2	2	2	6
Indonesia	2	2	1	5
Brazil	2	1	0	3
Greece	2	0	0	2
Sweden	1	7	4	12
New Zealand	1	4	5	10
Finland	1	2	2	5
Denmark	1	1	4	6
Morocco	1	1	1	3
Ireland	1	1	0	2
Ethiopia	1	0	2	3
Algeria	1	0	1	2
Estonia	1	0	1	2
Lithuania	1	0	1	2
Switzerland	1	0	0	1
Jamaica	0	3	1	4
Nigeria	0	3	1	4
Latvia	0	2	1	3
Austria	0	2	0	2
Namibia	0	2	0	2
South Africa	0	2	0	2
Belgium	0	1	2	3
Croatia	0	1	2	3
Independent Team	0	1	2	3
Iran	0	1	2	3
Israel	0	1	1	2
Mexico	0	1	0	1
Peru	0	1	0	1
Taiwan	0	1	0	1
Mongolia	0	0	2	2
Slovenia	0	0	2	2
Argentina	0	0	1	1
Bahamas	0	0	1	1
Columbia	0	0	1	1
Ghana	0	0	1	1
Malaysia	0	0	1	1
Pakistan	0	0	1	1
Philippines	0	0	1	1
Puerto Rico	0	0	1	1
Qatar	0	0	1	1
Surinam	0	0	1	1
Thailand	0	0	1	1
	259	258	298	815

Sports Records

WORLD ATHLETICS RECORDS

As at 7 September 1992, all the world records given below have been accepted by the International Amateur Athletic Federation except those marked with an asterisk* which are awaiting homologation. Fully automatic timing to 1/100th second is mandatory up to and including 400 metres. For distances up to and including 10,000 metres, records will be accepted to 1/10th second if timed automatically, and to 1/10th if hand timing is used.

MEN'S EVENTS

TRACK EVENTS	hr.	min.	sec.
100 metres C. Lewis, USA, 1991			9.86
200 metres P. Mennea, Italy, 1979			19.72
400 metres H.Reynolds, USA, 1988			43.29
800 metres S. Coe, GB, 1981		1	41.73
1,000 metres S. Coe, GB, 1981		2	12.18
1,500 metres N. Morceli, Algeria, 1992		3	28.86
1 mile S. Cram, GB, 1985		3	46.32
2,000 metres S. Aouita, Morocco, 1987		4	50.81
3,000 metres M. Kiptanui, Kenya, 1992		7	28.96
5,000 metres S. Aouita, Morocco, 1987		12	58.39
10,000 metres A. Barrios, Mexico, 1989		27	08.23
20,000 metres A. Barrios, Mexico, 1991		56	55.6
21,101 metres (13 miles 196 yards 1 foot) A. Barrios, Mexico, 1991	1	00	00.0
25,000 metres T. Seko, Japan, 1981	1	13	55.8
30,000 metres T. Seko, Japan, 1981	1	29	18.8
110 metres hurdles (3 ft 6 in) R. Kingdom, USA, 1989			12.92
400 metres hurdles (3 ft 0 in) K. Young, USA, 1992			46.78
3,000 metres steeplechase M. Kiptanui, Kenya, 1992		8	02.08

RELAYS	min.	sec.
4 × 100 metres USA, 1992		37.40
4 × 200 metres Santa Monica TC, 1992	1	19.11
4 × 400 metres USA, 1992	2	55.74
4 × 800 metres GB, 1982	7	03.89
4 × 1,500 metres Federal Republic of Germany, 1977	14	38.8

FIELD EVENTS	metres	ft	in
High jump J. Sotomayor, Cuba, 1989	2.44	8	0
Pole vault S. Bubka, CIS, 1992	6.12	20	0½
Long jump M. Powell, USA, 1991	8.95	29	4½
Triple jump W. Banks, USA, 1985	17.97	58	11½
Shot R. Barnes, USA, 1990	23.12	75	10¼
Discus J. Schult, GDR, 1986	74.08	243	0
Hammer Y. Sedykh, USSR, 1986	86.74	284	7
Javelin S. Backley, GB, 1992	91.46	300	1
Decathlon† D. O'Brien, USA, 1992		8,891 pts	

† Ten events comprising 100 m, long jump, shot, high jump, 400 m, 110 m hurdles, discus, pole vault, javelin, 1500 m

WALKING (TRACK)	hr.	min.	sec.
20,000 metres S. Johansson, Sweden, 1992	1	18	35
28,800* metres (17 miles 1576 yards) G. Leblanc, Canada, 1990	2	00	00.0
30,000 metres G. Leblanc, Canada, 1990	2	04	55.7
50,000 metres R. Gonzalez, Mexico, 1979	3	41	39.00

WOMEN'S EVENTS

TRACK EVENTS	min.	sec.
100 metres F. Griffith-Joyner, USA, 1988		10.49
200 metres F. Griffith-Joyner, USA, 1988		21.34
400 metres M. Koch, GDR, 1985		47.60
800 metres J. Kratochvilova, Czechoslovakia, 1983	1	53.28
1,500 metres T. Kazankina, USSR, 1980	3	52.47
1 mile P. Ivan, Romania, 1989	4	15.61
3,000 metres T. Kazankina, USSR, 1984	8	22.62
5,000 metres I. Kristiansen, Norway, 1986	14	37.33
10,000 metres I. Kristiansen, Norway, 1986	30	13.74
100 metres hurdles (2 ft 9 in) Y. Donkova, Bulgaria, 1988		12.21
400 metres hurdles (2 ft 6 in) M. Stepanova, USSR, 1986		52.94

RELAYS

	min.	sec.
4 × 100 metres GDR, 1985		41.37
4 × 200 metres GDR, 1980	1	28.15
4 × 400 metres USSR, 1988	3	15.17
4 × 800 metres USSR, 1984	7	50.17

FIELD EVENTS

	metres	ft	in
High jump S. Kostadinova, Bulgaria, 1987	2.09	6	10¼
Long jump G. Chistiakova, USSR, 1988	7.52	24	8¼
Triple jump I. Kravets, USSR, 1991	14.95	49	0¾
Shot N. Lisovskaya, USSR, 1987	22.63	74	3
Discus G. Reinsch, GDR, 1988	76.80	252	0
Javelin P. Felke, GDR, 1988	80.00	262	5
Heptathlon† J. Joyner–Kersee, USA, 1988	7,291 pts		

†Seven events comprising 100 m hurdles, shot, high jump, 200 m, long jump, javelin, 800 m

UNITED KINGDOM (NATIONAL) RECORDS

As at 15 September 1992; records set anywhere by athletes eligible to represent Great Britain and Northern Ireland

Men

TRACK EVENTS

	hr.	min.	sec.
100 metres L. Christie, 1991			9.92
200 metres L. Christie, 1988 J. Regis, 1992			20.09
400 metres D. Grindley, 1992			44.47
800 metres S. Coe, 1981		1	41.73
1,000 metres S. Coe, 1981		2	12.18
1,500 metres S. Coe, 1985		3	29.67
1 mile S. Cram, 1985		3	46.32
2,000 metres S. Cram, 1985		4	51.39
3,000 metres D. Moorcroft, 1982		7	32.79
5,000 metres D. Moorcroft, 1982		13	00.41
10,000 metres E. Martin, 1988		27	23.06
20,000 metres C. Thackery, 1990		57	28.7
20,855 metres C. Thackery, 1990	1		
25,000 metres R. Hill, 1965	1	15	22.6
30,000 metres J. Alder, 1970	1	31	30.4
3,000 metres steeplechase M. Rowland, 1988		8	07.96
110 metres hurdles C. Jackson, 1992			13.04
400 metres hurdles K. Akabusi, 1992			47.82

RELAYS

	min.	sec.
4 × 100 metres GB team, 1990		37.98
4 × 200 metres GB team, 1989	1	21.29
4 × 400 metres GB team, 1991	2	57.53
4 × 800 metres GB team, 1982	7	03.89

FIELD EVENTS

	metres	ft	in
High jump D. Grant, 1991	2.36	7	8¾
Pole vault K. Stock, 1981	5.65	18	6½
Long jump L. Davies, 1968	8.23	27	0
Triple jump K. Connor, 1982	17.57	57	7¾
Shot G. Capes, 1980	21.68	71	1½
Discus W. Tancred, 1974	64.32	211	0
Hammer M. Girvan, 1984	77.54	254	5
Javelin S. Backley, 1992	91.46	300	1
Decathlon D. Thompson, 1984	8,847 points		

WALKING (TRACK)

	hr.	min.	sec.
20,000 metres I. McCombie, 1990	1	23	26.5
30,000 metres C. Maddocks, 1984	2	19	18
50,000 metres P. Blagg, 1990	4	05	44.6
2 hours R. Wallwork, 1971	16 miles 315 yards		

Women

TRACK EVENTS

	min.	sec.
100 metres K. Cook, 1981		11.10
200 metres K. Cook, 1984		22.10
400 metres K. Cook, 1984		49.43
800 metres K. Wade, 1985	1	57.42
1,500 metres Z. Budd, 1985	3	59.96
1 mile Z. Budd, 1985	4	17.57

	min.	sec.
3,000 metres Z. Budd, 1985	8	28.83
5,000 metres Z. Budd, 1985	14	48.07
10,000 metres E. McColgan, 1991	30	57.07
100 metres hurdles S. Gunnell, 1988		12.82
400 metres hurdles S. Gunnell, 1991		53.16

RELAYS	min.	sec.
4 × 100 metres GB team, 1980		42.43
4 × 200 metres GB team, 1977	1	31.57
4 × 400 metres GB team, 1991	3	22.01
4 × 800 metres GB team, 1971	8	23.8

FIELD EVENTS	metres	ft	in
High jump D. Elliott, 1982	1.95	6	4¾
Long jump B. Kinch, 1983	6.90	22	7¾
Triple jump M. Berkeley, 1992	13.56	44	6
Shot J. Oakes, 1988	19.36	63	6¼
Discus M. Ritchie, 1981	67.48	221	5
Javelin F. Whitbread, 1986	77.44	254	1
Heptathlon J. Simpson, 1986	6,623 points		

SWIMMING WORLD RECORDS

As at 31 August 1992

Men	min.	sec.
50 metres freestyle T. Jager, USA		21.81
100 metres freestyle M. Biondi, USA		48.42
200 metres freestyle G. Lamberti, Italy	1	46.69
400 metres freestyle Y. Sadovyi, CIS	3	45.00
800 metres freestyle K. Perkins, Australia	7	46.60
1,500 metres freestyle K. Perkins, Australia	14	43.48
100 metres breaststroke N. Rosza, Hungary	1	01.29
200 metres breaststroke M. Barrowman, USA	2	10.16
100 metres butterfly P. Morales, USA		52.84
200 metres butterfly M. Stewart, USA	1	55.69
100 metres backstroke J. Rouse, USA		53.86
200 metres backstroke M. Lopez-Zubero, Spain	1	57.30
200 metres medley T. Darnyi, Hungary	1	59.36
400 metres medley T. Darnyi, Hungary	4	12.36
4 × 100 metres freestyle relay USA	3	16.53
4 × 200 metres freestyle relay CIS	7	11.95
4 × 100 metres medley relay USA	3	36.93

Women	min.	sec.
50 metres freestyle Yang Wenyi, China		24.79
100 metres freestyle J. Thompson, USA		54.48
200 metres freestyle H. Friedrich, GDR	1	57.55
400 metres freestyle J. Evans, USA	4	03.85
800 metres freestyle J. Evans, USA	8	16.22
1,500 metres freestyle J. Evans, USA	15	52.10
100 metres breaststroke S. Hörner, GDR	1	07.91
200 metres breaststroke A. Nall, USA	2	25.35
100 metres butterfly M. Meagher, USA		57.93
200 metres butterfly M. Meagher, USA	2	05.96
100 metres backstroke K. Egerszegi, Hungary	1	00.31
200 metres backstroke K. Egerszegi, Hungary	2	06.62
200 metres medley Li Lin, China	2	11.65
400 metres medley P. Schneider, GDR	4	36.10
4 × 100 metres freestyle relay USA	3	39.46
4 × 200 metres freestyle relay GDR	7	55.47
4 × 100 metres medley relay USA	4	02.54

WEIGHTLIFTING WORLD RECORDS (TOTALS)

As at 31 August 1992

Class	kg
52 kg I. Ivanov, Bulgaria, 1989	272.5
56 kg N. Shalamanov, Bulgaria, 1984	300
60 kg N. Suleymanoglu, Turkey, 1988	342.5
67.5 kg M. Petrov, Bulgaria, 1987	355
75 kg A. Varbanov, Bulgaria, 1988	382.5
82.5 kg Y. Vardanyan, USSR, 1984	405

CLASS	kg
90 kg	422.5
V. Solodov, USSR, 1984	
100 kg	440
Y. Zakharevich, USSR, 1983	
110 kg	455
Y. Zakharevich, USSR, 1988	
Over 110 kg	475
L. Taranenko, USSR, 1988	

The Olympic Games

The modern Olympic Games have been held as follows:

I	Athens, Greece	1896
II	Paris, France	1900
III	St Louis, USA	1904
IV	London, Britain	1908
V	Stockholm, Sweden	1912
VII	Antwerp, Belgium	1920
VIII	Paris, France	1924
IX	Amsterdam, Netherlands	1928
X	Los Angeles, USA	1932
XI	Berlin, Germany	1936
XIV	London, Britain	1948
XV	Helsinki, Finland	1952
XVI	Melbourne, Australia	1956
XVII	Rome, Italy	1960
XVIII	Tokyo, Japan	1964
XIX	Mexico City, Mexico	1968
XX	Munich, West Germany	1972
XXI	Montreal, Canada	1976
XXII	Moscow, USSR	1980
XXIII	Los Angeles, USA	1984
XXIV	Seoul, South Korea	1988
XXV	Barcelona, Spain	1992
XXVI	Atlanta, USA	1996

The following Games were scheduled but did not take place owing to World Wars:

VI	Berlin, Germany	1916
XII	Tokyo, Japan, then Helsinki, Finland	1940
XIII	London, Britain	1944

WINTER OLYMPIC GAMES

I	Chamonix, France	1924
II	St Moritz, Switzerland	1928
III	Lake Placid, USA	1932
IV	Garmisch-Partenkirchen, Germany	1936
V	St Moritz, Switzerland	1948
VI	Oslo, Norway	1952
VII	Cortina d'Ampezzo, Italy	1956
VIII	Squaw Valley, USA	1960
IX	Innsbruck, Austria	1964
X	Grenoble, France	1968
XI	Sapporo, Japan	1972
XII	Innsbruck, Austria	1976
XIII	Lake Placid, USA	1980
XIV	Sarajevo, Yugoslavia	1984
XV	Calgary, Canada	1988
XVI	Albertville, France	1992
XVII	Lillehammer, Norway	1994

The Commonwealth Games

The Games were originally called the British Empire Games. From 1954 to 1966 the Games were known as the British Empire and Commonwealth Games, and from 1970 to 1974 as the British Commonwealth Games. Since 1978 the Games have been called the Commonwealth Games.

BRITISH EMPIRE GAMES

I	Hamilton, Canada	1930
II	London, England	1934
III	Sydney, Australia	1938
IV	Auckland, New Zealand	1950

BRITISH EMPIRE AND COMMONWEALTH GAMES

V	Vancouver, Canada	1954
VI	Cardiff, Wales	1958
VII	Perth, Australia	1962
VIII	Kingston, Jamaica	1966

BRITISH COMMONWEALTH GAMES

IX	Edinburgh, Scotland	1970
X	Christchurch, New Zealand	1974

COMMONWEALTH GAMES

XI	Edmonton, Canada	1978
XII	Brisbane, Australia	1982
XIII	Edinburgh, Scotland	1986
XIV	Auckland, New Zealand	1990
XV	Victoria, Canada	1994

Television

The result of the latest franchise auction for Channel 3 (ITV) licences was announced on 16 October 1991, after five months of deliberations following the submission of bids and prospectuses to the Independent Television Commission (ITC). The terms for the awarding of franchises were laid down in the Broadcasting Act 1990; the main requirement was that each licence would be awarded to the highest bidder, who would first have to pass a quality test.

Speaking about the franchise auction at a meeting held by the Royal Television Society in September 1991, the Home Secretary, Kenneth Baker, said, 'I continue to believe that the overall effect of the Broadcasting Act will be to improve the quality and audience appeal of the programming, and also improve creativity and new talent. ITV's current success in the ratings bears witness to the fact that quality and efficiency are not mutually exclusive'.

Of the sixteen franchises, only half were in fact awarded to the highest bidders. There were four casualties among existing companies: Thames was the most significant loser, as one of the main providers, with Granada, of programmes for the ITV network. The company's bid of £32.5 million was surpassed by Carlton's £43.2 million bid. Thames, which makes programmes such as the twice-weekly police series *The Bill*, *Minder*, *Strike It Lucky* and *French Fields*, had made contingency plans in the event of losing its broadcasting licence and determined to carry on as an independent producer of programmes.

The breakfast service TV-AM, once threatened with closure by the Independent Broadcasting Authority unless it improved programme quality, was also outbid, its £14.2 million offer being substantially less than the £34.6 million of Sunrise TV. Sunrise later changed its name to GMTV, as British Sky Broadcasting had already laid claim to the Sunrise title for its early morning show.

TVS, which appeared to have survived a troublesome period when its purchase of the American MTM programme company caused it severe financial difficulty, was controversially deprived of its licence by an underbidder, Meridian Broadcasting. The ITC ruled that TVS would not be able to sustain its level of programme-making or profitability with its bid of £59.8 million. TSW lost out for the same reason to Westcountry Television, which bid £7.8 million against TSW's £16.1 million.

Somewhat surprisingly, North-West Television, headed by Phil Redmond of Mersey TV, makers of *Brookside* for Channel 4, was defeated in its attempt to oust Granada. Although NWTV outbid Granada with £35.3 million as against £9 million, it failed to pass the quality hurdle.

The farcical nature of the franchise process was demonstrated by the fact that the profitable Central television company, having realized that it was sole bidder for its franchise area, was able to succeed with a bid of only £2,000. The less profitable Scottish TV was also able to retain its franchise unopposed with a bid of £2,000, while Channel successfully bid £1,000, its only rival (with a bid of £102,000) having been ruled out on quality grounds. Border bid £52,000 and was unopposed. Yorkshire TV retained its licence with a bid of £37.7 million, which was generally considered to have been high.

If all the franchises been awarded to the highest bidders in each case, originally the Government's intention by throwing the whole process open to market forces, the Government would have benefited by an extra £200 million a year. It will receive an extra £40 million a year in revenue from the accepted bids but the folly of not establishing a bottom limit for bids (perhaps related to the sums paid by the incumbent companies, as suggested by the Peacock Committee) was apparent from the almost derisory offers accepted from some companies, which were nevertheless entirely within the rules.

Richard Dunn, chairman of Thames, commented, 'Cash has beaten quality . . . our contribution to the network has been unequalled and we have been a pioneer on many fronts for the network'. TSW, having passed the quality threshold, was aggrieved at having been defeated for bidding too much: 'They appear to have moved the goalposts', said Harry Turner, managing director.

The Times, in a leading article headed 'ITV Auction Fiasco', commented that 'Just four of the 16 incumbent television franchise-holders were sacrificed to shake up the industry, let in new blood, and warn the others against complacency . . . As this year's equally chaotic award of commercial radio franchises showed, Britain is no nearer a coherent broadcasting policy. With the BBC's franchise next in line for renewal, that lacuna must soon be filled'.

There were complaints from some of the unsuccessful applicants that the ITC had not seen fit to query any points in their applications. The system was, said Richard Dunn, 'an almost unintelligible mixture of objective and subjective judgements, with practically no viewer involvement'. Thames was left to look for a future in satellite broadcasting; however, with the moratorium on take-overs of independent television companies ending in 1994, it is possible that Thames could re-enter the scene.

Further controversy arose when Bruce Gyngell of TV-AM released the text of a letter he had received from the former Prime Minister Margaret Thatcher, whose determination to end 'the last bastion of restrictive practices' in the television industry had brought about the franchise auction. Mrs Thatcher wrote that she was 'mystified' that TV-AM had not received a licence: 'You of all people have done so much for the whole of television – there seems to have been no attention to that. I am only too painfully aware that *I* was responsible for the legislation'.

The ITC declared itself confident that its decisions would withstand judicial review: 'We have not made any perverse or unreasonable judgments', it said. TSW was the first to challenge the ruling in the High Court; its application for judicial review was rejected by the judge, who also refused leave to appeal, saying it was 'doomed to failure'. The case was later heard by the Court of Appeal, which turned it down, and TSW appealed to the House of Lords, 'in view of the importance of the case to TSW and the shortcomings in the Independent Television Commission's decision-making process'. TVS also sought judicial review, but neither company was successful.

Finance

After losing its franchise Thames announced that it would reduce its regional programming to the minimum requirement of six hours a week. TVS followed suit, cutting its regional output to 12 hours a week. Thames also offered to sell some of its popular programmes to the BBC, making it clear that it intended to exploit its earning potential to the full in the last months of its broadcasting licence. Thames later reached agreement with the BBC to set up a satellite channel, UK Gold, which would exploit both companies' substantial catalogue of programmes. The service is scheduled to begin broadcasting in autumn 1992. The ITC, concerned about the effect on programming of the ousted companies deciding to cut costs, warned that their licences could be revoked immediately if there was a serious decline in programme quality or variety.

In the aftermath of the franchise auction, White Rose TV, unsuccessful underbidder for Yorkshire TV's licence, attempted to stage a coup by urging YTV's shareholders to reject the offered licence. White Rose, which had bid £17.4 million, argued that Yorkshire's bid of £37.7 million was excessive, hoping that if the YTV shareholders agreed White Rose would be awarded the licence and would have a far better chance of operating profitably by being required to pay £20 million less to the Treasury each year. The ITC said that if YTV did refuse the licence it would not automatically pass to White Rose. The deal was rejected. In June, YTV agreed to merge with Tyne Tees TV, to which ITC agreed.

There were worries that TVS might not be able to continue operating because of financial problems. Central, which holds a 20 per cent stake in Meridian, the successor company to TVS, offered to step in to provide programmes should TVS collapse. However, the company was able to agree a refinancing deal with its bankers that would guarantee its future until the termination of its licence.

Relief was provided for the ITV companies in November 1991, when the Government agreed to relax the levy paid by them for 1992, the final year of the existing franchises. The reduction meant that they had an extra £100 million available.

In February 1992 the dismissal of David Plowright, executive chairman of Granada Television, was widely criticized. He had joined the company in 1957 and his reputation in the industry played a major part in Granada's successful retention of its licence.

Scheduling

In July, Andrew Quinn, chief executive of Granada, was appointed chief executive of the ITV network. He said that in future, current affairs programmes would not be shown at peak viewing times unless they drew audiences of over eight million viewers, and he did not rule out the possibility of moving ITN's *News at Ten* to another time. 'It would be foolish to disrupt viewers' relationship with ITV', he said, 'but it is a more commercial enterprise and programmes are going to hold their own in the schedule'.

Under the new system of central scheduling, a network director will also be appointed to determine all programming for the ITV companies. Delays in making the appointment began to cause problems by summer 1992 because companies were reluctant to commission programmes too far ahead in case they could not sell them to the network. Independent producers will also be able to compete directly with the ITV companies for airtime, but the Office of Fair Trading, which was required to approve the new arrangements, was concerned that they might be anti-competitive. The companies will retain control of the network budget and will approve the commissioning of programmes, which could work against the independent producers.

Attempts by ITV companies to prevent other broadcasters showing repeats of ITV programmes for ten or 15 years was also a matter for concern. Thames refused to surrender rights to repeats of its programmes; it threatened to cancel the broadcasting of all networked programmes and replace them with repeats of its own shows if the other companies insisted that it give up repeat rights to *The Bill* on other channels, such as Channel 5 or UK Gold. Thames eventually won its point.

Independent Television News is required under the Broadcasting Act 1990 to negotiate a new contract with the Channel 3 companies for 1993. The companies are also required to divest themselves of 51 per cent of their holdings in ITN, a condition which the ITC hope to persuade the Government to reverse.

In August, ITV agreed to pay £40 million for a four-year contract to screen Football League and Rumbelows Cup matches, having lost out to BSkyB and the BBC on Premier League and FA Cup matches. Channel 4 negotiated to screen Italian league matches on Sundays. ITV also signed an agreement to screen the 1995 Rugby Union World Cup series for £10 million.

BBC's Future

The focus on the ITV companies in the early part of 1992 kept the BBC out of the limelight but subsequently the expiry of its charter in 1996 provoked debate about its future. The Home Secretary, Kenneth Baker, speaking at the Royal Television Society meeting in September 1991, said that a Home Office committee would seek ideas on the Corporation's role; however, he ruled out a Royal Commission. Mr Baker said that a discussion document would be issued in 1992 setting out alternatives for the BBC. He wanted 'to involve [viewers] in this debate about its future'. Mr Baker continued: 'The central question is, what exactly do we mean by universality and how do we justify it? Do we mean simply the technical reach of the BBC's reception or do we mean that the BBC has to produce a range of programmes which cover everything from soaps to the Proms? If the full range of services is provided, then how should it be paid for? We cannot assume – and nor does the BBC – that things should inevitably continue as they are. Clearly there is a role for public service broadcasting, but that role will have to be defined more specifically. It's obvious that the BBC is going to be a different body in the next two or three years'.

Sir Michael Checkland, the director-general of the BBC, commented, 'The BBC is asking itself hard questions about its future. No issues are being avoided and no questions are being dodged'.

The BBC held a weekend meeting of its governors and senior managers in May 1992 to discuss the Corporation's future structure and strategy. The reports of the 15 task forces set up in 1991 to examine all aspects of the BBC's activities and to suggest a blueprint for the future were amalgamated into a discussion paper. There was a call for a 'more distinctive BBC with range, but without some of the programme areas it now covers.

Following widespread rumours about job losses and doubts over the future direction of the Corporation, Sir Michael Checkland, in a letter to staff in June 1992, reaffirmed its commitment to public service broadcasting up to and beyond the renewal of its royal charter in 1996. The BBC would, he said, be focusing on four key objectives for the next century, based on accurate and impartial news reporting, high standards of entertainment and cultural programmes, formal and informal educational programmes, and international services. The wide range of services that the public expected from the BBC could not be met by advertising or other revenues, and the BBC would urge the continuation of the licence fee. He said, 'Clearly the BBC is going through considerable internal change at the moment, coupled with uncertainty associated with the forthcoming debate about our future. Inevitably it will be a difficult time for all staff but we cannot expect these issues to be resolved early. We know already that questions will be asked about the range and scope of our services. The BBC intends to put up a vigorous case for its future'.

Although the BBC had not intended to publish its own policy document before the Government issued its green paper, a copy of the document was leaked to the press in September 1992. The document said that the BBC would 'withdraw from areas in which it is no longer able or needed to make an original contribution', but would not cease making popular programmes, as this would 'preclude the majority of licence payers from viewing and listening to programmes and services which they value and appreciate'. It declared that the BBC should aim to offer 'distinctive, high quality programmes in each of the major genres . . . That range should encompass programming that appeals to a broad viewing and listening audience, as well as programming which meets the specific needs and interests of smaller audiences.'

BBC2 should 'challenge and surprise and set out to change the general public perception of what television can do', showing innovative programmes at peak times and 'stimulating the development of British culture and entertainment'.

Competition

In October 1991 the BBC launched its 'producer choice' scheme, which is intended to save some £50 million over four years by cutting costs and overheads of television production. As from April 1993 the scheme will force direct competition with outside commercial companies for all services provided by the BBC. Producers will be able to buy from the BBC or outside sources including ITV, to give them 'greater scope to make quality programmes while ensuring maximum value for money for licence payers'.

By becoming fully competitive, the BBC would then be able to concentrate on 'the real debate', according to Sir Michael Checkland: 'the role and purpose of BBC services, what the viewers and listeners want'. The more commercial outlook of the Corporation was a reaction in part to the new commercial climate prevalent in independent companies, which had cut down costs and reduced staff numbers dramatically as they prepared their bids for the franchise auction.

John Birt, the deputy director-general and Sir Michael's designated successor, said the new scheme 'should invigorate the management of the BBC – ensuring greater clarity of role and responsibility; and far wider discretion . . . jibes about bloated bureaucracy and over-manning will end. We shall have a programme-driven BBC, with a lean and competitive resource base – but a BBC still very much a centre of craft excellence'.

In October 1991 the BBC announced that 3,000 jobs would be cut over the next four years. In November it announced the loss of 300 production jobs, included in the October figure of 3,000, and savings of an estimated £25 million over four years. The cuts are necessary because the BBC is required to meet the Government's target of commissioning at least 25 per cent of its output from independent producers.

Programming

The BBC also announced increased funding for drama and entertainment, with an extra £160 million earmarked for the next four years, plus £1 million for 'prestige documentaries'. It was announced later in the year that with effect from autumn 1992 the BBC would no longer screen repeats, American series or game shows in peak hours.

Details were disclosed of a proposed new soap opera, to be screened three times a week, based on an expatriate community and filmed in southern Spain. Provisionally entitled 'Little England', the project cost £10 million for the first year's production of 156 episodes. The programme was devised by Julia Smith, producer of the successful *EastEnders*, and produced by Verity Lambert. The BBC hoped it would rival *Coronation Street* in popularity, with viewing figures of up to 20 million. The programme was later renamed *Eldorado*, and became a *cause célèbre* which raised questions about the role of the BBC and the direction it should be taking.

The programme opened in July 1992, two months earlier than expected; although not scheduled in direct competition with *Coronation Street*, ITV met the challenge to its early evening viewing audience by showing a double-length episode of *Coronation Street* beginning at the same time as *Eldorado*. Although early viewing figures were said to be around 10 million, the show was criticized for poor standards of acting and ratings plummeted. There were reports that Julia Smith had gone on extended leave, one of the young stars was sacked, and the controller of BBC1, Jonathan Powell, flew to Spain to attempt to restore cast morale. 'I have real faith in this show' he said, 'although there is room for some improvement'. There were reports, however, that John Birt felt that *Eldorado* and the bad publicity it had attracted were not consistent with his ideas about the future of the Corporation or the upmarket image he hoped to promote. In some quarters it was suggested that he would cancel the show as soon as he became director-general.

The BBC again developed subscription services, which it tried briefly in 1991 with a night-time service for doctors which was not a success. BBC Select will offer up to 25 pay services, aimed at professionals, special interest groups and ethnic communities. Launched in the spring of 1992, the first service was the Executive Business Club, with a target of 80,000 subscribers in order for it to be profitable. The programmes are screened at night and carry advertising. Viewers have to purchase decoders to unscramble the pictures, having recorded them on video machines. Sir Michael Checkland said the venture would provide revenue to 'strengthen existing services'. The BBC later sold airtime to companies such as Nuclear Electric, Cable and Wireless and Scottish Power, so that they could broadcast reports of their annual general meetings and financial results at 5.30 a.m. The reports are not scrambled as in BBC Select.

In October 1991 the BBC aroused the wrath of the Conservative Party by what it felt was biased coverage of its party conference. As with the dispute with ITN the following year, the row concerned the reporting of a speech by the Health Secretary, William Waldegrave. John Birt refuted the allegations and praised his reporters' 'manifest dedication to impartiality'. However, the BBC later conceded that its report in the *Nine O'Clock News* 'was not up to our normal standards' but said that 'overall we are satisfied that our coverage of the health service issue has been impartial and fair'.

The Conservatives later complained about the BBC's coverage of their campaign in the run-up to the election in April 1992. The BBC was not, however, the only broadcaster to be accused of bias during the campaign. The Conservatives also complained about an ITN report on the National Health Service, in which statistics quoted by the Health Secretary William Waldegrave were countered by a London doctor who, it transpired, was a member of the Labour Party.

Licence Fees

On 1 April 1992 the fees for television licences were increased by 4 per cent, with the colour licence increasing from £77 to £80 and black and white from £25.50 to £26.50.

In February 1992 the BBC announced that it intended to launch a 24-hour satellite news service in direct competition with *Sky News*. It will be funded by subscriptions and will consist of television news supplemented by world news from BBC World Service Television, which was launched in 1991. Later, the BBC said that it would launch four satellite channels over the next three years, covering news, documentaries, natural history and children's programmes.

In May 1992, the BBC joined BSkyB in a deal worth £304 million over five years, to show matches from the new Premier Football League. BSkyB will show 60 live matches a season, while the BBC will restore its Saturday night programme *Match of the Day* to show highlights of matches. ITV sought to have the arrangement overruled in the High Court because it believed that the BBC and BSkyB had unfairly increased their final bid after learning that ITV had offered £262 million. However, its action was unsuccessful.

In August 1992 the BBC's controversial policy of promoting its own magazines was ended: following a Monopolies and Mergers Commission investigation into cross-media promotion, the BBC was told that it could not give free air time to promote its own products without offering similar time to rival publications in the same field. The Copyright Tribunal also ruled that the BBC and ITP (publishers of *TV Times*) should only receive £2 million, instead of the £13 million they had been seeking, for providing their listings for newspapers and magazines. Many newspapers brought out weekly television listings supplements in direct competition with *Radio Times* and *TV Times*.

Channel 4

Channel 4 was set up in 1982 with the remit of providing a 'suitable proportion of programmes calculated to appeal to tastes and interests not generally catered for by the existing ITV channel', to 'encourage innovation and experiment' and to have 'a distinctive character'. At the Edinburgh Television Festival in October 1991, Channel 4 was criticized for having lost its way; it was said that the channel now relied too much on imported American comedy shows and repeats of ITV programmes, and that minority interest and innovative shows were being cancelled.

Channel 4 was also criticized for the 'golden handcuff' payments made to its chief executive Michael Grade and other senior executives to dissuade them from joining any of the various consortia bidding for the Channel 3 franchises. Grade was reported to have been paid £500,000, with a similar amount shared by seven other staff. It was felt by some that the payments were insensitive at a time when programme budgets had been cut by 8 per cent, Channel 4 had lost £5 million in the collapse of the BCCI, and it was committed to spending £35 million on new headquarters although there was no shortage of empty office blocks in London.

In August 1992 Channel 4 and Box Productions were fined £75,000 for contempt of court. The companies refused to reveal the identity of an informant who had alleged in a documentary, *The Committee*, that a secret organization consisting of members of the Royal Ulster Constabulary and loyalist groups had carried out sectarian killings in Northern Ireland. The RUC denied the allegations, claiming that Channel 4 had been hoaxed.

Under the new regime for independent television instituted by the Broadcasting Act 1990, Channel 4 will be operating under new conditions from 1993. It will no longer be funded by a subscription levied on the ITV companies which sold its advertising in their respective regions. In future Channel 4 will sell its own advertising and will be in direct competition with the Channel 3 companies for revenue.

BSkyB

The annual report of the News Corporation in September 1991 stated that BSkyB had reduced its losses from an estimated £10 million a week at the time of the merger between Sky and BSB to £1.5 million a week. Chairman and chief executive Rupert Murdoch said, 'The break-even point is at last in sight'. The cost of contracts for the purchase of films was the satellite station's largest single item of expenditure, but BSkyB was able to renegotiate its film contracts with three major Hollywood film studios, securing substantial discounts. In their competition for major film libraries and new releases in the run-up to their respective launches, Sky and BSB had helped to force prices to unnaturally high levels.

Nearly one year after the two channels merged it appeared that the move, although controversial, was beginning to make commercial sense. In March 1992 BSkyB revealed that it was achieving a weekly operating profit of £100,000 a year earlier than it had forecast. However, £1.28 billion was still owed to shareholders. Subscription revenue had reached £3.8 million a week and it was now reaching 2.9 million, or 13 per cent of all homes in Britain. In homes with satellite or cable services, BSkyB had 31.7 per cent of the ratings.

Cable

In September 1991 the Independent Television Commission reported that over one million homes now had access to broadband cable networks, and that of these nearly 20 per cent subscribed. There was, however, still concern that of the 137 cable franchises awarded, only 49 had begun constructing their systems. Companies were warned that if they did not begin work by the end of January 1992, their licences might be withdrawn.

Channel 5

The licence for the proposed new independent television station, Channel 5, was advertised for auction, with a closing date for applications of 7 July 1992. Doubts remained about the viability of the new service. The requirement that the successful bidder should arrange and finance the retuning of video recorders, televisions and computers was variously estimated at a cost of between £50 and £200 million. Further, some 30 per cent of the country would not be able to receive the service, including the south coast of England, East Anglia, Wales, Scotland and the north-west. The ITC requires that the service should reach 30 per cent of the population by the end of its first year of broadcasting and its potential audience of 74 per cent within six years.

As with the Channel 3 licences, bidders had to pass a quality test, the highest bid then prevailing. However, the ITC said that it 'cannot guarantee we will award it to anyone or that if we do it will be a commercial success'. It was reported that the only applicant was Five TV Consortium, consisting of Thames TV and Moses Znaimer of Toronto's City TV, which bid £1,000 a year. However, there were doubts about the funding of the consortium, which still had to raise 85 per cent of the £150 million it needed. There appeared to be a strong possibility that the ITC would not award the licence when it reached its decision in November.

Suspect Award

In the BAFTA Awards, the award for best drama serial was won by *Prime Suspect*, a police thriller made by Granada. However, four of the judging panel of seven later said that they had chosen Alan Bleasdale's drama about political corruption, *GBH*. After an inquiry the award was allowed to stand.

Weights and Measures

SI UNITS

The Système International d'Unités (SI) is an international and coherent system of units devised to meet all known needs for measurement in science and technology. The system was adopted by the eleventh Conférence Générale des Poids et Mesures (CGPM) in 1960. A comprehensive description of the system is given in *SI The International System of Units*, HMSO. The British Standards describing the essential features of the International System of Units are *Specifications for SI Units* (BS 5555:1981) and *Conversion Factors and Tables* (BS 350, Part 1:1974).

The system consists of seven base units and the derived units formed as products or quotients of various powers of the base units. Together the base units and the derived units make up the coherent system of units. In the UK the SI base units, and almost all important derived units, are realized at the National Physical Laboratory and disseminated through the National Measurement System.

BASE UNITS

METRE (m) = unit of length
KILOGRAM (kg) = unit of mass
SECOND (s) = unit of time
AMPERE (A) = unit of electric current
KELVIN (K) = unit of thermodynamic temperature
MOLE (mol) = unit of amount of substance
CANDELA (cd) = unit of luminous intensity

DERIVED UNITS

For some of the derived SI units, special names and symbols exist; those approved by the CGPM are listed below.

HERTZ (Hz) = unit of frequency
NEWTON (N) = unit of force
PASCAL (Pa) = unit of pressure, stress
JOULE (J) = unit of energy, work, quantity of heat
WATT (W) = unit of power, radiant flux
COULOMB (C) = unit of electric charge, quantity of electricity
VOLT (V) = unit of electric potential, potential difference, electromotive force
FARAD (F) = unit of electric capacitance
OHM (Ω) = unit of electric resistance
SIEMENS (S) = unit of electric conductance
WEBER (Wb) = unit of magnetic flux
TESLA (T) = unit of magnetic flux density
HENRY (H) = unit of inductance
DEGREE Celsius (°C) = unit of Celsius temperature
LUMEN (lm) = unit of luminous flux
LUX (lx) = unit of illuminance
BECQUEREL (Bq) = unit of activity (of a radionuclide)
GRAY (Gy) = unit of absorbed dose, specific energy imparted, kerma, absorbed dose index
SIEVERT (Sv) = unit of dose equivalent, dose equivalent index

SUPPLEMENTARY UNITS

The derived units include, as a special case, the supplementary units which may be treated as dimensionless within the SI.

RADIAN (rad) = unit of plane angle
STERADIAN (sr) = unit of solid angle

Other derived units are expressed in terms of base units and/or supplementary units. Some of the more commonly-used derived units are the following:

Unit of area = square metre (m^2)
Unit of volume = cubic metre (m^3)
Unit of velocity = metre per second ($m\ s^{-1}$)
Unit of acceleration = metre per second squared ($m\ s^{-2}$)
Unit of density = kilogram per cubic metre ($kg\ m^{-3}$)
Unit of momentum = kilogram metre per second ($kg\ m\ s^{-1}$)
Unit of magnetic field strength = ampere per metre ($A\ m^{-1}$)
Unit of surface tension = newton per metre ($N\ m^{-1}$)
Unit of dynamic viscosity = pascal second (Pa s)
Unit of heat capacity = joule per kelvin ($J\ K^{-1}$)
Unit of specific heat capacity = joule per kilogram kelvin ($J\ kg^{-1}\ K^{-1}$)
Unit of heat flux density, irradiance = watt per square metre ($W\ m^{-2}$)
Unit of thermal conductivity = watt per metre kelvin ($W\ m^{-1}\ K^{-1}$)
Unit of electric field strength = volt per metre ($V\ m^{-1}$)
Unit of luminance = candela per square metre ($cd\ m^{-2}$)

SI PREFIXES

Decimal multiples and submultiples of the SI units are indicated by SI prefixes. These are as follows:

multiples	*submultiples*
yotta (Y) × 10^{24}	deci (d) × 10^{-1}
zetta (Z) × 10^{21}	centi (c) × 10^{-2}
exa (E) × 10^{18}	milli (m) × 10^{-3}
peta (P) × 10^{15}	micro (μ) × 10^{-6}
tera (T) × 10^{12}	nano (n) × 10^{-9}
giga (G) × 10^{9}	pico (p) × 10^{-12}
mega (M) × 10^{6}	femto (f) × 10^{-15}
kilo (k) × 10^{3}	atto (a) × 10^{-18}
hecto (h) × 10^{2}	zepto (z) × 10^{-21}
deca (da) × 10	yocto (y) × 10^{-24}

UK UNITS

The legal units for the United Kingdom are enacted in the Weights and Measures Act 1985. The United Kingdom primary standards are the yard or the metre as the unit of measurement of length, and the pound or the kilogram as the unit of measurement of mass. Other units of measurement are defined by reference to the primary standards.

Responsibility for the maintenance of the primary standards and for the determination or redetermination of their value rests with the Secretary of State for Trade and Industry.

The definition of the UK primary standards is as follows:

YARD = 0.9144 metre
METRE is the length of the path travelled by light in vacuum during a time interval of 1/299 792 458 of a second.
POUND = 0.453 592 37 kilogram
KILOGRAM is equal to the mass of the international prototype of the kilogram

The following list shows the definitions of measures set out in Schedule 1 of the Weights and Measures Act 1985.

MEASUREMENT OF LENGTH

Imperial Units
Mile = 1760 yards
Yard (yd) = 0.9144 metre
Foot (ft) = 1/3 yard
Inch (in) = 1/36 yard

Metric Units
Kilometre (km) = 1000 metres
Metre (m) is the length of the path travelled by light in vacuum during a time interval of 1/299 792 458 of a second
Decimetre (dm) = 1/10 metre
Centimetre (cm) = 1/100 metre
Millimetre (mm) = 1/1000 metre

MEASUREMENT OF AREA

Imperial Units
Acre = 4840 square yards
Square Yard = a superficial area equal to that of a square each side of which measures one yard
Square foot = 1/9 square yard

Metric Units
Hectare (ha) = 100 ares
Decare = 10 ares
Are (a) = 100 square metres
Square Metre = a superficial area equal to that of a square each side of which measures one metre
Square decimetre = 1/100 square metre
Square centimetre = 1/100 square decimetre
Square millimetre = 1/100 square centimetre

MEASUREMENT OF VOLUME

Metric Units
Cubic Metre (m^3) = a volume equal to that of a cube each edge of which measures one metre
Cubic decimetre = 1/1000 cubic metre
Cubic centimetre (cc) = 1/1000 cubic decimetre
Hectolitre = 100 litres
Litre = a cubic decimetre
Decilitre = 1/10 litre
Centilitre = 1/100 litre
Millilitre = 1/1000 litre

MEASUREMENT OF CAPACITY

Imperial Units
Gallon = 4.546 09 cubic decimetres
Quart = 1/4 gallon
Pint (pt) = 1/2 quart
Gill = 1/4 pint
Fluid ounce (fl oz) = 1/20 pint

Metric Units
Hectolitre (hl) = 100 litres
Litre (l or L) = a cubic decimetre
Decilitre (dl) = 1/10 litre
Centilitre (cl) = 1/100 litre
Millilitre (ml) = 1/1000 litre

MEASUREMENT OF MASS OR WEIGHT

Imperial Units
Pound (lb) = 0.453 592 37 kilogram
Ounce (oz) = 1/16 pound
*Ounce troy = 12/175 pound

Metric Units
Tonne, metric tonne (t) = 1000 kilograms
Kilogram (kg) is the unit of mass; it is equal to the mass of the international prototype of the kilogram
Hectogram (hg) = 1/10 kilogram
Gram (g) = 1/1000 kilogram
†Carat (metric) = 1/5 gram
Milligram (mg) = 1/1000 gram

*Used only for transactions in gold, silver or other precious metals, and articles made therefrom.
†Used only for transactions in precious stones or pearls.

OBSOLESCENT UNITS OF MEASUREMENT

Certain units of measurement may no longer be used for trade although the measure may still be used, e.g. it is legal to sell a 112 lb quantity of a commodity but it must be referred to in invoices, etc., as 112 lb, not as 1 cwt. These units are defined as follows:

Measurement of Length
Furlong = 220 yards
Chain = 22 yards

Measurement of Area
Square mile = 640 acres
Rood = 1210 square yards
Square inch = 1/144 square foot

Measurement of Volume
Cubic yard = a volume equal to that of a cube each edge of which measures one yard
Cubic foot = 1/27 cubic yard
Cubic inch = 1/1728 cubic foot

Measurement of Capacity
Bushel = 8 gallons
Peck = 2 gallons
Fluid drachm = 1/8 fluid ounce
Minim (min) = 1/60 fluid drachm

Measurement of Mass or Weight
Ton = 2240 pounds
Hundredweight (cwt) = 112 pounds
Cental = 100 pounds
Quarter = 28 pounds
Stone = 14 pounds
Dram (dr) = 1/16 ounce
Grain (gr) = 1/7000 pound
Pennyweight (dwt) = 24 grains
Ounce apothecaries = 480 grains
Drachm (ʒ1) = 1/8 ounce apothecaries
Scruple(℈1) = 1/3 drachm
Metric tonne = 1000 kilograms
Quintal (q) = 100 kilograms

MEASUREMENT OF ELECTRICITY

Units of measurement of electricity are defined by the Weights and Measures Act 1985, as follows:

AMPERE (A) = that constant current which, if maintained in two straight parallel conductors of infinite length, of negligible circular cross-section and placed 1 metre apart in vacuum, would produce between these conductors a force equal to 2×10^{-7} newton per metre of length.
OHM (Ω) = the electric resistance between two points of a conductor when a constant potential difference of 1 volt, applied between the two points, produces in the conductor a current of 1 ampere, the conductor not being the seat of any electromotive force.

VOLT (V) = the difference of electric potential between two points of a conducting wire carrying a constant current of 1 ampere when the power dissipated between these points is equal to 1 watt.
WATT (W) = the power which in one second gives rise to energy of 1 joule
Kilowatt (kW) = 1000 watts
Megawatt (MW) = one million watts

WATER MEASURES (approximate)

1 cubic foot = 62.32 lb
1 gallon = 10 lb
1 cubic cm = 1 gram
1000 cubic cm = 1 litre; 1 kilogram
1 cubic metre = 1000 litres; 1000 kg; 1 tonne
An inch of rain on the surface of an acre (43560 sq. ft) = 3630 cubic ft = 100.992 tons
Cisterns: A cistern 4 × 2½ feet and 3 feet deep will hold brimful 186.963 gallons, weighing 1869.63 lb in addition to its own weight

Water for Ships
Kilderkin = 18 gallons
Barrel = 36 gallons
Puncheon = 72 gallons
Butt = 110 gallons
Tun = 210 gallons

WINE MEASURES

Under the Weights and Measures (Intoxicating Liquor) Order 1988, as amended by the Weights and Measures (Various Foods) (Amendment) Order 1990, still wines may be pre-packed only in the following quantities: 10, 25, 37.5, 50 and 75 cl; 1, 1.5, 2, 3, 4, 5, 6, 8, 9 and 10 litres. In addition, the 18.7 cl size is permitted for consumption on board aircraft, ships and trains or for sale duty-free, and all quantities up to and including 25 cl are allowed when for consumption on the premises of the seller.

The Intoxicating Liquor Order also provides that sparkling wines (including champagne) may be pre-packed only in the following quantities: 12.5, 20, 37.5 and 75 cl; 1.5, 3, 4.5, 6 and 9 litres. However, all quantities are allowed when for consumption on board aircraft, ships and trains or for sale duty free.

Spirits and liqueurs may be pre-packed only in the following quantities: 2, 3, 4, 5, 7.1, 10, 20, 35, 50 and 70 cl; 1, 1.5, 2, 2.5, 3 and 4.5 litres. In addition, 1.125, 5 and 10 litres are permitted for non-retail sales and all quantities are allowed when for consumption on board aircraft, ships and trains or for sale duty free.

Bottles of Wine
Traditional equivalents in standard champagne bottles:

Magnum = 2 bottles
Jeroboam = 4 bottles
Rehoboam = 6 bottles
Methuselah = 8 bottles
Salmanazar = 12 bottles
Balthazar = 16 bottles
Nebuchadnezzar = 20 bottles
A quarter of a bottle is known as a ***nip***.
An eighth of a bottle is known as a ***baby***.

ANGULAR AND CIRCULAR MEASURES

60 seconds (″) = 1 minute (′)
60 minutes = 1 degree (°)
90 degrees = 1 right angle or quadrant
Diameter of circle × 3.141 6 = circumference
Diameter squared × 0.7854 = area of circle
Diameter squared × 3.141 6 = surface of sphere
Diameter cubed × 0.523 = solidity of sphere
One degree of circumference × 57.3 = radius*
Diameter of cylinder × 3.141 6; product by length or height, gives the surface
Diameter squared × 0.7854; product by length or height, gives solid content.

*Or, one radian (the angle subtended at the centre of a circle by an arc of the circumference equal in length to the radius) = 57.3 degrees.

MILLION, BILLION, ETC.

Value in the United Kingdom

Million	thousand × thousand	10^6
Billion	million × million	10^{12}
Trillion	million × billion	10^{18}
Quadrillion	million × trillion	10^{24}

Value in USA

Million	thousand × thousand	10^6
Billion	thousand × million	10^9
Trillion	million × million	10^{12}
Quadrillion	million × billion US	10^{15}

The American usage of billion (i.e. 10^9) is increasingly common, and is now universally used by statisticians.

NAUTICAL MEASURES

Distance
Distance at sea is measured in nautical miles. The British standard nautical mile was 6080 feet (the length of a minute of an arc of a great circle of the earth, rounded off to a mean value to allow for the length varying at different latitudes). This measure has been obsolete since 1970 when the international nautical mile of 1852 metres was adopted by the Hydrographic Department of the Ministry of Defence as a result of a recommendation by the International Hydrographic Bureau.

The cable (600 feet or 100 fathoms) was a measure approximately one-tenth of a nautical mile. Such distances are now expressed in decimal parts of a sea mile or in metres.

Soundings at sea were recorded in fathoms (6 feet). Depths are now expressed in metres on new Admiralty charts.

Speed
Speed is measured in nautical miles per hour, called knots. A ship moving at the rate of 30 nautical miles per hour is said to be doing 30 knots.

knots	*m.p.h.*	*knots*	*m.p.h.*
1	1.1515	9	10.3636
2	2.3030	10	11.5151
3	3.4545	15	17.2727
4	4.6060	20	23.0303
5	5.7575	25	28.7878
6	6.9090	30	34.5454
7	8.0606	35	40.3030
8	9.2121	40	46.0606

Tonnage

The tonnage of a vessel is measured in tons of 100 cubic feet.

Gross tonnage = the total volume of all the enclosed spaces of a vessel

Net tonnage = gross tonnage less deductions for crew space, engine room, water ballast and other spaces not used for passengers or cargo

DISTANCE OF THE HORIZON

The limit of distance to which one can see varies with the height of the spectator. The greatest distance at which an object on the surface of the sea, or of a level plain, can be seen by a person whose eyes are at a height of five feet from the same level is nearly three miles. At a height of 20 feet the range is increased to nearly six miles, and an approximate rule for finding the range of vision for small heights is to increase the square root of the number of feet that the eye is above the level surface by a third of itself. The result is the distance of the horizon in miles, but is slightly in excess of that in the table below, which is computed by a more precise formula. The table may be used conversely to show the distance of an object of given height that is just visible from a point on the surface of the earth or sea. Refraction is taken into account both in the approximate rule and in the table.

Height in feet	*range in miles*
5	2.9
20	5.9
50	9.3
100	13.2
500	29.5
1,000	41.6
2,000	58.9
3,000	72.1
4,000	83.3
5,000	93.1
20,000	186.2

TEMPERATURE SCALES

The Celsius scale is the SI name for the Centigrade scale. The Fahrenheit scale is related to it by the relationships:

$$C = (F - 32) \div 1.8$$

$$F = (C \times 1.8) + 32$$

The normal temperature of the human body is 36.9 °C or 98.4 °F. The freezing point of water is 0 °C = 32 °F. The boiling point is 99.974 °C (on adoption of the International Temperature Scale, ITS-90, from 1 January 1990) = 212 °F approximately.

On the kelvin temperature scale, the kelvin unit is 1/273.16 of the triple point of water (i.e. where ice, water and water vapour are in equilibrium). Absolute zero is zero K, the freezing point of water is 273.15 K and the boiling point is 373.124 K.

Conversion between scales

°C	°F	°C	°F	°C	°F
100	212	60	140	20	68
99	210.2	59	138.2	19	66.2
98	208.4	58	136.4	18	64.4
97	206.6	57	134.6	17	62.6
96	204.8	56	132.8	16	60.8
95	203	55	131	15	59
94	201.2	54	129.2	14	57.2
93	199.4	53	127.4	13	55.4
92	197.6	52	125.6	12	53.6
91	195.8	51	123.8	11	51.8
90	194	50	122	10	50
89	192.2	49	120.2	9	48.2
88	190.4	48	118.4	8	46.4
87	188.6	47	116.6	7	44.6
86	186.8	46	114.8	6	42.8
85	185	45	113	5	41
84	183.2	44	111.2	4	39.2
83	181.4	43	109.4	3	37.4
82	179.6	42	107.6	2	35.6
81	177.8	41	105.8	1	33.8
80	176	40	104	*zero*	32
79	174.2	39	102.2	−1	30.2
78	172.4	38	100.4	−2	28.4
77	170.6	37	98.6	−3	26.6
76	168.8	36	96.8	−4	24.8
75	167	35	95	−5	23
74	165.2	34	93.2	−6	21.2
73	163.4	33	91.4	−7	19.4
72	161.6	32	89.6	−8	17.6
71	159.8	31	87.8	−9	15.8
70	158	30	86	−10	14
69	156.2	29	84.2	−11	12.2
68	154.4	28	82.4	−12	10.4
67	152.6	27	80.6	−13	8.6
66	150.8	26	78.8	−14	6.8
65	149	25	77	−15	5
64	147.2	24	75.2	−16	3.2
63	145.4	23	73.4	−17	1.4
62	143.6	22	71.6	−18	0.4
61	141.8	21	69.8	−19	−2.2

PAPER MEASURES

Printing Paper

516 sheets = 1 ream
2 reams = 1 bundle
5 bundles = 1 bale

Writing Paper

480 sheets = 1 ream
24 sheets = 1 quire
20 quires = 1 ream

PRINTING PAPERS

	inches		*inches*
Foolscap	17 × 13½	Double Large Post	33 × 21
Double Foolscap	27 × 17	Demy	22½ × 17½
Quad Foolscap	34 × 27	Double Demy	35 × 22½
Crown	20 × 15	Quad Demy	45 × 35
Double Crown	30 × 20	Music Demy	20 × 15½
Quad Crown	40 × 30	Medium	23 × 18
Double Quad Crown	60 × 40	Royal	25 × 20
Post	19¼ × 15½	Super Royal	27½ × 20½
Double Post	31½ × 19½	Elephant	28 × 23
		Imperial	30 × 22

WRITING AND DRAWING PAPERS

	inches		inches
Emperor	72 × 48	Copy or Draft	20 × 16
Antiquarian	53 × 31	Demy	20 × 15½
Double Elephant	40 × 27	Post	19 × 15¼
Grand Eagle	42 × 28¾	Pinched Post	18½ × 14¾
Atlas	34 × 26	Foolscap	17 × 13½
Colombier	34½ × 23½	Double Foolscap	26½ × 16½
Imperial	30 × 22	Double Post	30½ × 19
Elephant	28 × 23	Double Large Post	33 × 21
Cartridge	26 × 21	Double Demy	31 × 20
Super Royal	27 × 19	Brief	16½ × 13¼
Royal	24 × 19	Pott	15 × 12½
Medium	22 × 17½		
Large Post	21 × 16½		

BROWN PAPERS

	inches		inches
Casing	46 × 36	Imperial Cap	29 × 22
Double Imperial	45 × 29	Haven Cap	26 × 21
Elephant	34 × 24	Bag Cap	24 × 19½
Double Four Pound	31 × 21	Kent Cap	21 × 18

INTERNATIONAL PAPER SIZES

The basis of the international series of paper sizes is a rectangle having an area of one square metre, the sides of which are in the proportion of 1:√2. The proportions 1:√2 have a geometrical relationship, the side and diagonal of any square being in this proportion. The effect of this arrangement is that if the area of the sheet of paper is doubled or halved, the shorter side and the longer side of the new sheet are still in the same proportion 1:√2. This feature is useful where photographic enlargement or reduction is used, as the proportions remain the same.

Description of the A series is by capital A followed by a figure. The basic size has the description A0 and the higher the figure following the letter, the greater is the number of sub-divisions and therefore the smaller the sheet. Half A0 is A1 and half A1 is A2. Where larger dimensions are required the A is preceded by a figure. Thus 2A means twice the size A0; 4A is four times the size of A0.

Subsidiary Series

A series of B sizes has been devised for use in exceptional circumstances when sizes intermediate between any two adjacent sizes of the A series are needed.

In addition there is a series of C sizes which is used much less. A is for magazines and books, B for posters, wall charts and other large items, C for envelopes particularly where it is necessary for an envelope (in C series) to fit into another envelope. The size recommended for business correspondence is A4.

Long Sizes

Long sizes (DL) are obtainable by dividing any appropriate sizes from the two series above into three, four or eight equal parts parallel with the shorter side in such a manner that the proportions mentioned in paragraph two are not maintained, the ratio between the longer and the shorter sides being greater than √ 2:1. In practice long sizes should be produced from the A series only.

It is an essential feature of these series that the dimensions are of the trimmed or finished size.

A Series

	mm		mm
A0	841 × 1189	A6	105 × 148
A1	594 × 841	A7	74 × 105
A2	420 × 594	A8	52 × 74
A3	297 × 420	A9	37 × 52
A4	210 × 297	A10	26 × 37
A5	148 × 210		

B Series

	mm		mm
B0	1000 × 1414	B6	125 × 176
B1	707 × 1000	B7	88 × 125
B2	500 × 707	B8	62 × 88
B3	353 × 500	B9	44 × 62
B4	250 × 353	B10	31 × 44
B5	176 × 250		

C Series / DL

C Series	mm	DL	mm
C4	324 × 229	DL	110 × 220
C5	229 × 162		
C6	114 × 162		

BOUND BOOKS

The book sizes most commonly used are listed below. Approximate centimetre equivalents are also shown. International sizes are converted to their nearest imperial size, e.g. A4 = D4; A5 = D8.

		inches	cm
Crown 32mo	C32	2½ × 3¾	6 × 9
Crown 16mo	C16	3¾ × 5	9 × 13
Foolscap 8vo	F8	4¼ × 6¾	11 × 17
Demy 16mo	D16	4⅜ × 5⅝	11 × 14
Crown 8vo	C8	5 × 7½	13 × 19
Demy 8vo	D8	5⅝ × 8¾	14 × 22
Medium 8vo	M8	5¾ × 9	15 × 23
Royal 8vo	R8	6¼ × 10	16 × 25
Super Royal 8vo	suR8	6¾ × 10	17 × 25
Foolscap 4to	F4	6¾ × 8½	17 × 22
Crown 4to	C4	7½ × 10	19 × 25
Imperial 8vo	Imp8	7½ × 11	19 × 28
Demy 4to	D4	8¾ × 11¼	22 × 29
Royal 4to	R4	10 × 12½	25 × 31
Super Royal 4to	suR4	10 × 13½	25 × 34
Crown Folio	Cfol	10 × 15	25 × 38
Imperial Folio	Impfol	11 × 15	28 × 38

Folio = a sheet folded in half
Quarto (4to) = a sheet folded into four
Octavo (8vo) = a sheet folded into eight
Books are usually bound up in sheets of 16 or 32 pages. Octavo books are generally printed 64 pages at a time, 32 pages on each side of a sheet of quad.

CONVERSION TABLES FOR WEIGHTS AND MEASURES

Bold figures equal units of either of the columns beside them; thus: 1 cm = 0.394″ and 1″ = 2.540 cm

LENGTH

Centimetres		*Inches*
2.540	**1**	0.394
5.080	**2**	0.787
7.620	**3**	1.181
10.160	**4**	1.575
12.700	**5**	1.969
15.240	**6**	2.362
17.780	**7**	2.756
20.320	**8**	3.150
22.860	**9**	3.543
25.400	**10**	3.937
50.800	**20**	7.874
76.200	**30**	11.811
101.600	**40**	15.748
127.000	**50**	19.685
152.400	**60**	23.622
177.800	**70**	27.559
203.200	**80**	31.496
228.600	**90**	35.433
254.000	**100**	39.370

Metres		*Yards*
0.914	**1**	1.094
1.829	**2**	2.187
2.743	**3**	3.281
3.658	**4**	4.374
4.572	**5**	5.468
5.486	**6**	6.562
6.401	**7**	7.655
7.315	**8**	8.749
8.230	**9**	9.843
9.144	**10**	10.936
18.288	**20**	21.872
27.432	**30**	32.808
36.576	**40**	43.745
45.720	**50**	54.681
54.864	**60**	65.617
64.008	**70**	76.553
73.152	**80**	87.489
82.296	**90**	98.425
91.440	**100**	109.361

Kilometres		*Miles*
1.609	**1**	0.621
3.219	**2**	1.243
4.828	**3**	1.864
6.437	**4**	2.485
8.047	**5**	3.107
9.656	**6**	3.728
11.265	**7**	4.350
12.875	**8**	4.971
14.484	**9**	5.592
16.093	**10**	6.214
32.187	**20**	12.427
48.280	**30**	18.641
64.374	**40**	24.855
80.467	**50**	31.069
96.561	**60**	37.282
112.654	**70**	43.496
128.748	**80**	49.710
144.841	**90**	55.923
160.934	**100**	62.137

AREA

Square cm		*Square in*
6.452	**1**	0.155
12.903	**2**	0.310
19.355	**3**	0.465
25.806	**4**	0.620
32.258	**5**	0.775
38.710	**6**	0.930
45.161	**7**	1.085
51.613	**8**	1.240
58.064	**9**	1.395
64.516	**10**	1.550
129.032	**20**	3.100
193.548	**30**	4.650
258.064	**40**	6.200
322.580	**50**	7.750
387.096	**60**	9.300
451.612	**70**	10.850
516.128	**80**	12.400
580.644	**90**	13.950
645.160	**100**	15.500

Square m		*Square yd*
0.836	**1**	1.196
1.672	**2**	2.392
2.508	**3**	3.588
3.345	**4**	4.784
4.181	**5**	5.980
5.017	**6**	7.176
5.853	**7**	8.372
6.689	**8**	9.568
7.525	**9**	10.764
8.361	**10**	11.960
16.723	**20**	23.920
25.084	**30**	35.880
33.445	**40**	47.840
41.806	**50**	59.799
50.168	**60**	71.759
58.529	**70**	83.719
66.890	**80**	95.679
75.251	**90**	107.639
83.613	**100**	119.599

Hectares		*Acres*
0.405	**1**	2.471
0.809	**2**	4.942
1.214	**3**	7.413
1.619	**4**	9.844
2.023	**5**	12.355
2.428	**6**	14.826
2.833	**7**	17.297
3.327	**8**	19.769
3.642	**9**	22.240
4.047	**10**	24.711
8.094	**20**	49.421
12.140	**30**	74.132
16.187	**40**	98.842
20.234	**50**	123.555
24.281	**60**	148.263
28.328	**70**	172.974
32.375	**80**	197.684
36.422	**90**	222.395
40.469	**100**	247.105

VOLUME

Cubic cm		*Cubic in*
16.387	**1**	0.061
32.774	**2**	0.122
49.161	**3**	0.183
65.548	**4**	0.244
81.936	**5**	0.305
98.323	**6**	0.366
114.710	**7**	0.427
131.097	**8**	0.488
147.484	**9**	0.549
163.871	**10**	0.610
327.742	**20**	1.220
491.613	**30**	1.831
655.484	**40**	2.441
819.355	**50**	3.051
983.226	**60**	3.661
1147.097	**70**	4.272
1310.968	**80**	4.882
1474.839	**90**	5.492
1638.710	**100**	6.102

Cubic m		*Cubic yd*
0.765	**1**	1.308
1.529	**2**	2.616
2.294	**3**	3.924
3.058	**4**	5.232
3.823	**5**	6.540
4.587	**6**	7.848
5.352	**7**	9.156
6.116	**8**	10.464
6.881	**9**	11.772
7.646	**10**	13.080
15.291	**20**	26.159
22.937	**30**	39.239
30.582	**40**	52.318
38.228	**50**	65.398
45.873	**60**	78.477
53.519	**70**	91.557
61.164	**80**	104.636
68.810	**90**	117.716
76.455	**100**	130.795

Litres		*Gallons*
4.546	**1**	0.220
9.092	**2**	0.440
13.638	**3**	0.660
18.184	**4**	0.880
22.730	**5**	1.100
27.276	**6**	1.320
31.822	**7**	1.540
36.368	**8**	1.760
40.914	**9**	1.980
45.460	**10**	2.200
90.919	**20**	4.400
136.379	**30**	6.599
181.839	**40**	8.799
227.298	**50**	10.999
272.758	**60**	13.199
318.217	**70**	15.398
363.677	**80**	17.598
409.137	**90**	19.798
454.596	**100**	21.998

WEIGHT (MASS)

Kilograms		*Pounds*
0.454	**1**	2.205
0.907	**2**	4.409
1.361	**3**	6.614
1.814	**4**	8.819
2.268	**5**	11.023
2.722	**6**	13.228
3.175	**7**	15.432
3.629	**8**	17.637
4.082	**9**	19.842
4.536	**10**	22.046
9.072	**20**	44.092
13.608	**30**	66.139
18.144	**40**	88.185
22.680	**50**	110.231
27.216	**60**	132.277
31.752	**70**	154.324
36.287	**80**	176.370
40.823	**90**	198.416
45.359	**100**	220.464

Metric tonnes		*Tons (UK)*
1.016	**1**	0.984
2.032	**2**	1.968
3.048	**3**	2.953
4.064	**4**	3.937
5.080	**5**	4.921
6.096	**6**	5.905
7.112	**7**	6.889
8.128	**8**	7.874
9.144	**9**	8.858
10.161	**10**	9.842
20.321	**20**	19.684
30.481	**30**	29.526
40.642	**40**	39.368
50.802	**50**	49.210
60.963	**60**	59.052
71.123	**70**	68.894
81.284	**80**	78.737
91.444	**90**	88.579
101.605	**100**	98.421

Metric tonnes		*Tons (US)*
0.907	**1**	1.102
1.814	**2**	2.205
2.722	**3**	3.305
3.629	**4**	4.409
4.536	**5**	5.521
5.443	**6**	6.614
6.350	**7**	7.716
7.257	**8**	8.818
8.165	**9**	9.921
9.072	**10**	11.023
18.144	**20**	22.046
27.216	**30**	33.069
36.287	**40**	44.092
45.359	**50**	55.116
54.431	**60**	66.139
63.503	**70**	77.162
72.575	**80**	88.185
81.647	**90**	99.208
90.719	**100**	110.231

Abbreviations

A	Associate of
AA	Alcoholics Anonymous
	Anti-Aircraft
	Automobile Association
AAA	Amateur Athletic Association
AB	Able-bodied seaman
ABA	Amateur Boxing Association
abbr(ev)	abbreviation
ABM	Anti-ballistic missile defence system
abr	abridged
ac	alternating current
a/c	account
AC	Aircraftman
	(*Ante Christum*) Before Christ
	Companion, Order of Australia
ACAS	Advisory, Conciliation and Arbitration Service
ACT	Australian Capital Territory
ACTT	Association of Cinematograph, Television and Allied Technicians
AD	(*Anno Domini*) In the year of our Lord
ADC	Aide-de-Camp
ADC (P)	Personal ADC to The Queen
adj	adjective
Adj	Adjutant
ad lib	(*ad libitum*) at pleasure
Adm	Admiral
	Admission
adv	adverb
	advocate
AE	Air Efficiency Award
AEA	Atomic Energy Authority
AEM	Air Efficiency Medal
AERE	Atomic Energy Research Establishment
AEU	Amalgamated Engineering Union
AFC	Air Force Cross
	Association Football Club
AFM	Air Force Medal
AFRC	Agricultural and Food Research Council
AFV	Armoured fighting vehicle
AG	Adjutant-General
	Attorney-General
AGM	air-to-ground missile
	annual general meeting
AH	(*Anno Hegirae*) In the year of the Hegira
AIDS	Acquired Immune Deficiency Syndrome
alt	altitude
am	(*ante meridiem*) before noon
AM	(*Anno mundi*) In the year of the world
amp	ampere
	amplifier
ANC	African National Congress
anon	anonymous(ly)
ANZAC	Australian and New Zealand Army Corps
AO	Air Officer
	Officer, Order of Australia
AOC	Air Officer Commanding
APEX	Association of Professional, Executive, Clerical and Computer Staff
AS	Anglo-Saxon
ASA	Advertising Standards Authority
	Amateur Swimming Association
ASB	*Alternative Service Book*
ASEAN	Association of South East Asian Nations
ASH	Action on Smoking and Health
ASLEF	Associated Society of Locomotive Engineers and Firemen
ASLIB	Association for Information Management
ASTMS	Association of Scientific, Technical and Managerial Staffs
ATC	Air Training Corps
AUC	(*ab urbe condita*) In the year from the foundation of Rome
	(*anno urbis conditae*) In the year of the founding of the city
AUT	Association of University Teachers
AV	Audio-visual
	Authorized Version (*of Bible*)
AVR	Army Volunteer Reserve
AWOL	Absent without leave
b	born
	bowled
BA	Bachelor of Arts
BAA	British Airports Authority
	British Astronomical Association
BAFTA	British Academy of Film and Television Arts
BAOR	British Army of the Rhine
Bart	Baronet
BAS	Bachelor in Agricultural Science
	British Antarctic Survey
BB	Boys' Brigade
BBC	British Broadcasting Corporation
BC	Before Christ
	British Columbia
BCCI	Bank of Credit and Commerce International
B Ch (D)	Bachelor of (Dental) Surgery
BCL	Bachelor of Civil Law
B Com	Bachelor of Commerce
BD	Bachelor of Divinity
BDA	British Dental Association
BDS	Bachelor of Dental Surgery
B Ed	Bachelor of Education
BEM	British Empire Medal
B Eng	Bachelor of Engineering
BFI	British Film Institute
BFPO	British Forces Post Office
BIM	British Institute of Management
B Litt	Bachelor of Letters *or* of Literature
BM	Bachelor of Medicine
	British Museum
BMA	British Medical Association
B Mus	Bachelor of Music
BOTB	British Overseas Trade Board
Bp	Bishop
B Pharm	Bachelor of Pharmacy
B Phil	Bachelor of Philosophy
Br	Britain
	British
BR	British Rail
BRCS	British Red Cross Society
Brig	Brigadier
Brit	Britain
	British
BSc	Bachelor of Science
BSC	British Steel Corporation
BSI	British Standards Institution
BST	British Summer Time
Bt	Baronet
BTEC	Business and Technician Education Council
B Th	Bachelor of Theology
Btu	British thermal unit
BVM	(*Beata Virgo Maria*) Blessed Virgin Mary
BVMS	Bachelor of Veterinary Medicine and Surgery
BWB	British Waterways Board
c	(*circa*) about
C	Celsius
	Centigrade
	Conservative
CA	Chartered Accountant (*Scotland*)
CAA	Civil Aviation Authority
CAB	Citizens' Advice Bureau
Cantab	(of) Cambridge
Cantuar:	of Canterbury (*Archbishop*)
CAP	Common Agricultural Policy
Capt	Captain
Caricom	Caribbean Community and Common Market
Carliol:	of Carlisle (*Bishop*)
CB	Companion, Order of the Bath
CBE	Commander, Order of the British Empire
CBI	Confederation of British Industry
CC	Chamber of Commerce
	Companion, Order of Canada
	City Council
	County Council
	County Court
CCC	County Cricket Club
C Chem	Chartered Chemist
CD	Civil Defence
	Compact Disc
	Corps Diplomatique
Cdr	Commander
Cdre	Commodore
CDS	Chief of the Defence Staff
CE	Civil Engineer
C Eng	Chartered Engineer
Cento	Central Treaty Organization
Cestr:	of Chester (*Bishop*)
CET	Central European Time
	Common External Tariff
cf	(*confer*) compare
CF	Chaplain to the Forces
CFC	Chlorofluorocarbon
CGM	Conspicuous Gallantry Medal
CGS	Centimetre-gramme-second (*system*)
	Chief of General Staff
CH	Companion of Honour
ChB/M	Bachelor/Master of Surgery
CI	Channel Islands
	The Imperial Order of the Crown of India
CIA	Central Intelligence Agency
Cicestr:	of Chichester (*Bishop*)
CID	Criminal Investigation Department
CIE	Companion, Order of the Indian Empire
cif	cost, insurance and freight

C-in-C	Commander-in-Chief
CIPFA	Chartered Institute of Public Finance and Accountancy
C Lit	Companion of Literature
CLJ	Commander, Order of St Lazarus of Jerusalem
CM	(*Chirurgiae Magister*) Master of Surgery
CMEA	Council for Mutual Economic Assistance (Comecon)
CMG	Companion, Order of St Michael and St George
CNAA	Council for National Academic Awards
CND	Campaign for Nuclear Disarmament
c/o	care of
CO	Commanding Officer
	conscientious objector
COD	Cash on delivery
C of E	Church of England
COHSE	Confederation of Health Service Employees
COI	Central Office of Information
Col	Colonel
Con	Conservative
Cpl	Corporal
CPM	Colonial Police Medal
CPRE	Council for the Protection of Rural England
CPVE	Certificate of Pre-Vocational Education
CRE	Council for Racial Equality
CSCE	Conference on Security and Co-operation in Europe
CSE	Certificate of Secondary Education
CSI	Companion, Order of the Star of India
CVO	Commander, Royal Victorian Order
d	(*denarius*) penny
DBE	Dame Commander, Order of the British Empire
dc	direct current
DC	District Council
	District of Columbia
DCB	Dame Commander, Order of the Bath
D Ch	(*Doctor Chirurgiae*) Doctor of Surgery
DCL	Doctor of Civil Law
DCM	Distinguished Conduct Medal
DCMG	Dame Commander, Order of St Michael and St George
DCVO	Dame Commander, Royal Victorian Order
DD	Doctor of Divinity
DDS	Doctor of Dental Surgery
DDT	dichlorodiphenyl-trichloroethane
del	(*delineavit*) he/she drew it
DFC	Distinguished Flying Cross
DFS	Department for Education
DFM	Distinguished Flying Medal
DG	(*Dei gratia*) By the grace of God
	Director-General
DH	Department of Health
DHA	District Health Authority
DHSS	Department of Health and Social Security
Dip Ed	Diploma in Education
Dip H E	Diploma in Higher Education
Dip Tech	Diploma in Technology
DJ	Disc jockey
DL	Deputy Lieutenant
D Litt	Doctor of Letters *or* of Literature
D Mus	Doctor of Music
DNA	deoxyribonucleic acid
DNB	*Dictionary of National Biography*
do	(*ditto*) the same
DoE	Department of the Environment
DOS	Disk operating system (*computer*)
DP	Data processing
D Ph *or* D Phil	Doctor of Philosophy
DPP	Director of Public Prosecutions
Dr	Doctor
DSc	Doctor of Science
DSC	Distinguished Service Cross
DSM	Distinguished Service Medal
DSO	Companion, Distinguished Service Order
DSS	Department of Social Security
DTI	Department of Trade and Industry
Dunelm:	of Durham (*Bishop*)
DV	(*Deo volente*) God willing
E	East
Ebor:	of York (*Archbishop*)
EBRD	European Bank of Reconstruction and Development
EC	European Community
ECG	Electrocardiogram
ECSC	European Coal and Steel Community
ECU	European Currency Unit
ED	Efficiency Decoration
EEC	European Economic Community
EEG	Electroencephalogram
EETPU	Electrical, Electronic, Telecommunication and Plumbing Union
EFA	European Fighter Aircraft
EFTA	European Free Trade Association
eg	(*exempli gratia*) for the sake of example
EMS	European Monetary System
ENEA	European Nuclear Energy Agency
ER	(*Elizabetha Regina*) Queen Elizabeth
ERD	Emergency Reserve Decoration
ERM	Exchange Rate Mechanism
ERNIE	Electronic random number indicator equipment
ESA	European Space Agency
ESP	Extra-sensory perception
ESRC	Economic and Social Research Council
ETA	Euzkadi ta Askatasuna (*Basque separatist organization*)
et al	(*et alibi*) and elsewhere
	(*et alii*) and others
etc	(*et cetera*) and the other things/and so forth
et seq	(*et sequentia*) and the following
Euratom	European Atomic Energy Commission
Exon:	of Exeter (*Bishop*)
f	(*forte*) loud
F	Fahrenheit
	Fellow of
FA	Football Association
FANY	First Aid Nursing Yeomanry
FAO	Food and Agriculture Organization
FBA	Fellow, British Academy
FBAA	Fellow, British Association of Accountants and Auditors
FBI	Federal Bureau of Investigation
FBIM	Fellow, British Institute of Management
FBS	Fellow, Botanical Society
FCA	Fellow, Institute of Chartered Accountants (*of England and Wales*)
FCCA	Fellow, Chartered Association of Certified Accountants
FCGI	Fellow, City and Guilds of London Institute
FCIA	Fellow, Corporation of Insurance Agents
FCIArb	Fellow, Chartered Institute of Arbitrators
FCIB	Fellow, Chartered Institute of Bankers
	Fellow, Corporation of Insurance Brokers
FCIBSE	Fellow, Chartered Institution of Building Services Engineers
FCII	Fellow, Chartered Insurance Institute
FCIS	Fellow, Institute of Chartered Secretaries and Administrators
FCIT	Fellow, Chartered Institute of Transport
FCMA	Fellow, Chartered Institute of Management Accountants
FCO	Foreign and Commonwealth Office
FCP	Fellow, College of Preceptors
FD	(*Fidei Defensor*) Defender of the Faith
fec	(*fecit*) made this
FEng	Fellow, Fellowship of Engineering
ff	(*fecerunt*) made this (*pl*)
	(*fortissimo*) very loud
FFA	Fellow, Faculty of Actuaries (*Scotland*)
	Fellow, Institute of Financial Accountants
FFAS	Fellow, Faculty of Architects and Surveyors
FGS	Fellow, Geological Society
FHS	Fellow, Heraldry Society
FHSM	Fellow, Institute of Health Service Management
FIA	Fellow, Institute of Actuaries
FIBiol	Fellow, Institute of Biology
FICE	Fellow, Institution of Civil Engineers
FICS	Fellow, Institution of Chartered Shipbrokers
FIEE	Fellow, Institution of Electrical Engineers
FIERE	Fellow, Institution of Electronic and Radio Engineers
FIFA	International Association Football Federation
FIM	Fellow, Institute of Metals
FIMM	Fellow, Institution of Mining and Metallurgy
FInstF	Fellow, Institute of Fuel
FInstP	Fellow, Institute of Physics
FIQS	Fellow, Institute of Quantity Surveyors
FIS	Fellow, Institute of Statisticians
FJI	Fellow, Institute of Journalists
fl	(*floruit*) flourished
FLA	Fellow, Library Association
FLS	Fellow, Linnean Society

FM	Field Marshal frequency modulation
fo	folio
FO	Flying Officer
fob	free on board
FPA	Family Planning Association
FPhS	Fellow, Philosophical Society
FRAD	Fellow, Royal Academy of Dancing
FRAeS	Fellow, Royal Aeronautical Society
FRAI	Fellow, Royal Anthropological Institute
FRAM	Fellow, Royal Academy of Music
FRAS	Fellow, Royal Astronomical Society
FRBS	Fellow, Royal Botanical Society Fellow, Royal Society of British Sculptors
FRCGP	Fellow, Royal College of General Practitioners
FRCM	Fellow, Royal College of Music
FRCO	Fellow, Royal College of Organists
FRCOG	Fellow, Royal College of Obstetricians and Gynaecologists
FRCP	Fellow, Royal College of Physicians, London
FRCPath	Fellow, Royal College of Pathologists
FRCPE(d)	Fellow, Royal College of Physicians, Edinburgh
FRCPI	Fellow, Royal College of Physicians, Ireland
FRCPsych	Fellow, Royal College of Psychiatrists
FRCR	Fellow, Royal College of Radiologists
FRCS	Fellow, Royal College of Surgeons of England
FRCSE(d)	Fellow, Royal College of Surgeons of Edinburgh
FRCSGlas	Fellow, Royal College of Physicians and Surgeons of Glasgow
FRCSI	Fellow, Royal College of Surgeons in Ireland
FRCVS	Fellow, Royal College of Veterinary Surgeons
FREconS	Fellow, Royal Economic Society
FRGS	Fellow, Royal Geographical Society
FRHistS	Fellow, Royal Historical Society
FRHS	Fellow, Royal Horticultural Society
FRIBA	Fellow, Royal Institute of British Architects
FRICS	Fellow, Royal Institution of Chartered Surveyors
FRMetS	Fellow, Royal Meteorological Society
FRMS	Fellow, Royal Microscopical Society
FRNS	Fellow, Royal Numismatic Society
FRPharmS	Fellow, Royal Pharmaceutical Society
FRPS	Fellow, Royal Photographic Society
FRS	Fellow, Royal Society
FRSA	Fellow, Royal Society of Arts
FRSC	Fellow, Royal Society of Chemistry
FRSE	Fellow, Royal Society of Edinburgh
FRSL	Fellow, Royal Society of Literature
FRTPI	Fellow, Royal Town Planning Institute
FSA	Fellow, Society of Antiquaries
FSS	Fellow, Statistical Society
FSVA	Fellow, Incorporated Society of Valuers and Auctioneers
FT	*Financial Times*
FTI	Fellow, Textile Institute
FTII	Fellow, Institute of Taxation
FZS	Fellow, Zoological Society
GATT	General Agreement on Tariffs and Trade
GBE	Dame/Knight Grand Cross, Order of the British Empire
GC	George Cross
GCB	Dame/Knight Grand Cross, Order of the Bath
GCE	General Certificate of Education
GCHQ	Government Communications Headquarters
GCIE	Knight Grand Commander, Order of the Indian Empire
GCLJ	Knight Grand Cross, Order of St Lazarus of Jerusalem
GCMG	Dame/Knight Grand Cross, Order of St Michael and St George
GCSE	General Certificate of Secondary Education
GCSI	Knight Grand Commander, Order of the Star of India
GCVO	Dame/Knight Grand Cross, Royal Victorian Order
GDP	Gross domestic product
Gen	General
GHQ	General Headquarters
GM	George Medal
GMB	General, Municipal, Boilermakers and Allied Trades Union
GMT	Greenwich Mean Time
GNP	Gross national product
GOC	General Officer Commanding
GP	General Practitioner
Gp Capt	Group Captain
GSO	General Staff Officer
HAC	Honourable Artillery Company
HBM	Her/His Britannic Majesty('s)
HCF	Highest common factor Honorary Chaplain to the Forces
HE	Her/His Excellency His Eminence
HGV	Heavy Goods Vehicle
HH	Her/His Highness Her/His Honour His Holiness
HIM	Her/His Imperial Majesty
HIV	Human Immunodeficiency Virus
HJS	(*hic jacet sepultus*) here lies buried
HM	Her/His Majesty('s)
HMAS	Her/His Majesty's Australian Ship
HMC	Headmasters' Conference
HMI	Her/His Majesty's Inspector
HML	Her/His Majesty's Lieutenant
HMS	Her/His Majesty's Ship
HMSO	Her/His Majesty's Stationery Office
HNC	Higher National Certificate
HND	Higher National Diploma
HOLMES	Home Office Large Major Enquiry System
Hon	Honorary Honourable
hp	horse power
HP	Hire purchase
HQ	Headquarters
HRH	Her/His Royal Highness
HSE	Health and Safety Executive (*hic sepultus est*) here lies buried
HSH	Her/His Serene Highness
HTR	High temperature reactor
HWM	High water mark
I	Island
IAAS	Incorporated Association of Architects and Surveyors
IAEA	International Atomic Energy Agency
IATA	International Air Transport Association
Ibid	(*ibidem*) in the same place
IBRD	International Bank for Reconstruction and Development
ICAO	International Civil Aviation Organization
ICBM	Inter-continental ballistic missile
ICFTU	International Confederation of Free Trade Unions
ICJ	International Court of Justice
ICRC	International Committee of the Red Cross
Id	(*idem*) the same
IDA	International Development Association
ie	(*id est*) that is
IEA	International Energy Agency
IFAD	International Fund for Agricultural Development
IFC	International Finance Corporation
IHS	(*Iesus Hominum Salvator*) Jesus the Saviour of Mankind
ILEA	Inner London Education Authority
ILO	International Labour Office/Organization
ILR	Independent local radio
IMF	International Monetary Fund
IMO	International Maritime Organization
Inc	Incorporated
Incog	(*incognito*) unknown, unrecognized
INF	International Nuclear Force
INLA	Irish National Liberation Army
In loc	(*in loco*) in its place
Inmarsat	International Maritime Satellite Organization
INRI	(*Iesus Nazarenus Rex Iudaeorum*) Jesus of Nazareth, King of the Jews
Inst	(*instant*) current month
Intelsat	International Telecommunications Satellite Consortium
Interpol	International Criminal Police Commission
IOC	International Olympic Committee
IOM	Isle of Man
IOU	I owe you
IOW	Isle of Wight
IPLO	Irish People's Liberation Organization
IQ	Intelligence quotient
IRA	Irish Republican Army
IRC	International Red Cross
Is	Islands

ISBN International Standard Book Number
ISO Imperial Service Order
ITC Independent Television Commission
ITU International Telecommunication Union
ITV Independent Television

JP Justice of the Peace

K Köchel numeration (*of Mozart's works*)
KANU Kenyan African National Union
KBE Knight Commander, Order of the British Empire
KCB Knight Commander, Order of the Bath
KCIE Knight Commander, Order of the Indian Empire
KCLJ Knight Commander, Order of St Lazarus of Jerusalem
KCMG Knight Commander, Order of St Michael and St George
KCSI Knight Commander, Order of the Star of India
KCVO Knight Commander, Royal Victorian Order
KG Knight of the Garter
KGB (*Komitet Gosudarstvennoi Besopasnosti*) Committee of State Security (USSR)
KKK Ku Klux Klan
KLJ Knight, Order of St Lazarus of Jerusalem
ko knock out (*boxing*)
KP Knight, Order of St Patrick
KStJ Knight, Order of St John of Jerusalem
Kt Knight
KT Knight of the Thistle
kV Kilovolt
kW Kilowatt
kWh Kilowatt hour

L Liberal
Lab Labour
Lat Latitude
lbw leg before wicket
lc lower case (*printing*)
LCJ Lord Chief Justice
LCM Least/lowest common multiple
LD Liberal Democrat
LDS Licentiate in Dental Surgery
LEA Local Education Authority
LHD (*Literarum Humaniorum Doctor*) Doctor of Humane Letters/ Literature
Lib Liberal
Lic (*Licenciado*) lawyer (*Spanish*)
Lic Med Licentiate in Medicine
Lit Literary
Lit Hum (*Literae Humaniores*) Faculty of classics and philosophy, Oxford
Litt D Doctor of Letters
LJ Lord Justice
LLB Bachelor of Laws
LLD Doctor of Laws
LLM Master of Laws
LM Licentiate in Midwifery
LMSSA Licentiate in Medicine and Surgery, Society of Apothecaries
loc cit (*loco citato*) in the place cited
log logarithm
Londin: of London (*Bishop*)
Long Longitude
LS (*loco sigilli*) place of the seal
LSA Licentiate of Society of Apothecaries
Lsd (*Librae, solidi, denarii*) £, shillings and pence
LSE London School of Economics and Political Science
Lt Lieutenant
LTA Lawn Tennis Association
Ltd Limited (liability)
LTh *or* L Theol Licentiate in Theology
LVO Lieutenant, Royal Victorian Order
LWM Low water mark

M Member of
Monsieur
MA Master of Arts
MAFF Ministry of Agriculture, Fisheries and Food
Maj Major
max maximum
MB/D Bachelor/Doctor of Medicine
MBA Master of Business Administration
MBE Member, Order of the British Empire
MC Master of Ceremonies
Military Cross
MCC Marylebone Cricket Club.
Maxwell Communications Corporation
MCh(D) Master of (Dental) Surgery
MD Managing Director
MDS Master of Dental Surgery
ME Middle English
MEC Member of Executive Council
MEd Master of Education
mega one million times
MEP Member of the European Parliament
MFH Master of Foxhounds
MGN Mirror Group Newspapers
Mgr Monsignor
MI Military Intelligence
micro one-millionth part
milli one-thousandth part
min minimum
MIRAS Mortgage Interest Relief at Source
MLA Member of Legislative Assembly
MLC Member of Legislative Council
Mlle Mademoiselle
MLR Minimum lending rate
MM Military Medal
Mme Madame
MN Merchant Navy
MO Medical Officer/Orderly
MoD Ministry of Defence
MoT Ministry of Transport
MP Member of Parliament
Military Police
mph miles per hour
MR Master of the Rolls
MRC Medical Research Council
MS Master of Surgery
Manuscript (*pl* MSS)
MSc Master of Science
MSF Manufacturing, Science and Finance Union
MTh Master of Theology
Mus B/D Bachelor/Doctor of Music
MV Merchant Vessel
Motor Vessel
MVO Member, Royal Victorian Order
MW Medium Wave

N North
n/a not applicable
not available
NAAFI Navy, Army and Air Force Institutes
NALGO National and Local Government Officers' Association
NASA National Aeronautics and Space Administration
NAS/UWT National Association of Schoolmasters/Union of Women Teachers
NATO North Atlantic Treaty Organization
NB New Brunswick
(*Nota bene*) note well
NCO Non-commissioned officer
NEB New English Bible
NEDC National Economic Development Council
Nem con (*Nemine contradicente*) no one contradicting
NERC Natural Environment Research Council
nes not elsewhere specified
NFT National Film Theatre
NFU National Farmers' Union
NGA '82 National Graphical Association 1982
NHS National Health Service
NI National Insurance
Northern Ireland
No (*numero*) number
Non seq (*Non sequitur*) it does not follow
Norvic: of Norwich (*Bishop*)
NP Notary Public
NRA National Rifle Association
NS New Style (*calendar*)
Nova Scotia
NSPCC National Society for the Prevention of Cruelty to Children
NSW New South Wales
NT National Theatre
National Trust
New Testament
NUCPS National Union of Civil and Public Servants
NUJ National Union of Journalists
NUM National Union of Mineworkers
NUPE National Union of Public Employees
NUR National Union of Railwaymen
NUS National Union of Seamen
National Union of Students
NUT National Union of Teachers
NVQ National Vocational Qualification
NWT Northwest Territory
NY New York
NZ New Zealand

OAPEC Organization of Arab Petroleum Exporting Countries
OAS Organization of American States
OAU Organization of African Unity
Ob *or* obit died
OBE Officer, Order of the British Empire
OC Officer Commanding
ODA Overseas Development Administration
OE Old English
omissions excepted

OECD Organization for Economic Co-operation and Development
OED *Oxford English Dictionary*
Ofgas Office of Gas Supply
OFM Order of Friars Minor (*Franciscans*)
Oftel Office of Telecommunications
OHMS On Her/His Majesty's Service
OM Order of Merit
OND Ordinary National Diploma
op (*opus*) work
OP Opposite prompt side (*of theatre*)
Order of Preachers (*Dominicans*)
out of print (*books*)
op cit (*opere citato*) in the work cited
OPCS Office of Population Censuses and Surveys
OPEC Organization of Petroleum Exporting Countries
OS Old Style (*calendar*)
Ordnance Survey
OSA Order of St Augustine
OSB Order of St Benedict
O St J Officer, Order of St John of Jerusalem
OT Old Testament
OTC Officers' Training Corps
Oxon (of) Oxford
Oxfordshire

p page (pp pages)
p (*piano*) softly
PA Personal Assistant
Press Association
PAYE Pay as You Earn
pc (*per centum*) in the hundred
PC Personal Computer
Police Constable
Privy Counsellor
PCAS Polytechnics Central Admissions System
PCFC Polytechnics' and Colleges' Funding Council
PDSA People's Dispensary for Sick Animals
PE Physical Education
Petriburg: of Peterborough (*Bishop*)
PhD Doctor of Philosophy
pinx(it) he/she painted it
pl plural
PLA Port of London Authority
PLC Public Limited Company
PLO Palestine Liberation Organization
pm (*post meridiem*) after noon
PM Prime Minister
PMRAFNS Princess Mary's Royal Air Force Nursing Service
PO Petty Officer
Pilot Officer
Post Office
postal order
POW Prisoner of War
pp (*per procurationem*) by proxy
PPS Parliamentary Private Secretary
PR Proportional Representation
Public Relations
PRA President of the Royal Academy
Pro tem (*pro tempore*) for the time being
Prox (*proximo*) next month
PRS President of the Royal Society
PRSE President of the Royal Society of Edinburgh
Ps Psalm
PS (*Post scriptum*) postscript
PSBR Public sector borrowing requirement
psc passed Staff College
PSV Public Service Vehicle
Pte Private
PTO Please turn over

QARANC Queen Alexandra's Royal Army Nursing Corps
QARNNS Queen Alexandra's Royal Naval Nursing Service
QB Queen's Bench
QC Queen's Counsel
QED (*quod erat demonstrandum*) which was to be proved
QGM Queen's Gallantry Medal
QHC Queen's Honorary Chaplain
QHDS Queen's Honorary Dental Surgeon
QHNS Queen's Honorary Nursing Sister
QHP Queen's Honorary Physician
QHS Queen's Honorary Surgeon
QMG Quartermaster General
QPM Queen's Police Medal
QS Quarter Sessions
QSO Quasi-stellar object (quasar)
Queen's Service Order
quango quasi-autonomous non-governmental organization
qv (*quod vide*) which see

R (*Regina*) Queen
(*Rex*) King
RA Royal Academy/Academician
Royal Artillery
RAC Royal Armoured Corps
Royal Automobile Club
RADA Royal Academy of Dramatic Art
RADC Royal Army Dental Corps
RAE Royal Aerospace Establishment
RAEC Royal Army Educational Corps
RAeS Royal Aeronautical Society
RAF Royal Air Force
RAM Random-access memory (*computer*)
Royal Academy of Music
RAMC Royal Army Medical Corps
RAN Royal Australian Navy
RAOC Royal Army Ordnance Corps
RAPC Royal Army Pay Corps
RAVC Royal Army Veterinary Corps
RBA Royal Society of British Artists
RBS Royal Society of British Sculptors
RC Red Cross
Roman Catholic
RCM Royal College of Music
RCN Royal Canadian Navy
RCT Royal Corps of Transport
RD Refer to drawer (*banking*)
Royal Naval and Royal Marine Forces Reserve Decoration
Rural Dean
RDI Royal Designer for Industry
RE Religious Education
Royal Engineers
REME Royal Electrical and Mechanical Engineers
Rep Representative
Republican
Rev(d) Reverend
RGN Registered General Nurse
RGS Royal Geographical Society
RHA Regional Health Authority
RHS Royal Horticultural Society
Royal Humane Society
RI Rhode Island
Royal Institute of Painters in Watercolours
Royal Institution
RIBA Royal Institute of British Architects
RIP (*Requiescat in pace*) May he/she rest in peace
RL Rugby League
RM Registered Midwife
Royal Marines
RMA Royal Military Academy
RMN Registered Mental Nurse
RN Royal Navy
RNIB Royal National Institute for the Blind
RNID Royal National Institute for the Deaf
RNLI Royal National Lifeboat Institution
RNR Royal Naval Reserve
RNVR Royal Naval Volunteer Reserve
RNXS Royal Naval Auxiliary Service
RNZN Royal New Zealand Navy
Ro (*Recto*) on the right-hand page
ROC Royal Observer Corps
Roffen: of Rochester (*Bishop*)
ROI Royal Institute of Oil Painters
ROM Read-only memory (*computer*)
RoSPA Royal Society for the Prevention of Accidents
RP Royal Society of Portrait Painters
rpm revolutions per minute
RRC Lady of Royal Red Cross
RSA Republic of South Africa
Royal Scottish Academician
Royal Society of Arts
RSC Royal Shakespeare Company
RSCN Registered Sick Children's Nurse
RSE Royal Society of Edinburgh
RSM Regimental Sergeant Major
RSPB Royal Society for the Protection of Birds
RSPCA Royal Society for the Prevention of Cruelty to Animals
RSV Revised Standard Version (*of Bible*)
RSVP (*Répondez, s'il vous plaît*) Please reply
RSW Royal Scottish Society of Painters in Watercolours
RTPI Royal Town Planning Institute
RU Rugby Union
RUC Royal Ulster Constabulary
RV Revised Version (*of Bible*)
RVM Royal Victorian Medal
RWS Royal Water Colour Society
RYS Royal Yacht Squadron

s second
(*solidus*) shilling
S South
SA Salvation Army
South Africa
South America
South Australia
SAE Stamped addressed envelope
Salop Shropshire
Sarum: of Salisbury (*Bishop*)
SAS Special Air Service Regiment
SBS Special Boat Squadron
SBN Standard Book Number
ScD Doctor of Science
SCM State Certified Midwife
SDLP Social Democratic and Labour Party

SDP	Social Democratic Party
SEAQ	Stock Exchange Automated Quotations system
SEN	State Enrolled Nurse
SERC	Science and Engineering Research Council
SERPS	State Earnings Related Pension Scheme
SFO	Serious Fraud Office
SI	(*Système Internationale d'Unités*) International System of Units Statutory Instrument
Sic	So written
Sig	Signature Signor
SJ	Society of Jesus (*Jesuits*)
SLD	Social and Liberal Democrats
SMP	Statutory Maternity Pay
SNP	Scottish National Party
SOGAT	Society of Graphical and Allied Trades
SOS	Save Our Souls (*distress signal*)
sp	(*sine prole*) without issue
spgr	specific gravity
SPQR	(*Senatus Populusque Romanus*) The Senate and People of Rome
SRN	State Registered Nurse
SRO	Self Regulating Organizations
SS	Saints Steamship
SSC	Solicitor before Supreme Court (*Scotland*)
SSF	Society of St Francis
SSP	Statutory Sick Pay
SSSI	Site of special scientific interest
stet	let it stand (*printing*)
STD	(*Sacrae Theologiae Doctor*) Doctor of Sacred Theology Subscriber trunk dialling
stp	Standard temperature and pressure
STP	(*Sacrae Theologiae Professor*) Professor of Sacred Theology
Sub Lt	Sub-Lieutenant
SVQ	Scottish Vocational Qualification
SWAPO	South West Africa People's Organization
SWET	Society of West End Theatres
TA	Territorial Army
TB	Tuberculosis
TCCB	Test and County Cricket Board
TD	Territorial Efficiency Decoration
temp	temperature temporary employee
TES	*Times Educational Supplement*
TGWU	Transport and General Workers' Union
THES	*Times Higher Education Supplement*
TLS	*Times Literary Supplement*
TNT	trinitrotoluene (*explosive*)
trs	transpose (*printing*)
TRH	Their Royal Highnesses
TT	Teetotal Tuberculin tested
TUC	Trades Union Congress
TVEI	Technical and Vocational Education Initiative
U	Unionist
UAE	United Arab Emirates
uc	upper case (*printing*)
UCATT	Union of Construction, Allied Trades and Technicians
UCCA	Universities' Central Council on Admissions
UDA	Ulster Defence Association
UDI	Unilateral Declaration of Independence
UDM	Union of Democratic Mineworkers
UDR	Ulster Defence Regiment
UEFA	Union of European Football Associations
UFC	Universities' Funding Council
UFF	Ulster Freedom Fighters
UFO	Unidentified flying object
UHF	ultra-high frequency
UK	United Kingdom
UKAEA	UK Atomic Energy Authority
UN	United Nations
UNESCO	United Nations Educational, Scientific and Cultural Organization
UNICEF	United Nations Children's Fund
UNIDO	United Nations Industrial Development Organization
Unita	National Union for the Total Independence of Angola
UPU	Universal Postal Union
URC	United Reformed Church
US(A)	United States (of America)
USDAW	Union of Shop, Distributive and Allied Workers
USM	Unlisted Securities Market
USSR	Union of Soviet Socialist Republics
UTC	Co-ordinated Universal Time system
UVF	Ulster Volunteer Force
v	(*versus*) against
VA	Vicar Apostolic Victoria and Albert Order
VAD	Voluntary Aid Detachment
VAT	Value added tax
VC	Victoria Cross
VD	Venereal disease Volunteer Officers' Decoration
VDU	Visual display unit
Ven	Venerable
VHF	very high frequency
VIP	Very important person
Vo	(*Verso*) on the left-hand page
VRD	Royal Naval Volunteer Reserve Officers' Decoration
VSO	Voluntary Service Overseas
VTOL	Vertical take-off and landing (*aircraft*)
W	West
WCC	World Council of Churches
WEA	Workers' Educational Association
WEU	Western European Union
WFTU	World Federation of Trade Unions
WHO	World Health Organization
WI	West Indies Women's Institute
Winton:	of Winchester (*Bishop*)
WIPO	World Intellectual Property Organization
WMO	World Meteorological Organization
WO	Warrant Officer
WRAC	Women's Royal Army Corps
WRAF	Women's Royal Air Force
WRNS	Women's Royal Naval Service
WRVS	Women's Royal Voluntary Service
WS	Writer to the Signet
YMCA	Young Men's Christian Association
YWCA	Young Women's Christian Association
ZANU	Zimbabwe African National Union

Ψ = seaport

Index

J. WHITAKER AND SONS LTD
12 Dyott Street, London WC1A 1DF

Whitaker's Almanack published annually since 1868
© 125th edition J. Whitaker and Sons Ltd 1992
Standard edition (1280 pages)
Cloth covers
0 85021 231 6

Leather binding
0 85021 233 2

Designed by Douglas Martin
Jacket design by Carroll Associates
Typeset by Clowes Computer Composition
Printed in Great Britain by
William Clowes Ltd, Beccles, Suffolk
Bound in Great Britain by
William Clowes Ltd, Beccles, Suffolk
and Clays Ltd, Bungay, Suffolk,
part of St Ives PLC

BORDERS REGIONAL LIBRARY

ACCESSION No.	CLASS No.
219079	R032-02

Whitaker's Almanack

1993

J. WHITAKER & SONS LTD

12 DYOTT STREET · LONDON WCIA IDF

Stop-press

CHANGES SINCE PAGES WENT TO PRESS

Royal Family
Daughter born to the Earl and Countess of St Andrews on 30 September 1992 (20th in order of succession)

The Queen's Household
Adviser for The Queen's Works of Art, Sir Francis Watson died
Chaplain in Scotland, Revd J. A. Simpson appointed

Peerage
Duke of Roxburghe married
Life barony conferred on Dafydd Elis Elis-Thomas gazetted – now Baron Elis-Thomas
Baroness Ewart-Biggs married

Baronetage and Knightage
Rear Adm. Sir Paul Greening appointed GCVO

Died
Sir Kenneth Anderson, KBE; Sir Geraint Evans, CBE; Adm. Sir Guy Grantham, GCB, CBE, DSO; Sir Walter Howard, MBE; Sir Maynard Jenour, TD; Sir Robert Micklethwait, QC; Sir Edward Nichols, TD; Sir Edward Singleton; Sir Eric Tansley, CMG; Sir Francis Watson, KCVO, FBA, FSA

Victoria Cross and George Cross Holders
Col. Fred Tilston, VC, CD, died
Lt.-Cdr Dennis Copperwheat, GC, died

Government Departments and Public Offices
National Portrait Gallery, Mrs C. Tomalin and Sir David Scholey replace the Duke of Grafton and Lord Sieff as trustees
British Council, Timothy Renton, MP, appointed vice-chairman
Parole Board, Lord Belstead appointed chairman
Public Health Laboratory Service, Dr Diana Walford appointed director

Law Courts and Offices

Lords of Appeal in Ordinary
Retired: Lord Ackner
Appointed: Sir Harry Woolf

Lord Justices of Appeal
Retired: Sir Michael Fox, Sir Roger Parker, Sir John Stocker
Appointed: Sir Simon Brown, Sir Anthony Evans, Sir David Hirst, Sir Leonard Hoffman, Sir Christopher Rose

High Court Judges
Retired: Sir Leslie Boreham
Appointed: R. H. Curtis, C. J. Holland, J. W. Kay, J. E. F. Lindsay, S. J. Sedley

Circuit Judges
Died: A. Jolly
Retired: H. Kershaw, A. Owen, K. Rubin
Appointed: M. R. Burr, G. M. Clifton, S. P. Grenfell, Miss G. Hallon, W. D. Matthews

Stipendiary Magistrates
Appointed: J. A. Browne (S. Yorks), P. C. Tain (E. and W. Sussex), H. Gott, M. Kelly (Metropolitan)

Churches
Graham James to be Suffragan Bishop of St Germans (diocese of Truro)

Local Government
London, Alderman Francis McWilliams becomes Lord Mayor on 13 November 1992

Media
ITV network director, M. Plantin appointed

Trade Unions
National Union of Journalists, J. Foster appointed general secretary

Countries of the World
Afghanistan – The Hezb-i-Islami party left the coalition government and Prime Minister Abdul Sabur Fareed was sacked
Bahamas – Hubert Ingraham replaced Sir Lynden Pindling as Prime Minister
Ukraine – Prime Minister Vitold Fokin was replaced by Valentyn Simonenko

Sport
World pole vault record – 6.13 m, S. Bubka, September 1992
British high jump record – 2.37 m, S. Smith, September 1992

EVENTS

September 1992
2. A Briton, Michael Wainwright, was sentenced in Iraq to ten years imprisonment for illegally entering the country. **3.** The Government borrowed £7.2 billion in foreign currencies to try to maintain the pound's position within the ERM. Kevin Maxwell was declared bankrupt. **7.** At least 28 people were killed by troops in Ciskei during an ANC demonstration there. David Gower was omitted from the England cricket team for the winter tour of India and Sri Lanka. **10.** The Prime Minister reiterated the Government's commitment to membership of the ERM. **13.** Pro-democracy parties were victorious in the Thai general election; Chuan Leekpai became Prime Minister at the head of a five-party coalition. **16.** The bank base rate was raised to 12 per cent, and a few hours later to 15 per cent, but was reduced to 12 per cent by the end of the day. The pound was suspended from the ERM after it fell below the permitted lowest level against the mark and was allowed to float; it fell to DM2.740. The Prime Minister recalled Parliament. **17.** The bank base rate was lowered to 10 per cent and the pound closed at DM2.6323. **20.** The French voted narrowly in favour of ratifying the Maastricht Treaty in a national referendum. **21.** The pound fell to DM2.5456. **22.** The bank base rate was cut to 9 per cent. Violent storms and heavy rain caused flooding in south-east France. **24.** Parliament held an emergency debate on the economic crisis. David Mellor resigned as Secretary of State for National Heritage. **25.** An emergency debate on foreign policy was held, after which Parliament went back into recess. **27.** Bryan Gould, the Opposition national heritage spokesman, resigned from the Shadow Cabinet in order to be able to voice his support for a national referendum on the Maastricht Treaty. **28.** An air crash in Nepal killed all 167 passengers and crew. **29.** The Brazilian House of Representatives suspended President Collor de Mello pending an impeachment trial; Vice-President Itamar Franco was sworn in as acting President three days later. **30.** A letter from the president of the German Bundesbank to the

Treasury, denying that the bank's actions had contributed to the sterling crisis, was leaked to the press by the German Embassy in London; the pound closed at DM2.5046.

OCTOBER 1992

1. The Prime Minister said that the bill ratifying the Maastricht Treaty would be introduced in the next session of Parliament. Russia launched its first-ever mass privatization scheme. The independent candidate Ross Perot announced that he would stand in the USA presidential election. **2.** The pound fell to DM2.4450. **4.** An El Al cargo jet crashed into blocks of flats in a suburb of Amsterdam.

DEATHS

SEPTEMBER 1992

5. Christopher Trace, *Blue Peter* presenter 1958–67, aged 59
6. Mervyn Johns, actor, aged 93
12. Anthony Perkins, American film actor, aged 60
19. Sir Geraint Evans, CBE, opera singer, aged 70
23. Gen. James Van Fleet, American Second World War general, aged 100
28. William Douglas Home, playwright and author, aged 80

BORDERS REGIONAL LIBRARY